THE
ISRAEL
BIBLE
™

Edited by Rabbi Tuly Weisz

ISRAEL
365

The Israel Bible
First Edition, 2018
Second Edition, 2021

The Israel Bible was produced by Israel365 in cooperation with
Teach for Israel and is used with permission from
Teach for Israel. All rights reserved.

The English translation was adapted by Israel365 from the JPS Tanakh.
Copyright © 1985 by the Jewish Publication Society. All rights reserved.

Cover images: © David Rubinger, Kluger Zoltan

All rights reserved. No part of this publication may be reproduced,
stored in a retrieval system or transmitted in any form or by
any means, electronic, mechanical, photocopying, or otherwise,
without the prior permission of the publisher, except in the case
of brief quotations embedded in critical articles or reviews.

ISBN 978-1-7333010-1-5, *hardcover*

A CIP catalogue record for this title is
available from the British Library

The Israel Bible is a holy book that contains the
name of God and should be treated with respect.

Printed and bound in Italy

It is with profound appreciation that
The Israel Bible
is dedicated to

Chanita and Michael Weisz

As pillars of their beloved community in Columbus, Ohio,
they are dedicated to the vibrancy of the Jewish people.
Daily, they have faced life's challenges with
unwavering trust and faith in God.

They serve as role models to many,
but primarily to their admiring children who they raised
to love the Land of Israel, the People of Israel
and the God of Israel.

May the Almighty bless them with continued years
of health and happiness.

Rabbi Tuly and Abby Weisz
Shaindee, Bella, Dovid, Tzofia and Amitai

Leah and Uriel Sturm
Alexandra Meira and Clarie

Ariella and Jonathan Eltes
Eliana, Nava, Daria, Yakov and David

Mina and Steven Stieglitz
Natalie, Ariana, and Georgie Naomi

In appreciation of

Dr. Helena Igra and Marc Singer

who have generously dedicated their time
and resources to strengthening *Eretz Yisrael* through
their remarkable support of groundbreaking initiatives.

Helena and Marc are true visionaries
who have always been quick to lend a hand,
offer an encouraging word or wise counsel
throughout the development of *The Israel Bible*.

In appreciation of

Donna Marie Jollay

for her unbridled enthusiasm for *The Israel Bible*
and other holy works that celebrate the miracles *Hashem*
has bestowed upon the Land and the People of Israel.

Donna is pioneering a new generation of
genuine friends of Israel from the nations of the world
who honor the *Torah* going forth from Zion.

Table of Contents

viii	Credits
ix	Acknowledgements
xii	Aleph Bet Chart
xiv	List of Weekly *Torah* portions and their *Haftarot*
xvi	List of *Torah* Readings for Special Occasions
xix	Introduction
xxv	Foreword
xxvii	Blessings Recited Before and After Reading the *Torah*
1	***Torah* (Five Books of Moses)**
3	*Bereishit* (Genesis)
135	*Shemot* (Exodus)
243	*Vayikra* (Leviticus)
323	*Bamidbar* (Numbers)
433	*Devarim* (Deuteronomy)
527	***Neviim* (Prophets)**
527	*Yehoshua* (Joshua)
593	*Shoftim* (Judges)
655	*Shmuel* (Samuel)
801	*Melachim* (Kings)
951	*Yeshayahu* (Isaiah)
1073	*Yirmiyahu* (Jeremiah)
1207	*Yechezkel* (Ezekiel)
1331	*Trei Asar* (Twelve Prophets)
1335	– *Hoshea* (Hosea)
1357	– *Yoel* (Joel)
1367	– *Amos* (Amos)
1383	– *Ovadya* (Obadiah)
1389	– *Yona* (Jonah)

1397	– *Micha* (Micah)
1411	– *Nachum* (Nahum)
1419	– *Chavakuk* (Habakkuk)
1427	– *Tzefanya* (Zephaniah)
1435	– *Chagai* (Haggai)
1441	– *Zecharya* (Zechariah)
1465	– *Malachi* (Malachi)
1471	***Ketuvim* (Writings)**
1471	*Tehillim* (Psalms)
1651	*Mishlei* (Proverbs)
1709	*Iyov* (Job)
1783	*Shir Hashirim* (Song of Songs)
1799	*Rut* (Ruth)
1815	*Eicha* (Lamentations)
1835	*Kohelet* (Ecclesiastes)
1859	*Esther* (Esther)
1879	*Daniel* (Daniel)
1919	*Ezra v'Nechemya* (Ezra and Nehemiah)
1985	*Divrei Hayamim* (Chronicles)
2143	Biographies of *The Israel Bible* Scholars
2145	Bibliography
2155	List of Transliterated Words in *The Israel Bible*
2169	Index
2174	Photo Credits
2178	Chart of the Hebrew Months and their Holidays
2181	Map of Modern-Day Israel and its Neighbors
2182	List of Prime Ministers of the State of Israel
2183	Prayer for the State of Israel
2186	Prayer for the Welfare of Israel's Soldiers
2188	Hatikvah

Maps, Charts and Lists

5	Map of the Journey of *Avraham* (Abraham)
137	Map of the Journey from Egypt to Mount Sinai
244	Chart of the *Korbanot Yachid* (Offerings Brought by an Individual)
325	Map of the Journey of the Spies
435	Map of the Cities of Refuge
529	Map of 12 Tribal Allotments
595	Chart of the Judges of Israel
657	Map of the Journey of the *Aron* (Ark of the Covenant)
803	Chart of the Kings of Israel
953	Chart of the Empires that Ruled the Land of Israel
1075	Map of the Two Kingdoms of Israel
1209	Map of the Ancient Near East
1332	Chart of the Twelve Prophets and When They Lived
1473	Map of Places Mentioned in *The Israel Bible* Commentary to *Sefer Tehillim* (Psalms)
1652	List of Opinions Regarding When *Shlomo* (Solomon) Authored his Biblical Books
1711	List of Opinions Regarding When *Iyov* (Job) lived
1784	Map of Places in *Shir Hashirim*
1798	Map of *Beit Lechem* (Beth-lehem) and Moab
1811	Chart of Israel's Exiles, Persecutions and Wars
1833	Map of Ancient *Yerushalayim* (Jerusalem)
1857	List of the *Neviim* (Prophets) and *Neviot* (Prophetesses)
1881	Chart of the 70 Years of Babylonian Exile
1921	Chart of Important Milestones in the Settlement of the Land of Israel
1987	List of the Generations from *Adam* to King *David*

Credits

Commentary and introductions for *The Israel Bible* were written by the following scholars:

Bereishit (Genesis):	Rabbi Tuly Weisz
Shemot (Exodus):	Rabbi Tuly Weisz
Vayikra (Leviticus):	Shira Schechter
Bamidbar (Numbers):	Shira Schechter
Devarim (Deuteronomy):	Shira Schechter
Yehoshua (Joshua):	Rabbi Shmuel Jablon
Shoftim (Judges):	Rabbi Shmuel Jablon
Shmuel (Samuel):	Rabbi Shmuel Jablon
Melachim (Kings):	Rabbi Shmuel Jablon
Yeshayahu (Isaiah):	Rabbi Yaakov Beasley
Yirmiyahu (Jeremiah):	Rabbi Yaakov Beasley
Yechezkel (Ezekiel):	Rabbi Yaakov Beasley
Trei Asar (Twelve Prophets):	Rabbi Yaakov Beasley
Tehillim (Psalms):	Rabbi Avi Baumol
Mishlei (Proverbs):	Ahuva Balofsky
Iyov (Job):	Alexander Jacob Tsykin
Shir Hashirim (Song of Songs):	Batya Markowitz
Rut (Ruth):	Rabbi Tuly Weisz
Eicha (Lamentations):	Rabbi Noam Shapiro
Kohelet (Ecclesiastes):	Batya Markowitz
Esther (Esther):	Batya Markowitz
Daniel (Daniel):	Batya Markowitz
Ezra v'Nechemya (Ezra and Nehemiah):	Josh Even-Chen
Divrei Hayamim (Chronicles):	Alexander Jacob Tsykin
Maps Editor:	Lorien Balofsky
Associate Editor:	Shira Schechter
Editor:	Rabbi Tuly Weisz
Production Management:	Avishai Magence
Commentary Editor:	Rabbi Alan Haber
Copy Editing:	Efrat Gross
Typesetting:	Estie Dishon
Cover Design:	Tani Bayer
Icon Design:	Eliyahu Misgav

Acknowledgements

Producing a *Tanakh* is a massive undertaking that requires a tremendous team of "wise students," as the Hebrew expression goes. *The Israel Bible* would never have seen the light of day without the herculean efforts of numerous contributors.

First and foremost, SHIRA SCHECHTER dedicated several years as associate editor of *The Israel Bible* and saw the project through from beginning till end. With a perfect balance of meticulousness and fear of Heaven, she carefully supervised all aspects of research, development, editing and production. Shira's innate appreciation for Hebrew grammar along with her sharp eye and love for the subject matter, can be felt on every page.

Thank you to the esteemed scholars who contributed their immense *Tanakh* knowledge to this groundbreaking initiative: RABBIS AVI BAUMOL, YAAKOV BEASLEY, SHMUEL JABLON and ALEXANDER JACOB TSYKIN, AHUVA BALOFSKY, JOSH EVEN-CHEN, and BATYA MARKOWITZ. The breadth of your *Torah* scholarship, along with your love for Israel, served as a constant inspiration.

I would like to thank the devoted staff of Israel365 for their vast and varied contributions to *The Israel Bible* in the five years since we naively asked each other, "How hard could it be to create a brand new *Tanakh*?"

First, to LORIEN BALOFSKY who was there in the beginning and designed the first versions of *The Israel Bible* along with many features of this volume, including the maps. And to all the other creative geniuses: MAAYAN HOFFMAN, TSIVYA FOX, ORLY GIBSON, SHLOMO VILE and ELISHEVA SOLOMON. To the brilliant strategic team SHIFRA GOLDMEIER, AYAL KELLMAN, STEVEN GOLDSTEIN, SIMONE SOMERS, GILA HALPERN, MAZZ WHITE and CLARINDA YUVIENCO. To the truth-seeking reporters and editors of Breaking Israel News, ABRA FORMAN, ELIYAHU ADAM BERKOWITZ, JONATHAN BENEDEK, RIVKAH LAMBERT ADLER and ELIANA RUDEE. And a special *yasher koach* to SHLOMO SCHREIBMAN whose acumen enabled this important effort to continue.

I would also like to acknowledge our "alumni" whose skills and personalities shaped *The Israel Bible* over the years: JILLIAN EZEKIEL, RACHAEL PLATT and ALIZA ABRAHAMOVITZ.

A major debt of gratitude is owed to my trusted friends and advisors ROBERT FROHLINGER, RAFI COHEN and ARIEL GOLDBERG, whose wise counsel continues to guide Israel365.

Thank you to the faculty of the Yeshiva for the Nations RABBIS SHIMON APISDORF, ELAN ADLER, YISHAI FLEISHER and MOSHE LICHTMAN who taught me a deep appreciation for *Eretz Yisrael* when I was his student, and SHARON NIV.

Teach for Israel made possible the research and writing of *The Israel Bible* and I would like to thank the board of directors for their years of friendship and encouragement: NOAM LIPSHITZ, SCOTT OSBORNE, MARC SINGER and DAVID SWAGGERTY.

I am indebted to the spiritual mentorship of RABBI SHLOMO RISKIN and DAVID NEKRUTMAN of the Center for Jewish Christian Understanding and Cooperation for their pioneering work and for contributing the foreward to *The Israel Bible*.

Thanks to RABBI BARRY SCHWARTZ and LEIF MILLIKEN for their assistance in providing the well respected New Jewish Publication Society English translation for inclusion in this volume.

In addition to its many unique features, *The Israel Bible* is the first *Tanakh* to be financed through crowdfunding. I can't thank enough the close to 1,000 contributors of our online campaign who enthusiastically supported our idea and waited patiently for its publication. While many Jews and non-Jews from all over the world eagerly participated with great generosity, a sincere thank you is to a special and humble friend of Israel from Nigeria. I am greatly appreciative of the gift in honor of EKPE NDIYO EKPE by his loving son.

Over the years, I have had many mentors, teachers and rabbis who deeply impacted me and taught me a love for *Torah*. I have been fortunate to benefit from many, yet would like to thank RABBI ZEVULUN CHARLOP, dean of the Rabbi Isaac Elchanan Theological Seminary for our private study sessions and his enthusiasm for my work in general and this initiative in particular.

I would like to acknowledge the influence of my two grandfathers, RABBI DAVID STAVSKY and GEORGE WEISZ, both of blessed memory. In very different ways, my grandfathers equally taught invaluable lessons of hard work and self-sacrifice on behalf of *Torah*. My grandmothers, PEPPI WEISZ and RUTH STAVSKY and ROSALIND DOMBROFF have assumed the role of beloved matriarchs to our family, and should be blessed with longevity.

My in-laws, RHONDA and DR. TOM WEISS, are like parents to me and have provided loving encouragement and much appreciated support. They should see much *"nachas"* from all their children and grandchildren.

I would like to thank my own precious children who were my real inspiration for *The Israel Bible*. Feeding off their wide-eyed enthusiasm in learning the holy words of the *Torah* in school – and in Hebrew no less – I felt invigorated to immerse myself in our ancient heritage. With eternal gratitude to *Hashem*, I am fortunate for the opportunity each day "to teach these words to my children," SHAINDEE, BELLA, DOVID, TZOFIA and AMITAI.

My ultimate thanks are reserved for my beloved wife, ABBY, for her steadfast support. Anything I have achieved is to her credit. Certainly, that is true for *The Israel Bible*, which only came about through her guiding our family to fulfilling our dream of making *aliyah*. May all the blessings that emerge from the study of *The Israel Bible* reward her with her innermost prayer: that our children always embrace the eternal values of the *Torah* of Israel.

Finally, all my colleagues in producing this volume join me in offering our profound thanksgiving to the Almighty for permitting us to help spread love for the Land and the People of Israel. May the God of Israel continue His blessings so that *The Israel Bible* shapes the minds and hearts of all His children for generations to come.

Naphtali "Tuly" Weisz
Ramat Beit Shemesh, Israel
Shevat 5778 / February 2018

PHABET CHART

3 ג **Gimel** 'G'	2 בּ **Vet** 'V'	2 בּ **Bet** 'B'	1 א **Aleph** Silent[1]
20 כ **Kaf** 'K'	10 י **Yud** 'Y'	9 ט **Tet** 'T'	8 ח **Chet** 'KH'
60 ס **Samekh** 'S'	50 ן **Final Nun** 'N'	50 נ **Nun** 'N'	40 ם **Final Mem** 'M'
200 ר **Raysh** 'R'	100 ק **Kuf** 'K'	90 ץ **Final Tzadi** 'TZ'	90 צ **Tzadi** 'TZ'

Vowels: The Aleph is silent[1] so we will use it in the example for each sound

אִ **Kheerik Khasayr** 'i' in igloo	אָ **Kamatz Katan**[3] 'o' in host	אַ **Patakh** 'a' in hurrah	אָ **Kamatz** 'a' in hurrah
אִי **Kheerik Malay** 'ee' in street	אֹ/אוֹ **Kholam** 'o' in host	אַי **Patakh + Yud** 'ai' in aisle	אָי **Kamatz + Yud** 'ai' in aisle

xii

Aleph Bet Chart

THE ISRAEL BIBLE	HEBREW AL		
7 **ז** Zayin 'Z'	6 **ו** Vav 'V'	5 **ה** Hay 'H'	4 **ד** Dalet 'D'
40 **מ** Mem 'M'	30 **ל** Lamed 'L'	20 **ך** Final Khaf 'KH'	20 **כ** Khaf 'KH'
80 **ף** Final Pey 'F'	80 **פ** Fay 'F'	80 **פּ** Pay 'P'	70 **ע** Ayin Silent[1]
400 **ת** Sav 'T'	400 **תּ** Tav 'T'	300 **שׂ** Sin 'S'	300 **שׁ** Shin 'SH'

Notes:

[1] If there is a vowel underneath the letter, the sound of the vowel is pronounced. If there is no vowel underneath, the letter remains silent.

[2] In Hebrew there are two types of Sh'vas. A sh'va na is considered a vowel and is pronounced. This is represented in our transliteration by the apostrophe (') and pronounced like the 'e' in father. The other sh'va, the sh'va nakh, indicates the end of a syllable. It does not have its own sound, and therefore no phonetic representation.

[3] A kamatz katan looks like a regular kamatz but is pronounced like a kholam.

[4] The Hebrew alphabet has a unique feature known as *gematriya*, in which every letter is assigned a numerical value.

Above each letter is its numeric value[4]

אוּ/אֻ Shuruk/Kubutz 'u' in junior	אֶ Segol 'e' in Edward
אְ Sh'va[2] ' (apostrophe)	אֵ Tzayray 'ay' in day

List of Weekly *Torah* Portions and their *Haftarot*

Every *Shabbat*, the weekly *Torah* portion, or *parasha*, is read out loud in the synagogue, as well as a related section from the *Neviim* (Prophets) known as the *haftarah*. Below is a list of the weekly *parshiot* and their corresponding *haftarot* according to Ashkenazi practice.

Torah Portion	Scope	Page Number	Haftarah	Page Number
The Book of Genesis				
Bereishit	Genesis 1:1–6:8	7	Isaiah 42:5–43:10	1028
Noach	Genesis 6:9–11:32	18	Isaiah 54:1–55:5	1050
Lech Lecha	Genesis 12:1–17:27	30	Isaiah 40:27–41:16	1025
Vayeira	Genesis 18:1–22:24	41	II Kings 4:1–37	887
Chayei Sara	Genesis 23:1–25:18	54	I Kings 1:1–31	805
Toldot	Genesis 25:19–28:9	62	Malachi 1:1–2:7	1465
Vayeitzei	Genesis 28:10–32:3	71	Hosea 12:13–14:10	1350
Vayishlach	Genesis 32:4–36:43	83	Obadiah 1:1–21	1383
Vayeishev	Genesis 37:1–40:23	95	Amos 2:6–3:8	1369
Mikeitz	Genesis 41:1–44:17	104	I Kings 3:15–4:1	814
Vayigash	Genesis 44:18–47:27	117	Ezekiel 37:15–28	1297
Vayechi	Genesis 47:28–50:26	125	I Kings 2:1–12	809
The Book of Exodus				
Shemot	Exodus 1:1–6:1	139	Isaiah 27:6–28:13, 29:22–23	998, 1004
Va'eira	Exodus 6:2–9:35	150	Ezekiel 28:25–29:21	1275
Bo	Exodus 10:1–13:16	161	Jeremiah 46:13–28	1184
Beshalach	Exodus 13:17–17:16	171	Judges 4:4–5:31	605
Yitro	Exodus 18:1–20:22	181	Isaiah 6:1–7:6, 9:5–6	964, 970
Mishpatim	Exodus 21:1–24:18	188	Jeremiah 34:8–22, 33:25–26	1157, 1156
Terumah	Exodus 25:1–27:19	197	I Kings 5:26–6:13	819
Tetzaveh	Exodus 27:20–30:10	205	Ezekiel 43:10–27	1313
Ki Tisa	Exodus 30:11–34:35	213	I Kings 18:1–39	861
Vayakhel	Exodus 35:1–38:20	225	I Kings 7:40–50	827
Pekudei	Exodus 38:21–40:38	235	I Kings 7:51–8:21	828

Torah Portion	Scope	Page Number	Haftarah	Page Number
The Book of Leviticus				
Vayikra	Leviticus 1:1–5:26	245	Isaiah 43:21–44:23	1031
Tzav	Leviticus 6:1–8:36	255	Jeremiah 7:21–8:3, 9:22–23	1093, 1098
Shemini	Leviticus 9:1–11:47	264	II Samuel 6:1–7:17	748
Tazria	Leviticus 12:1–13:59	271	II Kings 4:42–5:19	890
Metzora	Leviticus 14:1–15:33	277	II Kings 7:3–20	897
Acharei-Mot	Leviticus 16:1–18:30	285	Amos 9:7–15	1379
Kedoshim	Leviticus 19:1–20:27	292	Ezekiel 22:1–16	1258
Emor	Leviticus 21:1–24:23	298	Ezekiel 44:15–31	1317
Behar	Leviticus 25:1–26:2	310	Jeremiah 32:6–27	1151
Bechukotai	Leviticus 26:3–27:34	314	Jeremiah 16:19–17:14	1114
The Book of Numbers				
Bamidbar	Numbers 1:1–4:20	327	Hosea 2:1–22	1336
Naso	Numbers 4:21–7:89	339	Judges 13:2–25	631
Beha'alotcha	Numbers 8:1–12:16	352	Zechariah 2:14–4:7	1443
Shelach	Numbers 13:1–15:41	364	Joshua 2:1–24	533
Korach	Numbers 16:1–18:32	374	I Samuel 11:14–12:22	683
Chukat	Numbers 19:1–22:1	383	Judges 11:1–33	626
Balak	Numbers 22:2–25:9	391	Micah 5:6–6:8	1403
Pinchas	Numbers 25:10–30:1	399	I Kings 18:46–19:21	866
Matot	Numbers 30:2–32:42	412	Jeremiah 1:1–2:3	1077
Masei	Numbers 33:1–36:13	422	Jeremiah 2:4–28, 3:4	1078
The Book of Deuteronomy				
Devarim	Deuteronomy 1:1–3:22	437	Isaiah 1:1–27	955
Va'etchanan	Deuteronomy 3:23–7:11	446	Isaiah 40:1–26	1023
Eikev	Deuteronomy 7:12–11:25	457	Isaiah 49:14–51:3	1042
Re'eih	Deuteronomy 11:26–16:17	468	Isaiah 54:11–55:5	1051
Shoftim	Deuteronomy 16:18–21:9	481	Isaiah 51:12–52:12	1046
Ki Teitzei	Deuteronomy 21:10–25:19	490	Isaiah 54:1–10	1050
Ki Tavo	Deuteronomy 26:1–29:8	500	Isaiah 60:1–22	1060
Nitzavim	Deuteronomy 29:9–30:20	511	Isaiah 61:10–63:9	1063
Vayeilech	Deuteronomy 31:1–31:30	516	Hosea 14:2–10, Joel 2:11–27, Micah 7:18–20	1352, 1359, 1407
Ha'azinu	Deuteronomy 32:1–32:52	519	II Samuel 22:1–51	790
Vezot Haberachah	Deuteronomy 33:1–34:12	523	Joshua 1:1–18	531

List of *Torah* Readings for Special Occasions

In addition to *Shabbat*, the *Torah* is read out loud in the synagogue on holidays and other special occasions. Below is a list of *Torah* readings for special occasions as well as their corresponding *haftarot*. The *maftir* is a section of *Torah* read between the *parasha* and the *haftarah*. On a regular *Shabbat*, it consists of the last few verses of the week's *Torah* portion. On special occasions, it is often taken from a different section of the *Torah*.

Occasion	Torah Reading	Page Number	Maftir	Page Number	Haftarah	Page Number
Rosh Chodesh	Numbers 28:1–15	406				
Shabbat the day before Rosh Chodesh	Weekly *Parasha*		Weekly *Maftir*		I Samuel 20:18–42	709
Shabbat Rosh Chodesh	Weekly *Parasha*		Numbers 28:1–15	406	Isaiah 66:1–24	1070
Rosh Hashana – First Day	Genesis 21	49	Numbers 29:1–6	409	I Samuel 1:1–2:10	659
Rosh Hashana – Second Day	Genesis 22	51	Numbers 29:1–6	409	Jeremiah 31:1–19	1146
Yom Kippur – morning service	Leviticus 16	285	Numbers 29:7–11	410	Isaiah 57:14–58:4	1055
Yom Kippur – afternoon service	Leviticus 18	290			Book of Jonah	1389
Sukkot – First Day	Leviticus 22:26–23:44	302	Numbers 29:12–16	410	Zechariah 14:1–21	1459
Sukkot – Second Day	In Israel: Numbers 29:17–19 Outside of Israel: Leviticus 22:26–23:44	410, 302	Outside of Israel: Numbers 29:12–16	410	Outside of Israel: I Kings 8:2–21	828
Sukkot – Shabbat Chol Hamoed	Exodus 33:12–34:26	221	Day 1 – Numbers 29:17–22, Day 2 – Numbers 29:20–25, Day 4 – Numbers 29:26–31	410, 411, 411	Ezekiel 38:18–39:16	1301
Shemini Atzeret/ Simchat Torah	In Israel: Deuteronomy 33:1–34:12, Genesis 1:1–2:3 Outside of Israel: Deuteronomy 14:22–16:17	523, 7, 476	Numbers 29:35–30:1	412	In Israel: Joshua 1:1–18 Outside of Israel: I Kings 8:54–9:1	531, 833
Simchat Torah Outside of Israel	Deuteronomy 33:1–34:12, Genesis 1:1–2:3	523, 7	Numbers 29:35–30:1	412	Joshua 1:1–18	531
Shabbat Chanuka (1)	Weekly *Parasha*		Numbers 7:1–53	346	Zechariah 2:14–4:7	1443
Shabbat Chanuka (2)	Weekly *Parasha*		Numbers 7:54–8:4	350	I Kings 7:40–50	827
Parashat Shekalim	Weekly *Parasha*		Exodus 30:11–16	213	II Kings 11:17–12:17	911

Occasion	Torah Reading	Page Number	Maftir	Page Number	Haftarah	Page Number
Parashat Shekalim/ Rosh Chodesh	First 6 aliyot – Weekly Parasha, Seventh aliyah – Numbers 28:9–15	407	Exodus 30:11–16	213	II Kings 11:17–12:17	911
Parashat Zachor	Weekly Parasha		Deuteronomy 25:17–19	499	I Samuel 15:1–34	692
Purim	Exodus 17:8–16	180				
Parashat Parah	Weekly Parasha		Numbers 19:1–22	383	Ezekiel 36:16–38	1294
Parashat Hachodesh	Weekly Parasha		Exodus 12:1–20	165	Ezekiel 45:16–46:18	1320
Parashat Hachodesh/ Rosh Chodesh	First 6 aliyot – Weekly Parasha, Seventh aliyah – Numbers 28:9–15	407	Exodus 12:1–20	165	Ezekiel 45:16–46:18	1320
Shabbat Hagadol	Weekly Parasha		Regular weekly Maftir		Malachi 3:4–24	1468
Pesach – First Day	Exodus 12:21–51	167	Numbers 28:16–25	408	Joshua 3:5–7, 5:2–6:1, 6:27	536, 539, 544
Pesach – Second Day	In Israel: Leviticus 22:26–23:44, Numbers 28:19–25 Outside of Israel: Leviticus 22:26–23:44	302, 408, 302	Outside of Israel: Numbers 28:16–25	408	Outside of Israel: II Kings 23:1–9, 21–25	941, 944
Pesach – Shabbat Chol Hamoed	Exodus 33:12–34:26	221	Numbers 28:19–25	408	Ezekiel 37:1–14	1296
Pesach – Seventh Day	Exodus 13:17–15:26	171	Numbers 28:19–25	408	II Samuel 22:1–51	790
Outside of Israel – Pesach – Eighth Day (Weekday)	Deuteronomy 15:19–16:17	478	Numbers 28:19–25	408	Isaiah 10:32:-12:6	974
Outside of Israel – Pesach – Eighth Day (Shabbat)	Deuteronomy 14:22–16:17	476	Numbers 28:19–25	408	Isaiah 10:32:-12:6	974
Shavuot	Exodus 19:1–20:23	183	Numbers 28:26–31	409	Ezekiel 1:1–28, 3:12	1211, 1215
Shavuot – Second Day outside of Israel (Weekday)	Deuteronomy 15:19–16:17	478	Numbers 28:26–31	409	Habakkuk 2:20–3:19	1422
Shavuot – Second Day outside of Israel (Shabbat)	Deuteronomy 14:22–16:17	476	Numbers 28:26–31	409	Habakkuk 2:20–3:19	1422
Tisha B'Av – morning	Deuteronomy 4:25–40	449			Jeremiah 8:13–9:23	1096
Tisha B'Av – afternoon	Exodus 32:11–14, 34:1–10	217			Isaiah 55:6–56:8	1052

Introduction

The Hebrew Bible is commonly known as the *Tanakh* which stands for *Torah* (the Five Books of Moses), *Neviim* (the Prophets) and *Ketuvim* (the Writings). The *Tanakh* consists of 24 books that are considered by Jews to be the word of God. While these books have been referred to as the "Old Testament," many Jews reject this label since it implies the replacement of the Hebrew Bible with something newer and prefer the more authentic Jewish name.

The *Tanakh* is not only the most important book known to man, it is God's word that is perfect and absolute. It is therefore a daunting undertaking to publish an edition of the *Tanakh*, and the responsibilities are awesome. There is no room for error or carelessness in dealing with the eternal word of God. Further, upon embarking on such a serious initiative, we ask ourselves if our efforts are gratuitous. Considering the many editions of the Bible in print, is there truly a need for yet another one?

While there are numerous Bibles in circulation today, its most central aspect – the Land of Israel – has often been overlooked. References to Israel appear on nearly every page, and the city of Jerusalem is specifically referred to hundreds of times throughout the Bible. The essential link between Israel and *Torah* is emphasized repeatedly in verses such as, "For instruction (*Torah*) shall come forth from *Tzion*, the word of *Hashem* from *Yerushalayim*" (Micah 4:2).

The miraculous return of the People of Israel to the Land of Israel in our own generation provides the perfect moment for a new volume to fill this void in biblical literature. The Israel Bible includes many special features elucidating God's focus on Israel throughout *Tanakh* and there are many additional, multimedia features available on our website **www.theisraelbible.com**.

Ordering and Presentation – In presenting *The Israel Bible*, our goal is to spread awareness of the biblical significance of the Land of Israel as well as the Jewish people's eternal connection to the land, based on the text of the *Tanakh*, the Hebrew Bible. We aim to honor "the God, the People and the Land of Israel" from an Orthodox Jewish perspective. To that end, *The Israel Bible* follows the traditional Jewish ordering of the books and the customary Hebrew division of chapters. Therefore, for example, we count 24 books of *Tanakh* with *Sefer Divrei Hayamim* (Chronicles) appearing last. It is our hope that our rich content will speak to all Jews and non-Jews who appreciate Israel as the God given land of the Jewish people.

English Translation – Throughout history, Jews have studied the Bible in Hebrew, as any form of translation would miss much of the nuance of the original holy tongue in which *Torah* has been transmitted since the days of Moses. However, as many Jews settled in America in the 19th Century, the need for an English translation became necessary. To be sure, there were already English translations prepared over the centuries by Christians, but in the words of the original editors of the Jewish Publication Society (JPS), "The Jew cannot afford to have his Bible translation prepared for him by others. He cannot have it as a gift, even as he cannot borrow his soul from others."

JPS set out in the late 1800s to publish an authoritative English translation "in the spirit of Jewish tradition." It was compiled over decades by some of the leading Jewish scholars of the time. They formed committees and subcommittees to compare existing English versions, considering medieval and modern Jewish commentators. The monumental JPS translation, originally published in 1917, has been updated in recent years, and *The Israel Bible* is proud to utilize the 1984 New Jewish Publication Society (NJPS) version with its modern, clear language, as well as its wide-ranging acceptance as an accurate and high-quality translation. We applied the NJPS translation verbatim, except for a select list of nouns which we replaced with their traditional Hebrew names. This is true even when we found the NJPS translation to be different than the popular translation of a word or phrase and when the NJPS switched the order of the text for the sake of clarity (see, for example, Ezekiel 24:22–24).

Hebrew Transliteration – To give our readers an authentic *Tanakh* experience, every verse that has commentary is transliterated from Hebrew into English. The Hebrew alphabet chart includes our standards for transliteration and pronunciation of Hebrew verses, enabling readers of *The Israel Bible* to decipher key biblical passages in the holy language. Readers can hear the entire Bible read in Hebrew on our website **www.theisraelbible.com**.

There are various standards when it comes to transliterating Hebrew words into English letters. While we have relied primarily on the classical Hebrew transliteration, we have occasionally deviated for the sake of simplicity, clarity and to reflect common usage.

In addition to whole verses, we have also transliterated many proper nouns in the English translation so that our readers can learn the names of key biblical figures and locations in their Hebrew form. As a rule, we chose to transliterate names of people that were central in the establishment and functioning of the nation of Israel, as well as significant places in the Holy Land. Therefore, regarding Adam's sons, for example, only *Shet* (Seth) is transliterated since it was from him that *Noach* (Noah), and ultimately *Avraham* (Abraham), descended. For this reason, there might be verses or sections of *The Israel Bible* that contains multiple names and only some of them are transliterated.

For the same reason, we have transliterated the names of the books of *Tanakh* when referring to them in our introductions and commentary. When referencing a specific chapter or verse, however, we use the English names of the books in our citations for clarity. We also transliterated ideas and concepts that are central to Judaism such as *Shabbat* (Sabbath), the names of the Jewish holidays and the *Beit Hamikdash* (Temple), as well as biblical measurements. Finally, the name of God is transliterated. Out of respect, Orthodox Jews generally refer to the Lord as *Hashem*, which literally means 'the Name.' Referring to God as *Hashem* reminds us that we feel close to Him but also recognize our distance at the same time. To stress this moniker, we transliterated both the Tetragrammaton as well as the name *Elohim* as *Hashem*.

Study Notes – Our unique commentary was compiled by Orthodox Jewish scholars who live in Israel. It is an anthology in the sense that most of the commentary is not original, but draws from traditional teachings of early Jewish Sages and modern rabbinic commentators. We also include quotations from individuals who have played a significant part in the past century of modern Israeli history including Israeli prime ministers, poets and military leaders.

Our commentary can be broken into four categories, three of which are identified by an icon at the beginning of the study note:

 Israel lessons are indicated with an icon bearing the map of Israel and focus on the Land of Israel and the modern State of Israel.

 Jewish lessons are indicated with a *Torah* scroll and teach a concept in Judaism or a classic idea from rabbinic thought.

 Hebrew lessons are represented by an icon bearing the letter *aleph* and focus on the meaning of a Hebrew word or phrase.

All other comments are considered general comments and are not assigned an icon.

Supplemental Material – In addition to our unique translation and original commentary, *The Israel Bible* offers supplementary material to enrich the learning experience of our readers. Before every book of *Tanakh*, we provide an introduction, as well as information, generally in the form of a map, a chart or a list, which is central to the specific book.

Maps – As the purpose of *The Israel Bible* is to highlight the biblical significance of the Land of Israel, significant time was spent researching and preparing maps to bring the physical contours of the holy land to life with great accuracy. However, since there is a lack of information regarding the precise locations of certain ancient cities, some of the places on our maps are approximate or subject to debate. In these cases, we followed the opinion that we are most comfortable with, but acknowledge that there is room for disagreement. We continue to produce new maps, which are available on our website **www.theisraelbible.com/maps**.

Torah Readings – The *Torah* is not just a work that is studied privately, it is also read out loud in synagogue. Every *Shabbat* and holiday a portion of the *Torah* is read, as well as a related section from *Neviim*, the prophets, called the *haftarah*. We included the blessings recited before and after the reading of the *Torah*, a list of the weekly *Torah* portions and their corresponding *haftarot*, and a chart of the *Torah* readings for special days with their corresponding *haftarot*. Readers can always find the current week's *Torah* portion by visiting **www.theisraelbible.com/weekly-torah-portion**. In this volume, we indicate where a new *Torah* portion begins by highlighting the Hebrew verse number with a gray box so readers can follow along with the communal

Torah readings. Furthermore, we have included prayers for the State of Israel and the soldiers of the Israel Defense Forces (IDF) that are generally recited following the *Torah* reading in synagogue. It is our constant prayer that God watch over the State of Israel and the members of the IDF, who defend Israel every hour of every day.

In 1948, the State of Israel was created providing a modern answer to Isaiah's ancient question, "Is a nation born all at once?" (Isaiah 66:8). *The Israel Bible* was first published in the 70th year of God's miraculous restoration of the People of Israel to the Land of Israel. Jewish wisdom teaches that 70 is a significant number: *Moshe* (Moses) translated the *Torah* into 70 languages for all 70 nations of the world. From our very origins, the Jewish people were meant to be a light unto the 70 nations, spreading God's truth to the masses.

In the seven decades since the modern rebirth of the State of Israel, God's plan has been unfolding with unprecedented speed, dramatic highs and heartbreaking lows. Never has Israel been at the forefront of the world's attention as it is in our generation. Efforts to vilify the Jewish State seem to spread every day across the globe. At the same time, so does the growing movement of millions of non-Jewish biblical Zionists who stand with the nation of Israel as an expression of their commitment to God's word. As we seek to understand the clash of these two conflicting worldviews, the need for *The Israel Bible* has never been so important.

Standing on the great shoulders of those who came before us and emanating from the land that has always served as the birthplace for the Bible, we conclude with a heartfelt prayer: May the Almighty bless our efforts in offering this *Tanakh* to influence the hearts, minds and actions of its readers. In this way, it is our hope to spread God's name so that the publication of *The Israel Bible* brings us one step closer to the final redemption of Israel and the entire world.

Rabbi Tuly Weisz
Editor, *The Israel Bible*

Foreword

The mandate to study God's word daily is interestingly not found in the Five Books of Moses (Pentateuch), but rather in the first book of our prophetic writings: "Let not this Book of the Teaching cease from your lips, but recite it day and night, so that you may observe faithfully all that is written in it. Only then will you prosper in your undertakings and only then will you be successful" (Joshua 1:8). Charged with bringing the Israelites into the land covenantally promised to Abraham, Isaac and Jacob, God ensures Joshua of His protection if the nation observes His ways as dictated in the Divine constitution known as the Torah.

In Jewish tradition, Joshua (1:8) is directly linked with Deuteronomy (11:14), "You shall gather in your new grain and wine, and oil."[1] Our Sages deduced from this scriptural combination the importance of merging *Torah* study with a profession. Completely dedicating oneself to the study of *Torah* without having the financial means to sustain this lifestyle can lead one to eventually straying from observance of God's will. Poverty and crime can have an intimate relationship.

We must also be careful that our work does not affect our daily study of Scripture. The addiction of becoming a workaholic and not making *Torah* study a priority can also lead one into temptations that can violate our personal relationship with Him as well as our fellow human beings. The goal is to achieve a healthy balance between our study of God's word and our daily work.

The Deuteronomic verse quoted above is part of the second section of the Shema[2] that discusses the concept of reward and punishment. Sanctifying God by fulfilling His commandments results in the Land of Israel practically benefitting from rains that occur in the right season and reaping the abundance

---

1. Talmud Bavli Berachot 35b
2. Consisting of three sections within the Five Books of Moses (Deut. 6:4–8; 11:13–22 and Numbers 15:37–42), the *Shema* is proclamation of accepting God's Kingdom in our lives, loyalty to His commandments and remembering His redemptive act of liberating us from Egypt. Jews recite the *Shema* twice a day as stated in Deut. 6:7.

from the fields. However, if the nation follows pagan gods and practices, the consequences are devastating – famine and death. The Land of Israel is intrinsically linked with the keeping of the *Torah*. Covenant Land comes with covenant responsibility.

Born into slavery, Joshua is now leading His people into the Promised Land. More than 500 years separates him from his ancestral forefather Abraham. The historical narratives that took place between Abraham leaving everything behind to follow God in Genesis 12 and the death of Moses in the last chapter of Deuteronomy are filled with intrigue, suspense, joy, sorrow and hope. What began as a family is now a nation actualizing its mission to be a kingdom of priests to the world. However, for the Israelites to succeed in the Land of Israel, they must see the *Torah* as the only compass to direct their lives.

The biblical episodes after our first entry into the land are well known. Our ancestors' triumphs and sins are all on public record. We learned the harsh reality of Leviticus (18:28) "So let not the land spew you out for defiling it as it spewed out the nation that came before you." Twice, we lost the privilege to be stewards of the Land of Israel and to fulfill our nation state mandate to be a light to the world. However, when the annals of history were ready to archive the Jewish people after the Holocaust, God kept His covenantal promise and gathered us from the four corners of the globe to come home. The year 1948 was a game changer. Biblical prophecies were and are being realized. We are now living in the birth pangs of the messianic era.

In our morning prayers, we recite a series of blessings over the *Torah* that include petitioning God to have a sweet tooth for His word, to study it without any ulterior motive and to have Him to teach it to us. They are some congregations that invoke the following liturgical prayer after the completion of these blessings: *May the Torah be my faith and El Shaddai my help. Blessed be the name of His glorious kingdom forever and all time.*

According to Jewish tradition, the neglect of not blessing the *Torah* before engaging in its study was one of the reasons for the destruction of the Temple.[3] This is deduced from the redundancy of words in Jeremiah (9:12) that talks about Israel not following God: "…Because they forsook the teaching I had set before them. They did not obey Me and they did not follow it [did not make a blessing before studying it]." Our inability to properly cherish God's greatest gift to the world, the *Torah*, led to our eventual exile from our land.

---

3. Babylonian Talmud Nedarim 81a

On Israel's Independence Day, Jews around the world recite Psalms 113–118 to express our gratitude to God for His Divine hand in helping establish the State of Israel. We have learned from our past and realize the privilege to see firsthand the land, people and Torah operating all together in our generation.

When Rabbi Tuly Weisz approached me about his intent to publish *The Israel Bible* that would highlight commentary about the special relationship between the land and people, I saw this project as another way to publicly demonstrate our appreciation to God for having the State of Israel. In addition, it is another educational tool to ensure biblical literacy. If we are to truly enjoy the Land of Israel, it is incumbent upon us to continually study the *Torah*. Isaiah once prophesied that the Jewish people would return to Zion with songs, "crowned with everlasting joy" (35:10). *The Israel Bible* provides us the lyrical content to express our joy in living in the land that God calls holy.

Rabbi Shlomo Riskin
Chief Rabbi of Efrat
Founder of the Center for Jewish-Christian
Understanding & Cooperation (CJCUC)

Blessing Before Reading the *Torah*:

The one who has been called up to the *Torah* says:

| Bless *Hashem*, the one who is blessed | ba-r'-KHU et a-do-NAI ham-vo-RAKH | בָּרְכוּ אֶת יְיָ הַמְבֹרָךְ |

The Congregation responds:

| Blessed is *Hashem*, the one who is blessed, for all eternity | ba-RUKH a-do-NAI ham-vo-RAKH l'-o-LAM va-ED | בָּרוּךְ יְיָ הַמְבֹרָךְ לְעוֹלָם וָעֶד |

The one who has been called up to the *Torah* continues:

Blessed is *Hashem*, the one who is blessed, for all eternity	ba-RUKH a-do-NAI ham-vo-RAKH l'-o-LAM va-ED	בָּרוּךְ יְיָ הַמְבֹרָךְ לְעוֹלָם וָעֶד
Blessed are you, *Hashem*	ba-RUKH a-TAH a-do-NAI	בָּרוּךְ אַתָּה יְיָ
Our God, King of the universe	e-lo-HAY-nu ME-lekh ha-o-LAM	אֱלֹהֵינוּ מֶלֶךְ הָעוֹלָם
Who has chosen us	a-SHER BA-khar BA-nu	אֲשֶׁר בָּחַר בָּנוּ
From among all the nations	mi-KOL ha-a-MEEM	מִכָּל הָעַמִּים
And has given us	v'-NA-tan LA-nu	וְנָתַן לָנוּ
His *Torah*	et to-ra-TO	אֶת תּוֹרָתוֹ
Blessed are you, *Hashem*	ba-RUKH a-TAH a-do-NAI	בָּרוּךְ אַתָּה יְיָ
Giver of the *Torah*	no-TAYN ha-to-RAH	נוֹתֵן הַתּוֹרָה

Blessing After Reading the *Torah*:

Blessed are you, *Hashem*	ba-RUKH a-TAH a-do-NAI	בָּרוּךְ אַתָּה יְיָ
Our God, King of the universe	e-lo-HAY-nu ME-lekh ha-o-LAM	אֱלֹהֵינוּ מֶלֶךְ הָעוֹלָם
Who has given us	a-SHER NA-tan LA-nu	אֲשֶׁר נָתַן לָנוּ
The *Torah* of truth	to-RAT e-MET	תּוֹרַת אֱמֶת
And planted eternal life within us	v'-kha-YAY o-LAM na-TA b'-to-KHAY-nu	וְחַיֵּי עוֹלָם נָטַע בְּתוֹכֵנוּ
Blessed are you, *Hashem*	ba-RUKH a-TAH a-do-NAI	בָּרוּךְ אַתָּה יְיָ
Giver of the *Torah*	no-TAYN ha-to-RAH	נוֹתֵן הַתּוֹרָה

THE ISRAEL BIBLE
™

Sefer Bereishit
The Book of Genesis

Introduction and commentary by Rabbi Tuly Weisz

Sefer Bereishit (Genesis) is the first of the Five Books of *Moshe*. *Sefer Bereishit* begins with a detailed description of the creation of the world, and continues with a brief account of the generations from *Adam* through *Avraham*. The remainder of the book focuses on the lives of the matriarchs and patriarchs, culminating with the story of the departure of the family of *Yaakov* from the land of Israel and their descent to Egypt.

Rabbi Shlomo Yitzchaki, the famed medieval commentator known by his acronym *Rashi*, asks a compelling question. If the *Torah* is essentially a book of law, why did God choose to start it with the stories of creation? Would it not have made more sense to begin with the first commandment given to the Jewish people? Quoting the verse from *Sefer Tehillim* (Psalms 111:6), "He revealed to His people His powerful works, in giving them the heritage of nations." *Rashi* explains that the Lord began His *Torah* with the account of the creation of the world in order to give the People of Israel a response to anyone who would accuse them of stealing the Land of Israel: Since *Hashem* is the Creator of the world, it is His prerogative to give it to whomever He chooses. Though He initially gave it to the seven nations of Canaan, when they were no longer worthy He chose to take it from them and to give it to the Children of Israel.

This theme of choice and choosing is present throughout the book. *Sefer Bereishit* is known as the book of creation. Most obviously, this refers to the description of the creation of the world, but beyond that it is about the creation of a people, the nation chosen by *Hashem* to be His representatives in the world and to carry out His mission of being a light unto the nations. In every generation described in *Sefer Bereishit*, there is a person or a group that stands out from the rest, and is chosen by God due to their morality and recognition of God. Once a person is chosen, the continuation of the narrative focuses on him and his offspring, often emphasizing their positive qualities. Thus, *Shet* is the chosen son of *Adam*, *Noach* is chosen to survive his entire generation, and the Bible then focuses on the descendants of

Noach's son *Shem*. Ultimately, *Hashem* chooses *Avraham*, his son *Yitzchak* and *Yitzchak*'s son *Yaakov*. With *Yaakov*, the process of choosing is complete and a nation is born.

As *Rashi* implies, the *Torah* is much more than a book of laws; it is the legacy of the Jewish people. It tells of the creation of a nation, chosen by God to be His emissaries of kindness, justice, goodness and recognition of the one true Creator. It starts with the creation of the world so that there would be no question that *Eretz Yisrael* belongs to them. From the very beginning of the world, *Hashem* intended for the People of Israel to be holy, to do His holy work in the holy Land of Israel, and from there, for their light to emanate to the entire world. May our study of *Sefer Bereishit* strengthen the chosenness within each of us and our appreciation for *Eretz Yisrael*.

Map of *Avraham's* Journey

This map features *Avraham*'s journey to, and throughout, the Promised Land, as described in *Sefer Bereishit* (11:31–23:20).

1. *Avraham* is born in Ur of the Chaldeans (Genesis 11:26–31).
2. From Ur of the Chaldeans, *Avraham* travels with his family to Haran (Genesis 11:31–32).
3. From Haran, Avraham travels to Canaan, where he builds an altar to God in **Shechem** (Genesis 12:6–7).
4. In **Beit El**, Avraham builds an altar to God and calls out in His name (Genesis 12:8).
5. *Avraham* travels to Egypt in order to escape famine in Canaan (Genesis 12:10–20).
6. Upon returning from Egypt, Avraham moves to **Elonei Mamre**, just north of Chevron (Genesis 13:18).
7. *Avraham* moves once again and settles in Gerar (Genesis 20:1).
8. In **Be'er Sheva**, Avraham plants a tree and again calls out in God's name. He returns to Be'er Sheva after the binding of Isaac (Genesis 22:19).
9. When Sarah dies, Avraham buys the Cave of Machpelah, in **Chevron**, as a burial plot (Genesis 23:1–20).

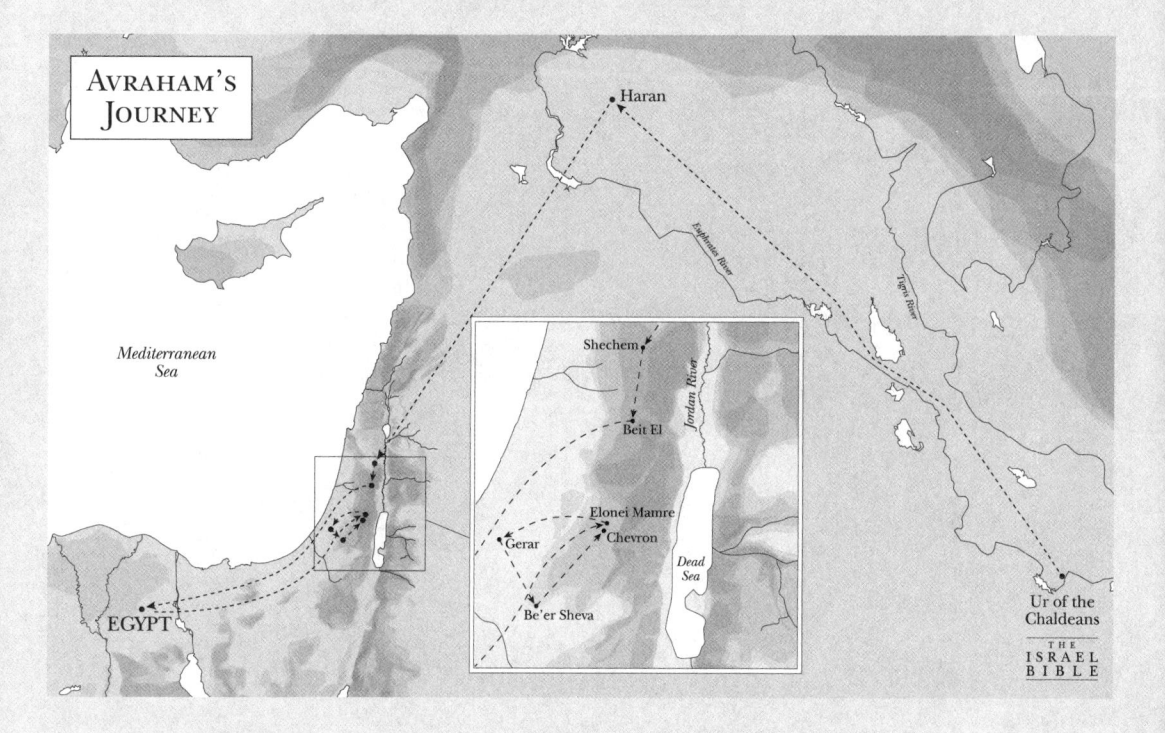

Bereishit/Genesis 1
Bereishit

בראשית א
בראשית

1:1 When *Hashem* began to create heaven and earth –

בְּרֵאשִׁ֖ית בָּרָ֣א אֱלֹהִ֑ים אֵ֥ת הַשָּׁמַ֖יִם וְאֵ֥ת הָאָֽרֶץ׃ א

b'-ray-SHEET ba-RA e-lo-HEEM AYT ha-sha-MA-yim v'-AYT ha-A-retz

2 the earth being unformed and void, with darkness over the surface of the deep and a wind from *Hashem* sweeping over the water –

וְהָאָ֗רֶץ הָיְתָ֥ה תֹ֙הוּ֙ וָבֹ֔הוּ וְחֹ֖שֶׁךְ עַל־פְּנֵ֣י תְה֑וֹם וְר֣וּחַ אֱלֹהִ֔ים מְרַחֶ֖פֶת עַל־פְּנֵ֥י הַמָּֽיִם׃ ב

3 *Hashem* said, "Let there be light"; and there was light.

וַיֹּ֥אמֶר אֱלֹהִ֖ים יְהִ֣י א֑וֹר וַֽיְהִי־אֽוֹר׃ ג

4 *Hashem* saw that the light was good, and *Hashem* separated the light from the darkness.

וַיַּ֧רְא אֱלֹהִ֛ים אֶת־הָא֖וֹר כִּי־ט֑וֹב וַיַּבְדֵּ֣ל אֱלֹהִ֔ים בֵּ֥ין הָא֖וֹר וּבֵ֥ין הַחֹֽשֶׁךְ׃ ד

5 *Hashem* called the light Day, and the darkness He called Night. And there was evening and there was morning, a first day.

וַיִּקְרָ֨א אֱלֹהִ֤ים ׀ לָאוֹר֙ י֔וֹם וְלַחֹ֖שֶׁךְ קָ֣רָא לָ֑יְלָה וַֽיְהִי־עֶ֥רֶב וַֽיְהִי־בֹ֖קֶר י֥וֹם אֶחָֽד׃ ה

6 *Hashem* said, "Let there be an expanse in the midst of the water, that it may separate water from water."

וַיֹּ֣אמֶר אֱלֹהִ֔ים יְהִ֥י רָקִ֖יעַ בְּת֣וֹךְ הַמָּ֑יִם וִיהִ֣י מַבְדִּ֔יל בֵּ֥ין מַ֖יִם לָמָֽיִם׃ ו

7 *Hashem* made the expanse, and it separated the water which was below the expanse from the water which was above the expanse. And it was so.

וַיַּ֣עַשׂ אֱלֹהִים֮ אֶת־הָרָקִיעַ֒ וַיַּבְדֵּ֗ל בֵּ֤ין הַמַּ֙יִם֙ אֲשֶׁר֙ מִתַּ֣חַת לָרָקִ֔יעַ וּבֵ֣ין הַמַּ֔יִם אֲשֶׁ֖ר מֵעַ֣ל לָרָקִ֑יעַ וַֽיְהִי־כֵֽן׃ ז

8 *Hashem* called the expanse Sky. And there was evening and there was morning, a second day.

וַיִּקְרָ֧א אֱלֹהִ֛ים לָֽרָקִ֖יעַ שָׁמָ֑יִם וַֽיְהִי־עֶ֥רֶב וַֽיְהִי־בֹ֖קֶר י֥וֹם שֵׁנִֽי׃ ח

9 *Hashem* said, "Let the water below the sky be gathered into one area, that the dry land may appear." And it was so.

וַיֹּ֣אמֶר אֱלֹהִ֗ים יִקָּו֨וּ הַמַּ֜יִם מִתַּ֤חַת הַשָּׁמַ֙יִם֙ אֶל־מָק֣וֹם אֶחָ֔ד וְתֵרָאֶ֖ה הַיַּבָּשָׁ֑ה וַֽיְהִי־כֵֽן׃ ט

10 *Hashem* called the dry land Earth, and the gathering of waters He called Seas. And *Hashem* saw that this was good.

וַיִּקְרָ֨א אֱלֹהִ֤ים ׀ לַיַּבָּשָׁה֙ אֶ֔רֶץ וּלְמִקְוֵ֥ה הַמַּ֖יִם קָרָ֣א יַמִּ֑ים וַיַּ֥רְא אֱלֹהִ֖ים כִּי־טֽוֹב׃ י

"Heaven and Earth" – Dead Sea landscape

1:1 When *Hashem* began to create heaven and earth If the Bible is essentially a book of law, why does it begin with stories of Genesis? Would it not make more sense to skip the stories and start with the legal sections of the *Torah*? Rashi, the famed medieval commentator, answers this question with an essential lesson that should inform our reading of the entire *Tanakh*. According to *Rashi*, one day the nations of the world would accuse the Jewish People of stealing *Eretz Yisrael*. In response, the Jews will point to the *Torah* which begins by telling us that God created the heaven and the earth. Since *Hashem* is the Creator of the world, He may give the land to whomever He wishes, and it is the divine will that the Land of Israel will belong to the People of Israel.

1:1 When *Hashem* began The first word in the *Torah* is *Bereishit* (בראשית), which begins with the letter *bet* (ב), while the last word in the *Torah* is *Yisrael* (ישראל), 'Israel,' which ends with the letter *lamed* (ל). Together, these two letters spell the word *lev* (לב), which means 'heart' in Hebrew. The first lesson hinted at in the very first letter of the *Tanakh* is that *Torah* is the heart of the People of Israel, and the ultimate expression of *Hashem's* love for us. By studying the *Torah*, from the first letter through the last, we can access the 'heart' of *Hashem*.

לב
ישראל
בראשית

Bereishit/Genesis 1
Bereishit

בראשית א
בראשית

11 And *Hashem* said, "Let the earth sprout vegetation: seed-bearing plants, fruit trees of every kind on earth that bear fruit with the seed in it." And it was so.

יא וַיֹּאמֶר אֱלֹהִים תַּדְשֵׁא הָאָרֶץ דֶּשֶׁא עֵשֶׂב מַזְרִיעַ זֶרַע עֵץ פְּרִי עֹשֶׂה פְּרִי לְמִינוֹ אֲשֶׁר זַרְעוֹ־בוֹ עַל־הָאָרֶץ וַיְהִי־כֵן:

12 The earth brought forth vegetation: seed-bearing plants of every kind, and trees of every kind bearing fruit with the seed in it. And *Hashem* saw that this was good.

יב וַתּוֹצֵא הָאָרֶץ דֶּשֶׁא עֵשֶׂב מַזְרִיעַ זֶרַע לְמִינֵהוּ וְעֵץ עֹשֶׂה־פְּרִי אֲשֶׁר זַרְעוֹ־בוֹ לְמִינֵהוּ וַיַּרְא אֱלֹהִים כִּי־טוֹב:

13 And there was evening and there was morning, a third day.

יג וַיְהִי־עֶרֶב וַיְהִי־בֹקֶר יוֹם שְׁלִישִׁי:

14 *Hashem* said, "Let there be lights in the expanse of the sky to separate day from night; they shall serve as signs for the set times – the days and the years;

יד וַיֹּאמֶר אֱלֹהִים יְהִי מְאֹרֹת בִּרְקִיעַ הַשָּׁמַיִם לְהַבְדִּיל בֵּין הַיּוֹם וּבֵין הַלָּיְלָה וְהָיוּ לְאֹתֹת וּלְמוֹעֲדִים וּלְיָמִים וְשָׁנִים:

15 and they serve as lights in the expanse of the sky to shine upon the earth." And it was so.

טו וְהָיוּ לִמְאוֹרֹת בִּרְקִיעַ הַשָּׁמַיִם לְהָאִיר עַל־הָאָרֶץ וַיְהִי־כֵן:

16 *Hashem* made the two great lights, the greater light to dominate the day and the lesser light to dominate the night, and the stars.

טז וַיַּעַשׂ אֱלֹהִים אֶת־שְׁנֵי הַמְּאֹרֹת הַגְּדֹלִים אֶת־הַמָּאוֹר הַגָּדֹל לְמֶמְשֶׁלֶת הַיּוֹם וְאֶת־הַמָּאוֹר הַקָּטֹן לְמֶמְשֶׁלֶת הַלַּיְלָה וְאֵת הַכּוֹכָבִים:

17 And *Hashem* set them in the expanse of the sky to shine upon the earth,

יז וַיִּתֵּן אֹתָם אֱלֹהִים בִּרְקִיעַ הַשָּׁמָיִם לְהָאִיר עַל־הָאָרֶץ:

18 to dominate the day and the night, and to separate light from darkness. And *Hashem* saw that this was good.

יח וְלִמְשֹׁל בַּיּוֹם וּבַלַּיְלָה וּלֲהַבְדִּיל בֵּין הָאוֹר וּבֵין הַחֹשֶׁךְ וַיַּרְא אֱלֹהִים כִּי־טוֹב:

19 And there was evening and there was morning, a fourth day.

יט וַיְהִי־עֶרֶב וַיְהִי־בֹקֶר יוֹם רְבִיעִי:

20 *Hashem* said, "Let the waters bring forth swarms of living creatures, and birds that fly above the earth across the expanse of the sky."

כ וַיֹּאמֶר אֱלֹהִים יִשְׁרְצוּ הַמַּיִם שֶׁרֶץ נֶפֶשׁ חַיָּה וְעוֹף יְעוֹפֵף עַל־הָאָרֶץ עַל־פְּנֵי רְקִיעַ הַשָּׁמָיִם:

21 *Hashem* created the great sea monsters, and all the living creatures of every kind that creep, which the waters brought forth in swarms, and all the winged birds of every kind. And *Hashem* saw that this was good.

כא וַיִּבְרָא אֱלֹהִים אֶת־הַתַּנִּינִם הַגְּדֹלִים וְאֵת כָּל־נֶפֶשׁ הַחַיָּה הָרֹמֶשֶׂת אֲשֶׁר שָׁרְצוּ הַמַּיִם לְמִינֵהֶם וְאֵת כָּל־עוֹף כָּנָף לְמִינֵהוּ וַיַּרְא אֱלֹהִים כִּי־טוֹב:

22 *Hashem* blessed them, saying, "Be fertile and increase, fill the waters in the seas, and let the birds increase on the earth."

כב וַיְבָרֶךְ אֹתָם אֱלֹהִים לֵאמֹר פְּרוּ וּרְבוּ וּמִלְאוּ אֶת־הַמַּיִם בַּיַּמִּים וְהָעוֹף יִרֶב בָּאָרֶץ:

23 And there was evening and there was morning, a fifth day.

כג וַיְהִי־עֶרֶב וַיְהִי־בֹקֶר יוֹם חֲמִישִׁי:

Bereishit/Genesis 2
Bereishit

24 *Hashem* said, "Let the earth bring forth every kind of living creature: cattle, creeping things, and wild beasts of every kind." And it was so.

25 *Hashem* made wild beasts of every kind and cattle of every kind, and all kinds of creeping things of the earth. And *Hashem* saw that this was good.

26 And *Hashem* said, "Let us make man in our image, after our likeness. They shall rule the fish of the sea, the birds of the sky, the cattle, the whole earth, and all the creeping things that creep on earth."

27 And *Hashem* created man in His image, in the image of *Hashem* He created him; male and female He created them.

28 *Hashem* blessed them and *Hashem* said to them, "Be fertile and increase, fill the earth and master it; and rule the fish of the sea, the birds of the sky, and all the living things that creep on earth."

29 *Hashem* said, "See, I give you every seed-bearing plant that is upon all the earth, and every tree that has seed-bearing fruit; they shall be yours for food.

30 And to all the animals on land, to all the birds of the sky, and to everything that creeps on earth, in which there is the breath of life, [I give] all the green plants for food." And it was so.

31 And *Hashem* saw all that He had made, and found it very good. And there was evening and there was morning, the sixth day.

2 1 The heaven and the earth were finished, and all their array.

2 On the seventh day *Hashem* finished the work that He had been doing, and He ceased on the seventh day from all the work that He had done.

3 And *Hashem* blessed the seventh day and declared it holy, because on it *Hashem* ceased from all the work of creation that He had done.

4 Such is the story of heaven and earth when they were created. When *Hashem* made earth and heaven –

Bereishit/Genesis 2
Bereishit

בראשית ב
בראשית

5	when no shrub of the field was yet on earth and no grasses of the field had yet sprouted, because *Hashem* had not sent rain upon the earth and there was no man to till the soil,	וְכֹל ׀ שִׂיחַ הַשָּׂדֶה טֶרֶם יִהְיֶה בָאָרֶץ וְכָל־עֵשֶׂב הַשָּׂדֶה טֶרֶם יִצְמָח כִּי לֹא הִמְטִיר יְהֹוָה אֱלֹהִים עַל־הָאָרֶץ וְאָדָם אַיִן לַעֲבֹד אֶת־הָאֲדָמָה: ה

v'-KHOL SEE-akh ha-sa-DEH TE-rem yih-YEH va-A-retz v'-khol AY-sev ha-sa-DEH TE-rem yitz-MAKH KEE LO him-TEER a-do-NAI e-lo-HEEM al ha-A-retz v'-a-DAM A-yin la-a-VOD et ha-a-da-MAH

6 but a flow would well up from the ground and water the whole surface of the earth –

ו וְאֵד יַעֲלֶה מִן־הָאָרֶץ וְהִשְׁקָה אֶת־כָּל־פְּנֵי־הָאֲדָמָה:

7 *Hashem* formed man from the dust of the earth. He blew into his nostrils the breath of life, and man became a living being.

ז וַיִּיצֶר יְהֹוָה אֱלֹהִים אֶת־הָאָדָם עָפָר מִן־הָאֲדָמָה וַיִּפַּח בְּאַפָּיו נִשְׁמַת חַיִּים וַיְהִי הָאָדָם לְנֶפֶשׁ חַיָּה:

8 *Hashem* planted a garden in Eden, in the east, and placed there the man whom He had formed.

ח וַיִּטַּע יְהֹוָה אֱלֹהִים גַּן־בְּעֵדֶן מִקֶּדֶם וַיָּשֶׂם שָׁם אֶת־הָאָדָם אֲשֶׁר יָצָר:

9 And from the ground *Hashem* caused to grow every tree that was pleasing to the sight and good for food, with the tree of life in the middle of the garden, and the tree of knowledge of good and bad.

ט וַיַּצְמַח יְהֹוָה אֱלֹהִים מִן־הָאֲדָמָה כָּל־עֵץ נֶחְמָד לְמַרְאֶה וְטוֹב לְמַאֲכָל וְעֵץ הַחַיִּים בְּתוֹךְ הַגָּן וְעֵץ הַדַּעַת טוֹב וָרָע:

10 A river issues from Eden to water the garden, and it then divides and becomes four branches.

י וְנָהָר יֹצֵא מֵעֵדֶן לְהַשְׁקוֹת אֶת־הַגָּן וּמִשָּׁם יִפָּרֵד וְהָיָה לְאַרְבָּעָה רָאשִׁים:

11 The name of the first is Pishon, the one that winds through the whole land of Havilah, where the gold is.

יא שֵׁם הָאֶחָד פִּישׁוֹן הוּא הַסֹּבֵב אֵת כָּל־אֶרֶץ הַחֲוִילָה אֲשֶׁר־שָׁם הַזָּהָב:

12 The gold of that land is good; bdellium is there, and lapis lazuli.

יב וּזֲהַב הָאָרֶץ הַהִוא טוֹב שָׁם הַבְּדֹלַח וְאֶבֶן הַשֹּׁהַם:

13 The name of the second river is Gichon, the one that winds through the whole land of Cush.

יג וְשֵׁם הַנָּהָר הַשֵּׁנִי גִּיחוֹן הוּא הַסּוֹבֵב אֵת כָּל־אֶרֶץ כּוּשׁ:

14 The name of the third river is Tigris, the one that flows east of Assyria. And the fourth river is the Euphrates.

יד וְשֵׁם הַנָּהָר הַשְּׁלִישִׁי חִדֶּקֶל הוּא הַהֹלֵךְ קִדְמַת אַשּׁוּר וְהַנָּהָר הָרְבִיעִי הוּא פְרָת:

Rashi (1040–1105)

2:5 Because *Hashem* had not sent rain upon the earth The land was poised to allow its seeds to sprout, but God did not bring forth rain to allow them to grow, because there was no man yet to work the land. *Hashem* did not bring rain until there was a person who could recognize the necessity for rain, and, says *Rashi*, pray for rain. During its short rainy season, *Eretz Yisrael* is dependent on adequate rainfall to produce yearly crops. It is God's design that the Jews living in Israel are to strengthen their relationship with Him through daily prayer requesting adequate rainfall and a successful agricultural season. Since *Hashem* desires a deep relationship with man, He incorporated the need for prayer, the ultimate form of dialogue between man and God, within the natural order.

Droplets on grass near Beit Shemesh

10

Bereishit/Genesis 3
Bereishit

15 *Hashem* took the man and placed him in the garden of Eden, to till it and tend it.

16 And *Hashem* commanded the man, saying, "Of every tree of the garden you are free to eat;

17 but as for the tree of knowledge of good and bad, you must not eat of it; for as soon as you eat of it, you shall die."

18 *Hashem* said, "It is not good for man to be alone; I will make a fitting helper for him."

19 And *Hashem* formed out of the earth all the wild beasts and all the birds of the sky, and brought them to the man to see what he would call them; and whatever the man called each living creature, that would be its name.

20 And the man gave names to all the cattle and to the birds of the sky and to all the wild beasts; but for *Adam* no fitting helper was found.

21 So *Hashem* cast a deep sleep upon the man; and, while he slept, He took one of his ribs and closed up the flesh at that spot.

22 And *Hashem* fashioned the rib that He had taken from the man into a woman; and He brought her to the man.

23 Then the man said, "This one at last Is bone of my bones And flesh of my flesh. This one shall be called Woman, For from man was she taken."

24 Hence a man leaves his father and mother and clings to his wife, so that they become one flesh.

25 The two of them were naked, the man and his wife, yet they felt no shame.

3 1 Now the serpent was the shrewdest of all the wild beasts that *Hashem* had made. He said to the woman, "Did *Hashem* really say: You shall not eat of any tree of the garden?"

2 The woman replied to the serpent, "We may eat of the fruit of the other trees of the garden.

3 It is only about fruit of the tree in the middle of the garden that *Hashem* said: 'You shall not eat of it or touch it, lest you die.'"

4 And the serpent said to the woman, "You are not going to die,

Bereishit/Genesis 3
Bereishit

5 but *Hashem* knows that as soon as you eat of it your eyes will be opened and you will be like divine beings who know good and bad."

6 When the woman saw that the tree was good for eating and a delight to the eyes, and that the tree was desirable as a source of wisdom, she took of its fruit and ate. She also gave some to her husband, and he ate.

7 Then the eyes of both of them were opened and they perceived that they were naked; and they sewed together fig leaves and made themselves loincloths.

8 They heard the sound of *Hashem* moving about in the garden at the breezy time of day; and the man and his wife hid from *Hashem* among the trees of the garden.

9 *Hashem* called out to the man and said to him, "Where are you?"

10 He replied, "I heard the sound of You in the garden, and I was afraid because I was naked, so I hid."

11 Then He asked, "Who told you that you were naked? Did you eat of the tree from which I had forbidden you to eat?"

12 The man said, "The woman You put at my side – she gave me of the tree, and I ate."

13 And *Hashem* said to the woman, "What is this you have done!" The woman replied, "The serpent duped me, and I ate."

14 Then *Hashem* said to the serpent, "Because you did this, More cursed shall you be Than all cattle And all the wild beasts: On your belly shall you crawl And dirt shall you eat All the days of your life.

15 I will put enmity Between you and the woman, And between your offspring and hers; They shall strike at your head, And you shall strike at their heel."

16 And to the woman He said, "I will make most severe Your pangs in childbearing; In pain shall you bear children. Yet your urge shall be for your husband, And he shall rule over you."

בראשית ג
בראשית

ה כִּי יֹדֵעַ אֱלֹהִים כִּי בְּיוֹם אֲכָלְכֶם מִמֶּנּוּ וְנִפְקְחוּ עֵינֵיכֶם וִהְיִיתֶם כֵּאלֹהִים יֹדְעֵי טוֹב וָרָע:

ו וַתֵּרֶא הָאִשָּׁה כִּי טוֹב הָעֵץ לְמַאֲכָל וְכִי תַאֲוָה־הוּא לָעֵינַיִם וְנֶחְמָד הָעֵץ לְהַשְׂכִּיל וַתִּקַּח מִפִּרְיוֹ וַתֹּאכַל וַתִּתֵּן גַּם־לְאִישָׁהּ עִמָּהּ וַיֹּאכַל:

ז וַתִּפָּקַחְנָה עֵינֵי שְׁנֵיהֶם וַיֵּדְעוּ כִּי עֵירֻמִּם הֵם וַיִּתְפְּרוּ עֲלֵה תְאֵנָה וַיַּעֲשׂוּ לָהֶם חֲגֹרֹת:

ח וַיִּשְׁמְעוּ אֶת־קוֹל יְהֹוָה אֱלֹהִים מִתְהַלֵּךְ בַּגָּן לְרוּחַ הַיּוֹם וַיִּתְחַבֵּא הָאָדָם וְאִשְׁתּוֹ מִפְּנֵי יְהֹוָה אֱלֹהִים בְּתוֹךְ עֵץ הַגָּן:

ט וַיִּקְרָא יְהֹוָה אֱלֹהִים אֶל־הָאָדָם וַיֹּאמֶר לוֹ אַיֶּכָּה:

י וַיֹּאמֶר אֶת־קֹלְךָ שָׁמַעְתִּי בַּגָּן וָאִירָא כִּי־עֵירֹם אָנֹכִי וָאֵחָבֵא:

יא וַיֹּאמֶר מִי הִגִּיד לְךָ כִּי עֵירֹם אָתָּה הֲמִן־הָעֵץ אֲשֶׁר צִוִּיתִיךָ לְבִלְתִּי אֲכָל־מִמֶּנּוּ אָכָלְתָּ:

יב וַיֹּאמֶר הָאָדָם הָאִשָּׁה אֲשֶׁר נָתַתָּה עִמָּדִי הִוא נָתְנָה־לִּי מִן־הָעֵץ וָאֹכֵל:

יג וַיֹּאמֶר יְהֹוָה אֱלֹהִים לָאִשָּׁה מַה־זֹּאת עָשִׂית וַתֹּאמֶר הָאִשָּׁה הַנָּחָשׁ הִשִּׁיאַנִי וָאֹכֵל:

יד וַיֹּאמֶר יְהֹוָה אֱלֹהִים אֶל־הַנָּחָשׁ כִּי עָשִׂיתָ זֹּאת אָרוּר אַתָּה מִכָּל־הַבְּהֵמָה וּמִכֹּל חַיַּת הַשָּׂדֶה עַל־גְּחֹנְךָ תֵלֵךְ וְעָפָר תֹּאכַל כָּל־יְמֵי חַיֶּיךָ:

טו וְאֵיבָה אָשִׁית בֵּינְךָ וּבֵין הָאִשָּׁה וּבֵין זַרְעֲךָ וּבֵין זַרְעָהּ הוּא יְשׁוּפְךָ רֹאשׁ וְאַתָּה תְּשׁוּפֶנּוּ עָקֵב:

טז אֶל־הָאִשָּׁה אָמַר הַרְבָּה אַרְבֶּה עִצְּבוֹנֵךְ וְהֵרֹנֵךְ בְּעֶצֶב תֵּלְדִי בָנִים וְאֶל־אִישֵׁךְ תְּשׁוּקָתֵךְ וְהוּא יִמְשָׁל־בָּךְ:

12

Bereishit/Genesis 4
Bereishit

בראשית ד
בראשית

17 To *Adam* He said, "Because you did as your wife said and ate of the tree about which I commanded you, 'You shall not eat of it,' Cursed be the ground because of you; By toil shall you eat of it All the days of your life:

יז וּלְאָדָם אָמַר כִּי־שָׁמַעְתָּ לְקוֹל אִשְׁתֶּךָ וַתֹּאכַל מִן־הָעֵץ אֲשֶׁר צִוִּיתִיךָ לֵאמֹר לֹא תֹאכַל מִמֶּנּוּ אֲרוּרָה הָאֲדָמָה בַּעֲבוּרֶךָ בְּעִצָּבוֹן תֹּאכֲלֶנָּה כֹּל יְמֵי חַיֶּיךָ:

ul-a-DAM a-MAR KEE sha-MA-ta l'-KOL ish-TE-kha va-TO-khal min ha-AYTZ a-SHER tzi-vee-TEE-kha lay-MOR LO to-KHAL mi-ME-nu a-ru-RAH ha-a-da-MAH ba-a-vu-RE-kha b'-i-tza-VON to-kh'-LE-na KOL y'-MAY kha-YE-kha

18 Thorns and thistles shall it sprout for you. But your food shall be the grasses of the field;

יח וְקוֹץ וְדַרְדַּר תַּצְמִיחַ לָךְ וְאָכַלְתָּ אֶת־עֵשֶׂב הַשָּׂדֶה:

19 By the sweat of your brow Shall you get bread to eat, Until you return to the ground – For from it you were taken. For dust you are, And to dust you shall return."

יט בְּזֵעַת אַפֶּיךָ תֹּאכַל לֶחֶם עַד שׁוּבְךָ אֶל־הָאֲדָמָה כִּי מִמֶּנָּה לֻקָּחְתָּ כִּי־עָפָר אַתָּה וְאֶל־עָפָר תָּשׁוּב:

20 The man named his wife *Chava*, because she was the mother of all the living.

כ וַיִּקְרָא הָאָדָם שֵׁם אִשְׁתּוֹ חַוָּה כִּי הִוא הָיְתָה אֵם כָּל־חָי:

21 And *Hashem* made garments of skins for *Adam* and his wife, and clothed them.

כא וַיַּעַשׂ יְהוָה אֱלֹהִים לְאָדָם וּלְאִשְׁתּוֹ כָּתְנוֹת עוֹר וַיַּלְבִּשֵׁם:

22 And *Hashem* said, "Now that the man has become like one of us, knowing good and bad, what if he should stretch out his hand and take also from the tree of life and eat, and live forever!"

כב וַיֹּאמֶר יְהוָה אֱלֹהִים הֵן הָאָדָם הָיָה כְּאַחַד מִמֶּנּוּ לָדַעַת טוֹב וָרָע וְעַתָּה פֶּן־יִשְׁלַח יָדוֹ וְלָקַח גַּם מֵעֵץ הַחַיִּים וְאָכַל וָחַי לְעֹלָם:

23 So *Hashem* banished him from the garden of Eden, to till the soil from which he was taken.

כג וַיְשַׁלְּחֵהוּ יְהוָה אֱלֹהִים מִגַּן־עֵדֶן לַעֲבֹד אֶת־הָאֲדָמָה אֲשֶׁר לֻקַּח מִשָּׁם:

24 He drove the man out, and stationed east of the garden of Eden the cherubim and the fiery ever-turning sword, to guard the way to the tree of life.

כד וַיְגָרֶשׁ אֶת־הָאָדָם וַיַּשְׁכֵּן מִקֶּדֶם לְגַן־עֵדֶן אֶת־הַכְּרֻבִים וְאֵת לַהַט הַחֶרֶב הַמִּתְהַפֶּכֶת לִשְׁמֹר אֶת־דֶּרֶךְ עֵץ הַחַיִּים:

4

1 Now the man knew his wife *Chava*, and she conceived and bore Cain, saying, "I have gained a male child with the help of *Hashem*."

ד א וְהָאָדָם יָדַע אֶת־חַוָּה אִשְׁתּוֹ וַתַּהַר וַתֵּלֶד אֶת־קַיִן וַתֹּאמֶר קָנִיתִי אִישׁ אֶת־יְהוָה:

Rabbi Samson R. Hirsch (1808–1888)

3:17 Cursed be the ground because of you The land is cursed *ba'avurecha* (בעבורך), translated here as 'because of you.' However, according to Rabbi Samson Raphael Hirsch, a prolific writer and leader of Orthodox Jewry in 19th century Germany, *ba'avurecha* means 'for your sake,' in order to rectify man's actions. Following *Adam's* sin, the land's prosperity became a means of measuring man's adherence to *Hashem*; for the Jewish nation, this means following the commandments and keeping God's *Torah*. When they do so, *Hashem* shows His approval through the land's flourishing. This is especially true in *Eretz Yisrael*. Scholars and historians alike note that while the Jews were in exile, the Land of Israel lay fallow and uninhabitable until they returned, and in just a short time the Jews of Israel, following the commandments set out in the *Torah*, have turned a wasteland into a blooming, prosperous country.

Bereishit/Genesis 4
Bereishit

בראשית ד
בראשית

2 She then bore his brother Abel. Abel became a keeper of sheep, and Cain became a tiller of the soil.

ב וַתֹּסֶף לָלֶדֶת אֶת־אָחִיו אֶת־הָבֶל וַיְהִי־הֶבֶל רֹעֵה צֹאן וְקַיִן הָיָה עֹבֵד אֲדָמָה׃

3 In the course of time, Cain brought an offering to *Hashem* from the fruit of the soil;

ג וַיְהִי מִקֵּץ יָמִים וַיָּבֵא קַיִן מִפְּרִי הָאֲדָמָה מִנְחָה לַיהוָה׃

4 and Abel, for his part, brought the choicest of the firstlings of his flock. *Hashem* paid heed to Abel and his offering,

ד וְהֶבֶל הֵבִיא גַם־הוּא מִבְּכֹרוֹת צֹאנוֹ וּמֵחֶלְבֵהֶן וַיִּשַׁע יְהוָה אֶל־הֶבֶל וְאֶל־מִנְחָתוֹ׃

5 but to Cain and his offering He paid no heed. Cain was much distressed and his face fell.

ה וְאֶל־קַיִן וְאֶל־מִנְחָתוֹ לֹא שָׁעָה וַיִּחַר לְקַיִן מְאֹד וַיִּפְּלוּ פָּנָיו׃

6 And *Hashem* said to Cain, "Why are you distressed, And why is your face fallen?

ו וַיֹּאמֶר יְהוָה אֶל־קָיִן לָמָּה חָרָה לָךְ וְלָמָּה נָפְלוּ פָנֶיךָ׃

7 Surely, if you do right, There is uplift. But if you do not do right Sin couches at the door; Its urge is toward you, Yet you can be its master."

ז הֲלוֹא אִם־תֵּיטִיב שְׂאֵת וְאִם לֹא תֵיטִיב לַפֶּתַח חַטָּאת רֹבֵץ וְאֵלֶיךָ תְּשׁוּקָתוֹ וְאַתָּה תִּמְשָׁל־בּוֹ׃

8 Cain said to his brother Abel and when they were in the field, Cain set upon his brother Abel and killed him.

ח וַיֹּאמֶר קַיִן אֶל־הֶבֶל אָחִיו וַיְהִי בִּהְיוֹתָם בַּשָּׂדֶה וַיָּקָם קַיִן אֶל־הֶבֶל אָחִיו וַיַּהַרְגֵהוּ׃

9 *Hashem* said to Cain, "Where is your brother Abel?" And he said, "I do not know. Am I my brother's keeper?"

ט וַיֹּאמֶר יְהוָה אֶל־קַיִן אֵי הֶבֶל אָחִיךָ וַיֹּאמֶר לֹא יָדַעְתִּי הֲשֹׁמֵר אָחִי אָנֹכִי׃

10 Then He said, "What have you done? Hark, your brother's blood cries out to Me from the ground!

י וַיֹּאמֶר מֶה עָשִׂיתָ קוֹל דְּמֵי אָחִיךָ צֹעֲקִים אֵלַי מִן־הָאֲדָמָה׃

11 Therefore, you shall be more cursed than the ground, which opened its mouth to receive your brother's blood from your hand.

יא וְעַתָּה אָרוּר אָתָּה מִן־הָאֲדָמָה אֲשֶׁר פָּצְתָה אֶת־פִּיהָ לָקַחַת אֶת־דְּמֵי אָחִיךָ מִיָּדֶךָ׃

12 If you till the soil, it shall no longer yield its strength to you. You shall become a ceaseless wanderer on earth."

יב כִּי תַעֲבֹד אֶת־הָאֲדָמָה לֹא־תֹסֵף תֵּת־כֹּחָהּ לָךְ נָע וָנָד תִּהְיֶה בָאָרֶץ׃

KEE ta-a-VOD et HA-a-da-MAH lo to-SAYF tayt ko-KHAH LAKH NA va-NAD tih-YEH va-A-retz

4:12 You shall become a ceaseless wanderer on earth The Hebrew for 'ceaseless wanderer' in this verse is *na v'nad* (נע ונד). Rabbi Samson Raphael Hirsch distinguishes the word *na* (נע) from *nad* (נד). *Na* refers to a wanderer who can find no physical resting place on Earth, whereas a *nad* is a wanderer whose connection to mankind has been severed. Cain's punishment isolated him from the land as well as from all of mankind; he was cursed with an inability to find a homeland or a society, and subsequently his sin was too much to bear. The privilege of living in a homeland among a society of people who share a common lineage is no small matter. The return of Jewish sovereignty to its biblical homeland in our time, after thousands of years of exile, is truly a mark of God's hand in this world.

נע
נד

Bereishit/Genesis 4
Bereishit

בראשית ד
בראשית

13 Cain said to *Hashem*, "My punishment is too great to bear!

יג וַיֹּאמֶר קַיִן אֶל־יְהוָה גָּדוֹל עֲוֹנִי מִנְּשֹׂא׃

14 Since You have banished me this day from the soil, and I must avoid Your presence and become a restless wanderer on earth – anyone who meets me may kill me!"

יד הֵן גֵּרַשְׁתָּ אֹתִי הַיּוֹם מֵעַל פְּנֵי הָאֲדָמָה וּמִפָּנֶיךָ אֶסָּתֵר וְהָיִיתִי נָע וָנָד בָּאָרֶץ וְהָיָה כָל־מֹצְאִי יַהַרְגֵנִי׃

15 *Hashem* said to him, "I promise, if anyone kills Cain, sevenfold vengeance shall be taken on him." And *Hashem* put a mark on Cain, lest anyone who met him should kill him.

טו וַיֹּאמֶר לוֹ יְהוָה לָכֵן כָּל־הֹרֵג קַיִן שִׁבְעָתַיִם יֻקָּם וַיָּשֶׂם יְהוָה לְקַיִן אוֹת לְבִלְתִּי הַכּוֹת־אֹתוֹ כָּל־מֹצְאוֹ׃

16 Cain left the presence of *Hashem* and settled in the land of Nod, east of Eden.

טז וַיֵּצֵא קַיִן מִלִּפְנֵי יְהוָה וַיֵּשֶׁב בְּאֶרֶץ־נוֹד קִדְמַת־עֵדֶן׃

17 Cain knew his wife, and she conceived and bore Enoch. And he then founded a city, and named the city after his son Enoch.

יז וַיֵּדַע קַיִן אֶת־אִשְׁתּוֹ וַתַּהַר וַתֵּלֶד אֶת־חֲנוֹךְ וַיְהִי בֹּנֶה עִיר וַיִּקְרָא שֵׁם הָעִיר כְּשֵׁם בְּנוֹ חֲנוֹךְ׃

18 To Enoch was born Irad, and Irad begot Mehujael, and Mehujael begot Methusael, and Methusael begot Lamech.

יח וַיִּוָּלֵד לַחֲנוֹךְ אֶת־עִירָד וְעִירָד יָלַד אֶת־מְחוּיָאֵל וּמְחִיָּיאֵל יָלַד אֶת־מְתוּשָׁאֵל וּמְתוּשָׁאֵל יָלַד אֶת־לָמֶךְ׃

19 Lamech took to himself two wives: the name of the one was Adah, and the name of the other was Zillah.

יט וַיִּקַּח־לוֹ לֶמֶךְ שְׁתֵּי נָשִׁים שֵׁם הָאַחַת עָדָה וְשֵׁם הַשֵּׁנִית צִלָּה׃

20 Adah bore Jabal; he was the ancestor of those who dwell in tents and amidst herds.

כ וַתֵּלֶד עָדָה אֶת־יָבָל הוּא הָיָה אֲבִי יֹשֵׁב אֹהֶל וּמִקְנֶה׃

21 And the name of his brother was Jubal; he was the ancestor of all who play the lyre and the pipe.

כא וְשֵׁם אָחִיו יוּבָל הוּא הָיָה אֲבִי כָּל־תֹּפֵשׂ כִּנּוֹר וְעוּגָב׃

22 As for Zillah, she bore Tubal-cain, who forged all implements of copper and iron. And the sister of Tubal-cain was Naamah.

כב וְצִלָּה גַם־הִוא יָלְדָה אֶת־תּוּבַל קַיִן לֹטֵשׁ כָּל־חֹרֵשׁ נְחֹשֶׁת וּבַרְזֶל וַאֲחוֹת תּוּבַל־קַיִן נַעֲמָה׃

23 And Lamech said to his wives, "Adah and Zillah, hear my voice; O wives of Lamech, give ear to my speech. I have slain a man for wounding me, a lad for bruising me.

כג וַיֹּאמֶר לֶמֶךְ לְנָשָׁיו עָדָה וְצִלָּה שְׁמַעַן קוֹלִי נְשֵׁי לֶמֶךְ הַאְזֵנָּה אִמְרָתִי כִּי אִישׁ הָרַגְתִּי לְפִצְעִי וְיֶלֶד לְחַבֻּרָתִי׃

24 If Cain is avenged sevenfold, Then Lamech seventy-sevenfold."

כד כִּי שִׁבְעָתַיִם יֻקַּם־קָיִן וְלֶמֶךְ שִׁבְעִים וְשִׁבְעָה׃

25 *Adam* knew his wife again, and she bore a son and named him *Shet*, meaning, "*Hashem* has provided me with another offspring in place of Abel," for Cain had killed him.

כה וַיֵּדַע אָדָם עוֹד אֶת־אִשְׁתּוֹ וַתֵּלֶד בֵּן וַתִּקְרָא אֶת־שְׁמוֹ שֵׁת כִּי שָׁת־לִי אֱלֹהִים זֶרַע אַחֵר תַּחַת הֶבֶל כִּי הֲרָגוֹ קָיִן׃

26 And to *Shet*, in turn, a son was born, and he named him *Enosh*. It was then that men began to invoke *Hashem* by name.

כו וּלְשֵׁת גַּם־הוּא יֻלַּד־בֵּן וַיִּקְרָא אֶת־שְׁמוֹ אֱנוֹשׁ אָז הוּחַל לִקְרֹא בְּשֵׁם יְהוָה׃

Bereishit/Genesis 5
Bereishit

בראשית ה
בראשית

5

1 This is the record of *Adam*'s line. When *Hashem* created man, He made him in the likeness of *Hashem*;

א זֶה סֵפֶר תּוֹלְדֹת אָדָם בְּיוֹם בְּרֹא אֱלֹהִים אָדָם בִּדְמוּת אֱלֹהִים עָשָׂה אֹתוֹ:

2 male and female He created them. And when they were created, He blessed them and called them Man.

ב זָכָר וּנְקֵבָה בְּרָאָם וַיְבָרֶךְ אֹתָם וַיִּקְרָא אֶת־שְׁמָם אָדָם בְּיוֹם הִבָּרְאָם:

3 When *Adam* had lived 130 years, he begot a son in his likeness after his image, and named him *Shet*.

ג וַיְחִי אָדָם שְׁלֹשִׁים וּמְאַת שָׁנָה וַיּוֹלֶד בִּדְמוּתוֹ כְּצַלְמוֹ וַיִּקְרָא אֶת־שְׁמוֹ שֵׁת:

vai-KHEE a-DAM sh'-lo-SHEEM um-AT sha-NAH va-YO-led bid-mu-TO k'-tzal-MO va-yik-RA et sh'-MO SHAYT

4 After the birth of *Shet*, *Adam* lived 800 years and begot sons and daughters.

ד וַיִּהְיוּ יְמֵי־אָדָם אַחֲרֵי הוֹלִידוֹ אֶת־שֵׁת שְׁמֹנֶה מֵאֹת שָׁנָה וַיּוֹלֶד בָּנִים וּבָנוֹת:

5 All the days that *Adam* lived came to 930 years; then he died.

ה וַיִּהְיוּ כָּל־יְמֵי אָדָם אֲשֶׁר־חַי תְּשַׁע מֵאוֹת שָׁנָה וּשְׁלֹשִׁים שָׁנָה וַיָּמֹת:

6 When *Shet* had lived 105 years, he begot *Enosh*.

ו וַיְחִי־שֵׁת חָמֵשׁ שָׁנִים וּמְאַת שָׁנָה וַיּוֹלֶד אֶת־אֱנוֹשׁ:

7 After the birth of *Enosh*, *Shet* lived 807 years and begot sons and daughters.

ז וַיְחִי־שֵׁת אַחֲרֵי הוֹלִידוֹ אֶת־אֱנוֹשׁ שֶׁבַע שָׁנִים וּשְׁמֹנֶה מֵאוֹת שָׁנָה וַיּוֹלֶד בָּנִים וּבָנוֹת:

8 All the days of *Shet* came to 912 years; then he died.

ח וַיִּהְיוּ כָּל־יְמֵי־שֵׁת שְׁתֵּים עֶשְׂרֵה שָׁנָה וּתְשַׁע מֵאוֹת שָׁנָה וַיָּמֹת:

9 When *Enosh* had lived 90 years, he begot *Keinan*.

ט וַיְחִי אֱנוֹשׁ תִּשְׁעִים שָׁנָה וַיּוֹלֶד אֶת־קֵינָן:

10 After the birth of *Keinan*, *Enosh* lived 815 years and begot sons and daughters.

י וַיְחִי אֱנוֹשׁ אַחֲרֵי הוֹלִידוֹ אֶת־קֵינָן חֲמֵשׁ עֶשְׂרֵה שָׁנָה וּשְׁמֹנֶה מֵאוֹת שָׁנָה וַיּוֹלֶד בָּנִים וּבָנוֹת:

11 All the days of *Enosh* came to 905 years; then he died.

יא וַיִּהְיוּ כָּל־יְמֵי אֱנוֹשׁ חָמֵשׁ שָׁנִים וּתְשַׁע מֵאוֹת שָׁנָה וַיָּמֹת:

12 When *Keinan* had lived 70 years, he begot *Mehalalel*.

יב וַיְחִי קֵינָן שִׁבְעִים שָׁנָה וַיּוֹלֶד אֶת־מַהֲלַלְאֵל:

5:3 In his likeness after his image Rabbi Yehuda Halevi, a medieval poet and philosopher who lived in Spain and later Jerusalem, states in his work *The Kuzari* that Cain killed Abel because he thought that Abel would inherit the Land of Israel and continue *Adam*'s lineage. When *Shet* was born in the likeness of *Adam*, he replaced Abel, and, therefore, became fitting to inherit the land in *Adam*'s stead. From the onset of history, *Eretz Yisrael* has been recognized as unique and chosen, and since then, many have sought to inherit it at all costs.

Rabbi Yehuda Halevi
(1075–1141)

Bereishit/Genesis 5
Bereishit

13 After the birth of *Mehalalel, Keinan* lived 840 years and begot sons and daughters.

14 All the days of *Keinan* came to 910 years; then he died.

15 When *Mehalalel* had lived 65 years, he begot *Yered*.

16 After the birth of *Yered, Mehalalel* lived 830 years and begot sons and daughters.

17 All the days of *Mehalalel* came to 895 years; then he died.

18 When *Yered* had lived 162 years, he begot Enoch.

19 After the birth of Enoch, *Yered* lived 800 years and begot sons and daughters.

20 All the days of *Yered* came to 962 years; then he died.

21 When Enoch had lived 65 years, he begot *Metushelach*.

22 After the birth of *Metushelach,* Enoch walked with *Hashem* 300 years; and he begot sons and daughters.

23 All the days of Enoch came to 365 years.

24 Enoch walked with *Hashem;* then he was no more, for *Hashem* took him.

25 When *Metushelach* had lived 187 years, he begot Lamech.

26 After the birth of Lamech, *Metushelach* lived 782 years and begot sons and daughters.

27 All the days of *Metushelach* came to 969 years; then he died.

28 When Lamech had lived 182 years, he begot a son.

29 And he named him *Noach*, saying, "This one will provide us relief from our work and from the toil of our hands, out of the very soil which *Hashem* placed under a curse."

יג וַיְחִי קֵינָן אַחֲרֵי הוֹלִידוֹ אֶת־מַהֲלַלְאֵל אַרְבָּעִים שָׁנָה וּשְׁמֹנֶה מֵאוֹת שָׁנָה וַיּוֹלֶד בָּנִים וּבָנוֹת:

יד וַיִּהְיוּ כָּל־יְמֵי קֵינָן עֶשֶׂר שָׁנִים וּתְשַׁע מֵאוֹת שָׁנָה וַיָּמֹת:

טו וַיְחִי מַהֲלַלְאֵל חָמֵשׁ שָׁנִים וְשִׁשִּׁים שָׁנָה וַיּוֹלֶד אֶת־יָרֶד:

טז וַיְחִי מַהֲלַלְאֵל אַחֲרֵי הוֹלִידוֹ אֶת־יֶרֶד שְׁלֹשִׁים שָׁנָה וּשְׁמֹנֶה מֵאוֹת שָׁנָה וַיּוֹלֶד בָּנִים וּבָנוֹת:

יז וַיִּהְיוּ כָּל־יְמֵי מַהֲלַלְאֵל חָמֵשׁ וְתִשְׁעִים שָׁנָה וּשְׁמֹנֶה מֵאוֹת שָׁנָה וַיָּמֹת:

יח וַיְחִי־יֶרֶד שְׁתַּיִם וְשִׁשִּׁים שָׁנָה וּמְאַת שָׁנָה וַיּוֹלֶד אֶת־חֲנוֹךְ:

יט וַיְחִי־יֶרֶד אַחֲרֵי הוֹלִידוֹ אֶת־חֲנוֹךְ שְׁמֹנֶה מֵאוֹת שָׁנָה וַיּוֹלֶד בָּנִים וּבָנוֹת:

כ וַיִּהְיוּ כָּל־יְמֵי־יֶרֶד שְׁתַּיִם וְשִׁשִּׁים שָׁנָה וּתְשַׁע מֵאוֹת שָׁנָה וַיָּמֹת:

כא וַיְחִי חֲנוֹךְ חָמֵשׁ וְשִׁשִּׁים שָׁנָה וַיּוֹלֶד אֶת־מְתוּשָׁלַח:

כב וַיִּתְהַלֵּךְ חֲנוֹךְ אֶת־הָאֱלֹהִים אַחֲרֵי הוֹלִידוֹ אֶת־מְתוּשֶׁלַח שְׁלֹשׁ מֵאוֹת שָׁנָה וַיּוֹלֶד בָּנִים וּבָנוֹת:

כג וַיְהִי כָּל־יְמֵי חֲנוֹךְ חָמֵשׁ וְשִׁשִּׁים שָׁנָה וּשְׁלֹשׁ מֵאוֹת שָׁנָה:

כד וַיִּתְהַלֵּךְ חֲנוֹךְ אֶת־הָאֱלֹהִים וְאֵינֶנּוּ כִּי־לָקַח אֹתוֹ אֱלֹהִים:

כה וַיְחִי מְתוּשֶׁלַח שֶׁבַע וּשְׁמֹנִים שָׁנָה וּמְאַת שָׁנָה וַיּוֹלֶד אֶת־לָמֶךְ:

כו וַיְחִי מְתוּשֶׁלַח אַחֲרֵי הוֹלִידוֹ אֶת־לֶמֶךְ שְׁתַּיִם וּשְׁמוֹנִים שָׁנָה וּשְׁבַע מֵאוֹת שָׁנָה וַיּוֹלֶד בָּנִים וּבָנוֹת:

כז וַיִּהְיוּ כָּל־יְמֵי מְתוּשֶׁלַח תֵּשַׁע וְשִׁשִּׁים שָׁנָה וּתְשַׁע מֵאוֹת שָׁנָה וַיָּמֹת:

כח וַיְחִי־לֶמֶךְ שְׁתַּיִם וּשְׁמֹנִים שָׁנָה וּמְאַת שָׁנָה וַיּוֹלֶד בֵּן:

כט וַיִּקְרָא אֶת־שְׁמוֹ נֹחַ לֵאמֹר זֶה יְנַחֲמֵנוּ מִמַּעֲשֵׂנוּ וּמֵעִצְּבוֹן יָדֵינוּ מִן־הָאֲדָמָה אֲשֶׁר אֵרְרָהּ יְהֹוָה:

Bereishit/Genesis 6
Noach

30 After the birth of *Noach*, Lamech lived 595 years and begot sons and daughters.

31 All the days of Lamech came to 777 years; then he died.

32 When *Noach* had lived 500 years, *Noach* begot *Shem*, Ham, and Japheth.

6 1 When men began to increase on earth and daughters were born to them,

2 the divine beings saw how beautiful the daughters of men were and took wives from among those that pleased them.

3 *Hashem* said, "My breath shall not abide in man forever, since he too is flesh; let the days allowed him be one hundred and twenty years."

4 It was then, and later too, that the Nephilim appeared on earth – when the divine beings cohabited with the daughters of men, who bore them offspring. They were the heroes of old, the men of renown.

5 *Hashem* saw how great was man's wickedness on earth, and how every plan devised by his mind was nothing but evil all the time.

6 And *Hashem* regretted that He had made man on earth, and His heart was saddened.

7 *Hashem* said, "I will blot out from the earth the men whom I created – men together with beasts, creeping things, and birds of the sky; for I regret that I made them."

8 But *Noach* found favor with *Hashem*.

9 This is the line of *Noach*. – *Noach* was a righteous man; he was blameless in his age; *Noach* walked with *Hashem*. –

10 *Noach* begot three sons: *Shem*, Ham, and Japheth.

11 The earth became corrupt before *Hashem*; the earth was filled with lawlessness.

12 When *Hashem* saw how corrupt the earth was, for all flesh had corrupted its ways on earth,

Bereishit/Genesis 6
Noach

בראשית ו
נח

13 *Hashem* said to *Noach*, "I have decided to put an end to all flesh, for the earth is filled with lawlessness because of them: I am about to destroy them with the earth.

יג וַיֹּאמֶר אֱלֹהִים לְנֹחַ קֵץ כָּל־בָּשָׂר בָּא לְפָנַי כִּי־מָלְאָה הָאָרֶץ חָמָס מִפְּנֵיהֶם וְהִנְנִי מַשְׁחִיתָם אֶת־הָאָרֶץ:

va-YO-mer e-lo-HEEM l'-NO-akh KAYTZ kol ba-SAR BA l'-fa-NAI kee ma-l'-AH ha-A-retz kha-MAS mi-p'-nay-HEM v'-hi-n'-NEE mash-khee-TAM et ha-A-retz

14 Make yourself an ark of gopher wood; make it an ark with compartments, and cover it inside and out with pitch.

יד עֲשֵׂה לְךָ תֵּבַת עֲצֵי־גֹפֶר קִנִּים תַּעֲשֶׂה אֶת־הַתֵּבָה וְכָפַרְתָּ אֹתָהּ מִבַּיִת וּמִחוּץ בַּכֹּפֶר:

15 This is how you shall make it: the length of the ark shall be three hundred *amot*, its width fifty *amot*, and its height thirty *amot*.

טו וְזֶה אֲשֶׁר תַּעֲשֶׂה אֹתָהּ שְׁלֹשׁ מֵאוֹת אַמָּה אֹרֶךְ הַתֵּבָה חֲמִשִּׁים אַמָּה רָחְבָּהּ וּשְׁלֹשִׁים אַמָּה קוֹמָתָהּ:

16 Make an opening for daylight in the ark, and terminate it within an *amah* of the top. Put the entrance to the ark in its side; make it with bottom, second, and third decks.

טז צֹהַר תַּעֲשֶׂה לַתֵּבָה וְאֶל־אַמָּה תְּכַלֶּנָּה מִלְמַעְלָה וּפֶתַח הַתֵּבָה בְּצִדָּהּ תָּשִׂים תַּחְתִּיִּם שְׁנִיִּם וּשְׁלִשִׁים תַּעֲשֶׂהָ:

17 "For My part, I am about to bring the Flood – waters upon the earth – to destroy all flesh under the sky in which there is breath of life; everything on earth shall perish.

יז וַאֲנִי הִנְנִי מֵבִיא אֶת־הַמַּבּוּל מַיִם עַל־הָאָרֶץ לְשַׁחֵת כָּל־בָּשָׂר אֲשֶׁר־בּוֹ רוּחַ חַיִּים מִתַּחַת הַשָּׁמָיִם כֹּל אֲשֶׁר־בָּאָרֶץ יִגְוָע:

18 But I will establish My covenant with you, and you shall enter the ark, with your sons, your wife, and your sons' wives.

יח וַהֲקִמֹתִי אֶת־בְּרִיתִי אִתָּךְ וּבָאתָ אֶל־הַתֵּבָה אַתָּה וּבָנֶיךָ וְאִשְׁתְּךָ וּנְשֵׁי־בָנֶיךָ אִתָּךְ:

19 And of all that lives, of all flesh, you shall take two of each into the ark to keep alive with you; they shall be male and female.

יט וּמִכָּל־הָחַי מִכָּל־בָּשָׂר שְׁנַיִם מִכֹּל תָּבִיא אֶל־הַתֵּבָה לְהַחֲיֹת אִתָּךְ זָכָר וּנְקֵבָה יִהְיוּ:

20 From birds of every kind, cattle of every kind, every kind of creeping thing on earth, two of each shall come to you to stay alive.

כ מֵהָעוֹף לְמִינֵהוּ וּמִן־הַבְּהֵמָה לְמִינָהּ מִכֹּל רֶמֶשׂ הָאֲדָמָה לְמִינֵהוּ שְׁנַיִם מִכֹּל יָבֹאוּ אֵלֶיךָ לְהַחֲיוֹת:

21 For your part, take of everything that is eaten and store it away, to serve as food for you and for them."

כא וְאַתָּה קַח־לְךָ מִכָּל־מַאֲכָל אֲשֶׁר יֵאָכֵל וְאָסַפְתָּ אֵלֶיךָ וְהָיָה לְךָ וְלָהֶם לְאָכְלָה:

22 *Noach* did so; just as *Hashem* commanded him, so he did.

כב וַיַּעַשׂ נֹחַ כְּכֹל אֲשֶׁר צִוָּה אֹתוֹ אֱלֹהִים כֵּן עָשָׂה:

Rabbi Shnuer Z. Liadi (1745–1813)

6:13 I am about to destroy them with the earth
According to one opinion in the Talmud (*Zevachim* 113b), the effects of the flood were less severe in the Land of Israel. Why did *Hashem* choose to spare this particular land? Rabbi Shneur Zalman of Liadi, the founder of the Chabad Hasidic dynasty in eighteenth century Russia, concludes that the purpose of the flood was to purify the world of its corruption. The flood, then, served as a kind of *mikveh*, a ritual bath, to bring about a process of purification. However, since *Eretz Yisrael* is intrinsically pure, it is impossible to corrupt and, therefore, did not need this type of purification. In fact, whenever the *Torah* discusses sins that can cause exile, it says that the land will purge itself of the sinners. *Eretz Yisrael* cannot be corrupted and does not tolerate impurity on its soil.

Bereishit/Genesis 7
Noach

בראשית ז
נח

1 Then *Hashem* said to *Noach*, "Go into the ark, with all your household, for you alone have I found righteous before Me in this generation.

2 Of every clean animal you shall take seven pairs, males and their mates, and of every animal that is not clean, two, a male and its mate;

3 of the birds of the sky also, seven pairs, male and female, to keep seed alive upon all the earth.

4 For in seven days' time I will make it rain upon the earth, forty days and forty nights, and I will blot out from the earth all existence that I created."

5 And *Noach* did just as *Hashem* commanded him.

6 *Noach* was six hundred years old when the Flood came, waters upon the earth.

7 *Noach*, with his sons, his wife, and his sons' wives, went into the ark because of the waters of the Flood.

8 Of the clean animals, of the animals that are not clean, of the birds, and of everything that creeps on the ground,

9 two of each, male and female, came to *Noach* into the ark, as *Hashem* had commanded *Noach*.

10 And on the seventh day the waters of the Flood came upon the earth.

11 In the six hundredth year of *Noach*'s life, in the second month, on the seventeenth day of the month, on that day All the fountains of the great deep burst apart, And the floodgates of the sky broke open.

12 The rain fell on the earth forty days and forty nights.

13 That same day *Noach* and *Noach*'s sons, *Shem*, Ham, and Japheth, went into the ark, with *Noach*'s wife and the three wives of his sons

14 they and all beasts of every kind, all cattle of every kind, all creatures of every kind that creep on the earth, and all birds of every kind, every bird, every winged thing.

15 They came to *Noach* into the ark, two each of all flesh in which there was breath of life.

Bereishit/Genesis 8
Noach

בראשית ח
נח

16 Thus they that entered comprised male and female of all flesh, as *Hashem* had commanded him. And *Hashem* shut him in.

טז וְהַבָּאִים זָכָר וּנְקֵבָה מִכָּל־בָּשָׂר בָּאוּ כַּאֲשֶׁר צִוָּה אֹתוֹ אֱלֹהִים וַיִּסְגֹּר יְהוָה בַּעֲדוֹ:

17 The Flood continued forty days on the earth, and the waters increased and raised the ark so that it rose above the earth.

יז וַיְהִי הַמַּבּוּל אַרְבָּעִים יוֹם עַל־הָאָרֶץ וַיִּרְבּוּ הַמַּיִם וַיִּשְׂאוּ אֶת־הַתֵּבָה וַתָּרָם מֵעַל הָאָרֶץ:

18 The waters swelled and increased greatly upon the earth, and the ark drifted upon the waters.

יח וַיִּגְבְּרוּ הַמַּיִם וַיִּרְבּוּ מְאֹד עַל־הָאָרֶץ וַתֵּלֶךְ הַתֵּבָה עַל־פְּנֵי הַמָּיִם:

19 When the waters had swelled much more upon the earth, all the highest mountains everywhere under the sky were covered.

יט וְהַמַּיִם גָּבְרוּ מְאֹד מְאֹד עַל־הָאָרֶץ וַיְכֻסּוּ כָּל־הֶהָרִים הַגְּבֹהִים אֲשֶׁר־תַּחַת כָּל־הַשָּׁמָיִם:

v'-ha-MA-yim ga-v'-RU m'-OD m'-OD al ha-A-retz vai-khu-SU kol he-ha-REEM ha-g'-vo-HEEM a-sher TA-khat kol ha-sha-MA-yim

20 Fifteen *amot* higher did the waters swell, as the mountains were covered.

כ חֲמֵשׁ עֶשְׂרֵה אַמָּה מִלְמַעְלָה גָּבְרוּ הַמָּיִם וַיְכֻסּוּ הֶהָרִים:

21 And all flesh that stirred on earth perished – birds, cattle, beasts, and all the things that swarmed upon the earth, and all mankind.

כא וַיִּגְוַע כָּל־בָּשָׂר הָרֹמֵשׂ עַל־הָאָרֶץ בָּעוֹף וּבַבְּהֵמָה וּבַחַיָּה וּבְכָל־הַשֶּׁרֶץ הַשֹּׁרֵץ עַל־הָאָרֶץ וְכֹל הָאָדָם:

22 All in whose nostrils was the merest breath of life, all that was on dry land, died.

כב כֹּל אֲשֶׁר נִשְׁמַת־רוּחַ חַיִּים בְּאַפָּיו מִכֹּל אֲשֶׁר בֶּחָרָבָה מֵתוּ:

23 All existence on earth was blotted out – man, cattle, creeping things, and birds of the sky; they were blotted out from the earth. Only *Noach* was left, and those with him in the ark.

כג וַיִּמַח אֶת־כָּל־הַיְקוּם אֲשֶׁר עַל־פְּנֵי הָאֲדָמָה מֵאָדָם עַד־בְּהֵמָה עַד־רֶמֶשׂ וְעַד־עוֹף הַשָּׁמַיִם וַיִּמָּחוּ מִן־הָאָרֶץ וַיִּשָּׁאֶר אַךְ־נֹחַ וַאֲשֶׁר אִתּוֹ בַּתֵּבָה:

24 And when the waters had swelled on the earth one hundred and fifty days,

כד וַיִּגְבְּרוּ הַמַּיִם עַל־הָאָרֶץ חֲמִשִּׁים וּמְאַת יוֹם:

8 1 *Hashem* remembered *Noach* and all the beasts and all the cattle that were with him in the ark, and *Hashem* caused a wind to blow across the earth, and the waters subsided.

ח א וַיִּזְכֹּר אֱלֹהִים אֶת־נֹחַ וְאֵת כָּל־הַחַיָּה וְאֶת־כָּל־הַבְּהֵמָה אֲשֶׁר אִתּוֹ בַּתֵּבָה וַיַּעֲבֵר אֱלֹהִים רוּחַ עַל־הָאָרֶץ וַיָּשֹׁכּוּ הַמָּיִם:

Dove of Peace, President's House, Jerusalem

7:19 All the highest mountains This verse seems to contradict the assertion that *Eretz Yisrael* was not affected by the flood. The *Ramban*, a leading scholar in medieval Spain, solves this contradiction by stating that rain did not fall over the Land of Israel, but nevertheless, as there was no barrier surrounding the land, the flood waters entered the land from the surrounding lands. Even though the land was flooded, the powerful rain did not fall directly on *Eretz Yisrael*. As a result, the trees were not affected and at the conclusion of the flood, the dove was able to find an olive leaf in bloom. The image of a dove grasping an olive branch has become a symbol of peace. This icon, which emerged at the re-initiation of the world, when God's anger was quenched and *Noach* was commanded to continue mankind anew, emerged from the Land of Israel, the land of peace.

Bereishit/Genesis 8
Noach

בראשית ח
נח

2 The fountains of the deep and the floodgates of the sky were stopped up, and the rain from the sky was held back;

ב וַיִּסָּכְרוּ מַעְיְנֹת תְּהוֹם וַאֲרֻבֹּת הַשָּׁמָיִם וַיִּכָּלֵא הַגֶּשֶׁם מִן־הַשָּׁמָיִם:

3 the waters then receded steadily from the earth. At the end of one hundred and fifty days the waters diminished,

ג וַיָּשֻׁבוּ הַמַּיִם מֵעַל הָאָרֶץ הָלוֹךְ וָשׁוֹב וַיַּחְסְרוּ הַמַּיִם מִקְצֵה חֲמִשִּׁים וּמְאַת יוֹם:

4 so that in the seventh month, on the seventeenth day of the month, the ark came to rest on the mountains of Ararat.

ד וַתָּנַח הַתֵּבָה בַּחֹדֶשׁ הַשְּׁבִיעִי בְּשִׁבְעָה־עָשָׂר יוֹם לַחֹדֶשׁ עַל הָרֵי אֲרָרָט:

5 The waters went on diminishing until the tenth month; in the tenth month, on the first of the month, the tops of the mountains became visible.

ה וְהַמַּיִם הָיוּ הָלוֹךְ וְחָסוֹר עַד הַחֹדֶשׁ הָעֲשִׂירִי בָּעֲשִׂירִי בְּאֶחָד לַחֹדֶשׁ נִרְאוּ רָאשֵׁי הֶהָרִים:

6 At the end of forty days, *Noach* opened the window of the ark that he had made

ו וַיְהִי מִקֵּץ אַרְבָּעִים יוֹם וַיִּפְתַּח נֹחַ אֶת־חַלּוֹן הַתֵּבָה אֲשֶׁר עָשָׂה:

7 and sent out the raven; it went to and fro until the waters had dried up from the earth.

ז וַיְשַׁלַּח אֶת־הָעֹרֵב וַיֵּצֵא יָצוֹא וָשׁוֹב עַד־יְבֹשֶׁת הַמַּיִם מֵעַל הָאָרֶץ:

8 Then he sent out the dove to see whether the waters had decreased from the surface of the ground.

ח וַיְשַׁלַּח אֶת־הַיּוֹנָה מֵאִתּוֹ לִרְאוֹת הֲקַלּוּ הַמַּיִם מֵעַל פְּנֵי הָאֲדָמָה:

9 But the dove could not find a resting place for its foot, and returned to him to the ark, for there was water over all the earth. So putting out his hand, he took it into the ark with him.

ט וְלֹא־מָצְאָה הַיּוֹנָה מָנוֹחַ לְכַף־רַגְלָהּ וַתָּשָׁב אֵלָיו אֶל־הַתֵּבָה כִּי־מַיִם עַל־פְּנֵי כָל־הָאָרֶץ וַיִּשְׁלַח יָדוֹ וַיִּקָּחֶהָ וַיָּבֵא אֹתָהּ אֵלָיו אֶל־הַתֵּבָה:

v'-lo ma-tz'-AH ha-yo-NAH ma-NO-akh l'-khaf rag-LAH va-TA-shov ay-LAV el ha-tay-VAH kee MA-yim al p'-NAY khol ha-A-retz va-yish-LAKH ya-DO va-yi-ka-KHE-ha va-ya-VAY o-TAH ay-LAV el ha-tay-VAH

10 He waited another seven days, and again sent out the dove from the ark.

י וַיָּחֶל עוֹד שִׁבְעַת יָמִים אֲחֵרִים וַיֹּסֶף שַׁלַּח אֶת־הַיּוֹנָה מִן־הַתֵּבָה:

11 The dove came back to him toward evening, and there in its bill was a plucked-off olive leaf! Then *Noach* knew that the waters had decreased on the earth.

יא וַתָּבֹא אֵלָיו הַיּוֹנָה לְעֵת עֶרֶב וְהִנֵּה עֲלֵה־זַיִת טָרָף בְּפִיהָ וַיֵּדַע נֹחַ כִּי־קַלּוּ הַמַּיִם מֵעַל הָאָרֶץ:

12 He waited still another seven days and sent the dove forth; and it did not return to him any more.

יב וַיִּיָּחֶל עוֹד שִׁבְעַת יָמִים אֲחֵרִים וַיְשַׁלַּח אֶת־הַיּוֹנָה וְלֹא־יָסְפָה שׁוּב־אֵלָיו עוֹד:

8:9 But the dove could not find a resting place Throughout Talmudic literature, the Jewish people are compared to the dove. Once a dove meets her mate, she never leaves him for another, and a dove, even when her offspring are taken, will never abandon her nest. In a similar fashion, the Children of Israel are faithful to God. The Sages of the *Midrash* comment that the dove that *Noach* sent foreshadows the journey of the Jewish people throughout history. Just as the dove found no rest for the sole of its foot, so the Jews will find no solace in exile. Just as the dove returned to the ark seeking shelter, so the Jews will return from exile to the Land of Israel. Like *Noach*'s dove, the people have remained faithful to *Hashem*, and now, after thousands of years of absence, have returned to His land.

Dove resting at the Western Wall

Bereishit/Genesis 9
Noach

בראשית ט
נח

13 In the six hundred and first year, in the first month, on the first of the month, the waters began to dry from the earth; and when *Noach* removed the covering of the ark, he saw that the surface of the ground was drying.

יג וַיְהִי בְּאַחַת וְשֵׁשׁ־מֵאוֹת שָׁנָה בָּרִאשׁוֹן בְּאֶחָד לַחֹדֶשׁ חָרְבוּ הַמַּיִם מֵעַל הָאָרֶץ וַיָּסַר נֹחַ אֶת־מִכְסֵה הַתֵּבָה וַיַּרְא וְהִנֵּה חָרְבוּ פְּנֵי הָאֲדָמָה׃

14 And in the second month, on the twenty-seventh day of the month, the earth was dry.

יד וּבַחֹדֶשׁ הַשֵּׁנִי בְּשִׁבְעָה וְעֶשְׂרִים יוֹם לַחֹדֶשׁ יָבְשָׁה הָאָרֶץ׃

15 *Hashem* spoke to *Noach*, saying,

טו וַיְדַבֵּר אֱלֹהִים אֶל־נֹחַ לֵאמֹר׃

16 "Come out of the ark, together with your wife, your sons, and your sons' wives.

טז צֵא מִן־הַתֵּבָה אַתָּה וְאִשְׁתְּךָ וּבָנֶיךָ וּנְשֵׁי־בָנֶיךָ אִתָּךְ׃

17 Bring out with you every living thing of all flesh that is with you: birds, animals, and everything that creeps on earth; and let them swarm on the earth and be fertile and increase on earth."

יז כָּל־הַחַיָּה אֲשֶׁר־אִתְּךָ מִכָּל־בָּשָׂר בָּעוֹף וּבַבְּהֵמָה וּבְכָל־הָרֶמֶשׂ הָרֹמֵשׂ עַל־הָאָרֶץ הוצא [הַיְצֵא] אִתָּךְ וְשָׁרְצוּ בָאָרֶץ וּפָרוּ וְרָבוּ עַל־הָאָרֶץ׃

18 So *Noach* came out, together with his sons, his wife, and his sons' wives.

יח וַיֵּצֵא־נֹחַ וּבָנָיו וְאִשְׁתּוֹ וּנְשֵׁי־בָנָיו אִתּוֹ׃

19 Every animal, every creeping thing, and every bird, everything that stirs on earth came out of the ark by families.

יט כָּל־הַחַיָּה כָּל־הָרֶמֶשׂ וְכָל־הָעוֹף כֹּל רוֹמֵשׂ עַל־הָאָרֶץ לְמִשְׁפְּחֹתֵיהֶם יָצְאוּ מִן־הַתֵּבָה׃

20 Then *Noach* built an altar to *Hashem* and, taking of every clean animal and of every clean bird, he offered burnt offerings on the altar.

כ וַיִּבֶן נֹחַ מִזְבֵּחַ לַיהֹוָה וַיִּקַּח מִכֹּל הַבְּהֵמָה הַטְּהוֹרָה וּמִכֹּל הָעוֹף הַטָּהֹר וַיַּעַל עֹלֹת בַּמִּזְבֵּחַ׃

21 *Hashem* smelled the pleasing odor, and *Hashem* said to Himself: "Never again will I doom the earth because of man, since the devisings of man's mind are evil from his youth; nor will I ever again destroy every living being, as I have done.

כא וַיָּרַח יְהֹוָה אֶת־רֵיחַ הַנִּיחֹחַ וַיֹּאמֶר יְהֹוָה אֶל־לִבּוֹ לֹא־אֹסִף לְקַלֵּל עוֹד אֶת־הָאֲדָמָה בַּעֲבוּר הָאָדָם כִּי יֵצֶר לֵב הָאָדָם רַע מִנְּעֻרָיו וְלֹא־אֹסִף עוֹד לְהַכּוֹת אֶת־כָּל־חַי כַּאֲשֶׁר עָשִׂיתִי׃

22 So long as the earth endures, Seedtime and harvest, Cold and heat, Summer and winter, Day and night Shall not cease."

כב עֹד כָּל־יְמֵי הָאָרֶץ זֶרַע וְקָצִיר וְקֹר וָחֹם וְקַיִץ וָחֹרֶף וְיוֹם וָלַיְלָה לֹא יִשְׁבֹּתוּ׃

9 1 *Hashem* blessed *Noach* and his sons, and said to them, "Be fertile and increase, and fill the earth.

ט א וַיְבָרֶךְ אֱלֹהִים אֶת־נֹחַ וְאֶת־בָּנָיו וַיֹּאמֶר לָהֶם פְּרוּ וּרְבוּ וּמִלְאוּ אֶת־הָאָרֶץ׃

2 The fear and the dread of you shall be upon all the beasts of the earth and upon all the birds of the sky – everything with which the earth is astir – and upon all the fish of the sea; they are given into your hand.

ב וּמוֹרַאֲכֶם וְחִתְּכֶם יִהְיֶה עַל כָּל־חַיַּת הָאָרֶץ וְעַל כָּל־עוֹף הַשָּׁמָיִם בְּכֹל אֲשֶׁר תִּרְמֹשׂ הָאֲדָמָה וּבְכָל־דְּגֵי הַיָּם בְּיֶדְכֶם נִתָּנוּ׃

3 Every creature that lives shall be yours to eat; as with the green grasses, I give you all these.

ג כָּל־רֶמֶשׂ אֲשֶׁר הוּא־חַי לָכֶם יִהְיֶה לְאָכְלָה כְּיֶרֶק עֵשֶׂב נָתַתִּי לָכֶם אֶת־כֹּל׃

4 You must not, however, eat flesh with its life-blood in it.

ד אַךְ־בָּשָׂר בְּנַפְשׁוֹ דָמוֹ לֹא תֹאכֵלוּ׃

23

Bereishit/Genesis 9
Noach

5 But for your own life-blood I will require a reckoning: I will require it of every beast; of man, too, will I require a reckoning for human life, of every man for that of his fellow man!

6 Whoever sheds the blood of man, By man shall his blood be shed; For in His image Did *Hashem* make man.

7 Be fertile, then, and increase; abound on the earth and increase on it."

8 And *Hashem* said to *Noach* and to his sons with him,

9 "I now establish My covenant with you and your offspring to come,

10 and with every living thing that is with you – birds, cattle, and every wild beast as well – all that have come out of the ark, every living thing on earth.

11 I will maintain My covenant with you: never again shall all flesh be cut off by the waters of a flood, and never again shall there be a flood to destroy the earth."

12 *Hashem* further said, "This is the sign that I set for the covenant between Me and you, and every living creature with you, for all ages to come.

13 I have set My bow in the clouds, and it shall serve as a sign of the covenant between Me and the earth.

14 When I bring clouds over the earth, and the bow appears in the clouds,

15 I will remember My covenant between Me and you and every living creature among all flesh, so that the waters shall never again become a flood to destroy all flesh.

16 When the bow is in the clouds, I will see it and remember the everlasting covenant between *Hashem* and all living creatures, all flesh that is on earth.

17 That," *Hashem* said to *Noach*, "shall be the sign of the covenant that I have established between Me and all flesh that is on earth."

18 The sons of *Noach* who came out of the ark were *Shem*, Ham, and Japheth – Ham being the father of Canaan.

בראשית ט
נח

ה וְאַ֨ךְ אֶת־דִּמְכֶ֤ם לְנַפְשֹֽׁתֵיכֶם֙ אֶדְרֹ֔שׁ מִיַּ֥ד כָּל־חַיָּ֖ה אֶדְרְשֶׁ֑נּוּ וּמִיַּ֣ד הָֽאָדָ֗ם מִיַּד֙ אִ֣ישׁ אָחִ֔יו אֶדְרֹ֖שׁ אֶת־נֶ֥פֶשׁ הָֽאָדָֽם׃

ו שֹׁפֵךְ֙ דַּ֣ם הָֽאָדָ֔ם בָּֽאָדָ֖ם דָּמ֣וֹ יִשָּׁפֵ֑ךְ כִּ֚י בְּצֶ֣לֶם אֱלֹהִ֔ים עָשָׂ֖ה אֶת־הָֽאָדָֽם׃

ז וְאַתֶּ֖ם פְּר֣וּ וּרְב֑וּ שִׁרְצ֥וּ בָאָ֖רֶץ וּרְבוּ־בָֽהּ׃

ח וַיֹּ֤אמֶר אֱלֹהִים֙ אֶל־נֹ֔חַ וְאֶל־בָּנָ֥יו אִתּ֖וֹ לֵאמֹֽר׃

ט וַאֲנִ֕י הִנְנִ֥י מֵקִ֛ים אֶת־בְּרִיתִ֖י אִתְּכֶ֑ם וְאֶֽת־זַרְעֲכֶ֖ם אַֽחֲרֵיכֶֽם׃

י וְאֵ֨ת כָּל־נֶ֤פֶשׁ הַֽחַיָּה֙ אֲשֶׁ֣ר אִתְּכֶ֔ם בָּע֧וֹף בַּבְּהֵמָ֛ה וּֽבְכָל־חַיַּ֥ת הָאָ֖רֶץ אִתְּכֶ֑ם מִכֹּל֙ יֹֽצְאֵ֣י הַתֵּבָ֔ה לְכֹ֖ל חַיַּ֥ת הָאָֽרֶץ׃

יא וַהֲקִֽמֹתִ֤י אֶת־בְּרִיתִי֙ אִתְּכֶ֔ם וְלֹֽא־יִכָּרֵ֧ת כָּל־בָּשָׂ֛ר ע֖וֹד מִמֵּ֣י הַמַּבּ֑וּל וְלֹֽא־יִֽהְיֶ֥ה ע֛וֹד מַבּ֖וּל לְשַׁחֵ֥ת הָאָֽרֶץ׃

יב וַיֹּ֣אמֶר אֱלֹהִ֗ים זֹ֤את אֽוֹת־הַבְּרִית֙ אֲשֶׁר־אֲנִ֣י נֹתֵ֗ן בֵּינִי֙ וּבֵ֣ינֵיכֶ֔ם וּבֵ֛ין כָּל־נֶ֥פֶשׁ חַיָּ֖ה אֲשֶׁ֣ר אִתְּכֶ֑ם לְדֹרֹ֖ת עוֹלָֽם׃

יג אֶת־קַשְׁתִּ֕י נָתַ֖תִּי בֶּֽעָנָ֑ן וְהָֽיְתָה֙ לְא֣וֹת בְּרִ֔ית בֵּינִ֖י וּבֵ֥ין הָאָֽרֶץ׃

יד וְהָיָ֕ה בְּעַֽנְנִ֥י עָנָ֖ן עַל־הָאָ֑רֶץ וְנִרְאֲתָ֥ה הַקֶּ֖שֶׁת בֶּעָנָֽן׃

טו וְזָֽכַרְתִּ֣י אֶת־בְּרִיתִ֗י אֲשֶׁ֤ר בֵּינִי֙ וּבֵ֣ינֵיכֶ֔ם וּבֵ֛ין כָּל־נֶ֥פֶשׁ חַיָּ֖ה בְּכָל־בָּשָׂ֑ר וְלֹֽא־יִֽהְיֶ֨ה ע֤וֹד הַמַּ֨יִם֙ לְמַבּ֔וּל לְשַׁחֵ֖ת כָּל־בָּשָֽׂר׃

טז וְהָֽיְתָ֥ה הַקֶּ֖שֶׁת בֶּֽעָנָ֑ן וּרְאִיתִ֗יהָ לִזְכֹּר֙ בְּרִ֣ית עוֹלָ֔ם בֵּ֣ין אֱלֹהִ֔ים וּבֵין֙ כָּל־נֶ֣פֶשׁ חַיָּ֔ה בְּכָל־בָּשָׂ֖ר אֲשֶׁ֥ר עַל־הָאָֽרֶץ׃

יז וַיֹּ֥אמֶר אֱלֹהִ֖ים אֶל־נֹ֑חַ זֹ֤את אֽוֹת־הַבְּרִית֙ אֲשֶׁ֣ר הֲקִמֹ֔תִי בֵּינִ֕י וּבֵ֥ין כָּל־בָּשָׂ֖ר אֲשֶׁ֥ר עַל־הָאָֽרֶץ׃

יח וַיִּֽהְי֣וּ בְנֵי־נֹ֗חַ הַיֹּֽצְאִים֙ מִן־הַתֵּבָ֔ה שֵׁ֖ם וְחָ֣ם וָיָ֑פֶת וְחָ֕ם ה֖וּא אֲבִ֥י כְנָֽעַן׃

Bereishit/Genesis 10
Noach

בראשית י
נח

19 These three were the sons of *Noach*, and from these the whole world branched out.

שְׁלֹשָׁה אֵלֶּה בְּנֵי־נֹחַ וּמֵאֵלֶּה נָפְצָה כָל־הָאָרֶץ:

20 *Noach*, the tiller of the soil, was the first to plant a vineyard.

וַיָּחֶל נֹחַ אִישׁ הָאֲדָמָה וַיִּטַּע כָּרֶם:

21 He drank of the wine and became drunk, and he uncovered himself within his tent.

וַיֵּשְׁתְּ מִן־הַיַּיִן וַיִּשְׁכָּר וַיִּתְגַּל בְּתוֹךְ אָהֳלֹה:

22 Ham, the father of Canaan, saw his father's nakedness and told his two brothers outside.

וַיַּרְא חָם אֲבִי כְנַעַן אֵת עֶרְוַת אָבִיו וַיַּגֵּד לִשְׁנֵי־אֶחָיו בַּחוּץ:

23 But *Shem* and Japheth took a cloth, placed it against both their backs and, walking backward, they covered their father's nakedness; their faces were turned the other way, so that they did not see their father's nakedness.

וַיִּקַּח שֵׁם וָיֶפֶת אֶת־הַשִּׂמְלָה וַיָּשִׂימוּ עַל־שְׁכֶם שְׁנֵיהֶם וַיֵּלְכוּ אֲחֹרַנִּית וַיְכַסּוּ אֵת עֶרְוַת אֲבִיהֶם וּפְנֵיהֶם אֲחֹרַנִּית וְעֶרְוַת אֲבִיהֶם לֹא רָאוּ:

24 When *Noach* woke up from his wine and learned what his youngest son had done to him,

וַיִּיקֶץ נֹחַ מִיֵּינוֹ וַיֵּדַע אֵת אֲשֶׁר־עָשָׂה־לוֹ בְּנוֹ הַקָּטָן:

25 he said, "Cursed be Canaan; The lowest of slaves Shall he be to his brothers."

וַיֹּאמֶר אָרוּר כְּנָעַן עֶבֶד עֲבָדִים יִהְיֶה לְאֶחָיו:

26 And he said, "Blessed be *Hashem*, The God of *Shem*; Let Canaan be a slave to them.

וַיֹּאמֶר בָּרוּךְ יְהוָֹה אֱלֹהֵי שֵׁם וִיהִי כְנַעַן עֶבֶד לָמוֹ:

va-YO-mer ba-RUKH a-do-NAI e-LO-hay SHAYM vee-HEE kh'-NA-an E-ved LA-mo

27 May *Hashem* enlarge Japheth, And let him dwell in the tents of *Shem*; And let Canaan be a slave to them."

יַפְתְּ אֱלֹהִים לְיֶפֶת וְיִשְׁכֹּן בְּאָהֳלֵי־שֵׁם וִיהִי כְנַעַן עֶבֶד לָמוֹ:

28 *Noach* lived after the Flood 350 years.

וַיְחִי־נֹחַ אַחַר הַמַּבּוּל שְׁלֹשׁ מֵאוֹת שָׁנָה וַחֲמִשִּׁים שָׁנָה:

29 And all the days of *Noach* came to 950 years; then he died.

וַיִּהְיוּ כָּל־יְמֵי־נֹחַ תְּשַׁע מֵאוֹת שָׁנָה וַחֲמִשִּׁים שָׁנָה וַיָּמֹת:

10

1 These are the lines of *Shem*, Ham, and Japheth, the sons of *Noach*: sons were born to them after the Flood.

וְאֵלֶּה תּוֹלְדֹת בְּנֵי־נֹחַ שֵׁם חָם וָיָפֶת וַיִּוָּלְדוּ לָהֶם בָּנִים אַחַר הַמַּבּוּל:

2 The descendants of Japheth: Gomer, Magog, Media, Javan, Tubal, Meshech, and Tiras.

בְּנֵי יֶפֶת גֹּמֶר וּמָגוֹג וּמָדַי וְיָוָן וְתֻבָל וּמֶשֶׁךְ וְתִירָס:

3 The descendants of Gomer: Ashkenaz, Riphath, and Togarmah.

וּבְנֵי גֹּמֶר אַשְׁכְּנַז וְרִיפַת וְתֹגַרְמָה:

9:26 Blessed be *Hashem*, The God of *Shem* Rashi comments that the God of *Shem* is blessed because He will eventually fulfill His promise to give the Land of Israel to *Shem*'s descendants. While not recorded explicitly in the verse, *Hashem* had revealed this plan to *Noach*, and *Noach*, in his righteousness, accepted it as fact even before the promise had been made. To bless God means to acknowledge that *Hashem* is the source of blessing. In this verse, *Noach* recognizes that *Eretz Yisrael* is a blessing and a gift, and thanks God for it.

Bereishit/Genesis 10
Noach

בראשית י
נח

4 The descendants of Javan: Elishah and Tarshish, the Kittim and the Dodanim.

ד וּבְנֵי יָוָן אֱלִישָׁה וְתַרְשִׁישׁ כִּתִּים וְדֹדָנִים:

5 From these the maritime nations branched out. [These are the descendants of Japheth] by their lands – each with its language – their clans and their nations.

ה מֵאֵלֶּה נִפְרְדוּ אִיֵּי הַגּוֹיִם בְּאַרְצֹתָם אִישׁ לִלְשֹׁנוֹ לְמִשְׁפְּחֹתָם בְּגוֹיֵהֶם:

may-AY-leh nif-r'-DU i-YAY ha-go-YIM b'-ar-tzo-TAM EESH lil-sho-NO l'-mish-p'-kho-TAM b'-go-yay-HEM

6 The descendants of Ham: Cush, Mizraim, Put, and Canaan.

ו וּבְנֵי חָם כּוּשׁ וּמִצְרַיִם וּפוּט וּכְנָעַן:

7 The descendants of Cush: Seba, Havilah, Sabtah, Raamah, and Sabteca. The descendants of Raamah: Sheba and Dedan.

ז וּבְנֵי כוּשׁ סְבָא וַחֲוִילָה וְסַבְתָּה וְרַעְמָה וְסַבְתְּכָא וּבְנֵי רַעְמָה שְׁבָא וּדְדָן:

8 Cush also begot Nimrod, who was the first man of might on earth.

ח וְכוּשׁ יָלַד אֶת־נִמְרֹד הוּא הֵחֵל לִהְיוֹת גִּבֹּר בָּאָרֶץ:

9 He was a mighty hunter by the grace of *Hashem*; hence the saying, "Like Nimrod a mighty hunter by the grace of *Hashem*."

ט הוּא־הָיָה גִבֹּר־צַיִד לִפְנֵי יְהֹוָה עַל־כֵּן יֵאָמַר כְּנִמְרֹד גִּבּוֹר צַיִד לִפְנֵי יְהֹוָה:

10 The mainstays of his kingdom were Babylon, Erech, Accad, and Calneh in the land of Shinar.

י וַתְּהִי רֵאשִׁית מַמְלַכְתּוֹ בָּבֶל וְאֶרֶךְ וְאַכַּד וְכַלְנֵה בְּאֶרֶץ שִׁנְעָר:

11 From that land Assyria went forth and built Nineveh, Rehoboth-ir, Calah,

יא מִן־הָאָרֶץ הַהִוא יָצָא אַשּׁוּר וַיִּבֶן אֶת־נִינְוֵה וְאֶת־רְחֹבֹת עִיר וְאֶת־כָּלַח:

12 and Resen between Nineveh and Calah, that is the great city.

יב וְאֶת־רֶסֶן בֵּין נִינְוֵה וּבֵין כָּלַח הִוא הָעִיר הַגְּדֹלָה:

13 And Mizraim begot the Ludim, the Anamim, the Lehabim, the Naphtuhim,

יג וּמִצְרַיִם יָלַד אֶת־לוּדִים וְאֶת־עֲנָמִים וְאֶת־לְהָבִים וְאֶת־נַפְתֻּחִים:

14 the Pathrusim, the Casluhim, and the Caphtorim,* whence the Philistines came forth.

יד וְאֶת־פַּתְרֻסִים וְאֶת־כַּסְלֻחִים אֲשֶׁר יָצְאוּ מִשָּׁם פְּלִשְׁתִּים וְאֶת־כַּפְתֹּרִים:

15 Canaan begot Sidon, his first-born, and Heth;

טו וּכְנַעַן יָלַד אֶת־צִידֹן בְּכֹרוֹ וְאֶת־חֵת:

---

* "and the Caphtorim" moved up from the end of the verse for clarity

10:5 From these the maritime nations branched out This chapter lists the generations that emerged from *Noach*'s sons after the flood, implying that the nations spread out as a result of natural population growth. Hence, the word *nifridu* (נפרדו), 'divided,' which connotes natural separation, is used here, as opposed to the term *vayafetz* (ויפץ), 'scattered,' used in the story of the Tower of Babel (11:8), which connotes forced dispersion. Similarly, the choice of the word *lashon* (לשון), 'tongue,' as opposed to *safa* (שפה), 'language,' which is used in chapter eleven, indicates a natural evolution of dialects as nations moved away from each other. Conceivably, new languages were not yet initiated, only dialects of Hebrew. Rabbi Zalman Sorotzkin, who fled Europe and arrived in Israel during World War II, points out that this verse mentions the three aspects that unite a nation; common ancestry, land and language. Although the Jewish people can be found all over the world, they are united by their common ancestry, their connection to *Eretz Yisrael* and their ability to converse in Hebrew.

נפרדו
ויפץ
שפה
לשון

Bereishit/Genesis 10
Noach

בראשית י
נח

16 and the Jebusites, the Amorites, the Girgashites,

טו וְאֶת־הַיְבוּסִי וְאֶת־הָאֱמֹרִי וְאֵת הַגִּרְגָּשִׁי:

17 the Hivites, the Arkites, the Sinites,

יז וְאֶת־הַחִוִּי וְאֶת־הַעַרְקִי וְאֶת־הַסִּינִי:

18 the Arvadites, the Zemarites, and the Hamathites. Afterward the clans of the Canaanites spread out.

יח וְאֶת־הָאַרְוָדִי וְאֶת־הַצְּמָרִי וְאֶת־הַחֲמָתִי וְאַחַר נָפֹצוּ מִשְׁפְּחוֹת הַכְּנַעֲנִי:

19 The [original] Canaanite territory extended from Sidon as far as Gerar, near *Azza*, and as far as Sodom, Gomorrah, Admah, and Zeboiim, near Lasha.

יט וַיְהִי גְּבוּל הַכְּנַעֲנִי מִצִּידֹן בֹּאֲכָה גְרָרָה עַד־עַזָּה בֹּאֲכָה סְדֹמָה וַעֲמֹרָה וְאַדְמָה וּצְבֹיִם עַד־לָשַׁע:

20 These are the descendants of Ham, according to their clans and languages, by their lands and nations.

כ אֵלֶּה בְנֵי־חָם לְמִשְׁפְּחֹתָם לִלְשֹׁנֹתָם בְּאַרְצֹתָם בְּגוֹיֵהֶם:

21 Sons were also born to *Shem*, ancestor of all the descendants of *Ever* and older brother of Japheth.

כא וּלְשֵׁם יֻלַּד גַּם־הוּא אֲבִי כָּל־בְּנֵי־עֵבֶר אֲחִי יֶפֶת הַגָּדוֹל:

22 The descendants of *Shem*: Elam, Assyria, *Arpachshad*, Lud, and Aram.

כב בְּנֵי שֵׁם עֵילָם וְאַשּׁוּר וְאַרְפַּכְשַׁד וְלוּד וַאֲרָם:

23 The descendants of Aram: Uz, Hul, Gether, and Mash.

כג וּבְנֵי אֲרָם עוּץ וְחוּל וְגֶתֶר וָמַשׁ:

24 *Arpachshad* begot *Sheila*, and *Sheila* begot *Ever*.

כד וְאַרְפַּכְשַׁד יָלַד אֶת־שָׁלַח וְשֶׁלַח יָלַד אֶת־עֵבֶר:

25 Two sons were born to *Ever*: the name of the first was *Peleg*, for in his days the earth was divided; and the name of his brother was Joktan.

כה וּלְעֵבֶר יֻלַּד שְׁנֵי בָנִים שֵׁם הָאֶחָד פֶּלֶג כִּי בְיָמָיו נִפְלְגָה הָאָרֶץ וְשֵׁם אָחִיו יָקְטָן:

26 Joktan begot Almodad, Sheleph, Hazarmaveth, Jerah,

כו וְיָקְטָן יָלַד אֶת־אַלְמוֹדָד וְאֶת־שָׁלֶף וְאֶת־חֲצַרְמָוֶת וְאֶת־יָרַח:

27 Hadoram, Uzal, Diklah,

כז וְאֶת־הֲדוֹרָם וְאֶת־אוּזָל וְאֶת־דִּקְלָה:

28 Obal, Abimael, Sheba,

כח וְאֶת־עוֹבָל וְאֶת־אֲבִימָאֵל וְאֶת־שְׁבָא:

29 Ophir, Havilah, and Jobab; all these were the descendants of Joktan.

כט וְאֶת־אוֹפִר וְאֶת־חֲוִילָה וְאֶת־יוֹבָב כָּל־אֵלֶּה בְּנֵי יָקְטָן:

30 Their settlements extended from Mesha as far as Sephar, the hill country to the east.

ל וַיְהִי מוֹשָׁבָם מִמֵּשָׁא בֹּאֲכָה סְפָרָה הַר הַקֶּדֶם:

31 These are the descendants of *Shem* according to their clans and languages, by their lands, according to their nations.

לא אֵלֶּה בְנֵי־שֵׁם לְמִשְׁפְּחֹתָם לִלְשֹׁנֹתָם בְּאַרְצֹתָם לְגוֹיֵהֶם:

32 These are the groupings of *Noach*'s descendants, according to their origins, by their nations; and from these the nations branched out over the earth after the Flood.

לב אֵלֶּה מִשְׁפְּחֹת בְּנֵי־נֹחַ לְתוֹלְדֹתָם בְּגוֹיֵהֶם וּמֵאֵלֶּה נִפְרְדוּ הַגּוֹיִם בָּאָרֶץ אַחַר הַמַּבּוּל:

Bereishit/Genesis 11
Noach

בראשית יא
נח

11 ¹ Everyone on earth had the same language and the same words.

א וַיְהִי כָל־הָאָרֶץ שָׂפָה אֶחָת וּדְבָרִים אֲחָדִים:

vai-HEE khol ha-A-retz sa-FAH e-KHAT ud-va-REEM a-kha-DEEM

² And as they migrated from the east, they came upon a valley in the land of Shinar and settled there.

ב וַיְהִי בְּנָסְעָם מִקֶּדֶם וַיִּמְצְאוּ בִקְעָה בְּאֶרֶץ שִׁנְעָר וַיֵּשְׁבוּ שָׁם:

³ They said to one another, "Come, let us make bricks and burn them hard." – Brick served them as stone, and bitumen served them as mortar.

ג וַיֹּאמְרוּ אִישׁ אֶל־רֵעֵהוּ הָבָה נִלְבְּנָה לְבֵנִים וְנִשְׂרְפָה לִשְׂרֵפָה וַתְּהִי לָהֶם הַלְּבֵנָה לְאָבֶן וְהַחֵמָר הָיָה לָהֶם לַחֹמֶר:

⁴ And they said, "Come, let us build us a city, and a tower with its top in the sky, to make a name for ourselves; else we shall be scattered all over the world."

ד וַיֹּאמְרוּ הָבָה ׀ נִבְנֶה־לָּנוּ עִיר וּמִגְדָּל וְרֹאשׁוֹ בַשָּׁמַיִם וְנַעֲשֶׂה־לָּנוּ שֵׁם פֶּן־נָפוּץ עַל־פְּנֵי כָל־הָאָרֶץ:

⁵ *Hashem* came down to look at the city and tower that man had built,

ה וַיֵּרֶד יְהֹוָה לִרְאֹת אֶת־הָעִיר וְאֶת־הַמִּגְדָּל אֲשֶׁר בָּנוּ בְּנֵי הָאָדָם:

⁶ and *Hashem* said, "If, as one people with one language for all, this is how they have begun to act, then nothing that they may propose to do will be out of their reach.

ו וַיֹּאמֶר יְהֹוָה הֵן עַם אֶחָד וְשָׂפָה אַחַת לְכֻלָּם וְזֶה הַחִלָּם לַעֲשׂוֹת וְעַתָּה לֹא־יִבָּצֵר מֵהֶם כֹּל אֲשֶׁר יָזְמוּ לַעֲשׂוֹת:

⁷ Let us, then, go down and confound their speech there, so that they shall not understand one another's speech."

ז הָבָה נֵרְדָה וְנָבְלָה שָׁם שְׂפָתָם אֲשֶׁר לֹא יִשְׁמְעוּ אִישׁ שְׂפַת רֵעֵהוּ:

⁸ Thus *Hashem* scattered them from there over the face of the whole earth; and they stopped building the city

ח וַיָּפֶץ יְהֹוָה אֹתָם מִשָּׁם עַל־פְּנֵי כָל־הָאָרֶץ וַיַּחְדְּלוּ לִבְנֹת הָעִיר:

⁹ That is why it was called Babel, because there *Hashem* confounded the speech of the whole earth; and from there *Hashem* scattered them over the face of the whole earth.

ט עַל־כֵּן קָרָא שְׁמָהּ בָּבֶל כִּי־שָׁם בָּלַל יְהֹוָה שְׂפַת כָּל־הָאָרֶץ וּמִשָּׁם הֱפִיצָם יְהֹוָה עַל־פְּנֵי כָּל־הָאָרֶץ:

¹⁰ This is the line of *Shem*. *Shem* was 100 years old when he begot *Arpachshad*, two years after the Flood.

י אֵלֶּה תּוֹלְדֹת שֵׁם שֵׁם בֶּן־מְאַת שָׁנָה וַיּוֹלֶד אֶת־אַרְפַּכְשָׁד שְׁנָתַיִם אַחַר הַמַּבּוּל:

¹¹ After the birth of *Arpachshad*, *Shem* lived 500 years and begot sons and daughters.

יא וַיְחִי־שֵׁם אַחֲרֵי הוֹלִידוֹ אֶת־אַרְפַּכְשָׁד חֲמֵשׁ מֵאוֹת שָׁנָה וַיּוֹלֶד בָּנִים וּבָנוֹת:

11:1 Everyone on earth had the same language The Hebrew word for 'language,' *safa* (שפה), also appears in *Sefer Tzefanya* (3:9) when the prophet describes a *safa b'rurah* (שפה ברורה), 'purity of speech,' that will be shared by all the nations of the world in the end of days: "For then I will make the peoples pure of speech, so that they all invoke *Hashem* by name and serve Him with one accord." Rabbi Avraham Ibn Ezra comments that the pure language that *Tzefanya* promises is the Hebrew language. In future times, the world will begin to learn Hebrew, the language of Creation. This promise has begun to come true in our age. Not only has the Hebrew language been revitalized over the past century as the spoken language in the Jewish homeland, but in more recent years, thousands of non-Jews have also begun to study Hebrew as a way to connect with their Creator and gain a deeper understanding of the Bible.

שפה ברורה

28

Bereishit/Genesis 11
Noach

12 When *Arpachshad* had lived 35 years, he begot *Shelach*.	יב וְאַרְפַּכְשַׁד חַי חָמֵשׁ וּשְׁלֹשִׁים שָׁנָה וַיּוֹלֶד אֶת־שָׁלַח:
13 After the birth of *Shelach*, *Arpachshad* lived 403 years and begot sons and daughters.	יג וַיְחִי אַרְפַּכְשַׁד אַחֲרֵי הוֹלִידוֹ אֶת־שֶׁלַח שָׁלֹשׁ שָׁנִים וְאַרְבַּע מֵאוֹת שָׁנָה וַיּוֹלֶד בָּנִים וּבָנוֹת:
14 When *Shelach* had lived 30 years, he begot *Ever*.	יד וְשֶׁלַח חַי שְׁלֹשִׁים שָׁנָה וַיּוֹלֶד אֶת־עֵבֶר:
15 After the birth of *Ever*, *Shelach* lived 403 years and begot sons and daughters.	טו וַיְחִי־שֶׁלַח אַחֲרֵי הוֹלִידוֹ אֶת־עֵבֶר שָׁלֹשׁ שָׁנִים וְאַרְבַּע מֵאוֹת שָׁנָה וַיּוֹלֶד בָּנִים וּבָנוֹת:
16 When *Ever* had lived 34 years, he begot *Peleg*.	טז וַיְחִי־עֵבֶר אַרְבַּע וּשְׁלֹשִׁים שָׁנָה וַיּוֹלֶד אֶת־פָּלֶג:
17 After the birth of *Peleg*, *Ever* lived 430 years and begot sons and daughters.	יז וַיְחִי־עֵבֶר אַחֲרֵי הוֹלִידוֹ אֶת־פֶּלֶג שְׁלֹשִׁים שָׁנָה וְאַרְבַּע מֵאוֹת שָׁנָה וַיּוֹלֶד בָּנִים וּבָנוֹת:
18 When *Peleg* had lived 30 years, he begot *Re'u*.	יח וַיְחִי־פֶלֶג שְׁלֹשִׁים שָׁנָה וַיּוֹלֶד אֶת־רְעוּ:
19 After the birth of *Re'u*, *Peleg* lived 209 years and begot sons and daughters.	יט וַיְחִי־פֶלֶג אַחֲרֵי הוֹלִידוֹ אֶת־רְעוּ תֵּשַׁע שָׁנִים וּמָאתַיִם שָׁנָה וַיּוֹלֶד בָּנִים וּבָנוֹת:
20 When *Re'u* had lived 32 years, he begot *Serug*.	כ וַיְחִי רְעוּ שְׁתַּיִם וּשְׁלֹשִׁים שָׁנָה וַיּוֹלֶד אֶת־שְׂרוּג:
21 After the birth of *Serug*, *Re'u* lived 207 years and begot sons and daughters.	כא וַיְחִי רְעוּ אַחֲרֵי הוֹלִידוֹ אֶת־שְׂרוּג שֶׁבַע שָׁנִים וּמָאתַיִם שָׁנָה וַיּוֹלֶד בָּנִים וּבָנוֹת:
22 When *Serug* had lived 30 years, he begot *Nachor*.	כב וַיְחִי שְׂרוּג שְׁלֹשִׁים שָׁנָה וַיּוֹלֶד אֶת־נָחוֹר:
23 After the birth of *Nachor*, *Serug* lived 200 years and begot sons and daughters.	כג וַיְחִי שְׂרוּג אַחֲרֵי הוֹלִידוֹ אֶת־נָחוֹר מָאתַיִם שָׁנָה וַיּוֹלֶד בָּנִים וּבָנוֹת:
24 When *Nachor* had lived 29 years, he begot *Terach*.	כד וַיְחִי נָחוֹר תֵּשַׁע וְעֶשְׂרִים שָׁנָה וַיּוֹלֶד אֶת־תָּרַח:
25 After the birth of *Terach*, *Nachor* lived 119 years and begot sons and daughters.	כה וַיְחִי נָחוֹר אַחֲרֵי הוֹלִידוֹ אֶת־תֶּרַח תְּשַׁע־עֶשְׂרֵה שָׁנָה וּמְאַת שָׁנָה וַיּוֹלֶד בָּנִים וּבָנוֹת:
26 When *Terach* had lived 70 years, he begot *Avram*, Nahor, and Haran.	כו וַיְחִי־תֶרַח שִׁבְעִים שָׁנָה וַיּוֹלֶד אֶת־אַבְרָם אֶת־נָחוֹר וְאֶת־הָרָן:
27 Now this is the line of *Terach*: *Terach* begot *Avram*, Nahor, and Haran; and Haran begot Lot.	כז וְאֵלֶּה תּוֹלְדֹת תֶּרַח תֶּרַח הוֹלִיד אֶת־אַבְרָם אֶת־נָחוֹר וְאֶת־הָרָן וְהָרָן הוֹלִיד אֶת־לוֹט:
28 Haran died in the lifetime of his father *Terach*, in his native land, Ur of the Chaldeans.	כח וַיָּמָת הָרָן עַל־פְּנֵי תֶּרַח אָבִיו בְּאֶרֶץ מוֹלַדְתּוֹ בְּאוּר כַּשְׂדִּים:

Bereishit/Genesis 12
Lech Lecha

בראשית יב
לך לך

29 Avram and Nahor took to themselves wives, the name of Avram's wife being Sarai and that of Nahor's wife Milcah, the daughter of Haran, the father of Milcah and Iscah.

כט וַיִּקַּח אַבְרָם וְנָחוֹר לָהֶם נָשִׁים שֵׁם אֵשֶׁת־אַבְרָם שָׂרָי וְשֵׁם אֵשֶׁת־נָחוֹר מִלְכָּה בַּת־הָרָן אֲבִי־מִלְכָּה וַאֲבִי יִסְכָּה:

30 Now Sarai was barren, she had no child.

ל וַתְּהִי שָׂרַי עֲקָרָה אֵין לָהּ וָלָד:

31 Terach took his son Avram, his grandson Lot the son of Haran, and his daughter-in-law Sarai, the wife of his son Avram, and they set out together from Ur of the Chaldeans for the land of Canaan; but when they had come as far as Haran, they settled there.

לא וַיִּקַּח תֶּרַח אֶת־אַבְרָם בְּנוֹ וְאֶת־לוֹט בֶּן־הָרָן בֶּן־בְּנוֹ וְאֵת שָׂרַי כַּלָּתוֹ אֵשֶׁת אַבְרָם בְּנוֹ וַיֵּצְאוּ אִתָּם מֵאוּר כַּשְׂדִּים לָלֶכֶת אַרְצָה כְּנַעַן וַיָּבֹאוּ עַד־חָרָן וַיֵּשְׁבוּ שָׁם:

32 The days of Terach came to 205 years; and Terach died in Haran.

לב וַיִּהְיוּ יְמֵי־תֶרַח חָמֵשׁ שָׁנִים וּמָאתַיִם שָׁנָה וַיָּמָת תֶּרַח בְּחָרָן:

12 1 Hashem said to Avram, "Go forth from your native land and from your father's house to the land that I will show you.

יב א וַיֹּאמֶר יְהוָה אֶל־אַבְרָם לֶךְ־לְךָ מֵאַרְצְךָ וּמִמּוֹלַדְתְּךָ וּמִבֵּית אָבִיךָ אֶל־הָאָרֶץ אֲשֶׁר אַרְאֶךָּ:

va-YO-mer a-do-NAI el av-RAM lekh l'-KHA may-ar-tz'-KHA u-mi-mo-lad-t'-KHA u-mi-BAYT a-VEE-kha el ha-A-retz a-SHER ar-E-ka

2 I will make of you a great nation, And I will bless you; I will make your name great, And you shall be a blessing.

ב וְאֶעֶשְׂךָ לְגוֹי גָּדוֹל וַאֲבָרֶכְךָ וַאֲגַדְּלָה שְׁמֶךָ וֶהְיֵה בְּרָכָה:

3 I will bless those who bless you And curse him that curses you; And all the families of the earth Shall bless themselves by you."

ג וַאֲבָרֲכָה מְבָרְכֶיךָ וּמְקַלֶּלְךָ אָאֹר וְנִבְרְכוּ בְךָ כֹּל מִשְׁפְּחֹת הָאֲדָמָה:

va-a-va-r'-KHA m'-VA-r'-KHE-kha um-ka-lel-KHA a-OR v'-niv-r'-KHU v'-KHA KOL mish-p'-KHOT ha-a-da-MAH

12:1 Go forth from your native land With the words *lech l'cha* (לֶךְ־לְךָ), literally 'go for yourself,' *Avraham* is commanded to leave everything behind and head to the Holy Land. It would have been enough for God to command him *lech* (לֶךְ), 'go'; what is added by the word *l'cha* (לְךָ), 'for yourself'? According to *Rashi*, the word *l'cha* implies that the travel was for *Avraham's* benefit. Though he is leaving his homeland, family, and father's house, God promises *Avraham* that the journey will be beneficial to him. As a result of his relocation, he will merit the children he has always wanted and will become influential throughout the world, so that he will be able to accomplish his mission to positively influence the world. A journey to *Eretz Yisrael* is not always simple, but the impact it can have is immeasurable.

12:3 I will bless those who bless you and curse him that curses you *Avraham* is commanded to travel to a land unknown to him. To assuage his fears that he would not find friends or supporters in his new home, *Hashem* promises that He will remain on *Avraham's* side by blessing those who bless him and cursing those who curse him. He concludes with the promise that *Avraham* and his descendants will become a source of blessing to the entire world. This promise has remained in effect through the generations. History has shown that whenever a nation persecutes the Jewish people, curses ultimately befall it. However, wherever the Children of Israel have been welcomed, they have made immeasurable contributions to society, thus earning divine favor for their host nation. On an individual level as well, many non-Jews look to this verse as an important reason to stand with the People of Israel and the Land of Israel.

לך לך

Bereishit/Genesis 12
Lech Lecha

בראשית יב
לך לך

4 *Avram* went forth as *Hashem* had commanded him, and Lot went with him. *Avram* was seventy-five years old when he left Haran.

ד וַיֵּלֶךְ אַבְרָם כַּאֲשֶׁר דִּבֶּר אֵלָיו יְהוָה וַיֵּלֶךְ אִתּוֹ לוֹט וְאַבְרָם בֶּן־חָמֵשׁ שָׁנִים וְשִׁבְעִים שָׁנָה בְּצֵאתוֹ מֵחָרָן׃

5 *Avram* took his wife *Sarai* and his brother's son Lot, and all the wealth that they had amassed, and the persons that they had acquired in Haran; and they set out for the land of Canaan. When they arrived in the land of Canaan,

ה וַיִּקַּח אַבְרָם אֶת־שָׂרַי אִשְׁתּוֹ וְאֶת־לוֹט בֶּן־אָחִיו וְאֶת־כָּל־רְכוּשָׁם אֲשֶׁר רָכָשׁוּ וְאֶת־הַנֶּפֶשׁ אֲשֶׁר־עָשׂוּ בְחָרָן וַיֵּצְאוּ לָלֶכֶת אַרְצָה כְּנַעַן וַיָּבֹאוּ אַרְצָה כְּנָעַן׃

6 *Avram* passed through the land as far as the site of Shechem, at the terebinth of Moreh. The Canaanites were then in the land.

ו וַיַּעֲבֹר אַבְרָם בָּאָרֶץ עַד מְקוֹם שְׁכֶם עַד אֵלוֹן מוֹרֶה וְהַכְּנַעֲנִי אָז בָּאָרֶץ׃

7 *Hashem* appeared to *Avram* and said, "I will assign this land to your offspring." And he built a *Mizbayach* there to *Hashem* who had appeared to him.

ז וַיֵּרָא יְהוָה אֶל־אַבְרָם וַיֹּאמֶר לְזַרְעֲךָ אֶתֵּן אֶת־הָאָרֶץ הַזֹּאת וַיִּבֶן שָׁם מִזְבֵּחַ לַיהוָה הַנִּרְאֶה אֵלָיו׃

va-yay-RA a-do-NAI el av-RAM va-YO-mer l'-ZAR-a-KHA e-TAYN et ha-A-retz ha-ZOT va-YI-ven SHAM miz-BAY-akh la-do-NAI ha-nir-EH ay-LAV

8 From there he moved on to the hill country east of *Beit El* and pitched his tent, with *Beit El* on the west and Ai on the east; and he built there a *Mizbayach* to *Hashem* and invoked *Hashem* by name.

ח וַיַּעְתֵּק מִשָּׁם הָהָרָה מִקֶּדֶם לְבֵית־אֵל וַיֵּט אָהֳלֹה בֵּית־אֵל מִיָּם וְהָעַי מִקֶּדֶם וַיִּבֶן־שָׁם מִזְבֵּחַ לַיהוָה וַיִּקְרָא בְּשֵׁם יְהוָה׃

9 Then *Avram* journeyed by stages toward the *Negev*.

ט וַיִּסַּע אַבְרָם הָלוֹךְ וְנָסוֹעַ הַנֶּגְבָּה׃

10 There was a famine in the land, and *Avram* went down to Egypt to sojourn there, for the famine was severe in the land.

י וַיְהִי רָעָב בָּאָרֶץ וַיֵּרֶד אַבְרָם מִצְרַיְמָה לָגוּר שָׁם כִּי־כָבֵד הָרָעָב בָּאָרֶץ׃

11 As he was about to enter Egypt, he said to his wife *Sarai*, "I know what a beautiful woman you are.

יא וַיְהִי כַּאֲשֶׁר הִקְרִיב לָבוֹא מִצְרָיְמָה וַיֹּאמֶר אֶל־שָׂרַי אִשְׁתּוֹ הִנֵּה־נָא יָדַעְתִּי כִּי אִשָּׁה יְפַת־מַרְאֶה אָתְּ׃

12 If the Egyptians see you, and think, 'She is his wife,' they will kill me and let you live.

יב וְהָיָה כִּי־יִרְאוּ אֹתָךְ הַמִּצְרִים וְאָמְרוּ אִשְׁתּוֹ זֹאת וְהָרְגוּ אֹתִי וְאֹתָךְ יְחַיּוּ׃

13 Please say that you are my sister, that it may go well with me because of you, and that I may remain alive thanks to you."

יג אִמְרִי־נָא אֲחֹתִי אָתְּ לְמַעַן יִיטַב־לִי בַעֲבוּרֵךְ וְחָיְתָה נַפְשִׁי בִּגְלָלֵךְ׃

12:7 Hashem appeared to Avram This is the first time that the Bible describes God revealing Himself to *Avraham*. Even at the beginning of this chapter when *Hashem* commanded *Avraham* to leave his land, it does not say that *Hashem* appeared to him. The *Kli Yakar*, a biblical commentator who lived in Prague in the early seventeenth century, explains this by reference to the principle that *Hashem* does not reveal Himself prophetically outside the Land of Israel. The command given in Haran at the start of this chapter was heard, but not seen. Only once he arrived in Israel did God actually appear to *Avraham*, which then prompted *Avraham* to build an altar to mark the occasion. God's presence is felt most intensely in *Eretz Yisrael*.

Bereishit/Genesis 13
Lech Lecha

בראשית יג
לך לך

14 When *Avram* entered Egypt, the Egyptians saw how very beautiful the woman was.

יד וַיְהִי כְּבוֹא אַבְרָם מִצְרָיְמָה וַיִּרְאוּ הַמִּצְרִים אֶת־הָאִשָּׁה כִּי־יָפָה הִוא מְאֹד:

15 Pharaoh's courtiers saw her and praised her to Pharaoh, and the woman was taken into Pharaoh's palace.

טו וַיִּרְאוּ אֹתָהּ שָׂרֵי פַרְעֹה וַיְהַלְלוּ אֹתָהּ אֶל־פַּרְעֹה וַתֻּקַּח הָאִשָּׁה בֵּית פַּרְעֹה:

16 And because of her, it went well with *Avram*; he acquired sheep, oxen, asses, male and female slaves, she-asses, and camels.

טז וּלְאַבְרָם הֵיטִיב בַּעֲבוּרָהּ וַיְהִי־לוֹ צֹאן וּבָקָר וַחֲמֹרִים וַעֲבָדִים וּשְׁפָחֹת וַאֲתֹנֹת וּגְמַלִּים:

17 But *Hashem* afflicted Pharaoh and his household with mighty plagues on account of *Sarai*, the wife of *Avram*.

יז וַיְנַגַּע יְהֹוָה אֶת־פַּרְעֹה נְגָעִים גְּדֹלִים וְאֶת־בֵּיתוֹ עַל־דְּבַר שָׂרַי אֵשֶׁת אַבְרָם:

18 Pharaoh sent for *Avram* and said, "What is this you have done to me! Why did you not tell me that she was your wife?

יח וַיִּקְרָא פַרְעֹה לְאַבְרָם וַיֹּאמֶר מַה־זֹּאת עָשִׂיתָ לִּי לָמָּה לֹא־הִגַּדְתָּ לִּי כִּי אִשְׁתְּךָ הִוא:

19 Why did you say, 'She is my sister,' so that I took her as my wife? Now, here is your wife; take her and begone!"

יט לָמָה אָמַרְתָּ אֲחֹתִי הִוא וָאֶקַּח אֹתָהּ לִי לְאִשָּׁה וְעַתָּה הִנֵּה אִשְׁתְּךָ קַח וָלֵךְ:

20 And Pharaoh put men in charge of him, and they sent him off with his wife and all that he possessed.

כ וַיְצַו עָלָיו פַּרְעֹה אֲנָשִׁים וַיְשַׁלְּחוּ אֹתוֹ וְאֶת־אִשְׁתּוֹ וְאֶת־כָּל־אֲשֶׁר־לוֹ:

13
1 From Egypt, *Avram* went up into the *Negev*, with his wife and all that he possessed, together with Lot.

יג א וַיַּעַל אַבְרָם מִמִּצְרַיִם הוּא וְאִשְׁתּוֹ וְכָל־אֲשֶׁר־לוֹ וְלוֹט עִמּוֹ הַנֶּגְבָּה:

2 Now *Avram* was very rich in cattle, silver, and gold.

ב וְאַבְרָם כָּבֵד מְאֹד בַּמִּקְנֶה בַּכֶּסֶף וּבַזָּהָב:

3 And he proceeded by stages from the *Negev* as far as *Beit El*, to the place where his tent had been formerly, between *Beit El* and Ai,

ג וַיֵּלֶךְ לְמַסָּעָיו מִנֶּגֶב וְעַד־בֵּית־אֵל עַד־הַמָּקוֹם אֲשֶׁר־הָיָה שָׁם אהלה [אָהֳלֹה] בַּתְּחִלָּה בֵּין בֵּית־אֵל וּבֵין הָעָי:

4 the site of the *Mizbayach* that he had built there at first; and there *Avram* invoked *Hashem* by name.

ד אֶל־מְקוֹם הַמִּזְבֵּחַ אֲשֶׁר־עָשָׂה שָׁם בָּרִאשֹׁנָה וַיִּקְרָא שָׁם אַבְרָם בְּשֵׁם יְהֹוָה:

5 Lot, who went with *Avram*, also had flocks and herds and tents,

ה וְגַם־לְלוֹט הַהֹלֵךְ אֶת־אַבְרָם הָיָה צֹאן וּבָקָר וְאֹהָלִים:

6 so that the land could not support them staying together; for their possessions were so great that they could not remain together.

ו וְלֹא־נָשָׂא אֹתָם הָאָרֶץ לָשֶׁבֶת יַחְדָּו כִּי־הָיָה רְכוּשָׁם רָב וְלֹא יָכְלוּ לָשֶׁבֶת יַחְדָּו:

7 And there was quarreling between the herdsmen of *Avram*'s cattle and those of Lot's cattle. – The Canaanites and Perizzites were then dwelling in the land.

ז וַיְהִי־רִיב בֵּין רֹעֵי מִקְנֵה־אַבְרָם וּבֵין רֹעֵי מִקְנֵה־לוֹט וְהַכְּנַעֲנִי וְהַפְּרִזִּי אָז יֹשֵׁב בָּאָרֶץ:

Bereishit/Genesis 13
Lech Lecha

בראשית יג
לך לך

8 *Avram* said to Lot, "Let there be no strife between you and me, between my herdsmen and yours, for we are kinsmen.

ח וַיֹּאמֶר אַבְרָם אֶל־לוֹט אַל־נָא תְהִי מְרִיבָה בֵּינִי וּבֵינֶךָ וּבֵין רֹעַי וּבֵין רֹעֶיךָ כִּי־אֲנָשִׁים אַחִים אֲנָחְנוּ׃

9 Is not the whole land before you? Let us separate: if you go north, I will go south; and if you go south, I will go north."

ט הֲלֹא כָל־הָאָרֶץ לְפָנֶיךָ הִפָּרֶד נָא מֵעָלָי אִם־הַשְּׂמֹאל וְאֵימִנָה וְאִם־הַיָּמִין וְאַשְׂמְאִילָה׃

10 Lot looked about him and saw how well watered was the whole plain of the *Yarden*, all of it – this was before *Hashem* had destroyed Sodom and Gomorrah – all the way to Zoar, like the garden of *Hashem*, like the land of Egypt.

י וַיִּשָּׂא־לוֹט אֶת־עֵינָיו וַיַּרְא אֶת־כָּל־כִּכַּר הַיַּרְדֵּן כִּי כֻלָּהּ מַשְׁקֶה לִפְנֵי שַׁחֵת יְהוָֹה אֶת־סְדֹם וְאֶת־עֲמֹרָה כְּגַן־יְהוָֹה כְּאֶרֶץ מִצְרַיִם בֹּאֲכָה צֹעַר׃

va-yi-sa LOT et ay-NAV va-YAR et kol ki-KAR ha-yar-DAYN KEE khu-LAH mash-KEH lif-NAY sha-KHAYT a-do-NAI et s'-DOM v'-et a-mo-RAH k'-gan a-do-NAI k'-E-retz mitz-RA-yim bo-a-KHA TZO-ar

11 So Lot chose for himself the whole plain of the *Yarden*, and Lot journeyed eastward. Thus they parted from each other;

יא וַיִּבְחַר־לוֹ לוֹט אֵת כָּל־כִּכַּר הַיַּרְדֵּן וַיִּסַּע לוֹט מִקֶּדֶם וַיִּפָּרְדוּ אִישׁ מֵעַל אָחִיו׃

12 *Avram* remained in the land of Canaan, while Lot settled in the cities of the Plain, pitching his tents near Sodom.

יב אַבְרָם יָשַׁב בְּאֶרֶץ־כְּנָעַן וְלוֹט יָשַׁב בְּעָרֵי הַכִּכָּר וַיֶּאֱהַל עַד־סְדֹם׃

13 Now the inhabitants of Sodom were very wicked sinners against *Hashem*.

יג וְאַנְשֵׁי סְדֹם רָעִים וְחַטָּאִים לַיהוָֹה מְאֹד׃

14 And *Hashem* said to *Avram*, after Lot had parted from him, "Raise your eyes and look out from where you are, to the north and south, to the east and west,

יד וַיהוָֹה אָמַר אֶל־אַבְרָם אַחֲרֵי הִפָּרֶד־לוֹט מֵעִמּוֹ שָׂא נָא עֵינֶיךָ וּרְאֵה מִן־הַמָּקוֹם אֲשֶׁר־אַתָּה שָׁם צָפֹנָה וָנֶגְבָּה וָקֵדְמָה וָיָמָּה׃

15 for I give all the land that you see to you and your offspring forever.

טו כִּי אֶת־כָּל־הָאָרֶץ אֲשֶׁר־אַתָּה רֹאֶה לְךָ אֶתְּנֶנָּה וּלְזַרְעֲךָ עַד־עוֹלָם׃

16 I will make your offspring as the dust of the earth, so that if one can count the dust of the earth, then your offspring too can be counted.

טז וְשַׂמְתִּי אֶת־זַרְעֲךָ כַּעֲפַר הָאָרֶץ אֲשֶׁר אִם־יוּכַל אִישׁ לִמְנוֹת אֶת־עֲפַר הָאָרֶץ גַּם־זַרְעֲךָ יִמָּנֶה׃

17 Up, walk about the land, through its length and its breadth, for I give it to you."

יז קוּם הִתְהַלֵּךְ בָּאָרֶץ לְאָרְכָּהּ וּלְרָחְבָּהּ כִּי לְךָ אֶתְּנֶנָּה׃

Jordan River

13:10 How well watered was the whole plain of the *Yarden* After conflict arises between their shepherds, it becomes clear that *Avraham* and Lot must separate. Lot chooses the fertile, well-watered plain of the *Yarden*, leaving Canaan, a land with meager water sources of its own, to *Avraham*. The area that Lot chooses, though lush and bountiful, was filled with cruel and corrupt inhabitants who are ultimately destroyed in Sodom and Gomorrah. *Avraham*, on the other hand, settles in the holy Land of Israel, where he begins to fulfill his spiritual calling. Though other places can be attractive, when it comes to sanctity and Godliness there is no better place on earth than *Eretz Yisrael*.

Bereishit/Genesis 14
Lech Lecha

בראשית יד
לך לך

18 And *Avram* moved his tent, and came to dwell at the terebinths of Mamre, which are in *Chevron*; and he built a *Mizbayach* there to *Hashem*.

יח וַיֶּאֱהַל אַבְרָם וַיָּבֹא וַיֵּשֶׁב בְּאֵלֹנֵי מַמְרֵא אֲשֶׁר בְּחֶבְרוֹן וַיִּבֶן־שָׁם מִזְבֵּחַ לַיהוָה:

14

1 Now, when King Amraphel of Shinar, King Arioch of Ellasar, King Chedorlaomer of Elam, and King Tidal of Goiim

יד א וַיְהִי בִּימֵי אַמְרָפֶל מֶלֶךְ־שִׁנְעָר אַרְיוֹךְ מֶלֶךְ אֶלָּסָר כְּדָרְלָעֹמֶר מֶלֶךְ עֵילָם וְתִדְעָל מֶלֶךְ גּוֹיִם:

2 made war on King Bera of Sodom, King Birsha of Gomorrah, King Shinab of Admah, King Shemeber of Zeboiim, and the king of Bela, which is Zoar,

ב עָשׂוּ מִלְחָמָה אֶת־בֶּרַע מֶלֶךְ סְדֹם וְאֶת־בִּרְשַׁע מֶלֶךְ עֲמֹרָה שִׁנְאָב מֶלֶךְ אַדְמָה וְשֶׁמְאֵבֶר מֶלֶךְ צְבִיִּים [צְבוֹיִים] וּמֶלֶךְ בֶּלַע הִיא־צֹעַר:

3 all the latter joined forces at the Valley of Siddim, now the Dead Sea.

ג כָּל־אֵלֶּה חָבְרוּ אֶל־עֵמֶק הַשִּׂדִּים הוּא יָם הַמֶּלַח:

4 Twelve years they served Chedorlaomer, and in the thirteenth year they rebelled.

ד שְׁתֵּים עֶשְׂרֵה שָׁנָה עָבְדוּ אֶת־כְּדָרְלָעֹמֶר וּשְׁלֹשׁ־עֶשְׂרֵה שָׁנָה מָרָדוּ:

5 In the fourteenth year Chedorlaomer and the kings who were with him came and defeated the Rephaim at Ashteroth-karnaim, the Zuzim at Ham, the Emim at Shaveh-kiriathaim,

ה וּבְאַרְבַּע עֶשְׂרֵה שָׁנָה בָּא כְדָרְלָעֹמֶר וְהַמְּלָכִים אֲשֶׁר אִתּוֹ וַיַּכּוּ אֶת־רְפָאִים בְּעַשְׁתְּרֹת קַרְנַיִם וְאֶת־הַזּוּזִים בְּהָם וְאֵת הָאֵימִים בְּשָׁוֵה קִרְיָתָיִם:

6 and the Horites in their hill country of Seir as far as *El*-paran, which is by the wilderness.

ו וְאֶת־הַחֹרִי בְּהַרְרָם שֵׂעִיר עַד אֵיל פָּארָן אֲשֶׁר עַל־הַמִּדְבָּר:

7 On their way back they came to En-mishpat, which is Kadesh, and subdued all the territory of the Amalekites, and also the Amorites who dwelt in Hazazon-tamar.

ז וַיָּשֻׁבוּ וַיָּבֹאוּ אֶל־עֵין מִשְׁפָּט הִוא קָדֵשׁ וַיַּכּוּ אֶת־כָּל־שְׂדֵה הָעֲמָלֵקִי וְגַם אֶת־הָאֱמֹרִי הַיֹּשֵׁב בְּחַצְצֹן תָּמָר:

8 Then the king of Sodom, the king of Gomorrah, the king of Admah, the king of Zeboiim, and the king of Bela, which is Zoar, went forth and engaged them in battle in the Valley of Siddim:

ח וַיֵּצֵא מֶלֶךְ־סְדֹם וּמֶלֶךְ עֲמֹרָה וּמֶלֶךְ אַדְמָה וּמֶלֶךְ צְבִיִּים [צְבוֹיִים] וּמֶלֶךְ בֶּלַע הִוא־צֹעַר וַיַּעַרְכוּ אִתָּם מִלְחָמָה בְּעֵמֶק הַשִּׂדִּים:

9 King Chedorlaomer of Elam, King Tidal of Goiim, King Amraphel of Shinar, and King Arioch of Ellasar – four kings against those five.

ט אֵת כְּדָרְלָעֹמֶר מֶלֶךְ עֵילָם וְתִדְעָל מֶלֶךְ גּוֹיִם וְאַמְרָפֶל מֶלֶךְ שִׁנְעָר וְאַרְיוֹךְ מֶלֶךְ אֶלָּסָר אַרְבָּעָה מְלָכִים אֶת־הַחֲמִשָּׁה:

10 Now the Valley of Siddim was dotted with bitumen pits; and the kings of Sodom and Gomorrah, in their flight, threw themselves into them, while the rest escaped to the hill country.

י וְעֵמֶק הַשִּׂדִּים בֶּאֱרֹת בֶּאֱרֹת חֵמָר וַיָּנֻסוּ מֶלֶךְ־סְדֹם וַעֲמֹרָה וַיִּפְּלוּ־שָׁמָּה וְהַנִּשְׁאָרִים הֶרָה נָּסוּ:

11 [The invaders] seized all the wealth of Sodom and Gomorrah and all their provisions, and went their way.

יא וַיִּקְחוּ אֶת־כָּל־רְכֻשׁ סְדֹם וַעֲמֹרָה וְאֶת־כָּל־אָכְלָם וַיֵּלֵכוּ:

12 They also took Lot, the son of *Avram*'s brother, and his possessions, and departed; for he had settled in Sodom.

יב וַיִּקְחוּ אֶת־לוֹט וְאֶת־רְכֻשׁוֹ בֶּן־אֲחִי אַבְרָם וַיֵּלֵכוּ וְהוּא יֹשֵׁב בִּסְדֹם:

Bereishit/Genesis 14
Lech Lecha

בראשית יד
לך לך

13 A fugitive brought the news to *Avram* the Hebrew, who was dwelling at the terebinths of Mamre the Amorite, kinsman of Eshkol and Aner, these being *Avram*'s allies.

יג וַיָּבֹא הַפָּלִיט וַיַּגֵּד לְאַבְרָם הָעִבְרִי וְהוּא שֹׁכֵן בְּאֵלֹנֵי מַמְרֵא הָאֱמֹרִי אֲחִי אֶשְׁכֹּל וַאֲחִי עָנֵר וְהֵם בַּעֲלֵי בְרִית־אַבְרָם:

14 When *Avram* heard that his kinsman had been taken captive, he mustered his retainers, born into his household, numbering three hundred and eighteen, and went in pursuit as far as *Dan*.

יד וַיִּשְׁמַע אַבְרָם כִּי נִשְׁבָּה אָחִיו וַיָּרֶק אֶת־חֲנִיכָיו יְלִידֵי בֵיתוֹ שְׁמֹנָה עָשָׂר וּשְׁלֹשׁ מֵאוֹת וַיִּרְדֹּף עַד־דָּן:

15 At night, he and his servants deployed against them and defeated them; and he pursued them as far as Hobah, which is north of Damascus.

טו וַיֵּחָלֵק עֲלֵיהֶם לַיְלָה הוּא וַעֲבָדָיו וַיַּכֵּם וַיִּרְדְּפֵם עַד־חוֹבָה אֲשֶׁר מִשְּׂמֹאל לְדַמָּשֶׂק:

16 He brought back all the possessions; he also brought back his kinsman Lot and his possessions, and the women and the rest of the people.

טז וַיָּשֶׁב אֵת כָּל־הָרְכֻשׁ וְגַם אֶת־לוֹט אָחִיו וּרְכֻשׁוֹ הֵשִׁיב וְגַם אֶת־הַנָּשִׁים וְאֶת־הָעָם:

17 When he returned from defeating Chedorlaomer and the kings with him, the king of Sodom came out to meet him in the Valley of Shaveh, which is the Valley of the King.

יז וַיֵּצֵא מֶלֶךְ־סְדֹם לִקְרָאתוֹ אַחֲרֵי שׁוּבוֹ מֵהַכּוֹת אֶת־כְּדָרְלָעֹמֶר וְאֶת־הַמְּלָכִים אֲשֶׁר אִתּוֹ אֶל־עֵמֶק שָׁוֵה הוּא עֵמֶק הַמֶּלֶךְ:

18 And King Melchizedek of *Shalem* brought out bread and wine; he was a priest of *Hashem* Most High.

יח וּמַלְכִּי־צֶדֶק מֶלֶךְ שָׁלֵם הוֹצִיא לֶחֶם וָיָיִן וְהוּא כֹהֵן לְאֵל עֶלְיוֹן:

u-mal-kee TZE-dek ME-lekh sha-LAYM ho-TZEE LE-khem va-ya-YIN v'-HU kho-HAYN l'-AYL el-YON

19 He blessed him, saying, "Blessed be *Avram* of *Hashem* Most High, Creator of heaven and earth.

יט וַיְבָרְכֵהוּ וַיֹּאמַר בָּרוּךְ אַבְרָם לְאֵל עֶלְיוֹן קֹנֵה שָׁמַיִם וָאָרֶץ:

20 And blessed be *Hashem* Most High, Who has delivered your foes into your hand." And [*Avram*] gave him a tenth of everything.

כ וּבָרוּךְ אֵל עֶלְיוֹן אֲשֶׁר־מִגֵּן צָרֶיךָ בְּיָדֶךָ וַיִּתֶּן־לוֹ מַעֲשֵׂר מִכֹּל:

21 Then the king of Sodom said to *Avram*, "Give me the persons, and take the possessions for yourself."

כא וַיֹּאמֶר מֶלֶךְ־סְדֹם אֶל־אַבְרָם תֶּן־לִי הַנֶּפֶשׁ וְהָרְכֻשׁ קַח־לָךְ:

22 But *Avram* said to the king of Sodom, "I swear to *Hashem*, *Hashem* Most High, Creator of heaven and earth:

כב וַיֹּאמֶר אַבְרָם אֶל־מֶלֶךְ סְדֹם הֲרִימֹתִי יָדִי אֶל־יְהֹוָה אֵל עֶלְיוֹן קֹנֵה שָׁמַיִם וָאָרֶץ:

23 I will not take so much as a thread or a sandal strap of what is yours; you shall not say, 'It is I who made *Avram* rich.'

כג אִם־מִחוּט וְעַד שְׂרוֹךְ־נַעַל וְאִם־אֶקַּח מִכָּל־אֲשֶׁר־לָךְ וְלֹא תֹאמַר אֲנִי הֶעֱשַׁרְתִּי אֶת־אַבְרָם:

14:18 And King Melchizedek of *Shalem* The Sages explain that Melchizedek, King of *Shalem*, is actually *Shem*, the son of *Noach*, and that *Shalem* is an early name for *Yerushalayim*. After *Avraham* emerges victorious from war, Melchizedek greets him with bread and wine and blesses him and the God who delivered him, thereby attributing *Avraham*'s success to divine justice. Even before knowledge of one God and His righteous ways had spread throughout the world, the concept of divine justice was present in *Shalem*, Israel's future capital.

Old City of Jerusalem

Bereishit/Genesis 15
Lech Lecha

בראשית טו
לך לך

24 For me, nothing but what my servants have used up; as for the share of the men who went with me – Aner, Eshkol, and Mamre – let them take their share."

כד בִּלְעָדַי רַק אֲשֶׁר אָכְלוּ הַנְּעָרִים וְחֵלֶק הָאֲנָשִׁים אֲשֶׁר הָלְכוּ אִתִּי עָנֵר אֶשְׁכֹּל וּמַמְרֵא הֵם יִקְחוּ חֶלְקָם:

15

1 Some time later, the word of *Hashem* came to *Avram* in a vision. He said, "Fear not, *Avram*, I am a shield to you; Your reward shall be very great."

טו א אַחַר הַדְּבָרִים הָאֵלֶּה הָיָה דְבַר־יְהוָה אֶל־אַבְרָם בַּמַּחֲזֶה לֵאמֹר אַל־תִּירָא אַבְרָם אָנֹכִי מָגֵן לָךְ שְׂכָרְךָ הַרְבֵּה מְאֹד:

2 But *Avram* said, "O *Hashem*, what can You give me, seeing that I shall die childless, and the one in charge of my household is Dammesek *Eliezer*!"

ב וַיֹּאמֶר אַבְרָם אֲדֹנָי יֱהֹוִה מַה־תִּתֶּן־לִי וְאָנֹכִי הוֹלֵךְ עֲרִירִי וּבֶן־מֶשֶׁק בֵּיתִי הוּא דַּמֶּשֶׂק אֱלִיעֶזֶר:

3 *Avram* said further, "Since You have granted me no offspring, my steward will be my heir."

ג וַיֹּאמֶר אַבְרָם הֵן לִי לֹא נָתַתָּה זָרַע וְהִנֵּה בֶן־בֵּיתִי יוֹרֵשׁ אֹתִי:

4 The word of *Hashem* came to him in reply, "That one shall not be your heir; none but your very own issue shall be your heir."

ד וְהִנֵּה דְבַר־יְהוָה אֵלָיו לֵאמֹר לֹא יִירָשְׁךָ זֶה כִּי־אִם אֲשֶׁר יֵצֵא מִמֵּעֶיךָ הוּא יִירָשֶׁךָ:

5 He took him outside and said, "Look toward heaven and count the stars, if you are able to count them." And He added, "So shall your offspring be."

ה וַיּוֹצֵא אֹתוֹ הַחוּצָה וַיֹּאמֶר הַבֶּט־נָא הַשָּׁמַיְמָה וּסְפֹר הַכּוֹכָבִים אִם־תּוּכַל לִסְפֹּר אֹתָם וַיֹּאמֶר לוֹ כֹּה יִהְיֶה זַרְעֶךָ:

6 And because he put his trust in *Hashem*, He reckoned it to his merit.

ו וְהֶאֱמִן בַּיהוָה וַיַּחְשְׁבֶהָ לּוֹ צְדָקָה:

7 Then He said to him, "I am *Hashem* who brought you out from Ur of the Chaldeans to assign this land to you as a possession."

ז וַיֹּאמֶר אֵלָיו אֲנִי יְהוָה אֲשֶׁר הוֹצֵאתִיךָ מֵאוּר כַּשְׂדִּים לָתֶת לְךָ אֶת־הָאָרֶץ הַזֹּאת לְרִשְׁתָּהּ:

8 And he said, "O *Hashem*, how shall I know that I am to possess it?"

ח וַיֹּאמַר אֲדֹנָי יֱהֹוִה בַּמָּה אֵדַע כִּי אִירָשֶׁנָּה:

9 He answered, "Bring Me a three-year-old heifer, a three-year-old she-goat, a three-year-old ram, a turtledove, and a young bird."

ט וַיֹּאמֶר אֵלָיו קְחָה לִי עֶגְלָה מְשֻׁלֶּשֶׁת וְעֵז מְשֻׁלֶּשֶׁת וְאַיִל מְשֻׁלָּשׁ וְתֹר וְגוֹזָל:

10 He brought Him all these and cut them in two, placing each half opposite the other; but he did not cut up the bird.

י וַיִּקַּח־לוֹ אֶת־כָּל־אֵלֶּה וַיְבַתֵּר אֹתָם בַּתָּוֶךְ וַיִּתֵּן אִישׁ־בִּתְרוֹ לִקְרַאת רֵעֵהוּ וְאֶת־הַצִּפֹּר לֹא בָתָר:

11 Birds of prey came down upon the carcasses, and *Avram* drove them away.

יא וַיֵּרֶד הָעַיִט עַל־הַפְּגָרִים וַיַּשֵּׁב אֹתָם אַבְרָם:

12 As the sun was about to set, a deep sleep fell upon *Avram*, and a great dark dread descended upon him.

יב וַיְהִי הַשֶּׁמֶשׁ לָבוֹא וְתַרְדֵּמָה נָפְלָה עַל־אַבְרָם וְהִנֵּה אֵימָה חֲשֵׁכָה גְדֹלָה נֹפֶלֶת עָלָיו:

13 And He said to *Avram*, "Know well that your offspring shall be strangers in a land not theirs, and they shall be enslaved and oppressed four hundred years;

יג וַיֹּאמֶר לְאַבְרָם יָדֹעַ תֵּדַע כִּי־גֵר יִהְיֶה זַרְעֲךָ בְּאֶרֶץ לֹא לָהֶם וַעֲבָדוּם וְעִנּוּ אֹתָם אַרְבַּע מֵאוֹת שָׁנָה:

Bereishit/Genesis 16
Lech Lecha

בראשית טז
לך לך

14 but I will execute judgment on the nation they shall serve, and in the end they shall go free with great wealth.

יד וְגַם אֶת־הַגּוֹי אֲשֶׁר יַעֲבֹדוּ דָּן אָנֹכִי וְאַחֲרֵי־כֵן יֵצְאוּ בִּרְכֻשׁ גָּדוֹל:

15 As for you, You shall go to your fathers in peace; You shall be buried at a ripe old age.

טו וְאַתָּה תָּבוֹא אֶל־אֲבֹתֶיךָ בְּשָׁלוֹם תִּקָּבֵר בְּשֵׂיבָה טוֹבָה:

16 And they shall return here in the fourth generation, for the iniquity of the Amorites is not yet complete."

טז וְדוֹר רְבִיעִי יָשׁוּבוּ הֵנָּה כִּי לֹא־שָׁלֵם עֲוֹן הָאֱמֹרִי עַד־הֵנָּה:

17 When the sun set and it was very dark, there appeared a smoking oven, and a flaming torch which passed between those pieces.

יז וַיְהִי הַשֶּׁמֶשׁ בָּאָה וַעֲלָטָה הָיָה וְהִנֵּה תַנּוּר עָשָׁן וְלַפִּיד אֵשׁ אֲשֶׁר עָבַר בֵּין הַגְּזָרִים הָאֵלֶּה:

18 On that day *Hashem* made a covenant with *Avram*, saying, "To your offspring I assign this land, from the river of Egypt to the great river, the river Euphrates:

יח בַּיּוֹם הַהוּא כָּרַת יְהוָה אֶת־אַבְרָם בְּרִית לֵאמֹר לְזַרְעֲךָ נָתַתִּי אֶת־הָאָרֶץ הַזֹּאת מִנְּהַר מִצְרַיִם עַד־הַנָּהָר הַגָּדֹל נְהַר־פְּרָת:

ba-YOM ha-HU ka-RAT a-do-NAI et av-RAM b'-REET lay-MOR l'-zar-a-KHA na-TA-tee et ha-A-retz ha-ZOT mi-n'-HAR mitz-RA-yim ad ha-na-HAR ha-ga-DOL n'-har p'-RAT

19 the Kenites, the Kenizzites, the Kadmonites,

יט אֶת־הַקֵּינִי וְאֶת־הַקְּנִזִּי וְאֵת הַקַּדְמֹנִי:

20 the Hittites, the Perizzites, the Rephaim,

כ וְאֶת־הַחִתִּי וְאֶת־הַפְּרִזִּי וְאֶת־הָרְפָאִים:

21 the Amorites, the Canaanites, the Girgashites, and the Jebusites."

כא וְאֶת־הָאֱמֹרִי וְאֶת־הַכְּנַעֲנִי וְאֶת־הַגִּרְגָּשִׁי וְאֶת־הַיְבוּסִי:

16

1 *Sarai*, *Avram*'s wife, had borne him no children. She had an Egyptian maidservant whose name was Hagar.

טז א וְשָׂרַי אֵשֶׁת אַבְרָם לֹא יָלְדָה לוֹ וְלָהּ שִׁפְחָה מִצְרִית וּשְׁמָהּ הָגָר:

2 And *Sarai* said to *Avram*, "Look, *Hashem* has kept me from bearing. Consort with my maid; perhaps I shall have a son through her." And *Avram* heeded *Sarai*'s request.

ב וַתֹּאמֶר שָׂרַי אֶל־אַבְרָם הִנֵּה־נָא עֲצָרַנִי יְהוָה מִלֶּדֶת בֹּא־נָא אֶל־שִׁפְחָתִי אוּלַי אִבָּנֶה מִמֶּנָּה וַיִּשְׁמַע אַבְרָם לְקוֹל שָׂרָי:

3 So *Sarai*, *Avram*'s wife, took her maid, Hagar the Egyptian – after *Avram* had dwelt in the land of Canaan ten years – and gave her to her husband *Avram* as concubine.

ג וַתִּקַּח שָׂרַי אֵשֶׁת־אַבְרָם אֶת־הָגָר הַמִּצְרִית שִׁפְחָתָהּ מִקֵּץ עֶשֶׂר שָׁנִים לְשֶׁבֶת אַבְרָם בְּאֶרֶץ כְּנָעַן וַתִּתֵּן אֹתָהּ לְאַבְרָם אִישָׁהּ לוֹ לְאִשָּׁה:

15:18 To your offspring I assign this land In this monumental covenant between *Hashem* and *Avraham*, God states that on this day He has given the Land of Israel to *Avraham*'s descendants. While *Hashem* uses the term *natatee* (נתתי), 'I have given,' in the past tense, in reference to generations that have not yet been born, *Rashi* explains that this is not a grammatical error. Since God's word is the ultimate truth, it is as if it has already been done. Though it took more than four hundred years until this promise was fulfilled, the children of *Avraham* waited with faith. This patient waiting served as good practice for the nearly two thousand years of waiting that preceded our present return to Zion. With the birth of the State of Israel, another promise to *Avraham* has been fulfilled.

Bereishit/Genesis 16
Lech Lecha

בראשית טז
לך לך

4 He cohabited with Hagar and she conceived; and when she saw that she had conceived, her mistress was lowered in her esteem.

ד וַיָּבֹא אֶל־הָגָר וַתַּהַר וַתֵּרֶא כִּי הָרָתָה וַתֵּקַל גְּבִרְתָּהּ בְּעֵינֶיהָ:

5 And *Sarai* said to *Avram*, "The wrong done me is your fault! I myself put my maid in your bosom; now that she sees that she is pregnant, I am lowered in her esteem. *Hashem* decide between you and me!"

ה וַתֹּאמֶר שָׂרַי אֶל־אַבְרָם חֲמָסִי עָלֶיךָ אָנֹכִי נָתַתִּי שִׁפְחָתִי בְּחֵיקֶךָ וַתֵּרֶא כִּי הָרָתָה וָאֵקַל בְּעֵינֶיהָ יִשְׁפֹּט יְהוָֹה בֵּינִי וּבֵינֶיךָ:

6 *Avram* said to *Sarai*, "Your maid is in your hands. Deal with her as you think right." Then *Sarai* treated her harshly, and she ran away from her.

ו וַיֹּאמֶר אַבְרָם אֶל־שָׂרַי הִנֵּה שִׁפְחָתֵךְ בְּיָדֵךְ עֲשִׂי־לָהּ הַטּוֹב בְּעֵינָיִךְ וַתְּעַנֶּהָ שָׂרַי וַתִּבְרַח מִפָּנֶיהָ:

7 An angel of *Hashem* found her by a spring of water in the wilderness, the spring on the road to Shur,

ז וַיִּמְצָאָהּ מַלְאַךְ יְהוָֹה עַל־עֵין הַמַּיִם בַּמִּדְבָּר עַל־הָעַיִן בְּדֶרֶךְ שׁוּר:

8 and said, "Hagar, slave of *Sarai*, where have you come from, and where are you going?" And she said, "I am running away from my mistress *Sarai*."

ח וַיֹּאמַר הָגָר שִׁפְחַת שָׂרַי אֵי־מִזֶּה בָאת וְאָנָה תֵלֵכִי וַתֹּאמֶר מִפְּנֵי שָׂרַי גְּבִרְתִּי אָנֹכִי בֹּרַחַת:

9 And the angel of *Hashem* said to her, "Go back to your mistress, and submit to her harsh treatment."

ט וַיֹּאמֶר לָהּ מַלְאַךְ יְהוָֹה שׁוּבִי אֶל־גְּבִרְתֵּךְ וְהִתְעַנִּי תַּחַת יָדֶיהָ:

10 And the angel of *Hashem* said to her, "I will greatly increase your offspring, And they shall be too many to count."

י וַיֹּאמֶר לָהּ מַלְאַךְ יְהוָֹה הַרְבָּה אַרְבֶּה אֶת־זַרְעֵךְ וְלֹא יִסָּפֵר מֵרֹב:

11 The angel of *Hashem* said to her further, "Behold, you are with child And shall bear a son; You shall call him Ishmael, For *Hashem* has paid heed to your suffering.

יא וַיֹּאמֶר לָהּ מַלְאַךְ יְהוָֹה הִנָּךְ הָרָה וְיֹלַדְתְּ בֵּן וְקָרָאת שְׁמוֹ יִשְׁמָעֵאל כִּי־שָׁמַע יְהוָֹה אֶל־עָנְיֵךְ:

12 He shall be a wild ass of a man; His hand against everyone, And everyone's hand against him; He shall dwell alongside of all his kinsmen."

יב וְהוּא יִהְיֶה פֶּרֶא אָדָם יָדוֹ בַכֹּל וְיַד כֹּל בּוֹ וְעַל־פְּנֵי כָל־אֶחָיו יִשְׁכֹּן:

13 And she called *Hashem* who spoke to her, "You Are El-roi," by which she meant, "Have I not gone on seeing after He saw me!"

יג וַתִּקְרָא שֵׁם־יְהוָֹה הַדֹּבֵר אֵלֶיהָ אַתָּה אֵל רֳאִי כִּי אָמְרָה הֲגַם הֲלֹם רָאִיתִי אַחֲרֵי רֹאִי:

14 Therefore the well was called Beer-lahai-roi; it is between Kadesh and Bered.

יד עַל־כֵּן קָרָא לַבְּאֵר בְּאֵר לַחַי רֹאִי הִנֵּה בֵין־קָדֵשׁ וּבֵין בָּרֶד:

al KAYN ka-RA la-b'-AYR b'-AYR la-KHAI ro-EE hi-NAY vayn ka-DAYSH u-VAYN BA-red

---

16:14 Therefore the well was called Beer-lahai-roi No longer able to bear her suffering in the home of her mistress *Sara*, Hagar runs to the desert in search of relief and solitude. According to Rabbi Samson Raphael Hirsch, when Hagar subsequently encounters the angel she realizes that one is never alone or out of God's sight. The well where this encounter takes place is therefore named *be'er lachai ro-ee* (באר לחי ראי), the 'well of the Living One who sees me.' Specifically in *Eretz Yisrael*, God's presence and watchful eye is felt strongly, as it says in *Devarim* (11:12) "on which *Hashem* your God always keeps His eye."

Rabbi Samson R. Hirsch (1808–1888)

Bereishit/Genesis 17
Lech Lecha

בראשית יז
לך לך

15 Hagar bore a son to *Avram*, and *Avram* gave the son that Hagar bore him the name Ishmael.

טו וַתֵּ֧לֶד הָגָ֛ר לְאַבְרָ֖ם בֵּ֑ן וַיִּקְרָ֨א אַבְרָ֧ם שֶׁם־בְּנ֛וֹ אֲשֶׁר־יָלְדָ֥ה הָגָ֖ר יִשְׁמָעֵֽאל׃

16 *Avram* was eighty-six years old when Hagar bore Ishmael to *Avram*.

טז וְאַבְרָ֕ם בֶּן־שְׁמֹנִ֥ים שָׁנָ֖ה וְשֵׁ֣שׁ שָׁנִ֑ים בְּלֶֽדֶת־הָגָ֥ר אֶת־יִשְׁמָעֵ֖אל לְאַבְרָֽם׃

17

1 When *Avram* was ninety-nine years old, *Hashem* appeared to *Avram* and said to him, "I am *El Shaddai*. Walk in My ways and be blameless.

יז א וַיְהִ֣י אַבְרָ֔ם בֶּן־תִּשְׁעִ֥ים שָׁנָ֖ה וְתֵ֣שַׁע שָׁנִ֑ים וַיֵּרָ֨א יְהוָ֜ה אֶל־אַבְרָ֗ם וַיֹּ֤אמֶר אֵלָיו֙ אֲנִי־אֵ֣ל שַׁדַּ֔י הִתְהַלֵּ֥ךְ לְפָנַ֖י וֶהְיֵ֥ה תָמִֽים׃

2 I will establish My covenant between Me and you, and I will make you exceedingly numerous."

ב וְאֶתְּנָ֥ה בְרִיתִ֖י בֵּינִ֣י וּבֵינֶ֑ךָ וְאַרְבֶּ֥ה אוֹתְךָ֖ בִּמְאֹ֥ד מְאֹֽד׃

3 *Avram* threw himself on his face; and *Hashem* spoke to him further,

ג וַיִּפֹּ֥ל אַבְרָ֖ם עַל־פָּנָ֑יו וַיְדַבֵּ֥ר אִתּ֛וֹ אֱלֹהִ֖ים לֵאמֹֽר׃

4 "As for Me, this is My covenant with you: You shall be the father of a multitude of nations.

ד אֲנִ֕י הִנֵּ֥ה בְרִיתִ֖י אִתָּ֑ךְ וְהָיִ֕יתָ לְאַ֖ב הֲמ֥וֹן גּוֹיִֽם׃

5 And you shall no longer be called *Avram*, but your name shall be *Avraham*, for I make you the father of a multitude of nations.

ה וְלֹא־יִקָּרֵ֥א ע֛וֹד אֶת־שִׁמְךָ֖ אַבְרָ֑ם וְהָיָ֤ה שִׁמְךָ֙ אַבְרָהָ֔ם כִּ֛י אַב־הֲמ֥וֹן גּוֹיִ֖ם נְתַתִּֽיךָ׃

6 I will make you exceedingly fertile, and make nations of you; and kings shall come forth from you.

ו וְהִפְרֵתִ֤י אֹֽתְךָ֙ בִּמְאֹ֣ד מְאֹ֔ד וּנְתַתִּ֖יךָ לְגוֹיִ֑ם וּמְלָכִ֖ים מִמְּךָ֥ יֵצֵֽאוּ׃

7 I will maintain My covenant between Me and you, and your offspring to come, as an everlasting covenant throughout the ages, to be *Hashem* to you and to your offspring to come.

ז וַהֲקִמֹתִ֨י אֶת־בְּרִיתִ֜י בֵּינִ֣י וּבֵינֶ֗ךָ וּבֵ֨ין זַרְעֲךָ֧ אַחֲרֶ֛יךָ לְדֹרֹתָ֖ם לִבְרִ֣ית עוֹלָ֑ם לִהְי֤וֹת לְךָ֙ לֵֽאלֹהִ֔ים וּֽלְזַרְעֲךָ֖ אַחֲרֶֽיךָ׃

8 I assign the land you sojourn in to you and your offspring to come, all the land of Canaan, as an everlasting holding. I will be their God."

ח וְנָתַתִּ֣י לְ֠ךָ וּלְזַרְעֲךָ֨ אַחֲרֶ֜יךָ אֵ֣ת ׀ אֶ֣רֶץ מְגֻרֶ֗יךָ אֵ֚ת כָּל־אֶ֣רֶץ כְּנַ֔עַן לַאֲחֻזַּ֖ת עוֹלָ֑ם וְהָיִ֥יתִי לָהֶ֖ם לֵאלֹהִֽים׃

v'-na-ta-TEE l'-KHA ul-zar-a-KHA a-kha-RE-kha AYT E-retz m'-gu-RE-kha AYT kol E-retz k'-NA-an la-a-khu-ZAT o-LAM v'-ha-YEE-tee la-HEM LAay-lo-HEEM

9 *Hashem* further said to *Avraham*, "As for you, you and your offspring to come throughout the ages shall keep My covenant.

ט וַיֹּ֤אמֶר אֱלֹהִים֙ אֶל־אַבְרָהָ֔ם וְאַתָּ֖ה אֶת־בְּרִיתִ֣י תִשְׁמֹ֑ר אַתָּ֛ה וְזַרְעֲךָ֥ אַֽחֲרֶ֖יךָ לְדֹרֹתָֽם׃

10 Such shall be the covenant between Me and you and your offspring to follow which you shall keep: every male among you shall be circumcised.

י זֹ֣את בְּרִיתִ֞י אֲשֶׁ֣ר תִּשְׁמְר֗וּ בֵּינִי֙ וּבֵ֣ינֵיכֶ֔ם וּבֵ֥ין זַרְעֲךָ֖ אַחֲרֶ֑יךָ הִמּ֥וֹל לָכֶ֖ם כָּל־זָכָֽר׃

11 You shall circumcise the flesh of your foreskin, and that shall be the sign of the covenant between Me and you.

יא וּנְמַלְתֶּ֕ם אֵ֖ת בְּשַׂ֣ר עָרְלַתְכֶ֑ם וְהָיָה֙ לְא֣וֹת בְּרִ֔ית בֵּינִ֖י וּבֵינֵיכֶֽם׃

12 And throughout the generations, every male among you shall be circumcised at the age of eight days. As for the homeborn slave and the one bought from an outsider who is not of your offspring,

יב וּבֶן־שְׁמֹנַ֣ת יָמִ֗ים יִמּ֥וֹל לָכֶ֛ם כָּל־זָכָ֖ר לְדֹרֹתֵיכֶ֑ם יְלִ֣יד בָּ֔יִת וּמִקְנַת־כֶּ֙סֶף֙ מִכֹּ֣ל בֶּן־נֵכָ֔ר אֲשֶׁ֛ר לֹ֥א מִזַּרְעֲךָ֖ הֽוּא׃

Bereishit/Genesis 17
Lech Lecha

בראשית יז
לך לך

13 they must be circumcised, homeborn, and purchased alike. Thus shall My covenant be marked in your flesh as an everlasting pact.

יג הִמּוֹל יִמּוֹל יְלִיד בֵּיתְךָ וּמִקְנַת כַּסְפֶּךָ וְהָיְתָה בְרִיתִי בִּבְשַׂרְכֶם לִבְרִית עוֹלָם׃

14 And if any male who is uncircumcised fails to circumcise the flesh of his foreskin, that person shall be cut off from his kin; he has broken My covenant."

יד וְעָרֵל זָכָר אֲשֶׁר לֹא־יִמּוֹל אֶת־בְּשַׂר עָרְלָתוֹ וְנִכְרְתָה הַנֶּפֶשׁ הַהִוא מֵעַמֶּיהָ אֶת־בְּרִיתִי הֵפַר׃

15 And *Hashem* said to *Avraham*, "As for your wife *Sarai*, you shall not call her *Sarai*, but her name shall be *Sara*.

טו וַיֹּאמֶר אֱלֹהִים אֶל־אַבְרָהָם שָׂרַי אִשְׁתְּךָ לֹא־תִקְרָא אֶת־שְׁמָהּ שָׂרָי כִּי שָׂרָה שְׁמָהּ׃

16 I will bless her; indeed, I will give you a son by her. I will bless her so that she shall give rise to nations; rulers of peoples shall issue from her."

טז וּבֵרַכְתִּי אֹתָהּ וְגַם נָתַתִּי מִמֶּנָּה לְךָ בֵּן וּבֵרַכְתִּיהָ וְהָיְתָה לְגוֹיִם מַלְכֵי עַמִּים מִמֶּנָּה יִהְיוּ׃

17 *Avraham* threw himself on his face and laughed, as he said to himself, "Can a child be born to a man a hundred years old, or can *Sara* bear a child at ninety?"

יז וַיִּפֹּל אַבְרָהָם עַל־פָּנָיו וַיִּצְחָק וַיֹּאמֶר בְּלִבּוֹ הַלְּבֶן מֵאָה־שָׁנָה יִוָּלֵד וְאִם־שָׂרָה הֲבַת־תִּשְׁעִים שָׁנָה תֵּלֵד׃

18 And *Avraham* said to *Hashem*, "O that Ishmael might live by Your favor!"

יח וַיֹּאמֶר אַבְרָהָם אֶל־הָאֱלֹהִים לוּ יִשְׁמָעֵאל יִחְיֶה לְפָנֶיךָ׃

19 *Hashem* said, "Nevertheless, *Sara* your wife shall bear you a son, and you shall name him *Yitzchak*; and I will maintain My covenant with him as an everlasting covenant for his offspring to come.

יט וַיֹּאמֶר אֱלֹהִים אֲבָל שָׂרָה אִשְׁתְּךָ יֹלֶדֶת לְךָ בֵּן וְקָרָאתָ אֶת־שְׁמוֹ יִצְחָק וַהֲקִמֹתִי אֶת־בְּרִיתִי אִתּוֹ לִבְרִית עוֹלָם לְזַרְעוֹ אַחֲרָיו׃

20 As for Ishmael, I have heeded you. I hereby bless him. I will make him fertile and exceedingly numerous. He shall be the father of twelve chieftains, and I will make of him a great nation.

כ וּלְיִשְׁמָעֵאל שְׁמַעְתִּיךָ הִנֵּה בֵּרַכְתִּי אֹתוֹ וְהִפְרֵיתִי אֹתוֹ וְהִרְבֵּיתִי אֹתוֹ בִּמְאֹד מְאֹד שְׁנֵים־עָשָׂר נְשִׂיאִם יוֹלִיד וּנְתַתִּיו לְגוֹי גָּדוֹל׃

21 But My covenant I will maintain with *Yitzchak*, whom *Sara* shall bear to you at this season next year."

כא וְאֶת־בְּרִיתִי אָקִים אֶת־יִצְחָק אֲשֶׁר תֵּלֵד לְךָ שָׂרָה לַמּוֹעֵד הַזֶּה בַּשָּׁנָה הָאַחֶרֶת׃

v'-et b'-ree-TEE a-KEEM et yitz-KHAK a-SHER tay-LAYD l'-KHA sa-RAH la-mo-AYD ha-ZEH ba-sha-NAH ha-a-KHE-ret

22 And when He was done speaking with him, *Hashem* was gone from *Avraham*.

כב וַיְכַל לְדַבֵּר אִתּוֹ וַיַּעַל אֱלֹהִים מֵעַל אַבְרָהָם׃

17:21 But My covenant I will maintain with *Yitzchak*
Avraham was chosen to be God's emissary in this world, to live in the Land of Israel, and to establish a nation with a unique mission. But who would be *Avraham*'s heir, Ishmael or *Yitzchak*? This ambiguity is eliminated when *Hashem* declares that, although a great nation will emerge from Ishmael's lineage, *Yitzchak* is the chosen heir to *Avraham*'s legacy and *Eretz Yisrael*.

Bereishit/Genesis 18
Vayeira

בראשית יח
וירא

23 Then *Avraham* took his son Ishmael, and all his homeborn slaves and all those he had bought, every male in *Avraham*'s household, and he circumcised the flesh of their foreskins on that very day, as *Hashem* had spoken to him.

כג וַיִּקַּח אַבְרָהָם אֶת־יִשְׁמָעֵאל בְּנוֹ וְאֵת כָּל־יְלִידֵי בֵיתוֹ וְאֵת כָּל־מִקְנַת כַּסְפּוֹ כָּל־זָכָר בְּאַנְשֵׁי בֵּית אַבְרָהָם וַיָּמָל אֶת־בְּשַׂר עָרְלָתָם בְּעֶצֶם הַיּוֹם הַזֶּה כַּאֲשֶׁר דִּבֶּר אִתּוֹ אֱלֹהִים:

24 *Avraham* was ninety-nine years old when he circumcised the flesh of his foreskin,

כד וְאַבְרָהָם בֶּן־תִּשְׁעִים וָתֵשַׁע שָׁנָה בְּהִמֹּלוֹ בְּשַׂר עָרְלָתוֹ:

25 and his son Ishmael was thirteen years old when he was circumcised in the flesh of his foreskin.

כה וְיִשְׁמָעֵאל בְּנוֹ בֶּן־שְׁלֹשׁ עֶשְׂרֵה שָׁנָה בְּהִמֹּלוֹ אֵת בְּשַׂר עָרְלָתוֹ:

26 Thus *Avraham* and his son Ishmael were circumcised on that very day;

כו בְּעֶצֶם הַיּוֹם הַזֶּה נִמּוֹל אַבְרָהָם וְיִשְׁמָעֵאל בְּנוֹ:

27 and all his household, his homeborn slaves and those that had been bought from outsiders, were circumcised with him.

כז וְכָל־אַנְשֵׁי בֵיתוֹ יְלִיד בָּיִת וּמִקְנַת־כֶּסֶף מֵאֵת בֶּן־נֵכָר נִמֹּלוּ אִתּוֹ:

18

1 *Hashem* appeared to him by the terebinths of Mamre; he was sitting at the entrance of the tent as the day grew hot.

יח א וַיֵּרָא אֵלָיו יְהֹוָה בְּאֵלֹנֵי מַמְרֵא וְהוּא יֹשֵׁב פֶּתַח־הָאֹהֶל כְּחֹם הַיּוֹם:

va-yay-RA ay-LAV a-do-NAI b'-ay-lo-NAY mam-RAY v'-HU yo-SHAYV pe-takh ha-O-hel k'-KHOM ha-YOM

2 Looking up, he saw three men standing near him. As soon as he saw them, he ran from the entrance of the tent to greet them and, bowing to the ground,

ב וַיִּשָּׂא עֵינָיו וַיַּרְא וְהִנֵּה שְׁלֹשָׁה אֲנָשִׁים נִצָּבִים עָלָיו וַיַּרְא וַיָּרָץ לִקְרָאתָם מִפֶּתַח הָאֹהֶל וַיִּשְׁתַּחוּ אָרְצָה:

3 he said, "My lords, if it please you, do not go on past your servant.

ג וַיֹּאמַר אֲדֹנָי אִם־נָא מָצָאתִי חֵן בְּעֵינֶיךָ אַל־נָא תַעֲבֹר מֵעַל עַבְדֶּךָ:

4 Let a little water be brought; bathe your feet and recline under the tree.

ד יֻקַּח־נָא מְעַט־מַיִם וְרַחֲצוּ רַגְלֵיכֶם וְהִשָּׁעֲנוּ תַּחַת הָעֵץ:

5 And let me fetch a morsel of bread that you may refresh yourselves; then go on – seeing that you have come your servant's way." They replied, "Do as you have said."

ה וְאֶקְחָה פַת־לֶחֶם וְסַעֲדוּ לִבְּכֶם אַחַר תַּעֲבֹרוּ כִּי־עַל־כֵּן עֲבַרְתֶּם עַל־עַבְדְּכֶם וַיֹּאמְרוּ כֵּן תַּעֲשֶׂה כַּאֲשֶׁר דִּבַּרְתָּ:

6 *Avraham* hastened into the tent to *Sara*, and said, "Quick, three *se'eem* of choice flour! Knead and make cakes!"

ו וַיְמַהֵר אַבְרָהָם הָאֹהֱלָה אֶל־שָׂרָה וַיֹּאמֶר מַהֲרִי שְׁלֹשׁ סְאִים קֶמַח סֹלֶת לוּשִׁי וַעֲשִׂי עֻגוֹת:

Terebinth tree at Nachal Sanin

18:1 By the terebinths of Mamre Mamre was the name of *Avraham*'s ally (Genesis 14:13). *Rashi* explains that of his three allies, Mamre was the only one who supported the idea of circumcision, and it was for this reason that *Hashem* reveals himself to *Avraham* in his territory. This teaches us an important lesson: A person should choose to live in a place conducive to spiritual growth. Choosing to live in the Land of Israel means choosing an environment that can foster a person's spiritual development and relationship with God.

Bereishit/Genesis 18
Vayeira

בראשית יח
וירא

7 Then *Avraham* ran to the herd, took a calf, tender and choice, and gave it to a servant-boy, who hastened to prepare it.

ז וְאֶל־הַבָּקָר רָץ אַבְרָהָם וַיִּקַּח בֶּן־בָּקָר רַךְ וָטוֹב וַיִּתֵּן אֶל־הַנַּעַר וַיְמַהֵר לַעֲשׂוֹת אֹתוֹ:

8 He took curds and milk and the calf that had been prepared and set these before them; and he waited on them under the tree as they ate.

ח וַיִּקַּח חֶמְאָה וְחָלָב וּבֶן־הַבָּקָר אֲשֶׁר עָשָׂה וַיִּתֵּן לִפְנֵיהֶם וְהוּא־עֹמֵד עֲלֵיהֶם תַּחַת הָעֵץ וַיֹּאכֵלוּ:

9 They said to him, "Where is your wife *Sara*?" And he replied, "There, in the tent."

ט וַיֹּאמְרוּ אֵלָיו אַיֵּה שָׂרָה אִשְׁתֶּךָ וַיֹּאמֶר הִנֵּה בָאֹהֶל:

10 Then one said, "I will return to you next year, and your wife *Sara* shall have a son!" *Sara* was listening at the entrance of the tent, which was behind him.

י וַיֹּאמֶר שׁוֹב אָשׁוּב אֵלֶיךָ כָּעֵת חַיָּה וְהִנֵּה־בֵן לְשָׂרָה אִשְׁתֶּךָ וְשָׂרָה שֹׁמַעַת פֶּתַח הָאֹהֶל וְהוּא אַחֲרָיו:

11 Now *Avraham* and *Sara* were old, advanced in years; *Sara* had stopped having the periods of women.

יא וְאַבְרָהָם וְשָׂרָה זְקֵנִים בָּאִים בַּיָּמִים חָדַל לִהְיוֹת לְשָׂרָה אֹרַח כַּנָּשִׁים:

12 And *Sara* laughed to herself, saying, "Now that I am withered, am I to have enjoyment – with my husband so old?"

יב וַתִּצְחַק שָׂרָה בְּקִרְבָּהּ לֵאמֹר אַחֲרֵי בְלֹתִי הָיְתָה־לִּי עֶדְנָה וַאדֹנִי זָקֵן:

13 Then *Hashem* said to *Avraham*, "Why did *Sara* laugh, saying, 'Shall I in truth bear a child, old as I am?'

יג וַיֹּאמֶר יְהֹוָה אֶל־אַבְרָהָם לָמָּה זֶּה צָחֲקָה שָׂרָה לֵאמֹר הַאַף אֻמְנָם אֵלֵד וַאֲנִי זָקַנְתִּי:

14 Is anything too wondrous for *Hashem*? I will return to you at the same season next year, and *Sara* shall have a son."

יד הֲיִפָּלֵא מֵיְהֹוָה דָּבָר לַמּוֹעֵד אָשׁוּב אֵלֶיךָ כָּעֵת חַיָּה וּלְשָׂרָה בֵן:

15 *Sara* lied, saying, "I did not laugh," for she was frightened. But He replied, "You did laugh."

טו וַתְּכַחֵשׁ שָׂרָה לֵאמֹר לֹא צָחַקְתִּי כִּי יָרֵאָה וַיֹּאמֶר לֹא כִּי צָחָקְתְּ:

16 The men set out from there and looked down toward Sodom, *Avraham* walking with them to see them off.

טז וַיָּקֻמוּ מִשָּׁם הָאֲנָשִׁים וַיַּשְׁקִפוּ עַל־פְּנֵי סְדֹם וְאַבְרָהָם הֹלֵךְ עִמָּם לְשַׁלְּחָם:

17 Now *Hashem* had said, "Shall I hide from *Avraham* what I am about to do,

יז וַיהֹוָה אָמָר הַמְכַסֶּה אֲנִי מֵאַבְרָהָם אֲשֶׁר אֲנִי עֹשֶׂה:

18 since *Avraham* is to become a great and populous nation and all the nations of the earth are to bless themselves by him?

יח וְאַבְרָהָם הָיוֹ יִהְיֶה לְגוֹי גָּדוֹל וְעָצוּם וְנִבְרְכוּ בוֹ כֹּל גּוֹיֵי הָאָרֶץ:

19 For I have singled him out, that he may instruct his children and his posterity to keep the way of *Hashem* by doing what is just and right, in order that *Hashem* may bring about for *Avraham* what He has promised him."

יט כִּי יְדַעְתִּיו לְמַעַן אֲשֶׁר יְצַוֶּה אֶת־בָּנָיו וְאֶת־בֵּיתוֹ אַחֲרָיו וְשָׁמְרוּ דֶּרֶךְ יְהֹוָה לַעֲשׂוֹת צְדָקָה וּמִשְׁפָּט לְמַעַן הָבִיא יְהֹוָה עַל־אַבְרָהָם אֵת אֲשֶׁר־דִּבֶּר עָלָיו:

20 Then *Hashem* said, "The outrage of Sodom and Gomorrah is so great, and their sin so grave!

כ וַיֹּאמֶר יְהֹוָה זַעֲקַת סְדֹם וַעֲמֹרָה כִּי־רָבָּה וְחַטָּאתָם כִּי כָבְדָה מְאֹד:

Bereishit/Genesis 18	בראשית יח
Vayeira	וירא

21 I will go down to see whether they have acted altogether according to the outcry that has reached Me; if not, I will take note."

כא אֵרֲדָה־נָּא וְאֶרְאֶה הַכְּצַעֲקָתָהּ הַבָּאָה אֵלַי עָשׂוּ ׀ כָּלָה וְאִם־לֹא אֵדָעָה׃

22 The men went on from there to Sodom, while *Avraham* remained standing before *Hashem*.

כב וַיִּפְנוּ מִשָּׁם הָאֲנָשִׁים וַיֵּלְכוּ סְדֹמָה וְאַבְרָהָם עוֹדֶנּוּ עֹמֵד לִפְנֵי יְהֹוָה׃

23 *Avraham* came forward and said, "Will You sweep away the innocent along with the guilty?

כג וַיִּגַּשׁ אַבְרָהָם וַיֹּאמַר הַאַף תִּסְפֶּה צַדִּיק עִם־רָשָׁע׃

24 What if there should be fifty innocent within the city; will You then wipe out the place and not forgive it for the sake of the innocent fifty who are in it?

כד אוּלַי יֵשׁ חֲמִשִּׁים צַדִּיקִם בְּתוֹךְ הָעִיר הַאַף תִּסְפֶּה וְלֹא־תִשָּׂא לַמָּקוֹם לְמַעַן חֲמִשִּׁים הַצַּדִּיקִם אֲשֶׁר בְּקִרְבָּהּ׃

25 Far be it from You to do such a thing, to bring death upon the innocent as well as the guilty, so that innocent and guilty fare alike. Far be it from You! Shall not the Judge of all the earth deal justly?"

כה חָלִלָה לְּךָ מֵעֲשֹׂת כַּדָּבָר הַזֶּה לְהָמִית צַדִּיק עִם־רָשָׁע וְהָיָה כַצַּדִּיק כָּרָשָׁע חָלִלָה לָּךְ הֲשֹׁפֵט כָּל־הָאָרֶץ לֹא יַעֲשֶׂה מִשְׁפָּט׃

26 And *Hashem* answered, "If I find within the city of Sodom fifty innocent ones, I will forgive the whole place for their sake."

כו וַיֹּאמֶר יְהֹוָה אִם־אֶמְצָא בִסְדֹם חֲמִשִּׁים צַדִּיקִם בְּתוֹךְ הָעִיר וְנָשָׂאתִי לְכָל־הַמָּקוֹם בַּעֲבוּרָם׃

27 *Avraham* spoke up, saying, "Here I venture to speak to my Lord, I who am but dust and ashes:

כז וַיַּעַן אַבְרָהָם וַיֹּאמַר הִנֵּה־נָא הוֹאַלְתִּי לְדַבֵּר אֶל־אֲדֹנָי וְאָנֹכִי עָפָר וָאֵפֶר׃

28 What if the fifty innocent should lack five? Will You destroy the whole city for want of the five?" And He answered, "I will not destroy if I find forty-five there."

כח אוּלַי יַחְסְרוּן חֲמִשִּׁים הַצַּדִּיקִם חֲמִשָּׁה הֲתַשְׁחִית בַּחֲמִשָּׁה אֶת־כָּל־הָעִיר וַיֹּאמֶר לֹא אַשְׁחִית אִם־אֶמְצָא שָׁם אַרְבָּעִים וַחֲמִשָּׁה׃

29 But he spoke to Him again, and said, "What if forty should be found there?" And He answered, "I will not do it, for the sake of the forty."

כט וַיֹּסֶף עוֹד לְדַבֵּר אֵלָיו וַיֹּאמַר אוּלַי יִמָּצְאוּן שָׁם אַרְבָּעִים וַיֹּאמֶר לֹא אֶעֱשֶׂה בַּעֲבוּר הָאַרְבָּעִים׃

30 And he said, "Let not my Lord be angry if I go on: What if thirty should be found there?" And He answered, "I will not do it if I find thirty there."

ל וַיֹּאמֶר אַל־נָא יִחַר לַאדֹנָי וַאֲדַבֵּרָה אוּלַי יִמָּצְאוּן שָׁם שְׁלֹשִׁים וַיֹּאמֶר לֹא אֶעֱשֶׂה אִם־אֶמְצָא שָׁם שְׁלֹשִׁים׃

31 And he said, "I venture again to speak to my Lord: What if twenty should be found there?" And He answered, "I will not destroy, for the sake of the twenty."

לא וַיֹּאמֶר הִנֵּה־נָא הוֹאַלְתִּי לְדַבֵּר אֶל־אֲדֹנָי אוּלַי יִמָּצְאוּן שָׁם עֶשְׂרִים וַיֹּאמֶר לֹא אַשְׁחִית בַּעֲבוּר הָעֶשְׂרִים׃

32 And he said, "Let not my Lord be angry if I speak but this last time: What if ten should be found there?" And He answered, "I will not destroy, for the sake of the ten."

לב וַיֹּאמֶר אַל־נָא יִחַר לַאדֹנָי וַאֲדַבְּרָה אַךְ־הַפַּעַם אוּלַי יִמָּצְאוּן שָׁם עֲשָׂרָה וַיֹּאמֶר לֹא אַשְׁחִית בַּעֲבוּר הָעֲשָׂרָה׃

33 When *Hashem* had finished speaking to *Avraham*, He departed; and *Avraham* returned to his place.

לג וַיֵּלֶךְ יְהֹוָה כַּאֲשֶׁר כִּלָּה לְדַבֵּר אֶל־אַבְרָהָם וְאַבְרָהָם שָׁב לִמְקֹמוֹ׃

Bereishit/Genesis 19
Vayeira

בראשית יט
וירא

19 1 The two angels arrived in Sodom in the evening, as Lot was sitting in the gate of Sodom. When Lot saw them, he rose to greet them and, bowing low with his face to the ground,

2 he said, "Please, my lords, turn aside to your servant's house to spend the night, and bathe your feet; then you may be on your way early." But they said, "No, we will spend the night in the square."

3 But he urged them strongly, so they turned his way and entered his house. He prepared a feast for them and baked unleavened bread, and they ate.

4 They had not yet lain down, when the townspeople, the men of Sodom, young and old – all the people to the last man – gathered about the house.

5 And they shouted to Lot and said to him, "Where are the men who came to you tonight? Bring them out to us, that we may be intimate with them."

6 So Lot went out to them to the entrance, shut the door behind him,

7 and said, "I beg you, my friends, do not commit such a wrong.

8 Look, I have two daughters who have not known a man. Let me bring them out to you, and you may do to them as you please; but do not do anything to these men, since they have come under the shelter of my roof."

9 But they said, "Stand back! The fellow," they said, "came here as an alien, and already he acts the ruler! Now we will deal worse with you than with them." And they pressed hard against the person of Lot, and moved forward to break the door.

10 But the men stretched out their hands and pulled Lot into the house with them, and shut the door.

11 And the people who were at the entrance of the house, young and old, they struck with blinding light, so that they were helpless to find the entrance.

12 Then the men said to Lot, "Whom else have you here? Sons-in-law, your sons and daughters, or anyone else that you have in the city – bring them out of the place.

א וַיָּבֹאוּ שְׁנֵי הַמַּלְאָכִים סְדֹמָה בָּעֶרֶב וְלוֹט יֹשֵׁב בְּשַׁעַר־סְדֹם וַיַּרְא־לוֹט וַיָּקָם לִקְרָאתָם וַיִּשְׁתַּחוּ אַפַּיִם אָרְצָה:

ב וַיֹּאמֶר הִנֶּה נָּא־אֲדֹנַי סוּרוּ נָא אֶל־בֵּית עַבְדְּכֶם וְלִינוּ וְרַחֲצוּ רַגְלֵיכֶם וְהִשְׁכַּמְתֶּם וַהֲלַכְתֶּם לְדַרְכְּכֶם וַיֹּאמְרוּ לֹּא כִּי בָרְחוֹב נָלִין:

ג וַיִּפְצַר־בָּם מְאֹד וַיָּסֻרוּ אֵלָיו וַיָּבֹאוּ אֶל־בֵּיתוֹ וַיַּעַשׂ לָהֶם מִשְׁתֶּה וּמַצּוֹת אָפָה וַיֹּאכֵלוּ:

ד טֶרֶם יִשְׁכָּבוּ וְאַנְשֵׁי הָעִיר אַנְשֵׁי סְדֹם נָסַבּוּ עַל־הַבַּיִת מִנַּעַר וְעַד־זָקֵן כָּל־הָעָם מִקָּצֶה:

ה וַיִּקְרְאוּ אֶל־לוֹט וַיֹּאמְרוּ לוֹ אַיֵּה הָאֲנָשִׁים אֲשֶׁר־בָּאוּ אֵלֶיךָ הַלָּיְלָה הוֹצִיאֵם אֵלֵינוּ וְנֵדְעָה אֹתָם:

ו וַיֵּצֵא אֲלֵהֶם לוֹט הַפֶּתְחָה וְהַדֶּלֶת סָגַר אַחֲרָיו:

ז וַיֹּאמַר אַל־נָא אַחַי תָּרֵעוּ:

ח הִנֵּה־נָא לִי שְׁתֵּי בָנוֹת אֲשֶׁר לֹא־יָדְעוּ אִישׁ אוֹצִיאָה־נָּא אֶתְהֶן אֲלֵיכֶם וַעֲשׂוּ לָהֶן כַּטּוֹב בְּעֵינֵיכֶם רַק לָאֲנָשִׁים הָאֵל אַל־תַּעֲשׂוּ דָבָר כִּי־עַל־כֵּן בָּאוּ בְּצֵל קֹרָתִי:

ט וַיֹּאמְרוּ גֶּשׁ־הָלְאָה וַיֹּאמְרוּ הָאֶחָד בָּא־לָגוּר וַיִּשְׁפֹּט שָׁפוֹט עַתָּה נָרַע לְךָ מֵהֶם וַיִּפְצְרוּ בָאִישׁ בְּלוֹט מְאֹד וַיִּגְּשׁוּ לִשְׁבֹּר הַדָּלֶת:

י וַיִּשְׁלְחוּ הָאֲנָשִׁים אֶת־יָדָם וַיָּבִיאוּ אֶת־לוֹט אֲלֵיהֶם הַבָּיְתָה וְאֶת־הַדֶּלֶת סָגָרוּ:

יא וְאֶת־הָאֲנָשִׁים אֲשֶׁר־פֶּתַח הַבַּיִת הִכּוּ בַּסַּנְוֵרִים מִקָּטֹן וְעַד־גָּדוֹל וַיִּלְאוּ לִמְצֹא הַפָּתַח:

יב וַיֹּאמְרוּ הָאֲנָשִׁים אֶל־לוֹט עֹד מִי־לְךָ פֹה חָתָן וּבָנֶיךָ וּבְנֹתֶיךָ וְכֹל אֲשֶׁר־לְךָ בָּעִיר הוֹצֵא מִן־הַמָּקוֹם:

44

Bereishit/Genesis 19
Vayeira

בראשית יט
וירא

13 For we are about to destroy this place; because the outcry against them before *Hashem* has become so great that *Hashem* has sent us to destroy it."

יג כִּי־מַשְׁחִתִים אֲנַחְנוּ אֶת־הַמָּקוֹם הַזֶּה כִּי־גָדְלָה צַעֲקָתָם אֶת־פְּנֵי יְהוָה וַיְשַׁלְּחֵנוּ יְהוָה לְשַׁחֲתָהּ:

14 So Lot went out and spoke to his sons-in-law, who had married his daughters, and said, "Up, get out of this place, for *Hashem* is about to destroy the city." But he seemed to his sons-in-law as one who jests.

יד וַיֵּצֵא לוֹט וַיְדַבֵּר אֶל־חֲתָנָיו לֹקְחֵי בְנֹתָיו וַיֹּאמֶר קוּמוּ צְּאוּ מִן־הַמָּקוֹם הַזֶּה כִּי־מַשְׁחִית יְהוָה אֶת־הָעִיר וַיְהִי כִמְצַחֵק בְּעֵינֵי חֲתָנָיו:

15 As dawn broke, the angels urged Lot on, saying, "Up, take your wife and your two remaining daughters, lest you be swept away because of the iniquity of the city."

טו וּכְמוֹ הַשַּׁחַר עָלָה וַיָּאִיצוּ הַמַּלְאָכִים בְּלוֹט לֵאמֹר קוּם קַח אֶת־אִשְׁתְּךָ וְאֶת־שְׁתֵּי בְנֹתֶיךָ הַנִּמְצָאֹת פֶּן־תִּסָּפֶה בַּעֲוֹן הָעִיר:

16 Still he delayed. So the men seized his hand, and the hands of his wife and his two daughters – in *Hashem*'s mercy on him – and brought him out and left him outside the city.

טז וַיִּתְמַהְמָהּ וַיַּחֲזִקוּ הָאֲנָשִׁים בְּיָדוֹ וּבְיַד־אִשְׁתּוֹ וּבְיַד שְׁתֵּי בְנֹתָיו בְּחֶמְלַת יְהוָה עָלָיו וַיֹּצִאֻהוּ וַיַּנִּחֻהוּ מִחוּץ לָעִיר:

17 When they had brought them outside, one said, "Flee for your life! Do not look behind you, nor stop anywhere in the Plain; flee to the hills, lest you be swept away."

יז וַיְהִי כְהוֹצִיאָם אֹתָם הַחוּצָה וַיֹּאמֶר הִמָּלֵט עַל־נַפְשֶׁךָ אַל־תַּבִּיט אַחֲרֶיךָ וְאַל־תַּעֲמֹד בְּכָל־הַכִּכָּר הָהָרָה הִמָּלֵט פֶּן־תִּסָּפֶה:

18 But Lot said to them, "Oh no, my lord!

יח וַיֹּאמֶר לוֹט אֲלֵהֶם אַל־נָא אֲדֹנָי:

19 You have been so gracious to your servant, and have already shown me so much kindness in order to save my life; but I cannot flee to the hills, lest the disaster overtake me and I die.

יט הִנֵּה־נָא מָצָא עַבְדְּךָ חֵן בְּעֵינֶיךָ וַתַּגְדֵּל חַסְדְּךָ אֲשֶׁר עָשִׂיתָ עִמָּדִי לְהַחֲיוֹת אֶת־נַפְשִׁי וְאָנֹכִי לֹא אוּכַל לְהִמָּלֵט הָהָרָה פֶּן־תִּדְבָּקַנִי הָרָעָה וָמַתִּי:

20 Look, that town there is near enough to flee to; it is such a little place! Let me flee there – it is such a little place – and let my life be saved."

כ הִנֵּה־נָא הָעִיר הַזֹּאת קְרֹבָה לָנוּס שָׁמָּה וְהִיא מִצְעָר אִמָּלְטָה נָּא שָׁמָּה הֲלֹא מִצְעָר הִוא וּתְחִי נַפְשִׁי:

21 He replied, "Very well, I will grant you this favor too, and I will not annihilate the town of which you have spoken.

כא וַיֹּאמֶר אֵלָיו הִנֵּה נָשָׂאתִי פָנֶיךָ גַּם לַדָּבָר הַזֶּה לְבִלְתִּי הָפְכִּי אֶת־הָעִיר אֲשֶׁר דִּבַּרְתָּ:

22 Hurry, flee there, for I cannot do anything until you arrive there." Hence the town came to be called Zoar.

כב מַהֵר הִמָּלֵט שָׁמָּה כִּי לֹא אוּכַל לַעֲשׂוֹת דָּבָר עַד־בֹּאֲךָ שָׁמָּה עַל־כֵּן קָרָא שֵׁם־הָעִיר צוֹעַר:

23 As the sun rose upon the earth and Lot entered Zoar,

כג הַשֶּׁמֶשׁ יָצָא עַל־הָאָרֶץ וְלוֹט בָּא צֹעֲרָה:

24 *Hashem* rained upon Sodom and Gomorrah sulfurous fire from *Hashem* out of heaven.

כד וַיהוָה הִמְטִיר עַל־סְדֹם וְעַל־עֲמֹרָה גָּפְרִית וָאֵשׁ מֵאֵת יְהוָה מִן־הַשָּׁמָיִם:

Bereishit/Genesis 19
Vayeira

בראשית יט
וירא

25 He annihilated those cities and the entire Plain, and all the inhabitants of the cities and the vegetation of the ground.

כה וַיַּהֲפֹךְ אֶת־הֶעָרִים הָאֵל וְאֵת כָּל־הַכִּכָּר וְאֵת כָּל־יֹשְׁבֵי הֶעָרִים וְצֶמַח הָאֲדָמָה:

va-ya-ha-FOKH et he-a-REEM ha-AYL v'-AYT kol ha-ki-KAR v'-AYT kol yo-sh'-VAY he-a-REEM v'-TZE-makh ha-a-da-MAH

26 Lot's wife looked back, and she thereupon turned into a pillar of salt.

כו וַתַּבֵּט אִשְׁתּוֹ מֵאַחֲרָיו וַתְּהִי נְצִיב מֶלַח:

27 Next morning, *Avraham* hurried to the place where he had stood before *Hashem*,

כז וַיַּשְׁכֵּם אַבְרָהָם בַּבֹּקֶר אֶל־הַמָּקוֹם אֲשֶׁר־עָמַד שָׁם אֶת־פְּנֵי יְהֹוָה:

28 and, looking down toward Sodom and Gomorrah and all the land of the Plain, he saw the smoke of the land rising like the smoke of a kiln.

כח וַיַּשְׁקֵף עַל־פְּנֵי סְדֹם וַעֲמֹרָה וְעַל־כָּל־פְּנֵי אֶרֶץ הַכִּכָּר וַיַּרְא וְהִנֵּה עָלָה קִיטֹר הָאָרֶץ כְּקִיטֹר הַכִּבְשָׁן:

29 Thus it was that, when *Hashem* destroyed the cities of the Plain and annihilated the cities where Lot dwelt, *Hashem* was mindful of *Avraham* and removed Lot from the midst of the upheaval.

כט וַיְהִי בְּשַׁחֵת אֱלֹהִים אֶת־עָרֵי הַכִּכָּר וַיִּזְכֹּר אֱלֹהִים אֶת־אַבְרָהָם וַיְשַׁלַּח אֶת־לוֹט מִתּוֹךְ הַהֲפֵכָה בַּהֲפֹךְ אֶת־הֶעָרִים אֲשֶׁר־יָשַׁב בָּהֵן לוֹט:

30 Lot went up from Zoar and settled in the hill country with his two daughters, for he was afraid to dwell in Zoar; and he and his two daughters lived in a cave.

ל וַיַּעַל לוֹט מִצּוֹעַר וַיֵּשֶׁב בָּהָר וּשְׁתֵּי בְנֹתָיו עִמּוֹ כִּי יָרֵא לָשֶׁבֶת בְּצוֹעַר וַיֵּשֶׁב בַּמְּעָרָה הוּא וּשְׁתֵּי בְנֹתָיו:

31 And the older one said to the younger, "Our father is old, and there is not a man on earth to consort with us in the way of all the world.

לא וַתֹּאמֶר הַבְּכִירָה אֶל־הַצְּעִירָה אָבִינוּ זָקֵן וְאִישׁ אֵין בָּאָרֶץ לָבוֹא עָלֵינוּ כְּדֶרֶךְ כָּל־הָאָרֶץ:

32 Come, let us make our father drink wine, and let us lie with him, that we may maintain life through our father."

לב לְכָה נַשְׁקֶה אֶת־אָבִינוּ יַיִן וְנִשְׁכְּבָה עִמּוֹ וּנְחַיֶּה מֵאָבִינוּ זָרַע:

33 That night they made their father drink wine, and the older one went in and lay with her father; he did not know when she lay down or when she rose.

לג וַתַּשְׁקֶיןָ אֶת־אֲבִיהֶן יַיִן בַּלַּיְלָה הוּא וַתָּבֹא הַבְּכִירָה וַתִּשְׁכַּב אֶת־אָבִיהָ וְלֹא־יָדַע בְּשִׁכְבָהּ וּבְקוּמָהּ:

34 The next day the older one said to the younger, "See, I lay with Father last night; let us make him drink wine tonight also, and you go and lie with him, that we may maintain life through our father."

לד וַיְהִי מִמָּחֳרָת וַתֹּאמֶר הַבְּכִירָה אֶל־הַצְּעִירָה הֵן־שָׁכַבְתִּי אֶמֶשׁ אֶת־אָבִי נַשְׁקֶנּוּ יַיִן גַּם־הַלַּיְלָה וּבֹאִי שִׁכְבִי עִמּוֹ וּנְחַיֶּה מֵאָבִינוּ זָרַע:

19:25 And the vegetation of the ground The destruction of Sodom is complete, total annihilation. The obliteration includes not just the people, but also the overturning of the city and the very earth they resided on. The *Ramban* comments that here, God set a precedent that the Land of Israel, which includes Sodom, does not tolerate corruption. This serves as a warning for future inhabitants of this holy place to guard their behavior. As it says in *Sefer Devarim* (29:22,24) "all its soil devastated by sulfur and salt, beyond sowing and producing, no grass growing in it, just like the upheaval of Sodom and Gomorrah… Because they forsook the covenant that the Lord, God of their fathers, made with them when He freed them from the land of Egypt… because they forsook the covenant of *Hashem*."

Ramban
(1194–1270)

Bereishit/Genesis 20
Vayeira

בראשית כ
ויֵרא

35 That night also they made their father drink wine, and the younger one went and lay with him; he did not know when she lay down or when she rose.

וַתַּשְׁקֶ֜יןָ גַּ֣ם בַּלַּ֧יְלָה הַה֛וּא אֶת־אֲבִיהֶ֖ן יָ֑יִן וַתָּ֤קָם הַצְּעִירָה֙ וַתִּשְׁכַּ֣ב עִמּ֔וֹ וְלֹֽא־יָדַ֥ע בְּשִׁכְבָ֖הּ וּבְקֻמָֽהּ׃ לה

36 Thus the two daughters of Lot came to be with child by their father.

וַתַּהֲרֶ֛יןָ שְׁתֵּ֥י בְנֽוֹת־ל֖וֹט מֵאֲבִיהֶֽן׃ לו

37 The older one bore a son and named him Moab; he is the father of the Moabites of today.

וַתֵּ֤לֶד הַבְּכִירָה֙ בֵּ֔ן וַתִּקְרָ֥א שְׁמ֖וֹ מוֹאָ֑ב ה֥וּא אֲבִֽי־מוֹאָ֖ב עַד־הַיּֽוֹם׃ לז

38 And the younger also bore a son, and she called him Ben-ammi; he is the father of the Ammonites of today.

וְהַצְּעִירָ֤ה גַם־הִוא֙ יָ֣לְדָה בֵּ֔ן וַתִּקְרָ֥א שְׁמ֖וֹ בֶּן־עַמִּ֑י ה֛וּא אֲבִ֥י בְנֵֽי־עַמּ֖וֹן עַד־הַיּֽוֹם׃ לח

20

1 *Avraham* journeyed from there to the region of the *Negev* and settled between Kadesh and Shur. While he was sojourning in Gerar,

וַיִּסַּ֨ע מִשָּׁ֤ם אַבְרָהָם֙ אַ֣רְצָה הַנֶּ֔גֶב וַיֵּ֥שֶׁב בֵּין־קָדֵ֖שׁ וּבֵ֣ין שׁ֑וּר וַיָּ֖גָר בִּגְרָֽר׃ א

va-yi-SA mi-SHAM av-ra-HAM AR-tzah ha-NE-gev va-YAY-shev bayn ka-DAYSH u-VAYN SHUR va-YA-gor big-RAR

2 *Avraham* said of *Sara* his wife, "She is my sister." So King Abimelech of Gerar had *Sara* brought to him.

וַיֹּ֧אמֶר אַבְרָהָ֛ם אֶל־שָׂרָ֥ה אִשְׁתּ֖וֹ אֲחֹ֣תִי הִ֑וא וַיִּשְׁלַ֗ח אֲבִימֶ֙לֶךְ֙ מֶ֣לֶךְ גְּרָ֔ר וַיִּקַּ֖ח אֶת־שָׂרָֽה׃ ב

va-YO-mer av-ra-HAM el sa-RAH ish-TO a-KHO-tee HEE va-yish-LAKH a-vee-ME-lekh ME-lekh g'-RAR va-yi-KAKH et sa-RAH

3 But *Hashem* came to Abimelech in a dream by night and said to him, "You are to die because of the woman that you have taken, for she is a married woman."

וַיָּבֹ֧א אֱלֹהִ֛ים אֶל־אֲבִימֶ֖לֶךְ בַּחֲל֣וֹם הַלָּ֑יְלָה וַיֹּ֣אמֶר ל֗וֹ הִנְּךָ֥ מֵת֙ עַל־הָאִשָּׁ֣ה אֲשֶׁר־לָקַ֔חְתָּ וְהִ֖וא בְּעֻ֥לַת בָּֽעַל׃ ג

20:1 *Avraham* journeyed from there Scripture does not provide any reason for *Avraham's* travels. Consequently, Rabbi David Kimchi, a medieval commentator and grammarian known as the *Radak*, posits that *Avraham* travels in order to dwell in the different parts of the land that *Hashem* gave to him. By residing in various places, even for short periods of time, *Avraham* thereby adds his own effort to acquire the breadth and width of the land promised to him. In this way, *Avraham* is fulfilling God's command "walk about the land" (Genesis 13:17). Saddened by the loss of the cities of Sodom and Gomorrah, *Avraham* wonders if the destruction could have been prevented by his presence there. He resolves to reach further areas in *Eretz Yisrael*.

20:2 So King Abimelech of Gerar had *Sara* brought to him Although *Sara* was taken captive by both Pharoah (Genesis 12:19) and Abimelech, her courage and bravery inspired many Jewish women over the centuries, especially those who carried her name. Sarah Braverman, the "first lady of the IDF," was born in Romania in 1918, and arrived in Israel when she was 20 years old. Upon her arrival, she immediately joined the Jewish liberation movement. Braverman was one of the first women to join "*Palmach*," the special fighting forces of the Haganah and one of the forerunners of the Israeli army. Braverman was chosen to be one of three women in a group of 37 Palmach fighters to take part in the 1943 parachuting mission behind enemy lines into Nazi Europe. After the creation of the State of Israel, Braverman helped establish the IDF Women's Corps. Sarah Braverman truly lived up to her namesake, the original *Sara*. She was a brave and devoted Jewish heroine, who put her life on the line time and again to protect and defend her people.

Sarah Braverman (1918–2013)

Bereishit/Genesis 20
Vayeira

בראשית כ
וירא

4 Now Abimelech had not approached her. He said, "O *Hashem*, will You slay people even though innocent?

ד וַאֲבִימֶ֕לֶךְ לֹ֥א קָרַ֖ב אֵלֶ֑יהָ וַיֹּאמַ֕ר אֲדֹנָ֕י הֲג֥וֹי גַּם־צַדִּ֖יק תַּהֲרֹֽג׃

5 He himself said to me, 'She is my sister!' And she also said, 'He is my brother.' When I did this, my heart was blameless and my hands were clean."

ה הֲלֹ֨א ה֤וּא אָֽמַר־לִי֙ אֲחֹ֣תִי הִ֔וא וְהִֽיא־גַם־הִ֥וא אָֽמְרָ֖ה אָחִ֣י ה֑וּא בְּתָם־לְבָבִ֛י וּבְנִקְיֹ֥ן כַּפַּ֖י עָשִׂ֥יתִי זֹֽאת׃

6 And *Hashem* said to him in the dream, "I knew that you did this with a blameless heart, and so I kept you from sinning against Me. That was why I did not let you touch her.

ו וַיֹּאמֶר֩ אֵלָ֨יו הָֽאֱלֹהִ֜ים בַּחֲלֹ֗ם גַּ֣ם אָנֹכִ֤י יָדַ֙עְתִּי֙ כִּ֤י בְתָם־לְבָבְךָ֙ עָשִׂ֣יתָ זֹּ֔את וָאֶחְשֹׂ֧ךְ גַּם־אָנֹכִ֛י אֽוֹתְךָ֖ מֵחֲטוֹ־לִ֑י עַל־כֵּ֥ן לֹא־נְתַתִּ֖יךָ לִנְגֹּ֥עַ אֵלֶֽיהָ׃

7 Therefore, restore the man's wife – since he is a *navi*, he will intercede for you – to save your life. If you fail to restore her, know that you shall die, you and all that are yours."

ז וְעַתָּ֗ה הָשֵׁ֤ב אֵֽשֶׁת־הָאִישׁ֙ כִּֽי־נָבִ֣יא ה֔וּא וְיִתְפַּלֵּ֥ל בַּֽעַדְךָ֖ וֶֽחְיֵ֑ה וְאִם־אֵֽינְךָ֣ מֵשִׁ֔יב דַּ֚ע כִּי־מ֣וֹת תָּמ֔וּת אַתָּ֖ה וְכָל־אֲשֶׁר־לָֽךְ׃

8 Early next morning, Abimelech called his servants and told them all that had happened; and the men were greatly frightened.

ח וַיַּשְׁכֵּ֨ם אֲבִימֶ֜לֶךְ בַּבֹּ֗קֶר וַיִּקְרָא֙ לְכָל־עֲבָדָ֔יו וַיְדַבֵּ֛ר אֶת־כָּל־הַדְּבָרִ֥ים הָאֵ֖לֶּה בְּאָזְנֵיהֶ֑ם וַיִּֽירְא֥וּ הָאֲנָשִׁ֖ים מְאֹֽד׃

9 Then Abimelech summoned *Avraham* and said to him, "What have you done to us? What wrong have I done that you should bring so great a guilt upon me and my kingdom? You have done to me things that ought not to be done.

ט וַיִּקְרָ֨א אֲבִימֶ֜לֶךְ לְאַבְרָהָ֗ם וַיֹּ֨אמֶר ל֜וֹ מֶֽה־עָשִׂ֤יתָ לָּ֙נוּ֙ וּמֶֽה־חָטָ֣אתִי לָ֔ךְ כִּֽי־הֵבֵ֧אתָ עָלַ֛י וְעַל־מַמְלַכְתִּ֖י חֲטָאָ֣ה גְדֹלָ֑ה מַעֲשִׂים֙ אֲשֶׁ֣ר לֹא־יֵֽעָשׂ֔וּ עָשִׂ֖יתָ עִמָּדִֽי׃

10 "What, then," Abimelech demanded of *Avraham*, "was your purpose in doing this thing?"

י וַיֹּ֥אמֶר אֲבִימֶ֖לֶךְ אֶל־אַבְרָהָ֑ם מָ֣ה רָאִ֔יתָ כִּ֥י עָשִׂ֖יתָ אֶת־הַדָּבָ֥ר הַזֶּֽה׃

11 "I thought," said *Avraham*, "surely there is no fear of *Hashem* in this place, and they will kill me because of my wife.

יא וַיֹּ֙אמֶר֙ אַבְרָהָ֔ם כִּ֣י אָמַ֗רְתִּי רַ֚ק אֵין־יִרְאַ֣ת אֱלֹהִ֔ים בַּמָּק֖וֹם הַזֶּ֑ה וַהֲרָג֖וּנִי עַל־דְּבַ֥ר אִשְׁתִּֽי׃

12 And besides, she is in truth my sister, my father's daughter though not my mother's; and she became my wife.

יב וְגַם־אָמְנָ֗ה אֲחֹתִ֤י בַת־אָבִי֙ הִ֔וא אַ֖ךְ לֹ֣א בַת־אִמִּ֑י וַתְּהִי־לִ֖י לְאִשָּֽׁה׃

13 So when *Hashem* made me wander from my father's house, I said to her, 'Let this be the kindness that you shall do me: whatever place we come to, say there of me: He is my brother.'"

יג וַיְהִ֞י כַּאֲשֶׁ֧ר הִתְע֣וּ אֹתִ֗י אֱלֹהִים֮ מִבֵּ֣ית אָבִי֒ וָאֹמַ֣ר לָ֔הּ זֶ֣ה חַסְדֵּ֔ךְ אֲשֶׁ֥ר תַּעֲשִׂ֖י עִמָּדִ֑י אֶ֤ל כָּל־הַמָּקוֹם֙ אֲשֶׁ֣ר נָב֣וֹא שָׁ֔מָּה אִמְרִי־לִ֖י אָחִ֥י הֽוּא׃

14 Abimelech took sheep and oxen, and male and female slaves, and gave them to *Avraham*; and he restored his wife *Sara* to him.

יד וַיִּקַּ֨ח אֲבִימֶ֜לֶךְ צֹ֣אן וּבָקָ֗ר וַעֲבָדִים֙ וּשְׁפָחֹ֔ת וַיִּתֵּ֖ן לְאַבְרָהָ֑ם וַיָּ֣שֶׁב ל֔וֹ אֵ֖ת שָׂרָ֥ה אִשְׁתּֽוֹ׃

15 And Abimelech said, "Here, my land is before you; settle wherever you please."

טו וַיֹּ֣אמֶר אֲבִימֶ֔לֶךְ הִנֵּ֥ה אַרְצִ֖י לְפָנֶ֑יךָ בַּטּ֥וֹב בְּעֵינֶ֖יךָ שֵֽׁב׃

16 And to *Sara* he said, "I herewith give your brother a thousand pieces of silver; this will serve you as vindication before all who are with you, and you are cleared before everyone."

טז וּלְשָׂרָ֣ה אָמַ֗ר הִנֵּ֨ה נָתַ֜תִּי אֶ֤לֶף כֶּ֙סֶף֙ לְאָחִ֔יךְ הִנֵּ֥ה הוּא־לָ֛ךְ כְּס֥וּת עֵינַ֖יִם לְכֹ֣ל אֲשֶׁ֣ר אִתָּ֑ךְ וְאֵ֥ת כֹּ֖ל וְנֹכָֽחַת׃

Bereishit/Genesis 21
Vayeira

בראשית כא
וירא

17 *Avraham* then prayed to *Hashem*, and *Hashem* healed Abimelech and his wife and his slave girls, so that they bore children;

יז וַיִּתְפַּלֵּל אַבְרָהָם אֶל־הָאֱלֹהִים וַיִּרְפָּא אֱלֹהִים אֶת־אֲבִימֶלֶךְ וְאֶת־אִשְׁתּוֹ וְאַמְהֹתָיו וַיֵּלֵדוּ:

18 for *Hashem* had closed fast every womb of the household of Abimelech because of *Sara*, the wife of *Avraham*.

יח כִּי־עָצֹר עָצַר יְהֹוָה בְּעַד כָּל־רֶחֶם לְבֵית אֲבִימֶלֶךְ עַל־דְּבַר שָׂרָה אֵשֶׁת אַבְרָהָם:

21

1 *Hashem* took note of *Sara* as He had promised, and *Hashem* did for *Sara* as He had spoken.

כא א וַיהֹוָה פָּקַד אֶת־שָׂרָה כַּאֲשֶׁר אָמָר וַיַּעַשׂ יְהֹוָה לְשָׂרָה כַּאֲשֶׁר דִּבֵּר:

2 *Sara* conceived and bore a son to *Avraham* in his old age, at the set time of which *Hashem* had spoken.

ב וַתַּהַר וַתֵּלֶד שָׂרָה לְאַבְרָהָם בֵּן לִזְקֻנָיו לַמּוֹעֵד אֲשֶׁר־דִּבֶּר אֹתוֹ אֱלֹהִים:

3 *Avraham* gave his newborn son, whom *Sara* had borne him, the name of *Yitzchak*.

ג וַיִּקְרָא אַבְרָהָם אֶת־שֶׁם־בְּנוֹ הַנּוֹלַד־לוֹ אֲשֶׁר־יָלְדָה־לּוֹ שָׂרָה יִצְחָק:

4 And when his son *Yitzchak* was eight days old, *Avraham* circumcised him, as *Hashem* had commanded him.

ד וַיָּמָל אַבְרָהָם אֶת־יִצְחָק בְּנוֹ בֶּן־שְׁמֹנַת יָמִים כַּאֲשֶׁר צִוָּה אֹתוֹ אֱלֹהִים:

5 Now *Avraham* was a hundred years old when his son *Yitzchak* was born to him.

ה וְאַבְרָהָם בֶּן־מְאַת שָׁנָה בְּהִוָּלֶד לוֹ אֵת יִצְחָק בְּנוֹ:

6 *Sara* said, "*Hashem* has brought me laughter; everyone who hears will laugh with me."

ו וַתֹּאמֶר שָׂרָה צְחֹק עָשָׂה לִי אֱלֹהִים כָּל־הַשֹּׁמֵעַ יִצְחַק־לִי:

7 And she added, "Who would have said to *Avraham* That *Sara* would suckle children! Yet I have borne a son in his old age."

ז וַתֹּאמֶר מִי מִלֵּל לְאַבְרָהָם הֵינִיקָה בָנִים שָׂרָה כִּי־יָלַדְתִּי בֵן לִזְקֻנָיו:

8 The child grew up and was weaned, and *Avraham* held a great feast on the day that *Yitzchak* was weaned.

ח וַיִּגְדַּל הַיֶּלֶד וַיִּגָּמַל וַיַּעַשׂ אַבְרָהָם מִשְׁתֶּה גָדוֹל בְּיוֹם הִגָּמֵל אֶת־יִצְחָק:

9 *Sara* saw the son whom Hagar the Egyptian had borne to *Avraham* playing.

ט וַתֵּרֶא שָׂרָה אֶת־בֶּן־הָגָר הַמִּצְרִית אֲשֶׁר־יָלְדָה לְאַבְרָהָם מְצַחֵק:

10 She said to *Avraham*, "Cast out that slave-woman and her son, for the son of that slave shall not share in the inheritance with my son *Yitzchak*."

י וַתֹּאמֶר לְאַבְרָהָם גָּרֵשׁ הָאָמָה הַזֹּאת וְאֶת־בְּנָהּ כִּי לֹא יִירַשׁ בֶּן־הָאָמָה הַזֹּאת עִם־בְּנִי עִם־יִצְחָק:

11 The matter distressed *Avraham* greatly, for it concerned a son of his.

יא וַיֵּרַע הַדָּבָר מְאֹד בְּעֵינֵי אַבְרָהָם עַל אוֹדֹת בְּנוֹ:

12 But *Hashem* said to *Avraham*, "Do not be distressed over the boy or your slave; whatever *Sara* tells you, do as she says, for it is through *Yitzchak* that offspring shall be continued for you.

יב וַיֹּאמֶר אֱלֹהִים אֶל־אַבְרָהָם אַל־יֵרַע בְּעֵינֶיךָ עַל־הַנַּעַר וְעַל־אֲמָתֶךָ כֹּל אֲשֶׁר תֹּאמַר אֵלֶיךָ שָׂרָה שְׁמַע בְּקֹלָהּ כִּי בְיִצְחָק יִקָּרֵא לְךָ זָרַע:

13 As for the son of the slave-woman, I will make a nation of him, too, for he is your seed."

יג וְגַם אֶת־בֶּן־הָאָמָה לְגוֹי אֲשִׂימֶנּוּ כִּי זַרְעֲךָ הוּא:

Bereishit/Genesis 21
Vayeira

בראשית כא
וירא

14 Early next morning *Avraham* took some bread and a skin of water, and gave them to Hagar. He placed them over her shoulder, together with the child, and sent her away. And she wandered about in the wilderness of *Be'er Sheva*.

יד וַיַּשְׁכֵּם אַבְרָהָם ׀ בַּבֹּקֶר וַיִּקַּח־לֶחֶם וְחֵמַת מַיִם וַיִּתֵּן אֶל־הָגָר שָׂם עַל־שִׁכְמָהּ וְאֶת־הַיֶּלֶד וַיְשַׁלְּחֶהָ וַתֵּלֶךְ וַתֵּתַע בְּמִדְבַּר בְּאֵר שָׁבַע:

15 When the water was gone from the skin, she left the child under one of the bushes,

טו וַיִּכְלוּ הַמַּיִם מִן־הַחֵמֶת וַתַּשְׁלֵךְ אֶת־הַיֶּלֶד תַּחַת אַחַד הַשִּׂיחִם:

16 and went and sat down at a distance, a bowshot away; for she thought, "Let me not look on as the child dies." And sitting thus afar, she burst into tears.

טז וַתֵּלֶךְ וַתֵּשֶׁב לָהּ מִנֶּגֶד הַרְחֵק כִּמְטַחֲוֵי קֶשֶׁת כִּי אָמְרָה אַל־אֶרְאֶה בְּמוֹת הַיָּלֶד וַתֵּשֶׁב מִנֶּגֶד וַתִּשָּׂא אֶת־קֹלָהּ וַתֵּבְךְּ:

17 *Hashem* heard the cry of the boy, and an angel of *Hashem* called to Hagar from heaven and said to her, "What troubles you, Hagar? Fear not, for *Hashem* has heeded the cry of the boy where he is.

יז וַיִּשְׁמַע אֱלֹהִים אֶת־קוֹל הַנַּעַר וַיִּקְרָא מַלְאַךְ אֱלֹהִים ׀ אֶל־הָגָר מִן־הַשָּׁמַיִם וַיֹּאמֶר לָהּ מַה־לָּךְ הָגָר אַל־תִּירְאִי כִּי־שָׁמַע אֱלֹהִים אֶל־קוֹל הַנַּעַר בַּאֲשֶׁר הוּא־שָׁם:

18 Come, lift up the boy and hold him by the hand, for I will make a great nation of him."

יח קוּמִי שְׂאִי אֶת־הַנַּעַר וְהַחֲזִיקִי אֶת־יָדֵךְ בּוֹ כִּי־לְגוֹי גָּדוֹל אֲשִׂימֶנּוּ:

19 Then *Hashem* opened her eyes and she saw a well of water. She went and filled the skin with water, and let the boy drink.

יט וַיִּפְקַח אֱלֹהִים אֶת־עֵינֶיהָ וַתֵּרֶא בְּאֵר מָיִם וַתֵּלֶךְ וַתְּמַלֵּא אֶת־הַחֵמֶת מַיִם וַתַּשְׁקְ אֶת־הַנָּעַר:

20 *Hashem* was with the boy and he grew up; he dwelt in the wilderness and became a bowman.

כ וַיְהִי אֱלֹהִים אֶת־הַנַּעַר וַיִּגְדָּל וַיֵּשֶׁב בַּמִּדְבָּר וַיְהִי רֹבֶה קַשָּׁת:

21 He lived in the wilderness of Paran; and his mother got a wife for him from the land of Egypt.

כא וַיֵּשֶׁב בְּמִדְבַּר פָּארָן וַתִּקַּח־לוֹ אִמּוֹ אִשָּׁה מֵאֶרֶץ מִצְרָיִם:

22 At that time Abimelech and Phicol, chief of his troops, said to *Avraham*, "*Hashem* is with you in everything that you do.

כב וַיְהִי בָּעֵת הַהִוא וַיֹּאמֶר אֲבִימֶלֶךְ וּפִיכֹל שַׂר־צְבָאוֹ אֶל־אַבְרָהָם לֵאמֹר אֱלֹהִים עִמְּךָ בְּכֹל אֲשֶׁר־אַתָּה עֹשֶׂה:

23 Therefore swear to me here by *Hashem* that you will not deal falsely with me or with my kith and kin, but will deal with me and with the land in which you have sojourned as loyally as I have dealt with you."

כג וְעַתָּה הִשָּׁבְעָה לִּי בֵאלֹהִים הֵנָּה אִם־תִּשְׁקֹר לִי וּלְנִינִי וּלְנֶכְדִּי כַּחֶסֶד אֲשֶׁר־עָשִׂיתִי עִמְּךָ תַּעֲשֶׂה עִמָּדִי וְעִם־הָאָרֶץ אֲשֶׁר־גַּרְתָּה בָּהּ:

24 And *Avraham* said, "I swear it."

כד וַיֹּאמֶר אַבְרָהָם אָנֹכִי אִשָּׁבֵעַ:

25 Then *Avraham* reproached Abimelech for the well of water which the servants of Abimelech had seized.

כה וְהוֹכִחַ אַבְרָהָם אֶת־אֲבִימֶלֶךְ עַל־אֹדוֹת בְּאֵר הַמַּיִם אֲשֶׁר גָּזְלוּ עַבְדֵי אֲבִימֶלֶךְ:

26 But Abimelech said, "I do not know who did this; you did not tell me, nor have I heard of it until today."

כו וַיֹּאמֶר אֲבִימֶלֶךְ לֹא יָדַעְתִּי מִי עָשָׂה אֶת־הַדָּבָר הַזֶּה וְגַם־אַתָּה לֹא־הִגַּדְתָּ לִּי וְגַם אָנֹכִי לֹא שָׁמַעְתִּי בִּלְתִּי הַיּוֹם:

27 *Avraham* took sheep and oxen and gave them to Abimelech, and the two of them made a pact.

כז וַיִּקַּח אַבְרָהָם צֹאן וּבָקָר וַיִּתֵּן לַאֲבִימֶלֶךְ וַיִּכְרְתוּ שְׁנֵיהֶם בְּרִית:

Bereishit/Genesis 22
Vayeira

בראשית כב
וירא

28 Avraham then set seven ewes of the flock by themselves,

וַיַּצֵּב אַבְרָהָם אֶת־שֶׁבַע כִּבְשֹׂת הַצֹּאן לְבַדְּהֶן:

29 and Abimelech said to *Avraham*, "What mean these seven ewes which you have set apart?"

וַיֹּאמֶר אֲבִימֶלֶךְ אֶל־אַבְרָהָם מָה הֵנָּה שֶׁבַע כְּבָשֹׂת הָאֵלֶּה אֲשֶׁר הִצַּבְתָּ לְבַדָּנָה:

30 He replied, "You are to accept these seven ewes from me as proof that I dug this well."

וַיֹּאמֶר כִּי אֶת־שֶׁבַע כְּבָשֹׂת תִּקַּח מִיָּדִי בַּעֲבוּר תִּהְיֶה־לִּי לְעֵדָה כִּי חָפַרְתִּי אֶת־הַבְּאֵר הַזֹּאת:

31 Hence that place was called *Be'er Sheva*, for there the two of them swore an oath.

עַל־כֵּן קָרָא לַמָּקוֹם הַהוּא בְּאֵר שָׁבַע כִּי שָׁם נִשְׁבְּעוּ שְׁנֵיהֶם:

al KAYN ka-RA la-ma-KOM ha-HU b'-AYR SHA-va KEE SHAM nish-b'-U sh'-nay-HEM

32 When they had concluded the pact at *Be'er Sheva*, Abimelech and Phicol, chief of his troops, departed and returned to the land of the Philistines.

וַיִּכְרְתוּ בְרִית בִּבְאֵר שָׁבַע וַיָּקָם אֲבִימֶלֶךְ וּפִיכֹל שַׂר־צְבָאוֹ וַיָּשֻׁבוּ אֶל־אֶרֶץ פְּלִשְׁתִּים:

33 [*Avraham*] planted a tamarisk at *Be'er Sheva*, and invoked there the name of *Hashem*, the Everlasting God.

וַיִּטַּע אֶשֶׁל בִּבְאֵר שָׁבַע וַיִּקְרָא־שָׁם בְּשֵׁם יְהוָה אֵל עוֹלָם:

va-yi-TA E-shel biv-AYR SHA-va va-YIK-ra SHAM b'-SHAYM a-do-NAI AYL o-LAM

34 And *Avraham* resided in the land of the Philistines a long time.

וַיָּגָר אַבְרָהָם בְּאֶרֶץ פְּלִשְׁתִּים יָמִים רַבִּים:

22 1 Some time afterward, *Hashem* put *Avraham* to the test. He said to him, "*Avraham*," and he answered, "Here I am."

כב וַיְהִי אַחַר הַדְּבָרִים הָאֵלֶּה וְהָאֱלֹהִים נִסָּה אֶת־אַבְרָהָם וַיֹּאמֶר אֵלָיו אַבְרָהָם וַיֹּאמֶר הִנֵּנִי:

באר שבע

Abraham's well in Beersheva

א 21:31 Hence that place was called *Be'er Sheva* *Avraham* names the place where he entered the covenant with Abimelech *Be'er Sheva*. The name *Be'er Sheva* (באר שבע), is made up of two Hebrew words. *Be'er* (באר), means 'well,' hinting to the fact that this covenant acknowledged *Avraham's* right to the water well. The second part of the word is made up of the root ש-ב-ע, which means both 'seven' and 'oath.' Thus, *Be'er Sheva* can mean either 'well of the seven' or 'well of the oath.' This double meaning hints both to the seven female sheep set aside by *Avraham* as verification of the oath, and to the oath taken with regard to the well itself.

א 21:33 The name of *Hashem*, the Everlasting God The Hebrew word used in this verse for everlasting is *olam* (עולם), which also means 'world' or 'universe.' The word *olam* is closely related to the word *ne'elam* (נעלם), meaning 'hidden.' The phrase "*El Olam*" (אל עולם), 'Everlasting God,' alludes to the fact that *Hashem* is also King over that which is hidden from us. God has specifically designed a world that is ruled by the laws of nature and hides His presence. It is up to man to see past His mask and reveal the Godliness that is hidden throughout the universe.

עולם

Bereishit/Genesis 22
Vayeira

בראשית כב
וירא

2 And He said, "Take your son, your favored one, *Yitzchak*, whom you love, and go to the land of *Moriah*, and offer him there as a burnt offering on one of the heights that I will point out to you."

ב וַיֹּאמֶר קַח־נָא אֶת־בִּנְךָ אֶת־יְחִידְךָ אֲשֶׁר־אָהַבְתָּ אֶת־יִצְחָק וְלֶךְ־לְךָ אֶל־אֶרֶץ הַמֹּרִיָּה וְהַעֲלֵהוּ שָׁם לְעֹלָה עַל אַחַד הֶהָרִים אֲשֶׁר אֹמַר אֵלֶיךָ:

va-YO-mer kakh NA et bin-KHA et y'-khee-d'-KHA a-sher a-HAV-ta et yitz-KHAK v'-LEKH l'-KHA el E-retz ha-mo-ri-YAH v'-ha-a-LAY-hu SHAM l'-o-LAH AL a-KHAD he-ha-REEM a-SHER o-MAR ay-LE-kha

3 So early next morning, *Avraham* saddled his ass and took with him two of his servants and his son *Yitzchak*. He split the wood for the burnt offering, and he set out for the place of which *Hashem* had told him.

ג וַיַּשְׁכֵּם אַבְרָהָם בַּבֹּקֶר וַיַּחֲבֹשׁ אֶת־חֲמֹרוֹ וַיִּקַּח אֶת־שְׁנֵי נְעָרָיו אִתּוֹ וְאֵת יִצְחָק בְּנוֹ וַיְבַקַּע עֲצֵי עֹלָה וַיָּקָם וַיֵּלֶךְ אֶל־הַמָּקוֹם אֲשֶׁר־אָמַר־לוֹ הָאֱלֹהִים:

4 On the third day *Avraham* looked up and saw the place from afar.

ד בַּיּוֹם הַשְּׁלִישִׁי וַיִּשָּׂא אַבְרָהָם אֶת־עֵינָיו וַיַּרְא אֶת־הַמָּקוֹם מֵרָחֹק:

5 Then *Avraham* said to his servants, "You stay here with the ass. The boy and I will go up there; we will worship and we will return to you."

ה וַיֹּאמֶר אַבְרָהָם אֶל־נְעָרָיו שְׁבוּ־לָכֶם פֹּה עִם־הַחֲמוֹר וַאֲנִי וְהַנַּעַר נֵלְכָה עַד־כֹּה וְנִשְׁתַּחֲוֶה וְנָשׁוּבָה אֲלֵיכֶם:

6 *Avraham* took the wood for the burnt offering and put it on his son *Yitzchak*. He himself took the firestone and the knife; and the two walked off together.

ו וַיִּקַּח אַבְרָהָם אֶת־עֲצֵי הָעֹלָה וַיָּשֶׂם עַל־יִצְחָק בְּנוֹ וַיִּקַּח בְּיָדוֹ אֶת־הָאֵשׁ וְאֶת־הַמַּאֲכֶלֶת וַיֵּלְכוּ שְׁנֵיהֶם יַחְדָּו:

7 Then *Yitzchak* said to his father *Avraham*, "Father!" And he answered, "Yes, my son." And he said, "Here are the firestone and the wood; but where is the sheep for the burnt offering?"

ז וַיֹּאמֶר יִצְחָק אֶל־אַבְרָהָם אָבִיו וַיֹּאמֶר אָבִי וַיֹּאמֶר הִנֶּנִּי בְנִי וַיֹּאמֶר הִנֵּה הָאֵשׁ וְהָעֵצִים וְאַיֵּה הַשֶּׂה לְעֹלָה:

8 And *Avraham* said, "*Hashem* will see to the sheep for His burnt offering, my son." And the two of them walked on together.

ח וַיֹּאמֶר אַבְרָהָם אֱלֹהִים יִרְאֶה־לּוֹ הַשֶּׂה לְעֹלָה בְּנִי וַיֵּלְכוּ שְׁנֵיהֶם יַחְדָּו:

9 They arrived at the place of which *Hashem* had told him. *Avraham* built a *Mizbayach* there; he laid out the wood; he bound his son *Yitzchak*; he laid him on the *Mizbayach*, on top of the wood.

ט וַיָּבֹאוּ אֶל־הַמָּקוֹם אֲשֶׁר אָמַר־לוֹ הָאֱלֹהִים וַיִּבֶן שָׁם אַבְרָהָם אֶת־הַמִּזְבֵּחַ וַיַּעֲרֹךְ אֶת־הָעֵצִים וַיַּעֲקֹד אֶת־יִצְחָק בְּנוֹ וַיָּשֶׂם אֹתוֹ עַל־הַמִּזְבֵּחַ מִמַּעַל לָעֵצִים:

10 And *Avraham* picked up the knife to slay his son.

י וַיִּשְׁלַח אַבְרָהָם אֶת־יָדוֹ וַיִּקַּח אֶת־הַמַּאֲכֶלֶת לִשְׁחֹט אֶת־בְּנוֹ:

11 Then an angel of *Hashem* called to him from heaven: "*Avraham! Avraham!*" And he answered, "Here I am."

יא וַיִּקְרָא אֵלָיו מַלְאַךְ יְהֹוָה מִן־הַשָּׁמַיִם וַיֹּאמֶר אַבְרָהָם אַבְרָהָם וַיֹּאמֶר הִנֵּנִי:

12 And he said, "Do not raise your hand against the boy, or do anything to him. For now I know that you fear *Hashem*, since you have not withheld your son, your favored one, from Me."

יב וַיֹּאמֶר אַל־תִּשְׁלַח יָדְךָ אֶל־הַנַּעַר וְאַל־תַּעַשׂ לוֹ מְאוּמָה כִּי עַתָּה יָדַעְתִּי כִּי־יְרֵא אֱלֹהִים אַתָּה וְלֹא חָשַׂכְתָּ אֶת־בִּנְךָ אֶת־יְחִידְךָ מִמֶּנִּי:

Bereishit/Genesis 22
Vayeira

בראשית כב
וירא

13 When *Avraham* looked up, his eye fell upon a ram, caught in the thicket by its horns. So *Avraham* went and took the ram and offered it up as a burnt offering in place of his son.

יג וַיִּשָּׂא אַבְרָהָם אֶת־עֵינָיו וַיַּרְא וְהִנֵּה־אַיִל אַחַר נֶאֱחַז בַּסְּבַךְ בְּקַרְנָיו וַיֵּלֶךְ אַבְרָהָם וַיִּקַּח אֶת־הָאַיִל וַיַּעֲלֵהוּ לְעֹלָה תַּחַת בְּנוֹ:

14 And *Avraham* named that site Adonai-yireh, whence the present saying, "On the mount of *Hashem* there is vision."

יד וַיִּקְרָא אַבְרָהָם שֵׁם־הַמָּקוֹם הַהוּא יְהֹוָה יִרְאֶה אֲשֶׁר יֵאָמֵר הַיּוֹם בְּהַר יְהֹוָה יֵרָאֶה:

15 The angel of *Hashem* called to *Avraham* a second time from heaven,

טו וַיִּקְרָא מַלְאַךְ יְהֹוָה אֶל־אַבְרָהָם שֵׁנִית מִן־הַשָּׁמָיִם:

16 and said, "By Myself I swear, *Hashem* declares: Because you have done this and have not withheld your son, your favored one,

טז וַיֹּאמֶר בִּי נִשְׁבַּעְתִּי נְאֻם־יְהֹוָה כִּי יַעַן אֲשֶׁר עָשִׂיתָ אֶת־הַדָּבָר הַזֶּה וְלֹא חָשַׂכְתָּ אֶת־בִּנְךָ אֶת־יְחִידֶךָ:

17 I will bestow My blessing upon you and make your descendants as numerous as the stars of heaven and the sands on the seashore; and your descendants shall seize the gates of their foes.

יז כִּי־בָרֵךְ אֲבָרֶכְךָ וְהַרְבָּה אַרְבֶּה אֶת־זַרְעֲךָ כְּכוֹכְבֵי הַשָּׁמַיִם וְכַחוֹל אֲשֶׁר עַל־שְׂפַת הַיָּם וְיִרַשׁ זַרְעֲךָ אֵת שַׁעַר אֹיְבָיו:

18 All the nations of the earth shall bless themselves by your descendants, because you have obeyed My command."

v'-hit-ba-r'-KHU v'-zar-a-KHA KOL go-YAY ha-A-retz AY-kev a-SHER sha-MA-ta b'-ko-LEE

יח וְהִתְבָּרֲכוּ בְזַרְעֲךָ כֹּל גּוֹיֵי הָאָרֶץ עֵקֶב אֲשֶׁר שָׁמַעְתָּ בְּקֹלִי:

19 *Avraham* then returned to his servants, and they departed together for *Be'er Sheva*; and *Avraham* stayed in *Be'er Sheva*.

יט וַיָּשָׁב אַבְרָהָם אֶל־נְעָרָיו וַיָּקֻמוּ וַיֵּלְכוּ יַחְדָּו אֶל־בְּאֵר שָׁבַע וַיֵּשֶׁב אַבְרָהָם בִּבְאֵר שָׁבַע:

20 Some time later, *Avraham* was told, "Milcah too has borne children to your brother Nahor:

כ וַיְהִי אַחֲרֵי הַדְּבָרִים הָאֵלֶּה וַיֻּגַּד לְאַבְרָהָם לֵאמֹר הִנֵּה יָלְדָה מִלְכָּה גַם־הִוא בָּנִים לְנָחוֹר אָחִיךָ:

21 Uz the first-born, and Buz his brother, and Kemuel the father of Aram;

כא אֶת־עוּץ בְּכֹרוֹ וְאֶת־בּוּז אָחִיו וְאֶת־קְמוּאֵל אֲבִי אֲרָם:

22 and Chesed, Hazo, Pildash, Jidlaph, and Bethuel"

כב וְאֶת־כֶּשֶׂד וְאֶת־חֲזוֹ וְאֶת־פִּלְדָּשׁ וְאֶת־יִדְלָף וְאֵת בְּתוּאֵל:

PM Ehud Barak visiting the NASDAQ

22:18 All the nations of the earth shall bless themselves by your descendants After *Avraham* demonstrates his unwavering faith in *Hashem* with the binding of *Yitzchak*, the Lord repeats His original promise found in *Sefer Bereishit* (12:3), and assures *Avraham* that all the nations of the world will be blessed through him. When we look at the many contributions that the State of Israel makes to the entire world even beyond its spiritual message – such as its technological, agricultural and humanitarian innovations – we see that the State of Israel is a fulfillment of this biblical promise. Contemporary Israel has come to be known as the "Start-up Nation," and there are actually more Israeli companies on the NASDAQ stock exchange than any foreign country besides China. Israel plays an outsized role in the global economy, proving this blessing's efficacy.

Bereishit/Genesis 23
Chayei Sara

בראשית כג

חיי שרה

23 Bethuel being the father of *Rivka*. These eight Milcah bore to Nahor, *Avraham*'s brother.

כג וּבְתוּאֵל יָלַד אֶת־רִבְקָה אֵלֶּה שְׁמֹנָה יָלְדָה מִלְכָּה לְנָחוֹר אֲחִי אַבְרָהָם׃

24 And his concubine, whose name was Reumah, also bore children: Tebah, Gaham, Tahash, and Maacah.

כד וּפִילַגְשׁוֹ וּשְׁמָהּ רְאוּמָה וַתֵּלֶד גַּם־הִוא אֶת־טֶבַח וְאֶת־גַּחַם וְאֶת־תַּחַשׁ וְאֶת־מַעֲכָה׃

23

1 *Sara*'s lifetime – the span of *Sara*'s life – came to one hundred and twenty-seven years.

א וַיִּהְיוּ חַיֵּי שָׂרָה מֵאָה שָׁנָה וְעֶשְׂרִים שָׁנָה וְשֶׁבַע שָׁנִים שְׁנֵי חַיֵּי שָׂרָה׃

2 *Sara* died in *Kiryat Arba* – now *Chevron* – in the land of Canaan; and *Avraham* proceeded to mourn for *Sara* and to bewail her.

ב וַתָּמָת שָׂרָה בְּקִרְיַת אַרְבַּע הִוא חֶבְרוֹן בְּאֶרֶץ כְּנָעַן וַיָּבֹא אַבְרָהָם לִסְפֹּד לְשָׂרָה וְלִבְכֹּתָהּ׃

3 Then *Avraham* rose from beside his dead, and spoke to the Hittites, saying,

ג וַיָּקָם אַבְרָהָם מֵעַל פְּנֵי מֵתוֹ וַיְדַבֵּר אֶל־בְּנֵי־חֵת לֵאמֹר׃

4 "I am a resident alien among you; sell me a burial site among you, that I may remove my dead for burial."

ד גֵּר־וְתוֹשָׁב אָנֹכִי עִמָּכֶם תְּנוּ לִי אֲחֻזַּת־קֶבֶר עִמָּכֶם וְאֶקְבְּרָה מֵתִי מִלְּפָנָי׃

5 And the Hittites replied to *Avraham*, saying to him,

ה וַיַּעֲנוּ בְנֵי־חֵת אֶת־אַבְרָהָם לֵאמֹר לוֹ׃

6 "Hear us, my lord: you are the elect of *Hashem* among us. Bury your dead in the choicest of our burial places; none of us will withhold his burial place from you for burying your dead."

ו שְׁמָעֵנוּ אֲדֹנִי נְשִׂיא אֱלֹהִים אַתָּה בְּתוֹכֵנוּ בְּמִבְחַר קְבָרֵינוּ קְבֹר אֶת־מֵתֶךָ אִישׁ מִמֶּנּוּ אֶת־קִבְרוֹ לֹא־יִכְלֶה מִמְּךָ מִקְּבֹר מֵתֶךָ׃

7 Thereupon *Avraham* bowed low to the people of the land, the Hittites,

ז וַיָּקָם אַבְרָהָם וַיִּשְׁתַּחוּ לְעַם־הָאָרֶץ לִבְנֵי־חֵת׃

8 and he said to them, "If it is your wish that I remove my dead for burial, you must agree to intercede for me with Ephron son of Zohar.

ח וַיְדַבֵּר אִתָּם לֵאמֹר אִם־יֵשׁ אֶת־נַפְשְׁכֶם לִקְבֹּר אֶת־מֵתִי מִלְּפָנַי שְׁמָעוּנִי וּפִגְעוּ־לִי בְּעֶפְרוֹן בֶּן־צֹחַר׃

9 Let him sell me the cave of Machpelah that he owns, which is at the edge of his land. Let him sell it to me, at the full price, for a burial site in your midst."

ט וְיִתֶּן־לִי אֶת־מְעָרַת הַמַּכְפֵּלָה אֲשֶׁר־לוֹ אֲשֶׁר בִּקְצֵה שָׂדֵהוּ בְּכֶסֶף מָלֵא יִתְּנֶנָּה לִי בְּתוֹכְכֶם לַאֲחֻזַּת־קָבֶר׃

10 Ephron was present among the Hittites; so Ephron the Hittite answered *Avraham* in the hearing of the Hittites, all who entered the gate of his town, saying,

י וְעֶפְרוֹן יֹשֵׁב בְּתוֹךְ בְּנֵי־חֵת וַיַּעַן עֶפְרוֹן הַחִתִּי אֶת־אַבְרָהָם בְּאָזְנֵי בְנֵי־חֵת לְכֹל בָּאֵי שַׁעַר־עִירוֹ לֵאמֹר׃

11 "No, my lord, hear me: I give you the field and I give you the cave that is in it; I give it to you in the presence of my people. Bury your dead."

יא לֹא־אֲדֹנִי שְׁמָעֵנִי הַשָּׂדֶה נָתַתִּי לָךְ וְהַמְּעָרָה אֲשֶׁר־בּוֹ לְךָ נְתַתִּיהָ לְעֵינֵי בְנֵי־עַמִּי נְתַתִּיהָ לָּךְ קְבֹר מֵתֶךָ׃

12 Then *Avraham* bowed low before the people of the land,

יב וַיִּשְׁתַּחוּ אַבְרָהָם לִפְנֵי עַם הָאָרֶץ׃

13 and spoke to Ephron in the hearing of the people of the land, saying, "If only you would hear me out! Let me pay the price of the land; accept it from me, that I may bury my dead there."

יג וַיְדַבֵּר אֶל־עֶפְרוֹן בְּאָזְנֵי עַם־הָאָרֶץ לֵאמֹר אַךְ אִם־אַתָּה לוּ שְׁמָעֵנִי נָתַתִּי כֶּסֶף הַשָּׂדֶה קַח מִמֶּנִּי וְאֶקְבְּרָה אֶת־מֵתִי שָׁמָּה׃

Bereishit/Genesis 24
Chayei Sara

בראשית כד
חיי שרה

14 And Ephron replied to *Avraham*, saying to him,

וַיַּעַן עֶפְרוֹן אֶת־אַבְרָהָם לֵאמֹר לוֹ:

15 "My lord, do hear me! A piece of land worth four hundred *shekalim* of silver — what is that between you and me? Go and bury your dead."

אֲדֹנִי שְׁמָעֵנִי אֶרֶץ אַרְבַּע מֵאֹת שֶׁקֶל־כֶּסֶף בֵּינִי וּבֵינְךָ מַה־הִוא וְאֶת־מֵתְךָ קְבֹר:

16 *Avraham* accepted Ephron's terms. *Avraham* paid out to Ephron the money that he had named in the hearing of the Hittites — four hundred *shekalim* of silver at the going merchants' rate.

וַיִּשְׁמַע אַבְרָהָם אֶל־עֶפְרוֹן וַיִּשְׁקֹל אַבְרָהָם לְעֶפְרֹן אֶת־הַכֶּסֶף אֲשֶׁר דִּבֶּר בְּאָזְנֵי בְנֵי־חֵת אַרְבַּע מֵאוֹת שֶׁקֶל כֶּסֶף עֹבֵר לַסֹּחֵר:

17 So Ephron's land in Machpelah, near Mamre — the field with its cave and all the trees anywhere within the confines of that field — passed

וַיָּקָם שְׂדֵה עֶפְרוֹן אֲשֶׁר בַּמַּכְפֵּלָה אֲשֶׁר לִפְנֵי מַמְרֵא הַשָּׂדֶה וְהַמְּעָרָה אֲשֶׁר־בּוֹ וְכָל־הָעֵץ אֲשֶׁר בַּשָּׂדֶה אֲשֶׁר בְּכָל־גְּבֻלוֹ סָבִיב:

18 to *Avraham* as his possession, in the presence of the Hittites, of all who entered the gate of his town.

לְאַבְרָהָם לְמִקְנָה לְעֵינֵי בְנֵי־חֵת בְּכֹל בָּאֵי שַׁעַר־עִירוֹ:

19 And then *Avraham* buried his wife *Sara* in the cave of the field of Machpelah, facing Mamre — now *Chevron* — in the land of Canaan.

וְאַחֲרֵי־כֵן קָבַר אַבְרָהָם אֶת־שָׂרָה אִשְׁתּוֹ אֶל־מְעָרַת שְׂדֵה הַמַּכְפֵּלָה עַל־פְּנֵי מַמְרֵא הִוא חֶבְרוֹן בְּאֶרֶץ כְּנָעַן:

v'-a-kha-ray KHAYN ka-VAR av-ra-HAM et sa-RAH ish-TO el m'-a-RAT s'-DAY ha-makh-pay-LAH al p'-NAY mam-RAY HEE khev-RON b'-E-retz k'-NA-an

20 Thus the field with its cave passed from the Hittites to *Avraham*, as a burial site.

וַיָּקָם הַשָּׂדֶה וְהַמְּעָרָה אֲשֶׁר־בּוֹ לְאַבְרָהָם לַאֲחֻזַּת־קָבֶר מֵאֵת בְּנֵי־חֵת:

va-YA-kom ha-sa-DEH v'-ha-m'-a-RAH a-sher BO l'-av-ra-HAM la-a-khu-zat KA-ver may-AYT b'-nay KHAYT

24

1 *Avraham* was now old, advanced in years, and *Hashem* had blessed *Avraham* in all things.

וְאַבְרָהָם זָקֵן בָּא בַּיָּמִים וַיהוָה בֵּרַךְ אֶת־אַבְרָהָם בַּכֹּל:

2 And *Avraham* said to the senior servant of his household, who had charge of all that he owned, "Put your hand under my thigh

וַיֹּאמֶר אַבְרָהָם אֶל־עַבְדּוֹ זְקַן בֵּיתוֹ הַמֹּשֵׁל בְּכָל־אֲשֶׁר־לוֹ שִׂים־נָא יָדְךָ תַּחַת יְרֵכִי:

חברון

23:19 Now *Chevron* The names of many Israeli cities have profound sigificance. According to a Midrash quoted by the *Ramban*, the Hebrew name for Hebron, '*Chevron*' (חברון), is a contraction of the word *chaver* (חבר), 'friend,' and the word *na-eh* (נאה) 'beloved.' Thus, the very name of the city of *Chevron* alludes to its most famous resident *Avraham*, who was the first beloved friend of the Lord, as *Hashem* says in *Sefer Yeshayahu* (41:8), "Seed of *Avraham* My friend."

Kiryat Arba with Chevron in the background

23:20 Passed from the Hittites to *Avraham*, as a burial site At the time of *Sara*'s death, *Avraham* had been living in the Land of Israel for over sixty years, yet this is the first mention of him actually purchasing land. Rabbi Moshe Lichtman, in his book *Eretz Yisrael in the Parasha*, notes that purchasing the land for *Sara*'s burial highlights the fundamental truth that one must sacrifice for *Eretz Yisrael*. It was only after *Avraham* experienced the hardship of the loss of his wife that he acquired his first piece of property. Lest this be discouraging, Jewish tradition teaches that "the reward is proportionate to the effort" (*Ethics of the Fathers*, 5:26). Because of the great sacrifice and effort the Jewish people have made in reclaiming *Eretz Yisrael*, we can be assured that the reward will likewise be great.

55

Bereishit/Genesis 24
Chayei Sara

בראשית כד
חיי שרה

3 and I will make you swear by *Hashem*, the God of heaven and the God of the earth, that you will not take a wife for my son from the daughters of the Canaanites among whom I dwell,

ג וְאַשְׁבִּיעֲךָ בַּיהוָה אֱלֹהֵי הַשָּׁמַיִם וֵאלֹהֵי הָאָרֶץ אֲשֶׁר לֹא־תִקַּח אִשָּׁה לִבְנִי מִבְּנוֹת הַכְּנַעֲנִי אֲשֶׁר אָנֹכִי יוֹשֵׁב בְּקִרְבּוֹ:

4 but will go to the land of my birth and get a wife for my son *Yitzchak*."

ד כִּי אֶל־אַרְצִי וְאֶל־מוֹלַדְתִּי תֵּלֵךְ וְלָקַחְתָּ אִשָּׁה לִבְנִי לְיִצְחָק:

5 And the servant said to him, "What if the woman does not consent to follow me to this land, shall I then take your son back to the land from which you came?"

ה וַיֹּאמֶר אֵלָיו הָעֶבֶד אוּלַי לֹא־תֹאבֶה הָאִשָּׁה לָלֶכֶת אַחֲרַי אֶל־הָאָרֶץ הַזֹּאת הֶהָשֵׁב אָשִׁיב אֶת־בִּנְךָ אֶל־הָאָרֶץ אֲשֶׁר־יָצָאתָ מִשָּׁם:

6 *Avraham* answered him, "On no account must you take my son back there!

ו וַיֹּאמֶר אֵלָיו אַבְרָהָם הִשָּׁמֶר לְךָ פֶּן־תָּשִׁיב אֶת־בְּנִי שָׁמָּה:

7 *Hashem*, the God of heaven, who took me from my father's house and from my native land, who promised me on oath, saying, 'I will assign this land to your offspring' – He will send His angel before you, and you will get a wife for my son from there.

ז יְהוָה אֱלֹהֵי הַשָּׁמַיִם אֲשֶׁר לְקָחַנִי מִבֵּית אָבִי וּמֵאֶרֶץ מוֹלַדְתִּי וַאֲשֶׁר דִּבֶּר־לִי וַאֲשֶׁר נִשְׁבַּע־לִי לֵאמֹר לְזַרְעֲךָ אֶתֵּן אֶת־הָאָרֶץ הַזֹּאת הוּא יִשְׁלַח מַלְאָכוֹ לְפָנֶיךָ וְלָקַחְתָּ אִשָּׁה לִבְנִי מִשָּׁם:

8 And if the woman does not consent to follow you, you shall then be clear of this oath to me; but do not take my son back there."

ח וְאִם־לֹא תֹאבֶה הָאִשָּׁה לָלֶכֶת אַחֲרֶיךָ וְנִקִּיתָ מִשְּׁבֻעָתִי זֹאת רַק אֶת־בְּנִי לֹא תָשֵׁב שָׁמָּה:

9 So the servant put his hand under the thigh of his master *Avraham* and swore to him as bidden.

ט וַיָּשֶׂם הָעֶבֶד אֶת־יָדוֹ תַּחַת יֶרֶךְ אַבְרָהָם אֲדֹנָיו וַיִּשָּׁבַע לוֹ עַל־הַדָּבָר הַזֶּה:

10 Then the servant took ten of his master's camels and set out, taking with him all the bounty of his master; and he made his way to Aram-Naharaim, to the city of Nahor.

י וַיִּקַּח הָעֶבֶד עֲשָׂרָה גְמַלִּים מִגְּמַלֵּי אֲדֹנָיו וַיֵּלֶךְ וְכָל־טוּב אֲדֹנָיו בְּיָדוֹ וַיָּקָם וַיֵּלֶךְ אֶל־אֲרַם נַהֲרַיִם אֶל־עִיר נָחוֹר:

va-yi-KAKH ha-E-ved a-sa-RAH g'-ma-LEEM mi-g'-ma-LAY a-do-NAV va-YAY-lekh v'-khol TUV a-do-NAV b'-ya-DO va-YA-kom va-YAY-lekh el a-RAM na-ha-RA-yim el EER na-KHOR

11 He made the camels kneel down by the well outside the city, at evening time, the time when women come out to draw water.

יא וַיַּבְרֵךְ הַגְּמַלִּים מִחוּץ לָעִיר אֶל־בְּאֵר הַמָּיִם לְעֵת עֶרֶב לְעֵת צֵאת הַשֹּׁאֲבֹת:

12 And he said, "*Hashem*, God of my master *Avraham*, grant me good fortune this day, and deal graciously with my master *Avraham*:

יב וַיֹּאמַר יְהוָה אֱלֹהֵי אֲדֹנִי אַבְרָהָם הַקְרֵה־נָא לְפָנַי הַיּוֹם וַעֲשֵׂה־חֶסֶד עִם אֲדֹנִי אַבְרָהָם:

גמל

24:10 Then the servant took ten of his master's camels The Hebrew word for 'camel' is *gamal* (גמל), which also means 'to be independent.' We find the usage of this word in a variety of contexts: "The child grew up, and was 'weaned' (*vayigamal*)" (Genesis 21:8); "and borne almonds" (*vayigmol* – i.e. 'became independent of the stalk'; Numbers 17:23). According to Rabbi Natan Slifkin, popularly known as the "Zoo Rabbi," the Hebrew name for camel refers to the animal's ability to survive without water for up to seven months. It is fitting that the independent camel was the method of transportation used by *Avraham*'s servant to bring back a wife for *Yitzchak*, as *Rivka* made the independent choice to leave her family in order to join *Yitzchak* in *Eretz Yisrael*.

A camel on the Mount of Olives

Bereishit/Genesis 24
Chayei Sara

13 Here I stand by the spring as the daughters of the townsmen come out to draw water;

14 let the maiden to whom I say, 'Please, lower your jar that I may drink,' and who replies, 'Drink, and I will also water your camels' – let her be the one whom You have decreed for Your servant *Yitzchak*. Thereby shall I know that You have dealt graciously with my master."

15 He had scarcely finished speaking, when *Rivka*, who was born to Bethuel, the son of Milcah the wife of *Avraham*'s brother Nahor, came out with her jar on her shoulder.

16 The maiden was very beautiful, a virgin whom no man had known. She went down to the spring, filled her jar, and came up.

17 The servant ran toward her and said, "Please, let me sip a little water from your jar."

18 "Drink, my lord," she said, and she quickly lowered her jar upon her hand and let him drink.

19 When she had let him drink his fill, she said, "I will also draw for your camels, until they finish drinking."

20 Quickly emptying her jar into the trough, she ran back to the well to draw, and she drew for all his camels.

21 The man, meanwhile, stood gazing at her, silently wondering whether *Hashem* had made his errand successful or not.

22 When the camels had finished drinking, the man took a gold nose-ring weighing a *beka*, and two gold bands for her arms, ten *shekalim* in weight.

23 "Pray tell me," he said, "whose daughter are you? Is there room in your father's house for us to spend the night?"

24 She replied, "I am the daughter of Bethuel the son of Milcah, whom she bore to Nahor."

25 And she went on, "There is plenty of straw and feed at home, and also room to spend the night."

26 The man bowed low in homage to *Hashem*

בראשית כד
חיי שרה

יג הִנֵּה אָנֹכִי נִצָּב עַל־עֵין הַמָּיִם וּבְנוֹת אַנְשֵׁי הָעִיר יֹצְאֹת לִשְׁאֹב מָיִם:

יד וְהָיָה הַנַּעֲרָ אֲשֶׁר אֹמַר אֵלֶיהָ הַטִּי־נָא כַדֵּךְ וְאֶשְׁתֶּה וְאָמְרָה שְׁתֵה וְגַם־גְּמַלֶּיךָ אַשְׁקֶה אֹתָהּ הֹכַחְתָּ לְעַבְדְּךָ לְיִצְחָק וּבָהּ אֵדַע כִּי־עָשִׂיתָ חֶסֶד עִם־אֲדֹנִי:

טו וַיְהִי־הוּא טֶרֶם כִּלָּה לְדַבֵּר וְהִנֵּה רִבְקָה יֹצֵאת אֲשֶׁר יֻלְּדָה לִבְתוּאֵל בֶּן־מִלְכָּה אֵשֶׁת נָחוֹר אֲחִי אַבְרָהָם וְכַדָּהּ עַל־שִׁכְמָהּ:

טז וְהַנַּעֲרָ טֹבַת מַרְאֶה מְאֹד בְּתוּלָה וְאִישׁ לֹא יְדָעָהּ וַתֵּרֶד הָעַיְנָה וַתְּמַלֵּא כַדָּהּ וַתָּעַל:

יז וַיָּרָץ הָעֶבֶד לִקְרָאתָהּ וַיֹּאמֶר הַגְמִיאִינִי נָא מְעַט־מַיִם מִכַּדֵּךְ:

יח וַתֹּאמֶר שְׁתֵה אֲדֹנִי וַתְּמַהֵר וַתֹּרֶד כַּדָּהּ עַל־יָדָהּ וַתַּשְׁקֵהוּ:

יט וַתְּכַל לְהַשְׁקֹתוֹ וַתֹּאמֶר גַּם לִגְמַלֶּיךָ אֶשְׁאָב עַד אִם־כִּלּוּ לִשְׁתֹּת:

כ וַתְּמַהֵר וַתְּעַר כַּדָּהּ אֶל־הַשֹּׁקֶת וַתָּרָץ עוֹד אֶל־הַבְּאֵר לִשְׁאֹב וַתִּשְׁאַב לְכָל־גְּמַלָּיו:

כא וְהָאִישׁ מִשְׁתָּאֵה לָהּ מַחֲרִישׁ לָדַעַת הַהִצְלִיחַ יְהֹוָה דַּרְכּוֹ אִם־לֹא:

כב וַיְהִי כַּאֲשֶׁר כִּלּוּ הַגְּמַלִּים לִשְׁתּוֹת וַיִּקַּח הָאִישׁ נֶזֶם זָהָב בֶּקַע מִשְׁקָלוֹ וּשְׁנֵי צְמִידִים עַל־יָדֶיהָ עֲשָׂרָה זָהָב מִשְׁקָלָם:

כג וַיֹּאמֶר בַּת־מִי אַתְּ הַגִּידִי נָא לִי הֲיֵשׁ בֵּית־אָבִיךְ מָקוֹם לָנוּ לָלִין:

כד וַתֹּאמֶר אֵלָיו בַּת־בְּתוּאֵל אָנֹכִי בֶּן־מִלְכָּה אֲשֶׁר יָלְדָה לְנָחוֹר:

כה וַתֹּאמֶר אֵלָיו גַּם־תֶּבֶן גַּם־מִסְפּוֹא רַב עִמָּנוּ גַּם־מָקוֹם לָלוּן:

כו וַיִּקֹּד הָאִישׁ וַיִּשְׁתַּחוּ לַיהֹוָה:

Bereishit/Genesis 24
Chayei Sara

בראשית כד
חיי שרה

27 and said, "Blessed be *Hashem*, the God of my master *Avraham*, who has not withheld His steadfast faithfulness from my master. For I have been guided on my errand by *Hashem*, to the house of my master's kinsmen."

כז וַיֹּאמֶר בָּרוּךְ יְהֹוָה אֱלֹהֵי אֲדֹנִי אַבְרָהָם אֲשֶׁר לֹא־עָזַב חַסְדּוֹ וַאֲמִתּוֹ מֵעִם אֲדֹנִי אָנֹכִי בַּדֶּרֶךְ נָחַנִי יְהֹוָה בֵּית אֲחֵי אֲדֹנִי׃

28 The maiden ran and told all this to her mother's household.

כח וַתָּרָץ הַנַּעֲרָ וַתַּגֵּד לְבֵית אִמָּהּ כַּדְּבָרִים הָאֵלֶּה׃

29 Now *Rivka* had a brother whose name was Laban. Laban ran out to the man at the spring

כט וּלְרִבְקָה אָח וּשְׁמוֹ לָבָן וַיָּרָץ לָבָן אֶל־הָאִישׁ הַחוּצָה אֶל־הָעָיִן׃

30 when he saw the nose-ring and the bands on his sister's arms, and when he heard his sister *Rivka* say, "Thus the man spoke to me." He went up to the man, who was still standing beside the camels at the spring.

ל וַיְהִי כִּרְאֹת אֶת־הַנֶּזֶם וְאֶת־הַצְּמִדִים עַל־יְדֵי אֲחֹתוֹ וּכְשָׁמְעוֹ אֶת־דִּבְרֵי רִבְקָה אֲחֹתוֹ לֵאמֹר כֹּה־דִבֶּר אֵלַי הָאִישׁ וַיָּבֹא אֶל־הָאִישׁ וְהִנֵּה עֹמֵד עַל־הַגְּמַלִּים עַל־הָעָיִן׃

31 "Come in, O blessed of *Hashem*," he said, "why do you remain outside, when I have made ready the house and a place for the camels?"

לא וַיֹּאמֶר בּוֹא בְּרוּךְ יְהֹוָה לָמָּה תַעֲמֹד בַּחוּץ וְאָנֹכִי פִּנִּיתִי הַבַּיִת וּמָקוֹם לַגְּמַלִּים׃

32 So the man entered the house, and the camels were unloaded. The camels were given straw and feed, and water was brought to bathe his feet and the feet of the men with him.

לב וַיָּבֹא הָאִישׁ הַבַּיְתָה וַיְפַתַּח הַגְּמַלִּים וַיִּתֵּן תֶּבֶן וּמִסְפּוֹא לַגְּמַלִּים וּמַיִם לִרְחֹץ רַגְלָיו וְרַגְלֵי הָאֲנָשִׁים אֲשֶׁר אִתּוֹ׃

33 But when food was set before him, he said, "I will not eat until I have told my tale." He said, "Speak, then."

לג וַיּוּשָׂם [וַיּוּשַׂם] לְפָנָיו לֶאֱכֹל וַיֹּאמֶר לֹא אֹכַל עַד אִם־דִּבַּרְתִּי דְּבָרָי וַיֹּאמֶר דַּבֵּר׃

34 "I am *Avraham*'s servant," he began.

לד וַיֹּאמַר עֶבֶד אַבְרָהָם אָנֹכִי׃

35 "*Hashem* has greatly blessed my master, and he has become rich: He has given him sheep and cattle, silver and gold, male and female slaves, camels and asses.

לה וַיהֹוָה בֵּרַךְ אֶת־אֲדֹנִי מְאֹד וַיִּגְדָּל וַיִּתֶּן־לוֹ צֹאן וּבָקָר וְכֶסֶף וְזָהָב וַעֲבָדִם וּשְׁפָחֹת וּגְמַלִּים וַחֲמֹרִים׃

36 And *Sara*, my master's wife, bore my master a son in her old age, and he has assigned to him everything he owns.

לו וַתֵּלֶד שָׂרָה אֵשֶׁת אֲדֹנִי בֵן לַאדֹנִי אַחֲרֵי זִקְנָתָהּ וַיִּתֶּן־לוֹ אֶת־כָּל־אֲשֶׁר־לוֹ׃

37 Now my master made me swear, saying, 'You shall not get a wife for my son from the daughters of the Canaanites in whose land I dwell;

לז וַיַּשְׁבִּעֵנִי אֲדֹנִי לֵאמֹר לֹא־תִקַּח אִשָּׁה לִבְנִי מִבְּנוֹת הַכְּנַעֲנִי אֲשֶׁר אָנֹכִי יֹשֵׁב בְּאַרְצוֹ׃

38 but you shall go to my father's house, to my kindred, and get a wife for my son.'

לח אִם־לֹא אֶל־בֵּית־אָבִי תֵּלֵךְ וְאֶל־מִשְׁפַּחְתִּי וְלָקַחְתָּ אִשָּׁה לִבְנִי׃

39 And I said to my master, 'What if the woman does not follow me?'

לט וָאֹמַר אֶל־אֲדֹנִי אֻלַי לֹא־תֵלֵךְ הָאִשָּׁה אַחֲרָי׃

Bereishit/Genesis 24
Chayei Sara

בראשית כד
חיי שרה

40 He replied to me, '*Hashem*, whose ways I have followed, will send His angel with you and make your errand successful; and you will get a wife for my son from my kindred, from my father's house.

מ וַיֹּאמֶר אֵלָי יְהוָה אֲשֶׁר־הִתְהַלַּכְתִּי לְפָנָיו יִשְׁלַח מַלְאָכוֹ אִתָּךְ וְהִצְלִיחַ דַּרְכֶּךָ וְלָקַחְתָּ אִשָּׁה לִבְנִי מִמִּשְׁפַּחְתִּי וּמִבֵּית אָבִי:

41 Thus only shall you be freed from my adjuration: if, when you come to my kindred, they refuse you – only then shall you be freed from my adjuration.'

מא אָז תִּנָּקֶה מֵאָלָתִי כִּי תָבוֹא אֶל־מִשְׁפַּחְתִּי וְאִם־לֹא יִתְּנוּ לָךְ וְהָיִיתָ נָקִי מֵאָלָתִי:

42 "I came today to the spring, and I said: *Hashem*, God of my master *Avraham*, if You would indeed grant success to the errand on which I am engaged!

מב וָאָבֹא הַיּוֹם אֶל־הָעָיִן וָאֹמַר יְהוָה אֱלֹהֵי אֲדֹנִי אַבְרָהָם אִם־יֶשְׁךָ־נָּא מַצְלִיחַ דַּרְכִּי אֲשֶׁר אָנֹכִי הֹלֵךְ עָלֶיהָ:

43 As I stand by the spring of water, let the young woman who comes out to draw and to whom I say, 'Please, let me drink a little water from your jar,'

מג הִנֵּה אָנֹכִי נִצָּב עַל־עֵין הַמָּיִם וְהָיָה הָעַלְמָה הַיֹּצֵאת לִשְׁאֹב וְאָמַרְתִּי אֵלֶיהָ הַשְׁקִינִי־נָא מְעַט־מַיִם מִכַּדֵּךְ:

44 and who answers, 'You may drink, and I will also draw for your camels' – let her be the wife whom *Hashem* has decreed for my master's son.'

מד וְאָמְרָה אֵלַי גַּם־אַתָּה שְׁתֵה וְגַם לִגְמַלֶּיךָ אֶשְׁאָב הִוא הָאִשָּׁה אֲשֶׁר־הֹכִיחַ יְהוָה לְבֶן־אֲדֹנִי:

45 I had scarcely finished praying in my heart, when *Rivka* came out with her jar on her shoulder, and went down to the spring and drew. And I said to her, 'Please give me a drink.'

מה אֲנִי טֶרֶם אֲכַלֶּה לְדַבֵּר אֶל־לִבִּי וְהִנֵּה רִבְקָה יֹצֵאת וְכַדָּהּ עַל־שִׁכְמָהּ וַתֵּרֶד הָעַיְנָה וַתִּשְׁאָב וָאֹמַר אֵלֶיהָ הַשְׁקִינִי נָא:

46 She quickly lowered her jar and said, 'Drink, and I will also water your camels.' So I drank, and she also watered the camels.

מו וַתְּמַהֵר וַתּוֹרֶד כַּדָּהּ מֵעָלֶיהָ וַתֹּאמֶר שְׁתֵה וְגַם־גְּמַלֶּיךָ אַשְׁקֶה וָאֵשְׁתְּ וְגַם הַגְּמַלִּים הִשְׁקָתָה:

47 I inquired of her, 'Whose daughter are you?' And she said, 'The daughter of Bethuel, son of Nahor, whom Milcah bore to him.' And I put the ring on her nose and the bands on her arms.

מז וָאֶשְׁאַל אֹתָהּ וָאֹמַר בַּת־מִי אַתְּ וַתֹּאמֶר בַּת־בְּתוּאֵל בֶּן־נָחוֹר אֲשֶׁר יָלְדָה־לּוֹ מִלְכָּה וָאָשִׂם הַנֶּזֶם עַל־אַפָּהּ וְהַצְּמִידִים עַל־יָדֶיהָ:

48 Then I bowed low in homage to *Hashem* and blessed *Hashem*, the God of my master *Avraham*, who led me on the right way to get the daughter of my master's brother for his son.

מח וָאֶקֹּד וָאֶשְׁתַּחֲוֶה לַיהוָה וָאֲבָרֵךְ אֶת־יְהוָה אֱלֹהֵי אֲדֹנִי אַבְרָהָם אֲשֶׁר הִנְחַנִי בְּדֶרֶךְ אֱמֶת לָקַחַת אֶת־בַּת־אֲחִי אֲדֹנִי לִבְנוֹ:

49 And now, if you mean to treat my master with true kindness, tell me; and if not, tell me also, that I may turn right or left."

מט וְעַתָּה אִם־יֶשְׁכֶם עֹשִׂים חֶסֶד וֶאֱמֶת אֶת־אֲדֹנִי הַגִּידוּ לִי וְאִם־לֹא הַגִּידוּ לִי וְאֶפְנֶה עַל־יָמִין אוֹ עַל־שְׂמֹאל:

50 Then Laban and Bethuel answered, "The matter was decreed by *Hashem*; we cannot speak to you bad or good.

נ וַיַּעַן לָבָן וּבְתוּאֵל וַיֹּאמְרוּ מֵיְהוָה יָצָא הַדָּבָר לֹא נוּכַל דַּבֵּר אֵלֶיךָ רַע אוֹ־טוֹב:

51 Here is *Rivka* before you; take her and go, and let her be a wife to your master's son, as *Hashem* has spoken."

נא הִנֵּה־רִבְקָה לְפָנֶיךָ קַח וָלֵךְ וּתְהִי אִשָּׁה לְבֶן־אֲדֹנֶיךָ כַּאֲשֶׁר דִּבֶּר יְהוָה:

52 When *Avraham*'s servant heard their words, he bowed low to the ground before *Hashem*.

נב וַיְהִי כַּאֲשֶׁר שָׁמַע עֶבֶד אַבְרָהָם אֶת־דִּבְרֵיהֶם וַיִּשְׁתַּחוּ אַרְצָה לַיהוָה:

59

Bereishit/Genesis 24
Chayei Sara

בראשית כד
חיי שרה

53 The servant brought out objects of silver and gold, and garments, and gave them to *Rivka*; and he gave presents to her brother and her mother.

נג וַיּוֹצֵא הָעֶבֶד כְּלֵי־כֶסֶף וּכְלֵי זָהָב וּבְגָדִים וַיִּתֵּן לְרִבְקָה וּמִגְדָּנֹת נָתַן לְאָחִיהָ וּלְאִמָּהּ:

54 Then he and the men with him ate and drank, and they spent the night. When they arose next morning, he said, "Give me leave to go to my master."

נד וַיֹּאכְלוּ וַיִּשְׁתּוּ הוּא וְהָאֲנָשִׁים אֲשֶׁר־עִמּוֹ וַיָּלִינוּ וַיָּקוּמוּ בַבֹּקֶר וַיֹּאמֶר שַׁלְּחֻנִי לַאדֹנִי:

55 But her brother and her mother said, "Let the maiden remain with us some ten days; then you may go."

נה וַיֹּאמֶר אָחִיהָ וְאִמָּהּ תֵּשֵׁב הַנַּעֲרָ אִתָּנוּ יָמִים אוֹ עָשׂוֹר אַחַר תֵּלֵךְ:

56 He said to them, "Do not delay me, now that *Hashem* has made my errand successful. Give me leave that I may go to my master."

נו וַיֹּאמֶר אֲלֵהֶם אַל־תְּאַחֲרוּ אֹתִי וַיהֹוָה הִצְלִיחַ דַּרְכִּי שַׁלְּחוּנִי וְאֵלְכָה לַאדֹנִי:

57 And they said, "Let us call the girl and ask for her reply."

נז וַיֹּאמְרוּ נִקְרָא לַנַּעֲרָ וְנִשְׁאֲלָה אֶת־פִּיהָ:

58 They called *Rivka* and said to her, "Will you go with this man?" And she said, "I will."

נח וַיִּקְרְאוּ לְרִבְקָה וַיֹּאמְרוּ אֵלֶיהָ הֲתֵלְכִי עִם־הָאִישׁ הַזֶּה וַתֹּאמֶר אֵלֵךְ:

59 So they sent off their sister *Rivka* and her nurse along with *Avraham*'s servant and his men.

נט וַיְשַׁלְּחוּ אֶת־רִבְקָה אֲחֹתָם וְאֶת־מֵנִקְתָּהּ וְאֶת־עֶבֶד אַבְרָהָם וְאֶת־אֲנָשָׁיו:

60 And they blessed *Rivka* and said to her, "O sister! May you grow Into thousands of myriads; May your offspring seize he gates of their foes."

ס וַיְבָרֲכוּ אֶת־רִבְקָה וַיֹּאמְרוּ לָהּ אֲחֹתֵנוּ אַתְּ הֲיִי לְאַלְפֵי רְבָבָה וְיִירַשׁ זַרְעֵךְ אֵת שַׁעַר שֹׂנְאָיו:

61 Then *Rivka* and her maids arose, mounted the camels, and followed the man. So the servant took *Rivka* and went his way.

סא וַתָּקָם רִבְקָה וְנַעֲרֹתֶיהָ וַתִּרְכַּבְנָה עַל־הַגְּמַלִּים וַתֵּלַכְנָה אַחֲרֵי הָאִישׁ וַיִּקַּח הָעֶבֶד אֶת־רִבְקָה וַיֵּלַךְ:

62 *Yitzchak* had just come back from the vicinity of Beer-lahai-roi, for he was settled in the region of the *Negev*.

סב וְיִצְחָק בָּא מִבּוֹא בְּאֵר לַחַי רֹאִי וְהוּא יוֹשֵׁב בְּאֶרֶץ הַנֶּגֶב:

63 And *Yitzchak* went out walking in the field toward evening and, looking up, he saw camels approaching.

סג וַיֵּצֵא יִצְחָק לָשׂוּחַ בַּשָּׂדֶה לִפְנוֹת עָרֶב וַיִּשָּׂא עֵינָיו וַיַּרְא וְהִנֵּה גְמַלִּים בָּאִים:

64 Raising her eyes, *Rivka* saw *Yitzchak*. She alighted from the camel

סד וַתִּשָּׂא רִבְקָה אֶת־עֵינֶיהָ וַתֵּרֶא אֶת־יִצְחָק וַתִּפֹּל מֵעַל הַגָּמָל:

65 and said to the servant, "Who is that man walking in the field toward us?" And the servant said, "That is my master." So she took her veil and covered herself.

סה וַתֹּאמֶר אֶל־הָעֶבֶד מִי־הָאִישׁ הַלָּזֶה הַהֹלֵךְ בַּשָּׂדֶה לִקְרָאתֵנוּ וַיֹּאמֶר הָעֶבֶד הוּא אֲדֹנִי וַתִּקַּח הַצָּעִיף וַתִּתְכָּס:

66 The servant told *Yitzchak* all the things that he had done.

סו וַיְסַפֵּר הָעֶבֶד לְיִצְחָק אֵת כָּל־הַדְּבָרִים אֲשֶׁר עָשָׂה:

Bereishit/Genesis 25
Chayei Sara

בראשית כה
חיי שרה

67 *Yitzchak* then brought her into the tent of his mother *Sara*, and he took *Rivka* as his wife. *Yitzchak* loved her, and thus found comfort after his mother's death.

וַיְבִאֶהָ יִצְחָק הָאֹהֱלָה שָׂרָה אִמּוֹ וַיִּקַּח אֶת־רִבְקָה וַתְּהִי־לוֹ לְאִשָּׁה וַיֶּאֱהָבֶהָ וַיִּנָּחֵם יִצְחָק אַחֲרֵי אִמּוֹ׃

25

1 *Avraham* took another wife, whose name was Keturah.

וַיֹּסֶף אַבְרָהָם וַיִּקַּח אִשָּׁה וּשְׁמָהּ קְטוּרָה׃

2 She bore him Zimran, Jokshan, Medan, Midian, Ishbak, and Shuah.

וַתֵּלֶד לוֹ אֶת־זִמְרָן וְאֶת־יָקְשָׁן וְאֶת־מְדָן וְאֶת־מִדְיָן וְאֶת־יִשְׁבָּק וְאֶת־שׁוּחַ׃

3 Jokshan begot Sheba and Dedan. The descendants of Dedan were the Assyrians, the Letushim, and the Leummim.

וְיָקְשָׁן יָלַד אֶת־שְׁבָא וְאֶת־דְּדָן וּבְנֵי דְדָן הָיוּ אַשּׁוּרִם וּלְטוּשִׁם וּלְאֻמִּים׃

4 The descendants of Midian were Ephah, Epher, Enoch, Abida, and Eldaah. All these were descendants of Keturah.

וּבְנֵי מִדְיָן עֵיפָה וָעֵפֶר וַחֲנֹךְ וַאֲבִידָע וְאֶלְדָּעָה כָּל־אֵלֶּה בְּנֵי קְטוּרָה׃

5 *Avraham* willed all that he owned to *Yitzchak*;

וַיִּתֵּן אַבְרָהָם אֶת־כָּל־אֲשֶׁר־לוֹ לְיִצְחָק׃

6 but to *Avraham*'s sons by concubines *Avraham* gave gifts while he was still living, and he sent them away from his son *Yitzchak* eastward, to the land of the East.

וְלִבְנֵי הַפִּילַגְשִׁים אֲשֶׁר לְאַבְרָהָם נָתַן אַבְרָהָם מַתָּנֹת וַיְשַׁלְּחֵם מֵעַל יִצְחָק בְּנוֹ בְּעוֹדֶנּוּ חַי קֵדְמָה אֶל־אֶרֶץ קֶדֶם׃

7 This was the total span of *Avraham*'s life: one hundred and seventy-five years.

וְאֵלֶּה יְמֵי שְׁנֵי־חַיֵּי אַבְרָהָם אֲשֶׁר־חָי מְאַת שָׁנָה וְשִׁבְעִים שָׁנָה וְחָמֵשׁ שָׁנִים׃

8 And *Avraham* breathed his last, dying at a good ripe age, old and contented; and he was gathered to his kin.

וַיִּגְוַע וַיָּמָת אַבְרָהָם בְּשֵׂיבָה טוֹבָה זָקֵן וְשָׂבֵעַ וַיֵּאָסֶף אֶל־עַמָּיו׃

9 His sons *Yitzchak* and Ishmael buried him in the cave of Machpelah, in the field of Ephron son of Zohar the Hittite, facing Mamre,

וַיִּקְבְּרוּ אֹתוֹ יִצְחָק וְיִשְׁמָעֵאל בָּנָיו אֶל־מְעָרַת הַמַּכְפֵּלָה אֶל־שְׂדֵה עֶפְרֹן בֶּן־צֹחַר הַחִתִּי אֲשֶׁר עַל־פְּנֵי מַמְרֵא׃

va-yik-b'-RU o-TO yitz-KHAK v'-yish-ma-AYL ba-NAV el m'-a-RAT ha-makh-pay-LAH el s'-DAY ef-RON ben TZO-khar ha-khi-TEE a-SHER al p'-NAY mam-RAY

10 the field that *Avraham* had bought from the Hittites; there *Avraham* was buried, and *Sara* his wife.

הַשָּׂדֶה אֲשֶׁר־קָנָה אַבְרָהָם מֵאֵת בְּנֵי־חֵת שָׁמָּה קֻבַּר אַבְרָהָם וְשָׂרָה אִשְׁתּוֹ׃

25:9 His sons *Yitzchak* and Ishmael buried him in the cave of *Machpelah* The *Torah* states that *Avraham*, *Sara*, *Yitzchak*, *Rivka*, *Yaakov* and *Leah* are all buried in *Machpelah* Cave. According to tradition, *Adam* and *Chava* were buried there as well. *Avraham*'s purchase of this property to bury *Sara* was the first concrete action that established a Jewish connection with a particular site in *Eretz Yisrael*, and upon his death he is also buried in this place. Although the entire Land of Israel was promised to the Children of Israel, there are three key places that were actually purchased, in order that they could never be accused of having taken possession of them inappropriately. *Avraham* purchased the Cave of *Machpelah*, *Yaakov* bought *Yosef*'s burial plot in *Shechem* (Genesis 33:19) and King *David* paid for the site of the *Beit Hamikdash* (II Samuel 24:24). While we are fortunate that we can actually visit the Cave of *Machpelah* today, sadly, Jewish authority over *Chevron*, *Shechem* and *Har Habayit*, is disputed by much of the world. We pray for the time when the biblical record will be recognized and respected by the nations.

Cave of the Machpelah in Chevron

Bereishit/Genesis 25
Toldot

בראשית כה
תולדות

11 After the death of *Avraham*, *Hashem* blessed his son *Yitzchak*. And *Yitzchak* settled near Beer-lahai-roi.

יא וַיְהִי אַחֲרֵי מוֹת אַבְרָהָם וַיְבָרֶךְ אֱלֹהִים אֶת־יִצְחָק בְּנוֹ וַיֵּשֶׁב יִצְחָק עִם־בְּאֵר לַחַי רֹאִי:

12 This is the line of Ishmael, *Avraham*'s son, whom Hagar the Egyptian, *Sara*'s slave, bore to *Avraham*.

יב וְאֵלֶּה תֹּלְדֹת יִשְׁמָעֵאל בֶּן־אַבְרָהָם אֲשֶׁר יָלְדָה הָגָר הַמִּצְרִית שִׁפְחַת שָׂרָה לְאַבְרָהָם:

13 These are the names of the sons of Ishmael, by their names, in the order of their birth: Nebaioth, the first-born of Ishmael, Kedar, Adbeel, Mibsam,

יג וְאֵלֶּה שְׁמוֹת בְּנֵי יִשְׁמָעֵאל בִּשְׁמֹתָם לְתוֹלְדֹתָם בְּכֹר יִשְׁמָעֵאל נְבָיֹת וְקֵדָר וְאַדְבְּאֵל וּמִבְשָׂם:

14 Mishma, Dumah, Massa,

יד וּמִשְׁמָע וְדוּמָה וּמַשָּׂא:

15 Hadad, Tema, Jetur, Naphish, and Kedmah.

טו חֲדַד וְתֵימָא יְטוּר נָפִישׁ וָקֵדְמָה:

16 These are the sons of Ishmael and these are their names by their villages and by their encampments: twelve chieftains of as many tribes.

טז אֵלֶּה הֵם בְּנֵי יִשְׁמָעֵאל וְאֵלֶּה שְׁמֹתָם בְּחַצְרֵיהֶם וּבְטִירֹתָם שְׁנֵים־עָשָׂר נְשִׂיאִם לְאֻמֹּתָם:

17 These were the years of the life of Ishmael: one hundred and thirty-seven years; then he breathed his last and died, and was gathered to his kin.

יז וְאֵלֶּה שְׁנֵי חַיֵּי יִשְׁמָעֵאל מְאַת שָׁנָה וּשְׁלֹשִׁים שָׁנָה וְשֶׁבַע שָׁנִים וַיִּגְוַע וַיָּמָת וַיֵּאָסֶף אֶל־עַמָּיו:

18 They dwelt from Havilah, by Shur, which is close to Egypt, all the way to Assyria; they camped alongside all their kinsmen.

יח וַיִּשְׁכְּנוּ מֵחֲוִילָה עַד־שׁוּר אֲשֶׁר עַל־פְּנֵי מִצְרַיִם בֹּאֲכָה אַשּׁוּרָה עַל־פְּנֵי כָל־אֶחָיו נָפָל:

19 This is the story of *Yitzchak*, son of *Avraham*. *Avraham* begot *Yitzchak*.

יט וְאֵלֶּה תּוֹלְדֹת יִצְחָק בֶּן־אַבְרָהָם אַבְרָהָם הוֹלִיד אֶת־יִצְחָק:

20 *Yitzchak* was forty years old when he took to wife *Rivka*, daughter of Bethuel the Aramean of Paddan-aram, sister of Laban the Aramean.

כ וַיְהִי יִצְחָק בֶּן־אַרְבָּעִים שָׁנָה בְּקַחְתּוֹ אֶת־רִבְקָה בַּת־בְּתוּאֵל הָאֲרַמִּי מִפַּדַּן אֲרָם אֲחוֹת לָבָן הָאֲרַמִּי לוֹ לְאִשָּׁה:

21 *Yitzchak* pleaded with *Hashem* on behalf of his wife, because she was barren; and *Hashem* responded to his plea, and his wife *Rivka* conceived.

כא וַיֶּעְתַּר יִצְחָק לַיהוָה לְנֹכַח אִשְׁתּוֹ כִּי עֲקָרָה הִוא וַיֵּעָתֶר לוֹ יְהוָה וַתַּהַר רִבְקָה אִשְׁתּוֹ:

22 But the children struggled in her womb, and she said, "If so, why do I exist?" She went to inquire of *Hashem*,

כב וַיִּתְרֹצְצוּ הַבָּנִים בְּקִרְבָּהּ וַתֹּאמֶר אִם־כֵּן לָמָּה זֶּה אָנֹכִי וַתֵּלֶךְ לִדְרֹשׁ אֶת־יְהוָה:

23 and *Hashem* answered her, "Two nations are in your womb, Two separate peoples shall issue from your body; One people shall be mightier than the other, And the older shall serve the younger."

כג וַיֹּאמֶר יְהוָה לָהּ שְׁנֵי גיים [גוֹיִם] בְּבִטְנֵךְ וּשְׁנֵי לְאֻמִּים מִמֵּעַיִךְ יִפָּרֵדוּ וּלְאֹם מִלְאֹם יֶאֱמָץ וְרַב יַעֲבֹד צָעִיר:

24 When her time to give birth was at hand, there were twins in her womb.

כד וַיִּמְלְאוּ יָמֶיהָ לָלֶדֶת וְהִנֵּה תוֹמִם בְּבִטְנָהּ:

25 The first one emerged red, like a hairy mantle all over; so they named him Esau.

כה וַיֵּצֵא הָרִאשׁוֹן אַדְמוֹנִי כֻּלּוֹ כְּאַדֶּרֶת שֵׂעָר וַיִּקְרְאוּ שְׁמוֹ עֵשָׂו:

Bereishit/Genesis 26
Toldot

26 Then his brother emerged, holding on to the heel of Esau; so they named him *Yaakov*. *Yitzchak* was sixty years old when they were born.

27 When the boys grew up, Esau became a skillful hunter, a man of the outdoors; but *Yaakov* was a mild man who stayed in camp.

28 *Yitzchak* favored Esau because he had a taste for game; but *Rivka* favored *Yaakov*.

29 Once when *Yaakov* was cooking a stew, Esau came in from the open, famished.

30 And Esau said to *Yaakov*, "Give me some of that red stuff to gulp down, for I am famished" – which is why he was named Edom.

31 *Yaakov* said, "First sell me your birthright."

32 And Esau said, "I am at the point of death, so of what use is my birthright to me?"

33 But *Yaakov* said, "Swear to me first." So he swore to him, and sold his birthright to *Yaakov*.

34 *Yaakov* then gave Esau bread and lentil stew; he ate and drank, and he rose and went away. Thus did Esau spurn the birthright.

בראשית כו
תולדות

כו וְאַחֲרֵי־כֵן יָצָא אָחִיו וְיָדוֹ אֹחֶזֶת בַּעֲקֵב עֵשָׂו וַיִּקְרָא שְׁמוֹ יַעֲקֹב וְיִצְחָק בֶּן־שִׁשִּׁים שָׁנָה בְּלֶדֶת אֹתָם:

כז וַיִּגְדְּלוּ הַנְּעָרִים וַיְהִי עֵשָׂו אִישׁ יֹדֵעַ צַיִד אִישׁ שָׂדֶה וְיַעֲקֹב אִישׁ תָּם יֹשֵׁב אֹהָלִים:

כח וַיֶּאֱהַב יִצְחָק אֶת־עֵשָׂו כִּי־צַיִד בְּפִיו וְרִבְקָה אֹהֶבֶת אֶת־יַעֲקֹב:

כט וַיָּזֶד יַעֲקֹב נָזִיד וַיָּבֹא עֵשָׂו מִן־הַשָּׂדֶה וְהוּא עָיֵף:

ל וַיֹּאמֶר עֵשָׂו אֶל־יַעֲקֹב הַלְעִיטֵנִי נָא מִן־הָאָדֹם הָאָדֹם הַזֶּה כִּי עָיֵף אָנֹכִי עַל־כֵּן קָרָא־שְׁמוֹ אֱדוֹם:

לא וַיֹּאמֶר יַעֲקֹב מִכְרָה כַיּוֹם אֶת־בְּכֹרָתְךָ לִי:

לב וַיֹּאמֶר עֵשָׂו הִנֵּה אָנֹכִי הוֹלֵךְ לָמוּת וְלָמָּה־זֶּה לִי בְּכֹרָה:

לג וַיֹּאמֶר יַעֲקֹב הִשָּׁבְעָה לִּי כַּיּוֹם וַיִּשָּׁבַע לוֹ וַיִּמְכֹּר אֶת־בְּכֹרָתוֹ לְיַעֲקֹב:

לד וְיַעֲקֹב נָתַן לְעֵשָׂו לֶחֶם וּנְזִיד עֲדָשִׁים וַיֹּאכַל וַיֵּשְׁתְּ וַיָּקָם וַיֵּלַךְ וַיִּבֶז עֵשָׂו אֶת־הַבְּכֹרָה:

26
1 There was a famine in the land – aside from the previous famine that had occurred in the days of *Avraham* – and *Yitzchak* went to Abimelech, king of the Philistines, in Gerar.

2 *Hashem* had appeared to him and said, "Do not go down to Egypt; stay in the land which I point out to you.

3 Reside in this land, and I will be with you and bless you; I will assign all these lands to you and to your heirs, fulfilling the oath that I swore to your father *Avraham*.

GUR ba-A-retz ha-ZOT v'-eh-YEH i-m'-KHA va-a-va-r'-KHE-ka kee l'-KHA ul-zar-a-KHA e-TAYN et kol ha-a-ra-TZOT ha-AYL va-ha-ki-mo-TEE et ha-sh'-vu-AH a-SHER nish-BA-tee l'-av-ra-HAM a-VEE-kha

כו א וַיְהִי רָעָב בָּאָרֶץ מִלְּבַד הָרָעָב הָרִאשׁוֹן אֲשֶׁר הָיָה בִּימֵי אַבְרָהָם וַיֵּלֶךְ יִצְחָק אֶל־אֲבִימֶלֶךְ מֶלֶךְ־פְּלִשְׁתִּים גְּרָרָה:

ב וַיֵּרָא אֵלָיו יְהוָה וַיֹּאמֶר אַל־תֵּרֵד מִצְרָיְמָה שְׁכֹן בָּאָרֶץ אֲשֶׁר אֹמַר אֵלֶיךָ:

ג גּוּר בָּאָרֶץ הַזֹּאת וְאֶהְיֶה עִמְּךָ וַאֲבָרְכֶךָּ כִּי־לְךָ וּלְזַרְעֲךָ אֶתֵּן אֶת־כָּל־הָאֲרָצֹת הָאֵל וַהֲקִמֹתִי אֶת־הַשְּׁבֻעָה אֲשֶׁר נִשְׁבַּעְתִּי לְאַבְרָהָם אָבִיךָ:

26:3 Reside in this land, and I will be with you and bless you *Yitzchak* is warned that despite the famine in *Eretz Yisrael*, he is not to escape the hardship by fleeing to Egypt. Though *Avraham* went down to Egypt when there was a plague in Israel, and *Yaakov* likewise descended to Egypt towards the end of his life, God told *Yitzchak* not to leave the Land of Israel. Due to the unique spiritual status he acquired after being offered on the altar, *Yitzchak* was the only one of the three forefathers to never step foot outside of the Holy Land.

Bereishit/Genesis 26
Toldot

בראשית כו
תולדות

4 I will make your heirs as numerous as the stars of heaven, and assign to your heirs all these lands, so that all the nations of the earth shall bless themselves by your heirs

ד וְהִרְבֵּיתִי אֶת־זַרְעֲךָ כְּכוֹכְבֵי הַשָּׁמַיִם וְנָתַתִּי לְזַרְעֲךָ אֵת כָּל־הָאֲרָצֹת הָאֵל וְהִתְבָּרֲכוּ בְזַרְעֲךָ כֹּל גּוֹיֵי הָאָרֶץ׃

v'-hir-bay-TEE et zar-a-KHA k'-kho-kh'-VAY ha-sha-MA-yim v'-na-ta-TEE l'-zar-a-KHA AYT kol ha-a-ra-TZOT ha-AYL v'-hit-ba-r'-KHU v'-zar-a-KHA KOL go-YAY ha-A-retz

5 inasmuch as *Avraham* obeyed Me and kept My charge: My commandments, My laws, and My teachings."

ה עֵקֶב אֲשֶׁר־שָׁמַע אַבְרָהָם בְּקֹלִי וַיִּשְׁמֹר מִשְׁמַרְתִּי מִצְוֹתַי חֻקּוֹתַי וְתוֹרֹתָי׃

6 So *Yitzchak* stayed in Gerar.

ו וַיֵּשֶׁב יִצְחָק בִּגְרָר׃

7 When the men of the place asked him about his wife, he said, "She is my sister," for he was afraid to say "my wife," thinking, "The men of the place might kill me on account of *Rivka*, for she is beautiful."

ז וַיִּשְׁאֲלוּ אַנְשֵׁי הַמָּקוֹם לְאִשְׁתּוֹ וַיֹּאמֶר אֲחֹתִי הִוא כִּי יָרֵא לֵאמֹר אִשְׁתִּי פֶּן־יַהַרְגֻנִי אַנְשֵׁי הַמָּקוֹם עַל־רִבְקָה כִּי־טוֹבַת מַרְאֶה הִיא׃

8 When some time had passed, Abimelech king of the Philistines, looking out of the window, saw *Yitzchak* fondling his wife *Rivka*.

ח וַיְהִי כִּי אָרְכוּ־לוֹ שָׁם הַיָּמִים וַיַּשְׁקֵף אֲבִימֶלֶךְ מֶלֶךְ פְּלִשְׁתִּים בְּעַד הַחַלּוֹן וַיַּרְא וְהִנֵּה יִצְחָק מְצַחֵק אֵת רִבְקָה אִשְׁתּוֹ׃

9 Abimelech sent for *Yitzchak* and said, "So she is your wife! Why then did you say: 'She is my sister?'" *Yitzchak* said to him, "Because I thought I might lose my life on account of her."

ט וַיִּקְרָא אֲבִימֶלֶךְ לְיִצְחָק וַיֹּאמֶר אַךְ הִנֵּה אִשְׁתְּךָ הִוא וְאֵיךְ אָמַרְתָּ אֲחֹתִי הִוא וַיֹּאמֶר אֵלָיו יִצְחָק כִּי אָמַרְתִּי פֶּן־אָמוּת עָלֶיהָ׃

10 Abimelech said, "What have you done to us! One of the people might have lain with your wife, and you would have brought guilt upon us."

י וַיֹּאמֶר אֲבִימֶלֶךְ מַה־זֹּאת עָשִׂיתָ לָּנוּ כִּמְעַט שָׁכַב אַחַד הָעָם אֶת־אִשְׁתֶּךָ וְהֵבֵאתָ עָלֵינוּ אָשָׁם׃

11 Abimelech then charged all the people, saying, "Anyone who molests this man or his wife shall be put to death."

יא וַיְצַו אֲבִימֶלֶךְ אֶת־כָּל־הָעָם לֵאמֹר הַנֹּגֵעַ בָּאִישׁ הַזֶּה וּבְאִשְׁתּוֹ מוֹת יוּמָת׃

12 *Yitzchak* sowed in that land and reaped a hundredfold the same year. *Hashem* blessed him,

יב וַיִּזְרַע יִצְחָק בָּאָרֶץ הַהִוא וַיִּמְצָא בַּשָּׁנָה הַהִוא מֵאָה שְׁעָרִים וַיְבָרֲכֵהוּ יְהֹוָה׃

26:4 I will make your heirs as numerous as the stars of heaven Why are the children of *Avraham* compared to the stars? The poetess Chana Senesh was born in Hungary in 1921 and in 1939 she emigrated to what was then the British Mandate of Palestine. Senesh was a brave heroine who volunteered to leave her beloved Palestine in 1944 in order to fight with the partisans against the Nazis. Unfortunately, she was caught, tried for treason and eventually executed. In one of her beautiful poems she wrote, "There are stars whose radiance is visible on earth though they have long been extinct. There are people whose brilliance continues to light the world though they are no longer among the living. These lights are particularly bright when the night is dark. They light the way for mankind." Like the stars in Senesh's poem, the Jew's role in this world is to light the way for mankind, despite the darkness we have encountered throughout our history.

Chana Senesh (1921–1944)

Bereishit/Genesis 26
Toldot

בראשית כו
תולדות

13 and the man grew richer and richer until he was very wealthy:

יג וַיִּגְדַּל הָאִישׁ וַיֵּלֶךְ הָלוֹךְ וְגָדֵל עַד כִּי־גָדַל מְאֹד:

14 he acquired flocks and herds, and a large household, so that the Philistines envied him.

יד וַיְהִי־לוֹ מִקְנֵה־צֹאן וּמִקְנֵה בָקָר וַעֲבֻדָּה רַבָּה וַיְקַנְאוּ אֹתוֹ פְּלִשְׁתִּים:

15 And the Philistines stopped up all the wells which his father's servants had dug in the days of his father *Avraham*, filling them with earth.

טו וְכָל־הַבְּאֵרֹת אֲשֶׁר חָפְרוּ עַבְדֵי אָבִיו בִּימֵי אַבְרָהָם אָבִיו סִתְּמוּם פְּלִשְׁתִּים וַיְמַלְאוּם עָפָר:

16 And Abimelech said to *Yitzchak*, "Go away from us, for you have become far too big for us."

טז וַיֹּאמֶר אֲבִימֶלֶךְ אֶל־יִצְחָק לֵךְ מֵעִמָּנוּ כִּי־עָצַמְתָּ מִמֶּנּוּ מְאֹד:

va-YO-mer a-vee-ME-lekh el yitz-KHAK LAYKH may-i-MA-nu kee a-TZAM-ta mi-ME-nu m'-OD

17 So *Yitzchak* departed from there and encamped in the wadi of Gerar, where he settled.

יז וַיֵּלֶךְ מִשָּׁם יִצְחָק וַיִּחַן בְּנַחַל־גְּרָר וַיֵּשֶׁב שָׁם:

18 *Yitzchak* dug anew the wells which had been dug in the days of his father *Avraham* and which the Philistines had stopped up after *Avraham*'s death; and he gave them the same names that his father had given them.

יח וַיָּשָׁב יִצְחָק וַיַּחְפֹּר אֶת־בְּאֵרֹת הַמַּיִם אֲשֶׁר חָפְרוּ בִּימֵי אַבְרָהָם אָבִיו וַיְסַתְּמוּם פְּלִשְׁתִּים אַחֲרֵי מוֹת אַבְרָהָם וַיִּקְרָא לָהֶן שֵׁמוֹת כַּשֵּׁמֹת אֲשֶׁר־קָרָא לָהֶן אָבִיו:

19 But when *Yitzchak*'s servants, digging in the wadi, found there a well of spring water,

יט וַיַּחְפְּרוּ עַבְדֵי־יִצְחָק בַּנָּחַל וַיִּמְצְאוּ־שָׁם בְּאֵר מַיִם חַיִּים:

20 the herdsmen of Gerar quarreled with *Yitzchak*'s herdsmen, saying, "The water is ours." He named that well Esek, because they contended with him.

כ וַיָּרִיבוּ רֹעֵי גְרָר עִם־רֹעֵי יִצְחָק לֵאמֹר לָנוּ הַמָּיִם וַיִּקְרָא שֵׁם־הַבְּאֵר עֵשֶׂק כִּי הִתְעַשְּׂקוּ עִמּוֹ:

21 And when they dug another well, they disputed over that one also; so he named it Sitnah.

כא וַיַּחְפְּרוּ בְּאֵר אַחֶרֶת וַיָּרִיבוּ גַּם־עָלֶיהָ וַיִּקְרָא שְׁמָהּ שִׂטְנָה:

22 He moved from there and dug yet another well, and they did not quarrel over it; so he called it Rehoboth, saying, "Now at last *Hashem* has granted us ample space to increase in the land."

כב וַיַּעְתֵּק מִשָּׁם וַיַּחְפֹּר בְּאֵר אַחֶרֶת וְלֹא רָבוּ עָלֶיהָ וַיִּקְרָא שְׁמָהּ רְחֹבוֹת וַיֹּאמֶר כִּי־עַתָּה הִרְחִיב יְהוָה לָנוּ וּפָרִינוּ בָאָרֶץ:

va-ya-TAYK mi-SHAM va-yakh-POR b'-AYR a-KHE-ret v'-LO ra-VU a-LE-ha va-yik-RA sh'-MAH r'-kho-VOT va-YO-mer kee a-TAH hir-KHEEV a-do-NAI LA-nu u-fa-REE-nu va-A-retz

23 From there he went up to *Be'er Sheva*.

כג וַיַּעַל מִשָּׁם בְּאֵר שָׁבַע:

26:16 Go away from us, for you have become far too big for us The story of *Yitzchak* among the Philistines alludes to the history of the Jewish people during their lengthy exile, hosted by various foreign nations. Rabbi Zalman Sorotzkin points out that *Yitzchak* is one Jew in an entire country, yet the Philistines claim that there is no room for him. As a successful farmer, *Yitzchak* is not an economic burden on his hosts, and yet the Philistines banish him. They could have learned agricultural techniques and benefitted from his water, but they instead choose to ignore the valuable contributions he could make, and they clog the wells he has dug. Similarly, many Jewish inventors and innovators have been expelled from their host nations throughout history. The only safe place where the Children of Israel can flourish is in the Land of Israel.

Bereishit/Genesis 27
Toldot

בראשית כז
תולדות

24 That night *Hashem* appeared to him and said, "I am the God of your father *Avraham*. Fear not, for I am with you, and I will bless you and increase your offspring for the sake of My servant *Avraham*."

כד וַיֵּרָא אֵלָיו יְהֹוָה בַּלַּיְלָה הַהוּא וַיֹּאמֶר אָנֹכִי אֱלֹהֵי אַבְרָהָם אָבִיךָ אַל־תִּירָא כִּי־אִתְּךָ אָנֹכִי וּבֵרַכְתִּיךָ וְהִרְבֵּיתִי אֶת־זַרְעֲךָ בַּעֲבוּר אַבְרָהָם עַבְדִּי:

25 So he built a *Mizbayach* there and invoked *Hashem* by name. *Yitzchak* pitched his tent there and his servants started digging a well.

כה וַיִּבֶן שָׁם מִזְבֵּחַ וַיִּקְרָא בְּשֵׁם יְהֹוָה וַיֶּט־שָׁם אָהֳלוֹ וַיִּכְרוּ־שָׁם עַבְדֵי־יִצְחָק בְּאֵר:

26 And Abimelech came to him from Gerar, with Ahuzzath his councilor and Phicol chief of his troops.

כו וַאֲבִימֶלֶךְ הָלַךְ אֵלָיו מִגְּרָר וַאֲחֻזַּת מֵרֵעֵהוּ וּפִיכֹל שַׂר־צְבָאוֹ:

27 *Yitzchak* said to them, "Why have you come to me, seeing that you have been hostile to me and have driven me away from you?"

כז וַיֹּאמֶר אֲלֵהֶם יִצְחָק מַדּוּעַ בָּאתֶם אֵלָי וְאַתֶּם שְׂנֵאתֶם אֹתִי וַתְּשַׁלְּחוּנִי מֵאִתְּכֶם:

28 And they said, "We now see plainly that *Hashem* has been with you, and we thought: Let there be a sworn treaty between our two parties, between you and us. Let us make a pact with you

כח וַיֹּאמְרוּ רָאוֹ רָאִינוּ כִּי־הָיָה יְהֹוָה עִמָּךְ וַנֹּאמֶר תְּהִי נָא אָלָה בֵּינוֹתֵינוּ בֵּינֵינוּ וּבֵינֶךָ וְנִכְרְתָה בְרִית עִמָּךְ:

29 that you will not do us harm, just as we have not molested you but have always dealt kindly with you and sent you away in peace. From now on, be you blessed of *Hashem*!"

כט אִם־תַּעֲשֵׂה עִמָּנוּ רָעָה כַּאֲשֶׁר לֹא נְגַעֲנוּךָ וְכַאֲשֶׁר עָשִׂינוּ עִמְּךָ רַק־טוֹב וַנְּשַׁלֵּחֲךָ בְּשָׁלוֹם אַתָּה עַתָּה בְּרוּךְ יְהֹוָה:

30 Then he made for them a feast, and they ate and drank.

ל וַיַּעַשׂ לָהֶם מִשְׁתֶּה וַיֹּאכְלוּ וַיִּשְׁתּוּ:

31 Early in the morning, they exchanged oaths. *Yitzchak* then bade them farewell, and they departed from him in peace.

לא וַיַּשְׁכִּימוּ בַבֹּקֶר וַיִּשָּׁבְעוּ אִישׁ לְאָחִיו וַיְשַׁלְּחֵם יִצְחָק וַיֵּלְכוּ מֵאִתּוֹ בְּשָׁלוֹם:

32 That same day *Yitzchak*'s servants came and told him about the well they had dug, and said to him, "We have found water!"

לב וַיְהִי בַּיּוֹם הַהוּא וַיָּבֹאוּ עַבְדֵי יִצְחָק וַיַּגִּדוּ לוֹ עַל־אֹדוֹת הַבְּאֵר אֲשֶׁר חָפָרוּ וַיֹּאמְרוּ לוֹ מָצָאנוּ מָיִם:

33 He named it Shibah; therefore the name of the city is *Be'er Sheva* to this day.

לג וַיִּקְרָא אֹתָהּ שִׁבְעָה עַל־כֵּן שֵׁם־הָעִיר בְּאֵר שֶׁבַע עַד הַיּוֹם הַזֶּה:

34 When Esau was forty years old, he took to wife Judith daughter of *Be'eri* the Hittite, and Basemath daughter of Elon the Hittite;

לד וַיְהִי עֵשָׂו בֶּן־אַרְבָּעִים שָׁנָה וַיִּקַּח אִשָּׁה אֶת־יְהוּדִית בַּת־בְּאֵרִי הַחִתִּי וְאֶת־בָּשְׂמַת בַּת־אֵילֹן הַחִתִּי:

35 and they were a source of bitterness to *Yitzchak* and *Rivka*.

לה וַתִּהְיֶיןָ מֹרַת רוּחַ לְיִצְחָק וּלְרִבְקָה:

27

1 When *Yitzchak* was old and his eyes were too dim to see, he called his older son Esau and said to him, "My son." He answered, "Here I am."

כז א וַיְהִי כִּי־זָקֵן יִצְחָק וַתִּכְהֶיןָ עֵינָיו מֵרְאֹת וַיִּקְרָא אֶת־עֵשָׂו בְּנוֹ הַגָּדֹל וַיֹּאמֶר אֵלָיו בְּנִי וַיֹּאמֶר אֵלָיו הִנֵּנִי:

2 And he said, "I am old now, and I do not know how soon I may die.

ב וַיֹּאמֶר הִנֵּה־נָא זָקַנְתִּי לֹא יָדַעְתִּי יוֹם מוֹתִי:

66

Bereishit/Genesis 27
Toldot

בראשית כז
תולדות

3 Take your gear, your quiver and bow, and go out into the open and hunt me some game.

ג וְעַתָּה שָׂא־נָא כֵלֶיךָ תֶּלְיְךָ וְקַשְׁתֶּךָ וְצֵא הַשָּׂדֶה וְצוּדָה לִּי צידה [צָיִד]:

4 Then prepare a dish for me such as I like, and bring it to me to eat, so that I may give you my innermost blessing before I die."

ד וַעֲשֵׂה־לִי מַטְעַמִּים כַּאֲשֶׁר אָהַבְתִּי וְהָבִיאָה לִּי וְאֹכֵלָה בַּעֲבוּר תְּבָרֶכְךָ נַפְשִׁי בְּטֶרֶם אָמוּת:

5 Rivka had been listening as Yitzchak spoke to his son Esau. When Esau had gone out into the open to hunt game to bring home,

ה וְרִבְקָה שֹׁמַעַת בְּדַבֵּר יִצְחָק אֶל־עֵשָׂו בְּנוֹ וַיֵּלֶךְ עֵשָׂו הַשָּׂדֶה לָצוּד צַיִד לְהָבִיא:

6 Rivka said to her son Yaakov, "I overheard your father speaking to your brother Esau, saying,

ו וְרִבְקָה אָמְרָה אֶל־יַעֲקֹב בְּנָהּ לֵאמֹר הִנֵּה שָׁמַעְתִּי אֶת־אָבִיךָ מְדַבֵּר אֶל־עֵשָׂו אָחִיךָ לֵאמֹר:

7 'Bring me some game and prepare a dish for me to eat, that I may bless you, with Hashem's approval, before I die.'

ז הָבִיאָה לִּי צַיִד וַעֲשֵׂה־לִי מַטְעַמִּים וְאֹכֵלָה וַאֲבָרֶכְכָה לִפְנֵי יְהֹוָה לִפְנֵי מוֹתִי:

8 Now, my son, listen carefully as I instruct you.

ח וְעַתָּה בְנִי שְׁמַע בְּקֹלִי לַאֲשֶׁר אֲנִי מְצַוָּה אֹתָךְ:

9 Go to the flock and fetch me two choice kids, and I will make of them a dish for your father, such as he likes.

ט לֶךְ־נָא אֶל־הַצֹּאן וְקַח־לִי מִשָּׁם שְׁנֵי גְּדָיֵי עִזִּים טֹבִים וְאֶעֱשֶׂה אֹתָם מַטְעַמִּים לְאָבִיךָ כַּאֲשֶׁר אָהֵב:

10 Then take it to your father to eat, in order that he may bless you before he dies."

י וְהֵבֵאתָ לְאָבִיךָ וְאָכָל בַּעֲבֻר אֲשֶׁר יְבָרֶכְךָ לִפְנֵי מוֹתוֹ:

11 Yaakov answered his mother Rivka, "But my brother Esau is a hairy man and I am smooth-skinned.

יא וַיֹּאמֶר יַעֲקֹב אֶל־רִבְקָה אִמּוֹ הֵן עֵשָׂו אָחִי אִישׁ שָׂעִר וְאָנֹכִי אִישׁ חָלָק:

12 If my father touches me, I shall appear to him as a trickster and bring upon myself a curse, not a blessing."

יב אוּלַי יְמֻשֵּׁנִי אָבִי וְהָיִיתִי בְעֵינָיו כִּמְתַעְתֵּעַ וְהֵבֵאתִי עָלַי קְלָלָה וְלֹא בְרָכָה:

13 But his mother said to him, "Your curse, my son, be upon me! Just do as I say and go fetch them for me."

יג וַתֹּאמֶר לוֹ אִמּוֹ עָלַי קִלְלָתְךָ בְּנִי אַךְ שְׁמַע בְּקֹלִי וְלֵךְ קַח־לִי:

14 He got them and brought them to his mother, and his mother prepared a dish such as his father liked.

יד וַיֵּלֶךְ וַיִּקַּח וַיָּבֵא לְאִמּוֹ וַתַּעַשׂ אִמּוֹ מַטְעַמִּים כַּאֲשֶׁר אָהֵב אָבִיו:

15 Rivka then took the best clothes of her older son Esau, which were there in the house, and had her younger son Yaakov put them on;

טו וַתִּקַּח רִבְקָה אֶת־בִּגְדֵי עֵשָׂו בְּנָהּ הַגָּדֹל הַחֲמֻדֹת אֲשֶׁר אִתָּהּ בַּבָּיִת וַתַּלְבֵּשׁ אֶת־יַעֲקֹב בְּנָהּ הַקָּטָן:

16 and she covered his hands and the hairless part of his neck with the skins of the kids.

טז וְאֵת עֹרֹת גְּדָיֵי הָעִזִּים הִלְבִּישָׁה עַל־יָדָיו וְעַל חֶלְקַת צַוָּארָיו:

17 Then she put in the hands of her son Yaakov the dish and the bread that she had prepared.

יז וַתִּתֵּן אֶת־הַמַּטְעַמִּים וְאֶת־הַלֶּחֶם אֲשֶׁר עָשָׂתָה בְּיַד יַעֲקֹב בְּנָהּ:

18 He went to his father and said, "Father." And he said, "Yes, which of my sons are you?"

יח וַיָּבֹא אֶל־אָבִיו וַיֹּאמֶר אָבִי וַיֹּאמֶר הִנֶּנִּי מִי אַתָּה בְּנִי:

Bereishit/Genesis 27
Toldot

בראשית כז
תולדות

19 Yaakov said to his father, "I am Esau, your firstborn; I have done as you told me. Pray sit up and eat of my game, that you may give me your innermost blessing."

יט וַיֹּאמֶר יַעֲקֹב אֶל־אָבִיו אָנֹכִי עֵשָׂו בְּכֹרֶךָ עָשִׂיתִי כַּאֲשֶׁר דִּבַּרְתָּ אֵלָי קוּם־נָא שְׁבָה וְאָכְלָה מִצֵּידִי בַּעֲבוּר תְּבָרֲכַנִּי נַפְשֶׁךָ:

20 Yitzchak said to his son, "How did you succeed so quickly, my son?" And he said, "Because *Hashem* your God granted me good fortune."

כ וַיֹּאמֶר יִצְחָק אֶל־בְּנוֹ מַה־זֶּה מִהַרְתָּ לִמְצֹא בְּנִי וַיֹּאמֶר כִּי הִקְרָה יְהוָה אֱלֹהֶיךָ לְפָנָי:

21 Yitzchak said to Yaakov, "Come closer that I may feel you, my son – whether you are really my son Esau or not."

כא וַיֹּאמֶר יִצְחָק אֶל־יַעֲקֹב גְּשָׁה־נָּא וַאֲמֻשְׁךָ בְּנִי הַאַתָּה זֶה בְּנִי עֵשָׂו אִם־לֹא:

22 So Yaakov drew close to his father Yitzchak, who felt him and wondered. "The voice is the voice of Yaakov, yet the hands are the hands of Esau."

כב וַיִּגַּשׁ יַעֲקֹב אֶל־יִצְחָק אָבִיו וַיְמֻשֵּׁהוּ וַיֹּאמֶר הַקֹּל קוֹל יַעֲקֹב וְהַיָּדַיִם יְדֵי עֵשָׂו:

23 He did not recognize him, because his hands were hairy like those of his brother Esau; and so he blessed him.

כג וְלֹא הִכִּירוֹ כִּי־הָיוּ יָדָיו כִּידֵי עֵשָׂו אָחִיו שְׂעִרֹת וַיְבָרֲכֵהוּ:

24 He asked, "Are you really my son Esau?" And when he said, "I am,"

כד וַיֹּאמֶר אַתָּה זֶה בְּנִי עֵשָׂו וַיֹּאמֶר אָנִי:

25 he said, "Serve me and let me eat of my son's game that I may give you my innermost blessing." So he served him and he ate, and he brought him wine and he drank.

כה וַיֹּאמֶר הַגִּשָׁה לִּי וְאֹכְלָה מִצֵּיד בְּנִי לְמַעַן תְּבָרֶכְךָ נַפְשִׁי וַיַּגֶּשׁ־לוֹ וַיֹּאכַל וַיָּבֵא לוֹ יַיִן וַיֵּשְׁתְּ:

26 Then his father Yitzchak said to him, "Come close and kiss me, my son";

כו וַיֹּאמֶר אֵלָיו יִצְחָק אָבִיו גְּשָׁה־נָּא וּשְׁקָה־לִּי בְּנִי:

27 and he went up and kissed him. And he smelled his clothes and he blessed him, saying, "Ah, the smell of my son is like the smell of the fields that *Hashem* has blessed.

כז וַיִּגַּשׁ וַיִּשַּׁק־לוֹ וַיָּרַח אֶת־רֵיחַ בְּגָדָיו וַיְבָרֲכֵהוּ וַיֹּאמֶר רְאֵה רֵיחַ בְּנִי כְּרֵיחַ שָׂדֶה אֲשֶׁר בֵּרֲכוֹ יְהוָה:

28 "May *Hashem* give you Of the dew of heaven and the fat of the earth, Abundance of new grain and wine.

v'-yi-ten l'-KHA ha-e-lo-HEEM mi-TAL ha-sha-MA-yim u-mish-ma-NAY ha-A-retz v'-ROV da-GAN v'-ti-ROSH

כח וְיִתֶּן־לְךָ הָאֱלֹהִים מִטַּל הַשָּׁמַיִם וּמִשְׁמַנֵּי הָאָרֶץ וְרֹב דָּגָן וְתִירֹשׁ:

27:28 May *Hashem* give you of the dew of heaven and the fat of the earth The *Zohar*, our primary mystical text, says that this blessing is what has sustained the People of Israel throughout the millennia. If so, why was *Yitzchak* the one who gave the blessing and not *Avraham* or *Yaakov*? Rabbi Shlomo Carlebach, the influential Hebrew songwriter of the 20th century, explained that both *Avraham* and *Yaakov* spent part of their lives outside Israel. Therefore it was only *Yitzchak*, who never once left the Holy Land, who was worthy of bestowing this powerful blessing.

Rabbi Shlomo Carlebach (1925–1994)

Bereishit/Genesis 27
Toldot

בראשית כז
תולדות

כט Let peoples serve you, And nations bow to you; Be master over your brothers, And let your mother's sons bow to you. Cursed be they who curse you, Blessed they who bless you."

יַעַבְדוּךָ עַמִּים וישתחו [וְיִשְׁתַּחֲווּ] לְךָ לְאֻמִּים הֱוֵה גְבִיר לְאַחֶיךָ וְיִשְׁתַּחֲווּ לְךָ בְּנֵי אִמֶּךָ אֹרְרֶיךָ אָרוּר וּמְבָרֲכֶיךָ בָּרוּךְ:

ל No sooner had *Yaakov* left the presence of his father *Yitzchak* – after *Yitzchak* had finished blessing *Yaakov* – than his brother Esau came back from his hunt.

וַיְהִי כַּאֲשֶׁר כִּלָּה יִצְחָק לְבָרֵךְ אֶת־יַעֲקֹב וַיְהִי אַךְ יָצֹא יָצָא יַעֲקֹב מֵאֵת פְּנֵי יִצְחָק אָבִיו וְעֵשָׂו אָחִיו בָּא מִצֵּידוֹ:

לא He too prepared a dish and brought it to his father. And he said to his father, "Let my father sit up and eat of his son's game, so that you may give me your innermost blessing."

וַיַּעַשׂ גַּם־הוּא מַטְעַמִּים וַיָּבֵא לְאָבִיו וַיֹּאמֶר לְאָבִיו יָקֻם אָבִי וְיֹאכַל מִצֵּיד בְּנוֹ בַּעֲבֻר תְּבָרֲכַנִּי נַפְשֶׁךָ:

לב His father *Yitzchak* said to him, "Who are you?" And he said, "I am your son, Esau, your first-born!"

וַיֹּאמֶר לוֹ יִצְחָק אָבִיו מִי־אָתָּה וַיֹּאמֶר אֲנִי בִּנְךָ בְכֹרְךָ עֵשָׂו:

לג *Yitzchak* was seized with very violent trembling. "Who was it then," he demanded, "that hunted game and brought it to me? Moreover, I ate of it before you came, and I blessed him; now he must remain blessed!"

וַיֶּחֱרַד יִצְחָק חֲרָדָה גְּדֹלָה עַד־מְאֹד וַיֹּאמֶר מִי־אֵפוֹא הוּא הַצָּד־צַיִד וַיָּבֵא לִי וָאֹכַל מִכֹּל בְּטֶרֶם תָּבוֹא וָאֲבָרֲכֵהוּ גַּם־בָּרוּךְ יִהְיֶה:

לד When Esau heard his father's words, he burst into wild and bitter sobbing, and said to his father, "Bless me too, Father!"

כִּשְׁמֹעַ עֵשָׂו אֶת־דִּבְרֵי אָבִיו וַיִּצְעַק צְעָקָה גְּדֹלָה וּמָרָה עַד־מְאֹד וַיֹּאמֶר לְאָבִיו בָּרֲכֵנִי גַם־אָנִי אָבִי:

לה But he answered, "Your brother came with guile and took away your blessing."

וַיֹּאמֶר בָּא אָחִיךָ בְּמִרְמָה וַיִּקַּח בִּרְכָתֶךָ:

לו [Esau] said, "Was he, then, named *Yaakov* that he might supplant me these two times? First he took away my birthright and now he has taken away my blessing!" And he added, "Have you not reserved a blessing for me?"

וַיֹּאמֶר הֲכִי קָרָא שְׁמוֹ יַעֲקֹב וַיַּעְקְבֵנִי זֶה פַעֲמַיִם אֶת־בְּכֹרָתִי לָקָח וְהִנֵּה עַתָּה לָקַח בִּרְכָתִי וַיֹּאמַר הֲלֹא־אָצַלְתָּ לִּי בְּרָכָה:

לז *Yitzchak* answered, saying to Esau, "But I have made him master over you: I have given him all his brothers for servants, and sustained him with grain and wine. What, then, can I still do for you, my son?"

וַיַּעַן יִצְחָק וַיֹּאמֶר לְעֵשָׂו הֵן גְּבִיר שַׂמְתִּיו לָךְ וְאֶת־כָּל־אֶחָיו נָתַתִּי לוֹ לַעֲבָדִים וְדָגָן וְתִירֹשׁ סְמַכְתִּיו וּלְכָה אֵפוֹא מָה אֶעֱשֶׂה בְּנִי:

לח And Esau said to his father, "Have you but one blessing, Father? Bless me too, Father!" And Esau wept aloud.

וַיֹּאמֶר עֵשָׂו אֶל־אָבִיו הַבְרָכָה אַחַת הִוא־לְךָ אָבִי בָּרֲכֵנִי גַם־אָנִי אָבִי וַיִּשָּׂא עֵשָׂו קֹלוֹ וַיֵּבְךְּ:

לט And his father *Yitzchak* answered, saying to him, "See, your abode shall enjoy the fat of the earth And the dew of heaven above.

וַיַּעַן יִצְחָק אָבִיו וַיֹּאמֶר אֵלָיו הִנֵּה מִשְׁמַנֵּי הָאָרֶץ יִהְיֶה מוֹשָׁבֶךָ וּמִטַּל הַשָּׁמַיִם מֵעָל:

מ Yet by your sword you shall live, And you shall serve your brother; But when you grow restive, You shall break his yoke from your neck."

וְעַל־חַרְבְּךָ תִחְיֶה וְאֶת־אָחִיךָ תַּעֲבֹד וְהָיָה כַּאֲשֶׁר תָּרִיד וּפָרַקְתָּ עֻלּוֹ מֵעַל צַוָּארֶךָ:

Bereishit/Genesis 28
Toldot

בראשית כח
תולדות

41 Now Esau harbored a grudge against *Yaakov* because of the blessing which his father had given him, and Esau said to himself, "Let but the mourning period of my father come, and I will kill my brother *Yaakov*."

מא וַיִּשְׂטֹם עֵשָׂו אֶת־יַעֲקֹב עַל־הַבְּרָכָה אֲשֶׁר בֵּרֲכוֹ אָבִיו וַיֹּאמֶר עֵשָׂו בְּלִבּוֹ יִקְרְבוּ יְמֵי אֵבֶל אָבִי וְאַהַרְגָה אֶת־יַעֲקֹב אָחִי:

42 When the words of her older son Esau were reported to *Rivka*, she sent for her younger son *Yaakov* and said to him, "Your brother Esau is consoling himself by planning to kill you.

מב וַיֻּגַּד לְרִבְקָה אֶת־דִּבְרֵי עֵשָׂו בְּנָהּ הַגָּדֹל וַתִּשְׁלַח וַתִּקְרָא לְיַעֲקֹב בְּנָהּ הַקָּטָן וַתֹּאמֶר אֵלָיו הִנֵּה עֵשָׂו אָחִיךָ מִתְנַחֵם לְךָ לְהָרְגֶךָ:

43 Now, my son, listen to me. Flee at once to Haran, to my brother Laban.

מג וְעַתָּה בְנִי שְׁמַע בְּקֹלִי וְקוּם בְּרַח־לְךָ אֶל־לָבָן אָחִי חָרָנָה:

44 Stay with him a while, until your brother's fury subsides

מד וְיָשַׁבְתָּ עִמּוֹ יָמִים אֲחָדִים עַד אֲשֶׁר־תָּשׁוּב חֲמַת אָחִיךָ:

45 until your brother's anger against you subsides – and he forgets what you have done to him. Then I will fetch you from there. Let me not lose you both in one day!"

מה עַד־שׁוּב אַף־אָחִיךָ מִמְּךָ וְשָׁכַח אֵת אֲשֶׁר־עָשִׂיתָ לּוֹ וְשָׁלַחְתִּי וּלְקַחְתִּיךָ מִשָּׁם לָמָה אֶשְׁכַּל גַּם־שְׁנֵיכֶם יוֹם אֶחָד:

46 *Rivka* said to *Yitzchak*, "I am disgusted with my life because of the Hittite women. If *Yaakov* marries a Hittite woman like these, from among the native women, what good will life be to me?"

מו וַתֹּאמֶר רִבְקָה אֶל־יִצְחָק קַצְתִּי בְחַיַּי מִפְּנֵי בְּנוֹת חֵת אִם־לֹקֵחַ יַעֲקֹב אִשָּׁה מִבְּנוֹת־חֵת כָּאֵלֶּה מִבְּנוֹת הָאָרֶץ לָמָה לִי חַיִּים:

28 1 So *Yitzchak* sent for *Yaakov* and blessed him. He instructed him, saying, "You shall not take a wife from among the Canaanite women.

כח א וַיִּקְרָא יִצְחָק אֶל־יַעֲקֹב וַיְבָרֶךְ אֹתוֹ וַיְצַוֵּהוּ וַיֹּאמֶר לוֹ לֹא־תִקַּח אִשָּׁה מִבְּנוֹת כְּנָעַן:

2 Up, go to Paddan-aram, to the house of Bethuel, your mother's father, and take a wife there from among the daughters of Laban, your mother's brother,

ב קוּם לֵךְ פַּדֶּנָה אֲרָם בֵּיתָה בְתוּאֵל אֲבִי אִמֶּךָ וְקַח־לְךָ מִשָּׁם אִשָּׁה מִבְּנוֹת לָבָן אֲחִי אִמֶּךָ:

3 May *El Shaddai* bless you, make you fertile and numerous, so that you become an assembly of peoples.

ג וְאֵל שַׁדַּי יְבָרֵךְ אֹתְךָ וְיַפְרְךָ וְיַרְבֶּךָ וְהָיִיתָ לִקְהַל עַמִּים:

4 May He grant the blessing of *Avraham* to you and your offspring, that you may possess the land where you are sojourning, which *Hashem* assigned to *Avraham*."

ד וְיִתֶּן־לְךָ אֶת־בִּרְכַּת אַבְרָהָם לְךָ וּלְזַרְעֲךָ אִתָּךְ לְרִשְׁתְּךָ אֶת־אֶרֶץ מְגֻרֶיךָ אֲשֶׁר־נָתַן אֱלֹהִים לְאַבְרָהָם:

v'-yi-ten l'-KHA et bir-KAT av-ra-HAM l'-KHA ul-zar-a-KHA i-TAKH l'-rish-t'-KHA et E-retz m'-gu-RE-kha a-sher na-TAN e-lo-HEEM l'-av-ra-HAM

5 Then *Yitzchak* sent *Yaakov* off, and he went to Paddan-aram, to Laban the son of Bethuel the Aramean, the brother of *Rivka*, mother of *Yaakov* and Esau.

ה וַיִּשְׁלַח יִצְחָק אֶת־יַעֲקֹב וַיֵּלֶךְ פַּדֶּנָה אֲרָם אֶל־לָבָן בֶּן־בְּתוּאֵל הָאֲרַמִּי אֲחִי רִבְקָה אֵם יַעֲקֹב וְעֵשָׂו:

Bereishit/Genesis 28
Vayeitzei

בראשית כח
ויצא

6 When Esau saw that *Yitzchak* had blessed *Yaakov* and sent him off to Paddan-aram to take a wife from there, charging him, as he blessed him, "You shall not take a wife from among the Canaanite women,"

ו וַיַּ֣רְא עֵשָׂ֗ו כִּֽי־בֵרַ֣ךְ יִצְחָק֮ אֶֽת־יַעֲקֹב֒ וְשִׁלַּ֤ח אֹתוֹ֙ פַּדֶּ֣נָֽה אֲרָ֔ם לָקַֽחַת־ל֥וֹ מִשָּׁ֖ם אִשָּׁ֑ה בְּבָרֲכ֣וֹ אֹת֔וֹ וַיְצַ֤ו עָלָיו֙ לֵאמֹ֔ר לֹֽא־תִקַּ֥ח אִשָּׁ֖ה מִבְּנ֥וֹת כְּנָֽעַן:

7 and that *Yaakov* had obeyed his father and mother and gone to Paddan-aram,

ז וַיִּשְׁמַ֣ע יַעֲקֹ֔ב אֶל־אָבִ֖יו וְאֶל־אִמּ֑וֹ וַיֵּ֖לֶךְ פַּדֶּ֥נָה אֲרָֽם:

8 Esau realized that the Canaanite women displeased his father *Yitzchak*.

ח וַיַּ֣רְא עֵשָׂ֔ו כִּ֥י רָע֖וֹת בְּנ֣וֹת כְּנָ֑עַן בְּעֵינֵ֖י יִצְחָ֥ק אָבִֽיו:

9 So Esau went to Ishmael and took to wife, in addition to the wives he had, Mahalath the daughter of Ishmael son of *Avraham*, sister of Nebaioth.

ט וַיֵּ֥לֶךְ עֵשָׂ֖ו אֶל־יִשְׁמָעֵ֑אל וַיִּקַּ֡ח אֶֽת־מָחֲלַ֣ת ׀ בַּת־יִשְׁמָעֵ֨אל בֶּן־אַבְרָהָ֜ם אֲח֧וֹת נְבָי֛וֹת עַל־נָשָׁ֖יו ל֥וֹ לְאִשָּֽׁה:

10 *Yaakov* left *Be'er Sheva*, and set out for Haran.

י וַיֵּצֵ֥א יַעֲקֹ֖ב מִבְּאֵ֣ר שָׁ֑בַע וַיֵּ֖לֶךְ חָרָֽנָה:

11 He came upon a certain place and stopped there for the night, for the sun had set. Taking one of the stones of that place, he put it under his head and lay down in that place.

יא וַיִּפְגַּ֨ע בַּמָּק֜וֹם וַיָּ֤לֶן שָׁם֙ כִּי־בָ֣א הַשֶּׁ֔מֶשׁ וַיִּקַּח֙ מֵאַבְנֵ֣י הַמָּק֔וֹם וַיָּ֖שֶׂם מְרַֽאֲשֹׁתָ֑יו וַיִּשְׁכַּ֖ב בַּמָּק֥וֹם הַהֽוּא:

va-yif-GA ba-ma-KOHM va-ya-LAYN shahm ki va ha-SHE-mesh va-yi-KAKH me-ahv-NAY ha-ma-KOME va-ya-SAYM m'-ra-sho-TAV va-yish-KAHV ba-ma-KOHM ha-HU

12 He had a dream; a stairway was set on the ground and its top reached to the sky, and angels of *Hashem* were going up and down on it.

יב וַֽיַּחֲלֹ֗ם וְהִנֵּ֤ה סֻלָּם֙ מֻצָּ֣ב אַ֔רְצָה וְרֹאשׁ֖וֹ מַגִּ֣יעַ הַשָּׁמָ֑יְמָה וְהִנֵּה֙ מַלְאֲכֵ֣י אֱלֹהִ֔ים עֹלִ֥ים וְיֹרְדִ֖ים בּֽוֹ:

13 And *Hashem* was standing beside him and He said, "I am *Hashem*, the God of your father *Avraham* and the God of *Yitzchak*: the ground on which you are lying I will assign to you and to your offspring.

יג וְהִנֵּ֨ה יְהוָ֜ה נִצָּ֣ב עָלָיו֘ וַיֹּאמַר֒ אֲנִ֣י יְהוָ֗ה אֱלֹהֵי֙ אַבְרָהָ֣ם אָבִ֔יךָ וֵאלֹהֵ֖י יִצְחָ֑ק הָאָ֗רֶץ אֲשֶׁ֤ר אַתָּה֙ שֹׁכֵ֣ב עָלֶ֔יהָ לְךָ֥ אֶתְּנֶ֖נָּה וּלְזַרְעֶֽךָ:

14 Your descendants shall be as the dust of the earth; you shall spread out to the west and to the east, to the north and to the south. All the families of the earth shall bless themselves by you and your descendants.

יד וְהָיָ֤ה זַרְעֲךָ֙ כַּעֲפַ֣ר הָאָ֔רֶץ וּפָרַצְתָּ֛ יָ֥מָּה וָקֵ֖דְמָה וְצָפֹ֣נָה וָנֶ֑גְבָּה וְנִבְרְכ֥וּ בְךָ֛ כָּל־מִשְׁפְּחֹ֥ת הָאֲדָמָ֖ה וּבְזַרְעֶֽךָ:

Rabbi David Stavsky (1929–2004)

28:11 He came upon a certain place Where is the place that *Yaakov* slept? American congregational Rabbi David Stavsky explained in one of his High Holy Day sermons that the Hebrew word used in this verse is *ba-makom* (במקום), 'upon *the* place,' and not *bi-makom* (במקום), 'upon *a* place.' The use of the definite article means this refers to the most important spot in the entire world. As Rabbi Stavsky said, *Yaakov* came upon "the place where Jacob's father Isaac, and his grandfather Abraham, had built an altar. The place where Isaac was bound to the altar. The place which, for centuries, has tied us to *Hashem*. *Hamakom*, 'the place,' was Mount *Moriah*, eventually to become the heart and soul of Jerusalem, and it was as if a magnet had drawn young Jacob to wander the hot Mesopotamian desert that night, to that particular place. And dear friends, I dare say that whatever force pulled Jacob to that place that night, pulls you and me to that place. It is a deep mystical pull. It is holiness."

Bereishit/Genesis 28
Vayeitzei

בראשית כח
ויצא

15 Remember, I am with you: I will protect you wherever you go and will bring you back to this land. I will not leave you until I have done what I have promised you."

טו וְהִנֵּה אָנֹכִי עִמָּךְ וּשְׁמַרְתִּיךָ בְּכֹל אֲשֶׁר־תֵּלֵךְ וַהֲשִׁבֹתִיךָ אֶל־הָאֲדָמָה הַזֹּאת כִּי לֹא אֶעֱזָבְךָ עַד אֲשֶׁר אִם־עָשִׂיתִי אֵת אֲשֶׁר־דִּבַּרְתִּי לָךְ׃

16 Yaakov awoke from his sleep and said, "Surely Hashem is present in this place, and I did not know it!"

טז וַיִּיקַץ יַעֲקֹב מִשְּׁנָתוֹ וַיֹּאמֶר אָכֵן יֵשׁ יְהֹוָה בַּמָּקוֹם הַזֶּה וְאָנֹכִי לֹא יָדָעְתִּי׃

17 Shaken, he said, "How awesome is this place! This is none other than the abode of *Hashem*, and that is the gateway to heaven."

יז וַיִּירָא וַיֹּאמַר מַה־נּוֹרָא הַמָּקוֹם הַזֶּה אֵין זֶה כִּי אִם־בֵּית אֱלֹהִים וְזֶה שַׁעַר הַשָּׁמָיִם׃

va-yee-RA va-yo-MAR mah no-RA ha-ma-KOM ha-ZEH AYN ZEH KEE im BAYT e-lo-HEEM v'-ZEH SHA-ar ha-sha-MA-yim

18 Early in the morning, Yaakov took the stone that he had put under his head and set it up as a pillar and poured oil on the top of it.

יח וַיַּשְׁכֵּם יַעֲקֹב בַּבֹּקֶר וַיִּקַּח אֶת־הָאֶבֶן אֲשֶׁר־שָׂם מְרַאֲשֹׁתָיו וַיָּשֶׂם אֹתָהּ מַצֵּבָה וַיִּצֹק שֶׁמֶן עַל־רֹאשָׁהּ׃

19 He named that site Beit El; but previously the name of the city had been Luz.

יט וַיִּקְרָא אֶת־שֵׁם־הַמָּקוֹם הַהוּא בֵּית־אֵל וְאוּלָם לוּז שֵׁם־הָעִיר לָרִאשֹׁנָה׃

va-yik-RA et shaym ha-ma-KOM ha-HU bayt EL v'-u-LAM LUZ shaym ha-EER la-ri-sho-NAH

20 Yaakov then made a vow, saying, "If Hashem remains with me, if He protects me on this journey that I am making, and gives me bread to eat and clothing to wear,

כ וַיִּדַּר יַעֲקֹב נֶדֶר לֵאמֹר אִם־יִהְיֶה אֱלֹהִים עִמָּדִי וּשְׁמָרַנִי בַּדֶּרֶךְ הַזֶּה אֲשֶׁר אָנֹכִי הוֹלֵךְ וְנָתַן־לִי לֶחֶם לֶאֱכֹל וּבֶגֶד לִלְבֹּשׁ׃

21 and if I return safe to my father's house – Hashem shall be my God.

כא וְשַׁבְתִּי בְשָׁלוֹם אֶל־בֵּית אָבִי וְהָיָה יְהֹוָה לִי לֵאלֹהִים׃

22 And this stone, which I have set up as a pillar, shall be Hashem's abode; and of all that You give me, I will set aside a tithe for You."

כב וְהָאֶבֶן הַזֹּאת אֲשֶׁר־שַׂמְתִּי מַצֵּבָה יִהְיֶה בֵּית אֱלֹהִים וְכֹל אֲשֶׁר תִּתֶּן־לִי עַשֵּׂר אֲעַשְּׂרֶנּוּ לָךְ׃

28:17 This is none other than the abode of Hashem According to Rashi, these words refer to the Temple Mount in Yerushalayim. He explains that the foot of the ladder in Yaakov's dream was in Be'er Sheva, and its head was in Beit El. Therefore the middle of the ladder hung over Mount Moriah and the intensity of the encounter with Hashem occurred in that spot. When Yaakov awakens, he realizes that he has seen no ordinary place, but "the abode of Hashem," the most intimate spot for prayers to ascend heavenward and the site where the Beit Hamikdash would later stand. The Beit Hamikdash is referred to here as 'abode' or 'house' because in the Temple, Hashem's revealed presence – the shechina (שכינה) – dwells with His people, just as a husband dwells intimately with his wife in their home.

28:19 He named that site Beit El When Yaakov arrives in Beit El, the city near which his grandfather Avraham called to Hashem for the first time in the Land of Israel (Genesis 12:8), he recognizes its unique spiritual character. From that moment on, Beit El appears throughout the Bible as a special location for prayer. The Hebrew name Beit El means "The House of the Lord," and signifies its powerful purpose. Rabbi Zalman Sorotzkin explains that a home protects a person from the elements, extreme temperatures and rain. Similarly, we are meant to view "The House of the Lord" as a safe haven, protecting us from danger and therefore an ideal location for coming close to God.

Ariel view of the Temple Mount

Ariel view of Beit El

Bereishit/Genesis 29
Vayeitzei

בראשית כט
ויצא

29 1 *Yaakov* resumed his journey and came to the land of the Easterners.

א וַיִּשָּׂא יַעֲקֹב רַגְלָיו וַיֵּלֶךְ אַרְצָה בְנֵי־קֶדֶם:

va-yi-SA ya-a-KOV rag-LAV va-YAY-lekh AR-tzah v'-nay KE-dem

2 There before his eyes was a well in the open. Three flocks of sheep were lying there beside it, for the flocks were watered from that well. The stone on the mouth of the well was large.

ב וַיַּרְא וְהִנֵּה בְאֵר בַּשָּׂדֶה וְהִנֵּה־שָׁם שְׁלֹשָׁה עֶדְרֵי־צֹאן רֹבְצִים עָלֶיהָ כִּי מִן־הַבְּאֵר הַהִוא יַשְׁקוּ הָעֲדָרִים וְהָאֶבֶן גְּדֹלָה עַל־פִּי הַבְּאֵר:

3 When all the flocks were gathered there, the stone would be rolled from the mouth of the well and the sheep watered; then the stone would be put back in its place on the mouth of the well.

ג וְנֶאֶסְפוּ־שָׁמָּה כָל־הָעֲדָרִים וְגָלֲלוּ אֶת־הָאֶבֶן מֵעַל פִּי הַבְּאֵר וְהִשְׁקוּ אֶת־הַצֹּאן וְהֵשִׁיבוּ אֶת־הָאֶבֶן עַל־פִּי הַבְּאֵר לִמְקֹמָהּ:

4 *Yaakov* said to them, "My friends, where are you from?" And they said, "We are from Haran."

ד וַיֹּאמֶר לָהֶם יַעֲקֹב אַחַי מֵאַיִן אַתֶּם וַיֹּאמְרוּ מֵחָרָן אֲנָחְנוּ:

5 He said to them, "Do you know Laban the son of Nahor?" And they said, "Yes, we do."

ה וַיֹּאמֶר לָהֶם הַיְדַעְתֶּם אֶת־לָבָן בֶּן־נָחוֹר וַיֹּאמְרוּ יָדָעְנוּ:

6 He continued, "Is he well?" They answered, "Yes, he is; and there is his daughter *Rachel*, coming with the flock."

ו וַיֹּאמֶר לָהֶם הֲשָׁלוֹם לוֹ וַיֹּאמְרוּ שָׁלוֹם וְהִנֵּה רָחֵל בִּתּוֹ בָּאָה עִם־הַצֹּאן:

7 He said, "It is still broad daylight, too early to round up the animals; water the flock and take them to pasture."

ז וַיֹּאמֶר הֵן עוֹד הַיּוֹם גָּדוֹל לֹא־עֵת הֵאָסֵף הַמִּקְנֶה הַשְׁקוּ הַצֹּאן וּלְכוּ רְעוּ:

8 But they said, "We cannot, until all the flocks are rounded up; then the stone is rolled off the mouth of the well and we water the sheep."

ח וַיֹּאמְרוּ לֹא נוּכַל עַד אֲשֶׁר יֵאָסְפוּ כָּל־הָעֲדָרִים וְגָלֲלוּ אֶת־הָאֶבֶן מֵעַל פִּי הַבְּאֵר וְהִשְׁקִינוּ הַצֹּאן:

9 While he was still speaking with them, *Rachel* came with her father's flock; for she was a shepherdess.

ט עוֹדֶנּוּ מְדַבֵּר עִמָּם וְרָחֵל בָּאָה עִם־הַצֹּאן אֲשֶׁר לְאָבִיהָ כִּי רֹעָה הִוא:

10 And when *Yaakov* saw *Rachel*, the daughter of his uncle Laban, and the flock of his uncle Laban, *Yaakov* went up and rolled the stone off the mouth of the well, and watered the flock of his uncle Laban.

י וַיְהִי כַּאֲשֶׁר רָאָה יַעֲקֹב אֶת־רָחֵל בַּת־לָבָן אֲחִי אִמּוֹ וְאֶת־צֹאן לָבָן אֲחִי אִמּוֹ וַיִּגַּשׁ יַעֲקֹב וַיָּגֶל אֶת־הָאֶבֶן מֵעַל פִּי הַבְּאֵר וַיַּשְׁקְ אֶת־צֹאן לָבָן אֲחִי אִמּוֹ:

11 Then *Yaakov* kissed *Rachel*, and broke into tears.

יא וַיִּשַּׁק יַעֲקֹב לְרָחֵל וַיִּשָּׂא אֶת־קֹלוֹ וַיֵּבְךְּ:

12 *Yaakov* told *Rachel* that he was her father's kinsman, that he was *Rivka*'s son; and she ran and told her father.

יב וַיַּגֵּד יַעֲקֹב לְרָחֵל כִּי אֲחִי אָבִיהָ הוּא וְכִי בֶן־רִבְקָה הוּא וַתָּרָץ וַתַּגֵּד לְאָבִיהָ:

Rashi (1040–1105)

29:1 To the land of the Easterners The distinction between *Eretz Yisrael* and other lands becomes clear to *Yaakov* as he enters the "land of the Easterners," where he immediately encounters jealous shepherds and later the crooked Lavan. This new land stands in stark contrast to the Land of Israel where *Yaakov*'s grandfather *Avraham* had sought to bring righteousness and Godliness to the world.

Bereishit/Genesis 29
Vayeitzei

בראשית כט
ויצא

13 On hearing the news of his sister's son *Yaakov*, Laban ran to greet him; he embraced him and kissed him, and took him into his house. He told Laban all that had happened,

יג וַיְהִי כִשְׁמֹעַ לָבָן אֶת־שֵׁמַע יַעֲקֹב בֶּן־אֲחֹתוֹ וַיָּרָץ לִקְרָאתוֹ וַיְחַבֶּק־לוֹ וַיְנַשֶּׁק־לוֹ וַיְבִיאֵהוּ אֶל־בֵּיתוֹ וַיְסַפֵּר לְלָבָן אֵת כָּל־הַדְּבָרִים הָאֵלֶּה׃

14 and Laban said to him, "You are truly my bone and flesh." When he had stayed with him a month's time,

יד וַיֹּאמֶר לוֹ לָבָן אַךְ עַצְמִי וּבְשָׂרִי אָתָּה וַיֵּשֶׁב עִמּוֹ חֹדֶשׁ יָמִים׃

15 Laban said to *Yaakov*, "Just because you are a kinsman, should you serve me for nothing? Tell me, what shall your wages be?"

טו וַיֹּאמֶר לָבָן לְיַעֲקֹב הֲכִי־אָחִי אַתָּה וַעֲבַדְתַּנִי חִנָּם הַגִּידָה לִּי מַה־מַּשְׂכֻּרְתֶּךָ׃

16 Now Laban had two daughters; the name of the older one was *Leah*, and the name of the younger was *Rachel*.

טז וּלְלָבָן שְׁתֵּי בָנוֹת שֵׁם הַגְּדֹלָה לֵאָה וְשֵׁם הַקְּטַנָּה רָחֵל׃

17 *Leah* had weak eyes; *Rachel* was shapely and beautiful.

יז וְעֵינֵי לֵאָה רַכּוֹת וְרָחֵל הָיְתָה יְפַת־תֹּאַר וִיפַת מַרְאֶה׃

18 *Yaakov* loved *Rachel*; so he answered, "I will serve you seven years for your younger daughter *Rachel*."

יח וַיֶּאֱהַב יַעֲקֹב אֶת־רָחֵל וַיֹּאמֶר אֶעֱבָדְךָ שֶׁבַע שָׁנִים בְּרָחֵל בִּתְּךָ הַקְּטַנָּה׃

19 Laban said, "Better that I give her to you than that I should give her to an outsider. Stay with me."

יט וַיֹּאמֶר לָבָן טוֹב תִּתִּי אֹתָהּ לָךְ מִתִּתִּי אֹתָהּ לְאִישׁ אַחֵר שְׁבָה עִמָּדִי׃

20 So *Yaakov* served seven years for *Rachel* and they seemed to him but a few days because of his love for her.

כ וַיַּעֲבֹד יַעֲקֹב בְּרָחֵל שֶׁבַע שָׁנִים וַיִּהְיוּ בְעֵינָיו כְּיָמִים אֲחָדִים בְּאַהֲבָתוֹ אֹתָהּ׃

21 Then *Yaakov* said to Laban, "Give me my wife, for my time is fulfilled, that I may cohabit with her."

כא וַיֹּאמֶר יַעֲקֹב אֶל־לָבָן הָבָה אֶת־אִשְׁתִּי כִּי מָלְאוּ יָמָי וְאָבוֹאָה אֵלֶיהָ׃

22 And Laban gathered all the people of the place and made a feast.

כב וַיֶּאֱסֹף לָבָן אֶת־כָּל־אַנְשֵׁי הַמָּקוֹם וַיַּעַשׂ מִשְׁתֶּה׃

23 When evening came, he took his daughter *Leah* and brought her to him; and he cohabited with her.

כג וַיְהִי בָעֶרֶב וַיִּקַּח אֶת־לֵאָה בִתּוֹ וַיָּבֵא אֹתָהּ אֵלָיו וַיָּבֹא אֵלֶיהָ׃

24 Laban had given his maidservant *Zilpa* to his daughter *Leah* as her maid.

כד וַיִּתֵּן לָבָן לָהּ אֶת־זִלְפָּה שִׁפְחָתוֹ לְלֵאָה בִתּוֹ שִׁפְחָה׃

25 When morning came, there was *Leah*! So he said to Laban, "What is this you have done to me? I was in your service for *Rachel*! Why did you deceive me?"

כה וַיְהִי בַבֹּקֶר וְהִנֵּה־הִוא לֵאָה וַיֹּאמֶר אֶל־לָבָן מַה־זֹּאת עָשִׂיתָ לִּי הֲלֹא בְרָחֵל עָבַדְתִּי עִמָּךְ וְלָמָּה רִמִּיתָנִי׃

26 Laban said, "It is not the practice in our place to marry off the younger before the older.

כו וַיֹּאמֶר לָבָן לֹא־יֵעָשֶׂה כֵן בִּמְקוֹמֵנוּ לָתֵת הַצְּעִירָה לִפְנֵי הַבְּכִירָה׃

27 Wait until the bridal week of this one is over and we will give you that one too, provided you serve me another seven years."

כז מַלֵּא שְׁבֻעַ זֹאת וְנִתְּנָה לְךָ גַּם־אֶת־זֹאת בַּעֲבֹדָה אֲשֶׁר תַּעֲבֹד עִמָּדִי עוֹד שֶׁבַע־שָׁנִים אֲחֵרוֹת׃

28 *Yaakov* did so; he waited out the bridal week of the one, and then he gave him his daughter *Rachel* as wife. –

כח וַיַּעַשׂ יַעֲקֹב כֵּן וַיְמַלֵּא שְׁבֻעַ זֹאת וַיִּתֶּן־לוֹ אֶת־רָחֵל בִּתּוֹ לוֹ לְאִשָּׁה׃

Bereishit/Genesis 30
Vayeitzei

בראשית ל
ויצא

29 Laban had given his maidservant *Bilha* to his daughter *Rachel* as her maid.

כט וַיִּתֵּן לָבָן לְרָחֵל בִּתּוֹ אֶת־בִּלְהָה שִׁפְחָתוֹ לָהּ לְשִׁפְחָה׃

30 And *Yaakov* cohabited with *Rachel* also; indeed, he loved *Rachel* more than *Leah*. And he served him another seven years.

ל וַיָּבֹא גַּם אֶל־רָחֵל וַיֶּאֱהַב גַּם־אֶת־רָחֵל מִלֵּאָה וַיַּעֲבֹד עִמּוֹ עוֹד שֶׁבַע־שָׁנִים אֲחֵרוֹת׃

31 *Hashem* saw that *Leah* was unloved and he opened her womb; but *Rachel* was barren.

לא וַיַּרְא יְהֹוָה כִּי־שְׂנוּאָה לֵאָה וַיִּפְתַּח אֶת־רַחְמָהּ וְרָחֵל עֲקָרָה׃

32 *Leah* conceived and bore a son, and named him *Reuven*; for she declared, "It means: '*Hashem* has seen my affliction'; it also means: 'Now my husband will love me.'"

לב וַתַּהַר לֵאָה וַתֵּלֶד בֵּן וַתִּקְרָא שְׁמוֹ רְאוּבֵן כִּי אָמְרָה כִּי־רָאָה יְהֹוָה בְּעָנְיִי כִּי עַתָּה יֶאֱהָבַנִי אִישִׁי׃

33 She conceived again and bore a son, and declared, "This is because *Hashem* heard that I was unloved and has given me this one also"; so she named him *Shimon*.

לג וַתַּהַר עוֹד וַתֵּלֶד בֵּן וַתֹּאמֶר כִּי־שָׁמַע יְהֹוָה כִּי־שְׂנוּאָה אָנֹכִי וַיִּתֶּן־לִי גַּם־אֶת־זֶה וַתִּקְרָא שְׁמוֹ שִׁמְעוֹן׃

34 Again she conceived and bore a son and declared, "This time my husband will become attached to me, for I have borne him three sons." Therefore he was named *Levi*.

לד וַתַּהַר עוֹד וַתֵּלֶד בֵּן וַתֹּאמֶר עַתָּה הַפַּעַם יִלָּוֶה אִישִׁי אֵלַי כִּי־יָלַדְתִּי לוֹ שְׁלֹשָׁה בָנִים עַל־כֵּן קָרָא־שְׁמוֹ לֵוִי׃

35 She conceived again and bore a son, and declared, "This time I will praise *Hashem*." Therefore she named him *Yehuda*. Then she stopped bearing.

לה וַתַּהַר עוֹד וַתֵּלֶד בֵּן וַתֹּאמֶר הַפַּעַם אוֹדֶה אֶת־יְהֹוָה עַל־כֵּן קָרְאָה שְׁמוֹ יְהוּדָה וַתַּעֲמֹד מִלֶּדֶת׃

30

1 When *Rachel* saw that she had borne *Yaakov* no children, she became envious of her sister; and *Rachel* said to *Yaakov*, "Give me children, or I shall die."

ל א וַתֵּרֶא רָחֵל כִּי לֹא יָלְדָה לְיַעֲקֹב וַתְּקַנֵּא רָחֵל בַּאֲחֹתָהּ וַתֹּאמֶר אֶל־יַעֲקֹב הָבָה־לִּי בָנִים וְאִם־אַיִן מֵתָה אָנֹכִי׃

2 *Yaakov* was incensed at *Rachel*, and said, "Can I take the place of *Hashem*, who has denied you fruit of the womb?"

ב וַיִּחַר־אַף יַעֲקֹב בְּרָחֵל וַיֹּאמֶר הֲתַחַת אֱלֹהִים אָנֹכִי אֲשֶׁר־מָנַע מִמֵּךְ פְּרִי־בָטֶן׃

3 She said, "Here is my maid *Bilha*. Consort with her, that she may bear on my knees and that through her I too may have children."

ג וַתֹּאמֶר הִנֵּה אֲמָתִי בִלְהָה בֹּא אֵלֶיהָ וְתֵלֵד עַל־בִּרְכַּי וְאִבָּנֶה גַם־אָנֹכִי מִמֶּנָּה׃

4 So she gave him her maid *Bilha* as concubine, and *Yaakov* cohabited with her.

ד וַתִּתֶּן־לוֹ אֶת־בִּלְהָה שִׁפְחָתָהּ לְאִשָּׁה וַיָּבֹא אֵלֶיהָ יַעֲקֹב׃

5 *Bilha* conceived and bore *Yaakov* a son.

ה וַתַּהַר בִּלְהָה וַתֵּלֶד לְיַעֲקֹב בֵּן׃

6 And *Rachel* said, "*Hashem* has vindicated me; indeed, He has heeded my plea and given me a son." Therefore she named him *Dan*.

ו וַתֹּאמֶר רָחֵל דָּנַנִּי אֱלֹהִים וְגַם שָׁמַע בְּקֹלִי וַיִּתֶּן־לִי בֵּן עַל־כֵּן קָרְאָה שְׁמוֹ דָּן׃

7 *Rachel*'s maid *Bilha* conceived again and bore *Yaakov* a second son.

ז וַתַּהַר עוֹד וַתֵּלֶד בִּלְהָה שִׁפְחַת רָחֵל בֵּן שֵׁנִי לְיַעֲקֹב׃

Bereishit/Genesis 30
Vayeitzei

8 And *Rachel* said, "A fateful contest I waged with my sister; yes, and I have prevailed." So she named him *Naftali*.

9 When *Leah* saw that she had stopped bearing, she took her maid *Zilpa* and gave her to *Yaakov* as concubine.

10 And when *Leah*'s maid *Zilpa* bore *Yaakov* a son,

11 *Leah* said, "What luck!" So she named him *Gad*.

12 When *Leah*'s maid *Zilpa* bore *Yaakov* a second son,

13 *Leah* declared, "What fortune!" meaning, "Women will deem me fortunate." So she named him *Asher*.

14 Once, at the time of the wheat harvest, *Reuven* came upon some mandrakes in the field and brought them to his mother *Leah*. *Rachel* said to *Leah*, "Please give me some of your son's mandrakes."

15 But she said to her, "Was it not enough for you to take away my husband, that you would also take my son's mandrakes?" *Rachel* replied, "I promise, he shall lie with you tonight, in return for your son's mandrakes."

16 When *Yaakov* came home from the field in the evening, *Leah* went out to meet him and said, "You are to sleep with me, for I have hired you with my son's mandrakes." And he lay with her that night.

17 *Hashem* heeded *Leah*, and she conceived and bore him a fifth son.

18 And *Leah* said, "*Hashem* has given me my reward for having given my maid to my husband." So she named him *Yissachar*.

19 When *Leah* conceived again and bore *Yaakov* a sixth son,

20 *Leah* said, "*Hashem* has given me a choice gift; this time my husband will exalt me, for I have borne him six sons." So she named him *Zevulun*.

21 Last, she bore him a daughter, and named her *Dina*.

22 Now *Hashem* remembered *Rachel*; *Hashem* heeded her and opened her womb.

Bereishit/Genesis 30
Vayeitzei

בראשית ל
ויצא

23 She conceived and bore a son, and said, "*Hashem* has taken away my disgrace."

כג וַתַּ֥הַר וַתֵּ֖לֶד בֵּ֑ן וַתֹּ֕אמֶר אָסַ֥ף אֱלֹהִ֖ים אֶת־חֶרְפָּתִֽי׃

24 So she named him *Yosef*, which is to say, "May *Hashem* add another son for me."

כד וַתִּקְרָ֧א אֶת־שְׁמ֛וֹ יוֹסֵ֖ף לֵאמֹ֑ר יֹסֵ֧ף יְהֹוָ֛ה לִ֖י בֵּ֥ן אַחֵֽר׃

25 After *Rachel* had borne *Yosef*, *Yaakov* said to Laban, "Give me leave to go back to my own homeland.

כה וַיְהִ֕י כַּאֲשֶׁ֛ר יָלְדָ֥ה רָחֵ֖ל אֶת־יוֹסֵ֑ף וַיֹּ֤אמֶר יַעֲקֹב֙ אֶל־לָבָ֔ן שַׁלְּחֵ֙נִי֙ וְאֵ֣לְכָ֔ה אֶל־מְקוֹמִ֖י וּלְאַרְצִֽי׃

vai-HEE ka-a-SHER ya-l'-DAH ra-KHAYL et yo-SAYF va-YO-mer ya-a-KOV el la-VAN sha-l'-KHAY-nee v'-AY-l'-KHAH el m'-ko-MEE ul-ar-TZEE

26 Give me my wives and my children, for whom I have served you, that I may go; for well you know what services I have rendered you."

כו תְּנָ֞ה אֶת־נָשַׁ֣י וְאֶת־יְלָדַ֗י אֲשֶׁ֨ר עָבַ֧דְתִּי אֹֽתְךָ֛ בָּהֵ֖ן וְאֵלֵ֑כָה כִּ֚י אַתָּ֣ה יָדַ֔עְתָּ אֶת־עֲבֹדָתִ֖י אֲשֶׁ֥ר עֲבַדְתִּֽיךָ׃

27 But Laban said to him, "If you will indulge me, I have learned by divination that *Hashem* has blessed me on your account."

כז וַיֹּ֤אמֶר אֵלָיו֙ לָבָ֔ן אִם־נָ֛א מָצָ֥אתִי חֵ֖ן בְּעֵינֶ֑יךָ נִחַ֕שְׁתִּי וַיְבָרְכֵ֥נִי יְהֹוָ֖ה בִּגְלָלֶֽךָ׃

28 And he continued, "Name the wages due from me, and I will pay you."

כח וַיֹּאמַ֑ר נׇקְבָ֧ה שְׂכָרְךָ֛ עָלַ֖י וְאֶתֵּֽנָה׃

29 But he said, "You know well how I have served you and how your livestock has fared with me.

כט וַיֹּ֣אמֶר אֵלָ֔יו אַתָּ֣ה יָדַ֔עְתָּ אֵ֥ת אֲשֶׁ֖ר עֲבַדְתִּ֑יךָ וְאֵ֛ת אֲשֶׁר־הָיָ֥ה מִקְנְךָ֖ אִתִּֽי׃

30 For the little you had before I came has grown to much, since *Hashem* has blessed you wherever I turned. And now, when shall I make provision for my own household?"

ל כִּ֡י מְעַט֩ אֲשֶׁר־הָיָ֨ה לְךָ֤ לְפָנַי֙ וַיִּפְרֹ֣ץ לָרֹ֔ב וַיְבָ֧רֶךְ יְהֹוָ֛ה אֹתְךָ֖ לְרַגְלִ֑י וְעַתָּ֗ה מָתַ֛י אֶֽעֱשֶׂ֥ה גַם־אָנֹכִ֖י לְבֵיתִֽי׃

31 He said, "What shall I pay you?" And *Yaakov* said, "Pay me nothing! If you will do this thing for me, I will again pasture and keep your flocks:

לא וַיֹּ֖אמֶר מָ֣ה אֶתֶּן־לָ֑ךְ וַיֹּ֤אמֶר יַעֲקֹב֙ לֹא־תִתֶּן־לִ֣י מְא֔וּמָה אִם־תַּעֲשֶׂה־לִּי֙ הַדָּבָ֣ר הַזֶּ֔ה אָשׁ֛וּבָה אֶרְעֶ֥ה צֹאנְךָ֖ אֶשְׁמֹֽר׃

32 let me pass through your whole flock today, removing from there every speckled and spotted animal – every dark-colored sheep and every spotted and speckled goat. Such shall be my wages.

לב אֶֽעֱבֹ֨ר בְּכׇל־צֹֽאנְךָ֜ הַיּ֗וֹם הָסֵ֨ר מִשָּׁ֜ם כׇּל־שֶׂ֣ה ׀ נָקֹ֣ד וְטָל֗וּא וְכׇל־שֶׂה־חוּם֙ בַּכְּשָׂבִ֔ים וְטָל֥וּא וְנָקֹ֖ד בָּעִזִּ֑ים וְהָיָ֖ה שְׂכָרִֽי׃

33 In the future when you go over my wages, let my honesty toward you testify for me: if there are among my goats any that are not speckled or spotted or any sheep that are not dark-colored, they got there by theft."

לג וְעָֽנְתָה־בִּ֤י צִדְקָתִי֙ בְּי֣וֹם מָחָ֔ר כִּֽי־תָב֥וֹא עַל־שְׂכָרִ֖י לְפָנֶ֑יךָ כֹּ֣ל אֲשֶׁר־אֵינֶ֩נּוּ֩ נָקֹ֨ד וְטָל֜וּא בָּֽעִזִּ֗ים וְחוּם֙ בַּכְּשָׂבִ֔ים גָּנ֥וּב ה֖וּא אִתִּֽי׃

Rashi (1040–1105)

30:25 To go back to my own homeland Once *Rachel* has finally been blessed with a son, *Yosef*, *Yaakov* concludes that his time in exile has ended and he begins to prepare to return to the Land of Israel. Later in the Bible, *Rashi* explains that *Yosef* is referred to as a "flame" who will extinguish Esau who "shall be straw" (Obadiah 1:18). Once Esau's defeater is born, *Yaakov* is free to return to the Land of Israel, from which he fled out of fear of Esau. The birth of *Yosef* reinforces *Yaakov*'s faith in *Hashem* and urges him to return home. *Yaakov* understands that his "own homeland" is only in *Eretz Yisrael*.

Bereishit/Genesis 31
Vayeitzei

לד **And Laban said, "Very well, let it be as you say."**

וַיֹּאמֶר לָבָן הֵן לוּ יְהִי כִדְבָרֶךָ׃

לה **But that same day he removed the streaked and spotted he-goats and all the speckled and spotted she-goats – every one that had white on it – and all the dark-colored sheep, and left them in the charge of his sons.**

וַיָּסַר בַּיּוֹם הַהוּא אֶת־הַתְּיָשִׁים הָעֲקֻדִּים וְהַטְּלֻאִים וְאֵת כָּל־הָעִזִּים הַנְּקֻדּוֹת וְהַטְּלֻאֹת כֹּל אֲשֶׁר־לָבָן בּוֹ וְכָל־חוּם בַּכְּשָׂבִים וַיִּתֵּן בְּיַד־בָּנָיו׃

לו **And he put a distance of three days' journey between himself and Yaakov, while Yaakov was pasturing the rest of Laban's flock.**

וַיָּשֶׂם דֶּרֶךְ שְׁלֹשֶׁת יָמִים בֵּינוֹ וּבֵין יַעֲקֹב וְיַעֲקֹב רֹעֶה אֶת־צֹאן לָבָן הַנּוֹתָרֹת׃

לז **Yaakov then got fresh shoots of poplar, and of almond and plane, and peeled white stripes in them, laying bare the white of the shoots.**

וַיִּקַּח־לוֹ יַעֲקֹב מַקַּל לִבְנֶה לַח וְלוּז וְעַרְמוֹן וַיְפַצֵּל בָּהֵן פְּצָלוֹת לְבָנוֹת מַחְשֹׂף הַלָּבָן אֲשֶׁר עַל־הַמַּקְלוֹת׃

לח **The rods that he had peeled he set up in front of the goats in the troughs, the water receptacles, that the goats came to drink from. Their mating occurred when they came to drink,**

וַיַּצֵּג אֶת־הַמַּקְלוֹת אֲשֶׁר פִּצֵּל בָּרֳהָטִים בְּשִׁקֲתוֹת הַמָּיִם אֲשֶׁר תָּבֹאןָ הַצֹּאן לִשְׁתּוֹת לְנֹכַח הַצֹּאן וַיֵּחַמְנָה בְּבֹאָן לִשְׁתּוֹת׃

לט **and since the goats mated by the rods, the goats brought forth streaked, speckled, and spotted young.**

וַיֶּחֱמוּ הַצֹּאן אֶל־הַמַּקְלוֹת וַתֵּלַדְןָ הַצֹּאן עֲקֻדִּים נְקֻדִּים וּטְלֻאִים׃

מ **But Yaakov dealt separately with the sheep; he made these animals face the streaked or wholly dark-colored animals in Laban's flock. And so he produced special flocks for himself, which he did not put with Laban's flocks.**

וְהַכְּשָׂבִים הִפְרִיד יַעֲקֹב וַיִּתֵּן פְּנֵי הַצֹּאן אֶל־עָקֹד וְכָל־חוּם בְּצֹאן לָבָן וַיָּשֶׁת־לוֹ עֲדָרִים לְבַדּוֹ וְלֹא שָׁתָם עַל־צֹאן לָבָן׃

מא **Moreover, when the sturdier animals were mating, Yaakov would place the rods in the troughs, in full view of the animals, so that they mated by the rods;**

וְהָיָה בְּכָל־יַחֵם הַצֹּאן הַמְקֻשָּׁרוֹת וְשָׂם יַעֲקֹב אֶת־הַמַּקְלוֹת לְעֵינֵי הַצֹּאן בָּרֳהָטִים לְיַחְמֵנָּה בַּמַּקְלוֹת׃

מב **but with the feebler animals he would not place them there. Thus the feeble ones went to Laban and the sturdy to Yaakov.**

וּבְהַעֲטִיף הַצֹּאן לֹא יָשִׂים וְהָיָה הָעֲטֻפִים לְלָבָן וְהַקְּשֻׁרִים לְיַעֲקֹב׃

מג **So the man grew exceedingly prosperous, and came to own large flocks, maidservants and menservants, camels and asses.**

וַיִּפְרֹץ הָאִישׁ מְאֹד מְאֹד וַיְהִי־לוֹ צֹאן רַבּוֹת וּשְׁפָחוֹת וַעֲבָדִים וּגְמַלִּים וַחֲמֹרִים׃

31

א **Now he heard the things that Laban's sons were saying: "Yaakov has taken all that was our father's, and from that which was our father's he has built up all this wealth."**

וַיִּשְׁמַע אֶת־דִּבְרֵי בְנֵי־לָבָן לֵאמֹר לָקַח יַעֲקֹב אֵת כָּל־אֲשֶׁר לְאָבִינוּ וּמֵאֲשֶׁר לְאָבִינוּ עָשָׂה אֵת כָּל־הַכָּבֹד הַזֶּה׃

ב **Yaakov also saw that Laban's manner toward him was not as it had been in the past.**

וַיַּרְא יַעֲקֹב אֶת־פְּנֵי לָבָן וְהִנֵּה אֵינֶנּוּ עִמּוֹ כִּתְמוֹל שִׁלְשׁוֹם׃

Bereishit/Genesis 31
Vayeitzei

בראשית לא
ויצא

3 Then *Hashem* said to *Yaakov*, "Return to the land of your fathers where you were born, and I will be with you."

וַיֹּאמֶר יְהֹוָה אֶל־יַעֲקֹב שׁוּב אֶל־אֶרֶץ אֲבוֹתֶיךָ וּלְמוֹלַדְתֶּךָ וְאֶהְיֶה עִמָּךְ:

va-YO-mer a-do-NAI el ya-a-KOV SHUV el E-retz a-vo-TE-kha ul-mo-lad-TE-kha v'-eh-YEH i-MAKH

4 *Yaakov* had *Rachel* and *Leah* called to the field, where his flock was,

וַיִּשְׁלַח יַעֲקֹב וַיִּקְרָא לְרָחֵל וּלְלֵאָה הַשָּׂדֶה אֶל־צֹאנוֹ:

5 and said to them, "I see that your father's manner toward me is not as it has been in the past. But the God of my father has been with me.

וַיֹּאמֶר לָהֶן רֹאֶה אָנֹכִי אֶת־פְּנֵי אֲבִיכֶן כִּי־אֵינֶנּוּ אֵלַי כִּתְמֹל שִׁלְשֹׁם וֵאלֹהֵי אָבִי הָיָה עִמָּדִי:

6 As you know, I have served your father with all my might;

וְאַתֵּנָה יְדַעְתֶּן כִּי בְּכָל־כֹּחִי עָבַדְתִּי אֶת־אֲבִיכֶן:

7 but your father has cheated me, changing my wages time and again. *Hashem*, however, would not let him do me harm.

וַאֲבִיכֶן הֵתֶל בִּי וְהֶחֱלִף אֶת־מַשְׂכֻּרְתִּי עֲשֶׂרֶת מֹנִים וְלֹא־נְתָנוֹ אֱלֹהִים לְהָרַע עִמָּדִי:

8 If he said thus, 'The speckled shall be your wages,' then all the flocks would drop speckled young; and if he said thus, 'The streaked shall be your wages,' then all the flocks would drop streaked young.

אִם־כֹּה יֹאמַר נְקֻדִּים יִהְיֶה שְׂכָרֶךָ וְיָלְדוּ כָל־הַצֹּאן נְקֻדִּים וְאִם־כֹּה יֹאמַר עֲקֻדִּים יִהְיֶה שְׂכָרֶךָ וְיָלְדוּ כָל־הַצֹּאן עֲקֻדִּים:

9 *Hashem* has taken away your father's livestock and given it to me.

וַיַּצֵּל אֱלֹהִים אֶת־מִקְנֵה אֲבִיכֶם וַיִּתֶּן־לִי:

10 "Once, at the mating time of the flocks, I had a dream in which I saw that the he-goats mating with the flock were streaked, speckled, and mottled.

וַיְהִי בְּעֵת יַחֵם הַצֹּאן וָאֶשָּׂא עֵינַי וָאֵרֶא בַּחֲלוֹם וְהִנֵּה הָעַתֻּדִים הָעֹלִים עַל־הַצֹּאן עֲקֻדִּים נְקֻדִּים וּבְרֻדִּים:

11 And in the dream an angel of *Hashem* said to me, '*Yaakov*!' 'Here,' I answered.

וַיֹּאמֶר אֵלַי מַלְאַךְ הָאֱלֹהִים בַּחֲלוֹם יַעֲקֹב וָאֹמַר הִנֵּנִי:

12 And he said, 'Note well that all the he-goats which are mating with the flock are streaked, speckled, and mottled; for I have noted all that Laban has been doing to you.

וַיֹּאמֶר שָׂא־נָא עֵינֶיךָ וּרְאֵה כָּל־הָעַתֻּדִים הָעֹלִים עַל־הַצֹּאן עֲקֻדִּים נְקֻדִּים וּבְרֻדִּים כִּי רָאִיתִי אֵת כָּל־אֲשֶׁר לָבָן עֹשֶׂה לָּךְ:

13 I am the God of *Beit El*, where you anointed a pillar and where you made a vow to Me. Now, arise and leave this land and return to your native land.'"

אָנֹכִי הָאֵל בֵּית־אֵל אֲשֶׁר מָשַׁחְתָּ שָּׁם מַצֵּבָה אֲשֶׁר נָדַרְתָּ לִּי שָׁם נֶדֶר עַתָּה קוּם צֵא מִן־הָאָרֶץ הַזֹּאת וְשׁוּב אֶל־אֶרֶץ מוֹלַדְתֶּךָ:

Malbim (1809–1879)

31:3 Return to the land of your fathers With these words, *Hashem* implies that He will be with *Yaakov* only if he returns to the land of his fathers, the Land of Israel, but not if he stays with *Lavan* in Haran. Rabbi Meir Leibush Weiser, a Bible commentator and Hebrew grammarian commonly known by the acronym *Malbim*, explains that *Hashem* intentionally removed His protection from *Yaakov* in order to motivate him to return to *Eretz Yisrael*. After spending so much time outside the Holy Land, it is time for *Yaakov* to go home.

Bereishit/Genesis 31
Vayeitzei

בראשית לא
ויצא

14 Then *Rachel* and *Leah* answered him, saying, "Have we still a share in the inheritance of our father's house?

יד וַתַּעַן רָחֵל וְלֵאָה וַתֹּאמַרְנָה לוֹ הַעוֹד לָנוּ חֵלֶק וְנַחֲלָה בְּבֵית אָבִינוּ׃

15 Surely, he regards us as outsiders, now that he has sold us and has used up our purchase price.

טו הֲלוֹא נָכְרִיּוֹת נֶחְשַׁבְנוּ לוֹ כִּי מְכָרָנוּ וַיֹּאכַל גַּם־אָכוֹל אֶת־כַּסְפֵּנוּ׃

16 Truly, all the wealth that *Hashem* has taken away from our father belongs to us and to our children. Now then, do just as *Hashem* has told you."

טז כִּי כָל־הָעֹשֶׁר אֲשֶׁר הִצִּיל אֱלֹהִים מֵאָבִינוּ לָנוּ הוּא וּלְבָנֵינוּ וְעַתָּה כֹּל אֲשֶׁר אָמַר אֱלֹהִים אֵלֶיךָ עֲשֵׂה׃

17 Thereupon *Yaakov* put his children and wives on camels;

יז וַיָּקָם יַעֲקֹב וַיִּשָּׂא אֶת־בָּנָיו וְאֶת־נָשָׁיו עַל־הַגְּמַלִּים׃

18 and he drove off all his livestock and all the wealth that he had amassed, the livestock in his possession that he had acquired in Paddan-aram, to go to his father *Yitzchak* in the land of Canaan.

יח וַיִּנְהַג אֶת־כָּל־מִקְנֵהוּ וְאֶת־כָּל־רְכֻשׁוֹ אֲשֶׁר רָכָשׁ מִקְנֵה קִנְיָנוֹ אֲשֶׁר רָכַשׁ בְּפַדַּן אֲרָם לָבוֹא אֶל־יִצְחָק אָבִיו אַרְצָה כְּנָעַן׃

19 Meanwhile Laban had gone to shear his sheep, and *Rachel* stole her father's household idols.

יט וְלָבָן הָלַךְ לִגְזֹז אֶת־צֹאנוֹ וַתִּגְנֹב רָחֵל אֶת־הַתְּרָפִים אֲשֶׁר לְאָבִיהָ׃

20 *Yaakov* kept Laban the Aramean in the dark, not telling him that he was fleeing,

כ וַיִּגְנֹב יַעֲקֹב אֶת־לֵב לָבָן הָאֲרַמִּי עַל־בְּלִי הִגִּיד לוֹ כִּי בֹרֵחַ הוּא׃

21 and fled with all that he had. Soon he was across the Euphrates and heading toward the hill country of *Gilad*.

כא וַיִּבְרַח הוּא וְכָל־אֲשֶׁר־לוֹ וַיָּקָם וַיַּעֲבֹר אֶת־הַנָּהָר וַיָּשֶׂם אֶת־פָּנָיו הַר הַגִּלְעָד׃

22 On the third day, Laban was told that *Yaakov* had fled.

כב וַיֻּגַּד לְלָבָן בַּיּוֹם הַשְּׁלִישִׁי כִּי בָרַח יַעֲקֹב׃

23 So he took his kinsmen with him and pursued him a distance of seven days, catching up with him in the hill country of *Gilad*.

כג וַיִּקַּח אֶת־אֶחָיו עִמּוֹ וַיִּרְדֹּף אַחֲרָיו דֶּרֶךְ שִׁבְעַת יָמִים וַיַּדְבֵּק אֹתוֹ בְּהַר הַגִּלְעָד׃

24 But *Hashem* appeared to Laban the Aramean in a dream by night and said to him, "Beware of attempting anything with *Yaakov*, good or bad."

כד וַיָּבֹא אֱלֹהִים אֶל־לָבָן הָאֲרַמִּי בַּחֲלֹם הַלָּיְלָה וַיֹּאמֶר לוֹ הִשָּׁמֶר לְךָ פֶּן־תְּדַבֵּר עִם־יַעֲקֹב מִטּוֹב עַד־רָע׃

25 Laban overtook *Yaakov*. *Yaakov* had pitched his tent on the Height, and Laban with his kinsmen encamped in the hill country of *Gilad*.

כה וַיַּשֵּׂג לָבָן אֶת־יַעֲקֹב וְיַעֲקֹב תָּקַע אֶת־אָהֳלוֹ בָּהָר וְלָבָן תָּקַע אֶת־אֶחָיו בְּהַר הַגִּלְעָד׃

26 And Laban said to *Yaakov*, "What did you mean by keeping me in the dark and carrying off my daughters like captives of the sword?

כו וַיֹּאמֶר לָבָן לְיַעֲקֹב מֶה עָשִׂיתָ וַתִּגְנֹב אֶת־לְבָבִי וַתְּנַהֵג אֶת־בְּנֹתַי כִּשְׁבֻיוֹת חָרֶב׃

27 Why did you flee in secrecy and mislead me and not tell me? I would have sent you off with festive music, with timbrel and lyre.

כז לָמָּה נַחְבֵּאתָ לִבְרֹחַ וַתִּגְנֹב אֹתִי וְלֹא־הִגַּדְתָּ לִּי וָאֲשַׁלֵּחֲךָ בְּשִׂמְחָה וּבְשִׁרִים בְּתֹף וּבְכִנּוֹר׃

28 You did not even let me kiss my sons and daughters good-by! It was a foolish thing for you to do.

כח וְלֹא נְטַשְׁתַּנִי לְנַשֵּׁק לְבָנַי וְלִבְנֹתָי עַתָּה הִסְכַּלְתָּ עֲשׂוֹ׃

Bereishit/Genesis 31
Vayeitzei

בראשית לא
ויצא

29 I have it in my power to do you harm; but the God of your father said to me last night, 'Beware of attempting anything with *Yaakov*, good or bad.'

כט יֶשׁ־לְאֵל יָדִי לַעֲשׂוֹת עִמָּכֶם רָע וֵאלֹהֵי אֲבִיכֶם אֶמֶשׁ אָמַר אֵלַי לֵאמֹר הִשָּׁמֶר לְךָ מִדַּבֵּר עִם־יַעֲקֹב מִטּוֹב עַד־רָע:

30 Very well, you had to leave because you were longing for your father's house; but why did you steal my gods?"

ל וְעַתָּה הָלֹךְ הָלַכְתָּ כִּי־נִכְסֹף נִכְסַפְתָּה לְבֵית אָבִיךָ לָמָּה גָנַבְתָּ אֶת־אֱלֹהָי:

31 *Yaakov* answered Laban, saying, "I was afraid because I thought you would take your daughters from me by force.

לא וַיַּעַן יַעֲקֹב וַיֹּאמֶר לְלָבָן כִּי יָרֵאתִי כִּי אָמַרְתִּי פֶּן־תִּגְזֹל אֶת־בְּנוֹתֶיךָ מֵעִמִּי:

32 But anyone with whom you find your gods shall not remain alive! In the presence of our kinsmen, point out what I have of yours and take it." *Yaakov*, of course, did not know that *Rachel* had stolen them.

לב עִם אֲשֶׁר תִּמְצָא אֶת־אֱלֹהֶיךָ לֹא יִחְיֶה נֶגֶד אַחֵינוּ הַכֶּר־לְךָ מָה עִמָּדִי וְקַח־לָךְ וְלֹא־יָדַע יַעֲקֹב כִּי רָחֵל גְּנָבָתַם:

33 So Laban went into *Yaakov*'s tent and *Leah*'s tent and the tents of the two maidservants; but he did not find them. Leaving *Leah*'s tent, he entered *Rachel*'s tent.

לג וַיָּבֹא לָבָן בְּאֹהֶל יַעֲקֹב וּבְאֹהֶל לֵאָה וּבְאֹהֶל שְׁתֵּי הָאֲמָהֹת וְלֹא מָצָא וַיֵּצֵא מֵאֹהֶל לֵאָה וַיָּבֹא בְּאֹהֶל רָחֵל:

34 *Rachel*, meanwhile, had taken the idols and placed them in the camel cushion and sat on them; and Laban rummaged through the tent without finding them.

לד וְרָחֵל לָקְחָה אֶת־הַתְּרָפִים וַתְּשִׂמֵם בְּכַר הַגָּמָל וַתֵּשֶׁב עֲלֵיהֶם וַיְמַשֵּׁשׁ לָבָן אֶת־כָּל־הָאֹהֶל וְלֹא מָצָא:

35 For she said to her father, "Let not my lord take it amiss that I cannot rise before you, for the period of women is upon me." Thus he searched, but could not find the household idols.

לה וַתֹּאמֶר אֶל־אָבִיהָ אַל־יִחַר בְּעֵינֵי אֲדֹנִי כִּי לוֹא אוּכַל לָקוּם מִפָּנֶיךָ כִּי־דֶרֶךְ נָשִׁים לִי וַיְחַפֵּשׂ וְלֹא מָצָא אֶת־הַתְּרָפִים:

36 Now *Yaakov* became incensed and took up his grievance with Laban. *Yaakov* spoke up and said to Laban, "What is my crime, what is my guilt that you should pursue me?

לו וַיִּחַר לְיַעֲקֹב וַיָּרֶב בְּלָבָן וַיַּעַן יַעֲקֹב וַיֹּאמֶר לְלָבָן מַה־פִּשְׁעִי מַה חַטָּאתִי כִּי דָלַקְתָּ אַחֲרָי:

37 You rummaged through all my things; what have you found of all your household objects? Set it here, before my kinsmen and yours, and let them decide between us two.

לז כִּי־מִשַּׁשְׁתָּ אֶת־כָּל־כֵּלַי מַה־מָּצָאתָ מִכֹּל כְּלֵי־בֵיתֶךָ שִׂים כֹּה נֶגֶד אַחַי וְאַחֶיךָ וְיוֹכִיחוּ בֵּין שְׁנֵינוּ:

38 "These twenty years I have spent in your service, your ewes and she-goats never miscarried, nor did I feast on rams from your flock.

לח זֶה עֶשְׂרִים שָׁנָה אָנֹכִי עִמָּךְ רְחֵלֶיךָ וְעִזֶּיךָ לֹא שִׁכֵּלוּ וְאֵילֵי צֹאנְךָ לֹא אָכָלְתִּי:

39 That which was torn by beasts I never brought to you; I myself made good the loss; you exacted it of me, whether snatched by day or snatched by night.

לט טְרֵפָה לֹא־הֵבֵאתִי אֵלֶיךָ אָנֹכִי אֲחַטֶּנָּה מִיָּדִי תְּבַקְשֶׁנָּה גְּנֻבְתִי יוֹם וּגְנֻבְתִי לָיְלָה:

40 Often, scorching heat ravaged me by day and frost by night; and sleep fled from my eyes.

מ הָיִיתִי בַיּוֹם אֲכָלַנִי חֹרֶב וְקֶרַח בַּלָּיְלָה וַתִּדַּד שְׁנָתִי מֵעֵינָי:

Bereishit/Genesis 31
Vayeitzei

בראשית לא
ויצא

41 Of the twenty years that I spent in your household, I served you fourteen years for your two daughters, and six years for your flocks; and you changed my wages time and again.

מא זֶה־לִּי עֶשְׂרִים שָׁנָה בְּבֵיתֶךָ עֲבַדְתִּיךָ אַרְבַּע־עֶשְׂרֵה שָׁנָה בִּשְׁתֵּי בְנֹתֶיךָ וְשֵׁשׁ שָׁנִים בְּצֹאנֶךָ וַתַּחֲלֵף אֶת־מַשְׂכֻּרְתִּי עֲשֶׂרֶת מֹנִים:

42 Had not the God of my father, the God of *Avraham* and the Fear of *Yitzchak*, been with me, you would have sent me away empty-handed. But *Hashem* took notice of my plight and the toil of my hands, and He gave judgment last night."

מב לוּלֵי אֱלֹהֵי אָבִי אֱלֹהֵי אַבְרָהָם וּפַחַד יִצְחָק הָיָה לִי כִּי עַתָּה רֵיקָם שִׁלַּחְתָּנִי אֶת־עָנְיִי וְאֶת־יְגִיעַ כַּפַּי רָאָה אֱלֹהִים וַיּוֹכַח אָמֶשׁ:

43 Then Laban spoke up and said to *Yaakov*, "The daughters are my daughters, the children are my children, and the flocks are my flocks; all that you see is mine. Yet what can I do now about my daughters or the children they have borne?

מג וַיַּעַן לָבָן וַיֹּאמֶר אֶל־יַעֲקֹב הַבָּנוֹת בְּנֹתַי וְהַבָּנִים בָּנַי וְהַצֹּאן צֹאנִי וְכֹל אֲשֶׁר־אַתָּה רֹאֶה לִי־הוּא וְלִבְנֹתַי מָה־אֶעֱשֶׂה לָאֵלֶּה הַיּוֹם אוֹ לִבְנֵיהֶן אֲשֶׁר יָלָדוּ:

44 Come, then, let us make a pact, you and I, that there may be a witness between you and me."

מד וְעַתָּה לְכָה נִכְרְתָה בְרִית אֲנִי וָאָתָּה וְהָיָה לְעֵד בֵּינִי וּבֵינֶךָ:

45 Thereupon *Yaakov* took a stone and set it up as a pillar.

מה וַיִּקַּח יַעֲקֹב אָבֶן וַיְרִימֶהָ מַצֵּבָה:

46 And *Yaakov* said to his kinsmen, "Gather stones." So they took stones and made a mound; and they partook of a meal there by the mound.

מו וַיֹּאמֶר יַעֲקֹב לְאֶחָיו לִקְטוּ אֲבָנִים וַיִּקְחוּ אֲבָנִים וַיַּעֲשׂוּ־גָל וַיֹּאכְלוּ שָׁם עַל־הַגָּל:

47 Laban named it Yegar-sahadutha, but *Yaakov* named it Gal-ed.

מז וַיִּקְרָא־לוֹ לָבָן יְגַר שָׂהֲדוּתָא וְיַעֲקֹב קָרָא לוֹ גַּלְעֵד:

48 And Laban declared, "This mound is a witness between you and me this day." That is why it was named Gal-ed;

מח וַיֹּאמֶר לָבָן הַגַּל הַזֶּה עֵד בֵּינִי וּבֵינְךָ הַיּוֹם עַל־כֵּן קָרָא־שְׁמוֹ גַּלְעֵד:

49 and [it was called] *Mitzpa*, because he said, "May *Hashem* watch between you and me, when we are out of sight of each other.

מט וְהַמִּצְפָּה אֲשֶׁר אָמַר יִצֶף יְהוָה בֵּינִי וּבֵינֶךָ כִּי נִסָּתֵר אִישׁ מֵרֵעֵהוּ:

50 If you ill-treat my daughters or take other wives besides my daughters – though no one else be about, remember, *Hashem* Himself will be witness between you and me."

נ אִם־תְּעַנֶּה אֶת־בְּנֹתַי וְאִם־תִּקַּח נָשִׁים עַל־בְּנֹתַי אֵין אִישׁ עִמָּנוּ רְאֵה אֱלֹהִים עֵד בֵּינִי וּבֵינֶךָ:

51 And Laban said to *Yaakov*, "Here is this mound and here the pillar which I have set up between you and me:

נא וַיֹּאמֶר לָבָן לְיַעֲקֹב הִנֵּה הַגַּל הַזֶּה וְהִנֵּה הַמַּצֵּבָה אֲשֶׁר יָרִיתִי בֵּינִי וּבֵינֶךָ:

52 this mound shall be witness and this pillar shall be witness that I am not to cross to you past this mound, and that you are not to cross to me past this mound and this pillar, with hostile intent.

נב עֵד הַגַּל הַזֶּה וְעֵדָה הַמַּצֵּבָה אִם־אָנִי לֹא־אֶעֱבֹר אֵלֶיךָ אֶת־הַגַּל הַזֶּה וְאִם־אַתָּה לֹא־תַעֲבֹר אֵלַי אֶת־הַגַּל הַזֶּה וְאֶת־הַמַּצֵּבָה הַזֹּאת לְרָעָה:

53 May the God of *Avraham* and the god of Nahor" – their ancestral deities – "judge between us." And *Yaakov* swore by the Fear of his father *Yitzchak*.

נג אֱלֹהֵי אַבְרָהָם וֵאלֹהֵי נָחוֹר יִשְׁפְּטוּ בֵינֵינוּ אֱלֹהֵי אֲבִיהֶם וַיִּשָּׁבַע יַעֲקֹב בְּפַחַד אָבִיו יִצְחָק:

Bereishit/Genesis 32
Vayishlach

בראשית לב
וישלח

54 Yaakov then offered up a sacrifice on the Height, and invited his kinsmen to partake of the meal. After the meal, they spent the night on the Height.

נד וַיִּזְבַּח יַעֲקֹב זֶבַח בָּהָר וַיִּקְרָא לְאֶחָיו לֶאֱכָל־לָחֶם וַיֹּאכְלוּ לֶחֶם וַיָּלִינוּ בָּהָר:

32

1 Early in the morning, Laban kissed his sons and daughters and bade them good-by; then Laban left on his journey homeward.

לב א וַיַּשְׁכֵּם לָבָן בַּבֹּקֶר וַיְנַשֵּׁק לְבָנָיו וְלִבְנוֹתָיו וַיְבָרֶךְ אֶתְהֶם וַיֵּלֶךְ וַיָּשָׁב לָבָן לִמְקֹמוֹ:

2 Yaakov went on his way, and angels of *Hashem* encountered him.

ב וְיַעֲקֹב הָלַךְ לְדַרְכּוֹ וַיִּפְגְּעוּ־בוֹ מַלְאֲכֵי אֱלֹהִים:

3 When he saw them, Yaakov said, "This is *Hashem*'s camp." So he named that place Mahanaim.

ג וַיֹּאמֶר יַעֲקֹב כַּאֲשֶׁר רָאָם מַחֲנֵה אֱלֹהִים זֶה וַיִּקְרָא שֵׁם־הַמָּקוֹם הַהוּא מַחֲנָיִם:

4 Yaakov sent messengers ahead to his brother Esau in the land of Seir, the country of Edom,

ד וַיִּשְׁלַח יַעֲקֹב מַלְאָכִים לְפָנָיו אֶל־עֵשָׂו אָחִיו אַרְצָה שֵׂעִיר שְׂדֵה אֱדוֹם:

5 and instructed them as follows, "Thus shall you say, 'To my lord Esau, thus says your servant *Yaakov*: I stayed with Laban and remained until now;

ה וַיְצַו אֹתָם לֵאמֹר כֹּה תֹאמְרוּן לַאדֹנִי לְעֵשָׂו כֹּה אָמַר עַבְדְּךָ יַעֲקֹב עִם־לָבָן גַּרְתִּי וָאֵחַר עַד־עָתָּה:

6 I have acquired cattle, asses, sheep, and male and female slaves; and I send this message to my lord in the hope of gaining your favor.'"

ו וַיְהִי־לִי שׁוֹר וַחֲמוֹר צֹאן וְעֶבֶד וְשִׁפְחָה וָאֶשְׁלְחָה לְהַגִּיד לַאדֹנִי לִמְצֹא־חֵן בְּעֵינֶיךָ:

7 The messengers returned to *Yaakov*, saying, "We came to your brother Esau; he himself is coming to meet you, and there are four hundred men with him."

ז וַיָּשֻׁבוּ הַמַּלְאָכִים אֶל־יַעֲקֹב לֵאמֹר בָּאנוּ אֶל־אָחִיךָ אֶל־עֵשָׂו וְגַם הֹלֵךְ לִקְרָאתְךָ וְאַרְבַּע־מֵאוֹת אִישׁ עִמּוֹ:

8 Yaakov was greatly frightened; in his anxiety, he divided the people with him, and the flocks and herds and camels, into two camps,

ח וַיִּירָא יַעֲקֹב מְאֹד וַיֵּצֶר לוֹ וַיַּחַץ אֶת־הָעָם אֲשֶׁר־אִתּוֹ וְאֶת־הַצֹּאן וְאֶת־הַבָּקָר וְהַגְּמַלִּים לִשְׁנֵי מַחֲנוֹת:

9 thinking, "If Esau comes to the one camp and attacks it, the other camp may yet escape."

ט וַיֹּאמֶר אִם־יָבוֹא עֵשָׂו אֶל־הַמַּחֲנֶה הָאַחַת וְהִכָּהוּ וְהָיָה הַמַּחֲנֶה הַנִּשְׁאָר לִפְלֵיטָה:

va-YO-mer im ya-VO ay-SAV el ha-ma-kha-NEH ha-a-KHAT v'-hi-KA-hu v'-ha-YAH ha-ma-kha-NEH ha-nish-AR lif-lay-TAH

פליטה

32:9 The other camp may yet escape Whenever the same Hebrew word is used to describe unrelated events, the Bible is drawing a deep connection between the two events. The word for 'escape' in this verse is *playta* (פליטה), the same word used by the Prophet *Ovadya* (1:17) "But on Mount Zion a remnant (*playta*) shall survive, and it shall be holy. The house of *Yaakov* shall dispossess those who had dispossessed them. The house of *Yaakov* shall be fire, and the house of *Yosef* a flame, and the house of Esau shall be straw." As he prepares for war with his brother Esau, *Yaakov* alludes to the fact that Zion is the only real refuge for the Jewish people from all future battles with the descendants of Esau.

Bereishit/Genesis 32
Vayishlach

בראשית לב
וישלח

10 Then *Yaakov* said, "O God of my father *Avraham* and God of my father *Yitzchak*, *Hashem*, who said to me, 'Return to your native land and I will deal bountifully with you'!

י וַיֹּאמֶר יַעֲקֹב אֱלֹהֵי אָבִי אַבְרָהָם וֵאלֹהֵי אָבִי יִצְחָק יְהֹוָה הָאֹמֵר אֵלַי שׁוּב לְאַרְצְךָ וּלְמוֹלַדְתְּךָ וְאֵיטִיבָה עִמָּךְ:

11 I am unworthy of all the kindness that You have so steadfastly shown Your servant: with my staff alone I crossed this *Yarden*, and now I have become two camps.

יא קָטֹנְתִּי מִכֹּל הַחֲסָדִים וּמִכָּל־הָאֱמֶת אֲשֶׁר עָשִׂיתָ אֶת־עַבְדֶּךָ כִּי בְמַקְלִי עָבַרְתִּי אֶת־הַיַּרְדֵּן הַזֶּה וְעַתָּה הָיִיתִי לִשְׁנֵי מַחֲנוֹת:

12 Deliver me, I pray, from the hand of my brother, from the hand of Esau; else, I fear, he may come and strike me down, mothers and children alike.

יב הַצִּילֵנִי נָא מִיַּד אָחִי מִיַּד עֵשָׂו כִּי־יָרֵא אָנֹכִי אֹתוֹ פֶּן־יָבוֹא וְהִכַּנִי אֵם עַל־בָּנִים:

13 Yet You have said, 'I will deal bountifully with you and make your offspring as the sands of the sea, which are too numerous to count.'"

יג וְאַתָּה אָמַרְתָּ הֵיטֵב אֵיטִיב עִמָּךְ וְשַׂמְתִּי אֶת־זַרְעֲךָ כְּחוֹל הַיָּם אֲשֶׁר לֹא־יִסָּפֵר מֵרֹב:

14 After spending the night there, he selected from what was at hand these presents for his brother Esau:

יד וַיָּלֶן שָׁם בַּלַּיְלָה הַהוּא וַיִּקַּח מִן־הַבָּא בְיָדוֹ מִנְחָה לְעֵשָׂו אָחִיו:

15 200 she-goats and 20 he-goats; 200 ewes and 20 rams;

טו עִזִּים מָאתַיִם וּתְיָשִׁים עֶשְׂרִים רְחֵלִים מָאתַיִם וְאֵילִים עֶשְׂרִים:

16 30 milch camels with their colts; 40 cows and 10 bulls; 20 she-asses and 10 he-asses.

טז גְּמַלִּים מֵינִיקוֹת וּבְנֵיהֶם שְׁלֹשִׁים פָּרוֹת אַרְבָּעִים וּפָרִים עֲשָׂרָה אֲתֹנֹת עֶשְׂרִים וַעְיָרִם עֲשָׂרָה:

17 These he put in the charge of his servants, drove by drove, and he told his servants, "Go on ahead, and keep a distance between droves."

יז וַיִּתֵּן בְּיַד־עֲבָדָיו עֵדֶר עֵדֶר לְבַדּוֹ וַיֹּאמֶר אֶל־עֲבָדָיו עִבְרוּ לְפָנַי וְרֶוַח תָּשִׂימוּ בֵּין עֵדֶר וּבֵין עֵדֶר:

18 He instructed the one in front as follows, "When my brother Esau meets you and asks you, 'Whose man are you? Where are you going? And whose [animals] are these ahead of you?'

יח וַיְצַו אֶת־הָרִאשׁוֹן לֵאמֹר כִּי יִפְגָּשְׁךָ עֵשָׂו אָחִי וּשְׁאֵלְךָ לֵאמֹר לְמִי־אַתָּה וְאָנָה תֵלֵךְ וּלְמִי אֵלֶּה לְפָנֶיךָ:

19 you shall answer, 'Your servant *Yaakov*'s; they are a gift sent to my lord Esau; and [*Yaakov*] himself is right behind us.'"

יט וְאָמַרְתָּ לְעַבְדְּךָ לְיַעֲקֹב מִנְחָה הִוא שְׁלוּחָה לַאדֹנִי לְעֵשָׂו וְהִנֵּה גַם־הוּא אַחֲרֵינוּ:

20 He gave similar instructions to the second one, and the third, and all the others who followed the droves, namely, "Thus and so shall you say to Esau when you reach him.

כ וַיְצַו גַּם אֶת־הַשֵּׁנִי גַּם אֶת־הַשְּׁלִישִׁי גַּם אֶת־כָּל־הַהֹלְכִים אַחֲרֵי הָעֲדָרִים לֵאמֹר כַּדָּבָר הַזֶּה תְּדַבְּרוּן אֶל־עֵשָׂו בְּמֹצַאֲכֶם אֹתוֹ:

21 And you shall add, 'And your servant *Yaakov* himself is right behind us.'" For he reasoned, "If I propitiate him with presents in advance, and then face him, perhaps he will show me favor."

כא וַאֲמַרְתֶּם גַּם הִנֵּה עַבְדְּךָ יַעֲקֹב אַחֲרֵינוּ כִּי־אָמַר אֲכַפְּרָה פָנָיו בַּמִּנְחָה הַהֹלֶכֶת לְפָנָי וְאַחֲרֵי־כֵן אֶרְאֶה פָנָיו אוּלַי יִשָּׂא פָנָי:

22 And so the gift went on ahead, while he remained in camp that night.

כב וַתַּעֲבֹר הַמִּנְחָה עַל־פָּנָיו וְהוּא לָן בַּלַּיְלָה־הַהוּא בַּמַּחֲנֶה:

84

Bereishit/Genesis 33
Vayishlach

ברא שית לג
וישלח

23 That same night he arose, and taking his two wives, his two maidservants, and his eleven children, he crossed the ford of the Jabbok.

כג וַיָּקָם בַּלַּיְלָה הוּא וַיִּקַּח אֶת־שְׁתֵּי נָשָׁיו וְאֶת־שְׁתֵּי שִׁפְחֹתָיו וְאֶת־אַחַד עָשָׂר יְלָדָיו וַיַּעֲבֹר אֵת מַעֲבַר יַבֹּק׃

24 After taking them across the stream, he sent across all his possessions.

כד וַיִּקָּחֵם וַיַּעֲבִרֵם אֶת־הַנָּחַל וַיַּעֲבֵר אֶת־אֲשֶׁר־לוֹ׃

25 *Yaakov* was left alone. And a man wrestled with him until the break of dawn.

כה וַיִּוָּתֵר יַעֲקֹב לְבַדּוֹ וַיֵּאָבֵק אִישׁ עִמּוֹ עַד עֲלוֹת הַשָּׁחַר׃

26 When he saw that he had not prevailed against him, he wrenched *Yaakov*'s hip at its socket, so that the socket of his hip was strained as he wrestled with him.

כו וַיַּרְא כִּי לֹא יָכֹל לוֹ וַיִּגַּע בְּכַף־יְרֵכוֹ וַתֵּקַע כַּף־יֶרֶךְ יַעֲקֹב בְּהֵאָבְקוֹ עִמּוֹ׃

27 Then he said, "Let me go, for dawn is breaking." But he answered, "I will not let you go, unless you bless me."

כז וַיֹּאמֶר שַׁלְּחֵנִי כִּי עָלָה הַשָּׁחַר וַיֹּאמֶר לֹא אֲשַׁלֵּחֲךָ כִּי אִם־בֵּרַכְתָּנִי׃

28 Said the other, "What is your name?" He replied, "*Yaakov*."

כח וַיֹּאמֶר אֵלָיו מַה־שְּׁמֶךָ וַיֹּאמֶר יַעֲקֹב׃

29 Said he, "Your name shall no longer be *Yaakov*, but *Yisrael*, for you have striven with beings divine and human, and have prevailed."

כט וַיֹּאמֶר לֹא יַעֲקֹב יֵאָמֵר עוֹד שִׁמְךָ כִּי אִם־יִשְׂרָאֵל כִּי־שָׂרִיתָ עִם־אֱלֹהִים וְעִם־אֲנָשִׁים וַתּוּכָל׃

30 *Yaakov* asked, "Pray tell me your name." But he said, "You must not ask my name!" And he took leave of him there.

ל וַיִּשְׁאַל יַעֲקֹב וַיֹּאמֶר הַגִּידָה־נָּא שְׁמֶךָ וַיֹּאמֶר לָמָּה זֶּה תִּשְׁאַל לִשְׁמִי וַיְבָרֶךְ אֹתוֹ שָׁם׃

31 So *Yaakov* named the place Peniel, meaning, "I have seen a divine being face to face, yet my life has been preserved."

לא וַיִּקְרָא יַעֲקֹב שֵׁם הַמָּקוֹם פְּנִיאֵל כִּי־רָאִיתִי אֱלֹהִים פָּנִים אֶל־פָּנִים וַתִּנָּצֵל נַפְשִׁי׃

32 The sun rose upon him as he passed Penuel, limping on his hip.

לב וַיִּזְרַח־לוֹ הַשֶּׁמֶשׁ כַּאֲשֶׁר עָבַר אֶת־פְּנוּאֵל וְהוּא צֹלֵעַ עַל־יְרֵכוֹ׃

33 That is why the children of *Yisrael* to this day do not eat the thigh muscle that is on the socket of the hip, since *Yaakov*'s hip socket was wrenched at the thigh muscle.

לג עַל־כֵּן לֹא־יֹאכְלוּ בְנֵי־יִשְׂרָאֵל אֶת־גִּיד הַנָּשֶׁה אֲשֶׁר עַל־כַּף הַיָּרֵךְ עַד הַיּוֹם הַזֶּה כִּי נָגַע בְּכַף־יֶרֶךְ יַעֲקֹב בְּגִיד הַנָּשֶׁה׃

33

1 Looking up, *Yaakov* saw Esau coming, accompanied by four hundred men. He divided the children among *Leah*, *Rachel*, and the two maids,

לג א וַיִּשָּׂא יַעֲקֹב עֵינָיו וַיַּרְא וְהִנֵּה עֵשָׂו בָּא וְעִמּוֹ אַרְבַּע מֵאוֹת אִישׁ וַיַּחַץ אֶת־הַיְלָדִים עַל־לֵאָה וְעַל־רָחֵל וְעַל שְׁתֵּי הַשְּׁפָחוֹת׃

2 putting the maids and their children first, *Leah* and her children next, and *Rachel* and *Yosef* last.

ב וַיָּשֶׂם אֶת־הַשְּׁפָחוֹת וְאֶת־יַלְדֵיהֶן רִאשֹׁנָה וְאֶת־לֵאָה וִילָדֶיהָ אַחֲרֹנִים וְאֶת־רָחֵל וְאֶת־יוֹסֵף אַחֲרֹנִים׃

3 He himself went on ahead and bowed low to the ground seven times until he was near his brother.

ג וְהוּא עָבַר לִפְנֵיהֶם וַיִּשְׁתַּחוּ אַרְצָה שֶׁבַע פְּעָמִים עַד־גִּשְׁתּוֹ עַד־אָחִיו׃

Bereishit/Genesis 33
Vayishlach

בראשית לג
וישלח

4 Esau ran to greet him. He embraced him and, falling on his neck, he kissed him; and they wept.

ד וַיָּ֨רָץ עֵשָׂ֤ו לִקְרָאתוֹ֙ וַֽיְחַבְּקֵ֔הוּ וַיִּפֹּ֥ל עַל־צַוָּארָ֖ו וַׄיִּׄשָּׁׄקֵ֑ׄהׄוּׄ וַיִּבְכּֽוּ׃

5 Looking about, he saw the women and the children. "Who," he asked, "are these with you?" He answered, "The children with whom *Hashem* has favored your servant."

ה וַיִּשָּׂ֣א אֶת־עֵינָ֗יו וַיַּ֤רְא אֶת־הַנָּשִׁים֙ וְאֶת־הַיְלָדִ֔ים וַיֹּ֖אמֶר מִי־אֵ֣לֶּה לָּ֑ךְ וַיֹּאמַ֕ר הַיְלָדִ֕ים אֲשֶׁר־חָנַ֥ן אֱלֹהִ֖ים אֶת־עַבְדֶּֽךָ׃

6 Then the maids, with their children, came forward and bowed low;

ו וַתִּגַּ֧שְׁןָ הַשְּׁפָח֛וֹת הֵ֥נָּה וְיַלְדֵיהֶ֖ן וַתִּֽשְׁתַּחֲוֶֽיןָ׃

7 next *Leah*, with her children, came forward and bowed low; and last, *Yosef* and *Rachel* came forward and bowed low;

ז וַתִּגַּ֧שׁ גַּם־לֵאָ֛ה וִילָדֶ֖יהָ וַיִּֽשְׁתַּחֲו֑וּ וְאַחַ֗ר נִגַּ֥שׁ יוֹסֵ֛ף וְרָחֵ֖ל וַיִּֽשְׁתַּחֲוֽוּ׃

8 And he asked, "What do you mean by all this company which I have met?" He answered, "To gain my lord's favor."

ח וַיֹּ֕אמֶר מִ֥י לְךָ֛ כָּל־הַמַּחֲנֶ֥ה הַזֶּ֖ה אֲשֶׁ֣ר פָּגָ֑שְׁתִּי וַיֹּ֕אמֶר לִמְצֹא־חֵ֖ן בְּעֵינֵ֥י אֲדֹנִֽי׃

9 Esau said, "I have enough, my brother; let what you have remain yours."

ט וַיֹּ֥אמֶר עֵשָׂ֖ו יֶשׁ־לִ֣י רָ֑ב אָחִ֕י יְהִ֥י לְךָ֖ אֲשֶׁר־לָֽךְ׃

10 But *Yaakov* said, "No, I pray you; if you would do me this favor, accept from me this gift; for to see your face is like seeing the face of *Hashem*, and you have received me favorably.

י וַיֹּ֣אמֶר יַעֲקֹ֗ב אַל־נָא֙ אִם־נָ֨א מָצָ֤אתִי חֵן֙ בְּעֵינֶ֔יךָ וְלָקַחְתָּ֥ מִנְחָתִ֖י מִיָּדִ֑י כִּ֣י עַל־כֵּ֤ן רָאִ֨יתִי֙ פָנֶ֔יךָ כִּרְאֹ֖ת פְּנֵ֥י אֱלֹהִ֖ים וַתִּרְצֵֽנִי׃

11 Please accept my present which has been brought to you, for *Hashem* has favored me and I have plenty." And when he urged him, he accepted.

יא קַח־נָ֤א אֶת־בִּרְכָתִי֙ אֲשֶׁ֣ר הֻבָ֣את לָ֔ךְ כִּֽי־חַנַּ֥נִי אֱלֹהִ֖ים וְכִ֣י יֶשׁ־לִי־כֹ֑ל וַיִּפְצַר־בּ֖וֹ וַיִּקָּֽח׃

12 And [Esau] said, "Let us start on our journey, and I will proceed at your pace."

יב וַיֹּ֖אמֶר נִסְעָ֣ה וְנֵלֵ֑כָה וְאֵלְכָ֖ה לְנֶגְדֶּֽךָ׃

13 But he said to him, "My lord knows that the children are frail and that the flocks and herds, which are nursing, are a care to me; if they are driven hard a single day, all the flocks will die.

יג וַיֹּ֣אמֶר אֵלָ֗יו אֲדֹנִ֤י יֹדֵ֙עַ֙ כִּֽי־הַיְלָדִ֣ים רַכִּ֔ים וְהַצֹּ֥אן וְהַבָּקָ֖ר עָל֣וֹת עָלָ֑י וּדְפָקוּם֙ י֣וֹם אֶחָ֔ד וָמֵ֖תוּ כָּל־הַצֹּֽאן׃

14 Let my lord go on ahead of his servant, while I travel slowly, at the pace of the cattle before me and at the pace of the children, until I come to my lord in Seir."

יד יַעֲבָר־נָ֥א אֲדֹנִ֖י לִפְנֵ֣י עַבְדּ֑וֹ וַאֲנִ֞י אֶֽתְנָהֲלָ֣ה לְאִטִּ֗י לְרֶ֨גֶל הַמְּלָאכָ֤ה אֲשֶׁר־לְפָנַי֙ וּלְרֶ֣גֶל הַיְלָדִ֔ים עַ֛ד אֲשֶׁר־אָבֹ֥א אֶל־אֲדֹנִ֖י שֵׂעִֽירָה׃

15 Then Esau said, "Let me assign to you some of the men who are with me." But he said, "Oh no, my lord is too kind to me!"

טו וַיֹּ֣אמֶר עֵשָׂ֔ו אַצִּֽיגָה־נָּ֣א עִמְּךָ֔ מִן־הָעָ֖ם אֲשֶׁ֣ר אִתִּ֑י וַיֹּ֙אמֶר֙ לָ֣מָּה זֶּ֔ה אֶמְצָא־חֵ֖ן בְּעֵינֵ֥י אֲדֹנִֽי׃

16 So Esau started back that day on his way to Seir.

טז וַיָּשָׁב֩ בַּיּ֨וֹם הַה֥וּא עֵשָׂ֛ו לְדַרְכּ֖וֹ שֵׂעִֽירָה׃

17 But *Yaakov* journeyed on to Succoth, and built a house for himself and made stalls for his cattle; that is why the place was called Succoth.

יז וְיַעֲקֹב֙ נָסַ֣ע סֻכֹּ֔תָה וַיִּ֥בֶן ל֖וֹ בָּ֑יִת וּלְמִקְנֵ֙הוּ֙ עָשָׂ֣ה סֻכֹּ֔ת עַל־כֵּ֛ן קָרָ֥א שֵׁם־הַמָּק֖וֹם סֻכּֽוֹת׃

Bereishit/Genesis 34
Vayishlach

בראשית לד
וישלח

18 *Yaakov* arrived safe in the city of Shechem which is in the land of Canaan – having come thus from Paddan-aram – and he encamped before the city.

יח וַיָּבֹא יַעֲקֹב שָׁלֵם עִיר שְׁכֶם אֲשֶׁר בְּאֶרֶץ כְּנַעַן בְּבֹאוֹ מִפַּדַּן אֲרָם וַיִּחַן אֶת־פְּנֵי הָעִיר:

19 The parcel of land where he pitched his tent he purchased from the children of Hamor, Shechem's father, for a hundred *kesitah*.

יט וַיִּקֶן אֶת־חֶלְקַת הַשָּׂדֶה אֲשֶׁר נָטָה־שָׁם אָהֳלוֹ מִיַּד בְּנֵי־חֲמוֹר אֲבִי שְׁכֶם בְּמֵאָה קְשִׂיטָה:

va-YI-ken et khel-KAT ha-sa-DEH a-SHER na-tah SHAM a-ha-LO mi-YAD b'-nay kha-MOR a-VEE sh'-KHEM b'-may-AH k'-see-TAH

20 He set up a *Mizbayach* there, and called it *El-elohe-yisrael*.

כ וַיַּצֶּב־שָׁם מִזְבֵּחַ וַיִּקְרָא־לוֹ אֵל אֱלֹהֵי יִשְׂרָאֵל:

34

1 Now *Dina*, the daughter whom *Leah* had borne to *Yaakov*, went out to visit the daughters of the land.

א וַתֵּצֵא דִינָה בַּת־לֵאָה אֲשֶׁר יָלְדָה לְיַעֲקֹב לִרְאוֹת בִּבְנוֹת הָאָרֶץ:

2 Shechem son of Hamor the Hivite, chief of the country, saw her, and took her and lay with her by force.

ב וַיַּרְא אֹתָהּ שְׁכֶם בֶּן־חֲמוֹר הַחִוִּי נְשִׂיא הָאָרֶץ וַיִּקַּח אֹתָהּ וַיִּשְׁכַּב אֹתָהּ וַיְעַנֶּהָ:

3 Being strongly drawn to *Dina* daughter of *Yaakov*, and in love with the maiden, he spoke to the maiden tenderly.

ג וַתִּדְבַּק נַפְשׁוֹ בְּדִינָה בַּת־יַעֲקֹב וַיֶּאֱהַב אֶת־הַנַּעֲרָ וַיְדַבֵּר עַל־לֵב הַנַּעֲרָ:

4 So Shechem said to his father Hamor, "Get me this girl as a wife."

ד וַיֹּאמֶר שְׁכֶם אֶל־חֲמוֹר אָבִיו לֵאמֹר קַח־לִי אֶת־הַיַּלְדָּה הַזֹּאת לְאִשָּׁה:

5 *Yaakov* heard that he had defiled his daughter *Dina*; but since his sons were in the field with his cattle, *Yaakov* kept silent until they came home.

ה וְיַעֲקֹב שָׁמַע כִּי טִמֵּא אֶת־דִּינָה בִתּוֹ וּבָנָיו הָיוּ אֶת־מִקְנֵהוּ בַּשָּׂדֶה וְהֶחֱרִשׁ יַעֲקֹב עַד־בֹּאָם:

6 Then Shechem's father Hamor came out to *Yaakov* to speak to him.

ו וַיֵּצֵא חֲמוֹר אֲבִי־שְׁכֶם אֶל־יַעֲקֹב לְדַבֵּר אִתּוֹ:

7 Meanwhile *Yaakov*'s sons, having heard the news, came in from the field. The men were distressed and very angry, because he had committed an outrage in *Yisrael* by lying with *Yaakov*'s daughter – a thing not to be done.

ז וּבְנֵי יַעֲקֹב בָּאוּ מִן־הַשָּׂדֶה כְּשָׁמְעָם וַיִּתְעַצְּבוּ הָאֲנָשִׁים וַיִּחַר לָהֶם מְאֹד כִּי־נְבָלָה עָשָׂה בְיִשְׂרָאֵל לִשְׁכַּב אֶת־בַּת־יַעֲקֹב וְכֵן לֹא יֵעָשֶׂה:

8 And Hamor spoke with them, saying, "My son Shechem longs for your daughter. Please give her to him in marriage.

ח וַיְדַבֵּר חֲמוֹר אִתָּם לֵאמֹר שְׁכֶם בְּנִי חָשְׁקָה נַפְשׁוֹ בְּבִתְּכֶם תְּנוּ נָא אֹתָהּ לוֹ לְאִשָּׁה:

View of the landscape of Shechem

33:19 The parcel of land where he pitched his tent After escaping unscathed from Esau's clutches, *Yaakov* enters Canaan and purchases the land he has chosen to settle. This is a message for all of eternity. To ensure survival amidst countless enemies, the Children of Israel must build up their only true safe haven, the Land of Israel. Like his grandfather *Avraham*, *Yaakov* then builds an altar to *Hashem*. Rabbi Ovadya Seforno, a sixteenth century Italian commentator, points out that after spending time in exile, *Yaakov* appreciates that service of *Hashem* is most fitting in *Eretz Yisrael*, and he immediately makes every possible effort to worship the one true God of Israel there.

Bereishit/Genesis 34
Vayishlach

9 Intermarry with us: give your daughters to us, and take our daughters for yourselves:

10 You will dwell among us, and the land will be open before you; settle, move about, and acquire holdings in it."

11 Then Shechem said to her father and brothers, "Do me this favor, and I will pay whatever you tell me.

12 Ask of me a bride-price ever so high, as well as gifts, and I will pay what you tell me; only give me the maiden for a wife."

13 Yaakov's sons answered Shechem and his father Hamor – speaking with guile because he had defiled their sister *Dina*

14 and said to them, "We cannot do this thing, to give our sister to a man who is uncircumcised, for that is a disgrace among us.

15 Only on this condition will we agree with you; that you will become like us in that every male among you is circumcised.

16 Then we will give our daughters to you and take your daughters to ourselves; and we will dwell among you and become as one kindred.

17 But if you will not listen to us and become circumcised, we will take our daughter and go."

18 Their words pleased Hamor and Hamor's son Shechem.

19 And the youth lost no time in doing the thing, for he wanted *Yaakov*'s daughter. Now he was the most respected in his father's house.

20 So Hamor and his son Shechem went to the public place of their town and spoke to their fellow townsmen, saying,

21 "These people are our friends; let them settle in the land and move about in it, for the land is large enough for them; we will take their daughters to ourselves as wives and give our daughters to them.

22 But only on this condition will the men agree with us to dwell among us and be as one kindred: that all our males become circumcised as they are circumcised.

ט וְהִתְחַתְּנ֖וּ אֹתָ֑נוּ בְּנֹֽתֵיכֶם֙ תִּתְּנוּ־לָ֔נוּ וְאֶת־בְּנֹתֵ֖ינוּ תִּקְח֥וּ לָכֶֽם׃

י וְאִתָּ֖נוּ תֵּשֵׁ֑בוּ וְהָאָ֙רֶץ֙ תִּהְיֶ֣ה לִפְנֵיכֶ֔ם שְׁבוּ֙ וּסְחָר֔וּהָ וְהֵֽאָחֲז֖וּ בָּֽהּ׃

יא וַיֹּ֤אמֶר שְׁכֶם֙ אֶל־אָבִ֣יהָ וְאֶל־אַחֶ֔יהָ אֶמְצָא־חֵ֖ן בְּעֵֽינֵיכֶ֑ם וַאֲשֶׁ֧ר תֹּאמְר֛וּ אֵלַ֖י אֶתֵּֽן׃

יב הַרְבּ֙וּ עָלַ֤י מְאֹד֙ מֹ֣הַר וּמַתָּ֔ן וְאֶ֨תְּנָ֔ה כַּאֲשֶׁ֥ר תֹּאמְר֖וּ אֵלָ֑י וּתְנוּ־לִ֥י אֶת־הַֽנַּעֲרָ֖ לְאִשָּֽׁה׃

יג וַיַּעֲנ֨וּ בְנֵי־יַעֲקֹ֜ב אֶת־שְׁכֶ֨ם וְאֶת־חֲמ֥וֹר אָבִ֛יו בְּמִרְמָ֖ה וַיְדַבֵּ֑רוּ אֲשֶׁ֣ר טִמֵּ֔א אֵ֖ת דִּינָ֥ה אֲחֹתָֽם׃

יד וַיֹּאמְר֣וּ אֲלֵיהֶ֗ם לֹ֤א נוּכַל֙ לַעֲשׂוֹת֙ הַדָּבָ֣ר הַזֶּ֔ה לָתֵת֙ אֶת־אֲחֹתֵ֔נוּ לְאִ֖ישׁ אֲשֶׁר־ל֣וֹ עָרְלָ֑ה כִּֽי־חֶרְפָּ֥ה הִ֖וא לָֽנוּ׃

טו אַךְ־בְּזֹ֖את נֵא֣וֹת לָכֶ֑ם אִ֚ם תִּהְי֣וּ כָמֹ֔נוּ לְהִמֹּ֥ל לָכֶ֖ם כָּל־זָכָֽר׃

טז וְנָתַ֤נּוּ אֶת־בְּנֹתֵ֙ינוּ֙ לָכֶ֔ם וְאֶת־בְּנֹתֵיכֶ֖ם נִֽקַּֽח־לָ֑נוּ וְיָשַׁ֣בְנוּ אִתְּכֶ֔ם וְהָיִ֖ינוּ לְעַ֥ם אֶחָֽד׃

יז וְאִם־לֹ֧א תִשְׁמְע֛וּ אֵלֵ֖ינוּ לְהִמּ֑וֹל וְלָקַ֥חְנוּ אֶת־בִּתֵּ֖נוּ וְהָלָֽכְנוּ׃

יח וַיִּֽיטְב֥וּ דִבְרֵיהֶ֖ם בְּעֵינֵ֣י חֲמ֑וֹר וּבְעֵינֵ֖י שְׁכֶ֥ם בֶּן־חֲמֽוֹר׃

יט וְלֹֽא־אֵחַ֤ר הַנַּ֙עַר֙ לַעֲשׂ֣וֹת הַדָּבָ֔ר כִּ֥י חָפֵ֖ץ בְּבַֽת־יַעֲקֹ֑ב וְה֣וּא נִכְבָּ֔ד מִכֹּ֖ל בֵּ֥ית אָבִֽיו׃

כ וַיָּבֹ֥א חֲמ֛וֹר וּשְׁכֶ֥ם בְּנ֖וֹ אֶל־שַׁ֣עַר עִירָ֑ם וַֽיְדַבְּר֛וּ אֶל־אַנְשֵׁ֥י עִירָ֖ם לֵאמֹֽר׃

כא הָאֲנָשִׁ֨ים הָאֵ֜לֶּה שְׁלֵמִ֧ים הֵ֣ם אִתָּ֗נוּ וְיֵשְׁב֤וּ בָאָ֙רֶץ֙ וְיִסְחֲר֣וּ אֹתָ֔הּ וְהָאָ֛רֶץ הִנֵּ֥ה רַֽחֲבַת־יָדַ֖יִם לִפְנֵיהֶ֑ם אֶת־בְּנֹתָם֙ נִקַּֽח־לָ֣נוּ לְנָשִׁ֔ים וְאֶת־בְּנֹתֵ֖ינוּ נִתֵּ֥ן לָהֶֽם׃

כב אַךְ־בְּ֠זֹ֠את יֵאֹ֨תוּ לָ֤נוּ הָאֲנָשִׁים֙ לָשֶׁ֣בֶת אִתָּ֔נוּ לִהְי֖וֹת לְעַ֣ם אֶחָ֑ד בְּהִמּ֥וֹל לָ֙נוּ֙ כָּל־זָכָ֔ר כַּאֲשֶׁ֖ר הֵ֥ם נִמֹּלִֽים׃

Bereishit/Genesis 35
Vayishlach

בראשית לה
וישלח

23 Their cattle and substance and all their beasts will be ours, if we only agree to their terms, so that they will settle among us."

כג מִקְנֵהֶם וְקִנְיָנָם וְכָל־בְּהֶמְתָּם הֲלוֹא לָנוּ הֵם אַךְ נֵאוֹתָה לָהֶם וְיֵשְׁבוּ אִתָּנוּ׃

24 All who went out of the gate of his town heeded Hamor and his son Shechem, and all males, all those who went out of the gate of his town, were circumcised.

כד וַיִּשְׁמְעוּ אֶל־חֲמוֹר וְאֶל־שְׁכֶם בְּנוֹ כָּל־יֹצְאֵי שַׁעַר עִירוֹ וַיִּמֹּלוּ כָּל־זָכָר כָּל־יֹצְאֵי שַׁעַר עִירוֹ׃

25 On the third day, when they were in pain, *Shimon* and *Levi*, two of *Yaakov*'s sons, brothers of *Dina*, took each his sword, came upon the city unmolested, and slew all the males.

כה וַיְהִי בַיּוֹם הַשְּׁלִישִׁי בִּהְיוֹתָם כֹּאֲבִים וַיִּקְחוּ שְׁנֵי־בְנֵי־יַעֲקֹב שִׁמְעוֹן וְלֵוִי אֲחֵי דִינָה אִישׁ חַרְבּוֹ וַיָּבֹאוּ עַל־הָעִיר בֶּטַח וַיַּהַרְגוּ כָּל־זָכָר׃

26 They put Hamor and his son Shechem to the sword, took *Dina* out of Shechem's house, and went away.

כו וְאֶת־חֲמוֹר וְאֶת־שְׁכֶם בְּנוֹ הָרְגוּ לְפִי־חָרֶב וַיִּקְחוּ אֶת־דִּינָה מִבֵּית שְׁכֶם וַיֵּצֵאוּ׃

27 The other sons of *Yaakov* came upon the slain and plundered the town, because their sister had been defiled.

כז בְּנֵי יַעֲקֹב בָּאוּ עַל־הַחֲלָלִים וַיָּבֹזּוּ הָעִיר אֲשֶׁר טִמְּאוּ אֲחוֹתָם׃

28 They seized their flocks and herds and asses, all that was inside the town and outside;

כח אֶת־צֹאנָם וְאֶת־בְּקָרָם וְאֶת־חֲמֹרֵיהֶם וְאֵת אֲשֶׁר־בָּעִיר וְאֶת־אֲשֶׁר בַּשָּׂדֶה לָקָחוּ׃

29 all their wealth, all their children, and their wives, all that was in the houses, they took as captives and booty.

כט וְאֶת־כָּל־חֵילָם וְאֶת־כָּל־טַפָּם וְאֶת־נְשֵׁיהֶם שָׁבוּ וַיָּבֹזּוּ וְאֵת כָּל־אֲשֶׁר בַּבָּיִת׃

30 *Yaakov* said to *Shimon* and *Levi*, "You have brought trouble on me, making me odious among the inhabitants of the land, the Canaanites and the Perizzites; my men are few in number, so that if they unite against me and attack me, I and my house will be destroyed."

ל וַיֹּאמֶר יַעֲקֹב אֶל־שִׁמְעוֹן וְאֶל־לֵוִי עֲכַרְתֶּם אֹתִי לְהַבְאִישֵׁנִי בְּיֹשֵׁב הָאָרֶץ בַּכְּנַעֲנִי וּבַפְּרִזִּי וַאֲנִי מְתֵי מִסְפָּר וְנֶאֶסְפוּ עָלַי וְהִכּוּנִי וְנִשְׁמַדְתִּי אֲנִי וּבֵיתִי׃

31 But they answered, "Should our sister be treated like a whore?"

לא וַיֹּאמְרוּ הַכְזוֹנָה יַעֲשֶׂה אֶת־אֲחוֹתֵנוּ׃

va-yo-m'-RU hakh-zo-NAH ya-a-SEH et a-kho-TAY-nu

35

1 *Hashem* said to *Yaakov*, "Arise, go up to *Beit El* and remain there; and build a *Mizbayach* there to the God who appeared to you when you were fleeing from your brother Esau."

א וַיֹּאמֶר אֱלֹהִים אֶל־יַעֲקֹב קוּם עֲלֵה בֵית־אֵל וְשֶׁב־שָׁם וַעֲשֵׂה־שָׁם מִזְבֵּחַ לָאֵל הַנִּרְאֶה אֵלֶיךָ בְּבָרְחֲךָ מִפְּנֵי עֵשָׂו אָחִיךָ׃

Rabbi Samson R. Hirsch (1808–1888)

34:31 Should our sister be treated like a whore *Yaakov*'s sons argue with their father, who personifies peace and mercy, maintaining that in order to protect the family's honor, there are times when use of the sword is necessary. It is through the *Torah*'s education, says Rabbi Samson Raphael Hirsch, that the Jewish people have learned gentleness and humanity. But, this has not made the Jews a weak or cowardly nation. With *Hashem*'s help, the tiny State of Israel has time and again stood up successfully to her numerous enemies, through the courageous men and women of the Israel Defense Forces.

Bereishit/Genesis 35
Vayishlach

בראשית לה
וישלח

2 So *Yaakov* said to his household and to all who were with him, "Rid yourselves of the alien gods in your midst, purify yourselves, and change your clothes.

ב וַיֹּאמֶר יַעֲקֹב אֶל־בֵּיתוֹ וְאֶל כָּל־אֲשֶׁר עִמּוֹ הָסִרוּ אֶת־אֱלֹהֵי הַנֵּכָר אֲשֶׁר בְּתֹכְכֶם וְהִטַּהֲרוּ וְהַחֲלִיפוּ שִׂמְלֹתֵיכֶם:

3 Come, let us go up to *Beit El*, and I will build a *Mizbayach* there to the God who answered me when I was in distress and who has been with me wherever I have gone."

ג וְנָקוּמָה וְנַעֲלֶה בֵּית־אֵל וְאֶעֱשֶׂה־שָּׁם מִזְבֵּחַ לָאֵל הָעֹנֶה אֹתִי בְּיוֹם צָרָתִי וַיְהִי עִמָּדִי בַּדֶּרֶךְ אֲשֶׁר הָלָכְתִּי:

4 They gave to *Yaakov* all the alien gods that they had, and the rings that were in their ears, and *Yaakov* buried them under the terebinth that was near Shechem.

ד וַיִּתְּנוּ אֶל־יַעֲקֹב אֵת כָּל־אֱלֹהֵי הַנֵּכָר אֲשֶׁר בְּיָדָם וְאֶת־הַנְּזָמִים אֲשֶׁר בְּאָזְנֵיהֶם וַיִּטְמֹן אֹתָם יַעֲקֹב תַּחַת הָאֵלָה אֲשֶׁר עִם־שְׁכֶם:

5 As they set out, a terror from *Hashem* fell on the cities round about, so that they did not pursue the sons of *Yaakov*.

ה וַיִּסָּעוּ וַיְהִי חִתַּת אֱלֹהִים עַל־הֶעָרִים אֲשֶׁר סְבִיבֹתֵיהֶם וְלֹא רָדְפוּ אַחֲרֵי בְּנֵי יַעֲקֹב:

6 Thus *Yaakov* came to Luz – that is, *Beit El* – in the land of Canaan, he and all the people who were with him.

ו וַיָּבֹא יַעֲקֹב לוּזָה אֲשֶׁר בְּאֶרֶץ כְּנַעַן הִוא בֵּית־אֵל הוּא וְכָל־הָעָם אֲשֶׁר־עִמּוֹ:

7 There he built a *Mizbayach* and named the site *El-Beit El*, for it was there that *Hashem* had revealed Himself to him when he was fleeing from his brother.

ז וַיִּבֶן שָׁם מִזְבֵּחַ וַיִּקְרָא לַמָּקוֹם אֵל בֵּית־אֵל כִּי שָׁם נִגְלוּ אֵלָיו הָאֱלֹהִים בְּבָרְחוֹ מִפְּנֵי אָחִיו:

8 *Devora*, *Rivka*'s nurse, died, and was buried under the oak below *Beit El*; so it was named Allon-bacuth.

ח וַתָּמָת דְּבֹרָה מֵינֶקֶת רִבְקָה וַתִּקָּבֵר מִתַּחַת לְבֵית־אֵל תַּחַת הָאַלּוֹן וַיִּקְרָא שְׁמוֹ אַלּוֹן בָּכוּת:

9 *Hashem* appeared again to *Yaakov* on his arrival from Paddan-aram, and He blessed him.

ט וַיֵּרָא אֱלֹהִים אֶל־יַעֲקֹב עוֹד בְּבֹאוֹ מִפַּדַּן אֲרָם וַיְבָרֶךְ אֹתוֹ:

10 *Hashem* said to him, "You whose name is *Yaakov*, You shall be called *Yaakov* no more, But *Yisrael* shall be your name." Thus He named him *Yisrael*.

י וַיֹּאמֶר־לוֹ אֱלֹהִים שִׁמְךָ יַעֲקֹב לֹא־יִקָּרֵא שִׁמְךָ עוֹד יַעֲקֹב כִּי אִם־יִשְׂרָאֵל יִהְיֶה שְׁמֶךָ וַיִּקְרָא אֶת־שְׁמוֹ יִשְׂרָאֵל:

11 And *Hashem* said to him, "I am *El Shaddai*. Be fertile and increase; A nation, yea an assembly of nations, Shall descend from you. Kings shall issue from your loins.

יא וַיֹּאמֶר לוֹ אֱלֹהִים אֲנִי אֵל שַׁדַּי פְּרֵה וּרְבֵה גּוֹי וּקְהַל גּוֹיִם יִהְיֶה מִמֶּךָּ וּמְלָכִים מֵחֲלָצֶיךָ יֵצֵאוּ:

12 The land that I assigned to *Avraham* and *Yitzchak* I assign to you; And to your offspring to come Will I assign the land."

יב וְאֶת־הָאָרֶץ אֲשֶׁר נָתַתִּי לְאַבְרָהָם וּלְיִצְחָק לְךָ אֶתְּנֶנָּה וּלְזַרְעֲךָ אַחֲרֶיךָ אֶתֵּן אֶת־הָאָרֶץ:

v'-et ha-A-retz a-SHER na-TA-tee l'-av-ra-HAM ul-yitz-KHAK l'-KHA e-t'-NE-nah ul-zar-a-KHA a-kha-RE-kha e-TAYN et ha-A-retz

13 *Hashem* parted from him at the spot where He had spoken to him;

יג וַיַּעַל מֵעָלָיו אֱלֹהִים בַּמָּקוֹם אֲשֶׁר־דִּבֶּר אִתּוֹ:

Bereishit/Genesis 35
Vayishlach

בראשית לה
וישלח

14 and *Yaakov* set up a pillar at the site where He had spoken to him, a pillar of stone, and he offered a libation on it and poured oil upon it.

יד וַיַּצֵּב יַעֲקֹב מַצֵּבָה בַּמָּקוֹם אֲשֶׁר־דִּבֶּר אִתּוֹ מַצֶּבֶת אָבֶן וַיַּסֵּךְ עָלֶיהָ נֶסֶךְ וַיִּצֹק עָלֶיהָ שָׁמֶן:

15 *Yaakov* gave the site, where *Hashem* had spoken to him, the name of *Beit El*.

טו וַיִּקְרָא יַעֲקֹב אֶת־שֵׁם הַמָּקוֹם אֲשֶׁר דִּבֶּר אִתּוֹ שָׁם אֱלֹהִים בֵּית־אֵל:

16 They set out from *Beit El*; but when they were still some distance short of *Efrat*, *Rachel* was in childbirth, and she had hard labor.

טז וַיִּסְעוּ מִבֵּית אֵל וַיְהִי־עוֹד כִּבְרַת־הָאָרֶץ לָבוֹא אֶפְרָתָה וַתֵּלֶד רָחֵל וַתְּקַשׁ בְּלִדְתָּהּ:

17 When her labor was at its hardest, the midwife said to her, "Have no fear, for it is another boy for you."

יז וַיְהִי בְהַקְשֹׁתָהּ בְּלִדְתָּהּ וַתֹּאמֶר לָהּ הַמְיַלֶּדֶת אַל־תִּירְאִי כִּי־גַם־זֶה לָךְ בֵּן:

18 But as she breathed her last – for she was dying – she named him Ben-oni; but his father called him *Binyamin*.

יח וַיְהִי בְּצֵאת נַפְשָׁהּ כִּי מֵתָה וַתִּקְרָא שְׁמוֹ בֶּן־אוֹנִי וְאָבִיו קָרָא־לוֹ בִנְיָמִין:

19 Thus *Rachel* died. She was buried on the road to *Efrat* – now *Beit Lechem*.

יט וַתָּמָת רָחֵל וַתִּקָּבֵר בְּדֶרֶךְ אֶפְרָתָה הִוא בֵּית לָחֶם:

va-TA-mot ra-KHAYL va-ti-ka-VAYR b'-DE-rekh ef-RA-tah HEE BAYT LA-khem

20 Over her grave *Yaakov* set up a pillar; it is the pillar at *Rachel*'s grave to this day.

כ וַיַּצֵּב יַעֲקֹב מַצֵּבָה עַל־קְבֻרָתָהּ הִוא מַצֶּבֶת קְבֻרַת־רָחֵל עַד־הַיּוֹם:

21 *Yisrael* journeyed on, and pitched his tent beyond Migdal-eder.

כא וַיִּסַּע יִשְׂרָאֵל וַיֵּט אָהֳלֹה מֵהָלְאָה לְמִגְדַּל־עֵדֶר:

22 While *Yisrael* stayed in that land, *Reuven* went and lay with *Bilha*, his father's concubine; and *Yisrael* found out. Now the sons of *Yaakov* were twelve in number.

כב וַיְהִי בִּשְׁכֹּן יִשְׂרָאֵל בָּאָרֶץ הַהִוא וַיֵּלֶךְ רְאוּבֵן וַיִּשְׁכַּב אֶת־בִּלְהָה פִּילֶגֶשׁ אָבִיו וַיִּשְׁמַע יִשְׂרָאֵל וַיִּהְיוּ בְנֵי־יַעֲקֹב שְׁנֵים עָשָׂר:

23 The sons of *Leah*: Reuven – *Yaakov*'s first-born – Shimon, Levi, Yehuda, Yissachar, and Zevulun.

כג בְּנֵי לֵאָה בְּכוֹר יַעֲקֹב רְאוּבֵן וְשִׁמְעוֹן וְלֵוִי וִיהוּדָה וְיִשָּׂשכָר וּזְבֻלֻן:

24 The sons of *Rachel*: Yosef and Binyamin.

כד בְּנֵי רָחֵל יוֹסֵף וּבִנְיָמִן:

25 The sons of *Bilha*, *Rachel*'s maid: Dan and Naftali.

כה וּבְנֵי בִלְהָה שִׁפְחַת רָחֵל דָּן וְנַפְתָּלִי:

Rachel's Tomb in Beit Lechem, c. 1890

35:19 She was buried on the road to *Efrat* *Yaakov* did not bury his beloved wife *Rachel* in the family plot in *Chevron*, but rather in nearby *Beit Lechem*. Rashi explains that *Rachel* was intentionally buried there in *Beit Lechem*, on the side of the road on which the Jews were forcibly marched into exile following the destruction of the first *Beit Hamikdash*. At that devastating moment in Jewish history, the downtrodden people found comfort in *Rachel*'s holy resting spot as she entreated God's mercy towards His people. This is alluded to in *Yirmiyahu*'s prophecy (Jeremiah 31:15–17) "A cry is heard in *Rama* – wailing, bitter weeping – *Rachel* is weeping for her children." According to the *Zohar*, the *Mashiach* will ultimately lead the dispersed Jews along that same route, again passing *Rachel*'s grave as they are led back to their land and thus fulfilling the continuation of *Yirmiyahu*'s prophecy, "they shall return from the enemy's land … the children shall return to their country." Today, *Rachel*'s Tomb on the outskirts of contemporary Bethlehem remains a popular destination for people to pour out their hearts in prayer for the day when all of *Rachel*'s descendants will pass her grave, on their way back home into *Eretz Yisrael*.

Bereishit/Genesis 36
Vayishlach

בראשית לו
וישלח

26 And the sons of *Zilpa*, *Leah*'s maid: *Gad* and *Asher*. These are the sons of *Yaakov* who were born to him in Paddan-aram.

כו וּבְנֵי זִלְפָּה שִׁפְחַת לֵאָה גָּד וְאָשֵׁר אֵלֶּה בְּנֵי יַעֲקֹב אֲשֶׁר יֻלַּד־לוֹ בְּפַדַּן אֲרָם:

27 And *Yaakov* came to his father *Yitzchak* at Mamre, at *Kiryat Arba* – now *Chevron* – where *Avraham* and *Yitzchak* had sojourned.

כז וַיָּבֹא יַעֲקֹב אֶל־יִצְחָק אָבִיו מַמְרֵא קִרְיַת הָאַרְבַּע הִוא חֶבְרוֹן אֲשֶׁר־גָּר־שָׁם אַבְרָהָם וְיִצְחָק:

28 *Yitzchak* was a hundred and eighty years old

כח וַיִּהְיוּ יְמֵי יִצְחָק מְאַת שָׁנָה וּשְׁמֹנִים שָׁנָה:

29 when he breathed his last and died. He was gathered to his kin in ripe old age; and he was buried by his sons Esau and *Yaakov*.

כט וַיִּגְוַע יִצְחָק וַיָּמָת וַיֵּאָסֶף אֶל־עַמָּיו זָקֵן וּשְׂבַע יָמִים וַיִּקְבְּרוּ אֹתוֹ עֵשָׂו וְיַעֲקֹב בָּנָיו:

36 1 This is the line of Esau – that is, Edom.

לו א וְאֵלֶּה תֹּלְדוֹת עֵשָׂו הוּא אֱדוֹם:

2 Esau took his wives from among the Canaanite women – Adah daughter of Elon the Hittite, and Oholibamah daughter of Anah daughter of Zibeon the Hivite

ב עֵשָׂו לָקַח אֶת־נָשָׁיו מִבְּנוֹת כְּנָעַן אֶת־עָדָה בַּת־אֵילוֹן הַחִתִּי וְאֶת־אָהֳלִיבָמָה בַּת־עֲנָה בַּת־צִבְעוֹן הַחִוִּי:

3 and also Basemath daughter of Ishmael and sister of Nebaioth.

ג וְאֶת־בָּשְׂמַת בַּת־יִשְׁמָעֵאל אֲחוֹת נְבָיוֹת:

4 Adah bore to Esau Eliphaz; Basemath bore Reuel;

ד וַתֵּלֶד עָדָה לְעֵשָׂו אֶת־אֱלִיפָז וּבָשְׂמַת יָלְדָה אֶת־רְעוּאֵל:

5 and Oholibamah bore Jeush, Jalam, and Korah. Those were the sons of Esau, who were born to him in the land of Canaan.

ה וְאָהֳלִיבָמָה יָלְדָה אֶת־יעיש [יְעוּשׁ] וְאֶת־יַעְלָם וְאֶת־קֹרַח אֵלֶּה בְּנֵי עֵשָׂו אֲשֶׁר יֻלְּדוּ־לוֹ בְּאֶרֶץ כְּנָעַן:

6 Esau took his wives, his sons and daughters, and all the members of his household, his cattle and all his livestock, and all the property that he had acquired in the land of Canaan, and went to another land because of his brother *Yaakov*.

ו וַיִּקַּח עֵשָׂו אֶת־נָשָׁיו וְאֶת־בָּנָיו וְאֶת־בְּנֹתָיו וְאֶת־כָּל־נַפְשׁוֹת בֵּיתוֹ וְאֶת־מִקְנֵהוּ וְאֶת־כָּל־בְּהֶמְתּוֹ וְאֵת כָּל־קִנְיָנוֹ אֲשֶׁר רָכַשׁ בְּאֶרֶץ כְּנָעַן וַיֵּלֶךְ אֶל־אֶרֶץ מִפְּנֵי יַעֲקֹב אָחִיו:

va-yi-KAKH ay-SAV et na-SHAV v'-et ba-NAV v'-et b'-no-TAV v'-et kol naf-SHOT bay-TO v'-et mik-NAY-hu v'-et kol b'-hem-TO v'-AYT kol kin-ya-NO a-SHER ra-KHASH b'-E-retz k'-NA-an va-YAY-lekh el E-retz mi-p'-NAY ya-a-KOV a-KHEEV

36:6 Went to another land because of his brother *Yaakov* *Esau* moves away from *Yaakov* and the Land of Israel to a foreign land. Rabbi Zalman Sorotzkin explains that Esau is interested in "a land," meaning a physical territory. He does not want the spiritual and moral responsibilities that come with *Eretz Yisrael*, since he understands the unique spiritual sensitivity of the land, and wants to live without worry that the land may "vomit" him out (see Leviticus 18:28) The Sages comment that Esau deferred to his brother in recognition of *Yaakov*'s rightful acquisition of the birthright, thereby acknowledging his right to the Promised Land. With this fateful decision, Esau decided to release himself of the responsibilities inherent in ownership of the Land of Israel and relinquished them to *Yaakov*.

Bereishit/Genesis 36
Vayishlach

7 For their possessions were too many for them to dwell together, and the land where they sojourned could not support them because of their livestock.

8 So Esau settled in the hill country of Seir – Esau being Edom.

9 This, then, is the line of Esau, the ancestor of the Edomites, in the hill country of Seir.

10 These are the names of Esau's sons: Eliphaz, the son of Esau's wife Adah; Reuel, the son of Esau's wife Basemath.

11 The sons of Eliphaz were Teman, Omar, Zepho, Gatam, and Kenaz.

12 Timna was a concubine of Esau's son Eliphaz; she bore Amalek to Eliphaz. Those were the descendants of Esau's wife Adah.

13 And these were the sons of Reuel: Nahath, Zerah, Shammah, and Mizzah. Those were the descendants of Esau's wife Basemath.

14 And these were the sons of Esau's wife Oholibamah, daughter of Anah daughter of Zibeon: she bore to Esau Jeush, Jalam, and Korah.

15 These are the clans of the children of Esau. The descendants of Esau's first-born Eliphaz: the clans Teman, Omar, Zepho, Kenaz,

16 Korah, Gatam, and Amalek; these are the clans of Eliphaz in the land of Edom. Those are the descendants of Adah.

17 And these are the descendants of Esau's son Reuel: the clans Nahath, Zerah, Shammah, and Mizzah; these are the clans of Reuel in the land of Edom. Those are the descendants of Esau's wife Basemath.

18 And these are the descendants of Esau's wife Oholibamah: the clans Jeush, Jalam, and Korah; these are the clans of Esau's wife Oholibamah, the daughter of Anah.

19 Those were the sons of Esau – that is, Edom – and those are their clans.

20 These were the sons of Seir the Horite, who were settled in the land: Lotan, Shobal, Zibeon, Anah,

Bereishit/Genesis 36
Vayishlach

21 Dishon, Ezer, and Dishan. Those are the clans of the Horites, the descendants of Seir, in the land of Edom.

22 The sons of Lotan were Hori and Hemam; and Lotan's sister was Timna.

23 The sons of Shobal were these: Alvan, Manahath, Ebal, Shepho, and Onam.

24 The sons of Zibeon were these: Aiah and Anah – that was the Anah who discovered the hot springs in the wilderness while pasturing the asses of his father Zibeon.

25 The children of Anah were these: Dishon and Anah's daughter Oholibamah.

26 The sons of Dishon were these: Hemdan, Eshban, Ithran, and Cheran.

27 The sons of Ezer were these: Bilhan, Zaavan, and Akan.

28 And the sons of Dishan were these: Uz and Aran.

29 These are the clans of the Horites: the clans Lotan, Shobal, Zibeon, Anah,

30 Dishon, Ezer, and Dishan. Those are the clans of the Horites, clan by clan, in the land of Seir.

31 These are the kings who reigned in the land of Edom before any king reigned over the Israelites.

32 Bela son of Beor reigned in Edom, and the name of his city was Dinhabah.

33 When Bela died, Jobab son of Zerah, from Bozrah, succeeded him as king.

34 When Jobab died, Husham of the land of the Temanites succeeded him as king.

35 When Husham died, Hadad son of Bedad, who defeated the Midianites in the country of Moab, succeeded him as king; the name of his city was Avith.

36 When Hadad died, Samlah of Masrekah succeeded him as king.

37 When Samlah died, Saul of Rehoboth-on-the-river succeeded him as king.

38 When Saul died, Baal-hanan son of Achbor succeeded him as king.

Bereishit/Genesis 37
Vayeishev

בראשית לז
וישב

39 And when Baal-hanan son of Achbor died, Hadar succeeded him as king; the name of his city was Pau, and his wife's name was Mehetabel daughter of Matred daughter of Me-zahab.

לט וַיָּמָת בַּעַל חָנָן בֶּן־עַכְבּוֹר וַיִּמְלֹךְ תַּחְתָּיו הֲדַר וְשֵׁם עִירוֹ פָּעוּ וְשֵׁם אִשְׁתּוֹ מְהֵיטַבְאֵל בַּת־מַטְרֵד בַּת מֵי זָהָב:

40 These are the names of the clans of Esau, each with its families and locality, name by name: the clans Timna, Alvah, Jetheth,

מ וְאֵלֶּה שְׁמוֹת אַלּוּפֵי עֵשָׂו לְמִשְׁפְּחֹתָם לִמְקֹמֹתָם בִּשְׁמֹתָם אַלּוּף תִּמְנָע אַלּוּף עַלְוָה אַלּוּף יְתֵת:

41 Oholibamah, Elah, Pinon,

מא אַלּוּף אָהֳלִיבָמָה אַלּוּף אֵלָה אַלּוּף פִּינֹן:

42 Kenaz, Teman, Mibzar,

מב אַלּוּף קְנַז אַלּוּף תֵּימָן אַלּוּף מִבְצָר:

43 Magdiel, and Iram. Those are the clans of Edom – that is, of Esau, father of the Edomites – by their settlements in the land which they hold.

מג אַלּוּף מַגְדִּיאֵל אַלּוּף עִירָם אֵלֶּה אַלּוּפֵי אֱדוֹם לְמֹשְׁבֹתָם בְּאֶרֶץ אֲחֻזָּתָם הוּא עֵשָׂו אֲבִי אֱדוֹם:

37 1 Now *Yaakov* was settled in the land where his father had sojourned, the land of Canaan.

לז א וַיֵּשֶׁב יַעֲקֹב בְּאֶרֶץ מְגוּרֵי אָבִיו בְּאֶרֶץ כְּנָעַן:

2 This, then, is the line of *Yaakov*: At seventeen years of age, *Yosef* tended the flocks with his brothers, as a helper to the sons of his father's wives *Bilha* and *Zilpa*. And *Yosef* brought bad reports of them to their father.

ב אֵלֶּה תֹּלְדוֹת יַעֲקֹב יוֹסֵף בֶּן־שְׁבַע־עֶשְׂרֵה שָׁנָה הָיָה רֹעֶה אֶת־אֶחָיו בַּצֹּאן וְהוּא נַעַר אֶת־בְּנֵי בִלְהָה וְאֶת־בְּנֵי זִלְפָּה נְשֵׁי אָבִיו וַיָּבֵא יוֹסֵף אֶת־דִּבָּתָם רָעָה אֶל־אֲבִיהֶם:

AY-leh tol-DOT ya-a-KOV yo-SAYF ben sh'-va es-RAY sha-NAH ha-YAH ro-EH et e-KHAV ba-TZON v'-HU NA-ar et b'-NAY bil-HAH v'-et b'-NAY zil-PAH n'-SHAY a-VEEV va-ya-VAY yo-SAYF et di-ba-TAM ra-AH el a-vee-HEM

3 Now *Yisrael* loved *Yosef* best of all his sons, for he was the child of his old age; and he had made him an ornamented tunic.

ג וְיִשְׂרָאֵל אָהַב אֶת־יוֹסֵף מִכָּל־בָּנָיו כִּי־בֶן־זְקֻנִים הוּא לוֹ וְעָשָׂה לוֹ כְּתֹנֶת פַּסִּים:

4 And when his brothers saw that their father loved him more than any of his brothers, they hated him so that they could not speak a friendly word to him.

ד וַיִּרְאוּ אֶחָיו כִּי־אֹתוֹ אָהַב אֲבִיהֶם מִכָּל־אֶחָיו וַיִּשְׂנְאוּ אֹתוֹ וְלֹא יָכְלוּ דַּבְּרוֹ לְשָׁלֹם:

5 Once *Yosef* had a dream which he told to his brothers; and they hated him even more.

ה וַיַּחֲלֹם יוֹסֵף חֲלוֹם וַיַּגֵּד לְאֶחָיו וַיּוֹסִפוּ עוֹד שְׂנֹא אֹתוֹ:

6 He said to them, "Hear this dream which I have dreamed:

ו וַיֹּאמֶר אֲלֵיהֶם שִׁמְעוּ־נָא הַחֲלוֹם הַזֶּה אֲשֶׁר חָלָמְתִּי:

"Mikve Yisrael" Agricultural School, 1970

37:2 *Yosef* tended the flocks with his brothers It is no coincidence that so many biblical heroes are shepherds. The Sages point out that this simple profession is excellent spiritually, for two reasons. On one hand, the abundance of time for quiet reflection and meditation allows the shepherd to develop an intimate relationship with *Hashem*. On the other hand, a shepherd who excels in his work acquires a deep sensitivity to the needs of each and every sheep in his flock. What *Yosef* learns as a young shepherd enables him to become a paradigm of leadership for all future generations in the service of God and the service of man.

Bereishit/Genesis 37
Vayeishev

בראשית לז
וישב

7 There we were binding sheaves in the field, when suddenly my sheaf stood up and remained upright; then your sheaves gathered around and bowed low to my sheaf."

ז וְהִנֵּה אֲנַחְנוּ מְאַלְּמִים אֲלֻמִּים בְּתוֹךְ הַשָּׂדֶה וְהִנֵּה קָמָה אֲלֻמָּתִי וְגַם־נִצָּבָה וְהִנֵּה תְסֻבֶּינָה אֲלֻמֹּתֵיכֶם וַתִּשְׁתַּחֲוֶיןָ לַאֲלֻמָּתִי:

8 His brothers answered, "Do you mean to reign over us? Do you mean to rule over us?" And they hated him even more for his talk about his dreams.

ח וַיֹּאמְרוּ לוֹ אֶחָיו הֲמָלֹךְ תִּמְלֹךְ עָלֵינוּ אִם־מָשׁוֹל תִּמְשֹׁל בָּנוּ וַיּוֹסִפוּ עוֹד שְׂנֹא אֹתוֹ עַל־חֲלֹמֹתָיו וְעַל־דְּבָרָיו:

9 He dreamed another dream and told it to his brothers, saying, "Look, I have had another dream: And this time, the sun, the moon, and eleven stars were bowing down to me."

ט וַיַּחֲלֹם עוֹד חֲלוֹם אַחֵר וַיְסַפֵּר אֹתוֹ לְאֶחָיו וַיֹּאמֶר הִנֵּה חָלַמְתִּי חֲלוֹם עוֹד וְהִנֵּה הַשֶּׁמֶשׁ וְהַיָּרֵחַ וְאַחַד עָשָׂר כּוֹכָבִים מִשְׁתַּחֲוִים לִי:

10 And when he told it to his father and brothers, his father berated him. "What," he said to him, "is this dream you have dreamed? Are we to come, I and your mother and your brothers, and bow low to you to the ground?"

י וַיְסַפֵּר אֶל־אָבִיו וְאֶל־אֶחָיו וַיִּגְעַר־בּוֹ אָבִיו וַיֹּאמֶר לוֹ מָה הַחֲלוֹם הַזֶּה אֲשֶׁר חָלָמְתָּ הֲבוֹא נָבוֹא אֲנִי וְאִמְּךָ וְאַחֶיךָ לְהִשְׁתַּחֲוֹת לְךָ אָרְצָה:

11 So his brothers were wrought up at him, and his father kept the matter in mind.

יא וַיְקַנְאוּ־בוֹ אֶחָיו וְאָבִיו שָׁמַר אֶת־הַדָּבָר:

12 One time, when his brothers had gone to pasture their father's flock at Shechem,

יב וַיֵּלְכוּ אֶחָיו לִרְעוֹת אֶת־צֹאן אֲבִיהֶם בִּשְׁכֶם:

13 Yisrael said to Yosef, "Your brothers are pasturing at Shechem. Come, I will send you to them." He answered, "I am ready."

יג וַיֹּאמֶר יִשְׂרָאֵל אֶל־יוֹסֵף הֲלוֹא אַחֶיךָ רֹעִים בִּשְׁכֶם לְכָה וְאֶשְׁלָחֲךָ אֲלֵיהֶם וַיֹּאמֶר לוֹ הִנֵּנִי:

14 And he said to him, "Go and see how your brothers are and how the flocks are faring, and bring me back word." So he sent him from the valley of Chevron. When he reached Shechem,

יד וַיֹּאמֶר לוֹ לֶךְ־נָא רְאֵה אֶת־שְׁלוֹם אַחֶיךָ וְאֶת־שְׁלוֹם הַצֹּאן וַהֲשִׁבֵנִי דָּבָר וַיִּשְׁלָחֵהוּ מֵעֵמֶק חֶבְרוֹן וַיָּבֹא שְׁכֶמָה:

15 a man came upon him wandering in the fields. The man asked him, "What are you looking for?"

טו וַיִּמְצָאֵהוּ אִישׁ וְהִנֵּה תֹעֶה בַּשָּׂדֶה וַיִּשְׁאָלֵהוּ הָאִישׁ לֵאמֹר מַה־תְּבַקֵּשׁ:

16 He answered, "I am looking for my brothers. Could you tell me where they are pasturing?"

טז וַיֹּאמֶר אֶת־אַחַי אָנֹכִי מְבַקֵּשׁ הַגִּידָה־נָּא לִי אֵיפֹה הֵם רֹעִים:

17 The man said, "They have gone from here, for I heard them say: Let us go to Dothan." So Yosef followed his brothers and found them at Dothan.

יז וַיֹּאמֶר הָאִישׁ נָסְעוּ מִזֶּה כִּי שָׁמַעְתִּי אֹמְרִים נֵלְכָה דֹּתָיְנָה וַיֵּלֶךְ יוֹסֵף אַחַר אֶחָיו וַיִּמְצָאֵם בְּדֹתָן:

18 They saw him from afar, and before he came close to them they conspired to kill him.

יח וַיִּרְאוּ אֹתוֹ מֵרָחֹק וּבְטֶרֶם יִקְרַב אֲלֵיהֶם וַיִּתְנַכְּלוּ אֹתוֹ לַהֲמִיתוֹ:

19 They said to one another, "Here comes that dreamer!

יט וַיֹּאמְרוּ אִישׁ אֶל־אָחִיו הִנֵּה בַּעַל הַחֲלֹמוֹת הַלָּזֶה בָּא:

20 Come now, let us kill him and throw him into one of the pits; and we can say, 'A savage beast devoured him.' We shall see what comes of his dreams!"

כ וְעַתָּה לְכוּ וְנַהַרְגֵהוּ וְנַשְׁלִכֵהוּ בְּאַחַד הַבֹּרוֹת וְאָמַרְנוּ חַיָּה רָעָה אֲכָלָתְהוּ וְנִרְאֶה מַה־יִּהְיוּ חֲלֹמֹתָיו:

Bereishit/Genesis 37
Vayeishev

בראשית לז
וישב

21 But when *Reuven* heard it, he tried to save him from them. He said, "Let us not take his life."

וַיִּשְׁמַע רְאוּבֵן וַיַּצִּלֵהוּ מִיָּדָם וַיֹּאמֶר לֹא נַכֶּנּוּ נָפֶשׁ׃

22 And *Reuven* went on, "Shed no blood! Cast him into that pit out in the wilderness, but do not touch him yourselves" – intending to save him from them and restore him to his father.

וַיֹּאמֶר אֲלֵהֶם רְאוּבֵן אַל־תִּשְׁפְּכוּ־דָם הַשְׁלִיכוּ אֹתוֹ אֶל־הַבּוֹר הַזֶּה אֲשֶׁר בַּמִּדְבָּר וְיָד אַל־תִּשְׁלְחוּ־בוֹ לְמַעַן הַצִּיל אֹתוֹ מִיָּדָם לַהֲשִׁיבוֹ אֶל־אָבִיו׃

va-YO-mer a-lay-HEM r'-u-VAYN al tish-p'-khu DAM hash-LEE-khu o-TO el ha-BOR ha-ZEH a-SHER ba-mid-BAR v'-YAD al tish-l'-khu VO l'-MA-an ha-TZEEL o-TO mi-ya-DAM la-ha-shee-VO el a-VEEV

23 When *Yosef* came up to his brothers, they stripped *Yosef* of his tunic, the ornamented tunic that he was wearing,

וַיְהִי כַּאֲשֶׁר־בָּא יוֹסֵף אֶל־אֶחָיו וַיַּפְשִׁיטוּ אֶת־יוֹסֵף אֶת־כֻּתָּנְתּוֹ אֶת־כְּתֹנֶת הַפַּסִּים אֲשֶׁר עָלָיו׃

24 and took him and cast him into the pit. The pit was empty; there was no water in it.

וַיִּקָּחֻהוּ וַיַּשְׁלִכוּ אֹתוֹ הַבֹּרָה וְהַבּוֹר רֵק אֵין בּוֹ מָיִם׃

25 Then they sat down to a meal. Looking up, they saw a caravan of Ishmaelites coming from *Gilad*, their camels bearing gum, balm, and ladanum to be taken to Egypt.

וַיֵּשְׁבוּ לֶאֱכָל־לֶחֶם וַיִּשְׂאוּ עֵינֵיהֶם וַיִּרְאוּ וְהִנֵּה אֹרְחַת יִשְׁמְעֵאלִים בָּאָה מִגִּלְעָד וּגְמַלֵּיהֶם נֹשְׂאִים נְכֹאת וּצְרִי וָלֹט הוֹלְכִים לְהוֹרִיד מִצְרָיְמָה׃

26 Then *Yehuda* said to his brothers, "What do we gain by killing our brother and covering up his blood?

וַיֹּאמֶר יְהוּדָה אֶל־אֶחָיו מַה־בֶּצַע כִּי נַהֲרֹג אֶת־אָחִינוּ וְכִסִּינוּ אֶת־דָּמוֹ׃

27 Come, let us sell him to the Ishmaelites, but let us not do away with him ourselves. After all, he is our brother, our own flesh." His brothers agreed.

לְכוּ וְנִמְכְּרֶנּוּ לַיִּשְׁמְעֵאלִים וְיָדֵנוּ אַל־תְּהִי־בוֹ כִּי־אָחִינוּ בְשָׂרֵנוּ הוּא וַיִּשְׁמְעוּ אֶחָיו׃

28 When Midianite traders passed by, they pulled *Yosef* up out of the pit. They sold *Yosef* for twenty pieces of silver to the Ishmaelites, who brought *Yosef* to Egypt.

וַיַּעַבְרוּ אֲנָשִׁים מִדְיָנִים סֹחֲרִים וַיִּמְשְׁכוּ וַיַּעֲלוּ אֶת־יוֹסֵף מִן־הַבּוֹר וַיִּמְכְּרוּ אֶת־יוֹסֵף לַיִּשְׁמְעֵאלִים בְּעֶשְׂרִים כָּסֶף וַיָּבִיאוּ אֶת־יוֹסֵף מִצְרָיְמָה׃

29 When *Reuven* returned to the pit and saw that *Yosef* was not in the pit, he rent his clothes.

וַיָּשָׁב רְאוּבֵן אֶל־הַבּוֹר וְהִנֵּה אֵין־יוֹסֵף בַּבּוֹר וַיִּקְרַע אֶת־בְּגָדָיו׃

30 Returning to his brothers, he said, "The boy is gone! Now, what am I to do?"

וַיָּשָׁב אֶל־אֶחָיו וַיֹּאמַר הַיֶּלֶד אֵינֶנּוּ וַאֲנִי אָנָה אֲנִי־בָא׃

31 Then they took *Yosef*'s tunic, slaughtered a kid, and dipped the tunic in the blood.

וַיִּקְחוּ אֶת־כְּתֹנֶת יוֹסֵף וַיִּשְׁחֲטוּ שְׂעִיר עִזִּים וַיִּטְבְּלוּ אֶת־הַכֻּתֹּנֶת בַּדָּם׃

37:22 Cast him into that pit *Reuven* suggests throwing *Yosef* into a pit filled with dangerous snakes and scorpions, whereas *Yehuda* recommends selling *Yosef* to merchants. It would seem that *Yehuda*'s plan was likelier to save *Yosef*'s life and ensure a better outcome. Nevertheless, Rabbi Chaim of Volozhin, the nineteenth century author of *Nefesh Hachaim* and founder of the Volozhin Yeshiva, explains that one is safer in *Eretz Yisrael*, despite apparent imminent dangers, than in a foreign land with the illusion of physical security.

Bereishit/Genesis 38
Vayeishev

בראשית לח
וישב

32 They had the ornamented tunic taken to their father, and they said, "We found this. Please examine it; is it your son's tunic or not?"

לב וַיְשַׁלְּחוּ אֶת־כְּתֹנֶת הַפַּסִּים וַיָּבִיאוּ אֶל־אֲבִיהֶם וַיֹּאמְרוּ זֹאת מָצָאנוּ הַכֶּר־נָא הַכְּתֹנֶת בִּנְךָ הִוא אִם־לֹא:

33 He recognized it, and said, "My son's tunic! A savage beast devoured him! *Yosef* was torn by a beast!"

לג וַיַּכִּירָהּ וַיֹּאמֶר כְּתֹנֶת בְּנִי חַיָּה רָעָה אֲכָלָתְהוּ טָרֹף טֹרַף יוֹסֵף:

34 *Yaakov* rent his clothes, put sackcloth on his loins, and observed mourning for his son many days.

לד וַיִּקְרַע יַעֲקֹב שִׂמְלֹתָיו וַיָּשֶׂם שַׂק בְּמָתְנָיו וַיִּתְאַבֵּל עַל־בְּנוֹ יָמִים רַבִּים:

35 All his sons and daughters sought to comfort him; but he refused to be comforted, saying, "No, I will go down mourning to my son in Sheol." Thus his father bewailed him.

לה וַיָּקֻמוּ כָל־בָּנָיו וְכָל־בְּנֹתָיו לְנַחֲמוֹ וַיְמָאֵן לְהִתְנַחֵם וַיֹּאמֶר כִּי־אֵרֵד אֶל־בְּנִי אָבֵל שְׁאֹלָה וַיֵּבְךְּ אֹתוֹ אָבִיו:

36 The Midianites, meanwhile, sold him in Egypt to Potiphar, a courtier of Pharaoh and his chief steward.

לו וְהַמְּדָנִים מָכְרוּ אֹתוֹ אֶל־מִצְרָיִם לְפוֹטִיפַר סְרִיס פַּרְעֹה שַׂר הַטַּבָּחִים:

38 1 About that time *Yehuda* left his brothers and camped near a certain Adullamite whose name was Hirah.

לח א וַיְהִי בָּעֵת הַהִוא וַיֵּרֶד יְהוּדָה מֵאֵת אֶחָיו וַיֵּט עַד־אִישׁ עֲדֻלָּמִי וּשְׁמוֹ חִירָה:

vai-HEE ba-AYT ha-HEE va-YAY-red y'-hu-DAH may-AYT e-KHAV va-YAYT ad EESH a-du-la-MEE ush-MO khee-RAH

2 There *Yehuda* saw the daughter of a certain Canaanite whose name was Shua, and he married her and cohabited with her.

ב וַיַּרְא־שָׁם יְהוּדָה בַּת־אִישׁ כְּנַעֲנִי וּשְׁמוֹ שׁוּעַ וַיִּקָּחֶהָ וַיָּבֹא אֵלֶיהָ:

3 She conceived and bore a son, and he named him *Er*.

ג וַתַּהַר וַתֵּלֶד בֵּן וַיִּקְרָא אֶת־שְׁמוֹ עֵר:

4 She conceived again and bore a son, and named him *Onan*.

ד וַתַּהַר עוֹד וַתֵּלֶד בֵּן וַתִּקְרָא אֶת־שְׁמוֹ אוֹנָן:

5 Once again she bore a son, and named him *Sheila*; he was at Chezib when she bore him.

ה וַתֹּסֶף עוֹד וַתֵּלֶד בֵּן וַתִּקְרָא אֶת־שְׁמוֹ שֵׁלָה וְהָיָה בִכְזִיב בְּלִדְתָּהּ אֹתוֹ:

6 *Yehuda* got a wife for *Er* his first-born; her name was *Tamar*.

ו וַיִּקַּח יְהוּדָה אִשָּׁה לְעֵר בְּכוֹרוֹ וּשְׁמָהּ תָּמָר:

38:1 *Yehuda* left his brothers Though the story of *Yehuda* and his daughter-in-law *Tamar* seems to interrupt the narrative of the *Yosef* stories, Jewish tradition teaches that its placement here is deliberate. In beautiful shorthand, the Midrash explains the connection: "While the tribes were busy with the sale of *Yosef*, *Reuven*, *Yosef* and *Yaakov* were busy with their sackcloth and mourning; *Yehuda* was busy taking a wife; and God was busy creating the light of the *Mashiach*." Like a puppet master operating behind the scenes and hidden from view, *Hashem* is pulling the strings and directing events without the knowledge or understanding of the participants themselves. From the union between *Yehuda* and *Tamar*, the Davidic dynasty and ultimately the *Mashiach* himself would emerge. Precisely when life seems to be completely unraveling, *Hashem* is directing events with His infinite wisdom, and is carefully nurturing our redemption.

Bereishit/Genesis 38
Vayeishev

7 But *Er*, *Yehuda*'s first-born, was displeasing to *Hashem*, and *Hashem* took his life.

וַיְהִ֗י עֵ֚ר בְּכ֣וֹר יְהוּדָ֔ה רַ֖ע בְּעֵינֵ֣י יְהוָ֑ה וַיְמִתֵ֖הוּ יְהוָֽה׃

8 Then *Yehuda* said to *Onan*, "Join with your brother's wife and do your duty by her as a brother-in-law, and provide offspring for your brother."

וַיֹּ֤אמֶר יְהוּדָה֙ לְאוֹנָ֔ן בֹּ֛א אֶל־אֵ֥שֶׁת אָחִ֖יךָ וְיַבֵּ֣ם אֹתָ֑הּ וְהָקֵ֥ם זֶ֖רַע לְאָחִֽיךָ׃

9 But *Onan*, knowing that the seed would not count as his, let it go to waste whenever he joined with his brother's wife, so as not to provide offspring for his brother.

וַיֵּ֣דַע אוֹנָ֔ן כִּ֛י לֹּ֥א ל֖וֹ יִהְיֶ֣ה הַזָּ֑רַע וְהָיָ֞ה אִם־בָּ֨א אֶל־אֵ֤שֶׁת אָחִיו֙ וְשִׁחֵ֣ת אַ֔רְצָה לְבִלְתִּ֥י נְתָן־זֶ֖רַע לְאָחִֽיו׃

10 What he did was displeasing to *Hashem*, and He took his life also.

וַיֵּ֛רַע בְּעֵינֵ֥י יְהוָ֖ה אֲשֶׁ֣ר עָשָׂ֑ה וַיָּ֖מֶת גַּם־אֹתֽוֹ׃

11 Then *Yehuda* said to his daughter-in-law *Tamar*, "Stay as a widow in your father's house until my son *Sheila* grows up" – for he thought, "He too might die like his brothers." So *Tamar* went to live in her father's house.

וַיֹּ֣אמֶר יְהוּדָה֩ לְתָמָ֨ר כַּלָּת֜וֹ שְׁבִ֧י אַלְמָנָ֣ה בֵית־אָבִ֗יךְ עַד־יִגְדַּל֙ שֵׁלָ֣ה בְנִ֔י כִּ֣י אָמַ֔ר פֶּן־יָמ֥וּת גַּם־ה֖וּא כְּאֶחָ֑יו וַתֵּ֣לֶךְ תָּמָ֔ר וַתֵּ֖שֶׁב בֵּ֥ית אָבִֽיהָ׃

12 A long time afterward, Shua's daughter, the wife of *Yehuda*, died. When his period of mourning was over, *Yehuda* went up to Timnah to his sheepshearers, together with his friend Hirah the Adullamite.

וַיִּרְבּוּ֙ הַיָּמִ֔ים וַתָּ֖מָת בַּת־שׁ֣וּעַ אֵֽשֶׁת־יְהוּדָ֑ה וַיִּנָּ֣חֶם יְהוּדָ֗ה וַיַּ֜עַל עַל־גֹּֽזֲזֵ֤י צֹאנוֹ֙ ה֗וּא וְחִירָ֛ה רֵעֵ֥הוּ הָעֲדֻלָּמִ֖י תִּמְנָֽתָה׃

13 And *Tamar* was told, "Your father-in-law is coming up to Timnah for the sheepshearing."

וַיֻּגַּ֥ד לְתָמָ֖ר לֵאמֹ֑ר הִנֵּ֥ה חָמִ֛יךְ עֹלֶ֥ה תִמְנָ֖תָה לָגֹ֥ז צֹאנֽוֹ׃

14 So she took off her widow's garb, covered her face with a veil, and, wrapping herself up, sat down at the entrance to Enaim, which is on the road to Timnah; for she saw that *Sheila* was grown up, yet she had not been given to him as wife.

וַתָּסַר֩ בִּגְדֵ֨י אַלְמְנוּתָ֜הּ מֵֽעָלֶ֗יהָ וַתְּכַ֤ס בַּצָּעִיף֙ וַתִּתְעַלָּ֔ף וַתֵּ֨שֶׁב֙ בְּפֶ֣תַח עֵינַ֔יִם אֲשֶׁ֖ר עַל־דֶּ֣רֶךְ תִּמְנָ֑תָה כִּ֤י רָאֲתָה֙ כִּֽי־גָדַ֣ל שֵׁלָ֔ה וְהִ֕וא לֹֽא־נִתְּנָ֥ה ל֖וֹ לְאִשָּֽׁה׃

15 When *Yehuda* saw her, he took her for a harlot; for she had covered her face.

וַיִּרְאֶ֣הָ יְהוּדָ֔ה וַֽיַּחְשְׁבֶ֖הָ לְזוֹנָ֑ה כִּ֥י כִסְּתָ֖ה פָּנֶֽיהָ׃

16 So he turned aside to her by the road and said, "Here, let me sleep with you" – for he did not know that she was his daughter-in-law. "What," she asked, "will you pay for sleeping with me?"

וַיֵּ֨ט אֵלֶ֜יהָ אֶל־הַדֶּ֗רֶךְ וַיֹּ֨אמֶר֙ הָֽבָה־נָּא֙ אָב֣וֹא אֵלַ֔יִךְ כִּ֚י לֹ֣א יָדַ֔ע כִּ֥י כַלָּת֖וֹ הִ֑וא וַתֹּ֨אמֶר֙ מַה־תִּתֶּן־לִ֔י כִּ֥י תָב֖וֹא אֵלָֽי׃

17 He replied, "I will send a kid from my flock." But she said, "You must leave a pledge until you have sent it."

וַיֹּ֕אמֶר אָנֹכִ֛י אֲשַׁלַּ֥ח גְּדִֽי־עִזִּ֖ים מִן־הַצֹּ֑אן וַתֹּ֕אמֶר אִם־תִּתֵּ֥ן עֵרָב֖וֹן עַ֥ד שָׁלְחֶֽךָ׃

18 And he said, "What pledge shall I give you?" She replied, "Your seal and cord, and the staff which you carry." So he gave them to her and slept with her, and she conceived by him.

וַיֹּ֗אמֶר מָ֣ה הָעֵֽרָבוֹן֮ אֲשֶׁ֣ר אֶתֶּן־לָךְ֒ וַתֹּ֗אמֶר חֹתָֽמְךָ֙ וּפְתִילֶ֔ךָ וּמַטְּךָ֖ אֲשֶׁ֣ר בְּיָדֶ֑ךָ וַיִּתֶּן־לָ֛הּ וַיָּבֹ֥א אֵלֶ֖יהָ וַתַּ֥הַר לֽוֹ׃

19 Then she went on her way. She took off her veil and again put on her widow's garb.

וַתָּ֣קָם וַתֵּ֔לֶךְ וַתָּ֥סַר צְעִיפָ֖הּ מֵעָלֶ֑יהָ וַתִּלְבַּ֖שׁ בִּגְדֵ֥י אַלְמְנוּתָֽהּ׃

Bereishit/Genesis 39
Vayeishev

בראשית לט
וישב

20 *Yehuda* sent the kid by his friend the Adullamite, to redeem the pledge from the woman; but he could not find her.

וַיִּשְׁלַח יְהוּדָה אֶת־גְּדִי הָעִזִּים בְּיַד רֵעֵהוּ הָעֲדֻלָּמִי לָקַחַת הָעֵרָבוֹן מִיַּד הָאִשָּׁה וְלֹא מְצָאָהּ׃

21 He inquired of the people of that town, "Where is the cult prostitute, the one at Enaim, by the road?" But they said, "There has been no prostitute here."

וַיִּשְׁאַל אֶת־אַנְשֵׁי מְקֹמָהּ לֵאמֹר אַיֵּה הַקְּדֵשָׁה הִוא בָעֵינַיִם עַל־הַדָּרֶךְ וַיֹּאמְרוּ לֹא־הָיְתָה בָזֶה קְדֵשָׁה׃

22 So he returned to *Yehuda* and said, "I could not find her; moreover, the townspeople said: There has been no prostitute here."

וַיָּשָׁב אֶל־יְהוּדָה וַיֹּאמֶר לֹא מְצָאתִיהָ וְגַם אַנְשֵׁי הַמָּקוֹם אָמְרוּ לֹא־הָיְתָה בָזֶה קְדֵשָׁה׃

23 *Yehuda* said, "Let her keep them, lest we become a laughingstock. I did send her this kid, but you did not find her."

וַיֹּאמֶר יְהוּדָה תִּקַּח־לָהּ פֶּן נִהְיֶה לָבוּז הִנֵּה שָׁלַחְתִּי הַגְּדִי הַזֶּה וְאַתָּה לֹא מְצָאתָהּ׃

24 About three months later, *Yehuda* was told, "Your daughter-in-law *Tamar* has played the harlot; in fact, she is with child by harlotry." "Bring her out," said *Yehuda*, "and let her be burned."

וַיְהִי כְּמִשְׁלֹשׁ חֳדָשִׁים וַיֻּגַּד לִיהוּדָה לֵאמֹר זָנְתָה תָּמָר כַּלָּתֶךָ וְגַם הִנֵּה הָרָה לִזְנוּנִים וַיֹּאמֶר יְהוּדָה הוֹצִיאוּהָ וְתִשָּׂרֵף׃

25 As she was being brought out, she sent this message to her father-in-law, "I am with child by the man to whom these belong." And she added, "Examine these: whose seal and cord and staff are these?"

הִוא מוּצֵאת וְהִיא שָׁלְחָה אֶל־חָמִיהָ לֵאמֹר לְאִישׁ אֲשֶׁר־אֵלֶּה לּוֹ אָנֹכִי הָרָה וַתֹּאמֶר הַכֶּר־נָא לְמִי הַחֹתֶמֶת וְהַפְּתִילִים וְהַמַּטֶּה הָאֵלֶּה׃

26 *Yehuda* recognized them, and said, "She is more in the right than I, inasmuch as I did not give her to my son *Sheila*." And he was not intimate with her again.

וַיַּכֵּר יְהוּדָה וַיֹּאמֶר צָדְקָה מִמֶּנִּי כִּי־עַל־כֵּן לֹא־נְתַתִּיהָ לְשֵׁלָה בְנִי וְלֹא־יָסַף עוֹד לְדַעְתָּהּ׃

27 When the time came for her to give birth, there were twins in her womb!

וַיְהִי בְּעֵת לִדְתָּהּ וְהִנֵּה תְאוֹמִים בְּבִטְנָהּ׃

28 While she was in labor, one of them put out his hand, and the midwife tied a crimson thread on that hand, to signify: This one came out first.

וַיְהִי בְלִדְתָּהּ וַיִּתֶּן־יָד וַתִּקַּח הַמְיַלֶּדֶת וַתִּקְשֹׁר עַל־יָדוֹ שָׁנִי לֵאמֹר זֶה יָצָא רִאשֹׁנָה׃

29 But just then he drew back his hand, and out came his brother; and she said, "What a breach you have made for yourself!" So he was named *Peretz*.

וַיְהִי כְּמֵשִׁיב יָדוֹ וְהִנֵּה יָצָא אָחִיו וַתֹּאמֶר מַה־פָּרַצְתָּ עָלֶיךָ פָּרֶץ וַיִּקְרָא שְׁמוֹ פָּרֶץ׃

30 Afterward his brother came out, on whose hand was the crimson thread; he was named *Zerach*.

וְאַחַר יָצָא אָחִיו אֲשֶׁר עַל־יָדוֹ הַשָּׁנִי וַיִּקְרָא שְׁמוֹ זָרַח׃

39 1 When *Yosef* was taken down to Egypt, a certain Egyptian, Potiphar, a courtier of Pharaoh and his chief steward, bought him from the Ishmaelites who had brought him there.

לט וְיוֹסֵף הוּרַד מִצְרָיְמָה וַיִּקְנֵהוּ פּוֹטִיפַר סְרִיס פַּרְעֹה שַׂר הַטַּבָּחִים אִישׁ מִצְרִי מִיַּד הַיִּשְׁמְעֵאלִים אֲשֶׁר הוֹרִדֻהוּ שָׁמָּה׃

Bereishit/Genesis 39
Vayeishev

בראשית לט
וישב

v'-yo-SAYF hu-RAD mitz-RA-y'-mah va-yik-NAY-hu po-tee-FAR s'-REES par-OH SAR ha-ta-ba-KHEEM EESH mitz-REE mi-YAD ha-yish-m'-ay-LEEM a-SHER ho-ri-DU-hu SHA-mah

2 *Hashem* was with *Yosef*, and he was a successful man; and he stayed in the house of his Egyptian master.

ב וַיְהִי יְהֹוָה אֶת־יוֹסֵף וַיְהִי אִישׁ מַצְלִיחַ וַיְהִי בְּבֵית אֲדֹנָיו הַמִּצְרִי׃

3 And when his master saw that *Hashem* was with him and that *Hashem* lent success to everything he undertook,

ג וַיַּרְא אֲדֹנָיו כִּי יְהֹוָה אִתּוֹ וְכֹל אֲשֶׁר־הוּא עֹשֶׂה יְהֹוָה מַצְלִיחַ בְּיָדוֹ׃

4 he took a liking to *Yosef*. He made him his personal attendant and put him in charge of his household, placing in his hands all that he owned.

ד וַיִּמְצָא יוֹסֵף חֵן בְּעֵינָיו וַיְשָׁרֶת אֹתוֹ וַיַּפְקִדֵהוּ עַל־בֵּיתוֹ וְכָל־יֶשׁ־לוֹ נָתַן בְּיָדוֹ׃

5 And from the time that the Egyptian put him in charge of his household and of all that he owned, *Hashem* blessed his house for *Yosef*'s sake, so that the blessing of *Hashem* was upon everything that he owned, in the house and outside.

ה וַיְהִי מֵאָז הִפְקִיד אֹתוֹ בְּבֵיתוֹ וְעַל כָּל־אֲשֶׁר יֶשׁ־לוֹ וַיְבָרֶךְ יְהֹוָה אֶת־בֵּית הַמִּצְרִי בִּגְלַל יוֹסֵף וַיְהִי בִּרְכַּת יְהֹוָה בְּכָל־אֲשֶׁר יֶשׁ־לוֹ בַּבַּיִת וּבַשָּׂדֶה׃

6 He left all that he had in *Yosef*'s hands and, with him there, he paid attention to nothing save the food that he ate. Now *Yosef* was well built and handsome.

ו וַיַּעֲזֹב כָּל־אֲשֶׁר־לוֹ בְּיַד־יוֹסֵף וְלֹא־יָדַע אִתּוֹ מְאוּמָה כִּי אִם־הַלֶּחֶם אֲשֶׁר־הוּא אוֹכֵל וַיְהִי יוֹסֵף יְפֵה־תֹאַר וִיפֵה מַרְאֶה׃

7 After a time, his master's wife cast her eyes upon *Yosef* and said, "Lie with me."

ז וַיְהִי אַחַר הַדְּבָרִים הָאֵלֶּה וַתִּשָּׂא אֵשֶׁת־אֲדֹנָיו אֶת־עֵינֶיהָ אֶל־יוֹסֵף וַתֹּאמֶר שִׁכְבָה עִמִּי׃

8 But he refused. He said to his master's wife, "Look, with me here, my master gives no thought to anything in this house, and all that he owns he has placed in my hands.

ח וַיְמָאֵן וַיֹּאמֶר אֶל־אֵשֶׁת אֲדֹנָיו הֵן אֲדֹנִי לֹא־יָדַע אִתִּי מַה־בַּבָּיִת וְכֹל אֲשֶׁר־יֶשׁ־לוֹ נָתַן בְּיָדִי׃

9 He wields no more authority in this house than I, and he has withheld nothing from me except yourself, since you are his wife. How then could I do this most wicked thing, and sin before *Hashem*?"

ט אֵינֶנּוּ גָדוֹל בַּבַּיִת הַזֶּה מִמֶּנִּי וְלֹא־חָשַׂךְ מִמֶּנִּי מְאוּמָה כִּי אִם־אוֹתָךְ בַּאֲשֶׁר אַתְּ־אִשְׁתּוֹ וְאֵיךְ אֶעֱשֶׂה הָרָעָה הַגְּדֹלָה הַזֹּאת וְחָטָאתִי לֵאלֹהִים׃

39:1 A certain Egyptian The verse here labels Potiphar *ish mitzree* (איש מצרי), 'an Egyptian,' in contrast to *Yosef*, who is called *Ha'Ivri* (העברי), 'the Hebrew' (verse 14). Since we already know the nationalities of these individuals, why are the labels necessary? The Egyptians were known for their arrogance and condescension towards the nomadic tribes. Despite their prejudice, *Yosef* will rise in rank among them. He will succeed at every task presented to him, and subsequently find favor in the eyes of Potiphar, the Egyptian royal official. Only Divine Providence could bring about the success of a mere "Hebrew," as the next verse says *"Hashem* was with *Yosef*, and he was a successful man." *Yosef* demonstrates that when a person puts himself in the hands of God, he can succeed beyond expectation.

Bereishit/Genesis 39
Vayeishev

בראשית לט
וישב

10 And much as she coaxed *Yosef* day after day, he did not yield to her request to lie beside her, to be with her.

י וַיְהִי כְּדַבְּרָהּ אֶל־יוֹסֵף יוֹם יוֹם וְלֹא־שָׁמַע אֵלֶיהָ לִשְׁכַּב אֶצְלָהּ לִהְיוֹת עִמָּהּ׃

11 One such day, he came into the house to do his work. None of the household being there inside,

יא וַיְהִי כְּהַיּוֹם הַזֶּה וַיָּבֹא הַבַּיְתָה לַעֲשׂוֹת מְלַאכְתּוֹ וְאֵין אִישׁ מֵאַנְשֵׁי הַבַּיִת שָׁם בַּבָּיִת׃

12 she caught hold of him by his garment and said, "Lie with me!" But he left his garment in her hand and got away and fled outside.

יב וַתִּתְפְּשֵׂהוּ בְּבִגְדוֹ לֵאמֹר שִׁכְבָה עִמִּי וַיַּעֲזֹב בִּגְדוֹ בְּיָדָהּ וַיָּנָס וַיֵּצֵא הַחוּצָה׃

13 When she saw that he had left it in her hand and had fled outside,

יג וַיְהִי כִּרְאוֹתָהּ כִּי־עָזַב בִּגְדוֹ בְּיָדָהּ וַיָּנָס הַחוּצָה׃

14 she called out to her servants and said to them, "Look, he had to bring us a Hebrew to dally with us! This one came to lie with me; but I screamed loud.

יד וַתִּקְרָא לְאַנְשֵׁי בֵיתָהּ וַתֹּאמֶר לָהֶם לֵאמֹר רְאוּ הֵבִיא לָנוּ אִישׁ עִבְרִי לְצַחֶק בָּנוּ בָּא אֵלַי לִשְׁכַּב עִמִּי וָאֶקְרָא בְּקוֹל גָּדוֹל׃

15 And when he heard me screaming at the top of my voice, he left his garment with me and got away and fled outside."

טו וַיְהִי כְשָׁמְעוֹ כִּי־הֲרִימֹתִי קוֹלִי וָאֶקְרָא וַיַּעֲזֹב בִּגְדוֹ אֶצְלִי וַיָּנָס וַיֵּצֵא הַחוּצָה׃

16 She kept his garment beside her, until his master came home.

טז וַתַּנַּח בִּגְדוֹ אֶצְלָהּ עַד־בּוֹא אֲדֹנָיו אֶל־בֵּיתוֹ׃

17 Then she told him the same story, saying, "The Hebrew slave whom you brought into our house came to me to dally with me;

יז וַתְּדַבֵּר אֵלָיו כַּדְּבָרִים הָאֵלֶּה לֵאמֹר בָּא־אֵלַי הָעֶבֶד הָעִבְרִי אֲשֶׁר־הֵבֵאתָ לָּנוּ לְצַחֶק בִּי׃

18 but when I screamed at the top of my voice, he left his garment with me and fled outside."

יח וַיְהִי כַּהֲרִימִי קוֹלִי וָאֶקְרָא וַיַּעֲזֹב בִּגְדוֹ אֶצְלִי וַיָּנָס הַחוּצָה׃

19 When his master heard the story that his wife told him, namely, "Thus and so your slave did to me," he was furious.

יט וַיְהִי כִשְׁמֹעַ אֲדֹנָיו אֶת־דִּבְרֵי אִשְׁתּוֹ אֲשֶׁר דִּבְּרָה אֵלָיו לֵאמֹר כַּדְּבָרִים הָאֵלֶּה עָשָׂה לִי עַבְדֶּךָ וַיִּחַר אַפּוֹ׃

20 So *Yosef*'s master had him put in prison, where the king's prisoners were confined. But even while he was there in prison,

כ וַיִּקַּח אֲדֹנֵי יוֹסֵף אֹתוֹ וַיִּתְּנֵהוּ אֶל־בֵּית הַסֹּהַר מְקוֹם אֲשֶׁר־אסורי [אֲסִירֵי] הַמֶּלֶךְ אֲסוּרִים וַיְהִי־שָׁם בְּבֵית הַסֹּהַר׃

21 *Hashem* was with *Yosef*: He extended kindness to him and disposed the chief jailer favorably toward him.

כא וַיְהִי יְהֹוָה אֶת־יוֹסֵף וַיֵּט אֵלָיו חָסֶד וַיִּתֵּן חִנּוֹ בְּעֵינֵי שַׂר בֵּית־הַסֹּהַר׃

22 The chief jailer put in *Yosef*'s charge all the prisoners who were in that prison, and he was the one to carry out everything that was done there.

כב וַיִּתֵּן שַׂר בֵּית־הַסֹּהַר בְּיַד־יוֹסֵף אֵת כָּל־הָאֲסִירִם אֲשֶׁר בְּבֵית הַסֹּהַר וְאֵת כָּל־אֲשֶׁר עֹשִׂים שָׁם הוּא הָיָה עֹשֶׂה׃

23 The chief jailer did not supervise anything that was in *Yosef*'s charge, because *Hashem* was with him, and whatever he did *Hashem* made successful.

כג אֵין שַׂר בֵּית־הַסֹּהַר רֹאֶה אֶת־כָּל־מְאוּמָה בְּיָדוֹ בַּאֲשֶׁר יְהֹוָה אִתּוֹ וַאֲשֶׁר־הוּא עֹשֶׂה יְהֹוָה מַצְלִיחַ׃

Bereishit/Genesis 40
Vayeishev

בראשית מ
וישב

מ א וַיְהִ֗י אַחַר֙ הַדְּבָרִ֣ים הָאֵ֔לֶּה חָטְא֛וּ מַשְׁקֵ֥ה מֶֽלֶךְ־מִצְרַ֖יִם וְהָאֹפֶ֑ה לַאֲדֹנֵיהֶ֖ם לְמֶ֥לֶךְ מִצְרָֽיִם׃

ב וַיִּקְצֹ֣ף פַּרְעֹ֔ה עַ֖ל שְׁנֵ֣י סָרִיסָ֑יו עַ֚ל שַׂ֣ר הַמַּשְׁקִ֔ים וְעַ֖ל שַׂ֥ר הָאוֹפִֽים׃

ג וַיִּתֵּ֨ן אֹתָ֜ם בְּמִשְׁמַ֗ר בֵּ֛ית שַׂ֥ר הַטַּבָּחִ֖ים אֶל־בֵּ֣ית הַסֹּ֑הַר מְק֕וֹם אֲשֶׁ֥ר יוֹסֵ֖ף אָס֥וּר שָֽׁם׃

ד וַ֠יִּפְקֹ֠ד שַׂ֣ר הַטַּבָּחִ֧ים אֶת־יוֹסֵ֛ף אִתָּ֖ם וַיְשָׁ֣רֶת אֹתָ֑ם וַיִּהְי֥וּ יָמִ֖ים בְּמִשְׁמָֽר׃

ה וַיַּֽחַלְמוּ֩ חֲל֨וֹם שְׁנֵיהֶ֜ם אִ֤ישׁ חֲלֹמוֹ֙ בְּלַ֣יְלָה אֶחָ֔ד אִ֖ישׁ כְּפִתְר֣וֹן חֲלֹמ֑וֹ הַמַּשְׁקֶ֣ה וְהָאֹפֶ֗ה אֲשֶׁר֙ לְמֶ֣לֶךְ מִצְרַ֔יִם אֲשֶׁ֥ר אֲסוּרִ֖ים בְּבֵ֥ית הַסֹּֽהַר׃

ו וַיָּבֹ֧א אֲלֵיהֶ֛ם יוֹסֵ֖ף בַּבֹּ֑קֶר וַיַּ֣רְא אֹתָ֔ם וְהִנָּ֖ם זֹעֲפִֽים׃

ז וַיִּשְׁאַ֞ל אֶת־סְרִיסֵ֣י פַרְעֹ֗ה אֲשֶׁ֨ר אִתּ֧וֹ בְמִשְׁמַ֛ר בֵּ֥ית אֲדֹנָ֖יו לֵאמֹ֑ר מַדּ֛וּעַ פְּנֵיכֶ֥ם רָעִ֖ים הַיּֽוֹם׃

ח וַיֹּאמְר֣וּ אֵלָ֔יו חֲל֣וֹם חָלַ֔מְנוּ וּפֹתֵ֖ר אֵ֣ין אֹת֑וֹ וַיֹּ֨אמֶר אֲלֵהֶ֜ם יוֹסֵ֗ף הֲל֤וֹא לֵֽאלֹהִים֙ פִּתְרֹנִ֔ים סַפְּרוּ־נָ֖א לִֽי׃

ט וַיְסַפֵּ֧ר שַֽׂר־הַמַּשְׁקִ֛ים אֶת־חֲלֹמ֖וֹ לְיוֹסֵ֑ף וַיֹּ֣אמֶר ל֔וֹ בַּחֲלוֹמִ֕י וְהִנֵּה־גֶ֖פֶן לְפָנָֽי׃

י וּבַגֶּ֖פֶן שְׁלֹשָׁ֣ה שָׂרִיגִ֑ם וְהִ֤וא כְפֹרַ֙חַת֙ עָלְתָ֣ה נִצָּ֔הּ הִבְשִׁ֥ילוּ אַשְׁכְּלֹתֶ֖יהָ עֲנָבִֽים׃

יא וְכ֥וֹס פַּרְעֹ֖ה בְּיָדִ֑י וָאֶקַּ֣ח אֶת־הָֽעֲנָבִ֗ים וָֽאֶשְׂחַ֤ט אֹתָם֙ אֶל־כּ֣וֹס פַּרְעֹ֔ה וָאֶתֵּ֥ן אֶת־הַכּ֖וֹס עַל־כַּ֥ף פַּרְעֹֽה׃

יב וַיֹּ֤אמֶר לוֹ֙ יוֹסֵ֔ף זֶ֖ה פִּתְרֹנ֑וֹ שְׁלֹ֙שֶׁת֙ הַשָּׂ֣רִגִ֔ים שְׁלֹ֥שֶׁת יָמִ֖ים הֵֽם׃

יג בְּע֣וֹד ׀ שְׁלֹ֣שֶׁת יָמִ֗ים יִשָּׂ֤א פַרְעֹה֙ אֶת־רֹאשֶׁ֔ךָ וַהֲשִֽׁיבְךָ֖ עַל־כַּנֶּ֑ךָ וְנָתַתָּ֤ כוֹס־פַּרְעֹה֙ בְּיָד֔וֹ כַּמִּשְׁפָּט֙ הָרִאשׁ֔וֹן אֲשֶׁ֥ר הָיִ֖יתָ מַשְׁקֵֽהוּ׃

יד כִּ֧י אִם־זְכַרְתַּ֣נִי אִתְּךָ֗ כַּאֲשֶׁר֙ יִ֣יטַב לָ֔ךְ וְעָשִֽׂיתָ־נָּ֥א עִמָּדִ֖י חָ֑סֶד וְהִזְכַּרְתַּ֙נִי֙ אֶל־פַּרְעֹ֔ה וְהוֹצֵאתַ֖נִי מִן־הַבַּ֥יִת הַזֶּֽה׃

40 ¹ Some time later, the cupbearer and the baker of the king of Egypt gave offense to their lord the king of Egypt.

² Pharaoh was angry with his two courtiers, the chief cupbearer and the chief baker,

³ and put them in custody, in the house of the chief steward, in the same prison house where *Yosef* was confined.

⁴ The chief steward assigned *Yosef* to them, and he attended them. When they had been in custody for some time,

⁵ both of them – the cupbearer and the baker of the king of Egypt, who were confined in the prison – dreamed in the same night, each his own dream and each dream with its own meaning.

⁶ When *Yosef* came to them in the morning, he saw that they were distraught.

⁷ He asked Pharaoh's courtiers, who were with him in custody in his master's house, saying, "Why do you appear downcast today?"

⁸ And they said to him, "We had dreams, and there is no one to interpret them." So *Yosef* said to them, "Surely *Hashem* can interpret! Tell me [your dreams]."

⁹ Then the chief cupbearer told his dream to *Yosef*. He said to him, "In my dream, there was a vine in front of me.

¹⁰ On the vine were three branches. It had barely budded, when out came its blossoms and its clusters ripened into grapes.

¹¹ Pharaoh's cup was in my hand, and I took the grapes, pressed them into Pharaoh's cup, and placed the cup in Pharaoh's hand."

¹² *Yosef* said to him, "This is its interpretation: The three branches are three days.

¹³ In three days Pharaoh will pardon you and restore you to your post; you will place Pharaoh's cup in his hand, as was your custom formerly when you were his cupbearer.

¹⁴ But think of me when all is well with you again, and do me the kindness of mentioning me to Pharaoh, so as to free me from this place.

Bereishit/Genesis 41
Mikeitz

בראשית מא
מקץ

15 For in truth, I was kidnapped from the land of the Hebrews; nor have I done anything here that they should have put me in the dungeon."

טו כִּי־גֻנֹּב גֻּנַּבְתִּי מֵאֶרֶץ הָעִבְרִים וְגַם־פֹּה לֹא־עָשִׂיתִי מְאוּמָה כִּי־שָׂמוּ אֹתִי בַּבּוֹר׃

kee gu-NOV gu-NAV-tee may-E-retz ha-iv-REEM v'-gam POH lo a-SEE-tee m'-U-mah kee sa-MU o-TEE ba-BOR

16 When the chief baker saw how favorably he had interpreted, he said to *Yosef*, "In my dream, similarly, there were three openwork baskets on my head.

טז וַיַּרְא שַׂר־הָאֹפִים כִּי טוֹב פָּתָר וַיֹּאמֶר אֶל־יוֹסֵף אַף־אֲנִי בַּחֲלוֹמִי וְהִנֵּה שְׁלֹשָׁה סַלֵּי חֹרִי עַל־רֹאשִׁי׃

17 In the uppermost basket were all kinds of food for Pharaoh that a baker prepares; and the birds were eating it out of the basket above my head."

יז וּבַסַּל הָעֶלְיוֹן מִכֹּל מַאֲכַל פַּרְעֹה מַעֲשֵׂה אֹפֶה וְהָעוֹף אֹכֵל אֹתָם מִן־הַסַּל מֵעַל רֹאשִׁי׃

18 *Yosef* answered, "This is its interpretation: The three baskets are three days.

יח וַיַּעַן יוֹסֵף וַיֹּאמֶר זֶה פִּתְרֹנוֹ שְׁלֹשֶׁת הַסַּלִּים שְׁלֹשֶׁת יָמִים הֵם׃

19 In three days Pharaoh will lift off your head and impale you upon a pole; and the birds will pick off your flesh."

יט בְּעוֹד שְׁלֹשֶׁת יָמִים יִשָּׂא פַרְעֹה אֶת־רֹאשְׁךָ מֵעָלֶיךָ וְתָלָה אוֹתְךָ עַל־עֵץ וְאָכַל הָעוֹף אֶת־בְּשָׂרְךָ מֵעָלֶיךָ׃

20 On the third day – his birthday – Pharaoh made a banquet for all his officials, and he singled out his chief cupbearer and his chief baker from among his officials.

כ וַיְהִי ׀ בַּיּוֹם הַשְּׁלִישִׁי יוֹם הֻלֶּדֶת אֶת־פַּרְעֹה וַיַּעַשׂ מִשְׁתֶּה לְכָל־עֲבָדָיו וַיִּשָּׂא אֶת־רֹאשׁ ׀ שַׂר הַמַּשְׁקִים וְאֶת־רֹאשׁ שַׂר הָאֹפִים בְּתוֹךְ עֲבָדָיו׃

21 He restored the chief cupbearer to his cupbearing, and he placed the cup in Pharaoh's hand;

כא וַיָּשֶׁב אֶת־שַׂר הַמַּשְׁקִים עַל־מַשְׁקֵהוּ וַיִּתֵּן הַכּוֹס עַל־כַּף פַּרְעֹה׃

22 but the chief baker he impaled – just as *Yosef* had interpreted to them.

כב וְאֵת שַׂר הָאֹפִים תָּלָה כַּאֲשֶׁר פָּתַר לָהֶם יוֹסֵף׃

23 Yet the chief cupbearer did not think of *Yosef*; he forgot him.

כג וְלֹא־זָכַר שַׂר־הַמַּשְׁקִים אֶת־יוֹסֵף וַיִּשְׁכָּחֵהוּ׃

41 1 After two years' time, Pharaoh dreamed that he was standing by the Nile,

מא א וַיְהִי מִקֵּץ שְׁנָתַיִם יָמִים וּפַרְעֹה חֹלֵם וְהִנֵּה עֹמֵד עַל־הַיְאֹר׃

2 when out of the Nile there came up seven cows, handsome and sturdy, and they grazed in the reed grass.

ב וְהִנֵּה מִן־הַיְאֹר עֹלֹת שֶׁבַע פָּרוֹת יְפוֹת מַרְאֶה וּבְרִיאֹת בָּשָׂר וַתִּרְעֶינָה בָּאָחוּ׃

40:15 I was kidnapped from the land of the Hebrews It is remarkable, notes Rabbi Samson Raphael Hirsch, that at this early date, the Land of Israel was already known as the 'Land of the Hebrews.' While the *Torah* chronicles and elaborates on events in the lives of the Patriarchs and other monumental occurrences that influence all of Jewish history, it provides little commentary on the surrounding nations' reactions to these events. Through this reference, though, it becomes clear that the Hebrew people was emerging as a recognized entity, important enough for the land to be referenced as theirs.

Rabbi Samson R. Hirsch (1808–1888)

Bereishit/Genesis 41
Mikeitz

בראשית מא
מקץ

3 But presently, seven other cows came up from the Nile close behind them, ugly and gaunt, and stood beside the cows on the bank of the Nile;

ג וְהִנֵּה שֶׁבַע פָּרוֹת אֲחֵרוֹת עֹלוֹת אַחֲרֵיהֶן מִן־הַיְאֹר רָעוֹת מַרְאֶה וְדַקּוֹת בָּשָׂר וַתַּעֲמֹדְנָה אֵצֶל הַפָּרוֹת עַל־שְׂפַת הַיְאֹר:

4 and the ugly gaunt cows ate up the seven handsome sturdy cows. And Pharaoh awoke.

ד וַתֹּאכַלְנָה הַפָּרוֹת רָעוֹת הַמַּרְאֶה וְדַקֹּת הַבָּשָׂר אֵת שֶׁבַע הַפָּרוֹת יְפֹת הַמַּרְאֶה וְהַבְּרִיאֹת וַיִּיקַץ פַּרְעֹה:

5 He fell asleep and dreamed a second time: Seven ears of grain, solid and healthy, grew on a single stalk.

ה וַיִּישָׁן וַיַּחֲלֹם שֵׁנִית וְהִנֵּה שֶׁבַע שִׁבֳּלִים עֹלוֹת בְּקָנֶה אֶחָד בְּרִיאוֹת וְטֹבוֹת:

6 But close behind them sprouted seven ears, thin and scorched by the east wind.

ו וְהִנֵּה שֶׁבַע שִׁבֳּלִים דַּקּוֹת וּשְׁדוּפֹת קָדִים צֹמְחוֹת אַחֲרֵיהֶן:

7 And the thin ears swallowed up the seven solid and full ears. Then Pharaoh awoke: it was a dream!

ז וַתִּבְלַעְנָה הַשִּׁבֳּלִים הַדַּקּוֹת אֵת שֶׁבַע הַשִּׁבֳּלִים הַבְּרִיאוֹת וְהַמְּלֵאוֹת וַיִּיקַץ פַּרְעֹה וְהִנֵּה חֲלוֹם:

8 Next morning, his spirit was agitated, and he sent for all the magicians of Egypt, and all its wise men; and Pharaoh told them his dreams, but none could interpret them for Pharaoh.

ח וַיְהִי בַבֹּקֶר וַתִּפָּעֶם רוּחוֹ וַיִּשְׁלַח וַיִּקְרָא אֶת־כָּל־חַרְטֻמֵּי מִצְרַיִם וְאֶת־כָּל־חֲכָמֶיהָ וַיְסַפֵּר פַּרְעֹה לָהֶם אֶת־חֲלֹמוֹ וְאֵין־פּוֹתֵר אוֹתָם לְפַרְעֹה:

9 The chief cupbearer then spoke up and said to Pharaoh, "I must make mention today of my offenses.

ט וַיְדַבֵּר שַׂר הַמַּשְׁקִים אֶת־פַּרְעֹה לֵאמֹר אֶת־חֲטָאַי אֲנִי מַזְכִּיר הַיּוֹם:

10 Once Pharaoh was angry with his servants, and placed me in custody in the house of the chief steward, together with the chief baker.

י פַּרְעֹה קָצַף עַל־עֲבָדָיו וַיִּתֵּן אֹתִי בְּמִשְׁמַר בֵּית שַׂר הַטַּבָּחִים אֹתִי וְאֵת שַׂר הָאֹפִים:

11 We had dreams the same night, he and I, each of us a dream with a meaning of its own.

יא וַנַּחַלְמָה חֲלוֹם בְּלַיְלָה אֶחָד אֲנִי וָהוּא אִישׁ כְּפִתְרוֹן חֲלֹמוֹ חָלָמְנוּ:

12 A Hebrew youth was there with us, a servant of the chief steward; and when we told him our dreams, he interpreted them for us, telling each of the meaning of his dream.

יב וְשָׁם אִתָּנוּ נַעַר עִבְרִי עֶבֶד לְשַׂר הַטַּבָּחִים וַנְּסַפֶּר־לוֹ וַיִּפְתָּר־לָנוּ אֶת־חֲלֹמֹתֵינוּ אִישׁ כַּחֲלֹמוֹ פָּתָר:

13 And as he interpreted for us, so it came to pass: I was restored to my post, and the other was impaled."

יג וַיְהִי כַּאֲשֶׁר פָּתַר־לָנוּ כֵּן הָיָה אֹתִי הֵשִׁיב עַל־כַּנִּי וְאֹתוֹ תָלָה:

14 Thereupon Pharaoh sent for *Yosef*, and he was rushed from the dungeon. He had his hair cut and changed his clothes, and he appeared before Pharaoh.

יד וַיִּשְׁלַח פַּרְעֹה וַיִּקְרָא אֶת־יוֹסֵף וַיְרִיצֻהוּ מִן־הַבּוֹר וַיְגַלַּח וַיְחַלֵּף שִׂמְלֹתָיו וַיָּבֹא אֶל־פַּרְעֹה:

15 And Pharaoh said to *Yosef*, "I have had a dream, but no one can interpret it. Now I have heard it said of you that for you to hear a dream is to tell its meaning."

טו וַיֹּאמֶר פַּרְעֹה אֶל־יוֹסֵף חֲלוֹם חָלַמְתִּי וּפֹתֵר אֵין אֹתוֹ וַאֲנִי שָׁמַעְתִּי עָלֶיךָ לֵאמֹר תִּשְׁמַע חֲלוֹם לִפְתֹּר אֹתוֹ:

Bereishit/Genesis 41
Mikeitz

16 *Yosef* answered Pharaoh, saying, "Not I! *Hashem* will see to Pharaoh's welfare."

17 Then Pharaoh said to *Yosef*, "In my dream, I was standing on the bank of the Nile,

18 when out of the Nile came up seven sturdy and well-formed cows and grazed in the reed grass.

19 Presently there followed them seven other cows, scrawny, ill-formed, and emaciated – never had I seen their likes for ugliness in all the land of Egypt!

20 And the seven lean and ugly cows ate up the first seven cows, the sturdy ones;

21 but when they had consumed them, one could not tell that they had consumed them, for they looked just as bad as before. And I awoke.

22 In my other dream, I saw seven ears of grain, full and healthy, growing on a single stalk;

23 but right behind them sprouted seven ears, shriveled, thin, and scorched by the east wind.

24 And the thin ears swallowed the seven healthy ears. I have told my magicians, but none has an explanation for me."

25 And *Yosef* said to Pharaoh, "Pharaoh's dreams are one and the same: *Hashem* has told Pharaoh what He is about to do.

26 The seven healthy cows are seven years, and the seven healthy ears are seven years; it is the same dream.

27 The seven lean and ugly cows that followed are seven years, as are also the seven empty ears scorched by the east wind; they are seven years of famine.

28 It is just as I have told Pharaoh: *Hashem* has revealed to Pharaoh what He is about to do.

29 Immediately ahead are seven years of great abundance in all the land of Egypt.

30 After them will come seven years of famine, and all the abundance in the land of Egypt will be forgotten. As the land is ravaged by famine,

בראשית מא
מקץ

טז וַיַּעַן יוֹסֵף אֶת־פַּרְעֹה לֵאמֹר בִּלְעָדָי אֱלֹהִים יַעֲנֶה אֶת־שְׁלוֹם פַּרְעֹה:

יז וַיְדַבֵּר פַּרְעֹה אֶל־יוֹסֵף בַּחֲלֹמִי הִנְנִי עֹמֵד עַל־שְׂפַת הַיְאֹר:

יח וְהִנֵּה מִן־הַיְאֹר עֹלֹת שֶׁבַע פָּרוֹת בְּרִיאוֹת בָּשָׂר וִיפֹת תֹּאַר וַתִּרְעֶינָה בָּאָחוּ:

יט וְהִנֵּה שֶׁבַע־פָּרוֹת אֲחֵרוֹת עֹלוֹת אַחֲרֵיהֶן דַּלּוֹת וְרָעוֹת תֹּאַר מְאֹד וְרַקּוֹת בָּשָׂר לֹא־רָאִיתִי כָהֵנָּה בְּכָל־אֶרֶץ מִצְרַיִם לָרֹעַ:

כ וַתֹּאכַלְנָה הַפָּרוֹת הָרַקּוֹת וְהָרָעוֹת אֵת שֶׁבַע הַפָּרוֹת הָרִאשֹׁנוֹת הַבְּרִיאֹת:

כא וַתָּבֹאנָה אֶל־קִרְבֶּנָה וְלֹא נוֹדַע כִּי־בָאוּ אֶל־קִרְבֶּנָה וּמַרְאֵיהֶן רַע כַּאֲשֶׁר בַּתְּחִלָּה וָאִיקָץ:

כב וָאֵרֶא בַּחֲלֹמִי וְהִנֵּה שֶׁבַע שִׁבֳּלִים עֹלֹת בְּקָנֶה אֶחָד מְלֵאֹת וְטֹבוֹת:

כג וְהִנֵּה שֶׁבַע שִׁבֳּלִים צְנֻמוֹת דַּקּוֹת שְׁדֻפוֹת קָדִים צֹמְחוֹת אַחֲרֵיהֶם:

כד וַתִּבְלַעְןָ הַשִּׁבֳּלִים הַדַּקֹּת אֵת שֶׁבַע הַשִּׁבֳּלִים הַטֹּבוֹת וָאֹמַר אֶל־הַחַרְטֻמִּים וְאֵין מַגִּיד לִי:

כה וַיֹּאמֶר יוֹסֵף אֶל־פַּרְעֹה חֲלוֹם פַּרְעֹה אֶחָד הוּא אֵת אֲשֶׁר הָאֱלֹהִים עֹשֶׂה הִגִּיד לְפַרְעֹה:

כו שֶׁבַע פָּרֹת הַטֹּבֹת שֶׁבַע שָׁנִים הֵנָּה וְשֶׁבַע הַשִּׁבֳּלִים הַטֹּבֹת שֶׁבַע שָׁנִים הֵנָּה חֲלוֹם אֶחָד הוּא:

כז וְשֶׁבַע הַפָּרוֹת הָרַקּוֹת וְהָרָעֹת הָעֹלֹת אַחֲרֵיהֶן שֶׁבַע שָׁנִים הֵנָּה וְשֶׁבַע הַשִּׁבֳּלִים הָרֵקוֹת שְׁדֻפוֹת הַקָּדִים יִהְיוּ שֶׁבַע שְׁנֵי רָעָב:

כח הוּא הַדָּבָר אֲשֶׁר דִּבַּרְתִּי אֶל־פַּרְעֹה אֲשֶׁר הָאֱלֹהִים עֹשֶׂה הֶרְאָה אֶת־פַּרְעֹה:

כט הִנֵּה שֶׁבַע שָׁנִים בָּאוֹת שָׂבָע גָּדוֹל בְּכָל־אֶרֶץ מִצְרָיִם:

ל וְקָמוּ שֶׁבַע שְׁנֵי רָעָב אַחֲרֵיהֶן וְנִשְׁכַּח כָּל־הַשָּׂבָע בְּאֶרֶץ מִצְרָיִם וְכִלָּה הָרָעָב אֶת־הָאָרֶץ:

Bereishit/Genesis 41
Mikeitz

בראשית מא
מקץ

31 no trace of the abundance will be left in the land because of the famine thereafter, for it will be very severe.

לא וְלֹא־יִוָּדַע הַשָּׂבָע בָּאָרֶץ מִפְּנֵי הָרָעָב הַהוּא אַחֲרֵי־כֵן כִּי־כָבֵד הוּא מְאֹד:

32 As for Pharaoh having had the same dream twice, it means that the matter has been determined by *Hashem*, and that *Hashem* will soon carry it out.

לב וְעַל הִשָּׁנוֹת הַחֲלוֹם אֶל־פַּרְעֹה פַּעֲמָיִם כִּי־נָכוֹן הַדָּבָר מֵעִם הָאֱלֹהִים וּמְמַהֵר הָאֱלֹהִים לַעֲשֹׂתוֹ:

33 "Accordingly, let Pharaoh find a man of discernment and wisdom, and set him over the land of Egypt.

לג וְעַתָּה יֵרֶא פַרְעֹה אִישׁ נָבוֹן וְחָכָם וִישִׁיתֵהוּ עַל־אֶרֶץ מִצְרָיִם:

34 And let Pharaoh take steps to appoint overseers over the land, and organize the land of Egypt in the seven years of plenty.

לד יַעֲשֶׂה פַרְעֹה וְיַפְקֵד פְּקִדִים עַל־הָאָרֶץ וְחִמֵּשׁ אֶת־אֶרֶץ מִצְרַיִם בְּשֶׁבַע שְׁנֵי הַשָּׂבָע:

35 Let all the food of these good years that are coming be gathered, and let the grain be collected under Pharaoh's authority as food to be stored in the cities.

לה וְיִקְבְּצוּ אֶת־כָּל־אֹכֶל הַשָּׁנִים הַטֹּבֹת הַבָּאֹת הָאֵלֶּה וְיִצְבְּרוּ־בָר תַּחַת יַד־פַּרְעֹה אֹכֶל בֶּעָרִים וְשָׁמָרוּ:

36 Let that food be a reserve for the land for the seven years of famine which will come upon the land of Egypt, so that the land may not perish in the famine."

לו וְהָיָה הָאֹכֶל לְפִקָּדוֹן לָאָרֶץ לְשֶׁבַע שְׁנֵי הָרָעָב אֲשֶׁר תִּהְיֶיןָ בְּאֶרֶץ מִצְרָיִם וְלֹא־תִכָּרֵת הָאָרֶץ בָּרָעָב:

37 The plan pleased Pharaoh and all his court

לז וַיִּיטַב הַדָּבָר בְּעֵינֵי פַרְעֹה וּבְעֵינֵי כָּל־עֲבָדָיו:

38 And Pharaoh said to his courtiers, "Could we find another like him, a man in whom is the spirit of *Hashem*?"

לח וַיֹּאמֶר פַּרְעֹה אֶל־עֲבָדָיו הֲנִמְצָא כָזֶה אִישׁ אֲשֶׁר רוּחַ אֱלֹהִים בּוֹ:

39 So Pharaoh said to *Yosef*, "Since *Hashem* has made all this known to you, there is none so discerning and wise as you.

לט וַיֹּאמֶר פַּרְעֹה אֶל־יוֹסֵף אַחֲרֵי הוֹדִיעַ אֱלֹהִים אוֹתְךָ אֶת־כָּל־זֹאת אֵין־נָבוֹן וְחָכָם כָּמוֹךָ:

40 You shall be in charge of my court, and by your command shall all my people be directed; only with respect to the throne shall I be superior to you."

מ אַתָּה תִּהְיֶה עַל־בֵּיתִי וְעַל־פִּיךָ יִשַּׁק כָּל־עַמִּי רַק הַכִּסֵּא אֶגְדַּל מִמֶּךָּ:

41 Pharaoh further said to *Yosef*, "See, I put you in charge of all the land of Egypt."

מא וַיֹּאמֶר פַּרְעֹה אֶל־יוֹסֵף רְאֵה נָתַתִּי אֹתְךָ עַל כָּל־אֶרֶץ מִצְרָיִם:

42 And removing his signet ring from his hand, Pharaoh put it on *Yosef*'s hand; and he had him dressed in robes of fine linen, and put a gold chain about his neck.

מב וַיָּסַר פַּרְעֹה אֶת־טַבַּעְתּוֹ מֵעַל יָדוֹ וַיִּתֵּן אֹתָהּ עַל־יַד יוֹסֵף וַיַּלְבֵּשׁ אֹתוֹ בִּגְדֵי־שֵׁשׁ וַיָּשֶׂם רְבִד הַזָּהָב עַל־צַוָּארוֹ:

43 He had him ride in the chariot of his second-in-command, and they cried before him, "Abrek!" Thus he placed him over all the land of Egypt.

מג וַיַּרְכֵּב אֹתוֹ בְּמִרְכֶּבֶת הַמִּשְׁנֶה אֲשֶׁר־לוֹ וַיִּקְרְאוּ לְפָנָיו אַבְרֵךְ וְנָתוֹן אֹתוֹ עַל כָּל־אֶרֶץ מִצְרָיִם:

44 Pharaoh said to *Yosef*, "I am Pharaoh; yet without you, no one shall lift up hand or foot in all the land of Egypt."

מד וַיֹּאמֶר פַּרְעֹה אֶל־יוֹסֵף אֲנִי פַרְעֹה וּבִלְעָדֶיךָ לֹא־יָרִים אִישׁ אֶת־יָדוֹ וְאֶת־רַגְלוֹ בְּכָל־אֶרֶץ מִצְרָיִם:

Bereishit/Genesis 41
Mikeitz

בראשית מא
מקץ

45 Pharaoh then gave *Yosef* the name Zaphenath-paneah; and he gave him for a wife Asenath daughter of Poti-phera, priest of On. Thus *Yosef* emerged in charge of the land of Egypt.

מה וַיִּקְרָא פַרְעֹה שֵׁם־יוֹסֵף צָפְנַת פַּעְנֵחַ וַיִּתֶּן־לוֹ אֶת־אָסְנַת בַּת־פּוֹטִי פֶרַע כֹּהֵן אֹן לְאִשָּׁה וַיֵּצֵא יוֹסֵף עַל־אֶרֶץ מִצְרָיִם:

46 *Yosef* was thirty years old when he entered the service of Pharaoh king of Egypt. – Leaving Pharaoh's presence, *Yosef* traveled through all the land of Egypt.

מו וְיוֹסֵף בֶּן־שְׁלֹשִׁים שָׁנָה בְּעָמְדוֹ לִפְנֵי פַּרְעֹה מֶלֶךְ־מִצְרָיִם וַיֵּצֵא יוֹסֵף מִלִּפְנֵי פַרְעֹה וַיַּעֲבֹר בְּכָל־אֶרֶץ מִצְרָיִם:

47 During the seven years of plenty, the land produced in abundance.

מז וַתַּעַשׂ הָאָרֶץ בְּשֶׁבַע שְׁנֵי הַשָּׂבָע לִקְמָצִים:

48 And he gathered all the grain of the seven years that the land of Egypt was enjoying, and stored the grain in the cities; he put in each city the grain of the fields around it.

מח וַיִּקְבֹּץ אֶת־כָּל־אֹכֶל שֶׁבַע שָׁנִים אֲשֶׁר הָיוּ בְּאֶרֶץ מִצְרַיִם וַיִּתֶּן־אֹכֶל בֶּעָרִים אֹכֶל שְׂדֵה־הָעִיר אֲשֶׁר סְבִיבֹתֶיהָ נָתַן בְּתוֹכָהּ:

49 So *Yosef* collected produce in very large quantity, like the sands of the sea, until he ceased to measure it, for it could not be measured.

מט וַיִּצְבֹּר יוֹסֵף בָּר כְּחוֹל הַיָּם הַרְבֵּה מְאֹד עַד כִּי־חָדַל לִסְפֹּר כִּי־אֵין מִסְפָּר:

50 Before the years of famine came, *Yosef* became the father of two sons, whom Asenath daughter of Poti-phera, priest of On, bore to him.

נ וּלְיוֹסֵף יֻלַּד שְׁנֵי בָנִים בְּטֶרֶם תָּבוֹא שְׁנַת הָרָעָב אֲשֶׁר יָלְדָה־לּוֹ אָסְנַת בַּת־פּוֹטִי פֶרַע כֹּהֵן אוֹן:

51 *Yosef* named the first-born *Menashe*, meaning, "Hashem has made me forget completely my hardship and my parental home."

נא וַיִּקְרָא יוֹסֵף אֶת־שֵׁם הַבְּכוֹר מְנַשֶּׁה כִּי־נַשַּׁנִי אֱלֹהִים אֶת־כָּל־עֲמָלִי וְאֵת כָּל־בֵּית אָבִי:

52 And the second he named *Efraim*, meaning, "Hashem has made me fertile in the land of my affliction."

נב וְאֵת שֵׁם הַשֵּׁנִי קָרָא אֶפְרָיִם כִּי־הִפְרַנִי אֱלֹהִים בְּאֶרֶץ עָנְיִי:

v'-AYT SHAYM ha-shay-NEE ka-RA ef-RA-yim kee hif-RA-nee e-lo-HEEM b'-E-retz on-YEE

53 The seven years of abundance that the land of Egypt enjoyed came to an end,

נג וַתִּכְלֶינָה שֶׁבַע שְׁנֵי הַשָּׂבָע אֲשֶׁר הָיָה בְּאֶרֶץ מִצְרָיִם:

54 and the seven years of famine set in, just as *Yosef* had foretold. There was famine in all lands, but throughout the land of Egypt there was bread.

נד וַתְּחִלֶּינָה שֶׁבַע שְׁנֵי הָרָעָב לָבוֹא כַּאֲשֶׁר אָמַר יוֹסֵף וַיְהִי רָעָב בְּכָל־הָאֲרָצוֹת וּבְכָל־אֶרֶץ מִצְרַיִם הָיָה לָחֶם:

41:52 *Hashem has made me forget completely my hardship* As the name of his first son indicates, *Yosef* is finally comforted after his troubling experience with his brothers. Yet, with the name of his second son, *Yosef* indicates that even after being appointed viceroy to Pharaoh, Egypt is still a land of affliction to him. Rabbi Yitzchak Abrabanel, a fifteenth century Bible commentator, points out that despite his elevated status, *Yosef* never forgot where he truly belonged. Though he was comforted over his loss, *Yosef* still yearned to return to his father's household in Eretz Yisrael.

Rabbi Yitzchak Abarbanel (1437–1508)

Bereishit/Genesis 42
Mikeitz

בראשית מב
מקץ

55 And when all the land of Egypt felt the hunger, the people cried out to Pharaoh for bread; and Pharaoh said to all the Egyptians, "Go to Joseph; whatever he tells you, you shall do."

נה וַתִּרְעַב כָּל־אֶרֶץ מִצְרַיִם וַיִּצְעַק הָעָם אֶל־פַּרְעֹה לַלָּחֶם וַיֹּאמֶר פַּרְעֹה לְכָל־מִצְרַיִם לְכוּ אֶל־יוֹסֵף אֲשֶׁר־יֹאמַר לָכֶם תַּעֲשֽׂוּ׃

56 Accordingly, when the famine became severe in the land of Egypt, *Yosef* laid open all that was within, and rationed out grain to the Egyptians. The famine, however, spread over the whole world.

נו וְהָרָעָב הָיָה עַל כָּל־פְּנֵי הָאָרֶץ וַיִּפְתַּח יוֹסֵף אֶת־כָּל־אֲשֶׁר בָּהֶם וַיִּשְׁבֹּר לְמִצְרַיִם וַיֶּחֱזַק הָרָעָב בְּאֶרֶץ מִצְרָיִם׃

57 So all the world came to *Yosef* in Egypt to procure rations, for the famine had become severe throughout the world.

נז וְכָל־הָאָרֶץ בָּאוּ מִצְרַיְמָה לִשְׁבֹּר אֶל־יוֹסֵף כִּי־חָזַק הָרָעָב בְּכָל־הָאָרֶץ׃

42 1 When *Yaakov* saw that there were food rations to be had in Egypt, he said to his sons, "Why do you keep looking at one another?"

מב א וַיַּרְא יַעֲקֹב כִּי יֶשׁ־שֶׁבֶר בְּמִצְרָיִם וַיֹּאמֶר יַעֲקֹב לְבָנָיו לָמָּה תִּתְרָאוּ׃

2 "Now I hear," he went on, "that there are rations to be had in Egypt. Go down and procure rations for us there, that we may live and not die."

ב וַיֹּאמֶר הִנֵּה שָׁמַעְתִּי כִּי יֶשׁ־שֶׁבֶר בְּמִצְרָיִם רְדוּ־שָׁמָּה וְשִׁבְרוּ־לָנוּ מִשָּׁם וְנִחְיֶה וְלֹא נָמֽוּת׃

3 So ten of *Yosef*'s brothers went down to get grain rations in Egypt;

ג וַיֵּרְדוּ אֲחֵי־יוֹסֵף עֲשָׂרָה לִשְׁבֹּר בָּר מִמִּצְרָיִם׃

4 for *Yaakov* did not send *Yosef*'s brother *Binyamin* with his brothers, since he feared that he might meet with disaster.

ד וְאֶת־בִּנְיָמִין אֲחִי יוֹסֵף לֹא־שָׁלַח יַעֲקֹב אֶת־אֶחָיו כִּי אָמַר פֶּן־יִקְרָאֶנּוּ אָסֽוֹן׃

5 Thus the sons of *Yisrael* were among those who came to procure rations, for the famine extended to the land of Canaan.

ה וַיָּבֹאוּ בְּנֵי יִשְׂרָאֵל לִשְׁבֹּר בְּתוֹךְ הַבָּאִים כִּי־הָיָה הָרָעָב בְּאֶרֶץ כְּנָֽעַן׃

6 Now *Yosef* was the vizier of the land; it was he who dispensed rations to all the people of the land. And *Yosef*'s brothers came and bowed low to him, with their faces to the ground.

ו וְיוֹסֵף הוּא הַשַּׁלִּיט עַל־הָאָרֶץ הוּא הַמַּשְׁבִּיר לְכָל־עַם הָאָרֶץ וַיָּבֹאוּ אֲחֵי יוֹסֵף וַיִּשְׁתַּחֲווּ־לוֹ אַפַּיִם אָֽרְצָה׃

7 When *Yosef* saw his brothers, he recognized them; but he acted like a stranger toward them and spoke harshly to them. He asked them, "Where do you come from?" And they said, "From the land of Canaan, to procure food."

ז וַיַּרְא יוֹסֵף אֶת־אֶחָיו וַיַּכִּרֵם וַיִּתְנַכֵּר אֲלֵיהֶם וַיְדַבֵּר אִתָּם קָשׁוֹת וַיֹּאמֶר אֲלֵהֶם מֵאַיִן בָּאתֶם וַיֹּאמְרוּ מֵאֶרֶץ כְּנַעַן לִשְׁבָּר־אֹֽכֶל׃

va-YAR yo-SAYF et e-KHAV va-ya-ki-RAYM va-yit-na-KAYR a-lay-HEM vai-da-BAYR i-TAM ka-SHOT va-YO-mer a-lay-HEM may-A-yin ba-TEM va-YO-m'-RU may-E-retz k'-NA-an lish-bor O-khel

---

42:7 From the land of *Canaan*, to procure food Many commentators point out the incongruity between *Yosef*'s question and the brothers' answer. *Yosef* asked only about their origin; why, then, did the brothers supply a reason for their travels? The question is strengthened by the fact that assumedly, their reason for coming to Egypt was self-evident. Rabbi Zalman Sorotzkin answers that the brothers were accustomed to the need to apologize and offer an explanation for leaving the holy Land of Israel. Al-

Bereishit/Genesis 42
Mikeitz

בראשית מב
מקץ

8 For though *Yosef* recognized his brothers, they did not recognize him.

ח וַיַּכֵּר יוֹסֵף אֶת־אֶחָיו וְהֵם לֹא הִכִּרֻהוּ׃

9 Recalling the dreams that he had dreamed about them, *Yosef* said to them, "You are spies, you have come to see the land in its nakedness."

ט וַיִּזְכֹּר יוֹסֵף אֵת הַחֲלֹמוֹת אֲשֶׁר חָלַם לָהֶם וַיֹּאמֶר אֲלֵהֶם מְרַגְּלִים אַתֶּם לִרְאוֹת אֶת־עֶרְוַת הָאָרֶץ בָּאתֶם׃

10 But they said to him, "No, my lord! Truly, your servants have come to procure food.

י וַיֹּאמְרוּ אֵלָיו לֹא אֲדֹנִי וַעֲבָדֶיךָ בָּאוּ לִשְׁבָּר־אֹכֶל׃

11 We are all of us sons of the same man; we are honest men; your servants have never been spies!

יא כֻּלָּנוּ בְּנֵי אִישׁ־אֶחָד נָחְנוּ כֵּנִים אֲנַחְנוּ לֹא־הָיוּ עֲבָדֶיךָ מְרַגְּלִים׃

12 And he said to them, "No, you have come to see the land in its nakedness!"

יב וַיֹּאמֶר אֲלֵהֶם לֹא כִּי־עֶרְוַת הָאָרֶץ בָּאתֶם לִרְאוֹת׃

13 And they replied, "We your servants were twelve brothers, sons of a certain man in the land of Canaan; the youngest, however, is now with our father, and one is no more."

יג וַיֹּאמְרוּ שְׁנֵים עָשָׂר עֲבָדֶיךָ אַחִים אֲנַחְנוּ בְּנֵי אִישׁ־אֶחָד בְּאֶרֶץ כְּנָעַן וְהִנֵּה הַקָּטֹן אֶת־אָבִינוּ הַיּוֹם וְהָאֶחָד אֵינֶנּוּ׃

14 But *Yosef* said to them, "It is just as I have told you: You are spies!

יד וַיֹּאמֶר אֲלֵהֶם יוֹסֵף הוּא אֲשֶׁר דִּבַּרְתִּי אֲלֵכֶם לֵאמֹר מְרַגְּלִים אַתֶּם׃

15 By this you shall be put to the test: unless your youngest brother comes here, by Pharaoh, you shall not depart from this place!

טו בְּזֹאת תִּבָּחֵנוּ חֵי פַרְעֹה אִם־תֵּצְאוּ מִזֶּה כִּי אִם־בְּבוֹא אֲחִיכֶם הַקָּטֹן הֵנָּה׃

16 Let one of you go and bring your brother, while the rest of you remain confined, that your words may be put to the test whether there is truth in you. Else, by Pharaoh, you are nothing but spies!"

טז שִׁלְחוּ מִכֶּם אֶחָד וְיִקַּח אֶת־אֲחִיכֶם וְאַתֶּם הֵאָסְרוּ וְיִבָּחֲנוּ דִּבְרֵיכֶם הַאֱמֶת אִתְּכֶם וְאִם־לֹא חֵי פַרְעֹה כִּי מְרַגְּלִים אַתֶּם׃

17 And he confined them in the guardhouse for three days.

יז וַיֶּאֱסֹף אֹתָם אֶל־מִשְׁמָר שְׁלֹשֶׁת יָמִים׃

18 On the third day *Yosef* said to them, "Do this and you shall live, for I am a *Hashem*-fearing man.

יח וַיֹּאמֶר אֲלֵהֶם יוֹסֵף בַּיּוֹם הַשְּׁלִישִׁי זֹאת עֲשׂוּ וִחְיוּ אֶת־הָאֱלֹהִים אֲנִי יָרֵא׃

19 If you are honest men, let one of you brothers be held in your place of detention, while the rest of you go and take home rations for your starving households;

יט אִם־כֵּנִים אַתֶּם אֲחִיכֶם אֶחָד יֵאָסֵר בְּבֵית מִשְׁמַרְכֶם וְאַתֶּם לְכוּ הָבִיאוּ שֶׁבֶר רַעֲבוֹן בָּתֵּיכֶם׃

20 but you must bring me your youngest brother, that your words may be verified and that you may not die." And they did accordingly.

כ וְאֶת־אֲחִיכֶם הַקָּטֹן תָּבִיאוּ אֵלַי וְיֵאָמְנוּ דִבְרֵיכֶם וְלֹא תָמוּתוּ וַיַּעֲשׂוּ־כֵן׃

---

though they could presume that the Egyptian would not think in these terms, they nevertheless felt the need to excuse their absence from their spiritual homeland.

Bereishit/Genesis 42
Mikeitz

בראשית מב
מקץ

21 They said to one another, "Alas, we are being punished on account of our brother, because we looked on at his anguish, yet paid no heed as he pleaded with us. That is why this distress has come upon us."

כא וַיֹּאמְרוּ אִישׁ אֶל־אָחִיו אֲבָל אֲשֵׁמִים אֲנַחְנוּ עַל־אָחִינוּ אֲשֶׁר רָאִינוּ צָרַת נַפְשׁוֹ בְּהִתְחַנְנוֹ אֵלֵינוּ וְלֹא שָׁמָעְנוּ עַל־כֵּן בָּאָה אֵלֵינוּ הַצָּרָה הַזֹּאת:

22 Then *Reuven* spoke up and said to them, "Did I not tell you, 'Do no wrong to the boy'? But you paid no heed. Now comes the reckoning for his blood."

כב וַיַּעַן רְאוּבֵן אֹתָם לֵאמֹר הֲלוֹא אָמַרְתִּי אֲלֵיכֶם לֵאמֹר אַל־תֶּחֶטְאוּ בַיֶּלֶד וְלֹא שְׁמַעְתֶּם וְגַם־דָּמוֹ הִנֵּה נִדְרָשׁ:

23 They did not know that *Yosef* understood, for there was an interpreter between him and them.

כג וְהֵם לֹא יָדְעוּ כִּי שֹׁמֵעַ יוֹסֵף כִּי הַמֵּלִיץ בֵּינֹתָם:

24 He turned away from them and wept. But he came back to them and spoke to them; and he took *Shimon* from among them and had him bound before their eyes.

כד וַיִּסֹּב מֵעֲלֵיהֶם וַיֵּבְךְּ וַיָּשָׁב אֲלֵהֶם וַיְדַבֵּר אֲלֵהֶם וַיִּקַּח מֵאִתָּם אֶת־שִׁמְעוֹן וַיֶּאֱסֹר אֹתוֹ לְעֵינֵיהֶם:

25 Then *Yosef* gave orders to fill their bags with grain, return each one's money to his sack, and give them provisions for the journey; and this was done for them.

כה וַיְצַו יוֹסֵף וַיְמַלְאוּ אֶת־כְּלֵיהֶם בָּר וּלְהָשִׁיב כַּסְפֵּיהֶם אִישׁ אֶל־שַׂקּוֹ וְלָתֵת לָהֶם צֵדָה לַדָּרֶךְ וַיַּעַשׂ לָהֶם כֵּן:

26 So they loaded their asses with the rations and departed from there.

כו וַיִּשְׂאוּ אֶת־שִׁבְרָם עַל־חֲמֹרֵיהֶם וַיֵּלְכוּ מִשָּׁם:

27 As one of them was opening his sack to give feed to his ass at the night encampment, he saw his money right there at the mouth of his bag.

כז וַיִּפְתַּח הָאֶחָד אֶת־שַׂקּוֹ לָתֵת מִסְפּוֹא לַחֲמֹרוֹ בַּמָּלוֹן וַיַּרְא אֶת־כַּסְפּוֹ וְהִנֵּה־הוּא בְּפִי אַמְתַּחְתּוֹ:

28 And he said to his brothers, "My money has been returned! It is here in my bag!" Their hearts sank; and, trembling, they turned to one another, saying, "What is this that *Hashem* has done to us?"

כח וַיֹּאמֶר אֶל־אֶחָיו הוּשַׁב כַּסְפִּי וְגַם הִנֵּה בְאַמְתַּחְתִּי וַיֵּצֵא לִבָּם וַיֶּחֶרְדוּ אִישׁ אֶל־אָחִיו לֵאמֹר מַה־זֹּאת עָשָׂה אֱלֹהִים לָנוּ:

29 When they came to their father *Yaakov* in the land of Canaan, they told him all that had befallen them, saying,

כט וַיָּבֹאוּ אֶל־יַעֲקֹב אֲבִיהֶם אַרְצָה כְּנָעַן וַיַּגִּידוּ לוֹ אֵת כָּל־הַקֹּרֹת אֹתָם לֵאמֹר:

30 "The man who is lord of the land spoke harshly to us and accused us of spying on the land.

ל דִּבֶּר הָאִישׁ אֲדֹנֵי הָאָרֶץ אִתָּנוּ קָשׁוֹת וַיִּתֵּן אֹתָנוּ כִּמְרַגְּלִים אֶת־הָאָרֶץ:

31 We said to him, 'We are honest men; we have never been spies!

לא וַנֹּאמֶר אֵלָיו כֵּנִים אֲנָחְנוּ לֹא הָיִינוּ מְרַגְּלִים:

32 There were twelve of us brothers, sons by the same father; but one is no more, and the youngest is now with our father in the land of Canaan.'

לב שְׁנֵים־עָשָׂר אֲנַחְנוּ אַחִים בְּנֵי אָבִינוּ הָאֶחָד אֵינֶנּוּ וְהַקָּטֹן הַיּוֹם אֶת־אָבִינוּ בְּאֶרֶץ כְּנָעַן:

33 But the man who is lord of the land said to us, 'By this I shall know that you are honest men: leave one of your brothers with me, and take something for your starving households and be off.

לג וַיֹּאמֶר אֵלֵינוּ הָאִישׁ אֲדֹנֵי הָאָרֶץ בְּזֹאת אֵדַע כִּי כֵנִים אַתֶּם אֲחִיכֶם הָאֶחָד הַנִּיחוּ אִתִּי וְאֶת־רַעֲבוֹן בָּתֵּיכֶם קְחוּ וָלֵכוּ:

Bereishit/Genesis 43
Mikeitz

בראשית מג
מקץ

34 And bring your youngest brother to me, that I may know that you are not spies but honest men. I will then restore your brother to you, and you shall be free to move about in the land.'"

לד וְהָבִיאוּ אֶת־אֲחִיכֶם הַקָּטֹן אֵלַי וְאֵדְעָה כִּי לֹא מְרַגְּלִים אַתֶּם כִּי כֵנִים אַתֶּם אֶת־אֲחִיכֶם אֶתֵּן לָכֶם וְאֶת־הָאָרֶץ תִּסְחָרוּ׃

35 As they were emptying their sacks, there, in each one's sack, was his money-bag! When they and their father saw their money-bags, they were dismayed.

לה וַיְהִי הֵם מְרִיקִים שַׂקֵּיהֶם וְהִנֵּה־אִישׁ צְרוֹר־כַּסְפּוֹ בְּשַׂקּוֹ וַיִּרְאוּ אֶת־צְרֹרוֹת כַּסְפֵּיהֶם הֵמָּה וַאֲבִיהֶם וַיִּירָאוּ׃

36 Their father *Yaakov* said to them, "It is always me that you bereave: *Yosef* is no more and *Shimon* is no more, and now you would take away *Binyamin*. These things always happen to me!"

לו וַיֹּאמֶר אֲלֵהֶם יַעֲקֹב אֲבִיהֶם אֹתִי שִׁכַּלְתֶּם יוֹסֵף אֵינֶנּוּ וְשִׁמְעוֹן אֵינֶנּוּ וְאֶת־בִּנְיָמִן תִּקָּחוּ עָלַי הָיוּ כֻלָּנָה׃

37 Then *Reuven* said to his father, "You may kill my two sons if I do not bring him back to you. Put him in my care, and I will return him to you."

לז וַיֹּאמֶר רְאוּבֵן אֶל־אָבִיו לֵאמֹר אֶת־שְׁנֵי בָנַי תָּמִית אִם־לֹא אֲבִיאֶנּוּ אֵלֶיךָ תְּנָה אֹתוֹ עַל־יָדִי וַאֲנִי אֲשִׁיבֶנּוּ אֵלֶיךָ׃

38 But he said, "My son must not go down with you, for his brother is dead and he alone is left. If he meets with disaster on the journey you are taking, you will send my white head down to Sheol in grief."

לח וַיֹּאמֶר לֹא־יֵרֵד בְּנִי עִמָּכֶם כִּי־אָחִיו מֵת וְהוּא לְבַדּוֹ נִשְׁאָר וּקְרָאָהוּ אָסוֹן בַּדֶּרֶךְ אֲשֶׁר תֵּלְכוּ־בָהּ וְהוֹרַדְתֶּם אֶת־שֵׂיבָתִי בְּיָגוֹן שְׁאוֹלָה׃

43 1 But the famine in the land was severe.

מג א וְהָרָעָב כָּבֵד בָּאָרֶץ׃

2 And when they had eaten up the rations which they had brought from Egypt, their father said to them, "Go again and procure some food for us."

ב וַיְהִי כַּאֲשֶׁר כִּלּוּ לֶאֱכֹל אֶת־הַשֶּׁבֶר אֲשֶׁר הֵבִיאוּ מִמִּצְרָיִם וַיֹּאמֶר אֲלֵיהֶם אֲבִיהֶם שֻׁבוּ שִׁבְרוּ־לָנוּ מְעַט־אֹכֶל׃

3 But *Yehuda* said to him, "The man warned us, 'Do not let me see your faces unless your brother is with you.'

ג וַיֹּאמֶר אֵלָיו יְהוּדָה לֵאמֹר הָעֵד הֵעִד בָּנוּ הָאִישׁ לֵאמֹר לֹא־תִרְאוּ פָנַי בִּלְתִּי אֲחִיכֶם אִתְּכֶם׃

4 If you will let our brother go with us, we will go down and procure food for you;

ד אִם־יֶשְׁךָ מְשַׁלֵּחַ אֶת־אָחִינוּ אִתָּנוּ נֵרְדָה וְנִשְׁבְּרָה לְךָ אֹכֶל׃

5 but if you will not let him go, we will not go down, for the man said to us, 'Do not let me see your faces unless your brother is with you.'"

ה וְאִם־אֵינְךָ מְשַׁלֵּחַ לֹא נֵרֵד כִּי־הָאִישׁ אָמַר אֵלֵינוּ לֹא־תִרְאוּ פָנַי בִּלְתִּי אֲחִיכֶם אִתְּכֶם׃

6 And *Yisrael* said, "Why did you serve me so ill as to tell the man that you had another brother?"

ו וַיֹּאמֶר יִשְׂרָאֵל לָמָה הֲרֵעֹתֶם לִי לְהַגִּיד לָאִישׁ הַעוֹד לָכֶם אָח׃

7 They replied, "But the man kept asking about us and our family, saying, 'Is your father still living? Have you another brother?' And we answered him accordingly. How were we to know that he would say, 'Bring your brother here'?"

ז וַיֹּאמְרוּ שָׁאוֹל שָׁאַל־הָאִישׁ לָנוּ וּלְמוֹלַדְתֵּנוּ לֵאמֹר הַעוֹד אֲבִיכֶם חַי הֲיֵשׁ לָכֶם אָח וַנַּגֶּד־לוֹ עַל־פִּי הַדְּבָרִים הָאֵלֶּה הֲיָדוֹעַ נֵדַע כִּי יֹאמַר הוֹרִידוּ אֶת־אֲחִיכֶם׃

8 Then *Yehuda* said to his father *Yisrael*, "Send the boy in my care, and let us be on our way, that we may live and not die – you and we and our children.

ח וַיֹּאמֶר יְהוּדָה אֶל־יִשְׂרָאֵל אָבִיו שִׁלְחָה הַנַּעַר אִתִּי וְנָקוּמָה וְנֵלֵכָה וְנִחְיֶה וְלֹא נָמוּת גַּם־אֲנַחְנוּ גַם־אַתָּה גַּם־טַפֵּנוּ׃

Bereishit/Genesis 43
Mikeitz

בראשית מג
מקץ

9 I myself will be surety for him; you may hold me responsible: if I do not bring him back to you and set him before you, I shall stand guilty before you forever.

ט אָנֹכִי אֶעֶרְבֶנּוּ מִיָּדִי תְּבַקְשֶׁנּוּ אִם־לֹא הֲבִיאֹתִיו אֵלֶיךָ וְהִצַּגְתִּיו לְפָנֶיךָ וְחָטָאתִי לְךָ כָּל־הַיָּמִים:

10 For we could have been there and back twice if we had not dawdled."

י כִּי לוּלֵא הִתְמַהְמָהְנוּ כִּי־עַתָּה שַׁבְנוּ זֶה פַעֲמָיִם:

11 Then their father *Yisrael* said to them, "If it must be so, do this: take some of the choice products of the land in your baggage, and carry them down as a gift for the man – some balm and some honey, gum, ladanum, pistachio nuts, and almonds.

יא וַיֹּאמֶר אֲלֵהֶם יִשְׂרָאֵל אֲבִיהֶם אִם־כֵּן אֵפוֹא זֹאת עֲשׂוּ קְחוּ מִזִּמְרַת הָאָרֶץ בִּכְלֵיכֶם וְהוֹרִידוּ לָאִישׁ מִנְחָה מְעַט צֳרִי וּמְעַט דְּבַשׁ נְכֹאת וָלֹט בָּטְנִים וּשְׁקֵדִים:

va-YO-mer a-lay-HEM yis-ra-AYL a-vee-HEM im KAYN ay-FO ZOT a-SU k'-KHU mi-zim-RAT ha-A-retz bikh-lay-KHEM v'-ho-REE-du la-EESH min-KHAH m'-AT tzo-REE um-AT d'-VASH n'-KHOT va-LOT bo-t'-NEEM ush-kay-DEEM

12 And take with you double the money, carrying back with you the money that was replaced in the mouths of your bags; perhaps it was a mistake.

יב וְכֶסֶף מִשְׁנֶה קְחוּ בְיֶדְכֶם וְאֶת־הַכֶּסֶף הַמּוּשָׁב בְּפִי אַמְתְּחֹתֵיכֶם תָּשִׁיבוּ בְיֶדְכֶם אוּלַי מִשְׁגֶּה הוּא:

13 Take your brother too; and go back at once to the man.

יג וְאֶת־אֲחִיכֶם קָחוּ וְקוּמוּ שׁוּבוּ אֶל־הָאִישׁ:

14 And may *El Shaddai* dispose the man to mercy toward you, that he may release to you your other brother, as well as *Binyamin*. As for me, if I am to be bereaved, I shall be bereaved."

יד וְאֵל שַׁדַּי יִתֵּן לָכֶם רַחֲמִים לִפְנֵי הָאִישׁ וְשִׁלַּח לָכֶם אֶת־אֲחִיכֶם אַחֵר וְאֶת־בִּנְיָמִין וַאֲנִי כַּאֲשֶׁר שָׁכֹלְתִּי שָׁכָלְתִּי:

15 So the men took that gift, and they took with them double the money, as well as *Binyamin*. They made their way down to Egypt, where they presented themselves to *Yosef*.

טו וַיִּקְחוּ הָאֲנָשִׁים אֶת־הַמִּנְחָה הַזֹּאת וּמִשְׁנֶה־כֶּסֶף לָקְחוּ בְיָדָם וְאֶת־בִּנְיָמִן וַיָּקֻמוּ וַיֵּרְדוּ מִצְרַיִם וַיַּעַמְדוּ לִפְנֵי יוֹסֵף:

16 When *Yosef* saw *Binyamin* with them, he said to his house steward, "Take the men into the house; slaughter and prepare an animal, for the men will dine with me at noon."

טז וַיַּרְא יוֹסֵף אִתָּם אֶת־בִּנְיָמִין וַיֹּאמֶר לַאֲשֶׁר עַל־בֵּיתוֹ הָבֵא אֶת־הָאֲנָשִׁים הַבָּיְתָה וּטְבֹחַ טֶבַח וְהָכֵן כִּי אִתִּי יֹאכְלוּ הָאֲנָשִׁים בַּצָּהֳרָיִם:

17 The man did as *Yosef* said, and he brought the men into *Yosef*'s house.

יז וַיַּעַשׂ הָאִישׁ כַּאֲשֶׁר אָמַר יוֹסֵף וַיָּבֵא הָאִישׁ אֶת־הָאֲנָשִׁים בֵּיתָה יוֹסֵף:

Fruit and nut stand in Jerusalem

43:11 Carry them down as a gift for the man *Yaakov* commands his sons to bring an offering to Pharaoh's viceroy of some choice fruits from the land. A *mincha* (מנחה), 'gift,' says Rabbi Samson Raphael Hirsch, indicates a present that benefits the giver more than the receiver. Obviously, a gift could provide a great benefit to the sons of *Yaakov*, if it will cause the viceroy to view them with favor. In addition, as they again descend to Egypt, this particular gift carries the added benefit of reminding them of their homeland and its many blessings. Though it is sometimes necessary to leave *Eretz Yisrael*, it should always be on the forefront of one's mind.

Bereishit/Genesis 43
Mikeitz

בראשית מג
מקץ

18 But the men were frightened at being brought into Yosef's house. "It must be," they thought, "because of the money replaced in our bags the first time that we have been brought inside, as a pretext to attack us and seize us as slaves, with our pack animals."

יח וַיִּירְאוּ הָאֲנָשִׁים כִּי הוּבְאוּ בֵּית יוֹסֵף וַיֹּאמְרוּ עַל־דְּבַר הַכֶּסֶף הַשָּׁב בְּאַמְתְּחֹתֵינוּ בַּתְּחִלָּה אֲנַחְנוּ מוּבָאִים לְהִתְגֹּלֵל עָלֵינוּ וּלְהִתְנַפֵּל עָלֵינוּ וְלָקַחַת אֹתָנוּ לַעֲבָדִים וְאֶת־חֲמֹרֵינוּ:

19 So they went up to Yosef's house steward and spoke to him at the entrance of the house.

יט וַיִּגְּשׁוּ אֶל־הָאִישׁ אֲשֶׁר עַל־בֵּית יוֹסֵף וַיְדַבְּרוּ אֵלָיו פֶּתַח הַבָּיִת:

20 "If you please, my lord," they said, "we came down once before to procure food.

כ וַיֹּאמְרוּ בִּי אֲדֹנִי יָרֹד יָרַדְנוּ בַּתְּחִלָּה לִשְׁבָּר־אֹכֶל:

21 But when we arrived at the night encampment and opened our bags, there was each one's money in the mouth of his bag, our money in full. So we have brought it back with us.

כא וַיְהִי כִּי־בָאנוּ אֶל־הַמָּלוֹן וַנִּפְתְּחָה אֶת־אַמְתְּחֹתֵינוּ וְהִנֵּה כֶסֶף־אִישׁ בְּפִי אַמְתַּחְתּוֹ כַּסְפֵּנוּ בְּמִשְׁקָלוֹ וַנָּשֶׁב אֹתוֹ בְּיָדֵנוּ:

22 And we have brought down with us other money to procure food. We do not know who put the money in our bags."

כב וְכֶסֶף אַחֵר הוֹרַדְנוּ בְיָדֵנוּ לִשְׁבָּר־אֹכֶל לֹא יָדַעְנוּ מִי־שָׂם כַּסְפֵּנוּ בְּאַמְתְּחֹתֵינוּ:

23 He replied, "All is well with you; do not be afraid. Your God, the God of your father, must have put treasure in your bags for you. I got your payment." And he brought out Shimon to them.

כג וַיֹּאמֶר שָׁלוֹם לָכֶם אַל־תִּירָאוּ אֱלֹהֵיכֶם וֵאלֹהֵי אֲבִיכֶם נָתַן לָכֶם מַטְמוֹן בְּאַמְתְּחֹתֵיכֶם כַּסְפְּכֶם בָּא אֵלָי וַיּוֹצֵא אֲלֵהֶם אֶת־שִׁמְעוֹן:

24 Then the man brought the men into Yosef's house; he gave them water to bathe their feet, and he provided feed for their asses.

כד וַיָּבֵא הָאִישׁ אֶת־הָאֲנָשִׁים בֵּיתָה יוֹסֵף וַיִּתֶּן־מַיִם וַיִּרְחֲצוּ רַגְלֵיהֶם וַיִּתֵּן מִסְפּוֹא לַחֲמֹרֵיהֶם:

25 They laid out their gifts to await Yosef's arrival at noon, for they had heard that they were to dine there.

כה וַיָּכִינוּ אֶת־הַמִּנְחָה עַד־בּוֹא יוֹסֵף בַּצָּהֳרָיִם כִּי שָׁמְעוּ כִּי־שָׁם יֹאכְלוּ לָחֶם:

26 When Yosef came home, they presented to him the gifts that they had brought with them into the house, bowing low before him to the ground.

כו וַיָּבֹא יוֹסֵף הַבַּיְתָה וַיָּבִיאוּ לוֹ אֶת־הַמִּנְחָה אֲשֶׁר־בְּיָדָם הַבָּיְתָה וַיִּשְׁתַּחֲווּ־לוֹ אָרְצָה:

27 He greeted them, and he said, "How is your aged father of whom you spoke? Is he still in good health?"

כז וַיִּשְׁאַל לָהֶם לְשָׁלוֹם וַיֹּאמֶר הֲשָׁלוֹם אֲבִיכֶם הַזָּקֵן אֲשֶׁר אֲמַרְתֶּם הַעוֹדֶנּוּ חָי:

28 They replied, "It is well with your servant our father; he is still in good health." And they bowed and made obeisance.

כח וַיֹּאמְרוּ שָׁלוֹם לְעַבְדְּךָ לְאָבִינוּ עוֹדֶנּוּ חָי וַיִּקְּדוּ וישתחו [וַיִּשְׁתַּחֲוּוּ]:

29 Looking about, he saw his brother Binyamin, his mother's son, and asked, "Is this your youngest brother of whom you spoke to me?" And he went on, "May Hashem be gracious to you, my boy."

כט וַיִּשָּׂא עֵינָיו וַיַּרְא אֶת־בִּנְיָמִין אָחִיו בֶּן־אִמּוֹ וַיֹּאמֶר הֲזֶה אֲחִיכֶם הַקָּטֹן אֲשֶׁר אֲמַרְתֶּם אֵלָי וַיֹּאמַר אֱלֹהִים יָחְנְךָ בְּנִי:

Bereishit/Genesis 44
Mikeitz

בראשית מד
מקץ

30 With that, *Yosef* hurried out, for he was overcome with feeling toward his brother and was on the verge of tears; he went into a room and wept there.

ל וַיְמַהֵר יוֹסֵף כִּי־נִכְמְרוּ רַחֲמָיו אֶל־אָחִיו וַיְבַקֵּשׁ לִבְכּוֹת וַיָּבֹא הַחַדְרָה וַיֵּבְךְּ שָׁמָּה׃

31 Then he washed his face, reappeared, and – now in control of himself – gave the order, "Serve the meal."

לא וַיִּרְחַץ פָּנָיו וַיֵּצֵא וַיִּתְאַפַּק וַיֹּאמֶר שִׂימוּ לָחֶם׃

32 They served him by himself, and them by themselves, and the Egyptians who ate with him by themselves; for the Egyptians could not dine with the Hebrews, since that would be abhorrent to the Egyptians.

לב וַיָּשִׂימוּ לוֹ לְבַדּוֹ וְלָהֶם לְבַדָּם וְלַמִּצְרִים הָאֹכְלִים אִתּוֹ לְבַדָּם כִּי לֹא יוּכְלוּן הַמִּצְרִים לֶאֱכֹל אֶת־הָעִבְרִים לֶחֶם כִּי־תוֹעֵבָה הִוא לְמִצְרָיִם׃

33 As they were seated by his direction, from the oldest in the order of his seniority to the youngest in the order of his youth, the men looked at one another in astonishment.

לג וַיֵּשְׁבוּ לְפָנָיו הַבְּכֹר כִּבְכֹרָתוֹ וְהַצָּעִיר כִּצְעִרָתוֹ וַיִּתְמְהוּ הָאֲנָשִׁים אִישׁ אֶל־רֵעֵהוּ׃

34 Portions were served them from his table; but *Binyamin*'s portion was several times that of anyone else. And they drank their fill with him.

לד וַיִּשָּׂא מַשְׂאֹת מֵאֵת פָּנָיו אֲלֵהֶם וַתֵּרֶב מַשְׂאַת בִּנְיָמִן מִמַּשְׂאֹת כֻּלָּם חָמֵשׁ יָדוֹת וַיִּשְׁתּוּ וַיִּשְׁכְּרוּ עִמּוֹ׃

44 1 Then he instructed his house steward as follows, "Fill the men's bags with food, as much as they can carry, and put each one's money in the mouth of his bag.

מד א וַיְצַו אֶת־אֲשֶׁר עַל־בֵּיתוֹ לֵאמֹר מַלֵּא אֶת־אַמְתְּחֹת הָאֲנָשִׁים אֹכֶל כַּאֲשֶׁר יוּכְלוּן שְׂאֵת וְשִׂים כֶּסֶף־אִישׁ בְּפִי אַמְתַּחְתּוֹ׃

2 Put my silver goblet in the mouth of the bag of the youngest one, together with his money for the rations." And he did as *Yosef* told him.

ב וְאֶת־גְּבִיעִי גְּבִיעַ הַכֶּסֶף תָּשִׂים בְּפִי אַמְתַּחַת הַקָּטֹן וְאֵת כֶּסֶף שִׁבְרוֹ וַיַּעַשׂ כִּדְבַר יוֹסֵף אֲשֶׁר דִּבֵּר׃

3 With the first light of morning, the men were sent off with their pack animals.

ג הַבֹּקֶר אוֹר וְהָאֲנָשִׁים שֻׁלְּחוּ הֵמָּה וַחֲמֹרֵיהֶם׃

4 They had just left the city and had not gone far, when *Yosef* said to his steward, "Up, go after the men! And when you overtake them, say to them, 'Why did you repay good with evil?

ד הֵם יָצְאוּ אֶת־הָעִיר לֹא הִרְחִיקוּ וְיוֹסֵף אָמַר לַאֲשֶׁר עַל־בֵּיתוֹ קוּם רְדֹף אַחֲרֵי הָאֲנָשִׁים וְהִשַּׂגְתָּם וְאָמַרְתָּ אֲלֵהֶם לָמָּה שִׁלַּמְתֶּם רָעָה תַּחַת טוֹבָה׃

5 It is the very one from which my master drinks and which he uses for divination. It was a wicked thing for you to do!'"

ה הֲלוֹא זֶה אֲשֶׁר יִשְׁתֶּה אֲדֹנִי בּוֹ וְהוּא נַחֵשׁ יְנַחֵשׁ בּוֹ הֲרֵעֹתֶם אֲשֶׁר עֲשִׂיתֶם׃

6 He overtook them and spoke those words to them.

ו וַיַּשִּׂגֵם וַיְדַבֵּר אֲלֵהֶם אֶת־הַדְּבָרִים הָאֵלֶּה׃

7 And they said to him, "Why does my lord say such things? Far be it from your servants to do anything of the kind!

ז וַיֹּאמְרוּ אֵלָיו לָמָּה יְדַבֵּר אֲדֹנִי כַּדְּבָרִים הָאֵלֶּה חָלִילָה לַעֲבָדֶיךָ מֵעֲשׂוֹת כַּדָּבָר הַזֶּה׃

Bereishit/Genesis 44
Mikeitz

בראשית מד
מקץ

8 Here we brought back to you from the land of Canaan the money that we found in the mouths of our bags. How then could we have stolen any silver or gold from your master's house!

הֵן כֶּסֶף אֲשֶׁר מָצָאנוּ בְּפִי אַמְתְּחֹתֵינוּ הֱשִׁיבֹנוּ אֵלֶיךָ מֵאֶרֶץ כְּנָעַן וְאֵיךְ נִגְנֹב מִבֵּית אֲדֹנֶיךָ כֶּסֶף אוֹ זָהָב:

HAYN KE-sef a-SHER ma-TZA-nu b'-FEE am-t'-kho-TAY-nu he-shee-VO-nu ay-LE-kha may-E-retz k'-NA-an v'-AYKH nig-NOV mi-BAYT a-do-NE-kha KE-sef O za-HAV

9 Whichever of your servants it is found with shall die; the rest of us, moreover, shall become slaves to my lord."

אֲשֶׁר יִמָּצֵא אִתּוֹ מֵעֲבָדֶיךָ וָמֵת וְגַם־אֲנַחְנוּ נִהְיֶה לַאדֹנִי לַעֲבָדִים:

10 He replied, "Although what you are proposing is right, only the one with whom it is found shall be my slave; but the rest of you shall go free."

וַיֹּאמֶר גַּם־עַתָּה כְדִבְרֵיכֶם כֶּן־הוּא אֲשֶׁר יִמָּצֵא אִתּוֹ יִהְיֶה־לִּי עָבֶד וְאַתֶּם תִּהְיוּ נְקִיִּם:

11 So each one hastened to lower his bag to the ground, and each one opened his bag.

וַיְמַהֲרוּ וַיּוֹרִדוּ אִישׁ אֶת־אַמְתַּחְתּוֹ אָרְצָה וַיִּפְתְּחוּ אִישׁ אַמְתַּחְתּוֹ:

12 He searched, beginning with the oldest and ending with the youngest; and the goblet turned up in Binyamin's bag.

וַיְחַפֵּשׂ בַּגָּדוֹל הֵחֵל וּבַקָּטֹן כִּלָּה וַיִּמָּצֵא הַגָּבִיעַ בְּאַמְתַּחַת בִּנְיָמִן:

13 At this they rent their clothes. Each reloaded his pack animal, and they returned to the city.

וַיִּקְרְעוּ שִׂמְלֹתָם וַיַּעֲמֹס אִישׁ עַל־חֲמֹרוֹ וַיָּשֻׁבוּ הָעִירָה:

14 When *Yehuda* and his brothers reentered the house of *Yosef*, who was still there, they threw themselves on the ground before him.

וַיָּבֹא יְהוּדָה וְאֶחָיו בֵּיתָה יוֹסֵף וְהוּא עוֹדֶנּוּ שָׁם וַיִּפְּלוּ לְפָנָיו אָרְצָה:

15 *Yosef* said to them, "What is this deed that you have done? Do you not know that a man like me practices divination?"

וַיֹּאמֶר לָהֶם יוֹסֵף מָה־הַמַּעֲשֶׂה הַזֶּה אֲשֶׁר עֲשִׂיתֶם הֲלוֹא יְדַעְתֶּם כִּי־נַחֵשׁ יְנַחֵשׁ אִישׁ אֲשֶׁר כָּמֹנִי:

16 *Yehuda* replied, "What can we say to my lord? How can we plead, how can we prove our innocence? *Hashem* has uncovered the crime of your servants. Here we are, then, slaves of my lord, the rest of us as much as he in whose possession the goblet was found."

וַיֹּאמֶר יְהוּדָה מַה־נֹּאמַר לַאדֹנִי מַה־נְּדַבֵּר וּמַה־נִּצְטַדָּק הָאֱלֹהִים מָצָא אֶת־עֲוֹן עֲבָדֶיךָ הִנֶּנּוּ עֲבָדִים לַאדֹנִי גַּם־אֲנַחְנוּ גַּם אֲשֶׁר־נִמְצָא הַגָּבִיעַ בְּיָדוֹ:

17 But he replied, "Far be it from me to act thus! Only he in whose possession the goblet was found shall be my slave; the rest of you go back in peace to your father."

וַיֹּאמֶר חָלִילָה לִּי מֵעֲשׂוֹת זֹאת הָאִישׁ אֲשֶׁר נִמְצָא הַגָּבִיעַ בְּיָדוֹ הוּא יִהְיֶה־לִּי עָבֶד וְאַתֶּם עֲלוּ לְשָׁלוֹם אֶל־אֲבִיכֶם:

44:8 From the land of Canaan The brothers attempt to exonerate themselves from the accusations of theft by mentioning that they had already returned the extra money they found in their sacks after the previous trip. Why must the brothers specify that they returned the money from the land of Canaan? It seems that in the brothers' minds, this detail adds a further verification of their honesty. As they brought the money back from the Land of Israel, known for its spiritual heights, they must surely have noble intentions. Since antiquity, *Eretz Yisrael* has been synonymous with morality, and the land itself demands a high level of ethical responsibility from its inhabitants.

Bereishit/Genesis 44
Vayigash

בראשית מד
ויגש

18 Then *Yehuda* went up to him and said, "Please, my lord, let your servant appeal to my lord, and do not be impatient with your servant, you who are the equal of Pharaoh.

יח וַיִּגַּ֨שׁ אֵלָ֜יו יְהוּדָ֗ה וַיֹּאמֶר֮ בִּ֣י אֲדֹנִי֒ יְדַבֶּר־נָ֨א עַבְדְּךָ֤ דָבָר֙ בְּאָזְנֵ֣י אֲדֹנִ֔י וְאַל־יִ֥חַר אַפְּךָ֖ בְּעַבְדֶּ֑ךָ כִּ֥י כָמ֖וֹךָ כְּפַרְעֹֽה:

19 My lord asked his servants, 'Have you a father or another brother?'

יט אֲדֹנִ֣י שָׁאַ֔ל אֶת־עֲבָדָ֖יו לֵאמֹ֑ר הֲיֵשׁ־לָכֶ֥ם אָ֖ב אוֹ־אָֽח:

20 We told my lord, 'We have an old father, and there is a child of his old age, the youngest; his full brother is dead, so that he alone is left of his mother, and his father dotes on him.'

כ וַנֹּ֨אמֶר֙ אֶל־אֲדֹנִ֔י יֶשׁ־לָ֨נוּ֙ אָ֣ב זָקֵ֔ן וְיֶ֥לֶד זְקֻנִ֖ים קָטָ֑ן וְאָחִ֨יו מֵ֜ת וַיִּוָּתֵ֨ר ה֧וּא לְבַדּ֛וֹ לְאִמּ֖וֹ וְאָבִ֥יו אֲהֵבֽוֹ:

21 Then you said to your servants, 'Bring him down to me, that I may set eyes on him.'

כא וַתֹּ֨אמֶר֙ אֶל־עֲבָדֶ֔יךָ הוֹרִדֻ֖הוּ אֵלָ֑י וְאָשִׂ֥ימָה עֵינִ֖י עָלָֽיו:

22 We said to my lord, 'The boy cannot leave his father; if he were to leave him, his father would die.'

כב וַנֹּ֨אמֶר֙ אֶל־אֲדֹנִ֔י לֹא־יוּכַ֥ל הַנַּ֖עַר לַעֲזֹ֣ב אֶת־אָבִ֑יו וְעָזַ֥ב אֶת־אָבִ֖יו וָמֵֽת:

23 But you said to your servants, 'Unless your youngest brother comes down with you, do not let me see your faces.'

כג וַתֹּ֨אמֶר֙ אֶל־עֲבָדֶ֔יךָ אִם־לֹ֥א יֵרֵ֛ד אֲחִיכֶ֥ם הַקָּטֹ֖ן אִתְּכֶ֑ם לֹ֥א תֹסִפ֖וּן לִרְא֥וֹת פָּנָֽי:

24 When we came back to your servant my father, we reported my lord's words to him.

כד וַֽיְהִי֙ כִּ֣י עָלִ֔ינוּ אֶֽל־עַבְדְּךָ֖ אָבִ֑י וַנַּ֨גֶּד־ל֔וֹ אֵ֖ת דִּבְרֵ֥י אֲדֹנִֽי:

25 "Later our father said, 'Go back and procure some food for us.'

כה וַיֹּ֖אמֶר אָבִ֑ינוּ שֻׁ֖בוּ שִׁבְרוּ־לָ֥נוּ מְעַט־אֹֽכֶל:

26 We answered, 'We cannot go down; only if our youngest brother is with us can we go down, for we may not show our faces to the man unless our youngest brother is with us.'

כו וַנֹּ֕אמֶר לֹ֥א נוּכַ֖ל לָרֶ֑דֶת אִם־יֵשׁ֩ אָחִ֨ינוּ הַקָּטֹ֤ן אִתָּ֨נוּ֙ וְיָרַ֔דְנוּ כִּי־לֹ֣א נוּכַ֗ל לִרְאוֹת֙ פְּנֵ֣י הָאִ֔ישׁ וְאָחִ֥ינוּ הַקָּטֹ֖ן אֵינֶ֥נּוּ אִתָּֽנוּ:

27 Your servant my father said to us, 'As you know, my wife bore me two sons.

כז וַיֹּ֛אמֶר עַבְדְּךָ֥ אָבִ֖י אֵלֵ֑ינוּ אַתֶּ֣ם יְדַעְתֶּ֔ם כִּ֥י שְׁנַ֖יִם יָֽלְדָה־לִּ֥י אִשְׁתִּֽי:

28 But one is gone from me, and I said: Alas, he was torn by a beast! And I have not seen him since.

כח וַיֵּצֵ֤א הָֽאֶחָד֙ מֵֽאִתִּ֔י וָאֹמַ֕ר אַ֖ךְ טָרֹ֣ף טֹרָ֑ף וְלֹ֥א רְאִיתִ֖יו עַד־הֵֽנָּה:

29 If you take this one from me, too, and he meets with disaster, you will send my white head down to Sheol in sorrow.'

כט וּלְקַחְתֶּ֧ם גַּם־אֶת־זֶ֛ה מֵעִ֥ם פָּנַ֖י וְקָרָ֣הוּ אָס֑וֹן וְהֽוֹרַדְתֶּ֧ם אֶת־שֵׂיבָתִ֛י בְּרָעָ֖ה שְׁאֹֽלָה:

30 "Now, if I come to your servant my father and the boy is not with us – since his own life is so bound up with his

ל וְעַתָּ֗ה כְּבֹאִי֙ אֶל־עַבְדְּךָ֣ אָבִ֔י וְהַנַּ֖עַר אֵינֶ֣נּוּ אִתָּ֑נוּ וְנַפְשׁ֖וֹ קְשׁוּרָ֥ה בְנַפְשֽׁוֹ:

31 when he sees that the boy is not with us, he will die, and your servants will send the white head of your servant our father down to Sheol in grief.

לא וְהָיָ֗ה כִּרְאוֹת֛וֹ כִּי־אֵ֥ין הַנַּ֖עַר וָמֵ֑ת וְהוֹרִ֨ידוּ עֲבָדֶ֜יךָ אֶת־שֵׂיבַ֨ת עַבְדְּךָ֥ אָבִ֛ינוּ בְּיָג֖וֹן שְׁאֹֽלָה:

32 Now your servant has pledged himself for the boy to my father, saying, 'If I do not bring him back to you, I shall stand guilty before my father forever.'

לב כִּ֤י עַבְדְּךָ֙ עָרַ֣ב אֶת־הַנַּ֔עַר מֵעִ֥ם אָבִ֖י לֵאמֹ֑ר אִם־לֹ֤א אֲבִיאֶ֨נּוּ֙ אֵלֶ֔יךָ וְחָטָ֥אתִי לְאָבִ֖י כָּל־הַיָּמִֽים:

Bereishit/Genesis 45
Vayigash

בראשית מה
ויגש

33 Therefore, please let your servant remain as a slave to my lord instead of the boy, and let the boy go back with his brothers.

לג וְעַתָּ֗ה יֵֽשֶׁב־נָ֤א עַבְדְּךָ֙ תַּ֣חַת הַנַּ֔עַר עֶ֖בֶד לַֽאדֹנִ֑י וְהַנַּ֖עַר יַ֥עַל עִם־אֶחָֽיו:

34 For how can I go back to my father unless the boy is with me? Let me not be witness to the woe that would overtake my father!"

לד כִּי־אֵיךְ֙ אֶֽעֱלֶ֣ה אֶל־אָבִ֔י וְהַנַּ֖עַר אֵינֶ֣נּוּ אִתִּ֑י פֶּ֚ן אֶרְאֶ֣ה בָרָ֔ע אֲשֶׁ֥ר יִמְצָ֖א אֶת־אָבִֽי:

45 1 Yosef could no longer control himself before all his attendants, and he cried out, "Have everyone withdraw from me!" So there was no one else about when Yosef made himself known to his brothers.

מה א וְלֹֽא־יָכֹ֨ל יוֹסֵ֜ף לְהִתְאַפֵּ֗ק לְכֹ֤ל הַנִּצָּבִים֙ עָלָ֔יו וַיִּקְרָ֕א הוֹצִ֥יאוּ כָל־אִ֖ישׁ מֵֽעָלָ֑י וְלֹא־עָ֤מַד אִישׁ֙ אִתּ֔וֹ בְּהִתְוַדַּ֥ע יוֹסֵ֖ף אֶל־אֶחָֽיו:

2 His sobs were so loud that the Egyptians could hear, and so the news reached Pharaoh's palace.

ב וַיִּתֵּ֥ן אֶת־קֹל֖וֹ בִּבְכִ֑י וַיִּשְׁמְע֣וּ מִצְרַ֔יִם וַיִּשְׁמַ֖ע בֵּ֥ית פַּרְעֹֽה:

3 Yosef said to his brothers, "I am Yosef. Is my father still well?" But his brothers could not answer him, so dumfounded were they on account of him.

ג וַיֹּ֨אמֶר יוֹסֵ֤ף אֶל־אֶחָיו֙ אֲנִ֣י יוֹסֵ֔ף הַע֥וֹד אָבִ֖י חָ֑י וְלֹֽא־יָכְל֤וּ אֶחָיו֙ לַֽעֲנ֣וֹת אֹת֔וֹ כִּ֥י נִבְהֲל֖וּ מִפָּנָֽיו:

4 Then Yosef said to his brothers, "Come forward to me." And when they came forward, he said, "I am your brother Yosef, he whom you sold into Egypt.

ד וַיֹּ֨אמֶר יוֹסֵ֧ף אֶל־אֶחָ֛יו גְּשׁוּ־נָ֥א אֵלַ֖י וַיִּגָּ֑שׁוּ וַיֹּ֗אמֶר אֲנִי֙ יוֹסֵ֣ף אֲחִיכֶ֔ם אֲשֶׁר־מְכַרְתֶּ֥ם אֹתִ֖י מִצְרָֽיְמָה:

5 Now, do not be distressed or reproach yourselves because you sold me hither; it was to save life that Hashem sent me ahead of you.

ה וְעַתָּ֣ה אַל־תֵּעָ֣צְב֗וּ וְאַל־יִ֨חַר֙ בְּעֵ֣ינֵיכֶ֔ם כִּֽי־מְכַרְתֶּ֥ם אֹתִ֖י הֵ֑נָּה כִּ֣י לְמִֽחְיָ֔ה שְׁלָחַ֥נִי אֱלֹהִ֖ים לִפְנֵיכֶֽם:

6 It is now two years that there has been famine in the land, and there are still five years to come in which there shall be no yield from tilling.

ו כִּי־זֶ֛ה שְׁנָתַ֥יִם הָֽרָעָ֖ב בְּקֶ֣רֶב הָאָ֑רֶץ וְעוֹד֙ חָמֵ֣שׁ שָׁנִ֔ים אֲשֶׁ֥ר אֵֽין־חָרִ֖ישׁ וְקָצִֽיר:

7 Hashem has sent me ahead of you to ensure your survival on earth, and to save your lives in an extraordinary deliverance.

ז וַיִּשְׁלָחֵ֤נִי אֱלֹהִים֙ לִפְנֵיכֶ֔ם לָשׂ֥וּם לָכֶ֛ם שְׁאֵרִ֖ית בָּאָ֑רֶץ וּלְהַֽחֲי֣וֹת לָכֶ֔ם לִפְלֵיטָ֖ה גְּדֹלָֽה:

va-yish-la-KHAY-nee e-lo-HEEM lif-nay-KHEM la-SUM la-KHEM sh'-ay-REET ba-A-retz ul-ha-kha-YOT la-KHEM lif-lay-TAH g'-do-LAH

8 So, it was not you who sent me here, but Hashem; and He has made me a father to Pharaoh, lord of all his household, and ruler over the whole land of Egypt.

ח וְעַתָּ֗ה לֹֽא־אַתֶּ֞ם שְׁלַחְתֶּ֤ם אֹתִי֙ הֵ֔נָּה כִּ֖י הָֽאֱלֹהִ֑ים וַיְשִׂימֵ֨נִי לְאָ֜ב לְפַרְעֹ֗ה וּלְאָדוֹן֙ לְכָל־בֵּית֔וֹ וּמֹשֵׁ֖ל בְּכָל־אֶ֥רֶץ מִצְרָֽיִם:

45:7 To save your lives in an extraordinary deliverance To allay his brothers' fears that he will take revenge for selling him into slavery, Yosef observes that their actions were part of the divine plan, and will undoubtedly bring great salvation. The short term benefit is already clear in that, due to his position, Yosef will be able to save his family and the entire region from the famine which has just begun. Further, in the great scheme of history, the sale of Yosef brought the entire family down to Egypt, thus beginning the fulfillment of God's promise (Genesis 15:13–14) that Avraham's descendants will be strangers in a strange land. It follows that after the period of enslavement in Egypt specified by the prophecy, they will merit a 'great deliverance,' and ultimately return to the Promised Land.

Bereishit/Genesis 45
Vayigash

9 "Now, hurry back to my father and say to him: Thus says your son *Yosef*, '*Hashem* has made me lord of all Egypt; come down to me without delay.

10 You will dwell in the region of Goshen, where you will be near me – you and your children and your grandchildren, your flocks and herds, and all that is yours.

11 There I will provide for you – for there are yet five years of famine to come – that you and your household and all that is yours may not suffer want.'

12 You can see for yourselves, and my brother *Binyamin* for himself, that it is indeed I who am speaking to you.

13 And you must tell my father everything about my high station in Egypt and all that you have seen; and bring my father here with all speed."

14 With that he embraced his brother *Binyamin* around the neck and wept, and *Binyamin* wept on his neck.

15 He kissed all his brothers and wept upon them; only then were his brothers able to talk to him.

16 The news reached Pharaoh's palace: "*Yosef*'s brothers have come." Pharaoh and his courtiers were pleased.

17 And Pharaoh said to *Yosef*, "Say to your brothers, 'Do as follows: load up your beasts and go at once to the land of Canaan.

18 Take your father and your households and come to me; I will give you the best of the land of Egypt and you shall live off the fat of the land.'

19 And you are bidden [to add], 'Do as follows: take from the land of Egypt wagons for your children and your wives, and bring your father here.

20 And never mind your belongings, for the best of all the land of Egypt shall be yours.'"

21 The sons of *Yisrael* did so; *Yosef* gave them wagons as Pharaoh had commanded, and he supplied them with provisions for the journey.

22 To each of them, moreover, he gave a change of clothing; but to *Binyamin* he gave three hundred pieces of silver and several changes of clothing.

בראשית מה
ויגש

ט מַהֲרוּ֮ וַעֲל֣וּ אֶל־אָבִי֒ וַאֲמַרְתֶּ֣ם אֵלָ֗יו כֹּ֤ה אָמַר֙ בִּנְךָ֣ יוֹסֵ֔ף שָׂמַ֧נִי אֱלֹהִ֛ים לְאָד֖וֹן לְכָל־מִצְרָ֑יִם רְדָ֥ה אֵלַ֖י אַֽל־תַּעֲמֹֽד:

י וְיָשַׁבְתָּ֣ בְאֶֽרֶץ־גֹּ֗שֶׁן וְהָיִ֤יתָ קָרוֹב֙ אֵלַ֔י אַתָּ֕ה וּבָנֶ֖יךָ וּבְנֵ֣י בָנֶ֑יךָ וְצֹֽאנְךָ֥ וּבְקָרְךָ֖ וְכָל־אֲשֶׁר־לָֽךְ:

יא וְכִלְכַּלְתִּ֤י אֹֽתְךָ֙ שָׁ֔ם כִּי־ע֛וֹד חָמֵ֥שׁ שָׁנִ֖ים רָעָ֑ב פֶּן־תִּוָּרֵ֛שׁ אַתָּ֥ה וּבֵֽיתְךָ֖ וְכָל־אֲשֶׁר־לָֽךְ:

יב וְהִנֵּ֤ה עֵֽינֵיכֶם֙ רֹא֔וֹת וְעֵינֵ֖י אָחִ֣י בִנְיָמִ֑ין כִּי־פִ֖י הַֽמְדַבֵּ֥ר אֲלֵיכֶֽם:

יג וְהִגַּדְתֶּ֣ם לְאָבִ֗י אֶת־כָּל־כְּבוֹדִי֙ בְּמִצְרַ֔יִם וְאֵ֖ת כָּל־אֲשֶׁ֣ר רְאִיתֶ֑ם וּמִֽהַרְתֶּ֥ם וְהוֹרַדְתֶּ֛ם אֶת־אָבִ֖י הֵֽנָּה:

יד וַיִּפֹּ֛ל עַל־צַוְּארֵ֥י בִנְיָמִֽן־אָחִ֖יו וַיֵּ֑בְךְּ וּבִ֨נְיָמִ֔ן בָּכָ֖ה עַל־צַוָּארָֽיו:

טו וַיְנַשֵּׁ֥ק לְכָל־אֶחָ֖יו וַיֵּ֣בְךְּ עֲלֵיהֶ֑ם וְאַ֣חֲרֵי כֵ֔ן דִּבְּר֥וּ אֶחָ֖יו אִתּֽוֹ:

טז וְהַקֹּ֣ל נִשְׁמַ֗ע בֵּ֤ית פַּרְעֹה֙ לֵאמֹ֔ר בָּ֖אוּ אֲחֵ֣י יוֹסֵ֑ף וַיִּיטַב֙ בְּעֵינֵ֣י פַרְעֹ֔ה וּבְעֵינֵ֖י עֲבָדָֽיו:

יז וַיֹּ֤אמֶר פַּרְעֹה֙ אֶל־יוֹסֵ֔ף אֱמֹ֥ר אֶל־אַחֶ֖יךָ זֹ֣את עֲשׂ֑וּ טַֽעֲנוּ֙ אֶת־בְּעִ֣ירְכֶ֔ם וּלְכוּ־בֹ֖אוּ אַ֥רְצָה כְּנָֽעַן:

יח וּקְח֧וּ אֶת־אֲבִיכֶ֛ם וְאֶת־בָּתֵּיכֶ֖ם וּבֹ֣אוּ אֵלָ֑י וְאֶתְּנָ֣ה לָכֶ֗ם אֶת־טוּב֙ אֶ֣רֶץ מִצְרַ֔יִם וְאִכְל֖וּ אֶת־חֵ֥לֶב הָאָֽרֶץ:

יט וְאַתָּ֥ה צֻוֵּ֖יתָה זֹ֣את עֲשׂ֑וּ קְחֽוּ־לָכֶם֩ מֵאֶ֨רֶץ מִצְרַ֜יִם עֲגָל֗וֹת לְטַפְּכֶם֙ וְלִנְשֵׁיכֶ֔ם וּנְשָׂאתֶ֥ם אֶת־אֲבִיכֶ֖ם וּבָאתֶֽם:

כ וְעֵ֣ינְכֶ֔ם אַל־תָּחֹ֖ס עַל־כְּלֵיכֶ֑ם כִּי־ט֛וּב כָּל־אֶ֥רֶץ מִצְרַ֖יִם לָכֶ֥ם הֽוּא:

כא וַיַּֽעֲשׂוּ־כֵן֙ בְּנֵ֣י יִשְׂרָאֵ֔ל וַיִּתֵּ֨ן לָהֶ֥ם יוֹסֵ֛ף עֲגָל֖וֹת עַל־פִּ֣י פַרְעֹ֑ה וַיִּתֵּ֥ן לָהֶ֛ם צֵדָ֖ה לַדָּֽרֶךְ:

כב לְכֻלָּ֥ם נָתַ֛ן לָאִ֖ישׁ חֲלִפ֣וֹת שְׂמָלֹ֑ת וּלְבִנְיָמִ֤ן נָתַן֙ שְׁלֹ֣שׁ מֵא֣וֹת כֶּ֔סֶף וְחָמֵ֖שׁ חֲלִפֹ֥ת שְׂמָלֹֽת:

Bereishit/Genesis 46
Vayigash

בראשית מו
ויגש

23 And to his father he sent the following: ten he-asses laden with the best things of Egypt, and ten she-asses laden with grain, bread, and provisions for his father on the journey.

כג וּלְאָבִיו שָׁלַח כְּזֹאת עֲשָׂרָה חֲמֹרִים נֹשְׂאִים מִטּוּב מִצְרָיִם וְעֶשֶׂר אֲתֹנֹת נֹשְׂאֹת בָּר וָלֶחֶם וּמָזוֹן לְאָבִיו לַדָּרֶךְ׃

24 As he sent his brothers off on their way, he told them, "Do not be quarrelsome on the way."

כד וַיְשַׁלַּח אֶת־אֶחָיו וַיֵּלֵכוּ וַיֹּאמֶר אֲלֵהֶם אַל־תִּרְגְּזוּ בַּדָּרֶךְ׃

25 They went up from Egypt and came to their father Yaakov in the land of Canaan.

כה וַיַּעֲלוּ מִמִּצְרָיִם וַיָּבֹאוּ אֶרֶץ כְּנַעַן אֶל־יַעֲקֹב אֲבִיהֶם׃

26 And they told him, "Yosef is still alive; yes, he is ruler over the whole land of Egypt." His heart went numb, for he did not believe them.

כו וַיַּגִּדוּ לוֹ לֵאמֹר עוֹד יוֹסֵף חַי וְכִי־הוּא מֹשֵׁל בְּכָל־אֶרֶץ מִצְרָיִם וַיָּפָג לִבּוֹ כִּי לֹא־הֶאֱמִין לָהֶם׃

27 But when they recounted all that Yosef had said to them, and when he saw the wagons that Yosef had sent to transport him, the spirit of their father Yaakov revived.

כז וַיְדַבְּרוּ אֵלָיו אֵת כָּל־דִּבְרֵי יוֹסֵף אֲשֶׁר דִּבֶּר אֲלֵהֶם וַיַּרְא אֶת־הָעֲגָלוֹת אֲשֶׁר־שָׁלַח יוֹסֵף לָשֵׂאת אֹתוֹ וַתְּחִי רוּחַ יַעֲקֹב אֲבִיהֶם׃

28 "Enough!" said Yisrael. "My son Yosef is still alive! I must go and see him before I die."

כח וַיֹּאמֶר יִשְׂרָאֵל רַב עוֹד־יוֹסֵף בְּנִי חָי אֵלְכָה וְאֶרְאֶנּוּ בְּטֶרֶם אָמוּת׃

46

1 So Yisrael set out with all that was his, and he came to Be'er Sheva, where he offered sacrifices to the God of his father Yitzchak.

מו א וַיִּסַּע יִשְׂרָאֵל וְכָל־אֲשֶׁר־לוֹ וַיָּבֹא בְּאֵרָה שָּׁבַע וַיִּזְבַּח זְבָחִים לֵאלֹהֵי אָבִיו יִצְחָק׃

2 Hashem called to Yisrael in a vision by night: "Yaakov! Yaakov!" He answered, "Here."

ב וַיֹּאמֶר אֱלֹהִים לְיִשְׂרָאֵל בְּמַרְאֹת הַלַּיְלָה וַיֹּאמֶר יַעֲקֹב יַעֲקֹב וַיֹּאמֶר הִנֵּנִי׃

3 And He said, "I am Hashem, the God of your father. Fear not to go down to Egypt, for I will make you there into a great nation.

ג וַיֹּאמֶר אָנֹכִי הָאֵל אֱלֹהֵי אָבִיךָ אַל־תִּירָא מֵרְדָה מִצְרַיְמָה כִּי־לְגוֹי גָּדוֹל אֲשִׂימְךָ שָׁם׃

4 I Myself will go down with you to Egypt, and I Myself will also bring you back; and Yosef's hand shall close your eyes."

ד אָנֹכִי אֵרֵד עִמְּךָ מִצְרַיְמָה וְאָנֹכִי אַעַלְךָ גַם־עָלֹה וְיוֹסֵף יָשִׁית יָדוֹ עַל־עֵינֶיךָ׃

a-no-KHEE ay-RAYD i-m'-KHA mitz-RAI-ma v'-a-no-KHEE a-al-KHA gam a-LO v'-yo-SAYF ya-SHEET ya-DO al ay-NE-kha

5 So Yaakov set out from Be'er Sheva. The sons of Yisrael put their father Yaakov and their children and their wives in the wagons that Pharaoh had sent to transport him;

ה וַיָּקָם יַעֲקֹב מִבְּאֵר שָׁבַע וַיִּשְׂאוּ בְנֵי־יִשְׂרָאֵל אֶת־יַעֲקֹב אֲבִיהֶם וְאֶת־טַפָּם וְאֶת־נְשֵׁיהֶם בָּעֲגָלוֹת אֲשֶׁר־שָׁלַח פַּרְעֹה לָשֵׂאת אֹתוֹ׃

46:4 | I Myself will go down with you to Egypt *Yaakov*'s family descends to Egypt to escape the famine in *Eretz Yisrael*. In this verse, *Hashem* assures *Yaakov* that when the Children of Israel are in exile, *Hashem*'s presence will accompany them. Rabbi Yehuda Lowe, a sixteenth century Talmudic scholar known as the *Maharal*, points out that the word 'descend' in this verse was carefully chosen. It conveys the idea that spiritually speaking, *Eretz Yisrael* is the highest of all places, and hence one who leaves that land is descending. Of course, the opposite is also true. Travel to Israel is repeatedly referred to in the Bible as an 'ascension.' Whenever one enters the land Israel, he or she experiences an elevated spiritual state.

Statue of the Maharal in Prague

Bereishit/Genesis 46
Vayigash

בראשית מו
ויגש

6 and they took along their livestock and the wealth that they had amassed in the land of Canaan. Thus *Yaakov* and all his offspring with him came to Egypt:

ו וַיִּקְחוּ אֶת־מִקְנֵיהֶם וְאֶת־רְכוּשָׁם אֲשֶׁר רָכְשׁוּ בְּאֶרֶץ כְּנַעַן וַיָּבֹאוּ מִצְרָיְמָה יַעֲקֹב וְכָל־זַרְעוֹ אִתּוֹ:

7 he brought with him to Egypt his sons and grandsons, his daughters and granddaughters – all his offspring.

ז בָּנָיו וּבְנֵי בָנָיו אִתּוֹ בְּנֹתָיו וּבְנוֹת בָּנָיו וְכָל־זַרְעוֹ הֵבִיא אִתּוֹ מִצְרָיְמָה:

8 These are the names of the Israelites, *Yaakov* and his descendants, who came to Egypt. *Yaakov*'s firstborn *Reuven*;

ח וְאֵלֶּה שְׁמוֹת בְּנֵי־יִשְׂרָאֵל הַבָּאִים מִצְרַיְמָה יַעֲקֹב וּבָנָיו בְּכֹר יַעֲקֹב רְאוּבֵן:

9 *Reuven*'s sons: Enoch, Pallu, *Chetzron*, and Carmi.

ט וּבְנֵי רְאוּבֵן חֲנוֹךְ וּפַלּוּא וְחֶצְרוֹן וְכַרְמִי:

10 *Shimon*'s sons: Jemuel, Jamin, Ohad, Jachin, Zohar, and *Shaul* the son of a Canaanite woman.

י וּבְנֵי שִׁמְעוֹן יְמוּאֵל וְיָמִין וְאֹהַד וְיָכִין וְצֹחַר וְשָׁאוּל בֶּן־הַכְּנַעֲנִית:

11 *Levi*'s sons: *Gershon*, *Kehat*, and *Merari*.

יא וּבְנֵי לֵוִי גֵּרְשׁוֹן קְהָת וּמְרָרִי:

12 *Yehuda*'s sons: *Er*, *Onan*, *Sheila*, *Peretz*, and *Zerach* – but *Er* and *Onan* had died in the land of Canaan; and *Peretz*'s sons were *Chetzron* and Hamul.

יב וּבְנֵי יְהוּדָה עֵר וְאוֹנָן וְשֵׁלָה וָפֶרֶץ וָזָרַח וַיָּמָת עֵר וְאוֹנָן בְּאֶרֶץ כְּנַעַן וַיִּהְיוּ בְנֵי־פֶרֶץ חֶצְרוֹן וְחָמוּל:

13 *Yissachar*'s sons: *Tola*, Puvah, Iob, and Shimron.

יג וּבְנֵי יִשָּׂשכָר תּוֹלָע וּפֻוָּה וְיוֹב וְשִׁמְרוֹן:

14 *Zevulun*'s sons: Sered, *Eilon*, and Jahleel.

יד וּבְנֵי זְבוּלֻן סֶרֶד וְאֵלוֹן וְיַחְלְאֵל:

15 Those were the sons whom *Leah* bore to *Yaakov* in Paddan-aram, in addition to his daughter *Dina*. Persons in all, male and female: 33.

טו אֵלֶּה בְּנֵי לֵאָה אֲשֶׁר יָלְדָה לְיַעֲקֹב בְּפַדַּן אֲרָם וְאֵת דִּינָה בִתּוֹ כָּל־נֶפֶשׁ בָּנָיו וּבְנוֹתָיו שְׁלֹשִׁים וְשָׁלֹשׁ:

16 *Gad*'s sons: Ziphion, Haggi, Shuni, Ezbon, Eri, Arodi, and Areli.

טז וּבְנֵי גָד צִפְיוֹן וְחַגִּי שׁוּנִי וְאֶצְבֹּן עֵרִי וַאֲרוֹדִי וְאַרְאֵלִי:

17 *Asher*'s sons: Imnah, Ishvah, Ishvi, and Beriah, and their sister Serah. Beriah's sons: *Chever* and Malchiel.

יז וּבְנֵי אָשֵׁר יִמְנָה וְיִשְׁוָה וְיִשְׁוִי וּבְרִיעָה וְשֶׂרַח אֲחֹתָם וּבְנֵי בְרִיעָה חֶבֶר וּמַלְכִּיאֵל:

18 These were the descendants of *Zilpa*, whom Laban had given to his daughter *Leah*. These she bore to *Yaakov* – 16 persons.

יח אֵלֶּה בְּנֵי זִלְפָּה אֲשֶׁר־נָתַן לָבָן לְלֵאָה בִתּוֹ וַתֵּלֶד אֶת־אֵלֶּה לְיַעֲקֹב שֵׁשׁ עֶשְׂרֵה נָפֶשׁ:

19 The sons of *Yaakov*'s wife *Rachel* were *Yosef* and *Binyamin*.

יט בְּנֵי רָחֵל אֵשֶׁת יַעֲקֹב יוֹסֵף וּבִנְיָמִן:

20 To *Yosef* were born in the land of Egypt *Menashe* and *Efraim*, whom Asenath daughter of Poti-phera priest of On bore to him.

כ וַיִּוָּלֵד לְיוֹסֵף בְּאֶרֶץ מִצְרַיִם אֲשֶׁר יָלְדָה־לּוֹ אָסְנַת בַּת־פּוֹטִי פֶרַע כֹּהֵן אֹן אֶת־מְנַשֶּׁה וְאֶת־אֶפְרָיִם:

21 *Binyamin*'s sons: Bela, Becher, Ashbel, Gera, Naaman, Ehi, Rosh, Muppim, Huppim, and Ard.

כא וּבְנֵי בִנְיָמִן בֶּלַע וָבֶכֶר וְאַשְׁבֵּל גֵּרָא וְנַעֲמָן אֵחִי וָרֹאשׁ מֻפִּים וְחֻפִּים וָאָרְדְּ:

22 These were the descendants of *Rachel* who were born to *Yaakov* – 14 persons in all.

כב אֵלֶּה בְּנֵי רָחֵל אֲשֶׁר יֻלַּד לְיַעֲקֹב כָּל־נֶפֶשׁ אַרְבָּעָה עָשָׂר:

23 *Dan*'s son: Hushim.

כג וּבְנֵי־דָן חֻשִׁים:

Bereishit/Genesis 47
Vayigash

24 *Naftali*'s sons: Jahzeel, Guni, Jezer, and Shillem.

25 These were the descendants of *Bilha*, whom Laban had given to his daughter *Rachel*. These she bore to *Yaakov* – 7 persons in all.

26 All the persons belonging to *Yaakov* who came to Egypt – his own issue, aside from the wives of *Yaakov*'s sons – all these persons numbered 66.

27 And *Yosef*'s sons who were born to him in Egypt were two in number. Thus the total of *Yaakov*'s household who came to Egypt was seventy persons.

28 He had sent *Yehuda* ahead of him to *Yosef*, to point the way before him to Goshen. So when they came to the region of Goshen,

29 *Yosef* ordered his chariot and went to Goshen to meet his father *Yisrael*; he presented himself to him and, embracing him around the neck, he wept on his neck a good while.

30 Then *Yisrael* said to *Yosef*, "Now I can die, having seen for myself that you are still alive."

31 Then *Yosef* said to his brothers and to his father's household, "I will go up and tell the news to Pharaoh, and say to him, 'My brothers and my father's household, who were in the land of Canaan, have come to me.

32 The men are shepherds; they have always been breeders of livestock, and they have brought with them their flocks and herds and all that is theirs.'

33 So when Pharaoh summons you and asks, 'What is your occupation?'

34 you shall answer, 'Your servants have been breeders of livestock from the start until now, both we and our fathers' – so that you may stay in the region of Goshen. For all shepherds are abhorrent to Egyptians."

47

1 Then *Yosef* came and reported to Pharaoh, saying, "My father and my brothers, with their flocks and herds and all that is theirs, have come from the land of Canaan and are now in the region of Goshen."

2 And selecting a few of his brothers, he presented them to Pharaoh.

Bereishit/Genesis 47
Vayigash

בראשית מז
ויגש

3 Pharaoh said to his brothers, "What is your occupation?" They answered Pharaoh, "We your servants are shepherds, as were also our fathers.

ג וַיֹּאמֶר פַּרְעֹה אֶל־אֶחָיו מַה־מַּעֲשֵׂיכֶם וַיֹּאמְרוּ אֶל־פַּרְעֹה רֹעֵה צֹאן עֲבָדֶיךָ גַּם־אֲנַחְנוּ גַּם־אֲבוֹתֵינוּ:

4 We have come," they told Pharaoh, "to sojourn in this land, for there is no pasture for your servants' flocks, the famine being severe in the land of Canaan. Pray, then, let your servants stay in the region of Goshen."

ד וַיֹּאמְרוּ אֶל־פַּרְעֹה לָגוּר בָּאָרֶץ בָּאנוּ כִּי־אֵין מִרְעֶה לַצֹּאן אֲשֶׁר לַעֲבָדֶיךָ כִּי־כָבֵד הָרָעָב בְּאֶרֶץ כְּנָעַן וְעַתָּה יֵשְׁבוּ־נָא עֲבָדֶיךָ בְּאֶרֶץ גֹּשֶׁן:

5 Then Pharaoh said to *Yosef*, "As regards your father and your brothers who have come to you,

ה וַיֹּאמֶר פַּרְעֹה אֶל־יוֹסֵף לֵאמֹר אָבִיךָ וְאַחֶיךָ בָּאוּ אֵלֶיךָ:

6 the land of Egypt is open before you: settle your father and your brothers in the best part of the land; let them stay in the region of Goshen. And if you know any capable men among them, put them in charge of my livestock."

ו אֶרֶץ מִצְרַיִם לְפָנֶיךָ הִוא בְּמֵיטַב הָאָרֶץ הוֹשֵׁב אֶת־אָבִיךָ וְאֶת־אַחֶיךָ יֵשְׁבוּ בְּאֶרֶץ גֹּשֶׁן וְאִם־יָדַעְתָּ וְיֶשׁ־בָּם אַנְשֵׁי־חַיִל וְשַׂמְתָּם שָׂרֵי מִקְנֶה עַל־אֲשֶׁר־לִי:

7 *Yosef* then brought his father *Yaakov* and presented him to Pharaoh; and *Yaakov* greeted Pharaoh.

ז וַיָּבֵא יוֹסֵף אֶת־יַעֲקֹב אָבִיו וַיַּעֲמִדֵהוּ לִפְנֵי פַרְעֹה וַיְבָרֶךְ יַעֲקֹב אֶת־פַּרְעֹה:

8 Pharaoh asked *Yaakov*, "How many are the years of your life?"

ח וַיֹּאמֶר פַּרְעֹה אֶל־יַעֲקֹב כַּמָּה יְמֵי שְׁנֵי חַיֶּיךָ:

9 And *Yaakov* answered Pharaoh, "The years of my sojourn [on earth] are one hundred and thirty. Few and hard have been the years of my life, nor do they come up to the life spans of my fathers during their sojourns."

ט וַיֹּאמֶר יַעֲקֹב אֶל־פַּרְעֹה יְמֵי שְׁנֵי מְגוּרַי שְׁלֹשִׁים וּמְאַת שָׁנָה מְעַט וְרָעִים הָיוּ יְמֵי שְׁנֵי חַיַּי וְלֹא הִשִּׂיגוּ אֶת־יְמֵי שְׁנֵי חַיֵּי אֲבֹתַי בִּימֵי מְגוּרֵיהֶם:

10 Then *Yaakov* bade Pharaoh farewell, and left Pharaoh's presence.

י וַיְבָרֶךְ יַעֲקֹב אֶת־פַּרְעֹה וַיֵּצֵא מִלִּפְנֵי פַרְעֹה:

11 So *Yosef* settled his father and his brothers, giving them holdings in the choicest part of the land of Egypt, in the region of Rameses, as Pharaoh had commanded.

יא וַיּוֹשֵׁב יוֹסֵף אֶת־אָבִיו וְאֶת־אֶחָיו וַיִּתֵּן לָהֶם אֲחֻזָּה בְּאֶרֶץ מִצְרַיִם בְּמֵיטַב הָאָרֶץ בְּאֶרֶץ רַעְמְסֵס כַּאֲשֶׁר צִוָּה פַרְעֹה:

12 *Yosef* sustained his father, and his brothers, and all his father's household with bread, down to the little ones.

יב וַיְכַלְכֵּל יוֹסֵף אֶת־אָבִיו וְאֶת־אֶחָיו וְאֵת כָּל־בֵּית אָבִיו לֶחֶם לְפִי הַטָּף:

13 Now there was no bread in all the world, for the famine was very severe; both the land of Egypt and the land of Canaan languished because of the famine.

יג וְלֶחֶם אֵין בְּכָל־הָאָרֶץ כִּי־כָבֵד הָרָעָב מְאֹד וַתֵּלַהּ אֶרֶץ מִצְרַיִם וְאֶרֶץ כְּנַעַן מִפְּנֵי הָרָעָב:

14 *Yosef* gathered in all the money that was to be found in the land of Egypt and in the land of Canaan, as payment for the rations that were being procured, and *Yosef* brought the money into Pharaoh's palace.

יד וַיְלַקֵּט יוֹסֵף אֶת־כָּל־הַכֶּסֶף הַנִּמְצָא בְאֶרֶץ־מִצְרַיִם וּבְאֶרֶץ כְּנַעַן בַּשֶּׁבֶר אֲשֶׁר־הֵם שֹׁבְרִים וַיָּבֵא יוֹסֵף אֶת־הַכֶּסֶף בֵּיתָה פַרְעֹה:

Bereishit/Genesis 47
Vayigash

בראשית מז
ויגש

15 And when the money gave out in the land of Egypt and in the land of Canaan, all the Egyptians came to *Yosef* and said, "Give us bread, lest we die before your very eyes; for the money is gone!"

טו וַיִּתֹּם הַכֶּסֶף מֵאֶרֶץ מִצְרַיִם וּמֵאֶרֶץ כְּנַעַן וַיָּבֹאוּ כָל־מִצְרַיִם אֶל־יוֹסֵף לֵאמֹר הָבָה־לָּנוּ לֶחֶם וְלָמָּה נָמוּת נֶגְדֶּךָ כִּי אָפֵס כָּסֶף:

16 And *Yosef* said, "Bring your livestock, and I will sell to you against your livestock, if the money is gone."

טז וַיֹּאמֶר יוֹסֵף הָבוּ מִקְנֵיכֶם וְאֶתְּנָה לָכֶם בְּמִקְנֵיכֶם אִם־אָפֵס כָּסֶף:

17 So they brought their livestock to *Yosef*, and *Yosef* gave them bread in exchange for the horses, for the stocks of sheep and cattle, and the asses; thus he provided them with bread that year in exchange for all their livestock.

יז וַיָּבִיאוּ אֶת־מִקְנֵיהֶם אֶל־יוֹסֵף וַיִּתֵּן לָהֶם יוֹסֵף לֶחֶם בַּסּוּסִים וּבְמִקְנֵה הַצֹּאן וּבְמִקְנֵה הַבָּקָר וּבַחֲמֹרִים וַיְנַהֲלֵם בַּלֶּחֶם בְּכָל־מִקְנֵהֶם בַּשָּׁנָה הַהִוא:

18 And when that year was ended, they came to him the next year and said to him, "We cannot hide from my lord that, with all the money and animal stocks consigned to my lord, nothing is left at my lord's disposal save our persons and our farmland.

יח וַתִּתֹּם הַשָּׁנָה הַהִוא וַיָּבֹאוּ אֵלָיו בַּשָּׁנָה הַשֵּׁנִית וַיֹּאמְרוּ לוֹ לֹא־נְכַחֵד מֵאֲדֹנִי כִּי אִם־תַּם הַכֶּסֶף וּמִקְנֵה הַבְּהֵמָה אֶל־אֲדֹנִי לֹא נִשְׁאַר לִפְנֵי אֲדֹנִי בִּלְתִּי אִם־גְּוִיָּתֵנוּ וְאַדְמָתֵנוּ:

19 Let us not perish before your eyes, both we and our land. Take us and our land in exchange for bread, and we with our land will be serfs to Pharaoh; provide the seed, that we may live and not die, and that the land may not become a waste."

יט לָמָּה נָמוּת לְעֵינֶיךָ גַּם־אֲנַחְנוּ גַּם אַדְמָתֵנוּ קְנֵה־אֹתָנוּ וְאֶת־אַדְמָתֵנוּ בַּלָּחֶם וְנִהְיֶה אֲנַחְנוּ וְאַדְמָתֵנוּ עֲבָדִים לְפַרְעֹה וְתֶן־זֶרַע וְנִחְיֶה וְלֹא נָמוּת וְהָאֲדָמָה לֹא תֵשָׁם:

20 So *Yosef* gained possession of all the farm land of Egypt for Pharaoh, every Egyptian having sold his field because the famine was too much for them; thus the land passed over to Pharaoh.

כ וַיִּקֶן יוֹסֵף אֶת־כָּל־אַדְמַת מִצְרַיִם לְפַרְעֹה כִּי־מָכְרוּ מִצְרַיִם אִישׁ שָׂדֵהוּ כִּי־חָזַק עֲלֵהֶם הָרָעָב וַתְּהִי הָאָרֶץ לְפַרְעֹה:

21 And he removed the population town by town, from one end of Egypt's border to the other.

כא וְאֶת־הָעָם הֶעֱבִיר אֹתוֹ לֶעָרִים מִקְצֵה גְבוּל־מִצְרַיִם וְעַד־קָצֵהוּ:

22 Only the land of the priests he did not take over, for the priests had an allotment from Pharaoh, and they lived off the allotment which Pharaoh had made to them; therefore they did not sell their land.

כב רַק אַדְמַת הַכֹּהֲנִים לֹא קָנָה כִּי חֹק לַכֹּהֲנִים מֵאֵת פַּרְעֹה וְאָכְלוּ אֶת־חֻקָּם אֲשֶׁר נָתַן לָהֶם פַּרְעֹה עַל־כֵּן לֹא מָכְרוּ אֶת־אַדְמָתָם:

23 Then *Yosef* said to the people, "Whereas I have this day acquired you and your land for Pharaoh, here is seed for you to sow the land.

כג וַיֹּאמֶר יוֹסֵף אֶל־הָעָם הֵן קָנִיתִי אֶתְכֶם הַיּוֹם וְאֶת־אַדְמַתְכֶם לְפַרְעֹה הֵא־לָכֶם זֶרַע וּזְרַעְתֶּם אֶת־הָאֲדָמָה:

24 And when harvest comes, you shall give one-fifth to Pharaoh, and four-fifths shall be yours as seed for the fields and as food for you and those in your households, and as nourishment for your children."

כד וְהָיָה בַּתְּבוּאֹת וּנְתַתֶּם חֲמִישִׁית לְפַרְעֹה וְאַרְבַּע הַיָּדֹת יִהְיֶה לָכֶם לְזֶרַע הַשָּׂדֶה וּלְאָכְלְכֶם וְלַאֲשֶׁר בְּבָתֵּיכֶם וְלֶאֱכֹל לְטַפְּכֶם:

25 And they said, "You have saved our lives! We are grateful to my lord, and we shall be serfs to Pharaoh."

כה וַיֹּאמְרוּ הֶחֱיִתָנוּ נִמְצָא־חֵן בְּעֵינֵי אֲדֹנִי וְהָיִינוּ עֲבָדִים לְפַרְעֹה:

Bereishit/Genesis 48
Vayechi

בראשית מח
ויחי

26 And *Yosef* made it into a land law in Egypt, which is still valid, that a fifth should be Pharaoh's; only the land of the priests did not become Pharaoh's.

כו וַיָּשֶׂם אֹתָהּ יוֹסֵף לְחֹק עַד־הַיּוֹם הַזֶּה עַל־אַדְמַת מִצְרַיִם לְפַרְעֹה לַחֹמֶשׁ רַק אַדְמַת הַכֹּהֲנִים לְבַדָּם לֹא הָיְתָה לְפַרְעֹה:

27 Thus *Yisrael* settled in the country of Egypt, in the region of Goshen; they acquired holdings in it, and were fertile and increased greatly.

כז וַיֵּשֶׁב יִשְׂרָאֵל בְּאֶרֶץ מִצְרַיִם בְּאֶרֶץ גֹּשֶׁן וַיֵּאָחֲזוּ בָהּ וַיִּפְרוּ וַיִּרְבּוּ מְאֹד:

28 *Yaakov* lived seventeen years in the land of Egypt, so that the span of *Yaakov*'s life came to one hundred and forty-seven years.

כח וַיְחִי יַעֲקֹב בְּאֶרֶץ מִצְרַיִם שְׁבַע עֶשְׂרֵה שָׁנָה וַיְהִי יְמֵי־יַעֲקֹב שְׁנֵי חַיָּיו שֶׁבַע שָׁנִים וְאַרְבָּעִים וּמְאַת שָׁנָה:

29 And when the time approached for *Yisrael* to die, he summoned his son *Yosef* and said to him, "Do me this favor, place your hand under my thigh as a pledge of your steadfast loyalty: please do not bury me in Egypt.

כט וַיִּקְרְבוּ יְמֵי־יִשְׂרָאֵל לָמוּת וַיִּקְרָא לִבְנוֹ לְיוֹסֵף וַיֹּאמֶר לוֹ אִם־נָא מָצָאתִי חֵן בְּעֵינֶיךָ שִׂים־נָא יָדְךָ תַּחַת יְרֵכִי וְעָשִׂיתָ עִמָּדִי חֶסֶד וֶאֱמֶת אַל־נָא תִקְבְּרֵנִי בְּמִצְרָיִם:

30 When I lie down with my fathers, take me up from Egypt and bury me in their burial-place." He replied, "I will do as you have spoken."

ל וְשָׁכַבְתִּי עִם־אֲבֹתַי וּנְשָׂאתַנִי מִמִּצְרַיִם וּקְבַרְתַּנִי בִּקְבֻרָתָם וַיֹּאמַר אָנֹכִי אֶעֱשֶׂה כִדְבָרֶךָ:

v'-sha-khav-TEE im a-vo-TAI un-sa-TA-nee mi-mitz-RA-yim uk-var-TA-nee bik-vu-ra-TAM va-yo-MAR a-no-KHEE e-SEH khid-va-RE-kha

31 And he said, "Swear to me." And he swore to him. Then *Yisrael* bowed at the head of the bed.

לא וַיֹּאמֶר הִשָּׁבְעָה לִי וַיִּשָּׁבַע לוֹ וַיִּשְׁתַּחוּ יִשְׂרָאֵל עַל־רֹאשׁ הַמִּטָּה:

48

1 Some time afterward, *Yosef* was told, "Your father is ill." So he took with him his two sons, *Menashe* and *Efraim*.

מח א וַיְהִי אַחֲרֵי הַדְּבָרִים הָאֵלֶּה וַיֹּאמֶר לְיוֹסֵף הִנֵּה אָבִיךָ חֹלֶה וַיִּקַּח אֶת־שְׁנֵי בָנָיו עִמּוֹ אֶת־מְנַשֶּׁה וְאֶת־אֶפְרָיִם:

2 When *Yaakov* was told, "Your son *Yosef* has come to see you," *Yisrael* summoned his strength and sat up in bed.

ב וַיַּגֵּד לְיַעֲקֹב וַיֹּאמֶר הִנֵּה בִּנְךָ יוֹסֵף בָּא אֵלֶיךָ וַיִּתְחַזֵּק יִשְׂרָאֵל וַיֵּשֶׁב עַל־הַמִּטָּה:

3 And *Yaakov* said to *Yosef*, "*El Shaddai* appeared to me at Luz in the land of Canaan, and He blessed me,

ג וַיֹּאמֶר יַעֲקֹב אֶל־יוֹסֵף אֵל שַׁדַּי נִרְאָה־אֵלַי בְּלוּז בְּאֶרֶץ כְּנָעַן וַיְבָרֶךְ אֹתִי:

Ariel view of Yosef's tomb in Shechem

47:30 Take me up from Egypt In requesting that he be buried in *Eretz Yisrael* with his father and grandfather, *Yaakov* is instilling in *Yosef* a message to carry through the ages. Though he journeyed to Egypt with God's blessing, *Yaakov* longs to return to the Holy Land – if not during his lifetime then at least after death. No matter how comfortable life may be at this historical juncture, *Yaakov* recognizes that Egypt is not where he belongs. He wants only to return to the land of his fathers. *Yosef* takes his father's message to heart, and later insists that his own bones also be carried back to the Land of Israel when the nation will ultimately be redeemed from Egypt (Genesis 50:25).

Bereishit/Genesis 48
Vayechi

בראשית מח
ויחי

4 and said to me, 'I will make you fertile and numerous, making of you a community of peoples; and I will assign this land to your offspring to come for an everlasting possession.'

וַיֹּאמֶר אֵלַי הִנְנִי מַפְרְךָ וְהִרְבִּיתִךָ וּנְתַתִּיךָ לִקְהַל עַמִּים וְנָתַתִּי אֶת־הָאָרֶץ הַזֹּאת לְזַרְעֲךָ אַחֲרֶיךָ אֲחֻזַּת עוֹלָם:

va-YO-mer ay-LAI hi-n'-NEE maf-r'-KHA v'-hir-bee-TI-kha un-ta-TEE-kha lik-HAL a-MEEM v'-NA-ta-TEE et ha-A-retz ha-ZOT l'-zar-a-KHA a-kha-RE-kha a-khu-ZAT o-LAM

5 Now, your two sons, who were born to you in the land of Egypt before I came to you in Egypt, shall be mine; *Efraim* and *Menashe* shall be mine no less than *Reuven* and *Shimon*.

וְעַתָּה שְׁנֵי־בָנֶיךָ הַנּוֹלָדִים לְךָ בְּאֶרֶץ מִצְרַיִם עַד־בֹּאִי אֵלֶיךָ מִצְרַיְמָה לִי־הֵם אֶפְרַיִם וּמְנַשֶּׁה כִּרְאוּבֵן וְשִׁמְעוֹן יִהְיוּ־לִי:

6 But progeny born to you after them shall be yours; they shall be recorded instead of their brothers in their inheritance.

וּמוֹלַדְתְּךָ אֲשֶׁר־הוֹלַדְתָּ אַחֲרֵיהֶם לְךָ יִהְיוּ עַל שֵׁם אֲחֵיהֶם יִקָּרְאוּ בְּנַחֲלָתָם:

7 I [do this because], when I was returning from *Paddan*, *Rachel* died, to my sorrow, while I was journeying in the land of Canaan, when still some distance short of *Efrat*; and I buried her there on the road to *Efrat* – now *Beit Lechem*.

וַאֲנִי בְּבֹאִי מִפַּדָּן מֵתָה עָלַי רָחֵל בְּאֶרֶץ כְּנַעַן בַּדֶּרֶךְ בְּעוֹד כִּבְרַת־אֶרֶץ לָבֹא אֶפְרָתָה וָאֶקְבְּרֶהָ שָּׁם בְּדֶרֶךְ אֶפְרָת הִוא בֵּית לָחֶם:

8 Noticing *Yosef*'s sons, *Yisrael* asked, "Who are these?"

וַיַּרְא יִשְׂרָאֵל אֶת־בְּנֵי יוֹסֵף וַיֹּאמֶר מִי־אֵלֶּה:

9 And *Yosef* said to his father, "They are my sons, whom *Hashem* has given me here." "Bring them up to me," he said, "that I may bless them."

וַיֹּאמֶר יוֹסֵף אֶל־אָבִיו בָּנַי הֵם אֲשֶׁר־נָתַן־לִי אֱלֹהִים בָּזֶה וַיֹּאמַר קָחֶם־נָא אֵלַי וַאֲבָרֲכֵם:

10 Now *Yisrael*'s eyes were dim with age; he could not see. So [*Yosef*] brought them close to him, and he kissed them and embraced them.

וְעֵינֵי יִשְׂרָאֵל כָּבְדוּ מִזֹּקֶן לֹא יוּכַל לִרְאוֹת וַיַּגֵּשׁ אֹתָם אֵלָיו וַיִּשַּׁק לָהֶם וַיְחַבֵּק לָהֶם:

11 And *Yisrael* said to *Yosef*, "I never expected to see you again, and here *Hashem* has let me see your children as well."

וַיֹּאמֶר יִשְׂרָאֵל אֶל־יוֹסֵף רְאֹה פָנֶיךָ לֹא פִלָּלְתִּי וְהִנֵּה הֶרְאָה אֹתִי אֱלֹהִים גַּם אֶת־זַרְעֶךָ:

12 *Yosef* then removed them from his knees, and bowed low with his face to the ground.

וַיּוֹצֵא יוֹסֵף אֹתָם מֵעִם בִּרְכָּיו וַיִּשְׁתַּחוּ לְאַפָּיו אָרְצָה:

13 *Yosef* took the two of them, *Efraim* with his right hand – to *Yisrael*'s left – and *Menashe* with his left hand – to *Yisrael*'s right – and brought them close to him.

וַיִּקַּח יוֹסֵף אֶת־שְׁנֵיהֶם אֶת־אֶפְרַיִם בִּימִינוֹ מִשְּׂמֹאל יִשְׂרָאֵל וְאֶת־מְנַשֶּׁה בִשְׂמֹאלוֹ מִימִין יִשְׂרָאֵל וַיַּגֵּשׁ אֵלָיו:

14 But *Yisrael* stretched out his right hand and laid it on *Efraim*'s head, though he was the younger, and his left hand on *Menashe*'s head – thus crossing his hands – although *Menashe* was the first-born.

וַיִּשְׁלַח יִשְׂרָאֵל אֶת־יְמִינוֹ וַיָּשֶׁת עַל־רֹאשׁ אֶפְרַיִם וְהוּא הַצָּעִיר וְאֶת־שְׂמֹאלוֹ עַל־רֹאשׁ מְנַשֶּׁה שִׂכֵּל אֶת־יָדָיו כִּי מְנַשֶּׁה הַבְּכוֹר:

Bereishit/Genesis 48
Vayechi

בראשית מח
ויחי

15 And he blessed *Yosef*, saying, "The *Hashem* in whose ways my fathers *Avraham* and *Yitzchak* walked, The *Hashem* who has been my shepherd from my birth to this day –

טו וַיְבָרֶךְ אֶת־יוֹסֵף וַיֹּאמַר הָאֱלֹהִים אֲשֶׁר הִתְהַלְּכוּ אֲבֹתַי לְפָנָיו אַבְרָהָם וְיִצְחָק הָאֱלֹהִים הָרֹעֶה אֹתִי מֵעוֹדִי עַד־הַיּוֹם הַזֶּה׃

16 The Angel who has redeemed me from all harm – the lads. In them may my name be recalled, And the names of my fathers *Avraham* and *Yitzchak*, And may they be teeming multitudes upon the earth."

טז הַמַּלְאָךְ הַגֹּאֵל אֹתִי מִכָּל־רָע יְבָרֵךְ אֶת־הַנְּעָרִים וְיִקָּרֵא בָהֶם שְׁמִי וְשֵׁם אֲבֹתַי אַבְרָהָם וְיִצְחָק וְיִדְגּוּ לָרֹב בְּקֶרֶב הָאָרֶץ׃

ha-mal-AKH ha-go-AYL o-TEE mi-kol RA y'-va-RAYKH et ha-n'-a-REEM v'-yi-ka-RAY va-HEM sh'-MEE v'-SHAYM a-vo-TAI av-ra-HAM v'-yitz-KHAK v'-yid-GU la-ROV b'-KE-rev ha-A-retz

17 When *Yosef* saw that his father was placing his right hand on *Efraim*'s head, he thought it wrong; so he took hold of his father's hand to move it from *Efraim*'s head to *Menashe*'s.

יז וַיַּרְא יוֹסֵף כִּי־יָשִׁית אָבִיו יַד־יְמִינוֹ עַל־רֹאשׁ אֶפְרַיִם וַיֵּרַע בְּעֵינָיו וַיִּתְמֹךְ יַד־אָבִיו לְהָסִיר אֹתָהּ מֵעַל רֹאשׁ־אֶפְרַיִם עַל־רֹאשׁ מְנַשֶּׁה׃

18 "Not so, Father," *Yosef* said to his father, "for the other is the first-born; place your right hand on his head."

יח וַיֹּאמֶר יוֹסֵף אֶל־אָבִיו לֹא־כֵן אָבִי כִּי־זֶה הַבְּכֹר שִׂים יְמִינְךָ עַל־רֹאשׁוֹ׃

19 But his father objected, saying, "I know, my son, I know. He too shall become a people, and he too shall be great. Yet his younger brother shall be greater than he, and his offspring shall be plentiful enough for nations."

יט וַיְמָאֵן אָבִיו וַיֹּאמֶר יָדַעְתִּי בְנִי יָדַעְתִּי גַּם־הוּא יִהְיֶה־לְּעָם וְגַם־הוּא יִגְדָּל וְאוּלָם אָחִיו הַקָּטֹן יִגְדַּל מִמֶּנּוּ וְזַרְעוֹ יִהְיֶה מְלֹא־הַגּוֹיִם׃

20 So he blessed them that day, saying, "By you shall *Yisrael* invoke blessings, saying: *Hashem* make you like *Efraim* and *Menashe*." Thus he put *Efraim* before *Menashe*.

כ וַיְבָרֲכֵם בַּיּוֹם הַהוּא לֵאמוֹר בְּךָ יְבָרֵךְ יִשְׂרָאֵל לֵאמֹר יְשִׂמְךָ אֱלֹהִים כְּאֶפְרַיִם וְכִמְנַשֶּׁה וַיָּשֶׂם אֶת־אֶפְרַיִם לִפְנֵי מְנַשֶּׁה׃

vai-VA-r'-KHAYM ba-YOM ha-HU lay-MOR b'-KHA y'-va-RAYKH yis-ra-AYL lay-MOR y'-sim-KHA e-lo-HEEM k'-ef-RA-yim v'-khim-na-SHEH va-YA-sem et ef-RA-yim lif-NAY m'-na-SHEH

שם

48:16 May my name be recalled The Hebrew word for 'name' is *shem* (שם). The great master of the Hebrew language, Rabbi Samson Raphael Hirsch, explains that the word *shem* is related to the word *sham* (שם), meaning 'there.' Rabbi Hirsch explains that by naming and defining something, one puts it in its proper 'place.' Here, *Yaakov* blesses his grandsons *Efraim* and *Menashe*, by placing their ancestors' names upon them, thereby establishing their 'place' within the spiritual legacy of their forbears.

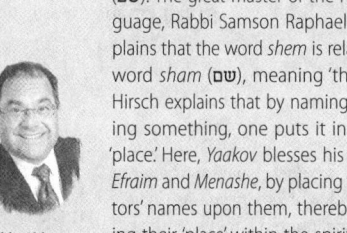

Rabbi Shlomo Riskin (b. 1940)

48:20 By you shall *Yisrael* invoke blessings As dictated by this verse, to this day Jewish parents bless their sons each *Shabbat* with the words, "May *Hashem* make you like *Efraim* and *Menashe*." Out of all the biblical heroes possible to emulate, what is special about *Efraim* and *Menashe*? Rabbi Shlomo Riskin, Chief Rabbi of *Efrat*, explains that the two sons of *Yosef* play a very significant role in the formation of the Jewish people. They are the first of *Avraham's* family to be born in Egypt, yet despite their physical disconnection from *Eretz Yisrael*, they remain loyal to the traditions of their ancestors. *Efraim* and *Menashe*, therefore, represent a key to the survival of the Jewish people and their return to Israel in the future. For this reason, they are chosen as special role models for the Children of Israel.

Bereishit/Genesis 49
Vayechi

בראשית מט
ויחי

21 Then *Yisrael* said to *Yosef*, "I am about to die; but *Hashem* will be with you and bring you back to the land of your fathers.

כא וַיֹּאמֶר יִשְׂרָאֵל אֶל־יוֹסֵף הִנֵּה אָנֹכִי מֵת וְהָיָה אֱלֹהִים עִמָּכֶם וְהֵשִׁיב אֶתְכֶם אֶל־אֶרֶץ אֲבֹתֵיכֶם:

22 And now, I assign to you one portion more than to your brothers, which I wrested from the Amorites with my sword and bow."

כב וַאֲנִי נָתַתִּי לְךָ שְׁכֶם אַחַד עַל־אַחֶיךָ אֲשֶׁר לָקַחְתִּי מִיַּד הָאֱמֹרִי בְּחַרְבִּי וּבְקַשְׁתִּי:

49 1 And *Yaakov* called his sons and said, "Come together that I may tell you what is to befall you in days to come.

מט א וַיִּקְרָא יַעֲקֹב אֶל־בָּנָיו וַיֹּאמֶר הֵאָסְפוּ וְאַגִּידָה לָכֶם אֵת אֲשֶׁר־יִקְרָא אֶתְכֶם בְּאַחֲרִית הַיָּמִים:

2 Assemble and hearken, O sons of *Yaakov*; Hearken to *Yisrael* your father:

ב הִקָּבְצוּ וְשִׁמְעוּ בְּנֵי יַעֲקֹב וְשִׁמְעוּ אֶל־יִשְׂרָאֵל אֲבִיכֶם:

3 *Reuven*, you are my first-born, My might and first fruit of my vigor, Exceeding in rank And exceeding in honor.

ג רְאוּבֵן בְּכֹרִי אַתָּה כֹּחִי וְרֵאשִׁית אוֹנִי יֶתֶר שְׂאֵת וְיֶתֶר עָז:

4 Unstable as water, you shall excel no longer; For when you mounted your father's bed, You brought disgrace – my couch he mounted!

ד פַּחַז כַּמַּיִם אַל־תּוֹתַר כִּי עָלִיתָ מִשְׁכְּבֵי אָבִיךָ אָז חִלַּלְתָּ יְצוּעִי עָלָה:

5 *Shimon* and *Levi* are a pair; Their weapons are tools of lawlessness.

ה שִׁמְעוֹן וְלֵוִי אַחִים כְּלֵי חָמָס מְכֵרֹתֵיהֶם:

6 Let not my person be included in their council, Let not my being be counted in their assembly. For when angry they slay men, And when pleased they maim oxen.

ו בְּסֹדָם אַל־תָּבֹא נַפְשִׁי בִּקְהָלָם אַל־תֵּחַד כְּבֹדִי כִּי בְאַפָּם הָרְגוּ אִישׁ וּבִרְצֹנָם עִקְּרוּ־שׁוֹר:

7 Cursed be their anger so fierce, And their wrath so relentless. I will divide them in *Yaakov*, Scatter them in *Yisrael*.

ז אָרוּר אַפָּם כִּי עָז וְעֶבְרָתָם כִּי קָשָׁתָה אֲחַלְּקֵם בְּיַעֲקֹב וַאֲפִיצֵם בְּיִשְׂרָאֵל:

8 You, O *Yehuda*, your brothers shall praise; Your hand shall be on the nape of your foes; Your father's sons shall bow low to you.

ח יְהוּדָה אַתָּה יוֹדוּךָ אַחֶיךָ יָדְךָ בְּעֹרֶף אֹיְבֶיךָ יִשְׁתַּחֲווּ לְךָ בְּנֵי אָבִיךָ:

9 *Yehuda* is a lion's whelp; On prey, my son, have you grown. He crouches, lies down like a lion, Like the king of beasts – who dare rouse him?

ט גּוּר אַרְיֵה יְהוּדָה מִטֶּרֶף בְּנִי עָלִיתָ כָּרַע רָבַץ כְּאַרְיֵה וּכְלָבִיא מִי יְקִימֶנּוּ:

10 The scepter shall not depart from *Yehuda*, Nor the ruler's staff from between his feet; So that tribute shall come to him And the homage of peoples be his.

י לֹא־יָסוּר שֵׁבֶט מִיהוּדָה וּמְחֹקֵק מִבֵּין רַגְלָיו עַד כִּי־יָבֹא שִׁילֹה [שִׁילוֹ] וְלוֹ יִקְּהַת עַמִּים:

49:10 So that tribute shall come to him The Hebrew word for tribute in this verse is *Shilo* (שילה). Fourteenth century scholar Rabbi Yaakov ben Asher, known by the name of his Bible commentary as the *Baal Haturim*, reveals a hidden connection between the word *Shilo* (שילה) and *Mashiach* (משיח), the Hebrew word for 'Messiah.' According to the mystical study of *gematriya*, every Hebrew letter corresponds to a differ-

שילה
משיח

128

Bereishit/Genesis 49
Vayechi

בראשית מט
ויחי

lo ya-SUR SHAY-vet mee-hu-DAH um-kho-KAYK mi-BAYN rag-LAV AD kee ya-VO shee-LOH v'-LO yi-k-HAHT a-MEEM

11 He tethers his ass to a vine, His ass's foal to a choice vine; He washes his garment in wine, His robe in blood of grapes.

יא אֹסְרִי לַגֶּפֶן עִירֹה [עִירוֹ] וְלַשֹּׂרֵקָה בְּנִי אֲתֹנוֹ כִּבֵּס בַּיַּיִן לְבֻשׁוֹ וּבְדַם־עֲנָבִים סוּתֹה [סוּתוֹ]:

12 His eyes are darker than wine; His teeth are whiter than milk.

יב חַכְלִילִי עֵינַיִם מִיָּיִן וּלְבֶן־שִׁנַּיִם מֵחָלָב:

13 *Zevulun* shall dwell by the seashore; He shall be a haven for ships, And his flank shall rest on Sidon.

יג זְבוּלֻן לְחוֹף יַמִּים יִשְׁכֹּן וְהוּא לְחוֹף אֳנִיּוֹת וְיַרְכָתוֹ עַל־צִידֹן:

z'-vu-LUN l'-KHOF ya-MEEM yish-KON v'-HU l'-KHOF a-ni-YOT v'-yar-kha-TO al tzee-DON

14 *Yissachar* is a strong-boned ass, Crouching among the sheepfolds.

יד יִשָּׂשכָר חֲמֹר גָּרֶם רֹבֵץ בֵּין הַמִּשְׁפְּתָיִם:

15 When he saw how good was security, And how pleasant was the country, He bent his shoulder to the burden, And became a toiling serf.

טו וַיַּרְא מְנֻחָה כִּי טוֹב וְאֶת־הָאָרֶץ כִּי נָעֵמָה וַיֵּט שִׁכְמוֹ לִסְבֹּל וַיְהִי לְמַס־עֹבֵד:

16 *Dan* shall govern his people, As one of the tribes of *Yisrael*.

טז דָּן יָדִין עַמּוֹ כְּאַחַד שִׁבְטֵי יִשְׂרָאֵל:

17 *Dan* shall be a serpent by the road, A viper by the path, That bites the horse's heels So that his rider is thrown backward.

יז יְהִי־דָן נָחָשׁ עֲלֵי־דֶרֶךְ שְׁפִיפֹן עֲלֵי־אֹרַח הַנֹּשֵׁךְ עִקְּבֵי־סוּס וַיִּפֹּל רֹכְבוֹ אָחוֹר:

18 I wait for Your deliverance, *Hashem*!

יח לִישׁוּעָתְךָ קִוִּיתִי יְהוָה:

19 *Gad* shall be raided by raiders, But he shall raid at their heels.

יט גָּד גְּדוּד יְגוּדֶנּוּ וְהוּא יָגֻד עָקֵב:

20 *Asher*'s bread shall be rich, And he shall yield royal dainties.

כ מֵאָשֵׁר שְׁמֵנָה לַחְמוֹ וְהוּא יִתֵּן מַעֲדַנֵּי־מֶלֶךְ:

---

ent number. With this understanding, if the numerical values of diverse words and ideas match each other, this means they are secretly connected. Amazingly, the numerical value of the words *yavo shilo* (יבא שילה), '*Shilo* shall come,' is to 358 which is exactly the same value as the word *Mashiach*. With prophetic foresight, *Yaakov* blesses *Yehuda* not only with the monarchy, but with the eventual emergence of the Messiah through his lineage.

49:13 *Zevulun* shall dwell by the seashore Each of the twelve tribes of Israel is to receive a specific portion of the land, corresponding to that tribe's unique spiritual attributes. According to Jewish tradition, the sons of *Zevulun*, who were given a coastal territory as their inheritance, became successful sea merchants and entered into a special partnership with the tribe of *Yissachar*, descendants of *Zevulun*'s closest brother. According to the arrangement they forged, members of the tribe of *Zevulun* would use some of their commercial profits to financially support the sons of *Yissachar*, noted scholars who would devote their energies to full time *Torah* study. In turn, they would share the spiritual revenue and heavenly reward of the joint venture with their brethren from *Zevulun*. Today as well, in many Israeli communities it is a common practice for business people to seek out a spiritual partner, supporting the learning of a Torah scholar in a mutually-beneficial partnership modeled after the original *Yissachar-Zevulun* agreement.

Mediterranean Sea

Bereishit/Genesis 49
Vayechi

בראשית מט
ויחי

21 *Naftali* is a hind let loose, Which yields lovely fawns.

כא נַפְתָּלִ֖י אַיָּלָ֣ה שְׁלֻחָ֑ה הַנֹּתֵ֖ן אִמְרֵי־שָֽׁפֶר׃

22 *Yosef* is a wild ass, A wild ass by a spring – Wild colts on a hillside.

כב בֵּ֤ן פֹּרָת֙ יוֹסֵ֔ף בֵּ֥ן פֹּרָ֖ת עֲלֵי־עָ֑יִן בָּנ֕וֹת צָעֲדָ֖ה עֲלֵי־שֽׁוּר׃

23 Archers bitterly assailed him; They shot at him and harried him.

כג וַֽיְמָרֲרֻ֖הוּ וָרֹ֑בּוּ וַֽיִּשְׂטְמֻ֖הוּ בַּעֲלֵ֥י חִצִּֽים׃

24 Yet his bow stayed taut, And his arms were made firm By the hands of the Mighty One of *Yaakov* – There, the Shepherd, the Rock of *Yisrael* –

כד וַתֵּ֤שֶׁב בְּאֵיתָן֙ קַשְׁתּ֔וֹ וַיָּפֹ֖זּוּ זְרֹעֵ֣י יָדָ֑יו מִידֵי֙ אֲבִ֣יר יַעֲקֹ֔ב מִשָּׁ֥ם רֹעֶ֖ה אֶ֥בֶן יִשְׂרָאֵֽל׃

25 The God of your father who helps you, And *Shaddai* who blesses you With blessings of heaven above, Blessings of the deep that couches below, Blessings of the breast and womb.

כה מֵאֵ֨ל אָבִ֜יךָ וְיַעְזְרֶ֗ךָּ וְאֵ֤ת שַׁדַּי֙ וִיבָ֣רְכֶ֔ךָּ בִּרְכֹ֤ת שָׁמַ֙יִם֙ מֵעָ֔ל בִּרְכֹ֥ת תְּה֖וֹם רֹבֶ֣צֶת תָּ֑חַת בִּרְכֹ֥ת שָׁדַ֖יִם וָרָֽחַם׃

26 The blessings of your father Surpass the blessings of my ancestors, To the utmost bounds of the eternal hills. May they rest on the head of *Yosef*, On the brow of the elect of his brothers.

כו בִּרְכֹ֣ת אָבִ֗יךָ גָּֽבְרוּ֙ עַל־בִּרְכֹ֣ת הוֹרַ֔י עַד־תַּאֲוַ֖ת גִּבְעֹ֣ת עוֹלָ֑ם תִּֽהְיֶ֙יןָ֙ לְרֹ֣אשׁ יוֹסֵ֔ף וּלְקָדְקֹ֖ד נְזִ֥יר אֶחָֽיו׃

27 *Binyamin* is a ravenous wolf; In the morning he consumes the foe, And in the evening he divides the spoil."

כז בִּנְיָמִין֙ זְאֵ֣ב יִטְרָ֔ף בַּבֹּ֖קֶר יֹ֣אכַל עַ֑ד וְלָעֶ֖רֶב יְחַלֵּ֥ק שָׁלָֽל׃

28 All these were the tribes of *Yisrael*, twelve in number, and this is what their father said to them as he bade them farewell, addressing to each a parting word appropriate to him.

כח כָּל־אֵ֛לֶּה שִׁבְטֵ֥י יִשְׂרָאֵ֖ל שְׁנֵ֣ים עָשָׂ֑ר וְ֠זֹאת אֲשֶׁר־דִּבֶּ֨ר לָהֶ֤ם אֲבִיהֶם֙ וַיְבָ֣רֶךְ אוֹתָ֔ם אִ֛ישׁ אֲשֶׁ֥ר כְּבִרְכָת֖וֹ בֵּרַ֥ךְ אֹתָֽם׃

29 Then he instructed them, saying to them, "I am about to be gathered to my kin. Bury me with my fathers in the cave which is in the field of Ephron the Hittite,

כט וַיְצַ֣ו אוֹתָ֗ם וַיֹּ֤אמֶר אֲלֵהֶם֙ אֲנִי֙ נֶאֱסָ֣ף אֶל־עַמִּ֔י קִבְר֥וּ אֹתִ֖י אֶל־אֲבֹתָ֑י אֶל־הַ֨מְּעָרָ֔ה אֲשֶׁ֥ר בִּשְׂדֵ֖ה עֶפְר֥וֹן הַֽחִתִּֽי׃

30 the cave which is in the field of Machpelah, facing Mamre, in the land of Canaan, the field that *Avraham* bought from Ephron the Hittite for a burial site

ל בַּמְּעָרָ֞ה אֲשֶׁ֨ר בִּשְׂדֵ֧ה הַמַּכְפֵּלָ֛ה אֲשֶׁ֥ר עַל־פְּנֵי־מַמְרֵ֖א בְּאֶ֣רֶץ כְּנָ֑עַן אֲשֶׁר֩ קָנָ֨ה אַבְרָהָ֜ם אֶת־הַשָּׂדֶ֗ה מֵאֵ֛ת עֶפְרֹ֥ן הַחִתִּ֖י לַאֲחֻזַּת־קָֽבֶר׃

31 there *Avraham* and his wife *Sara* were buried; there *Yitzchak* and his wife *Rivka* were buried; and there I buried *Leah*

לא שָׁ֣מָּה קָֽבְר֞וּ אֶת־אַבְרָהָ֗ם וְאֵת֙ שָׂרָ֣ה אִשְׁתּ֔וֹ שָׁ֥מָּה קָבְר֛וּ אֶת־יִצְחָ֖ק וְאֵ֣ת רִבְקָ֣ה אִשְׁתּ֑וֹ וְשָׁ֥מָּה קָבַ֖רְתִּי אֶת־לֵאָֽה׃

32 the field and the cave in it, bought from the Hittites."

לב מִקְנֵ֧ה הַשָּׂדֶ֛ה וְהַמְּעָרָ֥ה אֲשֶׁר־בּ֖וֹ מֵאֵ֥ת בְּנֵי־חֵֽת׃

33 When *Yaakov* finished his instructions to his sons, he drew his feet into the bed and, breathing his last, he was gathered to his people.

לג וַיְכַ֤ל יַעֲקֹב֙ לְצַוֺּ֣ת אֶת־בָּנָ֔יו וַיֶּאֱסֹ֥ף רַגְלָ֖יו אֶל־הַמִּטָּ֑ה וַיִּגְוַ֖ע וַיֵּאָ֥סֶף אֶל־עַמָּֽיו׃

130

Bereishit/Genesis 50
Vayechi

50 1 *Yosef* flung himself upon his father's face and wept over him and kissed him.

2 Then *Yosef* ordered the physicians in his service to embalm his father, and the physicians embalmed *Yisrael*.

3 It required forty days, for such is the full period of embalming. The Egyptians bewailed him seventy days;

4 and when the wailing period was over, *Yosef* spoke to Pharaoh's court, saying, "Do me this favor, and lay this appeal before Pharaoh:

5 'My father made me swear, saying, "I am about to die. Be sure to bury me in the grave which I made ready for myself in the land of Canaan." Now, therefore, let me go up and bury my father; then I shall return.'"

6 And Pharaoh said, "Go up and bury your father, as he made you promise on oath."

7 So *Yosef* went up to bury his father; and with him went up all the officials of Pharaoh, the senior members of his court, and all of Egypt's dignitaries,

8 together with all of *Yosef*'s household, his brothers, and his father's household; only their children, their flocks, and their herds were left in the region of Goshen.

9 Chariots, too, and horsemen went up with him; it was a very large troop.

10 When they came to Goren ha-Atad, which is beyond the *Yarden*, they held there a very great and solemn lamentation; and he observed a mourning period of seven days for his father.

11 And when the Canaanite inhabitants of the land saw the mourning at Goren ha-Atad, they said, "This is a solemn mourning on the part of the Egyptians." That is why it was named Abel-mizraim, which is beyond the *Yarden*.

12 Thus his sons did for him as he had instructed them.

13 His sons carried him to the land of Canaan, and buried him in the cave of the field of Machpelah, the field near Mamre, which *Avraham* had bought for a burial site from Ephron the Hittite.

בראשית נ

ויחי

א וַיִּפֹּל יוֹסֵף עַל־פְּנֵי אָבִיו וַיֵּבְךְּ עָלָיו וַיִּשַּׁק־לוֹ:

ב וַיְצַו יוֹסֵף אֶת־עֲבָדָיו אֶת־הָרֹפְאִים לַחֲנֹט אֶת־אָבִיו וַיַּחַנְטוּ הָרֹפְאִים אֶת־יִשְׂרָאֵל:

ג וַיִּמְלְאוּ־לוֹ אַרְבָּעִים יוֹם כִּי כֵּן יִמְלְאוּ יְמֵי הַחֲנֻטִים וַיִּבְכּוּ אֹתוֹ מִצְרַיִם שִׁבְעִים יוֹם:

ד וַיַּעַבְרוּ יְמֵי בְכִיתוֹ וַיְדַבֵּר יוֹסֵף אֶל־בֵּית פַּרְעֹה לֵאמֹר אִם־נָא מָצָאתִי חֵן בְּעֵינֵיכֶם דַּבְּרוּ־נָא בְּאָזְנֵי פַרְעֹה לֵאמֹר:

ה אָבִי הִשְׁבִּיעַנִי לֵאמֹר הִנֵּה אָנֹכִי מֵת בְּקִבְרִי אֲשֶׁר כָּרִיתִי לִי בְּאֶרֶץ כְּנַעַן שָׁמָּה תִּקְבְּרֵנִי וְעַתָּה אֶעֱלֶה־נָּא וְאֶקְבְּרָה אֶת־אָבִי וְאָשׁוּבָה:

ו וַיֹּאמֶר פַּרְעֹה עֲלֵה וּקְבֹר אֶת־אָבִיךָ כַּאֲשֶׁר הִשְׁבִּיעֶךָ:

ז וַיַּעַל יוֹסֵף לִקְבֹּר אֶת־אָבִיו וַיַּעֲלוּ אִתּוֹ כָּל־עַבְדֵי פַרְעֹה זִקְנֵי בֵיתוֹ וְכֹל זִקְנֵי אֶרֶץ־מִצְרָיִם:

ח וְכֹל בֵּית יוֹסֵף וְאֶחָיו וּבֵית אָבִיו רַק טַפָּם וְצֹאנָם וּבְקָרָם עָזְבוּ בְּאֶרֶץ גֹּשֶׁן:

ט וַיַּעַל עִמּוֹ גַּם־רֶכֶב גַּם־פָּרָשִׁים וַיְהִי הַמַּחֲנֶה כָּבֵד מְאֹד:

י וַיָּבֹאוּ עַד־גֹּרֶן הָאָטָד אֲשֶׁר בְּעֵבֶר הַיַּרְדֵּן וַיִּסְפְּדוּ־שָׁם מִסְפֵּד גָּדוֹל וְכָבֵד מְאֹד וַיַּעַשׂ לְאָבִיו אֵבֶל שִׁבְעַת יָמִים:

יא וַיַּרְא יוֹשֵׁב הָאָרֶץ הַכְּנַעֲנִי אֶת־הָאֵבֶל בְּגֹרֶן הָאָטָד וַיֹּאמְרוּ אֵבֶל־כָּבֵד זֶה לְמִצְרָיִם עַל־כֵּן קָרָא שְׁמָהּ אָבֵל מִצְרַיִם אֲשֶׁר בְּעֵבֶר הַיַּרְדֵּן:

יב וַיַּעֲשׂוּ בָנָיו לוֹ כֵּן כַּאֲשֶׁר צִוָּם:

יג וַיִּשְׂאוּ אֹתוֹ בָנָיו אַרְצָה כְּנַעַן וַיִּקְבְּרוּ אֹתוֹ בִּמְעָרַת שְׂדֵה הַמַּכְפֵּלָה אֲשֶׁר קָנָה אַבְרָהָם אֶת־הַשָּׂדֶה לַאֲחֻזַּת־קֶבֶר מֵאֵת עֶפְרֹן הַחִתִּי עַל־פְּנֵי מַמְרֵא:

Bereishit/Genesis 50
Vayechi

בראשית נ
ויחי

14 After burying his father, *Yosef* returned to Egypt, he and his brothers and all who had gone up with him to bury his father.

יד וַיָּשָׁב יוֹסֵף מִצְרַיְמָה הוּא וְאֶחָיו וְכָל־הָעֹלִים אִתּוֹ לִקְבֹּר אֶת־אָבִיו אַחֲרֵי קָבְרוֹ אֶת־אָבִיו:

15 When *Yosef*'s brothers saw that their father was dead, they said, "What if *Yosef* still bears a grudge against us and pays us back for all the wrong that we did him!"

טו וַיִּרְאוּ אֲחֵי־יוֹסֵף כִּי־מֵת אֲבִיהֶם וַיֹּאמְרוּ לוּ יִשְׂטְמֵנוּ יוֹסֵף וְהָשֵׁב יָשִׁיב לָנוּ אֵת כָּל־הָרָעָה אֲשֶׁר גָּמַלְנוּ אֹתוֹ:

16 So they sent this message to *Yosef*, "Before his death your father left this instruction:

טז וַיְצַוּוּ אֶל־יוֹסֵף לֵאמֹר אָבִיךָ צִוָּה לִפְנֵי מוֹתוֹ לֵאמֹר:

17 So shall you say to *Yosef*, 'Forgive, I urge you, the offense and guilt of your brothers who treated you so harshly.' Therefore, please forgive the offense of the servants of the God of your father." And *Yosef* was in tears as they spoke to him.

יז כֹּה־תֹאמְרוּ לְיוֹסֵף אָנָּא שָׂא נָא פֶּשַׁע אַחֶיךָ וְחַטָּאתָם כִּי־רָעָה גְמָלוּךָ וְעַתָּה שָׂא נָא לְפֶשַׁע עַבְדֵי אֱלֹהֵי אָבִיךָ וַיֵּבְךְּ יוֹסֵף בְּדַבְּרָם אֵלָיו:

18 His brothers went to him themselves, flung themselves before him, and said, "We are prepared to be your slaves."

יח וַיֵּלְכוּ גַּם־אֶחָיו וַיִּפְּלוּ לְפָנָיו וַיֹּאמְרוּ הִנֶּנּוּ לְךָ לַעֲבָדִים:

19 But *Yosef* said to them, "Have no fear! Am I a substitute for *Hashem*?

יט וַיֹּאמֶר אֲלֵהֶם יוֹסֵף אַל־תִּירָאוּ כִּי הֲתַחַת אֱלֹהִים אָנִי:

20 Besides, although you intended me harm, *Hashem* intended it for good, so as to bring about the present result – the survival of many people.

כ וְאַתֶּם חֲשַׁבְתֶּם עָלַי רָעָה אֱלֹהִים חֲשָׁבָהּ לְטֹבָה לְמַעַן עֲשֹׂה כַּיּוֹם הַזֶּה לְהַחֲיֹת עַם־רָב:

21 And so, fear not. I will sustain you and your children." Thus he reassured them, speaking kindly to them.

כא וְעַתָּה אַל־תִּירָאוּ אָנֹכִי אֲכַלְכֵּל אֶתְכֶם וְאֶת־טַפְּכֶם וַיְנַחֵם אוֹתָם וַיְדַבֵּר עַל־לִבָּם:

22 So *Yosef* and his father's household remained in Egypt. *Yosef* lived one hundred and ten years.

כב וַיֵּשֶׁב יוֹסֵף בְּמִצְרַיִם הוּא וּבֵית אָבִיו וַיְחִי יוֹסֵף מֵאָה וָעֶשֶׂר שָׁנִים:

23 *Yosef* lived to see children of the third generation of *Efraim*; the children of Machir son of *Menashe* were likewise born upon *Yosef*'s knees.

כג וַיַּרְא יוֹסֵף לְאֶפְרַיִם בְּנֵי שִׁלֵּשִׁים גַּם בְּנֵי מָכִיר בֶּן־מְנַשֶּׁה יֻלְּדוּ עַל־בִּרְכֵּי יוֹסֵף:

24 At length, *Yosef* said to his brothers, "I am about to die. *Hashem* will surely take notice of you and bring you up from this land to the land that He promised on oath to *Avraham*, to *Yitzchak*, and to *Yaakov*."

כד וַיֹּאמֶר יוֹסֵף אֶל־אֶחָיו אָנֹכִי מֵת וֵאלֹהִים פָּקֹד יִפְקֹד אֶתְכֶם וְהֶעֱלָה אֶתְכֶם מִן־הָאָרֶץ הַזֹּאת אֶל־הָאָרֶץ אֲשֶׁר נִשְׁבַּע לְאַבְרָהָם לְיִצְחָק וּלְיַעֲקֹב:

50:24 ***Hashem* will surely take notice of you** These words are spoken by *Yosef* to reassure his brothers that *Hashem* will one day bring the Israelites out of Egypt and into *Eretz Yisrael*. The Sages point out that the phrase used by *Yosef*, "surely take notice," is repeated many years later by *Moshe* when he tells the Jewish people that the time had come for their redemption (see Exodus 3:16). *Yosef* initiated an oral tradition among the descendants of *Yaakov*; the words "surely take notice" became a code for their national redemp-

Bereishit/Genesis 50
Vayechi

בראשית נ
ויחי

> va-YO-mer yo-SAYF el e-KHAV a-no-KHEE MAYT vay-lo-HEEM pa-KOD
> yif-KOD et-KHEM v'-he-e-LAH et-KHEM min ha-A-retz ha-ZOT el ha-A-retz
> a-SHER nish-BA l'-av-ra-HAM l'-yitz-KHAHK ul-ya-a-KOV

25 So *Yosef* made the sons of *Yisrael* swear, saying, "When *Hashem* has taken notice of you, you shall carry up my bones from here."

וַיַּשְׁבַּע יוֹסֵף אֶת־בְּנֵי יִשְׂרָאֵל לֵאמֹר פָּקֹד יִפְקֹד אֱלֹהִים אֶתְכֶם וְהַעֲלִתֶם אֶת־עַצְמֹתַי מִזֶּה: כה

26 *Yosef* died at the age of one hundred and ten years; and he was embalmed and placed in a coffin in Egypt.

וַיָּמָת יוֹסֵף בֶּן־מֵאָה וָעֶשֶׂר שָׁנִים וַיַּחַנְטוּ אֹתוֹ וַיִּישֶׂם בָּאָרוֹן בְּמִצְרָיִם: כו

tion. When later generations hear this phrase uttered by *Moshe*, they understand that their redemption is imminent.

50:24 To *Avraham*, to *Yitzchak*, and to *Yaakov*. The story of the origins of the Jewish nation through God's selection of *Avraham*, *Yitzchak*, and *Yaakov* is timeless. Though God indeed fulfilled His promise redeem *Avraham*'s children from Egypt, the story does not end there; it continues to unfold over thousands of years. *Hashem* made an eternal promise to *Avraham* and to his descendants, the Jewish people. While there are many difficult times along the way – persecution, slavery, exile, pogroms, and even the horrors of the twentieth century – the Jewish people will ultimately emerge as a great nation residing in *Eretz Yisrael*.

Sefer Shemot
The Book of Exodus

Introduction and commentary by Rabbi Tuly Weisz

Location and geography are central to *Sefer Shemot* (Exodus). Ancient Egypt and the barren wilderness form the essential backdrop to the drama which unfolds in the second book of the Bible. While all of the events recorded in *Sefer Shemot* take place outside of the Land of Israel, this does not mean that *Eretz Yisrael* is unimportant in this book. On the contrary, the Land of Israel is a central theme and primary focus of *Sefer Shemot*.

The Hebrew name for the Book of Exodus is *Sefer Shemot*, the 'Book of Names,' taken from the opening words of the first verse. Continuing the narrative from the point where *Sefer Bereishit* (Genesis) ended, it transitions from a family's individual story to the birth of an entire nation. The opening chapters of *Sefer Shemot* describe the trials experienced by the Children of Israel in the fiery furnace of slavery. This brutal oppression in a foreign land has been explained by Jewish commentators as a process of national purification, necessary in order to prepare the Israelites for entry into the "land flowing with milk and honey" (Exodus 3:8).

Sefer Shemot goes on to describe the exodus from Egypt and offers timeless insight into God's loving relationship with humanity as their ultimate Redeemer. With each step they take in the wilderness, the Israelites are marching towards, and getting closer to, *Eretz Yisrael*, which becomes the ultimate ideal for which they strive.

It is no wonder then, that the Book of *Shemot* has served throughout the ages as an inspiration for those who have longed for *Eretz Yisrael*. Wandering through the bitter exile, Jews have always seen themselves as following in the footsteps of the ancient Israelites. In the darkest moments of Jewish history, we have borne the burden of persecution with the knowledge that we are always getting closer to deliverance and redemption, and to Israel. *Sefer Shemot* causes us to realize that the destiny of the People of Israel always leads towards the Land of Israel.

Map of the Journey from Egypt to Mount Sinai

This map traces the journey of the Children of Israel from Egypt to Mount Sinai as described in *Sefer Shemot* (12:37–19:2).

1. The Children of Israel leave Egypt from **Ramses** (Exodus 12:37).
2. The first stop on their journey is **Succoth** (Exodus 12:37).
3. From Succoth they travel to **Etham** (Exodus 13:19).
4. They camp between **Midgol** and the sea while the Egyptian army pursues them (Exodus 14:1–14).
5. The **Sea of Reeds** splits, allowing the Jews to cross on dry land (Exodus 14:15–31).
6. The people travel to **Marah** where they find bitter water (Exodus 15:23–26).
7. In **Elim**, they find 12 springs of water and 70 palm trees (Exodus 15:27).
8. In the **wilderness of Sin**, they complain about the lack of food (Exodus 16:1–36).
9. They again lack water in **Rephidim**. God provides water from a rock and Amalek attacks (Exodus 17:1–16).
10. From Rephidim, they travel to **Mount Sinai** (Exodus 19:1–2).

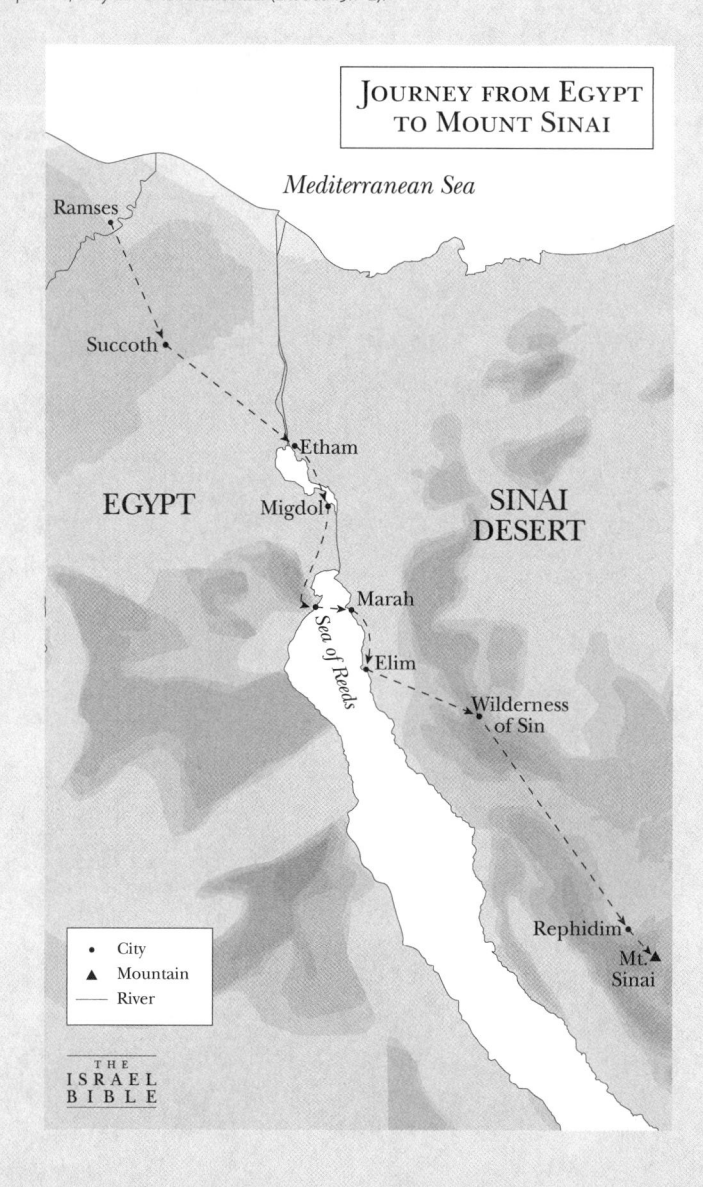

Shemot/Exodus 1

Shemot

שמות א
שמות

1 **1** These are the names of the sons of *Yisrael* who came to Egypt with *Yaakov*, each coming with his household:

א וְאֵ֗לֶּה שְׁמוֹת֙ בְּנֵ֣י יִשְׂרָאֵ֔ל הַבָּאִ֖ים מִצְרָ֑יְמָה אֵ֣ת יַעֲקֹ֔ב אִ֥ישׁ וּבֵית֖וֹ בָּֽאוּ׃

v'-AY-leh sh'-MOT b'-NAY yis-ra-AYL ha-ba-EEM mitz-RA-y'-mah AYT ya-a-KOV EESH u'-vay-TO BA-u

2 *Reuven, Shimon, Levi,* and *Yehuda;*

ב רְאוּבֵ֣ן שִׁמְע֔וֹן לֵוִ֖י וִיהוּדָֽה׃

3 *Yissachar, Zevulun,* and *Binyamin;*

ג יִשָּׂשכָ֥ר זְבוּלֻ֖ן וּבִנְיָמִֽן׃

4 *Dan* and *Naftali, Gad* and *Asher.*

ד דָּ֥ן וְנַפְתָּלִ֖י גָּ֥ד וְאָשֵֽׁר׃

5 The total number of persons that were of *Yaakov's* issue came to seventy, *Yosef* being already in Egypt.

ה וַֽיְהִ֗י כָּל־נֶ֛פֶשׁ יֹצְאֵ֥י יֶֽרֶךְ־יַעֲקֹ֖ב שִׁבְעִ֣ים נָ֑פֶשׁ וְיוֹסֵ֖ף הָיָ֥ה בְמִצְרָֽיִם׃

6 *Yosef* died, and all his brothers, and all that generation.

ו וַיָּ֤מָת יוֹסֵף֙ וְכָל־אֶחָ֔יו וְכֹ֖ל הַדּ֥וֹר הַהֽוּא׃

7 But the Israelites were fertile and prolific; they multiplied and increased very greatly, so that the land was filled with them.

ז וּבְנֵ֣י יִשְׂרָאֵ֗ל פָּר֧וּ וַֽיִּשְׁרְצ֛וּ וַיִּרְבּ֥וּ וַיַּֽעַצְמ֖וּ בִּמְאֹ֣ד מְאֹ֑ד וַתִּמָּלֵ֥א הָאָ֖רֶץ אֹתָֽם׃

8 A new king arose over Egypt who did not know *Yosef*.

ח וַיָּ֥קָם מֶֽלֶךְ־חָדָ֖שׁ עַל־מִצְרָ֑יִם אֲשֶׁ֥ר לֹֽא־יָדַ֖ע אֶת־יוֹסֵֽף׃

9 And he said to his people, "Look, *B'nei Yisrael* are much too numerous for us.

ט וַיֹּ֖אמֶר אֶל־עַמּ֑וֹ הִנֵּ֗ה עַ֚ם בְּנֵ֣י יִשְׂרָאֵ֔ל רַ֥ב וְעָצ֖וּם מִמֶּֽנּוּ׃

10 Let us deal shrewdly with them, so that they may not increase; otherwise in the event of war they may join our enemies in fighting against us and rise from the ground."

י הָ֥בָה נִֽתְחַכְּמָ֖ה ל֑וֹ פֶּן־יִרְבֶּ֗ה וְהָיָ֞ה כִּֽי־תִקְרֶ֤אנָה מִלְחָמָה֙ וְנוֹסַ֤ף גַּם־הוּא֙ עַל־שֹׂ֣נְאֵ֔ינוּ וְנִלְחַם־בָּ֖נוּ וְעָלָ֥ה מִן־הָאָֽרֶץ׃

11 So they set taskmasters over them to oppress them with forced labor; and they built garrison cities for Pharaoh: Pithom and Raamses.

יא וַיָּשִׂ֤ימוּ עָלָיו֙ שָׂרֵ֣י מִסִּ֔ים לְמַ֥עַן עַנֹּת֖וֹ בְּסִבְלֹתָ֑ם וַיִּ֜בֶן עָרֵ֤י מִסְכְּנוֹת֙ לְפַרְעֹ֔ה אֶת־פִּתֹ֖ם וְאֶת־רַֽעַמְסֵֽס׃

12 But the more they were oppressed, the more they increased and spread out, so that the [Egyptians] came to dread the Israelites.

יב וְכַאֲשֶׁר֙ יְעַנּ֣וּ אֹת֔וֹ כֵּ֥ן יִרְבֶּ֖ה וְכֵ֣ן יִפְרֹ֑ץ וַיָּקֻ֕צוּ מִפְּנֵ֖י בְּנֵ֥י יִשְׂרָאֵֽל׃

13 The Egyptians ruthlessly imposed upon the Israelites

יג וַיַּעֲבִ֧דוּ מִצְרַ֛יִם אֶת־בְּנֵ֥י יִשְׂרָאֵ֖ל בְּפָֽרֶךְ׃

ואלה **1:1 These are the names** *Sefer Shemot* starts with the letter *vav* (ו), which signifies the conjunction 'and,' thus connecting it to the end of *Sefer Bereishit*. In fact, the passages beginning with *Shemot* 1:1 and *Bereishit* 46:8 are practically identical, each containing a list of *Yaakov's* descendants who accompanied him to Egypt. The end of *Sefer Bereishit* describes the children of *Yaakov* leaving their homeland and descending to Egypt. *Sefer Shemot* continues the story of the exile and the subsequent miraculous redemption, and is therefore a direct continuation of *Sefer Bereishit*. However, the story does not end with the conclusion of *Sefer Shemot*. While the slavery itself comes to an end with the exodus from Egypt, the ultimate redemption comes only with the reunification of the Children of Israel and their homeland, as described in *Sefer Yehoshua*.

Shemot/Exodus 1
Shemot

שמות א
שמות

14 the various labors that they made them perform. Ruthlessly* they made life bitter for them with harsh labor at mortar and bricks and with all sorts of tasks in the field.

יד וַיְמָרְרוּ אֶת־חַיֵּיהֶם בַּעֲבֹדָה קָשָׁה בְּחֹמֶר וּבִלְבֵנִים וּבְכָל־עֲבֹדָה בַּשָּׂדֶה אֵת כָּל־עֲבֹדָתָם אֲשֶׁר־עָבְדוּ בָהֶם בְּפָרֶךְ:

15 The king of Egypt spoke to the Hebrew midwives, one of whom was named Shiphrah and the other Puah,

טו וַיֹּאמֶר מֶלֶךְ מִצְרַיִם לַמְיַלְּדֹת הָעִבְרִיֹּת אֲשֶׁר שֵׁם הָאַחַת שִׁפְרָה וְשֵׁם הַשֵּׁנִית פּוּעָה:

va-YO-mer ME-lekh mitz-RA-yim lam-ya-l'-DOT ha-iv-ri-YOT a-SHER SHAYM ha-a-KHAT shif-RAH v'-SHAYM ha-shay-NEET pu-AH

16 saying, "When you deliver the Hebrew women, look at the birthstool: if it is a boy, kill him; if it is a girl, let her live."

טז וַיֹּאמֶר בְּיַלֶּדְכֶן אֶת־הָעִבְרִיּוֹת וּרְאִיתֶן עַל־הָאָבְנָיִם אִם־בֵּן הוּא וַהֲמִתֶּן אֹתוֹ וְאִם־בַּת הִיא וָחָיָה:

17 The midwives, fearing *Hashem*, did not do as the king of Egypt had told them; they let the boys live.

יז וַתִּירֶאןָ הַמְיַלְּדֹת אֶת־הָאֱלֹהִים וְלֹא עָשׂוּ כַּאֲשֶׁר דִּבֶּר אֲלֵיהֶן מֶלֶךְ מִצְרָיִם וַתְּחַיֶּיןָ אֶת־הַיְלָדִים:

18 So the king of Egypt summoned the midwives and said to them, "Why have you done this thing, letting the boys live?"

יח וַיִּקְרָא מֶלֶךְ־מִצְרַיִם לַמְיַלְּדֹת וַיֹּאמֶר לָהֶן מַדּוּעַ עֲשִׂיתֶן הַדָּבָר הַזֶּה וַתְּחַיֶּיןָ אֶת־הַיְלָדִים:

19 The midwives said to Pharaoh, "Because the Hebrew women are not like the Egyptian women: they are vigorous. Before the midwife can come to them, they have given birth."

יט וַתֹּאמַרְןָ הַמְיַלְּדֹת אֶל־פַּרְעֹה כִּי לֹא כַנָּשִׁים הַמִּצְרִיֹּת הָעִבְרִיֹּת כִּי־חָיוֹת הֵנָּה בְּטֶרֶם תָּבוֹא אֲלֵהֶן הַמְיַלֶּדֶת וְיָלָדוּ:

20 And *Hashem* dealt well with the midwives; and the people multiplied and increased greatly.

כ וַיֵּיטֶב אֱלֹהִים לַמְיַלְּדֹת וַיִּרֶב הָעָם וַיַּעַצְמוּ מְאֹד:

21 And because the midwives feared *Hashem*, He established households for them.

כא וַיְהִי כִּי־יָרְאוּ הַמְיַלְּדֹת אֶת־הָאֱלֹהִים וַיַּעַשׂ לָהֶם בָּתִּים:

22 Then Pharaoh charged all his people, saying, "Every boy that is born you shall throw into the Nile, but let every girl live."

כב וַיְצַו פַּרְעֹה לְכָל־עַמּוֹ לֵאמֹר כָּל־הַבֵּן הַיִּלּוֹד הַיְאֹרָה תַּשְׁלִיכֻהוּ וְכָל־הַבַּת תְּחַיּוּן:

---

* "the various labors that they made them perform. Ruthlessly" moved up from the end of the verse for clarity

---

1:15 The Hebrew midwives The identity of these 'Hebrew midwives,' *meyalot haivriyot* (מילדות העבריות), is debated by Rabbinic commentators. Many have assumed, as the literal reading implies, that they were Jewish women. But other commentators, such as the *Abrabanel*, suggest that the midwives Shiphrah and Puah were Egyptians. This interpretation is primarily based on the use of the phrase "fear of God," a phrase often used to describe the behavior of exceptional gentiles, in reference to their heroic actions. According to these interpreters, the phrase *meyalot haivriyot*, 'Hebrew midwives,' is deliberately ambiguous, and it actually refers to the "midwives for the Hebrew women." If so, Shiphrah and Puah were the first gentiles in history to risk their lives in order to rescue a Jew. Israeli Bible scholar and teacher *par excellence*, Nechama Leibowitz, remarked about this passage, "If we accept that the midwives were Egyptian, a... very vital message becomes apparent. The *Torah* indicates how the individual can resist evil. He need not shirk his moral responsibility under cover of 'superior orders'... Neither moral courage nor sheer wickedness are ethnically or nationally determined qualities. Moab and Ammon produced a Ruth and Naamah respectively; Egypt two righteous midwives."

Nechama Leibowitz (1905–1997)

Shemot/Exodus 2
Shemot

שמות ב
שמות

2 ¹ A certain man of the house of *Levi* went and married a Levite woman.

א וַיֵּלֶךְ אִישׁ מִבֵּית לֵוִי וַיִּקַּח אֶת־בַּת־לֵוִי׃

² The woman conceived and bore a son; and when she saw how beautiful he was, she hid him for three months.

ב וַתַּהַר הָאִשָּׁה וַתֵּלֶד בֵּן וַתֵּרֶא אֹתוֹ כִּי־טוֹב הוּא וַתִּצְפְּנֵהוּ שְׁלֹשָׁה יְרָחִים׃

³ When she could hide him no longer, she got a wicker basket for him and caulked it with bitumen and pitch. She put the child into it and placed it among the reeds by the bank of the Nile.

ג וְלֹא־יָכְלָה עוֹד הַצְּפִינוֹ וַתִּקַּח־לוֹ תֵּבַת גֹּמֶא וַתַּחְמְרָה בַחֵמָר וּבַזָּפֶת וַתָּשֶׂם בָּהּ אֶת־הַיֶּלֶד וַתָּשֶׂם בַּסּוּף עַל־שְׂפַת הַיְאֹר׃

⁴ And his sister stationed herself at a distance, to learn what would befall him.

ד וַתֵּתַצַּב אֲחֹתוֹ מֵרָחֹק לְדֵעָה מַה־יֵּעָשֶׂה לוֹ׃

⁵ The daughter of Pharaoh came down to bathe in the Nile, while her maidens walked along the Nile. She spied the basket among the reeds and sent her slave girl to fetch it.

ה וַתֵּרֶד בַּת־פַּרְעֹה לִרְחֹץ עַל־הַיְאֹר וְנַעֲרֹתֶיהָ הֹלְכֹת עַל־יַד הַיְאֹר וַתֵּרֶא אֶת־הַתֵּבָה בְּתוֹךְ הַסּוּף וַתִּשְׁלַח אֶת־אֲמָתָהּ וַתִּקָּחֶהָ׃

⁶ When she opened it, she saw that it was a child, a boy crying. She took pity on it and said, "This must be a Hebrew child."

ו וַתִּפְתַּח וַתִּרְאֵהוּ אֶת־הַיֶּלֶד וְהִנֵּה־נַעַר בֹּכֶה וַתַּחְמֹל עָלָיו וַתֹּאמֶר מִיַּלְדֵי הָעִבְרִים זֶה׃

⁷ Then his sister said to Pharaoh's daughter, "Shall I go and get you a Hebrew nurse to suckle the child for you?"

ז וַתֹּאמֶר אֲחֹתוֹ אֶל־בַּת־פַּרְעֹה הַאֵלֵךְ וְקָרָאתִי לָךְ אִשָּׁה מֵינֶקֶת מִן הָעִבְרִיֹּת וְתֵינִק לָךְ אֶת־הַיָּלֶד׃

⁸ And Pharaoh's daughter answered, "Yes." So the girl went and called the child's mother.

ח וַתֹּאמֶר־לָהּ בַּת־פַּרְעֹה לֵכִי וַתֵּלֶךְ הָעַלְמָה וַתִּקְרָא אֶת־אֵם הַיָּלֶד׃

⁹ And Pharaoh's daughter said to her, "Take this child and nurse it for me, and I will pay your wages." So the woman took the child and nursed it.

ט וַתֹּאמֶר לָהּ בַּת־פַּרְעֹה הֵילִיכִי אֶת־הַיֶּלֶד הַזֶּה וְהֵינִקִהוּ לִי וַאֲנִי אֶתֵּן אֶת־שְׂכָרֵךְ וַתִּקַּח הָאִשָּׁה הַיֶּלֶד וַתְּנִיקֵהוּ׃

¹⁰ When the child grew up, she brought him to Pharaoh's daughter, who made him her son. She named him *Moshe*, explaining, "I drew him out of the water."

י וַיִּגְדַּל הַיֶּלֶד וַתְּבִאֵהוּ לְבַת־פַּרְעֹה וַיְהִי־לָהּ לְבֵן וַתִּקְרָא שְׁמוֹ מֹשֶׁה וַתֹּאמֶר כִּי מִן־הַמַּיִם מְשִׁיתִהוּ׃

va-yig-DAL ha-YE-led va-t'-vi-AY-hu l'-vat par-OH vai-hee LAH l'-VAYN va-tik-RA sh'-MO mo-SHEH va-TO-mer KEE min ha-MA-yim m'-shee-TI-hu

---

משה

2:10 She named him *Moshe* *Moshe* was the greatest of all of Israel's leaders, who is known with affection in Jewish tradition as *Moshe Rabbeinu* (משה רבינו), '*Moshe* our Teacher.' Although *Moshe* speaks directly with *Hashem*, he is identified as the most humble person to ever live (Numbers 12:3). The name *Moshe* is a constant reminder of his modest origins. According to the Sages of the *Midrash*, *Moshe* actually had ten names, but out of appreciation to Pharaoh's daughter who saved him, he is referred to by the name she gave him: *Moshe*, which means 'I have drawn him from the water.'

Shemot/Exodus 2
Shemot

שמות ב
שמות

11 Some time after that, when *Moshe* had grown up, he went out to his kinsfolk and witnessed their labors. He saw an Egyptian beating a Hebrew, one of his kinsmen.

יא וַיְהִי בַּיָּמִים הָהֵם וַיִּגְדַּל מֹשֶׁה וַיֵּצֵא אֶל־אֶחָיו וַיַּרְא בְּסִבְלֹתָם וַיַּרְא אִישׁ מִצְרִי מַכֶּה אִישׁ־עִבְרִי מֵאֶחָיו:

12 He turned this way and that and, seeing no one about, he struck down the Egyptian and hid him in the sand.

יב וַיִּפֶן כֹּה וָכֹה וַיַּרְא כִּי אֵין אִישׁ וַיַּךְ אֶת־הַמִּצְרִי וַיִּטְמְנֵהוּ בַּחוֹל:

13 When he went out the next day, he found two Hebrews fighting; so he said to the offender, "Why do you strike your fellow?"

יג וַיֵּצֵא בַּיּוֹם הַשֵּׁנִי וְהִנֵּה שְׁנֵי־אֲנָשִׁים עִבְרִים נִצִּים וַיֹּאמֶר לָרָשָׁע לָמָּה תַכֶּה רֵעֶךָ:

14 He retorted, "Who made you chief and ruler over us? Do you mean to kill me as you killed the Egyptian?" *Moshe* was frightened, and thought: Then the matter is known!

יד וַיֹּאמֶר מִי שָׂמְךָ לְאִישׁ שַׂר וְשֹׁפֵט עָלֵינוּ הַלְהָרְגֵנִי אַתָּה אֹמֵר כַּאֲשֶׁר הָרַגְתָּ אֶת־הַמִּצְרִי וַיִּירָא מֹשֶׁה וַיֹּאמַר אָכֵן נוֹדַע הַדָּבָר:

15 When Pharaoh learned of the matter, he sought to kill *Moshe*; but *Moshe* fled from Pharaoh. He arrived in the land of Midian, and sat down beside a well.

טו וַיִּשְׁמַע פַּרְעֹה אֶת־הַדָּבָר הַזֶּה וַיְבַקֵּשׁ לַהֲרֹג אֶת־מֹשֶׁה וַיִּבְרַח מֹשֶׁה מִפְּנֵי פַרְעֹה וַיֵּשֶׁב בְּאֶרֶץ־מִדְיָן וַיֵּשֶׁב עַל־הַבְּאֵר:

16 Now the priest of Midian had seven daughters. They came to draw water, and filled the troughs to water their father's flock;

טז וּלְכֹהֵן מִדְיָן שֶׁבַע בָּנוֹת וַתָּבֹאנָה וַתִּדְלֶנָה וַתְּמַלֶּאנָה אֶת־הָרְהָטִים לְהַשְׁקוֹת צֹאן אֲבִיהֶן:

17 but shepherds came and drove them off. *Moshe* rose to their defense, and he watered their flock.

יז וַיָּבֹאוּ הָרֹעִים וַיְגָרְשׁוּם וַיָּקָם מֹשֶׁה וַיּוֹשִׁעָן וַיַּשְׁקְ אֶת־צֹאנָם:

18 When they returned to their father Reuel, he said, "How is it that you have come back so soon today?"

יח וַתָּבֹאנָה אֶל־רְעוּאֵל אֲבִיהֶן וַיֹּאמֶר מַדּוּעַ מִהַרְתֶּן בֹּא הַיּוֹם:

19 They answered, "An Egyptian rescued us from the shepherds; he even drew water for us and watered the flock."

יט וַתֹּאמַרְןָ אִישׁ מִצְרִי הִצִּילָנוּ מִיַּד הָרֹעִים וְגַם־דָּלֹה דָלָה לָנוּ וַיַּשְׁקְ אֶת־הַצֹּאן:

va-to-MAR-na ish mitz-RI hi-tzi-LA-nu mi-YAD ha-RO-eem v'-GAM da-LO LA-nu va-YASHK et ha-TZON

20 He said to his daughters, "Where is he then? Why did you leave the man? Ask him in to break bread."

כ וַיֹּאמֶר אֶל־בְּנֹתָיו וְאַיּוֹ לָמָּה זֶּה עֲזַבְתֶּן אֶת־הָאִישׁ קִרְאֶן לוֹ וְיֹאכַל לָחֶם:

21 *Moshe* consented to stay with the man, and he gave *Moshe* his daughter *Tzipora* as wife.

כא וַיּוֹאֶל מֹשֶׁה לָשֶׁבֶת אֶת־הָאִישׁ וַיִּתֵּן אֶת־צִפֹּרָה בִתּוֹ לְמֹשֶׁה:

2:19 An Egyptian rescued us from the shepherds Based on this verse, the Sages of the *Midrash* contrast *Yosef* and *Moshe*. *Yosef* identified himself with *Eretz Yisrael*, as he says, "I was kidnapped from the land of the Hebrews" (Genesis 40:15), whereas *Moshe* does not protest when Jethro's daughters refer to him as an Egyptian. *Yosef* therefore merits to be buried in the Land of Israel, while *Moshe* does not. Rabbi Zalman Sorotzkin points out that *Moshe's* behavior is understandable, as he was not born in Israel nor had he ever been there. However, once *Hashem* had promised *Avraham* that his descendants would inherit the land, it became their homeland. No matter where in the world a Jew may find himself, he is called upon to identify with *Eretz Yisrael*.

142

Shemot/Exodus 3
Shemot

22 She bore a son whom he named *Gershom*, for he said, "I have been a stranger in a foreign land."

23 A long time after that, the king of Egypt died. The Israelites were groaning under the bondage and cried out; and their cry for help from the bondage rose up to *Hashem*.

24 *Hashem* heard their moaning, and *Hashem* remembered His covenant with *Avraham* and *Yitzchak* and *Yaakov*.

25 *Hashem* looked upon the Israelites, and *Hashem* took notice of them.

3 1 Now *Moshe*, tending the flock of his father-in-law Jethro, the priest of Midian, drove the flock into the wilderness, and came to Horeb, the mountain of *Hashem*.

2 An angel of *Hashem* appeared to him in a blazing fire out of a bush. He gazed, and there was a bush all aflame, yet the bush was not consumed.

3 *Moshe* said, "I must turn aside to look at this marvelous sight; why doesn't the bush burn up?"

4 When *Hashem* saw that he had turned aside to look, *Hashem* called to him out of the bush: "*Moshe! Moshe!*" He answered, "Here I am."

5 And He said, "Do not come closer. Remove your sandals from your feet, for the place on which you stand is holy ground.

6 I am," He said, "the God of your father, the God of *Avraham*, the God of *Yitzchak*, and the God of *Yaakov*." And *Moshe* hid his face, for he was afraid to look at *Hashem*.

7 And *Hashem* continued, "I have marked well the plight of My people in Egypt and have heeded their outcry because of their taskmasters; yes, I am mindful of their sufferings.

8 I have come down to rescue them from the Egyptians and to bring them out of that land to a good and spacious land, a land flowing with milk and honey, the region of the Canaanites, the Hittites, the Amorites, the Perizzites, the Hivites, and the Jebusites.

שמות ג
שמות

כב וַתֵּ֣לֶד בֵּ֔ן וַיִּקְרָ֥א אֶת־שְׁמ֖וֹ גֵּרְשֹׁ֑ם כִּ֣י אָמַ֔ר גֵּ֣ר הָיִ֔יתִי בְּאֶ֖רֶץ נָכְרִיָּֽה׃

כג וַיְהִי֩ בַיָּמִ֨ים הָֽרַבִּ֜ים הָהֵ֗ם וַיָּ֨מׇת֙ מֶ֣לֶךְ מִצְרַ֔יִם וַיֵּאָנְח֧וּ בְנֵֽי־יִשְׂרָאֵ֛ל מִן־הָֽעֲבֹדָ֖ה וַיִּזְעָ֑קוּ וַתַּ֧עַל שַׁוְעָתָ֛ם אֶל־הָֽאֱלֹהִ֖ים מִן־הָעֲבֹדָֽה׃

כד וַיִּשְׁמַ֥ע אֱלֹהִ֖ים אֶת־נַֽאֲקָתָ֑ם וַיִּזְכֹּ֤ר אֱלֹהִים֙ אֶת־בְּרִית֔וֹ אֶת־אַבְרָהָ֖ם אֶת־יִצְחָ֥ק וְאֶֽת־יַעֲקֹֽב׃

כה וַיַּ֥רְא אֱלֹהִ֖ים אֶת־בְּנֵ֣י יִשְׂרָאֵ֑ל וַיֵּ֖דַע אֱלֹהִֽים׃

ג א וּמֹשֶׁ֗ה הָיָ֥ה רֹעֶ֛ה אֶת־צֹ֛אן יִתְר֥וֹ חֹתְנ֖וֹ כֹּהֵ֣ן מִדְיָ֑ן וַיִּנְהַ֤ג אֶת־הַצֹּאן֙ אַחַ֣ר הַמִּדְבָּ֔ר וַיָּבֹ֛א אֶל־הַ֥ר הָאֱלֹהִ֖ים חֹרֵֽבָה׃

ב וַ֠יֵּרָ֠א מַלְאַ֨ךְ יְהֹוָ֥ה אֵלָ֛יו בְּלַבַּת־אֵ֖שׁ מִתּ֣וֹךְ הַסְּנֶ֑ה וַיַּ֗רְא וְהִנֵּ֤ה הַסְּנֶה֙ בֹּעֵ֣ר בָּאֵ֔שׁ וְהַסְּנֶ֖ה אֵינֶ֥נּוּ אֻכָּֽל׃

ג וַיֹּ֣אמֶר מֹשֶׁ֔ה אָסֻֽרָה־נָּ֣א וְאֶרְאֶ֔ה אֶת־הַמַּרְאֶ֥ה הַגָּדֹ֖ל הַזֶּ֑ה מַדּ֖וּעַ לֹא־יִבְעַ֥ר הַסְּנֶֽה׃

ד וַיַּ֥רְא יְהֹוָ֖ה כִּ֣י סָ֣ר לִרְא֑וֹת וַיִּקְרָא֩ אֵלָ֨יו אֱלֹהִ֜ים מִתּ֣וֹךְ הַסְּנֶ֗ה וַיֹּ֛אמֶר מֹשֶׁ֥ה מֹשֶׁ֖ה וַיֹּ֥אמֶר הִנֵּֽנִי׃

ה וַיֹּ֖אמֶר אַל־תִּקְרַ֣ב הֲלֹ֑ם שַׁל־נְעָלֶ֨יךָ֙ מֵעַ֣ל רַגְלֶ֔יךָ כִּ֣י הַמָּק֗וֹם אֲשֶׁ֤ר אַתָּה֙ עוֹמֵ֣ד עָלָ֔יו אַדְמַת־קֹ֖דֶשׁ הֽוּא׃

ו וַיֹּ֗אמֶר אָנֹכִי֙ אֱלֹהֵ֣י אָבִ֔יךָ אֱלֹהֵ֧י אַבְרָהָ֛ם אֱלֹהֵ֥י יִצְחָ֖ק וֵֽאלֹהֵ֣י יַעֲקֹ֑ב וַיַּסְתֵּ֤ר מֹשֶׁה֙ פָּנָ֔יו כִּ֣י יָרֵ֔א מֵהַבִּ֖יט אֶל־הָאֱלֹהִֽים׃

ז וַיֹּ֣אמֶר יְהֹוָ֔ה רָאֹ֥ה רָאִ֛יתִי אֶת־עֳנִ֥י עַמִּ֖י אֲשֶׁ֣ר בְּמִצְרָ֑יִם וְאֶת־צַעֲקָתָ֤ם שָׁמַ֙עְתִּי֙ מִפְּנֵ֣י נֹֽגְשָׂ֔יו כִּ֥י יָדַ֖עְתִּי אֶת־מַכְאֹבָֽיו׃

ח וָאֵרֵ֞ד לְהַצִּיל֣וֹ ׀ מִיַּ֣ד מִצְרַ֗יִם וּֽלְהַעֲלֹתוֹ֮ מִן־הָאָ֣רֶץ הַהִוא֒ אֶל־אֶ֤רֶץ טוֹבָה֙ וּרְחָבָ֔ה אֶל־אֶ֛רֶץ זָבַ֥ת חָלָ֖ב וּדְבָ֑שׁ אֶל־מְק֤וֹם הַֽכְּנַעֲנִי֙ וְהַ֣חִתִּ֔י וְהָֽאֱמֹרִי֙ וְהַפְּרִזִּ֔י וְהַחִוִּ֖י וְהַיְבוּסִֽי׃

143

Shemot/Exodus 3
Shemot

שמות ג
שמות

9 Now the cry of the Israelites has reached Me; moreover, I have seen how the Egyptians oppress them.

ט וְעַתָּה הִנֵּה צַעֲקַת בְּנֵי־יִשְׂרָאֵל בָּאָה אֵלָי וְגַם־רָאִיתִי אֶת־הַלַּחַץ אֲשֶׁר מִצְרַיִם לֹחֲצִים אֹתָם׃

10 Come, therefore, I will send you to Pharaoh, and you shall free My people, the Israelites, from Egypt."

י וְעַתָּה לְכָה וְאֶשְׁלָחֲךָ אֶל־פַּרְעֹה וְהוֹצֵא אֶת־עַמִּי בְנֵי־יִשְׂרָאֵל מִמִּצְרָיִם׃

11 But *Moshe* said to *Hashem*, "Who am I that I should go to Pharaoh and free the Israelites from Egypt?"

יא וַיֹּאמֶר מֹשֶׁה אֶל־הָאֱלֹהִים מִי אָנֹכִי כִּי אֵלֵךְ אֶל־פַּרְעֹה וְכִי אוֹצִיא אֶת־בְּנֵי יִשְׂרָאֵל מִמִּצְרָיִם׃

12 And He said, "I will be with you; that shall be your sign that it was I who sent you. And when you have freed the people from Egypt, you shall worship *Hashem* at this mountain."

יב וַיֹּאמֶר כִּי־אֶהְיֶה עִמָּךְ וְזֶה־לְּךָ הָאוֹת כִּי אָנֹכִי שְׁלַחְתִּיךָ בְּהוֹצִיאֲךָ אֶת־הָעָם מִמִּצְרַיִם תַּעַבְדוּן אֶת־הָאֱלֹהִים עַל הָהָר הַזֶּה׃

13 *Moshe* said to *Hashem*, "When I come to the Israelites and say to them, 'The God of your fathers has sent me to you,' and they ask me, 'What is His name?' what shall I say to them?"

יג וַיֹּאמֶר מֹשֶׁה אֶל־הָאֱלֹהִים הִנֵּה אָנֹכִי בָא אֶל־בְּנֵי יִשְׂרָאֵל וְאָמַרְתִּי לָהֶם אֱלֹהֵי אֲבוֹתֵיכֶם שְׁלָחַנִי אֲלֵיכֶם וְאָמְרוּ־לִי מַה־שְּׁמוֹ מָה אֹמַר אֲלֵהֶם׃

14 And *Hashem* said to *Moshe*, "*Ehyeh-Asher-Ehyeh*". He continued, "Thus shall you say to the Israelites, '*Ehyeh* sent me to you'".

יד וַיֹּאמֶר אֱלֹהִים אֶל־מֹשֶׁה אֶהְיֶה אֲשֶׁר אֶהְיֶה וַיֹּאמֶר כֹּה תֹאמַר לִבְנֵי יִשְׂרָאֵל אֶהְיֶה שְׁלָחַנִי אֲלֵיכֶם׃

15 And *Hashem* said further to *Moshe*, "Thus shall you speak to the Israelites: *Hashem*, the God of your fathers, the God of *Avraham*, the God of *Yitzchak*, and the God of *Yaakov*, has sent me to you: This shall be My name forever, This My appellation for all eternity.

טו וַיֹּאמֶר עוֹד אֱלֹהִים אֶל־מֹשֶׁה כֹּה־תֹאמַר אֶל־בְּנֵי יִשְׂרָאֵל יְהֹוָה אֱלֹהֵי אֲבֹתֵיכֶם אֱלֹהֵי אַבְרָהָם אֱלֹהֵי יִצְחָק וֵאלֹהֵי יַעֲקֹב שְׁלָחַנִי אֲלֵיכֶם זֶה־שְּׁמִי לְעֹלָם וְזֶה זִכְרִי לְדֹר דֹּר׃

16 "Go and assemble the elders of *Yisrael* and say to them: *Hashem*, the God of your fathers, the God of *Avraham*, *Yitzchak*, and *Yaakov*, has appeared to me and said, 'I have taken note of you and of what is being done to you in Egypt,

טז לֵךְ וְאָסַפְתָּ אֶת־זִקְנֵי יִשְׂרָאֵל וְאָמַרְתָּ אֲלֵהֶם יְהֹוָה אֱלֹהֵי אֲבֹתֵיכֶם נִרְאָה אֵלַי אֱלֹהֵי אַבְרָהָם יִצְחָק וְיַעֲקֹב לֵאמֹר פָּקֹד פָּקַדְתִּי אֶתְכֶם וְאֶת־הֶעָשׂוּי לָכֶם בְּמִצְרָיִם׃

17 and I have declared: I will take you out of the misery of Egypt to the land of the Canaanites, the Hittites, the Amorites, the Perizzites, the Hivites, and the Jebusites, to a land flowing with milk and honey.'

יז וָאֹמַר אַעֲלֶה אֶתְכֶם מֵעֳנִי מִצְרַיִם אֶל־אֶרֶץ הַכְּנַעֲנִי וְהַחִתִּי וְהָאֱמֹרִי וְהַפְּרִזִּי וְהַחִוִּי וְהַיְבוּסִי אֶל־אֶרֶץ זָבַת חָלָב וּדְבָשׁ׃

va-o-MAR a-a-LEH et-KHEM may-o-NEE mitz-RA-yim el E-retz ha-k'-na-a-NEE v'-ha-khee-TEE v'-ha-e-mo-REE v'-ha-p'-ree-ZEE v'-ha-khi-VEE v'-hai-vu-SEE el E-retz za-VAT kha-LAV ud-VASH

3:17 Out of the misery of Egypt. The Hebrew word for 'Egypt,' *Mitzrayim* (מצרים), is connected to two Hebrew words which offer insight into the nature of that country. The name *Mitzrayim* is related to the Hebrew word *tzara* (צרה), meaning 'tragedy' or 'distress.' This connection teaches that Egypt was a land of suffering for the Children of Israel, who suffered in slavery for hundreds of years before being redeemed

מצרים

Shemot/Exodus 4
Shemot

שמות ד
שמות

18 They will listen to you; then you shall go with the elders of *Yisrael* to the king of Egypt and you shall say to him, '*Hashem*, the God of the Hebrews, manifested Himself to us. Now therefore, let us go a distance of three days into the wilderness to sacrifice to *Hashem* our God.'

יח וְשָׁמְעוּ לְקֹלֶךָ וּבָאתָ אַתָּה וְזִקְנֵי יִשְׂרָאֵל אֶל־מֶלֶךְ מִצְרַיִם וַאֲמַרְתֶּם אֵלָיו יְהֹוָה אֱלֹהֵי הָעִבְרִיִּים נִקְרָה עָלֵינוּ וְעַתָּה נֵלֲכָה־נָּא דֶּרֶךְ שְׁלֹשֶׁת יָמִים בַּמִּדְבָּר וְנִזְבְּחָה לַיהֹוָה אֱלֹהֵינוּ:

19 Yet I know that the king of Egypt will let you go only because of a greater might.

יט וַאֲנִי יָדַעְתִּי כִּי לֹא־יִתֵּן אֶתְכֶם מֶלֶךְ מִצְרַיִם לַהֲלֹךְ וְלֹא בְּיָד חֲזָקָה:

20 So I will stretch out My hand and smite Egypt with various wonders which I will work upon them; after that he shall let you go.

כ וְשָׁלַחְתִּי אֶת־יָדִי וְהִכֵּיתִי אֶת־מִצְרָיִם בְּכֹל נִפְלְאֹתַי אֲשֶׁר אֶעֱשֶׂה בְּקִרְבּוֹ וְאַחֲרֵי־כֵן יְשַׁלַּח אֶתְכֶם:

21 And I will dispose the Egyptians favorably toward this people, so that when you go, you will not go away empty-handed.

כא וְנָתַתִּי אֶת־חֵן הָעָם־הַזֶּה בְּעֵינֵי מִצְרָיִם וְהָיָה כִּי תֵלֵכוּן לֹא תֵלְכוּ רֵיקָם:

22 Each woman shall borrow from her neighbor and the lodger in her house objects of silver and gold, and clothing, and you shall put these on your sons and daughters, thus stripping the Egyptians."

כב וְשָׁאֲלָה אִשָּׁה מִשְּׁכֶנְתָּהּ וּמִגָּרַת בֵּיתָהּ כְּלֵי־כֶסֶף וּכְלֵי זָהָב וּשְׂמָלֹת וְשַׂמְתֶּם עַל־בְּנֵיכֶם וְעַל־בְּנֹתֵיכֶם וְנִצַּלְתֶּם אֶת־מִצְרָיִם:

4 1 But *Moshe* spoke up and said, "What if they do not believe me and do not listen to me, but say: *Hashem* did not appear to you?"

ד א וַיַּעַן מֹשֶׁה וַיֹּאמֶר וְהֵן לֹא־יַאֲמִינוּ לִי וְלֹא יִשְׁמְעוּ בְּקֹלִי כִּי יֹאמְרוּ לֹא־נִרְאָה אֵלֶיךָ יְהֹוָה:

2 *Hashem* said to him, "What is that in your hand?" And he replied, "A rod."

ב וַיֹּאמֶר אֵלָיו יְהֹוָה מַזֶּה [מַה־] [זֶּה] בְיָדֶךָ וַיֹּאמֶר מַטֶּה:

3 He said, "Cast it on the ground." He cast it on the ground and it became a snake; and *Moshe* recoiled from it.

ג וַיֹּאמֶר הַשְׁלִיכֵהוּ אַרְצָה וַיַּשְׁלִיכֵהוּ אַרְצָה וַיְהִי לְנָחָשׁ וַיָּנָס מֹשֶׁה מִפָּנָיו:

4 Then *Hashem* said to *Moshe*, "Put out your hand and grasp it by the tail" – he put out his hand and seized it, and it became a rod in his hand

ד וַיֹּאמֶר יְהֹוָה אֶל־מֹשֶׁה שְׁלַח יָדְךָ וֶאֱחֹז בִּזְנָבוֹ וַיִּשְׁלַח יָדוֹ וַיַּחֲזֶק בּוֹ וַיְהִי לְמַטֶּה בְּכַפּוֹ:

5 "that they may believe that *Hashem*, the God of their fathers, the God of *Avraham*, the God of *Yitzchak*, and the God of *Yaakov*, did appear to you."

ה לְמַעַן יַאֲמִינוּ כִּי־נִרְאָה אֵלֶיךָ יְהֹוָה אֱלֹהֵי אֲבֹתָם אֱלֹהֵי אַבְרָהָם אֱלֹהֵי יִצְחָק וֵאלֹהֵי יַעֲקֹב:

6 *Hashem* said to him further, "Put your hand into your bosom." He put his hand into his bosom; and when he took it out, his hand was encrusted with snowy scales!

ו וַיֹּאמֶר יְהֹוָה לוֹ עוֹד הָבֵא־נָא יָדְךָ בְּחֵיקֶךָ וַיָּבֵא יָדוֹ בְּחֵיקוֹ וַיּוֹצִאָהּ וְהִנֵּה יָדוֹ מְצֹרַעַת כַּשָּׁלֶג:

by the Almighty. And the word *Mitzrayim* (מצרים) is also connected to the word *tzar* (צר), meaning 'narrow.' On a metaphorical level, a person is enslaved when he feels constricted and limited, and thereby unable to actualize his unique potential.

Shemot/Exodus 4
Shemot

שמות ד
שמות

7 And He said, "Put your hand back into your bosom." – He put his hand back into his bosom; and when he took it out of his bosom, there it was again like the rest of his body.

ז וַיֹּאמֶר הָשֵׁב יָדְךָ אֶל־חֵיקֶךָ וַיָּשֶׁב יָדוֹ אֶל־חֵיקוֹ וַיּוֹצִאָהּ מֵחֵיקוֹ וְהִנֵּה־שָׁבָה כִּבְשָׂרוֹ׃

8 "And if they do not believe you or pay heed to the first sign, they will believe the second.

ח וְהָיָה אִם־לֹא יַאֲמִינוּ לָךְ וְלֹא יִשְׁמְעוּ לְקֹל הָאֹת הָרִאשׁוֹן וְהֶאֱמִינוּ לְקֹל הָאֹת הָאַחֲרוֹן׃

9 And if they are not convinced by both these signs and still do not heed you, take some water from the Nile and pour it on the dry ground, and it – the water that you take from the Nile – will turn to blood on the dry ground."

ט וְהָיָה אִם־לֹא יַאֲמִינוּ גַּם לִשְׁנֵי הָאֹתוֹת הָאֵלֶּה וְלֹא יִשְׁמְעוּן לְקֹלֶךָ וְלָקַחְתָּ מִמֵּימֵי הַיְאֹר וְשָׁפַכְתָּ הַיַּבָּשָׁה וְהָיוּ הַמַּיִם אֲשֶׁר תִּקַּח מִן־הַיְאֹר וְהָיוּ לְדָם בַּיַּבָּשֶׁת׃

10 But *Moshe* said to *Hashem*, "Please, O *Hashem*, I have never been a man of words, either in times past or now that You have spoken to Your servant; I am slow of speech and slow of tongue."

י וַיֹּאמֶר מֹשֶׁה אֶל־יְהוָה בִּי אֲדֹנָי לֹא אִישׁ דְּבָרִים אָנֹכִי גַּם מִתְּמוֹל גַּם מִשִּׁלְשֹׁם גַּם מֵאָז דַּבֶּרְךָ אֶל־עַבְדֶּךָ כִּי כְבַד־פֶּה וּכְבַד לָשׁוֹן אָנֹכִי׃

11 And *Hashem* said to him, "Who gives man speech? Who makes him dumb or deaf, seeing or blind? Is it not I, *Hashem*?

יא וַיֹּאמֶר יְהוָה אֵלָיו מִי שָׂם פֶּה לָאָדָם אוֹ מִי־יָשׂוּם אִלֵּם אוֹ חֵרֵשׁ אוֹ פִקֵּחַ אוֹ עִוֵּר הֲלֹא אָנֹכִי יְהוָה׃

12 Now go, and I will be with you as you speak and will instruct you what to say."

יב וְעַתָּה לֵךְ וְאָנֹכִי אֶהְיֶה עִם־פִּיךָ וְהוֹרֵיתִיךָ אֲשֶׁר תְּדַבֵּר׃

13 But he said, "Please, O *Hashem*, make someone else Your agent."

יג וַיֹּאמֶר בִּי אֲדֹנָי שְׁלַח־נָא בְּיַד־תִּשְׁלָח׃

14 *Hashem* became angry with *Moshe*, and He said, "There is your brother *Aharon* the Levite. He, I know, speaks readily. Even now he is setting out to meet you, and he will be happy to see you.

יד וַיִּחַר־אַף יְהוָה בְּמֹשֶׁה וַיֹּאמֶר הֲלֹא אַהֲרֹן אָחִיךָ הַלֵּוִי יָדַעְתִּי כִּי־דַבֵּר יְדַבֵּר הוּא וְגַם הִנֵּה־הוּא יֹצֵא לִקְרָאתֶךָ וְרָאֲךָ וְשָׂמַח בְּלִבּוֹ׃

15 You shall speak to him and put the words in his mouth – I will be with you and with him as you speak, and tell both of you what to do

טו וְדִבַּרְתָּ אֵלָיו וְשַׂמְתָּ אֶת־הַדְּבָרִים בְּפִיו וְאָנֹכִי אֶהְיֶה עִם־פִּיךָ וְעִם־פִּיהוּ וְהוֹרֵיתִי אֶתְכֶם אֵת אֲשֶׁר תַּעֲשׂוּן׃

16 and he shall speak for you to the people. Thus he shall serve as your spokesman, with you playing the role of *Hashem* to him,

טז וְדִבֶּר־הוּא לְךָ אֶל־הָעָם וְהָיָה הוּא יִהְיֶה־לְּךָ לְפֶה וְאַתָּה תִּהְיֶה־לּוֹ לֵאלֹהִים׃

17 and take with you this rod, with which you shall perform the signs."

יז וְאֶת־הַמַּטֶּה הַזֶּה תִּקַּח בְּיָדֶךָ אֲשֶׁר תַּעֲשֶׂה־בּוֹ אֶת־הָאֹתֹת׃

18 *Moshe* went back to his father-in-law Jether and said to him, "Let me go back to my kinsmen in Egypt and see how they are faring." And Jethro said to *Moshe*, "Go in peace."

יח וַיֵּלֶךְ מֹשֶׁה וַיָּשָׁב אֶל־יֶתֶר חֹתְנוֹ וַיֹּאמֶר לוֹ אֵלְכָה נָּא וְאָשׁוּבָה אֶל־אַחַי אֲשֶׁר־בְּמִצְרַיִם וְאֶרְאֶה הַעוֹדָם חַיִּים וַיֹּאמֶר יִתְרוֹ לְמֹשֶׁה לֵךְ לְשָׁלוֹם׃

19 *Hashem* said to *Moshe* in Midian, "Go back to Egypt, for all the men who sought to kill you are dead."

יט וַיֹּאמֶר יְהוָה אֶל־מֹשֶׁה בְּמִדְיָן לֵךְ שֻׁב מִצְרָיִם כִּי־מֵתוּ כָּל־הָאֲנָשִׁים הַמְבַקְשִׁים אֶת־נַפְשֶׁךָ׃

Shemot/Exodus 4
Shemot

שמות ד
שמות

20 So *Moshe* took his wife and sons, mounted them on an ass, and went back to the land of Egypt; and *Moshe* took the rod of *Hashem* with him.

וַיִּקַּ֨ח מֹשֶׁ֜ה אֶת־אִשְׁתּ֣וֹ וְאֶת־בָּנָ֗יו וַיַּרְכִּבֵם֙ עַֽל־הַחֲמֹ֔ר וַיָּ֖שָׁב אַ֣רְצָה מִצְרָ֑יִם וַיִּקַּ֥ח מֹשֶׁ֛ה אֶת־מַטֵּ֥ה הָאֱלֹהִ֖ים בְּיָדֽוֹ׃

21 And *Hashem* said to *Moshe*, "When you return to Egypt, see that you perform before Pharaoh all the marvels that I have put within your power. I, however, will stiffen his heart so that he will not let the people go.

וַיֹּ֣אמֶר יְהֹוָה֮ אֶל־מֹשֶׁה֒ בְּלֶכְתְּךָ֙ לָשׁ֣וּב מִצְרַ֔יְמָה רְאֵ֗ה כׇּל־הַמֹּֽפְתִים֙ אֲשֶׁר־שַׂ֣מְתִּי בְיָדֶ֔ךָ וַעֲשִׂיתָ֖ם לִפְנֵ֣י פַרְעֹ֑ה וַאֲנִי֙ אֲחַזֵּ֣ק אֶת־לִבּ֔וֹ וְלֹ֥א יְשַׁלַּ֖ח אֶת־הָעָֽם׃

22 Then you shall say to Pharaoh, 'Thus says *Hashem*: *Yisrael* is My first-born son.

וְאָמַרְתָּ֖ אֶל־פַּרְעֹ֑ה כֹּ֚ה אָמַ֣ר יְהֹוָ֔ה בְּנִ֥י בְכֹרִ֖י יִשְׂרָאֵֽל׃

v'-a-mar-TA el par-OH KOH a-MAR a-do-NAI b'-NEE v'-kho-REE yis-ra-AYL

23 I have said to you, "Let My son go, that he may worship Me," yet you refuse to let him go. Now I will slay your first-born son.'"

וָאֹמַ֣ר אֵלֶ֗יךָ שַׁלַּ֤ח אֶת־בְּנִי֙ וְיַֽעַבְדֵ֔נִי וַתְּמָאֵ֖ן לְשַׁלְּח֑וֹ הִנֵּה֙ אָנֹכִ֣י הֹרֵ֔ג אֶת־בִּנְךָ֖ בְּכֹרֶֽךָ׃

24 At a night encampment on the way, *Hashem* encountered him and sought to kill him.

וַיְהִ֥י בַדֶּ֖רֶךְ בַּמָּל֑וֹן וַיִּפְגְּשֵׁ֣הוּ יְהֹוָ֔ה וַיְבַקֵּ֖שׁ הֲמִיתֽוֹ׃

25 So *Tzipora* took a flint and cut off her son's foreskin, and touched his legs with it, saying, "You are truly a bridegroom of blood to me!"

וַתִּקַּ֨ח צִפֹּרָ֜ה צֹ֗ר וַתִּכְרֹת֙ אֶת־עׇרְלַ֣ת בְּנָ֔הּ וַתַּגַּ֖ע לְרַגְלָ֑יו וַתֹּ֕אמֶר כִּ֧י חֲתַן־דָּמִ֛ים אַתָּ֖ה לִֽי׃

26 And when He let him alone, she added, "A bridegroom of blood because of the circumcision."

וַיִּ֖רֶף מִמֶּ֑נּוּ אָ֚ז אָֽמְרָ֔ה חֲתַ֥ן דָּמִ֖ים לַמּוּלֹֽת׃

27 *Hashem* said to *Aharon*, "Go to meet *Moshe* in the wilderness." He went and met him at the mountain of *Hashem*, and he kissed him.

וַיֹּ֤אמֶר יְהֹוָה֙ אֶֽל־אַהֲרֹ֔ן לֵ֛ךְ לִקְרַ֥את מֹשֶׁ֖ה הַמִּדְבָּ֑רָה וַיֵּ֗לֶךְ וַֽיִּפְגְּשֵׁ֛הוּ בְּהַ֥ר הָאֱלֹהִ֖ים וַיִּשַּׁק־לֽוֹ׃

28 *Moshe* told *Aharon* about all the things that *Hashem* had committed to him and all the signs about which He had instructed him.

וַיַּגֵּ֤ד מֹשֶׁה֙ לְאַֽהֲרֹ֔ן אֵ֛ת כׇּל־דִּבְרֵ֥י יְהֹוָ֖ה אֲשֶׁ֣ר שְׁלָח֑וֹ וְאֵ֥ת כׇּל־הָאֹתֹ֖ת אֲשֶׁ֥ר צִוָּֽהוּ׃

29 Then *Moshe* and *Aharon* went and assembled all the elders of the Israelites.

וַיֵּ֥לֶךְ מֹשֶׁ֖ה וְאַהֲרֹ֑ן וַיַּ֣אַסְפ֔וּ אֶת־כׇּל־זִקְנֵ֖י בְּנֵ֥י יִשְׂרָאֵֽל׃

30 *Aharon* repeated all the words that *Hashem* had spoken to *Moshe*, and he performed the signs in the sight of the people,

וַיְדַבֵּ֣ר אַהֲרֹ֔ן אֵ֚ת כׇּל־הַדְּבָרִ֔ים אֲשֶׁר־דִּבֶּ֥ר יְהֹוָ֖ה אֶל־מֹשֶׁ֑ה וַיַּ֥עַשׂ הָאֹתֹ֖ת לְעֵינֵ֥י הָעָֽם׃

4:22 My first-born son God refers to the Children of Israel as His first-born son. A firstborn is not the only child, yet his status is unique and therefore carries extra responsibility. Similarly, all nations of the world are *Hashem*'s children; anyone can form a meaningful relationship with Him. However, He chose the Jewish people as a "firstborn" to fulfill a unique role; to be His representatives to bring Godliness into this world. Similarly, He also chose *Eretz Yisrael* as the place where they are to fulfill that responsibility.

Shemot/Exodus 5
Shemot

שמות ה
שמות

31 and the people were convinced. When they heard that *Hashem* had taken note of the Israelites and that He had seen their plight, they bowed low in homage.

לא וַיַּאֲמֵן הָעָם וַיִּשְׁמְעוּ כִּי־פָקַד יְהֹוָה אֶת־בְּנֵי יִשְׂרָאֵל וְכִי רָאָה אֶת־עָנְיָם וַיִּקְּדוּ וַיִּשְׁתַּחֲוֽוּ׃

5

1 Afterward *Moshe* and *Aharon* went and said to Pharaoh, "Thus says *Hashem*, the God of *Yisrael*: Let My people go that they may celebrate a festival for Me in the wilderness."

א וְאַחַר בָּאוּ מֹשֶׁה וְאַהֲרֹן וַיֹּאמְרוּ אֶל־פַּרְעֹה כֹּה־אָמַר יְהֹוָה אֱלֹהֵי יִשְׂרָאֵל שַׁלַּח אֶת־עַמִּי וְיָחֹגּוּ לִי בַּמִּדְבָּר׃

2 But Pharaoh said, "Who is *Hashem* that I should heed Him and let *Yisrael* go? I do not know *Hashem*, nor will I let *Yisrael* go."

ב וַיֹּאמֶר פַּרְעֹה מִי יְהֹוָה אֲשֶׁר אֶשְׁמַע בְּקֹלוֹ לְשַׁלַּח אֶת־יִשְׂרָאֵל לֹא יָדַעְתִּי אֶת־יְהֹוָה וְגַם אֶת־יִשְׂרָאֵל לֹא אֲשַׁלֵּחַ׃

va-YO-mer par-OH MEE a-do-NAI a-SHER esh-MA b'-ko-LO l'-sha-LAKH et yis-ra-AYL LO ya-DA-tee et a-do-NAI v'-GAM et yis-ra-AYL LO a-sha-LAY-akh

3 They answered, "The God of the Hebrews has manifested Himself to us. Let us go, we pray, a distance of three days into the wilderness to sacrifice to *Hashem* our God, lest He strike us with pestilence or sword."

ג וַיֹּאמְרוּ אֱלֹהֵי הָעִבְרִים נִקְרָא עָלֵינוּ נֵלְכָה נָּא דֶּרֶךְ שְׁלֹשֶׁת יָמִים בַּמִּדְבָּר וְנִזְבְּחָה לַיהֹוָה אֱלֹהֵינוּ פֶּן־יִפְגָּעֵנוּ בַּדֶּבֶר אוֹ בֶחָֽרֶב׃

4 But the king of Egypt said to them, "*Moshe* and *Aharon*, why do you distract the people from their tasks? Get to your labors!"

ד וַיֹּאמֶר אֲלֵהֶם מֶלֶךְ מִצְרַיִם לָמָּה מֹשֶׁה וְאַהֲרֹן תַּפְרִיעוּ אֶת־הָעָם מִמַּעֲשָׂיו לְכוּ לְסִבְלֹתֵיכֶֽם׃

5 And Pharaoh continued, "The people of the land are already so numerous, and you would have them cease from their labors!"

ה וַיֹּאמֶר פַּרְעֹה הֵן־רַבִּים עַתָּה עַם הָאָרֶץ וְהִשְׁבַּתֶּם אֹתָם מִסִּבְלֹתָֽם׃

6 That same day Pharaoh charged the taskmasters and foremen of the people, saying,

ו וַיְצַו פַּרְעֹה בַּיּוֹם הַהוּא אֶת־הַנֹּגְשִׂים בָּעָם וְאֶת־שֹׁטְרָיו לֵאמֹֽר׃

7 "You shall no longer provide the people with straw for making bricks as heretofore; let them go and gather straw for themselves.

ז לֹא תֹאסִפוּן לָתֵת תֶּבֶן לָעָם לִלְבֹּן הַלְּבֵנִים כִּתְמוֹל שִׁלְשֹׁם הֵם יֵלְכוּ וְקֹשְׁשׁוּ לָהֶם תֶּֽבֶן׃

8 But impose upon them the same quota of bricks as they have been making heretofore; do not reduce it, for they are shirkers; that is why they cry, 'Let us go and sacrifice to our God!'

ח וְאֶת־מַתְכֹּנֶת הַלְּבֵנִים אֲשֶׁר הֵם עֹשִׂים תְּמוֹל שִׁלְשֹׁם תָּשִׂימוּ עֲלֵיהֶם לֹא תִגְרְעוּ מִמֶּנּוּ כִּי־נִרְפִּים הֵם עַל־כֵּן הֵם צֹעֲקִים לֵאמֹר נֵלְכָה נִזְבְּחָה לֵאלֹהֵֽינוּ׃

9 Let heavier work be laid upon the men; let them keep at it and not pay attention to deceitful promises."

ט תִּכְבַּד הָעֲבֹדָה עַל־הָאֲנָשִׁים וְיַעֲשׂוּ־בָהּ וְאַל־יִשְׁעוּ בְּדִבְרֵי־שָֽׁקֶר׃

5:2 I do not know *Hashem*. Only in complete absence of recognition of *Hashem* and His ways can one treat others the way Pharaoh treated the Israelites. Had he acknowledged the Lord, Pharaoh would not have been able to treat them that way. Therefore, God emphasizes (Exodus 7:5) that the purpose of the ten plagues is to prove to the Egyptians and the entire world that He is the one and only omnipotent God.

Shemot/Exodus 5
Shemot

שמות ה
שמות

10 So the taskmasters and foremen of the people went out and said to the people, "Thus says Pharaoh: I will not give you any straw.

וַיֵּצְאוּ נֹגְשֵׂי הָעָם וְשֹׁטְרָיו וַיֹּאמְרוּ אֶל־הָעָם לֵאמֹר כֹּה אָמַר פַּרְעֹה אֵינֶנִּי נֹתֵן לָכֶם תֶּבֶן׃

11 You must go and get the straw yourselves wherever you can find it; but there shall be no decrease whatever in your work."

אַתֶּם לְכוּ קְחוּ לָכֶם תֶּבֶן מֵאֲשֶׁר תִּמְצָאוּ כִּי אֵין נִגְרָע מֵעֲבֹדַתְכֶם דָּבָר׃

12 Then the people scattered throughout the land of Egypt to gather stubble for straw.

וַיָּפֶץ הָעָם בְּכָל־אֶרֶץ מִצְרָיִם לְקֹשֵׁשׁ קַשׁ לַתֶּבֶן׃

13 And the taskmasters pressed them, saying, "You must complete the same work assignment each day as when you had straw."

וְהַנֹּגְשִׂים אָצִים לֵאמֹר כַּלּוּ מַעֲשֵׂיכֶם דְּבַר־יוֹם בְּיוֹמוֹ כַּאֲשֶׁר בִּהְיוֹת הַתֶּבֶן׃

14 And the foremen of the Israelites, whom Pharaoh's taskmasters had set over them, were beaten. "Why," they were asked, "did you not complete the prescribed amount of bricks, either yesterday or today, as you did before?"

וַיֻּכּוּ שֹׁטְרֵי בְּנֵי יִשְׂרָאֵל אֲשֶׁר־שָׂמוּ עֲלֵהֶם נֹגְשֵׂי פַרְעֹה לֵאמֹר מַדּוּעַ לֹא כִלִּיתֶם חָקְכֶם לִלְבֹּן כִּתְמוֹל שִׁלְשֹׁם גַּם־תְּמוֹל גַּם־הַיּוֹם׃

15 Then the foremen of the Israelites came to Pharaoh and cried: "Why do you deal thus with your servants?

וַיָּבֹאוּ שֹׁטְרֵי בְּנֵי יִשְׂרָאֵל וַיִּצְעֲקוּ אֶל־פַּרְעֹה לֵאמֹר לָמָּה תַעֲשֶׂה כֹה לַעֲבָדֶיךָ׃

16 No straw is issued to your servants, yet they demand of us: Make bricks! Thus your servants are being beaten, when the fault is with your own people."

תֶּבֶן אֵין נִתָּן לַעֲבָדֶיךָ וּלְבֵנִים אֹמְרִים לָנוּ עֲשׂוּ וְהִנֵּה עֲבָדֶיךָ מֻכִּים וְחָטָאת עַמֶּךָ׃

17 He replied, "You are shirkers, shirkers! That is why you say, 'Let us go and sacrifice to *Hashem*.'

וַיֹּאמֶר נִרְפִּים אַתֶּם נִרְפִּים עַל־כֵּן אַתֶּם אֹמְרִים נֵלְכָה נִזְבְּחָה לַיהוָֹה׃

18 Be off now to your work! No straw shall be issued to you, but you must produce your quota of bricks!"

וְעַתָּה לְכוּ עִבְדוּ וְתֶבֶן לֹא־יִנָּתֵן לָכֶם וְתֹכֶן לְבֵנִים תִּתֵּנּוּ׃

19 Now the foremen of the Israelites found themselves in trouble because of the order, "You must not reduce your daily quantity of bricks."

וַיִּרְאוּ שֹׁטְרֵי בְנֵי־יִשְׂרָאֵל אֹתָם בְּרָע לֵאמֹר לֹא־תִגְרְעוּ מִלִּבְנֵיכֶם דְּבַר־יוֹם בְּיוֹמוֹ׃

20 As they left Pharaoh's presence, they came upon *Moshe* and *Aharon* standing in their path,

וַיִּפְגְּעוּ אֶת־מֹשֶׁה וְאֶת־אַהֲרֹן נִצָּבִים לִקְרָאתָם בְּצֵאתָם מֵאֵת פַּרְעֹה׃

21 and they said to them, "May *Hashem* look upon you and punish you for making us loathsome to Pharaoh and his courtiers – putting a sword in their hands to slay us."

וַיֹּאמְרוּ אֲלֵהֶם יֵרֶא יְהוָֹה עֲלֵיכֶם וְיִשְׁפֹּט אֲשֶׁר הִבְאַשְׁתֶּם אֶת־רֵיחֵנוּ בְּעֵינֵי פַרְעֹה וּבְעֵינֵי עֲבָדָיו לָתֶת־חֶרֶב בְּיָדָם לְהָרְגֵנוּ׃

22 Then *Moshe* returned to *Hashem* and said, "O *Hashem*, why did You bring harm upon this people? Why did You send me?

וַיָּשָׁב מֹשֶׁה אֶל־יְהוָֹה וַיֹּאמַר אֲדֹנָי לָמָה הֲרֵעֹתָה לָעָם הַזֶּה לָמָּה זֶּה שְׁלַחְתָּנִי׃

23 Ever since I came to Pharaoh to speak in Your name, he has dealt worse with this people; and still You have not delivered Your people."

וּמֵאָז בָּאתִי אֶל־פַּרְעֹה לְדַבֵּר בִּשְׁמֶךָ הֵרַע לָעָם הַזֶּה וְהַצֵּל לֹא־הִצַּלְתָּ אֶת־עַמֶּךָ׃

Shemot/Exodus 6
Va'eira

שמות ו
וארא

6 **1** Then *Hashem* said to *Moshe*, "You shall soon see what I will do to Pharaoh: he shall let them go because of a greater might; indeed, because of a greater might he shall drive them from his land."

וַיֹּאמֶר יְהֹוָה אֶל־מֹשֶׁה עַתָּה תִרְאֶה אֲשֶׁר אֶעֱשֶׂה לְפַרְעֹה כִּי בְיָד חֲזָקָה יְשַׁלְּחֵם וּבְיָד חֲזָקָה יְגָרְשֵׁם מֵאַרְצוֹ׃

2 *Hashem* spoke to *Moshe* and said to him, "I am *Hashem*.

וַיְדַבֵּר אֱלֹהִים אֶל־מֹשֶׁה וַיֹּאמֶר אֵלָיו אֲנִי יְהֹוָה׃

3 I appeared to *Avraham*, *Yitzchak*, and *Yaakov* as *El Shaddai*, but I did not make Myself known to them by My name *Hashem*

וָאֵרָא אֶל־אַבְרָהָם אֶל־יִצְחָק וְאֶל־יַעֲקֹב בְּאֵל שַׁדָּי וּשְׁמִי יְהֹוָה לֹא נוֹדַעְתִּי לָהֶם׃

4 I also established My covenant with them, to give them the land of Canaan, the land in which they lived as sojourners.

וְגַם הֲקִמֹתִי אֶת־בְּרִיתִי אִתָּם לָתֵת לָהֶם אֶת־אֶרֶץ כְּנָעַן אֵת אֶרֶץ מְגֻרֵיהֶם אֲשֶׁר־גָּרוּ בָהּ׃

v'-GAM ha-ki-MO-tee et b'-ree-TEE i-TAM la-TAYT la-HEM et E-retz k'-NA-an AYT E-retz m'-gu-ray-HEM a-sher GA-ru VAH

5 I have now heard the moaning of the Israelites because the Egyptians are holding them in bondage, and I have remembered My covenant.

וְגַם אֲנִי שָׁמַעְתִּי אֶת־נַאֲקַת בְּנֵי יִשְׂרָאֵל אֲשֶׁר מִצְרַיִם מַעֲבִדִים אֹתָם וָאֶזְכֹּר אֶת־בְּרִיתִי׃

6 Say, therefore, to *B'nei Yisrael*: I am *Hashem*. I will free you from the labors of the Egyptians and deliver you from their bondage. I will redeem you with an outstretched arm and through extraordinary chastisements.

לָכֵן אֱמֹר לִבְנֵי־יִשְׂרָאֵל אֲנִי יְהֹוָה וְהוֹצֵאתִי אֶתְכֶם מִתַּחַת סִבְלֹת מִצְרַיִם וְהִצַּלְתִּי אֶתְכֶם מֵעֲבֹדָתָם וְגָאַלְתִּי אֶתְכֶם בִּזְרוֹעַ נְטוּיָה וּבִשְׁפָטִים גְּדֹלִים׃

7 And I will take you to be My people, and I will be your God. And you shall know that I, *Hashem*, am your God who freed you from the labors of the Egyptians.

וְלָקַחְתִּי אֶתְכֶם לִי לְעָם וְהָיִיתִי לָכֶם לֵאלֹהִים וִידַעְתֶּם כִּי אֲנִי יְהֹוָה אֱלֹהֵיכֶם הַמּוֹצִיא אֶתְכֶם מִתַּחַת סִבְלוֹת מִצְרָיִם׃

8 I will bring you into the land which I swore to give to *Avraham*, *Yitzchak*, and *Yaakov*, and I will give it to you for a possession, I *Hashem*."

וְהֵבֵאתִי אֶתְכֶם אֶל־הָאָרֶץ אֲשֶׁר נָשָׂאתִי אֶת־יָדִי לָתֵת אֹתָהּ לְאַבְרָהָם לְיִצְחָק וּלְיַעֲקֹב וְנָתַתִּי אֹתָהּ לָכֶם מוֹרָשָׁה אֲנִי יְהֹוָה׃

v'-hay-vay-TEE et-KHEM el ha-A-retz a-SHER na-SA-tee et ya-DEE la-TAYT o-TAH l'-av-ra-HAM l'-yitz-KHAK ul-ya-a-KOV v'-na-ta-TEE o-TAH la-KHEM mo-ra-SHAH a-NEE a-do-NAI

6:8 I will bring you into the land Four cups of wine are drunk at the Passover Seder, corresponding to the four expressions of redemption used in this verse to describe the exodus from Egypt: "Free," "deliver," "redeem," and "take" (verses 6–8). A close reading of this chapter, however, uncovers that there is a fifth expression, "I will bring you," found in the following verse. Why, then, do we not have five cups of wine at the Seder? The Talmud (*Pesachim* 118) explain that while the first four expressions of redemption from Egypt have in fact been realized, the fifth expression, "I will bring you into the land" has not yet been completely fulfilled. Only when all the Jews return to Israel and *Mashiach* comes to Jerusalem will we rejoice with a fifth cup.

Four cups of wine for the Pesach seder

6:8 I will give it to you for a possession Biblical Hebrew has two words relating to bequests:

Shemot/Exodus 6
Va'eira

שמות ו
וארא

9 But when *Moshe* told this to the Israelites, they would not listen to *Moshe*, their spirits crushed by cruel bondage.

ט וַיְדַבֵּר מֹשֶׁה כֵּן אֶל־בְּנֵי יִשְׂרָאֵל וְלֹא שָׁמְעוּ אֶל־מֹשֶׁה מִקֹּצֶר רוּחַ וּמֵעֲבֹדָה קָשָׁה׃

10 *Hashem* spoke to *Moshe*, saying,

י וַיְדַבֵּר יְהֹוָה אֶל־מֹשֶׁה לֵּאמֹר׃

11 "Go and tell Pharaoh king of Egypt to let the Israelites depart from his land."

יא בֹּא דַבֵּר אֶל־פַּרְעֹה מֶלֶךְ מִצְרָיִם וִישַׁלַּח אֶת־בְּנֵי־יִשְׂרָאֵל מֵאַרְצוֹ׃

12 But *Moshe* appealed to *Hashem*, saying, "The Israelites would not listen to me; how then should Pharaoh heed me, a man of impeded speech!"

יב וַיְדַבֵּר מֹשֶׁה לִפְנֵי יְהֹוָה לֵאמֹר הֵן בְּנֵי־יִשְׂרָאֵל לֹא־שָׁמְעוּ אֵלַי וְאֵיךְ יִשְׁמָעֵנִי פַרְעֹה וַאֲנִי עֲרַל שְׂפָתָיִם׃

13 So *Hashem* spoke to both *Moshe* and *Aharon* in regard to the Israelites and Pharaoh king of Egypt, instructing them to deliver the Israelites from the land of Egypt.

יג וַיְדַבֵּר יְהֹוָה אֶל־מֹשֶׁה וְאֶל־אַהֲרֹן וַיְצַוֵּם אֶל־בְּנֵי יִשְׂרָאֵל וְאֶל־פַּרְעֹה מֶלֶךְ מִצְרָיִם לְהוֹצִיא אֶת־בְּנֵי־יִשְׂרָאֵל מֵאֶרֶץ מִצְרָיִם׃

14 The following are the heads of their respective clans. The sons of *Reuven*, *Yisrael*'s first-born: Enoch and Pallu, *Chetzron* and Carmi; those are the families of *Reuven*.

יד אֵלֶּה רָאשֵׁי בֵית־אֲבֹתָם בְּנֵי רְאוּבֵן בְּכֹר יִשְׂרָאֵל חֲנוֹךְ וּפַלּוּא חֶצְרֹן וְכַרְמִי אֵלֶּה מִשְׁפְּחֹת רְאוּבֵן׃

15 The sons of *Shimon*: Jemuel, Jamin, Ohad, Jachin, Zohar, and *Shaul* the son of a Canaanite woman; those are the families of *Shimon*.

טו וּבְנֵי שִׁמְעוֹן יְמוּאֵל וְיָמִין וְאֹהַד וְיָכִין וְצֹחַר וְשָׁאוּל בֶּן־הַכְּנַעֲנִית אֵלֶּה מִשְׁפְּחֹת שִׁמְעוֹן׃

16 These are the names of *Levi*'s sons by their lineage: *Gershon*, *Kehat*, and *Merari*; and the span of *Levi*'s life was 137 years.

טז וְאֵלֶּה שְׁמוֹת בְּנֵי־לֵוִי לְתֹלְדֹתָם גֵּרְשׁוֹן וּקְהָת וּמְרָרִי וּשְׁנֵי חַיֵּי לֵוִי שֶׁבַע וּשְׁלֹשִׁים וּמְאַת שָׁנָה׃

17 The sons of *Gershon*: Libni and *Shim'i*, by their families.

יז בְּנֵי גֵרְשׁוֹן לִבְנִי וְשִׁמְעִי לְמִשְׁפְּחֹתָם׃

18 The sons of *Kehat*: *Amram*, Izhar, *Chevron*, and Uzziel; and the span of *Kehat*'s life was 133 years.

יח וּבְנֵי קְהָת עַמְרָם וְיִצְהָר וְחֶבְרוֹן וְעֻזִּיאֵל וּשְׁנֵי חַיֵּי קְהָת שָׁלֹשׁ וּשְׁלֹשִׁים וּמְאַת שָׁנָה׃

19 The sons of *Merari*: Mahli and Mushi. These are the families of the *Leviim* by their lineage.

יט וּבְנֵי מְרָרִי מַחְלִי וּמוּשִׁי אֵלֶּה מִשְׁפְּחֹת הַלֵּוִי לְתֹלְדֹתָם׃

מורשה
ירושה

Morasha (מורשה), and *yerusha* (ירושה). *Morasha*, the Hebrew word for 'possession' in this verse, is generally translated as 'heritage,' while *yerusha* is translated as 'inheritance.' The use of different words suggests a difference in meaning. An inheritance is simply passed on from the previous generation, while a heritage requires the receiver's active involvement and participation, like a family business which the founder's children must work hard to maintain. An inheritance may be squandered; a heritage must be preserved intact for the next generation. This certainly explains why the verse uses the word *morasha* with regard to *Eretz Yisrael*. The land requires our active involvement to maintain and preserve it, and it is not ours to squander.

Shemot/Exodus 7
Va'eira

שמות ז
וארא

20 *Amram* took to wife his father's sister *Yocheved*, and she bore him *Aharon* and *Moshe*; and the span of *Amram's* life was 137 years.

כ וַיִּקַּח עַמְרָם אֶת־יוֹכֶבֶד דֹּדָתוֹ לוֹ לְאִשָּׁה וַתֵּלֶד לוֹ אֶת־אַהֲרֹן וְאֶת־מֹשֶׁה וּשְׁנֵי חַיֵּי עַמְרָם שֶׁבַע וּשְׁלֹשִׁים וּמְאַת שָׁנָה:

21 The sons of *Izhar*: *Korach*, Nepheg, and Zichri.

כא וּבְנֵי יִצְהָר קֹרַח וָנֶפֶג וְזִכְרִי:

22 The sons of *Uzziel*: *Mishael*, Elzaphan, and Sithri.

כב וּבְנֵי עֻזִּיאֵל מִישָׁאֵל וְאֶלְצָפָן וְסִתְרִי:

23 *Aharon* took to wife *Elisheva*, daughter of *Aminadav* and sister of *Nachshon*, and she bore him *Nadav* and *Avihu*, *Elazar* and *Itamar*.

כג וַיִּקַּח אַהֲרֹן אֶת־אֱלִישֶׁבַע בַּת־עַמִּינָדָב אֲחוֹת נַחְשׁוֹן לוֹ לְאִשָּׁה וַתֵּלֶד לוֹ אֶת־נָדָב וְאֶת־אֲבִיהוּא אֶת־אֶלְעָזָר וְאֶת־אִיתָמָר:

24 The sons of *Korach*: Assir, Elkana, and Abiasaph. Those are the families of the Korahites.

כד וּבְנֵי קֹרַח אַסִּיר וְאֶלְקָנָה וַאֲבִיאָסָף אֵלֶּה מִשְׁפְּחֹת הַקָּרְחִי:

25 And *Aharon's* son *Elazar* took to wife one of Putiel's daughters, and she bore him *Pinchas*. Those are the heads of the fathers' houses of the *Leviim* by their families.

כה וְאֶלְעָזָר בֶּן־אַהֲרֹן לָקַח־לוֹ מִבְּנוֹת פּוּטִיאֵל לוֹ לְאִשָּׁה וַתֵּלֶד לוֹ אֶת־פִּינְחָס אֵלֶּה רָאשֵׁי אֲבוֹת הַלְוִיִּם לְמִשְׁפְּחֹתָם:

26 It is the same *Aharon* and *Moshe* to whom *Hashem* said, "Bring forth the Israelites from the land of Egypt, troop by troop."

כו הוּא אַהֲרֹן וּמֹשֶׁה אֲשֶׁר אָמַר יְהוָה לָהֶם הוֹצִיאוּ אֶת־בְּנֵי יִשְׂרָאֵל מֵאֶרֶץ מִצְרַיִם עַל־צִבְאֹתָם:

27 It was they who spoke to Pharaoh king of Egypt to free the Israelites from the Egyptians; these are the same *Moshe* and *Aharon*.

כז הֵם הַמְדַבְּרִים אֶל־פַּרְעֹה מֶלֶךְ־מִצְרַיִם לְהוֹצִיא אֶת־בְּנֵי־יִשְׂרָאֵל מִמִּצְרָיִם הוּא מֹשֶׁה וְאַהֲרֹן:

28 For when *Hashem* spoke to *Moshe* in the land of Egypt

כח וַיְהִי בְּיוֹם דִּבֶּר יְהוָה אֶל־מֹשֶׁה בְּאֶרֶץ מִצְרָיִם:

29 and *Hashem* said to *Moshe*, "I am *Hashem*; speak to Pharaoh king of Egypt all that I will tell you,"

כט וַיְדַבֵּר יְהוָה אֶל־מֹשֶׁה לֵּאמֹר אֲנִי יְהוָה דַּבֵּר אֶל־פַּרְעֹה מֶלֶךְ מִצְרַיִם אֵת כָּל־אֲשֶׁר אֲנִי דֹּבֵר אֵלֶיךָ:

30 *Moshe* appealed to *Hashem*, saying, "See, I am of impeded speech; how then should Pharaoh heed me!"

ל וַיֹּאמֶר מֹשֶׁה לִפְנֵי יְהוָה הֵן אֲנִי עֲרַל שְׂפָתַיִם וְאֵיךְ יִשְׁמַע אֵלַי פַּרְעֹה:

7 1 *Hashem* replied to *Moshe*, "See, I place you in the role of *Hashem* to Pharaoh, with your brother *Aharon* as your *navi*.

ז א וַיֹּאמֶר יְהוָה אֶל־מֹשֶׁה רְאֵה נְתַתִּיךָ אֱלֹהִים לְפַרְעֹה וְאַהֲרֹן אָחִיךָ יִהְיֶה נְבִיאֶךָ:

2 You shall repeat all that I command you, and your brother *Aharon* shall speak to Pharaoh to let the Israelites depart from his land.

ב אַתָּה תְדַבֵּר אֵת כָּל־אֲשֶׁר אֲצַוֶּךָּ וְאַהֲרֹן אָחִיךָ יְדַבֵּר אֶל־פַּרְעֹה וְשִׁלַּח אֶת־בְּנֵי־יִשְׂרָאֵל מֵאַרְצוֹ:

3 But I will harden Pharaoh's heart, that I may multiply My signs and marvels in the land of Egypt.

ג וַאֲנִי אַקְשֶׁה אֶת־לֵב פַּרְעֹה וְהִרְבֵּיתִי אֶת־אֹתֹתַי וְאֶת־מוֹפְתַי בְּאֶרֶץ מִצְרָיִם:

Shemot/Exodus 7
Va'eira

שמות ז
וארא

4 When Pharaoh does not heed you, I will lay My hand upon Egypt and deliver My ranks, My people the Israelites, from the land of Egypt with extraordinary chastisements.

ד וְלֹא־יִשְׁמַע אֲלֵכֶם פַּרְעֹה וְנָתַתִּי אֶת־יָדִי בְּמִצְרָיִם וְהוֹצֵאתִי אֶת־צִבְאֹתַי אֶת־עַמִּי בְנֵי־יִשְׂרָאֵל מֵאֶרֶץ מִצְרַיִם בִּשְׁפָטִים גְּדֹלִים׃

5 And the Egyptians shall know that I am *Hashem*, when I stretch out My hand over Egypt and bring out the Israelites from their midst."

ה וְיָדְעוּ מִצְרַיִם כִּי־אֲנִי יְהֹוָה בִּנְטֹתִי אֶת־יָדִי עַל־מִצְרָיִם וְהוֹצֵאתִי אֶת־בְּנֵי־יִשְׂרָאֵל מִתּוֹכָם׃

6 This *Moshe* and *Aharon* did; as *Hashem* commanded them, so they did.

ו וַיַּעַשׂ מֹשֶׁה וְאַהֲרֹן כַּאֲשֶׁר צִוָּה יְהֹוָה אֹתָם כֵּן עָשׂוּ׃

7 *Moshe* was eighty years old and *Aharon* eighty-three, when they made their demand on Pharaoh.

ז וּמֹשֶׁה בֶּן־שְׁמֹנִים שָׁנָה וְאַהֲרֹן בֶּן־שָׁלֹשׁ וּשְׁמֹנִים שָׁנָה בְּדַבְּרָם אֶל־פַּרְעֹה׃

8 *Hashem* said to *Moshe* and *Aharon*,

ח וַיֹּאמֶר יְהֹוָה אֶל־מֹשֶׁה וְאֶל־אַהֲרֹן לֵאמֹר׃

9 "When Pharaoh speaks to you and says, 'Produce your marvel,' you shall say to *Aharon*, 'Take your rod and cast it down before Pharaoh.' It shall turn into a serpent."

ט כִּי יְדַבֵּר אֲלֵכֶם פַּרְעֹה לֵאמֹר תְּנוּ לָכֶם מוֹפֵת וְאָמַרְתָּ אֶל־אַהֲרֹן קַח אֶת־מַטְּךָ וְהַשְׁלֵךְ לִפְנֵי־פַרְעֹה יְהִי לְתַנִּין׃

10 So *Moshe* and *Aharon* came before Pharaoh and did just as *Hashem* had commanded: *Aharon* cast down his rod in the presence of Pharaoh and his courtiers, and it turned into a serpent.

י וַיָּבֹא מֹשֶׁה וְאַהֲרֹן אֶל־פַּרְעֹה וַיַּעֲשׂוּ כֵן כַּאֲשֶׁר צִוָּה יְהֹוָה וַיַּשְׁלֵךְ אַהֲרֹן אֶת־מַטֵּהוּ לִפְנֵי פַרְעֹה וְלִפְנֵי עֲבָדָיו וַיְהִי לְתַנִּין׃

11 Then Pharaoh, for his part, summoned the wise men and the sorcerers; and the Egyptian magicians, in turn, did the same with their spells;

יא וַיִּקְרָא גַּם־פַּרְעֹה לַחֲכָמִים וְלַמְכַשְּׁפִים וַיַּעֲשׂוּ גַם־הֵם חַרְטֻמֵּי מִצְרַיִם בְּלַהֲטֵיהֶם כֵּן׃

12 each cast down his rod, and they turned into serpents. But *Aharon*'s rod swallowed their rods.

יב וַיַּשְׁלִיכוּ אִישׁ מַטֵּהוּ וַיִּהְיוּ לְתַנִּינִם וַיִּבְלַע מַטֵּה־אַהֲרֹן אֶת־מַטֹּתָם׃

13 Yet Pharaoh's heart stiffened and he did not heed them, as *Hashem* had said.

יג וַיֶּחֱזַק לֵב פַּרְעֹה וְלֹא שָׁמַע אֲלֵהֶם כַּאֲשֶׁר דִּבֶּר יְהֹוָה׃

14 And *Hashem* said to *Moshe*, "Pharaoh is stubborn; he refuses to let the people go.

יד וַיֹּאמֶר יְהֹוָה אֶל־מֹשֶׁה כָּבֵד לֵב פַּרְעֹה מֵאֵן לְשַׁלַּח הָעָם׃

15 Go to Pharaoh in the morning, as he is coming out to the water, and station yourself before him at the edge of the Nile, taking with you the rod that turned into a snake.

טו לֵךְ אֶל־פַּרְעֹה בַּבֹּקֶר הִנֵּה יֹצֵא הַמַּיְמָה וְנִצַּבְתָּ לִקְרָאתוֹ עַל־שְׂפַת הַיְאֹר וְהַמַּטֶּה אֲשֶׁר־נֶהְפַּךְ לְנָחָשׁ תִּקַּח בְּיָדֶךָ׃

16 And say to him, '*Hashem*, the God of the Hebrews, sent me to you to say, "Let My people go that they may worship Me in the wilderness." But you have paid no heed until now.

טז וְאָמַרְתָּ אֵלָיו יְהֹוָה אֱלֹהֵי הָעִבְרִים שְׁלָחַנִי אֵלֶיךָ לֵאמֹר שַׁלַּח אֶת־עַמִּי וְיַעַבְדֻנִי בַּמִּדְבָּר וְהִנֵּה לֹא־שָׁמַעְתָּ עַד־כֹּה׃

Shemot/Exodus 7
Va'eira

שמות ז
וארא

17 Thus says *Hashem*, "By this you shall know that I am *Hashem*." See, I shall strike the water in the Nile with the rod that is in my hand, and it will be turned into blood;

יז כֹּה אָמַר יְהֹוָה בְּזֹאת תֵּדַע כִּי אֲנִי יְהֹוָה הִנֵּה אָנֹכִי מַכֶּה ׀ בַּמַּטֶּה אֲשֶׁר־בְּיָדִי עַל־הַמַּיִם אֲשֶׁר בַּיְאֹר וְנֶהֶפְכוּ לְדָם׃

KO a-MAR a-do-NAI b'-ZOT tay-DA KEE a-NEE a-do-NAI hi-NAY a-no-KHEE ma-KEH ba-ma-TEH a-sher b'-ya-DEE al ha-MA-yim a-SHER bai-OR v'-ne-hef-KHU l'-DAM

18 and the fish in the Nile will die. The Nile will stink so that the Egyptians will find it impossible to drink the water of the Nile.'"

יח וְהַדָּגָה אֲשֶׁר־בַּיְאֹר תָּמוּת וּבָאַשׁ הַיְאֹר וְנִלְאוּ מִצְרַיִם לִשְׁתּוֹת מַיִם מִן־הַיְאֹר׃

19 And *Hashem* said to *Moshe*, "Say to *Aharon*: Take your rod and hold out your arm over the waters of Egypt – its rivers, its canals, its ponds, all its bodies of water – that they may turn to blood; there shall be blood throughout the land of Egypt, even in vessels of wood and stone."

יט וַיֹּאמֶר יְהֹוָה אֶל־מֹשֶׁה אֱמֹר אֶל־אַהֲרֹן קַח מַטְּךָ וּנְטֵה־יָדְךָ עַל־מֵימֵי מִצְרַיִם עַל־נַהֲרֹתָם ׀ עַל־יְאֹרֵיהֶם וְעַל־אַגְמֵיהֶם וְעַל כָּל־מִקְוֵה מֵימֵיהֶם וְיִהְיוּ־דָם וְהָיָה דָם בְּכָל־אֶרֶץ מִצְרַיִם וּבָעֵצִים וּבָאֲבָנִים׃

20 *Moshe* and *Aharon* did just as *Hashem* commanded: he lifted up the rod and struck the water in the Nile in the sight of Pharaoh and his courtiers, and all the water in the Nile was turned into blood

כ וַיַּעֲשׂוּ־כֵן מֹשֶׁה וְאַהֲרֹן כַּאֲשֶׁר ׀ צִוָּה יְהֹוָה וַיָּרֶם בַּמַּטֶּה וַיַּךְ אֶת־הַמַּיִם אֲשֶׁר בַּיְאֹר לְעֵינֵי פַרְעֹה וּלְעֵינֵי עֲבָדָיו וַיֵּהָפְכוּ כָּל־הַמַּיִם אֲשֶׁר־בַּיְאֹר לְדָם׃

21 and the fish in the Nile died. The Nile stank so that the Egyptians could not drink water from the Nile; and there was blood throughout the land of Egypt.

כא וְהַדָּגָה אֲשֶׁר־בַּיְאֹר מֵתָה וַיִּבְאַשׁ הַיְאֹר וְלֹא־יָכְלוּ מִצְרַיִם לִשְׁתּוֹת מַיִם מִן־הַיְאֹר וַיְהִי הַדָּם בְּכָל־אֶרֶץ מִצְרָיִם׃

22 But when the Egyptian magicians did the same with their spells, Pharaoh's heart stiffened and he did not heed them – as *Hashem* had spoken.

כב וַיַּעֲשׂוּ־כֵן חַרְטֻמֵּי מִצְרַיִם בְּלָטֵיהֶם וַיֶּחֱזַק לֵב־פַּרְעֹה וְלֹא־שָׁמַע אֲלֵהֶם כַּאֲשֶׁר דִּבֶּר יְהֹוָה׃

23 Pharaoh turned and went into his palace, paying no regard even to this.

כג וַיִּפֶן פַּרְעֹה וַיָּבֹא אֶל־בֵּיתוֹ וְלֹא־שָׁת לִבּוֹ גַּם־לָזֹאת׃

24 And all the Egyptians had to dig round about the Nile for drinking water, because they could not drink the water of the Nile.

כד וַיַּחְפְּרוּ כָל־מִצְרַיִם סְבִיבֹת הַיְאֹר מַיִם לִשְׁתּוֹת כִּי לֹא יָכְלוּ לִשְׁתֹּת מִמֵּימֵי הַיְאֹר׃

7:17 The water in the Nile The first two of the ten plagues that *Hashem* inflicts upon Egypt specifically affect the Nile. When describing the attack on the Nile, *Yechezkel* says: "Thus said *Hashem*: I am going to deal with you, O Pharaoh king of Egypt, mighty monster, sprawling in your channels, who said, 'My Nile is my own; I made it for myself'." (Ezekiel 29:3). Unlike *Eretz Yisrael* which is dependent upon rain water, Egypt has the Nile as a reliable water source, and that is the key to its economic success. Since the Egyptians did not require rain, they saw themselves as self-sufficient and not dependent on God for their sustenance. Consequently, *Hashem* struck the Nile first. By contrast, the Land of Israel has no such water source, and therefore, its inhabitants are aware of their dependence on God and forge a relationship with Him through their daily prayers for rain. This spiritual relationship is built into the very geography of the *Eretz Yisrael*, in contrast with its neighbors.

Shemot/Exodus 8
Va'eira

25 When seven days had passed after *Hashem* struck the Nile,

26 *Hashem* said to *Moshe*, "Go to Pharaoh and say to him, 'Thus says *Hashem*: Let My people go that they may worship Me.

27 If you refuse to let them go, then I will plague your whole country with frogs.

28 The Nile shall swarm with frogs, and they shall come up and enter your palace, your bedchamber and your bed, the houses of your courtiers and your people, and your ovens and your kneading bowls.

29 The frogs shall come up on you and on your people and on all your courtiers.'"

8 1 And *Hashem* said to *Moshe*, "Say to *Aharon*: Hold out your arm with the rod over the rivers, the canals, and the ponds, and bring up the frogs on the land of Egypt."

2 *Aharon* held out his arm over the waters of Egypt, and the frogs came up and covered the land of Egypt.

3 But the magicians did the same with their spells, and brought frogs upon the land of Egypt.

4 Then Pharaoh summoned *Moshe* and *Aharon* and said, "Plead with *Hashem* to remove the frogs from me and my people, and I will let the people go to sacrifice to *Hashem*."

5 And *Moshe* said to Pharaoh, "You may have this triumph over me: for what time shall I plead in behalf of you and your courtiers and your people, that the frogs be cut off from you and your houses, to remain only in the Nile?"

6 "For tomorrow," he replied. And [*Moshe*] said, "As you say – that you may know that there is none like *Hashem* our God;

7 the frogs shall retreat from you and your courtiers and your people; they shall remain only in the Nile."

8 Then *Moshe* and *Aharon* left Pharaoh's presence, and *Moshe* cried out to *Hashem* in the matter of the frogs which He had inflicted upon Pharaoh.

שמות ח
וארא

כה וַיִּמָּלֵא שִׁבְעַת יָמִים אַחֲרֵי הַכּוֹת־יְהֹוָה אֶת־הַיְאֹר׃

כו וַיֹּאמֶר יְהֹוָה אֶל־מֹשֶׁה בֹּא אֶל־פַּרְעֹה וְאָמַרְתָּ אֵלָיו כֹּה אָמַר יְהֹוָה שַׁלַּח אֶת־עַמִּי וְיַעַבְדֻנִי׃

כז וְאִם־מָאֵן אַתָּה לְשַׁלֵּחַ הִנֵּה אָנֹכִי נֹגֵף אֶת־כׇּל־גְּבוּלְךָ בַּצְפַרְדְּעִים׃

כח וְשָׁרַץ הַיְאֹר צְפַרְדְּעִים וְעָלוּ וּבָאוּ בְּבֵיתֶךָ וּבַחֲדַר מִשְׁכָּבְךָ וְעַל־מִטָּתֶךָ וּבְבֵית עֲבָדֶיךָ וּבְעַמֶּךָ וּבְתַנּוּרֶיךָ וּבְמִשְׁאֲרוֹתֶיךָ׃

כט וּבְכָה וּבְעַמְּךָ וּבְכׇל־עֲבָדֶיךָ יַעֲלוּ הַצְפַרְדְּעִים׃

א וַיֹּאמֶר יְהֹוָה אֶל־מֹשֶׁה אֱמֹר אֶל־אַהֲרֹן נְטֵה אֶת־יָדְךָ בְּמַטֶּךָ עַל־הַנְּהָרֹת עַל־הַיְאֹרִים וְעַל־הָאֲגַמִּים וְהַעַל אֶת־הַצְפַרְדְּעִים עַל־אֶרֶץ מִצְרָיִם׃

ב וַיֵּט אַהֲרֹן אֶת־יָדוֹ עַל מֵימֵי מִצְרָיִם וַתַּעַל הַצְּפַרְדֵּעַ וַתְּכַס אֶת־אֶרֶץ מִצְרָיִם׃

ג וַיַּעֲשׂוּ־כֵן הַחַרְטֻמִּים בְּלָטֵיהֶם וַיַּעֲלוּ אֶת־הַצְפַרְדְּעִים עַל־אֶרֶץ מִצְרָיִם׃

ד וַיִּקְרָא פַרְעֹה לְמֹשֶׁה וּלְאַהֲרֹן וַיֹּאמֶר הַעְתִּירוּ אֶל־יְהֹוָה וְיָסֵר הַצְפַרְדְּעִים מִמֶּנִּי וּמֵעַמִּי וַאֲשַׁלְּחָה אֶת־הָעָם וְיִזְבְּחוּ לַיהֹוָה׃

ה וַיֹּאמֶר מֹשֶׁה לְפַרְעֹה הִתְפָּאֵר עָלַי לְמָתַי ׀ אַעְתִּיר לְךָ וְלַעֲבָדֶיךָ וּלְעַמְּךָ לְהַכְרִית הַצְפַרְדְּעִים מִמְּךָ וּמִבָּתֶּיךָ רַק בַּיְאֹר תִּשָּׁאַרְנָה׃

ו וַיֹּאמֶר לְמָחָר וַיֹּאמֶר כִּדְבָרְךָ לְמַעַן תֵּדַע כִּי־אֵין כַּיהֹוָה אֱלֹהֵינוּ׃

ז וְסָרוּ הַצְפַרְדְּעִים מִמְּךָ וּמִבָּתֶּיךָ וּמֵעֲבָדֶיךָ וּמֵעַמֶּךָ רַק בַּיְאֹר תִּשָּׁאַרְנָה׃

ח וַיֵּצֵא מֹשֶׁה וְאַהֲרֹן מֵעִם פַּרְעֹה וַיִּצְעַק מֹשֶׁה אֶל־יְהֹוָה עַל־דְּבַר הַצְפַרְדְּעִים אֲשֶׁר־שָׂם לְפַרְעֹה׃

Shemot/Exodus 8
Va'eira

שמות ח
וארא

9 And *Hashem* did as *Moshe* asked; the frogs died out in the houses, the courtyards, and the fields.

ט וַיַּעַשׂ יְהֹוָה כִּדְבַר מֹשֶׁה וַיָּמֻתוּ הַצְפַרְדְּעִים מִן־הַבָּתִּים מִן־הַחֲצֵרֹת וּמִן־הַשָּׂדֹת׃

10 And they piled them up in heaps, till the land stank.

י וַיִּצְבְּרוּ אֹתָם חֳמָרִם חֳמָרִם וַתִּבְאַשׁ הָאָרֶץ׃

11 But when Pharaoh saw that there was relief, he became stubborn and would not heed them, as *Hashem* had spoken.

יא וַיַּרְא פַּרְעֹה כִּי הָיְתָה הָרְוָחָה וְהַכְבֵּד אֶת־לִבּוֹ וְלֹא שָׁמַע אֲלֵהֶם כַּאֲשֶׁר דִּבֶּר יְהֹוָה׃

12 Then *Hashem* said to *Moshe*, "Say to *Aharon*: Hold out your rod and strike the dust of the earth, and it shall turn to lice throughout the land of Egypt."

יב וַיֹּאמֶר יְהֹוָה אֶל־מֹשֶׁה אֱמֹר אֶל־אַהֲרֹן נְטֵה אֶת־מַטְּךָ וְהַךְ אֶת־עֲפַר הָאָרֶץ וְהָיָה לְכִנִּם בְּכָל־אֶרֶץ מִצְרָיִם׃

13 And they did so. *Aharon* held out his arm with the rod and struck the dust of the earth, and vermin came upon man and beast; all the dust of the earth turned to lice throughout the land of Egypt.

יג וַיַּעֲשׂוּ־כֵן וַיֵּט אַהֲרֹן אֶת־יָדוֹ בְמַטֵּהוּ וַיַּךְ אֶת־עֲפַר הָאָרֶץ וַתְּהִי הַכִּנָּם בָּאָדָם וּבַבְּהֵמָה כָּל־עֲפַר הָאָרֶץ הָיָה כִנִּים בְּכָל־אֶרֶץ מִצְרָיִם׃

14 The magicians did the like with their spells to produce lice, but they could not. The vermin remained upon man and beast;

יד וַיַּעֲשׂוּ־כֵן הַחַרְטֻמִּים בְּלָטֵיהֶם לְהוֹצִיא אֶת־הַכִּנִּים וְלֹא יָכֹלוּ וַתְּהִי הַכִּנָּם בָּאָדָם וּבַבְּהֵמָה׃

15 and the magicians said to Pharaoh, "This is the finger of *Hashem*!" But Pharaoh's heart stiffened and he would not heed them, as *Hashem* had spoken.

טו וַיֹּאמְרוּ הַחַרְטֻמִּים אֶל־פַּרְעֹה אֶצְבַּע אֱלֹהִים הִוא וַיֶּחֱזַק לֵב־פַּרְעֹה וְלֹא־שָׁמַע אֲלֵהֶם כַּאֲשֶׁר דִּבֶּר יְהֹוָה׃

va-yo-m'-RU ha-khar-tu-MEEM el par-OH ETZ-ba e-lo-HEEM HEE va-ye-khe-ZAK layv par-OH v'-lo sha-MA a-lay-HEM ka-a-SHER di-BER a-do-NAI

16 And *Hashem* said to *Moshe*, "Early in the morning present yourself to Pharaoh, as he is coming out to the water, and say to him, 'Thus says *Hashem*: Let My people go that they may worship Me.

טז וַיֹּאמֶר יְהֹוָה אֶל־מֹשֶׁה הַשְׁכֵּם בַּבֹּקֶר וְהִתְיַצֵּב לִפְנֵי פַרְעֹה הִנֵּה יוֹצֵא הַמָּיְמָה וְאָמַרְתָּ אֵלָיו כֹּה אָמַר יְהֹוָה שַׁלַּח עַמִּי וְיַעַבְדֻנִי׃

8:15 This is the finger of *Hashem* The plague of lice had theological implications for the Egyptians, as it was the first time that Pharaoh's magicians recognized the "finger of *Hashem*." According to *Rashi*, this plague was also one of three reasons why *Yaakov* made his son *Yosef* promise to bury him in in the Land of Israel (Genesis 47:29–31). *Yaakov* did not want to be buried in the Egyptian soil which would crawl with lice, as described in verse 13. *Rashi* further explains that when *Mashiach* comes and the dead are resurrected from their graves, the remains of those buried outside *Eretz Yisrael* will need to painfully roll great distances to get to Israel. To avoid this, *Yosef* asks to be buried in the Holy Land. Finally, *Rashi* writes that *Yaakov* did not want to be deified by the Egyptians after his death. Rabbi Samson Raphael Hirsch, however, suggests a fourth reason. Though he had lived in Egypt for seventeen years, he longed to be back in his homeland and wanted to impress upon his descendants that the Land of Israel is where they really belong. To this day, there are many who follow *Yaakov's* example. Appreciating the value and significance of the land, they ask their descendants to bury them in Israel even if they are unable to live there.

Yaakov's grave inside the Machpelah cave

Shemot/Exodus 8
Va'eira

17 For if you do not let My people go, I will let loose swarms of insects against you and your courtiers and your people and your houses; the houses of the Egyptians, and the very ground they stand on, shall be filled with swarms of insects.

18 But on that day I will set apart the region of Goshen, where My people dwell, so that no swarms of insects shall be there, that you may know that I *Hashem* am in the midst of the land.

19 And I will make a distinction between My people and your people. Tomorrow this sign shall come to pass.'"

20 And *Hashem* did so. Heavy swarms of insects invaded Pharaoh's palace and the houses of his courtiers; throughout the country of Egypt the land was ruined because of the swarms of insects.

21 Then Pharaoh summoned *Moshe* and *Aharon* and said, "Go and sacrifice to your God within the land."

22 But *Moshe* replied, "It would not be right to do this, for what we sacrifice to *Hashem* our God is untouchable to the Egyptians. If we sacrifice that which is untouchable to the Egyptians before their very eyes, will they not stone us!

23 So we must go a distance of three days into the wilderness and sacrifice to *Hashem* our God as He may command us."

24 Pharaoh said, "I will let you go to sacrifice to *Hashem* your God in the wilderness; but do not go very far. Plead, then, for me."

25 And *Moshe* said, "When I leave your presence, I will plead with *Hashem* that the swarms of insects depart tomorrow from Pharaoh and his courtiers and his people; but let not Pharaoh again act deceitfully, not letting the people go to sacrifice to *Hashem*."

26 So *Moshe* left Pharaoh's presence and pleaded with *Hashem*.

27 And *Hashem* did as *Moshe* asked: He removed the swarms of insects from Pharaoh, from his courtiers, and from his people; not one remained.

28 But Pharaoh became stubborn this time also, and would not let the people go.

שמות ח
וארא

יז כִּי אִם־אֵינְךָ מְשַׁלֵּחַ אֶת־עַמִּי הִנְנִי מַשְׁלִיחַ בְּךָ וּבַעֲבָדֶיךָ וּבְעַמְּךָ וּבְבָתֶּיךָ אֶת־הֶעָרֹב וּמָלְאוּ בָּתֵּי מִצְרַיִם אֶת־הֶעָרֹב וְגַם הָאֲדָמָה אֲשֶׁר־הֵם עָלֶיהָ:

יח וְהִפְלֵיתִי בַיּוֹם הַהוּא אֶת־אֶרֶץ גֹּשֶׁן אֲשֶׁר עַמִּי עֹמֵד עָלֶיהָ לְבִלְתִּי הֱיוֹת־שָׁם עָרֹב לְמַעַן תֵּדַע כִּי אֲנִי יְהוָה בְּקֶרֶב הָאָרֶץ:

יט וְשַׂמְתִּי פְדֻת בֵּין עַמִּי וּבֵין עַמֶּךָ לְמָחָר יִהְיֶה הָאֹת הַזֶּה:

כ וַיַּעַשׂ יְהוָה כֵּן וַיָּבֹא עָרֹב כָּבֵד בֵּיתָה פַרְעֹה וּבֵית עֲבָדָיו וּבְכָל־אֶרֶץ מִצְרַיִם תִּשָּׁחֵת הָאָרֶץ מִפְּנֵי הֶעָרֹב:

כא וַיִּקְרָא פַרְעֹה אֶל־מֹשֶׁה וּלְאַהֲרֹן וַיֹּאמֶר לְכוּ זִבְחוּ לֵאלֹהֵיכֶם בָּאָרֶץ:

כב וַיֹּאמֶר מֹשֶׁה לֹא נָכוֹן לַעֲשׂוֹת כֵּן כִּי תּוֹעֲבַת מִצְרַיִם נִזְבַּח לַיהוָה אֱלֹהֵינוּ הֵן נִזְבַּח אֶת־תּוֹעֲבַת מִצְרַיִם לְעֵינֵיהֶם וְלֹא יִסְקְלֻנוּ:

כג דֶּרֶךְ שְׁלֹשֶׁת יָמִים נֵלֵךְ בַּמִּדְבָּר וְזָבַחְנוּ לַיהוָה אֱלֹהֵינוּ כַּאֲשֶׁר יֹאמַר אֵלֵינוּ:

כד וַיֹּאמֶר פַּרְעֹה אָנֹכִי אֲשַׁלַּח אֶתְכֶם וּזְבַחְתֶּם לַיהוָה אֱלֹהֵיכֶם בַּמִּדְבָּר רַק הַרְחֵק לֹא־תַרְחִיקוּ לָלֶכֶת הַעְתִּירוּ בַּעֲדִי:

כה וַיֹּאמֶר מֹשֶׁה הִנֵּה אָנֹכִי יוֹצֵא מֵעִמָּךְ וְהַעְתַּרְתִּי אֶל־יְהוָה וְסָר הֶעָרֹב מִפַּרְעֹה מֵעֲבָדָיו וּמֵעַמּוֹ מָחָר רַק אַל־יֹסֵף פַּרְעֹה הָתֵל לְבִלְתִּי שַׁלַּח אֶת־הָעָם לִזְבֹּחַ לַיהוָה:

כו וַיֵּצֵא מֹשֶׁה מֵעִם פַּרְעֹה וַיֶּעְתַּר אֶל־יְהוָה:

כז וַיַּעַשׂ יְהוָה כִּדְבַר מֹשֶׁה וַיָּסַר הֶעָרֹב מִפַּרְעֹה מֵעֲבָדָיו וּמֵעַמּוֹ לֹא נִשְׁאַר אֶחָד:

כח וַיַּכְבֵּד פַּרְעֹה אֶת־לִבּוֹ גַּם בַּפַּעַם הַזֹּאת וְלֹא שִׁלַּח אֶת־הָעָם:

Shemot/Exodus 9
Va'eira

שמות ט
וארא

9 1 *Hashem* said to *Moshe*, "Go to Pharaoh and say to him, 'Thus says *Hashem*, the God of the Hebrews: Let My people go to worship Me.

א וַיֹּאמֶר יְהֹוָה אֶל־מֹשֶׁה בֹּא אֶל־פַּרְעֹה וְדִבַּרְתָּ אֵלָיו כֹּה־אָמַר יְהֹוָה אֱלֹהֵי הָעִבְרִים שַׁלַּח אֶת־עַמִּי וְיַעַבְדֻנִי׃

va-YO-mer a-do-NAI el mo-SHEH BO el par-OH v'-di-bar-TA ay-LAV koh a-MAR a-do-NAI e-lo-HAY ha-iv-REEM sha-LAKH et a-MEE v'-ya-av-DU-nee

2 For if you refuse to let them go, and continue to hold them,

ב כִּי אִם־מָאֵן אַתָּה לְשַׁלֵּחַ וְעוֹדְךָ מַחֲזִיק בָּם׃

3 then the hand of *Hashem* will strike your livestock in the fields – the horses, the asses, the camels, the cattle, and the sheep – with a very severe pestilence.

ג הִנֵּה יַד־יְהֹוָה הוֹיָה בְּמִקְנְךָ אֲשֶׁר בַּשָּׂדֶה בַּסּוּסִים בַּחֲמֹרִים בַּגְּמַלִּים בַּבָּקָר וּבַצֹּאן דֶּבֶר כָּבֵד מְאֹד׃

4 But *Hashem* will make a distinction between the livestock of *Yisrael* and the livestock of the Egyptians, so that nothing shall die of all that belongs to the Israelites.

ד וְהִפְלָה יְהֹוָה בֵּין מִקְנֵה יִשְׂרָאֵל וּבֵין מִקְנֵה מִצְרָיִם וְלֹא יָמוּת מִכָּל־לִבְנֵי יִשְׂרָאֵל דָּבָר׃

5 *Hashem* has fixed the time: tomorrow *Hashem* will do this thing in the land.'"

ה וַיָּשֶׂם יְהֹוָה מוֹעֵד לֵאמֹר מָחָר יַעֲשֶׂה יְהֹוָה הַדָּבָר הַזֶּה בָּאָרֶץ׃

6 And *Hashem* did so the next day: all the livestock of the Egyptians died, but of the livestock of the Israelites not a beast died.

ו וַיַּעַשׂ יְהֹוָה אֶת־הַדָּבָר הַזֶּה מִמָּחֳרָת וַיָּמָת כֹּל מִקְנֵה מִצְרָיִם וּמִמִּקְנֵה בְנֵי־יִשְׂרָאֵל לֹא־מֵת אֶחָד׃

7 When Pharaoh inquired, he found that not a head of the livestock of *Yisrael* had died; yet Pharaoh remained stubborn, and he would not let the people go.

ז וַיִּשְׁלַח פַּרְעֹה וְהִנֵּה לֹא־מֵת מִמִּקְנֵה יִשְׂרָאֵל עַד־אֶחָד וַיִּכְבַּד לֵב פַּרְעֹה וְלֹא שִׁלַּח אֶת־הָעָם׃

8 Then *Hashem* said to *Moshe* and *Aharon*, "Each of you take handfuls of soot from the kiln, and let *Moshe* throw it toward the sky in the sight of Pharaoh.

ח וַיֹּאמֶר יְהֹוָה אֶל־מֹשֶׁה וְאֶל־אַהֲרֹן קְחוּ לָכֶם מְלֹא חָפְנֵיכֶם פִּיחַ כִּבְשָׁן וּזְרָקוֹ מֹשֶׁה הַשָּׁמַיְמָה לְעֵינֵי פַרְעֹה׃

9 It shall become a fine dust all over the land of Egypt, and cause an inflammation breaking out in boils on man and beast throughout the land of Egypt."

ט וְהָיָה לְאָבָק עַל כָּל־אֶרֶץ מִצְרָיִם וְהָיָה עַל־הָאָדָם וְעַל־הַבְּהֵמָה לִשְׁחִין פֹּרֵחַ אֲבַעְבֻּעֹת בְּכָל־אֶרֶץ מִצְרָיִם׃

9:1 Let My people go Unfortunately, the bondage of Jews was not limited to the period of slavery in Egypt. There have been many other such incidents in history, even in the 20th and 21st centuries. Golda Meir (1898–1978), while serving as Israel's first ambassador to the Soviet Union, worked tirelessly to facilitate the immigration to Israel of Jews trapped behind the "Iron Curtain." Upon her arrival, some 50,000 Jews greeted Golda for the *Shabbat*, despite fear of the Soviet regime. She was astonished. "I prayed together with them, Oh, how I prayed. I was caught up in a torrent of love so strong it literally took my breath away!" The 10,000 old Israeli Shekel banknote, followed by the first 10 New Israeli Shekel banknote, honored Golda Meir with her image on one side and on the other, an illustration of the mass of Russian Jews and the expression, taken from this verse, "Let My people go."

Prime Minister Golda Meir (1898–1978)

Shemot/Exodus 9
Va'eira

שמות ט
וארא

10 So they took soot of the kiln and appeared before Pharaoh; *Moshe* threw it toward the sky, and it caused an inflammation breaking out in boils on man and beast.

י וַיִּקְחוּ אֶת־פִּיחַ הַכִּבְשָׁן וַיַּעַמְדוּ לִפְנֵי פַרְעֹה וַיִּזְרֹק אֹתוֹ מֹשֶׁה הַשָּׁמָיְמָה וַיְהִי שְׁחִין אֲבַעְבֻּעֹת פֹּרֵחַ בָּאָדָם וּבַבְּהֵמָה׃

11 The magicians were unable to confront *Moshe* because of the inflammation, for the inflammation afflicted the magicians as well as all the other Egyptians.

יא וְלֹא־יָכְלוּ הַחַרְטֻמִּים לַעֲמֹד לִפְנֵי מֹשֶׁה מִפְּנֵי הַשְּׁחִין כִּי־הָיָה הַשְּׁחִין בַּחַרְטֻמִּם וּבְכָל־מִצְרָיִם׃

12 But *Hashem* stiffened the heart of Pharaoh, and he would not heed them, just as *Hashem* had told *Moshe*.

יב וַיְחַזֵּק יְהוָה אֶת־לֵב פַּרְעֹה וְלֹא שָׁמַע אֲלֵהֶם כַּאֲשֶׁר דִּבֶּר יְהוָה אֶל־מֹשֶׁה׃

13 *Hashem* said to *Moshe*, "Early in the morning present yourself to Pharaoh and say to him, 'Thus says *Hashem*, the God of the Hebrews: Let My people go to worship Me.

יג וַיֹּאמֶר יְהוָה אֶל־מֹשֶׁה הַשְׁכֵּם בַּבֹּקֶר וְהִתְיַצֵּב לִפְנֵי פַרְעֹה וְאָמַרְתָּ אֵלָיו כֹּה־אָמַר יְהוָה אֱלֹהֵי הָעִבְרִים שַׁלַּח אֶת־עַמִּי וְיַעַבְדֻנִי׃

14 For this time I will send all My plagues upon your person, and your courtiers, and your people, in order that you may know that there is none like Me in all the world.

יד כִּי בַּפַּעַם הַזֹּאת אֲנִי שֹׁלֵחַ אֶת־כָּל־מַגֵּפֹתַי אֶל־לִבְּךָ וּבַעֲבָדֶיךָ וּבְעַמֶּךָ בַּעֲבוּר תֵּדַע כִּי אֵין כָּמֹנִי בְּכָל־הָאָרֶץ׃

15 I could have stretched forth My hand and stricken you and your people with pestilence, and you would have been effaced from the earth.

טו כִּי עַתָּה שָׁלַחְתִּי אֶת־יָדִי וָאַךְ אוֹתְךָ וְאֶת־עַמְּךָ בַּדָּבֶר וַתִּכָּחֵד מִן־הָאָרֶץ׃

16 Nevertheless I have spared you for this purpose: in order to show you My power, and in order that My fame may resound throughout the world.

טז וְאוּלָם בַּעֲבוּר זֹאת הֶעֱמַדְתִּיךָ בַּעֲבוּר הַרְאֹתְךָ אֶת־כֹּחִי וּלְמַעַן סַפֵּר שְׁמִי בְּכָל־הָאָרֶץ׃

17 Yet you continue to thwart My people, and do not let them go!

יז עוֹדְךָ מִסְתּוֹלֵל בְּעַמִּי לְבִלְתִּי שַׁלְּחָם׃

18 This time tomorrow I will rain down a very heavy hail, such as has not been in Egypt from the day it was founded until now.

יח הִנְנִי מַמְטִיר כָּעֵת מָחָר בָּרָד כָּבֵד מְאֹד אֲשֶׁר לֹא־הָיָה כָמֹהוּ בְּמִצְרַיִם לְמִן־הַיּוֹם הִוָּסְדָה וְעַד־עָתָּה׃

19 Therefore, order your livestock and everything you have in the open brought under shelter; every man and beast that is found outside, not having been brought indoors, shall perish when the hail comes down upon them!'"

יט וְעַתָּה שְׁלַח הָעֵז אֶת־מִקְנְךָ וְאֵת כָּל־אֲשֶׁר לְךָ בַּשָּׂדֶה כָּל־הָאָדָם וְהַבְּהֵמָה אֲשֶׁר־יִמָּצֵא בַשָּׂדֶה וְלֹא יֵאָסֵף הַבַּיְתָה וְיָרַד עֲלֵהֶם הַבָּרָד וָמֵתוּ׃

20 Those among Pharaoh's courtiers who feared *Hashem*'s word brought their slaves and livestock indoors to safety;

כ הַיָּרֵא אֶת־דְּבַר יְהוָה מֵעַבְדֵי פַּרְעֹה הֵנִיס אֶת־עֲבָדָיו וְאֶת־מִקְנֵהוּ אֶל־הַבָּתִּים׃

21 but those who paid no regard to the word of *Hashem* left their slaves and livestock in the open.

כא וַאֲשֶׁר לֹא־שָׂם לִבּוֹ אֶל־דְּבַר יְהוָה וַיַּעֲזֹב אֶת־עֲבָדָיו וְאֶת־מִקְנֵהוּ בַּשָּׂדֶה׃

Shemot/Exodus 9
Va'eira

שמות ט
וארא

22 Hashem said to Moshe, "Hold out your arm toward the sky that hail may fall on all the land of Egypt, upon man and beast and all the grasses of the field in the land of Egypt."

כב וַיֹּאמֶר יְהֹוָה אֶל־מֹשֶׁה נְטֵה אֶת־יָדְךָ עַל־הַשָּׁמַיִם וִיהִי בָרָד בְּכָל־אֶרֶץ מִצְרָיִם עַל־הָאָדָם וְעַל־הַבְּהֵמָה וְעַל כָּל־עֵשֶׂב הַשָּׂדֶה בְּאֶרֶץ מִצְרָיִם:

23 So Moshe held out his rod toward the sky, and Hashem sent thunder and hail, and fire streamed down to the ground, as Hashem rained down hail upon the land of Egypt.

כג וַיֵּט מֹשֶׁה אֶת־מַטֵּהוּ עַל־הַשָּׁמַיִם וַיהֹוָה נָתַן קֹלֹת וּבָרָד וַתִּהֲלַךְ אֵשׁ אָרְצָה וַיַּמְטֵר יְהֹוָה בָּרָד עַל־אֶרֶץ מִצְרָיִם:

24 The hail was very heavy – fire flashing in the midst of the hail – such as had not fallen on the land of Egypt since it had become a nation.

כד וַיְהִי בָרָד וְאֵשׁ מִתְלַקַּחַת בְּתוֹךְ הַבָּרָד כָּבֵד מְאֹד אֲשֶׁר לֹא־הָיָה כָמֹהוּ בְּכָל־אֶרֶץ מִצְרַיִם מֵאָז הָיְתָה לְגוֹי:

vai-HEE va-RAD v'-AYSH mit-la-KA-khat b'-TOKH ha-ba-RAD ka-VAYD m'-OD a-SHER lo ha-YAH kha-MO-hu b'-khol E-retz mitz-RA-yim may-AZ ha-y'-TAH l'-GOY

25 Throughout the land of Egypt the hail struck down all that were in the open, both man and beast; the hail also struck down all the grasses of the field and shattered all the trees of the field.

כה וַיַּךְ הַבָּרָד בְּכָל־אֶרֶץ מִצְרַיִם אֵת כָּל־אֲשֶׁר בַּשָּׂדֶה מֵאָדָם וְעַד־בְּהֵמָה וְאֵת כָּל־עֵשֶׂב הַשָּׂדֶה הִכָּה הַבָּרָד וְאֶת־כָּל־עֵץ הַשָּׂדֶה שִׁבֵּר:

26 Only in the region of Goshen, where the Israelites were, there was no hail.

כו רַק בְּאֶרֶץ גֹּשֶׁן אֲשֶׁר־שָׁם בְּנֵי יִשְׂרָאֵל לֹא הָיָה בָּרָד:

27 Thereupon Pharaoh sent for Moshe and Aharon and said to them, "I stand guilty this time. Hashem is in the right, and I and my people are in the wrong.

כז וַיִּשְׁלַח פַּרְעֹה וַיִּקְרָא לְמֹשֶׁה וּלְאַהֲרֹן וַיֹּאמֶר אֲלֵהֶם חָטָאתִי הַפָּעַם יְהֹוָה הַצַּדִּיק וַאֲנִי וְעַמִּי הָרְשָׁעִים:

28 Plead with Hashem that there may be an end of Hashem's thunder and of hail. I will let you go; you need stay no longer."

כח הַעְתִּירוּ אֶל־יְהֹוָה וְרַב מִהְיֹת קֹלֹת אֱלֹהִים וּבָרָד וַאֲשַׁלְּחָה אֶתְכֶם וְלֹא תֹסִפוּן לַעֲמֹד:

29 Moshe said to him, "As I go out of the city, I shall spread out my hands to Hashem; the thunder will cease and the hail will fall no more, so that you may know that the earth is Hashem's.

כט וַיֹּאמֶר אֵלָיו מֹשֶׁה כְּצֵאתִי אֶת־הָעִיר אֶפְרֹשׂ אֶת־כַּפַּי אֶל־יְהֹוָה הַקֹּלוֹת יֶחְדָּלוּן וְהַבָּרָד לֹא יִהְיֶה־עוֹד לְמַעַן תֵּדַע כִּי לַיהֹוָה הָאָרֶץ:

30 But I know that you and your courtiers do not yet fear Hashem."

ל וְאַתָּה וַעֲבָדֶיךָ יָדַעְתִּי כִּי טֶרֶם תִּירְאוּן מִפְּנֵי יְהֹוָה אֱלֹהִים:

9:24 The hail was very heavy The hail contains both fire and ice coming down together to smite the Egyptians. Miraculously, the fire does not melt the ice and the ice does not extinguish the fire. The two ordinarily opposing forces work together harmoniously for the purpose of fulfilling God's will. Similarly, Rashi comments (Genesis 1:8) that the Hebrew word for 'heaven,' *shamayim* (שמים), comes from the Hebrew words *aish* (אש), 'fire,' and *mayim* (מים), 'water,' as the two came together in harmony to make up the heavens. This overruling of the laws of nature serves as a powerful lesson and is referenced in the daily Jewish prayer service. The following supplication appears multiple times in the liturgy: "He Who makes peace in His heights, may He make peace upon us and upon all Israel." With this request, humankind is reminded that the common goal of serving Hashem should override all differences between people and unite us in peace.

אש
שמים
מים

Shemot/Exodus 10
Bo

שמות י
בא

31 Now the flax and barley were ruined, for the barley was in the ear and the flax was in bud;

לא וְהַפִּשְׁתָּה וְהַשְּׂעֹרָה נֻכָּתָה כִּי הַשְּׂעֹרָה אָבִיב וְהַפִּשְׁתָּה גִּבְעֹל:

32 but the wheat and the emmer were not hurt, for they ripen late.

לב וְהַחִטָּה וְהַכֻּסֶּמֶת לֹא נֻכּוּ כִּי אֲפִילֹת הֵנָּה:

33 Leaving Pharaoh, *Moshe* went outside the city and spread out his hands to *Hashem*: the thunder and the hail ceased, and no rain came pouring down upon the earth.

לג וַיֵּצֵא מֹשֶׁה מֵעִם פַּרְעֹה אֶת־הָעִיר וַיִּפְרֹשׂ כַּפָּיו אֶל־יְהוָה וַיַּחְדְּלוּ הַקֹּלוֹת וְהַבָּרָד וּמָטָר לֹא־נִתַּךְ אָרְצָה:

34 But when Pharaoh saw that the rain and the hail and the thunder had ceased, he became stubborn and reverted to his guilty ways, as did his courtiers.

לד וַיַּרְא פַּרְעֹה כִּי־חָדַל הַמָּטָר וְהַבָּרָד וְהַקֹּלֹת וַיֹּסֶף לַחֲטֹא וַיַּכְבֵּד לִבּוֹ הוּא וַעֲבָדָיו:

35 So Pharaoh's heart stiffened and he would not let the Israelites go, just as *Hashem* had foretold through *Moshe*.

לה וַיֶּחֱזַק לֵב פַּרְעֹה וְלֹא שִׁלַּח אֶת־בְּנֵי יִשְׂרָאֵל כַּאֲשֶׁר דִּבֶּר יְהוָה בְּיַד־מֹשֶׁה:

10
1 Then *Hashem* said to *Moshe*, "Go to Pharaoh. For I have hardened his heart and the hearts of his courtiers, in order that I may display these My signs among them,

א וַיֹּאמֶר יְהוָה אֶל־מֹשֶׁה בֹּא אֶל־פַּרְעֹה כִּי־אֲנִי הִכְבַּדְתִּי אֶת־לִבּוֹ וְאֶת־לֵב עֲבָדָיו לְמַעַן שִׁתִי אֹתֹתַי אֵלֶּה בְּקִרְבּוֹ:

2 and that you may recount in the hearing of your sons and of your sons' sons how I made a mockery of the Egyptians and how I displayed My signs among them – in order that you may know that I am *Hashem*."

ב וּלְמַעַן תְּסַפֵּר בְּאָזְנֵי בִנְךָ וּבֶן־בִּנְךָ אֵת אֲשֶׁר הִתְעַלַּלְתִּי בְּמִצְרַיִם וְאֶת־אֹתֹתַי אֲשֶׁר־שַׂמְתִּי בָם וִידַעְתֶּם כִּי־אֲנִי יְהוָה:

ul-MA-an t'-sa-PAYR b'-oz-NAY vin-kha u-VEN bin-KHA AYT a-SHER hit-a-LAL-tee b'-mitz-RA-yim v'-et o-to-TAI a-sher SAM-tee VAM vee-da-TEM kee a-NEE a-do-NAI

3 So *Moshe* and *Aharon* went to Pharaoh and said to him, "Thus says *Hashem*, the God of the Hebrews, 'How long will you refuse to humble yourself before Me? Let My people go that they may worship Me.

ג וַיָּבֹא מֹשֶׁה וְאַהֲרֹן אֶל־פַּרְעֹה וַיֹּאמְרוּ אֵלָיו כֹּה־אָמַר יְהוָה אֱלֹהֵי הָעִבְרִים עַד־מָתַי מֵאַנְתָּ לֵעָנֹת מִפָּנָי שַׁלַּח עַמִּי וְיַעַבְדֻנִי:

4 For if you refuse to let My people go, tomorrow I will bring locusts on your territory.

ד כִּי אִם־מָאֵן אַתָּה לְשַׁלֵּחַ אֶת־עַמִּי הִנְנִי מֵבִיא מָחָר אַרְבֶּה בִּגְבֻלֶךָ:

10:2 In order that you may know that I am Hashem Until now, *Hashem* has said that the ten plagues are meant to teach the Egyptians that He is the true God. At this point, He adds another dimension: The plagues are also intended to cause the Children of Israel to recognize God. Sometimes, even people of faith need a spiritual boost. After living in Egypt for generations, the Jewish people have been influenced by their idolatrous surroundings. The plagues serve to remind them that *Hashem* runs the world, as they demonstrate God's control over everything: Water, earth, the animal kingdom, health, flying insects, light and human life. This lesson is especially important as the Children of Israel are about to follow God into the wilderness on their journey to the Promised Land. Jews are commanded to remember the exodus every day of their lives. The memory of the miracles that took place then, helps strengthen our faith and ability to meet life's constant challenges.

Shemot/Exodus 10
Bo

שמות י
בא

5 They shall cover the surface of the land, so that no one will be able to see the land. They shall devour the surviving remnant that was left to you after the hail; and they shall eat away all your trees that grow in the field.

ה וְכִסָּה אֶת־עֵין הָאָרֶץ וְלֹא יוּכַל לִרְאֹת אֶת־הָאָרֶץ וְאָכַל אֶת־יֶתֶר הַפְּלֵטָה הַנִּשְׁאֶרֶת לָכֶם מִן־הַבָּרָד וְאָכַל אֶת־כָּל־הָעֵץ הַצֹּמֵחַ לָכֶם מִן־הַשָּׂדֶה:

6 Moreover, they shall fill your palaces and the houses of all your courtiers and of all the Egyptians – something that neither your fathers nor fathers' fathers have seen from the day they appeared on earth to this day." With that he turned and left Pharaoh's presence.

ו וּמָלְאוּ בָתֶּיךָ וּבָתֵּי כָל־עֲבָדֶיךָ וּבָתֵּי כָל־מִצְרַיִם אֲשֶׁר לֹא־רָאוּ אֲבֹתֶיךָ וַאֲבוֹת אֲבֹתֶיךָ מִיּוֹם הֱיוֹתָם עַל־הָאֲדָמָה עַד הַיּוֹם הַזֶּה וַיִּפֶן וַיֵּצֵא מֵעִם פַּרְעֹה:

7 Pharaoh's courtiers said to him, "How long shall this one be a snare to us? Let the men go to worship Hashem their God! Are you not yet aware that Egypt is lost?"

ז וַיֹּאמְרוּ עַבְדֵי פַרְעֹה אֵלָיו עַד־מָתַי יִהְיֶה זֶה לָנוּ לְמוֹקֵשׁ שַׁלַּח אֶת־הָאֲנָשִׁים וְיַעַבְדוּ אֶת־יְהוָֹה אֱלֹהֵיהֶם הֲטֶרֶם תֵּדַע כִּי אָבְדָה מִצְרָיִם:

8 So Moshe and Aharon were brought back to Pharaoh and he said to them, "Go, worship Hashem your God! Who are the ones to go?"

ח וַיּוּשַׁב אֶת־מֹשֶׁה וְאֶת־אַהֲרֹן אֶל־פַּרְעֹה וַיֹּאמֶר אֲלֵהֶם לְכוּ עִבְדוּ אֶת־יְהוָֹה אֱלֹהֵיכֶם מִי וָמִי הַהֹלְכִים:

9 Moshe replied, "We will all go, young and old: we will go with our sons and daughters, our flocks and herds; for we must observe Hashem's festival."

ט וַיֹּאמֶר מֹשֶׁה בִּנְעָרֵינוּ וּבִזְקֵנֵינוּ נֵלֵךְ בְּבָנֵינוּ וּבִבְנוֹתֵנוּ בְּצֹאנֵנוּ וּבִבְקָרֵנוּ נֵלֵךְ כִּי חַג־יְהוָֹה לָנוּ:

10 But he said to them, "Hashem be with you the same as I mean to let your children go with you! Clearly, you are bent on mischief.

י וַיֹּאמֶר אֲלֵהֶם יְהִי כֵן יְהוָֹה עִמָּכֶם כַּאֲשֶׁר אֲשַׁלַּח אֶתְכֶם וְאֶת־טַפְּכֶם רְאוּ כִּי רָעָה נֶגֶד פְּנֵיכֶם:

11 No! You menfolk go and worship Hashem, since that is what you want." And they were expelled from Pharaoh's presence.

יא לֹא כֵן לְכוּ־נָא הַגְּבָרִים וְעִבְדוּ אֶת־יְהוָֹה כִּי אֹתָהּ אַתֶּם מְבַקְשִׁים וַיְגָרֶשׁ אֹתָם מֵאֵת פְּנֵי פַרְעֹה:

12 Then Hashem said to Moshe, "Hold out your arm over the land of Egypt for the locusts, that they may come upon the land of Egypt and eat up all the grasses in the land, whatever the hail has left."

יב וַיֹּאמֶר יְהוָֹה אֶל־מֹשֶׁה נְטֵה יָדְךָ עַל־אֶרֶץ מִצְרַיִם בָּאַרְבֶּה וְיַעַל עַל־אֶרֶץ מִצְרָיִם וְיֹאכַל אֶת־כָּל־עֵשֶׂב הָאָרֶץ אֵת כָּל־אֲשֶׁר הִשְׁאִיר הַבָּרָד:

13 So Moshe held out his rod over the land of Egypt, and Hashem drove an east wind over the land all that day and all night; and when morning came, the east wind had brought the locusts.

יג וַיֵּט מֹשֶׁה אֶת־מַטֵּהוּ עַל־אֶרֶץ מִצְרַיִם וַיהוָֹה נִהַג רוּחַ קָדִים בָּאָרֶץ כָּל־הַיּוֹם הַהוּא וְכָל־הַלָּיְלָה הַבֹּקֶר הָיָה וְרוּחַ הַקָּדִים נָשָׂא אֶת־הָאַרְבֶּה:

14 Locusts invaded all the land of Egypt and settled within all the territory of Egypt in a thick mass; never before had there been so many, nor will there ever be so many again.

יד וַיַּעַל הָאַרְבֶּה עַל כָּל־אֶרֶץ מִצְרַיִם וַיָּנַח בְּכֹל גְּבוּל מִצְרָיִם כָּבֵד מְאֹד לְפָנָיו לֹא־הָיָה כֵן אַרְבֶּה כָּמֹהוּ וְאַחֲרָיו לֹא יִהְיֶה־כֵּן:

Shemot/Exodus 10
Bo

15 They hid all the land from view, and the land was darkened; and they ate up all the grasses of the field and all the fruit of the trees which the hail had left, so that nothing green was left, of tree or grass of the field, in all the land of Egypt.

16 Pharaoh hurriedly summoned *Moshe* and *Aharon* and said, "I stand guilty before *Hashem* your God and before you.

17 Forgive my offense just this once, and plead with *Hashem* your God that He but remove this death from me."

18 So he left Pharaoh's presence and pleaded with *Hashem*.

19 *Hashem* caused a shift to a very strong west wind, which lifted the locusts and hurled them into the Sea of Reeds; not a single locust remained in all the territory of Egypt.

20 But *Hashem* stiffened Pharaoh's heart, and he would not let the Israelites go.

21 Then *Hashem* said to *Moshe*, "Hold out your arm toward the sky that there may be darkness upon the land of Egypt, a darkness that can be touched."

22 *Moshe* held out his arm toward the sky and thick darkness descended upon all the land of Egypt for three days.

23 People could not see one another, and for three days no one could get up from where he was; but all the Israelites enjoyed light in their dwellings.

24 Pharaoh then summoned *Moshe* and said, "Go, worship *Hashem*! Only your flocks and your herds shall be left behind; even your children may go with you."

25 But *Moshe* said, "You yourself must provide us with sacrifices and burnt offerings to offer up to *Hashem* our God;

26 our own livestock, too, shall go along with us – not a hoof shall remain behind: for we must select from it for the worship of *Hashem* our God; and we shall not know with what we are to worship *Hashem* until we arrive there."

27 But *Hashem* stiffened Pharaoh's heart and he would not agree to let them go.

שמות י
בא

טו וַיְכַס אֶת־עֵין כָּל־הָאָרֶץ וַתֶּחְשַׁךְ הָאָרֶץ וַיֹּאכַל אֶת־כָּל־עֵשֶׂב הָאָרֶץ וְאֵת כָּל־פְּרִי הָעֵץ אֲשֶׁר הוֹתִיר הַבָּרָד וְלֹא־נוֹתַר כָּל־יֶרֶק בָּעֵץ וּבְעֵשֶׂב הַשָּׂדֶה בְּכָל־אֶרֶץ מִצְרָיִם:

טז וַיְמַהֵר פַּרְעֹה לִקְרֹא לְמֹשֶׁה וּלְאַהֲרֹן וַיֹּאמֶר חָטָאתִי לַיהֹוָה אֱלֹהֵיכֶם וְלָכֶם:

יז וְעַתָּה שָׂא נָא חַטָּאתִי אַךְ הַפַּעַם וְהַעְתִּירוּ לַיהֹוָה אֱלֹהֵיכֶם וְיָסֵר מֵעָלַי רַק אֶת־הַמָּוֶת הַזֶּה:

יח וַיֵּצֵא מֵעִם פַּרְעֹה וַיֶּעְתַּר אֶל־יְהֹוָה:

יט וַיַּהֲפֹךְ יְהֹוָה רוּחַ־יָם חָזָק מְאֹד וַיִּשָּׂא אֶת־הָאַרְבֶּה וַיִּתְקָעֵהוּ יָמָּה סּוּף לֹא נִשְׁאַר אַרְבֶּה אֶחָד בְּכֹל גְּבוּל מִצְרָיִם:

כ וַיְחַזֵּק יְהֹוָה אֶת־לֵב פַּרְעֹה וְלֹא שִׁלַּח אֶת־בְּנֵי יִשְׂרָאֵל:

כא וַיֹּאמֶר יְהֹוָה אֶל־מֹשֶׁה נְטֵה יָדְךָ עַל־הַשָּׁמַיִם וִיהִי חֹשֶׁךְ עַל־אֶרֶץ מִצְרָיִם וְיָמֵשׁ חֹשֶׁךְ:

כב וַיֵּט מֹשֶׁה אֶת־יָדוֹ עַל־הַשָּׁמָיִם וַיְהִי חֹשֶׁךְ־אֲפֵלָה בְּכָל־אֶרֶץ מִצְרַיִם שְׁלֹשֶׁת יָמִים:

כג לֹא־רָאוּ אִישׁ אֶת־אָחִיו וְלֹא־קָמוּ אִישׁ מִתַּחְתָּיו שְׁלֹשֶׁת יָמִים וּלְכָל־בְּנֵי יִשְׂרָאֵל הָיָה אוֹר בְּמוֹשְׁבֹתָם:

כד וַיִּקְרָא פַרְעֹה אֶל־מֹשֶׁה וַיֹּאמֶר לְכוּ עִבְדוּ אֶת־יְהֹוָה רַק צֹאנְכֶם וּבְקַרְכֶם יֻצָּג גַּם־טַפְּכֶם יֵלֵךְ עִמָּכֶם:

כה וַיֹּאמֶר מֹשֶׁה גַּם־אַתָּה תִּתֵּן בְּיָדֵנוּ זְבָחִים וְעֹלֹת וְעָשִׂינוּ לַיהֹוָה אֱלֹהֵינוּ:

כו וְגַם־מִקְנֵנוּ יֵלֵךְ עִמָּנוּ לֹא תִשָּׁאֵר פַּרְסָה כִּי מִמֶּנּוּ נִקַּח לַעֲבֹד אֶת־יְהֹוָה אֱלֹהֵינוּ וַאֲנַחְנוּ לֹא־נֵדַע מַה־נַּעֲבֹד אֶת־יְהֹוָה עַד־בֹּאֵנוּ שָׁמָּה:

כז וַיְחַזֵּק יְהֹוָה אֶת־לֵב פַּרְעֹה וְלֹא אָבָה לְשַׁלְּחָם:

Shemot/Exodus 11
Bo

שמות יא
בא

28 Pharaoh said to him, "Be gone from me! Take care not to see me again, for the moment you look upon my face you shall die."

כח וַיֹּאמֶר־לוֹ פַרְעֹה לֵךְ מֵעָלָי הִשָּׁמֶר לְךָ אַל־תֹּסֶף רְאוֹת פָּנַי כִּי בְּיוֹם רְאֹתְךָ פָנַי תָּמוּת:

29 And *Moshe* replied, "You have spoken rightly. I shall not see your face again!"

כט וַיֹּאמֶר מֹשֶׁה כֵּן דִּבַּרְתָּ לֹא־אֹסִף עוֹד רְאוֹת פָּנֶיךָ:

11 1 And *Hashem* said to *Moshe*, "I will bring but one more plague upon Pharaoh and upon Egypt; after that he shall let you go from here; indeed, when he lets you go, he will drive you out of here one and all.

יא א וַיֹּאמֶר יְהֹוָה אֶל־מֹשֶׁה עוֹד נֶגַע אֶחָד אָבִיא עַל־פַּרְעֹה וְעַל־מִצְרַיִם אַחֲרֵי־כֵן יְשַׁלַּח אֶתְכֶם מִזֶּה כְּשַׁלְּחוֹ כָּלָה גָּרֵשׁ יְגָרֵשׁ אֶתְכֶם מִזֶּה:

2 Tell the people to borrow, each man from his neighbor and each woman from hers, objects of silver and gold."

ב דַּבֶּר־נָא בְּאָזְנֵי הָעָם וְיִשְׁאֲלוּ אִישׁ מֵאֵת רֵעֵהוּ וְאִשָּׁה מֵאֵת רְעוּתָהּ כְּלֵי־כֶסֶף וּכְלֵי זָהָב:

3 *Hashem* disposed the Egyptians favorably toward the people. Moreover, *Moshe* himself was much esteemed in the land of Egypt, among Pharaoh's courtiers and among the people.

ג וַיִּתֵּן יְהֹוָה אֶת־חֵן הָעָם בְּעֵינֵי מִצְרָיִם גַּם הָאִישׁ מֹשֶׁה גָּדוֹל מְאֹד בְּאֶרֶץ מִצְרַיִם בְּעֵינֵי עַבְדֵי־פַרְעֹה וּבְעֵינֵי הָעָם:

va-yi-TAYN a-do-NAI et KHAYN ha-AM b'-ay-NAY mitz-RA-yim GAM ha-EESH mo-SHEH ga-DOL m'-OD b'-E-retz mitz-RA-yim b'-ay-NAY av-DAY far-OH uv-ay-NAY ha-AM

4 *Moshe* said, "Thus says *Hashem*: Toward midnight I will go forth among the Egyptians,

ד וַיֹּאמֶר מֹשֶׁה כֹּה אָמַר יְהֹוָה כַּחֲצֹת הַלַּיְלָה אֲנִי יוֹצֵא בְּתוֹךְ מִצְרָיִם:

5 and every first-born in the land of Egypt shall die, from the first-born of Pharaoh who sits on his throne to the first-born of the slave girl who is behind the millstones; and all the first-born of the cattle.

ה וּמֵת כָּל־בְּכוֹר בְּאֶרֶץ מִצְרַיִם מִבְּכוֹר פַּרְעֹה הַיֹּשֵׁב עַל־כִּסְאוֹ עַד בְּכוֹר הַשִּׁפְחָה אֲשֶׁר אַחַר הָרֵחָיִם וְכֹל בְּכוֹר בְּהֵמָה:

6 And there shall be a loud cry in all the land of Egypt, such as has never been or will ever be again;

ו וְהָיְתָה צְעָקָה גְדֹלָה בְּכָל־אֶרֶץ מִצְרָיִם אֲשֶׁר כָּמֹהוּ לֹא נִהְיָתָה וְכָמֹהוּ לֹא תֹסִף:

7 but not a dog shall snarl at any of the Israelites, at man or beast – in order that you may know that *Hashem* makes a distinction between Egypt and *Yisrael*.

ז וּלְכֹל בְּנֵי יִשְׂרָאֵל לֹא יֶחֱרַץ־כֶּלֶב לְשֹׁנוֹ לְמֵאִישׁ וְעַד־בְּהֵמָה לְמַעַן תֵּדְעוּן אֲשֶׁר יַפְלֶה יְהֹוָה בֵּין מִצְרַיִם וּבֵין יִשְׂרָאֵל:

11:3 *Hashem* **disposed the Egyptians favorably toward the people** What transpires at this time that causes the Egyptians to finally find value in the Jewish nation and *Moshe*? Rabbi Samson Raphael Hirsch posits that after the plague of darkness, when the Egyptians were able to see again, they finally acknowledge the morality of the people they have cruelly enslaved. For three days, Egypt was blind and immobilized; the Jews could have easily taken advantage of this situation. Yet, when the light returns at the conclusion of the plague, the Egyptians discover that nothing has been moved from its rightful place. At this juncture, the Egyptians stand in awe of the Jewish people and *Moshe*, their leader. The Jewish mission is to be a light unto the nations, an example of honesty, morality and closeness to *Hashem*. When the People of Israel live up to this mission, the world is in awe.

Rabbi Samson R. Hirsch (1808–1888)

Shemot/Exodus 12
Bo

שמות יב
בא

8 Then all these courtiers of yours shall come down to me and bow low to me, saying, 'Depart, you and all the people who follow you!' After that I will depart." And he left Pharaoh's presence in hot anger.

ח וְיָרְדוּ כָל־עֲבָדֶיךָ אֵלֶּה אֵלַי וְהִשְׁתַּחֲווּ־לִי לֵאמֹר צֵא אַתָּה וְכָל־הָעָם אֲשֶׁר־בְּרַגְלֶיךָ וְאַחֲרֵי־כֵן אֵצֵא וַיֵּצֵא מֵעִם־פַּרְעֹה בָּחֳרִי־אָף׃

9 Now *Hashem* had said to *Moshe*, "Pharaoh will not heed you, in order that My marvels may be multiplied in the land of Egypt."

ט וַיֹּאמֶר יְהוָה אֶל־מֹשֶׁה לֹא־יִשְׁמַע אֲלֵיכֶם פַּרְעֹה לְמַעַן רְבוֹת מוֹפְתַי בְּאֶרֶץ מִצְרָיִם׃

10 *Moshe* and *Aharon* had performed all these marvels before Pharaoh, but *Hashem* had stiffened the heart of Pharaoh so that he would not let the Israelites go from his land.

י וּמֹשֶׁה וְאַהֲרֹן עָשׂוּ אֶת־כָּל־הַמֹּפְתִים הָאֵלֶּה לִפְנֵי פַרְעֹה וַיְחַזֵּק יְהוָה אֶת־לֵב פַּרְעֹה וְלֹא־שִׁלַּח אֶת־בְּנֵי־יִשְׂרָאֵל מֵאַרְצוֹ׃

12 1 *Hashem* said to *Moshe* and *Aharon* in the land of Egypt:

יב א וַיֹּאמֶר יְהוָה אֶל־מֹשֶׁה וְאֶל־אַהֲרֹן בְּאֶרֶץ מִצְרַיִם לֵאמֹר׃

2 This month shall mark for you the beginning of the months; it shall be the first of the months of the year for you.

ב הַחֹדֶשׁ הַזֶּה לָכֶם רֹאשׁ חֳדָשִׁים רִאשׁוֹן הוּא לָכֶם לְחָדְשֵׁי הַשָּׁנָה׃

ha-KHO-desh ha-ZEH la-KHEM ROSH kho-da-SHEEM ri-SHON HU la-KHEM l'-khod-SHAY ha-sha-NAH

3 Speak to the whole community of *Yisrael* and say that on the tenth of this month each of them shall take a lamb to a family, a lamb to a household.

ג דַּבְּרוּ אֶל־כָּל־עֲדַת יִשְׂרָאֵל לֵאמֹר בֶּעָשֹׂר לַחֹדֶשׁ הַזֶּה וְיִקְחוּ לָהֶם אִישׁ שֶׂה לְבֵית־אָבֹת שֶׂה לַבָּיִת׃

4 But if the household is too small for a lamb, let him share one with a neighbor who dwells nearby, in proportion to the number of persons: you shall contribute for the lamb according to what each household will eat.

ד וְאִם־יִמְעַט הַבַּיִת מִהְיֹת מִשֶּׂה וְלָקַח הוּא וּשְׁכֵנוֹ הַקָּרֹב אֶל־בֵּיתוֹ בְּמִכְסַת נְפָשֹׁת אִישׁ לְפִי אָכְלוֹ תָּכֹסּוּ עַל־הַשֶּׂה׃

5 Your lamb shall be without blemish, a yearling male; you may take it from the sheep or from the goats.

ה שֶׂה תָמִים זָכָר בֶּן־שָׁנָה יִהְיֶה לָכֶם מִן־הַכְּבָשִׂים וּמִן־הָעִזִּים תִּקָּחוּ׃

6 You shall keep watch over it until the fourteenth day of this month; and all the assembled congregation of the Israelites shall slaughter it at twilight.

ו וְהָיָה לָכֶם לְמִשְׁמֶרֶת עַד אַרְבָּעָה עָשָׂר יוֹם לַחֹדֶשׁ הַזֶּה וְשָׁחֲטוּ אֹתוֹ כֹּל קְהַל עֲדַת־יִשְׂרָאֵל בֵּין הָעַרְבָּיִם׃

12:2 The beginning of the months *Rosh Chodesh* (ראש חודש), literally 'head of the month,' is celebrated when the first sliver of the new moon appears. In this verse, *Hashem* declares that the Hebrew month of *Nisan* is to be considered the first month in the Jewish calendar. It was in the month of *Nisan* that the Children of Israel were redeemed from Egypt and became a nation, and therefore God refers to this month as "the beginning of the months." Even though the Jewish year begins with the Hebrew month of *Tishrei* (when *Rosh Hashana* is celebrated), the months are numbered starting with the month of redemption. According to the Sages, just as Israel was originally redeemed during *Nisan*, so too, *Nisan* will also be the month in which our final redemption occurs.

Shemot/Exodus 12
Bo

שמות יב
בא

7 They shall take some of the blood and put it on the two doorposts and the lintel of the houses in which they are to eat it.

ז וְלָקְחוּ מִן־הַדָּם וְנָתְנוּ עַל־שְׁתֵּי הַמְּזוּזֹת וְעַל־הַמַּשְׁקוֹף עַל הַבָּתִּים אֲשֶׁר־יֹאכְלוּ אֹתוֹ בָּהֶם:

8 They shall eat the flesh that same night; they shall eat it roasted over the fire, with unleavened bread and with bitter herbs.

ח וְאָכְלוּ אֶת־הַבָּשָׂר בַּלַּיְלָה הַזֶּה צְלִי־אֵשׁ וּמַצּוֹת עַל־מְרֹרִים יֹאכְלֻהוּ:

9 Do not eat any of it raw, or cooked in any way with water, but roasted – head, legs, and entrails – over the fire.

ט אַל־תֹּאכְלוּ מִמֶּנּוּ נָא וּבָשֵׁל מְבֻשָּׁל בַּמָּיִם כִּי אִם־צְלִי־אֵשׁ רֹאשׁוֹ עַל־כְּרָעָיו וְעַל־קִרְבּוֹ:

10 You shall not leave any of it over until morning; if any of it is left until morning, you shall burn it.

י וְלֹא־תוֹתִירוּ מִמֶּנּוּ עַד־בֹּקֶר וְהַנֹּתָר מִמֶּנּוּ עַד־בֹּקֶר בָּאֵשׁ תִּשְׂרֹפוּ:

11 This is how you shall eat it: your loins girded, your sandals on your feet, and your staff in your hand; and you shall eat it hurriedly: it is a *Pesach* offering to *Hashem*.

יא וְכָכָה תֹּאכְלוּ אֹתוֹ מָתְנֵיכֶם חֲגֻרִים נַעֲלֵיכֶם בְּרַגְלֵיכֶם וּמַקֶּלְכֶם בְּיֶדְכֶם וַאֲכַלְתֶּם אֹתוֹ בְּחִפָּזוֹן פֶּסַח הוּא לַיהֹוָה:

12 For that night I will go through the land of Egypt and strike down every first-born in the land of Egypt, both man and beast; and I will mete out punishments to all the gods of Egypt, I *Hashem*.

יב וְעָבַרְתִּי בְאֶרֶץ־מִצְרַיִם בַּלַּיְלָה הַזֶּה וְהִכֵּיתִי כָל־בְּכוֹר בְּאֶרֶץ מִצְרַיִם מֵאָדָם וְעַד־בְּהֵמָה וּבְכָל־אֱלֹהֵי מִצְרַיִם אֶעֱשֶׂה שְׁפָטִים אֲנִי יְהֹוָה:

13 And the blood on the houses where you are staying shall be a sign for you: when I see the blood I will pass over you, so that no plague will destroy you when I strike the land of Egypt.

יג וְהָיָה הַדָּם לָכֶם לְאֹת עַל הַבָּתִּים אֲשֶׁר אַתֶּם שָׁם וְרָאִיתִי אֶת־הַדָּם וּפָסַחְתִּי עֲלֵכֶם וְלֹא־יִהְיֶה בָכֶם נֶגֶף לְמַשְׁחִית בְּהַכֹּתִי בְּאֶרֶץ מִצְרָיִם:

14 This day shall be to you one of remembrance: you shall celebrate it as a festival to *Hashem* throughout the ages; you shall celebrate it as an institution for all time.

יד וְהָיָה הַיּוֹם הַזֶּה לָכֶם לְזִכָּרוֹן וְחַגֹּתֶם אֹתוֹ חַג לַיהֹוָה לְדֹרֹתֵיכֶם חֻקַּת עוֹלָם תְּחָגֻּהוּ:

15 Seven days you shall eat unleavened bread; on the very first day you shall remove leaven from your houses, for whoever eats leavened bread from the first day to the seventh day, that person shall be cut off from *Yisrael*.

טו שִׁבְעַת יָמִים מַצּוֹת תֹּאכֵלוּ אַךְ בַּיּוֹם הָרִאשׁוֹן תַּשְׁבִּיתוּ שְּׂאֹר מִבָּתֵּיכֶם כִּי כָּל־אֹכֵל חָמֵץ וְנִכְרְתָה הַנֶּפֶשׁ הַהִוא מִיִּשְׂרָאֵל מִיּוֹם הָרִאשֹׁן עַד־יוֹם הַשְּׁבִעִי:

16 You shall celebrate a sacred occasion on the first day, and a sacred occasion on the seventh day; no work at all shall be done on them; only what every person is to eat, that alone may be prepared for you.

טז וּבַיּוֹם הָרִאשׁוֹן מִקְרָא־קֹדֶשׁ וּבַיּוֹם הַשְּׁבִיעִי מִקְרָא־קֹדֶשׁ יִהְיֶה לָכֶם כָּל־מְלָאכָה לֹא־יֵעָשֶׂה בָהֶם אַךְ אֲשֶׁר יֵאָכֵל לְכָל־נֶפֶשׁ הוּא לְבַדּוֹ יֵעָשֶׂה לָכֶם:

17 You shall observe the [Feast of] Unleavened Bread, for on this very day I brought your ranks out of the land of Egypt; you shall observe this day throughout the ages as an institution for all time.

יז וּשְׁמַרְתֶּם אֶת־הַמַּצּוֹת כִּי בְּעֶצֶם הַיּוֹם הַזֶּה הוֹצֵאתִי אֶת־צִבְאוֹתֵיכֶם מֵאֶרֶץ מִצְרָיִם וּשְׁמַרְתֶּם אֶת־הַיּוֹם הַזֶּה לְדֹרֹתֵיכֶם חֻקַּת עוֹלָם:

Shemot/Exodus 12
Bo

שמות יב
בא

18 In the first month, from the fourteenth day of the month at evening, you shall eat unleavened bread until the twenty-first day of the month at evening.

יח בָּרִאשֹׁן בְּאַרְבָּעָה עָשָׂר יוֹם לַחֹדֶשׁ בָּעֶרֶב תֹּאכְלוּ מַצֹּת עַד יוֹם הָאֶחָד וְעֶשְׂרִים לַחֹדֶשׁ בָּעָרֶב:

19 No leaven shall be found in your houses for seven days. For whoever eats what is leavened, that person shall be cut off from the community of *Yisrael*, whether he is a stranger or a citizen of the country.

יט שִׁבְעַת יָמִים שְׂאֹר לֹא יִמָּצֵא בְּבָתֵּיכֶם כִּי כָּל־אֹכֵל מַחְמֶצֶת וְנִכְרְתָה הַנֶּפֶשׁ הַהִוא מֵעֲדַת יִשְׂרָאֵל בַּגֵּר וּבְאֶזְרַח הָאָרֶץ:

20 You shall eat nothing leavened; in all your settlements you shall eat unleavened bread.

כ כָּל־מַחְמֶצֶת לֹא תֹאכֵלוּ בְּכֹל מוֹשְׁבֹתֵיכֶם תֹּאכְלוּ מַצּוֹת:

21 *Moshe* then summoned all the elders of *Yisrael* and said to them, "Go, pick out lambs for your families, and slaughter the *Pesach* offering.

כא וַיִּקְרָא מֹשֶׁה לְכָל־זִקְנֵי יִשְׂרָאֵל וַיֹּאמֶר אֲלֵהֶם מִשְׁכוּ וּקְחוּ לָכֶם צֹאן לְמִשְׁפְּחֹתֵיכֶם וְשַׁחֲטוּ הַפָּסַח:

22 Take a bunch of hyssop, dip it in the blood that is in the basin, and apply some of the blood that is in the basin to the lintel and to the two doorposts. None of you shall go outside the door of his house until morning.

כב וּלְקַחְתֶּם אֲגֻדַּת אֵזוֹב וּטְבַלְתֶּם בַּדָּם אֲשֶׁר־בַּסַּף וְהִגַּעְתֶּם אֶל־הַמַּשְׁקוֹף וְאֶל־שְׁתֵּי הַמְּזוּזֹת מִן־הַדָּם אֲשֶׁר בַּסָּף וְאַתֶּם לֹא תֵצְאוּ אִישׁ מִפֶּתַח־בֵּיתוֹ עַד־בֹּקֶר:

23 For when *Hashem* goes through to smite the Egyptians, He will see the blood on the lintel and the two doorposts, and *Hashem* will pass over the door and not let the Destroyer enter and smite your home.

כג וְעָבַר יְהֹוָה לִנְגֹּף אֶת־מִצְרַיִם וְרָאָה אֶת־הַדָּם עַל־הַמַּשְׁקוֹף וְעַל שְׁתֵּי הַמְּזוּזֹת וּפָסַח יְהֹוָה עַל־הַפֶּתַח וְלֹא יִתֵּן הַמַּשְׁחִית לָבֹא אֶל־בָּתֵּיכֶם לִנְגֹּף:

24 "You shall observe this as an institution for all time, for you and for your descendants.

כד וּשְׁמַרְתֶּם אֶת־הַדָּבָר הַזֶּה לְחָק־לְךָ וּלְבָנֶיךָ עַד־עוֹלָם:

25 And when you enter the land that *Hashem* will give you, as He has promised, you shall observe this rite.

כה וְהָיָה כִּי־תָבֹאוּ אֶל־הָאָרֶץ אֲשֶׁר יִתֵּן יְהֹוָה לָכֶם כַּאֲשֶׁר דִּבֵּר וּשְׁמַרְתֶּם אֶת־הָעֲבֹדָה הַזֹּאת:

26 And when your children ask you, 'What do you mean by this rite?'

כו וְהָיָה כִּי־יֹאמְרוּ אֲלֵיכֶם בְּנֵיכֶם מָה הָעֲבֹדָה הַזֹּאת לָכֶם:

27 you shall say, 'It is the *Pesach* sacrifice to *Hashem*, because He passed over the houses of the Israelites in Egypt when He smote the Egyptians, but saved our houses.'" The people then bowed low in homage.

כז וַאֲמַרְתֶּם זֶבַח־פֶּסַח הוּא לַיהֹוָה אֲשֶׁר פָּסַח עַל־בָּתֵּי בְנֵי־יִשְׂרָאֵל בְּמִצְרַיִם בְּנָגְפּוֹ אֶת־מִצְרַיִם וְאֶת־בָּתֵּינוּ הִצִּיל וַיִּקֹּד הָעָם וַיִּשְׁתַּחֲוּוּ:

28 And the Israelites went and did so; just as *Hashem* had commanded *Moshe* and *Aharon*, so they did.

כח וַיֵּלְכוּ וַיַּעֲשׂוּ בְּנֵי יִשְׂרָאֵל כַּאֲשֶׁר צִוָּה יְהֹוָה אֶת־מֹשֶׁה וְאַהֲרֹן כֵּן עָשׂוּ:

29 In the middle of the night *Hashem* struck down all the first-born in the land of Egypt, from the first-born of Pharaoh who sat on the throne to the first-born of the captive who was in the dungeon, and all the first-born of the cattle.

כט וַיְהִי בַּחֲצִי הַלַּיְלָה וַיהֹוָה הִכָּה כָל־בְּכוֹר בְּאֶרֶץ מִצְרַיִם מִבְּכֹר פַּרְעֹה הַיֹּשֵׁב עַל־כִּסְאוֹ עַד בְּכוֹר הַשְּׁבִי אֲשֶׁר בְּבֵית הַבּוֹר וְכֹל בְּכוֹר בְּהֵמָה:

Shemot/Exodus 12
Bo

שמות יב
בא

30 And Pharaoh arose in the night, with all his courtiers and all the Egyptians – because there was a loud cry in Egypt; for there was no house where there was not someone dead.

ל וַיָּקָם פַּרְעֹה לַיְלָה הוּא וְכָל־עֲבָדָיו וְכָל־מִצְרַיִם וַתְּהִי צְעָקָה גְדֹלָה בְּמִצְרָיִם כִּי־אֵין בַּיִת אֲשֶׁר אֵין־שָׁם מֵת׃

31 He summoned *Moshe* and *Aharon* in the night and said, "Up, depart from among my people, you and the Israelites with you! Go, worship *Hashem* as you said!

לא וַיִּקְרָא לְמֹשֶׁה וּלְאַהֲרֹן לַיְלָה וַיֹּאמֶר קוּמוּ צְּאוּ מִתּוֹךְ עַמִּי גַּם־אַתֶּם גַּם־בְּנֵי יִשְׂרָאֵל וּלְכוּ עִבְדוּ אֶת־יְהוָה כְּדַבֶּרְכֶם׃

32 Take also your flocks and your herds, as you said, and begone! And may you bring a blessing upon me also!"

לב גַּם־צֹאנְכֶם גַּם־בְּקַרְכֶם קְחוּ כַּאֲשֶׁר דִּבַּרְתֶּם וָלֵכוּ וּבֵרַכְתֶּם גַּם־אֹתִי׃

33 The Egyptians urged the people on, impatient to have them leave the country, for they said, "We shall all be dead."

לג וַתֶּחֱזַק מִצְרַיִם עַל־הָעָם לְמַהֵר לְשַׁלְּחָם מִן־הָאָרֶץ כִּי אָמְרוּ כֻּלָּנוּ מֵתִים׃

34 So the people took their dough before it was leavened, their kneading bowls wrapped in their cloaks upon their shoulders.

לד וַיִּשָּׂא הָעָם אֶת־בְּצֵקוֹ טֶרֶם יֶחְמָץ מִשְׁאֲרֹתָם צְרֻרֹת בְּשִׂמְלֹתָם עַל־שִׁכְמָם׃

35 The Israelites had done *Moshe*'s bidding and borrowed from the Egyptians objects of silver and gold, and clothing.

לה וּבְנֵי־יִשְׂרָאֵל עָשׂוּ כִּדְבַר מֹשֶׁה וַיִּשְׁאֲלוּ מִמִּצְרַיִם כְּלֵי־כֶסֶף וּכְלֵי זָהָב וּשְׂמָלֹת׃

36 And *Hashem* had disposed the Egyptians favorably toward the people, and they let them have their request; thus they stripped the Egyptians.

לו וַיהוָה נָתַן אֶת־חֵן הָעָם בְּעֵינֵי מִצְרַיִם וַיַּשְׁאִלוּם וַיְנַצְּלוּ אֶת־מִצְרָיִם׃

37 The Israelites journeyed from Raamses to Succoth, about six hundred thousand men on foot, aside from children.

לז וַיִּסְעוּ בְנֵי־יִשְׂרָאֵל מֵרַעְמְסֵס סֻכֹּתָה כְּשֵׁשׁ־מֵאוֹת אֶלֶף רַגְלִי הַגְּבָרִים לְבַד מִטָּף׃

38 Moreover, a mixed multitude went up with them, and very much livestock, both flocks and herds.

לח וְגַם־עֵרֶב רַב עָלָה אִתָּם וְצֹאן וּבָקָר מִקְנֶה כָּבֵד מְאֹד׃

39 And they baked unleavened cakes of the dough that they had taken out of Egypt, for it was not leavened, since they had been driven out of Egypt and could not delay; nor had they prepared any provisions for themselves.

לט וַיֹּאפוּ אֶת־הַבָּצֵק אֲשֶׁר הוֹצִיאוּ מִמִּצְרַיִם עֻגֹת מַצּוֹת כִּי לֹא חָמֵץ כִּי־גֹרְשׁוּ מִמִּצְרַיִם וְלֹא יָכְלוּ לְהִתְמַהְמֵהַּ וְגַם־צֵדָה לֹא־עָשׂוּ לָהֶם׃

40 The length of time that the Israelites lived in Egypt was four hundred and thirty years;

מ וּמוֹשַׁב בְּנֵי יִשְׂרָאֵל אֲשֶׁר יָשְׁבוּ בְּמִצְרָיִם שְׁלֹשִׁים שָׁנָה וְאַרְבַּע מֵאוֹת שָׁנָה׃

41 at the end of the four hundred and thirtieth year, to the very day, all the ranks of *Hashem* departed from the land of Egypt.

מא וַיְהִי מִקֵּץ שְׁלֹשִׁים שָׁנָה וְאַרְבַּע מֵאוֹת שָׁנָה וַיְהִי בְּעֶצֶם הַיּוֹם הַזֶּה יָצְאוּ כָּל־צִבְאוֹת יְהוָה מֵאֶרֶץ מִצְרָיִם׃

42 That was for *Hashem* a night of vigil to bring them out of the land of Egypt; that same night is *Hashem*'s, one of vigil for all the children of *Yisrael* throughout the ages.

מב לֵיל שִׁמֻּרִים הוּא לַיהוָה לְהוֹצִיאָם מֵאֶרֶץ מִצְרָיִם הוּא־הַלַּיְלָה הַזֶּה לַיהוָה שִׁמֻּרִים לְכָל־בְּנֵי יִשְׂרָאֵל לְדֹרֹתָם׃

168

Shemot/Exodus 13
Bo

שמות יג
בא

43 *Hashem* said to *Moshe* and *Aharon*: This is the law of the *Pesach* offering: No foreigner shall eat of it.

מג וַיֹּאמֶר יְהֹוָה אֶל־מֹשֶׁה וְאַהֲרֹן זֹאת חֻקַּת הַפָּסַח כָּל־בֶּן־נֵכָר לֹא־יֹאכַל בּוֹ:

44 But any slave a man has bought may eat of it once he has been circumcised.

מד וְכָל־עֶבֶד אִישׁ מִקְנַת־כָּסֶף וּמַלְתָּה אֹתוֹ אָז יֹאכַל בּוֹ:

45 No bound or hired laborer shall eat of it.

מה תּוֹשָׁב וְשָׂכִיר לֹא־יֹאכַל־בּוֹ:

46 It shall be eaten in one house: you shall not take any of the flesh outside the house; nor shall you break a bone of it.

מו בְּבַיִת אֶחָד יֵאָכֵל לֹא־תוֹצִיא מִן־הַבַּיִת מִן־הַבָּשָׂר חוּצָה וְעֶצֶם לֹא תִשְׁבְּרוּ־בוֹ:

47 The whole community of *Yisrael* shall offer it.

מז כָּל־עֲדַת יִשְׂרָאֵל יַעֲשׂוּ אֹתוֹ:

48 If a stranger who dwells with you would offer the *Pesach* to *Hashem*, all his males must be circumcised; then he shall be admitted to offer it; he shall then be as a citizen of the country. But no uncircumcised person may eat of it.

מח וְכִי־יָגוּר אִתְּךָ גֵּר וְעָשָׂה פֶסַח לַיהֹוָה הִמּוֹל לוֹ כָל־זָכָר וְאָז יִקְרַב לַעֲשֹׂתוֹ וְהָיָה כְּאֶזְרַח הָאָרֶץ וְכָל־עָרֵל לֹא־יֹאכַל בּוֹ:

49 There shall be one law for the citizen and for the stranger who dwells among you.

מט תּוֹרָה אַחַת יִהְיֶה לָאֶזְרָח וְלַגֵּר הַגָּר בְּתוֹכְכֶם:

50 And all the Israelites did so; as *Hashem* had commanded *Moshe* and *Aharon*, so they did.

נ וַיַּעֲשׂוּ כָּל־בְּנֵי יִשְׂרָאֵל כַּאֲשֶׁר צִוָּה יְהֹוָה אֶת־מֹשֶׁה וְאֶת־אַהֲרֹן כֵּן עָשׂוּ:

51 That very day *Hashem* freed the Israelites from the land of Egypt, troop by troop.

נא וַיְהִי בְּעֶצֶם הַיּוֹם הַזֶּה הוֹצִיא יְהֹוָה אֶת־בְּנֵי יִשְׂרָאֵל מֵאֶרֶץ מִצְרַיִם עַל־צִבְאֹתָם:

13

1 *Hashem* spoke further to *Moshe*, saying,

יג א וַיְדַבֵּר יְהֹוָה אֶל־מֹשֶׁה לֵּאמֹר:

2 "Consecrate to Me every first-born; man and beast, the first issue of every womb among the Israelites is Mine."

ב קַדֶּשׁ־לִי כָל־בְּכוֹר פֶּטֶר כָּל־רֶחֶם בִּבְנֵי יִשְׂרָאֵל בָּאָדָם וּבַבְּהֵמָה לִי הוּא:

3 And *Moshe* said to the people, "Remember this day, on which you went free from Egypt, the house of bondage, how *Hashem* freed you from it with a mighty hand: no leavened bread shall be eaten.

ג וַיֹּאמֶר מֹשֶׁה אֶל־הָעָם זָכוֹר אֶת־הַיּוֹם הַזֶּה אֲשֶׁר יְצָאתֶם מִמִּצְרַיִם מִבֵּית עֲבָדִים כִּי בְּחֹזֶק יָד הוֹצִיא יְהֹוָה אֶתְכֶם מִזֶּה וְלֹא יֵאָכֵל חָמֵץ:

4 You go free on this day, in the month of Abib.

ד הַיּוֹם אַתֶּם יֹצְאִים בְּחֹדֶשׁ הָאָבִיב:

ha-YOM a-TEM yo-tz'-EEM b'-KHO-desh ha-a-VEEV

13:4 In the month of Abib 'Abib' in Hebrew is *Aviv* (אביב), meaning 'springtime.' The *Torah* has already stated that the redemption from Egypt took place in the first month, the month of *Nisan*, which is in the springtime. Why is it necessary to state explicitly that in happened in the month of *Aviv*? Emphasizing that the redemption took place in the spring highlights *Hashem*'s love and compassion for His children. He made sure to free the Israelites and set them on their journey through the desert when the weather was most pleasant; not too hot, too cold or too rainy. Furthermore, as springtime symbolizes the rebirth of the land, there was no better time to experience the rebirth of the nation than the spring.

אביב

Spring flowers in the Negev

Shemot/Exodus 13
Bo

שמות יג
בא

5 So, when *Hashem* has brought you into the land of the Canaanites, the Hittites, the Amorites, the Hivites, and the Jebusites, which He swore to your fathers to give you, a land flowing with milk and honey, you shall observe in this month the following practice:

ה וְהָיָה כִי־יְבִיאֲךָ יְהֹוָה אֶל־אֶרֶץ הַכְּנַעֲנִי וְהַחִתִּי וְהָאֱמֹרִי וְהַחִוִּי וְהַיְבוּסִי אֲשֶׁר נִשְׁבַּע לַאֲבֹתֶיךָ לָתֶת לָךְ אֶרֶץ זָבַת חָלָב וּדְבָשׁ וְעָבַדְתָּ אֶת־הָעֲבֹדָה הַזֹּאת בַּחֹדֶשׁ הַזֶּה:

v'-ha-YA ki y'-vee-ah-KHA el eh-RETZ ha-k'-na-a'-nee v'-ha-khi-TEE v'-ha-eh-mo-REE v'-ha-khee-VEE v'-ha-y'-vu-SEE a-SHER nish-BA la-a-vo-te-KHA la-TAYT lakh eh-RETZ za-VAT kha-LAV u-d'-VASH v'-a-va-d'-TA et ha-a-vo-DA ha-ZOHT ba-kho-DESH ha-ZE

6 "Seven days you shall eat unleavened bread, and on the seventh day there shall be a festival of *Hashem*.

ו שִׁבְעַת יָמִים תֹּאכַל מַצֹּת וּבַיּוֹם הַשְּׁבִיעִי חַג לַיהֹוָה:

7 Throughout the seven days unleavened bread shall be eaten; no leavened bread shall be found with you, and no leaven shall be found in all your territory.

ז מַצּוֹת יֵאָכֵל אֵת שִׁבְעַת הַיָּמִים וְלֹא־יֵרָאֶה לְךָ חָמֵץ וְלֹא־יֵרָאֶה לְךָ שְׂאֹר בְּכָל־גְּבֻלֶךָ:

8 And you shall explain to your son on that day, 'It is because of what *Hashem* did for me when I went free from Egypt.'

ח וְהִגַּדְתָּ לְבִנְךָ בַּיּוֹם הַהוּא לֵאמֹר בַּעֲבוּר זֶה עָשָׂה יְהֹוָה לִי בְּצֵאתִי מִמִּצְרָיִם:

9 "And this shall serve you as a sign on your hand and as a reminder on your forehead – in order that the Teaching of *Hashem* may be in your mouth – that with a mighty hand *Hashem* freed you from Egypt.

ט וְהָיָה לְךָ לְאוֹת עַל־יָדְךָ וּלְזִכָּרוֹן בֵּין עֵינֶיךָ לְמַעַן תִּהְיֶה תּוֹרַת יְהֹוָה בְּפִיךָ כִּי בְּיָד חֲזָקָה הוֹצִאֲךָ יְהֹוָה מִמִּצְרָיִם:

10 You shall keep this institution at its set time from year to year.

י וְשָׁמַרְתָּ אֶת־הַחֻקָּה הַזֹּאת לְמוֹעֲדָהּ מִיָּמִים יָמִימָה:

11 "And when *Hashem* has brought you into the land of the Canaanites, as He swore to you and to your fathers, and has given it to you,

יא וְהָיָה כִּי־יְבִאֲךָ יְהֹוָה אֶל־אֶרֶץ הַכְּנַעֲנִי כַּאֲשֶׁר נִשְׁבַּע לְךָ וְלַאֲבֹתֶיךָ וּנְתָנָהּ לָךְ:

12 you shall set apart for *Hashem* every first issue of the womb: every male firstling that your cattle drop shall be *Hashem*'s.

יב וְהַעֲבַרְתָּ כָל־פֶּטֶר־רֶחֶם לַיהֹוָה וְכָל־פֶּטֶר שֶׁגֶר בְּהֵמָה אֲשֶׁר יִהְיֶה לְךָ הַזְּכָרִים לַיהֹוָה:

13 But every firstling ass you shall redeem with a sheep; if you do not redeem it, you must break its neck. And you must redeem every first-born male among your children.

יג וְכָל־פֶּטֶר חֲמֹר תִּפְדֶּה בְשֶׂה וְאִם־לֹא תִפְדֶּה וַעֲרַפְתּוֹ וְכֹל בְּכוֹר אָדָם בְּבָנֶיךָ תִּפְדֶּה:

13:5 A land flowing with milk and honey *Eretz Yisrael* is described many times throughout the Bible as a land flowing with milk and honey. *Rashi* explains this expression quite literally: Milk flows from the goats, and honey comes from the dates and figs that Israel is known for. *Ramban* adds that the word "flowing" is used, which indicates exceptional fertility and abundance. On a metaphorical level, the *Midrash* explains that milk is a nutritional necessity whereas honey is a savory delicacy. *Hashem* promises that the Land of Israel will provide not only the essential things needed to survive, but also sweet luxuries.

Ripe dates in northern Israel

Shemot/Exodus 14
Beshalach

שמות יד
בשלח

14 And when, in time to come, your son asks you, saying, 'What does this mean?' you shall say to him, 'It was with a mighty hand that *Hashem* brought us out from Egypt, the house of bondage.

יד וְהָיָה כִּי־יִשְׁאָלְךָ בִנְךָ מָחָר לֵאמֹר מַה־זֹּאת וְאָמַרְתָּ אֵלָיו בְּחֹזֶק יָד הוֹצִיאָנוּ יְהֹוָה מִמִּצְרַיִם מִבֵּית עֲבָדִים:

15 When Pharaoh stubbornly refused to let us go, *Hashem* slew every first-born in the land of Egypt, the first-born of both man and beast. Therefore I sacrifice to *Hashem* every first male issue of the womb, but redeem every first-born among my sons.'

טו וַיְהִי כִּי־הִקְשָׁה פַרְעֹה לְשַׁלְּחֵנוּ וַיַּהֲרֹג יְהֹוָה כָּל־בְּכוֹר בְּאֶרֶץ מִצְרַיִם מִבְּכֹר אָדָם וְעַד־בְּכוֹר בְּהֵמָה עַל־כֵּן אֲנִי זֹבֵחַ לַיהֹוָה כָּל־פֶּטֶר רֶחֶם הַזְּכָרִים וְכָל־בְּכוֹר בָּנַי אֶפְדֶּה:

16 "And so it shall be as a sign upon your hand and as a symbol on your forehead that with a mighty hand *Hashem* freed us from Egypt."

טז וְהָיָה לְאוֹת עַל־יָדְכָה וּלְטוֹטָפֹת בֵּין עֵינֶיךָ כִּי בְּחֹזֶק יָד הוֹצִיאָנוּ יְהֹוָה מִמִּצְרָיִם:

17 Now when Pharaoh let the people go, *Hashem* did not lead them by way of the land of the Phillistines, although it was nearer; for *Hashem* said, "The people may have a change of heart when they see war, and return to Egypt."

יז וַיְהִי בְּשַׁלַּח פַּרְעֹה אֶת־הָעָם וְלֹא־נָחָם אֱלֹהִים דֶּרֶךְ אֶרֶץ פְּלִשְׁתִּים כִּי קָרוֹב הוּא כִּי אָמַר אֱלֹהִים פֶּן־יִנָּחֵם הָעָם בִּרְאֹתָם מִלְחָמָה וְשָׁבוּ מִצְרָיְמָה:

18 So *Hashem* led the people roundabout, by way of the wilderness at the Sea of Reeds. Now the Israelites went up armed out of the land of Egypt.

יח וַיַּסֵּב אֱלֹהִים אֶת־הָעָם דֶּרֶךְ הַמִּדְבָּר יַם־סוּף וַחֲמֻשִׁים עָלוּ בְנֵי־יִשְׂרָאֵל מֵאֶרֶץ מִצְרָיִם:

19 And *Moshe* took with him the bones of *Yosef*, who had exacted an oath from the children of *Yisrael*, saying, "*Hashem* will be sure to take notice of you: then you shall carry up my bones from here with you."

יט וַיִּקַּח מֹשֶׁה אֶת־עַצְמוֹת יוֹסֵף עִמּוֹ כִּי הַשְׁבֵּעַ הִשְׁבִּיעַ אֶת־בְּנֵי יִשְׂרָאֵל לֵאמֹר פָּקֹד יִפְקֹד אֱלֹהִים אֶתְכֶם וְהַעֲלִיתֶם אֶת־עַצְמֹתַי מִזֶּה אִתְּכֶם:

20 They set out from Succoth, and encamped at Etham, at the edge of the wilderness.

כ וַיִּסְעוּ מִסֻּכֹּת וַיַּחֲנוּ בְאֵתָם בִּקְצֵה הַמִּדְבָּר:

21 *Hashem* went before them in a pillar of cloud by day, to guide them along the way, and in a pillar of fire by night, to give them light, that they might travel day and night.

כא וַיהֹוָה הֹלֵךְ לִפְנֵיהֶם יוֹמָם בְּעַמּוּד עָנָן לַנְחֹתָם הַדֶּרֶךְ וְלַיְלָה בְּעַמּוּד אֵשׁ לְהָאִיר לָהֶם לָלֶכֶת יוֹמָם וָלָיְלָה:

22 The pillar of cloud by day and the pillar of fire by night did not depart from before the people.

כב לֹא־יָמִישׁ עַמּוּד הֶעָנָן יוֹמָם וְעַמּוּד הָאֵשׁ לָיְלָה לִפְנֵי הָעָם:

14
1 *Hashem* said to *Moshe*:

יד א וַיְדַבֵּר יְהֹוָה אֶל־מֹשֶׁה לֵּאמֹר:

2 Tell the Israelites to turn back and encamp before Pi-hahiroth, between Migdol and the sea, before Baal-zephon; you shall encamp facing it, by the sea.

ב דַּבֵּר אֶל־בְּנֵי יִשְׂרָאֵל וְיָשֻׁבוּ וְיַחֲנוּ לִפְנֵי פִּי הַחִירֹת בֵּין מִגְדֹּל וּבֵין הַיָּם לִפְנֵי בַּעַל צְפֹן נִכְחוֹ תַחֲנוּ עַל־הַיָּם:

3 Pharaoh will say of the Israelites, "They are astray in the land; the wilderness has closed in on them."

ג וְאָמַר פַּרְעֹה לִבְנֵי יִשְׂרָאֵל נְבֻכִים הֵם בָּאָרֶץ סָגַר עֲלֵיהֶם הַמִּדְבָּר:

4 Then I will stiffen Pharaoh's heart and he will pursue them, that I may gain glory through Pharaoh and all his host; and the Egyptians shall know that I am *Hashem*. And they did so.

ד וְחִזַּקְתִּי אֶת־לֵב־פַּרְעֹה וְרָדַף אַחֲרֵיהֶם וְאִכָּבְדָה בְּפַרְעֹה וּבְכָל־חֵילוֹ וְיָדְעוּ מִצְרַיִם כִּי־אֲנִי יְהֹוָה וַיַּעֲשׂוּ־כֵן:

Shemot/Exodus 14
Beshalach

שמות יד
בשלח

5 When the king of Egypt was told that the people had fled, Pharaoh and his courtiers had a change of heart about the people and said, "What is this we have done, releasing *Yisrael* from our service?"

ה וַיֻּגַּד לְמֶלֶךְ מִצְרַיִם כִּי בָרַח הָעָם וַיֵּהָפֵךְ לְבַב פַּרְעֹה וַעֲבָדָיו אֶל־הָעָם וַיֹּאמְרוּ מַה־זֹּאת עָשִׂינוּ כִּי־שִׁלַּחְנוּ אֶת־יִשְׂרָאֵל מֵעָבְדֵנוּ׃

6 He ordered his chariot and took his men with him;

ו וַיֶּאְסֹר אֶת־רִכְבּוֹ וְאֶת־עַמּוֹ לָקַח עִמּוֹ׃

7 he took six hundred of his picked chariots, and the rest of the chariots of Egypt, with officers in all of them.

ז וַיִּקַּח שֵׁשׁ־מֵאוֹת רֶכֶב בָּחוּר וְכֹל רֶכֶב מִצְרָיִם וְשָׁלִשִׁם עַל־כֻּלּוֹ׃

8 *Hashem* stiffened the heart of Pharaoh king of Egypt, and he gave chase to the Israelites. As the Israelites were departing defiantly,

ח וַיְחַזֵּק יְהֹוָה אֶת־לֵב פַּרְעֹה מֶלֶךְ מִצְרַיִם וַיִּרְדֹּף אַחֲרֵי בְּנֵי יִשְׂרָאֵל וּבְנֵי יִשְׂרָאֵל יֹצְאִים בְּיָד רָמָה׃

9 the Egyptians gave chase to them, and all the chariot horses of Pharaoh, his horsemen, and his warriors overtook them encamped by the sea, near Pi-hahiroth, before Baal-zephon.

ט וַיִּרְדְּפוּ מִצְרַיִם אַחֲרֵיהֶם וַיַּשִּׂיגוּ אוֹתָם חֹנִים עַל־הַיָּם כָּל־סוּס רֶכֶב פַּרְעֹה וּפָרָשָׁיו וְחֵילוֹ עַל־פִּי הַחִירֹת לִפְנֵי בַּעַל צְפֹן׃

10 As Pharaoh drew near, the Israelites caught sight of the Egyptians advancing upon them. Greatly frightened, the Israelites cried out to *Hashem*.

י וּפַרְעֹה הִקְרִיב וַיִּשְׂאוּ בְנֵי־יִשְׂרָאֵל אֶת־עֵינֵיהֶם וְהִנֵּה מִצְרַיִם נֹסֵעַ אַחֲרֵיהֶם וַיִּירְאוּ מְאֹד וַיִּצְעֲקוּ בְנֵי־יִשְׂרָאֵל אֶל־יְהֹוָה׃

11 And they said to *Moshe*, "Was it for want of graves in Egypt that you brought us to die in the wilderness? What have you done to us, taking us out of Egypt?

יא וַיֹּאמְרוּ אֶל־מֹשֶׁה הַמִבְּלִי אֵין־קְבָרִים בְּמִצְרַיִם לְקַחְתָּנוּ לָמוּת בַּמִּדְבָּר מַה־זֹּאת עָשִׂיתָ לָּנוּ לְהוֹצִיאָנוּ מִמִּצְרָיִם׃

12 Is this not the very thing we told you in Egypt, saying, 'Let us be, and we will serve the Egyptians, for it is better for us to serve the Egyptians than to die in the wilderness'?"

יב הֲלֹא־זֶה הַדָּבָר אֲשֶׁר דִּבַּרְנוּ אֵלֶיךָ בְמִצְרַיִם לֵאמֹר חֲדַל מִמֶּנּוּ וְנַעַבְדָה אֶת־מִצְרָיִם כִּי טוֹב לָנוּ עֲבֹד אֶת־מִצְרַיִם מִמֻּתֵנוּ בַּמִּדְבָּר׃

13 But *Moshe* said to the people, "Have no fear! Stand by, and witness the deliverance which *Hashem* will work for you today; for the Egyptians whom you see today you will never see again.

יג וַיֹּאמֶר מֹשֶׁה אֶל־הָעָם אַל־תִּירָאוּ הִתְיַצְּבוּ וּרְאוּ אֶת־יְשׁוּעַת יְהֹוָה אֲשֶׁר־יַעֲשֶׂה לָכֶם הַיּוֹם כִּי אֲשֶׁר רְאִיתֶם אֶת־מִצְרַיִם הַיּוֹם לֹא תֹסִפוּ לִרְאֹתָם עוֹד עַד־עוֹלָם׃

14 *Hashem* will battle for you; you hold your peace!"

יד יְהֹוָה יִלָּחֵם לָכֶם וְאַתֶּם תַּחֲרִשׁוּן׃

15 Then *Hashem* said to *Moshe*, "Why do you cry out to Me? Tell the Israelites to go forward.

טו וַיֹּאמֶר יְהֹוָה אֶל־מֹשֶׁה מַה־תִּצְעַק אֵלָי דַּבֵּר אֶל־בְּנֵי־יִשְׂרָאֵל וְיִסָּעוּ׃

16 And you lift up your rod and hold out your arm over the sea and split it, so that the Israelites may march into the sea on dry ground.

טז וְאַתָּה הָרֵם אֶת־מַטְּךָ וּנְטֵה אֶת־יָדְךָ עַל־הַיָּם וּבְקָעֵהוּ וְיָבֹאוּ בְנֵי־יִשְׂרָאֵל בְּתוֹךְ הַיָּם בַּיַּבָּשָׁה׃

17 And I will stiffen the hearts of the Egyptians so that they go in after them; and I will gain glory through Pharaoh and all his warriors, his chariots and his horsemen.

יז וַאֲנִי הִנְנִי מְחַזֵּק אֶת־לֵב מִצְרַיִם וְיָבֹאוּ אַחֲרֵיהֶם וְאִכָּבְדָה בְּפַרְעֹה וּבְכָל־חֵילוֹ בְּרִכְבּוֹ וּבְפָרָשָׁיו׃

172

Shemot/Exodus 14
Beshalach
שמות יד
בשלח

18 Let the Egyptians know that I am *Hashem*, when I gain glory through Pharaoh, his chariots, and his horsemen."

יח וְיָדְעוּ מִצְרַיִם כִּי־אֲנִי יְהוָה בְּהִכָּבְדִי בְּפַרְעֹה בְּרִכְבּוֹ וּבְפָרָשָׁיו׃

19 The angel of *Hashem*, who had been going ahead of the Israelite army, now moved and followed behind them; and the pillar of cloud shifted from in front of them and took up a place behind them,

יט וַיִּסַּע מַלְאַךְ הָאֱלֹהִים הַהֹלֵךְ לִפְנֵי מַחֲנֵה יִשְׂרָאֵל וַיֵּלֶךְ מֵאַחֲרֵיהֶם וַיִּסַּע עַמּוּד הֶעָנָן מִפְּנֵיהֶם וַיַּעֲמֹד מֵאַחֲרֵיהֶם׃

va-yi-SA mal-AKH ha-e-lo-HEEM ha-ho-LAYKH lif-NAY ma-kha-NAY yis-ra-AYL va-YAY-lekh may-a-kha-ray-HEM va-yi-SA a-MUD he-a-NAN mi-p'-nay-HEM va-ya-a-MOD may-a-kha-ray-HEM

20 and it came between the army of the Egyptians and the army of *Yisrael*. Thus there was the cloud with the darkness, and it cast a spell upon the night, so that the one could not come near the other all through the night.

כ וַיָּבֹא בֵּין מַחֲנֵה מִצְרַיִם וּבֵין מַחֲנֵה יִשְׂרָאֵל וַיְהִי הֶעָנָן וְהַחֹשֶׁךְ וַיָּאֶר אֶת־הַלָּיְלָה וְלֹא־קָרַב זֶה אֶל־זֶה כָּל־הַלָּיְלָה׃

21 Then *Moshe* held out his arm over the sea and *Hashem* drove back the sea with a strong east wind all that night, and turned the sea into dry ground. The waters were split,

כא וַיֵּט מֹשֶׁה אֶת־יָדוֹ עַל־הַיָּם וַיּוֹלֶךְ יְהוָה אֶת־הַיָּם בְּרוּחַ קָדִים עַזָּה כָּל־הַלַּיְלָה וַיָּשֶׂם אֶת־הַיָּם לֶחָרָבָה וַיִּבָּקְעוּ הַמָּיִם׃

22 and the Israelites went into the sea on dry ground, the waters forming a wall for them on their right and on their left.

כב וַיָּבֹאוּ בְנֵי־יִשְׂרָאֵל בְּתוֹךְ הַיָּם בַּיַּבָּשָׁה וְהַמַּיִם לָהֶם חֹמָה מִימִינָם וּמִשְּׂמֹאלָם׃

23 The Egyptians came in pursuit after them into the sea, all of Pharaoh's horses, chariots, and horsemen.

כג וַיִּרְדְּפוּ מִצְרַיִם וַיָּבֹאוּ אַחֲרֵיהֶם כֹּל סוּס פַּרְעֹה רִכְבּוֹ וּפָרָשָׁיו אֶל־תּוֹךְ הַיָּם׃

24 At the morning watch, *Hashem* looked down upon the Egyptian army from a pillar of fire and cloud, and threw the Egyptian army into panic.

כד וַיְהִי בְּאַשְׁמֹרֶת הַבֹּקֶר וַיַּשְׁקֵף יְהוָה אֶל־מַחֲנֵה מִצְרַיִם בְּעַמּוּד אֵשׁ וְעָנָן וַיָּהָם אֵת מַחֲנֵה מִצְרָיִם׃

25 He locked the wheels of their chariots so that they moved forward with difficulty. And the Egyptians said, "Let us flee from the Israelites, for *Hashem* is fighting for them against Egypt."

כה וַיָּסַר אֵת אֹפַן מַרְכְּבֹתָיו וַיְנַהֲגֵהוּ בִּכְבֵדֻת וַיֹּאמֶר מִצְרַיִם אָנוּסָה מִפְּנֵי יִשְׂרָאֵל כִּי יְהוָה נִלְחָם לָהֶם בְּמִצְרָיִם׃

26 Then *Hashem* said to *Moshe*, "Hold out your arm over the sea, that the waters may come back upon the Egyptians and upon their chariots and upon their horsemen."

כו וַיֹּאמֶר יְהוָה אֶל־מֹשֶׁה נְטֵה אֶת־יָדְךָ עַל־הַיָּם וְיָשֻׁבוּ הַמַּיִם עַל־מִצְרַיִם עַל־רִכְבּוֹ וְעַל־פָּרָשָׁיו׃

Israel Defense Forces insignia

14:19 And the pillar of cloud shifted from in front of them According to *Rashi*, the pillar of cloud that led the Jewish people in the desert during the day moved behind the camp, and obscured the Egyptians' vision as they progressed in their bloodthirsty pursuit of the Jewish people. The cloud protected Israel as they fled and absorbed the arrows shot by the Egyptians at the fleeing nation. Today, the soldiers of the Israeli Defense Forces are a pillar of defense, shielding Israel from her enemies. May the God of Israel continue to protect His people through His modern-day pillar of defense, just as He did long ago.

Shemot/Exodus 15
Beshalach

שמות טו
בשלח

27 *Moshe* held out his arm over the sea, and at daybreak the sea returned to its normal state, and the Egyptians fled at its approach. But *Hashem* hurled the Egyptians into the sea.

כז וַיֵּט מֹשֶׁה אֶת־יָדוֹ עַל־הַיָּם וַיָּשָׁב הַיָּם לִפְנוֹת בֹּקֶר לְאֵיתָנוֹ וּמִצְרַיִם נָסִים לִקְרָאתוֹ וַיְנַעֵר יְהֹוָה אֶת־מִצְרַיִם בְּתוֹךְ הַיָּם:

28 The waters turned back and covered the chariots and the horsemen – Pharaoh's entire army that followed them into the sea; not one of them remained.

כח וַיָּשֻׁבוּ הַמַּיִם וַיְכַסּוּ אֶת־הָרֶכֶב וְאֶת־הַפָּרָשִׁים לְכֹל חֵיל פַּרְעֹה הַבָּאִים אַחֲרֵיהֶם בַּיָּם לֹא־נִשְׁאַר בָּהֶם עַד־אֶחָד:

29 But the Israelites had marched through the sea on dry ground, the waters forming a wall for them on their right and on their left.

כט וּבְנֵי יִשְׂרָאֵל הָלְכוּ בַיַּבָּשָׁה בְּתוֹךְ הַיָּם וְהַמַּיִם לָהֶם חֹמָה מִימִינָם וּמִשְּׂמֹאלָם:

30 Thus *Hashem* delivered *Yisrael* that day from the Egyptians. *Yisrael* saw the Egyptians dead on the shore of the sea.

ל וַיּוֹשַׁע יְהֹוָה בַּיּוֹם הַהוּא אֶת־יִשְׂרָאֵל מִיַּד מִצְרָיִם וַיַּרְא יִשְׂרָאֵל אֶת־מִצְרַיִם מֵת עַל־שְׂפַת הַיָּם:

31 And when *Yisrael* saw the wondrous power which *Hashem* had wielded against the Egyptians, the people feared *Hashem*; they had faith in *Hashem* and His servant *Moshe*.

לא וַיַּרְא יִשְׂרָאֵל אֶת־הַיָּד הַגְּדֹלָה אֲשֶׁר עָשָׂה יְהֹוָה בְּמִצְרַיִם וַיִּירְאוּ הָעָם אֶת־יְהֹוָה וַיַּאֲמִינוּ בַּיהֹוָה וּבְמֹשֶׁה עַבְדּוֹ:

15

1 Then *Moshe* and the Israelites sang this song to *Hashem*. They said: I will sing to *Hashem*, for He has triumphed gloriously; Horse and driver He has hurled into the sea.

טו א אָז יָשִׁיר־מֹשֶׁה וּבְנֵי יִשְׂרָאֵל אֶת־הַשִּׁירָה הַזֹּאת לַיהֹוָה וַיֹּאמְרוּ לֵאמֹר אָשִׁירָה לַיהֹוָה כִּי־גָאֹה גָּאָה סוּס וְרֹכְבוֹ רָמָה בַיָּם:

2 *Hashem* is my strength and might; He is become my deliverance. This is my God and I will enshrine Him; The God of my father, and I will exalt Him.

ב עָזִּי וְזִמְרָת יָהּ וַיְהִי־לִי לִישׁוּעָה זֶה אֵלִי וְאַנְוֵהוּ אֱלֹהֵי אָבִי וַאֲרֹמְמֶנְהוּ:

3 *Hashem*, the Warrior – *Hashem* is His name!

ג יְהֹוָה אִישׁ מִלְחָמָה יְהֹוָה שְׁמוֹ:

4 Pharaoh's chariots and his army He has cast into the sea; And the pick of his officers Are drowned in the Sea of Reeds.

ד מַרְכְּבֹת פַּרְעֹה וְחֵילוֹ יָרָה בַיָּם וּמִבְחַר שָׁלִשָׁיו טֻבְּעוּ בְיַם־סוּף:

5 The deeps covered them; They went down into the depths like a stone.

ה תְּהֹמֹת יְכַסְיֻמוּ יָרְדוּ בִמְצוֹלֹת כְּמוֹ־אָבֶן:

6 Your right hand, *Hashem*, glorious in power, Your right hand, *Hashem*, shatters the foe!

ו יְמִינְךָ יְהֹוָה נֶאְדָּרִי בַּכֹּחַ יְמִינְךָ יְהֹוָה תִּרְעַץ אוֹיֵב:

7 In Your great triumph You break Your opponents; You send forth Your fury, it consumes them like straw.

ז וּבְרֹב גְּאוֹנְךָ תַּהֲרֹס קָמֶיךָ תְּשַׁלַּח חֲרֹנְךָ יֹאכְלֵמוֹ כַּקַּשׁ:

8 At the blast of Your nostrils the waters piled up, The floods stood straight like a wall; The deeps froze in the heart of the sea.

ח וּבְרוּחַ אַפֶּיךָ נֶעֶרְמוּ מַיִם נִצְּבוּ כְמוֹ־נֵד נֹזְלִים קָפְאוּ תְהֹמֹת בְּלֶב־יָם:

9 The foe said, "I will pursue, I will overtake, I will divide the spoil; My desire shall have its fill of them. I will bare my sword – My hand shall subdue them."

ט אָמַר אוֹיֵב אֶרְדֹּף אַשִּׂיג אֲחַלֵּק שָׁלָל תִּמְלָאֵמוֹ נַפְשִׁי אָרִיק חַרְבִּי תּוֹרִישֵׁמוֹ יָדִי:

174

Shemot/Exodus 15
Beshalach

שמות טו
בשלח

10 You made Your wind blow, the sea covered them; They sank like lead in the majestic waters.

י נָשַׁפְתָּ בְרוּחֲךָ כִּסָּמוֹ יָם צָלְלוּ כַּעוֹפֶרֶת בְּמַיִם אַדִּירִים:

11 Who is like You, *Hashem*, among the celestials; Who is like You, majestic in holiness, Awesome in splendor, working wonders!

יא מִי־כָמֹכָה בָּאֵלִם יְהֹוָה מִי כָּמֹכָה נֶאְדָּר בַּקֹּדֶשׁ נוֹרָא תְהִלֹּת עֹשֵׂה פֶלֶא:

mee kha-MO-khah ba-ay-LEEM a-do-NAI MEE ka-MO-khah ne-DAR ba-KO-desh no-RA t'-hi-LOT O-say FE-le

12 You put out Your right hand, The earth swallowed them.

יב נָטִיתָ יְמִינְךָ תִּבְלָעֵמוֹ אָרֶץ:

13 In Your love You lead the people You redeemed; In Your strength You guide them to Your holy abode.

יג נָחִיתָ בְחַסְדְּךָ עַם־זוּ גָּאָלְתָּ נֵהַלְתָּ בְעָזְּךָ אֶל־נְוֵה קָדְשֶׁךָ:

14 The peoples hear, they tremble; Agony grips the dwellers in Philistia.

יד שָׁמְעוּ עַמִּים יִרְגָּזוּן חִיל אָחַז יֹשְׁבֵי פְּלָשֶׁת:

15 Now are the clans of Edom dismayed; The tribes of Moab – trembling grips them; All the dwellers in Canaan are aghast.

טו אָז נִבְהֲלוּ אַלּוּפֵי אֱדוֹם אֵילֵי מוֹאָב יֹאחֲזֵמוֹ רָעַד נָמֹגוּ כֹּל יֹשְׁבֵי כְנָעַן:

16 Terror and dread descend upon them; Through the might of Your arm they are still as stone – Till Your people cross over, *Hashem*, Till Your people cross whom You have ransomed.

טז תִּפֹּל עֲלֵיהֶם אֵימָתָה וָפַחַד בִּגְדֹל זְרוֹעֲךָ יִדְּמוּ כָּאָבֶן עַד־יַעֲבֹר עַמְּךָ יְהֹוָה עַד־יַעֲבֹר עַם־זוּ קָנִיתָ:

17 You will bring them and plant them in Your own mountain, The place You made to dwell in, *Hashem*, The sanctuary, *Hashem*, which Your hands established.

יז תְּבִאֵמוֹ וְתִטָּעֵמוֹ בְּהַר נַחֲלָתְךָ מָכוֹן לְשִׁבְתְּךָ פָּעַלְתָּ יְהֹוָה מִקְּדָשׁ אֲדֹנָי כּוֹנְנוּ יָדֶיךָ:

t'-vi-AY-mo v'-ti-ta-AY-mo b'-HAR na-kha-la-t'-KHA ma-KHON l'-shiv'-t'-KHA pa-al-TA ah-do-NAI mik'-DASH ah-do-NAI ko-n'-NU ya-de-KHA

18 *Hashem* will reign for ever and ever!

יח יְהֹוָה יִמְלֹךְ לְעֹלָם וָעֶד:

19 For the horses of Pharaoh, with his chariots and horsemen, went into the sea; and *Hashem* turned back on them the waters of the sea; but the Israelites marched on dry ground in the midst of the sea.

יט כִּי בָא סוּס פַּרְעֹה בְּרִכְבּוֹ וּבְפָרָשָׁיו בַּיָּם וַיָּשֶׁב יְהֹוָה עֲלֵהֶם אֶת־מֵי הַיָּם וּבְנֵי יִשְׂרָאֵל הָלְכוּ בַיַּבָּשָׁה בְּתוֹךְ הַיָּם:

20 Then Miriam the *Neviah*, *Aharon*'s sister, took a timbrel in her hand, and all the women went out after her in dance with timbrels.

כ וַתִּקַּח מִרְיָם הַנְּבִיאָה אֲחוֹת אַהֲרֹן אֶת־הַתֹּף בְּיָדָהּ וַתֵּצֶאןָ כָל־הַנָּשִׁים אַחֲרֶיהָ בְּתֻפִּים וּבִמְחֹלֹת:

15:17 And plant them in Your own mountain
"And plant them in Your own mountain" is understood as a reference either to *Har Habayit* or to the entire Land of Israel. When *Hashem* says that the Jewish people will be planted in *Eretz Yisrael*, He means that they will establish roots there and flourish. The *Midrash* explains that this is a reference to the time of *Mashiach*, when the Children of Israel will be brought back to the Land of Israel, never to be uprooted again. For two thousand years, Jews have been asking for the fulfillment of this verse each week as part of the *Shabbat* prayers, "bring us with happiness to our land and plant us in our borders."

Shemot/Exodus 16
Beshalach

שמות טז
בשלח

21 And *Miriam* chanted for them: Sing to *Hashem*, for He has triumphed gloriously; Horse and driver He has hurled into the sea.

כא וַתַּ֥עַן לָהֶ֖ם מִרְיָ֑ם שִׁ֤ירוּ לַֽיהֹוָה֙ כִּֽי־גָאֹ֣ה גָּאָ֔ה ס֥וּס וְרֹכְב֖וֹ רָמָ֥ה בַיָּֽם׃

22 Then *Moshe* caused *Yisrael* to set out from the Sea of Reeds. They went on into the wilderness of Shur; they traveled three days in the wilderness and found no water.

כב וַיַּסַּ֨ע מֹשֶׁ֤ה אֶת־יִשְׂרָאֵל֙ מִיַּם־ס֔וּף וַיֵּצְא֖וּ אֶל־מִדְבַּר־שׁ֑וּר וַיֵּלְכ֧וּ שְׁלֹֽשֶׁת־יָמִ֛ים בַּמִּדְבָּ֖ר וְלֹא־מָ֥צְאוּ מָֽיִם׃

23 They came to Marah, but they could not drink the water of Marah because it was bitter; that is why it was named Marah.

כג וַיָּבֹ֣אוּ מָרָ֔תָה וְלֹ֣א יָֽכְל֗וּ לִשְׁתֹּ֥ת מַ֙יִם֙ מִמָּרָ֔ה כִּ֥י מָרִ֖ים הֵ֑ם עַל־כֵּ֥ן קָרָֽא־שְׁמָ֖הּ מָרָֽה׃

24 And the people grumbled against *Moshe*, saying, "What shall we drink?"

כד וַיִּלֹּ֧נוּ הָעָ֛ם עַל־מֹשֶׁ֖ה לֵּאמֹ֥ר מַה־נִּשְׁתֶּֽה׃

25 So he cried out to *Hashem*, and *Hashem* showed him a piece of wood; he threw it into the water and the water became sweet. There He made for them a fixed rule, and there He put them to the test.

כה וַיִּצְעַ֣ק אֶל־יְהֹוָ֗ה וַיּוֹרֵ֤הוּ יְהֹוָה֙ עֵ֔ץ וַיַּשְׁלֵךְ֙ אֶל־הַמַּ֔יִם וַֽיִּמְתְּק֖וּ הַמָּ֑יִם שָׁ֣ם שָׂ֥ם ל֛וֹ חֹ֥ק וּמִשְׁפָּ֖ט וְשָׁ֥ם נִסָּֽהוּ׃

26 He said, "If you will heed *Hashem* your God diligently, doing what is upright in His sight, giving ear to His commandments and keeping all His laws, then I will not bring upon you any of the diseases that I brought upon the Egyptians, for I *Hashem* am your healer."

כו וַיֹּאמֶר֩ אִם־שָׁמ֨וֹעַ תִּשְׁמַ֜ע לְק֣וֹל ׀ יְהֹוָ֣ה אֱלֹהֶ֗יךָ וְהַיָּשָׁ֤ר בְּעֵינָיו֙ תַּֽעֲשֶׂ֔ה וְהַֽאֲזַנְתָּ֙ לְמִצְוֺתָ֔יו וְשָֽׁמַרְתָּ֖ כָּל־חֻקָּ֑יו כָּל־הַמַּֽחֲלָ֞ה אֲשֶׁר־שַׂ֤מְתִּי בְמִצְרַ֙יִם֙ לֹא־אָשִׂ֣ים עָלֶ֔יךָ כִּ֛י אֲנִ֥י יְהֹוָ֖ה רֹפְאֶֽךָ׃

va-YO-mer im sha-MO-a tish-MA l'-KOL a-do-NAI e-lo-HE-kha v'-ha-ya-SHAR b'-ay-NAV ta-a-SEH v'-ha-a-zan-TA l'-mitz-vo-TAV v'-sha-mar-TA kol khu-KAV kol ha-ma-kha-LAH a-sher SAM-tee v'-mitz-RA-yim lo a-SEEM a-LE-kha kee a-NEE a-do-NAI ro-f'-E-kha

27 And they came to Elim, where there were twelve springs of water and seventy palm trees; and they encamped there beside the water.

כז וַיָּבֹ֣אוּ אֵילִ֔מָה וְשָׁ֗ם שְׁתֵּ֥ים עֶשְׂרֵ֛ה עֵינֹ֥ת מַ֖יִם וְשִׁבְעִ֣ים תְּמָרִ֑ים וַיַּחֲנוּ־שָׁ֖ם עַל־הַמָּֽיִם׃

16 1 Setting out from Elim, the whole Israelite community came to the wilderness of Sin, which is between Elim and Sinai, on the fifteenth day of the second month after their departure from the land of Egypt.

טז א וַיִּסְעוּ֙ מֵֽאֵילִ֔ם וַיָּבֹ֜אוּ כׇּל־עֲדַ֤ת בְּנֵֽי־יִשְׂרָאֵל֙ אֶל־מִדְבַּר־סִ֔ין אֲשֶׁ֥ר בֵּין־אֵילִ֖ם וּבֵ֣ין סִינָ֑י בַּחֲמִשָּׁ֨ה עָשָׂ֥ר יוֹם֙ לַחֹ֣דֶשׁ הַשֵּׁנִ֔י לְצֵאתָ֖ם מֵאֶ֥רֶץ מִצְרָֽיִם׃

2 In the wilderness, the whole Israelite community grumbled against *Moshe* and *Aharon*.

ב וילינו [וַיִּלּ֜וֹנוּ] כׇּל־עֲדַ֧ת בְּנֵי־יִשְׂרָאֵ֛ל עַל־מֹשֶׁ֥ה וְעַֽל־אַהֲרֹ֖ן בַּמִּדְבָּֽר׃

3 The Israelites said to them, "If only we had died by the hand of *Hashem* in the land of Egypt, when we sat by the fleshpots, when we ate our fill of bread! For you have brought us out into this wilderness to starve this whole congregation to death."

ג וַיֹּאמְר֨וּ אֲלֵהֶ֜ם בְּנֵ֣י יִשְׂרָאֵ֗ל מִֽי־יִתֵּ֨ן מוּתֵ֤נוּ בְיַד־יְהֹוָה֙ בְּאֶ֣רֶץ מִצְרַ֔יִם בְּשִׁבְתֵּ֙נוּ֙ עַל־סִ֣יר הַבָּשָׂ֔ר בְּאׇכְלֵ֥נוּ לֶ֖חֶם לָשֹׂ֑בַע כִּֽי־הוֹצֵאתֶ֤ם אֹתָ֙נוּ֙ אֶל־הַמִּדְבָּ֣ר הַזֶּ֔ה לְהָמִ֛ית אֶת־כׇּל־הַקָּהָ֥ל הַזֶּ֖ה בָּרָעָֽב׃

176

Shemot/Exodus 16
Beshalach

שמות טז
בשלח

4 And *Hashem* said to *Moshe*, "I will rain down bread for you from the sky, and the people shall go out and gather each day that day's portion – that I may thus test them, to see whether they will follow My instructions or not.

ד וַיֹּאמֶר יְהֹוָה אֶל־מֹשֶׁה הִנְנִי מַמְטִיר לָכֶם לֶחֶם מִן־הַשָּׁמָיִם וְיָצָא הָעָם וְלָקְטוּ דְּבַר־יוֹם בְּיוֹמוֹ לְמַעַן אֲנַסֶּנּוּ הֲיֵלֵךְ בְּתוֹרָתִי אִם־לֹא:

5 But on the sixth day, when they apportion what they have brought in, it shall prove to be double the amount they gather each day."

ה וְהָיָה בַּיּוֹם הַשִּׁשִּׁי וְהֵכִינוּ אֵת אֲשֶׁר־יָבִיאוּ וְהָיָה מִשְׁנֶה עַל אֲשֶׁר־יִלְקְטוּ יוֹם יוֹם:

6 So *Moshe* and *Aharon* said to all the Israelites, "By evening you shall know it was *Hashem* who brought you out from the land of Egypt;

ו וַיֹּאמֶר מֹשֶׁה וְאַהֲרֹן אֶל־כָּל־בְּנֵי יִשְׂרָאֵל עֶרֶב וִידַעְתֶּם כִּי יְהֹוָה הוֹצִיא אֶתְכֶם מֵאֶרֶץ מִצְרָיִם:

7 and in the morning you shall behold the Presence of *Hashem*, because He has heard your grumblings against *Hashem*. For who are we that you should grumble against us?

ז וּבֹקֶר וּרְאִיתֶם אֶת־כְּבוֹד יְהֹוָה בְּשָׁמְעוֹ אֶת־תְּלֻנֹּתֵיכֶם עַל־יְהֹוָה וְנַחְנוּ מָה כִּי תלונו [תַלִּינוּ] עָלֵינוּ:

8 Since it is *Hashem*," *Moshe* continued, "who will give you flesh to eat in the evening and bread in the morning to the full, because *Hashem* has heard the grumblings you utter against Him, what is our part? Your grumbling is not against us, but against *Hashem*!"

ח וַיֹּאמֶר מֹשֶׁה בְּתֵת יְהֹוָה לָכֶם בָּעֶרֶב בָּשָׂר לֶאֱכֹל וְלֶחֶם בַּבֹּקֶר לִשְׂבֹּעַ בִּשְׁמֹעַ יְהֹוָה אֶת־תְּלֻנֹּתֵיכֶם אֲשֶׁר־אַתֶּם מַלִּינִם עָלָיו וְנַחְנוּ מָה לֹא־עָלֵינוּ תְלֻנֹּתֵיכֶם כִּי עַל־יְהֹוָה:

9 Then *Moshe* said to *Aharon*, "Say to the whole Israelite community: Advance toward *Hashem*, for He has heard your grumbling."

ט וַיֹּאמֶר מֹשֶׁה אֶל־אַהֲרֹן אֱמֹר אֶל־כָּל־עֲדַת בְּנֵי יִשְׂרָאֵל קִרְבוּ לִפְנֵי יְהֹוָה כִּי שָׁמַע אֵת תְּלֻנֹּתֵיכֶם:

10 And as *Aharon* spoke to the whole Israelite community, they turned toward the wilderness, and there, in a cloud, appeared the Presence of *Hashem*.

י וַיְהִי כְּדַבֵּר אַהֲרֹן אֶל־כָּל־עֲדַת בְּנֵי־יִשְׂרָאֵל וַיִּפְנוּ אֶל־הַמִּדְבָּר וְהִנֵּה כְּבוֹד יְהֹוָה נִרְאָה בֶּעָנָן:

11 *Hashem* spoke to *Moshe*:

יא וַיְדַבֵּר יְהֹוָה אֶל־מֹשֶׁה לֵּאמֹר:

12 "I have heard the grumbling of the Israelites. Speak to them and say: By evening you shall eat flesh, and in the morning you shall have your fill of bread; and you shall know that I *Hashem* am your God."

יב שָׁמַעְתִּי אֶת־תְּלוּנֹּת בְּנֵי יִשְׂרָאֵל דַּבֵּר אֲלֵהֶם לֵאמֹר בֵּין הָעַרְבַּיִם תֹּאכְלוּ בָשָׂר וּבַבֹּקֶר תִּשְׂבְּעוּ־לָחֶם וִידַעְתֶּם כִּי אֲנִי יְהֹוָה אֱלֹהֵיכֶם:

13 In the evening quail appeared and covered the camp; in the morning there was a fall of dew about the camp.

יג וַיְהִי בָעֶרֶב וַתַּעַל הַשְּׂלָו וַתְּכַס אֶת־הַמַּחֲנֶה וּבַבֹּקֶר הָיְתָה שִׁכְבַת הַטַּל סָבִיב לַמַּחֲנֶה:

14 When the fall of dew lifted, there, over the surface of the wilderness, lay a fine and flaky substance, as fine as frost on the ground.

יד וַתַּעַל שִׁכְבַת הַטָּל וְהִנֵּה עַל־פְּנֵי הַמִּדְבָּר דַּק מְחֻסְפָּס דַּק כַּכְּפֹר עַל־הָאָרֶץ:

15 When the Israelites saw it, they said to one another, "What is it?" – for they did not know what it was. And *Moshe* said to them, "That is the bread which *Hashem* has given you to eat.

טו וַיִּרְאוּ בְנֵי־יִשְׂרָאֵל וַיֹּאמְרוּ אִישׁ אֶל־אָחִיו מָן הוּא כִּי לֹא יָדְעוּ מַה־הוּא וַיֹּאמֶר מֹשֶׁה אֲלֵהֶם הוּא הַלֶּחֶם אֲשֶׁר נָתַן יְהֹוָה לָכֶם לְאָכְלָה:

Shemot/Exodus 16
Beshalach

שמות טז
בשלח

16 This is what *Hashem* has commanded: Gather as much of it as each of you requires to eat, an *omer* to a person for as many of you as there are; each of you shall fetch for those in his tent."

טז זֶ֤ה הַדָּבָר֙ אֲשֶׁ֣ר צִוָּ֣ה יְהֹוָ֔ה לִקְט֣וּ מִמֶּ֔נּוּ אִ֖ישׁ לְפִ֣י אׇכְל֑וֹ עֹ֣מֶר לַגֻּלְגֹּ֗לֶת מִסְפַּר֙ נַפְשֹׁ֣תֵיכֶ֔ם אִ֛ישׁ לַאֲשֶׁ֥ר בְּאׇהֳל֖וֹ תִּקָּֽחוּ׃

17 The Israelites did so, some gathering much, some little.

יז וַיַּעֲשׂוּ־כֵ֖ן בְּנֵ֣י יִשְׂרָאֵ֑ל וַֽיִּלְקְט֔וּ הַמַּרְבֶּ֖ה וְהַמַּמְעִֽיט׃

18 But when they measured it by the *omer*, he who had gathered much had no excess, and he who had gathered little had no deficiency: they had gathered as much as they needed to eat.

יח וַיָּמֹ֣דּוּ בָעֹ֔מֶר וְלֹ֤א הֶעְדִּיף֙ הַמַּרְבֶּ֔ה וְהַמַּמְעִ֖יט לֹ֣א הֶחְסִ֑יר אִ֥ישׁ לְפִֽי־אׇכְל֖וֹ לָקָֽטוּ׃

19 And *Moshe* said to them, "Let no one leave any of it over until morning."

יט וַיֹּ֥אמֶר מֹשֶׁ֖ה אֲלֵהֶ֑ם אִ֕ישׁ אַל־יוֹתֵ֥ר מִמֶּ֖נּוּ עַד־בֹּֽקֶר׃

20 But they paid no attention to *Moshe*; some of them left of it until morning, and it became infested with maggots and stank. And *Moshe* was angry with them.

כ וְלֹא־שָׁמְע֣וּ אֶל־מֹשֶׁ֗ה וַיּוֹתִ֨רוּ אֲנָשִׁ֤ים מִמֶּ֙נּוּ֙ עַד־בֹּ֔קֶר וַיָּ֥רֻם תּוֹלָעִ֖ים וַיִּבְאַ֑שׁ וַיִּקְצֹ֥ף עֲלֵהֶ֖ם מֹשֶֽׁה׃

21 So they gathered it every morning, each as much as he needed to eat; for when the sun grew hot, it would melt.

כא וַיִּלְקְט֤וּ אֹתוֹ֙ בַּבֹּ֣קֶר בַּבֹּ֔קֶר אִ֖ישׁ כְּפִ֣י אׇכְל֑וֹ וְחַ֥ם הַשֶּׁ֖מֶשׁ וְנָמָֽס׃

22 On the sixth day they gathered double the amount of food, two *omers* for each; and when all the chieftains of the community came and told *Moshe*,

כב וַיְהִ֣י ׀ בַּיּ֣וֹם הַשִּׁשִּׁ֗י לָֽקְט֥וּ לֶ֙חֶם֙ מִשְׁנֶ֔ה שְׁנֵ֥י הָעֹ֖מֶר לָאֶחָ֑ד וַיָּבֹ֙אוּ֙ כׇּל־נְשִׂיאֵ֣י הָעֵדָ֔ה וַיַּגִּ֖ידוּ לְמֹשֶֽׁה׃

23 he said to them, "This is what *Hashem* meant: Tomorrow is a day of rest, a holy *Shabbat* of *Hashem*. Bake what you would bake and boil what you would boil; and all that is left put aside to be kept until morning."

כג וַיֹּ֣אמֶר אֲלֵהֶ֗ם ה֚וּא אֲשֶׁ֣ר דִּבֶּ֣ר יְהֹוָ֔ה שַׁבָּת֧וֹן שַׁבַּת־קֹ֛דֶשׁ לַיהֹוָ֖ה מָחָ֑ר אֵ֣ת אֲשֶׁר־תֹּאפ֞וּ אֵפ֗וּ וְאֵ֤ת אֲשֶֽׁר־תְּבַשְּׁלוּ֙ בַּשֵּׁ֔לוּ וְאֵת֙ כׇּל־הָ֣עֹדֵ֔ף הַנִּ֧יחוּ לָכֶ֛ם לְמִשְׁמֶ֖רֶת עַד־הַבֹּֽקֶר׃

24 So they put it aside until morning, as *Moshe* had ordered; and it did not turn foul, and there were no maggots in it.

כד וַיַּנִּ֤יחוּ אֹתוֹ֙ עַד־הַבֹּ֔קֶר כַּאֲשֶׁ֖ר צִוָּ֣ה מֹשֶׁ֑ה וְלֹ֣א הִבְאִ֔ישׁ וְרִמָּ֖ה לֹא־הָ֥יְתָה בּֽוֹ׃

25 Then *Moshe* said, "Eat it today, for today is a *Shabbat* of *Hashem*; you will not find it today on the plain.

כה וַיֹּ֤אמֶר מֹשֶׁה֙ אִכְלֻ֣הוּ הַיּ֔וֹם כִּֽי־שַׁבָּ֥ת הַיּ֖וֹם לַיהֹוָ֑ה הַיּ֕וֹם לֹ֥א תִמְצָאֻ֖הוּ בַּשָּׂדֶֽה׃

26 Six days you shall gather it; on the seventh day, the *Shabbat*, there will be none."

כו שֵׁ֥שֶׁת יָמִ֖ים תִּלְקְטֻ֑הוּ וּבַיּ֧וֹם הַשְּׁבִיעִ֛י שַׁבָּ֖ת לֹ֥א יִֽהְיֶה־בּֽוֹ׃

27 Yet some of the people went out on the seventh day to gather, but they found nothing.

כז וַֽיְהִי֙ בַּיּ֣וֹם הַשְּׁבִיעִ֔י יָצְא֥וּ מִן־הָעָ֖ם לִלְקֹ֑ט וְלֹ֖א מָצָֽאוּ׃

28 And *Hashem* said to *Moshe*, "How long will you men refuse to obey My commandments and My teachings?

כח וַיֹּ֥אמֶר יְהֹוָ֖ה אֶל־מֹשֶׁ֑ה עַד־אָ֙נָה֙ מֵֽאַנְתֶּ֔ם לִשְׁמֹ֥ר מִצְוֺתַ֖י וְתוֹרֹתָֽי׃

Shemot/Exodus 17
Beshalach

שמות יז
בשלח

29 Mark that *Hashem* has given you the *Shabbat*; therefore He gives you two days' food on the sixth day. Let everyone remain where he is: let no one leave his place on the seventh day."

כט רְאוּ כִּי־יְהֹוָה נָתַן לָכֶם הַשַּׁבָּת עַל־כֵּן הוּא נֹתֵן לָכֶם בַּיּוֹם הַשִּׁשִּׁי לֶחֶם יוֹמָיִם שְׁבוּ אִישׁ תַּחְתָּיו אַל־יֵצֵא אִישׁ מִמְּקֹמוֹ בַּיּוֹם הַשְּׁבִיעִי:

30 So the people remained inactive on the seventh day.

ל וַיִּשְׁבְּתוּ הָעָם בַּיּוֹם הַשְּׁבִעִי:

31 The house of *Yisrael* named it manna; it was like coriander seed, white, and it tasted like wafers in honey.

לא וַיִּקְרְאוּ בֵית־יִשְׂרָאֵל אֶת־שְׁמוֹ מָן וְהוּא כְּזֶרַע גַּד לָבָן וְטַעְמוֹ כְּצַפִּיחִת בִּדְבָשׁ:

32 *Moshe* said, "This is what *Hashem* has commanded: Let one *omer* of it be kept throughout the ages, in order that they may see the bread that I fed you in the wilderness when I brought you out from the land of Egypt."

לב וַיֹּאמֶר מֹשֶׁה זֶה הַדָּבָר אֲשֶׁר צִוָּה יְהֹוָה מְלֹא הָעֹמֶר מִמֶּנּוּ לְמִשְׁמֶרֶת לְדֹרֹתֵיכֶם לְמַעַן יִרְאוּ אֶת־הַלֶּחֶם אֲשֶׁר הֶאֱכַלְתִּי אֶתְכֶם בַּמִּדְבָּר בְּהוֹצִיאִי אֶתְכֶם מֵאֶרֶץ מִצְרָיִם:

33 And *Moshe* said to *Aharon*, "Take a jar, put one *omer* of manna in it, and place it before *Hashem*, to be kept throughout the ages."

לג וַיֹּאמֶר מֹשֶׁה אֶל־אַהֲרֹן קַח צִנְצֶנֶת אַחַת וְתֶן־שָׁמָּה מְלֹא־הָעֹמֶר מָן וְהַנַּח אֹתוֹ לִפְנֵי יְהֹוָה לְמִשְׁמֶרֶת לְדֹרֹתֵיכֶם:

34 As *Hashem* had commanded *Moshe*, *Aharon* placed it before the Pact, to be kept.

לד כַּאֲשֶׁר צִוָּה יְהֹוָה אֶל־מֹשֶׁה וַיַּנִּיחֵהוּ אַהֲרֹן לִפְנֵי הָעֵדֻת לְמִשְׁמָרֶת:

35 And the Israelites ate manna forty years, until they came to a settled land; they ate the manna until they came to the border of the land of Canaan.

לה וּבְנֵי יִשְׂרָאֵל אָכְלוּ אֶת־הַמָּן אַרְבָּעִים שָׁנָה עַד־בֹּאָם אֶל־אֶרֶץ נוֹשָׁבֶת אֶת־הַמָּן אָכְלוּ עַד־בֹּאָם אֶל־קְצֵה אֶרֶץ כְּנָעַן:

uv-NAY yis-ra-AYL a-kh'-LU et ha-MAN ar-ba-EEM sha-NAH ad bo-AM el E-retz no-SHA-vet et ha-MAN a-kh'-LU ad bo-AM el k'-TZAY E-retz k'-NA-an

36 The *omer* is a tenth of an *efah*.

לו וְהָעֹמֶר עֲשִׂרִית הָאֵיפָה הוּא:

17 1 From the wilderness of Sin the whole Israelite community continued by stages as *Hashem* would command. They encamped at Rephidim, and there was no water for the people to drink.

יז א וַיִּסְעוּ כָּל־עֲדַת בְּנֵי־יִשְׂרָאֵל מִמִּדְבַּר־סִין לְמַסְעֵיהֶם עַל־פִּי יְהֹוָה וַיַּחֲנוּ בִּרְפִידִים וְאֵין מַיִם לִשְׁתֹּת הָעָם:

2 The people quarreled with *Moshe*. "Give us water to drink," they said; and *Moshe* replied to them, "Why do you quarrel with me? Why do you try *Hashem*?"

ב וַיָּרֶב הָעָם עִם־מֹשֶׁה וַיֹּאמְרוּ תְּנוּ־לָנוּ מַיִם וְנִשְׁתֶּה וַיֹּאמֶר לָהֶם מֹשֶׁה מַה־תְּרִיבוּן עִמָּדִי מַה־תְּנַסּוּן אֶת־יְהֹוָה:

"Produce of the land" Wheat field near Tiveria

16:35 Until they came to a settled land The Children of Israel were fed manna from heaven during the entire period of forty years of wandering in the desert, until they were within sight of the Promised Land. At that point, they went from being directly sustained by the manna to being nourished by the bountiful produce of *Eretz Yisrael*. Rabbi Samson Raphael Hirsch notes that *Hashem* intended for the produce of the land to be enjoyed as though it, too, is like the miraculous manna, provided directly by God.

Shemot/Exodus 17
Beshalach

שמות יז
בשלח

3 But the people thirsted there for water; and the people grumbled against *Moshe* and said, "Why did you bring us up from Egypt, to kill us and our children and livestock with thirst?"

ג וַיִּצְמָא שָׁם הָעָם לַמַּיִם וַיָּלֶן הָעָם עַל־מֹשֶׁה וַיֹּאמֶר לָמָּה זֶּה הֶעֱלִיתָנוּ מִמִּצְרַיִם לְהָמִית אֹתִי וְאֶת־בָּנַי וְאֶת־מִקְנַי בַּצָּמָא:

4 *Moshe* cried out to *Hashem*, saying, "What shall I do with this people? Before long they will be stoning me!"

ד וַיִּצְעַק מֹשֶׁה אֶל־יְהוָה לֵאמֹר מָה אֶעֱשֶׂה לָעָם הַזֶּה עוֹד מְעַט וּסְקָלֻנִי:

5 Then *Hashem* said to *Moshe*, "Pass before the people; take with you some of the elders of *Yisrael*, and take along the rod with which you struck the Nile, and set out.

ה וַיֹּאמֶר יְהוָה אֶל־מֹשֶׁה עֲבֹר לִפְנֵי הָעָם וְקַח אִתְּךָ מִזִּקְנֵי יִשְׂרָאֵל וּמַטְּךָ אֲשֶׁר הִכִּיתָ בּוֹ אֶת־הַיְאֹר קַח בְּיָדְךָ וְהָלָכְתָּ:

6 I will be standing there before you on the rock at Horeb. Strike the rock and water will issue from it, and the people will drink." And *Moshe* did so in the sight of the elders of *Yisrael*.

ו הִנְנִי עֹמֵד לְפָנֶיךָ שָּׁם עַל־הַצּוּר בְּחֹרֵב וְהִכִּיתָ בַצּוּר וְיָצְאוּ מִמֶּנּוּ מַיִם וְשָׁתָה הָעָם וַיַּעַשׂ כֵּן מֹשֶׁה לְעֵינֵי זִקְנֵי יִשְׂרָאֵל:

7 The place was named Massah and Meribah, because the Israelites quarreled and because they tried *Hashem*, saying, "Is *Hashem* present among us or not?"

ז וַיִּקְרָא שֵׁם הַמָּקוֹם מַסָּה וּמְרִיבָה עַל־רִיב בְּנֵי יִשְׂרָאֵל וְעַל נַסֹּתָם אֶת־יְהוָה לֵאמֹר הֲיֵשׁ יְהוָה בְּקִרְבֵּנוּ אִם־אָיִן:

va-yik-RA SHAYM ha-ma-KOM ma-SAH um-ree-VAH al REEV b'-NAY yis-ra-AYL v'-AL na-so-TAM et a-do-NAI lay-MOR ha-YAYSH a-do-NAI b'-kir-BAY-nu im A-yin

8 Amalek came and fought with *Yisrael* at Rephidim.

ח וַיָּבֹא עֲמָלֵק וַיִּלָּחֶם עִם־יִשְׂרָאֵל בִּרְפִידִם:

9 *Moshe* said to *Yehoshua*, "Pick some men for us, and go out and do battle with Amalek. Tomorrow I will station myself on the top of the hill, with the rod of *Hashem* in my hand."

ט וַיֹּאמֶר מֹשֶׁה אֶל־יְהוֹשֻׁעַ בְּחַר־לָנוּ אֲנָשִׁים וְצֵא הִלָּחֵם בַּעֲמָלֵק מָחָר אָנֹכִי נִצָּב עַל־רֹאשׁ הַגִּבְעָה וּמַטֵּה הָאֱלֹהִים בְּיָדִי:

10 *Yehoshua* did as *Moshe* told him and fought with Amalek, while *Moshe*, *Aharon*, and *Chur* went up to the top of the hill.

י וַיַּעַשׂ יְהוֹשֻׁעַ כַּאֲשֶׁר אָמַר־לוֹ מֹשֶׁה לְהִלָּחֵם בַּעֲמָלֵק וּמֹשֶׁה אַהֲרֹן וְחוּר עָלוּ רֹאשׁ הַגִּבְעָה:

11 Then, whenever *Moshe* held up his hand, *Yisrael* prevailed; but whenever he let down his hand, Amalek prevailed.

יא וְהָיָה כַּאֲשֶׁר יָרִים מֹשֶׁה יָדוֹ וְגָבַר יִשְׂרָאֵל וְכַאֲשֶׁר יָנִיחַ יָדוֹ וְגָבַר עֲמָלֵק:

17:7 Is *Hashem* present among us or not? The People of Israel are not questioning their faith in *Hashem*. Rather, they are wondering to what extent He is involved in their everyday lives. In Egypt, and in other civilizations at that time, God was understood as a static force, and nature as governed by unchanging rules. The newly freed Children of Israel are therefore questioning God's involvement in their day-to-day affairs. In turn, *Hashem* is educating the Nation about His supremacy and control over nature and all the workings of the world. Not only did *Hashem* create water, but He also controls its supply, providing it or withholding it as He sees fit. This message becomes embedded in the psyche of the Chosen Nation and its practical application bears fruit in the Chosen Land where the Jews pray daily to God for water and see His active involvement in everyday life.

Shemot/Exodus 18
Yitro

שמות יח
יתרו

12 But *Moshe*'s hands grew heavy; so they took a stone and put it under him and he sat on it, while *Aharon* and *Chur*, one on each side, supported his hands; thus his hands remained steady until the sun set.

יב וִידֵ֤י מֹשֶׁה֙ כְּבֵדִ֔ים וַיִּקְחוּ־אֶ֛בֶן וַיָּשִׂ֥ימוּ תַחְתָּ֖יו וַיֵּ֣שֶׁב עָלֶ֑יהָ וְאַהֲרֹ֨ן וְח֜וּר תָּמְכ֣וּ בְיָדָ֗יו מִזֶּ֤ה אֶחָד֙ וּמִזֶּ֣ה אֶחָ֔ד וַיְהִ֥י יָדָ֛יו אֱמוּנָ֖ה עַד־בֹּ֥א הַשָּֽׁמֶשׁ׃

13 And *Yehoshua* overwhelmed the people of Amalek with the sword.

יג וַיַּחֲלֹ֧שׁ יְהוֹשֻׁ֛עַ אֶת־עֲמָלֵ֥ק וְאֶת־עַמּ֖וֹ לְפִי־חָֽרֶב׃

14 Then *Hashem* said to *Moshe*, "Inscribe this in a document as a reminder, and read it aloud to *Yehoshua*: I will utterly blot out the memory of Amalek from under heaven!"

יד וַיֹּ֨אמֶר יְהֹוָ֜ה אֶל־מֹשֶׁ֗ה כְּתֹ֨ב זֹ֤את זִכָּרוֹן֙ בַּסֵּ֔פֶר וְשִׂ֖ים בְּאׇזְנֵ֣י יְהוֹשֻׁ֑עַ כִּֽי־מָחֹ֤ה אֶמְחֶה֙ אֶת־זֵ֣כֶר עֲמָלֵ֔ק מִתַּ֖חַת הַשָּׁמָֽיִם׃

15 And *Moshe* built a *Mizbayach* and named it Adonai-nissi.

טו וַיִּ֥בֶן מֹשֶׁ֖ה מִזְבֵּ֑חַ וַיִּקְרָ֥א שְׁמ֖וֹ יְהֹוָ֥ה ׀ נִסִּֽי׃

16 He said, "It means, 'Hand upon the throne of *Hashem*!' *Hashem* will be at war with Amalek throughout the ages."

טז וַיֹּ֗אמֶר כִּֽי־יָד֙ עַל־כֵּ֣ס יָ֔הּ מִלְחָמָ֥ה לַיהֹוָ֖ה בַּֽעֲמָלֵ֑ק מִדֹּ֖ר דֹּֽר׃

18
1 Jethro priest of Midian, *Moshe*'s father-in-law, heard all that *Hashem* had done for *Moshe* and for *Yisrael* His people, how *Hashem* had brought *Yisrael* out from Egypt.

יח א וַיִּשְׁמַ֞ע יִתְר֨וֹ כֹהֵ֤ן מִדְיָן֙ חֹתֵ֣ן מֹשֶׁ֔ה אֵת֩ כׇּל־אֲשֶׁ֨ר עָשָׂ֤ה אֱלֹהִים֙ לְמֹשֶׁ֔ה וּלְיִשְׂרָאֵ֖ל עַמּ֑וֹ כִּֽי־הוֹצִ֧יא יְהֹוָ֛ה אֶת־יִשְׂרָאֵ֖ל מִמִּצְרָֽיִם׃

2 So Jethro, *Moshe*'s father-in-law, took *Tzipora*, *Moshe*'s wife, after she had been sent home,

ב וַיִּקַּ֗ח יִתְרוֹ֙ חֹתֵ֣ן מֹשֶׁ֔ה אֶת־צִפֹּרָ֖ה אֵ֣שֶׁת מֹשֶׁ֑ה אַחַ֖ר שִׁלּוּחֶֽיהָ׃

3 and her two sons – of whom one was named *Gershom*, that is to say, "I have been a stranger in a foreign land";

ג וְאֵ֖ת שְׁנֵ֣י בָנֶ֑יהָ אֲשֶׁ֨ר שֵׁ֤ם הָֽאֶחָד֙ גֵּֽרְשֹׁ֔ם כִּ֣י אָמַ֔ר גֵּ֣ר הָיִ֔יתִי בְּאֶ֖רֶץ נׇכְרִיָּֽה׃

4 and the other was named *Eliezer*, meaning, "The God of my father was my help, and He delivered me from the sword of Pharaoh."

ד וְשֵׁ֥ם הָאֶחָ֖ד אֱלִיעֶ֑זֶר כִּֽי־אֱלֹהֵ֤י אָבִי֙ בְּעֶזְרִ֔י וַיַּצִּלֵ֖נִי מֵחֶ֥רֶב פַּרְעֹֽה׃

5 Jethro, *Moshe*'s father-in-law, brought *Moshe*'s sons and wife to him in the wilderness, where he was encamped at the mountain of *Hashem*.

ה וַיָּבֹ֞א יִתְר֨וֹ חֹתֵ֥ן מֹשֶׁ֛ה וּבָנָ֥יו וְאִשְׁתּ֖וֹ אֶל־מֹשֶׁ֑ה אֶל־הַמִּדְבָּ֕ר אֲשֶׁר־ה֛וּא חֹנֶ֥ה שָׁ֖ם הַ֥ר הָאֱלֹהִֽים׃

6 He sent word to *Moshe*, "I, your father-in-law Jethro, am coming to you, with your wife and her two sons."

ו וַיֹּ֙אמֶר֙ אֶל־מֹשֶׁ֔ה אֲנִ֛י חֹתֶנְךָ֥ יִתְר֖וֹ בָּ֣א אֵלֶ֑יךָ וְאִ֨שְׁתְּךָ֔ וּשְׁנֵ֥י בָנֶ֖יהָ עִמָּֽהּ׃

7 *Moshe* went out to meet his father-in-law; he bowed low and kissed him; each asked after the other's welfare, and they went into the tent.

ז וַיֵּצֵ֨א מֹשֶׁ֜ה לִקְרַ֣את חֹֽתְנ֗וֹ וַיִּשְׁתַּ֙חוּ֙ וַיִּשַּׁק־ל֔וֹ וַיִּשְׁאֲל֥וּ אִישׁ־לְרֵעֵ֖הוּ לְשָׁל֑וֹם וַיָּבֹ֖אוּ הָאֹֽהֱלָה׃

8 *Moshe* then recounted to his father-in-law everything that *Hashem* had done to Pharaoh and to the Egyptians for *Yisrael*'s sake, all the hardships that had befallen them on the way, and how *Hashem* had delivered them.

ח וַיְסַפֵּ֤ר מֹשֶׁה֙ לְחֹ֣תְנ֔וֹ אֵת֩ כׇּל־אֲשֶׁ֨ר עָשָׂ֤ה יְהֹוָה֙ לְפַרְעֹ֣ה וּלְמִצְרַ֔יִם עַ֖ל אוֹדֹ֣ת יִשְׂרָאֵ֑ל אֵ֤ת כׇּל־הַתְּלָאָה֙ אֲשֶׁ֣ר מְצָאָ֣תַם בַּדֶּ֔רֶךְ וַיַּצִּלֵ֖ם יְהֹוָֽה׃

Shemot/Exodus 18
Yitro

שמות יח
יתרו

9 And Jethro rejoiced over all the kindness that *Hashem* had shown *Yisrael* when He delivered them from the Egyptians.

ט וַיִּחַדְּ יִתְרוֹ עַל כָּל־הַטּוֹבָה אֲשֶׁר־עָשָׂה יְהֹוָה לְיִשְׂרָאֵל אֲשֶׁר הִצִּילוֹ מִיַּד מִצְרָיִם:

10 "Blessed be *Hashem*," Jethro said, "who delivered you from the Egyptians and from Pharaoh, and who delivered the people from under the hand of the Egyptians.

י וַיֹּאמֶר יִתְרוֹ בָּרוּךְ יְהֹוָה אֲשֶׁר הִצִּיל אֶתְכֶם מִיַּד מִצְרַיִם וּמִיַּד פַּרְעֹה אֲשֶׁר הִצִּיל אֶת־הָעָם מִתַּחַת יַד־מִצְרָיִם:

11 Now I know that *Hashem* is greater than all gods, yes, by the result of their very schemes against [the people]."

יא עַתָּה יָדַעְתִּי כִּי־גָדוֹל יְהֹוָה מִכָּל־הָאֱלֹהִים כִּי בַדָּבָר אֲשֶׁר זָדוּ עֲלֵיהֶם:

12 And Jethro, *Moshe*'s father-in-law, brought a burnt offering and sacrifices for *Hashem*; and *Aharon* came with all the elders of *Yisrael* to partake of the meal before *Hashem* with *Moshe*'s father-in-law.

יב וַיִּקַּח יִתְרוֹ חֹתֵן מֹשֶׁה עֹלָה וּזְבָחִים לֵאלֹהִים וַיָּבֹא אַהֲרֹן וְכֹל זִקְנֵי יִשְׂרָאֵל לֶאֱכָל־לֶחֶם עִם־חֹתֵן מֹשֶׁה לִפְנֵי הָאֱלֹהִים:

13 Next day, *Moshe* sat as magistrate among the people, while the people stood about *Moshe* from morning until evening.

יג וַיְהִי מִמָּחֳרָת וַיֵּשֶׁב מֹשֶׁה לִשְׁפֹּט אֶת־הָעָם וַיַּעֲמֹד הָעָם עַל־מֹשֶׁה מִן־הַבֹּקֶר עַד־הָעָרֶב:

14 But when *Moshe*'s father-in-law saw how much he had to do for the people, he said, "What is this thing that you are doing to the people? Why do you act alone, while all the people stand about you from morning until evening?"

יד וַיַּרְא חֹתֵן מֹשֶׁה אֵת כָּל־אֲשֶׁר־הוּא עֹשֶׂה לָעָם וַיֹּאמֶר מָה־הַדָּבָר הַזֶּה אֲשֶׁר אַתָּה עֹשֶׂה לָעָם מַדּוּעַ אַתָּה יוֹשֵׁב לְבַדֶּךָ וְכָל־הָעָם נִצָּב עָלֶיךָ מִן־בֹּקֶר עַד־עָרֶב:

15 *Moshe* replied to his father-in-law, "It is because the people come to me to inquire of *Hashem*.

טו וַיֹּאמֶר מֹשֶׁה לְחֹתְנוֹ כִּי־יָבֹא אֵלַי הָעָם לִדְרֹשׁ אֱלֹהִים:

16 When they have a dispute, it comes before me, and I decide between one person and another, and I make known the laws and teachings of *Hashem*."

טז כִּי־יִהְיֶה לָהֶם דָּבָר בָּא אֵלַי וְשָׁפַטְתִּי בֵּין אִישׁ וּבֵין רֵעֵהוּ וְהוֹדַעְתִּי אֶת־חֻקֵּי הָאֱלֹהִים וְאֶת־תּוֹרֹתָיו:

17 But *Moshe*'s father-in-law said to him, "The thing you are doing is not right;

יז וַיֹּאמֶר חֹתֵן מֹשֶׁה אֵלָיו לֹא־טוֹב הַדָּבָר אֲשֶׁר אַתָּה עֹשֶׂה:

18 you will surely wear yourself out, and these people as well. For the task is too heavy for you; you cannot do it alone.

יח נָבֹל תִּבֹּל גַּם־אַתָּה גַּם־הָעָם הַזֶּה אֲשֶׁר עִמָּךְ כִּי־כָבֵד מִמְּךָ הַדָּבָר לֹא־תוּכַל עֲשֹׂהוּ לְבַדֶּךָ:

19 Now listen to me. I will give you counsel, and *Hashem* be with you! You represent the people before *Hashem*: you bring the disputes before *Hashem*,

יט עַתָּה שְׁמַע בְּקֹלִי אִיעָצְךָ וִיהִי אֱלֹהִים עִמָּךְ הֱיֵה אַתָּה לָעָם מוּל הָאֱלֹהִים וְהֵבֵאתָ אַתָּה אֶת־הַדְּבָרִים אֶל־הָאֱלֹהִים:

20 and enjoin upon them the laws and the teachings, and make known to them the way they are to go and the practices they are to follow.

כ וְהִזְהַרְתָּה אֶתְהֶם אֶת־הַחֻקִּים וְאֶת־הַתּוֹרֹת וְהוֹדַעְתָּ לָהֶם אֶת־הַדֶּרֶךְ יֵלְכוּ בָהּ וְאֶת־הַמַּעֲשֶׂה אֲשֶׁר יַעֲשׂוּן:

Shemot/Exodus 19
Yitro

שמות יט
יתרו

כא 21 You shall also seek out from among all the people capable men who fear *Hashem*, trustworthy men who spurn ill-gotten gain. Set these over them as chiefs of thousands, hundreds, fifties, and tens, and

וְאַתָּה תֶחֱזֶה מִכָּל־הָעָם אַנְשֵׁי־חַיִל יִרְאֵי אֱלֹהִים אַנְשֵׁי אֱמֶת שֹׂנְאֵי בָצַע וְשַׂמְתָּ עֲלֵהֶם שָׂרֵי אֲלָפִים שָׂרֵי מֵאוֹת שָׂרֵי חֲמִשִּׁים וְשָׂרֵי עֲשָׂרֹת:

כב 22 let them judge the people at all times. Have them bring every major dispute to you, but let them decide every minor dispute themselves. Make it easier for yourself by letting them share the burden with you.

וְשָׁפְטוּ אֶת־הָעָם בְּכָל־עֵת וְהָיָה כָּל־הַדָּבָר הַגָּדֹל יָבִיאוּ אֵלֶיךָ וְכָל־הַדָּבָר הַקָּטֹן יִשְׁפְּטוּ־הֵם וְהָקֵל מֵעָלֶיךָ וְנָשְׂאוּ אִתָּךְ:

כג 23 If you do this – and *Hashem* so commands you – you will be able to bear up; and all these people too will go home unwearied."

אִם אֶת־הַדָּבָר הַזֶּה תַּעֲשֶׂה וְצִוְּךָ אֱלֹהִים וְיָכָלְתָּ עֲמֹד וְגַם כָּל־הָעָם הַזֶּה עַל־מְקֹמוֹ יָבֹא בְשָׁלוֹם:

IM et ha-da-VAR ha-ZEH ta-a-SEH v'-tzi-v'-KHA e-lo-HEEM v'-ya-khol-TA a-MOD v'-GAM kol ha-AM ha-ZEH al m'-ko-MO ya-VO v'-sha-LOM

כד 24 *Moshe* heeded his father-in-law and did just as he had said.

וַיִּשְׁמַע מֹשֶׁה לְקוֹל חֹתְנוֹ וַיַּעַשׂ כֹּל אֲשֶׁר אָמָר:

כה 25 *Moshe* chose capable men out of all *Yisrael*, and appointed them heads over the people – chiefs of thousands, hundreds, fifties, and tens;

וַיִּבְחַר מֹשֶׁה אַנְשֵׁי־חַיִל מִכָּל־יִשְׂרָאֵל וַיִּתֵּן אֹתָם רָאשִׁים עַל־הָעָם שָׂרֵי אֲלָפִים שָׂרֵי מֵאוֹת שָׂרֵי חֲמִשִּׁים וְשָׂרֵי עֲשָׂרֹת:

כו 26 and they judged the people at all times: the difficult matters they would bring to *Moshe*, and all the minor matters they would decide themselves.

וְשָׁפְטוּ אֶת־הָעָם בְּכָל־עֵת אֶת־הַדָּבָר הַקָּשֶׁה יְבִיאוּן אֶל־מֹשֶׁה וְכָל־הַדָּבָר הַקָּטֹן יִשְׁפּוּטוּ הֵם:

כז 27 Then *Moshe* bade his father-in-law farewell, and he went his way to his own land.

וַיְשַׁלַּח מֹשֶׁה אֶת־חֹתְנוֹ וַיֵּלֶךְ לוֹ אֶל־אַרְצוֹ:

19

א 1 On the third new moon after the Israelites had gone forth from the land of Egypt, on that very day, they entered the wilderness of Sinai.

בַּחֹדֶשׁ הַשְּׁלִישִׁי לְצֵאת בְּנֵי־יִשְׂרָאֵל מֵאֶרֶץ מִצְרָיִם בַּיּוֹם הַזֶּה בָּאוּ מִדְבַּר סִינָי:

ב 2 Having journeyed from Rephidim, they entered the wilderness of Sinai and encamped in the wilderness. *Yisrael* encamped there in front of the mountain,

וַיִּסְעוּ מֵרְפִידִים וַיָּבֹאוּ מִדְבַּר סִינַי וַיַּחֲנוּ בַּמִּדְבָּר וַיִּחַן־שָׁם יִשְׂרָאֵל נֶגֶד הָהָר:

18:23 All these people too will go home unwearied A simple reading of this verse implies that after the implementation of Jethro's suggestion for expediting the judicial process, every individual would be able to return to their homes much sooner. Based on a careful reading of the Hebrew words, however, the *Kli Yakar* explains that the verse does not refer to individuals returning to their private homes, but rather, to the Nation of Israel arriving in their national home, *Eretz Yisrael*. Improving their system of justice was a vital step towards entering the land. Similarly, a renewed commitment to justice will ultimately lead to the final return of the People of Israel to the Land of Israel, as it says (Isaiah 1:27), "*Tzion* shall be saved in the judgement."

Shemot/Exodus 19
Yitro

שמות יט
יתרו

3 and *Moshe* went up to *Hashem*. *Hashem* called to him from the mountain, saying, "Thus shall you say to the house of *Yaakov* and declare to the children of *Yisrael*:

ג וּמֹשֶׁה עָלָה אֶל־הָאֱלֹהִים וַיִּקְרָא אֵלָיו יְהוָה מִן־הָהָר לֵאמֹר כֹּה תֹאמַר לְבֵית יַעֲקֹב וְתַגֵּיד לִבְנֵי יִשְׂרָאֵל:

4 'You have seen what I did to the Egyptians, how I bore you on eagles' wings and brought you to Me.

ד אַתֶּם רְאִיתֶם אֲשֶׁר עָשִׂיתִי לְמִצְרָיִם וָאֶשָּׂא אֶתְכֶם עַל־כַּנְפֵי נְשָׁרִים וָאָבִא אֶתְכֶם אֵלָי:

a-TEM r'-ee-TEM a-SHER a-SEE-tee l'-mitz-RA-yim va-e-SA et-KHEM al kan-FAY n'-sha-REEM va-a-VEE et-KHEM ay-LAI

5 Now then, if you will obey Me faithfully and keep My covenant, you shall be My treasured possession among all the peoples. Indeed, all the earth is Mine,

ה וְעַתָּה אִם־שָׁמוֹעַ תִּשְׁמְעוּ בְּקֹלִי וּשְׁמַרְתֶּם אֶת־בְּרִיתִי וִהְיִיתֶם לִי סְגֻלָּה מִכָּל־הָעַמִּים כִּי־לִי כָּל־הָאָרֶץ:

6 but you shall be to Me a kingdom of priests and a holy nation.' These are the words that you shall speak to the children of *Yisrael*."

ו וְאַתֶּם תִּהְיוּ־לִי מַמְלֶכֶת כֹּהֲנִים וְגוֹי קָדוֹשׁ אֵלֶּה הַדְּבָרִים אֲשֶׁר תְּדַבֵּר אֶל־בְּנֵי יִשְׂרָאֵל:

v'-a-TEM tih-yu LEE mam-LE-khet ko-ha-NEEM v'-GOY ka-DOSH AY-leh ha-d'-va-REEM a-SHER t'-da-BAYR el b'-NAY yis-ra-AYL

7 *Moshe* came and summoned the elders of the people and put before them all that *Hashem* had commanded him.

ז וַיָּבֹא מֹשֶׁה וַיִּקְרָא לְזִקְנֵי הָעָם וַיָּשֶׂם לִפְנֵיהֶם אֵת כָּל־הַדְּבָרִים הָאֵלֶּה אֲשֶׁר צִוָּהוּ יְהוָה:

8 All the people answered as one, saying, "All that *Hashem* has spoken we will do!" And *Moshe* brought back the people's words to *Hashem*.

ח וַיַּעֲנוּ כָל־הָעָם יַחְדָּו וַיֹּאמְרוּ כֹּל אֲשֶׁר־דִּבֶּר יְהוָה נַעֲשֶׂה וַיָּשֶׁב מֹשֶׁה אֶת־דִּבְרֵי הָעָם אֶל־יְהוָה:

9 And *Hashem* said to *Moshe*, "I will come to you in a thick cloud, in order that the people may hear when I speak with you and so trust you ever after." Then *Moshe* reported the people's words to *Hashem*,

ט וַיֹּאמֶר יְהוָה אֶל־מֹשֶׁה הִנֵּה אָנֹכִי בָּא אֵלֶיךָ בְּעַב הֶעָנָן בַּעֲבוּר יִשְׁמַע הָעָם בְּדַבְּרִי עִמָּךְ וְגַם־בְּךָ יַאֲמִינוּ לְעוֹלָם וַיַּגֵּד מֹשֶׁה אֶת־דִּבְרֵי הָעָם אֶל־יְהוָה:

10 and *Hashem* said to *Moshe*, "Go to the people and warn them to stay pure today and tomorrow. Let them wash their clothes.

י וַיֹּאמֶר יְהוָה אֶל־מֹשֶׁה לֵךְ אֶל־הָעָם וְקִדַּשְׁתָּם הַיּוֹם וּמָחָר וְכִבְּסוּ שִׂמְלֹתָם:

11 Let them be ready for the third day; for on the third day *Hashem* will come down, in the sight of all the people, on *Har Sinai*.

יא וְהָיוּ נְכֹנִים לַיּוֹם הַשְּׁלִישִׁי כִּי בַּיּוֹם הַשְּׁלִישִׁי יֵרֵד יְהוָה לְעֵינֵי כָל־הָעָם עַל־הַר סִינָי:

19:4 How I bore you on eagles' wings "Operation Magic Carpet", also called "Operation On Wings of Eagles" based on this verse, secretly airlifted almost fifty thousand Yemenite Jews to Israel between June 1949 and September 1950. Many of the Yemenite Jews had never seen an airplane before, and they likened the ride from Yemen to Israel as a fulfillment of this verse, "I bore you on eagles' wings." This Operation was just one example of the fulfillment of the State of Israel's responsibility toward all Jews worldwide, summarized by Prime Minister Yitzhak Rabin in a speech he delivered to the Zionist Congress in 1992: "Our responsibility also extends to all Jews throughout the world... World Jewry should know that we are responsible for them and will do all we can to assist them when they are in need."

Operation on Wings of Eagles, 1949

Shemot/Exodus 19
Yitro

שמות יט
יתרו

12 You shall set bounds for the people round about, saying, 'Beware of going up the mountain or touching the border of it. Whoever touches the mountain shall be put to death:

יב וְהִגְבַּלְתָּ אֶת־הָעָם סָבִיב לֵאמֹר הִשָּׁמְרוּ לָכֶם עֲלוֹת בָּהָר וּנְגֹעַ בְּקָצֵהוּ כָּל־הַנֹּגֵעַ בָּהָר מוֹת יוּמָת:

13 no hand shall touch him, but he shall be either stoned or shot; beast or man, he shall not live.' When the ram's horn sounds a long blast, they may go up on the mountain."

יג לֹא־תִגַּע בּוֹ יָד כִּי־סָקוֹל יִסָּקֵל אוֹ־יָרֹה יִיָּרֶה אִם־בְּהֵמָה אִם־אִישׁ לֹא יִחְיֶה בִּמְשֹׁךְ הַיֹּבֵל הֵמָּה יַעֲלוּ בָהָר:

14 *Moshe* came down from the mountain to the people and warned the people to stay pure, and they washed their clothes.

יד וַיֵּרֶד מֹשֶׁה מִן־הָהָר אֶל־הָעָם וַיְקַדֵּשׁ אֶת־הָעָם וַיְכַבְּסוּ שִׂמְלֹתָם:

15 And he said to the people, "Be ready for the third day: do not go near a woman."

טו וַיֹּאמֶר אֶל־הָעָם הֱיוּ נְכֹנִים לִשְׁלֹשֶׁת יָמִים אַל־תִּגְּשׁוּ אֶל־אִשָּׁה:

16 On the third day, as morning dawned, there was thunder, and lightning, and a dense cloud upon the mountain, and a very loud blast of the *shofar*; and all the people who were in the camp trembled.

טז וַיְהִי בַיּוֹם הַשְּׁלִישִׁי בִּהְיֹת הַבֹּקֶר וַיְהִי קֹלֹת וּבְרָקִים וְעָנָן כָּבֵד עַל־הָהָר וְקֹל שֹׁפָר חָזָק מְאֹד וַיֶּחֱרַד כָּל־הָעָם אֲשֶׁר בַּמַּחֲנֶה:

17 *Moshe* led the people out of the camp toward *Hashem*, and they took their places at the foot of the mountain.

יז וַיּוֹצֵא מֹשֶׁה אֶת־הָעָם לִקְרַאת הָאֱלֹהִים מִן־הַמַּחֲנֶה וַיִּתְיַצְּבוּ בְּתַחְתִּית הָהָר:

18 Now *Har Sinai* was all in smoke, for *Hashem* had come down upon it in fire; the smoke rose like the smoke of a kiln, and the whole mountain trembled violently.

יח וְהַר סִינַי עָשַׁן כֻּלּוֹ מִפְּנֵי אֲשֶׁר יָרַד עָלָיו יְהוָה בָּאֵשׁ וַיַּעַל עֲשָׁנוֹ כְּעֶשֶׁן הַכִּבְשָׁן וַיֶּחֱרַד כָּל־הָהָר מְאֹד:

19 The blare of the *shofar* grew louder and louder. As *Moshe* spoke, *Hashem* answered him in thunder.

יט וַיְהִי קוֹל הַשּׁוֹפָר הוֹלֵךְ וְחָזֵק מְאֹד מֹשֶׁה יְדַבֵּר וְהָאֱלֹהִים יַעֲנֶנּוּ בְקוֹל:

20 *Hashem* came down upon *Har Sinai*, on the top of the mountain, and *Hashem* called *Moshe* to the top of the mountain and *Moshe* went up.

כ וַיֵּרֶד יְהוָה עַל־הַר סִינַי אֶל־רֹאשׁ הָהָר וַיִּקְרָא יְהוָה לְמֹשֶׁה אֶל־רֹאשׁ הָהָר וַיַּעַל מֹשֶׁה:

21 *Hashem* said to *Moshe*, "Go down, warn the people not to break through to *Hashem* to gaze, lest many of them perish.

כא וַיֹּאמֶר יְהוָה אֶל־מֹשֶׁה רֵד הָעֵד בָּעָם פֶּן־יֶהֶרְסוּ אֶל־יְהוָה לִרְאוֹת וְנָפַל מִמֶּנּוּ רָב:

22 The *Kohanim* also, who come near *Hashem*, must stay pure, lest *Hashem* break out against them."

כב וְגַם הַכֹּהֲנִים הַנִּגָּשִׁים אֶל־יְהוָה יִתְקַדָּשׁוּ פֶּן־יִפְרֹץ בָּהֶם יְהוָה:

23 But *Moshe* said to *Hashem*, "The people cannot come up to *Har Sinai*, for You warned us saying, 'Set bounds about the mountain and sanctify it.'"

כג וַיֹּאמֶר מֹשֶׁה אֶל־יְהוָה לֹא־יוּכַל הָעָם לַעֲלֹת אֶל־הַר סִינָי כִּי־אַתָּה הַעֵדֹתָה בָּנוּ לֵאמֹר הַגְבֵּל אֶת־הָהָר וְקִדַּשְׁתּוֹ:

24 So *Hashem* said to him, "Go down, and come back together with *Aharon*; but let not the *Kohanim* or the people break through to come up to *Hashem*, lest He break out against them."

כד וַיֹּאמֶר אֵלָיו יְהוָה לֶךְ־רֵד וְעָלִיתָ אַתָּה וְאַהֲרֹן עִמָּךְ וְהַכֹּהֲנִים וְהָעָם אַל־יֶהֶרְסוּ לַעֲלֹת אֶל־יְהוָה פֶּן־יִפְרָץ־בָּם:

25 And *Moshe* went down to the people and spoke to them.

כה וַיֵּרֶד מֹשֶׁה אֶל־הָעָם וַיֹּאמֶר אֲלֵהֶם:

Shemot/Exodus 20
Yitro

שמות כ
יתרו

20 1 *Hashem* spoke all these words, saying:

2 I *Hashem* am your God who brought you out of the land of Egypt, the house of bondage:

3 You shall have no other gods besides Me.

4 You shall not make for yourself a sculptured image, or any likeness of what is in the heavens above, or on the earth below, or in the waters under the earth.

5 You shall not bow down to them or serve them. For I *Hashem* your God am an impassioned God, visiting the guilt of the parents upon the children, upon the third and upon the fourth generations of those who reject Me,

6 but showing kindness to the thousandth generation of those who love Me and keep My commandments.

7 You shall not swear falsely by the name of *Hashem* your God; for *Hashem* will not clear one who swears falsely by His name.

8 Remember the *Shabbat* day and keep it holy.

9 Six days you shall labor and do all your work,

10 but the seventh day is a *Shabbat* of *Hashem* your God: you shall not do any work – you, your son or daughter, your male or female slave, or your cattle, or the stranger who is within your settlements.

11 For in six days *Hashem* made heaven and earth and sea, and all that is in them, and He rested on the seventh day; therefore *Hashem* blessed the *Shabbat* day and hallowed it.

12 Honor your father and your mother, that you may long endure on the land that *Hashem* your God is assigning to you.

13 You shall not murder. You shall not commit adultery. You shall not steal. You shall not bear false witness against your neighbor.

14 You shall not covet your neighbor's house: you shall not covet your neighbor's wife, or his male or female slave, or his ox or his ass, or anything that is your neighbor's.

כ א וַיְדַבֵּר אֱלֹהִים אֵת כָּל־הַדְּבָרִים הָאֵלֶּה לֵאמֹר:

ב אָנֹכִי יְהֹוָה אֱלֹהֶיךָ אֲשֶׁר הוֹצֵאתִיךָ מֵאֶרֶץ מִצְרַיִם מִבֵּית עֲבָדִים:

ג לֹא יִהְיֶה־לְךָ אֱלֹהִים אֲחֵרִים עַל־פָּנָי:

ד לֹא תַעֲשֶׂה־לְךָ פֶסֶל וְכָל־תְּמוּנָה אֲשֶׁר בַּשָּׁמַיִם מִמַּעַל וַאֲשֶׁר בָּאָרֶץ מִתָּחַת וַאֲשֶׁר בַּמַּיִם מִתַּחַת לָאָרֶץ:

ה לֹא־תִשְׁתַּחֲוֶה לָהֶם וְלֹא תָעָבְדֵם כִּי אָנֹכִי יְהֹוָה אֱלֹהֶיךָ אֵל קַנָּא פֹּקֵד עֲוֹן אָבֹת עַל־בָּנִים עַל־שִׁלֵּשִׁים וְעַל־רִבֵּעִים לְשֹׂנְאָי:

ו וְעֹשֶׂה חֶסֶד לַאֲלָפִים לְאֹהֲבַי וּלְשֹׁמְרֵי מִצְוֹתָי:

ז לֹא תִשָּׂא אֶת־שֵׁם־יְהֹוָה אֱלֹהֶיךָ לַשָּׁוְא כִּי לֹא יְנַקֶּה יְהֹוָה אֵת אֲשֶׁר־יִשָּׂא אֶת־שְׁמוֹ לַשָּׁוְא:

ח זָכוֹר אֶת־יוֹם הַשַּׁבָּת לְקַדְּשׁוֹ:

ט שֵׁשֶׁת יָמִים תַּעֲבֹד וְעָשִׂיתָ כָּל־מְלַאכְתֶּךָ:

י וְיוֹם הַשְּׁבִיעִי שַׁבָּת לַיהֹוָה אֱלֹהֶיךָ לֹא־תַעֲשֶׂה כָל־מְלָאכָה אַתָּה וּבִנְךָ וּבִתֶּךָ עַבְדְּךָ וַאֲמָתְךָ וּבְהֶמְתֶּךָ וְגֵרְךָ אֲשֶׁר בִּשְׁעָרֶיךָ:

יא כִּי שֵׁשֶׁת־יָמִים עָשָׂה יְהֹוָה אֶת־הַשָּׁמַיִם וְאֶת־הָאָרֶץ אֶת־הַיָּם וְאֶת־כָּל־אֲשֶׁר־בָּם וַיָּנַח בַּיּוֹם הַשְּׁבִיעִי עַל־כֵּן בֵּרַךְ יְהֹוָה אֶת־יוֹם הַשַּׁבָּת וַיְקַדְּשֵׁהוּ:

יב כַּבֵּד אֶת־אָבִיךָ וְאֶת־אִמֶּךָ לְמַעַן יַאֲרִכוּן יָמֶיךָ עַל הָאֲדָמָה אֲשֶׁר־יְהֹוָה אֱלֹהֶיךָ נֹתֵן לָךְ:

יג לֹא תִּרְצָח: לֹא תִּנְאָף: לֹא תִגְנֹב: לֹא־תַעֲנֶה בְרֵעֲךָ עֵד שָׁקֶר:

יד לֹא תַחְמֹד בֵּית רֵעֶךָ לֹא־תַחְמֹד אֵשֶׁת רֵעֶךָ וְעַבְדּוֹ וַאֲמָתוֹ וְשׁוֹרוֹ וַחֲמֹרוֹ וְכֹל אֲשֶׁר לְרֵעֶךָ:

Shemot/Exodus 20
Yitro

שמות כ
יתרו

15 All the people witnessed the thunder and lightning, the blare of the *shofar* and the mountain smoking; and when the people saw it, they fell back and stood at a distance.

וְכָל־הָעָם רֹאִים אֶת־הַקּוֹלֹת וְאֶת־הַלַּפִּידִם וְאֵת קוֹל הַשֹּׁפָר וְאֶת־הָהָר עָשֵׁן וַיַּרְא הָעָם וַיָּנֻעוּ וַיַּעַמְדוּ מֵרָחֹק:

16 "You speak to us," they said to *Moshe*, "and we will obey; but let not *Hashem* speak to us, lest we die."

וַיֹּאמְרוּ אֶל־מֹשֶׁה דַּבֵּר־אַתָּה עִמָּנוּ וְנִשְׁמָעָה וְאַל־יְדַבֵּר עִמָּנוּ אֱלֹהִים פֶּן־נָמוּת:

17 *Moshe* answered the people, "Be not afraid; for *Hashem* has come only in order to test you, and in order that the fear of Him may be ever with you, so that you do not go astray."

וַיֹּאמֶר מֹשֶׁה אֶל־הָעָם אַל־תִּירָאוּ כִּי לְבַעֲבוּר נַסּוֹת אֶתְכֶם בָּא הָאֱלֹהִים וּבַעֲבוּר תִּהְיֶה יִרְאָתוֹ עַל־פְּנֵיכֶם לְבִלְתִּי תֶחֱטָאוּ:

18 So the people remained at a distance, while *Moshe* approached the thick cloud where *Hashem* was.

וַיַּעֲמֹד הָעָם מֵרָחֹק וּמֹשֶׁה נִגַּשׁ אֶל־הָעֲרָפֶל אֲשֶׁר־שָׁם הָאֱלֹהִים:

19 *Hashem* said to *Moshe*: Thus shall you say to the Israelites: You yourselves saw that I spoke to you from the very heavens:

וַיֹּאמֶר יְהֹוָה אֶל־מֹשֶׁה כֹּה תֹאמַר אֶל־בְּנֵי יִשְׂרָאֵל אַתֶּם רְאִיתֶם כִּי מִן־הַשָּׁמַיִם דִּבַּרְתִּי עִמָּכֶם:

20 With Me, therefore, you shall not make any gods of silver, nor shall you make for yourselves any gods of gold.

לֹא תַעֲשׂוּן אִתִּי אֱלֹהֵי כֶסֶף וֵאלֹהֵי זָהָב לֹא תַעֲשׂוּ לָכֶם:

miz-BAKH a-da-MAH ta-a-seh LEE v'-za-vakh-TA a-LAV et o-lo-TE-kha v'-et sh'-la-ME-kha et tzo-n'-KHA v'-et b'-ka-RE-kha b'-khol ha-ma-KOM a-SHER az-KEER et sh'-MEE a-VO ay-LE-kha u-vay-rakh-TEE-kha

21 Make for Me a *Mizbayach* of earth and sacrifice on it your burnt offerings and your sacrifices of well-being, your sheep and your oxen; in every place where I cause My name to be mentioned I will come to you and bless you.

מִזְבַּח אֲדָמָה תַּעֲשֶׂה־לִּי וְזָבַחְתָּ עָלָיו אֶת־עֹלֹתֶיךָ וְאֶת־שְׁלָמֶיךָ אֶת־צֹאנְךָ וְאֶת־בְּקָרֶךָ בְּכָל־הַמָּקוֹם אֲשֶׁר אַזְכִּיר אֶת־שְׁמִי אָבוֹא אֵלֶיךָ וּבֵרַכְתִּיךָ:

miz-BAKH a-da-MAH ta-a-SEH lee v'-za-vakh-TA a-LAV et o-lo-TE-kha v'-ET sh'-la-ME-kha et tzo-n'-KHA v'-ET b'-ka-RE-kha b'-KHOL ha-ma-KOM a-SHER az-KEER et sh'-MEE a-VO ay-LE-kha u-vay-rakh-TEE-kha

22 And if you make for Me a *Mizbayach* of stones, do not build it of hewn stones; for by wielding your tool upon them you have profaned them.

וְאִם־מִזְבַּח אֲבָנִים תַּעֲשֶׂה־לִּי לֹא־תִבְנֶה אֶתְהֶן גָּזִית כִּי חַרְבְּךָ הֵנַפְתָּ עָלֶיהָ וַתְּחַלְלֶהָ:

The Priestly Blessing at the Western Wall

20:21 In every place where I cause My name to be mentioned Based on this verse, *Rashi* explains that God's forty-two letter name can only be uttered where the Divine Presence resides. The *Beit Hamikdash* in *Yerushalayim* was, therefore, the only place where the *Kohanim* could use this special name when giving the priestly blessing to the people. The description of the blessing, found in *Sefer Bamidbar* (6:23–27), ends with the following verse: "Thus they shall link My name with the People of Israel, and I will bless them." Even though the *Kohanim* were the ones standing in front of the people and invoking *Hashem*'s name to bless them, the blessing itself comes from *Hashem*. To this day, the priestly blessing is recited daily throughout Israel. In the rest of the world, this blessing is only recited a few times a year, on holidays. The recitation of the Priestly Blessing is a constant reminder that all blessing in our lives ultimately comes from *Hashem*.

Shemot/Exodus 21
Mishpatim

שמות כא
משפטים

23 Do not ascend My *Mizbayach* by steps, that your nakedness may not be exposed upon it.

כג וְלֹא־תַעֲלֶה בְמַעֲלֹת עַל־מִזְבְּחִי אֲשֶׁר לֹא־תִגָּלֶה עֶרְוָתְךָ עָלָיו:

21

1 These are the rules that you shall set before them:

כא א וְאֵלֶּה הַמִּשְׁפָּטִים אֲשֶׁר תָּשִׂים לִפְנֵיהֶם:

v'-AY-leh ha-mish-pa-TEEM a-SHER ta-SEEM lif-nay-HEM

2 When you acquire a Hebrew slave, he shall serve six years; in the seventh year he shall go free, without payment.

ב כִּי תִקְנֶה עֶבֶד עִבְרִי שֵׁשׁ שָׁנִים יַעֲבֹד וּבַשְּׁבִעִת יֵצֵא לַחָפְשִׁי חִנָּם:

3 If he came single, he shall leave single; if he had a wife, his wife shall leave with him.

ג אִם־בְּגַפּוֹ יָבֹא בְּגַפּוֹ יֵצֵא אִם־בַּעַל אִשָּׁה הוּא וְיָצְאָה אִשְׁתּוֹ עִמּוֹ:

4 If his master gave him a wife, and she has borne him children, the wife and her children shall belong to the master, and he shall leave alone.

ד אִם־אֲדֹנָיו יִתֶּן־לוֹ אִשָּׁה וְיָלְדָה־לוֹ בָנִים אוֹ בָנוֹת הָאִשָּׁה וִילָדֶיהָ תִּהְיֶה לַאדֹנֶיהָ וְהוּא יֵצֵא בְגַפּוֹ:

5 But if the slave declares, "I love my master, and my wife and children: I do not wish to go free,"

ה וְאִם־אָמֹר יֹאמַר הָעֶבֶד אָהַבְתִּי אֶת־אֲדֹנִי אֶת־אִשְׁתִּי וְאֶת־בָּנָי לֹא אֵצֵא חָפְשִׁי:

6 his master shall take him before *Hashem*. He shall be brought to the door or the doorpost, and his master shall pierce his ear with an awl; and he shall then remain his slave for life.

ו וְהִגִּישׁוֹ אֲדֹנָיו אֶל־הָאֱלֹהִים וְהִגִּישׁוֹ אֶל־הַדֶּלֶת אוֹ אֶל־הַמְּזוּזָה וְרָצַע אֲדֹנָיו אֶת־אָזְנוֹ בַּמַּרְצֵעַ וַעֲבָדוֹ לְעֹלָם:

7 When a man sells his daughter as a slave, she shall not be freed as male slaves are.

ז וְכִי־יִמְכֹּר אִישׁ אֶת־בִּתּוֹ לְאָמָה לֹא תֵצֵא כְּצֵאת הָעֲבָדִים:

8 If she proves to be displeasing to her master, who designated her for himself, he must let her be redeemed; he shall not have the right to sell her to outsiders, since he broke faith with her.

ח אִם־רָעָה בְּעֵינֵי אֲדֹנֶיהָ אֲשֶׁר־לֹא [לוֹ] יְעָדָהּ וְהֶפְדָּהּ לְעַם נָכְרִי לֹא־יִמְשֹׁל לְמָכְרָהּ בְּבִגְדוֹ־בָהּ:

9 And if he designated her for his son, he shall deal with her as is the practice with free maidens.

ט וְאִם־לִבְנוֹ יִיעָדֶנָּה כְּמִשְׁפַּט הַבָּנוֹת יַעֲשֶׂה־לָּהּ:

10 If he marries another, he must not withhold from this one her food, her clothing, or her conjugal rights.

י אִם־אַחֶרֶת יִקַּח־לוֹ שְׁאֵרָהּ כְּסוּתָהּ וְעֹנָתָהּ לֹא יִגְרָע:

11 If he fails her in these three ways, she shall go free, without payment.

יא וְאִם־שְׁלָשׁ־אֵלֶּה לֹא יַעֲשֶׂה לָהּ וְיָצְאָה חִנָּם אֵין כָּסֶף:

12 He who fatally strikes a man shall be put to death.

יב מַכֵּה אִישׁ וָמֵת מוֹת יוּמָת:

21:1 These are the rules Following the giving of the Ten Commandments, the *Torah* discusses numerous civil laws dealing with honest and ethical business practices and interpersonal relationships. These laws precede the dictates regulating our relationship with *Hashem*, teaching us that religion demands not just belief, but ethical conduct as well. In fact, there is an oft-quoted adage, *"derech eretz kadma laTorah"* (דרך ארץ קדמה לתורה), which means that 'ethics precedes *Torah.*' Decency and common courtesy serve as the foundation for keeping the rest of the *Torah's* commandments.

Shemot/Exodus 21
Mishpatim

שמות כא
משפטים

13 If he did not do it by design, but it came about by an act of *Hashem*, I will assign you a place to which he can flee.

יג וַאֲשֶׁר לֹא צָדָה וְהָאֱלֹהִים אִנָּה לְיָדוֹ וְשַׂמְתִּי לְךָ מָקוֹם אֲשֶׁר יָנוּס שָׁמָּה:

14 When a man schemes against another and kills him treacherously, you shall take him from My very *Mizbayach* to be put to death.

יד וְכִי־יָזִד אִישׁ עַל־רֵעֵהוּ לְהָרְגוֹ בְעָרְמָה מֵעִם מִזְבְּחִי תִּקָּחֶנּוּ לָמוּת:

15 He who strikes his father or his mother shall be put to death.

טו וּמַכֵּה אָבִיו וְאִמּוֹ מוֹת יוּמָת:

16 He who kidnaps a man – whether he has sold him or is still holding him – shall be put to death.

טז וְגֹנֵב אִישׁ וּמְכָרוֹ וְנִמְצָא בְיָדוֹ מוֹת יוּמָת:

17 He who insults his father or his mother shall be put to death.

יז וּמְקַלֵּל אָבִיו וְאִמּוֹ מוֹת יוּמָת:

18 When men quarrel and one strikes the other with stone or fist, and he does not die but has to take to his bed

יח וְכִי־יְרִיבֻן אֲנָשִׁים וְהִכָּה־אִישׁ אֶת־רֵעֵהוּ בְּאֶבֶן אוֹ בְאֶגְרֹף וְלֹא יָמוּת וְנָפַל לְמִשְׁכָּב:

19 if he then gets up and walks outdoors upon his staff, the assailant shall go unpunished, except that he must pay for his idleness and his cure.

יט אִם־יָקוּם וְהִתְהַלֵּךְ בַּחוּץ עַל־מִשְׁעַנְתּוֹ וְנִקָּה הַמַּכֶּה רַק שִׁבְתּוֹ יִתֵּן וְרַפֹּא יְרַפֵּא:

20 When a man strikes his slave, male or female, with a rod, and he dies there and then, he must be avenged.

כ וְכִי־יַכֶּה אִישׁ אֶת־עַבְדּוֹ אוֹ אֶת־אֲמָתוֹ בַּשֵּׁבֶט וּמֵת תַּחַת יָדוֹ נָקֹם יִנָּקֵם:

21 But if he survives a day or two, he is not to be avenged, since he is the other's property.

כא אַךְ אִם־יוֹם אוֹ יוֹמַיִם יַעֲמֹד לֹא יֻקַּם כִּי כַסְפּוֹ הוּא:

22 When men fight, and one of them pushes a pregnant woman and a miscarriage results, but no other damage ensues, the one responsible shall be fined according as the woman's husband may exact from him, the payment to be based on reckoning.

כב וְכִי־יִנָּצוּ אֲנָשִׁים וְנָגְפוּ אִשָּׁה הָרָה וְיָצְאוּ יְלָדֶיהָ וְלֹא יִהְיֶה אָסוֹן עָנוֹשׁ יֵעָנֵשׁ כַּאֲשֶׁר יָשִׁית עָלָיו בַּעַל הָאִשָּׁה וְנָתַן בִּפְלִלִים:

23 But if other damage ensues, the penalty shall be life for life,

כג וְאִם־אָסוֹן יִהְיֶה וְנָתַתָּה נֶפֶשׁ תַּחַת נָפֶשׁ:

24 eye for eye, tooth for tooth, hand for hand, foot for foot,

כד עַיִן תַּחַת עַיִן שֵׁן תַּחַת שֵׁן יָד תַּחַת יָד רֶגֶל תַּחַת רָגֶל:

25 burn for burn, wound for wound, bruise for bruise.

כה כְּוִיָּה תַּחַת כְּוִיָּה פֶּצַע תַּחַת פָּצַע חַבּוּרָה תַּחַת חַבּוּרָה:

26 When a man strikes the eye of his slave, male or female, and destroys it, he shall let him go free on account of his eye.

כו וְכִי־יַכֶּה אִישׁ אֶת־עֵין עַבְדּוֹ אוֹ־אֶת־עֵין אֲמָתוֹ וְשִׁחֲתָהּ לַחָפְשִׁי יְשַׁלְּחֶנּוּ תַּחַת עֵינוֹ:

27 If he knocks out the tooth of his slave, male or female, he shall let him go free on account of his tooth.

כז וְאִם־שֵׁן עַבְדּוֹ אוֹ־שֵׁן אֲמָתוֹ יַפִּיל לַחָפְשִׁי יְשַׁלְּחֶנּוּ תַּחַת שִׁנּוֹ:

Shemot/Exodus 22
Mishpatim

שמות כב
משפטים

28 When an ox gores a man or a woman to death, the ox shall be stoned and its flesh shall not be eaten, but the owner of the ox is not to be punished.

כח וְכִֽי־יִגַּ֥ח שׁ֛וֹר אֶת־אִ֥ישׁ א֛וֹ אֶת־אִשָּׁ֖ה וָמֵ֑ת סָק֨וֹל יִסָּקֵ֜ל הַשּׁ֗וֹר וְלֹ֤א יֵֽאָכֵל֙ אֶת־בְּשָׂר֔וֹ וּבַ֥עַל הַשּׁ֖וֹר נָקִֽי׃

29 If, however, that ox has been in the habit of goring, and its owner, though warned, has failed to guard it, and it kills a man or a woman — the ox shall be stoned and its owner, too, shall be put to death.

כט וְאִ֡ם שׁוֹר֩ נַגָּ֨ח ה֜וּא מִתְּמֹ֣ל שִׁלְשֹׁ֗ם וְהוּעַ֤ד בִּבְעָלָיו֙ וְלֹ֣א יִשְׁמְרֶ֔נּוּ וְהֵמִ֥ית אִ֖ישׁ א֣וֹ אִשָּׁ֑ה הַשּׁוֹר֙ יִסָּקֵ֔ל וְגַם־בְּעָלָ֖יו יוּמָֽת׃

30 If ransom is laid upon him, he must pay whatever is laid upon him to redeem his life.

ל אִם־כֹּ֖פֶר יוּשַׁ֣ת עָלָ֑יו וְנָתַן֙ פִּדְיֹ֣ן נַפְשׁ֔וֹ כְּכֹ֥ל אֲשֶׁר־יוּשַׁ֖ת עָלָֽיו׃

31 So, too, if it gores a minor, male or female, [the owner] shall be dealt with according to the same rule.

לא אוֹ־בֵ֥ן יִגָּ֖ח אוֹ־בַ֣ת יִגָּ֑ח כַּמִּשְׁפָּ֥ט הַזֶּ֖ה יֵעָ֥שֶׂה לּֽוֹ׃

32 But if the ox gores a slave, male or female, he shall pay thirty *shekalim* of silver to the master, and the ox shall be stoned.

לב אִם־עֶ֛בֶד יִגַּ֥ח הַשּׁ֖וֹר א֣וֹ אָמָ֑ה כֶּ֣סֶף ׀ שְׁלֹשִׁ֣ים שְׁקָלִ֗ים יִתֵּן֙ לַֽאדֹנָ֔יו וְהַשּׁ֖וֹר יִסָּקֵֽל׃

33 When a man opens a pit, or digs a pit and does not cover it, and an ox or an ass falls into it,

לג וְכִֽי־יִפְתַּ֨ח אִ֜ישׁ בּ֗וֹר א֠וֹ כִּֽי־יִכְרֶ֥ה אִ֛ישׁ בֹּ֖ר וְלֹ֣א יְכַסֶּ֑נּוּ וְנָֽפַל־שָׁ֥מָּה שּׁ֖וֹר א֥וֹ חֲמֽוֹר׃

34 the one responsible for the pit must make restitution; he shall pay the price to the owner, but shall keep the dead animal.

לד בַּ֤עַל הַבּוֹר֙ יְשַׁלֵּ֔ם כֶּ֖סֶף יָשִׁ֣יב לִבְעָלָ֑יו וְהַמֵּ֖ת יִֽהְיֶה־לּֽוֹ׃

35 When a man's ox injures his neighbor's ox and it dies, they shall sell the live ox and divide its price; they shall also divide the dead animal.

לה וְכִֽי־יִגֹּ֧ף שֽׁוֹר־אִ֛ישׁ אֶת־שׁ֥וֹר רֵעֵ֖הוּ וָמֵ֑ת וּמָ֨כְר֜וּ אֶת־הַשּׁ֤וֹר הַחַי֙ וְחָצ֣וּ אֶת־כַּסְפּ֔וֹ וְגַ֥ם אֶת־הַמֵּ֖ת יֶֽחֱצֽוּן׃

36 If, however, it is known that the ox was in the habit of goring, and its owner has failed to guard it, he must restore ox for ox, but shall keep the dead animal.

לו א֣וֹ נוֹדַ֗ע כִּ֠י שׁ֣וֹר נַגָּ֥ח הוּא֙ מִתְּמ֣וֹל שִׁלְשֹׁ֔ם וְלֹ֥א יִשְׁמְרֶ֖נּוּ בְּעָלָ֑יו שַׁלֵּ֨ם יְשַׁלֵּ֥ם שׁוֹר֙ תַּ֣חַת הַשּׁ֔וֹר וְהַמֵּ֖ת יִֽהְיֶה־לּֽוֹ׃

37 When a man steals an ox or a sheep, and slaughters it or sells it, he shall pay five oxen for the ox, and four sheep for the sheep

לז כִּ֤י יִגְנֹֽב־אִישׁ֙ שׁ֣וֹר אוֹ־שֶׂ֔ה וּטְבָח֖וֹ א֣וֹ מְכָר֑וֹ חֲמִשָּׁ֣ה בָקָ֗ר יְשַׁלֵּם֙ תַּ֣חַת הַשּׁ֔וֹר וְאַרְבַּע־צֹ֖אן תַּ֥חַת הַשֶּֽׂה׃

22
1 If the thief is seized while tunneling, and he is beaten to death, there is no bloodguilt in his case.

כב א אִם־בַּמַּחְתֶּ֛רֶת יִמָּצֵ֥א הַגַּנָּ֖ב וְהֻכָּ֣ה וָמֵ֑ת אֵ֥ין ל֖וֹ דָּמִֽים׃

2 If the sun has risen on him, there is bloodguilt in that case. — He must make restitution; if he lacks the means, he shall be sold for his theft.

ב אִם־זָרְחָ֥ה הַשֶּׁ֛מֶשׁ עָלָ֖יו דָּמִ֣ים ל֑וֹ שַׁלֵּ֣ם יְשַׁלֵּ֔ם אִם־אֵ֣ין ל֔וֹ וְנִמְכַּ֖ר בִּגְנֵבָתֽוֹ׃

Shemot/Exodus 22
Mishpatim

שמות כב
משפטים

3 But if what he stole – whether ox or ass or sheep – is found alive in his possession, he shall pay double.

ג אִם־הִמָּצֵא תִמָּצֵא בְיָדוֹ הַגְּנֵבָה מִשּׁוֹר עַד־חֲמוֹר עַד־שֶׂה חַיִּים שְׁנַיִם יְשַׁלֵּם׃

im hi-ma-TZAY ti-ma-TZAY v'-ya-DO ha-g'-nay-VAH mi-SHOR ad kha-MOR ad SEH kha-YEEM sh'-NA-yim y'-sha-LAYM

4 When a man lets his livestock loose to graze in another's land, and so allows a field or a vineyard to be grazed bare, he must make restitution for the impairment of that field or vineyard.

ד כִּי יַבְעֶר־אִישׁ שָׂדֶה אוֹ־כֶרֶם וְשִׁלַּח אֶת־בְּעִירוֹ [בְּעִירֹה] וּבִעֵר בִּשְׂדֵה אַחֵר מֵיטַב שָׂדֵהוּ וּמֵיטַב כַּרְמוֹ יְשַׁלֵּם׃

5 When a fire is started and spreads to thorns, so that stacked, standing, or growing grain is consumed, he who started the fire must make restitution.

ה כִּי־תֵצֵא אֵשׁ וּמָצְאָה קֹצִים וְנֶאֱכַל גָּדִישׁ אוֹ הַקָּמָה אוֹ הַשָּׂדֶה שַׁלֵּם יְשַׁלֵּם הַמַּבְעִר אֶת־הַבְּעֵרָה׃

6 When a man gives money or goods to another for safekeeping, and they are stolen from the man's house – if the thief is caught, he shall pay double;

ו כִּי־יִתֵּן אִישׁ אֶל־רֵעֵהוּ כֶּסֶף אוֹ־כֵלִים לִשְׁמֹר וְגֻנַּב מִבֵּית הָאִישׁ אִם־יִמָּצֵא הַגַּנָּב יְשַׁלֵּם שְׁנָיִם׃

7 if the thief is not caught, the owner of the house shall depose before *Hashem* that he has not laid hands on the other's property.

ז אִם־לֹא יִמָּצֵא הַגַּנָּב וְנִקְרַב בַּעַל־הַבַּיִת אֶל־הָאֱלֹהִים אִם־לֹא שָׁלַח יָדוֹ בִּמְלֶאכֶת רֵעֵהוּ׃

8 In all charges of misappropriation – pertaining to an ox, an ass, a sheep, a garment, or any other loss, whereof one party alleges, "This is it" – the case of both parties shall come before *Hashem*: he whom *Hashem* declares guilty shall pay double to the other.

ח עַל־כָּל־דְּבַר־פֶּשַׁע עַל־שׁוֹר עַל־חֲמוֹר עַל־שֶׂה עַל־שַׂלְמָה עַל־כָּל־אֲבֵדָה אֲשֶׁר יֹאמַר כִּי־הוּא זֶה עַד הָאֱלֹהִים יָבֹא דְּבַר־שְׁנֵיהֶם אֲשֶׁר יַרְשִׁיעֻן אֱלֹהִים יְשַׁלֵּם שְׁנַיִם לְרֵעֵהוּ׃

9 When a man gives to another an ass, an ox, a sheep or any other animal to guard, and it dies or is injured or is carried off, with no witness about,

ט כִּי־יִתֵּן אִישׁ אֶל־רֵעֵהוּ חֲמוֹר אוֹ־שׁוֹר אוֹ־שֶׂה וְכָל־בְּהֵמָה לִשְׁמֹר וּמֵת אוֹ־נִשְׁבַּר אוֹ־נִשְׁבָּה אֵין רֹאֶה׃

10 an oath before *Hashem* shall decide between the two of them that the one has not laid hands on the property of the other; the owner must acquiesce, and no restitution shall be made.

י שְׁבֻעַת יְהוָה תִּהְיֶה בֵּין שְׁנֵיהֶם אִם־לֹא שָׁלַח יָדוֹ בִּמְלֶאכֶת רֵעֵהוּ וְלָקַח בְּעָלָיו וְלֹא יְשַׁלֵּם׃

11 But if [the animal] was stolen from him, he shall make restitution to its owner.

יא וְאִם־גָּנֹב יִגָּנֵב מֵעִמּוֹ יְשַׁלֵּם לִבְעָלָיו׃

12 If it was torn by beasts, he shall bring it as evidence; he need not replace what has been torn by beasts.

יב אִם־טָרֹף יִטָּרֵף יְבִאֵהוּ עֵד הַטְּרֵפָה לֹא יְשַׁלֵּם׃

Rambam (1135–1204)

22:3 He shall pay double The double payment for damages commanded in this verse is considered a penalty. Rabbi Moshe Lichtman, in his book *Eretz Yisrael* in the *Parsha*, reflects that according to Jewish Law, the authority for implementation of this penalty, and many others, rests only upon judges who have been ordained with a special authorization that was passed down from teacher to student beginning with *Moshe*. This chain of ordination was unfortunately broken at the time of the Bar Kochba revolt in the second century CE. However, Maimonides, a medieval scholar, philosopher and physician known by his Hebrew acronym *Rambam*, rules that once the masses of Jews reside in *Eretz Yisrael* and the rabbinic authorities there agree, this special ordination can be reinstated.

Shemot/Exodus 22
Mishpatim

שמות כב
משפטים

#	English	#	Hebrew
13	When a man borrows [an animal] from another and it dies or is injured, its owner not being with it, he must make restitution.	יג	וְכִי־יִשְׁאַל אִישׁ מֵעִם רֵעֵהוּ וְנִשְׁבַּר אוֹ־מֵת בְּעָלָיו אֵין־עִמּוֹ שַׁלֵּם יְשַׁלֵּם:
14	If its owner was with it, no restitution need be made; but if it was hired, he is entitled to the hire.	יד	אִם־בְּעָלָיו עִמּוֹ לֹא יְשַׁלֵּם אִם־שָׂכִיר הוּא בָּא בִּשְׂכָרוֹ:
15	If a man seduces a virgin for whom the bride-price has not been paid, and lies with her, he must make her his wife by payment of a bride-price.	טו	וְכִי־יְפַתֶּה אִישׁ בְּתוּלָה אֲשֶׁר לֹא־אֹרָשָׂה וְשָׁכַב עִמָּהּ מָהֹר יִמְהָרֶנָּה לּוֹ לְאִשָּׁה:
16	If her father refuses to give her to him, he must still weigh out silver in accordance with the bride-price for virgins.	טז	אִם־מָאֵן יְמָאֵן אָבִיהָ לְתִתָּהּ לוֹ כֶּסֶף יִשְׁקֹל כְּמֹהַר הַבְּתוּלֹת:
17	You shall not tolerate a sorceress.	יז	מְכַשֵּׁפָה לֹא תְחַיֶּה:
18	Whoever lies with a beast shall be put to death.	יח	כָּל־שֹׁכֵב עִם־בְּהֵמָה מוֹת יוּמָת:
19	Whoever sacrifices to a god other than *Hashem* alone shall be proscribed.	יט	זֹבֵחַ לָאֱלֹהִים יָחֳרָם בִּלְתִּי לַיהוָה לְבַדּוֹ:
20	You shall not wrong a stranger or oppress him, for you were strangers in the land of Egypt.	כ	וְגֵר לֹא־תוֹנֶה וְלֹא תִלְחָצֶנּוּ כִּי־גֵרִים הֱיִיתֶם בְּאֶרֶץ מִצְרָיִם:
21	You shall not ill-treat any widow or orphan.	כא	כָּל־אַלְמָנָה וְיָתוֹם לֹא תְעַנּוּן:
22	If you do mistreat them, I will heed their outcry as soon as they cry out to Me,	כב	אִם־עַנֵּה תְעַנֶּה אֹתוֹ כִּי אִם־צָעֹק יִצְעַק אֵלַי שָׁמֹעַ אֶשְׁמַע צַעֲקָתוֹ:
23	and My anger shall blaze forth and I will put you to the sword, and your own wives shall become widows and your children orphans.	כג	וְחָרָה אַפִּי וְהָרַגְתִּי אֶתְכֶם בֶּחָרֶב וְהָיוּ נְשֵׁיכֶם אַלְמָנוֹת וּבְנֵיכֶם יְתֹמִים:
24	If you lend money to My people, to the poor among you, do not act toward them as a creditor; exact no interest from them.	כד	אִם־כֶּסֶף תַּלְוֶה אֶת־עַמִּי אֶת־הֶעָנִי עִמָּךְ לֹא־תִהְיֶה לוֹ כְּנֹשֶׁה לֹא־תְשִׂימוּן עָלָיו נֶשֶׁךְ:
25	If you take your neighbor's garment in pledge, you must return it to him before the sun sets;	כה	אִם־חָבֹל תַּחְבֹּל שַׂלְמַת רֵעֶךָ עַד־בֹּא הַשֶּׁמֶשׁ תְּשִׁיבֶנּוּ לוֹ:
26	it is his only clothing, the sole covering for his skin. In what else shall he sleep? Therefore, if he cries out to Me, I will pay heed, for I am compassionate.	כו	כִּי הִוא כְסוּתֹה [כְסוּתוֹ] לְבַדָּהּ הִוא שִׂמְלָתוֹ לְעֹרוֹ בַּמֶּה יִשְׁכָּב וְהָיָה כִּי־יִצְעַק אֵלַי וְשָׁמַעְתִּי כִּי־חַנּוּן אָנִי:
27	You shall not revile *Hashem*, nor put a curse upon a chieftain among your people.	כז	אֱלֹהִים לֹא תְקַלֵּל וְנָשִׂיא בְעַמְּךָ לֹא תָאֹר:
28	You shall not put off the skimming of the first yield of your vats. You shall give Me the first-born among your sons.	כח	מְלֵאָתְךָ וְדִמְעֲךָ לֹא תְאַחֵר בְּכוֹר בָּנֶיךָ תִּתֶּן־לִי:
29	You shall do the same with your cattle and your flocks: seven days it shall remain with its mother; on the eighth day you shall give it to Me.	כט	כֵּן־תַּעֲשֶׂה לְשֹׁרְךָ לְצֹאנֶךָ שִׁבְעַת יָמִים יִהְיֶה עִם־אִמּוֹ בַּיּוֹם הַשְּׁמִינִי תִּתְּנוֹ־לִי:

Shemot/Exodus 23
Mishpatim

שמות כג
משפטים

30 You shall be holy people to Me: you must not eat flesh torn by beasts in the field; you shall cast it to the dogs.

ל וְאַנְשֵׁי־קֹדֶשׁ תִּהְיוּן לִי וּבָשָׂר בַּשָּׂדֶה טְרֵפָה לֹא תֹאכֵלוּ לַכֶּלֶב תַּשְׁלִכוּן אֹתוֹ:

23 1 You must not carry false rumors; you shall not join hands with the guilty to act as a malicious witness:

כג א לֹא תִשָּׂא שֵׁמַע שָׁוְא אַל־תָּשֶׁת יָדְךָ עִם־רָשָׁע לִהְיֹת עֵד חָמָס:

2 You shall neither side with the mighty to do wrong – you shall not give perverse testimony in a dispute so as to pervert it in favor of the mighty

ב לֹא־תִהְיֶה אַחֲרֵי־רַבִּים לְרָעֹת וְלֹא־תַעֲנֶה עַל־רִב לִנְטֹת אַחֲרֵי רַבִּים לְהַטֹּת:

3 nor shall you show deference to a poor man in his dispute.

ג וְדָל לֹא תֶהְדַּר בְּרִיבוֹ:

4 When you encounter your enemy's ox or ass wandering, you must take it back to him.

ד כִּי תִפְגַּע שׁוֹר אֹיִבְךָ אוֹ חֲמֹרוֹ תֹּעֶה הָשֵׁב תְּשִׁיבֶנּוּ לוֹ:

5 When you see the ass of your enemy lying under its burden and would refrain from raising it, you must nevertheless raise it with him.

ה כִּי־תִרְאֶה חֲמוֹר שֹׂנַאֲךָ רֹבֵץ תַּחַת מַשָּׂאוֹ וְחָדַלְתָּ מֵעֲזֹב לוֹ עָזֹב תַּעֲזֹב עִמּוֹ:

6 You shall not subvert the rights of your needy in their disputes.

ו לֹא תַטֶּה מִשְׁפַּט אֶבְיֹנְךָ בְּרִיבוֹ:

7 Keep far from a false charge; do not bring death on those who are innocent and in the right, for I will not acquit the wrongdoer.

ז מִדְּבַר־שֶׁקֶר תִּרְחָק וְנָקִי וְצַדִּיק אַל־תַּהֲרֹג כִּי לֹא־אַצְדִּיק רָשָׁע:

8 Do not take bribes, for bribes blind the clear-sighted and upset the pleas of those who are in the right.

ח וְשֹׁחַד לֹא תִקָּח כִּי הַשֹּׁחַד יְעַוֵּר פִּקְחִים וִיסַלֵּף דִּבְרֵי צַדִּיקִים:

9 You shall not oppress a stranger, for you know the feelings of the stranger, having yourselves been strangers in the land of Egypt.

ט וְגֵר לֹא תִלְחָץ וְאַתֶּם יְדַעְתֶּם אֶת־נֶפֶשׁ הַגֵּר כִּי־גֵרִים הֱיִיתֶם בְּאֶרֶץ מִצְרָיִם:

10 Six years you shall sow your land and gather in its yield;

י וְשֵׁשׁ שָׁנִים תִּזְרַע אֶת־אַרְצֶךָ וְאָסַפְתָּ אֶת־תְּבוּאָתָהּ:

11 but in the seventh you shall let it rest and lie fallow. Let the needy among your people eat of it, and what they leave let the wild beasts eat. You shall do the same with your vineyards and your olive groves.

יא וְהַשְּׁבִיעִת תִּשְׁמְטֶנָּה וּנְטַשְׁתָּהּ וְאָכְלוּ אֶבְיֹנֵי עַמֶּךָ וְיִתְרָם תֹּאכַל חַיַּת הַשָּׂדֶה כֵּן־תַּעֲשֶׂה לְכַרְמְךָ לְזֵיתֶךָ:

v'-ha-sh'-vee-IT tish-m'-TE-nah un-tash-TAH v'-a-kh'-LU ev-yo-NAY a-ME-kha v'-yit-RAM to-KHAL kha-YAT ha-sa-DEH kayn ta-a-SEH l'-khar-m'-KHA l'-zay-TE-kha

23:11 In the seventh you shall let it rest and lie fallow Every seventh year, all farms, fields, orchards and vineyards in *Eretz Yisrael* are left untended and unharvested. To this very day, the Sabbatical year is kept in Israel. The message of this unique commandment is similar to that of *Shabbat*. Just as we are commanded to keep *Shabbat* and cease our daily activities every seventh day, we are similarly to rest from working the fields every seventh year. Just as *Shabbat* reminds us that *Hashem* created the world (Exodus 20:10) and everything in it belongs to Him, the Sabbatical year reminds us that our economic success and all that we produce is in the hands of our Creator.

Shemot/Exodus 23
Mishpatim

שמות כג
משפטים

12 Six days you shall do work, but on the seventh day you shall cease from labor, in order that your ox and your ass may rest, and that your bondman and the stranger may be refreshed.

יב שֵׁ֣שֶׁת יָמִים֮ תַּעֲשֶׂ֣ה מַעֲשֶׂיךָ֒ וּבַיּ֣וֹם הַשְּׁבִיעִ֖י תִּשְׁבֹּ֑ת לְמַ֣עַן יָנ֗וּחַ שֽׁוֹרְךָ֙ וַחֲמֹרֶ֔ךָ וְיִנָּפֵ֥שׁ בֶּן־אֲמָתְךָ֖ וְהַגֵּֽר׃

13 Be on guard concerning all that I have told you. Make no mention of the names of other gods; they shall not be heard on your lips.

יג וּבְכֹ֛ל אֲשֶׁר־אָמַ֥רְתִּי אֲלֵיכֶ֖ם תִּשָּׁמֵ֑רוּ וְשֵׁ֨ם אֱלֹהִ֤ים אֲחֵרִים֙ לֹ֣א תַזְכִּ֔ירוּ לֹ֥א יִשָּׁמַ֖ע עַל־פִּֽיךָ׃

14 Three times a year you shall hold a festival for Me:

יד שָׁלֹ֣שׁ רְגָלִ֔ים תָּחֹ֥ג לִ֖י בַּשָּׁנָֽה׃

15 You shall observe the Feast of Unleavened Bread – eating unleavened bread for seven days as I have commanded you – at the set time in the month of Abib, for in it you went forth from Egypt; and none shall appear before Me empty-handed;

טו אֶת־חַ֣ג הַמַּצּוֹת֮ תִּשְׁמֹר֒ שִׁבְעַ֣ת יָמִים֩ תֹּאכַ֨ל מַצּ֜וֹת כַּֽאֲשֶׁ֣ר צִוִּיתִ֗ךָ לְמוֹעֵד֙ חֹ֣דֶשׁ הָֽאָבִ֔יב כִּי־ב֖וֹ יָצָ֣אתָ מִמִּצְרָ֑יִם וְלֹא־יֵרָא֥וּ פָנַ֖י רֵיקָֽם׃

16 and the Feast of the Harvest, of the first fruits of your work, of what you sow in the field; and the Feast of Ingathering at the end of the year, when you gather in the results of your work from the field.

טז וְחַ֤ג הַקָּצִיר֙ בִּכּוּרֵ֣י מַעֲשֶׂ֔יךָ אֲשֶׁ֥ר תִּזְרַ֖ע בַּשָּׂדֶ֑ה וְחַ֤ג הָֽאָסִף֙ בְּצֵ֣את הַשָּׁנָ֔ה בְּאָסְפְּךָ֥ אֶֽת־מַעֲשֶׂ֖יךָ מִן־הַשָּׂדֶֽה׃

17 Three times a year all your males shall appear before the Sovereign, *Hashem*.

יז שָׁלֹ֥שׁ פְּעָמִ֖ים בַּשָּׁנָ֑ה יֵרָאֶה֙ כָּל־זְכ֣וּרְךָ֔ אֶל־פְּנֵ֖י הָֽאָדֹ֥ן ׀ יְהוָֽה׃

18 You shall not offer the blood of My sacrifice with anything leavened; and the fat of My festal offering shall not be left lying until morning.

יח לֹֽא־תִזְבַּ֥ח עַל־חָמֵ֖ץ דַּם־זִבְחִ֑י וְלֹֽא־יָלִ֥ין חֵֽלֶב־חַגִּ֖י עַד־בֹּֽקֶר׃

19 The choice first fruits of your soil you shall bring to the house of *Hashem* your God. You shall not boil a kid in its mother's milk.

יט רֵאשִׁ֗ית בִּכּוּרֵי֙ אַדְמָ֣תְךָ֔ תָּבִ֕יא בֵּ֖ית יְהוָ֣ה אֱלֹהֶ֑יךָ לֹֽא־תְבַשֵּׁ֥ל גְּדִ֖י בַּחֲלֵ֥ב אִמּֽוֹ׃

20 I am sending an angel before you to guard you on the way and to bring you to the place that I have made ready.

כ הִנֵּ֨ה אָנֹכִ֜י שֹׁלֵ֤חַ מַלְאָךְ֙ לְפָנֶ֔יךָ לִשְׁמָרְךָ֖ בַּדָּ֑רֶךְ וְלַהֲבִ֣יאֲךָ֔ אֶל־הַמָּק֖וֹם אֲשֶׁ֥ר הֲכִנֹֽתִי׃

hi-NAY a-no-KHEE sho-LAY-akh mal-AKH l'-fa-NE-kha lish-mor-KHA ba-DA-rekh v'-la-ha-VEE-a-KHA el ha-ma-KOM a-SHER ha-khi-NO-tee

21 Pay heed to him and obey him. Do not defy him, for he will not pardon your offenses, since My Name is in him;

כא הִשָּׁ֧מֶר מִפָּנָ֛יו וּשְׁמַ֥ע בְּקֹל֖וֹ אַל־תַּמֵּ֣ר בּ֑וֹ כִּ֣י לֹ֤א יִשָּׂא֙ לְפִשְׁעֲכֶ֔ם כִּ֥י שְׁמִ֖י בְּקִרְבּֽוֹ׃

22 but if you obey him and do all that I say, I will be an enemy to your enemies and a foe to your foes.

כב כִּ֣י אִם־שָׁמ֤וֹעַ תִּשְׁמַע֙ בְּקֹל֔וֹ וְעָשִׂ֕יתָ כֹּ֖ל אֲשֶׁ֣ר אֲדַבֵּ֑ר וְאָֽיַבְתִּי֙ אֶת־אֹ֣יְבֶ֔יךָ וְצַרְתִּ֖י אֶת־צֹרְרֶֽיךָ׃

23 When My angel goes before you and brings you to the Amorites, the Hittites, the Perizzites, the Canaanites, the Hivites, and the Jebusites, and I annihilate them,

כג כִּֽי־יֵלֵ֣ךְ מַלְאָכִי֮ לְפָנֶיךָ֒ וֶהֱבִֽיאֲךָ֗ אֶל־הָֽאֱמֹרִי֙ וְהַ֣חִתִּ֔י וְהַפְּרִזִּי֙ וְהַֽכְּנַעֲנִ֔י הַחִוִּ֖י וְהַיְבוּסִ֑י וְהִכְחַדְתִּֽיו׃

24 you shall not bow down to their gods in worship or follow their practices, but shall tear them down and smash their pillars to bits.

כד לֹֽא־תִשְׁתַּחֲוֶ֤ה לֵאלֹֽהֵיהֶם֙ וְלֹ֣א תָֽעָבְדֵ֔ם וְלֹ֥א תַעֲשֶׂ֖ה כְּמַֽעֲשֵׂיהֶ֑ם כִּ֤י הָרֵס֙ תְּהָ֣רְסֵ֔ם וְשַׁבֵּ֥ר תְּשַׁבֵּ֖ר מַצֵּבֹתֵיהֶֽם׃

194

Shemot/Exodus 24
Mishpatim

שמות כד
משפטים

25 You shall serve *Hashem* your God, and He will bless your bread and your water. And I will remove sickness from your midst.

כה וַעֲבַדְתֶּם אֵת יְהֹוָה אֱלֹהֵיכֶם וּבֵרַךְ אֶת־לַחְמְךָ וְאֶת־מֵימֶיךָ וַהֲסִרֹתִי מַחֲלָה מִקִּרְבֶּךָ׃

26 No woman in your land shall miscarry or be barren. I will let you enjoy the full count of your days.

כו לֹא תִהְיֶה מְשַׁכֵּלָה וַעֲקָרָה בְּאַרְצֶךָ אֶת־מִסְפַּר יָמֶיךָ אֲמַלֵּא׃

27 I will send forth My terror before you, and I will throw into panic all the people among whom you come, and I will make all your enemies turn tail before you.

כז אֶת־אֵימָתִי אֲשַׁלַּח לְפָנֶיךָ וְהַמֹּתִי אֶת־כָּל־הָעָם אֲשֶׁר תָּבֹא בָּהֶם וְנָתַתִּי אֶת־כָּל־אֹיְבֶיךָ אֵלֶיךָ עֹרֶף׃

28 I will send a plague ahead of you, and it shall drive out before you the Hivites, the Canaanites, and the Hittites.

כח וְשָׁלַחְתִּי אֶת־הַצִּרְעָה לְפָנֶיךָ וְגֵרְשָׁה אֶת־הַחִוִּי אֶת־הַכְּנַעֲנִי וְאֶת־הַחִתִּי מִלְּפָנֶיךָ׃

29 I will not drive them out before you in a single year, lest the land become desolate and the wild beasts multiply to your hurt.

כט לֹא אֲגָרְשֶׁנּוּ מִפָּנֶיךָ בְּשָׁנָה אֶחָת פֶּן־תִּהְיֶה הָאָרֶץ שְׁמָמָה וְרַבָּה עָלֶיךָ חַיַּת הַשָּׂדֶה׃

30 I will drive them out before you little by little, until you have increased and possess the land.

ל מְעַט מְעַט אֲגָרְשֶׁנּוּ מִפָּנֶיךָ עַד אֲשֶׁר תִּפְרֶה וְנָחַלְתָּ אֶת־הָאָרֶץ׃

m'-AT m'-AT a-ga-r'-SHE-nu mi-pa-NE-kha AD a-SHER tif-REH v'-na-khal-TA et ha-A-retz

31 I will set your borders from the Sea of Reeds to the Sea of Philistia, and from the wilderness to the Euphrates; for I will deliver the inhabitants of the land into your hands, and you will drive them out before you.

לא וְשַׁתִּי אֶת־גְּבֻלְךָ מִיַּם־סוּף וְעַד־יָם פְּלִשְׁתִּים וּמִמִּדְבָּר עַד־הַנָּהָר כִּי אֶתֵּן בְּיֶדְכֶם אֵת יֹשְׁבֵי הָאָרֶץ וְגֵרַשְׁתָּמוֹ מִפָּנֶיךָ׃

32 You shall make no covenant with them and their gods.

לב לֹא־תִכְרֹת לָהֶם וְלֵאלֹהֵיהֶם בְּרִית׃

33 They shall not remain in your land, lest they cause you to sin against Me; for you will serve their gods – and it will prove a snare to you.

לג לֹא יֵשְׁבוּ בְּאַרְצְךָ פֶּן־יַחֲטִיאוּ אֹתְךָ לִי כִּי תַעֲבֹד אֶת־אֱלֹהֵיהֶם כִּי־יִהְיֶה לְךָ לְמוֹקֵשׁ׃

24 1 Then He said to *Moshe*, "Come up to *Hashem*, with *Aharon*, *Nadav* and *Avihu*, and seventy elders of *Yisrael*, and bow low from afar.

כד א וְאֶל־מֹשֶׁה אָמַר עֲלֵה אֶל־יְהֹוָה אַתָּה וְאַהֲרֹן נָדָב וַאֲבִיהוּא וְשִׁבְעִים מִזִּקְנֵי יִשְׂרָאֵל וְהִשְׁתַּחֲוִיתֶם מֵרָחֹק׃

Rabbi Avraham Ibn Ezra (1089–1167)

23:30 until you have increased and possess the land In these verses, *Hashem* describes a precise plan to inherit the Land of Israel through a gradual process. Rabbi Avraham Ibn Ezra, a well-known medieval commentator, poet and philosopher, explains that although God could have destroyed the inhabitants of Canaan instantaneously, He gave the Jewish people time to increase and take over the land in an incremental, natural way. We are privileged to live in an era in which we can see this verse being fulfilled before our eyes. The once desolate land has warmly embraced the gradual return of the Jewish people and has become a source of spiritual blessing and economic success. Israel is known around the world for its scientific, medical, economic, technological and agricultural research and innovation.

Shemot/Exodus 24
Mishpatim

שמות כד
משפטים

2 *Moshe* alone shall come near *Hashem*; but the others shall not come near, nor shall the people come up with him."

ב וְנִגַּשׁ מֹשֶׁה לְבַדּוֹ אֶל־יְהֹוָה וְהֵם לֹא יִגָּשׁוּ וְהָעָם לֹא יַעֲלוּ עִמּוֹ׃

3 *Moshe* went and repeated to the people all the commands of *Hashem* and all the rules; and all the people answered with one voice, saying, "All the things that *Hashem* has commanded we will do!"

ג וַיָּבֹא מֹשֶׁה וַיְסַפֵּר לָעָם אֵת כָּל־דִּבְרֵי יְהֹוָה וְאֵת כָּל־הַמִּשְׁפָּטִים וַיַּעַן כָּל־הָעָם קוֹל אֶחָד וַיֹּאמְרוּ כָּל־הַדְּבָרִים אֲשֶׁר־דִּבֶּר יְהֹוָה נַעֲשֶׂה׃

4 *Moshe* then wrote down all the commands of *Hashem*. Early in the morning, he set up a *Mizbayach* at the foot of the mountain, with twelve pillars for the twelve tribes of *Yisrael*.

ד וַיִּכְתֹּב מֹשֶׁה אֵת כָּל־דִּבְרֵי יְהֹוָה וַיַּשְׁכֵּם בַּבֹּקֶר וַיִּבֶן מִזְבֵּחַ תַּחַת הָהָר וּשְׁתֵּים עֶשְׂרֵה מַצֵּבָה לִשְׁנֵים עָשָׂר שִׁבְטֵי יִשְׂרָאֵל׃

va-yikh-TOV mo-SHEH AYT kol div-RAY a-do-NAI va-yash-KAYM ba-BO-ker va-YI-ven miz-BAY-akh TA-khat ha-HAR u-sh'-TAYM es-RAY ma-tzay-VAH lish-NAYM a-SAR shiv-TAY yis-ra-AYL

5 He designated some young men among the Israelites, and they offered burnt offerings and sacrificed bulls as offerings of well-being to *Hashem*.

ה וַיִּשְׁלַח אֶת־נַעֲרֵי בְּנֵי יִשְׂרָאֵל וַיַּעֲלוּ עֹלֹת וַיִּזְבְּחוּ זְבָחִים שְׁלָמִים לַיהֹוָה פָּרִים׃

6 *Moshe* took one part of the blood and put it in basins, and the other part of the blood he dashed against the *Mizbayach*.

ו וַיִּקַּח מֹשֶׁה חֲצִי הַדָּם וַיָּשֶׂם בָּאַגָּנֹת וַחֲצִי הַדָּם זָרַק עַל־הַמִּזְבֵּחַ׃

7 Then he took the record of the covenant and read it aloud to the people. And they said, "All that *Hashem* has spoken we will faithfully do!"

ז וַיִּקַּח סֵפֶר הַבְּרִית וַיִּקְרָא בְּאָזְנֵי הָעָם וַיֹּאמְרוּ כֹּל אֲשֶׁר־דִּבֶּר יְהֹוָה נַעֲשֶׂה וְנִשְׁמָע׃

8 *Moshe* took the blood and dashed it on the people and said, "This is the blood of the covenant that *Hashem* now makes with you concerning all these commands."

ח וַיִּקַּח מֹשֶׁה אֶת־הַדָּם וַיִּזְרֹק עַל־הָעָם וַיֹּאמֶר הִנֵּה דַם־הַבְּרִית אֲשֶׁר כָּרַת יְהֹוָה עִמָּכֶם עַל כָּל־הַדְּבָרִים הָאֵלֶּה׃

9 Then *Moshe* and *Aharon*, *Nadav* and *Avihu*, and seventy elders of *Yisrael* ascended;

ט וַיַּעַל מֹשֶׁה וְאַהֲרֹן נָדָב וַאֲבִיהוּא וְשִׁבְעִים מִזִּקְנֵי יִשְׂרָאֵל׃

10 and they saw the God of *Yisrael*: under His feet there was the likeness of a pavement of sapphire, like the very sky for purity.

י וַיִּרְאוּ אֵת אֱלֹהֵי יִשְׂרָאֵל וְתַחַת רַגְלָיו כְּמַעֲשֵׂה לִבְנַת הַסַּפִּיר וּכְעֶצֶם הַשָּׁמַיִם לָטֹהַר׃

11 Yet He did not raise His hand against the leaders of the Israelites; they beheld *Hashem*, and they ate and drank.

יא וְאֶל־אֲצִילֵי בְּנֵי יִשְׂרָאֵל לֹא שָׁלַח יָדוֹ וַיֶּחֱזוּ אֶת־הָאֱלֹהִים וַיֹּאכְלוּ וַיִּשְׁתּוּ׃

24:4 With twelve pillars If the Twelve Tribes are physically present at the foot of the mountain, what is the meaning behind the symbolic representation of the tribes through the twelve pillars erected by *Moshe*? Commentators reflect that these pillars are meant to represent all future descendants of the nation alongside the generation that exited Egypt. Based on this verse, the Sages of the *Midrash* teach that, in a sense, all the future souls of the Jewish nation were present at Sinai; they too witnessed the revelation of God and personally accepted the *Torah* and its laws upon themselves.

Shemot/Exodus 25
Terumah

12 *Hashem* said to *Moshe*, "Come up to Me on the mountain and wait there, and I will give you the stone tablets with the teachings and commandments which I have inscribed to instruct them."

13 So *Moshe* and his attendant *Yehoshua* arose, and *Moshe* ascended the mountain of *Hashem*.

14 To the elders he had said, "Wait here for us until we return to you. You have *Aharon* and *Chur* with you; let anyone who has a legal matter approach them."

15 When *Moshe* had ascended the mountain, the cloud covered the mountain.

16 The Presence of *Hashem* abode on *Har Sinai*, and the cloud hid it for six days. On the seventh day He called to *Moshe* from the midst of the cloud.

17 Now the Presence of *Hashem* appeared in the sight of the Israelites as a consuming fire on the top of the mountain.

18 *Moshe* went inside the cloud and ascended the mountain; and *Moshe* remained on the mountain forty days and forty nights.

25
1 *Hashem* spoke to *Moshe*, saying:

2 Tell *B'nei Yisrael* to bring Me gifts; you shall accept gifts for Me from every person whose heart so moves him.

3 And these are the gifts that you shall accept from them: gold, silver, and copper;

4 blue, purple, and crimson yarns, fine linen, goats' hair;

5 tanned ram skins, dolphin skins, and acacia wood;

6 oil for lighting, spices for the anointing oil and for the aromatic incense;

7 lapis lazuli and other stones for setting, for the ephod and for the breastpiece.

שמות כה
תרומה

יב וַיֹּאמֶר יְהֹוָה אֶל־מֹשֶׁה עֲלֵה אֵלַי הָהָרָה וֶהְיֵה־שָׁם וְאֶתְּנָה לְךָ אֶת־לֻחֹת הָאֶבֶן וְהַתּוֹרָה וְהַמִּצְוָה אֲשֶׁר כָּתַבְתִּי לְהוֹרֹתָם:

יג וַיָּקָם מֹשֶׁה וִיהוֹשֻׁעַ מְשָׁרְתוֹ וַיַּעַל מֹשֶׁה אֶל־הַר הָאֱלֹהִים:

יד וְאֶל־הַזְּקֵנִים אָמַר שְׁבוּ־לָנוּ בָזֶה עַד אֲשֶׁר־נָשׁוּב אֲלֵיכֶם וְהִנֵּה אַהֲרֹן וְחוּר עִמָּכֶם מִי־בַעַל דְּבָרִים יִגַּשׁ אֲלֵהֶם:

טו וַיַּעַל מֹשֶׁה אֶל־הָהָר וַיְכַס הֶעָנָן אֶת־הָהָר:

טז וַיִּשְׁכֹּן כְּבוֹד־יְהֹוָה עַל־הַר סִינַי וַיְכַסֵּהוּ הֶעָנָן שֵׁשֶׁת יָמִים וַיִּקְרָא אֶל־מֹשֶׁה בַּיּוֹם הַשְּׁבִיעִי מִתּוֹךְ הֶעָנָן:

יז וּמַרְאֵה כְּבוֹד יְהֹוָה כְּאֵשׁ אֹכֶלֶת בְּרֹאשׁ הָהָר לְעֵינֵי בְּנֵי יִשְׂרָאֵל:

יח וַיָּבֹא מֹשֶׁה בְּתוֹךְ הֶעָנָן וַיַּעַל אֶל־הָהָר וַיְהִי מֹשֶׁה בָּהָר אַרְבָּעִים יוֹם וְאַרְבָּעִים לָיְלָה:

כה א וַיְדַבֵּר יְהֹוָה אֶל־מֹשֶׁה לֵּאמֹר:

ב דַּבֵּר אֶל־בְּנֵי יִשְׂרָאֵל וְיִקְחוּ־לִי תְּרוּמָה מֵאֵת כָּל־אִישׁ אֲשֶׁר יִדְּבֶנּוּ לִבּוֹ תִּקְחוּ אֶת־תְּרוּמָתִי:

ג וְזֹאת הַתְּרוּמָה אֲשֶׁר תִּקְחוּ מֵאִתָּם זָהָב וָכֶסֶף וּנְחֹשֶׁת:

ד וּתְכֵלֶת וְאַרְגָּמָן וְתוֹלַעַת שָׁנִי וְשֵׁשׁ וְעִזִּים:

ה וְעֹרֹת אֵילִם מְאָדָּמִים וְעֹרֹת תְּחָשִׁים וַעֲצֵי שִׁטִּים:

ו שֶׁמֶן לַמָּאֹר בְּשָׂמִים לְשֶׁמֶן הַמִּשְׁחָה וְלִקְטֹרֶת הַסַּמִּים:

ז אַבְנֵי־שֹׁהַם וְאַבְנֵי מִלֻּאִים לָאֵפֹד וְלַחֹשֶׁן:

Shemot/Exodus 25
Terumah

שמות כה
תרומה

8 And let them make Me a sanctuary that I may dwell among them.

וְעָשׂוּ לִי מִקְדָּשׁ וְשָׁכַנְתִּי בְּתוֹכָם: ח

v'-a-SU LEE mik-DASH v'-sha-khan-TEE b'-to-KHAM

9 Exactly as I show you – the pattern of the *Mishkan* and the pattern of all its furnishings – so shall you make it.

כְּכֹל אֲשֶׁר אֲנִי מַרְאֶה אוֹתְךָ אֵת תַּבְנִית הַמִּשְׁכָּן וְאֵת תַּבְנִית כָּל־כֵּלָיו וְכֵן תַּעֲשׂוּ: ט

10 They shall make an ark of acacia wood, two and a half *amot* long, an *amah* and a half wide, and an *amah* and a half high.

וְעָשׂוּ אֲרוֹן עֲצֵי שִׁטִּים אַמָּתַיִם וָחֵצִי אָרְכּוֹ וְאַמָּה וָחֵצִי רָחְבּוֹ וְאַמָּה וָחֵצִי קֹמָתוֹ: י

11 Overlay it with pure gold – overlay it inside and out – and make upon it a gold molding round about.

וְצִפִּיתָ אֹתוֹ זָהָב טָהוֹר מִבַּיִת וּמִחוּץ תְּצַפֶּנּוּ וְעָשִׂיתָ עָלָיו זֵר זָהָב סָבִיב: יא

12 Cast four gold rings for it, to be attached to its four feet, two rings on one of its side walls and two on the other.

וְיָצַקְתָּ לּוֹ אַרְבַּע טַבְּעֹת זָהָב וְנָתַתָּה עַל אַרְבַּע פַּעֲמֹתָיו וּשְׁתֵּי טַבָּעֹת עַל־צַלְעוֹ הָאֶחָת וּשְׁתֵּי טַבָּעֹת עַל־צַלְעוֹ הַשֵּׁנִית: יב

13 Make poles of acacia wood and overlay them with gold;

וְעָשִׂיתָ בַדֵּי עֲצֵי שִׁטִּים וְצִפִּיתָ אֹתָם זָהָב: יג

14 then insert the poles into the rings on the side walls of the ark, for carrying the ark.

וְהֵבֵאתָ אֶת־הַבַּדִּים בַּטַּבָּעֹת עַל צַלְעֹת הָאָרֹן לָשֵׂאת אֶת־הָאָרֹן בָּהֶם: יד

15 The poles shall remain in the rings of the ark: they shall not be removed from it.

בְּטַבְּעֹת הָאָרֹן יִהְיוּ הַבַּדִּים לֹא יָסֻרוּ מִמֶּנּוּ: טו

16 And deposit in the *Aron* [the tablets of] the Pact which I will give you.

וְנָתַתָּ אֶל־הָאָרֹן אֵת הָעֵדֻת אֲשֶׁר אֶתֵּן אֵלֶיךָ: טז

17 You shall make a cover of pure gold, two and a half *amot* long and an *amah* and a half wide.

וְעָשִׂיתָ כַפֹּרֶת זָהָב טָהוֹר אַמָּתַיִם וָחֵצִי אָרְכָּהּ וְאַמָּה וָחֵצִי רָחְבָּהּ: יז

18 Make two cherubim of gold – make them of hammered work – at the two ends of the cover.

וְעָשִׂיתָ שְׁנַיִם כְּרֻבִים זָהָב מִקְשָׁה תַּעֲשֶׂה אֹתָם מִשְּׁנֵי קְצוֹת הַכַּפֹּרֶת: יח

19 Make one cherub at one end and the other cherub at the other end; of one piece with the cover shall you make the cherubim at its two ends.

וַעֲשֵׂה כְּרוּב אֶחָד מִקָּצָה מִזֶּה וּכְרוּב־אֶחָד מִקָּצָה מִזֶּה מִן־הַכַּפֹּרֶת תַּעֲשׂוּ אֶת־הַכְּרֻבִים עַל־שְׁנֵי קְצוֹתָיו: יט

25:8 That I may dwell among them Significantly, the verse does not say "that I may dwell within it." The *Mishkan* is not intended to physically contain *Hashem* within its walls. Rather, the *Seforno* explains, it is a place which enables *Hashem* to dwell "among them," meaning in the midst of the Children of Israel. Unlike pagan places of worship, the *Mishkan* is not meant to provide a home on earth for a god. Rather, the *Mishkan*, and ultimately the *Beit Hamikdash* in *Yerushahlayim*, are designed to facilitate the relationship between *Hashem* and His children, where every person can go to elevate himself or herself spiritually.

Shemot/Exodus 25
Terumah

שמות כה
תרומה

20 The cherubim shall have their wings spread out above, shielding the cover with their wings. They shall confront each other, the faces of the cherubim being turned toward the cover.

כ וְהָיוּ הַכְּרֻבִים פֹּרְשֵׂי כְנָפַיִם לְמַעְלָה סֹכְכִים בְּכַנְפֵיהֶם עַל־הַכַּפֹּרֶת וּפְנֵיהֶם אִישׁ אֶל־אָחִיו אֶל־הַכַּפֹּרֶת יִהְיוּ פְּנֵי הַכְּרֻבִים׃

21 Place the cover on top of the *Aron*, after depositing inside the *Aron* the Pact that I will give you.

כא וְנָתַתָּ אֶת־הַכַּפֹּרֶת עַל־הָאָרֹן מִלְמָעְלָה וְאֶל־הָאָרֹן תִּתֵּן אֶת־הָעֵדֻת אֲשֶׁר אֶתֵּן אֵלֶיךָ׃

22 There I will meet with you, and I will impart to you – from above the cover, from between the two cherubim that are on top of the *Aron HaBrit* – all that I will command you concerning *B'nei Yisrael*.

כב וְנוֹעַדְתִּי לְךָ שָׁם וְדִבַּרְתִּי אִתְּךָ מֵעַל הַכַּפֹּרֶת מִבֵּין שְׁנֵי הַכְּרֻבִים אֲשֶׁר עַל־אֲרֹן הָעֵדֻת אֵת כָּל־אֲשֶׁר אֲצַוֶּה אוֹתְךָ אֶל־בְּנֵי יִשְׂרָאֵל׃

23 You shall make a table of acacia wood, two *amot* long, one *amah* wide, and an *amah* and a half high.

כג וְעָשִׂיתָ שֻׁלְחָן עֲצֵי שִׁטִּים אַמָּתַיִם אָרְכּוֹ וְאַמָּה רָחְבּוֹ וְאַמָּה וָחֵצִי קֹמָתוֹ׃

24 Overlay it with pure gold, and make a gold molding around it.

כד וְצִפִּיתָ אֹתוֹ זָהָב טָהוֹר וְעָשִׂיתָ לּוֹ זֵר זָהָב סָבִיב׃

25 Make a rim of a hand's breadth around it, and make a gold molding for its rim round about.

כה וְעָשִׂיתָ לּוֹ מִסְגֶּרֶת טֹפַח סָבִיב וְעָשִׂיתָ זֵר־זָהָב לְמִסְגַּרְתּוֹ סָבִיב׃

26 Make four gold rings for it, and attach the rings to the four corners at its four legs.

כו וְעָשִׂיתָ לּוֹ אַרְבַּע טַבְּעֹת זָהָב וְנָתַתָּ אֶת־הַטַּבָּעֹת עַל אַרְבַּע הַפֵּאֹת אֲשֶׁר לְאַרְבַּע רַגְלָיו׃

27 The rings shall be next to the rim, as holders for poles to carry the table.

כז לְעֻמַּת הַמִּסְגֶּרֶת תִּהְיֶיןָ הַטַּבָּעֹת לְבָתִּים לְבַדִּים לָשֵׂאת אֶת־הַשֻּׁלְחָן׃

28 Make the poles of acacia wood, and overlay them with gold; by these the table shall be carried.

כח וְעָשִׂיתָ אֶת־הַבַּדִּים עֲצֵי שִׁטִּים וְצִפִּיתָ אֹתָם זָהָב וְנִשָּׂא־בָם אֶת־הַשֻּׁלְחָן׃

29 Make its bowls, ladles, jars and jugs with which to offer libations; make them of pure gold.

כט וְעָשִׂיתָ קְּעָרֹתָיו וְכַפֹּתָיו וּקְשׂוֹתָיו וּמְנַקִּיֹּתָיו אֲשֶׁר יֻסַּךְ בָּהֵן זָהָב טָהוֹר תַּעֲשֶׂה אֹתָם׃

30 And on the table you shall set the bread of display, to be before Me always.

ל וְנָתַתָּ עַל־הַשֻּׁלְחָן לֶחֶם פָּנִים לְפָנַי תָּמִיד׃

31 You shall make a *menorah* of pure gold; the *menorah* shall be made of hammered work; its base and its shaft, its cups, calyxes, and petals shall be of one piece.

לא וְעָשִׂיתָ מְנֹרַת זָהָב טָהוֹר מִקְשָׁה תֵּעָשֶׂה הַמְּנוֹרָה יְרֵכָהּ וְקָנָהּ גְּבִיעֶיהָ כַּפְתֹּרֶיהָ וּפְרָחֶיהָ מִמֶּנָּה יִהְיוּ׃

32 Six branches shall issue from its sides; three branches from one side of the *menorah* and three branches from the other side of the *menorah*.

לב וְשִׁשָּׁה קָנִים יֹצְאִים מִצִּדֶּיהָ שְׁלֹשָׁה קְנֵי מְנֹרָה מִצִּדָּהּ הָאֶחָד וּשְׁלֹשָׁה קְנֵי מְנֹרָה מִצִּדָּהּ הַשֵּׁנִי׃

33 On one branch there shall be three cups shaped like almond-blossoms, each with calyx and petals, and on the next branch there shall be three cups shaped like almond-blossoms, each with calyx and petals; so for all six branches issuing from the *menorah*.

לג שְׁלֹשָׁה גְבִעִים מְשֻׁקָּדִים בַּקָּנֶה הָאֶחָד כַּפְתֹּר וָפֶרַח וּשְׁלֹשָׁה גְבִעִים מְשֻׁקָּדִים בַּקָּנֶה הָאֶחָד כַּפְתֹּר וָפָרַח כֵּן לְשֵׁשֶׁת הַקָּנִים הַיֹּצְאִים מִן־הַמְּנֹרָה׃

Shemot/Exodus 26
Terumah

שמות כו
תרומה

34 And on the *menorah* itself there shall be four cups shaped like almond-blossoms, each with calyx and petals:

לד וּבַמְּנֹרָה אַרְבָּעָה גְבִעִים מְשֻׁקָּדִים כַּפְתֹּרֶיהָ וּפְרָחֶיהָ:

35 a calyx, of one piece with it, under a pair of branches; and a calyx, of one piece with it, under the second pair of branches, and a calyx, of one piece with it, under the last pair of branches; so for all six branches issuing from the *menorah*.

לה וְכַפְתֹּר תַּחַת שְׁנֵי הַקָּנִים מִמֶּנָּה וְכַפְתֹּר תַּחַת שְׁנֵי הַקָּנִים מִמֶּנָּה וְכַפְתֹּר תַּחַת־שְׁנֵי הַקָּנִים מִמֶּנָּה לְשֵׁשֶׁת הַקָּנִים הַיֹּצְאִים מִן־הַמְּנֹרָה:

36 Their calyxes and their stems shall be of one piece with it, the whole of it a single hammered piece of pure gold.

לו כַּפְתֹּרֵיהֶם וּקְנֹתָם מִמֶּנָּה יִהְיוּ כֻּלָּהּ מִקְשָׁה אַחַת זָהָב טָהוֹר:

37 Make its seven lamps – the lamps shall be so mounted as to give the light on its front side

לז וְעָשִׂיתָ אֶת־נֵרֹתֶיהָ שִׁבְעָה וְהֶעֱלָה אֶת־נֵרֹתֶיהָ וְהֵאִיר עַל־עֵבֶר פָּנֶיהָ:

38 and its tongs and fire pans of pure gold.

לח וּמַלְקָחֶיהָ וּמַחְתֹּתֶיהָ זָהָב טָהוֹר:

39 It shall be made, with all these furnishings, out of a *kikar* of pure gold.

לט כִּכַּר זָהָב טָהוֹר יַעֲשֶׂה אֹתָהּ אֵת כָּל־הַכֵּלִים הָאֵלֶּה:

40 Note well, and follow the patterns for them that are being shown you on the mountain.

מ וּרְאֵה וַעֲשֵׂה בְּתַבְנִיתָם אֲשֶׁר־אַתָּה מָרְאֶה בָּהָר:

26

1 As for the *Mishkan*, make it of ten strips of cloth; make these of fine twisted linen, of blue, purple, and crimson yarns, with a design of cherubim worked into them.

א וְאֶת־הַמִּשְׁכָּן תַּעֲשֶׂה עֶשֶׂר יְרִיעֹת שֵׁשׁ מָשְׁזָר וּתְכֵלֶת וְאַרְגָּמָן וְתֹלַעַת שָׁנִי כְּרֻבִים מַעֲשֵׂה חֹשֵׁב תַּעֲשֶׂה אֹתָם:

2 The length of each cloth shall be twenty-eight *amot*, and the width of each cloth shall be four *amot*, all the cloths to have the same measurements.

ב אֹרֶךְ הַיְרִיעָה הָאַחַת שְׁמֹנֶה וְעֶשְׂרִים בָּאַמָּה וְרֹחַב אַרְבַּע בָּאַמָּה הַיְרִיעָה הָאֶחָת מִדָּה אַחַת לְכָל־הַיְרִיעֹת:

3 Five of the cloths shall be joined to one another, and the other five cloths shall be joined to one another.

ג חֲמֵשׁ הַיְרִיעֹת תִּהְיֶיןָ חֹבְרֹת אִשָּׁה אֶל־אֲחֹתָהּ וְחָמֵשׁ יְרִיעֹת חֹבְרֹת אִשָּׁה אֶל־אֲחֹתָהּ:

4 Make loops of blue wool on the edge of the outermost cloth of the one set; and do likewise on the edge of the outermost cloth of the other set:

ד וְעָשִׂיתָ לֻלְאֹת תְּכֵלֶת עַל שְׂפַת הַיְרִיעָה הָאֶחָת מִקָּצָה בַּחֹבָרֶת וְכֵן תַּעֲשֶׂה בִּשְׂפַת הַיְרִיעָה הַקִּיצוֹנָה בַּמַּחְבֶּרֶת הַשֵּׁנִית:

5 make fifty loops on the one cloth, and fifty loops on the edge of the end cloth of the other set, the loops to be opposite one another.

ה חֲמִשִּׁים לֻלָאֹת תַּעֲשֶׂה בַּיְרִיעָה הָאֶחָת וַחֲמִשִּׁים לֻלָאֹת תַּעֲשֶׂה בִּקְצֵה הַיְרִיעָה אֲשֶׁר בַּמַּחְבֶּרֶת הַשֵּׁנִית מַקְבִּילֹת הַלֻּלָאֹת אִשָּׁה אֶל־אֲחֹתָהּ:

6 And make fifty gold clasps, and couple the cloths to one another with the clasps, so that the *Mishkan* becomes one whole.

ו וְעָשִׂיתָ חֲמִשִּׁים קַרְסֵי זָהָב וְחִבַּרְתָּ אֶת־הַיְרִיעֹת אִשָּׁה אֶל־אֲחֹתָהּ בַּקְּרָסִים וְהָיָה הַמִּשְׁכָּן אֶחָד:

7 You shall then make cloths of goats' hair for a tent over the *Mishkan*; make the cloths eleven in number.

ז וְעָשִׂיתָ יְרִיעֹת עִזִּים לְאֹהֶל עַל־הַמִּשְׁכָּן עַשְׁתֵּי־עֶשְׂרֵה יְרִיעֹת תַּעֲשֶׂה אֹתָם:

200

Shemot/Exodus 26
Terumah

שמות כו
תרומה

8 The length of each cloth shall be thirty *amot*, and the width of each cloth shall be four *amot*, the eleven cloths to have the same measurements.

אֹ֗רֶךְ הַיְרִיעָ֣ה הָֽאַחַ֗ת שְׁלֹשִׁים֙ בָּֽאַמָּ֔ה וְרֹ֙חַב֙ אַרְבַּ֣ע בָּֽאַמָּ֔ה הַיְרִיעָ֖ה הָֽאֶחָ֑ת מִדָּ֣ה אַחַ֔ת לְעַשְׁתֵּ֥י עֶשְׂרֵ֖ה יְרִיעֹֽת:

9 Join five of the cloths by themselves, and the other six cloths by themselves; and fold over the sixth cloth at the front of the tent.

וְחִבַּרְתָּ֞ אֶת־חֲמֵ֤שׁ הַיְרִיעֹת֙ לְבָ֔ד וְאֶת־שֵׁ֥שׁ הַיְרִיעֹ֖ת לְבָ֑ד וְכָֽפַלְתָּ֙ אֶת־הַיְרִיעָ֣ה הַשִּׁשִּׁ֔ית אֶל־מ֖וּל פְּנֵ֥י הָאֹֽהֶל:

10 Make fifty loops on the edge of the outermost cloth of the one set, and fifty loops on the edge of the cloth of the other set.

וְעָשִׂ֜יתָ חֲמִשִּׁ֣ים לֻֽלָאֹ֗ת עַ֣ל שְׂפַ֤ת הַיְרִיעָה֙ הָֽאֶחָ֔ת הַקִּֽיצֹנָ֖ה בַּֽחֹבָ֑רֶת וַֽחֲמִשִּׁ֣ים לֻֽלָאֹ֗ת עַ֚ל שְׂפַ֣ת הַיְרִיעָ֔ה הַֽחֹבֶ֖רֶת הַשֵּׁנִֽית:

11 Make fifty copper clasps, and fit the clasps into the loops, and couple the tent together so that it becomes one whole.

וְעָשִׂ֛יתָ קַרְסֵ֥י נְחֹ֖שֶׁת חֲמִשִּׁ֑ים וְהֵֽבֵאתָ֤ אֶת־הַקְּרָסִים֙ בַּלֻּ֣לָאֹ֔ת וְחִבַּרְתָּ֥ אֶת־הָאֹ֖הֶל וְהָיָ֥ה אֶחָֽד:

12 As for the overlapping excess of the cloths of the tent, the extra half-cloth shall overlap the back of the *Mishkan*,

וְסֶ֙רַח֙ הָֽעֹדֵ֔ף בִּֽירִיעֹ֖ת הָאֹ֑הֶל חֲצִ֤י הַיְרִיעָה֙ הָֽעֹדֶ֔פֶת תִּסְרַ֕ח עַ֖ל אֲחֹרֵ֥י הַמִּשְׁכָּֽן:

13 while the extra *amah* at either end of each length of tent cloth shall hang down to the bottom of the two sides of the *Mishkan* and cover it.

וְהָֽאַמָּ֨ה מִזֶּ֜ה וְהָֽאַמָּ֤ה מִזֶּה֙ בָּֽעֹדֵ֔ף בְּאֹ֖רֶךְ יְרִיעֹ֣ת הָאֹ֑הֶל יִֽהְיֶ֨ה סָר֜וּחַ עַל־צִדֵּ֧י הַמִּשְׁכָּ֛ן מִזֶּ֥ה וּמִזֶּ֖ה לְכַסֹּתֽוֹ:

14 And make for the tent a covering of tanned ram skins, and a covering of dolphin skins above.

וְעָשִׂ֤יתָ מִכְסֶה֙ לָאֹ֔הֶל עֹרֹ֥ת אֵילִ֖ם מְאָדָּמִ֑ים וּמִכְסֵ֛ה עֹרֹ֥ת תְּחָשִׁ֖ים מִלְמָֽעְלָה:

15 You shall make the planks for the *Mishkan* of acacia wood, upright.

וְעָשִׂ֥יתָ אֶת־הַקְּרָשִׁ֖ים לַמִּשְׁכָּ֑ן עֲצֵ֥י שִׁטִּ֖ים עֹֽמְדִֽים:

v'-a-SEE-ta et ha-k'-ra-SHEEM la-mish-KAN a-TZAY shi-TEEM o-m'-DEEM

16 The length of each plank shall be ten *amot* and the width of each plank an *amah* and a half.

עֶ֥שֶׂר אַמּ֖וֹת אֹ֣רֶךְ הַקָּ֑רֶשׁ וְאַמָּה֙ וַֽחֲצִ֣י הָֽאַמָּ֔ה רֹ֖חַב הַקֶּ֥רֶשׁ הָֽאֶחָֽד:

17 Each plank shall have two tenons, parallel to each other; do the same with all the planks of the *Mishkan*.

שְׁתֵּ֣י יָד֗וֹת לַקֶּ֙רֶשׁ֙ הָֽאֶחָ֔ד מְשֻׁלָּבֹ֔ת אִשָּׁ֖ה אֶל־אֲחֹתָ֑הּ כֵּ֣ן תַּֽעֲשֶׂ֔ה לְכֹ֖ל קַרְשֵׁ֥י הַמִּשְׁכָּֽן:

Acacia tree growing in the Negev

26:15 You shall make the planks Why is the definite article 'the' used in reference to the planks used in the construction of the *Mishkan*? Rashi answers that this refers to specific planks with great significance. He cites the tradition that *Yaakov* planted acacia trees in Egypt in preparation for the redemption, and commanded his sons to take these trees with them upon exiting Egypt hundreds of years in the future. In this way, *Yaakov* was not only preparing the materials for the future building of the *Mishkan*, but also imparting a message, teaching the coming generations of his descendants that their exile is temporary. Later in history, throughout the bitter exile, the children of *Yaakov* have similarly longed continuously and prepared for their redemption and return to their homeland. How fortunate are we to witness the beginning of this final redemption.

Shemot/Exodus 26
Terumah

שמות כו
תרומה

18 Of the planks of the *Mishkan*, make twenty planks on the south side:

יח וְעָשִׂיתָ אֶת־הַקְּרָשִׁים לַמִּשְׁכָּן עֶשְׂרִים קֶרֶשׁ לִפְאַת נֶגְבָּה תֵימָנָה׃

19 making forty silver sockets under the twenty planks, two sockets under the one plank for its two tenons and two sockets under each following plank for its two tenons;

יט וְאַרְבָּעִים אַדְנֵי־כֶסֶף תַּעֲשֶׂה תַּחַת עֶשְׂרִים הַקָּרֶשׁ שְׁנֵי אֲדָנִים תַּחַת־הַקֶּרֶשׁ הָאֶחָד לִשְׁתֵּי יְדֹתָיו וּשְׁנֵי אֲדָנִים תַּחַת־הַקֶּרֶשׁ הָאֶחָד לִשְׁתֵּי יְדֹתָיו׃

20 and for the other side wall of the *Mishkan*, on the north side, twenty planks.

כ וּלְצֶלַע הַמִּשְׁכָּן הַשֵּׁנִית לִפְאַת צָפוֹן עֶשְׂרִים קָרֶשׁ׃

21 with forty silver sockets, two sockets under the one plank and two sockets under each following plank.

כא וְאַרְבָּעִים אַדְנֵיהֶם כָּסֶף שְׁנֵי אֲדָנִים תַּחַת הַקֶּרֶשׁ הָאֶחָד וּשְׁנֵי אֲדָנִים תַּחַת הַקֶּרֶשׁ הָאֶחָד׃

22 And for the rear of the *Mishkan*, to the west, make six planks;

כב וּלְיַרְכְּתֵי הַמִּשְׁכָּן יָמָּה תַּעֲשֶׂה שִׁשָּׁה קְרָשִׁים׃

23 and make two planks for the corners of the *Mishkan* at the rear.

כג וּשְׁנֵי קְרָשִׁים תַּעֲשֶׂה לִמְקֻצְעֹת הַמִּשְׁכָּן בַּיַּרְכָתָיִם׃

24 They shall match at the bottom, and terminate alike at the top inside one ring; thus shall it be with both of them: they shall form the two corners.

כד וְיִהְיוּ תֹאֲמִם מִלְּמַטָּה וְיַחְדָּו יִהְיוּ תַמִּים עַל־רֹאשׁוֹ אֶל־הַטַּבַּעַת הָאֶחָת כֵּן יִהְיֶה לִשְׁנֵיהֶם לִשְׁנֵי הַמִּקְצֹעֹת יִהְיוּ׃

25 Thus there shall be eight planks with their sockets of silver: sixteen sockets, two sockets under the first plank, and two sockets under each of the other planks.

כה וְהָיוּ שְׁמֹנָה קְרָשִׁים וְאַדְנֵיהֶם כֶּסֶף שִׁשָּׁה עָשָׂר אֲדָנִים שְׁנֵי אֲדָנִים תַּחַת הַקֶּרֶשׁ הָאֶחָד וּשְׁנֵי אֲדָנִים תַּחַת הַקֶּרֶשׁ הָאֶחָד׃

26 You shall make bars of acacia wood: five for the planks of the one side wall of the *Mishkan*,

כו וְעָשִׂיתָ בְרִיחִם עֲצֵי שִׁטִּים חֲמִשָּׁה לְקַרְשֵׁי צֶלַע־הַמִּשְׁכָּן הָאֶחָד׃

27 five bars for the planks of the other side wall of the *Mishkan*, and five bars for the planks of the wall of the *Mishkan* at the rear to the west.

כז וַחֲמִשָּׁה בְרִיחִם לְקַרְשֵׁי צֶלַע־הַמִּשְׁכָּן הַשֵּׁנִית וַחֲמִשָּׁה בְרִיחִם לְקַרְשֵׁי צֶלַע הַמִּשְׁכָּן לַיַּרְכָתַיִם יָמָּה׃

28 The center bar halfway up the planks shall run from end to end.

כח וְהַבְּרִיחַ הַתִּיכֹן בְּתוֹךְ הַקְּרָשִׁים מַבְרִחַ מִן־הַקָּצֶה אֶל־הַקָּצֶה׃

29 Overlay the planks with gold, and make their rings of gold, as holders for the bars; and overlay the bars with gold.

כט וְאֶת־הַקְּרָשִׁים תְּצַפֶּה זָהָב וְאֶת־טַבְּעֹתֵיהֶם תַּעֲשֶׂה זָהָב בָּתִּים לַבְּרִיחִם וְצִפִּיתָ אֶת־הַבְּרִיחִם זָהָב׃

30 Then set up the *Mishkan* according to the manner of it that you were shown on the mountain.

ל וַהֲקֵמֹתָ אֶת־הַמִּשְׁכָּן כְּמִשְׁפָּטוֹ אֲשֶׁר הָרְאֵיתָ בָּהָר׃

31 You shall make a curtain of blue, purple, and crimson yarns, and fine twisted linen; it shall have a design of cherubim worked into it.

לא וְעָשִׂיתָ פָרֹכֶת תְּכֵלֶת וְאַרְגָּמָן וְתוֹלַעַת שָׁנִי וְשֵׁשׁ מָשְׁזָר מַעֲשֵׂה חֹשֵׁב יַעֲשֶׂה אֹתָהּ כְּרֻבִים׃

Shemot/Exodus 27
Terumah

32 Hang it upon four posts of acacia wood overlaid with gold and having hooks of gold, [set] in four sockets of silver.

33 Hang the curtain under the clasps, and carry the *Aron HaBrit* there, behind the curtain, so that the curtain shall serve you as a partition between the Holy and the Holy of Holies.

34 Place the cover upon the *Aron HaBrit* in the Holy of Holies.

35 Place the table outside the curtain, and the *menorah* by the south wall of the *Mishkan* opposite the table, which is to be placed by the north wall.

36 You shall make a screen for the entrance of the Tent, of blue, purple, and crimson yarns, and fine twisted linen, done in embroidery.

37 Make five posts of acacia wood for the screen and overlay them with gold – their hooks being of gold – and cast for them five sockets of copper.

27 1 You shall make the *Mizbayach* of acacia wood, five *amot* long and five *amot* wide – the *Mizbayach* is to be square – and three *amot* high.

2 Make its horns on the four corners, the horns to be of one piece with it; and overlay it with copper.

3 Make the pails for removing its ashes, as well as its scrapers, basins, flesh hooks, and fire pans – make all its utensils of copper.

4 Make for it a grating of meshwork in copper; and on the mesh make four copper rings at its four corners.

5 Set the mesh below, under the ledge of the *Mizbayach*, so that it extends to the middle of the *Mizbayach*.

6 And make poles for the *Mizbayach*, poles of acacia wood, and overlay them with copper.

7 The poles shall be inserted into the rings, so that the poles remain on the two sides of the *Mizbayach* when it is carried.

שמות כז
תרומה

לב וְנָתַתָּה אֹתָהּ עַל־אַרְבָּעָה עַמּוּדֵי שִׁטִּים מְצֻפִּים זָהָב וָוֵיהֶם זָהָב עַל־אַרְבָּעָה אַדְנֵי־כָסֶף:

לג וְנָתַתָּה אֶת־הַפָּרֹכֶת תַּחַת הַקְּרָסִים וְהֵבֵאתָ שָׁמָּה מִבֵּית לַפָּרֹכֶת אֵת אֲרוֹן הָעֵדוּת וְהִבְדִּילָה הַפָּרֹכֶת לָכֶם בֵּין הַקֹּדֶשׁ וּבֵין קֹדֶשׁ הַקֳּדָשִׁים:

לד וְנָתַתָּ אֶת־הַכַּפֹּרֶת עַל אֲרוֹן הָעֵדֻת בְּקֹדֶשׁ הַקֳּדָשִׁים:

לה וְשַׂמְתָּ אֶת־הַשֻּׁלְחָן מִחוּץ לַפָּרֹכֶת וְאֶת־הַמְּנֹרָה נֹכַח הַשֻּׁלְחָן עַל צֶלַע הַמִּשְׁכָּן תֵּימָנָה וְהַשֻּׁלְחָן תִּתֵּן עַל־צֶלַע צָפוֹן:

לו וְעָשִׂיתָ מָסָךְ לְפֶתַח הָאֹהֶל תְּכֵלֶת וְאַרְגָּמָן וְתוֹלַעַת שָׁנִי וְשֵׁשׁ מָשְׁזָר מַעֲשֵׂה רֹקֵם:

לז וְעָשִׂיתָ לַמָּסָךְ חֲמִשָּׁה עַמּוּדֵי שִׁטִּים וְצִפִּיתָ אֹתָם זָהָב וָוֵיהֶם זָהָב וְיָצַקְתָּ לָהֶם חֲמִשָּׁה אַדְנֵי נְחֹשֶׁת:

כז א וְעָשִׂיתָ אֶת־הַמִּזְבֵּחַ עֲצֵי שִׁטִּים חָמֵשׁ אַמּוֹת אֹרֶךְ וְחָמֵשׁ אַמּוֹת רֹחַב רָבוּעַ יִהְיֶה הַמִּזְבֵּחַ וְשָׁלֹשׁ אַמּוֹת קֹמָתוֹ:

ב וְעָשִׂיתָ קַרְנֹתָיו עַל אַרְבַּע פִּנֹּתָיו מִמֶּנּוּ תִּהְיֶיןָ קַרְנֹתָיו וְצִפִּיתָ אֹתוֹ נְחֹשֶׁת:

ג וְעָשִׂיתָ סִּירֹתָיו לְדַשְּׁנוֹ וְיָעָיו וּמִזְרְקֹתָיו וּמִזְלְגֹתָיו וּמַחְתֹּתָיו לְכָל־כֵּלָיו תַּעֲשֶׂה נְחֹשֶׁת:

ד וְעָשִׂיתָ לּוֹ מִכְבָּר מַעֲשֵׂה רֶשֶׁת נְחֹשֶׁת וְעָשִׂיתָ עַל־הָרֶשֶׁת אַרְבַּע טַבְּעֹת נְחֹשֶׁת עַל אַרְבַּע קְצוֹתָיו:

ה וְנָתַתָּה אֹתָהּ תַּחַת כַּרְכֹּב הַמִּזְבֵּחַ מִלְּמָטָּה וְהָיְתָה הָרֶשֶׁת עַד חֲצִי הַמִּזְבֵּחַ:

ו וְעָשִׂיתָ בַדִּים לַמִּזְבֵּחַ בַּדֵּי עֲצֵי שִׁטִּים וְצִפִּיתָ אֹתָם נְחֹשֶׁת:

ז וְהוּבָא אֶת־בַּדָּיו בַּטַּבָּעֹת וְהָיוּ הַבַּדִּים עַל־שְׁתֵּי צַלְעֹת הַמִּזְבֵּחַ בִּשְׂאֵת אֹתוֹ:

Shemot/Exodus 27
Terumah

שמות כז
תרומה

8 Make it hollow, of boards. As you were shown on the mountain, so shall they be made.

נְבוּב לֻחֹת תַּעֲשֶׂה אֹתוֹ כַּאֲשֶׁר הֶרְאָה אֹתְךָ בָּהָר כֵּן יַעֲשׂוּ: ח

n'-VUV lu-KHOT ta-a-SEH o-TO ka-a-SHER her-AH o-t'-KHA ba-HAR KAYN ya-a-SU

9 You shall make the enclosure of the *Mishkan*: On the south side, a hundred *amot* of hangings of fine twisted linen for the length of the enclosure on that side

וְעָשִׂיתָ אֵת חֲצַר הַמִּשְׁכָּן לִפְאַת נֶגֶב־תֵּימָנָה קְלָעִים לֶחָצֵר שֵׁשׁ מָשְׁזָר מֵאָה בָאַמָּה אֹרֶךְ לַפֵּאָה הָאֶחָת: ט

10 with its twenty posts and their twenty sockets of copper, the hooks and bands of the posts to be of silver.

וְעַמֻּדָיו עֶשְׂרִים וְאַדְנֵיהֶם עֶשְׂרִים נְחֹשֶׁת וָוֵי הָעַמֻּדִים וַחֲשֻׁקֵיהֶם כָּסֶף: י

11 Again a hundred *amot* of hangings for its length along the north side – with its twenty posts and their twenty sockets of copper, the hooks and bands of the posts to be of silver.

וְכֵן לִפְאַת צָפוֹן בָּאֹרֶךְ קְלָעִים מֵאָה אֹרֶךְ וְעַמֻּדוֹ [וְעַמּוּדָיו] עֶשְׂרִים וְאַדְנֵיהֶם עֶשְׂרִים נְחֹשֶׁת וָוֵי הָעַמֻּדִים וַחֲשֻׁקֵיהֶם כָּסֶף: יא

12 For the width of the enclosure, on the west side, fifty *amot* of hangings, with their ten posts and their ten sockets.

וְרֹחַב הֶחָצֵר לִפְאַת־יָם קְלָעִים חֲמִשִּׁים אַמָּה עַמֻּדֵיהֶם עֲשָׂרָה וְאַדְנֵיהֶם עֲשָׂרָה: יב

13 For the width of the enclosure on the front, or east side, fifty *amot*:

וְרֹחַב הֶחָצֵר לִפְאַת קֵדְמָה מִזְרָחָה חֲמִשִּׁים אַמָּה: יג

14 fifteen *amot* of hangings on the one flank, with their three posts and their three sockets;

וַחֲמֵשׁ עֶשְׂרֵה אַמָּה קְלָעִים לַכָּתֵף עַמֻּדֵיהֶם שְׁלֹשָׁה וְאַדְנֵיהֶם שְׁלֹשָׁה: יד

15 fifteen *amot* of hangings on the other flank, with their three posts and their three sockets;

וְלַכָּתֵף הַשֵּׁנִית חֲמֵשׁ עֶשְׂרֵה קְלָעִים עַמֻּדֵיהֶם שְׁלֹשָׁה וְאַדְנֵיהֶם שְׁלֹשָׁה: טו

16 and for the gate of the enclosure, a screen of twenty *amot*, of blue, purple, and crimson yarns, and fine twisted linen, done in embroidery, with their four posts and their four sockets.

וּלְשַׁעַר הֶחָצֵר מָסָךְ עֶשְׂרִים אַמָּה תְּכֵלֶת וְאַרְגָּמָן וְתוֹלַעַת שָׁנִי וְשֵׁשׁ מָשְׁזָר מַעֲשֵׂה רֹקֵם עַמֻּדֵיהֶם אַרְבָּעָה וְאַדְנֵיהֶם אַרְבָּעָה: טז

17 All the posts round the enclosure shall be banded with silver and their hooks shall be of silver; their sockets shall be of copper.

כָּל־עַמּוּדֵי הֶחָצֵר סָבִיב מְחֻשָּׁקִים כֶּסֶף וָוֵיהֶם כָּסֶף וְאַדְנֵיהֶם נְחֹשֶׁת: יז

18 The length of the enclosure shall be a hundred *amot*, and the width fifty throughout; and the height five *amot* – [with hangings] of fine twisted linen. The sockets shall be of copper:

אֹרֶךְ הֶחָצֵר מֵאָה בָאַמָּה וְרֹחַב חֲמִשִּׁים בַּחֲמִשִּׁים וְקֹמָה חָמֵשׁ אַמּוֹת שֵׁשׁ מָשְׁזָר וְאַדְנֵיהֶם נְחֹשֶׁת: יח

27:8 Hollow, of boards The altar is constructed from hollow boards that are filled with earth whenever the Israelites camp and reassemble the *Mishkan* in the desert. Only once the nation reaches *Eretz Yisrael* is a permanent, solid altar of stone constructed. These hollow planks reflect the transitory life of the Israelites in the desert. Only once they reach the Land of Israel can they finally settle into their permanent home. This is a timeless message to Jews in exile: Life outside of Israel should be seen as temporary, and homes and businesses should be built accordingly. The Land of Israel is the only truly permanent home for the People of Israel.

Shemot/Exodus 28
Tetzaveh

שמות כח
תצוה

19 all the utensils of the *Mishkan*, for all its service, as well as all its pegs and all the pegs of the court, shall be of copper.

לְכֹל כְּלֵי הַמִּשְׁכָּן בְּכֹל עֲבֹדָתוֹ וְכָל־יְתֵדֹתָיו וְכָל־יִתְדֹת הֶחָצֵר נְחֹשֶׁת:

20 You shall further instruct the Israelites to bring you clear oil of beaten olives for lighting, for kindling lamps regularly.

וְאַתָּה תְּצַוֶּה אֶת־בְּנֵי יִשְׂרָאֵל וְיִקְחוּ אֵלֶיךָ שֶׁמֶן זַיִת זָךְ כָּתִית לַמָּאוֹר לְהַעֲלֹת נֵר תָּמִיד:

21 *Aharon* and his sons shall set them up in the Tent of Meeting, outside the curtain which is over [the *Aron* of] the Pact, [to burn] from evening to morning before *Hashem*. It shall be a due from the Israelites for all time, throughout the ages.

בְּאֹהֶל מוֹעֵד מִחוּץ לַפָּרֹכֶת אֲשֶׁר עַל־הָעֵדֻת יַעֲרֹךְ אֹתוֹ אַהֲרֹן וּבָנָיו מֵעֶרֶב עַד־בֹּקֶר לִפְנֵי יְהוָה חֻקַּת עוֹלָם לְדֹרֹתָם מֵאֵת בְּנֵי יִשְׂרָאֵל:

28

1 You shall bring forward your brother *Aharon*, with his sons, from among the Israelites, to serve Me as *Kohanim*: *Aharon*, *Nadav* and *Avihu*, *Elazar* and *Itamar*, the sons of *Aharon*.

וְאַתָּה הַקְרֵב אֵלֶיךָ אֶת־אַהֲרֹן אָחִיךָ וְאֶת־בָּנָיו אִתּוֹ מִתּוֹךְ בְּנֵי יִשְׂרָאֵל לְכַהֲנוֹ־לִי אַהֲרֹן נָדָב וַאֲבִיהוּא אֶלְעָזָר וְאִיתָמָר בְּנֵי אַהֲרֹן:

2 Make sacral vestments for your brother *Aharon*, for dignity and adornment.

וְעָשִׂיתָ בִגְדֵי־קֹדֶשׁ לְאַהֲרֹן אָחִיךָ לְכָבוֹד וּלְתִפְאָרֶת:

v'-a-SEE-ta vig-day KO-desh l'-a-ha-RON a-KHEE-kha l'-kha-VOD ul-tif-A-ret

3 Next you shall instruct all who are skillful, whom I have endowed with the gift of skill, to make *Aharon*'s vestments, for consecrating him to serve Me as *Kohen*.

וְאַתָּה תְּדַבֵּר אֶל־כָּל־חַכְמֵי־לֵב אֲשֶׁר מִלֵּאתִיו רוּחַ חָכְמָה וְעָשׂוּ אֶת־בִּגְדֵי אַהֲרֹן לְקַדְּשׁוֹ לְכַהֲנוֹ־לִי:

4 These are the vestments they are to make: a breastpiece, an ephod, a robe, a fringed tunic, a headdress, and a sash. They shall make those sacral vestments for your brother *Aharon* and his sons, for priestly service to Me;

וְאֵלֶּה הַבְּגָדִים אֲשֶׁר יַעֲשׂוּ חֹשֶׁן וְאֵפוֹד וּמְעִיל וּכְתֹנֶת תַּשְׁבֵּץ מִצְנֶפֶת וְאַבְנֵט וְעָשׂוּ בִגְדֵי־קֹדֶשׁ לְאַהֲרֹן אָחִיךָ וּלְבָנָיו לְכַהֲנוֹ־לִי:

5 they, therefore, shall receive the gold, the blue, purple, and crimson yarns, and the fine linen.

וְהֵם יִקְחוּ אֶת־הַזָּהָב וְאֶת־הַתְּכֵלֶת וְאֶת־הָאַרְגָּמָן וְאֶת־תּוֹלַעַת הַשָּׁנִי וְאֶת־הַשֵּׁשׁ:

6 They shall make the ephod of gold, of blue, purple, and crimson yarns, and of fine twisted linen, worked into designs.

וְעָשׂוּ אֶת־הָאֵפֹד זָהָב תְּכֵלֶת וְאַרְגָּמָן תּוֹלַעַת שָׁנִי וְשֵׁשׁ מָשְׁזָר מַעֲשֵׂה חֹשֵׁב:

7 It shall have two shoulder-pieces attached; they shall be attached at its two ends.

שְׁתֵּי כְתֵפֹת חֹבְרֹת יִהְיֶה־לּוֹ אֶל־שְׁנֵי קְצוֹתָיו וְחֻבָּר:

כבוד
תפארת

28:2 For dignity and adornment The verse says that the purpose of the priestly garments is for *kavod* (כבוד), 'dignity,' and *tiferet* (תפארת), 'adornment.' What is the difference between these two words? The **Malbim** explains that *kavod* is the honor a person gets for the things that are part of his inherent nature. *Tiferet*, on the other hand, is the glory one receives as a result of his own efforts and accomplishments. The special priestly garments signify both the dignity of their God-given position as well as the "adornment" of the accomplishments the priests would achieve by investing effort and energy in their elevated spiritual position.

Shemot/Exodus 28
Tetzaveh

שמות כח
תצוה

8 And the decorated band that is upon it shall be made like it, of one piece with it: of gold, of blue, purple, and crimson yarns, and of fine twisted linen.

ח וְחֵ֨שֶׁב אֲפֻדָּת֜וֹ אֲשֶׁ֧ר עָלָ֛יו כְּמַעֲשֵׂ֖הוּ מִמֶּ֣נּוּ יִהְיֶ֑ה זָהָ֗ב תְּכֵ֧לֶת וְאַרְגָּמָ֛ן וְתוֹלַ֥עַת שָׁנִ֖י וְשֵׁ֥שׁ מָשְׁזָֽר׃

9 Then take two lazuli stones and engrave on them the names of the sons of *Yisrael*:

ט וְלָ֣קַחְתָּ֔ אֶת־שְׁתֵּ֖י אַבְנֵי־שֹׁ֑הַם וּפִתַּחְתָּ֣ עֲלֵיהֶ֔ם שְׁמ֖וֹת בְּנֵ֥י יִשְׂרָאֵֽל׃

10 six of their names on the one stone, and the names of the remaining six on the other stone, in the order of their birth.

י שִׁשָּׁה֙ מִשְּׁמֹתָ֔ם עַ֖ל הָאֶ֣בֶן הָאֶחָ֑ת וְאֶת־שְׁמ֞וֹת הַשִּׁשָּׁ֧ה הַנּוֹתָרִ֛ים עַל־הָאֶ֥בֶן הַשֵּׁנִ֖ית כְּתוֹלְדֹתָֽם׃

11 On the two stones you shall make seal engravings – the work of a lapidary – of the names of the sons of *Yisrael*. Having bordered them with frames of gold,

יא מַעֲשֵׂ֣ה חָרַשׁ֘ אֶבֶן֒ פִּתּוּחֵ֣י חֹתָ֗ם תְּפַתַּח֙ אֶת־שְׁתֵּ֣י הָאֲבָנִ֔ים עַל־שְׁמֹ֖ת בְּנֵ֣י יִשְׂרָאֵ֑ל מֻסַבֹּ֛ת מִשְׁבְּצ֥וֹת זָהָ֖ב תַּעֲשֶׂ֥ה אֹתָֽם׃

12 attach the two stones to the shoulder-pieces of the ephod, as stones for remembrance of *B'nei Yisrael*, whose names *Aharon* shall carry upon his two shoulder-pieces for remembrance before *Hashem*.

יב וְשַׂמְתָּ֞ אֶת־שְׁתֵּ֣י הָאֲבָנִ֗ים עַ֚ל כִּתְפֹ֣ת הָאֵפֹ֔ד אַבְנֵ֥י זִכָּרֹ֖ן לִבְנֵ֣י יִשְׂרָאֵ֑ל וְנָשָׂא֩ אַהֲרֹ֨ן אֶת־שְׁמוֹתָ֜ם לִפְנֵ֧י יְהֹוָ֛ה עַל־שְׁתֵּ֥י כְתֵפָ֖יו לְזִכָּרֹֽן׃

13 Then make frames of gold

יג וְעָשִׂ֥יתָ מִשְׁבְּצֹ֖ת זָהָֽב׃

14 and two chains of pure gold; braid these like corded work, and fasten the corded chains to the frames.

יד וּשְׁתֵּ֤י שַׁרְשְׁרֹת֙ זָהָ֣ב טָה֔וֹר מִגְבָּלֹ֛ת תַּעֲשֶׂ֥ה אֹתָ֖ם מַעֲשֵׂ֣ה עֲבֹ֑ת וְנָתַתָּ֛ה אֶת־שַׁרְשְׁרֹ֥ת הָעֲבֹתֹ֖ת עַל־הַֽמִּשְׁבְּצֹֽת׃

15 You shall make a breastpiece of decision, worked into a design; make it in the style of the ephod: make it of gold, of blue, purple, and crimson yarns, and of fine twisted linen.

טו וְעָשִׂ֜יתָ חֹ֤שֶׁן מִשְׁפָּט֙ מַעֲשֵׂ֣ה חֹשֵׁ֔ב כְּמַעֲשֵׂ֥ה אֵפֹ֖ד תַּעֲשֶׂ֑נּוּ זָ֠הָ֠ב תְּכֵ֨לֶת וְאַרְגָּמָ֜ן וְתוֹלַ֧עַת שָׁנִ֛י וְשֵׁ֥שׁ מָשְׁזָ֖ר תַּעֲשֶׂ֥ה אֹתֽוֹ׃

16 It shall be square and doubled, a *zeret* in length and a *zeret* in width.

טז רָב֥וּעַ יִֽהְיֶ֖ה כָּפ֑וּל זֶ֥רֶת אָרְכּ֖וֹ וְזֶ֥רֶת רָחְבּֽוֹ׃

17 Set in it mounted stones, in four rows of stones. The first row shall be a row of carnelian, chrysolite, and emerald;

יז וּמִלֵּאתָ֥ ב֛וֹ מִלֻּ֥אַת אֶ֖בֶן אַרְבָּעָ֣ה טוּרִ֣ים אָ֑בֶן ט֗וּר אֹ֤דֶם פִּטְדָה֙ וּבָרֶ֔קֶת הַטּ֖וּר הָאֶחָֽד׃

18 the second row: a turquoise, a sapphire, and an amethyst;

יח וְהַטּ֖וּר הַשֵּׁנִ֑י נֹ֥פֶךְ סַפִּ֖יר וְיָהֲלֹֽם׃

19 the third row: a jacinth, an agate, and a crystal;

יט וְהַטּ֖וּר הַשְּׁלִישִׁ֑י לֶ֥שֶׁם שְׁב֖וֹ וְאַחְלָֽמָה׃

20 and the fourth row: a beryl, a lapis lazuli, and a jasper. They shall be framed with gold in their mountings.

כ וְהַטּוּר֙ הָרְבִיעִ֔י תַּרְשִׁ֥ישׁ וְשֹׁ֖הַם וְיָשְׁפֵ֑ה מְשֻׁבָּצִ֥ים זָהָ֛ב יִהְי֖וּ בְּמִלּוּאֹתָֽם׃

21 The stones shall correspond [in number] to the names of the sons of *Yisrael*: twelve, corresponding to their names. They shall be engraved like seals, each with its name, for the twelve tribes.

כא וְ֠הָאֲבָנִ֠ים תִּֽהְיֶ֜יןָ עַל־שְׁמֹ֧ת בְּנֵֽי־יִשְׂרָאֵ֛ל שְׁתֵּ֥ים עֶשְׂרֵ֖ה עַל־שְׁמֹתָ֑ם פִּתּוּחֵ֤י חוֹתָם֙ אִ֣ישׁ עַל־שְׁמ֔וֹ תִּֽהְיֶ֕יןָ לִשְׁנֵ֥י עָשָׂ֖ר שָֽׁבֶט׃

22 On the breastpiece make braided chains of corded work in pure gold.

כב וְעָשִׂ֧יתָ עַל־הַחֹ֛שֶׁן שַׁרְשֹׁ֥ת גַּבְלֻ֖ת מַעֲשֵׂ֥ה עֲבֹ֖ת זָהָ֥ב טָהֽוֹר׃

206

Shemot/Exodus 28
Tetzaveh

23 Make two rings of gold on the breastpiece, and fasten the two rings at the two ends of the breastpiece,

24 attaching the two golden cords to the two rings at the ends of the breastpiece.

25 Then fasten the two ends of the cords to the two frames, which you shall attach to the shoulder-pieces of the ephod, at the front.

26 Make two rings of gold and attach them to the two ends of the breastpiece, at its inner edge, which faces the ephod.

27 And make two other rings of gold and fasten them on the front of the ephod, low on the two shoulder-pieces, close to its seam above the decorated band.

28 The breastpiece shall be held in place by a cord of blue from its rings to the rings of the ephod, so that the breastpiece rests on the decorated band and does not come loose from the ephod.

29 Aharon shall carry the names of the sons of Yisrael on the breastpiece of decision over his heart, when he enters the sanctuary, for remembrance before Hashem at all times.

30 Inside the breastpiece of decision you shall place the Urim and Thummim, so that they are over Aharon's heart when he comes before Hashem. Thus Aharon shall carry the instrument of decision for the Israelites over his heart before Hashem at all times.

31 You shall make the robe of the ephod of pure blue.

32 The opening for the head shall be in the middle of it; the opening shall have a binding of woven work round about – it shall be like the opening of a coat of mail – so that it does not tear.

33 On its hem make pomegranates of blue, purple, and crimson yarns, all around the hem, with bells of gold between them all around:

34 a golden bell and a pomegranate, a golden bell and a pomegranate, all around the hem of the robe.

35 Aharon shall wear it while officiating, so that the sound of it is heard when he comes into the sanctuary before Hashem and when he goes out – that he may not die.

שמות כח
תצוה

כג וְעָשִׂיתָ עַל־הַחֹשֶׁן שְׁתֵּי טַבְּעוֹת זָהָב וְנָתַתָּ אֶת־שְׁתֵּי הַטַּבָּעוֹת עַל־שְׁנֵי קְצוֹת הַחֹשֶׁן:

כד וְנָתַתָּה אֶת־שְׁתֵּי עֲבֹתֹת הַזָּהָב עַל־שְׁתֵּי הַטַּבָּעֹת אֶל־קְצוֹת הַחֹשֶׁן:

כה וְאֵת שְׁתֵּי קְצוֹת שְׁתֵּי הָעֲבֹתֹת תִּתֵּן עַל־שְׁתֵּי הַמִּשְׁבְּצוֹת וְנָתַתָּה עַל־כִּתְפוֹת הָאֵפֹד אֶל־מוּל פָּנָיו:

כו וְעָשִׂיתָ שְׁתֵּי טַבְּעוֹת זָהָב וְשַׂמְתָּ אֹתָם עַל־שְׁנֵי קְצוֹת הַחֹשֶׁן עַל־שְׂפָתוֹ אֲשֶׁר אֶל־עֵבֶר הָאֵפֹד בָּיְתָה:

כז וְעָשִׂיתָ שְׁתֵּי טַבְּעוֹת זָהָב וְנָתַתָּה אֹתָם עַל־שְׁתֵּי כִתְפוֹת הָאֵפוֹד מִלְּמַטָּה מִמּוּל פָּנָיו לְעֻמַּת מֶחְבַּרְתּוֹ מִמַּעַל לְחֵשֶׁב הָאֵפוֹד:

כח וְיִרְכְּסוּ אֶת־הַחֹשֶׁן מטבעתו [מִטַּבְּעֹתָיו] אֶל־טַבְּעֹת הָאֵפֹד בִּפְתִיל תְּכֵלֶת לִהְיוֹת עַל־חֵשֶׁב הָאֵפוֹד וְלֹא־יִזַּח הַחֹשֶׁן מֵעַל הָאֵפוֹד:

כט וְנָשָׂא אַהֲרֹן אֶת־שְׁמוֹת בְּנֵי־יִשְׂרָאֵל בְּחֹשֶׁן הַמִּשְׁפָּט עַל־לִבּוֹ בְּבֹאוֹ אֶל־הַקֹּדֶשׁ לְזִכָּרֹן לִפְנֵי־יְהוָֹה תָּמִיד:

ל וְנָתַתָּ אֶל־חֹשֶׁן הַמִּשְׁפָּט אֶת־הָאוּרִים וְאֶת־הַתֻּמִּים וְהָיוּ עַל־לֵב אַהֲרֹן בְּבֹאוֹ לִפְנֵי יְהוָֹה וְנָשָׂא אַהֲרֹן אֶת־מִשְׁפַּט בְּנֵי־יִשְׂרָאֵל עַל־לִבּוֹ לִפְנֵי יְהוָֹה תָּמִיד:

לא וְעָשִׂיתָ אֶת־מְעִיל הָאֵפוֹד כְּלִיל תְּכֵלֶת:

לב וְהָיָה פִי־רֹאשׁוֹ בְּתוֹכוֹ שָׂפָה יִהְיֶה לְפִיו סָבִיב מַעֲשֵׂה אֹרֵג כְּפִי תַחְרָא יִהְיֶה־לּוֹ לֹא יִקָּרֵעַ:

לג וְעָשִׂיתָ עַל־שׁוּלָיו רִמֹּנֵי תְּכֵלֶת וְאַרְגָּמָן וְתוֹלַעַת שָׁנִי עַל־שׁוּלָיו סָבִיב וּפַעֲמֹנֵי זָהָב בְּתוֹכָם סָבִיב:

לד פַּעֲמֹן זָהָב וְרִמּוֹן פַּעֲמֹן זָהָב וְרִמּוֹן עַל־שׁוּלֵי הַמְּעִיל סָבִיב:

לה וְהָיָה עַל־אַהֲרֹן לְשָׁרֵת וְנִשְׁמַע קוֹלוֹ בְּבֹאוֹ אֶל־הַקֹּדֶשׁ לִפְנֵי יְהוָֹה וּבְצֵאתוֹ וְלֹא יָמוּת:

Shemot/Exodus 29
Tetzaveh

שמות כט
תצוה

36 You shall make a frontlet of pure gold and engrave on it the seal inscription: "Holy to *Hashem*."

לו וְעָשִׂיתָ צִּיץ זָהָב טָהוֹר וּפִתַּחְתָּ עָלָיו פִּתּוּחֵי חֹתָם קֹדֶשׁ לַיהוָה׃

37 Suspend it on a cord of blue, so that it may remain on the headdress; it shall remain on the front of the headdress.

לז וְשַׂמְתָּ אֹתוֹ עַל־פְּתִיל תְּכֵלֶת וְהָיָה עַל־הַמִּצְנָפֶת אֶל־מוּל פְּנֵי־הַמִּצְנֶפֶת יִהְיֶה׃

38 It shall be on *Aharon*'s forehead, that *Aharon* may take away any sin arising from the holy things that the Israelites consecrate, from any of their sacred donations; it shall be on his forehead at all times, to win acceptance for them before *Hashem*.

לח וְהָיָה עַל־מֵצַח אַהֲרֹן וְנָשָׂא אַהֲרֹן אֶת־עֲוֹן הַקֳּדָשִׁים אֲשֶׁר יַקְדִּישׁוּ בְּנֵי יִשְׂרָאֵל לְכָל־מַתְּנֹת קָדְשֵׁיהֶם וְהָיָה עַל־מִצְחוֹ תָּמִיד לְרָצוֹן לָהֶם לִפְנֵי יְהוָה׃

39 You shall make the fringed tunic of fine linen. You shall make the headdress of fine linen. You shall make the sash of embroidered work.

לט וְשִׁבַּצְתָּ הַכְּתֹנֶת שֵׁשׁ וְעָשִׂיתָ מִצְנֶפֶת שֵׁשׁ וְאַבְנֵט תַּעֲשֶׂה מַעֲשֵׂה רֹקֵם׃

40 And for *Aharon*'s sons also you shall make tunics, and make sashes for them, and make turbans for them, for dignity and adornment.

מ וְלִבְנֵי אַהֲרֹן תַּעֲשֶׂה כֻתֳּנֹת וְעָשִׂיתָ לָהֶם אַבְנֵטִים וּמִגְבָּעוֹת תַּעֲשֶׂה לָהֶם לְכָבוֹד וּלְתִפְאָרֶת׃

41 Put these on your brother *Aharon* and on his sons as well; anoint them, and ordain them and consecrate them to serve Me as *Kohanim*.

מא וְהִלְבַּשְׁתָּ אֹתָם אֶת־אַהֲרֹן אָחִיךָ וְאֶת־בָּנָיו אִתּוֹ וּמָשַׁחְתָּ אֹתָם וּמִלֵּאתָ אֶת־יָדָם וְקִדַּשְׁתָּ אֹתָם וְכִהֲנוּ לִי׃

42 You shall also make for them linen breeches to cover their nakedness; they shall extend from the hips to the thighs.

מב וַעֲשֵׂה לָהֶם מִכְנְסֵי־בָד לְכַסּוֹת בְּשַׂר עֶרְוָה מִמָּתְנַיִם וְעַד־יְרֵכַיִם יִהְיוּ׃

43 They shall be worn by *Aharon* and his sons when they enter the Tent of Meeting or when they approach the *Mizbayach* to officiate in the sanctuary, so that they do not incur punishment and die. It shall be a law for all time for him and for his offspring to come.

מג וְהָיוּ עַל־אַהֲרֹן וְעַל־בָּנָיו בְּבֹאָם אֶל־אֹהֶל מוֹעֵד אוֹ בְגִשְׁתָּם אֶל־הַמִּזְבֵּחַ לְשָׁרֵת בַּקֹּדֶשׁ וְלֹא־יִשְׂאוּ עָוֹן וָמֵתוּ חֻקַּת עוֹלָם לוֹ וּלְזַרְעוֹ אַחֲרָיו׃

29

1 This is what you shall do to them in consecrating them to serve Me as *Kohanim*: Take a young bull of the herd and two rams without blemish;

כט א וְזֶה הַדָּבָר אֲשֶׁר־תַּעֲשֶׂה לָהֶם לְקַדֵּשׁ אֹתָם לְכַהֵן לִי לְקַח פַּר אֶחָד בֶּן־בָּקָר וְאֵילִם שְׁנַיִם תְּמִימִם׃

v'-ZEH ha-da-VAR a-SHER ta-a-SEH la-HEM l'-ka-DAYSH o-TAM l'-kha-HAYN LEE l'-KAKH PAR e-KHAD ben ba-KAR v'-ay-LEEM sh'-NA-yim t'-mee-MIM

הדבר

29:1 This is what you shall do to them This verse starts with the words *v'zeh hadavar asher ta'aseh lahem* (וזה הדבר אשר תעשה להם), 'this is what you shall do to them.' In the context of this verse, the Hebrew word *hadavar* (הדבר) means 'the thing.' However, *hadavar* can also mean 'the word.' According to the Sages, the use of this term in the chapter describing the inauguration ritual of the *Mishkan* alludes to an important lesson. *Hashem* is not found exclusively in the *Mishkan*, nor is the *Mishkan* service the only way to access Him. Even when there is no longer a Holy Temple and sacrifices are not brought, *Hashem* is still accessible through words, the words of our prayers.

Praying at the Western Wall

208

Shemot/Exodus 29
Tetzaveh

שמות כט
תצוה

2 also unleavened bread, unleavened cakes with oil mixed in, and unleavened wafers spread with oil – make these of choice wheat flour.

ב וְלֶ֣חֶם מַצּ֗וֹת וְחַלֹּ֤ת מַצֹּת֙ בְּלוּלֹ֣ת בַּשֶּׁ֔מֶן וּרְקִיקֵ֥י מַצּ֖וֹת מְשֻׁחִ֣ים בַּשָּׁ֑מֶן סֹ֥לֶת חִטִּ֖ים תַּעֲשֶׂ֥ה אֹתָֽם׃

3 Place these in one basket and present them in the basket, along with the bull and the two rams.

ג וְנָתַתָּ֤ אוֹתָם֙ עַל־סַ֣ל אֶחָ֔ד וְהִקְרַבְתָּ֥ אֹתָ֖ם בַּסָּ֑ל וְאֶ֨ת־הַפָּ֔ר וְאֵ֖ת שְׁנֵ֥י הָאֵילִֽם׃

4 Lead *Aharon* and his sons up to the entrance of the Tent of Meeting, and wash them with water.

ד וְאֶת־אַהֲרֹ֤ן וְאֶת־בָּנָיו֙ תַּקְרִ֔יב אֶל־פֶּ֖תַח אֹ֣הֶל מוֹעֵ֑ד וְרָחַצְתָּ֥ אֹתָ֖ם בַּמָּֽיִם׃

5 Then take the vestments, and clothe *Aharon* with the tunic, the robe of the ephod, the ephod, and the breastpiece, and gird him with the decorated band of the ephod.

ה וְלָקַחְתָּ֣ אֶת־הַבְּגָדִ֗ים וְהִלְבַּשְׁתָּ֤ אֶֽת־אַהֲרֹן֙ אֶת־הַכֻּתֹּ֔נֶת וְאֵת֙ מְעִ֣יל הָאֵפֹ֔ד וְאֶת־הָאֵפֹ֖ד וְאֶת־הַחֹ֑שֶׁן וְאָפַדְתָּ֣ ל֔וֹ בְּחֵ֖שֶׁב הָאֵפֹֽד׃

6 Put the headdress on his head, and place the holy diadem upon the headdress.

ו וְשַׂמְתָּ֥ הַמִּצְנֶ֖פֶת עַל־רֹאשׁ֑וֹ וְנָתַתָּ֛ אֶת־נֵ֥זֶר הַקֹּ֖דֶשׁ עַל־הַמִּצְנָֽפֶת׃

7 Take the anointing oil and pour it on his head and anoint him.

ז וְלָֽקַחְתָּ֙ אֶת־שֶׁ֣מֶן הַמִּשְׁחָ֔ה וְיָצַקְתָּ֖ עַל־רֹאשׁ֑וֹ וּמָשַׁחְתָּ֖ אֹתֽוֹ׃

8 Then bring his sons forward; clothe them with tunics

ח וְאֶת־בָּנָ֖יו תַּקְרִ֑יב וְהִלְבַּשְׁתָּ֖ם כֻּתֳּנֹֽת׃

9 and wind turbans upon them. And gird both *Aharon* and his sons with sashes. And so they shall have priesthood as their right for all time. You shall then ordain *Aharon* and his sons.

ט וְחָגַרְתָּ֩ אֹתָ֨ם אַבְנֵ֜ט אַהֲרֹ֣ן וּבָנָ֗יו וְחָבַשְׁתָּ֤ לָהֶם֙ מִגְבָּעֹ֔ת וְהָיְתָ֥ה לָהֶ֛ם כְּהֻנָּ֖ה לְחֻקַּ֣ת עוֹלָ֑ם וּמִלֵּאתָ֥ יַֽד־אַהֲרֹ֖ן וְיַד־בָּנָֽיו׃

10 Lead the bull up to the front of the Tent of Meeting, and let *Aharon* and his sons lay their hands upon the head of the bull.

י וְהִקְרַבְתָּ֙ אֶת־הַפָּ֔ר לִפְנֵ֖י אֹ֣הֶל מוֹעֵ֑ד וְסָמַ֨ךְ אַהֲרֹ֧ן וּבָנָ֛יו אֶת־יְדֵיהֶ֖ם עַל־רֹ֥אשׁ הַפָּֽר׃

11 Slaughter the bull before *Hashem*, at the entrance of the Tent of Meeting,

יא וְשָׁחַטְתָּ֥ אֶת־הַפָּ֖ר לִפְנֵ֣י יְהוָ֑ה פֶּ֖תַח אֹ֥הֶל מוֹעֵֽד׃

12 and take some of the bull's blood and put it on the horns of the *Mizbayach* with your finger; then pour out the rest of the blood at the base of the *Mizbayach*.

יב וְלָֽקַחְתָּ֙ מִדַּ֣ם הַפָּ֔ר וְנָתַתָּ֛ה עַל־קַרְנֹ֥ת הַמִּזְבֵּ֖חַ בְּאֶצְבָּעֶ֑ךָ וְאֶת־כָּל־הַדָּ֣ם תִּשְׁפֹּ֔ךְ אֶל־יְס֖וֹד הַמִּזְבֵּֽחַ׃

13 Take all the fat that covers the entrails, the protuberance on the liver, and the two kidneys with the fat on them, and turn them into smoke upon the *Mizbayach*.

יג וְלָֽקַחְתָּ֗ אֶֽת־כָּל־הַחֵלֶב֮ הַֽמְכַסֶּ֣ה אֶת־הַקֶּרֶב֒ וְאֵ֗ת הַיֹּתֶ֙רֶת֙ עַל־הַכָּבֵ֔ד וְאֵת֙ שְׁתֵּ֣י הַכְּלָיֹ֔ת וְאֶת־הַחֵ֖לֶב אֲשֶׁ֣ר עֲלֵיהֶ֑ן וְהִקְטַרְתָּ֖ הַמִּזְבֵּֽחָה׃

14 The rest of the flesh of the bull, its hide, and its dung shall be put to the fire outside the camp; it is a sin offering.

יד וְאֶת־בְּשַׂ֤ר הַפָּר֙ וְאֶת־עֹר֣וֹ וְאֶת־פִּרְשׁ֔וֹ תִּשְׂרֹ֣ף בָּאֵ֔שׁ מִח֖וּץ לַֽמַּחֲנֶ֑ה חַטָּ֖את הֽוּא׃

15 Next take the one ram, and let *Aharon* and his sons lay their hands upon the ram's head.

טו וְאֶת־הָאַ֥יִל הָאֶחָ֖ד תִּקָּ֑ח וְסָ֨מְכ֜וּ אַהֲרֹ֧ן וּבָנָ֛יו אֶת־יְדֵיהֶ֖ם עַל־רֹ֥אשׁ הָאָֽיִל׃

16 Slaughter the ram, and take its blood and dash it against all sides of the *Mizbayach*.

טז וְשָׁחַטְתָּ֖ אֶת־הָאָ֑יִל וְלָֽקַחְתָּ֙ אֶת־דָּמ֔וֹ וְזָרַקְתָּ֥ עַל־הַמִּזְבֵּ֖חַ סָבִֽיב׃

Shemot/Exodus 29
Tetzaveh

שמות כט
תצוה

17 Cut up the ram into sections, wash its entrails and legs, and put them with its quarters and its head.

יז וְאֶת־הָאַ֙יִל֙ תְּנַתֵּ֣חַ לִנְתָחָ֔יו וְרָחַצְתָּ֥ קִרְבּ֖וֹ וּכְרָעָ֑יו וְנָתַתָּ֥ עַל־נְתָחָ֖יו וְעַל־רֹאשֽׁוֹ׃

18 Turn all of the ram into smoke upon the *Mizbayach*. It is a burnt offering to *Hashem*, a pleasing odor, an offering by fire to *Hashem*.

יח וְהִקְטַרְתָּ֤ אֶת־כָּל־הָאַ֙יִל֙ הַמִּזְבֵּ֔חָה עֹלָ֥ה ה֖וּא לַֽיהוָ֑ה רֵ֣יחַ נִיח֔וֹחַ אִשֶּׁ֥ה לַיהוָ֖ה הֽוּא׃

19 Then take the other ram, and let *Aharon* and his sons lay their hands upon the ram's head.

יט וְלָ֣קַחְתָּ֔ אֵ֖ת הָאַ֣יִל הַשֵּׁנִ֑י וְסָמַ֨ךְ אַהֲרֹ֧ן וּבָנָ֛יו אֶת־יְדֵיהֶ֖ם עַל־רֹ֥אשׁ הָאָֽיִל׃

20 Slaughter the ram, and take some of its blood and put it on the ridge of *Aharon*'s right ear and on the ridges of his sons' right ears, and on the thumbs of their right hands, and on the big toes of their right feet; and dash the rest of the blood against every side of the *Mizbayach* round about.

כ וְשָׁחַטְתָּ֣ אֶת־הָאַ֗יִל וְלָקַחְתָּ֤ מִדָּמוֹ֙ וְנָתַתָּ֡ה עַל־תְּנוּךְ֩ אֹ֨זֶן אַהֲרֹ֜ן וְעַל־תְּנ֨וּךְ אֹ֤זֶן בָּנָיו֙ הַיְמָנִ֔ית וְעַל־בֹּ֤הֶן יָדָם֙ הַיְמָנִ֔ית וְעַל־בֹּ֥הֶן רַגְלָ֖ם הַיְמָנִ֑ית וְזָרַקְתָּ֧ אֶת־הַדָּ֛ם עַל־הַמִּזְבֵּ֖חַ סָבִֽיב׃

21 Take some of the blood that is on the *Mizbayach* and some of the anointing oil and sprinkle upon *Aharon* and his vestments, and also upon his sons and his sons' vestments. Thus shall he and his vestments be holy, as well as his sons and his sons' vestments.

כא וְלָקַחְתָּ֞ מִן־הַדָּ֨ם אֲשֶׁ֤ר עַֽל־הַמִּזְבֵּ֙חַ֙ וּמִשֶּׁ֣מֶן הַמִּשְׁחָ֔ה וְהִזֵּיתָ֥ עַֽל־אַהֲרֹ֖ן וְעַל־בְּגָדָ֑יו וְעַל־בָּנָ֛יו וְעַל־בִּגְדֵ֥י בָנָ֖יו אִתּ֑וֹ וְקָדַ֥שׁ הוּא֙ וּבְגָדָ֔יו וּבָנָ֛יו וּבִגְדֵ֥י בָנָ֖יו אִתּֽוֹ׃

22 You shall take from the ram the fat parts – the broad tail, the fat that covers the entrails, the protuberance on the liver, the two kidneys with the fat on them – and the right thigh; for this is a ram of ordination.

כב וְלָקַחְתָּ֣ מִן־הָ֠אַיִל הַחֵ֨לֶב וְהָֽאַלְיָ֜ה וְאֶת־הַחֵ֣לֶב ׀ הַֽמְכַסֶּ֣ה אֶת־הַקֶּ֗רֶב וְאֵ֨ת יֹתֶ֤רֶת הַכָּבֵד֙ וְאֵ֣ת ׀ שְׁתֵּ֣י הַכְּלָיֹ֗ת וְאֶת־הַחֵ֙לֶב֙ אֲשֶׁ֣ר עֲלֵהֶ֔ן וְאֵ֖ת שׁ֣וֹק הַיָּמִ֑ין כִּ֛י אֵ֥יל מִלֻּאִ֖ים הֽוּא׃

23 Add one flat loaf of bread, one cake of oil bread, and one wafer, from the basket of unleavened bread that is before *Hashem*.

כג וְכִכַּ֨ר לֶ֜חֶם אַחַ֗ת וְֽחַלַּ֨ת לֶ֥חֶם שֶׁ֛מֶן אַחַ֖ת וְרָקִ֣יק אֶחָ֑ד מִסַּל֙ הַמַּצּ֔וֹת אֲשֶׁ֖ר לִפְנֵ֥י יְהוָֽה׃

24 Place all these on the palms of *Aharon* and his sons, and offer them as an elevation offering before *Hashem*.

כד וְשַׂמְתָּ֣ הַכֹּ֔ל עַ֚ל כַּפֵּ֣י אַהֲרֹ֔ן וְעַ֖ל כַּפֵּ֣י בָנָ֑יו וְהֵנַפְתָּ֥ אֹתָ֛ם תְּנוּפָ֖ה לִפְנֵ֥י יְהוָֽה׃

25 Take them from their hands and turn them into smoke upon the *Mizbayach* with the burnt offering, as a pleasing odor before *Hashem*; it is an offering by fire to *Hashem*.

כה וְלָקַחְתָּ֤ אֹתָם֙ מִיָּדָ֔ם וְהִקְטַרְתָּ֥ הַמִּזְבֵּ֖חָה עַל־הָעֹלָ֑ה לְרֵ֤יחַ נִיחוֹחַ֙ לִפְנֵ֣י יְהוָ֔ה אִשֶּׁ֥ה ה֖וּא לַיהוָֽה׃

26 Then take the breast of *Aharon*'s ram of ordination and offer it as an elevation offering before *Hashem*; it shall be your portion.

כו וְלָקַחְתָּ֣ אֶת־הֶֽחָזֶ֗ה מֵאֵ֤יל הַמִּלֻּאִים֙ אֲשֶׁ֣ר לְאַהֲרֹ֔ן וְהֵנַפְתָּ֥ אֹת֛וֹ תְּנוּפָ֖ה לִפְנֵ֣י יְהוָ֑ה וְהָיָ֥ה לְךָ֖ לְמָנָֽה׃

27 You shall consecrate the breast that was offered as an elevation offering and the thigh that was offered as a gift offering from the ram of ordination – from that which was *Aharon*'s and from that which was his sons'

כז וְקִדַּשְׁתָּ֞ אֵ֣ת ׀ חֲזֵ֣ה הַתְּנוּפָ֗ה וְאֵת֙ שׁ֣וֹק הַתְּרוּמָ֔ה אֲשֶׁ֥ר הוּנַ֖ף וַאֲשֶׁ֣ר הוּרָ֑ם מֵאֵיל֙ הַמִּלֻּאִ֔ים מֵאֲשֶׁ֥ר לְאַהֲרֹ֖ן וּמֵאֲשֶׁ֥ר לְבָנָֽיו׃

210

Shemot/Exodus 29
Tetzaveh

28 and those parts shall be a due for all time from the Israelites to *Aharon* and his descendants. For they are a gift; and so shall they be a gift from the Israelites, their gift to *Hashem* out of their sacrifices of well-being.

29 The sacral vestments of *Aharon* shall pass on to his sons after him, for them to be anointed and ordained in.

30 He among his sons who becomes *Kohen* in his stead, who enters the Tent of Meeting to officiate within the sanctuary, shall wear them seven days.

31 You shall take the ram of ordination and boil its flesh in the sacred precinct;

32 and *Aharon* and his sons shall eat the flesh of the ram, and the bread that is in the basket, at the entrance of the Tent of Meeting.

33 These things shall be eaten only by those for whom expiation was made with them when they were ordained and consecrated; they may not be eaten by a layman, for they are holy.

34 And if any of the flesh of ordination, or any of the bread, is left until morning, you shall put what is left to the fire; it shall not be eaten, for it is holy.

35 Thus you shall do to *Aharon* and his sons, just as I have commanded you. You shall ordain them through seven days,

36 and each day you shall prepare a bull as a sin offering for expiation; you shall purge the *Mizbayach* by performing purification upon it, and you shall anoint it to consecrate it.

37 Seven days you shall perform purification for the *Mizbayach* to consecrate it, and the *Mizbayach* shall become most holy; whatever touches the *Mizbayach* shall become consecrated.

38 Now this is what you shall offer upon the *Mizbayach*: two yearling lambs each day, regularly.

39 You shall offer the one lamb in the morning, and you shall offer the other lamb at twilight.

40 There shall be a tenth of a measure of choice flour with a quarter of a *hin* of beaten oil mixed in, and a libation of a quarter *hin* of wine for one lamb;

שמות כט
תצוה

כח וְהָיָה לְאַהֲרֹן וּלְבָנָיו לְחָק־עוֹלָם מֵאֵת בְּנֵי יִשְׂרָאֵל כִּי תְרוּמָה הוּא וּתְרוּמָה יִהְיֶה מֵאֵת בְּנֵי־יִשְׂרָאֵל מִזִּבְחֵי שַׁלְמֵיהֶם תְּרוּמָתָם לַיהוָֹה:

כט וּבִגְדֵי הַקֹּדֶשׁ אֲשֶׁר לְאַהֲרֹן יִהְיוּ לְבָנָיו אַחֲרָיו לְמָשְׁחָה בָהֶם וּלְמַלֵּא־בָם אֶת־יָדָם:

ל שִׁבְעַת יָמִים יִלְבָּשָׁם הַכֹּהֵן תַּחְתָּיו מִבָּנָיו אֲשֶׁר יָבֹא אֶל־אֹהֶל מוֹעֵד לְשָׁרֵת בַּקֹּדֶשׁ:

לא וְאֵת אֵיל הַמִּלֻּאִים תִּקָּח וּבִשַּׁלְתָּ אֶת־בְּשָׂרוֹ בְּמָקֹם קָדֹשׁ:

לב וְאָכַל אַהֲרֹן וּבָנָיו אֶת־בְּשַׂר הָאַיִל וְאֶת־הַלֶּחֶם אֲשֶׁר בַּסָּל פֶּתַח אֹהֶל מוֹעֵד:

לג וְאָכְלוּ אֹתָם אֲשֶׁר כֻּפַּר בָּהֶם לְמַלֵּא אֶת־יָדָם לְקַדֵּשׁ אֹתָם וְזָר לֹא־יֹאכַל כִּי־קֹדֶשׁ הֵם:

לד וְאִם־יִוָּתֵר מִבְּשַׂר הַמִּלֻּאִים וּמִן־הַלֶּחֶם עַד־הַבֹּקֶר וְשָׂרַפְתָּ אֶת־הַנּוֹתָר בָּאֵשׁ לֹא יֵאָכֵל כִּי־קֹדֶשׁ הוּא:

לה וְעָשִׂיתָ לְאַהֲרֹן וּלְבָנָיו כָּכָה כְּכֹל אֲשֶׁר־צִוִּיתִי אֹתָכָה שִׁבְעַת יָמִים תְּמַלֵּא יָדָם:

לו וּפַר חַטָּאת תַּעֲשֶׂה לַיּוֹם עַל־הַכִּפֻּרִים וְחִטֵּאתָ עַל־הַמִּזְבֵּחַ בְּכַפֶּרְךָ עָלָיו וּמָשַׁחְתָּ אֹתוֹ לְקַדְּשׁוֹ:

לז שִׁבְעַת יָמִים תְּכַפֵּר עַל־הַמִּזְבֵּחַ וְקִדַּשְׁתָּ אֹתוֹ וְהָיָה הַמִּזְבֵּחַ קֹדֶשׁ קָדָשִׁים כָּל־הַנֹּגֵעַ בַּמִּזְבֵּחַ יִקְדָּשׁ:

לח וְזֶה אֲשֶׁר תַּעֲשֶׂה עַל־הַמִּזְבֵּחַ כְּבָשִׂים בְּנֵי־שָׁנָה שְׁנַיִם לַיּוֹם תָּמִיד:

לט אֶת־הַכֶּבֶשׂ הָאֶחָד תַּעֲשֶׂה בַבֹּקֶר וְאֵת הַכֶּבֶשׂ הַשֵּׁנִי תַּעֲשֶׂה בֵּין הָעַרְבָּיִם:

מ וְעִשָּׂרֹן סֹלֶת בָּלוּל בְּשֶׁמֶן כָּתִית רֶבַע הַהִין וְנֵסֶךְ רְבִיעִת הַהִין יָיִן לַכֶּבֶשׂ הָאֶחָד:

Shemot/Exodus 30
Tetzaveh

שמות ל
תצוה

41 and you shall offer the other lamb at twilight, repeating with it the meal offering of the morning with its libation – an offering by fire for a pleasing odor to *Hashem*,

מא וְאֵת הַכֶּבֶשׂ הַשֵּׁנִי תַּעֲשֶׂה בֵּין הָעַרְבָּיִם כְּמִנְחַת הַבֹּקֶר וּכְנִסְכָּהּ תַּעֲשֶׂה־לָּהּ לְרֵיחַ נִיחֹחַ אִשֶּׁה לַיהֹוָה:

42 a regular burnt offering throughout the generations, at the entrance of the Tent of Meeting before *Hashem*. For there I will meet with you, and there I will speak with you,

מב עֹלַת תָּמִיד לְדֹרֹתֵיכֶם פֶּתַח אֹהֶל־מוֹעֵד לִפְנֵי יְהֹוָה אֲשֶׁר אִוָּעֵד לָכֶם שָׁמָּה לְדַבֵּר אֵלֶיךָ שָׁם:

43 and there I will meet with the Israelites, and it shall be sanctified by My Presence.

מג וְנֹעַדְתִּי שָׁמָּה לִבְנֵי יִשְׂרָאֵל וְנִקְדַּשׁ בִּכְבֹדִי:

44 I will sanctify the Tent of Meeting and the *Mizbayach*, and I will consecrate *Aharon* and his sons to serve Me as *Kohanim*.

מד וְקִדַּשְׁתִּי אֶת־אֹהֶל מוֹעֵד וְאֶת־הַמִּזְבֵּחַ וְאֶת־אַהֲרֹן וְאֶת־בָּנָיו אֲקַדֵּשׁ לְכַהֵן לִי:

45 I will abide among the Israelites, and I will be their God.

מה וְשָׁכַנְתִּי בְּתוֹךְ בְּנֵי יִשְׂרָאֵל וְהָיִיתִי לָהֶם לֵאלֹהִים:

46 And they shall know that I *Hashem* am their God, who brought them out from the land of Egypt that I might abide among them, I *Hashem* their God.

מו וְיָדְעוּ כִּי אֲנִי יְהֹוָה אֱלֹהֵיהֶם אֲשֶׁר הוֹצֵאתִי אֹתָם מֵאֶרֶץ מִצְרַיִם לְשָׁכְנִי בְתוֹכָם אֲנִי יְהֹוָה אֱלֹהֵיהֶם:

30

1 You shall make a *Mizbayach* for burning incense; make it of acacia wood.

א וְעָשִׂיתָ מִזְבֵּחַ מִקְטַר קְטֹרֶת עֲצֵי שִׁטִּים תַּעֲשֶׂה אֹתוֹ:

2 It shall be an *amah* long and an *amah* wide – it shall be square – and two *amot* high, its horns of one piece with it.

ב אַמָּה אָרְכּוֹ וְאַמָּה רָחְבּוֹ רָבוּעַ יִהְיֶה וְאַמָּתַיִם קֹמָתוֹ מִמֶּנּוּ קַרְנֹתָיו:

3 Overlay it with pure gold: its top, its sides round about, and its horns; and make a gold molding for it round about.

ג וְצִפִּיתָ אֹתוֹ זָהָב טָהוֹר אֶת־גַּגּוֹ וְאֶת־קִירֹתָיו סָבִיב וְאֶת־קַרְנֹתָיו וְעָשִׂיתָ לּוֹ זֵר זָהָב סָבִיב:

4 And make two gold rings for it under its molding; make them on its two side walls, on opposite sides. They shall serve as holders for poles with which to carry it.

ד וּשְׁתֵּי טַבְּעֹת זָהָב תַּעֲשֶׂה־לּוֹ מִתַּחַת לְזֵרוֹ עַל שְׁתֵּי צַלְעֹתָיו תַּעֲשֶׂה עַל־שְׁנֵי צִדָּיו וְהָיָה לְבָתִּים לְבַדִּים לָשֵׂאת אֹתוֹ בָּהֵמָּה:

5 Make the poles of acacia wood, and overlay them with gold.

ה וְעָשִׂיתָ אֶת־הַבַּדִּים עֲצֵי שִׁטִּים וְצִפִּיתָ אֹתָם זָהָב:

6 Place it in front of the curtain that is over the *Aron HaBrit* – in front of the cover that is over the Pact – where I will meet with you.

ו וְנָתַתָּה אֹתוֹ לִפְנֵי הַפָּרֹכֶת אֲשֶׁר עַל־אֲרֹן הָעֵדֻת לִפְנֵי הַכַּפֹּרֶת אֲשֶׁר עַל־הָעֵדֻת אֲשֶׁר אִוָּעֵד לְךָ שָׁמָּה:

7 On it *Aharon* shall burn aromatic incense: he shall burn it every morning when he tends the lamps,

ז וְהִקְטִיר עָלָיו אַהֲרֹן קְטֹרֶת סַמִּים בַּבֹּקֶר בַּבֹּקֶר בְּהֵיטִיבוֹ אֶת־הַנֵּרֹת יַקְטִירֶנָּה:

8 and *Aharon* shall burn it at twilight when he lights the lamps – a regular incense offering before *Hashem* throughout the ages.

ח וּבְהַעֲלֹת אַהֲרֹן אֶת־הַנֵּרֹת בֵּין הָעַרְבַּיִם יַקְטִירֶנָּה קְטֹרֶת תָּמִיד לִפְנֵי יְהֹוָה לְדֹרֹתֵיכֶם:

Shemot/Exodus 30
Ki Tisa

שמות ל
כי תשא

9 You shall not offer alien incense on it, or a burnt offering or a meal offering; neither shall you pour a libation on it.

ט לֹא־תַעֲלוּ עָלָיו קְטֹרֶת זָרָה וְעֹלָה וּמִנְחָה וְנֵסֶךְ לֹא תִסְּכוּ עָלָיו:

10 Once a year *Aharon* shall perform purification upon its horns with blood of the sin offering of purification; purification shall be performed upon it once a year throughout the ages. It is most holy to *Hashem*.

י וְכִפֶּר אַהֲרֹן עַל־קַרְנֹתָיו אַחַת בַּשָּׁנָה מִדַּם חַטַּאת הַכִּפֻּרִים אַחַת בַּשָּׁנָה יְכַפֵּר עָלָיו לְדֹרֹתֵיכֶם קֹדֶשׁ־קָדָשִׁים הוּא לַיהוָֹה:

11 *Hashem* spoke to *Moshe*, saying:

יא וַיְדַבֵּר יְהוָֹה אֶל־מֹשֶׁה לֵּאמֹר:

12 When you take a census of *B'nei Yisrael* according to their enrollment, each shall pay *Hashem* a ransom for himself on being enrolled, that no plague may come upon them through their being enrolled.

יב כִּי תִשָּׂא אֶת־רֹאשׁ בְּנֵי־יִשְׂרָאֵל לִפְקֻדֵיהֶם וְנָתְנוּ אִישׁ כֹּפֶר נַפְשׁוֹ לַיהוָֹה בִּפְקֹד אֹתָם וְלֹא־יִהְיֶה בָהֶם נֶגֶף בִּפְקֹד אֹתָם:

kee ti-SA et ROSH b'-nay yis-ra-AYL lif-ku-day-HEM v'-na-t'-NU EESH KO-fer naf-SHO la-do-NAI bif-KOD o-TAM v'-lo yih-YEH va-HEM NE-gef bif-KOD o-TAM

13 This is what everyone who is entered in the records shall pay: a half-*shekel* by the sanctuary weight – twenty *giera* to the *shekel* – a half-*shekel* as an offering to *Hashem*.

יג זֶה יִתְּנוּ כָּל־הָעֹבֵר עַל־הַפְּקֻדִים מַחֲצִית הַשֶּׁקֶל בְּשֶׁקֶל הַקֹּדֶשׁ עֶשְׂרִים גֵּרָה הַשֶּׁקֶל מַחֲצִית הַשֶּׁקֶל תְּרוּמָה לַיהוָֹה:

14 Everyone who is entered in the records, from the age of twenty years up, shall give *Hashem*'s offering:

יד כֹּל הָעֹבֵר עַל־הַפְּקֻדִים מִבֶּן עֶשְׂרִים שָׁנָה וָמָעְלָה יִתֵּן תְּרוּמַת יְהוָֹה:

15 the rich shall not pay more and the poor shall not pay less than half a *shekel* when giving *Hashem*'s offering as expiation for your persons.

טו הֶעָשִׁיר לֹא־יַרְבֶּה וְהַדַּל לֹא יַמְעִיט מִמַּחֲצִית הַשָּׁקֶל לָתֵת אֶת־תְּרוּמַת יְהוָֹה לְכַפֵּר עַל־נַפְשֹׁתֵיכֶם:

16 You shall take the expiation money from the Israelites and assign it to the service of the Tent of Meeting; it shall serve the Israelites as a reminder before *Hashem*, as expiation for your persons.

טז וְלָקַחְתָּ אֶת־כֶּסֶף הַכִּפֻּרִים מֵאֵת בְּנֵי יִשְׂרָאֵל וְנָתַתָּ אֹתוֹ עַל־עֲבֹדַת אֹהֶל מוֹעֵד וְהָיָה לִבְנֵי יִשְׂרָאֵל לְזִכָּרוֹן לִפְנֵי יְהוָֹה לְכַפֵּר עַל־נַפְשֹׁתֵיכֶם:

17 *Hashem* spoke to *Moshe*, saying:

יז וַיְדַבֵּר יְהוָֹה אֶל־מֹשֶׁה לֵּאמֹר:

18 Make a laver of copper and a stand of copper for it, for washing; and place it between the Tent of Meeting and the *Mizbayach*. Put water in it,

יח וְעָשִׂיתָ כִּיּוֹר נְחֹשֶׁת וְכַנּוֹ נְחֹשֶׁת לְרָחְצָה וְנָתַתָּ אֹתוֹ בֵּין־אֹהֶל מוֹעֵד וּבֵין הַמִּזְבֵּחַ וְנָתַתָּ שָׁמָּה מָיִם:

Rabbi Samson R. Hirsch (1808–1888)

30:12 When you take a census of the *B'nei Yisrael* *Moshe* is commanded to count the Nation of Israel. However, he is not to count individuals. Instead, each person being counted is to make a donation of half a *shekel* to the *Mishkan*, and the half *shekel* coins are to then be counted. Rabbi Samson Raphael Hirsch explains the symbolism of this method: Merely existing among others does not make one an integral part of a society. In order to be counted as part of the nation, each member has to give of themselves and contribute to the community.

Shemot/Exodus 30
Ki Tisa

19 and let *Aharon* and his sons wash their hands and feet [in water drawn] from it.

20 When they enter the Tent of Meeting they shall wash with water, that they may not die; or when they approach the *Mizbayach* to serve, to turn into smoke an offering by fire to *Hashem*,

21 they shall wash their hands and feet, that they may not die. It shall be a law for all time for them – for him and his offspring – throughout the ages.

22 *Hashem* spoke to *Moshe*, saying:

23 Next take choice spices: five hundred weight of solidified myrrh, half as much – two hundred and fifty – of fragrant cinnamon, two hundred and fifty of aromatic cane,

24 five hundred – by the sanctuary weight – of cassia, and a *hin* of olive oil.

25 Make of this a sacred anointing oil, a compound of ingredients expertly blended, to serve as sacred anointing oil.

26 With it anoint the Tent of Meeting, the *Aron HaBrit*,

27 the table and all its utensils, the *menorah* and all its fittings, the *Mizbayach* of incense,

28 the *Mizbayach* of burnt offering and all its utensils, and the laver and its stand.

29 Thus you shall consecrate them so that they may be most holy; whatever touches them shall be consecrated.

30 You shall also anoint *Aharon* and his sons, consecrating them to serve Me as *Kohanim*.

31 And speak to *B'nei Yisrael*, as follows: This shall be an anointing oil sacred to Me throughout the ages.

32 It must not be rubbed on any person's body, and you must not make anything like it in the same proportions; it is sacred, to be held sacred by you.

33 Whoever compounds its like, or puts any of it on a layman, shall be cut off from his kin.

34 And *Hashem* said to *Moshe*: Take the herbs stacte, onycha, and galbanum – these herbs together with pure frankincense; let there be an equal part of each.

שמות ל
כי תשא

יט וְרָחֲצוּ אַהֲרֹן וּבָנָיו מִמֶּנּוּ אֶת־יְדֵיהֶם וְאֶת־רַגְלֵיהֶם:

כ בְּבֹאָם אֶל־אֹהֶל מוֹעֵד יִרְחֲצוּ־מַיִם וְלֹא יָמֻתוּ אוֹ בְגִשְׁתָּם אֶל־הַמִּזְבֵּחַ לְשָׁרֵת לְהַקְטִיר אִשֶּׁה לַיהוָה:

כא וְרָחֲצוּ יְדֵיהֶם וְרַגְלֵיהֶם וְלֹא יָמֻתוּ וְהָיְתָה לָהֶם חָק־עוֹלָם לוֹ וּלְזַרְעוֹ לְדֹרֹתָם:

כב וַיְדַבֵּר יְהוָה אֶל־מֹשֶׁה לֵּאמֹר:

כג וְאַתָּה קַח־לְךָ בְּשָׂמִים רֹאשׁ מָר־דְּרוֹר חֲמֵשׁ מֵאוֹת וְקִנְּמָן־בֶּשֶׂם מַחֲצִיתוֹ חֲמִשִּׁים וּמָאתָיִם וּקְנֵה־בֹשֶׂם חֲמִשִּׁים וּמָאתָיִם:

כד וְקִדָּה חֲמֵשׁ מֵאוֹת בְּשֶׁקֶל הַקֹּדֶשׁ וְשֶׁמֶן זַיִת הִין:

כה וְעָשִׂיתָ אֹתוֹ שֶׁמֶן מִשְׁחַת־קֹדֶשׁ רֹקַח מִרְקַחַת מַעֲשֵׂה רֹקֵחַ שֶׁמֶן מִשְׁחַת־קֹדֶשׁ יִהְיֶה:

כו וּמָשַׁחְתָּ בוֹ אֶת־אֹהֶל מוֹעֵד וְאֵת אֲרוֹן הָעֵדֻת:

כז וְאֶת־הַשֻּׁלְחָן וְאֶת־כָּל־כֵּלָיו וְאֶת־הַמְּנֹרָה וְאֶת־כֵּלֶיהָ וְאֵת מִזְבַּח הַקְּטֹרֶת:

כח וְאֶת־מִזְבַּח הָעֹלָה וְאֶת־כָּל־כֵּלָיו וְאֶת־הַכִּיֹּר וְאֶת־כַּנּוֹ:

כט וְקִדַּשְׁתָּ אֹתָם וְהָיוּ קֹדֶשׁ קָדָשִׁים כָּל־הַנֹּגֵעַ בָּהֶם יִקְדָּשׁ:

ל וְאֶת־אַהֲרֹן וְאֶת־בָּנָיו תִּמְשָׁח וְקִדַּשְׁתָּ אֹתָם לְכַהֵן לִי:

לא וְאֶל־בְּנֵי יִשְׂרָאֵל תְּדַבֵּר לֵאמֹר שֶׁמֶן מִשְׁחַת־קֹדֶשׁ יִהְיֶה זֶה לִי לְדֹרֹתֵיכֶם:

לב עַל־בְּשַׂר אָדָם לֹא יִיסָךְ וּבְמַתְכֻּנְתּוֹ לֹא תַעֲשׂוּ כָּמֹהוּ קֹדֶשׁ הוּא קֹדֶשׁ יִהְיֶה לָכֶם:

לג אִישׁ אֲשֶׁר יִרְקַח כָּמֹהוּ וַאֲשֶׁר יִתֵּן מִמֶּנּוּ עַל־זָר וְנִכְרַת מֵעַמָּיו:

לד וַיֹּאמֶר יְהוָה אֶל־מֹשֶׁה קַח־לְךָ סַמִּים נָטָף וּשְׁחֵלֶת וְחֶלְבְּנָה סַמִּים וּלְבֹנָה זַכָּה בַּד בְּבַד יִהְיֶה:

214

Shemot/Exodus 31
Ki Tisa

שמות לא
כי תשא

35 Make them into incense, a compound expertly blended, refined, pure, sacred.

לה וְעָשִׂיתָ אֹתָהּ קְטֹרֶת רֹקַח מַעֲשֵׂה רוֹקֵחַ מְמֻלָּח טָהוֹר קֹדֶשׁ׃

36 Beat some of it into powder, and put some before the Pact in the Tent of Meeting, where I will meet with you; it shall be most holy to you.

לו וְשָׁחַקְתָּ מִמֶּנָּה הָדֵק וְנָתַתָּה מִמֶּנָּה לִפְנֵי הָעֵדֻת בְּאֹהֶל מוֹעֵד אֲשֶׁר אִוָּעֵד לְךָ שָׁמָּה קֹדֶשׁ קָדָשִׁים תִּהְיֶה לָכֶם׃

37 But when you make this incense, you must not make any in the same proportions for yourselves; it shall be held by you sacred to *Hashem*.

לז וְהַקְּטֹרֶת אֲשֶׁר תַּעֲשֶׂה בְּמַתְכֻּנְתָּהּ לֹא תַעֲשׂוּ לָכֶם קֹדֶשׁ תִּהְיֶה לְךָ לַיהוָה׃

38 Whoever makes any like it, to smell of it, shall be cut off from his kin.

לח אִישׁ אֲשֶׁר־יַעֲשֶׂה כָמוֹהָ לְהָרִיחַ בָּהּ וְנִכְרַת מֵעַמָּיו׃

31 1 *Hashem* spoke to *Moshe*:

לא א וַיְדַבֵּר יְהוָה אֶל־מֹשֶׁה לֵּאמֹר׃

2 See, I have singled out by name *Betzalel* son of *Uri* son of *Chur*, of the tribe of *Yehuda*.

ב רְאֵה קָרָאתִי בְשֵׁם בְּצַלְאֵל בֶּן־אוּרִי בֶן־חוּר לְמַטֵּה יְהוּדָה׃

3 I have endowed him with a divine spirit of skill, ability, and knowledge in every kind of craft;

ג וָאֲמַלֵּא אֹתוֹ רוּחַ אֱלֹהִים בְּחָכְמָה וּבִתְבוּנָה וּבְדַעַת וּבְכָל־מְלָאכָה׃

4 to make designs for work in gold, silver, and copper,

ד לַחְשֹׁב מַחֲשָׁבֹת לַעֲשׂוֹת בַּזָּהָב וּבַכֶּסֶף וּבַנְּחֹשֶׁת׃

5 to cut stones for setting and to carve wood – to work in every kind of craft.

ה וּבַחֲרֹשֶׁת אֶבֶן לְמַלֹּאת וּבַחֲרֹשֶׁת עֵץ לַעֲשׂוֹת בְּכָל־מְלָאכָה׃

6 Moreover, I have assigned to him *Oholiav* son of *Achisamach*, of the tribe of *Dan*; and I have also granted skill to all who are skillful, that they may make everything that I have commanded you:

ו וַאֲנִי הִנֵּה נָתַתִּי אִתּוֹ אֵת אָהֳלִיאָב בֶּן־אֲחִיסָמָךְ לְמַטֵּה־דָן וּבְלֵב כָּל־חֲכַם־לֵב נָתַתִּי חָכְמָה וְעָשׂוּ אֵת כָּל־אֲשֶׁר צִוִּיתִךָ׃

7 the Tent of Meeting, the *Aron HaBrit* and the cover upon it, and all the furnishings of the Tent;

ז אֵת אֹהֶל מוֹעֵד וְאֶת־הָאָרֹן לָעֵדֻת וְאֶת־הַכַּפֹּרֶת אֲשֶׁר עָלָיו וְאֵת כָּל־כְּלֵי הָאֹהֶל׃

8 the table and its utensils, the pure *menorah* and all its fittings, and the *Mizbayach* of incense;

ח וְאֶת־הַשֻּׁלְחָן וְאֶת־כֵּלָיו וְאֶת־הַמְּנֹרָה הַטְּהֹרָה וְאֶת־כָּל־כֵּלֶיהָ וְאֵת מִזְבַּח הַקְּטֹרֶת׃

9 the *Mizbayach* of burnt offering and all its utensils, and the laver and its stand;

ט וְאֶת־מִזְבַּח הָעֹלָה וְאֶת־כָּל־כֵּלָיו וְאֶת־הַכִּיּוֹר וְאֶת־כַּנּוֹ׃

10 the service vestments, the sacral vestments of *Aharon* the *Kohen* and the vestments of his sons, for their service as *Kohanim*;

י וְאֵת בִּגְדֵי הַשְּׂרָד וְאֶת־בִּגְדֵי הַקֹּדֶשׁ לְאַהֲרֹן הַכֹּהֵן וְאֶת־בִּגְדֵי בָנָיו לְכַהֵן׃

11 as well as the anointing oil and the aromatic incense for the sanctuary. Just as I have commanded you, they shall do.

יא וְאֵת שֶׁמֶן הַמִּשְׁחָה וְאֶת־קְטֹרֶת הַסַּמִּים לַקֹּדֶשׁ כְּכֹל אֲשֶׁר־צִוִּיתִךָ יַעֲשׂוּ׃

Shemot/Exodus 32
Ki Tisa

שמות לב
כי תשא

12 And *Hashem* said to *Moshe*:

יב וַיֹּ֥אמֶר יְהֹוָ֖ה אֶל־מֹשֶׁ֥ה לֵּאמֹֽר׃

13 Speak to *B'nei Yisrael* and say: Nevertheless, you must keep My *Shabbatot*, for this is a sign between Me and you throughout the ages, that you may know that I *Hashem* have consecrated you.

יג וְאַתָּ֞ה דַּבֵּ֨ר אֶל־בְּנֵ֤י יִשְׂרָאֵל֙ לֵאמֹ֔ר אַ֥ךְ אֶת־שַׁבְּתֹתַ֖י תִּשְׁמֹ֑רוּ כִּי֩ א֨וֹת הִ֜וא בֵּינִ֤י וּבֵֽינֵיכֶם֙ לְדֹרֹ֣תֵיכֶ֔ם לָדַ֕עַת כִּ֛י אֲנִ֥י יְהֹוָ֖ה מְקַדִּשְׁכֶֽם׃

14 You shall keep the *Shabbat*, for it is holy for you. He who profanes it shall be put to death: whoever does work on it, that person shall be cut off from among his kin.

יד וּשְׁמַרְתֶּם֙ אֶת־הַשַּׁבָּ֔ת כִּ֛י קֹ֥דֶשׁ הִ֖וא לָכֶ֑ם מְחַֽלְלֶ֨יהָ֙ מ֣וֹת יוּמָ֔ת כִּ֗י כׇּל־הָֽעֹשֶׂ֥ה בָהּ֙ מְלָאכָ֔ה וְנִכְרְתָ֛ה הַנֶּ֥פֶשׁ הַהִ֖וא מִקֶּ֥רֶב עַמֶּֽיהָ׃

15 Six days may work be done, but on the seventh day there shall be a *Shabbat* of complete rest, holy to *Hashem*; whoever does work on the *Shabbat* day shall be put to death.

טו שֵׁ֣שֶׁת יָמִים֮ יֵעָשֶׂ֣ה מְלָאכָה֒ וּבַיּ֣וֹם הַשְּׁבִיעִ֗י שַׁבַּ֧ת שַׁבָּת֛וֹן קֹ֖דֶשׁ לַיהֹוָ֑ה כׇּל־הָעֹשֶׂ֧ה מְלָאכָ֛ה בְּי֥וֹם הַשַּׁבָּ֖ת מ֥וֹת יוּמָֽת׃

16 *B'nei Yisrael* shall keep the *Shabbat*, observing the *Shabbat* throughout the ages as a covenant for all time:

טז וְשָׁמְר֥וּ בְנֵֽי־יִשְׂרָאֵ֖ל אֶת־הַשַּׁבָּ֑ת לַעֲשׂ֧וֹת אֶת־הַשַּׁבָּ֛ת לְדֹרֹתָ֖ם בְּרִ֥ית עוֹלָֽם׃

17 it shall be a sign for all time between Me and the people of *Yisrael*. For in six days *Hashem* made heaven and earth, and on the seventh day He ceased from work and was refreshed.

יז בֵּינִ֗י וּבֵין֙ בְּנֵ֣י יִשְׂרָאֵ֔ל א֥וֹת הִ֖וא לְעֹלָ֑ם כִּי־שֵׁ֣שֶׁת יָמִ֗ים עָשָׂ֤ה יְהֹוָה֙ אֶת־הַשָּׁמַ֣יִם וְאֶת־הָאָ֔רֶץ וּבַיּוֹם֙ הַשְּׁבִיעִ֔י שָׁבַ֖ת וַיִּנָּפַֽשׁ׃

bay-NEE u-VAYN b'-NAY yis-ra-AYL OT HEE l'-o-LAM kee SHAY-shet ya-MEEM a-SAH a-do-NAI et ha-sha-MA-yim v'-ET ha-A-retz u-va-YOM ha-sh'-vee-EE sha-VAT va-yi-na-FASH

18 When He finished speaking with him on *Har Sinai*, He gave *Moshe* the two tablets of the Pact, stone tablets inscribed with the finger of *Hashem*.

יח וַיִּתֵּ֣ן אֶל־מֹשֶׁ֗ה כְּכַלֹּתוֹ֙ לְדַבֵּ֤ר אִתּוֹ֙ בְּהַ֣ר סִינַ֔י שְׁנֵ֖י לֻחֹ֣ת הָעֵדֻ֑ת לֻחֹ֣ת אֶ֔בֶן כְּתֻבִ֖ים בְּאֶצְבַּ֥ע אֱלֹהִֽים׃

32:1 When the people saw that *Moshe* was so long in coming down from the mountain, the people gathered against *Aharon* and said to him, "Come, make us a god who shall go before us, for that man *Moshe*, who brought us from the land of Egypt – we do not know what has happened to him."

לב א וַיַּ֣רְא הָעָ֔ם כִּֽי־בֹשֵׁ֥שׁ מֹשֶׁ֖ה לָרֶ֣דֶת מִן־הָהָ֑ר וַיִּקָּהֵ֨ל הָעָ֜ם עַֽל־אַהֲרֹ֗ן וַיֹּאמְר֤וּ אֵלָיו֙ ק֣וּם ׀ עֲשֵׂה־לָ֣נוּ אֱלֹהִ֗ים אֲשֶׁ֤ר יֵֽלְכוּ֙ לְפָנֵ֔ינוּ כִּי־זֶ֣ה ׀ מֹשֶׁ֣ה הָאִ֗ישׁ אֲשֶׁ֤ר הֶֽעֱלָ֙נוּ֙ מֵאֶ֣רֶץ מִצְרַ֔יִם לֹ֥א יָדַ֖עְנוּ מֶה־הָ֥יָה לֽוֹ׃

31:17 It shall be a sign for all time between Me and the people of *Yisrael* The *Shabbat* (שבת), 'Sabbath,' is designated as a sign between *Hashem* and the Children of Israel that *Hashem* created the world, and resting from work on *Shabbat* is the sign that the Jewish Nation recognizes God as the Creator. Each week, Jews reaffirm their submission to *Hashem* by sanctifying the *Shabbat*, and they recite this verse during the *Shabbat* prayers. Though the observance of *Shabbat* was commanded to the Children of Israel, the message of *Shabbat*, that God created the universe and everything in it, is a universal one.

Shabbat table, 1947

Shemot/Exodus 32
Ki Tisa

2 *Aharon* said to them, "Take off the gold rings that are on the ears of your wives, your sons, and your daughters, and bring them to me."

3 And all the people took off the gold rings that were in their ears and brought them to *Aharon*.

4 This he took from them and cast in a mold, and made it into a molten calf. And they exclaimed, "This is your god, O *Yisrael*, who brought you out of the land of Egypt!"

5 When *Aharon* saw this, he built a *Mizbayach* before it; and *Aharon* announced: "Tomorrow shall be a festival of *Hashem*!"

6 Early next day, the people offered up burnt offerings and brought sacrifices of well-being; they sat down to eat and drink, and then rose to dance.

7 *Hashem* spoke to *Moshe*, "Hurry down, for your people, whom you brought out of the land of Egypt, have acted basely.

8 They have been quick to turn aside from the way that I enjoined upon them. They have made themselves a molten calf and bowed low to it and sacrificed to it, saying: 'This is your god, O *Yisrael*, who brought you out of the land of Egypt!'"

9 *Hashem* further said to *Moshe*, "I see that this is a stiffnecked people.

10 Now, let Me be, that My anger may blaze forth against them and that I may destroy them, and make of you a great nation."

11 But *Moshe* implored *Hashem* his God, saying, "Let not Your anger, O *Hashem*, blaze forth against Your people, whom You delivered from the land of Egypt with great power and with a mighty hand.

12 Let not the Egyptians say, 'It was with evil intent that He delivered them, only to kill them off in the mountains and annihilate them from the face of the earth.' Turn from Your blazing anger, and renounce the plan to punish Your people.

שמות לב
כי תשא

ב וַיֹּאמֶר אֲלֵהֶם אַהֲרֹן פָּרְקוּ נִזְמֵי הַזָּהָב אֲשֶׁר בְּאָזְנֵי נְשֵׁיכֶם בְּנֵיכֶם וּבְנֹתֵיכֶם וְהָבִיאוּ אֵלָי:

ג וַיִּתְפָּרְקוּ כָּל־הָעָם אֶת־נִזְמֵי הַזָּהָב אֲשֶׁר בְּאָזְנֵיהֶם וַיָּבִיאוּ אֶל־אַהֲרֹן:

ד וַיִּקַּח מִיָּדָם וַיָּצַר אֹתוֹ בַּחֶרֶט וַיַּעֲשֵׂהוּ עֵגֶל מַסֵּכָה וַיֹּאמְרוּ אֵלֶּה אֱלֹהֶיךָ יִשְׂרָאֵל אֲשֶׁר הֶעֱלוּךָ מֵאֶרֶץ מִצְרָיִם:

ה וַיַּרְא אַהֲרֹן וַיִּבֶן מִזְבֵּחַ לְפָנָיו וַיִּקְרָא אַהֲרֹן וַיֹּאמַר חַג לַיהוָה מָחָר:

ו וַיַּשְׁכִּימוּ מִמָּחֳרָת וַיַּעֲלוּ עֹלֹת וַיַּגִּשׁוּ שְׁלָמִים וַיֵּשֶׁב הָעָם לֶאֱכֹל וְשָׁתוֹ וַיָּקֻמוּ לְצַחֵק:

ז וַיְדַבֵּר יְהוָה אֶל־מֹשֶׁה לֶךְ־רֵד כִּי שִׁחֵת עַמְּךָ אֲשֶׁר הֶעֱלֵיתָ מֵאֶרֶץ מִצְרָיִם:

ח סָרוּ מַהֵר מִן־הַדֶּרֶךְ אֲשֶׁר צִוִּיתִם עָשׂוּ לָהֶם עֵגֶל מַסֵּכָה וַיִּשְׁתַּחֲווּ־לוֹ וַיִּזְבְּחוּ־לוֹ וַיֹּאמְרוּ אֵלֶּה אֱלֹהֶיךָ יִשְׂרָאֵל אֲשֶׁר הֶעֱלוּךָ מֵאֶרֶץ מִצְרָיִם:

ט וַיֹּאמֶר יְהוָה אֶל־מֹשֶׁה רָאִיתִי אֶת־הָעָם הַזֶּה וְהִנֵּה עַם־קְשֵׁה־עֹרֶף הוּא:

י וְעַתָּה הַנִּיחָה לִּי וְיִחַר־אַפִּי בָהֶם וַאֲכַלֵּם וְאֶעֱשֶׂה אוֹתְךָ לְגוֹי גָּדוֹל:

יא וַיְחַל מֹשֶׁה אֶת־פְּנֵי יְהוָה אֱלֹהָיו וַיֹּאמֶר לָמָה יְהוָה יֶחֱרֶה אַפְּךָ בְּעַמֶּךָ אֲשֶׁר הוֹצֵאתָ מֵאֶרֶץ מִצְרַיִם בְּכֹחַ גָּדוֹל וּבְיָד חֲזָקָה:

יב לָמָּה יֹאמְרוּ מִצְרַיִם לֵאמֹר בְּרָעָה הוֹצִיאָם לַהֲרֹג אֹתָם בֶּהָרִים וּלְכַלֹּתָם מֵעַל פְּנֵי הָאֲדָמָה שׁוּב מֵחֲרוֹן אַפֶּךָ וְהִנָּחֵם עַל־הָרָעָה לְעַמֶּךָ:

Shemot/Exodus 32
Ki Tisa

שמות לב
כי תשא

13 Remember Your servants, *Avraham, Yitzchak,* and *Yisrael,* how You swore to them by Your Self and said to them: I will make your offspring as numerous as the stars of heaven, and I will give to your offspring this whole land of which I spoke, to possess forever."

יג זְכֹר לְאַבְרָהָם לְיִצְחָק וּלְיִשְׂרָאֵל עֲבָדֶיךָ אֲשֶׁר נִשְׁבַּעְתָּ לָהֶם בָּךְ וַתְּדַבֵּר אֲלֵהֶם אַרְבֶּה אֶת־זַרְעֲכֶם כְּכוֹכְבֵי הַשָּׁמָיִם וְכָל־הָאָרֶץ הַזֹּאת אֲשֶׁר אָמַרְתִּי אֶתֵּן לְזַרְעֲכֶם וְנָחֲלוּ לְעֹלָם:

z'-KHOR l'-av-ra-HAM l'-yitz-KHAK ul-yis-ra-AYL a-va-DE-kha a-SHER nish-BA-ta la-HEM BAKH va-t'-da-BAYR a-lay-HEM ar-BEH et zar-a-KHEM k'-kho-kh'-VAY ha-sha-MA-yim v'-khol ha-A-retz ha-ZOT a-SHER a-MAR-tee e-TAYN l'-zar-a-KHEM v'-na-kha-LU l'-o-LAM

14 And *Hashem* renounced the punishment He had planned to bring upon His people.

יד וַיִּנָּחֶם יְהֹוָה עַל־הָרָעָה אֲשֶׁר דִּבֶּר לַעֲשׂוֹת לְעַמּוֹ:

15 Thereupon *Moshe* turned and went down from the mountain bearing the two tablets of the Pact, tablets inscribed on both their surfaces: they were inscribed on the one side and on the other.

טו וַיִּפֶן וַיֵּרֶד מֹשֶׁה מִן־הָהָר וּשְׁנֵי לֻחֹת הָעֵדֻת בְּיָדוֹ לֻחֹת כְּתֻבִים מִשְּׁנֵי עֶבְרֵיהֶם מִזֶּה וּמִזֶּה הֵם כְּתֻבִים:

16 The tablets were *Hashem's* work, and the writing was *Hashem's* writing, incised upon the tablets.

טז וְהַלֻּחֹת מַעֲשֵׂה אֱלֹהִים הֵמָּה וְהַמִּכְתָּב מִכְתַּב אֱלֹהִים הוּא חָרוּת עַל־הַלֻּחֹת:

17 When *Yehoshua* heard the sound of the people in its boisterousness, he said to *Moshe,* There is a cry of war in the camp."

יז וַיִּשְׁמַע יְהוֹשֻׁעַ אֶת־קוֹל הָעָם בְּרֵעֹה וַיֹּאמֶר אֶל־מֹשֶׁה קוֹל מִלְחָמָה בַּמַּחֲנֶה:

18 But he answered, "It is not the sound of the tune of triumph, Or the sound of the tune of defeat; It is the sound of song that I hear!"

יח וַיֹּאמֶר אֵין קוֹל עֲנוֹת גְּבוּרָה וְאֵין קוֹל עֲנוֹת חֲלוּשָׁה קוֹל עַנּוֹת אָנֹכִי שֹׁמֵעַ:

19 As soon as *Moshe* came near the camp and saw the calf and the dancing, he became enraged; and he hurled the tablets from his hands and shattered them at the foot of the mountain.

יט וַיְהִי כַּאֲשֶׁר קָרַב אֶל־הַמַּחֲנֶה וַיַּרְא אֶת־הָעֵגֶל וּמְחֹלֹת וַיִּחַר־אַף מֹשֶׁה וַיַּשְׁלֵךְ מִיָּדָו [מִיָּדָיו] אֶת־הַלֻּחֹת וַיְשַׁבֵּר אֹתָם תַּחַת הָהָר:

20 He took the calf that they had made and burned it; he ground it to powder and strewed it upon the water and so made the Israelites drink it.

כ וַיִּקַּח אֶת־הָעֵגֶל אֲשֶׁר עָשׂוּ וַיִּשְׂרֹף בָּאֵשׁ וַיִּטְחַן עַד אֲשֶׁר־דָּק וַיִּזֶר עַל־פְּנֵי הַמַּיִם וַיַּשְׁקְ אֶת־בְּנֵי יִשְׂרָאֵל:

21 *Moshe* said to *Aharon,* "What did this people do to you that you have brought such great sin upon them?"

כא וַיֹּאמֶר מֹשֶׁה אֶל־אַהֲרֹן מֶה־עָשָׂה לְךָ הָעָם הַזֶּה כִּי־הֵבֵאתָ עָלָיו חֲטָאָה גְדֹלָה:

22 *Aharon* said, "Let not my lord be enraged. You know that this people is bent on evil.

כב וַיֹּאמֶר אַהֲרֹן אַל־יִחַר אַף אֲדֹנִי אַתָּה יָדַעְתָּ אֶת־הָעָם כִּי בְרָע הוּא:

32:13 To possess forever With this verse, *Moshe* attempts to convince *Hashem* to spare the Jewish nation, despite the egregious sin of the golden calf. He pleads with God to remember his oath to *Avraham, Yitzchak* and *Yaakov* that their progeny will inherit *Eretz Yisrael.* *Moshe* is concerned that if *Hashem* is to destroy the Nation and re-create a great nation from him alone, the promise of the Holy Land made to the Patriarchs would be lost. He therefore pleads with God to spare the people despite their transgressions.

Shemot/Exodus 32
Ki Tisa

23 They said to me, 'Make us a god to lead us; for that man *Moshe*, who brought us from the land of Egypt – we do not know what has happened to him.'

24 So I said to them, 'Whoever has gold, take it off!' They gave it to me and I hurled it into the fire and out came this calf!"

25 *Moshe* saw that the people were out of control – since *Aharon* had let them get out of control – so that they were a menace to any who might oppose them.

26 *Moshe* stood up in the gate of the camp and said, "Whoever is for *Hashem*, come here!" And all the *Leviim* rallied to him.

27 He said to them, "Thus says *Hashem*, the God of *Yisrael*: Each of you put sword on thigh, go back and forth from gate to gate throughout the camp, and slay brother, neighbor, and kin."

28 The *Leviim* did as *Moshe* had bidden; and some three thousand of the people fell that day.

29 And *Moshe* said, "Dedicate yourselves to *Hashem* this day – for each of you has been against son and brother – that He may bestow a blessing upon you today."

30 The next day *Moshe* said to the people, "You have been guilty of a great sin. Yet I will now go up to *Hashem*; perhaps I may win forgiveness for your sin."

31 *Moshe* went back to *Hashem* and said, "Alas, this people is guilty of a great sin in making for themselves a god of gold.

32 Now, if You will forgive their sin [well and good]; but if not, erase me from the record which You have written!"

33 But *Hashem* said to *Moshe*, "He who has sinned against Me, him only will I erase from My record.

34 Go now, lead the people where I told you. See, My angel shall go before you. But when I make an accounting, I will bring them to account for their sins."

35 Then *Hashem* sent a plague upon the people, for what they did with the calf that *Aharon* made.

Shemot/Exodus 33
Ki Tisa

שמות לג
כי תשא

33

1 Then *Hashem* said to *Moshe*, "Set out from here, you and the people that you have brought up from the land of Egypt, to the land of which I swore to *Avraham*, *Yitzchak*, and *Yaakov*, saying, 'To your offspring will I give it'

א וַיְדַבֵּר יְהֹוָה אֶל־מֹשֶׁה לֵךְ עֲלֵה מִזֶּה אַתָּה וְהָעָם אֲשֶׁר הֶעֱלִיתָ מֵאֶרֶץ מִצְרָיִם אֶל־הָאָרֶץ אֲשֶׁר נִשְׁבַּעְתִּי לְאַבְרָהָם לְיִצְחָק וּלְיַעֲקֹב לֵאמֹר לְזַרְעֲךָ אֶתְּנֶנָּה:

vai-da-BAYR a-do-NAI el mo-SHEH LAYKH a-LAY mi-ZEH a-TAH v'-ha-AM a-SHER he-e-LEE-ta may-E-retz mitz-RA-yim el ha-A-retz a-SHER nish-BA-tee l'-av-ra-HAM l'-yitz-KHAK ul-ya-a-KOV lay-MOR l'-zar-a-KHA e-t'-NE-nah

2 I will send an angel before you, and I will drive out the Canaanites, the Amorites, the Hittites, the Perizzites, the Hivites, and the Jebusites

ב וְשָׁלַחְתִּי לְפָנֶיךָ מַלְאָךְ וְגֵרַשְׁתִּי אֶת־הַכְּנַעֲנִי הָאֱמֹרִי וְהַחִתִּי וְהַפְּרִזִּי הַחִוִּי וְהַיְבוּסִי:

3 a land flowing with milk and honey. But I will not go in your midst, since you are a stiffnecked people, lest I destroy you on the way."

ג אֶל־אֶרֶץ זָבַת חָלָב וּדְבָשׁ כִּי לֹא אֶעֱלֶה בְּקִרְבְּךָ כִּי עַם־קְשֵׁה־עֹרֶף אַתָּה פֶּן־אֲכֶלְךָ בַּדָּרֶךְ:

4 When the people heard this harsh word, they went into mourning, and none put on his finery.

ד וַיִּשְׁמַע הָעָם אֶת־הַדָּבָר הָרָע הַזֶּה וַיִּתְאַבָּלוּ וְלֹא־שָׁתוּ אִישׁ עֶדְיוֹ עָלָיו:

5 *Hashem* said to *Moshe*, "Say to *B'nei Yisrael*, 'You are a stiffnecked people. If I were to go in your midst for one moment, I would destroy you. Now, then, leave off your finery, and I will consider what to do to you.'"

ה וַיֹּאמֶר יְהֹוָה אֶל־מֹשֶׁה אֱמֹר אֶל־בְּנֵי־יִשְׂרָאֵל אַתֶּם עַם־קְשֵׁה־עֹרֶף רֶגַע אֶחָד אֶעֱלֶה בְקִרְבְּךָ וְכִלִּיתִיךָ וְעַתָּה הוֹרֵד עֶדְיְךָ מֵעָלֶיךָ וְאֵדְעָה מָה אֶעֱשֶׂה־לָּךְ:

6 So the Israelites remained stripped of the finery from Mount Horeb on.

ו וַיִּתְנַצְּלוּ בְנֵי־יִשְׂרָאֵל אֶת־עֶדְיָם מֵהַר חוֹרֵב:

7 Now *Moshe* would take the Tent and pitch it outside the camp, at some distance from the camp. It was called the Tent of Meeting, and whoever sought *Hashem* would go out to the Tent of Meeting that was outside the camp.

ז וּמֹשֶׁה יִקַּח אֶת־הָאֹהֶל וְנָטָה־לוֹ מִחוּץ לַמַּחֲנֶה הַרְחֵק מִן־הַמַּחֲנֶה וְקָרָא לוֹ אֹהֶל מוֹעֵד וְהָיָה כָּל־מְבַקֵּשׁ יְהֹוָה יֵצֵא אֶל־אֹהֶל מוֹעֵד אֲשֶׁר מִחוּץ לַמַּחֲנֶה:

8 Whenever *Moshe* went out to the Tent, all the people would rise and stand, each at the entrance of his tent, and gaze after *Moshe* until he had entered the Tent.

ח וְהָיָה כְּצֵאת מֹשֶׁה אֶל־הָאֹהֶל יָקוּמוּ כָּל־הָעָם וְנִצְּבוּ אִישׁ פֶּתַח אָהֳלוֹ וְהִבִּיטוּ אַחֲרֵי מֹשֶׁה עַד־בֹּאוֹ הָאֹהֱלָה:

9 And when *Moshe* entered the Tent, the pillar of cloud would descend and stand at the entrance of the Tent, while He spoke with *Moshe*.

ט וְהָיָה כְּבֹא מֹשֶׁה הָאֹהֱלָה יֵרֵד עַמּוּד הֶעָנָן וְעָמַד פֶּתַח הָאֹהֶל וְדִבֶּר עִם־מֹשֶׁה:

33:1 Set out from here The Hebrew for 'set out from here' is *lech, aleh mizeh* (לך עלה מזה). The word *lech* means 'go' or 'set out,' and the word *aleh* means 'ascend.' It seems that it would have been enough for *Hashem* to simply tell *Moshe lech mizeh*, set out from here, and head to "the land of which I swore…" What is added by the word *aleh*, 'ascend'? *Rashi* finds a beautiful message in this seemingly extraneous word. He quotes the Talmud (*Zevachim* 54b) which teaches a precious lesson regarding the role of *Eretz Yisrael*: In a spiritual sense, the Holy Land is "the highest of all places on Earth" which is why the *Torah* uses an extra word, "to ascend."

לך עלה מזה

Shemot/Exodus 33
Ki Tisa

שמות לג
כי תשא

10 When all the people saw the pillar of cloud poised at the entrance of the Tent, all the people would rise and bow low, each at the entrance of his tent.

וְרָאָה כָל־הָעָם אֶת־עַמּוּד הֶעָנָן עֹמֵד פֶּתַח הָאֹהֶל וְקָם כָּל־הָעָם וְהִשְׁתַּחֲווּ אִישׁ פֶּתַח אָהֳלוֹ:

11 *Hashem* would speak to *Moshe* face to face, as one man speaks to another. And he would then return to the camp; but his attendant, *Yehoshua* son of *Nun*, a youth, would not stir out of the Tent.

וְדִבֶּר יְהֹוָה אֶל־מֹשֶׁה פָּנִים אֶל־פָּנִים כַּאֲשֶׁר יְדַבֵּר אִישׁ אֶל־רֵעֵהוּ וְשָׁב אֶל־הַמַּחֲנֶה וּמְשָׁרְתוֹ יְהוֹשֻׁעַ בִּן־נוּן נַעַר לֹא יָמִישׁ מִתּוֹךְ הָאֹהֶל:

12 *Moshe* said to *Hashem*, "See, You say to me, 'Lead this people forward,' but You have not made known to me whom You will send with me. Further, You have said, 'I have singled you out by name, and you have, indeed, gained My favor.'

וַיֹּאמֶר מֹשֶׁה אֶל־יְהֹוָה רְאֵה אַתָּה אֹמֵר אֵלַי הַעַל אֶת־הָעָם הַזֶּה וְאַתָּה לֹא הוֹדַעְתַּנִי אֵת אֲשֶׁר־תִּשְׁלַח עִמִּי וְאַתָּה אָמַרְתָּ יְדַעְתִּיךָ בְשֵׁם וְגַם־מָצָאתָ חֵן בְּעֵינָי:

13 Now, if I have truly gained Your favor, pray let me know Your ways, that I may know You and continue in Your favor. Consider, too, that this nation is Your people."

וְעַתָּה אִם־נָא מָצָאתִי חֵן בְּעֵינֶיךָ הוֹדִעֵנִי נָא אֶת־דְּרָכֶךָ וְאֵדָעֲךָ לְמַעַן אֶמְצָא־חֵן בְּעֵינֶיךָ וּרְאֵה כִּי עַמְּךָ הַגּוֹי הַזֶּה:

14 And He said, "I will go in the lead and will lighten your burden."

וַיֹּאמַר פָּנַי יֵלֵכוּ וַהֲנִחֹתִי לָךְ:

15 And he said to Him, "Unless You go in the lead, do not make us leave this place.

וַיֹּאמֶר אֵלָיו אִם־אֵין פָּנֶיךָ הֹלְכִים אַל־תַּעֲלֵנוּ מִזֶּה:

16 For how shall it be known that Your people have gained Your favor unless You go with us, so that we may be distinguished, Your people and I, from every people on the face of the earth?"

וּבַמֶּה יִוָּדַע אֵפוֹא כִּי־מָצָאתִי חֵן בְּעֵינֶיךָ אֲנִי וְעַמֶּךָ הֲלוֹא בְּלֶכְתְּךָ עִמָּנוּ וְנִפְלִינוּ אֲנִי וְעַמְּךָ מִכָּל־הָעָם אֲשֶׁר עַל־פְּנֵי הָאֲדָמָה:

17 And *Hashem* said to *Moshe*, "I will also do this thing that you have asked; for you have truly gained My favor and I have singled you out by name."

וַיֹּאמֶר יְהֹוָה אֶל־מֹשֶׁה גַּם אֶת־הַדָּבָר הַזֶּה אֲשֶׁר דִּבַּרְתָּ אֶעֱשֶׂה כִּי־מָצָאתָ חֵן בְּעֵינַי וָאֵדָעֲךָ בְּשֵׁם:

18 He said, "Oh, let me behold Your Presence!"

וַיֹּאמַר הַרְאֵנִי נָא אֶת־כְּבֹדֶךָ:

19 And He answered, "I will make all My goodness pass before you, and I will proclaim before you the name *Hashem*, and the grace that I grant and the compassion that I show.

וַיֹּאמֶר אֲנִי אַעֲבִיר כָּל־טוּבִי עַל־פָּנֶיךָ וְקָרָאתִי בְשֵׁם יְהֹוָה לְפָנֶיךָ וְחַנֹּתִי אֶת־אֲשֶׁר אָחֹן וְרִחַמְתִּי אֶת־אֲשֶׁר אֲרַחֵם:

20 But," He said, "you cannot see My face, for man may not see Me and live."

וַיֹּאמֶר לֹא תוּכַל לִרְאֹת אֶת־פָּנָי כִּי לֹא־יִרְאַנִי הָאָדָם וָחָי:

21 And *Hashem* said, "See, there is a place near Me. Station yourself on the rock

וַיֹּאמֶר יְהֹוָה הִנֵּה מָקוֹם אִתִּי וְנִצַּבְתָּ עַל־הַצּוּר:

22 and, as My Presence passes by, I will put you in a cleft of the rock and shield you with My hand until I have passed by.

וְהָיָה בַּעֲבֹר כְּבֹדִי וְשַׂמְתִּיךָ בְּנִקְרַת הַצּוּר וְשַׂכֹּתִי כַפִּי עָלֶיךָ עַד־עָבְרִי:

Shemot/Exodus 34
Ki Tisa

שמות לד
כי תשא

23 Then I will take My hand away and you will see My back; but My face must not be seen."

כג וַהֲסִרֹתִי֙ אֶת־כַּפִּ֔י וְרָאִ֖יתָ אֶת־אֲחֹרָ֑י וּפָנַ֖י לֹ֥א יֵרָאֽוּ׃

34 1 *Hashem* said to *Moshe*: "Carve two tablets of stone like the first, and I will inscribe upon the tablets the words that were on the first tablets, which you shattered.

לד א וַיֹּ֤אמֶר יְהֹוָה֙ אֶל־מֹשֶׁ֔ה פְּסׇל־לְךָ֛ שְׁנֵֽי־לֻחֹ֥ת אֲבָנִ֖ים כָּרִאשֹׁנִ֑ים וְכָתַבְתִּי֙ עַל־הַלֻּחֹ֔ת אֶת־הַדְּבָרִ֔ים אֲשֶׁ֥ר הָי֛וּ עַל־הַלֻּחֹ֥ת הָרִאשֹׁנִ֖ים אֲשֶׁ֥ר שִׁבַּֽרְתָּ׃

2 Be ready by morning, and in the morning come up to *Har Sinai* and present yourself there to Me, on the top of the mountain.

ב וֶהְיֵ֥ה נָכ֖וֹן לַבֹּ֑קֶר וְעָלִ֤יתָ בַבֹּ֙קֶר֙ אֶל־הַ֣ר סִינַ֔י וְנִצַּבְתָּ֥ לִ֛י שָׁ֖ם עַל־רֹ֥אשׁ הָהָֽר׃

3 No one else shall come up with you, and no one else shall be seen anywhere on the mountain; neither shall the flocks and the herds graze at the foot of this mountain."

ג וְאִישׁ֙ לֹֽא־יַעֲלֶ֣ה עִמָּ֔ךְ וְגַם־אִ֥ישׁ אַל־יֵרָ֖א בְּכׇל־הָהָ֑ר גַּם־הַצֹּ֤אן וְהַבָּקָר֙ אַל־יִרְע֔וּ אֶל־מ֖וּל הָהָ֥ר הַהֽוּא׃

4 So *Moshe* carved two tablets of stone, like the first, and early in the morning he went up on *Har Sinai*, as *Hashem* had commanded him, taking the two stone tablets with him.

ד וַיִּפְסֹ֡ל שְׁנֵֽי־לֻחֹ֨ת אֲבָנִ֜ים כָּרִאשֹׁנִ֗ים וַיַּשְׁכֵּ֨ם מֹשֶׁ֤ה בַבֹּ֙קֶר֙ וַיַּ֙עַל֙ אֶל־הַ֣ר סִינַ֔י כַּאֲשֶׁ֛ר צִוָּ֥ה יְהֹוָ֖ה אֹת֑וֹ וַיִּקַּ֣ח בְּיָד֔וֹ שְׁנֵ֖י לֻחֹ֥ת אֲבָנִֽים׃

5 *Hashem* came down in a cloud; He stood with him there, and proclaimed the name *Hashem*.

ה וַיֵּ֤רֶד יְהֹוָה֙ בֶּֽעָנָ֔ן וַיִּתְיַצֵּ֥ב עִמּ֖וֹ שָׁ֑ם וַיִּקְרָ֥א בְשֵׁ֖ם יְהֹוָֽה׃

6 *Hashem* passed before him and proclaimed: "*Hashem*! *Hashem*! a *Hashem* compassionate and gracious, slow to anger, abounding in kindness and faithfulness,

ו וַיַּעֲבֹ֨ר יְהֹוָ֥ה ׀ עַל־פָּנָיו֮ וַיִּקְרָא֒ יְהֹוָ֣ה ׀ יְהֹוָ֔ה אֵ֥ל רַח֖וּם וְחַנּ֑וּן אֶ֥רֶךְ אַפַּ֖יִם וְרַב־חֶ֥סֶד וֶאֱמֶֽת׃

7 extending kindness to the thousandth generation, forgiving iniquity, transgression, and sin; yet He does not remit all punishment, but visits the iniquity of parents upon children and children's children, upon the third and fourth generations."

ז נֹצֵ֥ר חֶ֙סֶד֙ לָאֲלָפִ֔ים נֹשֵׂ֥א עָוֺ֛ן וָפֶ֖שַׁע וְחַטָּאָ֑ה וְנַקֵּה֙ לֹ֣א יְנַקֶּ֔ה פֹּקֵ֣ד ׀ עֲוֺ֣ן אָב֗וֹת עַל־בָּנִים֙ וְעַל־בְּנֵ֣י בָנִ֔ים עַל־שִׁלֵּשִׁ֖ים וְעַל־רִבֵּעִֽים׃

8 *Moshe* hastened to bow low to the ground in homage,

ח וַיְמַהֵ֖ר מֹשֶׁ֑ה וַיִּקֹּ֥ד אַ֖רְצָה וַיִּשְׁתָּֽחוּ׃

9 and said, "If I have gained Your favor, O *Hashem*, pray, let *Hashem* go in our midst, even though this is a stiffnecked people. Pardon our iniquity and our sin, and take us for Your own!"

ט וַיֹּ֡אמֶר אִם־נָא֩ מָצָ֨אתִי חֵ֤ן בְּעֵינֶ֙יךָ֙ אֲדֹנָ֔י יֵֽלֶךְ־נָ֥א אֲדֹנָ֖י בְּקִרְבֵּ֑נוּ כִּ֤י עַם־קְשֵׁה־עֹ֙רֶף֙ ה֔וּא וְסָלַחְתָּ֛ לַעֲוֺנֵ֥נוּ וּלְחַטָּאתֵ֖נוּ וּנְחַלְתָּֽנוּ׃

10 He said: I hereby make a covenant. Before all your people I will work such wonders as have not been wrought on all the earth or in any nation; and all the people who are with you shall see how awesome are *Hashem*'s deeds which I will perform for you.

י וַיֹּ֗אמֶר הִנֵּ֣ה אָנֹכִי֮ כֹּרֵ֣ת בְּרִית֒ נֶ֤גֶד כׇּֽל־עַמְּךָ֙ אֶעֱשֶׂ֣ה נִפְלָאֹ֔ת אֲשֶׁ֛ר לֹֽא־נִבְרְא֥וּ בְכׇל־הָאָ֖רֶץ וּבְכׇל־הַגּוֹיִ֑ם וְרָאָ֣ה כׇל־הָ֠עָ֠ם אֲשֶׁר־אַתָּ֨ה בְקִרְבּ֜וֹ אֶת־מַעֲשֵׂ֤ה יְהֹוָה֙ כִּֽי־נוֹרָ֣א ה֔וּא אֲשֶׁ֥ר אֲנִ֖י עֹשֶׂ֥ה עִמָּֽךְ׃

Shemot/Exodus 34
Ki Tisa

שְׁמָר־לְךָ אֵת אֲשֶׁר אָנֹכִי מְצַוְּךָ הַיּוֹם הִנְנִי גֹרֵשׁ מִפָּנֶיךָ אֶת־הָאֱמֹרִי וְהַכְּנַעֲנִי וְהַחִתִּי וְהַפְּרִזִּי וְהַחִוִּי וְהַיְבוּסִי: יא

11 Mark well what I command you this day. I will drive out before you the Amorites, the Canaanites, the Hittites, the Perizzites, the Hivites, and the Jebusites.

הִשָּׁמֶר לְךָ פֶּן־תִּכְרֹת בְּרִית לְיוֹשֵׁב הָאָרֶץ אֲשֶׁר אַתָּה בָּא עָלֶיהָ פֶּן־יִהְיֶה לְמוֹקֵשׁ בְּקִרְבֶּךָ: יב

12 Beware of making a covenant with the inhabitants of the land against which you are advancing, lest they be a snare in your midst.

כִּי אֶת־מִזְבְּחֹתָם תִּתֹּצוּן וְאֶת־מַצֵּבֹתָם תְּשַׁבֵּרוּן וְאֶת־אֲשֵׁרָיו תִּכְרֹתוּן: יג

13 No, you must tear down their altars, smash their pillars, and cut down their sacred posts;

כִּי לֹא תִשְׁתַּחֲוֶה לְאֵל אַחֵר כִּי יְהֹוָה קַנָּא שְׁמוֹ אֵל קַנָּא הוּא: יד

14 for you must not worship any other god, because *Hashem*, whose name is Impassioned, is an impassioned God.

פֶּן־תִּכְרֹת בְּרִית לְיוֹשֵׁב הָאָרֶץ וְזָנוּ אַחֲרֵי אֱלֹהֵיהֶם וְזָבְחוּ לֵאלֹהֵיהֶם וְקָרָא לְךָ וְאָכַלְתָּ מִזִּבְחוֹ: טו

15 You must not make a covenant with the inhabitants of the land, for they will lust after their gods and sacrifice to their gods and invite you, and you will eat of their sacrifices.

וְלָקַחְתָּ מִבְּנֹתָיו לְבָנֶיךָ וְזָנוּ בְנֹתָיו אַחֲרֵי אֱלֹהֵיהֶן וְהִזְנוּ אֶת־בָּנֶיךָ אַחֲרֵי אֱלֹהֵיהֶן: טז

16 And when you take wives from among their daughters for your sons, their daughters will lust after their gods and will cause your sons to lust after their gods.

אֱלֹהֵי מַסֵּכָה לֹא תַעֲשֶׂה־לָּךְ: יז

17 You shall not make molten gods for yourselves.

אֶת־חַג הַמַּצּוֹת תִּשְׁמֹר שִׁבְעַת יָמִים תֹּאכַל מַצּוֹת אֲשֶׁר צִוִּיתִךָ לְמוֹעֵד חֹדֶשׁ הָאָבִיב כִּי בְּחֹדֶשׁ הָאָבִיב יָצָאתָ מִמִּצְרָיִם: יח

18 You shall observe the festival of *Pesach* – eating unleavened bread for seven days, as I have commanded you – at the set time of the month of Abib, for in the month of Abib you went forth from Egypt.

כָּל־פֶּטֶר רֶחֶם לִי וְכָל־מִקְנְךָ תִּזָּכָר פֶּטֶר שׁוֹר וָשֶׂה: יט

19 Every first issue of the womb is Mine, from all your livestock that drop a male as firstling, whether cattle or sheep.

וּפֶטֶר חֲמוֹר תִּפְדֶּה בְשֶׂה וְאִם־לֹא תִפְדֶּה וַעֲרַפְתּוֹ כֹּל בְּכוֹר בָּנֶיךָ תִּפְדֶּה וְלֹא־יֵרָאוּ פָנַי רֵיקָם: כ

20 But the firstling of an ass you shall redeem with a sheep; if you do not redeem it, you must break its neck. And you must redeem every first-born among your sons. None shall appear before Me empty-handed.

שֵׁשֶׁת יָמִים תַּעֲבֹד וּבַיּוֹם הַשְּׁבִיעִי תִּשְׁבֹּת בֶּחָרִישׁ וּבַקָּצִיר תִּשְׁבֹּת: כא

21 Six days you shall work, but on the seventh day you shall cease from labor; you shall cease from labor even at plowing time and harvest time.

וְחַג שָׁבֻעֹת תַּעֲשֶׂה לְךָ בִּכּוּרֵי קְצִיר חִטִּים וְחַג הָאָסִיף תְּקוּפַת הַשָּׁנָה: כב

22 You shall observe the festival of *Shavuot*, of the first fruits of the wheat harvest; and the Feast of Ingathering at the turn of the year.

שָׁלֹשׁ פְּעָמִים בַּשָּׁנָה יֵרָאֶה כָּל־זְכוּרְךָ אֶת־פְּנֵי הָאָדֹן יְהֹוָה אֱלֹהֵי יִשְׂרָאֵל: כג

23 Three times a year all your males shall appear before the Sovereign *Hashem*, the God of *Yisrael*.

Shemot/Exodus 34
Ki Tisa

24 I will drive out nations from your path and enlarge your territory; no one will covet your land when you go up to appear before *Hashem* your God three times a year.

כד כִּֽי־אוֹרִ֤ישׁ גּוֹיִם֙ מִפָּנֶ֔יךָ וְהִרְחַבְתִּ֖י אֶת־גְּבוּלֶ֑ךָ וְלֹא־יַחְמֹ֥ד אִישׁ֙ אֶֽת־אַרְצְךָ֔ בַּעֲלֹֽתְךָ֗ לֵרָאוֹת֙ אֶת־פְּנֵי֙ יְהֹוָ֣ה אֱלֹהֶ֔יךָ שָׁלֹ֥שׁ פְּעָמִ֖ים בַּשָּׁנָֽה׃

kee o-REESH go-YIM mi-pa-NE-kha v'-hir-khav-TEE et g'-vu-LE-kha v'-lo yakh-MOD EESH et ar-tz'-KHA ba-a-lo-t'-KHA lay-ra-OT et p'-NAY a-do-NAI e-lo-HE-kha sha-LOSH p'-a-MEEM ba-sha-NAH

25 You shall not offer the blood of My sacrifice with anything leavened; and the sacrifice of the festival of *Pesach* shall not be left lying until morning.

כה לֹֽא־תִשְׁחַ֥ט עַל־חָמֵ֖ץ דַּם־זִבְחִ֑י וְלֹא־יָלִ֣ין לַבֹּ֔קֶר זֶ֖בַח חַ֥ג הַפָּֽסַח׃

26 The choice first fruits of your soil you shall bring to the house of *Hashem* your God. You shall not boil a kid in its mother's milk.

כו רֵאשִׁ֗ית בִּכּוּרֵי֙ אַדְמָ֣תְךָ֔ תָּבִ֕יא בֵּ֖ית יְהֹוָ֣ה אֱלֹהֶ֑יךָ לֹֽא־תְבַשֵּׁ֥ל גְּדִ֖י בַּחֲלֵ֥ב אִמּֽוֹ׃

27 And *Hashem* said to *Moshe*: Write down these commandments, for in accordance with these commandments I make a covenant with you and with *Yisrael*.

כז וַיֹּ֤אמֶר יְהֹוָה֙ אֶל־מֹשֶׁ֔ה כְּתָב־לְךָ֖ אֶת־הַדְּבָרִ֣ים הָאֵ֑לֶּה כִּ֞י עַל־פִּ֣י ׀ הַדְּבָרִ֣ים הָאֵ֗לֶּה כָּרַ֧תִּי אִתְּךָ֛ בְּרִ֖ית וְאֶת־יִשְׂרָאֵֽל׃

28 And he was there with *Hashem* forty days and forty nights; he ate no bread and drank no water; and he wrote down on the tablets the terms of the covenant, the Ten Commandments.

כח וַיְהִי־שָׁ֣ם עִם־יְהֹוָ֗ה אַרְבָּעִ֥ים יוֹם֙ וְאַרְבָּעִ֣ים לַ֔יְלָה לֶ֚חֶם לֹ֣א אָכַ֔ל וּמַ֖יִם לֹ֣א שָׁתָ֑ה וַיִּכְתֹּ֣ב עַל־הַלֻּחֹ֗ת אֵ֚ת דִּבְרֵ֣י הַבְּרִ֔ית עֲשֶׂ֖רֶת הַדְּבָרִֽים׃

29 So *Moshe* came down from *Har Sinai*. And as *Moshe* came down from the mountain bearing the two tablets of the Pact, *Moshe* was not aware that the skin of his face was radiant, since he had spoken with Him.

כט וַיְהִ֗י בְּרֶ֤דֶת מֹשֶׁה֙ מֵהַ֣ר סִינַ֔י וּשְׁנֵ֨י לֻחֹ֤ת הָעֵדֻת֙ בְּיַד־מֹשֶׁ֔ה בְּרִדְתּ֖וֹ מִן־הָהָ֑ר וּמֹשֶׁ֣ה לֹֽא־יָדַ֗ע כִּ֥י קָרַ֛ן ע֥וֹר פָּנָ֖יו בְּדַבְּר֥וֹ אִתּֽוֹ׃

vai-HEE b'-RE-det mo-SHEH may-HAR see-NAI ush-NAY lu-KHOT ha-ay-DUT b'-yad mo-SHEH b'-rid-TO min ha-HAR u-mo-SHEH lo ya-DA KEE ka-RAN OR pa-NAV b'-da-b'-RO i-TO

30 *Aharon* and all the Israelites saw that the skin of *Moshe*'s face was radiant; and they shrank from coming near him.

ל וַיַּ֨רְא אַהֲרֹ֜ן וְכׇל־בְּנֵ֤י יִשְׂרָאֵל֙ אֶת־מֹשֶׁ֔ה וְהִנֵּ֥ה קָרַ֖ן ע֣וֹר פָּנָ֑יו וַיִּֽירְא֖וּ מִגֶּ֥שֶׁת אֵלָֽיו׃

31 But *Moshe* called to them, and *Aharon* and all the chieftains in the assembly returned to him, and *Moshe* spoke to them.

לא וַיִּקְרָ֤א אֲלֵהֶם֙ מֹשֶׁ֔ה וַיָּשֻׁ֧בוּ אֵלָ֛יו אַהֲרֹ֖ן וְכׇל־הַנְּשִׂאִ֣ים בָּעֵדָ֑ה וַיְדַבֵּ֥ר מֹשֶׁ֖ה אֲלֵהֶֽם׃

34:24 No one will covet your land when you go up to appear before *Hashem* This verse refers to the triannual festival pilgrimage to *Yerushalayim*. Based on this verse, the Talmud (*Pesachim* 8b) suggests that only people who owned property in the Land of Israel were required to make the pilgrimage, since the focus of the trip was to bring the first fruits and the second tithe produce to *Yerushalayim*, and only a person with farmland would have such produce to bring. In practice, however, everyone was required to make the journey. The pilgrimage was a joyous occasion, a celebration of thanks to God for the land and the rain that had provided the farmer with a harvest. To this day, Jews continue to make a point of visiting *Yerushalayim* and the site of the *Beit Hamikdash* during the three festivals: *Pesach*, *Shavuot* and *Sukkot*.

Praying at the Western Wall on Succot

Shemot/Exodus 35
Vayakhel

32 Afterward all the Israelites came near, and he instructed them concerning all that *Hashem* had imparted to him on *Har Sinai*.

33 And when *Moshe* had finished speaking with them, he put a veil over his face.

34 Whenever *Moshe* went in before *Hashem* to speak with Him, he would leave the veil off until he came out; and when he came out and told the Israelites what he had been commanded,

35 the Israelites would see how radiant the skin of *Moshe*'s face was. *Moshe* would then put the veil back over his face until he went in to speak with Him.

35

1 *Moshe* then convoked the whole Israelite community and said to them: These are the things that *Hashem* has commanded you to do:

2 On six days work may be done, but on the seventh day you shall have a *Shabbat* of complete rest, holy to *Hashem*; whoever does any work on it shall be put to death.

3 You shall kindle no fire throughout your settlements on the *Shabbat* day.

4 *Moshe* said further to the whole community of Israelites: This is what *Hashem* has commanded:

5 Take from among you gifts to *Hashem*; everyone whose heart so moves him shall bring them – gifts for *Hashem*: gold, silver, and copper;

6 blue, purple, and crimson yarns, fine linen, and goats' hair;

7 tanned ram skins, dolphin skins, and acacia wood;

8 oil for lighting, spices for the anointing oil and for the aromatic incense;

9 lapis lazuli and other stones for setting, for the ephod and the breastpiece.

10 And let all among you who are skilled come and make all that *Hashem* has commanded:

11 the *Mishkan*, its tent and its covering, its clasps and its planks, its bars, its posts, and its sockets;

Shemot/Exodus 35
Vayakhel

12 the ark and its poles, the cover, and the curtain for the screen;

13 the table, and its poles and all its utensils; and the bread of display;

14 the *menorah* for lighting, its furnishings and its lamps, and the oil for lighting;

15 the *Mizbayach* of incense and its poles; the anointing oil and the aromatic incense; and the entrance screen for the entrance of the *Mishkan*;

16 the *Mizbayach* of burnt offering, its copper grating, its poles, and all its furnishings; the laver and its stand;

17 the hangings of the enclosure, its posts and its sockets, and the screen for the gate of the court;

18 the pegs for the *Mishkan*, the pegs for the enclosure, and their cords;

19 the service vestments for officiating in the sanctuary, the sacral vestments of *Aharon* the *Kohen* and the vestments of his sons for priestly service.

20 So the whole community of the Israelites left *Moshe*'s presence.

21 And everyone who excelled in ability and everyone whose spirit moved him came, bringing to *Hashem* his offering for the work of the Tent of Meeting and for all its service and for the sacral vestments.

22 Men and women, all whose hearts moved them, all who would make an elevation offering of gold to *Hashem*, came bringing brooches, earrings, rings, and pendants – gold objects of all kinds.

23 And everyone who had in his possession blue, purple, and crimson yarns, fine linen, goats' hair, tanned ram skins, and dolphin skins, brought them;

24 everyone who would make gifts of silver or copper brought them as gifts for *Hashem*; and everyone who had in his possession acacia wood for any work of the service brought that.

25 And all the skilled women spun with their own hands, and brought what they had spun, in blue, purple, and crimson yarns, and in fine linen.

Shemot/Exodus 36
Vayakhel

שמות לו
ויקהל

26 And all the women who excelled in that skill spun the goats' hair.

כו וְכָל־הַנָּשִׁים אֲשֶׁר נָשָׂא לִבָּן אֹתָנָה בְּחָכְמָה טָווּ אֶת־הָעִזִּים:

27 And the chieftains brought lapis lazuli and other stones for setting, for the ephod and for the breastpiece;

כז וְהַנְּשִׂאִם הֵבִיאוּ אֵת אַבְנֵי הַשֹּׁהַם וְאֵת אַבְנֵי הַמִּלֻּאִים לָאֵפוֹד וְלַחֹשֶׁן:

28 and spices and oil for lighting, for the anointing oil, and for the aromatic incense.

כח וְאֶת־הַבֹּשֶׂם וְאֶת־הַשָּׁמֶן לְמָאוֹר וּלְשֶׁמֶן הַמִּשְׁחָה וְלִקְטֹרֶת הַסַּמִּים:

29 Thus the Israelites, all the men and women whose hearts moved them to bring anything for the work that *Hashem*, through *Moshe*, had commanded to be done, brought it as a freewill offering to *Hashem*.

כט כָּל־אִישׁ וְאִשָּׁה אֲשֶׁר נָדַב לִבָּם אֹתָם לְהָבִיא לְכָל־הַמְּלָאכָה אֲשֶׁר צִוָּה יְהֹוָה לַעֲשׂוֹת בְּיַד־מֹשֶׁה הֵבִיאוּ בְנֵי־יִשְׂרָאֵל נְדָבָה לַיהֹוָה:

kol EESH v'-i-SHAH a-SHER na-DAV li-BAM o-TAM l'-ha-VEE l'-khol ha-m'-la-KHAH a-SHER tzi-VAH a-do-NAI la-a-SOT b'-YAD mo-SHEH hay-VEE-u v'-nay yis-ra-AYL n'-da-VAH la-do-NAI

30 And *Moshe* said to the Israelites: See, *Hashem* has singled out by name *Betzalel*, son of *Uri* son of *Chur*, of the tribe of *Yehuda*.

ל וַיֹּאמֶר מֹשֶׁה אֶל־בְּנֵי יִשְׂרָאֵל רְאוּ קָרָא יְהֹוָה בְּשֵׁם בְּצַלְאֵל בֶּן־אוּרִי בֶן־חוּר לְמַטֵּה יְהוּדָה:

31 He has endowed him with a divine spirit of skill, ability, and knowledge in every kind of craft

לא וַיְמַלֵּא אֹתוֹ רוּחַ אֱלֹהִים בְּחָכְמָה בִּתְבוּנָה וּבְדַעַת וּבְכָל־מְלָאכָה:

32 and has inspired him* to make designs for work in gold, silver, and copper,

לב וְלַחְשֹׁב מַחֲשָׁבֹת לַעֲשֹׂת בַּזָּהָב וּבַכֶּסֶף וּבַנְּחֹשֶׁת:

33 to cut stones for setting and to carve wood – to work in every kind of designer's craft

לג וּבַחֲרֹשֶׁת אֶבֶן לְמַלֹּאת וּבַחֲרֹשֶׁת עֵץ לַעֲשׂוֹת בְּכָל־מְלֶאכֶת מַחֲשָׁבֶת:

34 and to give directions. He and *Oholiav* son of *Achisamach* of the tribe of *Dan*

לד וּלְהוֹרֹת נָתַן בְּלִבּוֹ הוּא וְאָהֳלִיאָב בֶּן־אֲחִיסָמָךְ לְמַטֵּה־דָן:

35 have been endowed with the skill to do any work – of the carver, the designer, the embroiderer in blue, purple, crimson yarns, and in fine linen, and of the weaver – as workers in all crafts and as makers of designs.

לה מִלֵּא אֹתָם חָכְמַת־לֵב לַעֲשׂוֹת כָּל־מְלֶאכֶת חָרָשׁ וְחֹשֵׁב וְרֹקֵם בַּתְּכֵלֶת וּבָאַרְגָּמָן בְּתוֹלַעַת הַשָּׁנִי וּבַשֵּׁשׁ וְאֹרֵג עֹשֵׂי כָּל־מְלָאכָה וְחֹשְׁבֵי מַחֲשָׁבֹת:

36
1 Let, then, *Betzalel* and *Oholiav* and all the skilled persons whom *Hashem* has endowed with skill and ability to perform expertly all the tasks connected with the service of the sanctuary carry out all that *Hashem* has commanded.

לו
א וְעָשָׂה בְצַלְאֵל וְאָהֳלִיאָב וְכֹל אִישׁ חֲכַם־לֵב אֲשֶׁר נָתַן יְהֹוָה חָכְמָה וּתְבוּנָה בָּהֵמָּה לָדַעַת לַעֲשֹׂת אֶת־כָּל־מְלֶאכֶת עֲבֹדַת הַקֹּדֶשׁ לְכֹל אֲשֶׁר־צִוָּה יְהֹוָה:

---

* "has inspired him" moved up from v. 34 for clarity

35:29 Whose hearts moved them The *Mishkan* is a glorious structure decorated with precious metals, tapestries and intricate designs. The raw materials for its constructions are donated by the nation itself, by every man and woman "whose hearts moved them" to give of themselves and their belongings to *Hashem*. Since this structure is meant to foster deep, meaningful relationships between man and God, it stands to reason that the construction materials were taken from those who donated with this highest of intentions.

Shemot/Exodus 36
Vayakhel

שמות לו
ויקהל

2 *Moshe* then called *Betzalel* and *Oholiav*, and every skilled person whom *Hashem* had endowed with skill, everyone who excelled in ability, to undertake the task and carry it out.

ב וַיִּקְרָא מֹשֶׁה אֶל־בְּצַלְאֵל וְאֶל־אָהֳלִיאָב וְאֶל כָּל־אִישׁ חֲכַם־לֵב אֲשֶׁר נָתַן יְהוָה חָכְמָה בְּלִבּוֹ כֹּל אֲשֶׁר נְשָׂאוֹ לִבּוֹ לְקָרְבָה אֶל־הַמְּלָאכָה לַעֲשֹׂת אֹתָהּ׃

3 They took over from *Moshe* all the gifts that the Israelites had brought, to carry out the tasks connected with the service of the sanctuary. But when these continued to bring freewill offerings to him morning after morning,

ג וַיִּקְחוּ מִלִּפְנֵי מֹשֶׁה אֵת כָּל־הַתְּרוּמָה אֲשֶׁר הֵבִיאוּ בְּנֵי יִשְׂרָאֵל לִמְלֶאכֶת עֲבֹדַת הַקֹּדֶשׁ לַעֲשֹׂת אֹתָהּ וְהֵם הֵבִיאוּ אֵלָיו עוֹד נְדָבָה בַּבֹּקֶר בַּבֹּקֶר׃

4 all the artisans who were engaged in the tasks of the sanctuary came, each from the task upon which he was engaged,

ד וַיָּבֹאוּ כָּל־הַחֲכָמִים הָעֹשִׂים אֵת כָּל־מְלֶאכֶת הַקֹּדֶשׁ אִישׁ־אִישׁ מִמְּלַאכְתּוֹ אֲשֶׁר־הֵמָּה עֹשִׂים׃

5 and said to *Moshe*, "The people are bringing more than is needed for the tasks entailed in the work that *Hashem* has commanded to be done."

ה וַיֹּאמְרוּ אֶל־מֹשֶׁה לֵּאמֹר מַרְבִּים הָעָם לְהָבִיא מִדֵּי הָעֲבֹדָה לַמְּלָאכָה אֲשֶׁר־צִוָּה יְהוָה לַעֲשֹׂת אֹתָהּ׃

6 *Moshe* thereupon had this proclamation made throughout the camp: "Let no man or woman make further effort toward gifts for the sanctuary!" So the people stopped bringing:

ו וַיְצַו מֹשֶׁה וַיַּעֲבִירוּ קוֹל בַּמַּחֲנֶה לֵאמֹר אִישׁ וְאִשָּׁה אַל־יַעֲשׂוּ־עוֹד מְלָאכָה לִתְרוּמַת הַקֹּדֶשׁ וַיִּכָּלֵא הָעָם מֵהָבִיא׃

7 their efforts had been more than enough for all the tasks to be done.

ז וְהַמְּלָאכָה הָיְתָה דַיָּם לְכָל־הַמְּלָאכָה לַעֲשׂוֹת אֹתָהּ וְהוֹתֵר׃

8 Then all the skilled among those engaged in the work made the *Mishkan* of ten strips of cloth, which they made of fine twisted linen, blue, purple, and crimson yarns; into these they worked a design of cherubim.

ח וַיַּעֲשׂוּ כָל־חֲכַם־לֵב בְּעֹשֵׂי הַמְּלָאכָה אֶת־הַמִּשְׁכָּן עֶשֶׂר יְרִיעֹת שֵׁשׁ מָשְׁזָר וּתְכֵלֶת וְאַרְגָּמָן וְתוֹלַעַת שָׁנִי כְּרֻבִים מַעֲשֵׂה חֹשֵׁב עָשָׂה אֹתָם׃

va-ya-a-SU khol kha-kham LAYV b'-o-SAY ha-m'-la-KHAH et ha-mish-KAN E-ser y'-ree-OT SHAYSH mosh-ZAR ut-KHAY-let v'-ar-ga-MAN v'-to-LA-at sha-NEE k'-ru-VEEM ma-a-SAY kho-SHAYV a-SAH o-TAM

9 The length of each cloth was twenty-eight *amot*, and the width of each cloth was four *amot*, all cloths having the same measurements.

ט אֹרֶךְ הַיְרִיעָה הָאַחַת שְׁמֹנֶה וְעֶשְׂרִים בָּאַמָּה וְרֹחַב אַרְבַּע בָּאַמָּה הַיְרִיעָה הָאֶחָת מִדָּה אַחַת לְכָל־הַיְרִיעֹת׃

36:8 Twisted linen, blue, purple The fine threads used to weave the curtains of the *Mishkan*, and later the *Beit Hamikdash*, were surely remarkable and unmistakable. In *Megillat Esther*, read on the holiday of *Purim* which marks the Jewish salvation from the evil Haman, the descriptions of the wall hangings in King Ahasuerus's palace are nearly identical to those of the *Mishkan*: "Hangings of white, fine cotton, and blue, bordered with cords of fine linen and purple" (Esther 1:6). This similarity prompted the Talmud (*Megillah* 12a) to understand that upon the exile from Israel after the destruction of the First *Beit Hamikdash*, the Temple's fine vessels and adornments were taken as booty, and later became part of the Persian king's treasury. It was these stolen items that were on display at King Ahasuerus's party. While most Jews ignored *Mordechai*'s warning not to participate, the Sages say that the notables fled, refusing to partake of a feast in which the holy vessels and adornments were displayed. In doing so, these Jews were declaring their loyalty to God and the fallen Temple in *Yerushalayim*.

Shemot/Exodus 36
Vayakhel

שמות לו
ויקהל

10 They joined five of the cloths to one another, and they joined the other five cloths to one another.

י וַיְחַבֵּר אֶת־חֲמֵשׁ הַיְרִיעֹת אַחַת אֶל־אֶחָת וְחָמֵשׁ יְרִיעֹת חִבַּר אַחַת אֶל־אֶחָת:

11 They made loops of blue wool on the edge of the outermost cloth of the one set, and did the same on the edge of the outermost cloth of the other set:

יא וַיַּעַשׂ לֻלְאֹת תְּכֵלֶת עַל שְׂפַת הַיְרִיעָה הָאֶחָת מִקָּצָה בַּמַּחְבָּרֶת כֵּן עָשָׂה בִּשְׂפַת הַיְרִיעָה הַקִּיצוֹנָה בַּמַּחְבֶּרֶת הַשֵּׁנִית:

12 they made fifty loops on the one cloth, and they made fifty loops on the edge of the end cloth of the other set, the loops being opposite one another.

יב חֲמִשִּׁים לֻלָאֹת עָשָׂה בַּיְרִיעָה הָאֶחָת וַחֲמִשִּׁים לֻלָאֹת עָשָׂה בִּקְצֵה הַיְרִיעָה אֲשֶׁר בַּמַּחְבֶּרֶת הַשֵּׁנִית מַקְבִּילֹת הַלֻּלָאֹת אַחַת אֶל־אֶחָת:

13 And they made fifty gold clasps and coupled the units to one another with the clasps, so that the *Mishkan* became one whole.

יג וַיַּעַשׂ חֲמִשִּׁים קַרְסֵי זָהָב וַיְחַבֵּר אֶת־הַיְרִיעֹת אַחַת אֶל־אַחַת בַּקְּרָסִים וַיְהִי הַמִּשְׁכָּן אֶחָד:

14 They made cloths of goats' hair for a tent over the *Mishkan*; they made the cloths eleven in number.

יד וַיַּעַשׂ יְרִיעֹת עִזִּים לְאֹהֶל עַל־הַמִּשְׁכָּן עַשְׁתֵּי־עֶשְׂרֵה יְרִיעֹת עָשָׂה אֹתָם:

15 The length of each cloth was thirty *amot*, and the width of each cloth was four *amot*, the eleven cloths having the same measurements.

טו אֹרֶךְ הַיְרִיעָה הָאַחַת שְׁלֹשִׁים בָּאַמָּה וְאַרְבַּע אַמּוֹת רֹחַב הַיְרִיעָה הָאֶחָת מִדָּה אַחַת לְעַשְׁתֵּי עֶשְׂרֵה יְרִיעֹת:

16 They joined five of the cloths by themselves, and the other six cloths by themselves.

טז וַיְחַבֵּר אֶת־חֲמֵשׁ הַיְרִיעֹת לְבָד וְאֶת־שֵׁשׁ הַיְרִיעֹת לְבָד:

17 They made fifty loops on the edge of the outermost cloth of the one set, and they made fifty loops on the edge of the end cloth of the other set.

יז וַיַּעַשׂ לֻלָאֹת חֲמִשִּׁים עַל שְׂפַת הַיְרִיעָה הַקִּיצֹנָה בַּמַּחְבָּרֶת וַחֲמִשִּׁים לֻלָאֹת עָשָׂה עַל־שְׂפַת הַיְרִיעָה הַחֹבֶרֶת הַשֵּׁנִית:

18 They made fifty copper clasps to couple the Tent together so that it might become one whole.

יח וַיַּעַשׂ קַרְסֵי נְחֹשֶׁת חֲמִשִּׁים לְחַבֵּר אֶת־הָאֹהֶל לִהְיֹת אֶחָד:

19 And they made a covering of tanned ram skins for the tent, and a covering of dolphin skins above.

יט וַיַּעַשׂ מִכְסֶה לָאֹהֶל עֹרֹת אֵלִים מְאָדָּמִים וּמִכְסֵה עֹרֹת תְּחָשִׁים מִלְמָעְלָה:

20 They made the planks for the *Mishkan* of acacia wood, upright.

כ וַיַּעַשׂ אֶת־הַקְּרָשִׁים לַמִּשְׁכָּן עֲצֵי שִׁטִּים עֹמְדִים:

21 The length of each plank was ten *amot*, the width of each plank an *amah* and a half.

כא עֶשֶׂר אַמֹּת אֹרֶךְ הַקָּרֶשׁ וְאַמָּה וַחֲצִי הָאַמָּה רֹחַב הַקֶּרֶשׁ הָאֶחָד:

22 Each plank had two tenons, parallel to each other; they did the same with all the planks of the *Mishkan*.

כב שְׁתֵּי יָדֹת לַקֶּרֶשׁ הָאֶחָד מְשֻׁלָּבֹת אַחַת אֶל־אֶחָת כֵּן עָשָׂה לְכֹל קַרְשֵׁי הַמִּשְׁכָּן:

23 Of the planks of the *Mishkan*, they made twenty planks for the south side,

כג וַיַּעַשׂ אֶת־הַקְּרָשִׁים לַמִּשְׁכָּן עֶשְׂרִים קְרָשִׁים לִפְאַת נֶגֶב תֵּימָנָה:

Shemot/Exodus 36
Vayakhel

שמות לו
ויקהל

24	making forty silver sockets under the twenty planks, two sockets under one plank for its two tenons and two sockets under each following plank for its two tenons;	וְאַרְבָּעִים אַדְנֵי־כֶסֶף עָשָׂה תַּחַת עֶשְׂרִים הַקְּרָשִׁים שְׁנֵי אֲדָנִים תַּחַת־הַקֶּרֶשׁ הָאֶחָד לִשְׁתֵּי יְדֹתָיו וּשְׁנֵי אֲדָנִים תַּחַת־הַקֶּרֶשׁ הָאֶחָד לִשְׁתֵּי יְדֹתָיו: כד
25	and for the other side wall of the *Mishkan*, the north side, twenty planks,	וּלְצֶלַע הַמִּשְׁכָּן הַשֵּׁנִית לִפְאַת צָפוֹן עָשָׂה עֶשְׂרִים קְרָשִׁים: כה
26	with their forty silver sockets, two sockets under one plank and two sockets under each following plank.	וְאַרְבָּעִים אַדְנֵיהֶם כָּסֶף שְׁנֵי אֲדָנִים תַּחַת הַקֶּרֶשׁ הָאֶחָד וּשְׁנֵי אֲדָנִים תַּחַת הַקֶּרֶשׁ הָאֶחָד: כו
27	And for the rear of the *Mishkan*, to the west, they made six planks;	וּלְיַרְכְּתֵי הַמִּשְׁכָּן יָמָּה עָשָׂה שִׁשָּׁה קְרָשִׁים: כז
28	and they made two planks for the corners of the *Mishkan* at the rear.	וּשְׁנֵי קְרָשִׁים עָשָׂה לִמְקֻצְעֹת הַמִּשְׁכָּן בַּיַּרְכָתָיִם: כח
29	They matched at the bottom, but terminated as one at the top into one ring; they did so with both of them at the two corners.	וְהָיוּ תוֹאֲמִם מִלְּמַטָּה וְיַחְדָּו יִהְיוּ תַמִּים אֶל־רֹאשׁוֹ אֶל־הַטַּבַּעַת הָאֶחָת כֵּן עָשָׂה לִשְׁנֵיהֶם לִשְׁנֵי הַמִּקְצֹעֹת: כט
30	Thus there were eight planks with their sockets of silver: sixteen sockets, two under each plank.	וְהָיוּ שְׁמֹנָה קְרָשִׁים וְאַדְנֵיהֶם כֶּסֶף שִׁשָּׁה עָשָׂר אֲדָנִים שְׁנֵי אֲדָנִים שְׁנֵי אֲדָנִים תַּחַת הַקֶּרֶשׁ הָאֶחָד: ל
31	They made bars of acacia wood, five for the planks of the one side wall of the *Mishkan*,	וַיַּעַשׂ בְּרִיחֵי עֲצֵי שִׁטִּים חֲמִשָּׁה לְקַרְשֵׁי צֶלַע־הַמִּשְׁכָּן הָאֶחָת: לא
32	five bars for the planks of the other side wall of the *Mishkan*, and five bars for the planks of the wall of the *Mishkan* at the rear, to the west;	וַחֲמִשָּׁה בְרִיחִם לְקַרְשֵׁי צֶלַע־הַמִּשְׁכָּן הַשֵּׁנִית וַחֲמִשָּׁה בְרִיחִם לְקַרְשֵׁי הַמִּשְׁכָּן לַיַּרְכָתַיִם יָמָּה: לב
33	they made the center bar to run, halfway up the planks, from end to end.	וַיַּעַשׂ אֶת־הַבְּרִיחַ הַתִּיכֹן לִבְרֹחַ בְּתוֹךְ הַקְּרָשִׁים מִן־הַקָּצֶה אֶל־הַקָּצֶה: לג
34	They overlaid the planks with gold, and made their rings of gold, as holders for the bars; and they overlaid the bars with gold.	וְאֶת־הַקְּרָשִׁים צִפָּה זָהָב וְאֶת־טַבְּעֹתָם עָשָׂה זָהָב בָּתִּים לַבְּרִיחִם וַיְצַף אֶת־הַבְּרִיחִם זָהָב: לד
35	They made the curtain of blue, purple, and crimson yarns, and fine twisted linen, working into it a design of cherubim.	וַיַּעַשׂ אֶת־הַפָּרֹכֶת תְּכֵלֶת וְאַרְגָּמָן וְתוֹלַעַת שָׁנִי וְשֵׁשׁ מָשְׁזָר מַעֲשֵׂה חֹשֵׁב עָשָׂה אֹתָהּ כְּרֻבִים: לה
36	They made for it four posts of acacia wood and overlaid them with gold, with their hooks of gold; and they cast for them four silver sockets.	וַיַּעַשׂ לָהּ אַרְבָּעָה עַמּוּדֵי שִׁטִּים וַיְצַפֵּם זָהָב וָוֵיהֶם זָהָב וַיִּצֹק לָהֶם אַרְבָּעָה אַדְנֵי־כָסֶף: לו
37	They made the screen for the entrance of the Tent, of blue, purple, and crimson yarns, and fine twisted linen, done in embroidery;	וַיַּעַשׂ מָסָךְ לְפֶתַח הָאֹהֶל תְּכֵלֶת וְאַרְגָּמָן וְתוֹלַעַת שָׁנִי וְשֵׁשׁ מָשְׁזָר מַעֲשֵׂה רֹקֵם: לז

Shemot/Exodus 37
Vayakhel

שמות לז
ויקהל

38 and five posts for it with their hooks. They overlaid their tops and their bands with gold; but the five sockets were of copper.

לח וְאֶת־עַמּוּדָיו חֲמִשָּׁה וְאֶת־וָוֵיהֶם וְצִפָּה רָאשֵׁיהֶם וַחֲשֻׁקֵיהֶם זָהָב וְאַדְנֵיהֶם חֲמִשָּׁה נְחֹֽשֶׁת׃

37 1 *Betzalel* made the ark of acacia wood, two and a half *amot* long, an *amah* and a half wide, and an *amah* and a half high.

לז א וַיַּעַשׂ בְּצַלְאֵל אֶת־הָאָרֹן עֲצֵי שִׁטִּים אַמָּתַיִם וָחֵצִי אָרְכּוֹ וְאַמָּה וָחֵצִי רָחְבּוֹ וְאַמָּה וָחֵצִי קֹמָתֽוֹ׃

2 He overlaid it with pure gold, inside and out; and he made a gold molding for it round about.

ב וַיְצַפֵּהוּ זָהָב טָהוֹר מִבַּיִת וּמִחוּץ וַיַּעַשׂ לוֹ זֵר זָהָב סָבִֽיב׃

3 He cast four gold rings for it, for its four feet: two rings on one of its side walls and two rings on the other.

ג וַיִּצֹק לוֹ אַרְבַּע טַבְּעֹת זָהָב עַל אַרְבַּע פַּעֲמֹתָיו וּשְׁתֵּי טַבָּעֹת עַל־צַלְעוֹ הָאֶחָת וּשְׁתֵּי טַבָּעוֹת עַל־צַלְעוֹ הַשֵּׁנִֽית׃

4 He made poles of acacia wood, overlaid them with gold,

ד וַיַּעַשׂ בַּדֵּי עֲצֵי שִׁטִּים וַיְצַף אֹתָם זָהָֽב׃

5 and inserted the poles into the rings on the side walls of the ark for carrying the ark.

ה וַיָּבֵא אֶת־הַבַּדִּים בַּטַּבָּעֹת עַל צַלְעֹת הָאָרֹן לָשֵׂאת אֶת־הָאָרֹֽן׃

6 He made a cover of pure gold, two and a half *amot* long and an *amah* and a half wide.

ו וַיַּעַשׂ כַּפֹּרֶת זָהָב טָהוֹר אַמָּתַיִם וָחֵצִי אָרְכָּהּ וְאַמָּה וָחֵצִי רָחְבָּֽהּ׃

7 He made two cherubim of gold; he made them of hammered work, at the two ends of the cover:

ז וַיַּעַשׂ שְׁנֵי כְרֻבִים זָהָב מִקְשָׁה עָשָׂה אֹתָם מִשְּׁנֵי קְצוֹת הַכַּפֹּֽרֶת׃

8 one cherub at one end and the other cherub at the other end; he made the cherubim of one piece with the cover, at its two ends.

ח כְּרוּב־אֶחָד מִקָּצָה מִזֶּה וּכְרוּב־אֶחָד מִקָּצָה מִזֶּה מִן־הַכַּפֹּרֶת עָשָׂה אֶת־הַכְּרֻבִים מִשְּׁנֵי קצוותו [קְצוֹתָֽיו׃]

9 The cherubim had their wings spread out above, shielding the cover with their wings. They faced each other; the faces of the cherubim were turned toward the cover.

ט וַיִּהְיוּ הַכְּרֻבִים פֹּרְשֵׂי כְנָפַיִם לְמַעְלָה סֹכְכִים בְּכַנְפֵיהֶם עַל־הַכַּפֹּרֶת וּפְנֵיהֶם אִישׁ אֶל־אָחִיו אֶל־הַכַּפֹּרֶת הָיוּ פְּנֵי הַכְּרֻבִֽים׃

10 He made the table of acacia wood, two *amot* long, one *amah* wide, and an *amah* and a half high;

י וַיַּעַשׂ אֶת־הַשֻּׁלְחָן עֲצֵי שִׁטִּים אַמָּתַיִם אָרְכּוֹ וְאַמָּה רָחְבּוֹ וְאַמָּה וָחֵצִי קֹמָתֽוֹ׃

11 he overlaid it with pure gold and made a gold molding around it.

יא וַיְצַף אֹתוֹ זָהָב טָהוֹר וַיַּעַשׂ לוֹ זֵר זָהָב סָבִֽיב׃

12 He made a rim of a hand's breadth around it and made a gold molding for its rim round about.

יב וַיַּעַשׂ לוֹ מִסְגֶּרֶת טֹפַח סָבִיב וַיַּעַשׂ זֵר־זָהָב לְמִסְגַּרְתּוֹ סָבִֽיב׃

13 He cast four gold rings for it and attached the rings to the four corners at its four legs.

יג וַיִּצֹק לוֹ אַרְבַּע טַבְּעֹת זָהָב וַיִּתֵּן אֶת־הַטַּבָּעֹת עַל אַרְבַּע הַפֵּאֹת אֲשֶׁר לְאַרְבַּע רַגְלָֽיו׃

14 The rings were next to the rim, as holders for the poles to carry the table.

יד לְעֻמַּת הַמִּסְגֶּרֶת הָיוּ הַטַּבָּעֹת בָּתִּים לַבַּדִּים לָשֵׂאת אֶת־הַשֻּׁלְחָֽן׃

Shemot/Exodus 37
Vayakhel

שמות לז
ויקהל

15 He made the poles of acacia wood for carrying the table, and overlaid them with gold.

טו וַיַּעַשׂ אֶת־הַבַּדִּים עֲצֵי שִׁטִּים וַיְצַף אֹתָם זָהָב לָשֵׂאת אֶת־הַשֻּׁלְחָן:

16 The utensils that were to be upon the table – its bowls, ladles, jugs, and jars with which to offer libations – he made of pure gold.

טז וַיַּעַשׂ אֶת־הַכֵּלִים ׀ אֲשֶׁר עַל־הַשֻּׁלְחָן אֶת־קְעָרֹתָיו וְאֶת־כַּפֹּתָיו וְאֵת מְנַקִּיֹּתָיו וְאֶת־הַקְּשָׂוֺת אֲשֶׁר יֻסַּךְ בָּהֵן זָהָב טָהוֹר:

17 He made the *menorah* of pure gold. He made the *menorah* – its base and its shaft – of hammered work; its cups, calyxes, and petals were of one piece with it.

יז וַיַּעַשׂ אֶת־הַמְּנֹרָה זָהָב טָהוֹר מִקְשָׁה עָשָׂה אֶת־הַמְּנֹרָה יְרֵכָהּ וְקָנָהּ גְּבִיעֶיהָ כַּפְתֹּרֶיהָ וּפְרָחֶיהָ מִמֶּנָּה הָיוּ:

va-YA-as et ha-m'-no-RAH za-HAV ta-HOR mik-SHAH a-SAH et ha-m'-no-RAH y'-ray-KHAH v'-ka-NAH g'-vee-E-ha kaf-to-RE-ha uf-ra-KHE-ha mi-ME-nah ha-YU

18 Six branches issued from its sides: three branches from one side of the *menorah*, and three branches from the other side of the *menorah*.

יח וְשִׁשָּׁה קָנִים יֹצְאִים מִצִּדֶּיהָ שְׁלֹשָׁה ׀ קְנֵי מְנֹרָה מִצִּדָּהּ הָאֶחָד וּשְׁלֹשָׁה קְנֵי מְנֹרָה מִצִּדָּהּ הַשֵּׁנִי:

19 There were three cups shaped like almond-blossoms, each with calyx and petals, on one branch; and there were three cups shaped like almond-blossoms, each with calyx and petals, on the next branch; so for all six branches issuing from the *menorah*.

יט שְׁלֹשָׁה גְבִעִים מְשֻׁקָּדִים בַּקָּנֶה הָאֶחָד כַּפְתֹּר וָפֶרַח וּשְׁלֹשָׁה גְבִעִים מְשֻׁקָּדִים בְּקָנֶה אֶחָד כַּפְתֹּר וָפָרַח כֵּן לְשֵׁשֶׁת הַקָּנִים הַיֹּצְאִים מִן־הַמְּנֹרָה:

20 On the *menorah* itself there were four cups shaped like almond-blossoms, each with calyx and petals:

כ וּבַמְּנֹרָה אַרְבָּעָה גְבִעִים מְשֻׁקָּדִים כַּפְתֹּרֶיהָ וּפְרָחֶיהָ:

21 a calyx, of one piece with it, under a pair of branches; and a calyx, of one piece with it, under the second pair of branches; and a calyx, of one piece with it, under the last pair of branches; so for all six branches issuing from it.

כא וְכַפְתֹּר תַּחַת שְׁנֵי הַקָּנִים מִמֶּנָּה וְכַפְתֹּר תַּחַת שְׁנֵי הַקָּנִים מִמֶּנָּה וְכַפְתֹּר תַּחַת־שְׁנֵי הַקָּנִים מִמֶּנָּה לְשֵׁשֶׁת הַקָּנִים הַיֹּצְאִים מִמֶּנָּה:

22 Their calyxes and their stems were of one piece with it, the whole of it a single hammered piece of pure gold.

כב כַּפְתֹּרֵיהֶם וּקְנֹתָם מִמֶּנָּה הָיוּ כֻּלָּהּ מִקְשָׁה אַחַת זָהָב טָהוֹר:

37:17 He made the *menorah* of pure gold The *menorah*, made of "pure gold," was lit with pure olive oil and gave off a radiant light. The light of the *menorah* is symbolic of the Jewish Nation's duty to spread the light of *Torah* and God's will. The pure gold and olive oil are reflective of the pure intentions necessary to influence the nations of the world for the sake of Heaven. Today, the *menorah* is the official symbol of the State of Israel, which represents the eternity of the Jewish People. The bronze *menorah*, located across from the Knesset, Israel's parliament in *Yerushalayim*, was modeled after the *menorah* of the Temple. The six side branches are engraved with depictions of events from the Bible, as well as the Jews in exile. The center branch of this impressive *menorah* tells the story of the return to *Eretz Yisrael*, up until the establishment of the State of Israel. Now that the People of Israel have returned home, they can again work together to spread light to the rest of the world.

Knesset Menorah in Jerusalem

Shemot/Exodus 38
Vayakhel

שמות לח
ויקהל

23 He made its seven lamps, its tongs, and its fire pans of pure gold.

כג וַיַּעַשׂ אֶת־נֵרֹתֶיהָ שִׁבְעָה וּמַלְקָחֶיהָ וּמַחְתֹּתֶיהָ זָהָב טָהוֹר:

24 He made it and all its furnishings out of a *kikar* of pure gold.

כד כִּכַּר זָהָב טָהוֹר עָשָׂה אֹתָהּ וְאֵת כָּל־כֵּלֶיהָ:

25 He made the incense *Mizbayach* of acacia wood, an *amah* long and an *amah* wide – square – and two *amot* high; its horns were of one piece with it.

כה וַיַּעַשׂ אֶת־מִזְבַּח הַקְּטֹרֶת עֲצֵי שִׁטִּים אַמָּה אָרְכּוֹ וְאַמָּה רָחְבּוֹ רָבוּעַ וְאַמָּתַיִם קֹמָתוֹ מִמֶּנּוּ הָיוּ קַרְנֹתָיו:

26 He overlaid it with pure gold: its top, its sides round about, and its horns; and he made a gold molding for it round about.

כו וַיְצַף אֹתוֹ זָהָב טָהוֹר אֶת־גַּגּוֹ וְאֶת־קִירֹתָיו סָבִיב וְאֶת־קַרְנֹתָיו וַיַּעַשׂ לוֹ זֵר זָהָב סָבִיב:

27 He made two gold rings for it under its molding, on its two walls – on opposite sides – as holders for the poles with which to carry it.

כז וּשְׁתֵּי טַבְּעֹת זָהָב עָשָׂה־לוֹ מִתַּחַת לְזֵרוֹ עַל שְׁתֵּי צַלְעֹתָיו עַל שְׁנֵי צִדָּיו לְבָתִּים לְבַדִּים לָשֵׂאת אֹתוֹ בָּהֶם:

28 He made the poles of acacia wood, and overlaid them with gold.

כח וַיַּעַשׂ אֶת־הַבַּדִּים עֲצֵי שִׁטִּים וַיְצַף אֹתָם זָהָב:

29 He prepared the sacred anointing oil and the pure aromatic incense, expertly blended.

כט וַיַּעַשׂ אֶת־שֶׁמֶן הַמִּשְׁחָה קֹדֶשׁ וְאֶת־קְטֹרֶת הַסַּמִּים טָהוֹר מַעֲשֵׂה רֹקֵחַ:

38

1 He made the *Mizbayach* for burnt offering of acacia wood, five *amot* long and five *amot* wide – square – and three *amot* high.

לח א וַיַּעַשׂ אֶת־מִזְבַּח הָעֹלָה עֲצֵי שִׁטִּים חָמֵשׁ אַמּוֹת אָרְכּוֹ וְחָמֵשׁ־אַמּוֹת רָחְבּוֹ רָבוּעַ וְשָׁלֹשׁ אַמּוֹת קֹמָתוֹ:

2 He made horns for it on its four corners, the horns being of one piece with it; and he overlaid it with copper.

ב וַיַּעַשׂ קַרְנֹתָיו עַל אַרְבַּע פִּנֹּתָיו מִמֶּנּוּ הָיוּ קַרְנֹתָיו וַיְצַף אֹתוֹ נְחֹשֶׁת:

3 He made all the utensils of the *Mizbayach* – the pails, the scrapers, the basins, the flesh hooks, and the fire pans; he made all these utensils of copper.

ג וַיַּעַשׂ אֶת־כָּל־כְּלֵי הַמִּזְבֵּחַ אֶת־הַסִּירֹת וְאֶת־הַיָּעִים וְאֶת־הַמִּזְרָקֹת אֶת־הַמִּזְלָגֹת וְאֶת־הַמַּחְתֹּת כָּל־כֵּלָיו עָשָׂה נְחֹשֶׁת:

4 He made for the *Mizbayach* a grating of meshwork in copper, extending below, under its ledge, to its middle.

ד וַיַּעַשׂ לַמִּזְבֵּחַ מִכְבָּר מַעֲשֵׂה רֶשֶׁת נְחֹשֶׁת תַּחַת כַּרְכֻּבּוֹ מִלְּמַטָּה עַד־חֶצְיוֹ:

5 He cast four rings, at the four corners of the copper grating, as holders for the poles.

ה וַיִּצֹק אַרְבַּע טַבָּעֹת בְּאַרְבַּע הַקְּצָוֹת לְמִכְבַּר הַנְּחֹשֶׁת בָּתִּים לַבַּדִּים:

6 He made the poles of acacia wood and overlaid them with copper;

ו וַיַּעַשׂ אֶת־הַבַּדִּים עֲצֵי שִׁטִּים וַיְצַף אֹתָם נְחֹשֶׁת:

7 and he inserted the poles into the rings on the side walls of the *Mizbayach*, to carry it by them. He made it hollow, of boards.

ז וַיָּבֵא אֶת־הַבַּדִּים בַּטַּבָּעֹת עַל צַלְעֹת הַמִּזְבֵּחַ לָשֵׂאת אֹתוֹ בָּהֶם נְבוּב לֻחֹת עָשָׂה אֹתוֹ:

Shemot/Exodus 38
Vayakhel

שמות לח
ויקהל

8 He made the laver of copper and its stand of copper, from the mirrors of the women who performed tasks at the entrance of the Tent of Meeting.

ח וַיַּעַשׂ אֵת הַכִּיּוֹר נְחֹשֶׁת וְאֵת כַּנּוֹ נְחֹשֶׁת בְּמַרְאֹת הַצֹּבְאֹת אֲשֶׁר צָבְאוּ פֶּתַח אֹהֶל מוֹעֵד:

va-YA-as AYT ha-kee-YOR n'-KHO-shet v'-AYT ka-NO n'-KHO-shet b'-mar-OT ha-TZO-v'-OT a-SHER tza-v'-U PE-takh O-hel mo-AYD

9 He made the enclosure: On the south side, a hundred *amot* of hangings of fine twisted linen for the enclosure

ט וַיַּעַשׂ אֶת־הֶחָצֵר לִפְאַת נֶגֶב תֵּימָנָה קַלְעֵי הֶחָצֵר שֵׁשׁ מָשְׁזָר מֵאָה בָּאַמָּה:

10 with their twenty posts and their twenty sockets of copper, the hooks and bands of the posts being silver.

י עַמּוּדֵיהֶם עֶשְׂרִים וְאַדְנֵיהֶם עֶשְׂרִים נְחֹשֶׁת וָוֵי הָעַמֻּדִים וַחֲשֻׁקֵיהֶם כָּסֶף:

11 On the north side, a hundred *amot* – with their twenty posts and their twenty sockets of copper, the hooks and bands of the posts being silver.

יא וְלִפְאַת צָפוֹן מֵאָה בָאַמָּה עַמּוּדֵיהֶם עֶשְׂרִים וְאַדְנֵיהֶם עֶשְׂרִים נְחֹשֶׁת וָוֵי הָעַמּוּדִים וַחֲשֻׁקֵיהֶם כָּסֶף:

12 On the west side, fifty *amot* of hangings – with their ten posts and their ten sockets, the hooks and bands of the posts being silver.

יב וְלִפְאַת־יָם קְלָעִים חֲמִשִּׁים בָּאַמָּה עַמּוּדֵיהֶם עֲשָׂרָה וְאַדְנֵיהֶם עֲשָׂרָה וָוֵי הָעַמֻּדִים וַחֲשׁוּקֵיהֶם כָּסֶף:

13 And on the front side, to the east, fifty *amot*:

יג וְלִפְאַת קֵדְמָה מִזְרָחָה חֲמִשִּׁים אַמָּה:

14 fifteen *amot* of hangings on the one flank, with their three posts and their three sockets,

יד קְלָעִים חֲמֵשׁ־עֶשְׂרֵה אַמָּה אֶל־הַכָּתֵף עַמּוּדֵיהֶם שְׁלֹשָׁה וְאַדְנֵיהֶם שְׁלֹשָׁה:

15 and fifteen *amot* of hangings on the other flank – on each side of the gate of the enclosure – with their three posts and their three sockets.

טו וְלַכָּתֵף הַשֵּׁנִית מִזֶּה וּמִזֶּה לְשַׁעַר הֶחָצֵר קְלָעִים חֲמֵשׁ עֶשְׂרֵה אַמָּה עַמֻּדֵיהֶם שְׁלֹשָׁה וְאַדְנֵיהֶם שְׁלֹשָׁה:

16 All the hangings around the enclosure were of fine twisted linen.

טז כָּל־קַלְעֵי הֶחָצֵר סָבִיב שֵׁשׁ מָשְׁזָר:

17 The sockets for the posts were of copper, the hooks and bands of the posts were of silver, the overlay of their tops was of silver; all the posts of the enclosure were banded with silver.

יז וְהָאֲדָנִים לָעַמֻּדִים נְחֹשֶׁת וָוֵי הָעַמּוּדִים וַחֲשׁוּקֵיהֶם כֶּסֶף וְצִפּוּי רָאשֵׁיהֶם כָּסֶף וְהֵם מְחֻשָּׁקִים כֶּסֶף כֹּל עַמֻּדֵי הֶחָצֵר:

18 The screen of the gate of the enclosure, done in embroidery, was of blue, purple, and crimson yarns, and fine twisted linen. It was twenty *amot* long. Its height – or width – was five *amot*, like that of the hangings of the enclosure.

יח וּמָסַךְ שַׁעַר הֶחָצֵר מַעֲשֵׂה רֹקֵם תְּכֵלֶת וְאַרְגָּמָן וְתוֹלַעַת שָׁנִי וְשֵׁשׁ מָשְׁזָר וְעֶשְׂרִים אַמָּה אֹרֶךְ וְקוֹמָה בְרֹחַב חָמֵשׁ אַמּוֹת לְעֻמַּת קַלְעֵי הֶחָצֵר:

38:8 From the mirrors of the women who performed tasks The women of the nation donate their mirrors to provide copper for the laver. The medieval commentator *Rashi* teaches that in Egypt, the women would use these mirrors to make themselves beautiful, in order to enliven the spirits of their husbands upon returning from the day's slave labor. These righteous women never lost faith in *Hashem* and in His promised redemption, and ensured the continuity of the Jewish people with these same mirrors. It is due to the merit of the righteous women in the generation of the exodus that their mirrors are used to construct a vessel in the holy *Mishkan*.

234

Shemot/Exodus 38
Pekudei

שמות לח
פקודי

19 The posts were four; their four sockets were of copper, their hooks of silver; and the overlay of their tops was of silver, as were also their bands.

יט וְעַמֻּדֵיהֶם אַרְבָּעָה וְאַדְנֵיהֶם אַרְבָּעָה נְחֹשֶׁת וָוֵיהֶם כֶּסֶף וְצִפּוּי רָאשֵׁיהֶם וַחֲשֻׁקֵיהֶם כָּסֶף:

20 All the pegs of the *Mishkan* and of the enclosure round about were of copper.

כ וְכָל־הַיְתֵדֹת לַמִּשְׁכָּן וְלֶחָצֵר סָבִיב נְחֹשֶׁת:

21 These are the records of the *Mishkan*, the *Mishkan* of the Pact, which were drawn up at *Moshe*'s bidding – the work of the *Leviim* under the direction of *Itamar* son of *Aharon* the *Kohen*.

כא אֵלֶּה פְקוּדֵי הַמִּשְׁכָּן מִשְׁכַּן הָעֵדֻת אֲשֶׁר פֻּקַּד עַל־פִּי מֹשֶׁה עֲבֹדַת הַלְוִיִּם בְּיַד אִיתָמָר בֶּן־אַהֲרֹן הַכֹּהֵן:

22 Now *Betzalel*, son of *Uri* son of *Chur*, of the tribe of *Yehuda*, had made all that *Hashem* had commanded *Moshe*;

כב וּבְצַלְאֵל בֶּן־אוּרִי בֶן־חוּר לְמַטֵּה יְהוּדָה עָשָׂה אֵת כָּל־אֲשֶׁר־צִוָּה יְהוָה אֶת־מֹשֶׁה:

23 at his side was *Oholiav* son of *Achisamach*, of the tribe of *Dan*, carver and designer, and embroiderer in blue, purple, and crimson yarns and in fine linen.

כג וְאִתּוֹ אָהֳלִיאָב בֶּן־אֲחִיסָמָךְ לְמַטֵּה־דָן חָרָשׁ וְחֹשֵׁב וְרֹקֵם בַּתְּכֵלֶת וּבָאַרְגָּמָן וּבְתוֹלַעַת הַשָּׁנִי וּבַשֵּׁשׁ:

24 All the gold that was used for the work, in all the work of the sanctuary – the elevation offering of gold – came to 29 *kikarot* and 730 *shekalim* by the sanctuary weight.

כד כָּל־הַזָּהָב הֶעָשׂוּי לַמְּלָאכָה בְּכֹל מְלֶאכֶת הַקֹּדֶשׁ וַיְהִי זְהַב הַתְּנוּפָה תֵּשַׁע וְעֶשְׂרִים כִּכָּר וּשְׁבַע מֵאוֹת וּשְׁלֹשִׁים שֶׁקֶל בְּשֶׁקֶל הַקֹּדֶשׁ:

25 The silver of those of the community who were recorded came to 100 *kikarot* and 1,775 *shekalim* by the sanctuary weight:

כה וְכֶסֶף פְּקוּדֵי הָעֵדָה מְאַת כִּכָּר וְאֶלֶף וּשְׁבַע מֵאוֹת וַחֲמִשָּׁה וְשִׁבְעִים שֶׁקֶל בְּשֶׁקֶל הַקֹּדֶשׁ:

26 a *beka* a head, half a *shekel* by the sanctuary weight, for each one who was entered in the records, from the age of twenty years up, 603,550 men.

כו בֶּקַע לַגֻּלְגֹּלֶת מַחֲצִית הַשֶּׁקֶל בְּשֶׁקֶל הַקֹּדֶשׁ לְכֹל הָעֹבֵר עַל־הַפְּקֻדִים מִבֶּן עֶשְׂרִים שָׁנָה וָמַעְלָה לְשֵׁשׁ־מֵאוֹת אֶלֶף וּשְׁלֹשֶׁת אֲלָפִים וַחֲמֵשׁ מֵאוֹת וַחֲמִשִּׁים:

27 The 100 *kikarot* of silver were for casting the sockets of the sanctuary and the sockets for the curtain, 100 sockets to the 100 *kikarot*, a *kikar* a socket.

כז וַיְהִי מְאַת כִּכַּר הַכֶּסֶף לָצֶקֶת אֵת אַדְנֵי הַקֹּדֶשׁ וְאֵת אַדְנֵי הַפָּרֹכֶת מְאַת אֲדָנִים לִמְאַת הַכִּכָּר כִּכָּר לָאָדֶן:

28 And of the 1,775 *shekalim* he made hooks for the posts, overlay for their tops, and bands around them.

כח וְאֶת־הָאֶלֶף וּשְׁבַע הַמֵּאוֹת וַחֲמִשָּׁה וְשִׁבְעִים עָשָׂה וָוִים לָעַמּוּדִים וְצִפָּה רָאשֵׁיהֶם וְחִשַּׁק אֹתָם:

29 The copper from the elevation offering came to 70 *kikarot* and 2,400 *shekalim*.

כט וּנְחֹשֶׁת הַתְּנוּפָה שִׁבְעִים כִּכָּר וְאַלְפַּיִם וְאַרְבַּע־מֵאוֹת שָׁקֶל:

30 Of it he made the sockets for the entrance of the Tent of Meeting; the copper *Mizbayach* and its copper grating and all the utensils of the *Mizbayach*;

ל וַיַּעַשׂ בָּהּ אֶת־אַדְנֵי פֶּתַח אֹהֶל מוֹעֵד וְאֵת מִזְבַּח הַנְּחֹשֶׁת וְאֶת־מִכְבַּר הַנְּחֹשֶׁת אֲשֶׁר־לוֹ וְאֵת כָּל־כְּלֵי הַמִּזְבֵּחַ:

31 the sockets of the enclosure round about and the sockets of the gate of the enclosure; and all the pegs of the *Mishkan* and all the pegs of the enclosure round about.

לא וְאֶת־אַדְנֵי הֶחָצֵר סָבִיב וְאֶת־אַדְנֵי שַׁעַר הֶחָצֵר וְאֵת כָּל־יִתְדֹת הַמִּשְׁכָּן וְאֶת־כָּל־יִתְדֹת הֶחָצֵר סָבִיב:

Shemot/Exodus 39
Pekudei

39 1 Of the blue, purple, and crimson yarns they also made the service vestments for officiating in the sanctuary; they made *Aharon*'s sacral vestments – as *Hashem* had commanded *Moshe*.

2 The ephod was made of gold, blue, purple, and crimson yarns, and fine twisted linen.

3 They hammered out sheets of gold and cut threads to be worked into designs among the blue, the purple, and the crimson yarns, and the fine linen.

4 They made for it attaching shoulder-pieces; they were attached at its two ends.

5 The decorated band that was upon it was made like it, of one piece with it; of gold, blue, purple, and crimson yarns, and fine twisted linen – as *Hashem* had commanded *Moshe*.

6 They bordered the lazuli stones with frames of gold, engraved with seal engravings of the names of the sons of *Yisrael*.

7 They were set on the shoulder-pieces of the ephod, as stones of remembrance for the Israelites – as *Hashem* had commanded *Moshe*.

8 The breastpiece was made in the style of the ephod: of gold, blue, purple, and crimson yarns, and fine twisted linen.

9 It was square; they made the breastpiece doubled – a *zeret* in length and a *zeret* in width, doubled.

10 They set in it four rows of stones. The first row was a row of carnelian, chrysolite, and emerald;

11 the second row: a turquoise, a sapphire, and an amethyst;

12 the third row: a jacinth, an agate, and a crystal;

13 and the fourth row: a beryl, a lapis lazuli, and a jasper. They were encircled in their mountings with frames of gold.

14 The stones corresponded [in number] to the names of the sons of *Yisrael*: twelve, corresponding to their names; engraved like seals, each with its name, for the twelve tribes.

שמות לט
פקודי

לט א וּמִן־הַתְּכֵ֤לֶת וְהָֽאַרְגָּמָן֙ וְתוֹלַ֣עַת הַשָּׁנִ֔י עָשׂ֥וּ בִגְדֵי־שְׂרָ֖ד לְשָׁרֵ֣ת בַּקֹּ֑דֶשׁ וַֽיַּעֲשׂ֞וּ אֶת־בִּגְדֵ֤י הַקֹּ֙דֶשׁ֙ אֲשֶׁ֣ר לְאַהֲרֹ֔ן כַּאֲשֶׁ֛ר צִוָּ֥ה יְהֹוָ֖ה אֶת־מֹשֶֽׁה׃

ב וַיַּ֖עַשׂ אֶת־הָאֵפֹ֑ד זָהָ֗ב תְּכֵ֧לֶת וְאַרְגָּמָ֛ן וְתוֹלַ֥עַת שָׁנִ֖י וְשֵׁ֥שׁ מָשְׁזָֽר׃

ג וַֽיְרַקְּע֞וּ אֶת־פַּחֵ֣י הַזָּהָב֮ וְקִצֵּ֣ץ פְּתִילִם֒ לַעֲשׂ֗וֹת בְּת֤וֹךְ הַתְּכֵ֙לֶת֙ וּבְת֣וֹךְ הָֽאַרְגָּמָ֔ן וּבְת֛וֹךְ תּוֹלַ֥עַת הַשָּׁנִ֖י וּבְת֣וֹךְ הַשֵּׁ֑שׁ מַעֲשֵׂ֖ה חֹשֵֽׁב׃

ד כְּתֵפֹ֥ת עָֽשׂוּ־ל֖וֹ חֹבְרֹ֑ת עַל־שְׁנֵ֥י קְצוֹותָ֖ו [קְצוֹתָ֖יו] חֻבָּֽר׃

ה וְחֵ֨שֶׁב אֲפֻדָּת֜וֹ אֲשֶׁ֣ר עָלָ֗יו מִמֶּ֣נּוּ הוּא֮ כְּמַעֲשֵׂהוּ֒ זָהָ֗ב תְּכֵ֧לֶת וְאַרְגָּמָ֛ן וְתוֹלַ֥עַת שָׁנִ֖י וְשֵׁ֣שׁ מָשְׁזָ֑ר כַּאֲשֶׁ֛ר צִוָּ֥ה יְהֹוָ֖ה אֶת־מֹשֶֽׁה׃

ו וַֽיַּעֲשׂוּ֙ אֶת־אַבְנֵ֣י הַשֹּׁ֔הַם מֻֽסַבֹּ֖ת מִשְׁבְּצֹ֣ת זָהָ֑ב מְפֻתָּחֹת֙ פִּתּוּחֵ֣י חוֹתָ֔ם עַל־שְׁמ֖וֹת בְּנֵ֥י יִשְׂרָאֵֽל׃

ז וַיָּ֣שֶׂם אֹתָ֗ם עַ֚ל כִּתְפֹ֣ת הָאֵפֹ֔ד אַבְנֵ֥י זִכָּר֖וֹן לִבְנֵ֣י יִשְׂרָאֵ֑ל כַּאֲשֶׁ֛ר צִוָּ֥ה יְהֹוָ֖ה אֶת־מֹשֶֽׁה׃

ח וַיַּ֧עַשׂ אֶת־הַחֹ֛שֶׁן מַעֲשֵׂ֥ה חֹשֵׁ֖ב כְּמַעֲשֵׂ֣ה אֵפֹ֑ד זָהָ֗ב תְּכֵ֧לֶת וְאַרְגָּמָ֛ן וְתוֹלַ֥עַת שָׁנִ֖י וְשֵׁ֥שׁ מָשְׁזָֽר׃

ט רָב֧וּעַ הָיָ֛ה כָּפ֖וּל עָשׂ֣וּ אֶת־הַחֹ֑שֶׁן זֶ֧רֶת אָרְכּ֛וֹ וְזֶ֥רֶת רָחְבּ֖וֹ כָּפֽוּל׃

י וַיְמַלְאוּ־ב֔וֹ אַרְבָּעָ֖ה ט֣וּרֵי אָ֑בֶן ט֗וּר אֹ֤דֶם פִּטְדָה֙ וּבָרֶ֔קֶת הַטּ֖וּר הָאֶחָֽד׃

יא וְהַטּ֖וּר הַשֵּׁנִ֑י נֹ֥פֶךְ סַפִּ֖יר וְיָהֲלֹֽם׃

יב וְהַטּ֖וּר הַשְּׁלִישִׁ֑י לֶ֥שֶׁם שְׁב֖וֹ וְאַחְלָֽמָה׃

יג וְהַטּוּר֙ הָֽרְבִיעִ֔י תַּרְשִׁ֥ישׁ שֹׁ֖הַם וְיָשְׁפֵ֑ה מֽוּסַבֹּ֛ת מִשְׁבְּצ֥וֹת זָהָ֖ב בְּמִלֻּאֹתָֽם׃

יד וְ֠הָאֲבָנִ֠ים עַל־שְׁמֹ֨ת בְּנֵֽי־יִשְׂרָאֵ֥ל הֵ֛נָּה שְׁתֵּ֥ים עֶשְׂרֵ֖ה עַל־שְׁמֹתָ֑ם פִּתּוּחֵ֤י חֹתָם֙ אִ֣ישׁ עַל־שְׁמ֔וֹ לִשְׁנֵ֥ים עָשָׂ֖ר שָֽׁבֶט׃

Shemot/Exodus 39
Pekudei

15 On the breastpiece they made braided chains of corded work in pure gold.

16 They made two frames of gold and two rings of gold, and fastened the two rings at the two ends of the breastpiece,

17 attaching the two golden cords to the two rings at the ends of the breastpiece.

18 They then fastened the two ends of the cords to the two frames, attaching them to the shoulder-pieces of the ephod, at the front.

19 They made two rings of gold and attached them to the two ends of the breastpiece, at its inner edge, which faced the ephod.

20 They made two other rings of gold and fastened them on the front of the ephod, low on the two shoulder-pieces, close to its seam above the decorated band.

21 The breastpiece was held in place by a cord of blue from its rings to the rings of the ephod, so that the breastpiece rested on the decorated band and did not come loose from the ephod – as *Hashem* had commanded *Moshe*.

22 The robe for the ephod was made of woven work, of pure blue.

23 The opening of the robe, in the middle of it, was like the opening of a coat of mail, with a binding around the opening, so that it would not tear.

24 On the hem of the robe they made pomegranates of blue, purple, and crimson yarns, twisted.

25 They also made bells of pure gold, and attached the bells between the pomegranates, all around the hem of the robe, between the pomegranates:

26 a bell and a pomegranate, a bell and a pomegranate, all around the hem of the robe for officiating in – as *Hashem* had commanded *Moshe*.

27 They made the tunics of fine linen, of woven work, for *Aharon* and his sons;

28 and the headdress of fine linen, and the decorated turbans of fine linen, and the linen breeches of fine twisted linen;

שמות לט
פקודי

טו וַיַּעֲשׂוּ עַל־הַחֹשֶׁן שַׁרְשְׁרֹת גַּבְלֻת מַעֲשֵׂה עֲבֹת זָהָב טָהוֹר:

טז וַיַּעֲשׂוּ שְׁתֵּי מִשְׁבְּצֹת זָהָב וּשְׁתֵּי טַבְּעֹת זָהָב וַיִּתְּנוּ אֶת־שְׁתֵּי הַטַּבָּעֹת עַל־שְׁנֵי קְצוֹת הַחֹשֶׁן:

יז וַיִּתְּנוּ שְׁתֵּי הָעֲבֹתֹת הַזָּהָב עַל־שְׁתֵּי הַטַּבָּעֹת עַל־קְצוֹת הַחֹשֶׁן:

יח וְאֵת שְׁתֵּי קְצוֹת שְׁתֵּי הָעֲבֹתֹת נָתְנוּ עַל־שְׁתֵּי הַמִּשְׁבְּצֹת וַיִּתְּנֻם עַל־כִּתְפֹת הָאֵפֹד אֶל־מוּל פָּנָיו:

יט וַיַּעֲשׂוּ שְׁתֵּי טַבְּעֹת זָהָב וַיָּשִׂימוּ עַל־שְׁנֵי קְצוֹת הַחֹשֶׁן עַל־שְׂפָתוֹ אֲשֶׁר אֶל־עֵבֶר הָאֵפֹד בָּיְתָה:

כ וַיַּעֲשׂוּ שְׁתֵּי טַבְּעֹת זָהָב וַיִּתְּנֻם עַל־שְׁתֵּי כִתְפֹת הָאֵפֹד מִלְמַטָּה מִמּוּל פָּנָיו לְעֻמַּת מֶחְבַּרְתּוֹ מִמַּעַל לְחֵשֶׁב הָאֵפֹד:

כא וַיִּרְכְּסוּ אֶת־הַחֹשֶׁן מִטַּבְּעֹתָיו אֶל־טַבְּעֹת הָאֵפֹד בִּפְתִיל תְּכֵלֶת לִהְיֹת עַל־חֵשֶׁב הָאֵפֹד וְלֹא־יִזַּח הַחֹשֶׁן מֵעַל הָאֵפֹד כַּאֲשֶׁר צִוָּה יְהֹוָה אֶת־מֹשֶׁה:

כב וַיַּעַשׂ אֶת־מְעִיל הָאֵפֹד מַעֲשֵׂה אֹרֵג כְּלִיל תְּכֵלֶת:

כג וּפִי־הַמְּעִיל בְּתוֹכוֹ כְּפִי תַחְרָא שָׂפָה לְפִיו סָבִיב לֹא יִקָּרֵעַ:

כד וַיַּעֲשׂוּ עַל־שׁוּלֵי הַמְּעִיל רִמּוֹנֵי תְּכֵלֶת וְאַרְגָּמָן וְתוֹלַעַת שָׁנִי מָשְׁזָר:

כה וַיַּעֲשׂוּ פַעֲמֹנֵי זָהָב טָהוֹר וַיִּתְּנוּ אֶת־הַפַּעֲמֹנִים בְּתוֹךְ הָרִמֹּנִים עַל־שׁוּלֵי הַמְּעִיל סָבִיב בְּתוֹךְ הָרִמֹּנִים:

כו פַּעֲמֹן וְרִמֹּן פַּעֲמֹן וְרִמֹּן עַל־שׁוּלֵי הַמְּעִיל סָבִיב לְשָׁרֵת כַּאֲשֶׁר צִוָּה יְהֹוָה אֶת־מֹשֶׁה:

כז וַיַּעֲשׂוּ אֶת־הַכָּתְנֹת שֵׁשׁ מַעֲשֵׂה אֹרֵג לְאַהֲרֹן וּלְבָנָיו:

כח וְאֵת הַמִּצְנֶפֶת שֵׁשׁ וְאֶת־פַּאֲרֵי הַמִּגְבָּעֹת שֵׁשׁ וְאֶת־מִכְנְסֵי הַבָּד שֵׁשׁ מָשְׁזָר:

Shemot/Exodus 39
Pekudei

שמות לט
פקודי

29 and sashes of fine twisted linen, blue, purple, and crimson yarns, done in embroidery – as *Hashem* had commanded *Moshe*.

כט וְאֶת־הָאַבְנֵט שֵׁשׁ מָשְׁזָר וּתְכֵלֶת וְאַרְגָּמָן וְתוֹלַעַת שָׁנִי מַעֲשֵׂה רֹקֵם כַּאֲשֶׁר צִוָּה יְהֹוָה אֶת־מֹשֶׁה׃

30 They made the frontlet for the holy diadem of pure gold, and incised upon it the seal inscription: "Holy to *Hashem*."

ל וַיַּעֲשׂוּ אֶת־צִיץ נֵזֶר־הַקֹּדֶשׁ זָהָב טָהוֹר וַיִּכְתְּבוּ עָלָיו מִכְתַּב פִּתּוּחֵי חוֹתָם קֹדֶשׁ לַיהֹוָה׃

31 They attached to it a cord of blue to fix it upon the headdress above – as *Hashem* had commanded *Moshe*.

לא וַיִּתְּנוּ עָלָיו פְּתִיל תְּכֵלֶת לָתֵת עַל־הַמִּצְנֶפֶת מִלְמָעְלָה כַּאֲשֶׁר צִוָּה יְהֹוָה אֶת־מֹשֶׁה׃

32 Thus was completed all the work of the *Mishkan* of the Tent of Meeting. The Israelites did so; just as *Hashem* had commanded *Moshe*, so they did.

לב וַתֵּכֶל כָּל־עֲבֹדַת מִשְׁכַּן אֹהֶל מוֹעֵד וַיַּעֲשׂוּ בְּנֵי יִשְׂרָאֵל כְּכֹל אֲשֶׁר צִוָּה יְהֹוָה אֶת־מֹשֶׁה כֵּן עָשׂוּ׃

33 Then they brought the *Mishkan* to *Moshe*, with the Tent and all its furnishings: its clasps, its planks, its bars, its posts, and its sockets;

לג וַיָּבִיאוּ אֶת־הַמִּשְׁכָּן אֶל־מֹשֶׁה אֶת־הָאֹהֶל וְאֶת־כָּל־כֵּלָיו קְרָסָיו קְרָשָׁיו בריחו [בְּרִיחָיו] וְעַמֻּדָיו וַאֲדָנָיו׃

34 the covering of tanned ram skins, the covering of dolphin skins, and the curtain for the screen;

לד וְאֶת־מִכְסֵה עוֹרֹת הָאֵילִם הַמְאָדָּמִים וְאֶת־מִכְסֵה עֹרֹת הַתְּחָשִׁים וְאֵת פָּרֹכֶת הַמָּסָךְ׃

35 the *Aron HaBrit* and its poles, and the cover;

לה אֶת־אֲרוֹן הָעֵדֻת וְאֶת־בַּדָּיו וְאֵת הַכַּפֹּרֶת׃

36 the table and all its utensils, and the bread of display;

לו אֶת־הַשֻּׁלְחָן אֶת־כָּל־כֵּלָיו וְאֵת לֶחֶם הַפָּנִים׃

37 the pure *menorah*, its lamps – lamps in due order – and all its fittings, and the oil for lighting;

לז אֶת־הַמְּנֹרָה הַטְּהֹרָה אֶת־נֵרֹתֶיהָ נֵרֹת הַמַּעֲרָכָה וְאֶת־כָּל־כֵּלֶיהָ וְאֵת שֶׁמֶן הַמָּאוֹר׃

38 the *Mizbayach* of gold, the oil for anointing, the aromatic incense, and the screen for the entrance of the Tent;

לח וְאֵת מִזְבַּח הַזָּהָב וְאֵת שֶׁמֶן הַמִּשְׁחָה וְאֵת קְטֹרֶת הַסַּמִּים וְאֵת מָסַךְ פֶּתַח הָאֹהֶל׃

39 the copper *Mizbayach* with its copper grating, its poles and all its utensils, and the laver and its stand;

לט אֵת מִזְבַּח הַנְּחֹשֶׁת וְאֶת־מִכְבַּר הַנְּחֹשֶׁת אֲשֶׁר־לוֹ אֶת־בַּדָּיו וְאֶת־כָּל־כֵּלָיו אֶת־הַכִּיֹּר וְאֶת־כַּנּוֹ׃

40 the hangings of the enclosure, its posts and its sockets, the screen for the gate of the enclosure, its cords and its pegs – all the furnishings for the service of the *Mishkan*, the Tent of Meeting;

מ אֵת קַלְעֵי הֶחָצֵר אֶת־עַמֻּדֶיהָ וְאֶת־אֲדָנֶיהָ וְאֶת־הַמָּסָךְ לְשַׁעַר הֶחָצֵר אֶת־מֵיתָרָיו וִיתֵדֹתֶיהָ וְאֵת כָּל־כְּלֵי עֲבֹדַת הַמִּשְׁכָּן לְאֹהֶל מוֹעֵד׃

41 the service vestments for officiating in the sanctuary, the sacral vestments of *Aharon* the *Kohen*, and the vestments of his sons for priestly service.

מא אֶת־בִּגְדֵי הַשְּׂרָד לְשָׁרֵת בַּקֹּדֶשׁ אֶת־בִּגְדֵי הַקֹּדֶשׁ לְאַהֲרֹן הַכֹּהֵן וְאֶת־בִּגְדֵי בָנָיו לְכַהֵן׃

42 Just as *Hashem* had commanded *Moshe*, so the Israelites had done all the work.

מב כְּכֹל אֲשֶׁר־צִוָּה יְהֹוָה אֶת־מֹשֶׁה כֵּן עָשׂוּ בְּנֵי יִשְׂרָאֵל אֵת כָּל־הָעֲבֹדָה׃

Shemot/Exodus 40
Pekudei

שמות מ
פקודי

43 And when *Moshe* saw that they had performed all the tasks – as *Hashem* had commanded, so they had done – *Moshe* blessed them.

מג וַיַּרְא מֹשֶׁה אֶת־כָּל־הַמְּלָאכָה וְהִנֵּה עָשׂוּ אֹתָהּ כַּאֲשֶׁר צִוָּה יְהֹוָה כֵּן עָשׂוּ וַיְבָרֶךְ אֹתָם מֹשֶׁה:

va-YAR mo-SHEH et kol ha-m'-la-KHAH v'-hi-NAY a-SU o-TAH ka-a-SHER tzi-VAH a-do-NAI KAYN a-SU vai-VA-rekh o-TAM mo-SHEH

40

1 And *Hashem* spoke to *Moshe*, saying:

א וַיְדַבֵּר יְהֹוָה אֶל־מֹשֶׁה לֵּאמֹר:

2 On the first day of the first month you shall set up the *Mishkan* of the Tent of Meeting.

ב בְּיוֹם־הַחֹדֶשׁ הָרִאשׁוֹן בְּאֶחָד לַחֹדֶשׁ תָּקִים אֶת־מִשְׁכַּן אֹהֶל מוֹעֵד:

3 Place there the *Aron HaBrit*, and screen off the ark with the curtain.

ג וְשַׂמְתָּ שָׁם אֵת אֲרוֹן הָעֵדוּת וְסַכֹּתָ עַל־הָאָרֹן אֶת־הַפָּרֹכֶת:

4 Bring in the table and lay out its due setting; bring in the *menorah* and light its lamps;

ד וְהֵבֵאתָ אֶת־הַשֻּׁלְחָן וְעָרַכְתָּ אֶת־עֶרְכּוֹ וְהֵבֵאתָ אֶת־הַמְּנֹרָה וְהַעֲלֵיתָ אֶת־נֵרֹתֶיהָ:

5 and place the gold *Mizbayach* of incense before the *Aron HaBrit*. Then put up the screen for the entrance of the *Mishkan*.

ה וְנָתַתָּה אֶת־מִזְבַּח הַזָּהָב לִקְטֹרֶת לִפְנֵי אֲרוֹן הָעֵדֻת וְשַׂמְתָּ אֶת־מָסַךְ הַפֶּתַח לַמִּשְׁכָּן:

6 You shall place the *Mizbayach* of burnt offering before the entrance of the *Mishkan* of the Tent of Meeting.

ו וְנָתַתָּה אֵת מִזְבַּח הָעֹלָה לִפְנֵי פֶּתַח מִשְׁכַּן אֹהֶל־מוֹעֵד:

7 Place the laver between the Tent of Meeting and the *Mizbayach*, and put water in it.

ז וְנָתַתָּ אֶת־הַכִּיֹּר בֵּין־אֹהֶל מוֹעֵד וּבֵין הַמִּזְבֵּחַ וְנָתַתָּ שָׁם מָיִם:

8 Set up the enclosure round about, and put in place the screen for the gate of the enclosure.

ח וְשַׂמְתָּ אֶת־הֶחָצֵר סָבִיב וְנָתַתָּ אֶת־מָסַךְ שַׁעַר הֶחָצֵר:

9 You shall take the anointing oil and anoint the *Mishkan* and all that is in it to consecrate it and all its furnishings, so that it shall be holy.

ט וְלָקַחְתָּ אֶת־שֶׁמֶן הַמִּשְׁחָה וּמָשַׁחְתָּ אֶת־הַמִּשְׁכָּן וְאֶת־כָּל־אֲשֶׁר־בּוֹ וְקִדַּשְׁתָּ אֹתוֹ וְאֶת־כָּל־כֵּלָיו וְהָיָה קֹדֶשׁ:

10 Then anoint the *Mizbayach* of burnt offering and all its utensils to consecrate the *Mizbayach*, so that the *Mizbayach* shall be most holy.

י וּמָשַׁחְתָּ אֶת־מִזְבַּח הָעֹלָה וְאֶת־כָּל־כֵּלָיו וְקִדַּשְׁתָּ אֶת־הַמִּזְבֵּחַ וְהָיָה הַמִּזְבֵּחַ קֹדֶשׁ קָדָשִׁים:

11 And anoint the laver and its stand to consecrate it.

יא וּמָשַׁחְתָּ אֶת־הַכִּיֹּר וְאֶת־כַּנּוֹ וְקִדַּשְׁתָּ אֹתוֹ:

12 You shall bring *Aharon* and his sons forward to the entrance of the Tent of Meeting and wash them with the water.

יב וְהִקְרַבְתָּ אֶת־אַהֲרֹן וְאֶת־בָּנָיו אֶל־פֶּתַח אֹהֶל מוֹעֵד וְרָחַצְתָּ אֹתָם בַּמָּיִם:

39:43 As *Hashem* had commanded Upon the completion of the building of the *Mishkan* and its vessels, *Moshe* inspects the work and rejoices, because it has been done exactly as *Hashem* has commanded. Many commentators note that particularly following the sin of the golden calf, when the nation initiated a new form of worship that was not in accordance with God's will, it was vital that the construction of the *Mishkan* followed the instructions down to the most minute detail. By doing so, the nation demonstrates its understanding that God's will is unchanging and does not yield to interpretation of individuals.

Shemot/Exodus 40
Pekudei

שמות מ
פקודי

13 Put the sacral vestments on *Aharon*, and anoint him and consecrate him, that he may serve Me as *Kohen*.

יג וְהִלְבַּשְׁתָּ֙ אֶֽת־אַהֲרֹ֔ן אֵ֖ת בִּגְדֵ֣י הַקֹּ֑דֶשׁ וּמָשַׁחְתָּ֥ אֹת֛וֹ וְקִדַּשְׁתָּ֥ אֹת֖וֹ וְכִהֵ֥ן לִֽי׃

14 Then bring his sons forward, put tunics on them,

יד וְאֶת־בָּנָ֖יו תַּקְרִ֑יב וְהִלְבַּשְׁתָּ֥ אֹתָ֖ם כֻּתֳּנֹֽת׃

15 and anoint them as you have anointed their father, that they may serve Me as *Kohanim*. This their anointing shall serve them for everlasting priesthood throughout the ages.

טו וּמָשַׁחְתָּ֣ אֹתָ֗ם כַּאֲשֶׁ֤ר מָשַׁ֙חְתָּ֙ אֶת־אֲבִיהֶ֔ם וְכִהֲנ֖וּ לִ֑י וְ֠הָיְתָ֠ה לִהְיֹ֨ת לָהֶ֧ם מָשְׁחָתָ֛ם לִכְהֻנַּ֥ת עוֹלָ֖ם לְדֹרֹתָֽם׃

16 This *Moshe* did; just as *Hashem* had commanded him, so he did.

טז וַיַּ֖עַשׂ מֹשֶׁ֑ה כְּ֠כֹ֠ל אֲשֶׁ֨ר צִוָּ֧ה יְהוָ֛ה אֹת֖וֹ כֵּ֥ן עָשָֽׂה׃

17 In the first month of the second year, on the first of the month, the *Mishkan* was set up.

יז וַיְהִ֞י בַּחֹ֧דֶשׁ הָרִאשׁ֛וֹן בַּשָּׁנָ֥ה הַשֵּׁנִ֖ית בְּאֶחָ֣ד לַחֹ֑דֶשׁ הוּקַ֖ם הַמִּשְׁכָּֽן׃

18 *Moshe* set up the *Mishkan*, placing its sockets, setting up its planks, inserting its bars, and erecting its posts.

יח וַיָּ֨קֶם מֹשֶׁ֜ה אֶת־הַמִּשְׁכָּ֗ן וַיִּתֵּן֙ אֶת־אֲדָנָ֔יו וַיָּ֙שֶׂם֙ אֶת־קְרָשָׁ֔יו וַיִּתֵּ֖ן אֶת־בְּרִיחָ֑יו וַיָּ֖קֶם אֶת־עַמּוּדָֽיו׃

19 He spread the tent over the *Mishkan*, placing the covering of the tent on top of it – just as *Hashem* had commanded *Moshe*.

יט וַיִּפְרֹ֤שׂ אֶת־הָאֹ֙הֶל֙ עַל־הַמִּשְׁכָּ֔ן וַיָּ֜שֶׂם אֶת־מִכְסֵ֥ה הָאֹ֛הֶל עָלָ֖יו מִלְמָ֑עְלָה כַּאֲשֶׁ֛ר צִוָּ֥ה יְהוָ֖ה אֶת־מֹשֶֽׁה׃

20 He took the Pact and placed it in the ark; he fixed the poles to the ark, placed the cover on top of the ark,

כ וַיִּקַּ֞ח וַיִּתֵּ֤ן אֶת־הָעֵדֻת֙ אֶל־הָ֣אָרֹ֔ן וַיָּ֥שֶׂם אֶת־הַבַּדִּ֖ים עַל־הָאָרֹ֑ן וַיִּתֵּ֧ן אֶת־הַכַּפֹּ֛רֶת עַל־הָאָרֹ֖ן מִלְמָֽעְלָה׃

21 and brought the ark inside the *Mishkan*. Then he put up the curtain for screening, and screened off the *Aron HaBrit* – just as *Hashem* had commanded *Moshe*.

כא וַיָּבֵ֣א אֶת־הָאָרֹן֮ אֶל־הַמִּשְׁכָּן֒ וַיָּ֗שֶׂם אֵ֚ת פָּרֹ֣כֶת הַמָּסָ֔ךְ וַיָּ֕סֶךְ עַ֖ל אֲר֣וֹן הָעֵד֑וּת כַּאֲשֶׁ֛ר צִוָּ֥ה יְהוָ֖ה אֶת־מֹשֶֽׁה׃

22 He placed the table in the Tent of Meeting, outside the curtain, on the north side of the *Mishkan*.

כב וַיִּתֵּ֤ן אֶת־הַשֻּׁלְחָן֙ בְּאֹ֣הֶל מוֹעֵ֔ד עַ֛ל יֶ֥רֶךְ הַמִּשְׁכָּ֖ן צָפֹ֑נָה מִח֖וּץ לַפָּרֹֽכֶת׃

23 Upon it he laid out the setting of bread before *Hashem* – as *Hashem* had commanded *Moshe*.

כג וַיַּעֲרֹ֥ךְ עָלָ֛יו עֵ֥רֶךְ לֶ֖חֶם לִפְנֵ֣י יְהוָ֑ה כַּאֲשֶׁ֛ר צִוָּ֥ה יְהוָ֖ה אֶת־מֹשֶֽׁה׃

24 He placed the *menorah* in the Tent of Meeting opposite the table, on the south side of the *Mishkan*.

כד וַיָּ֤שֶׂם אֶת־הַמְּנֹרָה֙ בְּאֹ֣הֶל מוֹעֵ֔ד נֹ֖כַח הַשֻּׁלְחָ֑ן עַ֛ל יֶ֥רֶךְ הַמִּשְׁכָּ֖ן נֶֽגְבָּה׃

25 And he lit the lamps before *Hashem* – as *Hashem* had commanded *Moshe*.

כה וַיַּ֥עַל הַנֵּרֹ֖ת לִפְנֵ֣י יְהוָ֑ה כַּאֲשֶׁ֛ר צִוָּ֥ה יְהוָ֖ה אֶת־מֹשֶֽׁה׃

26 He placed the *Mizbayach* of gold in the Tent of Meeting, before the curtain.

כו וַיָּ֛שֶׂם אֶת־מִזְבַּ֥ח הַזָּהָ֖ב בְּאֹ֣הֶל מוֹעֵ֑ד לִפְנֵ֖י הַפָּרֹֽכֶת׃

27 On it he burned aromatic incense – as *Hashem* had commanded *Moshe*.

כז וַיַּקְטֵ֥ר עָלָ֖יו קְטֹ֣רֶת סַמִּ֑ים כַּאֲשֶׁ֛ר צִוָּ֥ה יְהוָ֖ה אֶת־מֹשֶֽׁה׃

28 Then he put up the screen for the entrance of the *Mishkan*.

כח וַיָּ֛שֶׂם אֶת־מָסַ֥ךְ הַפֶּ֖תַח לַמִּשְׁכָּֽן׃

240

Shemot/Exodus 40
Pekudei

שמות מ
פקודי

29 At the entrance of the *Mishkan* of the Tent of Meeting he placed the *Mizbayach* of burnt offering. On it he offered up the burnt offering and the meal offering – as *Hashem* had commanded *Moshe*.

כט וְאֵת מִזְבַּח הָעֹלָה שָׂם פֶּתַח מִשְׁכַּן אֹהֶל־מוֹעֵד וַיַּעַל עָלָיו אֶת־הָעֹלָה וְאֶת־הַמִּנְחָה כַּאֲשֶׁר צִוָּה יְהוָה אֶת־מֹשֶׁה:

30 He placed the laver between the Tent of Meeting and the *Mizbayach*, and put water in it for washing.

ל וַיָּשֶׂם אֶת־הַכִּיֹּר בֵּין־אֹהֶל מוֹעֵד וּבֵין הַמִּזְבֵּחַ וַיִּתֵּן שָׁמָּה מַיִם לְרָחְצָה:

31 From it *Moshe* and *Aharon* and his sons would wash their hands and feet;

לא וְרָחֲצוּ מִמֶּנּוּ מֹשֶׁה וְאַהֲרֹן וּבָנָיו אֶת־יְדֵיהֶם וְאֶת־רַגְלֵיהֶם:

32 they washed when they entered the Tent of Meeting and when they approached the *Mizbayach* – as *Hashem* had commanded *Moshe*.

לב בְּבֹאָם אֶל־אֹהֶל מוֹעֵד וּבְקָרְבָתָם אֶל־הַמִּזְבֵּחַ יִרְחָצוּ כַּאֲשֶׁר צִוָּה יְהוָה אֶת־מֹשֶׁה:

33 And he set up the enclosure around the *Mishkan* and the *Mizbayach*, and put up the screen for the gate of the enclosure. When *Moshe* had finished the work,

לג וַיָּקֶם אֶת־הֶחָצֵר סָבִיב לַמִּשְׁכָּן וְלַמִּזְבֵּחַ וַיִּתֵּן אֶת־מָסַךְ שַׁעַר הֶחָצֵר וַיְכַל מֹשֶׁה אֶת־הַמְּלָאכָה:

34 the cloud covered the Tent of Meeting, and the Presence of *Hashem* filled the *Mishkan*.

לד וַיְכַס הֶעָנָן אֶת־אֹהֶל מוֹעֵד וּכְבוֹד יְהוָה מָלֵא אֶת־הַמִּשְׁכָּן:

35 *Moshe* could not enter the Tent of Meeting, because the cloud had settled upon it and the Presence of *Hashem* filled the *Mishkan*.

לה וְלֹא־יָכֹל מֹשֶׁה לָבוֹא אֶל־אֹהֶל מוֹעֵד כִּי־שָׁכַן עָלָיו הֶעָנָן וּכְבוֹד יְהוָה מָלֵא אֶת־הַמִּשְׁכָּן:

36 When the cloud lifted from the *Mishkan*, the Israelites would set out, on their various journeys;

לו וּבְהֵעָלוֹת הֶעָנָן מֵעַל הַמִּשְׁכָּן יִסְעוּ בְּנֵי יִשְׂרָאֵל בְּכֹל מַסְעֵיהֶם:

37 but if the cloud did not lift, they would not set out until such time as it did lift.

לז וְאִם־לֹא יֵעָלֶה הֶעָנָן וְלֹא יִסְעוּ עַד־יוֹם הֵעָלֹתוֹ:

38 For over the *Mishkan* a cloud of *Hashem* rested by day, and fire would appear in it by night, in the view of all the house of *Yisrael* throughout their journeys.

לח כִּי עֲנַן יְהוָה עַל־הַמִּשְׁכָּן יוֹמָם וְאֵשׁ תִּהְיֶה לַיְלָה בּוֹ לְעֵינֵי כָל־בֵּית־יִשְׂרָאֵל בְּכָל־מַסְעֵיהֶם:

KEE a-NAN a-do-NAI al ha-mish-KAN yo-MAM v'-AYSH tih-YEH LAI-lah bo l'-ay-NAY khol bayt yis-ra-AYL b'-KHOL mas-ay-HEM

40:38 A cloud of *Hashem* rested by day, and fire would appear in it by night The pillars of cloud and fire that accompanied the nation upon their exodus from Egypt now reposition themselves by hovering above the *Mishkan* at its completion. This manifestation of God's presence accompanies the Jews throughout their travels in the desert, reminding them that He continuously dwells in their midst. Similarly, when the *Beit Hamikdash* is built by King *Shlomo*, God's glory fills the Temple in the form of a cloud (I Kings 8:10–11), and a fire comes down from heaven (II Chronicles 7:1). Again, His presence among the people is manifest, this time in the holy city of *Yerushalayim*.

Sefer Vayikra
The Book of Leviticus

Introduction and commentary by Shira Schechter

Following the inspirational narrative of *Sefer Bereishit* (Genesis) and the exciting stories of *Sefer Shemot* (Exodus), it may appear at first glance that *Sefer Vayikra* (Leviticus) fails to live up to the standard set by its two dramatic predecessors. The name "Leviticus" comes from *Levi*, the father of the priestly tribe, and much of its 27 chapters are devoted to describing the priestly rituals in great detail. Since most of these practices are not observed today, some modern readers have difficulty in finding practical significance in *Sefer Vayikra*, and thus miss out on its eternal values.

To be sure, it is possible to get lost in all the nuances of the various rituals and offerings described in *Sefer Vayikra*, but it is imperative that the reader not lose sight of the big picture. As we study the intricate details of the offerings, we discover that their overarching purpose is to bring the people closer to *Hashem* through His earthly dwelling place, as it says, "Make for Me a sanctuary, that I may dwell among them" (Exodus 25:8). *Sefer Vayikra*'s intricate details are necessary for us to bring God's presence into our lives in a very physical way, by serving Him in a very specific manner.

The *Mishkan* was a temporary edifice that paved the way for the *Beit Hamikdash* in *Yerushalayim*, which served as the permanent structure for worshipping the God of Israel. Today, even though we don't have the *Mishkan* (Tabernacle) to uplift us or the Temple to pray in, *Yerushalayim* remains mankind's special gateway between heaven and earth. Nowadays, our connection to *Eretz Yisrael* is still able to uplift our service to *Hashem*.

By delving deeper into the meaning behind the *Torah*'s ancient rituals and discovering their many fundamental truths, and by highlighting the role of Zion throughout the Book of *Vayikra*, it is our hope that *The Israel Bible* helps us fulfill the purpose of the *Mishkan*: to bring God's presence into our lives.

May our study of *The Israel Bible* infuse us with sanctity as if we were bringing the offerings described in *Sefer Vayikra*, and prepare us for the day when the *Beit Hamikdash* is rebuilt in *Yerushalayim* and we are able to fully feel God's presence in this world.

Chart of the *Korbanot Yachid* (Offerings Brought by an Individual)

While the end of *Sefer Shemot* describes the construction of the *Mishkan* (Tabernacle) at the foot of Mount Sinai, *Sefer Vayikra* focuses on the service performed in the *Mishkan*. It begins with the laws of *korbanot* (offerings) brought on the *Mizbayach* (altar). The following chart outlines *Sefer Vayikra* chapters 1–5, which describe the *korbanot yachid*, or offerings brought by an individual.

Voluntary Offerings (Leviticus Chapters 1–3)

Type of *korban*	Description	What is brought	Relevant verses
Korban Olah – Burnt Offering	An offering of an animal – the entire *korban* is burnt on the *Mizbayach*	Cattle, Sheep, Goats, Fowl	Leviticus 1:1–17
Korban Mincha – Meal Offering	An offering from flour – part of the offering is burnt on the *Mizbayach* and part is eaten by the *kohanim*.	a. Flour mixed with oil and frankincense b. Flour mixture baked in an oven c. Flour mixture fried on a griddle d. Flour mixture fried in a pan e. Flour taken from the first harvest	Leviticus 2:1–16
Korban Shelamim – Peace Offering	An animal offering that is partially burnt on the *Mizbayach*, partially eaten by the *kohanim* and partially eaten by the owner.	Cattle, Sheep, Goats	Leviticus 3:1–17

Mandatory Offerings (Leviticus Chapters 4–5)

Type of *Korban*	Reason for the *Korban*	What is brought	Relevant Verses
Korban Chatat – Sin Offering	To atone for unintentional sins	**For General Transgressions:** a. *Kohen* – bull b. The High Court – bull c. Prince – male goat d. Layman – a female goat or a female lamb	Leviticus 4:1–35
		For Specific Transgressions: a. Wealthy Person – a female goat or lamb b. Poor Person – two birds c. Very Poor Person – a plain flour offering	Leviticus 5:1–13
Korban Asham – Guilt Offering	To atone for taking from Temple property, if one is unsure he sinned, or for stealing from someone else	Ram	Leviticus 5:14–26

Vayikra/Leviticus 1
Vayikra

ויקרא א
ויקרא

1 ¹ *Hashem* called to *Moshe* and spoke to him from the Tent of Meeting, saying:

א וַיִּקְרָא אֶל־מֹשֶׁה וַיְדַבֵּר יְהֹוָה אֵלָיו מֵאֹהֶל מוֹעֵד לֵאמֹר:

² Speak to *B'nei Yisrael*, and say to them: When any of you presents an offering of cattle to *Hashem*, he shall choose his offering from the herd or from the flock.

ב דַּבֵּר אֶל־בְּנֵי יִשְׂרָאֵל וְאָמַרְתָּ אֲלֵהֶם אָדָם כִּי־יַקְרִיב מִכֶּם קָרְבָּן לַיהֹוָה מִן־הַבְּהֵמָה מִן־הַבָּקָר וּמִן־הַצֹּאן תַּקְרִיבוּ אֶת־קָרְבַּנְכֶם:

da-BAYR el b'-NAY yis-ra-AYL v'-a-mar-TA a-lay-HEM a-DAM kee yak-REEV mi-KEM kor-BAN la-do-NAI min ha-b'-hay-MAH min ha-ba-KAR u-min ha-TZON tak-REE-vu et kor-ban-KHEM

³ If his offering is a burnt offering from the herd, he shall make his offering a male without blemish. He shall bring it to the entrance of the Tent of Meeting, for acceptance in his behalf before *Hashem*.

ג אִם־עֹלָה קָרְבָּנוֹ מִן־הַבָּקָר זָכָר תָּמִים יַקְרִיבֶנּוּ אֶל־פֶּתַח אֹהֶל מוֹעֵד יַקְרִיב אֹתוֹ לִרְצֹנוֹ לִפְנֵי יְהֹוָה:

⁴ He shall lay his hand upon the head of the burnt offering, that it may be acceptable in his behalf, in expiation for him.

ד וְסָמַךְ יָדוֹ עַל רֹאשׁ הָעֹלָה וְנִרְצָה לוֹ לְכַפֵּר עָלָיו:

⁵ The bull shall be slaughtered before *Hashem*; and *Aharon*'s sons, the *Kohanim*, shall offer the blood, dashing the blood against all sides of the *Mizbayach* which is at the entrance of the Tent of Meeting.

ה וְשָׁחַט אֶת־בֶּן הַבָּקָר לִפְנֵי יְהֹוָה וְהִקְרִיבוּ בְּנֵי אַהֲרֹן הַכֹּהֲנִים אֶת־הַדָּם וְזָרְקוּ אֶת־הַדָּם עַל־הַמִּזְבֵּחַ סָבִיב אֲשֶׁר־פֶּתַח אֹהֶל מוֹעֵד:

⁶ The burnt offering shall be flayed and cut up into sections.

ו וְהִפְשִׁיט אֶת־הָעֹלָה וְנִתַּח אֹתָהּ לִנְתָחֶיהָ:

⁷ The sons of *Aharon* the *Kohen* shall put fire on the *Mizbayach* and lay out wood upon the fire;

ז וְנָתְנוּ בְּנֵי אַהֲרֹן הַכֹּהֵן אֵשׁ עַל־הַמִּזְבֵּחַ וְעָרְכוּ עֵצִים עַל־הָאֵשׁ:

⁸ and *Aharon*'s sons, the *Kohanim*, shall lay out the sections, with the head and the suet, on the wood that is on the fire upon the *Mizbayach*.

ח וְעָרְכוּ בְּנֵי אַהֲרֹן הַכֹּהֲנִים אֵת הַנְּתָחִים אֶת־הָרֹאשׁ וְאֶת־הַפָּדֶר עַל־הָעֵצִים אֲשֶׁר עַל־הָאֵשׁ אֲשֶׁר עַל־הַמִּזְבֵּחַ:

⁹ Its entrails and legs shall be washed with water, and the *Kohen* shall turn the whole into smoke on the *Mizbayach* as a burnt offering, an offering by fire of pleasing odor to *Hashem*.

ט וְקִרְבּוֹ וּכְרָעָיו יִרְחַץ בַּמָּיִם וְהִקְטִיר הַכֹּהֵן אֶת־הַכֹּל הַמִּזְבֵּחָה עֹלָה אִשֵּׁה רֵיחַ־נִיחוֹחַ לַיהֹוָה:

¹⁰ If his offering for a burnt offering is from the flock, of sheep or of goats, he shall make his offering a male without blemish.

י וְאִם־מִן־הַצֹּאן קָרְבָּנוֹ מִן־הַכְּשָׂבִים אוֹ מִן־הָעִזִּים לְעֹלָה זָכָר תָּמִים יַקְרִיבֶנּוּ:

קרבן

1:2 When any of you presents an offering of cattle to *Hashem* *Sefer Vayikra* describes the various offerings that were brought in the *Beit Hamikdash* in great detail. The Hebrew term for 'offering,' *korban* (קרבן), comes from the word *karov* (ק-ר-ב), meaning 'close,' since the offerings are meant to bring people closer to the Eternal One. For this reason, the common English translation of *korban*, 'sacrifice,' is insufficient, as it does not accurately portray the essence of the word. While the person bringing the offering might be giving something from his personal possessions, he gains much more than he gives. Now that we no longer have *korbanot*, prayer is the primary vehicle through which we come close to our Father in Heaven.

Vayikra/Leviticus 2
Vayikra

ויקרא ב
ויקרא

11 It shall be slaughtered before *Hashem* on the north side of the *Mizbayach*, and *Aharon*'s sons, the *Kohanim*, shall dash its blood against all sides of the *Mizbayach*.

יא וְשָׁחַט אֹתוֹ עַל יֶרֶךְ הַמִּזְבֵּחַ צָפֹנָה לִפְנֵי יְהֹוָה וְזָרְקוּ בְּנֵי אַהֲרֹן הַכֹּהֲנִים אֶת־דָּמוֹ עַל־הַמִּזְבֵּחַ סָבִיב׃

12 When it has been cut up into sections, the *Kohen* shall lay them out, with the head and the suet, on the wood that is on the fire upon the *Mizbayach*.

יב וְנִתַּח אֹתוֹ לִנְתָחָיו וְאֶת־רֹאשׁוֹ וְאֶת־פִּדְרוֹ וְעָרַךְ הַכֹּהֵן אֹתָם עַל־הָעֵצִים אֲשֶׁר עַל־הָאֵשׁ אֲשֶׁר עַל־הַמִּזְבֵּחַ׃

13 The entrails and the legs shall be washed with water; the *Kohen* shall offer up and turn the whole into smoke on the *Mizbayach*. It is a burnt offering, an offering by fire, of pleasing odor to *Hashem*.

יג וְהַקֶּרֶב וְהַכְּרָעַיִם יִרְחַץ בַּמָּיִם וְהִקְרִיב הַכֹּהֵן אֶת־הַכֹּל וְהִקְטִיר הַמִּזְבֵּחָה עֹלָה הוּא אִשֵּׁה רֵיחַ־נִיחוֹחַ לַיהֹוָה׃

14 If his offering to *Hashem* is a burnt offering of birds, he shall choose his offering from turtledoves or pigeons.

יד וְאִם מִן־הָעוֹף עֹלָה קָרְבָּנוֹ לַיהֹוָה וְהִקְרִיב מִן־הַתֹּרִים אוֹ מִן־בְּנֵי הַיּוֹנָה אֶת־קָרְבָּנוֹ׃

15 The *Kohen* shall bring it to the *Mizbayach*, pinch off its head, and turn it into smoke on the *Mizbayach*; and its blood shall be drained out against the side of the *Mizbayach*.

טו וְהִקְרִיבוֹ הַכֹּהֵן אֶל־הַמִּזְבֵּחַ וּמָלַק אֶת־רֹאשׁוֹ וְהִקְטִיר הַמִּזְבֵּחָה וְנִמְצָה דָמוֹ עַל קִיר הַמִּזְבֵּחַ׃

16 He shall remove its crop with its contents, and cast it into the place of the ashes, at the east side of the *Mizbayach*.

טז וְהֵסִיר אֶת־מֻרְאָתוֹ בְּנֹצָתָהּ וְהִשְׁלִיךְ אֹתָהּ אֵצֶל הַמִּזְבֵּחַ קֵדְמָה אֶל־מְקוֹם הַדָּשֶׁן׃

17 The *Kohen* shall tear it open by its wings, without severing it, and turn it into smoke on the *Mizbayach*, upon the wood that is on the fire. It is a burnt offering, an offering by fire, of pleasing odor to *Hashem*.

יז וְשִׁסַּע אֹתוֹ בִכְנָפָיו לֹא יַבְדִּיל וְהִקְטִיר אֹתוֹ הַכֹּהֵן הַמִּזְבֵּחָה עַל־הָעֵצִים אֲשֶׁר עַל־הָאֵשׁ עֹלָה הוּא אִשֵּׁה רֵיחַ נִיחֹחַ לַיהֹוָה׃

2 1 When a person presents an offering of meal to *Hashem*, his offering shall be of choice flour; he shall pour oil upon it, lay frankincense on it,

ב א וְנֶפֶשׁ כִּי־תַקְרִיב קָרְבַּן מִנְחָה לַיהֹוָה סֹלֶת יִהְיֶה קָרְבָּנוֹ וְיָצַק עָלֶיהָ שֶׁמֶן וְנָתַן עָלֶיהָ לְבֹנָה׃

v'-NE-fesh kee tak-REEV kor-BAN min-KHAH la-do-NAI SO-let yih-YEH kor-ba-NO v'-ya-TZAK a-LE-ha SHE-men v'-na-TAN a-LE-ha l'-vo-NAH

2:1 When a person presents an offering of meal to *Hashem* In this verse, the Bible uses the word *nefesh* (נפש), 'soul,' to describe the person bringing this offering. The Talmud (*Menachot* 104b) explains that the word "soul" is specifically chosen for the voluntary meal-offering, as opposed to any of the other sacrifices, because the meal-offering is comprised of flour, oil and frankincense. These ingredients are much less expensive than the animals brought for the other offerings, and therefore, this offering is often brought specifically by poor people. When a poor person chooses to give from his meager means to *Hashem*, He considers it as if the person has offered his very soul. What matters to the Lord is not our material wealth, how much we have or even how much we give. It is the sincerity behind our actions that matters most.

Vayikra/Leviticus 2
Vayikra

2 and present it to *Aharon*'s sons, the *Kohanim*. The *Kohen* shall scoop out of it a handful of its choice flour and oil, as well as all of its frankincense; and this token portion he shall turn into smoke on the *Mizbayach*, as an offering by fire, of pleasing odor to *Hashem*.

3 And the remainder of the meal offering shall be for *Aharon* and his sons, a most holy portion from *Hashem*'s offerings by fire.

4 When you present an offering of meal baked in the oven, [it shall be of] choice flour: unleavened cakes with oil mixed in, or unleavened wafers spread with oil.

5 If your offering is a meal offering on a griddle, it shall be of choice flour with oil mixed in, unleavened.

6 Break it into bits and pour oil on it; it is a meal offering.

7 If your offering is a meal offering in a pan, it shall be made of choice flour in oil.

8 When you present to *Hashem* a meal offering that is made in any of these ways, it shall be brought to the *Kohen* who shall take it up to the *Mizbayach*.

9 The *Kohen* shall remove the token portion from the meal offering and turn it into smoke on the *Mizbayach* as an offering by fire, of pleasing odor to *Hashem*.

10 And the remainder of the meal offering shall be for *Aharon* and his sons, a most holy portion from *Hashem*'s offerings by fire.

11 No meal offering that you offer to *Hashem* shall be made with leaven, for no leaven or honey may be turned into smoke as an offering by fire to *Hashem*.

12 You may bring them to *Hashem* as an offering of choice products; but they shall not be offered up on the *Mizbayach* for a pleasing odor.

13 You shall season your every offering of meal with salt; you shall not omit from your meal offering the salt of your covenant with *Hashem*; with all your offerings you must offer salt.

14 If you bring a meal offering of first fruits to *Hashem*, you shall bring new ears parched with fire, grits of the fresh grain, as your meal offering of first fruits.

ויקרא ב
ויקרא

ב וֶהֱבִיאָהּ אֶל־בְּנֵי אַהֲרֹן הַכֹּהֲנִים וְקָמַץ מִשָּׁם מְלֹא קֻמְצוֹ מִסָּלְתָּהּ וּמִשַּׁמְנָהּ עַל כָּל־לְבֹנָתָהּ וְהִקְטִיר הַכֹּהֵן אֶת־אַזְכָּרָתָהּ הַמִּזְבֵּחָה אִשֵּׁה רֵיחַ נִיחֹחַ לַיהוָה:

ג וְהַנּוֹתֶרֶת מִן־הַמִּנְחָה לְאַהֲרֹן וּלְבָנָיו קֹדֶשׁ קָדָשִׁים מֵאִשֵּׁי יְהוָה:

ד וְכִי תַקְרִב קָרְבַּן מִנְחָה מַאֲפֵה תַנּוּר סֹלֶת חַלּוֹת מַצֹּת בְּלוּלֹת בַּשֶּׁמֶן וּרְקִיקֵי מַצּוֹת מְשֻׁחִים בַּשָּׁמֶן:

ה וְאִם־מִנְחָה עַל־הַמַּחֲבַת קָרְבָּנֶךָ סֹלֶת בְּלוּלָה בַשֶּׁמֶן מַצָּה תִהְיֶה:

ו פָּתוֹת אֹתָהּ פִּתִּים וְיָצַקְתָּ עָלֶיהָ שָׁמֶן מִנְחָה הִוא:

ז וְאִם־מִנְחַת מַרְחֶשֶׁת קָרְבָּנֶךָ סֹלֶת בַּשֶּׁמֶן תֵּעָשֶׂה:

ח וְהֵבֵאתָ אֶת־הַמִּנְחָה אֲשֶׁר יֵעָשֶׂה מֵאֵלֶּה לַיהוָה וְהִקְרִיבָהּ אֶל־הַכֹּהֵן וְהִגִּישָׁהּ אֶל־הַמִּזְבֵּחַ:

ט וְהֵרִים הַכֹּהֵן מִן־הַמִּנְחָה אֶת־אַזְכָּרָתָהּ וְהִקְטִיר הַמִּזְבֵּחָה אִשֵּׁה רֵיחַ נִיחֹחַ לַיהוָה:

י וְהַנּוֹתֶרֶת מִן־הַמִּנְחָה לְאַהֲרֹן וּלְבָנָיו קֹדֶשׁ קָדָשִׁים מֵאִשֵּׁי יְהוָה:

יא כָּל־הַמִּנְחָה אֲשֶׁר תַּקְרִיבוּ לַיהוָה לֹא תֵעָשֶׂה חָמֵץ כִּי כָל־שְׂאֹר וְכָל־דְּבַשׁ לֹא־תַקְטִירוּ מִמֶּנּוּ אִשֶּׁה לַיהוָה:

יב קָרְבַּן רֵאשִׁית תַּקְרִיבוּ אֹתָם לַיהוָה וְאֶל־הַמִּזְבֵּחַ לֹא־יַעֲלוּ לְרֵיחַ נִיחֹחַ:

יג וְכָל־קָרְבַּן מִנְחָתְךָ בַּמֶּלַח תִּמְלָח וְלֹא תַשְׁבִּית מֶלַח בְּרִית אֱלֹהֶיךָ מֵעַל מִנְחָתֶךָ עַל כָּל־קָרְבָּנְךָ תַּקְרִיב מֶלַח:

יד וְאִם־תַּקְרִיב מִנְחַת בִּכּוּרִים לַיהוָה אָבִיב קָלוּי בָּאֵשׁ גֶּרֶשׂ כַּרְמֶל תַּקְרִיב אֵת מִנְחַת בִּכּוּרֶיךָ:

Vayikra/Leviticus 3
Vayikra

ויקרא ג
ויקרא

15 You shall add oil to it and lay frankincense on it; it is a meal offering.

טו וְנָתַתָּ עָלֶיהָ שֶׁמֶן וְשַׂמְתָּ עָלֶיהָ לְבֹנָה מִנְחָה הִוא׃

16 And the *Kohen* shall turn a token portion of it into smoke: some of the grits and oil, with all of the frankincense, as an offering by fire to *Hashem*.

טז וְהִקְטִיר הַכֹּהֵן אֶת־אַזְכָּרָתָהּ מִגִּרְשָׂהּ וּמִשַּׁמְנָהּ עַל כָּל־לְבֹנָתָהּ אִשֶּׁה לַיהוָה׃

3

1 If his offering is a sacrifice of well-being – If he offers of the herd, whether a male or a female, he shall bring before *Hashem* one without blemish.

א וְאִם־זֶבַח שְׁלָמִים קָרְבָּנוֹ אִם מִן־הַבָּקָר הוּא מַקְרִיב אִם־זָכָר אִם־נְקֵבָה תָּמִים יַקְרִיבֶנּוּ לִפְנֵי יְהוָה׃

v'-im ZE-vakh sh'-la-MEEM kor-ba-NO im min ha-ba-KAR HU mak-REEV im za-KHAR im n'-kay-VAH ta-MEEM yak-ree-VE-nu lif-NAY a-do-NAI

2 He shall lay his hand upon the head of his offering and slaughter it at the entrance of the Tent of Meeting; and *Aharon*'s sons, the *Kohanim*, shall dash the blood against all sides of the *Mizbayach*.

ב וְסָמַךְ יָדוֹ עַל־רֹאשׁ קָרְבָּנוֹ וּשְׁחָטוֹ פֶּתַח אֹהֶל מוֹעֵד וְזָרְקוּ בְּנֵי אַהֲרֹן הַכֹּהֲנִים אֶת־הַדָּם עַל־הַמִּזְבֵּחַ סָבִיב׃

3 He shall then present from the sacrifice of well-being, as an offering by fire to *Hashem*, the fat that covers the entrails and all the fat that is about the entrails;

ג וְהִקְרִיב מִזֶּבַח הַשְּׁלָמִים אִשֶּׁה לַיהוָה אֶת־הַחֵלֶב הַמְכַסֶּה אֶת־הַקֶּרֶב וְאֵת כָּל־הַחֵלֶב אֲשֶׁר עַל־הַקֶּרֶב׃

4 the two kidneys and the fat that is on them, that is at the loins; and the protuberance on the liver, which he shall remove with the kidneys.

ד וְאֵת שְׁתֵּי הַכְּלָיֹת וְאֶת־הַחֵלֶב אֲשֶׁר עֲלֵהֶן אֲשֶׁר עַל־הַכְּסָלִים וְאֶת־הַיֹּתֶרֶת עַל־הַכָּבֵד עַל־הַכְּלָיוֹת יְסִירֶנָּה׃

5 *Aharon*'s sons shall turn these into smoke on the *Mizbayach*, with the burnt offering which is upon the wood that is on the fire, as an offering by fire, of pleasing odor to *Hashem*.

ה וְהִקְטִירוּ אֹתוֹ בְנֵי־אַהֲרֹן הַמִּזְבֵּחָה עַל־הָעֹלָה אֲשֶׁר עַל־הָעֵצִים אֲשֶׁר עַל־הָאֵשׁ אִשֵּׁה רֵיחַ נִיחֹחַ לַיהוָה׃

6 And if his offering for a sacrifice of well-being to *Hashem* is from the flock, whether a male or a female, he shall offer one without blemish.

ו וְאִם־מִן־הַצֹּאן קָרְבָּנוֹ לְזֶבַח שְׁלָמִים לַיהוָה זָכָר אוֹ נְקֵבָה תָּמִים יַקְרִיבֶנּוּ׃

7 If he presents a sheep as his offering, he shall bring it before *Hashem*

ז אִם־כֶּשֶׂב הוּא־מַקְרִיב אֶת־קָרְבָּנוֹ וְהִקְרִיב אֹתוֹ לִפְנֵי יְהוָה׃

שלמים

3:1 If his offering is a sacrifice of well-being The sacrifice of well-being is often called the 'peace-offering' based on its Hebrew name, *korban sh'lamim* (קרבן שלמים), which comes from the Hebrew word *shalom* (שלום), 'peace.' According to Jewish tradition, it is so called because the *korban sh'lamim* symbolizes peace and unity, as it is the only offering that is shared by everyone involved: *Hashem* (referring to the portions consumed on the altar), the priest and the owner of the sacrifice. It is perhaps not a coincidence that it is also the only offering that is not restricted to the *Beit Hamikdash*, but may be eaten anywhere in the city of *Yerushalayim*. *Yerushalayim*, the Hebrew name for Jerusalem, also has the word *shalom* at its root. It is known as the *eer shel shalom* (עיר של שלום), 'city of peace.' We pray for the time when peace and unity, symbolized by the *korban sh'lamim*, will return to Jerusalem, and to all of Israel.

Old City of Jerusalem, "city of peace"

Vayikra/Leviticus 4
Vayikra

8 and lay his hand upon the head of his offering. It shall be slaughtered before the Tent of Meeting, and *Aharon*'s sons shall dash its blood against all sides of the *Mizbayach*.

9 He shall then present, as an offering by fire to *Hashem*, the fat from the sacrifice of well-being: the whole broad tail, which shall be removed close to the backbone; the fat that covers the entrails and all the fat that is about the entrails;

10 the two kidneys and the fat that is on them, that is at the loins; and the protuberance on the liver, which he shall remove with the kidneys.

11 The *Kohen* shall turn these into smoke on the *Mizbayach* as food, an offering by fire to *Hashem*.

12 And if his offering is a goat, he shall bring it before *Hashem*

13 and lay his hand upon its head. It shall be slaughtered before the Tent of Meeting, and *Aharon*'s sons shall dash its blood against all sides of the *Mizbayach*.

14 He shall then present as his offering from it, as an offering by fire to *Hashem*, the fat that covers the entrails and all the fat that is about the entrails;

15 the two kidneys and the fat that is on them, that is at the loins; and the protuberance on the liver, which he shall remove with the kidneys.

16 The *Kohen* shall turn these into smoke on the *Mizbayach* as food, an offering by fire, of pleasing odor. All fat is *Hashem*'s.

17 It is a law for all time throughout the ages, in all your settlements: you must not eat any fat or any blood.

4

1 *Hashem* spoke to *Moshe*, saying:

2 Speak to *B'nei Yisrael* thus: When a person unwittingly incurs guilt in regard to any of *Hashem*'s commandments about things not to be done, and does one of them –

3 If it is the anointed *Kohen* who has incurred guilt, so that blame falls upon the people, he shall offer for the sin of which he is guilty a bull of the herd without blemish as a sin offering to *Hashem*.

Vayikra/Leviticus 4
Vayikra

ויקרא ד
ויקרא

4 He shall bring the bull to the entrance of the Tent of Meeting, before *Hashem*, and lay his hand upon the head of the bull. The bull shall be slaughtered before *Hashem*,

ד וְהֵבִיא אֶת־הַפָּר אֶל־פֶּתַח אֹהֶל מוֹעֵד לִפְנֵי יְהֹוָה וְסָמַךְ אֶת־יָדוֹ עַל־רֹאשׁ הַפָּר וְשָׁחַט אֶת־הַפָּר לִפְנֵי יְהֹוָה:

5 and the anointed *Kohen* shall take some of the bull's blood and bring it into the Tent of Meeting.

ה וְלָקַח הַכֹּהֵן הַמָּשִׁיחַ מִדַּם הַפָּר וְהֵבִיא אֹתוֹ אֶל־אֹהֶל מוֹעֵד:

6 The *Kohen* shall dip his finger in the blood, and sprinkle of the blood seven times before *Hashem*, in front of the curtain of the Shrine.

ו וְטָבַל הַכֹּהֵן אֶת־אֶצְבָּעוֹ בַּדָּם וְהִזָּה מִן־הַדָּם שֶׁבַע פְּעָמִים לִפְנֵי יְהֹוָה אֶת־פְּנֵי פָּרֹכֶת הַקֹּדֶשׁ:

7 The *Kohen* shall put some of the blood on the horns of the *Mizbayach* of aromatic incense, which is in the Tent of Meeting, before *Hashem*; and all the rest of the bull's blood he shall pour out at the base of the *Mizbayach* of burnt offering, which is at the entrance of the Tent of Meeting.

ז וְנָתַן הַכֹּהֵן מִן־הַדָּם עַל־קַרְנוֹת מִזְבַּח קְטֹרֶת הַסַּמִּים לִפְנֵי יְהֹוָה אֲשֶׁר בְּאֹהֶל מוֹעֵד וְאֵת כָּל־דַּם הַפָּר יִשְׁפֹּךְ אֶל־יְסוֹד מִזְבַּח הָעֹלָה אֲשֶׁר־פֶּתַח אֹהֶל מוֹעֵד:

8 He shall remove all the fat from the bull of sin offering: the fat that covers the entrails and all the fat that is about the entrails;

ח וְאֶת־כָּל־חֵלֶב פַּר הַחַטָּאת יָרִים מִמֶּנּוּ אֶת־הַחֵלֶב הַמְכַסֶּה עַל־הַקֶּרֶב וְאֵת כָּל־הַחֵלֶב אֲשֶׁר עַל־הַקֶּרֶב:

9 the two kidneys and the fat that is on them, that is at the loins; and the protuberance on the liver, which he shall remove with the kidneys

ט וְאֵת שְׁתֵּי הַכְּלָיֹת וְאֶת־הַחֵלֶב אֲשֶׁר עֲלֵיהֶן אֲשֶׁר עַל־הַכְּסָלִים וְאֶת־הַיֹּתֶרֶת עַל־הַכָּבֵד עַל־הַכְּלָיוֹת יְסִירֶנָּה:

10 just as it is removed from the ox of the sacrifice of well-being. The *Kohen* shall turn them into smoke on the *Mizbayach* of burnt offering.

י כַּאֲשֶׁר יוּרַם מִשּׁוֹר זֶבַח הַשְּׁלָמִים וְהִקְטִירָם הַכֹּהֵן עַל מִזְבַּח הָעֹלָה:

11 But the hide of the bull, and all its flesh, as well as its head and legs, its entrails and its dung

יא וְאֶת־עוֹר הַפָּר וְאֶת־כָּל־בְּשָׂרוֹ עַל־רֹאשׁוֹ וְעַל־כְּרָעָיו וְקִרְבּוֹ וּפִרְשׁוֹ:

12 all the rest of the bull – he shall carry to a clean place outside the camp, to the ash heap, and burn it up in a wood fire; it shall be burned on the ash heap.

יב וְהוֹצִיא אֶת־כָּל־הַפָּר אֶל־מִחוּץ לַמַּחֲנֶה אֶל־מָקוֹם טָהוֹר אֶל־שֶׁפֶךְ הַדֶּשֶׁן וְשָׂרַף אֹתוֹ עַל־עֵצִים בָּאֵשׁ עַל־שֶׁפֶךְ הַדֶּשֶׁן יִשָּׂרֵף:

13 If it is the whole community of *Yisrael* that has erred and the matter escapes the notice of the congregation, so that they do any of the things which by *Hashem*'s commandments ought not to be done, and they realize their guilt

יג וְאִם כָּל־עֲדַת יִשְׂרָאֵל יִשְׁגּוּ וְנֶעְלַם דָּבָר מֵעֵינֵי הַקָּהָל וְעָשׂוּ אַחַת מִכָּל־מִצְוֹת יְהֹוָה אֲשֶׁר לֹא־תֵעָשֶׂינָה וְאָשֵׁמוּ:

v'-IM kol a-DAT yis-ra-AYL yish-GU v'-ne-e-LAM da-VAR may-ay-NAY ha-ka-HAL v'-a-SU a-KHAT mi-kol mitz-VOT a-do-NAI a-SHER lo tay-a-SE-na v'-a-SHAY-mu

---

4:13 If it is the whole community of *Yisrael* that has erred As opposed to the previous three chapters which discuss the voluntary offerings meant for spiritual elevation, chapter four discusses sin-offerings, required to atone for unintentional transgressions, and lists different scenarios in which a person might

Vayikra/Leviticus 4
Vayikra

יד וְנוֹדְעָה הַחַטָּאת אֲשֶׁר חָטְאוּ עָלֶיהָ וְהִקְרִיבוּ הַקָּהָל פַּר בֶּן־בָּקָר לְחַטָּאת וְהֵבִיאוּ אֹתוֹ לִפְנֵי אֹהֶל מוֹעֵד:

טו וְסָמְכוּ זִקְנֵי הָעֵדָה אֶת־יְדֵיהֶם עַל־רֹאשׁ הַפָּר לִפְנֵי יְהוָה וְשָׁחַט אֶת־הַפָּר לִפְנֵי יְהוָה:

טז וְהֵבִיא הַכֹּהֵן הַמָּשִׁיחַ מִדַּם הַפָּר אֶל־אֹהֶל מוֹעֵד:

יז וְטָבַל הַכֹּהֵן אֶצְבָּעוֹ מִן־הַדָּם וְהִזָּה שֶׁבַע פְּעָמִים לִפְנֵי יְהוָה אֵת פְּנֵי הַפָּרֹכֶת:

יח וּמִן־הַדָּם יִתֵּן עַל־קַרְנֹת הַמִּזְבֵּחַ אֲשֶׁר לִפְנֵי יְהוָה אֲשֶׁר בְּאֹהֶל מוֹעֵד וְאֵת כָּל־הַדָּם יִשְׁפֹּךְ אֶל־יְסוֹד מִזְבַּח הָעֹלָה אֲשֶׁר־פֶּתַח אֹהֶל מוֹעֵד:

יט וְאֵת כָּל־חֶלְבּוֹ יָרִים מִמֶּנּוּ וְהִקְטִיר הַמִּזְבֵּחָה:

כ וְעָשָׂה לַפָּר כַּאֲשֶׁר עָשָׂה לְפַר הַחַטָּאת כֵּן יַעֲשֶׂה־לּוֹ וְכִפֶּר עֲלֵהֶם הַכֹּהֵן וְנִסְלַח לָהֶם:

כא וְהוֹצִיא אֶת־הַפָּר אֶל־מִחוּץ לַמַּחֲנֶה וְשָׂרַף אֹתוֹ כַּאֲשֶׁר שָׂרַף אֵת הַפָּר הָרִאשׁוֹן חַטַּאת הַקָּהָל הוּא:

כב אֲשֶׁר נָשִׂיא יֶחֱטָא וְעָשָׂה אַחַת מִכָּל־מִצְוֺת יְהוָה אֱלֹהָיו אֲשֶׁר לֹא־תֵעָשֶׂינָה בִּשְׁגָגָה וְאָשֵׁם:

כג אוֹ־הוֹדַע אֵלָיו חַטָּאתוֹ אֲשֶׁר חָטָא בָּהּ וְהֵבִיא אֶת־קָרְבָּנוֹ שְׂעִיר עִזִּים זָכָר תָּמִים:

14 when the sin through which they incurred guilt becomes known, the congregation shall offer a bull of the herd as a sin offering, and bring it before the Tent of Meeting.

15 The elders of the community shall lay their hands upon the head of the bull before *Hashem*, and the bull shall be slaughtered before *Hashem*.

16 The anointed *Kohen* shall bring some of the blood of the bull into the Tent of Meeting,

17 and the *Kohen* shall dip his finger in the blood and sprinkle of it seven times before *Hashem*, in front of the curtain.

18 Some of the blood he shall put on the horns of the *Mizbayach* which is before *Hashem* in the Tent of Meeting, and all the rest of the blood he shall pour out at the base of the *Mizbayach* of burnt offering, which is at the entrance of the Tent of Meeting.

19 He shall remove all its fat from it and turn it into smoke on the *Mizbayach*.

20 He shall do with this bull just as is done with the [*Kohen's*] bull of sin offering; he shall do the same with it. Thus the *Kohen* shall make expiation for them, and they shall be forgiven.

21 He shall carry the bull outside the camp and burn it as he burned the first bull; it is the sin offering of the congregation.

22 In case it is a chieftain who incurs guilt by doing unwittingly any of the things which by the commandment of *Hashem* his God ought not to be done, and he realizes his guilt

23 or the sin of which he is guilty is brought to his knowledge – he shall bring as his offering a male goat without blemish.

אם
כי

need to bring such an offering. The *Kli Yakar* points out that when introducing the offering brought to atone for a sin committed by the entire congregation, meaning the nation as a whole, the verse uses the Hebrew word *im* (אם), 'if,' implying that such a situation is somewhat unlikely to occur. However, when referring to the offering brought by an individual, the Bibe (verse 1) uses the word *kee* (כי), which can be translated as 'when,' suggesting that an individual person is much more likely to make a mistake. This underscores the fact that the Children of Israel are significantly strengthened when they join together as a people.

251

Vayikra/Leviticus 4
Vayikra

ויקרא ד
ויקרא

24 He shall lay his hand upon the goat's head, and it shall be slaughtered at the spot where the burnt offering is slaughtered before *Hashem*; it is a sin offering.

כד וְסָמַךְ יָדוֹ עַל־רֹאשׁ הַשָּׂעִיר וְשָׁחַט אֹתוֹ בִּמְקוֹם אֲשֶׁר־יִשְׁחַט אֶת־הָעֹלָה לִפְנֵי יְהֹוָה חַטָּאת הוּא:

25 The *Kohen* shall take with his finger some of the blood of the sin offering and put it on the horns of the *Mizbayach* of burnt offering; and the rest of its blood he shall pour out at the base of the *Mizbayach* of burnt offering.

כה וְלָקַח הַכֹּהֵן מִדַּם הַחַטָּאת בְּאֶצְבָּעוֹ וְנָתַן עַל־קַרְנֹת מִזְבַּח הָעֹלָה וְאֶת־דָּמוֹ יִשְׁפֹּךְ אֶל־יְסוֹד מִזְבַּח הָעֹלָה:

26 All its fat he shall turn into smoke on the *Mizbayach*, like the fat of the sacrifice of well-being. Thus the *Kohen* shall make expiation on his behalf for his sin, and he shall be forgiven.

כו וְאֶת־כָּל־חֶלְבּוֹ יַקְטִיר הַמִּזְבֵּחָה כְּחֵלֶב זֶבַח הַשְּׁלָמִים וְכִפֶּר עָלָיו הַכֹּהֵן מֵחַטָּאתוֹ וְנִסְלַח לוֹ:

27 If any person from among the populace unwittingly incurs guilt by doing any of the things which by *Hashem*'s commandments ought not to be done, and he realizes his guilt

כז וְאִם־נֶפֶשׁ אַחַת תֶּחֱטָא בִשְׁגָגָה מֵעַם הָאָרֶץ בַּעֲשֹׂתָהּ אַחַת מִמִּצְוֹת יְהֹוָה אֲשֶׁר לֹא־תֵעָשֶׂינָה וְאָשֵׁם:

28 or the sin of which he is guilty is brought to his knowledge – he shall bring a female goat without blemish as his offering for the sin of which he is guilty.

כח אוֹ הוֹדַע אֵלָיו חַטָּאתוֹ אֲשֶׁר חָטָא וְהֵבִיא קָרְבָּנוֹ שְׂעִירַת עִזִּים תְּמִימָה נְקֵבָה עַל־חַטָּאתוֹ אֲשֶׁר חָטָא:

29 He shall lay his hand upon the head of the sin offering, and the sin offering shall be slaughtered at the place of the burnt offering.

כט וְסָמַךְ אֶת־יָדוֹ עַל רֹאשׁ הַחַטָּאת וְשָׁחַט אֶת־הַחַטָּאת בִּמְקוֹם הָעֹלָה:

30 The *Kohen* shall take with his finger some of its blood and put it on the horns of the *Mizbayach* of burnt offering; and all the rest of its blood he shall pour out at the base of the *Mizbayach*.

ל וְלָקַח הַכֹּהֵן מִדָּמָהּ בְּאֶצְבָּעוֹ וְנָתַן עַל־קַרְנֹת מִזְבַּח הָעֹלָה וְאֶת־כָּל־דָּמָהּ יִשְׁפֹּךְ אֶל־יְסוֹד הַמִּזְבֵּחַ:

31 He shall remove all its fat, just as the fat is removed from the sacrifice of well-being; and the *Kohen* shall turn it into smoke on the *Mizbayach*, for a pleasing odor to *Hashem*. Thus the *Kohen* shall make expiation for him, and he shall be forgiven.

לא וְאֶת־כָּל־חֶלְבָּהּ יָסִיר כַּאֲשֶׁר הוּסַר חֵלֶב מֵעַל זֶבַח הַשְּׁלָמִים וְהִקְטִיר הַכֹּהֵן הַמִּזְבֵּחָה לְרֵיחַ נִיחֹחַ לַיהֹוָה וְכִפֶּר עָלָיו הַכֹּהֵן וְנִסְלַח לוֹ:

32 If the offering he brings as a sin offering is a sheep, he shall bring a female without blemish.

לב וְאִם־כֶּבֶשׂ יָבִיא קָרְבָּנוֹ לְחַטָּאת נְקֵבָה תְמִימָה יְבִיאֶנָּה:

33 He shall lay his hand upon the head of the sin offering, and it shall be slaughtered as a sin offering at the spot where the burnt offering is slaughtered.

לג וְסָמַךְ אֶת־יָדוֹ עַל רֹאשׁ הַחַטָּאת וְשָׁחַט אֹתָהּ לְחַטָּאת בִּמְקוֹם אֲשֶׁר יִשְׁחַט אֶת־הָעֹלָה:

34 The *Kohen* shall take with his finger some of the blood of the sin offering and put it on the horns of the *Mizbayach* of burnt offering, and all the rest of its blood he shall pour out at the base of the *Mizbayach*.

לד וְלָקַח הַכֹּהֵן מִדַּם הַחַטָּאת בְּאֶצְבָּעוֹ וְנָתַן עַל־קַרְנֹת מִזְבַּח הָעֹלָה וְאֶת־כָּל־דָּמָהּ יִשְׁפֹּךְ אֶל־יְסוֹד הַמִּזְבֵּחַ:

Vayikra/Leviticus 5
Vayikra

ויקרא ה
ויקרא

35 And all its fat he shall remove just as the fat of the sheep of the sacrifice of well-being is removed; and this the *Kohen* shall turn into smoke on the *Mizbayach*, over *Hashem*'s offering by fire. Thus the *Kohen* shall make expiation on his behalf for the sin of which he is guilty, and he shall be forgiven.

לה וְאֶת־כָּל־חֶלְבָּה יָסִיר כַּאֲשֶׁר יוּסַר חֵלֶב־הַכֶּשֶׂב מִזֶּבַח הַשְּׁלָמִים וְהִקְטִיר הַכֹּהֵן אֹתָם הַמִּזְבֵּחָה עַל אִשֵּׁי יְהוָה וְכִפֶּר עָלָיו הַכֹּהֵן עַל־חַטָּאתוֹ אֲשֶׁר־חָטָא וְנִסְלַח לוֹ:

5 1 If a person incurs guilt – When he has heard a public imprecation and – although able to testify as one who has either seen or learned of the matter – he does not give information, so that he is subject to punishment;

ה א וְנֶפֶשׁ כִּי־תֶחֱטָא וְשָׁמְעָה קוֹל אָלָה וְהוּא עֵד אוֹ רָאָה אוֹ יָדָע אִם־לוֹא יַגִּיד וְנָשָׂא עֲוֹנוֹ:

2 Or when a person touches any unclean thing – be it the carcass of an unclean beast or the carcass of unclean cattle or the carcass of an unclean creeping thing – and the fact has escaped him, and then, being unclean, he realizes his guilt;

ב אוֹ נֶפֶשׁ אֲשֶׁר תִּגַּע בְּכָל־דָּבָר טָמֵא אוֹ בְנִבְלַת חַיָּה טְמֵאָה אוֹ בְּנִבְלַת בְּהֵמָה טְמֵאָה אוֹ בְּנִבְלַת שֶׁרֶץ טָמֵא וְנֶעְלַם מִמֶּנּוּ וְהוּא טָמֵא וְאָשֵׁם:

3 Or when he touches human uncleanness – any such uncleanness whereby one becomes unclean – and, though he has known it, the fact has escaped him, but later he realizes his guilt;

ג אוֹ כִי יִגַּע בְּטֻמְאַת אָדָם לְכֹל טֻמְאָתוֹ אֲשֶׁר יִטְמָא בָּהּ וְנֶעְלַם מִמֶּנּוּ וְהוּא יָדַע וְאָשֵׁם:

4 Or when a person utters an oath to bad or good purpose – whatever a man may utter in an oath – and, though he has known it, the fact has escaped him, but later he realizes his guilt in any of these matters –

ד אוֹ נֶפֶשׁ כִּי תִשָּׁבַע לְבַטֵּא בִשְׂפָתַיִם לְהָרַע אוֹ לְהֵיטִיב לְכֹל אֲשֶׁר יְבַטֵּא הָאָדָם בִּשְׁבֻעָה וְנֶעְלַם מִמֶּנּוּ וְהוּא־יָדַע וְאָשֵׁם לְאַחַת מֵאֵלֶּה:

5 when he realizes his guilt in any of these matters, he shall confess that wherein he has sinned.

ה וְהָיָה כִי־יֶאְשַׁם לְאַחַת מֵאֵלֶּה וְהִתְוַדָּה אֲשֶׁר חָטָא עָלֶיהָ:

6 And he shall bring as his penalty to *Hashem*, for the sin of which he is guilty, a female from the flock, sheep or goat, as a sin offering; and the *Kohen* shall make expiation on his behalf for his sin.

ו וְהֵבִיא אֶת־אֲשָׁמוֹ לַיהוָה עַל חַטָּאתוֹ אֲשֶׁר חָטָא נְקֵבָה מִן־הַצֹּאן כִּשְׂבָּה אוֹ־שְׂעִירַת עִזִּים לְחַטָּאת וְכִפֶּר עָלָיו הַכֹּהֵן מֵחַטָּאתוֹ:

7 But if his means do not suffice for a sheep, he shall bring to *Hashem*, as his penalty for that of which he is guilty, two turtledoves or two pigeons, one for a sin offering and the other for a burnt offering.

ז וְאִם־לֹא תַגִּיעַ יָדוֹ דֵּי שֶׂה וְהֵבִיא אֶת־אֲשָׁמוֹ אֲשֶׁר חָטָא שְׁתֵּי תֹרִים אוֹ־שְׁנֵי בְנֵי־יוֹנָה לַיהוָה אֶחָד לְחַטָּאת וְאֶחָד לְעֹלָה:

8 He shall bring them to the *Kohen*, who shall offer first the one for the sin offering, pinching its head at the nape without severing it.

ח וְהֵבִיא אֹתָם אֶל־הַכֹּהֵן וְהִקְרִיב אֶת־אֲשֶׁר לַחַטָּאת רִאשׁוֹנָה וּמָלַק אֶת־רֹאשׁוֹ מִמּוּל עָרְפּוֹ וְלֹא יַבְדִּיל:

9 He shall sprinkle some of the blood of the sin offering on the side of the *Mizbayach*, and what remains of the blood shall be drained out at the base of the *Mizbayach*; it is a sin offering.

ט וְהִזָּה מִדַּם הַחַטָּאת עַל־קִיר הַמִּזְבֵּחַ וְהַנִּשְׁאָר בַּדָּם יִמָּצֵה אֶל־יְסוֹד הַמִּזְבֵּחַ חַטָּאת הוּא:

Vayikra/Leviticus 5
Vayikra

ויקרא ה
ויקרא

10 And the second he shall prepare as a burnt offering, according to regulation. Thus the *Kohen* shall make expiation on his behalf for the sin of which he is guilty, and he shall be forgiven.

י וְאֶת־הַשֵּׁנִי יַעֲשֶׂה עֹלָה כַּמִּשְׁפָּט וְכִפֶּר עָלָיו הַכֹּהֵן מֵחַטָּאתוֹ אֲשֶׁר־חָטָא וְנִסְלַח לוֹ:

11 And if his means do not suffice for two turtledoves or two pigeons, he shall bring as his offering for that of which he is guilty a tenth of an *efah* of choice flour for a sin offering; he shall not add oil to it or lay frankincense on it, for it is a sin offering.

יא וְאִם־לֹא תַשִּׂיג יָדוֹ לִשְׁתֵּי תֹרִים אוֹ לִשְׁנֵי בְנֵי־יוֹנָה וְהֵבִיא אֶת־קָרְבָּנוֹ אֲשֶׁר חָטָא עֲשִׂירִת הָאֵפָה סֹלֶת לְחַטָּאת לֹא־יָשִׂים עָלֶיהָ שֶׁמֶן וְלֹא־יִתֵּן עָלֶיהָ לְבֹנָה כִּי חַטָּאת הִיא:

12 He shall bring it to the *Kohen*, and the *Kohen* shall scoop out of it a handful as a token portion of it and turn it into smoke on the *Mizbayach*, with *Hashem*'s offerings by fire; it is a sin offering.

יב וֶהֱבִיאָהּ אֶל־הַכֹּהֵן וְקָמַץ הַכֹּהֵן מִמֶּנָּה מְלוֹא קֻמְצוֹ אֶת־אַזְכָּרָתָהּ וְהִקְטִיר הַמִּזְבֵּחָה עַל אִשֵּׁי יְהֹוָה חַטָּאת הִוא:

13 Thus the *Kohen* shall make expiation on his behalf for whichever of these sins he is guilty, and he shall be forgiven. It shall belong to the *Kohen*, like the meal offering.

יג וְכִפֶּר עָלָיו הַכֹּהֵן עַל־חַטָּאתוֹ אֲשֶׁר־חָטָא מֵאַחַת מֵאֵלֶּה וְנִסְלַח לוֹ וְהָיְתָה לַכֹּהֵן כַּמִּנְחָה:

14 And *Hashem* spoke to *Moshe*, saying:

יד וַיְדַבֵּר יְהֹוָה אֶל־מֹשֶׁה לֵּאמֹר:

15 When a person commits a trespass, being unwittingly remiss about any of *Hashem*'s sacred things, he shall bring as his penalty to *Hashem* a ram without blemish from the flock, convertible into payment in silver by the sanctuary weight, as a guilt offering.

טו נֶפֶשׁ כִּי־תִמְעֹל מַעַל וְחָטְאָה בִּשְׁגָגָה מִקָּדְשֵׁי יְהֹוָה וְהֵבִיא אֶת־אֲשָׁמוֹ לַיהֹוָה אַיִל תָּמִים מִן־הַצֹּאן בְּעֶרְכְּךָ כֶּסֶף־שְׁקָלִים בְּשֶׁקֶל־הַקֹּדֶשׁ לְאָשָׁם:

NE-fesh kee tim-OL MA-al v'-kha-t'-AH bish-ga-GAH mi-kod-SHAY a-do-NAI v'-hay-VEE et a-sha-MO la-do-NAI A-yil ta-MEEM min ha-TZON b'-er-k'-KHA KE-sef sh'-ka-LEEM b'-SHE-kel ha-KO-desh l'-a-SHAM

16 He shall make restitution for that wherein he was remiss about the sacred things, and he shall add a fifth part to it and give it to the *Kohen*. The *Kohen* shall make expiation on his behalf with the ram of the guilt offering, and he shall be forgiven.

טז וְאֵת אֲשֶׁר חָטָא מִן־הַקֹּדֶשׁ יְשַׁלֵּם וְאֶת־חֲמִישִׁתוֹ יוֹסֵף עָלָיו וְנָתַן אֹתוֹ לַכֹּהֵן וְהַכֹּהֵן יְכַפֵּר עָלָיו בְּאֵיל הָאָשָׁם וְנִסְלַח לוֹ:

17 And when a person, without knowing it, sins in regard to any of *Hashem*'s commandments about things not to be done, and then realizes his guilt, he shall be subject to punishment.

יז וְאִם־נֶפֶשׁ כִּי תֶחֱטָא וְעָשְׂתָה אַחַת מִכָּל־מִצְוֹת יְהֹוָה אֲשֶׁר לֹא תֵעָשֶׂינָה וְלֹא־יָדַע וְאָשֵׁם וְנָשָׂא עֲוֹנוֹ:

5:15 When a person commits a trespass Chapter five contains a list of sins for which one is required to bring a guilt-offering. Among those listed is the transgression of benefiting from an object belonging to the *Beit Hamikdash*. This refers to someone who eats or derives other personal gain from food or property that belongs to the Temple, including its wood or stones, or who improperly eats part of a sacrifice. The verse calls this sin 'a trespass', an improper use of something holy. We must be careful to honor the sanctity, not only of the *Beit Hamikdash*, but of the entire Holy Land, and not to misuse any part of it.

Vayikra/Leviticus 6
Tzav

18 He shall bring to the *Kohen* a ram without blemish from the flock, or the equivalent, as a guilt offering. The *Kohen* shall make expiation on his behalf for the error that he committed unwittingly, and he shall be forgiven.

19 It is a guilt offering; he has incurred guilt before *Hashem*.

20 *Hashem* spoke to *Moshe*, saying:

21 When a person sins and commits a trespass against *Hashem* by dealing deceitfully with his fellow in the matter of a deposit or a pledge, or through robbery, or by defrauding his fellow,

22 or by finding something lost and lying about it; if he swears falsely regarding any one of the various things that one may do and sin thereby

23 when one has thus sinned and, realizing his guilt, would restore that which he got through robbery or fraud, or the deposit that was entrusted to him, or the lost thing that he found,

24 or anything else about which he swore falsely, he shall repay the principal amount and add a fifth part to it. He shall pay it to its owner when he realizes his guilt.

25 Then he shall bring to the *Kohen*, as his penalty to *Hashem*, a ram without blemish from the flock, or the equivalent, as a guilt offering.

26 The *Kohen* shall make expiation on his behalf before *Hashem*, and he shall be forgiven for whatever he may have done to draw blame thereby.

6

1 *Hashem* spoke to *Moshe*, saying:

2 Command *Aharon* and his sons thus: This is the ritual of the burnt offering: The burnt offering itself shall remain where it is burned upon the *Mizbayach* all night until morning, while the fire on the *Mizbayach* is kept going on it.

3 The *Kohen* shall dress in linen raiment, with linen breeches next to his body; and he shall take up the ashes to which the fire has reduced the burnt offering on the *Mizbayach* and place them beside the *Mizbayach*.

Vayikra/Leviticus 6
Tzav

ויקרא ו
צו

4 He shall then take off his vestments and put on other vestments, and carry the ashes outside the camp to a clean place.

ד וּפָשַׁט אֶת־בְּגָדָיו וְלָבַשׁ בְּגָדִים אֲחֵרִים וְהוֹצִיא אֶת־הַדֶּשֶׁן אֶל־מִחוּץ לַמַּחֲנֶה אֶל־מָקוֹם טָהוֹר:

5 The fire on the *Mizbayach* shall be kept burning, not to go out: every morning the *Kohen* shall feed wood to it, lay out the burnt offering on it, and turn into smoke the fat parts of the offerings of well-being.

ה וְהָאֵשׁ עַל־הַמִּזְבֵּחַ תּוּקַד־בּוֹ לֹא תִכְבֶּה וּבִעֵר עָלֶיהָ הַכֹּהֵן עֵצִים בַּבֹּקֶר בַּבֹּקֶר וְעָרַךְ עָלֶיהָ הָעֹלָה וְהִקְטִיר עָלֶיהָ חֶלְבֵי הַשְּׁלָמִים:

v'-ha-AYSH al ha-miz-BAY-akh tu-kad BO LO tikh-BEH u-vi-AYR a-LE-ha ha-ko-HAYN ay-TZEEM ba-BO-ker ba-BO-ker v'-a-RAKH a-LE-ha ha-o-LAH v'-hik-TEER a-LE-ha khel-VAY ha-sh'-la-MEEM

6 A perpetual fire shall be kept burning on the *Mizbayach*, not to go out.

ו אֵשׁ תָּמִיד תּוּקַד עַל־הַמִּזְבֵּחַ לֹא תִכְבֶּה:

7 And this is the ritual of the meal offering: *Aharon's* sons shall present it before *Hashem*, in front of the *Mizbayach*.

ז וְזֹאת תּוֹרַת הַמִּנְחָה הַקְרֵב אֹתָהּ בְּנֵי־אַהֲרֹן לִפְנֵי יְהוָה אֶל־פְּנֵי הַמִּזְבֵּחַ:

8 A handful of the choice flour and oil of the meal offering shall be taken from it, with all the frankincense that is on the meal offering, and this token portion shall be turned into smoke on the *Mizbayach* as a pleasing odor to *Hashem*.

ח וְהֵרִים מִמֶּנּוּ בְּקֻמְצוֹ מִסֹּלֶת הַמִּנְחָה וּמִשַּׁמְנָהּ וְאֵת כָּל־הַלְּבֹנָה אֲשֶׁר עַל־הַמִּנְחָה וְהִקְטִיר הַמִּזְבֵּחַ רֵיחַ נִיחֹחַ אַזְכָּרָתָהּ לַיהוָה:

9 What is left of it shall be eaten by *Aharon* and his sons; it shall be eaten as unleavened cakes, in the sacred precinct; they shall eat it in the enclosure of the Tent of Meeting.

ט וְהַנּוֹתֶרֶת מִמֶּנָּה יֹאכְלוּ אַהֲרֹן וּבָנָיו מַצּוֹת תֵּאָכֵל בְּמָקוֹם קָדֹשׁ בַּחֲצַר אֹהֶל־מוֹעֵד יֹאכְלוּהָ:

10 It shall not be baked with leaven; I have given it as their portion from My offerings by fire; it is most holy, like the sin offering and the guilt offering.

י לֹא תֵאָפֶה חָמֵץ חֶלְקָם נָתַתִּי אֹתָהּ מֵאִשָּׁי קֹדֶשׁ קָדָשִׁים הִוא כַּחַטָּאת וְכָאָשָׁם:

11 Only the males among *Aharon's* descendants may eat of it, as their due for all time throughout the ages from *Hashem's* offerings by fire. Anything that touches these shall become holy.

יא כָּל־זָכָר בִּבְנֵי אַהֲרֹן יֹאכְלֶנָּה חָק־עוֹלָם לְדֹרֹתֵיכֶם מֵאִשֵּׁי יְהוָה כֹּל אֲשֶׁר־יִגַּע בָּהֶם יִקְדָּשׁ:

12 *Hashem* spoke to *Moshe*, saying:

יב וַיְדַבֵּר יְהוָה אֶל־מֹשֶׁה לֵּאמֹר:

6:5 The fire on the *Mizbayach* shall be kept burning The fire on the altar burns continuously, and is never extinguished. Although the priests were commanded to add two pieces of wood to the fire twice daily, the fire on the *Mizbayach* remained burning miraculously, lit by a heavenly fire. The Sages (*Ethics of the Fathers* 5:5) list this as one of ten miracles experienced each day in the *Beit Hamikdash*. The continual flame serves as a reminder of *Hashem's* constant presence among the People of Israel. While there is no longer a Temple nor an Altar, God's everlasting presence is signified today by hanging an eternal light above the ark in every synagogue, a reminder of the eternal flame first mentioned in this verse.

Eternal lamp above the ark, Petach Tikva

Vayikra/Leviticus 7
Tzav

ויקרא ז
צו

13 This is the offering that *Aharon* and his sons shall offer to *Hashem* on the occasion of his anointment: a tenth of an *efah* of choice flour as a regular meal offering, half of it in the morning and half of it in the evening,

יג זֶה קָרְבַּן אַהֲרֹן וּבָנָיו אֲשֶׁר־יַקְרִיבוּ לַיהֹוָה בְּיוֹם הִמָּשַׁח אֹתוֹ עֲשִׂירִת הָאֵפָה סֹלֶת מִנְחָה תָּמִיד מַחֲצִיתָהּ בַּבֹּקֶר וּמַחֲצִיתָהּ בָּעָרֶב:

14 shall be prepared with oil on a griddle. You shall bring it well soaked, and offer it as a meal offering of baked slices, of pleasing odor to *Hashem*.

יד עַל־מַחֲבַת בַּשֶּׁמֶן תֵּעָשֶׂה מֻרְבֶּכֶת תְּבִיאֶנָּה תֻּפִינֵי מִנְחַת פִּתִּים תַּקְרִיב רֵיחַ־נִיחֹחַ לַיהֹוָה:

15 And so shall the *Kohen*, anointed from among his sons to succeed him, prepare it; it is *Hashem*'s – a law for all time – to be turned entirely into smoke.

טו וְהַכֹּהֵן הַמָּשִׁיחַ תַּחְתָּיו מִבָּנָיו יַעֲשֶׂה אֹתָהּ חָק־עוֹלָם לַיהֹוָה כָּלִיל תָּקְטָר:

16 So, too, every meal offering of a *Kohen* shall be a whole offering: it shall not be eaten.

טז וְכָל־מִנְחַת כֹּהֵן כָּלִיל תִּהְיֶה לֹא תֵאָכֵל:

17 *Hashem* spoke to *Moshe*, saying:

יז וַיְדַבֵּר יְהֹוָה אֶל־מֹשֶׁה לֵּאמֹר:

18 Speak to *Aharon* and his sons thus: This is the ritual of the sin offering: the sin offering shall be slaughtered before *Hashem*, at the spot where the burnt offering is slaughtered: it is most holy.

יח דַּבֵּר אֶל־אַהֲרֹן וְאֶל־בָּנָיו לֵאמֹר זֹאת תּוֹרַת הַחַטָּאת בִּמְקוֹם אֲשֶׁר תִּשָּׁחֵט הָעֹלָה תִּשָּׁחֵט הַחַטָּאת לִפְנֵי יְהֹוָה קֹדֶשׁ קָדָשִׁים הִוא:

19 The *Kohen* who offers it as a sin offering shall eat of it; it shall be eaten in the sacred precinct, in the enclosure of the Tent of Meeting.

יט הַכֹּהֵן הַמְחַטֵּא אֹתָהּ יֹאכְלֶנָּה בְּמָקוֹם קָדֹשׁ תֵּאָכֵל בַּחֲצַר אֹהֶל מוֹעֵד:

20 Anything that touches its flesh shall become holy; and if any of its blood is spattered upon a garment, you shall wash the bespattered part in the sacred precinct.

כ כֹּל אֲשֶׁר־יִגַּע בִּבְשָׂרָהּ יִקְדָּשׁ וַאֲשֶׁר יִזֶּה מִדָּמָהּ עַל־הַבֶּגֶד אֲשֶׁר יִזֶּה עָלֶיהָ תְּכַבֵּס בְּמָקוֹם קָדֹשׁ:

21 An earthen vessel in which it was boiled shall be broken; if it was boiled in a copper vessel, [the vessel] shall be scoured and rinsed with water.

כא וּכְלִי־חֶרֶשׂ אֲשֶׁר תְּבֻשַּׁל־בּוֹ יִשָּׁבֵר וְאִם־בִּכְלִי נְחֹשֶׁת בֻּשָּׁלָה וּמֹרַק וְשֻׁטַּף בַּמָּיִם:

22 Only the males in the priestly line may eat of it: it is most holy.

כב כָּל־זָכָר בַּכֹּהֲנִים יֹאכַל אֹתָהּ קֹדֶשׁ קָדָשִׁים הִוא:

23 But no sin offering may be eaten from which any blood is brought into the Tent of Meeting for expiation in the sanctuary; any such shall be consumed in fire.

כג וְכָל־חַטָּאת אֲשֶׁר יוּבָא מִדָּמָהּ אֶל־אֹהֶל מוֹעֵד לְכַפֵּר בַּקֹּדֶשׁ לֹא תֵאָכֵל בָּאֵשׁ תִּשָּׂרֵף:

7 1 This is the ritual of the guilt offering: it is most holy.

ז א וְזֹאת תּוֹרַת הָאָשָׁם קֹדֶשׁ קָדָשִׁים הוּא:

2 The guilt offering shall be slaughtered at the spot where the burnt offering is slaughtered, and the blood shall be dashed on all sides of the *Mizbayach*.

ב בִּמְקוֹם אֲשֶׁר יִשְׁחֲטוּ אֶת־הָעֹלָה יִשְׁחֲטוּ אֶת־הָאָשָׁם וְאֶת־דָּמוֹ יִזְרֹק עַל־הַמִּזְבֵּחַ סָבִיב:

3 All its fat shall be offered: the broad tail; the fat that covers the entrails;

ג וְאֵת כָּל־חֶלְבּוֹ יַקְרִיב מִמֶּנּוּ אֵת הָאַלְיָה וְאֶת־הַחֵלֶב הַמְכַסֶּה אֶת־הַקֶּרֶב:

Vayikra/Leviticus 7
Tzav

ויקרא ז
צו

4 the two kidneys and the fat that is on them at the loins; and the protuberance on the liver, which shall be removed with the kidneys.

ד וְאֵת שְׁתֵּי הַכְּלָיֹת וְאֶת־הַחֵלֶב אֲשֶׁר עֲלֵיהֶן אֲשֶׁר עַל־הַכְּסָלִים וְאֶת־הַיֹּתֶרֶת עַל־הַכָּבֵד עַל־הַכְּלָיֹת יְסִירֶנָּה׃

5 The *Kohen* shall turn them into smoke on the *Mizbayach* as an offering by fire to *Hashem*; it is a guilt offering.

ה וְהִקְטִיר אֹתָם הַכֹּהֵן הַמִּזְבֵּחָה אִשֶּׁה לַיהֹוָה אָשָׁם הוּא׃

6 Only the males in the priestly line may eat of it; it shall be eaten in the sacred precinct: it is most holy.

ו כָּל־זָכָר בַּכֹּהֲנִים יֹאכְלֶנּוּ בְּמָקוֹם קָדוֹשׁ יֵאָכֵל קֹדֶשׁ קָדָשִׁים הוּא׃

7 The guilt offering is like the sin offering. The same rule applies to both: it shall belong to the *Kohen* who makes expiation thereby.

ז כַּחַטָּאת כָּאָשָׁם תּוֹרָה אַחַת לָהֶם הַכֹּהֵן אֲשֶׁר יְכַפֶּר־בּוֹ לוֹ יִהְיֶה׃

8 So, too, the *Kohen* who offers a man's burnt offering shall keep the skin of the burnt offering that he offered.

ח וְהַכֹּהֵן הַמַּקְרִיב אֶת־עֹלַת אִישׁ עוֹר הָעֹלָה אֲשֶׁר הִקְרִיב לַכֹּהֵן לוֹ יִהְיֶה׃

9 Further, any meal offering that is baked in an oven, and any that is prepared in a pan or on a griddle, shall belong to the *Kohen* who offers it.

ט וְכָל־מִנְחָה אֲשֶׁר תֵּאָפֶה בַּתַּנּוּר וְכָל־נַעֲשָׂה בַמַּרְחֶשֶׁת וְעַל־מַחֲבַת לַכֹּהֵן הַמַּקְרִיב אֹתָהּ לוֹ תִהְיֶה׃

10 But every other meal offering, with oil mixed in or dry, shall go to the sons of *Aharon* all alike.

י וְכָל־מִנְחָה בְלוּלָה־בַשֶּׁמֶן וַחֲרֵבָה לְכָל־בְּנֵי אַהֲרֹן תִּהְיֶה אִישׁ כְּאָחִיו׃

11 This is the ritual of the sacrifice of well-being that one may offer to *Hashem*:

יא וְזֹאת תּוֹרַת זֶבַח הַשְּׁלָמִים אֲשֶׁר יַקְרִיב לַיהֹוָה׃

12 If he offers it for thanksgiving, he shall offer together with the sacrifice of thanksgiving unleavened cakes with oil mixed in, unleavened wafers spread with oil, and cakes of choice flour with oil mixed in, well soaked.

יב אִם עַל־תּוֹדָה יַקְרִיבֶנּוּ וְהִקְרִיב עַל־זֶבַח הַתּוֹדָה חַלּוֹת מַצּוֹת בְּלוּלֹת בַּשֶּׁמֶן וּרְקִיקֵי מַצּוֹת מְשֻׁחִים בַּשָּׁמֶן וְסֹלֶת מֻרְבֶּכֶת חַלֹּת בְּלוּלֹת בַּשָּׁמֶן׃

IM al to-DAH yak-ree-VE-nu v'-hik-REEV al ZE-vakh ha-to-DAH kha-LOT ma-TZOT b'-lu-LOT ba-SHE-men u-r'-kee-KAY ma-TZOT m'-shu-KHIM ba-SHA-men v'-SO-let mur-BE-khet kha-LOT b'-lu-LOT ba-SHA-men

13 This offering, with cakes of leavened bread added, he shall offer along with his thanksgiving sacrifice of well-being.

יג עַל־חַלֹּת לֶחֶם חָמֵץ יַקְרִיב קָרְבָּנוֹ עַל־זֶבַח תּוֹדַת שְׁלָמָיו׃

7:12 If he offers it for thanksgiving When one survives a life-threatening situation, he or she naturally feels a tremendous amount of gratitude to *Hashem*. Therefore, the *Torah* commands such a person to offer a thanksgiving-offering to the Lord. The Talmud (*Berachot* 54b) lists the four dangerous situations whose survivors are required to bring this offering: a potentially dangerous journey, dangerous imprisonment, serious illness and a sea voyage. In the absence of the *Beit Hamikdash* and the thanksgiving offering, the Jewish people have a special blessing, called the *gomel* blessing, recited to express thanks to *Hashem* when one overcomes a life-threatening situation. This idea of thanksgiving and being grateful is ingrained in the DNA of the Nation of Israel. In fact, the term *yehudi* (יהודי), 'Jew,' comes from the name of the tribe of *Yehuda*, which derives from the word *hoda'ah* (הודאה), 'thanksgiving.'

Vayikra/Leviticus 7
Tzav

14 Out of this he shall offer one of each kind as a gift to *Hashem*; it shall go to the *Kohen* who dashes the blood of the offering of well-being.

15 And the flesh of his thanksgiving sacrifice of well-being shall be eaten on the day that it is offered; none of it shall be set aside until morning.

16 If, however, the sacrifice he offers is a votive or a freewill offering, it shall be eaten on the day that he offers his sacrifice, and what is left of it shall be eaten on the morrow.

17 What is then left of the flesh of the sacrifice shall be consumed in fire on the third day.

18 If any of the flesh of his sacrifice of well-being is eaten on the third day, it shall not be acceptable; it shall not count for him who offered it. It is an offensive thing, and the person who eats of it shall bear his guilt.

19 Flesh that touches anything unclean shall not be eaten; it shall be consumed in fire. As for other flesh, only he who is clean may eat such flesh.

20 But the person who, in a state of uncleanness, eats flesh from *Hashem's* sacrifices of well-being, that person shall be cut off from his kin.

21 When a person touches anything unclean, be it human uncleanness or an unclean animal or any unclean creature, and eats flesh from *Hashem's* sacrifices of well-being, that person shall be cut off from his kin.

22 And *Hashem* spoke to *Moshe*, saying:

23 Speak to *B'nei Yisrael* thus: You shall eat no fat of ox or sheep or goat.

24 Fat from animals that died or were torn by beasts may be put to any use, but you must not eat it.

25 If anyone eats the fat of animals from which offerings by fire may be made to *Hashem*, the person who eats it shall be cut off from his kin.

26 And you must not consume any blood, either of bird or of animal, in any of your settlements.

27 Anyone who eats blood shall be cut off from his kin.

28 And *Hashem* spoke to *Moshe*, saying:

ויקרא ז
צו

יד וְהִקְרִיב מִמֶּנּוּ אֶחָד מִכָּל־קָרְבָּן תְּרוּמָה לַיהֹוָה לַכֹּהֵן הַזֹּרֵק אֶת־דַּם הַשְּׁלָמִים לוֹ יִהְיֶה׃

טו וּבְשַׂר זֶבַח תּוֹדַת שְׁלָמָיו בְּיוֹם קָרְבָּנוֹ יֵאָכֵל לֹא־יַנִּיחַ מִמֶּנּוּ עַד־בֹּקֶר׃

טז וְאִם־נֶדֶר ׀ אוֹ נְדָבָה זֶבַח קָרְבָּנוֹ בְּיוֹם הַקְרִיבוֹ אֶת־זִבְחוֹ יֵאָכֵל וּמִמָּחֳרָת וְהַנּוֹתָר מִמֶּנּוּ יֵאָכֵל׃

יז וְהַנּוֹתָר מִבְּשַׂר הַזָּבַח בַּיּוֹם הַשְּׁלִישִׁי בָּאֵשׁ יִשָּׂרֵף׃

יח וְאִם הֵאָכֹל יֵאָכֵל מִבְּשַׂר־זֶבַח שְׁלָמָיו בַּיּוֹם הַשְּׁלִישִׁי לֹא יֵרָצֶה הַמַּקְרִיב אֹתוֹ לֹא יֵחָשֵׁב לוֹ פִּגּוּל יִהְיֶה וְהַנֶּפֶשׁ הָאֹכֶלֶת מִמֶּנּוּ עֲוֺנָהּ תִּשָּׂא׃

יט וְהַבָּשָׂר אֲשֶׁר־יִגַּע בְּכָל־טָמֵא לֹא יֵאָכֵל בָּאֵשׁ יִשָּׂרֵף וְהַבָּשָׂר כָּל־טָהוֹר יֹאכַל בָּשָׂר׃

כ וְהַנֶּפֶשׁ אֲשֶׁר־תֹּאכַל בָּשָׂר מִזֶּבַח הַשְּׁלָמִים אֲשֶׁר לַיהֹוָה וְטֻמְאָתוֹ עָלָיו וְנִכְרְתָה הַנֶּפֶשׁ הַהִוא מֵעַמֶּיהָ׃

כא וְנֶפֶשׁ כִּי־תִגַּע בְּכָל־טָמֵא בְּטֻמְאַת אָדָם אוֹ ׀ בִּבְהֵמָה טְמֵאָה אוֹ בְּכָל־שֶׁקֶץ טָמֵא וְאָכַל מִבְּשַׂר־זֶבַח הַשְּׁלָמִים אֲשֶׁר לַיהֹוָה וְנִכְרְתָה הַנֶּפֶשׁ הַהִוא מֵעַמֶּיהָ׃

כב וַיְדַבֵּר יְהֹוָה אֶל־מֹשֶׁה לֵּאמֹר׃

כג דַּבֵּר אֶל־בְּנֵי יִשְׂרָאֵל לֵאמֹר כָּל־חֵלֶב שׁוֹר וְכֶשֶׂב וָעֵז לֹא תֹאכֵלוּ׃

כד וְחֵלֶב נְבֵלָה וְחֵלֶב טְרֵפָה יֵעָשֶׂה לְכָל־מְלָאכָה וְאָכֹל לֹא תֹאכְלֻהוּ׃

כה כִּי כָּל־אֹכֵל חֵלֶב מִן־הַבְּהֵמָה אֲשֶׁר יַקְרִיב מִמֶּנָּה אִשֶּׁה לַיהֹוָה וְנִכְרְתָה הַנֶּפֶשׁ הָאֹכֶלֶת מֵעַמֶּיהָ׃

כו וְכָל־דָּם לֹא תֹאכְלוּ בְּכֹל מוֹשְׁבֹתֵיכֶם לָעוֹף וְלַבְּהֵמָה׃

כז כָּל־נֶפֶשׁ אֲשֶׁר־תֹּאכַל כָּל־דָּם וְנִכְרְתָה הַנֶּפֶשׁ הַהִוא מֵעַמֶּיהָ׃

כח וַיְדַבֵּר יְהֹוָה אֶל־מֹשֶׁה לֵּאמֹר׃

Vayikra/Leviticus 8
Tzav

ויקרא ח
צו

29 Speak to *B'nei Yisrael* thus: The offering to *Hashem* from a sacrifice of well-being must be presented by him who offers his sacrifice of well-being to *Hashem*:

כט דַּבֵּ֛ר אֶל־בְּנֵ֥י יִשְׂרָאֵ֖ל לֵאמֹ֑ר הַמַּקְרִ֞יב אֶת־זֶ֤בַח שְׁלָמָיו֙ לַֽיהֹוָ֔ה יָבִ֧יא אֶת־קׇרְבָּנ֛וֹ לַיהֹוָ֖ה מִזֶּ֥בַח שְׁלָמָֽיו׃

30 his own hands shall present *Hashem*'s offerings by fire. He shall present the fat with the breast, the breast to be elevated as an elevation offering before *Hashem*;

ל יָדָ֣יו תְּבִיאֶ֔ינָה אֵ֖ת אִשֵּׁ֣י יְהֹוָ֑ה אֶת־הַחֵ֤לֶב עַל־הֶֽחָזֶה֙ יְבִיאֶ֔נּוּ אֵ֣ת הֶחָזֶ֗ה לְהָנִ֥יף אֹת֛וֹ תְּנוּפָ֖ה לִפְנֵ֥י יְהֹוָֽה׃

31 the *Kohen* shall turn the fat into smoke on the *Mizbayach*, and the breast shall go to *Aharon* and his sons.

לא וְהִקְטִ֧יר הַכֹּהֵ֛ן אֶת־הַחֵ֖לֶב הַמִּזְבֵּ֑חָה וְהָיָה֙ הֶֽחָזֶ֔ה לְאַהֲרֹ֖ן וּלְבָנָֽיו׃

32 And the right thigh from your sacrifices of well-being you shall present to the *Kohen* as a gift;

לב וְאֵת֙ שׁ֣וֹק הַיָּמִ֔ין תִּתְּנ֥וּ תְרוּמָ֖ה לַכֹּהֵ֑ן מִזִּבְחֵ֖י שַׁלְמֵיכֶֽם׃

33 he from among *Aharon*'s sons who offers the blood and the fat of the offering of well-being shall get the right thigh as his portion.

לג הַמַּקְרִ֞יב אֶת־דַּ֧ם הַשְּׁלָמִ֛ים וְאֶת־הַחֵ֖לֶב מִבְּנֵ֣י אַהֲרֹ֑ן ל֧וֹ תִהְיֶ֛ה שׁ֥וֹק הַיָּמִ֖ין לְמָנָֽה׃

34 For I have taken the breast of elevation offering and the thigh of gift offering from the Israelites, from their sacrifices of well-being, and given them to *Aharon* the *Kohen* and to his sons as their due from the Israelites for all time.

לד כִּי֩ אֶת־חֲזֵ֨ה הַתְּנוּפָ֜ה וְאֵ֣ת ׀ שׁ֣וֹק הַתְּרוּמָ֗ה לָקַ֙חְתִּי֙ מֵאֵ֣ת בְּנֵֽי־יִשְׂרָאֵ֔ל מִזִּבְחֵ֖י שַׁלְמֵיהֶ֑ם וָאֶתֵּ֣ן אֹ֠תָ֠ם לְאַהֲרֹ֨ן הַכֹּהֵ֤ן וּלְבָנָיו֙ לְחׇק־עוֹלָ֔ם מֵאֵ֖ת בְּנֵ֥י יִשְׂרָאֵֽל׃

35 Those shall be the perquisites of *Aharon* and the perquisites of his sons from *Hashem*'s offerings by fire, once they have been inducted to serve *Hashem* as *Kohanim*;

לה זֹ֣את מִשְׁחַ֤ת אַהֲרֹן֙ וּמִשְׁחַ֣ת בָּנָ֔יו מֵאִשֵּׁ֖י יְהֹוָ֑ה בְּיוֹם֙ הִקְרִ֣יב אֹתָ֔ם לְכַהֵ֖ן לַיהֹוָֽה׃

36 these *Hashem* commanded to be given them, once they had been anointed, as a due from the Israelites for all time throughout the ages.

לו אֲשֶׁר֩ צִוָּ֨ה יְהֹוָ֜ה לָתֵ֣ת לָהֶ֗ם בְּיוֹם֙ מׇשְׁח֣וֹ אֹתָ֔ם מֵאֵ֖ת בְּנֵ֣י יִשְׂרָאֵ֑ל חֻקַּ֥ת עוֹלָ֖ם לְדֹרֹתָֽם׃

37 Such are the rituals of the burnt offering, the meal offering, the sin offering, the guilt offering, the offering of ordination, and the sacrifice of well-being,

לז זֹ֣את הַתּוֹרָ֗ה לָֽעֹלָה֙ לַמִּנְחָ֔ה וְלַֽחַטָּ֖את וְלָאָשָׁ֑ם וְלַ֨מִּלּוּאִ֔ים וּלְזֶ֖בַח הַשְּׁלָמִֽים׃

38 with which *Hashem* charged *Moshe* on *Har Sinai*, when He commanded that the Israelites present their offerings to *Hashem*, in the wilderness of Sinai.

לח אֲשֶׁ֨ר צִוָּ֧ה יְהֹוָ֛ה אֶת־מֹשֶׁ֖ה בְּהַ֣ר סִינָ֑י בְּי֣וֹם צַוֺּת֗וֹ אֶת־בְּנֵ֤י יִשְׂרָאֵל֙ לְהַקְרִ֣יב אֶת־קׇרְבְּנֵיהֶ֔ם לַיהֹוָ֖ה בְּמִדְבַּ֥ר סִינָֽי׃

8 1 *Hashem* spoke to *Moshe*, saying:

ח א וַיְדַבֵּ֥ר יְהֹוָ֖ה אֶל־מֹשֶׁ֥ה לֵּאמֹֽר׃

2 Take *Aharon* along with his sons, and the vestments, the anointing oil, the bull of sin offering, the two rams, and the basket of unleavened bread;

ב קַ֤ח אֶֽת־אַהֲרֹן֙ וְאֶת־בָּנָ֣יו אִתּ֔וֹ וְאֵת֙ הַבְּגָדִ֔ים וְאֵ֖ת שֶׁ֣מֶן הַמִּשְׁחָ֑ה וְאֵ֣ת ׀ פַּ֣ר הַֽחַטָּ֗את וְאֵת֙ שְׁנֵ֣י הָֽאֵילִ֔ים וְאֵ֖ת סַ֥ל הַמַּצּֽוֹת׃

260

Vayikra/Leviticus 8
Tzav

ויקרא ח
צו

3 and assemble the whole community at the entrance of the Tent of Meeting.

וְאֵת־כָּל־הָעֵדָה הַקְהֵל אֶל־פֶּתַח אֹהֶל מוֹעֵד: ג

v'-AYT kol ha-ay-DAH hak-HAYL el PE-takh O-hel mo-AYD

4 *Moshe* did as *Hashem* commanded him. And when the community was assembled at the entrance of the Tent of Meeting,

וַיַּעַשׂ מֹשֶׁה כַּאֲשֶׁר צִוָּה יְהֹוָה אֹתוֹ וַתִּקָּהֵל הָעֵדָה אֶל־פֶּתַח אֹהֶל מוֹעֵד: ד

5 *Moshe* said to the community, "This is what *Hashem* has commanded to be done."

וַיֹּאמֶר מֹשֶׁה אֶל־הָעֵדָה זֶה הַדָּבָר אֲשֶׁר־צִוָּה יְהֹוָה לַעֲשׂוֹת: ה

6 Then *Moshe* brought *Aharon* and his sons forward and washed them with water.

וַיַּקְרֵב מֹשֶׁה אֶת־אַהֲרֹן וְאֶת־בָּנָיו וַיִּרְחַץ אֹתָם בַּמָּיִם: ו

7 He put the tunic on him, girded him with the sash, clothed him with the robe, and put the ephod on him, girding him with the decorated band with which he tied it to him.

וַיִּתֵּן עָלָיו אֶת־הַכֻּתֹּנֶת וַיַּחְגֹּר אֹתוֹ בָּאַבְנֵט וַיַּלְבֵּשׁ אֹתוֹ אֶת־הַמְּעִיל וַיִּתֵּן עָלָיו אֶת־הָאֵפֹד וַיַּחְגֹּר אֹתוֹ בְּחֵשֶׁב הָאֵפֹד וַיֶּאְפֹּד לוֹ בּוֹ: ז

8 He put the breastpiece on him, and put into the breastpiece the Urim and Thummim.

וַיָּשֶׂם עָלָיו אֶת־הַחֹשֶׁן וַיִּתֵּן אֶל־הַחֹשֶׁן אֶת־הָאוּרִים וְאֶת־הַתֻּמִּים: ח

9 And he set the headdress on his head; and on the headdress, in front, he put the gold frontlet, the holy diadem – as *Hashem* had commanded *Moshe*.

וַיָּשֶׂם אֶת־הַמִּצְנֶפֶת עַל־רֹאשׁוֹ וַיָּשֶׂם עַל־הַמִּצְנֶפֶת אֶל־מוּל פָּנָיו אֵת צִיץ הַזָּהָב נֵזֶר הַקֹּדֶשׁ כַּאֲשֶׁר צִוָּה יְהֹוָה אֶת־מֹשֶׁה: ט

10 *Moshe* took the anointing oil and anointed the *Mishkan* and all that was in it, thus consecrating them.

וַיִּקַּח מֹשֶׁה אֶת־שֶׁמֶן הַמִּשְׁחָה וַיִּמְשַׁח אֶת־הַמִּשְׁכָּן וְאֶת־כָּל־אֲשֶׁר־בּוֹ וַיְקַדֵּשׁ אֹתָם: י

va-yi-KAKH mo-SHEH et SHE-men ha-mish-KHAH va-yim-SHAKH et ha-mish-KAN v'-et kol a-sher BO vai-ka-DAYSH o-TAM

11 He sprinkled some of it on the *Mizbayach* seven times, anointing the *Mizbayach*, all its utensils, and the laver with its stand, to consecrate them.

וַיַּז מִמֶּנּוּ עַל־הַמִּזְבֵּחַ שֶׁבַע פְּעָמִים וַיִּמְשַׁח אֶת־הַמִּזְבֵּחַ וְאֶת־כָּל־כֵּלָיו וְאֶת־הַכִּיֹּר וְאֶת־כַּנּוֹ לְקַדְּשָׁם: יא

12 He poured some of the anointing oil upon *Aharon*'s head and anointed him, to consecrate him.

וַיִּצֹק מִשֶּׁמֶן הַמִּשְׁחָה עַל רֹאשׁ אַהֲרֹן וַיִּמְשַׁח אֹתוֹ לְקַדְּשׁוֹ: יב

va-yi-TZOK mi-SHE-men ha-mish-KHAH AL ROSH a-ha-RON va-yim-SHAKH o-TO l'-ka-d'-SHO

8:3 And assemble the whole community at the entrance of the Tent of Meeting The entrance of the Tent of Meeting housed the *Mishkan*, the altar and the laver, and was not large enough to accommodate six hundred thousand people. *Rashi* comments that this is one of the miraculous instances where a small area contained many people. This miracle repeated itself daily in the *Beit Hamikdash*, and is one of the incredible features of *Eretz Yisrael* in general (see Ezekiel 20:6 and Daniel 11:41). The Sages (*Ethics of the Fathers* 5:7) recount that in the *Beit Hamikdash*, "the people stood pressed together, yet they found ample space to prostrate themselves…and no one ever said to his fellow, 'There is not enough room for me to spend the night in Jerusalem.'" One of the unique metaphysical properties of Israel in general, and *Yerushalayim* and the Temple Mount specifically, is that they expand to hold all their inhabitants and visitors.

Vayikra/Leviticus 8
Tzav

ויקרא ח
צו

13 Moshe then brought *Aharon*'s sons forward, clothed them in tunics, girded them with sashes, and wound turbans upon them, as *Hashem* had commanded *Moshe*.

יג וַיַּקְרֵב מֹשֶׁה אֶת־בְּנֵי אַהֲרֹן וַיַּלְבִּשֵׁם כֻּתֳּנֹת וַיַּחְגֹּר אֹתָם אַבְנֵט וַיַּחֲבֹשׁ לָהֶם מִגְבָּעוֹת כַּאֲשֶׁר צִוָּה יְהוָה אֶת־מֹשֶׁה:

14 He led forward the bull of sin offering. *Aharon* and his sons laid their hands upon the head of the bull of sin offering,

יד וַיַּגֵּשׁ אֵת פַּר הַחַטָּאת וַיִּסְמֹךְ אַהֲרֹן וּבָנָיו אֶת־יְדֵיהֶם עַל־רֹאשׁ פַּר הַחַטָּאת:

15 and it was slaughtered. *Moshe* took the blood and with his finger put some on each of the horns of the *Mizbayach*, cleansing the *Mizbayach*; then he poured out the blood at the base of the *Mizbayach*. Thus he consecrated it in order to make expiation upon it.

טו וַיִּשְׁחָט וַיִּקַּח מֹשֶׁה אֶת־הַדָּם וַיִּתֵּן עַל־קַרְנוֹת הַמִּזְבֵּחַ סָבִיב בְּאֶצְבָּעוֹ וַיְחַטֵּא אֶת־הַמִּזְבֵּחַ וְאֶת־הַדָּם יָצַק אֶל־יְסוֹד הַמִּזְבֵּחַ וַיְקַדְּשֵׁהוּ לְכַפֵּר עָלָיו:

16 *Moshe* then took all the fat that was about the entrails, and the protuberance of the liver, and the two kidneys and their fat, and turned them into smoke on the *Mizbayach*.

טז וַיִּקַּח אֶת־כָּל־הַחֵלֶב אֲשֶׁר עַל־הַקֶּרֶב וְאֵת יֹתֶרֶת הַכָּבֵד וְאֶת־שְׁתֵּי הַכְּלָיֹת וְאֶת־חֶלְבְּהֶן וַיַּקְטֵר מֹשֶׁה הַמִּזְבֵּחָה:

17 The rest of the bull, its hide, its flesh, and its dung, he put to the fire outside the camp – as *Hashem* had commanded *Moshe*.

יז וְאֶת־הַפָּר וְאֶת־עֹרוֹ וְאֶת־בְּשָׂרוֹ וְאֶת־פִּרְשׁוֹ שָׂרַף בָּאֵשׁ מִחוּץ לַמַּחֲנֶה כַּאֲשֶׁר צִוָּה יְהוָה אֶת־מֹשֶׁה:

18 Then he brought forward the ram of burnt offering. *Aharon* and his sons laid their hands upon the ram's head,

יח וַיַּקְרֵב אֵת אֵיל הָעֹלָה וַיִּסְמְכוּ אַהֲרֹן וּבָנָיו אֶת־יְדֵיהֶם עַל־רֹאשׁ הָאָיִל:

19 and it was slaughtered. *Moshe* dashed the blood against all sides of the *Mizbayach*.

יט וַיִּשְׁחָט וַיִּזְרֹק מֹשֶׁה אֶת־הַדָּם עַל־הַמִּזְבֵּחַ סָבִיב:

20 The ram was cut up into sections and *Moshe* turned the head, the sections, and the suet into smoke on the *Mizbayach*;

כ וְאֶת־הָאַיִל נִתַּח לִנְתָחָיו וַיַּקְטֵר מֹשֶׁה אֶת־הָרֹאשׁ וְאֶת־הַנְּתָחִים וְאֶת־הַפָּדֶר:

21 *Moshe* washed the entrails and the legs with water and turned all of the ram into smoke. That was a burnt offering for a pleasing odor, an offering by fire to *Hashem* – as *Hashem* had commanded *Moshe*.

כא וְאֶת־הַקֶּרֶב וְאֶת־הַכְּרָעַיִם רָחַץ בַּמָּיִם וַיַּקְטֵר מֹשֶׁה אֶת־כָּל־הָאַיִל הַמִּזְבֵּחָה עֹלָה הוּא לְרֵיחַ־נִיחֹחַ אִשֶּׁה הוּא לַיהוָה כַּאֲשֶׁר צִוָּה יְהוָה אֶת־מֹשֶׁה:

22 He brought forward the second ram, the ram of ordination. *Aharon* and his sons laid their hands upon the ram's head,

כב וַיַּקְרֵב אֶת־הָאַיִל הַשֵּׁנִי אֵיל הַמִּלֻּאִים וַיִּסְמְכוּ אַהֲרֹן וּבָנָיו אֶת־יְדֵיהֶם עַל־רֹאשׁ הָאָיִל:

23 and it was slaughtered. *Moshe* took some of its blood and put it on the ridge of *Aharon*'s right ear, and on the thumb of his right hand, and on the big toe of his right foot.

כג וַיִּשְׁחָט וַיִּקַּח מֹשֶׁה מִדָּמוֹ וַיִּתֵּן עַל־תְּנוּךְ אֹזֶן־אַהֲרֹן הַיְמָנִית וְעַל־בֹּהֶן יָדוֹ הַיְמָנִית וְעַל־בֹּהֶן רַגְלוֹ הַיְמָנִית:

24 *Moshe* then brought forward the sons of *Aharon*, and put some of the blood on the ridges of their right ears, and on the thumbs of their right hands, and on the big toes of their right feet; and the rest of the blood *Moshe* dashed against every side of the *Mizbayach*.

כד וַיַּקְרֵב אֶת־בְּנֵי אַהֲרֹן וַיִּתֵּן מֹשֶׁה מִן־הַדָּם עַל־תְּנוּךְ אָזְנָם הַיְמָנִית וְעַל־בֹּהֶן יָדָם הַיְמָנִית וְעַל־בֹּהֶן רַגְלָם הַיְמָנִית וַיִּזְרֹק מֹשֶׁה אֶת־הַדָּם עַל־הַמִּזְבֵּחַ סָבִיב:

Vayikra/Leviticus 8
Tzav

ויקרא ח
צו

25 He took the fat – the broad tail, all the fat about the entrails, the protuberance of the liver, and the two kidneys and their fat – and the right thigh.

כה וַיִּקַּח אֶת־הַחֵלֶב וְאֶת־הָאַלְיָה וְאֶת־כָּל־הַחֵלֶב אֲשֶׁר עַל־הַקֶּרֶב וְאֵת יֹתֶרֶת הַכָּבֵד וְאֶת־שְׁתֵּי הַכְּלָיֹת וְאֶת־חֶלְבְּהֶן וְאֵת שׁוֹק הַיָּמִין:

26 From the basket of unleavened bread that was before *Hashem*, he took one cake of unleavened bread, one cake of oil bread, and one wafer, and placed them on the fat parts and on the right thigh.

כו וּמִסַּל הַמַּצּוֹת אֲשֶׁר לִפְנֵי יְהוָה לָקַח חַלַּת מַצָּה אַחַת וְחַלַּת לֶחֶם שֶׁמֶן אַחַת וְרָקִיק אֶחָד וַיָּשֶׂם עַל־הַחֲלָבִים וְעַל שׁוֹק הַיָּמִין:

27 He placed all these on the palms of *Aharon* and on the palms of his sons, and elevated them as an elevation offering before *Hashem*.

כז וַיִּתֵּן אֶת־הַכֹּל עַל כַּפֵּי אַהֲרֹן וְעַל כַּפֵּי בָנָיו וַיָּנֶף אֹתָם תְּנוּפָה לִפְנֵי יְהוָה:

28 Then *Moshe* took them from their hands and turned them into smoke on the *Mizbayach* with the burnt offering. This was an ordination offering for a pleasing odor; it was an offering by fire to *Hashem*.

כח וַיִּקַּח מֹשֶׁה אֹתָם מֵעַל כַּפֵּיהֶם וַיַּקְטֵר הַמִּזְבֵּחָה עַל־הָעֹלָה מִלֻּאִים הֵם לְרֵיחַ נִיחֹחַ אִשֶּׁה הוּא לַיהוָה:

29 *Moshe* took the breast and elevated it as an elevation offering before *Hashem*; it was *Moshe*'s portion of the ram of ordination – as *Hashem* had commanded *Moshe*.

כט וַיִּקַּח מֹשֶׁה אֶת־הֶחָזֶה וַיְנִיפֵהוּ תְנוּפָה לִפְנֵי יְהוָה מֵאֵיל הַמִּלֻּאִים לְמֹשֶׁה הָיָה לְמָנָה כַּאֲשֶׁר צִוָּה יְהוָה אֶת־מֹשֶׁה:

30 And *Moshe* took some of the anointing oil and some of the blood that was on the *Mizbayach* and sprinkled it upon *Aharon* and upon his vestments, and also upon his sons and upon their vestments. Thus he consecrated *Aharon* and his vestments, and also his sons and their vestments.

ל וַיִּקַּח מֹשֶׁה מִשֶּׁמֶן הַמִּשְׁחָה וּמִן־הַדָּם אֲשֶׁר עַל־הַמִּזְבֵּחַ וַיַּז עַל־אַהֲרֹן עַל־בְּגָדָיו וְעַל־בָּנָיו וְעַל־בִּגְדֵי בָנָיו אִתּוֹ וַיְקַדֵּשׁ אֶת־אַהֲרֹן אֶת־בְּגָדָיו וְאֶת־בָּנָיו וְאֶת־בִּגְדֵי בָנָיו אִתּוֹ:

31 *Moshe* said to *Aharon* and his sons: Boil the flesh at the entrance of the Tent of Meeting and eat it there with the bread that is in the basket of ordination – as I commanded: *Aharon* and his sons shall eat it;

לא וַיֹּאמֶר מֹשֶׁה אֶל־אַהֲרֹן וְאֶל־בָּנָיו בַּשְּׁלוּ אֶת־הַבָּשָׂר פֶּתַח אֹהֶל מוֹעֵד וְשָׁם תֹּאכְלוּ אֹתוֹ וְאֶת־הַלֶּחֶם אֲשֶׁר בְּסַל הַמִּלֻּאִים כַּאֲשֶׁר צִוֵּיתִי לֵאמֹר אַהֲרֹן וּבָנָיו יֹאכְלֻהוּ:

32 and what is left over of the flesh and the bread you shall consume in fire.

לב וְהַנּוֹתָר בַּבָּשָׂר וּבַלָּחֶם בָּאֵשׁ תִּשְׂרֹפוּ:

33 You shall not go outside the entrance of the Tent of Meeting for seven days, until the day that your period of ordination is completed. For your ordination will require seven days.

לג וּמִפֶּתַח אֹהֶל מוֹעֵד לֹא תֵצְאוּ שִׁבְעַת יָמִים עַד יוֹם מְלֹאת יְמֵי מִלֻּאֵיכֶם כִּי שִׁבְעַת יָמִים יְמַלֵּא אֶת־יֶדְכֶם:

34 Everything done today, *Hashem* has commanded to be done [seven days], to make expiation for you.

לד כַּאֲשֶׁר עָשָׂה בַּיּוֹם הַזֶּה צִוָּה יְהוָה לַעֲשֹׂת לְכַפֵּר עֲלֵיכֶם:

35 You shall remain at the entrance of the Tent of Meeting day and night for seven days, keeping *Hashem*'s charge – that you may not die – for so I have been commanded.

לה וּפֶתַח אֹהֶל מוֹעֵד תֵּשְׁבוּ יוֹמָם וָלַיְלָה שִׁבְעַת יָמִים וּשְׁמַרְתֶּם אֶת־מִשְׁמֶרֶת יְהוָה וְלֹא תָמוּתוּ כִּי־כֵן צֻוֵּיתִי:

36 And *Aharon* and his sons did all the things that *Hashem* had commanded through *Moshe*.

לו וַיַּעַשׂ אַהֲרֹן וּבָנָיו אֵת כָּל־הַדְּבָרִים אֲשֶׁר־צִוָּה יְהוָה בְּיַד־מֹשֶׁה:

Vayikra/Leviticus 9
Shemini

ויקרא ט
שמיני

9 ¹ On the eighth day *Moshe* called *Aharon* and his sons, and the elders of *Yisrael*.

² He said to *Aharon*: "Take a calf of the herd for a sin offering and a ram for a burnt offering, without blemish, and bring them before *Hashem*.

³ And speak to the Israelites, saying: Take a he-goat for a sin offering; a calf and a lamb, yearlings without blemish, for a burnt offering;

⁴ and an ox and a ram for an offering of well-being to sacrifice before *Hashem*; and a meal offering with oil mixed in. For today *Hashem* will appear to you."

⁵ They brought to the front of the Tent of Meeting the things that *Moshe* had commanded, and the whole community came forward and stood before *Hashem*.

⁶ *Moshe* said: "This is what *Hashem* has commanded that you do, that the Presence of *Hashem* may appear to you."

⁷ Then *Moshe* said to *Aharon*: "Come forward to the *Mizbayach* and sacrifice your sin offering and your burnt offering, making expiation for yourself and for the people; and sacrifice the people's offering and make expiation for them, as *Hashem* has commanded."

⁸ *Aharon* came forward to the *Mizbayach* and slaughtered his calf of sin offering.

⁹ *Aharon*'s sons brought the blood to him; he dipped his finger in the blood and put it on the horns of the *Mizbayach*; and he poured out the rest of the blood at the base of the *Mizbayach*.

¹⁰ The fat, the kidneys, and the protuberance of the liver from the sin offering he turned into smoke on the *Mizbayach* – as *Hashem* had commanded *Moshe*;

¹¹ and the flesh and the skin were consumed in fire outside the camp.

¹² Then he slaughtered the burnt offering. *Aharon*'s sons passed the blood to him, and he dashed it against all sides of the *Mizbayach*.

¹³ They passed the burnt offering to him in sections, as well as the head, and he turned it into smoke on the *Mizbayach*.

א וַיְהִי בַּיּוֹם הַשְּׁמִינִי קָרָא מֹשֶׁה לְאַהֲרֹן וּלְבָנָיו וּלְזִקְנֵי יִשְׂרָאֵל:

ב וַיֹּאמֶר אֶל־אַהֲרֹן קַח־לְךָ עֵגֶל בֶּן־בָּקָר לְחַטָּאת וְאַיִל לְעֹלָה תְּמִימִם וְהַקְרֵב לִפְנֵי יְהֹוָה:

ג וְאֶל־בְּנֵי יִשְׂרָאֵל תְּדַבֵּר לֵאמֹר קְחוּ שְׂעִיר־עִזִּים לְחַטָּאת וְעֵגֶל וָכֶבֶשׂ בְּנֵי־שָׁנָה תְּמִימִם לְעֹלָה:

ד וְשׁוֹר וָאַיִל לִשְׁלָמִים לִזְבֹּחַ לִפְנֵי יְהֹוָה וּמִנְחָה בְּלוּלָה בַשָּׁמֶן כִּי הַיּוֹם יְהֹוָה נִרְאָה אֲלֵיכֶם:

ה וַיִּקְחוּ אֵת אֲשֶׁר צִוָּה מֹשֶׁה אֶל־פְּנֵי אֹהֶל מוֹעֵד וַיִּקְרְבוּ כָּל־הָעֵדָה וַיַּעַמְדוּ לִפְנֵי יְהֹוָה:

ו וַיֹּאמֶר מֹשֶׁה זֶה הַדָּבָר אֲשֶׁר־צִוָּה יְהֹוָה תַּעֲשׂוּ וְיֵרָא אֲלֵיכֶם כְּבוֹד יְהֹוָה:

ז וַיֹּאמֶר מֹשֶׁה אֶל־אַהֲרֹן קְרַב אֶל־הַמִּזְבֵּחַ וַעֲשֵׂה אֶת־חַטָּאתְךָ וְאֶת־עֹלָתֶךָ וְכַפֵּר בַּעַדְךָ וּבְעַד הָעָם וַעֲשֵׂה אֶת־קָרְבַּן הָעָם וְכַפֵּר בַּעֲדָם כַּאֲשֶׁר צִוָּה יְהֹוָה:

ח וַיִּקְרַב אַהֲרֹן אֶל־הַמִּזְבֵּחַ וַיִּשְׁחַט אֶת־עֵגֶל הַחַטָּאת אֲשֶׁר־לוֹ:

ט וַיַּקְרִבוּ בְּנֵי אַהֲרֹן אֶת־הַדָּם אֵלָיו וַיִּטְבֹּל אֶצְבָּעוֹ בַּדָּם וַיִּתֵּן עַל־קַרְנוֹת הַמִּזְבֵּחַ וְאֶת־הַדָּם יָצַק אֶל־יְסוֹד הַמִּזְבֵּחַ:

י וְאֶת־הַחֵלֶב וְאֶת־הַכְּלָיֹת וְאֶת־הַיֹּתֶרֶת מִן־הַכָּבֵד מִן־הַחַטָּאת הִקְטִיר הַמִּזְבֵּחָה כַּאֲשֶׁר צִוָּה יְהֹוָה אֶת־מֹשֶׁה:

יא וְאֶת־הַבָּשָׂר וְאֶת־הָעוֹר שָׂרַף בָּאֵשׁ מִחוּץ לַמַּחֲנֶה:

יב וַיִּשְׁחַט אֶת־הָעֹלָה וַיַּמְצִאוּ בְּנֵי אַהֲרֹן אֵלָיו אֶת־הַדָּם וַיִּזְרְקֵהוּ עַל־הַמִּזְבֵּחַ סָבִיב:

יג וְאֶת־הָעֹלָה הִמְצִיאוּ אֵלָיו לִנְתָחֶיהָ וְאֶת־הָרֹאשׁ וַיַּקְטֵר עַל־הַמִּזְבֵּחַ:

Vayikra/Leviticus 9
Shemini

14 He washed the entrails and the legs, and turned them into smoke on the *Mizbayach* with the burnt offering.

וַיִּרְחַץ אֶת־הַקֶּרֶב וְאֶת־הַכְּרָעָיִם וַיַּקְטֵר עַל־הָעֹלָה הַמִּזְבֵּחָה׃

15 Next he brought forward the people's offering. He took the goat for the people's sin offering, and slaughtered it, and presented it as a sin offering like the previous one.

וַיַּקְרֵב אֵת קָרְבַּן הָעָם וַיִּקַּח אֶת־שְׂעִיר הַחַטָּאת אֲשֶׁר לָעָם וַיִּשְׁחָטֵהוּ וַיְחַטְּאֵהוּ כָּרִאשׁוֹן׃

16 He brought forward the burnt offering and sacrificed it according to regulation.

וַיַּקְרֵב אֶת־הָעֹלָה וַיַּעֲשֶׂהָ כַּמִּשְׁפָּט׃

17 He then brought forward the meal offering and, taking a handful of it, he turned it into smoke on the *Mizbayach* – in addition to the burnt offering of the morning.

וַיַּקְרֵב אֶת־הַמִּנְחָה וַיְמַלֵּא כַפּוֹ מִמֶּנָּה וַיַּקְטֵר עַל־הַמִּזְבֵּחַ מִלְּבַד עֹלַת הַבֹּקֶר׃

18 He slaughtered the ox and the ram, the people's sacrifice of well-being. *Aharon*'s sons passed the blood to him – which he dashed against every side of the *Mizbayach*

וַיִּשְׁחַט אֶת־הַשּׁוֹר וְאֶת־הָאַיִל זֶבַח הַשְּׁלָמִים אֲשֶׁר לָעָם וַיַּמְצִאוּ בְּנֵי אַהֲרֹן אֶת־הַדָּם אֵלָיו וַיִּזְרְקֵהוּ עַל־הַמִּזְבֵּחַ סָבִיב׃

19 and the fat parts of the ox and the ram: the broad tail, the covering [fat], the kidneys, and the protuberances of the livers.

וְאֶת־הַחֲלָבִים מִן־הַשּׁוֹר וּמִן־הָאַיִל הָאַלְיָה וְהַמְכַסֶּה וְהַכְּלָיֹת וְיֹתֶרֶת הַכָּבֵד׃

20 They laid these fat parts over the breasts; and *Aharon** turned the fat parts into smoke on the *Mizbayach*,

וַיָּשִׂימוּ אֶת־הַחֲלָבִים עַל־הֶחָזוֹת וַיַּקְטֵר הַחֲלָבִים הַמִּזְבֵּחָה׃

21 and elevated the breasts and the right thighs as an elevation offering before *Hashem* – as *Moshe* had commanded.

וְאֵת הֶחָזוֹת וְאֵת שׁוֹק הַיָּמִין הֵנִיף אַהֲרֹן תְּנוּפָה לִפְנֵי יְהוָה כַּאֲשֶׁר צִוָּה מֹשֶׁה׃

22 *Aharon* lifted his hands toward the people and blessed them; and he stepped down after offering the sin offering, the burnt offering, and the offering of well-being.

וַיִּשָּׂא אַהֲרֹן אֶת־יָדָו [יָדָיו] אֶל־הָעָם וַיְבָרְכֵם וַיֵּרֶד מֵעֲשֹׂת הַחַטָּאת וְהָעֹלָה וְהַשְּׁלָמִים׃

23 *Moshe* and *Aharon* then went inside the Tent of Meeting. When they came out, they blessed the people; and the Presence of *Hashem* appeared to all the people.

וַיָּבֹא מֹשֶׁה וְאַהֲרֹן אֶל־אֹהֶל מוֹעֵד וַיֵּצְאוּ וַיְבָרְכוּ אֶת־הָעָם וַיֵּרָא כְבוֹד־יְהוָה אֶל־כָּל־הָעָם׃

va-ya-VO mo-SHEH v'-a-ha-RON el O-hel mo-AYD va-YAY-tz'-U vai-va-ra-KHU et ha-AM va-yay-RA kh'-vod a-do-NAI el kol ha-AM

---

* "*Aharon*" moved up from v. 21 for clarity

Model of the Mishkan in Timna Park

9:23 And the Presence of the Lord appeared to all the people The purpose of the *Mishkan* in the desert, and the *Beit Hamikdash* in *Yerushalayim*, is to serve as a fixed resting place for *Hashem*'s presence on earth. The commandment to build the *Mishkan* directly follows the revelation at Sinai, since, according to *Ramban*, the *Mishkan* constitutes the continuation of the revelation at Sinai. While the Divine Presence rested briefly on Mount Sinai, it found a long-term home in the *Mishkan*, and ultimately a permanent dwelling on the Temple Mount in *Yerushalayim*.

Vayikra/Leviticus 10
Shemini

ויקרא י
שמיני

24 Fire came forth from before *Hashem* and consumed the burnt offering and the fat parts on the *Mizbayach*. And all the people saw, and shouted, and fell on their faces.

כד וַתֵּצֵא אֵשׁ מִלִּפְנֵי יְהֹוָה וַתֹּאכַל עַל־הַמִּזְבֵּחַ אֶת־הָעֹלָה וְאֶת־הַחֲלָבִים וַיַּרְא כָּל־הָעָם וַיָּרֹנּוּ וַיִּפְּלוּ עַל־פְּנֵיהֶם׃

10 1 Now *Aharon*'s sons *Nadav* and *Avihu* each took his fire pan, put fire in it, and laid incense on it; and they offered before *Hashem* alien fire, which He had not enjoined upon them.

א וַיִּקְחוּ בְנֵי־אַהֲרֹן נָדָב וַאֲבִיהוּא אִישׁ מַחְתָּתוֹ וַיִּתְּנוּ בָהֵן אֵשׁ וַיָּשִׂימוּ עָלֶיהָ קְטֹרֶת וַיַּקְרִיבוּ לִפְנֵי יְהֹוָה אֵשׁ זָרָה אֲשֶׁר לֹא צִוָּה אֹתָם׃

2 And fire came forth from *Hashem* and consumed them; thus they died at the instance of *Hashem*.

ב וַתֵּצֵא אֵשׁ מִלִּפְנֵי יְהֹוָה וַתֹּאכַל אוֹתָם וַיָּמֻתוּ לִפְנֵי יְהֹוָה׃

3 Then *Moshe* said to *Aharon*, "This is what *Hashem* meant when He said: Through those near to Me I show Myself holy, And gain glory before all the people." And *Aharon* was silent.

ג וַיֹּאמֶר מֹשֶׁה אֶל־אַהֲרֹן הוּא אֲשֶׁר־דִּבֶּר יְהֹוָה לֵאמֹר בִּקְרֹבַי אֶקָּדֵשׁ וְעַל־פְּנֵי כָל־הָעָם אֶכָּבֵד וַיִּדֹּם אַהֲרֹן׃

va-YO-mer mo-SHEH el a-ha-RON HU a-sher di-BER a-do-NAI lay-MOR bik-ro-VAI e-ka-DAYSH v'-al p'-NAY khol ha-AM e-ka-VAYD va-yi-DOM a-ha-RON

4 *Moshe* called *Mishael* and Elzaphan, sons of Uzziel the uncle of *Aharon*, and said to them, "Come forward and carry your kinsmen away from the front of the sanctuary to a place outside the camp."

ד וַיִּקְרָא מֹשֶׁה אֶל־מִישָׁאֵל וְאֶל־אֶלְצָפָן בְּנֵי עֻזִּיאֵל דֹּד אַהֲרֹן וַיֹּאמֶר אֲלֵהֶם קִרְבוּ שְׂאוּ אֶת־אֲחֵיכֶם מֵאֵת פְּנֵי־הַקֹּדֶשׁ אֶל־מִחוּץ לַמַּחֲנֶה׃

5 They came forward and carried them out of the camp by their tunics, as *Moshe* had ordered.

ה וַיִּקְרְבוּ וַיִּשָּׂאֻם בְּכֻתֳּנֹתָם אֶל־מִחוּץ לַמַּחֲנֶה כַּאֲשֶׁר דִּבֶּר מֹשֶׁה׃

6 And *Moshe* said to *Aharon* and to his sons *Elazar* and *Itamar*, "Do not bare your heads and do not rend your clothes, lest you die and anger strike the whole community. But your kinsmen, all the house of *Yisrael*, shall bewail the burning that *Hashem* has wrought.

ו וַיֹּאמֶר מֹשֶׁה אֶל־אַהֲרֹן וּלְאֶלְעָזָר וּלְאִיתָמָר בָּנָיו רָאשֵׁיכֶם אַל־תִּפְרָעוּ וּבִגְדֵיכֶם לֹא־תִפְרֹמוּ וְלֹא תָמֻתוּ וְעַל כָּל־הָעֵדָה יִקְצֹף וַאֲחֵיכֶם כָּל־בֵּית יִשְׂרָאֵל יִבְכּוּ אֶת־הַשְּׂרֵפָה אֲשֶׁר שָׂרַף יְהֹוָה׃

7 And so do not go outside the entrance of the Tent of Meeting, lest you die, for *Hashem*'s anointing oil is upon you." And they did as *Moshe* had bidden.

ז וּמִפֶּתַח אֹהֶל מוֹעֵד לֹא תֵצְאוּ פֶּן־תָּמֻתוּ כִּי־שֶׁמֶן מִשְׁחַת יְהֹוָה עֲלֵיכֶם וַיַּעֲשׂוּ כִּדְבַר מֹשֶׁה׃

8 And *Hashem* spoke to *Aharon*, saying:

ח וַיְדַבֵּר יְהֹוָה אֶל־אַהֲרֹן לֵאמֹר׃

10:3 Through those near to Me I show Myself holy The death of *Aharon*'s sons, *Nadav* and *Avihu*, occurs in the midst of the joyous inauguration ceremony of the *Mishkan*. The Sages explain that they are so moved by the closeness they feel to *Hashem* at this moment of revelation, that *Nadav* and *Avihu* desire to get even closer with an offering of their own which they bring in the Holy of Holies. Though their intentions are pure, the offering is unauthorized and the entry into the Holy sanctuary forbidden, so they are punished. Their desire for closeness is reflected in *Moshe*'s words to *Aharon*, "Through those near to Me I show Myself holy." *Nadav* and *Avihu* are indeed close to God, but this closeness does not allow them to bend the rules. By punishing those who were closest to Him, God's name is sanctified, as He teaches the important lesson that everyone, even those who are most powerful and respected, must be held to the same standard.

Vayikra/Leviticus 10
Shemini

ויקרא י
שמיני

9 Drink no wine or other intoxicant, you or your sons, when you enter the Tent of Meeting, that you may not die. This is a law for all time throughout the ages,

ט יַ֣יִן וְשֵׁכָ֞ר אַל־תֵּ֣שְׁתְּ ׀ אַתָּ֣ה ׀ וּבָנֶ֣יךָ אִתָּ֗ךְ בְּבֹאֲכֶ֛ם אֶל־אֹ֥הֶל מוֹעֵ֖ד וְלֹ֣א תָמֻ֑תוּ חֻקַּ֥ת עוֹלָ֖ם לְדֹרֹתֵיכֶֽם׃

10 for you must distinguish between the sacred and the profane, and between the unclean and the clean;

י וּֽלֲהַבְדִּ֔יל בֵּ֥ין הַקֹּ֖דֶשׁ וּבֵ֣ין הַחֹ֑ל וּבֵ֥ין הַטָּמֵ֖א וּבֵ֥ין הַטָּהֽוֹר׃

11 and you must teach the Israelites all the laws which *Hashem* has imparted to them through *Moshe*.

יא וּלְהוֹרֹ֖ת אֶת־בְּנֵ֣י יִשְׂרָאֵ֑ל אֵ֚ת כׇּל־הַ֣חֻקִּ֔ים אֲשֶׁ֨ר דִּבֶּ֧ר יְהֹוָ֛ה אֲלֵיהֶ֖ם בְּיַד־מֹשֶֽׁה׃

12 *Moshe* spoke to *Aharon* and to his remaining sons, *Elazar* and *Itamar*: Take the meal offering that is left over from *Hashem's* offerings by fire and eat it unleavened beside the *Mizbayach*, for it is most holy.

יב וַיְדַבֵּ֨ר מֹשֶׁ֜ה אֶֽל־אַהֲרֹ֗ן וְאֶ֣ל אֶלְעָזָר֩ וְאֶל־אִ֨יתָמָ֥ר ׀ בָּנָיו֮ הַנּֽוֹתָרִים֒ קְח֣וּ אֶת־הַמִּנְחָ֗ה הַנּוֹתֶ֙רֶת֙ מֵאִשֵּׁ֣י יְהֹוָ֔ה וְאִכְל֥וּהָ מַצּ֖וֹת אֵ֣צֶל הַמִּזְבֵּ֑חַ כִּ֛י קֹ֥דֶשׁ קָֽדָשִׁ֖ים הִֽוא׃

13 You shall eat it in the sacred precinct, inasmuch as it is your due, and that of your children, from *Hashem's* offerings by fire; for so I have been commanded.

יג וַאֲכַלְתֶּ֤ם אֹתָהּ֙ בְּמָק֣וֹם קָדֹ֔שׁ כִּ֣י חׇקְךָ֤ וְחׇק־בָּנֶ֙יךָ֙ הִ֔וא מֵאִשֵּׁ֖י יְהֹוָ֑ה כִּי־כֵ֖ן צֻוֵּֽיתִי׃

14 But the breast of elevation offering and the thigh of gift offering you, and your sons and daughters with you, may eat in any clean place, for they have been assigned as a due to you and your children from the Israelites' sacrifices of well-being.

יד וְאֵת֩ חֲזֵ֨ה הַתְּנוּפָ֜ה וְאֵ֣ת ׀ שׁ֣וֹק הַתְּרוּמָ֗ה תֹּֽאכְלוּ֙ בְּמָק֣וֹם טָה֔וֹר אַתָּ֕ה וּבָנֶ֥יךָ וּבְנֹתֶ֖יךָ אִתָּ֑ךְ כִּֽי־חׇקְךָ֤ וְחׇק־בָּנֶ֙יךָ֙ נִתְּנ֔וּ מִזִּבְחֵ֥י שַׁלְמֵ֖י בְּנֵ֥י יִשְׂרָאֵֽל׃

15 Together with the fat of fire offering, they must present the thigh of gift offering and the breast of elevation offering, which are to be elevated as an elevation offering before *Hashem*, and which are to be your due and that of your children with you for all time – as *Hashem* has commanded.

טו שׁ֣וֹק הַתְּרוּמָ֞ה וַחֲזֵ֣ה הַתְּנוּפָ֗ה עַ֣ל אִשֵּׁ֤י הַחֲלָבִים֙ יָבִ֔יאוּ לְהָנִ֥יף תְּנוּפָ֖ה לִפְנֵ֣י יְהֹוָ֑ה וְהָיָ֨ה לְךָ֜ וּלְבָנֶ֤יךָ אִתְּךָ֙ לְחׇק־עוֹלָ֔ם כַּאֲשֶׁ֖ר צִוָּ֥ה יְהֹוָֽה׃

16 Then *Moshe* inquired about the goat of sin offering, and it had already been burned! He was angry with *Elazar* and *Itamar*, *Aharon's* remaining sons, and said,

טז וְאֵ֣ת ׀ שְׂעִ֣יר הַֽחַטָּ֗את דָּרֹ֥שׁ דָּרַ֛שׁ מֹשֶׁ֖ה וְהִנֵּ֣ה שֹׂרָ֑ף וַיִּקְצֹ֥ף עַל־אֶלְעָזָ֣ר וְעַל־אִֽיתָמָ֔ר בְּנֵ֥י אַהֲרֹ֖ן הַנּוֹתָרִ֥ם לֵאמֹֽר׃

17 "Why did you not eat the sin offering in the sacred area? For it is most holy, and He has given it to you to remove the guilt of the community and to make expiation for them before *Hashem*.

יז מַדּ֗וּעַ לֹֽא־אֲכַלְתֶּ֤ם אֶת־הַחַטָּאת֙ בִּמְק֣וֹם הַקֹּ֔דֶשׁ כִּ֛י קֹ֥דֶשׁ קָֽדָשִׁ֖ים הִ֑וא וְאֹתָ֣הּ ׀ נָתַ֣ן לָכֶ֗ם לָשֵׂאת֙ אֶת־עֲוֺ֣ן הָעֵדָ֔ה לְכַפֵּ֥ר עֲלֵיהֶ֖ם לִפְנֵ֥י יְהֹוָֽה׃

18 Since its blood was not brought inside the sanctuary, you should certainly have eaten it in the sanctuary, as I commanded."

יח הֵ֚ן לֹא־הוּבָ֣א אֶת־דָּמָ֔הּ אֶל־הַקֹּ֖דֶשׁ פְּנִ֑ימָה אָכ֨וֹל תֹּאכְל֥וּ אֹתָ֛הּ בַּקֹּ֖דֶשׁ כַּאֲשֶׁ֥ר צִוֵּֽיתִי׃

Vayikra/Leviticus 11
Shemini

ויקרא יא
שמיני

19 And *Aharon* spoke to *Moshe*, "See, this day they brought their sin offering and their burnt offering before *Hashem*, and such things have befallen me! Had I eaten sin offering today, would *Hashem* have approved?"

יט וַיְדַבֵּר אַהֲרֹן אֶל־מֹשֶׁה הֵן הַיּוֹם הִקְרִיבוּ אֶת־חַטָּאתָם וְאֶת־עֹלָתָם לִפְנֵי יְהֹוָה וַתִּקְרֶאנָה אֹתִי כָּאֵלֶּה וְאָכַלְתִּי חַטָּאת הַיּוֹם הַיִּיטַב בְּעֵינֵי יְהֹוָה׃

20 And when *Moshe* heard this, he approved.

כ וַיִּשְׁמַע מֹשֶׁה וַיִּיטַב בְּעֵינָיו׃

11 1 *Hashem* spoke to *Moshe* and *Aharon*, saying to them:

יא א וַיְדַבֵּר יְהֹוָה אֶל־מֹשֶׁה וְאֶל־אַהֲרֹן לֵאמֹר אֲלֵהֶם׃

2 Speak to *B'nei Yisrael* thus: These are the creatures that you may eat from among all the land animals:

ב דַּבְּרוּ אֶל־בְּנֵי יִשְׂרָאֵל לֵאמֹר זֹאת הַחַיָּה אֲשֶׁר תֹּאכְלוּ מִכָּל־הַבְּהֵמָה אֲשֶׁר עַל־הָאָרֶץ׃

3 any animal that has true hoofs, with clefts through the hoofs, and that chews the cud – such you may eat.

ג כֹּל מַפְרֶסֶת פַּרְסָה וְשֹׁסַעַת שֶׁסַע פְּרָסֹת מַעֲלַת גֵּרָה בַּבְּהֵמָה אֹתָהּ תֹּאכֵלוּ׃

4 The following, however, of those that either chew the cud or have true hoofs, you shall not eat: the camel – although it chews the cud, it has no true hoofs: it is unclean for you;

ד אַךְ אֶת־זֶה לֹא תֹאכְלוּ מִמַּעֲלֵי הַגֵּרָה וּמִמַּפְרִיסֵי הַפַּרְסָה אֶת־הַגָּמָל כִּי־מַעֲלֵה גֵרָה הוּא וּפַרְסָה אֵינֶנּוּ מַפְרִיס טָמֵא הוּא לָכֶם׃

5 the daman – although it chews the cud, it has no true hoofs: it is unclean for you;

ה וְאֶת־הַשָּׁפָן כִּי־מַעֲלֵה גֵרָה הוּא וּפַרְסָה לֹא יַפְרִיס טָמֵא הוּא לָכֶם׃

6 the hare – although it chews the cud, it has no true hoofs: it is unclean for you;

ו וְאֶת־הָאַרְנֶבֶת כִּי־מַעֲלַת גֵּרָה הִוא וּפַרְסָה לֹא הִפְרִיסָה טְמֵאָה הִוא לָכֶם׃

7 and the swine – although it has true hoofs, with the hoofs cleft through, it does not chew the cud: it is unclean for you.

ז וְאֶת־הַחֲזִיר כִּי־מַפְרִיס פַּרְסָה הוּא וְשֹׁסַע שֶׁסַע פַּרְסָה וְהוּא גֵּרָה לֹא־יִגָּר טָמֵא הוּא לָכֶם׃

8 You shall not eat of their flesh or touch their carcasses; they are unclean for you.

ח מִבְּשָׂרָם לֹא תֹאכֵלוּ וּבְנִבְלָתָם לֹא תִגָּעוּ טְמֵאִים הֵם לָכֶם׃

9 These you may eat of all that live in water: anything in water, whether in the seas or in the streams, that has fins and scales – these you may eat.

ט אֶת־זֶה תֹּאכְלוּ מִכֹּל אֲשֶׁר בַּמָּיִם כֹּל אֲשֶׁר־לוֹ סְנַפִּיר וְקַשְׂקֶשֶׂת בַּמַּיִם בַּיַּמִּים וּבַנְּחָלִים אֹתָם תֹּאכֵלוּ׃

10 But anything in the seas or in the streams that has no fins and scales, among all the swarming things of the water and among all the other living creatures that are in the water – they are an abomination for you

י וְכֹל אֲשֶׁר אֵין־לוֹ סְנַפִּיר וְקַשְׂקֶשֶׂת בַּיַּמִּים וּבַנְּחָלִים מִכֹּל שֶׁרֶץ הַמַּיִם וּמִכֹּל נֶפֶשׁ הַחַיָּה אֲשֶׁר בַּמָּיִם שֶׁקֶץ הֵם לָכֶם׃

11 and an abomination for you they shall remain: you shall not eat of their flesh and you shall abominate their carcasses.

יא וְשֶׁקֶץ יִהְיוּ לָכֶם מִבְּשָׂרָם לֹא תֹאכֵלוּ וְאֶת־נִבְלָתָם תְּשַׁקֵּצוּ׃

12 Everything in water that has no fins and scales shall be an abomination for you.

יב כֹּל אֲשֶׁר אֵין־לוֹ סְנַפִּיר וְקַשְׂקֶשֶׂת בַּמָּיִם שֶׁקֶץ הוּא לָכֶם׃

Vayikra/Leviticus 11
Shemini

13 The following you shall abominate among the birds – they shall not be eaten, they are an abomination: the eagle, the vulture, and the black vulture;

14 the kite, falcons of every variety;

15 all varieties of raven;

16 the ostrich, the nighthawk, the sea gull; hawks of every variety;

17 the little owl, the cormorant, and the great owl;

18 the white owl, the pelican, and the bustard;

19 the stork; herons of every variety; the hoopoe, and the bat.

20 All winged swarming things that walk on fours shall be an abomination for you.

21 But these you may eat among all the winged swarming things that walk on fours: all that have, above their feet, jointed legs to leap with on the ground

22 of these you may eat the following: locusts of every variety; all varieties of bald locust; crickets of every variety; and all varieties of grasshopper.

23 But all other winged swarming things that have four legs shall be an abomination for you.

24 And the following shall make you unclean – whoever touches their carcasses shall be unclean until evening,

25 and whoever carries the carcasses of any of them shall wash his clothes and be unclean until evening

26 every animal that has true hoofs but without clefts through the hoofs, or that does not chew the cud. They are unclean for you; whoever touches them shall be unclean.

27 Also all animals that walk on paws, among those that walk on fours, are unclean for you; whoever touches their carcasses shall be unclean until evening.

28 And anyone who carries their carcasses shall wash his clothes and remain unclean until evening. They are unclean for you.

Vayikra/Leviticus 11
Shemini

ויקרא יא
שמיני

29 The following shall be unclean for you from among the things that swarm on the earth: the mole, the mouse, and great lizards of every variety;

כט וְזֶה לָכֶם הַטָּמֵא בַּשֶּׁרֶץ עַל־הָאָרֶץ הַחֹלֶד וְהָעַכְבָּר וְהַצָּב לְמִינֵהוּ:

30 the gecko, the land crocodile, the lizard, the sand lizard, and the Hameleon.

ל וְהָאֲנָקָה וְהַכֹּחַ וְהַלְּטָאָה וְהַחֹמֶט וְהַתִּנְשָׁמֶת:

31 Those are for you the unclean among all the swarming things; whoever touches them when they are dead shall be unclean until evening.

לא אֵלֶּה הַטְּמֵאִים לָכֶם בְּכָל־הַשָּׁרֶץ כָּל־הַנֹּגֵעַ בָּהֶם בְּמֹתָם יִטְמָא עַד־הָעָרֶב:

32 And anything on which one of them falls when dead shall be unclean: be it any article of wood, or a cloth, or a skin, or a sack – any such article that can be put to use shall be dipped in water, and it shall remain unclean until evening; then it shall be clean.

לב וְכֹל אֲשֶׁר־יִפֹּל־עָלָיו מֵהֶם בְּמֹתָם יִטְמָא מִכָּל־כְּלִי־עֵץ אוֹ בֶגֶד אוֹ־עוֹר אוֹ שָׂק כָּל־כְּלִי אֲשֶׁר־יֵעָשֶׂה מְלָאכָה בָּהֶם בַּמַּיִם יוּבָא וְטָמֵא עַד־הָעֶרֶב וְטָהֵר:

33 And if any of those falls into an earthen vessel, everything inside it shall be unclean and [the vessel] itself you shall break.

לג וְכָל־כְּלִי־חֶרֶשׂ אֲשֶׁר־יִפֹּל מֵהֶם אֶל־תּוֹכוֹ כֹּל אֲשֶׁר בְּתוֹכוֹ יִטְמָא וְאֹתוֹ תִשְׁבֹּרוּ:

34 As to any food that may be eaten, it shall become unclean if it came in contact with water; as to any liquid that may be drunk, it shall become unclean if it was inside any vessel.

לד מִכָּל־הָאֹכֶל אֲשֶׁר יֵאָכֵל אֲשֶׁר יָבוֹא עָלָיו מַיִם יִטְמָא וְכָל־מַשְׁקֶה אֲשֶׁר יִשָּׁתֶה בְּכָל־כְּלִי יִטְמָא:

35 Everything on which the carcass of any of them falls shall be unclean: an oven or stove shall be smashed. They are unclean and unclean they shall remain for you.

לה וְכֹל אֲשֶׁר־יִפֹּל מִנִּבְלָתָם עָלָיו יִטְמָא תַּנּוּר וְכִירַיִם יֻתָּץ טְמֵאִים הֵם וּטְמֵאִים יִהְיוּ לָכֶם:

36 However, a spring or cistern in which water is collected shall be clean, but whoever touches such a carcass in it shall be unclean.

לו אַךְ מַעְיָן וּבוֹר מִקְוֵה־מַיִם יִהְיֶה טָהוֹר וְנֹגֵעַ בְּנִבְלָתָם יִטְמָא:

37 If such a carcass falls upon seed grain that is to be sown, it is clean;

לז וְכִי יִפֹּל מִנִּבְלָתָם עַל־כָּל־זֶרַע זֵרוּעַ אֲשֶׁר יִזָּרֵעַ טָהוֹר הוּא:

38 but if water is put on the seed and any part of a carcass falls upon it, it shall be unclean for you.

לח וְכִי יֻתַּן־מַיִם עַל־זֶרַע וְנָפַל מִנִּבְלָתָם עָלָיו טָמֵא הוּא לָכֶם:

39 If an animal that you may eat has died, anyone who touches its carcass shall be unclean until evening;

לט וְכִי יָמוּת מִן־הַבְּהֵמָה אֲשֶׁר־הִיא לָכֶם לְאָכְלָה הַנֹּגֵעַ בְּנִבְלָתָהּ יִטְמָא עַד־הָעָרֶב:

40 anyone who eats of its carcass shall wash his clothes and remain unclean until evening; and anyone who carries its carcass shall wash his clothes and remain unclean until evening.

מ וְהָאֹכֵל מִנִּבְלָתָהּ יְכַבֵּס בְּגָדָיו וְטָמֵא עַד־הָעָרֶב וְהַנֹּשֵׂא אֶת־נִבְלָתָהּ יְכַבֵּס בְּגָדָיו וְטָמֵא עַד־הָעָרֶב:

41 All the things that swarm upon the earth are an abomination; they shall not be eaten.

מא וְכָל־הַשֶּׁרֶץ הַשֹּׁרֵץ עַל־הָאָרֶץ שֶׁקֶץ הוּא לֹא יֵאָכֵל:

Vayikra/Leviticus 12
Tazria

ויקרא יב
תזריע

42 You shall not eat, among all things that swarm upon the earth, anything that crawls on its belly, or anything that walks on fours, or anything that has many legs; for they are an abomination.

מב כֹּל הוֹלֵךְ עַל־גָּחוֹן וְכֹל הוֹלֵךְ עַל־אַרְבַּע עַד כָּל־מַרְבֵּה רַגְלַיִם לְכָל־הַשֶּׁרֶץ הַשֹּׁרֵץ עַל־הָאָרֶץ לֹא תֹאכְלוּם כִּי־שֶׁקֶץ הֵם:

43 You shall not draw abomination upon yourselves through anything that swarms; you shall not make yourselves unclean therewith and thus become unclean.

מג אַל־תְּשַׁקְּצוּ אֶת־נַפְשֹׁתֵיכֶם בְּכָל־הַשֶּׁרֶץ הַשֹּׁרֵץ וְלֹא תִטַּמְּאוּ בָּהֶם וְנִטְמֵתֶם בָּם:

44 For I Hashem am your God: you shall sanctify yourselves and be holy, for I am holy. You shall not make yourselves unclean through any swarming thing that moves upon the earth.

מד כִּי אֲנִי יְהֹוָה אֱלֹהֵיכֶם וְהִתְקַדִּשְׁתֶּם וִהְיִיתֶם קְדֹשִׁים כִּי קָדוֹשׁ אָנִי וְלֹא תְטַמְּאוּ אֶת־נַפְשֹׁתֵיכֶם בְּכָל־הַשֶּׁרֶץ הָרֹמֵשׂ עַל־הָאָרֶץ:

45 For I Hashem am He who brought you up from the land of Egypt to be your God: you shall be holy, for I am holy.

מה כִּי אֲנִי יְהֹוָה הַמַּעֲלֶה אֶתְכֶם מֵאֶרֶץ מִצְרַיִם לִהְיֹת לָכֶם לֵאלֹהִים וִהְיִיתֶם קְדֹשִׁים כִּי קָדוֹשׁ אָנִי:

KEE a-NEE a-do-NAI ha-ma-a-LEH et-KHEM may-E-retz mitz-RA-yim lih-YOT la-KHEM lay-lo-HEEM vih-yee-TEM k'-do-SHEEM KEE ka-DOSH A-nee

46 These are the instructions concerning animals, birds, all living creatures that move in water, and all creatures that swarm on earth,

מו זֹאת תּוֹרַת הַבְּהֵמָה וְהָעוֹף וְכֹל נֶפֶשׁ הַחַיָּה הָרֹמֶשֶׂת בַּמָּיִם וּלְכָל־נֶפֶשׁ הַשֹּׁרֶצֶת עַל־הָאָרֶץ:

47 for distinguishing between the unclean and the clean, between the living things that may be eaten and the living things that may not be eaten.

מז לְהַבְדִּיל בֵּין הַטָּמֵא וּבֵין הַטָּהֹר וּבֵין הַחַיָּה הַנֶּאֱכֶלֶת וּבֵין הַחַיָּה אֲשֶׁר לֹא תֵאָכֵל:

12

1 Hashem spoke to Moshe, saying:

יב א וַיְדַבֵּר יְהֹוָה אֶל־מֹשֶׁה לֵּאמֹר:

2 Speak to B'nei Yisrael thus: When a woman at childbirth bears a male, she shall be unclean seven days; she shall be unclean as at the time of her menstrual infirmity.

ב דַּבֵּר אֶל־בְּנֵי יִשְׂרָאֵל לֵאמֹר אִשָּׁה כִּי תַזְרִיעַ וְיָלְדָה זָכָר וְטָמְאָה שִׁבְעַת יָמִים כִּימֵי נִדַּת דְּוֹתָהּ תִּטְמָא:

3 On the eighth day the flesh of his foreskin shall be circumcised.

ג וּבַיּוֹם הַשְּׁמִינִי יִמּוֹל בְּשַׂר עָרְלָתוֹ:

u-va-YOM ha-sh'-mee-NEE yi-MOL b'-SAR or-la-TO

President Ezer Weizman (R) at a Brit Milah ceremony

11:45 You shall be holy, for I am holy This verse appears towards the end of the description of the kosher dietary laws. God draws a clear connection between obeying the kosher laws and sustaining a status of holiness. The Bible instructs the Children of Israel to distinguish between things which may be eaten and things which are not to be eaten. In handing these requirements to the Jewish people, *Hashem* is requiring that they distinguish themselves from the other nations. They are charged with a great responsibility to live a holy life, to follow God's commandments and to come as close as possible to the holiness of *Hashem*. Through observance of the kosher dietary laws, the People of Israel are meant to have a positive influence on the rest of the world.

12:3 On the eighth day the flesh of his foreskin shall be circumcised This chapter deals with the laws of purity applying to a woman after childbirth. In this context, the Bible also mentions the law of circumcision, the removal of the baby boy's foreskin on the eighth day of his life. Circumcision was the first commandment

Vayikra/Leviticus 13
Tazria

ויקרא יג
תזריע

4 She shall remain in a state of blood purification for thirty-three days: she shall not touch any consecrated thing, nor enter the sanctuary until her period of purification is completed.

ד וּשְׁלֹשִׁים יוֹם וּשְׁלֹשֶׁת יָמִים תֵּשֵׁב בִּדְמֵי טָהֳרָה בְּכָל־קֹדֶשׁ לֹא־תִגָּע וְאֶל־הַמִּקְדָּשׁ לֹא תָבֹא עַד־מְלֹאת יְמֵי טָהֳרָהּ׃

5 If she bears a female, she shall be unclean two weeks as during her menstruation, and she shall remain in a state of blood purification for sixty-six days.

ה וְאִם־נְקֵבָה תֵלֵד וְטָמְאָה שְׁבֻעַיִם כְּנִדָּתָהּ וְשִׁשִּׁים יוֹם וְשֵׁשֶׁת יָמִים תֵּשֵׁב עַל־דְּמֵי טָהֳרָה׃

6 On the completion of her period of purification, for either son or daughter, she shall bring to the *Kohen*, at the entrance of the Tent of Meeting, a lamb in its first year for a burnt offering, and a pigeon or a turtledove for a sin offering.

ו וּבִמְלֹאת ׀ יְמֵי טָהֳרָהּ לְבֵן אוֹ לְבַת תָּבִיא כֶּבֶשׂ בֶּן־שְׁנָתוֹ לְעֹלָה וּבֶן־יוֹנָה אוֹ־תֹר לְחַטָּאת אֶל־פֶּתַח אֹהֶל־מוֹעֵד אֶל־הַכֹּהֵן׃

7 He shall offer it before *Hashem* and make expiation on her behalf; she shall then be clean from her flow of blood. Such are the rituals concerning her who bears a child, male or female.

ז וְהִקְרִיבוֹ לִפְנֵי יְהֹוָה וְכִפֶּר עָלֶיהָ וְטָהֲרָה מִמְּקֹר דָּמֶיהָ זֹאת תּוֹרַת הַיֹּלֶדֶת לַזָּכָר אוֹ לַנְּקֵבָה׃

8 If, however, her means do not suffice for a sheep, she shall take two turtledoves or two pigeons, one for a burnt offering and the other for a sin offering. The *Kohen* shall make expiation on her behalf, and she shall be clean.

ח וְאִם־לֹא תִמְצָא יָדָהּ דֵּי שֶׂה וְלָקְחָה שְׁתֵּי־תֹרִים אוֹ שְׁנֵי בְּנֵי יוֹנָה אֶחָד לְעֹלָה וְאֶחָד לְחַטָּאת וְכִפֶּר עָלֶיהָ הַכֹּהֵן וְטָהֵרָה׃

13 1 *Hashem* spoke to *Moshe* and *Aharon*, saying:

יג א וַיְדַבֵּר יְהֹוָה אֶל־מֹשֶׁה וְאֶל־אַהֲרֹן לֵאמֹר׃

2 When a person has on the skin of his body a swelling, a rash, or a discoloration, and it develops into a scaly affection on the skin of his body, it shall be reported to *Aharon* the *Kohen* or to one of his sons, the *Kohanim*.

ב אָדָם כִּי־יִהְיֶה בְעוֹר־בְּשָׂרוֹ שְׂאֵת אוֹ־סַפַּחַת אוֹ בַהֶרֶת וְהָיָה בְעוֹר־בְּשָׂרוֹ לְנֶגַע צָרָעַת וְהוּבָא אֶל־אַהֲרֹן הַכֹּהֵן אוֹ אֶל־אַחַד מִבָּנָיו הַכֹּהֲנִים׃

3 The *Kohen* shall examine the affection on the skin of his body: if hair in the affected patch has turned white and the affection appears to be deeper than the skin of his body, it is a leprous affection; when the *Kohen* sees it, he shall pronounce him unclean.

ג וְרָאָה הַכֹּהֵן אֶת־הַנֶּגַע בְּעוֹר־הַבָּשָׂר וְשֵׂעָר בַּנֶּגַע הָפַךְ ׀ לָבָן וּמַרְאֵה הַנֶּגַע עָמֹק מֵעוֹר בְּשָׂרוֹ נֶגַע צָרַעַת הוּא וְרָאָהוּ הַכֹּהֵן וְטִמֵּא אֹתוֹ׃

---

given to *Avraham*, as detailed in *Sefer Bereishit* chapter 17. That chapter begins with the covenant *Hashem* makes with *Avraham*, promising that He will be an everlasting God to *Avraham* and his descendants, that *Avraham* will merit numerous offspring, and that *Hashem* will give them the Land of Israel as an eternal inheritance. To this very day, the circumcision of a male descendant of *Avraham* draws the new child into the covenant with *Hashem*, and serves as a constant reminder of God's promise to remain with His people and give them *Eretz Yisrael*.

Vayikra/Leviticus 13
Tazria

ויקרא יג
תזריע

4 But if it is a white discoloration on the skin of his body which does not appear to be deeper than the skin and the hair in it has not turned white, the *Kohen* shall isolate the affected person for seven days.

ד וְאִם־בַּהֶרֶת לְבָנָה הִוא בְּעוֹר בְּשָׂרוֹ וְעָמֹק אֵין־מַרְאֶהָ מִן־הָעוֹר וּשְׂעָרָה לֹא־הָפַךְ לָבָן וְהִסְגִּיר הַכֹּהֵן אֶת־הַנֶּגַע שִׁבְעַת יָמִים:

5 On the seventh day the *Kohen* shall examine him, and if the affection has remained unchanged in color and the disease has not spread on the skin, the *Kohen* shall isolate him for another seven days.

ה וְרָאָהוּ הַכֹּהֵן בַּיּוֹם הַשְּׁבִיעִי וְהִנֵּה הַנֶּגַע עָמַד בְּעֵינָיו לֹא־פָשָׂה הַנֶּגַע בָּעוֹר וְהִסְגִּירוֹ הַכֹּהֵן שִׁבְעַת יָמִים שֵׁנִית:

6 On the seventh day the *Kohen* shall examine him again: if the affection has faded and has not spread on the skin, the *Kohen* shall pronounce him clean. It is a rash; he shall wash his clothes, and he shall be clean.

ו וְרָאָה הַכֹּהֵן אֹתוֹ בַּיּוֹם הַשְּׁבִיעִי שֵׁנִית וְהִנֵּה כֵּהָה הַנֶּגַע וְלֹא־פָשָׂה הַנֶּגַע בָּעוֹר וְטִהֲרוֹ הַכֹּהֵן מִסְפַּחַת הִיא וְכִבֶּס בְּגָדָיו וְטָהֵר:

7 But if the rash should spread on the skin after he has presented himself to the *Kohen* and been pronounced clean, he shall present himself again to the *Kohen*.

ז וְאִם־פָּשֹׂה תִפְשֶׂה הַמִּסְפַּחַת בָּעוֹר אַחֲרֵי הֵרָאֹתוֹ אֶל־הַכֹּהֵן לְטָהֳרָתוֹ וְנִרְאָה שֵׁנִית אֶל־הַכֹּהֵן:

8 And if the *Kohen* sees that the rash has spread on the skin, the *Kohen* shall pronounce him unclean; it is leprosy.

ח וְרָאָה הַכֹּהֵן וְהִנֵּה פָּשְׂתָה הַמִּסְפַּחַת בָּעוֹר וְטִמְּאוֹ הַכֹּהֵן צָרַעַת הִוא:

9 When a person has a scaly affection, it shall be reported to the *Kohen*.

ט נֶגַע צָרַעַת כִּי תִהְיֶה בְּאָדָם וְהוּבָא אֶל־הַכֹּהֵן:

10 If the *Kohen* finds on the skin a white swelling which has turned some hair white, with a patch of undiscolored flesh in the swelling,

י וְרָאָה הַכֹּהֵן וְהִנֵּה שְׂאֵת־לְבָנָה בָּעוֹר וְהִיא הָפְכָה שֵׂעָר לָבָן וּמִחְיַת בָּשָׂר חַי בַּשְׂאֵת:

11 it is chronic leprosy on the skin of his body, and the *Kohen* shall pronounce him unclean; he need not isolate him, for he is unclean.

יא צָרַעַת נוֹשֶׁנֶת הִוא בְּעוֹר בְּשָׂרוֹ וְטִמְּאוֹ הַכֹּהֵן לֹא יַסְגִּרֶנּוּ כִּי טָמֵא הוּא:

12 If the eruption spreads out over the skin so that it covers all the skin of the affected person from head to foot, wherever the *Kohen* can see

יב וְאִם־פָּרוֹחַ תִּפְרַח הַצָּרַעַת בָּעוֹר וְכִסְּתָה הַצָּרַעַת אֵת כָּל־עוֹר הַנֶּגַע מֵרֹאשׁוֹ וְעַד־רַגְלָיו לְכָל־מַרְאֵה עֵינֵי הַכֹּהֵן:

13 if the *Kohen* sees that the eruption has covered the whole body – he shall pronounce the affected person clean; he is clean, for he has turned all white.

יג וְרָאָה הַכֹּהֵן וְהִנֵּה כִסְּתָה הַצָּרַעַת אֶת־כָּל־בְּשָׂרוֹ וְטִהַר אֶת־הַנָּגַע כֻּלּוֹ הָפַךְ לָבָן טָהוֹר הוּא:

14 But as soon as undiscolored flesh appears in it, he shall be unclean;

יד וּבְיוֹם הֵרָאוֹת בּוֹ בָּשָׂר חַי יִטְמָא:

15 when the *Kohen* sees the undiscolored flesh, he shall pronounce him unclean. The undiscolored flesh is unclean; it is leprosy.

טו וְרָאָה הַכֹּהֵן אֶת־הַבָּשָׂר הַחַי וְטִמְּאוֹ הַבָּשָׂר הַחַי טָמֵא הוּא צָרַעַת הוּא:

16 But if the undiscolored flesh again turns white, he shall come to the *Kohen*,

טז אוֹ כִי יָשׁוּב הַבָּשָׂר הַחַי וְנֶהְפַּךְ לְלָבָן וּבָא אֶל־הַכֹּהֵן:

Vayikra/Leviticus 13
Tazria

ויקרא יג
תזריע

17 and the *Kohen* shall examine him: if the affection has turned white, the *Kohen* shall pronounce the affected person clean; he is clean.

יז וְרָאָהוּ הַכֹּהֵן וְהִנֵּה נֶהְפַּךְ הַנֶּגַע לְלָבָן וְטִהַר הַכֹּהֵן אֶת־הַנֶּגַע טָהוֹר הוּא׃

18 When an inflammation appears on the skin of one's body and it heals,

יח וּבָשָׂר כִּי־יִהְיֶה בוֹ־בְעֹרוֹ שְׁחִין וְנִרְפָּא׃

19 and a white swelling or a white discoloration streaked with red develops where the inflammation was, he shall present himself to the *Kohen*.

יט וְהָיָה בִּמְקוֹם הַשְּׁחִין שְׂאֵת לְבָנָה אוֹ בַהֶרֶת לְבָנָה אֲדַמְדָּמֶת וְנִרְאָה אֶל־הַכֹּהֵן׃

20 If the *Kohen* finds that it appears lower than the rest of the skin and that the hair in it has turned white, the *Kohen* shall pronounce him unclean; it is a leprous affection that has broken out in the inflammation.

כ וְרָאָה הַכֹּהֵן וְהִנֵּה מַרְאֶהָ שָׁפָל מִן־הָעוֹר וּשְׂעָרָהּ הָפַךְ לָבָן וְטִמְּאוֹ הַכֹּהֵן נֶגַע־צָרַעַת הִוא בַּשְּׁחִין פָּרָחָה׃

21 But if the *Kohen* finds that there is no white hair in it and it is not lower than the rest of the skin, and it is faded, the *Kohen* shall isolate him for seven days.

כא וְאִם יִרְאֶנָּה הַכֹּהֵן וְהִנֵּה אֵין־בָּהּ שֵׂעָר לָבָן וּשְׁפָלָה אֵינֶנָּה מִן־הָעוֹר וְהִיא כֵהָה וְהִסְגִּירוֹ הַכֹּהֵן שִׁבְעַת יָמִים׃

22 If it should spread in the skin, the *Kohen* shall pronounce him unclean; it is an affection.

כב וְאִם־פָּשֹׂה תִפְשֶׂה בָּעוֹר וְטִמֵּא הַכֹּהֵן אֹתוֹ נֶגַע הִוא׃

23 But if the discoloration remains stationary, not having spread, it is the scar of the inflammation; the *Kohen* shall pronounce him clean.

כג וְאִם־תַּחְתֶּיהָ תַּעֲמֹד הַבַּהֶרֶת לֹא פָשָׂתָה צָרֶבֶת הַשְּׁחִין הִוא וְטִהֲרוֹ הַכֹּהֵן׃

24 When the skin of one's body sustains a burn by fire, and the patch from the burn is a discoloration, either white streaked with red, or white,

כד אוֹ בָשָׂר כִּי־יִהְיֶה בְעֹרוֹ מִכְוַת־אֵשׁ וְהָיְתָה מִחְיַת הַמִּכְוָה בַּהֶרֶת לְבָנָה אֲדַמְדֶּמֶת אוֹ לְבָנָה׃

25 the *Kohen* shall examine it. If some hair has turned white in the discoloration, which itself appears to go deeper than the skin, it is leprosy that has broken out in the burn. The *Kohen* shall pronounce him unclean; it is a leprous affection.

כה וְרָאָה אֹתָהּ הַכֹּהֵן וְהִנֵּה נֶהְפַּךְ שֵׂעָר לָבָן בַּבַּהֶרֶת וּמַרְאֶהָ עָמֹק מִן־הָעוֹר צָרַעַת הִוא בַּמִּכְוָה פָּרָחָה וְטִמֵּא אֹתוֹ הַכֹּהֵן נֶגַע צָרַעַת הִוא׃

26 But if the *Kohen* finds that there is no white hair in the discoloration, and that it is not lower than the rest of the skin, and it is faded, the *Kohen* shall isolate him for seven days.

כו וְאִם יִרְאֶנָּה הַכֹּהֵן וְהִנֵּה אֵין־בַּבַּהֶרֶת שֵׂעָר לָבָן וּשְׁפָלָה אֵינֶנָּה מִן־הָעוֹר וְהִוא כֵהָה וְהִסְגִּירוֹ הַכֹּהֵן שִׁבְעַת יָמִים׃

27 On the seventh day the *Kohen* shall examine him: if it has spread in the skin, the *Kohen* shall pronounce him unclean; it is a leprous affection.

כז וְרָאָהוּ הַכֹּהֵן בַּיּוֹם הַשְּׁבִיעִי אִם־פָּשֹׂה תִפְשֶׂה בָּעוֹר וְטִמֵּא הַכֹּהֵן אֹתוֹ נֶגַע צָרַעַת הִוא׃

28 But if the discoloration has remained stationary, not having spread on the skin, and it is faded, it is the swelling from the burn. The *Kohen* shall pronounce him clean, for it is the scar of the burn.

כח וְאִם־תַּחְתֶּיהָ תַעֲמֹד הַבַּהֶרֶת לֹא־פָשְׂתָה בָעוֹר וְהִוא כֵהָה שְׂאֵת הַמִּכְוָה הִוא וְטִהֲרוֹ הַכֹּהֵן כִּי־צָרֶבֶת הַמִּכְוָה הִוא׃

29 If a man or a woman has an affection on the head or in the beard,

כט וְאִישׁ אוֹ אִשָּׁה כִּי־יִהְיֶה בוֹ נָגַע בְּרֹאשׁ אוֹ בְזָקָן׃

Vayikra/Leviticus 13
Tazria

30 the *Kohen* shall examine the affection. If it appears to go deeper than the skin and there is thin yellow hair in it, the *Kohen* shall pronounce him unclean; it is a scall, a scaly eruption in the hair or beard.

31 But if the *Kohen* finds that the scall affection does not appear to go deeper than the skin, yet there is no black hair in it, the *Kohen* shall isolate the person with the scall affection for seven days.

32 On the seventh day the *Kohen* shall examine the affection. If the scall has not spread and no yellow hair has appeared in it, and the scall does not appear to go deeper than the skin,

33 the person with the scall shall shave himself, but without shaving the scall; the *Kohen* shall isolate him for another seven days.

34 On the seventh day the *Kohen* shall examine the scall. If the scall has not spread on the skin, and does not appear to go deeper than the skin, the *Kohen* shall pronounce him clean; he shall wash his clothes, and he shall be clean.

35 If, however, the scall should spread on the skin after he has been pronounced clean,

36 the *Kohen* shall examine him. If the scall has spread on the skin, the *Kohen* need not look for yellow hair: he is unclean.

37 But if the scall has remained unchanged in color, and black hair has grown in it, the scall is healed; he is clean. The *Kohen* shall pronounce him clean.

38 If a man or a woman has the skin of the body streaked with white discolorations,

39 and the *Kohen* sees that the discolorations on the skin of the body are of a dull white, it is a tetter broken out on the skin; he is clean.

40 If a man loses the hair of his head and becomes bald, he is clean.

41 If he loses the hair on the front part of his head and becomes bald at the forehead, he is clean.

42 But if a white affection streaked with red appears on the bald part in the front or at the back of the head, it is a scaly eruption that is spreading over the bald part in the front or at the back of the head.

ויקרא יג
תזריע

ל וְרָאָה הַכֹּהֵן אֶת־הַנֶּגַע וְהִנֵּה מַרְאֵהוּ עָמֹק מִן־הָעוֹר וּבוֹ שֵׂעָר צָהֹב דָּק וְטִמֵּא אֹתוֹ הַכֹּהֵן נֶתֶק הוּא צָרַעַת הָרֹאשׁ אוֹ הַזָּקָן הוּא׃

לא וְכִי־יִרְאֶה הַכֹּהֵן אֶת־נֶגַע הַנֶּתֶק וְהִנֵּה אֵין־מַרְאֵהוּ עָמֹק מִן־הָעוֹר וְשֵׂעָר שָׁחֹר אֵין בּוֹ וְהִסְגִּיר הַכֹּהֵן אֶת־נֶגַע הַנֶּתֶק שִׁבְעַת יָמִים׃

לב וְרָאָה הַכֹּהֵן אֶת־הַנֶּגַע בַּיּוֹם הַשְּׁבִיעִי וְהִנֵּה לֹא־פָשָׂה הַנֶּתֶק וְלֹא־הָיָה בוֹ שֵׂעָר צָהֹב וּמַרְאֵה הַנֶּתֶק אֵין עָמֹק מִן־הָעוֹר׃

לג וְהִתְגַּלָּח וְאֶת־הַנֶּתֶק לֹא יְגַלֵּחַ וְהִסְגִּיר הַכֹּהֵן אֶת־הַנֶּתֶק שִׁבְעַת יָמִים שֵׁנִית׃

לד וְרָאָה הַכֹּהֵן אֶת־הַנֶּתֶק בַּיּוֹם הַשְּׁבִיעִי וְהִנֵּה לֹא־פָשָׂה הַנֶּתֶק בָּעוֹר וּמַרְאֵהוּ אֵינֶנּוּ עָמֹק מִן־הָעוֹר וְטִהַר אֹתוֹ הַכֹּהֵן וְכִבֶּס בְּגָדָיו וְטָהֵר׃

לה וְאִם־פָּשֹׂה יִפְשֶׂה הַנֶּתֶק בָּעוֹר אַחֲרֵי טָהֳרָתוֹ׃

לו וְרָאָהוּ הַכֹּהֵן וְהִנֵּה פָּשָׂה הַנֶּתֶק בָּעוֹר לֹא־יְבַקֵּר הַכֹּהֵן לַשֵּׂעָר הַצָּהֹב טָמֵא הוּא׃

לז וְאִם־בְּעֵינָיו עָמַד הַנֶּתֶק וְשֵׂעָר שָׁחֹר צָמַח־בּוֹ נִרְפָּא הַנֶּתֶק טָהוֹר הוּא וְטִהֲרוֹ הַכֹּהֵן׃

לח וְאִישׁ אוֹ־אִשָּׁה כִּי־יִהְיֶה בְעוֹר־בְּשָׂרָם בֶּהָרֹת בֶּהָרֹת לְבָנֹת׃

לט וְרָאָה הַכֹּהֵן וְהִנֵּה בְעוֹר־בְּשָׂרָם בֶּהָרֹת כֵּהוֹת לְבָנֹת בֹּהַק הוּא פָּרַח בָּעוֹר טָהוֹר הוּא׃

מ וְאִישׁ כִּי יִמָּרֵט רֹאשׁוֹ קֵרֵחַ הוּא טָהוֹר הוּא׃

מא וְאִם מִפְּאַת פָּנָיו יִמָּרֵט רֹאשׁוֹ גִּבֵּחַ הוּא טָהוֹר הוּא׃

מב וְכִי־יִהְיֶה בַקָּרַחַת אוֹ בַגַּבַּחַת נֶגַע לָבָן אֲדַמְדָּם צָרַעַת פֹּרַחַת הִוא בְּקָרַחְתּוֹ אוֹ בְגַבַּחְתּוֹ׃

Vayikra/Leviticus 13
Tazria

ויקרא יג
תזריע

43 The *Kohen* shall examine him: if the swollen affection on the bald part in the front or at the back of his head is white streaked with red, like the leprosy of body skin in appearance,

מג וְרָאָה אֹתוֹ הַכֹּהֵן וְהִנֵּה שְׂאֵת־הַנֶּגַע לְבָנָה אֲדַמְדֶּמֶת בְּקָרַחְתּוֹ אוֹ בְגַבַּחְתּוֹ כְּמַרְאֵה צָרַעַת עוֹר בָּשָׂר׃

44 the man is leprous; he is unclean. The *Kohen* shall pronounce him unclean; he has the affection on his head.

מד אִישׁ־צָרוּעַ הוּא טָמֵא הוּא טַמֵּא יְטַמְּאֶנּוּ הַכֹּהֵן בְּרֹאשׁוֹ נִגְעוֹ׃

45 As for the person with a leprous affection, his clothes shall be rent, his head shall be left bare, and he shall cover over his upper lip; and he shall call out, "Unclean! Unclean!"

מה וְהַצָּרוּעַ אֲשֶׁר־בּוֹ הַנֶּגַע בְּגָדָיו יִהְיוּ פְרֻמִים וְרֹאשׁוֹ יִהְיֶה פָרוּעַ וְעַל־שָׂפָם יַעְטֶה וְטָמֵא טָמֵא יִקְרָא׃

46 He shall be unclean as long as the disease is on him. Being unclean, he shall dwell apart; his dwelling shall be outside the camp.

מו כָּל־יְמֵי אֲשֶׁר הַנֶּגַע בּוֹ יִטְמָא טָמֵא הוּא בָּדָד יֵשֵׁב מִחוּץ לַמַּחֲנֶה מוֹשָׁבוֹ׃

47 When an eruptive affection occurs in a cloth of wool or linen fabric,

מז וְהַבֶּגֶד כִּי־יִהְיֶה בוֹ נֶגַע צָרָעַת בְּבֶגֶד צֶמֶר אוֹ בְּבֶגֶד פִּשְׁתִּים׃

48 in the warp or in the woof of the linen or the wool, or in a skin or in anything made of skin;

מח אוֹ בִשְׁתִי אוֹ בְעֵרֶב לַפִּשְׁתִּים וְלַצָּמֶר אוֹ בְעוֹר אוֹ בְּכָל־מְלֶאכֶת עוֹר׃

49 if the affection in the cloth or the skin, in the warp or the woof, or in any article of skin, is streaky green or red, it is an eruptive affection. It shall be shown to the *Kohen*;

מט וְהָיָה הַנֶּגַע יְרַקְרַק אוֹ אֲדַמְדָּם בַּבֶּגֶד אוֹ בָעוֹר אוֹ־בַשְּׁתִי אוֹ־בָעֵרֶב אוֹ בְכָל־כְּלִי־עוֹר נֶגַע צָרַעַת הוּא וְהָרְאָה אֶת־הַכֹּהֵן׃

50 and the *Kohen*, after examining the affection, shall isolate the affected article for seven days.

נ וְרָאָה הַכֹּהֵן אֶת־הַנָּגַע וְהִסְגִּיר אֶת־הַנֶּגַע שִׁבְעַת יָמִים׃

51 On the seventh day he shall examine the affection: if the affection has spread in the cloth – whether in the warp or the woof, or in the skin, for whatever purpose the skin may be used – the affection is a malignant eruption; it is unclean.

נא וְרָאָה אֶת־הַנֶּגַע בַּיּוֹם הַשְּׁבִיעִי כִּי־פָשָׂה הַנֶּגַע בַּבֶּגֶד אוֹ־בַשְּׁתִי אוֹ־בָעֵרֶב אוֹ בָעוֹר לְכֹל אֲשֶׁר־יֵעָשֶׂה הָעוֹר לִמְלָאכָה צָרַעַת מַמְאֶרֶת הַנֶּגַע טָמֵא הוּא׃

52 The cloth – whether warp or woof in wool or linen, or any article of skin – in which the affection is found, shall be burned, for it is a malignant eruption; it shall be consumed in fire.

נב וְשָׂרַף אֶת־הַבֶּגֶד אוֹ אֶת־הַשְּׁתִי אוֹ אֶת־הָעֵרֶב בַּצֶּמֶר אוֹ בַפִּשְׁתִּים אוֹ אֶת־כָּל־כְּלִי הָעוֹר אֲשֶׁר־יִהְיֶה בוֹ הַנָּגַע כִּי־צָרַעַת מַמְאֶרֶת הִוא בָּאֵשׁ תִּשָּׂרֵף׃

53 But if the *Kohen* sees that the affection in the cloth – whether in warp or in woof, or in any article of skin – has not spread,

נג וְאִם יִרְאֶה הַכֹּהֵן וְהִנֵּה לֹא־פָשָׂה הַנֶּגַע בַּבֶּגֶד אוֹ בַשְּׁתִי אוֹ בָעֵרֶב אוֹ בְּכָל־כְּלִי־עוֹר׃

54 the *Kohen* shall order the affected article washed, and he shall isolate it for another seven days.

נד וְצִוָּה הַכֹּהֵן וְכִבְּסוּ אֵת אֲשֶׁר־בּוֹ הַנָּגַע וְהִסְגִּירוֹ שִׁבְעַת־יָמִים שֵׁנִית׃

55 And if, after the affected article has been washed, the *Kohen* sees that the affection has not changed color and that it has not spread, it is unclean. It shall be consumed in fire; it is a fret, whether on its inner side or on its outer side.

נה וְרָאָה הַכֹּהֵן אַחֲרֵי הֻכַּבֵּס אֶת־הַנֶּגַע וְהִנֵּה לֹא־הָפַךְ הַנֶּגַע אֶת־עֵינוֹ וְהַנֶּגַע לֹא־פָשָׂה טָמֵא הוּא בָּאֵשׁ תִּשְׂרְפֶנּוּ פְּחֶתֶת הִוא בְּקָרַחְתּוֹ אוֹ בְגַבַּחְתּוֹ׃

Vayikra/Leviticus 14
Metzora

ויקרא יד
מצורע

56 But if the *Kohen* sees that the affected part, after it has been washed, is faded, he shall tear it out from the cloth or skin, whether in the warp or in the woof;

נו וְאִם רָאָה הַכֹּהֵן וְהִנֵּה כֵּהָה הַנֶּגַע אַחֲרֵי הֻכַּבֵּס אֹתוֹ וְקָרַע אֹתוֹ מִן־הַבֶּגֶד אוֹ מִן־הָעוֹר אוֹ מִן־הַשְּׁתִי אוֹ מִן־הָעֵרֶב:

57 and if it occurs again in the cloth – whether in warp or in woof – or in any article of skin, it is a wild growth; the affected article shall be consumed in fire.

נז וְאִם־תֵּרָאֶה עוֹד בַּבֶּגֶד אוֹ־בַשְּׁתִי אוֹ־בָעֵרֶב אוֹ בְכָל־כְּלִי־עוֹר פֹּרַחַת הִוא בָּאֵשׁ תִּשְׂרְפֶנּוּ אֵת אֲשֶׁר־בּוֹ הַנָּגַע:

58 If, however, the affection disappears from the cloth – warp or woof – or from any article of skin that has been washed, it shall be washed again, and it shall be clean.

נח וְהַבֶּגֶד אוֹ־הַשְּׁתִי אוֹ־הָעֵרֶב אוֹ־כָל־כְּלִי הָעוֹר אֲשֶׁר תְּכַבֵּס וְסָר מֵהֶם הַנָּגַע וְכֻבַּס שֵׁנִית וְטָהֵר:

59 Such is the procedure for eruptive affections of cloth, woolen or linen, in warp or in woof, or of any article of skin, for pronouncing it clean or unclean.

נט זֹאת תּוֹרַת נֶגַע־צָרַעַת בֶּגֶד הַצֶּמֶר אוֹ הַפִּשְׁתִּים אוֹ הַשְּׁתִי אוֹ הָעֵרֶב אוֹ כָּל־כְּלִי־עוֹר לְטַהֲרוֹ אוֹ לְטַמְּאוֹ:

ZOT to-RAT ne-ga tza-RA-at BE-ged ha-TZE-mer O ha-pish-TEEM O ha-sh'-TEE O ha-AY-rev O kol k'-lee OR l'-ta-ha-RO O l'-ta-m'-O

14

1 *Hashem* spoke to *Moshe*, saying:

יד א וַיְדַבֵּר יְהוָה אֶל־מֹשֶׁה לֵּאמֹר:

2 This shall be the ritual for a leper at the time that he is to be cleansed. When it has been reported to the *Kohen*,

ב זֹאת תִּהְיֶה תּוֹרַת הַמְּצֹרָע בְּיוֹם טָהֳרָתוֹ וְהוּבָא אֶל־הַכֹּהֵן:

3 the *Kohen* shall go outside the camp. If the *Kohen* sees that the leper has been healed of his scaly affection,

ג וְיָצָא הַכֹּהֵן אֶל־מִחוּץ לַמַּחֲנֶה וְרָאָה הַכֹּהֵן וְהִנֵּה נִרְפָּא נֶגַע־הַצָּרַעַת מִן־הַצָּרוּעַ:

4 the *Kohen* shall order two live clean birds, cedar wood, crimson stuff, and hyssop to be brought for him who is to be cleansed.

ד וְצִוָּה הַכֹּהֵן וְלָקַח לַמִּטַּהֵר שְׁתֵּי־צִפֳּרִים חַיּוֹת טְהֹרוֹת וְעֵץ אֶרֶז וּשְׁנִי תוֹלַעַת וְאֵזֹב:

5 The *Kohen* shall order one of the birds slaughtered over fresh water in an earthen vessel;

ה וְצִוָּה הַכֹּהֵן וְשָׁחַט אֶת־הַצִּפּוֹר הָאֶחָת אֶל־כְּלִי־חֶרֶשׂ עַל־מַיִם חַיִּים:

6 and he shall take the live bird, along with the cedar wood, the crimson stuff, and the hyssop, and dip them together with the live bird in the blood of the bird that was slaughtered over the fresh water.

ו אֶת־הַצִּפֹּר הַחַיָּה יִקַּח אֹתָהּ וְאֶת־עֵץ הָאֶרֶז וְאֶת־שְׁנִי הַתּוֹלַעַת וְאֶת־הָאֵזֹב וְטָבַל אוֹתָם וְאֵת הַצִּפֹּר הַחַיָּה בְּדַם הַצִּפֹּר הַשְּׁחֻטָה עַל הַמַּיִם הַחַיִּים:

Ramban (1194–1270)

13:59 Such is the procedure for eruptive affections This chapter details with the spiritual disease known as tzaraat (צרעת), similar in presentation to leprosy, and the subsequent process of purification from this ailment. *Tzaraat* is understood to be a punishment for a number of sins, most famously the sin of *lashon hara* (לשון הרע), or 'slander.' *Tzaraat* could appear on a person's skin, clothing or home. Ramban emphasizes that it is absolutely supernatural for inanimate objects to display signs of illness. Although *lashon hara* is a sin not restricted to the Land of Israel, the miraculous spiritual malady of *tzaraat* could occur only in the land where God's presence is manifest so clearly. This demonstrates that the spiritual stakes are higher for those who live in the Holy Land. We must always remember that one is held more accountable, and one's actions have greater significance, in *Eretz Yisrael*.

Vayikra/Leviticus 14
Metzora

7 He shall then sprinkle it seven times on him who is to be cleansed of the eruption and cleanse him; and he shall set the live bird free in the open country.

8 The one to be cleansed shall wash his clothes, shave off all his hair, and bathe in water; then he shall be clean. After that he may enter the camp, but he must remain outside his tent seven days.

9 On the seventh day he shall shave off all his hair – of head, beard, and eyebrows. When he has shaved off all his hair, he shall wash his clothes and bathe his body in water; then he shall be clean.

10 On the eighth day he shall take two male lambs without blemish, one ewe lamb in its first year without blemish, three-tenths of a measure of choice flour with oil mixed in for a meal offering, and one *log* of oil.

11 These shall be presented before *Hashem*, with the man to be cleansed, at the entrance of the Tent of Meeting, by the *Kohen* who performs the cleansing.

12 The *Kohen* shall take one of the male lambs and offer it with the *log* of oil as a guilt offering, and he shall elevate them as an elevation offering before *Hashem*.

13 The lamb shall be slaughtered at the spot in the sacred area where the sin offering and the burnt offering are slaughtered. For the guilt offering, like the sin offering, goes to the *Kohen*; it is most holy.

14 The *Kohen* shall take some of the blood of the guilt offering, and the *Kohen* shall put it on the ridge of the right ear of him who is being cleansed, and on the thumb of his right hand, and on the big toe of his right foot.

15 The *Kohen* shall then take some of the *log* of oil and pour it into the palm of his own left hand.

16 And the *Kohen* shall dip his right finger in the oil that is in the palm of his left hand and sprinkle some of the oil with his finger seven times before *Hashem*.

17 Some of the oil left in his palm shall be put by the *Kohen* on the ridge of the right ear of the one being cleansed, on the thumb of his right hand, and on the big toe of his right foot – over the blood of the guilt offering.

Vayikra/Leviticus 14
Metzora

ויקרא יד
מצורע

#	English	Hebrew
18	The rest of the oil in his palm the *Kohen* shall put on the head of the one being cleansed. Thus the *Kohen* shall make expiation for him before *Hashem*.	יח וְהַנּוֹתָ֗ר בַּשֶּׁ֙מֶן֙ אֲשֶׁר֙ עַל־כַּ֣ף הַכֹּהֵ֔ן יִתֵּ֖ן עַל־רֹ֣אשׁ הַמִּטַּהֵ֑ר וְכִפֶּ֥ר עָלָ֛יו הַכֹּהֵ֖ן לִפְנֵ֥י יְהֹוָֽה׃
19	The *Kohen* shall then offer the sin offering and make expiation for the one being cleansed of his uncleanness. Last, the burnt offering shall be slaughtered,	יט וְעָשָׂ֤ה הַכֹּהֵן֙ אֶת־הַ֣חַטָּ֔את וְכִפֶּ֕ר עַל־הַמִּטַּהֵ֖ר מִטֻּמְאָת֑וֹ וְאַחַ֥ר יִשְׁחַ֖ט אֶת־הָעֹלָֽה׃
20	and the *Kohen* shall offer the burnt offering and the meal offering on the *Mizbayach*, and the *Kohen* shall make expiation for him. Then he shall be clean.	כ וְהֶעֱלָ֧ה הַכֹּהֵ֛ן אֶת־הָעֹלָ֥ה וְאֶת־הַמִּנְחָ֖ה הַמִּזְבֵּ֑חָה וְכִפֶּ֥ר עָלָ֛יו הַכֹּהֵ֖ן וְטָהֵֽר׃
21	If, however, he is poor and his means are insufficient, he shall take one male lamb for a guilt offering, to be elevated in expiation for him, one-tenth of a measure of choice flour with oil mixed in for a meal offering, and a *log* of oil;	כא וְאִם־דַּ֣ל ה֗וּא וְאֵ֣ין יָדוֹ֮ מַשֶּׂגֶת֒ וְ֠לָקַ֠ח כֶּ֣בֶשׂ אֶחָ֥ד אָשָׁ֛ם לִתְנוּפָ֖ה לְכַפֵּ֣ר עָלָ֑יו וְעִשָּׂר֨וֹן סֹ֜לֶת אֶחָ֨ד בָּל֥וּל בַּשֶּׁ֛מֶן לְמִנְחָ֖ה וְלֹ֥ג שָֽׁמֶן׃
22	and two turtledoves or two pigeons, depending on his means, the one to be the sin offering and the other the burnt offering.	כב וּשְׁתֵּ֣י תֹרִ֗ים א֤וֹ שְׁנֵי֙ בְּנֵ֣י יוֹנָ֔ה אֲשֶׁ֥ר תַּשִּׂ֖יג יָד֑וֹ וְהָיָ֤ה אֶחָד֙ חַטָּ֔את וְהָאֶחָ֖ד עֹלָֽה׃
23	On the eighth day of his cleansing he shall bring them to the *Kohen* at the entrance of the Tent of Meeting, before *Hashem*.	כג וְהֵבִ֨יא אֹתָ֜ם בַּיּ֧וֹם הַשְּׁמִינִ֛י לְטׇהֳרָת֖וֹ אֶל־הַכֹּהֵ֑ן אֶל־פֶּ֥תַח אֹֽהֶל־מוֹעֵ֖ד לִפְנֵ֥י יְהֹוָֽה׃
24	The *Kohen* shall take the lamb of guilt offering and the *log* of oil, and elevate them as an elevation offering before *Hashem*.	כד וְלָקַ֧ח הַכֹּהֵ֛ן אֶת־כֶּ֥בֶשׂ הָאָשָׁ֖ם וְאֶת־לֹ֣ג הַשָּׁ֑מֶן וְהֵנִ֨יף אֹתָ֧ם הַכֹּהֵ֛ן תְּנוּפָ֖ה לִפְנֵ֥י יְהֹוָֽה׃
25	When the lamb of guilt offering has been slaughtered, the *Kohen* shall take some of the blood of the guilt offering and put it on the ridge of the right ear of the one being cleansed, on the thumb of his right hand, and on the big toe of his right foot.	כה וְשָׁחַט֮ אֶת־כֶּ֣בֶשׂ הָאָשָׁם֒ וְלָקַ֤ח הַכֹּהֵן֙ מִדַּ֣ם הָֽאָשָׁ֔ם וְנָתַ֛ן עַל־תְּנ֥וּךְ אֹֽזֶן־הַמִּטַּהֵ֖ר הַיְמָנִ֑ית וְעַל־בֹּ֤הֶן יָדוֹ֙ הַיְמָנִ֔ית וְעַל־בֹּ֥הֶן רַגְל֖וֹ הַיְמָנִֽית׃
26	The *Kohen* shall then pour some of the oil into the palm of his own left hand,	כו וּמִן־הַשֶּׁ֖מֶן יִצֹ֣ק הַכֹּהֵ֑ן עַל־כַּ֥ף הַכֹּהֵ֖ן הַשְּׂמָאלִֽית׃
27	and with the finger of his right hand the *Kohen* shall sprinkle some of the oil that is in the palm of his left hand seven times before *Hashem*.	כז וְהִזָּ֤ה הַכֹּהֵן֙ בְּאֶצְבָּע֣וֹ הַיְמָנִ֔ית מִן־הַשֶּׁ֕מֶן אֲשֶׁ֥ר עַל־כַּפּ֖וֹ הַשְּׂמָאלִ֑ית שֶׁ֥בַע פְּעָמִ֖ים לִפְנֵ֥י יְהֹוָֽה׃
28	Some of the oil in his palm shall be put by the *Kohen* on the ridge of the right ear of the one being cleansed, on the thumb of his right hand, and on the big toe of his right foot, over the same places as the blood of the guilt offering;	כח וְנָתַ֨ן הַכֹּהֵ֜ן מִן־הַשֶּׁ֣מֶן ׀ אֲשֶׁ֣ר עַל־כַּפּ֗וֹ עַל־תְּנ֞וּךְ אֹ֤זֶן הַמִּטַּהֵר֙ הַיְמָנִ֔ית וְעַל־בֹּ֤הֶן יָדוֹ֙ הַיְמָנִ֔ית וְעַל־בֹּ֥הֶן רַגְל֖וֹ הַיְמָנִ֑ית עַל־מְק֖וֹם דַּ֥ם הָאָשָֽׁם׃
29	and what is left of the oil in his palm the *Kohen* shall put on the head of the one being cleansed, to make expiation for him before *Hashem*.	כט וְהַנּוֹתָ֗ר מִן־הַשֶּׁ֙מֶן֙ אֲשֶׁר֙ עַל־כַּ֣ף הַכֹּהֵ֔ן יִתֵּ֖ן עַל־רֹ֣אשׁ הַמִּטַּהֵ֑ר לְכַפֵּ֥ר עָלָ֖יו לִפְנֵ֥י יְהֹוָֽה׃

Vayikra/Leviticus 14
Metzora

ויקרא יד
מצורע

30 He shall then offer one of the turtledoves or pigeons, depending on his means

ל וְעָשָׂה אֶת־הָאֶחָד מִן־הַתֹּרִים אוֹ מִן־בְּנֵי הַיּוֹנָה מֵאֲשֶׁר תַּשִּׂיג יָדוֹ:

31 whichever he can afford – the one as a sin offering and the other as a burnt offering, together with the meal offering. Thus the *Kohen* shall make expiation before *Hashem* for the one being cleansed.

לא אֵת אֲשֶׁר־תַּשִּׂיג יָדוֹ אֶת־הָאֶחָד חַטָּאת וְאֶת־הָאֶחָד עֹלָה עַל־הַמִּנְחָה וְכִפֶּר הַכֹּהֵן עַל הַמִּטַּהֵר לִפְנֵי יְהוָה:

32 Such is the ritual for him who has a scaly affection and whose means for his cleansing are limited.

לב זֹאת תּוֹרַת אֲשֶׁר־בּוֹ נֶגַע צָרָעַת אֲשֶׁר לֹא־תַשִּׂיג יָדוֹ בְּטָהֳרָתוֹ:

33 *Hashem* spoke to *Moshe* and *Aharon*, saying:

לג וַיְדַבֵּר יְהוָה אֶל־מֹשֶׁה וְאֶל־אַהֲרֹן לֵאמֹר:

34 When you enter the land of Canaan that I give you as a possession, and I inflict an eruptive plague upon a house in the land you possess,

לד כִּי תָבֹאוּ אֶל־אֶרֶץ כְּנַעַן אֲשֶׁר אֲנִי נֹתֵן לָכֶם לַאֲחֻזָּה וְנָתַתִּי נֶגַע צָרַעַת בְּבֵית אֶרֶץ אֲחֻזַּתְכֶם:

KEE ta-VO-u el E-retz k'-NA-an a-SHER a-NEE no-TAYN la-KHEM la-a-khu-ZAH v'-na-ta-TEE NE-ga tza-RA-at b'-VAYT E-retz a-khu-zat-KHEM

35 the owner of the house shall come and tell the *Kohen*, saying, "Something like a plague has appeared upon my house."

לה וּבָא אֲשֶׁר־לוֹ הַבַּיִת וְהִגִּיד לַכֹּהֵן לֵאמֹר כְּנֶגַע נִרְאָה לִי בַּבָּיִת:

36 The *Kohen* shall order the house cleared before the *Kohen* enters to examine the plague, so that nothing in the house may become unclean; after that the *Kohen* shall enter to examine the house.

לו וְצִוָּה הַכֹּהֵן וּפִנּוּ אֶת־הַבַּיִת בְּטֶרֶם יָבֹא הַכֹּהֵן לִרְאוֹת אֶת־הַנֶּגַע וְלֹא יִטְמָא כָּל־אֲשֶׁר בַּבָּיִת וְאַחַר כֵּן יָבֹא הַכֹּהֵן לִרְאוֹת אֶת־הַבָּיִת:

37 If, when he examines the plague, the plague in the walls of the house is found to consist of greenish or reddish streaks that appear to go deep into the wall,

לז וְרָאָה אֶת־הַנֶּגַע וְהִנֵּה הַנֶּגַע בְּקִירֹת הַבַּיִת שְׁקַעֲרוּרֹת יְרַקְרַקֹּת אוֹ אֲדַמְדַּמֹּת וּמַרְאֵיהֶן שָׁפָל מִן־הַקִּיר:

38 the *Kohen* shall come out of the house to the entrance of the house, and close up the house for seven days.

לח וְיָצָא הַכֹּהֵן מִן־הַבַּיִת אֶל־פֶּתַח הַבָּיִת וְהִסְגִּיר אֶת־הַבַּיִת שִׁבְעַת יָמִים:

14:34 When you enter the land of *Canaan* that I give you as a possession In addition to the sin of *lashon hara*, speaking negatively about others, lacking generosity and being unwilling to give to other could also cause *tzaraat* to appear on one's home. The *Kli Yakar* points out that once they took possession of the land, the Israelites found many homes filled with riches. If they failed to share what they had, *Hashem* would afflict those homes. *Hashem* bequeathed the Jewish people the Land of Israel with the expectation that they would share its bounty with others. From its inception, the contemporary State of Israel internalized this message; it is often the first to volunteer its resources and knowledge to help countries in need. In his book *Altneuland*, Theodor Herzl wrote that following the establishment of a Jewish national home, Jews would come to the aid of the suffering people in Africa, whose "problem, in all its horror, only a Jew can fathom." Israel's founding leaders took this admonition to heart and, in 1958, Golda Meir, then Israel's Foreign Minister, created a department whose mission was to help Africa overcome problems of water, irrigation, agriculture and education.

Theodor Herzl (1860–1904)

Vayikra/Leviticus 14
Metzora

39 On the seventh day the *Kohen* shall return. If he sees that the plague has spread on the walls of the house,

40 the *Kohen* shall order the stones with the plague in them to be pulled out and cast outside the city into an unclean place.

41 The house shall be scraped inside all around, and the coating that is scraped off shall be dumped outside the city in an unclean place.

42 They shall take other stones and replace those stones with them, and take other coating and plaster the house.

43 If the plague again breaks out in the house, after the stones have been pulled out and after the house has been scraped and replastered,

44 the *Kohen* shall come to examine: if the plague has spread in the house, it is a malignant eruption in the house; it is unclean.

45 The house shall be torn down – its stones and timber and all the coating on the house – and taken to an unclean place outside the city.

46 Whoever enters the house while it is closed up shall be unclean until evening.

47 Whoever sleeps in the house must wash his clothes, and whoever eats in the house must wash his clothes.

48 If, however, the *Kohen* comes and sees that the plague has not spread in the house after the house was replastered, the *Kohen* shall pronounce the house clean, for the plague has healed.

49 To purge the house, he shall take two birds, cedar wood, crimson stuff, and hyssop.

50 He shall slaughter the one bird over fresh water in an earthen vessel.

51 He shall take the cedar wood, the hyssop, the crimson stuff, and the live bird, and dip them in the blood of the slaughtered bird and the fresh water, and sprinkle on the house seven times.

ויקרא יד
מצורע

לט וְשָׁב הַכֹּהֵן בַּיּוֹם הַשְּׁבִיעִי וְרָאָה וְהִנֵּה פָּשָׂה הַנֶּגַע בְּקִירֹת הַבָּיִת:

מ וְצִוָּה הַכֹּהֵן וְחִלְּצוּ אֶת־הָאֲבָנִים אֲשֶׁר בָּהֵן הַנָּגַע וְהִשְׁלִיכוּ אֶתְהֶן אֶל־מִחוּץ לָעִיר אֶל־מָקוֹם טָמֵא:

מא וְאֶת־הַבַּיִת יַקְצִעַ מִבַּיִת סָבִיב וְשָׁפְכוּ אֶת־הֶעָפָר אֲשֶׁר הִקְצוּ אֶל־מִחוּץ לָעִיר אֶל־מָקוֹם טָמֵא:

מב וְלָקְחוּ אֲבָנִים אֲחֵרוֹת וְהֵבִיאוּ אֶל־תַּחַת הָאֲבָנִים וְעָפָר אַחֵר יִקַּח וְטָח אֶת־הַבָּיִת:

מג וְאִם־יָשׁוּב הַנֶּגַע וּפָרַח בַּבַּיִת אַחַר חִלֵּץ אֶת־הָאֲבָנִים וְאַחֲרֵי הִקְצוֹת אֶת־הַבַּיִת וְאַחֲרֵי הִטּוֹחַ:

מד וּבָא הַכֹּהֵן וְרָאָה וְהִנֵּה פָּשָׂה הַנֶּגַע בַּבָּיִת צָרַעַת מַמְאֶרֶת הִוא בַּבַּיִת טָמֵא הוּא:

מה וְנָתַץ אֶת־הַבַּיִת אֶת־אֲבָנָיו וְאֶת־עֵצָיו וְאֵת כָּל־עֲפַר הַבָּיִת וְהוֹצִיא אֶל־מִחוּץ לָעִיר אֶל־מָקוֹם טָמֵא:

מו וְהַבָּא אֶל־הַבַּיִת כָּל־יְמֵי הִסְגִּיר אֹתוֹ יִטְמָא עַד־הָעָרֶב:

מז וְהַשֹּׁכֵב בַּבַּיִת יְכַבֵּס אֶת־בְּגָדָיו וְהָאֹכֵל בַּבַּיִת יְכַבֵּס אֶת־בְּגָדָיו:

מח וְאִם־בֹּא יָבֹא הַכֹּהֵן וְרָאָה וְהִנֵּה לֹא־פָשָׂה הַנֶּגַע בַּבַּיִת אַחֲרֵי הִטֹּחַ אֶת־הַבָּיִת וְטִהַר הַכֹּהֵן אֶת־הַבַּיִת כִּי נִרְפָּא הַנָּגַע:

מט וְלָקַח לְחַטֵּא אֶת־הַבַּיִת שְׁתֵּי צִפֳּרִים וְעֵץ אֶרֶז וּשְׁנִי תוֹלַעַת וְאֵזֹב:

נ וְשָׁחַט אֶת־הַצִּפֹּר הָאֶחָת אֶל־כְּלִי־חֶרֶשׂ עַל־מַיִם חַיִּים:

נא וְלָקַח אֶת־עֵץ־הָאֶרֶז וְאֶת־הָאֵזֹב וְאֵת שְׁנִי הַתּוֹלַעַת וְאֵת הַצִּפֹּר הַחַיָּה וְטָבַל אֹתָם בְּדַם הַצִּפֹּר הַשְּׁחוּטָה וּבַמַּיִם הַחַיִּים וְהִזָּה אֶל־הַבַּיִת שֶׁבַע פְּעָמִים:

Vayikra/Leviticus 15
Metzora

ויקרא טו
מצורע

52 Having purged the house with the blood of the bird, the fresh water, the live bird, the cedar wood, the hyssop, and the crimson stuff,

נב וְחִטֵּא אֶת־הַבַּיִת בְּדַם הַצִּפּוֹר וּבַמַּיִם הַחַיִּים וּבַצִּפֹּר הַחַיָּה וּבְעֵץ הָאֶרֶז וּבָאֵזֹב וּבִשְׁנִי הַתּוֹלָעַת׃

53 he shall set the live bird free outside the city in the open country. Thus he shall make expiation for the house, and it shall be clean.

נג וְשִׁלַּח אֶת־הַצִּפֹּר הַחַיָּה אֶל־מִחוּץ לָעִיר אֶל־פְּנֵי הַשָּׂדֶה וְכִפֶּר עַל־הַבַּיִת וְטָהֵר׃

54 Such is the ritual for every eruptive affection – for scalls,

נד זֹאת הַתּוֹרָה לְכָל־נֶגַע הַצָּרַעַת וְלַנָּתֶק׃

55 for an eruption on a cloth or a house,

נה וּלְצָרַעַת הַבֶּגֶד וְלַבָּיִת׃

56 for swellings, for rashes, or for discolorations

נו וְלַשְׂאֵת וְלַסַּפַּחַת וְלַבֶּהָרֶת׃

57 to determine when they are unclean and when they are clean. Such is the ritual concerning eruptions.

נז לְהוֹרֹת בְּיוֹם הַטָּמֵא וּבְיוֹם הַטָּהֹר זֹאת תּוֹרַת הַצָּרָעַת׃

15 1 *Hashem* spoke to *Moshe* and *Aharon*, saying:

טו א וַיְדַבֵּר יְהוָה אֶל־מֹשֶׁה וְאֶל־אַהֲרֹן לֵאמֹר׃

2 Speak to *B'nei Yisrael* and say to them: When any man has a discharge issuing from his member, he is unclean.

ב דַּבְּרוּ אֶל־בְּנֵי יִשְׂרָאֵל וַאֲמַרְתֶּם אֲלֵהֶם אִישׁ אִישׁ כִּי יִהְיֶה זָב מִבְּשָׂרוֹ זוֹבוֹ טָמֵא הוּא׃

3 The uncleanness from his discharge shall mean the following – whether his member runs with the discharge or is stopped up so that there is no discharge, his uncleanness means this:

ג וְזֹאת תִּהְיֶה טֻמְאָתוֹ בְּזוֹבוֹ רָר בְּשָׂרוֹ אֶת־זוֹבוֹ אוֹ־הֶחְתִּים בְּשָׂרוֹ מִזּוֹבוֹ טֻמְאָתוֹ הִוא׃

4 Any bedding on which the one with the discharge lies shall be unclean, and every object on which he sits shall be unclean.

ד כָּל־הַמִּשְׁכָּב אֲשֶׁר יִשְׁכַּב עָלָיו הַזָּב יִטְמָא וְכָל־הַכְּלִי אֲשֶׁר־יֵשֵׁב עָלָיו יִטְמָא׃

5 Anyone who touches his bedding shall wash his clothes, bathe in water, and remain unclean until evening.

ה וְאִישׁ אֲשֶׁר יִגַּע בְּמִשְׁכָּבוֹ יְכַבֵּס בְּגָדָיו וְרָחַץ בַּמַּיִם וְטָמֵא עַד־הָעָרֶב׃

6 Whoever sits on an object on which the one with the discharge has sat shall wash his clothes, bathe in water, and remain unclean until evening.

ו וְהַיֹּשֵׁב עַל־הַכְּלִי אֲשֶׁר־יֵשֵׁב עָלָיו הַזָּב יְכַבֵּס בְּגָדָיו וְרָחַץ בַּמַּיִם וְטָמֵא עַד־הָעָרֶב׃

7 Whoever touches the body of the one with the discharge shall wash his clothes, bathe in water, and remain unclean until evening.

ז וְהַנֹּגֵעַ בִּבְשַׂר הַזָּב יְכַבֵּס בְּגָדָיו וְרָחַץ בַּמַּיִם וְטָמֵא עַד־הָעָרֶב׃

8 If one with a discharge spits on one who is clean, the latter shall wash his clothes, bathe in water, and remain unclean until evening.

ח וְכִי־יָרֹק הַזָּב בַּטָּהוֹר וְכִבֶּס בְּגָדָיו וְרָחַץ בַּמַּיִם וְטָמֵא עַד־הָעָרֶב׃

9 Any means for riding that one with a discharge has mounted shall be unclean;

ט וְכָל־הַמֶּרְכָּב אֲשֶׁר יִרְכַּב עָלָיו הַזָּב יִטְמָא׃

10 whoever touches anything that was under him shall be unclean until evening; and whoever carries such things shall wash his clothes, bathe in water, and remain unclean until evening.

י וְכָל־הַנֹּגֵעַ בְּכֹל אֲשֶׁר יִהְיֶה תַחְתָּיו יִטְמָא עַד־הָעָרֶב וְהַנּוֹשֵׂא אוֹתָם יְכַבֵּס בְּגָדָיו וְרָחַץ בַּמַּיִם וְטָמֵא עַד־הָעָרֶב׃

Vayikra/Leviticus 15
Metzora

ויקרא טו
מצורע

11 If one with a discharge, without having rinsed his hands in water, touches another person, that person shall wash his clothes, bathe in water, and remain unclean until evening.

וְכֹ֨ל אֲשֶׁ֤ר יִגַּע־בּוֹ֙ הַזָּ֔ב וְיָדָ֖יו לֹא־שָׁטַ֣ף בַּמָּ֑יִם וְכִבֶּ֧ס בְּגָדָ֛יו וְרָחַ֥ץ בַּמַּ֖יִם וְטָמֵ֥א עַד־הָעָֽרֶב׃ יא

12 An earthen vessel that one with a discharge touches shall be broken; and any wooden implement shall be rinsed with water.

וּכְלִי־חֶ֛רֶשׂ אֲשֶׁר־יִגַּע־בּ֥וֹ הַזָּ֖ב יִשָּׁבֵ֑ר וְכָל־כְּלִי־עֵ֔ץ יִשָּׁטֵ֖ף בַּמָּֽיִם׃ יב

13 When one with a discharge becomes clean of his discharge, he shall count off seven days for his cleansing, wash his clothes, and bathe his body in fresh water; then he shall be clean.

וְכִֽי־יִטְהַ֤ר הַזָּב֙ מִזּוֹב֔וֹ וְסָ֨פַר ל֜וֹ שִׁבְעַ֥ת יָמִ֛ים לְטָהֳרָת֖וֹ וְכִבֶּ֣ס בְּגָדָ֑יו וְרָחַ֧ץ בְּשָׂר֛וֹ בְּמַ֥יִם חַיִּ֖ים וְטָהֵֽר׃ יג

v'-khee yit-HAR ha-ZAV mi-zo-VO v'-SA-far LO shiv-AT ya-MEEM l'-ta-ho-ra-TO v'-khi-BES b'-ga-DAV v'-ra-KHATZ b'-sa-RO b'-MA-yim kha-YEEM v'-ta-HAYR

14 On the eighth day he shall take two turtledoves or two pigeons and come before *Hashem* at the entrance of the Tent of Meeting and give them to the *Kohen*.

וּבַיּ֣וֹם הַשְּׁמִינִ֗י יִֽקַּֽח־לוֹ֙ שְׁתֵּ֣י תֹרִ֔ים א֥וֹ שְׁנֵ֖י בְּנֵ֣י יוֹנָ֑ה וּבָ֣א ׀ לִפְנֵ֣י יְהֹוָ֗ה אֶל־פֶּ֙תַח֙ אֹ֣הֶל מוֹעֵ֔ד וּנְתָנָ֖ם אֶל־הַכֹּהֵֽן׃ יד

15 The *Kohen* shall offer them, the one as a sin offering and the other as a burnt offering. Thus the *Kohen* shall make expiation on his behalf, for his discharge, before *Hashem*.

וְעָשָׂ֤ה אֹתָם֙ הַכֹּהֵ֔ן אֶחָ֥ד חַטָּ֖את וְהָאֶחָ֣ד עֹלָ֑ה וְכִפֶּ֨ר עָלָ֧יו הַכֹּהֵ֛ן לִפְנֵ֥י יְהֹוָ֖ה מִזּוֹבֽוֹ׃ טו

16 When a man has an emission of semen, he shall bathe his whole body in water and remain unclean until evening.

וְאִ֕ישׁ כִּֽי־תֵצֵ֥א מִמֶּ֖נּוּ שִׁכְבַת־זָ֑רַע וְרָחַ֥ץ בַּמַּ֛יִם אֶת־כָּל־בְּשָׂר֖וֹ וְטָמֵ֥א עַד־הָעָֽרֶב׃ טז

17 All cloth or leather on which semen falls shall be washed in water and remain unclean until evening.

וְכָל־בֶּ֣גֶד וְכָל־ע֔וֹר אֲשֶׁר־יִהְיֶ֥ה עָלָ֖יו שִׁכְבַת־זָ֑רַע וְכֻבַּ֥ס בַּמַּ֖יִם וְטָמֵ֥א עַד־הָעָֽרֶב׃ יז

18 And if a man has carnal relations with a woman, they shall bathe in water and remain unclean until evening.

וְאִשָּׁ֕ה אֲשֶׁ֨ר יִשְׁכַּ֥ב אִ֛ישׁ אֹתָ֖הּ שִׁכְבַת־זָ֑רַע וְרָחֲצ֣וּ בַמַּ֔יִם וְטָמְא֖וּ עַד־הָעָֽרֶב׃ יח

19 When a woman has a discharge, her discharge being blood from her body, she shall remain in her impurity seven days; whoever touches her shall be unclean until evening.

וְאִשָּׁה֙ כִּֽי־תִהְיֶ֣ה זָבָ֔ה דָּ֛ם יִהְיֶ֥ה זֹבָ֖הּ בִּבְשָׂרָ֑הּ שִׁבְעַ֤ת יָמִים֙ תִּהְיֶ֣ה בְנִדָּתָ֔הּ וְכָל־הַנֹּגֵ֥עַ בָּ֖הּ יִטְמָ֥א עַד־הָעָֽרֶב׃ יט

Ancient ritual bath found in Qumran

15:13 And bathe his body in fresh water Chapter 15 discusses the different kinds of impurity that occur as a result of certain types of bodily discharges. As part of the purification process, the person who has become impure must immerse in a ritual bath. This immersion signifies an elevation in spiritual status, and it is no coincidence that water is the means through which this elevation occurs. Water is the source of life, and so it is appropriate to immerse in it during the process of spiritual rebirth and renewal. In addition, the fluid nature of water symbolizes that as spiritual beings, we are never fixed in one place. In life we have ups and downs, but there is always the potential for further growth.

Vayikra/Leviticus 15
Metzora

ויקרא טו
מצורע

20 Anything that she lies on during her impurity shall be unclean; and anything that she sits on shall be unclean.

כ וְכֹל אֲשֶׁר תִּשְׁכַּב עָלָיו בְּנִדָּתָהּ יִטְמָא וְכֹל אֲשֶׁר־תֵּשֵׁב עָלָיו יִטְמָא׃

21 Anyone who touches her bedding shall wash his clothes, bathe in water, and remain unclean until evening;

כא וְכָל־הַנֹּגֵעַ בְּמִשְׁכָּבָהּ יְכַבֵּס בְּגָדָיו וְרָחַץ בַּמַּיִם וְטָמֵא עַד־הָעָרֶב׃

22 and anyone who touches any object on which she has sat shall wash his clothes, bathe in water, and remain unclean until evening.

כב וְכָל־הַנֹּגֵעַ בְּכָל־כְּלִי אֲשֶׁר־תֵּשֵׁב עָלָיו יְכַבֵּס בְּגָדָיו וְרָחַץ בַּמַּיִם וְטָמֵא עַד־הָעָרֶב׃

23 Be it the bedding or be it the object on which she has sat, on touching it he shall be unclean until evening.

כג וְאִם עַל־הַמִּשְׁכָּב הוּא אוֹ עַל־הַכְּלִי אֲשֶׁר־הִוא יֹשֶׁבֶת־עָלָיו בְּנָגְעוֹ־בוֹ יִטְמָא עַד־הָעָרֶב׃

24 And if a man lies with her, her impurity is communicated to him; he shall be unclean seven days, and any bedding on which he lies shall become unclean.

כד וְאִם שָׁכֹב יִשְׁכַּב אִישׁ אֹתָהּ וּתְהִי נִדָּתָהּ עָלָיו וְטָמֵא שִׁבְעַת יָמִים וְכָל־הַמִּשְׁכָּב אֲשֶׁר־יִשְׁכַּב עָלָיו יִטְמָא׃

25 When a woman has had a discharge of blood for many days, not at the time of her impurity, or when she has a discharge beyond her period of impurity, she shall be unclean, as though at the time of her impurity, as long as her discharge lasts.

כה וְאִשָּׁה כִּי־יָזוּב זוֹב דָּמָהּ יָמִים רַבִּים בְּלֹא עֶת־נִדָּתָהּ אוֹ כִי־תָזוּב עַל־נִדָּתָהּ כָּל־יְמֵי זוֹב טֻמְאָתָהּ כִּימֵי נִדָּתָהּ תִּהְיֶה טְמֵאָה הִוא׃

26 Any bedding on which she lies while her discharge lasts shall be for her like bedding during her impurity; and any object on which she sits shall become unclean, as it does during her impurity:

כו כָּל־הַמִּשְׁכָּב אֲשֶׁר־תִּשְׁכַּב עָלָיו כָּל־יְמֵי זוֹבָהּ כְּמִשְׁכַּב נִדָּתָהּ יִהְיֶה־לָּהּ וְכָל־הַכְּלִי אֲשֶׁר תֵּשֵׁב עָלָיו טָמֵא יִהְיֶה כְּטֻמְאַת נִדָּתָהּ׃

27 whoever touches them shall be unclean; he shall wash his clothes, bathe in water, and remain unclean until evening.

כז וְכָל־הַנּוֹגֵעַ בָּם יִטְמָא וְכִבֶּס בְּגָדָיו וְרָחַץ בַּמַּיִם וְטָמֵא עַד־הָעָרֶב׃

28 When she becomes clean of her discharge, she shall count off seven days, and after that she shall be clean.

כח וְאִם־טָהֲרָה מִזּוֹבָהּ וְסָפְרָה לָּהּ שִׁבְעַת יָמִים וְאַחַר תִּטְהָר׃

29 On the eighth day she shall take two turtledoves or two pigeons, and bring them to the *Kohen* at the entrance of the Tent of Meeting.

כט וּבַיּוֹם הַשְּׁמִינִי תִּקַּח־לָהּ שְׁתֵּי תֹרִים אוֹ שְׁנֵי בְּנֵי יוֹנָה וְהֵבִיאָה אוֹתָם אֶל־הַכֹּהֵן אֶל־פֶּתַח אֹהֶל מוֹעֵד׃

30 The *Kohen* shall offer the one as a sin offering and the other as a burnt offering; and the *Kohen* shall make expiation on her behalf, for her unclean discharge, before *Hashem*.

ל וְעָשָׂה הַכֹּהֵן אֶת־הָאֶחָד חַטָּאת וְאֶת־הָאֶחָד עֹלָה וְכִפֶּר עָלֶיהָ הַכֹּהֵן לִפְנֵי יְהוָה מִזּוֹב טֻמְאָתָהּ׃

31 You shall put the Israelites on guard against their uncleanness, lest they die through their uncleanness by defiling My *Mishkan* which is among them.

לא וְהִזַּרְתֶּם אֶת־בְּנֵי־יִשְׂרָאֵל מִטֻּמְאָתָם וְלֹא יָמֻתוּ בְּטֻמְאָתָם בְּטַמְּאָם אֶת־מִשְׁכָּנִי אֲשֶׁר בְּתוֹכָם׃

v'-hiz-har-TEM et b'-nay yis-ra-AYL mi-tum-a-TAM v'-LO ya-MU-tu b'-tum-a-TAM b'-ta-m'-AM et mish-ka-NEE a-SHER b'-to-KHAM

Vayikra/Leviticus 16
Acharei Mot

ויקרא טז
אחרי מות

32 Such is the ritual concerning him who has a discharge: concerning him who has an emission of semen and becomes unclean thereby,

לב זֹאת תּוֹרַת הַזָּב וַאֲשֶׁר תֵּצֵא מִמֶּנּוּ שִׁכְבַת־זֶרַע לְטָמְאָה־בָהּ:

33 and concerning her who is in menstrual infirmity, and concerning anyone, male or female, who has a discharge, and concerning a man who lies with an unclean woman.

לג וְהַדָּוָה בְּנִדָּתָהּ וְהַזָּב אֶת־זוֹבוֹ לַזָּכָר וְלַנְּקֵבָה וּלְאִישׁ אֲשֶׁר יִשְׁכַּב עִם־טְמֵאָה:

16

1 *Hashem* spoke to *Moshe* after the death of the two sons of *Aharon* who died when they drew too close to the presence of *Hashem*.

טז א וַיְדַבֵּר יְהֹוָה אֶל־מֹשֶׁה אַחֲרֵי מוֹת שְׁנֵי בְּנֵי אַהֲרֹן בְּקָרְבָתָם לִפְנֵי־יְהֹוָה וַיָּמֻתוּ:

2 *Hashem* said to *Moshe*: Tell your brother *Aharon* that he is not to come at will into the Shrine behind the curtain, in front of the cover that is upon the ark, lest he die; for I appear in the cloud over the cover.

ב וַיֹּאמֶר יְהֹוָה אֶל־מֹשֶׁה דַּבֵּר אֶל־אַהֲרֹן אָחִיךָ וְאַל־יָבֹא בְכָל־עֵת אֶל־הַקֹּדֶשׁ מִבֵּית לַפָּרֹכֶת אֶל־פְּנֵי הַכַּפֹּרֶת אֲשֶׁר עַל־הָאָרֹן וְלֹא יָמוּת כִּי בֶּעָנָן אֵרָאֶה עַל־הַכַּפֹּרֶת:

va-YO-mer a-do-NAI el mo-SHEH da-BAYR el a-ha-RON a-KHEE-kha v'-al ya-VO v-khol AYT el ha-KO-desh mi-BAYT la-pa-RO-khet el p'-NAY ha-ka-PO-ret a-SHER al ha-a-RON v'-LO ya-MUT kee be-a-NAN ay-ra-EH al ha-ka-PO-ret

3 Thus only shall *Aharon* enter the Shrine: with a bull of the herd for a sin offering and a ram for a burnt offering.

ג בְּזֹאת יָבֹא אַהֲרֹן אֶל־הַקֹּדֶשׁ בְּפַר בֶּן־בָּקָר לְחַטָּאת וְאַיִל לְעֹלָה:

4 He shall be dressed in a sacral linen tunic, with linen breeches next to his flesh, and be girt with a linen sash, and he shall wear a linen turban. They are sacral vestments; he shall bathe his body in water and then put them on.

ד כְּתֹנֶת־בַּד קֹדֶשׁ יִלְבָּשׁ וּמִכְנְסֵי־בַד יִהְיוּ עַל־בְּשָׂרוֹ וּבְאַבְנֵט בַּד יַחְגֹּר וּבְמִצְנֶפֶת בַּד יִצְנֹף בִּגְדֵי־קֹדֶשׁ הֵם וְרָחַץ בַּמַּיִם אֶת־בְּשָׂרוֹ וּלְבֵשָׁם:

k'-to-net BAD KO-desh yil-BASH u-mikh-n'-say VAD yih-YU al b'-sa-RO uv-av-NAYT BAD yakh-GOR u-v'-mitz-NE-fet BAD yitz-NOF big-day KO-desh HAYM v'-ra-KHATZ ba-MA-yim et b'-sa-RO ul-vay-SHAM

Ariel view of the Temple Mount

16:2 He is not to come at will into the Shrine behind the curtain The service detailed in this chapter is performed by the *Kohen Gadol*, 'high priest,' in the Holy of Holies on *Yom Kippur*, the 'Day of Atonement.' This unique service represents a pinnacle of holiness, as it brings the holiest person to the holiest place on the holiest day of the year. Tradition tells us that the world was created from the stone that stands at the location of the Holy of Holies on the Temple Mount. When the *Kohen Gadol* enters this same spot, he atones for the sins of mankind beginning with the time of *Adam* and the creation of the world. *Adam* himself was formed from the earth at the spot of the *Mizbayach*, close to the area of the Holy of Holies. To this day, people from all over the world are drawn to the Temple Mount, the place from which all of mankind originated. Yet, on account of political pressures, currently only Muslims are granted full access to the Temple Mount; Jews are not even allowed to utter words of prayer at this holy site. We pray for the day when this holy mountain is restored to its vital role as a place of prayer for all nations.

16:4 He shall be dressed in a sacral linen tunic On a regular day the *Kohen Gadol* wears eight garments, four of which are decorated with gold. However, when he enters the Holy of Holies on *Yom Kippur* he wears only four white linen garments. The simplicity of his attire portrays feelings of humility as he approaches *Hashem* on the holiest day of the year, and the white color is symbolic of forgiveness. As the *Kohen Gadol* stands before God and begs forgiveness for himself, his family, and the entire nation, his clothing reminds him that he is at the mercy of God's benevolence, yet also instills confidence that God, in His compassion, will forgive His people.

Vayikra/Leviticus 16
Acharei Mot

ויקרא טז
אחרי מות

5 And from the Israelite community he shall take two he-goats for a sin offering and a ram for a burnt offering.

ה וּמֵאֵת עֲדַת בְּנֵי יִשְׂרָאֵל יִקַּח שְׁנֵי־שְׂעִירֵי עִזִּים לְחַטָּאת וְאַיִל אֶחָד לְעֹלָה׃

6 Aharon is to offer his own bull of sin offering, to make expiation for himself and for his household.

ו וְהִקְרִיב אַהֲרֹן אֶת־פַּר הַחַטָּאת אֲשֶׁר־לוֹ וְכִפֶּר בַּעֲדוֹ וּבְעַד בֵּיתוֹ׃

7 Aharon* shall take the two he-goats and let them stand before Hashem at the entrance of the Tent of Meeting;

ז וְלָקַח אֶת־שְׁנֵי הַשְּׂעִירִם וְהֶעֱמִיד אֹתָם לִפְנֵי יְהֹוָה פֶּתַח אֹהֶל מוֹעֵד׃

8 and he shall place lots upon the two goats, one marked for Hashem and the other marked for Azazel.

ח וְנָתַן אַהֲרֹן עַל־שְׁנֵי הַשְּׂעִירִם גֹּרָלוֹת גּוֹרָל אֶחָד לַיהֹוָה וְגוֹרָל אֶחָד לַעֲזָאזֵל׃

9 Aharon shall bring forward the goat designated by lot for Hashem, which he is to offer as a sin offering;

ט וְהִקְרִיב אַהֲרֹן אֶת־הַשָּׂעִיר אֲשֶׁר עָלָה עָלָיו הַגּוֹרָל לַיהֹוָה וְעָשָׂהוּ חַטָּאת׃

10 while the goat designated by lot for Azazel shall be left standing alive before Hashem, to make expiation with it and to send it off to the wilderness for Azazel.

י וְהַשָּׂעִיר אֲשֶׁר עָלָה עָלָיו הַגּוֹרָל לַעֲזָאזֵל יׇעֳמַד־חַי לִפְנֵי יְהֹוָה לְכַפֵּר עָלָיו לְשַׁלַּח אֹתוֹ לַעֲזָאזֵל הַמִּדְבָּרָה׃

11 Aharon shall then offer his bull of sin offering, to make expiation for himself and his household. He shall slaughter his bull of sin offering,

יא וְהִקְרִיב אַהֲרֹן אֶת־פַּר הַחַטָּאת אֲשֶׁר־לוֹ וְכִפֶּר בַּעֲדוֹ וּבְעַד בֵּיתוֹ וְשָׁחַט אֶת־פַּר הַחַטָּאת אֲשֶׁר־לוֹ׃

12 and he shall take a panful of glowing coals scooped from the Mizbayach before Hashem, and two handfuls of finely ground aromatic incense, and bring this behind the curtain.

יב וְלָקַח מְלֹא־הַמַּחְתָּה גַּחֲלֵי־אֵשׁ מֵעַל הַמִּזְבֵּחַ מִלִּפְנֵי יְהֹוָה וּמְלֹא חׇפְנָיו קְטֹרֶת סַמִּים דַּקָּה וְהֵבִיא מִבֵּית לַפָּרֹכֶת׃

13 He shall put the incense on the fire before Hashem, so that the cloud from the incense screens the cover that is over [the Aron of] the Pact, lest he die.

יג וְנָתַן אֶת־הַקְּטֹרֶת עַל־הָאֵשׁ לִפְנֵי יְהֹוָה וְכִסָּה עֲנַן הַקְּטֹרֶת אֶת־הַכַּפֹּרֶת אֲשֶׁר עַל־הָעֵדוּת וְלֹא יָמוּת׃

14 He shall take some of the blood of the bull and sprinkle it with his finger over the cover on the east side; and in front of the cover he shall sprinkle some of the blood with his finger seven times.

יד וְלָקַח מִדַּם הַפָּר וְהִזָּה בְאֶצְבָּעוֹ עַל־פְּנֵי הַכַּפֹּרֶת קֵדְמָה וְלִפְנֵי הַכַּפֹּרֶת יַזֶּה שֶׁבַע־פְּעָמִים מִן־הַדָּם בְּאֶצְבָּעוֹ׃

15 He shall then slaughter the people's goat of sin offering, bring its blood behind the curtain, and do with its blood as he has done with the blood of the bull: he shall sprinkle it over the cover and in front of the cover.

טו וְשָׁחַט אֶת־שְׂעִיר הַחַטָּאת אֲשֶׁר לָעָם וְהֵבִיא אֶת־דָּמוֹ אֶל־מִבֵּית לַפָּרֹכֶת וְעָשָׂה אֶת־דָּמוֹ כַּאֲשֶׁר עָשָׂה לְדַם הַפָּר וְהִזָּה אֹתוֹ עַל־הַכַּפֹּרֶת וְלִפְנֵי הַכַּפֹּרֶת׃

---

* "Aharon" moved up from v. 8 for clarity

Vayikra/Leviticus 16
Acharei Mot

ויקרא טז
אחרי מות

16 Thus he shall purge the Shrine of the uncleanness and transgression of the Israelites, whatever their sins; and he shall do the same for the Tent of Meeting, which abides with them in the midst of their uncleanness.

טז וְכִפֶּר עַל־הַקֹּדֶשׁ מִטֻּמְאֹת בְּנֵי יִשְׂרָאֵל וּמִפִּשְׁעֵיהֶם לְכָל־חַטֹּאתָם וְכֵן יַעֲשֶׂה לְאֹהֶל מוֹעֵד הַשֹּׁכֵן אִתָּם בְּתוֹךְ טֻמְאֹתָם׃

17 When he goes in to make expiation in the Shrine, nobody else shall be in the Tent of Meeting until he comes out. When he has made expiation for himself and his household, and for the whole congregation of *Yisrael*,

יז וְכָל־אָדָם לֹא־יִהְיֶה בְּאֹהֶל מוֹעֵד בְּבֹאוֹ לְכַפֵּר בַּקֹּדֶשׁ עַד־צֵאתוֹ וְכִפֶּר בַּעֲדוֹ וּבְעַד בֵּיתוֹ וּבְעַד כָּל־קְהַל יִשְׂרָאֵל׃

18 he shall go out to the *Mizbayach* that is before *Hashem* and purge it: he shall take some of the blood of the bull and of the goat and apply it to each of the horns of the *Mizbayach*;

יח וְיָצָא אֶל־הַמִּזְבֵּחַ אֲשֶׁר לִפְנֵי־יְהוָה וְכִפֶּר עָלָיו וְלָקַח מִדַּם הַפָּר וּמִדַּם הַשָּׂעִיר וְנָתַן עַל־קַרְנוֹת הַמִּזְבֵּחַ סָבִיב׃

19 and the rest of the blood he shall sprinkle on it with his finger seven times. Thus he shall cleanse it of the uncleanness of the Israelites and consecrate it.

יט וְהִזָּה עָלָיו מִן־הַדָּם בְּאֶצְבָּעוֹ שֶׁבַע פְּעָמִים וְטִהֲרוֹ וְקִדְּשׁוֹ מִטֻּמְאֹת בְּנֵי יִשְׂרָאֵל׃

20 When he has finished purging the Shrine, the Tent of Meeting, and the *Mizbayach*, the live goat shall be brought forward.

כ וְכִלָּה מִכַּפֵּר אֶת־הַקֹּדֶשׁ וְאֶת־אֹהֶל מוֹעֵד וְאֶת־הַמִּזְבֵּחַ וְהִקְרִיב אֶת־הַשָּׂעִיר הֶחָי׃

21 *Aharon* shall lay both his hands upon the head of the live goat and confess over it all the iniquities and transgressions of the Israelites, whatever their sins, putting them on the head of the goat; and it shall be sent off to the wilderness through a designated man.

כא וְסָמַךְ אַהֲרֹן אֶת־שְׁתֵּי ידו [יָדָיו] עַל רֹאשׁ הַשָּׂעִיר הַחַי וְהִתְוַדָּה עָלָיו אֶת־כָּל־עֲוֺנֹת בְּנֵי יִשְׂרָאֵל וְאֶת־כָּל־פִּשְׁעֵיהֶם לְכָל־חַטֹּאתָם וְנָתַן אֹתָם עַל־רֹאשׁ הַשָּׂעִיר וְשִׁלַּח בְּיַד־אִישׁ עִתִּי הַמִּדְבָּרָה׃

22 Thus the goat shall carry on it all their iniquities to an inaccessible region; and the goat shall be set free in the wilderness.

כב וְנָשָׂא הַשָּׂעִיר עָלָיו אֶת־כָּל־עֲוֺנֹתָם אֶל־אֶרֶץ גְּזֵרָה וְשִׁלַּח אֶת־הַשָּׂעִיר בַּמִּדְבָּר׃

23 And *Aharon* shall go into the Tent of Meeting, take off the linen vestments that he put on when he entered the Shrine, and leave them there.

כג וּבָא אַהֲרֹן אֶל־אֹהֶל מוֹעֵד וּפָשַׁט אֶת־בִּגְדֵי הַבָּד אֲשֶׁר לָבַשׁ בְּבֹאוֹ אֶל־הַקֹּדֶשׁ וְהִנִּיחָם שָׁם׃

24 He shall bathe his body in water in the holy precinct and put on his vestments; then he shall come out and offer his burnt offering and the burnt offering of the people, making expiation for himself and for the people.

כד וְרָחַץ אֶת־בְּשָׂרוֹ בַמַּיִם בְּמָקוֹם קָדוֹשׁ וְלָבַשׁ אֶת־בְּגָדָיו וְיָצָא וְעָשָׂה אֶת־עֹלָתוֹ וְאֶת־עֹלַת הָעָם וְכִפֶּר בַּעֲדוֹ וּבְעַד הָעָם׃

25 The fat of the sin offering he shall turn into smoke on the *Mizbayach*.

כה וְאֵת חֵלֶב הַחַטָּאת יַקְטִיר הַמִּזְבֵּחָה׃

Vayikra/Leviticus 17
Acharei Mot

ויקרא יז
אחרי מות

26 He who set the Azazel-goat free shall wash his clothes and bathe his body in water; after that he may reenter the camp.

כו וְהַמְשַׁלֵּחַ אֶת־הַשָּׂעִיר לַעֲזָאזֵל יְכַבֵּס בְּגָדָיו וְרָחַץ אֶת־בְּשָׂרוֹ בַּמָּיִם וְאַחֲרֵי־כֵן יָבוֹא אֶל־הַמַּחֲנֶה׃

27 The bull of sin offering and the goat of sin offering whose blood was brought in to purge the Shrine shall be taken outside the camp; and their hides, flesh, and dung shall be consumed in fire.

כז וְאֵת פַּר הַחַטָּאת וְאֵת שְׂעִיר הַחַטָּאת אֲשֶׁר הוּבָא אֶת־דָּמָם לְכַפֵּר בַּקֹּדֶשׁ יוֹצִיא אֶל־מִחוּץ לַמַּחֲנֶה וְשָׂרְפוּ בָאֵשׁ אֶת־עֹרֹתָם וְאֶת־בְּשָׂרָם וְאֶת־פִּרְשָׁם׃

28 He who burned them shall wash his clothes and bathe his body in water; after that he may re-enter the camp.

כח וְהַשֹּׂרֵף אֹתָם יְכַבֵּס בְּגָדָיו וְרָחַץ אֶת־בְּשָׂרוֹ בַּמָּיִם וְאַחֲרֵי־כֵן יָבוֹא אֶל־הַמַּחֲנֶה׃

29 And this shall be to you a law for all time: In the seventh month, on the tenth day of the month, you shall practice self-denial; and you shall do no manner of work, neither the citizen nor the alien who resides among you.

כט וְהָיְתָה לָכֶם לְחֻקַּת עוֹלָם בַּחֹדֶשׁ הַשְּׁבִיעִי בֶּעָשׂוֹר לַחֹדֶשׁ תְּעַנּוּ אֶת־נַפְשֹׁתֵיכֶם וְכָל־מְלָאכָה לֹא תַעֲשׂוּ הָאֶזְרָח וְהַגֵּר הַגָּר בְּתוֹכְכֶם׃

30 For on this day atonement shall be made for you to cleanse you of all your sins; you shall be clean before *Hashem*.

ל כִּי־בַיּוֹם הַזֶּה יְכַפֵּר עֲלֵיכֶם לְטַהֵר אֶתְכֶם מִכֹּל חַטֹּאתֵיכֶם לִפְנֵי יְהוָה תִּטְהָרוּ׃

kee va-YOM ha-ZEH y'-kha-PAYR a-lay-KHEM l'-ta-HAYR et-KHEM mi-KOL kha-TO-tay-KHEM lif-NAY a-do-NAI tit-HA-ru

31 It shall be a *Shabbat* of complete rest for you, and you shall practice self-denial; it is a law for all time.

לא שַׁבַּת שַׁבָּתוֹן הִיא לָכֶם וְעִנִּיתֶם אֶת־נַפְשֹׁתֵיכֶם חֻקַּת עוֹלָם׃

32 The *Kohen* who has been anointed and ordained to serve as *Kohen* in place of his father shall make expiation. He shall put on the linen vestments, the sacral vestments.

לב וְכִפֶּר הַכֹּהֵן אֲשֶׁר־יִמְשַׁח אֹתוֹ וַאֲשֶׁר יְמַלֵּא אֶת־יָדוֹ לְכַהֵן תַּחַת אָבִיו וְלָבַשׁ אֶת־בִּגְדֵי הַבָּד בִּגְדֵי הַקֹּדֶשׁ׃

33 He shall purge the innermost Shrine; he shall purge the Tent of Meeting and the *Mizbayach*; and he shall make expiation for the *Kohanim* and for all the people of the congregation.

לג וְכִפֶּר אֶת־מִקְדַּשׁ הַקֹּדֶשׁ וְאֶת־אֹהֶל מוֹעֵד וְאֶת־הַמִּזְבֵּחַ יְכַפֵּר וְעַל הַכֹּהֲנִים וְעַל־כָּל־עַם הַקָּהָל יְכַפֵּר׃

34 This shall be to you a law for all time: to make atonement for the Israelites for all their sins once a year. And *Moshe* did as *Hashem* had commanded him.

לד וְהָיְתָה־זֹּאת לָכֶם לְחֻקַּת עוֹלָם לְכַפֵּר עַל־בְּנֵי יִשְׂרָאֵל מִכָּל־חַטֹּאתָם אַחַת בַּשָּׁנָה וַיַּעַשׂ כַּאֲשֶׁר צִוָּה יְהוָה אֶת־מֹשֶׁה׃

17

1 *Hashem* spoke to *Moshe*, saying:

יז א וַיְדַבֵּר יְהוָה אֶל־מֹשֶׁה לֵּאמֹר׃

2 Speak to *Aharon* and his sons and to all *B'nei Yisrael* and say to them: This is what *Hashem* has commanded:

ב דַּבֵּר אֶל־אַהֲרֹן וְאֶל־בָּנָיו וְאֶל כָּל־בְּנֵי יִשְׂרָאֵל וְאָמַרְתָּ אֲלֵיהֶם זֶה הַדָּבָר אֲשֶׁר־צִוָּה יְהוָה לֵאמֹר׃

3 if anyone of the house of *Yisrael* slaughters an ox or sheep or goat in the camp, or does so outside the camp,

ג אִישׁ אִישׁ מִבֵּית יִשְׂרָאֵל אֲשֶׁר יִשְׁחַט שׁוֹר אוֹ־כֶשֶׂב אוֹ־עֵז בַּמַּחֲנֶה אוֹ אֲשֶׁר יִשְׁחַט מִחוּץ לַמַּחֲנֶה׃

Vayikra/Leviticus 17
Acharei Mot

ויקרא יז
אחרי מות

4 and does not bring it to the entrance of the Tent of Meeting to present it as an offering to *Hashem*, before *Hashem*'s *Mishkan*, bloodguilt shall be imputed to that man: he has shed blood; that man shall be cut off from among his people.

ד וְאֶל־פֶּתַח אֹהֶל מוֹעֵד לֹא הֱבִיאוֹ לְהַקְרִיב קָרְבָּן לַיהוָֹה לִפְנֵי מִשְׁכַּן יְהוָֹה דָּם יֵחָשֵׁב לָאִישׁ הַהוּא דָּם שָׁפָךְ וְנִכְרַת הָאִישׁ הַהוּא מִקֶּרֶב עַמּוֹ:

v'-el PE-takh O-hel mo-AYD LO he-vee-O l'-hak-REEV kor-BAN la-do-NAI lif-NAY mish-KAN a-do-NAI DAM yay-kha-SHAYV la-EESH ha-HU DAM sha-FAKH v'-nikh-RAT ha-EESH ha-HU mi-KE-rev a-MO

5 This is in order that the Israelites may bring the sacrifices which they have been making in the open – that they may bring them before *Hashem*, to the *Kohen*, at the entrance of the Tent of Meeting, and offer them as sacrifices of well-being to *Hashem*;

ה לְמַעַן אֲשֶׁר יָבִיאוּ בְּנֵי יִשְׂרָאֵל אֶת־זִבְחֵיהֶם אֲשֶׁר הֵם זֹבְחִים עַל־פְּנֵי הַשָּׂדֶה וֶהֱבִיאֻם לַיהוָֹה אֶל־פֶּתַח אֹהֶל מוֹעֵד אֶל־הַכֹּהֵן וְזָבְחוּ זִבְחֵי שְׁלָמִים לַיהוָֹה אוֹתָם:

6 that the *Kohen* may dash the blood against the *Mizbayach* of *Hashem* at the entrance of the Tent of Meeting, and turn the fat into smoke as a pleasing odor to *Hashem*;

ו וְזָרַק הַכֹּהֵן אֶת־הַדָּם עַל־מִזְבַּח יְהוָֹה פֶּתַח אֹהֶל מוֹעֵד וְהִקְטִיר הַחֵלֶב לְרֵיחַ נִיחֹחַ לַיהוָֹה:

7 and that they may offer their sacrifices no more to the goat-demons after whom they stray. This shall be to them a law for all time, throughout the ages.

ז וְלֹא־יִזְבְּחוּ עוֹד אֶת־זִבְחֵיהֶם לַשְּׂעִירִם אֲשֶׁר הֵם זֹנִים אַחֲרֵיהֶם חֻקַּת עוֹלָם תִּהְיֶה־זֹּאת לָהֶם לְדֹרֹתָם:

8 Say to them further: If anyone of the house of *Yisrael* or of the strangers who reside among them offers a burnt offering or a sacrifice,

ח וַאֲלֵהֶם תֹּאמַר אִישׁ אִישׁ מִבֵּית יִשְׂרָאֵל וּמִן־הַגֵּר אֲשֶׁר־יָגוּר בְּתוֹכָם אֲשֶׁר־יַעֲלֶה עֹלָה אוֹ־זָבַח:

9 and does not bring it to the entrance of the Tent of Meeting to offer it to *Hashem*, that person shall be cut off from his people.

ט וְאֶל־פֶּתַח אֹהֶל מוֹעֵד לֹא יְבִיאֶנּוּ לַעֲשׂוֹת אֹתוֹ לַיהוָֹה וְנִכְרַת הָאִישׁ הַהוּא מֵעַמָּיו:

10 And if anyone of the house of *Yisrael* or of the strangers who reside among them partakes of any blood, I will set My face against the person who partakes of the blood, and I will cut him off from among his kin.

י וְאִישׁ אִישׁ מִבֵּית יִשְׂרָאֵל וּמִן־הַגֵּר הַגָּר בְּתוֹכָם אֲשֶׁר יֹאכַל כָּל־דָּם וְנָתַתִּי פָנַי בַּנֶּפֶשׁ הָאֹכֶלֶת אֶת־הַדָּם וְהִכְרַתִּי אֹתָהּ מִקֶּרֶב עַמָּהּ:

Model of the Second Beit Hamikdash

17:4 And does not bring it to the entrance of the Tent of Meeting Once the *Mishkan* is constructed, and again after the *Beit Hamikdash* is built in *Yerushalayim*, it becomes forbidden to offer sacrifices anywhere else. This is because *Hashem* wants the acts of worshipping Him to bring unity among the people, and is also designed to minimize the danger of changes being introduced to the manner of worship. In addition, the mandate that sacrifices be brought only in the *Beit Hamikdash* requires everyone to travel to *Yerushalayim* at least three times a year. God's system ensures that everyone will have the triannual opportunity to be uplifted by the holiness of the *Beit Hamikdash* and the holy city of *Yerushalayim*.

Vayikra/Leviticus 18
Acharei Mot

ויקרא יח
אחרי מות

11 For the life of the flesh is in the blood, and I have assigned it to you for making expiation for your lives upon the *Mizbayach*; it is the blood, as life, that effects expiation.

יא כִּי נֶפֶשׁ הַבָּשָׂר בַּדָּם הִוא וַאֲנִי נְתַתִּיו לָכֶם עַל־הַמִּזְבֵּחַ לְכַפֵּר עַל־נַפְשֹׁתֵיכֶם כִּי־הַדָּם הוּא בַּנֶּפֶשׁ יְכַפֵּר׃

12 Therefore I say to *B'nei Yisrael*: No person among you shall partake of blood, nor shall the stranger who resides among you partake of blood.

יב עַל־כֵּן אָמַרְתִּי לִבְנֵי יִשְׂרָאֵל כָּל־נֶפֶשׁ מִכֶּם לֹא־תֹאכַל דָּם וְהַגֵּר הַגָּר בְּתוֹכְכֶם לֹא־יֹאכַל דָּם׃

13 And if any Israelite or any stranger who resides among them hunts down an animal or a bird that may be eaten, he shall pour out its blood and cover it with earth.

יג וְאִישׁ אִישׁ מִבְּנֵי יִשְׂרָאֵל וּמִן־הַגֵּר הַגָּר בְּתוֹכָם אֲשֶׁר יָצוּד צֵיד חַיָּה אוֹ־עוֹף אֲשֶׁר יֵאָכֵל וְשָׁפַךְ אֶת־דָּמוֹ וְכִסָּהוּ בֶּעָפָר׃

14 For the life of all flesh – its blood is its life. Therefore I say to *B'nei Yisrael*: You shall not partake of the blood of any flesh, for the life of all flesh is its blood. Anyone who partakes of it shall be cut off.

יד כִּי־נֶפֶשׁ כָּל־בָּשָׂר דָּמוֹ בְנַפְשׁוֹ הוּא וָאֹמַר לִבְנֵי יִשְׂרָאֵל דַּם כָּל־בָּשָׂר לֹא תֹאכֵלוּ כִּי נֶפֶשׁ כָּל־בָּשָׂר דָּמוֹ הִוא כָּל־אֹכְלָיו יִכָּרֵת׃

15 Any person, whether citizen or stranger, who eats what has died or has been torn by beasts shall wash his clothes, bathe in water, and remain unclean until evening; then he shall be clean.

טו וְכָל־נֶפֶשׁ אֲשֶׁר תֹּאכַל נְבֵלָה וּטְרֵפָה בָּאֶזְרָח וּבַגֵּר וְכִבֶּס בְּגָדָיו וְרָחַץ בַּמַּיִם וְטָמֵא עַד־הָעֶרֶב וְטָהֵר׃

16 But if he does not wash [his clothes] and bathe his body, he shall bear his guilt.

טז וְאִם לֹא יְכַבֵּס וּבְשָׂרוֹ לֹא יִרְחָץ וְנָשָׂא עֲוֹנוֹ׃

18

1 *Hashem* spoke to *Moshe*, saying:

יח א וַיְדַבֵּר יְהֹוָה אֶל־מֹשֶׁה לֵּאמֹר׃

2 Speak to *B'nei Yisrael* and say to them: I *Hashem* am your God.

ב דַּבֵּר אֶל־בְּנֵי יִשְׂרָאֵל וְאָמַרְתָּ אֲלֵהֶם אֲנִי יְהֹוָה אֱלֹהֵיכֶם׃

3 You shall not copy the practices of the land of Egypt where you dwelt, or of the land of Canaan to which I am taking you; nor shall you follow their laws.

ג כְּמַעֲשֵׂה אֶרֶץ־מִצְרַיִם אֲשֶׁר יְשַׁבְתֶּם־בָּהּ לֹא תַעֲשׂוּ וּכְמַעֲשֵׂה אֶרֶץ־כְּנַעַן אֲשֶׁר אֲנִי מֵבִיא אֶתְכֶם שָׁמָּה לֹא תַעֲשׂוּ וּבְחֻקֹּתֵיהֶם לֹא תֵלֵכוּ׃

k'-ma-a-SAY e-retz mitz-RA-yim a-SHER y'-shav-tem BA LO ta-a-SU uk'-ma-a-SAY e-retz k'-NA-an a-SHER a-NEE may-VEE et-KHEM SHA-ma LO ta-a-SU uv-khu-ko-tay-HEM lo tay-LAY-khu

---

18:3 Or of the land of Canaan This verse warns the Israelites to avoid the negative behaviors (such as incest and child sacrifices) that were prevalent in Canaan. The chapter ends with an incredible, spiritual statement. It warns that *Eretz Yisrael* itself is so pure that it cannot tolerate abominable behavior, and will therefore expel any nation that defiles itself and the land, including the Jewish people. Ultimately, the Jews were indeed expelled from the land because of their sins. In modern times, even as we are grateful that *Hashem* has returned the Children of Israel to the land, this warning must be taken to heart. The land must be kept pure, and the people's behavior must adhere to the teachings of the Bible.

Vayikra/Leviticus 18
Acharei Mot

ויקרא יח
אחרי מות

4 My rules alone shall you observe, and faithfully follow My laws: I *Hashem* am your God.

ד אֶת־מִשְׁפָּטַי תַּעֲשׂוּ וְאֶת־חֻקֹּתַי תִּשְׁמְרוּ לָלֶכֶת בָּהֶם אֲנִי יְהֹוָה אֱלֹהֵיכֶם:

5 You shall keep My laws and My rules, by the pursuit of which man shall live: I am *Hashem*.

ה וּשְׁמַרְתֶּם אֶת־חֻקֹּתַי וְאֶת־מִשְׁפָּטַי אֲשֶׁר יַעֲשֶׂה אֹתָם הָאָדָם וָחַי בָּהֶם אֲנִי יְהֹוָה:

6 None of you shall come near anyone of his own flesh to uncover nakedness: I am *Hashem*.

ו אִישׁ אִישׁ אֶל־כָּל־שְׁאֵר בְּשָׂרוֹ לֹא תִקְרְבוּ לְגַלּוֹת עֶרְוָה אֲנִי יְהֹוָה:

7 Your father's nakedness, that is, the nakedness of your mother, you shall not uncover; she is your mother – you shall not uncover her nakedness.

ז עֶרְוַת אָבִיךָ וְעֶרְוַת אִמְּךָ לֹא תְגַלֵּה אִמְּךָ הִוא לֹא תְגַלֶּה עֶרְוָתָהּ:

8 Do not uncover the nakedness of your father's wife; it is the nakedness of your father.

ח עֶרְוַת אֵשֶׁת־אָבִיךָ לֹא תְגַלֵּה עֶרְוַת אָבִיךָ הִוא:

9 The nakedness of your sister – your father's daughter or your mother's, whether born into the household or outside – do not uncover their nakedness.

ט עֶרְוַת אֲחוֹתְךָ בַת־אָבִיךָ אוֹ בַת־אִמֶּךָ מוֹלֶדֶת בַּיִת אוֹ מוֹלֶדֶת חוּץ לֹא תְגַלֶּה עֶרְוָתָן:

10 The nakedness of your son's daughter, or of your daughter's daughter – do not uncover their nakedness; for their nakedness is yours.

י עֶרְוַת בַּת־בִּנְךָ אוֹ בַת־בִּתְּךָ לֹא תְגַלֶּה עֶרְוָתָן כִּי עֶרְוָתְךָ הֵנָּה:

11 The nakedness of your father's wife's daughter, who has born into your father's household – she is your sister; do not uncover her nakedness.

יא עֶרְוַת בַּת־אֵשֶׁת אָבִיךָ מוֹלֶדֶת אָבִיךָ אֲחוֹתְךָ הִוא לֹא תְגַלֶּה עֶרְוָתָהּ:

12 Do not uncover the nakedness of your father's sister; she is your father's flesh.

יב עֶרְוַת אֲחוֹת־אָבִיךָ לֹא תְגַלֵּה שְׁאֵר אָבִיךָ הִוא:

13 Do not uncover the nakedness of your mother's sister; for she is your mother's flesh.

יג עֶרְוַת אֲחוֹת־אִמְּךָ לֹא תְגַלֵּה כִּי־שְׁאֵר אִמְּךָ הִוא:

14 Do not uncover the nakedness of your father's brother: do not approach his wife; she is your aunt.

יד עֶרְוַת אֲחִי־אָבִיךָ לֹא תְגַלֵּה אֶל־אִשְׁתּוֹ לֹא תִקְרָב דֹּדָתְךָ הִוא:

15 Do not uncover the nakedness of your daughter-in-law: she is your son's wife; you shall not uncover her nakedness.

טו עֶרְוַת כַּלָּתְךָ לֹא תְגַלֵּה אֵשֶׁת בִּנְךָ הִוא לֹא תְגַלֶּה עֶרְוָתָהּ:

16 Do not uncover the nakedness of your brother's wife; it is the nakedness of your brother.

טז עֶרְוַת אֵשֶׁת־אָחִיךָ לֹא תְגַלֵּה עֶרְוַת אָחִיךָ הִוא:

17 Do not uncover the nakedness of a woman and her daughter; nor shall you marry her son's daughter or her daughter's daughter and uncover her nakedness: they are kindred; it is depravity.

יז עֶרְוַת אִשָּׁה וּבִתָּהּ לֹא תְגַלֵּה אֶת־בַּת־בְּנָהּ וְאֶת־בַּת־בִּתָּהּ לֹא תִקַּח לְגַלּוֹת עֶרְוָתָהּ שַׁאֲרָה הֵנָּה זִמָּה הִוא:

18 Do not marry a woman as a rival to her sister and uncover her nakedness in the other's lifetime.

יח וְאִשָּׁה אֶל־אֲחֹתָהּ לֹא תִקָּח לִצְרֹר לְגַלּוֹת עֶרְוָתָהּ עָלֶיהָ בְּחַיֶּיהָ:

Vayikra/Leviticus 19
Kedoshim

ויקרא יט
קדושים

19 Do not come near a woman during her period of uncleanness to uncover her nakedness.

יט וְאֶל־אִשָּׁה בְּנִדַּת טֻמְאָתָהּ לֹא תִקְרַב לְגַלּוֹת עֶרְוָתָהּ׃

20 Do not have carnal relations with your neighbor's wife and defile yourself with her.

כ וְאֶל־אֵשֶׁת עֲמִיתְךָ לֹא־תִתֵּן שְׁכָבְתְּךָ לְזָרַע לְטָמְאָה־בָהּ׃

21 Do not allow any of your offspring to be offered up to Molech, and do not profane the name of your God: I am *Hashem*.

כא וּמִזַּרְעֲךָ לֹא־תִתֵּן לְהַעֲבִיר לַמֹּלֶךְ וְלֹא תְחַלֵּל אֶת־שֵׁם אֱלֹהֶיךָ אֲנִי יְהֹוָה׃

22 Do not lie with a male as one lies with a woman; it is an abhorrence.

כב וְאֶת־זָכָר לֹא תִשְׁכַּב מִשְׁכְּבֵי אִשָּׁה תּוֹעֵבָה הִוא׃

23 Do not have carnal relations with any beast and defile yourself thereby; and let no woman lend herself to a beast to mate with it; it is perversion.

כג וּבְכָל־בְּהֵמָה לֹא־תִתֵּן שְׁכָבְתְּךָ לְטָמְאָה־בָהּ וְאִשָּׁה לֹא־תַעֲמֹד לִפְנֵי בְהֵמָה לְרִבְעָהּ תֶּבֶל הוּא׃

24 Do not defile yourselves in any of those ways, for it is by such that the nations that I am casting out before you defiled themselves.

כד אַל־תִּטַּמְּאוּ בְּכָל־אֵלֶּה כִּי בְכָל־אֵלֶּה נִטְמְאוּ הַגּוֹיִם אֲשֶׁר־אֲנִי מְשַׁלֵּחַ מִפְּנֵיכֶם׃

25 Thus the land became defiled; and I called it to account for its iniquity, and the land spewed out its inhabitants.

כה וַתִּטְמָא הָאָרֶץ וָאֶפְקֹד עֲוֺנָהּ עָלֶיהָ וַתָּקִא הָאָרֶץ אֶת־יֹשְׁבֶיהָ׃

26 But you must keep My laws and My rules, and you must not do any of those abhorrent things, neither the citizen nor the stranger who resides among you;

כו וּשְׁמַרְתֶּם אַתֶּם אֶת־חֻקֹּתַי וְאֶת־מִשְׁפָּטַי וְלֹא תַעֲשׂוּ מִכֹּל הַתּוֹעֵבֹת הָאֵלֶּה הָאֶזְרָח וְהַגֵּר הַגָּר בְּתוֹכְכֶם׃

27 for all those abhorrent things were done by the people who were in the land before you, and the land became defiled.

כז כִּי אֶת־כָּל־הַתּוֹעֵבֹת הָאֵל עָשׂוּ אַנְשֵׁי־הָאָרֶץ אֲשֶׁר לִפְנֵיכֶם וַתִּטְמָא הָאָרֶץ׃

28 So let not the land spew you out for defiling it, as it spewed out the nation that came before you.

כח וְלֹא־תָקִיא הָאָרֶץ אֶתְכֶם בְּטַמַּאֲכֶם אֹתָהּ כַּאֲשֶׁר קָאָה אֶת־הַגּוֹי אֲשֶׁר לִפְנֵיכֶם׃

29 All who do any of those abhorrent things – such persons shall be cut off from their people.

כט כִּי כָּל־אֲשֶׁר יַעֲשֶׂה מִכֹּל הַתּוֹעֵבֹת הָאֵלֶּה וְנִכְרְתוּ הַנְּפָשׁוֹת הָעֹשֹׂת מִקֶּרֶב עַמָּם׃

30 You shall keep My charge not to engage in any of the abhorrent practices that were carried on before you, and you shall not defile yourselves through them: I *Hashem* am your God.

ל וּשְׁמַרְתֶּם אֶת־מִשְׁמַרְתִּי לְבִלְתִּי עֲשׂוֹת מֵחֻקּוֹת הַתּוֹעֵבֹת אֲשֶׁר נַעֲשׂוּ לִפְנֵיכֶם וְלֹא תִטַּמְּאוּ בָּהֶם אֲנִי יְהֹוָה אֱלֹהֵיכֶם׃

19 1 *Hashem* spoke to *Moshe*, saying:

יט א וַיְדַבֵּר יְהֹוָה אֶל־מֹשֶׁה לֵּאמֹר׃

2 Speak to the whole Israelite community and say to them: You shall be holy, for I, *Hashem* your God, am holy.

ב דַּבֵּר אֶל־כָּל־עֲדַת בְּנֵי־יִשְׂרָאֵל וְאָמַרְתָּ אֲלֵהֶם קְדֹשִׁים תִּהְיוּ כִּי קָדוֹשׁ אֲנִי יְהֹוָה אֱלֹהֵיכֶם׃

3 You shall each revere his mother and his father, and keep My *Shabbatot*: I *Hashem* am your God.

ג אִישׁ אִמּוֹ וְאָבִיו תִּירָאוּ וְאֶת־שַׁבְּתֹתַי תִּשְׁמֹרוּ אֲנִי יְהֹוָה אֱלֹהֵיכֶם׃

Vayikra/Leviticus 19
Kedoshim

ויקרא יט
קדושים

4 Do not turn to idols or make molten gods for yourselves: I *Hashem* am your God.

ד אַל־תִּפְנוּ אֶל־הָאֱלִילִים וֵאלֹהֵי מַסֵּכָה לֹא תַעֲשׂוּ לָכֶם אֲנִי יְהֹוָה אֱלֹהֵיכֶם:

5 When you sacrifice an offering of well-being to *Hashem*, sacrifice it so that it may be accepted on your behalf.

ה וְכִי תִזְבְּחוּ זֶבַח שְׁלָמִים לַיהֹוָה לִרְצֹנְכֶם תִּזְבָּחֻהוּ:

6 It shall be eaten on the day you sacrifice it, or on the day following; but what is left by the third day must be consumed in fire.

ו בְּיוֹם זִבְחֲכֶם יֵאָכֵל וּמִמָּחֳרָת וְהַנּוֹתָר עַד־יוֹם הַשְּׁלִישִׁי בָּאֵשׁ יִשָּׂרֵף:

7 If it should be eaten on the third day, it is an offensive thing, it will not be acceptable.

ז וְאִם הֵאָכֹל יֵאָכֵל בַּיּוֹם הַשְּׁלִישִׁי פִּגּוּל הוּא לֹא יֵרָצֶה:

8 And he who eats of it shall bear his guilt, for he has profaned what is sacred to *Hashem*; that person shall be cut off from his kin.

ח וְאֹכְלָיו עֲוֺנוֹ יִשָּׂא כִּי־אֶת־קֹדֶשׁ יְהֹוָה חִלֵּל וְנִכְרְתָה הַנֶּפֶשׁ הַהִוא מֵעַמֶּיהָ:

9 When you reap the harvest of your land, you shall not reap all the way to the edges of your field, or gather the gleanings of your harvest.

ט וּבְקֻצְרְכֶם אֶת־קְצִיר אַרְצְכֶם לֹא תְכַלֶּה פְּאַת שָׂדְךָ לִקְצֹר וְלֶקֶט קְצִירְךָ לֹא תְלַקֵּט:

uv-kutz-r'-KHEM et k'-TZEER ar-tz'-KHEM LO t'-kha-LE p'-AT sa-d'-KHA lik-TZOR v'-LE-ket k'-tzee-r'-KHA LO t'-la-KAYT

10 You shall not pick your vineyard bare, or gather the fallen fruit of your vineyard; you shall leave them for the poor and the stranger: I *Hashem* am your God.

י וְכַרְמְךָ לֹא תְעוֹלֵל וּפֶרֶט כַּרְמְךָ לֹא תְלַקֵּט לֶעָנִי וְלַגֵּר תַּעֲזֹב אֹתָם אֲנִי יְהֹוָה אֱלֹהֵיכֶם:

11 You shall not steal; you shall not deal deceitfully or falsely with one another.

יא לֹא תִּגְנֹבוּ וְלֹא־תְכַחֲשׁוּ וְלֹא־תְשַׁקְּרוּ אִישׁ בַּעֲמִיתוֹ:

12 You shall not swear falsely by My name, profaning the name of your God: I am *Hashem*.

יב וְלֹא־תִשָּׁבְעוּ בִשְׁמִי לַשָּׁקֶר וְחִלַּלְתָּ אֶת־שֵׁם אֱלֹהֶיךָ אֲנִי יְהֹוָה:

13 You shall not defraud your fellow. You shall not commit robbery. The wages of a laborer shall not remain with you until morning.

יג לֹא־תַעֲשֹׁק אֶת־רֵעֲךָ וְלֹא תִגְזֹל לֹא־תָלִין פְּעֻלַּת שָׂכִיר אִתְּךָ עַד־בֹּקֶר:

14 You shall not insult the deaf, or place a stumbling block before the blind. You shall fear your God: I am *Hashem*.

יד לֹא־תְקַלֵּל חֵרֵשׁ וְלִפְנֵי עִוֵּר לֹא תִתֵּן מִכְשֹׁל וְיָרֵאתָ מֵּאֱלֹהֶיךָ אֲנִי יְהֹוָה:

15 You shall not render an unfair decision: do not favor the poor or show deference to the rich; judge your kinsman fairly.

טו לֹא־תַעֲשׂוּ עָוֶל בַּמִּשְׁפָּט לֹא־תִשָּׂא פְנֵי־דָל וְלֹא תֶהְדַּר פְּנֵי גָדוֹל בְּצֶדֶק תִּשְׁפֹּט עֲמִיתֶךָ:

16 Do not deal basely with your countrymen. Do not profit by the blood of your fellow: I am *Hashem*.

טז לֹא־תֵלֵךְ רָכִיל בְּעַמֶּיךָ לֹא תַעֲמֹד עַל־דַּם רֵעֶךָ אֲנִי יְהֹוָה:

17 You shall not hate your kinsfolk in your heart. Reprove your kinsman but incur no guilt because of him.

יז לֹא־תִשְׂנָא אֶת־אָחִיךָ בִּלְבָבֶךָ הוֹכֵחַ תּוֹכִיחַ אֶת־עֲמִיתֶךָ וְלֹא־תִשָּׂא עָלָיו חֵטְא:

Vayikra/Leviticus 19
Kedoshim

ויקרא יט
קדושים

18 You shall not take vengeance or bear a grudge against your countrymen. Love your fellow as yourself: I am *Hashem*.

לֹא־תִקֹּם וְלֹא־תִטֹּר אֶת־בְּנֵי עַמֶּךָ וְאָהַבְתָּ לְרֵעֲךָ כָּמוֹךָ אֲנִי יְהוָה: יח

lo ti-KOM v'-lo ti-TOR et b'-NAY a-ME-kha v'-a-hav-TA l'-ray-a-KHA ka-MO-kha a-NEE a-do-NAI

19 You shall observe My laws. You shall not let your cattle mate with a different kind; you shall not sow your field with two kinds of seed; you shall not put on cloth from a mixture of two kinds of material.

אֶת־חֻקֹּתַי תִּשְׁמֹרוּ בְּהֶמְתְּךָ לֹא־תַרְבִּיעַ כִּלְאַיִם שָׂדְךָ לֹא־תִזְרַע כִּלְאָיִם וּבֶגֶד כִּלְאַיִם שַׁעַטְנֵז לֹא יַעֲלֶה עָלֶיךָ: יט

20 If a man has carnal relations with a woman who is a slave and has been designated for another man, but has not been redeemed or given her freedom, there shall be an indemnity; they shall not, however, be put to death, since she has not been freed.

וְאִישׁ כִּי־יִשְׁכַּב אֶת־אִשָּׁה שִׁכְבַת־זֶרַע וְהִוא שִׁפְחָה נֶחֱרֶפֶת לְאִישׁ וְהָפְדֵּה לֹא נִפְדָּתָה אוֹ חֻפְשָׁה לֹא נִתַּן־לָהּ בִּקֹּרֶת תִּהְיֶה לֹא יוּמְתוּ כִּי־לֹא חֻפָּשָׁה: כ

21 But he must bring to the entrance of the Tent of Meeting, as his guilt offering to *Hashem*, a ram of guilt offering.

וְהֵבִיא אֶת־אֲשָׁמוֹ לַיהוָה אֶל־פֶּתַח אֹהֶל מוֹעֵד אֵיל אָשָׁם: כא

22 With the ram of guilt offering the *Kohen* shall make expiation for him before *Hashem* for the sin that he committed; and the sin that he committed will be forgiven him.

וְכִפֶּר עָלָיו הַכֹּהֵן בְּאֵיל הָאָשָׁם לִפְנֵי יְהוָה עַל־חַטָּאתוֹ אֲשֶׁר חָטָא וְנִסְלַח לוֹ מֵחַטָּאתוֹ אֲשֶׁר חָטָא: כב

23 When you enter the land and plant any tree for food, you shall regard its fruit as forbidden. Three years it shall be forbidden for you, not to be eaten.

וְכִי־תָבֹאוּ אֶל־הָאָרֶץ וּנְטַעְתֶּם כָּל־עֵץ מַאֲכָל וַעֲרַלְתֶּם עָרְלָתוֹ אֶת־פִּרְיוֹ שָׁלֹשׁ שָׁנִים יִהְיֶה לָכֶם עֲרֵלִים לֹא יֵאָכֵל: כג

v'-khee ta-VO-u el ha-A-retz u-n'-ta-TEM kol AYTZ ma-a-KHAL va-a-ral-TEM or-la-TO et pir-YO sha-LOSH sha-NEEM yih-YEH la-KHEM a-ray-LEEM LO yay-a-KHAYL

24 In the fourth year all its fruit shall be set aside for jubilation before *Hashem*;

וּבַשָּׁנָה הָרְבִיעִת יִהְיֶה כָּל־פִּרְיוֹ קֹדֶשׁ הִלּוּלִים לַיהוָה: כד

19:18 Love your fellow as yourself In a speech given in 1944 to a gathering of youth groups in Haifa, Prime Minister David Ben Gurion referred to these words as an example of how Judaism serves as a paradigm of a society built on morality, peace and love: "Ours was a tiny nation inhabiting a small country, and there have been many tiny nations and many small countries, but ours was a tiny nation possessed of a great spirit; an inspired people that believed in its pioneering mission to all men, in the mission that had been preached by the prophets of Israel. This people gave the world great and eternal moral truths and commandments. This people rose to prophetic visions of the unity of the Creator with His creation, of the dignity and infinite worth of the individual because every man is created in the divine image, of social justice, universal peace, and love: 'Thou shalt love thy neighbor as thyself.' This people was the first to prophesy about 'the end of days,' the first to see the vision of a new human society." Even though Ben Gurion was not a religious Jew, he was deeply influenced by the Bible, which had a profound impact on his outlook and his actions on behalf of the Jewish State.

Prime Minister David Ben Gurion (1886–1973)

Vayikra/Leviticus 20
Kedoshim

25 and only in the fifth year may you use its fruit – that its yield to you may be increased: I *Hashem* am your God.

כה וּבַשָּׁנָה הַחֲמִישִׁת תֹּאכְלוּ אֶת־פִּרְיוֹ לְהוֹסִיף לָכֶם תְּבוּאָתוֹ אֲנִי יְהֹוָה אֱלֹהֵיכֶם׃

26 You shall not eat anything with its blood. You shall not practice divination or soothsaying.

כו לֹא תֹאכְלוּ עַל־הַדָּם לֹא תְנַחֲשׁוּ וְלֹא תְעוֹנֵנוּ׃

27 You shall not round off the side-growth on your head, or destroy the side-growth of your beard.

כז לֹא תַקִּפוּ פְּאַת רֹאשְׁכֶם וְלֹא תַשְׁחִית אֵת פְּאַת זְקָנֶךָ׃

28 You shall not make gashes in your flesh for the dead, or incise any marks on yourselves: I am *Hashem*.

כח וְשֶׂרֶט לָנֶפֶשׁ לֹא תִתְּנוּ בִּבְשַׂרְכֶם וּכְתֹבֶת קַעֲקַע לֹא תִתְּנוּ בָּכֶם אֲנִי יְהֹוָה׃

29 Do not degrade your daughter and make her a harlot, lest the land fall into harlotry and the land be filled with depravity.

כט אַל־תְּחַלֵּל אֶת־בִּתְּךָ לְהַזְנוֹתָהּ וְלֹא־תִזְנֶה הָאָרֶץ וּמָלְאָה הָאָרֶץ זִמָּה׃

30 You shall keep My *Shabbatot* and venerate My sanctuary: I am *Hashem*.

ל אֶת־שַׁבְּתֹתַי תִּשְׁמֹרוּ וּמִקְדָּשִׁי תִּירָאוּ אֲנִי יְהֹוָה׃

31 Do not turn to ghosts and do not inquire of familiar spirits, to be defiled by them: I *Hashem* am your God.

לא אַל־תִּפְנוּ אֶל־הָאֹבֹת וְאֶל־הַיִּדְּעֹנִים אַל־תְּבַקְשׁוּ לְטָמְאָה בָהֶם אֲנִי יְהֹוָה אֱלֹהֵיכֶם׃

32 You shall rise before the aged and show deference to the old; you shall fear your God: I am *Hashem*.

לב מִפְּנֵי שֵׂיבָה תָּקוּם וְהָדַרְתָּ פְּנֵי זָקֵן וְיָרֵאתָ מֵּאֱלֹהֶיךָ אֲנִי יְהֹוָה׃

33 When a stranger resides with you in your land, you shall not wrong him.

לג וְכִי־יָגוּר אִתְּךָ גֵּר בְּאַרְצְכֶם לֹא תוֹנוּ אֹתוֹ׃

34 The stranger who resides with you shall be to you as one of your citizens; you shall love him as yourself, for you were strangers in the land of Egypt: I *Hashem* am your God.

לד כְּאֶזְרָח מִכֶּם יִהְיֶה לָכֶם הַגֵּר הַגָּר אִתְּכֶם וְאָהַבְתָּ לוֹ כָּמוֹךָ כִּי־גֵרִים הֱיִיתֶם בְּאֶרֶץ מִצְרָיִם אֲנִי יְהֹוָה אֱלֹהֵיכֶם׃

35 You shall not falsify measures of length, weight, or capacity.

לה לֹא־תַעֲשׂוּ עָוֶל בַּמִּשְׁפָּט בַּמִּדָּה בַּמִּשְׁקָל וּבַמְּשׂוּרָה׃

36 You shall have an honest balance, honest weights, an honest *efah*, and an honest *hin*. I *Hashem* am your God who freed you from the land of Egypt.

לו מֹאזְנֵי צֶדֶק אַבְנֵי־צֶדֶק אֵיפַת צֶדֶק וְהִין צֶדֶק יִהְיֶה לָכֶם אֲנִי יְהֹוָה אֱלֹהֵיכֶם אֲשֶׁר־הוֹצֵאתִי אֶתְכֶם מֵאֶרֶץ מִצְרָיִם׃

37 You shall faithfully observe all My laws and all My rules: I am *Hashem*.

לז וּשְׁמַרְתֶּם אֶת־כָּל־חֻקֹּתַי וְאֶת־כָּל־מִשְׁפָּטַי וַעֲשִׂיתֶם אֹתָם אֲנִי יְהֹוָה׃

20 1 And *Hashem* spoke to *Moshe*:

כ א וַיְדַבֵּר יְהֹוָה אֶל־מֹשֶׁה לֵּאמֹר׃

2 Say further to *B'nei Yisrael*: Anyone among the Israelites, or among the strangers residing in *Yisrael*, who gives any of his offspring to Molech, shall be put to death; the people of the land shall pelt him with stones.

ב וְאֶל־בְּנֵי יִשְׂרָאֵל תֹּאמַר אִישׁ אִישׁ מִבְּנֵי יִשְׂרָאֵל וּמִן־הַגֵּר הַגָּר בְּיִשְׂרָאֵל אֲשֶׁר יִתֵּן מִזַּרְעוֹ לַמֹּלֶךְ מוֹת יוּמָת עַם הָאָרֶץ יִרְגְּמֻהוּ בָאָבֶן׃

Vayikra/Leviticus 20
Kedoshim

ויקרא כ
קדושים

3 And I will set My face against that man and will cut him off from among his people, because he gave of his offspring to Molech and so defiled My sanctuary and profaned My holy name.

ג וַאֲנִי אֶתֵּן אֶת־פָּנַי בָּאִישׁ הַהוּא וְהִכְרַתִּי אֹתוֹ מִקֶּרֶב עַמּוֹ כִּי מִזַּרְעוֹ נָתַן לַמֹּלֶךְ לְמַעַן טַמֵּא אֶת־מִקְדָּשִׁי וּלְחַלֵּל אֶת־שֵׁם קָדְשִׁי:

4 And if the people of the land should shut their eyes to that man when he gives of his offspring to Molech, and should not put him to death,

ד וְאִם הַעְלֵם יַעְלִימוּ עַם הָאָרֶץ אֶת־עֵינֵיהֶם מִן־הָאִישׁ הַהוּא בְּתִתּוֹ מִזַּרְעוֹ לַמֹּלֶךְ לְבִלְתִּי הָמִית אֹתוֹ:

5 I Myself will set My face against that man and his kin, and will cut off from among their people both him and all who follow him in going astray after Molech.

ה וְשַׂמְתִּי אֲנִי אֶת־פָּנַי בָּאִישׁ הַהוּא וּבְמִשְׁפַּחְתּוֹ וְהִכְרַתִּי אֹתוֹ וְאֵת כָּל־הַזֹּנִים אַחֲרָיו לִזְנוֹת אַחֲרֵי הַמֹּלֶךְ מִקֶּרֶב עַמָּם:

6 And if any person turns to ghosts and familiar spirits and goes astray after them, I will set My face against that person and cut him off from among his people.

ו וְהַנֶּפֶשׁ אֲשֶׁר תִּפְנֶה אֶל־הָאֹבֹת וְאֶל־הַיִּדְּעֹנִים לִזְנוֹת אַחֲרֵיהֶם וְנָתַתִּי אֶת־פָּנַי בַּנֶּפֶשׁ הַהִוא וְהִכְרַתִּי אֹתוֹ מִקֶּרֶב עַמּוֹ:

7 You shall sanctify yourselves and be holy, for I *Hashem* am your God.

ז וְהִתְקַדִּשְׁתֶּם וִהְיִיתֶם קְדֹשִׁים כִּי אֲנִי יְהֹוָה אֱלֹהֵיכֶם:

8 You shall faithfully observe My laws: I *Hashem* make you holy.

ח וּשְׁמַרְתֶּם אֶת־חֻקֹּתַי וַעֲשִׂיתֶם אֹתָם אֲנִי יְהֹוָה מְקַדִּשְׁכֶם:

9 If anyone insults his father or his mother, he shall be put to death; he has insulted his father and his mother – his bloodguilt is upon him.

ט כִּי־אִישׁ אִישׁ אֲשֶׁר יְקַלֵּל אֶת־אָבִיו וְאֶת־אִמּוֹ מוֹת יוּמָת אָבִיו וְאִמּוֹ קִלֵּל דָּמָיו בּוֹ:

10 If a man commits adultery with a married woman, committing adultery with another man's wife, the adulterer and the adulteress shall be put to death.

י וְאִישׁ אֲשֶׁר יִנְאַף אֶת־אֵשֶׁת אִישׁ אֲשֶׁר יִנְאַף אֶת־אֵשֶׁת רֵעֵהוּ מוֹת־יוּמַת הַנֹּאֵף וְהַנֹּאָפֶת:

11 If a man lies with his father's wife, it is the nakedness of his father that he has uncovered; the two shall be put to death – their bloodguilt is upon them.

יא וְאִישׁ אֲשֶׁר יִשְׁכַּב אֶת־אֵשֶׁת אָבִיו עֶרְוַת אָבִיו גִּלָּה מוֹת־יוּמְתוּ שְׁנֵיהֶם דְּמֵיהֶם בָּם:

12 If a man lies with his daughter-in-law, both of them shall be put to death; they have committed incest – their bloodguilt is upon them.

יב וְאִישׁ אֲשֶׁר יִשְׁכַּב אֶת־כַּלָּתוֹ מוֹת יוּמְתוּ שְׁנֵיהֶם תֶּבֶל עָשׂוּ דְּמֵיהֶם בָּם:

13 If a man lies with a male as one lies with a woman, the two of them have done an abhorrent thing; they shall be put to death – their bloodguilt is upon them.

יג וְאִישׁ אֲשֶׁר יִשְׁכַּב אֶת־זָכָר מִשְׁכְּבֵי אִשָּׁה תּוֹעֵבָה עָשׂוּ שְׁנֵיהֶם מוֹת יוּמָתוּ דְּמֵיהֶם בָּם:

14 If a man marries a woman and her mother, it is depravity; both he and they shall be put to the fire, that there be no depravity among you.

יד וְאִישׁ אֲשֶׁר יִקַּח אֶת־אִשָּׁה וְאֶת־אִמָּהּ זִמָּה הִוא בָּאֵשׁ יִשְׂרְפוּ אֹתוֹ וְאֶתְהֶן וְלֹא־תִהְיֶה זִמָּה בְּתוֹכְכֶם:

15 If a man has carnal relations with a beast, he shall be put to death; and you shall kill the beast.

טו וְאִישׁ אֲשֶׁר יִתֵּן שְׁכָבְתּוֹ בִּבְהֵמָה מוֹת יוּמָת וְאֶת־הַבְּהֵמָה תַּהֲרֹגוּ:

Vayikra/Leviticus 20
Kedoshim

ויקרא כ
קדושים

16 If a woman approaches any beast to mate with it, you shall kill the woman and the beast; they shall be put to death – their bloodguilt is upon them.

טז וְאִשָּׁה אֲשֶׁר תִּקְרַב אֶל־כָּל־בְּהֵמָה לְרִבְעָה אֹתָהּ וְהָרַגְתָּ אֶת־הָאִשָּׁה וְאֶת־הַבְּהֵמָה מוֹת יוּמָתוּ דְּמֵיהֶם בָּם:

17 If a man marries his sister, the daughter of either his father or his mother, so that he sees her nakedness and she sees his nakedness, it is a disgrace; they shall be excommunicated in the sight of their kinsfolk. He has uncovered the nakedness of his sister, he shall bear his guilt.

יז וְאִישׁ אֲשֶׁר־יִקַּח אֶת־אֲחֹתוֹ בַּת־אָבִיו אוֹ בַת־אִמּוֹ וְרָאָה אֶת־עֶרְוָתָהּ וְהִיא־תִרְאֶה אֶת־עֶרְוָתוֹ חֶסֶד הוּא וְנִכְרְתוּ לְעֵינֵי בְּנֵי עַמָּם עֶרְוַת אֲחֹתוֹ גִּלָּה עֲוֹנוֹ יִשָּׂא:

18 If a man lies with a woman in her infirmity and uncovers her nakedness, he has laid bare her flow and she has exposed her blood flow; both of them shall be cut off from among their people.

יח וְאִישׁ אֲשֶׁר־יִשְׁכַּב אֶת־אִשָּׁה דָּוָה וְגִלָּה אֶת־עֶרְוָתָהּ אֶת־מְקֹרָהּ הֶעֱרָה וְהִיא גִּלְּתָה אֶת־מְקוֹר דָּמֶיהָ וְנִכְרְתוּ שְׁנֵיהֶם מִקֶּרֶב עַמָּם:

19 You shall not uncover the nakedness of your mother's sister or of your father's sister, for that is laying bare one's own flesh; they shall bear their guilt.

יט וְעֶרְוַת אֲחוֹת אִמְּךָ וַאֲחוֹת אָבִיךָ לֹא תְגַלֵּה כִּי אֶת־שְׁאֵרוֹ הֶעֱרָה עֲוֹנָם יִשָּׂאוּ:

20 If a man lies with his uncle's wife, it is his uncle's nakedness that he has uncovered. They shall bear their guilt: they shall die childless.

כ וְאִישׁ אֲשֶׁר יִשְׁכַּב אֶת־דֹּדָתוֹ עֶרְוַת דֹּדוֹ גִּלָּה חֶטְאָם יִשָּׂאוּ עֲרִירִים יָמֻתוּ:

21 If a man marries the wife of his brother, it is indecency. It is the nakedness of his brother that he has uncovered; they shall remain childless.

כא וְאִישׁ אֲשֶׁר יִקַּח אֶת־אֵשֶׁת אָחִיו נִדָּה הִוא עֶרְוַת אָחִיו גִּלָּה עֲרִירִים יִהְיוּ:

22 You shall faithfully observe all My laws and all My regulations, lest the land to which I bring you to settle in spew you out.

כב וּשְׁמַרְתֶּם אֶת־כָּל־חֻקֹּתַי וְאֶת־כָּל־מִשְׁפָּטַי וַעֲשִׂיתֶם אֹתָם וְלֹא־תָקִיא אֶתְכֶם הָאָרֶץ אֲשֶׁר אֲנִי מֵבִיא אֶתְכֶם שָׁמָּה לָשֶׁבֶת בָּהּ:

ush-mar-TEM et kol khu-ko-TAI v'-et kol mish-pa-TAI va-a-see-TEM o-TAM v'-lo ta-KEE et-KHEM ha-A-retz a-SHER a-NEE may-VEE et-KHEM SHA-mah la-SHE-vet BAH

23 You shall not follow the practices of the nation that I am driving out before you. For it is because they did all these things that I abhorred them

כג וְלֹא תֵלְכוּ בְּחֻקֹּת הַגּוֹי אֲשֶׁר־אֲנִי מְשַׁלֵּחַ מִפְּנֵיכֶם כִּי אֶת־כָּל־אֵלֶּה עָשׂוּ וָאָקֻץ בָּם:

20:22 Lest the land to which I bring you to settle in spew you out Following the warning in Chapter 18 against embracing the abominations of the Canaanites lest the Children of Israel be expelled from their land, Chapter 20 gives an example of such abominable behavior, containing a list of forbidden relationships that are detestable in *Hashem*'s eyes. This verse then says that they must follow the commandments, "lest the land to which I bring you to settle in spew you out." This expression attributes human-like sensitivity to the Land of Israel; it cannot stomach impurity and abomination, and thus engaging in illicit relationships will result in exile from the land. This is a further example of the reality that the gift of *Eretz Yisrael* is dependent on maintaining a high level of purity and faith, since the land's sanctity cannot tolerate immorality.

Vayikra/Leviticus 21
Emor

ויקרא כא
אמור

24 and said to you: You shall possess their land, for I will give it to you to possess, a land flowing with milk and honey. I *Hashem* am your God who has set you apart from other peoples.

כד וָאֹמַר לָכֶם אַתֶּם תִּירְשׁוּ אֶת־אַדְמָתָם וַאֲנִי אֶתְּנֶנָּה לָכֶם לָרֶשֶׁת אֹתָהּ אֶרֶץ זָבַת חָלָב וּדְבָשׁ אֲנִי יְהֹוָה אֱלֹהֵיכֶם אֲשֶׁר־הִבְדַּלְתִּי אֶתְכֶם מִן־הָעַמִּים׃

va-o-MAR la-KHEM a-TEM tee-r'-SHU et ad-ma-TAM va-a-NEE et-NE-na la-KHEM la-RE-shet o-TAH E-retz za-VAT kha-LAV ud-VASH a-NEE a-do-NAI e-lo-hay-KHEM a-sher hiv-DAL-tee et-KHEM min ha-a-MEEM

25 So you shall set apart the clean beast from the unclean, the unclean bird from the clean. You shall not draw abomination upon yourselves through beast or bird or anything with which the ground is alive, which I have set apart for you to treat as unclean.

כה וְהִבְדַּלְתֶּם בֵּין־הַבְּהֵמָה הַטְּהֹרָה לַטְּמֵאָה וּבֵין־הָעוֹף הַטָּמֵא לַטָּהֹר וְלֹא־תְשַׁקְּצוּ אֶת־נַפְשֹׁתֵיכֶם בַּבְּהֵמָה וּבָעוֹף וּבְכֹל אֲשֶׁר תִּרְמֹשׂ הָאֲדָמָה אֲשֶׁר־הִבְדַּלְתִּי לָכֶם לְטַמֵּא׃

26 You shall be holy to Me, for I *Hashem* am holy, and I have set you apart from other peoples to be Mine.

כו וִהְיִיתֶם לִי קְדֹשִׁים כִּי קָדוֹשׁ אֲנִי יְהֹוָה וָאַבְדִּל אֶתְכֶם מִן־הָעַמִּים לִהְיוֹת לִי׃

27 A man or a woman who has a ghost or a familiar spirit shall be put to death; they shall be pelted with stones – their bloodguilt shall be upon them.

כז וְאִישׁ אוֹ־אִשָּׁה כִּי־יִהְיֶה בָהֶם אוֹב אוֹ יִדְּעֹנִי מוֹת יוּמָתוּ בָּאֶבֶן יִרְגְּמוּ אֹתָם דְּמֵיהֶם בָּם׃

21 1 *Hashem* said to *Moshe*: Speak to the *Kohanim*, the sons of *Aharon*, and say to them: None shall defile himself for any [dead] person among his kin,

כא א וַיֹּאמֶר יְהֹוָה אֶל־מֹשֶׁה אֱמֹר אֶל־הַכֹּהֲנִים בְּנֵי אַהֲרֹן וְאָמַרְתָּ אֲלֵהֶם לְנֶפֶשׁ לֹא־יִטַּמָּא בְּעַמָּיו׃

va-YO-mer a-do-NAI el mo-SHEH e-MOR el ha-ko-ha-NEEM b'-NAY a-ha-RON v'-a-mar-TA a-lay-HEM l'-NE-fesh lo yi-ta-MA b'-a-MAV

2 except for the relatives that are closest to him: his mother, his father, his son, his daughter, and his brother;

ב כִּי אִם־לִשְׁאֵרוֹ הַקָּרֹב אֵלָיו לְאִמּוֹ וּלְאָבִיו וְלִבְנוֹ וּלְבִתּוֹ וּלְאָחִיו׃

3 also for a virgin sister, close to him because she has not married, for her he may defile himself.

ג וְלַאֲחֹתוֹ הַבְּתוּלָה הַקְּרוֹבָה אֵלָיו אֲשֶׁר לֹא־הָיְתָה לְאִישׁ לָהּ יִטַּמָּא׃

4 But he shall not defile himself as a kinsman by marriage, and so profane himself.

ד לֹא יִטַּמָּא בַּעַל בְּעַמָּיו לְהֵחַלּוֹ׃

21:1 None shall defile himself for any [dead] person among his kin While the entire Nation of Israel is commanded to maintain a certain level of holiness, the *Kohanim* were held to an even higher standard. For example, a priest may not become ritually impure through contact with a dead body. Therefore, he may not participate in the burial of anyone other than his immediate relatives. However, *Rashi* teaches that there is an exception to this rule. If there is no one else to bury the person, then even the *Kohen Gadol* is obligated to perform the burial, even if the deceased is not "among his kin." This is particularly striking, since under normal circumstances, unlike ordinary *Kohanim*, the *Kohen Gadol* may not participate in the burial of even his closest relatives. In this way, the Bible teaches that an elevated status must not make one oblivious to the needs of people. On the contrary, it is the obligation of those with heightened responsibility to see to it that everyone is taken care of, even at the expense of their own personal state of holiness.

Vayikra/Leviticus 21
Emor

5 They shall not shave smooth any part of their heads, or cut the side-growth of their beards, or make gashes in their flesh.

6 They shall be holy to their God and not profane the name of their God; for they offer *Hashem*'s offerings by fire, the food of their God, and so must be holy.

7 They shall not marry a woman defiled by harlotry, nor shall they marry one divorced from her husband. For they are holy to their God

8 and you must treat them as holy, since they offer the food of your God; they shall be holy to you, for I *Hashem* who sanctify you am holy.

9 When the daughter of a *Kohen* defiles herself through harlotry, it is her father whom she defiles; she shall be put to the fire.

10 The *Kohen* who is exalted above his fellows, on whose head the anointing oil has been poured and who has been ordained to wear the vestments, shall not bare his head or rend his vestments.

11 He shall not go in where there is any dead body; he shall not defile himself even for his father or mother.

12 He shall not go outside the sanctuary and profane the sanctuary of his God, for upon him is the distinction of the anointing oil of his God, Mine *Hashem*'s.

13 He may marry only a woman who is a virgin.

14 A widow, or a divorced woman, or one who is degraded by harlotry – such he may not marry. Only a virgin of his own kin may he take to wife –

15 that he may not profane his offspring among his kin, for I *Hashem* have sanctified him.

16 *Hashem* spoke further to *Moshe*:

17 Speak to *Aharon* and say: No man of your offspring throughout the ages who has a defect shall be qualified to offer the food of his God.

18 No one at all who has a defect shall be qualified: no man who is blind, or lame, or has a limb too short or too long;

19 no man who has a broken leg or a broken arm;

ויקרא כא
אמור

ה לֹא־יִקְרְח֤וּ [יִקְרְחוּ֙] קָרְחָה֙ בְּרֹאשָׁ֔ם וּפְאַ֥ת זְקָנָ֖ם לֹ֣א יְגַלֵּ֑חוּ וּבִ֨בְשָׂרָ֔ם לֹ֥א יִשְׂרְט֖וּ שָׂרָֽטֶת׃

ו קְדֹשִׁ֤ים יִהְיוּ֙ לֵאלֹ֣הֵיהֶ֔ם וְלֹ֣א יְחַלְּל֔וּ שֵׁ֖ם אֱלֹהֵיהֶ֑ם כִּי֩ אֶת־אִשֵּׁ֨י יְהוָ֜ה לֶ֧חֶם אֱלֹהֵיהֶ֛ם הֵ֥ם מַקְרִיבִ֖ם וְהָ֥יוּ קֹֽדֶשׁ׃

ז אִשָּׁ֨ה זֹנָ֤ה וַחֲלָלָה֙ לֹ֣א יִקָּ֔חוּ וְאִשָּׁ֛ה גְּרוּשָׁ֥ה מֵאִישָׁ֖הּ לֹ֣א יִקָּ֑חוּ כִּֽי־קָדֹ֥שׁ ה֖וּא לֵאלֹהָֽיו׃

ח וְקִדַּשְׁתּ֔וֹ כִּֽי־אֶת־לֶ֥חֶם אֱלֹהֶ֖יךָ ה֣וּא מַקְרִ֑יב קָדֹשׁ֙ יִֽהְיֶה־לָּ֔ךְ כִּ֣י קָד֔וֹשׁ אֲנִ֥י יְהוָ֖ה מְקַדִּשְׁכֶֽם׃

ט וּבַת֙ אִ֣ישׁ כֹּהֵ֔ן כִּ֥י תֵחֵ֖ל לִזְנ֑וֹת אֶת־אָבִ֨יהָ֙ הִ֣יא מְחַלֶּ֔לֶת בָּאֵ֖שׁ תִּשָּׂרֵֽף׃

י וְהַכֹּהֵן֩ הַגָּד֨וֹל מֵאֶחָ֜יו אֲ‍ֽשֶׁר־יוּצַ֥ק עַל־רֹאשׁ֣וֹ ׀ שֶׁ֤מֶן הַמִּשְׁחָה֙ וּמִלֵּ֣א אֶת־יָד֔וֹ לִלְבֹּ֖שׁ אֶת־הַבְּגָדִ֑ים אֶת־רֹאשׁוֹ֙ לֹ֣א יִפְרָ֔ע וּבְגָדָ֖יו לֹ֥א יִפְרֹֽם׃

יא וְעַ֛ל כָּל־נַפְשֹׁ֥ת מֵ֖ת לֹ֣א יָבֹ֑א לְאָבִ֥יו וּלְאִמּ֖וֹ לֹ֥א יִטַּמָּֽא׃

יב וּמִן־הַמִּקְדָּשׁ֙ לֹ֣א יֵצֵ֔א וְלֹ֣א יְחַלֵּ֔ל אֵ֖ת מִקְדַּ֣שׁ אֱלֹהָ֑יו כִּ֡י נֵ֠זֶר שֶׁ֣מֶן מִשְׁחַ֧ת אֱלֹהָ֛יו עָלָ֖יו אֲנִ֥י יְהוָֽה׃

יג וְה֕וּא אִשָּׁ֥ה בִבְתוּלֶ֖יהָ יִקָּֽח׃

יד אַלְמָנָ֤ה וּגְרוּשָׁה֙ וַחֲלָלָ֣ה זֹנָ֔ה אֶת־אֵ֖לֶּה לֹ֣א יִקָּ֑ח כִּ֛י אִם־בְּתוּלָ֥ה מֵעַמָּ֖יו יִקַּ֥ח אִשָּֽׁה׃

טו וְלֹֽא־יְחַלֵּ֥ל זַרְע֖וֹ בְּעַמָּ֑יו כִּ֛י אֲנִ֥י יְהוָ֖ה מְקַדְּשֽׁוֹ׃

טז וַיְדַבֵּ֥ר יְהוָ֖ה אֶל־מֹשֶׁ֥ה לֵּאמֹֽר׃

יז דַּבֵּ֥ר אֶֽל־אַהֲרֹ֖ן לֵאמֹ֑ר אִ֣ישׁ מִֽזַּרְעֲךָ֞ לְדֹרֹתָ֗ם אֲשֶׁ֨ר יִהְיֶ֥ה בוֹ֙ מ֔וּם לֹ֣א יִקְרַ֔ב לְהַקְרִ֖יב לֶ֥חֶם אֱלֹהָֽיו׃

יח כִּ֥י כָל־אִ֛ישׁ אֲשֶׁר־בּ֥וֹ מ֖וּם לֹ֣א יִקְרָ֑ב אִ֤ישׁ עִוֵּר֙ א֣וֹ פִסֵּ֔חַ א֥וֹ חָרֻ֖ם א֥וֹ שָׂרֽוּעַ׃

יט א֣וֹ אִ֔ישׁ אֲשֶׁר־יִהְיֶ֥ה ב֖וֹ שֶׁ֣בֶר רָ֑גֶל א֖וֹ שֶׁ֥בֶר יָֽד׃

Vayikra/Leviticus 22
Emor

ויקרא כב
אמור

20 or who is a hunchback, or a dwarf, or who has a growth in his eye, or who has a boil-scar, or scurvy, or crushed testes.

כ אוֹ־גִבֵּ֣ן אוֹ־דַ֔ק אוֹ תְּבַלֻּ֖ל בְּעֵינ֑וֹ א֤וֹ גָרָב֙ א֣וֹ יַלֶּ֔פֶת א֖וֹ מְר֥וֹחַ אָֽשֶׁךְ׃

21 No man among the offspring of *Aharon* the *Kohen* who has a defect shall be qualified to offer *Hashem*'s offering by fire; having a defect, he shall not be qualified to offer the food of his God.

כא כָּל־אִ֞ישׁ אֲשֶׁר־בּ֣וֹ מ֗וּם מִזֶּ֙רַע֙ אַהֲרֹ֣ן הַכֹּהֵ֔ן לֹ֣א יִגַּ֔שׁ לְהַקְרִ֖יב אֶת־אִשֵּׁ֣י יְהוָ֑ה מ֣וּם בּ֔וֹ אֵ֚ת לֶ֣חֶם אֱלֹהָ֔יו לֹ֥א יִגַּ֖שׁ לְהַקְרִֽיב׃

22 He may eat of the food of his God, of the most holy as well as of the holy;

כב לֶ֣חֶם אֱלֹהָ֔יו מִקָּדְשֵׁ֥י הַקֳּדָשִׁ֖ים וּמִן־הַקֳּדָשִׁ֥ים יֹאכֵֽל׃

23 but he shall not enter behind the curtain or come near the *Mizbayach*, for he has a defect. He shall not profane these places sacred to Me, for I *Hashem* have sanctified them.

כג אַ֣ךְ אֶל־הַפָּרֹ֜כֶת לֹ֣א יָבֹ֗א וְאֶל־הַמִּזְבֵּ֛חַ לֹ֥א יִגַּ֖שׁ כִּי־מ֣וּם בּ֑וֹ וְלֹ֤א יְחַלֵּל֙ אֶת־מִקְדָּשַׁ֔י כִּ֛י אֲנִ֥י יְהוָ֖ה מְקַדְּשָֽׁם׃

24 Thus *Moshe* spoke to *Aharon* and his sons and to all the Israelites.

כד וַיְדַבֵּ֣ר מֹשֶׁ֔ה אֶֽל־אַהֲרֹ֖ן וְאֶל־בָּנָ֑יו וְאֶֽל־כָּל־בְּנֵ֥י יִשְׂרָאֵֽל׃

22 1 *Hashem* spoke to *Moshe*, saying:

כב א וַיְדַבֵּ֥ר יְהוָ֖ה אֶל־מֹשֶׁ֥ה לֵּאמֹֽר׃

2 Instruct *Aharon* and his sons to be scrupulous about the sacred donations that *B'nei Yisrael* consecrate to Me, lest they profane My holy name, Mine *Hashem*'s.

ב דַּבֵּ֨ר אֶֽל־אַהֲרֹ֜ן וְאֶל־בָּנָ֗יו וְיִנָּֽזְרוּ֙ מִקָּדְשֵׁ֣י בְנֵֽי־יִשְׂרָאֵ֔ל וְלֹ֥א יְחַלְּל֖וּ אֶת־שֵׁ֣ם קָדְשִׁ֑י אֲשֶׁ֨ר הֵ֧ם מַקְדִּשִׁ֛ים לִ֖י אֲנִ֥י יְהוָֽה׃

3 Say to them: Throughout the ages, if any man among your offspring, while in a state of uncleanness, partakes of any sacred donation that *B'nei Yisrael* may consecrate to *Hashem*, that person shall be cut off from before Me: I am *Hashem*.

ג אֱמֹ֣ר אֲלֵהֶ֗ם לְדֹרֹ֨תֵיכֶ֜ם כָּל־אִ֣ישׁ ׀ אֲשֶׁר־יִקְרַ֣ב מִכָּל־זַרְעֲכֶ֗ם אֶל־הַקֳּדָשִׁים֙ אֲשֶׁ֨ר יַקְדִּ֤ישׁוּ בְנֵֽי־יִשְׂרָאֵל֙ לַֽיהוָ֔ה וְטֻמְאָת֖וֹ עָלָ֑יו וְנִכְרְתָ֞ה הַנֶּ֧פֶשׁ הַהִ֛וא מִלְּפָנַ֖י אֲנִ֥י יְהוָֽה׃

4 No man of *Aharon*'s offspring who has an eruption or a discharge shall eat of the sacred donations until he is clean. If one touches anything made unclean by a corpse, or if a man has an emission of semen,

ד אִ֣ישׁ אִ֞ישׁ מִזֶּ֣רַע אַהֲרֹ֗ן וְה֤וּא צָר֙וּעַ֙ א֣וֹ זָ֔ב בַּקֳּדָשִׁים֙ לֹ֣א יֹאכַ֔ל עַ֖ד אֲשֶׁ֣ר יִטְהָ֑ר וְהַנֹּגֵ֙עַ֙ בְּכָל־טְמֵא־נֶ֔פֶשׁ א֣וֹ אִ֔ישׁ אֲשֶׁר־תֵּצֵ֥א מִמֶּ֖נּוּ שִׁכְבַת־זָֽרַע׃

5 or if a man touches any swarming thing by which he is made unclean or any human being by whom he is made unclean – whatever his uncleanness –

ה אוֹ־אִישׁ֙ אֲשֶׁ֣ר יִגַּ֔ע בְּכָל־שֶׁ֖רֶץ אֲשֶׁ֣ר יִטְמָא־ל֑וֹ א֤וֹ בְאָדָם֙ אֲשֶׁ֣ר יִטְמָא־ל֔וֹ לְכֹ֖ל טֻמְאָתֽוֹ׃

6 the person who touches such shall be unclean until evening and shall not eat of the sacred donations unless he has washed his body in water.

ו נֶ֚פֶשׁ אֲשֶׁ֣ר תִּגַּע־בּ֔וֹ וְטָמְאָ֖ה עַד־הָעָ֑רֶב וְלֹ֤א יֹאכַל֙ מִן־הַקֳּדָשִׁ֔ים כִּ֛י אִם־רָחַ֥ץ בְּשָׂר֖וֹ בַּמָּֽיִם׃

7 As soon as the sun sets, he shall be clean; and afterward he may eat of the sacred donations, for they are his food.

ז וּבָ֥א הַשֶּׁ֖מֶשׁ וְטָהֵ֑ר וְאַחַר֙ יֹאכַ֣ל מִן־הַקֳּדָשִׁ֔ים כִּ֥י לַחְמ֖וֹ הֽוּא׃

8 He shall not eat anything that died or was torn by beasts, thereby becoming unclean: I am *Hashem*.

ח נְבֵלָ֧ה וּטְרֵפָ֛ה לֹ֥א יֹאכַ֖ל לְטָמְאָה־בָ֑הּ אֲנִ֖י יְהוָֽה׃

Vayikra/Leviticus 22
Emor

9 They shall keep My charge, lest they incur guilt thereby and die for it, having committed profanation: I *Hashem* consecrate them.

ט וְשָׁמְרוּ אֶת־מִשְׁמַרְתִּי וְלֹא־יִשְׂאוּ עָלָיו חֵטְא וּמֵתוּ בוֹ כִּי יְחַלְּלֻהוּ אֲנִי יְהֹוָה מְקַדְּשָׁם:

10 No lay person shall eat of the sacred donations. No bound or hired laborer of a *Kohen* shall eat of the sacred donations;

י וְכָל־זָר לֹא־יֹאכַל קֹדֶשׁ תּוֹשַׁב כֹּהֵן וְשָׂכִיר לֹא־יֹאכַל קֹדֶשׁ:

11 but a person who is a *Kohen*'s property by purchase may eat of them; and those that are born into his household may eat of his food.

יא וְכֹהֵן כִּי־יִקְנֶה נֶפֶשׁ קִנְיַן כַּסְפּוֹ הוּא יֹאכַל בּוֹ וִילִיד בֵּיתוֹ הֵם יֹאכְלוּ בְלַחְמוֹ:

12 If a *Kohen*'s daughter marries a layman, she may not eat of the sacred gifts;

יב וּבַת־כֹּהֵן כִּי תִהְיֶה לְאִישׁ זָר הִוא בִּתְרוּמַת הַקֳּדָשִׁים לֹא תֹאכֵל:

13 but if the *Kohen*'s daughter is widowed or divorced and without offspring, and is back in her father's house as in her youth, she may eat of her father's food. No lay person may eat of it:

יג וּבַת־כֹּהֵן כִּי תִהְיֶה אַלְמָנָה וּגְרוּשָׁה וְזֶרַע אֵין לָהּ וְשָׁבָה אֶל־בֵּית אָבִיהָ כִּנְעוּרֶיהָ מִלֶּחֶם אָבִיהָ תֹּאכֵל וְכָל־זָר לֹא־יֹאכַל בּוֹ:

14 but if a man eats of a sacred donation unwittingly, he shall pay the *Kohen* for the sacred donation, adding one-fifth of its value.

יד וְאִישׁ כִּי־יֹאכַל קֹדֶשׁ בִּשְׁגָגָה וְיָסַף חֲמִשִׁיתוֹ עָלָיו וְנָתַן לַכֹּהֵן אֶת־הַקֹּדֶשׁ:

15 But [the *Kohanim*] must not allow the Israelites to profane the sacred donations that they set aside for *Hashem*,

טו וְלֹא יְחַלְּלוּ אֶת־קָדְשֵׁי בְּנֵי יִשְׂרָאֵל אֵת אֲשֶׁר־יָרִימוּ לַיהוָה:

16 or to incur guilt requiring a penalty payment, by eating such sacred donations: for it is I *Hashem* who make them sacred.

טז וְהִשִּׂיאוּ אוֹתָם עֲוֹן אַשְׁמָה בְּאָכְלָם אֶת־קָדְשֵׁיהֶם כִּי אֲנִי יְהֹוָה מְקַדְּשָׁם:

17 *Hashem* spoke to *Moshe*, saying:

יז וַיְדַבֵּר יְהֹוָה אֶל־מֹשֶׁה לֵּאמֹר:

18 Speak to *Aharon* and his sons, and to all *B'nei Yisrael*, and say to them: When any man of the house of *Yisrael* or of the strangers in *Yisrael* presents a burnt offering as his offering for any of the votive or any of the freewill offerings that they offer to *Hashem*,

יח דַּבֵּר אֶל־אַהֲרֹן וְאֶל־בָּנָיו וְאֶל כָּל־בְּנֵי יִשְׂרָאֵל וְאָמַרְתָּ אֲלֵהֶם אִישׁ אִישׁ מִבֵּית יִשְׂרָאֵל וּמִן־הַגֵּר בְּיִשְׂרָאֵל אֲשֶׁר יַקְרִיב קָרְבָּנוֹ לְכָל־נִדְרֵיהֶם וּלְכָל־נִדְבוֹתָם אֲשֶׁר־יַקְרִיבוּ לַיהוָה לְעֹלָה:

19 it must, to be acceptable in your favor, be a male without blemish, from cattle or sheep or goats.

יט לִרְצֹנְכֶם תָּמִים זָכָר בַּבָּקָר בַּכְּשָׂבִים וּבָעִזִּים:

20 You shall not offer any that has a defect, for it will not be accepted in your favor.

כ כֹּל אֲשֶׁר־בּוֹ מוּם לֹא תַקְרִיבוּ כִּי־לֹא לְרָצוֹן יִהְיֶה לָכֶם:

21 And when a man offers, from the herd or the flock, a sacrifice of well-being to *Hashem* for an explicit vow or as a freewill offering, it must, to be acceptable, be without blemish; there must be no defect in it.

כא וְאִישׁ כִּי־יַקְרִיב זֶבַח־שְׁלָמִים לַיהוָה לְפַלֵּא־נֶדֶר אוֹ לִנְדָבָה בַּבָּקָר אוֹ בַצֹּאן תָּמִים יִהְיֶה לְרָצוֹן כָּל־מוּם לֹא יִהְיֶה־בּוֹ:

Vayikra/Leviticus 22
Emor

ויקרא כב
אמור

22 Anything blind, or injured, or maimed, or with a wen, boil-scar, or scurvy – such you shall not offer to *Hashem*; you shall not put any of them on the *Mizbayach* as offerings by fire to *Hashem*.

כב עַוֶּרֶת אוֹ שָׁבוּר אוֹ־חָרוּץ אוֹ־יַבֶּלֶת אוֹ גָרָב אוֹ יַלֶּפֶת לֹא־תַקְרִיבוּ אֵלֶּה לַיהוָה וְאִשֶּׁה לֹא־תִתְּנוּ מֵהֶם עַל־הַמִּזְבֵּחַ לַיהוָה׃

23 You may, however, present as a freewill offering an ox or a sheep with a limb extended or contracted; but it will not be accepted for a vow.

כג וְשׁוֹר וָשֶׂה שָׂרוּעַ וְקָלוּט נְדָבָה תַּעֲשֶׂה אֹתוֹ וּלְנֵדֶר לֹא יֵרָצֶה׃

24 You shall not offer to *Hashem* anything [with its testes] bruised or crushed or torn or cut. You shall have no such practices in your own land,

כד וּמָעוּךְ וְכָתוּת וְנָתוּק וְכָרוּת לֹא תַקְרִיבוּ לַיהוָה וּבְאַרְצְכֶם לֹא תַעֲשׂוּ׃

25 nor shall you accept such [animals] from a foreigner for offering as food for your God, for they are mutilated, they have a defect; they shall not be accepted in your favor.

כה וּמִיַּד בֶּן־נֵכָר לֹא תַקְרִיבוּ אֶת־לֶחֶם אֱלֹהֵיכֶם מִכָּל־אֵלֶּה כִּי מָשְׁחָתָם בָּהֶם מוּם בָּם לֹא יֵרָצוּ לָכֶם׃

26 *Hashem* spoke to *Moshe*, saying:

כו וַיְדַבֵּר יְהוָה אֶל־מֹשֶׁה לֵּאמֹר׃

27 When an ox or a sheep or a goat is born, it shall stay seven days with its mother, and from the eighth day on it shall be acceptable as an offering by fire to *Hashem*.

כז שׁוֹר אוֹ־כֶשֶׂב אוֹ־עֵז כִּי יִוָּלֵד וְהָיָה שִׁבְעַת יָמִים תַּחַת אִמּוֹ וּמִיּוֹם הַשְּׁמִינִי וָהָלְאָה יֵרָצֶה לְקָרְבַּן אִשֶּׁה לַיהוָה׃

28 However, no animal from the herd or from the flock shall be slaughtered on the same day with its young.

כח וְשׁוֹר אוֹ־שֶׂה אֹתוֹ וְאֶת־בְּנוֹ לֹא תִשְׁחֲטוּ בְּיוֹם אֶחָד׃

29 When you sacrifice a thanksgiving offering to *Hashem*, sacrifice it so that it may be acceptable in your favor.

כט וְכִי־תִזְבְּחוּ זֶבַח־תּוֹדָה לַיהוָה לִרְצֹנְכֶם תִּזְבָּחוּ׃

30 It shall be eaten on the same day; you shall not leave any of it until morning: I am *Hashem*.

ל בַּיּוֹם הַהוּא יֵאָכֵל לֹא־תוֹתִירוּ מִמֶּנּוּ עַד־בֹּקֶר אֲנִי יְהוָה׃

31 You shall faithfully observe My commandments: I am *Hashem*.

לא וּשְׁמַרְתֶּם מִצְוֹתַי וַעֲשִׂיתֶם אֹתָם אֲנִי יְהוָה׃

32 You shall not profane My holy name, that I may be sanctified in the midst of *B'nei Yisrael* – I *Hashem* who sanctify you,

לב וְלֹא תְחַלְּלוּ אֶת־שֵׁם קָדְשִׁי וְנִקְדַּשְׁתִּי בְּתוֹךְ בְּנֵי יִשְׂרָאֵל אֲנִי יְהוָה מְקַדִּשְׁכֶם׃

v'-LO t'-kha-l'-LU et SHAYM ko-d'-SHEE v'-NIK-dash-TEE b'-TOKH b'-NAY yis-ra-AYL a-NEE a-do-NAI m'-ka-dish-KHEM

22:32 That I may be sanctified in the midst of the *B'nei Yisrael* This verse addresses the imperative to sanctify the name of *Hashem*. *Rashi* comments that the juxtaposition of the command to make *Hashem*'s name holy with the statement "I am *Hashem*... Who brought you out of the land of Egypt" implies that God took the Children of Israel out of Egypt on condition that they sanctify His name. According to the Talmud (*Yoma* 86a), the primary way to sanctify *Hashem*'s name is through ensuring that one's behavior reflects positively upon *Hashem*. One must act in accordance with His commandments and treat others with kindness, consideration and honesty. The mandate to sanctify God's name guides the State of Israel, and the IDF in particular, to hold itself to the highest standards of morality.

Rashi
(1040–1105)

Vayikra/Leviticus 23
Emor

ויקרא כג
אמור

33 I who brought you out of the land of Egypt to be your God, I *Hashem*.

לו הַמּוֹצִיא אֶתְכֶם מֵאֶרֶץ מִצְרַיִם לִהְיוֹת לָכֶם לֵאלֹהִים אֲנִי יְהוָה:

ha-mo-TZEE at-KHEM may-E-retz mitz-RA-yim lih-YOT la-KHEM lay-lo-HEEM a-NEE a-do-NAI

23

1 *Hashem* spoke to *Moshe*, saying:

כג א וַיְדַבֵּר יְהוָה אֶל־מֹשֶׁה לֵּאמֹר:

2 Speak to *B'nei Yisrael* and say to them: These are My fixed times, the fixed times of *Hashem*, which you shall proclaim as sacred occasions.

ב דַּבֵּר אֶל־בְּנֵי יִשְׂרָאֵל וְאָמַרְתָּ אֲלֵהֶם מוֹעֲדֵי יְהוָה אֲשֶׁר־תִּקְרְאוּ אֹתָם מִקְרָאֵי קֹדֶשׁ אֵלֶּה הֵם מוֹעֲדָי:

3 On six days work may be done, but on the seventh day there shall be a *Shabbat* of complete rest, a sacred occasion. You shall do no work; it shall be a *Shabbat* of *Hashem* throughout your settlements.

ג שֵׁשֶׁת יָמִים תֵּעָשֶׂה מְלָאכָה וּבַיּוֹם הַשְּׁבִיעִי שַׁבַּת שַׁבָּתוֹן מִקְרָא־קֹדֶשׁ כָּל־מְלָאכָה לֹא תַעֲשׂוּ שַׁבָּת הִוא לַיהוָה בְּכֹל מוֹשְׁבֹתֵיכֶם:

4 These are the set times of *Hashem*, the sacred occasions, which you shall celebrate each at its appointed time:

ד אֵלֶּה מוֹעֲדֵי יְהוָה מִקְרָאֵי קֹדֶשׁ אֲשֶׁר־תִּקְרְאוּ אֹתָם בְּמוֹעֲדָם:

5 In the first month, on the fourteenth day of the month, at twilight, there shall be a *Pesach* offering to *Hashem*,

ה בַּחֹדֶשׁ הָרִאשׁוֹן בְּאַרְבָּעָה עָשָׂר לַחֹדֶשׁ בֵּין הָעַרְבָּיִם פֶּסַח לַיהוָה:

6 and on the fifteenth day of that month *Hashem*'s Feast of Unleavened Bread. You shall eat unleavened bread for seven days.

ו וּבַחֲמִשָּׁה עָשָׂר יוֹם לַחֹדֶשׁ הַזֶּה חַג הַמַּצּוֹת לַיהוָה שִׁבְעַת יָמִים מַצּוֹת תֹּאכֵלוּ:

7 On the first day you shall celebrate a sacred occasion: you shall not work at your occupations.

ז בַּיּוֹם הָרִאשׁוֹן מִקְרָא־קֹדֶשׁ יִהְיֶה לָכֶם כָּל־מְלֶאכֶת עֲבֹדָה לֹא תַעֲשׂוּ:

8 Seven days you shall make offerings by fire to *Hashem*. The seventh day shall be a sacred occasion: you shall not work at your occupations.

ח וְהִקְרַבְתֶּם אִשֶּׁה לַיהוָה שִׁבְעַת יָמִים בַּיּוֹם הַשְּׁבִיעִי מִקְרָא־קֹדֶשׁ כָּל־מְלֶאכֶת עֲבֹדָה לֹא תַעֲשׂוּ:

9 *Hashem* spoke to *Moshe*, saying:

ט וַיְדַבֵּר יְהוָה אֶל־מֹשֶׁה לֵּאמֹר:

10 Speak to *B'nei Yisrael* and say to them: When you enter the land that I am giving to you and you reap its harvest, you shall bring the first sheaf of your harvest to the *Kohen*.

י דַּבֵּר אֶל־בְּנֵי יִשְׂרָאֵל וְאָמַרְתָּ אֲלֵהֶם כִּי־תָבֹאוּ אֶל־הָאָרֶץ אֲשֶׁר אֲנִי נֹתֵן לָכֶם וּקְצַרְתֶּם אֶת־קְצִירָהּ וַהֲבֵאתֶם אֶת־עֹמֶר רֵאשִׁית קְצִירְכֶם אֶל־הַכֹּהֵן:

da-BAYR el b'-NAY yis-ra-AYL v'-a-mar-TA a-lay-HEM kee ta-VO-u el ha-A-retz a-SHER a-NEE no-TAYN la-KHEM uk-tzar-TEM et k'-tzee-RA va-ha-vay-TEM et O-mer ray-SHEET k'-tzee-r'-KHEM el ha-ko-HAYN

Barley growing in the Western Negev

23:10 You shall bring the first sheaf of your harvest The *omer* is an offering of barley brought to the *Beit Hamikdash* in *Yerushalayim* on the second day of *Pesach*, corresponding to the sixteenth day of the month of *Nisan*. Only once this offering was brought, all grain that had taken root prior to the time of the offering may be eaten. According to the Sages (*Kiddushin* 38a), it was on the sixteenth of *Nisan* that the Israelites ran out of manna after it ceased to fall following the death of *Moshe*. The offering of the first grain in the *Beit Hamikdash* on that day each year reminds us of the eternal lesson of the manna. We dedicate a portion of our crops to our

Vayikra/Leviticus 23
Emor

ויקרא כג
אמור

11 He shall elevate the sheaf before *Hashem* for acceptance in your behalf; the *Kohen* shall elevate it on the day after the *Shabbat*.

יא וְהֵנִיף אֶת־הָעֹמֶר לִפְנֵי יְהֹוָה לִרְצֹנְכֶם מִמׇּחֳרַת הַשַּׁבָּת יְנִיפֶנּוּ הַכֹּהֵן׃

12 On the day that you elevate the sheaf, you shall offer as a burnt offering to *Hashem* a lamb of the first year without blemish.

יב וַעֲשִׂיתֶם בְּיוֹם הֲנִיפְכֶם אֶת־הָעֹמֶר כֶּבֶשׂ תָּמִים בֶּן־שְׁנָתוֹ לְעֹלָה לַיהֹוָה׃

13 The meal offering with it shall be two-tenths of a measure of choice flour with oil mixed in, an offering by fire of pleasing odor to *Hashem*; and the libation with it shall be of wine, a quarter of a *hin*.

יג וּמִנְחָתוֹ שְׁנֵי עֶשְׂרֹנִים סֹלֶת בְּלוּלָה בַשֶּׁמֶן אִשֶּׁה לַיהֹוָה רֵיחַ נִיחֹחַ וְנִסְכֹּה יַיִן רְבִיעִת הַהִין׃

14 Until that very day, until you have brought the offering of your God, you shall eat no bread or parched grain or fresh ears; it is a law for all time throughout the ages in all your settlements.

יד וְלֶחֶם וְקָלִי וְכַרְמֶל לֹא תֹאכְלוּ עַד־עֶצֶם הַיּוֹם הַזֶּה עַד הֲבִיאֲכֶם אֶת־קׇרְבַּן אֱלֹהֵיכֶם חֻקַּת עוֹלָם לְדֹרֹתֵיכֶם בְּכֹל מֹשְׁבֹתֵיכֶם׃

15 And from the day on which you bring the sheaf of elevation offering – the day after the *Shabbat* – you shall count off seven weeks. They must be complete:

טו וּסְפַרְתֶּם לָכֶם מִמׇּחֳרַת הַשַּׁבָּת מִיּוֹם הֲבִיאֲכֶם אֶת־עֹמֶר הַתְּנוּפָה שֶׁבַע שַׁבָּתוֹת תְּמִימֹת תִּהְיֶינָה׃

16 you must count until the day after the seventh week – fifty days; then you shall bring an offering of new grain to *Hashem*.

טז עַד מִמׇּחֳרַת הַשַּׁבָּת הַשְּׁבִיעִת תִּסְפְּרוּ חֲמִשִּׁים יוֹם וְהִקְרַבְתֶּם מִנְחָה חֲדָשָׁה לַיהֹוָה׃

17 You shall bring from your settlements two loaves of bread as an elevation offering; each shall be made of two-tenths of a measure of choice flour, baked after leavening, as first fruits to *Hashem*.

יז מִמּוֹשְׁבֹתֵיכֶם תָּבִיאוּ לֶחֶם תְּנוּפָה שְׁתַּיִם שְׁנֵי עֶשְׂרֹנִים סֹלֶת תִּהְיֶינָה חָמֵץ תֵּאָפֶינָה בִּכּוּרִים לַיהֹוָה׃

18 With the bread you shall present, as burnt offerings to *Hashem*, seven yearling lambs without blemish, one bull of the herd, and two rams, with their meal offerings and libations, an offering by fire of pleasing odor to *Hashem*.

יח וְהִקְרַבְתֶּם עַל־הַלֶּחֶם שִׁבְעַת כְּבָשִׂים תְּמִימִם בְּנֵי שָׁנָה וּפַר בֶּן־בָּקָר אֶחָד וְאֵילִם שְׁנָיִם יִהְיוּ עֹלָה לַיהֹוָה וּמִנְחָתָם וְנִסְכֵּיהֶם אִשֵּׁה רֵיחַ־נִיחֹחַ לַיהֹוָה׃

19 You shall also offer one he-goat as a sin offering and two yearling lambs as a sacrifice of well-being.

יט וַעֲשִׂיתֶם שְׂעִיר־עִזִּים אֶחָד לְחַטָּאת וּשְׁנֵי כְבָשִׂים בְּנֵי שָׁנָה לְזֶבַח שְׁלָמִים׃

20 The *Kohen* shall elevate these – the two lambs – together with the bread of first fruits as an elevation offering before *Hashem*; they shall be holy to *Hashem*, for the *Kohen*.

כ וְהֵנִיף הַכֹּהֵן אֹתָם עַל לֶחֶם הַבִּכֻּרִים תְּנוּפָה לִפְנֵי יְהֹוָה עַל־שְׁנֵי כְּבָשִׂים קֹדֶשׁ יִהְיוּ לַיהֹוָה לַכֹּהֵן׃

Creator before we eat from them ourselves, to remind us that no matter how hard we work the land, and despite the tremendous human effort required to produce it, our sustenance is really a gift from God in heaven.

Vayikra/Leviticus 23
Emor

ויקרא כג
אמור

21 On that same day you shall hold a celebration; it shall be a sacred occasion for you; you shall not work at your occupations. This is a law for all time in all your settlements, throughout the ages.

וּקְרָאתֶם בְּעֶצֶם הַיּוֹם הַזֶּה מִקְרָא־קֹדֶשׁ יִהְיֶה לָכֶם כָּל־מְלֶאכֶת עֲבֹדָה לֹא תַעֲשׂוּ חֻקַּת עוֹלָם בְּכָל־מוֹשְׁבֹתֵיכֶם לְדֹרֹתֵיכֶם׃

22 And when you reap the harvest of your land, you shall not reap all the way to the edges of your field, or gather the gleanings of your harvest; you shall leave them for the poor and the stranger: I *Hashem* am your God.

וּבְקֻצְרְכֶם אֶת־קְצִיר אַרְצְכֶם לֹא־תְכַלֶּה פְּאַת שָׂדְךָ בְּקֻצְרֶךָ וְלֶקֶט קְצִירְךָ לֹא תְלַקֵּט לֶעָנִי וְלַגֵּר תַּעֲזֹב אֹתָם אֲנִי יְהֹוָה אֱלֹהֵיכֶם׃

uv-kutz-r'-KHEM et k'-TZEER ar-tz'-KHEM lo t'-kha-LE p'-AT sa-d'-KHA b'-kutz-RE-kha v'-LE-ket k'-tzee-r'-KHA LO te-la-KAYT le-a-NEE v'-la-GAYR ta-a-ZOV o-TAM a-NEE a-do-NAI e-LO-hay-khem

23 *Hashem* spoke to *Moshe,* saying:

וַיְדַבֵּר יְהֹוָה אֶל־מֹשֶׁה לֵּאמֹר׃

24 Speak to *B'nei Yisrael* thus: In the seventh month, on the first day of the month, you shall observe complete rest, a sacred occasion commemorated with loud blasts.

דַּבֵּר אֶל־בְּנֵי יִשְׂרָאֵל לֵאמֹר בַּחֹדֶשׁ הַשְּׁבִיעִי בְּאֶחָד לַחֹדֶשׁ יִהְיֶה לָכֶם שַׁבָּתוֹן זִכְרוֹן תְּרוּעָה מִקְרָא־קֹדֶשׁ׃

da-BAYR el b'-NAY yis-ra-AYL lay-MOR ba-KHO-desh ha-sh'-vee-EE b'-e-KHAD la-KHO-desh yih-YEH la-KHEM sha-ba-TON zikh-RON t'-ru-AH mik-ra KO-desh

25 You shall not work at your occupations; and you shall bring an offering by fire to *Hashem*.

כָּל־מְלֶאכֶת עֲבֹדָה לֹא תַעֲשׂוּ וְהִקְרַבְתֶּם אִשֶּׁה לַיהֹוָה׃

26 *Hashem* spoke to *Moshe,* saying:

וַיְדַבֵּר יְהֹוָה אֶל־מֹשֶׁה לֵּאמֹר׃

27 Mark, the tenth day of this seventh month is *Yom Kippur*. It shall be a sacred occasion for you: you shall practice self-denial, and you shall bring an offering by fire to *Hashem;*

אַךְ בֶּעָשׂוֹר לַחֹדֶשׁ הַשְּׁבִיעִי הַזֶּה יוֹם הַכִּפֻּרִים הוּא מִקְרָא־קֹדֶשׁ יִהְיֶה לָכֶם וְעִנִּיתֶם אֶת־נַפְשֹׁתֵיכֶם וְהִקְרַבְתֶּם אִשֶּׁה לַיהֹוָה׃

23:22 You shall not reap all the way to the edges of your field This verse describes some of the agricultural laws reflecting the biblical notion of charity. A farmer must leave a corner of his field unharvested, and may also not collect stalks of grain that fall during harvesting. Similarly, forgotten sheaves of grain and small grapes left on the vine must not be collected. Instead, each of these portions of the harvest must be left for the poor. These commandments only apply to farmers in Israel. Farmers outside of *Eretz Yisrael* may harvest their entire field, as reflected in the words "of your land," which refer specifically to the Land of Israel. This biblical imperative is still practiced in Israel today. Each season, farmers throughout Israel leave over millions of pounds of produce from the fields, which are collected by volunteers and distributed to poor people all over the country.

23:24 In the seventh month, on the first day of the month This verse refers to the celebration of the holiday of *Rosh Hashana*, the Jewish New Year and the first of the High Holidays. The story is told of a small, uneducated child who did not know Hebrew, and thus could not participate in the *Rosh Hashana* services. He desperately wanted to pray with the congregation on such a holy day, and so he entered the synagogue and hesitantly approached the Holy Ark. As the congregants looked at him in confusion, he called out to *Hashem* by simply reciting the letters of the Hebrew alphabet, the only Hebrew familiar to him. There was not a person in the room who wasn't moved by his pure desire to return to *Hashem*, and the gates of Heaven immediately opened to accept his prayers. Do not think that the road to heaven is closed to you, God is always ready to welcome anyone who sincerely desires to approach Him.

Vayikra/Leviticus 23
Emor

28 you shall do no work throughout that day. For it is *Yom Kippur*, on which expiation is made on your behalf before *Hashem* your God.

כח וְכָל־מְלָאכָה לֹא תַעֲשׂוּ בְּעֶצֶם הַיּוֹם הַזֶּה כִּי יוֹם כִּפֻּרִים הוּא לְכַפֵּר עֲלֵיכֶם לִפְנֵי יהוה אֱלֹהֵיכֶם:

29 Indeed, any person who does not practice self-denial throughout that day shall be cut off from his kin;

כט כִּי כָל־הַנֶּפֶשׁ אֲשֶׁר לֹא־תְעֻנֶּה בְּעֶצֶם הַיּוֹם הַזֶּה וְנִכְרְתָה מֵעַמֶּיהָ:

30 and whoever does any work throughout that day, I will cause that person to perish from among his people.

ל וְכָל־הַנֶּפֶשׁ אֲשֶׁר תַּעֲשֶׂה כָּל־מְלָאכָה בְּעֶצֶם הַיּוֹם הַזֶּה וְהַאֲבַדְתִּי אֶת־הַנֶּפֶשׁ הַהִוא מִקֶּרֶב עַמָּהּ:

31 Do no work whatever; it is a law for all time, throughout the ages in all your settlements.

לא כָּל־מְלָאכָה לֹא תַעֲשׂוּ חֻקַּת עוֹלָם לְדֹרֹתֵיכֶם בְּכֹל מֹשְׁבֹתֵיכֶם:

32 It shall be a *Shabbat* of complete rest for you, and you shall practice self-denial; on the ninth day of the month at evening, from evening to evening, you shall observe this your *Shabbat*.

לב שַׁבַּת שַׁבָּתוֹן הוּא לָכֶם וְעִנִּיתֶם אֶת־נַפְשֹׁתֵיכֶם בְּתִשְׁעָה לַחֹדֶשׁ בָּעֶרֶב מֵעֶרֶב עַד־עֶרֶב תִּשְׁבְּתוּ שַׁבַּתְּכֶם:

33 *Hashem* spoke to *Moshe*, saying:

לג וַיְדַבֵּר יהוה אֶל־מֹשֶׁה לֵּאמֹר:

34 Say to *B'nei Yisrael*: On the fifteenth day of this seventh month there shall be the festival of *Sukkot* to *Hashem*, [to last] seven days.

לד דַּבֵּר אֶל־בְּנֵי יִשְׂרָאֵל לֵאמֹר בַּחֲמִשָּׁה עָשָׂר יוֹם לַחֹדֶשׁ הַשְּׁבִיעִי הַזֶּה חַג הַסֻּכּוֹת שִׁבְעַת יָמִים לַיהוה:

35 The first day shall be a sacred occasion: you shall not work at your occupations;

לה בַּיּוֹם הָרִאשׁוֹן מִקְרָא־קֹדֶשׁ כָּל־מְלֶאכֶת עֲבֹדָה לֹא תַעֲשׂוּ:

36 seven days you shall bring offerings by fire to *Hashem*. On the eighth day you shall observe a sacred occasion and bring an offering by fire to *Hashem*; it is a solemn gathering: you shall not work at your occupations.

לו שִׁבְעַת יָמִים תַּקְרִיבוּ אִשֶּׁה לַיהוה בַּיּוֹם הַשְּׁמִינִי מִקְרָא־קֹדֶשׁ יִהְיֶה לָכֶם וְהִקְרַבְתֶּם אִשֶּׁה לַיהוה עֲצֶרֶת הִוא כָּל־מְלֶאכֶת עֲבֹדָה לֹא תַעֲשׂוּ:

37 Those are the set times of *Hashem* that you shall celebrate as sacred occasions, bringing offerings by fire to *Hashem* – burnt offerings, meal offerings, sacrifices, and libations, on each day what is proper to it –

לז אֵלֶּה מוֹעֲדֵי יהוה אֲשֶׁר־תִּקְרְאוּ אֹתָם מִקְרָאֵי קֹדֶשׁ לְהַקְרִיב אִשֶּׁה לַיהוה עֹלָה וּמִנְחָה זֶבַח וּנְסָכִים דְּבַר־יוֹם בְּיוֹמוֹ:

38 apart from the *Shabbatot* of *Hashem*, and apart from your gifts and from all your votive offerings and from all your freewill offerings that you give to *Hashem*.

לח מִלְּבַד שַׁבְּתֹת יהוה וּמִלְּבַד מַתְּנוֹתֵיכֶם וּמִלְּבַד כָּל־נִדְרֵיכֶם וּמִלְּבַד כָּל־נִדְבוֹתֵיכֶם אֲשֶׁר תִּתְּנוּ לַיהוה:

39 Mark, on the fifteenth day of the seventh month, when you have gathered in the yield of your land,

לט אַךְ בַּחֲמִשָּׁה עָשָׂר יוֹם לַחֹדֶשׁ הַשְּׁבִיעִי בְּאָסְפְּכֶם אֶת־תְּבוּאַת הָאָרֶץ תָּחֹגּוּ

23:39 On the first day you shall take One of the unique practices of the holiday of *Sukkot* is the taking of the four species. The Sages of the *Midrash* tell us that these four species symbolize four different personality types. The *etrog* (אתרוג), 'citron,' which is both fragrant and tasty, represents a person who knows *Torah*

Vayikra/Leviticus 23
Emor

ויקרא כג
אמור

you shall observe the festival of *Hashem* [to last] seven days: a complete rest on the first day, and a complete rest on the eighth day.

אֶת־חַג־יְהוָה שִׁבְעַת יָמִים בַּיּוֹם הָרִאשׁוֹן שַׁבָּתוֹן וּבַיּוֹם הַשְּׁמִינִי שַׁבָּתוֹן:

AKH ba-kha-mi-SHAH a-SAR YOM la-KHO-desh ha-sh'-vee-EE b'os-p'-KHEM et t'-vu-at ha-A-retz ta-KHO-gu et khag a-do-NAI shiv-AT ya-MEEM ba-YOM ha-ri-SHON sha-ba-TON u-va-YOM ha-sh'-mee-NEE sha-ba-TON

40 On the first day you shall take the product of hadar trees, branches of palm trees, boughs of leafy trees, and willows of the brook, and you shall rejoice before *Hashem* your God seven days.

מ וּלְקַחְתֶּם לָכֶם בַּיּוֹם הָרִאשׁוֹן פְּרִי עֵץ הָדָר כַּפֹּת תְּמָרִים וַעֲנַף עֵץ־עָבֹת וְעַרְבֵי־נָחַל וּשְׂמַחְתֶּם לִפְנֵי יְהוָה אֱלֹהֵיכֶם שִׁבְעַת יָמִים:

ul-kakh-TEM la-KHEM ba-YOM ha-ri-SHON p'-REE AYTZ ha-DAR ka-POT t'-ma-REEM va-a-NAF aytz a-VOT v'-ar-VAY NA-khal us-makh-TEM lif-NAY a-do-NAI e-lo-hay-KHEM shiv-AT ya-MEEM

41 You shall observe it as a festival of *Hashem* for seven days in the year; you shall observe it in the seventh month as a law for all time, throughout the ages.

מא וְחַגֹּתֶם אֹתוֹ חַג לַיהוָה שִׁבְעַת יָמִים בַּשָּׁנָה חֻקַּת עוֹלָם לְדֹרֹתֵיכֶם בַּחֹדֶשׁ הַשְּׁבִיעִי תָּחֹגּוּ אֹתוֹ:

42 You shall live in booths seven days; all citizens in *Yisrael* shall live in booths,

מב בַּסֻּכֹּת תֵּשְׁבוּ שִׁבְעַת יָמִים כָּל־הָאֶזְרָח בְּיִשְׂרָאֵל יֵשְׁבוּ בַּסֻּכֹּת:

43 in order that future generations may know that I made *B'nei Yisrael* live in booths when I brought them out of the land of Egypt, I *Hashem* your God.

מג לְמַעַן יֵדְעוּ דֹרֹתֵיכֶם כִּי בַסֻּכּוֹת הוֹשַׁבְתִּי אֶת־בְּנֵי יִשְׂרָאֵל בְּהוֹצִיאִי אוֹתָם מֵאֶרֶץ מִצְרָיִם אֲנִי יְהוָה אֱלֹהֵיכֶם:

l'-MA-an yay-d'-U do-ro-tay-KHEM KEE va-su-KOT ho-SHAV-tee et b'-NAY yis-ra-AYL b'-ho-tzee-EE o-TAM may-E-retz mitz-RA-yim a-NEE a-do-NAI e-lo-hay-KHEM

The four species

A sukkah in Kibbutz Ein Hanatziv

and also performs good deeds. The *lulav* (לולב), 'palm branch,' has tasty fruit but no aroma, and thus represents a person who has knowledge of *Torah*, but does not perform good deeds. Conversely, the *hadas* (הדס), 'myrtle branch,' has a pleasant smell but no taste, representing a person who does good deeds, but lacks *Torah* knowledge. And the *arava* (ערבה), 'willow branch,' which lacks both smell and taste, represents a person who has neither *Torah* nor good deeds. By taking these different species and holding them together, we emphasize the importance of everyone, with all of their strengths and weaknesses, coming together and uniting in the service of the one true God.

23:40 You shall rejoice before *Hashem* your God seven days *Sukkot*, the Feast of Tabernacles, was the most joyous of the festivals observed in the *Beit Hamikdash*. However, according to the Sages (*Rosh Hashana* 16a), *Hashem* judges the people for water and determines how much rain will fall in the coming year on *Sukkot*. Given the fact that *Eretz Yisrael* is very dependent on rainfall, it seems that *Sukkot* should be a solemn time and not one of joyous celebration. What is the reason for such festivity? By making His people dependent on rainfall which comes from heaven, *Hashem* ensures that they must maintain a close connection with Him through prayer at all times. It is the constant connection with the Almighty, by virtue of His children's continued dependence on Him, which is the cause for great celebration on *Sukkot*.

23:43 In order that future generations may know The holiday of *Sukkot* recalls the protective shelter *Hashem* provided to the People of Israel in the desert. By following Him into the wilderness, they demonstrated their unshakable faith in the Lord and their unwavering love for Him, as it says in *Yirmiyahu* (2:2) "Thus said *Hashem*: I accounted to your favor the devotion of your youth, your love as a bride, how you followed Me in the wilderness, in a land not sown." By leaving their sturdy homes and

307

Vayikra/Leviticus 24
Emor

ויקרא כד
אמור

44 So *Moshe* declared to the Israelites the set times of *Hashem*.

מד וַיְדַבֵּר מֹשֶׁה אֶת־מֹעֲדֵי יְהֹוָה אֶל־בְּנֵי יִשְׂרָאֵל׃

24

1 *Hashem* spoke to *Moshe*, saying:

א וַיְדַבֵּר יְהֹוָה אֶל־מֹשֶׁה לֵּאמֹר׃

2 Command *B'nei Yisrael* to bring you clear oil of beaten olives for lighting, for kindling lamps regularly.

ב צַו אֶת־בְּנֵי יִשְׂרָאֵל וְיִקְחוּ אֵלֶיךָ שֶׁמֶן זַיִת זָךְ כָּתִית לַמָּאוֹר לְהַעֲלֹת נֵר תָּמִיד׃

3 *Aharon* shall set them up in the Tent of Meeting outside the curtain of the Pact [to burn] from evening to morning before *Hashem* regularly; it is a law for all time throughout the ages.

ג מִחוּץ לְפָרֹכֶת הָעֵדֻת בְּאֹהֶל מוֹעֵד יַעֲרֹךְ אֹתוֹ אַהֲרֹן מֵעֶרֶב עַד־בֹּקֶר לִפְנֵי יְהֹוָה תָּמִיד חֻקַּת עוֹלָם לְדֹרֹתֵיכֶם׃

4 He shall set up the lamps on the pure *menorah* before *Hashem* [to burn] regularly.

ד עַל הַמְּנֹרָה הַטְּהֹרָה יַעֲרֹךְ אֶת־הַנֵּרוֹת לִפְנֵי יְהֹוָה תָּמִיד׃

5 You shall take choice flour and bake of it twelve loaves, two-tenths of a measure for each loaf.

ה וְלָקַחְתָּ סֹלֶת וְאָפִיתָ אֹתָהּ שְׁתֵּים עֶשְׂרֵה חַלּוֹת שְׁנֵי עֶשְׂרֹנִים יִהְיֶה הַחַלָּה הָאֶחָת׃

6 Place them on the pure table before *Hashem* in two rows, six to a row.

ו וְשַׂמְתָּ אוֹתָם שְׁתַּיִם מַעֲרָכוֹת שֵׁשׁ הַמַּעֲרָכֶת עַל הַשֻּׁלְחָן הַטָּהֹר לִפְנֵי יְהֹוָה׃

7 With each row you shall place pure frankincense, which is to be a token offering for the bread, as an offering by fire to *Hashem*.

ז וְנָתַתָּ עַל־הַמַּעֲרֶכֶת לְבֹנָה זַכָּה וְהָיְתָה לַלֶּחֶם לְאַזְכָּרָה אִשֶּׁה לַיהֹוָה׃

8 **He shall arrange them before *Hashem* regularly every *Shabbat* day – it is a commitment for all time on the part of the Israelites.**

ח בְּיוֹם הַשַּׁבָּת בְּיוֹם הַשַּׁבָּת יַעַרְכֶנּוּ לִפְנֵי יְהֹוָה תָּמִיד מֵאֵת בְּנֵי־יִשְׂרָאֵל בְּרִית עוֹלָם׃

b'-YOM ha-sha-BAT b'-YOM ha-sha-BAT ya-ar-KHE-nu lif-NAY a-do-NAI ta-MEED may-AYT b'nay yis-ra-AYL b'-REET o-LAM

9 They shall belong to *Aharon* and his sons, who shall eat them in the sacred precinct; for they are his as most holy things from *Hashem*'s offerings by fire, a due for all time.

ט וְהָיְתָה לְאַהֲרֹן וּלְבָנָיו וַאֲכָלֻהוּ בְּמָקוֹם קָדֹשׁ כִּי קֹדֶשׁ קָדָשִׁים הוּא לוֹ מֵאִשֵּׁי יְהֹוָה חָק־עוֹלָם׃

---

eating and sleeping in a *sukkah* for the seven days of the holiday, future generations demonstrate their unshakeable trust in *Hashem* and their faith that He will continue to take care of them throughout all of their challenges and tribulations, just as He did in the wilderness.

24:8 He shall arrange them before *Hashem* regularly Just as *Aharon* arranges the candles of the Temple *menorah* (Numbers 8:2–3), he is to arrange the twelve loaves of bread every *Shabbat* as a "commitment for all time." On the day that the Children of Israel desist from activities related to earning their livelihood and focus instead on their relationship with the Almighty, *Aharon* sets the bread before *Hashem*, reflecting the understanding that it is He who ultimately provides mankind with their physical sustenance. Both the *menorah* and the *lechem hapanim* (לחם הפנים) 'bread of display,' or 'shewbread,' are a constant presence in the *Beit Hamikdash*. The light of the lamp symbolizes the spiritual life of the people, while bread symbolizes the physical realm. When the People of Israel rest on the *Shabbat* and focus on matters of the soul, God ensures that their physical well-being will be taken care of as well.

Vayikra/Leviticus 24
Emor

ויקרא כד
אמור

10 There came out among the Israelites one whose mother was Israelite and whose father was Egyptian. And a fight broke out in the camp between that half-Israelite and a certain Israelite.

י וַיֵּצֵא בֶּן־אִשָּׁה יִשְׂרְאֵלִית וְהוּא בֶּן־אִישׁ מִצְרִי בְּתוֹךְ בְּנֵי יִשְׂרָאֵל וַיִּנָּצוּ בַּמַּחֲנֶה בֶּן הַיִּשְׂרְאֵלִית וְאִישׁ הַיִּשְׂרְאֵלִי׃

11 The son of the Israelite woman pronounced the Name in blasphemy, and he was brought to *Moshe* – now his mother's name was Shelomith daughter of Dibri of the tribe of *Dan* –

יא וַיִּקֹּב בֶּן־הָאִשָּׁה הַיִּשְׂרְאֵלִית אֶת־הַשֵּׁם וַיְקַלֵּל וַיָּבִיאוּ אֹתוֹ אֶל־מֹשֶׁה וְשֵׁם אִמּוֹ שְׁלֹמִית בַּת־דִּבְרִי לְמַטֵּה־דָן׃

12 and he was placed in custody, until the decision of *Hashem* should be made clear to them.

יב וַיַּנִּיחֻהוּ בַּמִּשְׁמָר לִפְרֹשׁ לָהֶם עַל־פִּי יְהוָה׃

13 And *Hashem* spoke to *Moshe*, saying:

יג וַיְדַבֵּר יְהוָה אֶל־מֹשֶׁה לֵּאמֹר׃

14 Take the blasphemer outside the camp; and let all who were within hearing lay their hands upon his head, and let the whole community stone him.

יד הוֹצֵא אֶת־הַמְקַלֵּל אֶל־מִחוּץ לַמַּחֲנֶה וְסָמְכוּ כָל־הַשֹּׁמְעִים אֶת־יְדֵיהֶם עַל־רֹאשׁוֹ וְרָגְמוּ אֹתוֹ כָּל־הָעֵדָה׃

15 And to *B'nei Yisrael* speak thus: Anyone who blasphemes his God shall bear his guilt;

טו וְאֶל־בְּנֵי יִשְׂרָאֵל תְּדַבֵּר לֵאמֹר אִישׁ אִישׁ כִּי־יְקַלֵּל אֱלֹהָיו וְנָשָׂא חֶטְאוֹ׃

16 if he also pronounces the name *Hashem*, he shall be put to death. The whole community shall stone him; stranger or citizen, if he has thus pronounced the Name, he shall be put to death.

טז וְנֹקֵב שֵׁם־יְהוָה מוֹת יוּמָת רָגוֹם יִרְגְּמוּ־בוֹ כָּל־הָעֵדָה כַּגֵּר כָּאֶזְרָח בְּנָקְבוֹ־שֵׁם יוּמָת׃

17 If anyone kills any human being, he shall be put to death.

יז וְאִישׁ כִּי יַכֶּה כָּל־נֶפֶשׁ אָדָם מוֹת יוּמָת׃

18 One who kills a beast shall make restitution for it: life for life.

יח וּמַכֵּה נֶפֶשׁ־בְּהֵמָה יְשַׁלְּמֶנָּה נֶפֶשׁ תַּחַת נָפֶשׁ׃

19 If anyone maims his fellow, as he has done so shall it be done to him:

יט וְאִישׁ כִּי־יִתֵּן מוּם בַּעֲמִיתוֹ כַּאֲשֶׁר עָשָׂה כֵּן יֵעָשֶׂה לּוֹ׃

20 fracture for fracture, eye for eye, tooth for tooth. The injury he inflicted on another shall be inflicted on him.

כ שֶׁבֶר תַּחַת שֶׁבֶר עַיִן תַּחַת עַיִן שֵׁן תַּחַת שֵׁן כַּאֲשֶׁר יִתֵּן מוּם בָּאָדָם כֵּן יִנָּתֶן בּוֹ׃

21 One who kills a beast shall make restitution for it; but one who kills a human being shall be put to death.

כא וּמַכֵּה בְהֵמָה יְשַׁלְּמֶנָּה וּמַכֵּה אָדָם יוּמָת׃

22 You shall have one standard for stranger and citizen alike: for I *Hashem* am your God.

כב מִשְׁפַּט אֶחָד יִהְיֶה לָכֶם כַּגֵּר כָּאֶזְרָח יִהְיֶה כִּי אֲנִי יְהוָה אֱלֹהֵיכֶם׃

23 *Moshe* spoke thus to the Israelites. And they took the blasphemer outside the camp and pelted him with stones. The Israelites did as *Hashem* had commanded *Moshe*.

כג וַיְדַבֵּר מֹשֶׁה אֶל־בְּנֵי יִשְׂרָאֵל וַיּוֹצִיאוּ אֶת־הַמְקַלֵּל אֶל־מִחוּץ לַמַּחֲנֶה וַיִּרְגְּמוּ אֹתוֹ אָבֶן וּבְנֵי־יִשְׂרָאֵל עָשׂוּ כַּאֲשֶׁר צִוָּה יְהוָה אֶת־מֹשֶׁה׃

Vayikra/Leviticus 25
Behar

ויקרא כה
בהר

25 1 *Hashem* spoke to *Moshe* on *Har Sinai*:

א וַיְדַבֵּר יְהֹוָה אֶל־מֹשֶׁה בְּהַר סִינַי לֵאמֹר:

2 Speak to *B'nei Yisrael* and say to them: When you enter the land that I assign to you, the land shall observe a *Shabbat* of *Hashem*.

ב דַּבֵּר אֶל־בְּנֵי יִשְׂרָאֵל וְאָמַרְתָּ אֲלֵהֶם כִּי תָבֹאוּ אֶל־הָאָרֶץ אֲשֶׁר אֲנִי נֹתֵן לָכֶם וְשָׁבְתָה הָאָרֶץ שַׁבָּת לַיהֹוָה:

3 Six years you may sow your field and six years you may prune your vineyard and gather in the yield.

ג שֵׁשׁ שָׁנִים תִּזְרַע שָׂדֶךָ וְשֵׁשׁ שָׁנִים תִּזְמֹר כַּרְמֶךָ וְאָסַפְתָּ אֶת־תְּבוּאָתָהּ:

4 But in the seventh year the land shall have a *Shabbat* of complete rest, a *Shabbat* of *Hashem*: you shall not sow your field or prune your vineyard.

ד וּבַשָּׁנָה הַשְּׁבִיעִת שַׁבַּת שַׁבָּתוֹן יִהְיֶה לָאָרֶץ שַׁבָּת לַיהֹוָה שָׂדְךָ לֹא תִזְרָע וְכַרְמְךָ לֹא תִזְמֹר:

5 You shall not reap the aftergrowth of your harvest or gather the grapes of your untrimmed vines; it shall be a year of complete rest for the land.

ה אֵת סְפִיחַ קְצִירְךָ לֹא תִקְצוֹר וְאֶת־עִנְּבֵי נְזִירֶךָ לֹא תִבְצֹר שְׁנַת שַׁבָּתוֹן יִהְיֶה לָאָרֶץ:

6 But you may eat whatever the land during its *Shabbat* will produce – you, your male and female slaves, the hired and bound laborers who live with you,

ו וְהָיְתָה שַׁבַּת הָאָרֶץ לָכֶם לְאָכְלָה לְךָ וּלְעַבְדְּךָ וְלַאֲמָתֶךָ וְלִשְׂכִירְךָ וּלְתוֹשָׁבְךָ הַגָּרִים עִמָּךְ:

7 and your cattle and the beasts in your land may eat all its yield.

ז וְלִבְהֶמְתְּךָ וְלַחַיָּה אֲשֶׁר בְּאַרְצֶךָ תִּהְיֶה כָל־תְּבוּאָתָהּ לֶאֱכֹל:

8 You shall count off seven weeks of years – seven times seven years – so that the period of seven weeks of years gives you a total of forty-nine years.

ח וְסָפַרְתָּ לְךָ שֶׁבַע שַׁבְּתֹת שָׁנִים שֶׁבַע שָׁנִים שֶׁבַע פְּעָמִים וְהָיוּ לְךָ יְמֵי שֶׁבַע שַׁבְּתֹת הַשָּׁנִים תֵּשַׁע וְאַרְבָּעִים שָׁנָה:

9 Then you shall sound the *shofar* loud; in the seventh month, on the tenth day of the month – the Day of Atonement – you shall have the *shofar* sounded throughout your land

ט וְהַעֲבַרְתָּ שׁוֹפַר תְּרוּעָה בַּחֹדֶשׁ הַשְּׁבִעִי בֶּעָשׂוֹר לַחֹדֶשׁ בְּיוֹם הַכִּפֻּרִים תַּעֲבִירוּ שׁוֹפָר בְּכָל־אַרְצְכֶם:

10 and you shall hallow the fiftieth year. You shall proclaim release throughout the land for all its inhabitants. It shall be a jubilee for you: each of you shall return to his holding and each of you shall return to his family.

י וְקִדַּשְׁתֶּם אֵת שְׁנַת הַחֲמִשִּׁים שָׁנָה וּקְרָאתֶם דְּרוֹר בָּאָרֶץ לְכָל־יֹשְׁבֶיהָ יוֹבֵל הִוא תִּהְיֶה לָכֶם וְשַׁבְתֶּם אִישׁ אֶל־אֲחֻזָּתוֹ וְאִישׁ אֶל־מִשְׁפַּחְתּוֹ תָּשֻׁבוּ:

v'-ki-dash-TEM AYT sh'-NAT ha-kha-mi-SHEEM sha-NAH uk-ra-TEM d'-ROR ba-A-retz l'-khol yo-sh'-VE-ha yo-VAYL HEE tih-YEH la-KHEM v'-shav-TEM EESH el a-khu-za-TO v'-EESH el mish-pakh-TO ta-SHU-vu

---

25:10 You shall proclaim release throughout the land The Liberty Bell is an icon of American independence. Commissioned in 1751 for the Pennsylvania State House, the bell was cast with the words "proclaim liberty throughout all the land unto all the inhabitants thereof," taken from this verse. Because of this inscription, it was made a symbol of freedom by the abolitionists in the 1830s, when it was also given the name 'Liberty Bell.' It has remained a symbol of freedom and liberty ever since. In recognition of their shared Judeo-Christian values, the State of Israel built a replica of the Liberty Bell and placed it in the center of Jerusalem as a symbol the special bond between the two countries.

Liberty Bell Park in Jerusalem

310

Vayikra/Leviticus 25
Behar

ויקרא כה
בהר

11 That fiftieth year shall be a jubilee for you: you shall not sow, neither shall you reap the aftergrowth or harvest the untrimmed vines,

יא יוֹבֵל הִוא שְׁנַת הַחֲמִשִּׁים שָׁנָה תִּהְיֶה לָכֶם לֹא תִזְרָעוּ וְלֹא תִקְצְרוּ אֶת־סְפִיחֶיהָ וְלֹא תִבְצְרוּ אֶת־נְזִרֶיהָ׃

12 for it is a jubilee. It shall be holy to you: you may only eat the growth direct from the field.

יב כִּי יוֹבֵל הִוא קֹדֶשׁ תִּהְיֶה לָכֶם מִן־הַשָּׂדֶה תֹּאכְלוּ אֶת־תְּבוּאָתָהּ׃

13 In this year of jubilee, each of you shall return to his holding.

יג בִּשְׁנַת הַיּוֹבֵל הַזֹּאת תָּשֻׁבוּ אִישׁ אֶל־אֲחֻזָּתוֹ׃

14 When you sell property to your neighbor, or buy any from your neighbor, you shall not wrong one another.

יד וְכִי־תִמְכְּרוּ מִמְכָּר לַעֲמִיתֶךָ אוֹ קָנֹה מִיַּד עֲמִיתֶךָ אַל־תּוֹנוּ אִישׁ אֶת־אָחִיו׃

15 In buying from your neighbor, you shall deduct only for the number of years since the jubilee; and in selling to you, he shall charge you only for the remaining crop years:

טו בְּמִסְפַּר שָׁנִים אַחַר הַיּוֹבֵל תִּקְנֶה מֵאֵת עֲמִיתֶךָ בְּמִסְפַּר שְׁנֵי־תְבוּאֹת יִמְכָּר־לָךְ׃

16 the more such years, the higher the price you pay; the fewer such years, the lower the price; for what he is selling you is a number of harvests.

טז לְפִי רֹב הַשָּׁנִים תַּרְבֶּה מִקְנָתוֹ וּלְפִי מְעֹט הַשָּׁנִים תַּמְעִיט מִקְנָתוֹ כִּי מִסְפַּר תְּבוּאֹת הוּא מֹכֵר לָךְ׃

17 Do not wrong one another, but fear your God; for I *Hashem* am your God.

יז וְלֹא תוֹנוּ אִישׁ אֶת־עֲמִיתוֹ וְיָרֵאתָ מֵאֱלֹהֶיךָ כִּי אֲנִי יְהֹוָה אֱלֹהֵיכֶם׃

18 You shall observe My laws and faithfully keep My rules, that you may live upon the land in security;

יח וַעֲשִׂיתֶם אֶת־חֻקֹּתַי וְאֶת־מִשְׁפָּטַי תִּשְׁמְרוּ וַעֲשִׂיתֶם אֹתָם וִישַׁבְתֶּם עַל־הָאָרֶץ לָבֶטַח׃

19 the land shall yield its fruit and you shall eat your fill, and you shall live upon it in security.

יט וְנָתְנָה הָאָרֶץ פִּרְיָהּ וַאֲכַלְתֶּם לָשֹׂבַע וִישַׁבְתֶּם לָבֶטַח עָלֶיהָ׃

20 And should you ask, "What are we to eat in the seventh year, if we may neither sow nor gather in our crops?"

כ וְכִי תֹאמְרוּ מַה־נֹּאכַל בַּשָּׁנָה הַשְּׁבִיעִת הֵן לֹא נִזְרָע וְלֹא נֶאֱסֹף אֶת־תְּבוּאָתֵנוּ׃

21 I will ordain My blessing for you in the sixth year, so that it shall yield a crop sufficient for three years.

כא וְצִוִּיתִי אֶת־בִּרְכָתִי לָכֶם בַּשָּׁנָה הַשִּׁשִּׁית וְעָשָׂת אֶת־הַתְּבוּאָה לִשְׁלֹשׁ הַשָּׁנִים׃

v'-tzi-VEE-tee et bir-kha-TEE la-KHEM ba-sha-NAH ha-shi-SHEET v'-a-SAT et ha-t'-vu-AH lish-LOSH ha-sha-NEEM

25:21 I will ordain My blessing for you in the sixth year Chapter 25 describes the blessing of the Sabbatical year, which is often cited as one of the proofs of the Divinity of the Bible. Verses 20–21 state, "And should you ask, 'What are we to eat in the seventh year, if we may neither sow nor gather in our crops?' I will ordain My blessing for you in the sixth year, so that it shall yield a crop sufficient for three years." No human being would ever make such an audacious guarantee – essentially sentencing the entire nation to starve every seventh year. Certainly, after one failed cycle, no one would obey the Sabbatical restrictions again. Only the one true God could make and keep such a grandiose promise.

Vayikra/Leviticus 25
Behar

22 When you sow in the eighth year, you will still be eating old grain of that crop; you will be eating the old until the ninth year, until its crops come in.

23 But the land must not be sold beyond reclaim, for the land is Mine; you are but strangers resident with Me.

24 Throughout the land that you hold, you must provide for the redemption of the land.

25 If your kinsman is in straits and has to sell part of his holding, his nearest redeemer shall come and redeem what his kinsman has sold.

26 If a man has no one to redeem for him, but prospers and acquires enough to redeem with,

27 he shall compute the years since its sale, refund the difference to the man to whom he sold it, and return to his holding.

28 If he lacks sufficient means to recover it, what he sold shall remain with the purchaser until the jubilee; in the jubilee year it shall be released, and he shall return to his holding.

29 If a man sells a dwelling house in a walled city, it may be redeemed until a year has elapsed since its sale; the redemption period shall be a year.

30 If it is not redeemed before a full year has elapsed, the house in the walled city shall pass to the purchaser beyond reclaim throughout the ages; it shall not be released in the jubilee.

31 But houses in villages that have no encircling walls shall be classed as open country: they may be redeemed, and they shall be released through the jubilee.

32 As for the cities of the *Leviim*, the houses in the cities they hold – the *Leviim* shall forever have the right of redemption.

33 Such property as may be redeemed from the *Leviim* – houses sold in a city they hold – shall be released through the jubilee; for the houses in the cities of the *Leviim* are their holding among the Israelites.

Vayikra/Leviticus 25
Behar

ויקרא כה
בהר

34 But the unenclosed land about their cities cannot be sold, for that is their holding for all time.

לד וּשְׂדֵה מִגְרַשׁ עָרֵיהֶם לֹא יִמָּכֵר כִּי־אֲחֻזַּת עוֹלָם הוּא לָהֶם:

35 If your kinsman, being in straits, comes under your authority, and you hold him as though a resident alien, let him live by your side:

לה וְכִי־יָמוּךְ אָחִיךָ וּמָטָה יָדוֹ עִמָּךְ וְהֶחֱזַקְתָּ בּוֹ גֵּר וְתוֹשָׁב וָחַי עִמָּךְ:

36 do not exact from him advance or accrued interest, but fear your God. Let him live by your side as your kinsman.

לו אַל־תִּקַּח מֵאִתּוֹ נֶשֶׁךְ וְתַרְבִּית וְיָרֵאתָ מֵאֱלֹהֶיךָ וְחֵי אָחִיךָ עִמָּךְ:

37 Do not lend him your money at advance interest, or give him your food at accrued interest.

לז אֶת־כַּסְפְּךָ לֹא־תִתֵּן לוֹ בְּנֶשֶׁךְ וּבְמַרְבִּית לֹא־תִתֵּן אָכְלֶךָ:

38 I *Hashem* am your God, who brought you out of the land of Egypt, to give you the land of Canaan, to be your God.

לח אֲנִי יְהוָה אֱלֹהֵיכֶם אֲשֶׁר־הוֹצֵאתִי אֶתְכֶם מֵאֶרֶץ מִצְרָיִם לָתֵת לָכֶם אֶת־אֶרֶץ כְּנַעַן לִהְיוֹת לָכֶם לֵאלֹהִים:

39 If your kinsman under you continues in straits and must give himself over to you, do not subject him to the treatment of a slave.

לט וְכִי־יָמוּךְ אָחִיךָ עִמָּךְ וְנִמְכַּר־לָךְ לֹא־תַעֲבֹד בּוֹ עֲבֹדַת עָבֶד:

40 He shall remain with you as a hired or bound laborer; he shall serve with you only until the jubilee year.

מ כְּשָׂכִיר כְּתוֹשָׁב יִהְיֶה עִמָּךְ עַד־שְׁנַת הַיֹּבֵל יַעֲבֹד עִמָּךְ:

41 Then he and his children with him shall be free of your authority; he shall go back to his family and return to his ancestral holding. –

מא וְיָצָא מֵעִמָּךְ הוּא וּבָנָיו עִמּוֹ וְשָׁב אֶל־מִשְׁפַּחְתּוֹ וְאֶל־אֲחֻזַּת אֲבֹתָיו יָשׁוּב:

42 For they are My servants, whom I freed from the land of Egypt; they may not give themselves over into servitude. –

מב כִּי־עֲבָדַי הֵם אֲשֶׁר־הוֹצֵאתִי אֹתָם מֵאֶרֶץ מִצְרָיִם לֹא יִמָּכְרוּ מִמְכֶּרֶת עָבֶד:

43 You shall not rule over him ruthlessly; you shall fear your God.

מג לֹא־תִרְדֶּה בוֹ בְּפָרֶךְ וְיָרֵאתָ מֵאֱלֹהֶיךָ:

44 Such male and female slaves as you may have – it is from the nations round about you that you may acquire male and female slaves.

מד וְעַבְדְּךָ וַאֲמָתְךָ אֲשֶׁר יִהְיוּ־לָךְ מֵאֵת הַגּוֹיִם אֲשֶׁר סְבִיבֹתֵיכֶם מֵהֶם תִּקְנוּ עֶבֶד וְאָמָה:

45 You may also buy them from among the children of aliens resident among you, or from their families that are among you, whom they begot in your land. These shall become your property:

מה וְגַם מִבְּנֵי הַתּוֹשָׁבִים הַגָּרִים עִמָּכֶם מֵהֶם תִּקְנוּ וּמִמִּשְׁפַּחְתָּם אֲשֶׁר עִמָּכֶם אֲשֶׁר הוֹלִידוּ בְּאַרְצְכֶם וְהָיוּ לָכֶם לַאֲחֻזָּה:

46 you may keep them as a possession for your children after you, for them to inherit as property for all time. Such you may treat as slaves. But as for your Israelite kinsmen, no one shall rule ruthlessly over the other.

מו וְהִתְנַחַלְתֶּם אֹתָם לִבְנֵיכֶם אַחֲרֵיכֶם לָרֶשֶׁת אֲחֻזָּה לְעֹלָם בָּהֶם תַּעֲבֹדוּ וּבְאַחֵיכֶם בְּנֵי־יִשְׂרָאֵל אִישׁ בְּאָחִיו לֹא־תִרְדֶּה בוֹ בְּפָרֶךְ:

Vayikra/Leviticus 26
Bechukotai

ויקרא כו
בחקתי

47 If a resident alien among you has prospered, and your kinsman being in straits, comes under his authority and gives himself over to the resident alien among you, or to an offshoot of an alien's family,

מז וְכִי תַשִּׂיג יַד גֵּר וְתוֹשָׁב עִמָּךְ וּמָךְ אָחִיךָ עִמּוֹ וְנִמְכַּר לְגֵר תּוֹשָׁב עִמָּךְ אוֹ לְעֵקֶר מִשְׁפַּחַת גֵּר:

48 he shall have the right of redemption even after he has given himself over. One of his kinsmen shall redeem him,

מח אַחֲרֵי נִמְכַּר גְּאֻלָּה תִּהְיֶה־לּוֹ אֶחָד מֵאֶחָיו יִגְאָלֶנּוּ:

49 or his uncle or his uncle's son shall redeem him, or anyone of his family who is of his own flesh shall redeem him; or, if he prospers, he may redeem himself.

מט אוֹ־דֹדוֹ אוֹ בֶן־דֹּדוֹ יִגְאָלֶנּוּ אוֹ־מִשְּׁאֵר בְּשָׂרוֹ מִמִּשְׁפַּחְתּוֹ יִגְאָלֶנּוּ אוֹ־הִשִּׂיגָה יָדוֹ וְנִגְאָל:

50 He shall compute with his purchaser the total from the year he gave himself over to him until the jubilee year; the price of his sale shall be applied to the number of years, as though it were for a term as a hired laborer under the other's authority.

נ וְחִשַּׁב עִם־קֹנֵהוּ מִשְּׁנַת הִמָּכְרוֹ לוֹ עַד שְׁנַת הַיֹּבֵל וְהָיָה כֶּסֶף מִמְכָּרוֹ בְּמִסְפַּר שָׁנִים כִּימֵי שָׂכִיר יִהְיֶה עִמּוֹ:

51 If many years remain, he shall pay back for his redemption in proportion to his purchase price;

נא אִם־עוֹד רַבּוֹת בַּשָּׁנִים לְפִיהֶן יָשִׁיב גְּאֻלָּתוֹ מִכֶּסֶף מִקְנָתוֹ:

52 and if few years remain until the jubilee year, he shall so compute: he shall make payment for his redemption according to the years involved.

נב וְאִם־מְעַט נִשְׁאַר בַּשָּׁנִים עַד־שְׁנַת הַיֹּבֵל וְחִשַּׁב־לוֹ כְּפִי שָׁנָיו יָשִׁיב אֶת־גְּאֻלָּתוֹ:

53 He shall be under his authority as a laborer hired by the year; he shall not rule ruthlessly over him in your sight.

נג כִּשְׂכִיר שָׁנָה בְּשָׁנָה יִהְיֶה עִמּוֹ לֹא־יִרְדֶּנּוּ בְּפֶרֶךְ לְעֵינֶיךָ:

54 If he has not been redeemed in any of those ways, he and his children with him shall go free in the jubilee year.

נד וְאִם־לֹא יִגָּאֵל בְּאֵלֶּה וְיָצָא בִּשְׁנַת הַיֹּבֵל הוּא וּבָנָיו עִמּוֹ:

55 For it is to Me that the Israelites are servants: they are My servants, whom I freed from the land of Egypt, I *Hashem* your God.

נה כִּי־לִי בְנֵי־יִשְׂרָאֵל עֲבָדִים עֲבָדַי הֵם אֲשֶׁר־הוֹצֵאתִי אוֹתָם מֵאֶרֶץ מִצְרָיִם אֲנִי יְהוָה אֱלֹהֵיכֶם:

26 1 You shall not make idols for yourselves, or set up for yourselves carved images or pillars, or place figured stones in your land to worship upon, for I *Hashem* am your God.

כו א לֹא־תַעֲשׂוּ לָכֶם אֱלִילִם וּפֶסֶל וּמַצֵּבָה לֹא־תָקִימוּ לָכֶם וְאֶבֶן מַשְׂכִּית לֹא תִתְּנוּ בְּאַרְצְכֶם לְהִשְׁתַּחֲוֹת עָלֶיהָ כִּי אֲנִי יְהוָה אֱלֹהֵיכֶם:

2 You shall keep My *Shabbatot* and venerate My sanctuary, Mine, *Hashem*'s.

ב אֶת־שַׁבְּתֹתַי תִּשְׁמֹרוּ וּמִקְדָּשִׁי תִּירָאוּ אֲנִי יְהוָה:

3 If you follow My laws and faithfully observe My commandments,

ג אִם־בְּחֻקֹּתַי תֵּלֵכוּ וְאֶת־מִצְוֹתַי תִּשְׁמְרוּ וַעֲשִׂיתֶם אֹתָם:

im b'-khu-ko-TAI tay-LAY-khu v'-et mitz-vo-TAI tish-m'-RU va-a-see-TEM o-TAM

Vayikra/Leviticus 26
Bechukotai

ויקרא כו
בחקתי

4 I will grant your rains in their season, so that the earth shall yield its produce and the trees of the field their fruit.

ד וְנָתַתִּי גִשְׁמֵיכֶם בְּעִתָּם וְנָתְנָה הָאָרֶץ יְבוּלָהּ וְעֵץ הַשָּׂדֶה יִתֵּן פִּרְיוֹ:

v'-na-ta-TEE gish-may-KHEM b'-i-TAM v'-na-t'-NAH ha-A-retz y'-vu-LAH v'-AYTZ ha-sa-DEH yi-TAYN pir-YO

5 Your threshing shall overtake the vintage, and your vintage shall overtake the sowing; you shall eat your fill of bread and dwell securely in your land.

ה וְהִשִּׂיג לָכֶם דַּיִשׁ אֶת־בָּצִיר וּבָצִיר יַשִּׂיג אֶת־זָרַע וַאֲכַלְתֶּם לַחְמְכֶם לָשֹׂבַע וִישַׁבְתֶּם לָבֶטַח בְּאַרְצְכֶם:

6 I will grant peace in the land, and you shall lie down untroubled by anyone; I will give the land respite from vicious beasts, and no sword shall cross your land.

ו וְנָתַתִּי שָׁלוֹם בָּאָרֶץ וּשְׁכַבְתֶּם וְאֵין מַחֲרִיד וְהִשְׁבַּתִּי חַיָּה רָעָה מִן־הָאָרֶץ וְחֶרֶב לֹא־תַעֲבֹר בְּאַרְצְכֶם:

v'-na-ta-TEE sha-LOM ba-A-retz ush-khav-TEM v'-AYN ma-kha-REED v'-hish-ba-TEE kha-YAH ra-AH min ha-A-retz v'-KHE-rev lo ta-a-VOR b'-ar-tz'-KHEM

7 You shall give chase to your enemies, and they shall fall before you by the sword.

ז וּרְדַפְתֶּם אֶת־אֹיְבֵיכֶם וְנָפְלוּ לִפְנֵיכֶם לֶחָרֶב:

8 Five of you shall give chase to a hundred, and a hundred of you shall give chase to ten thousand; your enemies shall fall before you by the sword.

ח וְרָדְפוּ מִכֶּם חֲמִשָּׁה מֵאָה וּמֵאָה מִכֶּם רְבָבָה יִרְדֹּפוּ וְנָפְלוּ אֹיְבֵיכֶם לִפְנֵיכֶם לֶחָרֶב:

9 I will look with favor upon you, and make you fertile and multiply you; and I will maintain My covenant with you.

ט וּפָנִיתִי אֲלֵיכֶם וְהִפְרֵיתִי אֶתְכֶם וְהִרְבֵּיתִי אֶתְכֶם וַהֲקִימֹתִי אֶת־בְּרִיתִי אִתְּכֶם:

10 You shall eat old grain long stored, and you shall have to clear out the old to make room for the new.

י וַאֲכַלְתֶּם יָשָׁן נוֹשָׁן וְיָשָׁן מִפְּנֵי חָדָשׁ תּוֹצִיאוּ:

11 I will establish My abode in your midst, and I will not spurn you.

יא וְנָתַתִּי מִשְׁכָּנִי בְּתוֹכְכֶם וְלֹא־תִגְעַל נַפְשִׁי אֶתְכֶם:

12 I will be ever present in your midst: I will be your God, and you shall be My people.

יב וְהִתְהַלַּכְתִּי בְּתוֹכְכֶם וְהָיִיתִי לָכֶם לֵאלֹהִים וְאַתֶּם תִּהְיוּ־לִי לְעָם:

13 I *Hashem* am your God who brought you out from the land of the Egyptians to be their slaves no more, who broke the bars of your yoke and made you walk erect.

יג אֲנִי יְהוָה אֱלֹהֵיכֶם אֲשֶׁר הוֹצֵאתִי אֶתְכֶם מֵאֶרֶץ מִצְרַיִם מִהְיֹת לָהֶם עֲבָדִים וָאֶשְׁבֹּר מֹטֹת עֻלְּכֶם וָאוֹלֵךְ אֶתְכֶם קוֹמְמִיּוּת:

14 But if you do not obey Me and do not observe all these commandments,

יד וְאִם־לֹא תִשְׁמְעוּ לִי וְלֹא תַעֲשׂוּ אֵת כָּל־הַמִּצְוֹת הָאֵלֶּה:

26:4 I will grant your rains in their season Israel depends heavily on rain in order to grow its crops, as it does not have an independent body of water which can provide sufficient irrigation. Water can be the source of great blessing, but at the wrong times, too much or too little water can also be a curse. In this verse, *Hashem* promises that if the Children of Israel follow His commandments and do what He asks of them, He will bless them with the right amount of water at the right times, in order to provide an abundance of crops. In Hebrew, this rain is called *gishmay b'racha* (גשמי ברכה), 'rain of blessing' (Ezekiel 34:26).

Vayikra/Leviticus 26
Bechukotai

ויקרא כו
בחקתי

15 if you reject My laws and spurn My rules, so that you do not observe all My commandments and you break My covenant,

טו וְאִם־בְּחֻקֹּתַי תִּמְאָסוּ וְאִם אֶת־מִשְׁפָּטַי תִּגְעַל נַפְשְׁכֶם לְבִלְתִּי עֲשׂוֹת אֶת־כָּל־מִצְוֺתַי לְהַפְרְכֶם אֶת־בְּרִיתִי:

16 I in turn will do this to you: I will wreak misery upon you – consumption and fever, which cause the eyes to pine and the body to languish; you shall sow your seed to no purpose, for your enemies shall eat it.

טז אַף־אֲנִי אֶעֱשֶׂה־זֹּאת לָכֶם וְהִפְקַדְתִּי עֲלֵיכֶם בֶּהָלָה אֶת־הַשַּׁחֶפֶת וְאֶת־הַקַּדַּחַת מְכַלּוֹת עֵינַיִם וּמְדִיבֹת נָפֶשׁ וּזְרַעְתֶּם לָרִיק זַרְעֲכֶם וַאֲכָלֻהוּ אֹיְבֵיכֶם:

17 I will set My face against you: you shall be routed by your enemies, and your foes shall dominate you. You shall flee though none pursues.

יז וְנָתַתִּי פָנַי בָּכֶם וְנִגַּפְתֶּם לִפְנֵי אֹיְבֵיכֶם וְרָדוּ בָכֶם שֹׂנְאֵיכֶם וְנַסְתֶּם וְאֵין־רֹדֵף אֶתְכֶם:

18 And if, for all that, you do not obey Me, I will go on to discipline you sevenfold for your sins,

יח וְאִם־עַד־אֵלֶּה לֹא תִשְׁמְעוּ לִי וְיָסַפְתִּי לְיַסְּרָה אֶתְכֶם שֶׁבַע עַל־חַטֹּאתֵיכֶם:

19 and I will break your proud glory. I will make your skies like iron and your earth like copper,

יט וְשָׁבַרְתִּי אֶת־גְּאוֹן עֻזְּכֶם וְנָתַתִּי אֶת־שְׁמֵיכֶם כַּבַּרְזֶל וְאֶת־אַרְצְכֶם כַּנְּחֻשָׁה:

20 so that your strength shall be spent to no purpose. Your land shall not yield its produce, nor shall the trees of the land yield their fruit.

כ וְתַם לָרִיק כֹּחֲכֶם וְלֹא־תִתֵּן אַרְצְכֶם אֶת־יְבוּלָהּ וְעֵץ הָאָרֶץ לֹא יִתֵּן פִּרְיוֹ:

21 And if you remain hostile toward Me and refuse to obey Me, I will go on smiting you sevenfold for your sins.

כא וְאִם־תֵּלְכוּ עִמִּי קֶרִי וְלֹא תֹאבוּ לִשְׁמֹעַ לִי וְיָסַפְתִּי עֲלֵיכֶם מַכָּה שֶׁבַע כְּחַטֹּאתֵיכֶם:

22 I will loose wild beasts against you, and they shall bereave you of your children and wipe out your cattle. They shall decimate you, and your roads shall be deserted.

כב וְהִשְׁלַחְתִּי בָכֶם אֶת־חַיַּת הַשָּׂדֶה וְשִׁכְּלָה אֶתְכֶם וְהִכְרִיתָה אֶת־בְּהֶמְתְּכֶם וְהִמְעִיטָה אֶתְכֶם וְנָשַׁמּוּ דַּרְכֵיכֶם:

23 And if these things fail to discipline you for Me, and you remain hostile to Me,

כג וְאִם־בְּאֵלֶּה לֹא תִוָּסְרוּ לִי וַהֲלַכְתֶּם עִמִּי קֶרִי:

24 I too will remain hostile to you: I in turn will smite you sevenfold for your sins.

כד וְהָלַכְתִּי אַף־אֲנִי עִמָּכֶם בְּקֶרִי וְהִכֵּיתִי אֶתְכֶם גַּם־אָנִי שֶׁבַע עַל־חַטֹּאתֵיכֶם:

25 I will bring a sword against you to wreak vengeance for the covenant; and if you withdraw into your cities, I will send pestilence among you, and you shall be delivered into enemy hands.

כה וְהֵבֵאתִי עֲלֵיכֶם חֶרֶב נֹקֶמֶת נְקַם־בְּרִית וְנֶאֱסַפְתֶּם אֶל־עָרֵיכֶם וְשִׁלַּחְתִּי דֶבֶר בְּתוֹכְכֶם וְנִתַּתֶּם בְּיַד־אוֹיֵב:

26 When I break your staff of bread, ten women shall bake your bread in a single oven; they shall dole out your bread by weight, and though you eat, you shall not be satisfied.

כו בְּשִׁבְרִי לָכֶם מַטֵּה־לֶחֶם וְאָפוּ עֶשֶׂר נָשִׁים לַחְמְכֶם בְּתַנּוּר אֶחָד וְהֵשִׁיבוּ לַחְמְכֶם בַּמִּשְׁקָל וַאֲכַלְתֶּם וְלֹא תִשְׂבָּעוּ:

27 But if, despite this, you disobey Me and remain hostile to Me,

כז וְאִם־בְּזֹאת לֹא תִשְׁמְעוּ לִי וַהֲלַכְתֶּם עִמִּי בְּקֶרִי:

28 I will act against you in wrathful hostility; I, for My part, will discipline you sevenfold for your sins.

כח וְהָלַכְתִּי עִמָּכֶם בַּחֲמַת־קֶרִי וְיִסַּרְתִּי אֶתְכֶם אַף־אָנִי שֶׁבַע עַל־חַטֹּאתֵיכֶם:

Vayikra/Leviticus 26
Bechukotai

ויקרא כו
בחקתי

29 You shall eat the flesh of your sons and the flesh of your daughters.

וַאֲכַלְתֶּם בְּשַׂר בְּנֵיכֶם וּבְשַׂר בְּנֹתֵיכֶם תֹּאכֵלוּ: כט

30 I will destroy your cult places and cut down your incense stands, and I will heap your carcasses upon your lifeless fetishes. I will spurn you.

וְהִשְׁמַדְתִּי אֶת־בָּמֹתֵיכֶם וְהִכְרַתִּי אֶת־חַמָּנֵיכֶם וְנָתַתִּי אֶת־פִּגְרֵיכֶם עַל־פִּגְרֵי גִלּוּלֵיכֶם וְגָעֲלָה נַפְשִׁי אֶתְכֶם: ל

31 I will lay your cities in ruin and make your sanctuaries desolate, and I will not savor your pleasing odors.

וְנָתַתִּי אֶת־עָרֵיכֶם חָרְבָּה וַהֲשִׁמּוֹתִי אֶת־מִקְדְּשֵׁיכֶם וְלֹא אָרִיחַ בְּרֵיחַ נִיחֹחֲכֶם: לא

32 I will make the land desolate, so that your enemies who settle in it shall be appalled by it.

וַהֲשִׁמֹּתִי אֲנִי אֶת־הָאָרֶץ וְשָׁמְמוּ עָלֶיהָ אֹיְבֵיכֶם הַיֹּשְׁבִים בָּהּ: לב

va-ha-shi-mo-TEE a-NEE et ha-A-retz v'-sha-ma-MU a-LE-ha o-y'-vay-KHEM ha-yo-sh'-VEEM bah

33 And you I will scatter among the nations, and I will unsheath the sword against you. Your land shall become a desolation and your cities a ruin.

וְאֶתְכֶם אֱזָרֶה בַגּוֹיִם וַהֲרִיקֹתִי אַחֲרֵיכֶם חָרֶב וְהָיְתָה אַרְצְכֶם שְׁמָמָה וְעָרֵיכֶם יִהְיוּ חָרְבָּה: לג

34 Then shall the land make up for its *Shabbat* years throughout the time that it is desolate and you are in the land of your enemies; then shall the land rest and make up for its *Shabbat* years.

אָז תִּרְצֶה הָאָרֶץ אֶת־שַׁבְּתֹתֶיהָ כֹּל יְמֵי הָשַּׁמָּה וְאַתֶּם בְּאֶרֶץ אֹיְבֵיכֶם אָז תִּשְׁבַּת הָאָרֶץ וְהִרְצָת אֶת־שַׁבְּתֹתֶיהָ: לד

35 Throughout the time that it is desolate, it shall observe the rest that it did not observe in your *Shabbat* years while you were dwelling upon it.

כָּל־יְמֵי הָשַּׁמָּה תִּשְׁבֹּת אֵת אֲשֶׁר לֹא־שָׁבְתָה בְּשַׁבְּתֹתֵיכֶם בְּשִׁבְתְּכֶם עָלֶיהָ: לה

36 As for those of you who survive, I will cast a faintness into their hearts in the land of their enemies. The sound of a driven leaf shall put them to flight. Fleeing as though from the sword, they shall fall though none pursues.

וְהַנִּשְׁאָרִים בָּכֶם וְהֵבֵאתִי מֹרֶךְ בִּלְבָבָם בְּאַרְצֹת אֹיְבֵיהֶם וְרָדַף אֹתָם קוֹל עָלֶה נִדָּף וְנָסוּ מְנֻסַת־חֶרֶב וְנָפְלוּ וְאֵין רֹדֵף: לו

37 With no one pursuing, they shall stumble over one another as before the sword. You shall not be able to stand your ground before your enemies,

וְכָשְׁלוּ אִישׁ־בְּאָחִיו כְּמִפְּנֵי־חֶרֶב וְרֹדֵף אָיִן וְלֹא־תִהְיֶה לָכֶם תְּקוּמָה לִפְנֵי אֹיְבֵיכֶם: לז

38 but shall perish among the nations; and the land of your enemies shall consume you.

וַאֲבַדְתֶּם בַּגּוֹיִם וְאָכְלָה אֶתְכֶם אֶרֶץ אֹיְבֵיכֶם: לח

Mark Twain (1835–1910)

26:32 I will make the land desolate Though this verse is frightening, *Nachmanides* explains that it is actually a blessing in disguise. "I will make the land desolate; so that your enemies who settle in it will be appalled by it" implies that throughout the ages, no matter how many foreign empires occupy Israel, the land will not cooperate to bring forth its bounty. Indeed, in his book *Innocents Abroad*, Mark Twain wrote about his visit to Palestine in the 1860s: "A desolation is here that not even imagination can grace with the pomp of life and action.... Palestine is desolate and unlovely." Only when the Jewish People return to the Land of Israel does it give forth its blessing and return to its former glory. Today, thanks to the return of its indigenous Jewish population, *Eretz Yisrael* is once again thriving and prosperous.

Vayikra/Leviticus 27
Bechukotai

ויקרא כז
בחקתי

39 Those of you who survive shall be heartsick over their iniquity in the land of your enemies; more, they shall be heartsick over the iniquities of their fathers;

לט וְהַנִּשְׁאָרִים בָּכֶם יִמַּקּוּ בַּעֲוֺנָם בְּאַרְצֹת אֹיְבֵיכֶם וְאַף בַּעֲוֺנֹת אֲבֹתָם אִתָּם יִמָּקּוּ׃

40 and they shall confess their iniquity and the iniquity of their fathers, in that they trespassed against Me, yea, were hostile to Me.

מ וְהִתְוַדּוּ אֶת־עֲוֺנָם וְאֶת־עֲוֺן אֲבֹתָם בְּמַעֲלָם אֲשֶׁר מָעֲלוּ־בִי וְאַף אֲשֶׁר־הָלְכוּ עִמִּי בְּקֶרִי׃

41 When I, in turn, have been hostile to them and have removed them into the land of their enemies, then at last shall their obdurate heart humble itself, and they shall atone for their iniquity.

מא אַף־אֲנִי אֵלֵךְ עִמָּם בְּקֶרִי וְהֵבֵאתִי אֹתָם בְּאֶרֶץ אֹיְבֵיהֶם אוֹ־אָז יִכָּנַע לְבָבָם הֶעָרֵל וְאָז יִרְצוּ אֶת־עֲוֺנָם׃

42 Then will I remember My covenant with *Yaakov*; I will remember also My covenant with *Yitzchak*, and also My covenant with *Avraham*; and I will remember the land.

מב וְזָכַרְתִּי אֶת־בְּרִיתִי יַעֲקוֹב וְאַף אֶת־בְּרִיתִי יִצְחָק וְאַף אֶת־בְּרִיתִי אַבְרָהָם אֶזְכֹּר וְהָאָרֶץ אֶזְכֹּר׃

v'-za-khar-TEE et b'-ree-TEE ya-a-KOV v'-AF et b'-ree-TEE yitz-KHAK v'-AF et b'-ree-TEE av-ra-HAM ez-KOR v'-ha-A-retz ez-KOR

43 For the land shall be forsaken of them, making up for its *Shabbat* years by being desolate of them, while they atone for their iniquity; for the abundant reason that they rejected My rules and spurned My laws.

מג וְהָאָרֶץ תֵּעָזֵב מֵהֶם וְתִרֶץ אֶת־שַׁבְּתֹתֶיהָ בָּהְשַׁמָּה מֵהֶם וְהֵם יִרְצוּ אֶת־עֲוֺנָם יַעַן וּבְיַעַן בְּמִשְׁפָּטַי מָאָסוּ וְאֶת־חֻקֹּתַי גָּעֲלָה נַפְשָׁם׃

44 Yet, even then, when they are in the land of their enemies, I will not reject them or spurn them so as to destroy them, annulling My covenant with them: for I *Hashem* am their God.

מד וְאַף־גַּם־זֹאת בִּהְיוֹתָם בְּאֶרֶץ אֹיְבֵיהֶם לֹא־מְאַסְתִּים וְלֹא־גְעַלְתִּים לְכַלֹּתָם לְהָפֵר בְּרִיתִי אִתָּם כִּי אֲנִי יְהוָה אֱלֹהֵיהֶם׃

45 I will remember in their favor the covenant with the ancients, whom I freed from the land of Egypt in the sight of the nations to be their God: I, *Hashem*.

מה וְזָכַרְתִּי לָהֶם בְּרִית רִאשֹׁנִים אֲשֶׁר הוֹצֵאתִי־אֹתָם מֵאֶרֶץ מִצְרַיִם לְעֵינֵי הַגּוֹיִם לִהְיוֹת לָהֶם לֵאלֹהִים אֲנִי יְהוָה׃

46 These are the laws, rules, and instructions that *Hashem* established, through *Moshe* on *Har Sinai*, between Himself and *B'nei Yisrael*.

מו אֵלֶּה הַחֻקִּים וְהַמִּשְׁפָּטִים וְהַתּוֹרֹת אֲשֶׁר נָתַן יְהוָה בֵּינוֹ וּבֵין בְּנֵי יִשְׂרָאֵל בְּהַר סִינַי בְּיַד־מֹשֶׁה׃

27 1 *Hashem* spoke to *Moshe*, saying:

כז א וַיְדַבֵּר יְהוָה אֶל־מֹשֶׁה לֵּאמֹר׃

26:42 And I will remember the land This passage lists the curses that will be brought upon the People of Israel if they fail to follow *Hashem*'s commandments. If His children's sins become too great, God promises to exile the people from the Promised Land, and to destroy the land itself. Following these curses, however, *Hashem* promises that He will never give up on His people and that ultimately, there will be a redemption. In this verse, He promises that he will remember not only the People of Israel, but also the Land of Israel itself. He will return His chosen people to the chosen land, and this land will flourish. How fortunate is our generation to witness *Hashem* "remembering the land" as this verse promises.

Vayikra/Leviticus 27
Bechukotai

2 Speak to *B'nei Yisrael* and say to them: When anyone explicitly vows to *Hashem* the equivalent for a human being,

3 the following scale shall apply: If it is a male from twenty to sixty years of age, the equivalent is fifty *shekalim* of silver by the sanctuary weight;

4 if it is a female, the equivalent is thirty *shekalim*.

5 If the age is from five years to twenty years, the equivalent is twenty *shekalim* for a male and ten *shekalim* for a female.

6 If the age is from one month to five years, the equivalent for a male is five *shekalim* of silver, and the equivalent for a female is three *shekalim* of silver.

7 If the age is sixty years or over, the equivalent is fifteen *shekalim* in the case of a male and ten *shekalim* for a female.

8 But if one cannot afford the equivalent, he shall be presented before the *Kohen*, and the *Kohen* shall assess him; the *Kohen* shall assess him according to what the vower can afford.

9 If [the vow concerns] any animal that may be brought as an offering to *Hashem*, any such that may be given to *Hashem* shall be holy.

10 One may not exchange or substitute another for it, either good for bad, or bad for good; if one does substitute one animal for another, the thing vowed and its substitute shall both be holy.

11 If [the vow concerns] any unclean animal that may not be brought as an offering to *Hashem*, the animal shall be presented before the *Kohen*,

12 and the *Kohen* shall assess it. Whether high or low, whatever assessment is set by the *Kohen* shall stand;

13 and if he wishes to redeem it, he must add one-fifth to its assessment.

14 If anyone consecrates his house to *Hashem*, the *Kohen* shall assess it. Whether high or low, as the *Kohen* assesses it, so it shall stand;

15 and if he who has consecrated his house wishes to redeem it, he must add one-fifth to the sum at which it was assessed, and it shall be his.

ויקרא כז
בחקתי

ב דַּבֵּר אֶל־בְּנֵי יִשְׂרָאֵל וְאָמַרְתָּ אֲלֵהֶם אִישׁ כִּי יַפְלִא נֶדֶר בְּעֶרְכְּךָ נְפָשֹׁת לַיהוָה:

ג וְהָיָה עֶרְכְּךָ הַזָּכָר מִבֶּן עֶשְׂרִים שָׁנָה וְעַד בֶּן־שִׁשִּׁים שָׁנָה וְהָיָה עֶרְכְּךָ חֲמִשִּׁים שֶׁקֶל כֶּסֶף בְּשֶׁקֶל הַקֹּדֶשׁ:

ד וְאִם־נְקֵבָה הִוא וְהָיָה עֶרְכְּךָ שְׁלֹשִׁים שָׁקֶל:

ה וְאִם מִבֶּן־חָמֵשׁ שָׁנִים וְעַד בֶּן־עֶשְׂרִים שָׁנָה וְהָיָה עֶרְכְּךָ הַזָּכָר עֶשְׂרִים שְׁקָלִים וְלַנְּקֵבָה עֲשֶׂרֶת שְׁקָלִים:

ו וְאִם מִבֶּן־חֹדֶשׁ וְעַד בֶּן־חָמֵשׁ שָׁנִים וְהָיָה עֶרְכְּךָ הַזָּכָר חֲמִשָּׁה שְׁקָלִים כָּסֶף וְלַנְּקֵבָה עֶרְכְּךָ שְׁלֹשֶׁת שְׁקָלִים כָּסֶף:

ז וְאִם מִבֶּן־שִׁשִּׁים שָׁנָה וָמַעְלָה אִם־זָכָר וְהָיָה עֶרְכְּךָ חֲמִשָּׁה עָשָׂר שָׁקֶל וְלַנְּקֵבָה עֲשָׂרָה שְׁקָלִים:

ח וְאִם־מָךְ הוּא מֵעֶרְכֶּךָ וְהֶעֱמִידוֹ לִפְנֵי הַכֹּהֵן וְהֶעֱרִיךְ אֹתוֹ הַכֹּהֵן עַל־פִּי אֲשֶׁר תַּשִּׂיג יַד הַנֹּדֵר יַעֲרִיכֶנּוּ הַכֹּהֵן:

ט וְאִם־בְּהֵמָה אֲשֶׁר יַקְרִיבוּ מִמֶּנָּה קָרְבָּן לַיהוָה כֹּל אֲשֶׁר יִתֵּן מִמֶּנּוּ לַיהוָה יִהְיֶה־קֹּדֶשׁ:

י לֹא יַחֲלִיפֶנּוּ וְלֹא־יָמִיר אֹתוֹ טוֹב בְּרָע אוֹ־רַע בְּטוֹב וְאִם־הָמֵר יָמִיר בְּהֵמָה בִּבְהֵמָה וְהָיָה־הוּא וּתְמוּרָתוֹ יִהְיֶה־קֹּדֶשׁ:

יא וְאִם כָּל־בְּהֵמָה טְמֵאָה אֲשֶׁר לֹא־יַקְרִיבוּ מִמֶּנָּה קָרְבָּן לַיהוָה וְהֶעֱמִיד אֶת־הַבְּהֵמָה לִפְנֵי הַכֹּהֵן:

יב וְהֶעֱרִיךְ הַכֹּהֵן אֹתָהּ בֵּין טוֹב וּבֵין רָע כְּעֶרְכְּךָ הַכֹּהֵן כֵּן יִהְיֶה:

יג וְאִם־גָּאֹל יִגְאָלֶנָּה וְיָסַף חֲמִישִׁתוֹ עַל־עֶרְכֶּךָ:

יד וְאִישׁ כִּי־יַקְדִּשׁ אֶת־בֵּיתוֹ קֹדֶשׁ לַיהוָה וְהֶעֱרִיכוֹ הַכֹּהֵן בֵּין טוֹב וּבֵין רָע כַּאֲשֶׁר יַעֲרִיךְ אֹתוֹ הַכֹּהֵן כֵּן יָקוּם:

טו וְאִם־הַמַּקְדִּישׁ יִגְאַל אֶת־בֵּיתוֹ וְיָסַף חֲמִישִׁית כֶּסֶף־עֶרְכְּךָ עָלָיו וְהָיָה לוֹ:

Vayikra/Leviticus 27
Bechukotai

ויקרא כז
בחקתי

16 If anyone consecrates to *Hashem* any land that he holds, its assessment shall be in accordance with its seed requirement: fifty *shekalim* of silver to a *chomer* of barley seed.

טז וְאִם מִשְּׂדֵ֣ה אֲחֻזָּתוֹ֮ יַקְדִּ֣ישׁ אִישׁ֒ לַיהוָ֔ה וְהָיָ֥ה עֶרְכְּךָ֖ לְפִ֣י זַרְע֑וֹ זֶ֚רַע חֹ֣מֶר שְׂעֹרִ֔ים בַּחֲמִשִּׁ֖ים שֶׁ֥קֶל כָּֽסֶף׃

17 If he consecrates his land as of the jubilee year, its assessment stands.

יז אִם־מִשְּׁנַ֥ת הַיֹּבֵ֖ל יַקְדִּ֣ישׁ שָׂדֵ֑הוּ כְּעֶרְכְּךָ֖ יָקֽוּם׃

18 But if he consecrates his land after the jubilee, the *Kohen* shall compute the price according to the years that are left until the jubilee year, and its assessment shall be so reduced;

יח וְאִם־אַחַ֣ר הַיֹּבֵל֮ יַקְדִּ֣ישׁ שָׂדֵהוּ֒ וְחִשַּׁב־ל֨וֹ הַכֹּהֵ֜ן אֶת־הַכֶּ֗סֶף עַל־פִּ֤י הַשָּׁנִים֙ הַנּ֣וֹתָרֹ֔ת עַ֖ד שְׁנַ֣ת הַיֹּבֵ֑ל וְנִגְרַ֖ע מֵֽעֶרְכֶּֽךָ׃

19 and if he who consecrated the land wishes to redeem it, he must add one-fifth to the sum at which it was assessed, and it shall pass to him.

יט וְאִם־גָּאֹ֤ל יִגְאַל֙ אֶת־הַשָּׂדֶ֔ה הַמַּקְדִּ֖ישׁ אֹת֑וֹ וְ֠יָסַף חֲמִשִׁ֧ית כֶּֽסֶף־עֶרְכְּךָ֛ עָלָ֖יו וְקָ֥ם לֽוֹ׃

20 But if he does not redeem the land, and the land is sold to another, it shall no longer be redeemable:

כ וְאִם־לֹ֤א יִגְאַל֙ אֶת־הַשָּׂדֶ֔ה וְאִם־מָכַ֥ר אֶת־הַשָּׂדֶ֖ה לְאִ֣ישׁ אַחֵ֑ר לֹ֥א יִגָּאֵ֖ל עֽוֹד׃

21 when it is released in the jubilee, the land shall be holy to *Hashem*, as land proscribed; it becomes the *Kohen*'s holding.

כא וְהָיָ֨ה הַשָּׂדֶ֜ה בְּצֵאת֣וֹ בַיֹּבֵ֗ל קֹ֛דֶשׁ לַיהוָ֖ה כִּשְׂדֵ֣ה הַחֵ֑רֶם לַכֹּהֵ֖ן תִּהְיֶ֥ה אֲחֻזָּתֽוֹ׃

22 If he consecrates to *Hashem* land that he purchased, which is not land of his holding,

כב וְאִם֙ אֶת־שְׂדֵ֣ה מִקְנָת֔וֹ אֲשֶׁ֕ר לֹ֖א מִשְּׂדֵ֣ה אֲחֻזָּת֑וֹ יַקְדִּ֖ישׁ לַֽיהוָֽה׃

23 the *Kohen* shall compute for him the proportionate assessment up to the jubilee year, and he shall pay the assessment as of that day, a sacred donation to *Hashem*.

כג וְחִשַּׁב־ל֣וֹ הַכֹּהֵ֗ן אֵ֚ת מִכְסַ֣ת הָֽעֶרְכְּךָ֔ עַ֖ד שְׁנַ֣ת הַיֹּבֵ֑ל וְנָתַ֤ן אֶת־הָעֶרְכְּךָ֙ בַּיּ֣וֹם הַה֔וּא קֹ֖דֶשׁ לַֽיהוָֽה׃

24 In the jubilee year the land shall revert to him from whom it was bought, whose holding the land is.

כד בִּשְׁנַ֤ת הַיּוֹבֵל֙ יָשׁ֣וּב הַשָּׂדֶ֔ה לַאֲשֶׁ֥ר קָנָ֖הוּ מֵאִתּ֑וֹ לַאֲשֶׁר־ל֖וֹ אֲחֻזַּ֥ת הָאָֽרֶץ׃

25 All assessments shall be by the sanctuary weight, the *shekel* being twenty *geira*.

כה וְכָ֨ל־עֶרְכְּךָ֔ יִהְיֶ֖ה בְּשֶׁ֣קֶל הַקֹּ֑דֶשׁ עֶשְׂרִ֥ים גֵּרָ֖ה יִהְיֶ֥ה הַשָּֽׁקֶל׃

26 A firstling of animals, however, which – as a firstling – is *Hashem*'s, cannot be consecrated by anybody; whether ox or sheep, it is *Hashem*'s.

כו אַךְ־בְּכ֞וֹר אֲשֶׁר־יְבֻכַּ֤ר לַֽיהוָה֙ בִּבְהֵמָ֔ה לֹא־יַקְדִּ֥ישׁ אִ֖ישׁ אֹת֑וֹ אִם־שׁ֣וֹר אִם־שֶׂ֔ה לַֽיהוָ֖ה הֽוּא׃

27 But if it is of unclean animals, it may be ransomed as its assessment, with one-fifth added; if it is not redeemed, it shall be sold at its assessment.

כז וְאִ֤ם בַּבְּהֵמָה֙ הַטְּמֵאָ֔ה וּפָדָ֥ה בְעֶרְכְּךָ֖ וְיָסַ֣ף חֲמִשִׁת֣וֹ עָלָ֑יו וְאִם־לֹ֥א יִגָּאֵ֖ל וְנִמְכַּ֥ר בְּעֶרְכֶּֽךָ׃

28 But of all that anyone owns, be it man or beast or land of his holding, nothing that he has proscribed for *Hashem* may be sold or redeemed; every proscribed thing is totally consecrated to *Hashem*.

כח אַךְ־כָּל־חֵ֡רֶם אֲשֶׁ֣ר יַחֲרִם֩ אִ֨ישׁ לַֽיהוָ֜ה מִכָּל־אֲשֶׁר־ל֗וֹ מֵאָדָ֤ם וּבְהֵמָה֙ וּמִשְּׂדֵ֣ה אֲחֻזָּת֔וֹ לֹ֥א יִמָּכֵ֖ר וְלֹ֣א יִגָּאֵ֑ל כָּל־חֵ֕רֶם קֹֽדֶשׁ־קָֽדָשִׁ֥ים ה֖וּא לַיהוָֽה׃

29 No human being who has been proscribed can be ransomed: he shall be put to death.

כט כָּל־חֵ֗רֶם אֲשֶׁ֧ר יָחֳרַ֛ם מִן־הָאָדָ֖ם לֹ֣א יִפָּדֶ֑ה מ֖וֹת יוּמָֽת׃

Vayikra/Leviticus 27
Bechukotai

ויקרא כז
בחקתי

30 All tithes from the land, whether seed from the ground or fruit from the tree, are *Hashem*'s; they are holy to *Hashem*.

v'-khol ma-SAR ha-A-retz mi-ZE-ra ha-A-retz mi-p'-REE ha-AYTZ la-do-NAI HU KO-desh la-do-NAI

ל וְכָל־מַעְשַׂר הָאָרֶץ מִזֶּרַע הָאָרֶץ מִפְּרִי הָעֵץ לַיהֹוָה הוּא קֹדֶשׁ לַיהֹוָה׃

31 If anyone wishes to redeem any of his tithes, he must add one-fifth to them.

לא וְאִם־גָּאֹל יִגְאַל אִישׁ מִמַּעַשְׂרוֹ חֲמִשִׁיתוֹ יֹסֵף עָלָיו׃

32 All tithes of the herd or flock – of all that passes under the shepherd's staff, every tenth one – shall be holy to *Hashem*.

לב וְכָל־מַעְשַׂר בָּקָר וָצֹאן כֹּל אֲשֶׁר־יַעֲבֹר תַּחַת הַשָּׁבֶט הָעֲשִׂירִי יִהְיֶה־קֹּדֶשׁ לַיהֹוָה׃

33 He must not look out for good as against bad, or make substitution for it. If he does make substitution for it, then it and its substitute shall both be holy: it cannot be redeemed.

לג לֹא יְבַקֵּר בֵּין־טוֹב לָרַע וְלֹא יְמִירֶנּוּ וְאִם־הָמֵר יְמִירֶנּוּ וְהָיָה־הוּא וּתְמוּרָתוֹ יִהְיֶה־קֹּדֶשׁ לֹא יִגָּאֵל׃

34 These are the commandments that *Hashem* gave *Moshe* for *B'nei Yisrael* on *Har Sinai*.

לד אֵלֶּה הַמִּצְוֹת אֲשֶׁר צִוָּה יְהֹוָה אֶת־מֹשֶׁה אֶל־בְּנֵי יִשְׂרָאֵל בְּהַר סִינָי׃

27:30 All tithes from the land The laws of the tithes serve as another reminder that our successes in life should be attributed to *Hashem*, the source of everything in this world. This verse describes the second tithe, one tenth of a farmer's produce that is to be separated after the first tithe is set aside for the *Leviim*. This tithe must be eaten in *Yerushalayim*, or redeemed for coins with which to purchase and eat food in the holy city. By separating one tenth of his produce and bringing it to *Hashem*'s capital city, the farmer is forced to remember that all of his produce is a gift from God; not merely the result of his own efforts.

Sefer Bamidbar
The Book of Numbers

Introduction and commentary by Shira Schechter

When *Sefer Bamidbar* (literally, 'in the wilderness') begins, the Israelites are in the wilderness, having left Egypt and received the *Torah*, and are preparing to travel to Israel. They are preparing militarily, and hence the English name of this fourth book of the Bible is 'Numbers,' since it begins with a census in which they organize and count their ranks. At the same time, they are also preparing spiritually for their life as a nation, following the laws of the *Torah* in their ancestral homeland.

However, during the course of *Sefer Bamidbar*, the plan becomes derailed. The people complain, turn against *Hashem* and His servant *Moshe*, and arouse the anger of the Almighty. Instead of heading immediately into the land, they are sentenced to wander the desert for forty years. These people lost their chance to enter Israel; only the next generation would be given that opportunity. *Hashem*, Who is merciful and compassionate, suddenly cannot forgive them. What did the people do to deserve such a harsh punishment?

Jewish tradition teaches that the generation of the wilderness committed an inexcusable infraction, in that they rejected *Eretz Yisrael*. In Chapter 14, they cry out, "Why is *Hashem* taking us to that land to fall by the sword?" Instead of eagerly claiming their ancestral heritage and assuming their divine mission, the people second-guess God, cynically call His will into question, and critically reject the greatest of all gifts.

The rest of *Sefer Bamidbar* continues to depict this downward spiral. In Chapter 16, they call into question the legitimacy and qualifications for leadership of *Moshe* and *Aharon*, and rebellion is launched against their leadership. Later, in Chapter 20, the people complain about the lack of water in the wilderness, and in yet another affront to *Hashem*, become involved in idolatry and immoral relations in Chapter 25.

This all started with a rejection of the land. In fact, Jewish tradition teaches that a lack of honor towards the Land of Israel is the source of many calamities throughout history, including the destruction of both Temples in *Yerushalyim*.

The lessons of the Bible are as relevant today as ever before. When studying *Bamidbar*, we must learn the lessons of the incident of the spies, in order to constantly re-evaluate our own relationship with the Land of Israel.

Map of the Journey of the Spies

This map features the places visited by the twelve spies on their mission to scout out the Land of Israel as described in *Sefer Bamidbar* chapter 13.

1. The spies were sent to scout out the Land of Israel from **Kadesh-barnea** in the wilderness of Paran (see Numbers 13:3, 32:8, Deuteronomy 1:19).
2. Moshe commanded the spies to enter Israel from the south, in Hebrew, the **Negev** (Numbers 13:17).
3. After entering from the Negev, the spies came to **Chevron** where they encountered the Anakites, or giants (Numbers 13:22). Wadi Eshcol, where the spies cut a cluster of grapes, pomegranates and figs to bring back to Moshe, was in the area of Chevron (Numbers 13:23–24).
4. The spies walked the length and width of the borders as far north as **Lebo-hamath** (Numbers 13:21).

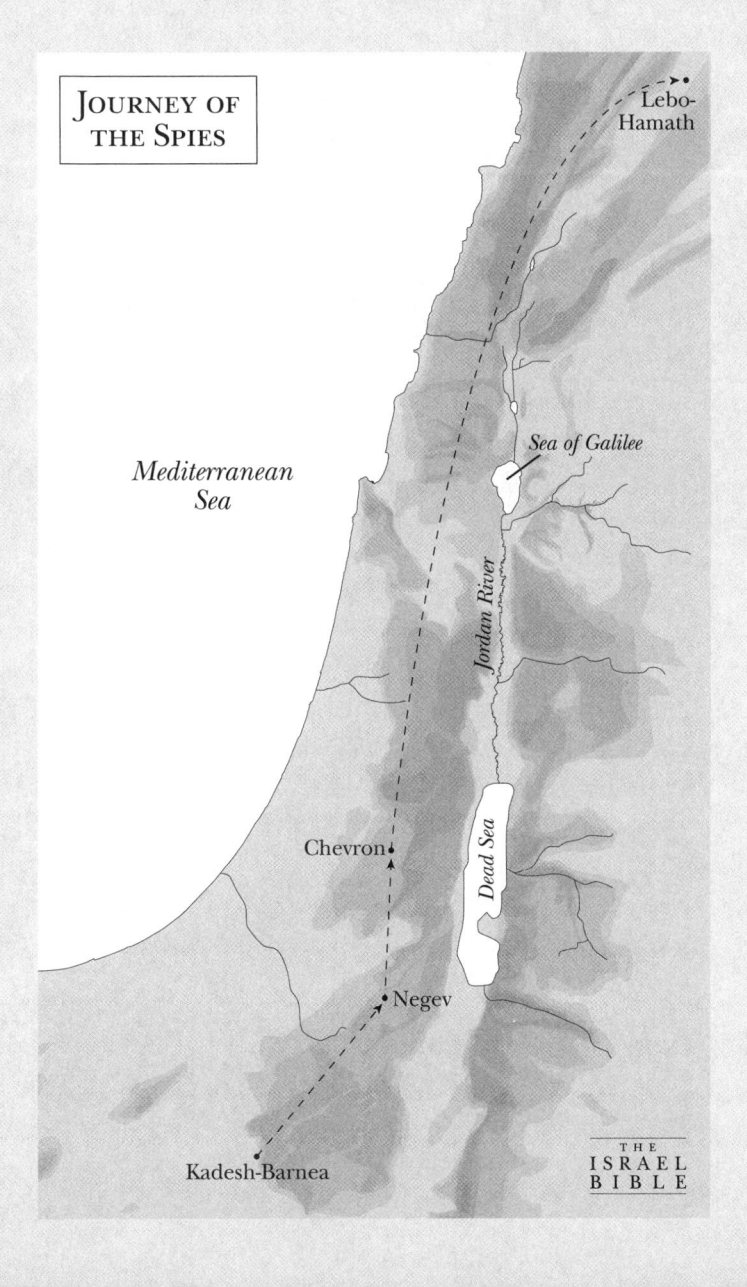

Bamidbar/Numbers 1
Bamidbar

במדבר א
במדבר

1 ¹ On the first day of the second month, in the second year following the exodus from the land of Egypt, *Hashem* spoke to *Moshe* in the wilderness of Sinai, in the Tent of Meeting, saying:

וַיְדַבֵּר יְהֹוָה אֶל־מֹשֶׁה בְּמִדְבַּר סִינַי בְּאֹהֶל מוֹעֵד בְּאֶחָד לַחֹדֶשׁ הַשֵּׁנִי בַּשָּׁנָה הַשֵּׁנִית לְצֵאתָם מֵאֶרֶץ מִצְרַיִם לֵאמֹר:

vai-da-BAYR a-do-NAI el mo-SHEH b'-mid-BAR see-NAI b'-O-hel mo-AYD b'-e-KHAD la-KHO-desh ha-shay-NEE ba-sha-NAH ha-shay-NEET l'-tzay-TAM may-E-retz mitz-RA-yim lay-MOR

² Take a census of the whole Israelite community by the clans of its ancestral houses, listing the names, every male, head by head.

שְׂאוּ אֶת־רֹאשׁ כָּל־עֲדַת בְּנֵי־יִשְׂרָאֵל לְמִשְׁפְּחֹתָם לְבֵית אֲבֹתָם בְּמִסְפַּר שֵׁמוֹת כָּל־זָכָר לְגֻלְגְּלֹתָם:

s'-U et ROSH kol a-DAT b'-nay yis-ra-AYL l'-mish-p'-kho-TAM l'-VAYT a-vo-TAM b'-mis-PAR shay-MOT kol za-KHAR l'-gul-g'-lo-TAM

³ You and *Aharon* shall record them by their groups, from the age of twenty years up, all those in *Yisrael* who are able to bear arms.

⁴ Associated with you shall be a man from each tribe, each one the head of his ancestral house.

⁵ These are the names of the men who shall assist you: From *Reuven*, Elitzur son of Shedeur.

⁶ From *Shimon*, Shelumiel son of Zurishaddai.

⁷ From *Yehuda*, Nachshon son of *Aminadav*.

⁸ From *Yissachar*, Netanel son of Zuar.

⁹ From *Zevulun*, Eliav son of Helon.

¹⁰ From the sons of *Yosef*: from *Efraim*, Elishama son of Ammihud; from *Menashe*, Gamliel son of Pedahzur.

Ramban (1194–1270)

1:1 In the wilderness of *Sinai*, in the Tent of Meeting After a stay of almost a year in the Sinai Desert where the people received the *Torah*, constructed the *Mishkan* and studied some of their new laws, *Sefer Bamidbar* opens with the preparations to leave the desert and head to the Promised Land. The *Ramban* explains that their entry into *Eretz Yisrael* with the *Torah* in hand was the ultimate goal of the exodus from Egypt. The *Mishkan*, where *Hashem* reveals Himself on a daily basis, will allow the people to carry the experience of revelation at Mount Sinai with them on their journey, and He will ultimately find His permanent resting place on earth in the *Beit Hamikdash* in *Yerushalayim*. In this way, God remains permanently in their midst.

1:2 Take a census of the whole Israelite community The foremost commandment given by *Hashem* to *Moshe* and *Aharon* in preparation for travel to the Land of Israel is to count the people. This is one of several censuses described in the Bible, and the first of two in *Sefer Bamidbar*. In fact, the English name of this book, Numbers, derives from these two countings. Since the Israelites are heading toward the Promised Land to conquer and settle it, the census serves to inform the leadership of how many soldiers they have available for their army and among how many people the land would then need to be divided. *Rashi*, however, gives another reason for the count. He explains that *Hashem* counts His people repeatedly, simply because they are precious to Him. Just as someone with a valuable collection will count its contents over and over, so too *Hashem* frequently counts His people, to teach us that every individual is precious to Him.

Bamidbar/Numbers 1
Bamidbar

11 From *Binyamin*, *Avidan* son of Gideoni.

12 From *Dan*, *Achiezer* son of Ammishaddai.

13 From *Asher*, *Pagiel* son of Ochran.

14 From *Gad*, *Elyasaf* son of Deuel.

15 From *Naftali*, *Achira* son of Enan.

16 Those are the elected of the assembly, the chieftains of their ancestral tribes: they are the heads of the contingents of *Yisrael*.

17 So *Moshe* and *Aharon* took those men, who were designated by name,

18 and on the first day of the second month they convoked the whole community, who were registered by the clans of their ancestral houses – the names of those aged twenty years and over being listed head by head.

19 As *Hashem* had commanded *Moshe*, so he recorded them in the wilderness of Sinai.

20 They totaled as follows: The descendants of *Reuven*, *Yisrael*'s first-born, the registration of the clans of their ancestral house, as listed by name, head by head, all males aged twenty years and over, all who were able to bear arms –

21 those enrolled from the tribe of *Reuven*: 46,500.

22 Of the descendants of *Shimon*, the registration of the clans of their ancestral house, their enrollment as listed by name, head by head, all males aged twenty years and over, all who were able to bear arms –

23 those enrolled from the tribe of *Shimon*: 59,300.

24 Of the descendants of *Gad*, the registration of the clans of their ancestral house, as listed by name, aged twenty years and over, all who were able to bear arms –

25 those enrolled from the tribe of *Gad*: 45,650.

26 Of the descendants of *Yehuda*, the registration of the clans of their ancestral house, as listed by name, aged twenty years and over, all who were able to bear arms –

Bamidbar/Numbers 1
Bamidbar

27 those enrolled from the tribe of *Yehuda*: 74,600.

פְּקֻדֵיהֶם לְמַטֵּה יְהוּדָה אַרְבָּעָה וְשִׁבְעִים אֶלֶף וְשֵׁשׁ מֵאוֹת: כז

28 Of the descendants of *Yissachar*, the registration of the clans of their ancestral house, as listed by name, aged twenty years and over, all who were able to bear arms –

לִבְנֵי יִשָּׂשכָר תּוֹלְדֹתָם לְמִשְׁפְּחֹתָם לְבֵית אֲבֹתָם בְּמִסְפַּר שֵׁמֹת מִבֶּן עֶשְׂרִים שָׁנָה וָמַעְלָה כֹּל יֹצֵא צָבָא: כח

29 those enrolled from the tribe of *Yissachar*: 54,400.

פְּקֻדֵיהֶם לְמַטֵּה יִשָּׂשכָר אַרְבָּעָה וַחֲמִשִּׁים אֶלֶף וְאַרְבַּע מֵאוֹת: כט

30 Of the descendants of *Zevulun*, the registration of the clans of their ancestral house, as listed by name, aged twenty years and over, all who were able to bear arms –

לִבְנֵי זְבוּלֻן תּוֹלְדֹתָם לְמִשְׁפְּחֹתָם לְבֵית אֲבֹתָם בְּמִסְפַּר שֵׁמֹת מִבֶּן עֶשְׂרִים שָׁנָה וָמַעְלָה כֹּל יֹצֵא צָבָא: ל

31 those enrolled from the tribe of *Zevulun*: 57,400.

פְּקֻדֵיהֶם לְמַטֵּה זְבוּלֻן שִׁבְעָה וַחֲמִשִּׁים אֶלֶף וְאַרְבַּע מֵאוֹת: לא

32 Of the descendants of *Yosef*: Of the descendants of *Efraim*, the registration of the clans of their ancestral house, as listed by name, aged twenty years and over, all who were able to bear arms –

לִבְנֵי יוֹסֵף לִבְנֵי אֶפְרַיִם תּוֹלְדֹתָם לְמִשְׁפְּחֹתָם לְבֵית אֲבֹתָם בְּמִסְפַּר שֵׁמֹת מִבֶּן עֶשְׂרִים שָׁנָה וָמַעְלָה כֹּל יֹצֵא צָבָא: לב

33 those enrolled from the tribe of *Efraim*: 40,500.

פְּקֻדֵיהֶם לְמַטֵּה אֶפְרָיִם אַרְבָּעִים אֶלֶף וַחֲמֵשׁ מֵאוֹת: לג

34 Of the descendants of *Menashe*, the registration of the clans of their ancestral house, as listed by name, aged twenty years and over, all who were able to bear arms –

לִבְנֵי מְנַשֶּׁה תּוֹלְדֹתָם לְמִשְׁפְּחֹתָם לְבֵית אֲבֹתָם בְּמִסְפַּר שֵׁמוֹת מִבֶּן עֶשְׂרִים שָׁנָה וָמַעְלָה כֹּל יֹצֵא צָבָא: לד

35 those enrolled from the tribe of *Menashe*: 32,200.

פְּקֻדֵיהֶם לְמַטֵּה מְנַשֶּׁה שְׁנַיִם וּשְׁלֹשִׁים אֶלֶף וּמָאתָיִם: לה

36 Of the descendants of *Binyamin*, the registration of the clans of their ancestral house, as listed by name, aged twenty years and over, all who were able to bear arms –

לִבְנֵי בִנְיָמִן תּוֹלְדֹתָם לְמִשְׁפְּחֹתָם לְבֵית אֲבֹתָם בְּמִסְפַּר שֵׁמֹת מִבֶּן עֶשְׂרִים שָׁנָה וָמַעְלָה כֹּל יֹצֵא צָבָא: לו

37 those enrolled from the tribe of *Binyamin*: 35,400.

פְּקֻדֵיהֶם לְמַטֵּה בִנְיָמִן חֲמִשָּׁה וּשְׁלֹשִׁים אֶלֶף וְאַרְבַּע מֵאוֹת: לז

38 Of the descendants of *Dan*, the registration of the clans of their ancestral house, as listed by name, aged twenty years and over, all who were able to bear arms –

לִבְנֵי דָן תּוֹלְדֹתָם לְמִשְׁפְּחֹתָם לְבֵית אֲבֹתָם בְּמִסְפַּר שֵׁמֹת מִבֶּן עֶשְׂרִים שָׁנָה וָמַעְלָה כֹּל יֹצֵא צָבָא: לח

39 those enrolled from the tribe of *Dan*: 62,700.

פְּקֻדֵיהֶם לְמַטֵּה דָן שְׁנַיִם וְשִׁשִּׁים אֶלֶף וּשְׁבַע מֵאוֹת: לט

40 Of the descendants of *Asher*, the registration of the clans of their ancestral house, as listed by name, aged twenty years and over, all who were able to bear arms –

לִבְנֵי אָשֵׁר תּוֹלְדֹתָם לְמִשְׁפְּחֹתָם לְבֵית אֲבֹתָם בְּמִסְפַּר שֵׁמֹת מִבֶּן עֶשְׂרִים שָׁנָה וָמַעְלָה כֹּל יֹצֵא צָבָא: מ

Bamidbar/Numbers 1
Bamidbar

במדבר א
במדבר

41 those enrolled from the tribe of *Asher*: 41,500.

מא פְּקֻדֵיהֶם לְמַטֵּה אָשֵׁר אֶחָד וְאַרְבָּעִים אֶלֶף וַחֲמֵשׁ מֵאוֹת:

42 [Of] the descendants of *Naftali*, the registration of the clans of their ancestral house as listed by name, aged twenty years and over, all who were able to bear arms –

מב בְּנֵי נַפְתָּלִי תּוֹלְדֹתָם לְמִשְׁפְּחֹתָם לְבֵית אֲבֹתָם בְּמִסְפַּר שֵׁמֹת מִבֶּן עֶשְׂרִים שָׁנָה וָמַעְלָה כֹּל יֹצֵא צָבָא:

43 those enrolled from the tribe of *Naftali*: 53,400.

מג פְּקֻדֵיהֶם לְמַטֵּה נַפְתָּלִי שְׁלֹשָׁה וַחֲמִשִּׁים אֶלֶף וְאַרְבַּע מֵאוֹת:

44 Those are the enrollments recorded by *Moshe* and *Aharon* and by the chieftains of *Yisrael*, who were twelve in number, one man to each ancestral house.

מד אֵלֶּה הַפְּקֻדִים אֲשֶׁר פָּקַד מֹשֶׁה וְאַהֲרֹן וּנְשִׂיאֵי יִשְׂרָאֵל שְׁנֵים עָשָׂר אִישׁ אִישׁ־אֶחָד לְבֵית־אֲבֹתָיו הָיוּ:

45 All the Israelites, aged twenty years and over, enrolled by ancestral houses, all those in *Yisrael* who were able to bear arms –

מה וַיִּהְיוּ כָּל־פְּקוּדֵי בְנֵי־יִשְׂרָאֵל לְבֵית אֲבֹתָם מִבֶּן עֶשְׂרִים שָׁנָה וָמַעְלָה כָּל־יֹצֵא צָבָא בְּיִשְׂרָאֵל:

46 all who were enrolled came to 603,550.

מו וַיִּהְיוּ כָּל־הַפְּקֻדִים שֵׁשׁ־מֵאוֹת אֶלֶף וּשְׁלֹשֶׁת אֲלָפִים וַחֲמֵשׁ מֵאוֹת וַחֲמִשִּׁים:

47 The *Leviim*, however, were not recorded among them by their ancestral tribe.

מז וְהַלְוִיִּם לְמַטֵּה אֲבֹתָם לֹא הָתְפָּקְדוּ בְּתוֹכָם:

48 For *Hashem* had spoken to *Moshe*, saying:

מח וַיְדַבֵּר יְהֹוָה אֶל־מֹשֶׁה לֵּאמֹר:

49 Do not on any account enroll the tribe of *Levi* or take a census of them with the Israelites.

מט אַךְ אֶת־מַטֵּה לֵוִי לֹא תִפְקֹד וְאֶת־רֹאשָׁם לֹא תִשָּׂא בְּתוֹךְ בְּנֵי יִשְׂרָאֵל:

50 You shall put the *Leviim* in charge of the *Mishkan* of the Pact, all its furnishings, and everything that pertains to it: they shall carry the *Mishkan* and all its furnishings, and they shall tend it; and they shall camp around the *Mishkan*.

נ וְאַתָּה הַפְקֵד אֶת־הַלְוִיִּם עַל־מִשְׁכַּן הָעֵדֻת וְעַל כָּל־כֵּלָיו וְעַל כָּל־אֲשֶׁר־לוֹ הֵמָּה יִשְׂאוּ אֶת־הַמִּשְׁכָּן וְאֶת־כָּל־כֵּלָיו וְהֵם יְשָׁרְתֻהוּ וְסָבִיב לַמִּשְׁכָּן יַחֲנוּ:

51 When the *Mishkan* is to set out, the *Leviim* shall take it down, and when the *Mishkan* is to be pitched, the *Leviim* shall set it up; any outsider who encroaches shall be put to death.

נא וּבִנְסֹעַ הַמִּשְׁכָּן יוֹרִידוּ אֹתוֹ הַלְוִיִּם וּבַחֲנֹת הַמִּשְׁכָּן יָקִימוּ אֹתוֹ הַלְוִיִּם וְהַזָּר הַקָּרֵב יוּמָת:

52 The Israelites shall encamp troop by troop, each man with his division and each under his standard.

נב וְחָנוּ בְּנֵי יִשְׂרָאֵל אִישׁ עַל־מַחֲנֵהוּ וְאִישׁ עַל־דִּגְלוֹ לְצִבְאֹתָם:

v'-kha-NU b'-NAY yis-ra-AYL EESH al ma-kha-NAY-hu v'-EESH al dig-LO l'-tziv-o-TAM

1:52 Each under his standard Following the census depicted at the beginning of *Bamidbar*, the Bible describes the layout of the Israelite camp in the desert. At the center of the camp is the *Mishkan*, a reminder that *Hashem* is always at the center of our lives. The *Leviim* surround the *Mishkan*, and the remaining tribes, organized into groups of three, surround the *Leviim*. Each tribe has its own flag featuring an insignia representative of the tribe's unique character; each group of tribes also possessed a distinctive banner. At the First Zionist Congress in 1897, a flag was needed to represent the new movement being formed. David

Flag of Israel

Bamidbar/Numbers 2
Bamidbar

במדבר ב
במדבר

53 The *Leviim*, however, shall camp around the *Mishkan* of the Pact, that wrath may not strike the Israelite community; the *Leviim* shall stand guard around the *Mishkan* of the Pact.

נג וְהַלְוִיִּם יַחֲנוּ סָבִיב לְמִשְׁכַּן הָעֵדֻת וְלֹא־יִהְיֶה קֶצֶף עַל־עֲדַת בְּנֵי יִשְׂרָאֵל וְשָׁמְרוּ הַלְוִיִּם אֶת־מִשְׁמֶרֶת מִשְׁכַּן הָעֵדוּת:

54 The Israelites did accordingly; just as *Hashem* had commanded *Moshe*, so they did.

נד וַיַּעֲשׂוּ בְּנֵי יִשְׂרָאֵל כְּכֹל אֲשֶׁר צִוָּה יְהֹוָה אֶת־מֹשֶׁה כֵּן עָשׂוּ:

2

1 *Hashem* spoke to *Moshe* and *Aharon*, saying:

ב א וַיְדַבֵּר יְהֹוָה אֶל־מֹשֶׁה וְאֶל־אַהֲרֹן לֵאמֹר:

2 The Israelites shall camp each with his standard, under the banners of their ancestral house; they shall camp around the Tent of Meeting at a distance.

ב אִישׁ עַל־דִּגְלוֹ בְאֹתֹת לְבֵית אֲבֹתָם יַחֲנוּ בְּנֵי יִשְׂרָאֵל מִנֶּגֶד סָבִיב לְאֹהֶל־מוֹעֵד יַחֲנוּ:

3 Camped on the front, or east side: the standard of the division of *Yehuda*, troop by troop. Chieftain of the Judites: *Nachshon* son of *Aminadav*.

ג וְהַחֹנִים קֵדְמָה מִזְרָחָה דֶּגֶל מַחֲנֵה יְהוּדָה לְצִבְאֹתָם וְנָשִׂיא לִבְנֵי יְהוּדָה נַחְשׁוֹן בֶּן־עַמִּינָדָב:

v'-ha-kho-NEEM KAY-d'-mah miz-RA-khah DE-gel ma-kha-NAY y'-hu-DAH l'-tziv-o-TAM v'-na-SEE liv-NAY y'-hu-DAH nakh-SHON ben a-mee-na-DAV

4 His troop, as enrolled: 74,600.

ד וּצְבָאוֹ וּפְקֻדֵיהֶם אַרְבָּעָה וְשִׁבְעִים אֶלֶף וְשֵׁשׁ מֵאוֹת:

5 Camping next to it: The tribe of *Yissachar*. Chieftain of the Issacharites: *Netanel* son of Zuar.

ה וְהַחֹנִים עָלָיו מַטֵּה יִשָּׂשכָר וְנָשִׂיא לִבְנֵי יִשָּׂשכָר נְתַנְאֵל בֶּן־צוּעָר:

6 His troop, as enrolled: 54,400.

ו וּצְבָאוֹ וּפְקֻדָיו אַרְבָּעָה וַחֲמִשִּׁים אֶלֶף וְאַרְבַּע מֵאוֹת:

7 The tribe of *Zevulun*. Chieftain of the Zebulunites: *Eliav* son of Helon.

ז מַטֵּה זְבוּלֻן וְנָשִׂיא לִבְנֵי זְבוּלֻן אֱלִיאָב בֶּן־חֵלֹן:

8 His troop, as enrolled: 57,400.

ח וּצְבָאוֹ וּפְקֻדָיו שִׁבְעָה וַחֲמִשִּׁים אֶלֶף וְאַרְבַּע מֵאוֹת:

9 The total enrolled in the division of *Yehuda*: 186,400, for all troops. These shall march first.

ט כָּל־הַפְּקֻדִים לְמַחֲנֵה יְהוּדָה מְאַת אֶלֶף וּשְׁמֹנִים אֶלֶף וְשֵׁשֶׁת־אֲלָפִים וְאַרְבַּע־מֵאוֹת לְצִבְאֹתָם רִאשֹׁנָה יִסָּעוּ:

The emblem of Jerusalem bearing the lion of Yehuda

Wolfsohn, a prominent member of the early Zionist movement, described how he came up with the design they ultimately adopted: "What flag would we hang in the Congress Hall? Then an idea struck me. We [already] have a flag – and it is blue and white. The *Tallit* (prayer shawl) with which we wrap ourselves when we pray: that is our symbol. Let us take this *Tallit* from its bag and unroll it before the eyes of Israel and the eyes of all nations. So I ordered a blue and white flag with the Shield of David painted upon it. That is how the national flag, that flew over Congress Hall, came into being."

2:3 The standard of the division of *Yehuda* As the forebear of the Davidic dynasty, *Yehuda* is given a place of honor in the Israelite camp. When the camp is not in motion, the tribe of *Yehuda* camps to the east of the *Mishkan*, which is considered the front, as it is the direction of the rising sun. And when they travel, the tribe of *Yehuda* goes in front, leading the Nation on its journey through the desert. As *Yehuda* led the Nation of Israel to the Promised Land, his descendant, the *Mashiach ben David*, will similarly gather the Children of Israel from all over the world and bring them back to *Eretz Yisrael*.

Bamidbar/Numbers 2
Bamidbar

במדבר ב
במדבר

10 On the south: the standard of the division of *Reuven*, troop by troop. Chieftain of the Reubenites: *Elitzur* son of Shedeur.

י דֶּ֣גֶל מַחֲנֵ֥ה רְאוּבֵ֛ן תֵּימָ֖נָה לְצִבְאֹתָ֑ם וְנָשִׂיא֙ לִבְנֵ֣י רְאוּבֵ֔ן אֱלִיצ֖וּר בֶּן־שְׁדֵיאֽוּר׃

11 His troop, as enrolled: 46,500.

יא וּצְבָא֖וֹ וּפְקֻדֵיהֶ֑ם שִׁשָּׁ֧ה וְאַרְבָּעִ֛ים אֶ֖לֶף וַחֲמֵ֥שׁ מֵאֽוֹת׃

12 Camping next to it: The tribe of *Shimon*. Chieftain of the Simeonites: *Shelumiel* son of Zurishaddai.

יב וְהַחֹנִ֥ם עָלָ֖יו מַטֵּ֣ה שִׁמְע֑וֹן וְנָשִׂיא֙ לִבְנֵ֣י שִׁמְע֔וֹן שְׁלֻמִיאֵ֖ל בֶּן־צוּרִֽישַׁדָּֽי׃

13 His troop, as enrolled: 59,300.

יג וּצְבָא֖וֹ וּפְקֻדֵיהֶ֑ם תִּשְׁעָ֧ה וַחֲמִשִּׁ֛ים אֶ֖לֶף וּשְׁלֹ֥שׁ מֵאֽוֹת׃

14 And the tribe of *Gad*. Chieftain of the Gadites: *Elyasaf* son of Reuel.

יד וּמַטֵּ֖ה גָּ֑ד וְנָשִׂיא֙ לִבְנֵ֣י גָ֔ד אֶלְיָסָ֖ף בֶּן־רְעוּאֵֽל׃

15 His troop, as enrolled: 45,650.

טו וּצְבָא֖וֹ וּפְקֻדֵיהֶ֑ם חֲמִשָּׁ֧ה וְאַרְבָּעִ֛ים אֶ֖לֶף וְשֵׁ֥שׁ מֵא֖וֹת וַחֲמִשִּֽׁים׃

16 The total enrolled in the division of *Reuven*: 151,450, for all troops. These shall march second.

טז כׇּֽל־הַפְּקֻדִ֞ים לְמַחֲנֵ֣ה רְאוּבֵ֗ן מְאַ֨ת אֶ֜לֶף וְאֶחָ֨ד וַחֲמִשִּׁ֥ים אֶ֛לֶף וְאַרְבַּע־מֵא֥וֹת וַחֲמִשִּׁ֖ים לְצִבְאֹתָ֑ם וּשְׁנִיִּ֖ם יִסָּֽעוּ׃

17 Then, midway between the divisions, the Tent of Meeting, the division of the *Leviim*, shall move. As they camp, so they shall march, each in position, by their standards.

יז וְנָסַ֧ע אֹֽהֶל־מוֹעֵ֛ד מַחֲנֵ֥ה הַלְוִיִּ֖ם בְּת֣וֹךְ הַֽמַּחֲנֹ֑ת כַּאֲשֶׁ֤ר יַחֲנוּ֙ כֵּ֣ן יִסָּ֔עוּ אִ֥ישׁ עַל־יָד֖וֹ לְדִגְלֵיהֶֽם׃

18 On the west: the standard of the division of *Efraim*, troop by troop. Chieftain of the Ephraimites: *Elishama* son of Ammihud.

יח דֶּ֣גֶל מַחֲנֵ֥ה אֶפְרַ֛יִם לְצִבְאֹתָ֖ם יָ֑מָּה וְנָשִׂיא֙ לִבְנֵ֣י אֶפְרַ֔יִם אֱלִישָׁמָ֖ע בֶּן־עַמִּיהֽוּד׃

19 His troop, as enrolled: 40,500.

יט וּצְבָא֖וֹ וּפְקֻדֵיהֶ֑ם אַרְבָּעִ֥ים אֶ֖לֶף וַחֲמֵ֥שׁ מֵאֽוֹת׃

20 Next to it: The tribe of *Menashe*. Chieftain of the Manassites: *Gamliel* son of Pedahzur.

כ וְעָלָ֖יו מַטֵּ֣ה מְנַשֶּׁ֑ה וְנָשִׂיא֙ לִבְנֵ֣י מְנַשֶּׁ֔ה גַּמְלִיאֵ֖ל בֶּן־פְּדָהצֽוּר׃

21 His troop, as enrolled: 32,200.

כא וּצְבָא֖וֹ וּפְקֻדֵיהֶ֑ם שְׁנַ֧יִם וּשְׁלֹשִׁ֛ים אֶ֖לֶף וּמָאתָֽיִם׃

22 And the tribe of *Binyamin*. Chieftain of the Benjaminites: *Avidan* son of Gideoni.

כב וּמַטֵּ֖ה בִּנְיָמִ֑ן וְנָשִׂיא֙ לִבְנֵ֣י בִנְיָמִ֔ן אֲבִידָ֖ן בֶּן־גִּדְעֹנִֽי׃

23 His troop, as enrolled: 35,400.

כג וּצְבָא֖וֹ וּפְקֻדֵיהֶ֑ם חֲמִשָּׁ֧ה וּשְׁלֹשִׁ֛ים אֶ֖לֶף וְאַרְבַּ֥ע מֵאֽוֹת׃

24 The total enrolled in the division of *Efraim*: 108,100 for all troops. These shall march third.

כד כׇּֽל־הַפְּקֻדִ֞ים לְמַחֲנֵ֣ה אֶפְרַ֗יִם מְאַ֥ת אֶ֛לֶף וּשְׁמֹֽנַת־אֲלָפִ֥ים וּמֵאָ֖ה לְצִבְאֹתָ֑ם וּשְׁלִשִׁ֖ים יִסָּֽעוּ׃

25 On the north: the standard of the division of *Dan*, troop by troop. Chieftain of the Danites: *Achiezer* son of Ammishaddai.

כה דֶּ֣גֶל מַחֲנֵ֥ה דָ֛ן צָפֹ֖נָה לְצִבְאֹתָ֑ם וְנָשִׂיא֙ לִבְנֵ֣י דָ֔ן אֲחִיעֶ֖זֶר בֶּן־עַמִּישַׁדָּֽי׃

Bamidbar/Numbers 3
Bamidbar

במדבר ג
במדבר

26 His troop, as enrolled: 62,700.

כו וּצְבָא֖וֹ וּפְקֻדֵיהֶ֑ם שְׁנַ֧יִם וְשִׁשִּׁ֛ים אֶ֖לֶף וּשְׁבַ֥ע מֵאֽוֹת׃

27 Camping next to it: The tribe of *Asher*. Chieftain of the Asherites: *Pagiel* son of Ochran.

כז וְהַחֹנִ֥ים עָלָ֖יו מַטֵּ֣ה אָשֵׁ֑ר וְנָשִׂיא֙ לִבְנֵ֣י אָשֵׁ֔ר פַּגְעִיאֵ֖ל בֶּן־עָכְרָֽן׃

28 His troop, as enrolled: 41,500.

כח וּצְבָא֖וֹ וּפְקֻדֵיהֶ֑ם אֶחָ֧ד וְאַרְבָּעִ֛ים אֶ֖לֶף וַחֲמֵ֥שׁ מֵאֽוֹת׃

29 And the tribe of *Naftali*. Chieftain of the Naphtalites: *Achira* son of Enan.

כט וּמַטֵּ֖ה נַפְתָּלִ֑י וְנָשִׂיא֙ לִבְנֵ֣י נַפְתָּלִ֔י אֲחִירַ֖ע בֶּן־עֵינָֽן׃

30 His troop, as enrolled: 53,400.

ל וּצְבָא֖וֹ וּפְקֻדֵיהֶ֑ם שְׁלֹשָׁ֧ה וַחֲמִשִּׁ֛ים אֶ֖לֶף וְאַרְבַּ֥ע מֵאֽוֹת׃

31 The total enrolled in the division of *Dan*: 157,600. These shall march last, by their standards.

לא כׇּל־הַפְּקֻדִ֞ים לְמַ֣חֲנֵה דָ֗ן מְאַ֥ת אֶ֙לֶף֙ וְשִׁבְעָ֧ה וַחֲמִשִּׁ֛ים אֶ֖לֶף וְשֵׁ֣שׁ מֵא֑וֹת לָאַחֲרֹנָ֥ה יִסְע֖וּ לְדִגְלֵיהֶֽם׃

32 Those are the enrollments of the Israelites by ancestral houses. The total enrolled in the divisions, for all troops: 603,550.

לב אֵ֛לֶּה פְּקוּדֵ֥י בְנֵֽי־יִשְׂרָאֵ֖ל לְבֵ֣ית אֲבֹתָ֑ם כׇּל־פְּקוּדֵ֤י הַֽמַּחֲנֹת֙ לְצִבְאֹתָ֔ם שֵׁשׁ־מֵא֥וֹת אֶ֙לֶף֙ וּשְׁלֹ֣שֶׁת אֲלָפִ֔ים וַחֲמֵ֥שׁ מֵא֖וֹת וַחֲמִשִּֽׁים׃

33 The *Leviim*, however, were not recorded among the Israelites, as *Hashem* had commanded *Moshe*.

לג וְהַ֨לְוִיִּ֔ם לֹ֣א הׇתְפָּקְד֔וּ בְּת֖וֹךְ בְּנֵ֣י יִשְׂרָאֵ֑ל כַּאֲשֶׁ֛ר צִוָּ֥ה יְהֹוָ֖ה אֶת־מֹשֶֽׁה׃

34 The Israelites did accordingly; just as *Hashem* had commanded *Moshe*, so they camped by their standards, and so they marched, each with his clan according to his ancestral house.

לד וַֽיַּעֲשׂ֖וּ בְּנֵ֣י יִשְׂרָאֵ֑ל כְּ֠כֹ֠ל אֲשֶׁר־צִוָּ֨ה יְהֹוָ֜ה אֶת־מֹשֶׁ֗ה כֵּֽן־חָנ֤וּ לְדִגְלֵיהֶם֙ וְכֵ֣ן נָסָ֔עוּ אִ֥ישׁ לְמִשְׁפְּחֹתָ֖יו עַל־בֵּ֥ית אֲבֹתָֽיו׃

3
1 This is the line of *Aharon* and *Moshe* at the time that *Hashem* spoke with *Moshe* on *Har Sinai*.

ג א וְאֵ֛לֶּה תּוֹלְדֹ֥ת אַהֲרֹ֖ן וּמֹשֶׁ֑ה בְּי֗וֹם דִּבֶּ֧ר יְהֹוָ֛ה אֶת־מֹשֶׁ֖ה בְּהַ֥ר סִינָֽי׃

v'-AY-leh to-l'-DOT a-ha-RON u-mo-SHEH b'-YOM di-BER a-do-NAI et mo-SHEH b'-HAR see-NAI

2 These were the names of *Aharon*'s sons: *Nadav*, the first-born, and *Avihu*, *Elazar* and *Itamar*;

ב וְאֵ֛לֶּה שְׁמ֥וֹת בְּֽנֵי־אַהֲרֹ֖ן הַבְּכֹ֣ר ׀ נָדָ֑ב וַאֲבִיה֕וּא אֶלְעָזָ֖ר וְאִיתָמָֽר׃

3 those were the names of *Aharon*'s sons, the anointed *Kohanim* who were ordained for priesthood.

ג אֵ֗לֶּה שְׁמוֹת֙ בְּנֵ֣י אַהֲרֹ֔ן הַכֹּהֲנִ֖ים הַמְּשֻׁחִ֑ים אֲשֶׁר־מִלֵּ֥א יָדָ֖ם לְכַהֵֽן׃

3:1 This is the line of *Aharon* and *Moshe* Following these words which introduce the census of the tribe of *Levi*, the Bible goes on to list only the descendants of *Aharon* and not those of *Moshe*, *Levi*'s most famous offspring. According to *Rashi*, *Aharon*'s descendants were considered to be *Moshe*'s as well, since *Moshe* was the one who taught them God's word. Although *Aharon* was their biological father, providing them with physical life, *Moshe* became their spiritual father, providing for them a life of fulfillment and holiness. Without this spiritual life, their physical lives would have been lacking, devoid of meaning and purpose. How great it is to spread *Hashem*'s message to others, for in doing so you are giving them life, just as *Moshe* did.

Bamidbar/Numbers 3
Bamidbar

במדבר ג
במדבר

4 But *Nadav* and *Avihu* died by the will of *Hashem*, when they offered alien fire before *Hashem* in the wilderness of Sinai; and they left no sons. So it was *Elazar* and *Itamar* who served as *Kohanim* in the lifetime of their father *Aharon*.

ד וַיָּמָת נָדָב וַאֲבִיהוּא לִפְנֵי יְהוָה בְּהַקְרִבָם אֵשׁ זָרָה לִפְנֵי יְהוָה בְּמִדְבַּר סִינַי וּבָנִים לֹא־הָיוּ לָהֶם וַיְכַהֵן אֶלְעָזָר וְאִיתָמָר עַל־פְּנֵי אַהֲרֹן אֲבִיהֶם:

5 *Hashem* spoke to *Moshe*, saying:

ה וַיְדַבֵּר יְהוָה אֶל־מֹשֶׁה לֵּאמֹר:

6 Advance the tribe of *Levi* and place them in attendance upon *Aharon* the *Kohen* to serve him.

ו הַקְרֵב אֶת־מַטֵּה לֵוִי וְהַעֲמַדְתָּ אֹתוֹ לִפְנֵי אַהֲרֹן הַכֹּהֵן וְשֵׁרְתוּ אֹתוֹ:

7 They shall perform duties for him and for the whole community before the Tent of Meeting, doing the work of the *Mishkan*.

ז וְשָׁמְרוּ אֶת־מִשְׁמַרְתּוֹ וְאֶת־מִשְׁמֶרֶת כָּל־הָעֵדָה לִפְנֵי אֹהֶל מוֹעֵד לַעֲבֹד אֶת־עֲבֹדַת הַמִּשְׁכָּן:

8 They shall take charge of all the furnishings of the Tent of Meeting – a duty on behalf of the Israelites – doing the work of the *Mishkan*.

ח וְשָׁמְרוּ אֶת־כָּל־כְּלֵי אֹהֶל מוֹעֵד וְאֶת־מִשְׁמֶרֶת בְּנֵי יִשְׂרָאֵל לַעֲבֹד אֶת־עֲבֹדַת הַמִּשְׁכָּן:

9 You shall assign the *Leviim* to *Aharon* and to his sons: they are formally assigned to him from among the Israelites.

ט וְנָתַתָּה אֶת־הַלְוִיִּם לְאַהֲרֹן וּלְבָנָיו נְתוּנִם נְתוּנִם הֵמָּה לוֹ מֵאֵת בְּנֵי יִשְׂרָאֵל:

10 You shall make *Aharon* and his sons responsible for observing their priestly duties; and any outsider who encroaches shall be put to death.

י וְאֶת־אַהֲרֹן וְאֶת־בָּנָיו תִּפְקֹד וְשָׁמְרוּ אֶת־כְּהֻנָּתָם וְהַזָּר הַקָּרֵב יוּמָת:

11 *Hashem* spoke to *Moshe*, saying:

יא וַיְדַבֵּר יְהוָה אֶל־מֹשֶׁה לֵּאמֹר:

12 I hereby take the *Leviim* from among the Israelites in place of all the first-born, the first issue of the womb among the Israelites: the *Leviim* shall be Mine.

יב וַאֲנִי הִנֵּה לָקַחְתִּי אֶת־הַלְוִיִּם מִתּוֹךְ בְּנֵי יִשְׂרָאֵל תַּחַת כָּל־בְּכוֹר פֶּטֶר רֶחֶם מִבְּנֵי יִשְׂרָאֵל וְהָיוּ לִי הַלְוִיִּם:

13 For every first-born is Mine: at the time that I smote every first-born in the land of Egypt, I consecrated every first-born in *Yisrael*, man and beast, to Myself, to be Mine, *Hashem*'s.

יג כִּי לִי כָּל־בְּכוֹר בְּיוֹם הַכֹּתִי כָל־בְּכוֹר בְּאֶרֶץ מִצְרַיִם הִקְדַּשְׁתִּי לִי כָל־בְּכוֹר בְּיִשְׂרָאֵל מֵאָדָם עַד־בְּהֵמָה לִי יִהְיוּ אֲנִי יְהוָה:

14 *Hashem* spoke to *Moshe* in the wilderness of Sinai, saying:

יד וַיְדַבֵּר יְהוָה אֶל־מֹשֶׁה בְּמִדְבַּר סִינַי לֵאמֹר:

15 Record the *Leviim* by ancestral house and by clan; record every male among them from the age of one month up.

טו פְּקֹד אֶת־בְּנֵי לֵוִי לְבֵית אֲבֹתָם לְמִשְׁפְּחֹתָם כָּל־זָכָר מִבֶּן־חֹדֶשׁ וָמַעְלָה תִּפְקְדֵם:

16 So *Moshe* recorded them at the command of *Hashem*, as he was bidden.

טז וַיִּפְקֹד אֹתָם מֹשֶׁה עַל־פִּי יְהוָה כַּאֲשֶׁר צֻוָּה:

17 These were the sons of *Levi* by name: *Gershon*, *Kehat*, and *Merari*.

יז וַיִּהְיוּ־אֵלֶּה בְנֵי־לֵוִי בִּשְׁמֹתָם גֵּרְשׁוֹן וּקְהָת וּמְרָרִי:

18 These were the names of the sons of *Gershon* by clan: Libni and *Shim'i*.

יח וְאֵלֶּה שְׁמוֹת בְּנֵי־גֵרְשׁוֹן לְמִשְׁפְּחֹתָם לִבְנִי וְשִׁמְעִי:

Bamidbar/Numbers 3
Bamidbar

19 The sons of *Kehat* by clan: *Amram* and Izhar, *Chevron* and Uzziel.

20 The sons of *Merari* by clan: Mahli and Mushi. These were the clans of the *Leviim* within their ancestral houses:

21 To *Gershon* belonged the clan of the Libnites and the clan of the Shim'ites; those were the clans of the Gershonites.

22 The recorded entries of all their males from the age of one month up, as recorded, came to 7,500.

23 The clans of the Gershonites were to camp behind the *Mishkan*, to the west.

24 The chieftain of the ancestral house of the Gershonites was *Elyasaf* son of Lael.

25 The duties of the Gershonites in the Tent of Meeting comprised: the *Mishkan*, the tent, its covering, and the screen for the entrance of the Tent of Meeting;

26 the hangings of the enclosure, the screen for the entrance of the enclosure which surrounds the *Mishkan*, the cords thereof, and the *Mizbayach* – all the service connected with these.

27 To *Kehat* belonged the clan of the Amramites, the clan of the Izharites, the clan of the Chevronites, and the clan of the Uzzielites; those were the clans of the Kohathites.

28 All the listed males from the age of one month up came to 8,600, attending to the duties of the sanctuary.

29 The clans of the Kohathites were to camp along the south side of the *Mishkan*.

30 The chieftain of the ancestral house of the Kohathite clans was *Elitzafan* son of Uzziel.

31 Their duties comprised: the ark, the table, the *menorah*, the *mizbachot*, and the sacred utensils that were used with them, and the screen – all the service connected with these.

32 The head chieftain of the *Leviim* was *Elazar* son of *Aharon* the *Kohen*, in charge of those attending to the duties of the sanctuary.

במדבר ג
במדבר

יט וּבְנֵי קְהָת לְמִשְׁפְּחֹתָם עַמְרָם וְיִצְהָר חֶבְרוֹן וְעֻזִּיאֵל:

כ וּבְנֵי מְרָרִי לְמִשְׁפְּחֹתָם מַחְלִי וּמוּשִׁי אֵלֶּה הֵם מִשְׁפְּחֹת הַלֵּוִי לְבֵית אֲבֹתָם:

כא לְגֵרְשׁוֹן מִשְׁפַּחַת הַלִּבְנִי וּמִשְׁפַּחַת הַשִּׁמְעִי אֵלֶּה הֵם מִשְׁפְּחֹת הַגֵּרְשֻׁנִּי:

כב פְּקֻדֵיהֶם בְּמִסְפַּר כָּל־זָכָר מִבֶּן־חֹדֶשׁ וָמָעְלָה פְּקֻדֵיהֶם שִׁבְעַת אֲלָפִים וַחֲמֵשׁ מֵאוֹת:

כג מִשְׁפְּחֹת הַגֵּרְשֻׁנִּי אַחֲרֵי הַמִּשְׁכָּן יַחֲנוּ יָמָּה:

כד וּנְשִׂיא בֵית־אָב לַגֵּרְשֻׁנִּי אֶלְיָסָף בֶּן־לָאֵל:

כה וּמִשְׁמֶרֶת בְּנֵי־גֵרְשׁוֹן בְּאֹהֶל מוֹעֵד הַמִּשְׁכָּן וְהָאֹהֶל מִכְסֵהוּ וּמָסַךְ פֶּתַח אֹהֶל מוֹעֵד:

כו וְקַלְעֵי הֶחָצֵר וְאֶת־מָסַךְ פֶּתַח הֶחָצֵר אֲשֶׁר עַל־הַמִּשְׁכָּן וְעַל־הַמִּזְבֵּחַ סָבִיב וְאֵת מֵיתָרָיו לְכֹל עֲבֹדָתוֹ:

כז וְלִקְהָת מִשְׁפַּחַת הַעַמְרָמִי וּמִשְׁפַּחַת הַיִּצְהָרִי וּמִשְׁפַּחַת הַחֶבְרֹנִי וּמִשְׁפַּחַת הָעָזִּיאֵלִי אֵלֶּה הֵם מִשְׁפְּחֹת הַקְּהָתִי:

כח בְּמִסְפַּר כָּל־זָכָר מִבֶּן־חֹדֶשׁ וָמָעְלָה שְׁמֹנַת אֲלָפִים וְשֵׁשׁ מֵאוֹת שֹׁמְרֵי מִשְׁמֶרֶת הַקֹּדֶשׁ:

כט מִשְׁפְּחֹת בְּנֵי־קְהָת יַחֲנוּ עַל יֶרֶךְ הַמִּשְׁכָּן תֵּימָנָה:

ל וּנְשִׂיא בֵית־אָב לְמִשְׁפְּחֹת הַקְּהָתִי אֱלִיצָפָן בֶּן־עֻזִּיאֵל:

לא וּמִשְׁמַרְתָּם הָאָרֹן וְהַשֻּׁלְחָן וְהַמְּנֹרָה וְהַמִּזְבְּחֹת וּכְלֵי הַקֹּדֶשׁ אֲשֶׁר יְשָׁרְתוּ בָּהֶם וְהַמָּסָךְ וְכֹל עֲבֹדָתוֹ:

לב וּנְשִׂיא נְשִׂיאֵי הַלֵּוִי אֶלְעָזָר בֶּן־אַהֲרֹן הַכֹּהֵן פְּקֻדַּת שֹׁמְרֵי מִשְׁמֶרֶת הַקֹּדֶשׁ:

Bamidbar/Numbers 3
Bamidbar

33 To *Merari* belonged the clan of the Mahlites and the clan of the Mushites; those were the clans of *Merari*.

34 The recorded entries of all their males from the age of one month up came to 6,200.

35 The chieftain of the ancestral house of the clans of *Merari* was *Tzuriel* son of *Avichayil*. They were to camp along the north side of the *Mishkan*.

36 The assigned duties of the Merarites comprised: the planks of the *Mishkan*, its bars, posts, and sockets, and all its furnishings – all the service connected with these;

37 also the posts around the enclosure and their sockets, pegs, and cords.

38 Those who were to camp before the *Mishkan*, in front – before the Tent of Meeting, on the east – were *Moshe* and *Aharon* and his sons, attending to the duties of the sanctuary, as a duty on behalf of the Israelites; and any outsider who encroached was to be put to death.

39 All the *Leviim* who were recorded, whom at *Hashem*'s command *Moshe* and *Aharon* recorded by their clans, all the males from the age of one month up, came to 22,000.

40 *Hashem* said to *Moshe*: Record every first-born male of *B'nei Yisrael* from the age of one month up, and make a list of their names;

41 and take the *Leviim* for Me, *Hashem*, in place of every first-born among *B'nei Yisrael*, and the cattle of the *Leviim* in place of every first-born among the cattle of the Israelites.

42 So *Moshe* recorded all the first-born among the Israelites, as *Hashem* had commanded him.

43 All the first-born males as listed by name, recorded from the age of one month up, came to 22,273.

44 *Hashem* spoke to *Moshe*, saying:

45 Take the *Leviim* in place of all the first-born among *B'nei Yisrael*, and the cattle of the *Leviim* in place of their cattle; and the *Leviim* shall be Mine, *Hashem*'s.

46 And as the redemption price of the 273 Israelite first-born over and above the number of the *Leviim*,

Bamidbar/Numbers 4
Bamidbar

47 take five *shekalim* per head – take this by the sanctuary weight, twenty *geira* to the *shekel* –

48 and give the money to *Aharon* and his sons as the redemption price for those who are in excess.

49 So *Moshe* took the redemption money from those over and above the ones redeemed by the *Leviim*;

50 he took the money from the first-born of the Israelites, 1,365 sanctuary *shekalim*.

51 And *Moshe* gave the redemption money to *Aharon* and his sons at *Hashem*'s bidding, as *Hashem* had commanded *Moshe*.

4

1 *Hashem* spoke to *Moshe* and *Aharon*, saying:

2 Take a [separate] census of the Kohathites among the *Leviim*, by the clans of their ancestral house,

3 from the age of thirty years up to the age of fifty, all who are subject to service, to perform tasks for the Tent of Meeting.

4 This is the responsibility of the Kohathites in the Tent of Meeting: the most sacred objects.

5 At the breaking of camp, *Aharon* and his sons shall go in and take down the screening curtain and cover the *Aron HaBrit* with it.

6 They shall lay a covering of dolphin skin over it and spread a cloth of pure blue on top; and they shall put its poles in place.

7 Over the table of display they shall spread a blue cloth; they shall place upon it the bowls, the ladles, the jars, and the libation jugs; and the regular bread shall rest upon it.

8 They shall spread over these a crimson cloth which they shall cover with a covering of dolphin skin; and they shall put the poles in place.

9 Then they shall take a blue cloth and cover the *menorah* for lighting, with its lamps, its tongs, and its fire pans, as well as all the oil vessels that are used in its service.

10 They shall put it and all its furnishings into a covering of dolphin skin, which they shall then place on a carrying frame.

במדבר ד
במדבר

מז וְלָקַחְתָּ֗ חֲמֵ֧שֶׁת שְׁקָלִ֛ים לַגֻּלְגֹּ֖לֶת בְּשֶׁ֣קֶל הַקֹּ֑דֶשׁ תִּקָּ֔ח עֶשְׂרִ֥ים גֵּרָ֖ה הַשָּֽׁקֶל׃

מח וְנָתַתָּ֣ה הַכֶּ֔סֶף לְאַהֲרֹ֖ן וּלְבָנָ֑יו פְּדוּיֵ֖י הָעֹדְפִ֥ים בָּהֶֽם׃

מט וַיִּקַּ֣ח מֹשֶׁ֔ה אֵ֖ת כֶּ֣סֶף הַפִּדְי֑וֹם מֵאֵת֙ הָעֹ֣דְפִ֔ים עַ֖ל פְּדוּיֵ֥י הַלְוִיִּֽם׃

נ מֵאֵ֗ת בְּכ֛וֹר בְּנֵ֥י יִשְׂרָאֵ֖ל לָקַ֣ח אֶת־הַכָּ֑סֶף חֲמִשָּׁ֨ה וְשִׁשִּׁ֜ים וּשְׁלֹ֥שׁ מֵא֛וֹת וָאֶ֖לֶף בְּשֶׁ֥קֶל הַקֹּֽדֶשׁ׃

נא וַיִּתֵּ֨ן מֹשֶׁ֜ה אֶת־כֶּ֧סֶף הַפְּדֻיִ֛ם לְאַהֲרֹ֥ן וּלְבָנָ֖יו עַל־פִּ֣י יְהֹוָ֑ה כַּאֲשֶׁ֛ר צִוָּ֥ה יְהֹוָ֖ה אֶת־מֹשֶֽׁה׃

ד א וַיְדַבֵּ֣ר יְהֹוָ֔ה אֶל־מֹשֶׁ֥ה וְאֶֽל־אַהֲרֹ֖ן לֵאמֹֽר׃

ב נָשֹׂ֗א אֶת־רֹאשׁ֙ בְּנֵ֣י קְהָ֔ת מִתּ֖וֹךְ בְּנֵ֣י לֵוִ֑י לְמִשְׁפְּחֹתָ֖ם לְבֵ֥ית אֲבֹתָֽם׃

ג מִבֶּ֨ן שְׁלֹשִׁ֤ים שָׁנָה֙ וָמַ֔עְלָה וְעַ֖ד בֶּן־חֲמִשִּׁ֣ים שָׁנָ֑ה כׇּל־בָּא֙ לַצָּבָ֔א לַעֲשׂ֥וֹת מְלָאכָ֖ה בְּאֹ֥הֶל מוֹעֵֽד׃

ד זֹ֛את עֲבֹדַ֥ת בְּנֵי־קְהָ֖ת בְּאֹ֣הֶל מוֹעֵ֑ד קֹ֖דֶשׁ הַקֳּדָשִֽׁים׃

ה וּבָ֨א אַהֲרֹ֤ן וּבָנָיו֙ בִּנְסֹ֣עַ הַֽמַּחֲנֶ֔ה וְהוֹרִ֕דוּ אֵ֖ת פָּרֹ֣כֶת הַמָּסָ֑ךְ וְכִ֨סּוּ־בָ֔הּ אֵ֖ת אֲרֹ֥ן הָעֵדֻֽת׃

ו וְנָתְנ֣וּ עָלָ֗יו כְּסוּי֙ ע֣וֹר תַּ֔חַשׁ וּפָרְשׂ֧וּ בֶֽגֶד־כְּלִ֛יל תְּכֵ֖לֶת מִלְמָ֑עְלָה וְשָׂמ֖וּ בַּדָּֽיו׃

ז וְעַ֣ל ׀ שֻׁלְחַ֣ן הַפָּנִ֗ים יִפְרְשׂוּ֙ בֶּ֣גֶד תְּכֵ֔לֶת וְנָתְנ֣וּ עָ֠לָ֠יו אֶת־הַקְּעָרֹ֤ת וְאֶת־הַכַּפֹּת֙ וְאֶת־הַמְּנַקִּיֹּ֔ת וְאֵ֖ת קְשׂ֣וֹת הַנָּ֑סֶךְ וְלֶ֥חֶם הַתָּמִ֖יד עָלָ֥יו יִהְיֶֽה׃

ח וּפָרְשׂ֣וּ עֲלֵיהֶ֗ם בֶּ֚גֶד תּוֹלַ֣עַת שָׁנִ֔י וְכִסּ֣וּ אֹת֔וֹ בְּמִכְסֵ֖ה ע֣וֹר תָּ֑חַשׁ וְשָׂמ֖וּ אֶת־בַּדָּֽיו׃

ט וְלָקְח֣וּ ׀ בֶּ֣גֶד תְּכֵ֗לֶת וְכִסּ֞וּ אֶת־מְנֹרַ֤ת הַמָּאוֹר֙ וְאֶת־נֵ֣רֹתֶ֔יהָ וְאֶת־מַלְקָחֶ֖יהָ וְאֶת־מַחְתֹּתֶ֑יהָ וְאֵת֙ כׇּל־כְּלֵ֣י שַׁמְנָ֔הּ אֲשֶׁ֥ר יְשָׁרְתוּ־לָ֖הּ בָּהֶֽם׃

י וְנָתְנ֤וּ אֹתָהּ֙ וְאֶת־כׇּל־כֵּלֶ֔יהָ אֶל־מִכְסֵ֖ה ע֣וֹר תָּ֑חַשׁ וְנָתְנ֖וּ עַל־הַמּֽוֹט׃

Bamidbar/Numbers 4
Bamidbar

במדבר ד
במדבר

11 Next they shall spread a blue cloth over the *Mizbayach* of gold and cover it with a covering of dolphin skin; and they shall put its poles in place.

יא וְעַל מִזְבַּח הַזָּהָב יִפְרְשׂוּ בֶּגֶד תְּכֵלֶת וְכִסּוּ אֹתוֹ בְּמִכְסֵה עוֹר תָּחַשׁ וְשָׂמוּ אֶת־בַּדָּיו:

12 They shall take all the service vessels with which the service in the sanctuary is performed, put them into a blue cloth and cover them with a covering of dolphin skin, which they shall then place on a carrying frame.

יב וְלָקְחוּ אֶת־כָּל־כְּלֵי הַשָּׁרֵת אֲשֶׁר יְשָׁרְתוּ־בָם בַּקֹּדֶשׁ וְנָתְנוּ אֶל־בֶּגֶד תְּכֵלֶת וְכִסּוּ אוֹתָם בְּמִכְסֵה עוֹר תָּחַשׁ וְנָתְנוּ עַל־הַמּוֹט:

13 They shall remove the ashes from the [copper] *Mizbayach* and spread a purple cloth over it.

יג וְדִשְּׁנוּ אֶת־הַמִּזְבֵּחַ וּפָרְשׂוּ עָלָיו בֶּגֶד אַרְגָּמָן:

14 Upon it they shall place all the vessels that are used in its service: the fire pans, the flesh hooks, the scrapers, and the basins – all the vessels of the *Mizbayach* – and over it they shall spread a covering of dolphin skin; and they shall put its poles in place.

יד וְנָתְנוּ עָלָיו אֶת־כָּל־כֵּלָיו אֲשֶׁר יְשָׁרְתוּ עָלָיו בָּהֶם אֶת־הַמַּחְתֹּת אֶת־הַמִּזְלָגֹת וְאֶת־הַיָּעִים וְאֶת־הַמִּזְרָקֹת כֹּל כְּלֵי הַמִּזְבֵּחַ וּפָרְשׂוּ עָלָיו כְּסוּי עוֹר תַּחַשׁ וְשָׂמוּ בַדָּיו:

15 When *Aharon* and his sons have finished covering the sacred objects and all the furnishings of the sacred objects at the breaking of camp, only then shall the Kohathites come and lift them, so that they do not come in contact with the sacred objects and die. These things in the Tent of Meeting shall be the porterage of the Kohathites.

טו וְכִלָּה אַהֲרֹן־וּבָנָיו לְכַסֹּת אֶת־הַקֹּדֶשׁ וְאֶת־כָּל־כְּלֵי הַקֹּדֶשׁ בִּנְסֹעַ הַמַּחֲנֶה וְאַחֲרֵי־כֵן יָבֹאוּ בְנֵי־קְהָת לָשֵׂאת וְלֹא־יִגְּעוּ אֶל־הַקֹּדֶשׁ וָמֵתוּ אֵלֶּה מַשָּׂא בְנֵי־קְהָת בְּאֹהֶל מוֹעֵד:

16 Responsibility shall rest with *Elazar* son of *Aharon* the *Kohen* for the lighting oil, the aromatic incense, the regular meal offering, and the anointing oil – responsibility for the whole *Mishkan* and for everything consecrated that is in it or in its vessels.

טז וּפְקֻדַּת אֶלְעָזָר בֶּן־אַהֲרֹן הַכֹּהֵן שֶׁמֶן הַמָּאוֹר וּקְטֹרֶת הַסַּמִּים וּמִנְחַת הַתָּמִיד וְשֶׁמֶן הַמִּשְׁחָה פְּקֻדַּת כָּל־הַמִּשְׁכָּן וְכָל־אֲשֶׁר־בּוֹ בְּקֹדֶשׁ וּבְכֵלָיו:

17 *Hashem* spoke to *Moshe* and *Aharon*, saying:

יז וַיְדַבֵּר יְהֹוָה אֶל־מֹשֶׁה וְאֶל־אַהֲרֹן לֵאמֹר:

18 Do not let the group of Kohathite clans be cut off from the *Leviim*.

יח אַל־תַּכְרִיתוּ אֶת־שֵׁבֶט מִשְׁפְּחֹת הַקְּהָתִי מִתּוֹךְ הַלְוִיִּם:

al takh-REE-tu et SHAY-vet mish-p'-KHOT ha-k'-ha-TEE mi-TOKH hal-vi-YIM

4:18 Do not let the group of Kohathites clans be cut off from the *Leviim* The children of *Kehat*, one of the three sons of *Levi*, are responsible for the most sacred parts of the *Mishkan*, including the Holy of Holies and the *Aron*. When the people break camp and begin a new journey, the Kohathites must dismantle the Holy of Holies and cover the *Aron*. However, due to its elevated holiness they are required to do so without viewing the inside of the Holy of Holies, since merely looking at it carries the strictest of penalties. Interestingly, *Moshe* and *Aharon* are the ones who are commanded, "Do not let the group of Kohathite clans be cut off…" They are the ones responsible for making sure that the Kohathites do not mistakenly look into the Holy of Holies and incur the death penalty. Not only does *Hashem* care about the life of every individual, He holds us all responsible for looking out for, and caring about, each other.

Bamidbar/Numbers 4
Naso

במדבר ד
נשא

19 Do this with them, that they may live and not die when they approach the most sacred objects: let *Aharon* and his sons go in and assign each of them to his duties and to his porterage.

יט וְזֹאת ׀ עֲשׂוּ לָהֶם וְחָיוּ וְלֹא יָמֻתוּ בְּגִשְׁתָּם אֶת־קֹדֶשׁ הַקֳּדָשִׁים אַהֲרֹן וּבָנָיו יָבֹאוּ וְשָׂמוּ אוֹתָם אִישׁ אִישׁ עַל־עֲבֹדָתוֹ וְאֶל־מַשָּׂאוֹ:

20 But let not [the Kohathites] go inside and witness the dismantling of the sanctuary, lest they die.

כ וְלֹא־יָבֹאוּ לִרְאוֹת כְּבַלַּע אֶת־הַקֹּדֶשׁ וָמֵתוּ:

21 *Hashem* spoke to *Moshe*:

כא וַיְדַבֵּר יְהֹוָה אֶל־מֹשֶׁה לֵּאמֹר:

22 Take a census of the Gershonites also, by their ancestral house and by their clans.

כב נָשֹׂא אֶת־רֹאשׁ בְּנֵי גֵרְשׁוֹן גַּם־הֵם לְבֵית אֲבֹתָם לְמִשְׁפְּחֹתָם:

23 Record them from the age of thirty years up to the age of fifty, all who are subject to service in the performance of tasks for the Tent of Meeting.

כג מִבֶּן שְׁלֹשִׁים שָׁנָה וָמַעְלָה עַד בֶּן־חֲמִשִּׁים שָׁנָה תִּפְקֹד אוֹתָם כָּל־הַבָּא לִצְבֹא צָבָא לַעֲבֹד עֲבֹדָה בְּאֹהֶל מוֹעֵד:

24 These are the duties of the Gershonite clans as to labor and porterage:

כד זֹאת עֲבֹדַת מִשְׁפְּחֹת הַגֵּרְשֻׁנִּי לַעֲבֹד וּלְמַשָּׂא:

25 they shall carry the cloths of the *Mishkan*, the Tent of Meeting with its covering, the covering of dolphin skin that is on top of it, and the screen for the entrance of the Tent of Meeting;

כה וְנָשְׂאוּ אֶת־יְרִיעֹת הַמִּשְׁכָּן וְאֶת־אֹהֶל מוֹעֵד מִכְסֵהוּ וּמִכְסֵה הַתַּחַשׁ אֲשֶׁר־עָלָיו מִלְמָעְלָה וְאֶת־מָסַךְ פֶּתַח אֹהֶל מוֹעֵד:

26 the hangings of the enclosure, the screen at the entrance of the gate of the enclosure that surrounds the *Mishkan*, the cords thereof, and the *Mizbayach*, and all their service equipment and all their accessories; and they shall perform the service.

כו וְאֵת קַלְעֵי הֶחָצֵר וְאֶת־מָסַךְ ׀ פֶּתַח ׀ שַׁעַר הֶחָצֵר אֲשֶׁר עַל־הַמִּשְׁכָּן וְעַל־הַמִּזְבֵּחַ סָבִיב וְאֵת מֵיתְרֵיהֶם וְאֶת־כָּל־כְּלֵי עֲבֹדָתָם וְאֵת כָּל־אֲשֶׁר יֵעָשֶׂה לָהֶם וְעָבָדוּ:

27 All the duties of the Gershonites, all their porterage and all their service, shall be performed on orders from *Aharon* and his sons; you shall make them responsible for attending to all their porterage.

כז עַל־פִּי אַהֲרֹן וּבָנָיו תִּהְיֶה כָּל־עֲבֹדַת בְּנֵי הַגֵּרְשֻׁנִּי לְכָל־מַשָּׂאָם וּלְכֹל עֲבֹדָתָם וּפְקַדְתֶּם עֲלֵהֶם בְּמִשְׁמֶרֶת אֵת כָּל־מַשָּׂאָם:

28 Those are the duties of the Gershonite clans for the Tent of Meeting; they shall attend to them under the direction of *Itamar* son of *Aharon* the *Kohen*.

כח זֹאת עֲבֹדַת מִשְׁפְּחֹת בְּנֵי הַגֵּרְשֻׁנִּי בְּאֹהֶל מוֹעֵד וּמִשְׁמַרְתָּם בְּיַד אִיתָמָר בֶּן־אַהֲרֹן הַכֹּהֵן:

29 As for the Merarites, you shall record them by the clans of their ancestral house;

כט בְּנֵי מְרָרִי לְמִשְׁפְּחֹתָם לְבֵית־אֲבֹתָם תִּפְקֹד אֹתָם:

30 you shall record them from the age of thirty years up to the age of fifty, all who are subject to service in the performance of the duties for the Tent of Meeting.

ל מִבֶּן שְׁלֹשִׁים שָׁנָה וָמַעְלָה וְעַד בֶּן־חֲמִשִּׁים שָׁנָה תִּפְקְדֵם כָּל־הַבָּא לַצָּבָא לַעֲבֹד אֶת־עֲבֹדַת אֹהֶל מוֹעֵד:

31 These are their porterage tasks in connection with their various duties for the Tent of Meeting: the planks, the bars, the posts, and the sockets of the *Mishkan*;

לא וְזֹאת מִשְׁמֶרֶת מַשָּׂאָם לְכָל־עֲבֹדָתָם בְּאֹהֶל מוֹעֵד קַרְשֵׁי הַמִּשְׁכָּן וּבְרִיחָיו וְעַמּוּדָיו וַאֲדָנָיו:

Bamidbar/Numbers 4
Naso

32 the posts around the enclosure and their sockets, pegs, and cords – all these furnishings and their service: you shall list by name the objects that are their porterage tasks.

33 Those are the duties of the Merarite clans, pertaining to their various duties in the Tent of Meeting under the direction of *Itamar* son of *Aharon* the *Kohen*.

34 So *Moshe, Aharon,* and the chieftains of the community recorded the Kohathites by the clans of their ancestral house,

35 from the age of thirty years up to the age of fifty, all who were subject to service for work relating to the Tent of Meeting.

36 Those recorded by their clans came to 2,750.

37 That was the enrollment of the Kohathite clans, all those who performed duties relating to the Tent of Meeting, whom *Moshe* and *Aharon* recorded at the command of *Hashem* through *Moshe*.

38 The Gershonites who were recorded by the clans of their ancestral house,

39 from the age of thirty years up to the age of fifty, all who were subject to service for work relating to the Tent of Meeting –

40 those recorded by the clans of their ancestral house came to 2,630.

41 That was the enrollment of the Gershonite clans, all those performing duties relating to the Tent of Meeting whom *Moshe* and *Aharon* recorded at the command of *Hashem*.

42 The enrollment of the Merarite clans by the clans of their ancestral house,

43 from the age of thirty years up to the age of fifty, all who were subject to service for work relating to the Tent of Meeting –

44 those recorded by their clans came to 3,200.

45 That was the enrollment of the Merarite clans which *Moshe* and *Aharon* recorded at the command of *Hashem* through *Moshe*.

במדבר ד
נשא

לב וְעַמּוּדֵי הֶחָצֵר סָבִיב וְאַדְנֵיהֶם וִיתֵדֹתָם וּמֵיתְרֵיהֶם לְכָל־כְּלֵיהֶם וּלְכֹל עֲבֹדָתָם וּבְשֵׁמֹת תִּפְקְדוּ אֶת־כְּלֵי מִשְׁמֶרֶת מַשָּׂאָם׃

לג זֹאת עֲבֹדַת מִשְׁפְּחֹת בְּנֵי מְרָרִי לְכָל־עֲבֹדָתָם בְּאֹהֶל מוֹעֵד בְּיַד אִיתָמָר בֶּן־אַהֲרֹן הַכֹּהֵן׃

לד וַיִּפְקֹד מֹשֶׁה וְאַהֲרֹן וּנְשִׂיאֵי הָעֵדָה אֶת־בְּנֵי הַקְּהָתִי לְמִשְׁפְּחֹתָם וּלְבֵית אֲבֹתָם׃

לה מִבֶּן שְׁלֹשִׁים שָׁנָה וָמַעְלָה וְעַד בֶּן־חֲמִשִּׁים שָׁנָה כָּל־הַבָּא לַצָּבָא לַעֲבֹדָה בְּאֹהֶל מוֹעֵד׃

לו וַיִּהְיוּ פְקֻדֵיהֶם לְמִשְׁפְּחֹתָם אַלְפַּיִם שְׁבַע מֵאוֹת וַחֲמִשִּׁים׃

לז אֵלֶּה פְקוּדֵי מִשְׁפְּחֹת הַקְּהָתִי כָּל־הָעֹבֵד בְּאֹהֶל מוֹעֵד אֲשֶׁר פָּקַד מֹשֶׁה וְאַהֲרֹן עַל־פִּי יְהֹוָה בְּיַד־מֹשֶׁה׃

לח וּפְקוּדֵי בְּנֵי גֵרְשׁוֹן לְמִשְׁפְּחוֹתָם וּלְבֵית אֲבֹתָם׃

לט מִבֶּן שְׁלֹשִׁים שָׁנָה וָמַעְלָה וְעַד בֶּן־חֲמִשִּׁים שָׁנָה כָּל־הַבָּא לַצָּבָא לַעֲבֹדָה בְּאֹהֶל מוֹעֵד׃

מ וַיִּהְיוּ פְּקֻדֵיהֶם לְמִשְׁפְּחֹתָם לְבֵית אֲבֹתָם אַלְפַּיִם וְשֵׁשׁ מֵאוֹת וּשְׁלֹשִׁים׃

מא אֵלֶּה פְקוּדֵי מִשְׁפְּחֹת בְּנֵי גֵרְשׁוֹן כָּל־הָעֹבֵד בְּאֹהֶל מוֹעֵד אֲשֶׁר פָּקַד מֹשֶׁה וְאַהֲרֹן עַל־פִּי יְהֹוָה׃

מב וּפְקוּדֵי מִשְׁפְּחֹת בְּנֵי מְרָרִי לְמִשְׁפְּחֹתָם לְבֵית אֲבֹתָם׃

מג מִבֶּן שְׁלֹשִׁים שָׁנָה וָמַעְלָה וְעַד בֶּן־חֲמִשִּׁים שָׁנָה כָּל־הַבָּא לַצָּבָא לַעֲבֹדָה בְּאֹהֶל מוֹעֵד׃

מד וַיִּהְיוּ פְקֻדֵיהֶם לְמִשְׁפְּחֹתָם שְׁלֹשֶׁת אֲלָפִים וּמָאתָיִם׃

מה אֵלֶּה פְקוּדֵי מִשְׁפְּחֹת בְּנֵי מְרָרִי אֲשֶׁר פָּקַד מֹשֶׁה וְאַהֲרֹן עַל־פִּי יְהֹוָה בְּיַד־מֹשֶׁה׃

Bamidbar/Numbers 5
Naso

46 All the *Leviim* whom *Moshe*, *Aharon*, and the chieftains of *Yisrael* recorded by the clans of their ancestral houses,

מו כׇּל־הַפְּקֻדִים אֲשֶׁר פָּקַד מֹשֶׁה וְאַהֲרֹן וּנְשִׂיאֵי יִשְׂרָאֵל אֶת־הַלְוִיִּם לְמִשְׁפְּחֹתָם וּלְבֵית אֲבֹתָם׃

47 from the age of thirty years up to the age of fifty, all who were subject to duties of service and porterage relating to the Tent of Meeting –

מז מִבֶּן שְׁלֹשִׁים שָׁנָה וָמַעְלָה וְעַד בֶּן־חֲמִשִּׁים שָׁנָה כׇּל־הַבָּא לַעֲבֹד עֲבֹדַת עֲבֹדָה וַעֲבֹדַת מַשָּׂא בְּאֹהֶל מוֹעֵד׃

48 those recorded came to 8,580.

מח וַיִּהְיוּ פְּקֻדֵיהֶם שְׁמֹנַת אֲלָפִים וַחֲמֵשׁ מֵאוֹת וּשְׁמֹנִים׃

49 Each one was given responsibility for his service and porterage at the command of *Hashem* through *Moshe*, and each was recorded as *Hashem* had commanded *Moshe*.

מט עַל־פִּי יְהֹוָה פָּקַד אוֹתָם בְּיַד־מֹשֶׁה אִישׁ אִישׁ עַל־עֲבֹדָתוֹ וְעַל־מַשָּׂאוֹ וּפְקֻדָיו אֲשֶׁר־צִוָּה יְהֹוָה אֶת־מֹשֶׁה׃

5

1 *Hashem* spoke to *Moshe*, saying:

א וַיְדַבֵּר יְהֹוָה אֶל־מֹשֶׁה לֵּאמֹר׃

2 Instruct the Israelites to remove from camp anyone with an eruption or a discharge and anyone defiled by a corpse.

ב צַו אֶת־בְּנֵי יִשְׂרָאֵל וִישַׁלְּחוּ מִן־הַמַּחֲנֶה כׇּל־צָרוּעַ וְכׇל־זָב וְכֹל טָמֵא לָנָפֶשׁ׃

3 Remove male and female alike; put them outside the camp so that they do not defile the camp of those in whose midst I dwell.

ג מִזָּכָר עַד־נְקֵבָה תְּשַׁלֵּחוּ אֶל־מִחוּץ לַמַּחֲנֶה תְּשַׁלְּחוּם וְלֹא יְטַמְּאוּ אֶת־מַחֲנֵיהֶם אֲשֶׁר אֲנִי שֹׁכֵן בְּתוֹכָם׃

4 The Israelites did so, putting them outside the camp; as *Hashem* had spoken to *Moshe*, so the Israelites did.

ד וַיַּעֲשׂוּ־כֵן בְּנֵי יִשְׂרָאֵל וַיְשַׁלְּחוּ אוֹתָם אֶל־מִחוּץ לַמַּחֲנֶה כַּאֲשֶׁר דִּבֶּר יְהֹוָה אֶל־מֹשֶׁה כֵּן עָשׂוּ בְּנֵי יִשְׂרָאֵל׃

5 *Hashem* spoke to *Moshe*, saying:

ה וַיְדַבֵּר יְהֹוָה אֶל־מֹשֶׁה לֵּאמֹר׃

6 Speak to the Israelites: When a man or woman commits any wrong toward a fellow man, thus breaking faith with *Hashem*, and that person realizes his guilt,

ו דַּבֵּר אֶל־בְּנֵי יִשְׂרָאֵל אִישׁ אוֹ־אִשָּׁה כִּי יַעֲשׂוּ מִכׇּל־חַטֹּאת הָאָדָם לִמְעֹל מַעַל בַּיהֹוָה וְאָשְׁמָה הַנֶּפֶשׁ הַהִוא׃

da-BAYR el b'-NAY yis-ra-AYL EESH o i-SHAH KEE ya-a-SU mi-kol kha-TOT ha-a-DAM lim-OL MA-al ba-a-do-NAI v'-a-sh'-MAH ha-NE-fesh ha-HEE

5:6 When a man or woman commits any wrong toward a fellow man After describing the camp of Israel in the desert with the *Mishkan* at its center, the *Torah* continues by detailing a series of laws that are seemingly unrelated to the camp, or to each other: Laws concerning theft, the wayward wife, and the nazirite. The connection between these different topics may be that all of these laws have to do with the high level of holiness and morality that the Children of Israel are expected to maintain, not only in their relationship with *Hashem*, but also in their human interactions. These laws represent three different types of relationships that require this type of sensitivity: Relations between a person and his fellow (theft), between a person and his family (the wayward wife), and between a person and himself (nazirite). Those who desire to ensure that *Hashem*'s presence will continue to rest among them must ensure that all their interpersonal interactions are characterized by respect and sensitivity.

Bamidbar/Numbers 5
Naso

במדבר ה
נשא

7 he shall confess the wrong that he has done. He shall make restitution in the principal amount and add one-fifth to it, giving it to him whom he has wronged.

ז וְהִתְוַדּוּ אֶת־חַטָּאתָם אֲשֶׁר עָשׂוּ וְהֵשִׁיב אֶת־אֲשָׁמוֹ בְּרֹאשׁוֹ וַחֲמִישִׁתוֹ יֹסֵף עָלָיו וְנָתַן לַאֲשֶׁר אָשַׁם לוֹ:

8 If the man has no kinsman to whom restitution can be made, the amount repaid shall go to *Hashem* for the *Kohen* – in addition to the ram of expiation with which expiation is made on his behalf.

ח וְאִם־אֵין לָאִישׁ גֹּאֵל לְהָשִׁיב הָאָשָׁם אֵלָיו הָאָשָׁם הַמּוּשָׁב לַיהוָה לַכֹּהֵן מִלְּבַד אֵיל הַכִּפֻּרִים אֲשֶׁר יְכַפֶּר־בּוֹ עָלָיו:

9 So, too, any gift among the sacred donations that the Israelites offer shall be the *Kohen*'s.

ט וְכָל־תְּרוּמָה לְכָל־קָדְשֵׁי בְנֵי־יִשְׂרָאֵל אֲשֶׁר־יַקְרִיבוּ לַכֹּהֵן לוֹ יִהְיֶה:

10 And each shall retain his sacred donations: each *Kohen* shall keep what is given to him.

י וְאִישׁ אֶת־קֳדָשָׁיו לוֹ יִהְיוּ אִישׁ אֲשֶׁר־יִתֵּן לַכֹּהֵן לוֹ יִהְיֶה:

11 *Hashem* spoke to *Moshe*, saying:

יא וַיְדַבֵּר יְהוָה אֶל־מֹשֶׁה לֵּאמֹר:

12 Speak to *B'nei Yisrael* and say to them: If any man's wife has gone astray and broken faith with him

יב דַּבֵּר אֶל־בְּנֵי יִשְׂרָאֵל וְאָמַרְתָּ אֲלֵהֶם אִישׁ אִישׁ כִּי־תִשְׂטֶה אִשְׁתּוֹ וּמָעֲלָה בוֹ מָעַל:

13 in that a man has had carnal relations with her unbeknown to her husband, and she keeps secret the fact that she has defiled herself without being forced, and there is no witness against her –

יג וְשָׁכַב אִישׁ אֹתָהּ שִׁכְבַת־זֶרַע וְנֶעְלַם מֵעֵינֵי אִישָׁהּ וְנִסְתְּרָה וְהִיא נִטְמָאָה וְעֵד אֵין בָּהּ וְהִוא לֹא נִתְפָּשָׂה:

14 but a fit of jealousy comes over him and he is wrought up about the wife who has defiled herself; or if a fit of jealousy comes over one and he is wrought up about his wife although she has not defiled herself –

יד וְעָבַר עָלָיו רוּחַ־קִנְאָה וְקִנֵּא אֶת־אִשְׁתּוֹ וְהִוא נִטְמָאָה אוֹ־עָבַר עָלָיו רוּחַ־קִנְאָה וְקִנֵּא אֶת־אִשְׁתּוֹ וְהִיא לֹא נִטְמָאָה:

15 the man shall bring his wife to the *Kohen*. And he shall bring as an offering for her one-tenth of an *efah* of barley flour. No oil shall be poured upon it and no frankincense shall be laid on it, for it is a meal offering of jealousy, a meal offering of remembrance which recalls wrongdoing.

טו וְהֵבִיא הָאִישׁ אֶת־אִשְׁתּוֹ אֶל־הַכֹּהֵן וְהֵבִיא אֶת־קָרְבָּנָהּ עָלֶיהָ עֲשִׂירִת הָאֵיפָה קֶמַח שְׂעֹרִים לֹא־יִצֹק עָלָיו שֶׁמֶן וְלֹא־יִתֵּן עָלָיו לְבֹנָה כִּי־מִנְחַת קְנָאֹת הוּא מִנְחַת זִכָּרוֹן מַזְכֶּרֶת עָוֹן:

16 The *Kohen* shall bring her forward and have her stand before *Hashem*.

טז וְהִקְרִיב אֹתָהּ הַכֹּהֵן וְהֶעֱמִדָהּ לִפְנֵי יְהוָה:

17 The *Kohen* shall take sacral water in an earthen vessel and, taking some of the earth that is on the floor of the *Mishkan*, the *Kohen* shall put it into the water.

יז וְלָקַח הַכֹּהֵן מַיִם קְדֹשִׁים בִּכְלִי־חָרֶשׂ וּמִן־הֶעָפָר אֲשֶׁר יִהְיֶה בְּקַרְקַע הַמִּשְׁכָּן יִקַּח הַכֹּהֵן וְנָתַן אֶל־הַמָּיִם:

18 After he has made the woman stand before *Hashem*, the *Kohen* shall bare the woman's head and place upon her hands the meal offering of remembrance, which is a meal offering of jealousy. And in the *Kohen*'s hands shall be the water of bitterness that induces the spell.

יח וְהֶעֱמִיד הַכֹּהֵן אֶת־הָאִשָּׁה לִפְנֵי יְהוָה וּפָרַע אֶת־רֹאשׁ הָאִשָּׁה וְנָתַן עַל־כַּפֶּיהָ אֵת מִנְחַת הַזִּכָּרוֹן מִנְחַת קְנָאֹת הִוא וּבְיַד הַכֹּהֵן יִהְיוּ מֵי הַמָּרִים הַמְאָרֲרִים:

Bamidbar/Numbers 5
Naso

במדבר ה
נשא

19 The *Kohen* shall adjure the woman, saying to her, "If no man has lain with you, if you have not gone astray in defilement while married to your husband, be immune to harm from this water of bitterness that induces the spell.

יט וְהִשְׁבִּיעַ אֹתָהּ הַכֹּהֵן וְאָמַר אֶל־הָאִשָּׁה אִם־לֹא שָׁכַב אִישׁ אֹתָךְ וְאִם־לֹא שָׂטִית טֻמְאָה תַּחַת אִישֵׁךְ הִנָּקִי מִמֵּי הַמָּרִים הַמְאָרֲרִים הָאֵלֶּה:

20 But if you have gone astray while married to your husband and have defiled yourself, if a man other than your husband has had carnal relations with you" –

כ וְאַתְּ כִּי שָׂטִית תַּחַת אִישֵׁךְ וְכִי נִטְמֵאת וַיִּתֵּן אִישׁ בָּךְ אֶת־שְׁכָבְתּוֹ מִבַּלְעֲדֵי אִישֵׁךְ:

21 here the *Kohen* shall administer the curse of adjuration to the woman, as the *Kohen* goes on to say to the woman – "may *Hashem* make you a curse and an imprecation among your people, as *Hashem* causes your thigh to sag and your belly to distend;

כא וְהִשְׁבִּיעַ הַכֹּהֵן אֶת־הָאִשָּׁה בִּשְׁבֻעַת הָאָלָה וְאָמַר הַכֹּהֵן לָאִשָּׁה יִתֵּן יְהוָה אוֹתָךְ לְאָלָה וְלִשְׁבֻעָה בְּתוֹךְ עַמֵּךְ בְּתֵת יְהוָה אֶת־יְרֵכֵךְ נֹפֶלֶת וְאֶת־בִּטְנֵךְ צָבָה:

22 may this water that induces the spell enter your body, causing the belly to distend and the thigh to sag." And the woman shall say, "*Amen, Amen!*"

כב וּבָאוּ הַמַּיִם הַמְאָרֲרִים הָאֵלֶּה בְּמֵעַיִךְ לַצְבּוֹת בֶּטֶן וְלַנְפִּל יָרֵךְ וְאָמְרָה הָאִשָּׁה אָמֵן אָמֵן:

23 The *Kohen* shall put these curses down in writing and rub it off into the water of bitterness.

כג וְכָתַב אֶת־הָאָלֹת הָאֵלֶּה הַכֹּהֵן בַּסֵּפֶר וּמָחָה אֶל־מֵי הַמָּרִים:

24 He is to make the woman drink the water of bitterness that induces the spell, so that the spell-inducing water may enter into her to bring on bitterness.

כד וְהִשְׁקָה אֶת־הָאִשָּׁה אֶת־מֵי הַמָּרִים הַמְאָרֲרִים וּבָאוּ בָהּ הַמַּיִם הַמְאָרֲרִים לְמָרִים:

25 Then the *Kohen* shall take from the woman's hand the meal offering of jealousy, elevate the meal offering before *Hashem*, and present it on the *Mizbayach*.

כה וְלָקַח הַכֹּהֵן מִיַּד הָאִשָּׁה אֵת מִנְחַת הַקְּנָאֹת וְהֵנִיף אֶת־הַמִּנְחָה לִפְנֵי יְהוָה וְהִקְרִיב אֹתָהּ אֶל־הַמִּזְבֵּחַ:

26 The *Kohen* shall scoop out of the meal offering a token part of it and turn it into smoke on the *Mizbayach*. Last, he shall make the woman drink the water.

כו וְקָמַץ הַכֹּהֵן מִן־הַמִּנְחָה אֶת־אַזְכָּרָתָהּ וְהִקְטִיר הַמִּזְבֵּחָה וְאַחַר יַשְׁקֶה אֶת־הָאִשָּׁה אֶת־הַמָּיִם:

27 Once he has made her drink the water – if she has defiled herself by breaking faith with her husband, the spell-inducing water shall enter into her to bring on bitterness, so that her belly shall distend and her thigh shall sag; and the woman shall become a curse among her people.

כז וְהִשְׁקָהּ אֶת־הַמַּיִם וְהָיְתָה אִם־נִטְמְאָה וַתִּמְעֹל מַעַל בְּאִישָׁהּ וּבָאוּ בָהּ הַמַּיִם הַמְאָרֲרִים לְמָרִים וְצָבְתָה בִטְנָהּ וְנָפְלָה יְרֵכָהּ וְהָיְתָה הָאִשָּׁה לְאָלָה בְּקֶרֶב עַמָּהּ:

28 But if the woman has not defiled herself and is pure, she shall be unharmed and able to retain seed.

כח וְאִם־לֹא נִטְמְאָה הָאִשָּׁה וּטְהֹרָה הִוא וְנִקְּתָה וְנִזְרְעָה זָרַע:

29 This is the ritual in cases of jealousy, when a woman goes astray while married to her husband and defiles herself,

כט זֹאת תּוֹרַת הַקְּנָאֹת אֲשֶׁר תִּשְׂטֶה אִשָּׁה תַּחַת אִישָׁהּ וְנִטְמָאָה:

Bamidbar/Numbers 6
Naso

במדבר ו
נשא

30 or when a fit of jealousy comes over a man and he is wrought up over his wife: the woman shall be made to stand before *Hashem* and the *Kohen* shall carry out all this ritual with her.

ל אוֹ אִישׁ אֲשֶׁר תַּעֲבֹר עָלָיו רוּחַ קִנְאָה וְקִנֵּא אֶת־אִשְׁתּוֹ וְהֶעֱמִיד אֶת־הָאִשָּׁה לִפְנֵי יְהֹוָה וְעָשָׂה לָהּ הַכֹּהֵן אֵת כָּל־הַתּוֹרָה הַזֹּאת׃

31 The man shall be clear of guilt; but that woman shall suffer for her guilt.

לא וְנִקָּה הָאִישׁ מֵעָוֺן וְהָאִשָּׁה הַהִוא תִּשָּׂא אֶת־עֲוֺנָהּ׃

6 1 *Hashem* spoke to *Moshe*, saying:

ו א וַיְדַבֵּר יְהֹוָה אֶל־מֹשֶׁה לֵּאמֹר׃

2 Speak to the Israelites and say to them: If anyone, man or woman, explicitly utters a nazirite's vow, to set himself apart for *Hashem*,

ב דַּבֵּר אֶל־בְּנֵי יִשְׂרָאֵל וְאָמַרְתָּ אֲלֵהֶם אִישׁ אוֹ־אִשָּׁה כִּי יַפְלִא לִנְדֹּר נֶדֶר נָזִיר לְהַזִּיר לַיהֹוָה׃

3 he shall abstain from wine and any other intoxicant; he shall not drink vinegar of wine or of any other intoxicant, neither shall he drink anything in which grapes have been steeped, nor eat grapes fresh or dried.

ג מִיַּיִן וְשֵׁכָר יַזִּיר חֹמֶץ יַיִן וְחֹמֶץ שֵׁכָר לֹא יִשְׁתֶּה וְכָל־מִשְׁרַת עֲנָבִים לֹא יִשְׁתֶּה וַעֲנָבִים לַחִים וִיבֵשִׁים לֹא יֹאכֵל׃

4 Throughout his term as nazirite, he may not eat anything that is obtained from the grapevine, even seeds or skin.

ד כֹּל יְמֵי נִזְרוֹ מִכֹּל אֲשֶׁר יֵעָשֶׂה מִגֶּפֶן הַיַּיִן מֵחַרְצַנִּים וְעַד־זָג לֹא יֹאכֵל׃

5 Throughout the term of his vow as nazirite, no razor shall touch his head; it shall remain consecrated until the completion of his term as nazirite of *Hashem*, the hair of his head being left to grow untrimmed.

ה כָּל־יְמֵי נֶדֶר נִזְרוֹ תַּעַר לֹא־יַעֲבֹר עַל־רֹאשׁוֹ עַד־מְלֹאת הַיָּמִם אֲשֶׁר־יַזִּיר לַיהֹוָה קָדֹשׁ יִהְיֶה גַּדֵּל פֶּרַע שְׂעַר רֹאשׁוֹ׃

6 Throughout the term that he has set apart for *Hashem*, he shall not go in where there is a dead person.

ו כָּל־יְמֵי הַזִּירוֹ לַיהֹוָה עַל־נֶפֶשׁ מֵת לֹא יָבֹא׃

7 Even if his father or mother, or his brother or sister should die, he must not defile himself for them, since hair set apart for his God is upon his head:

ז לְאָבִיו וּלְאִמּוֹ לְאָחִיו וּלְאַחֹתוֹ לֹא־יִטַּמָּא לָהֶם בְּמֹתָם כִּי נֵזֶר אֱלֹהָיו עַל־רֹאשׁוֹ׃

8 throughout his term as nazirite he is consecrated to *Hashem*.

ח כֹּל יְמֵי נִזְרוֹ קָדֹשׁ הוּא לַיהֹוָה׃

9 If a person dies suddenly near him, defiling his consecrated hair, he shall shave his head on the day he becomes clean; he shall shave it on the seventh day.

ט וְכִי־יָמוּת מֵת עָלָיו בְּפֶתַע פִּתְאֹם וְטִמֵּא רֹאשׁ נִזְרוֹ וְגִלַּח רֹאשׁוֹ בְּיוֹם טָהֳרָתוֹ בַּיּוֹם הַשְּׁבִיעִי יְגַלְּחֶנּוּ׃

10 On the eighth day he shall bring two turtledoves or two pigeons to the *Kohen*, at the entrance of the Tent of Meeting.

י וּבַיּוֹם הַשְּׁמִינִי יָבִא שְׁתֵּי תֹרִים אוֹ שְׁנֵי בְּנֵי יוֹנָה אֶל־הַכֹּהֵן אֶל־פֶּתַח אֹהֶל מוֹעֵד׃

11 The *Kohen* shall offer one as a sin offering and the other as a burnt offering, and make expiation on his behalf for the guilt that he incurred through the corpse. That same day he shall reconsecrate his head

יא וְעָשָׂה הַכֹּהֵן אֶחָד לְחַטָּאת וְאֶחָד לְעֹלָה וְכִפֶּר עָלָיו מֵאֲשֶׁר חָטָא עַל־הַנָּפֶשׁ וְקִדַּשׁ אֶת־רֹאשׁוֹ בַּיּוֹם הַהוּא׃

Bamidbar/Numbers 6
Naso

12 and rededicate to *Hashem* his term as nazirite; and he shall bring a lamb in its first year as a penalty offering. The previous period shall be void, since his consecrated hair was defiled.

וְהִזִּיר לַיהוָה אֶת־יְמֵי נִזְרוֹ וְהֵבִיא כֶּבֶשׂ בֶּן־שְׁנָתוֹ לְאָשָׁם וְהַיָּמִים הָרִאשֹׁנִים יִפְּלוּ כִּי טָמֵא נִזְרוֹ׃

13 This is the ritual for the nazirite: On the day that his term as nazirite is completed, he shall be brought to the entrance of the Tent of Meeting.

וְזֹאת תּוֹרַת הַנָּזִיר בְּיוֹם מְלֹאת יְמֵי נִזְרוֹ יָבִיא אֹתוֹ אֶל־פֶּתַח אֹהֶל מוֹעֵד׃

14 As his offering to *Hashem* he shall present: one male lamb in its first year, without blemish, for a burnt offering; one ewe lamb in its first year, without blemish, for a sin offering; one ram without blemish for an offering of well-being;

וְהִקְרִיב אֶת־קָרְבָּנוֹ לַיהוָה כֶּבֶשׂ בֶּן־שְׁנָתוֹ תָמִים אֶחָד לְעֹלָה וְכַבְשָׂה אַחַת בַּת־שְׁנָתָהּ תְּמִימָה לְחַטָּאת וְאַיִל־אֶחָד תָּמִים לִשְׁלָמִים׃

v'-hik-REEV et kor-ba-NO la-a-do-NAI KE-ves ben sh'-na-TO ta-MEEM e-KHAD l'-o-LAH v'-khav-SAH a-KHAT bat sh'-na-TAH t'-mee-MAH l'-kha-TAT v'-a-yil e-KHAD ta-MEEM lish-la-MEEM

15 a basket of unleavened cakes of choice flour with oil mixed in, and unleavened wafers spread with oil; and the proper meal offerings and libations.

וְסַל מַצּוֹת סֹלֶת חַלֹּת בְּלוּלֹת בַּשֶּׁמֶן וּרְקִיקֵי מַצּוֹת מְשֻׁחִים בַּשָּׁמֶן וּמִנְחָתָם וְנִסְכֵּיהֶם׃

16 The *Kohen* shall present them before *Hashem* and offer the sin offering and the burnt offering.

וְהִקְרִיב הַכֹּהֵן לִפְנֵי יְהוָה וְעָשָׂה אֶת־חַטָּאתוֹ וְאֶת־עֹלָתוֹ׃

17 He shall offer the ram as a sacrifice of well-being to *Hashem*, together with the basket of unleavened cakes; the *Kohen* shall also offer the meal offerings and the libations.

וְאֶת־הָאַיִל יַעֲשֶׂה זֶבַח שְׁלָמִים לַיהוָה עַל סַל הַמַּצּוֹת וְעָשָׂה הַכֹּהֵן אֶת־מִנְחָתוֹ וְאֶת־נִסְכּוֹ׃

18 The nazirite shall then shave his consecrated hair, at the entrance of the Tent of Meeting, and take the locks of his consecrated hair and put them on the fire that is under the sacrifice of well-being.

וְגִלַּח הַנָּזִיר פֶּתַח אֹהֶל מוֹעֵד אֶת־רֹאשׁ נִזְרוֹ וְלָקַח אֶת־שְׂעַר רֹאשׁ נִזְרוֹ וְנָתַן עַל־הָאֵשׁ אֲשֶׁר־תַּחַת זֶבַח הַשְּׁלָמִים׃

19 The *Kohen* shall take the shoulder of the ram when it has been boiled, one unleavened cake from the basket, and one unleavened wafer, and place them on the hands of the nazirite after he has shaved his consecrated hair.

וְלָקַח הַכֹּהֵן אֶת־הַזְּרֹעַ בְּשֵׁלָה מִן־הָאַיִל וְחַלַּת מַצָּה אַחַת מִן־הַסַּל וּרְקִיק מַצָּה אֶחָד וְנָתַן עַל־כַּפֵּי הַנָּזִיר אַחַר הִתְגַּלְּחוֹ אֶת־נִזְרוֹ׃

6:14 For a sin offering The nazirite is someone who takes it upon himself to abstain from wine, from cutting his hair and from contracting spiritual impurity from a dead body. He accepts these voluntary restrictions for the purpose of coming closer to *Hashem* and elevating himself spiritually. In essence, a nazirite removes himself from the ills of society so that he can remain pure and holy. At first glance, this seems admirable, something to be lauded and emulated. Indeed, the verse refers to the nazirite as "consecrated to *Hashem*" (verse 8). However, at the completion of his period of abstinence, the nazirite is required to bring a sin-offering. What is his sin? The Talmud (*Taanit* 11a) explains that while it is important to set aside time to work on oneself and one's personal growth, the ideal is not to remove oneself from society completely. Rather, we must try to elevate ourselves within society and bring the rest of the world up with us.

Bamidbar/Numbers 7
Naso

במדבר ז
נשא

20 The *Kohen* shall elevate them as an elevation offering before *Hashem*; and this shall be a sacred donation for the *Kohen*, in addition to the breast of the elevation offering and the thigh of gift offering. After that the nazirite may drink wine.

כ וְהֵנִיף אוֹתָם הַכֹּהֵן תְּנוּפָה לִפְנֵי יְהֹוָה קֹדֶשׁ הוּא לַכֹּהֵן עַל חֲזֵה הַתְּנוּפָה וְעַל שׁוֹק הַתְּרוּמָה וְאַחַר יִשְׁתֶּה הַנָּזִיר יָיִן:

21 Such is the obligation of a nazirite; except that he who vows an offering to God of what he can afford, beyond his nazirite requirements, must do exactly according to the vow that he has made beyond his obligation as a nazirite.

כא זֹאת תּוֹרַת הַנָּזִיר אֲשֶׁר יִדֹּר קָרְבָּנוֹ לַיהֹוָה עַל נִזְרוֹ מִלְּבַד אֲשֶׁר תַּשִּׂיג יָדוֹ כְּפִי נִדְרוֹ אֲשֶׁר יִדֹּר כֵּן יַעֲשֶׂה עַל תּוֹרַת נִזְרוֹ:

22 *Hashem* spoke to *Moshe*:

כב וַיְדַבֵּר יְהֹוָה אֶל מֹשֶׁה לֵּאמֹר:

23 Speak to *Aharon* and his sons: Thus shall you bless the people of *Yisrael*. Say to them:

כג דַּבֵּר אֶל אַהֲרֹן וְאֶל בָּנָיו לֵאמֹר כֹּה תְבָרְכוּ אֶת בְּנֵי יִשְׂרָאֵל אָמוֹר לָהֶם:

da-BAYR el ah-ha-RON v'-el ba-NAV lay-MOR KOH t'-va-r'-KHU et b'-NAY yis-ra-AYL a-MOR la-HEM

24 *Hashem* bless you and protect you!

כד יְבָרֶכְךָ יְהֹוָה וְיִשְׁמְרֶךָ:

y'-va-re-kh'-KHA a-do-NAI v'-yish-m'-RE-kha

25 *Hashem* deal kindly and graciously with you!

כה יָאֵר יְהֹוָה פָּנָיו אֵלֶיךָ וִיחֻנֶּךָּ:

ya-AYR a-do-NAI pa-NAV ay-LE-kha vee-khu-NE-ka

26 *Hashem* bestow His favor upon you and grant you peace!

כו יִשָּׂא יְהֹוָה פָּנָיו אֵלֶיךָ וְיָשֵׂם לְךָ שָׁלוֹם:

yi-SA a-do-NAI pa-NAV ay-LE-kha v'-ya-SAYM l'-KHA sha-LOM

27 Thus they shall link My name with the people of *Yisrael*, and I will bless them.

כז וְשָׂמוּ אֶת שְׁמִי עַל בְּנֵי יִשְׂרָאֵל וַאֲנִי אֲבָרֲכֵם:

7 1 On the day that *Moshe* finished setting up the *Mishkan*, he anointed and consecrated it and all its furnishings, as well as the *Mizbayach* and its utensils. When he had anointed and consecrated them,

ז א וַיְהִי בְּיוֹם כַּלּוֹת מֹשֶׁה לְהָקִים אֶת הַמִּשְׁכָּן וַיִּמְשַׁח אֹתוֹ וַיְקַדֵּשׁ אֹתוֹ וְאֶת כָּל כֵּלָיו וְאֶת הַמִּזְבֵּחַ וְאֶת כָּל כֵּלָיו וַיִּמְשָׁחֵם וַיְקַדֵּשׁ אֹתָם:

2 the chieftains of *Yisrael*, the heads of ancestral houses, namely, the chieftains of the tribes, those who were in charge of enrollment, drew near

ב וַיַּקְרִיבוּ נְשִׂיאֵי יִשְׂרָאֵל רָאשֵׁי בֵּית אֲבֹתָם הֵם נְשִׂיאֵי הַמַּטֹּת הֵם הָעֹמְדִים עַל הַפְּקֻדִים:

6:26 Bestow His favor upon you and grant you peace The Priestly Blessing uttered by the *Kohanim* contains three parts. It begins with a blessing for prosperity and safety, continues with a blessing for *Hashem*'s grace, and climaxes with a blessing of peace. Indeed, the Sages of the *Mishna* (*Oktzin* 3:12) taught that "God found no vessel to contain His blessings, other than peace." In Israel, the Priestly Blessing is recited publicly each day by individuals possessing a family tradition that they are among the descendants of *Aharon*, a group whose lineage has been verified in recent years by DNA testing. We pray every day for the total fulfillment of the Priestly Blessing, when the Jewish people will live peacefully in *Eretz Yisrael*.

The Priestly Blessing at the Western Wall

Bamidbar/Numbers 7
Naso

במדבר ז
נשא

3 and brought their offering before *Hashem*: six draught carts and twelve oxen, a cart for every two chieftains and an ox for each one. When they had brought them before the *Mishkan*,

ג וַיָּבִיאוּ אֶת־קָרְבָּנָם לִפְנֵי יְהֹוָה שֵׁשׁ־עֶגְלֹת צָב וּשְׁנֵי עָשָׂר בָּקָר עֲגָלָה עַל־שְׁנֵי הַנְּשִׂאִים וְשׁוֹר לְאֶחָד וַיַּקְרִיבוּ אוֹתָם לִפְנֵי הַמִּשְׁכָּן:

4 *Hashem* said to *Moshe*:

ד וַיֹּאמֶר יְהֹוָה אֶל־מֹשֶׁה לֵּאמֹר:

5 Accept these from them for use in the service of the Tent of Meeting, and give them to the *Leviim* according to their respective services.

ה קַח מֵאִתָּם וְהָיוּ לַעֲבֹד אֶת־עֲבֹדַת אֹהֶל מוֹעֵד וְנָתַתָּה אוֹתָם אֶל־הַלְוִיִּם אִישׁ כְּפִי עֲבֹדָתוֹ:

6 *Moshe* took the carts and the oxen and gave them to the *Leviim*.

ו וַיִּקַּח מֹשֶׁה אֶת־הָעֲגָלֹת וְאֶת־הַבָּקָר וַיִּתֵּן אוֹתָם אֶל־הַלְוִיִּם:

7 Two carts and four oxen he gave to the Gershonites, as required for their service,

ז אֵת שְׁתֵּי הָעֲגָלֹת וְאֵת אַרְבַּעַת הַבָּקָר נָתַן לִבְנֵי גֵרְשׁוֹן כְּפִי עֲבֹדָתָם:

8 and four carts and eight oxen he gave to the Merarites, as required for their service – under the direction of *Itamar* son of *Aharon* the *Kohen*.

ח וְאֵת אַרְבַּע הָעֲגָלֹת וְאֵת שְׁמֹנַת הַבָּקָר נָתַן לִבְנֵי מְרָרִי כְּפִי עֲבֹדָתָם בְּיַד אִיתָמָר בֶּן־אַהֲרֹן הַכֹּהֵן:

9 But to the Kohathites he did not give any; since theirs was the service of the [most] sacred objects, their porterage was by shoulder.

ט וְלִבְנֵי קְהָת לֹא נָתָן כִּי־עֲבֹדַת הַקֹּדֶשׁ עֲלֵהֶם בַּכָּתֵף יִשָּׂאוּ:

10 The chieftains also brought the dedication offering for the *Mizbayach* upon its being anointed. As the chieftains were presenting their offerings before the *Mizbayach*,

י וַיַּקְרִיבוּ הַנְּשִׂאִים אֵת חֲנֻכַּת הַמִּזְבֵּחַ בְּיוֹם הִמָּשַׁח אֹתוֹ וַיַּקְרִיבוּ הַנְּשִׂיאִם אֶת־קָרְבָּנָם לִפְנֵי הַמִּזְבֵּחַ:

va-yak-REE-vu han-si-EEM AYT kha-nu-KAT ha-miz-BAY-akh b'-YOM hi-ma-SHAKH o-TO va-yak-REE-vu ha-n'-see-IM et kor-ba-NAM lif-NAY ha-miz-BAY-akh

11 *Hashem* said to *Moshe*: Let them present their offerings for the dedication of the *Mizbayach*, one chieftain each day.

יא וַיֹּאמֶר יְהֹוָה אֶל־מֹשֶׁה נָשִׂיא אֶחָד לַיּוֹם נָשִׂיא אֶחָד לַיּוֹם יַקְרִיבוּ אֶת־קָרְבָּנָם לַחֲנֻכַּת הַמִּזְבֵּחַ:

12 The one who presented his offering on the first day was *Nachshon* son of *Aminadav* of the tribe of *Yehuda*.

יב וַיְהִי הַמַּקְרִיב בַּיּוֹם הָרִאשׁוֹן אֶת־קָרְבָּנוֹ נַחְשׁוֹן בֶּן־עַמִּינָדָב לְמַטֵּה יְהוּדָה:

13 His offering: one silver bowl weighing 130 *shekalim* and one silver basin of 70 *shekalim* by the sanctuary weight, both filled with choice flour with oil mixed in, for a meal offering;

יג וְקָרְבָּנוֹ קַעֲרַת־כֶּסֶף אַחַת שְׁלֹשִׁים וּמֵאָה מִשְׁקָלָהּ מִזְרָק אֶחָד כֶּסֶף שִׁבְעִים שֶׁקֶל בְּשֶׁקֶל הַקֹּדֶשׁ שְׁנֵיהֶם מְלֵאִים סֹלֶת בְּלוּלָה בַשֶּׁמֶן לְמִנְחָה:

7:10 The chieftains also brought the dedication offering for the *Mizbayach* Chapter 7 describes the donations given by the tribal leaders in celebration of the sanctification of the *Mishkan*. After the donations of the chieftains are accepted, they are inspired to bring offerings in celebration of the dedication of the altar. Following this example, the inaugurations of the First and Second Temples were also celebrated with an abundance of offerings (I Kings 8:62–63, Ezra 6:17). We await the day on which we will celebrate the inauguration of the third *Beit Hamikdash* in this same manner.

Bamidbar/Numbers 7
Naso

במדבר ז
נשא

14 one gold ladle of 10 *shekalim*, filled with incense;

יד כַּף אַחַת עֲשָׂרָה זָהָב מְלֵאָה קְטֹרֶת:

15 one bull of the herd, one ram, and one lamb in its first year, for a burnt offering;

טו פַּר אֶחָד בֶּן־בָּקָר אַיִל אֶחָד כֶּבֶשׂ־אֶחָד בֶּן־שְׁנָתוֹ לְעֹלָה:

16 one goat for a sin offering;

טז שְׂעִיר־עִזִּים אֶחָד לְחַטָּאת:

17 and for his sacrifice of well-being: two oxen, five rams, five he-goats, and five yearling lambs. That was the offering of *Nachshon* son of *Aminadav*.

יז וּלְזֶבַח הַשְּׁלָמִים בָּקָר שְׁנַיִם אֵילִם חֲמִשָּׁה עַתּוּדִים חֲמִשָּׁה כְּבָשִׂים בְּנֵי־שָׁנָה חֲמִשָּׁה זֶה קָרְבַּן נַחְשׁוֹן בֶּן־עַמִּינָדָב:

18 On the second day, *Netanel* son of Zuar, chieftain of *Yissachar*, made his offering.

יח בַּיּוֹם הַשֵּׁנִי הִקְרִיב נְתַנְאֵל בֶּן־צוּעָר נְשִׂיא יִשָּׂשכָר:

19 He presented as his offering: one silver bowl weighing 130 *shekalim* and one silver basin of 70 *shekalim* by the sanctuary weight, both filled with choice flour with oil mixed in, for a meal offering;

יט הִקְרִב אֶת־קָרְבָּנוֹ קַעֲרַת־כֶּסֶף אַחַת שְׁלֹשִׁים וּמֵאָה מִשְׁקָלָהּ מִזְרָק אֶחָד כֶּסֶף שִׁבְעִים שֶׁקֶל בְּשֶׁקֶל הַקֹּדֶשׁ שְׁנֵיהֶם מְלֵאִים סֹלֶת בְּלוּלָה בַשֶּׁמֶן לְמִנְחָה:

20 one gold ladle of 10 *shekalim*, filled with incense;

כ כַּף אַחַת עֲשָׂרָה זָהָב מְלֵאָה קְטֹרֶת:

21 one bull of the herd, one ram, and one lamb in its first year, for a burnt offering;

כא פַּר אֶחָד בֶּן־בָּקָר אַיִל אֶחָד כֶּבֶשׂ־אֶחָד בֶּן־שְׁנָתוֹ לְעֹלָה:

22 one goat for a sin offering;

כב שְׂעִיר־עִזִּים אֶחָד לְחַטָּאת:

23 and for his sacrifice of well-being: two oxen, five rams, five he-goats, and five yearling lambs. That was the offering of *Netanel* son of Zuar.

כג וּלְזֶבַח הַשְּׁלָמִים בָּקָר שְׁנַיִם אֵילִם חֲמִשָּׁה עַתֻּדִים חֲמִשָּׁה כְּבָשִׂים בְּנֵי־שָׁנָה חֲמִשָּׁה זֶה קָרְבַּן נְתַנְאֵל בֶּן־צוּעָר:

24 On the third day, it was the chieftain of the Zebulunites, *Eliav* son of Helon.

כד בַּיּוֹם הַשְּׁלִישִׁי נָשִׂיא לִבְנֵי זְבוּלֻן אֱלִיאָב בֶּן־חֵלֹן:

25 His offering: one silver bowl weighing 130 *shekalim* and one silver basin of 70 *shekalim* by the sanctuary weight, both filled with choice flour with oil mixed in, for a meal offering;

כה קָרְבָּנוֹ קַעֲרַת־כֶּסֶף אַחַת שְׁלֹשִׁים וּמֵאָה מִשְׁקָלָהּ מִזְרָק אֶחָד כֶּסֶף שִׁבְעִים שֶׁקֶל בְּשֶׁקֶל הַקֹּדֶשׁ שְׁנֵיהֶם מְלֵאִים סֹלֶת בְּלוּלָה בַשֶּׁמֶן לְמִנְחָה:

26 one gold ladle of 10 *shekalim*, filled with incense;

כו כַּף אַחַת עֲשָׂרָה זָהָב מְלֵאָה קְטֹרֶת:

27 one bull of the herd, one ram, and one lamb in its first year, for a burnt offering;

כז פַּר אֶחָד בֶּן־בָּקָר אַיִל אֶחָד כֶּבֶשׂ־אֶחָד בֶּן־שְׁנָתוֹ לְעֹלָה:

28 one goat for a sin offering;

כח שְׂעִיר־עִזִּים אֶחָד לְחַטָּאת:

29 and for his sacrifice of well-being: two oxen, five rams, five he-goats, and five yearling lambs. That was the offering of *Eliav* son of Helon.

כט וּלְזֶבַח הַשְּׁלָמִים בָּקָר שְׁנַיִם אֵילִם חֲמִשָּׁה עַתֻּדִים חֲמִשָּׁה כְּבָשִׂים בְּנֵי־שָׁנָה חֲמִשָּׁה זֶה קָרְבַּן אֱלִיאָב בֶּן־חֵלֹן:

30 On the fourth day, it was the chieftain of the Reubenites, *Elitzur* son of Shedeur.

ל בַּיּוֹם הָרְבִיעִי נָשִׂיא לִבְנֵי רְאוּבֵן אֱלִיצוּר בֶּן־שְׁדֵיאוּר:

Bamidbar/Numbers 7
Naso

31 His offering: one silver bowl weighing 130 *shekalim* and one silver basin of 70 *shekalim* by the sanctuary weight, both filled with choice flour with oil mixed in, for a meal offering;

32 one gold ladle of 10 *shekalim*, filled with incense;

33 one bull of the herd, one ram, and one lamb in its first year, for a burnt offering;

34 one goat for a sin offering;

35 and for his sacrifice of well-being: two oxen, five rams, five he-goats, and five yearling lambs. That was the offering of *Elitzur* son of Shedeur.

36 On the fifth day, it was the chieftain of the Simeonites, *Shelumiel* son of Zurishaddai.

37 His offering: one silver bowl weighing 130 *shekalim* and one silver basin of 70 *shekalim* by the sanctuary weight, both filled with choice flour with oil mixed in, for a meal offering;

38 one gold ladle of 10 *shekalim*, filled with incense;

39 one bull of the herd, one ram, and one lamb in its first year, for a burnt offering;

40 one goat for a sin offering;

41 and for his sacrifice of well-being: two oxen, five rams, five he-goats, and five yearling lambs. That was the offering of *Shelumiel* son of Zurishaddai.

42 On the sixth day, it was the chieftain of the Gadites, *Elyasaf* son of Deuel.

43 His offering: one silver bowl weighing 130 *shekalim* and one silver basin of 70 *shekalim* by the sanctuary weight, both filled with choice flour with oil mixed in, for a meal offering;

44 one gold ladle of 10 *shekalim*, filled with incense;

45 one bull of the herd, one ram, and one lamb in its first year, for a burnt offering;

46 one goat for a sin offering;

47 and for his sacrifice of well-being: two oxen, five rams, five he-goats, and five yearling lambs. That was the offering of *Elyasaf* son of Deuel.

במדבר ז
נשא

לא קׇרְבָּנוֹ קַעֲרַת־כֶּסֶף אַחַת שְׁלֹשִׁים וּמֵאָה מִשְׁקָלָהּ מִזְרָק אֶחָד כֶּסֶף שִׁבְעִים שֶׁקֶל בְּשֶׁקֶל הַקֹּדֶשׁ שְׁנֵיהֶם מְלֵאִים סֹלֶת בְּלוּלָה בַשֶּׁמֶן לְמִנְחָה:

לב כַּף אַחַת עֲשָׂרָה זָהָב מְלֵאָה קְטֹרֶת׃

לג פַּר אֶחָד בֶּן־בָּקָר אַיִל אֶחָד כֶּבֶשׂ־אֶחָד בֶּן־שְׁנָתוֹ לְעֹלָה׃

לד שְׂעִיר־עִזִּים אֶחָד לְחַטָּאת׃

לה וּלְזֶבַח הַשְּׁלָמִים בָּקָר שְׁנַיִם אֵילִם חֲמִשָּׁה עַתֻּדִים חֲמִשָּׁה כְּבָשִׂים בְּנֵי־שָׁנָה חֲמִשָּׁה זֶה קׇרְבַּן אֱלִיצוּר בֶּן־שְׁדֵיאוּר׃

לו בַּיּוֹם הַחֲמִישִׁי נָשִׂיא לִבְנֵי שִׁמְעוֹן שְׁלֻמִיאֵל בֶּן־צוּרִישַׁדָּי׃

לז קׇרְבָּנוֹ קַעֲרַת־כֶּסֶף אַחַת שְׁלֹשִׁים וּמֵאָה מִשְׁקָלָהּ מִזְרָק אֶחָד כֶּסֶף שִׁבְעִים שֶׁקֶל בְּשֶׁקֶל הַקֹּדֶשׁ שְׁנֵיהֶם מְלֵאִים סֹלֶת בְּלוּלָה בַשֶּׁמֶן לְמִנְחָה׃

לח כַּף אַחַת עֲשָׂרָה זָהָב מְלֵאָה קְטֹרֶת׃

לט פַּר אֶחָד בֶּן־בָּקָר אַיִל אֶחָד כֶּבֶשׂ־אֶחָד בֶּן־שְׁנָתוֹ לְעֹלָה׃

מ שְׂעִיר־עִזִּים אֶחָד לְחַטָּאת

מא וּלְזֶבַח הַשְּׁלָמִים בָּקָר שְׁנַיִם אֵילִם חֲמִשָּׁה עַתֻּדִים חֲמִשָּׁה כְּבָשִׂים בְּנֵי־שָׁנָה חֲמִשָּׁה זֶה קׇרְבַּן שְׁלֻמִיאֵל בֶּן־צוּרִישַׁדָּי׃

מב בַּיּוֹם הַשִּׁשִּׁי נָשִׂיא לִבְנֵי גָד אֶלְיָסָף בֶּן־דְּעוּאֵל׃

מג קׇרְבָּנוֹ קַעֲרַת־כֶּסֶף אַחַת שְׁלֹשִׁים וּמֵאָה מִשְׁקָלָהּ מִזְרָק אֶחָד כֶּסֶף שִׁבְעִים שֶׁקֶל בְּשֶׁקֶל הַקֹּדֶשׁ שְׁנֵיהֶם מְלֵאִים סֹלֶת בְּלוּלָה בַשֶּׁמֶן לְמִנְחָה׃

מד כַּף אַחַת עֲשָׂרָה זָהָב מְלֵאָה קְטֹרֶת׃

מה פַּר אֶחָד בֶּן־בָּקָר אַיִל אֶחָד כֶּבֶשׂ־אֶחָד בֶּן־שְׁנָתוֹ לְעֹלָה׃

מו שְׂעִיר־עִזִּים אֶחָד לְחַטָּאת׃

מז וּלְזֶבַח הַשְּׁלָמִים בָּקָר שְׁנַיִם אֵילִם חֲמִשָּׁה עַתֻּדִים חֲמִשָּׁה כְּבָשִׂים בְּנֵי־שָׁנָה חֲמִשָּׁה זֶה קׇרְבַּן אֶלְיָסָף בֶּן־דְּעוּאֵל׃

Bamidbar/Numbers 7
Naso

במדבר ז
נשא

48 On the seventh day, it was the chieftain of the Ephraimites, *Elishama* son of Ammihud.

מח בַּיּוֹם הַשְּׁבִיעִי נָשִׂיא לִבְנֵי אֶפְרָיִם אֱלִישָׁמָע בֶּן־עַמִּיהוּד:

49 His offering: one silver bowl weighing 130 *shekalim* and one silver basin of 70 *shekalim* by the sanctuary weight, both filled with choice flour with oil mixed in, for a meal offering;

מט קָרְבָּנוֹ קַעֲרַת־כֶּסֶף אַחַת שְׁלֹשִׁים וּמֵאָה מִשְׁקָלָהּ מִזְרָק אֶחָד כֶּסֶף שִׁבְעִים שֶׁקֶל בְּשֶׁקֶל הַקֹּדֶשׁ שְׁנֵיהֶם מְלֵאִים סֹלֶת בְּלוּלָה בַשֶּׁמֶן לְמִנְחָה:

50 one gold ladle of 10 *shekalim*, filled with incense;

נ כַּף אַחַת עֲשָׂרָה זָהָב מְלֵאָה קְטֹרֶת:

51 one bull of the herd, one ram, and one lamb in its first year, for a burnt offering;

נא פַּר אֶחָד בֶּן־בָּקָר אַיִל אֶחָד כֶּבֶשׂ־אֶחָד בֶּן־שְׁנָתוֹ לְעֹלָה:

52 one goat for a sin offering;

נב שְׂעִיר־עִזִּים אֶחָד לְחַטָּאת:

53 and for his sacrifice of well-being: two oxen, five rams, five he-goats, and five yearling lambs. That was the offering of *Elishama* son of Ammihud.

נג וּלְזֶבַח הַשְּׁלָמִים בָּקָר שְׁנַיִם אֵילִם חֲמִשָּׁה עַתֻּדִים חֲמִשָּׁה כְּבָשִׂים בְּנֵי־שָׁנָה חֲמִשָּׁה זֶה קָרְבַּן אֱלִישָׁמָע בֶּן־עַמִּיהוּד:

54 On the eighth day, it was the chieftain of the Manassites, *Gamliel* son of Pedahzur.

נד בַּיּוֹם הַשְּׁמִינִי נָשִׂיא לִבְנֵי מְנַשֶּׁה גַּמְלִיאֵל בֶּן־פְּדָהצוּר:

55 His offering: one silver bowl weighing 130 *shekalim* and one silver basin of 70 *shekalim* by the sanctuary weight, both filled with choice flour with oil mixed in, for a meal offering;

נה קָרְבָּנוֹ קַעֲרַת־כֶּסֶף אַחַת שְׁלֹשִׁים וּמֵאָה מִשְׁקָלָהּ מִזְרָק אֶחָד כֶּסֶף שִׁבְעִים שֶׁקֶל בְּשֶׁקֶל הַקֹּדֶשׁ שְׁנֵיהֶם מְלֵאִים סֹלֶת בְּלוּלָה בַשֶּׁמֶן לְמִנְחָה:

56 one gold ladle of 10 *shekalim*, filled with incense;

נו כַּף אַחַת עֲשָׂרָה זָהָב מְלֵאָה קְטֹרֶת:

57 one bull of the herd, one ram, and one lamb in its first year, for a burnt offering;

נז פַּר אֶחָד בֶּן־בָּקָר אַיִל אֶחָד כֶּבֶשׂ־אֶחָד בֶּן־שְׁנָתוֹ לְעֹלָה:

58 one goat for a sin offering;

נח שְׂעִיר־עִזִּים אֶחָד לְחַטָּאת:

59 and for his sacrifice of well-being: two oxen, five rams, five he-goats, and five yearling lambs. That was the offering of *Gamliel* son of Pedahzur.

נט וּלְזֶבַח הַשְּׁלָמִים בָּקָר שְׁנַיִם אֵילִם חֲמִשָּׁה עַתֻּדִים חֲמִשָּׁה כְּבָשִׂים בְּנֵי־שָׁנָה חֲמִשָּׁה זֶה קָרְבַּן גַּמְלִיאֵל בֶּן־פְּדָהצוּר:

60 On the ninth day, it was the chieftain of the Benjaminites, *Avidan* son of Gideoni.

ס בַּיּוֹם הַתְּשִׁיעִי נָשִׂיא לִבְנֵי בִנְיָמִן אֲבִידָן בֶּן־גִּדְעֹנִי:

61 His offering: one silver bowl weighing 130 *shekalim* and one silver basin of 70 *shekalim* by the sanctuary weight, both filled with choice flour with oil mixed in, for a meal offering;

סא קָרְבָּנוֹ קַעֲרַת־כֶּסֶף אַחַת שְׁלֹשִׁים וּמֵאָה מִשְׁקָלָהּ מִזְרָק אֶחָד כֶּסֶף שִׁבְעִים שֶׁקֶל בְּשֶׁקֶל הַקֹּדֶשׁ שְׁנֵיהֶם מְלֵאִים סֹלֶת בְּלוּלָה בַשֶּׁמֶן לְמִנְחָה:

62 one gold ladle of 10 *shekalim*, filled with incense;

סב כַּף אַחַת עֲשָׂרָה זָהָב מְלֵאָה קְטֹרֶת:

63 one bull of the herd, one ram, and one lamb in its first year, for a burnt offering;

סג פַּר אֶחָד בֶּן־בָּקָר אַיִל אֶחָד כֶּבֶשׂ־אֶחָד בֶּן־שְׁנָתוֹ לְעֹלָה:

64 one goat for a sin offering;

סד שְׂעִיר־עִזִּים אֶחָד לְחַטָּאת:

Bamidbar/Numbers 7
Naso

65 and for his sacrifice of well-being: two oxen, five rams, five he-goats, and five yearling lambs. That was the offering of *Avidan* son of Gideoni.

סה וּלְזֶבַח הַשְּׁלָמִים בָּקָר שְׁנַיִם אֵילִם חֲמִשָּׁה עַתֻּדִים חֲמִשָּׁה כְּבָשִׂים בְּנֵי־שָׁנָה חֲמִשָּׁה זֶה קָרְבַּן אֲבִידָן בֶּן־גִּדְעֹנִי׃

66 On the tenth day, it was the chieftain of the Danites, *Achiezer* son of Ammishaddai.

סו בַּיּוֹם הָעֲשִׂירִי נָשִׂיא לִבְנֵי דָן אֲחִיעֶזֶר בֶּן־עַמִּישַׁדָּי׃

67 His offering: one silver bowl weighing 130 *shekalim* and one silver basin of 70 *shekalim* by the sanctuary weight, both filled with choice flour with oil mixed in, for a meal offering;

סז קָרְבָּנוֹ קַעֲרַת־כֶּסֶף אַחַת שְׁלֹשִׁים וּמֵאָה מִשְׁקָלָהּ מִזְרָק אֶחָד כֶּסֶף שִׁבְעִים שֶׁקֶל בְּשֶׁקֶל הַקֹּדֶשׁ שְׁנֵיהֶם מְלֵאִים סֹלֶת בְּלוּלָה בַשֶּׁמֶן לְמִנְחָה׃

68 one gold ladle of 10 *shekalim*, filled with incense;

סח כַּף אַחַת עֲשָׂרָה זָהָב מְלֵאָה קְטֹרֶת׃

69 one bull of the herd, one ram, and one lamb in its first year, for a burnt offering;

סט פַּר אֶחָד בֶּן־בָּקָר אַיִל אֶחָד כֶּבֶשׂ־אֶחָד בֶּן־שְׁנָתוֹ לְעֹלָה׃

70 one goat for a sin offering;

ע שְׂעִיר־עִזִּים אֶחָד לְחַטָּאת׃

71 and for his sacrifice of well-being: two oxen, five rams, five he-goats, and five yearling lambs. That was the offering of *Achiezer* son of Ammishaddai.

עא וּלְזֶבַח הַשְּׁלָמִים בָּקָר שְׁנַיִם אֵילִם חֲמִשָּׁה עַתֻּדִים חֲמִשָּׁה כְּבָשִׂים בְּנֵי־שָׁנָה חֲמִשָּׁה זֶה קָרְבַּן אֲחִיעֶזֶר בֶּן־עַמִּישַׁדָּי׃

72 On the eleventh day, it was the chieftain of the Asherites, *Pagiel* son of Ochran.

עב בְּיוֹם עַשְׁתֵּי עָשָׂר יוֹם נָשִׂיא לִבְנֵי אָשֵׁר פַּגְעִיאֵל בֶּן־עָכְרָן׃

73 His offering: one silver bowl weighing 130 *shekalim* and one silver basin of 70 *shekalim* by the sanctuary weight, both filled with choice flour with oil mixed in, for a meal offering;

עג קָרְבָּנוֹ קַעֲרַת־כֶּסֶף אַחַת שְׁלֹשִׁים וּמֵאָה מִשְׁקָלָהּ מִזְרָק אֶחָד כֶּסֶף שִׁבְעִים שֶׁקֶל בְּשֶׁקֶל הַקֹּדֶשׁ שְׁנֵיהֶם מְלֵאִים סֹלֶת בְּלוּלָה בַשֶּׁמֶן לְמִנְחָה׃

74 one gold ladle of 10 *shekalim*, filled with incense;

עד כַּף אַחַת עֲשָׂרָה זָהָב מְלֵאָה קְטֹרֶת׃

75 one bull of the herd, one ram, and one lamb in its first year, for a burnt offering;

עה פַּר אֶחָד בֶּן־בָּקָר אַיִל אֶחָד כֶּבֶשׂ־אֶחָד בֶּן־שְׁנָתוֹ לְעֹלָה׃

76 one goat for a sin offering;

עו שְׂעִיר־עִזִּים אֶחָד לְחַטָּאת׃

77 and for his sacrifice of well-being: two oxen, five rams, five he-goats, and five yearling lambs. That was the offering of *Pagiel* son of Ochran.

עז וּלְזֶבַח הַשְּׁלָמִים בָּקָר שְׁנַיִם אֵילִם חֲמִשָּׁה עַתֻּדִים חֲמִשָּׁה כְּבָשִׂים בְּנֵי־שָׁנָה חֲמִשָּׁה זֶה קָרְבַּן פַּגְעִיאֵל בֶּן־עָכְרָן׃

78 On the twelfth day, it was the chieftain of the Naphtalites, *Achira* son of Enan.

עח בְּיוֹם שְׁנֵים עָשָׂר יוֹם נָשִׂיא לִבְנֵי נַפְתָּלִי אֲחִירַע בֶּן־עֵינָן׃

79 His offering: one silver bowl weighing 130 *shekalim* and one silver basin of 70 *shekalim* by the sanctuary weight, both filled with choice flour with oil mixed in, for a meal offering;

עט קָרְבָּנוֹ קַעֲרַת־כֶּסֶף אַחַת שְׁלֹשִׁים וּמֵאָה מִשְׁקָלָהּ מִזְרָק אֶחָד כֶּסֶף שִׁבְעִים שֶׁקֶל בְּשֶׁקֶל הַקֹּדֶשׁ שְׁנֵיהֶם מְלֵאִים סֹלֶת בְּלוּלָה בַשֶּׁמֶן לְמִנְחָה׃

80 one gold ladle of 10 *shekalim*, filled with incense;

פ כַּף אַחַת עֲשָׂרָה זָהָב מְלֵאָה קְטֹרֶת׃

81 one bull of the herd, one ram, and one lamb in its first year, for a burnt offering;

פא פַּר אֶחָד בֶּן־בָּקָר אַיִל אֶחָד כֶּבֶשׂ־אֶחָד בֶּן־שְׁנָתוֹ לְעֹלָה׃

Bamidbar/Numbers 8
Beha'alotcha

במדבר ח
בהעלתך

82 one goat for a sin offering;

פב שְׂעִיר־עִזִּים אֶחָד לְחַטָּאת:

83 and for his sacrifice of well-being: two oxen, five rams, five he-goats, and five yearling lambs. That was the offering of *Achira* son of Enan.

פג וּלְזֶבַח הַשְּׁלָמִים בָּקָר שְׁנַיִם אֵילִם חֲמִשָּׁה עַתּוּדִים חֲמִשָּׁה כְּבָשִׂים בְּנֵי־שָׁנָה חֲמִשָּׁה זֶה קׇרְבַּן אֲחִירַע בֶּן־עֵינָן:

84 This was the dedication offering for the *Mizbayach* from the chieftains of *Yisrael* upon its being anointed: silver bowls, 12; silver basins, 12; gold ladles, 12.

פד זֹאת ׀ חֲנֻכַּת הַמִּזְבֵּחַ בְּיוֹם הִמָּשַׁח אֹתוֹ מֵאֵת נְשִׂיאֵי יִשְׂרָאֵל קַעֲרֹת כֶּסֶף שְׁתֵּים עֶשְׂרֵה מִזְרְקֵי־כֶסֶף שְׁנֵים עָשָׂר כַּפּוֹת זָהָב שְׁתֵּים עֶשְׂרֵה:

85 Silver per bowl, 130; per basin, 70. Total silver of vessels, 2,400 sanctuary *shekalim*.

פה שְׁלֹשִׁים וּמֵאָה הַקְּעָרָה הָאַחַת כֶּסֶף וְשִׁבְעִים הַמִּזְרָק הָאֶחָד כֹּל כֶּסֶף הַכֵּלִים אַלְפַּיִם וְאַרְבַּע־מֵאוֹת בְּשֶׁקֶל הַקֹּדֶשׁ:

86 The 12 gold ladles filled with incense – 10 sanctuary *shekalim* per ladle – total gold of the ladles, 120.

פו כַּפּוֹת זָהָב שְׁתֵּים־עֶשְׂרֵה מְלֵאֹת קְטֹרֶת עֲשָׂרָה עֲשָׂרָה הַכַּף בְּשֶׁקֶל הַקֹּדֶשׁ כׇּל־זְהַב הַכַּפּוֹת עֶשְׂרִים וּמֵאָה:

87 Total of herd animals for burnt offerings, 12 bulls; of rams, 12; of yearling lambs, 12 – with their proper meal offerings; of goats for sin offerings, 12.

פז כׇּל־הַבָּקָר לָעֹלָה שְׁנֵים עָשָׂר פָּרִים אֵילִם שְׁנֵים־עָשָׂר כְּבָשִׂים בְּנֵי־שָׁנָה שְׁנֵים עָשָׂר וּמִנְחָתָם וּשְׂעִירֵי עִזִּים שְׁנֵים עָשָׂר לְחַטָּאת:

88 Total of herd animals for sacrifices of well-being, 24 bulls; of rams, 60; of he-goats, 60; of yearling lambs, 60. That was the dedication offering for the *Mizbayach* after its anointing.

פח וְכֹל בְּקַר ׀ זֶבַח הַשְּׁלָמִים עֶשְׂרִים וְאַרְבָּעָה פָּרִים אֵילִם שִׁשִּׁים עַתֻּדִים שִׁשִּׁים כְּבָשִׂים בְּנֵי־שָׁנָה שִׁשִּׁים זֹאת חֲנֻכַּת הַמִּזְבֵּחַ אַחֲרֵי הִמָּשַׁח אֹתוֹ:

89 When *Moshe* went into the Tent of Meeting to speak with Him, he would hear the Voice addressing him from above the cover that was on top of the *Aron HaBrit* between the two cherubim; thus He spoke to him.

פט וּבְבֹא מֹשֶׁה אֶל־אֹהֶל מוֹעֵד לְדַבֵּר אִתּוֹ וַיִּשְׁמַע אֶת־הַקּוֹל מִדַּבֵּר אֵלָיו מֵעַל הַכַּפֹּרֶת אֲשֶׁר עַל־אֲרֹן הָעֵדֻת מִבֵּין שְׁנֵי הַכְּרֻבִים וַיְדַבֵּר אֵלָיו:

8 1 *Hashem* spoke to *Moshe*, saying:

ח א וַיְדַבֵּר יְהֹוָה אֶל־מֹשֶׁה לֵּאמֹר:

2 Speak to *Aharon* and say to him, "When you mount the lamps, let the seven lamps give light at the front of the *menorah*."

ב דַּבֵּר אֶל־אַהֲרֹן וְאָמַרְתָּ אֵלָיו בְּהַעֲלֹתְךָ אֶת־הַנֵּרֹת אֶל־מוּל פְּנֵי הַמְּנוֹרָה יָאִירוּ שִׁבְעַת הַנֵּרוֹת:

da-BAYR el a-ha-RON v'-a-mar-TA ay-LAV b'-ha-a-lo-t'-KHA et ha-nay-ROT el MUL p'-NAY ha-m'-no-RAH ya-EE-ru shiv-AT ha-nay-ROT

8:2 When you mount the lamps *Aharon* is charged with the daily task of lighting the lamps of the *menorah* in the *Mishkan*. The *Ramban* adds that many centuries later, a small group of priests who descended from the family of *Aharon* boldly led a revolt against the mighty Syrian-Greek army. After miraculously defeating the enemy, the Maccabees reclaimed the *Beit Hamikdash* and sought pure olive oil to kindle the *menorah* which had been extinguished. Due to the scarcity of pure oil to be found in the *Beit Hamikdash*, *Hashem* performed a second miracle, causing one day's supply of oil to burn for a full eight days, until new oil

PM Netanyahu lighting a menorah at the Western Wall

Bamidbar/Numbers 8
Beha'alotcha

במדבר ח
בהעלתך

3 *Aharon* did so; he mounted the lamps at the front of the *menorah*, as *Hashem* had commanded *Moshe*. –

ג וַיַּעַשׂ כֵּן אַהֲרֹן אֶל־מוּל פְּנֵי הַמְּנוֹרָה הֶעֱלָה נֵרֹתֶיהָ כַּאֲשֶׁר צִוָּה יְהוָה אֶת־מֹשֶׁה:

4 Now this is how the *menorah* was made: it was hammered work of gold, hammered from base to petal. According to the pattern that *Hashem* had shown *Moshe*, so was the *menorah* made.

ד וְזֶה מַעֲשֵׂה הַמְּנֹרָה מִקְשָׁה זָהָב עַד־יְרֵכָהּ עַד־פִּרְחָהּ מִקְשָׁה הִוא כַּמַּרְאֶה אֲשֶׁר הֶרְאָה יְהוָה אֶת־מֹשֶׁה כֵּן עָשָׂה אֶת־הַמְּנֹרָה:

5 *Hashem* spoke to *Moshe*, saying:

ה וַיְדַבֵּר יְהוָה אֶל־מֹשֶׁה לֵּאמֹר:

6 Take the *Leviim* from among the Israelites and cleanse them.

ו קַח אֶת־הַלְוִיִּם מִתּוֹךְ בְּנֵי יִשְׂרָאֵל וְטִהַרְתָּ אֹתָם:

7 This is what you shall do to them to cleanse them: sprinkle on them water of purification, and let them go over their whole body with a razor, and wash their clothes; thus they shall be cleansed.

ז וְכֹה־תַעֲשֶׂה לָהֶם לְטַהֲרָם הַזֵּה עֲלֵיהֶם מֵי חַטָּאת וְהֶעֱבִירוּ תַעַר עַל־כָּל־בְּשָׂרָם וְכִבְּסוּ בִגְדֵיהֶם וְהִטֶּהָרוּ:

8 Let them take a bull of the herd, and with it a meal offering of choice flour with oil mixed in, and you take a second bull of the herd for a sin offering.

ח וְלָקְחוּ פַּר בֶּן־בָּקָר וּמִנְחָתוֹ סֹלֶת בְּלוּלָה בַשָּׁמֶן וּפַר־שֵׁנִי בֶן־בָּקָר תִּקַּח לְחַטָּאת:

9 You shall bring the *Leviim* forward before the Tent of Meeting. Assemble the whole Israelite community,

ט וְהִקְרַבְתָּ אֶת־הַלְוִיִּם לִפְנֵי אֹהֶל מוֹעֵד וְהִקְהַלְתָּ אֶת־כָּל־עֲדַת בְּנֵי יִשְׂרָאֵל:

10 and bring the *Leviim* forward before *Hashem*. Let the Israelites lay their hands upon the *Leviim*,

י וְהִקְרַבְתָּ אֶת־הַלְוִיִּם לִפְנֵי יְהוָה וְסָמְכוּ בְנֵי־יִשְׂרָאֵל אֶת־יְדֵיהֶם עַל־הַלְוִיִּם:

11 and let *Aharon* designate the *Leviim* before *Hashem* as an elevation offering from the Israelites, that they may perform the service of *Hashem*.

יא וְהֵנִיף אַהֲרֹן אֶת־הַלְוִיִּם תְּנוּפָה לִפְנֵי יְהוָה מֵאֵת בְּנֵי יִשְׂרָאֵל וְהָיוּ לַעֲבֹד אֶת־עֲבֹדַת יְהוָה:

12 The *Leviim* shall now lay their hands upon the heads of the bulls; one shall be offered to *Hashem* as a sin offering and the other as a burnt offering, to make expiation for the *Leviim*.

יב וְהַלְוִיִּם יִסְמְכוּ אֶת־יְדֵיהֶם עַל רֹאשׁ הַפָּרִים וַעֲשֵׂה אֶת־הָאֶחָד חַטָּאת וְאֶת־הָאֶחָד עֹלָה לַיהוָה לְכַפֵּר עַל־הַלְוִיִּם:

13 You shall place the *Leviim* in attendance upon *Aharon* and his sons, and designate them as an elevation offering to *Hashem*.

יג וְהַעֲמַדְתָּ אֶת־הַלְוִיִּם לִפְנֵי אַהֲרֹן וְלִפְנֵי בָנָיו וְהֵנַפְתָּ אֹתָם תְּנוּפָה לַיהוָה:

14 Thus you shall set the *Leviim* apart from the Israelites, and the *Leviim* shall be Mine.

יד וְהִבְדַּלְתָּ אֶת־הַלְוִיִּם מִתּוֹךְ בְּנֵי יִשְׂרָאֵל וְהָיוּ לִי הַלְוִיִּם:

15 Thereafter the *Leviim* shall be qualified for the service of the Tent of Meeting, once you have cleansed them and designated them as an elevation offering.

טו וְאַחֲרֵי־כֵן יָבֹאוּ הַלְוִיִּם לַעֲבֹד אֶת־אֹהֶל מוֹעֵד וְטִהַרְתָּ אֹתָם וְהֵנַפְתָּ אֹתָם תְּנוּפָה:

was produced. In perpetual commemoration of these miracles, the Jewish people light their own menorah lamps for eight nights every year, when they celebrate *Chanukah*.

Bamidbar/Numbers 9
Beha'alotcha

16 For they are formally assigned to Me from among the Israelites: I have taken them for Myself in place of all the first issue of the womb, of all the first-born of the Israelites.

17 For every first-born among the Israelites, man as well as beast, is Mine; I consecrated them to Myself at the time that I smote every first-born in the land of Egypt.

18 Now I take the *Leviim* instead of every first-born of the Israelites;

19 and from among the Israelites I formally assign the *Leviim* to *Aharon* and his sons, to perform the service for the Israelites in the Tent of Meeting and to make expiation for the Israelites, so that no plague may afflict the Israelites for coming too near the sanctuary.

20 *Moshe*, *Aharon*, and the whole Israelite community did with the *Leviim* accordingly; just as *Hashem* had commanded *Moshe* in regard to the *Leviim*, so the Israelites did with them.

21 The *Leviim* purified themselves and washed their clothes; and *Aharon* designated them as an elevation offering before *Hashem*, and *Aharon* made expiation for them to cleanse them.

22 Thereafter the *Leviim* were qualified to perform their service in the Tent of Meeting, under *Aharon* and his sons. As *Hashem* had commanded *Moshe* in regard to the *Leviim*, so they did to them.

23 *Hashem* spoke to *Moshe*, saying:

24 This is the rule for the *Leviim*. From twenty-five years of age up they shall participate in the work force in the service of the Tent of Meeting;

25 but at the age of fifty they shall retire from the work force and shall serve no more.

26 They may assist their brother *Leviim* at the Tent of Meeting by standing guard, but they shall perform no labor. Thus you shall deal with the *Leviim* in regard to their duties.

9
1 *Hashem* spoke to *Moshe* in the wilderness of Sinai, on the first new moon of the second year following the exodus from the land of Egypt, saying:

2 Let *B'nei Yisrael* offer the *Pesach* sacrifice at its set time:

Bamidbar/Numbers 9
Beha'alotcha

במדבר ט
בהעלתך

3 you shall offer it on the fourteenth day of this month, at twilight, at its set time; you shall offer it in accordance with all its rules and rites.

ג בְּאַרְבָּעָה עָשָׂר־יוֹם בַּחֹדֶשׁ הַזֶּה בֵּין הָעַרְבַּיִם תַּעֲשׂוּ אֹתוֹ בְּמוֹעֲדוֹ כְּכָל־חֻקֹּתָיו וּכְכָל־מִשְׁפָּטָיו תַּעֲשׂוּ אֹתוֹ:

4 *Moshe* instructed the Israelites to offer the *Pesach* sacrifice;

ד וַיְדַבֵּר מֹשֶׁה אֶל־בְּנֵי יִשְׂרָאֵל לַעֲשֹׂת הַפָּסַח:

5 and they offered the *Pesach* sacrifice in the first month, on the fourteenth day of the month, at twilight, in the wilderness of Sinai. Just as *Hashem* had commanded *Moshe*, so the Israelites did.

ה וַיַּעֲשׂוּ אֶת־הַפֶּסַח בָּרִאשׁוֹן בְּאַרְבָּעָה עָשָׂר יוֹם לַחֹדֶשׁ בֵּין הָעַרְבַּיִם בְּמִדְבַּר סִינָי כְּכֹל אֲשֶׁר צִוָּה יְהוָה אֶת־מֹשֶׁה כֵּן עָשׂוּ בְּנֵי יִשְׂרָאֵל:

va-ya-a-SU et ha-PE-sakh ba-ri-SHON b'-ar-ba-AH a-SAR YOM la-KHO-desh BAYN ha-ar-BA-yim b'-mid-BAR see-NAI k'-KHOL a-SHER tzi-VAH a-do-NAI et mo-SHEH KAYN a-SU b'-NAY yis-ra-AYL

6 But there were some men who were unclean by reason of a corpse and could not offer the *Pesach* sacrifice on that day. Appearing that same day before *Moshe* and *Aharon*,

ו וַיְהִי אֲנָשִׁים אֲשֶׁר הָיוּ טְמֵאִים לְנֶפֶשׁ אָדָם וְלֹא־יָכְלוּ לַעֲשֹׂת־הַפֶּסַח בַּיּוֹם הַהוּא וַיִּקְרְבוּ לִפְנֵי מֹשֶׁה וְלִפְנֵי אַהֲרֹן בַּיּוֹם הַהוּא:

7 those men said to them, "Unclean though we are by reason of a corpse, why must we be debarred from presenting *Hashem*'s offering at its set time with the rest of the Israelites?"

ז וַיֹּאמְרוּ הָאֲנָשִׁים הָהֵמָּה אֵלָיו אֲנַחְנוּ טְמֵאִים לְנֶפֶשׁ אָדָם לָמָּה נִגָּרַע לְבִלְתִּי הַקְרִיב אֶת־קָרְבַּן יְהוָה בְּמֹעֲדוֹ בְּתוֹךְ בְּנֵי יִשְׂרָאֵל:

8 *Moshe* said to them, "Stand by, and let me hear what instructions *Hashem* gives about you."

ח וַיֹּאמֶר אֲלֵהֶם מֹשֶׁה עִמְדוּ וְאֶשְׁמְעָה מַה־יְצַוֶּה יְהוָה לָכֶם:

9 And *Hashem* spoke to *Moshe*, saying:

ט וַיְדַבֵּר יְהוָה אֶל־מֹשֶׁה לֵּאמֹר:

10 Speak to *B'nei Yisrael*, saying: When any of you or of your posterity who are defiled by a corpse or are on a long journey would offer a *Pesach* sacrifice to *Hashem*,

י דַּבֵּר אֶל־בְּנֵי יִשְׂרָאֵל לֵאמֹר אִישׁ אִישׁ כִּי־יִהְיֶה־טָמֵא לָנֶפֶשׁ אוֹ בְדֶרֶךְ רְחֹקָה לָכֶם אוֹ לְדֹרֹתֵיכֶם וְעָשָׂה פֶסַח לַיהוָה:

11 they shall offer it in the second month, on the fourteenth day of the month, at twilight. They shall eat it with unleavened bread and bitter herbs,

יא בַּחֹדֶשׁ הַשֵּׁנִי בְּאַרְבָּעָה עָשָׂר יוֹם בֵּין הָעַרְבַּיִם יַעֲשׂוּ אֹתוֹ עַל־מַצּוֹת וּמְרֹרִים יֹאכְלֻהוּ:

12 and they shall not leave any of it over until morning. They shall not break a bone of it. They shall offer it in strict accord with the law of the *Pesach* sacrifice.

יב לֹא־יַשְׁאִירוּ מִמֶּנּוּ עַד־בֹּקֶר וְעֶצֶם לֹא יִשְׁבְּרוּ־בוֹ כְּכָל־חֻקַּת הַפֶּסַח יַעֲשׂוּ אֹתוֹ:

9:5 And they offered the *Pesach* sacrifice in the first month Before embarking on their journey through the desert, the Children of Israel observed the holiday of *Pesach*, commemorating the day they had left Egypt one year previously. Although the Israelites were already able to celebrate their release from bondage, their ultimate freedom was still to come; it would be realized only once they were settled in their own land. A nation is truly free only when it inhabits its own land under its own leadership. For this reason, the *Pesach seder* meal ends with the declaration, "Next year in *Yerushalayim*." The Jewish people can only be truly free when they are all living in *Eretz Yisrael*.

A table set for the Pesach seder

Bamidbar/Numbers 9
Beha'alotcha

במדבר ט
בהעלתך

13 But if a man who is clean and not on a journey refrains from offering the *Pesach* sacrifice, that person shall be cut off from his kin, for he did not present *Hashem*'s offering at its set time; that man shall bear his guilt.

יג וְהָאִישׁ אֲשֶׁר־הוּא טָהוֹר וּבְדֶרֶךְ לֹא־הָיָה וְחָדַל לַעֲשׂוֹת הַפֶּסַח וְנִכְרְתָה הַנֶּפֶשׁ הַהִוא מֵעַמֶּיהָ כִּי קָרְבַּן יְהֹוָה לֹא הִקְרִיב בְּמֹעֲדוֹ חֶטְאוֹ יִשָּׂא הָאִישׁ הַהוּא:

14 And when a stranger who resides with you would offer a *Pesach* sacrifice to *Hashem*, he must offer it in accordance with the rules and rites of the *Pesach* sacrifice. There shall be one law for you, whether stranger or citizen of the country.

יד וְכִי־יָגוּר אִתְּכֶם גֵּר וְעָשָׂה פֶסַח לַיהֹוָה כְּחֻקַּת הַפֶּסַח וּכְמִשְׁפָּטוֹ כֵּן יַעֲשֶׂה חֻקָּה אַחַת יִהְיֶה לָכֶם וְלַגֵּר וּלְאֶזְרַח הָאָרֶץ:

15 On the day that the *Mishkan* was set up, the cloud covered the *Mishkan*, the Tent of the Pact; and in the evening it rested over the *Mishkan* in the likeness of fire until morning.

טו וּבְיוֹם הָקִים אֶת־הַמִּשְׁכָּן כִּסָּה הֶעָנָן אֶת־הַמִּשְׁכָּן לְאֹהֶל הָעֵדֻת וּבָעֶרֶב יִהְיֶה עַל־הַמִּשְׁכָּן כְּמַרְאֵה־אֵשׁ עַד־בֹּקֶר:

16 It was always so: the cloud covered it, appearing as fire by night.

טז כֵּן יִהְיֶה תָמִיד הֶעָנָן יְכַסֶּנּוּ וּמַרְאֵה־אֵשׁ לָיְלָה:

17 And whenever the cloud lifted from the Tent, the Israelites would set out accordingly; and at the spot where the cloud settled, there the Israelites would make camp.

יז וּלְפִי הֵעָלוֹת הֶעָנָן מֵעַל הָאֹהֶל וְאַחֲרֵי־כֵן יִסְעוּ בְּנֵי יִשְׂרָאֵל וּבִמְקוֹם אֲשֶׁר יִשְׁכָּן־שָׁם הֶעָנָן שָׁם יַחֲנוּ בְּנֵי יִשְׂרָאֵל:

18 At a command of *Hashem* the Israelites broke camp, and at a command of *Hashem* they made camp: they remained encamped as long as the cloud stayed over the *Mishkan*.

יח עַל־פִּי יְהֹוָה יִסְעוּ בְּנֵי יִשְׂרָאֵל וְעַל־פִּי יְהֹוָה יַחֲנוּ כָּל־יְמֵי אֲשֶׁר יִשְׁכֹּן הֶעָנָן עַל־הַמִּשְׁכָּן יַחֲנוּ:

al PEE a-do-NAI yis-U b'-NAY yis-ra-AYL v'-al PEE a-do-NAI ya-kha-NU kol y'-MAY a-SHER yish-KON he-a-NAN al ha-mish-KAN ya-kha-NU

19 When the cloud lingered over the *Mishkan* many days, the Israelites observed *Hashem*'s mandate and did not journey on.

יט וּבְהַאֲרִיךְ הֶעָנָן עַל־הַמִּשְׁכָּן יָמִים רַבִּים וְשָׁמְרוּ בְנֵי־יִשְׂרָאֵל אֶת־מִשְׁמֶרֶת יְהֹוָה וְלֹא יִסָּעוּ:

20 At such times as the cloud rested over the *Mishkan* for but a few days, they remained encamped at a command of *Hashem*, and broke camp at a command of *Hashem*.

כ וְיֵשׁ אֲשֶׁר יִהְיֶה הֶעָנָן יָמִים מִסְפָּר עַל־הַמִּשְׁכָּן עַל־פִּי יְהֹוָה יַחֲנוּ וְעַל־פִּי יְהֹוָה יִסָּעוּ:

21 And at such times as the cloud stayed from evening until morning, they broke camp as soon as the cloud lifted in the morning. Day or night, whenever the cloud lifted, they would break camp.

כא וְיֵשׁ אֲשֶׁר־יִהְיֶה הֶעָנָן מֵעֶרֶב עַד־בֹּקֶר וְנַעֲלָה הֶעָנָן בַּבֹּקֶר וְנָסָעוּ אוֹ יוֹמָם וָלַיְלָה וְנַעֲלָה הֶעָנָן וְנָסָעוּ:

22 Whether it was two days or a month or a year – however long the cloud lingered over the *Mishkan* – the Israelites remained encamped and did not set out; only when it lifted did they break camp.

כב אוֹ־יֹמַיִם אוֹ־חֹדֶשׁ אוֹ־יָמִים בְּהַאֲרִיךְ הֶעָנָן עַל־הַמִּשְׁכָּן לִשְׁכֹּן עָלָיו יַחֲנוּ בְנֵי־יִשְׂרָאֵל וְלֹא יִסָּעוּ וּבְהֵעָלֹתוֹ יִסָּעוּ:

Bamidbar/Numbers 10
Beha'alotcha

23 On a sign from *Hashem* they made camp and on a sign from *Hashem* they broke camp; they observed *Hashem*'s mandate at *Hashem*'s bidding through *Moshe*.

10 1 *Hashem* spoke to *Moshe*, saying:

2 Have two silver trumpets made; make them of hammered work. They shall serve you to summon the community and to set the divisions in motion.

3 When both are blown in long blasts, the whole community shall assemble before you at the entrance of the Tent of Meeting;

4 and if only one is blown, the chieftains, heads of *Yisrael*'s contingents, shall assemble before you.

5 But when you sound short blasts, the divisions encamped on the east shall move forward;

6 and when you sound short blasts a second time, those encamped on the south shall move forward. Thus short blasts shall be blown for setting them in motion,

7 while to convoke the congregation you shall blow long blasts, not short ones.

8 The trumpets shall be blown by *Aharon*'s sons, the *Kohanim*; they shall be for you an institution for all time throughout the ages.

9 When you are at war in your land against an aggressor who attacks you, you shall sound short blasts on the trumpets, that you may be remembered before *Hashem* your God and be delivered from your enemies.

10 And on your joyous occasions – your fixed festivals and new moon days – you shall sound the trumpets over your burnt offerings and your sacrifices of well-being. They shall be a reminder of you before your God: I, *Hashem*, am your God.

11 In the second year, on the twentieth day of the second month, the cloud lifted from the *Mishkan* of the Pact

12 and the Israelites set out on their journeys from the wilderness of Sinai. The cloud came to rest in the wilderness of Paran.

13 When the march was to begin, at *Hashem*'s command through *Moshe*,

במדבר י
בהעלתך

כג עַל־פִּי יְהֹוָה יַחֲנוּ וְעַל־פִּי יְהֹוָה יִסָּעוּ אֶת־מִשְׁמֶרֶת יְהֹוָה שָׁמָרוּ עַל־פִּי יְהֹוָה בְּיַד־מֹשֶׁה׃

י א וַיְדַבֵּר יְהֹוָה אֶל־מֹשֶׁה לֵּאמֹר׃

ב עֲשֵׂה לְךָ שְׁתֵּי חֲצוֹצְרֹת כֶּסֶף מִקְשָׁה תַּעֲשֶׂה אֹתָם וְהָיוּ לְךָ לְמִקְרָא הָעֵדָה וּלְמַסַּע אֶת־הַמַּחֲנוֹת׃

ג וְתָקְעוּ בָּהֵן וְנוֹעֲדוּ אֵלֶיךָ כָּל־הָעֵדָה אֶל־פֶּתַח אֹהֶל מוֹעֵד׃

ד וְאִם־בְּאַחַת יִתְקָעוּ וְנוֹעֲדוּ אֵלֶיךָ הַנְּשִׂיאִים רָאשֵׁי אַלְפֵי יִשְׂרָאֵל׃

ה וּתְקַעְתֶּם תְּרוּעָה וְנָסְעוּ הַמַּחֲנוֹת הַחֹנִים קֵדְמָה׃

ו וּתְקַעְתֶּם תְּרוּעָה שֵׁנִית וְנָסְעוּ הַמַּחֲנוֹת הַחֹנִים תֵּימָנָה תְּרוּעָה יִתְקְעוּ לְמַסְעֵיהֶם׃

ז וּבְהַקְהִיל אֶת־הַקָּהָל תִּתְקְעוּ וְלֹא תָרִיעוּ׃

ח וּבְנֵי אַהֲרֹן הַכֹּהֲנִים יִתְקְעוּ בַּחֲצֹצְרוֹת וְהָיוּ לָכֶם לְחֻקַּת עוֹלָם לְדֹרֹתֵיכֶם׃

ט וְכִי־תָבֹאוּ מִלְחָמָה בְּאַרְצְכֶם עַל־הַצַּר הַצֹּרֵר אֶתְכֶם וַהֲרֵעֹתֶם בַּחֲצֹצְרוֹת וְנִזְכַּרְתֶּם לִפְנֵי יְהֹוָה אֱלֹהֵיכֶם וְנוֹשַׁעְתֶּם מֵאֹיְבֵיכֶם׃

י וּבְיוֹם שִׂמְחַתְכֶם וּבְמוֹעֲדֵיכֶם וּבְרָאשֵׁי חָדְשֵׁיכֶם וּתְקַעְתֶּם בַּחֲצֹצְרֹת עַל עֹלֹתֵיכֶם וְעַל זִבְחֵי שַׁלְמֵיכֶם וְהָיוּ לָכֶם לְזִכָּרוֹן לִפְנֵי אֱלֹהֵיכֶם אֲנִי יְהֹוָה אֱלֹהֵיכֶם׃

יא וַיְהִי בַּשָּׁנָה הַשֵּׁנִית בַּחֹדֶשׁ הַשֵּׁנִי בְּעֶשְׂרִים בַּחֹדֶשׁ נַעֲלָה הֶעָנָן מֵעַל מִשְׁכַּן הָעֵדֻת׃

יב וַיִּסְעוּ בְנֵי־יִשְׂרָאֵל לְמַסְעֵיהֶם מִמִּדְבַּר סִינָי וַיִּשְׁכֹּן הֶעָנָן בְּמִדְבַּר פָּארָן׃

יג וַיִּסְעוּ בָּרִאשֹׁנָה עַל־פִּי יְהֹוָה בְּיַד־מֹשֶׁה׃

Bamidbar/Numbers 10
Beha'alotcha

במדבר י
בהעלתך

14 the first standard to set out, troop by troop, was the division of *Yehuda*. In command of its troops was *Nachshon* son of *Aminadav*;

יד וַיִּסַּע דֶּגֶל מַחֲנֵה בְנֵי־יְהוּדָה בָּרִאשֹׁנָה לְצִבְאֹתָם וְעַל־צְבָאוֹ נַחְשׁוֹן בֶּן־עַמִּינָדָב:

15 in command of the tribal troop of *Yissachar*, *Netanel* son of Zuar;

טו וְעַל־צְבָא מַטֵּה בְּנֵי יִשָּׂשכָר נְתַנְאֵל בֶּן־צוּעָר:

16 and in command of the tribal troop of *Zevulun*, *Eliav* son of Helon.

טז וְעַל־צְבָא מַטֵּה בְּנֵי זְבוּלֻן אֱלִיאָב בֶּן־חֵלֹן:

17 Then the *Mishkan* would be taken apart; and the Gershonites and the Merarites, who carried the *Mishkan*, would set out.

יז וְהוּרַד הַמִּשְׁכָּן וְנָסְעוּ בְנֵי־גֵרְשׁוֹן וּבְנֵי מְרָרִי נֹשְׂאֵי הַמִּשְׁכָּן:

18 The next standard to set out, troop by troop, was the division of *Reuven*. In command of its troop was *Elitzur* son of Shedeur;

יח וְנָסַע דֶּגֶל מַחֲנֵה רְאוּבֵן לְצִבְאֹתָם וְעַל־צְבָאוֹ אֱלִיצוּר בֶּן־שְׁדֵיאוּר:

19 in command of the tribal troop of *Shimon*, *Shelumiel* son of Zurishaddai;

יט וְעַל־צְבָא מַטֵּה בְּנֵי שִׁמְעוֹן שְׁלֻמִיאֵל בֶּן־צוּרִי שַׁדָּי:

20 and in command of the tribal troop of *Gad*, *Elyasaf* son of Deuel.

כ וְעַל־צְבָא מַטֵּה בְּנֵי־גָד אֶלְיָסָף בֶּן־דְּעוּאֵל:

21 Then the Kohathites, who carried the sacred objects, would set out; and by the time they arrived, the *Mishkan* would be set up again.

כא וְנָסְעוּ הַקְּהָתִים נֹשְׂאֵי הַמִּקְדָּשׁ וְהֵקִימוּ אֶת־הַמִּשְׁכָּן עַד־בֹּאָם:

22 The next standard to set out, troop by troop, was the division of *Efraim*. In command of its troop was *Elishama* son of Ammihud;

כב וְנָסַע דֶּגֶל מַחֲנֵה בְנֵי־אֶפְרַיִם לְצִבְאֹתָם וְעַל־צְבָאוֹ אֱלִישָׁמָע בֶּן־עַמִּיהוּד:

23 in command of the tribal troop of *Menashe*, *Gamliel* son of Pedahzur;

כג וְעַל־צְבָא מַטֵּה בְּנֵי מְנַשֶּׁה גַּמְלִיאֵל בֶּן־פְּדָה־צוּר:

24 and in command of the tribal troop of *Binyamin*, *Avidan* son of Gideoni.

כד וְעַל־צְבָא מַטֵּה בְּנֵי בִנְיָמִן אֲבִידָן בֶּן־גִּדְעוֹנִי:

25 Then, as the rear guard of all the divisions, the standard of the division of *Dan* would set out, troop by troop. In command of its troop was *Achiezer* son of Ammishaddai;

כה וְנָסַע דֶּגֶל מַחֲנֵה בְנֵי־דָן מְאַסֵּף לְכָל־הַמַּחֲנֹת לְצִבְאֹתָם וְעַל־צְבָאוֹ אֲחִיעֶזֶר בֶּן־עַמִּישַׁדָּי:

26 in command of the tribal troop of *Asher*, *Pagiel* son of Ochran;

כו וְעַל־צְבָא מַטֵּה בְּנֵי אָשֵׁר פַּגְעִיאֵל בֶּן־עָכְרָן:

27 and in command of the tribal troop of *Naftali*, *Achira* son of Enan.

כז וְעַל־צְבָא מַטֵּה בְּנֵי נַפְתָּלִי אֲחִירַע בֶּן־עֵינָן:

28 Such was the order of march of the Israelites, as they marched troop by troop.

כח אֵלֶּה מַסְעֵי בְנֵי־יִשְׂרָאֵל לְצִבְאֹתָם וַיִּסָּעוּ:

Bamidbar/Numbers 11
Beha'alotcha

במדבר יא
בהעלתך

29 *Moshe* said to Hobab son of Reuel the Midianite, *Moshe*'s father-in-law, "We are setting out for the place of which *Hashem* has said, 'I will give it to you.' Come with us and we will be generous with you; for *Hashem* has promised to be generous to *Yisrael*."

כט וַיֹּאמֶר מֹשֶׁה לְחֹבָב בֶּן־רְעוּאֵל הַמִּדְיָנִי חֹתֵן מֹשֶׁה נֹסְעִים אֲנַחְנוּ אֶל־הַמָּקוֹם אֲשֶׁר אָמַר יְהוָה אֹתוֹ אֶתֵּן לָכֶם לְכָה אִתָּנוּ וְהֵטַבְנוּ לָךְ כִּי־יְהוָה דִּבֶּר־טוֹב עַל־יִשְׂרָאֵל:

va-YO-mer mo-SHEH l'-kho-VAV ben r'-u-AYL ha-mid-ya-NEE kho-TAYN mo-SHEH no-s'-EEM a-NAKH-nu el ha-ma-KOM a-SHER a-MAR a-do-NAI o-TO e-TAYN la-KHEM l'-KHAH i-TA-nu v'-hay-TAV-nu LAKH kee a-do-NAI di-ber TOV al yis-ra-AYL

30 "I will not go," he replied to him, "but will return to my native land."

ל וַיֹּאמֶר אֵלָיו לֹא אֵלֵךְ כִּי אִם־אֶל־אַרְצִי וְאֶל־מוֹלַדְתִּי אֵלֵךְ:

31 He said, "Please do not leave us, inasmuch as you know where we should camp in the wilderness and can be our guide.

לא וַיֹּאמֶר אַל־נָא תַּעֲזֹב אֹתָנוּ כִּי עַל־כֵּן יָדַעְתָּ חֲנֹתֵנוּ בַּמִּדְבָּר וְהָיִיתָ לָּנוּ לְעֵינָיִם:

32 So if you come with us, we will extend to you the same bounty that *Hashem* grants us."

לב וְהָיָה כִּי־תֵלֵךְ עִמָּנוּ וְהָיָה הַטּוֹב הַהוּא אֲשֶׁר יֵיטִיב יְהוָה עִמָּנוּ וְהֵטַבְנוּ לָךְ:

33 They marched from the mountain of *Hashem* a distance of three days. The *Aron Brit Hashem* traveled in front of them on that three days' journey to seek out a resting place for them;

לג וַיִּסְעוּ מֵהַר יְהוָה דֶּרֶךְ שְׁלֹשֶׁת יָמִים וַאֲרוֹן בְּרִית־יְהוָה נֹסֵעַ לִפְנֵיהֶם דֶּרֶךְ שְׁלֹשֶׁת יָמִים לָתוּר לָהֶם מְנוּחָה:

34 and *Hashem*'s cloud kept above them by day, as they moved on from camp.

לד וַעֲנַן יְהוָה עֲלֵיהֶם יוֹמָם בְּנָסְעָם מִן־הַמַּחֲנֶה:

35 When the *Aron* was to set out, *Moshe* would say: Advance, *Hashem*! May Your enemies be scattered, And may Your foes flee before You!

לה וַיְהִי בִּנְסֹעַ הָאָרֹן וַיֹּאמֶר מֹשֶׁה קוּמָה יְהוָה וְיָפֻצוּ אֹיְבֶיךָ וְיָנֻסוּ מְשַׂנְאֶיךָ מִפָּנֶיךָ:

vai-HEE bin-SO-a ha-a-RON va-YO-mer mo-SHEH ku-MAH a-do-NAI v'-ya-FU-tzu o-y'-VE-kka v'-ya-NU-su m'-san-E-khah mi-pa-NE-khah

36 And when it halted, he would say: Return, *Hashem*, You who are *Yisrael*'s myriads of thousands!

לו וּבְנֻחֹה יֹאמַר שׁוּבָה יְהוָה רִבְבוֹת אַלְפֵי יִשְׂרָאֵל:

uv-nu-KHOH yo-MAR shu-VAH a-do-NAI ri-v'-VOT al-FAY yis-ra-AYL

11 1 The people took to complaining bitterly before *Hashem*. *Hashem* heard and was incensed: a fire of *Hashem* broke out against them, ravaging the outskirts of the camp.

יא א וַיְהִי הָעָם כְּמִתְאֹנְנִים רַע בְּאָזְנֵי יְהוָה וַיִּשְׁמַע יְהוָה וַיִּחַר אַפּוֹ וַתִּבְעַר־בָּם אֵשׁ יְהוָה וַתֹּאכַל בִּקְצֵה הַמַּחֲנֶה:

10:35–36 When the *Aron* was to set out The Holy Ark travels with the Jewish people throughout their journey to the Promised Land, reminding them of God's presence within their camp. The Ark of the Covenant contained the Tablets of the Law – concretizing and symbolizing the entire *Torah* given to *Moshe* by *Hashem*. Just as the *Aron* was the focal point of the Israelites' existence in the desert, so too the Bible must always be the central focus of our own lives.

Bamidbar/Numbers 11
Beha'alotcha

2 The people cried out to *Moshe*. *Moshe* prayed to *Hashem*, and the fire died down.

3 That place was named Taberah, because a fire of *Hashem* had broken out against them.

4 The riffraff in their midst felt a gluttonous craving; and then the Israelites wept and said, "If only we had meat to eat!

5 We remember the fish that we used to eat free in Egypt, the cucumbers, the melons, the leeks, the onions, and the garlic.

6 Now our gullets are shriveled. There is nothing at all! Nothing but this manna to look to!"

7 Now the manna was like coriander seed, and in color it was like bdellium.

8 The people would go about and gather it, grind it between millstones or pound it in a mortar, boil it in a pot, and make it into cakes. It tasted like rich cream.

9 When the dew fell on the camp at night, the manna would fall upon it.

10 *Moshe* heard the people weeping, every clan apart, each person at the entrance of his tent. *Hashem* was very angry, and *Moshe* was distressed.

11 And *Moshe* said to *Hashem*, "Why have You dealt ill with Your servant, and why have I not enjoyed Your favor, that You have laid the burden of all this people upon me?

12 Did I conceive all this people, did I bear them, that You should say to me, 'Carry them in your bosom as a nurse carries an infant,' to the land that You have promised on oath to their fathers?

13 Where am I to get meat to give to all this people, when they whine before me and say, 'Give us meat to eat!'

14 I cannot carry all this people by myself, for it is too much for me.

15 If You would deal thus with me, kill me rather, I beg You, and let me see no more of my wretchedness!"

Bamidbar/Numbers 11
Beha'alotcha

במדבר יא
בהעלתך

16 Then *Hashem* said to *Moshe*, "Gather for Me seventy of *Yisrael*'s elders of whom you have experience as elders and officers of the people, and bring them to the Tent of Meeting and let them take their place there with you.

טז וַיֹּאמֶר יְהוָה אֶל־מֹשֶׁה אֶסְפָה־לִּי שִׁבְעִים אִישׁ מִזִּקְנֵי יִשְׂרָאֵל אֲשֶׁר יָדַעְתָּ כִּי־הֵם זִקְנֵי הָעָם וְשֹׁטְרָיו וְלָקַחְתָּ אֹתָם אֶל־אֹהֶל מוֹעֵד וְהִתְיַצְּבוּ שָׁם עִמָּךְ:

17 I will come down and speak with you there, and I will draw upon the spirit that is on you and put it upon them; they shall share the burden of the people with you, and you shall not bear it alone.

יז וְיָרַדְתִּי וְדִבַּרְתִּי עִמְּךָ שָׁם וְאָצַלְתִּי מִן־הָרוּחַ אֲשֶׁר עָלֶיךָ וְשַׂמְתִּי עֲלֵיהֶם וְנָשְׂאוּ אִתְּךָ בְּמַשָּׂא הָעָם וְלֹא־תִשָּׂא אַתָּה לְבַדֶּךָ:

v'-ya-rad-TEE v'-di-bar-TEE i-m'-KHA SHAM v'-a-tzal-TEE min ha-RU-akh a-SHER a-LE-kha v'-sam-TEE a-lay-HEM v'-na-s'-U i-t'-KHA b'-ma-SA ha-AM v'-lo ti-SA a-TAH l'-va-DE-kha

18 And say to the people: Purify yourselves for tomorrow and you shall eat meat, for you have kept whining before *Hashem* and saying, 'If only we had meat to eat! Indeed, we were better off in Egypt!' *Hashem* will give you meat and you shall eat.

יח וְאֶל־הָעָם תֹּאמַר הִתְקַדְּשׁוּ לְמָחָר וַאֲכַלְתֶּם בָּשָׂר כִּי בְּכִיתֶם בְּאָזְנֵי יְהוָה לֵאמֹר מִי יַאֲכִלֵנוּ בָּשָׂר כִּי־טוֹב לָנוּ בְּמִצְרָיִם וְנָתַן יְהוָה לָכֶם בָּשָׂר וַאֲכַלְתֶּם:

19 You shall eat not one day, not two, not even five days or ten or twenty,

יט לֹא יוֹם אֶחָד תֹּאכְלוּן וְלֹא יוֹמָיִם וְלֹא חֲמִשָּׁה יָמִים וְלֹא עֲשָׂרָה יָמִים וְלֹא עֶשְׂרִים יוֹם:

20 but a whole month, until it comes out of your nostrils and becomes loathsome to you. For you have rejected *Hashem* who is among you, by whining before Him and saying, 'Oh, why did we ever leave Egypt!'"

כ עַד חֹדֶשׁ יָמִים עַד אֲשֶׁר־יֵצֵא מֵאַפְּכֶם וְהָיָה לָכֶם לְזָרָא יַעַן כִּי־מְאַסְתֶּם אֶת־יְהוָה אֲשֶׁר בְּקִרְבְּכֶם וַתִּבְכּוּ לְפָנָיו לֵאמֹר לָמָּה זֶּה יָצָאנוּ מִמִּצְרָיִם:

21 But *Moshe* said, "The people who are with me number six hundred thousand men; yet You say, 'I will give them enough meat to eat for a whole month.'

כא וַיֹּאמֶר מֹשֶׁה שֵׁשׁ־מֵאוֹת אֶלֶף רַגְלִי הָעָם אֲשֶׁר אָנֹכִי בְּקִרְבּוֹ וְאַתָּה אָמַרְתָּ בָּשָׂר אֶתֵּן לָהֶם וְאָכְלוּ חֹדֶשׁ יָמִים:

Replica of the Temple menorah

11:17 And I will draw upon the spirit that is on you and put it upon them In his commentary to this verse, *Rashi*, compares *Moshe* to a candle. Just as one candle can light many others without diminishing its own flame, *Moshe*'s spirit will inspire the seventy elders he is about to gather, but his own spirit will not become lacking as a result. Candles are often thought of as a symbol of spirituality. The *Shabbat* is brought in with the lighting of candles, and its completion is marked with the *havdala* ceremony, which also features a lit candle. Just as the flame of a candle can illuminate a dark room, the holiness of *Shabbat* is meant to radiate and illuminate the rest of the week. Similarly, candles were lit daily on the *menorah*, 'lamp,' in the *Beit Hamikdash*. According to the Sages of the *Midrash*, the *menorah* was not designed to provide light in the sanctuary, but rather to spread light and holiness to the rest of the world. For this reason, the windows of the *Beit Hamikdash* were constructed with a unique design, narrow on the inside and wide on the outside (see I Kings 6:4). The *Beit Hamikdash* in *Yerushalayim* is the source of holiness in the world; it is the duty of the Children of Israel to spread that holiness and serve as a "light unto the nations" (Isaiah 42:6, 49:6).

Bamidbar/Numbers 11
Beha'alotcha

22 Could enough flocks and herds be slaughtered to suffice them? Or could all the fish of the sea be gathered for them to suffice them?"

23 And *Hashem* answered *Moshe*, "Is there a limit to *Hashem*'s power? You shall soon see whether what I have said happens to you or not!"

24 *Moshe* went out and reported the words of *Hashem* to the people. He gathered seventy of the people's elders and stationed them around the Tent.

25 Then *Hashem* came down in a cloud and spoke to him; He drew upon the spirit that was on him and put it upon the seventy elders. And when the spirit rested upon them, they spoke in ecstasy, but did not continue.

26 Two men, one named Eldad and the other Medad, had remained in camp; yet the spirit rested upon them – they were among those recorded, but they had not gone out to the Tent – and they spoke in ecstasy in the camp.

27 A youth ran out and told *Moshe*, saying, "Eldad and Medad are acting the *navi* in the camp!"

28 And *Yehoshua* son of *Nun*, *Moshe*'s attendant from his youth, spoke up and said, "My lord *Moshe*, restrain them!"

29 But *Moshe* said to him, "Are you wrought up on my account? Would that all *Hashem*'s people were *Neviim*, that *Hashem* put His spirit upon them!"

30 *Moshe* then reentered the camp together with the elders of *Yisrael*.

31 A wind from *Hashem* started up, swept quail from the sea and strewed them over the camp, about a day's journey on this side and about a day's journey on that side, all around the camp, and some two *amot* deep on the ground.

32 The people set to gathering quail all that day and night and all the next day – even he who gathered least had ten *chomarim* – and they spread them out all around the camp.

33 The meat was still between their teeth, nor yet chewed, when the anger of *Hashem* blazed forth against the people and *Hashem* struck the people with a very severe plague.

במדבר יא
בהעלתך

כב הֲצֹאן וּבָקָר יִשָּׁחֵט לָהֶם וּמָצָא לָהֶם אִם אֶת־כָּל־דְּגֵי הַיָּם יֵאָסֵף לָהֶם וּמָצָא לָהֶם׃

כג וַיֹּאמֶר יְהֹוָה אֶל־מֹשֶׁה הֲיַד יְהֹוָה תִּקְצָר עַתָּה תִרְאֶה הֲיִקְרְךָ דְבָרִי אִם־לֹא׃

כד וַיֵּצֵא מֹשֶׁה וַיְדַבֵּר אֶל־הָעָם אֵת דִּבְרֵי יְהֹוָה וַיֶּאֱסֹף שִׁבְעִים אִישׁ מִזִּקְנֵי הָעָם וַיַּעֲמֵד אֹתָם סְבִיבֹת הָאֹהֶל׃

כה וַיֵּרֶד יְהֹוָה בֶּעָנָן וַיְדַבֵּר אֵלָיו וַיָּאצֶל מִן־הָרוּחַ אֲשֶׁר עָלָיו וַיִּתֵּן עַל־שִׁבְעִים אִישׁ הַזְּקֵנִים וַיְהִי כְּנוֹחַ עֲלֵיהֶם הָרוּחַ וַיִּתְנַבְּאוּ וְלֹא יָסָפוּ׃

כו וַיִּשָּׁאֲרוּ שְׁנֵי־אֲנָשִׁים בַּמַּחֲנֶה שֵׁם הָאֶחָד אֶלְדָּד וְשֵׁם הַשֵּׁנִי מֵידָד וַתָּנַח עֲלֵהֶם הָרוּחַ וְהֵמָּה בַּכְּתֻבִים וְלֹא יָצְאוּ הָאֹהֱלָה וַיִּתְנַבְּאוּ בַּמַּחֲנֶה׃

כז וַיָּרָץ הַנַּעַר וַיַּגֵּד לְמֹשֶׁה וַיֹּאמַר אֶלְדָּד וּמֵידָד מִתְנַבְּאִים בַּמַּחֲנֶה׃

כח וַיַּעַן יְהוֹשֻׁעַ בִּן־נוּן מְשָׁרֵת מֹשֶׁה מִבְּחֻרָיו וַיֹּאמַר אֲדֹנִי מֹשֶׁה כְּלָאֵם׃

כט וַיֹּאמֶר לוֹ מֹשֶׁה הַמְקַנֵּא אַתָּה לִי וּמִי יִתֵּן כָּל־עַם יְהֹוָה נְבִיאִים כִּי־יִתֵּן יְהֹוָה אֶת־רוּחוֹ עֲלֵיהֶם׃

ל וַיֵּאָסֵף מֹשֶׁה אֶל־הַמַּחֲנֶה הוּא וְזִקְנֵי יִשְׂרָאֵל׃

לא וְרוּחַ נָסַע מֵאֵת יְהֹוָה וַיָּגָז שַׂלְוִים מִן־הַיָּם וַיִּטֹּשׁ עַל־הַמַּחֲנֶה כְּדֶרֶךְ יוֹם כֹּה וּכְדֶרֶךְ יוֹם כֹּה סְבִיבוֹת הַמַּחֲנֶה וּכְאַמָּתַיִם עַל־פְּנֵי הָאָרֶץ׃

לב וַיָּקָם הָעָם כָּל־הַיּוֹם הַהוּא וְכָל־הַלַּיְלָה וְכֹל ׀ יוֹם הַמָּחֳרָת וַיַּאַסְפוּ אֶת־הַשְּׂלָו הַמַּמְעִיט אָסַף עֲשָׂרָה חֳמָרִים וַיִּשְׁטְחוּ לָהֶם שָׁטוֹחַ סְבִיבוֹת הַמַּחֲנֶה׃

לג הַבָּשָׂר עוֹדֶנּוּ בֵּין שִׁנֵּיהֶם טֶרֶם יִכָּרֵת וְאַף יְהֹוָה חָרָה בָעָם וַיַּךְ יְהֹוָה בָּעָם מַכָּה רַבָּה מְאֹד׃

Bamidbar/Numbers 12
Beha'alotcha

במדבר יב
בהעלתך

34 That place was named Kibroth-hattaavah, because the people who had the craving were buried there.

וַיִּקְרָא אֶת־שֵׁם־הַמָּקוֹם הַהוּא קִבְרוֹת הַתַּאֲוָה כִּי־שָׁם קָבְרוּ אֶת־הָעָם הַמִּתְאַוִּים:

35 Then the people set out from Kibroth-hattaavah for Hazeroth. When they were in Hazeroth,

מִקִּבְרוֹת הַתַּאֲוָה נָסְעוּ הָעָם חֲצֵרוֹת וַיִּהְיוּ בַּחֲצֵרוֹת:

12 1 *Miriam* and *Aharon* spoke against *Moshe* because of the Cushite woman he had married: "He married a Cushite woman!"

וַתְּדַבֵּר מִרְיָם וְאַהֲרֹן בְּמֹשֶׁה עַל־אֹדוֹת הָאִשָּׁה הַכֻּשִׁית אֲשֶׁר לָקָח כִּי־אִשָּׁה כֻשִׁית לָקָח:

2 They said, "Has *Hashem* spoken only through *Moshe*? Has He not spoken through us as well?" *Hashem* heard it.

וַיֹּאמְרוּ הֲרַק אַךְ־בְּמֹשֶׁה דִּבֶּר יְהוָה הֲלֹא גַּם־בָּנוּ דִבֵּר וַיִּשְׁמַע יְהוָה:

3 Now *Moshe* was a very humble man, more so than any other man on earth.

וְהָאִישׁ מֹשֶׁה עָנָו [עָנָיו] מְאֹד מִכֹּל הָאָדָם אֲשֶׁר עַל־פְּנֵי הָאֲדָמָה:

4 Suddenly *Hashem* called to *Moshe*, *Aharon*, and *Miriam*, "Come out, you three, to the Tent of Meeting." So the three of them went out.

וַיֹּאמֶר יְהוָה פִּתְאֹם אֶל־מֹשֶׁה וְאֶל־אַהֲרֹן וְאֶל־מִרְיָם צְאוּ שְׁלָשְׁתְּכֶם אֶל־אֹהֶל מוֹעֵד וַיֵּצְאוּ שְׁלָשְׁתָּם:

5 *Hashem* came down in a pillar of cloud, stopped at the entrance of the Tent, and called out, "*Aharon* and *Miriam*!" The two of them came forward;

וַיֵּרֶד יְהוָה בְּעַמּוּד עָנָן וַיַּעֲמֹד פֶּתַח הָאֹהֶל וַיִּקְרָא אַהֲרֹן וּמִרְיָם וַיֵּצְאוּ שְׁנֵיהֶם:

6 and He said, "Hear these My words: When a *navi* of *Hashem* arises among you, I make Myself known to him in a vision, I speak with him in a dream.

וַיֹּאמֶר שִׁמְעוּ־נָא דְבָרָי אִם־יִהְיֶה נְבִיאֲכֶם יְהוָה בַּמַּרְאָה אֵלָיו אֶתְוַדָּע בַּחֲלוֹם אֲדַבֶּר־בּוֹ:

7 Not so with My servant *Moshe*; he is trusted throughout My household.

לֹא־כֵן עַבְדִּי מֹשֶׁה בְּכָל־בֵּיתִי נֶאֱמָן הוּא:

8 With him I speak mouth to mouth, plainly and not in riddles, and he beholds the likeness of *Hashem*. How then did you not shrink from speaking against My servant *Moshe*!"

פֶּה אֶל־פֶּה אֲדַבֶּר־בּוֹ וּמַרְאֶה וְלֹא בְחִידֹת וּתְמֻנַת יְהוָה יַבִּיט וּמַדּוּעַ לֹא יְרֵאתֶם לְדַבֵּר בְּעַבְדִּי בְמֹשֶׁה:

PEH el PEH a-da-bayr BO u-mar-EH v'-LO v'-khee-DOT ut-mu-NAT a-do-NAI ya-BEET u-ma-DU-a LO y'-ray-TEM l'-da-BAYR b'-av-DEE v'-mo-SHEH

9 Still incensed with them, *Hashem* departed.

וַיִּחַר אַף יְהוָה בָּם וַיֵּלַךְ:

12:8 With him I speak mouth to mouth The prophecy of *Moshe* was qualitatively different than that of any other prophet to have ever lived. According to Jewish teachings, prophets generally received their prophecy in a dream or trance, and were given a message that they needed to decode before they could deliver it to the people. They expressed and wrote these messages in their own words, though the messages themselves were divine. *Moshe's* prophecy, though, was different. As the verse indicates, he spoke to God, as it were, "face to face." When receiving his prophecy, *Moshe* was fully conscious, and he heard *Hashem's* messages word for word. It is through this level of prophecy that the Five Books of *Moshe* were written; not only are the messages of the books divine, but the words themselves were given directly by *Hashem*.

Bamidbar/Numbers 13
Shelach

10 As the cloud withdrew from the Tent, there was *Miriam* stricken with snow-white scales! When *Aharon* turned toward *Miriam*, he saw that she was stricken with scales.

11 And *Aharon* said to *Moshe*, "O my lord, account not to us the sin which we committed in our folly.

12 Let her not be as one dead, who emerges from his mother's womb with half his flesh eaten away."

13 So *Moshe* cried out to *Hashem*, saying, "O *Hashem*, pray heal her!"

14 But *Hashem* said to *Moshe*, "If her father spat in her face, would she not bear her shame for seven days? Let her be shut out of camp for seven days, and then let her be readmitted."

15 So *Miriam* was shut out of camp seven days; and the people did not march on until *Miriam* was readmitted.

16 After that the people set out from Hazeroth and encamped in the wilderness of Paran.

13

1 *Hashem* spoke to *Moshe*, saying,

2 "Send men to scout the land of Canaan, which I am giving to *B'nei Yisrael*; send one man from each of their ancestral tribes, each one a chieftain among them."

3 So *Moshe*, by *Hashem*'s command, sent them out from the wilderness of Paran, all the men being leaders of the Israelites.

4 And these were their names: From the tribe of *Reuven*, *Shamua* son of Zaccur.

5 From the tribe of *Shimon*, *Shafat* son of Hori.

6 From the tribe of *Yehuda*, *Kalev* son of Jephunneh.

7 From the tribe of *Yissachar*, *Yigal* son of *Yosef*.

8 From the tribe of *Efraim*, *Hoshea* son of Nun.

9 From the tribe of *Binyamin*, *Palti* son of Rafu.

10 From the tribe of *Zevulun*, *Gadiel* son of Sodi.

11 From the tribe of *Yosef*, namely, the tribe of *Menashe*, *Gadi* son of Susi.

במדבר יג
שלח

י וְהֶעָנָן סָר מֵעַל הָאֹהֶל וְהִנֵּה מִרְיָם מְצֹרַעַת כַּשָּׁלֶג וַיִּפֶן אַהֲרֹן אֶל־מִרְיָם וְהִנֵּה מְצֹרָעַת:

יא וַיֹּאמֶר אַהֲרֹן אֶל־מֹשֶׁה בִּי אֲדֹנִי אַל־נָא תָשֵׁת עָלֵינוּ חַטָּאת אֲשֶׁר נוֹאַלְנוּ וַאֲשֶׁר חָטָאנוּ:

יב אַל־נָא תְהִי כַּמֵּת אֲשֶׁר בְּצֵאתוֹ מֵרֶחֶם אִמּוֹ וַיֵּאָכֵל חֲצִי בְשָׂרוֹ:

יג וַיִּצְעַק מֹשֶׁה אֶל־יְהֹוָה לֵאמֹר אֵל נָא רְפָא נָא לָהּ:

יד וַיֹּאמֶר יְהֹוָה אֶל־מֹשֶׁה וְאָבִיהָ יָרֹק יָרַק בְּפָנֶיהָ הֲלֹא תִכָּלֵם שִׁבְעַת יָמִים תִּסָּגֵר שִׁבְעַת יָמִים מִחוּץ לַמַּחֲנֶה וְאַחַר תֵּאָסֵף:

טו וַתִּסָּגֵר מִרְיָם מִחוּץ לַמַּחֲנֶה שִׁבְעַת יָמִים וְהָעָם לֹא נָסַע עַד־הֵאָסֵף מִרְיָם:

טז וְאַחַר נָסְעוּ הָעָם מֵחֲצֵרוֹת וַיַּחֲנוּ בְּמִדְבַּר פָּארָן:

יג

א וַיְדַבֵּר יְהֹוָה אֶל־מֹשֶׁה לֵּאמֹר:

ב שְׁלַח־לְךָ אֲנָשִׁים וְיָתֻרוּ אֶת־אֶרֶץ כְּנַעַן אֲשֶׁר־אֲנִי נֹתֵן לִבְנֵי יִשְׂרָאֵל אִישׁ אֶחָד אִישׁ אֶחָד לְמַטֵּה אֲבֹתָיו תִּשְׁלָחוּ כֹּל נָשִׂיא בָהֶם:

ג וַיִּשְׁלַח אֹתָם מֹשֶׁה מִמִּדְבַּר פָּארָן עַל־פִּי יְהֹוָה כֻּלָּם אֲנָשִׁים רָאשֵׁי בְנֵי־יִשְׂרָאֵל הֵמָּה:

ד וְאֵלֶּה שְׁמוֹתָם לְמַטֵּה רְאוּבֵן שַׁמּוּעַ בֶּן־זַכּוּר:

ה לְמַטֵּה שִׁמְעוֹן שָׁפָט בֶּן־חוֹרִי:

ו לְמַטֵּה יְהוּדָה כָּלֵב בֶּן־יְפֻנֶּה:

ז לְמַטֵּה יִשָּׂשכָר יִגְאָל בֶּן־יוֹסֵף:

ח לְמַטֵּה אֶפְרָיִם הוֹשֵׁעַ בִּן־נוּן:

ט לְמַטֵּה בִנְיָמִן פַּלְטִי בֶּן־רָפוּא:

י לְמַטֵּה זְבוּלֻן גַּדִּיאֵל בֶּן־סוֹדִי:

יא לְמַטֵּה יוֹסֵף לְמַטֵּה מְנַשֶּׁה גַּדִּי בֶּן־סוּסִי:

Bamidbar/Numbers 13
Shelach

במדבר יג
שלח

12 From the tribe of *Dan*, *Amiel* son of Gemalli.

יב לְמַטֵּה דָן עַמִּיאֵל בֶּן־גְּמַלִּי:

13 From the tribe of *Asher*, *Setur* son of Michael.

יג לְמַטֵּה אָשֵׁר סְתוּר בֶּן־מִיכָאֵל:

14 From the tribe of *Naftali*, *Nachbi* son of Vophsi.

יד לְמַטֵּה נַפְתָּלִי נַחְבִּי בֶּן־וָפְסִי:

15 From the tribe of *Gad*, *Geuel* son of Machi.

טו לְמַטֵּה גָד גְּאוּאֵל בֶּן־מָכִי:

16 Those were the names of the men whom *Moshe* sent to scout the land; but *Moshe* changed the name of *Hoshea* son of *Nun* to *Yehoshua*.

טז אֵלֶּה שְׁמוֹת הָאֲנָשִׁים אֲשֶׁר־שָׁלַח מֹשֶׁה לָתוּר אֶת־הָאָרֶץ וַיִּקְרָא מֹשֶׁה לְהוֹשֵׁעַ בִּן־נוּן יְהוֹשֻׁעַ:

17 When *Moshe* sent them to scout the land of Canaan, he said to them, "Go up there into the *Negev* and on into the hill country,

יז וַיִּשְׁלַח אֹתָם מֹשֶׁה לָתוּר אֶת־אֶרֶץ כְּנָעַן וַיֹּאמֶר אֲלֵהֶם עֲלוּ זֶה בַּנֶּגֶב וַעֲלִיתֶם אֶת־הָהָר:

18 and see what kind of country it is. Are the people who dwell in it strong or weak, few or many?

יח וּרְאִיתֶם אֶת־הָאָרֶץ מַה־הִוא וְאֶת־הָעָם הַיֹּשֵׁב עָלֶיהָ הֶחָזָק הוּא הֲרָפֶה הַמְעַט הוּא אִם־רָב:

19 Is the country in which they dwell good or bad? Are the towns they live in open or fortified?

יט וּמָה הָאָרֶץ אֲשֶׁר־הוּא יֹשֵׁב בָּהּ הֲטוֹבָה הִוא אִם־רָעָה וּמָה הֶעָרִים אֲשֶׁר־הוּא יוֹשֵׁב בָּהֵנָּה הַבְּמַחֲנִים אִם בְּמִבְצָרִים:

20 Is the soil rich or poor? Is it wooded or not? And take pains to bring back some of the fruit of the land." – Now it happened to be the season of the first ripe grapes.

כ וּמָה הָאָרֶץ הַשְּׁמֵנָה הִוא אִם־רָזָה הֲיֵשׁ־בָּהּ עֵץ אִם־אַיִן וְהִתְחַזַּקְתֶּם וּלְקַחְתֶּם מִפְּרִי הָאָרֶץ וְהַיָּמִים יְמֵי בִּכּוּרֵי עֲנָבִים:

21 They went up and scouted the land, from the wilderness of Zin to Rehob, at Lebo-hamath.

כא וַיַּעֲלוּ וַיָּתֻרוּ אֶת־הָאָרֶץ מִמִּדְבַּר־צִן עַד־רְחֹב לְבֹא חֲמָת:

22 They went up into the *Negev* and came to *Chevron*, where lived Ahiman, Sheshai, and Talmai, the Anakites. – Now *Chevron* was founded seven years before Zoan of Egypt. –

כב וַיַּעֲלוּ בַנֶּגֶב וַיָּבֹא עַד־חֶבְרוֹן וְשָׁם אֲחִימַן שֵׁשַׁי וְתַלְמַי יְלִידֵי הָעֲנָק וְחֶבְרוֹן שֶׁבַע שָׁנִים נִבְנְתָה לִפְנֵי צֹעַן מִצְרָיִם:

va-ya-a-LU va-NE-gev va-ya-VO ad khev-RON v'-SHAM a-khi-MAN shay-SHAI v'-tal-MAI y'-lee-DAY ha-a-NAK v'-khev-RON SHE-va sha-NEEM niv-ni-TAH lif-NAY TZO-an mitz-RA-yim

23 They reached the wadi Eshcol, and there they cut down a branch with a single cluster of grapes – it had to be borne on a carrying frame by two of them – and some pomegranates and figs.

כג וַיָּבֹאוּ עַד־נַחַל אֶשְׁכֹּל וַיִּכְרְתוּ מִשָּׁם זְמוֹרָה וְאֶשְׁכּוֹל עֲנָבִים אֶחָד וַיִּשָּׂאֻהוּ בַמּוֹט בִּשְׁנָיִם וּמִן־הָרִמֹּנִים וּמִן־הַתְּאֵנִים:

24 That place was named the wadi Eshcol because of the cluster that the Israelites cut down there.

כד לַמָּקוֹם הַהוּא קָרָא נַחַל אֶשְׁכּוֹל עַל אֹדוֹת הָאֶשְׁכּוֹל אֲשֶׁר־כָּרְתוּ מִשָּׁם בְּנֵי יִשְׂרָאֵל:

25 At the end of forty days they returned from scouting the land.

כה וַיָּשֻׁבוּ מִתּוּר הָאָרֶץ מִקֵּץ אַרְבָּעִים יוֹם:

Bamidbar/Numbers 13
Shelach

במדבר יג
שלח

26 They went straight to *Moshe* and *Aharon* and the whole Israelite community at Kadesh in the wilderness of Paran, and they made their report to them and to the whole community, as they showed them the fruit of the land.

כו וַיֵּלְכוּ וַיָּבֹאוּ אֶל־מֹשֶׁה וְאֶל־אַהֲרֹן וְאֶל־כָּל־עֲדַת בְּנֵי־יִשְׂרָאֵל אֶל־מִדְבַּר פָּארָן קָדֵשָׁה וַיָּשִׁיבוּ אוֹתָם דָּבָר וְאֶת־כָּל־הָעֵדָה וַיַּרְאוּם אֶת־פְּרִי הָאָרֶץ:

27 This is what they told him: "We came to the land you sent us to; it does indeed flow with milk and honey, and this is its fruit.

כז וַיְסַפְּרוּ־לוֹ וַיֹּאמְרוּ בָּאנוּ אֶל־הָאָרֶץ אֲשֶׁר שְׁלַחְתָּנוּ וְגַם זָבַת חָלָב וּדְבַשׁ הִוא וְזֶה־פִּרְיָהּ:

vai-sa-p'-ru LO va-YO-m'-RU BA-nu el ha-A-retz a-SHER sh'-lakh-TA-nu v'-GAM za-VAT kha-LAV u-d'-VASH HEE v'-zeh pir-YAH

28 However, the people who inhabit the country are powerful, and the cities are fortified and very large; moreover, we saw the Anakites there.

כח אֶפֶס כִּי־עַז הָעָם הַיֹּשֵׁב בָּאָרֶץ וְהֶעָרִים בְּצֻרוֹת גְּדֹלֹת מְאֹד וְגַם־יְלִדֵי הָעֲנָק רָאִינוּ שָׁם:

29 Amalekites dwell in the *Negev* region; Hittites, Jebusites, and Amorites inhabit the hill country; and Canaanites dwell by the Sea and along the Yarden."

כט עֲמָלֵק יוֹשֵׁב בְּאֶרֶץ הַנֶּגֶב וְהַחִתִּי וְהַיְבוּסִי וְהָאֱמֹרִי יוֹשֵׁב בָּהָר וְהַכְּנַעֲנִי יוֹשֵׁב עַל־הַיָּם וְעַל יַד הַיַּרְדֵּן:

30 *Kalev* hushed the people before *Moshe* and said, "Let us by all means go up, and we shall gain possession of it, for we shall surely overcome it."

ל וַיַּהַס כָּלֵב אֶת־הָעָם אֶל־מֹשֶׁה וַיֹּאמֶר עָלֹה נַעֲלֶה וְיָרַשְׁנוּ אֹתָהּ כִּי־יָכוֹל נוּכַל לָהּ:

va-ya-HAS ka-LAYV et ha-AM el mo-SHEH va-YO-mer a-LOH na-a-LEH v'-ya-RASH-nu o-TAH kee ya-KHOL nu-KHAL LAH

31 But the men who had gone up with him said, "We cannot attack that people, for it is stronger than we."

לא וְהָאֲנָשִׁים אֲשֶׁר־עָלוּ עִמּוֹ אָמְרוּ לֹא נוּכַל לַעֲלוֹת אֶל־הָעָם כִּי־חָזָק הוּא מִמֶּנּוּ:

32 Thus they spread calumnies among the Israelites about the land they had scouted, saying, "The country that we traversed and scouted is one that devours its settlers. All the people that we saw in it are men of great size;

לב וַיּוֹצִיאוּ דִּבַּת הָאָרֶץ אֲשֶׁר תָּרוּ אֹתָהּ אֶל־בְּנֵי יִשְׂרָאֵל לֵאמֹר הָאָרֶץ אֲשֶׁר עָבַרְנוּ בָהּ לָתוּר אֹתָהּ אֶרֶץ אֹכֶלֶת יוֹשְׁבֶיהָ הִוא וְכָל־הָעָם אֲשֶׁר־רָאִינוּ בְתוֹכָהּ אַנְשֵׁי מִדּוֹת:

13:27 This is what they told him The spies' slanderous report against *Eretz Yisrael* is one of the worst, if not the single gravest, sin described in the Bible. *Moshe* sends one representative from each tribe to scout out the land, and ten of the twelve return with a negative report. Only *Kalev* and *Yehoshua* have faith in *Hashem* and speak positively about the Land of Israel. Whereas *Hashem* forgives many sins throughout the Bible, slandering *Eretz Yisrael* is unacceptable, and the entire generation is punished for accepting the report. They are condemned to wander in the desert for forty years until the entire generation of the spies dies, as they no longer deserve to enter the Promised Land. Like *Kalev* and *Yehoshua*, we must not fall into the trap of criticizing the greatest of all God's gifts. Rather, we must speak positively about Israel at every opportunity.

Bamidbar/Numbers 14
Shelach

במדבר יד
שלח

33 we saw the Nephilim there – the Anakites are part of the Nephilim – and we looked like grasshoppers to ourselves, and so we must have looked to them."

לג וְשָׁם רָאִינוּ אֶת־הַנְּפִילִים בְּנֵי עֲנָק מִן־הַנְּפִלִים וַנְּהִי בְעֵינֵינוּ כַּחֲגָבִים וְכֵן הָיִינוּ בְּעֵינֵיהֶם:

v'-SHAM ra-EE-nu et ha-n'-fee-LEEM b'-NAY a-NAK min ha-n'-fee-LEEM va-n'-HEE v'-ay-NAY-nu ka-kha-ga-VEEM v'-KHAYN ha-YEE-nu b'-ay-nay-HEM

14

1 The whole community broke into loud cries, and the people wept that night.

יד א וַתִּשָּׂא כָּל־הָעֵדָה וַיִּתְּנוּ אֶת־קוֹלָם וַיִּבְכּוּ הָעָם בַּלַּיְלָה הַהוּא:

va-ti-SA kol HA-ay-DAH va-yi-t'-NU et ko-LAM va-yiv-KU ha-AM ba-LAI-lah ha-HU

2 All the Israelites railed against *Moshe* and *Aharon*. "If only we had died in the land of Egypt," the whole community shouted at them, "or if only we might die in this wilderness!

ב וַיִּלֹּנוּ עַל־מֹשֶׁה וְעַל־אַהֲרֹן כֹּל בְּנֵי יִשְׂרָאֵל וַיֹּאמְרוּ אֲלֵהֶם כָּל־הָעֵדָה לוּ־מַתְנוּ בְּאֶרֶץ מִצְרַיִם אוֹ בַּמִּדְבָּר הַזֶּה לוּ־מָתְנוּ:

3 Why is *Hashem* taking us to that land to fall by the sword? Our wives and children will be carried off! It would be better for us to go back to Egypt!"

ג וְלָמָה יְהֹוָה מֵבִיא אֹתָנוּ אֶל־הָאָרֶץ הַזֹּאת לִנְפֹּל בַּחֶרֶב נָשֵׁינוּ וְטַפֵּנוּ יִהְיוּ לָבַז הֲלוֹא טוֹב לָנוּ שׁוּב מִצְרָיְמָה:

4 And they said to one another, "Let us head back for Egypt."

ד וַיֹּאמְרוּ אִישׁ אֶל־אָחִיו נִתְּנָה רֹאשׁ וְנָשׁוּבָה מִצְרָיְמָה:

5 Then *Moshe* and *Aharon* fell on their faces before all the assembled congregation of the Israelites.

ה וַיִּפֹּל מֹשֶׁה וְאַהֲרֹן עַל־פְּנֵיהֶם לִפְנֵי כָּל־קְהַל עֲדַת בְּנֵי יִשְׂרָאֵל:

6 And *Yehoshua* son of *Nun* and *Kalev* son of Jephunneh, of those who had scouted the land, rent their clothes

ו וִיהוֹשֻׁעַ בִּן־נוּן וְכָלֵב בֶּן־יְפֻנֶּה מִן־הַתָּרִים אֶת־הָאָרֶץ קָרְעוּ בִּגְדֵיהֶם:

Rabbi Menachem Mendel of Kotzk (1787–1859)

13:33 And so we must have looked to them. In comparison to the giants living in Canaan, the spies report that "we looked like grasshoppers to ourselves, and so we must have looked to them." Rabbi Menachem Mendel of Kotzk, a Hasidic leader in the nineteenth century, suggests that the sin of the spies was that they worried about what others thought of them. As emissaries of *Hashem*, they should have been concerned only with fulfilling their mission, despite how they might be perceived by the people around them. We all have a special mission, to spread God's messages to the world. Since we know we are fulfilling *Hashem*'s work, we should not worry about what others will think about us.

Mourning on the 9th of Av

14:1 And the people wept that night The Sages explain that *Hashem* intentionally selected the ninth day of the month of *Av* as the day upon which both the first and second Temples would be destroyed. According to Jewish tradition, this is because it was on this day that the twelve spies returned from their mission to scout out *Eretz Yisrael*. As reported in the coming verses, following their pessimistic and libelous report, the people cried out to God in fear: "If only we had died in the land of Egypt… or if only we might die in this wilderness! Why is *Hashem* taking us to that land to fall by the sword? Our wives and children will be carried off! It would be better for us to go back to Egypt!" (Numbers 14:2–3). The Talmud (*Taanit* 29a) records that *Hashem* reprimanded the people for their lack of faith and said: "As you cried on the ninth of *Av* for no reason, this day will become a day of crying for all future generations." The events surrounding the destruction of the *Beit Hamikdash* are linked back to the biblical account of the twelve spies, to illustrate that all of Jewish history is inexorably interwoven, and is the unfolding of *Hashem*'s plan. We must never forget that one of the keys to the rebuilding of the *Beit Hamikdash* and the heralding in of the Messianic Era is our unquestioning trust in God, and appreciation of *Eretz Yisrael*.

Bamidbar/Numbers 14
Shelach

במדבר יד
שלח

7 and exhorted the whole Israelite community: "The land that we traversed and scouted is an exceedingly good land.

ז וַיֹּאמְרוּ אֶל־כָּל־עֲדַת בְּנֵי־יִשְׂרָאֵל לֵאמֹר הָאָרֶץ אֲשֶׁר עָבַרְנוּ בָהּ לָתוּר אֹתָהּ טוֹבָה הָאָרֶץ מְאֹד מְאֹד:

va-YO-m'-RU el kol a-DAT b'-nay yis-ra-AYL lay-MOR ha-A-retz a-SHER a-VAR-nu VAH la-TUR o-TAH to-VAH ha-A-retz m'-OD m'-OD

8 If *Hashem* is pleased with us, He will bring us into that land, a land that flows with milk and honey, and give it to us;

ח אִם־חָפֵץ בָּנוּ יְהֹוָה וְהֵבִיא אֹתָנוּ אֶל־הָאָרֶץ הַזֹּאת וּנְתָנָהּ לָנוּ אֶרֶץ אֲשֶׁר־הִוא זָבַת חָלָב וּדְבָשׁ:

im kha-FAYTZ BA-nu a-do-NAI v'-hay-VEE o-TA-nu el ha-A-retz ha-ZOT u-n'-ta-NAH LA-nu E-retz a-sher HEE za-VAT kha-LAV u-d'-VASH

9 only you must not rebel against *Hashem*. Have no fear then of the people of the country, for they are our prey: their protection has departed from them, but *Hashem* is with us. Have no fear of them!"

ט אַךְ בַּיהֹוָה אַל־תִּמְרֹדוּ וְאַתֶּם אַל־תִּירְאוּ אֶת־עַם הָאָרֶץ כִּי לַחְמֵנוּ הֵם סָר צִלָּם מֵעֲלֵיהֶם וַיהֹוָה אִתָּנוּ אַל־תִּירָאֻם:

10 As the whole community threatened to pelt them with stones, the Presence of *Hashem* appeared in the Tent of Meeting to all the Israelites.

י וַיֹּאמְרוּ כָּל־הָעֵדָה לִרְגּוֹם אֹתָם בָּאֲבָנִים וּכְבוֹד יְהֹוָה נִרְאָה בְּאֹהֶל מוֹעֵד אֶל־כָּל־בְּנֵי יִשְׂרָאֵל:

11 And *Hashem* said to *Moshe*, "How long will this people spurn Me, and how long will they have no faith in Me despite all the signs that I have performed in their midst?

יא וַיֹּאמֶר יְהֹוָה אֶל־מֹשֶׁה עַד־אָנָה יְנַאֲצֻנִי הָעָם הַזֶּה וְעַד־אָנָה לֹא־יַאֲמִינוּ בִי בְּכֹל הָאֹתוֹת אֲשֶׁר עָשִׂיתִי בְּקִרְבּוֹ:

12 I will strike them with pestilence and disown them, and I will make of you a nation far more numerous than they!"

יב אַכֶּנּוּ בַדֶּבֶר וְאוֹרִשֶׁנּוּ וְאֶעֱשֶׂה אֹתְךָ לְגוֹי־גָּדוֹל וְעָצוּם מִמֶּנּוּ:

13 But *Moshe* said to *Hashem*, "When the Egyptians, from whose midst You brought up this people in Your might, hear the news,

יג וַיֹּאמֶר מֹשֶׁה אֶל־יְהֹוָה וְשָׁמְעוּ מִצְרַיִם כִּי־הֶעֱלִיתָ בְכֹחֲךָ אֶת־הָעָם הַזֶּה מִקִּרְבּוֹ:

14 they will tell it to the inhabitants of that land. Now they have heard that You, *Hashem*, are in the midst of this people; that You, *Hashem*, appear in plain sight when Your cloud rests over them and when You go before them in a pillar of cloud by day and in a pillar of fire by night.

יד וְאָמְרוּ אֶל־יוֹשֵׁב הָאָרֶץ הַזֹּאת שָׁמְעוּ כִּי־אַתָּה יְהֹוָה בְּקֶרֶב הָעָם הַזֶּה אֲשֶׁר־עַיִן בְּעַיִן נִרְאָה אַתָּה יְהֹוָה וַעֲנָנְךָ עֹמֵד עֲלֵהֶם וּבְעַמֻּד עָנָן אַתָּה הֹלֵךְ לִפְנֵיהֶם יוֹמָם וּבְעַמּוּד אֵשׁ לָיְלָה:

14:7–8 If *Hashem* is pleased with us After the negative report of ten of the twelve spies, *Kalev* responds by saying that if *Hashem* desires that the People of Israel live in *Eretz Yisrael*, He will make sure that they will inherit it, despite the many obstacles. *Hashem* desired to give the land to His chosen nation then, and He desires for them to have it now. There are certainly deterrents from living in, and loving, the land of Israel. For example, it is surrounded by hostile neighbors and there are constant security threats. Nevertheless, God has returned the land to the Children of Israel. Let us not repeat the mistake of the ten spies by minimizing God's great gift to our generation.

Bamidbar/Numbers 14
Shelach

15 If then You slay this people to a man, the nations who have heard Your fame will say,

טו וְהֵמַתָּה אֶת־הָעָם הַזֶּה כְּאִישׁ אֶחָד וְאָמְרוּ הַגּוֹיִם אֲשֶׁר־שָׁמְעוּ אֶת־שִׁמְעֲךָ לֵאמֹר:

16 'It must be because *Hashem* was powerless to bring that people into the land He had promised them on oath that He slaughtered them in the wilderness.'

טז מִבִּלְתִּי יְכֹלֶת יְהֹוָה לְהָבִיא אֶת־הָעָם הַזֶּה אֶל־הָאָרֶץ אֲשֶׁר־נִשְׁבַּע לָהֶם וַיִּשְׁחָטֵם בַּמִּדְבָּר:

17 Therefore, I pray, let my Lord's forbearance be great, as You have declared, saying,

יז וְעַתָּה יִגְדַּל־נָא כֹּחַ אֲדֹנָי כַּאֲשֶׁר דִּבַּרְתָּ לֵאמֹר:

18 '*Hashem*! slow to anger and abounding in kindness; forgiving iniquity and transgression; yet not remitting all punishment, but visiting the iniquity of fathers upon children, upon the third and fourth generations.'

יח יְהֹוָה אֶרֶךְ אַפַּיִם וְרַב־חֶסֶד נֹשֵׂא עָוֹן וָפָשַׁע וְנַקֵּה לֹא יְנַקֶּה פֹּקֵד עֲוֹן אָבוֹת עַל־בָּנִים עַל־שִׁלֵּשִׁים וְעַל־רִבֵּעִים:

19 Pardon, I pray, the iniquity of this people according to Your great kindness, as You have forgiven this people ever since Egypt."

יט סְלַח־נָא לַעֲוֹן הָעָם הַזֶּה כְּגֹדֶל חַסְדֶּךָ וְכַאֲשֶׁר נָשָׂאתָה לָעָם הַזֶּה מִמִּצְרַיִם וְעַד־הֵנָּה:

20 And *Hashem* said, "I pardon, as you have asked.

כ וַיֹּאמֶר יְהֹוָה סָלַחְתִּי כִּדְבָרֶךָ:

21 Nevertheless, as I live and as *Hashem*'s Presence fills the whole world,

כא וְאוּלָם חַי־אָנִי וְיִמָּלֵא כְבוֹד־יְהֹוָה אֶת־כָּל־הָאָרֶץ:

22 none of the men who have seen My Presence and the signs that I have performed in Egypt and in the wilderness, and who have tried Me these many times and have disobeyed Me,

כב כִּי כָל־הָאֲנָשִׁים הָרֹאִים אֶת־כְּבֹדִי וְאֶת־אֹתֹתַי אֲשֶׁר־עָשִׂיתִי בְמִצְרַיִם וּבַמִּדְבָּר וַיְנַסּוּ אֹתִי זֶה עֶשֶׂר פְּעָמִים וְלֹא שָׁמְעוּ בְּקוֹלִי:

23 shall see the land that I promised on oath to their fathers; none of those who spurn Me shall see it.

כג אִם־יִרְאוּ אֶת־הָאָרֶץ אֲשֶׁר נִשְׁבַּעְתִּי לַאֲבֹתָם וְכָל־מְנַאֲצַי לֹא יִרְאוּהָ:

24 But My servant *Kalev*, because he was imbued with a different spirit and remained loyal to Me – him will I bring into the land that he entered, and his offspring shall hold it as a possession.

כד וְעַבְדִּי כָלֵב עֵקֶב הָיְתָה רוּחַ אַחֶרֶת עִמּוֹ וַיְמַלֵּא אַחֲרָי וַהֲבִיאֹתִיו אֶל־הָאָרֶץ אֲשֶׁר־בָּא שָׁמָּה וְזַרְעוֹ יוֹרִשֶׁנָּה:

25 Now the Amalekites and the Canaanites occupy the valleys. Start out, then, tomorrow and march into the wilderness by way of the Sea of Reeds."

כה וְהָעֲמָלֵקִי וְהַכְּנַעֲנִי יוֹשֵׁב בָּעֵמֶק מָחָר פְּנוּ וּסְעוּ לָכֶם הַמִּדְבָּר דֶּרֶךְ יַם־סוּף:

26 *Hashem* spoke further to *Moshe* and *Aharon*,

כו וַיְדַבֵּר יְהֹוָה אֶל־מֹשֶׁה וְאֶל־אַהֲרֹן לֵאמֹר:

27 "How much longer shall that wicked community keep muttering against Me? Very well, I have heeded the incessant muttering of the Israelites against Me.

כז עַד־מָתַי לָעֵדָה הָרָעָה הַזֹּאת אֲשֶׁר הֵמָּה מַלִּינִים עָלָי אֶת־תְּלֻנּוֹת בְּנֵי יִשְׂרָאֵל אֲשֶׁר הֵמָּה מַלִּינִים עָלַי שָׁמָעְתִּי:

28 Say to them: 'As I live,' says *Hashem*, 'I will do to you just as you have urged Me.

כח אֱמֹר אֲלֵהֶם חַי־אָנִי נְאֻם־יְהֹוָה אִם־לֹא כַּאֲשֶׁר דִּבַּרְתֶּם בְּאָזְנָי כֵּן אֶעֱשֶׂה לָכֶם:

Bamidbar/Numbers 14
Shelach

29 In this very wilderness shall your carcasses drop. Of all of you who were recorded in your various lists from the age of twenty years up, you who have muttered against Me,

30 not one shall enter the land in which I swore to settle you – save *Kalev* son of Jephunneh and *Yehoshua* son of *Nun*.

31 Your children who, you said, would be carried off – these will I allow to enter; they shall know the land that you have rejected.

32 But your carcasses shall drop in this wilderness,

33 while your children roam the wilderness for forty years, suffering for your faithlessness, until the last of your carcasses is down in the wilderness.

34 You shall bear your punishment for forty years, corresponding to the number of days – forty days – that you scouted the land: a year for each day. Thus you shall know what it means to thwart Me.

35 I *Hashem* have spoken: Thus will I do to all that wicked band that has banded together against Me: in this very wilderness they shall die to the last man.'"

36 As for the men whom *Moshe* sent to scout the land, those who came back and caused the whole community to mutter against him by spreading calumnies about the land –

37 those who spread such calumnies about the land died of plague, by the will of *Hashem*.

38 Of those men who had gone to scout the land, only *Yehoshua* son of *Nun* and *Kalev* son of Jephunneh survived.

39 When *Moshe* repeated these words to all the Israelites, the people were overcome by grief.

40 Early next morning they set out toward the crest of the hill country, saying, "We are prepared to go up to the place that *Hashem* has spoken of, for we were wrong."

41 But *Moshe* said, "Why do you transgress *Hashem*'s command? This will not succeed.

42 Do not go up, lest you be routed by your enemies, for *Hashem* is not in your midst.

במדבר יד
שלח

כט בַּמִּדְבָּ֣ר הַ֠זֶּה יִפְּל֨וּ פִגְרֵיכֶ֜ם וְכָל־פְּקֻדֵיכֶם֙ לְכָל־מִסְפַּרְכֶ֔ם מִבֶּ֛ן עֶשְׂרִ֥ים שָׁנָ֖ה וָמָ֑עְלָה אֲשֶׁ֥ר הֲלִֽינֹתֶ֖ם עָלָֽי׃

ל אִם־אַתֶּם֙ תָּבֹ֣אוּ אֶל־הָאָ֔רֶץ אֲשֶׁ֤ר נָשָׂ֙אתִי֙ אֶת־יָדִ֔י לְשַׁכֵּ֥ן אֶתְכֶ֖ם בָּ֑הּ כִּ֚י אִם־כָּלֵ֣ב בֶּן־יְפֻנֶּ֔ה וִיהוֹשֻׁ֖עַ בִּן־נֽוּן׃

לא וְטַ֨פְּכֶ֔ם אֲשֶׁ֥ר אֲמַרְתֶּ֖ם לָבַ֣ז יִהְיֶ֑ה וְהֵבֵיאתִ֣י אֹתָ֔ם וְיָֽדְעוּ֙ אֶת־הָאָ֔רֶץ אֲשֶׁ֥ר מְאַסְתֶּ֖ם בָּֽהּ׃

לב וּפִגְרֵיכֶ֖ם אַתֶּ֑ם יִפְּל֖וּ בַּמִּדְבָּ֥ר הַזֶּֽה׃

לג וּבְנֵיכֶ֜ם יִהְי֣וּ רֹעִ֣ים בַּמִּדְבָּר֮ אַרְבָּעִ֣ים שָׁנָה֒ וְנָשְׂא֖וּ אֶת־זְנוּתֵיכֶ֑ם עַד־תֹּ֥ם פִּגְרֵיכֶ֖ם בַּמִּדְבָּֽר׃

לד בְּמִסְפַּ֨ר הַיָּמִ֜ים אֲשֶׁר־תַּרְתֶּ֣ם אֶת־הָאָרֶץ֮ אַרְבָּעִ֣ים יוֹם֒ י֣וֹם לַשָּׁנָ֞ה י֣וֹם לַשָּׁנָ֗ה תִּשְׂאוּ֙ אֶת־עֲוֺנֹ֣תֵיכֶ֔ם אַרְבָּעִ֖ים שָׁנָ֑ה וִֽידַעְתֶּ֖ם אֶת־תְּנוּאָתִֽי׃

לה אֲנִ֣י יְהֹוָה֮ דִּבַּרְתִּי֒ אִם־לֹ֣א ׀ זֹ֣את אֶֽעֱשֶׂ֗ה לְכָל־הָעֵדָ֤ה הָֽרָעָה֙ הַזֹּ֔את הַנּוֹעָדִ֖ים עָלָ֑י בַּמִּדְבָּ֥ר הַזֶּ֛ה יִתַּ֖מּוּ וְשָׁ֥ם יָמֻֽתוּ׃

לו וְהָ֣אֲנָשִׁ֔ים אֲשֶׁר־שָׁלַ֥ח מֹשֶׁ֖ה לָת֣וּר אֶת־הָאָ֑רֶץ וַיָּשֻׁ֗בוּ וילונו [וַיַּלִּ֤ינוּ] עָלָיו֙ אֶת־כָּל־הָ֣עֵדָ֔ה לְהוֹצִ֥יא דִבָּ֖ה עַל־הָאָֽרֶץ׃

לז וַיָּמֻ֙תוּ֙ הָֽאֲנָשִׁ֔ים מוֹצִאֵ֥י דִבַּת־הָאָ֖רֶץ רָעָ֑ה בַּמַּגֵּפָ֖ה לִפְנֵ֥י יְהֹוָֽה׃

לח וִיהוֹשֻׁ֣עַ בִּן־נ֔וּן וְכָלֵ֖ב בֶּן־יְפֻנֶּ֑ה חָיוּ֙ מִן־הָאֲנָשִׁ֣ים הָהֵ֔ם הַהֹלְכִ֖ים לָת֥וּר אֶת־הָאָֽרֶץ׃

לט וַיְדַבֵּ֤ר מֹשֶׁה֙ אֶת־הַדְּבָרִ֣ים הָאֵ֔לֶּה אֶֽל־כָּל־בְּנֵ֖י יִשְׂרָאֵ֑ל וַיִּֽתְאַבְּל֥וּ הָעָ֖ם מְאֹֽד׃

מ וַיַּשְׁכִּ֣מוּ בַבֹּ֔קֶר וַיַּֽעֲל֥וּ אֶל־רֹאשׁ־הָהָ֖ר לֵאמֹ֑ר הִנֶּ֗נּוּ וְעָלִ֛ינוּ אֶל־הַמָּק֛וֹם אֲשֶׁר־אָמַ֥ר יְהֹוָ֖ה כִּ֥י חָטָֽאנוּ׃

מא וַיֹּ֣אמֶר מֹשֶׁ֔ה לָ֥מָּה זֶּ֛ה אַתֶּ֥ם עֹבְרִ֖ים אֶת־פִּ֣י יְהֹוָ֑ה וְהִ֖וא לֹ֥א תִצְלָֽח׃

מב אַֽל־תַּעֲל֔וּ כִּ֛י אֵ֥ין יְהֹוָ֖ה בְּקִרְבְּכֶ֑ם וְלֹא֙ תִּנָּ֣גְפ֔וּ לִפְנֵ֖י אֹיְבֵיכֶֽם׃

Bamidbar/Numbers 15
Shelach

43 For the Amalekites and the Canaanites will be there to face you, and you will fall by the sword, inasmuch as you have turned from following *Hashem* and *Hashem* will not be with you."

44 Yet defiantly they marched toward the crest of the hill country, though neither *Hashem's Aron HaBrit* nor *Moshe* stirred from the camp.

45 And the Amalekites and the Canaanites who dwelt in that hill country came down and dealt them a shattering blow at Hormah.

15 1 *Hashem* spoke to *Moshe*, saying:

2 Speak to *B'nei Yisrael* and say to them: When you enter the land that I am giving you to settle in,

3 and would present an offering by fire to *Hashem* from the herd or from the flock, be it burnt offering or sacrifice, in fulfillment of a vow explicitly uttered, or as a freewill offering, or at your fixed occasions, producing an odor pleasing to *Hashem*:

4 The person who presents the offering to *Hashem* shall bring as a meal offering: a tenth of a measure of choice flour with a quarter of a *hin* of oil mixed in.

5 You shall also offer, with the burnt offering or the sacrifice, a quarter of a *hin* of wine as a libation for each sheep.

6 In the case of a ram, you shall present as a meal offering: two-tenths of a measure of choice flour with a third of a *hin* of oil mixed in;

7 and a third of a *hin* of wine as a libation – as an offering of pleasing odor to *Hashem*.

8 And if it is an animal from the herd that you offer to *Hashem* as a burnt offering or as a sacrifice, in fulfillment of a vow explicitly uttered or as an offering of well-being,

9 there shall be offered a meal offering along with the animal: three-tenths of a measure of choice flour with half a *hin* of oil mixed in;

10 and as libation you shall offer half a *hin* of wine – these being offerings by fire of pleasing odor to *Hashem*.

במדבר טו
שלח

מג כִּי הָעֲמָלֵקִי וְהַכְּנַעֲנִי שָׁם לִפְנֵיכֶם וּנְפַלְתֶּם בֶּחָרֶב כִּי־עַל־כֵּן שַׁבְתֶּם מֵאַחֲרֵי יְהֹוָה וְלֹא־יִהְיֶה יְהֹוָה עִמָּכֶם:

מד וַיַּעְפִּלוּ לַעֲלוֹת אֶל־רֹאשׁ הָהָר וַאֲרוֹן בְּרִית־יְהֹוָה וּמֹשֶׁה לֹא־מָשׁוּ מִקֶּרֶב הַמַּחֲנֶה:

מה וַיֵּרֶד הָעֲמָלֵקִי וְהַכְּנַעֲנִי הַיֹּשֵׁב בָּהָר הַהוּא וַיַּכּוּם וַיַּכְּתוּם עַד־הַחָרְמָה:

טו א וַיְדַבֵּר יְהֹוָה אֶל־מֹשֶׁה לֵּאמֹר:

ב דַּבֵּר אֶל־בְּנֵי יִשְׂרָאֵל וְאָמַרְתָּ אֲלֵהֶם כִּי תָבֹאוּ אֶל־אֶרֶץ מוֹשְׁבֹתֵיכֶם אֲשֶׁר אֲנִי נֹתֵן לָכֶם:

ג וַעֲשִׂיתֶם אִשֶּׁה לַיהֹוָה עֹלָה אוֹ־זֶבַח לְפַלֵּא־נֶדֶר אוֹ בִנְדָבָה אוֹ בְּמֹעֲדֵיכֶם לַעֲשׂוֹת רֵיחַ נִיחֹחַ לַיהֹוָה מִן־הַבָּקָר אוֹ מִן־הַצֹּאן:

ד וְהִקְרִיב הַמַּקְרִיב קָרְבָּנוֹ לַיהֹוָה מִנְחָה סֹלֶת עִשָּׂרוֹן בָּלוּל בִּרְבִעִית הַהִין שָׁמֶן:

ה וְיַיִן לַנֶּסֶךְ רְבִיעִית הַהִין תַּעֲשֶׂה עַל־הָעֹלָה אוֹ לַזָּבַח לַכֶּבֶשׂ הָאֶחָד:

ו אוֹ לָאַיִל תַּעֲשֶׂה מִנְחָה סֹלֶת שְׁנֵי עֶשְׂרֹנִים בְּלוּלָה בַשֶּׁמֶן שְׁלִשִׁית הַהִין:

ז וְיַיִן לַנֶּסֶךְ שְׁלִשִׁית הַהִין תַּקְרִיב רֵיחַ־נִיחֹחַ לַיהֹוָה:

ח וְכִי־תַעֲשֶׂה בֶן־בָּקָר עֹלָה אוֹ־זָבַח לְפַלֵּא־נֶדֶר אוֹ־שְׁלָמִים לַיהֹוָה:

ט וְהִקְרִיב עַל־בֶּן־הַבָּקָר מִנְחָה סֹלֶת שְׁלֹשָׁה עֶשְׂרֹנִים בָּלוּל בַּשֶּׁמֶן חֲצִי הַהִין:

י וְיַיִן תַּקְרִיב לַנֶּסֶךְ חֲצִי הַהִין אִשֵּׁה רֵיחַ־נִיחֹחַ לַיהֹוָה:

Bamidbar/Numbers 15
Shelach

11 Thus shall be done with each ox, with each ram, and with any sheep or goat,

יא כָּכָה יֵעָשֶׂה לַשּׁוֹר הָאֶחָד אוֹ לָאַיִל הָאֶחָד אוֹ־לַשֶּׂה בַכְּבָשִׂים אוֹ בָעִזִּים:

12 as many as you offer; you shall do thus with each one, as many as there are.

יב כַּמִּסְפָּר אֲשֶׁר תַּעֲשׂוּ כָּכָה תַּעֲשׂוּ לָאֶחָד כְּמִסְפָּרָם:

13 Every citizen, when presenting an offering by fire of pleasing odor to *Hashem*, shall do so with them.

יג כָּל־הָאֶזְרָח יַעֲשֶׂה־כָּכָה אֶת־אֵלֶּה לְהַקְרִיב אִשֵּׁה רֵיחַ־נִיחֹחַ לַיהוָה:

14 And when, throughout the ages, a stranger who has taken up residence with you, or one who lives among you, would present an offering by fire of pleasing odor to *Hashem* – as you do, so shall it be done by

יד וְכִי־יָגוּר אִתְּכֶם גֵּר אוֹ אֲשֶׁר־בְּתוֹכְכֶם לְדֹרֹתֵיכֶם וְעָשָׂה אִשֵּׁה רֵיחַ־נִיחֹחַ לַיהוָה כַּאֲשֶׁר תַּעֲשׂוּ כֵּן יַעֲשֶׂה:

15 the rest of the congregation. There shall be one law for you and for the resident stranger; it shall be a law for all time throughout the ages. You and the stranger shall be alike before *Hashem*;

טו הַקָּהָל חֻקָּה אַחַת לָכֶם וְלַגֵּר הַגָּר חֻקַּת עוֹלָם לְדֹרֹתֵיכֶם כָּכֶם כַּגֵּר יִהְיֶה לִפְנֵי יְהוָה:

16 the same ritual and the same rule shall apply to you and to the stranger who resides among you.

טז תּוֹרָה אַחַת וּמִשְׁפָּט אֶחָד יִהְיֶה לָכֶם וְלַגֵּר הַגָּר אִתְּכֶם:

17 *Hashem* spoke to *Moshe*, saying:

יז וַיְדַבֵּר יְהוָה אֶל־מֹשֶׁה לֵּאמֹר:

18 Speak to *B'nei Yisrael* and say to them: When you enter the land to which I am taking you

יח דַּבֵּר אֶל־בְּנֵי יִשְׂרָאֵל וְאָמַרְתָּ אֲלֵהֶם בְּבֹאֲכֶם אֶל־הָאָרֶץ אֲשֶׁר אֲנִי מֵבִיא אֶתְכֶם שָׁמָּה:

19 and you eat of the bread of the land, you shall set some aside as a gift to *Hashem*:

יט וְהָיָה בַּאֲכָלְכֶם מִלֶּחֶם הָאָרֶץ תָּרִימוּ תְרוּמָה לַיהוָה:

20 as the first yield of your baking, you shall set aside a loaf as a gift; you shall set it aside as a gift like the gift from the threshing floor.

כ רֵאשִׁית עֲרִסֹתֵכֶם חַלָּה תָּרִימוּ תְרוּמָה כִּתְרוּמַת גֹּרֶן כֵּן תָּרִימוּ אֹתָהּ:

21 You shall make a gift to *Hashem* from the first yield of your baking, throughout the ages.

כא מֵרֵאשִׁית עֲרִסֹתֵיכֶם תִּתְּנוּ לַיהוָה תְּרוּמָה לְדֹרֹתֵיכֶם:

may-ray-SHEET a-ri-so-tay-KHEM ti-t'-NU la-do-NAI t'-ru-MAH l'-do-RO-tay-KHEM

22 If you unwittingly fail to observe any one of the commandments that *Hashem* has declared to *Moshe* –

כב וְכִי תִשְׁגּוּ וְלֹא תַעֲשׂוּ אֵת כָּל־הַמִּצְוֹת הָאֵלֶּה אֲשֶׁר־דִּבֶּר יְהוָה אֶל־מֹשֶׁה:

15:21 You shall make a gift to *Hashem* from the first yield of your baking The commandment to separate a portion of dough for the *Kohanim*, known as *challah* (חלה), went into effect only once the people entered the Land of Israel. This dough is given to the *Kohanim*, since they did not receive their own portion of land through which they could sustain themselves. The job of the *Kohanim* is to educate the people and work in the *Beit Hamikdash*, thereby providing the Nation with spiritual sustenance. In turn, they are provided with physical sustenance from the portions of the other tribes. Such is one's existence in *Eretz Yisrael* – the physical and spiritual are continuously intertwined.

Bamidbar/Numbers 15
Shelach

23 anything that *Hashem* has enjoined upon you through *Moshe* – from the day that *Hashem* gave the commandment and on through the ages:

24 If this was done unwittingly, through the inadvertence of the community, the whole community shall present one bull of the herd as a burnt offering of pleasing odor to *Hashem*, with its proper meal offering and libation, and one he-goat as a sin offering.

25 The *Kohen* shall make expiation for the whole Israelite community and they shall be forgiven; for it was an error, and for their error they have brought their offering, an offering by fire to *Hashem* and their sin offering before *Hashem*.

26 The whole Israelite community and the stranger residing among them shall be forgiven, for it happened to the entire people through error.

27 In case it is an individual who has sinned unwittingly, he shall offer a she-goat in its first year as a sin offering.

28 The *Kohen* shall make expiation before *Hashem* on behalf of the person who erred, for he sinned unwittingly, making such expiation for him that he may be forgiven.

29 For the citizen among the Israelites and for the stranger who resides among them – you shall have one ritual for anyone who acts in error.

30 But the person, be he citizen or stranger, who acts defiantly reviles *Hashem*; that person shall be cut off from among his people.

31 Because he has spurned the word of *Hashem* and violated His commandment, that person shall be cut off – he bears his guilt.

32 Once, when the Israelites were in the wilderness, they came upon a man gathering wood on the *Shabbat* day.

33 Those who found him as he was gathering wood brought him before *Moshe, Aharon*, and the whole community.

34 He was placed in custody, for it had not been specified what should be done to him.

כג אֵת כָּל־אֲשֶׁר צִוָּה יְהֹוָה אֲלֵיכֶם בְּיַד־מֹשֶׁה מִן־הַיּוֹם אֲשֶׁר צִוָּה יְהֹוָה וָהָלְאָה לְדֹרֹתֵיכֶם:

כד וְהָיָה אִם מֵעֵינֵי הָעֵדָה נֶעֶשְׂתָה לִשְׁגָגָה וְעָשׂוּ כָל־הָעֵדָה פַּר בֶּן־בָּקָר אֶחָד לְעֹלָה לְרֵיחַ נִיחֹחַ לַיהֹוָה וּמִנְחָתוֹ וְנִסְכּוֹ כַּמִּשְׁפָּט וּשְׂעִיר־עִזִּים אֶחָד לְחַטָּת:

כה וְכִפֶּר הַכֹּהֵן עַל־כָּל־עֲדַת בְּנֵי יִשְׂרָאֵל וְנִסְלַח לָהֶם כִּי־שְׁגָגָה הִוא וְהֵם הֵבִיאוּ אֶת־קָרְבָּנָם אִשֶּׁה לַיהֹוָה וְחַטָּאתָם לִפְנֵי יְהֹוָה עַל־שִׁגְגָתָם:

כו וְנִסְלַח לְכָל־עֲדַת בְּנֵי יִשְׂרָאֵל וְלַגֵּר הַגָּר בְּתוֹכָם כִּי לְכָל־הָעָם בִּשְׁגָגָה:

כז וְאִם־נֶפֶשׁ אַחַת תֶּחֱטָא בִשְׁגָגָה וְהִקְרִיבָה עֵז בַּת־שְׁנָתָהּ לְחַטָּאת:

כח וְכִפֶּר הַכֹּהֵן עַל־הַנֶּפֶשׁ הַשֹּׁגֶגֶת בְּחֶטְאָה בִשְׁגָגָה לִפְנֵי יְהֹוָה לְכַפֵּר עָלָיו וְנִסְלַח לוֹ:

כט הָאֶזְרָח בִּבְנֵי יִשְׂרָאֵל וְלַגֵּר הַגָּר בְּתוֹכָם תּוֹרָה אַחַת יִהְיֶה לָכֶם לָעֹשֶׂה בִּשְׁגָגָה:

ל וְהַנֶּפֶשׁ אֲשֶׁר־תַּעֲשֶׂה בְּיָד רָמָה מִן־הָאֶזְרָח וּמִן־הַגֵּר אֶת־יְהֹוָה הוּא מְגַדֵּף וְנִכְרְתָה הַנֶּפֶשׁ הַהִוא מִקֶּרֶב עַמָּהּ:

לא כִּי דְבַר־יְהֹוָה בָּזָה וְאֶת־מִצְוָתוֹ הֵפַר הִכָּרֵת תִּכָּרֵת הַנֶּפֶשׁ הַהִוא עֲוֹנָה בָהּ:

לב וַיִּהְיוּ בְנֵי־יִשְׂרָאֵל בַּמִּדְבָּר וַיִּמְצְאוּ אִישׁ מְקֹשֵׁשׁ עֵצִים בְּיוֹם הַשַּׁבָּת:

לג וַיַּקְרִיבוּ אֹתוֹ הַמֹּצְאִים אֹתוֹ מְקֹשֵׁשׁ עֵצִים אֶל־מֹשֶׁה וְאֶל־אַהֲרֹן וְאֶל כָּל־הָעֵדָה:

לד וַיַּנִּיחוּ אֹתוֹ בַּמִּשְׁמָר כִּי לֹא פֹרַשׁ מַה־יֵּעָשֶׂה לוֹ:

Bamidbar/Numbers 16
Korach

35 Then *Hashem* said to *Moshe*, "The man shall be put to death: the whole community shall pelt him with stones outside the camp."

לה וַיֹּאמֶר יְהוָה אֶל־מֹשֶׁה מוֹת יוּמַת הָאִישׁ רָגוֹם אֹתוֹ בָאֲבָנִים כָּל־הָעֵדָה מִחוּץ לַמַּחֲנֶה:

36 So the whole community took him outside the camp and stoned him to death – as *Hashem* had commanded *Moshe*.

לו וַיֹּצִיאוּ אֹתוֹ כָּל־הָעֵדָה אֶל־מִחוּץ לַמַּחֲנֶה וַיִּרְגְּמוּ אֹתוֹ בָּאֲבָנִים וַיָּמֹת כַּאֲשֶׁר צִוָּה יְהוָה אֶת־מֹשֶׁה:

37 *Hashem* said to *Moshe* as follows:

לז וַיֹּאמֶר יְהוָה אֶל־מֹשֶׁה לֵּאמֹר:

38 Speak to *B'nei Yisrael* and instruct them to make for themselves fringes on the corners of their garments throughout the ages; let them attach a cord of blue to the fringe at each corner.

לח דַּבֵּר אֶל־בְּנֵי יִשְׂרָאֵל וְאָמַרְתָּ אֲלֵהֶם וְעָשׂוּ לָהֶם צִיצִת עַל־כַּנְפֵי בִגְדֵיהֶם לְדֹרֹתָם וְנָתְנוּ עַל־צִיצִת הַכָּנָף פְּתִיל תְּכֵלֶת:

da-BAYR el b'-NAY yis-ra-AYL v'-a-mar-TA a-lay-HEM v'-a-SU la-HEM tzee-TZIT al kan-FAY vig-day-HEM l'-do-ro-TAM v'-na-t'-NU al tzee-TZIT ha-ka-NAF p'-TEEL t'-KHAY-let

39 That shall be your fringe; look at it and recall all the commandments of *Hashem* and observe them, so that you do not follow your heart and eyes in your lustful urge.

לט וְהָיָה לָכֶם לְצִיצִת וּרְאִיתֶם אֹתוֹ וּזְכַרְתֶּם אֶת־כָּל־מִצְוֹת יְהוָה וַעֲשִׂיתֶם אֹתָם וְלֹא־תָתֻרוּ אַחֲרֵי לְבַבְכֶם וְאַחֲרֵי עֵינֵיכֶם אֲשֶׁר־אַתֶּם זֹנִים אַחֲרֵיהֶם:

40 Thus you shall be reminded to observe all My commandments and to be holy to your God.

מ לְמַעַן תִּזְכְּרוּ וַעֲשִׂיתֶם אֶת־כָּל־מִצְוֹתָי וִהְיִיתֶם קְדֹשִׁים לֵאלֹהֵיכֶם:

41 I *Hashem* am your God, who brought you out of the land of Egypt to be your God: I, *Hashem* your God.

מא אֲנִי יְהוָה אֱלֹהֵיכֶם אֲשֶׁר הוֹצֵאתִי אֶתְכֶם מֵאֶרֶץ מִצְרַיִם לִהְיוֹת לָכֶם לֵאלֹהִים אֲנִי יְהוָה אֱלֹהֵיכֶם:

16 1 Now *Korach*, son of Izhar son of *Kehat* son of *Levi*, betook himself, along with *Datan* and *Aviram* sons of *Eliav*, and On son of Peleth – descendants of *Reuven* –

טז א וַיִּקַּח קֹרַח בֶּן־יִצְהָר בֶּן־קְהָת בֶּן־לֵוִי וְדָתָן וַאֲבִירָם בְּנֵי אֱלִיאָב וְאוֹן בֶּן־פֶּלֶת בְּנֵי רְאוּבֵן:

2 to rise up against *Moshe*, together with two hundred and fifty Israelites, chieftains of the community, chosen in the assembly, men of repute.

ב וַיָּקֻמוּ לִפְנֵי מֹשֶׁה וַאֲנָשִׁים מִבְּנֵי־יִשְׂרָאֵל חֲמִשִּׁים וּמָאתָיִם נְשִׂיאֵי עֵדָה קְרִאֵי מוֹעֵד אַנְשֵׁי־שֵׁם:

15:38 A cord of blue The biblical blue color *techelet* (תכלת) is mentioned numerous times in the Bible. *Rashi* explains that this color, worn on the fringes known as *tzitzit* (ציצית) placed on the corners of four-cornered garments, is meant to remind us of the sky, and, by extension, of *Hashem* and His constant presence in our lives. For close to fifteen hundred years, the source of this special blue dye had been lost to the world. In an exciting discovery in recent years, marine biologists together with Talmudic researchers have identified the source of *techelet* as a small snail found off the coast of northern Israel, near Haifa. Today, for the first time in centuries, people are once again wearing *techelet* on their *tzitzit*. From even the smallest sea creature, we continue to see the wonders of the Bible come to life in *Eretz Yisrael*.

Tzitzit strings with techelet

Bamidbar/Numbers 16
Korach

במדבר טז
קרח

3 They combined against *Moshe* and *Aharon* and said to them, "You have gone too far! For all the community are holy, all of them, and *Hashem* is in their midst. Why then do you raise yourselves above *Hashem*'s congregation?"

ג וַיִּקָּהֲלוּ עַל־מֹשֶׁה וְעַל־אַהֲרֹן וַיֹּאמְרוּ אֲלֵהֶם רַב־לָכֶם כִּי כָל־הָעֵדָה כֻּלָּם קְדֹשִׁים וּבְתוֹכָם יְהֹוָה וּמַדּוּעַ תִּתְנַשְּׂאוּ עַל־קְהַל יְהֹוָה:

va-yi-ka-ha-LU al mo-SHEH v'-al a-ha-RON va-yo-m'-RU a-lay-HEM rav la-KHEM KEE khol ha-ay-DAH ku-LAM k'do-SHEEM uv-to-KHAM a-do-NAI u-ma-DU-a tit-na-s'-U al k'-HAL a-do-NAI

4 When *Moshe* heard this, he fell on his face.

ד וַיִּשְׁמַע מֹשֶׁה וַיִּפֹּל עַל־פָּנָיו:

5 Then he spoke to *Korach* and all his company, saying, "Come morning, *Hashem* will make known who is His and who is holy, and will grant him access to Himself; He will grant access to the one He has chosen.

ה וַיְדַבֵּר אֶל־קֹרַח וְאֶל־כָּל־עֲדָתוֹ לֵאמֹר בֹּקֶר וְיֹדַע יְהֹוָה אֶת־אֲשֶׁר־לוֹ וְאֶת־הַקָּדוֹשׁ וְהִקְרִיב אֵלָיו וְאֵת אֲשֶׁר יִבְחַר־בּוֹ יַקְרִיב אֵלָיו:

6 Do this: You, *Korach* and all your band, take fire pans,

ו זֹאת עֲשׂוּ קְחוּ־לָכֶם מַחְתּוֹת קֹרַח וְכָל־עֲדָתוֹ:

7 and tomorrow put fire in them and lay incense on them before *Hashem*. Then the man whom *Hashem* chooses, he shall be the holy one. You have gone too far, sons of *Levi*!"

ז וּתְנוּ בָהֵן אֵשׁ וְשִׂימוּ עֲלֵיהֶן קְטֹרֶת לִפְנֵי יְהֹוָה מָחָר וְהָיָה הָאִישׁ אֲשֶׁר־יִבְחַר יְהֹוָה הוּא הַקָּדוֹשׁ רַב־לָכֶם בְּנֵי לֵוִי:

8 *Moshe* said further to *Korach*, "Hear me, sons of *Levi*.

ח וַיֹּאמֶר מֹשֶׁה אֶל־קֹרַח שִׁמְעוּ־נָא בְּנֵי לֵוִי:

9 Is it not enough for you that the God of *Yisrael* has set you apart from the community of *Yisrael* and given you access to Him, to perform the duties of *Hashem*'s *Mishkan* and to minister to the community and serve them?

ט הַמְעַט מִכֶּם כִּי־הִבְדִּיל אֱלֹהֵי יִשְׂרָאֵל אֶתְכֶם מֵעֲדַת יִשְׂרָאֵל לְהַקְרִיב אֶתְכֶם אֵלָיו לַעֲבֹד אֶת־עֲבֹדַת מִשְׁכַּן יְהֹוָה וְלַעֲמֹד לִפְנֵי הָעֵדָה לְשָׁרְתָם:

10 Now that He has advanced you and all your fellow *Leviim* with you, do you seek the priesthood too?

י וַיַּקְרֵב אֹתְךָ וְאֶת־כָּל־אַחֶיךָ בְנֵי־לֵוִי אִתָּךְ וּבִקַּשְׁתֶּם גַּם־כְּהֻנָּה:

11 Truly, it is against *Hashem* that you and all your company have banded together. For who is *Aharon* that you should rail against him?"

יא לָכֵן אַתָּה וְכָל־עֲדָתְךָ הַנֹּעָדִים עַל־יְהֹוָה וְאַהֲרֹן מַה־הוּא כִּי תלונו [תַלִּינוּ] עָלָיו:

16:3 Why then do you raise yourselves above *Hashem*'s congregation? *Korach* rebels against his cousins *Moshe* and *Aharon*, accusing them of taking positions of power for themselves. He declares that the entire Nation of Israel is holy, and therefore questions why *Moshe* and *Aharon* have raised themselves above the rest of the congregation. In making this claim, *Korach* not only implies that *Moshe* and *Aharon* inappropriately chose the leadership positions for themselves, thereby denying *Hashem*'s role in their appointment. He also makes the erroneous claim that every individual in the nation is on the same level of holiness. While it is true that everyone is endowed with an element of Godliness, it is up to each person to elevate himself or herself to even greater levels of holiness. The exact degree of a person's holiness, therefore, depends on their individual achievements.

Bamidbar/Numbers 16
Korach

במדבר טז
קרח

12	*Moshe* sent for *Datan* and *Aviram*, sons of *Eliav*; but they said, "We will not come!	יב וַיִּשְׁלַ֣ח מֹשֶׁ֔ה לִקְרֹ֛א לְדָתָ֥ן וְלַאֲבִירָ֖ם בְּנֵ֣י אֱלִיאָ֑ב וַיֹּאמְר֖וּ לֹ֥א נַעֲלֶֽה:
13	Is it not enough that you brought us from a land flowing with milk and honey to have us die in the wilderness, that you would also lord it over us?	יג הַמְעַ֗ט כִּ֤י הֶֽעֱלִיתָ֨נוּ֙ מֵאֶ֨רֶץ זָבַ֤ת חָלָב֙ וּדְבַ֔שׁ לַהֲמִיתֵ֖נוּ בַּמִּדְבָּ֑ר כִּֽי־תִשְׂתָּרֵ֥ר עָלֵ֖ינוּ גַּם־הִשְׂתָּרֵֽר:
14	Even if you had brought us to a land flowing with milk and honey, and given us possession of fields and vineyards, should you gouge out those men's eyes? We will not come!"	יד אַ֡ף לֹ֣א אֶל־אֶרֶץ֩ זָבַ֨ת חָלָ֤ב וּדְבַשׁ֙ הֲבִ֣יאֹתָ֔נוּ וַתִּ֨תֶּן־לָ֔נוּ נַחֲלַ֖ת שָׂדֶ֣ה וָכָ֑רֶם הַעֵינֵ֞י הָאֲנָשִׁ֥ים הָהֵ֛ם תְּנַקֵּ֖ר לֹ֥א נַעֲלֶֽה:
15	*Moshe* was much aggrieved and he said to *Hashem*, "Pay no regard to their oblation. I have not taken the ass of any one of them, nor have I wronged any one of them."	טו וַיִּ֤חַר לְמֹשֶׁה֙ מְאֹ֔ד וַיֹּ֨אמֶר֙ אֶל־יְהֹוָ֔ה אַל־תֵּ֖פֶן אֶל־מִנְחָתָ֑ם לֹ֠א חֲמ֨וֹר אֶחָ֤ד מֵהֶם֙ נָשָׂ֔אתִי וְלֹ֥א הֲרֵעֹ֖תִי אֶת־אַחַ֥ד מֵהֶֽם:
16	And *Moshe* said to *Korach*, "Tomorrow, you and all your company appear before *Hashem*, you and they and *Aharon*.	טז וַיֹּ֤אמֶר מֹשֶׁה֙ אֶל־קֹ֔רַח אַתָּה֙ וְכָל־עֲדָ֣תְךָ֔ הֱי֖וּ לִפְנֵ֣י יְהֹוָ֑ה אַתָּ֥ה וָהֵ֛ם וְאַהֲרֹ֖ן מָחָֽר:
17	Each of you take his fire pan and lay incense on it, and each of you bring his fire pan before *Hashem*, two hundred and fifty fire pans; you and *Aharon* also [bring] your fire pans."	יז וּקְח֣וּ ׀ אִ֣ישׁ מַחְתָּת֗וֹ וּנְתַתֶּ֤ם עֲלֵיהֶם֙ קְטֹ֔רֶת וְהִקְרַבְתֶּ֞ם לִפְנֵ֤י יְהֹוָה֙ אִ֣ישׁ מַחְתָּת֔וֹ חֲמִשִּׁ֥ים וּמָאתַ֖יִם מַחְתֹּ֑ת וְאַתָּ֥ה וְאַהֲרֹ֖ן אִ֥ישׁ מַחְתָּתֽוֹ:
18	Each of them took his fire pan, put fire in it, laid incense on it, and took his place at the entrance of the Tent of Meeting, as did *Moshe* and *Aharon*.	יח וַיִּקְח֞וּ אִ֣ישׁ מַחְתָּת֗וֹ וַיִּתְּנ֤וּ עֲלֵיהֶם֙ אֵ֔שׁ וַיָּשִׂ֥ימוּ עֲלֵיהֶ֖ם קְטֹ֑רֶת וַיַּעַמְד֗וּ פֶּ֛תַח אֹ֥הֶל מוֹעֵ֖ד וּמֹשֶׁ֥ה וְאַהֲרֹֽן:
19	*Korach* gathered the whole community against them at the entrance of the Tent of Meeting. Then the Presence of *Hashem* appeared to the whole community,	יט וַיַּקְהֵ֨ל עֲלֵיהֶ֥ם קֹ֨רַח֙ אֶת־כָּל־הָ֣עֵדָ֔ה אֶל־פֶּ֖תַח אֹ֣הֶל מוֹעֵ֑ד וַיֵּרָ֥א כְבוֹד־יְהֹוָ֖ה אֶל־כָּל־הָעֵדָֽה:
20	and *Hashem* spoke to *Moshe* and *Aharon*, saying,	כ וַיְדַבֵּ֣ר יְהֹוָ֔ה אֶל־מֹשֶׁ֥ה וְאֶל־אַהֲרֹ֖ן לֵאמֹֽר:
21	"Stand back from this community that I may annihilate them in an instant!"	כא הִבָּ֣דְל֔וּ מִתּ֖וֹךְ הָעֵדָ֣ה הַזֹּ֑את וַאֲכַלֶּ֥ה אֹתָ֖ם כְּרָֽגַע:
22	But they fell on their faces and said, "O *Hashem*, Source of the breath of all flesh! When one man sins, will You be wrathful with the whole community?"	כב וַיִּפְּל֤וּ עַל־פְּנֵיהֶם֙ וַיֹּ֣אמְר֔וּ אֵ֕ל אֱלֹהֵ֥י הָרוּחֹ֖ת לְכָל־בָּשָׂ֑ר הָאִ֤ישׁ אֶחָד֙ יֶחֱטָ֔א וְעַ֥ל כָּל־הָעֵדָ֖ה תִּקְצֹֽף:
23	*Hashem* spoke to *Moshe*, saying,	כג וַיְדַבֵּ֥ר יְהֹוָ֖ה אֶל־מֹשֶׁ֥ה לֵּאמֹֽר:
24	"Speak to the community and say: Withdraw from about the abodes of *Korach*, *Datan*, and *Aviram*."	כד דַּבֵּ֥ר אֶל־הָעֵדָ֖ה לֵאמֹ֑ר הֵֽעָלוּ֙ מִסָּבִ֔יב לְמִשְׁכַּן־קֹ֖רַח דָּתָ֥ן וַאֲבִירָֽם:
25	*Moshe* rose and went to *Datan* and *Aviram*, the elders of *Yisrael* following him.	כה וַיָּ֣קָם מֹשֶׁ֔ה וַיֵּ֖לֶךְ אֶל־דָּתָ֣ן וַאֲבִירָ֑ם וַיֵּלְכ֥וּ אַחֲרָ֖יו זִקְנֵ֥י יִשְׂרָאֵֽל:

Bamidbar/Numbers 17
Korach

במדבר יז
קרח

26 He addressed the community, saying, "Move away from the tents of these wicked men and touch nothing that belongs to them, lest you be wiped out for all their sins."

כו וַיְדַבֵּר אֶל־הָעֵדָה לֵאמֹר סוּרוּ נָא מֵעַל אָהֳלֵי הָאֲנָשִׁים הָרְשָׁעִים הָאֵלֶּה וְאַל־תִּגְּעוּ בְּכָל־אֲשֶׁר לָהֶם פֶּן־תִּסָּפוּ בְּכָל־חַטֹּאתָם:

27 So they withdrew from about the abodes of *Korach*, *Datan*, and *Aviram*. Now *Datan* and *Aviram* had come out and they stood at the entrance of their tents, with their wives, their children, and their little ones.

כז וַיֵּעָלוּ מֵעַל מִשְׁכַּן־קֹרַח דָּתָן וַאֲבִירָם מִסָּבִיב וְדָתָן וַאֲבִירָם יָצְאוּ נִצָּבִים פֶּתַח אָהֳלֵיהֶם וּנְשֵׁיהֶם וּבְנֵיהֶם וְטַפָּם:

28 And *Moshe* said, "By this you shall know that it was *Hashem* who sent me to do all these things; that they are not of my own devising:

כח וַיֹּאמֶר מֹשֶׁה בְּזֹאת תֵּדְעוּן כִּי־יְהֹוָה שְׁלָחַנִי לַעֲשׂוֹת אֵת כָּל־הַמַּעֲשִׂים הָאֵלֶּה כִּי־לֹא מִלִּבִּי:

29 if these men die as all men do, if their lot be the common fate of all mankind, it was not *Hashem* who sent me.

כט אִם־כְּמוֹת כָּל־הָאָדָם יְמֻתוּן אֵלֶּה וּפְקֻדַּת כָּל־הָאָדָם יִפָּקֵד עֲלֵיהֶם לֹא יְהֹוָה שְׁלָחָנִי:

30 But if *Hashem* brings about something unheard-of, so that the ground opens its mouth and swallows them up with all that belongs to them, and they go down alive into Sheol, you shall know that these men have spurned *Hashem*."

ל וְאִם־בְּרִיאָה יִבְרָא יְהֹוָה וּפָצְתָה הָאֲדָמָה אֶת־פִּיהָ וּבָלְעָה אֹתָם וְאֶת־כָּל־אֲשֶׁר לָהֶם וְיָרְדוּ חַיִּים שְׁאֹלָה וִידַעְתֶּם כִּי נִאֲצוּ הָאֲנָשִׁים הָאֵלֶּה אֶת־יְהֹוָה:

31 Scarcely had he finished speaking all these words when the ground under them burst asunder,

לא וַיְהִי כְּכַלֹּתוֹ לְדַבֵּר אֵת כָּל־הַדְּבָרִים הָאֵלֶּה וַתִּבָּקַע הָאֲדָמָה אֲשֶׁר תַּחְתֵּיהֶם:

32 and the earth opened its mouth and swallowed them up with their households, all *Korach*'s people and all their possessions.

לב וַתִּפְתַּח הָאָרֶץ אֶת־פִּיהָ וַתִּבְלַע אֹתָם וְאֶת־בָּתֵּיהֶם וְאֵת כָּל־הָאָדָם אֲשֶׁר לְקֹרַח וְאֵת כָּל־הָרְכוּשׁ:

33 They went down alive into Sheol, with all that belonged to them; the earth closed over them and they vanished from the midst of the congregation.

לג וַיֵּרְדוּ הֵם וְכָל־אֲשֶׁר לָהֶם חַיִּים שְׁאֹלָה וַתְּכַס עֲלֵיהֶם הָאָרֶץ וַיֹּאבְדוּ מִתּוֹךְ הַקָּהָל:

34 All *Yisrael* around them fled at their shrieks, for they said, "The earth might swallow us!"

לד וְכָל־יִשְׂרָאֵל אֲשֶׁר סְבִיבֹתֵיהֶם נָסוּ לְקֹלָם כִּי אָמְרוּ פֶּן־תִּבְלָעֵנוּ הָאָרֶץ:

35 And a fire went forth from *Hashem* and consumed the two hundred and fifty men offering the incense.

לה וְאֵשׁ יָצְאָה מֵאֵת יְהֹוָה וַתֹּאכַל אֵת הַחֲמִשִּׁים וּמָאתַיִם אִישׁ מַקְרִיבֵי הַקְּטֹרֶת:

17 1 *Hashem* spoke to *Moshe*, saying:

יז א וַיְדַבֵּר יְהֹוָה אֶל־מֹשֶׁה לֵּאמֹר:

2 Order *Elazar* son of *Aharon* the *Kohen* to remove the fire pans – for they have become sacred – from among the charred remains; and scatter the coals abroad.

ב אֱמֹר אֶל־אֶלְעָזָר בֶּן־אַהֲרֹן הַכֹּהֵן וְיָרֵם אֶת־הַמַּחְתֹּת מִבֵּין הַשְּׂרֵפָה וְאֶת־הָאֵשׁ זְרֵה־הָלְאָה כִּי קָדֵשׁוּ:

Bamidbar/Numbers 17
Korach

במדבר יז
קרח

3 [Remove] the fire pans of those who have sinned at the cost of their lives, and let them be made into hammered sheets as plating for the *Mizbayach* – for once they have been used for offering to *Hashem*, they have become sacred – and let them serve as a warning to the people of *Yisrael*.

ג אֵת מַחְתּוֹת הַחַטָּאִים הָאֵלֶּה בְּנַפְשֹׁתָם וְעָשׂוּ אֹתָם רִקֻּעֵי פַחִים צִפּוּי לַמִּזְבֵּחַ כִּי־הִקְרִיבֻם לִפְנֵי־יְהֹוָה וַיִּקְדָּשׁוּ וְיִהְיוּ לְאוֹת לִבְנֵי יִשְׂרָאֵל:

4 *Elazar* the *Kohen* took the copper fire pans which had been used for offering by those who died in the fire; and they were hammered into plating for the *Mizbayach*,

ד וַיִּקַּח אֶלְעָזָר הַכֹּהֵן אֵת מַחְתּוֹת הַנְּחֹשֶׁת אֲשֶׁר הִקְרִיבוּ הַשְּׂרֻפִים וַיְרַקְּעוּם צִפּוּי לַמִּזְבֵּחַ:

5 as *Hashem* had ordered him through *Moshe*. It was to be a reminder to the Israelites, so that no outsider – one not of *Aharon*'s offspring – should presume to offer incense before *Hashem* and suffer the fate of *Korach* and his band.

ה זִכָּרוֹן לִבְנֵי יִשְׂרָאֵל לְמַעַן אֲשֶׁר לֹא־יִקְרַב אִישׁ זָר אֲשֶׁר לֹא מִזֶּרַע אַהֲרֹן הוּא לְהַקְטִיר קְטֹרֶת לִפְנֵי יְהֹוָה וְלֹא־יִהְיֶה כְקֹרַח וְכַעֲדָתוֹ כַּאֲשֶׁר דִּבֶּר יְהֹוָה בְּיַד־מֹשֶׁה לוֹ:

6 Next day the whole Israelite community railed against *Moshe* and *Aharon*, saying, "You two have brought death upon *Hashem*'s people!"

ו וַיִּלֹּנוּ כָּל־עֲדַת בְּנֵי־יִשְׂרָאֵל מִמָּחֳרָת עַל־מֹשֶׁה וְעַל־אַהֲרֹן לֵאמֹר אַתֶּם הֲמִתֶּם אֶת־עַם יְהֹוָה:

7 But as the community gathered against them, *Moshe* and *Aharon* turned toward the Tent of Meeting; the cloud had covered it and the Presence of *Hashem* appeared.

ז וַיְהִי בְּהִקָּהֵל הָעֵדָה עַל־מֹשֶׁה וְעַל־אַהֲרֹן וַיִּפְנוּ אֶל־אֹהֶל מוֹעֵד וְהִנֵּה כִסָּהוּ הֶעָנָן וַיֵּרָא כְּבוֹד יְהֹוָה:

8 When *Moshe* and *Aharon* reached the Tent of Meeting,

ח וַיָּבֹא מֹשֶׁה וְאַהֲרֹן אֶל־פְּנֵי אֹהֶל מוֹעֵד:

9 *Hashem* spoke to *Moshe*, saying,

ט וַיְדַבֵּר יְהֹוָה אֶל־מֹשֶׁה לֵּאמֹר:

10 "Remove yourselves from this community, that I may annihilate them in an instant." They fell on their faces.

י הֵרֹמּוּ מִתּוֹךְ הָעֵדָה הַזֹּאת וַאֲכַלֶּה אֹתָם כְּרָגַע וַיִּפְּלוּ עַל־פְּנֵיהֶם:

11 Then *Moshe* said to *Aharon*, "Take the fire pan, and put on it fire from the *Mizbayach*. Add incense and take it quickly to the community and make expiation for them. For wrath has gone forth from *Hashem*: the plague has begun!"

יא וַיֹּאמֶר מֹשֶׁה אֶל־אַהֲרֹן קַח אֶת־הַמַּחְתָּה וְתֶן־עָלֶיהָ אֵשׁ מֵעַל הַמִּזְבֵּחַ וְשִׂים קְטֹרֶת וְהוֹלֵךְ מְהֵרָה אֶל־הָעֵדָה וְכַפֵּר עֲלֵיהֶם כִּי־יָצָא הַקֶּצֶף מִלִּפְנֵי יְהֹוָה הֵחֵל הַנָּגֶף:

12 *Aharon* took it, as *Moshe* had ordered, and ran to the midst of the congregation, where the plague had begun among the people. He put on the incense and made expiation for the people;

יב וַיִּקַּח אַהֲרֹן כַּאֲשֶׁר דִּבֶּר מֹשֶׁה וַיָּרָץ אֶל־תּוֹךְ הַקָּהָל וְהִנֵּה הֵחֵל הַנֶּגֶף בָּעָם וַיִּתֵּן אֶת־הַקְּטֹרֶת וַיְכַפֵּר עַל־הָעָם:

13 he stood between the dead and the living until the plague was checked.

יג וַיַּעֲמֹד בֵּין־הַמֵּתִים וּבֵין הַחַיִּים וַתֵּעָצַר הַמַּגֵּפָה:

14 Those who died of the plague came to fourteen thousand and seven hundred, aside from those who died on account of *Korach*.

יד וַיִּהְיוּ הַמֵּתִים בַּמַּגֵּפָה אַרְבָּעָה עָשָׂר אֶלֶף וּשְׁבַע מֵאוֹת מִלְּבַד הַמֵּתִים עַל־דְּבַר־קֹרַח:

Bamidbar/Numbers 17
Korach

במדבר יז
קרח

15 *Aharon* then returned to *Moshe* at the entrance of the Tent of Meeting, since the plague was checked.

טו וַיָּשָׁב אַהֲרֹן אֶל־מֹשֶׁה אֶל־פֶּתַח אֹהֶל מוֹעֵד וְהַמַּגֵּפָה נֶעֱצָרָה:

16 *Hashem* spoke to *Moshe*, saying:

טז וַיְדַבֵּר יְהֹוָה אֶל־מֹשֶׁה לֵּאמֹר:

17 Speak to *B'nei Yisrael* and take from them – from the chieftains of their ancestral houses – one staff for each chieftain of an ancestral house: twelve staffs in all. Inscribe each man's name on his staff,

יז דַּבֵּר אֶל־בְּנֵי יִשְׂרָאֵל וְקַח מֵאִתָּם מַטֶּה מַטֶּה לְבֵית אָב מֵאֵת כָּל־נְשִׂיאֵהֶם לְבֵית אֲבֹתָם שְׁנֵים עָשָׂר מַטּוֹת אִישׁ אֶת־שְׁמוֹ תִּכְתֹּב עַל־מַטֵּהוּ:

18 there being one staff for each head of an ancestral house; also inscribe *Aharon*'s name on the staff of *Levi*.

יח וְאֵת שֵׁם אַהֲרֹן תִּכְתֹּב עַל־מַטֵּה לֵוִי כִּי מַטֶּה אֶחָד לְרֹאשׁ בֵּית אֲבוֹתָם:

19 Deposit them in the Tent of Meeting before the Pact, where I meet with you.

יט וְהִנַּחְתָּם בְּאֹהֶל מוֹעֵד לִפְנֵי הָעֵדוּת אֲשֶׁר אִוָּעֵד לָכֶם שָׁמָּה:

20 The staff of the man whom I choose shall sprout, and I will rid Myself of the incessant mutterings of the Israelites against you.

כ וְהָיָה הָאִישׁ אֲשֶׁר אֶבְחַר־בּוֹ מַטֵּהוּ יִפְרָח וַהֲשִׁכֹּתִי מֵעָלַי אֶת־תְּלֻנּוֹת בְּנֵי יִשְׂרָאֵל אֲשֶׁר הֵם מַלִּינִם עֲלֵיכֶם:

21 *Moshe* spoke thus to the Israelites. Their chieftains gave him a staff for each chieftain of an ancestral house, twelve staffs in all; among these staffs was that of *Aharon*.

כא וַיְדַבֵּר מֹשֶׁה אֶל־בְּנֵי יִשְׂרָאֵל וַיִּתְּנוּ אֵלָיו כָּל־נְשִׂיאֵיהֶם מַטֶּה לְנָשִׂיא אֶחָד מַטֶּה לְנָשִׂיא אֶחָד לְבֵית אֲבֹתָם שְׁנֵים עָשָׂר מַטּוֹת וּמַטֵּה אַהֲרֹן בְּתוֹךְ מַטּוֹתָם:

22 *Moshe* deposited the staffs before *Hashem*, in the Tent of the Pact.

כב וַיַּנַּח מֹשֶׁה אֶת־הַמַּטֹּת לִפְנֵי יְהֹוָה בְּאֹהֶל הָעֵדֻת:

23 The next day *Moshe* entered the Tent of the Pact, and there the staff of *Aharon* of the house of *Levi* had sprouted: it had brought forth sprouts, produced blossoms, and borne almonds.

כג וַיְהִי מִמָּחֳרָת וַיָּבֹא מֹשֶׁה אֶל־אֹהֶל הָעֵדוּת וְהִנֵּה פָּרַח מַטֵּה־אַהֲרֹן לְבֵית לֵוִי וַיֹּצֵא פֶרַח וַיָּצֵץ צִיץ וַיִּגְמֹל שְׁקֵדִים:

vai-HEE mi-ma-kha-RAT va-ya-VO mo-SHEH el O-hel ha-ay-DUT v'-hi-NAY pa-RAKH ma-tay a-ha-RON l'-VAYT lay-VEE va-YO-tzay FE-rakh va-YA-tzaytz TZEETZ va-yig-MOL sh'-kay-DEEM

Mount Zion

17:23 The staff of *Aharon* of the house of *Levi* had sprouted Legendary Israeli storyteller Rabbi S.Z. Kahana tells a story about three clergymen who were on a visit to Mount Zion in 1965. When they asked the Jewish curator of Mt. Zion why the Jews insist on claiming Jerusalem as the capital of the Israel instead of letting it remain an international city, he replied with an example from this chapter. When *Moshe* appointed *Aharon* as the *Kohen Gadol*, 'High Priest,' the people objected and murmured. Neither the earthquake that swallowed *Korach* and his followers nor the plague that followed were enough to convince the people that *Aharon* had been appointed by God. It was only once his staff blossomed, showing the vitality of life, that they accepted *Aharon* as the *Kohen*. The curator invited the visiting clergymen to climb up with him to the mountain's observation tower. "From here, you can see both the old and new Jerusalem. In the old Arab-controlled section of the city, as you can observe, there is desolation: ruins, desert, and rocks. On our side is the new Jerusalem, where over 150,000 Jews have settled. You can see our new homes and schools, the new hospital and the new university. Everywhere you look, you see life, growth, and vitality. You ask: To whom does Jerusalem belong? It belongs to those who make it bud and blossom, to those who make it live and grow." Half a century later, Jewish Jerusalem continues to show even more incredible signs of life and vitality. *Yerushalayim* in Jewish hands is indeed ordained by *Hashem*, just as the budding of *Aharon*'s staff demonstrated his divine selection.

Bamidbar/Numbers 18
Korach

24 *Moshe* then brought out all the staffs from before *Hashem* to all the Israelites; each identified and recovered his staff.

25 *Hashem* said to *Moshe*, "Put *Aharon*'s staff back before the Pact, to be kept as a lesson to rebels, so that their mutterings against Me may cease, lest they die."

26 This *Moshe* did; just as *Hashem* had commanded him, so he did.

27 But the Israelites said to *Moshe*, "Lo, we perish! We are lost, all of us lost!

28 Everyone who so much as ventures near *Hashem*'s *Mishkan* must die. Alas, we are doomed to perish!"

18 1 *Hashem* said to *Aharon*: You and your sons and the ancestral house under your charge shall bear any guilt connected with the sanctuary; you and your sons alone shall bear any guilt connected with your priesthood.

2 You shall also associate with yourself your kinsmen the tribe of *Levi*, your ancestral tribe, to be attached to you and to minister to you, while you and your sons under your charge are before the Tent of the Pact.

3 They shall discharge their duties to you and to the Tent as a whole, but they must not have any contact with the furnishings of the Shrine or with the *Mizbayach*, lest both they and you die.

4 They shall be attached to you and discharge the duties of the Tent of Meeting, all the service of the Tent; but no outsider shall intrude upon you

5 as you discharge the duties connected with the Shrine and the *Mizbayach*, that wrath may not again strike the Israelites.

6 I hereby take your fellow *Leviim* from among the Israelites; they are assigned to you in dedication to *Hashem*, to do the work of the Tent of Meeting;

7 while you and your sons shall be careful to perform your priestly duties in everything pertaining to the *Mizbayach* and to what is behind the curtain. I make your priesthood a service of dedication; any outsider who encroaches shall be put to death.

במדבר יח
קרח

כד וַיֹּצֵא מֹשֶׁה אֶת־כָּל־הַמַּטֹּת מִלִּפְנֵי יְהֹוָה אֶל־כָּל־בְּנֵי יִשְׂרָאֵל וַיִּרְאוּ וַיִּקְחוּ אִישׁ מַטֵּהוּ׃

כה וַיֹּאמֶר יְהֹוָה אֶל־מֹשֶׁה הָשֵׁב אֶת־מַטֵּה אַהֲרֹן לִפְנֵי הָעֵדוּת לְמִשְׁמֶרֶת לְאוֹת לִבְנֵי־מֶרִי וּתְכַל תְּלוּנֹּתָם מֵעָלַי וְלֹא יָמֻתוּ׃

כו וַיַּעַשׂ מֹשֶׁה כַּאֲשֶׁר צִוָּה יְהֹוָה אֹתוֹ כֵּן עָשָׂה׃

כז וַיֹּאמְרוּ בְּנֵי יִשְׂרָאֵל אֶל־מֹשֶׁה לֵאמֹר הֵן גָּוַעְנוּ אָבַדְנוּ כֻּלָּנוּ אָבָדְנוּ׃

כח כֹּל הַקָּרֵב הַקָּרֵב אֶל־מִשְׁכַּן יְהֹוָה יָמוּת הַאִם תַּמְנוּ לִגְוֺעַ׃

יח א וַיֹּאמֶר יְהֹוָה אֶל־אַהֲרֹן אַתָּה וּבָנֶיךָ וּבֵית־אָבִיךָ אִתָּךְ תִּשְׂאוּ אֶת־עֲוֺן הַמִּקְדָּשׁ וְאַתָּה וּבָנֶיךָ אִתָּךְ תִּשְׂאוּ אֶת־עֲוֺן כְּהֻנַּתְכֶם׃

ב וְגַם אֶת־אַחֶיךָ מַטֵּה לֵוִי שֵׁבֶט אָבִיךָ הַקְרֵב אִתָּךְ וְיִלָּווּ עָלֶיךָ וִישָׁרְתוּךָ וְאַתָּה וּבָנֶיךָ אִתָּךְ לִפְנֵי אֹהֶל הָעֵדֻת׃

ג וְשָׁמְרוּ מִשְׁמַרְתְּךָ וּמִשְׁמֶרֶת כָּל־הָאֹהֶל אַךְ אֶל־כְּלֵי הַקֹּדֶשׁ וְאֶל־הַמִּזְבֵּחַ לֹא יִקְרָבוּ וְלֹא־יָמֻתוּ גַם־הֵם גַּם־אַתֶּם׃

ד וְנִלְווּ עָלֶיךָ וְשָׁמְרוּ אֶת־מִשְׁמֶרֶת אֹהֶל מוֹעֵד לְכֹל עֲבֹדַת הָאֹהֶל וְזָר לֹא־יִקְרַב אֲלֵיכֶם׃

ה וּשְׁמַרְתֶּם אֵת מִשְׁמֶרֶת הַקֹּדֶשׁ וְאֵת מִשְׁמֶרֶת הַמִּזְבֵּחַ וְלֹא־יִהְיֶה עוֹד קֶצֶף עַל־בְּנֵי יִשְׂרָאֵל׃

ו וַאֲנִי הִנֵּה לָקַחְתִּי אֶת־אֲחֵיכֶם הַלְוִיִּם מִתּוֹךְ בְּנֵי יִשְׂרָאֵל לָכֶם מַתָּנָה נְתֻנִים לַיהֹוָה לַעֲבֹד אֶת־עֲבֹדַת אֹהֶל מוֹעֵד׃

ז וְאַתָּה וּבָנֶיךָ אִתְּךָ תִּשְׁמְרוּ אֶת־כְּהֻנַּתְכֶם לְכָל־דְּבַר הַמִּזְבֵּחַ וּלְמִבֵּית לַפָּרֹכֶת וַעֲבַדְתֶּם עֲבֹדַת מַתָּנָה אֶתֵּן אֶת־כְּהֻנַּתְכֶם וְהַזָּר הַקָּרֵב יוּמָת׃

Bamidbar/Numbers 18
Korach

במדבר יח
קרח

8 *Hashem* spoke further to *Aharon*: I hereby give you charge of My gifts, all the sacred donations of the Israelites; I grant them to you and to your sons as a perquisite, a due for all time.

ח וַיְדַבֵּר יְהֹוָה אֶל־אַהֲרֹן וַאֲנִי הִנֵּה נָתַתִּי לְךָ אֶת־מִשְׁמֶרֶת תְּרוּמֹתָי לְכָל־קָדְשֵׁי בְנֵי־יִשְׂרָאֵל לְךָ נְתַתִּים לְמָשְׁחָה וּלְבָנֶיךָ לְחָק־עוֹלָם:

vai-da-BAYR a-do-NAI el a-ha-RON v-a-NEE hi-NAY na-TA-tee l'-KHA et mish-ME-ret t'-ru-mo-TAI l'-khol kod-SHAY v'-nay yis-ra-AYL l'-KHA n'-ta-TEEM l'-mosh-KHAH ul-va-NE-kha l'-khok o-LAM

9 This shall be yours from the most holy sacrifices, the offerings by fire: every such offering that they render to Me as most holy sacrifices, namely, every meal offering, sin offering, and guilt offering of theirs, shall belong to you and your sons.

ט זֶה־יִהְיֶה לְךָ מִקֹּדֶשׁ הַקֳּדָשִׁים מִן־הָאֵשׁ כָּל־קָרְבָּנָם לְכָל־מִנְחָתָם וּלְכָל־חַטָּאתָם וּלְכָל־אֲשָׁמָם אֲשֶׁר יָשִׁיבוּ לִי קֹדֶשׁ קָדָשִׁים לְךָ הוּא וּלְבָנֶיךָ:

10 You shall partake of them as most sacred donations: only males may eat them; you shall treat them as consecrated.

י בְּקֹדֶשׁ הַקֳּדָשִׁים תֹּאכְלֶנּוּ כָּל־זָכָר יֹאכַל אֹתוֹ קֹדֶשׁ יִהְיֶה־לָּךְ:

11 This, too, shall be yours: the gift offerings of their contributions, all the elevation offerings of the Israelites, I give to you, to your sons, and to the daughters that are with you, as a due for all time; everyone of your household who is clean may eat it.

יא וְזֶה־לְּךָ תְּרוּמַת מַתָּנָם לְכָל־תְּנוּפֹת בְּנֵי יִשְׂרָאֵל לְךָ נְתַתִּים וּלְבָנֶיךָ וְלִבְנֹתֶיךָ אִתְּךָ לְחָק־עוֹלָם כָּל־טָהוֹר בְּבֵיתְךָ יֹאכַל אֹתוֹ:

12 All the best of the new oil, wine, and grain – the choice parts that they present to *Hashem* – I give to you.

יב כֹּל חֵלֶב יִצְהָר וְכָל־חֵלֶב תִּירוֹשׁ וְדָגָן רֵאשִׁיתָם אֲשֶׁר־יִתְּנוּ לַיהֹוָה לְךָ נְתַתִּים:

13 The first fruits of everything in their land, that they bring to *Hashem*, shall be yours; everyone of your household who is clean may eat them.

יג בִּכּוּרֵי כָּל־אֲשֶׁר בְּאַרְצָם אֲשֶׁר־יָבִיאוּ לַיהֹוָה לְךָ יִהְיֶה כָּל־טָהוֹר בְּבֵיתְךָ יֹאכֲלֶנּוּ:

14 Everything that has been proscribed in *Yisrael* shall be yours.

יד כָּל־חֵרֶם בְּיִשְׂרָאֵל לְךָ יִהְיֶה:

15 The first issue of the womb of every being, man or beast, that is offered to *Hashem*, shall be yours; but you shall have the first-born of man redeemed, and you shall also have the firstling of unclean animals redeemed.

טו כָּל־פֶּטֶר רֶחֶם לְכָל־בָּשָׂר אֲשֶׁר־יַקְרִיבוּ לַיהֹוָה בָּאָדָם וּבַבְּהֵמָה יִהְיֶה־לָּךְ אַךְ פָּדֹה תִפְדֶּה אֵת בְּכוֹר הָאָדָם וְאֵת בְּכוֹר־הַבְּהֵמָה הַטְּמֵאָה תִּפְדֶּה:

16 Take as their redemption price, from the age of one month up, the money equivalent of five *shekalim* by the sanctuary weight, which is twenty *geira*.

טז וּפְדוּיָו מִבֶּן־חֹדֶשׁ תִּפְדֶּה בְּעֶרְכְּךָ כֶּסֶף חֲמֵשֶׁת שְׁקָלִים בְּשֶׁקֶל הַקֹּדֶשׁ עֶשְׂרִים גֵּרָה הוּא:

18:8 I grant them to you and to your sons as a perquisite The gifts and tithes presented to the *Kohanim* and *Leviim* are additional examples of commandments that apply only in the Land of Israel. Like the portion of *challah* (Numbers 15:17–21), these are gifts given to the spiritual leaders of Israel to provide for their physical sustenance in exchange for the spiritual sustenance they offered to the people. Since they have no portion of land of their own, the *Kohanim* and *Leviim* are dependent on the rest of the nation for their physical nourishment, while the spiritual work that they do elevates everyone else's existence in the land.

Bamidbar/Numbers 18
Korach

במדבר יח
קרח

17 But the firstlings of cattle, sheep, or goats may not be redeemed; they are consecrated. You shall dash their blood against the *Mizbayach*, and turn their fat into smoke as an offering by fire for a pleasing odor to *Hashem*.

יז אַ֣ךְ בְּכֽוֹר־שׁ֡וֹר אֽוֹ־בְכ֨וֹר כֶּ֜שֶׂב אֽוֹ־בְכ֥וֹר עֵ֛ז לֹ֥א תִפְדֶּ֖ה קֹ֣דֶשׁ הֵ֑ם אֶת־דָּמָ֞ם תִּזְרֹ֤ק עַל־הַמִּזְבֵּ֨חַ֙ וְאֶת־חֶלְבָּ֣ם תַּקְטִ֔יר אִשֶּׁ֛ה לְרֵ֥יחַ נִיחֹ֖חַ לַֽיהוָֽה׃

18 But their meat shall be yours: it shall be yours like the breast of elevation offering and like the right thigh.

יח וּבְשָׂרָ֖ם יִֽהְיֶה־לָּ֑ךְ כַּחֲזֵ֧ה הַתְּנוּפָ֛ה וּכְשׁ֥וֹק הַיָּמִ֖ין לְךָ֥ יִהְיֶֽה׃

19 All the sacred gifts that the Israelites set aside for *Hashem* I give to you, to your sons, and to the daughters that are with you, as a due for all time. It shall be an everlasting covenant of salt before *Hashem* for you and for your offspring as well.

יט כֹּ֣ל ׀ תְּרוּמֹ֣ת הַקֳּדָשִׁ֗ים אֲשֶׁ֨ר יָרִ֥ימוּ בְנֵֽי־יִשְׂרָאֵל֮ לַֽיהוָה֒ נָתַ֣תִּי לְךָ֗ וּלְבָנֶ֧יךָ וְלִבְנֹתֶ֛יךָ אִתְּךָ֖ לְחָק־עוֹלָ֑ם בְּרִית֩ מֶ֨לַח עוֹלָ֥ם הִוא֙ לִפְנֵ֣י יְהוָ֔ה לְךָ֖ וּלְזַרְעֲךָ֥ אִתָּֽךְ׃

20 And *Hashem* said to *Aharon*: You shall, however, have no territorial share among them or own any portion in their midst; I am your portion and your share among the Israelites.

כ וַיֹּ֨אמֶר יְהוָ֜ה אֶֽל־אַהֲרֹ֗ן בְּאַרְצָם֙ לֹ֣א תִנְחָ֔ל וְחֵ֕לֶק לֹא־יִהְיֶ֥ה לְךָ֖ בְּתוֹכָ֑ם אֲנִ֤י חֶלְקְךָ֙ וְנַחֲלָ֣תְךָ֔ בְּת֖וֹךְ בְּנֵ֥י יִשְׂרָאֵֽל׃

21 And to the *Leviim* I hereby give all the tithes in *Yisrael* as their share in return for the services that they perform, the services of the Tent of Meeting.

כא וְלִבְנֵ֣י לֵוִ֔י הִנֵּ֥ה נָתַ֛תִּי כָּל־מַֽעֲשֵׂ֥ר בְּיִשְׂרָאֵ֖ל לְנַחֲלָ֑ה חֵ֤לֶף עֲבֹֽדָתָם֙ אֲשֶׁר־הֵ֣ם עֹֽבְדִ֔ים אֶת־עֲבֹדַ֖ת אֹ֥הֶל מוֹעֵֽד׃

22 Henceforth, Israelites shall not trespass on the Tent of Meeting, and thus incur guilt and die:

כב וְלֹא־יִקְרְב֥וּ ע֛וֹד בְּנֵ֥י יִשְׂרָאֵ֖ל אֶל־אֹ֣הֶל מוֹעֵ֑ד לָשֵׂ֥את חֵ֖טְא לָמֽוּת׃

23 only *Leviim* shall perform the services of the Tent of Meeting; others would incur guilt. It is the law for all time throughout the ages. But they shall have no territorial share among the Israelites;

כג וְעָבַ֨ד הַלֵּוִ֜י ה֗וּא אֶת־עֲבֹדַת֙ אֹ֣הֶל מוֹעֵ֔ד וְהֵ֖ם יִשְׂא֣וּ עֲוֺנָ֑ם חֻקַּ֤ת עוֹלָם֙ לְדֹרֹ֣תֵיכֶ֔ם וּבְתוֹךְ֙ בְּנֵ֣י יִשְׂרָאֵ֔ל לֹ֥א יִנְחֲל֖וּ נַחֲלָֽה׃

24 for it is the tithes set aside by the Israelites as a gift to *Hashem* that I give to the *Leviim* as their share. Therefore I have said concerning them: They shall have no territorial share among the Israelites.

כד כִּ֞י אֶת־מַעְשַׂ֣ר בְּנֵֽי־יִשְׂרָאֵ֗ל אֲשֶׁ֨ר יָרִ֤ימוּ לַֽיהוָה֙ תְּרוּמָ֔ה נָתַ֥תִּי לַלְוִיִּ֖ם לְנַחֲלָ֑ה עַל־כֵּן֙ אָמַ֣רְתִּי לָהֶ֔ם בְּתוֹךְ֙ בְּנֵ֣י יִשְׂרָאֵ֔ל לֹ֥א יִנְחֲל֖וּ נַחֲלָֽה׃

25 *Hashem* spoke to *Moshe*, saying:

כה וַיְדַבֵּ֥ר יְהוָ֖ה אֶל־מֹשֶׁ֥ה לֵּאמֹֽר׃

26 Speak to the *Leviim* and say to them: When you receive from the Israelites their tithes, which I have assigned to you as your share, you shall set aside from them one-tenth of the tithe as a gift to *Hashem*.

כו וְאֶל־הַלְוִיִּ֣ם תְּדַבֵּר֮ וְאָמַרְתָּ֣ אֲלֵהֶם֒ כִּֽי־תִ֠קְח֠וּ מֵאֵ֨ת בְּנֵֽי־יִשְׂרָאֵ֜ל אֶת־הַֽמַּעֲשֵׂ֗ר אֲשֶׁ֨ר נָתַ֧תִּי לָכֶ֛ם מֵאִתָּ֖ם בְּנַחֲלַתְכֶ֑ם וַהֲרֵמֹתֶ֤ם מִמֶּ֨נּוּ֙ תְּרוּמַ֣ת יְהוָ֔ה מַעֲשֵׂ֖ר מִן־הַֽמַּעֲשֵֽׂר׃

27 This shall be accounted to you as your gift. As with the new grain from the threshing floor or the flow from the vat,

כז וְנֶחְשַׁ֥ב לָכֶ֖ם תְּרֽוּמַתְכֶ֑ם כַּדָּגָן֙ מִן־הַגֹּ֔רֶן וְכַֽמְלֵאָ֖ה מִן־הַיָּֽקֶב׃

28 so shall you on your part set aside a gift for *Hashem* from all the tithes that you receive from the Israelites; and from them you shall bring the gift for *Hashem* to *Aharon* the *Kohen*.

כח כֵּ֣ן תָּרִ֤ימוּ גַם־אַתֶּם֙ תְּרוּמַ֣ת יְהוָ֔ה מִכֹּל֙ מַעְשְׂרֹ֣תֵיכֶ֔ם אֲשֶׁ֣ר תִּקְח֔וּ מֵאֵ֖ת בְּנֵ֣י יִשְׂרָאֵ֑ל וּנְתַתֶּ֤ם מִמֶּ֨נּוּ֙ אֶת־תְּרוּמַ֣ת יְהוָ֔ה לְאַהֲרֹ֖ן הַכֹּהֵֽן׃

Bamidbar/Numbers 19
Chukat

במדבר יט
חקת

29 You shall set aside all gifts due to *Hashem* from everything that is donated to you, from each thing its best portion, the part thereof that is to be consecrated.

כט מִכֹּל מַתְּנֹתֵיכֶם תָּרִימוּ אֵת כָּל־תְּרוּמַת יְהוָה מִכָּל־חֶלְבּוֹ אֶת־מִקְדְּשׁוֹ מִמֶּנּוּ:

30 Say to them further: When you have removed the best part from it, you *Leviim* may consider it the same as the yield of threshing floor or vat.

ל וְאָמַרְתָּ אֲלֵהֶם בַּהֲרִימְכֶם אֶת־חֶלְבּוֹ מִמֶּנּוּ וְנֶחְשַׁב לַלְוִיִּם כִּתְבוּאַת גֹּרֶן וְכִתְבוּאַת יָקֶב:

31 You and your households may eat it anywhere, for it is your recompense for your services in the Tent of Meeting.

לא וַאֲכַלְתֶּם אֹתוֹ בְּכָל־מָקוֹם אַתֶּם וּבֵיתְכֶם כִּי־שָׂכָר הוּא לָכֶם חֵלֶף עֲבֹדַתְכֶם בְּאֹהֶל מוֹעֵד:

32 You will incur no guilt through it, once you have removed the best part from it; but you must not profane the sacred donations of the Israelites, lest you die.

לב וְלֹא־תִשְׂאוּ עָלָיו חֵטְא בַּהֲרִימְכֶם אֶת־חֶלְבּוֹ מִמֶּנּוּ וְאֶת־קָדְשֵׁי בְנֵי־יִשְׂרָאֵל לֹא תְחַלְּלוּ וְלֹא תָמוּתוּ:

19

1 *Hashem* spoke to *Moshe* and *Aharon*, saying:

יט א וַיְדַבֵּר יְהוָה אֶל־מֹשֶׁה וְאֶל־אַהֲרֹן לֵאמֹר:

2 This is the ritual law that *Hashem* has commanded: Instruct *B'nei Yisrael* to bring you a red cow without blemish, in which there is no defect and on which no yoke has been laid.

ב זֹאת חֻקַּת הַתּוֹרָה אֲשֶׁר־צִוָּה יְהוָה לֵאמֹר דַּבֵּר ׀ אֶל־בְּנֵי יִשְׂרָאֵל וְיִקְחוּ אֵלֶיךָ פָרָה אֲדֻמָּה תְּמִימָה אֲשֶׁר אֵין־בָּהּ מוּם אֲשֶׁר לֹא־עָלָה עָלֶיהָ עֹל:

3 You shall give it to *Elazar* the *Kohen*. It shall be taken outside the camp and slaughtered in his presence.

ג וּנְתַתֶּם אֹתָהּ אֶל־אֶלְעָזָר הַכֹּהֵן וְהוֹצִיא אֹתָהּ אֶל־מִחוּץ לַמַּחֲנֶה וְשָׁחַט אֹתָהּ לְפָנָיו:

4 *Elazar* the *Kohen* shall take some of its blood with his finger and sprinkle it seven times toward the front of the Tent of Meeting.

ד וְלָקַח אֶלְעָזָר הַכֹּהֵן מִדָּמָהּ בְּאֶצְבָּעוֹ וְהִזָּה אֶל־נֹכַח פְּנֵי אֹהֶל־מוֹעֵד מִדָּמָהּ שֶׁבַע פְּעָמִים:

5 The cow shall be burned in his sight – its hide, flesh, and blood shall be burned, its dung included –

ה וְשָׂרַף אֶת־הַפָּרָה לְעֵינָיו אֶת־עֹרָהּ וְאֶת־בְּשָׂרָהּ וְאֶת־דָּמָהּ עַל־פִּרְשָׁהּ יִשְׂרֹף:

6 and the *Kohen* shall take cedar wood, hyssop, and crimson stuff, and throw them into the fire consuming the cow.

ו וְלָקַח הַכֹּהֵן עֵץ אֶרֶז וְאֵזוֹב וּשְׁנִי תוֹלָעַת וְהִשְׁלִיךְ אֶל־תּוֹךְ שְׂרֵפַת הַפָּרָה:

7 The *Kohen* shall wash his garments and bathe his body in water; after that the *Kohen* may reenter the camp, but he shall be unclean until evening.

ז וְכִבֶּס בְּגָדָיו הַכֹּהֵן וְרָחַץ בְּשָׂרוֹ בַּמַּיִם וְאַחַר יָבוֹא אֶל־הַמַּחֲנֶה וְטָמֵא הַכֹּהֵן עַד־הָעָרֶב:

8 He who performed the burning shall also wash his garments in water, bathe his body in water, and be unclean until evening.

ח וְהַשֹּׂרֵף אֹתָהּ יְכַבֵּס בְּגָדָיו בַּמַּיִם וְרָחַץ בְּשָׂרוֹ בַּמָּיִם וְטָמֵא עַד־הָעָרֶב:

9 A man who is clean shall gather up the ashes of the cow and deposit them outside the camp in a clean place, to be kept for water of lustration for the Israelite community. It is for cleansing.

ט וְאָסַף ׀ אִישׁ טָהוֹר אֵת אֵפֶר הַפָּרָה וְהִנִּיחַ מִחוּץ לַמַּחֲנֶה בְּמָקוֹם טָהוֹר וְהָיְתָה לַעֲדַת בְּנֵי־יִשְׂרָאֵל לְמִשְׁמֶרֶת לְמֵי נִדָּה חַטָּאת הִוא:

Bamidbar/Numbers 19
Chukat

במדבר יט
חקת

10 He who gathers up the ashes of the cow shall also wash his clothes and be unclean until evening. This shall be a permanent law for the Israelites and for the strangers who reside among you.

י וְכִבֶּס הָאֹסֵף אֶת־אֵפֶר הַפָּרָה אֶת־בְּגָדָיו וְטָמֵא עַד־הָעָרֶב וְהָיְתָה לִבְנֵי יִשְׂרָאֵל וְלַגֵּר הַגָּר בְּתוֹכָם לְחֻקַּת עוֹלָם׃

11 He who touches the corpse of any human being shall be unclean for seven days.

יא הַנֹּגֵעַ בְּמֵת לְכָל־נֶפֶשׁ אָדָם וְטָמֵא שִׁבְעַת יָמִים׃

ha-no-GAY-a b'-MAYT l'-khol NE-fesh a-DAM v'-ta-MAY shiv-AT ya-MEEM

12 He shall cleanse himself with it on the third day and on the seventh day, and then be clean; if he fails to cleanse himself on the third and seventh days, he shall not be clean.

יב הוּא יִתְחַטָּא־בוֹ בַּיּוֹם הַשְּׁלִישִׁי וּבַיּוֹם הַשְּׁבִיעִי יִטְהָר וְאִם־לֹא יִתְחַטָּא בַּיּוֹם הַשְּׁלִישִׁי וּבַיּוֹם הַשְּׁבִיעִי לֹא יִטְהָר׃

13 Whoever touches a corpse, the body of a person who has died, and does not cleanse himself, defiles *Hashem*'s *Mishkan*; that person shall be cut off from *Yisrael*. Since the water of lustration was not dashed on him, he remains unclean; his uncleanness is still upon him.

יג כָּל־הַנֹּגֵעַ בְּמֵת בְּנֶפֶשׁ הָאָדָם אֲשֶׁר־יָמוּת וְלֹא יִתְחַטָּא אֶת־מִשְׁכַּן יְהֹוָה טִמֵּא וְנִכְרְתָה הַנֶּפֶשׁ הַהִוא מִיִּשְׂרָאֵל כִּי מֵי נִדָּה לֹא־זֹרַק עָלָיו טָמֵא יִהְיֶה עוֹד טֻמְאָתוֹ בוֹ׃

14 This is the ritual: When a person dies in a tent, whoever enters the tent and whoever is in the tent shall be unclean seven days;

יד זֹאת הַתּוֹרָה אָדָם כִּי־יָמוּת בְּאֹהֶל כָּל־הַבָּא אֶל־הָאֹהֶל וְכָל־אֲשֶׁר בָּאֹהֶל יִטְמָא שִׁבְעַת יָמִים׃

15 and every open vessel, with no lid fastened down, shall be unclean.

טו וְכֹל כְּלִי פָתוּחַ אֲשֶׁר אֵין־צָמִיד פָּתִיל עָלָיו טָמֵא הוּא׃

16 And in the open, anyone who touches a person who was killed or who died naturally, or human bone, or a grave, shall be unclean seven days.

טז וְכֹל אֲשֶׁר־יִגַּע עַל־פְּנֵי הַשָּׂדֶה בַּחֲלַל־חֶרֶב אוֹ בְמֵת אוֹ־בְעֶצֶם אָדָם אוֹ בְקָבֶר יִטְמָא שִׁבְעַת יָמִים׃

17 Some of the ashes from the fire of cleansing shall be taken for the unclean person, and fresh water shall be added to them in a vessel.

יז וְלָקְחוּ לַטָּמֵא מֵעֲפַר שְׂרֵפַת הַחַטָּאת וְנָתַן עָלָיו מַיִם חַיִּים אֶל־כֶּלִי׃

18 A person who is clean shall take hyssop, dip it in the water, and sprinkle on the tent and on all the vessels and people who were there, or on him who touched the bones or the person who was killed or died naturally or the grave.

יח וְלָקַח אֵזוֹב וְטָבַל בַּמַּיִם אִישׁ טָהוֹר וְהִזָּה עַל־הָאֹהֶל וְעַל־כָּל־הַכֵּלִים וְעַל־הַנְּפָשׁוֹת אֲשֶׁר הָיוּ־שָׁם וְעַל־הַנֹּגֵעַ בַּעֶצֶם אוֹ בֶחָלָל אוֹ בַמֵּת אוֹ בַקָּבֶר׃

19:11 He who touches the corpse of any human being shall be unclean Chapter 19 discusses the laws of ritual impurity that result from coming into contact, directly or indirectly, with a dead body. Unlike other rituals that were performed inside the *Mishkan* or its courtyard, the purification process for these ritually impure individuals takes place outside the camp, in the place farthest from the *Mishkan*. When a person passes from this world, his body is left bereft of its soul, its Godliness. The absence of the soul is the antithesis of the spirituality of the *Mishkan*, where God's presence is most intensely concentrated. Entering the holy sanctuary after having encountered the absence of Godliness is incongruous. It is only after a person has become purified that he can regain entry into such a holy place.

384

Bamidbar/Numbers 20
Chukat

במדבר כ
חקת

19 The clean person shall sprinkle it upon the unclean person on the third day and on the seventh day, thus cleansing him by the seventh day. He shall then wash his clothes and bathe in water, and at nightfall he shall be clean.

יט וְהִזָּה הַטָּהֹר עַל־הַטָּמֵא בַּיּוֹם הַשְּׁלִישִׁי וּבַיּוֹם הַשְּׁבִיעִי וְחִטְּאוֹ בַּיּוֹם הַשְּׁבִיעִי וְכִבֶּס בְּגָדָיו וְרָחַץ בַּמַּיִם וְטָהֵר בָּעָרֶב:

20 If anyone who has become unclean fails to cleanse himself, that person shall be cut off from the congregation, for he has defiled *Hashem*'s sanctuary. The water of lustration was not dashed on him: he is unclean.

כ וְאִישׁ אֲשֶׁר־יִטְמָא וְלֹא יִתְחַטָּא וְנִכְרְתָה הַנֶּפֶשׁ הַהִוא מִתּוֹךְ הַקָּהָל כִּי אֶת־מִקְדַּשׁ יְהֹוָה טִמֵּא מֵי נִדָּה לֹא־זֹרַק עָלָיו טָמֵא הוּא:

21 That shall be for them a law for all time. Further, he who sprinkled the water of lustration shall wash his clothes; and whoever touches the water of lustration shall be unclean until evening.

כא וְהָיְתָה לָהֶם לְחֻקַּת עוֹלָם וּמַזֵּה מֵי־הַנִּדָּה יְכַבֵּס בְּגָדָיו וְהַנֹּגֵעַ בְּמֵי הַנִּדָּה יִטְמָא עַד־הָעָרֶב:

22 Whatever that unclean person touches shall be unclean; and the person who touches him shall be unclean until evening.

כב וְכֹל אֲשֶׁר־יִגַּע־בּוֹ הַטָּמֵא יִטְמָא וְהַנֶּפֶשׁ הַנֹּגַעַת תִּטְמָא עַד־הָעָרֶב:

20 1 The Israelites arrived in a body at the wilderness of Zin on the first new moon, and the people stayed at Kadesh. *Miriam* died there and was buried there.

כ א וַיָּבֹאוּ בְנֵי־יִשְׂרָאֵל כָּל־הָעֵדָה מִדְבַּר־צִן בַּחֹדֶשׁ הָרִאשׁוֹן וַיֵּשֶׁב הָעָם בְּקָדֵשׁ וַתָּמָת שָׁם מִרְיָם וַתִּקָּבֵר שָׁם:

2 The community was without water, and they joined against *Moshe* and *Aharon*.

ב וְלֹא־הָיָה מַיִם לָעֵדָה וַיִּקָּהֲלוּ עַל־מֹשֶׁה וְעַל־אַהֲרֹן:

3 The people quarreled with *Moshe*, saying, "If only we had perished when our brothers perished at the instance of *Hashem*!

ג וַיָּרֶב הָעָם עִם־מֹשֶׁה וַיֹּאמְרוּ לֵאמֹר וְלוּ גָוַעְנוּ בִּגְוַע אַחֵינוּ לִפְנֵי יְהֹוָה:

4 Why have you brought *Hashem*'s congregation into this wilderness for us and our beasts to die there?

ד וְלָמָה הֲבֵאתֶם אֶת־קְהַל יְהֹוָה אֶל־הַמִּדְבָּר הַזֶּה לָמוּת שָׁם אֲנַחְנוּ וּבְעִירֵנוּ:

5 Why did you make us leave Egypt to bring us to this wretched place, a place with no grain or figs or vines or pomegranates? There is not even water to drink!"

ה וְלָמָה הֶעֱלִיתֻנוּ מִמִּצְרַיִם לְהָבִיא אֹתָנוּ אֶל־הַמָּקוֹם הָרָע הַזֶּה לֹא מְקוֹם זֶרַע וּתְאֵנָה וְגֶפֶן וְרִמּוֹן וּמַיִם אַיִן לִשְׁתּוֹת:

6 *Moshe* and *Aharon* came away from the congregation to the entrance of the Tent of Meeting, and fell on their faces. The Presence of *Hashem* appeared to them,

ו וַיָּבֹא מֹשֶׁה וְאַהֲרֹן מִפְּנֵי הַקָּהָל אֶל־פֶּתַח אֹהֶל מוֹעֵד וַיִּפְּלוּ עַל־פְּנֵיהֶם וַיֵּרָא כְבוֹד־יְהֹוָה אֲלֵיהֶם:

7 and *Hashem* spoke to *Moshe*, saying,

ז וַיְדַבֵּר יְהֹוָה אֶל־מֹשֶׁה לֵּאמֹר:

8 "You and your brother *Aharon* take the rod and assemble the community, and before their very eyes order the rock to yield its water. Thus you shall produce water for them from the rock and provide drink for the congregation and their beasts."

ח קַח אֶת־הַמַּטֶּה וְהַקְהֵל אֶת־הָעֵדָה אַתָּה וְאַהֲרֹן אָחִיךָ וְדִבַּרְתֶּם אֶל־הַסֶּלַע לְעֵינֵיהֶם וְנָתַן מֵימָיו וְהוֹצֵאתָ לָהֶם מַיִם מִן־הַסֶּלַע וְהִשְׁקִיתָ אֶת־הָעֵדָה וְאֶת־בְּעִירָם:

9 *Moshe* took the rod from before *Hashem*, as He had commanded him.

ט וַיִּקַּח מֹשֶׁה אֶת־הַמַּטֶּה מִלִּפְנֵי יְהֹוָה כַּאֲשֶׁר צִוָּהוּ:

Bamidbar/Numbers 20
Chukat

במדבר כ
חקת

10 *Moshe* and *Aharon* assembled the congregation in front of the rock; and he said to them, "Listen, you rebels, shall we get water for you out of this rock?"

י וַיַּקְהִ֜לוּ מֹשֶׁ֧ה וְאַהֲרֹ֛ן אֶת־הַקָּהָ֖ל אֶל־פְּנֵ֣י הַסָּ֑לַע וַיֹּ֣אמֶר לָהֶ֗ם שִׁמְעוּ־נָא֙ הַמֹּרִ֔ים הֲמִן־הַסֶּ֣לַע הַזֶּ֔ה נוֹצִ֥יא לָכֶ֖ם מָֽיִם׃

11 And *Moshe* raised his hand and struck the rock twice with his rod. Out came copious water, and the community and their beasts drank.

יא וַיָּ֨רֶם מֹשֶׁ֜ה אֶת־יָד֗וֹ וַיַּ֧ךְ אֶת־הַסֶּ֛לַע בְּמַטֵּ֖הוּ פַּעֲמָ֑יִם וַיֵּצְאוּ֙ מַ֣יִם רַבִּ֔ים וַתֵּ֥שְׁתְּ הָעֵדָ֖ה וּבְעִירָֽם׃

12 But *Hashem* said to *Moshe* and *Aharon*, "Because you did not trust Me enough to affirm My sanctity in the sight of *B'nei Yisrael*, therefore you shall not lead this congregation into the land that I have given them."

יב וַיֹּ֣אמֶר יְהוָה֮ אֶל־מֹשֶׁ֣ה וְאֶֽל־אַהֲרֹן֒ יַ֚עַן לֹא־הֶאֱמַנְתֶּ֣ם בִּ֔י לְהַ֨קְדִּישֵׁ֔נִי לְעֵינֵ֖י בְּנֵ֣י יִשְׂרָאֵ֑ל לָכֵ֗ן לֹ֤א תָבִ֨יאוּ֙ אֶת־הַקָּהָ֣ל הַזֶּ֔ה אֶל־הָאָ֖רֶץ אֲשֶׁר־נָתַ֥תִּי לָהֶֽם׃

va-YO-mer a-do-NAI el mo-SHEH v'-el a-ha-RON YA-an lo he-e-man-TEM BEE l'-HAK-dee-SHAY-nee l'-ay-NAY b'-NAY yis-ra-AYL la-KHAYN LO ta-VEE-u et ha-ka-HAL ha-ZEH el ha-A-retz a-sher na-TA-tee la-HEM

13 Those are the Waters of Meribah – meaning that the Israelites quarreled with *Hashem* – through which He affirmed His sanctity.

יג הֵ֚מָּה מֵ֣י מְרִיבָ֔ה אֲשֶׁר־רָב֥וּ בְנֵֽי־יִשְׂרָאֵ֖ל אֶת־יְהוָ֑ה וַיִּקָּדֵ֖שׁ בָּֽם׃

14 From Kadesh, *Moshe* sent messengers to the king of Edom: "Thus says your brother *Yisrael*: You know all the hardships that have befallen us;

יד וַיִּשְׁלַ֨ח מֹשֶׁ֧ה מַלְאָכִ֛ים מִקָּדֵ֖שׁ אֶל־מֶ֣לֶךְ אֱד֑וֹם כֹּ֤ה אָמַר֙ אָחִ֣יךָ יִשְׂרָאֵ֔ל אַתָּ֣ה יָדַ֔עְתָּ אֵ֥ת כָּל־הַתְּלָאָ֖ה אֲשֶׁ֥ר מְצָאָֽתְנוּ׃

15 that our ancestors went down to Egypt, that we dwelt in Egypt a long time, and that the Egyptians dealt harshly with us and our ancestors.

טו וַיֵּרְד֤וּ אֲבֹתֵ֨ינוּ֙ מִצְרַ֔יְמָה וַנֵּ֥שֶׁב בְּמִצְרַ֖יִם יָמִ֣ים רַבִּ֑ים וַיָּרֵ֥עוּ לָ֛נוּ מִצְרַ֖יִם וְלַאֲבֹתֵֽינוּ׃

16 We cried to *Hashem* and He heard our plea, and He sent a messenger who freed us from Egypt. Now we are in Kadesh, the town on the border of your territory.

טז וַנִּצְעַ֤ק אֶל־יְהוָה֙ וַיִּשְׁמַ֣ע קֹלֵ֔נוּ וַיִּשְׁלַ֣ח מַלְאָ֔ךְ וַיֹּצִאֵ֖נוּ מִמִּצְרָ֑יִם וְהִנֵּה֙ אֲנַ֣חְנוּ בְקָדֵ֔שׁ עִ֖יר קְצֵ֥ה גְבוּלֶֽךָ׃

17 Allow us, then, to cross your country. We will not pass through fields or vineyards, and we will not drink water from wells. We will follow the king's highway, turning off neither to the right nor to the left until we have crossed your territory."

יז נַעְבְּרָה־נָּ֣א בְאַרְצֶ֗ךָ לֹ֤א נַעֲבֹר֙ בְּשָׂדֶ֣ה וּבְכֶ֔רֶם וְלֹ֥א נִשְׁתֶּ֖ה מֵ֣י בְאֵ֑ר דֶּ֧רֶךְ הַמֶּ֣לֶךְ נֵלֵ֗ךְ לֹ֤א נִטֶּה֙ יָמִ֣ין וּשְׂמֹ֔אול עַ֥ד אֲשֶֽׁר־נַעֲבֹ֖ר גְּבוּלֶֽךָ׃

20:12 Because you did not trust Me The account of *Moshe* hitting the rock to get water for his people is one of the most perplexing stories in the entire Bible. *Hashem* tells him to speak to the rock in order to bring forth water, but *Moshe* hits the rock instead and is punished by being prevented from entering the Land of Israel, "because you did not trust Me enough to affirm My sanctity in the sight of the *B'nei Yisrael*." What could be so terrible about hitting the rock instead of speaking to it? One explanation, given by *Rashi*, is that while *Moshe* understood that the water flowing from the rock was God's doing, he did not make this sufficiently clear to the rest of the Children of Israel. Instead of hitting the rock, which implied that it was his own power that brought forth the water, *Moshe* should have spoken to it. By failing to do this, he missed an opportunity to attribute greatness to *Hashem*. It is not enough for us to recognize *Hashem* in our lives or within history; we have a duty to make sure others recognize Him as well.

Rashi
(1040–1105)

Bamidbar/Numbers 21
Chukat

במדבר כא
חקת

18 But Edom answered him, "You shall not pass through us, else we will go out against you with the sword."

יח וַיֹּאמֶר אֵלָיו אֱדוֹם לֹא תַעֲבֹר בִּי פֶּן־בַּחֶרֶב אֵצֵא לִקְרָאתֶךָ׃

19 "We will keep to the beaten track," the Israelites said to them, "and if we or our cattle drink your water, we will pay for it. We ask only for passage on foot – it is but a small matter."

יט וַיֹּאמְרוּ אֵלָיו בְּנֵי־יִשְׂרָאֵל בַּמְסִלָּה נַעֲלֶה וְאִם־מֵימֶיךָ נִשְׁתֶּה אֲנִי וּמִקְנַי וְנָתַתִּי מִכְרָם רַק אֵין־דָּבָר בְּרַגְלַי אֶעֱבֹרָה׃

20 But they replied, "You shall not pass through!" And Edom went out against them in heavy force, strongly armed.

כ וַיֹּאמֶר לֹא תַעֲבֹר וַיֵּצֵא אֱדוֹם לִקְרָאתוֹ בְּעַם כָּבֵד וּבְיָד חֲזָקָה׃

21 So Edom would not let *Yisrael* cross their territory, and *Yisrael* turned away from them.

כא וַיְמָאֵן אֱדוֹם נְתֹן אֶת־יִשְׂרָאֵל עֲבֹר בִּגְבֻלוֹ וַיֵּט יִשְׂרָאֵל מֵעָלָיו׃

22 Setting out from Kadesh, the Israelites arrived in a body at Mount Hor.

כב וַיִּסְעוּ מִקָּדֵשׁ וַיָּבֹאוּ בְנֵי־יִשְׂרָאֵל כָּל־הָעֵדָה הֹר הָהָר׃

23 At Mount Hor, on the boundary of the land of Edom, *Hashem* said to *Moshe* and *Aharon*,

כג וַיֹּאמֶר יְהֹוָה אֶל־מֹשֶׁה וְאֶל־אַהֲרֹן בְּהֹר הָהָר עַל־גְּבוּל אֶרֶץ־אֱדוֹם לֵאמֹר׃

24 "Let *Aharon* be gathered to his kin: he is not to enter the land that I have assigned to *B'nei Yisrael*, because you disobeyed my command about the waters of Meribah.

כד יֵאָסֵף אַהֲרֹן אֶל־עַמָּיו כִּי לֹא יָבֹא אֶל־הָאָרֶץ אֲשֶׁר נָתַתִּי לִבְנֵי יִשְׂרָאֵל עַל אֲשֶׁר־מְרִיתֶם אֶת־פִּי לְמֵי מְרִיבָה׃

25 Take *Aharon* and his son *Elazar* and bring them up on Mount Hor.

כה קַח אֶת־אַהֲרֹן וְאֶת־אֶלְעָזָר בְּנוֹ וְהַעַל אֹתָם הֹר הָהָר׃

KAKH et a-ha-RON v'-et el-a-ZAR b'-NO v'-HA-al o-TAM hor ha-HAR

26 Strip *Aharon* of his vestments and put them on his son *Elazar*. There *Aharon* shall be gathered unto the dead."

כו וְהַפְשֵׁט אֶת־אַהֲרֹן אֶת־בְּגָדָיו וְהִלְבַּשְׁתָּם אֶת־אֶלְעָזָר בְּנוֹ וְאַהֲרֹן יֵאָסֵף וּמֵת שָׁם׃

27 *Moshe* did as *Hashem* had commanded. They ascended Mount Hor in the sight of the whole community.

כז וַיַּעַשׂ מֹשֶׁה כַּאֲשֶׁר צִוָּה יְהֹוָה וַיַּעֲלוּ אֶל־הֹר הָהָר לְעֵינֵי כָּל־הָעֵדָה׃

28 *Moshe* stripped *Aharon* of his vestments and put them on his son *Elazar*, and *Aharon* died there on the summit of the mountain. When *Moshe* and *Elazar* came down from the mountain,

כח וַיַּפְשֵׁט מֹשֶׁה אֶת־אַהֲרֹן אֶת־בְּגָדָיו וַיַּלְבֵּשׁ אֹתָם אֶת־אֶלְעָזָר בְּנוֹ וַיָּמָת אַהֲרֹן שָׁם בְּרֹאשׁ הָהָר וַיֵּרֶד מֹשֶׁה וְאֶלְעָזָר מִן־הָהָר׃

29 the whole community knew that *Aharon* had breathed his last. All the house of *Yisrael* bewailed *Aharon* thirty days.

כט וַיִּרְאוּ כָּל־הָעֵדָה כִּי גָוַע אַהֲרֹן וַיִּבְכּוּ אֶת־אַהֲרֹן שְׁלֹשִׁים יוֹם כֹּל בֵּית יִשְׂרָאֵל׃

21 1 When the Canaanite, king of Arad, who dwelt in the *Negev*, learned that *Yisrael* was coming by the way of Atharim, he engaged *Yisrael* in battle and took some of them captive.

כא א וַיִּשְׁמַע הַכְּנַעֲנִי מֶלֶךְ־עֲרָד יֹשֵׁב הַנֶּגֶב כִּי בָּא יִשְׂרָאֵל דֶּרֶךְ הָאֲתָרִים וַיִּלָּחֶם בְּיִשְׂרָאֵל וַיִּשְׁבְּ מִמֶּנּוּ שֶׁבִי׃

Bamidbar/Numbers 21
Chukat

במדבר כא
חקת

2 Then *Yisrael* made a vow to *Hashem* and said, "If You deliver this people into our hand, we will proscribe their towns."

ב וַיִּדַּר יִשְׂרָאֵל נֶדֶר לַיהוָה וַיֹּאמַר אִם־נָתֹן תִּתֵּן אֶת־הָעָם הַזֶּה בְּיָדִי וְהַחֲרַמְתִּי אֶת־עָרֵיהֶם:

3 *Hashem* heeded *Yisrael*'s plea and delivered up the Canaanites; and they and their cities were proscribed. So that place was named Hormah.

ג וַיִּשְׁמַע יְהוָה בְּקוֹל יִשְׂרָאֵל וַיִּתֵּן אֶת־הַכְּנַעֲנִי וַיַּחֲרֵם אֶתְהֶם וְאֶת־עָרֵיהֶם וַיִּקְרָא שֵׁם־הַמָּקוֹם חָרְמָה:

4 They set out from Mount Hor by way of the Sea of Reeds to skirt the land of Edom. But the people grew restive on the journey,

ד וַיִּסְעוּ מֵהֹר הָהָר דֶּרֶךְ יַם־סוּף לִסְבֹב אֶת־אֶרֶץ אֱדוֹם וַתִּקְצַר נֶפֶשׁ־הָעָם בַּדָּרֶךְ:

5 and the people spoke against *Hashem* and against *Moshe*, "Why did you make us leave Egypt to die in the wilderness? There is no bread and no water, and we have come to loathe this miserable food."

ה וַיְדַבֵּר הָעָם בֵּאלֹהִים וּבְמֹשֶׁה לָמָה הֶעֱלִיתֻנוּ מִמִּצְרַיִם לָמוּת בַּמִּדְבָּר כִּי אֵין לֶחֶם וְאֵין מַיִם וְנַפְשֵׁנוּ קָצָה בַּלֶּחֶם הַקְּלֹקֵל:

va-y'-da-BER ha-AM be-e-lo-HEEM u-v'-mo-SHE la-MA he-e'-lee-TU-nu mi-mitz-RA-yim la-MOOT ba-mid-BAR kee ayn LEH-khem v'-AYN MA-yim v'-naf-SHAY-nu ka-TZA ba-LE-khem ha-k'-lo-KEL

6 *Hashem* sent seraph serpents against the people. They bit the people and many of the Israelites died.

ו וַיְשַׁלַּח יְהוָה בָּעָם אֵת הַנְּחָשִׁים הַשְּׂרָפִים וַיְנַשְּׁכוּ אֶת־הָעָם וַיָּמָת עַם־רָב מִיִּשְׂרָאֵל:

7 The people came to *Moshe* and said, "We sinned by speaking against *Hashem* and against you. Intercede with *Hashem* to take away the serpents from us!" And *Moshe* interceded for the people.

ז וַיָּבֹא הָעָם אֶל־מֹשֶׁה וַיֹּאמְרוּ חָטָאנוּ כִּי־דִבַּרְנוּ בַיהוָה וָבָךְ הִתְפַּלֵּל אֶל־יְהוָה וְיָסֵר מֵעָלֵינוּ אֶת־הַנָּחָשׁ וַיִּתְפַּלֵּל מֹשֶׁה בְּעַד הָעָם:

8 Then *Hashem* said to *Moshe*, "Make a seraph figure and mount it on a standard. And if anyone who is bitten looks at it, he shall recover."

ח וַיֹּאמֶר יְהוָה אֶל־מֹשֶׁה עֲשֵׂה לְךָ שָׂרָף וְשִׂים אֹתוֹ עַל־נֵס וְהָיָה כָּל־הַנָּשׁוּךְ וְרָאָה אֹתוֹ וָחָי:

9 *Moshe* made a copper serpent and mounted it on a standard; and when anyone was bitten by a serpent, he would look at the copper serpent and recover.

ט וַיַּעַשׂ מֹשֶׁה נְחַשׁ נְחֹשֶׁת וַיְשִׂמֵהוּ עַל־הַנֵּס וְהָיָה אִם־נָשַׁךְ הַנָּחָשׁ אֶת־אִישׁ וְהִבִּיט אֶל־נְחַשׁ הַנְּחֹשֶׁת וָחָי:

va-YA-as mo-SHEH n'-KHASH n'-KHO-shet va-y'-si-MAY-hu al ha-NAYS v'-ha-YAH im na-SHAKH ha-na-KHASH et EESH v'-hi-BEET el n'-KHASH ha-n'-KHO-shet va-KHAI

10 The Israelites marched on and encamped at Oboth.

י וַיִּסְעוּ בְּנֵי יִשְׂרָאֵל וַיַּחֲנוּ בְּאֹבֹת:

11 They set out from Oboth and encamped at Iye-abarim, in the wilderness bordering on Moab to the east.

יא וַיִּסְעוּ מֵאֹבֹת וַיַּחֲנוּ בְּעִיֵּי הָעֲבָרִים בַּמִּדְבָּר אֲשֶׁר עַל־פְּנֵי מוֹאָב מִמִּזְרַח הַשָּׁמֶשׁ:

21:5 We have come to loathe this miserable food According to the Sages, the manna was a miraculous and wonderful food that tasted like anything a person would wish. If so, why did the Children of Israel complain so bitterly about it, and call it, "this miserable food"? According to the 13th century French scholar Rabbi Hezekiah ben Manoah, and known as *Chizkuni*, the Israelites were not complaining about the quality of the manna. Rather, they were expressing their impatience and eagerness to enter the Land of Israel where they would finally be able to eat the fruit of their own hands from the soil of the Holy Land.

Fruit of the land from Kibbutz Alumot

Bamidbar/Numbers 21
Chukat

12 From there they set out and encamped at the wadi Zered.

יב מִשָּׁם נָסָעוּ וַיַּחֲנוּ בְּנַחַל זָרֶד:

13 From there they set out and encamped beyond the Arnon, that is, in the wilderness that extends from the territory of the Amorites. For the Arnon is the boundary of Moab, between Moab and the Amorites.

יג מִשָּׁם נָסָעוּ וַיַּחֲנוּ מֵעֵבֶר אַרְנוֹן אֲשֶׁר בַּמִּדְבָּר הַיֹּצֵא מִגְּבוּל הָאֱמֹרִי כִּי אַרְנוֹן גְּבוּל מוֹאָב בֵּין מוֹאָב וּבֵין הָאֱמֹרִי:

14 Therefore the Book of the Wars of *Hashem* speaks of "...Waheb in Suphah, and the wadis: the Arnon

יד עַל־כֵּן יֵאָמַר בְּסֵפֶר מִלְחֲמֹת יְהֹוָה אֶת־וָהֵב בְּסוּפָה וְאֶת־הַנְּחָלִים אַרְנוֹן:

15 with its tributary wadis, stretched along the settled country of Ar, hugging the territory of Moab..."

טו וְאֶשֶׁד הַנְּחָלִים אֲשֶׁר נָטָה לְשֶׁבֶת עָר וְנִשְׁעַן לִגְבוּל מוֹאָב:

16 And from there to Beer, which is the well where *Hashem* said to *Moshe*, "Assemble the people that I may give them water."

טז וּמִשָּׁם בְּאֵרָה הִוא הַבְּאֵר אֲשֶׁר אָמַר יְהֹוָה לְמֹשֶׁה אֱסֹף אֶת־הָעָם וְאֶתְּנָה לָהֶם מָיִם:

17 Then *Yisrael* sang this song: Spring up, O well – sing to it –

יז אָז יָשִׁיר יִשְׂרָאֵל אֶת־הַשִּׁירָה הַזֹּאת עֲלִי בְאֵר עֱנוּ־לָהּ:

18 The well which the chieftains dug, Which the nobles of the people started With maces, with their own staffs. And from Midbar to Mattanah,

יח בְּאֵר חֲפָרוּהָ שָׂרִים כָּרוּהָ נְדִיבֵי הָעָם בִּמְחֹקֵק בְּמִשְׁעֲנֹתָם וּמִמִּדְבָּר מַתָּנָה:

19 and from Mattanah to Nahaliel, and from Nahaliel to Bamoth,

יט וּמִמַּתָּנָה נַחֲלִיאֵל וּמִנַּחֲלִיאֵל בָּמוֹת:

20 and from Bamoth to the valley that is in the country of Moab, at the peak of Pisgah, overlooking the wasteland.

כ וּמִבָּמוֹת הַגַּיְא אֲשֶׁר בִּשְׂדֵה מוֹאָב רֹאשׁ הַפִּסְגָּה וְנִשְׁקָפָה עַל־פְּנֵי הַיְשִׁימֹן:

21 *Yisrael* now sent messengers to Sihon king of the Amorites, saying,

כא וַיִּשְׁלַח יִשְׂרָאֵל מַלְאָכִים אֶל־סִיחֹן מֶלֶךְ־הָאֱמֹרִי לֵאמֹר:

22 Let me pass through your country. We will not turn off into fields or vineyards, and we will not drink water from wells. We will follow the king's highway until we have crossed your territory."

כב אֶעְבְּרָה בְאַרְצֶךָ לֹא נִטֶּה בְּשָׂדֶה וּבְכֶרֶם לֹא נִשְׁתֶּה מֵי בְאֵר בְּדֶרֶךְ הַמֶּלֶךְ נֵלֵךְ עַד אֲשֶׁר־נַעֲבֹר גְּבֻלֶךָ:

23 But Sihon would not let *Yisrael* pass through his territory. Sihon gathered all his people and went out against *Yisrael* in the wilderness. He came to Jahaz and engaged *Yisrael* in battle.

כג וְלֹא־נָתַן סִיחֹן אֶת־יִשְׂרָאֵל עֲבֹר בִּגְבֻלוֹ וַיֶּאֱסֹף סִיחֹן אֶת־כָּל־עַמּוֹ וַיֵּצֵא לִקְרַאת יִשְׂרָאֵל הַמִּדְבָּרָה וַיָּבֹא יָהְצָה וַיִּלָּחֶם בְּיִשְׂרָאֵל:

24 But *Yisrael* put them to the sword, and took possession of their land, from the Arnon to the Jabbok, as far as [Az] of the Ammonites, for Az marked the boundary of the Ammonites.

כד וַיַּכֵּהוּ יִשְׂרָאֵל לְפִי־חָרֶב וַיִּירַשׁ אֶת־אַרְצוֹ מֵאַרְנֹן עַד־יַבֹּק עַד־בְּנֵי עַמּוֹן כִּי עַז גְּבוּל בְּנֵי עַמּוֹן:

25 *Yisrael* took all those towns. And *Yisrael* settled in all the towns of the Amorites, in Heshbon and all its dependencies.

כה וַיִּקַּח יִשְׂרָאֵל אֵת כָּל־הֶעָרִים הָאֵלֶּה וַיֵּשֶׁב יִשְׂרָאֵל בְּכָל־עָרֵי הָאֱמֹרִי בְּחֶשְׁבּוֹן וּבְכָל־בְּנֹתֶיהָ:

Bamidbar/Numbers 21
Chukat

במדבר כא
חקת

26 Now Heshbon was the city of Sihon king of the Amorites, who had fought against a former king of Moab and taken all his land from him as far as the Arnon.

כו כִּי חֶשְׁבּוֹן עִיר סִיחֹן מֶלֶךְ הָאֱמֹרִי הִוא וְהוּא נִלְחַם בְּמֶלֶךְ מוֹאָב הָרִאשׁוֹן וַיִּקַּח אֶת־כָּל־אַרְצוֹ מִיָּדוֹ עַד־אַרְנֹן׃

27 Therefore the bards would recite: "Come to Heshbon; firmly built And well founded is Sihon's city.

כז עַל־כֵּן יֹאמְרוּ הַמֹּשְׁלִים בֹּאוּ חֶשְׁבּוֹן תִּבָּנֶה וְתִכּוֹנֵן עִיר סִיחוֹן׃

28 For fire went forth from Heshbon, Flame from Sihon's city, Consuming Ar of Moab, The lords of Bamoth by the Arnon.

כח כִּי־אֵשׁ יָצְאָה מֵחֶשְׁבּוֹן לֶהָבָה מִקִּרְיַת סִיחֹן אָכְלָה עָר מוֹאָב בַּעֲלֵי בָּמוֹת אַרְנֹן׃

29 Woe to you, O Moab! You are undone, O people of Chemosh! His sons are rendered fugitive And his daughters captive By an Amorite king, Sihon."

כט אוֹי־לְךָ מוֹאָב אָבַדְתָּ עַם־כְּמוֹשׁ נָתַן בָּנָיו פְּלֵיטִם וּבְנֹתָיו בַּשְּׁבִית לְמֶלֶךְ אֱמֹרִי סִיחוֹן׃

30 Yet we have cast them down utterly, Heshbon along with Dibon; We have wrought desolation at Nophah, Which is hard by Medeba.

ל וַנִּירָם אָבַד חֶשְׁבּוֹן עַד־דִּיבֹן וַנַּשִּׁים עַד־נֹפַח אֲשֶׁר עַד־מֵידְבָא׃

31 So *Yisrael* occupied the land of the Amorites.

לא וַיֵּשֶׁב יִשְׂרָאֵל בְּאֶרֶץ הָאֱמֹרִי׃

32 Then *Moshe* sent to spy out Jazer, and they captured its dependencies and dispossessed the Amorites who were there.

לב וַיִּשְׁלַח מֹשֶׁה לְרַגֵּל אֶת־יַעְזֵר וַיִּלְכְּדוּ בְּנֹתֶיהָ וַיּוֹרֶשׁ [וַיּוֹרִישׁ] אֶת־הָאֱמֹרִי אֲשֶׁר־שָׁם׃

33 They marched on and went up the road to Bashan, and King Og of Bashan, with all his people, came out to Edrei to engage them in battle.

לג וַיִּפְנוּ וַיַּעֲלוּ דֶּרֶךְ הַבָּשָׁן וַיֵּצֵא עוֹג מֶלֶךְ־הַבָּשָׁן לִקְרָאתָם הוּא וְכָל־עַמּוֹ לַמִּלְחָמָה אֶדְרֶעִי׃

34 But *Hashem* said to *Moshe*, "Do not fear him, for I give him and all his people and his land into your hand. You shall do to him as you did to Sihon king of the Amorites who dwelt in Heshbon."

לד וַיֹּאמֶר יְהֹוָה אֶל־מֹשֶׁה אַל־תִּירָא אֹתוֹ כִּי בְיָדְךָ נָתַתִּי אֹתוֹ וְאֶת־כָּל־עַמּוֹ וְאֶת־אַרְצוֹ וְעָשִׂיתָ לּוֹ כַּאֲשֶׁר עָשִׂיתָ לְסִיחֹן מֶלֶךְ הָאֱמֹרִי אֲשֶׁר יוֹשֵׁב בְּחֶשְׁבּוֹן׃

35 They defeated him and his sons and all his people, until no remnant was left him; and they took possession of his country.

לה וַיַּכּוּ אֹתוֹ וְאֶת־בָּנָיו וְאֶת־כָּל־עַמּוֹ עַד־בִּלְתִּי הִשְׁאִיר־לוֹ שָׂרִיד וַיִּירְשׁוּ אֶת־אַרְצוֹ׃

va-ya-KU o-TO v'-et ba-NAV v'-et kol a-MO ad bil-TEE hish-eer LO sa-REED va-yee-r'-SHU et ar-TZO

21:35 They defeated him In this section, the Israelites capture the lands of Sihon, king of the Amorites and Og, king of Bashan. *Moshe* initially asks these two kings for permission to pass peacefully through their lands in order to reach the Land of Israel. Instead of agreeing to the request, however, the Israelites were greeted with swords and spears. They thus had no choice but to go to war, from which they emerged victorious. While these lands were not included within the original borders of *Eretz Yisrael*, the capture of this territory marks the beginning of the successful conquest of the Promised Land.

390

Bamidbar/Numbers 22
Balak

במדבר כב
בלק

22

1 The Israelites then marched on and encamped in the steppes of Moab, across the *Yarden* from *Yericho*.

2 Balak son of Zippor saw all that *Yisrael* had done to the Amorites.

3 Moab was alarmed because that people was so numerous. Moab dreaded the Israelites,

4 and Moab said to the elders of Midian, "Now this horde will lick clean all that is about us as an ox licks up the grass of the field." Balak son of Zippor, who was king of Moab at that time,

5 sent messengers to Balaam son of Beor in Pethor, which is by the Euphrates, in the land of his kinsfolk, to invite him, saying, "There is a people that came out of Egypt; it hides the earth from view, and it is settled next to me.

6 Come then, put a curse upon this people for me, since they are too numerous for me; perhaps I can thus defeat them and drive them out of the land. For I know that he whom you bless is blessed indeed, and he whom you curse is cursed."

7 The elders of Moab and the elders of Midian, versed in divination, set out. They came to Balaam and gave him Balak's message.

8 He said to them, "Spend the night here, and I shall reply to you as *Hashem* may instruct me." So the Moabite dignitaries stayed with Balaam.

9 *Hashem* came to Balaam and said, "What do these people want of you?"

10 Balaam said to *Hashem*, "Balak son of Zippor, king of Moab, sent me this message:

11 Here is a people that came out from Egypt and hides the earth from view. Come now and curse them for me; perhaps I can engage them in battle and drive them off."

hi-NAY ha-AM ha-yo-TZAY mi-mitz-RA-yim vai-KHAS et AYN ha-A-retz a-TAH l'-KHAH ka-vah LEE o-TO u-LAI u-KHAL l'-hi-la-KHEM BO v'-gay-rash-TEEV

22:11 Here is a people that came out from Egypt and hides the earth from view As a result of the defeat of the Amorites led by Sihon and Og, king of Bashan, the people of Moab become afraid of the People of Israel. In an effort to stop the Israelites, their king, Balak, sends for the prophet Balaam to curse them. *Hashem*, however, has a different idea and puts a blessing into Balaam's mouth instead of his intended curses. This verse highlights Balaam's typically prejudicial attitude, in his description of the Israelites as a nation that

Bamidbar/Numbers 22
Balak

במדבר כב
בלק

12 But *Hashem* said to Balaam, "Do not go with them. You must not curse that people, for they are blessed."

יב וַיֹּאמֶר אֱלֹהִים אֶל־בִּלְעָם לֹא תֵלֵךְ עִמָּהֶם לֹא תָאֹר אֶת־הָעָם כִּי בָרוּךְ הוּא׃

13 Balaam arose in the morning and said to Balak's dignitaries, "Go back to your own country, for *Hashem* will not let me go with you."

יג וַיָּקָם בִּלְעָם בַּבֹּקֶר וַיֹּאמֶר אֶל־שָׂרֵי בָלָק לְכוּ אֶל־אַרְצְכֶם כִּי מֵאֵן יְהֹוָה לְתִתִּי לַהֲלֹךְ עִמָּכֶם׃

14 The Moabite dignitaries left, and they came to Balak and said, "Balaam refused to come with us."

יד וַיָּקוּמוּ שָׂרֵי מוֹאָב וַיָּבֹאוּ אֶל־בָּלָק וַיֹּאמְרוּ מֵאֵן בִּלְעָם הֲלֹךְ עִמָּנוּ׃

15 Then Balak sent other dignitaries, more numerous and distinguished than the first.

טו וַיֹּסֶף עוֹד בָּלָק שְׁלֹחַ שָׂרִים רַבִּים וְנִכְבָּדִים מֵאֵלֶּה׃

16 They came to Balaam and said to him, "Thus says Balak son of Zippor: Please do not refuse to come to me.

טז וַיָּבֹאוּ אֶל־בִּלְעָם וַיֹּאמְרוּ לוֹ כֹּה אָמַר בָּלָק בֶּן־צִפּוֹר אַל־נָא תִמָּנַע מֵהֲלֹךְ אֵלָי׃

17 I will reward you richly and I will do anything you ask of me. Only come and damn this people for me."

יז כִּי־כַבֵּד אֲכַבֶּדְךָ מְאֹד וְכֹל אֲשֶׁר־תֹּאמַר אֵלַי אֶעֱשֶׂה וּלְכָה־נָּא קָבָה־לִּי אֵת הָעָם הַזֶּה׃

18 Balaam replied to Balak's officials, "Though Balak were to give me his house full of silver and gold, I could not do anything, big or little, contrary to the command of *Hashem* my God.

יח וַיַּעַן בִּלְעָם וַיֹּאמֶר אֶל־עַבְדֵי בָלָק אִם־יִתֶּן־לִי בָלָק מְלֹא בֵיתוֹ כֶּסֶף וְזָהָב לֹא אוּכַל לַעֲבֹר אֶת־פִּי יְהֹוָה אֱלֹהָי לַעֲשׂוֹת קְטַנָּה אוֹ גְדוֹלָה׃

19 So you, too, stay here overnight, and let me find out what else *Hashem* may say to me."

יט וְעַתָּה שְׁבוּ נָא בָזֶה גַּם־אַתֶּם הַלָּיְלָה וְאֵדְעָה מַה־יֹּסֵף יְהֹוָה דַּבֵּר עִמִּי׃

20 That night *Hashem* came to Balaam and said to him, "If these men have come to invite you, you may go with them. But whatever I command you, that you shall do."

כ וַיָּבֹא אֱלֹהִים אֶל־בִּלְעָם לַיְלָה וַיֹּאמֶר לוֹ אִם־לִקְרֹא לְךָ בָּאוּ הָאֲנָשִׁים קוּם לֵךְ אִתָּם וְאַךְ אֶת־הַדָּבָר אֲשֶׁר־אֲדַבֵּר אֵלֶיךָ אֹתוֹ תַעֲשֶׂה׃

21 When he arose in the morning, Balaam saddled his ass and departed with the Moabite dignitaries.

כא וַיָּקָם בִּלְעָם בַּבֹּקֶר וַיַּחֲבֹשׁ אֶת־אֲתֹנוֹ וַיֵּלֶךְ עִם־שָׂרֵי מוֹאָב׃

22 But *Hashem* was incensed at his going; so an angel of *Hashem* placed himself in his way as an adversary. He was riding on his she-ass, with his two servants alongside,

כב וַיִּחַר־אַף אֱלֹהִים כִּי־הוֹלֵךְ הוּא וַיִּתְיַצֵּב מַלְאַךְ יְהֹוָה בַּדֶּרֶךְ לְשָׂטָן לוֹ וְהוּא רֹכֵב עַל־אֲתֹנוֹ וּשְׁנֵי נְעָרָיו עִמּוֹ׃

---

covers the entire earth. Even today, the Jewish people comprise less than 0.2% of the world population, yet they are often thought of as a nuisance that threatens the world. This story, however, also underscores the fact that anti-Semitism will not prevail. *Hashem* tells Balaam that the Jewish people "are blessed," and that those who try to curse them will not succeed, just as *Hashem* had promised *Avraham* long before, "I will bless those who bless you and curse him that curses you" (Genesis 12:3). The Jewish nation is indeed blessed, and has made enormous contributions to the world, as evidenced by the fact that despite their small number, between 1901 and 2015 over 20% of all Nobel laureates have either been Jewish, or of Jewish descent.

Bamidbar/Numbers 22
Balak

23 when the ass caught sight of the angel of *Hashem* standing in the way, with his drawn sword in his hand. The ass swerved from the road and went into the fields; and Balaam beat the ass to turn her back onto the road.

24 The angel of *Hashem* then stationed himself in a lane between the vineyards, with a fence on either side.

25 The ass, seeing the angel of *Hashem*, pressed herself against the wall and squeezed Balaam's foot against the wall; so he beat her again.

26 Once more the angel of *Hashem* moved forward and stationed himself on a spot so narrow that there was no room to swerve right or left.

27 When the ass now saw the angel of *Hashem*, she lay down under Balaam; and Balaam was furious and beat the ass with his stick.

28 Then *Hashem* opened the ass's mouth, and she said to Balaam, "What have I done to you that you have beaten me these three times?"

29 Balaam said to the ass, "You have made a mockery of me! If I had a sword with me, I'd kill you."

30 The ass said to Balaam, "Look, I am the ass that you have been riding all along until this day! Have I been in the habit of doing thus to you?" And he answered, "No."

31 Then *Hashem* uncovered Balaam's eyes, and he saw the angel of *Hashem* standing in the way, his drawn sword in his hand; thereupon he bowed right down to the ground.

32 The angel of *Hashem* said to him, "Why have you beaten your ass these three times? It is I who came out as an adversary, for the errand is obnoxious to me.

33 And when the ass saw me, she shied away because of me those three times. If she had not shied away from me, you are the one I should have killed, while sparing her."

34 Balaam said to the angel of *Hashem*, "I erred because I did not know that you were standing in my way. If you still disapprove, I will turn back."

במדבר כב
בלק

כג וַתֵּ֣רֶא הָאָתוֹן֩ אֶת־מַלְאַ֨ךְ יְהֹוָ֜ה נִצָּ֣ב בַּדֶּ֗רֶךְ וְחַרְבּ֤וֹ שְׁלוּפָה֙ בְּיָד֔וֹ וַתֵּ֤ט הָֽאָתוֹן֙ מִן־הַדֶּ֔רֶךְ וַתֵּ֖לֶךְ בַּשָּׂדֶ֑ה וַיַּ֤ךְ בִּלְעָם֙ אֶת־הָ֣אָת֔וֹן לְהַטֹּתָ֖הּ הַדָּֽרֶךְ׃

כד וַֽיַּעֲמֹד֙ מַלְאַ֣ךְ יְהֹוָ֔ה בְּמִשְׁע֖וֹל הַכְּרָמִ֑ים גָּדֵ֥ר מִזֶּ֖ה וְגָדֵ֥ר מִזֶּֽה׃

כה וַתֵּ֨רֶא הָאָת֜וֹן אֶת־מַלְאַ֣ךְ יְהֹוָ֗ה וַתִּלָּחֵץ֙ אֶל־הַקִּ֔יר וַתִּלְחַ֛ץ אֶת־רֶ֥גֶל בִּלְעָ֖ם אֶל־הַקִּ֑יר וַיֹּ֖סֶף לְהַכֹּתָֽהּ׃

כו וַיּ֥וֹסֶף מַלְאַךְ־יְהֹוָ֖ה עֲב֑וֹר וַֽיַּעֲמֹד֙ בְּמָק֣וֹם צָ֔ר אֲשֶׁ֛ר אֵֽין־דֶּ֥רֶךְ לִנְט֖וֹת יָמִ֥ין וּשְׂמֹֽאול׃

כז וַתֵּ֤רֶא הָֽאָתוֹן֙ אֶת־מַלְאַ֣ךְ יְהֹוָ֔ה וַתִּרְבַּ֖ץ תַּ֣חַת בִּלְעָ֑ם וַיִּֽחַר־אַ֣ף בִּלְעָ֔ם וַיַּ֥ךְ אֶת־הָאָת֖וֹן בַּמַּקֵּֽל׃

כח וַיִּפְתַּ֥ח יְהֹוָ֖ה אֶת־פִּ֣י הָאָת֑וֹן וַתֹּ֤אמֶר לְבִלְעָם֙ מֶה־עָשִׂ֣יתִֽי לְךָ֔ כִּ֣י הִכִּיתַ֔נִי זֶ֖ה שָׁלֹ֥שׁ רְגָלִֽים׃

כט וַיֹּ֤אמֶר בִּלְעָם֙ לָֽאָת֔וֹן כִּ֥י הִתְעַלַּ֖לְתְּ בִּ֑י ל֤וּ יֶשׁ־חֶ֙רֶב֙ בְּיָדִ֔י כִּ֥י עַתָּ֖ה הֲרַגְתִּֽיךְ׃

ל וַתֹּ֨אמֶר הָאָת֜וֹן אֶל־בִּלְעָ֗ם הֲלוֹא֩ אָנֹכִ֨י אֲתֹֽנְךָ֜ אֲשֶׁר־רָכַ֣בְתָּ עָלַ֗י מֵעֽוֹדְךָ֙ עַד־הַיּ֣וֹם הַזֶּ֔ה הַֽהַסְכֵּ֣ן הִסְכַּ֔נְתִּי לַעֲשׂ֥וֹת לְךָ֖ כֹּ֑ה וַיֹּ֖אמֶר לֹֽא׃

לא וַיְגַ֣ל יְהֹוָה֮ אֶת־עֵינֵ֣י בִלְעָם֒ וַיַּ֞רְא אֶת־מַלְאַ֤ךְ יְהֹוָה֙ נִצָּ֣ב בַּדֶּ֔רֶךְ וְחַרְבּ֥וֹ שְׁלֻפָ֖ה בְּיָד֑וֹ וַיִּקֹּ֥ד וַיִּשְׁתַּ֖חוּ לְאַפָּֽיו׃

לב וַיֹּ֤אמֶר אֵלָיו֙ מַלְאַ֣ךְ יְהֹוָ֔ה עַל־מָ֗ה הִכִּ֙יתָ֙ אֶת־אֲתֹ֣נְךָ֔ זֶ֖ה שָׁל֣וֹשׁ רְגָלִ֑ים הִנֵּ֤ה אָנֹכִי֙ יָצָ֣אתִי לְשָׂטָ֔ן כִּֽי־יָרַ֥ט הַדֶּ֖רֶךְ לְנֶגְדִּֽי׃

לג וַתִּרְאַ֙נִי֙ הָֽאָת֔וֹן וַתֵּ֣ט לְפָנַ֔י זֶ֖ה שָׁלֹ֣שׁ רְגָלִ֑ים אוּלַי֙ נָטְתָ֣ה מִפָּנַ֔י כִּ֥י עַתָּ֛ה גַּם־אֹתְכָ֥ה הָרַ֖גְתִּי וְאוֹתָ֥הּ הֶחֱיֵֽיתִי׃

לד וַיֹּ֨אמֶר בִּלְעָ֜ם אֶל־מַלְאַ֤ךְ יְהֹוָה֙ חָטָ֔אתִי כִּ֚י לֹ֣א יָדַ֔עְתִּי כִּ֥י אַתָּ֛ה נִצָּ֥ב לִקְרָאתִ֖י בַּדָּ֑רֶךְ וְעַתָּ֛ה אִם־רַ֥ע בְּעֵינֶ֖יךָ אָשׁ֥וּבָה לִּֽי׃

Bamidbar/Numbers 23
Balak

במדבר כג
בלק

35 But the angel of *Hashem* said to Balaam, "Go with the men. But you must say nothing except what I tell you." So Balaam went on with Balak's dignitaries.

לה וַיֹּאמֶר מַלְאַךְ יְהֹוָה אֶל־בִּלְעָם לֵךְ עִם־הָאֲנָשִׁים וְאֶפֶס אֶת־הַדָּבָר אֲשֶׁר־אֲדַבֵּר אֵלֶיךָ אֹתוֹ תְדַבֵּר וַיֵּלֶךְ בִּלְעָם עִם־שָׂרֵי בָלָק׃

36 When Balak heard that Balaam was coming, he went out to meet him at Ir-moab, which is on the Arnon border, at its farthest point.

לו וַיִּשְׁמַע בָּלָק כִּי בָא בִלְעָם וַיֵּצֵא לִקְרָאתוֹ אֶל־עִיר מוֹאָב אֲשֶׁר עַל־גְּבוּל אַרְנֹן אֲשֶׁר בִּקְצֵה הַגְּבוּל׃

37 Balak said to Balaam, "When I first sent to invite you, why didn't you come to me? Am I really unable to reward you?"

לז וַיֹּאמֶר בָּלָק אֶל־בִּלְעָם הֲלֹא שָׁלֹחַ שָׁלַחְתִּי אֵלֶיךָ לִקְרֹא־לָךְ לָמָּה לֹא־הָלַכְתָּ אֵלָי הַאֻמְנָם לֹא אוּכַל כַּבְּדֶךָ׃

38 But Balaam said to Balak, "And now that I have come to you, have I the power to speak freely? I can utter only the word that *Hashem* puts into my mouth."

לח וַיֹּאמֶר בִּלְעָם אֶל־בָּלָק הִנֵּה־בָאתִי אֵלֶיךָ עַתָּה הֲיָכוֹל אוּכַל דַּבֵּר מְאוּמָה הַדָּבָר אֲשֶׁר יָשִׂים אֱלֹהִים בְּפִי אֹתוֹ אֲדַבֵּר׃

39 Balaam went with Balak and they came to Kiriath-huzoth.

לט וַיֵּלֶךְ בִּלְעָם עִם־בָּלָק וַיָּבֹאוּ קִרְיַת חֻצוֹת׃

40 Balak sacrificed oxen and sheep, and had them served to Balaam and the dignitaries with him.

מ וַיִּזְבַּח בָּלָק בָּקָר וָצֹאן וַיְשַׁלַּח לְבִלְעָם וְלַשָּׂרִים אֲשֶׁר אִתּוֹ׃

41 In the morning Balak took Balaam up to Bamoth-baal. From there he could see a portion of the people.

מא וַיְהִי בַבֹּקֶר וַיִּקַּח בָּלָק אֶת־בִּלְעָם וַיַּעֲלֵהוּ בָּמוֹת בָּעַל וַיַּרְא מִשָּׁם קְצֵה הָעָם׃

23 1 Balaam said to Balak, "Build me seven altars here and have seven bulls and seven rams ready here for me."

כג א וַיֹּאמֶר בִּלְעָם אֶל־בָּלָק בְּנֵה־לִי בָזֶה שִׁבְעָה מִזְבְּחֹת וְהָכֵן לִי בָּזֶה שִׁבְעָה פָרִים וְשִׁבְעָה אֵילִים׃

2 Balak did as Balaam directed; and Balak and Balaam offered up a bull and a ram on each altar.

ב וַיַּעַשׂ בָּלָק כַּאֲשֶׁר דִּבֶּר בִּלְעָם וַיַּעַל בָּלָק וּבִלְעָם פָּר וָאַיִל בַּמִּזְבֵּחַ׃

3 Then Balaam said to Balak, "Stay here beside your offerings while I am gone. Perhaps *Hashem* will grant me a manifestation, and whatever He reveals to me I will tell you." And he went off alone.

ג וַיֹּאמֶר בִּלְעָם לְבָלָק הִתְיַצֵּב עַל־עֹלָתֶךָ וְאֵלְכָה אוּלַי יִקָּרֵה יְהֹוָה לִקְרָאתִי וּדְבַר מַה־יַּרְאֵנִי וְהִגַּדְתִּי לָךְ וַיֵּלֶךְ שֶׁפִי׃

4 *Hashem* manifested Himself to Balaam, who said to Him, "I have set up the seven altars and offered up a bull and a ram on each altar."

ד וַיִּקָּר אֱלֹהִים אֶל־בִּלְעָם וַיֹּאמֶר אֵלָיו אֶת־שִׁבְעַת הַמִּזְבְּחֹת עָרַכְתִּי וָאַעַל פָּר וָאַיִל בַּמִּזְבֵּחַ׃

5 And *Hashem* put a word in Balaam's mouth and said, "Return to Balak and speak thus."

ה וַיָּשֶׂם יְהֹוָה דָּבָר בְּפִי בִלְעָם וַיֹּאמֶר שׁוּב אֶל־בָּלָק וְכֹה תְדַבֵּר׃

6 So he returned to him and found him standing beside his offerings, and all the Moabite dignitaries with him.

ו וַיָּשָׁב אֵלָיו וְהִנֵּה נִצָּב עַל־עֹלָתוֹ הוּא וְכָל־שָׂרֵי מוֹאָב׃

7 He took up his theme, and said: From Aram has Balak brought me, Moab's king from the hills of the East: Come, curse me *Yaakov*, Come, tell *Yisrael*'s doom!

ז וַיִּשָּׂא מְשָׁלוֹ וַיֹּאמַר מִן־אֲרָם יַנְחֵנִי בָלָק מֶלֶךְ־מוֹאָב מֵהַרְרֵי־קֶדֶם לְכָה אָרָה־לִּי יַעֲקֹב וּלְכָה זֹעֲמָה יִשְׂרָאֵל׃

Bamidbar/Numbers 23
Balak

במדבר כג
בלק

8 How can I damn whom *Hashem* has not damned, How doom when *Hashem* has not doomed?

ח מָה אֶקֹּב לֹא קַבֹּה אֵל וּמָה אֶזְעֹם לֹא זָעַם יְהוָה:

9 As I see them from the mountain tops, Gaze on them from the heights, There is a people that dwells apart, Not reckoned among the nations,

ט כִּי־מֵרֹאשׁ צֻרִים אֶרְאֶנּוּ וּמִגְּבָעוֹת אֲשׁוּרֶנּוּ הֶן־עָם לְבָדָד יִשְׁכֹּן וּבַגּוֹיִם לֹא יִתְחַשָּׁב:

kee may-ROSH tzu-REEM er-E-nu u-mig-va-OT a-shu-RE-nu hen AM l'-va-DAD yish-KON u-va-go-YEEM LO yit-kha-SHAV

10 Who can count the dust of *Yaakov*, Number the dust-cloud of *Yisrael*? May I die the death of the upright, May my fate be like theirs!

י מִי מָנָה עֲפַר יַעֲקֹב וּמִסְפָּר אֶת־רֹבַע יִשְׂרָאֵל תָּמֹת נַפְשִׁי מוֹת יְשָׁרִים וּתְהִי אַחֲרִיתִי כָּמֹהוּ:

11 Then Balak said to Balaam, "What have you done to me? Here I brought you to damn my enemies, and instead you have blessed them!"

יא וַיֹּאמֶר בָּלָק אֶל־בִּלְעָם מֶה עָשִׂיתָ לִי לָקֹב אֹיְבַי לְקַחְתִּיךָ וְהִנֵּה בֵּרַכְתָּ בָרֵךְ:

12 He replied, "I can only repeat faithfully what *Hashem* puts in my mouth."

יב וַיַּעַן וַיֹּאמַר הֲלֹא אֵת אֲשֶׁר יָשִׂים יְהוָה בְּפִי אֹתוֹ אֶשְׁמֹר לְדַבֵּר:

13 Then Balak said to him, "Come with me to another place from which you can see them – you will see only a portion of them; you will not see all of them – and damn them for me from there."

יג וַיֹּאמֶר אֵלָיו בָּלָק לְךָ־[לְכָה־]נָּא אִתִּי אֶל־מָקוֹם אַחֵר אֲשֶׁר תִּרְאֶנּוּ מִשָּׁם אֶפֶס קָצֵהוּ תִרְאֶה וְכֻלּוֹ לֹא תִרְאֶה וְקָבְנוֹ־לִי מִשָּׁם:

14 With that, he took him to Sedehzophim, on the summit of Pisgah. He built seven altars and offered a bull and a ram on each altar.

יד וַיִּקָּחֵהוּ שְׂדֵה צֹפִים אֶל־רֹאשׁ הַפִּסְגָּה וַיִּבֶן שִׁבְעָה מִזְבְּחֹת וַיַּעַל פָּר וָאַיִל בַּמִּזְבֵּחַ:

15 And [Balaam] said to Balak, "Stay here beside your offerings, while I seek a manifestation yonder."

טו וַיֹּאמֶר אֶל־בָּלָק הִתְיַצֵּב כֹּה עַל־עֹלָתֶךָ וְאָנֹכִי אִקָּרֶה כֹּה:

16 *Hashem* manifested Himself to Balaam and put a word in his mouth, saying, "Return to Balak and speak thus."

טז וַיִּקָּר יְהוָה אֶל־בִּלְעָם וַיָּשֶׂם דָּבָר בְּפִיו וַיֹּאמֶר שׁוּב אֶל־בָּלָק וְכֹה תְדַבֵּר:

17 He went to him and found him standing beside his offerings, and the Moabite dignitaries with him. Balak asked him, "What did *Hashem* say?"

יז וַיָּבֹא אֵלָיו וְהִנּוֹ נִצָּב עַל־עֹלָתוֹ וְשָׂרֵי מוֹאָב אִתּוֹ וַיֹּאמֶר לוֹ בָּלָק מַה־דִּבֶּר יְהוָה:

23:9 There is a people that dwells apart, not reckoned among the nations This chapter is one of three that describe the failed attempt by Balaam to curse the People of Israel. His plan is foiled by *Hashem*, and instead of a curse, Balaam utters a reluctant compliment, "There is a people that dwells apart, not reckoned among the nations." For better or for worse, the Jews have always been set aside from among the nations and singled out for special treatment. Today, Israel receives a disproportionate amount of coverage by the media, most of it negative. However, we must recognize the inherent lesson of this solitude: the People of Israel have been singled out for a holy purpose. They were chosen by *Hashem* to remain faithful to Him and to fulfill the biblical mandate of teaching His truths to the world. While for most of history, the Jewish Nation has indeed been an isolated "people that dwells apart," that reality began to change with the establishment of the State of Israel. For the first time, millions of non-Jews have started to stand together with the People of Israel, rejecting the curse of Balaam.

Bamidbar/Numbers 24
Balak

במדבר כד
בלק

18 And he took up his theme, and said: Up, Balak, attend, Give ear unto me, son of Zippor!

יח וַיִּשָּׂא מְשָׁלוֹ וַיֹּאמַר קוּם בָּלָק וּשֲׁמָע הַאֲזִינָה עָדַי בְּנוֹ צִפֹּר:

19 *Hashem* is not man to be capricious, Or mortal to change His mind. Would He speak and not act, Promise and not fulfill?

יט לֹא אִישׁ אֵל וִיכַזֵּב וּבֶן־אָדָם וְיִתְנֶחָם הַהוּא אָמַר וְלֹא יַעֲשֶׂה וְדִבֶּר וְלֹא יְקִימֶנָּה:

20 My message was to bless: When He blesses, I cannot reverse it.

כ הִנֵּה בָרֵךְ לָקָחְתִּי וּבֵרֵךְ וְלֹא אֲשִׁיבֶנָּה:

21 No harm is in sight for *Yaakov*, No woe in view for *Yisrael*. *Hashem* their God is with them, And their King's acclaim in their midst.

כא לֹא־הִבִּיט אָוֶן בְּיַעֲקֹב וְלֹא־רָאָה עָמָל בְּיִשְׂרָאֵל יְהֹוָה אֱלֹהָיו עִמּוֹ וּתְרוּעַת מֶלֶךְ בּוֹ:

22 *Hashem* who freed them from Egypt Is for them like the horns of the wild ox.

כב אֵל מוֹצִיאָם מִמִּצְרָיִם כְּתוֹעֲפֹת רְאֵם לוֹ:

23 Lo, there is no augury in *Yaakov*, No divining in *Yisrael*: *Yaakov* is told at once, Yea *Yisrael*, what *Hashem* has planned.

כג כִּי לֹא־נַחַשׁ בְּיַעֲקֹב וְלֹא־קֶסֶם בְּיִשְׂרָאֵל כָּעֵת יֵאָמֵר לְיַעֲקֹב וּלְיִשְׂרָאֵל מַה־פָּעַל אֵל:

24 Lo, a people that rises like a lion, Leaps up like the king of beasts, Rests not till it has feasted on prey And drunk the blood of the slain.

כד הֶן־עָם כְּלָבִיא יָקוּם וְכַאֲרִי יִתְנַשָּׂא לֹא יִשְׁכַּב עַד־יֹאכַל טֶרֶף וְדַם־חֲלָלִים יִשְׁתֶּה:

25 Thereupon Balak said to Balaam, "Don't curse them and don't bless them!"

כה וַיֹּאמֶר בָּלָק אֶל־בִּלְעָם גַּם־קֹב לֹא תִקֳּבֶנּוּ גַּם־בָּרֵךְ לֹא תְבָרֲכֶנּוּ:

26 In reply, Balaam said to Balak, "But I told you: Whatever *Hashem* says, that I must do."

כו וַיַּעַן בִּלְעָם וַיֹּאמֶר אֶל־בָּלָק הֲלֹא דִּבַּרְתִּי אֵלֶיךָ לֵאמֹר כֹּל אֲשֶׁר־יְדַבֵּר יְהֹוָה אֹתוֹ אֶעֱשֶׂה:

27 Then Balak said to Balaam, "Come now, I will take you to another place. Perhaps *Hashem* will deem it right that you damn them for me there."

כז וַיֹּאמֶר בָּלָק אֶל־בִּלְעָם לְכָה־נָּא אֶקָּחֲךָ אֶל־מָקוֹם אַחֵר אוּלַי יִישַׁר בְּעֵינֵי הָאֱלֹהִים וְקַבֹּתוֹ לִי מִשָּׁם:

28 Balak took Balaam to the peak of Peor, which overlooks the wasteland.

כח וַיִּקַּח בָּלָק אֶת־בִּלְעָם רֹאשׁ הַפְּעוֹר הַנִּשְׁקָף עַל־פְּנֵי הַיְשִׁימֹן:

29 Balaam said to Balak, "Build me here seven altars, and have seven bulls and seven rams ready for me here."

כט וַיֹּאמֶר בִּלְעָם אֶל־בָּלָק בְּנֵה־לִי בָזֶה שִׁבְעָה מִזְבְּחֹת וְהָכֵן לִי בָּזֶה שִׁבְעָה פָרִים וְשִׁבְעָה אֵילִים:

30 Balak did as Balaam said: he offered up a bull and a ram on each altar.

ל וַיַּעַשׂ בָּלָק כַּאֲשֶׁר אָמַר בִּלְעָם וַיַּעַל פָּר וָאַיִל בַּמִּזְבֵּחַ:

24

1 Now Balaam, seeing that it pleased *Hashem* to bless *Yisrael*, did not, as on previous occasions, go in search of omens, but turned his face toward the wilderness.

א וַיַּרְא בִּלְעָם כִּי טוֹב בְּעֵינֵי יְהֹוָה לְבָרֵךְ אֶת־יִשְׂרָאֵל וְלֹא־הָלַךְ כְּפַעַם־בְּפַעַם לִקְרַאת נְחָשִׁים וַיָּשֶׁת אֶל־הַמִּדְבָּר פָּנָיו:

2 As Balaam looked up and saw *Yisrael* encamped tribe by tribe, the spirit of *Hashem* came upon him.

ב וַיִּשָּׂא בִלְעָם אֶת־עֵינָיו וַיַּרְא אֶת־יִשְׂרָאֵל שֹׁכֵן לִשְׁבָטָיו וַתְּהִי עָלָיו רוּחַ אֱלֹהִים:

Bamidbar/Numbers 24
Balak

במדבר כד
בלק

3 Taking up his theme, he said: Word of Balaam son of Beor, Word of the man whose eye is true,

ג וַיִּשָּׂא מְשָׁלוֹ וַיֹּאמַר נְאֻם בִּלְעָם בְּנוֹ בְעֹר וּנְאֻם הַגֶּבֶר שְׁתֻם הָעָיִן:

4 Word of him who hears *Hashem*'s speech, Who beholds visions from the Almighty, Prostrate, but with eyes unveiled:

ד נְאֻם שֹׁמֵעַ אִמְרֵי־אֵל אֲשֶׁר מַחֲזֵה שַׁדַּי יֶחֱזֶה נֹפֵל וּגְלוּי עֵינָיִם:

5 How fair are your tents, O *Yaakov*, Your dwellings, O *Yisrael*!

מַה־טֹּבוּ אֹהָלֶיךָ יַעֲקֹב מִשְׁכְּנֹתֶיךָ יִשְׂרָאֵל:

ma TO-vu o-ha-LE-kha ya-a-KOV mish-k'-no-TE-kha yis-ra-AYL

6 Like palm-groves that stretch out, Like gardens beside a river, Like aloes planted by *Hashem*, Like cedars beside the water;

ו כִּנְחָלִים נִטָּיוּ כְּגַנֹּת עֲלֵי נָהָר כַּאֲהָלִים נָטַע יְהֹוָה כַּאֲרָזִים עֲלֵי־מָיִם:

7 Their boughs drip with moisture, Their roots have abundant water. Their king shall rise above Agag, Their kingdom shall be exalted.

ז יִזַּל־מַיִם מִדָּלְיָו וְזַרְעוֹ בְּמַיִם רַבִּים וְיָרֹם מֵאֲגַג מַלְכּוֹ וְתִנַּשֵּׂא מַלְכֻתוֹ:

8 *Hashem* who freed them from Egypt Is for them like the horns of the wild ox. They shall devour enemy nations, Crush their bones, And smash their arrows.

ח אֵל מוֹצִיאוֹ מִמִּצְרַיִם כְּתוֹעֲפֹת רְאֵם לוֹ יֹאכַל גּוֹיִם צָרָיו וְעַצְמֹתֵיהֶם יְגָרֵם וְחִצָּיו יִמְחָץ:

9 They crouch, they lie down like a lion, Like the king of beasts; who dare rouse them? Blessed are they who bless you, Accursed they who curse you!

ט כָּרַע שָׁכַב כַּאֲרִי וּכְלָבִיא מִי יְקִימֶנּוּ מְבָרֲכֶיךָ בָרוּךְ וְאֹרְרֶיךָ אָרוּר:

10 Enraged at Balaam, Balak struck his hands together. "I called you," Balak said to Balaam, "to damn my enemies, and instead you have blessed them these three times!

י וַיִּחַר־אַף בָּלָק אֶל־בִּלְעָם וַיִּסְפֹּק אֶת־כַּפָּיו וַיֹּאמֶר בָּלָק אֶל־בִּלְעָם לָקֹב אֹיְבַי קְרָאתִיךָ וְהִנֵּה בֵּרַכְתָּ בָרֵךְ זֶה שָׁלֹשׁ פְּעָמִים:

11 Back with you at once to your own place! I was going to reward you richly, but *Hashem* has denied you the reward."

יא וְעַתָּה בְּרַח־לְךָ אֶל־מְקוֹמֶךָ אָמַרְתִּי כַּבֵּד אֲכַבֶּדְךָ וְהִנֵּה מְנָעֲךָ יְהֹוָה מִכָּבוֹד:

12 Balaam replied to Balak, "But I even told the messengers you sent to me,

יב וַיֹּאמֶר בִּלְעָם אֶל־בָּלָק הֲלֹא גַּם אֶל־מַלְאָכֶיךָ אֲשֶׁר־שָׁלַחְתָּ אֵלַי דִּבַּרְתִּי לֵאמֹר:

13 'Though Balak were to give me his house full of silver and gold, I could not of my own accord do anything good or bad contrary to *Hashem*'s command. What *Hashem* says, that I must say.'

יג אִם־יִתֶּן־לִי בָלָק מְלֹא בֵיתוֹ כֶּסֶף וְזָהָב לֹא אוּכַל לַעֲבֹר אֶת־פִּי יְהֹוָה לַעֲשׂוֹת טוֹבָה אוֹ רָעָה מִלִּבִּי אֲשֶׁר־יְדַבֵּר יְהֹוָה אֹתוֹ אֲדַבֵּר:

Ramban (1194–1270)

24:5 How fair are your tents, O *Yaakov*, your dwellings, O *Yisrael* Ramban points out that when referring to the homes of the Children of Israel, the verse first mentions tents of *Yaakov* and then dwellings of Israel. He explains that "tents" are temporary living quarters, referring to Israel's sojourn in the desert, while "dwellings" implies a permanent living space, hinting to the established life of the Jews in the Holy Land. Just as they are taken care of and protected in the desert, the Children of Israel will ultimately be blessed with success, prosperity and security in *Eretz Yisrael*.

397

Bamidbar/Numbers 25
Balak

במדבר כה
בלק

14 And now, as I go back to my people, let me inform you of what this people will do to your people in days to come."

יד וְעַתָּה הִנְנִי הוֹלֵךְ לְעַמִּי לְכָה אִיעָצְךָ אֲשֶׁר יַעֲשֶׂה הָעָם הַזֶּה לְעַמְּךָ בְּאַחֲרִית הַיָּמִים׃

15 He took up his theme, and said: Word of Balaam son of Beor, Word of the man whose eye is true,

טו וַיִּשָּׂא מְשָׁלוֹ וַיֹּאמַר נְאֻם בִּלְעָם בְּנוֹ בְעֹר וּנְאֻם הַגֶּבֶר שְׁתֻם הָעָיִן׃

16 Word of him who hears *Hashem*'s speech, Who obtains knowledge from the Most High, And beholds visions from the Almighty, Prostrate, but with eyes unveiled:

טז נְאֻם שֹׁמֵעַ אִמְרֵי־אֵל וְיֹדֵעַ דַּעַת עֶלְיוֹן מַחֲזֵה שַׁדַּי יֶחֱזֶה נֹפֵל וּגְלוּי עֵינָיִם׃

17 What I see for them is not yet, What I behold will not be soon: A star rises from *Yaakov*, A scepter comes forth from *Yisrael*; It smashes the brow of Moab, The foundation of all children of *Shet*.

יז אֶרְאֶנּוּ וְלֹא עַתָּה אֲשׁוּרֶנּוּ וְלֹא קָרוֹב דָּרַךְ כּוֹכָב מִיַּעֲקֹב וְקָם שֵׁבֶט מִיִּשְׂרָאֵל וּמָחַץ פַּאֲתֵי מוֹאָב וְקַרְקַר כָּל־בְּנֵי־שֵׁת׃

18 Edom becomes a possession, Yea, Seir a possession of its enemies; But *Yisrael* is triumphant.

יח וְהָיָה אֱדוֹם יְרֵשָׁה וְהָיָה יְרֵשָׁה שֵׂעִיר אֹיְבָיו וְיִשְׂרָאֵל עֹשֶׂה חָיִל׃

19 A victor issues from *Yaakov* To wipe out what is left of Ir.

יט וְיֵרְדְּ מִיַּעֲקֹב וְהֶאֱבִיד שָׂרִיד מֵעִיר׃

20 He saw Amalek and, taking up his theme, he said: A leading nation is Amalek; But its fate is to perish forever.

כ וַיַּרְא אֶת־עֲמָלֵק וַיִּשָּׂא מְשָׁלוֹ וַיֹּאמַר רֵאשִׁית גּוֹיִם עֲמָלֵק וְאַחֲרִיתוֹ עֲדֵי אֹבֵד׃

21 He saw the Kenites and, taking up his theme, he said: Though your abode be secure, And your nest be set among cliffs,

כא וַיַּרְא אֶת־הַקֵּינִי וַיִּשָּׂא מְשָׁלוֹ וַיֹּאמַר אֵיתָן מוֹשָׁבֶךָ וְשִׂים בַּסֶּלַע קִנֶּךָ׃

22 Yet shall Kain be consumed, When Assyria takes you captive.

כב כִּי אִם־יִהְיֶה לְבָעֵר קָיִן עַד־מָה אַשּׁוּר תִּשְׁבֶּךָּ׃

23 He took up his theme and said: Alas, who can survive except *Hashem* has willed it!

כג וַיִּשָּׂא מְשָׁלוֹ וַיֹּאמַר אוֹי מִי יִחְיֶה מִשֻּׂמוֹ אֵל׃

24 Ships come from the quarter of Kittim; They subject Assyria, subject Eber. They, too, shall perish forever.

כד וְצִים מִיַּד כִּתִּים וְעִנּוּ אַשּׁוּר וְעִנּוּ־עֵבֶר וְגַם־הוּא עֲדֵי אֹבֵד׃

25 Then Balaam set out on his journey back home; and Balak also went his way.

כה וַיָּקָם בִּלְעָם וַיֵּלֶךְ וַיָּשָׁב לִמְקֹמוֹ וְגַם־בָּלָק הָלַךְ לְדַרְכּוֹ׃

25

1 While *Yisrael* was staying at Shittim, the people profaned themselves by whoring with the Moabite women,

כה א וַיֵּשֶׁב יִשְׂרָאֵל בַּשִּׁטִּים וַיָּחֶל הָעָם לִזְנוֹת אֶל־בְּנוֹת מוֹאָב׃

2 who invited the people to the sacrifices for their god. The people partook of them and worshiped that god.

ב וַתִּקְרֶאןָ לָעָם לְזִבְחֵי אֱלֹהֵיהֶן וַיֹּאכַל הָעָם וַיִּשְׁתַּחֲווּ לֵאלֹהֵיהֶן׃

3 Thus *Yisrael* attached itself to Baal-peor, and *Hashem* was incensed with *Yisrael*.

ג וַיִּצָּמֶד יִשְׂרָאֵל לְבַעַל פְּעוֹר וַיִּחַר־אַף יְהֹוָה בְּיִשְׂרָאֵל׃

Bamidbar/Numbers 25
Pinchas

4 *Hashem* said to *Moshe*, "Take all the ringleaders and have them publicly impaled before *Hashem*, so that *Hashem*'s wrath may turn away from *Yisrael*."

ד וַיֹּאמֶר יְהֹוָה אֶל־מֹשֶׁה קַח אֶת־כָּל־רָאשֵׁי הָעָם וְהוֹקַע אוֹתָם לַיהֹוָה נֶגֶד הַשָּׁמֶשׁ וְיָשֹׁב חֲרוֹן אַף־יְהֹוָה מִיִּשְׂרָאֵל׃

5 So *Moshe* said to *Yisrael*'s officials, "Each of you slay those of his men who attached themselves to Baal-peor."

ה וַיֹּאמֶר מֹשֶׁה אֶל־שֹׁפְטֵי יִשְׂרָאֵל הִרְגוּ אִישׁ אֲנָשָׁיו הַנִּצְמָדִים לְבַעַל פְּעוֹר׃

6 Just then one of the Israelites came and brought a Midianite woman over to his companions, in the sight of *Moshe* and of the whole Israelite community who were weeping at the entrance of the Tent of Meeting.

ו וְהִנֵּה אִישׁ מִבְּנֵי יִשְׂרָאֵל בָּא וַיַּקְרֵב אֶל־אֶחָיו אֶת־הַמִּדְיָנִית לְעֵינֵי מֹשֶׁה וּלְעֵינֵי כָּל־עֲדַת בְּנֵי־יִשְׂרָאֵל וְהֵמָּה בֹכִים פֶּתַח אֹהֶל מוֹעֵד׃

7 When *Pinchas*, son of *Elazar* son of *Aharon* the *Kohen*, saw this, he left the assembly and, taking a spear in his hand,

ז וַיַּרְא פִּינְחָס בֶּן־אֶלְעָזָר בֶּן־אַהֲרֹן הַכֹּהֵן וַיָּקָם מִתּוֹךְ הָעֵדָה וַיִּקַּח רֹמַח בְּיָדוֹ׃

8 he followed the Israelite into the Hamber and stabbed both of them, the Israelite and the woman, through the belly. Then the plague against the Israelites was checked.

ח וַיָּבֹא אַחַר אִישׁ־יִשְׂרָאֵל אֶל־הַקֻּבָּה וַיִּדְקֹר אֶת־שְׁנֵיהֶם אֵת אִישׁ יִשְׂרָאֵל וְאֶת־הָאִשָּׁה אֶל־קֳבָתָהּ וַתֵּעָצַר הַמַּגֵּפָה מֵעַל בְּנֵי יִשְׂרָאֵל׃

9 Those who died of the plague numbered twenty-four thousand.

ט וַיִּהְיוּ הַמֵּתִים בַּמַּגֵּפָה אַרְבָּעָה וְעֶשְׂרִים אָלֶף׃

10 *Hashem* spoke to *Moshe*, saying,

י וַיְדַבֵּר יְהֹוָה אֶל־מֹשֶׁה לֵּאמֹר׃

11 "*Pinchas*, son of *Elazar* son of *Aharon* the *Kohen*, has turned back My wrath from the Israelites by displaying among them his passion for Me, so that I did not wipe out *B'nei Yisrael* in My passion.

יא פִּינְחָס בֶּן־אֶלְעָזָר בֶּן־אַהֲרֹן הַכֹּהֵן הֵשִׁיב אֶת־חֲמָתִי מֵעַל בְּנֵי־יִשְׂרָאֵל בְּקַנְאוֹ אֶת־קִנְאָתִי בְּתוֹכָם וְלֹא־כִלִּיתִי אֶת־בְּנֵי־יִשְׂרָאֵל בְּקִנְאָתִי׃

12 Say, therefore, 'I grant him My pact of friendship.

יב לָכֵן אֱמֹר הִנְנִי נֹתֵן לוֹ אֶת־בְּרִיתִי שָׁלוֹם׃

la-KHAYN e-MOR hin-NEE no-TAYN LO et b'-ree-TEE sha-LOM

13 It shall be for him and his descendants after him a pact of priesthood for all time, because he took impassioned action for his God, thus making expiation for the Israelites.'"

יג וְהָיְתָה לּוֹ וּלְזַרְעוֹ אַחֲרָיו בְּרִית כְּהֻנַּת עוֹלָם תַּחַת אֲשֶׁר קִנֵּא לֵאלֹהָיו וַיְכַפֵּר עַל־בְּנֵי יִשְׂרָאֵל׃

ברית שלום

25:12 I grant him My pact of friendship The zealot, *Pinchas*, sees immoral behavior among the camp of Israel, and immediately responds with an iron fist and a sharp spear. Ironically, *Pinchas* is rewarded for his violent action with Hashem's "pact of friendship," known in Hebrew as *brit shalom* (ברית שלום), literally 'covenant of peace.' With this striking detail, the *Torah* illustrates a vital lesson. Genuine peace is not merely the absence of conflict. *Pinchas* did not negotiate with the perpetrators and attempt to achieve a compromise solution. By standing up for his principles, *Pinchas* demonstrated that only when based on eternal principles of truth and justice can true peace be achieved. A person who internalizes this idea and acts accordingly is a true "friend" of God.

Bamidbar/Numbers 26
Pinchas

במדבר כו
פינחס

14 The name of the Israelite who killed, the one who was killed with the Midianite woman, was *Zimri* son of *Salu*, chieftain of a Simeonite ancestral house.

יד וְשֵׁם אִישׁ יִשְׂרָאֵל הַמֻּכֶּה אֲשֶׁר הֻכָּה אֶת־הַמִּדְיָנִית זִמְרִי בֶּן־סָלוּא נְשִׂיא בֵית־אָב לַשִּׁמְעֹנִי׃

15 The name of the Midianite woman who was killed was *Cozbi* daughter of *Zur*; he was the tribal head of an ancestral house in *Midian*.

טו וְשֵׁם הָאִשָּׁה הַמֻּכָּה הַמִּדְיָנִית כָּזְבִּי בַת־צוּר רֹאשׁ אֻמּוֹת בֵּית־אָב בְּמִדְיָן הוּא׃

16 *Hashem* spoke to *Moshe*, saying,

טז וַיְדַבֵּר יְהֹוָה אֶל־מֹשֶׁה לֵּאמֹר׃

17 "Assail the Midianites and defeat them

יז צָרוֹר אֶת־הַמִּדְיָנִים וְהִכִּיתֶם אוֹתָם׃

18 for they assailed you by the trickery they practiced against you – because of the affair of Peor and because of the affair of their kinswoman Cozbi, daughter of the Midianite chieftain, who was killed at the time of the plague on account of Peor."

יח כִּי צֹרְרִים הֵם לָכֶם בְּנִכְלֵיהֶם אֲשֶׁר־נִכְּלוּ לָכֶם עַל־דְּבַר־פְּעוֹר וְעַל־דְּבַר כָּזְבִּי בַת־נְשִׂיא מִדְיָן אֲחֹתָם הַמֻּכָּה בְיוֹם־הַמַּגֵּפָה עַל־דְּבַר־פְּעוֹר׃

26 1 When the plague was over, *Hashem* said to *Moshe* and to *Elazar* son of *Aharon* the *Kohen*,

כו א וַיְהִי אַחֲרֵי הַמַּגֵּפָה וַיֹּאמֶר יְהֹוָה אֶל־מֹשֶׁה וְאֶל אֶלְעָזָר בֶּן־אַהֲרֹן הַכֹּהֵן לֵאמֹר׃

2 "Take a census of the whole Israelite community from the age of twenty years up, by their ancestral houses, all Israelites able to bear arms."

ב שְׂאוּ אֶת־רֹאשׁ כָּל־עֲדַת בְּנֵי־יִשְׂרָאֵל מִבֶּן עֶשְׂרִים שָׁנָה וָמַעְלָה לְבֵית אֲבֹתָם כָּל־יֹצֵא צָבָא בְּיִשְׂרָאֵל׃

s'-U et ROSH kol a-DAT b'-nay yis-ra-AYL mi-BEN es-REEM sha-NAH va-MA-lah l'-VAYT a-vo-TAM kol yo-TZAY tza-VA b'-yis-ra-AYL

3 So *Moshe* and *Elazar* the *Kohen*, on the steppes of Moab, at the *Yarden* near *Yericho*, gave instructions about them, namely,

ג וַיְדַבֵּר מֹשֶׁה וְאֶלְעָזָר הַכֹּהֵן אֹתָם בְּעַרְבֹת מוֹאָב עַל־יַרְדֵּן יְרֵחוֹ לֵאמֹר׃

4 those from twenty years up, as *Hashem* had commanded *Moshe*. The descendants of the Israelites who came out of the land of Egypt were:

ד מִבֶּן עֶשְׂרִים שָׁנָה וָמָעְלָה כַּאֲשֶׁר צִוָּה יְהֹוָה אֶת־מֹשֶׁה וּבְנֵי יִשְׂרָאֵל הַיֹּצְאִים מֵאֶרֶץ מִצְרָיִם׃

5 *Reuven*, *Yisrael*'s first-born. Descendants of *Reuven*: [Of] Enoch, the clan of the Enochites; of Pallu, the clan of the Palluites;

ה רְאוּבֵן בְּכוֹר יִשְׂרָאֵל בְּנֵי רְאוּבֵן חֲנוֹךְ מִשְׁפַּחַת הַחֲנֹכִי לְפַלּוּא מִשְׁפַּחַת הַפַּלֻּאִי׃

6 of *Chetzron*, the clan of the Chetzronites; of Carmi, the clan of the Carmites.

ו לְחֶצְרֹן מִשְׁפַּחַת הַחֶצְרוֹנִי לְכַרְמִי מִשְׁפַּחַת הַכַּרְמִי׃

26:2 Take a census of the whole Israelite community This chapter discusses the second census found in the book of *Bamidbar*. The forty years of wandering in the desert are now over, and the people are finally going to conquer, inherit and divide the land. A count is now necessary, to determine how big their army will be and among how many people the land must be divided. By counting each individual, *Hashem* conveys the message that each person's role in conquering and inhabiting the Promised Land is vital. Each person receives his portion, and with it a responsibility to contribute his part to *Hashem*, the country and the nation.

IDF recruits at their swearing in ceremony

400

Bamidbar/Numbers 26
Pinchas

במדבר כו
פינחס

7 Those are the clans of the Reubenites. The persons enrolled came to 43,730.

ז אֵ֖לֶּה מִשְׁפְּחֹ֣ת הָרֽאוּבֵנִ֑י וַיִּהְי֣וּ פְקֻדֵיהֶ֗ם שְׁלֹשָׁ֧ה וְאַרְבָּעִ֛ים אֶ֖לֶף וּשְׁבַ֥ע מֵא֖וֹת וּשְׁלֹשִֽׁים:

8 Born to Pallu: Eliav.

ח וּבְנֵ֥י פַלּ֖וּא אֱלִיאָֽב:

9 The sons of Eliav were Nemuel, and Datan and Aviram. These are the same Datan and Aviram, chosen in the assembly, who agitated against Moshe and Aharon as part of Korach's band when they agitated against Hashem.

ט וּבְנֵ֣י אֱלִיאָ֔ב נְמוּאֵ֖ל וְדָתָ֣ן וַאֲבִירָ֑ם הֽוּא־דָתָ֨ן וַאֲבִירָ֜ם [קְרוּאֵ֣י] (קריאי) הָֽעֵדָ֗ה אֲשֶׁ֨ר הִצּ֜וּ עַל־מֹשֶׁ֤ה וְעַֽל־אַהֲרֹן֙ בַּעֲדַת־קֹ֔רַח בְּהַצֹּתָ֖ם עַל־יְהוָֽה:

10 Whereupon the earth opened its mouth and swallowed them up with Korach – when that band died, when the fire consumed the two hundred and fifty men – and they became an example.

י וַתִּפְתַּ֨ח הָאָ֜רֶץ אֶת־פִּ֗יהָ וַתִּבְלַ֥ע אֹתָ֛ם וְאֶת־קֹ֖רַח בְּמ֣וֹת הָעֵדָ֑ה בַּאֲכֹ֣ל הָאֵ֗שׁ אֵ֣ת חֲמִשִּׁ֤ים וּמָאתַ֙יִם֙ אִ֔ישׁ וַיִּהְי֖וּ לְנֵֽס:

11 The sons of Korach, however, did not die.

יא וּבְנֵי־קֹ֖רַח לֹא־מֵֽתוּ:

12 Descendants of Shimon by their clans: Of Nemuel, the clan of the Nemuelites; of Jamin, the clan of the Jaminites; of Jachin, the clan of the Jachinites;

יב בְּנֵ֣י שִׁמְעוֹן֮ לְמִשְׁפְּחֹתָם֒ לִנְמוּאֵ֗ל מִשְׁפַּ֙חַת֙ הַנְּמ֣וּאֵלִ֔י לְיָמִ֕ין מִשְׁפַּ֖חַת הַיָּמִינִ֑י לְיָכִ֕ין מִשְׁפַּ֖חַת הַיָּכִינִֽי:

13 of Zerach, the clan of the Zerahites; of Shaul, the clan of the Shaulites.

יג לְזֶ֕רַח מִשְׁפַּ֖חַת הַזַּרְחִ֑י לְשָׁא֕וּל מִשְׁפַּ֖חַת הַשָּׁאוּלִֽי:

14 Those are the clans of the Simeonites; [persons enrolled:] 22,200.

יד אֵ֖לֶּה מִשְׁפְּחֹ֣ת הַשִּׁמְעֹנִ֑י שְׁנַ֧יִם וְעֶשְׂרִ֛ים אֶ֖לֶף וּמָאתָֽיִם:

15 Descendants of Gad by their clans: Of Zephon, the clan of the Zephonites; of Haggi, the clan of the Haggites; of Shuni, the clan of the Shunites;

טו בְּנֵ֣י גָד֮ לְמִשְׁפְּחֹתָם֒ לִצְפ֗וֹן מִשְׁפַּ֙חַת֙ הַצְּפוֹנִ֔י לְחַגִּ֕י מִשְׁפַּ֖חַת הַֽחַגִּ֑י לְשׁוּנִ֕י מִשְׁפַּ֖חַת הַשּׁוּנִֽי:

16 of Ozni, the clan of the Oznites; of Eri, the clan of the Erites;

טז לְאָזְנִ֕י מִשְׁפַּ֖חַת הָאָזְנִ֑י לְעֵרִ֕י מִשְׁפַּ֖חַת הָעֵרִֽי:

17 of Arod, the clan of the Arodites; of Areli, the clan of the Arelites.

יז לַאֲר֕וֹד מִשְׁפַּ֖חַת הָאֲרוֹדִ֑י לְאַ֨רְאֵלִ֔י מִשְׁפַּ֖חַת הָאַרְאֵלִֽי:

18 Those are the clans of Gad's descendants; persons enrolled: 40,500.

יח אֵ֛לֶּה מִשְׁפְּחֹ֥ת בְּנֵי־גָ֖ד לִפְקֻדֵיהֶ֑ם אַרְבָּעִ֥ים אֶ֖לֶף וַחֲמֵ֥שׁ מֵאֽוֹת:

19 Born to Yehuda: Er and Onan. Er and Onan died in the land of Canaan.

יט בְּנֵ֥י יְהוּדָ֖ה עֵ֣ר וְאוֹנָ֑ן וַיָּ֥מָת עֵ֛ר וְאוֹנָ֖ן בְּאֶ֥רֶץ כְּנָֽעַן:

20 Descendants of Yehuda by their clans: Of Sheilah, the clan of the Shelanites; of Peretz, the clan of the Peretzites; of Zerach, the clan of the Zerahites.

כ וַיִּהְי֣וּ בְנֵֽי־יְהוּדָה֮ לְמִשְׁפְּחֹתָם֒ לְשֵׁלָ֗ה מִשְׁפַּ֙חַת֙ הַשֵּׁ֣לָנִ֔י לְפֶ֕רֶץ מִשְׁפַּ֖חַת הַפַּרְצִ֑י לְזֶ֕רַח מִשְׁפַּ֖חַת הַזַּרְחִֽי:

21 Descendants of Peretz: of Chetzron, the clan of the Chetzronites; of Hamul, the clan of the Hamulites.

כא וַיִּהְי֣וּ בְנֵי־פֶ֔רֶץ לְחֶצְרֹ֕ן מִשְׁפַּ֖חַת הַֽחֶצְרֹנִ֑י לְחָמ֕וּל מִשְׁפַּ֖חַת הֶחָמוּלִֽי:

22 Those are the clans of Yehuda; persons enrolled: 76,500.

כב אֵ֛לֶּה מִשְׁפְּחֹ֥ת יְהוּדָ֖ה לִפְקֻדֵיהֶ֑ם שִׁשָּׁ֧ה וְשִׁבְעִ֛ים אֶ֖לֶף וַחֲמֵ֥שׁ מֵאֽוֹת:

Bamidbar/Numbers 26
Pinchas

במדבר כו
פינחס

23 Descendants of *Yissachar* by their clans: [Of] *Tola*, the clan of the Tolaites; of Puvah, the clan of the Punites;

כג בְּנֵי יִשָּׂשכָר לְמִשְׁפְּחֹתָם תּוֹלָע מִשְׁפַּחַת הַתּוֹלָעִי לְפֻוָּה מִשְׁפַּחַת הַפּוּנִי:

24 of Yashuv, the clan of the Yashuvites; of Shimron, the clan of the Shimronites.

כד לְיָשׁוּב מִשְׁפַּחַת הַיָּשׁוּבִי לְשִׁמְרֹן מִשְׁפַּחַת הַשִּׁמְרֹנִי:

25 Those are the clans of *Yissachar*; persons enrolled: 64,300.

כה אֵלֶּה מִשְׁפְּחֹת יִשָּׂשכָר לִפְקֻדֵיהֶם אַרְבָּעָה וְשִׁשִּׁים אֶלֶף וּשְׁלֹשׁ מֵאוֹת:

26 Descendants of *Zevulun* by their clans: Of Sered, the clan of the Seredites; of *Eilon*, the clan of the Elonites; of Jahleel, the clan of the Jahleelites.

כו בְּנֵי זְבוּלֻן לְמִשְׁפְּחֹתָם לְסֶרֶד מִשְׁפַּחַת הַסַּרְדִּי לְאֵלוֹן מִשְׁפַּחַת הָאֵלֹנִי לְיַחְלְאֵל מִשְׁפַּחַת הַיַּחְלְאֵלִי:

27 Those are the clans of the Zebulunites; persons enrolled: 60,500.

כז אֵלֶּה מִשְׁפְּחֹת הַזְּבוּלֹנִי לִפְקֻדֵיהֶם שִׁשִּׁים אֶלֶף וַחֲמֵשׁ מֵאוֹת:

28 The sons of *Yosef* were *Menashe* and *Efraim* – by their clans.

כח בְּנֵי יוֹסֵף לְמִשְׁפְּחֹתָם מְנַשֶּׁה וְאֶפְרָיִם:

29 Descendants of *Menashe*: Of Machir, the clan of the Machirites. – Machir begot *Gilad*. – Of *Gilad*, the clan of the Giladites.

כט בְּנֵי מְנַשֶּׁה לְמָכִיר מִשְׁפַּחַת הַמָּכִירִי וּמָכִיר הוֹלִיד אֶת־גִּלְעָד לְגִלְעָד מִשְׁפַּחַת הַגִּלְעָדִי:

30 These were the descendants of *Gilad*: [Of] Iezer, the clan of the Iezerites; of Helek, the clan of the Helekites;

ל אֵלֶּה בְּנֵי גִלְעָד אִיעֶזֶר מִשְׁפַּחַת הָאִיעֶזְרִי לְחֵלֶק מִשְׁפַּחַת הַחֶלְקִי:

31 [of] Asriel, the clan of the Asrielites; [of] *Shechem*, the clan of the Sh'chemites;

לא וְאַשְׂרִיאֵל מִשְׁפַּחַת הָאַשְׂרִאֵלִי וְשֶׁכֶם מִשְׁפַּחַת הַשִּׁכְמִי:

32 [of] Shemida, the clan of the Shemidaites; [of] Hepher, the clan of the Hepherites. –

לב וּשְׁמִידָע מִשְׁפַּחַת הַשְּׁמִידָעִי וְחֵפֶר מִשְׁפַּחַת הַחֶפְרִי:

33 Now *Tzelofchad* son of Hepher had no sons, only daughters. The names of *Tzelofchad*'s daughters were *Machla, Noa, Chagla, Milka,* and *Tirtza.*

לג וּצְלָפְחָד בֶּן־חֵפֶר לֹא־הָיוּ לוֹ בָּנִים כִּי אִם־בָּנוֹת וְשֵׁם בְּנוֹת צְלָפְחָד מַחְלָה וְנֹעָה חָגְלָה מִלְכָּה וְתִרְצָה:

34 Those are the clans of *Menashe*; persons enrolled: 52,700.

לד אֵלֶּה מִשְׁפְּחֹת מְנַשֶּׁה וּפְקֻדֵיהֶם שְׁנַיִם וַחֲמִשִּׁים אֶלֶף וּשְׁבַע מֵאוֹת:

35 These are the descendants of *Efraim* by their clans: Of Shuthelah, the clan of the Shuthelahites; of Becher, the clan of the Becherites; of Tahan, the clan of the Tahanites.

לה אֵלֶּה בְנֵי־אֶפְרַיִם לְמִשְׁפְּחֹתָם לְשׁוּתֶלַח מִשְׁפַּחַת הַשֻּׁתַלְחִי לְבֶכֶר מִשְׁפַּחַת הַבַּכְרִי לְתַחַן מִשְׁפַּחַת הַתַּחֲנִי:

36 These are the descendants of Shuthelah: Of Eran, the clan of the Eranites.

לו וְאֵלֶּה בְּנֵי שׁוּתָלַח לְעֵרָן מִשְׁפַּחַת הָעֵרָנִי:

37 Those are the clans of *Efraim*'s descendants; persons enrolled: 32,500. Those are the descendants of *Yosef* by their clans.

לז אֵלֶּה מִשְׁפְּחֹת בְּנֵי־אֶפְרַיִם לִפְקֻדֵיהֶם שְׁנַיִם וּשְׁלֹשִׁים אֶלֶף וַחֲמֵשׁ מֵאוֹת אֵלֶּה בְנֵי־יוֹסֵף לְמִשְׁפְּחֹתָם:

38 The descendants of *Binyamin* by their clans: Of Bela, the clan of the Belaites; of Ashbel, the clan of the Ashbelites; of Ahiram, the clan of the Ahiramites;

לח בְּנֵי בִנְיָמִן לְמִשְׁפְּחֹתָם לְבֶלַע מִשְׁפַּחַת הַבַּלְעִי לְאַשְׁבֵּל מִשְׁפַּחַת הָאַשְׁבֵּלִי לַאֲחִירָם מִשְׁפַּחַת הָאֲחִירָמִי:

402

Bamidbar/Numbers 26
Pinchas

39 of Shephupham, the clan of the Shuphamites; of Hupham, the clan of the Huphamites.

40 The sons of Bela were Ard and Naaman: [Of Ard,] the clan of the Ardites; of Naaman, the clan of the Naamanites.

41 Those are the descendants of *Binyamin* by their clans; persons enrolled: 45,600.

42 These are the descendants of *Dan* by their clans: Of Shuham, the clan of the Shuhamites. Those are the clans of *Dan*, by their clans.

43 All the clans of the Shuhamites; persons enrolled: 64,400.

44 Descendants of *Asher* by their clans: Of Imnah, the clan of the Imnites; of Ishvi, the clan of the Ishvites; of Beriah, the clan of the Beriites.

45 Of the descendants of Beriah: Of *Chever*, the clan of the Heberites; of Malchiel, the clan of the Malchielites.

46 The name of *Asher*'s daughter was Serah.

47 These are the clans of *Asher*'s descendants; persons enrolled: 53,400.

48 Descendants of *Naftali* by their clans: Of Jahzeel, the clan of the Jahzeelites; of Guni, the clan of the Gunites;

49 of Jezer, the clan of the Jezerites; of Shillem, the clan of the Shillemites.

50 Those are the clans of the Naphtalites, clan by clan; persons enrolled: 45,400.

51 This is the enrollment of the Israelites: 601,730.

52 *Hashem* spoke to *Moshe*, saying,

53 "Among these shall the land be apportioned as shares, according to the listed names:

54 with larger groups increase the share, with smaller groups reduce the share. Each is to be assigned its share according to its enrollment.

55 The land, moreover, is to be apportioned by lot; and the allotment shall be made according to the listings of their ancestral tribes.

במדבר כו
פינחס

לט לִשְׁפוּפָם מִשְׁפַּחַת הַשּׁוּפָמִי לְחוּפָם מִשְׁפַּחַת הַחוּפָמִי׃

מ וַיִּהְיוּ בְנֵי־בֶלַע אַרְדְּ וְנַעֲמָן מִשְׁפַּחַת הָאַרְדִּי לְנַעֲמָן מִשְׁפַּחַת הַנַּעֲמִי׃

מא אֵלֶּה בְנֵי־בִנְיָמִן לְמִשְׁפְּחֹתָם וּפְקֻדֵיהֶם חֲמִשָּׁה וְאַרְבָּעִים אֶלֶף וְשֵׁשׁ מֵאוֹת׃

מב אֵלֶּה בְנֵי־דָן לְמִשְׁפְּחֹתָם לְשׁוּחָם מִשְׁפַּחַת הַשּׁוּחָמִי אֵלֶּה מִשְׁפְּחֹת דָּן לְמִשְׁפְּחֹתָם׃

מג כׇּל־מִשְׁפְּחֹת הַשּׁוּחָמִי לִפְקֻדֵיהֶם אַרְבָּעָה וְשִׁשִּׁים אֶלֶף וְאַרְבַּע מֵאוֹת׃

מד בְּנֵי אָשֵׁר לְמִשְׁפְּחֹתָם לְיִמְנָה מִשְׁפַּחַת הַיִּמְנָה לְיִשְׁוִי מִשְׁפַּחַת הַיִּשְׁוִי לִבְרִיעָה מִשְׁפַּחַת הַבְּרִיעִי׃

מה לִבְנֵי בְרִיעָה לְחֶבֶר מִשְׁפַּחַת הַחֶבְרִי לְמַלְכִּיאֵל מִשְׁפַּחַת הַמַּלְכִּיאֵלִי׃

מו וְשֵׁם בַּת־אָשֵׁר שָׂרַח׃

מז אֵלֶּה מִשְׁפְּחֹת בְּנֵי־אָשֵׁר לִפְקֻדֵיהֶם שְׁלֹשָׁה וַחֲמִשִּׁים אֶלֶף וְאַרְבַּע מֵאוֹת׃

מח בְּנֵי נַפְתָּלִי לְמִשְׁפְּחֹתָם לְיַחְצְאֵל מִשְׁפַּחַת הַיַּחְצְאֵלִי לְגוּנִי מִשְׁפַּחַת הַגּוּנִי׃

מט לְיֵצֶר מִשְׁפַּחַת הַיִּצְרִי לְשִׁלֵּם מִשְׁפַּחַת הַשִּׁלֵּמִי׃

נ אֵלֶּה מִשְׁפְּחֹת נַפְתָּלִי לְמִשְׁפְּחֹתָם וּפְקֻדֵיהֶם חֲמִשָּׁה וְאַרְבָּעִים אֶלֶף וְאַרְבַּע מֵאוֹת׃

נא אֵלֶּה פְּקוּדֵי בְּנֵי יִשְׂרָאֵל שֵׁשׁ־מֵאוֹת אֶלֶף וָאָלֶף שְׁבַע מֵאוֹת וּשְׁלֹשִׁים׃

נב וַיְדַבֵּר יְהֹוָה אֶל־מֹשֶׁה לֵּאמֹר׃

נג לָאֵלֶּה תֵּחָלֵק הָאָרֶץ בְּנַחֲלָה בְּמִסְפַּר שֵׁמוֹת׃

נד לָרַב תַּרְבֶּה נַחֲלָתוֹ וְלַמְעַט תַּמְעִיט נַחֲלָתוֹ אִישׁ לְפִי פְקֻדָיו יֻתַּן נַחֲלָתוֹ׃

נה אַךְ־בְּגוֹרָל יֵחָלֵק אֶת־הָאָרֶץ לִשְׁמוֹת מַטּוֹת־אֲבֹתָם יִנְחָלוּ׃

Bamidbar/Numbers 27
Pinchas

56 Each portion shall be assigned by lot, whether for larger or smaller groups."

57 This is the enrollment of the *Leviim* by their clans: Of *Gershon*, the clan of the Gershonites; of *Kehat*, the clan of the Kohathites; of *Merari*, the clan of the Merarites.

58 These are the clans of *Levi*: The clan of the Libnites, the clan of the Chevronites, the clan of the Mahlites, the clan of the Mushites, the clan of the Korahites. – *Kehat* begot *Amram*.

59 The name of *Amram*'s wife was *Yocheved* daughter of *Levi*, who was born to *Levi* in Egypt; she bore to *Amram Aharon* and *Moshe* and their sister *Miriam*.

60 To *Aharon* were born *Nadav* and *Avihu*, *Elazar* and *Itamar*.

61 *Nadav* and *Avihu* died when they offered alien fire before *Hashem*.

62 Their enrollment of 23,000 comprised all males from a month up. They were not part of the regular enrollment of the Israelites, since no share was assigned to them among the Israelites.

63 These are the persons enrolled by *Moshe* and *Elazar* the *Kohen* who registered the Israelites on the steppes of Moab, at the *Yarden* near *Yericho*.

64 Among these there was not one of those enrolled by *Moshe* and *Aharon* the *Kohen* when they recorded the Israelites in the wilderness of Sinai.

65 For *Hashem* had said of them, "They shall die in the wilderness." Not one of them survived, except *Kalev* son of Jephunneh and *Yehoshua* son of *Nun*.

27 1 The daughters of *Tzelofchad*, of Manassite family – son of Hepher son of *Gilad* son of Machir son of *Menashe* son of *Yosef* – came forward. The names of the daughters were *Machla*, *Noa*, *Chagla*, *Milka*, and *Tirtza*.

2 They stood before *Moshe*, *Elazar* the *Kohen*, the chieftains, and the whole assembly, at the entrance of the Tent of Meeting, and they said,

3 "Our father died in the wilderness. He was not one of the faction, *Korach*'s faction, which banded together against *Hashem*, but died for his own sin; and he has left no sons.

במדבר כז
פינחס

נו עַל־פִּי הַגּוֹרָל תֵּחָלֵק נַחֲלָתוֹ בֵּין רַב לִמְעָט:

נז וְאֵלֶּה פְקוּדֵי הַלֵּוִי לְמִשְׁפְּחֹתָם לְגֵרְשׁוֹן מִשְׁפַּחַת הַגֵּרְשֻׁנִּי לִקְהָת מִשְׁפַּחַת הַקְּהָתִי לִמְרָרִי מִשְׁפַּחַת הַמְּרָרִי:

נח אֵלֶּה מִשְׁפְּחֹת לֵוִי מִשְׁפַּחַת הַלִּבְנִי מִשְׁפַּחַת הַחֶבְרֹנִי מִשְׁפַּחַת הַמַּחְלִי מִשְׁפַּחַת הַמּוּשִׁי מִשְׁפַּחַת הַקָּרְחִי וּקְהָת הוֹלִד אֶת־עַמְרָם:

נט וְשֵׁם ׀ אֵשֶׁת עַמְרָם יוֹכֶבֶד בַּת־לֵוִי אֲשֶׁר יָלְדָה אֹתָהּ לְלֵוִי בְּמִצְרָיִם וַתֵּלֶד לְעַמְרָם אֶת־אַהֲרֹן וְאֶת־מֹשֶׁה וְאֵת מִרְיָם אֲחֹתָם:

ס וַיִּוָּלֵד לְאַהֲרֹן אֶת־נָדָב וְאֶת־אֲבִיהוּא אֶת־אֶלְעָזָר וְאֶת־אִיתָמָר:

סא וַיָּמָת נָדָב וַאֲבִיהוּא בְּהַקְרִיבָם אֵשׁ־זָרָה לִפְנֵי יְהוָה:

סב וַיִּהְיוּ פְקֻדֵיהֶם שְׁלֹשָׁה וְעֶשְׂרִים אֶלֶף כָּל־זָכָר מִבֶּן־חֹדֶשׁ וָמָעְלָה כִּי ׀ לֹא הָתְפָּקְדוּ בְּתוֹךְ בְּנֵי יִשְׂרָאֵל כִּי לֹא־נִתַּן לָהֶם נַחֲלָה בְּתוֹךְ בְּנֵי יִשְׂרָאֵל:

סג אֵלֶּה פְּקוּדֵי מֹשֶׁה וְאֶלְעָזָר הַכֹּהֵן אֲשֶׁר פָּקְדוּ אֶת־בְּנֵי יִשְׂרָאֵל בְּעַרְבֹת מוֹאָב עַל יַרְדֵּן יְרֵחוֹ:

סד וּבְאֵלֶּה לֹא־הָיָה אִישׁ מִפְּקוּדֵי מֹשֶׁה וְאַהֲרֹן הַכֹּהֵן אֲשֶׁר פָּקְדוּ אֶת־בְּנֵי יִשְׂרָאֵל בְּמִדְבַּר סִינָי:

סה כִּי־אָמַר יְהוָה לָהֶם מוֹת יָמֻתוּ בַּמִּדְבָּר וְלֹא־נוֹתַר מֵהֶם אִישׁ כִּי אִם־כָּלֵב בֶּן־יְפֻנֶּה וִיהוֹשֻׁעַ בִּן־נוּן:

כז א וַתִּקְרַבְנָה בְּנוֹת צְלָפְחָד בֶּן־חֵפֶר בֶּן־גִּלְעָד בֶּן־מָכִיר בֶּן־מְנַשֶּׁה לְמִשְׁפְּחֹת מְנַשֶּׁה בֶן־יוֹסֵף וְאֵלֶּה שְׁמוֹת בְּנֹתָיו מַחְלָה נֹעָה וְחָגְלָה וּמִלְכָּה וְתִרְצָה:

ב וַתַּעֲמֹדְנָה לִפְנֵי מֹשֶׁה וְלִפְנֵי אֶלְעָזָר הַכֹּהֵן וְלִפְנֵי הַנְּשִׂיאִם וְכָל־הָעֵדָה פֶּתַח אֹהֶל־מוֹעֵד לֵאמֹר:

ג אָבִינוּ מֵת בַּמִּדְבָּר וְהוּא לֹא־הָיָה בְּתוֹךְ הָעֵדָה הַנּוֹעָדִים עַל־יְהוָה בַּעֲדַת־קֹרַח כִּי־בְחֶטְאוֹ מֵת וּבָנִים לֹא־הָיוּ לוֹ:

404

Bamidbar/Numbers 27
Pinchas

במדבר כז
פינחס

4 Let not our father's name be lost to his clan just because he had no son! Give us a holding among our father's kinsmen!"

ד לָמָּה יִגָּרַע שֵׁם־אָבִינוּ מִתּוֹךְ מִשְׁפַּחְתּוֹ כִּי אֵין לוֹ בֵּן תְּנָה־לָּנוּ אֲחֻזָּה בְּתוֹךְ אֲחֵי אָבִינוּ׃

LA-mah yi-ga-RA shaym a-VEE-nu mi-TOKH mish-pakh-TO KEE AYN LO BAYN t'-NAH LA-nu a-khu-ZAH b'-TOKH a-KHAY a-VEE-nu

5 *Moshe* brought their case before *Hashem*.

ה וַיַּקְרֵב מֹשֶׁה אֶת־מִשְׁפָּטָן לִפְנֵי יְהֹוָה׃

6 And *Hashem* said to *Moshe*,

ו וַיֹּאמֶר יְהֹוָה אֶל־מֹשֶׁה לֵּאמֹר׃

7 "The plea of *Tzelofchad*'s daughters is just: you should give them a hereditary holding among their father's kinsmen; transfer their father's share to them.

ז כֵּן בְּנוֹת צְלׇפְחָד דֹּבְרֹת נָתֹן תִּתֵּן לָהֶם אֲחֻזַּת נַחֲלָה בְּתוֹךְ אֲחֵי אֲבִיהֶם וְהַעֲבַרְתָּ אֶת־נַחֲלַת אֲבִיהֶן לָהֶן׃

8 "Further, speak to *B'nei Yisrael* as follows: 'If a man dies without leaving a son, you shall transfer his property to his daughter.

ח וְאֶל־בְּנֵי יִשְׂרָאֵל תְּדַבֵּר לֵאמֹר אִישׁ כִּי־יָמוּת וּבֵן אֵין לוֹ וְהַעֲבַרְתֶּם אֶת־נַחֲלָתוֹ לְבִתּוֹ׃

9 If he has no daughter, you shall assign his property to his brothers.

ט וְאִם־אֵין לוֹ בַּת וּנְתַתֶּם אֶת־נַחֲלָתוֹ לְאֶחָיו׃

10 If he has no brothers, you shall assign his property to his father's brothers.

י וְאִם־אֵין לוֹ אַחִים וּנְתַתֶּם אֶת־נַחֲלָתוֹ לַאֲחֵי אָבִיו׃

11 If his father had no brothers, you shall assign his property to his nearest relative in his own clan, and he shall inherit it.' This shall be the law of procedure for the Israelites, in accordance with *Hashem*'s command to *Moshe*."

יא וְאִם־אֵין אַחִים לְאָבִיו וּנְתַתֶּם אֶת־נַחֲלָתוֹ לִשְׁאֵרוֹ הַקָּרֹב אֵלָיו מִמִּשְׁפַּחְתּוֹ וְיָרַשׁ אֹתָהּ וְהָיְתָה לִבְנֵי יִשְׂרָאֵל לְחֻקַּת מִשְׁפָּט כַּאֲשֶׁר צִוָּה יְהֹוָה אֶת־מֹשֶׁה׃

12 *Hashem* said to *Moshe*, "Ascend these heights of Abarim and view the land that I have given to *B'nei Yisrael*.

יב וַיֹּאמֶר יְהֹוָה אֶל־מֹשֶׁה עֲלֵה אֶל־הַר הָעֲבָרִים הַזֶּה וּרְאֵה אֶת־הָאָרֶץ אֲשֶׁר נָתַתִּי לִבְנֵי יִשְׂרָאֵל׃

va-YO-mer a-do-NAI el mo-SHEH a-LAY el HAR ha-a-va-REEM ha-ZEH ur-AY et ha-A-RETZ a-SHER na-TA-tee liv-NAY yis-ra-AYL

27:4 Give us a holding among our father's kinsmen After it is determined among whom *Eretz Yisrael* will be divided, the daughters of a deceased man named *Tzelofchad* approach *Moshe* with a complaint. The rule of inheritance is that a father's land is inherited by his sons, but the late *Tzelofchad* had no sons who could inherit his portion. Moved by a deep love for the Land of Israel, *Tzelofchad*'s daughters complain that if nothing is done, their family will forever lose its portion of land. *Rashi* points out that it is no coincidence that the verse traces their lineage back to their forefather *Yosef*, who served as a model of love for the Promised Land when he made his brothers promise that they would take his remains with them out of Egypt, for burial in *Eretz Yisrael*. The women are relieved when *Hashem* clarifies to *Moshe* that in the absence of sons, a man's land is to be inherited by his daughters. The passion for Israel exhibited by the daughters of *Tzelofchad* serves as a model for the special role that women have always played in settling *Eretz Yisrael*.

27:12 And view the land Though *Moshe* was not allowed to enter the Land of Israel, he is given an opportunity to see the land from atop the mountain of *Avarim*. In verse 12, *Hashem* tells him to go up to the mountain and "view the land", and in verse 13 He repeats "when you have seen it." The double language reflects the notion that *Moshe* saw beyond the land's physical beauty. In addition, he was able to perceive its spiritual grandeur as well.

Bamidbar/Numbers 28
Pinchas

13	When you have seen it, you too shall be gathered to your kin, just as your brother *Aharon* was.	יג וְרָאִיתָה אֹתָהּ וְנֶאֱסַפְתָּ אֶל־עַמֶּיךָ גַּם־אָתָּה כַּאֲשֶׁר נֶאֱסַף אַהֲרֹן אָחִיךָ:
14	For, in the wilderness of Zin, when the community was contentious, you disobeyed My command to uphold My sanctity in their sight by means of the water." Those are the Waters of Meribath-kadesh, in the wilderness of Zin.	יד כַּאֲשֶׁר מְרִיתֶם פִּי בְּמִדְבַּר־צִן בִּמְרִיבַת הָעֵדָה לְהַקְדִּישֵׁנִי בַמַּיִם לְעֵינֵיהֶם הֵם מֵי־מְרִיבַת קָדֵשׁ מִדְבַּר־צִן:
15	*Moshe* spoke to *Hashem*, saying,	טו וַיְדַבֵּר מֹשֶׁה אֶל־יְהֹוָה לֵאמֹר:
16	"Let *Hashem*, Source of the breath of all flesh, appoint someone over the community	טז יִפְקֹד יְהֹוָה אֱלֹהֵי הָרוּחֹת לְכָל־בָּשָׂר אִישׁ עַל־הָעֵדָה:
17	who shall go out before them and come in before them, and who shall take them out and bring them in, so that *Hashem*'s community may not be like sheep that have no shepherd."	יז אֲשֶׁר־יֵצֵא לִפְנֵיהֶם וַאֲשֶׁר יָבֹא לִפְנֵיהֶם וַאֲשֶׁר יוֹצִיאֵם וַאֲשֶׁר יְבִיאֵם וְלֹא תִהְיֶה עֲדַת יְהֹוָה כַּצֹּאן אֲשֶׁר אֵין־לָהֶם רֹעֶה:
18	And *Hashem* answered *Moshe*, "Single out *Yehoshua* son of *Nun*, an inspired man, and lay your hand upon him.	יח וַיֹּאמֶר יְהֹוָה אֶל־מֹשֶׁה קַח־לְךָ אֶת־יְהוֹשֻׁעַ בִּן־נוּן אִישׁ אֲשֶׁר־רוּחַ בּוֹ וְסָמַכְתָּ אֶת־יָדְךָ עָלָיו:
19	Have him stand before *Elazar* the *Kohen* and before the whole community, and commission him in their sight.	יט וְהַעֲמַדְתָּ אֹתוֹ לִפְנֵי אֶלְעָזָר הַכֹּהֵן וְלִפְנֵי כָּל־הָעֵדָה וְצִוִּיתָה אֹתוֹ לְעֵינֵיהֶם:
20	Invest him with some of your authority, so that the whole Israelite community may obey.	כ וְנָתַתָּה מֵהוֹדְךָ עָלָיו לְמַעַן יִשְׁמְעוּ כָּל־עֲדַת בְּנֵי יִשְׂרָאֵל:
21	But he shall present himself to *Elazar* the *Kohen*, who shall on his behalf seek the decision of the Urim before *Hashem*. By such instruction they shall go out and by such instruction they shall come in, he and all the Israelites, the whole community."	כא וְלִפְנֵי אֶלְעָזָר הַכֹּהֵן יַעֲמֹד וְשָׁאַל לוֹ בְּמִשְׁפַּט הָאוּרִים לִפְנֵי יְהֹוָה עַל־פִּיו יֵצְאוּ וְעַל־פִּיו יָבֹאוּ הוּא וְכָל־בְּנֵי־יִשְׂרָאֵל אִתּוֹ וְכָל־הָעֵדָה:
22	*Moshe* did as *Hashem* commanded him. He took *Yehoshua* and had him stand before *Elazar* the *Kohen* and before the whole community.	כב וַיַּעַשׂ מֹשֶׁה כַּאֲשֶׁר צִוָּה יְהֹוָה אֹתוֹ וַיִּקַּח אֶת־יְהוֹשֻׁעַ וַיַּעֲמִדֵהוּ לִפְנֵי אֶלְעָזָר הַכֹּהֵן וְלִפְנֵי כָּל־הָעֵדָה:
23	He laid his hands upon him and commissioned him – as *Hashem* had spoken through *Moshe*.	כג וַיִּסְמֹךְ אֶת־יָדָיו עָלָיו וַיְצַוֵּהוּ כַּאֲשֶׁר דִּבֶּר יְהֹוָה בְּיַד־מֹשֶׁה:

28

1	*Hashem* spoke to *Moshe*, saying:	א וַיְדַבֵּר יְהֹוָה אֶל־מֹשֶׁה לֵּאמֹר:
2	Command *B'nei Yisrael* and say to them: Be punctilious in presenting to Me at stated times the offerings of food due Me, as offerings by fire of pleasing odor to Me.	ב צַו אֶת־בְּנֵי יִשְׂרָאֵל וְאָמַרְתָּ אֲלֵהֶם אֶת־קָרְבָּנִי לַחְמִי לְאִשַּׁי רֵיחַ נִיחֹחִי תִּשְׁמְרוּ לְהַקְרִיב לִי בְּמוֹעֲדוֹ:
3	Say to them: These are the offerings by fire that you are to present to *Hashem*: As a regular burnt offering every day, two yearling lambs without blemish.	ג וְאָמַרְתָּ לָהֶם זֶה הָאִשֶּׁה אֲשֶׁר תַּקְרִיבוּ לַיהֹוָה כְּבָשִׂים בְּנֵי־שָׁנָה תְמִימִם שְׁנַיִם לַיּוֹם עֹלָה תָמִיד:

Bamidbar/Numbers 28
Pinchas

במדבר כח
פינחס

4 You shall offer one lamb in the morning, and the other lamb you shall offer at twilight.

ד אֶת־הַכֶּבֶשׂ אֶחָד תַּעֲשֶׂה בַבֹּקֶר וְאֵת הַכֶּבֶשׂ הַשֵּׁנִי תַּעֲשֶׂה בֵּין הָעַרְבָּיִם:

5 And as a meal offering, there shall be a tenth of an *efah* of choice flour with a quarter of a *hin* of beaten oil mixed in

ה וַעֲשִׂירִית הָאֵיפָה סֹלֶת לְמִנְחָה בְּלוּלָה בְּשֶׁמֶן כָּתִית רְבִיעִת הַהִין:

6 the regular burnt offering instituted at *Har Sinai* – an offering by fire of pleasing odor to *Hashem*.

ו עֹלַת תָּמִיד הָעֲשֻׂיָה בְּהַר סִינַי לְרֵיחַ נִיחֹחַ אִשֶּׁה לַיהוָה:

7 The libation with it shall be a quarter of a *hin* for each lamb, to be poured in the sacred precinct as an offering of fermented drink to *Hashem*.

ז וְנִסְכּוֹ רְבִיעִת הַהִין לַכֶּבֶשׂ הָאֶחָד בַּקֹּדֶשׁ הַסֵּךְ נֶסֶךְ שֵׁכָר לַיהוָה:

8 The other lamb you shall offer at twilight, preparing the same meal offering and libation as in the morning – an offering by fire of pleasing odor to *Hashem*.

ח וְאֵת הַכֶּבֶשׂ הַשֵּׁנִי תַּעֲשֶׂה בֵּין הָעַרְבָּיִם כְּמִנְחַת הַבֹּקֶר וּכְנִסְכּוֹ תַּעֲשֶׂה אִשֵּׁה רֵיחַ נִיחֹחַ לַיהוָה:

9 On the *Shabbat* day: two yearling lambs without blemish, together with two-tenths of a measure of choice flour with oil mixed in as a meal offering, and with the proper libation –

ט וּבְיוֹם הַשַּׁבָּת שְׁנֵי־כְבָשִׂים בְּנֵי־שָׁנָה תְּמִימִם וּשְׁנֵי עֶשְׂרֹנִים סֹלֶת מִנְחָה בְּלוּלָה בַשֶּׁמֶן וְנִסְכּוֹ:

uv-YOM ha-sha-BAT sh'-nay kh'-va-SEEM b'-nay sha-NAH t'-mee-MIM u-sh'-NAY es-ro-NEEM SO-let min-KHAH b'-lu-LAH va-SHE-men v'-nis-KO

10 a burnt offering for every *Shabbat*, in addition to the regular burnt offering and its libation.

י עֹלַת שַׁבַּת בְּשַׁבַּתּוֹ עַל־עֹלַת הַתָּמִיד וְנִסְכָּהּ:

11 On your new moons you shall present a burnt offering to *Hashem*: two bulls of the herd, one ram, and seven yearling lambs, without blemish.

יא וּבְרָאשֵׁי חָדְשֵׁיכֶם תַּקְרִיבוּ עֹלָה לַיהוָה פָּרִים בְּנֵי־בָקָר שְׁנַיִם וְאַיִל אֶחָד כְּבָשִׂים בְּנֵי־שָׁנָה שִׁבְעָה תְּמִימִם:

uv-ro-SHAY khod-shay-KHEM tak-REE-vu o-LAH la-do-NAI pa-REEM b'-nay va-KAR sh'-NA-yim v'-A-yil e-KHAD k'-va-SEEM b'-NAY sha-NAH shiv-AH t'-mee-MIM

Shabbat candles, wine and Challah

28:9 On the Shabbat day *Shabbat*, the seventh day of the week, is a reminder that God is the creator of the entire world. Just as He created the world in six days and rested on the seventh, we use our creative powers to work for six days, but rest on the seventh. *Shabbat* also serves as a remembrance of the exodus from Egypt (see Deuteronomy 5:14). Through the miracles associated with the exodus, *Hashem* demonstrated that He is still very much involved in the world, though He generally works behind the scenes. By keeping the *Shabbat*, we affirm our belief in *Hashem* as the Creator who is continuously responsible for everything that happens in the world. The Land of Israel also has a *Shabbat* of its own, once every seven years.

By abandoning the fields during the Sabbatical year and putting our sustenance in the hands of the Lord, we affirm our belief that He is intimately involved in everything that happens in our lives. We owe all of our success to Him, and we believe that He will provide for us, even if we are not working the land.

28:11 On your new moons Judaism follows a calendar with both lunar and solar components. The months are determined by the cycle of the moon, with the new month beginning when the first sliver of moon reappears in the sky at the beginning of a new lunar cycle. At the same time, though, the Jewish calendar has a solar component. Each of the

Bamidbar/Numbers 28
Pinchas

במדבר כח
פינחס

12 As meal offering for each bull: three-tenths of a measure of choice flour with oil mixed in. As meal offering for each ram: two-tenths of a measure of choice flour with oil mixed in.

יב וּשְׁלֹשָׁה עֶשְׂרֹנִים סֹלֶת מִנְחָה בְּלוּלָה בַשֶּׁמֶן לַפָּר הָאֶחָד וּשְׁנֵי עֶשְׂרֹנִים סֹלֶת מִנְחָה בְּלוּלָה בַשֶּׁמֶן לָאַיִל הָאֶחָד:

13 As meal offering for each lamb: a tenth of a measure of fine flour with oil mixed in. Such shall be the burnt offering of pleasing odor, an offering by fire to *Hashem*.

יג וְעִשָּׂרֹן עִשָּׂרוֹן סֹלֶת מִנְחָה בְּלוּלָה בַשֶּׁמֶן לַכֶּבֶשׂ הָאֶחָד עֹלָה רֵיחַ נִיחֹחַ אִשֶּׁה לַיהוָה:

14 Their libations shall be: half a *hin* of wine for a bull, a third of a *hin* for a ram, and a quarter of a *hin* for a lamb. That shall be the monthly burnt offering for each new moon of the year.

יד וְנִסְכֵּיהֶם חֲצִי הַהִין יִהְיֶה לַפָּר וּשְׁלִישִׁת הַהִין לָאַיִל וּרְבִיעִת הַהִין לַכֶּבֶשׂ יָיִן זֹאת עֹלַת חֹדֶשׁ בְּחָדְשׁוֹ לְחָדְשֵׁי הַשָּׁנָה:

15 And there shall be one goat as a sin offering to *Hashem*, to be offered in addition to the regular burnt offering and its libation.

טו וּשְׂעִיר עִזִּים אֶחָד לְחַטָּאת לַיהוָה עַל־עֹלַת הַתָּמִיד יֵעָשֶׂה וְנִסְכּוֹ:

16 In the first month, on the fourteenth day of the month, there shall be a *Pesach* sacrifice to *Hashem*,

טז וּבַחֹדֶשׁ הָרִאשׁוֹן בְּאַרְבָּעָה עָשָׂר יוֹם לַחֹדֶשׁ פֶּסַח לַיהוָה:

17 and on the fifteenth day of that month a festival. Unleavened bread shall be eaten for seven days.

יז וּבַחֲמִשָּׁה עָשָׂר יוֹם לַחֹדֶשׁ הַזֶּה חָג שִׁבְעַת יָמִים מַצּוֹת יֵאָכֵל:

18 The first day shall be a sacred occasion: you shall not work at your occupations.

יח בַּיּוֹם הָרִאשׁוֹן מִקְרָא־קֹדֶשׁ כָּל־מְלֶאכֶת עֲבֹדָה לֹא תַעֲשׂוּ:

19 You shall present an offering by fire, a burnt offering, to *Hashem*: two bulls of the herd, one ram, and seven yearling lambs – see that they are without blemish.

יט וְהִקְרַבְתֶּם אִשֶּׁה עֹלָה לַיהוָה פָּרִים בְּנֵי־בָקָר שְׁנַיִם וְאַיִל אֶחָד וְשִׁבְעָה כְבָשִׂים בְּנֵי שָׁנָה תְּמִימִם יִהְיוּ לָכֶם:

20 The meal offering with them shall be of choice flour with oil mixed in: prepare three-tenths of a measure for a bull, two-tenths for a ram;

כ וּמִנְחָתָם סֹלֶת בְּלוּלָה בַשֶּׁמֶן שְׁלֹשָׁה עֶשְׂרֹנִים לַפָּר וּשְׁנֵי עֶשְׂרֹנִים לָאַיִל תַּעֲשׂוּ:

21 and for each of the seven lambs prepare one-tenth of a measure.

כא עִשָּׂרוֹן עִשָּׂרוֹן תַּעֲשֶׂה לַכֶּבֶשׂ הָאֶחָד לְשִׁבְעַת הַכְּבָשִׂים:

22 And there shall be one goat for a sin offering, to make expiation in your behalf.

כב וּשְׂעִיר חַטָּאת אֶחָד לְכַפֵּר עֲלֵיכֶם:

23 You shall present these in addition to the morning portion of the regular burnt offering.

כג מִלְּבַד עֹלַת הַבֹּקֶר אֲשֶׁר לְעֹלַת הַתָּמִיד תַּעֲשׂוּ אֶת־אֵלֶּה:

---

festivals are supposed to fall out during a specific season in Israel, reflected in the agricultural aspects of the holiday. *Pesach* must fall out during the springtime as the grain begins to ripen, *Shavuot* celebrates the wheat harvest and the beginning of the fruit harvest in early summer, and *Sukkot* is celebrated in the beginning of the autumn, at the end of the harvest season.

There is, however, an eleven-day discrepancy between the number of days in twelve lunar months and a solar year. To enable the months to follow the cycle of the moon while also ensuring that the holidays are celebrated in the appropriate seasons, a thirteenth month is added to the year seven times in every nineteen-year cycle.

Bamidbar/Numbers 29
Pinchas

במדבר כט
פינחס

24 You shall offer the like daily for seven days as food, an offering by fire of pleasing odor to *Hashem*; they shall be offered, with their libations, in addition to the regular burnt offering.

כד כָּאֵ֨לֶּה תַּעֲשׂ֤וּ לַיּוֹם֙ שִׁבְעַ֣ת יָמִ֔ים לֶ֛חֶם אִשֵּׁ֥ה רֵֽיחַ־נִיחֹ֖חַ לַיהוָ֑ה עַל־עוֹלַ֧ת הַתָּמִ֛יד יֵעָשֶׂ֖ה וְנִסְכּֽוֹ׃

25 And the seventh day shall be a sacred occasion for you: you shall not work at your occupations.

כה וּבַיּוֹם֙ הַשְּׁבִיעִ֔י מִקְרָא־קֹ֖דֶשׁ יִהְיֶ֣ה לָכֶ֑ם כָּל־מְלֶ֥אכֶת עֲבֹדָ֖ה לֹ֥א תַעֲשֽׂוּ׃

26 On the day of the first fruits, your festival of *Shavuot*, when you bring an offering of new grain to *Hashem*, you shall observe a sacred occasion: you shall not work at your occupations.

כו וּבְי֣וֹם הַבִּכּוּרִ֗ים בְּהַקְרִֽיבְכֶ֞ם מִנְחָ֤ה חֲדָשָׁה֙ לַֽיהוָ֔ה בְּשָׁבֻעֹ֖תֵיכֶ֑ם מִֽקְרָא־קֹ֙דֶשׁ֙ יִהְיֶ֣ה לָכֶ֔ם כָּל־מְלֶ֥אכֶת עֲבֹדָ֖ה לֹ֥א תַעֲשֽׂוּ׃

27 You shall present a burnt offering of pleasing odor to *Hashem*: two bulls of the herd, one ram, seven yearling lambs.

כז וְהִקְרַבְתֶּ֨ם עוֹלָ֜ה לְרֵ֤יחַ נִיחֹ֙חַ֙ לַֽיהוָ֔ה פָּרִ֧ים בְּנֵֽי־בָקָ֛ר שְׁנַ֖יִם אַ֣יִל אֶחָ֑ד שִׁבְעָ֥ה כְבָשִׂ֖ים בְּנֵ֥י שָׁנָֽה׃

28 The meal offering with them shall be of choice flour with oil mixed in, three-tenths of a measure for a bull, two-tenths for a ram,

כח וּמִנְחָתָ֔ם סֹ֖לֶת בְּלוּלָ֣ה בַשָּׁ֑מֶן שְׁלֹשָׁ֨ה עֶשְׂרֹנִ֜ים לַפָּ֣ר הָֽאֶחָ֗ד שְׁנֵי֙ עֶשְׂרֹנִ֔ים לָאַ֖יִל הָאֶחָֽד׃

29 and one-tenth for each of the seven lambs.

כט עִשָּׂר֤וֹן עִשָּׂרוֹן֙ לַכֶּ֣בֶשׂ הָֽאֶחָ֔ד לְשִׁבְעַ֖ת הַכְּבָשִֽׂים׃

30 And there shall be one goat for expiation in your behalf.

ל שְׂעִ֥יר עִזִּ֖ים אֶחָ֑ד לְכַפֵּ֖ר עֲלֵיכֶֽם׃

31 You shall present them – see that they are without blemish – with their libations, in addition to the regular burnt offering and its meal offering.

לא מִלְּבַ֞ד עֹלַ֧ת הַתָּמִ֛יד וּמִנְחָת֖וֹ תַּעֲשׂ֑וּ תְּמִימִ֥ם יִהְיוּ־לָכֶ֖ם וְנִסְכֵּיהֶֽם׃

29

1 In the seventh month, on the first day of the month, you shall observe a sacred occasion: you shall not work at your occupations. You shall observe it as a day when the *shofar* is sounded.

כט א וּבַחֹ֨דֶשׁ הַשְּׁבִיעִ֜י בְּאֶחָ֣ד לַחֹ֗דֶשׁ מִֽקְרָא־קֹ֙דֶשׁ֙ יִהְיֶ֣ה לָכֶ֔ם כָּל־מְלֶ֥אכֶת עֲבֹדָ֖ה לֹ֣א תַעֲשׂ֑וּ י֥וֹם תְּרוּעָ֖ה יִהְיֶ֥ה לָכֶֽם׃

2 You shall present a burnt offering of pleasing odor to *Hashem*: one bull of the herd, one ram, and seven yearling lambs, without blemish.

ב וַעֲשִׂיתֶ֨ם עֹלָ֜ה לְרֵ֤יחַ נִיחֹ֙חַ֙ לַֽיהוָ֔ה פַּ֧ר בֶּן־בָּקָ֛ר אֶחָ֖ד אַ֣יִל אֶחָ֑ד כְּבָשִׂ֧ים בְּנֵֽי־שָׁנָ֛ה שִׁבְעָ֖ה תְּמִימִֽם׃

3 The meal offering with them – choice flour with oil mixed in – shall be: three-tenths of a measure for a bull, two-tenths for a ram,

ג וּמִנְחָתָ֔ם סֹ֖לֶת בְּלוּלָ֣ה בַשָּׁ֑מֶן שְׁלֹשָׁ֤ה עֶשְׂרֹנִים֙ לַפָּ֔ר שְׁנֵ֥י עֶשְׂרֹנִ֖ים לָאָֽיִל׃

4 and one-tenth for each of the seven lambs.

ד וְעִשָּׂר֣וֹן אֶחָ֔ד לַכֶּ֖בֶשׂ הָאֶחָ֑ד לְשִׁבְעַ֖ת הַכְּבָשִֽׂים׃

5 And there shall be one goat for a sin offering, to make expiation in your behalf

ה וּשְׂעִיר־עִזִּ֥ים אֶחָ֖ד חַטָּ֑את לְכַפֵּ֖ר עֲלֵיכֶֽם׃

6 in addition to the burnt offering of the new moon with its meal offering and the regular burnt offering with its meal offering, each with its libation as prescribed, offerings by fire of pleasing odor to *Hashem*.

ו מִלְּבַד֩ עֹלַ֨ת הַחֹ֜דֶשׁ וּמִנְחָתָ֗הּ וְעֹלַ֤ת הַתָּמִיד֙ וּמִנְחָתָ֔הּ וְנִסְכֵּיהֶ֖ם כְּמִשְׁפָּטָ֑ם לְרֵ֣יחַ נִיחֹ֔חַ אִשֶּׁ֖ה לַיהוָֽה׃

409

Bamidbar/Numbers 29
Pinchas

7 On the tenth day of the same seventh month you shall observe a sacred occasion when you shall practice self-denial. You shall do no work.

8 You shall present to *Hashem* a burnt offering of pleasing odor: one bull of the herd, one ram, seven yearling lambs; see that they are without blemish.

9 The meal offering with them – of choice flour with oil mixed in – shall be: three-tenths of a measure for a bull, two-tenths for the one ram,

10 one-tenth for each of the seven lambs.

11 And there shall be one goat for a sin offering, in addition to the sin offering of expiation and the regular burnt offering with its meal offering, each with its libation.

12 On the fifteenth day of the seventh month, you shall observe a sacred occasion: you shall not work at your occupations. – Seven days you shall observe a festival of *Hashem*.

13 You shall present a burnt offering, an offering by fire of pleasing odor to *Hashem*: Thirteen bulls of the herd, two rams, fourteen yearling lambs; they shall be without blemish.

14 The meal offerings with them – of choice flour with oil mixed in – shall be: three-tenths of a measure for each of the thirteen bulls, two-tenths for each of the two rams,

15 and one-tenth for each of the fourteen lambs.

16 And there shall be one goat for a sin offering – in addition to the regular burnt offering, its meal offering and libation.

17 Second day: Twelve bulls of the herd, two rams, fourteen yearling lambs, without blemish;

18 the meal offerings and libations for the bulls, rams, and lambs, in the quantities prescribed;

19 and one goat for a sin offering – in addition to the regular burnt offering, its meal offering and libations.

במדבר כט
פינחס

ז וּבֶעָשׂוֹר לַחֹדֶשׁ הַשְּׁבִיעִי הַזֶּה מִקְרָא־קֹדֶשׁ יִהְיֶה לָכֶם וְעִנִּיתֶם אֶת־נַפְשֹׁתֵיכֶם כָּל־מְלָאכָה לֹא תַעֲשׂוּ:

ח וְהִקְרַבְתֶּם עֹלָה לַיהוָה רֵיחַ נִיחֹחַ פַּר בֶּן־בָּקָר אֶחָד אַיִל אֶחָד כְּבָשִׂים בְּנֵי־שָׁנָה שִׁבְעָה תְּמִימִם יִהְיוּ לָכֶם:

ט וּמִנְחָתָם סֹלֶת בְּלוּלָה בַשָּׁמֶן שְׁלֹשָׁה עֶשְׂרֹנִים לַפָּר שְׁנֵי עֶשְׂרֹנִים לָאַיִל הָאֶחָד:

י עִשָּׂרוֹן עִשָּׂרוֹן לַכֶּבֶשׂ הָאֶחָד לְשִׁבְעַת הַכְּבָשִׂים:

יא שְׂעִיר־עִזִּים אֶחָד חַטָּאת מִלְּבַד חַטַּאת הַכִּפֻּרִים וְעֹלַת הַתָּמִיד וּמִנְחָתָהּ וְנִסְכֵּיהֶם:

יב וּבַחֲמִשָּׁה עָשָׂר יוֹם לַחֹדֶשׁ הַשְּׁבִיעִי מִקְרָא־קֹדֶשׁ יִהְיֶה לָכֶם כָּל־מְלֶאכֶת עֲבֹדָה לֹא תַעֲשׂוּ וְחַגֹּתֶם חַג לַיהוָה שִׁבְעַת יָמִים:

יג וְהִקְרַבְתֶּם עֹלָה אִשֵּׁה רֵיחַ נִיחֹחַ לַיהוָה פָּרִים בְּנֵי־בָקָר שְׁלֹשָׁה עָשָׂר אֵילִם שְׁנָיִם כְּבָשִׂים בְּנֵי־שָׁנָה אַרְבָּעָה עָשָׂר תְּמִימִם יִהְיוּ:

יד וּמִנְחָתָם סֹלֶת בְּלוּלָה בַשֶּׁמֶן שְׁלֹשָׁה עֶשְׂרֹנִים לַפָּר הָאֶחָד לִשְׁלֹשָׁה עָשָׂר פָּרִים שְׁנֵי עֶשְׂרֹנִים לָאַיִל הָאֶחָד לִשְׁנֵי הָאֵילִם:

טו וְעִשָּׂרוֹן עִשָּׂרוֹן לַכֶּבֶשׂ הָאֶחָד לְאַרְבָּעָה עָשָׂר כְּבָשִׂים:

טז וּשְׂעִיר־עִזִּים אֶחָד חַטָּאת מִלְּבַד עֹלַת הַתָּמִיד מִנְחָתָהּ וְנִסְכָּהּ:

יז וּבַיּוֹם הַשֵּׁנִי פָּרִים בְּנֵי־בָקָר שְׁנֵים עָשָׂר אֵילִם שְׁנָיִם כְּבָשִׂים בְּנֵי־שָׁנָה אַרְבָּעָה עָשָׂר תְּמִימִם:

יח וּמִנְחָתָם וְנִסְכֵּיהֶם לַפָּרִים לָאֵילִם וְלַכְּבָשִׂים בְּמִסְפָּרָם כַּמִּשְׁפָּט:

יט וּשְׂעִיר־עִזִּים אֶחָד חַטָּאת מִלְּבַד עֹלַת הַתָּמִיד וּמִנְחָתָהּ וְנִסְכֵּיהֶם:

410

Bamidbar/Numbers 29
Pinchas

במדבר כט
פינחס

20	Third day: Eleven bulls, two rams, fourteen yearling lambs, without blemish;	וּבַיּוֹם הַשְּׁלִישִׁי פָּרִים עַשְׁתֵּי־עָשָׂר אֵילִם שְׁנָיִם כְּבָשִׂים בְּנֵי־שָׁנָה אַרְבָּעָה עָשָׂר תְּמִימִם: כ
21	the meal offerings and libations for the bulls, rams, and lambs, in the quantities prescribed;	וּמִנְחָתָם וְנִסְכֵּיהֶם לַפָּרִים לָאֵילִם וְלַכְּבָשִׂים בְּמִסְפָּרָם כַּמִּשְׁפָּט: כא
22	and one goat for a sin offering – in addition to the regular burnt offering, its meal offering and libation.	וּשְׂעִיר חַטָּאת אֶחָד מִלְּבַד עֹלַת הַתָּמִיד וּמִנְחָתָהּ וְנִסְכָּהּ: כב
23	Fourth day: Ten bulls, two rams, fourteen yearling lambs, without blemish;	וּבַיּוֹם הָרְבִיעִי פָּרִים עֲשָׂרָה אֵילִם שְׁנָיִם כְּבָשִׂים בְּנֵי־שָׁנָה אַרְבָּעָה עָשָׂר תְּמִימִם: כג
24	the meal offerings and libations for the bulls, rams, and lambs, in the quantities prescribed;	מִנְחָתָם וְנִסְכֵּיהֶם לַפָּרִים לָאֵילִם וְלַכְּבָשִׂים בְּמִסְפָּרָם כַּמִּשְׁפָּט: כד
25	and one goat for a sin offering – in addition to the regular burnt offering, its meal offering and libation.	וּשְׂעִיר־עִזִּים אֶחָד חַטָּאת מִלְּבַד עֹלַת הַתָּמִיד מִנְחָתָהּ וְנִסְכָּהּ: כה
26	Fifth day: Nine bulls, two rams, fourteen yearling lambs, without blemish;	וּבַיּוֹם הַחֲמִישִׁי פָּרִים תִּשְׁעָה אֵילִם שְׁנָיִם כְּבָשִׂים בְּנֵי־שָׁנָה אַרְבָּעָה עָשָׂר תְּמִימִם: כו
27	the meal offerings and libations for the bulls, rams, and lambs, in the quantities prescribed;	וּמִנְחָתָם וְנִסְכֵּיהֶם לַפָּרִים לָאֵילִם וְלַכְּבָשִׂים בְּמִסְפָּרָם כַּמִּשְׁפָּט: כז
28	and one goat for a sin offering – in addition to the regular burnt offering, its meal offering and libation.	וּשְׂעִיר חַטָּאת אֶחָד מִלְּבַד עֹלַת הַתָּמִיד וּמִנְחָתָהּ וְנִסְכָּהּ: כח
29	Sixth day: Eight bulls, two rams, fourteen yearling lambs, without blemish;	וּבַיּוֹם הַשִּׁשִּׁי פָּרִים שְׁמֹנָה אֵילִם שְׁנָיִם כְּבָשִׂים בְּנֵי־שָׁנָה אַרְבָּעָה עָשָׂר תְּמִימִם: כט
30	the meal offerings and libations for the bulls, rams, and lambs, in the quantities prescribed;	וּמִנְחָתָם וְנִסְכֵּיהֶם לַפָּרִים לָאֵילִם וְלַכְּבָשִׂים בְּמִסְפָּרָם כַּמִּשְׁפָּט: ל
31	and one goat for a sin offering – in addition to the regular burnt offering, its meal offering and libations.	וּשְׂעִיר חַטָּאת אֶחָד מִלְּבַד עֹלַת הַתָּמִיד מִנְחָתָהּ וּנְסָכֶיהָ: לא
32	Seventh day: Seven bulls, two rams, fourteen yearling lambs, without blemish;	וּבַיּוֹם הַשְּׁבִיעִי פָּרִים שִׁבְעָה אֵילִם שְׁנָיִם כְּבָשִׂים בְּנֵי־שָׁנָה אַרְבָּעָה עָשָׂר תְּמִימִם: לב
33	the meal offerings and libations for the bulls, rams, and lambs, in the quantities prescribed;	וּמִנְחָתָם וְנִסְכֵּהֶם לַפָּרִים לָאֵילִם וְלַכְּבָשִׂים בְּמִסְפָּרָם כְּמִשְׁפָּטָם: לג
34	and one goat for a sin offering – in addition to the regular burnt offering, its meal offering and libation.	וּשְׂעִיר חַטָּאת אֶחָד מִלְּבַד עֹלַת הַתָּמִיד מִנְחָתָהּ וְנִסְכָּהּ: לד

Bamidbar/Numbers 30
Matot

במדבר ל
מטות

35 On the eighth day you shall hold a solemn gathering; you shall not work at your occupations.

לה בַּיּוֹם הַשְּׁמִינִי עֲצֶרֶת תִּהְיֶה לָכֶם כָּל־מְלֶאכֶת עֲבֹדָה לֹא תַעֲשׂוּ׃

ba-YOM ha-sh'-mee-NEE a-TZE-ret tih-YEH la-KHEM kol m'-LE-khet a-vo-DAH LO ta-a-SU

36 You shall present a burnt offering, an offering by fire of pleasing odor to *Hashem*; one bull, one ram, seven yearling lambs, without blemish;

לו וְהִקְרַבְתֶּם עֹלָה אִשֵּׁה רֵיחַ נִיחֹחַ לַיהוָה פַּר אֶחָד אַיִל אֶחָד כְּבָשִׂים בְּנֵי־שָׁנָה שִׁבְעָה תְּמִימִם׃

37 the meal offerings and libations for the bull, the ram, and the lambs, in the quantities prescribed;

לז מִנְחָתָם וְנִסְכֵּיהֶם לַפָּר לָאַיִל וְלַכְּבָשִׂים בְּמִסְפָּרָם כַּמִּשְׁפָּט׃

38 and one goat for a sin offering – in addition to the regular burnt offering, its meal offering and libation.

לח וּשְׂעִיר חַטָּאת אֶחָד מִלְּבַד עֹלַת הַתָּמִיד וּמִנְחָתָהּ וְנִסְכָּהּ׃

39 All these you shall offer to *Hashem* at the stated times, in addition to your votive and freewill offerings, be they burnt offerings, meal offerings, libations, or offerings of well-being.

לט אֵלֶּה תַּעֲשׂוּ לַיהוָה בְּמוֹעֲדֵיכֶם לְבַד מִנִּדְרֵיכֶם וְנִדְבֹתֵיכֶם לְעֹלֹתֵיכֶם וּלְמִנְחֹתֵיכֶם וּלְנִסְכֵּיכֶם וּלְשַׁלְמֵיכֶם׃

30

1 So *Moshe* spoke to the Israelites just as *Hashem* had commanded *Moshe*.

א וַיֹּאמֶר מֹשֶׁה אֶל־בְּנֵי יִשְׂרָאֵל כְּכֹל אֲשֶׁר־צִוָּה יְהוָה אֶת־מֹשֶׁה׃

2 *Moshe* spoke to the heads of the Israelite tribes, saying: This is what *Hashem* has commanded:

ב וַיְדַבֵּר מֹשֶׁה אֶל־רָאשֵׁי הַמַּטּוֹת לִבְנֵי יִשְׂרָאֵל לֵאמֹר זֶה הַדָּבָר אֲשֶׁר צִוָּה יְהוָה׃

3 If a man makes a vow to *Hashem* or takes an oath imposing an obligation on himself, he shall not break his pledge; he must carry out all that has crossed his lips.

ג אִישׁ כִּי־יִדֹּר נֶדֶר לַיהוָה אוֹ־הִשָּׁבַע שְׁבֻעָה לֶאְסֹר אִסָּר עַל־נַפְשׁוֹ לֹא יַחֵל דְּבָרוֹ כְּכָל־הַיֹּצֵא מִפִּיו יַעֲשֶׂה׃

EESH kee yi-DOR NE-der la-do-NAI o hi-SHA-va sh'-vu-AH le-SOR i-SAR al naf-SHO LO ya-KHAYL d'-va-RO k'-khol ha-yo-TZAY mi-PEEV ya-a-SEH

29:35 On the eighth day you shall hold a solemn gathering This verse mandates an additional "solemn gathering" to be held on the day immediately following the seven days of *Sukkot*. According to the Sages (*Sukkah* 55b), the festival of *Sukkot* has a universal message, demonstrated by the fact that over the course of these seven days, seventy special sacrifices were brought in the *Beit Hamikdash*, corresponding to the seventy primordial nations of the world. At the completion of the *Sukkot* holiday, *Hashem* adds an extra day, as if to say to His people "I don't want you to leave yet. Let us celebrate one more day together so I can enjoy your exclusive, intimate company." After celebrating *Rosh Hashana*, *Yom Kippur* and finally *Sukkot*, *Hashem* doesn't want the special time to end. He asks His chosen nation to celebrate with Him alone for one more day. This final day is known as *Shemini Atzeret*, the 'eighth day of assembly.'

30:3 He shall not break his pledge This chapter elaborates on the laws regarding vows and oaths. *Hashem* takes these matters very seriously, and commands that any commitment to do something must be fulfilled. In fact, violating one's vows is a sin. This commandment teaches how important it is to be true to one's word: *Hashem* expects us to keep our word, just as He keeps His. Today, we are witness to *Hashem*'s fulfillment of His promise, made through His prophets, to return His people to the Promised Land. We hope to see the fulfillment of the rest of the divine promise, that the People of Israel will live peacefully in the Promised Land, very soon.

Bamidbar/Numbers 30
Matot

4 If a woman makes a vow to *Hashem* or assumes an obligation while still in her father's household by reason of her youth,

5 and her father learns of her vow or her self-imposed obligation and offers no objection, all her vows shall stand and every self-imposed obligation shall stand.

6 But if her father restrains her on the day he finds out, none of her vows or self-imposed obligations shall stand; and *Hashem* will forgive her, since her father restrained her.

7 If she should marry while her vow or the commitment to which she bound herself is still in force,

8 and her husband learns of it and offers no objection on the day he finds out, her vows shall stand and her self-imposed obligations shall stand.

9 But if her husband restrains her on the day that he learns of it, he thereby annuls her vow which was in force or the commitment to which she bound herself; and *Hashem* will forgive her.

10 The vow of a widow or of a divorced woman, however, whatever she has imposed on herself, shall be binding upon her.

11 So, too, if, while in her husband's household, she makes a vow or imposes an obligation on herself by oath,

12 and her husband learns of it, yet offers no objection – thus failing to restrain her – all her vows shall stand and all her self-imposed obligations shall stand.

13 But if her husband does annul them on the day he finds out, then nothing that has crossed her lips shall stand, whether vows or self-imposed obligations. Her husband has annulled them, and *Hashem* will forgive her.

14 Every vow and every sworn obligation of self-denial may be upheld by her husband or annulled by her husband.

15 If her husband offers no objection from that day to the next, he has upheld all the vows or obligations she has assumed: he has upheld them by offering no objection on the day he found out.

במדבר ל
מטות

ד וְאִשָּׁה כִּי־תִדֹּר נֶדֶר לַיהוָה וְאָסְרָה אִסָּר בְּבֵית אָבִיהָ בִּנְעֻרֶיהָ׃

ה וְשָׁמַע אָבִיהָ אֶת־נִדְרָהּ וֶאֱסָרָהּ אֲשֶׁר אָסְרָה עַל־נַפְשָׁהּ וְהֶחֱרִישׁ לָהּ אָבִיהָ וְקָמוּ כָּל־נְדָרֶיהָ וְכָל־אִסָּר אֲשֶׁר־אָסְרָה עַל־נַפְשָׁהּ יָקוּם׃

ו וְאִם־הֵנִיא אָבִיהָ אֹתָהּ בְּיוֹם שָׁמְעוֹ כָּל־נְדָרֶיהָ וֶאֱסָרֶיהָ אֲשֶׁר־אָסְרָה עַל־נַפְשָׁהּ לֹא יָקוּם וַיהוָה יִסְלַח־לָהּ כִּי־הֵנִיא אָבִיהָ אֹתָהּ׃

ז וְאִם־הָיוֹ תִהְיֶה לְאִישׁ וּנְדָרֶיהָ עָלֶיהָ אוֹ מִבְטָא שְׂפָתֶיהָ אֲשֶׁר אָסְרָה עַל־נַפְשָׁהּ׃

ח וְשָׁמַע אִישָׁהּ בְּיוֹם שָׁמְעוֹ וְהֶחֱרִישׁ לָהּ וְקָמוּ נְדָרֶיהָ וֶאֱסָרֶהָ אֲשֶׁר־אָסְרָה עַל־נַפְשָׁהּ יָקֻמוּ׃

ט וְאִם בְּיוֹם שְׁמֹעַ אִישָׁהּ יָנִיא אוֹתָהּ וְהֵפֵר אֶת־נִדְרָהּ אֲשֶׁר עָלֶיהָ וְאֵת מִבְטָא שְׂפָתֶיהָ אֲשֶׁר אָסְרָה עַל־נַפְשָׁהּ וַיהוָה יִסְלַח־לָהּ׃

י וְנֵדֶר אַלְמָנָה וּגְרוּשָׁה כֹּל אֲשֶׁר־אָסְרָה עַל־נַפְשָׁהּ יָקוּם עָלֶיהָ׃

יא וְאִם־בֵּית אִישָׁהּ נָדָרָה אוֹ־אָסְרָה אִסָּר עַל־נַפְשָׁהּ בִּשְׁבֻעָה׃

יב וְשָׁמַע אִישָׁהּ וְהֶחֱרִשׁ לָהּ לֹא הֵנִיא אֹתָהּ וְקָמוּ כָּל־נְדָרֶיהָ וְכָל־אִסָּר אֲשֶׁר־אָסְרָה עַל־נַפְשָׁהּ יָקוּם׃

יג וְאִם־הָפֵר יָפֵר אֹתָם אִישָׁהּ בְּיוֹם שָׁמְעוֹ כָּל־מוֹצָא שְׂפָתֶיהָ לִנְדָרֶיהָ וּלְאִסַּר נַפְשָׁהּ לֹא יָקוּם אִישָׁהּ הֲפֵרָם וַיהוָה יִסְלַח־לָהּ׃

יד כָּל־נֵדֶר וְכָל־שְׁבֻעַת אִסָּר לְעַנֹּת נָפֶשׁ אִישָׁהּ יְקִימֶנּוּ וְאִישָׁהּ יְפֵרֶנּוּ׃

טו וְאִם־הַחֲרֵשׁ יַחֲרִישׁ לָהּ אִישָׁהּ מִיּוֹם אֶל־יוֹם וְהֵקִים אֶת־כָּל־נְדָרֶיהָ אוֹ אֶת־כָּל־אֱסָרֶיהָ אֲשֶׁר עָלֶיהָ הֵקִים אֹתָם כִּי־הֶחֱרִשׁ לָהּ בְּיוֹם שָׁמְעוֹ׃

Bamidbar/Numbers 31
Matot

16 But if he annuls them after [the day] he finds out, he shall bear her guilt.

17 Those are the laws that *Hashem* enjoined upon *Moshe* between a man and his wife, and as between a father and his daughter while in her father's household by reason of her youth.

31

1 *Hashem* spoke to *Moshe*, saying,

2 "Avenge *B'nei Yisrael* on the Midianites; then you shall be gathered to your kin."

3 *Moshe* spoke to the people, saying, "Let men be picked out from among you for a campaign, and let them fall upon Midian to wreak *Hashem*'s vengeance on Midian.

4 You shall dispatch on the campaign a thousand from every one of the tribes of *Yisrael*."

5 So a thousand from each tribe were furnished from the divisions of *Yisrael*, twelve thousand picked for the campaign.

6 *Moshe* dispatched them on the campaign, a thousand from each tribe, with *Pinchas* son of *Elazar* serving as a *Kohen* on the campaign, equipped with the sacred utensils and the trumpets for sounding the blasts.

7 They took the field against Midian, as *Hashem* had commanded *Moshe*, and slew every male.

8 Along with their other victims, they slew the kings of Midian: Evi, Rekem, Zur, Hur, and Reba, the five kings of Midian. They also put Balaam son of Beor to the sword.

9 The Israelites took the women and children of the Midianites captive, and seized as booty all their beasts, all their herds, and all their wealth.

10 And they destroyed by fire all the towns in which they were settled, and their encampments.

11 They gathered all the spoil and all the booty, man and beast,

12 and they brought the captives, the booty, and the spoil to *Moshe*, *Elazar* the *Kohen*, and the whole Israelite community, at the camp in the steppes of Moab, at the *Yarden* near *Yericho*.

במדבר לא
מטות

טז וְאִם־הָפֵר יָפֵר אֹתָם אַחֲרֵי שָׁמְעוֹ וְנָשָׂא אֶת־עֲוֺנָהּ:

יז אֵלֶּה הַחֻקִּים אֲשֶׁר צִוָּה יְהֹוָה אֶת־מֹשֶׁה בֵּין אִישׁ לְאִשְׁתּוֹ בֵּין־אָב לְבִתּוֹ בִּנְעֻרֶיהָ בֵּית אָבִיהָ:

לא

א וַיְדַבֵּר יְהֹוָה אֶל־מֹשֶׁה לֵּאמֹר:

ב נְקֹם נִקְמַת בְּנֵי יִשְׂרָאֵל מֵאֵת הַמִּדְיָנִים אַחַר תֵּאָסֵף אֶל־עַמֶּיךָ:

ג וַיְדַבֵּר מֹשֶׁה אֶל־הָעָם לֵאמֹר הֵחָלְצוּ מֵאִתְּכֶם אֲנָשִׁים לַצָּבָא וְיִהְיוּ עַל־מִדְיָן לָתֵת נִקְמַת־יְהֹוָה בְּמִדְיָן:

ד אֶלֶף לַמַּטֶּה אֶלֶף לַמַּטֶּה לְכֹל מַטּוֹת יִשְׂרָאֵל תִּשְׁלְחוּ לַצָּבָא:

ה וַיִּמָּסְרוּ מֵאַלְפֵי יִשְׂרָאֵל אֶלֶף לַמַּטֶּה שְׁנֵים־עָשָׂר אֶלֶף חֲלוּצֵי צָבָא:

ו וַיִּשְׁלַח אֹתָם מֹשֶׁה אֶלֶף לַמַּטֶּה לַצָּבָא אֹתָם וְאֶת־פִּינְחָס בֶּן־אֶלְעָזָר הַכֹּהֵן לַצָּבָא וּכְלֵי הַקֹּדֶשׁ וַחֲצֹצְרוֹת הַתְּרוּעָה בְּיָדוֹ:

ז וַיִּצְבְּאוּ עַל־מִדְיָן כַּאֲשֶׁר צִוָּה יְהֹוָה אֶת־מֹשֶׁה וַיַּהַרְגוּ כָּל־זָכָר:

ח וְאֶת־מַלְכֵי מִדְיָן הָרְגוּ עַל־חַלְלֵיהֶם אֶת־אֱוִי וְאֶת־רֶקֶם וְאֶת־צוּר וְאֶת־חוּר וְאֶת־רֶבַע חֲמֵשֶׁת מַלְכֵי מִדְיָן וְאֵת בִּלְעָם בֶּן־בְּעוֹר הָרְגוּ בֶּחָרֶב:

ט וַיִּשְׁבּוּ בְנֵי־יִשְׂרָאֵל אֶת־נְשֵׁי מִדְיָן וְאֶת־טַפָּם וְאֵת כָּל־בְּהֶמְתָּם וְאֶת־כָּל־מִקְנֵהֶם וְאֶת־כָּל־חֵילָם בָּזָזוּ:

י וְאֵת כָּל־עָרֵיהֶם בְּמוֹשְׁבֹתָם וְאֵת כָּל־טִירֹתָם שָׂרְפוּ בָּאֵשׁ:

יא וַיִּקְחוּ אֶת־כָּל־הַשָּׁלָל וְאֵת כָּל־הַמַּלְקוֹחַ בָּאָדָם וּבַבְּהֵמָה:

יב וַיָּבִאוּ אֶל־מֹשֶׁה וְאֶל־אֶלְעָזָר הַכֹּהֵן וְאֶל־עֲדַת בְּנֵי־יִשְׂרָאֵל אֶת־הַשְּׁבִי וְאֶת־הַמַּלְקוֹחַ וְאֶת־הַשָּׁלָל אֶל־הַמַּחֲנֶה אֶל־עַרְבֹת מוֹאָב אֲשֶׁר עַל־יַרְדֵּן יְרֵחוֹ:

Bamidbar/Numbers 31
Matot

13 Moshe, Elazar the Kohen, and all the chieftains of the community came out to meet them outside the camp.

14 Moshe became angry with the commanders of the army, the officers of thousands and the officers of hundreds, who had come back from the military campaign.

15 Moshe said to them, "You have spared every female!

16 Yet they are the very ones who, at the bidding of Balaam, induced the Israelites to trespass against Hashem in the matter of Peor, so that Hashem's community was struck by the plague.

17 Now, therefore, slay every male among the children, and slay also every woman who has known a man carnally;

18 but spare every young woman who has not had carnal relations with a man.

19 "You shall then stay outside the camp seven days; every one among you or among your captives who has slain a person or touched a corpse shall cleanse himself on the third and seventh days.

20 You shall also cleanse every cloth, every article of skin, everything made of goats' hair, and every object of wood."

21 Elazar the Kohen said to the troops who had taken part in the fighting, "This is the ritual law that Hashem has enjoined upon Moshe:

22 Gold and silver, copper, iron, tin, and lead

23 any article that can withstand fire – these you shall pass through fire and they shall be clean, except that they must be cleansed with water of lustration; and anything that cannot withstand fire you must pass through water.

24 On the seventh day you shall wash your clothes and be clean, and after that you may enter the camp."

25 Hashem said to Moshe:

26 "You and Elazar the Kohen and the family heads of the community take an inventory of the booty that was captured, man and beast,

במדבר לא
מטות

יג וַיֵּצְאוּ מֹשֶׁה וְאֶלְעָזָר הַכֹּהֵן וְכָל־נְשִׂיאֵי הָעֵדָה לִקְרָאתָם אֶל־מִחוּץ לַמַּחֲנֶה:

יד וַיִּקְצֹף מֹשֶׁה עַל פְּקוּדֵי הֶחָיִל שָׂרֵי הָאֲלָפִים וְשָׂרֵי הַמֵּאוֹת הַבָּאִים מִצְּבָא הַמִּלְחָמָה:

טו וַיֹּאמֶר אֲלֵיהֶם מֹשֶׁה הַחִיִּיתֶם כָּל־נְקֵבָה:

טז הֵן הֵנָּה הָיוּ לִבְנֵי יִשְׂרָאֵל בִּדְבַר בִּלְעָם לִמְסָר־מַעַל בַּיהוָה עַל־דְּבַר־פְּעוֹר וַתְּהִי הַמַּגֵּפָה בַּעֲדַת יְהוָה:

יז וְעַתָּה הִרְגוּ כָל־זָכָר בַּטָּף וְכָל־אִשָּׁה יֹדַעַת אִישׁ לְמִשְׁכַּב זָכָר הֲרֹגוּ:

יח וְכֹל הַטַּף בַּנָּשִׁים אֲשֶׁר לֹא־יָדְעוּ מִשְׁכַּב זָכָר הַחֲיוּ לָכֶם:

יט וְאַתֶּם חֲנוּ מִחוּץ לַמַּחֲנֶה שִׁבְעַת יָמִים כֹּל הֹרֵג נֶפֶשׁ וְכֹל נֹגֵעַ בֶּחָלָל תִּתְחַטְּאוּ בַּיּוֹם הַשְּׁלִישִׁי וּבַיּוֹם הַשְּׁבִיעִי אַתֶּם וּשְׁבִיכֶם:

כ וְכָל־בֶּגֶד וְכָל־כְּלִי־עוֹר וְכָל־מַעֲשֵׂה עִזִּים וְכָל־כְּלִי־עֵץ תִּתְחַטָּאוּ:

כא וַיֹּאמֶר אֶלְעָזָר הַכֹּהֵן אֶל־אַנְשֵׁי הַצָּבָא הַבָּאִים לַמִּלְחָמָה זֹאת חֻקַּת הַתּוֹרָה אֲשֶׁר־צִוָּה יְהוָה אֶת־מֹשֶׁה:

כב אַךְ אֶת־הַזָּהָב וְאֶת־הַכָּסֶף אֶת־הַנְּחֹשֶׁת אֶת־הַבַּרְזֶל אֶת־הַבְּדִיל וְאֶת־הָעֹפָרֶת:

כג כָּל־דָּבָר אֲשֶׁר־יָבֹא בָאֵשׁ תַּעֲבִירוּ בָאֵשׁ וְטָהֵר אַךְ בְּמֵי נִדָּה יִתְחַטָּא וְכֹל אֲשֶׁר לֹא־יָבֹא בָּאֵשׁ תַּעֲבִירוּ בַמָּיִם:

כד וְכִבַּסְתֶּם בִּגְדֵיכֶם בַּיּוֹם הַשְּׁבִיעִי וּטְהַרְתֶּם וְאַחַר תָּבֹאוּ אֶל־הַמַּחֲנֶה:

כה וַיֹּאמֶר יְהוָה אֶל־מֹשֶׁה לֵּאמֹר:

כו שָׂא אֵת רֹאשׁ מַלְקוֹחַ הַשְּׁבִי בָּאָדָם וּבַבְּהֵמָה אַתָּה וְאֶלְעָזָר הַכֹּהֵן וְרָאשֵׁי אֲבוֹת הָעֵדָה:

Bamidbar/Numbers 31
Matot

במדבר לא
מטות

27 and divide the booty equally between the combatants who engaged in the campaign and the rest of the community.

כז וְחָצִיתָ אֶת־הַמַּלְקוֹחַ בֵּין תֹּפְשֵׂי הַמִּלְחָמָה הַיֹּצְאִים לַצָּבָא וּבֵין כָּל־הָעֵדָה:

v'-kha-TZEE-ta et ha-mal-KO-akh BAYN to-f'-SAY ha-mil-kha-MAH ha-yo-tz'-EEM la-tza-VA u-VAYN kol ha-ay-DAH

28 You shall exact a levy for *Hashem*: in the case of the warriors who engaged in the campaign, one item in five hundred, of persons, oxen, asses, and sheep,

כח וַהֲרֵמֹתָ מֶכֶס לַיהוָה מֵאֵת אַנְשֵׁי הַמִּלְחָמָה הַיֹּצְאִים לַצָּבָא אֶחָד נֶפֶשׁ מֵחֲמֵשׁ הַמֵּאוֹת מִן־הָאָדָם וּמִן־הַבָּקָר וּמִן־הַחֲמֹרִים וּמִן־הַצֹּאן:

29 shall be taken from their half-share and given to *Elazar* the *Kohen* as a contribution to *Hashem*;

כט מִמַּחֲצִיתָם תִּקָּחוּ וְנָתַתָּה לְאֶלְעָזָר הַכֹּהֵן תְּרוּמַת יְהוָה:

30 and from the half-share of the other Israelites you shall withhold one in every fifty human beings as well as cattle, asses, and sheep – all the animals – and give them to the *Leviim*, who attend to the duties of *Hashem*'s *Mishkan*."

ל וּמִמַּחֲצִת בְּנֵי־יִשְׂרָאֵל תִּקַּח אֶחָד אָחֻז מִן־הַחֲמִשִּׁים מִן־הָאָדָם מִן־הַבָּקָר מִן־הַחֲמֹרִים וּמִן־הַצֹּאן מִכָּל־הַבְּהֵמָה וְנָתַתָּה אֹתָם לַלְוִיִּם שֹׁמְרֵי מִשְׁמֶרֶת מִשְׁכַּן יְהוָה:

31 *Moshe* and *Elazar* the *Kohen* did as *Hashem* commanded *Moshe*.

לא וַיַּעַשׂ מֹשֶׁה וְאֶלְעָזָר הַכֹּהֵן כַּאֲשֶׁר צִוָּה יְהוָה אֶת־מֹשֶׁה:

32 The amount of booty, other than the spoil that the troops had plundered, came to 675,000 sheep,

לב וַיְהִי הַמַּלְקוֹחַ יֶתֶר הַבָּז אֲשֶׁר בָּזְזוּ עַם הַצָּבָא צֹאן שֵׁשׁ־מֵאוֹת אֶלֶף וְשִׁבְעִים אֶלֶף וַחֲמֵשֶׁת־אֲלָפִים:

33 72,000 head of cattle,

לג וּבָקָר שְׁנַיִם וְשִׁבְעִים אָלֶף:

34 61,000 asses,

לד וַחֲמֹרִים אֶחָד וְשִׁשִּׁים אָלֶף:

35 and a total of 32,000 human beings, namely, the women who had not had carnal relations.

לה וְנֶפֶשׁ אָדָם מִן־הַנָּשִׁים אֲשֶׁר לֹא־יָדְעוּ מִשְׁכַּב זָכָר כָּל־נֶפֶשׁ שְׁנַיִם וּשְׁלֹשִׁים אָלֶף:

36 Thus, the half-share of those who had engaged in the campaign [was as follows]: The number of sheep was 337,500,

לו וַתְּהִי הַמֶּחֱצָה חֵלֶק הַיֹּצְאִים בַּצָּבָא מִסְפַּר הַצֹּאן שְׁלֹשׁ־מֵאוֹת אֶלֶף וּשְׁלֹשִׁים אֶלֶף וְשִׁבְעַת אֲלָפִים וַחֲמֵשׁ מֵאוֹת:

37 and *Hashem*'s levy from the sheep was 675;

לז וַיְהִי הַמֶּכֶס לַיהוָה מִן־הַצֹּאן שֵׁשׁ מֵאוֹת חָמֵשׁ וְשִׁבְעִים:

31:27 And the rest of the community Chapter 31 describes the war waged by the Israelites against the Midianites as retribution for the immorality and idolatry that the Midianites caused, which lead to the death of twenty-four thousand Israelites. *Moshe* commands that an equal number of men from each tribe be chosen to fight, and at the conclusion of the battle, the spoils of war are divided among the entire congregation. The fact that each tribe is equally represented in battle, and that everyone, even those who did not fight, is given a share in the spoils, highlights the unity of the congregation of Israel. Since they are functioning as one cohesive unit, united in the service of *Hashem*, they are finally ready to enter the Land of Israel and complete the journey their parents had started forty years earlier.

Bamidbar/Numbers 31
Matot

38 the cattle came to 36,000, from which *Hashem*'s levy was 72;

39 the asses came to 30,500, from which *Hashem*'s levy was 61.

40 And the number of human beings was 16,000, from which *Hashem*'s levy was 32.

41 *Moshe* gave the contributions levied for *Hashem* to *Elazar* the *Kohen*, as *Hashem* had commanded *Moshe*.

42 As for the half-share of the other Israelites, which *Moshe* withdrew from the men who had taken the field,

43 that half-share of the community consisted of 337,500 sheep,

44 36,000 head of cattle,

45 30,500 asses,

46 and 16,000 human beings.

47 From this half-share of the Israelites, *Moshe* withheld one in every fifty humans and animals; and he gave them to the *Leviim*, who attended to the duties of *Hashem*'s *Mishkan*, as *Hashem* had commanded *Moshe*.

48 The commanders of the troop divisions, the officers of thousands and the officers of hundreds, approached *Moshe*.

49 They said to *Moshe*, "Your servants have made a check of the warriors in our charge, and not one of us is missing.

50 So we have brought as an offering to *Hashem* such articles of gold as each of us came upon: armlets, bracelets, signet rings, earrings, and pendants, that expiation may be made for our persons before *Hashem*."

51 *Moshe* and *Elazar* the *Kohen* accepted the gold from them, all kinds of wrought articles.

52 All the gold that was offered by the officers of thousands and the officers of hundreds as a contribution to *Hashem* came to 16,750 *shekalim*.

במדבר לא
מטות

לח וְהַבָּקָר שִׁשָּׁה וּשְׁלֹשִׁים אָלֶף וּמִכְסָם לַיהוָה שְׁנַיִם וְשִׁבְעִים:

לט וַחֲמֹרִים שְׁלֹשִׁים אֶלֶף וַחֲמֵשׁ מֵאוֹת וּמִכְסָם לַיהוָה אֶחָד וְשִׁשִּׁים:

מ וְנֶפֶשׁ אָדָם שִׁשָּׁה עָשָׂר אָלֶף וּמִכְסָם לַיהוָה שְׁנַיִם וּשְׁלֹשִׁים נָפֶשׁ:

מא וַיִּתֵּן מֹשֶׁה אֶת־מֶכֶס תְּרוּמַת יְהוָה לְאֶלְעָזָר הַכֹּהֵן כַּאֲשֶׁר צִוָּה יְהוָה אֶת־מֹשֶׁה:

מב וּמִמַּחֲצִית בְּנֵי יִשְׂרָאֵל אֲשֶׁר חָצָה מֹשֶׁה מִן־הָאֲנָשִׁים הַצֹּבְאִים:

מג וַתְּהִי מֶחֱצַת הָעֵדָה מִן־הַצֹּאן שְׁלֹשׁ־מֵאוֹת אֶלֶף וּשְׁלֹשִׁים אֶלֶף שִׁבְעַת אֲלָפִים וַחֲמֵשׁ מֵאוֹת:

מד וּבָקָר שִׁשָּׁה וּשְׁלֹשִׁים אָלֶף:

מה וַחֲמֹרִים שְׁלֹשִׁים אֶלֶף וַחֲמֵשׁ מֵאוֹת:

מו וְנֶפֶשׁ אָדָם שִׁשָּׁה עָשָׂר אָלֶף:

מז וַיִּקַּח מֹשֶׁה מִמַּחֲצִת בְּנֵי־יִשְׂרָאֵל אֶת־הָאָחֻז אֶחָד מִן־הַחֲמִשִּׁים מִן־הָאָדָם וּמִן־הַבְּהֵמָה וַיִּתֵּן אֹתָם לַלְוִיִּם שֹׁמְרֵי מִשְׁמֶרֶת מִשְׁכַּן יְהוָה כַּאֲשֶׁר צִוָּה יְהוָה אֶת־מֹשֶׁה:

מח וַיִּקְרְבוּ אֶל־מֹשֶׁה הַפְּקֻדִים אֲשֶׁר לְאַלְפֵי הַצָּבָא שָׂרֵי הָאֲלָפִים וְשָׂרֵי הַמֵּאוֹת:

מט וַיֹּאמְרוּ אֶל־מֹשֶׁה עֲבָדֶיךָ נָשְׂאוּ אֶת־רֹאשׁ אַנְשֵׁי הַמִּלְחָמָה אֲשֶׁר בְּיָדֵנוּ וְלֹא־נִפְקַד מִמֶּנּוּ אִישׁ:

נ וַנַּקְרֵב אֶת־קָרְבַּן יְהוָה אִישׁ אֲשֶׁר מָצָא כְלִי־זָהָב אֶצְעָדָה וְצָמִיד טַבַּעַת עָגִיל וְכוּמָז לְכַפֵּר עַל־נַפְשֹׁתֵינוּ לִפְנֵי יְהוָה:

נא וַיִּקַּח מֹשֶׁה וְאֶלְעָזָר הַכֹּהֵן אֶת־הַזָּהָב מֵאִתָּם כֹּל כְּלִי מַעֲשֶׂה:

נב וַיְהִי כָּל־זְהַב הַתְּרוּמָה אֲשֶׁר הֵרִימוּ לַיהוָה שִׁשָּׁה עָשָׂר אֶלֶף שְׁבַע־מֵאוֹת וַחֲמִשִּׁים שָׁקֶל מֵאֵת שָׂרֵי הָאֲלָפִים וּמֵאֵת שָׂרֵי הַמֵּאוֹת:

Bamidbar/Numbers 32
Matot

במדבר לב
מטות

53 But in the ranks, everyone kept his booty for himself.

נג אַנְשֵׁי הַצָּבָא בָּזְזוּ אִישׁ לוֹ:

54 So *Moshe* and *Elazar* the *Kohen* accepted the gold from the officers of thousands and the officers of hundreds and brought it to the Tent of Meeting, as a reminder in behalf of the Israelites before *Hashem*.

נד וַיִּקַּח מֹשֶׁה וְאֶלְעָזָר הַכֹּהֵן אֶת־הַזָּהָב מֵאֵת שָׂרֵי הָאֲלָפִים וְהַמֵּאוֹת וַיָּבִאוּ אֹתוֹ אֶל־אֹהֶל מוֹעֵד זִכָּרוֹן לִבְנֵי־יִשְׂרָאֵל לִפְנֵי יְהוָה:

32

1 The Reubenites and the Gadites owned cattle in very great numbers. Noting that the lands of Jazer and *Gilad* were a region suitable for cattle,

לב א וּמִקְנֶה רַב הָיָה לִבְנֵי רְאוּבֵן וְלִבְנֵי־גָד עָצוּם מְאֹד וַיִּרְאוּ אֶת־אֶרֶץ יַעְזֵר וְאֶת־אֶרֶץ גִּלְעָד וְהִנֵּה הַמָּקוֹם מְקוֹם מִקְנֶה:

2 the Gadites and the Reubenites came to *Moshe*, *Elazar* the *Kohen*, and the chieftains of the community, and said,

ב וַיָּבֹאוּ בְנֵי־גָד וּבְנֵי רְאוּבֵן וַיֹּאמְרוּ אֶל־מֹשֶׁה וְאֶל־אֶלְעָזָר הַכֹּהֵן וְאֶל־נְשִׂיאֵי הָעֵדָה לֵאמֹר:

3 "Ataroth, Dibon, Jazer, Nimrah, Heshbon, Elealeh, Sebam, Nebo, and Beon

ג עֲטָרוֹת וְדִיבֹן וְיַעְזֵר וְנִמְרָה וְחֶשְׁבּוֹן וְאֶלְעָלֵה וּשְׂבָם וּנְבוֹ וּבְעֹן:

4 the land that *Hashem* has conquered for the community of *Yisrael* is cattle country, and your servants have cattle.

ד הָאָרֶץ אֲשֶׁר הִכָּה יְהוָה לִפְנֵי עֲדַת יִשְׂרָאֵל אֶרֶץ מִקְנֶה הִוא וְלַעֲבָדֶיךָ מִקְנֶה:

5 It would be a favor to us," they continued, "if this land were given to your servants as a holding; do not move us across the *Yarden*."

ה וַיֹּאמְרוּ אִם־מָצָאנוּ חֵן בְּעֵינֶיךָ יֻתַּן אֶת־הָאָרֶץ הַזֹּאת לַעֲבָדֶיךָ לַאֲחֻזָּה אַל־תַּעֲבִרֵנוּ אֶת־הַיַּרְדֵּן:

6 *Moshe* replied to the Gadites and the Reubenites, "Are your brothers to go to war while you stay here?

ו וַיֹּאמֶר מֹשֶׁה לִבְנֵי־גָד וְלִבְנֵי רְאוּבֵן הַאַחֵיכֶם יָבֹאוּ לַמִּלְחָמָה וְאַתֶּם תֵּשְׁבוּ פֹה:

7 Why will you turn the minds of the Israelites from crossing into the land that *Hashem* has given them?

ז וְלָמָּה תנואון [תְנִיאוּן] אֶת־לֵב בְּנֵי יִשְׂרָאֵל מֵעֲבֹר אֶל־הָאָרֶץ אֲשֶׁר־נָתַן לָהֶם יְהוָה:

8 That is what your fathers did when I sent them from Kadesh-barnea to survey the land.

ח כֹּה עָשׂוּ אֲבֹתֵיכֶם בְּשָׁלְחִי אֹתָם מִקָּדֵשׁ בַּרְנֵעַ לִרְאוֹת אֶת־הָאָרֶץ:

KO a-SU a-vo-tay-KHEM b'-shol-KHEE o-TAM mi-ka-DAYSH bar-NAY-a lir-OT et ha-A-retz

---

32:8 That is what your fathers did When the tribes of *Reuven* and *Gad* request to settle in the lands conquered from Sihon and Og on the east bank of the Jordan River, instead of settling in the Land of Israel proper, *Moshe*'s reaction is very strong and negative. In his eyes, they are rejecting the land given to them by God, and he fears that they will influence others to also refrain from crossing into the land of Israel. He wonders: Have they learned nothing from the sin of the spies? *Moshe* acquiesces only when he becomes convinced that the request stems neither from a rejection of God's land, nor from a desire to be relieved of the long and hard upcoming struggle to conquer the Promised Land. That mistake had already been made once and the people suffered the consequences; they have learned not to make the same mistake again. Let us make sure that neither our actions nor our speech in anyway rejects or belittles *Eretz Yisrael*.

Bamidbar/Numbers 32
Matot

9 After going up to the wadi Eshcol and surveying the land, they turned the minds of the Israelites from invading the land that *Hashem* had given them.

10 Thereupon *Hashem* was incensed and He swore,

11 'None of the men from twenty years up who came out of Egypt shall see the land that I promised on oath to *Avraham*, *Yitzchak*, and *Yaakov*, for they did not remain loyal to Me –

12 none except *Kalev* son of Jephunneh the Kenizzite and *Yehoshua* son of *Nun*, for they remained loyal to *Hashem*.'

13 *Hashem* was incensed at *Yisrael*, and for forty years He made them wander in the wilderness, until the whole generation that had provoked *Hashem's* displeasure was gone.

14 And now you, a breed of sinful men, have replaced your fathers, to add still further to *Hashem's* wrath against *Yisrael*.

15 If you turn away from Him and He abandons them once more in the wilderness, you will bring calamity upon all this people."

16 Then they stepped up to him and said, "We will build here sheepfolds for our flocks and towns for our children.

17 And we will hasten as shock-troops in the van of the Israelites until we have established them in their home, while our children stay in the fortified towns because of the inhabitants of the land.

18 We will not return to our homes until every one of the Israelites is in possession of his portion.

19 But we will not have a share with them in the territory beyond the *Yarden*, for we have received our share on the east side of the *Yarden*."

20 *Moshe* said to them, "If you do this, if you go to battle as shock-troops, at the instance of *Hashem*,

במדבר לב
מטות

ט וַיַּעֲל֣וּ עַד־נַ֣חַל אֶשְׁכּוֹל֮ וַיִּרְאוּ֮ אֶת־הָאָ֒רֶץ֒ וַיָּנִ֕יאוּ אֶת־לֵ֖ב בְּנֵ֣י יִשְׂרָאֵ֑ל לְבִלְתִּי־בֹא֙ אֶל־הָאָ֔רֶץ אֲשֶׁר־נָתַ֥ן לָהֶ֖ם יְהֹוָֽה׃

י וַיִּֽחַר־אַ֥ף יְהֹוָ֖ה בַּיּ֣וֹם הַה֑וּא וַיִּשָּׁבַ֖ע לֵאמֹֽר׃

יא אִם־יִרְא֨וּ הָאֲנָשִׁ֜ים הָעֹלִ֣ים מִמִּצְרַ֗יִם מִבֶּ֨ן עֶשְׂרִ֤ים שָׁנָה֙ וָמַ֔עְלָה אֵ֚ת הָאֲדָמָ֔ה אֲשֶׁ֥ר נִשְׁבַּ֛עְתִּי לְאַבְרָהָ֥ם לְיִצְחָ֖ק וּֽלְיַעֲקֹ֑ב כִּ֥י לֹא־מִלְא֖וּ אַחֲרָֽי׃

יב בִּלְתִּ֞י כָּלֵ֤ב בֶּן־יְפֻנֶּה֙ הַקְּנִזִּ֔י וִיהוֹשֻׁ֖עַ בִּן־נ֑וּן כִּ֥י מִלְא֖וּ אַחֲרֵ֥י יְהֹוָֽה׃

יג וַיִּֽחַר־אַ֤ף יְהֹוָה֙ בְּיִשְׂרָאֵ֔ל וַיְנִעֵם֙ בַּמִּדְבָּ֔ר אַרְבָּעִ֖ים שָׁנָ֑ה עַד־תֹּם֙ כָּל־הַדּ֔וֹר הָעֹשֶׂ֥ה הָרַ֖ע בְּעֵינֵ֥י יְהֹוָֽה׃

יד וְהִנֵּ֣ה קַמְתֶּ֗ם תַּ֚חַת אֲבֹתֵיכֶ֔ם תַּרְבּ֖וּת אֲנָשִׁ֣ים חַטָּאִ֑ים לִסְפּ֣וֹת ע֗וֹד עַ֛ל חֲר֥וֹן אַף־יְהֹוָ֖ה אֶל־יִשְׂרָאֵֽל׃

טו כִּ֤י תְשׁוּבֻן֙ מֵֽאַחֲרָ֔יו וְיָסַ֣ף ע֔וֹד לְהַנִּיח֖וֹ בַּמִּדְבָּ֑ר וְשִֽׁחַתֶּ֖ם לְכָל־הָעָ֥ם הַזֶּֽה׃

טז וַיִּגְּשׁ֤וּ אֵלָיו֙ וַ֣יֹּאמְר֔וּ גִּדְרֹ֥ת צֹ֛אן נִבְנֶ֥ה לְמִקְנֵ֖נוּ פֹּ֑ה וְעָרִ֖ים לְטַפֵּֽנוּ׃

יז וַאֲנַ֜חְנוּ נֵחָלֵ֣ץ חֻשִׁ֗ים לִפְנֵי֙ בְּנֵ֣י יִשְׂרָאֵ֔ל עַ֛ד אֲשֶׁ֥ר אִם־הֲבִֽיאֹנֻ֖ם אֶל־מְקוֹמָ֑ם וְיָשַׁ֤ב טַפֵּ֙נוּ֙ בְּעָרֵ֣י הַמִּבְצָ֔ר מִפְּנֵ֖י יֹשְׁבֵ֥י הָאָֽרֶץ׃

יח לֹ֥א נָשׁ֖וּב אֶל־בָּתֵּ֑ינוּ עַ֗ד הִתְנַחֵל֙ בְּנֵ֣י יִשְׂרָאֵ֔ל אִ֖ישׁ נַחֲלָתֽוֹ׃

יט כִּ֣י לֹ֤א נִנְחַל֙ אִתָּ֔ם מֵעֵ֥בֶר לַיַּרְדֵּ֖ן וָהָ֑לְאָה כִּ֣י בָ֤אָה נַחֲלָתֵ֙נוּ֙ אֵלֵ֔ינוּ מֵעֵ֥בֶר הַיַּרְדֵּ֖ן מִזְרָֽחָה׃

כ וַיֹּ֤אמֶר אֲלֵיהֶם֙ מֹשֶׁ֔ה אִֽם־תַּעֲשׂ֖וּן אֶת־הַדָּבָ֣ר הַזֶּ֑ה אִם־תֵּחָ֥לְצ֛וּ לִפְנֵ֥י יְהֹוָ֖ה לַמִּלְחָמָֽה׃

Bamidbar/Numbers 32
Matot

במדבר לב
מטות

21 and every shock-fighter among you crosses the *Yarden*, at the instance of *Hashem*, until He has dispossessed His enemies before Him,

וְעָבַ֨ר לָכֶ֧ם כָּל־חָל֛וּץ אֶת־הַיַּרְדֵּ֖ן לִפְנֵ֣י יְהֹוָ֑ה עַ֧ד הוֹרִישׁ֛וֹ אֶת־אֹיְבָ֖יו מִפָּנָֽיו׃ כא

v'-a-VAR la-KHEM kol kha-LUTZ et ha-yar-DAYN lif-NAY a-do-NAI AD ho-ree-SHO et o-y'-VAV mi-pa-NAV

22 and the land has been subdued, at the instance of *Hashem*, and then you return – you shall be clear before *Hashem* and before *Yisrael*; and this land shall be your holding under *Hashem*.

וְנִכְבְּשָׁ֨ה הָאָ֜רֶץ לִפְנֵ֤י יְהֹוָה֙ וְאַחַ֣ר תָּשֻׁ֔בוּ וִהְיִיתֶ֧ם נְקִיִּ֛ם מֵיְהֹוָ֖ה וּמִיִּשְׂרָאֵ֑ל וְ֠הָיְתָ֠ה הָאָ֨רֶץ הַזֹּ֥את לָכֶ֛ם לַאֲחֻזָּ֖ה לִפְנֵ֥י יְהֹוָֽה׃ כב

23 But if you do not do so, you will have sinned against *Hashem*; and know that your sin will overtake you.

וְאִם־לֹ֤א תַעֲשׂוּן֙ כֵּ֔ן הִנֵּ֥ה חֲטָאתֶ֖ם לַיהֹוָ֑ה וּדְעוּ֙ חַטַּאתְכֶ֔ם אֲשֶׁ֥ר תִּמְצָ֖א אֶתְכֶֽם׃ כג

24 Build towns for your children and sheepfolds for your flocks, but do what you have promised."

בְּנֽוּ־לָכֶ֤ם עָרִים֙ לְטַפְּכֶ֔ם וּגְדֵרֹ֖ת לְצֹנַאֲכֶ֑ם וְהַיֹּצֵ֥א מִפִּיכֶ֖ם תַּעֲשֽׂוּ׃ כד

25 The Gadites and the Reubenites answered *Moshe*, "Your servants will do as my lord commands.

וַיֹּ֤אמֶר בְּנֵי־גָד֙ וּבְנֵ֣י רְאוּבֵ֔ן אֶל־מֹשֶׁ֖ה לֵאמֹ֑ר עֲבָדֶ֣יךָ יַעֲשׂ֔וּ כַּאֲשֶׁ֥ר אֲדֹנִ֖י מְצַוֶּֽה׃ כה

26 Our children, our wives, our flocks, and all our other livestock will stay behind in the towns of *Gilad*;

טַפֵּ֣נוּ נָשֵׁ֔ינוּ מִקְנֵ֖נוּ וְכָל־בְּהֶמְתֵּ֑נוּ יִֽהְיוּ־שָׁ֖ם בְּעָרֵ֥י הַגִּלְעָֽד׃ כו

27 while your servants, all those recruited for war, cross over, at the instance of *Hashem*, to engage in battle – as my lord orders."

וַעֲבָדֶ֨יךָ יַֽעַבְר֜וּ כָּל־חֲל֥וּץ צָבָ֛א לִפְנֵ֥י יְהֹוָ֖ה לַמִּלְחָמָ֑ה כַּאֲשֶׁ֥ר אֲדֹנִ֖י דֹּבֵֽר׃ כז

28 Then *Moshe* gave instructions concerning them to *Elazar* the *Kohen*, *Yehoshua* son of *Nun*, and the family heads of the Israelite tribes.

וַיְצַ֤ו לָהֶם֙ מֹשֶׁ֔ה אֵ֚ת אֶלְעָזָ֣ר הַכֹּהֵ֔ן וְאֵ֖ת יְהוֹשֻׁ֣עַ בִּן־נ֑וּן וְאֶת־רָאשֵׁ֛י אֲב֥וֹת הַמַּטּ֖וֹת לִבְנֵ֥י יִשְׂרָאֵֽל׃ כח

29 *Moshe* said to them, "If every shock-fighter among the Gadites and the Reubenites crosses the *Yarden* with you to do battle, at the instance of *Hashem*, and the land is subdued before you, you shall give them the land of *Gilad* as a holding.

וַיֹּ֨אמֶר מֹשֶׁ֜ה אֲלֵהֶ֗ם אִם־יַעַבְר֣וּ בְנֵי־גָ֣ד וּבְנֵי־רְאוּבֵ֣ן ׀ אִ֠תְּכֶ֠ם אֶֽת־הַיַּרְדֵּ֞ן כָּל־חָל֤וּץ לַמִּלְחָמָה֙ לִפְנֵ֣י יְהֹוָ֔ה וְנִכְבְּשָׁ֥ה הָאָ֖רֶץ לִפְנֵיכֶ֑ם וּנְתַתֶּ֥ם לָהֶ֛ם אֶת־אֶ֥רֶץ הַגִּלְעָ֖ד לַאֲחֻזָּֽה׃ כט

32:21 And every shock-fighter among you crosses the Yarden *Moshe* was willing to accept the request of *Reuven* and *Gad* to settle on the east of the *Yarden* River only after they promised to help fight to inherit the Land of Israel. We learn a powerful lesson of responsibility from this story. While they already possess the land that was going to be their home, these tribes are not allowed to settle down until every other tribe in Israel also has land of their own in which to settle. Life in *Eretz Yisrael* demands and engenders the concept that everyone is responsible for his fellow. This spirit of collective cooperation can be seen in the *Kibbutz* movement formed by the original Zionist pioneers. These unique farms, known as *Kibbutzim*, took collective responsibility so far that members didn't even own their own clothing or personal property. Everything was shared equally among the members.

Members of Kibbutz Amir heading to work, 1940

420

Bamidbar/Numbers 32
Matot

במדבר לב
מטות

30 But if they do not cross over with you as shock-troops, they shall receive holdings among you in the land of Canaan."

ל וְאִם־לֹא יַעַבְרוּ חֲלוּצִים אִתְּכֶם וְנֹאחֲזוּ בְתֹכְכֶם בְּאֶרֶץ כְּנָעַן:

31 The Gadites and the Reubenites said in reply, "Whatever *Hashem* has spoken concerning your servants, that we will do.

לא וַיַּעֲנוּ בְנֵי־גָד וּבְנֵי רְאוּבֵן לֵאמֹר אֵת אֲשֶׁר דִּבֶּר יְהוָה אֶל־עֲבָדֶיךָ כֵּן נַעֲשֶׂה:

32 We ourselves will cross over as shock-troops, at the instance of *Hashem*, into the land of Canaan; and we shall keep our hereditary holding across the *Yarden.*"

לב נַחְנוּ נַעֲבֹר חֲלוּצִים לִפְנֵי יְהוָה אֶרֶץ כְּנָעַן וְאִתָּנוּ אֲחֻזַּת נַחֲלָתֵנוּ מֵעֵבֶר לַיַּרְדֵּן:

33 So *Moshe* assigned to them – to the Gadites, the Reubenites, and the half-tribe of *Menashe* son of *Yosef* – the kingdom of Sihon king of the Amorites and the kingdom of King Og of Bashan, the land with its various cities and the territories of their surrounding towns.

לג וַיִּתֵּן לָהֶם מֹשֶׁה לִבְנֵי־גָד וְלִבְנֵי רְאוּבֵן וְלַחֲצִי שֵׁבֶט מְנַשֶּׁה בֶן־יוֹסֵף אֶת־מַמְלֶכֶת סִיחֹן מֶלֶךְ הָאֱמֹרִי וְאֶת־מַמְלֶכֶת עוֹג מֶלֶךְ הַבָּשָׁן הָאָרֶץ לְעָרֶיהָ בִּגְבֻלֹת עָרֵי הָאָרֶץ סָבִיב:

34 The Gadites rebuilt Dibon, Ataroth, Aroer,

לד וַיִּבְנוּ בְנֵי־גָד אֶת־דִּיבֹן וְאֶת־עֲטָרֹת וְאֵת עֲרֹעֵר:

35 Atroth-shophan, Jazer, Jogbehah,

לה וְאֶת־עַטְרֹת שׁוֹפָן וְאֶת־יַעְזֵר וְיָגְבְּהָה:

36 Beth-nimrah, and Beth-haran as fortified towns or as enclosures for flocks.

לו וְאֶת־בֵּית נִמְרָה וְאֶת־בֵּית הָרָן עָרֵי מִבְצָר וְגִדְרֹת צֹאן:

37 The Reubenites rebuilt Heshbon, Elealeh, Kiriathaim,

לז וּבְנֵי רְאוּבֵן בָּנוּ אֶת־חֶשְׁבּוֹן וְאֶת־אֶלְעָלֵא וְאֵת קִרְיָתָיִם:

38 Nebo, Baal-meon – some names being changed – and Sibmah; they gave [their own] names to towns that they rebuilt.

לח וְאֶת־נְבוֹ וְאֶת־בַּעַל מְעוֹן מוּסַבֹּת שֵׁם וְאֶת־שִׂבְמָה וַיִּקְרְאוּ בְשֵׁמֹת אֶת־שְׁמוֹת הֶעָרִים אֲשֶׁר בָּנוּ:

39 The descendants of Machir son of *Menashe* went to *Gilad* and captured it, dispossessing the Amorites who were there;

לט וַיֵּלְכוּ בְּנֵי מָכִיר בֶּן־מְנַשֶּׁה גִּלְעָדָה וַיִּלְכְּדֻהָ וַיּוֹרֶשׁ אֶת־הָאֱמֹרִי אֲשֶׁר־בָּהּ:

40 so *Moshe* gave *Gilad* to Machir son of *Menashe*, and he settled there.

מ וַיִּתֵּן מֹשֶׁה אֶת־הַגִּלְעָד לְמָכִיר בֶּן־מְנַשֶּׁה וַיֵּשֶׁב בָּהּ:

41 *Yair* son of *Menashe* went and captured their villages, which he renamed Havvoth-jair.

מא וְיָאִיר בֶּן־מְנַשֶּׁה הָלַךְ וַיִּלְכֹּד אֶת־חַוֹּתֵיהֶם וַיִּקְרָא אֶתְהֶן חַוֹּת יָאִיר:

42 And Nobah went and captured Kenath and its dependencies, renaming it Nobah after himself.

מב וְנֹבַח הָלַךְ וַיִּלְכֹּד אֶת־קְנָת וְאֶת־בְּנֹתֶיהָ וַיִּקְרָא לָה נֹבַח בִּשְׁמוֹ:

Bamidbar/Numbers 33
Masei

במדבר לג
מסעי

33 1 These were the marches of the Israelites who started out from the land of Egypt, troop by troop, in the charge of *Moshe* and *Aharon*.

א אֵ֜לֶּה מַסְעֵ֣י בְנֵֽי־יִשְׂרָאֵ֗ל אֲשֶׁ֥ר יָצְא֛וּ מֵאֶ֥רֶץ מִצְרַ֖יִם לְצִבְאֹתָ֑ם בְּיַד־מֹשֶׁ֖ה וְאַהֲרֹֽן׃

AY-leh mas-AY v'-nay yis-ra-AYL a-SHER ya-tz'-U may-E-retz mitz-RA-yim l'-tziv-o-TAM b'-yad mo-SHEH v'-a-ha-RON

2 *Moshe* recorded the starting points of their various marches as directed by *Hashem*. Their marches, by starting points, were as follows:

ב וַיִּכְתֹּ֨ב מֹשֶׁ֜ה אֶת־מוֹצָאֵיהֶ֛ם לְמַסְעֵיהֶ֖ם עַל־פִּ֣י יְהֹוָ֑ה וְאֵ֥לֶּה מַסְעֵיהֶ֖ם לְמוֹצָאֵיהֶֽם׃

3 They set out from Rameses in the first month, on the fifteenth day of the first month. It was on the morrow of the *Pesach* offering that the Israelites started out defiantly, in plain view of all the Egyptians.

ג וַיִּסְע֤וּ מֵרַעְמְסֵס֙ בַּחֹ֣דֶשׁ הָרִאשׁ֔וֹן בַּחֲמִשָּׁ֥ה עָשָׂ֛ר י֖וֹם לַחֹ֣דֶשׁ הָרִאשׁ֑וֹן מִמָּחֳרַ֣ת הַפֶּ֗סַח יָצְא֤וּ בְנֵֽי־יִשְׂרָאֵל֙ בְּיָ֣ד רָמָ֔ה לְעֵינֵ֖י כׇּל־מִצְרָֽיִם׃

4 The Egyptians meanwhile were burying those among them whom *Hashem* had struck down, every first-born – whereby *Hashem* executed judgment on their gods.

ד וּמִצְרַ֣יִם מְקַבְּרִ֗ים אֵת֩ אֲשֶׁ֨ר הִכָּ֧ה יְהֹוָ֛ה בָּהֶ֖ם כׇּל־בְּכ֑וֹר וּבֵאלֹ֣הֵיהֶ֔ם עָשָׂ֥ה יְהֹוָ֖ה שְׁפָטִֽים׃

5 The Israelites set out from Rameses and encamped at Succoth.

ה וַיִּסְע֥וּ בְנֵֽי־יִשְׂרָאֵ֖ל מֵרַעְמְסֵ֑ס וַֽיַּחֲנ֖וּ בְּסֻכֹּֽת׃

6 They set out from Succoth and encamped at Etham, which is on the edge of the wilderness.

ו וַיִּסְע֖וּ מִסֻּכֹּ֑ת וַיַּחֲנ֣וּ בְאֵתָ֔ם אֲשֶׁ֖ר בִּקְצֵ֥ה הַמִּדְבָּֽר׃

7 They set out from Etham and turned about toward Pi-hahiroth, which faces Baal-zephon, and they encamped before Migdol.

ז וַיִּסְעוּ֙ מֵֽאֵתָ֔ם וַיָּ֨שׇׁב֙ עַל־פִּ֣י הַחִירֹ֔ת אֲשֶׁ֥ר עַל־פְּנֵ֖י בַּ֣עַל צְפ֑וֹן וַֽיַּחֲנ֖וּ לִפְנֵ֥י מִגְדֹּֽל׃

8 They set out from Pene-hahiroth and passed through the sea into the wilderness; and they made a three-days' journey in the wilderness of Etham and encamped at Marah.

ח וַיִּסְעוּ֙ מִפְּנֵ֣י הַֽחִירֹ֔ת וַיַּֽעַבְר֥וּ בְתוֹךְ־הַיָּ֖ם הַמִּדְבָּ֑רָה וַיֵּ֨לְכ֜וּ דֶּ֣רֶךְ שְׁלֹ֤שֶׁת יָמִים֙ בְּמִדְבַּ֣ר אֵתָ֔ם וַֽיַּחֲנ֖וּ בְּמָרָֽה׃

9 They set out from Marah and came to Elim. There were twelve springs in Elim and seventy palm trees, so they encamped there.

ט וַיִּסְעוּ֙ מִמָּרָ֔ה וַיָּבֹ֖אוּ אֵילִ֑מָה וּ֠בְאֵילִ֠ם שְׁתֵּ֣ים עֶשְׂרֵ֞ה עֵינֹ֥ת מַ֛יִם וְשִׁבְעִ֥ים תְּמָרִ֖ים וַיַּחֲנוּ־שָֽׁם׃

10 They set out from Elim and encamped by the Sea of Reeds.

י וַיִּסְע֖וּ מֵאֵילִ֑ם וַֽיַּחֲנ֖וּ עַל־יַם־סֽוּף׃

33:1 These were the marches of the Israelites This chapter summarizes the journey that the People of Israel took to the Promised Land, starting with the flight from Egypt until they stood on the bank of the *Yarden* River, ready to enter the land. Overall, there were forty-two encampments in the desert: fourteen before the sin of the spies which took place in the second year, and eight in the fortieth year, leaving only twenty stops during the thirty-eight years in between. *Rashi* points out that this highlights *Hashem*'s compassion for His people. Although they were punished with forty years of wandering in the desert, He did not force them to continuously move around, as this would have been too physically grueling. Instead, they were allowed much opportunity to rest between their wanderings.

Bamidbar/Numbers 33
Masei

11 They set out from the Sea of Reeds and encamped in the wilderness of Sin.

יא וַיִּסְעוּ מִיַּם־סוּף וַיַּחֲנוּ בְּמִדְבַּר־סִין:

12 They set out from the wilderness of Sin and encamped at Dophkah.

יב וַיִּסְעוּ מִמִּדְבַּר־סִין וַיַּחֲנוּ בְּדָפְקָה:

13 They set out from Dophkah and encamped at Alush.

יג וַיִּסְעוּ מִדָּפְקָה וַיַּחֲנוּ בְּאָלוּשׁ:

14 They set out from Alush and encamped at Rephidim; it was there that the people had no water to drink.

יד וַיִּסְעוּ מֵאָלוּשׁ וַיַּחֲנוּ בִּרְפִידִם וְלֹא־הָיָה שָׁם מַיִם לָעָם לִשְׁתּוֹת:

15 They set out from Rephidim and encamped in the wilderness of Sinai.

טו וַיִּסְעוּ מֵרְפִידִם וַיַּחֲנוּ בְּמִדְבַּר סִינָי:

16 They set out from the wilderness of Sinai and encamped at Kibroth-hattaavah.

טז וַיִּסְעוּ מִמִּדְבַּר סִינָי וַיַּחֲנוּ בְּקִבְרֹת הַתַּאֲוָה:

17 They set out from Kibroth-hattaavah and encamped at Hazeroth.

יז וַיִּסְעוּ מִקִּבְרֹת הַתַּאֲוָה וַיַּחֲנוּ בַּחֲצֵרֹת:

18 They set out from Hazeroth and encamped at Rithmah.

יח וַיִּסְעוּ מֵחֲצֵרֹת וַיַּחֲנוּ בְּרִתְמָה:

19 They set out from Rithmah and encamped at Rimmon-perez.

יט וַיִּסְעוּ מֵרִתְמָה וַיַּחֲנוּ בְּרִמֹּן פָּרֶץ:

20 They set out from Rimmon-perez and encamped at Libnah.

כ וַיִּסְעוּ מֵרִמֹּן פָּרֶץ וַיַּחֲנוּ בְּלִבְנָה:

21 They set out from Libnah and encamped at Rissah.

כא וַיִּסְעוּ מִלִּבְנָה וַיַּחֲנוּ בְּרִסָּה:

22 They set out from Rissah and encamped at Kehelath.

כב וַיִּסְעוּ מֵרִסָּה וַיַּחֲנוּ בִּקְהֵלָתָה:

23 They set out from Kehelath and encamped at Mount Shepher.

כג וַיִּסְעוּ מִקְּהֵלָתָה וַיַּחֲנוּ בְּהַר־שָׁפֶר:

24 They set out from Mount Shepher and encamped at Haradah.

כד וַיִּסְעוּ מֵהַר־שָׁפֶר וַיַּחֲנוּ בַּחֲרָדָה:

25 They set out from Haradah and encamped at Makheloth.

כה וַיִּסְעוּ מֵחֲרָדָה וַיַּחֲנוּ בְּמַקְהֵלֹת:

26 They set out from Makheloth and encamped at Tahath.

כו וַיִּסְעוּ מִמַּקְהֵלֹת וַיַּחֲנוּ בְּתָחַת:

27 They set out from Tahath and encamped at Terah.

כז וַיִּסְעוּ מִתָּחַת וַיַּחֲנוּ בְּתָרַח:

28 They set out from Terah and encamped at Mithkah.

כח וַיִּסְעוּ מִתָּרַח וַיַּחֲנוּ בְּמִתְקָה:

29 They set out from Mithkah and encamped at Hashmonah.

כט וַיִּסְעוּ מִמִּתְקָה וַיַּחֲנוּ בְּחַשְׁמֹנָה:

30 They set out from Hashmonah and encamped at Moseroth.

ל וַיִּסְעוּ מֵחַשְׁמֹנָה וַיַּחֲנוּ בְּמֹסֵרוֹת:

31 They set out from Moseroth and encamped at Bene-jaakan.

לא וַיִּסְעוּ מִמֹּסֵרוֹת וַיַּחֲנוּ בִּבְנֵי יַעֲקָן:

Bamidbar/Numbers 33
Masei

32 They set out from Bene-jaakan and encamped at Hor-haggidgad.

לב וַיִּסְעוּ מִבְּנֵי יַעֲקָן וַיַּחֲנוּ בְּחֹר הַגִּדְגָּד:

33 They set out from Hor-haggidgad and encamped at Jotbath.

לג וַיִּסְעוּ מֵחֹר הַגִּדְגָּד וַיַּחֲנוּ בְּיָטְבָתָה:

34 They set out from Jotbath and encamped at Abronah.

לד וַיִּסְעוּ מִיָּטְבָתָה וַיַּחֲנוּ בְּעַבְרֹנָה:

35 They set out from Abronah and encamped at Ezion-geber.

לה וַיִּסְעוּ מֵעַבְרֹנָה וַיַּחֲנוּ בְּעֶצְיוֹן גָּבֶר:

36 They set out from Ezion-geber and encamped in the wilderness of Zin, that is, Kadesh.

לו וַיִּסְעוּ מֵעֶצְיוֹן גָּבֶר וַיַּחֲנוּ בְמִדְבַּר־צִן הִוא קָדֵשׁ:

37 They set out from Kadesh and encamped at Mount Hor, on the edge of the land of Edom.

לז וַיִּסְעוּ מִקָּדֵשׁ וַיַּחֲנוּ בְּהֹר הָהָר בִּקְצֵה אֶרֶץ אֱדוֹם:

38 *Aharon* the *Kohen* ascended Mount Hor at the command of *Hashem* and died there, in the fortieth year after the Israelites had left the land of Egypt, on the first day of the fifth month.

לח וַיַּעַל אַהֲרֹן הַכֹּהֵן אֶל־הֹר הָהָר עַל־פִּי יְהוָה וַיָּמָת שָׁם בִּשְׁנַת הָאַרְבָּעִים לְצֵאת בְּנֵי־יִשְׂרָאֵל מֵאֶרֶץ מִצְרַיִם בַּחֹדֶשׁ הַחֲמִישִׁי בְּאֶחָד לַחֹדֶשׁ:

39 *Aharon* was a hundred and twenty-three years old when he died on Mount Hor.

לט וְאַהֲרֹן בֶּן־שָׁלֹשׁ וְעֶשְׂרִים וּמְאַת שָׁנָה בְּמֹתוֹ בְּהֹר הָהָר:

40 And the Canaanite, king of Arad, who dwelt in the *Negev*, in the land of Canaan, learned of the coming of the Israelites.

מ וַיִּשְׁמַע הַכְּנַעֲנִי מֶלֶךְ עֲרָד וְהוּא־יֹשֵׁב בַּנֶּגֶב בְּאֶרֶץ כְּנָעַן בְּבֹא בְּנֵי יִשְׂרָאֵל:

41 They set out from Mount Hor and encamped at Zalmonah.

מא וַיִּסְעוּ מֵהֹר הָהָר וַיַּחֲנוּ בְּצַלְמֹנָה:

42 They set out from Zalmonah and encamped at Punon.

מב וַיִּסְעוּ מִצַּלְמֹנָה וַיַּחֲנוּ בְּפוּנֹן:

43 They set out from Punon and encamped at Oboth.

מג וַיִּסְעוּ מִפּוּנֹן וַיַּחֲנוּ בְּאֹבֹת:

44 They set out from Oboth and encamped at Iye-abarim, in the territory of Moab.

מד וַיִּסְעוּ מֵאֹבֹת וַיַּחֲנוּ בְּעִיֵּי הָעֲבָרִים בִּגְבוּל מוֹאָב:

45 They set out from Iyim and encamped at Dibon-gad.

מה וַיִּסְעוּ מֵעִיִּים וַיַּחֲנוּ בְּדִיבֹן גָּד:

46 They set out from Dibon-gad and encamped at Almon-diblathaim.

מו וַיִּסְעוּ מִדִּיבֹן גָּד וַיַּחֲנוּ בְּעַלְמֹן דִּבְלָתָיְמָה:

47 They set out from Almon-diblathaim and encamped in the hills of Abarim, before Nebo.

מז וַיִּסְעוּ מֵעַלְמֹן דִּבְלָתָיְמָה וַיַּחֲנוּ בְּהָרֵי הָעֲבָרִים לִפְנֵי נְבוֹ:

48 They set out from the hills of Abarim and encamped in the steppes of Moab, at the *Yarden* near *Yericho*;

מח וַיִּסְעוּ מֵהָרֵי הָעֲבָרִים וַיַּחֲנוּ בְּעַרְבֹת מוֹאָב עַל יַרְדֵּן יְרֵחוֹ:

49 they encamped by the *Yarden* from Beth-jeshimoth as far as Abel-shittim, in the steppes of Moab.

מט וַיַּחֲנוּ עַל־הַיַּרְדֵּן מִבֵּית הַיְשִׁמֹת עַד אָבֵל הַשִּׁטִּים בְּעַרְבֹת מוֹאָב:

Bamidbar/Numbers 34
Masei

במדבר לד
מסעי

50 In the steppes of Moab, at the *Yarden* near *Yericho*, *Hashem* spoke to *Moshe*, saying:

נ וַיְדַבֵּר יְהֹוָה אֶל־מֹשֶׁה בְּעַרְבֹת מוֹאָב עַל־יַרְדֵּן יְרֵחוֹ לֵאמֹר:

51 Speak to *B'nei Yisrael* and say to them: When you cross the *Yarden* into the land of Canaan,

נא דַּבֵּר אֶל־בְּנֵי יִשְׂרָאֵל וְאָמַרְתָּ אֲלֵהֶם כִּי אַתֶּם עֹבְרִים אֶת־הַיַּרְדֵּן אֶל־אֶרֶץ כְּנָעַן:

52 you shall dispossess all the inhabitants of the land; you shall destroy all their figured objects; you shall destroy all their molten images, and you shall demolish all their cult places.

נב וְהוֹרַשְׁתֶּם אֶת־כָּל־יֹשְׁבֵי הָאָרֶץ מִפְּנֵיכֶם וְאִבַּדְתֶּם אֵת כָּל־מַשְׂכִּיֹּתָם וְאֵת כָּל־צַלְמֵי מַסֵּכֹתָם תְּאַבֵּדוּ וְאֵת כָּל־בָּמֹתָם תַּשְׁמִידוּ:

53 And you shall take possession of the land and settle in it, for I have assigned the land to you to possess.

נג וְהוֹרַשְׁתֶּם אֶת־הָאָרֶץ וִישַׁבְתֶּם־בָּהּ כִּי לָכֶם נָתַתִּי אֶת־הָאָרֶץ לָרֶשֶׁת אֹתָהּ:

v'-ho-rash-TEM et ha-A-retz vee-shav-tem BAH KEE la-KHEM na-TA-tee et ha-A-retz la-RE-shet o-TAH

54 You shall apportion the land among yourselves by lot, clan by clan: with larger groups increase the share, with smaller groups reduce the share. Wherever the lot falls for anyone, that shall be his. You shall have your portions according to your ancestral tribes.

נד וְהִתְנַחַלְתֶּם אֶת־הָאָרֶץ בְּגוֹרָל לְמִשְׁפְּחֹתֵיכֶם לָרַב תַּרְבּוּ אֶת־נַחֲלָתוֹ וְלַמְעַט תַּמְעִיט אֶת־נַחֲלָתוֹ אֶל אֲשֶׁר־יֵצֵא לוֹ שָׁמָּה הַגּוֹרָל לוֹ יִהְיֶה לְמַטּוֹת אֲבֹתֵיכֶם תִּתְנֶחָלוּ:

v'-hit-na-khal-TEM et ha-A-retz b'-go-RAL l'-mish-p'-kho-tay-KHEM la-RAV tar-BU et na-kha-la-TO v'-lam-AT tam-EET et na-kha-la-TO EL a-sher yay-TZAY LO SHA-mah ha-go-RAL LO yih-YEH l'-ma-TOT a-vo-TAY-khem tit-ne-KHA-lu

55 But if you do not dispossess the inhabitants of the land, those whom you allow to remain shall be stings in your eyes and thorns in your sides, and they shall harass you in the land in which you live;

נה וְאִם־לֹא תוֹרִישׁוּ אֶת־יֹשְׁבֵי הָאָרֶץ מִפְּנֵיכֶם וְהָיָה אֲשֶׁר תּוֹתִירוּ מֵהֶם לְשִׂכִּים בְּעֵינֵיכֶם וְלִצְנִינִם בְּצִדֵּיכֶם וְצָרֲרוּ אֶתְכֶם עַל־הָאָרֶץ אֲשֶׁר אַתֶּם יֹשְׁבִים בָּהּ:

56 so that I will do to you what I planned to do to them.

נו וְהָיָה כַּאֲשֶׁר דִּמִּיתִי לַעֲשׂוֹת לָהֶם אֶעֱשֶׂה לָכֶם:

34

1 *Hashem* spoke to *Moshe*, saying:

לד א וַיְדַבֵּר יְהֹוָה אֶל־מֹשֶׁה לֵּאמֹר:

Holocaust survivors yearning for Israel

33:53 I have assigned the land to you to possess This verse is the source for the biblical command to settle and inhabit the Land of Israel. It emphasizes the importance of living in the land and, according to many, hints to a prohibition of leaving Israel without a compelling reason. As *Sefer Bamidbar* draws to a close, the people are on the verge of entering the Promised Land and fulfilling these words. They would remain in the land for hundreds of years, but sin and transgression eventually led to their exile. For centuries, the Jewish people yearned to return and resettle their land. While over the centuries, some individuals were able to fulfill these dreams, the founding of the State of Israel in 1948 made it possible for any Jew who wishes to return to come and settle in their homeland. Today, there are approximately six million Jews and eight million total residents in *Eretz Yisrael*. How fortunate we are to live in a time when the Land of Israel is so accessible to all.

Bamidbar/Numbers 34
Masei

במדבר לד
מסעי

2 Instruct *B'nei Yisrael* and say to them: When you enter the land of Canaan, this is the land that shall fall to you as your portion, the land of Canaan with its various boundaries:

ב צַו אֶת־בְּנֵי יִשְׂרָאֵל וְאָמַרְתָּ אֲלֵהֶם כִּי־אַתֶּם בָּאִים אֶל־הָאָרֶץ כְּנָעַן זֹאת הָאָרֶץ אֲשֶׁר תִּפֹּל לָכֶם בְּנַחֲלָה אֶרֶץ כְּנַעַן לִגְבֻלֹתֶיהָ:

TZAV et b'-NAY yis-ra-AYL v'-a-mar-TA a-lay-HEM kee a-TEM ba-EEM el ha-A-retz k'-NA-an ZOT ha-A-retz a-SHER ti-POL la-KHEM b'-na-kha-LAH E-retz k'-NA-an lig-vu-lo-TE-ha

3 Your southern sector shall extend from the wilderness of Zin alongside Edom. Your southern boundary shall start on the east from the tip of the Dead Sea.

ג וְהָיָה לָכֶם פְּאַת־נֶגֶב מִמִּדְבַּר־צִן עַל־יְדֵי אֱדוֹם וְהָיָה לָכֶם גְּבוּל נֶגֶב מִקְצֵה יָם־הַמֶּלַח קֵדְמָה:

4 Your boundary shall then turn to pass south of the ascent of Akrabbim and continue to Zin, and its limits shall be south of Kadesh-barnea, reaching Hazar-addar and continuing to Azmon.

ד וְנָסַב לָכֶם הַגְּבוּל מִנֶּגֶב לְמַעֲלֵה עַקְרַבִּים וְעָבַר צִנָה והיה [וְהָיוּ] תּוֹצְאֹתָיו מִנֶּגֶב לְקָדֵשׁ בַּרְנֵעַ וְיָצָא חֲצַר־אַדָּר וְעָבַר עַצְמֹנָה:

5 From Azmon the boundary shall turn toward the Wadi of Egypt and terminate at the Sea.

ה וְנָסַב הַגְּבוּל מֵעַצְמוֹן נַחְלָה מִצְרָיִם וְהָיוּ תוֹצְאֹתָיו הַיָּמָּה:

6 For the western boundary you shall have the coast of the Great Sea; that shall serve as your western boundary.

ו וּגְבוּל יָם וְהָיָה לָכֶם הַיָּם הַגָּדוֹל וּגְבוּל זֶה־יִהְיֶה לָכֶם גְּבוּל יָם:

7 This shall be your northern boundary: Draw a line from the Great Sea to Mount Hor;

ז וְזֶה־יִהְיֶה לָכֶם גְּבוּל צָפוֹן מִן־הַיָּם הַגָּדֹל תְּתָאוּ לָכֶם הֹר הָהָר:

8 from Mount Hor draw a line to Lebo-hamath, and let the boundary reach Zedad.

ח מֵהֹר הָהָר תְּתָאוּ לְבֹא חֲמָת וְהָיוּ תּוֹצְאֹת הַגְּבֻל צְדָדָה:

9 The boundary shall then run to Ziphron and terminate at Hazar-enan. That shall be your northern boundary.

ט וְיָצָא הַגְּבֻל זִפְרֹנָה וְהָיוּ תוֹצְאֹתָיו חֲצַר עֵינָן זֶה־יִהְיֶה לָכֶם גְּבוּל צָפוֹן:

10 For your eastern boundary you shall draw a line from Hazar-enan to Shepham.

י וְהִתְאַוִּיתֶם לָכֶם לִגְבוּל קֵדְמָה מֵחֲצַר עֵינָן שְׁפָמָה:

11 From Shepham the boundary shall descend to Riblah on the east side of Ain; from there the boundary shall continue downward and abut on the eastern slopes of the Sea of Chinnereth.

יא וְיָרַד הַגְּבֻל מִשְּׁפָם הָרִבְלָה מִקֶּדֶם לָעָיִן וְיָרַד הַגְּבוּל וּמָחָה עַל־כֶּתֶף יָם־כִּנֶּרֶת קֵדְמָה:

34:2 The land of Canaan with its various boundaries Chapter 34 describes the biblical boundaries of the Land of Israel. These boundaries are important, since a number of *mitzvot* (מצוות), 'commandments,' apply only within these borders. Many of the biblical laws that apply specifically inside *Eretz Yisrael* are agricultural ones that are intrinsically connected to the land. Many of them mandate providing for those who cannot provide for themselves, either because they are poor or because they do not have their own portion of land. How special is the Land of Israel: Caring for others is inherent in living there.

Bamidbar/Numbers 34
Masei

במדבר לד
מסעי

12 The boundary shall then descend along the *Yarden* and terminate at the Dead Sea. That shall be your land as defined by its boundaries on all sides.

יב וְיָרַד הַגְּבוּל הַיַּרְדֵּנָה וְהָיוּ תוֹצְאֹתָיו יָם הַמֶּלַח זֹאת תִּהְיֶה לָכֶם הָאָרֶץ לִגְבֻלֹתֶיהָ סָבִיב:

13 *Moshe* instructed the Israelites, saying: This is the land you are to receive by lot as your hereditary portion, which *Hashem* has commanded to be given to the nine and a half tribes.

יג וַיְצַו מֹשֶׁה אֶת־בְּנֵי יִשְׂרָאֵל לֵאמֹר זֹאת הָאָרֶץ אֲשֶׁר תִּתְנַחֲלוּ אֹתָהּ בְּגוֹרָל אֲשֶׁר צִוָּה יְהֹוָה לָתֵת לְתִשְׁעַת הַמַּטּוֹת וַחֲצִי הַמַּטֶּה:

14 For the Reubenite tribe by its ancestral houses, the Gadite tribe by its ancestral houses, and the half-tribe of *Menashe* have already received their portions:

יד כִּי לָקְחוּ מַטֵּה בְנֵי הָראוּבֵנִי לְבֵית אֲבֹתָם וּמַטֵּה בְנֵי־הַגָּדִי לְבֵית אֲבֹתָם וַחֲצִי מַטֵּה מְנַשֶּׁה לָקְחוּ נַחֲלָתָם:

15 those two and a half tribes have received their portions across the *Yarden*, opposite *Yericho*, on the east, the orient side.

טו שְׁנֵי הַמַּטּוֹת וַחֲצִי הַמַּטֶּה לָקְחוּ נַחֲלָתָם מֵעֵבֶר לְיַרְדֵּן יְרֵחוֹ קֵדְמָה מִזְרָחָה:

16 *Hashem* spoke to *Moshe*, saying:

טז וַיְדַבֵּר יְהֹוָה אֶל־מֹשֶׁה לֵּאמֹר:

17 These are the names of the men through whom the land shall be apportioned for you: *Elazar* the *Kohen* and *Yehoshua* son of *Nun*.

יז אֵלֶּה שְׁמוֹת הָאֲנָשִׁים אֲשֶׁר־יִנְחֲלוּ לָכֶם אֶת־הָאָרֶץ אֶלְעָזָר הַכֹּהֵן וִיהוֹשֻׁעַ בִּן־נוּן:

18 And you shall also take a chieftain from each tribe through whom the land shall be apportioned.

יח וְנָשִׂיא אֶחָד נָשִׂיא אֶחָד מִמַּטֶּה תִּקְחוּ לִנְחֹל אֶת־הָאָרֶץ:

19 These are the names of the men: from the tribe of *Yehuda*: *Kalev* son of Jephunneh.

יט וְאֵלֶּה שְׁמוֹת הָאֲנָשִׁים לְמַטֵּה יְהוּדָה כָּלֵב בֶּן־יְפֻנֶּה:

20 From the Simeonite tribe: *Shmuel* son of Ammihud.

כ וּלְמַטֵּה בְּנֵי שִׁמְעוֹן שְׁמוּאֵל בֶּן־עַמִּיהוּד:

21 From the tribe of *Binyamin*: *Elidad* son of Chislon.

כא לְמַטֵּה בִנְיָמִן אֱלִידָד בֶּן־כִּסְלוֹן:

22 From the Danite tribe: a chieftain, *Buki* son of Jogli.

כב וּלְמַטֵּה בְנֵי־דָן נָשִׂיא בֻּקִּי בֶּן־יָגְלִי:

23 For the descendants of *Yosef*: from the Manassite tribe: a chieftain, *Chaniel* son of Ephod;

כג לִבְנֵי יוֹסֵף לְמַטֵּה בְנֵי־מְנַשֶּׁה נָשִׂיא חַנִּיאֵל בֶּן־אֵפֹד:

24 and from the Ephraimite tribe: a chieftain, *Kemuel* son of Shiphtan.

כד וּלְמַטֵּה בְנֵי־אֶפְרַיִם נָשִׂיא קְמוּאֵל בֶּן־שִׁפְטָן:

25 From the Zebulunite tribe: a chieftain, *Elitzafan* son of Parnach.

כה וּלְמַטֵּה בְנֵי־זְבוּלֻן נָשִׂיא אֱלִיצָפָן בֶּן־פַּרְנָךְ:

26 From the Issacharite tribe: a chieftain, *Paltiel* son of Azzan.

כו וּלְמַטֵּה בְנֵי־יִשָּׂשכָר נָשִׂיא פַּלְטִיאֵל בֶּן־עַזָּן:

27 From the Asherite tribe: a chieftain, *Achihud* son of Shelomi.

כז וּלְמַטֵּה בְנֵי־אָשֵׁר נָשִׂיא אֲחִיהוּד בֶּן־שְׁלֹמִי:

28 From the Naphtalite tribe: a chieftain, *Pedahel* son of Ammihud.

כח וּלְמַטֵּה בְנֵי־נַפְתָּלִי נָשִׂיא פְּדַהְאֵל בֶּן־עַמִּיהוּד:

Bamidbar/Numbers 35
Masei

במדבר לה
מסעי

29 It was these whom *Hashem* designated to allot portions to the Israelites in the land of Canaan.

כט אֵ֚לֶּה אֲשֶׁ֣ר צִוָּ֣ה יְהֹוָ֔ה לְנַחֵ֥ל אֶת־בְּנֵֽי־יִשְׂרָאֵ֖ל בְּאֶ֥רֶץ כְּנָֽעַן׃

35

1 *Hashem* spoke to *Moshe* in the steppes of Moab at the *Yarden* near *Yericho*, saying:

א וַיְדַבֵּ֧ר יְהֹוָ֛ה אֶל־מֹשֶׁ֖ה בְּעַֽרְבֹ֣ת מוֹאָ֑ב עַל־יַרְדֵּ֥ן יְרֵח֖וֹ לֵאמֹֽר׃

2 Instruct *B'nei Yisrael* to assign, out of the holdings apportioned to them, towns for the *Leviim* to dwell in; you shall also assign to the *Leviim* pasture land around their towns.

ב צַו֮ אֶת־בְּנֵ֣י יִשְׂרָאֵל֒ וְנָתְנ֣וּ לַלְוִיִּ֗ם מִֽנַּחֲלַ֛ת אֲחֻזָּתָ֖ם עָרִ֣ים לָשָׁ֑בֶת וּמִגְרָ֗שׁ לֶֽעָרִים֙ סְבִיבֹ֣תֵיהֶ֔ם תִּתְּנ֖וּ לַלְוִיִּֽם׃

TZAV et b'-NAY yis-ra-AYL v'-na-t'-NU lal-vee-YIM mi-na-kha-LAT a-khu-za-TAM a-REEM la-SHA-vet u-mig-RASH le-a-REEM s'-vee-vo-tay-HEM ti-t'-NU lal-vee-YIM

3 The towns shall be theirs to dwell in, and the pasture shall be for the cattle they own and all their other beasts.

ג וְהָי֧וּ הֶֽעָרִ֛ים לָהֶ֖ם לָשָׁ֑בֶת וּמִגְרְשֵׁיהֶ֗ם יִהְי֤וּ לִבְהֶמְתָּם֙ וְלִרְכֻשָׁ֔ם וּלְכֹ֖ל חַיָּתָֽם׃

4 The town pasture that you are to assign to the *Leviim* shall extend a thousand *amot* outside the town wall all around.

ד וּמִגְרְשֵׁי֙ הֶֽעָרִ֔ים אֲשֶׁ֥ר תִּתְּנ֖וּ לַלְוִיִּ֑ם מִקִּ֤יר הָעִיר֙ וָח֔וּצָה אֶ֥לֶף אַמָּ֖ה סָבִֽיב׃

5 You shall measure off two thousand *amot* outside the town on the east side, two thousand on the south side, two thousand on the west side, and two thousand on the north side, with the town in the center. That shall be the pasture for their towns.

ה וּמַדֹּתֶ֞ם מִח֣וּץ לָעִ֗יר אֶת־פְּאַת־קֵ֣דְמָה אַלְפַּ֪יִם בָּאַמָּ֟ה וְאֶת־פְּאַת־נֶ֩גֶב֩ אַלְפַּ֨יִם בָּאַמָּ֜ה וְאֶת־פְּאַת־יָ֣ם ׀ אַלְפַּ֣יִם בָּאַמָּ֗ה וְאֵ֨ת פְּאַ֥ת צָפ֛וֹן אַלְפַּ֥יִם בָּאַמָּ֖ה וְהָעִ֣יר בַּתָּ֑וֶךְ זֶ֚ה יִהְיֶ֣ה לָהֶ֔ם מִגְרְשֵׁ֖י הֶעָרִֽים׃

6 The towns that you assign to the *Leviim* shall comprise the six cities of refuge that you are to designate for a manslayer to flee to, to which you shall add forty-two towns.

ו וְאֵ֣ת הֶֽעָרִ֗ים אֲשֶׁ֤ר תִּתְּנוּ֙ לַלְוִיִּ֔ם אֵ֚ת שֵׁשׁ־עָרֵ֣י הַמִּקְלָ֔ט אֲשֶׁ֣ר תִּתְּנ֔וּ לָנֻ֥ס שָׁ֖מָּה הָרֹצֵ֑חַ וַעֲלֵיהֶ֣ם תִּתְּנ֔וּ אַרְבָּעִ֥ים וּשְׁתַּ֖יִם עִֽיר׃

7 Thus the total of the towns that you assign to the *Leviim* shall be forty-eight towns, with their pasture.

ז כׇּל־הֶעָרִ֗ים אֲשֶׁ֤ר תִּתְּנוּ֙ לַלְוִיִּ֔ם אַרְבָּעִ֥ים וּשְׁמֹנֶ֖ה עִ֑יר אֶתְהֶ֖ן וְאֶת־מִגְרְשֵׁיהֶֽן׃

8 In assigning towns from the holdings of the Israelites, take more from the larger groups and less from the smaller, so that each assigns towns to the *Leviim* in proportion to the share it receives.

ח וְהֶֽעָרִ֗ים אֲשֶׁ֤ר תִּתְּנוּ֙ מֵאֲחֻזַּ֣ת בְּנֵי־יִשְׂרָאֵ֔ל מֵאֵ֤ת הָרַב֙ תַּרְבּ֔וּ וּמֵאֵ֥ת הַמְעַ֖ט תַּמְעִ֑יטוּ אִ֗ישׁ כְּפִ֤י נַחֲלָתוֹ֙ אֲשֶׁ֣ר יִנְחָ֔לוּ יִתֵּ֥ן מֵעָרָ֖יו לַלְוִיִּֽם׃

9 *Hashem* spoke further to *Moshe*:

ט וַיְדַבֵּ֥ר יְהֹוָ֖ה אֶל־מֹשֶׁ֥ה לֵּאמֹֽר׃

10 Speak to *B'nei Yisrael* and say to them: When you cross the *Yarden* into the land of Canaan,

י דַּבֵּר֙ אֶל־בְּנֵ֣י יִשְׂרָאֵ֔ל וְאָמַרְתָּ֖ אֲלֵהֶ֑ם כִּ֥י אַתֶּ֛ם עֹבְרִ֥ים אֶת־הַיַּרְדֵּ֖ן אַ֥רְצָה כְּנָֽעַן׃

35:2 Towns for the *Leviim* to dwell in The Children of Israel are commanded to set aside forty-eight cities throughout the length and breadth of the Land of Israel as residences for the *Leviim* (Levites). The people are required to live holy lives in the Promised Land, and it is the *Leviim* who are given the task of instructing them about how to live this way. By scattering the *Leviim* among the nation instead of giving them their own portion of land, *Hashem* ensures that everyone will have the opportunity to be exposed to the spiritual leaders of the people and to learn from them and by their example.

Bamidbar/Numbers 35
Masei

במדבר לה
מסעי

11 you shall provide yourselves with places to serve you as cities of refuge to which a manslayer who has killed a person unintentionally may flee.

יא וְהִקְרִיתֶם לָכֶם עָרִים עָרֵי מִקְלָט תִּהְיֶינָה לָכֶם וְנָס שָׁמָּה רֹצֵחַ מַכֵּה־נֶפֶשׁ בִּשְׁגָגָה:

12 The cities shall serve you as a refuge from the avenger, so that the manslayer may not die unless he has stood trial before the assembly.

יב וְהָיוּ לָכֶם הֶעָרִים לְמִקְלָט מִגֹּאֵל וְלֹא יָמוּת הָרֹצֵחַ עַד־עָמְדוֹ לִפְנֵי הָעֵדָה לַמִּשְׁפָּט:

13 The towns that you thus assign shall be six cities of refuge in all.

יג וְהֶעָרִים אֲשֶׁר תִּתֵּנוּ שֵׁשׁ־עָרֵי מִקְלָט תִּהְיֶינָה לָכֶם:

14 Three cities shall be designated beyond the *Yarden*, and the other three shall be designated in the land of Canaan: they shall serve as cities of refuge.

יד אֵת שְׁלֹשׁ הֶעָרִים תִּתְּנוּ מֵעֵבֶר לַיַּרְדֵּן וְאֵת שְׁלֹשׁ הֶעָרִים תִּתְּנוּ בְּאֶרֶץ כְּנָעַן עָרֵי מִקְלָט תִּהְיֶינָה:

15 These six cities shall serve the Israelites and the resident aliens among them for refuge, so that anyone who kills a person unintentionally may flee there.

טו לִבְנֵי יִשְׂרָאֵל וְלַגֵּר וְלַתּוֹשָׁב בְּתוֹכָם תִּהְיֶינָה שֵׁשׁ־הֶעָרִים הָאֵלֶּה לְמִקְלָט לָנוּס שָׁמָּה כָּל־מַכֵּה־נֶפֶשׁ בִּשְׁגָגָה:

16 Anyone, however, who strikes another with an iron object so that death results is a murderer; the murderer must be put to death.

טז וְאִם־בִּכְלִי בַרְזֶל הִכָּהוּ וַיָּמֹת רֹצֵחַ הוּא מוֹת יוּמַת הָרֹצֵחַ:

17 If he struck him with a stone tool that could cause death, and death resulted, he is a murderer; the murderer must be put to death.

יז וְאִם בְּאֶבֶן יָד אֲשֶׁר־יָמוּת בָּהּ הִכָּהוּ וַיָּמֹת רֹצֵחַ הוּא מוֹת יוּמַת הָרֹצֵחַ:

18 Similarly, if the object with which he struck him was a wooden tool that could cause death, and death resulted, he is a murderer; the murderer must be put to death.

יח אוֹ בִּכְלִי עֵץ־יָד אֲשֶׁר־יָמוּת בּוֹ הִכָּהוּ וַיָּמֹת רֹצֵחַ הוּא מוֹת יוּמַת הָרֹצֵחַ:

19 The blood-avenger himself shall put the murderer to death; it is he who shall put him to death upon encounter.

יט גֹּאֵל הַדָּם הוּא יָמִית אֶת־הָרֹצֵחַ בְּפִגְעוֹ־בוֹ הוּא יְמִיתֶנּוּ:

20 So, too, if he pushed him in hate or hurled something at him on purpose and death resulted,

כ וְאִם־בְּשִׂנְאָה יֶהְדֳּפֶנּוּ אוֹ־הִשְׁלִיךְ עָלָיו בִּצְדִיָּה וַיָּמֹת:

21 or if he struck him with his hand in enmity and death resulted, the assailant shall be put to death; he is a murderer. The blood-avenger shall put the murderer to death upon encounter.

כא אוֹ בְאֵיבָה הִכָּהוּ בְיָדוֹ וַיָּמֹת מוֹת־יוּמַת הַמַּכֶּה רֹצֵחַ הוּא גֹּאֵל הַדָּם יָמִית אֶת־הָרֹצֵחַ בְּפִגְעוֹ־בוֹ:

22 But if he pushed him without malice aforethought or hurled any object at him unintentionally,

כב וְאִם־בְּפֶתַע בְּלֹא־אֵיבָה הֲדָפוֹ אוֹ־הִשְׁלִיךְ עָלָיו כָּל־כְּלִי בְּלֹא צְדִיָּה:

23 or inadvertently dropped upon him any deadly object of stone, and death resulted – though he was not an enemy of his and did not seek his harm

כג אוֹ בְכָל־אֶבֶן אֲשֶׁר־יָמוּת בָּהּ בְּלֹא רְאוֹת וַיַּפֵּל עָלָיו וַיָּמֹת וְהוּא לֹא־אוֹיֵב לוֹ וְלֹא מְבַקֵּשׁ רָעָתוֹ:

24 in such cases the assembly shall decide between the slayer and the blood-avenger.

כד וְשָׁפְטוּ הָעֵדָה בֵּין הַמַּכֶּה וּבֵין גֹּאֵל הַדָּם עַל הַמִּשְׁפָּטִים הָאֵלֶּה:

Bamidbar/Numbers 36
Masei

25 The assembly shall protect the manslayer from the blood-avenger, and the assembly shall restore him to the city of refuge to which he fled, and there he shall remain until the death of the *Kohen Gadol* who was anointed with the sacred oil.

26 But if the manslayer ever goes outside the limits of the city of refuge to which he has fled,

27 and the blood-avenger comes upon him outside the limits of his city of refuge, and the blood-avenger kills the manslayer, there is no bloodguilt on his account.

28 For he must remain inside his city of refuge until the death of the *Kohen Gadol*; after the death of the *Kohen Gadol*, the manslayer may return to his land holding.

29 Such shall be your law of procedure throughout the ages in all your settlements.

30 If anyone kills a person, the manslayer may be executed only on the evidence of witnesses; the testimony of a single witness against a person shall not suffice for a sentence of death.

31 You may not accept a ransom for the life of a murderer who is guilty of a capital crime; he must be put to death.

32 Nor may you accept ransom in lieu of flight to a city of refuge, enabling one to return to live on his land before the death of the *Kohen*.

33 You shall not pollute the land in which you live; for blood pollutes the land, and the land can have no expiation for blood that is shed on it, except by the blood of him who shed it.

34 You shall not defile the land in which you live, in which I Myself abide, for I *Hashem* abide among *B'nei Yisrael*.

36 1 The family heads in the clan of the descendants of *Gilad* son of Machir son of *Menashe*, one of the Yosefite clans, came forward and appealed to *Moshe* and the chieftains, family heads of the Israelites.

2 They said, "*Hashem* commanded my lord to assign the land to the Israelites as shares by lot, and my lord was further commanded by *Hashem* to assign the share of our kinsman *Tzelofchad* to his daughters.

במדבר לו
מסעי

כה וְהִצִּילוּ הָעֵדָה אֶת־הָרֹצֵחַ מִיַּד גֹּאֵל הַדָּם וְהֵשִׁיבוּ אֹתוֹ הָעֵדָה אֶל־עִיר מִקְלָטוֹ אֲשֶׁר־נָס שָׁמָּה וְיָשַׁב בָּהּ עַד־מוֹת הַכֹּהֵן הַגָּדֹל אֲשֶׁר־מָשַׁח אֹתוֹ בְּשֶׁמֶן הַקֹּדֶשׁ:

כו וְאִם־יָצֹא יֵצֵא הָרֹצֵחַ אֶת־גְּבוּל עִיר מִקְלָטוֹ אֲשֶׁר יָנוּס שָׁמָּה:

כז וּמָצָא אֹתוֹ גֹּאֵל הַדָּם מִחוּץ לִגְבוּל עִיר מִקְלָטוֹ וְרָצַח גֹּאֵל הַדָּם אֶת־הָרֹצֵחַ אֵין לוֹ דָּם:

כח כִּי בְעִיר מִקְלָטוֹ יֵשֵׁב עַד־מוֹת הַכֹּהֵן הַגָּדֹל וְאַחֲרֵי מוֹת הַכֹּהֵן הַגָּדֹל יָשׁוּב הָרֹצֵחַ אֶל־אֶרֶץ אֲחֻזָּתוֹ:

כט וְהָיוּ אֵלֶּה לָכֶם לְחֻקַּת מִשְׁפָּט לְדֹרֹתֵיכֶם בְּכֹל מוֹשְׁבֹתֵיכֶם:

ל כָּל־מַכֵּה־נֶפֶשׁ לְפִי עֵדִים יִרְצַח אֶת־הָרֹצֵחַ וְעֵד אֶחָד לֹא־יַעֲנֶה בְנֶפֶשׁ לָמוּת:

לא וְלֹא־תִקְחוּ כֹפֶר לְנֶפֶשׁ רֹצֵחַ אֲשֶׁר־הוּא רָשָׁע לָמוּת כִּי־מוֹת יוּמָת:

לב וְלֹא־תִקְחוּ כֹפֶר לָנוּס אֶל־עִיר מִקְלָטוֹ לָשׁוּב לָשֶׁבֶת בָּאָרֶץ עַד־מוֹת הַכֹּהֵן:

לג וְלֹא־תַחֲנִיפוּ אֶת־הָאָרֶץ אֲשֶׁר אַתֶּם בָּהּ כִּי הַדָּם הוּא יַחֲנִיף אֶת־הָאָרֶץ וְלָאָרֶץ לֹא־יְכֻפַּר לַדָּם אֲשֶׁר שֻׁפַּךְ־בָּהּ כִּי־אִם בְּדַם שֹׁפְכוֹ:

לד וְלֹא תְטַמֵּא אֶת־הָאָרֶץ אֲשֶׁר אַתֶּם יֹשְׁבִים בָּהּ אֲשֶׁר אֲנִי שֹׁכֵן בְּתוֹכָהּ כִּי אֲנִי יְהֹוָה שֹׁכֵן בְּתוֹךְ בְּנֵי יִשְׂרָאֵל:

לו א וַיִּקְרְבוּ רָאשֵׁי הָאָבוֹת לְמִשְׁפַּחַת בְּנֵי־גִלְעָד בֶּן־מָכִיר בֶּן־מְנַשֶּׁה מִמִּשְׁפְּחֹת בְּנֵי יוֹסֵף וַיְדַבְּרוּ לִפְנֵי מֹשֶׁה וְלִפְנֵי הַנְּשִׂאִים רָאשֵׁי אָבוֹת לִבְנֵי יִשְׂרָאֵל:

ב וַיֹּאמְרוּ אֶת־אֲדֹנִי צִוָּה יְהֹוָה לָתֵת אֶת־הָאָרֶץ בְּנַחֲלָה בְּגוֹרָל לִבְנֵי יִשְׂרָאֵל וַאדֹנִי צֻוָּה בַיהֹוָה לָתֵת אֶת־נַחֲלַת צְלָפְחָד אָחִינוּ לִבְנֹתָיו:

430

Bamidbar/Numbers 36
Masei

במדבר לו
מסעי

3 Now, if they marry persons from another Israelite tribe, their share will be cut off from our ancestral portion and be added to the portion of the tribe into which they marry; thus our allotted portion will be diminished.

ג וְהָיוּ לְאֶחָד מִבְּנֵי שִׁבְטֵי בְנֵי־יִשְׂרָאֵל לְנָשִׁים וְנִגְרְעָה נַחֲלָתָן מִנַּחֲלַת אֲבֹתֵינוּ וְנוֹסַף עַל נַחֲלַת הַמַּטֶּה אֲשֶׁר תִּהְיֶינָה לָהֶם וּמִגֹּרַל נַחֲלָתֵנוּ יִגָּרֵעַ:

v'-ha-YU l'-e-KHAD mi-b'-NAY shiv-TAY v'-nay yis-ra-AYL l'-na-SHEEM v'-nig-r'-AH na-kha-la-TAN mi-na-kha-LAT a-vo-TAY-nu v'-no-SAF AL na-kha-LAT ha-ma-TEH a-SHER tih-YE-nah la-HEM u-mi-go-RAL na-kha-la-TAY-nu yi-ga-RAY-a

4 And even when the Israelites observe the jubilee, their share will be added to that of the tribe into which they marry, and their share will be cut off from the ancestral portion of our tribe."

ד וְאִם־יִהְיֶה הַיֹּבֵל לִבְנֵי יִשְׂרָאֵל וְנוֹסְפָה נַחֲלָתָן עַל נַחֲלַת הַמַּטֶּה אֲשֶׁר תִּהְיֶינָה לָהֶם וּמִנַּחֲלַת מַטֵּה אֲבֹתֵינוּ יִגָּרַע נַחֲלָתָן:

5 So *Moshe*, at *Hashem*'s bidding, instructed the Israelites, saying: "The plea of the Josephite tribe is just.

ה וַיְצַו מֹשֶׁה אֶת־בְּנֵי יִשְׂרָאֵל עַל־פִּי יְהוָה לֵאמֹר כֵּן מַטֵּה בְנֵי־יוֹסֵף דֹּבְרִים:

6 This is what *Hashem* has commanded concerning the daughters of *Tzelofchad*: They may marry anyone they wish, provided they marry into a clan of their father's tribe.

ו זֶה הַדָּבָר אֲשֶׁר־צִוָּה יְהוָה לִבְנוֹת צְלָפְחָד לֵאמֹר לַטּוֹב בְּעֵינֵיהֶם תִּהְיֶינָה לְנָשִׁים אַךְ לְמִשְׁפַּחַת מַטֵּה אֲבִיהֶם תִּהְיֶינָה לְנָשִׁים:

7 No inheritance of the Israelites may pass over from one tribe to another, but the Israelites must remain bound each to the ancestral portion of his tribe.

ז וְלֹא־תִסֹּב נַחֲלָה לִבְנֵי יִשְׂרָאֵל מִמַּטֶּה אֶל־מַטֶּה כִּי אִישׁ בְּנַחֲלַת מַטֵּה אֲבֹתָיו יִדְבְּקוּ בְּנֵי יִשְׂרָאֵל:

8 Every daughter among the Israelite tribes who inherits a share must marry someone from a clan of her father's tribe, in order that every Israelite may keep his ancestral share.

ח וְכָל־בַּת יֹרֶשֶׁת נַחֲלָה מִמַּטּוֹת בְּנֵי יִשְׂרָאֵל לְאֶחָד מִמִּשְׁפַּחַת מַטֵּה אָבִיהָ תִּהְיֶה לְאִשָּׁה לְמַעַן יִירְשׁוּ בְּנֵי יִשְׂרָאֵל אִישׁ נַחֲלַת אֲבֹתָיו:

9 Thus no inheritance shall pass over from one tribe to another, but the Israelite tribes shall remain bound each to its portion."

ט וְלֹא־תִסֹּב נַחֲלָה לְמַטֶּה אַחֵר כִּי־אִישׁ בְּנַחֲלָתוֹ יִדְבְּקוּ מַטּוֹת בְּנֵי יִשְׂרָאֵל:

36:3 Their share will be cut off from our ancestral portion Motivated by a deep sense of passion for the Land of Israel, *Tzelofchad*'s daughters pleaded with *Moshe* for the right to inherit their father's land in the absence of sons, and their request was granted (see Chapter 27). Now, the elders of the tribe of *Menashe*, who share the same love of the land, approach *Moshe* concerned that this ruling could adversely affect their tribe. The Land of Israel will soon be divided among the tribes through lots, for eternal inheritance. If *Tzelofchad*'s daughters would marry men from other tribes, their father's land that they inherit, which will ultimately be inherited by their husbands and sons, will be permanently transferred to other tribes. The prospect of their tribe losing title to a piece of *Eretz Yisrael* is distressing to the tribal leaders, and they approach *Moshe* with their dilemma. To resolve the issue, the daughters of *Tzelofchad* are instructed to marry men from their own tribe, thus guaranteeing that the tribe of *Menashe* will maintain every inch of the precious land in its possession. The Book of *Bamidbar* tells the story of many times that the Children of Israel provoked *Hashem* in the desert. The most unsettling of these was the sin of the spies, the rejection of the Promised Land that led to forty years of wandering in the desert and the death of an entire generation. However, in contrast, the book concludes with an inspiring example of deep love for *Eretz Yisrael*.

Bamidbar/Numbers 36
Masei

במדבר לו
מסעי

10 The daughters of *Tzelofchad* did as *Hashem* had commanded *Moshe*:

י כַּאֲשֶׁר צִוָּה יְהֹוָה אֶת־מֹשֶׁה כֵּן עָשׂוּ בְּנוֹת צְלָפְחָד׃

11 *Machla*, *Tirtza*, *Chagla*, *Milka*, and *Noa*, *Tzelofchad's* daughters, were married to sons of their uncles,

יא וַתִּהְיֶינָה מַחְלָה תִרְצָה וְחָגְלָה וּמִלְכָּה וְנֹעָה בְּנוֹת צְלָפְחָד לִבְנֵי דֹדֵיהֶן לְנָשִׁים׃

12 marrying into clans of descendants of *Menashe* son of *Yosef*; and so their share remained in the tribe of their father's clan.

יב מִמִּשְׁפְּחֹת בְּנֵי־מְנַשֶּׁה בֶן־יוֹסֵף הָיוּ לְנָשִׁים וַתְּהִי נַחֲלָתָן עַל־מַטֵּה מִשְׁפַּחַת אֲבִיהֶן׃

13 These are the commandments and regulations that *Hashem* enjoined upon the Israelites, through *Moshe*, on the steppes of Moab, at the *Yarden* near *Yericho*.

יג אֵלֶּה הַמִּצְוֺת וְהַמִּשְׁפָּטִים אֲשֶׁר צִוָּה יְהֹוָה בְּיַד־מֹשֶׁה אֶל־בְּנֵי יִשְׂרָאֵל בְּעַרְבֹת מוֹאָב עַל יַרְדֵּן יְרֵחוֹ׃

Sefer Devarim
The Book of Deuteronomy

Introduction and commentary by Shira Schechter

While Jews believe that all twenty-four books comprising the *Tanakh* (Hebrew Bible) are the word of *Hashem*, there is a distinction between the first five, the books of *Moshe*, and the others. Known in Hebrew as *Chumash* (חומש), meaning 'five', *Sefer Bereishit* (Genesis), *Sefer Shemot* (Exodus), *Sefer Vayikra* (Leviticus), *Sefer Bamidbar* (Numbers) and *Sefer Devarim* (Deuteronomy) are on a higher level of holiness than the rest of the Bible, since *Hashem* communicated each word of these books directly to *Moshe*. In contrast, the nineteen books of the *Neviim* (Prophets) and *Ketuvim* (Writings) are based on God's prophetic communications to His individual messengers, but are written in their own language. This underscores the idea that *Moshe*'s prophecy was unparalleled, based on his particularly close relationship with the Almighty, as the Bible states explicitly, "Never again did there arise in *Yisrael* a prophet like *Moshe* – whom *Hashem* singled out, face to face" (Deuteronomy 34:10). As such, the Book of Deuteronomy, or *Sefer Devarim*, marks the conclusion of the Torah portion of the *Tanakh*, and with it the end of God's direct word to *Moshe*. It must therefore be mined carefully for its precious lessons.

Written in the last weeks of *Moshe*'s life, *Sefer Devarim* is a summary of his final lessons to the people in the wilderness, before they enter the Land of Israel. Hundreds of commandments are taught or reviewed, some with minor differences that teach important lessons. The quantity and diversity of the various commandments does not distract from one primary theme that is repeated multiple times throughout *Sefer Devarim*: The primacy of *Eretz Yisrael*. In one of the most beautiful and incisive descriptions, *Moshe* describes the Land of Israel as being unlike any other place on earth:

> For the land that you are about to enter and possess is not like the land of Egypt from which you have come. There, the grain you sowed had to be watered by your own labors, like a vegetable garden; but the land you are about to cross into and possess, a land of hills and valleys,

soaks up its water from the rains of heaven. It is a land which *Hashem* your God looks after, on which *Hashem* your God always keeps His eye, from year's beginning to year's end. (Deuteronomy 11:10–12)

The Israel Bible elucidates the uniqueness of the land featured repeatedly in the Book of *Devarim*, a land where God's presence is fully manifest, and where our relationship with Him is more profound and more complete. May our study of *Sefer Devarim* contribute to our own deeper love for *Hashem* and the Land of Israel.

Map of the Cities of Refuge

This map features the cities of refuge set aside by *Moshe* and *Yehoshua* as described in *Sefer Devarim* (4:41–43) and *Sefer Yehoshua* (20:7). A city of refuge is a place where someone who murdered unintentionally can seek asylum. God commanded the Israelites to set aside six Levitical cities in the Land of Israel to be cities of refuge. Three of those cities were to be on the west side of the Jordan River, and three on the east side (Numbers 35:9–15).

The three cities of refuge on the east of the Jordan River, set aside by *Moshe*, were:

1. **Bezer** in the land of *Reuven*
2. **Ramoth-Gilead** in the land of *Gad*
3. **Golan** in the land of *Menashe*

The three cities of refuge on the west side of the Jordan River, set aside by *Yehoshua*, were:

4. **Kedesh** in the land of *Naftali*
5. **Shechem** in the land of *Efraim*
6. **Kiryat Arba/Chevron** in the land of *Yehuda*

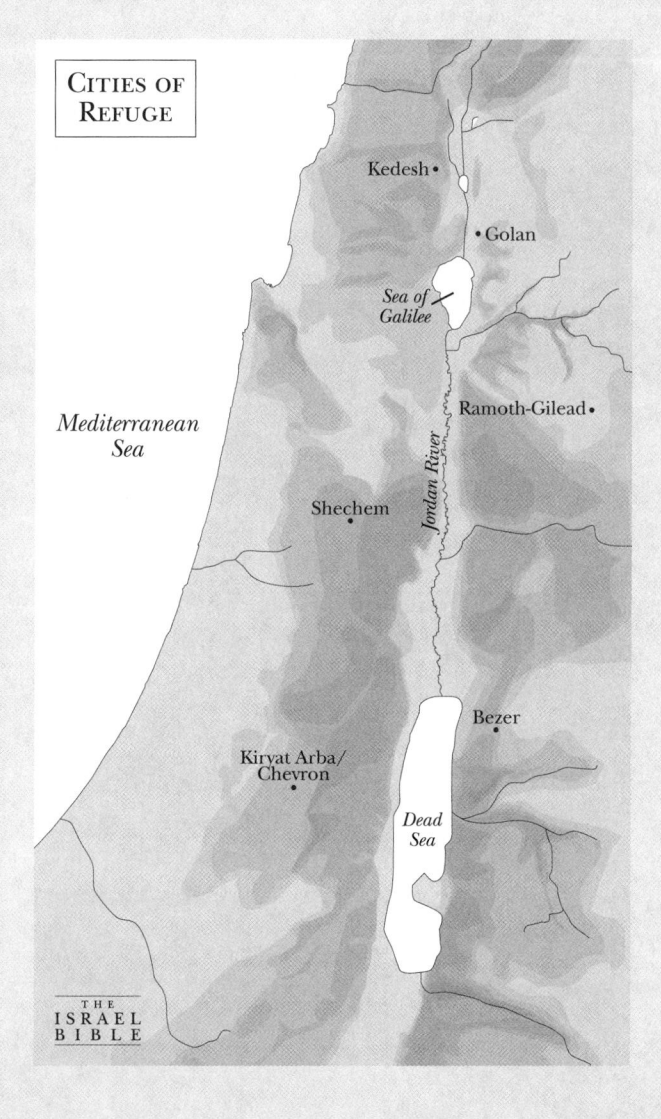

Devarim/Deuteronomy 1
Devarim

דברים א
דברים

1 **1** These are the words that *Moshe* addressed to all *Yisrael* on the other side of the *Yarden*. Through the wilderness, in the Arabah near Suph, between Paran and Tophel, Laban, Hazeroth, and Di-zahab,

א אֵ֣לֶּה הַדְּבָרִ֗ים אֲשֶׁ֨ר דִּבֶּ֤ר מֹשֶׁה֙ אֶל־כׇּל־יִשְׂרָאֵ֔ל בְּעֵ֖בֶר הַיַּרְדֵּ֑ן בַּמִּדְבָּ֡ר בָּֽעֲרָבָה֩ מ֨וֹל ס֜וּף בֵּֽין־פָּארָ֧ן וּבֵֽין־תֹּ֛פֶל וְלָבָ֥ן וַחֲצֵרֹ֖ת וְדִ֥י זָהָֽב׃

AY-leh ha-d'-va-REEM a-SHER di-BER mo-SHEH el kol yis-ra-AYL b'-AY-ver ha-yar-DAYN ba-mid-BAR ba-a-ra-VAH MOL SUF bayn pa-RAN u-vayn TO-fel v'-la-VAN va-kha-tzay-ROT v'-DEE za-HAV

2 it is eleven days from Horeb to Kadesh-barnea by the Mount Seir route.

ב אַחַ֨ד עָשָׂ֥ר יוֹם֙ מֵֽחֹרֵ֔ב דֶּ֖רֶךְ הַר־שֵׂעִ֑יר עַ֖ד קָדֵ֥שׁ בַּרְנֵֽעַ׃

3 It was in the fortieth year, on the first day of the eleventh month, that *Moshe* addressed the Israelites in accordance with the instructions that *Hashem* had given him for them,

ג וַיְהִי֙ בְּאַרְבָּעִ֣ים שָׁנָ֔ה בְּעַשְׁתֵּֽי־עָשָׂ֥ר חֹ֖דֶשׁ בְּאֶחָ֣ד לַחֹ֑דֶשׁ דִּבֶּ֤ר מֹשֶׁה֙ אֶל־בְּנֵ֣י יִשְׂרָאֵ֔ל כְּ֠כֹ֠ל אֲשֶׁ֨ר צִוָּ֧ה יְהֹוָ֛ה אֹת֖וֹ אֲלֵהֶֽם׃

4 after he had defeated Sihon king of the Amorites, who dwelt in Heshbon, and King Og of Bashan, who dwelt at Ashtaroth [and]

ד אַחֲרֵ֣י הַכֹּת֗וֹ אֵ֚ת סִיחֹן֙ מֶ֣לֶךְ הָֽאֱמֹרִ֔י אֲשֶׁ֥ר יוֹשֵׁ֖ב בְּחֶשְׁבּ֑וֹן וְאֵ֗ת ע֚וֹג מֶ֣לֶךְ הַבָּשָׁ֔ן אֲשֶׁר־יוֹשֵׁ֥ב בְּעַשְׁתָּרֹ֖ת בְּאֶדְרֶֽעִי׃

5 On the other side of the *Yarden*, in the land of Moab, *Moshe* undertook to expound this Teaching. He said:

ה בְּעֵ֥בֶר הַיַּרְדֵּ֖ן בְּאֶ֣רֶץ מוֹאָ֑ב הוֹאִ֣יל מֹשֶׁ֔ה בֵּאֵ֛ר אֶת־הַתּוֹרָ֥ה הַזֹּ֖את לֵאמֹֽר׃

6 *Hashem* our God spoke to us at Horeb, saying: You have stayed long enough at this mountain.

ו יְהֹוָ֧ה אֱלֹהֵ֛ינוּ דִּבֶּ֥ר אֵלֵ֖ינוּ בְּחֹרֵ֣ב לֵאמֹ֑ר רַב־לָכֶ֥ם שֶׁ֖בֶת בָּהָ֥ר הַזֶּֽה׃

7 Start out and make your way to the hill country of the Amorites and to all their neighbors in the Arabah, the hill country, the Shephelah, the *Negev*, the seacoast, the land of the Canaanites, and the Lebanon, as far as the Great River, the river Euphrates.

ז פְּנ֣וּ ׀ וּסְע֣וּ לָכֶ֗ם וּבֹ֨אוּ הַ֥ר הָֽאֱמֹרִי֮ וְאֶל־כׇּל־שְׁכֵנָיו֒ בָּעֲרָבָ֥ה בָהָ֛ר וּבַשְּׁפֵלָ֥ה וּבַנֶּ֖גֶב וּבְח֣וֹף הַיָּ֑ם אֶ֤רֶץ הַֽכְּנַעֲנִי֙ וְהַלְּבָנ֔וֹן עַד־הַנָּהָ֥ר הַגָּדֹ֖ל נְהַר־פְּרָֽת׃

8 See, I place the land at your disposal. Go, take possession of the land that *Hashem* swore to your fathers, *Avraham*, *Yitzchak*, and *Yaakov*, to assign to them and to their heirs after them.

ח רְאֵ֛ה נָתַ֥תִּי לִפְנֵיכֶ֖ם אֶת־הָאָ֑רֶץ בֹּ֚אוּ וּרְשׁ֣וּ אֶת־הָאָ֔רֶץ אֲשֶׁ֣ר נִשְׁבַּ֣ע יְ֠הֹוָ֠ה לַאֲבֹ֨תֵיכֶ֜ם לְאַבְרָהָ֨ם לְיִצְחָ֤ק וּֽלְיַעֲקֹב֙ לָתֵ֣ת לָהֶ֔ם וּלְזַרְעָ֖ם אַחֲרֵיהֶֽם׃

r'-AY na-TA-tee lif-nay-KHEM et ha-A-retz BO-u ur-SHU et ha-A-retz a-SHER nish-BA ah-do-NAI la-a-VO-tay-KHEM l'-av-ra-HAM l'-yitz-KHAK ul-ya-a-KOV la-TAYT la-HEM ul-zar-AM a-kha-ray-HEM

1:1 These are the words that *Moshe* addressed to all *Yisrael* *Sefer Devarim* contains *Moshe's* farewell speeches to the People of Israel. They are camped on the banks of the Jordan River, finally ready to cross over and inherit the land that *Hashem* promised to their forefathers. Since *Moshe* is not allowed to enter the land, he takes this opportunity to impart to them the thoughts, laws and ideas that he wants them to consider as they prepare for their entry into the land. *Moshe* makes sure to speak to the entire nation, as the Land of Israel belongs to everyone. Young and old, rich and poor – everyone can find his or her place in this special land.

Devarim/Deuteronomy 1
Devarim

דברים א
דברים

9 Thereupon I said to you, "I cannot bear the burden of you by myself.

ט וָאֹמַ֣ר אֲלֵכֶ֔ם בָּעֵ֥ת הַהִ֖וא לֵאמֹ֑ר לֹא־אוּכַ֥ל לְבַדִּ֖י שְׂאֵ֥ת אֶתְכֶֽם׃

10 *Hashem* your God has multiplied you until you are today as numerous as the stars in the sky.

י יְהֹוָ֥ה אֱלֹהֵיכֶ֖ם הִרְבָּ֣ה אֶתְכֶ֑ם וְהִנְּכֶ֣ם הַיּ֔וֹם כְּכוֹכְבֵ֥י הַשָּׁמַ֖יִם לָרֹֽב׃

11 May *Hashem*, the God of your fathers, increase your numbers a thousandfold, and bless you as He promised you.

יא יְהֹוָ֞ה אֱלֹהֵ֣י אֲבֽוֹתֵכֶ֗ם יֹסֵ֧ף עֲלֵיכֶ֛ם כָּכֶ֖ם אֶ֣לֶף פְּעָמִ֑ים וִיבָרֵ֣ךְ אֶתְכֶ֔ם כַּאֲשֶׁ֖ר דִּבֶּ֥ר לָכֶֽם׃

12 How can I bear unaided the trouble of you, and the burden, and the bickering!

יב אֵיכָ֥ה אֶשָּׂ֖א לְבַדִּ֑י טָרְחֲכֶ֥ם וּמַֽשַּׂאֲכֶ֖ם וְרִֽיבְכֶֽם׃

13 Pick from each of your tribes men who are wise, discerning, and experienced, and I will appoint them as your heads."

יג הָב֣וּ לָ֠כֶ֠ם אֲנָשִׁ֨ים חֲכָמִ֧ים וּנְבֹנִ֛ים וִידֻעִ֖ים לְשִׁבְטֵיכֶ֑ם וַאֲשִׂימֵ֖ם בְּרָאשֵׁיכֶֽם׃

14 You answered me and said, "What you propose to do is good."

יד וַֽתַּעֲנ֖וּ אֹתִ֑י וַתֹּ֣אמְר֔וּ טֽוֹב־הַדָּבָ֥ר אֲשֶׁר־דִּבַּ֖רְתָּ לַעֲשֽׂוֹת׃

15 So I took your tribal leaders, wise and experienced men, and appointed them heads over you: chiefs of thousands, chiefs of hundreds, chiefs of fifties, and chiefs of tens, and officials for your tribes.

טו וָאֶקַּ֞ח אֶת־רָאשֵׁ֣י שִׁבְטֵיכֶ֗ם אֲנָשִׁ֤ים חֲכָמִים֙ וִֽידֻעִ֔ים וָאֶתֵּ֥ן אֹתָ֖ם רָאשִׁ֣ים עֲלֵיכֶ֑ם שָׂרֵ֨י אֲלָפִ֜ים וְשָׂרֵ֣י מֵא֗וֹת וְשָׂרֵ֤י חֲמִשִּׁים֙ וְשָׂרֵ֣י עֲשָׂרֹ֔ת וְשֹׁטְרִ֖ים לְשִׁבְטֵיכֶֽם׃

16 I charged your magistrates at that time as follows, "Hear out your fellow men, and decide justly between any man and a fellow Israelite or a stranger.

טז וָאֲצַוֶּה֙ אֶת־שֹׁ֣פְטֵיכֶ֔ם בָּעֵ֥ת הַהִ֖וא לֵאמֹ֑ר שָׁמֹ֤עַ בֵּין־אֲחֵיכֶם֙ וּשְׁפַטְתֶּ֣ם צֶ֔דֶק בֵּֽין־אִ֥ישׁ וּבֵין־אָחִ֖יו וּבֵ֥ין גֵּרֽוֹ׃

17 You shall not be partial in judgment: hear out low and high alike. Fear no man, for judgment is *Hashem*'s. And any matter that is too difficult for you, you shall bring to me and I will hear it."

יז לֹֽא־תַכִּ֨ירוּ פָנִ֜ים בַּמִּשְׁפָּ֗ט כַּקָּטֹ֤ן כַּגָּדֹל֙ תִּשְׁמָע֔וּן לֹ֤א תָג֙וּרוּ֙ מִפְּנֵי־אִ֔ישׁ כִּ֥י הַמִּשְׁפָּ֖ט לֵאלֹהִ֣ים ה֑וּא וְהַדָּבָר֙ אֲשֶׁ֣ר יִקְשֶׁ֣ה מִכֶּ֔ם תַּקְרִב֥וּן אֵלַ֖י וּשְׁמַעְתִּֽיו׃

18 Thus I instructed you, at that time, about the various things that you should do.

יח וָאֲצַוֶּ֥ה אֶתְכֶ֖ם בָּעֵ֣ת הַהִ֑וא אֵ֥ת כׇּל־הַדְּבָרִ֖ים אֲשֶׁ֥ר תַּעֲשֽׂוּן׃

19 We set out from Horeb and traveled the great and terrible wilderness that you saw, along the road to the hill country of the Amorites, as *Hashem* our God had commanded us. When we reached Kadesh-barnea,

יט וַנִּסַּ֣ע מֵחֹרֵ֗ב וַנֵּ֡לֶךְ אֵ֣ת כׇּל־הַמִּדְבָּ֣ר הַגָּד֣וֹל וְהַנּוֹרָא֩ הַה֨וּא אֲשֶׁ֤ר רְאִיתֶם֙ דֶּ֚רֶךְ הַ֣ר הָֽאֱמֹרִ֔י כַּאֲשֶׁ֥ר צִוָּ֛ה יְהֹוָ֥ה אֱלֹהֵ֖ינוּ אֹתָ֑נוּ וַנָּבֹ֕א עַ֖ד קָדֵ֥שׁ בַּרְנֵֽעַ׃

20 I said to you, "You have come to the hill country of the Amorites which *Hashem* our God is giving to us.

כ וָאֹמַ֖ר אֲלֵכֶ֑ם בָּאתֶם֙ עַד־הַ֣ר הָאֱמֹרִ֔י אֲשֶׁר־יְהֹוָ֥ה אֱלֹהֵ֖ינוּ נֹתֵ֥ן לָֽנוּ׃

21 See, *Hashem* your God has placed the land at your disposal. Go up, take possession, as *Hashem*, the God of your fathers, promised you. Fear not and be not dismayed."

כא רְ֠אֵ֠ה נָתַ֨ן יְהֹוָ֧ה אֱלֹהֶ֛יךָ לְפָנֶ֖יךָ אֶת־הָאָ֑רֶץ עֲלֵ֣ה רֵ֗שׁ כַּאֲשֶׁר֩ דִּבֶּ֨ר יְהֹוָ֜ה אֱלֹהֵ֤י אֲבֹתֶ֙יךָ֙ לָ֔ךְ אַל־תִּירָ֖א וְאַל־תֵּחָֽת׃

r'-AY na-TAN a-do-NAI e-lo-HE-kha l'-fa-NE-kha et ha-A-retz a-LAY RAYSH ka-a-SHER di-BER a-do-NAI e-lo-HAY a-vo-TE-kha LAKH al tee-RAH v'-al tay-KHAT

438

Devarim/Deuteronomy 1
Devarim

דברים א
דברים

22 Then all of you came to me and said, "Let us send men ahead to reconnoiter the land for us and bring back word on the route we shall follow and the cities we shall come to."

כב וַתִּקְרְבוּן אֵלַי כֻּלְּכֶם וַתֹּאמְרוּ נִשְׁלְחָה אֲנָשִׁים לְפָנֵינוּ וְיַחְפְּרוּ־לָנוּ אֶת־הָאָרֶץ וְיָשִׁבוּ אֹתָנוּ דָּבָר אֶת־הַדֶּרֶךְ אֲשֶׁר נַעֲלֶה־בָּהּ וְאֵת הֶעָרִים אֲשֶׁר נָבֹא אֲלֵיהֶן:

23 I approved of the plan, and so I selected twelve of your men, one from each tribe.

כג וַיִּיטַב בְּעֵינַי הַדָּבָר וָאֶקַּח מִכֶּם שְׁנֵים עָשָׂר אֲנָשִׁים אִישׁ אֶחָד לַשָּׁבֶט:

24 They made for the hill country, came to the wadi Eshcol, and spied it out.

כד וַיִּפְנוּ וַיַּעֲלוּ הָהָרָה וַיָּבֹאוּ עַד־נַחַל אֶשְׁכֹּל וַיְרַגְּלוּ אֹתָהּ:

25 They took some of the fruit of the land with them and brought it down to us. And they gave us this report: "It is a good land that *Hashem* our God is giving to us."

כה וַיִּקְחוּ בְיָדָם מִפְּרִי הָאָרֶץ וַיּוֹרִדוּ אֵלֵינוּ וַיָּשִׁבוּ אֹתָנוּ דָבָר וַיֹּאמְרוּ טוֹבָה הָאָרֶץ אֲשֶׁר־יְהוָה אֱלֹהֵינוּ נֹתֵן לָנוּ:

va-yik-KHU v'-ya-DAM mi-p'-REE ha-A-retz va-yo-RI-du ay-LAY-nu va-ya-SHI-vu o-TA-nu da-VAR va-YO-m'-RU to-VAH ha-A-retz a-sher a-do-NAI e-lo-HAY-nu no-TAYN LA-nu

26 Yet you refused to go up, and flouted the command of *Hashem* your God.

כו וְלֹא אֲבִיתֶם לַעֲלֹת וַתַּמְרוּ אֶת־פִּי יְהוָה אֱלֹהֵיכֶם:

27 You sulked in your tents and said, "It is because *Hashem* hates us that He brought us out of the land of Egypt, to hand us over to the Amorites to wipe us out.

כז וַתֵּרָגְנוּ בְאָהֳלֵיכֶם וַתֹּאמְרוּ בְּשִׂנְאַת יְהוָה אֹתָנוּ הוֹצִיאָנוּ מֵאֶרֶץ מִצְרָיִם לָתֵת אֹתָנוּ בְּיַד הָאֱמֹרִי לְהַשְׁמִידֵנוּ:

28 What kind of place are we going to? Our kinsmen have taken the heart out of us, saying, 'We saw there a people stronger and taller than we, large cities with walls sky-high, and even Anakites.'"

כח אָנָה ׀ אֲנַחְנוּ עֹלִים אַחֵינוּ הֵמַסּוּ אֶת־לְבָבֵנוּ לֵאמֹר עַם גָּדוֹל וָרָם מִמֶּנּוּ עָרִים גְּדֹלֹת וּבְצוּרֹת בַּשָּׁמָיִם וְגַם־בְּנֵי עֲנָקִים רָאִינוּ שָׁם:

29 I said to you, "Have no dread or fear of them.

כט וָאֹמַר אֲלֵכֶם לֹא־תַעַרְצוּן וְלֹא־תִירְאוּן מֵהֶם:

30 None other than *Hashem* your God, who goes before you, will fight for you, just as He did for you in Egypt before your very eyes,

ל יְהוָה אֱלֹהֵיכֶם הַהֹלֵךְ לִפְנֵיכֶם הוּא יִלָּחֵם לָכֶם כְּכֹל אֲשֶׁר עָשָׂה אִתְּכֶם בְּמִצְרַיִם לְעֵינֵיכֶם:

31 and in the wilderness, where you saw how *Hashem* your God carried you, as a man carries his son, all the way that you traveled until you came to this place.

לא וּבַמִּדְבָּר אֲשֶׁר רָאִיתָ אֲשֶׁר נְשָׂאֲךָ יְהוָה אֱלֹהֶיךָ כַּאֲשֶׁר יִשָּׂא־אִישׁ אֶת־בְּנוֹ בְּכָל־הַדֶּרֶךְ אֲשֶׁר הֲלַכְתֶּם עַד־בֹּאֲכֶם עַד־הַמָּקוֹם הַזֶּה:

Clusters of grapes near Beit Shemesh

1:25 It is a good land that *Hashem* our God is giving to us. The spies committed a grave sin by rejecting the Land of Israel. But despite their rejection of the land, even they could not deny its beauty and its bounty. The spies carried back a cluster of grapes, a fig and a pomegranate. Upon their return, they reported "We came to the land you sent us to; it does indeed flow with milk and honey, and this is its fruit" (Numbers 13:27). How magnificent is *Eretz Yisrael* – even those who slight it cannot help but be struck by its grandeur!

Devarim/Deuteronomy 1
Devarim

דברים א
דברים

32 Yet for all that, you have no faith in *Hashem* your God,

לב וּבַדָּבָר הַזֶּה אֵינְכֶם מַאֲמִינִם בַּיהוָה אֱלֹהֵיכֶם:

33 who goes before you on your journeys – to scout the place where you are to encamp – in fire by night and in cloud by day, in order to guide you on the route you are to follow."

לג הַהֹלֵךְ לִפְנֵיכֶם בַּדֶּרֶךְ לָתוּר לָכֶם מָקוֹם לַחֲנֹתְכֶם בָּאֵשׁ ׀ לַיְלָה לַרְאֹתְכֶם בַּדֶּרֶךְ אֲשֶׁר תֵּלְכוּ־בָהּ וּבֶעָנָן יוֹמָם:

34 When *Hashem* heard your loud complaint, He was angry. He vowed:

לד וַיִּשְׁמַע יְהוָה אֶת־קוֹל דִּבְרֵיכֶם וַיִּקְצֹף וַיִּשָּׁבַע לֵאמֹר:

35 Not one of these men, this evil generation, shall see the good land that I swore to give to your fathers

לה אִם־יִרְאֶה אִישׁ בָּאֲנָשִׁים הָאֵלֶּה הַדּוֹר הָרָע הַזֶּה אֵת הָאָרֶץ הַטּוֹבָה אֲשֶׁר נִשְׁבַּעְתִּי לָתֵת לַאֲבֹתֵיכֶם:

36 none except *Kalev* son of Jephunneh; he shall see it, and to him and his descendants will I give the land on which he set foot, because he remained loyal to *Hashem*.

לו זוּלָתִי כָּלֵב בֶּן־יְפֻנֶּה הוּא יִרְאֶנָּה וְלוֹ־אֶתֵּן אֶת־הָאָרֶץ אֲשֶׁר דָּרַךְ־בָּהּ וּלְבָנָיו יַעַן אֲשֶׁר מִלֵּא אַחֲרֵי יְהוָה:

37 Because of you *Hashem* was incensed with me too, and He said: You shall not enter it either.

לז גַּם־בִּי הִתְאַנַּף יְהוָה בִּגְלַלְכֶם לֵאמֹר גַּם־אַתָּה לֹא־תָבֹא שָׁם:

38 *Yehoshua* son of *Nun*, who attends you, he shall enter it. Imbue him with strength, for he shall allot it to *Yisrael*.

לח יְהוֹשֻׁעַ בִּן־נוּן הָעֹמֵד לְפָנֶיךָ הוּא יָבֹא שָׁמָּה אֹתוֹ חַזֵּק כִּי־הוּא יַנְחִלֶנָּה אֶת־יִשְׂרָאֵל:

39 Moreover, your little ones who you said would be carried off, your children who do not yet know good from bad, they shall enter it; to them will I give it and they shall possess it.

לט וְטַפְּכֶם אֲשֶׁר אֲמַרְתֶּם לָבַז יִהְיֶה וּבְנֵיכֶם אֲשֶׁר לֹא־יָדְעוּ הַיּוֹם טוֹב וָרָע הֵמָּה יָבֹאוּ שָׁמָּה וְלָהֶם אֶתְּנֶנָּה וְהֵם יִירָשׁוּהָ:

40 As for you, turn about and march into the wilderness by the way of the Sea of Reeds.

מ וְאַתֶּם פְּנוּ לָכֶם וּסְעוּ הַמִּדְבָּרָה דֶּרֶךְ יַם־סוּף:

41 You replied to me, saying, "We stand guilty before *Hashem*. We will go up now and fight, just as *Hashem* our God commanded us." And you all girded yourselves with war gear and recklessly started for the hill country.

מא וַתַּעֲנוּ ׀ וַתֹּאמְרוּ אֵלַי חָטָאנוּ לַיהוָה אֲנַחְנוּ נַעֲלֶה וְנִלְחַמְנוּ כְּכֹל אֲשֶׁר־צִוָּנוּ יְהוָה אֱלֹהֵינוּ וַתַּחְגְּרוּ אִישׁ אֶת־כְּלֵי מִלְחַמְתּוֹ וַתָּהִינוּ לַעֲלֹת הָהָרָה:

42 But *Hashem* said to me, "Warn them: Do not go up and do not fight, since I am not in your midst; else you will be routed by your enemies."

מב וַיֹּאמֶר יְהוָה אֵלַי אֱמֹר לָהֶם לֹא תַעֲלוּ וְלֹא־תִלָּחֲמוּ כִּי אֵינֶנִּי בְּקִרְבְּכֶם וְלֹא תִּנָּגְפוּ לִפְנֵי אֹיְבֵיכֶם:

43 I spoke to you, but you would not listen; you flouted *Hashem*'s command and willfully marched into the hill country.

מג וָאֲדַבֵּר אֲלֵיכֶם וְלֹא שְׁמַעְתֶּם וַתַּמְרוּ אֶת־פִּי יְהוָה וַתָּזִדוּ וַתַּעֲלוּ הָהָרָה:

44 Then the Amorites who lived in those hills came out against you like so many bees and chased you, and they crushed you at Hormah in Seir.

מד וַיֵּצֵא הָאֱמֹרִי הַיֹּשֵׁב בָּהָר הַהוּא לִקְרַאתְכֶם וַיִּרְדְּפוּ אֶתְכֶם כַּאֲשֶׁר תַּעֲשֶׂינָה הַדְּבֹרִים וַיַּכְּתוּ אֶתְכֶם בְּשֵׂעִיר עַד־חָרְמָה:

Devarim/Deuteronomy 2
Devarim

45 Again you wept before *Hashem*; but *Hashem* would not heed your cry or give ear to you.

46 Thus, after you had remained at Kadesh all that long time,

2 1 we marched back into the wilderness by the way of the Sea of Reeds, as *Hashem* had spoken to me, and skirted the hill country of Seir a long time.

2 Then *Hashem* said to me:

3 You have been skirting this hill country long enough; now turn north.

4 And charge the people as follows: You will be passing through the territory of your kinsmen, the descendants of Esau, who live in Seir. Though they will be afraid of you, be very careful

5 not to provoke them. For I will not give you of their land so much as a foot can tread on; I have given the hill country of Seir as a possession to Esau.

6 What food you eat you shall obtain from them for money; even the water you drink you shall procure from them for money.

7 Indeed, *Hashem* your God has blessed you in all your undertakings. He has watched over your wanderings through this great wilderness; *Hashem* your God has been with you these past forty years: you have lacked nothing.

8 We then moved on, away from our kinsmen, the descendants of Esau, who live in Seir, away from the road of the Arabah, away from Eilat and Ezion-geber; and we marched on in the direction of the wilderness of Moab.

9 And *Hashem* said to me: Do not harass the Moabites or provoke them to war. For I will not give you any of their land as a possession; I have assigned Ar as a possession to the descendants of Lot. –

va-YO-mer a-do-NAI ay-LAI al ta-TZAR et mo-AV v'-al tit-GAR BAM mil-kha-MAH KEE lo e-TAYN l'-KHA may-ar-TZO y'-ru-SHAH KEE liv-nay LOT na-TA-tee et AR y'-ru-SHAH

2:9 I have assigned *Ar* as a possession to the descendants of *Lot* The people of Moab are descendants of Lot, nephew of *Avraham*. When *Avraham* went to Egypt to escape the famine, he told the Egyptians that *Sara* was his sister, instead of his wife, in order to save his life. The Sages of the *Midrash* explain that Lot, who was with them, maintained his silence and preserved the secret. As an expression of gratitude for this act of nobility, the children of *Avraham* are forbidden from attacking the children of Lot generations later, even for the purpose of expanding the borders of Israel.

Devarim/Deuteronomy 2
Devarim

10 It was formerly inhabited by the Emim, a people great and numerous, and as tall as the Anakites.

11 Like the Anakites, they are counted as Rephaim; but the Moabites call them Emim.

12 Similarly, Seir was formerly inhabited by the Horites; but the descendants of Esau dispossessed them, wiping them out and settling in their place, just as *Yisrael* did in the land they were to possess, which *Hashem* had given to them. –

13 Up now! Cross the wadi Zered! So we crossed the wadi Zered.

14 The time that we spent in travel from Kadesh-barnea until we crossed the wadi Zered was thirty-eight years, until that whole generation of warriors had perished from the camp, as *Hashem* had sworn concerning them.

15 Indeed, the hand of *Hashem* struck them, to root them out from the camp to the last man.

16 When all the warriors among the people had died off,

17 *Hashem* spoke to me, saying:

18 You are now passing through the territory of Moab, through Ar.

19 You will then be close to the Ammonites; do not harass them or start a fight with them. For I will not give any part of the land of the Ammonites to you as a possession; I have assigned it as a possession to the descendants of Lot. –

20 It, too, is counted as Rephaim country. It was formerly inhabited by Rephaim, whom the Ammonites call Zamzummim,

21 a people great and numerous and as tall as the Anakites. *Hashem* wiped them out, so that [the Ammonites] dispossessed them and settled in their place,

22 as He did for the descendants of Esau who live in Seir, when He wiped out the Horites before them, so that they dispossessed them and settled in their place, as is still the case.

23 So, too, with the Avvim who dwelt in villages in the vicinity of *Azza*: the Caphtorim, who came from Crete, wiped them out and settled in their place. –

Devarim/Deuteronomy 2
Devarim

24 Up! Set out across the wadi Arnon! See, I give into your power Sihon the Amorite, king of Heshbon, and his land. Begin the occupation: engage him in battle.

25 This day I begin to put the dread and fear of you upon the peoples everywhere under heaven, so that they shall tremble and quake because of you whenever they hear you mentioned.

26 Then I sent messengers from the wilderness of Kedemoth to King Sihon of Heshbon with an offer of peace, as follows,

27 "Let me pass through your country. I will keep strictly to the highway, turning off neither to the right nor to the left.

28 What food I eat you will supply for money, and what water I drink you will furnish for money; just let me pass through

29 as the descendants of Esau who dwell in Seir did for me, and the Moabites who dwell in Ar – that I may cross the *Yarden* into the land that *Hashem* our God is giving us."

30 But King Sihon of Heshbon refused to let us pass through, because *Hashem* had stiffened his will and hardened his heart in order to deliver him into your power – as is now the case.

31 And *Hashem* said to me: See, I begin by placing Sihon and his land at your disposal. Begin the occupation; take possession of his land.

32 Sihon with all his men took the field against us at Jahaz,

33 and *Hashem* our God delivered him to us and we defeated him and his sons and all his men.

34 At that time we captured all his towns, and we doomed every town – men, women, and children – leaving no survivor.

35 We retained as booty only the cattle and the spoil of the cities that we captured.

36 From Aroer on the edge of the Arnon valley, including the town in the valley itself, to *Gilad*, not a city was too mighty for us; *Hashem* our God delivered everything to us.

Devarim/Deuteronomy 3
Devarim

37 But you did not encroach upon the land of the Ammonites, all along the wadi Jabbok and the towns of the hill country, just as *Hashem* our God had commanded.

3 1 We made our way up the road toward Bashan, and King Og of Bashan with all his men took the field against us at Edrei.

2 But *Hashem* said to me: Do not fear him, for I am delivering him and all his men and his country into your power, and you will do to him as you did to Sihon king of the Amorites, who lived in Heshbon.

3 So *Hashem* our God also delivered into our power King Og of Bashan, with all his men, and we dealt them such a blow that no survivor was left.

4 At that time we captured all his towns; there was not a town that we did not take from them: sixty towns, the whole district of Argob, the kingdom of Og in Bashan

5 all those towns were fortified with high walls, gates, and bars – apart from a great number of unwalled towns.

6 We doomed them as we had done in the case of King Sihon of Heshbon; we doomed every town – men, women, and children –

7 and retained as booty all the cattle and the spoil of the towns.

8 Thus we seized, at that time, from the two Amorite kings, the country beyond the *Yarden*, from the wadi Arnon to Mount *Chermon*

9 Sidonians called *Chermon* Sirion, and the Amorites call it Senir

10 all the towns of the Tableland and the whole of *Gilad* and Bashan as far as Salcah and Edrei, the towns of Og's kingdom in Bashan.

11 Only King Og of Bashan was left of the remaining Rephaim. His bedstead, an iron bedstead, is now in Rabbah of the Ammonites; it is nine *amot* long and four *amot* wide, by the standard *amah*!

12 And this is the land which we apportioned at that time: The part from Aroer along the wadi Arnon, with part of the hill country of *Gilad* and its towns, I assigned to the Reubenites and the Gadites.

דברים ג
דברים

לז רַק אֶל־אֶרֶץ בְּנֵי־עַמּוֹן לֹא קָרָבְתָּ כָּל־יַד נַחַל יַבֹּק וְעָרֵי הָהָר וְכֹל אֲשֶׁר־צִוָּה יְהוָה אֱלֹהֵינוּ׃

ג א וַנֵּפֶן וַנַּעַל דֶּרֶךְ הַבָּשָׁן וַיֵּצֵא עוֹג מֶלֶךְ־הַבָּשָׁן לִקְרָאתֵנוּ הוּא וְכָל־עַמּוֹ לַמִּלְחָמָה אֶדְרֶעִי׃

ב וַיֹּאמֶר יְהוָה אֵלַי אַל־תִּירָא אֹתוֹ כִּי בְיָדְךָ נָתַתִּי אֹתוֹ וְאֶת־כָּל־עַמּוֹ וְאֶת־אַרְצוֹ וְעָשִׂיתָ לּוֹ כַּאֲשֶׁר עָשִׂיתָ לְסִיחֹן מֶלֶךְ הָאֱמֹרִי אֲשֶׁר יוֹשֵׁב בְּחֶשְׁבּוֹן׃

ג וַיִּתֵּן יְהוָה אֱלֹהֵינוּ בְּיָדֵנוּ גַּם אֶת־עוֹג מֶלֶךְ־הַבָּשָׁן וְאֶת־כָּל־עַמּוֹ וַנַּכֵּהוּ עַד־בִּלְתִּי הִשְׁאִיר־לוֹ שָׂרִיד׃

ד וַנִּלְכֹּד אֶת־כָּל־עָרָיו בָּעֵת הַהִוא לֹא הָיְתָה קִרְיָה אֲשֶׁר לֹא־לָקַחְנוּ מֵאִתָּם שִׁשִּׁים עִיר כָּל־חֶבֶל אַרְגֹּב מַמְלֶכֶת עוֹג בַּבָּשָׁן׃

ה כָּל־אֵלֶּה עָרִים בְּצֻרוֹת חוֹמָה גְבֹהָה דְּלָתַיִם וּבְרִיחַ לְבַד מֵעָרֵי הַפְּרָזִי הַרְבֵּה מְאֹד׃

ו וַנַּחֲרֵם אוֹתָם כַּאֲשֶׁר עָשִׂינוּ לְסִיחֹן מֶלֶךְ חֶשְׁבּוֹן הַחֲרֵם כָּל־עִיר מְתִם הַנָּשִׁים וְהַטָּף׃

ז וְכָל־הַבְּהֵמָה וּשְׁלַל הֶעָרִים בַּזּוֹנוּ לָנוּ׃

ח וַנִּקַּח בָּעֵת הַהִוא אֶת־הָאָרֶץ מִיַּד שְׁנֵי מַלְכֵי הָאֱמֹרִי אֲשֶׁר בְּעֵבֶר הַיַּרְדֵּן מִנַּחַל אַרְנֹן עַד־הַר חֶרְמוֹן׃

ט צִידֹנִים יִקְרְאוּ לְחֶרְמוֹן שִׂרְיֹן וְהָאֱמֹרִי יִקְרְאוּ־לוֹ שְׂנִיר׃

י כֹּל עָרֵי הַמִּישֹׁר וְכָל־הַגִּלְעָד וְכָל־הַבָּשָׁן עַד־סַלְכָה וְאֶדְרֶעִי עָרֵי מַמְלֶכֶת עוֹג בַּבָּשָׁן׃

יא כִּי רַק־עוֹג מֶלֶךְ הַבָּשָׁן נִשְׁאַר מִיֶּתֶר הָרְפָאִים הִנֵּה עַרְשׂוֹ עֶרֶשׂ בַּרְזֶל הֲלֹה הִוא בְּרַבַּת בְּנֵי עַמּוֹן תֵּשַׁע אַמּוֹת אָרְכָּהּ וְאַרְבַּע אַמּוֹת רָחְבָּהּ בְּאַמַּת־אִישׁ׃

יב וְאֶת־הָאָרֶץ הַזֹּאת יָרַשְׁנוּ בָּעֵת הַהִוא מֵעֲרֹעֵר אֲשֶׁר־עַל־נַחַל אַרְנֹן וַחֲצִי הַר־הַגִּלְעָד וְעָרָיו נָתַתִּי לָרֻאוּבֵנִי וְלַגָּדִי׃

444

Devarim/Deuteronomy 3
Devarim

דברים ג
דברים

13 The rest of *Gilad*, and all of Bashan under Og's rule – the whole Argob district, all that part of Bashan which is called Rephaim country – I assigned to the half-tribe of *Menashe*.

יג וְיֶ֤תֶר הַגִּלְעָד֙ וְכָל־הַבָּשָׁ֔ן מַמְלֶ֖כֶת ע֑וֹג נָתַ֕תִּי לַחֲצִ֖י שֵׁ֣בֶט הַֽמְנַשֶּׁ֑ה כֹּ֣ל חֶ֤בֶל הָֽאַרְגֹּב֙ לְכָל־הַבָּשָׁ֔ן הַה֥וּא יִקָּרֵ֖א אֶ֥רֶץ רְפָאִֽים:

14 *Yair* son of *Menashe* received the whole Argob district (that is, Bashan) as far as the boundary of the Geshurites and the Maacathites, and named it after himself: Havvoth-jair – as is still the case.

יד יָאִ֤יר בֶּן־מְנַשֶּׁה֙ לָקַח֙ אֶת־כָּל־חֶ֣בֶל אַרְגֹּ֔ב עַד־גְּב֥וּל הַגְּשׁוּרִ֖י וְהַמַּֽעֲכָתִ֑י וַיִּקְרָ֨א אֹתָ֤ם עַל־שְׁמוֹ֙ אֶת־הַבָּשָׁ֔ן חַוֺּ֣ת יָאִ֔יר עַ֖ד הַיּ֥וֹם הַזֶּֽה:

15 To Machir I assigned *Gilad*.

טו וּלְמָכִ֖יר נָתַ֥תִּי אֶת־הַגִּלְעָֽד:

16 And to the Reubenites and the Gadites I assigned the part from *Gilad* down to the wadi Arnon, the middle of the wadi being the boundary, and up to the wadi Jabbok, the boundary of the Ammonites.

טז וְלָרֽאוּבֵנִ֣י וְלַגָּדִ֗י נָתַ֙תִּי֙ מִן־הַגִּלְעָ֣ד וְעַד־נַ֣חַל אַרְנֹ֔ן תּ֥וֹךְ הַנַּ֖חַל וּגְבֻ֑ל וְעַד֙ יַבֹּ֣ק הַנַּ֔חַל גְּב֖וּל בְּנֵ֥י עַמּֽוֹן:

17 [We also seized] the Arabah, from the foot of the slopes of Pisgah on the east, to the edge of the *Yarden*, and from Chinnereth down to the sea of the Arabah, the Dead Sea.

יז וְהָ֣עֲרָבָ֔ה וְהַיַּרְדֵּ֖ן וּגְבֻ֑ל מִכִּנֶּ֗רֶת וְעַ֨ד יָ֤ם הָֽעֲרָבָה֙ יָ֣ם הַמֶּ֔לַח תַּ֛חַת אַשְׁדֹּ֥ת הַפִּסְגָּ֖ה מִזְרָֽחָה:

18 At that time I charged you, saying, "*Hashem* your God has given you this country to possess. You must go as shock-troops, warriors all, at the head of your Israelite kinsmen.

יח וָֽאֲצַ֣ו אֶתְכֶ֔ם בָּעֵ֥ת הַהִ֖וא לֵאמֹ֑ר יְהוָֹ֣ה אֱלֹֽהֵיכֶ֗ם נָתַ֨ן לָכֶ֜ם אֶת־הָאָ֤רֶץ הַזֹּאת֙ לְרִשְׁתָּ֔הּ חֲלוּצִ֣ים תַּֽעַבְר֗וּ לִפְנֵ֛י אֲחֵיכֶ֥ם בְּנֵֽי־יִשְׂרָאֵ֖ל כָּל־בְּנֵי־חָֽיִל:

va-a-TZAV et-KHEM ba-AYT ha-HEE lay-MOR a-do-NAI e-lo-hay-KHEM na-TAN la-KHEM et ha-A-retz ha-ZOT l'-rish-TAH kha-lu-TZEEM ta-av-RU lif-NAY a-khay-KHEM b'-nay yis-ra-AYL kol b'-nay KHA-yil

19 Only your wives, children, and livestock – I know that you have much livestock – shall be left in the towns I have assigned to you,

יט רַ֣ק נְשֵׁיכֶ֤ם וְטַפְּכֶם֙ וּמִקְנֵכֶ֔ם יָדַ֕עְתִּי כִּֽי־מִקְנֶ֥ה רַ֖ב לָכֶ֑ם יֵֽשְׁבוּ֙ בְּעָ֣רֵיכֶ֔ם אֲשֶׁ֥ר נָתַ֖תִּי לָכֶֽם:

20 until *Hashem* has granted your kinsmen a haven such as you have, and they too have taken possession of the land that *Hashem* your God is assigning them, beyond the *Yarden*. Then you may return each to the homestead that I have assigned to him."

כ עַ֠ד אֲשֶׁר־יָנִ֨יחַ יְהוָֹ֥ה ׀ לַֽאֲחֵיכֶם֮ כָּכֶם֒ וְיָֽרְשׁ֣וּ גַם־הֵ֔ם אֶת־הָאָ֕רֶץ אֲשֶׁ֨ר יְהוָֹ֧ה אֱלֹֽהֵיכֶ֛ם נֹתֵ֥ן לָהֶ֖ם בְּעֵ֣בֶר הַיַּרְדֵּ֑ן וְשַׁבְתֶּ֗ם אִ֚ישׁ לִֽירֻשָּׁת֔וֹ אֲשֶׁ֥ר נָתַ֖תִּי לָכֶֽם:

IDF raising a handmade flag in Eilat, 1949

3:18 You must go as shock-troops, warriors all The tribes of *Reuven* and *Gad* requested to settle on the eastern side of the *Yarden* in the lands conquered from Sihon and Og, rather than join their brethren on the western side. *Moshe* granted this request on condition that *Reuven* and *Gad* would fight alongside the other tribes in the conquest of the land. Here, *Moshe* reminds *Reuven* and *Gad* of their agreement. And, indeed, when *Yehoshua* succeeds *Moshe* and leads the nation into their land, he calls upon these tribes to fulfill their promise. The men of *Reuven* and *Gad* answer their call to duty and fight in the army until the battles are over. As in the days of *Yehoshua*, today the State of Israel calls upon all of its citizens to serve in the Israel Defense Forces. Military service typically lasts for three years, between the ages of eighteen to twenty-one, followed by several weeks of reserve duty each year until the age of forty-five. Similarly, Israel turns to those living outside the State for different, but also important, contributions to its vitality, growth and security.

Devarim/Deuteronomy 3
Va'etchanan

דברים ג
ואתחנן

21 I also charged *Yehoshua* at that time, saying, "You have seen with your own eyes all that *Hashem* your God has done to these two kings; so shall *Hashem* do to all the kingdoms into which you shall cross over.

כא וְאֶת־יְהוֹשׁוּעַ צִוֵּיתִי בָּעֵת הַהִוא לֵאמֹר עֵינֶיךָ הָרֹאֹת אֵת כָּל־אֲשֶׁר עָשָׂה יְהֹוָה אֱלֹהֵיכֶם לִשְׁנֵי הַמְּלָכִים הָאֵלֶּה כֵּן־יַעֲשֶׂה יְהֹוָה לְכָל־הַמַּמְלָכוֹת אֲשֶׁר אַתָּה עֹבֵר שָׁמָּה׃

22 Do not fear them, for it is *Hashem* your God who will battle for you."

כב לֹא תִּירָאוּם כִּי יְהֹוָה אֱלֹהֵיכֶם הוּא הַנִּלְחָם לָכֶם׃

23 I pleaded with *Hashem* at that time, saying,

כג וָאֶתְחַנַּן אֶל־יְהֹוָה בָּעֵת הַהִוא לֵאמֹר׃

24 "O *Hashem*, You who let Your servant see the first works of Your greatness and Your mighty hand, You whose powerful deeds no god in heaven or on earth can equal!

כד אֲדֹנָי יְהֹוִה אַתָּה הַחִלּוֹתָ לְהַרְאוֹת אֶת־עַבְדְּךָ אֶת־גָּדְלְךָ וְאֶת־יָדְךָ הַחֲזָקָה אֲשֶׁר מִי־אֵל בַּשָּׁמַיִם וּבָאָרֶץ אֲשֶׁר־יַעֲשֶׂה כְמַעֲשֶׂיךָ וְכִגְבוּרֹתֶךָ׃

25 Let me, I pray, cross over and see the good land on the other side of the *Yarden*, that good hill country, and the Lebanon."

כה אֶעְבְּרָה־נָּא וְאֶרְאֶה אֶת־הָאָרֶץ הַטּוֹבָה אֲשֶׁר בְּעֵבֶר הַיַּרְדֵּן הָהָר הַטּוֹב הַזֶּה וְהַלְּבָנֹן׃

e-b'-rah NA v'-er-EH et ha-A-retz ha-to-VAH a-SHER b'-AY-ver ha-yar-DAYN ha-HAR ha-TOV ha-ZEH v'-ha-l'-va-NON

26 But *Hashem* was wrathful with me on your account and would not listen to me. *Hashem* said to me, "Enough! Never speak to Me of this matter again!

כו וַיִּתְעַבֵּר יְהֹוָה בִּי לְמַעַנְכֶם וְלֹא שָׁמַע אֵלָי וַיֹּאמֶר יְהֹוָה אֵלַי רַב־לָךְ אַל־תּוֹסֶף דַּבֵּר אֵלַי עוֹד בַּדָּבָר הַזֶּה׃

27 Go up to the summit of Pisgah and gaze about, to the west, the north, the south, and the east. Look at it well, for you shall not go across yonder *Yarden*.

כז עֲלֵה רֹאשׁ הַפִּסְגָּה וְשָׂא עֵינֶיךָ יָמָּה וְצָפֹנָה וְתֵימָנָה וּמִזְרָחָה וּרְאֵה בְעֵינֶיךָ כִּי־לֹא תַעֲבֹר אֶת־הַיַּרְדֵּן הַזֶּה׃

28 Give *Yehoshua* his instructions, and imbue him with strength and courage, for he shall go across at the head of this people, and he shall allot to them the land that you may only see."

כח וְצַו אֶת־יְהוֹשֻׁעַ וְחַזְּקֵהוּ וְאַמְּצֵהוּ כִּי־הוּא יַעֲבֹר לִפְנֵי הָעָם הַזֶּה וְהוּא יַנְחִיל אוֹתָם אֶת־הָאָרֶץ אֲשֶׁר תִּרְאֶה׃

29 Meanwhile we stayed on in the valley near Beth-peor.

כט וַנֵּשֶׁב בַּגָּיְא מוּל בֵּית פְּעוֹר׃

3:25 Let me, I pray, cross over and see the good land In this verse, *Moshe* demonstrates his pure love for the Land of Israel. Though *Hashem* already forbade him from setting foot in the Promised Land, *Moshe* pleads with God to change His mind. The words "Let me, I pray, cross over and see the good land on the other side of the *Yarden*" highlight the motivation behind *Moshe's* request. It is not arrogance nor a desire for power that leads to his request, as he did not ask to lead the people into *Eretz Yisrael*. He simply wants to see the land, to breathe its air, to experience its goodness. Though *Moshe* wanted desperately to enter *Eretz Yisrael*, he could not. A visit to the Land of Israel has never been as easy as it is today, and the love for the land espoused by *Moshe* inspires millions of tourists to visit Israel each year. Visitors to Israel must remember that by entering the land, they are experiencing a blessing that even *Moshe* was not able to achieve.

Devarim/Deuteronomy 4
Va'etchanan

דברים ד
ואתחנן

4 **1** And now, O *Yisrael*, give heed to the laws and rules that I am instructing you to observe, so that you may live to enter and occupy the land that *Hashem*, the God of your fathers, is giving you.

וְעַתָּה יִשְׂרָאֵל שְׁמַע אֶל־הַחֻקִּים וְאֶל־הַמִּשְׁפָּטִים אֲשֶׁר אָנֹכִי מְלַמֵּד אֶתְכֶם לַעֲשׂוֹת לְמַעַן תִּחְיוּ וּבָאתֶם וִירִשְׁתֶּם אֶת־הָאָרֶץ אֲשֶׁר יְהֹוָה אֱלֹהֵי אֲבֹתֵיכֶם נֹתֵן לָכֶם׃

> v'-a-TAH yis-ra-AYL sh'-MA el ha-khu-KEEM v'-el ha-mish-pa-TEEM a-SHER a-no-KHEE m'-la-MAYD et-KHEM la-a-SOT l'-MA-an tikh-YU u-VA-tem vee-rish-TEM et ha-A-retz a-SHER a-do-NAI e-lo-HAY a-vo-tay-KHEM no-TAYN la-KHEM

2 You shall not add anything to what I command you or take anything away from it, but keep the commandments of *Hashem* your God that I enjoin upon you.

לֹא תֹסִפוּ עַל־הַדָּבָר אֲשֶׁר אָנֹכִי מְצַוֶּה אֶתְכֶם וְלֹא תִגְרְעוּ מִמֶּנּוּ לִשְׁמֹר אֶת־מִצְוֺת יְהֹוָה אֱלֹהֵיכֶם אֲשֶׁר אָנֹכִי מְצַוֶּה אֶתְכֶם׃

3 You saw with your own eyes what *Hashem* did in the matter of Baal-peor, that *Hashem* your God wiped out from among you every person who followed Baal-peor;

עֵינֵיכֶם הָרֹאֹת אֵת אֲשֶׁר־עָשָׂה יְהֹוָה בְּבַעַל פְּעוֹר כִּי כׇל־הָאִישׁ אֲשֶׁר הָלַךְ אַחֲרֵי בַעַל־פְּעוֹר הִשְׁמִידוֹ יְהֹוָה אֱלֹהֶיךָ מִקִּרְבֶּךָ׃

4 while you, who held fast to *Hashem* your God, are all alive today.

וְאַתֶּם הַדְּבֵקִים בַּיהֹוָה אֱלֹהֵיכֶם חַיִּים כֻּלְּכֶם הַיּוֹם׃

5 See, I have imparted to you laws and rules, as *Hashem* my God has commanded me, for you to abide by in the land that you are about to enter and occupy.

רְאֵה לִמַּדְתִּי אֶתְכֶם חֻקִּים וּמִשְׁפָּטִים כַּאֲשֶׁר צִוַּנִי יְהֹוָה אֱלֹהָי לַעֲשׂוֹת כֵּן בְּקֶרֶב הָאָרֶץ אֲשֶׁר אַתֶּם בָּאִים שָׁמָּה לְרִשְׁתָּהּ׃

6 Observe them faithfully, for that will be proof of your wisdom and discernment to other peoples, who on hearing of all these laws will say, "Surely, that great nation is a wise and discerning people."

וּשְׁמַרְתֶּם וַעֲשִׂיתֶם כִּי הִוא חׇכְמַתְכֶם וּבִינַתְכֶם לְעֵינֵי הָעַמִּים אֲשֶׁר יִשְׁמְעוּן אֵת כׇּל־הַחֻקִּים הָאֵלֶּה וְאָמְרוּ רַק עַם־חָכָם וְנָבוֹן הַגּוֹי הַגָּדוֹל הַזֶּה׃

7 For what great nation is there that has a god so close at hand as is *Hashem* our God whenever we call upon Him?

כִּי מִי־גוֹי גָּדוֹל אֲשֶׁר־לוֹ אֱלֹהִים קְרֹבִים אֵלָיו כַּיהֹוָה אֱלֹהֵינוּ בְּכׇל־קׇרְאֵנוּ אֵלָיו׃

8 Or what great nation has laws and rules as perfect as all this Teaching that I set before you this day?

וּמִי גּוֹי גָּדוֹל אֲשֶׁר־לוֹ חֻקִּים וּמִשְׁפָּטִים צַדִּיקִם כְּכֹל הַתּוֹרָה הַזֹּאת אֲשֶׁר אָנֹכִי נֹתֵן לִפְנֵיכֶם הַיּוֹם׃

9 But take utmost care and watch yourselves scrupulously, so that you do not forget the things that you saw with your own eyes and so that they do not fade from your mind as long as you live. And make them known to your children and to your children's children:

רַק הִשָּׁמֶר לְךָ וּשְׁמֹר נַפְשְׁךָ מְאֹד פֶּן־תִּשְׁכַּח אֶת־הַדְּבָרִים אֲשֶׁר־רָאוּ עֵינֶיךָ וּפֶן־יָסוּרוּ מִלְּבָבְךָ כֹּל יְמֵי חַיֶּיךָ וְהוֹדַעְתָּם לְבָנֶיךָ וְלִבְנֵי בָנֶיךָ׃

10 The day you stood before *Hashem* your God at Horeb, when *Hashem* said to Me, "Gather the people to Me that I may let them hear My words, in order that they may learn to revere Me as long as they live on earth, and may so teach their children."

יוֹם אֲשֶׁר עָמַדְתָּ לִפְנֵי יְהֹוָה אֱלֹהֶיךָ בְּחֹרֵב בֶּאֱמֹר יְהֹוָה אֵלַי הַקְהֶל־לִי אֶת־הָעָם וְאַשְׁמִעֵם אֶת־דְּבָרָי אֲשֶׁר יִלְמְדוּן לְיִרְאָה אֹתִי כׇּל־הַיָּמִים אֲשֶׁר הֵם חַיִּים עַל־הָאֲדָמָה וְאֶת־בְּנֵיהֶם יְלַמֵּדוּן׃

Devarim/Deuteronomy 4
Va'etchanan

דברים ד
ואתחנן

11 You came forward and stood at the foot of the mountain. The mountain was ablaze with flames to the very skies, dark with densest clouds.

יא וַתִּקְרְבוּן וַתַּעַמְדוּן תַּחַת הָהָר וְהָהָר בֹּעֵר בָּאֵשׁ עַד־לֵב הַשָּׁמַיִם חֹשֶׁךְ עָנָן וַעֲרָפֶל׃

12 *Hashem* spoke to you out of the fire; you heard the sound of words but perceived no shape – nothing but a voice.

יב וַיְדַבֵּר יְהֹוָה אֲלֵיכֶם מִתּוֹךְ הָאֵשׁ קוֹל דְּבָרִים אַתֶּם שֹׁמְעִים וּתְמוּנָה אֵינְכֶם רֹאִים זוּלָתִי קוֹל׃

13 He declared to you the covenant that He commanded you to observe, the Ten Commandments; and He inscribed them on two tablets of stone.

יג וַיַּגֵּד לָכֶם אֶת־בְּרִיתוֹ אֲשֶׁר צִוָּה אֶתְכֶם לַעֲשׂוֹת עֲשֶׂרֶת הַדְּבָרִים וַיִּכְתְּבֵם עַל־שְׁנֵי לֻחוֹת אֲבָנִים׃

14 At the same time *Hashem* commanded me to impart to you laws and rules for you to observe in the land that you are about to cross into and occupy.

יד וְאֹתִי צִוָּה יְהֹוָה בָּעֵת הַהִוא לְלַמֵּד אֶתְכֶם חֻקִּים וּמִשְׁפָּטִים לַעֲשֹׂתְכֶם אֹתָם בָּאָרֶץ אֲשֶׁר אַתֶּם עֹבְרִים שָׁמָּה לְרִשְׁתָּהּ׃

15 For your own sake, therefore, be most careful – since you saw no shape when *Hashem* your God spoke to you at Horeb out of the fire

טו וְנִשְׁמַרְתֶּם מְאֹד לְנַפְשֹׁתֵיכֶם כִּי לֹא רְאִיתֶם כָּל־תְּמוּנָה בְּיוֹם דִּבֶּר יְהֹוָה אֲלֵיכֶם בְּחֹרֵב מִתּוֹךְ הָאֵשׁ׃

16 not to act wickedly and make for yourselves a sculptured image in any likeness whatever: the form of a man or a woman,

טז פֶּן־תַּשְׁחִתוּן וַעֲשִׂיתֶם לָכֶם פֶּסֶל תְּמוּנַת כָּל־סָמֶל תַּבְנִית זָכָר אוֹ נְקֵבָה׃

17 the form of any beast on earth, the form of any winged bird that flies in the sky,

יז תַּבְנִית כָּל־בְּהֵמָה אֲשֶׁר בָּאָרֶץ תַּבְנִית כָּל־צִפּוֹר כָּנָף אֲשֶׁר תָּעוּף בַּשָּׁמָיִם׃

18 the form of anything that creeps on the ground, the form of any fish that is in the waters below the earth.

יח תַּבְנִית כָּל־רֹמֵשׂ בָּאֲדָמָה תַּבְנִית כָּל־דָּגָה אֲשֶׁר־בַּמַּיִם מִתַּחַת לָאָרֶץ׃

19 And when you look up to the sky and behold the sun and the moon and the stars, the whole heavenly host, you must not be lured into bowing down to them or serving them. These *Hashem* your God allotted to other peoples everywhere under heaven;

יט וּפֶן־תִּשָּׂא עֵינֶיךָ הַשָּׁמַיְמָה וְרָאִיתָ אֶת־הַשֶּׁמֶשׁ וְאֶת־הַיָּרֵחַ וְאֶת־הַכּוֹכָבִים כֹּל צְבָא הַשָּׁמַיִם וְנִדַּחְתָּ וְהִשְׁתַּחֲוִיתָ לָהֶם וַעֲבַדְתָּם אֲשֶׁר חָלַק יְהֹוָה אֱלֹהֶיךָ אֹתָם לְכֹל הָעַמִּים תַּחַת כָּל־הַשָּׁמָיִם׃

20 but you *Hashem* took and brought out of Egypt, that iron blast furnace, to be His very own people, as is now the case.

כ וְאֶתְכֶם לָקַח יְהֹוָה וַיּוֹצִא אֶתְכֶם מִכּוּר הַבַּרְזֶל מִמִּצְרָיִם לִהְיוֹת לוֹ לְעַם נַחֲלָה כַּיּוֹם הַזֶּה׃

21 Now *Hashem* was angry with me on your account and swore that I should not cross the *Yarden* and enter the good land that *Hashem* your God is assigning you as a heritage.

כא וַיהֹוָה הִתְאַנַּף־בִּי עַל־דִּבְרֵיכֶם וַיִּשָּׁבַע לְבִלְתִּי עָבְרִי אֶת־הַיַּרְדֵּן וּלְבִלְתִּי־בֹא אֶל־הָאָרֶץ הַטּוֹבָה אֲשֶׁר יְהֹוָה אֱלֹהֶיךָ נֹתֵן לְךָ נַחֲלָה׃

22 For I must die in this land; I shall not cross the *Yarden*. But you will cross and take possession of that good land.

כב כִּי אָנֹכִי מֵת בָּאָרֶץ הַזֹּאת אֵינֶנִּי עֹבֵר אֶת־הַיַּרְדֵּן וְאַתֶּם עֹבְרִים וִירִשְׁתֶּם אֶת־הָאָרֶץ הַטּוֹבָה הַזֹּאת׃

Devarim/Deuteronomy 4
Va'etchanan

דברים ד
ואתחנן

23 Take care, then, not to forget the covenant that *Hashem* your God concluded with you, and not to make for yourselves a sculptured image in any likeness, against which *Hashem* your God has enjoined you.

כג הִשָּׁמְר֣וּ לָכֶ֗ם פֶּֽן־תִּשְׁכְּחוּ֙ אֶת־בְּרִ֤ית יְהֹוָה֙ אֱלֹ֣הֵיכֶ֔ם אֲשֶׁ֥ר כָּרַ֖ת עִמָּכֶ֑ם וַעֲשִׂיתֶ֨ם לָכֶ֥ם פֶּ֙סֶל֙ תְּמ֣וּנַת כֹּ֔ל אֲשֶׁ֥ר צִוְּךָ֖ יְהֹוָ֥ה אֱלֹהֶֽיךָ׃

24 For *Hashem* your God is a consuming fire, an impassioned God.

כד כִּ֚י יְהֹוָ֣ה אֱלֹהֶ֔יךָ אֵ֥שׁ אֹכְלָ֖ה ה֑וּא אֵ֖ל קַנָּֽא׃

25 When you have begotten children and children's children and are long established in the land, should you act wickedly and make for yourselves a sculptured image in any likeness, causing *Hashem* your God displeasure and vexation,

כה כִּֽי־תוֹלִ֤יד בָּנִים֙ וּבְנֵ֣י בָנִ֔ים וְנוֹשַׁנְתֶּ֖ם בָּאָ֑רֶץ וְהִשְׁחַתֶּ֗ם וַעֲשִׂ֤יתֶם פֶּ֙סֶל֙ תְּמ֣וּנַת כֹּ֔ל וַעֲשִׂיתֶ֥ם הָרַ֛ע בְּעֵינֵ֥י יְהֹוָֽה־אֱלֹהֶ֖יךָ לְהַכְעִיסֽוֹ׃

26 I call heaven and earth this day to witness against you that you shall soon perish from the land that you are crossing the *Yarden* to possess; you shall not long endure in it, but shall be utterly wiped out.

כו הַעִידֹ֨תִי בָכֶ֣ם הַיּוֹם֮ אֶת־הַשָּׁמַ֣יִם וְאֶת־הָאָ֒רֶץ֒ כִּֽי־אָבֹ֣ד תֹּאבֵדוּן֮ מַהֵר֒ מֵעַ֣ל הָאָ֔רֶץ אֲשֶׁ֨ר אַתֶּ֜ם עֹבְרִ֧ים אֶת־הַיַּרְדֵּ֛ן שָׁ֖מָּה לְרִשְׁתָּ֑הּ לֹֽא־תַאֲרִיכֻ֤ן יָמִים֙ עָלֶ֔יהָ כִּ֥י הִשָּׁמֵ֖ד תִּשָּׁמֵדֽוּן׃

27 *Hashem* will scatter you among the peoples, and only a scant few of you shall be left among the nations to which *Hashem* will drive you.

כז וְהֵפִ֧יץ יְהֹוָ֛ה אֶתְכֶ֖ם בָּעַמִּ֑ים וְנִשְׁאַרְתֶּם֙ מְתֵ֣י מִסְפָּ֔ר בַּגּוֹיִ֕ם אֲשֶׁ֨ר יְנַהֵ֧ג יְהֹוָ֛ה אֶתְכֶ֖ם שָֽׁמָּה׃

28 There you will serve man-made gods of wood and stone, that cannot see or hear or eat or smell.

כח וַעֲבַדְתֶּם־שָׁ֣ם אֱלֹהִ֔ים מַעֲשֵׂ֖ה יְדֵ֣י אָדָ֑ם עֵ֣ץ וָאֶ֔בֶן אֲשֶׁ֤ר לֹֽא־יִרְאוּן֙ וְלֹ֣א יִשְׁמְע֔וּן וְלֹ֥א יֹאכְל֖וּן וְלֹ֥א יְרִיחֻֽן׃

29 But if you search there for *Hashem* your God, you will find Him, if only you seek Him with all your heart and soul

כט וּבִקַּשְׁתֶּ֥ם מִשָּׁ֛ם אֶת־יְהֹוָ֥ה אֱלֹהֶ֖יךָ וּמָצָ֑אתָ כִּ֣י תִדְרְשֶׁ֔נּוּ בְּכָל־לְבָבְךָ֖ וּבְכָל־נַפְשֶֽׁךָ׃

30 when you are in distress because all these things have befallen you and, in the end, return to *Hashem* your God and obey Him.

ל בַּצַּ֣ר לְךָ֔ וּמְצָא֕וּךָ כֹּ֖ל הַדְּבָרִ֣ים הָאֵ֑לֶּה בְּאַחֲרִית֙ הַיָּמִ֔ים וְשַׁבְתָּ֙ עַד־יְהֹוָ֣ה אֱלֹהֶ֔יךָ וְשָׁמַעְתָּ֖ בְּקֹלֽוֹ׃

31 For *Hashem* your God is a compassionate *Hashem*: He will not fail you nor will He let you perish; He will not forget the covenant which He made on oath with your fathers.

לא כִּ֣י אֵ֤ל רַחוּם֙ יְהֹוָ֣ה אֱלֹהֶ֔יךָ לֹ֥א יַרְפְּךָ֖ וְלֹ֣א יַשְׁחִיתֶ֑ךָ וְלֹ֤א יִשְׁכַּח֙ אֶת־בְּרִ֣ית אֲבֹתֶ֔יךָ אֲשֶׁ֥ר נִשְׁבַּ֖ע לָהֶֽם׃

32 You have but to inquire about bygone ages that came before you, ever since *Hashem* created man on earth, from one end of heaven to the other: has anything as grand as this ever happened, or has its like ever been known?

לב כִּ֣י שְׁאַל־נָא֩ לְיָמִ֨ים רִֽאשֹׁנִ֜ים אֲשֶׁר־הָי֣וּ לְפָנֶ֗יךָ לְמִן־הַיּוֹם֙ אֲשֶׁר֩ בָּרָ֨א אֱלֹהִ֤ים ׀ אָדָם֙ עַל־הָאָ֔רֶץ וּלְמִקְצֵ֥ה הַשָּׁמַ֖יִם וְעַד־קְצֵ֣ה הַשָּׁמָ֑יִם הֲנִֽהְיָ֗ה כַּדָּבָ֤ר הַגָּדוֹל֙ הַזֶּ֔ה א֖וֹ הֲנִשְׁמַ֥ע כָּמֹֽהוּ׃

33 Has any people heard the voice of a god speaking out of a fire, as you have, and survived?

לג הֲשָׁ֣מַֽע עָם֩ ק֨וֹל אֱלֹהִ֜ים מְדַבֵּ֧ר מִתּוֹךְ־הָאֵ֛שׁ כַּאֲשֶׁר־שָׁמַ֥עְתָּ אַתָּ֖ה וַיֶּֽחִי׃

Devarim/Deuteronomy 4
Va'etchanan

דברים ד
ואתחנן

34 Or has any god ventured to go and take for himself one nation from the midst of another by prodigious acts, by signs and portents, by war, by a mighty and an outstretched arm and awesome power, as *Hashem* your God did for you in Egypt before your very eyes?

לד אוֹ ׀ הֲנִסָּה אֱלֹהִים לָבוֹא לָקַחַת לוֹ גוֹי מִקֶּרֶב גּוֹי בְּמַסֹּת בְּאֹתֹת וּבְמוֹפְתִים וּבְמִלְחָמָה וּבְיָד חֲזָקָה וּבִזְרוֹעַ נְטוּיָה וּבְמוֹרָאִים גְּדֹלִים כְּכֹל אֲשֶׁר־עָשָׂה לָכֶם יְהֹוָה אֱלֹהֵיכֶם בְּמִצְרַיִם לְעֵינֶיךָ:

35 It has been clearly demonstrated to you that *Hashem* alone is God; there is none beside Him.

לה אַתָּה הָרְאֵתָ לָדַעַת כִּי יְהֹוָה הוּא הָאֱלֹהִים אֵין עוֹד מִלְּבַדּוֹ:

a-TAH ha-r'-ay-TA la-DA-at KEE a-do-NAI HU ha-e-lo-HEEM AYN OD mi-l'-va-DO

36 From the heavens He let you hear His voice to discipline you; on earth He let you see His great fire; and from amidst that fire you heard His words.

לו מִן־הַשָּׁמַיִם הִשְׁמִיעֲךָ אֶת־קֹלוֹ לְיַסְּרֶךָּ וְעַל־הָאָרֶץ הֶרְאֲךָ אֶת־אִשּׁוֹ הַגְּדוֹלָה וּדְבָרָיו שָׁמַעְתָּ מִתּוֹךְ הָאֵשׁ:

37 And because He loved your fathers, He chose their heirs after them; He Himself, in His great might, led you out of Egypt,

לז וְתַחַת כִּי אָהַב אֶת־אֲבֹתֶיךָ וַיִּבְחַר בְּזַרְעוֹ אַחֲרָיו וַיּוֹצִאֲךָ בְּפָנָיו בְּכֹחוֹ הַגָּדֹל מִמִּצְרָיִם:

38 to drive from your path nations greater and more populous than you, to take you into their land and assign it to you as a heritage, as is still the case.

לח לְהוֹרִישׁ גּוֹיִם גְּדֹלִים וַעֲצֻמִים מִמְּךָ מִפָּנֶיךָ לַהֲבִיאֲךָ לָתֶת־לְךָ אֶת־אַרְצָם נַחֲלָה כַּיּוֹם הַזֶּה:

39 Know therefore this day and keep in mind that *Hashem* alone is God in heaven above and on earth below; there is no other.

לט וְיָדַעְתָּ הַיּוֹם וַהֲשֵׁבֹתָ אֶל־לְבָבֶךָ כִּי יְהֹוָה הוּא הָאֱלֹהִים בַּשָּׁמַיִם מִמַּעַל וְעַל־הָאָרֶץ מִתָּחַת אֵין עוֹד:

40 Observe His laws and commandments, which I enjoin upon you this day, that it may go well with you and your children after you, and that you may long remain in the land that *Hashem* your God is assigning to you for all time.

מ וְשָׁמַרְתָּ אֶת־חֻקָּיו וְאֶת־מִצְוֺתָיו אֲשֶׁר אָנֹכִי מְצַוְּךָ הַיּוֹם אֲשֶׁר יִיטַב לְךָ וּלְבָנֶיךָ אַחֲרֶיךָ וּלְמַעַן תַּאֲרִיךְ יָמִים עַל־הָאֲדָמָה אֲשֶׁר יְהֹוָה אֱלֹהֶיךָ נֹתֵן לְךָ כָּל־הַיָּמִים:

v'-sha-mar-TA et khu-KAV v'-et mitz-vo-TAV a-SHER a-no-KHEE m'-tza-v'-KHA ha-YOM a-SHER yee-TAV l'-KHA ul-va-NE-kha a-kha-RE-kha ul-MA-an ta-a-REEKH ya-MEEM al ha-a-da-MAH a-SHER a-do-NAI e-lo-HE-kha no-TAYN l'-KHA kol ha-ya-MEEM

41 Then *Moshe* set aside three cities on the east side of the *Yarden*

מא אָז יַבְדִּיל מֹשֶׁה שָׁלֹשׁ עָרִים בְּעֵבֶר הַיַּרְדֵּן מִזְרְחָה שָׁמֶשׁ:

4:35 It has been clearly demonstrated to you that Hashem alone is God Our greatest ability as humans is our capacity to think and ponder. In this verse, we are told that we must recognize, or know about, the existence of the one true God. The Hebrew phrase in this verse for 'clearly demonstrated' is *har'eita lada'at* (הראת לדעת). However, in Biblical Hebrew, *da'at* also refers to a deep, intimate connection, as in, "Now the man knew his wife *Chava*" (Genesis 4:1). It therefore follows that the verse actually means that as humans, we are required not just to know about *Hashem*, but also to forge a deep connection with Him, the Almighty Creator.

דעת

Devarim/Deuteronomy 5
Va'etchanan

דברים ה
ואתחנן

42 to which a manslayer could escape, one who unwittingly slew a fellow man without having been hostile to him in the past; he could flee to one of these cities and live:

מב לָנֻס שָׁמָּה רוֹצֵחַ אֲשֶׁר יִרְצַח אֶת־רֵעֵהוּ בִּבְלִי־דַעַת וְהוּא לֹא־שֹׂנֵא לוֹ מִתְּמוֹל שִׁלְשֹׁם וְנָס אֶל־אַחַת מִן־הֶעָרִים הָאֵל וָחָי:

43 Bezer, in the wilderness in the Tableland, belonging to the Reubenites; Ramoth, in *Gilad*, belonging to the Gadites; and Golan, in Bashan, belonging to the Manassites.

מג אֶת־בֶּצֶר בַּמִּדְבָּר בְּאֶרֶץ הַמִּישֹׁר לָרֻאוּבֵנִי וְאֶת־רָאמֹת בַּגִּלְעָד לַגָּדִי וְאֶת־גּוֹלָן בַּבָּשָׁן לַמְנַשִּׁי:

44 This is the Teaching that *Moshe* set before the Israelites:

מד וְזֹאת הַתּוֹרָה אֲשֶׁר־שָׂם מֹשֶׁה לִפְנֵי בְּנֵי יִשְׂרָאֵל:

45 these are the decrees, laws, and rules that *Moshe* addressed to the people of *Yisrael*, after they had left Egypt,

מה אֵלֶּה הָעֵדֹת וְהַחֻקִּים וְהַמִּשְׁפָּטִים אֲשֶׁר דִּבֶּר מֹשֶׁה אֶל־בְּנֵי יִשְׂרָאֵל בְּצֵאתָם מִמִּצְרָיִם:

46 beyond the *Yarden*, in the valley at Beth-peor, in the land of King Sihon of the Amorites, who dwelt in Heshbon, whom *Moshe* and the Israelites defeated after they had left Egypt.

מו בְּעֵבֶר הַיַּרְדֵּן בַּגַּיְא מוּל בֵּית פְּעוֹר בְּאֶרֶץ סִיחֹן מֶלֶךְ הָאֱמֹרִי אֲשֶׁר יוֹשֵׁב בְּחֶשְׁבּוֹן אֲשֶׁר הִכָּה מֹשֶׁה וּבְנֵי יִשְׂרָאֵל בְּצֵאתָם מִמִּצְרָיִם:

47 They had taken possession of his country and that of King Og of Bashan – the two kings of the Amorites – which were on the east side of the *Yarden*

מז וַיִּירְשׁוּ אֶת־אַרְצוֹ וְאֶת־אֶרֶץ עוֹג מֶלֶךְ־הַבָּשָׁן שְׁנֵי מַלְכֵי הָאֱמֹרִי אֲשֶׁר בְּעֵבֶר הַיַּרְדֵּן מִזְרַח שָׁמֶשׁ:

48 from Aroer on the banks of the wadiArnon, as far as Mount Sion, that is, *Chermon*;

מח מֵעֲרֹעֵר אֲשֶׁר עַל־שְׂפַת־נַחַל אַרְנֹן וְעַד־הַר שִׂיאֹן הוּא חֶרְמוֹן:

49 also the whole Arabah on the east side of the *Yarden*, as far as the Sea of the Arabah, at the foot of the slopes of Pisgah.

מט וְכָל־הָעֲרָבָה עֵבֶר הַיַּרְדֵּן מִזְרָחָה וְעַד יָם הָעֲרָבָה תַּחַת אַשְׁדֹּת הַפִּסְגָּה:

5 1 *Moshe* summoned all the Israelites and said to them: Hear, O *Yisrael*, the laws and rules that I proclaim to you this day! Study them and observe them faithfully!

ה א וַיִּקְרָא מֹשֶׁה אֶל־כָּל־יִשְׂרָאֵל וַיֹּאמֶר אֲלֵהֶם שְׁמַע יִשְׂרָאֵל אֶת־הַחֻקִּים וְאֶת־הַמִּשְׁפָּטִים אֲשֶׁר אָנֹכִי דֹּבֵר בְּאָזְנֵיכֶם הַיּוֹם וּלְמַדְתֶּם אֹתָם וּשְׁמַרְתֶּם לַעֲשֹׂתָם:

2 *Hashem* our God made a covenant with us at Horeb.

ב יְהֹוָה אֱלֹהֵינוּ כָּרַת עִמָּנוּ בְּרִית בְּחֹרֵב:

3 It was not with our fathers that *Hashem* made this covenant, but with us, the living, every one of us who is here today.

ג לֹא אֶת־אֲבֹתֵינוּ כָּרַת יְהֹוָה אֶת־הַבְּרִית הַזֹּאת כִּי אִתָּנוּ אֲנַחְנוּ אֵלֶּה פֹה הַיּוֹם כֻּלָּנוּ חַיִּים:

4 Face to face *Hashem* spoke to you on the mountain out of the fire

ד פָּנִים בְּפָנִים דִּבֶּר יְהֹוָה עִמָּכֶם בָּהָר מִתּוֹךְ הָאֵשׁ:

5 I stood between *Hashem* and you at that time to convey *Hashem*'s words to you, for you were afraid of the fire and did not go up the mountain – saying:

ה אָנֹכִי עֹמֵד בֵּין־יְהֹוָה וּבֵינֵיכֶם בָּעֵת הַהִוא לְהַגִּיד לָכֶם אֶת־דְּבַר יְהֹוָה כִּי יְרֵאתֶם מִפְּנֵי הָאֵשׁ וְלֹא־עֲלִיתֶם בָּהָר לֵאמֹר:

Devarim/Deuteronomy 5
Va'etchanan

דברים ה
ואתחנן

6 I *Hashem* am your God who brought you out of the land of Egypt, the house of bondage:

ו אָנֹכִי יְהֹוָה אֱלֹהֶיךָ אֲשֶׁר הוֹצֵאתִיךָ מֵאֶרֶץ מִצְרַיִם מִבֵּית עֲבָדִים׃

7 You shall have no other gods beside Me.

ז לֹא יִהְיֶה־לְךָ אֱלֹהִים אֲחֵרִים עַל־פָּנָי׃

8 You shall not make for yourself a sculptured image, any likeness of what is in the heavens above, or on the earth below, or in the waters below the earth.

ח לֹא־תַעֲשֶׂה־לְךָ פֶסֶל כָּל־תְּמוּנָה אֲשֶׁר בַּשָּׁמַיִם מִמַּעַל וַאֲשֶׁר בָּאָרֶץ מִתָּחַת וַאֲשֶׁר בַּמַּיִם מִתַּחַת לָאָרֶץ׃

9 You shall not bow down to them or serve them. For I *Hashem* your God am an impassioned God, visiting the guilt of the parents upon the children, upon the third and upon the fourth generations of those who reject Me,

ט לֹא־תִשְׁתַּחֲוֶה לָהֶם וְלֹא תָעָבְדֵם כִּי אָנֹכִי יְהֹוָה אֱלֹהֶיךָ אֵל קַנָּא פֹּקֵד עֲוֺן אָבוֹת עַל־בָּנִים וְעַל־שִׁלֵּשִׁים וְעַל־רִבֵּעִים לְשֹׂנְאָי׃

10 but showing kindness to the thousandth generation of those who love Me and keep My commandments.

י וְעֹשֶׂה חֶסֶד לַאֲלָפִים לְאֹהֲבַי וּלְשֹׁמְרֵי מצותו [מִצְוֺתָי]׃

11 You shall not swear falsely by the name of *Hashem* your God; for *Hashem* will not clear one who swears falsely by His name.

יא לֹא תִשָּׂא אֶת־שֵׁם־יְהֹוָה אֱלֹהֶיךָ לַשָּׁוְא כִּי לֹא יְנַקֶּה יְהֹוָה אֵת אֲשֶׁר־יִשָּׂא אֶת־שְׁמוֹ לַשָּׁוְא׃

12 Observe the *Shabbat* day and keep it holy, as *Hashem* your God has commanded you.

יב שָׁמוֹר אֶת־יוֹם הַשַּׁבָּת לְקַדְּשׁוֹ כַּאֲשֶׁר צִוְּךָ יְהֹוָה אֱלֹהֶיךָ׃

13 Six days you shall labor and do all your work,

יג שֵׁשֶׁת יָמִים תַּעֲבֹד וְעָשִׂיתָ כָּל־מְלַאכְתֶּךָ׃

14 but the seventh day is a *Shabbat* of *Hashem* your God; you shall not do any work – you, your son or your daughter, your male or female slave, your ox or your ass, or any of your cattle, or the stranger in your settlements, so that your male and female slave may rest as you do.

יד וְיוֹם הַשְּׁבִיעִי שַׁבָּת לַיהֹוָה אֱלֹהֶיךָ לֹא תַעֲשֶׂה כָל־מְלָאכָה אַתָּה וּבִנְךָ־וּבִתֶּךָ וְעַבְדְּךָ־וַאֲמָתֶךָ וְשׁוֹרְךָ וַחֲמֹרְךָ וְכָל־בְּהֶמְתֶּךָ וְגֵרְךָ אֲשֶׁר בִּשְׁעָרֶיךָ לְמַעַן יָנוּחַ עַבְדְּךָ וַאֲמָתְךָ כָּמוֹךָ׃

15 Remember that you were a slave in the land of Egypt and *Hashem* your God freed you from there with a mighty hand and an outstretched arm; therefore *Hashem* your God has commanded you to observe the *Shabbat* day.

טו וְזָכַרְתָּ כִּי־עֶבֶד הָיִיתָ בְּאֶרֶץ מִצְרַיִם וַיֹּצִאֲךָ יְהֹוָה אֱלֹהֶיךָ מִשָּׁם בְּיָד חֲזָקָה וּבִזְרֹעַ נְטוּיָה עַל־כֵּן צִוְּךָ יְהֹוָה אֱלֹהֶיךָ לַעֲשׂוֹת אֶת־יוֹם הַשַּׁבָּת׃

16 Honor your father and your mother, as *Hashem* your God has commanded you, that you may long endure, and that you may fare well, in the land that *Hashem* your God is assigning to you.

טז כַּבֵּד אֶת־אָבִיךָ וְאֶת־אִמֶּךָ כַּאֲשֶׁר צִוְּךָ יְהֹוָה אֱלֹהֶיךָ לְמַעַן יַאֲרִיכֻן יָמֶיךָ וּלְמַעַן יִיטַב לָךְ עַל הָאֲדָמָה אֲשֶׁר־יְהֹוָה אֱלֹהֶיךָ נֹתֵן לָךְ׃

17 You shall not murder. You shall not commit adultery. You shall not steal. You shall not bear false witness against your neighbor.

יז לֹא תִּרְצָח׃ וְלֹא תִּנְאָף׃ וְלֹא תִּגְנֹב׃ וְלֹא־תַעֲנֶה בְרֵעֲךָ עֵד שָׁוְא׃

18 You shall not covet your neighbor's wife. You shall not crave your neighbor's house, or his field, or his male or female slave, or his ox, or his ass, or anything that is your neighbor's.

יח וְלֹא תַחְמֹד אֵשֶׁת רֵעֶךָ וְלֹא תִתְאַוֶּה בֵּית רֵעֲךָ שָׂדֵהוּ וְעַבְדּוֹ וַאֲמָתוֹ שׁוֹרוֹ וַחֲמֹרוֹ וְכֹל אֲשֶׁר לְרֵעֶךָ׃

Devarim/Deuteronomy 5
Va'etchanan

דברים ה
ואתחנן

19 *Hashem* spoke those words – those and no more – to your whole congregation at the mountain, with a mighty voice out of the fire and the dense clouds. He inscribed them on two tablets of stone, which He gave to me.

יט אֶת־הַדְּבָרִים הָאֵלֶּה דִּבֶּר יְהֹוָה אֶל־כָּל־קְהַלְכֶם בָּהָר מִתּוֹךְ הָאֵשׁ הֶעָנָן וְהָעֲרָפֶל קוֹל גָּדוֹל וְלֹא יָסָף וַיִּכְתְּבֵם עַל־שְׁנֵי לֻחֹת אֲבָנִים וַיִּתְּנֵם אֵלָי:

20 When you heard the voice out of the darkness, while the mountain was ablaze with fire, you came up to me, all your tribal heads and elders,

כ וַיְהִי כְּשָׁמְעֲכֶם אֶת־הַקּוֹל מִתּוֹךְ הַחֹשֶׁךְ וְהָהָר בֹּעֵר בָּאֵשׁ וַתִּקְרְבוּן אֵלַי כָּל־רָאשֵׁי שִׁבְטֵיכֶם וְזִקְנֵיכֶם:

21 and said, "*Hashem* our God has just shown us His majestic Presence, and we have heard His voice out of the fire; we have seen this day that man may live though *Hashem* has spoken to him.

כא וַתֹּאמְרוּ הֵן הֶרְאָנוּ יְהֹוָה אֱלֹהֵינוּ אֶת־כְּבֹדוֹ וְאֶת־גָּדְלוֹ וְאֶת־קֹלוֹ שָׁמַעְנוּ מִתּוֹךְ הָאֵשׁ הַיּוֹם הַזֶּה רָאִינוּ כִּי־יְדַבֵּר אֱלֹהִים אֶת־הָאָדָם וָחָי:

22 Let us not die, then, for this fearsome fire will consume us; if we hear the voice of *Hashem* our God any longer, we shall die.

כב וְעַתָּה לָמָּה נָמוּת כִּי תֹאכְלֵנוּ הָאֵשׁ הַגְּדֹלָה הַזֹּאת אִם־יֹסְפִים אֲנַחְנוּ לִשְׁמֹעַ אֶת־קוֹל יְהֹוָה אֱלֹהֵינוּ עוֹד וָמָתְנוּ:

23 For what mortal ever heard the voice of the living *Hashem* speak out of the fire, as we did, and lived?

כג כִּי מִי כָל־בָּשָׂר אֲשֶׁר שָׁמַע קוֹל אֱלֹהִים חַיִּים מְדַבֵּר מִתּוֹךְ־הָאֵשׁ כָּמֹנוּ וַיֶּחִי:

24 You go closer and hear all that *Hashem* our God says, and then you tell us everything that *Hashem* our God tells you, and we will willingly do it."

כד קְרַב אַתָּה וּשֲׁמָע אֵת כָּל־אֲשֶׁר יֹאמַר יְהֹוָה אֱלֹהֵינוּ וְאַתְּ תְּדַבֵּר אֵלֵינוּ אֵת כָּל־אֲשֶׁר יְדַבֵּר יְהֹוָה אֱלֹהֵינוּ אֵלֶיךָ וְשָׁמַעְנוּ וְעָשִׂינוּ:

25 *Hashem* heard the plea that you made to me, and *Hashem* said to me, "I have heard the plea that this people made to you; they did well to speak thus.

כה וַיִּשְׁמַע יְהֹוָה אֶת־קוֹל דִּבְרֵיכֶם בְּדַבֶּרְכֶם אֵלָי וַיֹּאמֶר יְהֹוָה אֵלַי שָׁמַעְתִּי אֶת־קוֹל דִּבְרֵי הָעָם הַזֶּה אֲשֶׁר דִּבְּרוּ אֵלֶיךָ הֵיטִיבוּ כָּל־אֲשֶׁר דִּבֵּרוּ:

26 May they always be of such mind, to revere Me and follow all My commandments, that it may go well with them and with their children forever!

כו מִי־יִתֵּן וְהָיָה לְבָבָם זֶה לָהֶם לְיִרְאָה אֹתִי וְלִשְׁמֹר אֶת־כָּל־מִצְוֹתַי כָּל־הַיָּמִים לְמַעַן יִיטַב לָהֶם וְלִבְנֵיהֶם לְעֹלָם:

27 Go, say to them, 'Return to your tents.'

כז לֵךְ אֱמֹר לָהֶם שׁוּבוּ לָכֶם לְאָהֳלֵיכֶם:

28 But you remain here with Me, and I will give you the whole Instruction – the laws and the rules – that you shall impart to them, for them to observe in the land that I am giving them to possess."

כח וְאַתָּה פֹּה עֲמֹד עִמָּדִי וַאֲדַבְּרָה אֵלֶיךָ אֵת כָּל־הַמִּצְוָה וְהַחֻקִּים וְהַמִּשְׁפָּטִים אֲשֶׁר תְּלַמְּדֵם וְעָשׂוּ בָאָרֶץ אֲשֶׁר אָנֹכִי נֹתֵן לָהֶם לְרִשְׁתָּהּ:

v'-a-TAH POH a-MOD i-ma-DEE va-a-da-b'-RA ay-LE-kha AYT kol ha-mitz-VAH v'-ha-khu-KEEM v'-ha-mish-pa-TEEM a-SHER t'-la-m'-DAYM v'-a-SU va-A-retz a-SHER a-no-KHEE no-TAYN la-HEM l'-rish-TAH

5:28 For them to observe in the land that I am giving them to possess Some of the commandments are unique to the Land of Israel, while others apply everywhere. However, according to the Sages, even those commandments that can be performed anywhere in the world carry greater weight when performed in *Eretz Yisrael*. Not only is the land itself special, but every good deed done there takes on added meaning and value.

Devarim/Deuteronomy 6
Va'etchanan

דברים ו
ואתחנן

29 Be careful, then, to do as *Hashem* your God has commanded you. Do not turn aside to the right or to the left:

כט וּשְׁמַרְתֶּם לַעֲשׂוֹת כַּאֲשֶׁר צִוָּה יְהֹוָה אֱלֹהֵיכֶם אֶתְכֶם לֹא תָסֻרוּ יָמִין וּשְׂמֹאל:

30 follow only the path that *Hashem* your God has enjoined upon you, so that you may thrive and that it may go well with you, and that you may long endure in the land you are to possess.

ל בְּכָל־הַדֶּרֶךְ אֲשֶׁר צִוָּה יְהֹוָה אֱלֹהֵיכֶם אֶתְכֶם תֵּלֵכוּ לְמַעַן תִּחְיוּן וְטוֹב לָכֶם וְהַאֲרַכְתֶּם יָמִים בָּאָרֶץ אֲשֶׁר תִּירָשׁוּן:

6 1 And this is the Instruction – the laws and the rules – that *Hashem* your God has commanded [me] to impart to you, to be observed in the land that you are about to cross into and occupy,

א וְזֹאת הַמִּצְוָה הַחֻקִּים וְהַמִּשְׁפָּטִים אֲשֶׁר צִוָּה יְהֹוָה אֱלֹהֵיכֶם לְלַמֵּד אֶתְכֶם לַעֲשׂוֹת בָּאָרֶץ אֲשֶׁר אַתֶּם עֹבְרִים שָׁמָּה לְרִשְׁתָּהּ:

2 so that you, your children, and your children's children may revere *Hashem* your God and follow, as long as you live, all His laws and commandments that I enjoin upon you, to the end that you may long endure.

ב לְמַעַן תִּירָא אֶת־יְהֹוָה אֱלֹהֶיךָ לִשְׁמֹר אֶת־כָּל־חֻקֹּתָיו וּמִצְוֹתָיו אֲשֶׁר אָנֹכִי מְצַוֶּךָ אַתָּה וּבִנְךָ וּבֶן־בִּנְךָ כֹּל יְמֵי חַיֶּיךָ וּלְמַעַן יַאֲרִכֻן יָמֶיךָ:

3 Obey, O *Yisrael*, willingly and faithfully, that it may go well with you and that you may increase greatly [in] a land flowing with milk and honey, as *Hashem*, the God of your fathers, spoke to you.

ג וְשָׁמַעְתָּ יִשְׂרָאֵל וְשָׁמַרְתָּ לַעֲשׂוֹת אֲשֶׁר יִיטַב לְךָ וַאֲשֶׁר תִּרְבּוּן מְאֹד כַּאֲשֶׁר דִּבֶּר יְהֹוָה אֱלֹהֵי אֲבֹתֶיךָ לָךְ אֶרֶץ זָבַת חָלָב וּדְבָשׁ:

4 Hear, O *Yisrael*! *Hashem* is our God, *Hashem* alone.

ד שְׁמַע יִשְׂרָאֵל יְהֹוָה אֱלֹהֵינוּ יְהֹוָה אֶחָד:

sh'-MA yis-ra-AYL a-do-NAI e-lo-HAY-nu a-do-NAI e-KHAD

5 You shall love *Hashem* your God with all your heart and with all your soul and with all your might.

ה וְאָהַבְתָּ אֵת יְהֹוָה אֱלֹהֶיךָ בְּכָל־לְבָבְךָ וּבְכָל־נַפְשְׁךָ וּבְכָל־מְאֹדֶךָ:

6 Take to heart these instructions with which I charge you this day.

ו וְהָיוּ הַדְּבָרִים הָאֵלֶּה אֲשֶׁר אָנֹכִי מְצַוְּךָ הַיּוֹם עַל־לְבָבֶךָ:

v'-ha-YU ha-d'-va-REEM ha-AY-leh a-SHER a-no-KHEE m'-tza-v'-KHA ha-YOM al l'-va-VE-kha

---

6:4 ***Hashem* is our God, *Hashem* alone** The single most important belief in Judaism is the belief in monotheism, the oneness of God. This key principle is attested to in this fundamental verse, known as the *Shema*, which is recited twice each day by Jews. In the unique system of *gematriya*, in which every Hebrew letter is assigned a numerical value, the word *echad* (אחד), which means 'one' and is translated here as 'alone,' adds up to 13: א equals 1, ח equals 8, and ד equals 4. Interestingly, 13 is also the numerical value of the word *ahava* (אהבה), 'love,' as א equals 1, ה equals 5, ב equals 2, and ה equals 5. The hidden message of this *gematriya* is that the greatest love a person can feel is the love of the one and only God, whose very essence is love.

6:6 These instructions with which I charge you this day *Rashi*, the great *Torah* commentator, asks why *Moshe* says that he is commanding the people the laws of the *Torah* "this day," since the *Torah* had actually been given thirty-eight years earlier. He explains that this expression indicates that we must always look at the teachings of the Bible as if they are new and exciting, as if they were given today, and not as outdated or relics of the past. New lessons of growth and inspiration relevant to our contemporary lives can always be found in the *Torah*, if we merely look for them.

אחד

Devarim/Deuteronomy 6
Va'etchanan

7 Impress them upon your children. Recite them when you stay at home and when you are away, when you lie down and when you get up.

8 Bind them as a sign on your hand and let them serve as a symbol on your forehead;

9 inscribe them on the doorposts of your house and on your gates.

10 When *Hashem* your God brings you into the land that He swore to your fathers, *Avraham*, *Yitzchak*, and *Yaakov*, to assign to you – great and flourishing cities that you did not build,

11 houses full of all good things that you did not fill, hewn cisterns that you did not hew, vineyards and olive groves that you did not plant – and you eat your fill,

12 take heed that you do not forget *Hashem* who freed you from the land of Egypt, the house of bondage.

13 Revere only *Hashem* your God and worship Him alone, and swear only by His name.

14 Do not follow other gods, any gods of the peoples about you

15 for *Hashem* your God in your midst is an impassioned God – lest the anger of *Hashem* your God blaze forth against you and He wipe you off the face of the earth.

16 Do not try *Hashem* your God, as you did at Massah.

17 Be sure to keep the commandments, decrees, and laws that *Hashem* your God has enjoined upon you.

18 Do what is right and good in the sight of *Hashem*, that it may go well with you and that you may be able to possess the good land that *Hashem* your God promised on oath to your fathers,

19 and that all your enemies may be driven out before you, as *Hashem* has spoken.

20 When, in time to come, your children ask you, "What mean the decrees, laws, and rules that *Hashem* our God has enjoined upon you?"

21 you shall say to your children, "We were slaves to Pharaoh in Egypt and *Hashem* freed us from Egypt with a mighty hand.

דברים ו
ואתחנן

ז וְשִׁנַּנְתָּ֣ם לְבָנֶ֔יךָ וְדִבַּרְתָּ֖ בָּ֑ם בְּשִׁבְתְּךָ֤ בְּבֵיתֶ֙ךָ֙ וּבְלֶכְתְּךָ֣ בַדֶּ֔רֶךְ וּֽבְשָׁכְבְּךָ֖ וּבְקוּמֶֽךָ׃

ח וּקְשַׁרְתָּ֥ם לְא֖וֹת עַל־יָדֶ֑ךָ וְהָי֥וּ לְטֹטָפֹ֖ת בֵּ֥ין עֵינֶֽיךָ׃

ט וּכְתַבְתָּ֛ם עַל־מְזֻז֥וֹת בֵּיתֶ֖ךָ וּבִשְׁעָרֶֽיךָ׃

י וְהָיָ֞ה כִּ֥י יְבִיאֲךָ֣ ׀ יְהֹוָ֣ה אֱלֹהֶ֗יךָ אֶל־הָאָ֜רֶץ אֲשֶׁ֨ר נִשְׁבַּ֧ע לַאֲבֹתֶ֛יךָ לְאַבְרָהָ֛ם לְיִצְחָ֥ק וּֽלְיַעֲקֹ֖ב לָ֣תֶת לָ֑ךְ עָרִ֛ים גְּדֹלֹ֥ת וְטֹבֹ֖ת אֲשֶׁ֥ר לֹא־בָנִֽיתָ׃

יא וּבָ֨תִּ֜ים מְלֵאִ֣ים כָּל־טוּב֮ אֲשֶׁ֣ר לֹא־מִלֵּאתָ֒ וּבֹרֹ֤ת חֲצוּבִים֙ אֲשֶׁ֣ר לֹא־חָצַ֔בְתָּ כְּרָמִ֥ים וְזֵיתִ֖ים אֲשֶׁ֣ר לֹא־נָטָ֑עְתָּ וְאָכַלְתָּ֖ וְשָׂבָֽעְתָּ׃

יב הִשָּׁ֣מֶר לְךָ֔ פֶּן־תִּשְׁכַּ֖ח אֶת־יְהֹוָ֑ה אֲשֶׁ֧ר הוֹצִיאֲךָ֛ מֵאֶ֥רֶץ מִצְרַ֖יִם מִבֵּ֥ית עֲבָדִֽים׃

יג אֶת־יְהֹוָ֧ה אֱלֹהֶ֛יךָ תִּירָ֖א וְאֹת֣וֹ תַעֲבֹ֑ד וּבִשְׁמ֖וֹ תִּשָּׁבֵֽעַ׃

יד לֹ֣א תֵֽלְכ֔וּן אַחֲרֵ֖י אֱלֹהִ֣ים אֲחֵרִ֑ים מֵאֱלֹהֵי֙ הָֽעַמִּ֔ים אֲשֶׁ֖ר סְבִיבוֹתֵיכֶֽם׃

טו כִּ֣י אֵ֥ל קַנָּ֛א יְהֹוָ֥ה אֱלֹהֶ֖יךָ בְּקִרְבֶּ֑ךָ פֶּן־יֶ֠חֱרֶ֠ה אַף־יְהֹוָ֤ה אֱלֹהֶ֙יךָ֙ בָּ֔ךְ וְהִשְׁמִ֣ידְךָ֔ מֵעַ֖ל פְּנֵ֥י הָאֲדָמָֽה׃

טז לֹ֣א תְנַסּ֔וּ אֶת־יְהֹוָ֖ה אֱלֹהֵיכֶ֑ם כַּאֲשֶׁ֥ר נִסִּיתֶ֖ם בַּמַּסָּֽה׃

יז שָׁמ֣וֹר תִּשְׁמְר֔וּן אֶת־מִצְוֺ֖ת יְהֹוָ֣ה אֱלֹהֵיכֶ֑ם וְעֵדֹתָ֥יו וְחֻקָּ֖יו אֲשֶׁ֥ר צִוָּֽךְ׃

יח וְעָשִׂ֛יתָ הַיָּשָׁ֥ר וְהַטּ֖וֹב בְּעֵינֵ֣י יְהֹוָ֑ה לְמַ֙עַן֙ יִ֣יטַב לָ֔ךְ וּבָ֗אתָ וְיָרַשְׁתָּ֙ אֶת־הָאָ֣רֶץ הַטֹּבָ֔ה אֲשֶׁר־נִשְׁבַּ֥ע יְהֹוָ֖ה לַאֲבֹתֶֽיךָ׃

יט לַהֲדֹ֥ף אֶת־כָּל־אֹיְבֶ֖יךָ מִפָּנֶ֑יךָ כַּאֲשֶׁ֖ר דִּבֶּ֥ר יְהֹוָֽה׃

כ כִּֽי־יִשְׁאָלְךָ֥ בִנְךָ֛ מָחָ֖ר לֵאמֹ֑ר מָ֣ה הָעֵדֹ֗ת וְהַֽחֻקִּים֙ וְהַמִּשְׁפָּטִ֔ים אֲשֶׁ֥ר צִוָּ֛ה יְהֹוָ֥ה אֱלֹהֵ֖ינוּ אֶתְכֶֽם׃

כא וְאָמַרְתָּ֣ לְבִנְךָ֔ עֲבָדִ֛ים הָיִ֥ינוּ לְפַרְעֹ֖ה בְּמִצְרָ֑יִם וַיּוֹצִיאֵ֧נוּ יְהֹוָ֛ה מִמִּצְרַ֖יִם בְּיָ֥ד חֲזָקָֽה׃

Devarim/Deuteronomy 7
Va'etchanan

דברים ז
ואתחנן

22 *Hashem* wrought before our eyes marvelous and destructive signs and portents in Egypt, against Pharaoh and all his household;

כב וַיִּתֵּן יְהֹוָה אוֹתֹת וּמֹפְתִים גְּדֹלִים וְרָעִים בְּמִצְרַיִם בְּפַרְעֹה וּבְכָל־בֵּיתוֹ לְעֵינֵינוּ:

23 and us He freed from there, that He might take us and give us the land that He had promised on oath to our fathers.

כג וְאוֹתָנוּ הוֹצִיא מִשָּׁם לְמַעַן הָבִיא אֹתָנוּ לָתֶת לָנוּ אֶת־הָאָרֶץ אֲשֶׁר נִשְׁבַּע לַאֲבֹתֵינוּ:

v'-o-TA-nu ho-TZEE mi-SHAM l'-MA-an ha-VEE o-TA-nu LA-tet LA-nu et ha-A-retz a-SHER nish-BA la-a-vo-TAY-nu

24 Then *Hashem* commanded us to observe all these laws, to revere *Hashem* our God, for our lasting good and for our survival, as is now the case.

כד וַיְצַוֵּנוּ יְהֹוָה לַעֲשׂוֹת אֶת־כָּל־הַחֻקִּים הָאֵלֶּה לְיִרְאָה אֶת־יְהֹוָה אֱלֹהֵינוּ לְטוֹב לָנוּ כָּל־הַיָּמִים לְחַיֹּתֵנוּ כְּהַיּוֹם הַזֶּה:

25 It will be therefore to our merit before *Hashem* our God to observe faithfully this whole Instruction, as He has commanded us."

כה וּצְדָקָה תִּהְיֶה־לָּנוּ כִּי־נִשְׁמֹר לַעֲשׂוֹת אֶת־כָּל־הַמִּצְוָה הַזֹּאת לִפְנֵי יְהֹוָה אֱלֹהֵינוּ כַּאֲשֶׁר צִוָּנוּ:

7

1 When *Hashem* your God brings you to the land that you are about to enter and possess, and He dislodges many nations before you – the Hittites, Girgashites, Amorites, Canaanites, Perizzites, Hivites, and Jebusites, seven nations much larger than you

א כִּי יְבִיאֲךָ יְהֹוָה אֱלֹהֶיךָ אֶל־הָאָרֶץ אֲשֶׁר־אַתָּה בָא־שָׁמָּה לְרִשְׁתָּהּ וְנָשַׁל גּוֹיִם־רַבִּים מִפָּנֶיךָ הַחִתִּי וְהַגִּרְגָּשִׁי וְהָאֱמֹרִי וְהַכְּנַעֲנִי וְהַפְּרִזִּי וְהַחִוִּי וְהַיְבוּסִי שִׁבְעָה גוֹיִם רַבִּים וַעֲצוּמִים מִמֶּךָּ:

2 and *Hashem* your God delivers them to you and you defeat them, you must doom them to destruction: grant them no terms and give them no quarter.

ב וּנְתָנָם יְהֹוָה אֱלֹהֶיךָ לְפָנֶיךָ וְהִכִּיתָם הַחֲרֵם תַּחֲרִים אֹתָם לֹא־תִכְרֹת לָהֶם בְּרִית וְלֹא תְחָנֵּם:

3 You shall not intermarry with them: do not give your daughters to their sons or take their daughters for your sons.

ג וְלֹא תִתְחַתֵּן בָּם בִּתְּךָ לֹא־תִתֵּן לִבְנוֹ וּבִתּוֹ לֹא־תִקַּח לִבְנֶךָ:

4 For they will turn your children away from Me to worship other gods, and *Hashem*'s anger will blaze forth against you and He will promptly wipe you out.

ד כִּי־יָסִיר אֶת־בִּנְךָ מֵאַחֲרַי וְעָבְדוּ אֱלֹהִים אֲחֵרִים וְחָרָה אַף־יְהֹוָה בָּכֶם וְהִשְׁמִידְךָ מַהֵר:

6:23 And us He freed from there Israel's first Prime Minister, David Ben Gurion, summed up this verse in a speech he gave to the Peel Commission in 1936. "Three-hundred years ago, there came to the New World a boat, and its name was the Mayflower. The Mayflower's landing on Plymouth Rock was one of the great historical events in the history of England and in the history of America. But I would like to ask any Englishman sitting here on the commission, what date did the Mayflower leave port? How many people were on the boat? Who were their leaders? What kind of food did they eat on the boat? More than three-thousand three-hundred years ago, long before the Mayflower, our people left Egypt, and every Jew in the world, wherever he is, knows what day they left. And he knows what food they ate. And we still eat that food with every anniversary. And we know who our leader was. And we sit down and tell the story to our children and grandchildren, in order to guarantee that it will never be forgotten. And we say our two slogans: 'Now we may be enslaved, but next year, we'll be a free people.' … Now we are in the prison of the Soviet Union. Now, we're in Germany where Hitler is destroying us. Now we're scattered throughout the world, but next year, we'll be in Jerusalem. There'll come a day that we'll come home to Zion, to the Land of Israel. That is the nature of the Jewish people."

Prime Minister David Ben Gurion (1886–1973)

Devarim/Deuteronomy 7
Eikev

דברים ז
עקב

5 Instead, this is what you shall do to them: you shall tear down their altars, smash their pillars, cut down their sacred posts, and consign their images to the fire.

ה כִּי־אִם־כֹּה תַעֲשׂוּ לָהֶם מִזְבְּחֹתֵיהֶם תִּתֹּצוּ וּמַצֵּבֹתָם תְּשַׁבֵּרוּ וַאֲשֵׁירֵהֶם תְּגַדֵּעוּן וּפְסִילֵיהֶם תִּשְׂרְפוּן בָּאֵשׁ:

6 For you are a people consecrated to *Hashem* your God: of all the peoples on earth *Hashem* your God chose you to be His treasured people.

ו כִּי עַם קָדוֹשׁ אַתָּה לַיהוָה אֱלֹהֶיךָ בְּךָ בָּחַר יְהוָה אֱלֹהֶיךָ לִהְיוֹת לוֹ לְעַם סְגֻלָּה מִכֹּל הָעַמִּים אֲשֶׁר עַל־פְּנֵי הָאֲדָמָה:

7 It is not because you are the most numerous of peoples that *Hashem* set His heart on you and chose you — indeed, you are the smallest of peoples;

ז לֹא מֵרֻבְּכֶם מִכָּל־הָעַמִּים חָשַׁק יְהוָה בָּכֶם וַיִּבְחַר בָּכֶם כִּי־אַתֶּם הַמְעַט מִכָּל־הָעַמִּים:

8 but it was because *Hashem* favored you and kept the oath He made to your fathers that *Hashem* freed you with a mighty hand and rescued you from the house of bondage, from the power of Pharaoh king of Egypt.

ח כִּי מֵאַהֲבַת יְהוָה אֶתְכֶם וּמִשָּׁמְרוֹ אֶת־הַשְּׁבֻעָה אֲשֶׁר נִשְׁבַּע לַאֲבֹתֵיכֶם הוֹצִיא יְהוָה אֶתְכֶם בְּיָד חֲזָקָה וַיִּפְדְּךָ מִבֵּית עֲבָדִים מִיַּד פַּרְעֹה מֶלֶךְ־מִצְרָיִם:

9 Know, therefore, that only *Hashem* your God is *Hashem*, the steadfast *Hashem* who keeps His covenant faithfully to the thousandth generation of those who love Him and keep His commandments,

ט וְיָדַעְתָּ כִּי־יְהוָה אֱלֹהֶיךָ הוּא הָאֱלֹהִים הָאֵל הַנֶּאֱמָן שֹׁמֵר הַבְּרִית וְהַחֶסֶד לְאֹהֲבָיו וּלְשֹׁמְרֵי מִצְוֹתוֹ [מִצְוֹתָיו] לְאֶלֶף דּוֹר:

10 but who instantly requites with destruction those who reject Him — never slow with those who reject Him, but requiting them instantly.

י וּמְשַׁלֵּם לְשֹׂנְאָיו אֶל־פָּנָיו לְהַאֲבִידוֹ לֹא יְאַחֵר לְשֹׂנְאוֹ אֶל־פָּנָיו יְשַׁלֶּם־לוֹ:

11 Therefore, observe faithfully the Instruction — the laws and the rules — with which I charge you today.

יא וְשָׁמַרְתָּ אֶת־הַמִּצְוָה וְאֶת־הַחֻקִּים וְאֶת־הַמִּשְׁפָּטִים אֲשֶׁר אָנֹכִי מְצַוְּךָ הַיּוֹם לַעֲשׂוֹתָם:

12 And if you do obey these rules and observe them carefully, *Hashem* your God will maintain faithfully for you the covenant that He made on oath with your fathers:

יב וְהָיָה עֵקֶב תִּשְׁמְעוּן אֵת הַמִּשְׁפָּטִים הָאֵלֶּה וּשְׁמַרְתֶּם וַעֲשִׂיתֶם אֹתָם וְשָׁמַר יְהוָה אֱלֹהֶיךָ לְךָ אֶת־הַבְּרִית וְאֶת־הַחֶסֶד אֲשֶׁר נִשְׁבַּע לַאֲבֹתֶיךָ:

v'-ha-YAH AY-kev tish-m'-UN AYT ha-mish-pa-TEEM ha-AY-leh ush-mar-TEM va-a-see-TEM o-TAM v'-sha-MAR a-do-NAI e-lo-HE-kha l'-KHA et ha-b'-REET v'-et ha-KHE-sed a-SHER nish-BA la-a-vo-TE-kha

---

עקב

7:12 And if you do obey these rules In this verse, *Hashem* promises that if we listen to His commandments, He will bless us and multiply us, and grant us success in the Land of Israel. The Hebrew word for 'and if you do,' *eikev* (עקב), also means 'heel.' *Rashi* quotes the Sages who teach that the use of the word *eikev* hints to the fact that we must keep all the commandments equally, even the ones that seem unimportant, which people tend to figuratively step on with their heels. If we are careful to follow all the commandments of *Hashem*, even the seemingly insignificant ones, then we will certainly be rewarded with great blessings in the Promised Land.

Devarim/Deuteronomy 7
Eikev

דברים ז
עקב

13 He will favor you and bless you and multiply you; He will bless the issue of your womb and the produce of your soil, your new grain and wine and oil, the calving of your herd and the lambing of your flock, in the land that He swore to your fathers to assign to you.

יג וַאֲהֵבְךָ וּבֵרַכְךָ וְהִרְבֶּךָ וּבֵרַךְ פְּרִי־בִטְנְךָ וּפְרִי־אַדְמָתֶךָ דְּגָנְךָ וְתִירֹשְׁךָ וְיִצְהָרֶךָ שְׁגַר־אֲלָפֶיךָ וְעַשְׁתְּרֹת צֹאנֶךָ עַל הָאֲדָמָה אֲשֶׁר־נִשְׁבַּע לַאֲבֹתֶיךָ לָתֶת לָךְ:

14 You shall be blessed above all other peoples: there shall be no sterile male or female among you or among your livestock.

יד בָּרוּךְ תִּהְיֶה מִכָּל־הָעַמִּים לֹא־יִהְיֶה בְךָ עָקָר וַעֲקָרָה וּבִבְהֶמְתֶּךָ:

15 *Hashem* will ward off from you all sickness; He will not bring upon you any of the dreadful diseases of Egypt, about which you know, but will inflict them upon all your enemies.

טו וְהֵסִיר יְהֹוָה מִמְּךָ כָּל־חֹלִי וְכָל־מַדְוֵי מִצְרַיִם הָרָעִים אֲשֶׁר יָדַעְתָּ לֹא יְשִׂימָם בָּךְ וּנְתָנָם בְּכָל־שֹׂנְאֶיךָ:

16 You shall destroy all the peoples that *Hashem* your God delivers to you, showing them no pity. And you shall not worship their gods, for that would be a snare to you.

טז וְאָכַלְתָּ אֶת־כָּל־הָעַמִּים אֲשֶׁר יְהֹוָה אֱלֹהֶיךָ נֹתֵן לָךְ לֹא־תָחֹס עֵינְךָ עֲלֵיהֶם וְלֹא תַעֲבֹד אֶת־אֱלֹהֵיהֶם כִּי־מוֹקֵשׁ הוּא לָךְ:

17 Should you say to yourselves, "These nations are more numerous than we; how can we dispossess them?"

יז כִּי תֹאמַר בִּלְבָבְךָ רַבִּים הַגּוֹיִם הָאֵלֶּה מִמֶּנִּי אֵיכָה אוּכַל לְהוֹרִישָׁם:

18 You need have no fear of them. You have but to bear in mind what *Hashem* your God did to Pharaoh and all the Egyptians:

יח לֹא תִירָא מֵהֶם זָכֹר תִּזְכֹּר אֵת אֲשֶׁר־עָשָׂה יְהֹוָה אֱלֹהֶיךָ לְפַרְעֹה וּלְכָל־מִצְרָיִם:

19 the wondrous acts that you saw with your own eyes, the signs and the portents, the mighty hand, and the outstretched arm by which *Hashem* your God liberated you. Thus will *Hashem* your God do to all the peoples you now fear.

יט הַמַּסֹּת הַגְּדֹלֹת אֲשֶׁר־רָאוּ עֵינֶיךָ וְהָאֹתֹת וְהַמֹּפְתִים וְהַיָּד הַחֲזָקָה וְהַזְּרֹעַ הַנְּטוּיָה אֲשֶׁר הוֹצִאֲךָ יְהֹוָה אֱלֹהֶיךָ כֵּן־יַעֲשֶׂה יְהֹוָה אֱלֹהֶיךָ לְכָל־הָעַמִּים אֲשֶׁר־אַתָּה יָרֵא מִפְּנֵיהֶם:

20 *Hashem* your God will also send a plague against them, until those who are left in hiding perish before you.

כ וְגַם אֶת־הַצִּרְעָה יְשַׁלַּח יְהֹוָה אֱלֹהֶיךָ בָּם עַד־אֲבֹד הַנִּשְׁאָרִים וְהַנִּסְתָּרִים מִפָּנֶיךָ:

21 Do not stand in dread of them, for *Hashem* your God is in your midst, a great and awesome God.

כא לֹא תַעֲרֹץ מִפְּנֵיהֶם כִּי־יְהֹוָה אֱלֹהֶיךָ בְּקִרְבֶּךָ אֵל גָּדוֹל וְנוֹרָא:

22 *Hashem* your God will dislodge those peoples before you little by little; you will not be able to put an end to them at once, else the wild beasts would multiply to your hurt.

כב וְנָשַׁל יְהֹוָה אֱלֹהֶיךָ אֶת־הַגּוֹיִם הָאֵל מִפָּנֶיךָ מְעַט מְעָט לֹא תוּכַל כַּלֹּתָם מַהֵר פֶּן־תִּרְבֶּה עָלֶיךָ חַיַּת הַשָּׂדֶה:

v'-na-SHAL a-do-NAI e-lo-HE-kha et ha-go-YIM ha-AYL mi-pa-NE-kha m'-AT m'-AT
LO tu-KHAL ka-lo-TAM ma-HAYR pen tir-BEH a-LE-kha kha-YAT ha-sa-DEH

7:22 Hashem your God will dislodge those peoples before you little by little In response to the concern that the People of Israel will not be able to drive the nations of Canaan out of their land, *Hashem* reassures them with a surprising promise: "*Hashem* your God will dislodge those peoples before you little by little." Would it not

Devarim/Deuteronomy 8
Eikev

דברים ח
עקב

23 *Hashem* your God will deliver them up to you, throwing them into utter panic until they are wiped out.

כג וּנְתָנָם יְהֹוָה אֱלֹהֶיךָ לְפָנֶיךָ וְהָמָם מְהוּמָה גְדֹלָה עַד הִשָּׁמְדָם:

24 He will deliver their kings into your hand, and you shall obliterate their name from under the heavens; no man shall stand up to you, until you have wiped them out.

כד וְנָתַן מַלְכֵיהֶם בְּיָדֶךָ וְהַאֲבַדְתָּ אֶת־שְׁמָם מִתַּחַת הַשָּׁמָיִם לֹא־יִתְיַצֵּב אִישׁ בְּפָנֶיךָ עַד הִשְׁמִדְךָ אֹתָם:

25 You shall consign the images of their gods to the fire; you shall not covet the silver and gold on them and keep it for yourselves, lest you be ensnared thereby; for that is abhorrent to *Hashem* your God.

כה פְּסִילֵי אֱלֹהֵיהֶם תִּשְׂרְפוּן בָּאֵשׁ לֹא־תַחְמֹד כֶּסֶף וְזָהָב עֲלֵיהֶם וְלָקַחְתָּ לָךְ פֶּן תִּוָּקֵשׁ בּוֹ כִּי תוֹעֲבַת יְהֹוָה אֱלֹהֶיךָ הוּא:

26 You must not bring an abhorrent thing into your house, or you will be proscribed like it; you must reject it as abominable and abhorrent, for it is proscribed.

כו וְלֹא־תָבִיא תוֹעֵבָה אֶל־בֵּיתֶךָ וְהָיִיתָ חֵרֶם כָּמֹהוּ שַׁקֵּץ תְּשַׁקְּצֶנּוּ וְתַעֵב תְּתַעֲבֶנּוּ כִּי־חֵרֶם הוּא:

8 1 You shall faithfully observe all the Instruction that I enjoin upon you today, that you may thrive and increase and be able to possess the land that *Hashem* promised on oath to your fathers.

א כָּל־הַמִּצְוָה אֲשֶׁר אָנֹכִי מְצַוְּךָ הַיּוֹם תִּשְׁמְרוּן לַעֲשׂוֹת לְמַעַן תִּחְיוּן וּרְבִיתֶם וּבָאתֶם וִירִשְׁתֶּם אֶת־הָאָרֶץ אֲשֶׁר־נִשְׁבַּע יְהֹוָה לַאֲבֹתֵיכֶם:

kol ha-mitz-VAH a-SHER a-no-KHEE m'-tza-v'-KHA ha-YOM tish-m'-RUN la-a-SOT l'-MA-an tikh-YUN ur-vee-TEM u-va-TEM vee-rish-TEM et ha-A-retz a-sher nish-BA a-do-NAI la-a-vo-tay-KHEM

2 Remember the long way that *Hashem* your God has made you travel in the wilderness these past forty years, that He might test you by hardships to learn what was in your hearts: whether you would keep His commandments or not.

ב וְזָכַרְתָּ אֶת־כָּל־הַדֶּרֶךְ אֲשֶׁר הוֹלִיכְךָ יְהֹוָה אֱלֹהֶיךָ זֶה אַרְבָּעִים שָׁנָה בַּמִּדְבָּר לְמַעַן עַנֹּתְךָ לְנַסֹּתְךָ לָדַעַת אֶת־אֲשֶׁר בִּלְבָבְךָ הֲתִשְׁמֹר מִצְוֺתָו [מִצְוֺתָיו] אִם־לֹא:

ח

be more comforting to know that the period of conquest would be quick, as opposed to long and drawn out? How is this promise of a, protracted military campaign of comfort to the people? The end of the verse provides the answer. If all of the people of *Canaan* would have fled at one time, large portions of land would have been left unpopulated, allowing for dangerous, wild beasts to enter and roam the land. In order to prevent this from happening, the Israelites were told that they would capture the land in stages. The modern era has also seen the remarkable return of Jewish people to their land, and it has again happened in stages, "little by little."

8:1 That you may thrive The *Kli Yakar* notes that in Hebrew this verse starts in the singular, "all the Instruction that I enjoin upon you today," but finishes in the plural, "that you may thrive and increase and be able to possess the land that *Hashem* promised on oath to your fathers." He suggests that this is because the positive actions of even a single person can benefit the entire world. An individual following one commandment can bring merit to many, and ensure that they live and thrive. Furthermore, the words in this verse, as in so many others throughout the Bible, directly connect the blessing of life to living in the Land of Israel. It is in every person's power not only to enable others to live, but to "thrive and increase and be able to possess the land that *Hashem* promised on oath to your fathers."

Devarim/Deuteronomy 8
Eikev

דברים ח
עקב

3 He subjected you to the hardship of hunger and then gave you manna to eat, which neither you nor your fathers had ever known, in order to teach you that man does not live on bread alone, but that man may live on anything that *Hashem* decrees.

ג וַיְעַנְּךָ וַיַּרְעִבֶךָ וַיַּאֲכִלְךָ אֶת הַמָּן אֲשֶׁר לֹא־יָדַעְתָּ וְלֹא יָדְעוּן אֲבֹתֶיךָ לְמַעַן הוֹדִיעֲךָ כִּי לֹא עַל־הַלֶּחֶם לְבַדּוֹ יִחְיֶה הָאָדָם כִּי עַל־כָּל־מוֹצָא פִי־יְהֹוָה יִחְיֶה הָאָדָם:

4 The clothes upon you did not wear out, nor did your feet swell these forty years.

ד שִׂמְלָתְךָ לֹא בָלְתָה מֵעָלֶיךָ וְרַגְלְךָ לֹא בָצֵקָה זֶה אַרְבָּעִים שָׁנָה:

5 Bear in mind that *Hashem* your God disciplines you just as a man disciplines his son.

ה וְיָדַעְתָּ עִם־לְבָבֶךָ כִּי כַּאֲשֶׁר יְיַסֵּר אִישׁ אֶת־בְּנוֹ יְהֹוָה אֱלֹהֶיךָ מְיַסְּרֶךָּ:

6 Therefore keep the commandments of *Hashem* your God: walk in His ways and revere Him.

ו וְשָׁמַרְתָּ אֶת־מִצְוֹת יְהֹוָה אֱלֹהֶיךָ לָלֶכֶת בִּדְרָכָיו וּלְיִרְאָה אֹתוֹ:

7 For *Hashem* your God is bringing you into a good land, a land with streams and springs and fountains issuing from plain and hill;

ז כִּי יְהֹוָה אֱלֹהֶיךָ מְבִיאֲךָ אֶל־אֶרֶץ טוֹבָה אֶרֶץ נַחֲלֵי מָיִם עֲיָנֹת וּתְהֹמֹת יֹצְאִים בַּבִּקְעָה וּבָהָר:

KEE a-do-NAI e-lo-HE-kha m'-vee-a-KHA el E-retz to-VAH E-retz NA-kha-lay MA-yim a-ya-NOT ut-ho-MOT yo-tz'-EEM ba-bik-AH u-va-HAR

8 a land of wheat and barley, of vines, figs, and pomegranates, a land of olive trees and honey;

ח אֶרֶץ חִטָּה וּשְׂעֹרָה וְגֶפֶן וּתְאֵנָה וְרִמּוֹן אֶרֶץ־זֵית שֶׁמֶן וּדְבָשׁ:

E-retz khi-TAH us-o-RAH v'-GE-fen ut-ay-NAH v'-ree-MON e-retz ZAYT SHE-men ud-VASH

9 a land where you may eat food without stint, where you will lack nothing; a land whose rocks are iron and from whose hills you can mine copper.

ט אֶרֶץ אֲשֶׁר לֹא בְמִסְכֵּנֻת תֹּאכַל־בָּהּ לֶחֶם לֹא־תֶחְסַר כֹּל בָּהּ אֶרֶץ אֲשֶׁר אֲבָנֶיהָ בַרְזֶל וּמֵהֲרָרֶיהָ תַּחְצֹב נְחֹשֶׁת:

E-retz a-SHER LO v'-mis-kay-NUT to-khal BA LE-khem lo tekh-SAR KOL BA E-retz a-SHER a-va-NE-ha var-ZEL u-may-ha-ra-RE-ha takh-TZOV n'-KHO-shet

10 When you have eaten your fill, give thanks to *Hashem* your God for the good land which He has given you.

י וְאָכַלְתָּ וְשָׂבָעְתָּ וּבֵרַכְתָּ אֶת־יְהֹוָה אֱלֹהֶיךָ עַל־הָאָרֶץ הַטֹּבָה אֲשֶׁר נָתַן־לָךְ:

11 Take care lest you forget *Hashem* your God and fail to keep His commandments, His rules, and His laws, which I enjoin upon you today.

יא הִשָּׁמֶר לְךָ פֶּן־תִּשְׁכַּח אֶת־יְהֹוָה אֱלֹהֶיךָ לְבִלְתִּי שְׁמֹר מִצְוֹתָיו וּמִשְׁפָּטָיו וְחֻקֹּתָיו אֲשֶׁר אָנֹכִי מְצַוְּךָ הַיּוֹם:

12 When you have eaten your fill, and have built fine houses to live in,

יב פֶּן־תֹּאכַל וְשָׂבָעְתָּ וּבָתִּים טוֹבִים תִּבְנֶה וְיָשָׁבְתָּ:

13 and your herds and flocks have multiplied, and your silver and gold have increased, and everything you own has prospered,

יג וּבְקָרְךָ וְצֹאנְךָ יִרְבְּיֻן וְכֶסֶף וְזָהָב יִרְבֶּה־לָךְ וְכֹל אֲשֶׁר־לְךָ יִרְבֶּה:

8:8 A land of wheat and barley, of vines, figs, and pomegranates The *Torah* names seven species as the special agricultural products of *Eretz Yisrael*. Even today, these seven crops can be seen growing all over Israel. In particular, the pomegranate has always been a symbol of beauty. Its unique shape was a favorite design element, appearing on the priestly garments and the pillars at the entrance to the *Beit Hamikdash* in *Yerushalayim*.

Pomegranates in Beit Dagan

Devarim/Deuteronomy 9
Eikev

דברים ט
עקב

14 beware lest* your heart grow haughty and you forget *Hashem* your God – who freed you from the land of Egypt, the house of bondage;

יד וְרָם לְבָבֶךָ וְשָׁכַחְתָּ אֶת־יְהֹוָה אֱלֹהֶיךָ הַמּוֹצִיאֲךָ מֵאֶרֶץ מִצְרַיִם מִבֵּית עֲבָדִים:

15 who led you through the great and terrible wilderness with its seraph serpents and scorpions, a parched land with no water in it, who brought forth water for you from the flinty rock;

טו הַמּוֹלִיכֲךָ בַּמִּדְבָּר ׀ הַגָּדֹל וְהַנּוֹרָא נָחָשׁ ׀ שָׂרָף וְעַקְרָב וְצִמָּאוֹן אֲשֶׁר אֵין־מָיִם הַמּוֹצִיא לְךָ מַיִם מִצּוּר הַחַלָּמִישׁ:

16 who fed you in the wilderness with manna, which your fathers had never known, in order to test you by hardships only to benefit you in the end

טז הַמַּאֲכִלְךָ מָן בַּמִּדְבָּר אֲשֶׁר לֹא־יָדְעוּן אֲבֹתֶיךָ לְמַעַן עַנֹּתְךָ וּלְמַעַן נַסֹּתֶךָ לְהֵיטִבְךָ בְּאַחֲרִיתֶךָ:

17 and you say to yourselves, "My own power and the might of my own hand have won this wealth for me."

יז וְאָמַרְתָּ בִּלְבָבֶךָ כֹּחִי וְעֹצֶם יָדִי עָשָׂה לִי אֶת־הַחַיִל הַזֶּה:

18 Remember that it is *Hashem* your God who gives you the power to get wealth, in fulfillment of the covenant that He made on oath with your fathers, as is still the case.

יח וְזָכַרְתָּ אֶת־יְהֹוָה אֱלֹהֶיךָ כִּי הוּא הַנֹּתֵן לְךָ כֹּחַ לַעֲשׂוֹת חָיִל לְמַעַן הָקִים אֶת־בְּרִיתוֹ אֲשֶׁר־נִשְׁבַּע לַאֲבֹתֶיךָ כַּיּוֹם הַזֶּה:

19 If you do forget *Hashem* your God and follow other gods to serve them or bow down to them, I warn you this day that you shall certainly perish;

יט וְהָיָה אִם־שָׁכֹחַ תִּשְׁכַּח אֶת־יְהֹוָה אֱלֹהֶיךָ וְהָלַכְתָּ אַחֲרֵי אֱלֹהִים אֲחֵרִים וַעֲבַדְתָּם וְהִשְׁתַּחֲוִיתָ לָהֶם הַעִדֹתִי בָכֶם הַיּוֹם כִּי אָבֹד תֹּאבֵדוּן:

20 like the nations that *Hashem* will cause to perish before you, so shall you perish – because you did not heed *Hashem* your God.

כ כַּגּוֹיִם אֲשֶׁר יְהֹוָה מַאֲבִיד מִפְּנֵיכֶם כֵּן תֹּאבֵדוּן עֵקֶב לֹא תִשְׁמְעוּן בְּקוֹל יְהֹוָה אֱלֹהֵיכֶם:

9

1 Hear, O *Yisrael*! You are about to cross the *Yarden* to go in and dispossess nations greater and more populous than you: great cities with walls sky-high;

א שְׁמַע יִשְׂרָאֵל אַתָּה עֹבֵר הַיּוֹם אֶת־הַיַּרְדֵּן לָבֹא לָרֶשֶׁת גּוֹיִם גְּדֹלִים וַעֲצֻמִים מִמֶּךָּ עָרִים גְּדֹלֹת וּבְצֻרֹת בַּשָּׁמָיִם:

sh'-MA yis-ra-AYL a-TAH o-VAYR ha-YOM et ha-yar-DAYN la-VO la-RE-shet go-YIM g'-do-LEEM va-a-tzu-MEEM mi-ME-ka a-REEM g'-do-LOT uv-tzu-ROT ba-sha-MA-yim

---

* Heb. "pen" (beware lest) moved down from v. 12 for clarity

עבר

9:1 Hear, O *Yisrael*! You are about to cross the *Yarden* The word for 'Hebrew', *Ivrit* (עברית), comes from the root *avar* (עבר), 'to cross over,' which appears in this verse. *Moshe* tells the people that they are about to cross into the land on the other side of the Jordan. Similarly, our forefather *Avraham* was called *Ha'Ivri* (Genesis 14:13) because he came from the other side of the river, and because his monotheistic views were on the "other side" compared to those of the rest of the world. *Avraham*'s heirs still carry the responsibility of being the world's moral compass, reminding others not to necessarily conform to popular norms and mores, but to do only what is right. Accordingly, the State of Israel has adopted this responsibility as its mission, to do what is right among the international community of nations even when it is not popular. Indeed, Israel comes under great scrutiny by the nations of the world. It is often viewed as being on the "other side," as a result of its historic mission to live by the principles of the Bible.

Devarim/Deuteronomy 9
Eikev

דברים ט
עקב

2 a people great and tall, the Anakites, of whom you have knowledge; for you have heard it said, "Who can stand up to the children of Anak?"

ב עַם־גָּדוֹל וָרָם בְּנֵי עֲנָקִים אֲשֶׁר אַתָּה יָדַעְתָּ וְאַתָּה שָׁמַעְתָּ מִי יִתְיַצֵּב לִפְנֵי בְּנֵי עֲנָק׃

3 Know then this day that none other than *Hashem* your God is crossing at your head, a devouring fire; it is He who will wipe them out. He will subdue them before you, that you may quickly dispossess and destroy them, as *Hashem* promised you.

ג וְיָדַעְתָּ הַיּוֹם כִּי יְהֹוָה אֱלֹהֶיךָ הוּא־הָעֹבֵר לְפָנֶיךָ אֵשׁ אֹכְלָה הוּא יַשְׁמִידֵם וְהוּא יַכְנִיעֵם לְפָנֶיךָ וְהוֹרַשְׁתָּם וְהַאֲבַדְתָּם מַהֵר כַּאֲשֶׁר דִּבֶּר יְהֹוָה לָךְ׃

4 And when *Hashem* your God has thrust them from your path, say not to yourselves, "*Hashem* has enabled us to possess this land because of our virtues"; it is rather because of the wickedness of those nations that *Hashem* is dispossessing them before you.

ד אַל־תֹּאמַר בִּלְבָבְךָ בַּהֲדֹף יְהֹוָה אֱלֹהֶיךָ אֹתָם מִלְּפָנֶיךָ לֵאמֹר בְּצִדְקָתִי הֱבִיאַנִי יְהֹוָה לָרֶשֶׁת אֶת־הָאָרֶץ הַזֹּאת וּבְרִשְׁעַת הַגּוֹיִם הָאֵלֶּה יְהֹוָה מוֹרִישָׁם מִפָּנֶיךָ׃

5 It is not because of your virtues and your rectitude that you will be able to possess their country; but it is because of their wickedness that *Hashem* your God is dispossessing those nations before you, and in order to fulfill the oath that *Hashem* made to your fathers, *Avraham*, *Yitzchak*, and *Yaakov*.

ה לֹא בְצִדְקָתְךָ וּבְיֹשֶׁר לְבָבְךָ אַתָּה בָא לָרֶשֶׁת אֶת־אַרְצָם כִּי בְּרִשְׁעַת הַגּוֹיִם הָאֵלֶּה יְהֹוָה אֱלֹהֶיךָ מוֹרִישָׁם מִפָּנֶיךָ וּלְמַעַן הָקִים אֶת־הַדָּבָר אֲשֶׁר נִשְׁבַּע יְהֹוָה לַאֲבֹתֶיךָ לְאַבְרָהָם לְיִצְחָק וּלְיַעֲקֹב׃

6 Know, then, that it is not for any virtue of yours that *Hashem* your God is giving you this good land to possess; for you are a stiffnecked people.

ו וְיָדַעְתָּ כִּי לֹא בְצִדְקָתְךָ יְהֹוָה אֱלֹהֶיךָ נֹתֵן לְךָ אֶת־הָאָרֶץ הַטּוֹבָה הַזֹּאת לְרִשְׁתָּהּ כִּי עַם־קְשֵׁה־עֹרֶף אָתָּה׃

7 Remember, never forget, how you provoked *Hashem* your God to anger in the wilderness: from the day that you left the land of Egypt until you reached this place, you have continued defiant toward *Hashem*.

ז זְכֹר אַל־תִּשְׁכַּח אֵת אֲשֶׁר־הִקְצַפְתָּ אֶת־יְהֹוָה אֱלֹהֶיךָ בַּמִּדְבָּר לְמִן־הַיּוֹם אֲשֶׁר־יָצָאתָ מֵאֶרֶץ מִצְרַיִם עַד־בֹּאֲכֶם עַד־הַמָּקוֹם הַזֶּה מַמְרִים הֱיִיתֶם עִם־יְהֹוָה׃

8 At Horeb you so provoked *Hashem* that *Hashem* was angry enough with you to have destroyed you.

ח וּבְחֹרֵב הִקְצַפְתֶּם אֶת־יְהֹוָה וַיִּתְאַנַּף יְהֹוָה בָּכֶם לְהַשְׁמִיד אֶתְכֶם׃

9 I had ascended the mountain to receive the tablets of stone, the Tablets of the Covenant that *Hashem* had made with you, and I stayed on the mountain forty days and forty nights, eating no bread and drinking no water.

ט בַּעֲלֹתִי הָהָרָה לָקַחַת לוּחֹת הָאֲבָנִים לוּחֹת הַבְּרִית אֲשֶׁר־כָּרַת יְהֹוָה עִמָּכֶם וָאֵשֵׁב בָּהָר אַרְבָּעִים יוֹם וְאַרְבָּעִים לַיְלָה לֶחֶם לֹא אָכַלְתִּי וּמַיִם לֹא שָׁתִיתִי׃

10 And *Hashem* gave me the two tablets of stone inscribed by the finger of *Hashem*, with the exact words that *Hashem* had addressed to you on the mountain out of the fire on the day of the Assembly.

י וַיִּתֵּן יְהֹוָה אֵלַי אֶת־שְׁנֵי לוּחֹת הָאֲבָנִים כְּתֻבִים בְּאֶצְבַּע אֱלֹהִים וַעֲלֵיהֶם כְּכָל־הַדְּבָרִים אֲשֶׁר דִּבֶּר יְהֹוָה עִמָּכֶם בָּהָר מִתּוֹךְ הָאֵשׁ בְּיוֹם הַקָּהָל׃

11 At the end of those forty days and forty nights, *Hashem* gave me the two tablets of stone, the Tablets of the Covenant.

יא וַיְהִי מִקֵּץ אַרְבָּעִים יוֹם וְאַרְבָּעִים לָיְלָה נָתַן יְהֹוָה אֵלַי אֶת־שְׁנֵי לֻחֹת הָאֲבָנִים לֻחוֹת הַבְּרִית׃

Devarim/Deuteronomy 9
Eikev

12 And *Hashem* said to me, "Hurry, go down from here at once, for the people whom you brought out of Egypt have acted wickedly; they have been quick to stray from the path that I enjoined upon them; they have made themselves a molten image."

13 *Hashem* further said to me, "I see that this is a stiffnecked people.

14 Let Me alone and I will destroy them and blot out their name from under heaven, and I will make you a nation far more numerous than they."

15 I started down the mountain, a mountain ablaze with fire, the two Tablets of the Covenant in my two hands.

16 I saw how you had sinned against *Hashem* your God: you had made yourselves a molten calf; you had been quick to stray from the path that *Hashem* had enjoined upon you.

17 Thereupon I gripped the two tablets and flung them away with both my hands, smashing them before your eyes.

18 I threw myself down before *Hashem* – eating no bread and drinking no water forty days and forty nights, as before – because of the great wrong you had committed, doing what displeased *Hashem* and vexing Him.

19 For I was in dread of *Hashem*'s fierce anger against you, which moved Him to wipe you out. And that time, too, *Hashem* gave heed to me.

20 Moreover, *Hashem* was angry enough with *Aharon* to have destroyed him; so I also interceded for *Aharon* at that time.

21 As for that sinful thing you had made, the calf, I took it and put it to the fire; I broke it to bits and ground it thoroughly until it was fine as dust, and I threw its dust into the brook that comes down from the mountain.

22 Again you provoked *Hashem* at Taberah, and at Massah, and at Kibroth-hattaavah.

23 And when *Hashem* sent you on from Kadesh-barnea, saying, "Go up and take possession of the land that I am giving you," you flouted the command of *Hashem* your God; you did not put your trust in Him and did not obey Him.

דברים ט
עקב

יב וַיֹּאמֶר יְהֹוָה אֵלַי קוּם רֵד מַהֵר מִזֶּה כִּי שִׁחֵת עַמְּךָ אֲשֶׁר הוֹצֵאתָ מִמִּצְרָיִם סָרוּ מַהֵר מִן־הַדֶּרֶךְ אֲשֶׁר צִוִּיתִם עָשׂוּ לָהֶם מַסֵּכָה:

יג וַיֹּאמֶר יְהֹוָה אֵלַי לֵאמֹר רָאִיתִי אֶת־הָעָם הַזֶּה וְהִנֵּה עַם־קְשֵׁה־עֹרֶף הוּא:

יד הֶרֶף מִמֶּנִּי וְאַשְׁמִידֵם וְאֶמְחֶה אֶת־שְׁמָם מִתַּחַת הַשָּׁמָיִם וְאֶעֱשֶׂה אוֹתְךָ לְגוֹי־עָצוּם וָרָב מִמֶּנּוּ:

טו וָאֵפֶן וָאֵרֵד מִן־הָהָר וְהָהָר בֹּעֵר בָּאֵשׁ וּשְׁנֵי לֻחֹת הַבְּרִית עַל שְׁתֵּי יָדָי:

טז וָאֵרֶא וְהִנֵּה חֲטָאתֶם לַיהֹוָה אֱלֹהֵיכֶם עֲשִׂיתֶם לָכֶם עֵגֶל מַסֵּכָה סַרְתֶּם מַהֵר מִן־הַדֶּרֶךְ אֲשֶׁר־צִוָּה יְהֹוָה אֶתְכֶם:

יז וָאֶתְפֹּשׂ בִּשְׁנֵי הַלֻּחֹת וָאַשְׁלִכֵם מֵעַל שְׁתֵּי יָדָי וָאֲשַׁבְּרֵם לְעֵינֵיכֶם:

יח וָאֶתְנַפַּל לִפְנֵי יְהֹוָה כָּרִאשֹׁנָה אַרְבָּעִים יוֹם וְאַרְבָּעִים לַיְלָה לֶחֶם לֹא אָכַלְתִּי וּמַיִם לֹא שָׁתִיתִי עַל כָּל־חַטַּאתְכֶם אֲשֶׁר חֲטָאתֶם לַעֲשׂוֹת הָרַע בְּעֵינֵי יְהֹוָה לְהַכְעִיסוֹ:

יט כִּי יָגֹרְתִּי מִפְּנֵי הָאַף וְהַחֵמָה אֲשֶׁר קָצַף יְהֹוָה עֲלֵיכֶם לְהַשְׁמִיד אֶתְכֶם וַיִּשְׁמַע יְהֹוָה אֵלַי גַּם בַּפַּעַם הַהִוא:

כ וּבְאַהֲרֹן הִתְאַנַּף יְהֹוָה מְאֹד לְהַשְׁמִידוֹ וָאֶתְפַּלֵּל גַּם־בְּעַד אַהֲרֹן בָּעֵת הַהִוא:

כא וְאֶת־חַטַּאתְכֶם אֲשֶׁר־עֲשִׂיתֶם אֶת־הָעֵגֶל לָקַחְתִּי וָאֶשְׂרֹף אֹתוֹ בָּאֵשׁ וָאֶכֹּת אֹתוֹ טָחוֹן הֵיטֵב עַד אֲשֶׁר־דַּק לְעָפָר וָאַשְׁלִךְ אֶת־עֲפָרוֹ אֶל־הַנַּחַל הַיֹּרֵד מִן־הָהָר:

כב וּבְתַבְעֵרָה וּבְמַסָּה וּבְקִבְרֹת הַתַּאֲוָה מַקְצִפִים הֱיִיתֶם אֶת־יְהֹוָה:

כג וּבִשְׁלֹחַ יְהֹוָה אֶתְכֶם מִקָּדֵשׁ בַּרְנֵעַ לֵאמֹר עֲלוּ וּרְשׁוּ אֶת־הָאָרֶץ אֲשֶׁר נָתַתִּי לָכֶם וַתַּמְרוּ אֶת־פִּי יְהֹוָה אֱלֹהֵיכֶם וְלֹא הֶאֱמַנְתֶּם לוֹ וְלֹא שְׁמַעְתֶּם בְּקֹלוֹ:

Devarim/Deuteronomy 10
Eikev

דברים י
עקב

24 As long as I have known you, you have been defiant toward *Hashem*.

כד מַמְרִ֥ים הֱיִיתֶ֖ם עִם־יְהֹוָ֑ה מִיּ֖וֹם דַּעְתִּ֥י אֶתְכֶֽם׃

25 When I lay prostrate before *Hashem* those forty days and forty nights, because *Hashem* was determined to destroy you,

כה וָֽאֶתְנַפַּ֞ל לִפְנֵ֣י יְהֹוָ֗ה אֵ֣ת אַרְבָּעִ֥ים הַיּ֛וֹם וְאֶת־אַרְבָּעִ֥ים הַלַּ֖יְלָה אֲשֶׁ֣ר הִתְנַפָּ֑לְתִּי כִּֽי־אָמַ֥ר יְהֹוָ֖ה לְהַשְׁמִ֥יד אֶתְכֶֽם׃

26 I prayed to *Hashem* and said, "O *Hashem*, do not annihilate Your very own people, whom You redeemed in Your majesty and whom You freed from Egypt with a mighty hand.

כו וָאֶתְפַּלֵּ֣ל אֶל־יְהֹוָה֮ וָאֹמַר֒ אֲדֹנָ֣י יֱהֹוִ֗ה אַל־תַּשְׁחֵ֤ת עַמְּךָ֙ וְנַחֲלָ֣תְךָ֔ אֲשֶׁ֥ר פָּדִ֖יתָ בְּגׇדְלֶ֑ךָ אֲשֶׁר־הוֹצֵ֥אתָ מִמִּצְרַ֖יִם בְּיָ֥ד חֲזָקָֽה׃

27 Give thought to Your servants, *Avraham*, *Yitzchak*, and *Yaakov*, and pay no heed to the stubbornness of this people, its wickedness, and its sinfulness.

כז זְכֹר֙ לַעֲבָדֶ֔יךָ לְאַבְרָהָ֥ם לְיִצְחָ֖ק וּֽלְיַעֲקֹ֑ב אַל־תֵּ֗פֶן אֶל־קְשִׁי֙ הָעָ֣ם הַזֶּ֔ה וְאֶל־רִשְׁע֖וֹ וְאֶל־חַטָּאתֽוֹ׃

28 Else the country from which You freed us will say, 'It was because *Hashem* was powerless to bring them into the land that He had promised them, and because He rejected them, that He brought them out to have them die in the wilderness.'

כח פֶּן־יֹאמְר֗וּ הָאָ֘רֶץ֮ אֲשֶׁ֣ר הוֹצֵאתָ֣נוּ מִשָּׁם֒ מִבְּלִי֙ יְכֹ֣לֶת יְהֹוָ֔ה לַהֲבִיאָ֕ם אֶל־הָאָ֖רֶץ אֲשֶׁר־דִּבֶּ֣ר לָהֶ֑ם וּמִשִּׂנְאָת֣וֹ אוֹתָ֔ם הוֹצִיאָ֖ם לַהֲמִתָ֥ם בַּמִּדְבָּֽר׃

29 Yet they are Your very own people, whom You freed with Your great might and Your outstretched arm."

כט וְהֵ֥ם עַמְּךָ֖ וְנַחֲלָתֶ֑ךָ אֲשֶׁ֤ר הוֹצֵ֙אתָ֙ בְּכֹחֲךָ֣ הַגָּדֹ֔ל וּבִֽזְרֹעֲךָ֖ הַנְּטוּיָֽה׃

10

1 Thereupon *Hashem* said to me, "Carve out two tablets of stone like the first, and come up to Me on the mountain; and make an ark of wood.

א בָּעֵ֨ת הַהִ֜וא אָמַ֧ר יְהֹוָ֣ה אֵלַ֗י פְּסׇל־לְךָ֞ שְׁנֵֽי־לוּחֹ֤ת אֲבָנִים֙ כָּרִ֣אשֹׁנִ֔ים וַעֲלֵ֥ה אֵלַ֖י הָהָ֑רָה וְעָשִׂ֥יתָ לְּךָ֖ אֲר֥וֹן עֵֽץ׃

2 I will inscribe on the tablets the commandments that were on the first tablets that you smashed, and you shall deposit them in the ark."

ב וְאֶכְתֹּב֙ עַל־הַלֻּחֹ֔ת אֶ֨ת־הַדְּבָרִ֔ים אֲשֶׁ֥ר הָי֛וּ עַל־הַלֻּחֹ֥ת הָרִאשֹׁנִ֖ים אֲשֶׁ֣ר שִׁבַּ֑רְתָּ וְשַׂמְתָּ֖ם בָּאָרֽוֹן׃

3 I made an ark of acacia wood and carved out two tablets of stone like the first; I took the two tablets with me and went up the mountain.

ג וָאַ֤עַשׂ אֲרוֹן֙ עֲצֵ֣י שִׁטִּ֔ים וָאֶפְסֹ֛ל שְׁנֵֽי־לֻחֹ֥ת אֲבָנִ֖ים כָּרִאשֹׁנִ֑ים וָאַ֣עַל הָהָ֔רָה וּשְׁנֵ֥י הַלֻּחֹ֖ת בְּיָדִֽי׃

4 *Hashem* inscribed on the tablets the same text as on the first, the Ten Commandments that He addressed to you on the mountain out of the fire on the day of the Assembly; and *Hashem* gave them to me.

ד וַיִּכְתֹּ֨ב עַֽל־הַלֻּחֹ֜ת כַּמִּכְתָּ֣ב הָרִאשׁ֗וֹן אֵ֚ת עֲשֶׂ֣רֶת הַדְּבָרִ֔ים אֲשֶׁ֣ר דִּבֶּר֩ יְהֹוָ֨ה אֲלֵיכֶ֥ם בָּהָ֛ר מִתּ֥וֹךְ הָאֵ֖שׁ בְּי֣וֹם הַקָּהָ֑ל וַיִּתְּנֵ֥ם יְהֹוָ֖ה אֵלָֽי׃

5 Then I left and went down from the mountain, and I deposited the tablets in the ark that I had made, where they still are, as *Hashem* had commanded me.

ה וָאֵ֗פֶן וָֽאֵרֵד֙ מִן־הָהָ֔ר וָֽאָשִׂם֙ אֶת־הַלֻּחֹ֔ת בָּאָר֖וֹן אֲשֶׁ֣ר עָשִׂ֑יתִי וַיִּ֣הְיוּ שָׁ֔ם כַּאֲשֶׁ֥ר צִוַּ֖נִי יְהֹוָֽה׃

6 From Beeroth-bene-jaakan the Israelites marched to Moserah. *Aharon* died there and was buried there; and his son *Elazar* became *Kohen* in his stead.

ו וּבְנֵ֣י יִשְׂרָאֵ֗ל נָֽסְע֛וּ מִבְּאֵרֹ֥ת בְּנֵי־יַעֲקָ֖ן מוֹסֵרָ֑ה שָׁ֣ם מֵ֤ת אַהֲרֹן֙ וַיִּקָּבֵ֣ר שָׁ֔ם וַיְכַהֵ֛ן אֶלְעָזָ֥ר בְּנ֖וֹ תַּחְתָּֽיו׃

7 From there they marched to Gudgod, and from Gudgod to Jotbath, a region of running brooks.

ז מִשָּׁ֥ם נָסְע֖וּ הַגֻּדְגֹּ֑דָה וּמִן־הַגֻּדְגֹּ֣דָה יׇטְבָ֔תָה אֶ֖רֶץ נַ֥חֲלֵי מָֽיִם׃

Devarim/Deuteronomy 10
Eikev

8 At that time *Hashem* set apart the tribe of *Levi* to carry the *Aron* Brit *Hashem*, to stand in attendance upon *Hashem*, and to bless in His name, as is still the case.

9 That is why the *Leviim* have received no hereditary portion along with their kinsmen: *Hashem* is their portion, as *Hashem* your God spoke concerning them.

10 I had stayed on the mountain, as I did the first time, forty days and forty nights; and *Hashem* heeded me once again: *Hashem* agreed not to destroy you.

11 And *Hashem* said to me, "Up, resume the march at the head of the people, that they may go in and possess the land that I swore to their fathers to give them."

12 And now, O *Yisrael*, what does *Hashem* your God demand of you? Only this: to revere *Hashem* your God, to walk only in His paths, to love Him, and to serve *Hashem* your God with all your heart and soul,

13 keeping *Hashem*'s commandments and laws, which I enjoin upon you today, for your good.

14 Mark, the heavens to their uttermost reaches belong to *Hashem* your God, the earth and all that is on it!

15 Yet it was to your fathers that *Hashem* was drawn in His love for them, so that He chose you, their lineal descendants, from among all peoples – as is now the case.

16 Cut away, therefore, the thickening about your hearts and stiffen your necks no more.

17 For *Hashem* your God is God supreme and Lord supreme, the great, the mighty, and the awesome *Hashem*, who shows no favor and takes no bribe,

18 but upholds the cause of the fatherless and the widow, and befriends the stranger, providing him with food and clothing.

דברים י
עקב

ח בָּעֵת הַהִוא הִבְדִּיל יְהֹוָה אֶת־שֵׁבֶט הַלֵּוִי לָשֵׂאת אֶת־אֲרוֹן בְּרִית־יְהֹוָה לַעֲמֹד לִפְנֵי יְהֹוָה לְשָׁרְתוֹ וּלְבָרֵךְ בִּשְׁמוֹ עַד הַיּוֹם הַזֶּה:

ט עַל־כֵּן לֹא־הָיָה לְלֵוִי חֵלֶק וְנַחֲלָה עִם־אֶחָיו יְהֹוָה הוּא נַחֲלָתוֹ כַּאֲשֶׁר דִּבֶּר יְהֹוָה אֱלֹהֶיךָ לוֹ:

י וְאָנֹכִי עָמַדְתִּי בָהָר כַּיָּמִים הָרִאשֹׁנִים אַרְבָּעִים יוֹם וְאַרְבָּעִים לָיְלָה וַיִּשְׁמַע יְהֹוָה אֵלַי גַּם בַּפַּעַם הַהִוא לֹא־אָבָה יְהֹוָה הַשְׁחִיתֶךָ:

יא וַיֹּאמֶר יְהֹוָה אֵלַי קוּם לֵךְ לְמַסַּע לִפְנֵי הָעָם וְיָבֹאוּ וְיִירְשׁוּ אֶת־הָאָרֶץ אֲשֶׁר־נִשְׁבַּעְתִּי לַאֲבֹתָם לָתֵת לָהֶם:

יב וְעַתָּה יִשְׂרָאֵל מָה יְהֹוָה אֱלֹהֶיךָ שֹׁאֵל מֵעִמָּךְ כִּי אִם־לְיִרְאָה אֶת־יְהֹוָה אֱלֹהֶיךָ לָלֶכֶת בְּכָל־דְּרָכָיו וּלְאַהֲבָה אֹתוֹ וְלַעֲבֹד אֶת־יְהֹוָה אֱלֹהֶיךָ בְּכָל־לְבָבְךָ וּבְכָל־נַפְשֶׁךָ:

יג לִשְׁמֹר אֶת־מִצְוֺת יְהֹוָה וְאֶת־חֻקֹּתָיו אֲשֶׁר אָנֹכִי מְצַוְּךָ הַיּוֹם לְטוֹב לָךְ:

יד הֵן לַיהֹוָה אֱלֹהֶיךָ הַשָּׁמַיִם וּשְׁמֵי הַשָּׁמָיִם הָאָרֶץ וְכָל־אֲשֶׁר־בָּהּ:

טו רַק בַּאֲבֹתֶיךָ חָשַׁק יְהֹוָה לְאַהֲבָה אוֹתָם וַיִּבְחַר בְּזַרְעָם אַחֲרֵיהֶם בָּכֶם מִכָּל־הָעַמִּים כַּיּוֹם הַזֶּה:

טז וּמַלְתֶּם אֵת עָרְלַת לְבַבְכֶם וְעָרְפְּכֶם לֹא תַקְשׁוּ עוֹד:

יז כִּי יְהֹוָה אֱלֹהֵיכֶם הוּא אֱלֹהֵי הָאֱלֹהִים וַאֲדֹנֵי הָאֲדֹנִים הָאֵל הַגָּדֹל הַגִּבֹּר וְהַנּוֹרָא אֲשֶׁר לֹא־יִשָּׂא פָנִים וְלֹא יִקַּח שֹׁחַד:

יח עֹשֶׂה מִשְׁפַּט יָתוֹם וְאַלְמָנָה וְאֹהֵב גֵּר לָתֶת לוֹ לֶחֶם וְשִׂמְלָה:

Devarim/Deuteronomy 11
Eikev

דברים יא
עקב

19 You too must befriend the stranger, for you were strangers in the land of Egypt.

יט וַאֲהַבְתֶּם אֶת־הַגֵּר כִּי־גֵרִים הֱיִיתֶם בְּאֶרֶץ מִצְרָיִם:

va-a-hav-TEM et ha-GAYR kee gay-REEM he-yee-TEM b'-E-retz mitz-RA-yim

20 You must revere *Hashem* your God: only Him shall you worship, to Him shall you hold fast, and by His name shall you swear.

כ אֶת־יְהֹוָה אֱלֹהֶיךָ תִּירָא אֹתוֹ תַעֲבֹד וּבוֹ תִדְבָּק וּבִשְׁמוֹ תִּשָּׁבֵעַ:

21 He is your glory and He is your God, who wrought for you those marvelous, awesome deeds that you saw with your own eyes.

כא הוּא תְהִלָּתְךָ וְהוּא אֱלֹהֶיךָ אֲשֶׁר־עָשָׂה אִתְּךָ אֶת־הַגְּדֹלֹת וְאֶת־הַנּוֹרָאֹת הָאֵלֶּה אֲשֶׁר רָאוּ עֵינֶיךָ:

22 Your ancestors went down to Egypt seventy persons in all; and now *Hashem* your God has made you as numerous as the stars of heaven.

כב בְּשִׁבְעִים נֶפֶשׁ יָרְדוּ אֲבֹתֶיךָ מִצְרָיְמָה וְעַתָּה שָׂמְךָ יְהֹוָה אֱלֹהֶיךָ כְּכוֹכְבֵי הַשָּׁמַיִם לָרֹב:

11 1 Love, therefore, *Hashem* your God, and always keep His charge, His laws, His rules, and His commandments.

יא א וְאָהַבְתָּ אֵת יְהֹוָה אֱלֹהֶיךָ וְשָׁמַרְתָּ מִשְׁמַרְתּוֹ וְחֻקֹּתָיו וּמִשְׁפָּטָיו וּמִצְוֹתָיו כָּל־הַיָּמִים:

2 Take thought this day that it was not your children, who neither experienced nor witnessed the lesson of *Hashem* your God – His majesty, His mighty hand, His outstretched arm;

ב וִידַעְתֶּם הַיּוֹם כִּי לֹא אֶת־בְּנֵיכֶם אֲשֶׁר לֹא־יָדְעוּ וַאֲשֶׁר לֹא־רָאוּ אֶת־מוּסַר יְהֹוָה אֱלֹהֵיכֶם אֶת־גָּדְלוֹ אֶת־יָדוֹ הַחֲזָקָה וּזְרֹעוֹ הַנְּטוּיָה:

3 the signs and the deeds that He performed in Egypt against Pharaoh king of Egypt and all his land;

ג וְאֶת־אֹתֹתָיו וְאֶת־מַעֲשָׂיו אֲשֶׁר עָשָׂה בְּתוֹךְ מִצְרָיִם לְפַרְעֹה מֶלֶךְ־מִצְרַיִם וּלְכָל־אַרְצוֹ:

4 what He did to Egypt's army, its horses and chariots; how *Hashem* rolled back upon them the waters of the Sea of Reeds when they were pursuing you, thus destroying them once and for all;

ד וַאֲשֶׁר עָשָׂה לְחֵיל מִצְרַיִם לְסוּסָיו וּלְרִכְבּוֹ אֲשֶׁר הֵצִיף אֶת־מֵי יַם־סוּף עַל־פְּנֵיהֶם בְּרָדְפָם אַחֲרֵיכֶם וַיְאַבְּדֵם יְהֹוָה עַד הַיּוֹם הַזֶּה:

5 what He did for you in the wilderness before you arrived in this place;

ה וַאֲשֶׁר עָשָׂה לָכֶם בַּמִּדְבָּר עַד־בֹּאֲכֶם עַד־הַמָּקוֹם הַזֶּה:

6 and what He did to *Datan* and *Aviram*, sons of *Eliav* son of *Reuven*, when the earth opened her mouth and swallowed them, along with their households, their tents, and every living thing in their train, from amidst all *Yisrael* –

ו וַאֲשֶׁר עָשָׂה לְדָתָן וְלַאֲבִירָם בְּנֵי אֱלִיאָב בֶּן־רְאוּבֵן אֲשֶׁר פָּצְתָה הָאָרֶץ אֶת־פִּיהָ וַתִּבְלָעֵם וְאֶת־בָּתֵּיהֶם וְאֶת־אָהֳלֵיהֶם וְאֵת כָּל־הַיְקוּם אֲשֶׁר בְּרַגְלֵיהֶם בְּקֶרֶב כָּל־יִשְׂרָאֵל:

10:19 For you were strangers in the land of Egypt *Hashem* instructs His People to love the stranger and the convert, and to take extra care of those who are new to the community and alone. This stands in contrast to the people's experience as strangers in Egypt, where they were viciously oppressed. The Talmud (*Bava Metzia* 59b) points out that this commandment is repeated no less than thirty-six times throughout the Bible, to emphasize that as the People of Israel prepare to enter the Land of Israel, where they will be the masters and no longer the strangers, they are warned not to forget what is was like to be outsiders. They must do whatever they can to ease the struggles of strangers in their land.

Devarim/Deuteronomy 11
Eikev

דברים יא
עקב

7 but that it was you who saw with your own eyes all the marvelous deeds that *Hashem* performed.

ז כִּי עֵינֵיכֶם הָרֹאֹת אֶת־כָּל־מַעֲשֵׂה יְהֹוָה הַגָּדֹל אֲשֶׁר עָשָׂה:

8 Keep, therefore, all the Instruction that I enjoin upon you today, so that you may have the strength to enter and take possession of the land that you are about to cross into and possess,

ח וּשְׁמַרְתֶּם אֶת־כָּל־הַמִּצְוָה אֲשֶׁר אָנֹכִי מְצַוְּךָ הַיּוֹם לְמַעַן תֶּחֶזְקוּ וּבָאתֶם וִירִשְׁתֶּם אֶת־הָאָרֶץ אֲשֶׁר אַתֶּם עֹבְרִים שָׁמָּה לְרִשְׁתָּהּ:

9 and that you may long endure upon the soil that *Hashem* swore to your fathers to assign to them and to their heirs, a land flowing with milk and honey.

ט וּלְמַעַן תַּאֲרִיכוּ יָמִים עַל־הָאֲדָמָה אֲשֶׁר נִשְׁבַּע יְהֹוָה לַאֲבֹתֵיכֶם לָתֵת לָהֶם וּלְזַרְעָם אֶרֶץ זָבַת חָלָב וּדְבָשׁ:

10 For the land that you are about to enter and possess is not like the land of Egypt from which you have come. There the grain you sowed had to be watered by your own labors, like a vegetable garden;

י כִּי הָאָרֶץ אֲשֶׁר אַתָּה בָא־שָׁמָּה לְרִשְׁתָּהּ לֹא כְאֶרֶץ מִצְרַיִם הִוא אֲשֶׁר יְצָאתֶם מִשָּׁם אֲשֶׁר תִּזְרַע אֶת־זַרְעֲךָ וְהִשְׁקִיתָ בְרַגְלְךָ כְּגַן הַיָּרָק:

11 but the land you are about to cross into and possess, a land of hills and valleys, soaks up its water from the rains of heaven.

יא וְהָאָרֶץ אֲשֶׁר אַתֶּם עֹבְרִים שָׁמָּה לְרִשְׁתָּהּ אֶרֶץ הָרִים וּבְקָעֹת לִמְטַר הַשָּׁמַיִם תִּשְׁתֶּה־מָּיִם:

12 It is a land which *Hashem* your God looks after, on which *Hashem* your God always keeps His eye, from year's beginning to year's end.

יב אֶרֶץ אֲשֶׁר־יְהֹוָה אֱלֹהֶיךָ דֹּרֵשׁ אֹתָהּ תָּמִיד עֵינֵי יְהֹוָה אֱלֹהֶיךָ בָּהּ מֵרֵשִׁית הַשָּׁנָה וְעַד אַחֲרִית שָׁנָה:

E-retz a-sher a-do-NAI e-lo-HE-kha do-RAYSH o-TAH ta-MEED ay-NAY a-do-NAI e-lo-HE-kha BA may-ray-SHEET ha-sha-NAH v'-AD a-kha-REET sha-NAH

13 If, then, you obey the commandments that I enjoin upon you this day, loving *Hashem* your God and serving Him with all your heart and soul,

יג וְהָיָה אִם־שָׁמֹעַ תִּשְׁמְעוּ אֶל־מִצְוֹתַי אֲשֶׁר אָנֹכִי מְצַוֶּה אֶתְכֶם הַיּוֹם לְאַהֲבָה אֶת־יְהֹוָה אֱלֹהֵיכֶם וּלְעָבְדוֹ בְּכָל־לְבַבְכֶם וּבְכָל־נַפְשְׁכֶם:

14 I will grant the rain for your land in season, the early rain and the late. You shall gather in your new grain and wine and oil

יד וְנָתַתִּי מְטַר־אַרְצְכֶם בְּעִתּוֹ יוֹרֶה וּמַלְקוֹשׁ וְאָסַפְתָּ דְגָנֶךָ וְתִירֹשְׁךָ וְיִצְהָרֶךָ:

15 I will also provide grass in the fields for your cattle – and thus you shall eat your fill.

טו וְנָתַתִּי עֵשֶׂב בְּשָׂדְךָ לִבְהֶמְתֶּךָ וְאָכַלְתָּ וְשָׂבָעְתָּ:

16 Take care not to be lured away to serve other gods and bow to them.

טז הִשָּׁמְרוּ לָכֶם פֶּן יִפְתֶּה לְבַבְכֶם וְסַרְתֶּם וַעֲבַדְתֶּם אֱלֹהִים אֲחֵרִים וְהִשְׁתַּחֲוִיתֶם לָהֶם:

11:12 From year's beginning to year's end This is the only time the Bible tells us how *Hashem* "spends His time." From the beginning of the year until the end, it says, the Creator of the universe focuses "His eyes" and attention on Israel. If we combine this idea with that mentioned in verse 22 instructing us to walk in *Hashem*'s ways and hold fast to Him, we must likewise keep our eyes focused on *Eretz Yisrael* "from year's beginning to year's end." This verse inspired Rabbi Tuly Weisz to start "Israel365," which enables hundreds of thousands of people all over the world to connect with Israel each and every day of the year.

Devarim/Deuteronomy 11
Re'eih

17 For *Hashem*'s anger will flare up against you, and He will shut up the skies so that there will be no rain and the ground will not yield its produce; and you will soon perish from the good land that *Hashem* is assigning to you.

18 Therefore impress these My words upon your very heart: bind them as a sign on your hand and let them serve as a symbol on your forehead,

19 and teach them to your children – reciting them when you stay at home and when you are away, when you lie down and when you get up;

20 and inscribe them on the doorposts of your house and on your gates

21 to the end that you and your children may endure, in the land that *Hashem* swore to your fathers to assign to them, as long as there is a heaven over the earth.

22 If, then, you faithfully keep all this Instruction that I command you, loving *Hashem* your God, walking in all His ways, and holding fast to Him,

23 *Hashem* will dislodge before you all these nations: you will dispossess nations greater and more numerous than you.

24 Every spot on which your foot treads shall be yours; your territory shall extend from the wilderness to the Lebanon and from the River – the Euphrates – to the Western Sea.

25 No man shall stand up to you: *Hashem* your God will put the dread and the fear of you over the whole land in which you set foot, as He promised you.

26 See, this day I set before you blessing and curse:

27 blessing, if you obey the commandments of *Hashem* your God that I enjoin upon you this day;

28 and curse, if you do not obey the commandments of *Hashem* your God, but turn away from the path that I enjoin upon you this day and follow other gods, whom you have not experienced.

דברים יא
ראה

יז וְחָרָה אַף־יְהֹוָה בָּכֶם וְעָצַר אֶת־הַשָּׁמַיִם וְלֹא־יִהְיֶה מָטָר וְהָאֲדָמָה לֹא תִתֵּן אֶת־יְבוּלָהּ וַאֲבַדְתֶּם מְהֵרָה מֵעַל הָאָרֶץ הַטֹּבָה אֲשֶׁר יְהֹוָה נֹתֵן לָכֶם׃

יח וְשַׂמְתֶּם אֶת־דְּבָרַי אֵלֶּה עַל־לְבַבְכֶם וְעַל־נַפְשְׁכֶם וּקְשַׁרְתֶּם אֹתָם לְאוֹת עַל־יֶדְכֶם וְהָיוּ לְטוֹטָפֹת בֵּין עֵינֵיכֶם׃

יט וְלִמַּדְתֶּם אֹתָם אֶת־בְּנֵיכֶם לְדַבֵּר בָּם בְּשִׁבְתְּךָ בְּבֵיתֶךָ וּבְלֶכְתְּךָ בַדֶּרֶךְ וּבְשָׁכְבְּךָ וּבְקוּמֶךָ׃

כ וּכְתַבְתָּם עַל־מְזוּזוֹת בֵּיתֶךָ וּבִשְׁעָרֶיךָ׃

כא לְמַעַן יִרְבּוּ יְמֵיכֶם וִימֵי בְנֵיכֶם עַל הָאֲדָמָה אֲשֶׁר נִשְׁבַּע יְהֹוָה לַאֲבֹתֵיכֶם לָתֵת לָהֶם כִּימֵי הַשָּׁמַיִם עַל־הָאָרֶץ׃

כב כִּי אִם־שָׁמֹר תִּשְׁמְרוּן אֶת־כָּל־הַמִּצְוָה הַזֹּאת אֲשֶׁר אָנֹכִי מְצַוֶּה אֶתְכֶם לַעֲשֹׂתָהּ לְאַהֲבָה אֶת־יְהֹוָה אֱלֹהֵיכֶם לָלֶכֶת בְּכָל־דְּרָכָיו וּלְדָבְקָה־בּוֹ׃

כג וְהוֹרִישׁ יְהֹוָה אֶת־כָּל־הַגּוֹיִם הָאֵלֶּה מִלִּפְנֵיכֶם וִירִשְׁתֶּם גּוֹיִם גְּדֹלִים וַעֲצֻמִים מִכֶּם׃

כד כָּל־הַמָּקוֹם אֲשֶׁר תִּדְרֹךְ כַּף־רַגְלְכֶם בּוֹ לָכֶם יִהְיֶה מִן־הַמִּדְבָּר וְהַלְּבָנוֹן מִן־הַנָּהָר נְהַר־פְּרָת וְעַד הַיָּם הָאַחֲרוֹן יִהְיֶה גְּבֻלְכֶם׃

כה לֹא־יִתְיַצֵּב אִישׁ בִּפְנֵיכֶם פַּחְדְּכֶם וּמוֹרַאֲכֶם יִתֵּן יְהֹוָה אֱלֹהֵיכֶם עַל־פְּנֵי כָל־הָאָרֶץ אֲשֶׁר תִּדְרְכוּ־בָהּ כַּאֲשֶׁר דִּבֶּר לָכֶם׃

כו רְאֵה אָנֹכִי נֹתֵן לִפְנֵיכֶם הַיּוֹם בְּרָכָה וּקְלָלָה׃

כז אֶת־הַבְּרָכָה אֲשֶׁר תִּשְׁמְעוּ אֶל־מִצְוֺת יְהֹוָה אֱלֹהֵיכֶם אֲשֶׁר אָנֹכִי מְצַוֶּה אֶתְכֶם הַיּוֹם׃

כח וְהַקְּלָלָה אִם־לֹא תִשְׁמְעוּ אֶל־מִצְוֺת יְהֹוָה אֱלֹהֵיכֶם וְסַרְתֶּם מִן־הַדֶּרֶךְ אֲשֶׁר אָנֹכִי מְצַוֶּה אֶתְכֶם הַיּוֹם לָלֶכֶת אַחֲרֵי אֱלֹהִים אֲחֵרִים אֲשֶׁר לֹא־יְדַעְתֶּם׃

Devarim/Deuteronomy 12
Re'eih

דברים יב
ראה

29 When *Hashem* your God brings you into the land that you are about to enter and possess, you shall pronounce the blessing at *Har Gerizim* and the curse at *Har Eival*.

כט וְהָיָ֡ה כִּֽי־יְבִֽיאֲךָ֩ יְהוָ֨ה אֱלֹהֶ֜יךָ אֶל־הָאָ֗רֶץ אֲשֶׁר־אַתָּ֥ה בָא־שָׁ֖מָּה לְרִשְׁתָּ֑הּ וְנָתַתָּ֤ה אֶת־הַבְּרָכָה֙ עַל־הַ֣ר גְּרִזִ֔ים וְאֶת־הַקְּלָלָ֖ה עַל־הַ֥ר עֵיבָֽל:

v'-ha-YA KEE y'-vee-a-KHA a-do-NAI e-lo-HE-kha el ha-A-retz a-sher a-TA va SHA-ma l'-rish-TA v'-na-ta-TA et ha-b'-ra-KHAH al HAR g'-ri-ZEEM v'-et ha-k'-la-LAH al HAR ay-VAL

30 Both are on the other side of the *Yarden*, beyond the west road that is in the land of the Canaanites who dwell in the Arabah – near *Gilgal*, by the terebinths of Moreh.

ל הֲלֹא־הֵ֜מָּה בְּעֵ֣בֶר הַיַּרְדֵּ֗ן אַֽחֲרֵי֙ דֶּ֚רֶךְ מְב֣וֹא הַשֶּׁ֔מֶשׁ בְּאֶ֨רֶץ֙ הַֽכְּנַעֲנִ֔י הַיֹּשֵׁ֖ב בָּֽעֲרָבָ֑ה מ֚וּל הַגִּלְגָּ֔ל אֵ֖צֶל אֵלוֹנֵ֥י מֹרֶֽה:

31 For you are about to cross the *Yarden* to enter and possess the land that *Hashem* your God is assigning to you. When you have occupied it and are settled in it,

לא כִּ֤י אַתֶּם֙ עֹֽבְרִ֣ים אֶת־הַיַּרְדֵּ֔ן לָבֹא֙ לָרֶ֣שֶׁת אֶת־הָאָ֔רֶץ אֲשֶׁר־יְהוָ֥ה אֱלֹֽהֵיכֶ֖ם נֹתֵ֣ן לָכֶ֑ם וִֽירִשְׁתֶּ֥ם אֹתָ֖הּ וִֽישַׁבְתֶּם־בָּֽהּ:

32 take care to observe all the laws and rules that I have set before you this day.

לב וּשְׁמַרְתֶּ֣ם לַֽעֲשׂ֔וֹת אֵ֥ת כָּל־הַֽחֻקִּ֖ים וְאֶת־הַמִּשְׁפָּטִ֑ים אֲשֶׁ֧ר אָֽנֹכִ֛י נֹתֵ֖ן לִפְנֵיכֶ֥ם הַיּֽוֹם:

12

1 These are the laws and rules that you must carefully observe in the land that *Hashem*, God of your fathers, is giving you to possess, as long as you live on earth.

א אֵ֠לֶּה הַֽחֻקִּ֣ים וְהַמִּשְׁפָּטִים֮ אֲשֶׁ֣ר תִּשְׁמְר֣וּן לַֽעֲשׂוֹת֒ בָּאָ֕רֶץ אֲשֶׁר֩ נָתַ֨ן יְהוָ֜ה אֱלֹהֵ֧י אֲבֹתֶ֛יךָ לְךָ֖ לְרִשְׁתָּ֑הּ כָּל־הַיָּמִ֔ים אֲשֶׁר־אַתֶּ֥ם חַיִּ֖ים עַל־הָֽאֲדָמָֽה:

2 You must destroy all the sites at which the nations you are to dispossess worshiped their gods, whether on lofty mountains and on hills or under any luxuriant tree.

ב אַבֵּ֣ד תְּ֠אַבְּד֠וּן אֶֽת־כָּל־הַמְּקֹמ֞וֹת אֲשֶׁ֧ר עָֽבְדוּ־שָׁ֣ם הַגּוֹיִ֗ם אֲשֶׁ֥ר אַתֶּ֛ם יֹֽרְשִׁ֥ים אֹתָ֖ם אֶת־אֱלֹֽהֵיהֶ֑ם עַל־הֶֽהָרִ֤ים הָֽרָמִים֙ וְעַל־הַגְּבָע֔וֹת וְתַ֖חַת כָּל־עֵ֥ץ רַֽעֲנָֽן:

3 Tear down their altars, smash their pillars, put their sacred posts to the fire, and cut down the images of their gods, obliterating their name from that site.

ג וְנִתַּצְתֶּ֣ם אֶת־מִזְבְּחֹתָ֗ם וְשִׁבַּרְתֶּם֙ אֶת־מַצֵּ֣בֹתָ֔ם וַֽאֲשֵֽׁרֵיהֶם֙ תִּשְׂרְפ֣וּן בָּאֵ֔שׁ וּפְסִילֵ֥י אֱלֹֽהֵיהֶ֖ם תְּגַדֵּע֑וּן וְאִבַּדְתֶּ֣ם אֶת־שְׁמָ֔ם מִן־הַמָּק֖וֹם הַהֽוּא:

4 Do not worship *Hashem* your God in like manner,

ד לֹֽא־תַֽעֲשׂ֣וּן כֵּ֔ן לַֽיהוָ֖ה אֱלֹֽהֵיכֶֽם:

5 but look only to the site that *Hashem* your God will choose amidst all your tribes as His habitation, to establish His name there. There you are to go,

ה כִּ֠י אִֽם־אֶל־הַמָּק֞וֹם אֲשֶׁר־יִבְחַ֨ר יְהוָ֤ה אֱלֹֽהֵיכֶם֙ מִכָּל־שִׁבְטֵיכֶ֔ם לָשׂ֥וּם אֶת־שְׁמ֖וֹ שָׁ֑ם לְשִׁכְנ֥וֹ תִדְרְשׁ֖וּ וּבָ֥אתָ שָֽׁמָּה:

KEE im el ha-ma-KOM a-sher yiv-KHAR a-do-NAI e-lo-hay-KHEM mi-kol shiv-tay-KHEM la-SUM et sh'-MO SHAM l'-shikh-NO tid-r'-SHU u-VA-ta SHA-ma

---

12:5 To establish His name there The Hebrew word for 'to establish His name' is *l'shichno* (לשכנו). The root of this word, *shachen* (ש-כ-נ), means 'to dwell', and is also the root of the word *shechina* (שכינה), used to refer to *Hashem*'s presence. The use of this word to refer to His presence alludes to our close, personal, relationship with the Almighty, as the name indicates that He dwells among us. Additionally, this verse reminds us that the place on earth where *Hashem*'s presence is perceived more than any other is the Temple Mount in *Yerushalayim*, the place where he chose "to establish His name."

שכינה

The Temple Mount and Western Wall

469

Devarim/Deuteronomy 12
Re'eih

דברים יב
ראה

6 and there you are to bring your burnt offerings and other sacrifices, your tithes and contributions, your votive and freewill offerings, and the firstlings of your herds and flocks.

ו וַהֲבֵאתֶ֣ם שָׁ֗מָּה עֹלֹתֵיכֶם֙ וְזִבְחֵיכֶ֔ם וְאֵת֙ מַעְשְׂרֹ֣תֵיכֶ֔ם וְאֵ֖ת תְּרוּמַ֣ת יֶדְכֶ֑ם וְנִדְרֵיכֶם֙ וְנִדְבֹ֣תֵיכֶ֔ם וּבְכֹרֹ֥ת בְּקַרְכֶ֖ם וְצֹאנְכֶֽם׃

7 Together with your households, you shall feast there before *Hashem* your God, happy in all the undertakings in which *Hashem* your God has blessed you.

ז וַאֲכַלְתֶּם־שָׁ֗ם לִפְנֵי֙ יְהֹוָ֣ה אֱלֹֽהֵיכֶ֔ם וּשְׂמַחְתֶּ֗ם בְּכֹל֙ מִשְׁלַ֣ח יֶדְכֶ֔ם אַתֶּ֖ם וּבָתֵּיכֶ֑ם אֲשֶׁ֥ר בֵּֽרַכְךָ֖ יְהֹוָ֥ה אֱלֹהֶֽיךָ׃

8 You shall not act at all as we now act here, every man as he pleases,

ח לֹ֣א תַעֲשׂ֔וּן כְּ֠כֹ֠ל אֲשֶׁ֨ר אֲנַ֧חְנוּ עֹשִׂ֛ים פֹּ֖ה הַיּ֑וֹם אִ֖ישׁ כׇּל־הַיָּשָׁ֥ר בְּעֵינָֽיו׃

9 because you have not yet come to the allotted haven that *Hashem* your God is giving you.

ט כִּ֥י לֹא־בָּאתֶ֖ם עַד־עָ֑תָּה אֶל־הַמְּנוּחָה֙ וְאֶל־הַֽנַּחֲלָ֔ה אֲשֶׁר־יְהֹוָ֥ה אֱלֹהֶ֖יךָ נֹתֵ֥ן לָֽךְ׃

10 When you cross the *Yarden* and settle in the land that *Hashem* your God is allotting to you, and He grants you safety from all your enemies around you and you live in security,

י וַעֲבַרְתֶּם֮ אֶת־הַיַּרְדֵּן֒ וִישַׁבְתֶּ֣ם בָּאָ֔רֶץ אֲשֶׁר־יְהֹוָ֥ה אֱלֹהֵיכֶ֖ם מַנְחִ֣יל אֶתְכֶ֑ם וְהֵנִ֨יחַ לָכֶ֧ם מִכׇּל־אֹיְבֵיכֶ֛ם מִסָּבִ֖יב וִֽישַׁבְתֶּם־בֶּֽטַח׃

va-a-var-TEM et ha-yar-DAYN vee-shav-TEM ba-A-retz a-sher a-do-NAI e-lo-hay-KHEM man-KHEEL et-KHEM v'-hay-NEE-akh la-KHEM mi-kol o-y'-vay-KHEM mi-sa-VEEV vee-shav-tem BE-takh

11 then you must bring everything that I command you to the site where *Hashem* your God will choose to establish His name: your burnt offerings and other sacrifices, your tithes and contributions, and all the choice votive offerings that you vow to *Hashem*.

יא וְהָיָ֣ה הַמָּק֗וֹם אֲשֶׁר־יִבְחַר֩ יְהֹוָ֨ה אֱלֹהֵיכֶ֥ם בּוֹ֙ לְשַׁכֵּ֤ן שְׁמוֹ֙ שָׁ֔ם שָׁ֣מָּה תָבִ֔יאוּ אֵ֛ת כׇּל־אֲשֶׁ֥ר אָנֹכִ֖י מְצַוֶּ֣ה אֶתְכֶ֑ם עוֹלֹתֵיכֶ֣ם וְזִבְחֵיכֶ֗ם מַעְשְׂרֹֽתֵיכֶם֙ וּתְרֻמַ֣ת יֶדְכֶ֔ם וְכֹל֙ מִבְחַ֣ר נִדְרֵיכֶ֔ם אֲשֶׁ֥ר תִּדְּר֖וּ לַֽיהֹוָֽה׃

12 And you shall rejoice before *Hashem* your God with your sons and daughters and with your male and female slaves, along with the Levite in your settlements, for he has no territorial allotment among you.

יב וּשְׂמַחְתֶּ֗ם לִפְנֵי֙ יְהֹוָ֣ה אֱלֹֽהֵיכֶ֔ם אַתֶּ֕ם וּבְנֵיכֶ֖ם וּבְנֹתֵיכֶ֑ם וְעַבְדֵיכֶ֖ם וְאַמְהֹתֵיכֶ֑ם וְהַלֵּוִי֙ אֲשֶׁ֣ר בְּשַׁעֲרֵיכֶ֔ם כִּ֣י אֵ֥ין ל֛וֹ חֵ֥לֶק וְנַחֲלָ֖ה אִתְּכֶֽם׃

13 Take care not to sacrifice your burnt offerings in any place you like,

יג הִשָּׁ֣מֶר לְךָ֔ פֶּֽן־תַּעֲלֶ֖ה עֹלֹתֶ֑יךָ בְּכׇל־מָק֖וֹם אֲשֶׁ֥ר תִּרְאֶֽה׃

12:10 He grants you safety from all your enemies around you *Moshe* promises the Children of Israel peace and security in the Land of Israel. Indeed, after conquering and dividing the land under the leadership of *Yehoshua*, the Children of Israel did dwell peacefully in the land, as the verse says "*Hashem* had given Israel rest from all the enemies around them" (Joshua 23:1). However, this peace was short-lived; it did not take long after the death of *Yehoshua* for enemy nations to begin harassing them in their land. Throughout history, there have been periods of relative quiet in the land, but none have lasted very long. We pray for the complete fulfillment of this verse, when we will be blessed with everlasting safety and security in *Eretz Yisrael*.

Devarim/Deuteronomy 12
Re'eih

דברים יב
ראה

14 but only in the place that *Hashem* will choose in one of your tribal territories. There you shall sacrifice your burnt offerings and there you shall observe all that I enjoin upon you.

יד כִּי אִם־בַּמָּקוֹם אֲשֶׁר־יִבְחַר יְהֹוָה בְּאַחַד שְׁבָטֶיךָ שָׁם תַּעֲלֶה עֹלֹתֶיךָ וְשָׁם תַּעֲשֶׂה כֹּל אֲשֶׁר אָנֹכִי מְצַוֶּךָּ׃

15 But whenever you desire, you may slaughter and eat meat in any of your settlements, according to the blessing that *Hashem* your God has granted you. The unclean and the clean alike may partake of it, as of the gazelle and the deer.

טו רַק בְּכׇל־אַוַּת נַפְשְׁךָ תִּזְבַּח וְאָכַלְתָּ בָשָׂר כְּבִרְכַּת יְהֹוָה אֱלֹהֶיךָ אֲשֶׁר נָתַן־לְךָ בְּכׇל־שְׁעָרֶיךָ הַטָּמֵא וְהַטָּהוֹר יֹאכְלֶנּוּ כַּצְּבִי וְכָאַיָּל׃

16 But you must not partake of the blood; you shall pour it out on the ground like water.

טז רַק הַדָּם לֹא תֹאכֵלוּ עַל־הָאָרֶץ תִּשְׁפְּכֶנּוּ כַּמָּיִם׃

17 You may not partake in your settlements of the tithes of your new grain or wine or oil, or of the firstlings of your herds and flocks, or of any of the votive offerings that you vow, or of your freewill offerings, or of your contributions.

יז לֹא־תוּכַל לֶאֱכֹל בִּשְׁעָרֶיךָ מַעְשַׂר דְּגָנְךָ וְתִירֹשְׁךָ וְיִצְהָרֶךָ וּבְכֹרֹת בְּקָרְךָ וְצֹאנֶךָ וְכׇל־נְדָרֶיךָ אֲשֶׁר תִּדֹּר וְנִדְבֹתֶיךָ וּתְרוּמַת יָדֶךָ׃

18 These you must consume before *Hashem* your God in the place that *Hashem* your God will choose – you and your sons and your daughters, your male and female slaves, and the Levite in your settlements – happy before *Hashem* your God in all your undertakings.

יח כִּי אִם־לִפְנֵי יְהֹוָה אֱלֹהֶיךָ תֹּאכְלֶנּוּ בַּמָּקוֹם אֲשֶׁר יִבְחַר יְהֹוָה אֱלֹהֶיךָ בּוֹ אַתָּה וּבִנְךָ וּבִתֶּךָ וְעַבְדְּךָ וַאֲמָתֶךָ וְהַלֵּוִי אֲשֶׁר בִּשְׁעָרֶיךָ וְשָׂמַחְתָּ לִפְנֵי יְהֹוָה אֱלֹהֶיךָ בְּכֹל מִשְׁלַח יָדֶךָ׃

19 Be sure not to neglect the Levite as long as you live in your land.

יט הִשָּׁמֶר לְךָ פֶּן־תַּעֲזֹב אֶת־הַלֵּוִי כׇּל־יָמֶיךָ עַל־אַדְמָתֶךָ׃

20 When *Hashem* enlarges your territory, as He has promised you, and you say, "I shall eat some meat," for you have the urge to eat meat, you may eat meat whenever you wish.

כ כִּי־יַרְחִיב יְהֹוָה אֱלֹהֶיךָ אֶת־גְּבֻלְךָ כַּאֲשֶׁר דִּבֶּר־לָךְ וְאָמַרְתָּ אֹכְלָה בָשָׂר כִּי־תְאַוֶּה נַפְשְׁךָ לֶאֱכֹל בָּשָׂר בְּכׇל־אַוַּת נַפְשְׁךָ תֹּאכַל בָּשָׂר׃

21 If the place where *Hashem* has chosen to establish His name is too far from you, you may slaughter any of the cattle or sheep that *Hashem* gives you, as I have instructed you; and you may eat to your heart's content in your settlements.

כא כִּי־יִרְחַק מִמְּךָ הַמָּקוֹם אֲשֶׁר יִבְחַר יְהֹוָה אֱלֹהֶיךָ לָשׂוּם שְׁמוֹ שָׁם וְזָבַחְתָּ מִבְּקָרְךָ וּמִצֹּאנְךָ אֲשֶׁר נָתַן יְהֹוָה לְךָ כַּאֲשֶׁר צִוִּיתִךָ וְאָכַלְתָּ בִּשְׁעָרֶיךָ בְּכֹל אַוַּת נַפְשֶׁךָ׃

22 Eat it, however, as the gazelle and the deer are eaten: the unclean may eat it together with the clean.

כב אַךְ כַּאֲשֶׁר יֵאָכֵל אֶת־הַצְּבִי וְאֶת־הָאַיָּל כֵּן תֹּאכְלֶנּוּ הַטָּמֵא וְהַטָּהוֹר יַחְדָּו יֹאכְלֶנּוּ׃

23 But make sure that you do not partake of the blood; for the blood is the life, and you must not consume the life with the flesh.

כג רַק חֲזַק לְבִלְתִּי אֲכֹל הַדָּם כִּי הַדָּם הוּא הַנָּפֶשׁ וְלֹא־תֹאכַל הַנֶּפֶשׁ עִם־הַבָּשָׂר׃

24 You must not partake of it; you must pour it out on the ground like water:

כד לֹא תֹּאכְלֶנּוּ עַל־הָאָרֶץ תִּשְׁפְּכֶנּוּ כַּמָּיִם׃

Devarim/Deuteronomy 13
Re'eih

25 you must not partake of it, in order that it may go well with you and with your descendants to come, for you will be doing what is right in the sight of *Hashem*.

כה לֹא תֹאכְלֶנּוּ לְמַעַן יִיטַב לְךָ וּלְבָנֶיךָ אַחֲרֶיךָ כִּי־תַעֲשֶׂה הַיָּשָׁר בְּעֵינֵי יְהֹוָה׃

26 But such sacred and votive donations as you may have shall be taken by you to the site that *Hashem* will choose.

כו רַק קָדָשֶׁיךָ אֲשֶׁר־יִהְיוּ לְךָ וּנְדָרֶיךָ תִּשָּׂא וּבָאתָ אֶל־הַמָּקוֹם אֲשֶׁר־יִבְחַר יְהֹוָה׃

27 You shall offer your burnt offerings, both the flesh and the blood, on the *Mizbayach* of *Hashem* your God; and of your other sacrifices, the blood shall be poured out on the *Mizbayach* of *Hashem* your God, and you shall eat the flesh.

כז וְעָשִׂיתָ עֹלֹתֶיךָ הַבָּשָׂר וְהַדָּם עַל־מִזְבַּח יְהֹוָה אֱלֹהֶיךָ וְדַם־זְבָחֶיךָ יִשָּׁפֵךְ עַל־מִזְבַּח יְהֹוָה אֱלֹהֶיךָ וְהַבָּשָׂר תֹּאכֵל׃

28 Be careful to heed all these commandments that I enjoin upon you; thus it will go well with you and with your descendants after you forever, for you will be doing what is good and right in the sight of *Hashem* your God.

כח שְׁמֹר וְשָׁמַעְתָּ אֵת כָּל־הַדְּבָרִים הָאֵלֶּה אֲשֶׁר אָנֹכִי מְצַוֶּךָּ לְמַעַן יִיטַב לְךָ וּלְבָנֶיךָ אַחֲרֶיךָ עַד־עוֹלָם כִּי תַעֲשֶׂה הַטּוֹב וְהַיָּשָׁר בְּעֵינֵי יְהֹוָה אֱלֹהֶיךָ׃

29 When *Hashem* your God has cut down before you the nations that you are about to enter and dispossess, and you have dispossessed them and settled in their land,

כט כִּי־יַכְרִית יְהֹוָה אֱלֹהֶיךָ אֶת־הַגּוֹיִם אֲשֶׁר אַתָּה בָא־שָׁמָּה לָרֶשֶׁת אוֹתָם מִפָּנֶיךָ וְיָרַשְׁתָּ אֹתָם וְיָשַׁבְתָּ בְּאַרְצָם׃

30 beware of being lured into their ways after they have been wiped out before you! Do not inquire about their gods, saying, "How did those nations worship their gods? I too will follow those practices."

ל הִשָּׁמֶר לְךָ פֶּן־תִּנָּקֵשׁ אַחֲרֵיהֶם אַחֲרֵי הִשָּׁמְדָם מִפָּנֶיךָ וּפֶן־תִּדְרֹשׁ לֵאלֹהֵיהֶם לֵאמֹר אֵיכָה יַעַבְדוּ הַגּוֹיִם הָאֵלֶּה אֶת־אֱלֹהֵיהֶם וְאֶעֱשֶׂה־כֵּן גַּם־אָנִי׃

31 You shall not act thus toward *Hashem* your God, for they perform for their gods every abhorrent act that *Hashem* detests; they even offer up their sons and daughters in fire to their gods.

לא לֹא־תַעֲשֶׂה כֵן לַיהֹוָה אֱלֹהֶיךָ כִּי כָל־תּוֹעֲבַת יְהֹוָה אֲשֶׁר שָׂנֵא עָשׂוּ לֵאלֹהֵיהֶם כִּי גַם אֶת־בְּנֵיהֶם וְאֶת־בְּנֹתֵיהֶם יִשְׂרְפוּ בָאֵשׁ לֵאלֹהֵיהֶם׃

13

1 Be careful to observe only that which I enjoin upon you: neither add to it nor take away from it.

יג א אֵת כָּל־הַדָּבָר אֲשֶׁר אָנֹכִי מְצַוֶּה אֶתְכֶם אֹתוֹ תִשְׁמְרוּ לַעֲשׂוֹת לֹא־תֹסֵף עָלָיו וְלֹא תִגְרַע מִמֶּנּוּ׃

2 If there appears among you a prophet or a dream-diviner and he gives you a sign or a portent,

ב כִּי־יָקוּם בְּקִרְבְּךָ נָבִיא אוֹ חֹלֵם חֲלוֹם וְנָתַן אֵלֶיךָ אוֹת אוֹ מוֹפֵת׃

3 saying, "Let us follow and worship another god" – whom you have not experienced – even if the sign or portent that he named to you comes true,

ג וּבָא הָאוֹת וְהַמּוֹפֵת אֲשֶׁר־דִּבֶּר אֵלֶיךָ לֵאמֹר נֵלְכָה אַחֲרֵי אֱלֹהִים אֲחֵרִים אֲשֶׁר לֹא־יְדַעְתָּם וְנָעָבְדֵם׃

4 do not heed the words of that prophet or that dream-diviner. For *Hashem* your God is testing you to see whether you really love *Hashem* your God with all your heart and soul.

ד לֹא תִשְׁמַע אֶל־דִּבְרֵי הַנָּבִיא הַהוּא אוֹ אֶל־חוֹלֵם הַחֲלוֹם הַהוּא כִּי מְנַסֶּה יְהֹוָה אֱלֹהֵיכֶם אֶתְכֶם לָדַעַת הֲיִשְׁכֶם אֹהֲבִים אֶת־יְהֹוָה אֱלֹהֵיכֶם בְּכָל־לְבַבְכֶם וּבְכָל־נַפְשְׁכֶם׃

Devarim/Deuteronomy 13
Re'eih

דברים יג
ראה

5 Follow none but *Hashem* your God, and revere none but Him; observe His commandments alone, and heed only His orders; worship none but Him, and hold fast to Him.

ה אַחֲרֵי יְהֹוָה אֱלֹהֵיכֶם תֵּלֵכוּ וְאֹתוֹ תִירָאוּ וְאֶת־מִצְוֺתָיו תִּשְׁמֹרוּ וּבְקֹלוֹ תִשְׁמָעוּ וְאֹתוֹ תַעֲבֹדוּ וּבוֹ תִדְבָּקוּן׃

a-kha-RAY a-do-NAI e-lo-hay-KHEM tay-LAY-khu v'-o-TO tee-RA-u v'-et mitz-vo-TAV tish-MO-ru uv-ko-LO tish-MA-u v'-o-TO ta-a-VO-du u-VO tid-ba-KUN

6 As for that prophet or dream-diviner, he shall be put to death; for he urged disloyalty to *Hashem* your God – who freed you from the land of Egypt and who redeemed you from the house of bondage – to make you stray from the path that *Hashem* your God commanded you to follow. Thus you will sweep out evil from your midst.

ו וְהַנָּבִיא הַהוּא אוֹ חֹלֵם הַחֲלוֹם הַהוּא יוּמָת כִּי דִבֶּר־סָרָה עַל־יְהֹוָה אֱלֹהֵיכֶם הַמּוֹצִיא אֶתְכֶם מֵאֶרֶץ מִצְרַיִם וְהַפֹּדְךָ מִבֵּית עֲבָדִים לְהַדִּיחֲךָ מִן־הַדֶּרֶךְ אֲשֶׁר צִוְּךָ יְהֹוָה אֱלֹהֶיךָ לָלֶכֶת בָּהּ וּבִעַרְתָּ הָרָע מִקִּרְבֶּךָ׃

7 If your brother, your own mother's son, or your son or daughter, or the wife of your bosom, or your closest friend entices you in secret, saying, "Come let us worship other gods" – whom neither you nor your fathers have experienced

ז כִּי יְסִיתְךָ אָחִיךָ בֶן־אִמֶּךָ אוֹ־בִנְךָ אוֹ־בִתְּךָ אוֹ ׀ אֵשֶׁת חֵיקֶךָ אוֹ רֵעֲךָ אֲשֶׁר כְּנַפְשְׁךָ בַּסֵּתֶר לֵאמֹר נֵלְכָה וְנַעַבְדָה אֱלֹהִים אֲחֵרִים אֲשֶׁר לֹא יָדַעְתָּ אַתָּה וַאֲבֹתֶיךָ׃

8 from among the gods of the peoples around you, either near to you or distant, anywhere from one end of the earth to the other:

ח מֵאֱלֹהֵי הָעַמִּים אֲשֶׁר סְבִיבֹתֵיכֶם הַקְּרֹבִים אֵלֶיךָ אוֹ הָרְחֹקִים מִמֶּךָּ מִקְצֵה הָאָרֶץ וְעַד־קְצֵה הָאָרֶץ׃

9 do not assent or give heed to him. Show him no pity or compassion, and do not shield him;

ט לֹא־תֹאבֶה לוֹ וְלֹא תִשְׁמַע אֵלָיו וְלֹא־תָחוֹס עֵינְךָ עָלָיו וְלֹא־תַחְמֹל וְלֹא־תְכַסֶּה עָלָיו׃

10 but take his life. Let your hand be the first against him to put him to death, and the hand of the rest of the people thereafter.

י כִּי הָרֹג תַּהַרְגֶנּוּ יָדְךָ תִּהְיֶה־בּוֹ בָרִאשׁוֹנָה לַהֲמִיתוֹ וְיַד כָּל־הָעָם בָּאַחֲרֹנָה׃

11 Stone him to death, for he sought to make you stray from *Hashem* your God, who brought you out of the land of Egypt, out of the house of bondage.

יא וּסְקַלְתּוֹ בָאֲבָנִים וָמֵת כִּי בִקֵּשׁ לְהַדִּיחֲךָ מֵעַל יְהֹוָה אֱלֹהֶיךָ הַמּוֹצִיאֲךָ מֵאֶרֶץ מִצְרַיִם מִבֵּית עֲבָדִים׃

12 Thus all *Yisrael* will hear and be afraid, and such evil things will not be done again in your midst.

יב וְכָל־יִשְׂרָאֵל יִשְׁמְעוּ וְיִרָאוּן וְלֹא־יוֹסִפוּ לַעֲשׂוֹת כַּדָּבָר הָרָע הַזֶּה בְּקִרְבֶּךָ׃

13:5 And hold fast to Him This verse concludes with the directive to cleave to *Hashem*. Since it is impossible to literally "hold fast" to a being that has no physical form, the Sages explain (*Sotah* 14a) that this commandment means we are required to emulate His ways. Just as *Hashem* performs kind deeds, buries the dead (Deuteronomy 33:6) and visits the sick (Genesis 18:1), so too must we be kind to others and take care of their needs. Contemporary Israel fulfills this mandate, and emulates God's compassion. It is often the first country to respond to natural disasters, providing medical aid and other assistance around the world. For example, when a devastating earthquake struck Haiti in 2010, the IDF was amongst the first responders on the scene. One woman who gave birth in an Israeli field hospital was so grateful to the Israeli medical team that she named her baby 'Israel.'

Israel, first baby born in the Israeli field hospital in Haiti

Devarim/Deuteronomy 14
Re'eih

דברים יד
ראה

13 If you hear it said, of one of the towns that *Hashem* your God is giving you to dwell in,

יג כִּי־תִשְׁמַע בְּאַחַת עָרֶיךָ אֲשֶׁר יְהֹוָה אֱלֹהֶיךָ נֹתֵן לְךָ לָשֶׁבֶת שָׁם לֵאמֹר:

14 that some scoundrels from among you have gone and subverted the inhabitants of their town, saying, "Come let us worship other gods" – whom you have not experienced

יד יָצְאוּ אֲנָשִׁים בְּנֵי־בְלִיַּעַל מִקִּרְבֶּךָ וַיַּדִּיחוּ אֶת־יֹשְׁבֵי עִירָם לֵאמֹר נֵלְכָה וְנַעַבְדָה אֱלֹהִים אֲחֵרִים אֲשֶׁר לֹא־יְדַעְתֶּם:

15 you shall investigate and inquire and interrogate thoroughly. If it is true, the fact is established – that abhorrent thing was perpetrated in your midst

טו וְדָרַשְׁתָּ וְחָקַרְתָּ וְשָׁאַלְתָּ הֵיטֵב וְהִנֵּה אֱמֶת נָכוֹן הַדָּבָר נֶעֶשְׂתָה הַתּוֹעֵבָה הַזֹּאת בְּקִרְבֶּךָ:

16 put the inhabitants of that town to the sword and put its cattle to the sword. Doom it and all that is in it to destruction:

טז הַכֵּה תַכֶּה אֶת־יֹשְׁבֵי הָעִיר הַהוּא [הַהִיא] לְפִי־חָרֶב הַחֲרֵם אֹתָהּ וְאֶת־כָּל־אֲשֶׁר־בָּהּ וְאֶת־בְּהֶמְתָּהּ לְפִי־חָרֶב:

17 gather all its spoil into the open square, and burn the town and all its spoil as a holocaust to *Hashem* your God. And it shall remain an everlasting ruin, never to be rebuilt.

יז וְאֶת־כָּל־שְׁלָלָהּ תִּקְבֹּץ אֶל־תּוֹךְ רְחֹבָהּ וְשָׂרַפְתָּ בָאֵשׁ אֶת־הָעִיר וְאֶת־כָּל־שְׁלָלָהּ כָּלִיל לַיהֹוָה אֱלֹהֶיךָ וְהָיְתָה תֵּל עוֹלָם לֹא תִבָּנֶה עוֹד:

18 Let nothing that has been doomed stick to your hand, in order that *Hashem* may turn from His blazing anger and show you compassion, and in His compassion increase you as He promised your fathers on oath

יח וְלֹא־יִדְבַּק בְּיָדְךָ מְאוּמָה מִן־הַחֵרֶם לְמַעַן יָשׁוּב יְהֹוָה מֵחֲרוֹן אַפּוֹ וְנָתַן־לְךָ רַחֲמִים וְרִחַמְךָ וְהִרְבֶּךָ כַּאֲשֶׁר נִשְׁבַּע לַאֲבֹתֶיךָ:

19 for you will be heeding *Hashem* your God, obeying all His commandments that I enjoin upon you this day, doing what is right in the sight of *Hashem* your God.

יט כִּי תִשְׁמַע בְּקוֹל יְהֹוָה אֱלֹהֶיךָ לִשְׁמֹר אֶת־כָּל־מִצְוֹתָיו אֲשֶׁר אָנֹכִי מְצַוְּךָ הַיּוֹם לַעֲשׂוֹת הַיָּשָׁר בְּעֵינֵי יְהֹוָה אֱלֹהֶיךָ:

14

1 You are children of *Hashem* your God. You shall not gash yourselves or shave the front of your heads because of the dead.

א בָּנִים אַתֶּם לַיהֹוָה אֱלֹהֵיכֶם לֹא תִתְגֹּדְדוּ וְלֹא־תָשִׂימוּ קָרְחָה בֵּין עֵינֵיכֶם לָמֵת:

ba-NEEM a-TEM la-do-NAI e-lo-hay-KHEM LO tit-go-d'-DU v'-lo ta-SEE-mu kor-KHAH BAYN ay-nay-KHEM la-MAYT

2 For you are a people consecrated to *Hashem* your God: *Hashem* your God chose you from among all other peoples on earth to be His treasured people.

ב כִּי עַם קָדוֹשׁ אַתָּה לַיהֹוָה אֱלֹהֶיךָ וּבְךָ בָּחַר יְהֹוָה לִהְיוֹת לוֹ לְעַם סְגֻלָּה מִכֹּל הָעַמִּים אֲשֶׁר עַל־פְּנֵי הָאֲדָמָה:

3 You shall not eat anything abhorrent.

ג לֹא תֹאכַל כָּל־תּוֹעֵבָה:

14:1 You are children of *Hashem* your God These words explain why the Nation of Israel is sometimes held to a higher standard. Since they are the children of *Hashem*, they cannot express their mourning by hurting themselves and they may eat only certain foods, as the chapter goes on to describe. This is not meant to imply that they are the only children of *Hashem*, but rather that their special status reflects the fact that they were chosen by God to be His ambassadors and to set an example for the rest of His creations. As such, *Hashem* chose the Land of Israel as the place from which the Israelites are to serve as "a light unto the nations."

Devarim/Deuteronomy 14
Re'eih

4 These are the animals that you may eat: the ox, the sheep, and the goat;

5 the deer, the gazelle, the roebuck, the wild goat, the ibex, the antelope, the mountain sheep,

6 and any other animal that has true hoofs which are cleft in two and brings up the cud – such you may eat.

7 But the following, which do bring up the cud or have true hoofs which are cleft through, you may not eat: the camel, the hare, and the daman – for although they bring up the cud, they have no true hoofs – they are unclean for you;

8 also the swine – for although it has true hoofs, it does not bring up the cud – is unclean for you. You shall not eat of their flesh or touch their carcasses.

9 These you may eat of all that live in water: you may eat anything that has fins and scales.

10 But you may not eat anything that has no fins and scales: it is unclean for you.

11 You may eat any clean bird.

12 The following you may not eat: the eagle, the vulture, and the black vulture;

13 the kite, the falcon, and the buzzard of any variety;

14 every variety of raven;

15 the ostrich, the nighthawk, the sea gull, and the hawk of any variety;

16 the little owl, the great owl, and the white owl;

17 the pelican, the bustard, and the cormorant;

18 the stork, any variety of heron, the hoopoe, and the bat.

19 All winged swarming things are unclean for you: they may not be eaten.

20 You may eat only clean winged creatures.

21 You shall not eat anything that has died a natural death; give it to the stranger in your community to eat, or you may sell it to a foreigner. For you are a people consecrated to *Hashem* your God. You shall not boil a kid in its mother's milk.

Devarim/Deuteronomy 15
Re'eih

דברים טו
ראה

22 You shall set aside every year a tenth part of all the yield of your sowing that is brought from the field.

כב עַשֵּׂר תְּעַשֵּׂר אֵת כׇּל־תְּבוּאַת זַרְעֶךָ הַיֹּצֵא הַשָּׂדֶה שָׁנָה שָׁנָה׃

23 You shall consume the tithes of your new grain and wine and oil, and the firstlings of your herds and flocks, in the presence of *Hashem* your God, in the place where He will choose to establish His name, so that you may learn to revere *Hashem* your God forever.

כג וְאָכַלְתָּ לִפְנֵי יְהֹוָה אֱלֹהֶיךָ בַּמָּקוֹם אֲשֶׁר־יִבְחַר לְשַׁכֵּן שְׁמוֹ שָׁם מַעְשַׂר דְּגָנְךָ תִּירֹשְׁךָ וְיִצְהָרֶךָ וּבְכֹרֹת בְּקָרְךָ וְצֹאנֶךָ לְמַעַן תִּלְמַד לְיִרְאָה אֶת־יְהֹוָה אֱלֹהֶיךָ כׇּל־הַיָּמִים׃

24 Should the distance be too great for you, should you be unable to transport them, because the place where *Hashem* your God has chosen to establish His name is far from you and because *Hashem* your God has blessed you,

כד וְכִי־יִרְבֶּה מִמְּךָ הַדֶּרֶךְ כִּי לֹא תוּכַל שְׂאֵתוֹ כִּי־יִרְחַק מִמְּךָ הַמָּקוֹם אֲשֶׁר יִבְחַר יְהֹוָה אֱלֹהֶיךָ לָשׂוּם שְׁמוֹ שָׁם כִּי יְבָרֶכְךָ יְהֹוָה אֱלֹהֶיךָ׃

25 you may convert them into money. Wrap up the money and take it with you to the place that *Hashem* your God has chosen,

כה וְנָתַתָּה בַּכָּסֶף וְצַרְתָּ הַכֶּסֶף בְּיָדְךָ וְהָלַכְתָּ אֶל־הַמָּקוֹם אֲשֶׁר יִבְחַר יְהֹוָה אֱלֹהֶיךָ בּוֹ׃

26 and spend the money on anything you want – cattle, sheep, wine, or other intoxicant, or anything you may desire. And you shall feast there, in the presence of *Hashem* your God, and rejoice with your household.

כו וְנָתַתָּה הַכֶּסֶף בְּכֹל אֲשֶׁר־תְּאַוֶּה נַפְשְׁךָ בַּבָּקָר וּבַצֹּאן וּבַיַּיִן וּבַשֵּׁכָר וּבְכֹל אֲשֶׁר תִּשְׁאָלְךָ נַפְשֶׁךָ וְאָכַלְתָּ שָּׁם לִפְנֵי יְהֹוָה אֱלֹהֶיךָ וְשָׂמַחְתָּ אַתָּה וּבֵיתֶךָ׃

27 But do not neglect the Levite in your community, for he has no hereditary portion as you have.

כז וְהַלֵּוִי אֲשֶׁר־בִּשְׁעָרֶיךָ לֹא תַעַזְבֶנּוּ כִּי אֵין לוֹ חֵלֶק וְנַחֲלָה עִמָּךְ׃

28 Every third year you shall bring out the full tithe of your yield of that year, but leave it within your settlements.

כח מִקְצֵה שָׁלֹשׁ שָׁנִים תּוֹצִיא אֶת־כׇּל־מַעְשַׂר תְּבוּאָתְךָ בַּשָּׁנָה הַהִוא וְהִנַּחְתָּ בִּשְׁעָרֶיךָ׃

29 Then the Levite, who has no hereditary portion as you have, and the stranger, the fatherless, and the widow in your settlements shall come and eat their fill, so that *Hashem* your God may bless you in all the enterprises you undertake.

כט וּבָא הַלֵּוִי כִּי אֵין־לוֹ חֵלֶק וְנַחֲלָה עִמָּךְ וְהַגֵּר וְהַיָּתוֹם וְהָאַלְמָנָה אֲשֶׁר בִּשְׁעָרֶיךָ וְאָכְלוּ וְשָׂבֵעוּ לְמַעַן יְבָרֶכְךָ יְהֹוָה אֱלֹהֶיךָ בְּכׇל־מַעֲשֵׂה יָדְךָ אֲשֶׁר תַּעֲשֶׂה׃

15 1 Every seventh year you shall practice remission of debts.

טו א מִקֵּץ שֶׁבַע־שָׁנִים תַּעֲשֶׂה שְׁמִטָּה׃

2 This shall be the nature of the remission: every creditor shall remit the due that he claims from his fellow; he shall not dun his fellow or kinsman, for the remission proclaimed is of *Hashem*.

ב וְזֶה דְּבַר הַשְּׁמִטָּה שָׁמוֹט כׇּל־בַּעַל מַשֵּׁה יָדוֹ אֲשֶׁר יַשֶּׁה בְּרֵעֵהוּ לֹא־יִגֹּשׂ אֶת־רֵעֵהוּ וְאֶת־אָחִיו כִּי־קָרָא שְׁמִטָּה לַיהֹוָה׃

Devarim/Deuteronomy 15
Re'eih

דברים טו
ראה

3 You may dun the foreigner; but you must remit whatever is due you from your kinsmen.

אֶת־הַנָּכְרִ֖י תִּגֹּ֑שׂ וַאֲשֶׁ֨ר יִהְיֶ֥ה לְךָ֛ אֶת־אָחִ֖יךָ תַּשְׁמֵ֥ט יָדֶֽךָ׃

4 There shall be no needy among you – since *Hashem* your God will bless you in the land that *Hashem* your God is giving you as a hereditary portion

אֶ֕פֶס כִּ֛י לֹ֥א יִֽהְיֶה־בְּךָ֖ אֶבְי֑וֹן כִּֽי־בָרֵ֤ךְ יְבָֽרֶכְךָ֙ יְהֹוָ֔ה בָּאָ֕רֶץ אֲשֶׁר֙ יְהֹוָ֣ה אֱלֹהֶ֔יךָ נֹֽתֵן־לְךָ֥ נַחֲלָ֖ה לְרִשְׁתָּֽהּ׃

E-fes KEE LO yih-yeh b'-KHA ev-YON kee va-RAYKH y'-va-re-kh'-kha a-do-NAI ba-A-retz a-SHER a-do-NAI e-lo-HE-kha no-tayn l'-KHA na-kha-LAH l'-rish-TAH

5 if only you heed *Hashem* your God and take care to keep all this Instruction that I enjoin upon you this day.

רַ֚ק אִם־שָׁמ֣וֹעַ תִּשְׁמַ֔ע בְּק֖וֹל יְהֹוָ֣ה אֱלֹהֶ֑יךָ לִשְׁמֹ֤ר לַעֲשׂוֹת֙ אֶת־כׇּל־הַמִּצְוָ֣ה הַזֹּ֔את אֲשֶׁ֛ר אָנֹכִ֥י מְצַוְּךָ֖ הַיּֽוֹם׃

6 For *Hashem* your God will bless you as He has promised you: you will extend loans to many nations, but require none yourself; you will dominate many nations, but they will not dominate you.

כִּֽי־יְהֹוָ֤ה אֱלֹהֶ֙יךָ֙ בֵּֽרַכְךָ֔ כַּאֲשֶׁ֖ר דִּבֶּר־לָ֑ךְ וְהַֽעֲבַטְתָּ֞ גּוֹיִ֣ם רַבִּ֗ים וְאַתָּה֙ לֹ֣א תַעֲבֹ֔ט וּמָֽשַׁלְתָּ֙ בְּגוֹיִ֣ם רַבִּ֔ים וּבְךָ֖ לֹ֥א יִמְשֹֽׁלוּ׃

7 If, however, there is a needy person among you, one of your kinsmen in any of your settlements in the land that *Hashem* your God is giving you, do not harden your heart and shut your hand against your needy kinsman.

כִּֽי־יִהְיֶה֩ בְךָ֨ אֶבְי֜וֹן מֵאַחַ֤ד אַחֶ֙יךָ֙ בְּאַחַ֣ד שְׁעָרֶ֔יךָ בְּאַ֨רְצְךָ֔ אֲשֶׁר־יְהֹוָ֥ה אֱלֹהֶ֖יךָ נֹתֵ֣ן לָ֑ךְ לֹ֧א תְאַמֵּ֣ץ אֶת־לְבָבְךָ֗ וְלֹ֤א תִקְפֹּץ֙ אֶת־יָ֣דְךָ֔ מֵאָחִ֖יךָ הָאֶבְיֽוֹן׃

8 Rather, you must open your hand and lend him sufficient for whatever he needs.

כִּֽי־פָתֹ֧חַ תִּפְתַּ֛ח אֶת־יָדְךָ֖ ל֑וֹ וְהַעֲבֵט֙ תַּעֲבִיטֶ֔נּוּ דֵּ֚י מַחְסֹר֔וֹ אֲשֶׁ֥ר יֶחְסַ֖ר לֽוֹ׃

9 Beware lest you harbor the base thought, "The seventh year, the year of remission, is approaching," so that you are mean to your needy kinsman and give him nothing. He will cry out to *Hashem* against you, and you will incur guilt.

הִשָּׁ֣מֶר לְךָ֡ פֶּן־יִהְיֶ֣ה דָבָר֩ עִם־לְבָבְךָ֨ בְלִיַּ֜עַל לֵאמֹ֗ר קָֽרְבָ֣ה שְׁנַֽת־הַשֶּׁ֘בַע֮ שְׁנַ֣ת הַשְּׁמִטָּה֒ וְרָעָ֣ה עֵֽינְךָ֗ בְּאָחִ֙יךָ֙ הָֽאֶבְי֔וֹן וְלֹ֥א תִתֵּ֖ן ל֑וֹ וְקָרָ֤א עָלֶ֙יךָ֙ אֶל־יְהֹוָ֔ה וְהָיָ֥ה בְךָ֖ חֵֽטְא׃

10 Give to him readily and have no regrets when you do so, for in return *Hashem* your God will bless you in all your efforts and in all your undertakings.

נָת֤וֹן תִּתֵּן֙ ל֔וֹ וְלֹא־יֵרַ֥ע לְבָבְךָ֖ בְּתִתְּךָ֣ ל֑וֹ כִּ֞י בִּגְלַ֣ל ׀ הַדָּבָ֣ר הַזֶּ֗ה יְבָרֶכְךָ֙ יְהֹוָ֣ה אֱלֹהֶ֔יךָ בְּכׇֽל־מַעֲשֶׂ֔ךָ וּבְכֹ֖ל מִשְׁלַ֥ח יָדֶֽךָ׃

ברכה

15:4 ***Hashem* your God will bless you in the land that *Hashem* your God is giving you** The Hebrew word for 'blessing,' *beracha* (ברכה), is very similar to the word for 'pool of water,' *bereicha* (בריכה). Water refreshes, nourishes and purifies. In fact, immersing in the special pool of water known as a *mikveh* (מקוה), 'ritual bath,' is the final stage of purification for those who have become ritually impure. Similarly, when we bless something, we raise it spiritually. The Bible repeatedly refers to the Land of Israel as a blessing, teaching us that Israel is the source of abundant blessings, both material and spiritual, for the entire world.

Devarim/Deuteronomy 15
Re'eih

דברים טו
ראה

11 For there will never cease to be needy ones in your land, which is why I command you: open your hand to the poor and needy kinsman in your land.

יא כִּי לֹא־יֶחְדַּל אֶבְיוֹן מִקֶּרֶב הָאָרֶץ עַל־כֵּן אָנֹכִי מְצַוְּךָ לֵאמֹר פָּתֹחַ תִּפְתַּח אֶת־יָדְךָ לְאָחִיךָ לַעֲנִיֶּךָ וּלְאֶבְיֹנְךָ בְּאַרְצֶךָ׃

KEE lo yekh-DAL ev-YON mi-KE-rev ha-A-retz al KAYN a-no-KHEE m'-tza-v'-KHA lay-MOR pa-TO-akh tif-TAKH at ya-d'-KHA l'-a-KHEE-kha la-a-nee-YE-kha ul-ev-yo-n'-KHA b'-ar-TZE-kha

12 If a fellow Hebrew, man or woman, is sold to you, he shall serve you six years, and in the seventh year you shall set him free.

יב כִּי־יִמָּכֵר לְךָ אָחִיךָ הָעִבְרִי אוֹ הָעִבְרִיָּה וַעֲבָדְךָ שֵׁשׁ שָׁנִים וּבַשָּׁנָה הַשְּׁבִיעִת תְּשַׁלְּחֶנּוּ חָפְשִׁי מֵעִמָּךְ׃

13 When you set him free, do not let him go empty-handed:

יג וְכִי־תְשַׁלְּחֶנּוּ חָפְשִׁי מֵעִמָּךְ לֹא תְשַׁלְּחֶנּוּ רֵיקָם׃

14 Furnish him out of the flock, threshing floor, and vat, with which *Hashem* your God has blessed you.

יד הַעֲנֵיק תַּעֲנִיק לוֹ מִצֹּאנְךָ וּמִגָּרְנְךָ וּמִיִּקְבֶךָ אֲשֶׁר בֵּרַכְךָ יְהֹוָה אֱלֹהֶיךָ תִּתֶּן־לוֹ׃

15 Bear in mind that you were slaves in the land of Egypt and *Hashem* your God redeemed you; therefore I enjoin this commandment upon you today.

טו וְזָכַרְתָּ כִּי עֶבֶד הָיִיתָ בְּאֶרֶץ מִצְרַיִם וַיִּפְדְּךָ יְהֹוָה אֱלֹהֶיךָ עַל־כֵּן אָנֹכִי מְצַוְּךָ אֶת־הַדָּבָר הַזֶּה הַיּוֹם׃

16 But should he say to you, "I do not want to leave you" – for he loves you and your household and is happy with you

טז וְהָיָה כִּי־יֹאמַר אֵלֶיךָ לֹא אֵצֵא מֵעִמָּךְ כִּי אֲהֵבְךָ וְאֶת־בֵּיתֶךָ כִּי־טוֹב לוֹ עִמָּךְ׃

17 you shall take an awl and put it through his ear into the door, and he shall become your slave in perpetuity. Do the same with your female slave.

יז וְלָקַחְתָּ אֶת־הַמַּרְצֵעַ וְנָתַתָּה בְאָזְנוֹ וּבַדֶּלֶת וְהָיָה לְךָ עֶבֶד עוֹלָם וְאַף לַאֲמָתְךָ תַּעֲשֶׂה־כֵּן׃

18 When you do set him free, do not feel aggrieved; for in the six years he has given you double the service of a hired man. Moreover, *Hashem* your God will bless you in all you do.

יח לֹא־יִקְשֶׁה בְעֵינֶךָ בְּשַׁלֵּחֲךָ אֹתוֹ חָפְשִׁי מֵעִמָּךְ כִּי מִשְׁנֶה שְׂכַר שָׂכִיר עֲבָדְךָ שֵׁשׁ שָׁנִים וּבֵרַכְךָ יְהֹוָה אֱלֹהֶיךָ בְּכֹל אֲשֶׁר תַּעֲשֶׂה׃

19 You shall consecrate to *Hashem* your God all male firstlings that are born in your herd and in your flock: you must not work your firstling ox or shear your firstling sheep.

יט כָּל־הַבְּכוֹר אֲשֶׁר יִוָּלֵד בִּבְקָרְךָ וּבְצֹאנְךָ הַזָּכָר תַּקְדִּישׁ לַיהֹוָה אֱלֹהֶיךָ לֹא תַעֲבֹד בִּבְכֹר שׁוֹרֶךָ וְלֹא תָגֹז בְּכוֹר צֹאנֶךָ׃

15:11 Open your hand to the poor and needy kinsman Strangely, the word *lechem* (לחם), 'bread,' is the root of the word *milchama* (מלחמה), which means 'war.' According to Rabbi Benjamin Blech in his book *The Secrets of Hebrew Words*, people usually do not go to war because they are wicked, but rather because they are deprived of basic necessities, such as bread. If we take care of those who are needy and provide for those who are hungry, we will be one step closer to bringing peace to the world. This is one of the reasons why the State of Israel allows for an enormous amount of supplies to cross over into Gaza each day, supplying the people living in Gaza with goods such as food, medical devices and construction materials. The Hamas-controlled area remains extremely hostile towards Israel, nevertheless, Israel hopes that the daily deliveries of bread and other supplies will lead to peace.

מלחמה

Devarim/Deuteronomy 16
Re'eih

20 You and your household shall eat it annually before *Hashem* your God in the place that *Hashem* will choose.

21 But if it has a defect, lameness or blindness, any serious defect, you shall not sacrifice it to *Hashem* your God.

22 Eat it in your settlements, the unclean among you no less than the clean, just like the gazelle and the deer.

23 Only you must not partake of its blood; you shall pour it out on the ground like water.

16 1 Observe the month of Abib and offer a *Pesach* sacrifice to *Hashem* your God, for it was in the month of Abib, at night, that *Hashem* your God freed you from Egypt.

2 You shall slaughter the *Pesach* sacrifice for *Hashem* your God, from the flock and the herd, in the place where *Hashem* will choose to establish His name.

3 You shall not eat anything leavened with it; for seven days thereafter you shall eat unleavened bread, bread of distress – for you departed from the land of Egypt hurriedly – so that you may remember the day of your departure from the land of Egypt as long as you live.

4 For seven days no leaven shall be found with you in all your territory, and none of the flesh of what you slaughter on the evening of the first day shall be left until morning.

5 You are not permitted to slaughter the *Pesach* sacrifice in any of the settlements that *Hashem* your God is giving you;

6 but at the place where *Hashem* your God will choose to establish His name, there alone shall you slaughter the *Pesach* sacrifice, in the evening, at sundown, the time of day when you departed from Egypt.

7 You shall cook and eat it at the place that *Hashem* your God will choose; and in the morning you may start back on your journey home.

8 After eating unleavened bread six days, you shall hold a solemn gathering for *Hashem* your God on the seventh day: you shall do no work.

דברים טז
ראה

כ לִפְנֵי יְהֹוָה אֱלֹהֶיךָ תֹאכְלֶנּוּ שָׁנָה בְשָׁנָה בַּמָּקוֹם אֲשֶׁר־יִבְחַר יְהֹוָה אַתָּה וּבֵיתֶךָ:

כא וְכִי־יִהְיֶה בוֹ מוּם פִּסֵּחַ אוֹ עִוֵּר כֹּל מוּם רָע לֹא תִזְבָּחֶנּוּ לַיהֹוָה אֱלֹהֶיךָ:

כב בִּשְׁעָרֶיךָ תֹּאכְלֶנּוּ הַטָּמֵא וְהַטָּהוֹר יַחְדָּו כַּצְּבִי וְכָאַיָּל:

כג רַק אֶת־דָּמוֹ לֹא תֹאכֵל עַל־הָאָרֶץ תִּשְׁפְּכֶנּוּ כַּמָּיִם:

טז א שָׁמוֹר אֶת־חֹדֶשׁ הָאָבִיב וְעָשִׂיתָ פֶּסַח לַיהֹוָה אֱלֹהֶיךָ כִּי בְּחֹדֶשׁ הָאָבִיב הוֹצִיאֲךָ יְהֹוָה אֱלֹהֶיךָ מִמִּצְרַיִם לָיְלָה:

ב וְזָבַחְתָּ פֶּסַח לַיהֹוָה אֱלֹהֶיךָ צֹאן וּבָקָר בַּמָּקוֹם אֲשֶׁר־יִבְחַר יְהֹוָה לְשַׁכֵּן שְׁמוֹ שָׁם:

ג לֹא־תֹאכַל עָלָיו חָמֵץ שִׁבְעַת יָמִים תֹּאכַל־עָלָיו מַצּוֹת לֶחֶם עֹנִי כִּי בְחִפָּזוֹן יָצָאתָ מֵאֶרֶץ מִצְרַיִם לְמַעַן תִּזְכֹּר אֶת־יוֹם צֵאתְךָ מֵאֶרֶץ מִצְרַיִם כֹּל יְמֵי חַיֶּיךָ:

ד וְלֹא־יֵרָאֶה לְךָ שְׂאֹר בְּכָל־גְּבֻלְךָ שִׁבְעַת יָמִים וְלֹא־יָלִין מִן־הַבָּשָׂר אֲשֶׁר תִּזְבַּח בָּעֶרֶב בַּיּוֹם הָרִאשׁוֹן לַבֹּקֶר:

ה לֹא תוּכַל לִזְבֹּחַ אֶת־הַפָּסַח בְּאַחַד שְׁעָרֶיךָ אֲשֶׁר־יְהֹוָה אֱלֹהֶיךָ נֹתֵן לָךְ:

ו כִּי אִם־אֶל־הַמָּקוֹם אֲשֶׁר־יִבְחַר יְהֹוָה אֱלֹהֶיךָ לְשַׁכֵּן שְׁמוֹ שָׁם תִּזְבַּח אֶת־הַפֶּסַח בָּעָרֶב כְּבוֹא הַשֶּׁמֶשׁ מוֹעֵד צֵאתְךָ מִמִּצְרָיִם:

ז וּבִשַּׁלְתָּ וְאָכַלְתָּ בַּמָּקוֹם אֲשֶׁר יִבְחַר יְהֹוָה אֱלֹהֶיךָ בּוֹ וּפָנִיתָ בַבֹּקֶר וְהָלַכְתָּ לְאֹהָלֶיךָ:

ח שֵׁשֶׁת יָמִים תֹּאכַל מַצּוֹת וּבַיּוֹם הַשְּׁבִיעִי עֲצֶרֶת לַיהֹוָה אֱלֹהֶיךָ לֹא תַעֲשֶׂה מְלָאכָה:

Devarim/Deuteronomy 16
Re'eih

דברים טז
ראה

9 You shall count off seven weeks; start to count the seven weeks when the sickle is first put to the standing grain.

ט שִׁבְעָה שָׁבֻעֹת תִּסְפָּר־לָךְ מֵהָחֵל חֶרְמֵשׁ בַּקָּמָה תָּחֵל לִסְפֹּר שִׁבְעָה שָׁבֻעוֹת:

10 Then you shall observe the festival of *Shavuot* for *Hashem* your God, offering your freewill contribution according as *Hashem* your God has blessed you.

י וְעָשִׂיתָ חַג שָׁבֻעוֹת לַיהֹוָה אֱלֹהֶיךָ מִסַּת נִדְבַת יָדְךָ אֲשֶׁר תִּתֵּן כַּאֲשֶׁר יְבָרֶכְךָ יְהֹוָה אֱלֹהֶיךָ:

11 You shall rejoice before *Hashem* your God with your son and daughter, your male and female slave, the Levite in your communities, and the stranger, the fatherless, and the widow in your midst, at the place where *Hashem* your God will choose to establish His name.

יא וְשָׂמַחְתָּ לִפְנֵי יְהֹוָה אֱלֹהֶיךָ אַתָּה וּבִנְךָ וּבִתֶּךָ וְעַבְדְּךָ וַאֲמָתֶךָ וְהַלֵּוִי אֲשֶׁר בִּשְׁעָרֶיךָ וְהַגֵּר וְהַיָּתוֹם וְהָאַלְמָנָה אֲשֶׁר בְּקִרְבֶּךָ בַּמָּקוֹם אֲשֶׁר יִבְחַר יְהֹוָה אֱלֹהֶיךָ לְשַׁכֵּן שְׁמוֹ שָׁם:

12 Bear in mind that you were slaves in Egypt, and take care to obey these laws.

יב וְזָכַרְתָּ כִּי־עֶבֶד הָיִיתָ בְּמִצְרָיִם וְשָׁמַרְתָּ וְעָשִׂיתָ אֶת־הַחֻקִּים הָאֵלֶּה:

13 After the ingathering from your threshing floor and your vat, you shall hold the festival of *Sukkot* for seven days.

יג חַג הַסֻּכֹּת תַּעֲשֶׂה לְךָ שִׁבְעַת יָמִים בְּאָסְפְּךָ מִגָּרְנְךָ וּמִיִּקְבֶךָ:

14 You shall rejoice in your festival, with your son and daughter, your male and female slave, the Levite, the stranger, the fatherless, and the widow in your communities.

יד וְשָׂמַחְתָּ בְּחַגֶּךָ אַתָּה וּבִנְךָ וּבִתֶּךָ וְעַבְדְּךָ וַאֲמָתֶךָ וְהַלֵּוִי וְהַגֵּר וְהַיָּתוֹם וְהָאַלְמָנָה אֲשֶׁר בִּשְׁעָרֶיךָ:

15 You shall hold a festival for *Hashem* your God seven days, in the place that *Hashem* will choose; for *Hashem* your God will bless all your crops and all your undertakings, and you shall have nothing but joy.

טו שִׁבְעַת יָמִים תָּחֹג לַיהֹוָה אֱלֹהֶיךָ בַּמָּקוֹם אֲשֶׁר־יִבְחַר יְהֹוָה כִּי יְבָרֶכְךָ יְהֹוָה אֱלֹהֶיךָ בְּכֹל תְּבוּאָתְךָ וּבְכֹל מַעֲשֵׂה יָדֶיךָ וְהָיִיתָ אַךְ שָׂמֵחַ:

16 Three times a year – on the festival of *Pesach*, on the festival of *Shavuot*, and on the festival of *Sukkot* – all your males shall appear before *Hashem* your God in the place that He will choose. They shall not appear before *Hashem* empty-handed,

טז שָׁלוֹשׁ פְּעָמִים בַּשָּׁנָה יֵרָאֶה כָל־זְכוּרְךָ אֶת־פְּנֵי יְהֹוָה אֱלֹהֶיךָ בַּמָּקוֹם אֲשֶׁר יִבְחָר בְּחַג הַמַּצּוֹת וּבְחַג הַשָּׁבֻעוֹת וּבְחַג הַסֻּכּוֹת וְלֹא יֵרָאֶה אֶת־פְּנֵי יְהֹוָה רֵיקָם:

sha-LOSH p'-a-MEEM ba-sha-NAH yay-ra-EH khol z'-khu-r'-KHA et p'-NAY a-do-NAI e-lo-HE-kha ba-ma-KOM a-SHER yiv-KHAR b'-KHAG ha-ma-TZOT u-v'-KHAG ha-sha-vu-OT u-v'-KHAG ha-su-KOT v'-LO yay-ra-EH et p'-NAY a-do-NAI ray-KAM

16:16 Three times a year The Hebrew word *shalosh* (שלוש) means 'three.' The number three indicates a strong unit or bond, as it says in *Megillat Kohelet* (4:12), "A threefold cord is not readily broken." Perhaps for this reason, there are three times a year when every Jew is commanded to make a pilgrimage to the *Beit Hamikdash* in *Yerushalayim* and to appear before *Hashem* in the Temple. This ensures that he will reconnect with his Creator at least three times a year, and that the bonds between them will remain strong.

שלוש

16:16 On the festival of *Sukkot* *Sukkot* stands out from the other pilgrimage festivals in that its celebration is not limited to the Jewish people.

Devarim/Deuteronomy 17
Shoftim

דברים יז
שופטים

17 but each with his own gift, according to the blessing that *Hashem* your God has bestowed upon you.

אִישׁ כְּמַתְּנַת יָדוֹ כְּבִרְכַּת יְהֹוָה אֱלֹהֶיךָ אֲשֶׁר נָתַן־לָךְ׃

18 You shall appoint magistrates and officials for your tribes, in all the settlements that *Hashem* your God is giving you, and they shall govern the people with due justice.

שֹׁפְטִים וְשֹׁטְרִים תִּתֶּן־לְךָ בְּכָל־שְׁעָרֶיךָ אֲשֶׁר יְהֹוָה אֱלֹהֶיךָ נֹתֵן לְךָ לִשְׁבָטֶיךָ וְשָׁפְטוּ אֶת־הָעָם מִשְׁפַּט־צֶדֶק׃

19 You shall not judge unfairly: you shall show no partiality; you shall not take bribes, for bribes blind the eyes of the discerning and upset the plea of the just.

לֹא־תַטֶּה מִשְׁפָּט לֹא תַכִּיר פָּנִים וְלֹא־תִקַּח שֹׁחַד כִּי הַשֹּׁחַד יְעַוֵּר עֵינֵי חֲכָמִים וִיסַלֵּף דִּבְרֵי צַדִּיקִם׃

20 Justice, justice shall you pursue, that you may thrive and occupy the land that *Hashem* your God is giving you.

צֶדֶק צֶדֶק תִּרְדֹּף לְמַעַן תִּחְיֶה וְיָרַשְׁתָּ אֶת־הָאָרֶץ אֲשֶׁר־יְהֹוָה אֱלֹהֶיךָ נֹתֵן לָךְ׃

TZE-dek TZE-dek tir-DOF l'-MA-an tikh-YEH v'-ya-rash-TA et ha-A-retz a-sher a-do-NAI e-lo-HE-kha no-TAYN LAKH

21 You shall not set up a sacred post – any kind of pole beside the *Mizbayach* of *Hashem* your God that you may make

לֹא־תִטַּע לְךָ אֲשֵׁרָה כָּל־עֵץ אֵצֶל מִזְבַּח יְהֹוָה אֱלֹהֶיךָ אֲשֶׁר תַּעֲשֶׂה־לָּךְ׃

22 or erect a stone pillar; for such *Hashem* your God detests.

וְלֹא־תָקִים לְךָ מַצֵּבָה אֲשֶׁר שָׂנֵא יְהֹוָה אֱלֹהֶיךָ׃

17

1 You shall not sacrifice to *Hashem* your God an ox or a sheep that has any defect of a serious kind, for that is abhorrent to *Hashem* your God.

לֹא־תִזְבַּח לַיהֹוָה אֱלֹהֶיךָ שׁוֹר וָשֶׂה אֲשֶׁר יִהְיֶה בוֹ מוּם כֹּל דָּבָר רָע כִּי תוֹעֲבַת יְהֹוָה אֱלֹהֶיךָ הוּא׃

2 If there is found among you, in one of the settlements that *Hashem* your God is giving you, a man or woman who has affronted *Hashem* your God and transgressed His covenant

כִּי־יִמָּצֵא בְקִרְבְּךָ בְּאַחַד שְׁעָרֶיךָ אֲשֶׁר־יְהֹוָה אֱלֹהֶיךָ נֹתֵן לָךְ אִישׁ אוֹ־אִשָּׁה אֲשֶׁר יַעֲשֶׂה אֶת־הָרַע בְּעֵינֵי יְהֹוָה־אֱלֹהֶיךָ לַעֲבֹר בְּרִיתוֹ׃

3 turning to the worship of other gods and bowing down to them, to the sun or the moon or any of the heavenly host, something I never commanded

וַיֵּלֶךְ וַיַּעֲבֹד אֱלֹהִים אֲחֵרִים וַיִּשְׁתַּחוּ לָהֶם וְלַשֶּׁמֶשׁ אוֹ לַיָּרֵחַ אוֹ לְכָל־צְבָא הַשָּׁמַיִם אֲשֶׁר לֹא־צִוִּיתִי׃

The Chinese delegation at the Jerusalem March, Sukkot 2013

Rather, the Sages explain (*Sukkah* 55b) that a total of seventy bulls were brought as burnt-offerings throughout the Feast of Booths, on behalf of all seventy nations of the world. This served as a mighty display of universal solidarity and worship of the one true God of Israel. The Sages of the *Midrash* conclude that had the Babylonians and Romans understood the universal benefit that the *Beit Hamikdash* provided, they would never have destroyed it and would even have built a protective fortress around it. The prophet *Zecharya* promises that in the time of *Mashiach*, *Sukkot* will once again be celebrated in *Yerushalayim* by all the nations of the world: "All who survive of all those nations that came up against *Yerushalayim* shall make a pilgrimage year by year to bow low to the King Lord of Hosts, and to observe the festival of *Sukkot*" (Zechariah 14:16). This prophecy has begun to be fulfilled through the thousands of non-Jewish visitors from all over the world who come to *Yerushalayim* each year for *Sukkot*.

Devarim/Deuteronomy 17
Shoftim

דברים יז
שופטים

4 and you have been informed or have learned of it, then you shall make a thorough inquiry. If it is true, the fact is established, that abhorrent thing was perpetrated in *Yisrael*,

ד וְהֻגַּד־לְךָ וְשָׁמָעְתָּ וְדָרַשְׁתָּ הֵיטֵב וְהִנֵּה אֱמֶת נָכוֹן הַדָּבָר נֶעֶשְׂתָה הַתּוֹעֵבָה הַזֹּאת בְּיִשְׂרָאֵל׃

5 you shall take the man or the woman who did that wicked thing out to the public place, and you shall stone them, man or woman, to death.

ה וְהוֹצֵאתָ אֶת־הָאִישׁ הַהוּא אוֹ אֶת־הָאִשָּׁה הַהִוא אֲשֶׁר עָשׂוּ אֶת־הַדָּבָר הָרָע הַזֶּה אֶל־שְׁעָרֶיךָ אֶת־הָאִישׁ אוֹ אֶת־הָאִשָּׁה וּסְקַלְתָּם בָּאֲבָנִים וָמֵתוּ׃

6 A person shall be put to death only on the testimony of two or more witnesses; he must not be put to death on the testimony of a single witness.

ו עַל־פִּי שְׁנַיִם עֵדִים אוֹ שְׁלֹשָׁה עֵדִים יוּמַת הַמֵּת לֹא יוּמַת עַל־פִּי עֵד אֶחָד׃

7 Let the hands of the witnesses be the first against him to put him to death, and the hands of the rest of the people thereafter. Thus you will sweep out evil from your midst.

ז יַד הָעֵדִים תִּהְיֶה־בּוֹ בָרִאשֹׁנָה לַהֲמִיתוֹ וְיַד כָּל־הָעָם בָּאַחֲרֹנָה וּבִעַרְתָּ הָרָע מִקִּרְבֶּךָ׃

8 If a case is too baffling for you to decide, be it a controversy over homicide, civil law, or assault – matters of dispute in your courts – you shall promptly repair to the place that *Hashem* your God will have chosen,

ח כִּי יִפָּלֵא מִמְּךָ דָבָר לַמִּשְׁפָּט בֵּין־דָּם לְדָם בֵּין־דִּין לְדִין וּבֵין נֶגַע לָנֶגַע דִּבְרֵי רִיבֹת בִּשְׁעָרֶיךָ וְקַמְתָּ וְעָלִיתָ אֶל־הַמָּקוֹם אֲשֶׁר יִבְחַר יְהוָה אֱלֹהֶיךָ בּוֹ׃

9 and appear before the levitical *Kohanim*, or the magistrate in charge at the time, and present your problem. When they have announced to you the verdict in the case,

ט וּבָאתָ אֶל־הַכֹּהֲנִים הַלְוִיִּם וְאֶל־הַשֹּׁפֵט אֲשֶׁר יִהְיֶה בַּיָּמִים הָהֵם וְדָרַשְׁתָּ וְהִגִּידוּ לְךָ אֵת דְּבַר הַמִּשְׁפָּט׃

10 you shall carry out the verdict that is announced to you from that place that *Hashem* chose, observing scrupulously all their instructions to you.

י וְעָשִׂיתָ עַל־פִּי הַדָּבָר אֲשֶׁר יַגִּידוּ לְךָ מִן־הַמָּקוֹם הַהוּא אֲשֶׁר יִבְחַר יְהוָה וְשָׁמַרְתָּ לַעֲשׂוֹת כְּכֹל אֲשֶׁר יוֹרוּךָ׃

11 You shall act in accordance with the instructions given you and the ruling handed down to you; you must not deviate from the verdict that they announce to you either to the right or to the left.

יא עַל־פִּי הַתּוֹרָה אֲשֶׁר יוֹרוּךָ וְעַל־הַמִּשְׁפָּט אֲשֶׁר־יֹאמְרוּ לְךָ תַּעֲשֶׂה לֹא תָסוּר מִן־הַדָּבָר אֲשֶׁר־יַגִּידוּ לְךָ יָמִין וּשְׂמֹאל׃

12 Should a man act presumptuously and disregard the *Kohen* charged with serving there *Hashem* your God, or the magistrate, that man shall die. Thus you will sweep out evil from *Yisrael*:

יב וְהָאִישׁ אֲשֶׁר־יַעֲשֶׂה בְזָדוֹן לְבִלְתִּי שְׁמֹעַ אֶל־הַכֹּהֵן הָעֹמֵד לְשָׁרֶת שָׁם אֶת־יְהוָה אֱלֹהֶיךָ אוֹ אֶל־הַשֹּׁפֵט וּמֵת הָאִישׁ הַהוּא וּבִעַרְתָּ הָרָע מִיִּשְׂרָאֵל׃

13 all the people will hear and be afraid and will not act presumptuously again.

יג וְכָל־הָעָם יִשְׁמְעוּ וְיִרָאוּ וְלֹא יְזִידוּן עוֹד׃

14 If, after you have entered the land that *Hashem* your God has assigned to you, and taken possession of it and settled in it, you decide, "I will set a king over me, as do all the nations about me,"

יד כִּי־תָבֹא אֶל־הָאָרֶץ אֲשֶׁר יְהוָה אֱלֹהֶיךָ נֹתֵן לָךְ וִירִשְׁתָּהּ וְיָשַׁבְתָּה בָּהּ וְאָמַרְתָּ אָשִׂימָה עָלַי מֶלֶךְ כְּכָל־הַגּוֹיִם אֲשֶׁר סְבִיבֹתָי׃

Devarim/Deuteronomy 18
Shoftim

15 you shall be free to set a king over yourself, one chosen by *Hashem* your God. Be sure to set as king over yourself one of your own people; you must not set a foreigner over you, one who is not your kinsman.

16 Moreover, he shall not keep many horses or send people back to Egypt to add to his horses, since *Hashem* has warned you, "You must not go back that way again."

17 And he shall not have many wives, lest his heart go astray; nor shall he amass silver and gold to excess.

18 When he is seated on his royal throne, he shall have a copy of this *Torah* written for him on a scroll by the levitical *Kohanim*.

19 Let it remain with him and let him read in it all his life, so that he may learn to revere *Hashem* his God, to observe faithfully every word of this Teaching as well as these laws.

20 Thus he will not act haughtily toward his fellows or deviate from the Instruction to the right or to the left, to the end that he and his descendants may reign long in the midst of *Yisrael*.

טו שׂוֹם תָּשִׂים עָלֶיךָ מֶלֶךְ אֲשֶׁר יִבְחַר יְהֹוָה אֱלֹהֶיךָ בּוֹ מִקֶּרֶב אַחֶיךָ תָּשִׂים עָלֶיךָ מֶלֶךְ לֹא תוּכַל לָתֵת עָלֶיךָ אִישׁ נָכְרִי אֲשֶׁר לֹא־אָחִיךָ הוּא:

טז רַק לֹא־יַרְבֶּה־לּוֹ סוּסִים וְלֹא־יָשִׁיב אֶת־הָעָם מִצְרַיְמָה לְמַעַן הַרְבּוֹת סוּס וַיהֹוָה אָמַר לָכֶם לֹא תֹסִפוּן לָשׁוּב בַּדֶּרֶךְ הַזֶּה עוֹד:

יז וְלֹא יַרְבֶּה־לּוֹ נָשִׁים וְלֹא יָסוּר לְבָבוֹ וְכֶסֶף וְזָהָב לֹא יַרְבֶּה־לּוֹ מְאֹד:

יח וְהָיָה כְשִׁבְתּוֹ עַל כִּסֵּא מַמְלַכְתּוֹ וְכָתַב לוֹ אֶת־מִשְׁנֵה הַתּוֹרָה הַזֹּאת עַל־סֵפֶר מִלִּפְנֵי הַכֹּהֲנִים הַלְוִיִּם:

יט וְהָיְתָה עִמּוֹ וְקָרָא בוֹ כָּל־יְמֵי חַיָּיו לְמַעַן יִלְמַד לְיִרְאָה אֶת־יְהֹוָה אֱלֹהָיו לִשְׁמֹר אֶת־כָּל־דִּבְרֵי הַתּוֹרָה הַזֹּאת וְאֶת־הַחֻקִּים הָאֵלֶּה לַעֲשֹׂתָם:

כ לְבִלְתִּי רוּם־לְבָבוֹ מֵאֶחָיו וּלְבִלְתִּי סוּר מִן־הַמִּצְוָה יָמִין וּשְׂמֹאול לְמַעַן יַאֲרִיךְ יָמִים עַל־מַמְלַכְתּוֹ הוּא וּבָנָיו בְּקֶרֶב יִשְׂרָאֵל:

l'-vil-TEE rum l'-va-VO may-e-KHAV u-l'-vil-TEE SUR min ha-mitz-VAH ya-MIN us-MOL l'-MA-an ya-a-REEKH ya-MEEM al mam-lakh-TO HU u-va-NAV b'-KE-rev yis-ra-AYL

18

1 The levitical *Kohanim*, the whole tribe of *Levi*, shall have no territorial portion with *Yisrael*. They shall live only off *Hashem*'s offerings by fire as their portion,

2 and shall have no portion among their brother tribes: *Hashem* is their portion, as He promised them.

יח א לֹא־יִהְיֶה לַכֹּהֲנִים הַלְוִיִּם כָּל־שֵׁבֶט לֵוִי חֵלֶק וְנַחֲלָה עִם־יִשְׂרָאֵל אִשֵּׁי יְהֹוָה וְנַחֲלָתוֹ יֹאכֵלוּן:

ב וְנַחֲלָה לֹא־יִהְיֶה־לּוֹ בְּקֶרֶב אֶחָיו יְהֹוָה הוּא נַחֲלָתוֹ כַּאֲשֶׁר דִּבֶּר־לוֹ:

17:20 Thus he will not act haughtily Verses 14–20 discuss the command for the People of Israel to appoint a king, and the subsequent restrictions the *Torah* places on the kings of Israel. Appointing a king is one of the three commandments that the Jews were instructed to perform after settling the land. Without leadership, chaos ensues, as the verse implies "In those days there was no king in *Yisrael*; everyone did as he pleased" (Judges 21:25). However, there is a risk that the king will forget the source of his strength and attribute his successes to his own wisdom and power. Therefore, the Bible places three special restrictions upon the kings, and also requires that they carry a copy of the *Torah* with them at all times. The laws of the kings remind us that we all must recognize the true source of blessing and success in our lives.

Devarim/Deuteronomy 18
Shoftim

דברים יח
שופטים

3 This then shall be the *Kohanim*'s due from the people: Everyone who offers a sacrifice, whether an ox or a sheep, must give the shoulder, the cheeks, and the stomach to the *Kohen*.

ג וְזֶה יִהְיֶה מִשְׁפַּט הַכֹּהֲנִים מֵאֵת הָעָם מֵאֵת זֹבְחֵי הַזֶּבַח אִם־שׁוֹר אִם־שֶׂה וְנָתַן לַכֹּהֵן הַזְּרֹעַ וְהַלְּחָיַיִם וְהַקֵּבָה׃

4 You shall also give him the first fruits of your new grain and wine and oil, and the first shearing of your sheep.

ד רֵאשִׁית דְּגָנְךָ תִּירֹשְׁךָ וְיִצְהָרֶךָ וְרֵאשִׁית גֵּז צֹאנְךָ תִּתֶּן־לוֹ׃

5 For *Hashem* your God has chosen him and his descendants, out of all your tribes, to be in attendance for service in the name of *Hashem* for all time.

ה כִּי בוֹ בָּחַר יְהֹוָה אֱלֹהֶיךָ מִכָּל־שְׁבָטֶיךָ לַעֲמֹד לְשָׁרֵת בְּשֵׁם־יְהֹוָה הוּא וּבָנָיו כָּל־הַיָּמִים׃

6 If a Levite would go, from any of the settlements throughout *Yisrael* where he has been residing, to the place that *Hashem* has chosen, he may do so whenever he pleases.

ו וְכִי־יָבֹא הַלֵּוִי מֵאַחַד שְׁעָרֶיךָ מִכָּל־יִשְׂרָאֵל אֲשֶׁר־הוּא גָּר שָׁם וּבָא בְּכָל־אַוַּת נַפְשׁוֹ אֶל־הַמָּקוֹם אֲשֶׁר־יִבְחַר יְהֹוָה׃

7 He may serve in the name of *Hashem* his God like all his fellow *Leviim* who are there in attendance before *Hashem*.

ז וְשֵׁרֵת בְּשֵׁם יְהֹוָה אֱלֹהָיו כְּכָל־אֶחָיו הַלְוִיִּם הָעֹמְדִים שָׁם לִפְנֵי יְהֹוָה׃

8 They shall receive equal shares of the dues, without regard to personal gifts or patrimonies.

ח חֵלֶק כְּחֵלֶק יֹאכֵלוּ לְבַד מִמְכָּרָיו עַל־הָאָבוֹת׃

9 When you enter the land that *Hashem* your God is giving you, you shall not learn to imitate the abhorrent practices of those nations.

ט כִּי אַתָּה בָּא אֶל־הָאָרֶץ אֲשֶׁר־יְהֹוָה אֱלֹהֶיךָ נֹתֵן לָךְ לֹא־תִלְמַד לַעֲשׂוֹת כְּתוֹעֲבֹת הַגּוֹיִם הָהֵם׃

KEE a-TAH BA el ha-A-retz a-sher a-do-NAI e-lo-HE-kha no-TAYN LAKH lo til-MAD la-a-SOT k'-to-a-VOT ha-go-YIM ha-HAYM

10 Let no one be found among you who consigns his son or daughter to the fire, or who is an augur, a soothsayer, a diviner, a sorcerer,

י לֹא־יִמָּצֵא בְךָ מַעֲבִיר בְּנוֹ־וּבִתּוֹ בָּאֵשׁ קֹסֵם קְסָמִים מְעוֹנֵן וּמְנַחֵשׁ וּמְכַשֵּׁף׃

11 one who casts spells, or one who consults ghosts or familiar spirits, or one who inquires of the dead.

יא וְחֹבֵר חָבֶר וְשֹׁאֵל אוֹב וְיִדְּעֹנִי וְדֹרֵשׁ אֶל־הַמֵּתִים׃

12 For anyone who does such things is abhorrent to *Hashem*, and it is because of these abhorrent things that *Hashem* your God is dispossessing them before you.

יב כִּי־תוֹעֲבַת יְהֹוָה כָּל־עֹשֵׂה אֵלֶּה וּבִגְלַל הַתּוֹעֵבֹת הָאֵלֶּה יְהֹוָה אֱלֹהֶיךָ מוֹרִישׁ אוֹתָם מִפָּנֶיךָ׃

18:9 The land that *Hashem* your God is giving you This verse teaches that *Hashem* promises the land to 'you,' written in the singular form *lach* (לך). Every individual in the nation has a place in the Land of Israel, and everyone needs to be mindful of the fact that remaining in the land depends on his or her moral character. Therefore, in the continuation of the verse, *Hashem* warns the people not to learn from and mimic the abominations of the peoples already living there, as doing so would jeopardize their right to be rulers of their land. The Jewish people are charged to live up to a high moral standard, and to serve as models of morality and ethics for the rest of the world.

Devarim/Deuteronomy 19
Shoftim

13 You must be wholehearted with *Hashem* your God.

14 Those nations that you are about to dispossess do indeed resort to soothsayers and augurs; to you, however, *Hashem* your God has not assigned the like.

15 *Hashem* your God will raise up for you a *navi* from among your own people, like myself; him you shall heed.

16 This is just what you asked of *Hashem* your God at Horeb, on the day of the Assembly, saying, "Let me not hear the voice of *Hashem* my God any longer or see this wondrous fire any more, lest I die."

17 Whereupon *Hashem* said to me, "They have done well in speaking thus.

18 I will raise up a *navi* for them from among their own people, like yourself: I will put My words in his mouth and he will speak to them all that I command him;

19 and if anybody fails to heed the words he speaks in My name, I Myself will call him to account.

20 But any *navi* who presumes to speak in My name an oracle that I did not command him to utter, or who speaks in the name of other gods – that *navi* shall die."

21 And should you ask yourselves, "How can we know that the oracle was not spoken by *Hashem*?"

22 if the *navi* speaks in the name of *Hashem* and the oracle does not come true, that oracle was not spoken by *Hashem*; the *navi* has uttered it presumptuously: do not stand in dread of him.

19
1 When *Hashem* your God has cut down the nations whose land *Hashem* your God is assigning to you, and you have dispossessed them and settled in their towns and homes,

2 you shall set aside three cities in the land that *Hashem* your God is giving you to possess.

3 You shall survey the distances, and divide into three parts the territory of the country that *Hashem* your God has allotted to you, so that any manslayer may have a place to flee to.

דברים יט
שופטים

יג תָּמִים תִּהְיֶה עִם יְהֹוָה אֱלֹהֶיךָ׃

יד כִּי הַגּוֹיִם הָאֵלֶּה אֲשֶׁר אַתָּה יוֹרֵשׁ אוֹתָם אֶל־מְעֹנְנִים וְאֶל־קֹסְמִים יִשְׁמָעוּ וְאַתָּה לֹא כֵן נָתַן לְךָ יְהֹוָה אֱלֹהֶיךָ׃

טו נָבִיא מִקִּרְבְּךָ מֵאַחֶיךָ כָּמֹנִי יָקִים לְךָ יְהֹוָה אֱלֹהֶיךָ אֵלָיו תִּשְׁמָעוּן׃

טז כְּכֹל אֲשֶׁר־שָׁאַלְתָּ מֵעִם יְהֹוָה אֱלֹהֶיךָ בְּחֹרֵב בְּיוֹם הַקָּהָל לֵאמֹר לֹא אֹסֵף לִשְׁמֹעַ אֶת־קוֹל יְהֹוָה אֱלֹהָי וְאֶת־הָאֵשׁ הַגְּדֹלָה הַזֹּאת לֹא־אֶרְאֶה עוֹד וְלֹא אָמוּת׃

יז וַיֹּאמֶר יְהֹוָה אֵלָי הֵיטִיבוּ אֲשֶׁר דִּבֵּרוּ׃

יח נָבִיא אָקִים לָהֶם מִקֶּרֶב אֲחֵיהֶם כָּמוֹךָ וְנָתַתִּי דְבָרַי בְּפִיו וְדִבֶּר אֲלֵיהֶם אֵת כָּל־אֲשֶׁר אֲצַוֶּנּוּ׃

יט וְהָיָה הָאִישׁ אֲשֶׁר לֹא־יִשְׁמַע אֶל־דְּבָרַי אֲשֶׁר יְדַבֵּר בִּשְׁמִי אָנֹכִי אֶדְרֹשׁ מֵעִמּוֹ׃

כ אַךְ הַנָּבִיא אֲשֶׁר יָזִיד לְדַבֵּר דָּבָר בִּשְׁמִי אֵת אֲשֶׁר לֹא־צִוִּיתִיו לְדַבֵּר וַאֲשֶׁר יְדַבֵּר בְּשֵׁם אֱלֹהִים אֲחֵרִים וּמֵת הַנָּבִיא הַהוּא׃

כא וְכִי תֹאמַר בִּלְבָבֶךָ אֵיכָה נֵדַע אֶת־הַדָּבָר אֲשֶׁר לֹא־דִבְּרוֹ יְהֹוָה׃

כב אֲשֶׁר יְדַבֵּר הַנָּבִיא בְּשֵׁם יְהֹוָה וְלֹא־יִהְיֶה הַדָּבָר וְלֹא יָבוֹא הוּא הַדָּבָר אֲשֶׁר לֹא־דִבְּרוֹ יְהֹוָה בְּזָדוֹן דִּבְּרוֹ הַנָּבִיא לֹא תָגוּר מִמֶּנּוּ׃

יט א כִּי־יַכְרִית יְהֹוָה אֱלֹהֶיךָ אֶת־הַגּוֹיִם אֲשֶׁר יְהֹוָה אֱלֹהֶיךָ נֹתֵן לְךָ אֶת־אַרְצָם וִירִשְׁתָּם וְיָשַׁבְתָּ בְעָרֵיהֶם וּבְבָתֵּיהֶם׃

ב שָׁלוֹשׁ עָרִים תַּבְדִּיל לָךְ בְּתוֹךְ אַרְצֶךָ אֲשֶׁר יְהֹוָה אֱלֹהֶיךָ נֹתֵן לְךָ לְרִשְׁתָּהּ׃

ג תָּכִין לְךָ הַדֶּרֶךְ וְשִׁלַּשְׁתָּ אֶת־גְּבוּל אַרְצְךָ אֲשֶׁר יַנְחִילְךָ יְהֹוָה אֱלֹהֶיךָ וְהָיָה לָנוּס שָׁמָּה כָּל־רֹצֵחַ׃

Devarim/Deuteronomy 19
Shoftim

דברים יט
שופטים

4 Now this is the case of the manslayer who may flee there and live: one who has killed another unwittingly, without having been his enemy in the past.

ד וְזֶה דְּבַר הָרֹצֵחַ אֲשֶׁר־יָנוּס שָׁמָּה וָחָי אֲשֶׁר יַכֶּה אֶת־רֵעֵהוּ בִּבְלִי־דַעַת וְהוּא לֹא־שֹׂנֵא לוֹ מִתְּמֹל שִׁלְשֹׁם׃

5 For instance, a man goes with his neighbor into a grove to cut wood; as his hand swings the ax to cut down a tree, the ax-head flies off the handle and strikes the other so that he dies. That man shall flee to one of these cities and live.

ה וַאֲשֶׁר יָבֹא אֶת־רֵעֵהוּ בַיַּעַר לַחְטֹב עֵצִים וְנִדְּחָה יָדוֹ בַגַּרְזֶן לִכְרֹת הָעֵץ וְנָשַׁל הַבַּרְזֶל מִן־הָעֵץ וּמָצָא אֶת־רֵעֵהוּ וָמֵת הוּא יָנוּס אֶל־אַחַת הֶעָרִים־הָאֵלֶּה וָחָי׃

6 Otherwise, when the distance is great, the blood-avenger, pursuing the manslayer in hot anger, may overtake him and kill him; yet he did not incur the death penalty, since he had never been the other's enemy.

ו פֶּן־יִרְדֹּף גֹּאֵל הַדָּם אַחֲרֵי הָרֹצֵחַ כִּי־יֵחַם לְבָבוֹ וְהִשִּׂיגוֹ כִּי־יִרְבֶּה הַדֶּרֶךְ וְהִכָּהוּ נָפֶשׁ וְלוֹ אֵין מִשְׁפַּט־מָוֶת כִּי לֹא שֹׂנֵא הוּא לוֹ מִתְּמוֹל שִׁלְשׁוֹם׃

7 That is why I command you: set aside three cities.

ז עַל־כֵּן אָנֹכִי מְצַוְּךָ לֵאמֹר שָׁלֹשׁ עָרִים תַּבְדִּיל לָךְ׃

8 And when *Hashem* your God enlarges your territory, as He swore to your fathers, and gives you all the land that He promised to give your fathers

ח וְאִם־יַרְחִיב יְהוָה אֱלֹהֶיךָ אֶת־גְּבֻלְךָ כַּאֲשֶׁר נִשְׁבַּע לַאֲבֹתֶיךָ וְנָתַן לְךָ אֶת־כָּל־הָאָרֶץ אֲשֶׁר דִּבֶּר לָתֵת לַאֲבֹתֶיךָ׃

v'-im yar-KHEEV a-do-NAI e-lo-HE-kha et g'-VU-l'-KHA ka-a-SHER nish-BA la-a-vo-TE-kha v'-na-TAN l'-KHA et kol ha-A-retz a-SHER di-BAYR la-TAYT la-a-vo-TE-kha

9 if you faithfully observe all this Instruction that I enjoin upon you this day, to love *Hashem* your God and to walk in His ways at all times – then you shall add three more towns to those three.

ט כִּי־תִשְׁמֹר אֶת־כָּל־הַמִּצְוָה הַזֹּאת לַעֲשֹׂתָהּ אֲשֶׁר אָנֹכִי מְצַוְּךָ הַיּוֹם לְאַהֲבָה אֶת־יְהוָה אֱלֹהֶיךָ וְלָלֶכֶת בִּדְרָכָיו כָּל־הַיָּמִים וְיָסַפְתָּ לְךָ עוֹד שָׁלֹשׁ עָרִים עַל הַשָּׁלֹשׁ הָאֵלֶּה׃

10 Thus blood of the innocent will not be shed, bringing bloodguilt upon you in the land that *Hashem* your God is allotting to you.

י וְלֹא יִשָּׁפֵךְ דָּם נָקִי בְּקֶרֶב אַרְצְךָ אֲשֶׁר יְהוָה אֱלֹהֶיךָ נֹתֵן לְךָ נַחֲלָה וְהָיָה עָלֶיךָ דָּמִים׃

11 If, however, a person who is the enemy of another lies in wait for him and sets upon him and strikes him a fatal blow and then flees to one of these towns,

יא וְכִי־יִהְיֶה אִישׁ שֹׂנֵא לְרֵעֵהוּ וְאָרַב לוֹ וְקָם עָלָיו וְהִכָּהוּ נֶפֶשׁ וָמֵת וְנָס אֶל־אַחַת הֶעָרִים הָאֵל׃

12 the elders of his town shall have him brought back from there and shall hand him over to the blood-avenger to be put to death;

יב וְשָׁלְחוּ זִקְנֵי עִירוֹ וְלָקְחוּ אֹתוֹ מִשָּׁם וְנָתְנוּ אֹתוֹ בְּיַד גֹּאֵל הַדָּם וָמֵת׃

13 you must show him no pity. Thus you will purge *Yisrael* of the blood of the innocent, and it will go well with you.

יג לֹא־תָחוֹס עֵינְךָ עָלָיו וּבִעַרְתָּ דַם־הַנָּקִי מִיִּשְׂרָאֵל וְטוֹב לָךְ׃

Devarim/Deuteronomy 20
Shoftim

דברים כ
שופטים

14 You shall not move your countryman's landmarks, set up by previous generations, in the property that will be allotted to you in the land that *Hashem* your God is giving you to possess.

לֹא תַסִּיג גְּבוּל רֵעֲךָ אֲשֶׁר גָּבְלוּ רִאשֹׁנִים בְּנַחֲלָתְךָ אֲשֶׁר תִּנְחַל בָּאָרֶץ אֲשֶׁר יְהוָה אֱלֹהֶיךָ נֹתֵן לְךָ לְרִשְׁתָּהּ׃

LO ta-SEEG g'-VUL ray-a-KHA a-SHER ga-v'-LU ri-sho-NEEM b'-na-kha-la-t'-KHA a-SHER tin-KHAL ba-A-retz a-SHER a-do-NAI e-lo-HE-kha no-TAYN l'-KHA l'-rish-TAH

15 A single witness may not validate against a person any guilt or blame for any offense that may be committed; a case can be valid only on the testimony of two witnesses or more.

לֹא־יָקוּם עֵד אֶחָד בְּאִישׁ לְכָל־עָוֹן וּלְכָל־חַטָּאת בְּכָל־חֵטְא אֲשֶׁר יֶחֱטָא עַל־פִּי שְׁנֵי עֵדִים אוֹ עַל־פִּי שְׁלֹשָׁה־עֵדִים יָקוּם דָּבָר׃

16 If a man appears against another to testify maliciously and gives false testimony against him,

כִּי־יָקוּם עֵד־חָמָס בְּאִישׁ לַעֲנוֹת בּוֹ סָרָה׃

17 the two parties to the dispute shall appear before *Hashem*, before the *Kohanim* or magistrates in authority at the time,

וְעָמְדוּ שְׁנֵי־הָאֲנָשִׁים אֲשֶׁר־לָהֶם הָרִיב לִפְנֵי יְהוָה לִפְנֵי הַכֹּהֲנִים וְהַשֹּׁפְטִים אֲשֶׁר יִהְיוּ בַּיָּמִים הָהֵם׃

18 and the magistrates shall make a thorough investigation. If the man who testified is a false witness, if he has testified falsely against his fellow,

וְדָרְשׁוּ הַשֹּׁפְטִים הֵיטֵב וְהִנֵּה עֵד־שֶׁקֶר הָעֵד שֶׁקֶר עָנָה בְאָחִיו׃

19 you shall do to him as he schemed to do to his fellow. Thus you will sweep out evil from your midst;

וַעֲשִׂיתֶם לוֹ כַּאֲשֶׁר זָמַם לַעֲשׂוֹת לְאָחִיו וּבִעַרְתָּ הָרָע מִקִּרְבֶּךָ׃

20 others will hear and be afraid, and such evil things will not again be done in your midst.

וְהַנִּשְׁאָרִים יִשְׁמְעוּ וְיִרָאוּ וְלֹא־יֹסִפוּ לַעֲשׂוֹת עוֹד כַּדָּבָר הָרָע הַזֶּה בְּקִרְבֶּךָ׃

21 Nor must you show pity: life for life, eye for eye, tooth for tooth, hand for hand, foot for foot.

וְלֹא תָחוֹס עֵינֶךָ נֶפֶשׁ בְּנֶפֶשׁ עַיִן בְּעַיִן שֵׁן בְּשֵׁן יָד בְּיָד רֶגֶל בְּרָגֶל׃

20 1 When you take the field against your enemies, and see horses and chariots – forces larger than yours – have no fear of them, for *Hashem* your God, who brought you from the land of Egypt, is with you.

כִּי־תֵצֵא לַמִּלְחָמָה עַל־אֹיְבֶיךָ וְרָאִיתָ סוּס וָרֶכֶב עַם רַב מִמְּךָ לֹא תִירָא מֵהֶם כִּי־יְהוָה אֱלֹהֶיךָ עִמָּךְ הַמַּעַלְךָ מֵאֶרֶץ מִצְרָיִם׃

2 Before you join battle, the *Kohen* shall come forward and address the troops.

וְהָיָה כְּקָרָבְכֶם אֶל־הַמִּלְחָמָה וְנִגַּשׁ הַכֹּהֵן וְדִבֶּר אֶל־הָעָם׃

19:14 You shall not move your countryman's landmarks In this verse, the *Torah* prohibits moving the borders of one's property in order to secretly and illegitimately incorporate some of his neighbor's land into his own. *Hashem* gave *Eretz Yisrael* to the Israelites, and He expects them to live in it fairly and justly, without taking even one inch of land that does not belong to them. It is therefore particularly painful today to see those who deny the Bible accuse the Jewish people of "occupation," and of stealing someone else's land. Over and over, the *Tanakh* establishes the deep connection between the Jewish People and *Eretz Yisrael*, yet this fundamental fact has been attacked in recent years with increasing hostility. It is incumbent upon students of the Bible to point to verses such as this as evidence of the fairness and honesty that underpins the historic relationship between the People of Israel and the Land of Israel.

Devarim/Deuteronomy 20
Shoftim

דברים כ
שופטים

3 He shall say to them, "Hear, O *Yisrael*! You are about to join battle with your enemy. Let not your courage falter. Do not be in fear, or in panic, or in dread of them.

ג וְאָמַר אֲלֵהֶם שְׁמַע יִשְׂרָאֵל אַתֶּם קְרֵבִים הַיּוֹם לַמִּלְחָמָה עַל־אֹיְבֵיכֶם אַל־יֵרַךְ לְבַבְכֶם אַל־תִּירְאוּ וְאַל־תַּחְפְּזוּ וְאַל־תַּעַרְצוּ מִפְּנֵיהֶם:

4 For it is *Hashem* your God who marches with you to do battle for you against your enemy, to bring you victory."

ד כִּי יְהֹוָה אֱלֹהֵיכֶם הַהֹלֵךְ עִמָּכֶם לְהִלָּחֵם לָכֶם עִם־אֹיְבֵיכֶם לְהוֹשִׁיעַ אֶתְכֶם:

KEE a-do-NAI e-lo-hay-KHEM ha-ho-LAYKH i-ma-KHEM l'-hi-la-KHAYM la-KHEM im o-y'-vay-KHEM l'-ho-SHEE-a et-KHEM

5 Then the officials shall address the troops, as follows: "Is there anyone who has built a new house but has not dedicated it? Let him go back to his home, lest he die in battle and another dedicate it.

ה וְדִבְּרוּ הַשֹּׁטְרִים אֶל־הָעָם לֵאמֹר מִי־הָאִישׁ אֲשֶׁר בָּנָה בַיִת־חָדָשׁ וְלֹא חֲנָכוֹ יֵלֵךְ וְיָשֹׁב לְבֵיתוֹ פֶּן־יָמוּת בַּמִּלְחָמָה וְאִישׁ אַחֵר יַחְנְכֶנּוּ:

6 Is there anyone who has planted a vineyard but has never harvested it? Let him go back to his home, lest he die in battle and another harvest it.

ו וּמִי־הָאִישׁ אֲשֶׁר־נָטַע כֶּרֶם וְלֹא חִלְּלוֹ יֵלֵךְ וְיָשֹׁב לְבֵיתוֹ פֶּן־יָמוּת בַּמִּלְחָמָה וְאִישׁ אַחֵר יְחַלְּלֶנּוּ:

7 Is there anyone who has paid the bride-price for a wife, but who has not yet married her? Let him go back to his home, lest he die in battle and another marry her."

ז וּמִי־הָאִישׁ אֲשֶׁר־אֵרַשׂ אִשָּׁה וְלֹא לְקָחָהּ יֵלֵךְ וְיָשֹׁב לְבֵיתוֹ פֶּן־יָמוּת בַּמִּלְחָמָה וְאִישׁ אַחֵר יִקָּחֶנָּה:

8 The officials shall go on addressing the troops and say, "Is there anyone afraid and disheartened? Let him go back to his home, lest the courage of his comrades flag like his."

ח וְיָסְפוּ הַשֹּׁטְרִים לְדַבֵּר אֶל־הָעָם וְאָמְרוּ מִי־הָאִישׁ הַיָּרֵא וְרַךְ הַלֵּבָב יֵלֵךְ וְיָשֹׁב לְבֵיתוֹ וְלֹא יִמַּס אֶת־לְבַב אֶחָיו כִּלְבָבוֹ:

9 When the officials have finished addressing the troops, army commanders shall assume command of the troops.

ט וְהָיָה כְּכַלֹּת הַשֹּׁטְרִים לְדַבֵּר אֶל־הָעָם וּפָקְדוּ שָׂרֵי צְבָאוֹת בְּרֹאשׁ הָעָם:

10 When you approach a town to attack it, you shall offer it terms of peace.

י כִּי־תִקְרַב אֶל־עִיר לְהִלָּחֵם עָלֶיהָ וְקָרָאתָ אֵלֶיהָ לְשָׁלוֹם:

kee tik-RAV el EER l'-hi-la-KHAYM a-LE-ha v'-ka-RA-ta ay-LE-ha l'-sha-LOM

11 If it responds peaceably and lets you in, all the people present there shall serve you at forced labor.

יא וְהָיָה אִם־שָׁלוֹם תַּעַנְךָ וּפָתְחָה לָךְ וְהָיָה כָּל־הָעָם הַנִּמְצָא־בָהּ יִהְיוּ לְךָ לָמַס וַעֲבָדוּךָ:

12 If it does not surrender to you, but would join battle with you, you shall lay siege to it;

יב וְאִם־לֹא תַשְׁלִים עִמָּךְ וְעָשְׂתָה עִמְּךָ מִלְחָמָה וְצַרְתָּ עָלֶיהָ:

20:10 You shall offer it terms of peace Before going to war, the Children of Israel are required to first offer their enemies the opportunity to make peace. According to some commentators, this applies even to the nations living in the parts of the Land of Israel promised to *B'nei Yisrael*. The land was given to the People of Israel as an inheritance, but first and foremost they must try to live there in peace with their neighbors. The State of Israel has taken the quest for peace very seriously. It has even returned land captured in a defensive war, and offered to return more, in exchange for peace with its neighbors.

Devarim/Deuteronomy 21
Shoftim

דברים כא
שופטים

13 and when *Hashem* your God delivers it into your hand, you shall put all its males to the sword.

יג וּנְתָנָהּ יְהֹוָה אֱלֹהֶיךָ בְּיָדֶךָ וְהִכִּיתָ אֶת־כָּל־זְכוּרָהּ לְפִי־חָרֶב׃

14 You may, however, take as your booty the women, the children, the livestock, and everything in the town – all its spoil – and enjoy the use of the spoil of your enemy, which *Hashem* your God gives you.

יד רַק הַנָּשִׁים וְהַטַּף וְהַבְּהֵמָה וְכֹל אֲשֶׁר יִהְיֶה בָעִיר כָּל־שְׁלָלָהּ תָּבֹז לָךְ וְאָכַלְתָּ אֶת־שְׁלַל אֹיְבֶיךָ אֲשֶׁר נָתַן יְהֹוָה אֱלֹהֶיךָ לָךְ׃

15 Thus you shall deal with all towns that lie very far from you, towns that do not belong to nations hereabout.

טו כֵּן תַּעֲשֶׂה לְכָל־הֶעָרִים הָרְחֹקֹת מִמְּךָ מְאֹד אֲשֶׁר לֹא־מֵעָרֵי הַגּוֹיִם־הָאֵלֶּה הֵנָּה׃

16 In the towns of the latter peoples, however, which *Hashem* your God is giving you as a heritage, you shall not let a soul remain alive.

טז רַק מֵעָרֵי הָעַמִּים הָאֵלֶּה אֲשֶׁר יְהֹוָה אֱלֹהֶיךָ נֹתֵן לְךָ נַחֲלָה לֹא תְחַיֶּה כָּל־נְשָׁמָה׃

17 No, you must proscribe them – the Hittites and the Amorites, the Canaanites and the Perizzites, the Hivites and the Jebusites – as *Hashem* your God has commanded you,

יז כִּי־הַחֲרֵם תַּחֲרִימֵם הַחִתִּי וְהָאֱמֹרִי הַכְּנַעֲנִי וְהַפְּרִזִּי הַחִוִּי וְהַיְבוּסִי כַּאֲשֶׁר צִוְּךָ יְהֹוָה אֱלֹהֶיךָ׃

18 lest they lead you into doing all the abhorrent things that they have done for their gods and you stand guilty before *Hashem* your God.

יח לְמַעַן אֲשֶׁר לֹא־יְלַמְּדוּ אֶתְכֶם לַעֲשׂוֹת כְּכֹל תּוֹעֲבֹתָם אֲשֶׁר עָשׂוּ לֵאלֹהֵיהֶם וַחֲטָאתֶם לַיהֹוָה אֱלֹהֵיכֶם׃

19 When in your war against a city you have to besiege it a long time in order to capture it, you must not destroy its trees, wielding the ax against them. You may eat of them, but you must not cut them down. Are trees of the field human to withdraw before you into the besieged city?

יט כִּי־תָצוּר אֶל־עִיר יָמִים רַבִּים לְהִלָּחֵם עָלֶיהָ לְתָפְשָׂהּ לֹא־תַשְׁחִית אֶת־עֵצָהּ לִנְדֹּחַ עָלָיו גַּרְזֶן כִּי מִמֶּנּוּ תֹאכֵל וְאֹתוֹ לֹא תִכְרֹת כִּי הָאָדָם עֵץ הַשָּׂדֶה לָבֹא מִפָּנֶיךָ בַּמָּצוֹר׃

20 Only trees that you know do not yield food may be destroyed; you may cut them down for constructing siegeworks against the city that is waging war on you, until it has been reduced.

כ רַק עֵץ אֲשֶׁר־תֵּדַע כִּי־לֹא־עֵץ מַאֲכָל הוּא אֹתוֹ תַשְׁחִית וְכָרָתָּ וּבָנִיתָ מָצוֹר עַל־הָעִיר אֲשֶׁר־הִוא עֹשָׂה עִמְּךָ מִלְחָמָה עַד רִדְתָּהּ׃

21

1 If, in the land that *Hashem* your God is assigning you to possess, someone slain is found lying in the open, the identity of the slayer not being known,

כא א כִּי־יִמָּצֵא חָלָל בָּאֲדָמָה אֲשֶׁר יְהֹוָה אֱלֹהֶיךָ נֹתֵן לְךָ לְרִשְׁתָּהּ נֹפֵל בַּשָּׂדֶה לֹא נוֹדַע מִי הִכָּהוּ׃

kee yi-ma-TZAY kha-LAL ba-a-da-MAH a-SHER a-do-NAI e-lo-HE-kha no-TAYN l'-KHA l'-rish-TAH no-FAYL ba-sa-DEH LO no-DA MEE hi-KA-hu

Rabbi Joseph B. Soloveitchik (1903–1993)

21:1 In the land that *Hashem* your God is assigning you The axed heifer is one of the few biblical commandments that can be performed only in *Eretz Yisrael* even though it is not an agricultural law. Rabbi Joseph B. Soloveitchik explains that the reason for this is that this law is incumbent on the 'Congregation of Israel,' not on individual members of the nation, and the Israelites are only considered the 'Congregation of Israel' when residing in their land. This highlights the centrality of the Land of Israel to the People of Israel: They are considered the Congregation of Israel in every sense of the term only when they live in their land. The ability to fulfill national biblical commands such as this is one of the reasons it is so important for Jews from all over the world to come on *aliyah*, to move to Israel.

Devarim/Deuteronomy 21
Ki Teitzei

2 your elders and magistrates shall go out and measure the distances from the corpse to the nearby towns.

3 The elders of the town nearest to the corpse shall then take a heifer which has never been worked, which has never pulled in a yoke;

4 and the elders of that town shall bring the heifer down to an everflowingwadi, which is not tilled or sown. There, in the wadi, they shall break the heifer's neck.

5 The *Kohanim*, sons of *Levi*, shall come forward; for *Hashem* your God has chosen them to minister to Him and to pronounce blessing in the name of *Hashem*, and every lawsuit and case of assault is subject to their ruling.

6 Then all the elders of the town nearest to the corpse shall wash their hands over the heifer whose neck was broken in the wadi.

7 And they shall make this declaration: "Our hands did not shed this blood, nor did our eyes see it done.

8 Absolve, *Hashem*, Your people *Yisrael* whom You redeemed, and do not let guilt for the blood of the innocent remain among Your people *Yisrael*." And they will be absolved of bloodguilt.

9 Thus you will remove from your midst guilt for the blood of the innocent, for you will be doing what is right in the sight of *Hashem*.

10 When you take the field against your enemies, and *Hashem* your God delivers them into your power and you take some of them captive,

11 and you see among the captives a beautiful woman and you desire her and would take her to wife,

12 you shall bring her into your house, and she shall trim her hair, pare her nails,

13 and discard her captive's garb. She shall spend a month's time in your house lamenting her father and mother; after that you may come to her and possess her, and she shall be your wife.

14 Then, should you no longer want her, you must release her outright. You must not sell her for money: since you had your will of her, you must not enslave her.

דברים כא
כי תצא

ב וְיָצְא֥וּ זְקֵנֶ֖יךָ וְשֹׁפְטֶ֑יךָ וּמָדְד֕וּ אֶל־הֶ֣עָרִ֔ים אֲשֶׁ֖ר סְבִיבֹ֥ת הֶחָלָֽל׃

ג וְהָיָ֣ה הָעִ֔יר הַקְּרֹבָ֖ה אֶל־הֶחָלָ֑ל וְלָקְח֡וּ זִקְנֵי֩ הָעִ֨יר הַהִ֜וא עֶגְלַ֣ת בָּקָ֗ר אֲשֶׁ֤ר לֹֽא־עֻבַּד֙ בָּ֔הּ אֲשֶׁ֥ר לֹא־מָשְׁכָ֖ה בְּעֹֽל׃

ד וְהוֹרִ֡דוּ זִקְנֵי֩ הָעִ֨יר הַהִ֤וא אֶת־הָֽעֶגְלָה֙ אֶל־נַ֣חַל אֵיתָ֔ן אֲשֶׁ֛ר לֹא־יֵעָבֵ֥ד בּ֖וֹ וְלֹ֣א יִזָּרֵ֑עַ וְעָֽרְפוּ־שָׁ֥ם אֶת־הָעֶגְלָ֖ה בַּנָּֽחַל׃

ה וְנִגְּשׁ֣וּ הַכֹּֽהֲנִים֮ בְּנֵ֣י לֵוִי֒ כִּ֣י בָ֗ם בָּחַ֞ר יְהוָ֤ה אֱלֹהֶ֨יךָ֙ לְשָׁ֣רְת֔וֹ וּלְבָרֵ֖ךְ בְּשֵׁ֣ם יְהוָ֑ה וְעַל־פִּיהֶ֥ם יִהְיֶ֖ה כָּל־רִ֥יב וְכָל־נָֽגַע׃

ו וְכֹ֗ל זִקְנֵי֙ הָעִ֣יר הַהִ֔וא הַקְּרֹבִ֖ים אֶל־הֶחָלָ֑ל יִרְחֲצוּ֙ אֶת־יְדֵיהֶ֔ם עַל־הָעֶגְלָ֖ה הָעֲרוּפָ֥ה בַנָּֽחַל׃

ז וְעָנ֖וּ וְאָמְר֑וּ יָדֵ֗ינוּ לֹ֤א שפכה [שָֽׁפְכוּ֙] אֶת־הַדָּ֣ם הַזֶּ֔ה וְעֵינֵ֖ינוּ לֹ֥א רָאֽוּ׃

ח כַּפֵּר֩ לְעַמְּךָ֨ יִשְׂרָאֵ֤ל אֲשֶׁר־פָּדִ֨יתָ֙ יְהוָ֔ה וְאַל־תִּתֵּן֙ דָּ֣ם נָקִ֔י בְּקֶ֖רֶב עַמְּךָ֣ יִשְׂרָאֵ֑ל וְנִכַּפֵּ֥ר לָהֶ֖ם הַדָּֽם׃

ט וְאַתָּ֗ה תְּבַעֵ֛ר הַדָּ֥ם הַנָּקִ֖י מִקִּרְבֶּ֑ךָ כִּֽי־תַעֲשֶׂ֥ה הַיָּשָׁ֖ר בְּעֵינֵ֥י יְהוָֽה׃

י כִּֽי־תֵצֵ֥א לַמִּלְחָמָ֖ה עַל־אֹיְבֶ֑יךָ וּנְתָנ֞וֹ יְהוָ֧ה אֱלֹהֶ֛יךָ בְּיָדֶ֖ךָ וְשָׁבִ֥יתָ שִׁבְיֽוֹ׃

יא וְרָאִ֨יתָ֙ בַּשִּׁבְיָ֔ה אֵ֖שֶׁת יְפַת־תֹּ֑אַר וְחָשַׁקְתָּ֣ בָ֔הּ וְלָקַחְתָּ֥ לְךָ֖ לְאִשָּֽׁה׃

יב וַהֲבֵאתָ֖הּ אֶל־תּ֣וֹךְ בֵּיתֶ֑ךָ וְגִלְּחָה֙ אֶת־רֹאשָׁ֔הּ וְעָשְׂתָ֖ה אֶת־צִפָּרְנֶֽיהָ׃

יג וְהֵסִ֩ירָה֩ אֶת־שִׂמְלַ֨ת שִׁבְיָ֜הּ מֵעָלֶ֗יהָ וְיָֽשְׁבָה֙ בְּבֵיתֶ֔ךָ וּבָֽכְתָ֛ה אֶת־אָבִ֥יהָ וְאֶת־אִמָּ֖הּ יֶ֣רַח יָמִ֑ים וְאַ֨חַר כֵּ֜ן תָּב֤וֹא אֵלֶ֨יהָ֙ וּבְעַלְתָּ֔הּ וְהָיְתָ֥ה לְךָ֖ לְאִשָּֽׁה׃

יד וְהָיָ֞ה אִם־לֹ֧א חָפַ֣צְתָּ בָּ֗הּ וְשִׁלַּחְתָּהּ֙ לְנַפְשָׁ֔הּ וּמָכֹ֥ר לֹא־תִמְכְּרֶ֖נָּה בַּכָּ֑סֶף לֹא־תִתְעַמֵּ֣ר בָּ֔הּ תַּ֖חַת אֲשֶׁ֥ר עִנִּיתָֽהּ׃

Devarim/Deuteronomy 22
Ki Teitzei

15 If a man has two wives, one loved and the other unloved, and both the loved and the unloved have borne him sons, but the first-born is the son of the unloved one

16 when he wills his property to his sons, he may not treat as first-born the son of the loved one in disregard of the son of the unloved one who is older.

17 Instead, he must accept the first-born, the son of the unloved one, and allot to him a double portion of all he possesses; since he is the first fruit of his vigor, the birthright is his due.

18 If a man has a wayward and defiant son, who does not heed his father or mother and does not obey them even after they discipline him,

19 his father and mother shall take hold of him and bring him out to the elders of his town at the public place of his community.

20 They shall say to the elders of his town, "This son of ours is disloyal and defiant; he does not heed us. He is a glutton and a drunkard."

21 Thereupon the men of his town shall stone him to death. Thus you will sweep out evil from your midst: all *Yisrael* will hear and be afraid.

22 If a man is guilty of a capital offense and is put to death, and you impale him on a stake,

23 you must not let his corpse remain on the stake overnight, but must bury him the same day. For an impaled body is an affront to *Hashem*: you shall not defile the land that *Hashem* your God is giving you to possess.

22 1 If you see your fellow's ox or sheep gone astray, do not ignore it; you must take it back to your fellow.

2 If your fellow does not live near you or you do not know who he is, you shall bring it home and it shall remain with you until your fellow claims it; then you shall give it back to him.

3 You shall do the same with his ass; you shall do the same with his garment; and so too shall you do with anything that your fellow loses and you find: you must not remain indifferent.

דברים כב
כי תצא

טו כִּי־תִהְיֶיןָ לְאִישׁ שְׁתֵּי נָשִׁים הָאַחַת אֲהוּבָה וְהָאַחַת שְׂנוּאָה וְיָלְדוּ־לוֹ בָנִים הָאֲהוּבָה וְהַשְּׂנוּאָה וְהָיָה הַבֵּן הַבְּכוֹר לַשְּׂנִיאָה׃

טז וְהָיָה בְּיוֹם הַנְחִילוֹ אֶת־בָּנָיו אֵת אֲשֶׁר־יִהְיֶה לוֹ לֹא יוּכַל לְבַכֵּר אֶת־בֶּן־הָאֲהוּבָה עַל־פְּנֵי בֶן־הַשְּׂנוּאָה הַבְּכֹר׃

יז כִּי אֶת־הַבְּכֹר בֶּן־הַשְּׂנוּאָה יַכִּיר לָתֶת לוֹ פִּי שְׁנַיִם בְּכֹל אֲשֶׁר־יִמָּצֵא לוֹ כִּי־הוּא רֵאשִׁית אֹנוֹ לוֹ מִשְׁפַּט הַבְּכֹרָה׃

יח כִּי־יִהְיֶה לְאִישׁ בֵּן סוֹרֵר וּמוֹרֶה אֵינֶנּוּ שֹׁמֵעַ בְּקוֹל אָבִיו וּבְקוֹל אִמּוֹ וְיִסְּרוּ אֹתוֹ וְלֹא יִשְׁמַע אֲלֵיהֶם׃

יט וְתָפְשׂוּ בוֹ אָבִיו וְאִמּוֹ וְהוֹצִיאוּ אֹתוֹ אֶל־זִקְנֵי עִירוֹ וְאֶל־שַׁעַר מְקֹמוֹ׃

כ וְאָמְרוּ אֶל־זִקְנֵי עִירוֹ בְּנֵנוּ זֶה סוֹרֵר וּמֹרֶה אֵינֶנּוּ שֹׁמֵעַ בְּקֹלֵנוּ זוֹלֵל וְסֹבֵא׃

כא וּרְגָמֻהוּ כָּל־אַנְשֵׁי עִירוֹ בָאֲבָנִים וָמֵת וּבִעַרְתָּ הָרָע מִקִּרְבֶּךָ וְכָל־יִשְׂרָאֵל יִשְׁמְעוּ וְיִרָאוּ׃

כב וְכִי־יִהְיֶה בְאִישׁ חֵטְא מִשְׁפַּט־מָוֶת וְהוּמָת וְתָלִיתָ אֹתוֹ עַל־עֵץ׃

כג לֹא־תָלִין נִבְלָתוֹ עַל־הָעֵץ כִּי־קָבוֹר תִּקְבְּרֶנּוּ בַּיּוֹם הַהוּא כִּי־קִלְלַת אֱלֹהִים תָּלוּי וְלֹא תְטַמֵּא אֶת־אַדְמָתְךָ אֲשֶׁר יְהוָה אֱלֹהֶיךָ נֹתֵן לְךָ נַחֲלָה׃

כב א לֹא־תִרְאֶה אֶת־שׁוֹר אָחִיךָ אוֹ אֶת־שֵׂיוֹ נִדָּחִים וְהִתְעַלַּמְתָּ מֵהֶם הָשֵׁב תְּשִׁיבֵם לְאָחִיךָ׃

ב וְאִם־לֹא קָרוֹב אָחִיךָ אֵלֶיךָ וְלֹא יְדַעְתּוֹ וַאֲסַפְתּוֹ אֶל־תּוֹךְ בֵּיתֶךָ וְהָיָה עִמְּךָ עַד דְּרֹשׁ אָחִיךָ אֹתוֹ וַהֲשֵׁבֹתוֹ לוֹ׃

ג וְכֵן תַּעֲשֶׂה לַחֲמֹרוֹ וְכֵן תַּעֲשֶׂה לְשִׂמְלָתוֹ וְכֵן תַּעֲשֶׂה לְכָל־אֲבֵדַת אָחִיךָ אֲשֶׁר־תֹּאבַד מִמֶּנּוּ וּמְצָאתָהּ לֹא תוּכַל לְהִתְעַלֵּם׃

Devarim/Deuteronomy 22
Ki Teitzei

דברים כב
כי תצא

4 If you see your fellow's ass or ox fallen on the road, do not ignore it; you must help him raise it.

ד לֹא־תִרְאֶה אֶת־חֲמוֹר אָחִיךָ אוֹ שׁוֹרוֹ נֹפְלִים בַּדֶּרֶךְ וְהִתְעַלַּמְתָּ מֵהֶם הָקֵם תָּקִים עִמּוֹ׃

5 A woman must not put on man's apparel, nor shall a man wear woman's clothing; for whoever does these things is abhorrent to *Hashem* your God.

ה לֹא־יִהְיֶה כְלִי־גֶבֶר עַל־אִשָּׁה וְלֹא־יִלְבַּשׁ גֶּבֶר שִׂמְלַת אִשָּׁה כִּי תוֹעֲבַת יְהוָה אֱלֹהֶיךָ כָּל־עֹשֵׂה אֵלֶּה׃

6 If, along the road, you chance upon a bird's nest, in any tree or on the ground, with fledglings or eggs and the mother sitting over the fledglings or on the eggs, do not take the mother together with her young.

ו כִּי יִקָּרֵא קַן־צִפּוֹר לְפָנֶיךָ בַּדֶּרֶךְ בְּכָל־עֵץ אוֹ עַל־הָאָרֶץ אֶפְרֹחִים אוֹ בֵיצִים וְהָאֵם רֹבֶצֶת עַל־הָאֶפְרֹחִים אוֹ עַל־הַבֵּיצִים לֹא־תִקַּח הָאֵם עַל־הַבָּנִים׃

7 Let the mother go, and take only the young, in order that you may fare well and have a long life.

ז שַׁלֵּחַ תְּשַׁלַּח אֶת־הָאֵם וְאֶת־הַבָּנִים תִּקַּח־לָךְ לְמַעַן יִיטַב לָךְ וְהַאֲרַכְתָּ יָמִים׃

sha-LAY-akh t'-sha-LAKH et ha-AYM v'-et ha-ba-NEEM ti-kakh LAKH l'-MA-an YEE-tav LAKH v'-ha-a-rakh-TA ya-MEEM

8 When you build a new house, you shall make a parapet for your roof, so that you do not bring bloodguilt on your house if anyone should fall from it.

ח כִּי תִבְנֶה בַּיִת חָדָשׁ וְעָשִׂיתָ מַעֲקֶה לְגַגֶּךָ וְלֹא־תָשִׂים דָּמִים בְּבֵיתֶךָ כִּי־יִפֹּל הַנֹּפֵל מִמֶּנּוּ׃

9 You shall not sow your vineyard with a second kind of seed, else the crop – from the seed you have sown – and the yield of the vineyard may not be used.

ט לֹא־תִזְרַע כַּרְמְךָ כִּלְאָיִם פֶּן־תִּקְדַּשׁ הַמְלֵאָה הַזֶּרַע אֲשֶׁר תִּזְרָע וּתְבוּאַת הַכָּרֶם׃

10 You shall not plow with an ox and an ass together.

י לֹא־תַחֲרֹשׁ בְּשׁוֹר־וּבַחֲמֹר יַחְדָּו׃

11 You shall not wear cloth combining wool and linen.

יא לֹא תִלְבַּשׁ שַׁעַטְנֵז צֶמֶר וּפִשְׁתִּים יַחְדָּו׃

12 You shall make tassels on the four corners of the garment with which you cover yourself.

יב גְּדִלִים תַּעֲשֶׂה־לָּךְ עַל־אַרְבַּע כַּנְפוֹת כְּסוּתְךָ אֲשֶׁר תְּכַסֶּה־בָּהּ׃

13 A man marries a woman and cohabits with her. Then he takes an aversion to her

יג כִּי־יִקַּח אִישׁ אִשָּׁה וּבָא אֵלֶיהָ וּשְׂנֵאָהּ׃

22:7 Let the mother go This verse instructs one to chase a mother bird from its nest before taking its fledglings. On a deeper level, this law reflects the state of the Jewish people in exile. According to the mystical work *Zohar*, the mother bird who has been chased away cries about the separation from her children. When her cries are heard on high, the angels ask *Hashem* why He has commanded that the mother bird suffer such a sad fate. God answers that He shares the same fate as the mother bird: His presence has been driven from the *Beit Hamikdash*, and His children have been taken into exile. God asks that the angels sympathize with His plight and the plight of the Jewish people. He demands that they pray for the return of the Jewish people to their homeland and for the restoration of the *Beit Hamikdash* so that His presence can once again dwell in *Yerushalayim*.

A mother and her chick in Ramat Gan

Devarim/Deuteronomy 22
Ki Teitzei

14 and makes up charges against her and defames her, saying, "I married this woman; but when I approached her, I found that she was not a virgin."

15 In such a case, the girl's father and mother shall produce the evidence of the girl's virginity before the elders of the town at the gate.

16 And the girl's father shall say to the elders, "I gave this man my daughter to wife, but he has taken an aversion to her;

17 so he has made up charges, saying, 'I did not find your daughter a virgin.' But here is the evidence of my daughter's virginity!" And they shall spread out the cloth before the elders of the town.

18 The elders of that town shall then take the man and flog him,

19 and they shall fine him a hundred [*shekalim* of] silver and give it to the girl's father; for the man has defamed a virgin in *Yisrael*. Moreover, she shall remain his wife; he shall never have the right to divorce her.

20 But if the charge proves true, the girl was found not to have been a virgin,

21 then the girl shall be brought out to the entrance of her father's house, and the men of her town shall stone her to death; for she did a shameful thing in *Yisrael*, committing fornication while under her father's authority. Thus you will sweep away evil from your midst.

22 If a man is found lying with another man's wife, both of them – the man and the woman with whom he lay – shall die. Thus you will sweep away evil from *Yisrael*.

23 In the case of a virgin who is engaged to a man – if a man comes upon her in town and lies with her,

24 you shall take the two of them out to the gate of that town and stone them to death: the girl because she did not cry for help in the town, and the man because he violated another man's wife. Thus you will sweep away evil from your midst.

דברים כב
כי תצא

יד וְשָׂם לָהּ עֲלִילֹת דְּבָרִים וְהוֹצִיא עָלֶיהָ שֵׁם רָע וְאָמַר אֶת־הָאִשָּׁה הַזֹּאת לָקַחְתִּי וָאֶקְרַב אֵלֶיהָ וְלֹא־מָצָאתִי לָהּ בְּתוּלִים:

טו וְלָקַח אֲבִי הנער [הַנַּעֲרָה] וְאִמָּהּ וְהוֹצִיאוּ אֶת־בְּתוּלֵי הנער [הַנַּעֲרָה] אֶל־זִקְנֵי הָעִיר הַשָּׁעְרָה:

טז וְאָמַר אֲבִי הנער [הַנַּעֲרָה] אֶל־הַזְּקֵנִים אֶת־בִּתִּי נָתַתִּי לָאִישׁ הַזֶּה לְאִשָּׁה וַיִּשְׂנָאֶהָ:

יז וְהִנֵּה־הוּא שָׂם עֲלִילֹת דְּבָרִים לֵאמֹר לֹא־מָצָאתִי לְבִתְּךָ בְּתוּלִים וְאֵלֶּה בְּתוּלֵי בִתִּי וּפָרְשׂוּ הַשִּׂמְלָה לִפְנֵי זִקְנֵי הָעִיר:

יח וְלָקְחוּ זִקְנֵי הָעִיר־הַהִוא אֶת־הָאִישׁ וְיִסְּרוּ אֹתוֹ:

יט וְעָנְשׁוּ אֹתוֹ מֵאָה כֶסֶף וְנָתְנוּ לַאֲבִי הַנַּעֲרָה כִּי הוֹצִיא שֵׁם רָע עַל בְּתוּלַת יִשְׂרָאֵל וְלוֹ־תִהְיֶה לְאִשָּׁה לֹא־יוּכַל לְשַׁלְּחָהּ כָּל־יָמָיו:

כ וְאִם־אֱמֶת הָיָה הַדָּבָר הַזֶּה לֹא־נִמְצְאוּ בְתוּלִים לנער [לַנַּעֲרָה:]

כא וְהוֹצִיאוּ אֶת־הנער [הַנַּעֲרָה] אֶל־פֶּתַח בֵּית־אָבִיהָ וּסְקָלוּהָ אַנְשֵׁי עִירָהּ בָּאֲבָנִים וָמֵתָה כִּי־עָשְׂתָה נְבָלָה בְּיִשְׂרָאֵל לִזְנוֹת בֵּית אָבִיהָ וּבִעַרְתָּ הָרָע מִקִּרְבֶּךָ:

כב כִּי־יִמָּצֵא אִישׁ שֹׁכֵב עִם־אִשָּׁה בְעֻלַת־בַּעַל וּמֵתוּ גַּם־שְׁנֵיהֶם הָאִישׁ הַשֹּׁכֵב עִם־הָאִשָּׁה וְהָאִשָּׁה וּבִעַרְתָּ הָרָע מִיִּשְׂרָאֵל:

כג כִּי יִהְיֶה נער [נַעֲרָה] בְתוּלָה מְאֹרָשָׂה לְאִישׁ וּמְצָאָהּ אִישׁ בָּעִיר וְשָׁכַב עִמָּהּ:

כד וְהוֹצֵאתֶם אֶת־שְׁנֵיהֶם אֶל־שַׁעַר הָעִיר הַהִוא וּסְקַלְתֶּם אֹתָם בָּאֲבָנִים וָמֵתוּ אֶת־הנער [הַנַּעֲרָה] עַל־דְּבַר אֲשֶׁר לֹא־צָעֲקָה בָעִיר וְאֶת־הָאִישׁ עַל־דְּבַר אֲשֶׁר־עִנָּה אֶת־אֵשֶׁת רֵעֵהוּ וּבִעַרְתָּ הָרָע מִקִּרְבֶּךָ:

Devarim/Deuteronomy 23
Ki Teitzei

25 But if the man comes upon the engaged girl in the open country, and the man lies with her by force, only the man who lay with her shall die,

26 but you shall do nothing to the girl. The girl did not incur the death penalty, for this case is like that of a man attacking another and murdering him.

27 He came upon her in the open; though the engaged girl cried for help, there was no one to save her.

28 If a man comes upon a virgin who is not engaged and he seizes her and lies with her, and they are discovered,

29 the man who lay with her shall pay the girl's father fifty [*shekalim* of] silver, and she shall be his wife. Because he has violated her, he can never have the right to divorce her.

23 1 No man shall marry his father's former wife, so as to remove his father's garment.

2 No one whose testes are crushed or whose member is cut off shall be admitted into the congregation of *Hashem*.

3 No one misbegotten shall be admitted into the congregation of *Hashem*; none of his descendants, even in the tenth generation, shall be admitted into the congregation of *Hashem*.

4 No Amonite or Moabite shall be admitted into the congregation of *Hashem*; none of their descendants, even in the tenth generation, shall ever be admitted into the congregation of *Hashem*,

5 because they did not meet you with food and water on your journey after you left Egypt, and because they hired Balaam son of Beor, from Pethor of Aram-Naharaim, to curse you.

6 But *Hashem* your God refused to heed Balaam; instead, *Hashem* your God turned the curse into a blessing for you, for *Hashem* your God loves you.

7 You shall never concern yourself with their welfare or benefit as long as you live.

כה וְאִם־בַּשָּׂדֶה יִמְצָא הָאִישׁ אֶת־הַנַּעֲרָ [הַנַּעֲרָה] הַמְאֹרָשָׂה וְהֶחֱזִיק־בָּהּ הָאִישׁ וְשָׁכַב עִמָּהּ וּמֵת הָאִישׁ אֲשֶׁר־שָׁכַב עִמָּהּ לְבַדּוֹ:

כו וְלַנַּעֲרָ [וְלַנַּעֲרָה] לֹא־תַעֲשֶׂה דָבָר אֵין לַנַּעֲרָ [לַנַּעֲרָה] חֵטְא מָוֶת כִּי כַּאֲשֶׁר יָקוּם אִישׁ עַל־רֵעֵהוּ וּרְצָחוֹ נֶפֶשׁ כֵּן הַדָּבָר הַזֶּה:

כז כִּי בַשָּׂדֶה מְצָאָהּ צָעֲקָה הַנַּעֲרָ [הַנַּעֲרָה] הַמְאֹרָשָׂה וְאֵין מוֹשִׁיעַ לָהּ:

כח כִּי־יִמְצָא אִישׁ נַעֲרָ [נַעֲרָה] בְתוּלָה אֲשֶׁר לֹא־אֹרָשָׂה וּתְפָשָׂהּ וְשָׁכַב עִמָּהּ וְנִמְצָאוּ:

כט וְנָתַן הָאִישׁ הַשֹּׁכֵב עִמָּהּ לַאֲבִי הַנַּעֲרָ [הַנַּעֲרָה] חֲמִשִּׁים כָּסֶף וְלוֹ־תִהְיֶה לְאִשָּׁה תַּחַת אֲשֶׁר עִנָּהּ לֹא־יוּכַל שַׁלְּחָהּ כָּל־יָמָיו:

כג א לֹא־יִקַּח אִישׁ אֶת־אֵשֶׁת אָבִיו וְלֹא יְגַלֶּה כְּנַף אָבִיו:

ב לֹא־יָבֹא פְצוּעַ־דַּכָּא וּכְרוּת שָׁפְכָה בִּקְהַל יְהֹוָה:

ג לֹא־יָבֹא מַמְזֵר בִּקְהַל יְהֹוָה גַּם דּוֹר עֲשִׂירִי לֹא־יָבֹא לוֹ בִּקְהַל יְהֹוָה:

ד לֹא־יָבֹא עַמּוֹנִי וּמוֹאָבִי בִּקְהַל יְהֹוָה גַּם דּוֹר עֲשִׂירִי לֹא־יָבֹא לָהֶם בִּקְהַל יְהֹוָה עַד־עוֹלָם:

ה עַל־דְּבַר אֲשֶׁר לֹא־קִדְּמוּ אֶתְכֶם בַּלֶּחֶם וּבַמַּיִם בַּדֶּרֶךְ בְּצֵאתְכֶם מִמִּצְרָיִם וַאֲשֶׁר שָׂכַר עָלֶיךָ אֶת־בִּלְעָם בֶּן־בְּעוֹר מִפְּתוֹר אֲרַם נַהֲרַיִם לְקַלְלֶךָּ:

ו וְלֹא־אָבָה יְהֹוָה אֱלֹהֶיךָ לִשְׁמֹעַ אֶל־בִּלְעָם וַיַּהֲפֹךְ יְהֹוָה אֱלֹהֶיךָ לְּךָ אֶת־הַקְּלָלָה לִבְרָכָה כִּי אֲהֵבְךָ יְהֹוָה אֱלֹהֶיךָ:

ז לֹא־תִדְרֹשׁ שְׁלֹמָם וְטֹבָתָם כָּל־יָמֶיךָ לְעוֹלָם:

Devarim/Deuteronomy 23
Ki Teitzei

דברים כג
כי תצא

8 You shall not abhor an Edomite, for he is your kinsman. You shall not abhor an Egyptian, for you were a stranger in his land.

ח לֹא־תְתַעֵב אֲדֹמִי כִּי אָחִיךָ הוּא לֹא־תְתַעֵב מִצְרִי כִּי־גֵר הָיִיתָ בְאַרְצוֹ:

lo t'-ta-AYV a-do-MEE KEE a-KHEE-kha HU lo t'-ta-AYV mitz-REE kee GAYR ha-YEE-ta v'-ar-TZO

9 Children born to them may be admitted into the congregation of *Hashem* in the third generation.

ט בָּנִים אֲשֶׁר־יִוָּלְדוּ לָהֶם דּוֹר שְׁלִישִׁי יָבֹא לָהֶם בִּקְהַל יְהוָה:

10 When you go out as a troop against your enemies, be on your guard against anything untoward.

י כִּי־תֵצֵא מַחֲנֶה עַל־אֹיְבֶיךָ וְנִשְׁמַרְתָּ מִכֹּל דָּבָר רָע:

11 If anyone among you has been rendered unclean by a nocturnal emission, he must leave the camp, and he must not reenter the camp.

יא כִּי־יִהְיֶה בְךָ אִישׁ אֲשֶׁר לֹא־יִהְיֶה טָהוֹר מִקְּרֵה־לָיְלָה וְיָצָא אֶל־מִחוּץ לַמַּחֲנֶה לֹא יָבֹא אֶל־תּוֹךְ הַמַּחֲנֶה:

12 Toward evening he shall bathe in water, and at sundown he may reenter the camp.

יב וְהָיָה לִפְנוֹת־עֶרֶב יִרְחַץ בַּמָּיִם וּכְבֹא הַשֶּׁמֶשׁ יָבֹא אֶל־תּוֹךְ הַמַּחֲנֶה:

13 Further, there shall be an area for you outside the camp, where you may relieve yourself.

יג וְיָד תִּהְיֶה לְךָ מִחוּץ לַמַּחֲנֶה וְיָצָאתָ שָׁמָּה חוּץ:

14 With your gear you shall have a spike, and when you have squatted you shall dig a hole with it and cover up your excrement.

יד וְיָתֵד תִּהְיֶה לְךָ עַל־אֲזֵנֶךָ וְהָיָה בְּשִׁבְתְּךָ חוּץ וְחָפַרְתָּה בָהּ וְשַׁבְתָּ וְכִסִּיתָ אֶת־צֵאָתֶךָ:

15 Since *Hashem* your God moves about in your camp to protect you and to deliver your enemies to you, let your camp be holy; let Him not find anything unseemly among you and turn away from you.

טו כִּי יְהוָה אֱלֹהֶיךָ מִתְהַלֵּךְ בְּקֶרֶב מַחֲנֶךָ לְהַצִּילְךָ וְלָתֵת אֹיְבֶיךָ לְפָנֶיךָ וְהָיָה מַחֲנֶיךָ קָדוֹשׁ וְלֹא־יִרְאֶה בְךָ עֶרְוַת דָּבָר וְשָׁב מֵאַחֲרֶיךָ:

KEE a-do-NAI e-lo-HE-kha mit-ha-LAYKH b'-KE-rev ma-kha-NE-kha l'-ha-TZEE-l'-kha v'-la-TAYT o-y'-VE-kha l'-fa-NE-kha v'-ha-YAH ma-kha-NE-khah ka-DOSH v'-lo yir-EH v'-KHA er-VAT da-VAR v'-SHAV may-a-kha-RE-kha

16 You shall not turn over to his master a slave who seeks refuge with you from his master.

טז לֹא־תַסְגִּיר עֶבֶד אֶל־אֲדֹנָיו אֲשֶׁר־יִנָּצֵל אֵלֶיךָ מֵעִם אֲדֹנָיו:

17 He shall live with you in any place he may choose among the settlements in your midst, wherever he pleases; you must not ill-treat him.

יז עִמְּךָ יֵשֵׁב בְּקִרְבְּךָ בַּמָּקוֹם אֲשֶׁר־יִבְחַר בְּאַחַד שְׁעָרֶיךָ בַּטּוֹב לוֹ לֹא תּוֹנֶנּוּ:

IDF field hospital for wounded Syrian civilians

23:8 You shall not abhor an *Egyptian* Despite the bitter slavery the nation suffered at the hand of the Egyptians, the *Torah* teaches that we must care for all of *Hashem*'s children, even our persecutors, and not treat them the same way they treated us. In fact, the *Torah* emphasizes universal feelings of sympathy and compassion for all, and warns against rejoicing at the downfall of our enemies. It is for this reason that at the *Seder* meal every *Pesach*, when the Jewish people celebrate their salvation from the hands of their Egyptian oppressors, they spill symbolic drops of wine from their cups while mentioning the ten plagues, to indicate that their joy is diminished due the suffering caused to their enemies. The State of Israel has also demonstrated great sympathy towards its military enemies and towards the civilian populations of neighboring countries, despite their hostility. The field hospitals the IDF has maintained for Syrian refugees provide one example of the fact that the Israeli army is the most humanitarian one in the world.

Devarim/Deuteronomy 24
Ki Teitzei

18 No Israelite woman shall be a cult prostitute, nor shall any Israelite man be a cult prostitute.

19 You shall not bring the fee of a whore or the pay of a dog into the house of *Hashem* your God in fulfillment of any vow, for both are abhorrent to *Hashem* your God.

20 You shall not deduct interest from loans to your countrymen, whether in money or food or anything else that can be deducted as interest;

21 but you may deduct interest from loans to foreigners. Do not deduct interest from loans to your countrymen, so that *Hashem* your God may bless you in all your undertakings in the land that you are about to enter and possess.

22 When you make a vow to *Hashem* your God, do not put off fulfilling it, for *Hashem* your God will require it of you, and you will have incurred guilt;

23 whereas you incur no guilt if you refrain from vowing.

24 You must fulfill what has crossed your lips and perform what you have voluntarily vowed to *Hashem* your God, having made the promise with your own mouth.

25 When you enter another man's vineyard, you may eat as many grapes as you want, until you are full, but you must not put any in your vessel.

26 When you enter another man's field of standing grain, you may pluck ears with your hand; but you must not put a sickle to your neighbor's grain.

24

1 A man takes a wife and possesses her. She fails to please him because he finds something obnoxious about her, and he writes her a bill of divorcement, hands it to her, and sends her away from his house;

2 she leaves his household and becomes the wife of another man;

3 then this latter man rejects her, writes her a bill of divorcement, hands it to her, and sends her away from his house; or the man who married her last dies.

4 Then the first husband who divorced her shall not take her to wife again, since she has been defiled – for that would be abhorrent to *Hashem*. You must not bring sin upon the land that *Hashem* your God is giving you as a heritage.

דברים כד
כי תצא

יח לֹא־תִהְיֶ֥ה קְדֵשָׁ֖ה מִבְּנ֣וֹת יִשְׂרָאֵ֑ל וְלֹֽא־יִהְיֶ֥ה קָדֵ֖שׁ מִבְּנֵ֥י יִשְׂרָאֵֽל׃

יט לֹא־תָבִיא֩ אֶתְנַ֨ן זוֹנָ֜ה וּמְחִ֣יר כֶּ֗לֶב בֵּ֛ית יְהֹוָ֥ה אֱלֹהֶ֖יךָ לְכׇל־נֶ֑דֶר כִּ֧י תוֹעֲבַ֛ת יְהֹוָ֥ה אֱלֹהֶ֖יךָ גַּם־שְׁנֵיהֶֽם׃

כ לֹא־תַשִּׁ֣יךְ לְאָחִ֔יךָ נֶ֥שֶׁךְ כֶּ֖סֶף נֶ֣שֶׁךְ אֹ֑כֶל נֶ֕שֶׁךְ כׇּל־דָּבָ֖ר אֲשֶׁ֥ר יִשָּֽׁךְ׃

כא לַנׇּכְרִ֣י תַשִּׁ֔יךְ וּלְאָחִ֖יךָ לֹ֣א תַשִּׁ֑יךְ לְמַ֨עַן יְבָרֶכְךָ֜ יְהֹוָ֣ה אֱלֹהֶ֗יךָ בְּכֹל֙ מִשְׁלַ֣ח יָדֶ֔ךָ עַל־הָאָ֕רֶץ אֲשֶׁר־אַתָּ֥ה בָא־שָׁ֖מָּה לְרִשְׁתָּֽהּ׃

כב כִּֽי־תִדֹּ֥ר נֶ֙דֶר֙ לַיהֹוָ֣ה אֱלֹהֶ֔יךָ לֹ֥א תְאַחֵ֖ר לְשַׁלְּמ֑וֹ כִּֽי־דָרֹ֨שׁ יִדְרְשֶׁ֜נּוּ יְהֹוָ֤ה אֱלֹהֶ֙יךָ֙ מֵֽעִמָּ֔ךְ וְהָיָ֥ה בְךָ֖ חֵֽטְא׃

כג וְכִ֥י תֶחְדַּ֖ל לִנְדֹּ֑ר לֹא־יִהְיֶ֥ה בְךָ֖ חֵֽטְא׃

כד מוֹצָ֥א שְׂפָתֶ֖יךָ תִּשְׁמֹ֣ר וְעָשִׂ֑יתָ כַּאֲשֶׁ֨ר נָדַ֜רְתָּ לַיהֹוָ֤ה אֱלֹהֶ֙יךָ֙ נְדָבָ֔ה אֲשֶׁ֥ר דִּבַּ֖רְתָּ בְּפִֽיךָ׃

כה כִּ֤י תָבֹא֙ בְּכֶ֣רֶם רֵעֶ֔ךָ וְאָכַלְתָּ֧ עֲנָבִ֛ים כְּנַפְשְׁךָ֖ שָׂבְעֶ֑ךָ וְאֶֽל־כֶּלְיְךָ֖ לֹ֥א תִתֵּֽן׃

כו כִּ֤י תָבֹא֙ בְּקָמַ֣ת רֵעֶ֔ךָ וְקָטַפְתָּ֥ מְלִילֹ֖ת בְּיָדֶ֑ךָ וְחֶרְמֵשׁ֙ לֹ֣א תָנִ֔יף עַ֖ל קָמַ֥ת רֵעֶֽךָ׃

כד

א כִּֽי־יִקַּ֥ח אִ֛ישׁ אִשָּׁ֖ה וּבְעָלָ֑הּ וְהָיָ֞ה אִם־לֹ֧א תִמְצָא־חֵ֣ן בְּעֵינָ֗יו כִּי־מָ֤צָא בָהּ֙ עֶרְוַ֣ת דָּבָ֔ר וְכָ֨תַב לָ֜הּ סֵ֤פֶר כְּרִיתֻת֙ וְנָתַ֣ן בְּיָדָ֔הּ וְשִׁלְּחָ֖הּ מִבֵּיתֽוֹ׃

ב וְיָצְאָ֖ה מִבֵּית֑וֹ וְהָלְכָ֖ה וְהָיְתָ֥ה לְאִישׁ־אַחֵֽר׃

ג וּשְׂנֵאָהּ֮ הָאִ֣ישׁ הָאַחֲרוֹן֒ וְכָ֨תַב לָ֜הּ סֵ֤פֶר כְּרִיתֻת֙ וְנָתַ֣ן בְּיָדָ֔הּ וְשִׁלְּחָ֖הּ מִבֵּית֑וֹ א֣וֹ כִ֤י יָמוּת֙ הָאִ֣ישׁ הָאַחֲר֔וֹן אֲשֶׁר־לְקָחָ֥הּ ל֖וֹ לְאִשָּֽׁה׃

ד לֹא־יוּכַ֣ל בַּעְלָ֣הּ הָרִאשׁ֣וֹן אֲשֶֽׁר־שִׁ֠לְּחָ֠הּ לָשׁ֨וּב לְקַחְתָּ֜הּ לִהְי֧וֹת ל֣וֹ לְאִשָּׁ֗ה אַחֲרֵי֙ אֲשֶׁ֣ר הֻטַּמָּ֔אָה כִּֽי־תוֹעֵבָ֥ה הִ֖וא לִפְנֵ֣י יְהֹוָ֑ה וְלֹ֤א תַחֲטִיא֙ אֶת־הָאָ֔רֶץ אֲשֶׁר֙ יְהֹוָ֣ה אֱלֹהֶ֔יךָ נֹתֵ֥ן לְךָ֖ נַחֲלָֽה׃

Devarim/Deuteronomy 24
Ki Teitzei

5 When a man has taken a bride, he shall not go out with the army or be assigned to it for any purpose; he shall be exempt one year for the sake of his household, to give happiness to the woman he has married.

6 A handmill or an upper millstone shall not be taken in pawn, for that would be taking someone's life in pawn.

7 If a man is found to have kidnapped a fellow Israelite, enslaving him or selling him, that kidnapper shall die; thus you will sweep out evil from your midst.

8 In cases of a skin affection be most careful to do exactly as the levitical *Kohanim* instruct you. Take care to do as I have commanded them.

9 Remember what *Hashem* your God did to *Miriam* on the journey after you left Egypt.

10 When you make a loan of any sort to your countryman, you must not enter his house to seize his pledge.

11 You must remain outside, while the man to whom you made the loan brings the pledge out to you.

12 If he is a needy man, you shall not go to sleep in his pledge;

13 you must return the pledge to him at sundown, that he may sleep in his cloth and bless you; and it will be to your merit before *Hashem* your God.

14 You shall not abuse a needy and destitute laborer, whether a fellow countryman or a stranger in one of the communities of your land.

15 You must pay him his wages on the same day, before the sun sets, for he is needy and urgently depends on it; else he will cry to *Hashem* against you and you will incur guilt.

16 Parents shall not be put to death for children, nor children be put to death for parents: a person shall be put to death only for his own crime.

17 You shall not subvert the rights of the stranger or the fatherless; you shall not take a widow's garment in pawn.

דברים כד
כי תצא

ה כִּי־יִקַּח אִישׁ אִשָּׁה חֲדָשָׁה לֹא יֵצֵא בַּצָּבָא וְלֹא־יַעֲבֹר עָלָיו לְכָל־דָּבָר נָקִי יִהְיֶה לְבֵיתוֹ שָׁנָה אֶחָת וְשִׂמַּח אֶת־אִשְׁתּוֹ אֲשֶׁר־לָקָח:

ו לֹא־יַחֲבֹל רֵחַיִם וָרָכֶב כִּי־נֶפֶשׁ הוּא חֹבֵל:

ז כִּי־יִמָּצֵא אִישׁ גֹּנֵב נֶפֶשׁ מֵאֶחָיו מִבְּנֵי יִשְׂרָאֵל וְהִתְעַמֶּר־בּוֹ וּמְכָרוֹ וּמֵת הַגַּנָּב הַהוּא וּבִעַרְתָּ הָרָע מִקִּרְבֶּךָ:

ח הִשָּׁמֶר בְּנֶגַע־הַצָּרַעַת לִשְׁמֹר מְאֹד וְלַעֲשׂוֹת כְּכֹל אֲשֶׁר־יוֹרוּ אֶתְכֶם הַכֹּהֲנִים הַלְוִיִּם כַּאֲשֶׁר צִוִּיתִם תִּשְׁמְרוּ לַעֲשׂוֹת:

ט זָכוֹר אֵת אֲשֶׁר־עָשָׂה יְהֹוָה אֱלֹהֶיךָ לְמִרְיָם בַּדֶּרֶךְ בְּצֵאתְכֶם מִמִּצְרָיִם:

י כִּי־תַשֶּׁה בְרֵעֲךָ מַשַּׁאת מְאוּמָה לֹא־תָבֹא אֶל־בֵּיתוֹ לַעֲבֹט עֲבֹטוֹ:

יא בַּחוּץ תַּעֲמֹד וְהָאִישׁ אֲשֶׁר אַתָּה נֹשֶׁה בוֹ יוֹצִיא אֵלֶיךָ אֶת־הָעֲבוֹט הַחוּצָה:

יב וְאִם־אִישׁ עָנִי הוּא לֹא תִשְׁכַּב בַּעֲבֹטוֹ:

יג הָשֵׁב תָּשִׁיב לוֹ אֶת־הָעֲבוֹט כְּבֹא הַשֶּׁמֶשׁ וְשָׁכַב בְּשַׂלְמָתוֹ וּבֵרֲכֶךָּ וּלְךָ תִּהְיֶה צְדָקָה לִפְנֵי יְהֹוָה אֱלֹהֶיךָ:

יד לֹא־תַעֲשֹׁק שָׂכִיר עָנִי וְאֶבְיוֹן מֵאַחֶיךָ אוֹ מִגֵּרְךָ אֲשֶׁר בְּאַרְצְךָ בִּשְׁעָרֶיךָ:

טו בְּיוֹמוֹ תִתֵּן שְׂכָרוֹ וְלֹא־תָבוֹא עָלָיו הַשֶּׁמֶשׁ כִּי עָנִי הוּא וְאֵלָיו הוּא נֹשֵׂא אֶת־נַפְשׁוֹ וְלֹא־יִקְרָא עָלֶיךָ אֶל־יְהֹוָה וְהָיָה בְךָ חֵטְא:

טז לֹא־יוּמְתוּ אָבוֹת עַל־בָּנִים וּבָנִים לֹא־יוּמְתוּ עַל־אָבוֹת אִישׁ בְּחֶטְאוֹ יוּמָתוּ:

יז לֹא תַטֶּה מִשְׁפַּט גֵּר יָתוֹם וְלֹא תַחֲבֹל בֶּגֶד אַלְמָנָה:

Devarim/Deuteronomy 25
Ki Teitzei

דברים כה
כי תצא

18 Remember that you were a slave in Egypt and that *Hashem* your God redeemed you from there; therefore do I enjoin you to observe this commandment.

יח וְזָכַרְתָּ֗ כִּ֣י עֶ֤בֶד הָיִ֨יתָ֙ בְּמִצְרַ֔יִם וַיִּפְדְּךָ֛ יְהֹוָ֥ה אֱלֹהֶ֖יךָ מִשָּׁ֑ם עַל־כֵּ֞ן אָנֹכִ֤י מְצַוְּךָ֙ לַעֲשׂ֔וֹת אֶת־הַדָּבָ֖ר הַזֶּֽה׃

19 When you reap the harvest in your field and overlook a sheaf in the field, do not turn back to get it; it shall go to the stranger, the fatherless, and the widow – in order that *Hashem* your God may bless you in all your undertakings.

יט כִּ֣י תִקְצֹר֩ קְצִֽירְךָ֨ בְשָׂדֶ֜ךָ וְשָׁכַחְתָּ֧ עֹ֣מֶר בַּשָּׂדֶ֗ה לֹ֤א תָשׁוּב֙ לְקַחְתּ֔וֹ לַגֵּ֛ר לַיָּת֥וֹם וְלָאַלְמָנָ֖ה יִהְיֶ֑ה לְמַ֤עַן יְבָרֶכְךָ֙ יְהֹוָ֣ה אֱלֹהֶ֔יךָ בְּכֹ֖ל מַעֲשֵׂ֥ה יָדֶֽיךָ׃

20 When you beat down the fruit of your olive trees, do not go over them again; that shall go to the stranger, the fatherless, and the widow.

כ כִּ֤י תַחְבֹּט֙ זֵֽיתְךָ֔ לֹ֥א תְפָאֵ֖ר אַחֲרֶ֑יךָ לַגֵּ֛ר לַיָּת֥וֹם וְלָאַלְמָנָ֖ה יִהְיֶֽה׃

KEE takh-BOT zay-t'-KHA LO t'-fa-AYR a-kha-RE-kha la-GAYR la-ya-TOM v'-la-al-ma-NAH yih-YEH

21 When you gather the grapes of your vineyard, do not pick it over again; that shall go to the stranger, the fatherless, and the widow.

כא כִּ֤י תִבְצֹר֙ כַּרְמְךָ֔ לֹ֥א תְעוֹלֵ֖ל אַחֲרֶ֑יךָ לַגֵּ֛ר לַיָּת֥וֹם וְלָאַלְמָנָ֖ה יִהְיֶֽה׃

22 Always remember that you were a slave in the land of Egypt; therefore do I enjoin you to observe this commandment.

כב וְזָ֣כַרְתָּ֔ כִּי־עֶ֥בֶד הָיִ֖יתָ בְּאֶ֣רֶץ מִצְרָ֑יִם עַל־כֵּ֞ן אָנֹכִ֤י מְצַוְּךָ֙ לַעֲשׂ֔וֹת אֶת־הַדָּבָ֖ר הַזֶּֽה׃

25 1 When there is a dispute between men and they go to law, and a decision is rendered declaring the one in the right and the other in the wrong

כה א כִּֽי־יִהְיֶ֥ה רִיב֙ בֵּ֣ין אֲנָשִׁ֔ים וְנִגְּשׁ֥וּ אֶל־הַמִּשְׁפָּ֖ט וּשְׁפָט֑וּם וְהִצְדִּ֨יקוּ֙ אֶת־הַצַּדִּ֔יק וְהִרְשִׁ֖יעוּ אֶת־הָרָשָֽׁע׃

2 if the guilty one is to be flogged, the magistrate shall have him lie down and be given lashes in his presence, by count, as his guilt warrants.

ב וְהָיָ֛ה אִם־בִּ֥ן הַכּ֖וֹת הָרָשָׁ֑ע וְהִפִּיל֤וֹ הַשֹּׁפֵט֙ וְהִכָּ֣הוּ לְפָנָ֔יו כְּדֵ֥י רִשְׁעָת֖וֹ בְּמִסְפָּֽר׃

3 He may be given up to forty lashes, but not more, lest being flogged further, to excess, your brother be degraded before your eyes.

ג אַרְבָּעִ֥ים יַכֶּ֖נּוּ לֹ֣א יֹסִ֑יף פֶּן־יֹסִ֨יף לְהַכֹּת֤וֹ עַל־אֵ֨לֶּה֙ מַכָּ֣ה רַבָּ֔ה וְנִקְלָ֥ה אָחִ֖יךָ לְעֵינֶֽיךָ׃

4 You shall not muzzle an ox while it is threshing.

ד לֹא־תַחְסֹ֥ם שׁ֖וֹר בְּדִישֽׁוֹ׃

5 When brothers dwell together and one of them dies and leaves no son, the wife of the deceased shall not be married to a stranger, outside the family. Her husband's brother shall unite with her: he shall take her as his wife and perform the levir's duty.

ה כִּֽי־יֵשְׁב֨וּ אַחִ֜ים יַחְדָּ֗ו וּמֵ֨ת אַחַ֤ד מֵהֶם֙ וּבֵ֣ן אֵֽין־ל֔וֹ לֹא־תִהְיֶ֧ה אֵֽשֶׁת־הַמֵּ֛ת הַח֖וּצָה לְאִ֣ישׁ זָ֑ר יְבָמָהּ֙ יָבֹ֣א עָלֶ֔יהָ וּלְקָחָ֥הּ ל֛וֹ לְאִשָּׁ֖ה וְיִבְּמָֽהּ׃

24:20 When you beat down the fruit of your olive trees Just as grain must be left in the fields for the poor during the time of the harvest, so too fruit must be left on the trees. In describing the process of removing the fruit from the olive tree, the verse says "when you beat down the fruit of your olive trees." In ancient times, olive trees were harvested by beating the branches with a stick, causing the olives to fall to the ground. According to Jewish tradition, this command hints to the blessing of abundance in the Land of Israel. There will be so much produce that the farmers will only need to harvest what falls off with the beating of the tree branches; they will not even need to bother climbing a ladder to reach the fruit at the top of the tree.

Harvesting olives in the Upper Galilee

Devarim/Deuteronomy 25
Ki Teitzei

6 The first son that she bears shall be accounted to the dead brother, that his name may not be blotted out in *Yisrael*.

7 But if the man does not want to marry his brother's widow, his brother's widow shall appear before the elders in the gate and declare, "My husband's brother refuses to establish a name in *Yisrael* for his brother; he will not perform the duty of a levir."

8 The elders of his town shall then summon him and talk to him. If he insists, saying, "I do not want to marry her,"

9 his brother's widow shall go up to him in the presence of the elders, pull the sandal off his foot, spit in his face, and make this declaration: Thus shall be done to the man who will not build up his brother's house!

10 And he shall go in *Yisrael* by the name of "the family of the unsandaled one."

11 If two men get into a fight with each other, and the wife of one comes up to save her husband from his antagonist and puts out her hand and seizes him by his genitals,

12 you shall cut off her hand; show no pity.

13 You shall not have in your pouch alternate weights, larger and smaller.

14 You shall not have in your house alternate measures, a larger and a smaller.

15 You must have completely honest weights and completely honest measures, if you are to endure long on the soil that *Hashem* your God is giving you.

16 For everyone who does those things, everyone who deals dishonestly, is abhorrent to *Hashem* your God.

17 Remember what Amalek did to you on your journey, after you left Egypt

18 how, undeterred by fear of *Hashem*, he surprised you on the march, when you were famished and weary, and cut down all the stragglers in your rear.

דברים כה
כי תצא

ו וְהָיָה הַבְּכוֹר אֲשֶׁר תֵּלֵד יָקוּם עַל־שֵׁם אָחִיו הַמֵּת וְלֹא־יִמָּחֶה שְׁמוֹ מִיִּשְׂרָאֵל:

ז וְאִם־לֹא יַחְפֹּץ הָאִישׁ לָקַחַת אֶת־יְבִמְתּוֹ וְעָלְתָה יְבִמְתּוֹ הַשַּׁעְרָה אֶל־הַזְּקֵנִים וְאָמְרָה מֵאֵין יְבָמִי לְהָקִים לְאָחִיו שֵׁם בְּיִשְׂרָאֵל לֹא אָבָה יַבְּמִי:

ח וְקָרְאוּ־לוֹ זִקְנֵי־עִירוֹ וְדִבְּרוּ אֵלָיו וְעָמַד וְאָמַר לֹא חָפַצְתִּי לְקַחְתָּהּ:

ט וְנִגְּשָׁה יְבִמְתּוֹ אֵלָיו לְעֵינֵי הַזְּקֵנִים וְחָלְצָה נַעֲלוֹ מֵעַל רַגְלוֹ וְיָרְקָה בְּפָנָיו וְעָנְתָה וְאָמְרָה כָּכָה יֵעָשֶׂה לָאִישׁ אֲשֶׁר לֹא־יִבְנֶה אֶת־בֵּית אָחִיו:

י וְנִקְרָא שְׁמוֹ בְּיִשְׂרָאֵל בֵּית חֲלוּץ הַנָּעַל:

יא כִּי־יִנָּצוּ אֲנָשִׁים יַחְדָּו אִישׁ וְאָחִיו וְקָרְבָה אֵשֶׁת הָאֶחָד לְהַצִּיל אֶת־אִישָׁהּ מִיַּד מַכֵּהוּ וְשָׁלְחָה יָדָהּ וְהֶחֱזִיקָה בִּמְבֻשָׁיו:

יב וְקַצֹּתָה אֶת־כַּפָּהּ לֹא תָחוֹס עֵינֶךָ:

יג לֹא־יִהְיֶה לְךָ בְּכִיסְךָ אֶבֶן וָאָבֶן גְּדוֹלָה וּקְטַנָּה:

יד לֹא־יִהְיֶה לְךָ בְּבֵיתְךָ אֵיפָה וְאֵיפָה גְּדוֹלָה וּקְטַנָּה:

טו אֶבֶן שְׁלֵמָה וָצֶדֶק יִהְיֶה־לָּךְ אֵיפָה שְׁלֵמָה וָצֶדֶק יִהְיֶה־לָּךְ לְמַעַן יַאֲרִיכוּ יָמֶיךָ עַל הָאֲדָמָה אֲשֶׁר־יְהֹוָה אֱלֹהֶיךָ נֹתֵן לָךְ:

טז כִּי תוֹעֲבַת יְהֹוָה אֱלֹהֶיךָ כָּל־עֹשֵׂה אֵלֶּה כֹּל עֹשֵׂה עָוֶל:

יז זָכוֹר אֵת אֲשֶׁר־עָשָׂה לְךָ עֲמָלֵק בַּדֶּרֶךְ בְּצֵאתְכֶם מִמִּצְרָיִם:

יח אֲשֶׁר קָרְךָ בַּדֶּרֶךְ וַיְזַנֵּב בְּךָ כָּל־הַנֶּחֱשָׁלִים אַחֲרֶיךָ וְאַתָּה עָיֵף וְיָגֵעַ וְלֹא יָרֵא אֱלֹהִים:

Devarim/Deuteronomy 26
Ki Tavo

דברים כו
כי תבוא

19 Therefore, when *Hashem* your God grants you safety from all your enemies around you, in the land that *Hashem* your God is giving you as a hereditary portion, you shall blot out the memory of Amalek from under heaven. Do not forget!

יט וְהָיָה בְּהָנִיחַ יְהֹוָה אֱלֹהֶיךָ לְךָ מִכָּל־אֹיְבֶיךָ מִסָּבִיב בָּאָרֶץ אֲשֶׁר יְהֹוָה אֱלֹהֶיךָ נֹתֵן לְךָ נַחֲלָה לְרִשְׁתָּהּ תִּמְחֶה אֶת־זֵכֶר עֲמָלֵק מִתַּחַת הַשָּׁמָיִם לֹא תִּשְׁכָּח:

v'-ha-YAH b'-ha-NEE-akh a-do-NAI e-lo-HE-kha l'-KHA mi-kol O-y'-VE-kha mi-sa-VEEV ba-A-retz a-sher a-do-NAI e-lo-HE-kha no-TAYN l'-KHA na-kha-LAH l'-rish-TAH tim-KHEH et ZAY-kher a-ma-LAYK mi-TA-khat ha-sh-MA-yim LO tish-KAKH

26

1 When you enter the land that *Hashem* your God is giving you as a heritage, and you possess it and settle in it,

כו א וְהָיָה כִּי־תָבוֹא אֶל־הָאָרֶץ אֲשֶׁר יְהֹוָה אֱלֹהֶיךָ נֹתֵן לְךָ נַחֲלָה וִירִשְׁתָּהּ וְיָשַׁבְתָּ בָּהּ:

v'-ha-YAH kee ta-VO el ha-A-retz a-SHER a-do-NAI e-lo-HE-kha no-TAYN l'-KHA na-kha-LAH vee-rish-TAH v'-ya-SHAV-ta BAH

2 you shall take some of every first fruit of the soil, which you harvest from the land that *Hashem* your God is giving you, put it in a basket and go to the place where *Hashem* your God will choose to establish His name.

ב וְלָקַחְתָּ מֵרֵאשִׁית כָּל־פְּרִי הָאֲדָמָה אֲשֶׁר תָּבִיא מֵאַרְצְךָ אֲשֶׁר יְהֹוָה אֱלֹהֶיךָ נֹתֵן לָךְ וְשַׂמְתָּ בַטֶּנֶא וְהָלַכְתָּ אֶל־הַמָּקוֹם אֲשֶׁר יִבְחַר יְהֹוָה אֱלֹהֶיךָ לְשַׁכֵּן שְׁמוֹ שָׁם:

v-la-kakh-TA may-ray-SHEET kol p'-REE ha-a-da-MAH a-SHER ta-VEE may-ar-tz'-KHA a-SHER a-do-NAY e-lo-HE-kha no-TAYN LKAH v'-sam-TA va-TE-ne v'-ha-lakh-TA el ha-ma-KOM a-SHER yiv-KHAR a-do-NAI e-lo-HE-kha l'-sha-KAYN sh'-MO SHAM

3 You shall go to the *Kohen* in charge at that time and say to him, "I acknowledge this day before *Hashem* your God that I have entered the land that *Hashem* swore to our fathers to assign us."

ג וּבָאתָ אֶל־הַכֹּהֵן אֲשֶׁר יִהְיֶה בַּיָּמִים הָהֵם וְאָמַרְתָּ אֵלָיו הִגַּדְתִּי הַיּוֹם לַיהֹוָה אֱלֹהֶיךָ כִּי־בָאתִי אֶל־הָאָרֶץ אֲשֶׁר נִשְׁבַּע יְהֹוָה לַאֲבֹתֵינוּ לָתֶת לָנוּ:

25:19 When *Hashem* your God grants you safety from all your enemies around you One of the three commandments that the People of Israel are to fulfill after successfully conquering the Land of Israel is the obliteration of the Amalekites. The Amalekites are descendants of Esau and were the first to attack the Children of Israel after the exodus from Egypt. Amalek is more than just a nation – it represents an ideology antithetical to that of Israel: Absolute denial of Godliness in this world and a total lack of morality. For this reason, once the land is conquered and the People of Israel are settled, Israel was required to wage war against Amalek, and against their system of belief.

26:1 The land that *Hashem* your God is giving you as a heritage The 1917 Balfour Declaration is one of the most significant documents in modern Jewish history, articulating the historic right of the Jewish people to reestablish their homeland in Israel. Written by foreign secretary Arthur James Balfour and approved by the government of Great Britain, the declaration states clearly and unequivocally that Britain's leaders "view with favor the establishment in Palestine of a national home for the Jewish people, and will use their best endeavors to facilitate the achievement of this object." Lord Balfour was a deeply religious Christian Zionist, whose biblical upbringing led to his pivotal support for the return of the Jewish people to the Land of Israel. This verse promises the Jewish people that *Eretz Yisrael* is their inheritance, their birthright and heritage forever. Throughout history, *Hashem* has used individuals such as Balfour as His agents in returning His people back to Israel.

Arthur James Balfour (1848–1930)

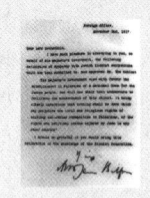

The Balfour Declaration

Devarim/Deuteronomy 26
Ki Tavo

דברים כו
כי תבוא

4 The *Kohen* shall take the basket from your hand and set it down in front of the *Mizbayach* of *Hashem* your God.

ד וְלָקַח הַכֹּהֵן הַטֶּנֶא מִיָּדֶךָ וְהִנִּיחוֹ לִפְנֵי מִזְבַּח יְהֹוָה אֱלֹהֶיךָ:

5 You shall then recite as follows before *Hashem* your God: "My father was a fugitive Aramean. He went down to Egypt with meager numbers and sojourned there; but there he became a great and very populous nation.

ה וְעָנִיתָ וְאָמַרְתָּ לִפְנֵי יְהֹוָה אֱלֹהֶיךָ אֲרַמִּי אֹבֵד אָבִי וַיֵּרֶד מִצְרַיְמָה וַיָּגָר שָׁם בִּמְתֵי מְעָט וַיְהִי־שָׁם לְגוֹי גָּדוֹל עָצוּם וָרָב:

6 The Egyptians dealt harshly with us and oppressed us; they imposed heavy labor upon us.

ו וַיָּרֵעוּ אֹתָנוּ הַמִּצְרִים וַיְעַנּוּנוּ וַיִּתְּנוּ עָלֵינוּ עֲבֹדָה קָשָׁה:

va-ya-RAY-u o-TA-nu ha-mitz-REEM vai-a-NU-nu va-yi-t'-NU a-LAY-nu a-vo-DAH ka-SHAH

7 We cried to *Hashem*, the God of our fathers, and *Hashem* heard our plea and saw our plight, our misery, and our oppression.

ז וַנִּצְעַק אֶל־יְהֹוָה אֱלֹהֵי אֲבֹתֵינוּ וַיִּשְׁמַע יְהֹוָה אֶת־קֹלֵנוּ וַיַּרְא אֶת־עָנְיֵנוּ וְאֶת־עֲמָלֵנוּ וְאֶת־לַחֲצֵנוּ:

8 *Hashem* freed us from Egypt by a mighty hand, by an outstretched arm and awesome power, and by signs and portents.

ח וַיּוֹצִאֵנוּ יְהֹוָה מִמִּצְרַיִם בְּיָד חֲזָקָה וּבִזְרֹעַ נְטוּיָה וּבְמֹרָא גָּדֹל וּבְאֹתוֹת וּבְמֹפְתִים:

9 He brought us to this place and gave us this land, a land flowing with milk and honey.

ט וַיְבִאֵנוּ אֶל־הַמָּקוֹם הַזֶּה וַיִּתֶּן־לָנוּ אֶת־הָאָרֶץ הַזֹּאת אֶרֶץ זָבַת חָלָב וּדְבָשׁ:

vai-vi-AY-nu el ha-ma-KOM ha-ZEH va-yi-ten LA-nu et ha-A-retz ha-ZOT E-retz za-VAT kha-LAV ud-VASH

10 Wherefore I now bring the first fruits of the soil which You, *Hashem*, have given me." You shall leave it before *Hashem* your God and bow low before *Hashem* your God.

י וְעַתָּה הִנֵּה הֵבֵאתִי אֶת־רֵאשִׁית פְּרִי הָאֲדָמָה אֲשֶׁר־נָתַתָּה לִּי יְהֹוָה וְהִנַּחְתּוֹ לִפְנֵי יְהֹוָה אֱלֹהֶיךָ וְהִשְׁתַּחֲוִיתָ לִפְנֵי יְהֹוָה אֱלֹהֶיךָ:

11 And you shall enjoy, together with the Levite and the stranger in your midst, all the bounty that *Hashem* your God has bestowed upon you and your household.

יא וְשָׂמַחְתָּ בְכָל־הַטּוֹב אֲשֶׁר נָתַן־לְךָ יְהֹוָה אֱלֹהֶיךָ וּלְבֵיתֶךָ אַתָּה וְהַלֵּוִי וְהַגֵּר אֲשֶׁר בְּקִרְבֶּךָ:

12 When you have set aside in full the tenth part of your yield – in the third year, the year of the tithe – and have given it to the Levite, the stranger, the fatherless, and the widow, that they may eat their fill in your settlements,

יב כִּי תְכַלֶּה לַעְשֵׂר אֶת־כָּל־מַעְשַׂר תְּבוּאָתְךָ בַּשָּׁנָה הַשְּׁלִישִׁת שְׁנַת הַמַּעֲשֵׂר וְנָתַתָּה לַלֵּוִי לַגֵּר לַיָּתוֹם וְלָאַלְמָנָה וְאָכְלוּ בִשְׁעָרֶיךָ וְשָׂבֵעוּ:

ויֵרעו

26:6 The Egyptians dealt harshly with us Ironically, the Hebrew word in this verse for 'dealt harshly with us,' *vayareiu* (וירעו), also contains the word for 'friendship,' *reiut* (רעות). By choosing this term, the *Torah* is making a subtle observation about the origins of Hebrew slavery. At first, the Egyptians befriended the Jews. It was only later on that they gradually began to institute discriminatory laws, persecution and finally slavery. This pattern, where a host nation invites Jews in and offers protection, but as time goes on the hospitality runs out and anti-Semitism creeps in, has repeated itself throughout Jewish history. Only in the State of Israel can safety and security be guaranteed to the Jewish people permanently.

Devarim/Deuteronomy 27
Ki Tavo

דברים כז
כי תבוא

13 you shall declare before *Hashem* your God: "I have cleared out the consecrated portion from the house; and I have given it to the Levite, the stranger, the fatherless, and the widow, just as You commanded me; I have neither transgressed nor neglected any of Your commandments:

וְאָמַרְתָּ֡ לִפְנֵי֩ יְהֹוָ֨ה אֱלֹהֶ֜יךָ בִּעַ֧רְתִּי הַקֹּ֣דֶשׁ מִן־הַבַּ֗יִת וְגַ֨ם נְתַתִּ֤יו לַלֵּוִי֙ וְלַגֵּ֣ר לַיָּת֣וֹם וְלָאַלְמָנָ֔ה כְּכׇל־מִצְוָתְךָ֖ אֲשֶׁ֣ר צִוִּיתָ֑נִי לֹֽא־עָבַ֥רְתִּי מִמִּצְוֺתֶ֖יךָ וְלֹ֥א שָׁכָֽחְתִּי:

14 I have not eaten of it while in mourning, I have not cleared out any of it while I was unclean, and I have not deposited any of it with the dead. I have obeyed *Hashem* my God; I have done just as You commanded me.

לֹא־אָכַ֨לְתִּי בְאֹנִ֜י מִמֶּ֗נּוּ וְלֹא־בִעַ֤רְתִּי מִמֶּ֙נּוּ֙ בְּטָמֵ֔א וְלֹא־נָתַ֥תִּי מִמֶּ֖נּוּ לְמֵ֑ת שָׁמַ֗עְתִּי בְּקוֹל֙ יְהֹוָ֣ה אֱלֹהָ֔י עָשִׂ֕יתִי כְּכֹ֖ל אֲשֶׁ֥ר צִוִּיתָֽנִי:

15 Look down from Your holy abode, from heaven, and bless Your people *Yisrael* and the soil You have given us, a land flowing with milk and honey, as You swore to our fathers."

הַשְׁקִ֩יפָה֩ מִמְּע֨וֹן קׇדְשְׁךָ֜ מִן־הַשָּׁמַ֗יִם וּבָרֵ֤ךְ אֶֽת־עַמְּךָ֙ אֶת־יִשְׂרָאֵ֔ל וְאֵת֙ הָאֲדָמָ֔ה אֲשֶׁ֥ר נָתַ֖תָּה לָ֑נוּ כַּאֲשֶׁ֤ר נִשְׁבַּ֙עְתָּ֙ לַאֲבֹתֵ֔ינוּ אֶ֛רֶץ זָבַ֥ת חָלָ֖ב וּדְבָֽשׁ:

hash-KEE-fah mi-m'-ON kod-sh'-KHA min ha-sha-MA-yim u-va-RAYKH et a-m'-KHA et yis-ra-AYL ve-AYT ha-a-da-MAH a-SHER na-TA-ta LA-nu ka-a-SHER nish-BA-ta la-a-vo-TAY-nu E-retz za-VAT kha-LAV ud-VASH

16 *Hashem* your God commands you this day to observe these laws and rules; observe them faithfully with all your heart and soul.

הַיּ֣וֹם הַזֶּ֗ה יְהֹוָ֤ה אֱלֹהֶ֙יךָ֙ מְצַוְּךָ֔ לַעֲשׂ֛וֹת אֶת־הַחֻקִּ֥ים הָאֵ֖לֶּה וְאֶת־הַמִּשְׁפָּטִ֑ים וְשָׁמַרְתָּ֤ וְעָשִׂ֙יתָ֙ אוֹתָ֔ם בְּכׇל־לְבָבְךָ֖ וּבְכׇל־נַפְשֶֽׁךָ:

17 You have affirmed this day that *Hashem* is your God, that you will walk in His ways, that you will observe His laws and commandments and rules, and that you will obey Him.

אֶת־יְהֹוָ֥ה הֶאֱמַ֖רְתָּ הַיּ֑וֹם לִהְי֨וֹת לְךָ֜ לֵֽאלֹהִ֗ים וְלָלֶ֣כֶת בִּדְרָכָ֗יו וְלִשְׁמֹ֨ר חֻקָּ֤יו וּמִצְוֺתָיו֙ וּמִשְׁפָּטָ֔יו וְלִשְׁמֹ֖עַ בְּקֹלֽוֹ:

18 And *Hashem* has affirmed this day that you are, as He promised you, His treasured people who shall observe all His commandments,

וַיהֹוָ֞ה הֶאֱמִֽירְךָ֣ הַיּ֗וֹם לִהְי֥וֹת לוֹ֙ לְעַ֣ם סְגֻלָּ֔ה כַּאֲשֶׁ֖ר דִּבֶּר־לָ֑ךְ וְלִשְׁמֹ֖ר כׇּל־מִצְוֺתָֽיו:

19 and that He will set you, in fame and renown and glory, high above all the nations that He has made; and that you shall be, as He promised, a holy people to *Hashem* your God.

וּלְתִתְּךָ֣ עֶלְי֗וֹן עַ֤ל כׇּל־הַגּוֹיִם֙ אֲשֶׁ֣ר עָשָׂ֔ה לִתְהִלָּ֖ה וּלְשֵׁ֣ם וּלְתִפְאָ֑רֶת וְלִֽהְיֹתְךָ֧ עַם־קָדֹ֛שׁ לַיהֹוָ֥ה אֱלֹהֶ֖יךָ כַּאֲשֶׁ֥ר דִּבֵּֽר:

27 1 *Moshe* and the elders of *Yisrael* charged the people, saying: Observe all the Instruction that I enjoin upon you this day.

כז א וַיְצַ֤ו מֹשֶׁה֙ וְזִקְנֵ֣י יִשְׂרָאֵ֔ל אֶת־הָעָ֖ם לֵאמֹ֑ר שָׁמֹר֙ אֶת־כׇּל־הַמִּצְוָ֔ה אֲשֶׁ֧ר אָנֹכִ֛י מְצַוֶּ֥ה אֶתְכֶ֖ם הַיּֽוֹם:

26:15 And bless Your people *Yisrael* and the soil You have given us In Hebrew, the name 'Israel,' *Yisrael* (ישראל), refers to both the land and the people. It also has a deeper meaning. In his book *The Secrets of Hebrew Words*, Rabbi Benjamin Blech points out that, "the smallest letter in the Hebrew alphabet is the *yud* (י). The largest letter is the *lamed* (ל). The very name of the Jewish people, *Yisrael* (ישראל), alludes to both its humble beginnings as well as its glorious destiny." There is no other language like Hebrew, where every word is infused with such deep meaning.

ישראל

Devarim/Deuteronomy 27
Ki Tavo

דברים כז
כי תבוא

2 As soon as you have crossed the *Yarden* into the land that *Hashem* your God is giving you, you shall set up large stones. Coat them with plaster

ב וְהָיָ֗ה בַּיּוֹם֮ אֲשֶׁ֣ר תַּעַבְר֣וּ אֶת־הַיַּרְדֵּן֒ אֶל־הָאָ֕רֶץ אֲשֶׁר־יְהֹוָ֥ה אֱלֹהֶ֖יךָ נֹתֵ֣ן לָ֑ךְ וַהֲקֵמֹתָ֤ לְךָ֙ אֲבָנִ֣ים גְּדֹל֔וֹת וְשַׂדְתָּ֥ אֹתָ֖ם בַּשִּֽׂיד׃

3 and inscribe upon them all the words of this Teaching. When you cross over to enter the land that *Hashem* your God is giving you, a land flowing with milk and honey, as *Hashem*, the God of your fathers, promised you

ג וְכָתַבְתָּ֣ עֲלֵיהֶ֗ן אֶֽת־כׇּל־דִּבְרֵ֛י הַתּוֹרָ֥ה הַזֹּ֖את בְּעׇבְרֶ֑ךָ לְמַ֡עַן אֲשֶׁר֩ תָּבֹ֨א אֶל־הָאָ֜רֶץ אֲ‍ֽשֶׁר־יְהֹוָ֥ה אֱלֹהֶ֣יךָ ׀ נֹתֵ֣ן לְךָ֗ אֶ֣רֶץ זָבַ֤ת חָלָב֙ וּדְבַ֔שׁ כַּאֲשֶׁ֥ר דִּבֶּ֛ר יְהֹוָ֥ה אֱלֹהֵֽי־אֲבֹתֶ֖יךָ לָֽךְ׃

4 upon crossing the *Yarden*, you shall set up these stones, about which I charge you this day, on *Har Eival*, and coat them with plaster.

ד וְהָיָה֮ בְּעׇבְרְכֶ֣ם אֶת־הַיַּרְדֵּן֒ תָּקִ֜ימוּ אֶת־הָאֲבָנִ֣ים הָאֵ֗לֶּה אֲשֶׁ֨ר אָנֹכִ֜י מְצַוֶּ֥ה אֶתְכֶ֛ם הַיּ֖וֹם בְּהַ֣ר עֵיבָ֑ל וְשַׂדְתָּ֥ אוֹתָ֖ם בַּשִּֽׂיד׃

5 There, too, you shall build a *Mizbayach* to *Hashem* your God, a *Mizbayach* of stones. Do not wield an iron tool over them;

ה וּבָנִ֤יתָ שָּׁם֙ מִזְבֵּ֔חַ לַיהֹוָ֖ה אֱלֹהֶ֑יךָ מִזְבַּ֣ח אֲבָנִ֔ים לֹא־תָנִ֥יף עֲלֵיהֶ֖ם בַּרְזֶֽל׃

u-va-NEE-ta SHAM miz-BAY-akh la-do-NAI e-lo-HE-kha miz-BAKH a-va-NEEM lo ta-NEEF a-lay-HEM bar-ZEL

6 you must build the *Mizbayach* of *Hashem* your God of unhewn stones. You shall offer on it burnt offerings to *Hashem* your God,

ו אֲבָנִ֤ים שְׁלֵמוֹת֙ תִּבְנֶ֔ה אֶת־מִזְבַּ֖ח יְהֹוָ֣ה אֱלֹהֶ֑יךָ וְהַעֲלִ֤יתָ עָלָיו֙ עוֹלֹ֔ת לַיהֹוָ֖ה אֱלֹהֶֽיךָ׃

7 and you shall sacrifice there offerings of well-being and eat them, rejoicing before *Hashem* your God.

ז וְזָבַחְתָּ֥ שְׁלָמִ֖ים וְאָכַ֣לְתָּ שָּׁ֑ם וְשָׂ֣מַחְתָּ֔ לִפְנֵ֖י יְהֹוָ֥ה אֱלֹהֶֽיךָ׃

8 And on those stones you shall inscribe every word of this Teaching most distinctly.

ח וְכָתַבְתָּ֣ עַל־הָאֲבָנִ֗ים אֶֽת־כׇּל־דִּבְרֵ֛י הַתּוֹרָ֥ה הַזֹּ֖את בַּאֵ֥ר הֵיטֵֽב׃

9 *Moshe* and the levitical *Kohanim* spoke to all *Yisrael*, saying: Silence! Hear, O *Yisrael*! Today you have become the people of *Hashem* your God:

ט וַיְדַבֵּ֤ר מֹשֶׁה֙ וְהַכֹּהֲנִ֣ים הַלְוִיִּ֔ם אֶ֥ל כׇּל־יִשְׂרָאֵ֖ל לֵאמֹ֑ר הַסְכֵּ֤ת ׀ וּשְׁמַע֙ יִשְׂרָאֵ֔ל הַיּ֤וֹם הַזֶּה֙ נִהְיֵ֣יתָֽ לְעָ֔ם לַיהֹוָ֖ה אֱלֹהֶֽיךָ׃

President Zalman Shazar, 1959

200 New Israeli Shekel banknote featuring Zalman Shazar

27:5 There, too, you shall build a *Mizbayach* *Moshe* commands the Israelites that upon entry into the land, they are to perform a ceremony recommitting themselves to *Hashem* and His *Torah*. This ceremony is to take place on Mount *Gerizim* and Mount *Eival*, located near the city of *Shechem*, also known today as Nablus. Indeed, the fulfilment of this command is documented in *Sefer Yehoshua* (8:30–35). In addition to the ceremony, the Jewish people are commanded to build an altar on Mount *Eival*. They are to inscribe the *Torah* on its stones and, according to the Sages, then dismantle the altar and place the stones in *Gilgal*, their first station in the Land of Israel (Sotah 36a). According to Rabbi Yitzchak Abrabanel, these stones inscribed with the *Torah* text, placed at the entry to the land, indicated to all that this is the land of the *Torah*. They served as a reminder that the purpose of living in *Eretz Yisrael* is to practice the *Torah*'s commandments, and that all success in the land comes from *Hashem*. In the modern State of Israel, Bible studies are a mandatory part of the curriculum in the state's educational system. As Zalman Shazar, third president of the State of Israel and then minister of education, said in his address to Knesset after the passing of the Compulsory Education Law in 1949, "Rich or poor, only children or large families, single or married – we must all carry the burden of *Torah* study." This quote, as well as a portrait of President Shazar, are featured on the 200 shekel bill first printed in 1999.

Devarim/Deuteronomy 27
Ki Tavo

דברים כז
כי תבוא

10 Heed *Hashem* your God and observe His commandments and His laws, which I enjoin upon you this day.

וְשָׁמַעְתָּ בְּקוֹל יְהֹוָה אֱלֹהֶיךָ וְעָשִׂיתָ אֶת־מִצְוֺתָו וְאֶת־חֻקָּיו אֲשֶׁר אָנֹכִי מְצַוְּךָ הַיּוֹם:

11 Thereupon *Moshe* charged the people, saying:

יא וַיְצַו מֹשֶׁה אֶת־הָעָם בַּיּוֹם הַהוּא לֵאמֹר:

12 After you have crossed the *Yarden*, the following shall stand on *Har Gerizim* when the blessing for the people is spoken: *Shimon, Levi, Yehuda, Yissachar, Yosef,* and *Binyamin.*

יב אֵלֶּה יַעַמְדוּ לְבָרֵךְ אֶת־הָעָם עַל־הַר גְּרִזִים בְּעָבְרְכֶם אֶת־הַיַּרְדֵּן שִׁמְעוֹן וְלֵוִי וִיהוּדָה וְיִשָּׂשכָר וְיוֹסֵף וּבִנְיָמִן:

13 And for the curse, the following shall stand on *Har Eival*: *Reuven, Gad, Asher, Zevulun, Dan,* and *Naftali.*

יג וְאֵלֶּה יַעַמְדוּ עַל־הַקְּלָלָה בְּהַר עֵיבָל רְאוּבֵן גָּד וְאָשֵׁר וּזְבוּלֻן דָּן וְנַפְתָּלִי:

14 The *Leviim* shall then proclaim in a loud voice to all the people of *Yisrael*:

יד וְעָנוּ הַלְוִיִּם וְאָמְרוּ אֶל־כָּל־אִישׁ יִשְׂרָאֵל קוֹל רָם:

15 Cursed be anyone who makes a sculptured or molten image, abhorred by *Hashem*, a craftsman's handiwork, and sets it up in secret. – And all the people shall respond, *Amen*.

טו אָרוּר הָאִישׁ אֲשֶׁר יַעֲשֶׂה פֶסֶל וּמַסֵּכָה תּוֹעֲבַת יְהֹוָה מַעֲשֵׂה יְדֵי חָרָשׁ וְשָׂם בַּסָּתֶר וְעָנוּ כָל־הָעָם וְאָמְרוּ אָמֵן:

16 Cursed be he who insults his father or mother. – And all the people shall say, *Amen*.

טז אָרוּר מַקְלֶה אָבִיו וְאִמּוֹ וְאָמַר כָּל־הָעָם אָמֵן:

17 Cursed be he who moves his fellow countryman's landmark. – And all the people shall say, *Amen*.

יז אָרוּר מַסִּיג גְּבוּל רֵעֵהוּ וְאָמַר כָּל־הָעָם אָמֵן:

18 Cursed be he who misdirects a blind person on his way. – And all the people shall say, *Amen*.

יח אָרוּר מַשְׁגֶּה עִוֵּר בַּדָּרֶךְ וְאָמַר כָּל־הָעָם אָמֵן:

19 Cursed be he who subverts the rights of the stranger, the fatherless, and the widow. – And all the people shall say, *Amen*.

יט אָרוּר מַטֶּה מִשְׁפַּט גֵּר־יָתוֹם וְאַלְמָנָה וְאָמַר כָּל־הָעָם אָמֵן:

20 Cursed be he who lies with his father's wife, for he has removed his father's garment. – And all the people shall say, *Amen*.

כ אָרוּר שֹׁכֵב עִם־אֵשֶׁת אָבִיו כִּי גִלָּה כְּנַף אָבִיו וְאָמַר כָּל־הָעָם אָמֵן:

21 Cursed be he who lies with any beast. – And all the people shall say, *Amen*.

כא אָרוּר שֹׁכֵב עִם־כָּל־בְּהֵמָה וְאָמַר כָּל־הָעָם אָמֵן:

22 Cursed be he who lies with his sister, whether daughter of his father or of his mother. – And all the people shall say, *Amen*.

כב אָרוּר שֹׁכֵב עִם־אֲחֹתוֹ בַּת־אָבִיו אוֹ בַת־אִמּוֹ וְאָמַר כָּל־הָעָם אָמֵן:

23 Cursed be he who lies with his mother-in-law. – And all the people shall say, *Amen*.

כג אָרוּר שֹׁכֵב עִם־חֹתַנְתּוֹ וְאָמַר כָּל־הָעָם אָמֵן:

24 Cursed be he who strikes down his fellow countryman in secret. – And all the people shall say, *Amen*.

כד אָרוּר מַכֵּה רֵעֵהוּ בַּסָּתֶר וְאָמַר כָּל־הָעָם אָמֵן:

Devarim/Deuteronomy 28
Ki Tavo

דברים כח
כי תבוא

25 Cursed be he who accepts a bribe in the case of the murder of an innocent person. – And all the people shall say, *Amen.*

כה אָר֗וּר לֹקֵ֥חַ שֹׁ֙חַד֙ לְהַכּ֣וֹת נֶ֣פֶשׁ דָּ֣ם נָקִ֑י וְאָמַ֥ר כָּל־הָעָ֖ם אָמֵֽן׃

26 Cursed be he who will not uphold the terms of this Teaching and observe them. – And all the people shall say, *Amen.*

כו אָר֗וּר אֲשֶׁ֧ר לֹא־יָקִ֛ים אֶת־דִּבְרֵ֥י הַתּוֹרָֽה־הַזֹּ֖את לַעֲשׂ֣וֹת אוֹתָ֑ם וְאָמַ֥ר כָּל־הָעָ֖ם אָמֵֽן׃

28 1 Now, if you obey *Hashem* your God, to observe faithfully all His commandments which I enjoin upon you this day, *Hashem* your God will set you high above all the nations of the earth.

כח א וְהָיָ֗ה אִם־שָׁמ֤וֹעַ תִּשְׁמַע֙ בְּקוֹל֙ יְהֹוָ֣ה אֱלֹהֶ֔יךָ לִשְׁמֹ֤ר לַעֲשׂוֹת֙ אֶת־כָּל־מִצְוֺתָ֔יו אֲשֶׁ֛ר אָנֹכִ֥י מְצַוְּךָ֖ הַיּ֑וֹם וּנְתָ֨נְךָ֜ יְהֹוָ֤ה אֱלֹהֶ֙יךָ֙ עֶלְי֔וֹן עַ֖ל כָּל־גּוֹיֵ֥י הָאָֽרֶץ׃

2 All these blessings shall come upon you and take effect, if you will but heed the word of *Hashem* your God:

ב וּבָ֧אוּ עָלֶ֛יךָ כָּל־הַבְּרָכ֥וֹת הָאֵ֖לֶּה וְהִשִּׂיגֻ֑ךָ כִּ֣י תִשְׁמַ֔ע בְּק֖וֹל יְהֹוָ֥ה אֱלֹהֶֽיךָ׃

3 Blessed shall you be in the city and blessed shall you be in the country.

ג בָּר֥וּךְ אַתָּ֖ה בָּעִ֑יר וּבָר֥וּךְ אַתָּ֖ה בַּשָּׂדֶֽה׃

4 Blessed shall be the issue of your womb, the produce of your soil, and the offspring of your cattle, the calving of your herd and the lambing of your flock.

ד בָּר֧וּךְ פְּרִֽי־בִטְנְךָ֛ וּפְרִ֥י אַדְמָתְךָ֖ וּפְרִ֣י בְהֶמְתֶּ֑ךָ שְׁגַ֥ר אֲלָפֶ֖יךָ וְעַשְׁתְּר֥וֹת צֹאנֶֽךָ׃

5 Blessed shall be your basket and your kneading bowl.

ה בָּר֥וּךְ טַנְאֲךָ֖ וּמִשְׁאַרְתֶּֽךָ׃

6 Blessed shall you be in your comings and blessed shall you be in your goings.

ו בָּר֥וּךְ אַתָּ֖ה בְּבֹאֶ֑ךָ וּבָר֥וּךְ אַתָּ֖ה בְּצֵאתֶֽךָ׃

7 *Hashem* will put to rout before you the enemies who attack you; they will march out against you by a single road, but flee from you by many roads.

ז יִתֵּ֨ן יְהֹוָ֤ה אֶת־אֹיְבֶ֙יךָ֙ הַקָּמִ֣ים עָלֶ֔יךָ נִגָּפִ֖ים לְפָנֶ֑יךָ בְּדֶ֤רֶךְ אֶחָד֙ יֵצְא֣וּ אֵלֶ֔יךָ וּבְשִׁבְעָ֥ה דְרָכִ֖ים יָנ֥וּסוּ לְפָנֶֽיךָ׃

8 *Hashem* will ordain blessings for you upon your barns and upon all your undertakings: He will bless you in the land that *Hashem* your God is giving you.

ח יְצַ֨ו יְהֹוָ֤ה אִתְּךָ֙ אֶת־הַבְּרָכָ֔ה בַּאֲסָמֶ֕יךָ וּבְכֹ֖ל מִשְׁלַ֣ח יָדֶ֑ךָ וּבֵ֣רַכְךָ֔ בָּאָ֕רֶץ אֲשֶׁר־יְהֹוָ֥ה אֱלֹהֶ֖יךָ נֹתֵ֥ן לָֽךְ׃

9 *Hashem* will establish you as His holy people, as He swore to you, if you keep the commandments of *Hashem* your God and walk in His ways.

ט יְקִֽימְךָ֨ יְהֹוָ֥ה לוֹ֙ לְעַ֣ם קָד֔וֹשׁ כַּאֲשֶׁ֖ר נִֽשְׁבַּֽע־לָ֑ךְ כִּ֣י תִשְׁמֹ֗ר אֶת־מִצְוֺת֙ יְהֹוָ֣ה אֱלֹהֶ֔יךָ וְהָלַכְתָּ֖ בִּדְרָכָֽיו׃

10 And all the peoples of the earth shall see that *Hashem*'s name is proclaimed over you, and they shall stand in fear of you.

י וְרָאוּ֙ כָּל־עַמֵּ֣י הָאָ֔רֶץ כִּ֛י שֵׁ֥ם יְהֹוָ֖ה נִקְרָ֣א עָלֶ֑יךָ וְיָֽרְא֖וּ מִמֶּֽךָּ׃

11 *Hashem* will give you abounding prosperity in the issue of your womb, the offspring of your cattle, and the produce of your soil in the land that *Hashem* swore to your fathers to assign to you.

יא וְהוֹתִֽרְךָ֤ יְהֹוָה֙ לְטוֹבָ֔ה בִּפְרִ֧י בִטְנְךָ֛ וּבִפְרִ֥י בְהֶמְתְּךָ֖ וּבִפְרִ֣י אַדְמָתֶ֑ךָ עַ֚ל הָֽאֲדָמָ֔ה אֲשֶׁ֨ר נִשְׁבַּ֧ע יְהֹוָ֛ה לַאֲבֹתֶ֖יךָ לָ֥תֶת לָֽךְ׃

Devarim/Deuteronomy 28
Ki Tavo

דברים כח
כי תבוא

12 *Hashem* will open for you His bounteous store, the heavens, to provide rain for your land in season and to bless all your undertakings. You will be creditor to many nations, but debtor to none.

יב יִפְתַּח יְהֹוָה לְךָ אֶת־אוֹצָרוֹ הַטּוֹב אֶת־הַשָּׁמַיִם לָתֵת מְטַר־אַרְצְךָ בְּעִתּוֹ וּלְבָרֵךְ אֵת כָּל־מַעֲשֵׂה יָדֶךָ וְהִלְוִיתָ גּוֹיִם רַבִּים וְאַתָּה לֹא תִלְוֶה:

yif-TAKH a-do-NAI l'-KHA et o-tza-RO ha-TOV et ha-sha-MA-yim la-TAYT m'-tar ar-tz'-KHA b'-i-TO u-l'-va-RAYKH AYT kol ma-a-SAY ya-DE-kha v'-hil-VEE-ta go-YIM ra-BEEM v'-a-TA lo til-VEH

13 *Hashem* will make you the head, not the tail; you will always be at the top and never at the bottom – if only you obey and faithfully observe the commandments of *Hashem* your God that I enjoin upon you this day,

יג וּנְתָנְךָ יְהֹוָה לְרֹאשׁ וְלֹא לְזָנָב וְהָיִיתָ רַק לְמַעְלָה וְלֹא תִהְיֶה לְמָטָּה כִּי־תִשְׁמַע אֶל־מִצְוֺת יְהֹוָה אֱלֹהֶיךָ אֲשֶׁר אָנֹכִי מְצַוְּךָ הַיּוֹם לִשְׁמֹר וְלַעֲשׂוֹת:

14 and do not deviate to the right or to the left from any of the commandments that I enjoin upon you this day and turn to the worship of other gods.

יד וְלֹא תָסוּר מִכָּל־הַדְּבָרִים אֲשֶׁר אָנֹכִי מְצַוֶּה אֶתְכֶם הַיּוֹם יָמִין וּשְׂמֹאול לָלֶכֶת אַחֲרֵי אֱלֹהִים אֲחֵרִים לְעָבְדָם:

15 But if you do not obey *Hashem* your God to observe faithfully all His commandments and laws which I enjoin upon you this day, all these curses shall come upon you and take effect:

טו וְהָיָה אִם־לֹא תִשְׁמַע בְּקוֹל יְהֹוָה אֱלֹהֶיךָ לִשְׁמֹר לַעֲשׂוֹת אֶת־כָּל־מִצְוֺתָיו וְחֻקֹּתָיו אֲשֶׁר אָנֹכִי מְצַוְּךָ הַיּוֹם וּבָאוּ עָלֶיךָ כָּל־הַקְּלָלוֹת הָאֵלֶּה וְהִשִּׂיגוּךָ:

16 Cursed shall you be in the city and cursed shall you be in the country.

טז אָרוּר אַתָּה בָּעִיר וְאָרוּר אַתָּה בַּשָּׂדֶה:

17 Cursed shall be your basket and your kneading bowl.

יז אָרוּר טַנְאֲךָ וּמִשְׁאַרְתֶּךָ:

18 Cursed shall be the issue of your womb and the produce of your soil, the calving of your herd and the lambing of your flock.

יח אָרוּר פְּרִי־בִטְנְךָ וּפְרִי אַדְמָתֶךָ שְׁגַר אֲלָפֶיךָ וְעַשְׁתְּרוֹת צֹאנֶךָ:

19 Cursed shall you be in your comings and cursed shall you be in your goings.

יט אָרוּר אַתָּה בְּבֹאֶךָ וְאָרוּר אַתָּה בְּצֵאתֶךָ:

20 *Hashem* will let loose against you calamity, panic, and frustration in all the enterprises you undertake, so that you shall soon be utterly wiped out because of your evildoing in forsaking Me.

כ יְשַׁלַּח יְהֹוָה בְּךָ אֶת־הַמְּאֵרָה אֶת־הַמְּהוּמָה וְאֶת־הַמִּגְעֶרֶת בְּכָל־מִשְׁלַח יָדְךָ אֲשֶׁר תַּעֲשֶׂה עַד הִשָּׁמֶדְךָ וְעַד־אֲבָדְךָ מַהֵר מִפְּנֵי רֹעַ מַעֲלָלֶיךָ אֲשֶׁר עֲזַבְתָּנִי:

28:12 To provide rain for your land in season One of the blessings promised as a reward for observing God's commandments in the Holy Land is the promise of rain *b'ito* (בעתו), 'in its time,' or 'in season.' While the Land of Israel is dependent on rainfall for water and irrigation, rain is valuable only if it falls at the right time. While at the right time, even a small amount of rain can be the source of much blessing, when it is not needed rain can be a curse, as it can ruin the crops. Because *Eretz Yisrael* does not have sufficient water sources, rain "in season" is a most significant blessing.

Devarim/Deuteronomy 28
Ki Tavo

דברים כח
כי תבוא

21 *Hashem* will make pestilence cling to you, until He has put an end to you in the land that you are entering to possess.

כא יַדְבֵּק יְהֹוָה בְּךָ אֶת־הַדָּבֶר עַד כַּלֹּתוֹ אֹתְךָ מֵעַל הָאֲדָמָה אֲשֶׁר־אַתָּה בָא־שָׁמָּה לְרִשְׁתָּהּ:

22 *Hashem* will strike you with consumption, fever, and inflammation, with scorching heat and drought, with blight and mildew; they shall hound you until you perish.

כב יַכְּכָה יְהֹוָה בַּשַּׁחֶפֶת וּבַקַּדַּחַת וּבַדַּלֶּקֶת וּבַחַרְחֻר וּבַחֶרֶב וּבַשִּׁדָּפוֹן וּבַיֵּרָקוֹן וּרְדָפוּךָ עַד אָבְדֶךָ:

23 The skies above your head shall be copper and the earth under you iron.

כג וְהָיוּ שָׁמֶיךָ אֲשֶׁר עַל־רֹאשְׁךָ נְחֹשֶׁת וְהָאָרֶץ אֲשֶׁר־תַּחְתֶּיךָ בַּרְזֶל:

24 *Hashem* will make the rain of your land dust, and sand shall drop on you from the sky, until you are wiped out.

כד יִתֵּן יְהֹוָה אֶת־מְטַר אַרְצְךָ אָבָק וְעָפָר מִן־הַשָּׁמַיִם יֵרֵד עָלֶיךָ עַד הִשָּׁמְדָךְ:

25 *Hashem* will put you to rout before your enemies; you shall march out against them by a single road, but flee from them by many roads; and you shall become a horror to all the kingdoms of the earth.

כה יִתֶּנְךָ יְהֹוָה נִגָּף לִפְנֵי אֹיְבֶיךָ בְּדֶרֶךְ אֶחָד תֵּצֵא אֵלָיו וּבְשִׁבְעָה דְרָכִים תָּנוּס לְפָנָיו וְהָיִיתָ לְזַעֲוָה לְכֹל מַמְלְכוֹת הָאָרֶץ:

26 Your carcasses shall become food for all the birds of the sky and all the beasts of the earth, with none to frighten them off.

כו וְהָיְתָה נִבְלָתְךָ לְמַאֲכָל לְכָל־עוֹף הַשָּׁמַיִם וּלְבֶהֱמַת הָאָרֶץ וְאֵין מַחֲרִיד:

27 *Hashem* will strike you with the Egyptian inflammation, with hemorrhoids, boil-scars, and itch, from which you shall never recover.

כז יַכְּכָה יְהֹוָה בִּשְׁחִין מִצְרַיִם וּבַעְפֹלִים [וּבַטְּחֹרִים] וּבַגָּרָב וּבֶחָרֶס אֲשֶׁר לֹא־תוּכַל לְהֵרָפֵא:

28 *Hashem* will strike you with madness, blindness, and dismay.

כח יַכְּכָה יְהֹוָה בְּשִׁגָּעוֹן וּבְעִוָּרוֹן וּבְתִמְהוֹן לֵבָב:

29 You shall grope at noon as a blind man gropes in the dark; you shall not prosper in your ventures, but shall be constantly abused and robbed, with none to give help.

כט וְהָיִיתָ מְמַשֵּׁשׁ בַּצָּהֳרַיִם כַּאֲשֶׁר יְמַשֵּׁשׁ הָעִוֵּר בָּאֲפֵלָה וְלֹא תַצְלִיחַ אֶת־דְּרָכֶיךָ וְהָיִיתָ אַךְ עָשׁוּק וְגָזוּל כָּל־הַיָּמִים וְאֵין מוֹשִׁיעַ:

30 If you pay the bride-price for a wife, another man shall enjoy her. If you build a house, you shall not live in it. If you plant a vineyard, you shall not harvest it.

ל אִשָּׁה תְאָרֵשׂ וְאִישׁ אַחֵר ישגלנה [יִשְׁכָּבֶנָּה] בַּיִת תִּבְנֶה וְלֹא־תֵשֵׁב בּוֹ כֶּרֶם תִּטַּע וְלֹא תְחַלְּלֶנּוּ:

31 Your ox shall be slaughtered before your eyes, but you shall not eat of it; your ass shall be seized in front of you, and it shall not be returned to you; your flock shall be delivered to your enemies, with none to help you.

לא שׁוֹרְךָ טָבוּחַ לְעֵינֶיךָ וְלֹא תֹאכַל מִמֶּנּוּ חֲמֹרְךָ גָּזוּל מִלְּפָנֶיךָ וְלֹא יָשׁוּב לָךְ צֹאנְךָ נְתֻנוֹת לְאֹיְבֶיךָ וְאֵין לְךָ מוֹשִׁיעַ:

32 Your sons and daughters shall be delivered to another people, while you look on; and your eyes shall strain for them constantly, but you shall be helpless.

לב בָּנֶיךָ וּבְנֹתֶיךָ נְתֻנִים לְעַם אַחֵר וְעֵינֶיךָ רֹאוֹת וְכָלוֹת אֲלֵיהֶם כָּל־הַיּוֹם וְאֵין לְאֵל יָדֶךָ:

Devarim/Deuteronomy 28
Ki Tavo

33 A people you do not know shall eat up the produce of your soil and all your gains; you shall be abused and downtrodden continually,

34 until you are driven mad by what your eyes behold.

35 *Hashem* will afflict you at the knees and thighs with a severe inflammation, from which you shall never recover – from the sole of your foot to the crown of your head.

36 *Hashem* will drive you, and the king you have set over you, to a nation unknown to you or your fathers, where you shall serve other gods, of wood and stone.

37 You shall be a consternation, a proverb, and a byword among all the peoples to which *Hashem* will drive you.

38 Though you take much seed out to the field, you shall gather in little, for the locust shall consume it.

39 Though you plant vineyards and till them, you shall have no wine to drink or store, for the worm shall devour them.

40 Though you have olive trees throughout your territory, you shall have no oil for anointment, for your olives shall drop off.

41 Though you beget sons and daughters, they shall not remain with you, for they shall go into captivity.

42 The cricket shall take over all the trees and produce of your land.

43 The stranger in your midst shall rise above you higher and higher, while you sink lower and lower:

44 he shall be your creditor, but you shall not be his; he shall be the head and you the tail.

45 All these curses shall befall you; they shall pursue you and overtake you, until you are wiped out, because you did not heed *Hashem* your God and keep the commandments and laws that He enjoined upon you.

46 They shall serve as signs and proofs against you and your offspring for all time.

47 Because you would not serve *Hashem* your God in joy and gladness over the abundance of everything,

דברים כח
כי תבוא

לג פְּרִי אַדְמָתְךָ וְכָל־יְגִיעֲךָ יֹאכַל עַם אֲשֶׁר לֹא־יָדָעְתָּ וְהָיִיתָ רַק עָשׁוּק וְרָצוּץ כָּל־הַיָּמִים:

לד וְהָיִיתָ מְשֻׁגָּע מִמַּרְאֵה עֵינֶיךָ אֲשֶׁר תִּרְאֶה:

לה יַכְּכָה יְהֹוָה בִּשְׁחִין רָע עַל־הַבִּרְכַּיִם וְעַל־הַשֹּׁקַיִם אֲשֶׁר לֹא־תוּכַל לְהֵרָפֵא מִכַּף רַגְלְךָ וְעַד קָדְקֳדֶךָ:

לו יוֹלֵךְ יְהֹוָה אֹתְךָ וְאֶת־מַלְכְּךָ אֲשֶׁר תָּקִים עָלֶיךָ אֶל־גּוֹי אֲשֶׁר לֹא־יָדַעְתָּ אַתָּה וַאֲבֹתֶיךָ וְעָבַדְתָּ שָּׁם אֱלֹהִים אֲחֵרִים עֵץ וָאָבֶן:

לז וְהָיִיתָ לְשַׁמָּה לְמָשָׁל וְלִשְׁנִינָה בְּכֹל הָעַמִּים אֲשֶׁר־יְנַהֶגְךָ יְהֹוָה שָׁמָּה:

לח זֶרַע רַב תּוֹצִיא הַשָּׂדֶה וּמְעַט תֶּאֱסֹף כִּי יַחְסְלֶנּוּ הָאַרְבֶּה:

לט כְּרָמִים תִּטַּע וְעָבָדְתָּ וְיַיִן לֹא־תִשְׁתֶּה וְלֹא תֶאֱגֹר כִּי תֹאכְלֶנּוּ הַתֹּלָעַת:

מ זֵיתִים יִהְיוּ לְךָ בְּכָל־גְּבוּלֶךָ וְשֶׁמֶן לֹא תָסוּךְ כִּי יִשַּׁל זֵיתֶךָ:

מא בָּנִים וּבָנוֹת תּוֹלִיד וְלֹא־יִהְיוּ לָךְ כִּי יֵלְכוּ בַּשֶּׁבִי:

מב כָּל־עֵצְךָ וּפְרִי אַדְמָתֶךָ יְיָרֵשׁ הַצְּלָצַל:

מג הַגֵּר אֲשֶׁר בְּקִרְבְּךָ יַעֲלֶה עָלֶיךָ מַעְלָה מָּעְלָה וְאַתָּה תֵרֵד מַטָּה מָּטָּה:

מד הוּא יַלְוְךָ וְאַתָּה לֹא תַלְוֶנּוּ הוּא יִהְיֶה לְרֹאשׁ וְאַתָּה תִּהְיֶה לְזָנָב:

מה וּבָאוּ עָלֶיךָ כָּל־הַקְּלָלוֹת הָאֵלֶּה וּרְדָפוּךָ וְהִשִּׂיגוּךָ עַד הִשָּׁמְדָךְ כִּי־לֹא שָׁמַעְתָּ בְּקוֹל יְהֹוָה אֱלֹהֶיךָ לִשְׁמֹר מִצְוֹתָיו וְחֻקֹּתָיו אֲשֶׁר צִוָּךְ:

מו וְהָיוּ בְךָ לְאוֹת וּלְמוֹפֵת וּבְזַרְעֲךָ עַד־עוֹלָם:

מז תַּחַת אֲשֶׁר לֹא־עָבַדְתָּ אֶת־יְהֹוָה אֱלֹהֶיךָ בְּשִׂמְחָה וּבְטוּב לֵבָב מֵרֹב כֹּל:

Devarim/Deuteronomy 28
Ki Tavo

דברים כח
כי תבוא

48 you shall have to serve – in hunger and thirst, naked and lacking everything – the enemies whom *Hashem* will let loose against you. He will put an iron yoke upon your neck until He has wiped you out.

מח וְעָבַדְתָּ אֶת־אֹיְבֶיךָ אֲשֶׁר יְשַׁלְּחֶנּוּ יְהֹוָה בָּךְ בְּרָעָב וּבְצָמָא וּבְעֵירֹם וּבְחֹסֶר כֹּל וְנָתַן עֹל בַּרְזֶל עַל־צַוָּארֶךָ עַד הִשְׁמִידוֹ אֹתָךְ:

49 *Hashem* will bring a nation against you from afar, from the end of the earth, which will swoop down like the eagle – a nation whose language you do not understand,

מט יִשָּׂא יְהֹוָה עָלֶיךָ גּוֹי מֵרָחוֹק מִקְצֵה הָאָרֶץ כַּאֲשֶׁר יִדְאֶה הַנָּשֶׁר גּוֹי אֲשֶׁר לֹא־תִשְׁמַע לְשֹׁנוֹ:

50 a ruthless nation, that will show the old no regard and the young no mercy.

נ גּוֹי עַז פָּנִים אֲשֶׁר לֹא־יִשָּׂא פָנִים לְזָקֵן וְנַעַר לֹא יָחֹן:

51 It shall devour the offspring of your cattle and the produce of your soil, until you have been wiped out, leaving you nothing of new grain, wine, or oil, of the calving of your herds and the lambing of your flocks, until it has brought you to ruin.

נא וְאָכַל פְּרִי בְהֶמְתְּךָ וּפְרִי־אַדְמָתְךָ עַד הִשָּׁמְדָךְ אֲשֶׁר לֹא־יַשְׁאִיר לְךָ דָּגָן תִּירוֹשׁ וְיִצְהָר שְׁגַר אֲלָפֶיךָ וְעַשְׁתְּרֹת צֹאנֶךָ עַד הַאֲבִידוֹ אֹתָךְ:

52 It shall shut you up in all your towns throughout your land until every mighty, towering wall in which you trust has come down. And when you are shut up in all your towns throughout your land that *Hashem* your God has assigned to you,

נב וְהֵצַר לְךָ בְּכָל־שְׁעָרֶיךָ עַד רֶדֶת חֹמֹתֶיךָ הַגְּבֹהֹת וְהַבְּצֻרוֹת אֲשֶׁר אַתָּה בֹּטֵחַ בָּהֵן בְּכָל־אַרְצֶךָ וְהֵצַר לְךָ בְּכָל־שְׁעָרֶיךָ בְּכָל־אַרְצְךָ אֲשֶׁר נָתַן יְהֹוָה אֱלֹהֶיךָ לָךְ:

53 you shall eat your own issue, the flesh of your sons and daughters that *Hashem* your God has assigned to you, because of the desperate straits to which your enemy shall reduce you.

נג וְאָכַלְתָּ פְרִי־בִטְנְךָ בְּשַׂר בָּנֶיךָ וּבְנֹתֶיךָ אֲשֶׁר נָתַן־לְךָ יְהֹוָה אֱלֹהֶיךָ בְּמָצוֹר וּבְמָצוֹק אֲשֶׁר־יָצִיק לְךָ אֹיְבֶךָ:

54 He who is most tender and fastidious among you shall be too mean to his brother and the wife of his bosom and the children he has spared

נד הָאִישׁ הָרַךְ בְּךָ וְהֶעָנֹג מְאֹד תֵּרַע עֵינוֹ בְאָחִיו וּבְאֵשֶׁת חֵיקוֹ וּבְיֶתֶר בָּנָיו אֲשֶׁר יוֹתִיר:

55 to share with any of them the flesh of the children that he eats, because he has nothing else left as a result of the desperate straits to which your enemy shall reduce you in all your towns.

נה מִתֵּת לְאַחַד מֵהֶם מִבְּשַׂר בָּנָיו אֲשֶׁר יֹאכֵל מִבְּלִי הִשְׁאִיר־לוֹ כֹּל בְּמָצוֹר וּבְמָצוֹק אֲשֶׁר יָצִיק לְךָ אֹיִבְךָ בְּכָל־שְׁעָרֶיךָ:

56 And she who is most tender and dainty among you, so tender and dainty that she would never venture to set a foot on the ground, shall begrudge the husband of her bosom, and her son and her daughter,

נו הָרַכָּה בְךָ וְהָעֲנֻגָּה אֲשֶׁר לֹא־נִסְּתָה כַף־רַגְלָהּ הַצֵּג עַל־הָאָרֶץ מֵהִתְעַנֵּג וּמֵרֹךְ תֵּרַע עֵינָהּ בְּאִישׁ חֵיקָהּ וּבִבְנָהּ וּבְבִתָּהּ:

57 the afterbirth that issues from between her legs and the babies she bears; she shall eat them secretly, because of utter want, in the desperate straits to which your enemy shall reduce you in your towns.

נז וּבְשִׁלְיָתָהּ הַיּוֹצֵת מִבֵּין רַגְלֶיהָ וּבְבָנֶיהָ אֲשֶׁר תֵּלֵד כִּי־תֹאכְלֵם בְּחֹסֶר־כֹּל בַּסָּתֶר בְּמָצוֹר וּבְמָצוֹק אֲשֶׁר יָצִיק לְךָ אֹיִבְךָ בִּשְׁעָרֶיךָ:

Devarim/Deuteronomy 28
Ki Tavo

58 If you fail to observe faithfully all the terms of this Teaching that are written in this book, to reverence this honored and awesome Name, *Hashem* your God,

59 *Hashem* will inflict extraordinary plagues upon you and your offspring, strange and lasting plagues, malignant and chronic diseases.

60 He will bring back upon you all the sicknesses of Egypt that you dreaded so, and they shall cling to you.

61 Moreover, *Hashem* will bring upon you all the other diseases and plagues that are not mentioned in this book of Teaching, until you are wiped out.

62 You shall be left a scant few, after having been as numerous as the stars in the skies, because you did not heed the command of *Hashem* your God.

63 And as *Hashem* once delighted in making you prosperous and many, so will *Hashem* now delight in causing you to perish and in wiping you out; you shall be torn from the land that you are about to enter and possess.

64 *Hashem* will scatter you among all the peoples from one end of the earth to the other, and there you shall serve other gods, wood and stone, whom neither you nor your ancestors have experienced.

65 Yet even among those nations you shall find no peace, nor shall your foot find a place to rest. *Hashem* will give you there an anguished heart and eyes that pine and a despondent spirit.

66 The life you face shall be precarious; you shall be in terror, night and day, with no assurance of survival.

67 In the morning you shall say, "If only it were evening!" and in the evening you shall say, "If only it were morning!" – because of what your heart shall dread and your eyes shall see.

68 *Hashem* will send you back to Egypt in galleys, by a route which I told you you should not see again. There you shall offer yourselves for sale to your enemies as male and female slaves, but none will buy.

69 These are the terms of the covenant which *Hashem* commanded *Moshe* to conclude with the Israelites in the land of Moab, in addition to the covenant which He had made with them at Horeb.

דברים כח
כי תבוא

נח אִם־לֹא תִשְׁמֹר לַעֲשׂוֹת אֶת־כָּל־דִּבְרֵי הַתּוֹרָה הַזֹּאת הַכְּתוּבִים בַּסֵּפֶר הַזֶּה לְיִרְאָה אֶת־הַשֵּׁם הַנִּכְבָּד וְהַנּוֹרָא הַזֶּה אֵת יְהֹוָה אֱלֹהֶיךָ:

נט וְהִפְלָא יְהֹוָה אֶת־מַכֹּתְךָ וְאֵת מַכּוֹת זַרְעֶךָ מַכּוֹת גְּדֹלוֹת וְנֶאֱמָנוֹת וָחֳלָיִם רָעִים וְנֶאֱמָנִים:

ס וְהֵשִׁיב בְּךָ אֵת כָּל־מַדְוֵה מִצְרַיִם אֲשֶׁר יָגֹרְתָּ מִפְּנֵיהֶם וְדָבְקוּ בָּךְ:

סא גַּם כָּל־חֳלִי וְכָל־מַכָּה אֲשֶׁר לֹא כָתוּב בְּסֵפֶר הַתּוֹרָה הַזֹּאת יַעְלֵם יְהֹוָה עָלֶיךָ עַד הִשָּׁמְדָךְ:

סב וְנִשְׁאַרְתֶּם בִּמְתֵי מְעָט תַּחַת אֲשֶׁר הֱיִיתֶם כְּכוֹכְבֵי הַשָּׁמַיִם לָרֹב כִּי־לֹא שָׁמַעְתָּ בְּקוֹל יְהֹוָה אֱלֹהֶיךָ:

סג וְהָיָה כַּאֲשֶׁר־שָׂשׂ יְהֹוָה עֲלֵיכֶם לְהֵיטִיב אֶתְכֶם וּלְהַרְבּוֹת אֶתְכֶם כֵּן יָשִׂישׂ יְהֹוָה עֲלֵיכֶם לְהַאֲבִיד אֶתְכֶם וּלְהַשְׁמִיד אֶתְכֶם וְנִסַּחְתֶּם מֵעַל הָאֲדָמָה אֲשֶׁר־אַתָּה בָא־שָׁמָּה לְרִשְׁתָּהּ:

סד וֶהֱפִיצְךָ יְהֹוָה בְּכָל־הָעַמִּים מִקְצֵה הָאָרֶץ וְעַד־קְצֵה הָאָרֶץ וְעָבַדְתָּ שָּׁם אֱלֹהִים אֲחֵרִים אֲשֶׁר לֹא־יָדַעְתָּ אַתָּה וַאֲבֹתֶיךָ עֵץ וָאָבֶן:

סה וּבַגּוֹיִם הָהֵם לֹא תַרְגִּיעַ וְלֹא־יִהְיֶה מָנוֹחַ לְכַף־רַגְלֶךָ וְנָתַן יְהֹוָה לְךָ שָׁם לֵב רַגָּז וְכִלְיוֹן עֵינַיִם וְדַאֲבוֹן נָפֶשׁ:

סו וְהָיוּ חַיֶּיךָ תְּלֻאִים לְךָ מִנֶּגֶד וּפָחַדְתָּ לַיְלָה וְיוֹמָם וְלֹא תַאֲמִין בְּחַיֶּיךָ:

סז בַּבֹּקֶר תֹּאמַר מִי־יִתֵּן עֶרֶב וּבָעֶרֶב תֹּאמַר מִי־יִתֵּן בֹּקֶר מִפַּחַד לְבָבְךָ אֲשֶׁר תִּפְחָד וּמִמַּרְאֵה עֵינֶיךָ אֲשֶׁר תִּרְאֶה:

סח וֶהֱשִׁיבְךָ יְהֹוָה מִצְרַיִם בָּאֳנִיּוֹת בַּדֶּרֶךְ אֲשֶׁר אָמַרְתִּי לְךָ לֹא־תֹסִיף עוֹד לִרְאֹתָהּ וְהִתְמַכַּרְתֶּם שָׁם לְאֹיְבֶיךָ לַעֲבָדִים וְלִשְׁפָחוֹת וְאֵין קֹנֶה:

סט אֵלֶּה דִבְרֵי הַבְּרִית אֲשֶׁר־צִוָּה יְהֹוָה אֶת־מֹשֶׁה לִכְרֹת אֶת־בְּנֵי יִשְׂרָאֵל בְּאֶרֶץ מוֹאָב מִלְּבַד הַבְּרִית אֲשֶׁר־כָּרַת אִתָּם בְּחֹרֵב:

Devarim/Deuteronomy 29
Nitzavim

29 1 *Moshe* summoned all *Yisrael* and said to them: You have seen all that *Hashem* did before your very eyes in the land of Egypt, to Pharaoh and to all his courtiers and to his whole country:

2 the wondrous feats that you saw with your own eyes, those prodigious signs and marvels.

3 Yet to this day *Hashem* has not given you a mind to understand or eyes to see or ears to hear.

4 I led you through the wilderness forty years; the clothes on your back did not wear out, nor did the sandals on your feet;

5 you had no bread to eat and no wine or other intoxicant to drink – that you might know that I *Hashem* am your God.

6 When you reached this place, King Sihon of Heshbon and King Og of Bashan came out to engage us in battle, but we defeated them.

7 We took their land and gave it to the Reubenites, the Gadites, and the half-tribe of *Menashe* as their heritage.

8 Therefore observe faithfully all the terms of this covenant, that you may succeed in all that you undertake.

9 You stand this day, all of you, before *Hashem* your God – your tribal heads, your elders and your officials, all the men of *Yisrael*,

10 your children, your wives, even the stranger within your camp, from woodchopper to water drawer

11 to enter into the covenant of *Hashem* your God, which *Hashem* your God is concluding with you this day, with its sanctions;

l'-av-r'-KHA biv-REET a-do-NAI e-lo-HE-kha uv-a-la-TO a-SHER a-do-NAI e-lo-HE-kha ko-RAYT i-m'-KHA ha-YOM

דברים כט
נצבים

א וַיִּקְרָ֥א מֹשֶׁ֛ה אֶל־כָּל־יִשְׂרָאֵ֖ל וַיֹּ֣אמֶר אֲלֵהֶ֑ם אַתֶּ֣ם רְאִיתֶ֗ם אֵ֤ת כָּל־אֲשֶׁר֙ עָשָׂ֤ה יְהֹוָה֙ לְעֵ֣ינֵיכֶ֔ם בְּאֶ֖רֶץ מִצְרָ֑יִם לְפַרְעֹ֥ה וּלְכָל־עֲבָדָ֖יו וּלְכָל־אַרְצֽוֹ׃

ב הַמַּסּוֹת֙ הַגְּדֹלֹ֔ת אֲשֶׁ֥ר רָא֖וּ עֵינֶ֑יךָ הָאֹתֹ֧ת וְהַמֹּפְתִ֛ים הַגְּדֹלִ֖ים הָהֵֽם׃

ג וְלֹֽא־נָתַן֩ יְהֹוָ֨ה לָכֶ֥ם לֵב֙ לָדַ֔עַת וְעֵינַ֥יִם לִרְא֖וֹת וְאָזְנַ֣יִם לִשְׁמֹ֑עַ עַ֖ד הַיּ֥וֹם הַזֶּֽה׃

ד וָאוֹלֵ֥ךְ אֶתְכֶ֛ם אַרְבָּעִ֥ים שָׁנָ֖ה בַּמִּדְבָּ֑ר לֹֽא־בָל֤וּ שַׂלְמֹֽתֵיכֶם֙ מֵעֲלֵיכֶ֔ם וְנַעַלְךָ֥ לֹֽא־בָלְתָ֖ה מֵעַ֥ל רַגְלֶֽךָ׃

ה לֶ֚חֶם לֹ֣א אֲכַלְתֶּ֔ם וְיַ֥יִן וְשֵׁכָ֖ר לֹ֣א שְׁתִיתֶ֑ם לְמַ֙עַן֙ תֵּֽדְע֔וּ כִּ֛י אֲנִ֥י יְהֹוָ֖ה אֱלֹהֵיכֶֽם׃

ו וַתָּבֹ֖אוּ אֶל־הַמָּק֣וֹם הַזֶּ֑ה וַיֵּצֵ֣א סִיחֹ֣ן מֶֽלֶךְ־חֶ֠שְׁבּ֠וֹן וְע֨וֹג מֶֽלֶךְ־הַבָּשָׁ֧ן לִקְרָאתֵ֛נוּ לַמִּלְחָמָ֖ה וַנַּכֵּֽם׃

ז וַנִּקַּח֙ אֶת־אַרְצָ֔ם וַנִּתְּנָ֖הּ לְנַחֲלָ֑ה לָרֽאוּבֵנִי֙ וְלַגָּדִ֔י וְלַחֲצִ֖י שֵׁ֥בֶט הַֽמְנַשִּֽׁי׃

ח וּשְׁמַרְתֶּ֗ם אֶת־דִּבְרֵי֙ הַבְּרִ֣ית הַזֹּ֔את וַעֲשִׂיתֶ֖ם אֹתָ֑ם לְמַ֣עַן תַּשְׂכִּ֔ילוּ אֵ֖ת כָּל־אֲשֶׁ֥ר תַּעֲשֽׂוּן׃

ט אַתֶּ֨ם נִצָּבִ֤ים הַיּוֹם֙ כֻּלְּכֶ֔ם לִפְנֵ֖י יְהֹוָ֣ה אֱלֹהֵיכֶ֑ם רָאשֵׁיכֶ֣ם שִׁבְטֵיכֶ֗ם זִקְנֵיכֶם֙ וְשֹׁ֣טְרֵיכֶ֔ם כֹּ֖ל אִ֥ישׁ יִשְׂרָאֵֽל׃

י טַפְּכֶ֣ם נְשֵׁיכֶ֔ם וְגֵ֣רְךָ֔ אֲשֶׁ֖ר בְּקֶ֣רֶב מַחֲנֶ֑יךָ מֵחֹטֵ֣ב עֵצֶ֔יךָ עַ֖ד שֹׁאֵ֥ב מֵימֶֽיךָ׃

יא לְעָבְרְךָ֗ בִּבְרִ֛ית יְהֹוָ֥ה אֱלֹהֶ֖יךָ וּבְאָלָת֑וֹ אֲשֶׁר֙ יְהֹוָ֣ה אֱלֹהֶ֔יךָ כֹּרֵ֥ת עִמְּךָ֖ הַיּֽוֹם׃

29:11 To enter into the covenant of *Hashem* your God As the People of Israel stand at the plains of Moab, ready to enter the Promised Land, *Moshe* leads them in reaffirming their covenant with *Hashem* for all generations. The Hebrew name for 'plains of Moab,' *Arvot Moav* (ערבות מואב), has a dual meaning, as the word *Arvot* is related to the term *areivut* (ערבות), which means 'mutual responsibility.' Rabbi Shlomo Riskin explains the significance: "I would submit that this covenant is that of mutuality, interdependent co-signership, but not necessarily between Jew and Jew – that was already incorporated into the previous covenants – but rather between Israel and the other nations of the world. After all, when *Avraham* was

Rabbi Shlomo Riskin (b. 1940)

Devarim/Deuteronomy 29

Nitzavim

דברים כט
נצבים

12 to the end that He may establish you this day as His people and be your God, as He promised you and as He swore to your fathers, *Avraham*, *Yitzchak*, and *Yaakov*.

יב לְמַעַן הָקִים־אֹתְךָ הַיּוֹם לוֹ לְעָם וְהוּא יִהְיֶה־לְּךָ לֵאלֹהִים כַּאֲשֶׁר דִּבֶּר־לָךְ וְכַאֲשֶׁר נִשְׁבַּע לַאֲבֹתֶיךָ לְאַבְרָהָם לְיִצְחָק וּלְיַעֲקֹב:

13 I make this covenant, with its sanctions, not with you alone,

יג וְלֹא אִתְּכֶם לְבַדְּכֶם אָנֹכִי כֹּרֵת אֶת־הַבְּרִית הַזֹּאת וְאֶת־הָאָלָה הַזֹּאת:

14 but both with those who are standing here with us this day before *Hashem* our God and with those who are not with us here this day.

יד כִּי אֶת־אֲשֶׁר יֶשְׁנוֹ פֹּה עִמָּנוּ עֹמֵד הַיּוֹם לִפְנֵי יְהוָֹה אֱלֹהֵינוּ וְאֵת אֲשֶׁר אֵינֶנּוּ פֹּה עִמָּנוּ הַיּוֹם:

15 Well you know that we dwelt in the land of Egypt and that we passed through the midst of various other nations through which you passed;

טו כִּי־אַתֶּם יְדַעְתֶּם אֵת אֲשֶׁר־יָשַׁבְנוּ בְּאֶרֶץ מִצְרָיִם וְאֵת אֲשֶׁר־עָבַרְנוּ בְּקֶרֶב הַגּוֹיִם אֲשֶׁר עֲבַרְתֶּם:

16 and you have seen the detestable things and the fetishes of wood and stone, silver and gold, that they keep.

טז וַתִּרְאוּ אֶת־שִׁקּוּצֵיהֶם וְאֵת גִּלֻּלֵיהֶם עֵץ וָאֶבֶן כֶּסֶף וְזָהָב אֲשֶׁר עִמָּהֶם:

17 Perchance there is among you some man or woman, or some clan or tribe, whose heart is even now turning away from *Hashem* our God to go and worship the gods of those nations – perchance there is among you a stock sprouting poison weed and wormwood.

יז פֶּן־יֵשׁ בָּכֶם אִישׁ אוֹ־אִשָּׁה אוֹ מִשְׁפָּחָה אוֹ־שֵׁבֶט אֲשֶׁר לְבָבוֹ פֹנֶה הַיּוֹם מֵעִם יְהוָֹה אֱלֹהֵינוּ לָלֶכֶת לַעֲבֹד אֶת־אֱלֹהֵי הַגּוֹיִם הָהֵם פֶּן־יֵשׁ בָּכֶם שֹׁרֶשׁ פֹּרֶה רֹאשׁ וְלַעֲנָה:

18 When such a one hears the words of these sanctions, he may fancy himself immune, thinking, "I shall be safe, though I follow my own willful heart" – to the utter ruin of moist and dry alike.

יח וְהָיָה בְּשָׁמְעוֹ אֶת־דִּבְרֵי הָאָלָה הַזֹּאת וְהִתְבָּרֵךְ בִּלְבָבוֹ לֵאמֹר שָׁלוֹם יִהְיֶה־לִּי כִּי בִּשְׁרִרוּת לִבִּי אֵלֵךְ לְמַעַן סְפוֹת הָרָוָה אֶת־הַצְּמֵאָה:

19 *Hashem* will never forgive him; rather will *Hashem's* anger and passion rage against that man, till every sanction recorded in this book comes down upon him, and *Hashem* blots out his name from under heaven.

יט לֹא־יֹאבֶה יְהוָֹה סְלֹחַ לוֹ כִּי אָז יֶעְשַׁן אַף־יְהוָֹה וְקִנְאָתוֹ בָּאִישׁ הַהוּא וְרָבְצָה בּוֹ כָּל־הָאָלָה הַכְּתוּבָה בַּסֵּפֶר הַזֶּה וּמָחָה יְהוָֹה אֶת־שְׁמוֹ מִתַּחַת הַשָּׁמָיִם:

20 *Hashem* will single them out from all the tribes of *Yisrael* for misfortune, in accordance with all the sanctions of the covenant recorded in this book of Teaching.

כ וְהִבְדִּילוֹ יְהוָֹה לְרָעָה מִכֹּל שִׁבְטֵי יִשְׂרָאֵל כְּכֹל אָלוֹת הַבְּרִית הַכְּתוּבָה בְּסֵפֶר הַתּוֹרָה הַזֶּה:

---

originally elected, God commanded that (Genesis 12:3) 'through you all the families of the world will be blessed' – through the message of ethical monotheism, the vision of a God who demands justice, compassion and peace, which *Avraham's* descendants must convey to the world. This is the true mission of Israel… This third covenant is the covenant of Israel's responsibility to the world."

Devarim/Deuteronomy 30
Nitzavim

דברים ל
נצבים

21 And later generations will ask – the children who succeed you, and foreigners who come from distant lands and see the plagues and diseases that *Hashem* has inflicted upon that land,

כא וְאָמַר הַדּוֹר הָאַחֲרוֹן בְּנֵיכֶם אֲשֶׁר יָקוּמוּ מֵאַחֲרֵיכֶם וְהַנָּכְרִי אֲשֶׁר יָבֹא מֵאֶרֶץ רְחוֹקָה וְרָאוּ אֶת־מַכּוֹת הָאָרֶץ הַהִוא וְאֶת־תַּחֲלֻאֶיהָ אֲשֶׁר־חִלָּה יְהֹוָה בָּהּ:

22 all its soil devastated by sulfur and salt, beyond sowing and producing, no grass growing in it, just like the upheaval of Sodom and Gomorrah, Admah and Zeboiim, which *Hashem* overthrew in His fierce anger

כב גָּפְרִית וָמֶלַח שְׂרֵפָה כָל־אַרְצָהּ לֹא תִזָּרַע וְלֹא תַצְמִחַ וְלֹא־יַעֲלֶה בָהּ כָּל־עֵשֶׂב כְּמַהְפֵּכַת סְדֹם וַעֲמֹרָה אַדְמָה וצביים [וּצְבֹיִים] אֲשֶׁר הָפַךְ יְהֹוָה בְּאַפּוֹ וּבַחֲמָתוֹ:

23 all nations will ask, "Why did *Hashem* do thus to this land? Wherefore that awful wrath?"

כג וְאָמְרוּ כָּל־הַגּוֹיִם עַל־מֶה עָשָׂה יְהֹוָה כָּכָה לָאָרֶץ הַזֹּאת מֶה חֳרִי הָאַף הַגָּדוֹל הַזֶּה:

24 They will be told, "Because they forsook the covenant that *Hashem*, God of their fathers, made with them when He freed them from the land of Egypt;

כד וְאָמְרוּ עַל אֲשֶׁר עָזְבוּ אֶת־בְּרִית יְהֹוָה אֱלֹהֵי אֲבֹתָם אֲשֶׁר כָּרַת עִמָּם בְּהוֹצִיאוֹ אֹתָם מֵאֶרֶץ מִצְרָיִם:

25 they turned to the service of other gods and worshiped them, gods whom they had not experienced and whom He had not allotted to them.

כה וַיֵּלְכוּ וַיַּעַבְדוּ אֱלֹהִים אֲחֵרִים וַיִּשְׁתַּחֲווּ לָהֶם אֱלֹהִים אֲשֶׁר לֹא־יְדָעוּם וְלֹא חָלַק לָהֶם:

26 So *Hashem* was incensed at that land and brought upon it all the curses recorded in this book.

כו וַיִּחַר־אַף יְהֹוָה בָּאָרֶץ הַהִוא לְהָבִיא עָלֶיהָ אֶת־כָּל־הַקְּלָלָה הַכְּתוּבָה בַּסֵּפֶר הַזֶּה:

27 *Hashem* uprooted them from their soil in anger, fury, and great wrath, and cast them into another land, as is still the case."

כז וַיִּתְּשֵׁם יְהֹוָה מֵעַל אַדְמָתָם בְּאַף וּבְחֵמָה וּבְקֶצֶף גָּדוֹל וַיַּשְׁלִכֵם אֶל־אֶרֶץ אַחֶרֶת כַּיּוֹם הַזֶּה:

28 Concealed acts concern *Hashem* our God; but with overt acts, it is for us and our children ever to apply all the provisions of this Teaching.

כח הַנִּסְתָּרֹת לַיהֹוָה אֱלֹהֵינוּ וְהַנִּגְלֹת לָנוּ וּלְבָנֵינוּ עַד־עוֹלָם לַעֲשׂוֹת אֶת־כָּל־דִּבְרֵי הַתּוֹרָה הַזֹּאת:

30
1 When all these things befall you – the blessing and the curse that I have set before you – and you take them to heart amidst the various nations to which *Hashem* your God has banished you,

ל א וְהָיָה כִי־יָבֹאוּ עָלֶיךָ כָּל־הַדְּבָרִים הָאֵלֶּה הַבְּרָכָה וְהַקְּלָלָה אֲשֶׁר נָתַתִּי לְפָנֶיךָ וַהֲשֵׁבֹתָ אֶל־לְבָבֶךָ בְּכָל־הַגּוֹיִם אֲשֶׁר הִדִּיחֲךָ יְהֹוָה אֱלֹהֶיךָ שָׁמָּה:

2 and you return to *Hashem* your God, and you and your children heed His command with all your heart and soul, just as I enjoin upon you this day,

ב וְשַׁבְתָּ עַד־יְהֹוָה אֱלֹהֶיךָ וְשָׁמַעְתָּ בְקֹלוֹ כְּכֹל אֲשֶׁר־אָנֹכִי מְצַוְּךָ הַיּוֹם אַתָּה וּבָנֶיךָ בְּכָל־לְבָבְךָ וּבְכָל־נַפְשֶׁךָ:

Devarim/Deuteronomy 30
Nitzavim

דברים ל
נצבים

3 then *Hashem* your God will restore your fortunes and take you back in love. He will bring you together again from all the peoples where *Hashem* your God has scattered you.

ג וְשָׁב יְהֹוָה אֱלֹהֶיךָ אֶת־שְׁבוּתְךָ וְרִחֲמֶךָ וְשָׁב וְקִבֶּצְךָ מִכָּל־הָעַמִּים אֲשֶׁר הֱפִיצְךָ יְהֹוָה אֱלֹהֶיךָ שָׁמָּה׃

v'-SHAV a-do-NAI e-lo-HE-kha et sh'-vu-t'-KHA v'-ri-kha-ME-kha v'-SHAV v'-ki-betz-KHA mi-kol HA-a-MEEM a-SHER he-fitz-KHA a-do-NAI e-lo-HE-kha SHA-mah

4 Even if your outcasts are at the ends of the world, from there *Hashem* your God will gather you, from there He will fetch you.

ד אִם־יִהְיֶה נִדַּחֲךָ בִּקְצֵה הַשָּׁמָיִם מִשָּׁם יְקַבֶּצְךָ יְהֹוָה אֱלֹהֶיךָ וּמִשָּׁם יִקָּחֶךָ׃

5 And *Hashem* your God will bring you to the land that your fathers possessed, and you shall possess it; and He will make you more prosperous and more numerous than your fathers.

ה וֶהֱבִיאֲךָ יְהֹוָה אֱלֹהֶיךָ אֶל־הָאָרֶץ אֲשֶׁר־יָרְשׁוּ אֲבֹתֶיךָ וִירִשְׁתָּהּ וְהֵיטִבְךָ וְהִרְבְּךָ מֵאֲבֹתֶיךָ׃

ve-he-vee-a-KHA a-do-NAI e-lo-HE-kha el ha-A-retz a-sher ya-r'-SHU a-vo-TE-kha vee-rish-TA v'-hay-tiv-KHA v'-hir-b'-KHA ear-be-KHA may-a-vo-TE-kha

6 Then *Hashem* your God will open up your heart and the hearts of your offspring to love *Hashem* your God with all your heart and soul, in order that you may live.

ו וּמָל יְהֹוָה אֱלֹהֶיךָ אֶת־לְבָבְךָ וְאֶת־לְבַב זַרְעֶךָ לְאַהֲבָה אֶת־יְהֹוָה אֱלֹהֶיךָ בְּכָל־לְבָבְךָ וּבְכָל־נַפְשְׁךָ לְמַעַן חַיֶּיךָ׃

7 *Hashem* your God will inflict all those curses upon the enemies and foes who persecuted you.

ז וְנָתַן יְהֹוָה אֱלֹהֶיךָ אֵת כָּל־הָאָלוֹת הָאֵלֶּה עַל־אֹיְבֶיךָ וְעַל־שֹׂנְאֶיךָ אֲשֶׁר רְדָפוּךָ׃

8 You, however, will again heed *Hashem* and obey all His commandments that I enjoin upon you this day.

ח וְאַתָּה תָשׁוּב וְשָׁמַעְתָּ בְּקוֹל יְהֹוָה וְעָשִׂיתָ אֶת־כָּל־מִצְוֺתָיו אֲשֶׁר אָנֹכִי מְצַוְּךָ הַיּוֹם׃

30:3 Then *Hashem* your God will restore your fortunes In his book *Meshech Chochma*, Rabbi Meir Simcha of Dvinsk (1843–1926) clarifies that this verse, foretelling the ingathering of the exiles, refers to two distinct groups of people. "God will restore your fortunes" alludes to the Jews who yearn to return to the Land of Israel. This group will be brought to *Eretz Yisrael* first. Subsequently, "He will bring you together again," and even those Jews who have become comfortable on foreign soil and lost their connection with Israel will be brought back. We are privileged to witness the first part of the verse being fulfilled, as thousands of Jews choose to make *aliyah* each year. In 2015, more than 31,000 Jewish immigrants left their homes worldwide and moved to the Land of Israel. Why do so many Jews choose to make *Eretz Yisrael* their home? According to Natan Sharansky, former Soviet "refusenik" and chairman of the Jewish Agency for Israel, "The high number of immigrants, particularly from western countries, attests to the drawing power of the Zionist idea. The fact that immigrants choose to come to Israel is a sign that Israel invests their lives with meaning that they cannot find elsewhere."

30:5 The land that your fathers possessed Customarily, this passage is read in synagogue every year prior to *Rosh Hashana*, the Jewish New Year and the first of the High Holidays. It describes the redemption of the Jewish people and their physical return to the Land of Israel. What is the connection between the return to the land and the High Holidays? One of the central themes of *Rosh Hashana* is the recognition of *Hashem*'s dominion over the whole world. Only at the time of the complete return of the People of Israel to *Eretz Yisrael* will all the world recognize *Hashem* as the King of the world. As it says "And *Hashem* shall be king over all the earth; in that day there shall be one *Hashem* with one name" (Zechariah 14:9).

Natan Sharansky (b. 1948)

Devarim/Deuteronomy 30
Nitzavim

דברים ל
נצבים

9 And *Hashem* your God will grant you abounding prosperity in all your undertakings, in the issue of your womb, the offspring of your cattle, and the produce of your soil. For *Hashem* will again delight in your well-being, as He did in that of your fathers,

ט וְהוֹתִירְךָ יְהֹוָה אֱלֹהֶיךָ בְּכֹל מַעֲשֵׂה יָדֶךָ בִּפְרִי בִטְנְךָ וּבִפְרִי בְהֶמְתְּךָ וּבִפְרִי אַדְמָתְךָ לְטֹבָה כִּי יָשׁוּב יְהֹוָה לָשׂוּשׂ עָלֶיךָ לְטוֹב כַּאֲשֶׁר־שָׂשׂ עַל־אֲבֹתֶיךָ:

10 since you will be heeding *Hashem* your God and keeping His commandments and laws that are recorded in this book of the Teaching – once you return to *Hashem* your God with all your heart and soul.

י כִּי תִשְׁמַע בְּקוֹל יְהֹוָה אֱלֹהֶיךָ לִשְׁמֹר מִצְוֹתָיו וְחֻקֹּתָיו הַכְּתוּבָה בְּסֵפֶר הַתּוֹרָה הַזֶּה כִּי תָשׁוּב אֶל־יְהֹוָה אֱלֹהֶיךָ בְּכָל־לְבָבְךָ וּבְכָל־נַפְשֶׁךָ:

11 Surely, this Instruction which I enjoin upon you this day is not too baffling for you, nor is it beyond reach.

יא כִּי הַמִּצְוָה הַזֹּאת אֲשֶׁר אָנֹכִי מְצַוְּךָ הַיּוֹם לֹא־נִפְלֵאת הִוא מִמְּךָ וְלֹא רְחֹקָה הִוא:

12 It is not in the heavens, that you should say, "Who among us can go up to the heavens and get it for us and impart it to us, that we may observe it?"

יב לֹא בַשָּׁמַיִם הִוא לֵאמֹר מִי יַעֲלֶה־לָּנוּ הַשָּׁמַיְמָה וְיִקָּחֶהָ לָּנוּ וְיַשְׁמִעֵנוּ אֹתָהּ וְנַעֲשֶׂנָּה:

13 Neither is it beyond the sea, that you should say, "Who among us can cross to the other side of the sea and get it for us and impart it to us, that we may observe it?"

יג וְלֹא־מֵעֵבֶר לַיָּם הִוא לֵאמֹר מִי יַעֲבָר־לָנוּ אֶל־עֵבֶר הַיָּם וְיִקָּחֶהָ לָּנוּ וְיַשְׁמִעֵנוּ אֹתָהּ וְנַעֲשֶׂנָּה:

14 No, the thing is very close to you, in your mouth and in your heart, to observe it.

יד כִּי־קָרוֹב אֵלֶיךָ הַדָּבָר מְאֹד בְּפִיךָ וּבִלְבָבְךָ לַעֲשֹׂתוֹ:

15 See, I set before you this day life and prosperity, death and adversity.

טו רְאֵה נָתַתִּי לְפָנֶיךָ הַיּוֹם אֶת־הַחַיִּים וְאֶת־הַטּוֹב וְאֶת־הַמָּוֶת וְאֶת־הָרָע:

16 For I command you this day, to love *Hashem* your God, to walk in His ways, and to keep His commandments, His laws, and His rules, that you may thrive and increase, and that *Hashem* your God may bless you in the land that you are about to enter and possess.

טז אֲשֶׁר אָנֹכִי מְצַוְּךָ הַיּוֹם לְאַהֲבָה אֶת־יְהֹוָה אֱלֹהֶיךָ לָלֶכֶת בִּדְרָכָיו וְלִשְׁמֹר מִצְוֹתָיו וְחֻקֹּתָיו וּמִשְׁפָּטָיו וְחָיִיתָ וְרָבִיתָ וּבֵרַכְךָ יְהֹוָה אֱלֹהֶיךָ בָּאָרֶץ אֲשֶׁר־אַתָּה בָא־שָׁמָּה לְרִשְׁתָּהּ:

a-SHER a-no-KHEE m'-tza-v'-KHA ha-YOM l'-a-ha-VAH et a-do-NAI e-lo-HE-kha la-LE-khet bid-ra-KHAV v'-lish-MOR mitz-vo-TAV v'khu-ko-TAV u-mish-pa-TAV v'-kha-YEE-ta v'-ra-VEE-ta u-vay-ra-kh'-KHA a-do-NAI e-lo-HE-kha ba-A-retz a-sher a-TAH va SHA-mah l'-rish-TAH

17 But if your heart turns away and you give no heed, and are lured into the worship and service of other gods,

יז וְאִם־יִפְנֶה לְבָבְךָ וְלֹא תִשְׁמָע וְנִדַּחְתָּ וְהִשְׁתַּחֲוִיתָ לֵאלֹהִים אֲחֵרִים וַעֲבַדְתָּם:

18 I declare to you this day that you shall certainly perish; you shall not long endure on the soil that you are crossing the *Yarden* to enter and possess.

יח הִגַּדְתִּי לָכֶם הַיּוֹם כִּי אָבֹד תֹּאבֵדוּן לֹא־תַאֲרִיכֻן יָמִים עַל־הָאֲדָמָה אֲשֶׁר אַתָּה עֹבֵר אֶת־הַיַּרְדֵּן לָבֹא שָׁמָּה לְרִשְׁתָּהּ:

19 I call heaven and earth to witness against you this day: I have put before you life and death, blessing and curse. Choose life – if you and your offspring would live

יט הַעִידֹתִי בָכֶם הַיּוֹם אֶת־הַשָּׁמַיִם וְאֶת־הָאָרֶץ הַחַיִּים וְהַמָּוֶת נָתַתִּי לְפָנֶיךָ הַבְּרָכָה וְהַקְּלָלָה וּבָחַרְתָּ בַּחַיִּים לְמַעַן תִּחְיֶה אַתָּה וְזַרְעֶךָ:

Devarim/Deuteronomy 31
Vayeilech

דברים לא
וילך

20 by loving *Hashem* your God, heeding His commands, and holding fast to Him. For thereby you shall have life and shall long endure upon the soil that *Hashem* swore to your ancestors, *Avraham*, *Yitzchak*, and *Yaakov*, to give to them.

לְאַהֲבָה אֶת־יְהוָה אֱלֹהֶיךָ לִשְׁמֹעַ בְּקֹלוֹ וּלְדָבְקָה־בוֹ כִּי הוּא חַיֶּיךָ וְאֹרֶךְ יָמֶיךָ לָשֶׁבֶת עַל־הָאֲדָמָה אֲשֶׁר נִשְׁבַּע יְהוָה לַאֲבֹתֶיךָ לְאַבְרָהָם לְיִצְחָק וּלְיַעֲקֹב לָתֵת לָהֶם׃

l'-a-ha-VAH et a-do-NAI e-lo-HE-kha lish-MO-a b'-ko-LO ul-dav-kah VO KEE HU kha-YE-kha v'-O-rekh ya-ME-kha la-SHE-vet al ha-a-da-MAH a-SHER nish-BA a-do-NAI la-a-vo-TE-kha l'-av-ra-HAM l'-yitz-KHAK ul-ya-a-KOV la-TAYT la-HEM

31

1 *Moshe* went and spoke these things to all *Yisrael*.

וַיֵּלֶךְ מֹשֶׁה וַיְדַבֵּר אֶת־הַדְּבָרִים הָאֵלֶּה אֶל־כָּל־יִשְׂרָאֵל׃ א

לא

2 He said to them: I am now one hundred and twenty years old, I can no longer be active. Moreover, *Hashem* has said to me, "You shall not go across yonder *Yarden*."

וַיֹּאמֶר אֲלֵהֶם בֶּן־מֵאָה וְעֶשְׂרִים שָׁנָה אָנֹכִי הַיּוֹם לֹא־אוּכַל עוֹד לָצֵאת וְלָבוֹא וַיהוָה אָמַר אֵלַי לֹא תַעֲבֹר אֶת־הַיַּרְדֵּן הַזֶּה׃ ב

3 *Hashem* your God Himself will cross over before you; and He Himself will wipe out those nations from your path and you shall dispossess them. – *Yehoshua* is the one who shall cross before you, as *Hashem* has spoken.

יְהוָה אֱלֹהֶיךָ הוּא עֹבֵר לְפָנֶיךָ הוּא־יַשְׁמִיד אֶת־הַגּוֹיִם הָאֵלֶּה מִלְּפָנֶיךָ וִירִשְׁתָּם יְהוֹשֻׁעַ הוּא עֹבֵר לְפָנֶיךָ כַּאֲשֶׁר דִּבֶּר יְהוָה׃ ג

4 *Hashem* will do to them as He did to Sihon and Og, kings of the Amorites, and to their countries, when He wiped them out.

וְעָשָׂה יְהוָה לָהֶם כַּאֲשֶׁר עָשָׂה לְסִיחוֹן וּלְעוֹג מַלְכֵי הָאֱמֹרִי וּלְאַרְצָם אֲשֶׁר הִשְׁמִיד אֹתָם׃ ד

5 *Hashem* will deliver them up to you, and you shall deal with them in full accordance with the Instruction that I have enjoined upon you.

וּנְתָנָם יְהוָה לִפְנֵיכֶם וַעֲשִׂיתֶם לָהֶם כְּכָל־הַמִּצְוָה אֲשֶׁר צִוִּיתִי אֶתְכֶם׃ ה

6 Be strong and resolute, be not in fear or in dread of them; for *Hashem* your God Himself marches with you: He will not fail you or forsake you.

חִזְקוּ וְאִמְצוּ אַל־תִּירְאוּ וְאַל־תַּעַרְצוּ מִפְּנֵיהֶם כִּי יְהוָה אֱלֹהֶיךָ הוּא הַהֹלֵךְ עִמָּךְ לֹא יַרְפְּךָ וְלֹא יַעַזְבֶךָּ׃ ו

khiz-KU v'-im-TZOO al tee-r'-U v'-al ta-ar-TZOO mi-p'-nay-HEM KEE a-do-NAI e-lo-HE-kha HU ha-ho-LAYKH i-MAKH LO yar-p'-KHA ve-LO ya-az-VE-ka

7 Then *Moshe* called *Yehoshua* and said to him in the sight of all *Yisrael*: "Be strong and resolute, for it is you who shall go with this people into the land that *Hashem* swore to their fathers to give them, and it is you who shall apportion it to them.

וַיִּקְרָא מֹשֶׁה לִיהוֹשֻׁעַ וַיֹּאמֶר אֵלָיו לְעֵינֵי כָל־יִשְׂרָאֵל חֲזַק וֶאֱמָץ כִּי אַתָּה תָּבוֹא אֶת־הָעָם הַזֶּה אֶל־הָאָרֶץ אֲשֶׁר נִשְׁבַּע יְהוָה לַאֲבֹתָם לָתֵת לָהֶם וְאַתָּה תַּנְחִילֶנָּה אוֹתָם׃ ז

va-yik-RA mo-SHEH lee-ho-SHU-ah va-YO-mer ay-LAV l'-ay-NAY khol yis-ra-AYL kha-ZAK ve-eh-MATZ KEE a-TAH ta-VO et ha-AM ha-ZEH el ha-A-retz a-SHER nish-BA a-do-NAI la-a-vo-TAM la-TAYT la-HEM ve-a-TAH tan-khee-LE-na o-TAM

31:7 Be strong and resolute In this verse, *Moshe* encourages *Yehoshua* to be "strong and resolute" in settling the Land of Israel. Rabbi Naftali Tzvi Yehuda Berlin, known as the *Netziv*, explains the double language used in this verse. *Yehoshua* will need to be "strong" to face the Canaanite enemy, and he will need

Devarim/Deuteronomy 31
Vayeilech

8 And *Hashem* Himself will go before you. He will be with you; He will not fail you or forsake you. Fear not and be not dismayed!"

9 *Moshe* wrote down this Teaching and gave it to the *Kohanim*, sons of *Levi*, who carried the *Aron* Brit *Hashem*, and to all the elders of *Yisrael*.

10 And *Moshe* instructed them as follows: Every seventh year, the year set for remission, at the festival of *Sukkot*,

11 when all *Yisrael* comes to appear before *Hashem* your God in the place that He will choose, you shall read this Teaching aloud in the presence of all *Yisrael*.

12 Gather the people – men, women, children, and the strangers in your communities – that they may hear and so learn to revere *Hashem* your God and to observe faithfully every word of this Teaching.

13 Their children, too, who have not had the experience, shall hear and learn to revere *Hashem* your God as long as they live in the land that you are about to cross the *Yarden* to possess.

14 *Hashem* said to *Moshe*: The time is drawing near for you to die. Call *Yehoshua* and present yourselves in the Tent of Meeting, that I may instruct him. *Moshe* and *Yehoshua* went and presented themselves in the Tent of Meeting.

15 *Hashem* appeared in the Tent, in a pillar of cloud, the pillar of cloud having come to rest at the entrance of the tent.

16 *Hashem* said to *Moshe*: You are soon to lie with your fathers. This people will thereupon go astray after the alien gods in their midst, in the land that they are about to enter; they will forsake Me and break My covenant that I made with them.

Rabbi Naftali Z.Y. Berlin (1816–1893)

to be "resolute" when dividing the land among the people. Though the battle for Israel might not be easy, it is well worth the fight. Three thousand years later, *Yehoshua's* spiritual heirs can be found among the ranks of the Israel Defense Forces, men and women who demonstrate strength and courage every day in serving their country and their nation.

Devarim/Deuteronomy 31
Vayeilech

17 Then My anger will flare up against them, and I will abandon them and hide My countenance from them. They shall be ready prey; and many evils and troubles shall befall them. And they shall say on that day, "Surely it is because our God is not in our midst that these evils have befallen us."

18 Yet I will keep My countenance hidden on that day, because of all the evil they have done in turning to other gods.

19 Therefore, write down this poem and teach it to the people of *Yisrael*; put it in their mouths, in order that this poem may be My witness against the people of *Yisrael*.

20 When I bring them into the land flowing with milk and honey that I promised on oath to their fathers, and they eat their fill and grow fat and turn to other gods and serve them, spurning Me and breaking My covenant,

21 and the many evils and troubles befall them – then this poem shall confront them as a witness, since it will never be lost from the mouth of their offspring. For I know what plans they are devising even now, before I bring them into the land that I promised on oath.

22 That day, *Moshe* wrote down this poem and taught it to the Israelites.

23 And He charged *Yehoshua* son of *Nun*: "Be strong and resolute: for you shall bring the Israelites into the land that I promised them on oath, and I will be with you."

24 When *Moshe* had put down in writing the words of this Teaching to the very end,

25 *Moshe* charged the *Leviim* who carried the *Aron* Brit Hashem, saying:

26 Take this book of Teaching and place it beside the *Aron* Brit Hashem your God, and let it remain there as a witness against you.

27 Well I know how defiant and stiffnecked you are: even now, while I am still alive in your midst, you have been defiant toward *Hashem*; how much more, then, when I am dead!

Devarim/Deuteronomy 32
Ha'azinu

דברים לב
האזינו

28 Gather to me all the elders of your tribes and your officials, that I may speak all these words to them and that I may call heaven and earth to witness against them.

כח הַקְהִילוּ אֵלַי אֶת־כָּל־זִקְנֵי שִׁבְטֵיכֶם וְשֹׁטְרֵיכֶם וַאֲדַבְּרָה בְאָזְנֵיהֶם אֵת הַדְּבָרִים הָאֵלֶּה וְאָעִידָה בָּם אֶת־הַשָּׁמַיִם וְאֶת־הָאָרֶץ:

29 For I know that, when I am dead, you will act wickedly and turn away from the path that I enjoined upon you, and that in time to come misfortune will befall you for having done evil in the sight of *Hashem* and vexed Him by your deeds.

כט כִּי יָדַעְתִּי אַחֲרֵי מוֹתִי כִּי־הַשְׁחֵת תַּשְׁחִתוּן וְסַרְתֶּם מִן־הַדֶּרֶךְ אֲשֶׁר צִוִּיתִי אֶתְכֶם וְקָרָאת אֶתְכֶם הָרָעָה בְּאַחֲרִית הַיָּמִים כִּי־תַעֲשׂוּ אֶת־הָרַע בְּעֵינֵי יְהוָה לְהַכְעִיסוֹ בְּמַעֲשֵׂה יְדֵיכֶם:

30 Then *Moshe* recited the words of this poem to the very end, in the hearing of the whole congregation of *Yisrael*:

ל וַיְדַבֵּר מֹשֶׁה בְּאָזְנֵי כָּל־קְהַל יִשְׂרָאֵל אֶת־דִּבְרֵי הַשִּׁירָה הַזֹּאת עַד תֻּמָּם:

32 1 Give ear, O heavens, let me speak; Let the earth hear the words I utter!

ha-a-ZEE-nu ha-sha-MA-yim va-a-da-BAY-ra v'-tish-MA ha-A-retz im-ray FEE

לב א הַאֲזִינוּ הַשָּׁמַיִם וַאֲדַבֵּרָה וְתִשְׁמַע הָאָרֶץ אִמְרֵי־פִי:

2 May my discourse come down as the rain, My speech distill as the dew, Like showers on young growth, Like droplets on the grass.

ב יַעֲרֹף כַּמָּטָר לִקְחִי תִּזַּל כַּטַּל אִמְרָתִי כִּשְׂעִירִם עֲלֵי־דֶשֶׁא וְכִרְבִיבִים עֲלֵי־עֵשֶׂב:

3 For the name of *Hashem* I proclaim; Give glory to our God!

ג כִּי שֵׁם יְהוָה אֶקְרָא הָבוּ גֹדֶל לֵאלֹהֵינוּ:

4 The Rock! – His deeds are perfect, Yea, all His ways are just; A faithful *Hashem*, never false, True and upright is He.

ד הַצּוּר תָּמִים פָּעֳלוֹ כִּי כָל־דְּרָכָיו מִשְׁפָּט אֵל אֱמוּנָה וְאֵין עָוֶל צַדִּיק וְיָשָׁר הוּא:

5 Children unworthy of Him – That crooked, perverse generation – Their baseness has played Him false.

ה שִׁחֵת לוֹ לֹא בָּנָיו מוּמָם דּוֹר עִקֵּשׁ וּפְתַלְתֹּל:

6 Do you thus requite *Hashem*, O dull and witless people? Is not He the Father who created you, Fashioned you and made you endure!

ו הֲ־לַיהוָה תִּגְמְלוּ־זֹאת עַם נָבָל וְלֹא חָכָם הֲלוֹא־הוּא אָבִיךָ קָּנֶךָ הוּא עָשְׂךָ וַיְכֹנְנֶךָ:

7 Remember the days of old, Consider the years of ages past; Ask your father, he will inform you, Your elders, they will tell you:

ז זְכֹר יְמוֹת עוֹלָם בִּינוּ שְׁנוֹת דֹּר־וָדֹר שְׁאַל אָבִיךָ וְיַגֵּדְךָ זְקֵנֶיךָ וְיֹאמְרוּ לָךְ:

"Heaven and Earth" in the Golan Heights

32:1 Give ear, O heavens *Devarim* 32 contains the song that *Moshe* teaches to the Israelites before his passing. In it, he reminds the people that if they sin in *Eretz Yisrael* they will be punished with exile. However, the song concludes with the promise that God will redeem His people and exact retribution from their enemies. *Moshe* starts his song by addressing heaven and earth, calling upon them as his witnesses for this covenant. Unlike humans who come and go, heaven and earth exist for eternity. Though it may take thousands of years, *Hashem* will keep His promise to redeem the entire Jewish people and return them to their land, and heaven and earth will be the loyal witnesses who see the process through to its complete fulfillment.

Devarim/Deuteronomy 32
Ha'azinu

דברים לב
האזינו

8 When the Most High gave nations their homes And set the divisions of man, He fixed the boundaries of peoples In relation to *Yisrael*'s numbers.

ח בְּהַנְחֵל עֶלְיוֹן גּוֹיִם בְּהַפְרִידוֹ בְּנֵי אָדָם יַצֵּב גְּבֻלֹת עַמִּים לְמִסְפַּר בְּנֵי יִשְׂרָאֵל:

9 For *Hashem*'s portion is His people, *Yaakov* His own allotment.

ט כִּי חֵלֶק יְהֹוָה עַמּוֹ יַעֲקֹב חֶבֶל נַחֲלָתוֹ:

10 He found him in a desert region, In an empty howling waste. He engirded him, watched over him, Guarded him as the pupil of His eye.

י יִמְצָאֵהוּ בְּאֶרֶץ מִדְבָּר וּבְתֹהוּ יְלֵל יְשִׁמֹן יְסֹבְבֶנְהוּ יְבוֹנְנֵהוּ יִצְּרֶנְהוּ כְּאִישׁוֹן עֵינוֹ:

11 Like an eagle who rouses his nestlings, Gliding down to his young, So did He spread His wings and take him, Bear him along on His pinions;

יא כְּנֶשֶׁר יָעִיר קִנּוֹ עַל־גּוֹזָלָיו יְרַחֵף יִפְרֹשׂ כְּנָפָיו יִקָּחֵהוּ יִשָּׂאֵהוּ עַל־אֶבְרָתוֹ:

12 *Hashem* alone did guide him, No alien god at His side.

יב יְהֹוָה בָּדָד יַנְחֶנּוּ וְאֵין עִמּוֹ אֵל נֵכָר:

13 He set him atop the highlands, To feast on the yield of the earth; He fed him honey from the crag, And oil from the flinty rock,

יג יַרְכִּבֵהוּ עַל־במותי [בָּמֳתֵי] אָרֶץ וַיֹּאכַל תְּנוּבֹת שָׂדָי וַיֵּנִקֵהוּ דְבַשׁ מִסֶּלַע וְשֶׁמֶן מֵחַלְמִישׁ צוּר:

14 Curd of kine and milk of flocks; With the best of lambs, And rams of Bashan, and he-goats; With the very finest wheat – And foaming grape-blood was your drink.

יד חֶמְאַת בָּקָר וַחֲלֵב צֹאן עִם־חֵלֶב כָּרִים וְאֵילִים בְּנֵי־בָשָׁן וְעַתּוּדִים עִם־חֵלֶב כִּלְיוֹת חִטָּה וְדַם־עֵנָב תִּשְׁתֶּה־חָמֶר:

15 So Jeshurun grew fat and kicked – You grew fat and gross and coarse – He forsook the God who made him And spurned the Rock of his support.

טו וַיִּשְׁמַן יְשֻׁרוּן וַיִּבְעָט שָׁמַנְתָּ עָבִיתָ כָּשִׂיתָ וַיִּטֹּשׁ אֱלוֹהַּ עָשָׂהוּ וַיְנַבֵּל צוּר יְשֻׁעָתוֹ:

16 They incensed Him with alien things, Vexed Him with abominations.

טז יַקְנִאֻהוּ בְּזָרִים בְּתוֹעֵבֹת יַכְעִיסֻהוּ:

17 They sacrificed to demons, no-gods, *Hashem*s they had never known, New ones, who came but lately, Who stirred not your fathers' fears.

יז יִזְבְּחוּ לַשֵּׁדִים לֹא אֱלֹהַּ אֱלֹהִים לֹא יְדָעוּם חֲדָשִׁים מִקָּרֹב בָּאוּ לֹא שְׂעָרוּם אֲבֹתֵיכֶם:

18 You neglected the Rock that begot you, Forgot the God who brought you forth.

יח צוּר יְלָדְךָ תֶּשִׁי וַתִּשְׁכַּח אֵל מְחֹלְלֶךָ:

19 *Hashem* saw and was vexed And spurned His sons and His daughters.

יט וַיַּרְא יְהֹוָה וַיִּנְאָץ מִכַּעַס בָּנָיו וּבְנֹתָיו:

20 He said: I will hide My countenance from them, And see how they fare in the end. For they are a treacherous breed, Children with no loyalty in them.

כ וַיֹּאמֶר אַסְתִּירָה פָנַי מֵהֶם אֶרְאֶה מָה אַחֲרִיתָם כִּי דוֹר תַּהְפֻּכֹת הֵמָּה בָּנִים לֹא־אֵמֻן בָּם:

21 They incensed Me with no-gods, Vexed Me with their futilities; I'll incense them with a no-folk, Vex them with a nation of fools.

כא הֵם קִנְאוּנִי בְלֹא־אֵל כִּעֲסוּנִי בְּהַבְלֵיהֶם וַאֲנִי אַקְנִיאֵם בְּלֹא־עָם בְּגוֹי נָבָל אַכְעִיסֵם:

22 For a fire has flared in My wrath And burned to the bottom of Sheol, Has consumed the earth and its increase, Eaten down to the base of the hills.

כב כִּי־אֵשׁ קָדְחָה בְאַפִּי וַתִּיקַד עַד־שְׁאוֹל תַּחְתִּית וַתֹּאכַל אֶרֶץ וִיבֻלָהּ וַתְּלַהֵט מוֹסְדֵי הָרִים:

Devarim/Deuteronomy 32
Ha'azinu

23 I will sweep misfortunes on them, Use up My arrows on them:

כג אַסְפֶּה עָלֵימוֹ רָעוֹת חִצַּי אֲכַלֶּה־בָּם:

24 Wasting famine, ravaging plague, Deadly pestilence, and fanged beasts Will I let loose against them, With venomous creepers in dust.

כד מְזֵי רָעָב וּלְחֻמֵי רֶשֶׁף וְקֶטֶב מְרִירִי וְשֶׁן־בְּהֵמֹת אֲשַׁלַּח־בָּם עִם־חֲמַת זֹחֲלֵי עָפָר:

25 The sword shall deal death without, As shall the terror within, To youth and maiden alike, The suckling as well as the aged.

כה מִחוּץ תְּשַׁכֶּל־חֶרֶב וּמֵחֲדָרִים אֵימָה גַּם־בָּחוּר גַּם־בְּתוּלָה יוֹנֵק עִם־אִישׁ שֵׂיבָה:

26 I might have reduced them to naught, Made their memory cease among men,

כו אָמַרְתִּי אַפְאֵיהֶם אַשְׁבִּיתָה מֵאֱנוֹשׁ זִכְרָם:

27 But for fear of the taunts of the foe, Their enemies who might misjudge And say "Our own hand has prevailed; None of this was wrought by *Hashem*!"

כז לוּלֵי כַּעַס אוֹיֵב אָגוּר פֶּן־יְנַכְּרוּ צָרֵימוֹ פֶּן־יֹאמְרוּ יָדֵינוּ רָמָה וְלֹא יְהֹוָה פָּעַל כָּל־זֹאת:

28 For they are a folk void of sense, Lacking in all discernment.

כח כִּי־גוֹי אֹבַד עֵצוֹת הֵמָּה וְאֵין בָּהֶם תְּבוּנָה:

29 ere they wise, they would think upon this, Gain insight into their future:

כט לוּ חָכְמוּ יַשְׂכִּילוּ זֹאת יָבִינוּ לְאַחֲרִיתָם:

30 "How could one have routed a thousand, Or two put ten thousand to flight, Unless their Rock had sold them, *Hashem* had given them up?"

ל אֵיכָה יִרְדֹּף אֶחָד אֶלֶף וּשְׁנַיִם יָנִיסוּ רְבָבָה אִם־לֹא כִּי־צוּרָם מְכָרָם וַיהֹוָה הִסְגִּירָם:

31 For their rock is not like our Rock, In our enemies' own estimation.

לא כִּי לֹא כְצוּרֵנוּ צוּרָם וְאֹיְבֵינוּ פְּלִילִים:

32 Ah! The vine for them is from Sodom, From the vineyards of Gomorrah; The grapes for them are poison, A bitter growth their clusters.

לב כִּי־מִגֶּפֶן סְדֹם גַּפְנָם וּמִשַּׁדְמֹת עֲמֹרָה עֲנָבֵמוֹ עִנְּבֵי־רוֹשׁ אַשְׁכְּלֹת מְרֹרֹת לָמוֹ:

33 Their wine is the venom of asps, The pitiless poison of vipers.

לג חֲמַת תַּנִּינִם יֵינָם וְרֹאשׁ פְּתָנִים אַכְזָר:

34 Lo, I have it all put away, Sealed up in My storehouses,

לד הֲלֹא־הוּא כָּמֻס עִמָּדִי חָתֻם בְּאוֹצְרֹתָי:

35 To be My vengeance and recompense, At the time that their foot falters. Yea, their day of disaster is near, And destiny rushes upon them.

לה לִי נָקָם וְשִׁלֵּם לְעֵת תָּמוּט רַגְלָם כִּי קָרוֹב יוֹם אֵידָם וְחָשׁ עֲתִדֹת לָמוֹ:

36 For *Hashem* will vindicate His people And take revenge for His servants, When He sees that their might is gone, And neither bond nor free is left.

לו כִּי־יָדִין יְהֹוָה עַמּוֹ וְעַל־עֲבָדָיו יִתְנֶחָם כִּי יִרְאֶה כִּי־אָזְלַת יָד וְאֶפֶס עָצוּר וְעָזוּב:

37 He will say: Where are their gods, The rock in whom they sought refuge,

לז וְאָמַר אֵי אֱלֹהֵימוֹ צוּר חָסָיוּ בוֹ:

38 Who ate the fat of their offerings And drank their libation wine? Let them rise up to your help, And let them be a shield unto you!

לח אֲשֶׁר חֵלֶב זְבָחֵימוֹ יֹאכֵלוּ יִשְׁתּוּ יֵין נְסִיכָם יָקוּמוּ וְיַעְזְרֻכֶם יְהִי עֲלֵיכֶם סִתְרָה:

Devarim/Deuteronomy 32
Ha'azinu

דברים לב
האזינו

39 See, then, that I, I am He; There is no god beside Me. I deal death and give life; I wounded and I will heal: None can deliver from My hand.

לט רְאוּ ׀ עַתָּה כִּי אֲנִי אֲנִי הוּא וְאֵין אֱלֹהִים עִמָּדִי אֲנִי אָמִית וַאֲחַיֶּה מָחַצְתִּי וַאֲנִי אֶרְפָּא וְאֵין מִיָּדִי מַצִּיל׃

40 Lo, I raise My hand to heaven And say: As I live forever,

מ כִּי־אֶשָּׂא אֶל־שָׁמַיִם יָדִי וְאָמַרְתִּי חַי אָנֹכִי לְעֹלָם׃

41 When I whet My flashing blade And My hand lays hold on judgment, Vengeance will I wreak on My foes, Will I deal to those who reject Me.

מא אִם־שַׁנּוֹתִי בְּרַק חַרְבִּי וְתֹאחֵז בְּמִשְׁפָּט יָדִי אָשִׁיב נָקָם לְצָרָי וְלִמְשַׂנְאַי אֲשַׁלֵּם׃

42 I will make My arrows drunk with blood – As My sword devours flesh – Blood of the slain and the captive From the long-haired enemy chiefs.

מב אַשְׁכִּיר חִצַּי מִדָּם וְחַרְבִּי תֹּאכַל בָּשָׂר מִדַּם חָלָל וְשִׁבְיָה מֵרֹאשׁ פַּרְעוֹת אוֹיֵב׃

43 O nations, acclaim His people! For He'll avenge the blood of His servants, Wreak vengeance on His foes, And cleanse the land of His people.

מג הַרְנִינוּ גוֹיִם עַמּוֹ כִּי דַם־עֲבָדָיו יִקּוֹם וְנָקָם יָשִׁיב לְצָרָיו וְכִפֶּר אַדְמָתוֹ עַמּוֹ׃

44 *Moshe* came, together with *Hoshea* son of *Nun*, and recited all the words of this poem in the hearing of the people.

מד וַיָּבֹא מֹשֶׁה וַיְדַבֵּר אֶת־כָּל־דִּבְרֵי הַשִּׁירָה־הַזֹּאת בְּאָזְנֵי הָעָם הוּא וְהוֹשֵׁעַ בִּן־נוּן׃

45 And when *Moshe* finished reciting all these words to all *Yisrael*,

מה וַיְכַל מֹשֶׁה לְדַבֵּר אֶת־כָּל־הַדְּבָרִים הָאֵלֶּה אֶל־כָּל־יִשְׂרָאֵל׃

46 he said to them: Take to heart all the words with which I have warned you this day. Enjoin them upon your children, that they may observe faithfully all the terms of this Teaching.

מו וַיֹּאמֶר אֲלֵהֶם שִׂימוּ לְבַבְכֶם לְכָל־הַדְּבָרִים אֲשֶׁר אָנֹכִי מֵעִיד בָּכֶם הַיּוֹם אֲשֶׁר תְּצַוֻּם אֶת־בְּנֵיכֶם לִשְׁמֹר לַעֲשׂוֹת אֶת־כָּל־דִּבְרֵי הַתּוֹרָה הַזֹּאת׃

47 For this is not a trifling thing for you: it is your very life; through it you shall long endure on the land that you are to possess upon crossing the *Yarden*.

מז כִּי לֹא־דָבָר רֵק הוּא מִכֶּם כִּי־הוּא חַיֵּיכֶם וּבַדָּבָר הַזֶּה תַּאֲרִיכוּ יָמִים עַל־הָאֲדָמָה אֲשֶׁר אַתֶּם עֹבְרִים אֶת־הַיַּרְדֵּן שָׁמָּה לְרִשְׁתָּהּ׃

KEE lo da-VAR RAYK HU mi-KEM kee HU kha-yay-KHEM u-va-da-VAR ha-ZEH ta-a-REE-khu ya-MEEM al ha-a-da-MAH a-SHER a-TEM o-v'-REEM et ha-yar-DAYN SHA-mah l'-rish-TAH

48 That very day *Hashem* spoke to *Moshe*:

מח וַיְדַבֵּר יְהֹוָה אֶל־מֹשֶׁה בְּעֶצֶם הַיּוֹם הַזֶּה לֵאמֹר׃

49 Ascend these heights of Abarim to Mount Nebo, which is in the land of Moab facing *Yericho*, and view the land of Canaan, which I am giving the Israelites as their holding.

מט עֲלֵה אֶל־הַר הָעֲבָרִים הַזֶּה הַר־נְבוֹ אֲשֶׁר בְּאֶרֶץ מוֹאָב אֲשֶׁר עַל־פְּנֵי יְרֵחוֹ וּרְאֵה אֶת־אֶרֶץ כְּנַעַן אֲשֶׁר אֲנִי נֹתֵן לִבְנֵי יִשְׂרָאֵל לַאֲחֻזָּה׃

50 You shall die on the mountain that you are about to ascend, and shall be gathered to your kin, as your brother *Aharon* died on Mount Hor and was gathered to his kin;

נ וּמֻת בָּהָר אֲשֶׁר אַתָּה עֹלֶה שָׁמָּה וְהֵאָסֵף אֶל־עַמֶּיךָ כַּאֲשֶׁר־מֵת אַהֲרֹן אָחִיךָ בְּהֹר הָהָר וַיֵּאָסֶף אֶל־עַמָּיו׃

Devarim/Deuteronomy 33
Vezot Haberachah

דברים לג
וזאת הברכה

51 for you both broke faith with Me among *B'nei Yisrael*, at the waters of Meribath-kadesh in the wilderness of Zin, by failing to uphold My sanctity among *B'nei Yisrael*.

נא עַל אֲשֶׁר מְעַלְתֶּם בִּי בְּתוֹךְ בְּנֵי יִשְׂרָאֵל בְּמֵי־מְרִיבַת קָדֵשׁ מִדְבַּר־צִן עַל אֲשֶׁר לֹא־קִדַּשְׁתֶּם אוֹתִי בְּתוֹךְ בְּנֵי יִשְׂרָאֵל:

52 You may view the land from a distance, but you shall not enter it – the land that I am giving to *B'nei Yisrael*.

נב כִּי מִנֶּגֶד תִּרְאֶה אֶת־הָאָרֶץ וְשָׁמָּה לֹא תָבוֹא אֶל־הָאָרֶץ אֲשֶׁר־אֲנִי נֹתֵן לִבְנֵי יִשְׂרָאֵל:

33 1 This is the blessing with which *Moshe*, the man of *Hashem*, bade the Israelites farewell before he died.

לג א וְזֹאת הַבְּרָכָה אֲשֶׁר בֵּרַךְ מֹשֶׁה אִישׁ הָאֱלֹהִים אֶת־בְּנֵי יִשְׂרָאֵל לִפְנֵי מוֹתוֹ:

2 He said: *Hashem* came from Sinai; He shone upon them from Seir; He appeared from Mount Paran, And approached from Ribeboth-kodesh, Lightning flashing at them from His right.

ב וַיֹּאמַר יְהֹוָה מִסִּינַי בָּא וְזָרַח מִשֵּׂעִיר לָמוֹ הוֹפִיעַ מֵהַר פָּארָן וְאָתָה מֵרִבְבֹת קֹדֶשׁ מִימִינוֹ אֵשְׁדָּת [אֵשׁ] [דָּת] לָמוֹ:

3 Lover, indeed, of the people, Their hallowed are all in Your hand. They followed in Your steps, Accepting Your pronouncements,

ג אַף חֹבֵב עַמִּים כָּל־קְדֹשָׁיו בְּיָדֶךָ וְהֵם תֻּכּוּ לְרַגְלֶךָ יִשָּׂא מִדַּבְּרֹתֶיךָ:

4 When *Moshe* charged us with the Teaching As the heritage of the congregation of *Yaakov*.

ד תּוֹרָה צִוָּה־לָנוּ מֹשֶׁה מוֹרָשָׁה קְהִלַּת יַעֲקֹב:

5 Then He became King in Jeshurun, When the heads of the people assembled, The tribes of *Yisrael* together.

ה וַיְהִי בִישֻׁרוּן מֶלֶךְ בְּהִתְאַסֵּף רָאשֵׁי עָם יַחַד שִׁבְטֵי יִשְׂרָאֵל:

6 May *Reuven* live and not die, Though few be his numbers.

ו יְחִי רְאוּבֵן וְאַל־יָמֹת וִיהִי מְתָיו מִסְפָּר:

7 And this he said of *Yehuda*: Hear, *Hashem* the voice of *Yehuda* And restore him to his people. Though his own hands strive for him, Help him against his foes.

ז וְזֹאת לִיהוּדָה וַיֹּאמַר שְׁמַע יְהֹוָה קוֹל יְהוּדָה וְאֶל־עַמּוֹ תְּבִיאֶנּוּ יָדָיו רָב לוֹ וְעֵזֶר מִצָּרָיו תִּהְיֶה:

8 And of *Levi* he said: Let Your Thummim and Urim Be with Your faithful one, Whom You tested at Massah, Challenged at the waters of Meribah;

ח וּלְלֵוִי אָמַר תֻּמֶּיךָ וְאוּרֶיךָ לְאִישׁ חֲסִידֶךָ אֲשֶׁר נִסִּיתוֹ בְּמַסָּה תְּרִיבֵהוּ עַל־מֵי מְרִיבָה:

9 Who said of his father and mother, "I consider them not." His brothers he disregarded, Ignored his own children. Your precepts alone they observed, And kept Your covenant.

ט הָאֹמֵר לְאָבִיו וּלְאִמּוֹ לֹא רְאִיתִיו וְאֶת־אֶחָיו לֹא הִכִּיר וְאֶת־בָּנוֹ [בָּנָיו] לֹא יָדָע כִּי שָׁמְרוּ אִמְרָתֶךָ וּבְרִיתְךָ יִנְצֹרוּ:

10 They shall teach Your laws to *Yaakov* And Your instructions to *Yisrael*. They shall offer You incense to savor And whole-offerings on Your *Mizbayach*.

י יוֹרוּ מִשְׁפָּטֶיךָ לְיַעֲקֹב וְתוֹרָתְךָ לְיִשְׂרָאֵל יָשִׂימוּ קְטוֹרָה בְּאַפֶּךָ וְכָלִיל עַל־מִזְבְּחֶךָ:

11 Bless, *Hashem*, his substance, And favor his undertakings. Smite the loins of his foes; Let his enemies rise no more.

יא בָּרֵךְ יְהֹוָה חֵילוֹ וּפֹעַל יָדָיו תִּרְצֶה מְחַץ מָתְנַיִם קָמָיו וּמְשַׂנְאָיו מִן־יְקוּמוּן:

523

Devarim/Deuteronomy 33
Vezot Haberachah

דברים לג
וזאת הברכה

12 Of *Binyamin* he said: Beloved of *Hashem*, He rests securely beside Him; Ever does He protect him, As he rests between His shoulders.

יב לְבִנְיָמִן אָמַר יְדִיד יְהֹוָה יִשְׁכֹּן לָבֶטַח עָלָיו חֹפֵף עָלָיו כָּל־הַיּוֹם וּבֵין כְּתֵיפָיו שָׁכֵן׃

l'-vin-ya-MIN a-MAR y'-DEED a-do-NAI yish-KON la-VE-takh a-LAV kho-FAYF a-LAV kol ha-YOM u-VAYN k'-tay-FAV sha-KHAYN

13 And of *Yosef* he said: Blessed of *Hashem* be his land With the bounty of dew from heaven, And of the deep that couches below;

יג וּלְיוֹסֵף אָמַר מְבֹרֶכֶת יְהֹוָה אַרְצוֹ מִמֶּגֶד שָׁמַיִם מִטָּל וּמִתְּהוֹם רֹבֶצֶת תָּחַת׃

14 With the bounteous yield of the sun, And the bounteous crop of the moons;

יד וּמִמֶּגֶד תְּבוּאֹת שָׁמֶשׁ וּמִמֶּגֶד גֶּרֶשׁ יְרָחִים׃

15 With the best from the ancient mountains, And the bounty of hills immemorial;

טו וּמֵרֹאשׁ הַרְרֵי־קֶדֶם וּמִמֶּגֶד גִּבְעוֹת עוֹלָם׃

16 With the bounty of earth and its fullness, And the favor of the Presence in the Bush. May these rest on the head of *Yosef*, On the crown of the elect of his brothers.

טז וּמִמֶּגֶד אֶרֶץ וּמְלֹאָהּ וּרְצוֹן שֹׁכְנִי סְנֶה תָּבוֹאתָה לְרֹאשׁ יוֹסֵף וּלְקָדְקֹד נְזִיר אֶחָיו׃

17 Like a firstling bull in his majesty, He has horns like the horns of the wild-ox; With them he gores the peoples, The ends of the earth one and all. These are the myriads of *Efraim*, Those are the thousands of *Menashe*.

יז בְּכוֹר שׁוֹרוֹ הָדָר לוֹ וְקַרְנֵי רְאֵם קַרְנָיו בָּהֶם עַמִּים יְנַגַּח יַחְדָּו אַפְסֵי־אָרֶץ וְהֵם רִבְבוֹת אֶפְרַיִם וְהֵם אַלְפֵי מְנַשֶּׁה׃

18 And of *Zevulun* he said: Rejoice, O *Zevulun*, on your journeys, And *Yissachar*, in your tents.

יח וְלִזְבוּלֻן אָמַר שְׂמַח זְבוּלֻן בְּצֵאתֶךָ וְיִשָּׂשכָר בְּאֹהָלֶיךָ׃

19 They invite their kin to the mountain, Where they offer sacrifices of success. For they draw from the riches of the sea And the hidden hoards of the sand.

יט עַמִּים הַר־יִקְרָאוּ שָׁם יִזְבְּחוּ זִבְחֵי־צֶדֶק כִּי שֶׁפַע יַמִּים יִינָקוּ וּשְׂפוּנֵי טְמוּנֵי חוֹל׃

20 And of *Gad* he said: Blessed be He who enlarges *Gad*! Poised is he like a lion To tear off arm and scalp.

כ וּלְגָד אָמַר בָּרוּךְ מַרְחִיב גָּד כְּלָבִיא שָׁכֵן וְטָרַף זְרוֹעַ אַף־קָדְקֹד׃

21 He chose for himself the best, For there is the portion of the revered chieftain, Where the heads of the people come. He executed *Hashem*'s judgments And His decisions for *Yisrael*.

כא וַיַּרְא רֵאשִׁית לוֹ כִּי־שָׁם חֶלְקַת מְחֹקֵק סָפוּן וַיֵּתֵא רָאשֵׁי עָם צִדְקַת יְהֹוָה עָשָׂה וּמִשְׁפָּטָיו עִם־יִשְׂרָאֵל׃

33:12 As he rests between His shoulders Immediately before his death, *Moshe* blesses each of the tribes with a blessing corresponding to its unique qualities. These words make reference to the fact that the *Beit Hamikdash* was built in the part of the city of *Yerushalayim* which belongs to the tribe of *Binyamin*. One reason offered to explain why *Binyamin* merited the *Beit Hamikdash* in his portion is that while all the other sons of *Yaakov* were born outside Israel, the youngest son, *Binyamin*, was born in the land (see Genesis 35:18). Therefore, he merited the special privilege of having the Temple in his territory.

Model of the Second Beit Hamikdash

Devarim/Deuteronomy 34
Vezot Haberachah

דברים לד
וזאת הברכה

22 And of *Dan* he said: *Dan* is a lion's whelp That leaps forth from Bashan.

כב וּלְדָ֣ן אָמַ֔ר דָּ֖ן גּ֣וּר אַרְיֵ֑ה יְזַנֵּ֖ק מִן־הַבָּשָֽׁן׃

23 And of *Naftali* he said: O *Naftali*, sated with favor And full of *Hashem*'s blessing, Take possession on the west and south.

כג וּלְנַפְתָּלִ֣י אָמַ֔ר נַפְתָּלִי֙ שְׂבַ֣ע רָצ֔וֹן וּמָלֵ֖א בִּרְכַּ֣ת יְהוָ֑ה יָ֥ם וְדָר֖וֹם יְרָֽשָׁה׃

24 And of *Asher* he said: Most blessed of sons be *Asher*; May he be the favorite of his brothers, May he dip his foot in oil.

כד וּלְאָשֵׁ֣ר אָמַ֔ר בָּר֥וּךְ מִבָּנִ֖ים אָשֵׁ֑ר יְהִ֤י רְצוּי֙ אֶחָ֔יו וְטֹבֵ֥ל בַּשֶּׁ֖מֶן רַגְלֽוֹ׃

25 May your doorbolts be iron and copper, And your security last all your days.

כה בַּרְזֶ֥ל וּנְחֹ֖שֶׁת מִנְעָלֶ֑יךָ וּכְיָמֶ֖יךָ דָּבְאֶֽךָ׃

26 O Jeshurun, there is none like *Hashem*, Riding through the heavens to help you, Through the skies in His majesty.

כו אֵ֥ין כָּאֵ֖ל יְשֻׁר֑וּן רֹכֵ֤ב שָׁמַ֙יִם֙ בְעֶזְרֶ֔ךָ וּבְגַאֲוָת֖וֹ שְׁחָקִֽים׃

27 The ancient *Hashem* is a refuge, A support are the arms everlasting. He drove out the enemy before you By His command: Destroy!

כז מְעֹנָה֙ אֱלֹ֣הֵי קֶ֔דֶם וּמִתַּ֖חַת זְרֹעֹ֣ת עוֹלָ֑ם וַיְגָ֧רֶשׁ מִפָּנֶ֛יךָ אוֹיֵ֖ב וַיֹּ֥אמֶר הַשְׁמֵֽד׃

28 Thus *Yisrael* dwells in safety, Untroubled is *Yaakov*'s abode, In a land of grain and wine, Under heavens dripping dew.

כח וַיִּשְׁכֹּן֩ יִשְׂרָאֵ֨ל בֶּ֤טַח בָּדָד֙ עֵ֣ין יַעֲקֹ֔ב אֶל־אֶ֖רֶץ דָּגָ֣ן וְתִיר֑וֹשׁ אַף־שָׁמָ֖יו יַעַ֥רְפוּ טָֽל׃

29 O happy *Yisrael*! Who is like you, A people delivered by *Hashem*, Your protecting Shield, your Sword triumphant! Your enemies shall come cringing before you, And you shall tread on their backs.

כט אַשְׁרֶ֨יךָ יִשְׂרָאֵ֜ל מִ֣י כָמ֗וֹךָ עַ֚ם נוֹשַׁ֣ע בַּיהוָ֔ה מָגֵ֣ן עֶזְרֶ֔ךָ וַאֲשֶׁר־חֶ֖רֶב גַּאֲוָתֶ֑ךָ וְיִכָּחֲשׁ֤וּ אֹיְבֶ֙יךָ֙ לָ֔ךְ וְאַתָּ֖ה עַל־בָּמוֹתֵ֥ימוֹ תִדְרֹֽךְ׃

34

1 *Moshe* went up from the steppes of Moab to Mount Nebo, to the summit of Pisgah, opposite *Yericho*, and *Hashem* showed him the whole land: *Gilad* as far as *Dan*;

לד א וַיַּ֨עַל מֹשֶׁ֜ה מֵעַֽרְבֹ֤ת מוֹאָב֙ אֶל־הַ֣ר נְב֔וֹ רֹ֚אשׁ הַפִּסְגָּ֔ה אֲשֶׁ֖ר עַל־פְּנֵ֣י יְרֵח֑וֹ וַיַּרְאֵ֨הוּ יְהוָ֧ה אֶת־כָּל־הָאָ֛רֶץ אֶת־הַגִּלְעָ֖ד עַד־דָּֽן׃

> va-YA-al mo-SHEH may-ar-VOT mo-AV el HAR n'-VO ROSH ha-pis-GAH a-SHER al p'-NAY y'-ray-KHO va-yar-AY-hu a-do-NAI et kol ha-A-retz et ha-gil-AD ad DAN

2 all *Naftali*; the land of *Efraim* and *Menashe*; the whole land of *Yehuda* as far as the Western Sea;

ב וְאֵת֙ כָּל־נַפְתָּלִ֔י וְאֶת־אֶ֥רֶץ אֶפְרַ֖יִם וּמְנַשֶּׁ֑ה וְאֵת֙ כָּל־אֶ֣רֶץ יְהוּדָ֔ה עַ֖ד הַיָּ֥ם הָאַחֲרֽוֹן׃

34:1 And *Hashem* showed him the whole land As the leader of the Jewish people, *Moshe* involved himself with all matters of concern to the nation. Yet, his final activity in this world was devoted to one area alone: *Moshe* ascends the mountain of *Nevo* and gazes upon the Land of Israel. The Talmud (*Sotah* 14a) asks: Why did *Moshe* desire to enter *Eretz Yisrael*? Was it to enjoy its fruits or to satiate himself of its bounty? The Talmud answers that *Moshe*'s desire was a spiritual one; he craved an opportunity to keep the commandments unique to the Land of Israel. While he was not permitted to enter, being allowed to view the land was a comfort to *Moshe*, as he understood that even just seeing it propels a person to new spiritual heights. Similarly, there are people today who access high balconies in the Old City of *Yerushalayim* in order to view *Har Habayit*, the Temple Mount. They appreciate the spiritual benefit they can get just from seeing this holy sight.

Devarim/Deuteronomy 34
Vezot Haberachah

דברים לד
וזאת הברכה

3 the *Negev*; and the Plain – the Valley of *Yericho*, the city of palm trees – as far as Zoar.

ג וְאֶת־הַנֶּגֶב וְאֶת־הַכִּכָּר בִּקְעַת יְרֵחוֹ עִיר הַתְּמָרִים עַד־צֹעַר׃

4 And *Hashem* said to him, "This is the land of which I swore to *Avraham*, *Yitzchak*, and *Yaakov*, 'I will assign it to your offspring.' I have let you see it with your own eyes, but you shall not cross there."

ד וַיֹּאמֶר יְהֹוָה אֵלָיו זֹאת הָאָרֶץ אֲשֶׁר נִשְׁבַּעְתִּי לְאַבְרָהָם לְיִצְחָק וּלְיַעֲקֹב לֵאמֹר לְזַרְעֲךָ אֶתְּנֶנָּה הֶרְאִיתִיךָ בְעֵינֶיךָ וְשָׁמָּה לֹא תַעֲבֹר׃

5 So *Moshe* the servant of *Hashem* died there, in the land of Moab, at the command of *Hashem*.

ה וַיָּמָת שָׁם מֹשֶׁה עֶבֶד־יְהֹוָה בְּאֶרֶץ מוֹאָב עַל־פִּי יְהֹוָה׃

6 He buried him in the valley in the land of Moab, near Beth-peor; and no one knows his burial place to this day.

ו וַיִּקְבֹּר אֹתוֹ בַגַּי בְּאֶרֶץ מוֹאָב מוּל בֵּית פְּעוֹר וְלֹא־יָדַע אִישׁ אֶת־קְבֻרָתוֹ עַד הַיּוֹם הַזֶּה׃

7 *Moshe* was a hundred and twenty years old when he died; his eyes were undimmed and his vigor unabated.

ז וּמֹשֶׁה בֶּן־מֵאָה וְעֶשְׂרִים שָׁנָה בְּמֹתוֹ לֹא־כָהֲתָה עֵינוֹ וְלֹא־נָס לֵחֹה׃

8 And the Israelites bewailed *Moshe* in the steppes of Moab for thirty days. The period of wailing and mourning for *Moshe* came to an end.

ח וַיִּבְכּוּ בְנֵי יִשְׂרָאֵל אֶת־מֹשֶׁה בְּעַרְבֹת מוֹאָב שְׁלֹשִׁים יוֹם וַיִּתְּמוּ יְמֵי בְכִי אֵבֶל מֹשֶׁה׃

9 Now *Yehoshua* son of *Nun* was filled with the spirit of wisdom because *Moshe* had laid his hands upon him; and the Israelites heeded him, doing as *Hashem* had commanded *Moshe*.

ט וִיהוֹשֻׁעַ בִּן־נוּן מָלֵא רוּחַ חָכְמָה כִּי־סָמַךְ מֹשֶׁה אֶת־יָדָיו עָלָיו וַיִּשְׁמְעוּ אֵלָיו בְּנֵי־יִשְׂרָאֵל וַיַּעֲשׂוּ כַּאֲשֶׁר צִוָּה יְהֹוָה אֶת־מֹשֶׁה׃

10 Never again did there arise in *Yisrael* a *navi* like *Moshe* – whom *Hashem* singled out, face to face,

י וְלֹא־קָם נָבִיא עוֹד בְּיִשְׂרָאֵל כְּמֹשֶׁה אֲשֶׁר יְדָעוֹ יְהֹוָה פָּנִים אֶל־פָּנִים׃

11 for the various signs and portents that *Hashem* sent him to display in the land of Egypt, against Pharaoh and all his courtiers and his whole country,

יא לְכָל־הָאֹתוֹת וְהַמּוֹפְתִים אֲשֶׁר שְׁלָחוֹ יְהֹוָה לַעֲשׂוֹת בְּאֶרֶץ מִצְרָיִם לְפַרְעֹה וּלְכָל־עֲבָדָיו וּלְכָל־אַרְצוֹ׃

12 and for all the great might and awesome power that *Moshe* displayed before all *Yisrael*.

יב וּלְכֹל הַיָּד הַחֲזָקָה וּלְכֹל הַמּוֹרָא הַגָּדוֹל אֲשֶׁר עָשָׂה מֹשֶׁה לְעֵינֵי כָּל־יִשְׂרָאֵל׃

Sefer Yehoshua
The Book of Joshua

Introduction and commentary by Rabbi Shmuel Jablon

Sefer Yehoshua (Joshua) is the first book of the Prophets. Though the People of Israel had many prophets, almost none of their writings are recorded. The rabbis of the Talmud (*Megillah* 14a) teach that only prophetic messages that would be relevant for later generations were written down and included in the *Tanakh*, the Hebrew Bible.

In his commentary to *Sefer Yehoshua*, Rabbi Shlomo Aviner notes that this does not mean that every prophecy in *Tanakh* is necessary in every period. Only the five books of the *Torah*, given by God Himself, have this eternal quality. The other prophecies written in the Bible, while relevant at some point in the future, are not relevant at all times.

Which future generation would need the messages of the book of *Yehoshua*? Rabbi Aviner answers that it is certainly our generation, which has witnessed the creation, building and flowering of the State of Israel, the ingathering of the exiles and the miraculous military victories. We are the ones who must derive inspiration and instruction from *Sefer Yehoshua*.

Sefer Yehoshua contains a number of central themes:

1. We are reminded that *Yehoshua* was *Moshe*'s loyal student, and that his leadership is a direct continuation of that of *Moshe*. The People of Israel are repeatedly instructed to remain loyal to the *Torah* of *Moshe*, and we are constantly reminded that *Yehoshua*'s actions and the nation's victories are due to the promises of the past.

2. We are taught that the entire Land of Israel belongs to the Children of Israel. We learn of the borders of the land, and of many key cities.

3. We learn that unlike the life the Israelites led in the desert, in the Land of Israel *Hashem* will not do all the work Himself. Whereas in the desert, *Hashem* fought their battles and sent them manna from heaven, the Children of Israel will have to engage in battles to take possession of the Promised Land and work the land in order to have food to eat.

Human actions, in addition to divine miracles, are necessary to survive and to thrive in *Eretz Yisrael*.

4. We are taught that the proper place for the Children of Israel is *Eretz Yisrael* under the reign of the Kingdom of Israel. Each tribe has its own inheritance, with the land divided according to divine lots, and they must all see themselves as sections of one great nation.

Each of these themes resonates with any contemporary person who feels a connection to the State of Israel. After more than two thousand years of bitter exile, the Jewish People have returned home and can serve *Hashem* as a free people in its own land. This dream of generations of Jewish history has now become a reality. *Sefer Yehoshua* surely speaks to our generation.

Map of 12 Tribal Allotments

This is a map of of the twelve tribal allotments in the Land of Israel, based of *Sefer Yehoshua* (chapters 14–19).

Yehoshua/Joshua
Chapter 1

יהושע
פרק א

1 ¹ After the death of *Moshe* the servant of *Hashem*, *Hashem* said to *Yehoshua* son of *Nun*, *Moshe*'s attendant:

א וַיְהִי אַחֲרֵי מוֹת מֹשֶׁה עֶבֶד יְהֹוָה וַיֹּאמֶר יְהֹוָה אֶל־יְהוֹשֻׁעַ בִּן־נוּן מְשָׁרֵת מֹשֶׁה לֵאמֹר:

vai-HEE a-kha-RAY MOT mo-SHEH E-ved a-do-NAI va-YO-mer a-do-NAI el y'-ho-SHU-a bin NUN m'-sha-RAYT mo-SHEH lay-MOR

² "My servant *Moshe* is dead. Prepare to cross the *Yarden*, together with all this people, into the land that I am giving to the Israelites.

ב מֹשֶׁה עַבְדִּי מֵת וְעַתָּה קוּם עֲבֹר אֶת־הַיַּרְדֵּן הַזֶּה אַתָּה וְכָל־הָעָם הַזֶּה אֶל־הָאָרֶץ אֲשֶׁר אָנֹכִי נֹתֵן לָהֶם לִבְנֵי יִשְׂרָאֵל:

mo-SHEH av-DEE MAYT v'-a-TAH KUM a-VOR et ha-yar-DAYN ha-ZEH a-TAH v'-khol ha-AM ha-ZEH el ha-A-retz a-SHER a-no-KHEE no-TAYN la-HEM liv-NAY yis-ra-AYL

³ Every spot on which your foot treads I give to you, as I promised *Moshe*.

ג כָּל־מָקוֹם אֲשֶׁר תִּדְרֹךְ כַּף־רַגְלְכֶם בּוֹ לָכֶם נְתַתִּיו כַּאֲשֶׁר דִּבַּרְתִּי אֶל־מֹשֶׁה:

⁴ Your territory shall extend from the wilderness and the Lebanon to the Great River, the River Euphrates [on the east] – the whole Hittite country – and up to the Mediterranean Sea on the west.

ד מֵהַמִּדְבָּר וְהַלְּבָנוֹן הַזֶּה וְעַד־הַנָּהָר הַגָּדוֹל נְהַר־פְּרָת כֹּל אֶרֶץ הַחִתִּים וְעַד־הַיָּם הַגָּדוֹל מְבוֹא הַשָּׁמֶשׁ יִהְיֶה גְּבוּלְכֶם:

⁵ No one shall be able to resist you as long as you live. As I was with *Moshe*, so I will be with you; I will not fail you or forsake you.

ה לֹא־יִתְיַצֵּב אִישׁ לְפָנֶיךָ כֹּל יְמֵי חַיֶּיךָ כַּאֲשֶׁר הָיִיתִי עִם־מֹשֶׁה אֶהְיֶה עִמָּךְ לֹא אַרְפְּךָ וְלֹא אֶעֶזְבֶךָּ:

⁶ "Be strong and resolute, for you shall apportion to this people the land that I swore to their fathers to assign to them.

ו חֲזַק וֶאֱמָץ כִּי אַתָּה תַּנְחִיל אֶת־הָעָם הַזֶּה אֶת־הָאָרֶץ אֲשֶׁר־נִשְׁבַּעְתִּי לַאֲבוֹתָם לָתֵת לָהֶם:

⁷ But you must be very strong and resolute to observe faithfully all the Teaching that My servant *Moshe* enjoined upon you. Do not deviate from it to the right or to the left, that you may be successful wherever you go.

ז רַק חֲזַק וֶאֱמַץ מְאֹד לִשְׁמֹר לַעֲשׂוֹת כְּכָל־הַתּוֹרָה אֲשֶׁר צִוְּךָ מֹשֶׁה עַבְדִּי אַל־תָּסוּר מִמֶּנּוּ יָמִין וּשְׂמֹאול לְמַעַן תַּשְׂכִּיל בְּכֹל אֲשֶׁר תֵּלֵךְ:

Jordan River

1:1 Hashem said to Yehoshua son of Nun The Talmud (*Nedarim* 22b) teaches that *Sefer Yehoshua* has a unique quality which sets it apart from all of the other books of the Prophets. Books like *Sefer Yeshayahu*, *Sefer Yirmiyahu*, *Sefer Melachim* and *Sefer Shoftim* were necessary only to rebuke the people as a response to their behavior. Had they not sinned, they would have needed only the five books of the *Torah* and *Sefer Yehoshua*, for it describes the borders and boundaries of Israel. May our study of *Sefer Yehoshua* increase our love for, and appreciation of, the Land of Israel.

1:2 Prepare to cross the Yarden *Hashem* instructs *Yehoshua*, the new leader of the Nation of Israel, to rise up and lead them across the *Yarden*, and to inhabit the land that *Hashem* is giving them. Taking possession of *Eretz Yisrael* will require human actions, which will be supported by God's miracles. At the very beginning of *Yehoshua*'s leadership, the nation is reminded that the entire *Eretz Yisrael* belongs to the Jewish people, and that they must do their part to take possession of this special gift from *Hashem*.

Yehoshua/Joshua
Chapter 1

יהושע
פרק א

8 Let not this Book of the Teaching cease from your lips, but recite it day and night, so that you may observe faithfully all that is written in it. Only then will you prosper in your undertakings and only then will you be successful.

ח לֹא־יָמוּשׁ סֵפֶר הַתּוֹרָה הַזֶּה מִפִּיךָ וְהָגִיתָ בּוֹ יוֹמָם וָלַיְלָה לְמַעַן תִּשְׁמֹר לַעֲשׂוֹת כְּכָל־הַכָּתוּב בּוֹ כִּי־אָז תַּצְלִיחַ אֶת־דְּרָכֶךָ וְאָז תַּשְׂכִּיל׃

9 "I charge you: Be strong and resolute; do not be terrified or dismayed, for *Hashem* your God is with you wherever you go."

ט הֲלוֹא צִוִּיתִיךָ חֲזַק וֶאֱמָץ אַל־תַּעֲרֹץ וְאַל־תֵּחָת כִּי עִמְּךָ יְהֹוָה אֱלֹהֶיךָ בְּכֹל אֲשֶׁר תֵּלֵךְ׃

10 *Yehoshua* thereupon gave orders to the officials of the people:

י וַיְצַו יְהוֹשֻׁעַ אֶת־שֹׁטְרֵי הָעָם לֵאמֹר׃

11 "Go through the camp and charge the people thus: Get provisions ready, for in three days' time you are to cross the *Yarden*, in order to enter and possess the land that *Hashem* your God is giving you as a possession."

יא עִבְרוּ בְּקֶרֶב הַמַּחֲנֶה וְצַוּוּ אֶת־הָעָם לֵאמֹר הָכִינוּ לָכֶם צֵידָה כִּי בְּעוֹד שְׁלֹשֶׁת יָמִים אַתֶּם עֹבְרִים אֶת־הַיַּרְדֵּן הַזֶּה לָבוֹא לָרֶשֶׁת אֶת־הָאָרֶץ אֲשֶׁר יְהֹוָה אֱלֹהֵיכֶם נֹתֵן לָכֶם לְרִשְׁתָּהּ׃

12 Then *Yehoshua* said to the Reubenites, the Gadites, and the half-tribe of *Menashe*,

יב וְלָרֽאוּבֵנִי וְלַגָּדִי וְלַחֲצִי שֵׁבֶט הַמְנַשֶּׁה אָמַר יְהוֹשֻׁעַ לֵאמֹר׃

13 "Remember what *Moshe* the servant of *Hashem* enjoined upon you, when he said: '*Hashem* your God is granting you a haven; He has assigned this territory to you.'

יג זָכוֹר אֶת־הַדָּבָר אֲשֶׁר צִוָּה אֶתְכֶם מֹשֶׁה עֶבֶד־יְהֹוָה לֵאמֹר יְהֹוָה אֱלֹהֵיכֶם מֵנִיחַ לָכֶם וְנָתַן לָכֶם אֶת־הָאָרֶץ הַזֹּאת׃

14 Let your wives, children, and livestock remain in the land that *Moshe* assigned to you on this side of the *Yarden*; but every one of your fighting men shall go across armed in the van of your kinsmen. And you shall assist them

יד נְשֵׁיכֶם טַפְּכֶם וּמִקְנֵיכֶם יֵשְׁבוּ בָּאָרֶץ אֲשֶׁר נָתַן לָכֶם מֹשֶׁה בְּעֵבֶר הַיַּרְדֵּן וְאַתֶּם תַּעַבְרוּ חֲמֻשִׁים לִפְנֵי אֲחֵיכֶם כֹּל גִּבּוֹרֵי הַחַיִל וַעֲזַרְתֶּם אוֹתָם׃

15 until *Hashem* has given your kinsmen a haven, such as you have, and they too have gained possession of the land that *Hashem* your God has assigned to them. Then you may return to the land on the east side of the *Yarden*, which *Moshe* the servant of *Hashem* assigned to you as your possession, and you may possess it."

טו עַד אֲשֶׁר־יָנִיחַ יְהֹוָה לַאֲחֵיכֶם כָּכֶם וְיָרְשׁוּ גַם־הֵמָּה אֶת־הָאָרֶץ אֲשֶׁר־יְהֹוָה אֱלֹהֵיכֶם נֹתֵן לָהֶם וְשַׁבְתֶּם לְאֶרֶץ יְרֻשַּׁתְכֶם וִירִשְׁתֶּם אוֹתָהּ אֲשֶׁר נָתַן לָכֶם מֹשֶׁה עֶבֶד יְהֹוָה בְּעֵבֶר הַיַּרְדֵּן מִזְרַח הַשָּׁמֶשׁ׃

16 They answered *Yehoshua*, "We will do everything you have commanded us and we will go wherever you send us.

טז וַיַּעֲנוּ אֶת־יְהוֹשֻׁעַ לֵאמֹר כֹּל אֲשֶׁר־צִוִּיתָנוּ נַעֲשֶׂה וְאֶל־כָּל־אֲשֶׁר תִּשְׁלָחֵנוּ נֵלֵךְ׃

17 We will obey you just as we obeyed *Moshe*; let but *Hashem* your God be with you as He was with *Moshe*!

יז כְּכֹל אֲשֶׁר־שָׁמַעְנוּ אֶל־מֹשֶׁה כֵּן נִשְׁמַע אֵלֶיךָ רַק יִהְיֶה יְהֹוָה אֱלֹהֶיךָ עִמָּךְ כַּאֲשֶׁר הָיָה עִם־מֹשֶׁה׃

18 Any man who flouts your commands and does not obey every order you give him shall be put to death. Only be strong and resolute!"

יח כָּל־אִישׁ אֲשֶׁר־יַמְרֶה אֶת־פִּיךָ וְלֹא־יִשְׁמַע אֶת־דְּבָרֶיךָ לְכֹל אֲשֶׁר־תְּצַוֶּנּוּ יוּמָת רַק חֲזַק וֶאֱמָץ׃

kol EESH a-sher yam-REH et PEE-kha v'-lo yish-MA et d'-va-RE-kha l'-KHOL a-sher t'-tza-VE-nu yu-MAT RAK kha-ZAK ve-e-MATZ

Yehoshua/Joshua
Chapter 2

יהושע
פרק ב

2 ¹ Yehoshua son of Nun secretly sent two spies from Shittim, saying, "Go, reconnoiter the region of Yericho." So they set out, and they came to the house of a harlot named Rahab and lodged there.

א וַיִּשְׁלַ֣ח יְהוֹשֻֽׁעַ־בִּן־נ֠וּן מִֽן־הַשִּׁטִּ֞ים שְׁנַֽיִם־אֲנָשִׁ֤ים מְרַגְּלִים֙ חֶ֣רֶשׁ לֵאמֹ֔ר לְכ֛וּ רְא֥וּ אֶת־הָאָ֖רֶץ וְאֶת־יְרִיח֑וֹ וַיֵּ֨לְכ֜וּ וַ֠יָּבֹ֠אוּ בֵּית־אִשָּׁ֥ה זוֹנָ֛ה וּשְׁמָ֥הּ רָחָ֖ב וַיִּשְׁכְּבוּ־שָֽׁמָּה:

² The king of Yericho was told, "Some men have come here tonight, Israelites, to spy out the country."

ב וַיֵּ֣אָמַ֔ר לְמֶ֥לֶךְ יְרִיח֖וֹ לֵאמֹ֑ר הִנֵּ֣ה אֲ֠נָשִׁים בָּ֣אוּ הֵ֧נָּה הַלַּ֛יְלָה מִבְּנֵ֥י יִשְׂרָאֵ֖ל לַחְפֹּ֥ר אֶת־הָאָֽרֶץ:

³ The king of Yericho thereupon sent orders to Rahab: "Produce the men who came to you and entered your house, for they have come to spy out the whole country."

ג וַיִּשְׁלַח֙ מֶ֣לֶךְ יְרִיח֔וֹ אֶל־רָחָ֖ב לֵאמֹ֑ר ה֠וֹצִ֠יאִי הָאֲנָשִׁ֨ים הַבָּאִ֤ים אֵלַ֙יִךְ֙ אֲשֶׁר־בָּ֣אוּ לְבֵיתֵ֔ךְ כִּ֛י לַחְפֹּ֥ר אֶת־כָּל־הָאָ֖רֶץ בָּֽאוּ:

⁴ The woman, however, had taken the two men and hidden them. "It is true," she said, "the men did come to me, but I didn't know where they were from.

ד וַתִּקַּ֧ח הָֽאִשָּׁ֛ה אֶת־שְׁנֵ֥י הָאֲנָשִׁ֖ים וַֽתִּצְפְּנ֑וֹ וַתֹּ֣אמֶר ׀ כֵּ֗ן בָּ֤אוּ אֵלַי֙ הָֽאֲנָשִׁ֔ים וְלֹ֥א יָדַ֖עְתִּי מֵאַ֥יִן הֵֽמָּה:

⁵ And at dark, when the gate was about to be closed, the men left; and I don't know where the men went. Quick, go after them, for you can overtake them."

ה וַיְהִ֨י הַשַּׁ֜עַר לִסְגּ֗וֹר בַּחֹ֙שֶׁךְ֙ וְהָֽאֲנָשִׁ֣ים יָצָ֔אוּ לֹ֣א יָדַ֔עְתִּי אָ֥נָה הָֽלְכ֖וּ הָֽאֲנָשִׁ֑ים רִדְפ֥וּ מַהֵ֛ר אַֽחֲרֵיהֶ֖ם כִּ֥י תַשִּׂיגֽוּם:

⁶ Now she had taken them up to the roof and hidden them under some stalks of flax which she had lying on the roof.

ו וְהִ֖יא הֶֽעֱלָ֣תַם הַגָּ֑גָה וַֽתִּטְמְנֵם֙ בְּפִשְׁתֵּ֣י הָעֵ֔ץ הָעֲרֻכ֥וֹת לָ֖הּ עַל־הַגָּֽג:

⁷ So the men pursued them in the direction of the Yarden down to the fords; and no sooner had the pursuers gone out than the gate was shut behind them.

ז וְהָאֲנָשִׁ֗ים רָדְפ֤וּ אַֽחֲרֵיהֶם֙ דֶּ֣רֶךְ הַיַּרְדֵּ֔ן עַ֖ל הַֽמַּעְבְּר֑וֹת וְהַשַּׁ֣עַר סָגָ֔רוּ אַֽחֲרֵ֕י כַּֽאֲשֶׁ֥ר יָֽצְא֛וּ הָרֹֽדְפִ֖ים אַֽחֲרֵיהֶֽם:

⁸ The spies had not yet gone to sleep when she came up to them on the roof.

ח וְהֵ֖מָּה טֶ֣רֶם יִשְׁכָּב֑וּן וְהִ֛יא עָֽלְתָ֥ה עֲלֵיהֶ֖ם עַל־הַגָּֽג:

⁹ She said to the men, "I know that Hashem has given the country to you, because dread of you has fallen upon us, and all the inhabitants of the land are quaking before you.

ט וַתֹּ֙אמֶר֙ אֶל־הָ֣אֲנָשִׁ֔ים יָדַ֕עְתִּי כִּֽי־נָתַ֧ן יְהוָ֛ה לָכֶ֖ם אֶת־הָאָ֑רֶץ וְכִֽי־נָֽפְלָ֤ה אֵֽימַתְכֶם֙ עָלֵ֔ינוּ וְכִ֥י נָמֹ֛גוּ כָּל־יֹֽשְׁבֵ֥י הָאָ֖רֶץ מִפְּנֵיכֶֽם:

va-TO-mer el ha-a-na-SHEEM ya-DA-tee kee na-TAN a-do-NAI la-KHEM et ha-A-retz v'-khee na-f'-LAH ay-mat-KHEM a-LAY-nu v'-KHEE na-MO-gu kol yo-sh'-VAY ha-A-retz mi-p'-nay-KHEM

2:9 I know that Hashem has given the country to you When Rahab speaks to the spies, she reports that the Canaanites are afraid of the Children of Israel. They are well aware of the miracles Hashem has done for the Israelites – both forty years earlier during the time of the exodus, and more recently in the battles against the Amorite kings Sihon and Og (Numbers 21). They know that God has given the land to the Children of Israel and therefore, they are afraid. Not only does Rahab report this to the spies, but she even casts her lot with the Israelites. Rahab is a prime example of a righteous gentile. Understanding that these men are representatives of Hashem's chosen people who will receive the chosen land, she singlehandedly undertakes to protect

Yehoshua/Joshua
Chapter 2

יהושע
פרק ב

10 For we have heard how *Hashem* dried up the waters of the Sea of Reeds for you when you left Egypt, and what you did to Sihon and Og, the two Amorite kings across the *Yarden*, whom you doomed.

י כִּי שָׁמַעְנוּ אֵת אֲשֶׁר־הוֹבִישׁ יְהֹוָה אֶת־מֵי יַם־סוּף מִפְּנֵיכֶם בְּצֵאתְכֶם מִמִּצְרָיִם וַאֲשֶׁר עֲשִׂיתֶם לִשְׁנֵי מַלְכֵי הָאֱמֹרִי אֲשֶׁר בְּעֵבֶר הַיַּרְדֵּן לְסִיחֹן וּלְעוֹג אֲשֶׁר הֶחֱרַמְתֶּם אוֹתָם:

11 When we heard about it, we lost heart, and no man had any more spirit left because of you; for *Hashem* your God is the only *Hashem* in heaven above and on earth below.

יא וַנִּשְׁמַע וַיִּמַּס לְבָבֵנוּ וְלֹא־קָמָה עוֹד רוּחַ בְּאִישׁ מִפְּנֵיכֶם כִּי יְהֹוָה אֱלֹהֵיכֶם הוּא אֱלֹהִים בַּשָּׁמַיִם מִמַּעַל וְעַל־הָאָרֶץ מִתָּחַת:

12 Now, since I have shown loyalty to you, swear to me by *Hashem* that you in turn will show loyalty to my family. Provide me with a reliable sign

יב וְעַתָּה הִשָּׁבְעוּ־נָא לִי בַּיהֹוָה כִּי־עָשִׂיתִי עִמָּכֶם חָסֶד וַעֲשִׂיתֶם גַּם־אַתֶּם עִם־בֵּית אָבִי חֶסֶד וּנְתַתֶּם לִי אוֹת אֱמֶת:

13 that you will spare the lives of my father and mother, my brothers and sisters, and all who belong to them, and save us from death."

יג וְהַחֲיִתֶם אֶת־אָבִי וְאֶת־אִמִּי וְאֶת־אַחַי וְאֶת־אַחוֹתַי [אַחְיוֹתַי] וְאֵת כָּל־אֲשֶׁר לָהֶם וְהִצַּלְתֶּם אֶת־נַפְשֹׁתֵינוּ מִמָּוֶת:

14 The men answered her, "Our persons are pledged for yours, even to death! If you do not disclose this mission of ours, we will show you true loyalty when *Hashem* gives us the land."

יד וַיֹּאמְרוּ לָהּ הָאֲנָשִׁים נַפְשֵׁנוּ תַחְתֵּיכֶם לָמוּת אִם לֹא תַגִּידוּ אֶת־דְּבָרֵנוּ זֶה וְהָיָה בְּתֵת־יְהֹוָה לָנוּ אֶת־הָאָרֶץ וְעָשִׂינוּ עִמָּךְ חֶסֶד וֶאֱמֶת:

va-YO-m'-ru LAH ha-a-na-SHEEM naf-SHAY-nu takh-tay-KHEM la-MUT IM LO ta-GEE-du et d'-va-RAY-nu ZEH v'-ha-YAH b'-tayt a-do-NAI LA-nu et ha-A-retz v'-a-SEE-nu i-MAKH KHE-sed ve-e-MET

15 She let them down by a rope through the window – for her dwelling was at the outer side of the city wall and she lived in the actual wall.

טו וַתּוֹרִדֵם בַּחֶבֶל בְּעַד הַחַלּוֹן כִּי בֵיתָהּ בְּקִיר הַחוֹמָה וּבַחוֹמָה הִיא יוֹשָׁבֶת:

16 She said to them, "Make for the hills, so that the pursuers may not come upon you. Stay there in hiding three days, until the pursuers return; then go your way."

טז וַתֹּאמֶר לָהֶם הָהָרָה לֵּכוּ פֶּן־יִפְגְּעוּ בָכֶם הָרֹדְפִים וְנַחְבֵּתֶם שָׁמָּה שְׁלֹשֶׁת יָמִים עַד שׁוֹב הָרֹדְפִים וְאַחַר תֵּלְכוּ לְדַרְכְּכֶם:

17 But the men warned her, "We will be released from this oath which you have made us take

יז וַיֹּאמְרוּ אֵלֶיהָ הָאֲנָשִׁים נְקִיִּם אֲנַחְנוּ מִשְּׁבֻעָתֵךְ הַזֶּה אֲשֶׁר הִשְׁבַּעְתָּנוּ:

---

the spies. The Children of Israel are not the only ones who understand that God is giving them the Promised Land; the righteous among the nations also recognize that this is the will of *Hashem*. God gave the Children of Israel the Land of Israel then, and He gives it to them now as well.

2:14 We will show you true loyalty The spies promise that they will repay Rahab with 'true loyalty,' *chesed v'emet* (חסד ואמת). Rabbi Benjamin Blech, in his book *The Secrets of Hebrew Words*, teaches that *emet* (אמת), the Hebrew word for 'truth,' contains a deep lesson. The word is comprised of three letters and "requires for its essence the first letter *alef* (א), the "One" standing for the Almighty. Remove the initial letter *alef* and all that remains is *met* (מת), meaning death. Without *Hashem* there can be no truth. In its place only death and destruction remain."

אמת

534

Yehoshua/Joshua
Chapter 3

יהושע
פרק ג

18 [unless,] when we invade the country, you tie this length of crimson cord to the window through which you let us down. Bring your father, your mother, your brothers, and all your family together in your house;

יח הִנֵּה אֲנַחְנוּ בָאִים בָּאָרֶץ אֶת־תִּקְוַת חוּט הַשָּׁנִי הַזֶּה תִּקְשְׁרִי בַּחַלּוֹן אֲשֶׁר הוֹרַדְתֵּנוּ בוֹ וְאֶת־אָבִיךְ וְאֶת־אִמֵּךְ וְאֶת־אַחַיִךְ וְאֵת כָּל־בֵּית אָבִיךְ תַּאַסְפִי אֵלַיִךְ הַבָּיְתָה׃

19 and if anyone ventures outside the doors of your house, his blood will be on his head, and we shall be clear. But if a hand is laid on anyone who remains in the house with you, his blood shall be on our heads.

יט וְהָיָה כֹּל אֲשֶׁר־יֵצֵא מִדַּלְתֵי בֵיתֵךְ הַחוּצָה דָּמוֹ בְרֹאשׁוֹ וַאֲנַחְנוּ נְקִיִּם וְכֹל אֲשֶׁר יִהְיֶה אִתָּךְ בַּבַּיִת דָּמוֹ בְרֹאשֵׁנוּ אִם־יָד תִּהְיֶה־בּוֹ׃

20 And if you disclose this mission of ours, we shall likewise be released from the oath which you made us take."

כ וְאִם־תַּגִּידִי אֶת־דְּבָרֵנוּ זֶה וְהָיִינוּ נְקִיִּם מִשְּׁבֻעָתֵךְ אֲשֶׁר הִשְׁבַּעְתָּנוּ׃

21 She replied, "Let it be as you say." She sent them on their way, and they left; and she tied the crimson cord to the window.

כא וַתֹּאמֶר כְּדִבְרֵיכֶם כֶּן־הוּא וַתְּשַׁלְּחֵם וַיֵּלֵכוּ וַתִּקְשֹׁר אֶת־תִּקְוַת הַשָּׁנִי בַּחַלּוֹן׃

22 They went straight to the hills and stayed there three days, until the pursuers turned back. And so the pursuers, searching all along the road, did not find them.

כב וַיֵּלְכוּ וַיָּבֹאוּ הָהָרָה וַיֵּשְׁבוּ שָׁם שְׁלֹשֶׁת יָמִים עַד־שָׁבוּ הָרֹדְפִים וַיְבַקְשׁוּ הָרֹדְפִים בְּכָל־הַדֶּרֶךְ וְלֹא מָצָאוּ׃

23 Then the two men came down again from the hills and crossed over. They came to Yehoshua son of Nun and reported to him all that had happened to them.

כג וַיָּשֻׁבוּ שְׁנֵי הָאֲנָשִׁים וַיֵּרְדוּ מֵהָהָר וַיַּעַבְרוּ וַיָּבֹאוּ אֶל־יְהוֹשֻׁעַ בִּן־נוּן וַיְסַפְּרוּ־לוֹ אֵת כָּל־הַמֹּצְאוֹת אוֹתָם׃

24 They said to Yehoshua, "Hashem has delivered the whole land into our power; in fact, all the inhabitants of the land are quaking before us."

כד וַיֹּאמְרוּ אֶל־יְהוֹשֻׁעַ כִּי־נָתַן יְהוָה בְּיָדֵנוּ אֶת־כָּל־הָאָרֶץ וְגַם־נָמֹגוּ כָּל־יֹשְׁבֵי הָאָרֶץ מִפָּנֵינוּ׃

3 1 Early next morning, Yehoshua and all the Israelites set out from Shittim and marched to the Yarden. They did not cross immediately, but spent the night there.

ג א וַיַּשְׁכֵּם יְהוֹשֻׁעַ בַּבֹּקֶר וַיִּסְעוּ מֵהַשִּׁטִּים וַיָּבֹאוּ עַד־הַיַּרְדֵּן הוּא וְכָל־בְּנֵי יִשְׂרָאֵל וַיָּלִנוּ שָׁם טֶרֶם יַעֲבֹרוּ׃

2 Three days later, the officials went through the camp

ב וַיְהִי מִקְצֵה שְׁלֹשֶׁת יָמִים וַיַּעַבְרוּ הַשֹּׁטְרִים בְּקֶרֶב הַמַּחֲנֶה׃

3 and charged the people as follows: "When you see the Aron Brit Hashem your God being borne by the levitical Kohanim, you shall move forward. Follow it

ג וַיְצַוּוּ אֶת־הָעָם לֵאמֹר כִּרְאוֹתְכֶם אֵת אֲרוֹן בְּרִית־יְהוָה אֱלֹהֵיכֶם וְהַכֹּהֲנִים הַלְוִיִּם נֹשְׂאִים אֹתוֹ וְאַתֶּם תִּסְעוּ מִמְּקוֹמְכֶם וַהֲלַכְתֶּם אַחֲרָיו׃

4 but keep a distance of some two thousand amot from it, never coming any closer to it – so that you may know by what route to march, since it is a road you have not traveled before."

ד אַךְ רָחוֹק יִהְיֶה בֵּינֵיכֶם וּבֵינוֹ [וּבֵינָיו] כְּאַלְפַּיִם אַמָּה בַּמִּדָּה אַל־תִּקְרְבוּ אֵלָיו לְמַעַן אֲשֶׁר־תֵּדְעוּ אֶת־הַדֶּרֶךְ אֲשֶׁר תֵּלְכוּ־בָהּ כִּי לֹא עֲבַרְתֶּם בַּדֶּרֶךְ מִתְּמוֹל שִׁלְשׁוֹם׃

Yehoshua/Joshua
Chapter 3

יהושע
פרק ג

ה 5 And *Yehoshua* said to the people, "Purify yourselves, for tomorrow *Hashem* will perform wonders in your midst."

וַיֹּאמֶר יְהוֹשֻׁעַ אֶל־הָעָם הִתְקַדָּשׁוּ כִּי מָחָר יַעֲשֶׂה יְהֹוָה בְּקִרְבְּכֶם נִפְלָאוֹת:

va-YO-mer y'-ho-SHU-a el ha-AM hit-ka-DA-shu KEE ma-KHAR ya-a-SEH a-do-NAI b'-kir-b'-KHEM nif-la-OT

ו 6 Then *Yehoshua* ordered the *Kohanim*, "Take up the *Aron HaBrit* and advance to the head of the people." And they took up the *Aron HaBrit* and marched at the head of the people.

וַיֹּאמֶר יְהוֹשֻׁעַ אֶל־הַכֹּהֲנִים לֵאמֹר שְׂאוּ אֶת־אֲרוֹן הַבְּרִית וְעִבְרוּ לִפְנֵי הָעָם וַיִּשְׂאוּ אֶת־אֲרוֹן הַבְּרִית וַיֵּלְכוּ לִפְנֵי הָעָם:

ז 7 *Hashem* said to *Yehoshua*, "This day, for the first time, I will exalt you in the sight of all *Yisrael*, so that they shall know that I will be with you as I was with *Moshe*.

וַיֹּאמֶר יְהֹוָה אֶל־יְהוֹשֻׁעַ הַיּוֹם הַזֶּה אָחֵל גַּדֶּלְךָ בְּעֵינֵי כָּל־יִשְׂרָאֵל אֲשֶׁר יֵדְעוּן כִּי כַּאֲשֶׁר הָיִיתִי עִם־מֹשֶׁה אֶהְיֶה עִמָּךְ:

ח 8 For your part, command the *Kohanim* who carry the *Aron HaBrit* as follows: When you reach the edge of the waters of the *Yarden*, make a halt in the *Yarden*."

וְאַתָּה תְּצַוֶּה אֶת־הַכֹּהֲנִים נֹשְׂאֵי אֲרוֹן־הַבְּרִית לֵאמֹר כְּבֹאֲכֶם עַד־קְצֵה מֵי הַיַּרְדֵּן בַּיַּרְדֵּן תַּעֲמֹדוּ:

ט 9 And *Yehoshua* said to the Israelites, "Come closer and listen to the words of *Hashem* your God.

וַיֹּאמֶר יְהוֹשֻׁעַ אֶל־בְּנֵי יִשְׂרָאֵל גֹּשׁוּ הֵנָּה וְשִׁמְעוּ אֶת־דִּבְרֵי יְהֹוָה אֱלֹהֵיכֶם:

י 10 By this," *Yehoshua* continued, "you shall know that a living *Hashem* is among you, and that He will dispossess for you the Canaanites, Hittites, Hivites, Perizzites, Girgashites, Amorites, and Jebusites:

וַיֹּאמֶר יְהוֹשֻׁעַ בְּזֹאת תֵּדְעוּן כִּי אֵל חַי בְּקִרְבְּכֶם וְהוֹרֵשׁ יוֹרִישׁ מִפְּנֵיכֶם אֶת־הַכְּנַעֲנִי וְאֶת־הַחִתִּי וְאֶת־הַחִוִּי וְאֶת־הַפְּרִזִּי וְאֶת־הַגִּרְגָּשִׁי וְהָאֱמֹרִי וְהַיְבוּסִי:

יא 11 the *Aron HaBrit* of the Sovereign of all the earth is advancing before you into the *Yarden*.

הִנֵּה אֲרוֹן הַבְּרִית אֲדוֹן כָּל־הָאָרֶץ עֹבֵר לִפְנֵיכֶם בַּיַּרְדֵּן:

יב 12 Now select twelve men from the tribes of *Yisrael*, one man from each tribe.

וְעַתָּה קְחוּ לָכֶם שְׁנֵי עָשָׂר אִישׁ מִשִּׁבְטֵי יִשְׂרָאֵל אִישׁ־אֶחָד אִישׁ־אֶחָד לַשָּׁבֶט:

יג 13 When the feet of the *Kohanim* bearing the *Aron* of *Hashem*, the Sovereign of all the earth, come to rest in the waters of the *Yarden*, the waters of the *Yarden* – the water coming from upstream – will be cut off and will stand in a single heap."

וְהָיָה כְּנוֹחַ כַּפּוֹת רַגְלֵי הַכֹּהֲנִים נֹשְׂאֵי אֲרוֹן יְהֹוָה אֲדוֹן כָּל־הָאָרֶץ בְּמֵי הַיַּרְדֵּן מֵי הַיַּרְדֵּן יִכָּרֵתוּן הַמַּיִם הַיֹּרְדִים מִלְמָעְלָה וְיַעַמְדוּ נֵד אֶחָד:

3:5 Tomorrow *Hashem* will perform wonders *Yehoshua* instructs the people to sanctify themselves, as *Hashem* will perform miracles for them. Typically, miracles require a partnership between God and man. Though ultimately *Hashem* performs the miracle, He expects us to do our part to merit His acting on our behalf. Hence, the Children of Israel need to prepare themselves spiritually and physically, in order to merit the miracles of the parting of the *Yarden* and the victories in the conquest of the Promised Land. In our own era as well, the partnership between man and *Hashem* has resulted in the rebirth and flourishing of the State of Israel. As a result of God's blessings, together with man's hard work, the desert literally blooms, the economy grows, the army defends and the nation continues to absorb countless immigrants from the four corners of the earth. As in the days of *Yehoshua*, the fulfillment of these miracles has demanded both spiritual and physical effort by human beings.

Yehoshua/Joshua
Chapter 4

יהושע
פרק ד

14 When the people set out from their encampment to cross the *Yarden*, the *Kohanim* bearing the *Aron HaBrit* were at the head of the people.

יד וַיְהִי בִּנְסֹעַ הָעָם מֵאָהֳלֵיהֶם לַעֲבֹר אֶת־הַיַּרְדֵּן וְהַכֹּהֲנִים נֹשְׂאֵי הָאָרוֹן הַבְּרִית לִפְנֵי הָעָם:

15 Now the *Yarden* keeps flowing over its entire bed throughout the harvest season. But as soon as the bearers of the *Aron* reached the *Yarden*, and the feet of the *Kohanim* bearing the *Aron* dipped into the water at its edge,

טו וּכְבוֹא נֹשְׂאֵי הָאָרוֹן עַד־הַיַּרְדֵּן וְרַגְלֵי הַכֹּהֲנִים נֹשְׂאֵי הָאָרוֹן נִטְבְּלוּ בִּקְצֵה הַמָּיִם וְהַיַּרְדֵּן מָלֵא עַל־כָּל־גְּדוֹתָיו כֹּל יְמֵי קָצִיר:

16 the waters coming down from upstream piled up in a single heap a great way off, at *Adam*, the town next to Zarethan; and those flowing away downstream to the Sea of the Arabah (the Dead Sea) ran out completely. So the people crossed near *Yericho*.

טז וַיַּעַמְדוּ הַמַּיִם הַיֹּרְדִים מִלְמַעְלָה קָמוּ נֵד־אֶחָד הַרְחֵק מְאֹד באדם [מֵאָדָם] הָעִיר אֲשֶׁר מִצַּד צָרְתָן וְהַיֹּרְדִים עַל יָם הָעֲרָבָה יָם־הַמֶּלַח תַּמּוּ נִכְרָתוּ וְהָעָם עָבְרוּ נֶגֶד יְרִיחוֹ:

17 The *Kohanim* who bore the *Aron Brit Hashem* stood on dry land exactly in the middle of the *Yarden*, while all *Yisrael* crossed over on dry land, until the entire nation had finished crossing the *Yarden*.

יז וַיַּעַמְדוּ הַכֹּהֲנִים נֹשְׂאֵי הָאָרוֹן בְּרִית־יְהוָה בֶּחָרָבָה בְּתוֹךְ הַיַּרְדֵּן הָכֵן וְכָל־יִשְׂרָאֵל עֹבְרִים בֶּחָרָבָה עַד אֲשֶׁר־תַּמּוּ כָּל־הַגּוֹי לַעֲבֹר אֶת־הַיַּרְדֵּן:

4
1 When the entire nation had finished crossing the *Yarden*, *Hashem* said to *Yehoshua*,

א וַיְהִי כַּאֲשֶׁר־תַּמּוּ כָל־הַגּוֹי לַעֲבוֹר אֶת־הַיַּרְדֵּן וַיֹּאמֶר יְהוָה אֶל־יְהוֹשֻׁעַ לֵאמֹר:

2 "Select twelve men from among the people, one from each tribe,

ב קְחוּ לָכֶם מִן־הָעָם שְׁנֵים עָשָׂר אֲנָשִׁים אִישׁ־אֶחָד אִישׁ־אֶחָד מִשָּׁבֶט:

3 and instruct them as follows: Pick up twelve stones from the spot exactly in the middle of the *Yarden*, where the *Kohanim*' feet are standing; take them along with you and deposit them in the place where you will spend the night."

ג וְצַוּוּ אוֹתָם לֵאמֹר שְׂאוּ־לָכֶם מִזֶּה מִתּוֹךְ הַיַּרְדֵּן מִמַּצַּב רַגְלֵי הַכֹּהֲנִים הָכִין שְׁתֵּים־עֶשְׂרֵה אֲבָנִים וְהַעֲבַרְתֶּם אוֹתָם עִמָּכֶם וְהִנַּחְתֶּם אוֹתָם בַּמָּלוֹן אֲשֶׁר־תָּלִינוּ בוֹ הַלָּיְלָה:

4 *Yehoshua* summoned the twelve men whom he had designated among the Israelites, one from each tribe;

ד וַיִּקְרָא יְהוֹשֻׁעַ אֶל־שְׁנֵים הֶעָשָׂר אִישׁ אֲשֶׁר הֵכִין מִבְּנֵי יִשְׂרָאֵל אִישׁ־אֶחָד אִישׁ־אֶחָד מִשָּׁבֶט:

5 and *Yehoshua* said to them, "Walk up to the *Aron* of *Hashem* your God, in the middle of the *Yarden*, and each of you lift a stone onto his shoulder – corresponding to the number of the tribes of *Yisrael*.

ה וַיֹּאמֶר לָהֶם יְהוֹשֻׁעַ עִבְרוּ לִפְנֵי אֲרוֹן יְהוָה אֱלֹהֵיכֶם אֶל־תּוֹךְ הַיַּרְדֵּן וְהָרִימוּ לָכֶם אִישׁ אֶבֶן אַחַת עַל־שִׁכְמוֹ לְמִסְפַּר שִׁבְטֵי בְנֵי־יִשְׂרָאֵל:

6 This shall serve as a symbol among you: in time to come, when your children ask, 'What is the meaning of these stones for you?'

ו לְמַעַן תִּהְיֶה זֹאת אוֹת בְּקִרְבְּכֶם כִּי־יִשְׁאָלוּן בְּנֵיכֶם מָחָר לֵאמֹר מָה הָאֲבָנִים הָאֵלֶּה לָכֶם:

7 you shall tell them, 'The waters of the *Yarden* were cut off because of the *Aron Brit Hashem*; when it passed through the *Yarden*, the waters of the *Yarden* were cut off.' And so these stones shall serve the people of *Yisrael* as a memorial for all time."

ז וַאֲמַרְתֶּם לָהֶם אֲשֶׁר נִכְרְתוּ מֵימֵי הַיַּרְדֵּן מִפְּנֵי אֲרוֹן בְּרִית־יְהוָה בְּעָבְרוֹ בַּיַּרְדֵּן נִכְרְתוּ מֵי הַיַּרְדֵּן וְהָיוּ הָאֲבָנִים הָאֵלֶּה לְזִכָּרוֹן לִבְנֵי יִשְׂרָאֵל עַד־עוֹלָם:

Yehoshua/Joshua
Chapter 4

יהושע
פרק ד

8 The Israelites did as *Yehoshua* ordered. They picked up twelve stones, corresponding to the number of the tribes of *Yisrael*, from the middle of the *Yarden* – as *Hashem* had charged *Yehoshua* – and they took them along with them to their night encampment and deposited them there.

ח וַיַּעֲשׂוּ־כֵן בְּנֵי־יִשְׂרָאֵל כַּאֲשֶׁר צִוָּה יְהוֹשֻׁעַ וַיִּשְׂאוּ שְׁתֵּי־עֶשְׂרֵה אֲבָנִים מִתּוֹךְ הַיַּרְדֵּן כַּאֲשֶׁר דִּבֶּר יְהֹוָה אֶל־יְהוֹשֻׁעַ לְמִסְפַּר שִׁבְטֵי בְנֵי־יִשְׂרָאֵל וַיַּעֲבִרוּם עִמָּם אֶל־הַמָּלוֹן וַיַּנִּחוּם שָׁם:

9 *Yehoshua* also set up twelve stones in the middle of the *Yarden*, at the spot where the feet of the *Kohanim* bearing the *Aron HaBrit* had stood; and they have remained there to this day.

ט וּשְׁתֵּים עֶשְׂרֵה אֲבָנִים הֵקִים יְהוֹשֻׁעַ בְּתוֹךְ הַיַּרְדֵּן תַּחַת מַצַּב רַגְלֵי הַכֹּהֲנִים נֹשְׂאֵי אֲרוֹן הַבְּרִית וַיִּהְיוּ שָׁם עַד הַיּוֹם הַזֶּה:

10 The *Kohanim* who bore the *Aron* remained standing in the middle of the *Yarden* until all the instructions that *Hashem* had ordered *Yehoshua* to convey to the people had been carried out. And so the people speedily crossed over, just as *Moshe* had assured *Yehoshua* in his charge to him.

י וְהַכֹּהֲנִים נֹשְׂאֵי הָאָרוֹן עֹמְדִים בְּתוֹךְ הַיַּרְדֵּן עַד תֹּם כָּל־הַדָּבָר אֲשֶׁר־צִוָּה יְהֹוָה אֶת־יְהוֹשֻׁעַ לְדַבֵּר אֶל־הָעָם כְּכֹל אֲשֶׁר־צִוָּה מֹשֶׁה אֶת־יְהוֹשֻׁעַ וַיְמַהֲרוּ הָעָם וַיַּעֲבֹרוּ:

11 And when all the people finished crossing, the *Aron* of *Hashem* and the *Kohanim* advanced to the head of the people.

יא וַיְהִי כַּאֲשֶׁר־תַּם כָּל־הָעָם לַעֲבוֹר וַיַּעֲבֹר אֲרוֹן־יְהֹוָה וְהַכֹּהֲנִים לִפְנֵי הָעָם:

12 The Reubenites, the Gadites, and the half-tribe of *Menashe* went across armed in the van of the Israelites, as *Moshe* had charged them.

יב וַיַּעַבְרוּ בְּנֵי־רְאוּבֵן וּבְנֵי־גָד וַחֲצִי שֵׁבֶט הַמְנַשֶּׁה חֲמֻשִׁים לִפְנֵי בְּנֵי יִשְׂרָאֵל כַּאֲשֶׁר דִּבֶּר אֲלֵיהֶם מֹשֶׁה:

13 About forty thousand shock troops went across, at the instance of *Hashem*, to the steppes of *Yericho* for battle.

יג כְּאַרְבָּעִים אֶלֶף חֲלוּצֵי הַצָּבָא עָבְרוּ לִפְנֵי יְהֹוָה לַמִּלְחָמָה אֶל עַרְבוֹת יְרִיחוֹ:

14 On that day *Hashem* exalted *Yehoshua* in the sight of all *Yisrael*, so that they revered him all his days as they had revered *Moshe*.

יד בַּיּוֹם הַהוּא גִּדַּל יְהֹוָה אֶת־יְהוֹשֻׁעַ בְּעֵינֵי כָּל־יִשְׂרָאֵל וַיִּרְאוּ אֹתוֹ כַּאֲשֶׁר יָרְאוּ אֶת־מֹשֶׁה כָּל־יְמֵי חַיָּיו:

15 *Hashem* said to *Yehoshua*,

טו וַיֹּאמֶר יְהֹוָה אֶל־יְהוֹשֻׁעַ לֵאמֹר:

16 "Command the *Kohanim* who bear the *Aron HaBrit* to come up out of the *Yarden*."

טז צַוֵּה אֶת־הַכֹּהֲנִים נֹשְׂאֵי אֲרוֹן הָעֵדוּת וְיַעֲלוּ מִן־הַיַּרְדֵּן:

17 So *Yehoshua* commanded the *Kohanim*, "Come up out of the *Yarden*."

יז וַיְצַו יְהוֹשֻׁעַ אֶת־הַכֹּהֲנִים לֵאמֹר עֲלוּ מִן־הַיַּרְדֵּן:

18 As soon as the *Kohanim* who bore the *Aron Brit Hashem* came up out of the *Yarden*, and the feet of the *Kohanim* stepped onto the dry ground, the waters of the *Yarden* resumed their course, flowing over its entire bed as before.

יח וַיְהִי בַּעֲלוֹת [כַּעֲלוֹת] הַכֹּהֲנִים נֹשְׂאֵי אֲרוֹן בְּרִית־יְהֹוָה מִתּוֹךְ הַיַּרְדֵּן נִתְּקוּ כַּפּוֹת רַגְלֵי הַכֹּהֲנִים אֶל הֶחָרָבָה וַיָּשֻׁבוּ מֵי־הַיַּרְדֵּן לִמְקוֹמָם וַיֵּלְכוּ כִתְמוֹל־שִׁלְשׁוֹם עַל־כָּל־גְּדוֹתָיו:

19 The people came up from the *Yarden* on the tenth day of the first month, and encamped at *Gilgal* on the eastern border of *Yericho*.

יט וְהָעָם עָלוּ מִן־הַיַּרְדֵּן בֶּעָשׂוֹר לַחֹדֶשׁ הָרִאשׁוֹן וַיַּחֲנוּ בַּגִּלְגָּל בִּקְצֵה מִזְרַח יְרִיחוֹ:

538

Yehoshua/Joshua
Chapter 5

יהושע
פרק ה

20 And *Yehoshua* set up in *Gilgal* the twelve stones they had taken from the *Yarden*.

כ וְאֵת שְׁתֵּים עֶשְׂרֵה הָאֲבָנִים הָאֵלֶּה אֲשֶׁר לָקְחוּ מִן־הַיַּרְדֵּן הֵקִים יְהוֹשֻׁעַ בַּגִּלְגָּל:

> *v'-AYT sh'-TAYM es-RAY ha-a-va-NEEM ha-AY-leh a-SHER la-k'-KHU min ha-yar-DAYN hay-KEEM y'-ho-SHU-a ba-gil-GAL*

21 He charged the Israelites as follows: "In time to come, when your children ask their fathers, 'What is the meaning of those stones?'

כא וַיֹּאמֶר אֶל־בְּנֵי יִשְׂרָאֵל לֵאמֹר אֲשֶׁר יִשְׁאָלוּן בְּנֵיכֶם מָחָר אֶת־אֲבוֹתָם לֵאמֹר מָה הָאֲבָנִים הָאֵלֶּה:

22 tell your children: 'Here the Israelites crossed the *Yarden* on dry land.'

כב וְהוֹדַעְתֶּם אֶת־בְּנֵיכֶם לֵאמֹר בַּיַּבָּשָׁה עָבַר יִשְׂרָאֵל אֶת־הַיַּרְדֵּן הַזֶּה:

23 For *Hashem* your God dried up the waters of the *Yarden* before you until you crossed, just as *Hashem* your God did to the Sea of Reeds, which He dried up before us until we crossed.

כג אֲשֶׁר־הוֹבִישׁ יְהֹוָה אֱלֹהֵיכֶם אֶת־מֵי הַיַּרְדֵּן מִפְּנֵיכֶם עַד־עָבְרְכֶם כַּאֲשֶׁר עָשָׂה יְהֹוָה אֱלֹהֵיכֶם לְיַם־סוּף אֲשֶׁר־הוֹבִישׁ מִפָּנֵינוּ עַד־עָבְרֵנוּ:

24 Thus all the peoples of the earth shall know how mighty is the hand of *Hashem*, and you shall fear *Hashem* your God always."

כד לְמַעַן דַּעַת כָּל־עַמֵּי הָאָרֶץ אֶת־יַד יְהֹוָה כִּי חֲזָקָה הִיא לְמַעַן יְרָאתֶם אֶת־יְהֹוָה אֱלֹהֵיכֶם כָּל־הַיָּמִים:

5 **1** When all the kings of the Amorites on the western side of the *Yarden*, and all the kings of the Canaanites near the Sea, heard how *Hashem* had dried up the waters of the *Yarden* for the sake of the Israelites until they crossed over, they lost heart, and no spirit was left in them because of the Israelites.

ה א וַיְהִי כִשְׁמֹעַ כָּל־מַלְכֵי הָאֱמֹרִי אֲשֶׁר בְּעֵבֶר הַיַּרְדֵּן יָמָּה וְכָל־מַלְכֵי הַכְּנַעֲנִי אֲשֶׁר עַל־הַיָּם אֵת אֲשֶׁר־הוֹבִישׁ יְהֹוָה אֶת־מֵי הַיַּרְדֵּן מִפְּנֵי בְנֵי־יִשְׂרָאֵל עַד־עברנו [עָבְרָם] וַיִּמַּס לְבָבָם וְלֹא־הָיָה בָם עוֹד רוּחַ מִפְּנֵי בְּנֵי־יִשְׂרָאֵל:

2 At that time *Hashem* said to *Yehoshua*, "Make flint knives and proceed with a second circumcision of the Israelites."

ב בָּעֵת הַהִיא אָמַר יְהֹוָה אֶל־יְהוֹשֻׁעַ עֲשֵׂה לְךָ חַרְבוֹת צֻרִים וְשׁוּב מֹל אֶת־בְּנֵי־יִשְׂרָאֵל שֵׁנִית:

3 So *Yehoshua* had flint knives made, and the Israelites were circumcised at Gibeath-haaraloth.

ג וַיַּעַשׂ־לוֹ יְהוֹשֻׁעַ חַרְבוֹת צֻרִים וַיָּמָל אֶת־בְּנֵי יִשְׂרָאֵל אֶל־גִּבְעַת הָעֲרָלוֹת:

4 This is the reason why *Yehoshua* had the circumcision performed: All the people who had come out of Egypt, all the males of military age, had died during the desert wanderings after leaving Egypt.

ד וְזֶה הַדָּבָר אֲשֶׁר־מָל יְהוֹשֻׁעַ כָּל־הָעָם הַיֹּצֵא מִמִּצְרַיִם הַזְּכָרִים כֹּל אַנְשֵׁי הַמִּלְחָמָה מֵתוּ בַמִּדְבָּר בַּדֶּרֶךְ בְּצֵאתָם מִמִּצְרָיִם:

Proposed location of biblical Gilgal

4:20 And *Yehoshua* set up in *Gilgal* the twelve stones *Yehoshua* establishes a monument from twelve stones taken from the *Yarden*, each representing one tribe. Rabbi Shlomo Aviner notes that this monument represents the "unity but not uniformity" of the Jewish people. There are twelve individual stones, which symbolize the diversity of the tribes. But the stones are not scattered. Together, they form a unified monument. This "unity but not uniformity" is one of the keys to Israel's success. Israel is an extremely diverse country. Yet her people have unified to create a society that is truly a "light unto the nations."

Yehoshua/Joshua
Chapter 5

5 Now, whereas all the people who came out of Egypt had been circumcised, none of the people born after the exodus, during the desert wanderings, had been circumcised.

6 For the Israelites had traveled in the wilderness forty years, until the entire nation – the men of military age who had left Egypt – had perished; because they had not obeyed *Hashem*, and *Hashem* had sworn never to let them see the land that *Hashem* had sworn to their fathers to assign to us, a land flowing with milk and honey.

7 But He had raised up their sons in their stead; and it was these that *Yehoshua* circumcised, for they were uncircumcised, not having been circumcised on the way.

8 After the circumcising of the whole nation was completed, they remained where they were, in the camp, until they recovered.

9 And *Hashem* said to *Yehoshua*, "Today I have rolled away from you the disgrace of Egypt." So that place was called *Gilgal*, as it still is.

10 Encamped at *Gilgal*, in the steppes of *Yericho*, the Israelites offered the *Pesach* sacrifice on the fourteenth day of the month, toward evening.

11 On the day after the *Pesach* offering, on that very day, they ate of the produce of the country, unleavened bread and parched grain.

12 On that same day, when they ate of the produce of the land, the manna ceased. The Israelites got no more manna; that year they ate of the yield of the land of Canaan.

13 Once, when *Yehoshua* was near *Yericho*, he looked up and saw a man standing before him, drawn sword in hand. *Yehoshua* went up to him and asked him, "Are you one of us or of our enemies?"

14 He replied, "No, I am captain of *Hashem*'s host. Now I have come!" *Yehoshua* threw himself face down to the ground and, prostrating himself, said to him, "What does my lord command his servant?"

יהושע
פרק ה

ה כִּי־מֻלִ֣ים הָי֔וּ כָּל־הָעָ֖ם הַיֹּצְאִ֑ים וְכָל־הָעָ֡ם הַיִּלֹּדִים֩ בַּמִּדְבָּ֨ר בַּדֶּ֜רֶךְ בְּצֵאתָ֧ם מִמִּצְרַ֛יִם לֹא־מָֽלוּ׃

ו כִּ֣י ׀ אַרְבָּעִ֣ים שָׁנָ֗ה הָלְכ֣וּ בְנֵֽי־יִשְׂרָאֵל֮ בַּמִּדְבָּר֒ עַד־תֹּ֨ם כָּל־הַגּ֜וֹי אַנְשֵׁ֤י הַמִּלְחָמָה֙ הַיֹּצְאִ֣ים מִמִּצְרַ֔יִם אֲשֶׁ֥ר לֹֽא־שָׁמְע֖וּ בְּק֣וֹל יְהֹוָ֑ה אֲשֶׁ֨ר נִשְׁבַּ֤ע יְהֹוָה֙ לָהֶ֔ם לְבִלְתִּ֞י הַרְאוֹתָ֣ם אֶת־הָאָ֗רֶץ אֲשֶׁר֩ נִשְׁבַּ֨ע יְהֹוָ֤ה לַאֲבוֹתָם֙ לָ֣תֶת לָ֔נוּ אֶ֛רֶץ זָבַ֥ת חָלָ֖ב וּדְבָֽשׁ׃

ז וְאֶת־בְּנֵיהֶם֙ הֵקִ֣ים תַּחְתָּ֔ם אֹתָ֖ם מָ֣ל יְהוֹשֻׁ֑עַ כִּֽי־עֲרֵלִ֣ים הָי֔וּ כִּ֛י לֹא־מָ֥לוּ אוֹתָ֖ם בַּדָּֽרֶךְ׃

ח וַיְהִ֛י כַּאֲשֶׁר־תַּ֥מּוּ כָל־הַגּ֖וֹי לְהִמּ֑וֹל וַיֵּשְׁב֥וּ תַחְתָּ֛ם בַּֽמַּחֲנֶ֖ה עַ֥ד חֲיוֹתָֽם׃

ט וַיֹּ֤אמֶר יְהֹוָה֙ אֶל־יְהוֹשֻׁ֔עַ הַיּ֗וֹם גַּלּ֛וֹתִי אֶת־חֶרְפַּ֥ת מִצְרַ֖יִם מֵעֲלֵיכֶ֑ם וַיִּקְרָ֞א שֵׁ֣ם הַמָּק֤וֹם הַהוּא֙ גִּלְגָּ֔ל עַ֖ד הַיּ֥וֹם הַזֶּֽה׃

י וַיַּחֲנ֥וּ בְנֵֽי־יִשְׂרָאֵ֖ל בַּגִּלְגָּ֑ל וַיַּעֲשׂ֣וּ אֶת־הַפֶּ֡סַח בְּאַרְבָּעָה֩ עָשָׂ֨ר י֥וֹם לַחֹ֛דֶשׁ בָּעֶ֖רֶב בְּעַרְב֥וֹת יְרִיחֽוֹ׃

יא וַיֹּ֨אכְל֜וּ מֵעֲב֥וּר הָאָ֛רֶץ מִמׇּחֳרַ֥ת הַפֶּ֖סַח מַצּ֣וֹת וְקָל֑וּי בְּעֶ֖צֶם הַיּ֥וֹם הַזֶּֽה׃

יב וַיִּשְׁבֹּ֨ת הַמָּ֜ן מִֽמָּחֳרָ֗ת בְּאָכְלָם֙ מֵעֲב֣וּר הָאָ֔רֶץ וְלֹא־הָ֥יָה ע֛וֹד לִבְנֵ֥י יִשְׂרָאֵ֖ל מָ֑ן וַיֹּאכְל֗וּ מִתְּבוּאַת֙ אֶ֣רֶץ כְּנַ֔עַן בַּשָּׁנָ֖ה הַהִֽיא׃

יג וַיְהִ֗י בִּֽהְי֣וֹת יְהוֹשֻׁ֘עַ֮ בִּירִיחוֹ֒ וַיִּשָּׂ֤א עֵינָיו֙ וַיַּ֔רְא וְהִנֵּה־אִישׁ֙ עֹמֵ֣ד לְנֶגְדּ֔וֹ וְחַרְבּ֥וֹ שְׁלוּפָ֖ה בְּיָד֑וֹ וַיֵּ֨לֶךְ יְהוֹשֻׁ֤עַ אֵלָיו֙ וַיֹּ֣אמֶר ל֔וֹ הֲלָ֥נוּ אַתָּ֖ה אִם־לְצָרֵֽינוּ׃

יד וַיֹּ֣אמֶר ׀ לֹ֗א כִּ֛י אֲנִ֥י שַׂר־צְבָֽא־יְהֹוָ֖ה עַתָּ֣ה בָ֑אתִי וַיִּפֹּל֩ יְהוֹשֻׁ֨עַ אֶל־פָּנָ֥יו אַ֙רְצָה֙ וַיִּשְׁתָּ֔חוּ וַיֹּ֣אמֶר ל֔וֹ מָ֥ה אֲדֹנִ֖י מְדַבֵּ֥ר אֶל־עַבְדּֽוֹ׃

Yehoshua/Joshua
Chapter 6

יהושע
פרק ו

15 The captain of *Hashem*'s host answered *Yehoshua*, "Remove your sandals from your feet, for the place where you stand is holy." And *Yehoshua* did so.

וַיֹּאמֶר שַׂר־צְבָא יְהוָה אֶל־יְהוֹשֻׁעַ שַׁל־נַעַלְךָ מֵעַל רַגְלֶךָ כִּי הַמָּקוֹם אֲשֶׁר אַתָּה עֹמֵד עָלָיו קֹדֶשׁ הוּא וַיַּעַשׂ יְהוֹשֻׁעַ כֵּן׃

va-YO-mer sar tz'-VA a-do-NAI el y'-ho-SHU-a shal na-al-KHA may-AL rag-LE-kha KEE ha-ma-KOM a-SHER a-TAH o-MAYD a-LAV KO-desh HU va-YA-as y'-ho-SHU-a KAYN

6 1 Now *Yericho* was shut up tight because of the Israelites; no one could leave or enter.

וִירִיחוֹ סֹגֶרֶת וּמְסֻגֶּרֶת מִפְּנֵי בְּנֵי יִשְׂרָאֵל אֵין יוֹצֵא וְאֵין בָּא׃

vee-ree-KHO so-GE-ret um-su-GE-ret mi-p'-NAY b'-NAY yis-ra-AYL AYN yo-TZAY v'-AYN ba

2 *Hashem* said to *Yehoshua*, "See, I will deliver *Yericho* and her king [and her] warriors into your hands.

וַיֹּאמֶר יְהוָה אֶל־יְהוֹשֻׁעַ רְאֵה נָתַתִּי בְיָדְךָ אֶת־יְרִיחוֹ וְאֶת־מַלְכָּהּ גִּבּוֹרֵי הֶחָיִל׃

3 Let all your troops march around the city and complete one circuit of the city. Do this six days,

וְסַבֹּתֶם אֶת־הָעִיר כֹּל אַנְשֵׁי הַמִּלְחָמָה הַקֵּיף אֶת־הָעִיר פַּעַם אֶחָת כֹּה תַעֲשֶׂה שֵׁשֶׁת יָמִים׃

4 with seven *Kohanim* carrying seven *shofarot* preceding the *Aron*. On the seventh day, march around the city seven times, with the *Kohanim* blowing the *shofarot*.

וְשִׁבְעָה כֹהֲנִים יִשְׂאוּ שִׁבְעָה שׁוֹפְרוֹת הַיּוֹבְלִים לִפְנֵי הָאָרוֹן וּבַיּוֹם הַשְּׁבִיעִי תָּסֹבּוּ אֶת־הָעִיר שֶׁבַע פְּעָמִים וְהַכֹּהֲנִים יִתְקְעוּ בַּשּׁוֹפָרוֹת׃

5 And when a long blast is sounded on the *shofar* – as soon as you hear that sound of the *shofar* – all the people shall give a mighty shout. Thereupon the city wall will collapse, and the people shall advance, every man straight ahead."

וְהָיָה בִּמְשֹׁךְ בְּקֶרֶן הַיּוֹבֵל בשמעכם [כְּשָׁמְעֲכֶם] אֶת־קוֹל הַשּׁוֹפָר יָרִיעוּ כָל־הָעָם תְּרוּעָה גְדוֹלָה וְנָפְלָה חוֹמַת הָעִיר תַּחְתֶּיהָ וְעָלוּ הָעָם אִישׁ נֶגְדּוֹ׃

6 *Yehoshua* son of *Nun* summoned the *Kohanim* and said to them, "Take up the *Aron HaBrit*, and let seven *Kohanim* carrying seven *shofarot* precede the *Aron* of *Hashem*."

וַיִּקְרָא יְהוֹשֻׁעַ בִּן־נוּן אֶל־הַכֹּהֲנִים וַיֹּאמֶר אֲלֵהֶם שְׂאוּ אֶת־אֲרוֹן הַבְּרִית וְשִׁבְעָה כֹהֲנִים יִשְׂאוּ שִׁבְעָה שׁוֹפְרוֹת יוֹבְלִים לִפְנֵי אֲרוֹן יְהוָה׃

5:15 Remove your sandals from your feet, for the place where you stand is holy *Yehoshua* is told to remove his shoes because the place where he is standing is holy. This is reminiscent of the similar command given to *Moshe* while standing at the burning bush on the mountain of God, Mount Sinai (Exodus 3:5). But there is a critical difference. Unlike Sinai, which attained only temporary holiness, the place upon which *Yehoshua* is standing is eternally sacred. He is standing upon the ground of *Eretz Yisrael*.

Yigael Yadin (1917–1984)

6:1 Now Yericho was shut up tight because of the Israelites Archeological finds of the past 150 years have granted significant understandings and insights into the world of the Bible, while also leaving us with many unanswered questions. In a 1983 interview, Israel's first Chief of Staff and renowned archaeologist, Yigael Yadin, addressed the limits of biblical archaeology. Describing this passage in *Sefer Yehoshua* about the miraculous nature of the tumbling walls of *Yericho*, Yadin opined: "That's beyond the realm of archaeology, and I think it's beyond the realm of history as well. It's a matter of faith… The fact is that there was a city there, in my opinion, and it was conquered. There can be no doubt." According to many ancient Jewish philosophers, science and nature are not meant to validate our faith, nor is archeology. However, they can serve as powerful tools in bolstering our faith to believe in the truth of God's word in a more complete and complex fashion.

Yehoshua/Joshua
Chapter 6

יהושע
פרק ו

7 And he instructed the people, "Go forward, march around the city, with the vanguard marching in front of the *Aron* of *Hashem*."

ז וַיֹּאמְרוּ [וַיֹּאמֶר] אֶל־הָעָם עִבְרוּ וְסֹבּוּ אֶת־הָעִיר וְהֶחָלוּץ יַעֲבֹר לִפְנֵי אֲרוֹן יְהוָה:

8 When *Yehoshua* had instructed the people, the seven *Kohanim* carrying seven *shofarot* advanced before *Hashem*, blowing their *shofarot*; and the *Aron Brit Hashem* followed them.

ח וַיְהִי כֶּאֱמֹר יְהוֹשֻׁעַ אֶל־הָעָם וְשִׁבְעָה הַכֹּהֲנִים נֹשְׂאִים שִׁבְעָה שׁוֹפְרוֹת הַיּוֹבְלִים לִפְנֵי יְהוָה עָבְרוּ וְתָקְעוּ בַּשּׁוֹפָרוֹת וַאֲרוֹן בְּרִית יְהוָה הֹלֵךְ אַחֲרֵיהֶם:

9 The vanguard marched in front of the *Kohanim* who were blowing the *shofarot*, and the rear guard marched behind the *Aron*, with the *shofarot* sounding all the time.

ט וְהֶחָלוּץ הֹלֵךְ לִפְנֵי הַכֹּהֲנִים תֹּקְעוּ [תֹּקְעֵי] הַשּׁוֹפָרוֹת וְהַמְאַסֵּף הֹלֵךְ אַחֲרֵי הָאָרוֹן הָלוֹךְ וְתָקוֹעַ בַּשּׁוֹפָרוֹת:

10 But *Yehoshua*'s orders to the rest of the people were, "Do not shout, do not let your voices be heard, and do not let a sound issue from your lips until the moment that I command you, 'Shout!' Then you shall shout."

י וְאֶת־הָעָם צִוָּה יְהוֹשֻׁעַ לֵאמֹר לֹא תָרִיעוּ וְלֹא־תַשְׁמִיעוּ אֶת־קוֹלְכֶם וְלֹא־יֵצֵא מִפִּיכֶם דָּבָר עַד יוֹם אָמְרִי אֲלֵיכֶם הָרִיעוּ וַהֲרִיעֹתֶם:

11 So he had the *Aron* of *Hashem* go around the city and complete one circuit; then they returned to camp and spent the night in camp.

יא וַיַּסֵּב אֲרוֹן־יְהוָה אֶת־הָעִיר הַקֵּף פַּעַם אֶחָת וַיָּבֹאוּ הַמַּחֲנֶה וַיָּלִינוּ בַּמַּחֲנֶה:

12 *Yehoshua* rose early the next day; and the *Kohanim* took up the *Aron* of *Hashem*,

יב וַיַּשְׁכֵּם יְהוֹשֻׁעַ בַּבֹּקֶר וַיִּשְׂאוּ הַכֹּהֲנִים אֶת־אֲרוֹן יְהוָה:

13 while the seven *Kohanim* bearing the seven *shofarot* marched in front of the *Aron* of *Hashem*, blowing the *shofarot* as they marched. The vanguard marched in front of them, and the rear guard marched behind the *Aron* of *Hashem*, with the *shofarot* sounding all the time.

יג וְשִׁבְעָה הַכֹּהֲנִים נֹשְׂאִים שִׁבְעָה שׁוֹפְרוֹת הַיֹּבְלִים לִפְנֵי אֲרוֹן יְהוָה הֹלְכִים הָלוֹךְ וְתָקְעוּ בַּשּׁוֹפָרוֹת וְהֶחָלוּץ הֹלֵךְ לִפְנֵיהֶם וְהַמְאַסֵּף הֹלֵךְ אַחֲרֵי אֲרוֹן יְהוָה הוֹלֵךְ [הָלוֹךְ] וְתָקוֹעַ בַּשּׁוֹפָרוֹת:

14 And so they marched around the city once on the second day and returned to the camp. They did this six days.

יד וַיָּסֹבּוּ אֶת־הָעִיר בַּיּוֹם הַשֵּׁנִי פַּעַם אַחַת וַיָּשֻׁבוּ הַמַּחֲנֶה כֹּה עָשׂוּ שֵׁשֶׁת יָמִים:

15 On the seventh day, they rose at daybreak and marched around the city, in the same manner, seven times; that was the only day that they marched around the city seven times.

טו וַיְהִי בַּיּוֹם הַשְּׁבִיעִי וַיַּשְׁכִּמוּ כַּעֲלוֹת הַשַּׁחַר וַיָּסֹבּוּ אֶת־הָעִיר כַּמִּשְׁפָּט הַזֶּה שֶׁבַע פְּעָמִים רַק בַּיּוֹם הַהוּא סָבְבוּ אֶת־הָעִיר שֶׁבַע פְּעָמִים:

vai-HEE ba-YOM ha-sh'-vee-EE va-yash-KI-mu ka-a-LOT ha-SHA-khar va-ya-SO-bu et ha-EER ka-mish-PAT ha-ZEH SHE-va p'-a-MEEM RAK ba-YOM ha-HU sa-v'-VU et ha-EER SHE-va p'-a-MEEM

6:15 On the seventh day On the seventh day, the Children of Israel walk around *Yericho* seven times. They blow the *shofarot* (שופרות), 'rams horns,' the walls miraculously fall, and they are able to take the city. The classical commentator *Rashi* notes that the seventh day of this process was *Shabbat*. This teaches us that war on behalf of defending the people and Land of Israel is permitted and required even on the peaceful and

Ancient Yericho

Yehoshua/Joshua
Chapter 6

16 On the seventh round, as the *Kohanim* blew the *shofarot*, *Yehoshua* commanded the people, "Shout! For *Hashem* has given you the city.

17 The city and everything in it are to be proscribed for *Hashem*; only Rahab the harlot is to be spared, and all who are with her in the house, because she hid the messengers we sent.

18 But you must beware of that which is proscribed, or else you will be proscribed: if you take anything from that which is proscribed, you will cause the camp of *Yisrael* to be proscribed; you will bring calamity upon it.

19 All the silver and gold and objects of copper and iron are consecrated to *Hashem*; they must go into the treasury of *Hashem*."

20 So the people shouted when the *shofarot* were sounded. When the people heard the sound of the *shofarot*, the people raised a mighty shout and the wall collapsed. The people rushed into the city, every man straight in front of him, and they captured the city.

21 They exterminated everything in the city with the sword: man and woman, young and old, ox and sheep and ass.

22 But *Yehoshua* bade the two men who had spied out the land, "Go into the harlot's house and bring out the woman and all that belong to her, as you swore to her."

23 So the young spies went in and brought out Rahab, her father and her mother, her brothers and all that belonged to her – they brought out her whole family and left them outside the camp of *Yisrael*.

24 They burned down the city and everything in it. But the silver and gold and the objects of copper and iron were deposited in the treasury of the House of *Hashem*.

---

holy Sabbath. Even today, though we honor *Shabbat* and keep it holy, the State of Israel is required to protect itself seven days a week. Thus, in the Israeli Army, essential tasks to protect the nation must and do continue, even on *Shabbat*.

Yehoshua/Joshua
Chapter 7

25 Only Rahab the harlot and her father's family were spared by *Yehoshua*, along with all that belonged to her, and she dwelt among the Israelites – as is still the case. For she had hidden the messengers that *Yehoshua* sent to spy out *Yericho*.

26 At that time *Yehoshua* pronounced this oath: "Cursed of *Hashem* be the man who shall undertake to fortify this city of *Yericho*: he shall lay its foundations at the cost of his first-born, and set up its gates at the cost of his youngest."

27 *Hashem* was with *Yehoshua*, and his fame spread throughout the land.

7

1 The Israelites, however, violated the proscription: *Achan* son of Carmi son of Zabdi son of *Zerach*, of the tribe of *Yehuda*, took of that which was proscribed, and *Hashem* was incensed with the Israelites.

2 *Yehoshua* sent men from *Yericho* to Ai, which lies close to *Beit Aven* – east of *Beit El* – with orders to go up and spy out the country. So the men went up and spied out Ai.

3 They returned to *Yehoshua* and reported to him, "Not all the troops need go up. Let two or three thousand men go and attack Ai; do not trouble all the troops to go up there, for [the people] there are few."

4 So about three thousand of the troops marched up there; but they were routed by the men of Ai.

5 The men of Ai killed about thirty-six of them, pursuing them outside the gate as far as Shebarim, and cutting them down along the descent. And the heart of the troops sank in utter dismay.

6 *Yehoshua* thereupon rent his clothes. He and the elders of *Yisrael* lay until evening with their faces to the ground in front of the *Aron* of *Hashem*; and they strewed earth on their heads.

7 "Ah, *Hashem*!" cried *Yehoshua*. "Why did You lead this people across the *Yarden* only to deliver us into the hands of the Amorites, to be destroyed by them? If only we had been content to remain on the other side of the *Yarden*!

8 O *Hashem*, what can I say after *Yisrael* has turned tail before its enemies?

Yehoshua/Joshua
Chapter 7

יהושע
פרק ז

9 When the Canaanites and all the inhabitants of the land hear of this, they will turn upon us and wipe out our very name from the earth. And what will You do about Your great name?"

ט וְיִשְׁמְעוּ הַכְּנַעֲנִי וְכֹל יֹשְׁבֵי הָאָרֶץ וְנָסַבּוּ עָלֵינוּ וְהִכְרִיתוּ אֶת־שְׁמֵנוּ מִן־הָאָרֶץ וּמַה־תַּעֲשֵׂה לְשִׁמְךָ הַגָּדוֹל׃

10 But *Hashem* answered *Yehoshua*: "Arise! Why do you lie prostrate?

י וַיֹּאמֶר יְהוָה אֶל־יְהוֹשֻׁעַ קֻם לָךְ לָמָּה זֶּה אַתָּה נֹפֵל עַל־פָּנֶיךָ׃

11 *Yisrael* has sinned! They have broken the covenant by which I bound them. They have taken of the proscribed and put it in their vessels; they have stolen; they have broken faith!

יא חָטָא יִשְׂרָאֵל וְגַם עָבְרוּ אֶת־בְּרִיתִי אֲשֶׁר צִוִּיתִי אוֹתָם וְגַם לָקְחוּ מִן־הַחֵרֶם וְגַם גָּנְבוּ וְגַם כִּחֲשׁוּ וְגַם שָׂמוּ בִכְלֵיהֶם׃

kha-TA yis-ra-AYL v'-GAM a-v'-RU et b'-ree-TEE a-SHER tzi-VEE-tee o-TAM v'-GAM la-k'-KHU min ha-KHAY-rem v'-GAM ga-n'-VU v'-GAM ki-kha-SHU v'-GAM SA-mu vikh-lay-HEM

12 Therefore, the Israelites will not be able to hold their ground against their enemies; they will have to turn tail before their enemies, for they have become proscribed. I will not be with you any more unless you root out from among you what is proscribed.

יב וְלֹא יֻכְלוּ בְּנֵי יִשְׂרָאֵל לָקוּם לִפְנֵי אֹיְבֵיהֶם עֹרֶף יִפְנוּ לִפְנֵי אֹיְבֵיהֶם כִּי הָיוּ לְחֵרֶם לֹא אוֹסִיף לִהְיוֹת עִמָּכֶם אִם־לֹא תַשְׁמִידוּ הַחֵרֶם מִקִּרְבְּכֶם׃

13 Go and purify the people. Order them: Purify yourselves for tomorrow. For thus says *Hashem*, the God of *Yisrael*: Something proscribed is in your midst, O *Yisrael*, and you will not be able to stand up to your enemies until you have purged the proscribed from among you.

יג קֻם קַדֵּשׁ אֶת־הָעָם וְאָמַרְתָּ הִתְקַדְּשׁוּ לְמָחָר כִּי כֹה אָמַר יְהוָה אֱלֹהֵי יִשְׂרָאֵל חֵרֶם בְּקִרְבְּךָ יִשְׂרָאֵל לֹא תוּכַל לָקוּם לִפְנֵי אֹיְבֶיךָ עַד־הֲסִירְכֶם הַחֵרֶם מִקִּרְבְּכֶם׃

14 Tomorrow morning you shall present yourselves by tribes. Whichever tribe *Hashem* indicates shall come forward by clans; the clan that *Hashem* indicates shall come forward by ancestral houses, and the ancestral house that *Hashem* indicates shall come forward man by man.

יד וְנִקְרַבְתֶּם בַּבֹּקֶר לְשִׁבְטֵיכֶם וְהָיָה הַשֵּׁבֶט אֲשֶׁר־יִלְכְּדֶנּוּ יְהוָה יִקְרַב לַמִּשְׁפָּחוֹת וְהַמִּשְׁפָּחָה אֲשֶׁר־יִלְכְּדֶנָּה יְהוָה תִּקְרַב לַבָּתִּים וְהַבַּיִת אֲשֶׁר יִלְכְּדֶנּוּ יְהוָה יִקְרַב לַגְּבָרִים׃

15 Then he who is indicated for proscription, and all that is his, shall be put to the fire, because he broke the Covenant of *Hashem* and because he committed an outrage in *Yisrael*."

טו וְהָיָה הַנִּלְכָּד בַּחֵרֶם יִשָּׂרֵף בָּאֵשׁ אֹתוֹ וְאֶת־כָּל־אֲשֶׁר־לוֹ כִּי עָבַר אֶת־בְּרִית יְהוָה וְכִי־עָשָׂה נְבָלָה בְּיִשְׂרָאֵל׃

Malbim
(1809–1879)

7:11 *Yisrael* has sinned On the surface, it seems odd that *Hashem* would say that the People of Israel had sinned. Wasn't it only *Achan*, the one who stole items from *Yericho*, who sinned? The *Malbim* points out that this verse teaches the critical principle of collective responsibility. The Children of Israel are not simply a collection of individuals. Rather, they are a spiritually united nation where the actions of one impact the fate of all. Therefore, when they entered *Eretz Yisrael* they became responsible for one another. This collective responsibility extends beyond simply avoiding negative things. All are also responsible for the positive welfare of their brothers and sisters, wherever they may be. Successfully meeting this collective responsibility is part of what makes the State of Israel great.

Yehoshua/Joshua
Chapter 7

16 Early next morning, *Yehoshua* had *Yisrael* come forward by tribes; and the tribe of *Yehuda* was indicated.

17 He then had the clans of *Yehuda* come forward, and the clan of *Zerach* was indicated. Then he had the clan of *Zerach* come forward by ancestral houses, and Zabdi was indicated.

18 Finally he had his ancestral house come forward man by man, and *Achan* son of Carmi, son of Zabdi, son of *Zerach*, of the tribe of *Yehuda*, was indicated.

19 Then *Yehoshua* said to *Achan*, "My son, pay honor to *Hashem*, the God of *Yisrael*, and make confession to Him. Tell me what you have done; do not hold anything back from me."

20 *Achan* answered *Yehoshua*, "It is true, I have sinned against *Hashem*, the God of *Yisrael*. This is what I did:

21 I saw among the spoil a fine Shinar mantle, two hundred *shekalim* of silver, and a wedge of gold weighing fifty *shekalim*, and I coveted them and took them. They are buried in the ground in my tent, with the silver under it."

22 *Yehoshua* sent messengers, who hurried to the tent; and there it was, buried in his tent, with the silver underneath.

23 They took them from the tent and brought them to *Yehoshua* and all the Israelites, and displayed them before *Hashem*.

24 Then *Yehoshua*, and all *Yisrael* with him, took *Achan* son of *Zerach* – and the silver, the mantle, and the wedge of gold – his sons and daughters, and his ox, his ass, and his flock, and his tent, and all his belongings, and brought them up to the Valley of Achor.

25 And *Yehoshua* said, "What calamity you have brought upon us! *Hashem* will bring calamity upon you this day." And all *Yisrael* pelted him with stones. They put them to the fire and stoned them.

26 They raised a huge mound of stones over him, which is still there. Then the anger of *Hashem* subsided. That is why that place was named the Valley of Achor – as is still the case.

יהושע
פרק ז

טז וַיַּשְׁכֵּם יְהוֹשֻׁעַ בַּבֹּקֶר וַיַּקְרֵב אֶת־יִשְׂרָאֵל לִשְׁבָטָיו וַיִּלָּכֵד שֵׁבֶט יְהוּדָה:

יז וַיַּקְרֵב אֶת־מִשְׁפַּחַת יְהוּדָה וַיִּלְכֹּד אֵת מִשְׁפַּחַת הַזַּרְחִי וַיַּקְרֵב אֶת־מִשְׁפַּחַת הַזַּרְחִי לַגְּבָרִים וַיִּלָּכֵד זַבְדִּי:

יח וַיַּקְרֵב אֶת־בֵּיתוֹ לַגְּבָרִים וַיִּלָּכֵד עָכָן בֶּן־כַּרְמִי בֶן־זַבְדִּי בֶן־זֶרַח לְמַטֵּה יְהוּדָה:

יט וַיֹּאמֶר יְהוֹשֻׁעַ אֶל־עָכָן בְּנִי שִׂים־נָא כָבוֹד לַיהוָה אֱלֹהֵי יִשְׂרָאֵל וְתֶן־לוֹ תוֹדָה וְהַגֶּד־נָא לִי מֶה עָשִׂיתָ אַל־תְּכַחֵד מִמֶּנִּי:

כ וַיַּעַן עָכָן אֶת־יְהוֹשֻׁעַ וַיֹּאמַר אָמְנָה אָנֹכִי חָטָאתִי לַיהוָה אֱלֹהֵי יִשְׂרָאֵל וְכָזֹאת וְכָזֹאת עָשִׂיתִי:

כא וָאֶרְאֶה [וָאֵרֶא] בַשָּׁלָל אַדֶּרֶת שִׁנְעָר אַחַת טוֹבָה וּמָאתַיִם שְׁקָלִים כֶּסֶף וּלְשׁוֹן זָהָב אֶחָד חֲמִשִּׁים שְׁקָלִים מִשְׁקָלוֹ וָאֶחְמְדֵם וָאֶקָּחֵם וְהִנָּם טְמוּנִים בָּאָרֶץ בְּתוֹךְ הָאָהֳלִי וְהַכֶּסֶף תַּחְתֶּיהָ:

כב וַיִּשְׁלַח יְהוֹשֻׁעַ מַלְאָכִים וַיָּרֻצוּ הָאֹהֱלָה וְהִנֵּה טְמוּנָה בְּאָהֳלוֹ וְהַכֶּסֶף תַּחְתֶּיהָ:

כג וַיִּקָּחוּם מִתּוֹךְ הָאֹהֶל וַיְבִאוּם אֶל־יְהוֹשֻׁעַ וְאֶל כָּל־בְּנֵי יִשְׂרָאֵל וַיַּצִּקֻם לִפְנֵי יְהוָה:

כד וַיִּקַּח יְהוֹשֻׁעַ אֶת־עָכָן בֶּן־זֶרַח וְאֶת־הַכֶּסֶף וְאֶת־הָאַדֶּרֶת וְאֶת־לְשׁוֹן הַזָּהָב וְאֶת־בָּנָיו וְאֶת־בְּנֹתָיו וְאֶת־שׁוֹרוֹ וְאֶת־חֲמֹרוֹ וְאֶת־צֹאנוֹ וְאֶת־אָהֳלוֹ וְאֶת־כָּל־אֲשֶׁר־לוֹ וְכָל־יִשְׂרָאֵל עִמּוֹ וַיַּעֲלוּ אֹתָם עֵמֶק עָכוֹר:

כה וַיֹּאמֶר יְהוֹשֻׁעַ מֶה עֲכַרְתָּנוּ יַעְכָּרְךָ יְהוָה בַּיּוֹם הַזֶּה וַיִּרְגְּמוּ אֹתוֹ כָל־יִשְׂרָאֵל אֶבֶן וַיִּשְׂרְפוּ אֹתָם בָּאֵשׁ וַיִּסְקְלוּ אֹתָם בָּאֲבָנִים:

כו וַיָּקִימוּ עָלָיו גַּל־אֲבָנִים גָּדוֹל עַד הַיּוֹם הַזֶּה וַיָּשָׁב יְהוָה מֵחֲרוֹן אַפּוֹ עַל־כֵּן קָרָא שֵׁם הַמָּקוֹם הַהוּא עֵמֶק עָכוֹר עַד הַיּוֹם הַזֶּה:

Yehoshua/Joshua
Chapter 8

8 1 *Hashem* said to *Yehoshua*, "Do not be frightened or dismayed. Take all the fighting troops with you, go and march against Ai. See, I will deliver the king of Ai, his people, his city, and his land into your hands.

2 You shall treat Ai and her king as you treated *Yericho* and her king; however, you may take the spoil and the cattle as booty for yourselves. Now set an ambush against the city behind it."

3 So *Yehoshua* and all the fighting troops prepared for the march on Ai. *Yehoshua* chose thirty thousand men, valiant warriors, and sent them ahead by night.

4 He instructed them as follows: "Mind, you are to lie in ambush behind the city; don't stay too far from the city, and all of you be on the alert.

5 I and all the troops with me will approach the city; and when they come out against us, as they did the first time, we will flee from them.

6 They will come rushing after us until we have drawn them away from the city. They will think, 'They are fleeing from us the same as last time'; but while we are fleeing before them,

7 you will dash out from your ambush and seize the city, and *Hashem* your God will deliver it into your hands.

8 And when you take the city, set it on fire. Do as *Hashem* has commanded. Mind, I have given you your orders."

9 *Yehoshua* then sent them off, and they proceeded to the ambush; they took up a position between Ai and *Beit El* – west of Ai – while *Yehoshua* spent the night with the rest of the troops.

10 Early in the morning, *Yehoshua* mustered the troops; then he and the elders of *Yisrael* marched upon Ai at the head of the troops.

11 All the fighting force that was with him advanced near the city and encamped to the north of Ai, with a hollow between them and Ai.

12 He selected about five thousand men and stationed them as an ambush between *Beit El* and Ai, west of the city.

יהושע
פרק ח

ח א וַיֹּאמֶר יְהֹוָה אֶל־יְהוֹשֻׁעַ אַל־תִּירָא וְאַל־תֵּחָת קַח עִמְּךָ אֵת כָּל־עַם הַמִּלְחָמָה וְקוּם עֲלֵה הָעָי רְאֵה נָתַתִּי בְיָדְךָ אֶת־מֶלֶךְ הָעַי וְאֶת־עַמּוֹ וְאֶת־עִירוֹ וְאֶת־אַרְצוֹ:

ב וְעָשִׂיתָ לָעַי וּלְמַלְכָּהּ כַּאֲשֶׁר עָשִׂיתָ לִירִיחוֹ וּלְמַלְכָּהּ רַק־שְׁלָלָהּ וּבְהֶמְתָּהּ תָּבֹזּוּ לָכֶם שִׂים־לְךָ אֹרֵב לָעִיר מֵאַחֲרֶיהָ:

ג וַיָּקָם יְהוֹשֻׁעַ וְכָל־עַם הַמִּלְחָמָה לַעֲלוֹת הָעָי וַיִּבְחַר יְהוֹשֻׁעַ שְׁלֹשִׁים אֶלֶף אִישׁ גִּבּוֹרֵי הַחַיִל וַיִּשְׁלָחֵם לָיְלָה:

ד וַיְצַו אֹתָם לֵאמֹר רְאוּ אַתֶּם אֹרְבִים לָעִיר מֵאַחֲרֵי הָעִיר אַל־תַּרְחִיקוּ מִן־הָעִיר מְאֹד וִהְיִיתֶם כֻּלְּכֶם נְכֹנִים:

ה וַאֲנִי וְכָל־הָעָם אֲשֶׁר אִתִּי נִקְרַב אֶל־הָעִיר וְהָיָה כִּי־יֵצְאוּ לִקְרָאתֵנוּ כַּאֲשֶׁר בָּרִאשֹׁנָה וְנַסְנוּ לִפְנֵיהֶם:

ו וְיָצְאוּ אַחֲרֵינוּ עַד הַתִּיקֵנוּ אוֹתָם מִן־הָעִיר כִּי יֹאמְרוּ נָסִים לְפָנֵינוּ כַּאֲשֶׁר בָּרִאשֹׁנָה וְנַסְנוּ לִפְנֵיהֶם:

ז וְאַתֶּם תָּקֻמוּ מֵהָאוֹרֵב וְהוֹרַשְׁתֶּם אֶת־הָעִיר וּנְתָנָהּ יְהֹוָה אֱלֹהֵיכֶם בְּיֶדְכֶם:

ח וְהָיָה כְּתָפְשְׂכֶם אֶת־הָעִיר תַּצִּיתוּ אֶת־הָעִיר בָּאֵשׁ כִּדְבַר יְהֹוָה תַּעֲשׂוּ רְאוּ צִוִּיתִי אֶתְכֶם:

ט וַיִּשְׁלָחֵם יְהוֹשֻׁעַ וַיֵּלְכוּ אֶל־הַמַּאְרָב וַיֵּשְׁבוּ בֵּין בֵּית־אֵל וּבֵין הָעַי מִיָּם לָעָי וַיָּלֶן יְהוֹשֻׁעַ בַּלַּיְלָה הַהוּא בְּתוֹךְ הָעָם:

י וַיַּשְׁכֵּם יְהוֹשֻׁעַ בַּבֹּקֶר וַיִּפְקֹד אֶת־הָעָם וַיַּעַל הוּא וְזִקְנֵי יִשְׂרָאֵל לִפְנֵי הָעָם הָעָי:

יא וְכָל־הָעָם הַמִּלְחָמָה אֲשֶׁר אִתּוֹ עָלוּ וַיִּגְּשׁוּ וַיָּבֹאוּ נֶגֶד הָעִיר וַיַּחֲנוּ מִצְּפוֹן לָעַי וְהַגַּי בֵּינוֹ [בֵּינָיו] וּבֵין הָעָי:

יב וַיִּקַּח כַּחֲמֵשֶׁת אֲלָפִים אִישׁ וַיָּשֶׂם אוֹתָם אֹרֵב בֵּין בֵּית־אֵל וּבֵין הָעַי מִיָּם לָעִיר:

Yehoshua/Joshua
Chapter 8

יהושע
פרק ח

13 Thus the main body of the army was disposed on the north of the city, but the far end of it was on the west. (This was after *Yehoshua* had spent the night in the valley.)

יג וַיָּשִׂימוּ הָעָם אֶת־כׇּל־הַמַּחֲנֶה אֲשֶׁר מִצְּפוֹן לָעִיר וְאֶת־עֲקֵבוֹ מִיָּם לָעִיר וַיֵּלֶךְ יְהוֹשֻׁעַ בַּלַּיְלָה הַהוּא בְּתוֹךְ הָעֵמֶק׃

14 When the king of Ai saw them, he and all his people, the inhabitants of the city, rushed out in the early morning to the meeting place, facing the Arabah, to engage the Israelites in battle; for he was unaware that a force was lying in ambush behind the city.

יד וַיְהִי כִּרְאוֹת מֶלֶךְ־הָעַי וַיְמַהֲרוּ וַיַּשְׁכִּימוּ וַיֵּצְאוּ אַנְשֵׁי־הָעִיר לִקְרַאת־יִשְׂרָאֵל לַמִּלְחָמָה הוּא וְכׇל־עַמּוֹ לַמּוֹעֵד לִפְנֵי הָעֲרָבָה וְהוּא לֹא יָדַע כִּי־אֹרֵב לוֹ מֵאַחֲרֵי הָעִיר׃

15 *Yehoshua* and all *Yisrael* fled in the direction of the wilderness, as though routed by them.

טו וַיִּנָּגְעוּ יְהוֹשֻׁעַ וְכׇל־יִשְׂרָאֵל לִפְנֵיהֶם וַיָּנֻסוּ דֶּרֶךְ הַמִּדְבָּר׃

16 All the troops in the city gathered to pursue them; pursuing *Yehoshua*, they were drawn out of the city.

טז וַיִּזָּעֲקוּ כׇּל־הָעָם אֲשֶׁר בָּעִיר [בָּעַי] לִרְדֹּף אַחֲרֵיהֶם וַיִּרְדְּפוּ אַחֲרֵי יְהוֹשֻׁעַ וַיִּנָּתְקוּ מִן־הָעִיר׃

17 Not a man was left in Ai or in *Beit El* who did not go out after *Yisrael*; they left the city open while they pursued *Yisrael*.

יז וְלֹא־נִשְׁאַר אִישׁ בָּעַי וּבֵית אֵל אֲשֶׁר לֹא־יָצְאוּ אַחֲרֵי יִשְׂרָאֵל וַיַּעַזְבוּ אֶת־הָעִיר פְּתוּחָה וַיִּרְדְּפוּ אַחֲרֵי יִשְׂרָאֵל׃

18 *Hashem* then said to *Yehoshua*, "Hold out the javelin in your hand toward Ai, for I will deliver it into your hands." So *Yehoshua* held out the javelin in his hand toward the city.

יח וַיֹּאמֶר יְהֹוָה אֶל־יְהוֹשֻׁעַ נְטֵה בַּכִּידוֹן אֲשֶׁר־בְּיָדְךָ אֶל־הָעַי כִּי בְיָדְךָ אֶתְּנֶנָּה וַיֵּט יְהוֹשֻׁעַ בַּכִּידוֹן אֲשֶׁר־בְּיָדוֹ אֶל־הָעִיר׃

19 As soon as he held out his hand, the ambush came rushing out of their station. They entered the city and captured it; and they swiftly set fire to the city.

יט וְהָאוֹרֵב קָם מְהֵרָה מִמְּקוֹמוֹ וַיָּרוּצוּ כִּנְטוֹת יָדוֹ וַיָּבֹאוּ הָעִיר וַיִּלְכְּדוּהָ וַיְמַהֲרוּ וַיַּצִּיתוּ אֶת־הָעִיר בָּאֵשׁ׃

20 The men of Ai looked back and saw the smoke of the city rising to the sky; they had no room for flight in any direction. The people who had been fleeing to the wilderness now became the pursuers.

כ וַיִּפְנוּ אַנְשֵׁי הָעַי אַחֲרֵיהֶם וַיִּרְאוּ וְהִנֵּה עָלָה עֲשַׁן הָעִיר הַשָּׁמַיְמָה וְלֹא־הָיָה בָהֶם יָדַיִם לָנוּס הֵנָּה וָהֵנָּה וְהָעָם הַנָּס הַמִּדְבָּר נֶהְפַּךְ אֶל־הָרוֹדֵף׃

21 For when *Yehoshua* and all *Yisrael* saw that the ambush had captured the city, and that smoke was rising from the city, they turned around and attacked the men of Ai.

כא וִיהוֹשֻׁעַ וְכׇל־יִשְׂרָאֵל רָאוּ כִּי־לָכַד הָאֹרֵב אֶת־הָעִיר וְכִי עָלָה עֲשַׁן הָעִיר וַיָּשֻׁבוּ וַיַּכּוּ אֶת־אַנְשֵׁי הָעָי׃

22 Now the other [Israelites] were coming out of the city against them, so that they were between two bodies of Israelites, one on each side of them. They were slaughtered, so that no one escaped or got away.

כב וְאֵלֶּה יָצְאוּ מִן־הָעִיר לִקְרָאתָם וַיִּהְיוּ לְיִשְׂרָאֵל בַּתָּוֶךְ אֵלֶּה מִזֶּה וְאֵלֶּה מִזֶּה וַיַּכּוּ אוֹתָם עַד־בִּלְתִּי הִשְׁאִיר־לוֹ שָׂרִיד וּפָלִיט׃

23 The king of Ai was taken alive and brought to *Yehoshua*.

כג וְאֶת־מֶלֶךְ הָעַי תָּפְשׂוּ חָי וַיַּקְרִבוּ אֹתוֹ אֶל־יְהוֹשֻׁעַ׃

548

Yehoshua/Joshua
Chapter 8

24 When *Yisrael* had killed all the inhabitants of Ai who had pursued them into the open wilderness, and all of them, to the last man, had fallen by the sword, all the Israelites turned back to Ai and put it to the sword.

25 The total of those who fell that day, men and women, the entire population of Ai, came to twelve thousand.

26 *Yehoshua* did not draw back the hand with which he held out his javelin until all the inhabitants of Ai had been exterminated.

27 However, the Israelites took the cattle and the spoil of the city as their booty, in accordance with the instructions that *Hashem* had given to *Yehoshua*.

28 Then *Yehoshua* burned down Ai, and turned it into a mound of ruins for all time, a desolation to this day.

29 And the king of Ai was impaled on a stake until the evening. At sunset, *Yehoshua* had the corpse taken down from the stake and it was left lying at the entrance to the city gate. They raised a great heap of stones over it, which is there to this day.

30 At that time *Yehoshua* built a *Mizbayach* to *Hashem*, the God of *Yisrael*, on *Har Eival*,

31 as *Moshe*, the servant of *Hashem*, had commanded the Israelites – as is written in the Book of the Teaching of *Moshe* – a *Mizbayach* of unhewn stone upon which no iron had been wielded. They offered on it burnt offerings to *Hashem*, and brought sacrifices of well-being.

32 And there, on the stones, he inscribed a copy of the Teaching that *Moshe* had written for the Israelites.

33 All *Yisrael* – stranger and citizen alike – with their elders, officials, and magistrates, stood on either side of the *Aron*, facing the levitical *Kohanim* who carried the *Aron Brit Hashem*. Half of them faced Mount Gerizim and half of them faced *Har Eival*, as *Moshe* the servant of *Hashem* had commanded them of old, in order to bless the people of *Yisrael*.

יהושע
פרק ח

כד וַיְהִי כְּכַלּוֹת יִשְׂרָאֵל לַהֲרֹג אֶת־כָּל־יֹשְׁבֵי הָעַי בַּשָּׂדֶה בַּמִּדְבָּר אֲשֶׁר רְדָפוּם בּוֹ וַיִּפְּלוּ כֻלָּם לְפִי־חֶרֶב עַד־תֻּמָּם וַיָּשֻׁבוּ כָל־יִשְׂרָאֵל הָעַי וַיַּכּוּ אֹתָהּ לְפִי־חָרֶב:

כה וַיְהִי כָל־הַנֹּפְלִים בַּיּוֹם הַהוּא מֵאִישׁ וְעַד־אִשָּׁה שְׁנֵים עָשָׂר אָלֶף כֹּל אַנְשֵׁי הָעָי:

כו וִיהוֹשֻׁעַ לֹא־הֵשִׁיב יָדוֹ אֲשֶׁר נָטָה בַּכִּידוֹן עַד אֲשֶׁר הֶחֱרִים אֵת כָּל־יֹשְׁבֵי הָעָי:

כז רַק הַבְּהֵמָה וּשְׁלַל הָעִיר הַהִיא בָּזְזוּ לָהֶם יִשְׂרָאֵל כִּדְבַר יְהֹוָה אֲשֶׁר צִוָּה אֶת־יְהוֹשֻׁעַ:

כח וַיִּשְׂרֹף יְהוֹשֻׁעַ אֶת־הָעָי וַיְשִׂימֶהָ תֵּל־עוֹלָם שְׁמָמָה עַד הַיּוֹם הַזֶּה:

כט וְאֶת־מֶלֶךְ הָעַי תָּלָה עַל־הָעֵץ עַד־עֵת הָעָרֶב וּכְבוֹא הַשֶּׁמֶשׁ צִוָּה יְהוֹשֻׁעַ וַיֹּרִידוּ אֶת־נִבְלָתוֹ מִן־הָעֵץ וַיַּשְׁלִיכוּ אוֹתָהּ אֶל־פֶּתַח שַׁעַר הָעִיר וַיָּקִימוּ עָלָיו גַּל־אֲבָנִים גָּדוֹל עַד הַיּוֹם הַזֶּה:

ל אָז יִבְנֶה יְהוֹשֻׁעַ מִזְבֵּחַ לַיהֹוָה אֱלֹהֵי יִשְׂרָאֵל בְּהַר עֵיבָל:

לא כַּאֲשֶׁר צִוָּה מֹשֶׁה עֶבֶד־יְהֹוָה אֶת־בְּנֵי יִשְׂרָאֵל כַּכָּתוּב בְּסֵפֶר תּוֹרַת מֹשֶׁה מִזְבַּח אֲבָנִים שְׁלֵמוֹת אֲשֶׁר לֹא־הֵנִיף עֲלֵיהֶן בַּרְזֶל וַיַּעֲלוּ עָלָיו עֹלוֹת לַיהֹוָה וַיִּזְבְּחוּ שְׁלָמִים:

לב וַיִּכְתָּב־שָׁם עַל־הָאֲבָנִים אֵת מִשְׁנֵה תּוֹרַת מֹשֶׁה אֲשֶׁר כָּתַב לִפְנֵי בְּנֵי יִשְׂרָאֵל:

לג וְכָל־יִשְׂרָאֵל וּזְקֵנָיו וְשֹׁטְרִים וְשֹׁפְטָיו עֹמְדִים מִזֶּה וּמִזֶּה לָאָרוֹן נֶגֶד הַכֹּהֲנִים הַלְוִיִּם נֹשְׂאֵי אֲרוֹן בְּרִית־יְהֹוָה כַּגֵּר כָּאֶזְרָח חֶצְיוֹ אֶל־מוּל הַר־גְּרִזִים וְהַחֶצְיוֹ אֶל־מוּל הַר־עֵיבָל כַּאֲשֶׁר צִוָּה מֹשֶׁה עֶבֶד־יְהֹוָה לְבָרֵךְ אֶת־הָעָם יִשְׂרָאֵל בָּרִאשֹׁנָה:

Yehoshua/Joshua
Chapter 9

יהושע
פרק ט

34 After that, he read all the words of the Teaching, the blessing and the curse, just as is written in the Book of the Teaching.

לד וְאַחֲרֵי־כֵן קָרָא אֶת־כָּל־דִּבְרֵי הַתּוֹרָה הַבְּרָכָה וְהַקְּלָלָה כְּכָל־הַכָּתוּב בְּסֵפֶר הַתּוֹרָה:

v'-a-kha-ray KHAYN ka-RA et kol div-RAY ha-to-RAH ha-b'-ra-KHAH v'-ha-k'-la-LAH k'-khol ha-ka-TUV b'-SAY-fer ha-to-RAH

35 There was not a word of all that *Moshe* had commanded that *Yehoshua* failed to read in the presence of the entire assembly of *Yisrael*, including the women and children and the strangers who accompanied them.

לה לֹא־הָיָה דָבָר מִכֹּל אֲשֶׁר־צִוָּה מֹשֶׁה אֲשֶׁר לֹא־קָרָא יְהוֹשֻׁעַ נֶגֶד כָּל־קְהַל יִשְׂרָאֵל וְהַנָּשִׁים וְהַטַּף וְהַגֵּר הַהֹלֵךְ בְּקִרְבָּם:

9 1 When all the kings west of the *Yarden* – in the hill country, in the Shephelah, and along the entire coast of the Mediterranean Sea up to the vicinity of Lebanon, the [land of the] Hittites, Amorites, Canaanites, Perizzites, Hivites, and Jebusites – learned of this,

ט א וַיְהִי כִשְׁמֹעַ כָּל־הַמְּלָכִים אֲשֶׁר בְּעֵבֶר הַיַּרְדֵּן בָּהָר וּבַשְּׁפֵלָה וּבְכֹל חוֹף הַיָּם הַגָּדוֹל אֶל־מוּל הַלְּבָנוֹן הַחִתִּי וְהָאֱמֹרִי הַכְּנַעֲנִי הַפְּרִזִּי הַחִוִּי וְהַיְבוּסִי:

2 they gathered with one accord to fight against *Yehoshua* and *Yisrael*.

ב וַיִּתְקַבְּצוּ יַחְדָּו לְהִלָּחֵם עִם־יְהוֹשֻׁעַ וְעִם־יִשְׂרָאֵל פֶּה אֶחָד:

3 But when the inhabitants of *Givon* learned how *Yehoshua* had treated *Yericho* and Ai,

ג וְיֹשְׁבֵי גִבְעוֹן שָׁמְעוּ אֵת אֲשֶׁר עָשָׂה יְהוֹשֻׁעַ לִירִיחוֹ וְלָעָי:

4 they for their part resorted to cunning. They set out in disguise: they took worn-out sacks for their asses, and worn-out waterskins that were cracked and patched;

ד וַיַּעֲשׂוּ גַם־הֵמָּה בְּעָרְמָה וַיֵּלְכוּ וַיִּצְטַיָּרוּ וַיִּקְחוּ שַׂקִּים בָּלִים לַחֲמוֹרֵיהֶם וְנֹאדוֹת יַיִן בָּלִים וּמְבֻקָּעִים וּמְצֹרָרִים:

5 they had worn-out, patched sandals on their feet, and threadbare clothes on their bodies; and all the bread they took as provision was dry and crumbly.

ה וּנְעָלוֹת בָּלוֹת וּמְטֻלָּאוֹת בְּרַגְלֵיהֶם וּשְׂלָמוֹת בָּלוֹת עֲלֵיהֶם וְכֹל לֶחֶם צֵידָם יָבֵשׁ הָיָה נִקֻּדִים:

6 And so they went to *Yehoshua* in the camp at *Gilgal* and said to him and to the men of *Yisrael*, "We come from a distant land; we propose that you make a pact with us."

ו וַיֵּלְכוּ אֶל־יְהוֹשֻׁעַ אֶל־הַמַּחֲנֶה הַגִּלְגָּל וַיֹּאמְרוּ אֵלָיו וְאֶל־אִישׁ יִשְׂרָאֵל מֵאֶרֶץ רְחוֹקָה בָּאנוּ וְעַתָּה כִּרְתוּ־לָנוּ בְרִית:

7 The men of *Yisrael* replied to the Hivites, "But perhaps you live among us; how then can we make a pact with you?"

ז וַיֹּאמְרוּ [וַיֹּאמֶר] אִישׁ־יִשְׂרָאֵל אֶל־הַחִוִּי אוּלַי בְּקִרְבִּי אַתָּה יוֹשֵׁב וְאֵיךְ אכרות־[אֶכְרָת־] לְךָ בְרִית:

8:34 He read all the words of the Teaching The goal of settling the Land of Israel is not simply for the Children of Israel to be a nation like all other nations. For that, any land would have been sufficient; the Holy Land would not be necessary. Rather, the purpose of being in *Eretz Yisrael* is to be a holy nation living freely in its land. Therefore, it stands to reason that *Yehoshua* would teach the entire *Torah* again to every man, woman and child at this early point of the nation's entrance into *Eretz Yisrael*. Rabbi Meir Bar Ilan, an early Religious Zionist, taught that the goal must be "the Land of Israel for the People of Israel according to the *Torah* of Israel." Similarly, commenting on the special relationship between the land and the Bible, former President and Prime Minister Shimon Peres said of his mentor David Ben Gurion, "he restored the Bible to its people, and he restored the people to the Bible."

Rabbi Meir Bar Ilan (1880–1949)

Yehoshua/Joshua
Chapter 9

8 They said to *Yehoshua*, "We will be your subjects." But *Yehoshua* asked them, "Who are you and where do you come from?"

9 They replied, "Your servants have come from a very distant country, because of the fame of *Hashem* your God. For we heard the report of Him: of all that He did in Egypt,

10 and of all that He did to the two Amorite kings on the other side of the *Yarden*, King Sihon of Heshbon and King Og of Bashan who lived in Ashtaroth.

11 So our elders and all the inhabitants of our country instructed us as follows, 'Take along provisions for a trip, and go to them and say: We will be your subjects; come make a pact with us.'

12 This bread of ours, which we took from our houses as provision, was still hot when we set out to come to you; and see how dry and crumbly it has become.

13 These wineskins were new when we filled them, and see how they have cracked. These clothes and sandals of ours are worn out from the very long journey."

14 The men took [their word] because of their provisions, and did not inquire of *Hashem*.

15 *Yehoshua* established friendship with them; he made a pact with them to spare their lives, and the chieftains of the community gave them their oath.

16 But when three days had passed after they made this pact with them, they learned that they were neighbors, living among them.

17 So the Israelites set out, and on the third day they came to their towns; these towns were *Givon*, Chephirah, Beeroth, and *Kiryat Ye'arim*.

18 But the Israelites did not attack them, since the chieftains of the community had sworn to them by *Hashem*, the God of *Yisrael*. The whole community muttered against the chieftains,

19 but all the chieftains answered the whole community, "We swore to them by *Hashem*, the God of *Yisrael*; therefore we cannot touch them.

Yehoshua/Joshua
Chapter 9

20 "This is what we will do to them: We will spare their lives, so that there may be no wrath against us because of the oath that we swore to them."

כ זֹאת נַעֲשֶׂה לָהֶם וְהַחֲיֵה אוֹתָם וְלֹא־יִהְיֶה עָלֵינוּ קֶצֶף עַל־הַשְּׁבוּעָה אֲשֶׁר־נִשְׁבַּעְנוּ לָהֶם:

21 And the chieftains declared concerning them, "They shall live!" And they became hewers of wood and drawers of water for the whole community, as the chieftains had decreed concerning them.

כא וַיֹּאמְרוּ אֲלֵיהֶם הַנְּשִׂיאִים יִחְיוּ וַיִּהְיוּ חֹטְבֵי עֵצִים וְשֹׁאֲבֵי־מַיִם לְכָל־הָעֵדָה כַּאֲשֶׁר דִּבְּרוּ לָהֶם הַנְּשִׂיאִים:

22 *Yehoshua* summoned them and spoke to them thus: "Why did you deceive us and tell us you lived very far from us, when in fact you live among us?

כב וַיִּקְרָא לָהֶם יְהוֹשֻׁעַ וַיְדַבֵּר אֲלֵיהֶם לֵאמֹר לָמָּה רִמִּיתֶם אֹתָנוּ לֵאמֹר רְחוֹקִים אֲנַחְנוּ מִכֶּם מְאֹד וְאַתֶּם בְּקִרְבֵּנוּ יֹשְׁבִים:

23 Therefore, be accursed! Never shall your descendants cease to be slaves, hewers of wood and drawers of water for the House of my God."

כג וְעַתָּה אֲרוּרִים אַתֶּם וְלֹא־יִכָּרֵת מִכֶּם עֶבֶד וְחֹטְבֵי עֵצִים וְשֹׁאֲבֵי־מַיִם לְבֵית אֱלֹהָי:

24 But they replied to *Yehoshua*, "You see, your servants had heard that *Hashem* your God had promised His servant *Moshe* to give you the whole land and to wipe out all the inhabitants of the country on your account; so we were in great fear for our lives on your account. That is why we did this thing.

כד וַיַּעֲנוּ אֶת־יְהוֹשֻׁעַ וַיֹּאמְרוּ כִּי הֻגֵּד הֻגַּד לַעֲבָדֶיךָ אֵת אֲשֶׁר צִוָּה יְהֹוָה אֱלֹהֶיךָ אֶת־מֹשֶׁה עַבְדּוֹ לָתֵת לָכֶם אֶת־כָּל־הָאָרֶץ וּלְהַשְׁמִיד אֶת־כָּל־יֹשְׁבֵי הָאָרֶץ מִפְּנֵיכֶם וַנִּירָא מְאֹד לְנַפְשֹׁתֵינוּ מִפְּנֵיכֶם וַנַּעֲשֵׂה אֶת־הַדָּבָר הַזֶּה:

25 And now we are at your mercy; do with us what you consider right and proper."

כה וְעַתָּה הִנְנוּ בְיָדֶךָ כַּטּוֹב וְכַיָּשָׁר בְּעֵינֶיךָ לַעֲשׂוֹת לָנוּ עֲשֵׂה:

26 And he did so; he saved them from being killed by the Israelites.

כו וַיַּעַשׂ לָהֶם כֵּן וַיַּצֵּל אוֹתָם מִיַּד בְּנֵי־יִשְׂרָאֵל וְלֹא הֲרָגוּם:

27 That day *Yehoshua* made them hewers of wood and drawers of water – as they still are – for the community and for the *Mizbayach* of *Hashem*, in the place that He would choose.

כז וַיִּתְּנֵם יְהוֹשֻׁעַ בַּיּוֹם הַהוּא חֹטְבֵי עֵצִים וְשֹׁאֲבֵי מַיִם לָעֵדָה וּלְמִזְבַּח יְהֹוָה עַד־הַיּוֹם הַזֶּה אֶל־הַמָּקוֹם אֲשֶׁר יִבְחָר:

va-yi-t'-NAYM y'-ho-SHU-a ba-YOM ha-HU kho-t'-VAY ay-TZEEM v'-SHO-a-vay MA-yim la-ay-DAH ul-miz-BAKH a-do-NAI ad ha-YOM ha-ZEH el ha-ma-KOM a-SHER yiv-KHAR

9:27 That day *Yehoshua* made them hewers of wood and drawers of water The Gibeonites trick *Yehoshua* into believing they are not Canaanites. Therefore, *Yehoshua* makes a treaty with them. Even after learning the truth, the Children of Israel do not violate their word. However, the Gibeonites are required to serve them and *Hashem*'s altar. The *Metzudat David*, a classic commentary on the books of the Prophets and Writings written in the late 17th and early 18th centuries, explains that this means they are to support the soldiers of Israel during war and to labor in the *Mishkan* in Shilo, and later in the *Beit Hamikdash* in *Yerushalayim*. Their service in the *Beit Hamikdash* would be important, as it would become the place for both Jews and non-Jews to direct their service of the one God.

Ancient well in Givon

Yehoshua/Joshua
Chapter 10

10 **1** When King Adoni-zedek of *Yerushalayim* learned that *Yehoshua* had captured Ai and proscribed it, treating Ai and its king as he had treated *Yericho* and its king, and that, moreover, the people of *Givon* had come to terms with *Yisrael* and remained among them,

> vai-HEE khish-MO-a a-do-nee TZE-dek ME-lekh y'-ru-sha-LA-yim kee la-KHAD y'-ho-SHU-a et ha-AI va-ya-kha-ree-MAH ka-a-SHER a-SAH lee-ree-KHO ul-mal-KAH kayn a-SAH la-AI ul-mal-KAH v'-KHEE hish-LEE-mu yo-sh'-VAY giv-ON et yis-ra-AYL va-yih-YU b'-kir-BAM

א וַיְהִי כִשְׁמֹעַ אֲדֹנִי־צֶדֶק מֶלֶךְ יְרוּשָׁלַםִ כִּי־לָכַד יְהוֹשֻׁעַ אֶת־הָעַי וַיַּחֲרִימָהּ כַּאֲשֶׁר עָשָׂה לִירִיחוֹ וּלְמַלְכָּהּ כֵּן־עָשָׂה לָעַי וּלְמַלְכָּהּ וְכִי הִשְׁלִימוּ יֹשְׁבֵי גִבְעוֹן אֶת־יִשְׂרָאֵל וַיִּהְיוּ בְּקִרְבָּם׃

2 he was very frightened. For *Givon* was a large city, like one of the royal cities – in fact, larger than Ai – and all its men were warriors.

ב וַיִּירְאוּ מְאֹד כִּי עִיר גְּדוֹלָה גִּבְעוֹן כְּאַחַת עָרֵי הַמַּמְלָכָה וְכִי הִיא גְדוֹלָה מִן־הָעַי וְכָל־אֲנָשֶׁיהָ גִּבֹּרִים׃

3 So King Adoni-zedek of *Yerushalayim* sent this message to King Hoham of *Chevron*, King Piram of *Yarmut*, King Japhia of *Lachish*, and King Debir of Eglon:

ג וַיִּשְׁלַח אֲדֹנִי־צֶדֶק מֶלֶךְ יְרוּשָׁלַםִ אֶל־הוֹהָם מֶלֶךְ־חֶבְרוֹן וְאֶל־פִּרְאָם מֶלֶךְ־יַרְמוּת וְאֶל־יָפִיעַ מֶלֶךְ־לָכִישׁ וְאֶל־דְּבִיר מֶלֶךְ־עֶגְלוֹן לֵאמֹר׃

4 "Come up and help me defeat *Givon*; for it has come to terms with *Yehoshua* and the Israelites."

ד עֲלוּ־אֵלַי וְעִזְרֻנִי וְנַכֶּה אֶת־גִּבְעוֹן כִּי־הִשְׁלִימָה אֶת־יְהוֹשֻׁעַ וְאֶת־בְּנֵי יִשְׂרָאֵל׃

5 The five Amorite kings – the king of *Yerushalayim*, the king of *Chevron*, the king of *Yarmut*, the king of *Lachish*, and the king of Eglon, with all their armies – joined forces and marched on *Givon*, and encamped against it and attacked it.

ה וַיֵּאָסְפוּ וַיַּעֲלוּ חֲמֵשֶׁת מַלְכֵי הָאֱמֹרִי מֶלֶךְ יְרוּשָׁלַםִ מֶלֶךְ־חֶבְרוֹן מֶלֶךְ־יַרְמוּת מֶלֶךְ־לָכִישׁ מֶלֶךְ־עֶגְלוֹן הֵם וְכָל־מַחֲנֵיהֶם וַיַּחֲנוּ עַל־גִּבְעוֹן וַיִּלָּחֲמוּ עָלֶיהָ׃

6 The people of *Givon* thereupon sent this message to *Yehoshua* in the camp at *Gilgal*: "Do not fail your servants; come up quickly and aid us and deliver us, for all the Amorite kings of the hill country have gathered against us."

ו וַיִּשְׁלְחוּ אַנְשֵׁי גִבְעוֹן אֶל־יְהוֹשֻׁעַ אֶל־הַמַּחֲנֶה הַגִּלְגָּלָה לֵאמֹר אַל־תֶּרֶף יָדֶיךָ מֵעֲבָדֶיךָ עֲלֵה אֵלֵינוּ מְהֵרָה וְהוֹשִׁיעָה לָּנוּ וְעָזְרֵנוּ כִּי נִקְבְּצוּ אֵלֵינוּ כָּל־מַלְכֵי הָאֱמֹרִי יֹשְׁבֵי הָהָר׃

7 So *Yehoshua* marched up from *Gilgal* with his whole fighting force, all the trained warriors.

ז וַיַּעַל יְהוֹשֻׁעַ מִן־הַגִּלְגָּל הוּא וְכָל־עַם הַמִּלְחָמָה עִמּוֹ וְכֹל גִּבּוֹרֵי הֶחָיִל׃

צדק

10:1 When King Adoni-zedek of *Yerushalayim* learned This is the first mention of the name *Yerushalayim* in the Bible. King Adoni-zedek, like Melchizedek King of *Shalem* (Genesis 14:18), gets his name *tzedek* (צדק), 'righteousness,' because he resides in *Yerushalayim*, the city of righteousness, as it says "righteousness lodged in her" (Isaiah 1:21). *Yerushayim* is not only filled with righteousness, it even causes its residents to be righteous and just. Adoni-zedek uses this virtue to stand up for moral justice by attacking the *Givonim* who had violated the Canaanite pact not to surrender to the Israelites. The *Ramban*, in his commentary (Genesis 14:18), points out that from time immemorial, the nations of the world have recognized the uniqueness of *Yerushalayim*. Physically, *Yerushalayim* is in a prime location at the center of the country. Spiritually, they knew it is aligned with the heavenly Temple where God's spirit dwells on high, and is the site He selected for the *Beit Hamikdash*.

Yehoshua/Joshua
Chapter 10

8 *Hashem* said to *Yehoshua*, "Do not be afraid of them, for I will deliver them into your hands; not one of them shall withstand you."

9 *Yehoshua* took them by surprise, marching all night from *Gilgal*.

10 *Hashem* threw them into a panic before *Yisrael*: [*Yehoshua*] inflicted a crushing defeat on them at *Givon*, pursued them in the direction of the Beth-horon ascent, and harried them all the way to *Azeika* and Makkedah.

11 While they were fleeing before *Yisrael* down the descent from Beth-horon, *Hashem* hurled huge stones on them from the sky, all the way to *Azeika*, and they perished; more perished from the hailstones than were killed by the Israelite weapons.

12 On that occasion, when *Hashem* routed the Amorites before the Israelites, *Yehoshua* addressed *Hashem*; he said in the presence of the Israelites: "Stand still, O sun, at *Givon*, O moon, in the Valley of Aijalon!"

13 And the sun stood still And the moon halted, While a nation wreaked judgment on its foes – as is written in the Book of Jashar. Thus the sun halted in midheaven, and did not press on to set, for a whole day;

14 for *Hashem* fought for *Yisrael*. Neither before nor since has there ever been such a day, when *Hashem* acted on words spoken by a man.

15 Then *Yehoshua* together with all *Yisrael* returned to the camp at *Gilgal*.

16 Meanwhile, those five kings fled and hid in a cave at Makkedah.

17 When it was reported to *Yehoshua* that the five kings had been found hiding in a cave at Makkedah,

18 *Yehoshua* ordered, "Roll large stones up against the mouth of the cave, and post men over it to keep guard over them.

19 But as for the rest of you, don't stop, but press on the heels of your enemies and harass them from the rear. Don't let them reach their towns, for *Hashem* your God has delivered them into your hands."

יהושע
פרק י

ח וַיֹּאמֶר יְהוָה אֶל־יְהוֹשֻׁעַ אַל־תִּירָא מֵהֶם כִּי בְיָדְךָ נְתַתִּים לֹא־יַעֲמֹד אִישׁ מֵהֶם בְּפָנֶיךָ:

ט וַיָּבֹא אֲלֵיהֶם יְהוֹשֻׁעַ פִּתְאֹם כָּל־הַלַּיְלָה עָלָה מִן־הַגִּלְגָּל:

י וַיְהֻמֵּם יְהוָה לִפְנֵי יִשְׂרָאֵל וַיַּכֵּם מַכָּה־גְדוֹלָה בְּגִבְעוֹן וַיִּרְדְּפֵם דֶּרֶךְ מַעֲלֵה בֵית־חוֹרֹן וַיַּכֵּם עַד־עֲזֵקָה וְעַד־מַקֵּדָה:

יא וַיְהִי בְּנֻסָם מִפְּנֵי יִשְׂרָאֵל הֵם בְּמוֹרַד בֵּית־חוֹרֹן וַיהוָה הִשְׁלִיךְ עֲלֵיהֶם אֲבָנִים גְּדֹלוֹת מִן־הַשָּׁמַיִם עַד־עֲזֵקָה וַיָּמֻתוּ רַבִּים אֲשֶׁר־מֵתוּ בְּאַבְנֵי הַבָּרָד מֵאֲשֶׁר הָרְגוּ בְּנֵי יִשְׂרָאֵל בֶּחָרֶב:

יב אָז יְדַבֵּר יְהוֹשֻׁעַ לַיהוָה בְּיוֹם תֵּת יְהוָה אֶת־הָאֱמֹרִי לִפְנֵי בְּנֵי יִשְׂרָאֵל וַיֹּאמֶר לְעֵינֵי יִשְׂרָאֵל שֶׁמֶשׁ בְּגִבְעוֹן דּוֹם וְיָרֵחַ בְּעֵמֶק אַיָּלוֹן:

יג וַיִּדֹּם הַשֶּׁמֶשׁ וְיָרֵחַ עָמָד עַד־יִקֹּם גּוֹי אֹיְבָיו הֲלֹא־הִיא כְתוּבָה עַל־סֵפֶר הַיָּשָׁר וַיַּעֲמֹד הַשֶּׁמֶשׁ בַּחֲצִי הַשָּׁמַיִם וְלֹא־אָץ לָבוֹא כְּיוֹם תָּמִים:

יד וְלֹא הָיָה כַּיּוֹם הַהוּא לְפָנָיו וְאַחֲרָיו לִשְׁמֹעַ יְהוָה בְּקוֹל אִישׁ כִּי יְהוָה נִלְחָם לְיִשְׂרָאֵל:

טו וַיָּשָׁב יְהוֹשֻׁעַ וְכָל־יִשְׂרָאֵל עִמּוֹ אֶל־הַמַּחֲנֶה הַגִּלְגָּלָה:

טז וַיָּנֻסוּ חֲמֵשֶׁת הַמְּלָכִים הָאֵלֶּה וַיֵּחָבְאוּ בַמְּעָרָה בְּמַקֵּדָה:

יז וַיֻּגַּד לִיהוֹשֻׁעַ לֵאמֹר נִמְצְאוּ חֲמֵשֶׁת הַמְּלָכִים נֶחְבְּאִים בַּמְּעָרָה בְּמַקֵּדָה:

יח וַיֹּאמֶר יְהוֹשֻׁעַ גֹּלּוּ אֲבָנִים גְּדֹלוֹת אֶל־פִּי הַמְּעָרָה וְהַפְקִידוּ עָלֶיהָ אֲנָשִׁים לְשָׁמְרָם:

יט וְאַתֶּם אַל־תַּעֲמֹדוּ רִדְפוּ אַחֲרֵי אֹיְבֵיכֶם וְזִנַּבְתֶּם אוֹתָם אַל־תִּתְּנוּם לָבוֹא אֶל־עָרֵיהֶם כִּי נְתָנָם יְהוָה אֱלֹהֵיכֶם בְּיֶדְכֶם:

Yehoshua/Joshua
Chapter 10

20 When *Yehoshua* and the Israelites had finished dealing them a deadly blow, they were wiped out, except for some fugitives who escaped into the fortified towns.

21 The whole army returned in safety to *Yehoshua* in the camp at Makkedah; no one so much as snarled at the Israelites.

22 And now *Yehoshua* ordered, "Open the mouth of the cave, and bring those five kings out of the cave to me."

23 This was done. Those five kings – the king of *Yerushalayim*, the king of *Chevron*, the king of *Yarmut*, the king of *Lachish*, and the king of Eglon – were brought out to him from the cave.

24 And when the kings were brought out to *Yehoshua*, *Yehoshua* summoned all the men of *Yisrael* and ordered the army officers who had accompanied him, "Come forward and place your feet on the necks of these kings." They came forward and placed their feet on their necks.

25 *Yehoshua* said to them, "Do not be frightened or dismayed; be firm and resolute. For this is what *Hashem* is going to do to all the enemies with whom you are at war."

26 After that, *Yehoshua* had them put to death and impaled on five stakes, and they remained impaled on the stakes until evening.

27 At sunset *Yehoshua* ordered them taken down from the poles and thrown into the cave in which they had hidden. Large stones were placed over the mouth of the cave, [and there they are] to this very day.

28 At that time *Yehoshua* captured Makkedah and put it and its king to the sword, proscribing it and every person in it and leaving none that escaped. And he treated the king of Makkedah as he had treated the king of *Yericho*.

29 From Makkedah, *Yehoshua* proceeded with all *Yisrael* to Libnah, and he attacked it.

Yehoshua/Joshua
Chapter 10

30 *Hashem* delivered it and its king into the hands of *Yisrael*; they put it and all the people in it to the sword, letting none escape. And he treated its king as he had treated the king of *Yericho*.

31 From Libnah, *Yehoshua* proceeded with all *Yisrael* to *Lachish*; he encamped against it and attacked it.

32 *Hashem* delivered *Lachish* into the hands of *Yisrael*. They captured it on the second day and put it and all the people in it to the sword, just as they had done to Libnah.

33 At that time King Horam of Gezer marched to the help of *Lachish*; but *Yehoshua* defeated him and his army, letting none of them escape.

34 From *Lachish*, *Yehoshua* proceeded with all *Yisrael* to Eglon; they encamped against it and attacked it.

35 They captured it on the same day and put it to the sword, proscribing all the people that were in it, as they had done to *Lachish*.

36 From Eglon, *Yehoshua* marched with all *Yisrael* to *Chevron* and attacked it.

37 They captured it and put it, its king, and all its towns, and all the people that were in it, to the sword. He let none escape, proscribing it and all the people in it, just as he had done in the case of Eglon.

38 *Yehoshua* and all *Yisrael* with him then turned back to Debir and attacked it.

39 He captured it and its king and all its towns. They put them to the sword and proscribed all the people in it. They let none escape; just as they had done to *Chevron*, and as they had done to Libnah and its king, so they did to Debir and its king.

40 Thus *Yehoshua* conquered the whole country: the hill country, the *Negev*, the Shephelah, and the slopes, with all their kings; he let none escape, but proscribed everything that breathed – as *Hashem*, the God of *Yisrael*, had commanded.

41 *Yehoshua* conquered them from Kadesh-barnea to *Azza*, all the land of Goshen, and up to *Givon*.

יהושע
פרק י

ל וַיִּתֵּן יְהוָה גַּם־אוֹתָהּ בְּיַד יִשְׂרָאֵל וְאֶת־מַלְכָּהּ וַיַּכֶּהָ לְפִי־חֶרֶב וְאֶת־כָּל־הַנֶּפֶשׁ אֲשֶׁר־בָּהּ לֹא־הִשְׁאִיר בָּהּ שָׂרִיד וַיַּעַשׂ לְמַלְכָּהּ כַּאֲשֶׁר עָשָׂה לְמֶלֶךְ יְרִיחוֹ׃

לא וַיַּעֲבֹר יְהוֹשֻׁעַ וְכָל־יִשְׂרָאֵל עִמּוֹ מִלִּבְנָה לָכִישָׁה וַיִּחַן עָלֶיהָ וַיִּלָּחֶם בָּהּ׃

לב וַיִּתֵּן יְהוָה אֶת־לָכִישׁ בְּיַד יִשְׂרָאֵל וַיִּלְכְּדָהּ בַּיּוֹם הַשֵּׁנִי וַיַּכֶּהָ לְפִי־חֶרֶב וְאֶת־כָּל־הַנֶּפֶשׁ אֲשֶׁר־בָּהּ כְּכֹל אֲשֶׁר־עָשָׂה לְלִבְנָה׃

לג אָז עָלָה הֹרָם מֶלֶךְ גֶּזֶר לַעְזֹר אֶת־לָכִישׁ וַיַּכֵּהוּ יְהוֹשֻׁעַ וְאֶת־עַמּוֹ עַד־בִּלְתִּי הִשְׁאִיר־לוֹ שָׂרִיד׃

לד וַיַּעֲבֹר יְהוֹשֻׁעַ וְכָל־יִשְׂרָאֵל עִמּוֹ מִלָּכִישׁ עֶגְלֹנָה וַיַּחֲנוּ עָלֶיהָ וַיִּלָּחֲמוּ עָלֶיהָ׃

לה וַיִּלְכְּדוּהָ בַּיּוֹם הַהוּא וַיַּכּוּהָ לְפִי־חֶרֶב וְאֵת כָּל־הַנֶּפֶשׁ אֲשֶׁר־בָּהּ בַּיּוֹם הַהוּא הֶחֱרִים כְּכֹל אֲשֶׁר־עָשָׂה לְלָכִישׁ׃

לו וַיַּעַל יְהוֹשֻׁעַ וְכָל־יִשְׂרָאֵל עִמּוֹ מֵעֶגְלוֹנָה חֶבְרוֹנָה וַיִּלָּחֲמוּ עָלֶיהָ׃

לז וַיִּלְכְּדוּהָ וַיַּכּוּהָ לְפִי־חֶרֶב וְאֶת־מַלְכָּהּ וְאֶת־כָּל־עָרֶיהָ וְאֶת־כָּל־הַנֶּפֶשׁ אֲשֶׁר־בָּהּ לֹא־הִשְׁאִיר שָׂרִיד כְּכֹל אֲשֶׁר־עָשָׂה לְעֶגְלוֹן וַיַּחֲרֵם אוֹתָהּ וְאֶת־כָּל־הַנֶּפֶשׁ אֲשֶׁר־בָּהּ׃

לח וַיָּשָׁב יְהוֹשֻׁעַ וְכָל־יִשְׂרָאֵל עִמּוֹ דְּבִרָה וַיִּלָּחֶם עָלֶיהָ׃

לט וַיִּלְכְּדָהּ וְאֶת־מַלְכָּהּ וְאֶת־כָּל־עָרֶיהָ וַיַּכּוּם לְפִי־חֶרֶב וַיַּחֲרִימוּ אֶת־כָּל־נֶפֶשׁ אֲשֶׁר־בָּהּ לֹא הִשְׁאִיר שָׂרִיד כַּאֲשֶׁר עָשָׂה לְחֶבְרוֹן כֵּן־עָשָׂה לִדְבִרָה וּלְמַלְכָּהּ וְכַאֲשֶׁר עָשָׂה לְלִבְנָה וּלְמַלְכָּהּ׃

מ וַיַּכֶּה יְהוֹשֻׁעַ אֶת־כָּל־הָאָרֶץ הָהָר וְהַנֶּגֶב וְהַשְּׁפֵלָה וְהָאֲשֵׁדוֹת וְאֵת כָּל־מַלְכֵיהֶם לֹא הִשְׁאִיר שָׂרִיד וְאֵת כָּל־הַנְּשָׁמָה הֶחֱרִים כַּאֲשֶׁר צִוָּה יְהוָה אֱלֹהֵי יִשְׂרָאֵל׃

מא וַיַּכֵּם יְהוֹשֻׁעַ מִקָּדֵשׁ בַּרְנֵעַ וְעַד־עַזָּה וְאֵת כָּל־אֶרֶץ גֹּשֶׁן וְעַד־גִּבְעוֹן׃

Yehoshua/Joshua
Chapter 11

42 All those kings and their lands were conquered by *Yehoshua* at a single stroke, for *Hashem*, the God of *Yisrael*, fought for *Yisrael*.

43 Then *Yehoshua*, with all *Yisrael*, returned to the camp at *Gilgal*.

11 1 When the news reached King Jabin of Hazor, he sent messages to King Jobab of Madon, to the king of Shimron, to the king of Achshaph,

2 and to the other kings in the north – in the hill country, in the Arabah south of Chinnereth, in the lowlands, and in the district of Dor on the west;

3 to the Canaanites in the east and in the west; to the Amorites, Hittites, Perizzites, and Jebusites in the hill country; and to the Hivites at the foot of *Chermon*, in the land of *Mitzpa*.

4 They took the field with all their armies – an enormous host, as numerous as the sands on the seashore – and a vast multitude of horses and chariots.

5 All these kings joined forces; they came and encamped together at the Waters of Merom to give battle to *Yisrael*.

6 But *Hashem* said to *Yehoshua*, "Do not be afraid of them; tomorrow at this time I will have them all lying slain before *Yisrael*. You shall hamstring their horses and burn their chariots."

7 So *Yehoshua*, with all his fighting men, came upon them suddenly at the Waters of Merom, and pounced upon them.

8 *Hashem* delivered them into the hands of *Yisrael*, and they defeated them and pursued them all the way to Great Sidon and Misrephothmaim, and all the way to the Valley of Mizpeh on the east; they crushed them, letting none escape.

9 And *Yehoshua* dealt with them as *Hashem* had ordered him; he hamstrung their horses and burned their chariots.

10 *Yehoshua* then turned back and captured Hazor and put her king to the sword. – Hazor was formerly the head of all those kingdoms.

יהושע
פרק יא

מב וְאֵת כָּל־הַמְּלָכִים הָאֵלֶּה וְאֶת־אַרְצָם לָכַד יְהוֹשֻׁעַ פַּעַם אֶחָת כִּי יְהוָה אֱלֹהֵי יִשְׂרָאֵל נִלְחָם לְיִשְׂרָאֵל׃

מג וַיָּשָׁב יְהוֹשֻׁעַ וְכָל־יִשְׂרָאֵל עִמּוֹ אֶל־הַמַּחֲנֶה הַגִּלְגָּלָה׃

יא א וַיְהִי כִּשְׁמֹעַ יָבִין מֶלֶךְ־חָצוֹר וַיִּשְׁלַח אֶל־יוֹבָב מֶלֶךְ מָדוֹן וְאֶל־מֶלֶךְ שִׁמְרוֹן וְאֶל־מֶלֶךְ אַכְשָׁף׃

ב וְאֶל־הַמְּלָכִים אֲשֶׁר מִצְּפוֹן בָּהָר וּבָעֲרָבָה נֶגֶב כִּנְרוֹת וּבַשְּׁפֵלָה וּבְנָפוֹת דּוֹר מִיָּם׃

ג הַכְּנַעֲנִי מִמִּזְרָח וּמִיָּם וְהָאֱמֹרִי וְהַחִתִּי וְהַפְּרִזִּי וְהַיְבוּסִי בָּהָר וְהַחִוִּי תַּחַת חֶרְמוֹן בְּאֶרֶץ הַמִּצְפָּה׃

ד וַיֵּצְאוּ הֵם וְכָל־מַחֲנֵיהֶם עִמָּם עַם־רָב כַּחוֹל אֲשֶׁר עַל־שְׂפַת־הַיָּם לָרֹב וְסוּס וָרֶכֶב רַב־מְאֹד׃

ה וַיִּוָּעֲדוּ כֹּל הַמְּלָכִים הָאֵלֶּה וַיָּבֹאוּ וַיַּחֲנוּ יַחְדָּו אֶל־מֵי מֵרוֹם לְהִלָּחֵם עִם־יִשְׂרָאֵל׃

ו וַיֹּאמֶר יְהוָה אֶל־יְהוֹשֻׁעַ אַל־תִּירָא מִפְּנֵיהֶם כִּי־מָחָר כָּעֵת הַזֹּאת אָנֹכִי נֹתֵן אֶת־כֻּלָּם חֲלָלִים לִפְנֵי יִשְׂרָאֵל אֶת־סוּסֵיהֶם תְּעַקֵּר וְאֶת־מַרְכְּבֹתֵיהֶם תִּשְׂרֹף בָּאֵשׁ׃

ז וַיָּבֹא יְהוֹשֻׁעַ וְכָל־עַם הַמִּלְחָמָה עִמּוֹ עֲלֵיהֶם עַל־מֵי מֵרוֹם פִּתְאֹם וַיִּפְּלוּ בָּהֶם׃

ח וַיִּתְּנֵם יְהוָה בְּיַד־יִשְׂרָאֵל וַיַּכּוּם וַיִּרְדְּפוּם עַד־צִידוֹן רַבָּה וְעַד מִשְׂרְפוֹת מַיִם וְעַד־בִּקְעַת מִצְפֶּה מִזְרָחָה וַיַּכֻּם עַד־בִּלְתִּי הִשְׁאִיר־לָהֶם שָׂרִיד׃

ט וַיַּעַשׂ לָהֶם יְהוֹשֻׁעַ כַּאֲשֶׁר אָמַר־לוֹ יְהוָה אֶת־סוּסֵיהֶם עִקֵּר וְאֶת־מַרְכְּבֹתֵיהֶם שָׂרַף בָּאֵשׁ׃

י וַיָּשָׁב יְהוֹשֻׁעַ בָּעֵת הַהִיא וַיִּלְכֹּד אֶת־חָצוֹר וְאֶת־מַלְכָּהּ הִכָּה בֶחָרֶב כִּי־חָצוֹר לְפָנִים הִיא רֹאשׁ כָּל־הַמַּמְלָכוֹת הָאֵלֶּה׃

Yehoshua/Joshua
Chapter 11

יהושע
פרק יא

11 They proscribed and put to the sword every person in it. Not a soul survived, and Hazor itself was burned down.

יא וַיַּכּוּ אֶת־כָּל־הַנֶּפֶשׁ אֲשֶׁר־בָּהּ לְפִי־חֶרֶב הַחֲרֵם לֹא נוֹתַר כָּל־נְשָׁמָה וְאֶת־חָצוֹר שָׂרַף בָּאֵשׁ׃

12 *Yehoshua* captured all those royal cities and their kings. He put them to the sword; he proscribed them in accordance with the charge of *Moshe*, the servant of *Hashem*.

יב וְאֶת־כָּל־עָרֵי הַמְּלָכִים־הָאֵלֶּה וְאֶת־כָּל־מַלְכֵיהֶם לָכַד יְהוֹשֻׁעַ וַיַּכֵּם לְפִי־חֶרֶב הֶחֱרִים אוֹתָם כַּאֲשֶׁר צִוָּה מֹשֶׁה עֶבֶד יְהוָה׃

v'-et kol a-RAY ha-m'-la-kheem ha-AY-leh v'-et kol mal-khay-HEM la-KHAD y'-ho-SHU-a va-ya-KAYM l'-fee KHE-rev he-khe-REEM o-TAM ka-a-SHER tzi-VAH mo-SHEH E-ved a-do-NAI

13 However, all those towns that are still standing on their mounds were not burned down by *Yisrael*; it was Hazor alone that *Yehoshua* burned down.

יג רַק כָּל־הֶעָרִים הָעֹמְדוֹת עַל־תִּלָּם לֹא שְׂרָפָם יִשְׂרָאֵל זוּלָתִי אֶת־חָצוֹר לְבַדָּהּ שָׂרַף יְהוֹשֻׁעַ׃

14 The Israelites kept all the spoil and cattle of the rest of those cities as booty. But they cut down their populations with the sword until they exterminated them; they did not spare a soul.

יד וְכֹל שְׁלַל הֶעָרִים הָאֵלֶּה וְהַבְּהֵמָה בָּזְזוּ לָהֶם בְּנֵי יִשְׂרָאֵל רַק אֶת־כָּל־הָאָדָם הִכּוּ לְפִי־חֶרֶב עַד־הִשְׁמִדָם אוֹתָם לֹא הִשְׁאִירוּ כָּל־נְשָׁמָה׃

15 Just as *Hashem* had commanded His servant *Moshe*, so *Moshe* had charged *Yehoshua*, and so *Yehoshua* did; he left nothing undone of all that *Hashem* had commanded *Moshe*.

טו כַּאֲשֶׁר צִוָּה יְהוָה אֶת־מֹשֶׁה עַבְדּוֹ כֵּן־צִוָּה מֹשֶׁה אֶת־יְהוֹשֻׁעַ וְכֵן עָשָׂה יְהוֹשֻׁעַ לֹא־הֵסִיר דָּבָר מִכֹּל אֲשֶׁר־צִוָּה יְהוָה אֶת־מֹשֶׁה׃

16 *Yehoshua* conquered the whole of this region: the hill country [of *Yehuda*], the *Negev*, the whole land of Goshen, the Shephelah, the Arabah, and the hill country and coastal plain of *Yisrael*

טז וַיִּקַּח יְהוֹשֻׁעַ אֶת־כָּל־הָאָרֶץ הַזֹּאת הָהָר וְאֶת־כָּל־הַנֶּגֶב וְאֵת כָּל־אֶרֶץ הַגֹּשֶׁן וְאֶת־הַשְּׁפֵלָה וְאֶת־הָעֲרָבָה וְאֶת־הַר יִשְׂרָאֵל וּשְׁפֵלָתֹה׃

17 [everything] from Mount Halak, which ascends to Seir, all the way to Baal-gad in the Valley of the Lebanon at the foot of Mount *Chermon*; and he captured all the kings there and executed them.

יז מִן־הָהָר הֶחָלָק הָעוֹלֶה שֵׂעִיר וְעַד־בַּעַל גָּד בְּבִקְעַת הַלְּבָנוֹן תַּחַת הַר־חֶרְמוֹן וְאֵת כָּל־מַלְכֵיהֶם לָכַד וַיַּכֵּם וַיְמִיתֵם׃

18 *Yehoshua* waged war with all those kings over a long period.

יח יָמִים רַבִּים עָשָׂה יְהוֹשֻׁעַ אֶת־כָּל־הַמְּלָכִים הָאֵלֶּה מִלְחָמָה׃

11:12 In accordance with the charge of *Moshe*, the servant of *Hashem* *Moshe* is described as being an *eved* (עבד) of *Hashem*. In Hebrew, *eved* can mean a 'slave.' However, it is also used to describe a servant, particularly one who faithfully serves his master. Therefore, one of the greatest praises that can be offered is to be called by the title "*Eved Hashem*," a 'faithful servant of God,' who always strives to fulfill His will. *Moshe* is the greatest example of this, but all human beings are to strive to achieve this high level of being a faithful servant to God.

עבד

Yehoshua/Joshua
Chapter 12

יט לֹא־הָיְתָה עִיר אֲשֶׁר הִשְׁלִימָה אֶל־בְּנֵי יִשְׂרָאֵל בִּלְתִּי הַחִוִּי יֹשְׁבֵי גִבְעוֹן אֶת־הַכֹּל לָקְחוּ בַמִּלְחָמָה׃

19 Apart from the Hivites who dwelt in *Givon*, not a single city made terms with the Israelites; all were taken in battle.

כ כִּי מֵאֵת יְהֹוָה הָיְתָה לְחַזֵּק אֶת־לִבָּם לִקְרַאת הַמִּלְחָמָה אֶת־יִשְׂרָאֵל לְמַעַן הַחֲרִימָם לְבִלְתִּי הֱיוֹת־לָהֶם תְּחִנָּה כִּי לְמַעַן הַשְׁמִידָם כַּאֲשֶׁר צִוָּה יְהֹוָה אֶת־מֹשֶׁה׃

20 For it was *Hashem*'s doing to stiffen their hearts to give battle to *Yisrael*, in order that they might be proscribed without quarter and wiped out, as *Hashem* had commanded *Moshe*.

כא וַיָּבֹא יְהוֹשֻׁעַ בָּעֵת הַהִיא וַיַּכְרֵת אֶת־הָעֲנָקִים מִן־הָהָר מִן־חֶבְרוֹן מִן־דְּבִר מִן־עֲנָב וּמִכֹּל הַר יְהוּדָה וּמִכֹּל הַר יִשְׂרָאֵל עִם־עָרֵיהֶם הֶחֱרִימָם יְהוֹשֻׁעַ׃

21 At that time, *Yehoshua* went and wiped out the Anakites from the hill country, from *Chevron*, Debir, and Anab, from the entire hill country of *Yehuda*, and from the entire hill country of *Yisrael*; *Yehoshua* proscribed them and their towns.

כב לֹא־נוֹתַר עֲנָקִים בְּאֶרֶץ בְּנֵי יִשְׂרָאֵל רַק בְּעַזָּה בְּגַת וּבְאַשְׁדּוֹד נִשְׁאָרוּ׃

22 No Anakites remained in the land of the Israelites; but some remained in *Azza*, Gath, and *Ashdod*.

כג וַיִּקַּח יְהוֹשֻׁעַ אֶת־כָּל־הָאָרֶץ כְּכֹל אֲשֶׁר דִּבֶּר יְהֹוָה אֶל־מֹשֶׁה וַיִּתְּנָהּ יְהוֹשֻׁעַ לְנַחֲלָה לְיִשְׂרָאֵל כְּמַחְלְקֹתָם לְשִׁבְטֵיהֶם וְהָאָרֶץ שָׁקְטָה מִמִּלְחָמָה׃

23 Thus *Yehoshua* conquered the whole country, just as *Hashem* had promised *Moshe*; and *Yehoshua* assigned it to *Yisrael* to share according to their tribal divisions. And the land had rest from war.

12

יב א וְאֵלֶּה מַלְכֵי הָאָרֶץ אֲשֶׁר הִכּוּ בְנֵי־יִשְׂרָאֵל וַיִּרְשׁוּ אֶת־אַרְצָם בְּעֵבֶר הַיַּרְדֵּן מִזְרְחָה הַשָּׁמֶשׁ מִנַּחַל אַרְנוֹן עַד־הַר חֶרְמוֹן וְכָל־הָעֲרָבָה מִזְרָחָה׃

1 The following are the local kings whom the Israelites defeated and whose territories they took possession of: East of the *Yarden*, from the Wadi Arnon to Mount *Chermon*, including the eastern half of the Arabah:

ב סִיחוֹן מֶלֶךְ הָאֱמֹרִי הַיּוֹשֵׁב בְּחֶשְׁבּוֹן מֹשֵׁל מֵעֲרוֹעֵר אֲשֶׁר עַל־שְׂפַת־נַחַל אַרְנוֹן וְתוֹךְ הַנַּחַל וַחֲצִי הַגִּלְעָד וְעַד יַבֹּק הַנַּחַל גְּבוּל בְּנֵי עַמּוֹן׃

2 King Sihon of the Amorites, who resided in Heshbon and ruled over part of *Gilad* – from Aroer on the bank of the Wadi Arnon and the wadi proper up to the Wadi Jabbok [and] the border of the Ammonites

ג וְהָעֲרָבָה עַד־יָם כִּנְרוֹת מִזְרָחָה וְעַד יָם הָעֲרָבָה יָם־הַמֶּלַח מִזְרָחָה דֶּרֶךְ בֵּית הַיְשִׁמוֹת וּמִתֵּימָן תַּחַת אַשְׁדּוֹת הַפִּסְגָּה׃

3 and over the eastern Arabah up to the Sea of Chinnereth and, southward by way of Beth-jeshimoth at the foot of the slopes of Pisgah on the east, down to the Sea of the Arabah, that is, the Dead Sea.

ד וּגְבוּל עוֹג מֶלֶךְ הַבָּשָׁן מִיֶּתֶר הָרְפָאִים הַיּוֹשֵׁב בְּעַשְׁתָּרוֹת וּבְאֶדְרֶעִי׃

4 Also the territory of King Og of Bashan – one of the last of the Rephaim – who resided in Ashtaroth and in Edrei

ה וּמֹשֵׁל בְּהַר חֶרְמוֹן וּבְסַלְכָה וּבְכָל־הַבָּשָׁן עַד־גְּבוּל הַגְּשׁוּרִי וְהַמַּעֲכָתִי וַחֲצִי הַגִּלְעָד גְּבוּל סִיחוֹן מֶלֶךְ־חֶשְׁבּוֹן׃

5 and ruled over Mount *Chermon*, Salcah, and all of Bashan up to the border of the Geshurites and the Maacathites, as also over part of *Gilad* [down to] the border of King Sihon of Heshbon.

Yehoshua/Joshua
Chapter 12

יהושע
פרק יב

6 These were vanquished by *Moshe*, the servant of *Hashem*, and the Israelites; and *Moshe*, the servant of *Hashem*, assigned that territory as a possession to the Reubenites, the Gadites, and the half-tribe of *Menashe*.

א מֹשֶׁה עֶבֶד־יְהֹוָה וּבְנֵי יִשְׂרָאֵל הִכּוּם וַיִּתְּנָהּ מֹשֶׁה עֶבֶד־יְהֹוָה יְרֻשָּׁה לָרֻאוּבֵנִי וְלַגָּדִי וְלַחֲצִי שֵׁבֶט הַמְנַשֶּׁה:

mo-SHEH e-ved a-do-NAI uv-NAY yis-ra-AYL hi-KUM va-yi-t'-NAH mo-SHEH e-ved a-do-NAI y'-ru-SHAH la-ru-vay-NEE v'-la-ga-DEE v'-la-kha-TZEE SHAY-vet ham-na-SHEH

7 And the following are the local kings whom *Yehoshua* and the Israelites defeated on the west side of the *Yarden* – from Baal-gad in the Valley of the Lebanon to Mount Halak, which ascends to Seir – which *Yehoshua* assigned as a possession to the tribal divisions of *Yisrael*:

ז וְאֵלֶּה מַלְכֵי הָאָרֶץ אֲשֶׁר הִכָּה יְהוֹשֻׁעַ וּבְנֵי יִשְׂרָאֵל בְּעֵבֶר הַיַּרְדֵּן יָמָּה מִבַּעַל גָּד בְּבִקְעַת הַלְּבָנוֹן וְעַד־הָהָר הֶחָלָק הָעֹלֶה שֵׂעִירָה וַיִּתְּנָהּ יְהוֹשֻׁעַ לְשִׁבְטֵי יִשְׂרָאֵל יְרֻשָּׁה כְּמַחְלְקֹתָם:

8 in the hill country, in the lowlands, in the Arabah, in the slopes, in the wilderness, and in the *Negev* – [in the land of] the Hittites, the Amorites, the Canaanites, the Perizzites, the Hivites, and the Jebusites.

ח בָּהָר וּבַשְּׁפֵלָה וּבָעֲרָבָה וּבָאֲשֵׁדוֹת וּבַמִּדְבָּר וּבַנֶּגֶב הַחִתִּי הָאֱמֹרִי וְהַכְּנַעֲנִי הַפְּרִזִּי הַחִוִּי וְהַיְבוּסִי:

9 They were: the king of *Yericho* 1. the king of Ai, near *Beit El*, 1.

ט מֶלֶךְ יְרִיחוֹ אֶחָד מֶלֶךְ הָעַי אֲשֶׁר־מִצַּד בֵּית־אֵל אֶחָד:

10 the king of *Yerushalayim* 1. the king of *Chevron* 1.

י מֶלֶךְ יְרוּשָׁלַםִ אֶחָד מֶלֶךְ חֶבְרוֹן אֶחָד:

11 the king of *Yarmut* 1. the king of *Lachish* 1.

יא מֶלֶךְ יַרְמוּת אֶחָד מֶלֶךְ לָכִישׁ אֶחָד:

12 the king of Eglon 1. the king of Gezer 1.

יב מֶלֶךְ עֶגְלוֹן אֶחָד מֶלֶךְ גֶּזֶר אֶחָד:

13 the king of *Debir* 1. the king of *Geder* 1.

יג מֶלֶךְ דְּבִר אֶחָד מֶלֶךְ גֶּדֶר אֶחָד:

14 the king of Hormah 1. the king of Arad 1.

יד מֶלֶךְ חָרְמָה אֶחָד מֶלֶךְ עֲרָד אֶחָד:

15 the king of Libnah 1. the king of *Adulam* 1.

טו מֶלֶךְ לִבְנָה אֶחָד מֶלֶךְ עֲדֻלָּם אֶחָד:

16 the king of Makkedah 1. the king of *Beit El* 1.

טז מֶלֶךְ מַקֵּדָה אֶחָד מֶלֶךְ בֵּית־אֵל אֶחָד:

17 the king of *Tapuach* 1. the king of Hepher 1.

יז מֶלֶךְ תַּפּוּחַ אֶחָד מֶלֶךְ חֵפֶר אֶחָד:

18 the king of Aphek 1. the king of Sharon 1.

יח מֶלֶךְ אֲפֵק אֶחָד מֶלֶךְ לַשָּׁרוֹן אֶחָד:

12:6 *Moshe*, the servant of *Hashem*, assigned that territory as a possession In this chapter, which summarizes the wars fought by the Children of Israel to take possession of the Promised Land, we are also reminded of the wars *Moshe* fought. *Moshe* led the people against Sihon and Og, and captured the Gilead and the Bashan. This area became the inheritance of the tribes of *Gad*, *Reuven* and half of *Menashe* (see Numbers 32:33). The Bashan is now known as the Golan Heights, which Israel conquered in the Six Day War from Syria. Towering over the north of the country, the Golan Heights provides an essential strategic perch that is vital for Israel's security. Coupled with its biblical significance, the Golan Heights remain an important part of the State of Israel. In his final interview before suffering a massive stroke in 2006, Prime Minister Ariel Sharon told Japanese reporters, "I am a Jew, and that is the most important thing for me. Therefore when it comes to the security of Israel I will not make any compromises... I don't see any situation where Israel will not be sitting on the Golan Heights."

Prime Minister Ariel Sharon (1928–2014)

Yehoshua/Joshua
Chapter 13

19 the king of Madon 1. the king of Hazor 1.

20 the king of Shimron-meron 1. the king of Achshaph 1.

21 the king of Taanach 1. the king of Megiddo 1.

22 the king of Kedesh 1. the king of Jokneam in the *Carmel* 1.

23 the king of Dor in the district of Dor 1. the king of Goiim in *Gilgal* 1.

24 the king of *Tirtza* 1. Total number of kings 31.

13 1 *Yehoshua* was now old, advanced in years. *Hashem* said to him, "You have grown old, you are advanced in years; and very much of the land still remains to be taken possession of.

2 This is the territory that remains: all the districts of the Philistines and all [those of] the Geshurites,

3 from the Shihor, which is close to Egypt, to the territory of Ekron on the north, are accounted Canaanite, namely, those of the five lords of the Philistines – the Gazites, the Ashdodites, the Ashkelonites, the Gittites, and the Ekronites – and those of the Avvim

4 on the south; further, all the Canaanite country from Mearah of the Sidonians to Aphek at the Amorite border

5 and the land of the Gebalites, with the whole [Valley of the] Lebanon, from Baal-gad at the foot of Mount *Chermon* to Lebo-hamath on the east,

6 with all the inhabitants of the hill country from the [Valley of the] Lebanon to Misrephoth-maim, namely, all the Sidonians. I Myself will dispossess those nations for the Israelites; you have only to apportion their lands by lot among *Yisrael*, as I have commanded you.

7 Therefore, divide this territory into hereditary portions for the nine tribes and the half-tribe of *Menashe*."

8 Now the Reubenites and the Gadites, along with the other half-tribe, had already received the shares which *Moshe* assigned to them on the east side of the *Yarden* – as assigned to them by *Moshe* the servant of *Hashem*:

יהושע
פרק יג

יט מֶלֶךְ מָדוֹן אֶחָד מֶלֶךְ חָצוֹר אֶחָד:

כ מֶלֶךְ שִׁמְרוֹן מְראוֹן אֶחָד מֶלֶךְ אַכְשָׁף אֶחָד:

כא מֶלֶךְ תַּעְנַךְ אֶחָד מֶלֶךְ מְגִדּוֹ אֶחָד:

כב מֶלֶךְ קֶדֶשׁ אֶחָד מֶלֶךְ־יָקְנֳעָם לַכַּרְמֶל אֶחָד:

כג מֶלֶךְ דּוֹר לְנָפַת דּוֹר אֶחָד מֶלֶךְ־גּוֹיִם לְגִלְגָּל אֶחָד:

כד מֶלֶךְ תִּרְצָה אֶחָד כָּל־מְלָכִים שְׁלֹשִׁים וְאֶחָד:

יג א וִיהוֹשֻׁעַ זָקֵן בָּא בַּיָּמִים וַיֹּאמֶר יְהוָה אֵלָיו אַתָּה זָקַנְתָּה בָּאתָ בַיָּמִים וְהָאָרֶץ נִשְׁאֲרָה הַרְבֵּה־מְאֹד לְרִשְׁתָּהּ:

ב זֹאת הָאָרֶץ הַנִּשְׁאָרֶת כָּל־גְּלִילוֹת הַפְּלִשְׁתִּים וְכָל־הַגְּשׁוּרִי:

ג מִן־הַשִּׁיחוֹר אֲשֶׁר עַל־פְּנֵי מִצְרַיִם וְעַד גְּבוּל עֶקְרוֹן צָפוֹנָה לַכְּנַעֲנִי תֵּחָשֵׁב חֲמֵשֶׁת סַרְנֵי פְלִשְׁתִּים הָעַזָּתִי וְהָאַשְׁדּוֹדִי הָאֶשְׁקְלוֹנִי הַגִּתִּי וְהָעֶקְרוֹנִי וְהָעַוִּים:

ד מִתֵּימָן כָּל־אֶרֶץ הַכְּנַעֲנִי וּמְעָרָה אֲשֶׁר לַצִּידֹנִים עַד־אֲפֵקָה עַד גְּבוּל הָאֱמֹרִי:

ה וְהָאָרֶץ הַגִּבְלִי וְכָל־הַלְּבָנוֹן מִזְרַח הַשֶּׁמֶשׁ מִבַּעַל גָּד תַּחַת הַר־חֶרְמוֹן עַד לְבוֹא חֲמָת:

ו כָּל־יֹשְׁבֵי הָהָר מִן־הַלְּבָנוֹן עַד־מִשְׂרְפֹת מַיִם כָּל־צִידֹנִים אָנֹכִי אוֹרִישֵׁם מִפְּנֵי בְּנֵי יִשְׂרָאֵל רַק הַפִּלֶהָ לְיִשְׂרָאֵל בְּנַחֲלָה כַּאֲשֶׁר צִוִּיתִיךָ:

ז וְעַתָּה חַלֵּק אֶת־הָאָרֶץ הַזֹּאת בְּנַחֲלָה לְתִשְׁעַת הַשְּׁבָטִים וַחֲצִי הַשֵּׁבֶט הַמְנַשֶּׁה:

ח עִמּוֹ הָראוּבֵנִי וְהַגָּדִי לָקְחוּ נַחֲלָתָם אֲשֶׁר נָתַן לָהֶם מֹשֶׁה בְּעֵבֶר הַיַּרְדֵּן מִזְרָחָה כַּאֲשֶׁר נָתַן לָהֶם מֹשֶׁה עֶבֶד יְהוָה:

Yehoshua/Joshua
Chapter 13

יהושע
פרק יג

9 from Aroer on the edge of the Wadi Arnon and the town in the middle of the wadi, the entire Tableland [from] Medeba to Dibon,

ט מֵעֲרוֹעֵ֡ר אֲשֶׁר֩ עַל־שְׂפַת־נַ֨חַל אַרְנ֜וֹן וְהָעִ֨יר אֲשֶׁ֧ר בְּתוֹךְ־הַנַּ֛חַל וְכָל־הַמִּישֹׁ֥ר מֵידְבָ֖א עַד־דִּיבֽוֹן׃

10 embracing all the towns of King Sihon of the Amorites, who had reigned in Heshbon, up to the border of the Ammonites;

י וְכֹ֗ל עָרֵי֙ סִיחוֹן֙ מֶ֣לֶךְ הָאֱמֹרִ֔י אֲשֶׁ֥ר מָלַ֖ךְ בְּחֶשְׁבּ֑וֹן עַד־גְּב֖וּל בְּנֵ֥י עַמּֽוֹן׃

11 further, *Gilad*, the territories of the Geshurites and the Maacathites, and all of Mount *Chermon*, and the whole of Bashan up to Salcah

יא וְהַגִּלְעָ֞ד וּגְב֧וּל הַגְּשׁוּרִ֣י וְהַמַּעֲכָתִ֗י וְכֹ֨ל הַ֥ר חֶרְמ֛וֹן וְכָל־הַבָּשָׁ֖ן עַד־סַלְכָֽה׃

12 the entire kingdom of Og, who had reigned over Bashan at Ashtaroth and at Edrei. (He was the last of the remaining Rephaim.) These were defeated and dispossessed by *Moshe*;

יב כָּל־מַמְלְכ֥וּת עוֹג֙ בַּבָּשָׁ֔ן אֲשֶׁר־מָלַ֥ךְ בְּעַשְׁתָּר֖וֹת וּבְאֶדְרֶ֑עִי ה֤וּא נִשְׁאַר֙ מִיֶּ֣תֶר הָרְפָאִ֔ים וַיַּכֵּ֥ם מֹשֶׁ֖ה וַיֹּרִשֵֽׁם׃

13 but the Israelites failed to dispossess the Geshurites and the Maacathites, and Geshur and Maacath remain among *Yisrael* to this day.

יג וְלֹ֤א הוֹרִ֙ישׁוּ֙ בְּנֵ֣י יִשְׂרָאֵ֔ל אֶת־הַגְּשׁוּרִ֖י וְאֶת־הַמַּעֲכָתִ֑י וַיֵּ֨שֶׁב גְּשׁ֤וּר וּמַֽעֲכָת֙ בְּקֶ֣רֶב יִשְׂרָאֵ֔ל עַ֖ד הַיּ֥וֹם הַזֶּֽה׃

14 No hereditary portion, however, was assigned to the tribe of *Levi*, their portion being the fire offerings of *Hashem*, the God of *Yisrael*, as He spoke concerning them.

יד רַ֚ק לְשֵׁ֣בֶט הַלֵּוִ֔י לֹ֥א נָתַ֖ן נַחֲלָ֑ה אִשֵּׁ֨י יְהֹוָ֜ה אֱלֹהֵ֤י יִשְׂרָאֵל֙ ה֣וּא נַחֲלָת֔וֹ כַּאֲשֶׁ֖ר דִּבֶּר־לֽוֹ׃

15 And so *Moshe* assigned [the following] to the tribe of the Reubenites, for their various clans,

טו וַיִּתֵּ֣ן מֹשֶׁ֔ה לְמַטֵּ֥ה בְנֵֽי־רְאוּבֵ֖ן לְמִשְׁפְּחֹתָֽם׃

16 and it became theirs: The territory from Aroer, on the edge of the Wadi Arnon and the town in the middle of the wadi, up to Medeba – the entire Tableland

טז וַיְהִ֨י לָהֶ֜ם הַגְּב֗וּל מֵעֲרוֹעֵ֡ר אֲשֶׁר֩ עַל־שְׂפַת־נַ֨חַל אַרְנ֜וֹן וְהָעִ֨יר אֲשֶׁ֧ר בְּתוֹךְ־הַנַּ֛חַל וְכָל־הַמִּישֹׁ֖ר עַל־מֵידְבָֽא׃

17 Heshbon and all its towns in the Tableland: Dibon, Bamoth-baal, Beth-baal-meon,

יז חֶשְׁבּ֥וֹן וְכָל־עָרֶ֖יהָ אֲשֶׁ֣ר בַּמִּישֹׁ֑ר דִּיבוֹן֙ וּבָמ֣וֹת בַּ֔עַל וּבֵ֖ית בַּ֥עַל מְעֽוֹן׃

18 Jahaz, Kedemoth, Mephaath,

יח וְיַ֥הְצָה וּקְדֵמֹ֖ת וּמֵפָֽעַת׃

19 Kiriathaim, Sibmah, and Zereth-shahar in the hill of the valley,

יט וְקִרְיָתַ֣יִם וְשִׂבְמָ֔ה וְצֶ֥רֶת הַשַּׁ֖חַר בְּהַ֥ר הָעֵֽמֶק׃

20 Beth-peor, the slopes of Pisgah, and Beth-jeshimoth

כ וּבֵ֥ית פְּע֛וֹר וְאַשְׁדּ֥וֹת הַפִּסְגָּ֖ה וּבֵ֥ית הַיְשִׁמֽוֹת׃

21 all the towns of the Tableland and the entire kingdom of Sihon, the king of the Amorites, who had reigned in Heshbon. (For *Moshe* defeated him and the Midianite chiefs Evi, Rekem, Zur, Hur, and Reba, who had dwelt in the land as princes of Sihon.

כא וְכֹל֙ עָרֵ֣י הַמִּישֹׁ֔ר וְכָֽל־מַמְלְכ֗וּת סִיחוֹן֙ מֶ֣לֶךְ הָאֱמֹרִ֔י אֲשֶׁ֥ר מָלַ֖ךְ בְּחֶשְׁבּ֑וֹן אֲשֶׁר֩ הִכָּ֨ה מֹשֶׁ֜ה אֹת֣וֹ ׀ וְאֶת־נְשִׂיאֵ֣י מִדְיָ֗ן אֶת־אֱוִ֤י וְאֶת־רֶ֙קֶם֙ וְאֶת־צ֤וּר וְאֶת־חוּר֙ וְאֶת־רֶ֔בַע נְסִיכֵ֣י סִיח֑וֹן יֹשְׁבֵ֖י הָאָֽרֶץ׃

22 Together with the others that they slew, the Israelites put Balaam son of Beor, the augur, to the sword.)

כב וְאֶת־בִּלְעָ֥ם בֶּן־בְּע֖וֹר הַקּוֹסֵ֑ם הָרְג֧וּ בְנֵֽי־יִשְׂרָאֵ֛ל בַּחֶ֖רֶב אֶל־חַלְלֵיהֶֽם׃

562

Yehoshua/Joshua
Chapter 13

יהושע
פרק יג

23 The boundary of the Reubenites was the edge of the *Yarden*. That was the portion of the Reubenites for their various clans – those towns with their villages.

כג וַיְהִי גְּבוּל בְּנֵי רְאוּבֵן הַיַּרְדֵּן וּגְבוּל זֹאת נַחֲלַת בְּנֵי־רְאוּבֵן לְמִשְׁפְּחֹתָם הֶעָרִים וְחַצְרֵיהֶן:

24 To the tribe of *Gad*, for the various Gadite clans, *Moshe* assigned [the following],

כד וַיִּתֵּן מֹשֶׁה לְמַטֵּה־גָד לִבְנֵי־גָד לְמִשְׁפְּחֹתָם:

25 and it became their territory: Jazer, all the towns of *Gilad*, part of the country of the Ammonites up to Aroer, which is close to Rabbah,

כה וַיְהִי לָהֶם הַגְּבוּל יַעְזֵר וְכָל־עָרֵי הַגִּלְעָד וַחֲצִי אֶרֶץ בְּנֵי עַמּוֹן עַד־עֲרוֹעֵר אֲשֶׁר עַל־פְּנֵי רַבָּה:

26 and from Heshbon to Ramath-mizpeh and Betonim, and from Mahanaim to the border of Lidbir;

כו וּמֵחֶשְׁבּוֹן עַד־רָמַת הַמִּצְפֶּה וּבְטֹנִים וּמִמַּחֲנַיִם עַד־גְּבוּל לִדְבִר:

27 and in the Valley, Beth-haram, Beth-nimrah, Succoth, and Zaphon – the rest of the kingdom of Sihon, the king of Heshbon – down to the edge of the *Yarden* and up to the tip of the Sea of Chinnereth on the east side of the *Yarden*.

כז וּבָעֵמֶק בֵּית הָרָם וּבֵית נִמְרָה וְסֻכּוֹת וְצָפוֹן יֶתֶר מַמְלְכוּת סִיחוֹן מֶלֶךְ חֶשְׁבּוֹן הַיַּרְדֵּן וּגְבֻל עַד־קְצֵה יָם־כִּנֶּרֶת עֵבֶר הַיַּרְדֵּן מִזְרָחָה:

28 That was the portion of the Gadites, for their various clans – those towns with their villages.

כח זֹאת נַחֲלַת בְּנֵי־גָד לְמִשְׁפְּחֹתָם הֶעָרִים וְחַצְרֵיהֶם:

29 And to the half-tribe of *Menashe Moshe* assigned [the following], so that it went to the half-tribe of *Menashe*, for its various clans,

כט וַיִּתֵּן מֹשֶׁה לַחֲצִי שֵׁבֶט מְנַשֶּׁה וַיְהִי לַחֲצִי מַטֵּה בְנֵי־מְנַשֶּׁה לְמִשְׁפְּחוֹתָם:

30 and became their territory: Mahanaim, all of Bashan, the entire kingdom of Og, king of Bashan, and all of Havvoth-jair in Bashan, sixty towns;

ל וַיְהִי גְבוּלָם מִמַּחֲנַיִם כָּל־הַבָּשָׁן כָּל־מַמְלְכוּת עוֹג מֶלֶךְ־הַבָּשָׁן וְכָל־חַוֹּת יָאִיר אֲשֶׁר בַּבָּשָׁן שִׁשִּׁים עִיר:

31 and part of *Gilad*, and Ashtaroth and Edrei, the royal cities of Og in Bashan, were assigned to the descendants of Machir son of *Menashe* – to a part of the descendants of Machir – for their various clans.

לא וַחֲצִי הַגִּלְעָד וְעַשְׁתָּרוֹת וְאֶדְרֶעִי עָרֵי מַמְלְכוּת עוֹג בַּבָּשָׁן לִבְנֵי מָכִיר בֶּן־מְנַשֶּׁה לַחֲצִי בְנֵי־מָכִיר לְמִשְׁפְּחוֹתָם:

32 Those, then, were the portions that *Moshe* assigned in the steppes of Moab, on the east side of the *Yarden*.

לב אֵלֶּה אֲשֶׁר־נִחַל מֹשֶׁה בְּעַרְבוֹת מוֹאָב מֵעֵבֶר לְיַרְדֵּן יְרִיחוֹ מִזְרָחָה:

33 But no portion was assigned by *Moshe* to the tribe of *Levi*; *Hashem*, the God of *Yisrael*, is their portion, as He spoke concerning them.

לג וּלְשֵׁבֶט הַלֵּוִי לֹא־נָתַן מֹשֶׁה נַחֲלָה יְהֹוָה אֱלֹהֵי יִשְׂרָאֵל הוּא נַחֲלָתָם כַּאֲשֶׁר דִּבֶּר לָהֶם:

ul-SHAY-vet ha-lay-VEE lo na-TAN mo-SHEH na-kha-LAH a-do-NAI e-lo-HAY yis-ra-AYL HU na-kha-la-TAM ka-a-SHER di-BER la-HEM

13:33 But no portion was assigned by *Moshe* to the tribe of *Levi* The tribe of *Levi* is the only one who was not assigned a portion of land. Instead of land, *Hashem* is to be their inheritance: The *Kohanim* (Priests) and the *Leviim* (Levites) are to perform the special task of serving in the Holy Temple and teaching *Hashem*'s

Yehoshua/Joshua
Chapter 14

יהושע
פרק יד

14 ¹ And these are the allotments of the Israelites in the land of Canaan, that were apportioned to them by the *Kohen Elazar*, by *Yehoshua* son of *Nun*, and by the heads of the ancestral houses of the Israelite tribes,

א וְאֵלֶּה אֲשֶׁר־נָחֲלוּ בְנֵי־יִשְׂרָאֵל בְּאֶרֶץ כְּנָעַן אֲשֶׁר נִחֲלוּ אוֹתָם אֶלְעָזָר הַכֹּהֵן וִיהוֹשֻׁעַ בִּן־נוּן וְרָאשֵׁי אֲבוֹת הַמַּטּוֹת לִבְנֵי יִשְׂרָאֵל:

² the portions that fell to them by lot, as *Hashem* had commanded through *Moshe* for the nine and a half tribes.

ב בְּגוֹרַל נַחֲלָתָם כַּאֲשֶׁר צִוָּה יְהֹוָה בְּיַד־מֹשֶׁה לְתִשְׁעַת הַמַּטּוֹת וַחֲצִי הַמַּטֶּה:

³ For the portion of the other two and a half tribes had been assigned to them by *Moshe* on the other side of the *Yarden*. He had not assigned any portion among them to the *Leviim*;

ג כִּי־נָתַן מֹשֶׁה נַחֲלַת שְׁנֵי הַמַּטּוֹת וַחֲצִי הַמַּטֶּה מֵעֵבֶר לַיַּרְדֵּן וְלַלְוִיִּם לֹא־נָתַן נַחֲלָה בְּתוֹכָם:

⁴ for whereas the descendants of *Yosef* constituted two tribes, *Menashe* and *Efraim*, the *Leviim* were assigned no share in the land, but only some towns to live in, with the pastures for their livestock and cattle.

ד כִּי־הָיוּ בְנֵי־יוֹסֵף שְׁנֵי מַטּוֹת מְנַשֶּׁה וְאֶפְרָיִם וְלֹא־נָתְנוּ חֵלֶק לַלְוִיִּם בָּאָרֶץ כִּי אִם־עָרִים לָשֶׁבֶת וּמִגְרְשֵׁיהֶם לְמִקְנֵיהֶם וּלְקִנְיָנָם:

⁵ Just as *Hashem* had commanded *Moshe*, so the Israelites did when they apportioned the land.

ה כַּאֲשֶׁר צִוָּה יְהֹוָה אֶת־מֹשֶׁה כֵּן עָשׂוּ בְנֵי יִשְׂרָאֵל וַיַּחְלְקוּ אֶת־הָאָרֶץ:

⁶ The Judites approached *Yehoshua* at *Gilgal*, and *Kalev* son of Jephunneh the Kenizzite said to him: "You know what instructions *Hashem* gave at Kadesh-barnea to *Moshe*, the man of *Hashem*, concerning you and me.

ו וַיִּגְּשׁוּ בְנֵי־יְהוּדָה אֶל־יְהוֹשֻׁעַ בַּגִּלְגָּל וַיֹּאמֶר אֵלָיו כָּלֵב בֶּן־יְפֻנֶּה הַקְּנִזִּי אַתָּה יָדַעְתָּ אֶת־הַדָּבָר אֲשֶׁר־דִּבֶּר יְהֹוָה אֶל־מֹשֶׁה אִישׁ־הָאֱלֹהִים עַל אֹדוֹתַי וְעַל אֹדוֹתֶיךָ בְּקָדֵשׁ בַּרְנֵעַ:

⁷ I was forty years old when *Moshe* the servant of *Hashem* sent me from Kadesh-barnea to spy out the land, and I gave him a forthright report.

ז בֶּן־אַרְבָּעִים שָׁנָה אָנֹכִי בִּשְׁלֹחַ מֹשֶׁה עֶבֶד־יְהֹוָה אֹתִי מִקָּדֵשׁ בַּרְנֵעַ לְרַגֵּל אֶת־הָאָרֶץ וָאָשֵׁב אֹתוֹ דָּבָר כַּאֲשֶׁר עִם־לְבָבִי:

⁸ While my companions who went up with me took the heart out of the people, I was loyal to *Hashem* my God.

ח וְאַחַי אֲשֶׁר עָלוּ עִמִּי הִמְסִיו אֶת־לֵב הָעָם וְאָנֹכִי מִלֵּאתִי אַחֲרֵי יְהֹוָה אֱלֹהָי:

⁹ On that day, *Moshe* promised on oath, 'The land on which your foot trod shall be a portion for you and your descendants forever, because you were loyal to *Hashem* my God.'

ט וַיִּשָּׁבַע מֹשֶׁה בַּיּוֹם הַהוּא לֵאמֹר אִם־לֹא הָאָרֶץ אֲשֶׁר דָּרְכָה רַגְלְךָ בָּהּ לְךָ תִהְיֶה לְנַחֲלָה וּלְבָנֶיךָ עַד־עוֹלָם כִּי מִלֵּאתָ אַחֲרֵי יְהֹוָה אֱלֹהָי:

Torah to the people. In return, the people, as a whole, are obligated to support them financially, by giving them special gifts from produce grown in *Eretz Yisrael*, as commanded in the *Torah*. In the case of the *Kohanim*, they are also to receive portions of certain sacrifices. Although in our era these gifts are not given, Jews still separate a small amount of all produce grown in Israel. The continuation of this practice is a constant reminder of the sacred obligation to make sure that all members of society are provided with a sufficient livelihood.

Yehoshua/Joshua
Chapter 15

יהושע
פרק טו

10 Now *Hashem* has preserved me, as He promised. It is forty-five years since *Hashem* made this promise to *Moshe*, when *Yisrael* was journeying through the wilderness; and here I am today, eighty-five years old.

י וְעַתָּה הִנֵּה הֶחֱיָה יְהֹוָה אוֹתִי כַּאֲשֶׁר דִּבֵּר זֶה אַרְבָּעִים וְחָמֵשׁ שָׁנָה מֵאָז דִּבֶּר יְהֹוָה אֶת־הַדָּבָר הַזֶּה אֶל־מֹשֶׁה אֲשֶׁר־הָלַךְ יִשְׂרָאֵל בַּמִּדְבָּר וְעַתָּה הִנֵּה אָנֹכִי הַיּוֹם בֶּן־חָמֵשׁ וּשְׁמוֹנִים שָׁנָה׃

11 I am still as strong today as on the day that *Moshe* sent me; my strength is the same now as it was then, for battle and for activity.

יא עוֹדֶנִּי הַיּוֹם חָזָק כַּאֲשֶׁר בְּיוֹם שְׁלֹחַ אוֹתִי מֹשֶׁה כְּכֹחִי אָז וּכְכֹחִי עָתָּה לַמִּלְחָמָה וְלָצֵאת וְלָבוֹא׃

12 So assign to me this hill country as *Hashem* promised on that day. Though you too heard on that day that Anakites are there and great fortified cities, if only *Hashem* is with me, I will dispossess them, as *Hashem* promised."

יב וְעַתָּה תְּנָה־לִּי אֶת־הָהָר הַזֶּה אֲשֶׁר־דִּבֶּר יְהֹוָה בַּיּוֹם הַהוּא כִּי אַתָּה־שָׁמַעְתָּ בַיּוֹם הַהוּא כִּי־עֲנָקִים שָׁם וְעָרִים גְּדֹלוֹת בְּצֻרוֹת אוּלַי יְהֹוָה אוֹתִי וְהוֹרַשְׁתִּים כַּאֲשֶׁר דִּבֶּר יְהֹוָה׃

13 So *Yehoshua* blessed *Kalev* son of Jephunneh and assigned *Chevron* to him as his portion.

יג וַיְבָרְכֵהוּ יְהוֹשֻׁעַ וַיִּתֵּן אֶת־חֶבְרוֹן לְכָלֵב בֶּן־יְפֻנֶּה לְנַחֲלָה׃

vai-va-r'-KHAY-hu y'-ho-SHU-a va-yi-TAYN et khev-RON l'-kha-LAYV ben y'-fu-NEH l'-na-kha-LAH

14 Thus *Chevron* became the portion of *Kalev* son of Jephunneh the Kenizzite, as it still is, because he was loyal to *Hashem*, the God of *Yisrael*.

יד עַל־כֵּן הָיְתָה־חֶבְרוֹן לְכָלֵב בֶּן־יְפֻנֶּה הַקְּנִזִּי לְנַחֲלָה עַד הַיּוֹם הַזֶּה יַעַן אֲשֶׁר מִלֵּא אַחֲרֵי יְהֹוָה אֱלֹהֵי יִשְׂרָאֵל׃

15 The name of *Chevron* was formerly *Kiryat Arba*: [Arba] was the great man among the Anakites. And the land had rest from war.

טו וְשֵׁם חֶבְרוֹן לְפָנִים קִרְיַת אַרְבַּע הָאָדָם הַגָּדוֹל בָּעֲנָקִים הוּא וְהָאָרֶץ שָׁקְטָה מִמִּלְחָמָה׃

15 ¹ The portion that fell by lot to the various clans of the tribe of *Yehuda* lay farthest south, down to the border of Edom, which is the Wilderness of Zin.

טז א וַיְהִי הַגּוֹרָל לְמַטֵּה בְנֵי יְהוּדָה לְמִשְׁפְּחֹתָם אֶל־גְּבוּל אֱדוֹם מִדְבַּר־צִן נֶגְבָּה מִקְצֵה תֵימָן׃

² Their southern boundary began from the tip of the Dead Sea, from the tongue that projects southward.

ב וַיְהִי לָהֶם גְּבוּל נֶגֶב מִקְצֵה יָם הַמֶּלַח מִן־הַלָּשֹׁן הַפֹּנֶה נֶגְבָּה׃

Cave of Machpelah in Chevron

14:13 So *Yehoshua* blessed *Kalev* son of Jephunneh
The ancient city of *Chevron* is also known as *Kiryat Arba* (although today, the name *Kiryat Arba* is used for a modern suburb next to the ancient holy city). There, *Avraham* bought the Cave of Machpelah to serve as the burial site of his wife, *Sara* (Genesis 23). This cave then became the burial site of all of the Patriarchs and three of the Matriarchs (*Rachel* is buried in *Beit Lechem*). *Yehoshua* gave this city, located within the territory of the tribe of *Yehuda*, as a special inheritance to *Kalev*, son of *Jephunneh*. Rashi (Numbers 13:22) explains that when *Kalev* was sent by *Moshe* to scout out the land, he prayed at the Cave Machpelah, asking God to help him avoid being influenced by the evil spies. Indeed, he remained loyal to *Hashem* and to His promise to give the Land of Israel to the Children of Israel. It is therefore fitting that he is rewarded with *Chevron* as his inheritance, and he bravely fights to claim it. Today, the Jewish residents of *Chevron* follow in *Kalev*'s footsteps. Despite many violent threats to their existence in the city – such as a brutal massacre in 1929 and many more recent terrorist attacks – they bravely preserve both their own community and the rights of the entire Jewish People to pray in the holy Cave of Machpelah.

Yehoshua/Joshua
Chapter 15

יהושע
פרק טו

3 It proceeded to the south of the Ascent of Akrabbim, passed on to Zin, ascended to the south of Kadesh-barnea, passed on to *Chetzron*, ascended to Addar, and made a turn to Karka.

ג וְיָצָא אֶל־מִנֶּגֶב לְמַעֲלֵה עַקְרַבִּים וְעָבַר צִנָה וְעָלָה מִנֶּגֶב לְקָדֵשׁ בַּרְנֵעַ וְעָבַר חֶצְרוֹן וְעָלָה אַדָּרָה וְנָסַב הַקַּרְקָעָה׃

4 From there it passed on to Azmon and proceeded to the Wadi of Egypt; and the boundary ran on to the Sea. That shall be your southern boundary.

ד וְעָבַר עַצְמוֹנָה וְיָצָא נַחַל מִצְרַיִם וְהָיָה [וְהָיוּ] תֹּצְאוֹת הַגְּבוּל יָמָּה זֶה־יִהְיֶה לָכֶם גְּבוּל נֶגֶב׃

5 The boundary on the east was the Dead Sea up to the mouth of the *Yarden*. On the northern side, the boundary began at the tongue of the Sea at the mouth of the *Yarden*.

ה וּגְבוּל קֵדְמָה יָם הַמֶּלַח עַד־קְצֵה הַיַּרְדֵּן וּגְבוּל לִפְאַת צָפוֹנָה מִלְּשׁוֹן הַיָּם מִקְצֵה הַיַּרְדֵּן׃

6 The boundary ascended to Beth-hoglah and passed north of Beth-arabah; then the boundary ascended to the Stone of Bohan son of *Reuven*.

ו וְעָלָה הַגְּבוּל בֵּית חָגְלָה וְעָבַר מִצְּפוֹן לְבֵית הָעֲרָבָה וְעָלָה הַגְּבוּל אֶבֶן בֹּהַן בֶּן־רְאוּבֵן׃

7 The boundary ascended from the Valley of Achor to Debir and turned north to *Gilgal*, facing the Ascent of Adummim which is south of the wadi; from there the boundary continued to the waters of En-shemesh and ran on to En-rogel.

ז וְעָלָה הַגְּבוּל דְּבִרָה מֵעֵמֶק עָכוֹר וְצָפוֹנָה פֹּנֶה אֶל־הַגִּלְגָּל אֲשֶׁר־נֹכַח לְמַעֲלֵה אֲדֻמִּים אֲשֶׁר מִנֶּגֶב לַנָּחַל וְעָבַר הַגְּבוּל אֶל־מֵי־עֵין שֶׁמֶשׁ וְהָיוּ תֹצְאֹתָיו אֶל־עֵין רֹגֵל׃

8 Then the boundary ascended into the Valley of Ben-hinnom, along the southern flank of the Jebusites – that is, *Yerushalayim*. The boundary then ran up to the top of the hill which flanks the Valley of Hinnom on the west, at the northern end of the Valley of Rephaim.

ח וְעָלָה הַגְּבוּל גֵּי בֶן־הִנֹּם אֶל־כֶּתֶף הַיְבוּסִי מִנֶּגֶב הִיא יְרוּשָׁלִָם וְעָלָה הַגְּבוּל אֶל־רֹאשׁ הָהָר אֲשֶׁר עַל־פְּנֵי גֵי־הִנֹּם יָמָּה אֲשֶׁר בִּקְצֵה עֵמֶק־רְפָאִים צָפוֹנָה׃

9 From that hilltop the boundary curved to the fountain of the Waters of Nephtoah and ran on to the towns of Mount Ephron; then the boundary curved to Baalah – that is, *Kiryat Ye'arim*.

ט וְתָאַר הַגְּבוּל מֵרֹאשׁ הָהָר אֶל־מַעְיַן מֵי נֶפְתּוֹחַ וְיָצָא אֶל־עָרֵי הַר־עֶפְרוֹן וְתָאַר הַגְּבוּל בַּעֲלָה הִיא קִרְיַת יְעָרִים׃

10 From Baalah the boundary turned westward to Mount Seir, passed north of the slope of Mount Jearim – that is, Chesalon – descended to *Beit Shemesh*, and passed on to Timnah.

י וְנָסַב הַגְּבוּל מִבַּעֲלָה יָמָּה אֶל־הַר שֵׂעִיר וְעָבַר אֶל־כֶּתֶף הַר־יְעָרִים מִצָּפוֹנָה הִיא כְסָלוֹן וְיָרַד בֵּית־שֶׁמֶשׁ וְעָבַר תִּמְנָה׃

11 The boundary then proceeded to the northern flank of Ekron; the boundary curved to Shikkeron, passed on to Mount Baalah, and proceeded to Jabneel; and the boundary ran on to the Sea.

יא וְיָצָא הַגְּבוּל אֶל־כֶּתֶף עֶקְרוֹן צָפוֹנָה וְתָאַר הַגְּבוּל שִׁכְּרוֹנָה וְעָבַר הַר־הַבַּעֲלָה וְיָצָא יַבְנְאֵל וְהָיוּ תֹּצְאוֹת הַגְּבוּל יָמָּה׃

12 And the western boundary was the edge of the Mediterranean Sea. Those were the boundaries of the various clans of the Judites on all sides.

יב וּגְבוּל יָם הַיָּמָּה הַגָּדוֹל וּגְבוּל זֶה גְּבוּל בְּנֵי־יְהוּדָה סָבִיב לְמִשְׁפְּחֹתָם׃

Yehoshua/Joshua
Chapter 15

יהושע
פרק טו

13 In accordance with *Hashem*'s command to *Yehoshua*, *Kalev* son of Jephunneh was given a portion among the Judites, namely, *Kiryat Arba* – that is, *Chevron*. ([Arba] was the father of Anak.)

וּלְכָלֵב בֶּן־יְפֻנֶּה נָתַן חֵלֶק בְּתוֹךְ בְּנֵי־יְהוּדָה אֶל־פִּי יְהֹוָה לִיהוֹשֻׁעַ אֶת־קִרְיַת אַרְבַּע אֲבִי הָעֲנָק הִיא חֶבְרוֹן׃

ul-kha-LAYV ben y'-fu-NEH na-TAN KHAY-lek b'-TOKH b'-nay y'-hu-DAH el PEE a-do-NAI lee-ho-SHU-a et kir-YAT ar-BA a-VEE ha-a-NAK HEE khev-RON

14 *Kalev* dislodged from there the three Anakites: Sheshai, Ahiman, and Talmai, descendants of Anak.

וַיֹּרֶשׁ מִשָּׁם כָּלֵב אֶת־שְׁלוֹשָׁה בְּנֵי הָעֲנָק אֶת־שֵׁשַׁי וְאֶת־אֲחִימַן וְאֶת־תַּלְמַי יְלִידֵי הָעֲנָק׃

15 From there he marched against the inhabitants of Debir – the name of Debir was formerly *Kiryat Sefer*.

וַיַּעַל מִשָּׁם אֶל־יֹשְׁבֵי דְּבִר וְשֵׁם־דְּבִר לְפָנִים קִרְיַת־סֵפֶר׃

16 and *Kalev* announced, "I will give my daughter Achsah in marriage to the man who attacks and captures *Kiryat Sefer*."

וַיֹּאמֶר כָּלֵב אֲשֶׁר־יַכֶּה אֶת־קִרְיַת־סֵפֶר וּלְכָדָהּ וְנָתַתִּי לוֹ אֶת־עַכְסָה בִתִּי לְאִשָּׁה׃

17 His kinsman *Otniel* the Kenizzite captured it; and *Kalev* gave him his daughter Achsah in marriage.

וַיִּלְכְּדָהּ עָתְנִיאֵל בֶּן־קְנַז אֲחִי כָלֵב וַיִּתֶּן־לוֹ אֶת־עַכְסָה בִתּוֹ לְאִשָּׁה׃

18 When she came [to him], she induced him to ask her father for some property. She dismounted from her donkey, and *Kalev* asked her, "What is the matter?"

וַיְהִי בְּבוֹאָהּ וַתְּסִיתֵהוּ לִשְׁאוֹל מֵאֵת־אָבִיהָ שָׂדֶה וַתִּצְנַח מֵעַל הַחֲמוֹר וַיֹּאמֶר־לָהּ כָּלֵב מַה־לָּךְ׃

19 She replied, "Give me a present; for you have given me away as *Negev*-land; so give me springs of water." And he gave her Upper and Lower Gulloth.

וַתֹּאמֶר תְּנָה־לִּי בְרָכָה כִּי אֶרֶץ הַנֶּגֶב נְתַתָּנִי וְנָתַתָּה לִי גֻּלֹּת מָיִם וַיִּתֶּן־לָהּ אֵת גֻּלֹּת עִלִּיּוֹת וְאֵת גֻּלֹּת תַּחְתִּיּוֹת׃

20 This was the portion of the tribe of the Judites by their clans:

זֹאת נַחֲלַת מַטֵּה בְנֵי־יְהוּדָה לְמִשְׁפְּחֹתָם׃

21 The towns at the far end of the tribe of *Yehuda*, near the border of Edom, in the *Negev*, were: Kabzeel, Eder, Jagur,

וַיִּהְיוּ הֶעָרִים מִקְצֵה לְמַטֵּה בְנֵי־יְהוּדָה אֶל־גְּבוּל אֱדוֹם בַּנֶּגְבָּה קַבְצְאֵל וְעֵדֶר וְיָגוּר׃

22 Kinah, Dimonah, Adadah,

וְקִינָה וְדִימוֹנָה וְעַדְעָדָה׃

23 Kedesh, Hazor, Ithnan,

וְקֶדֶשׁ וְחָצוֹר וְיִתְנָן׃

24 Ziph, Telem, Bealoth,

זִיף וָטֶלֶם וּבְעָלוֹת׃

25 Hazor-hadattah, Kerioth-hezron – that is, Hazor

וְחָצוֹר חֲדַתָּה וּקְרִיּוֹת חֶצְרוֹן הִיא חָצוֹר׃

Inside the Avraham Avinu synagogue in Chevron

15:13 *Kalev* son of *Jephunneh* was given Although *Eretz Yisrael* is divided among the tribes by divinely-directed lots, *Kalev* asks for, and receives, *Chevron*. He and *Yehoshua* had been the only scouts sent by *Moshe* who stayed loyal to God and promised the people that they could succeed in entering the land (Numbers 13:30). Therefore, he receives this reward. As Rabbi Shlomo Aviner writes, "He had something even greater than the determination of the divine lots – he had self-sacrifice." *Kalev* had risked his safety by speaking against the ten evil spies, and was also willing to risk his life by fighting the Canaanites for *Chevron*. Self-sacrifice for *Eretz Yisrael* is greatly rewarded.

Yehoshua/Joshua

Chapter 15

26 Amam, Shema, Moladah,

27 Hazar-gaddah, Heshmon, Beth-pelet,

28 Hazar-shual, *Be'er Sheva*, Biziothiah,

29 Baalah, Iim, Ezem,

30 Eltolad, Chesil, Hormah,

31 *Tziklag*, Madmannah, Sansannah,

32 Lebaoth, Shilhim, Ain and Rimmon. Total: 29 towns, with their villages.

33 In the Lowland: *Eshtaol*, *Tzora*, Ashnah,

34 *Zanoach*, En-gannim, *Tapuach*, Enam,

35 *Yarmut*, *Adulam*, Socoh, *Azeika*,

36 *Shaarayim*, Adithaim, *Gedera*, and Gederothaim – 14 towns, with their villages.

37 Zenan, Hadashah, Migdal-gad,

38 Dilan, Mizpeh, Joktheel,

39 *Lachish*, Bozkath, Eglon,

40 Cabbon, Lahmas, Chithlish,

41 Gederoth, Beth-dagon, Naamah, and Makkedah: 16 towns, with their villages.

42 Libnah, Ether, Ashan,

43 Iphtah, Ashnah, Nezib,

44 Keilah, Achzib, and Mareshah: 9 towns, with their villages.

45 Ekron, with its dependencies and villages.

46 From Ekron westward, all the towns in the vicinity of *Ashdod*, with their villages

47 *Ashdod*, its dependencies and its villages – *Azza*, its dependencies and its villages, all the way to the Wadi of Egypt and the edge of the Mediterranean Sea.

48 And in the hill country: Shamir, Jattir, Socoh,

49 Dannah, Kiriath-sannah – that is, Debir

50 Anab, Eshtemoh, Anim,

51 Goshen, Holon, and Giloh: 11 towns, with their villages.

Yehoshua/Joshua
Chapter 16

יהושע
פרק טז

52 Arab, Dumah, Eshan,

נב אֲרַב וְרוּמָה וְאֶשְׁעָן׃

53 Janum, Beth-tappuah, Aphekah,

נג וינים [וְיָנוּם] וּבֵית־תַּפּוּחַ וַאֲפֵקָה׃

54 Humtah, *Kiryat Arba* – that is, *Chevron* – and Zior: 9 towns, with their villages.

נד וְחֻמְטָה וְקִרְיַת אַרְבַּע הִיא חֶבְרוֹן וְצִיעֹר עָרִים תֵּשַׁע וְחַצְרֵיהֶן׃

55 Maon, *Carmel*, Ziph, Juttah,

נה מָעוֹן כַּרְמֶל וָזִיף וְיוּטָּה׃

56 *Yizrael*, Jokdeam, Zanoach,

נו וְיִזְרְעֶאל וְיָקְדְעָם וְזָנוֹחַ׃

57 Kain, *Giva*, and Timnah: 10 towns, with their villages.

נז הַקַּיִן גִּבְעָה וְתִמְנָה עָרִים עֶשֶׂר וְחַצְרֵיהֶן׃

58 Halhul, Beth-zur, Gedor,

נח חַלְחוּל בֵּית־צוּר וּגְדוֹר׃

59 Maarath, Beth-anoth, and Eltekon: 6 towns, with their villages.

נט וּמַעֲרָת וּבֵית־עֲנוֹת וְאֶלְתְּקֹן עָרִים שֵׁשׁ וְחַצְרֵיהֶן׃

60 Kiriath-baal – that is, *Kiryat Ye'arim* – and Rabbah: 2 towns, with their villages.

ס קִרְיַת־בַּעַל הִיא קִרְיַת יְעָרִים וְהָרַבָּה עָרִים שְׁתַּיִם וְחַצְרֵיהֶן׃

61 In the wilderness: Beth-arabah, Middin, Secacah,

סא בַּמִּדְבָּר בֵּית הָעֲרָבָה מִדִּין וּסְכָכָה׃

62 Nibshan, Ir-melah, and *Ein Gedi*: 6 towns, with their villages.

סב וְהַנִּבְשָׁן וְעִיר־הַמֶּלַח וְעֵין גֶּדִי עָרִים שֵׁשׁ וְחַצְרֵיהֶן׃

63 But the Judites could not dispossess the Jebusites, the inhabitants of *Yerushalayim*; so the Judites dwell with the Jebusites in *Yerushalayim* to this day.

סג וְאֶת־הַיְבוּסִי יוֹשְׁבֵי יְרוּשָׁלַםִ לֹא־יוכלו [יָכְלוּ] בְנֵי־יְהוּדָה לְהוֹרִישָׁם וַיֵּשֶׁב הַיְבוּסִי אֶת־בְּנֵי יְהוּדָה בִּירוּשָׁלַםִ עַד הַיּוֹם הַזֶּה׃

16

1 The portion that fell by lot to the Josephites ran from the *Yarden* at *Yericho* – from the waters of *Yericho* east of the wilderness. From *Yericho* it ascended through the hill country to *Beit El*.

טז א וַיֵּצֵא הַגּוֹרָל לִבְנֵי יוֹסֵף מִיַּרְדֵּן יְרִיחוֹ לְמֵי יְרִיחוֹ מִזְרָחָה הַמִּדְבָּר עֹלֶה מִירִיחוֹ בָּהָר בֵּית־אֵל׃

2 From *Beit El* it ran to Luz and passed on to the territory of the Archites at Ataroth,

v'-ya-TZA mi-bayt EL LU-zah v'-a-VAR el g'-VUL ha-ar-KEE a-ta-ROT

ב וְיָצָא מִבֵּית־אֵל לוּזָה וְעָבַר אֶל־גְּבוּל הָאַרְכִּי עֲטָרוֹת׃

3 descended westward to the territory of the Japhletites as far as the border of Lower Beth-horon and Gezer, and ran on to the Sea.

ג וְיָרַד־יָמָּה אֶל־גְּבוּל הַיַּפְלֵטִי עַד גְּבוּל בֵּית־חוֹרֹן תַּחְתּוֹן וְעַד־גָּזֶר וְהָיוּ תצאתו [תֹצְאֹתָיו] יָמָּה׃

16:2 From *Beit El* it ran *Beit El*, located in the territory of the tribe of *Binyamin*, near the border with *Efraim*, has an important place in Jewish history. It is near the site where *Avraham* built an altar and called out in *Hashem*'s name (Genesis 12:8). It is where *Yaakov* prayed, and dreamt about the angels ascending and descending a ladder that reached to the heavens (Genesis 28:12). It was also there that *Yaakov* received the promise that his children would inherit the Land of Israel (28:14). In 1838, the famous biblical archaeologist Edward Robinson identified the ancient site of *Beit El*. Following the Six Day War, a modern Jewish community was founded adjacent to the ancient site, and given the same name. Contemporary *Beit El* is the home of hundreds of Jewish families who are raising their children in the city of their forefathers.

Sign indentifying Yaakov's rock at Beit El

Yehoshua/Joshua
Chapter 17

יהושע
פרק יז

4 Thus the Josephites – that is, *Menashe* and *Efraim* – received their portion.

ד וַיִּנְחֲלוּ בְּנֵי־יוֹסֵף מְנַשֶּׁה וְאֶפְרָיִם׃

5 The territory of the Ephraimites, by their clans, was as follows: The boundary of their portion ran from Atroth-addar on the east to Upper Beth-horon,

ה וַיְהִי גְבוּל בְּנֵי־אֶפְרַיִם לְמִשְׁפְּחֹתָם וַיְהִי גְּבוּל נַחֲלָתָם מִזְרָחָה עַטְרוֹת אַדָּר עַד־בֵּית חוֹרֹן עֶלְיוֹן׃

6 and the boundary ran on to the Sea. And on the north, the boundary proceeded from Michmethath to the east of Taanath-shiloh and passed beyond it up to the east of Janoah;

ו וְיָצָא הַגְּבוּל הַיָּמָּה הַמִּכְמְתָת מִצָּפוֹן וְנָסַב הַגְּבוּל מִזְרָחָה תַּאֲנַת שִׁלֹה וְעָבַר אוֹתוֹ מִמִּזְרַח יָנוֹחָה׃

7 from Janoah it descended to Ataroth and Naarath, touched on *Yericho*, and ran on to the *Yarden*.

ז וְיָרַד מִיָּנוֹחָה עֲטָרוֹת וְנַעֲרָתָה וּפָגַע בִּירִיחוֹ וְיָצָא הַיַּרְדֵּן׃

8 Westward, the boundary proceeded from *Tapuach* to the Wadi Kanah and ran on to the Sea. This was the portion of the tribe of the Ephraimites, by their clans,

ח מִתַּפּוּחַ יֵלֵךְ הַגְּבוּל יָמָּה נַחַל קָנָה וְהָיוּ תֹצְאֹתָיו הַיָּמָּה זֹאת נַחֲלַת מַטֵּה בְנֵי־אֶפְרַיִם לְמִשְׁפְּחֹתָם׃

9 together with the towns marked off for the Ephraimites within the territory of the Manassites – all those towns with their villages.

ט וְהֶעָרִים הַמִּבְדָּלוֹת לִבְנֵי אֶפְרַיִם בְּתוֹךְ נַחֲלַת בְּנֵי־מְנַשֶּׁה כָּל־הֶעָרִים וְחַצְרֵיהֶן׃

10 However, they failed to dispossess the Canaanites who dwelt in Gezer; so the Canaanites remained in the midst of *Efraim*, as is still the case. But they had to perform forced labor.

י וְלֹא הוֹרִישׁוּ אֶת־הַכְּנַעֲנִי הַיּוֹשֵׁב בְּגָזֶר וַיֵּשֶׁב הַכְּנַעֲנִי בְּקֶרֶב אֶפְרַיִם עַד־הַיּוֹם הַזֶּה וַיְהִי לְמַס־עֹבֵד׃

17 1 And this is the portion that fell by lot to the tribe of *Menashe* – for he was *Yosef*'s first-born. Since Machir, the first-born of *Menashe* and the father of *Gilad*, was a valiant warrior, *Gilad* and Bashan were assigned to him.

יז א וַיְהִי הַגּוֹרָל לְמַטֵּה מְנַשֶּׁה כִּי־הוּא בְּכוֹר יוֹסֵף לְמָכִיר בְּכוֹר מְנַשֶּׁה אֲבִי הַגִּלְעָד כִּי הוּא הָיָה אִישׁ מִלְחָמָה וַיְהִי־לוֹ הַגִּלְעָד וְהַבָּשָׁן׃

2 And now assignments were made to the remaining Manassites, by their clans: the descendants of Abiezer, Helek, Asriel, *Shechem*, Hepher, and Shemida. Those were the male descendants of *Menashe* son of *Yosef*, by their clans.

ב וַיְהִי לִבְנֵי מְנַשֶּׁה הַנּוֹתָרִים לְמִשְׁפְּחֹתָם לִבְנֵי אֲבִיעֶזֶר וְלִבְנֵי־חֵלֶק וְלִבְנֵי אַשְׂרִיאֵל וְלִבְנֵי־שֶׁכֶם וְלִבְנֵי־חֵפֶר וְלִבְנֵי שְׁמִידָע אֵלֶּה בְּנֵי מְנַשֶּׁה בֶן־יוֹסֵף הַזְּכָרִים לְמִשְׁפְּחֹתָם׃

3 Now *Tzelofchad* son of Hepher son of *Gilad* son of Machir son of *Menashe* had no sons, but only daughters. The names of his daughters were *Machla*, *Noa*, *Chagla*, *Milka*, and *Tirtza*.

ג וְלִצְלָפְחָד בֶּן־חֵפֶר בֶּן־גִּלְעָד בֶּן־מָכִיר בֶּן־מְנַשֶּׁה לֹא־הָיוּ לוֹ בָּנִים כִּי אִם־בָּנוֹת וְאֵלֶּה שְׁמוֹת בְּנֹתָיו מַחְלָה וְנֹעָה חָגְלָה מִלְכָּה וְתִרְצָה׃

4 They appeared before the *Kohen Elazar*, *Yehoshua* son of *Nun*, and the chieftains, saying: "*Hashem* commanded *Moshe* to grant us a portion among our male kinsmen." So, in accordance with *Hashem*'s instructions, they were granted a portion among their father's kinsmen.

ד וַתִּקְרַבְנָה לִפְנֵי אֶלְעָזָר הַכֹּהֵן וְלִפְנֵי יְהוֹשֻׁעַ בִּן־נוּן וְלִפְנֵי הַנְּשִׂיאִים לֵאמֹר יְהוָה צִוָּה אֶת־מֹשֶׁה לָתֶת־לָנוּ נַחֲלָה בְּתוֹךְ אַחֵינוּ וַיִּתֵּן לָהֶם אֶל־פִּי יְהוָה נַחֲלָה בְּתוֹךְ אֲחֵי אֲבִיהֶן׃

Yehoshua/Joshua
Chapter 17

יהושע
פרק יז

va-tik-RAV-nah lif-NAY el-a-ZAR ha-ko-HAYN v'-lif-NAY y'-ho-SHU-a bin NUN v'-lif-NAY ha-n'-see-EEM lay-MOR a-do-NAI tzi-VAH et mo-SHEH la-tet LA-nu na-kha-LAH b'-TOKH a-KHAY-nu va-yi-TAYN la-HEM el PEE a-do-NAI na-kha-LAH b'-TOKH a-KHAY a-vee-HEN

5 Ten districts fell to *Menashe*, apart from the lands of *Gilad* and Bashan, which are across the *Yarden*.

ה וַיִּפְּלוּ חַבְלֵי־מְנַשֶּׁה עֲשָׂרָה לְבַד מֵאֶרֶץ הַגִּלְעָד וְהַבָּשָׁן אֲשֶׁר מֵעֵבֶר לַיַּרְדֵּן:

6 *Menashe*'s daughters inherited a portion in these together with his sons, while the land of *Gilad* was assigned to the rest of *Menashe*'s descendants.

ו כִּי בְּנוֹת מְנַשֶּׁה נָחֲלוּ נַחֲלָה בְּתוֹךְ בָּנָיו וְאֶרֶץ הַגִּלְעָד הָיְתָה לִבְנֵי־מְנַשֶּׁה הַנּוֹתָרִים:

7 The boundary of *Menashe* ran from *Asher* to Michmethath, which lies near *Shechem*. The boundary continued to the right, toward the inhabitants of En-tappuah.

ז וַיְהִי גְבוּל־מְנַשֶּׁה מֵאָשֵׁר הַמִּכְמְתָת אֲשֶׁר עַל־פְּנֵי שְׁכֶם וְהָלַךְ הַגְּבוּל אֶל־הַיָּמִין אֶל־יֹשְׁבֵי עֵין תַּפּוּחַ:

8 The region of *Tapuach* belonged to *Menashe*; but *Tapuach*, on the border of *Menashe*, belonged to the Ephraimites.

ח לִמְנַשֶּׁה הָיְתָה אֶרֶץ תַּפּוּחַ וְתַפּוּחַ אֶל־גְּבוּל מְנַשֶּׁה לִבְנֵי אֶפְרָיִם:

9 Then the boundary descended to the Wadi Kanah. Those towns to the south of the wadi belonged to *Efraim* as an enclave among the towns of *Menashe*. The boundary of *Menashe* lay north of the wadi and ran on to the Sea.

ט וְיָרַד הַגְּבוּל נַחַל קָנָה נֶגְבָּה לַנַּחַל עָרִים הָאֵלֶּה לְאֶפְרַיִם בְּתוֹךְ עָרֵי מְנַשֶּׁה וּגְבוּל מְנַשֶּׁה מִצְּפוֹן לַנַּחַל וַיְהִי תֹצְאֹתָיו הַיָּמָּה:

10 What lay to the south belonged to *Efraim*, and what lay to the north belonged to *Menashe*, with the Sea as its boundary. [This territory] was contiguous with *Asher* on the north and with *Yissachar* on the east.

י נֶגְבָּה לְאֶפְרַיִם וְצָפוֹנָה לִמְנַשֶּׁה וַיְהִי הַיָּם גְּבוּלוֹ וּבְאָשֵׁר יִפְגְּעוּן מִצָּפוֹן וּבְיִשָּׂשכָר מִמִּזְרָח:

11 Within *Yissachar* and *Asher*, *Menashe* possessed *Beit-Shean* and its dependencies, Ibleam and its dependencies, the inhabitants of Dor and its dependencies, the inhabitants of En-dor and its dependencies, the inhabitants of Taanach and its dependencies, and the inhabitants of Megiddo and its dependencies: these constituted three regions.

יא וַיְהִי לִמְנַשֶּׁה בְּיִשָּׂשכָר וּבְאָשֵׁר בֵּית־שְׁאָן וּבְנוֹתֶיהָ וְיִבְלְעָם וּבְנוֹתֶיהָ וְאֶת־יֹשְׁבֵי דֹאר וּבְנוֹתֶיהָ וְיֹשְׁבֵי עֵין־דֹּר וּבְנֹתֶיהָ וְיֹשְׁבֵי תַעְנַךְ וּבְנֹתֶיהָ וְיֹשְׁבֵי מְגִדּוֹ וּבְנוֹתֶיהָ שְׁלֹשֶׁת הַנָּפֶת:

Sarah Herzog (1898–1979)

17:4 Eleazer, Yehoshua son of Nun, and the chieftains During the division of the land, the daughters of *Tzelofchad* remind *Yehoshua* and *Elazar* the priest that since their father had no sons to inherit his portion of the Land of Israel, God had told *Moshe* that they, his daughters, were to receive his inheritance (Numbers 22:2–7). *Tzelofchad*'s daughters are exemplars of women in every generation who have had a special love for *Eretz Yisrael*. Two prominent twentieth-century women to epitomize the same characteristics of love and dedication to the Holy Land were Golda Meir and Sarah Herzog. Meir was Israel's first female Prime Minister, and Herzog, who was the wife of former Chief Rabbi Yitzchak Herzog, helped found the leading hospital for geriatrics and psychiatry in the Middle East, as well as the Jewish women's organization Emunah, one of the largest social service providers in Israel. Their great impact on Israeli society is still evident today, decades after their passing.

Yehoshua/Joshua
Chapter 18

יהושע
פרק יח

12 The Manassites could not dispossess [the inhabitants of] these towns, and the Canaanites stubbornly remained in this region.

יב וְלֹא יָכְלוּ בְּנֵי מְנַשֶּׁה לְהוֹרִישׁ אֶת־הֶעָרִים הָאֵלֶּה וַיּוֹאֶל הַכְּנַעֲנִי לָשֶׁבֶת בָּאָרֶץ הַזֹּאת׃

13 When the Israelites became stronger, they imposed tribute on the Canaanites; but they did not dispossess them.

יג וַיְהִי כִּי חָזְקוּ בְּנֵי יִשְׂרָאֵל וַיִּתְּנוּ אֶת־הַכְּנַעֲנִי לָמַס וְהוֹרֵשׁ לֹא הוֹרִישׁוֹ׃

14 The Josephites complained to *Yehoshua*, saying, "Why have you assigned as our portion a single allotment and a single district, seeing that we are a numerous people whom *Hashem* has blessed so greatly?"

יד וַיְדַבְּרוּ בְּנֵי יוֹסֵף אֶת־יְהוֹשֻׁעַ לֵאמֹר מַדּוּעַ נָתַתָּה לִּי נַחֲלָה גּוֹרָל אֶחָד וְחֶבֶל אֶחָד וַאֲנִי עַם־רָב עַד אֲשֶׁר־עַד־כֹּה בֵּרְכַנִי יְהוָה׃

15 "If you are a numerous people," *Yehoshua* answered them, "go up to the forest country and clear an area for yourselves there, in the territory of the Perizzites and the Rephaim, seeing that you are cramped in the hill country of *Efraim*."

טו וַיֹּאמֶר אֲלֵיהֶם יְהוֹשֻׁעַ אִם־עַם־רָב אַתָּה עֲלֵה לְךָ הַיַּעְרָה וּבֵרֵאתָ לְךָ שָׁם בְּאֶרֶץ הַפְּרִזִּי וְהָרְפָאִים כִּי־אָץ לְךָ הַר־אֶפְרָיִם׃

16 "The hill country is not enough for us," the Josephites replied, "and all the Canaanites who live in the valley area have iron chariots, both those in *Beit-Shean* and its dependencies and those in the Valley of *Yizrael*."

טז וַיֹּאמְרוּ בְּנֵי יוֹסֵף לֹא־יִמָּצֵא לָנוּ הָהָר וְרֶכֶב בַּרְזֶל בְּכָל־הַכְּנַעֲנִי הַיֹּשֵׁב בְּאֶרֶץ־הָעֵמֶק לַאֲשֶׁר בְּבֵית־שְׁאָן וּבְנוֹתֶיהָ וְלַאֲשֶׁר בְּעֵמֶק יִזְרְעֶאל׃

17 But *Yehoshua* declared to the House of *Yosef*, to *Efraim* and *Menashe*, "You are indeed a numerous people, possessed of great strength; you shall not have one allotment only.

יז וַיֹּאמֶר יְהוֹשֻׁעַ אֶל־בֵּית יוֹסֵף לְאֶפְרַיִם וְלִמְנַשֶּׁה לֵאמֹר עַם־רָב אַתָּה וְכֹחַ גָּדוֹל לָךְ לֹא־יִהְיֶה לְךָ גּוֹרָל אֶחָד׃

18 The hill country shall be yours as well; true, it is forest land, but you will clear it and possess it to its farthest limits. And you shall also dispossess the Canaanites, even though they have iron chariots and even though they are strong."

יח כִּי הַר יִהְיֶה־לָּךְ כִּי־יַעַר הוּא וּבֵרֵאתוֹ וְהָיָה לְךָ תֹצְאֹתָיו כִּי־תוֹרִישׁ אֶת־הַכְּנַעֲנִי כִּי רֶכֶב בַּרְזֶל לוֹ כִּי חָזָק הוּא׃

18

1 The whole community of *B'nei Yisrael* assembled at *Shilo*, and set up the Tent of Meeting there. The land was now under their control;

א וַיִּקָּהֲלוּ כָּל־עֲדַת בְּנֵי־יִשְׂרָאֵל שִׁלֹה וַיַּשְׁכִּינוּ שָׁם אֶת־אֹהֶל מוֹעֵד וְהָאָרֶץ נִכְבְּשָׁה לִפְנֵיהֶם׃

va-yi-ka-ha-LU kol a-DAT b'-nay yis-ra-AYL shi-LOH va-yash-KEE-nu SHAM et O-hel mo-AYD v'-ha-A-retz nikh-b'-SHAH lif-nay-HEM

18:1 The whole community of *B'nei Yisrael* assembled at *Shilo* The Jewish People bring the *Mishkan* to *Shilo*. This is meant to be its temporary location, until the *Beit Hamikdash* would be built in *Yerushalayim*. The *Mishkan* remains in *Shilo* for 369 years, serving as the central point for Israelite service to *Hashem* during that period, as is evident in the opening chapters of *Sefer Shmuel*. Like many biblical cities, the site of ancient *Shilo* has been identified and excavated, and a new Jewish community with the same name has been established adjacent to it. Today, hundreds of Jewish families live in the flourishing town of *Shilo*.

Ariel view of Shilo

Yehoshua/Joshua
Chapter 18

יהושע
פרק יח

2 but there remained seven tribes of the Israelites which had not yet received their portions.

ב וַיִּוָּתְרוּ בִּבְנֵי יִשְׂרָאֵל אֲשֶׁר לֹא־חָלְקוּ אֶת־נַחֲלָתָם שִׁבְעָה שְׁבָטִים׃

3 So *Yehoshua* said to the Israelites, "How long will you be slack about going and taking possession of the land which *Hashem*, the God of your fathers, has assigned to you?

ג וַיֹּאמֶר יְהוֹשֻׁעַ אֶל־בְּנֵי יִשְׂרָאֵל עַד־אָנָה אַתֶּם מִתְרַפִּים לָבוֹא לָרֶשֶׁת אֶת־הָאָרֶץ אֲשֶׁר נָתַן לָכֶם יְהוָה אֱלֹהֵי אֲבוֹתֵיכֶם׃

4 Appoint three men of each tribe; I will send them out to go through the country and write down a description of it for purposes of apportionment, and then come back to me.

ד הָבוּ לָכֶם שְׁלֹשָׁה אֲנָשִׁים לַשָּׁבֶט וְאֶשְׁלָחֵם וְיָקֻמוּ וְיִתְהַלְּכוּ בָאָרֶץ וְיִכְתְּבוּ אוֹתָהּ לְפִי נַחֲלָתָם וְיָבֹאוּ אֵלָי׃

5 They shall divide it into seven parts – *Yehuda* shall remain by its territory in the south, and the house of *Yosef* shall remain by its territory in the north.

ה וְהִתְחַלְּקוּ אֹתָהּ לְשִׁבְעָה חֲלָקִים יְהוּדָה יַעֲמֹד עַל־גְּבוּלוֹ מִנֶּגֶב וּבֵית יוֹסֵף יַעַמְדוּ עַל־גְּבוּלָם מִצָּפוֹן׃

6 When you have written down the description of the land in seven parts, bring it here to me. Then I will cast lots for you here before *Hashem* our God.

ו וְאַתֶּם תִּכְתְּבוּ אֶת־הָאָרֶץ שִׁבְעָה חֲלָקִים וַהֲבֵאתֶם אֵלַי הֵנָּה וְיָרִיתִי לָכֶם גּוֹרָל פֹּה לִפְנֵי יְהוָה אֱלֹהֵינוּ׃

7 For the *Leviim* have no share among you, since the priesthood of *Hashem* is their portion; and *Gad* and *Reuven* and the half-tribe of *Menashe* have received the portions which were assigned to them by *Moshe* the servant of *Hashem*, on the eastern side of the *Yarden*."

ז כִּי אֵין־חֵלֶק לַלְוִיִּם בְּקִרְבְּכֶם כִּי־כְהֻנַּת יְהוָה נַחֲלָתוֹ וְגָד וּרְאוּבֵן וַחֲצִי שֵׁבֶט הַמְנַשֶּׁה לָקְחוּ נַחֲלָתָם מֵעֵבֶר לַיַּרְדֵּן מִזְרָחָה אֲשֶׁר נָתַן לָהֶם מֹשֶׁה עֶבֶד יְהוָה׃

8 The men set out on their journeys. *Yehoshua* ordered the men who were leaving to write down a description of the land – "Go, traverse the country and write down a description of it. Then return to me, and I will cast lots for you here at *Shilo* before *Hashem*."

ח וַיָּקֻמוּ הָאֲנָשִׁים וַיֵּלֵכוּ וַיְצַו יְהוֹשֻׁעַ אֶת־הַהֹלְכִים לִכְתֹּב אֶת־הָאָרֶץ לֵאמֹר לְכוּ וְהִתְהַלְּכוּ בָאָרֶץ וְכִתְבוּ אוֹתָהּ וְשׁוּבוּ אֵלַי וּפֹה אַשְׁלִיךְ לָכֶם גּוֹרָל לִפְנֵי יְהוָה בְּשִׁלֹה׃

9 So the men went and traversed the land; they described it in a document, town by town, in seven parts, and they returned to *Yehoshua* in the camp at *Shilo*.

ט וַיֵּלְכוּ הָאֲנָשִׁים וַיַּעַבְרוּ בָאָרֶץ וַיִּכְתְּבוּהָ לֶעָרִים לְשִׁבְעָה חֲלָקִים עַל־סֵפֶר וַיָּבֹאוּ אֶל־יְהוֹשֻׁעַ אֶל־הַמַּחֲנֶה שִׁלֹה׃

10 *Yehoshua* cast lots for them at *Shilo* before *Hashem*, and there *Yehoshua* apportioned the land among the Israelites according to their divisions.

י וַיַּשְׁלֵךְ לָהֶם יְהוֹשֻׁעַ גּוֹרָל בְּשִׁלֹה לִפְנֵי יְהוָה וַיְחַלֶּק־שָׁם יְהוֹשֻׁעַ אֶת־הָאָרֶץ לִבְנֵי יִשְׂרָאֵל כְּמַחְלְקֹתָם׃

11 The lot of the tribe of the Benjaminites, by their clans, came out first. The territory which fell to their lot lay between the Judites and the Josephites.

יא וַיַּעַל גּוֹרַל מַטֵּה בְנֵי־בִנְיָמִן לְמִשְׁפְּחֹתָם וַיֵּצֵא גְּבוּל גּוֹרָלָם בֵּין בְּנֵי יְהוּדָה וּבֵין בְּנֵי יוֹסֵף׃

12 The boundary on their northern rim began at the *Yarden*; the boundary ascended to the northern flank of *Yericho*, ascended westward into the hill country and ran on to the Wilderness of *Beit Aven*.

יב וַיְהִי לָהֶם הַגְּבוּל לִפְאַת צָפוֹנָה מִן־הַיַּרְדֵּן וְעָלָה הַגְּבוּל אֶל־כֶּתֶף יְרִיחוֹ מִצָּפוֹן וְעָלָה בָהָר יָמָּה [וְהָיָה] וְהָיוּ תֹּצְאֹתָיו מִדְבַּרָה בֵּית אָוֶן׃

Yehoshua/Joshua
Chapter 18

יהושע
פרק יח

13 From there the boundary passed on southward to Luz, to the flank of Luz – that is, *Beit El*; then the boundary descended to Atroth-addar [and] to the hill south of Lower Beth-horon.

יג וְעָבַר מִשָּׁם הַגְּבוּל לוּזָה אֶל־כֶּתֶף לוּזָה נֶגְבָּה הִיא בֵּית־אֵל וְיָרַד הַגְּבוּל עַטְרוֹת אַדָּר עַל־הָהָר אֲשֶׁר מִנֶּגֶב לְבֵית־חֹרוֹן תַּחְתּוֹן:

14 The boundary now turned and curved onto the western rim; and the boundary ran southward from the hill on the south side of Beth-horon till it ended at Kiriath-baal – that is, *Kiryat Ye'arim* – a town of the Judites. That was the western rim.

יד וְתָאַר הַגְּבוּל וְנָסַב לִפְאַת־יָם נֶגְבָּה מִן־הָהָר אֲשֶׁר עַל־פְּנֵי בֵית־חֹרוֹן נֶגְבָּה והיה [וְהָיוּ] תֹצְאֹתָיו אֶל־קִרְיַת־בַּעַל הִיא קִרְיַת יְעָרִים עִיר בְּנֵי יְהוּדָה זֹאת פְּאַת־יָם:

15 The southern rim: From the outskirts of *Kiryat Ye'arim*, the boundary passed westward and ran on to the fountain of the Waters of Nephtoah.

טו וּפְאַת־נֶגְבָּה מִקְצֵה קִרְיַת יְעָרִים וְיָצָא הַגְּבוּל יָמָּה וְיָצָא אֶל־מַעְיַן מֵי נֶפְתּוֹחַ:

16 Then the boundary descended to the foot of the hill by the Valley of Ben-hinnom at the northern end of the Valley of Rephaim; then it ran down the Valley of Hinnom along the southern flank of the Jebusites to En-rogel.

טז וְיָרַד הַגְּבוּל אֶל־קְצֵה הָהָר אֲשֶׁר עַל־פְּנֵי גֵּי בֶן־הִנֹּם אֲשֶׁר בְּעֵמֶק רְפָאִים צָפוֹנָה וְיָרַד גֵּי הִנֹּם אֶל־כֶּתֶף הַיְבוּסִי נֶגְבָּה וְיָרַד עֵין רֹגֵל:

17 Curving northward, it ran on to En-shemesh and ran on to Geliloth, facing the Ascent of Adummim, and descended to the Stone of Bohan son of *Reuven*.

יז וְתָאַר מִצָּפוֹן וְיָצָא עֵין שֶׁמֶשׁ וְיָצָא אֶל־גְּלִילוֹת אֲשֶׁר־נֹכַח מַעֲלֵה אֲדֻמִּים וְיָרַד אֶבֶן בֹּהַן בֶּן־רְאוּבֵן:

18 It continued northward to the edge of the Arabah and descended into the Arabah.

יח וְעָבַר אֶל־כֶּתֶף מוּל־הָעֲרָבָה צָפוֹנָה וְיָרַד הָעֲרָבָתָה:

19 The boundary passed on to the northern flank of Beth-hoglah, and the boundary ended at the northern tongue of the Dead Sea, at the southern end of the *Yarden*. That was the southern boundary.

יט וְעָבַר הַגְּבוּל אֶל־כֶּתֶף בֵּית־חָגְלָה צָפוֹנָה והיה [וְהָיוּ] תצאותיו [תֹּצְאוֹת] הַגְּבוּל אֶל־לְשׁוֹן יָם־הַמֶּלַח צָפוֹנָה אֶל־קְצֵה הַיַּרְדֵּן נֶגְבָּה זֶה גְּבוּל נֶגֶב:

20 On their eastern rim, finally, the *Yarden* was their boundary. That was the portion of the Benjaminites, by their clans, according to its boundaries on all sides.

כ וְהַיַּרְדֵּן יִגְבֹּל־אֹתוֹ לִפְאַת־קֵדְמָה זֹאת נַחֲלַת בְּנֵי בִנְיָמִן לִגְבוּלֹתֶיהָ סָבִיב לְמִשְׁפְּחֹתָם:

21 And the towns of the tribe of the Benjaminites, by its clans, were: *Yericho*, Beth-hoglah, Emek-keziz,

כא וְהָיוּ הֶעָרִים לְמַטֵּה בְּנֵי בִנְיָמִן לְמִשְׁפְּחוֹתֵיהֶם יְרִיחוֹ וּבֵית־חָגְלָה וְעֵמֶק קְצִיץ:

22 Beth-arabah, Zemaraim, *Beit El*,

כב וּבֵית הָעֲרָבָה וּצְמָרַיִם וּבֵית־אֵל:

23 Avvim, Parah, Ophrah,

כג וְהָעַוִּים וְהַפָּרָה וְעָפְרָה:

24 Chephar-ammonah, Ophni, and Geba – 12 towns, with their villages.

כד וּכְפַר הָעַמֹּנִי [הָעַמֹּנָה] וְהָעָפְנִי וָגָבַע עָרִים שְׁתֵּים־עֶשְׂרֵה וְחַצְרֵיהֶן:

25 Also *Givon*, *Rama*, Beeroth,

כה גִּבְעוֹן וְהָרָמָה וּבְאֵרוֹת:

26 Mizpeh, Chephirah, Mozah,

כו וְהַמִּצְפֶּה וְהַכְּפִירָה וְהַמֹּצָה:

Yehoshua/Joshua
Chapter 19

27 Rekem, Irpeel, Taralah,

28 Zela, Eleph, and Jebus – that is, *Yerushalayim* – Gibeath [and] Kiriath: 14 towns, with their villages. That was the portion of the Benjaminites, by their clans.

19

1 The second lot fell to *Shimon*. The portion of the tribe of the Simeonites, by their clans, lay inside the portion of the Judites.

2 Their portion comprised: *Be'er Sheva* – or Sheba – Moladah,

3 Hazar-shual, Balah, Ezem,

4 Eltolad, Bethul, Hormah,

5 *Tziklag*, Beth-marcaboth, Hazar-susah,

6 Beth-lebaoth, and Sharuhen – 13 towns, with their villages.

7 Ain, Rimmon, Ether, and Ashan: 4 towns, with their villages

8 together with all the villages in the vicinity of those towns, down to Baalath-beer [and] Ramath-negeb. That was the portion of the tribe of the Simeonites, by their clans.

9 The portion of the Simeonites was part of the territory of the Judites; since the share of the Judites was larger than they needed, the Simeonites received a portion inside their portion.

10 The third lot emerged for the Zebulunites, by their clans. The boundary of their portion: Starting at Sarid,

11 their boundary ascended westward to Maralah, touching Dabbesheth and touching the wadi alongside Jokneam.

12 And it also ran from Sarid along the eastern side, where the sun rises, past the territory of Chisloth-tabor and on to Daberath and ascended to Japhia.

13 From there it ran [back] to the east, toward the sunrise, to Gath-hepher, to Eth-kazin, and on to Rimmon, where it curved to Neah.

14 Then it turned – that is, the boundary on the north – to Hannathon. Its extreme limits were the Valley of Iphtah-el,

Yehoshua/Joshua
Chapter 19

יהושע
פרק יט

15 Kattath, Nahalal, Shimron, Idalah, and *Beit Lechem*: 12 towns, with their villages.

טו וְקַטָּת וְנַהֲלָל וְשִׁמְרוֹן וְיִדְאֲלָה וּבֵית לָחֶם עָרִים שְׁתֵּים־עֶשְׂרֵה וְחַצְרֵיהֶן׃

16 That was the portion of the Zebulunites by their clans – those towns, with their villages.

טז זֹאת נַחֲלַת בְּנֵי־זְבוּלֻן לְמִשְׁפְּחוֹתָם הֶעָרִים הָאֵלֶּה וְחַצְרֵיהֶן׃

17 The fourth lot fell to *Yissachar*, the Issacharites by their clans.

יז לְיִשָּׂשכָר יָצָא הַגּוֹרָל הָרְבִיעִי לִבְנֵי יִשָּׂשכָר לְמִשְׁפְּחוֹתָם׃

18 Their territory comprised: *Yizrael*, Chesulloth, Shunem,

יח וַיְהִי גְבוּלָם יִזְרְעֶאלָה וְהַכְּסוּלֹת וְשׁוּנֵם׃

19 Hapharaim, Shion, Anaharath,

יט וַחֲפָרַיִם וְשִׁיאֹן וַאֲנָחֲרַת׃

20 Rabbith, Kishion, Ebez,

כ וְהָרַבִּית וְקִשְׁיוֹן וָאָבֶץ׃

21 Remeth, En-gannim, En-haddah, and Beth-pazzez.

כא וְרֶמֶת וְעֵין־גַּנִּים וְעֵין חַדָּה וּבֵית פַּצֵּץ׃

22 The boundary touched *Tavor*, Shahazimah, and *Beit Shemesh*; and their boundary ran to the *Yarden*: 16 towns, with their villages.

כב וּפָגַע הַגְּבוּל בְּתָבוֹר וְשַׁחֲצוּמָה [וְשַׁחֲצִימָה] וּבֵית שֶׁמֶשׁ וְהָיוּ תֹצְאוֹת גְּבוּלָם הַיַּרְדֵּן עָרִים שֵׁשׁ־עֶשְׂרֵה וְחַצְרֵיהֶן׃

23 That was the portion of the tribe of the Issacharites, by their clans – the towns with their villages.

כג זֹאת נַחֲלַת מַטֵּה בְנֵי־יִשָּׂשכָר לְמִשְׁפְּחֹתָם הֶעָרִים וְחַצְרֵיהֶן׃

24 The fifth lot fell to the tribe of the Asherites, by their clans.

כד וַיֵּצֵא הַגּוֹרָל הַחֲמִישִׁי לְמַטֵּה בְנֵי־אָשֵׁר לְמִשְׁפְּחוֹתָם׃

25 Their boundary ran along Helkath, Hali, Beten, Achshaph,

כה וַיְהִי גְּבוּלָם חֶלְקַת וַחֲלִי וָבֶטֶן וְאַכְשָׁף׃

26 Allammelech, Amad, and Mishal; and it touched *Carmel* on the west, and Shihor-libnath.

כו וְאַלַּמֶּלֶךְ וְעַמְעָד וּמִשְׁאָל וּפָגַע בְּכַרְמֶל הַיָּמָּה וּבְשִׁיחוֹר לִבְנָת׃

27 It also ran along the east side to Beth-dagon, and touched *Zevulun* and the Valley of Iphtah-el to the north, [as also] Beth-emek and Neiel; then it ran to Cabul on the north,

כז וְשָׁב מִזְרַח הַשֶּׁמֶשׁ בֵּית דָּגֹן וּפָגַע בִּזְבֻלוּן וּבְגֵי יִפְתַּח־אֵל צָפוֹנָה בֵּית הָעֵמֶק וּנְעִיאֵל וְיָצָא אֶל־כָּבוּל מִשְּׂמֹאל׃

28 Ebron, Rehob, Hammon, and Kanah, up to Great Sidon.

כח וְעֶבְרֹן וּרְחֹב וְחַמּוֹן וְקָנָה עַד צִידוֹן רַבָּה׃

29 The boundary turned to *Rama* and on to the fortified city of Tyre; then the boundary turned to Hosah and it ran on westward to Mehebel, Achzib,

כט וְשָׁב הַגְּבוּל הָרָמָה וְעַד־עִיר מִבְצַר־צֹר וְשָׁב הַגְּבוּל חֹסָה וְיִהְיוּ [וְהָיוּ] תֹצְאֹתָיו הַיָּמָּה מֵחֶבֶל אַכְזִיבָה׃

30 Ummah, Aphek, and Rehob: 22 towns, with their villages.

ל וְעֻמָה וַאֲפֵק וּרְחֹב עָרִים עֶשְׂרִים וּשְׁתַּיִם וְחַצְרֵיהֶן׃

31 That was the portion of the tribe of the Asherites, by their clans – those towns, with their villages.

לא זֹאת נַחֲלַת מַטֵּה בְנֵי־אָשֵׁר לְמִשְׁפְּחֹתָם הֶעָרִים הָאֵלֶּה וְחַצְרֵיהֶן׃

32 The sixth lot fell to the Naphtalites, the Naphtalites by their clans.

לב לִבְנֵי נַפְתָּלִי יָצָא הַגּוֹרָל הַשִּׁשִּׁי לִבְנֵי נַפְתָּלִי לְמִשְׁפְּחֹתָם׃

Yehoshua/Joshua
Chapter 19

33 Their boundary ran from Heleph, Elon-bezaanannim, Adaminekeb, and Jabneel to Lakkum, and it ended at the *Yarden*.

34 The boundary then turned westward to Aznoth-tabor and ran from there to Hukok. It touched *Zevulun* on the south, and it touched *Asher* on the west, and *Yehuda* at the *Yarden* on the east.

35 Its fortified towns were Ziddim, Zer, Hammath, Rakkath, Chinnereth,

36 Adamah, *Rama*, Hazor,

37 Kedesh, Edrei, En-hazor,

38 Iron, Migdal-el, Horem, Beth-anath, and *Beit Shemesh*: 19 towns, with their villages.

39 That was the portion of the tribe of the Naphtalites, by their clans – the towns, with their villages.

40 The seventh lot fell to the tribe of the Danites, by their clans.

41 Their allotted territory comprised: *Tzora*, *Eshtaol*, Ir-shemesh,

42 Shaalabbin, Aijalon, Ithlah,

43 Elon, Timnah, Ekron,

44 Eltekeh, Gibbethon, Baalath,

45 Jehud, Bene-berak, Gath-rimmon,

46 Me-jarkon, and Rakkon, at the border near *Yaffo*.

47 But the territory of the Danites slipped from their grasp. So the Danites migrated and made war on Leshem. They captured it and put it to the sword; they took possession of it and settled in it. And they changed the name of Leshem to *Dan*, after their ancestor *Dan*.

48 That was the portion of the tribe of the Danites, by their clans – those towns, with their villages.

49 When they had finished allotting the land by its boundaries, the Israelites gave a portion in their midst to *Yehoshua* son of *Nun*.

יהושע
פרק יט

לג וַיְהִי גְבוּלָם מֵחֵלֶף מֵאֵלוֹן בְּצַעֲנַנִּים וַאֲדָמִי הַנֶּקֶב וְיַבְנְאֵל עַד־לַקּוּם וַיְהִי תֹצְאֹתָיו הַיַּרְדֵּן:

לד וְשָׁב הַגְּבוּל יָמָּה אַזְנוֹת תָּבוֹר וְיָצָא מִשָּׁם חוּקֹקָה וּפָגַע בִּזְבֻלוּן מִנֶּגֶב וּבְאָשֵׁר פָּגַע מִיָּם וּבִיהוּדָה הַיַּרְדֵּן מִזְרַח הַשָּׁמֶשׁ:

לה וְעָרֵי מִבְצָר הַצִּדִּים צֵר וְחַמַּת רַקַּת וְכִנָּרֶת:

לו וַאֲדָמָה וְהָרָמָה וְחָצוֹר:

לז וְקֶדֶשׁ וְאֶדְרֶעִי וְעֵין חָצוֹר:

לח וְיִרְאוֹן וּמִגְדַּל־אֵל חֳרֵם וּבֵית־עֲנָת וּבֵית שָׁמֶשׁ עָרִים תְּשַׁע־עֶשְׂרֵה וְחַצְרֵיהֶן:

לט זֹאת נַחֲלַת מַטֵּה בְנֵי־נַפְתָּלִי לְמִשְׁפְּחֹתָם הֶעָרִים וְחַצְרֵיהֶן:

מ לְמַטֵּה בְנֵי־דָן לְמִשְׁפְּחֹתָם יָצָא הַגּוֹרָל הַשְּׁבִיעִי:

מא וַיְהִי גְּבוּל נַחֲלָתָם צָרְעָה וְאֶשְׁתָּאוֹל וְעִיר שָׁמֶשׁ:

מב וְשַׁעֲלַבִּין וְאַיָּלוֹן וְיִתְלָה:

מג וְאֵילוֹן וְתִמְנָתָה וְעֶקְרוֹן:

מד וְאֶלְתְּקֵה וְגִבְּתוֹן וּבַעֲלָת:

מה וִיהֻד וּבְנֵי־בְרַק וְגַת־רִמּוֹן:

מו וּמֵי הַיַּרְקוֹן וְהָרַקּוֹן עִם־הַגְּבוּל מוּל יָפוֹ:

מז וַיֵּצֵא גְבוּל־בְּנֵי־דָן מֵהֶם וַיַּעֲלוּ בְנֵי־דָן וַיִּלָּחֲמוּ עִם־לֶשֶׁם וַיִּלְכְּדוּ אוֹתָהּ וַיַּכּוּ אוֹתָהּ לְפִי־חֶרֶב וַיִּרְשׁוּ אוֹתָהּ וַיֵּשְׁבוּ בָהּ וַיִּקְרְאוּ לְלֶשֶׁם דָּן כְּשֵׁם דָּן אֲבִיהֶם:

מח זֹאת נַחֲלַת מַטֵּה בְנֵי־דָן לְמִשְׁפְּחֹתָם הֶעָרִים הָאֵלֶּה וְחַצְרֵיהֶן:

מט וַיְכַלּוּ לִנְחֹל־אֶת־הָאָרֶץ לִגְבוּלֹתֶיהָ וַיִּתְּנוּ בְנֵי־יִשְׂרָאֵל נַחֲלָה לִיהוֹשֻׁעַ בִּן־נוּן בְּתוֹכָם:

Yehoshua/Joshua
Chapter 20

יהושע
פרק כ

50 At the command of *Hashem* they gave him the town that he asked for, Timnath-serah in the hill country of *Efraim*; he fortified the town and settled in it.

נ עַל־פִּי יְהוָה נָתְנוּ לוֹ אֶת־הָעִיר אֲשֶׁר שָׁאָל אֶת־תִּמְנַת־סֶרַח בְּהַר אֶפְרָיִם וַיִּבְנֶה אֶת־הָעִיר וַיֵּשֶׁב בָּהּ:

al PEE a-do-NAI nat'-NU LO et ha-EER a-SHER sha-AL et tim-nat SE-rakh b'-HAR ef-RA-yim va-yiv-NEH et ha-EER va-YAY-shev bah

51 These are the portions assigned by lot to the tribes of *Yisrael* by the *Kohen Elazar*, *Yehoshua* son of *Nun*, and the heads of the ancestral houses, before *Hashem* at *Shilo*, at the entrance of the Tent of Meeting.

נא אֵלֶּה הַנְּחָלֹת אֲשֶׁר נִחֲלוּ אֶלְעָזָר הַכֹּהֵן וִיהוֹשֻׁעַ בִּן־נוּן וְרָאשֵׁי הָאָבוֹת לְמַטּוֹת בְּנֵי־יִשְׂרָאֵל בְּגוֹרָל בְּשִׁלֹה לִפְנֵי יְהוָה פֶּתַח אֹהֶל מוֹעֵד וַיְכַלּוּ מֵחַלֵּק אֶת־הָאָרֶץ:

20 1 When they had finished dividing the land, *Hashem* said to *Yehoshua*:

א וַיְדַבֵּר יְהוָה אֶל־יְהוֹשֻׁעַ לֵאמֹר:

2 "Speak to the Israelites: Designate the cities of refuge – about which I commanded you through *Moshe*

ב דַּבֵּר אֶל־בְּנֵי יִשְׂרָאֵל לֵאמֹר תְּנוּ לָכֶם אֶת־עָרֵי הַמִּקְלָט אֲשֶׁר־דִּבַּרְתִּי אֲלֵיכֶם בְּיַד־מֹשֶׁה:

da-BAYR el b'-NAY yis-ra-AYL lay-MOR t'-NU la-KHEM et a-RAY ha-mik-LAT a-sher di-BAR-tee a-lay-KHEM b'-yad mo-SHEH

3 to which a manslayer who kills a person by mistake, unintentionally, may flee. They shall serve you as a refuge from the blood avenger.

ג לָנוּס שָׁמָּה רוֹצֵחַ מַכֵּה־נֶפֶשׁ בִּשְׁגָגָה בִּבְלִי־דָעַת וְהָיוּ לָכֶם לְמִקְלָט מִגֹּאֵל הַדָּם:

4 He shall flee to one of those cities, present himself at the entrance to the city gate, and plead his case before the elders of that city; and they shall admit him into the city and give him a place in which to live among them.

ד וְנָס אֶל־אַחַת מֵהֶעָרִים הָאֵלֶּה וְעָמַד פֶּתַח שַׁעַר הָעִיר וְדִבֶּר בְּאָזְנֵי זִקְנֵי־הָעִיר הַהִיא אֶת־דְּבָרָיו וְאָסְפוּ אֹתוֹ הָעִירָה אֲלֵיהֶם וְנָתְנוּ־לוֹ מָקוֹם וְיָשַׁב עִמָּם:

19:50 They gave him the town that he asked for As the leader of the people, *Yehoshua* waits until the end of the process of dividing the land before receiving his own inheritance. He asks for *Timnat Serach* (Timnath-serah), in the mountains of *Efraim*, and through the lots, *Hashem* grants his request. However, unlike others who inherited existing towns built by the Canaanites, *Yehoshua* would not be able to simply move in; first, he needs to build the city. This is the task of leaders – to build something where nothing currently exists. In contemporary Israel, many modern religious, political and business leaders have followed this model, and like *Yehoshua*, have been blessed by *Hashem* with success. In the context of the miraculous growth of the State of Israel, many communities, schools, organizations and institutions, as well as fertile farmland and stunning landscapes, have risen out of nothingness.

20:2 Designate the cities of refuge The cities of refuge are places where people who are guilty of unintentional manslaughter must flee for protection from the relatives of their victims. The accidental killer must remain in the city of refuge until the death of the *Kohen Gadol*. This law, which subjects the unwitting murderer to exile from his home, teaches a powerful lesson. The section of the *Torah* which details these laws ends with words, "You shall not pollute the land in which you live; for blood pollutes the land … You shall not defile the land in which you live, in which I Myself abide, for I *Hashem* abide among *B'nei Yisrael*" (Numbers 35:33–34). Bloodshed, even unintentional, defiles the sanctity of the land. Therefore, the perpetrator must undergo a symbolic exile from the land which he has defiled. He can return only once atonement is achieved through the death of the *Kohen Gadol*. Similarly, the Jewish people were exiled from the Land of Israel because of their collective desecration of the land. And just as the unwitting murderer eventually returns home from the city of refuge, the People of Israel are now also returning home from their long and painful exile, to *Eretz Yisrael*.

Tomb of Yehoshua in Kifl Hares, biblical Timnat Serach

578

Yehoshua/Joshua
Chapter 21

5 Should the blood avenger pursue him, they shall not hand the manslayer over to him, since he killed the other person without intent and had not been his enemy in the past.

6 He shall live in that city until he can stand trial before the assembly, [and remain there] until the death of the *Kohen Gadol* who is in office at that time. Thereafter, the manslayer may go back to his home in his own town, to the town from which he fled."

7 So they set aside Kedesh in the hill country of *Naftali* in Galilee, *Shechem* in the hill country of *Efraim*, and *Kiryat Arba* – that is, *Chevron* – in the hill country of *Yehuda*.

8 And across the *Yarden*, east of *Yericho*, they assigned Bezer in the wilderness, in the Tableland, from the tribe of *Reuven*; Ramoth in *Gilad* from the tribe of *Gad*; and Golan in Bashan from the tribe of *Menashe*.

9 Those were the towns designated for all the Israelites and for aliens residing among them, to which anyone who killed a person unintentionally might flee, and not die by the hand of the blood avenger before standing trial by the assembly.

21

1 The heads of the ancestral houses of the *Leviim* approached the *Kohen Elazar, Yehoshua* son of *Nun*, and the heads of the ancestral houses of the Israelite tribes,

2 and spoke to them at *Shilo* in the land of Canaan, as follows: "*Hashem* commanded through *Moshe* that we be given towns to live in, along with their pastures for our livestock."

3 So the Israelites, in accordance with *Hashem*'s command, assigned to the *Leviim*, out of their own portions, the following towns with their pastures:

4 The [first] lot among the *Leviim* fell to the Kehatite clans. To the descendants of the *Kohen Aharon*, there fell by lot 13 towns from the tribe of *Yehuda*, the tribe of *Shimon*, and the tribe of *Binyamin*;

5 and to the remaining Kehatites [there fell] by lot 10 towns from the clans of the tribe of *Efraim*, the tribe of *Dan*, and the half-tribe of *Menashe*.

יהושע
פרק כא

ה וְכִי יִרְדֹּף גֹּאֵל הַדָּם אַחֲרָיו וְלֹא־יַסְגִּרוּ אֶת־הָרֹצֵחַ בְּיָדוֹ כִּי בִבְלִי־דַעַת הִכָּה אֶת־רֵעֵהוּ וְלֹא־שֹׂנֵא הוּא לוֹ מִתְּמוֹל שִׁלְשׁוֹם:

ו וְיָשַׁב בָּעִיר הַהִיא עַד־עָמְדוֹ לִפְנֵי הָעֵדָה לַמִּשְׁפָּט עַד־מוֹת הַכֹּהֵן הַגָּדוֹל אֲשֶׁר יִהְיֶה בַּיָּמִים הָהֵם אָז יָשׁוּב הָרוֹצֵחַ וּבָא אֶל־עִירוֹ וְאֶל־בֵּיתוֹ אֶל־הָעִיר אֲשֶׁר־נָס מִשָּׁם:

ז וַיַּקְדִּשׁוּ אֶת־קֶדֶשׁ בַּגָּלִיל בְּהַר נַפְתָּלִי וְאֶת־שְׁכֶם בְּהַר אֶפְרָיִם וְאֶת־קִרְיַת אַרְבַּע הִיא חֶבְרוֹן בְּהַר יְהוּדָה:

ח וּמֵעֵבֶר לְיַרְדֵּן יְרִיחוֹ מִזְרָחָה נָתְנוּ אֶת־בֶּצֶר בַּמִּדְבָּר בַּמִּישֹׁר מִמַּטֵּה רְאוּבֵן וְאֶת־רָאמֹת בַּגִּלְעָד מִמַּטֵּה־גָד וְאֶת־גֹּלָן [גּוֹלָן] בַּבָּשָׁן מִמַּטֵּה מְנַשֶּׁה:

ט אֵלֶּה הָיוּ עָרֵי הַמּוּעָדָה לְכֹל בְּנֵי יִשְׂרָאֵל וְלַגֵּר הַגָּר בְּתוֹכָם לָנוּס שָׁמָּה כָּל־מַכֵּה־נֶפֶשׁ בִּשְׁגָגָה וְלֹא יָמוּת בְּיַד גֹּאֵל הַדָּם עַד־עָמְדוֹ לִפְנֵי הָעֵדָה:

כא א וַיִּגְּשׁוּ רָאשֵׁי אֲבוֹת הַלְוִיִּם אֶל־אֶלְעָזָר הַכֹּהֵן וְאֶל־יְהוֹשֻׁעַ בִּן־נוּן וְאֶל־רָאשֵׁי אֲבוֹת הַמַּטּוֹת לִבְנֵי יִשְׂרָאֵל:

ב וַיְדַבְּרוּ אֲלֵיהֶם בְּשִׁלֹה בְּאֶרֶץ כְּנַעַן לֵאמֹר יְהוָה צִוָּה בְיַד־מֹשֶׁה לָתֶת־לָנוּ עָרִים לָשָׁבֶת וּמִגְרְשֵׁיהֶן לִבְהֶמְתֵּנוּ:

ג וַיִּתְּנוּ בְנֵי־יִשְׂרָאֵל לַלְוִיִּם מִנַּחֲלָתָם אֶל־פִּי יְהוָה אֶת־הֶעָרִים הָאֵלֶּה וְאֶת־מִגְרְשֵׁיהֶן:

ד וַיֵּצֵא הַגּוֹרָל לְמִשְׁפְּחֹת הַקְּהָתִי וַיְהִי לִבְנֵי אַהֲרֹן הַכֹּהֵן מִן־הַלְוִיִּם מִמַּטֵּה יְהוּדָה וּמִמַּטֵּה הַשִּׁמְעֹנִי וּמִמַּטֵּה בִנְיָמִן בַּגּוֹרָל עָרִים שְׁלֹשׁ עֶשְׂרֵה:

ה וְלִבְנֵי קְהָת הַנּוֹתָרִים מִמִּשְׁפְּחֹת מַטֵּה־אֶפְרַיִם וּמִמַּטֵּה־דָן וּמֵחֲצִי מַטֵּה מְנַשֶּׁה בַּגּוֹרָל עָרִים עָשֶׂר:

Yehoshua/Joshua
Chapter 21

6 To the Gershonites [there fell] by lot 13 towns from the clans of the tribe of *Yissachar*, the tribe of *Asher*, the tribe of *Naftali*, and the half-tribe of *Menashe* in Bashan.

7 [And] to the Merarites, by their clans – 12 towns from the tribe of *Reuven*, the tribe of *Gad*, and the tribe of *Zevulun*.

8 The Israelites assigned those towns with their pastures by lot to the *Leviim* – as *Hashem* had commanded through *Moshe*.

9 From the tribe of the Judites and the tribe of the Simeonites were assigned the following towns, which will be listed by name;

10 they went to the descendants of *Aharon* among the Kehatite clans of the *Leviim*, for the first lot had fallen to them.

11 To them were assigned in the hill country of *Yehuda Kiryat Arba* – that is, *Chevron* – together with the pastures around it. [Arba was] the father of the Anokites.

12 They gave the fields and the villages of the town to *Kalev* son of Jephunneh as his holding.

13 But to the descendants of *Aharon* the *Kohen* they assigned *Chevron* – the city of refuge for manslayers – together with its pastures, Libnah with its pastures,

14 Jattir with its pastures, Eshtemoa with its pastures,

15 Holon with its pastures, Debir with its pastures,

16 Ain with its pastures, Juttah with its pastures, and *Beit Shemesh* with its pastures – 9 towns from those two tribes.

17 And from the tribe of *Binyamin*: *Givon* with its pastures, Geba with its pastures,

18 *Anatot* with its pastures, and Almon with its pastures – 4 towns.

19 All the towns of the descendants of the *Kohen Aharon*, 13 towns with their pastures.

יהושע
פרק כא

ו וְלִבְנֵי גֵרְשׁוֹן מִמִּשְׁפְּחוֹת מַטֵּה־יִשָּׂשכָר וּמִמַּטֵּה־אָשֵׁר וּמִמַּטֵּה נַפְתָּלִי וּמֵחֲצִי מַטֵּה מְנַשֶּׁה בַבָּשָׁן בַּגּוֹרָל עָרִים שְׁלֹשׁ עֶשְׂרֵה:

ז לִבְנֵי מְרָרִי לְמִשְׁפְּחֹתָם מִמַּטֵּה רְאוּבֵן וּמִמַּטֵּה־גָד וּמִמַּטֵּה זְבוּלֻן עָרִים שְׁתֵּים עֶשְׂרֵה:

ח וַיִּתְּנוּ בְנֵי־יִשְׂרָאֵל לַלְוִיִּם אֶת־הֶעָרִים הָאֵלֶּה וְאֶת־מִגְרְשֵׁיהֶן כַּאֲשֶׁר צִוָּה יְהֹוָה בְּיַד־מֹשֶׁה בַּגּוֹרָל:

ט וַיִּתְּנוּ מִמַּטֵּה בְּנֵי יְהוּדָה וּמִמַּטֵּה בְּנֵי שִׁמְעוֹן אֵת הֶעָרִים הָאֵלֶּה אֲשֶׁר־יִקְרָא אֶתְהֶן בְּשֵׁם:

י וַיְהִי לִבְנֵי אַהֲרֹן מִמִּשְׁפְּחוֹת הַקְּהָתִי מִבְּנֵי לֵוִי כִּי לָהֶם הָיָה הַגּוֹרָל רִיאשֹׁנָה:

יא וַיִּתְּנוּ לָהֶם אֶת־קִרְיַת אַרְבַּע אֲבִי הָעֲנוֹק הִיא חֶבְרוֹן בְּהַר יְהוּדָה וְאֶת־מִגְרָשֶׁהָ סְבִיבֹתֶיהָ:

יב וְאֶת־שְׂדֵה הָעִיר וְאֶת־חֲצֵרֶיהָ נָתְנוּ לְכָלֵב בֶּן־יְפֻנֶּה בַּאֲחֻזָּתוֹ:

יג וְלִבְנֵי ׀ אַהֲרֹן הַכֹּהֵן נָתְנוּ אֶת־עִיר מִקְלַט הָרֹצֵחַ אֶת־חֶבְרוֹן וְאֶת־מִגְרָשֶׁהָ וְאֶת־לִבְנָה וְאֶת־מִגְרָשֶׁהָ:

יד וְאֶת־יַתִּר וְאֶת־מִגְרָשֶׁהָ וְאֶת־אֶשְׁתְּמֹעַ וְאֶת־מִגְרָשֶׁהָ:

טו וְאֶת־חֹלֹן וְאֶת־מִגְרָשֶׁהָ וְאֶת־דְּבִר וְאֶת־מִגְרָשֶׁהָ:

טז וְאֶת־עַיִן וְאֶת־מִגְרָשֶׁהָ וְאֶת־יֻטָּה וְאֶת־מִגְרָשֶׁהָ אֶת־בֵּית שֶׁמֶשׁ וְאֶת־מִגְרָשֶׁהָ עָרִים תֵּשַׁע מֵאֵת שְׁנֵי הַשְּׁבָטִים הָאֵלֶּה:

יז וּמִמַּטֵּה בִנְיָמִן אֶת־גִּבְעוֹן וְאֶת־מִגְרָשֶׁהָ אֶת־גֶּבַע וְאֶת־מִגְרָשֶׁהָ:

יח אֶת־עֲנָתוֹת וְאֶת־מִגְרָשֶׁהָ וְאֶת־עַלְמוֹן וְאֶת־מִגְרָשֶׁהָ עָרִים אַרְבַּע:

יט כָּל־עָרֵי בְנֵי־אַהֲרֹן הַכֹּהֲנִים שְׁלֹשׁ־עֶשְׂרֵה עָרִים וּמִגְרְשֵׁיהֶן:

Yehoshua/Joshua
Chapter 21

20	As for the other clans of the Kehatites, the remaining *Leviim* descended from *Kehat*, the towns in their lot were: From the tribe of *Efraim*
21	they were given, in the hill country of *Efraim*, *Shechem* – the city of refuge for manslayers – with its pastures, Gezer with its pastures,
22	Kibzaim with its pastures, and Beth-horon with its pastures – 4 towns.
23	From the tribe of *Dan*, Elteke with its pastures, Gibbethon with its pastures,
24	Aijalon with its pastures, and Gath-rimmon with its pastures – 4 towns.
25	And from the half-tribe of *Menashe*, Taanach with its pastures, and Gath-rimmon with its pastures – 2 towns.
26	All the towns for the remaining clans of the Kehatites came to 10, with their pastures.
27	To the Gershonites of the levitical clans: From the half-tribe of *Menashe*, Golan in Bashan – the city of refuge for manslayers – with its pastures, and Beeshterah with its pastures – 2 towns.
28	From the tribe of *Yissachar*: Kishion with its pastures, Dobrath with its pastures,
29	*Yarmut* with its pastures, and Engannim with its pastures – 4 towns.
30	From the tribe of *Asher*: Mishal with its pastures, *Avdon* with its pastures,
31	Helkath with its pastures, and Rehob with its pastures – 4 towns.
32	From the tribe of *Naftali*, Kedesh in Galilee – the city of refuge for manslayers – with its pastures, Hammoth-dor with its pastures, and Kartan with its pastures – 3 towns.
33	All the towns of the Gershonites, by their clans, came to 13 towns, with their pastures.
34	To the remaining *Leviim*, the clans of the Merarites: From the tribe of *Zevulun*, Jokneam with its pastures, Kartah with its pastures,

יהושע
פרק כא

כ וּלְמִשְׁפְּחוֹת בְּנֵי־קְהָת הַלְוִיִּם הַנּוֹתָרִים מִבְּנֵי קְהָת וַיְהִי עָרֵי גוֹרָלָם מִמַּטֵּה אֶפְרָיִם:

כא וַיִּתְּנוּ לָהֶם אֶת־עִיר מִקְלַט הָרֹצֵחַ אֶת־שְׁכֶם וְאֶת־מִגְרָשֶׁהָ בְּהַר אֶפְרָיִם וְאֶת־גֶּזֶר וְאֶת־מִגְרָשֶׁהָ:

כב וְאֶת־קִבְצַיִם וְאֶת־מִגְרָשֶׁהָ וְאֶת־בֵּית חוֹרֹן וְאֶת־מִגְרָשֶׁהָ עָרִים אַרְבַּע:

כג וּמִמַּטֵּה־דָן אֶת־אֶלְתְּקֵא וְאֶת־מִגְרָשֶׁהָ אֶת־גִּבְּתוֹן וְאֶת־מִגְרָשֶׁהָ:

כד אֶת־אַיָּלוֹן וְאֶת־מִגְרָשֶׁהָ אֶת־גַּת־רִמּוֹן וְאֶת־מִגְרָשֶׁהָ עָרִים אַרְבַּע:

כה וּמִמַּחֲצִית מַטֵּה מְנַשֶּׁה אֶת־תַּעְנַךְ וְאֶת־מִגְרָשֶׁהָ וְאֶת־גַּת־רִמּוֹן וְאֶת־מִגְרָשֶׁהָ עָרִים שְׁתָּיִם:

כו כָּל־עָרִים עֶשֶׂר וּמִגְרְשֵׁיהֶן לְמִשְׁפְּחוֹת בְּנֵי־קְהָת הַנּוֹתָרִים:

כז וְלִבְנֵי גֵרְשׁוֹן מִמִּשְׁפְּחֹת הַלְוִיִּם מֵחֲצִי מַטֵּה מְנַשֶּׁה אֶת־עִיר מִקְלַט הָרֹצֵחַ אֶת־גּלון [גּוֹלָן] בַּבָּשָׁן וְאֶת־מִגְרָשֶׁהָ וְאֶת־בְּעֶשְׁתְּרָה וְאֶת־מִגְרָשֶׁהָ עָרִים שְׁתָּיִם:

כח וּמִמַּטֵּה יִשָּׂשכָר אֶת־קִשְׁיוֹן וְאֶת־מִגְרָשֶׁהָ אֶת־דָּבְרַת וְאֶת־מִגְרָשֶׁהָ:

כט אֶת־יַרְמוּת וְאֶת־מִגְרָשֶׁהָ אֶת־עֵין גַּנִּים וְאֶת־מִגְרָשֶׁהָ עָרִים אַרְבַּע:

ל וּמִמַּטֵּה אָשֵׁר אֶת־מִשְׁאָל וְאֶת־מִגְרָשֶׁהָ אֶת־עַבְדּוֹן וְאֶת־מִגְרָשֶׁהָ:

לא אֶת־חֶלְקָת וְאֶת־מִגְרָשֶׁהָ וְאֶת־רְחֹב וְאֶת־מִגְרָשֶׁהָ עָרִים אַרְבַּע:

לב וּמִמַּטֵּה נַפְתָּלִי אֶת־עִיר מִקְלַט הָרֹצֵחַ אֶת־קֶדֶשׁ בַּגָּלִיל וְאֶת־מִגְרָשֶׁהָ וְאֶת־חַמֹּת דֹּאר וְאֶת־מִגְרָשֶׁהָ וְאֶת־קַרְתָּן וְאֶת־מִגְרָשֶׁהָ עָרִים שָׁלֹשׁ:

לג כָּל־עָרֵי הַגֵּרְשֻׁנִּי לְמִשְׁפְּחֹתָם שְׁלֹשׁ־עֶשְׂרֵה עִיר וּמִגְרְשֵׁיהֶן:

לד וּלְמִשְׁפְּחוֹת בְּנֵי־מְרָרִי הַלְוִיִּם הַנּוֹתָרִים מֵאֵת מַטֵּה זְבוּלֻן אֶת־יָקְנְעָם וְאֶת־מִגְרָשֶׁהָ אֶת־קַרְתָּה וְאֶת־מִגְרָשֶׁהָ:

Yehoshua/Joshua
Chapter 22

35 Dimnah with its pastures, and Nahalal with its pastures – 4 towns.

36 From the tribe of *Gad*, Ramoth in *Gilad* – the city of refuge for manslayers – with its pastures, Mahanaim with its pastures,

37 Heshbon with its pastures, and Jazer with its pastures – 4 towns in all.

38 All the towns which went by lot to the Merarites, by their clans – the rest of the levitical clans – came to 12 towns.

39 All the towns of the *Leviim* within the holdings of the Israelites came to 48 towns, with their pastures.

40 Thus those towns were assigned, every town with its surrounding pasture; and so it was with all those towns.

41 *Hashem* gave to *Yisrael* the whole country which He had sworn to their fathers that He would assign to them; they took possession of it and settled in it.

va-yi-TAYN a-do-NAI l'-yis-ra-AYL et kol ha-A-retz a-SHER nish-BA la-TAYT la-a-vo-TAM va-yi-ra-SHU-ha va-yay-sh'-VU VAH

42 *Hashem* gave them rest on all sides, just as He had promised to their fathers on oath. Not one man of all their enemies withstood them; *Hashem* delivered all their enemies into their hands.

43 Not one of the good things which *Hashem* had promised to the House of *Yisrael* was lacking. Everything was fulfilled.

22

1 Then *Yehoshua* summoned the Reubenites, the Gadites, and the half-tribe of *Menashe*,

2 and said to them, "You have observed all that *Moshe* the servant of *Hashem* commanded you, and have obeyed me in everything that I commanded you.

21:41 They took possession of it and settled in it *Hashem* fulfills His promise to the People of Israel, who live in and possess the Land of Israel. The *Ramban* notes that there are three aspects to the Jewish People's obligation regarding *Eretz Yisrael*: They are commanded to live in *Eretz Yisrael*, to build up the land through strengthening its Jewish community, and to maintain a sovereign government ruling over *Eretz Yisrael*. Thus, though it's important for individuals to live in the Land of Israel, it's also critically important that the Nation of Israel has "taken possession of it and settled in it." Former Prime Minister Yitzhak Shamir expressed how crucial it is to settle the land when he said that "the settlement of the Land of Israel is the essence of Zionism."

Ramban (1194–1270)

Yehoshua/Joshua
Chapter 22

3 You have not forsaken your kinsmen through the long years down to this day, but have faithfully observed the Instruction of *Hashem* your God.

4 Now *Hashem* your God has given your kinsmen rest, as He promised them. Therefore turn and go to your homes, to the land of your holdings beyond the *Yarden* that *Moshe* the servant of *Hashem* assigned to you.

5 But be very careful to fulfill the Instruction and the Teaching that *Moshe* the servant of *Hashem* enjoined upon you, to love *Hashem* your God and to walk in all His ways, and to keep His commandments and hold fast to Him, and to serve Him with all your heart and soul."

6 Then *Yehoshua* blessed them and dismissed them, and they went to their homes.

7 To the one half-tribe of *Menashe Moshe* had assigned territory in Bashan, and to the other *Yehoshua* assigned [territory] on the west side of the *Yarden*, with their kinsmen. Furthermore, when *Yehoshua* sent them off to their homes, he blessed them

8 and said to them, "Return to your homes with great wealth – with very much livestock, with silver and gold, with copper and iron, and with a great quantity of clothing. Share the spoil of your enemies with your kinsmen."

9 So the Reubenites, the Gadites, and the half-tribe of *Menashe* left the Israelites at *Shilo*, in the land of Canaan, and made their way back to the land of *Gilad*, the land of their own holding, which they had acquired by the command of *Hashem* through *Moshe*.

10 When they came to the region of the *Yarden* in the land of Canaan, the Reubenites and the Gadites and the half-tribe of *Menashe* built a *Mizbayach* there by the *Yarden*, a great conspicuous *Mizbayach*.

11 A report reached the Israelites: "The Reubenites, the Gadites, and the half-tribe of *Menashe* have built a *Mizbayach* opposite the land of Canaan, in the region of the *Yarden*, across from the Israelites."

יהושע
פרק כב

ג לֹא־עֲזַבְתֶּם אֶת־אֲחֵיכֶם זֶה יָמִים רַבִּים עַד הַיּוֹם הַזֶּה וּשְׁמַרְתֶּם אֶת־מִשְׁמֶרֶת מִצְוַת יְהֹוָה אֱלֹהֵיכֶם:

ד וְעַתָּה הֵנִיחַ יְהֹוָה אֱלֹהֵיכֶם לַאֲחֵיכֶם כַּאֲשֶׁר דִּבֶּר לָהֶם וְעַתָּה פְּנוּ וּלְכוּ לָכֶם לְאָהֳלֵיכֶם אֶל־אֶרֶץ אֲחֻזַּתְכֶם אֲשֶׁר נָתַן לָכֶם מֹשֶׁה עֶבֶד יְהֹוָה בְּעֵבֶר הַיַּרְדֵּן:

ה רַק שִׁמְרוּ מְאֹד לַעֲשׂוֹת אֶת־הַמִּצְוָה וְאֶת־הַתּוֹרָה אֲשֶׁר צִוָּה אֶתְכֶם מֹשֶׁה עֶבֶד־יְהֹוָה לְאַהֲבָה אֶת־יְהֹוָה אֱלֹהֵיכֶם וְלָלֶכֶת בְּכָל־דְּרָכָיו וְלִשְׁמֹר מִצְוֹתָיו וּלְדָבְקָה־בוֹ וּלְעָבְדוֹ בְּכָל־לְבַבְכֶם וּבְכָל־נַפְשְׁכֶם:

ו וַיְבָרְכֵם יְהוֹשֻׁעַ וַיְשַׁלְּחֵם וַיֵּלְכוּ אֶל־אָהֳלֵיהֶם:

ז וְלַחֲצִי שֵׁבֶט הַמְנַשֶּׁה נָתַן מֹשֶׁה בַּבָּשָׁן וּלְחֶצְיוֹ נָתַן יְהוֹשֻׁעַ עִם־אֲחֵיהֶם מֵעֵבֶר [בְּעֵבֶר] הַיַּרְדֵּן יָמָּה וְגַם כִּי שִׁלְּחָם יְהוֹשֻׁעַ אֶל־אָהֳלֵיהֶם וַיְבָרְכֵם:

ח וַיֹּאמֶר אֲלֵיהֶם לֵאמֹר בִּנְכָסִים רַבִּים שׁוּבוּ אֶל־אָהֳלֵיכֶם וּבְמִקְנֶה רַב־מְאֹד בְּכֶסֶף וּבְזָהָב וּבִנְחֹשֶׁת וּבְבַרְזֶל וּבִשְׂלָמוֹת הַרְבֵּה מְאֹד חִלְקוּ שְׁלַל־אֹיְבֵיכֶם עִם־אֲחֵיכֶם:

ט וַיָּשֻׁבוּ וַיֵּלְכוּ בְּנֵי־רְאוּבֵן וּבְנֵי־גָד וַחֲצִי שֵׁבֶט הַמְנַשֶּׁה מֵאֵת בְּנֵי יִשְׂרָאֵל מִשִּׁלֹה אֲשֶׁר בְּאֶרֶץ־כְּנָעַן לָלֶכֶת אֶל־אֶרֶץ הַגִּלְעָד אֶל־אֶרֶץ אֲחֻזָּתָם אֲשֶׁר נֹאחֲזוּ־בָהּ עַל־פִּי יְהֹוָה בְּיַד־מֹשֶׁה:

י וַיָּבֹאוּ אֶל־גְּלִילוֹת הַיַּרְדֵּן אֲשֶׁר בְּאֶרֶץ כְּנָעַן וַיִּבְנוּ בְנֵי־רְאוּבֵן וּבְנֵי־גָד וַחֲצִי שֵׁבֶט הַמְנַשֶּׁה שָׁם מִזְבֵּחַ עַל־הַיַּרְדֵּן מִזְבֵּחַ גָּדוֹל לְמַרְאֶה:

יא וַיִּשְׁמְעוּ בְנֵי־יִשְׂרָאֵל לֵאמֹר הִנֵּה בָנוּ בְנֵי־רְאוּבֵן וּבְנֵי־גָד וַחֲצִי שֵׁבֶט הַמְנַשֶּׁה אֶת־הַמִּזְבֵּחַ אֶל־מוּל אֶרֶץ כְּנַעַן אֶל־גְּלִילוֹת הַיַּרְדֵּן אֶל־עֵבֶר בְּנֵי יִשְׂרָאֵל:

Yehoshua/Joshua
Chapter 22

יהושע
פרק כב

12 When the Israelites heard this, the whole community of the Israelites assembled at *Shilo* to make war on them.

וַיִּשְׁמְעוּ בְּנֵי יִשְׂרָאֵל וַיִּקָּהֲלוּ כָּל־עֲדַת בְּנֵי־יִשְׂרָאֵל שִׁלֹה לַעֲלוֹת עֲלֵיהֶם לַצָּבָא׃

va-yish-m'-U b'-NAY yis-ra-AYL va-yi-ka-ha-LU kol a-DAT b'-nay yis-ra-AYL shi-LOH la-a-LOT a-lay-HEM la-tza-VA

13 But [first] the Israelites sent the *Kohen Pinchas* son of *Elazar* to the Reubenites, the Gadites, and the half-tribe of *Menashe* in the land of *Gilad*,

וַיִּשְׁלְחוּ בְנֵי־יִשְׂרָאֵל אֶל־בְּנֵי־רְאוּבֵן וְאֶל־בְּנֵי־גָד וְאֶל־חֲצִי שֵׁבֶט־מְנַשֶּׁה אֶל־אֶרֶץ הַגִּלְעָד אֶת־פִּינְחָס בֶּן־אֶלְעָזָר הַכֹּהֵן׃

14 accompanied by ten chieftains, one chieftain from each ancestral house of each of the tribes of *Yisrael*; they were every one of them heads of ancestral houses of the contingents of *Yisrael*.

וַעֲשָׂרָה נְשִׂאִים עִמּוֹ נָשִׂיא אֶחָד נָשִׂיא אֶחָד לְבֵית אָב לְכֹל מַטּוֹת יִשְׂרָאֵל וְאִישׁ רֹאשׁ בֵּית־אֲבוֹתָם הֵמָּה לְאַלְפֵי יִשְׂרָאֵל׃

15 When they came to the Reubenites, the Gadites, and the half-tribe of *Menashe* in the land of *Gilad*, they spoke to them as follows:

וַיָּבֹאוּ אֶל־בְּנֵי־רְאוּבֵן וְאֶל־בְּנֵי־גָד וְאֶל־חֲצִי שֵׁבֶט־מְנַשֶּׁה אֶל־אֶרֶץ הַגִּלְעָד וַיְדַבְּרוּ אִתָּם לֵאמֹר׃

16 "Thus said the whole community of *Hashem*: What is this treachery that you have committed this day against the God of *Yisrael*, turning away from *Hashem*, building yourselves a *Mizbayach* and rebelling this day against *Hashem*!

כֹּה אָמְרוּ כֹּל עֲדַת יְהֹוָה מָה־הַמַּעַל הַזֶּה אֲשֶׁר מְעַלְתֶּם בֵּאלֹהֵי יִשְׂרָאֵל לָשׁוּב הַיּוֹם מֵאַחֲרֵי יְהֹוָה בִּבְנוֹתְכֶם לָכֶם מִזְבֵּחַ לִמְרָדְכֶם הַיּוֹם בַּיהֹוָה׃

17 Is the sin of Peor, which brought a plague upon the community of *Hashem*, such a small thing to us? We have not cleansed ourselves from it to this very day;

הַמְעַט־לָנוּ אֶת־עֲוֺן פְּעוֹר אֲשֶׁר לֹא־הִטַּהַרְנוּ מִמֶּנּוּ עַד הַיּוֹם הַזֶּה וַיְהִי הַנֶּגֶף בַּעֲדַת יְהֹוָה׃

18 and now you would turn away from *Hashem*! If you rebel against *Hashem* today, tomorrow He will be angry with the whole community of *Yisrael*.

וְאַתֶּם תָּשֻׁבוּ הַיּוֹם מֵאַחֲרֵי יְהֹוָה וְהָיָה אַתֶּם תִּמְרְדוּ הַיּוֹם בַּיהֹוָה וּמָחָר אֶל־כָּל־עֲדַת יִשְׂרָאֵל יִקְצֹף׃

19 If it is because the land of your holding is unclean, cross over into the land of *Hashem*'s own holding, where the *Mishkan* of *Hashem* abides, and acquire holdings among us. But do not rebel against *Hashem*, and do not rebel against us by building for yourselves altar other than the *Mizbayach* of *Hashem* our God.

וְאַךְ אִם־טְמֵאָה אֶרֶץ אֲחֻזַּתְכֶם עִבְרוּ לָכֶם אֶל־אֶרֶץ אֲחֻזַּת יְהֹוָה אֲשֶׁר שָׁכַן־שָׁם מִשְׁכַּן יְהֹוָה וְהֵאָחֲזוּ בְּתוֹכֵנוּ וּבַיהֹוָה אַל־תִּמְרֹדוּ וְאֹתָנוּ אַל־תִּמְרֹדוּ בִּבְנֹתְכֶם לָכֶם מִזְבֵּחַ מִבַּלְעֲדֵי מִזְבַּח יְהֹוָה אֱלֹהֵינוּ׃

22:12 The whole community of the Israelites assembled at Shilo to make war on them When the 2½ tribes residing on the east bank of the *Yarden* set up an altar to *Hashem*, the other tribes react harshly and quickly. The 9½ other tribes threaten to make war if they do not put an end to this practice. Because the *Mishkan* stands, no other altars could be permitted. Similarly, once the *Beit Hamikdash* is built in *Yerushalayim*, no sacrifices are ever allowed anywhere else. Though the entire Land of Israel is holy, *Hashem* desires that His people join together to serve Him in one united center of worship, in the heart of the capital city *Yerushalayim*.

Tel Shilo, site of the Mishkan

Yehoshua/Joshua

Chapter 22

20 When *Achan* son of *Zerach* violated the proscription, anger struck the whole community of *Yisrael*; he was not the only one who perished for that sin."

21 The Reubenites, the Gadites, and the half-tribe of *Menashe* replied to the heads of the contingents of *Yisrael*: They said,

22 "*Hashem*, the Lord *Hashem*! *Hashem*, the Lord *Hashem*! He knows, and *Yisrael* too shall know! If we acted in rebellion or in treachery against *Hashem*, do not vindicate us this day!

23 If we built an altar to turn away from *Hashem*, if it was to offer burnt offerings or meal offerings upon it, or to present sacrifices of well-being upon it, may *Hashem* Himself demand [a reckoning]

24 We did this thing only out of our concern that, in time to come, your children might say to our children, 'What have you to do with *Hashem*, the God of *Yisrael*?

25 *Hashem* has made the *Yarden* a boundary between you and us, O Reubenites and Gadites; you have no share in *Hashem*!' Thus your children might prevent our children from worshiping *Hashem*.

26 So we decided to provide [a witness] for ourselves by building an altar – not for burnt offerings or [other] sacrifices,

27 but as a witness between you and us, and between the generations to come – that we may perform the service of *Hashem* before Him with our burnt offerings, our sacrifices, and our offerings of well-being; and that your children should not say to our children in time to come, 'You have no share in *Hashem*.'

28 We reasoned: should they speak thus to us and to our children in time to come, we would reply, 'See the replica of *Hashem*'s *Mizbayach*, which our fathers made – not for burnt offerings or sacrifices, but as a witness between you and us.'

29 Far be it from us to rebel against *Hashem*, or to turn away this day from *Hashem* and build a *Mizbayach* for burnt offerings, meal offerings, and sacrifices other than the *Mizbayach* of *Hashem* our God which stands before His *Mishkan*."

יהושע

פרק כב

כ הֲלוֹא ׀ עָכָן בֶּן־זֶרַח מָעַל מַעַל בַּחֵרֶם וְעַל־כָּל־עֲדַת יִשְׂרָאֵל הָיָה קָצֶף וְהוּא אִישׁ אֶחָד לֹא גָוַע בַּעֲוֹנְוֹ:

כא וַיַּעֲנוּ בְּנֵי־רְאוּבֵן וּבְנֵי־גָד וַחֲצִי שֵׁבֶט הַמְנַשֶּׁה וַיְדַבְּרוּ אֶת־רָאשֵׁי אַלְפֵי יִשְׂרָאֵל:

כב אֵל ׀ אֱלֹהִים ׀ יְהוָה אֵל ׀ אֱלֹהִים ׀ יְהוָה הוּא יֹדֵעַ וְיִשְׂרָאֵל הוּא יֵדָע אִם־בְּמֶרֶד וְאִם־בְּמַעַל בַּיהוָה אַל־תּוֹשִׁיעֵנוּ הַיּוֹם הַזֶּה:

כג לִבְנוֹת לָנוּ מִזְבֵּחַ לָשׁוּב מֵאַחֲרֵי יְהוָה וְאִם־לְהַעֲלוֹת עָלָיו עוֹלָה וּמִנְחָה וְאִם־לַעֲשׂוֹת עָלָיו זִבְחֵי שְׁלָמִים יְהוָה הוּא יְבַקֵּשׁ:

כד וְאִם־לֹא מִדְּאָגָה מִדָּבָר עָשִׂינוּ אֶת־זֹאת לֵאמֹר מָחָר יֹאמְרוּ בְנֵיכֶם לְבָנֵינוּ לֵאמֹר מַה־לָּכֶם וְלַיהוָה אֱלֹהֵי יִשְׂרָאֵל:

כה וּגְבוּל נָתַן־יְהוָה בֵּינֵנוּ וּבֵינֵיכֶם בְּנֵי־רְאוּבֵן וּבְנֵי־גָד אֶת־הַיַּרְדֵּן אֵין־לָכֶם חֵלֶק בַּיהוָה וְהִשְׁבִּיתוּ בְנֵיכֶם אֶת־בָּנֵינוּ לְבִלְתִּי יְרֹא אֶת־יְהוָה:

כו וַנֹּאמֶר נַעֲשֶׂה־נָּא לָנוּ לִבְנוֹת אֶת־הַמִּזְבֵּחַ לֹא לְעוֹלָה וְלֹא לְזָבַח:

כז כִּי עֵד הוּא בֵּינֵינוּ וּבֵינֵיכֶם וּבֵין דֹּרוֹתֵינוּ אַחֲרֵינוּ לַעֲבֹד אֶת־עֲבֹדַת יְהוָה לְפָנָיו בְּעֹלוֹתֵינוּ וּבִזְבָחֵינוּ וּבִשְׁלָמֵינוּ וְלֹא־יֹאמְרוּ בְנֵיכֶם מָחָר לְבָנֵינוּ אֵין־לָכֶם חֵלֶק בַּיהוָה:

כח וַנֹּאמֶר וְהָיָה כִּי־יֹאמְרוּ אֵלֵינוּ וְאֶל־דֹּרֹתֵינוּ מָחָר וְאָמַרְנוּ רְאוּ אֶת־תַּבְנִית מִזְבַּח יְהוָה אֲשֶׁר־עָשׂוּ אֲבוֹתֵינוּ לֹא לְעוֹלָה וְלֹא לְזֶבַח כִּי־עֵד הוּא בֵּינֵינוּ וּבֵינֵיכֶם:

כט חָלִילָה לָּנוּ מִמֶּנּוּ לִמְרֹד בַּיהוָה וְלָשׁוּב הַיּוֹם מֵאַחֲרֵי יְהוָה לִבְנוֹת מִזְבֵּחַ לְעֹלָה לְמִנְחָה וּלְזָבַח מִלְּבַד מִזְבַּח יְהוָה אֱלֹהֵינוּ אֲשֶׁר לִפְנֵי מִשְׁכָּנוֹ:

Yehoshua/Joshua
Chapter 23

30 When the *Kohen Pinchas* and the chieftains of the community – the heads of the contingents of *Yisrael* – who were with him heard the explanation given by the Reubenites, the Gadites, and the Manassites, they approved.

ל וַיִּשְׁמַע פִּינְחָס הַכֹּהֵן וּנְשִׂיאֵי הָעֵדָה וְרָאשֵׁי אַלְפֵי יִשְׂרָאֵל אֲשֶׁר אִתּוֹ אֶת־הַדְּבָרִים אֲשֶׁר דִּבְּרוּ בְּנֵי־רְאוּבֵן וּבְנֵי־גָד וּבְנֵי מְנַשֶּׁה וַיִּיטַב בְּעֵינֵיהֶם׃

31 The *Kohen Pinchas* son of *Elazar* said to the Reubenites, the Gadites, and the Manassites, "Now we know that *Hashem* is in our midst, since you have not committed such treachery against *Hashem*. You have indeed saved the Israelites from punishment by *Hashem*."

לא וַיֹּאמֶר פִּינְחָס בֶּן־אֶלְעָזָר הַכֹּהֵן אֶל־בְּנֵי־רְאוּבֵן וְאֶל־בְּנֵי־גָד וְאֶל־בְּנֵי מְנַשֶּׁה הַיּוֹם יָדַעְנוּ כִּי־בְתוֹכֵנוּ יְהֹוָה אֲשֶׁר לֹא־מְעַלְתֶּם בַּיהֹוָה הַמַּעַל הַזֶּה אָז הִצַּלְתֶּם אֶת־בְּנֵי יִשְׂרָאֵל מִיַּד יְהֹוָה׃

32 Then the *Kohen Pinchas* son of *Elazar* and the chieftains returned from the Reubenites and the Gadites in the land of *Gilad* to the Israelites in the land of Canaan, and gave them their report.

לב וַיָּשָׁב פִּינְחָס בֶּן־אֶלְעָזָר הַכֹּהֵן וְהַנְּשִׂיאִים מֵאֵת בְּנֵי־רְאוּבֵן וּמֵאֵת בְּנֵי־גָד מֵאֶרֶץ הַגִּלְעָד אֶל־אֶרֶץ כְּנַעַן אֶל־בְּנֵי יִשְׂרָאֵל וַיָּשִׁבוּ אוֹתָם דָּבָר׃

33 The Israelites were pleased, and the Israelites praised *Hashem*; and they spoke no more of going to war against them, to ravage the land in which the Reubenites and Gadites dwelt.

לג וַיִּיטַב הַדָּבָר בְּעֵינֵי בְּנֵי יִשְׂרָאֵל וַיְבָרְכוּ אֱלֹהִים בְּנֵי יִשְׂרָאֵל וְלֹא אָמְרוּ לַעֲלוֹת עֲלֵיהֶם לַצָּבָא לְשַׁחֵת אֶת־הָאָרֶץ אֲשֶׁר בְּנֵי־רְאוּבֵן וּבְנֵי־גָד יֹשְׁבִים בָּהּ׃

34 The Reubenites and the Gadites named the altar ["Witness"], meaning, "It is a witness between us and them that *Hashem* is [our] *Hashem*."

לד וַיִּקְרְאוּ בְּנֵי־רְאוּבֵן וּבְנֵי־גָד לַמִּזְבֵּחַ כִּי עֵד הוּא בֵּינֹתֵינוּ כִּי יְהֹוָה הָאֱלֹהִים׃

23

1 Much later, after *Hashem* had given *Yisrael* rest from all the enemies around them, and when *Yehoshua* was old and well advanced in years,

א וַיְהִי מִיָּמִים רַבִּים אַחֲרֵי אֲשֶׁר־הֵנִיחַ יְהֹוָה לְיִשְׂרָאֵל מִכָּל־אֹיְבֵיהֶם מִסָּבִיב וִיהוֹשֻׁעַ זָקֵן בָּא בַּיָּמִים׃

2 *Yehoshua* summoned all *Yisrael*, their elders and commanders, their magistrates and officials, and said to them: "I have grown old and am advanced in years.

ב וַיִּקְרָא יְהוֹשֻׁעַ לְכָל־יִשְׂרָאֵל לִזְקֵנָיו וּלְרָאשָׁיו וּלְשֹׁפְטָיו וּלְשֹׁטְרָיו וַיֹּאמֶר אֲלֵהֶם אֲנִי זָקַנְתִּי בָּאתִי בַּיָּמִים׃

3 You have seen all that *Hashem* your God has done to all those nations on your account, for it was *Hashem* your God who fought for you.

ג וְאַתֶּם רְאִיתֶם אֵת כָּל־אֲשֶׁר עָשָׂה יְהֹוָה אֱלֹהֵיכֶם לְכָל־הַגּוֹיִם הָאֵלֶּה מִפְּנֵיכֶם כִּי יְהֹוָה אֱלֹהֵיכֶם הוּא הַנִּלְחָם לָכֶם׃

4 See, I have allotted to you, by your tribes, [the territory of] these nations that still remain, and that of all the nations that I have destroyed, from the *Yarden* to the Mediterranean Sea in the west.

ד רְאוּ הִפַּלְתִּי לָכֶם אֶת־הַגּוֹיִם הַנִּשְׁאָרִים הָאֵלֶּה בְּנַחֲלָה לְשִׁבְטֵיכֶם מִן־הַיַּרְדֵּן וְכָל־הַגּוֹיִם אֲשֶׁר הִכְרַתִּי וְהַיָּם הַגָּדוֹל מְבוֹא הַשָּׁמֶשׁ׃

5 *Hashem* your God Himself will thrust them out on your account and drive them out to make way for you, and you shall possess their land as *Hashem* your God promised you.

ה וַיהֹוָה אֱלֹהֵיכֶם הוּא יֶהְדֳּפֵם מִפְּנֵיכֶם וְהוֹרִישׁ אֹתָם מִלִּפְנֵיכֶם וִירִשְׁתֶּם אֶת־אַרְצָם כַּאֲשֶׁר דִּבֶּר יְהֹוָה אֱלֹהֵיכֶם לָכֶם׃

Yehoshua/Joshua
Chapter 23

יהושע
פרק כג

6 "But be most resolute to observe faithfully all that is written in the Book of the Teaching of *Moshe*, without ever deviating from it to the right or to the left,

וַחֲזַקְתֶּם מְאֹד לִשְׁמֹר וְלַעֲשׂוֹת אֵת כָּל־הַכָּתוּב בְּסֵפֶר תּוֹרַת מֹשֶׁה לְבִלְתִּי סוּר־מִמֶּנּוּ יָמִין וּשְׂמֹאול: א

va-kha-zak-TEM m'-OD lish-MOR v'-la-a-SOT AYT kol ha-ka-TUV b'-SAY-fer to-RAT mo-SHEH l'-vil-TEE sur mi-ME-nu ya-MEEN us-MOL

7 and without intermingling with these nations that are left among you. Do not utter the names of their gods or swear by them; do not serve them or bow down to them.

לְבִלְתִּי־בוֹא בַּגּוֹיִם הָאֵלֶּה הַנִּשְׁאָרִים הָאֵלֶּה אִתְּכֶם וּבְשֵׁם אֱלֹהֵיהֶם לֹא־תַזְכִּירוּ וְלֹא תַשְׁבִּיעוּ וְלֹא תַעַבְדוּם וְלֹא תִשְׁתַּחֲווּ לָהֶם: ז

8 But hold fast to *Hashem* your God as you have done to this day.

כִּי אִם־בַּיהוָה אֱלֹהֵיכֶם תִּדְבָּקוּ כַּאֲשֶׁר עֲשִׂיתֶם עַד הַיּוֹם הַזֶּה: ח

9 "*Hashem* has driven out great, powerful nations on your account, and not a man has withstood you to this day.

וַיּוֹרֶשׁ יְהוָה מִפְּנֵיכֶם גּוֹיִם גְּדֹלִים וַעֲצוּמִים וְאַתֶּם לֹא־עָמַד אִישׁ בִּפְנֵיכֶם עַד הַיּוֹם הַזֶּה: ט

10 A single man of you would put a thousand to flight, for *Hashem* your God Himself has been fighting for you, as He promised you.

אִישׁ־אֶחָד מִכֶּם יִרְדָּף־אָלֶף כִּי יְהוָה אֱלֹהֵיכֶם הוּא הַנִּלְחָם לָכֶם כַּאֲשֶׁר דִּבֶּר לָכֶם: י

11 For your own sakes, therefore, be most mindful to love *Hashem* your God.

וְנִשְׁמַרְתֶּם מְאֹד לְנַפְשֹׁתֵיכֶם לְאַהֲבָה אֶת־יְהוָה אֱלֹהֵיכֶם: יא

12 For should you turn away and attach yourselves to the remnant of those nations – to those that are left among you – and intermarry with them, you joining them and they joining you,

כִּי אִם־שׁוֹב תָּשׁוּבוּ וּדְבַקְתֶּם בְּיֶתֶר הַגּוֹיִם הָאֵלֶּה הַנִּשְׁאָרִים הָאֵלֶּה אִתְּכֶם וְהִתְחַתַּנְתֶּם בָּהֶם וּבָאתֶם בָּהֶם וְהֵם בָּכֶם: יב

13 know for certain that *Hashem* your God will not continue to drive these nations out before you; they shall become a snare and a trap for you, a scourge to your sides and thorns in your eyes, until you perish from this good land that *Hashem* your God has given you.

יָדוֹעַ תֵּדְעוּ כִּי לֹא יוֹסִיף יְהוָה אֱלֹהֵיכֶם לְהוֹרִישׁ אֶת־הַגּוֹיִם הָאֵלֶּה מִלִּפְנֵיכֶם וְהָיוּ לָכֶם לְפַח וּלְמוֹקֵשׁ וּלְשֹׁטֵט בְּצִדֵּיכֶם וְלִצְנִינִם בְּעֵינֵיכֶם עַד־אֲבָדְכֶם מֵעַל הָאֲדָמָה הַטּוֹבָה הַזֹּאת אֲשֶׁר נָתַן לָכֶם יְהוָה אֱלֹהֵיכֶם: יג

Hesder students studying Torah in Shiloh

23:6 But be most resolute Throughout *Sefer Yehoshua*, the instructions to be "strong" and "resolute" are delivered repeatedly, both to *Yehoshua* himself and the Children of Israel as a whole. Significantly, this command applies both to spiritual tasks, such as the exhortation in this verse to observe the entire *Torah* of *Moshe*, and to physical tasks such as fighting battles to conquer the Land of Israel (see, e.g., Joshua 1:6). A complete national life requires both spiritual and physical fortitude. In today's Israeli army, many soldiers exemplify this devotion to both *Torah* study and military service by enlisting in the *Hesder* program that combines high level *Torah* study with mandatory army service. The students and graduates of these academies are exemplary soldiers as well as scholars, thereby serving as role models for all.

Yehoshua/Joshua
Chapter 24

14 "I am now going the way of all the earth. Acknowledge with all your heart and soul that not one of the good things that *Hashem* your God promised you has failed to happen; they have all come true for you, not a single one has failed.

15 But just as every good thing that *Hashem* your God promised you has been fulfilled for you, so *Hashem* can bring upon you every evil thing until He has wiped you off this good land that *Hashem* your God has given you.

16 If you break the covenant that *Hashem* your God enjoined upon you, and go and serve other gods and bow down to them, then *Hashem*'s anger will burn against you, and you shall quickly perish from the good land that He has given you."

24 1 *Yehoshua* assembled all the tribes of *Yisrael* at Schechem. He summoned *Yisrael*'s elders and commanders, magistrates and officers; and they presented themselves before *Hashem*.

2 Then *Yehoshua* said to all the people, "Thus said *Hashem*, the God of *Yisrael*: In olden times, your forefathers – *Terach*, father of *Avraham* and father of Nahor – lived beyond the Euphrates and worshiped other gods.

3 But I took your father *Avraham* from beyond the Euphrates and led him through the whole land of Canaan and multiplied his offspring. I gave him *Yitzchak*,

4 and to *Yitzchak* I gave *Yaakov* and Esau. I gave Esau the hill country of Seir as his possession, while *Yaakov* and his children went down to Egypt.

5 "Then I sent *Moshe* and *Aharon*, and I plagued Egypt with [the wonders] that I wrought in their midst, after which I freed you

6 I freed your fathers – from Egypt, and you came to the Sea. But the Egyptians pursued your fathers to the Sea of Reeds with chariots and horsemen.

7 They cried out to *Hashem*, and He put darkness between you and the Egyptians; then He brought the Sea upon them, and it covered them. Your own eyes saw what I did to the Egyptians. "After you had lived a long time in the wilderness,

יהושע
פרק כד

יד וְהִנֵּה אָנֹכִי הוֹלֵךְ הַיּוֹם בְּדֶרֶךְ כָּל־הָאָרֶץ וִידַעְתֶּם בְּכָל־לְבַבְכֶם וּבְכָל־נַפְשְׁכֶם כִּי לֹא־נָפַל דָּבָר אֶחָד מִכֹּל הַדְּבָרִים הַטּוֹבִים אֲשֶׁר דִּבֶּר יְהֹוָה אֱלֹהֵיכֶם עֲלֵיכֶם הַכֹּל בָּאוּ לָכֶם לֹא־נָפַל מִמֶּנּוּ דָּבָר אֶחָד:

טו וְהָיָה כַּאֲשֶׁר־בָּא עֲלֵיכֶם כָּל־הַדָּבָר הַטּוֹב אֲשֶׁר דִּבֶּר יְהֹוָה אֱלֹהֵיכֶם אֲלֵיכֶם כֵּן יָבִיא יְהֹוָה עֲלֵיכֶם אֵת כָּל־הַדָּבָר הָרָע עַד־הַשְׁמִידוֹ אוֹתְכֶם מֵעַל הָאֲדָמָה הַטּוֹבָה הַזֹּאת אֲשֶׁר נָתַן לָכֶם יְהֹוָה אֱלֹהֵיכֶם:

טז בְּעָבְרְכֶם אֶת־בְּרִית יְהֹוָה אֱלֹהֵיכֶם אֲשֶׁר צִוָּה אֶתְכֶם וַהֲלַכְתֶּם וַעֲבַדְתֶּם אֱלֹהִים אֲחֵרִים וְהִשְׁתַּחֲוִיתֶם לָהֶם וְחָרָה אַף־יְהֹוָה בָּכֶם וַאֲבַדְתֶּם מְהֵרָה מֵעַל הָאָרֶץ הַטּוֹבָה אֲשֶׁר נָתַן לָכֶם:

כד א וַיֶּאֱסֹף יְהוֹשֻׁעַ אֶת־כָּל־שִׁבְטֵי יִשְׂרָאֵל שְׁכֶמָה וַיִּקְרָא לְזִקְנֵי יִשְׂרָאֵל וּלְרָאשָׁיו וּלְשֹׁפְטָיו וּלְשֹׁטְרָיו וַיִּתְיַצְּבוּ לִפְנֵי הָאֱלֹהִים:

ב וַיֹּאמֶר יְהוֹשֻׁעַ אֶל־כָּל־הָעָם כֹּה־אָמַר יְהֹוָה אֱלֹהֵי יִשְׂרָאֵל בְּעֵבֶר הַנָּהָר יָשְׁבוּ אֲבוֹתֵיכֶם מֵעוֹלָם תֶּרַח אֲבִי אַבְרָהָם וַאֲבִי נָחוֹר וַיַּעַבְדוּ אֱלֹהִים אֲחֵרִים:

ג וָאֶקַּח אֶת־אֲבִיכֶם אֶת־אַבְרָהָם מֵעֵבֶר הַנָּהָר וָאוֹלֵךְ אוֹתוֹ בְּכָל־אֶרֶץ כְּנָעַן וארב [וָאַרְבֶּה] אֶת־זַרְעוֹ וָאֶתֶּן־לוֹ אֶת־יִצְחָק:

ד וָאֶתֵּן לְיִצְחָק אֶת־יַעֲקֹב וְאֶת־עֵשָׂו וָאֶתֵּן לְעֵשָׂו אֶת־הַר שֵׂעִיר לָרֶשֶׁת אוֹתוֹ וְיַעֲקֹב וּבָנָיו יָרְדוּ מִצְרָיִם:

ה וָאֶשְׁלַח אֶת־מֹשֶׁה וְאֶת־אַהֲרֹן וָאֶגֹּף אֶת־מִצְרַיִם כַּאֲשֶׁר עָשִׂיתִי בְּקִרְבּוֹ וְאַחַר הוֹצֵאתִי אֶתְכֶם:

ו וָאוֹצִיא אֶת־אֲבוֹתֵיכֶם מִמִּצְרַיִם וַתָּבֹאוּ הַיָּמָּה וַיִּרְדְּפוּ מִצְרַיִם אַחֲרֵי אֲבוֹתֵיכֶם בְּרֶכֶב וּבְפָרָשִׁים יַם־סוּף:

ז וַיִּצְעֲקוּ אֶל־יְהֹוָה וַיָּשֶׂם מַאֲפֵל בֵּינֵיכֶם וּבֵין הַמִּצְרִים וַיָּבֵא עָלָיו אֶת־הַיָּם וַיְכַסֵּהוּ וַתִּרְאֶינָה עֵינֵיכֶם אֵת אֲשֶׁר־עָשִׂיתִי בְּמִצְרָיִם וַתֵּשְׁבוּ בַמִּדְבָּר יָמִים רַבִּים:

Yehoshua/Joshua
Chapter 24

8 I brought you to the land of the Amorites who lived beyond the *Yarden*. They gave battle to you, but I delivered them into your hands; I annihilated them for you, and you took possession of their land.

9 Thereupon Balak son of Zippor, the king of Moab, made ready to attack *Yisrael*. He sent for Balaam son of Beor to curse you,

10 but I refused to listen to Balaam; he had to bless you, and thus I saved you from him.

11 "Then you crossed the *Yarden* and you came to *Yericho*. The citizens of *Yericho* and the Amorites, Perizzites, Canaanites, Hittites, Girgashites, Hivites, and Jebusites fought you, but I delivered them into your hands.

12 I sent a plague ahead of you, and it drove them out before you – [just like] the two Amorite kings – not by your sword or by your bow.

13 I have given you a land for which you did not labor and towns which you did not build, and you have settled in them; you are enjoying vineyards and olive groves which you did not plant.

va-e-TAYN la-KHEM E-retz a-SHER lo ya-GA-ta BAH v'-a-REEM a-SHER lo v'-nee-TEM va-tay-sh'-VU ba-HEM k'-ra-MEEM v'-zay-TEEM a-SHER lo n'-ta-TEM a-TEM o-kh'-LEEM

14 "Now, therefore, revere *Hashem* and serve Him with undivided loyalty; put away the gods that your forefathers served beyond the Euphrates and in Egypt, and serve *Hashem*.

15 Or, if you are loath to serve *Hashem*, choose this day which ones you are going to serve – the gods that your forefathers served beyond the Euphrates, or those of the Amorites in whose land you are settled; but I and my household will serve *Hashem*."

24:13 I have given you a land Yehoshua's final speech to the nation includes a review of their history, starting from before the birth of *Avraham*, continuing through the enslavement in Egypt and subsequent exodus, and concluding with their recent conquest and possession of the Promised Land. In addition to fostering loyalty to *Hashem*, this farewell address serves as a powerful reminder that what God wants is for the People of Israel to serve Him specifically in *Eretz Yisrael*. We, who live in an era that has seen the Jewish exiles gather from around the world to live together as a free nation in the State of Israel, are especially privileged to witness the words of *Yehoshua* realized before our very eyes.

Yehoshua/Joshua
Chapter 24

16 In reply, the people declared, "Far be it from us to forsake *Hashem* and serve other gods!

17 For it was *Hashem* our God who brought us and our fathers up from the land of Egypt, the house of bondage, and who wrought those wondrous signs before our very eyes, and guarded us all along the way that we traveled and among all the peoples through whose midst we passed.

18 And then *Hashem* drove out before us all the peoples – the Amorites – that inhabited the country. We too will serve *Hashem*, for He is our God."

19 *Yehoshua*, however, said to the people, "You will not be able to serve *Hashem*, for He is a holy *Hashem*. He is a jealous *Hashem*; He will not forgive your transgressions and your sins.

20 If you forsake *Hashem* and serve alien gods, He will turn and deal harshly with you and make an end of you, after having been gracious to you."

21 But the people replied to *Yehoshua*, "No, we will serve *Hashem*!"

22 Thereupon *Yehoshua* said to the people, "You are witnesses against yourselves that you have by your own act chosen to serve *Hashem*." "Yes, we are!" they responded.

23 "Then put away the alien gods that you have among you and direct your hearts to *Hashem*, the God of *Yisrael*."

24 And the people declared to *Yehoshua*, "We will serve none but *Hashem* our God, and we will obey none but Him."

25 On that day at *Shechem*, *Yehoshua* made a covenant for the people and he made a fixed rule for them.

26 *Yehoshua* recorded all this in a book of divine instruction. He took a great stone and set it up at the foot of the oak in the sacred precinct of *Hashem*;

27 and *Yehoshua* said to all the people, "See, this very stone shall be a witness against us, for it heard all the words that *Hashem* spoke to us; it shall be a witness against you, lest you break faith with your God."

Yehoshua/Joshua
Chapter 24

28 *Yehoshua* then dismissed the people to their allotted portions.

29 After these events, *Yehoshua* son of *Nun*, the servant of *Hashem*, died at the age of one hundred and ten years.

30 They buried him on his own property, at Timnath-serah in the hill country of *Efraim*, north of Mount Gaash.

31 *Yisrael* served *Hashem* during the lifetime of *Yehoshua* and the lifetime of the elders who lived on after *Yehoshua*, and who had experienced all the deeds that *Hashem* had wrought for *Yisrael*.

32 The bones of *Yosef*, which the Israelites had brought up from Egypt, were buried at *Shechem*, in the piece of ground which *Yaakov* had bought for a hundred *kesita* from the children of Hamor, *Shechem*'s father, and which had become a heritage of the Josephites.

33 *Elazar* son of *Aharon* also died, and they buried him on the hill of his son *Pinchas*, which had been assigned to him in the hill country of *Efraim*.

יהושע
פרק כד

כח וַיְשַׁלַּח יְהוֹשֻׁעַ אֶת־הָעָם אִישׁ לְנַחֲלָתֽוֹ׃

כט וַיְהִי אַחֲרֵי הַדְּבָרִים הָאֵלֶּה וַיָּמָת יְהוֹשֻׁעַ בִּן־נוּן עֶבֶד יְהֹוָה בֶּן־מֵאָה וָעֶשֶׂר שָׁנִֽים׃

ל וַיִּקְבְּרוּ אֹתוֹ בִּגְבוּל נַחֲלָתוֹ בְּתִמְנַת־סֶרַח אֲשֶׁר בְּהַר־אֶפְרָיִם מִצְּפוֹן לְהַר־גָּֽעַשׁ׃

לא וַיַּעֲבֹד יִשְׂרָאֵל אֶת־יְהֹוָה כֹּל יְמֵי יְהוֹשֻׁעַ וְכֹל ׀ יְמֵי הַזְּקֵנִים אֲשֶׁר הֶאֱרִיכוּ יָמִים אַחֲרֵי יְהוֹשֻׁעַ וַאֲשֶׁר יָדְעוּ אֵת כׇּל־מַעֲשֵׂה יְהֹוָה אֲשֶׁר עָשָׂה לְיִשְׂרָאֵֽל׃

לב וְאֶת־עַצְמוֹת יוֹסֵף אֲשֶׁר־הֶעֱלוּ בְנֵי־יִשְׂרָאֵל מִמִּצְרַיִם קָבְרוּ בִשְׁכֶם בְּחֶלְקַת הַשָּׂדֶה אֲשֶׁר קָנָה יַעֲקֹב מֵאֵת בְּנֵי־חֲמוֹר אֲבִי־שְׁכֶם בְּמֵאָה קְשִׂיטָה וַיִּהְיוּ לִבְנֵי־יוֹסֵף לְנַחֲלָֽה׃

לג וְאֶלְעָזָר בֶּן־אַהֲרֹן מֵת וַיִּקְבְּרוּ אֹתוֹ בְּגִבְעַת פִּינְחָס בְּנוֹ אֲשֶׁר נִתַּן־לוֹ בְּהַר אֶפְרָֽיִם׃

Sefer Shoftim
The Book of Judges

Introduction and Commentary by Rabbi Shmuel Jablon

The rabbis of the Talmud (*Bava Batra* 15b) teach that *Sefer Shoftim* (Judges), the second book of the Prophets, was written by the prophet *Shmuel*. This book tells the story of 390 difficult years of Israelite history, ending with the statement, "In those days there was no king in *Yisrael*; everyone did as he pleased" (Judges 21:24–25). This verse, which appears several times in the book of *Shoftim*, sums up this challenging era. During this period, the Children of Israel often turned away from *Hashem*'s *Torah*, and fell prey to the cardinal sins of idolatry, murder and sexual immorality. In return, God often allowed Israel's enemies to oppress them. In *Sefer Shoftim*, we read of the Israelites suffering at the hands of Moabites, Canaanites, Midianites, Ammonites and Philistines. All too often throughout this period, though they were living in their own land, the Children of Israel were not actually a free people.

However, not everything described in this book is tragic. After each descent into sin and subjugation, we learn about the judges who fostered spiritual reawakening and led the Israelites to military victories and salvation. In the era prior to Israel's kings, the judges provided leadership to all who were willing to follow.

These judges, drawn from various tribes of Israel, included some of the most heroic figures in Jewish history. For example, we learn about *Otniel*, who was both a *Torah* scholar and a warrior, about *Devora*, the prophetess and judge who sang to *Hashem* after Israel's miraculous victory, and about *Shimshon*, the symbol of great physical strength and willingness to sacrifice everything for the People of Israel. Throughout this book, we see that the judges served as both worldly and spiritual leaders. When the Israelites followed their guidance, they prospered.

Thus, *Sefer Shoftim* depicts a repeating cycle, in which sins, punishment and suffering are followed by repentance, military victory and spiritual growth. The lesson that success in the Land of Israel depends on following the God of Israel emerges as a consistent theme.

The books of the Prophets were written to teach lessons that would be needed to guide future generations. In his commentary to *Sefer Shoftim* (upon which much of the following commentary is based), Israeli scholar Rabbi Shlomo Aviner writes, "In the future there would be difficult and complicated situations faced by the People of Israel. Due to the prophecy of the *Shoftim*, the nation would be able to learn and strengthen itself."

Rabbi Aviner teaches that as our generation faces complicated challenges, we must look to *Sefer Shoftim* for inspiration and for lessons about how to muster the spiritual and physical strength necessary to cope with these challenges.

Chart of the Judges of Israel

The following is a chart of the Judges of Israel, the tribes they were from, and the amount of time they served, based on *Sefer Shoftim*.

Name	Tribe	Approximate Years	Relevant Verses
Otniel son of *Kenaz*	*Yehuda*	40	Judges 3:8–11
Ehud son of *Gera*	*Binyamin*	80	Judges 3:15–30
Shamgar son of *Anat*	Not recorded	1	Judges 3:31
Devora wife of *Lapidot*	*Efraim*	40	Judges 4–5
Gidon son of *Yoash*	*Menashe*	40	Judges 6–6
Avimelech son of *Gidon*	*Menashe*	3	Judges 9:1–56
Tola son of *Puah*	*Yissachar*	23	Judges 10:1–2
Yair the Giladite	*Menashe*	22	Judges 10:3–5
Yiftach the Giladite	*Menashe*	6	Judges 11:1–12:7
Ivtzan of *Beit Lechem*	*Yehuda*	7	Judges 12:8–10
Eilon the Zebulunite	*Zevulun*	10	Judges 12:11–12
Avdon son of *Hillel*	*Efraim*	8	Judges 12:13–15
Shimshon son of *Manoach*	*Dan*	20	Judges 13–16
Eli the *Kohen*	*Levi*	40	I Samuel 1–4
Shmuel the *Navi*	*Levi*	11	I Samuel 1–17

Shoftim/Judges
Chapter 1

1 ¹ After the death of *Yehoshua*, the Israelites inquired of *Hashem*, "Which of us shall be the first to go up against the Canaanites and attack them?"

² *Hashem* replied, "Let [the tribe of] *Yehuda* go up. I now deliver the land into their hands."

³ *Yehuda* then said to their brother-tribe *Shimon*, "Come up with us to our allotted territory and let us attack the Canaanites, and then we will go with you to your allotted territory." So *Shimon* joined them.

⁴ When *Yehuda* advanced, *Hashem* delivered the Canaanites and the Perizzites into their hands, and they defeated ten thousand of them at Bezek.

⁵ At Bezek, they encountered Adoni-bezek, engaged him in battle, and defeated the Canaanites and the Perizzites.

⁶ Adoni-bezek fled, but they pursued him and captured him; and they cut off his thumbs and his big toes.

⁷ And Adoni-bezek said, "Seventy kings, with thumbs and big toes cut off, used to pick up scraps under my table; as I have done, so *Hashem* has requited me." They brought him to *Yerushalayim* and he died there.

⁸ The Judites attacked *Yerushalayim* and captured it; they put it to the sword and set the city on fire.

⁹ After that the Judites went down to attack the Canaanites who inhabited the hill country, the *Negev*, and the Shephelah.

¹⁰ The Judites marched against the Canaanites who dwelt in *Chevron*, and they defeated Sheshai, Ahiman, and Talmai. (The name of *Chevron* was formerly *Kiryat Arba*.)

¹¹ From there they marched against the inhabitants of Debir (the name of Debir was formerly *Kiryat Sefer*).

¹² And *Kalev* announced, "I will give my daughter Achsah in marriage to the man who attacks and captures *Kiryat Sefer*."

שופטים
פרק א

א וַיְהִי אַחֲרֵי מוֹת יְהוֹשֻׁעַ וַיִּשְׁאֲלוּ בְּנֵי יִשְׂרָאֵל בַּיהֹוָה לֵאמֹר מִי יַעֲלֶה־לָּנוּ אֶל־הַכְּנַעֲנִי בַּתְּחִלָּה לְהִלָּחֶם בּוֹ:

ב וַיֹּאמֶר יְהֹוָה יְהוּדָה יַעֲלֶה הִנֵּה נָתַתִּי אֶת־הָאָרֶץ בְּיָדוֹ:

ג וַיֹּאמֶר יְהוּדָה לְשִׁמְעוֹן אָחִיו עֲלֵה אִתִּי בְגוֹרָלִי וְנִלָּחֲמָה בַּכְּנַעֲנִי וְהָלַכְתִּי גַם־אֲנִי אִתְּךָ בְּגוֹרָלֶךָ וַיֵּלֶךְ אִתּוֹ שִׁמְעוֹן:

ד וַיַּעַל יְהוּדָה וַיִּתֵּן יְהֹוָה אֶת־הַכְּנַעֲנִי וְהַפְּרִזִּי בְּיָדָם וַיַּכּוּם בְּבֶזֶק עֲשֶׂרֶת אֲלָפִים אִישׁ:

ה וַיִּמְצְאוּ אֶת־אֲדֹנִי בֶזֶק בְּבֶזֶק וַיִּלָּחֲמוּ בּוֹ וַיַּכּוּ אֶת־הַכְּנַעֲנִי וְאֶת־הַפְּרִזִּי:

ו וַיָּנָס אֲדֹנִי בֶזֶק וַיִּרְדְּפוּ אַחֲרָיו וַיֹּאחֲזוּ אֹתוֹ וַיְקַצְּצוּ אֶת־בְּהֹנוֹת יָדָיו וְרַגְלָיו:

ז וַיֹּאמֶר אֲדֹנִי־בֶזֶק שִׁבְעִים מְלָכִים בְּהֹנוֹת יְדֵיהֶם וְרַגְלֵיהֶם מְקֻצָּצִים הָיוּ מְלַקְּטִים תַּחַת שֻׁלְחָנִי כַּאֲשֶׁר עָשִׂיתִי כֵּן שִׁלַּם־לִי אֱלֹהִים וַיְבִיאֻהוּ יְרוּשָׁלַם וַיָּמָת שָׁם:

ח וַיִּלָּחֲמוּ בְנֵי־יְהוּדָה בִּירוּשָׁלַם וַיִּלְכְּדוּ אוֹתָהּ וַיַּכּוּהָ לְפִי־חָרֶב וְאֶת־הָעִיר שִׁלְּחוּ בָאֵשׁ:

ט וְאַחַר יָרְדוּ בְּנֵי יְהוּדָה לְהִלָּחֵם בַּכְּנַעֲנִי יוֹשֵׁב הָהָר וְהַנֶּגֶב וְהַשְּׁפֵלָה:

י וַיֵּלֶךְ יְהוּדָה אֶל־הַכְּנַעֲנִי הַיּוֹשֵׁב בְּחֶבְרוֹן וְשֵׁם־חֶבְרוֹן לְפָנִים קִרְיַת אַרְבַּע וַיַּכּוּ אֶת־שֵׁשַׁי וְאֶת־אֲחִימַן וְאֶת־תַּלְמָי:

יא וַיֵּלֶךְ מִשָּׁם אֶל־יוֹשְׁבֵי דְּבִיר וְשֵׁם־דְּבִיר לְפָנִים קִרְיַת־סֵפֶר:

יב וַיֹּאמֶר כָּלֵב אֲשֶׁר־יַכֶּה אֶת־קִרְיַת־סֵפֶר וּלְכָדָהּ וְנָתַתִּי לוֹ אֶת־עַכְסָה בִתִּי לְאִשָּׁה:

Shoftim/Judges
Chapter 1

שופטים
פרק א

13 His younger kinsman, *Otniel* the Kenizzite, captured it; and *Kalev* gave him his daughter Achsah in marriage.

יג וַיִּלְכְּדָהּ עָתְנִיאֵל בֶּן־קְנַז אֲחִי כָלֵב הַקָּטֹן מִמֶּנּוּ וַיִּתֶּן־לוֹ אֶת־עַכְסָה בִתּוֹ לְאִשָּׁה:

va-yil-k'-DAH ot-nee-AYL ben k'-NAZ a-KHEE kha-LAYV ha-ka-TON mi-ME-nu va-yi-ten LO et akh-SAH vi-TO l'-i-SHAH

14 When she came [to him], she induced him to ask her father for some property. She dismounted from her donkey, and *Kalev* asked her, "What is the matter?"

יד וַיְהִי בְּבוֹאָהּ וַתְּסִיתֵהוּ לִשְׁאוֹל מֵאֵת־אָבִיהָ הַשָּׂדֶה וַתִּצְנַח מֵעַל הַחֲמוֹר וַיֹּאמֶר־לָהּ כָּלֵב מַה־לָּךְ:

15 She replied, "Give me a present, for you have given me away as *Negev*-land; give me springs of water." And *Kalev* gave her Upper and Lower Gulloth.

טו וַתֹּאמֶר לוֹ הָבָה־לִּי בְרָכָה כִּי אֶרֶץ הַנֶּגֶב נְתַתָּנִי וְנָתַתָּה לִי גֻּלֹּת מָיִם וַיִּתֶּן־לָהּ כָּלֵב אֵת גֻּלֹּת עִלִּית וְאֵת גֻּלֹּת תַּחְתִּית:

16 The descendants of the Kenite, the father-in-law of *Moshe*, went up with the Judites from the City of Palms to the wilderness of *Yehuda*; and they went and settled among the people in the *Negev* of Arad.

טז וּבְנֵי קֵינִי חֹתֵן מֹשֶׁה עָלוּ מֵעִיר הַתְּמָרִים אֶת־בְּנֵי יְהוּדָה מִדְבַּר יְהוּדָה אֲשֶׁר בְּנֶגֶב עֲרָד וַיֵּלֶךְ וַיֵּשֶׁב אֶת־הָעָם:

17 And *Yehuda* with its brother-tribe *Shimon* went on and defeated the Canaanites who dwelt in Zephath. They proscribed it, and so the town was named Hormah.

יז וַיֵּלֶךְ יְהוּדָה אֶת־שִׁמְעוֹן אָחִיו וַיַּכּוּ אֶת־הַכְּנַעֲנִי יוֹשֵׁב צְפַת וַיַּחֲרִימוּ אוֹתָהּ וַיִּקְרָא אֶת־שֵׁם־הָעִיר חָרְמָה:

18 And *Yehuda* captured *Azza* and its territory, *Ashkelon* and its territory, and Ekron and its territory.

יח וַיִּלְכֹּד יְהוּדָה אֶת־עַזָּה וְאֶת־גְּבוּלָהּ וְאֶת־אַשְׁקְלוֹן וְאֶת־גְּבוּלָהּ וְאֶת־עֶקְרוֹן וְאֶת־גְּבוּלָהּ:

19 *Hashem* was with *Yehuda*, so that they took possession of the hill country; but they were not able to dispossess the inhabitants of the plain, for they had iron chariots.

יט וַיְהִי יְהֹוָה אֶת־יְהוּדָה וַיֹּרֶשׁ אֶת־הָהָר כִּי לֹא לְהוֹרִישׁ אֶת־יֹשְׁבֵי הָעֵמֶק כִּי־רֶכֶב בַּרְזֶל לָהֶם:

20 They gave *Chevron* to *Kalev*, as *Moshe* had promised; and he drove the three Anakites out of there.

כ וַיִּתְּנוּ לְכָלֵב אֶת־חֶבְרוֹן כַּאֲשֶׁר דִּבֶּר מֹשֶׁה וַיּוֹרֶשׁ מִשָּׁם אֶת־שְׁלֹשָׁה בְּנֵי הָעֲנָק:

21 The Benjaminites did not dispossess the Jebusite inhabitants of *Yerushalayim*; so the Jebusites have dwelt with the Benjaminites in *Yerushalayim* to this day.

כא וְאֶת־הַיְבוּסִי יֹשֵׁב יְרוּשָׁלַ͏ִם לֹא הוֹרִישׁוּ בְּנֵי בִנְיָמִן וַיֵּשֶׁב הַיְבוּסִי אֶת־בְּנֵי בִנְיָמִן בִּירוּשָׁלַ͏ִם עַד הַיּוֹם הַזֶּה:

1:13 His younger kinsman, *Otniel* the Kenizzite, captured it This verse, describing the conquest of *Kiryat Sefer*, demonstrates *Otniel* the Kenizzite's power as a military leader. However, *Otniel* is more than just a strategic tactician. The classic commentator *Rashi* (Joshua 15:15) notes that *Kiryat Sefer*, which means 'the city of the book,' gets its name from an incident that occurred after *Moshe*'s death. Due to the people's profound sadness, many biblical laws were forgotten. However, *Otniel*, with his great intellectual prowess, relearns and restores these commandments. Hence, we see that *Otniel* is not only a great warrior; he is also a great *Torah* scholar. Similarly, today's Israeli army has many soldier-scholars who combine "the book and the sword" in their service of God and the Jewish people.

Shoftim/Judges
Chapter 1

22 The House of *Yosef*, for their part, advanced against *Beit El*, and *Hashem* was with them.

23 While the House of *Yosef* were scouting at *Beit El* (the name of the town was formerly Luz),

24 their patrols saw a man leaving the town. They said to him, "Just show us how to get into the town, and we will treat you kindly."

25 He showed them how to get into the town; they put the town to the sword, but they let the man and all his relatives go free.

26 The man went to the Hittite country. He founded a city and named it Luz, and that has been its name to this day.

27 *Menashe* did not dispossess [the inhabitants of] *Beit-Shean* and its dependencies, or [of] Taanach and its dependencies, or the inhabitants of Dor and its dependencies, or the inhabitants of Ibleam and its dependencies, or the inhabitants of Megiddo and its dependencies. The Canaanites persisted in dwelling in this region.

28 And when *Yisrael* gained the upper hand, they subjected the Canaanites to forced labor; but they did not dispossess them.

29 Nor did *Efraim* dispossess the Canaanites who inhabited Gezer; so the Canaanites dwelt in their midst at Gezer.

30 *Zevulun* did not dispossess the inhabitants of Kitron or the inhabitants of Nahalol; so the Canaanites dwelt in their midst, but they were subjected to forced labor.

31 *Asher* did not dispossess the inhabitants of Acco or the inhabitants of Sidon, Ahlab, Achzib, Helbah, Aphik, and Rehob.

32 So the Asherites dwelt in the midst of the Canaanites, the inhabitants of the land, for they did not dispossess them.

33 *Naftali* did not dispossess the inhabitants of *Beit Shemesh* or the inhabitants of Beth-anath. But they settled in the midst of the Canaanite inhabitants of the land, and the inhabitants of *Beit Shemesh* and Beth-anath had to perform forced labor for them.

שופטים
פרק א

כב וַיַּעֲל֧וּ בֵית־יוֹסֵ֛ף גַּם־הֵ֖ם בֵּֽית־אֵ֑ל וַיהֹוָ֖ה עִמָּֽם׃

כג וַיָּתִ֥ירוּ בֵית־יוֹסֵ֖ף בְּבֵֽית־אֵ֑ל וְשֵׁם־הָעִ֥יר לְפָנִ֖ים לֽוּז׃

כד וַיִּרְאוּ֙ הַשֹּׁ֣מְרִ֔ים אִ֖ישׁ יוֹצֵ֣א מִן־הָעִ֑יר וַיֹּ֣אמְרוּ ל֗וֹ הַרְאֵ֤נוּ נָא֙ אֶת־מְב֣וֹא הָעִ֔יר וְעָשִׂ֥ינוּ עִמְּךָ֖ חָֽסֶד׃

כה וַיַּרְאֵם֙ אֶת־מְב֣וֹא הָעִ֔יר וַיַּכּ֥וּ אֶת־הָעִ֖יר לְפִי־חָ֑רֶב וְאֶת־הָאִ֥ישׁ וְאֶת־כׇּל־מִשְׁפַּחְתּ֖וֹ שִׁלֵּֽחוּ׃

כו וַיֵּ֣לֶךְ הָאִ֔ישׁ אֶ֖רֶץ הַחִתִּ֑ים וַיִּ֣בֶן עִ֗יר וַיִּקְרָ֤א שְׁמָהּ֙ ל֔וּז ה֣וּא שְׁמָ֔הּ עַ֖ד הַיּ֥וֹם הַזֶּֽה׃

כז וְלֹֽא־הוֹרִ֣ישׁ מְנַשֶּׁ֗ה אֶת־בֵּית־שְׁאָ֣ן וְאֶת־בְּנוֹתֶ֘יהָ֮ וְאֶת־תַּעְנַ֣ךְ וְאֶת־בְּנֹתֶיהָ֒ וְאֶת־יֹשֵׁ֨ב [יֹשְׁבֵ֨י] ד֤וֹר וְאֶת־בְּנוֹתֶ֙יהָ֙ וְאֶת־יוֹשְׁבֵ֤י יִבְלְעָם֙ וְאֶת־בְּנֹתֶ֔יהָ וְאֶת־יוֹשְׁבֵ֥י מְגִדּ֖וֹ וְאֶת־בְּנוֹתֶ֑יהָ וַיּ֙וֹאֶל֙ הַֽכְּנַעֲנִ֔י לָשֶׁ֖בֶת בָּאָ֥רֶץ הַזֹּֽאת׃

כח וַֽיְהִי֙ כִּֽי־חָזַ֣ק יִשְׂרָאֵ֔ל וַיָּ֥שֶׂם אֶת־הַֽכְּנַעֲנִ֖י לָמַ֑ס וְהוֹרֵ֖ישׁ לֹ֥א הוֹרִישֽׁוֹ׃

כט וְאֶפְרַ֙יִם֙ לֹ֣א הוֹרִ֔ישׁ אֶת־הַֽכְּנַעֲנִ֖י הַיּוֹשֵׁ֣ב בְּגָ֑זֶר וַיֵּ֧שֶׁב הַֽכְּנַעֲנִ֛י בְּקִרְבּ֖וֹ בְּגָֽזֶר׃

ל זְבוּלֻ֗ן לֹ֤א הוֹרִישׁ֙ אֶת־יוֹשְׁבֵ֣י קִטְר֔וֹן וְאֶת־יוֹשְׁבֵ֖י נַהֲלֹ֑ל וַיֵּ֤שֶׁב הַֽכְּנַעֲנִי֙ בְּקִרְבּ֔וֹ וַיִּֽהְי֖וּ לָמַֽס׃

לא אָשֵׁ֗ר לֹ֤א הוֹרִישׁ֙ אֶת־יֹשְׁבֵ֣י עַכּ֔וֹ וְאֶת־יוֹשְׁבֵ֖י צִיד֑וֹן וְאֶת־אַחְלָ֤ב וְאֶת־אַכְזִיב֙ וְאֶת־חֶלְבָּ֔ה וְאֶת־אֲפִ֖יק וְאֶת־רְחֹֽב׃

לב וַיֵּ֙שֶׁב֙ הָאָ֣שֵׁרִ֔י בְּקֶ֥רֶב הַֽכְּנַעֲנִ֖י יֹשְׁבֵ֣י הָאָ֑רֶץ כִּ֖י לֹ֥א הוֹרִישֽׁוֹ׃

לג נַפְתָּלִ֗י לֹֽא־הוֹרִ֞ישׁ אֶת־יֹשְׁבֵ֤י בֵֽית־שֶׁ֙מֶשׁ֙ וְאֶת־יֹשְׁבֵ֣י בֵית־עֲנָ֔ת וַיֵּ֕שֶׁב בְּקֶ֥רֶב הַֽכְּנַעֲנִ֖י יֹשְׁבֵ֣י הָאָ֑רֶץ וְיֹשְׁבֵ֤י בֵֽית־שֶׁ֙מֶשׁ֙ וּבֵ֣ית עֲנָ֔ת הָי֥וּ לָהֶ֖ם לָמַֽס׃

Shoftim/Judges
Chapter 2

שופטים
פרק ב

34 The Amorites pressed the Danites into the hill country; they would not let them come down to the plain.

לד וַיִּלְחֲצוּ הָאֱמֹרִי אֶת־בְּנֵי־דָן הָהָרָה כִּי־לֹא נְתָנוֹ לָרֶדֶת לָעֵמֶק׃

35 The Amorites also persisted in dwelling in Harheres, in Aijalon, and in Shaalbim. But the hand of the House of *Yosef* bore heavily on them and they had to perform forced labor.

לה וַיּוֹאֶל הָאֱמֹרִי לָשֶׁבֶת בְּהַר־חֶרֶס בְּאַיָּלוֹן וּבְשַׁעַלְבִים וַתִּכְבַּד יַד בֵּית־יוֹסֵף וַיִּהְיוּ לָמַס׃

36 The territory of the Amorites extended from the Ascent of Akrabbim – from Sela – onward.

לו וּגְבוּל הָאֱמֹרִי מִמַּעֲלֵה עַקְרַבִּים מֵהַסֶּלַע וָמָעְלָה׃

2 1 An angel of *Hashem* came up from *Gilgal* to Bochim and said, "I brought you up from Egypt and I took you into the land which I had promised on oath to your fathers. And I said, 'I will never break My covenant with you.

ב א וַיַּעַל מַלְאַךְ־יְהֹוָה מִן־הַגִּלְגָּל אֶל־הַבֹּכִים וַיֹּאמֶר אַעֲלֶה אֶתְכֶם מִמִּצְרַיִם וָאָבִיא אֶתְכֶם אֶל־הָאָרֶץ אֲשֶׁר נִשְׁבַּעְתִּי לַאֲבֹתֵיכֶם וָאֹמַר לֹא־אָפֵר בְּרִיתִי אִתְּכֶם לְעוֹלָם׃

va-YA-al mal-akh a-do-NAI min ha-gil-GAL el ha-bo-KHEEM va-YO-mer a-a-LEH et-KHEM mi-mitz-RA-yim va-a-VEE et-KHEM el ha-A-retz a-SHER nish-BA-tee la-a-VO-tay-KHEM va-o-MAR lo a-FAYR b'-ree-TEE i-t'-KHEM l'-o-LAM

2 And you, for your part, must make no covenant with the inhabitants of this land; you must tear down their altars.' But you have not obeyed Me – look what you have done!

ב וְאַתֶּם לֹא־תִכְרְתוּ בְרִית לְיוֹשְׁבֵי הָאָרֶץ הַזֹּאת מִזְבְּחוֹתֵיהֶם תִּתֹּצוּן וְלֹא־שְׁמַעְתֶּם בְּקֹלִי מַה־זֹּאת עֲשִׂיתֶם׃

3 Therefore, I have resolved not to drive them out before you; they shall become your oppressors, and their gods shall be a snare to you."

ג וְגַם אָמַרְתִּי לֹא־אֲגָרֵשׁ אוֹתָם מִפְּנֵיכֶם וְהָיוּ לָכֶם לְצִדִּים וֵאלֹהֵיהֶם יִהְיוּ לָכֶם לְמוֹקֵשׁ׃

4 As the angel of *Hashem* spoke these words to all the Israelites, the people broke into weeping.

ד וַיְהִי כְּדַבֵּר מַלְאַךְ יְהֹוָה אֶת־הַדְּבָרִים הָאֵלֶּה אֶל־כָּל־בְּנֵי יִשְׂרָאֵל וַיִּשְׂאוּ הָעָם אֶת־קוֹלָם וַיִּבְכּוּ׃

5 So they named that place Bochim, and they offered sacrifices there to *Hashem*.

ה וַיִּקְרְאוּ שֵׁם־הַמָּקוֹם הַהוּא בֹּכִים וַיִּזְבְּחוּ־שָׁם לַיהֹוָה׃

6 When *Yehoshua* dismissed the people, the Israelites went to their allotted territories and took possession of the land.

ו וַיְשַׁלַּח יְהוֹשֻׁעַ אֶת־הָעָם וַיֵּלְכוּ בְנֵי־יִשְׂרָאֵל אִישׁ לְנַחֲלָתוֹ לָרֶשֶׁת אֶת־הָאָרֶץ׃

2:1 An angel of *Hashem* came up from *Gilgal* to Bochim The angel, who is actually a human prophet according to *Metzudat David*, reiterates God's promise that He will never erase the covenant made with the Patriarchs, according to which the Land of Israel belongs to the Children of Israel. Rabbi Tzvi Yehuda Kook, who was dean of the Mercaz Harav Yeshiva and a prominent leader of Religious Zionism, teaches that whenever the Bible describes a covenant between *Hashem* and the People of Israel, it is not a mutual agreement. Rather, it is a promise that God makes, which the Jewish people must embrace. As this covenant is completely divine, it can never be changed or broken. The establishment of the State of Israel after thousands of years of exile is clearly a fulfillment of this divine covenant.

Rabbi Tzvi Yehuda Kook (1891–1982)

Shoftim/Judges — Chapter 2

7 The people served *Hashem* during the lifetime of *Yehoshua* and the lifetime of the older people who lived on after *Yehoshua* and who had witnessed all the marvelous deeds that *Hashem* had wrought for *Yisrael*.

8 *Yehoshua* son of *Nun*, the servant of *Hashem*, died at the age of one hundred and ten years,

9 and was buried on his own property, at Timnath-heres in the hill country of *Efraim*, north of Mount Gaash.

10 And all that generation were likewise gathered to their fathers. Another generation arose after them, which had not experienced [the deliverance of] *Hashem* or the deeds that He had wrought for *Yisrael*.

11 And the Israelites did what was offensive to *Hashem*. They worshiped the Baalim

12 and forsook *Hashem*, the God of their fathers, who had brought them out of the land of Egypt. They followed other gods, from among the gods of the peoples around them, and bowed down to them; they provoked *Hashem*.

13 They forsook *Hashem* and worshiped Baal and the Ashtaroth.

14 Then *Hashem* was incensed at *Yisrael*, and He handed them over to foes who plundered them. He surrendered them to their enemies on all sides, and they could no longer hold their own against their enemies.

15 In all their campaigns, the hand of *Hashem* was against them to their undoing, as *Hashem* had declared and as *Hashem* had sworn to them; and they were in great distress.

16 Then *Hashem* raised up chieftains who delivered them from those who plundered them.

17 But they did not heed their chieftains either; they went astray after other gods and bowed down to them. They were quick to turn aside from the way their fathers had followed in obedience to the commandments of *Hashem*; they did not do right.

Shoftim/Judges
Chapter 3

18 When *Hashem* raised up chieftains for them, *Hashem* would be with the chieftain and would save them from their enemies during the chieftain's lifetime; for *Hashem* would be moved to pity by their moanings because of those who oppressed and crushed them.

19 But when the chieftain died, they would again act basely, even more than the preceding generation – following other gods, worshiping them, and bowing down to them; they omitted none of their practices and stubborn ways.

20 Then *Hashem* became incensed against *Yisrael*, and He said, "Since that nation has transgressed the covenant that I enjoined upon their fathers and has not obeyed Me,

21 I for My part will no longer drive out before them any of the nations that *Yehoshua* left when he died."

22 For it was in order to test *Yisrael* by them – [to see] whether or not they would faithfully walk in the ways of *Hashem*, as their fathers had done –

23 that *Hashem* had left those nations, instead of driving them out at once, and had not delivered them into the hands of *Yehoshua*.

3 1 These are the nations that *Hashem* left so that He might test by them all the Israelites who had not known any of the wars of Canaan,

2 so that succeeding generations of Israelites might be made to experience war – but only those who had not known the former wars:

3 the five principalities of the Philistines and all the Canaanites, Sidonians, and Hivites who inhabited the hill country of the Lebanon from Mount Baal-hermon to Lebo-hamath.

4 These served as a means of testing *Yisrael*, to learn whether they would obey the commandments which *Hashem* had enjoined upon their fathers through *Moshe*.

5 The Israelites settled among the Canaanites, Hittites, Amorites, Perizzites, Hivites, and Jebusites;

שופטים
פרק ג

יח וְכִי־הֵקִים יְהֹוָה לָהֶם שֹׁפְטִים וְהָיָה יְהֹוָה עִם־הַשֹּׁפֵט וְהוֹשִׁיעָם מִיַּד אֹיְבֵיהֶם כֹּל יְמֵי הַשּׁוֹפֵט כִּי־יִנָּחֵם יְהֹוָה מִנַּאֲקָתָם מִפְּנֵי לֹחֲצֵיהֶם וְדֹחֲקֵיהֶם׃

יט וְהָיָה בְּמוֹת הַשּׁוֹפֵט יָשֻׁבוּ וְהִשְׁחִיתוּ מֵאֲבוֹתָם לָלֶכֶת אַחֲרֵי אֱלֹהִים אֲחֵרִים לְעָבְדָם וּלְהִשְׁתַּחֲוֺת לָהֶם לֹא הִפִּילוּ מִמַּעַלְלֵיהֶם וּמִדַּרְכָּם הַקָּשָׁה׃

כ וַיִּחַר־אַף יְהֹוָה בְּיִשְׂרָאֵל וַיֹּאמֶר יַעַן אֲשֶׁר עָבְרוּ הַגּוֹי הַזֶּה אֶת־בְּרִיתִי אֲשֶׁר צִוִּיתִי אֶת־אֲבוֹתָם וְלֹא שָׁמְעוּ לְקוֹלִי׃

כא גַּם־אֲנִי לֹא אוֹסִיף לְהוֹרִישׁ אִישׁ מִפְּנֵיהֶם מִן־הַגּוֹיִם אֲשֶׁר־עָזַב יְהוֹשֻׁעַ וַיָּמֹת׃

כב לְמַעַן נַסּוֹת בָּם אֶת־יִשְׂרָאֵל הֲשֹׁמְרִים הֵם אֶת־דֶּרֶךְ יְהֹוָה לָלֶכֶת בָּם כַּאֲשֶׁר שָׁמְרוּ אֲבוֹתָם אִם־לֹא׃

כג וַיַּנַּח יְהֹוָה אֶת־הַגּוֹיִם הָאֵלֶּה לְבִלְתִּי הוֹרִישָׁם מַהֵר וְלֹא נְתָנָם בְּיַד־יְהוֹשֻׁעַ׃

ג א וְאֵלֶּה הַגּוֹיִם אֲשֶׁר הִנִּיחַ יְהֹוָה לְנַסּוֹת בָּם אֶת־יִשְׂרָאֵל אֵת כָּל־אֲשֶׁר לֹא־יָדְעוּ אֵת כָּל־מִלְחֲמוֹת כְּנָעַן׃

ב רַק לְמַעַן דַּעַת דֹּרוֹת בְּנֵי־יִשְׂרָאֵל לְלַמְּדָם מִלְחָמָה רַק אֲשֶׁר־לְפָנִים לֹא יְדָעוּם׃

ג חֲמֵשֶׁת סַרְנֵי פְלִשְׁתִּים וְכָל־הַכְּנַעֲנִי וְהַצִּידֹנִי וְהַחִוִּי יֹשֵׁב הַר הַלְּבָנוֹן מֵהַר בַּעַל חֶרְמוֹן עַד לְבוֹא חֲמָת׃

ד וַיִּהְיוּ לְנַסּוֹת בָּם אֶת־יִשְׂרָאֵל לָדַעַת הֲיִשְׁמְעוּ אֶת־מִצְוֺת יְהֹוָה אֲשֶׁר־צִוָּה אֶת־אֲבוֹתָם בְּיַד־מֹשֶׁה׃

ה וּבְנֵי יִשְׂרָאֵל יָשְׁבוּ בְּקֶרֶב הַכְּנַעֲנִי הַחִתִּי וְהָאֱמֹרִי וְהַפְּרִזִּי וְהַחִוִּי וְהַיְבוּסִי׃

Shoftim/Judges
Chapter 3

6 they took their daughters to wife and gave their own daughters to their sons, and they worshiped their gods.

7 The Israelites did what was offensive to *Hashem*; they ignored *Hashem* their God and worshiped the Baalim and the Asheroth.

8 *Hashem* became incensed at *Yisrael* and surrendered them to King Cushan-rishathaim of Aram-Naharaim; and the Israelites were subject to Cushan-rishathaim for eight years.

9 The Israelites cried out to *Hashem*, and *Hashem* raised a champion for the Israelites to deliver them: *Otniel* the Kenizzite, a younger kinsman of *Kalev*.

10 The spirit of *Hashem* descended upon him and he became *Yisrael*'s chieftain. He went out to war, and *Hashem* delivered King Cushan-rishathaim of Aram into his hands. He prevailed over Cushan-rishathaim,

11 and the land had peace for forty years. When *Otniel* the Kenizzite died,

12 the Israelites again did what was offensive to *Hashem*. And because they did what was offensive to *Hashem*, *Hashem* let King Eglon of Moab prevail over *Yisrael*.

13 [Eglon] brought the Ammonites and the Amalekites together under his command, and went and defeated *Yisrael* and occupied the City of Palms.

14 The Israelites were subject to King Eglon of Moab for eighteen years.

15 Then the Israelites cried out to *Hashem*, and *Hashem* raised up a champion for them: the Benjaminite *Ehud* son of Gera, a left-handed man. It happened that the Israelites sent tribute to King Eglon of Moab through him.

16 So *Ehud* made for himself a two-edged dagger, a *gomed* in length, which he girded on his right side under his cloak.

17 He presented the tribute to King Eglon of Moab. Now Eglon was a very stout man.

שופטים
פרק ג

ו וַיִּקְח֨וּ אֶת־בְּנוֹתֵיהֶ֜ם לָהֶ֣ם לְנָשִׁ֗ים וְאֶת־בְּנוֹתֵיהֶ֖ם נָתְנ֣וּ לִבְנֵיהֶ֑ם וַיַּעַבְד֖וּ אֶת־אֱלֹהֵיהֶֽם׃

ז וַיַּעֲשׂ֨וּ בְנֵי־יִשְׂרָאֵ֤ל אֶת־הָרַע֙ בְּעֵינֵ֣י יְהֹוָ֔ה וַֽיִּשְׁכְּח֖וּ אֶת־יְהֹוָ֣ה אֱלֹהֵיהֶ֑ם וַיַּעַבְד֥וּ אֶת־הַבְּעָלִ֖ים וְאֶת־הָאֲשֵׁרֽוֹת׃

ח וַיִּחַר־אַ֤ף יְהֹוָה֙ בְּיִשְׂרָאֵ֔ל וַֽיִּמְכְּרֵ֗ם בְּיַד֙ כּוּשַׁ֣ן רִשְׁעָתַ֔יִם מֶ֖לֶךְ אֲרַ֣ם נַהֲרָ֑יִם וַיַּעַבְד֧וּ בְנֵי־יִשְׂרָאֵ֛ל אֶת־כּוּשַׁ֥ן רִשְׁעָתַ֖יִם שְׁמֹנֶ֥ה שָׁנִֽים׃

ט וַיִּזְעֲק֤וּ בְנֵֽי־יִשְׂרָאֵל֙ אֶל־יְהֹוָ֔ה וַיָּ֨קֶם יְהֹוָ֥ה מוֹשִׁ֛יעַ לִבְנֵ֥י יִשְׂרָאֵ֖ל וַיּֽוֹשִׁיעֵ֑ם אֵ֚ת עׇתְנִיאֵ֣ל בֶּן־קְנַ֔ז אֲחִ֥י כָלֵ֖ב הַקָּטֹ֥ן מִמֶּֽנּוּ׃

י וַתְּהִ֨י עָלָ֥יו רֽוּחַ־יְהֹוָה֮ וַיִּשְׁפֹּ֣ט אֶת־יִשְׂרָאֵל֒ וַיֵּצֵא֙ לַמִּלְחָמָ֔ה וַיִּתֵּ֤ן יְהֹוָה֙ בְּיָד֔וֹ אֶת־כּוּשַׁ֥ן רִשְׁעָתַ֖יִם מֶ֣לֶךְ אֲרָ֑ם וַתָּ֣עׇז יָד֔וֹ עַ֖ל כּוּשַׁ֥ן רִשְׁעָתָֽיִם׃

יא וַתִּשְׁקֹ֥ט הָאָ֖רֶץ אַרְבָּעִ֣ים שָׁנָ֑ה וַיָּ֖מׇת עׇתְנִיאֵ֥ל בֶּן־קְנַֽז׃

יב וַיֹּסִ֙פוּ֙ בְּנֵ֣י יִשְׂרָאֵ֔ל לַעֲשׂ֥וֹת הָרַ֖ע בְּעֵינֵ֣י יְהֹוָ֑ה וַיְחַזֵּ֨ק יְהֹוָ֜ה אֶת־עֶגְל֤וֹן מֶֽלֶךְ־מוֹאָב֙ עַל־יִשְׂרָאֵ֔ל עַ֛ל כִּֽי־עָשׂ֥וּ אֶת־הָרַ֖ע בְּעֵינֵ֥י יְהֹוָֽה׃

יג וַיֶּאֱסֹ֣ף אֵלָ֔יו אֶת־בְּנֵ֥י עַמּ֖וֹן וַעֲמָלֵ֑ק וַיֵּ֗לֶךְ וַיַּךְ֙ אֶת־יִשְׂרָאֵ֔ל וַיִּֽירְשׁ֖וּ אֶת־עִ֥יר הַתְּמָרִֽים׃

יד וַיַּעַבְד֤וּ בְנֵֽי־יִשְׂרָאֵל֙ אֶת־עֶגְל֣וֹן מֶלֶךְ־מוֹאָ֔ב שְׁמוֹנֶ֥ה עֶשְׂרֵ֖ה שָׁנָֽה׃

טו וַיִּזְעֲק֤וּ בְנֵֽי־יִשְׂרָאֵל֙ אֶל־יְהֹוָ֔ה וַיָּ֨קֶם יְהֹוָ֤ה לָהֶם֙ מוֹשִׁ֔יעַ אֶת־אֵה֥וּד בֶּן־גֵּרָ֖א בֶּן־הַיְמִינִ֑י אִ֥ישׁ אִטֵּ֖ר יַד־יְמִינ֑וֹ וַיִּשְׁלְח֨וּ בְנֵֽי־יִשְׂרָאֵ֤ל בְּיָדוֹ֙ מִנְחָ֔ה לְעֶגְל֖וֹן מֶ֥לֶךְ מוֹאָֽב׃

טז וַיַּ֩עַשׂ֩ ל֨וֹ אֵה֜וּד חֶ֗רֶב וְלָ֛הּ שְׁנֵ֥י פֵי֖וֹת גֹּ֣מֶד אׇרְכָּ֑הּ וַיַּחְגֹּ֤ר אוֹתָהּ֙ מִתַּ֣חַת לְמַדָּ֔יו עַ֖ל יֶ֥רֶךְ יְמִינֽוֹ׃

יז וַיַּקְרֵב֙ אֶת־הַמִּנְחָ֔ה לְעֶגְל֖וֹן מֶ֣לֶךְ מוֹאָ֑ב וְעֶגְל֕וֹן אִ֥ישׁ בָּרִ֖יא מְאֹֽד׃

Shoftim/Judges
Chapter 3

שופטים
פרק ג

18 When [*Ehud*] had finished presenting the tribute, he dismissed the people who had conveyed the tribute.

יח וַיְהִי כַּאֲשֶׁר כִּלָּה לְהַקְרִיב אֶת־הַמִּנְחָה וַיְשַׁלַּח אֶת־הָעָם נֹשְׂאֵי הַמִּנְחָה:

19 But he himself returned from Pesilim, near *Gilgal*, and said, "Your Majesty, I have a secret message for you." [Eglon] thereupon commanded, "Silence!" So all those in attendance left his presence;

יט וְהוּא שָׁב מִן־הַפְּסִילִים אֲשֶׁר אֶת־הַגִּלְגָּל וַיֹּאמֶר דְּבַר־סֵתֶר לִי אֵלֶיךָ הַמֶּלֶךְ וַיֹּאמֶר הָס וַיֵּצְאוּ מֵעָלָיו כָּל־הָעֹמְדִים עָלָיו:

20 and when *Ehud* approached him, he was sitting alone in his cool upper chamber. *Ehud* said, "I have a message for you from *Hashem*"; whereupon he rose from his seat.

כ וְאֵהוּד בָּא אֵלָיו וְהוּא־יֹשֵׁב בַּעֲלִיַּת הַמְּקֵרָה אֲשֶׁר־לוֹ לְבַדּוֹ וַיֹּאמֶר אֵהוּד דְּבַר־אֱלֹהִים לִי אֵלֶיךָ וַיָּקָם מֵעַל הַכִּסֵּא:

v'-ay-HUD BA ay-LAV v'-hu yo-SHAYV ba-a-li-YAT ha-m'-kay-RAH a-sher LO l'-va-DO va-YO-mer ay-HUD d'-var e-lo-HEEM LEE ay-LE-kha va-YA-kom may-AL ha-ki-SAY

21 Reaching with his left hand, *Ehud* drew the dagger from his right side and drove it into [Eglon's] belly.

כא וַיִּשְׁלַח אֵהוּד אֶת־יַד שְׂמֹאלוֹ וַיִּקַּח אֶת־הַחֶרֶב מֵעַל יֶרֶךְ יְמִינוֹ וַיִּתְקָעֶהָ בְּבִטְנוֹ:

22 The fat closed over the blade and the hilt went in after the blade – for he did not pull the dagger out of his belly – and the filth came out.

כב וַיָּבֹא גַם־הַנִּצָּב אַחַר הַלַּהַב וַיִּסְגֹּר הַחֵלֶב בְּעַד הַלַּהַב כִּי לֹא שָׁלַף הַחֶרֶב מִבִּטְנוֹ וַיֵּצֵא הַפַּרְשְׁדֹנָה:

23 Stepping out into the vestibule, *Ehud* shut the doors of the upper chamber on him and locked them.

כג וַיֵּצֵא אֵהוּד הַמִּסְדְּרוֹנָה וַיִּסְגֹּר דַּלְתוֹת הָעֲלִיָּה בַּעֲדוֹ וְנָעָל:

24 After he left, the courtiers returned. When they saw that the doors of the upper chamber were locked, they thought, "He must be relieving himself in the cool chamber."

כד וְהוּא יָצָא וַעֲבָדָיו בָּאוּ וַיִּרְאוּ וְהִנֵּה דַּלְתוֹת הָעֲלִיָּה נְעֻלוֹת וַיֹּאמְרוּ אַךְ מֵסִיךְ הוּא אֶת־רַגְלָיו בַּחֲדַר הַמְּקֵרָה:

25 They waited a long time; and when he did not open the doors of the chamber, they took the key and opened them – and there their master was lying dead on the floor!

כה וַיָּחִילוּ עַד־בּוֹשׁ וְהִנֵּה אֵינֶנּוּ פֹתֵחַ דַּלְתוֹת הָעֲלִיָּה וַיִּקְחוּ אֶת־הַמַּפְתֵּחַ וַיִּפְתָּחוּ וְהִנֵּה אֲדֹנֵיהֶם נֹפֵל אַרְצָה מֵת:

26 But *Ehud* had made good his escape while they delayed; he had passed Pesilim and escaped to Seirah.

כו וְאֵהוּד נִמְלַט עַד הִתְמַהְמְהָם וְהוּא עָבַר אֶת־הַפְּסִילִים וַיִּמָּלֵט הַשְּׂעִירָתָה:

3:20 And when *Ehud* approached him *Ehud* tells the Moabite king Eglon that he has a message for him from God. Eglon stands up, and *Ehud* stabs him, thereby killing the oppressor of the Israelites. Although he delivered no verbal message, *Ehud* told the truth: *Hashem* had instructed him to kill Eglon. At its core, God's message is that ultimately, even if it takes time, He will always save the People of Israel from their oppressors. This true message that *Ehud* delivered to Eglon remains equally true in our time. Often the enemies of the Jewish people appear strong, and even claim many innocent victims. But God continues to send the message that ultimately, those who oppress His people will always be destroyed. Over time, the Jews' persecutors all fade away, while the Nation of Israel lives forever.

Shoftim/Judges
Chapter 4

27 When he got there, he had the *shofar* sounded through the hill country of *Efraim*, and all the Israelites descended with him from the hill country; and he took the lead.

כז וַיְהִי בְּבוֹאוֹ וַיִּתְקַע בַּשּׁוֹפָר בְּהַר אֶפְרָיִם וַיֵּרְדוּ עִמּוֹ בְנֵי־יִשְׂרָאֵל מִן־הָהָר וְהוּא לִפְנֵיהֶם׃

28 "Follow me closely," he said, "for *Hashem* has delivered your enemies, the Moabites, into your hands." They followed him down and seized the fords of the *Yarden* against the Moabites; they let no one cross.

כח וַיֹּאמֶר אֲלֵהֶם רִדְפוּ אַחֲרַי כִּי־נָתַן יְהֹוָה אֶת־אֹיְבֵיכֶם אֶת־מוֹאָב בְּיֶדְכֶם וַיֵּרְדוּ אַחֲרָיו וַיִּלְכְּדוּ אֶת־מַעְבְּרוֹת הַיַּרְדֵּן לְמוֹאָב וְלֹא־נָתְנוּ אִישׁ לַעֲבֹר׃

29 On that occasion they slew about 10,000 Moabites; they were all robust and brave men, yet not one of them escaped.

כט וַיַּכּוּ אֶת־מוֹאָב בָּעֵת הַהִיא כַּעֲשֶׂרֶת אֲלָפִים אִישׁ כׇּל־שָׁמֵן וְכׇל־אִישׁ חָיִל וְלֹא נִמְלַט אִישׁ׃

30 On that day, Moab submitted to *Yisrael*; and the land was tranquil for eighty years.

ל וַתִּכָּנַע מוֹאָב בַּיּוֹם הַהוּא תַּחַת יַד יִשְׂרָאֵל וַתִּשְׁקֹט הָאָרֶץ שְׁמוֹנִים שָׁנָה׃

31 After him came *Shamgar* son of Anath, who slew six hundred Philistines with an ox-goad. He too was a champion of *Yisrael*.

לא וְאַחֲרָיו הָיָה שַׁמְגַּר בֶּן־עֲנָת וַיַּךְ אֶת־פְּלִשְׁתִּים שֵׁשׁ־מֵאוֹת אִישׁ בְּמַלְמַד הַבָּקָר וַיּוֹשַׁע גַּם־הוּא אֶת־יִשְׂרָאֵל׃

4

1 The Israelites again did what was offensive to *Hashem* – *Ehud* now being dead.

א וַיֹּסִפוּ בְּנֵי יִשְׂרָאֵל לַעֲשׂוֹת הָרַע בְּעֵינֵי יְהֹוָה וְאֵהוּד מֵת׃

2 And *Hashem* surrendered them to King Jabin of Canaan, who reigned in Hazor. His army commander was Sisera, whose base was Harosheth-goiim.

ב וַיִּמְכְּרֵם יְהֹוָה בְּיַד יָבִין מֶלֶךְ־כְּנַעַן אֲשֶׁר מָלַךְ בְּחָצוֹר וְשַׂר־צְבָאוֹ סִיסְרָא וְהוּא יוֹשֵׁב בַּחֲרֹשֶׁת הַגּוֹיִם׃

3 The Israelites cried out to *Hashem*; for he had nine hundred iron chariots, and he had oppressed *Yisrael* ruthlessly for twenty years.

ג וַיִּצְעֲקוּ בְנֵי־יִשְׂרָאֵל אֶל־יְהֹוָה כִּי תְּשַׁע מֵאוֹת רֶכֶב־בַּרְזֶל לוֹ וְהוּא לָחַץ אֶת־בְּנֵי יִשְׂרָאֵל בְּחׇזְקָה עֶשְׂרִים שָׁנָה׃

4 *Devora*, wife of Lappidoth, was a *Neviah*; she led *Yisrael* at that time.

ד וּדְבוֹרָה אִשָּׁה נְבִיאָה אֵשֶׁת לַפִּידוֹת הִיא שֹׁפְטָה אֶת־יִשְׂרָאֵל בָּעֵת הַהִיא׃

ud-vo-RAH i-SHAH n'-vee-AH AY-shet la-pee-DOT HEE sho-f'-TAH et yis-ra-AYL ba-AYT ha-HEE

Dona Gracia (1510–1569)

4:4 Now *Devora*, a prophetess Throughout Jewish history, many women have followed the example of *Devora*, described in this verse as both a prophetess and a judge, by taking positions of leadership on behalf of their people. One example dates to the early Renaissance period, when another Jewish woman emerged as a great leader of her people. At the time, the Jews of Spain faced the horrific persecutions of the Inquisition. But despite the strict prohibitions against practicing Judaism, many of the forced converts known as *Anussim* or "Crypto-Jews" continued to observe their religion in secret. Dona Gracia (1510–1569) discovered her Jewish identity only after she was married, but from that moment on, she was determined to bring respite to her people. As one of the wealthiest women in Europe, she was able to create an escape network for many of the *Anussim*, and eventually used her position of power to negotiate with Sultan Suleiman the Magnificent for a long term lease on the Tiberias region of the Land of Israel, of which she became the ruling authority. She began to rebuild the Galilee's abandoned towns for other *Anussim* to settle in, and aimed to turn Tiberias into a major center of Jewish settlement, trade and learning. Today, visitors to the

Shoftim/Judges
Chapter 4

שופטים
פרק ד

5 She used to sit under the Palm of *Devora*, between *Rama* and *Beit El* in the hill country of *Efraim*, and the Israelites would come to her for decisions.

ה וְהִיא יוֹשֶׁבֶת תַּחַת־תֹּמֶר דְּבוֹרָה בֵּין הָרָמָה וּבֵין בֵּית־אֵל בְּהַר אֶפְרָיִם וַיַּעֲלוּ אֵלֶיהָ בְּנֵי יִשְׂרָאֵל לַמִּשְׁפָּט:

6 She summoned *Barak* son of Abinoam, of Kedesh in *Naftali*, and said to him, "*Hashem*, the God of *Yisrael*, has commanded: Go, march up to Mount *Tavor*, and take with you ten thousand men of *Naftali* and *Zevulun*.

ו וַתִּשְׁלַח וַתִּקְרָא לְבָרָק בֶּן־אֲבִינֹעַם מִקֶּדֶשׁ נַפְתָּלִי וַתֹּאמֶר אֵלָיו הֲלֹא צִוָּה יְהֹוָה אֱלֹהֵי־יִשְׂרָאֵל לֵךְ וּמָשַׁכְתָּ בְּהַר תָּבוֹר וְלָקַחְתָּ עִמְּךָ עֲשֶׂרֶת אֲלָפִים אִישׁ מִבְּנֵי נַפְתָּלִי וּמִבְּנֵי זְבֻלוּן:

va-tish-LAKH va-tik-RA l'-va-RAK ben a-vee-NO-am mi-KE-desh naf-ta-LEE va-TO-mer ay-LAV ha-lo tzi-VAH a-do-NAI e-lo-hay yis-ra-AYL LAYKH u-ma-shakh-TA b'-HAR ta-VOR v'-la-kakh-TA i-m'-KHA a-SE-ret a-la-FEEM EESH mi-b'-NAY naf-ta-LEE u-mi-b'-NAY z'-vu-LUN

7 And I will draw Sisera, Jabin's army commander, with his chariots and his troops, toward you up to the Wadi Kishon; and I will deliver him into your hands."

ז וּמָשַׁכְתִּי אֵלֶיךָ אֶל־נַחַל קִישׁוֹן אֶת־סִיסְרָא שַׂר־צְבָא יָבִין וְאֶת־רִכְבּוֹ וְאֶת־הֲמוֹנוֹ וּנְתַתִּיהוּ בְּיָדֶךָ:

8 But *Barak* said to her, "If you will go with me, I will go; if not, I will not go."

ח וַיֹּאמֶר אֵלֶיהָ בָּרָק אִם־תֵּלְכִי עִמִּי וְהָלָכְתִּי וְאִם־לֹא תֵלְכִי עִמִּי לֹא אֵלֵךְ:

9 "Very well, I will go with you," she answered. "However, there will be no glory for you in the course you are taking, for then *Hashem* will deliver Sisera into the hands of a woman." So *Devora* went with *Barak* to Kedesh.

ט וַתֹּאמֶר הָלֹךְ אֵלֵךְ עִמָּךְ אֶפֶס כִּי לֹא תִהְיֶה תִּפְאַרְתְּךָ עַל־הַדֶּרֶךְ אֲשֶׁר אַתָּה הוֹלֵךְ כִּי בְיַד־אִשָּׁה יִמְכֹּר יְהֹוָה אֶת־סִיסְרָא וַתָּקָם דְּבוֹרָה וַתֵּלֶךְ עִם־בָּרָק קֶדְשָׁה:

10 *Barak* then mustered *Zevulun* and *Naftali* at Kedesh; ten thousand men marched up after him; and *Devora* also went up with him.

י וַיַּזְעֵק בָּרָק אֶת־זְבוּלֻן וְאֶת־נַפְתָּלִי קֶדְשָׁה וַיַּעַל בְּרַגְלָיו עֲשֶׂרֶת אַלְפֵי אִישׁ וַתַּעַל עִמּוֹ דְּבוֹרָה:

11 Now *Chever* the Kenite had separated from the other Kenites, descendants of Hobab, father-in-law of *Moshe*, and had pitched his tent at Elon-bezaanannim, which is near Kedesh.

יא וְחֶבֶר הַקֵּינִי נִפְרָד מִקַּיִן מִבְּנֵי חֹבָב חֹתֵן מֹשֶׁה וַיֵּט אָהֳלוֹ עַד־אֵלוֹן בְּצַעֲנִים [בְּצַעֲנַנִּים] אֲשֶׁר אֶת־קֶדֶשׁ:

12 Sisera was informed that *Barak* son of Abinoam had gone up to Mount *Tavor*.

יב וַיַּגִּדוּ לְסִיסְרָא כִּי עָלָה בָּרָק בֶּן־אֲבִינֹעַם הַר־תָּבוֹר:

---

contemporary city of *Teveria* (Tiberias) can visit the Dona Gracia museum to learn about this fascinating woman who pursued one of the earliest attempts to create a Zionist movement.

4:6 Go, march up to Mount *Tavor*, and take with you ten thousand men The prophetess and judge *Devora* instructs *Barak* in God's name that he is to "march up to Mount *Tavor*" and take ten thousand soldiers with him, to prepare to fight the enemy Sisera.

Metzudat David points out that taking the soldiers does not mean he was to simply draft them into service. Rather, it means to "draw at their hearts," so that they would overcome their natural fear of Sisera and fight courageously. Rabbi Shlomo Aviner notes that this teaches us an important lesson, which remains relevant to this day: the importance of paying attention to the emotional state of the soldiers of Israel. He writes, "The secret weapon of the Israeli Defense Forces is their morale, strength and courage."

Mount Tavor in Northern Israel

Shoftim / Judges
Chapter 4

שופטים
פרק ד

13 So Sisera ordered all his chariots – nine hundred iron chariots – and all the troops he had to move from Harosheth-goiim to the Wadi Kishon.

יג וַיַּזְעֵק סִיסְרָא אֶת־כָּל־רִכְבּוֹ תְּשַׁע מֵאוֹת רֶכֶב בַּרְזֶל וְאֶת־כָּל־הָעָם אֲשֶׁר אִתּוֹ מֵחֲרֹשֶׁת הַגּוֹיִם אֶל־נַחַל קִישׁוֹן:

14 Then *Devora* said to *Barak*, "Up! This is the day on which *Hashem* will deliver Sisera into your hands: *Hashem* is marching before you." *Barak* charged down Mount *Tavor*, followed by the ten thousand men,

יד וַתֹּאמֶר דְּבֹרָה אֶל־בָּרָק קוּם כִּי זֶה הַיּוֹם אֲשֶׁר נָתַן יְהוָה אֶת־סִיסְרָא בְּיָדֶךָ הֲלֹא יְהוָה יָצָא לְפָנֶיךָ וַיֵּרֶד בָּרָק מֵהַר תָּבוֹר וַעֲשֶׂרֶת אֲלָפִים אִישׁ אַחֲרָיו:

15 and *Hashem* threw Sisera and all his chariots and army into a panic before the onslaught of *Barak*. Sisera leaped from his chariot and fled on foot

טו וַיָּהָם יְהוָה אֶת־סִיסְרָא וְאֶת־כָּל־הָרֶכֶב וְאֶת־כָּל־הַמַּחֲנֶה לְפִי־חֶרֶב לִפְנֵי בָרָק וַיֵּרֶד סִיסְרָא מֵעַל הַמֶּרְכָּבָה וַיָּנָס בְּרַגְלָיו:

16 as *Barak* pursued the chariots and the soldiers as far as Harosheth-goiim. All of Sisera's soldiers fell by the sword; not a man was left.

טז וּבָרָק רָדַף אַחֲרֵי הָרֶכֶב וְאַחֲרֵי הַמַּחֲנֶה עַד חֲרֹשֶׁת הַגּוֹיִם וַיִּפֹּל כָּל־מַחֲנֵה סִיסְרָא לְפִי־חֶרֶב לֹא נִשְׁאַר עַד־אֶחָד:

17 Sisera, meanwhile, had fled on foot to the tent of *Yael*, wife of *Chever* the Kenite; for there was friendship between King Jabin of Hazor and the family of *Chever* the Kenite.

יז וְסִיסְרָא נָס בְּרַגְלָיו אֶל־אֹהֶל יָעֵל אֵשֶׁת חֶבֶר הַקֵּינִי כִּי שָׁלוֹם בֵּין יָבִין מֶלֶךְ־חָצוֹר וּבֵין בֵּית חֶבֶר הַקֵּינִי:

18 *Yael* came out to greet Sisera and said to him, "Come in, my lord, come in here, do not be afraid." So he entered her tent, and she covered him with a blanket.

יח וַתֵּצֵא יָעֵל לִקְרַאת סִיסְרָא וַתֹּאמֶר אֵלָיו סוּרָה אֲדֹנִי סוּרָה אֵלַי אַל־תִּירָא וַיָּסַר אֵלֶיהָ הָאֹהֱלָה וַתְּכַסֵּהוּ בַּשְּׂמִיכָה:

19 He said to her, "Please let me have some water; I am thirsty." She opened a skin of milk and gave him some to drink; and she covered him again.

יט וַיֹּאמֶר אֵלֶיהָ הַשְׁקִינִי־נָא מְעַט־מַיִם כִּי צָמֵאתִי וַתִּפְתַּח אֶת־נֹאוד הֶחָלָב וַתַּשְׁקֵהוּ וַתְּכַסֵּהוּ:

20 He said to her, "Stand at the entrance of the tent. If anybody comes and asks you if there is anybody here, say 'No.'"

כ וַיֹּאמֶר אֵלֶיהָ עֲמֹד פֶּתַח הָאֹהֶל וְהָיָה אִם־אִישׁ יָבוֹא וּשְׁאֵלֵךְ וְאָמַר הֲיֵשׁ־פֹּה אִישׁ וְאָמַרְתְּ אָיִן:

21 Then *Yael* wife of *Chever* took a tent pin and grasped the mallet. When he was fast asleep from exhaustion, she approached him stealthily and drove the pin through his temple till it went down to the ground. Thus he died.

כא וַתִּקַּח יָעֵל אֵשֶׁת־חֶבֶר אֶת־יְתַד הָאֹהֶל וַתָּשֶׂם אֶת־הַמַּקֶּבֶת בְּיָדָהּ וַתָּבוֹא אֵלָיו בַּלָּאט וַתִּתְקַע אֶת־הַיָּתֵד בְּרַקָּתוֹ וַתִּצְנַח בָּאָרֶץ וְהוּא־נִרְדָּם וַיָּעַף וַיָּמֹת:

va-ti-KAKH ya-AYL AY-shet KHE-ver et y'-TAD ha-O-hel va-TA-sem et ha-ma-KE-vet b'-ya-DAH va-ta-VO ay-LAV ba-LAT va-tit-KA et ha-ya-TAYD b'-ra-ka-TO va-titz-NAKH ba-A-retz v'-HU nir-DAM va-YA-af va-ya-MOT

Orna Barbavai (b. 1962)

4:21 Then *Yael* wife of *Chever* took a tent pin and grasped the mallet *Yael* is not the only great woman to act as a warrior on behalf of the Nation of Israel. Today, women form an important part of the Israel Defense Forces, serving at its highest levels. In 2011, Orna Barbavai made history, overcoming her underprivileged upbringing to become the first woman in IDF history to reach the rank of *Aluf* (אלוף), 'Major General'. "I am proud to be the first woman to become a major general, and to be part of an organization in which equality is a central principle," Barbavai said. The mother of three retired from the IDF in 2014, but serves as an

Shoftim/Judges
Chapter 5

שופטים
פרק ה

22 Now *Barak* appeared in pursuit of Sisera. *Yael* went out to greet him and said, "Come, I will show you the man you are looking for." He went inside with her, and there Sisera was lying dead, with the pin in his temple.

כב וְהִנֵּה בָרָק רֹדֵף אֶת־סִיסְרָא וַתֵּצֵא יָעֵל לִקְרָאתוֹ וַתֹּאמֶר לוֹ לֵךְ וְאַרְאֶךָּ אֶת־הָאִישׁ אֲשֶׁר־אַתָּה מְבַקֵּשׁ וַיָּבֹא אֵלֶיהָ וְהִנֵּה סִיסְרָא נֹפֵל מֵת וְהַיָּתֵד בְּרַקָּתוֹ:

23 On that day *Hashem* subdued King Jabin of Canaan before the Israelites.

כג וַיַּכְנַע אֱלֹהִים בַּיּוֹם הַהוּא אֵת יָבִין מֶלֶךְ־כְּנָעַן לִפְנֵי בְּנֵי יִשְׂרָאֵל:

24 The hand of the Israelites bore harder and harder on King Jabin of Canaan, until they destroyed King Jabin of Canaan.

כד וַתֵּלֶךְ יַד בְּנֵי־יִשְׂרָאֵל הָלוֹךְ וְקָשָׁה עַל יָבִין מֶלֶךְ־כְּנָעַן עַד אֲשֶׁר הִכְרִיתוּ אֵת יָבִין מֶלֶךְ־כְּנָעַן:

5 1 On that day *Devora* and *Barak* son of Abinoam sang:

ה א וַתָּשַׁר דְּבוֹרָה וּבָרָק בֶּן־אֲבִינֹעַם בַּיּוֹם הַהוּא לֵאמֹר:

2 When locks go untrimmed in *Yisrael*, When people dedicate themselves – Bless *Hashem*!

ב בִּפְרֹעַ פְּרָעוֹת בְּיִשְׂרָאֵל בְּהִתְנַדֵּב עָם בָּרֲכוּ יְהוָה:

3 Hear, O kings! Give ear, O potentates! I will sing, will sing to *Hashem*, Will hymn *Hashem*, the God of *Yisrael*.

ג שִׁמְעוּ מְלָכִים הַאֲזִינוּ רֹזְנִים אָנֹכִי לַיהוָה אָנֹכִי אָשִׁירָה אֲזַמֵּר לַיהוָה אֱלֹהֵי יִשְׂרָאֵל:

4 *Hashem*, when You came forth from Seir, Advanced from the country of Edom, The earth trembled; The heavens dripped, Yea, the clouds dripped water,

ד יְהוָה בְּצֵאתְךָ מִשֵּׂעִיר בְּצַעְדְּךָ מִשְּׂדֵה אֱדוֹם אֶרֶץ רָעָשָׁה גַּם־שָׁמַיִם נָטָפוּ גַּם־עָבִים נָטְפוּ מָיִם:

5 The mountains quaked – Before *Hashem*, Him of Sinai, Before *Hashem*, God of *Yisrael*.

ה הָרִים נָזְלוּ מִפְּנֵי יְהוָה זֶה סִינַי מִפְּנֵי יְהוָה אֱלֹהֵי יִשְׂרָאֵל:

6 In the days of *Shamgar* son of Anath, In the days of *Yael*, caravans ceased, And wayfarers went By roundabout paths.

ו בִּימֵי שַׁמְגַּר בֶּן־עֲנָת בִּימֵי יָעֵל חָדְלוּ אֳרָחוֹת וְהֹלְכֵי נְתִיבוֹת יֵלְכוּ אֳרָחוֹת עֲקַלְקַלּוֹת:

7 Deliverance ceased, Ceased in *Yisrael*, Till you arose, O *Devora*, Arose, O mother, in *Yisrael*!

ז חָדְלוּ פְרָזוֹן בְּיִשְׂרָאֵל חָדֵלּוּ עַד שַׁקַּמְתִּי דְּבוֹרָה שַׁקַּמְתִּי אֵם בְּיִשְׂרָאֵל:

kha-d'-LU f'-ra-ZON b'-yis-ra-AYL kha-DAY-lu AD sha-KAM-tee d'-vo-RAH sha-KAM-tee AYM b'-yis-ra-AYL

8 When they chose new gods, Was there a fighter then in the gates? No shield or spear was seen Among forty thousand in *Yisrael*!

ח יִבְחַר אֱלֹהִים חֲדָשִׁים אָז לָחֶם שְׁעָרִים מָגֵן אִם־יֵרָאֶה וָרֹמַח בְּאַרְבָּעִים אֶלֶף בְּיִשְׂרָאֵל:

5:7 Deliverance ceased, ceased in *Yisrael*, till you arose, O *Devora* Though one way of translating *f'razon* (פרזון) is 'deliverance,' Rashi explains it as "open towns without walls." According to this understanding, *Devora* is saying that prior to her leadership, the Children of Israel had ceased living in small, scattered, non-walled communities, due to fear of attack. However, the Canaanites continued living in such places, as they were not afraid of the Israelites. The miraculous military victory against Sisera would change this reality. It is interesting to note that in Israel today Jews have also not been afraid to establish small communities in all parts of the land. Miracles of biblical proportions continue in our era as communities of all sizes grow and thrive throughout the Land of Israel.

פרזון

inspiration to countless Israeli young women who enlist in the IDF each year and who know they can reach the highest levels not only in the IDF but throughout Israeli society.

Shoftim/Judges
Chapter 5

שׁוֹפְטִים
פרק ה

9 My heart is with *Yisrael*'s leaders, With the dedicated of the people – Bless *Hashem*!

ט לִבִּי לְחוֹקְקֵי יִשְׂרָאֵל הַמִּתְנַדְּבִים בָּעָם בָּרְכוּ יְהֹוָה׃

10 You riders on tawny she-asses, You who sit on saddle rugs, And you wayfarers, declare it!

י רֹכְבֵי אֲתֹנוֹת צְחֹרוֹת יֹשְׁבֵי עַל־מִדִּין וְהֹלְכֵי עַל־דֶּרֶךְ שִׂיחוּ׃

11 Louder than the sound of archers, There among the watering places Let them chant the gracious acts of *Hashem*, His gracious deliverance of *Yisrael*. Then did the people of *Hashem* March down to the gates!

יא מִקּוֹל מְחַצְצִים בֵּין מַשְׁאַבִּים שָׁם יְתַנּוּ צִדְקוֹת יְהֹוָה צִדְקֹת פִּרְזֹנוֹ בְּיִשְׂרָאֵל אָז יָרְדוּ לַשְּׁעָרִים עַם־יְהֹוָה׃

12 Awake, awake, O *Devora*! Awake, awake, strike up the chant! Arise, O *Barak*; Take your captives, O son of Abinoam!

יב עוּרִי עוּרִי דְּבוֹרָה עוּרִי עוּרִי דַּבְּרִי־שִׁיר קוּם בָּרָק וּשֲׁבֵה שֶׁבְיְךָ בֶּן־אֲבִינֹעַם׃

13 Then was the remnant made victor over the mighty, *Hashem*'s people won my victory over the warriors.

יג אָז יְרַד שָׂרִיד לְאַדִּירִים עָם יְהֹוָה יְרַד־לִי בַּגִּבּוֹרִים׃

14 From *Efraim* came they whose roots are in Amalek; After you, your kin *Binyamin*; From Machir came down leaders, From *Zevulun* such as hold the marshal's staff.

יד מִנִּי אֶפְרַיִם שָׁרְשָׁם בַּעֲמָלֵק אַחֲרֶיךָ בִנְיָמִין בַּעֲמָמֶיךָ מִנִּי מָכִיר יָרְדוּ מְחֹקְקִים וּמִזְּבוּלֻן מֹשְׁכִים בְּשֵׁבֶט סֹפֵר׃

15 And *Yissachar*'s chiefs were with *Devora*; As *Barak*, so was *Yissachar* – Rushing after him into the valley. Among the clans of *Reuven* Were great decisions of heart.

טו וְשָׂרַי בְּיִשָּׂשכָר עִם־דְּבֹרָה וְיִשָּׂשכָר כֵּן בָּרָק בָּעֵמֶק שֻׁלַּח בְּרַגְלָיו בִּפְלַגּוֹת רְאוּבֵן גְּדֹלִים חִקְקֵי־לֵב׃

16 Why then did you stay among the sheepfolds And listen as they pipe for the flocks? Among the clans of *Reuven* Were great searchings of heart!

טז לָמָּה יָשַׁבְתָּ בֵּין הַמִּשְׁפְּתַיִם לִשְׁמֹעַ שְׁרִקוֹת עֲדָרִים לִפְלַגּוֹת רְאוּבֵן גְּדוֹלִים חִקְרֵי־לֵב׃

17 *Gilad* tarried beyond the *Yarden*; And *Dan* – why did he linger by the ships? *Asher* remained at the seacoast And tarried at his landings.

יז גִּלְעָד בְּעֵבֶר הַיַּרְדֵּן שָׁכֵן וְדָן לָמָּה יָגוּר אֳנִיּוֹת אָשֵׁר יָשַׁב לְחוֹף יַמִּים וְעַל מִפְרָצָיו יִשְׁכּוֹן׃

18 *Zevulun* is a people that mocked at death, *Naftali* – on the open heights.

יח זְבֻלוּן עַם חֵרֵף נַפְשׁוֹ לָמוּת וְנַפְתָּלִי עַל מְרוֹמֵי שָׂדֶה׃

19 Then the kings came, they fought: The kings of Canaan fought At Taanach, by Megiddo's waters – They got no spoil of silver.

יט בָּאוּ מְלָכִים נִלְחָמוּ אָז נִלְחֲמוּ מַלְכֵי כְנַעַן בְּתַעְנַךְ עַל־מֵי מְגִדּוֹ בֶּצַע כֶּסֶף לֹא לָקָחוּ׃

20 The stars fought from heaven, From their courses they fought against Sisera.

כ מִן־שָׁמַיִם נִלְחָמוּ הַכּוֹכָבִים מִמְּסִלּוֹתָם נִלְחֲמוּ עִם־סִיסְרָא׃

21 The torrent Kishon swept them away, The raging torrent, the torrent Kishon. March on, my soul, with courage!
NA-khal kee-SHON g'-ra-FAM NA-khal k'-du-MEEM NA-khal kee-SHON tid-r'-KHEE naf-SHEE OZ

כא נַחַל קִישׁוֹן גְּרָפָם נַחַל קְדוּמִים נַחַל קִישׁוֹן תִּדְרְכִי נַפְשִׁי עֹז׃

5:21 The torrent Kishon swept them away According to this verse, the Kishon river swept away Sisera's army after it was defeated by the Israelites. Moshe Dayan, an important IDF general, loved

Shoftim/Judges
Chapter 5

שופטים
פרק ה

22 Then the horses' hoofs pounded As headlong galloped the steeds.

כב אָז הָלְמוּ עִקְּבֵי־סוּס מִדַּהֲרוֹת דַּהֲרוֹת אַבִּירָיו:

23 "Curse Meroz!" said the angel of *Hashem*. "Bitterly curse its inhabitants, Because they came not to the aid of *Hashem*, To the aid of *Hashem* among the warriors."

כג אוֹרוּ מֵרוֹז אָמַר מַלְאַךְ יְהוָה אֹרוּ אָרוֹר יֹשְׁבֶיהָ כִּי לֹא־בָאוּ לְעֶזְרַת יְהוָה לְעֶזְרַת יְהוָה בַּגִּבּוֹרִים:

24 Most blessed of women be *Yael*, Wife of *Chever* the Kenite, Most blessed of women in tents.

כד תְּבֹרַךְ מִנָּשִׁים יָעֵל אֵשֶׁת חֶבֶר הַקֵּינִי מִנָּשִׁים בָּאֹהֶל תְּבֹרָךְ:

25 He asked for water, she offered milk; In a princely bowl she brought him curds.

כה מַיִם שָׁאַל חָלָב נָתָנָה בְּסֵפֶל אַדִּירִים הִקְרִיבָה חֶמְאָה:

26 Her [left] hand reached for the tent pin, Her right for the workmen's hammer. She struck Sisera, crushed his head, Smashed and pierced his temple.

כו יָדָהּ לַיָּתֵד תִּשְׁלַחְנָה וִימִינָהּ לְהַלְמוּת עֲמֵלִים וְהָלְמָה סִיסְרָא מָחֲקָה רֹאשׁוֹ וּמָחֲצָה וְחָלְפָה רַקָּתוֹ:

27 At her feet he sank, lay outstretched, At her feet he sank, lay still; Where he sank, there he lay – destroyed.

כז בֵּין רַגְלֶיהָ כָּרַע נָפַל שָׁכָב בֵּין רַגְלֶיהָ כָּרַע נָפָל בַּאֲשֶׁר כָּרַע שָׁם נָפַל שָׁדוּד:

28 Through the window peered Sisera's mother, Behind the lattice she whined: "Why is his chariot so long in coming? Why so late the clatter of his wheels?"

כח בְּעַד הַחַלּוֹן נִשְׁקְפָה וַתְּיַבֵּב אֵם סִיסְרָא בְּעַד הָאֶשְׁנָב מַדּוּעַ בֹּשֵׁשׁ רִכְבּוֹ לָבוֹא מַדּוּעַ אֶחֱרוּ פַּעֲמֵי מַרְכְּבוֹתָיו:

29 The wisest of her ladies give answer; She, too, replies to herself:

כט חַכְמוֹת שָׂרוֹתֶיהָ תַּעֲנֶינָּה אַף־הִיא תָּשִׁיב אֲמָרֶיהָ לָהּ:

30 "They must be dividing the spoil they have found: A damsel or two for each man, Spoil of dyed cloths for Sisera, Spoil of embroidered cloths, A couple of embroidered cloths round every neck as spoil."

ל הֲלֹא יִמְצְאוּ יְחַלְּקוּ שָׁלָל רַחַם רַחֲמָתַיִם לְרֹאשׁ גֶּבֶר שְׁלַל צְבָעִים לְסִיסְרָא שְׁלַל צְבָעִים רִקְמָה צֶבַע רִקְמָתַיִם לְצַוְּארֵי שָׁלָל:

31 So may all Your enemies perish, *Hashem*! But may His friends be as the sun rising in might! And the land was tranquil forty years.

לא כֵּן יֹאבְדוּ כָל־אוֹיְבֶיךָ יְהוָה וְאֹהֲבָיו כְּצֵאת הַשֶּׁמֶשׁ בִּגְבֻרָתוֹ וַתִּשְׁקֹט הָאָרֶץ אַרְבָּעִים שָׁנָה:

---

the Land of Israel not only as his homeland, but also because it is the land of the Bible. In his book, "Living with the Bible," Dayan wrote about the Kishon: "To one who was born in Israel, love of the homeland was not an abstraction. The Rose of Sharon and Mount *Carmel* were very real to me, as were the sweet-scented blossom and the hills whose paths I climbed. Yet this was not enough. I was not content only with the Israel I could see and touch. I also longed for the Israel of antiquity, the Israel of the 'timeless verses' and the 'biblical names', and I wanted to give tangibility to that too. I wished to see not only the river Kishon marking off the fields of Nahalal from those of neighboring Kfar Yehoshua; I wished also to visualize the biblical Kishon sweeping away the Canaanite chariot forces of Sisera."

Moshe Dayan
(1915–1981)

Shoftim/Judges
Chapter 6

שופטים
פרק ו

6 1 Then the Israelites did what was offensive to *Hashem*, and *Hashem* delivered them into the hands of the Midianites for seven years.

א וַיַּעֲשׂוּ בְנֵי־יִשְׂרָאֵל הָרַע בְּעֵינֵי יְהֹוָה וַיִּתְּנֵם יְהֹוָה בְּיַד־מִדְיָן שֶׁבַע שָׁנִים:

2 The hand of the Midianites prevailed over *Yisrael*; and because of Midian, the Israelites provided themselves with refuges in the caves and strongholds of the mountains.

ב וַתָּעׇז יַד־מִדְיָן עַל־יִשְׂרָאֵל מִפְּנֵי מִדְיָן עָשׂוּ לָהֶם ׀ בְּנֵי יִשְׂרָאֵל אֶת־הַמִּנְהָרוֹת אֲשֶׁר בֶּהָרִים וְאֶת־הַמְּעָרוֹת וְאֶת־הַמְּצָדוֹת:

3 After the Israelites had done their sowing, Midian, Amalek, and the Kedemites would come up and raid them;

ג וְהָיָה אִם־זָרַע יִשְׂרָאֵל וְעָלָה מִדְיָן וַעֲמָלֵק וּבְנֵי־קֶדֶם וְעָלוּ עָלָיו:

4 they would attack them, destroy the produce of the land all the way to *Azza*, and leave no means of sustenance in *Yisrael*, not a sheep or an ox or an ass.

ד וַיַּחֲנוּ עֲלֵיהֶם וַיַּשְׁחִיתוּ אֶת־יְבוּל הָאָרֶץ עַד־בּוֹאֲךָ עַזָּה וְלֹא־יַשְׁאִירוּ מִחְיָה בְּיִשְׂרָאֵל וְשֶׂה וָשׁוֹר וַחֲמוֹר:

5 For they would come up with their livestock and their tents, swarming as thick as locusts; they and their camels were innumerable. Thus they would invade the land and ravage it.

ה כִּי הֵם וּמִקְנֵיהֶם יַעֲלוּ וְאׇהֳלֵיהֶם יבאו [וּבָאוּ] כְדֵי־אַרְבֶּה לָרֹב וְלָהֶם וְלִגְמַלֵּיהֶם אֵין מִסְפָּר וַיָּבֹאוּ בָאָרֶץ לְשַׁחֲתָהּ:

6 *Yisrael* was reduced to utter misery by the Midianites, and the Israelites cried out to *Hashem*.

ו וַיִּדַּל יִשְׂרָאֵל מְאֹד מִפְּנֵי מִדְיָן וַיִּזְעֲקוּ בְנֵי־יִשְׂרָאֵל אֶל־יְהֹוָה:

7 When the Israelites cried to *Hashem* on account of Midian,

ז וַיְהִי כִּי־זָעֲקוּ בְנֵי־יִשְׂרָאֵל אֶל־יְהֹוָה עַל אֹדוֹת מִדְיָן:

8 *Hashem* sent a *Navi* to the Israelites who said to them, "Thus said *Hashem*, the God of *Yisrael*: I brought you up out of Egypt and freed you from the house of bondage.

ח וַיִּשְׁלַח יְהֹוָה אִישׁ נָבִיא אֶל־בְּנֵי יִשְׂרָאֵל וַיֹּאמֶר לָהֶם כֹּה־אָמַר יְהֹוָה ׀ אֱלֹהֵי יִשְׂרָאֵל אָנֹכִי הֶעֱלֵיתִי אֶתְכֶם מִמִּצְרַיִם וָאֹצִיא אֶתְכֶם מִבֵּית עֲבָדִים:

9 I rescued you from the Egyptians and from all your oppressors; I drove them out before you, and gave you their land.

ט וָאַצִּל אֶתְכֶם מִיַּד מִצְרַיִם וּמִיַּד כׇּל־לֹחֲצֵיכֶם וָאֲגָרֵשׁ אוֹתָם מִפְּנֵיכֶם וָאֶתְּנָה לָכֶם אֶת־אַרְצָם:

va-a-TZIL et-KHEM mi-YAD mitz-RA-yim u-mi-YAD kol lo-kha-tzay-KHEM va-a-ga-RAYSH o-TAM mi-p'-nay-KHEM va-e-t'-NAH la-KHEM et ar-TZAM

10 And I said to you, 'I *Hashem* am your God. You must not worship the gods of the Amorites in whose land you dwell.' But you did not obey Me."

י וָאֹמְרָה לָכֶם אֲנִי יְהֹוָה אֱלֹהֵיכֶם לֹא תִירְאוּ אֶת־אֱלֹהֵי הָאֱמֹרִי אֲשֶׁר אַתֶּם יוֹשְׁבִים בְּאַרְצָם וְלֹא שְׁמַעְתֶּם בְּקוֹלִי:

Rabbi Abraham Isaac Kook (1865–1935)

6:9 I rescued you from the Egyptians When the Children of Israel cry out to *Hashem* due to the Midianite persecution, God sends a prophet to remind them that He is the one who brought them out from Egyptian oppression into *Eretz Yisrael*. Rabbi Abraham Isaac Kook, the first *Ashkenazi* chief rabbi of Palestine under the British Mandate and founder of the Mercaz Harav Yeshiva in the early twentieth century, teaches that the exodus was not simply a historical event. It was the beginning of a redemptive process which continues throughout Jewish history. Thus, all future redemptions, including *Gidon*'s defeat of Midian and including the State of Israel's defeat of its enemies in our generation, are all part of the ongoing redemption that will culminate with the coming of *Mashiach* and the rebuilding of the *Beit Hamikdash* in *Yerushalayim*.

Shoftim/Judges
Chapter 6

11 An angel of *Hashem* came and sat under the terebinth at Ophrah, which belonged to *Yoash* the Abiezrite. His son *Gidon* was then beating out wheat inside a winepress in order to keep it safe from the Midianites.

12 The angel of *Hashem* appeared to him and said to him, "*Hashem* is with you, valiant warrior!"

13 *Gidon* said to him, "Please, my lord, if *Hashem* is with us, why has all this befallen us? Where are all His wondrous deeds about which our fathers told us, saying, 'Truly *Hashem* brought us up from Egypt'? Now *Hashem* has abandoned us and delivered us into the hands of Midian!"

14 *Hashem* turned to him and said, "Go in this strength of yours and deliver *Yisrael* from the Midianites. I herewith make you My messenger."

15 He said to Him, "Please, my lord, how can I deliver *Yisrael*? Why, my clan is the humblest in *Menashe*, and I am the youngest in my father's household."

16 *Hashem* replied, "I will be with you, and you shall defeat Midian to a man."

17 And he said to Him, "If I have gained Your favor, give me a sign that it is You who are speaking to me:

18 do not leave this place until I come back to You and bring out my offering and place it before You." And He answered, "I will stay until you return."

19 So *Gidon* went in and prepared a kid, and [baked] unleavened bread from an ephah of flour. He put the meat in a basket and poured the broth into a pot, and he brought them out to Him under the terebinth. As he presented them,

20 the angel of *Hashem* said to him, "Take the meat and the unleavened bread, put them on yonder rock, and spill out the broth." He did so.

21 The angel of *Hashem* held out the staff that he carried, and touched the meat and the unleavened bread with its tip. A fire sprang up from the rock and consumed the meat and the unleavened bread. And the angel of *Hashem* vanished from his sight.

22 Then *Gidon* realized that it was an angel of *Hashem*; and *Gidon* said, "Alas, O *Hashem*! For I have seen an angel of *Hashem* face to face."

23 But *Hashem* said to him, "All is well; have no fear, you shall not die."

שופטים
פרק ו

יא וַיָּבֹא מַלְאַךְ יְהֹוָה וַיֵּשֶׁב תַּחַת הָאֵלָה אֲשֶׁר בְּעָפְרָה אֲשֶׁר לְיוֹאָשׁ אֲבִי הָעֶזְרִי וְגִדְעוֹן בְּנוֹ חֹבֵט חִטִּים בַּגַּת לְהָנִיס מִפְּנֵי מִדְיָן:

יב וַיֵּרָא אֵלָיו מַלְאַךְ יְהֹוָה וַיֹּאמֶר אֵלָיו יְהֹוָה עִמְּךָ גִּבּוֹר הֶחָיִל:

יג וַיֹּאמֶר אֵלָיו גִּדְעוֹן בִּי אֲדֹנִי וְיֵשׁ יְהֹוָה עִמָּנוּ וְלָמָּה מְצָאַתְנוּ כָּל־זֹאת וְאַיֵּה כָל־נִפְלְאֹתָיו אֲשֶׁר סִפְּרוּ־לָנוּ אֲבוֹתֵינוּ לֵאמֹר הֲלֹא מִמִּצְרַיִם הֶעֱלָנוּ יְהֹוָה וְעַתָּה נְטָשָׁנוּ יְהֹוָה וַיִּתְּנֵנוּ בְּכַף־מִדְיָן:

יד וַיִּפֶן אֵלָיו יְהֹוָה וַיֹּאמֶר לֵךְ בְּכֹחֲךָ זֶה וְהוֹשַׁעְתָּ אֶת־יִשְׂרָאֵל מִכַּף מִדְיָן הֲלֹא שְׁלַחְתִּיךָ:

טו וַיֹּאמֶר אֵלָיו בִּי אֲדֹנָי בַּמָּה אוֹשִׁיעַ אֶת־יִשְׂרָאֵל הִנֵּה אַלְפִּי הַדַּל בִּמְנַשֶּׁה וְאָנֹכִי הַצָּעִיר בְּבֵית אָבִי:

טז וַיֹּאמֶר אֵלָיו יְהֹוָה כִּי אֶהְיֶה עִמָּךְ וְהִכִּיתָ אֶת־מִדְיָן כְּאִישׁ אֶחָד:

יז וַיֹּאמֶר אֵלָיו אִם־נָא מָצָאתִי חֵן בְּעֵינֶיךָ וְעָשִׂיתָ לִּי אוֹת שָׁאַתָּה מְדַבֵּר עִמִּי:

יח אַל־נָא תָמֻשׁ מִזֶּה עַד־בֹּאִי אֵלֶיךָ וְהֹצֵאתִי אֶת־מִנְחָתִי וְהִנַּחְתִּי לְפָנֶיךָ וַיֹּאמַר אָנֹכִי אֵשֵׁב עַד שׁוּבֶךָ:

יט וְגִדְעוֹן בָּא וַיַּעַשׂ גְּדִי־עִזִּים וְאֵיפַת־קֶמַח מַצּוֹת הַבָּשָׂר שָׂם בַּסַּל וְהַמָּרַק שָׂם בַּפָּרוּר וַיּוֹצֵא אֵלָיו אֶל־תַּחַת הָאֵלָה וַיַּגַּשׁ:

כ וַיֹּאמֶר אֵלָיו מַלְאַךְ הָאֱלֹהִים קַח אֶת־הַבָּשָׂר וְאֶת־הַמַּצּוֹת וְהַנַּח אֶל־הַסֶּלַע הַלָּז וְאֶת־הַמָּרַק שְׁפוֹךְ וַיַּעַשׂ כֵּן:

כא וַיִּשְׁלַח מַלְאַךְ יְהֹוָה אֶת־קְצֵה הַמִּשְׁעֶנֶת אֲשֶׁר בְּיָדוֹ וַיִּגַּע בַּבָּשָׂר וּבַמַּצּוֹת וַתַּעַל הָאֵשׁ מִן־הַצּוּר וַתֹּאכַל אֶת־הַבָּשָׂר וְאֶת־הַמַּצּוֹת וּמַלְאַךְ יְהֹוָה הָלַךְ מֵעֵינָיו:

כב וַיַּרְא גִּדְעוֹן כִּי־מַלְאַךְ יְהֹוָה הוּא וַיֹּאמֶר גִּדְעוֹן אֲהָהּ אֲדֹנָי יֱהֹוִה כִּי־עַל־כֵּן רָאִיתִי מַלְאַךְ יְהֹוָה פָּנִים אֶל־פָּנִים:

כג וַיֹּאמֶר לוֹ יְהֹוָה שָׁלוֹם לְךָ אַל־תִּירָא לֹא תָמוּת:

Shoftim/Judges
Chapter 6

24 So *Gidon* built there a *Mizbayach* to *Hashem* and called it Adonaishalom. To this day it stands in Ophrah of the Abiezrites.

25 That night *Hashem* said to him: "Take the young bull belonging to your father and another bull seven years old; pull down the altar of Baal which belongs to your father, and cut down the sacred post which is beside it.

26 Then build a *Mizbayach* to *Hashem* your God, on the level ground on top of this stronghold. Take the other bull and offer it as a burnt offering, using the wood of the sacred post that you have cut down."

27 So *Gidon* took ten of his servants and did as *Hashem* had told him; but as he was afraid to do it by day, on account of his father's household and the townspeople, he did it by night.

28 Early the next morning, the townspeople found that the altar of Baal had been torn down and the sacred post beside it had been cut down, and that the second bull had been offered on the newly built *Mizbayach*.

29 They said to one another, "Who did this thing?" Upon inquiry and investigation, they were told, "*Gidon* son of *Yoash* did this thing!"

30 The townspeople said to *Yoash*, "Bring out your son, for he must die: he has torn down the altar of Baal and cut down the sacred post beside it!"

31 But *Yoash* said to all who had risen against him, "Do you have to contend for Baal? Do you have to vindicate him? Whoever fights his battles shall be dead by morning! If he is a god, let him fight his own battles, since it is his altar that has been torn down!"

32 That day they named him *Yerubaal*, meaning "Let Baal contend with him, since he tore down his altar."

33 All Midian, Amalek, and the Kedemites joined forces; they crossed over and encamped in the Valley of Yizrael.

34 The spirit of *Hashem* enveloped *Gidon*; he sounded the *shofar*, and the Abiezrites rallied behind him.

שופטים
פרק ו

כד וַיִּבֶן שָׁם גִּדְעוֹן מִזְבֵּחַ לַיהוָה וַיִּקְרָא־לוֹ יְהוָה שָׁלוֹם עַד הַיּוֹם הַזֶּה עוֹדֶנּוּ בְּעָפְרָת אֲבִי הָעֶזְרִי:

כה וַיְהִי בַּלַּיְלָה הַהוּא וַיֹּאמֶר לוֹ יְהוָה קַח אֶת־פַּר־הַשּׁוֹר אֲשֶׁר לְאָבִיךָ וּפַר הַשֵּׁנִי שֶׁבַע שָׁנִים וְהָרַסְתָּ אֶת־מִזְבַּח הַבַּעַל אֲשֶׁר לְאָבִיךָ וְאֶת־הָאֲשֵׁרָה אֲשֶׁר־עָלָיו תִּכְרֹת:

כו וּבָנִיתָ מִזְבֵּחַ לַיהוָה אֱלֹהֶיךָ עַל רֹאשׁ הַמָּעוֹז הַזֶּה בַּמַּעֲרָכָה וְלָקַחְתָּ אֶת־הַפָּר הַשֵּׁנִי וְהַעֲלִיתָ עוֹלָה בַּעֲצֵי הָאֲשֵׁרָה אֲשֶׁר תִּכְרֹת:

כז וַיִּקַּח גִּדְעוֹן עֲשָׂרָה אֲנָשִׁים מֵעֲבָדָיו וַיַּעַשׂ כַּאֲשֶׁר דִּבֶּר אֵלָיו יְהוָה וַיְהִי כַּאֲשֶׁר יָרֵא אֶת־בֵּית אָבִיו וְאֶת־אַנְשֵׁי הָעִיר מֵעֲשׂוֹת יוֹמָם וַיַּעַשׂ לָיְלָה:

כח וַיַּשְׁכִּימוּ אַנְשֵׁי הָעִיר בַּבֹּקֶר וְהִנֵּה נֻתַּץ מִזְבַּח הַבַּעַל וְהָאֲשֵׁרָה אֲשֶׁר־עָלָיו כֹּרָתָה וְאֵת הַפָּר הַשֵּׁנִי הֹעֲלָה עַל־הַמִּזְבֵּחַ הַבָּנוּי:

כט וַיֹּאמְרוּ אִישׁ אֶל־רֵעֵהוּ מִי עָשָׂה הַדָּבָר הַזֶּה וַיִּדְרְשׁוּ וַיְבַקְשׁוּ וַיֹּאמְרוּ גִּדְעוֹן בֶּן־יוֹאָשׁ עָשָׂה הַדָּבָר הַזֶּה:

ל וַיֹּאמְרוּ אַנְשֵׁי הָעִיר אֶל־יוֹאָשׁ הוֹצֵא אֶת־בִּנְךָ וְיָמֹת כִּי נָתַץ אֶת־מִזְבַּח הַבַּעַל וְכִי כָרַת הָאֲשֵׁרָה אֲשֶׁר־עָלָיו:

לא וַיֹּאמֶר יוֹאָשׁ לְכֹל אֲשֶׁר־עָמְדוּ עָלָיו הַאַתֶּם תְּרִיבוּן לַבַּעַל אִם־אַתֶּם תּוֹשִׁיעוּן אוֹתוֹ אֲשֶׁר יָרִיב לוֹ יוּמַת עַד־הַבֹּקֶר אִם־אֱלֹהִים הוּא יָרֶב לוֹ כִּי נָתַץ אֶת־מִזְבְּחוֹ:

לב וַיִּקְרָא־לוֹ בַיּוֹם־הַהוּא יְרֻבַּעַל לֵאמֹר יָרֶב בּוֹ הַבַּעַל כִּי נָתַץ אֶת־מִזְבְּחוֹ:

לג וְכָל־מִדְיָן וַעֲמָלֵק וּבְנֵי־קֶדֶם נֶאֶסְפוּ יַחְדָּו וַיַּעַבְרוּ וַיַּחֲנוּ בְּעֵמֶק יִזְרְעֶאל:

לד וְרוּחַ יְהוָה לָבְשָׁה אֶת־גִּדְעוֹן וַיִּתְקַע בַּשּׁוֹפָר וַיִּזָּעֵק אֲבִיעֶזֶר אַחֲרָיו:

Shoftim / Judges
Chapter 7

35 And he sent messengers throughout *Menashe*, and they too rallied behind him. He then sent messengers through *Asher*, *Zevulun*, and *Naftali*, and they came up to meet the Manassites.

36 And *Gidon* said to *Hashem*, "If You really intend to deliver *Yisrael* through me as You have said –

37 here I place a fleece of wool on the threshing floor. If dew falls only on the fleece and all the ground remains dry, I shall know that You will deliver *Yisrael* through me, as You have said."

38 And that is what happened. Early the next day, he squeezed the fleece and wrung out the dew from the fleece, a bowlful of water.

39 Then *Gidon* said to *Hashem*, "Do not be angry with me if I speak just once more. Let me make just one more test with the fleece: let the fleece alone be dry, while there is dew all over the ground."

40 *Hashem* did so that night: only the fleece was dry, while there was dew all over the ground.

7 1 Early next day, *Yerubaal* – that is, *Gidon* – and all the troops with him encamped above En-harod, while the camp of Midian was in the plain to the north of him, at Gibeath-moreh.

2 *Hashem* said to *Gidon*, "You have too many troops with you for Me to deliver Midian into their hands; *Yisrael* might claim for themselves the glory due to Me, thinking, 'Our own hand has brought us victory.'

3 Therefore, announce to the men, 'Let anybody who is timid and fearful turn back, as a bird flies from Mount *Gilad*.'" Thereupon, 22,000 of the troops turned back and 10,000 remained.

4 "There are still too many troops," *Hashem* said to *Gidon*. "Take them down to the water and I will sift them for you there. Anyone of whom I tell you, 'This one is to go with you,' that one shall go with you; and anyone of whom I tell you, 'This one is not to go with you,' that one shall not go."

שופטים
פרק ז

לה וּמַלְאָכִים שָׁלַח בְּכָל־מְנַשֶּׁה וַיִּזָּעֵק גַּם־הוּא אַחֲרָיו וּמַלְאָכִים שָׁלַח בְּאָשֵׁר וּבִזְבֻלוּן וּבְנַפְתָּלִי וַיַּעֲלוּ לִקְרָאתָם:

לו וַיֹּאמֶר גִּדְעוֹן אֶל־הָאֱלֹהִים אִם־יֶשְׁךָ מוֹשִׁיעַ בְּיָדִי אֶת־יִשְׂרָאֵל כַּאֲשֶׁר דִּבַּרְתָּ:

לז הִנֵּה אָנֹכִי מַצִּיג אֶת־גִּזַּת הַצֶּמֶר בַּגֹּרֶן אִם טַל יִהְיֶה עַל־הַגִּזָּה לְבַדָּהּ וְעַל־כָּל־הָאָרֶץ חֹרֶב וְיָדַעְתִּי כִּי־תוֹשִׁיעַ בְּיָדִי אֶת־יִשְׂרָאֵל כַּאֲשֶׁר דִּבַּרְתָּ:

לח וַיְהִי־כֵן וַיַּשְׁכֵּם מִמָּחֳרָת וַיָּזַר אֶת־הַגִּזָּה וַיִּמֶץ טַל מִן־הַגִּזָּה מְלוֹא הַסֵּפֶל מָיִם:

לט וַיֹּאמֶר גִּדְעוֹן אֶל־הָאֱלֹהִים אַל־יִחַר אַפְּךָ בִּי וַאֲדַבְּרָה אַךְ הַפָּעַם אֲנַסֶּה נָּא־רַק־הַפַּעַם בַּגִּזָּה יְהִי־נָא חֹרֶב אֶל־הַגִּזָּה לְבַדָּהּ וְעַל־כָּל־הָאָרֶץ יִהְיֶה־טָּל:

מ וַיַּעַשׂ אֱלֹהִים כֵּן בַּלַּיְלָה הַהוּא וַיְהִי־חֹרֶב אֶל־הַגִּזָּה לְבַדָּהּ וְעַל־כָּל־הָאָרֶץ הָיָה טָל:

ז א וַיַּשְׁכֵּם יְרֻבַּעַל הוּא גִדְעוֹן וְכָל־הָעָם אֲשֶׁר אִתּוֹ וַיַּחֲנוּ עַל־עֵין חֲרֹד וּמַחֲנֵה מִדְיָן הָיָה־לוֹ מִצָּפוֹן מִגִּבְעַת הַמּוֹרֶה בָּעֵמֶק:

ב וַיֹּאמֶר יְהוָה אֶל־גִּדְעוֹן רַב הָעָם אֲשֶׁר אִתָּךְ מִתִּתִּי אֶת־מִדְיָן בְּיָדָם פֶּן־יִתְפָּאֵר עָלַי יִשְׂרָאֵל לֵאמֹר יָדִי הוֹשִׁיעָה לִּי:

ג וְעַתָּה קְרָא נָא בְּאָזְנֵי הָעָם לֵאמֹר מִי־יָרֵא וְחָרֵד יָשֹׁב וְיִצְפֹּר מֵהַר הַגִּלְעָד וַיָּשָׁב מִן־הָעָם עֶשְׂרִים וּשְׁנַיִם אֶלֶף וַעֲשֶׂרֶת אֲלָפִים נִשְׁאָרוּ:

ד וַיֹּאמֶר יְהוָה אֶל־גִּדְעוֹן עוֹד הָעָם רָב הוֹרֵד אוֹתָם אֶל־הַמַּיִם וְאֶצְרְפֶנּוּ לְךָ שָׁם וְהָיָה אֲשֶׁר אֹמַר אֵלֶיךָ זֶה יֵלֵךְ אִתָּךְ הוּא יֵלֵךְ אִתָּךְ וְכֹל אֲשֶׁר־אֹמַר אֵלֶיךָ זֶה לֹא־יֵלֵךְ עִמָּךְ הוּא לֹא יֵלֵךְ:

Shoftim/Judges
Chapter 7

שופטים
פרק ז

5 So he took the troops down to the water. Then *Hashem* said to *Gidon*, "Set apart all those who lap up the water with their tongues like dogs from all those who get down on their knees to drink."

ה וַיּוֹרֶד אֶת־הָעָם אֶל־הַמָּיִם וַיֹּאמֶר יְהוָה אֶל־גִּדְעוֹן כֹּל אֲשֶׁר־יָלֹק בִּלְשׁוֹנוֹ מִן־הַמַּיִם כַּאֲשֶׁר יָלֹק הַכֶּלֶב תַּצִּיג אוֹתוֹ לְבָד וְכֹל אֲשֶׁר־יִכְרַע עַל־בִּרְכָּיו לִשְׁתּוֹת:

va-YO-red et ha-AM el ha-MA-yim va-YO-mer a-do-NAI el gid-ON KOL a-sher ya-LOK bil-sho-NO min ha-MA-yim ka-a-SHER ya-LOK ha-KE-lev ta-TZEEG o-TO l'-VAD v'-KHOL a-sher yikh-RA al bir-KAV lish-TOT

6 Now those who "lapped" the water into their mouths by hand numbered three hundred; all the rest of the troops got down on their knees to drink.

ו וַיְהִי מִסְפַּר הַמְלַקְקִים בְּיָדָם אֶל־פִּיהֶם שְׁלֹשׁ מֵאוֹת אִישׁ וְכֹל יֶתֶר הָעָם כָּרְעוּ עַל־בִּרְכֵיהֶם לִשְׁתּוֹת מָיִם:

7 Then *Hashem* said to *Gidon*, "I will deliver you and I will put Midian into your hands through the three hundred 'lappers'; let the rest of the troops go home."

ז וַיֹּאמֶר יְהוָה אֶל־גִּדְעוֹן בִּשְׁלֹשׁ מֵאוֹת הָאִישׁ הַמְלַקְקִים אוֹשִׁיעַ אֶתְכֶם וְנָתַתִּי אֶת־מִדְיָן בְּיָדֶךָ וְכָל־הָעָם יֵלְכוּ אִישׁ לִמְקֹמוֹ:

8 So [the lappers] took the provisions and *shofarot* that the other men had with them, and he sent the rest of the men of *Yisrael* back to their homes, retaining only the three hundred men. The Midianite camp was below him, in the plain.

ח וַיִּקְחוּ אֶת־צֵדָה הָעָם בְּיָדָם וְאֵת שׁוֹפְרֹתֵיהֶם וְאֵת כָּל־אִישׁ יִשְׂרָאֵל שִׁלַּח אִישׁ לְאֹהָלָיו וּבִשְׁלֹשׁ־מֵאוֹת הָאִישׁ הֶחֱזִיק וּמַחֲנֵה מִדְיָן הָיָה לוֹ מִתַּחַת בָּעֵמֶק:

9 That night *Hashem* said to him, "Come, attack the camp, for I have delivered it into your hands.

ט וַיְהִי בַּלַּיְלָה הַהוּא וַיֹּאמֶר אֵלָיו יְהוָה קוּם רֵד בַּמַּחֲנֶה כִּי נְתַתִּיו בְּיָדֶךָ:

10 And if you are afraid to attack, first go down to the camp with your attendant Purah

י וְאִם־יָרֵא אַתָּה לָרֶדֶת רֵד אַתָּה וּפֻרָה נַעַרְךָ אֶל־הַמַּחֲנֶה:

11 and listen to what they say; after that you will have the courage to attack the camp." So he went down with his attendant Purah to the outposts of the warriors who were in the camp.

יא וְשָׁמַעְתָּ מַה־יְדַבֵּרוּ וְאַחַר תֶּחֱזַקְנָה יָדֶיךָ וְיָרַדְתָּ בַּמַּחֲנֶה וַיֵּרֶד הוּא וּפֻרָה נַעֲרוֹ אֶל־קְצֵה הַחֲמֻשִׁים אֲשֶׁר בַּמַּחֲנֶה:

12 Now Midian, Amalek, and all the Kedemites were spread over the plain, as thick as locusts; and their camels were countless, as numerous as the sands on the seashore.

יב וּמִדְיָן וַעֲמָלֵק וְכָל־בְּנֵי־קֶדֶם נֹפְלִים בָּעֵמֶק כָּאַרְבֶּה לָרֹב וְלִגְמַלֵּיהֶם אֵין מִסְפָּר כַּחוֹל שֶׁעַל־שְׂפַת הַיָּם לָרֹב:

13 *Gidon* came there just as one man was narrating a dream to another. "Listen," he was saying, "I had this dream: There was a commotion – a loaf of barley bread was whirling through the Midianite camp. It came to a tent and struck it, and it fell; it turned it upside down, and the tent collapsed."

יג וַיָּבֹא גִדְעוֹן וְהִנֵּה־אִישׁ מְסַפֵּר לְרֵעֵהוּ חֲלוֹם וַיֹּאמֶר הִנֵּה חֲלוֹם חָלַמְתִּי וְהִנֵּה צְלִיל [צְלוּל] לֶחֶם שְׂעֹרִים מִתְהַפֵּךְ בְּמַחֲנֵה מִדְיָן וַיָּבֹא עַד־הָאֹהֶל וַיַּכֵּהוּ וַיִּפֹּל וַיַּהַפְכֵהוּ לְמַעְלָה וְנָפַל הָאֹהֶל:

7:5 Set apart all those who lap up the water with their tongues For it to be clear to all that the victory of the Israelites would be a miraculous one, *Hashem* orders *Gidon* to reduce the size of his army. He tells *Gidon* to send home all those who kneel down to drink water prior to the battle against Midian. *Rashi* says that the fact that they kneeled is proof that they had earlier knelt in worship of idols. *Eretz Yisrael* cannot tolerate idolatry (see Deuteronomy 29:24–27). Therefore, those soldiers who have previously engaged in such worship are the ones to be removed from this battle for control of the land.

14 To this the other responded, "That can only mean
the sword of the Israelite *Gidon* son of *Yoash*.
Hashem is delivering Midian and the entire camp
into his hands."

יד וַיַּעַן רֵעֵהוּ וַיֹּאמֶר אֵין זֹאת בִּלְתִּי
אִם־חֶרֶב גִּדְעוֹן בֶּן־יוֹאָשׁ אִישׁ יִשְׂרָאֵל
נָתַן הָאֱלֹהִים בְּיָדוֹ אֶת־מִדְיָן וְאֶת־כָּל־
הַמַּחֲנֶה׃

15 When *Gidon* heard the dream told and interpreted,
he bowed low. Returning to the camp of *Yisrael*,
he shouted, "Come on! *Hashem* has delivered the
Midianite camp into your hands!"

טו וַיְהִי כִשְׁמֹעַ גִּדְעוֹן אֶת־מִסְפַּר הַחֲלוֹם
וְאֶת־שִׁבְרוֹ וַיִּשְׁתָּחוּ וַיָּשָׁב אֶל־מַחֲנֵה
יִשְׂרָאֵל וַיֹּאמֶר קוּמוּ כִּי־נָתַן יְהֹוָה
בְּיֶדְכֶם אֶת־מַחֲנֵה מִדְיָן׃

16 He divided the three hundred men into three
columns and equipped every man with a *shofar* and
an empty jar, with a torch in each jar.

טז וַיַּחַץ אֶת־שְׁלֹשׁ־מֵאוֹת הָאִישׁ שְׁלֹשָׁה
רָאשִׁים וַיִּתֵּן שׁוֹפָרוֹת בְּיַד־כֻּלָּם וְכַדִּים
רֵקִים וְלַפִּדִים בְּתוֹךְ הַכַּדִּים׃

17 "Watch me," he said, "and do the same. When I get
to the outposts of the camp, do exactly as I do.

יז וַיֹּאמֶר אֲלֵיהֶם מִמֶּנִּי תִרְאוּ וְכֵן תַּעֲשׂוּ
וְהִנֵּה אָנֹכִי בָא בִּקְצֵה הַמַּחֲנֶה וְהָיָה
כַאֲשֶׁר־אֶעֱשֶׂה כֵּן תַּעֲשׂוּן׃

18 When I and all those with me blow our *shofarot*,
you too, all around the camp, will blow your
shofarot and shout, 'For *Hashem* and for *Gidon*!'"

יח וְתָקַעְתִּי בַּשּׁוֹפָר אָנֹכִי וְכָל־אֲשֶׁר אִתִּי
וּתְקַעְתֶּם בַּשּׁוֹפָרוֹת גַּם־אַתֶּם סְבִיבוֹת
כָּל־הַמַּחֲנֶה וַאֲמַרְתֶּם לַיהֹוָה וּלְגִדְעוֹן׃

19 *Gidon* and the hundred men with him arrived at
the outposts of the camp, at the beginning of the
middle watch, just after the sentries were posted.
They sounded the *shofarot* and smashed the jars
that they had with them,

יט וַיָּבֹא גִדְעוֹן וּמֵאָה־אִישׁ אֲשֶׁר־אִתּוֹ
בִּקְצֵה הַמַּחֲנֶה רֹאשׁ הָאַשְׁמֹרֶת
הַתִּיכוֹנָה אַךְ הָקֵם הֵקִימוּ אֶת־
הַשֹּׁמְרִים וַיִּתְקְעוּ בַּשּׁוֹפָרוֹת וְנָפוֹץ
הַכַּדִּים אֲשֶׁר בְּיָדָם׃

20 and the three columns blew their *shofarot* and broke
their jars. Holding the torches in their left hands and
the *shofarot* for blowing in their right hands, they
shouted, "A sword for *Hashem* and for *Gidon*!"

כ וַיִּתְקְעוּ שְׁלֹשֶׁת הָרָאשִׁים בַּשּׁוֹפָרוֹת
וַיִּשְׁבְּרוּ הַכַּדִּים וַיַּחֲזִיקוּ בְיַד־שְׂמֹאולָם
בַּלַּפִּדִים וּבְיַד־יְמִינָם הַשּׁוֹפָרוֹת לִתְקוֹעַ
וַיִּקְרְאוּ חֶרֶב לַיהֹוָה וּלְגִדְעוֹן׃

21 They remained standing where they were,
surrounding the camp; but the entire camp ran
about yelling, and took to flight.

כא וַיַּעַמְדוּ אִישׁ תַּחְתָּיו סָבִיב לַמַּחֲנֶה וַיָּרׇץ
כׇּל־הַמַּחֲנֶה וַיָּרִיעוּ ויניסו [וַיָּנוּסוּ׃]

22 For when the three hundred *shofarot* were sounded,
Hashem turned every man's sword against his
fellow, throughout the camp, and the entire host
fled as far as Beth-shittah and on to Zererah – as far
as the outskirts of Abel-meholah near Tabbath.

כב וַיִּתְקְעוּ שְׁלֹשׁ־מֵאוֹת הַשּׁוֹפָרוֹת וַיָּשֶׂם
יְהֹוָה אֵת חֶרֶב אִישׁ בְּרֵעֵהוּ וּבְכׇל־
הַמַּחֲנֶה וַיָּנׇס הַמַּחֲנֶה עַד־בֵּית הַשִּׁטָּה
צְרֵרָתָה עַד שְׂפַת־אָבֵל מְחוֹלָה עַל־
טַבָּת׃

23 And now the men of *Yisrael* from *Naftali* and *Asher*
and from all of *Menashe* rallied for the pursuit of
the Midianites.

כג וַיִּצָּעֵק אִישׁ־יִשְׂרָאֵל מִנַּפְתָּלִי וּמִן־אָשֵׁר
וּמִן־כׇּל־מְנַשֶּׁה וַיִּרְדְּפוּ אַחֲרֵי מִדְיָן׃

24 *Gidon* also sent messengers all through the hill
country of *Efraim* with this order: "Go down ahead
of the Midianites and seize their access to the water
all along the *Yarden* down to Beth-barah." So all
the men of *Efraim* rallied and seized the waterside
down to Beth-barah by the *Yarden*.

כד וּמַלְאָכִים שָׁלַח גִּדְעוֹן בְּכׇל־הַר אֶפְרַיִם
לֵאמֹר רְדוּ לִקְרַאת מִדְיָן וְלִכְדוּ לָהֶם
אֶת־הַמַּיִם עַד בֵּית בָּרָה וְאֶת־הַיַּרְדֵּן
וַיִּצָּעֵק כׇּל־אִישׁ אֶפְרַיִם וַיִּלְכְּדוּ אֶת־
הַמַּיִם עַד בֵּית בָּרָה וְאֶת־הַיַּרְדֵּן׃

Shoftim/Judges
Chapter 8

שופטים
פרק ח

25 They pursued the Midianites and captured Midian's two generals, Oreb and Zeeb. They killed Oreb at the Rock of Oreb and they killed Zeeb at the Winepress of Zeeb; and they brought the heads of Oreb and Zeeb from the other side of the *Yarden* to *Gidon*.

וַיִּלְכְּדוּ שְׁנֵי־שָׂרֵי מִדְיָן אֶת־עֹרֵב וְאֶת־זְאֵב וַיַּהַרְגוּ אֶת־עוֹרֵב בְּצוּר־עוֹרֵב וְאֶת־זְאֵב הָרְגוּ בְיֶקֶב־זְאֵב וַיִּרְדְּפוּ אֶל־מִדְיָן וְרֹאשׁ־עֹרֵב וּזְאֵב הֵבִיאוּ אֶל־גִּדְעוֹן מֵעֵבֶר לַיַּרְדֵּן: כה

8 1 And the men of *Efraim* said to him, "Why did you do that to us – not calling us when you went to fight the Midianites?" And they rebuked him severely.

וַיֹּאמְרוּ אֵלָיו אִישׁ אֶפְרַיִם מָה־הַדָּבָר הַזֶּה עָשִׂיתָ לָּנוּ לְבִלְתִּי קְרֹאות לָנוּ כִּי הָלַכְתָּ לְהִלָּחֵם בְּמִדְיָן וַיְרִיבוּן אִתּוֹ בְּחָזְקָה: א ח

2 But he answered them, "After all, what have I accomplished compared to you? Why, *Efraim*'s gleanings are better than Abiezer's vintage!

וַיֹּאמֶר אֲלֵיהֶם מֶה־עָשִׂיתִי עַתָּה כָּכֶם הֲלוֹא טוֹב עֹלְלוֹת אֶפְרַיִם מִבְצִיר אֲבִיעֶזֶר: ב

va-YO-mer a-lay-HEM meh a-SEE-tee a-TAH ka-KHEM ha-LO TOV o-l'-LOT ef-RA-yim miv-TZEER a-vee-E-zer

3 *Hashem* has delivered the Midianite generals Oreb and Zeeb into your hands, and what was I able to do compared to you?" And when he spoke in this fashion, their anger against him abated.

בְּיֶדְכֶם נָתַן אֱלֹהִים אֶת־שָׂרֵי מִדְיָן אֶת־עֹרֵב וְאֶת־זְאֵב וּמַה־יָּכֹלְתִּי עֲשׂוֹת כָּכֶם אָז רָפְתָה רוּחָם מֵעָלָיו בְּדַבְּרוֹ הַדָּבָר הַזֶּה: ג

4 *Gidon* came to the *Yarden* and crossed it. The three hundred men with him were famished, but still in pursuit.

וַיָּבֹא גִדְעוֹן הַיַּרְדֵּנָה עֹבֵר הוּא וּשְׁלֹשׁ־מֵאוֹת הָאִישׁ אֲשֶׁר אִתּוֹ עֲיֵפִים וְרֹדְפִים: ד

5 He said to the people of Succoth, "Please give some loaves of bread to the men who are following me, for they are famished, and I am pursuing Zebah and Zalmunna, the kings of Midian."

וַיֹּאמֶר לְאַנְשֵׁי סֻכּוֹת תְּנוּ־נָא כִּכְּרוֹת לֶחֶם לָעָם אֲשֶׁר בְּרַגְלָי כִּי־עֲיֵפִים הֵם וְאָנֹכִי רֹדֵף אַחֲרֵי זֶבַח וְצַלְמֻנָּע מַלְכֵי מִדְיָן: ה

6 But the officials of Succoth replied, "Are Zebah and Zalmunna already in your hands, that we should give bread to your troops?"

וַיֹּאמֶר שָׂרֵי סֻכּוֹת הֲכַף זֶבַח וְצַלְמֻנָּע עַתָּה בְּיָדֶךָ כִּי־נִתֵּן לִצְבָאֲךָ לָחֶם: ו

7 "I swear," declared *Gidon*, "when *Hashem* delivers Zebah and Zalmunna into my hands, I'll thresh your bodies upon desert thorns and briers!"

וַיֹּאמֶר גִּדְעוֹן לָכֵן בְּתֵת יְהֹוָה אֶת־זֶבַח וְאֶת־צַלְמֻנָּע בְּיָדִי וְדַשְׁתִּי אֶת־בְּשַׂרְכֶם אֶת־קוֹצֵי הַמִּדְבָּר וְאֶת־הַבַּרְקֳנִים: ז

Prime Minister Menachem Begin (1913–1992)

8:2 But he answered them, "After all, what have I accomplished" Though he has done nothing wrong, *Gidon* nevertheless attempts to pacify the men of *Efraim* who are angry with him, because he recognizes the essential need to avoid civil war. Infighting among the People of Israel always brings disastrous results, such as the destruction of the second *Beit Hamikdash*, which, according to the Talmud (*Yoma* 9b), was destroyed because of baseless hatred. On a number of occasions during the twentieth-century struggle for Jewish independence in the Land of Israel, the main Jewish defense group *Haganah* fought against the rival group *Irgun*, which used more extreme measures against the British authorities. Although it may have been against his own narrow interests, the *Irgun*'s leader, Menachem Begin, refused to escalate the violence, saying that civil war must be avoided at all costs. Begin later became Israel's sixth Prime Minister.

Shoftim/Judges
Chapter 8

שופטים
פרק ח

8 From there he went up to Penuel and made the same request of them; but the people of Penuel gave him the same reply as the people of Succoth.

ח וַיַּעַל מִשָּׁם פְּנוּאֵל וַיְדַבֵּר אֲלֵיהֶם כָּזֹאת וַיַּעֲנוּ אוֹתוֹ אַנְשֵׁי פְנוּאֵל כַּאֲשֶׁר עָנוּ אַנְשֵׁי סֻכּוֹת:

9 So he also threatened the people of Penuel: "When I come back safe, I'll tear down this tower!"

ט וַיֹּאמֶר גַּם־לְאַנְשֵׁי פְנוּאֵל לֵאמֹר בְּשׁוּבִי בְשָׁלוֹם אֶתֹּץ אֶת־הַמִּגְדָּל הַזֶּה:

10 Now Zebah and Zalmunna were at Karkor with their army of about 15,000; these were all that remained of the entire host of the Kedemites, for the slain numbered 120,000 fighting men.

י וְזֶבַח וְצַלְמֻנָּע בַּקַּרְקֹר וּמַחֲנֵיהֶם עִמָּם כַּחֲמֵשֶׁת עָשָׂר אֶלֶף כֹּל הַנּוֹתָרִים מִכֹּל מַחֲנֵה בְנֵי־קֶדֶם וְהַנֹּפְלִים מֵאָה וְעֶשְׂרִים אֶלֶף אִישׁ שֹׁלֵף חָרֶב:

11 *Gidon* marched up the road of the tent dwellers, up to east of Nobah and Jogbehah, and routed the camp, which was off guard.

יא וַיַּעַל גִּדְעוֹן דֶּרֶךְ הַשְּׁכוּנֵי בָאֳהָלִים מִקֶּדֶם לְנֹבַח וְיָגְבְּהָה וַיַּךְ אֶת־הַמַּחֲנֶה וְהַמַּחֲנֶה הָיָה בֶטַח:

12 Zebah and Zalmunna took to flight, with *Gidon* in pursuit. He captured Zebah and Zalmunna, the two kings of Midian, and threw the whole army into panic.

יב וַיָּנוּסוּ זֶבַח וְצַלְמֻנָּע וַיִּרְדֹּף אַחֲרֵיהֶם וַיִּלְכֹּד אֶת־שְׁנֵי מַלְכֵי מִדְיָן אֶת־זֶבַח וְאֶת־צַלְמֻנָּע וְכָל־הַמַּחֲנֶה הֶחֱרִיד:

13 On his way back from the battle at the Ascent of Heres, *Gidon* son of *Yoash*

יג וַיָּשָׁב גִּדְעוֹן בֶּן־יוֹאָשׁ מִן־הַמִּלְחָמָה מִלְמַעֲלֵה הֶחָרֶס:

14 captured a boy from among the people of Succoth and interrogated him. The latter drew up for him a list of the officials and elders of Succoth, seventy-seven in number.

יד וַיִּלְכָּד־נַעַר מֵאַנְשֵׁי סֻכּוֹת וַיִּשְׁאָלֵהוּ וַיִּכְתֹּב אֵלָיו אֶת־שָׂרֵי סֻכּוֹת וְאֶת־זְקֵנֶיהָ שִׁבְעִים וְשִׁבְעָה אִישׁ:

15 Then he came to the people of Succoth and said, "Here are Zebah and Zalmunna, about whom you mocked me, saying, 'Are Zebah and Zalmunna already in your hands, that we should give your famished men bread?'"

טו וַיָּבֹא אֶל־אַנְשֵׁי סֻכּוֹת וַיֹּאמֶר הִנֵּה זֶבַח וְצַלְמֻנָּע אֲשֶׁר חֵרַפְתֶּם אוֹתִי לֵאמֹר הֲכַף זֶבַח וְצַלְמֻנָּע עַתָּה בְּיָדֶךָ כִּי נִתֵּן לַאֲנָשֶׁיךָ הַיְּעֵפִים לָחֶם:

16 And he took the elders of the city and, [bringing] desert thorns and briers, he punished the people of Succoth with them.

טז וַיִּקַּח אֶת־זִקְנֵי הָעִיר וְאֶת־קוֹצֵי הַמִּדְבָּר וְאֶת־הַבַּרְקֳנִים וַיֹּדַע בָּהֶם אֵת אַנְשֵׁי סֻכּוֹת:

17 As for Penuel, he tore down its tower and killed the townspeople.

יז וְאֶת־מִגְדַּל פְּנוּאֵל נָתָץ וַיַּהֲרֹג אֶת־אַנְשֵׁי הָעִיר:

18 Then he asked Zebah and Zalmunna, "Those men you killed at *Tavor*, what were they like?" "They looked just like you," they replied, "like sons of a king."

יח וַיֹּאמֶר אֶל־זֶבַח וְאֶל־צַלְמֻנָּע אֵיפֹה הָאֲנָשִׁים אֲשֶׁר הֲרַגְתֶּם בְּתָבוֹר וַיֹּאמְרוּ כָּמוֹךָ כְמוֹהֶם אֶחָד כְּתֹאַר בְּנֵי הַמֶּלֶךְ:

19 "They were my brothers," he declared, "the sons of my mother. As *Hashem* lives, if you had spared them, I would not kill you."

יט וַיֹּאמַר אַחַי בְּנֵי־אִמִּי הֵם חַי־יְהֹוָה לוּ הַחֲיִתֶם אוֹתָם לֹא הָרַגְתִּי אֶתְכֶם:

20 And he commanded his oldest son Jether, "Go kill them!" But the boy did not draw his sword, for he was timid, being still a boy.

כ וַיֹּאמֶר לְיֶתֶר בְּכוֹרוֹ קוּם הֲרֹג אוֹתָם וְלֹא־שָׁלַף הַנַּעַר חַרְבּוֹ כִּי יָרֵא כִּי עוֹדֶנּוּ נָעַר:

618

Shoftim/Judges
Chapter 8

שופטים
פרק ח

21 Then Zebah and Zalmunna said, "Come, you slay us; for strength comes with manhood." So *Gidon* went over and killed Zebah and Zalmunna, and he took the crescents that were on the necks of their camels.

כא וַיֹּאמֶר זֶבַח וְצַלְמֻנָּע קוּם אַתָּה וּפְגַע־בָּנוּ כִּי כָאִישׁ גְּבוּרָתוֹ וַיָּקָם גִּדְעוֹן וַיַּהֲרֹג אֶת־זֶבַח וְאֶת־צַלְמֻנָּע וַיִּקַּח אֶת־הַשַּׂהֲרֹנִים אֲשֶׁר בְּצַוְּארֵי גְמַלֵּיהֶם:

22 Then the men of *Yisrael* said to *Gidon*, "Rule over us – you, your son, and your grandson as well; for you have saved us from the Midianites."

כב וַיֹּאמְרוּ אִישׁ־יִשְׂרָאֵל אֶל־גִּדְעוֹן מְשָׁל־בָּנוּ גַּם־אַתָּה גַּם־בִּנְךָ גַּם בֶּן־בְּנֶךָ כִּי הוֹשַׁעְתָּנוּ מִיַּד מִדְיָן:

23 But *Gidon* replied, "I will not rule over you myself, nor shall my son rule over you; *Hashem* alone shall rule over you."

כג וַיֹּאמֶר אֲלֵהֶם גִּדְעוֹן לֹא־אֶמְשֹׁל אֲנִי בָּכֶם וְלֹא־יִמְשֹׁל בְּנִי בָּכֶם יְהוָה יִמְשֹׁל בָּכֶם:

24 And *Gidon* said to them, "I have a request to make of you: Each of you give me the earring he received as booty." (They had golden earrings, for they were Ishmaelites.)

כד וַיֹּאמֶר אֲלֵהֶם גִּדְעוֹן אֶשְׁאֲלָה מִכֶּם שְׁאֵלָה וּתְנוּ־לִי אִישׁ נֶזֶם שְׁלָלוֹ כִּי־נִזְמֵי זָהָב לָהֶם כִּי יִשְׁמְעֵאלִים הֵם:

25 "Certainly!" they replied. And they spread out a cloth, and everyone threw onto it the earring he had received as booty.

כה וַיֹּאמְרוּ נָתוֹן נִתֵּן וַיִּפְרְשׂוּ אֶת־הַשִּׂמְלָה וַיַּשְׁלִיכוּ שָׁמָּה אִישׁ נֶזֶם שְׁלָלוֹ:

26 The weight of the golden earrings that he had requested came to 1,700 *shekalim* of gold; this was in addition to the crescents and the pendants and the purple robes worn by the kings of Midian and in addition to the collars on the necks of their camels.

כו וַיְהִי מִשְׁקַל נִזְמֵי הַזָּהָב אֲשֶׁר שָׁאָל אֶלֶף וּשְׁבַע־מֵאוֹת זָהָב לְבַד מִן־הַשַּׂהֲרֹנִים וְהַנְּטִפוֹת וּבִגְדֵי הָאַרְגָּמָן שֶׁעַל מַלְכֵי מִדְיָן וּלְבַד מִן־הָעֲנָקוֹת אֲשֶׁר בְּצַוְּארֵי גְמַלֵּיהֶם:

27 *Gidon* made an ephod of this gold and set it up in his own town of Ophrah. There all *Yisrael* went astray after it, and it became a snare to *Gidon* and his household.

כז וַיַּעַשׂ אוֹתוֹ גִדְעוֹן לְאֵפוֹד וַיַּצֵּג אוֹתוֹ בְעִירוֹ בְּעָפְרָה וַיִּזְנוּ כָל־יִשְׂרָאֵל אַחֲרָיו שָׁם וַיְהִי לְגִדְעוֹן וּלְבֵיתוֹ לְמוֹקֵשׁ:

28 Thus Midian submitted to the Israelites and did not raise its head again; and the land was tranquil for forty years in *Gidon*'s time.

כח וַיִּכָּנַע מִדְיָן לִפְנֵי בְּנֵי יִשְׂרָאֵל וְלֹא יָסְפוּ לָשֵׂאת רֹאשָׁם וַתִּשְׁקֹט הָאָרֶץ אַרְבָּעִים שָׁנָה בִּימֵי גִדְעוֹן:

29 So *Yerubaal* son of *Yoash* retired to his own house.

כט וַיֵּלֶךְ יְרֻבַּעַל בֶּן־יוֹאָשׁ וַיֵּשֶׁב בְּבֵיתוֹ:

30 *Gidon* had seventy sons of his own issue, for he had many wives.

ל וּלְגִדְעוֹן הָיוּ שִׁבְעִים בָּנִים יֹצְאֵי יְרֵכוֹ כִּי־נָשִׁים רַבּוֹת הָיוּ לוֹ:

31 A son was also born to him by his concubine in *Shechem*, and he named him *Avimelech*.

לא וּפִילַגְשׁוֹ אֲשֶׁר בִּשְׁכֶם יָלְדָה־לּוֹ גַם־הִיא בֵּן וַיָּשֶׂם אֶת־שְׁמוֹ אֲבִימֶלֶךְ:

32 *Gidon* son of *Yoash* died at a ripe old age, and was buried in the tomb of his father *Yoash* at Ophrah of the Abiezrites.

לב וַיָּמָת גִּדְעוֹן בֶּן־יוֹאָשׁ בְּשֵׂיבָה טוֹבָה וַיִּקָּבֵר בְּקֶבֶר יוֹאָשׁ אָבִיו בְּעָפְרָה אֲבִי הָעֶזְרִי:

33 After *Gidon* died, the Israelites again went astray after the Baalim, and they adopted Baal-berith as a god.

לג וַיְהִי כַּאֲשֶׁר מֵת גִּדְעוֹן וַיָּשׁוּבוּ בְּנֵי יִשְׂרָאֵל וַיִּזְנוּ אַחֲרֵי הַבְּעָלִים וַיָּשִׂימוּ לָהֶם בַּעַל בְּרִית לֵאלֹהִים:

Shoftim/Judges
Chapter 9

שופטים
פרק ט

34 The Israelites gave no thought to *Hashem* their God, who saved them from all the enemies around them.

לד וְלֹא זָכְרוּ בְּנֵי יִשְׂרָאֵל אֶת־יְהֹוָה אֱלֹהֵיהֶם הַמַּצִּיל אוֹתָם מִיַּד כָּל־אֹיְבֵיהֶם מִסָּבִיב׃

35 Nor did they show loyalty to the house of *Yerubaal-Gidon* in return for all the good that he had done for *Yisrael*.

לה וְלֹא־עָשׂוּ חֶסֶד עִם־בֵּית יְרֻבַּעַל גִּדְעוֹן כְּכָל־הַטּוֹבָה אֲשֶׁר עָשָׂה עִם־יִשְׂרָאֵל׃

9 1 *Avimelech* son of *Yerubaal* went to his mother's brothers in *Shechem* and spoke to them and to the whole clan of his mother's family. He said,

ט א וַיֵּלֶךְ אֲבִימֶלֶךְ בֶּן־יְרֻבַּעַל שְׁכֶמָה אֶל־אֲחֵי אִמּוֹ וַיְדַבֵּר אֲלֵיהֶם וְאֶל־כָּל־מִשְׁפַּחַת בֵּית־אֲבִי אִמּוֹ לֵאמֹר׃

va-YAY-lekh a-vee-ME-lekh ben y'-ru-BA-al sh'-KHE-mah el a-KHAY i-MO vai-da-BAYR a-lay-HEM v'-el kol mish-PA-khat bayt a-VEE i-MO lay-MOR

2 "Put this question to all the citizens of *Shechem*: Which is better for you, to be ruled by seventy men – by all the sons of *Yerubaal* – or to be ruled by one man? And remember, I am your own flesh and blood."

ב דַּבְּרוּ־נָא בְּאָזְנֵי כָל־בַּעֲלֵי שְׁכֶם מַה־טּוֹב לָכֶם הַמְשֹׁל בָּכֶם שִׁבְעִים אִישׁ כֹּל בְּנֵי יְרֻבַּעַל אִם־מְשֹׁל בָּכֶם אִישׁ אֶחָד וּזְכַרְתֶּם כִּי־עַצְמְכֶם וּבְשַׂרְכֶם אָנִי׃

3 His mother's brothers said all this in his behalf to all the citizens of *Shechem*, and they were won over to *Avimelech*; for they thought, "He is our kinsman."

ג וַיְדַבְּרוּ אֲחֵי־אִמּוֹ עָלָיו בְּאָזְנֵי כָּל־בַּעֲלֵי שְׁכֶם אֵת כָּל־הַדְּבָרִים הָאֵלֶּה וַיֵּט לִבָּם אַחֲרֵי אֲבִימֶלֶךְ כִּי אָמְרוּ אָחִינוּ הוּא׃

4 They gave him seventy *shekalim* from the temple of Baal-berith; and with this *Avimelech* hired some worthless and reckless fellows, and they followed him.

ד וַיִּתְּנוּ־לוֹ שִׁבְעִים כֶּסֶף מִבֵּית בַּעַל בְּרִית וַיִּשְׂכֹּר בָּהֶם אֲבִימֶלֶךְ אֲנָשִׁים רֵיקִים וּפֹחֲזִים וַיֵּלְכוּ אַחֲרָיו׃

5 Then he went to his father's house in Ophrah and killed his brothers, the sons of *Yerubaal*, seventy men on one stone. Only *Yotam*, the youngest son of *Yerubaal*, survived, because he went into hiding.

ה וַיָּבֹא בֵית־אָבִיו עָפְרָתָה וַיַּהֲרֹג אֶת־אֶחָיו בְּנֵי־יְרֻבַּעַל שִׁבְעִים אִישׁ עַל־אֶבֶן אֶחָת וַיִּוָּתֵר יוֹתָם בֶּן־יְרֻבַּעַל הַקָּטֹן כִּי נֶחְבָּא׃

6 All the citizens of *Shechem* and all Beth-millo convened, and they proclaimed *Avimelech* king at the terebinth of the pillar at *Shechem*.

ו וַיֵּאָסְפוּ כָּל־בַּעֲלֵי שְׁכֶם וְכָל־בֵּית מִלּוֹא וַיֵּלְכוּ וַיַּמְלִיכוּ אֶת־אֲבִימֶלֶךְ לְמֶלֶךְ עִם־אֵלוֹן מֻצָּב אֲשֶׁר בִּשְׁכֶם׃

7 When *Yotam* was informed, he went and stood on top of Mount Gerizim and called out to them in a loud voice. "Citizens of *Shechem*!" he cried, "listen to me, that *Hashem* may listen to you.

ז וַיַּגִּדוּ לְיוֹתָם וַיֵּלֶךְ וַיַּעֲמֹד בְּרֹאשׁ הַר־גְּרִזִים וַיִּשָּׂא קוֹלוֹ וַיִּקְרָא וַיֹּאמֶר לָהֶם שִׁמְעוּ אֵלַי בַּעֲלֵי שְׁכֶם וְיִשְׁמַע אֲלֵיכֶם אֱלֹהִים׃

9:1 *Avimelech* son of *Yerubaal* went to his mother's brothers in *Shechem* The city of *Shechem* appears many times in the Bible. *Yaakov* purchases part of the city (Genesis 33:18–20) and later gives it as a special gift to his son *Yosef* (ibid. 49:22–26). Later, when the Children of Israel enter the Land of Israel, they bury *Yosef* in *Shechem*. Other important sites in Israel were also acquired via purchase, such as the Temple Mount in *Yerushalayim* (II Samuel 24) and the cave of Machpelah in *Chevron* (Genesis 23). The Rabbis explain that because of the public nature of these sales, the entire world must recognize Jewish ownership over these three cities.

Tomb of Yosef in Shechem

Shoftim/Judges
Chapter 9

8 "Once the trees went to anoint a king over themselves. They said to the olive tree, 'Reign over us.'

9 But the olive tree replied, 'Have I, through whom *Hashem* and men are honored, stopped yielding my rich oil, that I should go and wave above the trees?'

10 So the trees said to the fig tree, 'You come and reign over us.'

11 But the fig tree replied, 'Have I stopped yielding my sweetness, my delicious fruit, that I should go and wave above the trees?'

12 So the trees said to the vine, 'You come and reign over us.'

13 But the vine replied, 'Have I stopped yielding my new wine, which gladdens *Hashem* and men, that I should go and wave above the trees?'

14 Then all the trees said to the thornbush, 'You come and reign over us.'

15 And the thornbush said to the trees, 'If you are acting honorably in anointing me king over you, come and take shelter in my shade; but if not, may fire issue from the thornbush and consume the cedars of Lebanon!'

16 "Now then, if you acted honorably and loyally in making *Avimelech* king, if you have done right by *Yerubaal* and his house and have requited him according to his deserts

17 considering that my father fought for you and saved you from the Midianites at the risk of his life,

18 and now you have turned on my father's household, killed his sons, seventy men on one stone, and set up *Avimelech*, the son of his handmaid, as king over the citizens of *Shechem* just because he is your kinsman

19 if, I say, you have this day acted honorably and loyally toward *Yerubaal* and his house, have joy in *Avimelech* and may he likewise have joy in you.

20 But if not, may fire issue from *Avimelech* and consume the citizens of *Shechem* and Beth-millo, and may fire issue from the citizens of *Shechem* and Beth-millo and consume *Avimelech*!"

שׁוֹפְטִים
פֶּרֶק ט

ח הָל֤וֹךְ הָֽלְכוּ֙ הָֽעֵצִ֔ים לִמְשֹׁ֥חַ עֲלֵיהֶ֖ם מֶ֑לֶךְ וַיֹּאמְר֥וּ לַזַּ֖יִת מלוכה [מָלְכָ֥ה] עָלֵֽינוּ:

ט וַיֹּ֤אמֶר לָהֶם֙ הַזַּ֔יִת הֶחֳדַ֨לְתִּי֙ אֶת־דִּשְׁנִ֔י אֲשֶׁר־בִּ֛י יְכַבְּד֥וּ אֱלֹהִ֖ים וַאֲנָשִׁ֑ים וְהָ֣לַכְתִּ֔י לָנ֖וּעַ עַל־הָעֵצִֽים:

י וַיֹּאמְר֥וּ הָעֵצִ֖ים לַתְּאֵנָ֑ה לְכִי־אַ֖תְּ מָלְכִ֥י עָלֵֽינוּ:

יא וַתֹּ֤אמֶר לָהֶם֙ הַתְּאֵנָ֔ה הֶחֳדַ֨לְתִּי֙ אֶת־מָתְקִ֔י וְאֶת־תְּנוּבָתִ֖י הַטּוֹבָ֑ה וְהָ֣לַכְתִּ֔י לָנ֖וּעַ עַל־הָעֵצִֽים:

יב וַיֹּאמְר֥וּ הָעֵצִ֖ים לַגָּ֑פֶן לְכִי־אַ֖תְּ מלוכי [מָלְכִ֥י] עָלֵֽינוּ:

יג וַתֹּ֤אמֶר לָהֶם֙ הַגֶּ֔פֶן הֶחֳדַ֨לְתִּי֙ אֶת־תִּ֣ירוֹשִׁ֔י הַֽמְשַׂמֵּ֥חַ אֱלֹהִ֖ים וַאֲנָשִׁ֑ים וְהָ֣לַכְתִּ֔י לָנ֖וּעַ עַל־הָעֵצִֽים:

יד וַיֹּאמְר֥וּ כָל־הָעֵצִ֖ים אֶל־הָאָטָ֑ד לֵ֥ךְ אַתָּ֖ה מְלָךְ־עָלֵֽינוּ:

טו וַיֹּ֣אמֶר הָאָטָד֮ אֶל־הָעֵצִים֒ אִ֡ם בֶּאֱמֶ֣ת אַתֶּם֩ מֹשְׁחִ֨ים אֹתִ֤י לְמֶ֙לֶךְ֙ עֲלֵיכֶ֔ם בֹּ֖אוּ חֲס֣וּ בְצִלִּ֑י וְאִם־אַ֕יִן תֵּ֤צֵא אֵשׁ֙ מִן־הָ֣אָטָ֔ד וְתֹאכַ֖ל אֶת־אַרְזֵ֥י הַלְּבָנֽוֹן:

טז וְעַתָּ֗ה אִם־בֶּאֱמֶ֤ת וּבְתָמִים֙ עֲשִׂיתֶ֔ם וַתַּמְלִ֖יכוּ אֶת־אֲבִימֶ֑לֶךְ וְאִם־טוֹבָ֤ה עֲשִׂיתֶם֙ עִם־יְרֻבַּ֣עַל וְעִם־בֵּית֔וֹ וְאִם־כִּגְמ֥וּל יָדָ֖יו עֲשִׂ֥יתֶם לֽוֹ:

יז אֲשֶׁר־נִלְחַ֥ם אָבִ֖י עֲלֵיכֶ֑ם וַיַּשְׁלֵ֤ךְ אֶת־נַפְשׁוֹ֙ מִנֶּ֔גֶד וַיַּצֵּ֥ל אֶתְכֶ֖ם מִיַּ֥ד מִדְיָֽן:

יח וְאַתֶּ֞ם קַמְתֶּ֨ם עַל־בֵּ֤ית אָבִי֙ הַיּ֔וֹם וַתַּהַרְג֧וּ אֶת־בָּנָ֛יו שִׁבְעִ֥ים אִ֖ישׁ עַל־אֶ֣בֶן אֶחָ֑ת וַתַּמְלִ֜יכוּ אֶת־אֲבִימֶ֤לֶךְ בֶּן־אֲמָתוֹ֙ עַל־בַּעֲלֵ֣י שְׁכֶ֔ם כִּ֥י אֲחִיכֶ֖ם הֽוּא:

יט וְאִם־בֶּאֱמֶ֧ת וּבְתָמִ֛ים עֲשִׂיתֶ֥ם עִם־יְרֻבַּ֖עַל וְעִם־בֵּית֑וֹ הַיּ֣וֹם הַזֶּ֑ה שִׂמְחוּ֙ בַּאֲבִימֶ֔לֶךְ וְיִשְׂמַ֥ח גַּם־ה֖וּא בָּכֶֽם:

כ וְאִם־אַ֕יִן תֵּ֤צֵא אֵשׁ֙ מֵאֲבִימֶ֔לֶךְ וְתֹאכַ֛ל אֶת־בַּעֲלֵ֥י שְׁכֶ֖ם וְאֶת־בֵּ֣ית מִלּ֑וֹא וְתֵצֵ֨א אֵ֜שׁ מִבַּעֲלֵ֤י שְׁכֶם֙ וּמִבֵּ֣ית מִלּ֔וֹא וְתֹאכַ֖ל אֶת־אֲבִימֶֽלֶךְ:

Shoftim/Judges
Chapter 9

שופטים
פרק ט

21 With that, *Yotam* fled. He ran to Beer and stayed there, because of his brother *Avimelech*.

כא וַיָּנָס יוֹתָם וַיִּבְרַח וַיֵּלֶךְ בְּאֵרָה וַיֵּשֶׁב שָׁם מִפְּנֵי אֲבִימֶלֶךְ אָחִיו׃

22 *Avimelech* held sway over *Yisrael* for three years.

כב וַיָּשַׂר אֲבִימֶלֶךְ עַל־יִשְׂרָאֵל שָׁלֹשׁ שָׁנִים׃

23 Then *Hashem* sent a spirit of discord between *Avimelech* and the citizens of *Shechem*, and the citizens of *Shechem* broke faith with *Avimelech*

כג וַיִּשְׁלַח אֱלֹהִים רוּחַ רָעָה בֵּין אֲבִימֶלֶךְ וּבֵין בַּעֲלֵי שְׁכֶם וַיִּבְגְּדוּ בַעֲלֵי־שְׁכֶם בַּאֲבִימֶלֶךְ׃

24 to the end that the crime committed against the seventy sons of *Yerubaal* might be avenged, and their blood recoil upon their brother *Avimelech*, who had slain them, and upon the citizens of *Shechem*, who had abetted him in the slaying of his brothers.

כד לָבוֹא חֲמַס שִׁבְעִים בְּנֵי־יְרֻבָּעַל וְדָמָם לָשׂוּם עַל־אֲבִימֶלֶךְ אֲחִיהֶם אֲשֶׁר הָרַג אוֹתָם וְעַל בַּעֲלֵי שְׁכֶם אֲשֶׁר־חִזְּקוּ אֶת־יָדָיו לַהֲרֹג אֶת־אֶחָיו׃

25 The citizens of *Shechem* planted ambuscades against him on the hilltops; and they robbed whoever passed by them on the road. Word of this reached *Avimelech*.

כה וַיָּשִׂימוּ לוֹ בַעֲלֵי שְׁכֶם מְאָרְבִים עַל רָאשֵׁי הֶהָרִים וַיִּגְזְלוּ אֵת כָּל־אֲשֶׁר־יַעֲבֹר עֲלֵיהֶם בַּדָּרֶךְ וַיֻּגַּד לַאֲבִימֶלֶךְ׃

26 Then Gaal son of Ebed and his companions came passing through *Shechem*, and the citizens of *Shechem* gave him their confidence.

כו וַיָּבֹא גַּעַל בֶּן־עֶבֶד וְאֶחָיו וַיַּעַבְרוּ בִּשְׁכֶם וַיִּבְטְחוּ־בוֹ בַּעֲלֵי שְׁכֶם׃

27 They went out into the fields, gathered and trod out the vintage of their vineyards, and made a festival. They entered the temple of their god, and as they ate and drank they reviled *Avimelech*.

כז וַיֵּצְאוּ הַשָּׂדֶה וַיִּבְצְרוּ אֶת־כַּרְמֵיהֶם וַיִּדְרְכוּ וַיַּעֲשׂוּ הִלּוּלִים וַיָּבֹאוּ בֵּית אֱלֹהֵיהֶם וַיֹּאכְלוּ וַיִּשְׁתּוּ וַיְקַלְלוּ אֶת־אֲבִימֶלֶךְ׃

28 Gaal son of Ebed said, "Who is *Avimelech* and who are [we] Sh'chemites, that we should serve him? This same son of *Yerubaal* and his lieutenant Zebul once served the men of Hamor, the father of *Shechem*; so why should we serve him?

כח וַיֹּאמֶר גַּעַל בֶּן־עֶבֶד מִי־אֲבִימֶלֶךְ וּמִי־שְׁכֶם כִּי נַעַבְדֶנּוּ הֲלֹא בֶן־יְרֻבַּעַל וּזְבֻל פְּקִידוֹ עִבְדוּ אֶת־אַנְשֵׁי חֲמוֹר אֲבִי שְׁכֶם וּמַדּוּעַ נַעַבְדֶנּוּ אֲנָחְנוּ׃

29 Oh, if only this people were under my command, I would get rid of *Avimelech*! One would challenge *Avimelech*, 'Fill up your ranks and come out here!'"

כט וּמִי יִתֵּן אֶת־הָעָם הַזֶּה בְּיָדִי וְאָסִירָה אֶת־אֲבִימֶלֶךְ וַיֹּאמֶר לַאֲבִימֶלֶךְ רַבֶּה צְבָאֲךָ וָצֵאָה׃

30 When Zebul, the governor of the city, heard the words of Gaal son of Ebed, he was furious.

ל וַיִּשְׁמַע זְבֻל שַׂר־הָעִיר אֶת־דִּבְרֵי גַּעַל בֶּן־עָבֶד וַיִּחַר אַפּוֹ׃

31 He sent messages to *Avimelech* at Tormah to say, "Gaal son of Ebed and his companions have come to *Shechem* and they are inciting the city against you.

לא וַיִּשְׁלַח מַלְאָכִים אֶל־אֲבִימֶלֶךְ בְּתָרְמָה לֵאמֹר הִנֵּה גַעַל בֶּן־עֶבֶד וְאֶחָיו בָּאִים שְׁכֶמָה וְהִנָּם צָרִים אֶת־הָעִיר עָלֶיךָ׃

32 Therefore, set out at night with the forces you have with you and conceal yourself in the fields.

לב וְעַתָּה קוּם לַיְלָה אַתָּה וְהָעָם אֲשֶׁר־אִתָּךְ וֶאֱרֹב בַּשָּׂדֶה׃

33 Early next morning, as the sun rises, advance on the city. He and his men will thereupon come out against you, and you will do to him whatever you find possible."

לג וְהָיָה בַבֹּקֶר כִּזְרֹחַ הַשֶּׁמֶשׁ תַּשְׁכִּים וּפָשַׁטְתָּ עַל־הָעִיר וְהִנֵּה־הוּא וְהָעָם אֲשֶׁר־אִתּוֹ יֹצְאִים אֵלֶיךָ וְעָשִׂיתָ לּוֹ כַּאֲשֶׁר תִּמְצָא יָדֶךָ׃

622

Shoftim/Judges
Chapter 9

34 *Avimelech* and all the men with him set out at night and disposed themselves against *Shechem* in four hiding places.

35 When Gaal son of Ebed came out and stood at the entrance to the city gate, *Avimelech* and the army with him emerged from concealment.

36 Gaal saw the army and said to Zebul, "That's an army marching down from the hilltops!" But Zebul said to him, "The shadows of the hills look to you like men."

37 Gaal spoke up again, "Look, an army is marching down from Tabbur-erez, and another column is coming from the direction of Elon-meonenim."

38 "Well," replied Zebul, "where is your boast, 'Who is *Avimelech* that we should serve him'? There is the army you sneered at; now go out and fight it!"

39 So Gaal went out at the head of the citizens of *Shechem* and gave battle to *Avimelech*.

40 But he had to flee before him, and *Avimelech* pursued him, and many fell slain, all the way to the entrance of the gate.

41 Then *Avimelech* stayed in Arumah, while Zebul expelled Gaal and his companions and kept them out of *Shechem*.

42 The next day, when people went out into the fields, *Avimelech* was informed.

43 Taking the army, he divided it into three columns and lay in ambush in the fields; and when he saw the people coming out of the city, he pounced upon them and struck them down.

44 While *Avimelech* and the column that followed him dashed ahead and took up a position at the entrance of the city gate, the other two columns rushed upon all that were in the open and struck them down.

45 *Avimelech* fought against the city all that day. He captured the city and massacred the people in it; he razed the town and sowed it with salt.

46 When all the citizens of the Tower of *Shechem* learned of this, they went into the tunnel of the temple of *El*-berith.

Shoftim/Judges
Chapter 10

שופטים
פרק י

47 When *Avimelech* was informed that all the citizens of the Tower of *Shechem* had gathered [there],

מז וַיֻּגַּד לַאֲבִימֶלֶךְ כִּי הִתְקַבְּצוּ כָּל־בַּעֲלֵי מִגְדַּל־שְׁכֶם:

48 *Avimelech* and all the troops he had with him went up on Mount Zalmon. Taking an ax in his hand, *Avimelech* lopped off a tree limb and lifted it onto his shoulder. Then he said to the troops that accompanied him, "What you saw me do – quick, do the same!"

מח וַיַּעַל אֲבִימֶלֶךְ הַר־צַלְמוֹן הוּא וְכָל־הָעָם אֲשֶׁר־אִתּוֹ וַיִּקַּח אֲבִימֶלֶךְ אֶת־הַקַּרְדֻּמּוֹת בְּיָדוֹ וַיִּכְרֹת שׂוֹכַת עֵצִים וַיִּשָּׂאֶהָ וַיָּשֶׂם עַל־שִׁכְמוֹ וַיֹּאמֶר אֶל־הָעָם אֲשֶׁר־עִמּוֹ מָה רְאִיתֶם עָשִׂיתִי מַהֲרוּ עֲשׂוּ כָמוֹנִי:

49 So each of the troops also lopped off a bough; then they marched behind *Avimelech* and laid them against the tunnel, and set fire to the tunnel over their heads. Thus all the people of the Tower of *Shechem* also perished, about a thousand men and women.

מט וַיִּכְרְתוּ גַם־כָּל־הָעָם אִישׁ שׂוֹכֹה וַיֵּלְכוּ אַחֲרֵי אֲבִימֶלֶךְ וַיָּשִׂימוּ עַל־הַצְּרִיחַ וַיַּצִּיתוּ עֲלֵיהֶם אֶת־הַצְּרִיחַ בָּאֵשׁ וַיָּמֻתוּ גַּם כָּל־אַנְשֵׁי מִגְדַּל־שְׁכֶם כְּאֶלֶף אִישׁ וְאִשָּׁה:

50 *Avimelech* proceeded to Thebez; he encamped at Thebez and occupied it.

נ וַיֵּלֶךְ אֲבִימֶלֶךְ אֶל־תֵּבֵץ וַיִּחַן בְּתֵבֵץ וַיִּלְכְּדָהּ:

51 Within the town was a fortified tower; and all the citizens of the town, men and women, took refuge there. They shut themselves in, and went up on the roof of the tower.

נא וּמִגְדַּל־עֹז הָיָה בְתוֹךְ־הָעִיר וַיָּנֻסוּ שָׁמָּה כָּל־הָאֲנָשִׁים וְהַנָּשִׁים וְכֹל בַּעֲלֵי הָעִיר וַיִּסְגְּרוּ בַּעֲדָם וַיַּעֲלוּ עַל־גַּג הַמִּגְדָּל:

52 *Avimelech* pressed forward to the tower and attacked it. He approached the door of the tower to set it on fire.

נב וַיָּבֹא אֲבִימֶלֶךְ עַד־הַמִּגְדָּל וַיִּלָּחֶם בּוֹ וַיִּגַּשׁ עַד־פֶּתַח הַמִּגְדָּל לְשָׂרְפוֹ בָאֵשׁ:

53 But a woman dropped an upper millstone on *Avimelech*'s head and cracked his skull.

נג וַתַּשְׁלֵךְ אִשָּׁה אַחַת פֶּלַח רֶכֶב עַל־רֹאשׁ אֲבִימֶלֶךְ וַתָּרִץ אֶת־גֻּלְגָּלְתּוֹ:

54 He immediately cried out to his attendant, his arms-bearer, "Draw your dagger and finish me off, that they may not say of me, 'A woman killed him!'" So his attendant stabbed him, and he died.

נד וַיִּקְרָא מְהֵרָה אֶל־הַנַּעַר נֹשֵׂא כֵלָיו וַיֹּאמֶר לוֹ שְׁלֹף חַרְבְּךָ וּמוֹתְתֵנִי פֶּן־יֹאמְרוּ לִי אִשָּׁה הֲרָגָתְהוּ וַיִּדְקְרֵהוּ נַעֲרוֹ וַיָּמֹת:

55 When the men of *Yisrael* saw that *Avimelech* was dead, everyone went home.

נה וַיִּרְאוּ אִישׁ־יִשְׂרָאֵל כִּי מֵת אֲבִימֶלֶךְ וַיֵּלְכוּ אִישׁ לִמְקֹמוֹ:

56 Thus *Hashem* repaid *Avimelech* for the evil he had done to his father by slaying his seventy brothers;

נו וַיָּשֶׁב אֱלֹהִים אֵת רָעַת אֲבִימֶלֶךְ אֲשֶׁר עָשָׂה לְאָבִיו לַהֲרֹג אֶת־שִׁבְעִים אֶחָיו:

57 and *Hashem* likewise repaid the men of *Shechem* for all their wickedness. And so the curse of *Yotam* son of *Yerubaal* was fulfilled upon them.

נז וְאֵת כָּל־רָעַת אַנְשֵׁי שְׁכֶם הֵשִׁיב אֱלֹהִים בְּרֹאשָׁם וַתָּבֹא אֲלֵיהֶם קִלֲלַת יוֹתָם בֶּן־יְרֻבָּעַל:

10 1 After *Avimelech*, *Tola* son of Puah son of Dodo, a man of *Yissachar*, arose to deliver *Yisrael*. He lived at Shamir in the hill country of *Efraim*.

י א וַיָּקָם אַחֲרֵי אֲבִימֶלֶךְ לְהוֹשִׁיעַ אֶת־יִשְׂרָאֵל תּוֹלָע בֶּן־פּוּאָה בֶּן־דּוֹדוֹ אִישׁ יִשָּׂשכָר וְהוּא־יֹשֵׁב בְּשָׁמִיר בְּהַר אֶפְרָיִם:

2 He led *Yisrael* for twenty-three years; then he died and was buried at Shamir.

ב וַיִּשְׁפֹּט אֶת־יִשְׂרָאֵל עֶשְׂרִים וְשָׁלֹשׁ שָׁנָה וַיָּמָת וַיִּקָּבֵר בְּשָׁמִיר:

624

Shoftim/Judges
Chapter 10

שופטים
פרק י

3 After him arose *Yair* the Giladite, and he led *Yisrael* for twenty-two years.

ג וַיָּקָם אַחֲרָיו יָאִיר הַגִּלְעָדִי וַיִּשְׁפֹּט אֶת־יִשְׂרָאֵל עֶשְׂרִים וּשְׁתַּיִם שָׁנָה:

4 (He had thirty sons, who rode on thirty burros and owned thirty boroughs in the region of *Gilad*; these are called Havvoth-jair to this day.)

ד וַיְהִי־לוֹ שְׁלֹשִׁים בָּנִים רֹכְבִים עַל־שְׁלֹשִׁים עֲיָרִים וּשְׁלֹשִׁים עֲיָרִים לָהֶם לָהֶם יִקְרְאוּ חַוֺּת יָאִיר עַד הַיּוֹם הַזֶּה אֲשֶׁר בְּאֶרֶץ הַגִּלְעָד:

5 Then *Yair* died and was buried at Kamon.

ה וַיָּמָת יָאִיר וַיִּקָּבֵר בְּקָמוֹן:

6 The Israelites again did what was offensive to *Hashem*. They served the Baalim and the Ashtaroth, and the gods of Aram, the gods of Sidon, the gods of Moab, the gods of the Ammonites, and the gods of the Philistines; they forsook *Hashem* and did not serve Him.

ו וַיֹּסִפוּ בְּנֵי יִשְׂרָאֵל לַעֲשׂוֹת הָרַע בְּעֵינֵי יְהֹוָה וַיַּעַבְדוּ אֶת־הַבְּעָלִים וְאֶת־הָעַשְׁתָּרוֹת וְאֶת־אֱלֹהֵי אֲרָם וְאֶת־אֱלֹהֵי צִידוֹן וְאֵת אֱלֹהֵי מוֹאָב וְאֵת אֱלֹהֵי בְנֵי־עַמּוֹן וְאֵת אֱלֹהֵי פְלִשְׁתִּים וַיַּעַזְבוּ אֶת־יְהֹוָה וְלֹא עֲבָדוּהוּ:

7 And *Hashem*, incensed with *Yisrael*, surrendered them to the Philistines and to the Ammonites.

ז וַיִּחַר־אַף יְהֹוָה בְּיִשְׂרָאֵל וַיִּמְכְּרֵם בְּיַד־פְּלִשְׁתִּים וּבְיַד בְּנֵי עַמּוֹן:

va-yi-khar AF a-do-NAI b'-yis-ra-AYL va-yim-k'-RAYM b'-yad p'-lish-TEEM u-v'-YAD b'-NAY a-MON

8 That year they battered and shattered the Israelites – for eighteen years – all the Israelites beyond the *Yarden*, in [what had been] the land of the Amorites in *Gilad*.

ח וַיִּרְעֲצוּ וַיְרֹצְצוּ אֶת־בְּנֵי יִשְׂרָאֵל בַּשָּׁנָה הַהִיא שְׁמֹנֶה עֶשְׂרֵה שָׁנָה אֶת־כָּל־בְּנֵי יִשְׂרָאֵל אֲשֶׁר בְּעֵבֶר הַיַּרְדֵּן בְּאֶרֶץ הָאֱמֹרִי אֲשֶׁר בַּגִּלְעָד:

9 The Ammonites also crossed the *Yarden* to make war on *Yehuda*, *Binyamin*, and the House of *Efraim*. *Yisrael* was in great distress.

ט וַיַּעַבְרוּ בְנֵי־עַמּוֹן אֶת־הַיַּרְדֵּן לְהִלָּחֵם גַּם־בִּיהוּדָה וּבְבִנְיָמִין וּבְבֵית אֶפְרָיִם וַתֵּצֶר לְיִשְׂרָאֵל מְאֹד:

10 Then the Israelites cried out to *Hashem*, "We stand guilty before You, for we have forsaken our God and served the Baalim."

י וַיִּזְעֲקוּ בְּנֵי יִשְׂרָאֵל אֶל־יְהֹוָה לֵאמֹר חָטָאנוּ לָךְ וְכִי עָזַבְנוּ אֶת־אֱלֹהֵינוּ וַנַּעֲבֹד אֶת־הַבְּעָלִים:

11 But *Hashem* said to the Israelites, "[I have rescued you] from the Egyptians, from the Amorites, from the Ammonites, and from the Philistines.

יא וַיֹּאמֶר יְהֹוָה אֶל־בְּנֵי יִשְׂרָאֵל הֲלֹא מִמִּצְרַיִם וּמִן־הָאֱמֹרִי וּמִן־בְּנֵי עַמּוֹן וּמִן־פְּלִשְׁתִּים:

12 The Sidonians, Amalek, and Maon also oppressed you; and when you cried out to Me, I saved you from them.

יב וְצִידוֹנִים וַעֲמָלֵק וּמָעוֹן לָחֲצוּ אֶתְכֶם וַתִּצְעֲקוּ אֵלַי וָאוֹשִׁיעָה אֶתְכֶם מִיָּדָם:

13 Yet you have forsaken Me and have served other gods. No, I will not deliver you again.

יג וְאַתֶּם עֲזַבְתֶּם אוֹתִי וַתַּעַבְדוּ אֱלֹהִים אֲחֵרִים לָכֵן לֹא־אוֹסִיף לְהוֹשִׁיעַ אֶתְכֶם:

10:7 Surrendered them to the Philistines The Philistines are one of the Israelites' long-term enemies. It is interesting to note, however, that they are not among the seven Canaanite nations who initially inhabited the land. Rather, they are a foreign nation that invaded *Eretz Yisrael* via sea. Yet despite being neither natives nor the recipients of God's promise of the land, they often succeed in persecuting the Children of Israel and holding large amounts of territory in its land. However, in every case, *Hashem* eventually saves the People of Israel from their enemy.

625

Shoftim/Judges
Chapter 11

14 Go cry to the gods you have chosen; let them deliver you in your time of distress!"

15 But the Israelites implored *Hashem*: "We stand guilty. Do to us as You see fit; only save us this day!"

16 They removed the alien gods from among them and served *Hashem*; and He could not bear the miseries of *Yisrael*.

17 The Ammonites mustered and they encamped in *Gilad*; and the Israelites massed and they encamped at *Mitzpa*.

18 The troops – the officers of *Gilad* – said to one another, "Let the man who is the first to fight the Ammonites be chieftain over all the inhabitants of *Gilad*."

11

1 *Yiftach* the Giladite was an able warrior, who was the son of a prostitute. *Yiftach*'s father was *Gilad*;

2 but *Gilad* also had sons by his wife, and when the wife's sons grew up, they drove *Yiftach* out. They said to him, "You shall have no share in our father's property, for you are the son of an outsider."

3 So *Yiftach* fled from his brothers and settled in the Tob country. Men of low character gathered about *Yiftach* and went out raiding with him.

4 Some time later, the Ammonites went to war against *Yisrael*.

5 And when the Ammonites attacked *Yisrael*, the elders of *Gilad* went to bring *Yiftach* back from the Tob country.

6 They said to *Yiftach*, "Come be our chief, so that we can fight the Ammonites."

7 *Yiftach* replied to the elders of *Gilad*, "You are the very people who rejected me and drove me out of my father's house. How can you come to me now when you are in trouble?"

8 The elders of *Gilad* said to *Yiftach*, "Honestly, we have now turned back to you. If you come with us and fight the Ammonites, you shall be our commander over all the inhabitants of *Gilad*."

Shoftim/Judges
Chapter 11

שופטים
פרק יא

9 *Yiftach* said to the elders of *Gilad*, "[Very well,] if you bring me back to fight the Ammonites and *Hashem* delivers them to me, I am to be your commander."

ט וַיֹּאמֶר יִפְתָּח אֶל־זִקְנֵי גִלְעָד אִם־מְשִׁיבִים אַתֶּם אוֹתִי לְהִלָּחֵם בִּבְנֵי עַמּוֹן וְנָתַן יְהֹוָה אוֹתָם לְפָנָי אָנֹכִי אֶהְיֶה לָכֶם לְרֹאשׁ:

10 And the elders of *Gilad* answered Jepthah, "*Hashem* Himself shall be witness between us: we will do just as you have said."

י וַיֹּאמְרוּ זִקְנֵי־גִלְעָד אֶל־יִפְתָּח יְהֹוָה יִהְיֶה שֹׁמֵעַ בֵּינוֹתֵינוּ אִם־לֹא כִדְבָרְךָ כֵּן נַעֲשֶׂה:

11 *Yiftach* went with the elders of *Gilad*, and the people made him their commander and chief. And *Yiftach* repeated all these terms before *Hashem* at *Mitzpa*.

יא וַיֵּלֶךְ יִפְתָּח עִם־זִקְנֵי גִלְעָד וַיָּשִׂימוּ הָעָם אוֹתוֹ עֲלֵיהֶם לְרֹאשׁ וּלְקָצִין וַיְדַבֵּר יִפְתָּח אֶת־כָּל־דְּבָרָיו לִפְנֵי יְהֹוָה בַּמִּצְפָּה:

12 *Yiftach* then sent messengers to the king of the Ammonites, saying, "What have you against me that you have come to make war on my country?"

יב וַיִּשְׁלַח יִפְתָּח מַלְאָכִים אֶל־מֶלֶךְ בְּנֵי־עַמּוֹן לֵאמֹר מַה־לִּי וָלָךְ כִּי־בָאתָ אֵלַי לְהִלָּחֵם בְּאַרְצִי:

va-yish-LAKH yif-TAKH mal-a-KHEEM el ME-lekh b'-nay a-MON lay-MOR mah LEE va-LAKH kee VA-ta ay-LAI l'-hi-la-KHAYM b'-ar-TZEE

13 The king of the Ammonites replied to *Yiftach's* messengers, "When *Yisrael* came from Egypt, they seized the land which is mine, from the Arnon to the Jabbok as far as the *Yarden*. Now, then, restore it peaceably."

יג וַיֹּאמֶר מֶלֶךְ בְּנֵי־עַמּוֹן אֶל־מַלְאֲכֵי יִפְתָּח כִּי־לָקַח יִשְׂרָאֵל אֶת־אַרְצִי בַּעֲלוֹתוֹ מִמִּצְרַיִם מֵאַרְנוֹן וְעַד־הַיַּבֹּק וְעַד־הַיַּרְדֵּן וְעַתָּה הָשִׁיבָה אֶתְהֶן בְּשָׁלוֹם:

14 *Yiftach* again sent messengers to the king of the Ammonites.

יד וַיּוֹסֶף עוֹד יִפְתָּח וַיִּשְׁלַח מַלְאָכִים אֶל־מֶלֶךְ בְּנֵי עַמּוֹן:

15 He said to him, "Thus said *Yiftach*: *Yisrael* did not seize the land of Moab or the land of the Ammonites.

טו וַיֹּאמֶר לוֹ כֹּה אָמַר יִפְתָּח לֹא־לָקַח יִשְׂרָאֵל אֶת־אֶרֶץ מוֹאָב וְאֶת־אֶרֶץ בְּנֵי עַמּוֹן:

16 When they left Egypt, *Yisrael* traveled through the wilderness to the Sea of Reeds and went on to Kadesh.

טז כִּי בַּעֲלוֹתָם מִמִּצְרָיִם וַיֵּלֶךְ יִשְׂרָאֵל בַּמִּדְבָּר עַד־יַם־סוּף וַיָּבֹא קָדֵשָׁה:

17 *Yisrael* then sent messengers to the king of Edom, saying, 'Allow us to cross your country.' But the king of Edom would not consent. They also sent a mission to the king of Moab, and he refused. So *Yisrael*, after staying at Kadesh,

יז וַיִּשְׁלַח יִשְׂרָאֵל מַלְאָכִים אֶל־מֶלֶךְ אֱדוֹם לֵאמֹר אֶעְבְּרָה־נָּא בְאַרְצֶךָ וְלֹא שָׁמַע מֶלֶךְ אֱדוֹם וְגַם אֶל־מֶלֶךְ מוֹאָב שָׁלַח וְלֹא אָבָה וַיֵּשֶׁב יִשְׂרָאֵל בְּקָדֵשׁ:

בארצי

11:12 Yiftach then sent messengers to the king of the Ammonites As *Moshe* and *Yehoshua* did before him, *Yiftach* tries to avoid war by sending a message to the enemy. The Children of Israel always offer their adversaries a choice between three options: make peace, flee the land, or fight. Although war is the least desirable choice, peace is not to be obtained at any price. In his message to the Ammonites, *Yiftach* emphasized that they were seeking to make war *b'artzee* (בארצי), meaning 'on my country' or, more literally, 'in my land.' *Hashem* has given the Land of Israel to the Children of Israel, and therefore their struggle to possess it is by divine right.

Shoftim/Judges
Chapter 11

שופטים
פרק יא

18 traveled on through the wilderness, skirting the land of Edom and the land of Moab. They kept to the east of the land of Moab until they encamped on the other side of the Arnon; and, since Moab ends at the Arnon, they never entered Moabite territory.

יח וַיֵּלֶךְ בַּמִּדְבָּר וַיָּסָב אֶת־אֶרֶץ אֱדוֹם וְאֶת־אֶרֶץ מוֹאָב וַיָּבֹא מִמִּזְרַח־שֶׁמֶשׁ לְאֶרֶץ מוֹאָב וַיַּחֲנוּן בְּעֵבֶר אַרְנוֹן וְלֹא־בָאוּ בִּגְבוּל מוֹאָב כִּי אַרְנוֹן גְּבוּל מוֹאָב׃

19 "Then *Yisrael* sent messengers to Sihon king of the Amorites, the king of Heshbon. *Yisrael* said to him, 'Allow us to cross through your country to our homeland.'

יט וַיִּשְׁלַח יִשְׂרָאֵל מַלְאָכִים אֶל־סִיחוֹן מֶלֶךְ־הָאֱמֹרִי מֶלֶךְ חֶשְׁבּוֹן וַיֹּאמֶר לוֹ יִשְׂרָאֵל נַעְבְּרָה־נָּא בְאַרְצְךָ עַד־מְקוֹמִי׃

20 But Sihon would not trust *Yisrael* to pass through his territory. Sihon mustered all his troops, and they encamped at Jahaz; he engaged *Yisrael* in battle.

כ וְלֹא־הֶאֱמִין סִיחוֹן אֶת־יִשְׂרָאֵל עֲבֹר בִּגְבֻלוֹ וַיֶּאֱסֹף סִיחוֹן אֶת־כָּל־עַמּוֹ וַיַּחֲנוּ בְּיָהְצָה וַיִּלָּחֶם עִם־יִשְׂרָאֵל׃

21 But *Hashem*, the God of *Yisrael*, delivered Sihon and all his troops into *Yisrael*'s hands, and they defeated them; and *Yisrael* took possession of all the land of the Amorites, the inhabitants of that land.

כא וַיִּתֵּן יְהוָה אֱלֹהֵי־יִשְׂרָאֵל אֶת־סִיחוֹן וְאֶת־כָּל־עַמּוֹ בְּיַד יִשְׂרָאֵל וַיַּכּוּם וַיִּירַשׁ יִשְׂרָאֵל אֵת כָּל־אֶרֶץ הָאֱמֹרִי יוֹשֵׁב הָאָרֶץ הַהִיא׃

22 Thus they possessed all the territory of the Amorites from the Arnon to the Jabbok and from the wilderness to the *Yarden*.

כב וַיִּירְשׁוּ אֵת כָּל־גְּבוּל הָאֱמֹרִי מֵאַרְנוֹן וְעַד־הַיַּבֹּק וּמִן־הַמִּדְבָּר וְעַד־הַיַּרְדֵּן׃

23 "Now, then, *Hashem*, the God of *Yisrael*, dispossessed the Amorites before His people *Yisrael*; and should you possess their land?

כג וְעַתָּה יְהוָה אֱלֹהֵי יִשְׂרָאֵל הוֹרִישׁ אֶת־הָאֱמֹרִי מִפְּנֵי עַמּוֹ יִשְׂרָאֵל וְאַתָּה תִּירָשֶׁנּוּ׃

24 Do you not hold what Chemosh your god gives you to possess? So we will hold on to everything that *Hashem* our God has given us to possess.

כד הֲלֹא אֵת אֲשֶׁר יוֹרִישְׁךָ כְּמוֹשׁ אֱלֹהֶיךָ אוֹתוֹ תִירָשׁ וְאֵת כָּל־אֲשֶׁר הוֹרִישׁ יְהוָה אֱלֹהֵינוּ מִפָּנֵינוּ אוֹתוֹ נִירָשׁ׃

25 "Besides, are you any better than Balak son of Zippor, king of Moab? Did he start a quarrel with *Yisrael* or go to war with them?

כה וְעַתָּה הֲטוֹב טוֹב אַתָּה מִבָּלָק בֶּן־צִפּוֹר מֶלֶךְ מוֹאָב הֲרוֹב רָב עִם־יִשְׂרָאֵל אִם־נִלְחֹם נִלְחַם בָּם׃

26 "While *Yisrael* has been inhabiting Heshbon and its dependencies, and Aroer and its dependencies, and all the towns along the Arnon for three hundred years, why have you not tried to recover them all this time?

כו בְּשֶׁבֶת יִשְׂרָאֵל בְּחֶשְׁבּוֹן וּבִבְנוֹתֶיהָ וּבְעַרְעוֹר וּבִבְנוֹתֶיהָ וּבְכָל־הֶעָרִים אֲשֶׁר עַל־יְדֵי אַרְנוֹן שְׁלֹשׁ מֵאוֹת שָׁנָה וּמַדּוּעַ לֹא־הִצַּלְתֶּם בָּעֵת הַהִיא׃

27 I have done you no wrong; yet you are doing me harm and making war on me. May *Hashem*, who judges, decide today between the Israelites and the Ammonites!"

כז וְאָנֹכִי לֹא־חָטָאתִי לָךְ וְאַתָּה עֹשֶׂה אִתִּי רָעָה לְהִלָּחֶם בִּי יִשְׁפֹּט יְהוָה הַשֹּׁפֵט הַיּוֹם בֵּין בְּנֵי יִשְׂרָאֵל וּבֵין בְּנֵי עַמּוֹן׃

28 But the king of the Ammonites paid no heed to the message that *Yiftach* sent him.

כח וְלֹא שָׁמַע מֶלֶךְ בְּנֵי עַמּוֹן אֶל־דִּבְרֵי יִפְתָּח אֲשֶׁר שָׁלַח אֵלָיו׃

628

Shoftim/Judges
Chapter 11

שופטים
פרק יא

29 Then the spirit of *Hashem* came upon *Yiftach*. He marched through *Gilad* and *Menashe*, passing Mizpeh of *Gilad*; and from Mizpeh of *Gilad* he crossed over [to] the Ammonites.

כט וַתְּהִ֤י עַל־יִפְתָּח֙ ר֣וּחַ יְהֹוָ֔ה וַיַּעֲבֹ֥ר אֶת־הַגִּלְעָ֖ד וְאֶת־מְנַשֶּׁ֑ה וַֽיַּעֲבֹר֙ אֶת־מִצְפֵּ֣ה גִלְעָ֔ד וּמִמִּצְפֵּ֣ה גִלְעָ֔ד עָבַ֖ר בְּנֵ֥י עַמּֽוֹן׃

30 And *Yiftach* made the following vow to *Hashem*: "If you deliver the Ammonites into my hands,

ל וַיִּדַּ֨ר יִפְתָּ֥ח נֶ֛דֶר לַיהֹוָ֖ה וַיֹּאמַ֑ר אִם־נָת֥וֹן תִּתֵּ֛ן אֶת־בְּנֵ֥י עַמּ֖וֹן בְּיָדִֽי׃

31 then whatever comes out of the door of my house to meet me on my safe return from the Ammonites shall be *Hashem*'s and shall be offered by me as a burnt offering."

לא וְהָיָ֣ה הַיּוֹצֵ֗א אֲשֶׁ֨ר יֵצֵ֜א מִדַּלְתֵ֤י בֵיתִי֙ לִקְרָאתִ֔י בְּשׁוּבִ֥י בְשָׁל֖וֹם מִבְּנֵ֣י עַמּ֑וֹן וְהָיָה֙ לַֽיהֹוָ֔ה וְהַעֲלִיתִ֖הוּ עוֹלָֽה׃

32 *Yiftach* crossed over to the Ammonites and attacked them, and *Hashem* delivered them into his hands.

לב וַיַּעֲבֹ֥ר יִפְתָּ֛ח אֶל־בְּנֵ֥י עַמּ֖וֹן לְהִלָּ֣חֶם בָּ֑ם וַיִּתְּנֵ֥ם יְהֹוָ֖ה בְּיָדֽוֹ׃

33 He utterly routed them – from Aroer as far as Minnith, twenty towns – all the way to Abel-cheramim. So the Ammonites submitted to the Israelites.

לג וַיַּכֵּ֡ם מֵעֲרוֹעֵר֩ וְעַד־בּוֹאֲךָ֨ מִנִּ֜ית עֶשְׂרִ֣ים עִ֗יר וְעַד֙ אָבֵ֣ל כְּרָמִ֔ים מַכָּ֖ה גְּדוֹלָ֣ה מְאֹ֑ד וַיִּכָּֽנְעוּ֙ בְּנֵ֣י עַמּ֔וֹן מִפְּנֵ֖י בְּנֵ֥י יִשְׂרָאֵֽל׃

34 When *Yiftach* arrived at his home in *Mitzpa*, there was his daughter coming out to meet him, with timbrel and dance! She was an only child; he had no other son or daughter.

לד וַיָּבֹ֨א יִפְתָּ֣ח הַמִּצְפָּה֮ אֶל־בֵּיתוֹ֒ וְהִנֵּ֤ה בִתּוֹ֙ יֹצֵ֣את לִקְרָאת֔וֹ בְּתֻפִּ֖ים וּבִמְחֹל֑וֹת וְרַק֙ הִ֣יא יְחִידָ֔ה אֵֽין־ל֥וֹ מִמֶּ֖נּוּ בֵּ֥ן אוֹ־בַֽת׃

35 On seeing her, he rent his clothes and said, "Alas, daughter! You have brought me low; you have become my troubler! For I have uttered a vow to *Hashem* and I cannot retract."

לה וַיְהִי֩ כִרְאוֹת֨וֹ אוֹתָ֜הּ וַיִּקְרַ֣ע אֶת־בְּגָדָ֗יו וַיֹּ֙אמֶר֙ אֲהָ֣הּ בִּתִּ֔י הַכְרֵ֥עַ הִכְרַעְתִּ֖נִי וְאַ֣תְּ הָיִ֣יתְ בְּעֹכְרָ֑י וְאָנֹכִ֗י פָּצִ֤יתִי־פִי֙ אֶל־יְהֹוָ֔ה וְלֹ֥א אוּכַ֖ל לָשֽׁוּב׃

36 "Father," she said, "you have uttered a vow to *Hashem*; do to me as you have vowed, seeing that *Hashem* has vindicated you against your enemies, the Ammonites."

לו וַתֹּ֣אמֶר אֵלָ֔יו אָבִ֕י פָּצִ֥יתָה אֶת־פִּ֖יךָ אֶל־יְהֹוָ֑ה עֲשֵׂ֣ה לִ֗י כַּאֲשֶׁ֤ר יָצָא֙ מִפִּ֔יךָ אַחֲרֵ֨י אֲשֶׁ֨ר עָ֤שָׂה לְךָ֙ יְהֹוָ֣ה נְקָמ֔וֹת מֵאֹיְבֶ֖יךָ מִבְּנֵ֥י עַמּֽוֹן׃

37 She further said to her father, "Let this be done for me: let me be for two months, and I will go with my companions and lament upon the hills and there bewail my maidenhood."

לז וַתֹּ֙אמֶר֙ אֶל־אָבִ֔יהָ יֵעָ֥שֶׂה לִּ֖י הַדָּבָ֣ר הַזֶּ֑ה הַרְפֵּ֣ה מִמֶּ֗נִּי שְׁנַ֤יִם חֳדָשִׁים֙ וְאֵֽלְכָה֙ וְיָרַדְתִּ֣י עַל־הֶהָרִ֔ים וְאֶבְכֶּה֙ עַל־בְּתוּלַ֔י אָנֹכִ֖י ורעיתי [וְרֵעוֹתָֽי]׃

38 "Go," he replied. He let her go for two months, and she and her companions went and bewailed her maidenhood upon the hills.

לח וַיֹּ֣אמֶר לֵ֔כִי וַיִּשְׁלַ֥ח אוֹתָ֖הּ שְׁנֵ֣י חֳדָשִׁ֑ים וַתֵּ֤לֶךְ הִיא֙ וְרֵ֣עוֹתֶ֔יהָ וַתֵּ֥בְךְּ עַל־בְּתוּלֶ֖יהָ עַל־הֶהָרִֽים׃

39 After two months' time, she returned to her father, and he did to her as he had vowed. She had never known a man. So it became a custom in *Yisrael*

לט וַיְהִ֞י מִקֵּ֣ץ ׀ שְׁנַ֣יִם חֳדָשִׁ֗ים וַתָּ֙שׇׁב֙ אֶל־אָבִ֔יהָ וַיַּ֣עַשׂ לָ֔הּ אֶת־נִדְר֖וֹ אֲשֶׁ֣ר נָדָ֑ר וְהִיא֙ לֹא־יָדְעָ֣ה אִ֔ישׁ וַתְּהִי־חֹ֖ק בְּיִשְׂרָאֵֽל׃

40 for the maidens of *Yisrael* to go every year, for four days in the year, and chant dirges for the daughter of *Yiftach* the Giladite.

מ מִיָּמִ֣ים ׀ יָמִ֗ימָה תֵּלַ֙כְנָה֙ בְּנ֣וֹת יִשְׂרָאֵ֔ל לְתַנּ֕וֹת לְבַת־יִפְתָּ֖ח הַגִּלְעָדִ֑י אַרְבַּ֥עַת יָמִ֖ים בַּשָּׁנָֽה׃

Shoftim/Judges
Chapter 12

שׁוֹפְטִים
פרק יב

12 1 The men of *Efraim* mustered and crossed [the *Yarden*] to Zaphon. They said to *Yiftach*, "Why did you march to fight the Ammonites without calling us to go with you? We'll burn your house down over you!"

א וַיִּצָּעֵק אִישׁ אֶפְרַיִם וַיַּעֲבֹר צָפוֹנָה וַיֹּאמְרוּ לְיִפְתָּח מַדּוּעַ עָבַרְתָּ לְהִלָּחֵם בִּבְנֵי־עַמּוֹן וְלָנוּ לֹא קָרָאתָ לָלֶכֶת עִמָּךְ בֵּיתְךָ נִשְׂרֹף עָלֶיךָ בָּאֵשׁ:

2 *Yiftach* answered them, "I and my people were in a bitter conflict with the Ammonites; and I summoned you, but you did not save me from them.

ב וַיֹּאמֶר יִפְתָּח אֲלֵיהֶם אִישׁ רִיב הָיִיתִי אֲנִי וְעַמִּי וּבְנֵי־עַמּוֹן מְאֹד וָאֶזְעַק אֶתְכֶם וְלֹא־הוֹשַׁעְתֶּם אוֹתִי מִיָּדָם:

3 When I saw that you were no saviors, I risked my life and advanced against the Ammonites; and *Hashem* delivered them into my hands. Why have you come here now to fight against me?"

ג וָאֶרְאֶה כִּי־אֵינְךָ מוֹשִׁיעַ וָאָשִׂימָה נַפְשִׁי בְכַפִּי וָאֶעְבְּרָה אֶל־בְּנֵי עַמּוֹן וַיִּתְּנֵם יְהוָה בְּיָדִי וְלָמָה עֲלִיתֶם אֵלַי הַיּוֹם הַזֶּה לְהִלָּחֶם בִּי:

4 And *Yiftach* gathered all the men of *Gilad* and fought the Ephraimites. The men of *Gilad* defeated the Ephraimites; for they had said, "You Giladites are nothing but fugitives from *Efraim* – being in *Menashe* is like being in *Efraim*."

ד וַיִּקְבֹּץ יִפְתָּח אֶת־כָּל־אַנְשֵׁי גִלְעָד וַיִּלָּחֶם אֶת־אֶפְרָיִם וַיַּכּוּ אַנְשֵׁי גִלְעָד אֶת־אֶפְרַיִם כִּי אָמְרוּ פְּלִיטֵי אֶפְרַיִם אַתֶּם גִּלְעָד בְּתוֹךְ אֶפְרַיִם בְּתוֹךְ מְנַשֶּׁה:

5 The Giladites held the fords of the *Yarden* against the Ephraimites. And when any fugitive from *Efraim* said, "Let me cross," the men of *Gilad* would ask him, "Are you an Ephraimites?"; if he said "No,"

ה וַיִּלְכֹּד גִּלְעָד אֶת־מַעְבְּרוֹת הַיַּרְדֵּן לְאֶפְרָיִם וְהָיָה כִּי יֹאמְרוּ פְּלִיטֵי אֶפְרַיִם אֶעֱבֹרָה וַיֹּאמְרוּ לוֹ אַנְשֵׁי־גִלְעָד הַאֶפְרָתִי אַתָּה וַיֹּאמֶר לֹא:

6 they would say to him, "Then say shibboleth"; but he would say "sibboleth," not being able to pronounce it correctly. Thereupon they would seize him and slay him by the fords of the *Yarden*. Forty-two thousand Ephraimites fell at that time.

ו וַיֹּאמְרוּ לוֹ אֱמָר־נָא שִׁבֹּלֶת וַיֹּאמֶר סִבֹּלֶת וְלֹא יָכִין לְדַבֵּר כֵּן וַיֹּאחֲזוּ אוֹתוֹ וַיִּשְׁחָטוּהוּ אֶל־מַעְבְּרוֹת הַיַּרְדֵּן וַיִּפֹּל בָּעֵת הַהִיא מֵאֶפְרַיִם אַרְבָּעִים וּשְׁנַיִם אָלֶף:

7 *Yiftach* led *Yisrael* six years. Then *Yiftach* the Giladite died and he was buried in one of the towns of *Gilad*.

ז וַיִּשְׁפֹּט יִפְתָּח אֶת־יִשְׂרָאֵל שֵׁשׁ שָׁנִים וַיָּמָת יִפְתָּח הַגִּלְעָדִי וַיִּקָּבֵר בְּעָרֵי גִלְעָד:

8 After him, *Ivtzan* of *Beit Lechem* led *Yisrael*.

ח וַיִּשְׁפֹּט אַחֲרָיו אֶת־יִשְׂרָאֵל אִבְצָן מִבֵּית לָחֶם:

va-yish-POT a-kha-RAV et yis-ra-AYL iv-TZAN mi-BAYT LA-khem

9 He had thirty sons, and he married off thirty daughters outside the clan and brought in thirty girls from outside the clan for his sons. He led *Yisrael* seven years.

ט וַיְהִי־לוֹ שְׁלֹשִׁים בָּנִים וּשְׁלֹשִׁים בָּנוֹת שִׁלַּח הַחוּצָה וּשְׁלֹשִׁים בָּנוֹת הֵבִיא לְבָנָיו מִן־הַחוּץ וַיִּשְׁפֹּט אֶת־יִשְׂרָאֵל שֶׁבַע שָׁנִים:

12:8 *Ivtzan* of *Beit Lechem* led *Yisrael* According to the Talmud (*Bava Batra* 91a), the judge called *Ivtzan* mentioned in this verse is none other than *Boaz*, one of the heroes of *Megillat Rut*. At the climax of that dramatic narrative, *Boaz* marries the poor Moabite convert *Rut*. Their descendants include King *David*, and will ultimately also include the righteous *Mashiach*. *Ivtzan* has sixty children. But it is a unique child, born as a result of his kindness to a poor convert, who is the ancestor of the redeemer of Israel. *Hashem* indeed finds many ways to take care of the People of Israel, and to reward acts of kindness.

Shoftim/Judges
Chapter 13

שׁוֹפְטִים
פרק יג

10 Then *Ivtzan* died and was buried in *Beit Lechem*.

י וַיָּמָת אִבְצָן וַיִּקָּבֵר בְּבֵית לָחֶם׃

11 After him, *Eilon* the Zebulunite led *Yisrael*; he led *Yisrael* for ten years.

יא וַיִּשְׁפֹּט אַחֲרָיו אֶת־יִשְׂרָאֵל אֵילוֹן הַזְּבוּלֹנִי וַיִּשְׁפֹּט אֶת־יִשְׂרָאֵל עֶשֶׂר שָׁנִים׃

12 Then *Eilon* the Zebulunite died and was buried in Aijalon, in the territory of *Zevulun*.

יב וַיָּמָת אֵלוֹן הַזְּבוּלֹנִי וַיִּקָּבֵר בְּאַיָּלוֹן בְּאֶרֶץ זְבוּלֻן׃

13 After him, *Avdon* son of Hillel the Pirathonite led *Yisrael*.

יג וַיִּשְׁפֹּט אַחֲרָיו אֶת־יִשְׂרָאֵל עַבְדּוֹן בֶּן־הִלֵּל הַפִּרְעָתוֹנִי׃

14 He had forty sons and thirty grandsons, who rode on seventy jackasses. He led *Yisrael* for eight years.

יד וַיְהִי־לוֹ אַרְבָּעִים בָּנִים וּשְׁלֹשִׁים בְּנֵי בָנִים רֹכְבִים עַל־שִׁבְעִים עֲיָרִם וַיִּשְׁפֹּט אֶת־יִשְׂרָאֵל שְׁמֹנֶה שָׁנִים׃

15 Then *Avdon* son of Hillel the Pirathonite died. He was buried in Pirathon, in the territory of *Efraim*, on the hill of the Amalekites.

טו וַיָּמָת עַבְדּוֹן בֶּן־הִלֵּל הַפִּרְעָתוֹנִי וַיִּקָּבֵר בְּפִרְעָתוֹן בְּאֶרֶץ אֶפְרַיִם בְּהַר הָעֲמָלֵקִי׃

13

1 *B'nei Yisrael* again did what was offensive to *Hashem*, and *Hashem* delivered them into the hands of the Philistines for forty years.

יג א וַיֹּסִפוּ בְּנֵי יִשְׂרָאֵל לַעֲשׂוֹת הָרַע בְּעֵינֵי יְהֹוָה וַיִּתְּנֵם יְהֹוָה בְּיַד־פְּלִשְׁתִּים אַרְבָּעִים שָׁנָה׃

2 There was a certain man from *Tzora*, of the stock of *Dan*, whose name was *Manoach*. His wife was barren and had borne no children.

ב וַיְהִי אִישׁ אֶחָד מִצָּרְעָה מִמִּשְׁפַּחַת הַדָּנִי וּשְׁמוֹ מָנוֹחַ וְאִשְׁתּוֹ עֲקָרָה וְלֹא יָלָדָה׃

3 An angel of *Hashem* appeared to the woman and said to her, "You are barren and have borne no children; but you shall conceive and bear a son.

ג וַיֵּרָא מַלְאַךְ־יְהֹוָה אֶל־הָאִשָּׁה וַיֹּאמֶר אֵלֶיהָ הִנֵּה־נָא אַתְּ־עֲקָרָה וְלֹא יָלַדְתְּ וְהָרִית וְיָלַדְתְּ בֵּן׃

4 Now be careful not to drink wine or other intoxicant, or to eat anything unclean.

ד וְעַתָּה הִשָּׁמְרִי נָא וְאַל־תִּשְׁתִּי יַיִן וְשֵׁכָר וְאַל־תֹּאכְלִי כָּל־טָמֵא׃

5 For you are going to conceive and bear a son; let no razor touch his head, for the boy is to be a nazirite to *Hashem* from the womb on. He shall be the first to deliver *Yisrael* from the Philistines."

ה כִּי הִנָּךְ הָרָה וְיֹלַדְתְּ בֵּן וּמוֹרָה לֹא־יַעֲלֶה עַל־רֹאשׁוֹ כִּי־נְזִיר אֱלֹהִים יִהְיֶה הַנַּעַר מִן־הַבָּטֶן וְהוּא יָחֵל לְהוֹשִׁיעַ אֶת־יִשְׂרָאֵל מִיַּד פְּלִשְׁתִּים׃

KEE hi-NAKH ha-RAH v'-yo-LAD-t' BAYN u-mo-RAH lo ya-a-LEH al ro-SHO kee n'-ZEER e-lo-HEEM yih-YEH ha-NA-ar min ha-BA-ten v'-HU ya-KHAYL l'-ho-SHEE-a et yis-ra-AYL mi-YAD p'-lish-TEEM

Rabbi David Cohen, Nazir of Jerusalem (1887–1972)

13:5 For the boy is to be a nazirite to *Hashem* from the womb on The promised child, who will be the strong and fearless judge *Shimshon*, is to be a nazirite from birth. This is an unusual situation; most nazirites choose this status temporarily, for a limited period. Though typically people do not take such vows nowadays, a famous exception was Rabbi David Cohen (1887–1972). Known as "The Nazir," 'nazirite,' he was a close student of Rabbi Abraham Isaac Kook, and was a nazirite for most of his life. Following his move to *Eretz Yisrael*, Rabbi Cohen also refused to leave Jerusalem. Along with Rabbi Tzvi Yehuda Kook, he was brought by his students serving in the Israeli Army to the Western Wall shortly after its liberation during the Six Day War. When secular Israeli soldiers saw Rabbis Cohen and Kook at the *Kotel* in the midst of the war, they gasped and pointed, assuming the two saintly rabbis were none other than the *Mashiach* and the Prophet *Eliyahu*. The *Nazir* of *Yerushalayim* was a reminder of the holiness that special people can achieve, even today.

Shoftim/Judges
Chapter 13

6 The woman went and told her husband, "A man of *Hashem* came to me; he looked like an angel of *Hashem*, very frightening. I did not ask him where he was from, nor did he tell me his name.

7 He said to me, 'You are going to conceive and bear a son. Drink no wine or other intoxicant, and eat nothing unclean, for the boy is to be a nazirite to *Hashem* from the womb to the day of his death!'"

8 *Manoach* pleaded with *Hashem*. "Oh, my Lord!" he said, "please let the man of *Hashem* that You sent come to us again, and let him instruct us how to act with the child that is to be born."

9 *Hashem* heeded *Manoach*'s plea, and the angel of *Hashem* came to the woman again. She was sitting in the field and her husband *Manoach* was not with her.

10 The woman ran in haste to tell her husband. She said to him, "The man who came to me before has just appeared to me."

11 *Manoach* promptly followed his wife. He came to the man and asked him: "Are you the man who spoke to my wife?" "Yes," he answered.

12 Then *Manoach* said, "May your words soon come true! What rules shall be observed for the boy?"

13 The angel of *Hashem* said to *Manoach*, "The woman must abstain from all the things against which I warned her.

14 She must not eat anything that comes from the grapevine, or drink wine or other intoxicant, or eat anything unclean. She must observe all that I commanded her."

15 *Manoach* said to the angel of *Hashem*, "Let us detain you and prepare a kid for you."

16 But the angel of *Hashem* said to *Manoach*, "If you detain me, I shall not eat your food; and if you present a burnt offering, offer it to *Hashem*." – For *Manoach* did not know that he was an angel of *Hashem*.

17 So *Manoach* said to the angel of *Hashem*, "What is your name? We should like to honor you when your words come true."

שׁוֹפְטִים
פרק יג

ו וַתָּבֹא הָאִשָּׁה וַתֹּאמֶר לְאִישָׁהּ לֵאמֹר אִישׁ הָאֱלֹהִים בָּא אֵלַי וּמַרְאֵהוּ כְּמַרְאֵה מַלְאַךְ הָאֱלֹהִים נוֹרָא מְאֹד וְלֹא שְׁאִלְתִּיהוּ אֵי־מִזֶּה הוּא וְאֶת־שְׁמוֹ לֹא־הִגִּיד לִי:

ז וַיֹּאמֶר לִי הִנָּךְ הָרָה וְיֹלַדְתְּ בֵּן וְעַתָּה אַל־תִּשְׁתִּי יַיִן וְשֵׁכָר וְאַל־תֹּאכְלִי כָּל־טֻמְאָה כִּי־נְזִיר אֱלֹהִים יִהְיֶה הַנַּעַר מִן־הַבֶּטֶן עַד־יוֹם מוֹתוֹ:

ח וַיֶּעְתַּר מָנוֹחַ אֶל־יְהוָה וַיֹּאמַר בִּי אֲדוֹנָי אִישׁ הָאֱלֹהִים אֲשֶׁר שָׁלַחְתָּ יָבוֹא־נָא עוֹד אֵלֵינוּ וְיוֹרֵנוּ מַה־נַּעֲשֶׂה לַנַּעַר הַיּוּלָּד:

ט וַיִּשְׁמַע הָאֱלֹהִים בְּקוֹל מָנוֹחַ וַיָּבֹא מַלְאַךְ הָאֱלֹהִים עוֹד אֶל־הָאִשָּׁה וְהִיא יוֹשֶׁבֶת בַּשָּׂדֶה וּמָנוֹחַ אִישָׁהּ אֵין עִמָּהּ:

י וַתְּמַהֵר הָאִשָּׁה וַתָּרָץ וַתַּגֵּד לְאִישָׁהּ וַתֹּאמֶר אֵלָיו הִנֵּה נִרְאָה אֵלַי הָאִישׁ אֲשֶׁר־בָּא בַיּוֹם אֵלָי:

יא וַיָּקָם וַיֵּלֶךְ מָנוֹחַ אַחֲרֵי אִשְׁתּוֹ וַיָּבֹא אֶל־הָאִישׁ וַיֹּאמֶר לוֹ הַאַתָּה הָאִישׁ אֲשֶׁר־דִּבַּרְתָּ אֶל־הָאִשָּׁה וַיֹּאמֶר אָנִי:

יב וַיֹּאמֶר מָנוֹחַ עַתָּה יָבֹא דְבָרֶיךָ מַה־יִּהְיֶה מִשְׁפַּט־הַנַּעַר וּמַעֲשֵׂהוּ:

יג וַיֹּאמֶר מַלְאַךְ יְהוָה אֶל־מָנוֹחַ מִכֹּל אֲשֶׁר־אָמַרְתִּי אֶל־הָאִשָּׁה תִּשָּׁמֵר:

יד מִכֹּל אֲשֶׁר־יֵצֵא מִגֶּפֶן הַיַּיִן לֹא תֹאכַל וְיַיִן וְשֵׁכָר אַל־תֵּשְׁתְּ וְכָל־טֻמְאָה אַל־תֹּאכַל כֹּל אֲשֶׁר־צִוִּיתִיהָ תִּשְׁמֹר:

טו וַיֹּאמֶר מָנוֹחַ אֶל־מַלְאַךְ יְהוָה נַעְצְרָה־נָּא אוֹתָךְ וְנַעֲשֶׂה לְפָנֶיךָ גְּדִי עִזִּים:

טז וַיֹּאמֶר מַלְאַךְ יְהוָה אֶל־מָנוֹחַ אִם־תַּעְצְרֵנִי לֹא־אֹכַל בְּלַחְמֶךָ וְאִם־תַּעֲשֶׂה עֹלָה לַיהוָה תַּעֲלֶנָּה כִּי לֹא־יָדַע מָנוֹחַ כִּי־מַלְאַךְ יְהוָה הוּא:

יז וַיֹּאמֶר מָנוֹחַ אֶל־מַלְאַךְ יְהוָה מִי שְׁמֶךָ כִּי־יָבֹא דבריך [דְבָרְךָ] וְכִבַּדְנוּךָ:

Shoftim/Judges
Chapter 14

שופטים
פרק יד

18 The angel said to him, "You must not ask for my name; it is unknowable!"

יח וַיֹּאמֶר לוֹ מַלְאַךְ יְהֹוָה לָמָּה זֶּה תִּשְׁאַל לִשְׁמִי וְהוּא־פֶּלִאי׃

19 *Manoach* took the kid and the meal offering and offered them up on the rock to *Hashem*; and a marvelous thing happened while *Manoach* and his wife looked on.

יט וַיִּקַּח מָנוֹחַ אֶת־גְּדִי הָעִזִּים וְאֶת־הַמִּנְחָה וַיַּעַל עַל־הַצּוּר לַיהֹוָה וּמַפְלִא לַעֲשׂוֹת וּמָנוֹחַ וְאִשְׁתּוֹ רֹאִים׃

20 As the flames leaped up from the *Mizbayach* toward the sky, the angel of *Hashem* ascended in the flames of the *Mizbayach*, while *Manoach* and his wife looked on; and they flung themselves on their faces to the ground.

כ וַיְהִי בַעֲלוֹת הַלַּהַב מֵעַל הַמִּזְבֵּחַ הַשָּׁמַיְמָה וַיַּעַל מַלְאַךְ־יְהֹוָה בְּלַהַב הַמִּזְבֵּחַ וּמָנוֹחַ וְאִשְׁתּוֹ רֹאִים וַיִּפְּלוּ עַל־פְּנֵיהֶם אָרְצָה׃

21 The angel of *Hashem* never appeared again to *Manoach* and his wife. – *Manoach* then realized that it had been an angel of *Hashem*.

כא וְלֹא־יָסַף עוֹד מַלְאַךְ יְהֹוָה לְהֵרָאֹה אֶל־מָנוֹחַ וְאֶל־אִשְׁתּוֹ אָז יָדַע מָנוֹחַ כִּי־מַלְאַךְ יְהֹוָה הוּא׃

22 And *Manoach* said to his wife, "We shall surely die, for we have seen a divine being."

כב וַיֹּאמֶר מָנוֹחַ אֶל־אִשְׁתּוֹ מוֹת נָמוּת כִּי אֱלֹהִים רָאִינוּ׃

23 But his wife said to him, "Had *Hashem* meant to take our lives, He would not have accepted a burnt offering and meal offering from us, nor let us see all these things; and He would not have made such an announcement to us."

כג וַתֹּאמֶר לוֹ אִשְׁתּוֹ לוּ חָפֵץ יְהֹוָה לַהֲמִיתֵנוּ לֹא־לָקַח מִיָּדֵנוּ עֹלָה וּמִנְחָה וְלֹא הֶרְאָנוּ אֶת־כָּל־אֵלֶּה וְכָעֵת לֹא הִשְׁמִיעָנוּ כָּזֹאת׃

24 The woman bore a son, and she named him *Shimshon*. The boy grew up, and *Hashem* blessed him.

כד וַתֵּלֶד הָאִשָּׁה בֵּן וַתִּקְרָא אֶת־שְׁמוֹ שִׁמְשׁוֹן וַיִּגְדַּל הַנַּעַר וַיְבָרְכֵהוּ יְהֹוָה׃

25 The spirit of *Hashem* first moved him in the encampment of *Dan*, between *Tzora* and *Eshtaol*.

כה וַתָּחֶל רוּחַ יְהֹוָה לְפַעֲמוֹ בְּמַחֲנֵה־דָן בֵּין צָרְעָה וּבֵין אֶשְׁתָּאֹל׃

14

1 Once *Shimshon* went down to Timnah; and while in Timnah, he noticed a girl among the Philistine women.

יד א וַיֵּרֶד שִׁמְשׁוֹן תִּמְנָתָה וַיַּרְא אִשָּׁה בְּתִמְנָתָה מִבְּנוֹת פְּלִשְׁתִּים׃

2 On his return, he told his father and mother, "I noticed one of the Philistine women in Timnah; please get her for me as a wife."

ב וַיַּעַל וַיַּגֵּד לְאָבִיו וּלְאִמּוֹ וַיֹּאמֶר אִשָּׁה רָאִיתִי בְתִמְנָתָה מִבְּנוֹת פְּלִשְׁתִּים וְעַתָּה קְחוּ־אוֹתָהּ לִּי לְאִשָּׁה׃

3 His father and mother said to him, "Is there no one among the daughters of your own kinsmen and among all our people, that you must go and take a wife from the uncircumcised Philistines?" But *Shimshon* answered his father, "Get me that one, for she is the one that pleases me."

ג וַיֹּאמֶר לוֹ אָבִיו וְאִמּוֹ הַאֵין בִּבְנוֹת אַחֶיךָ וּבְכָל־עַמִּי אִשָּׁה כִּי־אַתָּה הוֹלֵךְ לָקַחַת אִשָּׁה מִפְּלִשְׁתִּים הָעֲרֵלִים וַיֹּאמֶר שִׁמְשׁוֹן אֶל־אָבִיו אוֹתָהּ קַח־לִי כִּי־הִיא יָשְׁרָה בְעֵינָי׃

4 His father and mother did not realize that this was *Hashem*'s doing: He was seeking a pretext against the Philistines, for the Philistines were ruling over *Yisrael* at that time.

ד וְאָבִיו וְאִמּוֹ לֹא יָדְעוּ כִּי מֵיְהֹוָה הִיא כִּי־תֹאֲנָה הוּא־מְבַקֵּשׁ מִפְּלִשְׁתִּים וּבָעֵת הַהִיא פְּלִשְׁתִּים מֹשְׁלִים בְּיִשְׂרָאֵל׃

Shoftim/Judges
Chapter 14

5 So *Shimshon* and his father and mother went down to Timnah. When he came to the vineyards of Timnah [for the first time], a full-grown lion came roaring at him.

6 The spirit of *Hashem* gripped him, and he tore him asunder with his bare hands as one might tear a kid asunder; but he did not tell his father and mother what he had done.

7 Then he went down and spoke to the woman, and she pleased *Shimshon*.

8 Returning the following year to marry her, he turned aside to look at the remains of the lion; and in the lion's skeleton he found a swarm of bees, and honey.

9 He scooped it into his palms and ate it as he went along. When he rejoined his father and mother, he gave them some and they ate it; but he did not tell them that he had scooped the honey out of a lion's skeleton.

10 So his father came down to the woman, and *Shimshon* made a feast there, as young men used to do.

11 When they saw him, they designated thirty companions to be with him.

12 Then *Shimshon* said to them, "Let me propound a riddle to you. If you can give me the right answer during the seven days of the feast, I shall give you thirty linen tunics and thirty sets of clothing;

13 but if you are not able to tell it to me, you must give me thirty linen tunics and thirty sets of clothing." And they said to him, "Ask your riddle and we will listen."

14 So he said to them: "Out of the eater came something to eat, Out of the strong came something sweet." For three days they could not answer the riddle.

15 On the seventh day, they said to *Shimshon*'s wife, "Coax your husband to provide us with the answer to the riddle; else we shall put you and your father's household to the fire; have you invited us here in order to impoverish us?"

ה וַיֵּרֶד שִׁמְשׁוֹן וְאָבִיו וְאִמּוֹ תִּמְנָתָה וַיָּבֹאוּ עַד־כַּרְמֵי תִמְנָתָה וְהִנֵּה כְּפִיר אֲרָיוֹת שֹׁאֵג לִקְרָאתוֹ:

ו וַתִּצְלַח עָלָיו רוּחַ יְהֹוָה וַיְשַׁסְּעֵהוּ כְּשַׁסַּע הַגְּדִי וּמְאוּמָה אֵין בְּיָדוֹ וְלֹא הִגִּיד לְאָבִיו וּלְאִמּוֹ אֵת אֲשֶׁר עָשָׂה:

ז וַיֵּרֶד וַיְדַבֵּר לָאִשָּׁה וַתִּישַׁר בְּעֵינֵי שִׁמְשׁוֹן:

ח וַיָּשָׁב מִיָּמִים לְקַחְתָּהּ וַיָּסַר לִרְאוֹת אֵת מַפֶּלֶת הָאַרְיֵה וְהִנֵּה עֲדַת דְּבוֹרִים בִּגְוִיַּת הָאַרְיֵה וּדְבָשׁ:

ט וַיִּרְדֵּהוּ אֶל־כַּפָּיו וַיֵּלֶךְ הָלוֹךְ וְאָכֹל וַיֵּלֶךְ אֶל־אָבִיו וְאֶל־אִמּוֹ וַיִּתֵּן לָהֶם וַיֹּאכֵלוּ וְלֹא־הִגִּיד לָהֶם כִּי מִגְּוִיַּת הָאַרְיֵה רָדָה הַדְּבָשׁ:

י וַיֵּרֶד אָבִיהוּ אֶל־הָאִשָּׁה וַיַּעַשׂ שָׁם שִׁמְשׁוֹן מִשְׁתֶּה כִּי כֵּן יַעֲשׂוּ הַבַּחוּרִים:

יא וַיְהִי כִּרְאוֹתָם אוֹתוֹ וַיִּקְחוּ שְׁלֹשִׁים מֵרֵעִים וַיִּהְיוּ אִתּוֹ:

יב וַיֹּאמֶר לָהֶם שִׁמְשׁוֹן אָחוּדָה־נָּא לָכֶם חִידָה אִם־הַגֵּד תַּגִּידוּ אוֹתָהּ לִי שִׁבְעַת יְמֵי הַמִּשְׁתֶּה וּמְצָאתֶם וְנָתַתִּי לָכֶם שְׁלֹשִׁים סְדִינִים וּשְׁלֹשִׁים חֲלִפֹת בְּגָדִים:

יג וְאִם־לֹא תוּכְלוּ לְהַגִּיד לִי וּנְתַתֶּם אַתֶּם לִי שְׁלֹשִׁים סְדִינִים וּשְׁלֹשִׁים חֲלִיפוֹת בְּגָדִים וַיֹּאמְרוּ לוֹ חוּדָה חִידָתְךָ וְנִשְׁמָעֶנָּה:

יד וַיֹּאמֶר לָהֶם מֵהָאֹכֵל יָצָא מַאֲכָל וּמֵעַז יָצָא מָתוֹק וְלֹא יָכְלוּ לְהַגִּיד הַחִידָה שְׁלֹשֶׁת יָמִים:

טו וַיְהִי בַּיּוֹם הַשְּׁבִיעִי וַיֹּאמְרוּ לְאֵשֶׁת־שִׁמְשׁוֹן פַּתִּי אֶת־אִישֵׁךְ וְיַגֶּד־לָנוּ אֶת־הַחִידָה פֶּן־נִשְׂרֹף אוֹתָךְ וְאֶת־בֵּית אָבִיךְ בָּאֵשׁ הַלְיָרְשֵׁנוּ קְרָאתֶם לָנוּ הֲלֹא:

Shoftim/Judges
Chapter 15

שופטים
פרק טו

16 Then *Shimshon*'s wife harassed him with tears, and she said, "You really hate me, you don't love me. You asked my countrymen a riddle, and you didn't tell me the answer." He replied, "I haven't even told my father and mother; shall I tell you?"

טז וַתֵּבְךְּ אֵשֶׁת שִׁמְשׁוֹן עָלָיו וַתֹּאמֶר רַק־שְׂנֵאתַנִי וְלֹא אֲהַבְתָּנִי הַחִידָה חַדְתָּ לִבְנֵי עַמִּי וְלִי לֹא הִגַּדְתָּה וַיֹּאמֶר לָהּ הִנֵּה לְאָבִי וּלְאִמִּי לֹא הִגַּדְתִּי וְלָךְ אַגִּיד:

17 During the rest of the seven days of the feast she continued to harass him with her tears, and on the seventh day he told her, because she nagged him so. And she explained the riddle to her countrymen.

יז וַתֵּבְךְּ עָלָיו שִׁבְעַת הַיָּמִים אֲשֶׁר־הָיָה לָהֶם הַמִּשְׁתֶּה וַיְהִי בַּיּוֹם הַשְּׁבִיעִי וַיַּגֶּד־לָהּ כִּי הֱצִיקַתְהוּ וַתַּגֵּד הַחִידָה לִבְנֵי עַמָּהּ:

18 On the seventh day, before the sunset, the townsmen said to him: "What is sweeter than honey, And what is stronger than a lion?" He responded: "Had you not plowed with my heifer, You would not have guessed my riddle!"

יח וַיֹּאמְרוּ לוֹ אַנְשֵׁי הָעִיר בַּיּוֹם הַשְּׁבִיעִי בְּטֶרֶם יָבֹא הַחַרְסָה מַה־מָּתוֹק מִדְּבַשׁ וּמֶה עַז מֵאֲרִי וַיֹּאמֶר לָהֶם לוּלֵא חֲרַשְׁתֶּם בְּעֶגְלָתִי לֹא מְצָאתֶם חִידָתִי:

19 The spirit of *Hashem* gripped him. He went down to *Ashkelon* and killed thirty of its men. He stripped them and gave the sets of clothing to those who had answered the riddle. And he left in a rage for his father's house.

יט וַתִּצְלַח עָלָיו רוּחַ יְהֹוָה וַיֵּרֶד אַשְׁקְלוֹן וַיַּךְ מֵהֶם שְׁלֹשִׁים אִישׁ וַיִּקַּח אֶת־חֲלִיצוֹתָם וַיִּתֵּן הַחֲלִיפוֹת לְמַגִּידֵי הַחִידָה וַיִּחַר אַפּוֹ וַיַּעַל בֵּית אָבִיהוּ:

va-titz-LAKH a-LAV RU-akh a-do-NAI va-YAY-red ash-k'-LON va-YAKH may-HEM sh'-lo-SHEEM eesh va-yi-KAKH et kha-lee-tzo-TAM va-yi-TAYN ha-kha-lee-FOT l'-ma-gee-DAY ha-khee-DAH va-yi-KHAR a-PO va-YA-al BAYT a-VEE-hu

20 *Shimshon*'s wife then married one of those who had been his wedding companions.

כ וַתְּהִי אֵשֶׁת שִׁמְשׁוֹן לְמֵרֵעֵהוּ אֲשֶׁר רֵעָה לוֹ:

15

1 Some time later, in the season of the wheat harvest, *Shimshon* came to visit his wife, bringing a kid as a gift. He said, "Let me go into the chamber to my wife." But her father would not let him go in.

א וַיְהִי מִיָּמִים בִּימֵי קְצִיר־חִטִּים וַיִּפְקֹד שִׁמְשׁוֹן אֶת־אִשְׁתּוֹ בִּגְדִי עִזִּים וַיֹּאמֶר אָבֹאָה אֶל־אִשְׁתִּי הֶחָדְרָה וְלֹא־נְתָנוֹ אָבִיהָ לָבוֹא:

2 "I was sure," said her father, "that you had taken a dislike to her, so I gave her to your wedding companion. But her younger sister is more beautiful than she; let her become your wife instead."

ב וַיֹּאמֶר אָבִיהָ אָמֹר אָמַרְתִּי כִּי־שָׂנֹא שְׂנֵאתָהּ וָאֶתְּנֶנָּה לְמֵרֵעֶךָ הֲלֹא אֲחוֹתָהּ הַקְּטַנָּה טוֹבָה מִמֶּנָּה תְּהִי־נָא לְךָ תַּחְתֶּיהָ:

3 Thereupon *Shimshon* declared, "Now the Philistines can have no claim against me for the harm I shall do them."

ג וַיֹּאמֶר לָהֶם שִׁמְשׁוֹן נִקֵּיתִי הַפַּעַם מִפְּלִשְׁתִּים כִּי־עֹשֶׂה אֲנִי עִמָּם רָעָה:

14:19 The spirit of *Hashem* gripped him According to *Rashi*, when the Bible says that the "spirit of *Hashem*" rested upon *Shimshon*, it means that God gave him a strong, heroic spirit, meaning a type of spiritual strength that helps him recognize *Hashem*'s guidance and channel all of his powers into serving Him. Thus, it is this spiritual strength that enables *Shimshon* to use his great physical strength against the Philistines. There is a difference between the physical strength within our bodies and spiritual strength, which helps us meet all challenges to do God's will. *Shimshon* has both.

Shoftim/Judges
Chapter 15

4 *Shimshon* went and caught three hundred foxes. He took torches and, turning [the foxes] tail to tail, he placed a torch between each pair of tails.

ד וַיֵּלֶךְ שִׁמְשׁוֹן וַיִּלְכֹּד שְׁלֹשׁ־מֵאוֹת שׁוּעָלִים וַיִּקַּח לַפִּדִים וַיֶּפֶן זָנָב אֶל־זָנָב וַיָּשֶׂם לַפִּיד אֶחָד בֵּין־שְׁנֵי הַזְּנָבוֹת בַּתָּוֶךְ:

5 He lit the torches and turned [the foxes] loose among the standing grain of the Philistines, setting fire to stacked grain, standing grain, vineyards, [and] olive trees.

ה וַיַּבְעֶר־אֵשׁ בַּלַּפִּידִים וַיְשַׁלַּח בְּקָמוֹת פְּלִשְׁתִּים וַיַּבְעֵר מִגָּדִישׁ וְעַד־קָמָה וְעַד־כֶּרֶם זָיִת:

6 The Philistines asked, "Who did this?" And they were told, "It was *Shimshon*, the son-in-law of the Timnite, who took *Shimshon*'s wife and gave her to his wedding companion." Thereupon the Philistines came up and put her and her father to the fire.

ו וַיֹּאמְרוּ פְלִשְׁתִּים מִי עָשָׂה זֹאת וַיֹּאמְרוּ שִׁמְשׁוֹן חֲתַן הַתִּמְנִי כִּי לָקַח אֶת־אִשְׁתּוֹ וַיִּתְּנָהּ לְמֵרֵעֵהוּ וַיַּעֲלוּ פְלִשְׁתִּים וַיִּשְׂרְפוּ אוֹתָהּ וְאֶת־אָבִיהָ בָּאֵשׁ:

7 *Shimshon* said to them, "If that is how you act, I will not rest until I have taken revenge on you."

ז וַיֹּאמֶר לָהֶם שִׁמְשׁוֹן אִם־תַּעֲשׂוּן כָּזֹאת כִּי אִם־נִקַּמְתִּי בָכֶם וְאַחַר אֶחְדָּל:

8 He gave them a sound and thorough thrashing. Then he went down and stayed in the cave of the rock of Etam.

ח וַיַּךְ אוֹתָם שׁוֹק עַל־יָרֵךְ מַכָּה גְדוֹלָה וַיֵּרֶד וַיֵּשֶׁב בִּסְעִיף סֶלַע עֵיטָם:

9 The Philistines came up, pitched camp in *Yehuda* and spread out over Lehi.

ט וַיַּעֲלוּ פְלִשְׁתִּים וַיַּחֲנוּ בִּיהוּדָה וַיִּנָּטְשׁוּ בַּלֶּחִי:

va-ya-a-LU f'-lish-TEEM va-ya-kha-NU bee-hu-DAH va-yi-na-t'-SHU ba-LE-khee

10 The men of *Yehuda* asked, "Why have you come up against us?" They answered, "We have come to take *Shimshon* prisoner, and to do to him as he did to us."

י וַיֹּאמְרוּ אִישׁ יְהוּדָה לָמָה עֲלִיתֶם עָלֵינוּ וַיֹּאמְרוּ לֶאֱסוֹר אֶת־שִׁמְשׁוֹן עָלִינוּ לַעֲשׂוֹת לוֹ כַּאֲשֶׁר עָשָׂה לָנוּ:

11 Thereupon three thousand men of *Yehuda* went down to the cave of the rock of Etam, and they said to *Shimshon*, "You knew that the Philistines rule over us; why have you done this to us?" He replied, "As they did to me, so I did to them."

יא וַיֵּרְדוּ שְׁלֹשֶׁת אֲלָפִים אִישׁ מִיהוּדָה אֶל־סְעִיף סֶלַע עֵיטָם וַיֹּאמְרוּ לְשִׁמְשׁוֹן הֲלֹא יָדַעְתָּ כִּי־מֹשְׁלִים בָּנוּ פְלִשְׁתִּים וּמַה־זֹּאת עָשִׂיתָ לָּנוּ וַיֹּאמֶר לָהֶם כַּאֲשֶׁר עָשׂוּ לִי כֵּן עָשִׂיתִי לָהֶם:

12 "We have come down," they told him, "to take you prisoner and to hand you over to the Philistines." "But swear to me," said *Shimshon* to them, "that you yourselves will not attack me."

יב וַיֹּאמְרוּ לוֹ לֶאֱסָרְךָ יָרַדְנוּ לְתִתְּךָ בְּיַד־פְּלִשְׁתִּים וַיֹּאמֶר לָהֶם שִׁמְשׁוֹן הִשָּׁבְעוּ לִי פֶּן־תִּפְגְּעוּן בִּי אַתֶּם:

15:9 The Philistines came up, pitched camp in *Yehuda* The land of *Yehuda* encompasses much of the biblical heartland of *Eretz Yisrael*. *Chevron* and *Beit Lechem* are in the heart of the territory of *Yehuda*, while *Yerushalayim* is on its border. Though it borders both *Yehuda* and *Binyamin*, the Talmud (*Yoma* 12a) states that *Yerushalayim* was not given to a specific tribe; rather, it belongs to all of Israel. The holiness of the city chosen by God (Deuteronomy 12:5) is a unifying force that joins everyone together in the service of the Almighty.

Shoftim/Judges
Chapter 16

שופטים
פרק טז

13 "We won't," they replied. "We will only take you prisoner and hand you over to them; we will not slay you." So they bound him with two new ropes and brought him up from the rock.

יג וַיֹּאמְרוּ לוֹ לֵאמֹר לֹא כִּי־אָסֹר נֶאֱסָרְךָ וּנְתַנּוּךָ בְיָדָם וְהָמֵת לֹא נְמִיתֶךָ וַיַּאַסְרֻהוּ בִּשְׁנַיִם עֲבֹתִים חֲדָשִׁים וַיַּעֲלוּהוּ מִן־הַסָּלַע׃

14 When he reached Lehi, the Philistines came shouting to meet him. Thereupon the spirit of *Hashem* gripped him, and the ropes on his arms became like flax that catches fire; the bonds melted off his hands.

יד הוּא־בָא עַד־לֶחִי וּפְלִשְׁתִּים הֵרִיעוּ לִקְרָאתוֹ וַתִּצְלַח עָלָיו רוּחַ יְהוָה וַתִּהְיֶינָה הָעֲבֹתִים אֲשֶׁר עַל־זְרוֹעוֹתָיו כַּפִּשְׁתִּים אֲשֶׁר בָּעֲרוּ בָאֵשׁ וַיִּמַּסּוּ אֱסוּרָיו מֵעַל יָדָיו׃

15 He came upon a fresh jawbone of an ass and he picked it up; and with it he killed a thousand men.

טו וַיִּמְצָא לְחִי־חֲמוֹר טְרִיָּה וַיִּשְׁלַח יָדוֹ וַיִּקָּחֶהָ וַיַּךְ־בָּהּ אֶלֶף אִישׁ׃

16 Then *Shimshon* said: "With the jaw of an ass, Mass upon mass! With the jaw of an ass I have slain a thousand men."

טז וַיֹּאמֶר שִׁמְשׁוֹן בִּלְחִי הַחֲמוֹר חֲמוֹר חֲמֹרָתָיִם בִּלְחִי הַחֲמוֹר הִכֵּיתִי אֶלֶף אִישׁ׃

17 As he finished speaking, he threw the jawbone away; hence that place was called Ramath-lehi.

יז וַיְהִי כְּכַלֹּתוֹ לְדַבֵּר וַיַּשְׁלֵךְ הַלְּחִי מִיָּדוֹ וַיִּקְרָא לַמָּקוֹם הַהוּא רָמַת לֶחִי׃

18 He was very thirsty and he called to *Hashem*, "You Yourself have granted this great victory through Your servant; and must I now die of thirst and fall into the hands of the uncircumcised?"

יח וַיִּצְמָא מְאֹד וַיִּקְרָא אֶל־יְהוָה וַיֹּאמַר אַתָּה נָתַתָּ בְיַד־עַבְדְּךָ אֶת־הַתְּשׁוּעָה הַגְּדֹלָה הַזֹּאת וְעַתָּה אָמוּת בַּצָּמָא וְנָפַלְתִּי בְּיַד הָעֲרֵלִים׃

19 So *Hashem* split open the hollow which is at Lehi, and the water gushed out of it; he drank, regained his strength, and revived. That is why it is called to this day "En-hakkore of Lehi."

יט וַיִּבְקַע אֱלֹהִים אֶת־הַמַּכְתֵּשׁ אֲשֶׁר־בַּלֶּחִי וַיֵּצְאוּ מִמֶּנּוּ מַיִם וַיֵּשְׁתְּ וַתָּשָׁב רוּחוֹ וַיֶּחִי עַל־כֵּן קָרָא שְׁמָהּ עֵין הַקּוֹרֵא אֲשֶׁר בַּלֶּחִי עַד הַיּוֹם הַזֶּה׃

20 He led *Yisrael* in the days of the Philistines for twenty years.

כ וַיִּשְׁפֹּט אֶת־יִשְׂרָאֵל בִּימֵי פְלִשְׁתִּים עֶשְׂרִים שָׁנָה׃

16 1 Once *Shimshon* went to *Azza*; there he met a whore and slept with her.

טז א וַיֵּלֶךְ שִׁמְשׁוֹן עַזָּתָה וַיַּרְא־שָׁם אִשָּׁה זוֹנָה וַיָּבֹא אֵלֶיהָ׃

2 The Gazites [learned] that *Shimshon* had come there, so they gathered and lay in ambush for him in the town gate the whole night; and all night long they kept whispering to each other, "When daylight comes, we'll kill him."

ב לַעַזָּתִים לֵאמֹר בָּא שִׁמְשׁוֹן הֵנָּה וַיָּסֹבּוּ וַיֶּאֶרְבוּ־לוֹ כָל־הַלַּיְלָה בְּשַׁעַר הָעִיר וַיִּתְחָרְשׁוּ כָל־הַלַּיְלָה לֵאמֹר עַד־אוֹר הַבֹּקֶר וַהֲרַגְנֻהוּ׃

3 But *Shimshon* lay in bed only till midnight. At midnight he got up, grasped the doors of the town gate together with the two gateposts, and pulled them out along with the bar. He placed them on his shoulders and carried them off to the top of the hill that is near *Chevron*.

ג וַיִּשְׁכַּב שִׁמְשׁוֹן עַד־חֲצִי הַלַּיְלָה וַיָּקָם בַּחֲצִי הַלַּיְלָה וַיֶּאֱחֹז בְּדַלְתוֹת שַׁעַר־הָעִיר וּבִשְׁתֵּי הַמְּזוּזוֹת וַיִּסָּעֵם עִם־הַבְּרִיחַ וַיָּשֶׂם עַל־כְּתֵפָיו וַיַּעֲלֵם אֶל־רֹאשׁ הָהָר אֲשֶׁר עַל־פְּנֵי חֶבְרוֹן׃

4 After that, he fell in love with a woman in the Wadi Sorek, named Delilah.

ד וַיְהִי אַחֲרֵי־כֵן וַיֶּאֱהַב אִשָּׁה בְּנַחַל שֹׂרֵק וּשְׁמָהּ דְּלִילָה׃

Shoftim/Judges
Chapter 16

שופטים
פרק טז

5 The lords of the Philistines went up to her and said, "Coax him and find out what makes him so strong, and how we can overpower him, tie him up, and make him helpless; and we'll each give you eleven hundred *shekalim* of silver."

ה וַיַּעֲלוּ אֵלֶיהָ סַרְנֵי פְלִשְׁתִּים וַיֹּאמְרוּ לָהּ פַּתִּי אוֹתוֹ וּרְאִי בַּמֶּה כֹּחוֹ גָדוֹל וּבַמֶּה נוּכַל לוֹ וַאֲסַרְנֻהוּ לְעַנֹּתוֹ וַאֲנַחְנוּ נִתַּן־לָךְ אִישׁ אֶלֶף וּמֵאָה כָּסֶף׃

6 So Delilah said to *Shimshon*, "Tell me, what makes you so strong? And how could you be tied up and made helpless?"

ו וַתֹּאמֶר דְּלִילָה אֶל־שִׁמְשׁוֹן הַגִּידָה־נָּא לִי בַּמֶּה כֹּחֲךָ גָדוֹל וּבַמֶּה תֵאָסֵר לְעַנּוֹתֶךָ׃

7 *Shimshon* replied, "If I were to be tied with seven fresh tendons that had not been dried, I should become as weak as an ordinary man."

ז וַיֹּאמֶר אֵלֶיהָ שִׁמְשׁוֹן אִם־יַאַסְרֻנִי בְּשִׁבְעָה יְתָרִים לַחִים אֲשֶׁר לֹא־חֹרָבוּ וְחָלִיתִי וְהָיִיתִי כְּאַחַד הָאָדָם׃

8 So the lords of the Philistines brought up to her seven fresh tendons that had not been dried. She bound him with them,

ח וַיַּעֲלוּ־לָהּ סַרְנֵי פְלִשְׁתִּים שִׁבְעָה יְתָרִים לַחִים אֲשֶׁר לֹא־חֹרָבוּ וַתַּאַסְרֵהוּ בָּהֶם׃

9 while an ambush was waiting in her room. Then she called out to him, "*Shimshon*, the Philistines are upon you!" Whereat he pulled the tendons apart, as a strand of tow comes apart at the touch of fire. So the secret of his strength remained unknown.

ט וְהָאֹרֵב יֹשֵׁב לָהּ בַּחֶדֶר וַתֹּאמֶר אֵלָיו פְּלִשְׁתִּים עָלֶיךָ שִׁמְשׁוֹן וַיְנַתֵּק אֶת־הַיְתָרִים כַּאֲשֶׁר יִנָּתֵק פְּתִיל־הַנְּעֹרֶת בַּהֲרִיחוֹ אֵשׁ וְלֹא נוֹדַע כֹּחוֹ׃

10 Then Delilah said to *Shimshon*, "Oh, you deceived me; you lied to me! Do tell me now how you could be tied up."

י וַתֹּאמֶר דְּלִילָה אֶל־שִׁמְשׁוֹן הִנֵּה הֵתַלְתָּ בִּי וַתְּדַבֵּר אֵלַי כְּזָבִים עַתָּה הַגִּידָה־נָּא לִי בַּמֶּה תֵּאָסֵר׃

11 He said, "If I were to be bound with new ropes that had never been used, I would become as weak as an ordinary man."

יא וַיֹּאמֶר אֵלֶיהָ אִם־אָסוֹר יַאַסְרוּנִי בַּעֲבֹתִים חֲדָשִׁים אֲשֶׁר לֹא־נַעֲשָׂה בָהֶם מְלָאכָה וְחָלִיתִי וְהָיִיתִי כְּאַחַד הָאָדָם׃

12 So Delilah took new ropes and bound him with them, while an ambush was waiting in a room. And she cried, "*Shimshon*, the Philistines are upon you!" But he tore them off his arms like a thread.

יב וַתִּקַּח דְּלִילָה עֲבֹתִים חֲדָשִׁים וַתַּאַסְרֵהוּ בָהֶם וַתֹּאמֶר אֵלָיו פְּלִשְׁתִּים עָלֶיךָ שִׁמְשׁוֹן וְהָאֹרֵב יֹשֵׁב בֶּחָדֶר וַיְנַתְּקֵם מֵעַל זְרֹעֹתָיו כַּחוּט׃

13 Then Delilah said to *Shimshon*, "You have been deceiving me all along; you have been lying to me! Tell me, how could you be tied up?" He answered her, "If you weave seven locks of my head into the web."

יג וַתֹּאמֶר דְּלִילָה אֶל־שִׁמְשׁוֹן עַד־הֵנָּה הֵתַלְתָּ בִּי וַתְּדַבֵּר אֵלַי כְּזָבִים הַגִּידָה לִּי בַּמֶּה תֵּאָסֵר וַיֹּאמֶר אֵלֶיהָ אִם־תַּאַרְגִי אֶת־שֶׁבַע מַחְלְפוֹת רֹאשִׁי עִם־הַמַּסָּכֶת׃

14 And she pinned it with a peg and cried to him, "*Shimshon*, the Philistines are upon you!" Awaking from his sleep, he pulled out the peg, the loom, and the web.

יד וַתִּתְקַע בַּיָּתֵד וַתֹּאמֶר אֵלָיו פְּלִשְׁתִּים עָלֶיךָ שִׁמְשׁוֹן וַיִּיקַץ מִשְּׁנָתוֹ וַיִּסַּע אֶת־הַיְתַד הָאֶרֶג וְאֶת־הַמַּסָּכֶת׃

15 Then she said to him, "How can you say you love me, when you don't confide in me? This makes three times that you've deceived me and haven't told me what makes you so strong."

טו וַתֹּאמֶר אֵלָיו אֵיךְ תֹּאמַר אֲהַבְתִּיךְ וְלִבְּךָ אֵין אִתִּי זֶה שָׁלֹשׁ פְּעָמִים הֵתַלְתָּ בִּי וְלֹא־הִגַּדְתָּ לִּי בַּמֶּה כֹּחֲךָ גָדוֹל׃

Shoftim / Judges
Chapter 16

16 Finally, after she had nagged him and pressed him constantly, he was wearied to death

17 and he confided everything to her. He said to her, "No razor has ever touched my head, for I have been a nazirite to *Hashem* since I was in my mother's womb. If my hair were cut, my strength would leave me and I should become as weak as an ordinary man."

18 Sensing that he had confided everything to her, Delilah sent for the lords of the Philistines, with this message: "Come up once more, for he has confided everything to me." And the lords of the Philistines came up and brought the money with them.

19 She lulled him to sleep on her lap. Then she called in a man, and she had him cut off the seven locks of his head; thus she weakened him and made him helpless: his strength slipped away from him.

20 She cried, "*Shimshon*, the Philistines are upon you!" And he awoke from his sleep, thinking he would break loose and shake himself free as he had the other times. For he did not know that *Hashem* had departed from him.

21 The Philistines seized him and gouged out his eyes. They brought him down to *Azza* and shackled him in bronze fetters, and he became a mill slave in the prison.

22 After his hair was cut off, it began to grow back.

23 Now the lords of the Philistines gathered to offer a great sacrifice to their god Dagon and to make merry. They chanted, "Our god has delivered into our hands Our enemy *Shimshon*."

24 When the people saw him, they sang praises to their god, chanting, "Our god has delivered into our hands The enemy who devastated our land, And who slew so many of us."

25 As their spirits rose, they said, "Call *Shimshon* here and let him dance for us." *Shimshon* was fetched from the prison, and he danced for them. Then they put him between the pillars.

26 And *Shimshon* said to the boy who was leading him by the hand, "Let go of me and let me feel the pillars that the temple rests upon, that I may lean on them."

שופטים
פרק טז

טז וַיְהִי כִּי־הֵצִיקָה לּוֹ בִדְבָרֶיהָ כָּל־הַיָּמִים וַתְּאַלְצֵהוּ וַתִּקְצַר נַפְשׁוֹ לָמוּת:

יז וַיַּגֶּד־לָהּ אֶת־כָּל־לִבּוֹ וַיֹּאמֶר לָהּ מוֹרָה לֹא־עָלָה עַל־רֹאשִׁי כִּי־נְזִיר אֱלֹהִים אֲנִי מִבֶּטֶן אִמִּי אִם־גֻּלַּחְתִּי וְסָר מִמֶּנִּי כֹחִי וְחָלִיתִי וְהָיִיתִי כְּכָל־הָאָדָם:

יח וַתֵּרֶא דְלִילָה כִּי־הִגִּיד לָהּ אֶת־כָּל־לִבּוֹ וַתִּשְׁלַח וַתִּקְרָא לְסַרְנֵי פְלִשְׁתִּים לֵאמֹר עֲלוּ הַפַּעַם כִּי־הִגִּיד לָהּ [לִי] אֶת־כָּל־לִבּוֹ וְעָלוּ אֵלֶיהָ סַרְנֵי פְלִשְׁתִּים וַיַּעֲלוּ הַכֶּסֶף בְּיָדָם:

יט וַתְּיַשְּׁנֵהוּ עַל־בִּרְכֶּיהָ וַתִּקְרָא לָאִישׁ וַתְּגַלַּח אֶת־שֶׁבַע מַחְלְפוֹת רֹאשׁוֹ וַתָּחֶל לְעַנּוֹתוֹ וַיָּסַר כֹּחוֹ מֵעָלָיו:

כ וַתֹּאמֶר פְּלִשְׁתִּים עָלֶיךָ שִׁמְשׁוֹן וַיִּקַץ מִשְּׁנָתוֹ וַיֹּאמֶר אֵצֵא כְּפַעַם בְּפַעַם וְאִנָּעֵר וְהוּא לֹא יָדַע כִּי יְהוָה סָר מֵעָלָיו:

כא וַיֹּאחֲזוּהוּ פְלִשְׁתִּים וַיְנַקְּרוּ אֶת־עֵינָיו וַיּוֹרִידוּ אוֹתוֹ עַזָּתָה וַיַּאַסְרוּהוּ בַּנְחֻשְׁתַּיִם וַיְהִי טוֹחֵן בְּבֵית האסירים [הָאֲסוּרִים]:

כב וַיָּחֶל שְׂעַר־רֹאשׁוֹ לְצַמֵּחַ כַּאֲשֶׁר גֻּלָּח:

כג וְסַרְנֵי פְלִשְׁתִּים נֶאֶסְפוּ לִזְבֹּחַ זֶבַח־גָּדוֹל לְדָגוֹן אֱלֹהֵיהֶם וּלְשִׂמְחָה וַיֹּאמְרוּ נָתַן אֱלֹהֵינוּ בְּיָדֵנוּ אֵת שִׁמְשׁוֹן אוֹיְבֵינוּ:

כד וַיִּרְאוּ אֹתוֹ הָעָם וַיְהַלְלוּ אֶת־אֱלֹהֵיהֶם כִּי אָמְרוּ נָתַן אֱלֹהֵינוּ בְיָדֵנוּ אֶת־אוֹיְבֵנוּ וְאֵת מַחֲרִיב אַרְצֵנוּ וַאֲשֶׁר הִרְבָּה אֶת־חֲלָלֵינוּ:

כה וַיְהִי כי טוב [כְּטוֹב] לִבָּם וַיֹּאמְרוּ קִרְאוּ לְשִׁמְשׁוֹן וִישַׂחֶק־לָנוּ וַיִּקְרְאוּ לְשִׁמְשׁוֹן מִבֵּית האסירים [הָאֲסוּרִים] וַיְצַחֵק לִפְנֵיהֶם וַיַּעֲמִידוּ אוֹתוֹ בֵּין הָעַמּוּדִים:

כו וַיֹּאמֶר שִׁמְשׁוֹן אֶל־הַנַּעַר הַמַּחֲזִיק בְּיָדוֹ הַנִּיחָה אוֹתִי והימשני [וַהֲמִשֵׁנִי] אֶת־הָעַמֻּדִים אֲשֶׁר הַבַּיִת נָכוֹן עֲלֵיהֶם וְאֶשָּׁעֵן עֲלֵיהֶם:

Shoftim/Judges
Chapter 17

שופטים
פרק יז

27 Now the temple was full of men and women; all the lords of the Philistines were there, and there were some three thousand men and women on the roof watching *Shimshon* dance.

כז וְהַבַּיִת מָלֵא הָאֲנָשִׁים וְהַנָּשִׁים וְשָׁמָּה כֹּל סַרְנֵי פְלִשְׁתִּים וְעַל־הַגָּג כִּשְׁלֹשֶׁת אֲלָפִים אִישׁ וְאִשָּׁה הָרֹאִים בִּשְׂחוֹק שִׁמְשׁוֹן:

28 Then *Shimshon* called to *Hashem*, "O *Hashem*! Please remember me, and give me strength just this once, O *Hashem*, to take revenge of the Philistines, if only for one of my two eyes."

כח וַיִּקְרָא שִׁמְשׁוֹן אֶל־יְהֹוָה וַיֹּאמַר אֲדֹנָי יֱהֹוִה זָכְרֵנִי נָא וְחַזְּקֵנִי נָא אַךְ הַפַּעַם הַזֶּה הָאֱלֹהִים וְאִנָּקְמָה נְקַם־אַחַת מִשְּׁתֵי עֵינַי מִפְּלִשְׁתִּים:

29 He embraced the two middle pillars that the temple rested upon, one with his right arm and one with his left, and leaned against them;

כט וַיִּלְפֹּת שִׁמְשׁוֹן אֶת־שְׁנֵי עַמּוּדֵי הַתָּוֶךְ אֲשֶׁר הַבַּיִת נָכוֹן עֲלֵיהֶם וַיִּסָּמֵךְ עֲלֵיהֶם אֶחָד בִּימִינוֹ וְאֶחָד בִּשְׂמֹאלוֹ:

30 *Shimshon* cried, "Let me die with the Philistines!" and he pulled with all his might. The temple came crashing down on the lords and on all the people in it. Those who were slain by him as he died outnumbered those who had been slain by him when he lived.

ל וַיֹּאמֶר שִׁמְשׁוֹן תָּמוֹת נַפְשִׁי עִם־פְּלִשְׁתִּים וַיֵּט בְּכֹחַ וַיִּפֹּל הַבַּיִת עַל־הַסְּרָנִים וְעַל־כָּל־הָעָם אֲשֶׁר־בּוֹ וַיִּהְיוּ הַמֵּתִים אֲשֶׁר הֵמִית בְּמוֹתוֹ רַבִּים מֵאֲשֶׁר הֵמִית בְּחַיָּיו:

va-YO-mer shim-SHON ta-MOT naf-SHEE im p'-lish-TEEM va-YAYT b'-KHO-akh va-yi-POL ha-BA-yit al ha-s'-ra-NEEM v'-al kol ha-AM a-sher BO va-yih-YU ha-may-TEEM a-SHER hay-MEET b'-mo-TO ra-BEEM may-a-SHER hay-MEET b'-kha-YAV

31 His brothers and all his father's household came down and carried him up and buried him in the tomb of his father *Manoach*, between *Tzora* and *Eshtaol*. He had led *Yisrael* for twenty years.

לא וַיֵּרְדוּ אֶחָיו וְכָל־בֵּית אָבִיהוּ וַיִּשְׂאוּ אֹתוֹ וַיַּעֲלוּ וַיִּקְבְּרוּ אוֹתוֹ בֵּין צָרְעָה וּבֵין אֶשְׁתָּאֹל בְּקֶבֶר מָנוֹחַ אָבִיו וְהוּא שָׁפַט אֶת־יִשְׂרָאֵל עֶשְׂרִים שָׁנָה:

17 ¹ There was a man in the hill country of *Efraim* whose name was *Micha*.

יז א וַיְהִי־אִישׁ מֵהַר־אֶפְרָיִם וּשְׁמוֹ מִיכָיְהוּ:

² He said to his mother, "The eleven hundred *shekalim* of silver that were taken from you, so that you uttered an imprecation which you repeated in my hearing – I have that silver; I took it." "Blessed of *Hashem* be my son," said his mother.

ב וַיֹּאמֶר לְאִמּוֹ אֶלֶף וּמֵאָה הַכֶּסֶף אֲשֶׁר לֻקַּח־לָךְ וְאַתְּי [וְאַתְּ] אָלִית וְגַם אָמַרְתְּ בְּאָזְנַי הִנֵּה־הַכֶּסֶף אִתִּי אֲנִי לְקַחְתִּיו וַתֹּאמֶר אִמּוֹ בָּרוּךְ בְּנִי לַיהֹוָה:

16:30 *Shimshon* cried, "Let me die with the Philistines!" *Shimshon*'s prayer to die among his Philistine oppressors, taking his own life for the sake of his people, is one of the most stirring scenes in the Bible. *Shimshon* has served as a model for soldiers of Israel who have been willing to give up their lives to save the Jewish people. A moving modern example is the story of Major Ro'i Klein, who, during the Second Lebanon War in 2006, jumped on a grenade, shielding his comrades from the explosion with his own body. Dying with the holy words of *Shema Yisrael* (שמע ישראל), "Hear O Israel, *Hashem* is Our God, *Hashem* is One" on his lips, Ro'i Klein sacrificed his life to save other soldiers who were fighting for *Eretz Yisrael*.

Major Roi Klein (1975–2006)

640

Shoftim/Judges
Chapter 17

שופטים
פרק יז

3 He returned the eleven hundred *shekalim* of silver to his mother; but his mother said, "I herewith consecrate the silver to *Hashem*, transferring it to my son to make a sculptured image and a molten image. I now return it to you."

ג וַיָּשֶׁב אֶת־אֶלֶף־וּמֵאָה הַכֶּסֶף לְאִמּוֹ וַתֹּאמֶר אִמּוֹ הַקְדֵּשׁ הִקְדַּשְׁתִּי אֶת־הַכֶּסֶף לַיהוָה מִיָּדִי לִבְנִי לַעֲשׂוֹת פֶּסֶל וּמַסֵּכָה וְעַתָּה אֲשִׁיבֶנּוּ לָךְ:

4 So when he gave the silver back to his mother, his mother took two hundred *shekalim* of silver and gave it to a smith. He made of it a sculptured image and a molten image, which were kept in the house of *Micha*.

ד וַיָּשֶׁב אֶת־הַכֶּסֶף לְאִמּוֹ וַתִּקַּח אִמּוֹ מָאתַיִם כֶּסֶף וַתִּתְּנֵהוּ לַצּוֹרֵף וַיַּעֲשֵׂהוּ פֶּסֶל וּמַסֵּכָה וַיְהִי בְּבֵית מִיכָיְהוּ:

5 Now the man *Micha* had a house of *Hashem*; he had made an ephod and teraphim and he had inducted one of his sons to be his *Kohen*.

ה וְהָאִישׁ מִיכָה לוֹ בֵּית אֱלֹהִים וַיַּעַשׂ אֵפוֹד וּתְרָפִים וַיְמַלֵּא אֶת־יַד אַחַד מִבָּנָיו וַיְהִי־לוֹ לְכֹהֵן:

6 **In those days there was no king in *Yisrael*; every man did as he pleased.**

ו בַּיָּמִים הָהֵם אֵין מֶלֶךְ בְּיִשְׂרָאֵל אִישׁ הַיָּשָׁר בְּעֵינָיו יַעֲשֶׂה:

ba-ya-MEEM ha-HAYM AYN ME-lekh b'-yis-ra-AYL EESH ha-ya-SHAR b'-ay-NAV ya-a-SEH

7 There was a young man from *Beit Lechem* of *Yehuda*, from the clan seat of *Yehuda*; he was a Levite and had resided there as a sojourner.

ז וַיְהִי־נַעַר מִבֵּית לֶחֶם יְהוּדָה מִמִּשְׁפַּחַת יְהוּדָה וְהוּא לֵוִי וְהוּא גָר־שָׁם:

8 This man had left the town of *Beit Lechem* of *Yehuda* to take up residence wherever he could find a place. On his way, he came to the house of *Micha* in the hill country of *Efraim*.

ח וַיֵּלֶךְ הָאִישׁ מֵהָעִיר מִבֵּית לֶחֶם יְהוּדָה לָגוּר בַּאֲשֶׁר יִמְצָא וַיָּבֹא הַר־אֶפְרַיִם עַד־בֵּית מִיכָה לַעֲשׂוֹת דַּרְכּוֹ:

9 "Where do you come from?" *Micha* asked him. He replied, "I am a Levite from *Beit Lechem* of *Yehuda*, and I am traveling to take up residence wherever I can find a place."

ט וַיֹּאמֶר־לוֹ מִיכָה מֵאַיִן תָּבוֹא וַיֹּאמֶר אֵלָיו לֵוִי אָנֹכִי מִבֵּית לֶחֶם יְהוּדָה וְאָנֹכִי הֹלֵךְ לָגוּר בַּאֲשֶׁר אֶמְצָא:

10 "Stay with me," *Micha* said to him, "and be a father and a *Kohen* to me, and I will pay you ten *shekalim* of silver a year, an allowance of clothing, and your food." The Levite went.

י וַיֹּאמֶר לוֹ מִיכָה שְׁבָה עִמָּדִי וֶהְיֵה־לִי לְאָב וּלְכֹהֵן וְאָנֹכִי אֶתֶּן־לְךָ עֲשֶׂרֶת כֶּסֶף לַיָּמִים וְעֵרֶךְ בְּגָדִים וּמִחְיָתֶךָ וַיֵּלֶךְ הַלֵּוִי:

11 The Levite agreed to stay with the man, and the youth became like one of his own sons.

יא וַיּוֹאֶל הַלֵּוִי לָשֶׁבֶת אֶת־הָאִישׁ וַיְהִי הַנַּעַר לוֹ כְּאַחַד מִבָּנָיו:

12 *Micha* inducted the Levite, and the young man became his *Kohen* and remained in *Micha*'s shrine.

יב וַיְמַלֵּא מִיכָה אֶת־יַד הַלֵּוִי וַיְהִי־לוֹ הַנַּעַר לְכֹהֵן וַיְהִי בְּבֵית מִיכָה:

17:6 In those days there was no king in *Yisrael*; every man did as he pleased. *Sefer Shoftim* repeatedly teaches that the lack of a king, enabling everyone to do whatever was right in their eyes, is the preeminent problem of this era. According to the Bible, the king should not be responsible only for the legal, military and economic affairs of the nation. He should also be responsible for ensuring that the society is moral and follows *Hashem*'s *Torah*. Having a righteous king in *Yerushalayim* will be part of the complete redemption.

641

Shoftim/Judges
Chapter 18

שופטים
פרק יח

13 "Now I know," *Micha* told himself, "that *Hashem* will prosper me, since the Levite has become my *Kohen*."

יג וַיֹּאמֶר מִיכָה עַתָּה יָדַעְתִּי כִּי־יֵיטִיב יְהוָה לִי כִּי הָיָה־לִי הַלֵּוִי לְכֹהֵן׃

18 1 In those days there was no king in *Yisrael*, and in those days the tribe of *Dan* was seeking a territory in which to settle; for to that day no territory had fallen to their lot among the tribes of *Yisrael*.

יח א בַּיָּמִים הָהֵם אֵין מֶלֶךְ בְּיִשְׂרָאֵל וּבַיָּמִים הָהֵם שֵׁבֶט הַדָּנִי מְבַקֶּשׁ־לוֹ נַחֲלָה לָשֶׁבֶת כִּי לֹא־נָפְלָה לּוֹ עַד־הַיּוֹם הַהוּא בְּתוֹךְ־שִׁבְטֵי יִשְׂרָאֵל בְּנַחֲלָה׃

2 The Danites sent out five of their number, from their clan seat at *Tzora* and *Eshtaol* – valiant men – to spy out the land and explore it. "Go," they told them, "and explore the land." When they had advanced into the hill country of *Efraim* as far as the house of *Micha*, they stopped there for the night.

ב וַיִּשְׁלְחוּ בְנֵי־דָן מִמִּשְׁפַּחְתָּם חֲמִשָּׁה אֲנָשִׁים מִקְצוֹתָם אֲנָשִׁים בְּנֵי־חַיִל מִצָּרְעָה וּמֵאֶשְׁתָּאֹל לְרַגֵּל אֶת־הָאָרֶץ וּלְחָקְרָהּ וַיֹּאמְרוּ אֲלֵהֶם לְכוּ חִקְרוּ אֶת־הָאָרֶץ וַיָּבֹאוּ הַר־אֶפְרַיִם עַד־בֵּית מִיכָה וַיָּלִינוּ שָׁם׃

3 While in the vicinity of *Micha*'s house, they recognized the speech of the young Levite, so they went over and asked him, "Who brought you to these parts? What are you doing in this place? What is your business here?"

ג הֵמָּה עִם־בֵּית מִיכָה וְהֵמָּה הִכִּירוּ אֶת־קוֹל הַנַּעַר הַלֵּוִי וַיָּסוּרוּ שָׁם וַיֹּאמְרוּ לוֹ מִי־הֱבִיאֲךָ הֲלֹם וּמָה־אַתָּה עֹשֶׂה בָּזֶה וּמַה־לְּךָ פֹה׃

4 He replied, "Thus and thus *Micha* did for me – he hired me and I became his *Kohen*."

ד וַיֹּאמֶר אֲלֵהֶם כָּזֹה וְכָזֶה עָשָׂה לִי מִיכָה וַיִּשְׂכְּרֵנִי וָאֱהִי־לוֹ לְכֹהֵן׃

5 They said to him, "Please, inquire of *Hashem*; we would like to know if the mission on which we are going will be successful."

ה וַיֹּאמְרוּ לוֹ שְׁאַל־נָא בֵאלֹהִים וְנֵדְעָה הֲתַצְלִיחַ דַּרְכֵּנוּ אֲשֶׁר אֲנַחְנוּ הֹלְכִים עָלֶיהָ׃

6 "Go in peace," the *Kohen* said to them, "*Hashem* views with favor the mission you are going on."

ו וַיֹּאמֶר לָהֶם הַכֹּהֵן לְכוּ לְשָׁלוֹם נֹכַח יְהוָה דַּרְכְּכֶם אֲשֶׁר תֵּלְכוּ־בָהּ׃

7 The five men went on and came to Laish. They observed the people in it dwelling carefree, after the manner of the Sidonians, a tranquil and unsuspecting people, with no one in the land to molest them and with no hereditary ruler. Moreover, they were distant from the Sidonians and had no dealings with anybody.

ז וַיֵּלְכוּ חֲמֵשֶׁת הָאֲנָשִׁים וַיָּבֹאוּ לָיְשָׁה וַיִּרְאוּ אֶת־הָעָם אֲשֶׁר־בְּקִרְבָּהּ יוֹשֶׁבֶת־לָבֶטַח כְּמִשְׁפַּט צִדֹנִים שֹׁקֵט וּבֹטֵחַ וְאֵין־מַכְלִים דָּבָר בָּאָרֶץ יוֹרֵשׁ עֶצֶר וּרְחֹקִים הֵמָּה מִצִּדֹנִים וְדָבָר אֵין־לָהֶם עִם־אָדָם׃

8 When [the men] came back to their kinsmen at *Tzora* and *Eshtaol*, their kinsmen asked them, "How did you fare?"

ח וַיָּבֹאוּ אֶל־אֲחֵיהֶם צָרְעָה וְאֶשְׁתָּאֹל וַיֹּאמְרוּ לָהֶם אֲחֵיהֶם מָה אַתֶּם׃

9 They replied, "Let us go at once and attack them! For we found that the land was very good, and you are sitting idle! Don't delay; go and invade the land and take possession of it,

ט וַיֹּאמְרוּ קוּמָה וְנַעֲלֶה עֲלֵיהֶם כִּי רָאִינוּ אֶת־הָאָרֶץ וְהִנֵּה טוֹבָה מְאֹד וְאַתֶּם מַחְשִׁים אַל־תֵּעָצְלוּ לָלֶכֶת לָבֹא לָרֶשֶׁת אֶת־הָאָרֶץ׃

10 for *Hashem* has delivered it into your hand. When you come, you will come to an unsuspecting people; and the land is spacious and nothing on earth is lacking there."

י כְּבֹאֲכֶם תָּבֹאוּ אֶל־עַם בֹּטֵחַ וְהָאָרֶץ רַחֲבַת יָדַיִם כִּי־נְתָנָהּ אֱלֹהִים בְּיֶדְכֶם מָקוֹם אֲשֶׁר אֵין־שָׁם מַחְסוֹר כָּל־דָּבָר אֲשֶׁר בָּאָרֶץ׃

Shoftim / Judges
Chapter 18

שופטים
פרק יח

11 They departed from there, from the clan seat of the Danites, from *Tzora* and *Eshtaol*, six hundred strong, girt with weapons of war.

יא וַיִּסְעוּ מִשָּׁם מִמִּשְׁפַּחַת הַדָּנִי מִצָּרְעָה וּמֵאֶשְׁתָּאֹל שֵׁשׁ־מֵאוֹת אִישׁ חָגוּר כְּלֵי מִלְחָמָה:

12 They went up and encamped at *Kiryat Ye'arim* in *Yehuda*. That is why that place is called "the Camp of *Dan*" to this day; it lies west of *Kiryat Ye'arim*.

יב וַיַּעֲלוּ וַיַּחֲנוּ בְּקִרְיַת יְעָרִים בִּיהוּדָה עַל־כֵּן קָרְאוּ לַמָּקוֹם הַהוּא מַחֲנֵה־דָן עַד הַיּוֹם הַזֶּה הִנֵּה אַחֲרֵי קִרְיַת יְעָרִים:

13 From there they passed on to the hill country of *Efraim* and arrived at the house of *Micha*.

יג וַיַּעַבְרוּ מִשָּׁם הַר־אֶפְרָיִם וַיָּבֹאוּ עַד־בֵּית מִיכָה:

14 Here the five men who had gone to spy out the Laish region remarked to their kinsmen, "Do you know, there is an ephod in these houses, and teraphim, and a sculptured image and a molten image? Now you know what you have to do."

יד וַיַּעֲנוּ חֲמֵשֶׁת הָאֲנָשִׁים הַהֹלְכִים לְרַגֵּל אֶת־הָאָרֶץ לַיִשׁ וַיֹּאמְרוּ אֶל־אֲחֵיהֶם הַיְדַעְתֶּם כִּי יֵשׁ בַּבָּתִּים הָאֵלֶּה אֵפוֹד וּתְרָפִים וּפֶסֶל וּמַסֵּכָה וְעַתָּה דְּעוּ מַה־תַּעֲשׂוּ:

15 So they turned off there and entered the home of the young Levite at *Micha*'s house and greeted him.

טו וַיָּסוּרוּ שָׁמָּה וַיָּבֹאוּ אֶל־בֵּית־הַנַּעַר הַלֵּוִי בֵּית מִיכָה וַיִּשְׁאֲלוּ־לוֹ לְשָׁלוֹם:

16 The six hundred Danite men, girt with their weapons of war, stood at the entrance of the gate,

טז וְשֵׁשׁ־מֵאוֹת אִישׁ חֲגוּרִים כְּלֵי מִלְחַמְתָּם נִצָּבִים פֶּתַח הַשָּׁעַר אֲשֶׁר מִבְּנֵי־דָן:

17 while the five men who had gone to spy out the land went inside and took the sculptured image, the ephod, the teraphim, and the molten image. The *Kohen* was standing at the entrance of the gate, and the six hundred men girt with their weapons of war,

יז וַיַּעֲלוּ חֲמֵשֶׁת הָאֲנָשִׁים הַהֹלְכִים לְרַגֵּל אֶת־הָאָרֶץ בָּאוּ שָׁמָּה לָקְחוּ אֶת־הַפֶּסֶל וְאֶת־הָאֵפוֹד וְאֶת־הַתְּרָפִים וְאֶת־הַמַּסֵּכָה וְהַכֹּהֵן נִצָּב פֶּתַח הַשַּׁעַר וְשֵׁשׁ־מֵאוֹת הָאִישׁ הֶחָגוּר כְּלֵי הַמִּלְחָמָה:

18 while those men entered *Micha*'s house and took the sculptured image, the molten image, the ephod, and the household gods. The *Kohen* said to them, "What are you doing?"

יח וְאֵלֶּה בָּאוּ בֵּית מִיכָה וַיִּקְחוּ אֶת־פֶּסֶל הָאֵפוֹד וְאֶת־הַתְּרָפִים וְאֶת־הַמַּסֵּכָה וַיֹּאמֶר אֲלֵיהֶם הַכֹּהֵן מָה אַתֶּם עֹשִׂים:

19 But they said to him, "Be quiet; put your hand on your mouth! Come with us and be our father and *Kohen*. Would you rather be *Kohen* to one man's household or be *Kohen* to a tribe and clan in *Yisrael*?"

יט וַיֹּאמְרוּ לוֹ הַחֲרֵשׁ שִׂים־יָדְךָ עַל־פִּיךָ וְלֵךְ עִמָּנוּ וֶהְיֵה־לָנוּ לְאָב וּלְכֹהֵן הֲטוֹב הֱיוֹתְךָ כֹהֵן לְבֵית אִישׁ אֶחָד אוֹ הֱיוֹתְךָ כֹהֵן לְשֵׁבֶט וּלְמִשְׁפָּחָה בְּיִשְׂרָאֵל:

20 The *Kohen* was delighted. He took the ephod, the household gods, and the sculptured image, and he joined the people.

כ וַיִּיטַב לֵב הַכֹּהֵן וַיִּקַּח אֶת־הָאֵפוֹד וְאֶת־הַתְּרָפִים וְאֶת־הַפָּסֶל וַיָּבֹא בְּקֶרֶב הָעָם:

21 They set out again, placing the children, the cattle, and their household goods in front.

כא וַיִּפְנוּ וַיֵּלֵכוּ וַיָּשִׂימוּ אֶת־הַטַּף וְאֶת־הַמִּקְנֶה וְאֶת־הַכְּבוּדָּה לִפְנֵיהֶם:

22 They had already gone some distance from *Micha*'s house, when the men in the houses near *Micha*'s mustered and caught up with the Danites.

כב הֵמָּה הִרְחִיקוּ מִבֵּית מִיכָה וְהָאֲנָשִׁים אֲשֶׁר בַּבָּתִּים אֲשֶׁר עִם־בֵּית מִיכָה נִזְעֲקוּ וַיַּדְבִּיקוּ אֶת־בְּנֵי־דָן:

Shoftim/Judges
Chapter 18

שופטים
פרק יח

23 They called out to the Danites, who turned around and said to *Micha*, "What's the matter? Why have you mustered?"

כג וַיִּקְרְאוּ אֶל־בְּנֵי־דָן וַיַּסֵּבּוּ פְּנֵיהֶם וַיֹּאמְרוּ לְמִיכָה מַה־לְּךָ כִּי נִזְעָקְתָּ׃

24 He said, "You have taken my *Kohen* and the gods that I made, and walked off! What do I have left? How can you ask, 'What's the matter'?"

כד וַיֹּאמֶר אֶת־אֱלֹהַי אֲשֶׁר־עָשִׂיתִי לְקַחְתֶּם וְאֶת־הַכֹּהֵן וַתֵּלְכוּ וּמַה־לִּי עוֹד וּמַה־זֶּה תֹּאמְרוּ אֵלַי מַה־לָּךְ׃

25 But the Danites replied, "Don't do any shouting at us, or some desperate men might attack you, and you and your family would lose your lives."

כה וַיֹּאמְרוּ אֵלָיו בְּנֵי־דָן אַל־תַּשְׁמַע קוֹלְךָ עִמָּנוּ פֶּן־יִפְגְּעוּ בָכֶם אֲנָשִׁים מָרֵי נֶפֶשׁ וְאָסַפְתָּה נַפְשְׁךָ וְנֶפֶשׁ בֵּיתֶךָ׃

26 So *Micha*, realizing that they were stronger than he, turned back and went home; and the Danites went on their way,

כו וַיֵּלְכוּ בְנֵי־דָן לְדַרְכָּם וַיַּרְא מִיכָה כִּי־חֲזָקִים הֵמָּה מִמֶּנּוּ וַיִּפֶן וַיָּשָׁב אֶל־בֵּיתוֹ׃

27 taking the things *Micha* had made and the *Kohen* he had acquired. They proceeded to Laish, a people tranquil and unsuspecting, and they put them to the sword and burned down the town.

כז וְהֵמָּה לָקְחוּ אֵת אֲשֶׁר־עָשָׂה מִיכָה וְאֶת־הַכֹּהֵן אֲשֶׁר הָיָה־לוֹ וַיָּבֹאוּ עַל־לַיִשׁ עַל־עַם שֹׁקֵט וּבֹטֵחַ וַיַּכּוּ אוֹתָם לְפִי־חָרֶב וְאֶת־הָעִיר שָׂרְפוּ בָאֵשׁ׃

28 There was none to come to the rescue, for it was distant from Sidon and they had no dealings with anyone; it lay in the valley of Beth-rehob. They rebuilt the town and settled there,

כח וְאֵין מַצִּיל כִּי רְחוֹקָה־הִיא מִצִּידוֹן וְדָבָר אֵין־לָהֶם עִם־אָדָם וְהִיא בָּעֵמֶק אֲשֶׁר לְבֵית־רְחוֹב וַיִּבְנוּ אֶת־הָעִיר וַיֵּשְׁבוּ בָהּ׃

29 and they named the town *Dan*, after their ancestor *Dan* who was *Yisrael*'s son. Originally, however, the name of the town was Laish.

כט וַיִּקְרְאוּ שֵׁם־הָעִיר דָּן בְּשֵׁם דָּן אֲבִיהֶם אֲשֶׁר יוּלַּד לְיִשְׂרָאֵל וְאוּלָם לַיִשׁ שֵׁם־הָעִיר לָרִאשֹׁנָה׃

30 The Danites set up the sculptured image for themselves; and *Yonatan* son of *Gershom* son of *Menashe*, and his descendants, served as *Kohanim* to the Danite tribe until the land went into exile.

ל וַיָּקִימוּ לָהֶם בְּנֵי־דָן אֶת־הַפָּסֶל וִיהוֹנָתָן בֶּן־גֵּרְשֹׁם בֶּן־מְנַשֶּׁה הוּא וּבָנָיו הָיוּ כֹהֲנִים לְשֵׁבֶט הַדָּנִי עַד־יוֹם גְּלוֹת הָאָרֶץ׃

va-ya-KEE-mu la-HEM b'-nay DAN et ha-PA-sel vee-ho-na-TAN ben gay-r'-SHOM ben m'-na-SHEH HU u-va-NAV ha-YU kho-ha-NEEM l'-SHAY-vet ha-da-NEE ad yom g'-LOT ha-A-retz

---

18:30 *Yonatan* son of *Gershom* son of *Menashe* The idolatrous priest *Yonatan* is identified as being the son of *Gershom*, the son of *Menashe* (מנשה). However, *Rashi* writes that *Yonatan*'s actual grandfather was *Moshe* (משה). Out of respect for the greatest prophet in history, the prophet *Shmuel* (who authored this book) disguised *Moshe*'s name, inserting the letter *nun* (נ) between the first two letters, *mem* (מ) and *shin* (ש). The sad fact is that the grandson of *Moshe* left the ways of the *Torah*. This tragic betrayal was the result of living in a society that was spiritually adrift. Clearly, if this can happen to a grandchild of the greatest prophet in history, it can happen to any person, in any family. *Moshe*'s grandson *Yonatan* is a sobering reminder of the importance of making sure that our children are surrounded by positive role models, have a strong religious education and grow up in a just society that seeks to do *Hashem*'s will.

Shoftim/Judges
Chapter 19

31 They maintained the sculptured image that *Micha* had made throughout the time that the House of *Hashem* stood at *Shilo*.

19 1 In those days, when there was no king in *Yisrael*, a Levite residing at the other end of the hill country of *Efraim* took to himself a concubine from *Beit Lechem* in *Yehuda*.

2 Once his concubine deserted him, leaving him for her father's house in *Beit Lechem* in *Yehuda*; and she stayed there a full four months.

3 Then her husband set out, with an attendant and a pair of donkeys, and went after her to woo her and to win her back. She admitted him into her father's house; and when the girl's father saw him, he received him warmly.

4 His father-in-law, the girl's father, pressed him, and he stayed with him three days; they ate and drank and lodged there.

5 Early in the morning of the fourth day, he started to leave; but the girl's father said to his son-in-law, "Eat something to give you strength, then you can leave."

6 So the two of them sat down and they feasted together. Then the girl's father said to the man, "Won't you stay overnight and enjoy yourself?"

7 The man started to leave, but his father-in-law kept urging him until he turned back and spent the night there.

8 Early in the morning of the fifth day, he was about to leave, when the girl's father said, "Come, have a bite." The two of them ate, dawdling until past noon.

9 Then the man, his concubine, and his attendant started to leave. His father-in-law, the girl's father, said to him, "Look, the day is waning toward evening; do stop for the night. See, the day is declining; spend the night here and enjoy yourself. You can start early tomorrow on your journey and head for home."

10 But the man refused to stay for the night. He set out and traveled as far as the vicinity of Jebus – that is, *Yerushalayim*; he had with him a pair of laden donkeys, and his concubine was with him.

שופטים
פרק יט

לא וַיָּשִׂימוּ לָהֶם אֶת־פֶּסֶל מִיכָה אֲשֶׁר עָשָׂה כָּל־יְמֵי הֱיוֹת בֵּית־הָאֱלֹהִים בְּשִׁלֹה:

יט א וַיְהִי בַּיָּמִים הָהֵם וּמֶלֶךְ אֵין בְּיִשְׂרָאֵל וַיְהִי אִישׁ לֵוִי גָּר בְּיַרְכְּתֵי הַר־אֶפְרַיִם וַיִּקַּח־לוֹ אִשָּׁה פִילֶגֶשׁ מִבֵּית לֶחֶם יְהוּדָה:

ב וַתִּזְנֶה עָלָיו פִּילַגְשׁוֹ וַתֵּלֶךְ מֵאִתּוֹ אֶל־בֵּית אָבִיהָ אֶל־בֵּית לֶחֶם יְהוּדָה וַתְּהִי־שָׁם יָמִים אַרְבָּעָה חֳדָשִׁים:

ג וַיָּקָם אִישָׁהּ וַיֵּלֶךְ אַחֲרֶיהָ לְדַבֵּר עַל־לִבָּהּ לַהֲשִׁיבוֹ [לַהֲשִׁיבָהּ] וְנַעֲרוֹ עִמּוֹ וְצֶמֶד חֲמֹרִים וַתְּבִיאֵהוּ בֵּית אָבִיהָ וַיִּרְאֵהוּ אֲבִי הַנַּעֲרָה וַיִּשְׂמַח לִקְרָאתוֹ:

ד וַיֶּחֱזַק־בּוֹ חֹתְנוֹ אֲבִי הַנַּעֲרָה וַיֵּשֶׁב אִתּוֹ שְׁלֹשֶׁת יָמִים וַיֹּאכְלוּ וַיִּשְׁתּוּ וַיָּלִינוּ שָׁם:

ה וַיְהִי בַּיּוֹם הָרְבִיעִי וַיַּשְׁכִּימוּ בַבֹּקֶר וַיָּקָם לָלֶכֶת וַיֹּאמֶר אֲבִי הַנַּעֲרָה אֶל־חֲתָנוֹ סְעָד לִבְּךָ פַּת־לֶחֶם וְאַחַר תֵּלֵכוּ:

ו וַיֵּשְׁבוּ וַיֹּאכְלוּ שְׁנֵיהֶם יַחְדָּו וַיִּשְׁתּוּ וַיֹּאמֶר אֲבִי הַנַּעֲרָה אֶל־הָאִישׁ הוֹאֶל־נָא וְלִין וְיִטַב לִבֶּךָ:

ז וַיָּקָם הָאִישׁ לָלֶכֶת וַיִּפְצַר־בּוֹ חֹתְנוֹ וַיָּשָׁב וַיָּלֶן שָׁם:

ח וַיַּשְׁכֵּם בַּבֹּקֶר בַּיּוֹם הַחֲמִישִׁי לָלֶכֶת וַיֹּאמֶר אֲבִי הַנַּעֲרָה סְעָד־נָא לְבָבְךָ וְהִתְמַהְמְהוּ עַד־נְטוֹת הַיּוֹם וַיֹּאכְלוּ שְׁנֵיהֶם:

ט וַיָּקָם הָאִישׁ לָלֶכֶת הוּא וּפִילַגְשׁוֹ וְנַעֲרוֹ וַיֹּאמֶר לוֹ חֹתְנוֹ אֲבִי הַנַּעֲרָה הִנֵּה נָא רָפָה הַיּוֹם לַעֲרֹב לִינוּ־נָא הִנֵּה חֲנוֹת הַיּוֹם לִין פֹּה וְיִיטַב לְבָבֶךָ וְהִשְׁכַּמְתֶּם מָחָר לְדַרְכְּכֶם וְהָלַכְתָּ לְאֹהָלֶךָ:

י וְלֹא־אָבָה הָאִישׁ לָלוּן וַיָּקָם וַיֵּלֶךְ וַיָּבֹא עַד־נֹכַח יְבוּס הִיא יְרוּשָׁלָ͏ִם וְעִמּוֹ צֶמֶד חֲמוֹרִים חֲבוּשִׁים וּפִילַגְשׁוֹ עִמּוֹ:

Shoftim / Judges
Chapter 19

11 Since they were close to Jebus, and the day was very far spent, the attendant said to his master, "Let us turn aside to this town of the Jebusites and spend the night in it."

12 But his master said to him, "We will not turn aside to a town of aliens who are not of *Yisrael*, but will continue to *Giva*.

13 Come," he said to his attendant, "let us approach one of those places and spend the night either in *Giva* or in *Rama*."

14 So they traveled on, and the sun set when they were near *Giva* of *Binyamin*.

15 They turned off there and went in to spend the night in *Giva*. He went and sat down in the town square, but nobody took them indoors to spend the night.

16 In the evening, an old man came along from his property outside the town. (This man hailed from the hill country of *Efraim* and resided at *Giva*, where the townspeople were Benjaminites.)

17 He happened to see the wayfarer in the town square. "Where," the old man inquired, "are you going to, and where do you come from?"

18 He replied, "We are traveling from *Beit Lechem* in *Yehuda* to the other end of the hill country of *Efraim*. That is where I live. I made a journey to *Beit Lechem* of *Yehuda*, and now I am on my way to the House of *Hashem*, and nobody has taken me indoors.

19 We have both bruised straw and feed for our donkeys, and bread and wine for me and your handmaid, and for the attendant with your servants. We lack nothing."

20 "Rest easy," said the old man. "Let me take care of all your needs. Do not on any account spend the night in the square."

21 And he took him into his house. He mixed fodder for the donkeys; then they bathed their feet and ate and drank.

22 While they were enjoying themselves, the men of the town, a depraved lot, had gathered about the house and were pounding on the door. They called

שופטים
פרק יט

יא הֵם עִם־יְבוּס וְהַיּוֹם רַד מְאֹד וַיֹּאמֶר הַנַּעַר אֶל־אֲדֹנָיו לְכָה־נָּא וְנָסוּרָה אֶל־עִיר־הַיְבוּסִי הַזֹּאת וְנָלִין בָּהּ׃

יב וַיֹּאמֶר אֵלָיו אֲדֹנָיו לֹא נָסוּר אֶל־עִיר נָכְרִי אֲשֶׁר לֹא־מִבְּנֵי יִשְׂרָאֵל הֵנָּה וְעָבַרְנוּ עַד־גִּבְעָה׃

יג וַיֹּאמֶר לְנַעֲרוֹ לְךָ וְנִקְרְבָה בְּאַחַד הַמְּקֹמוֹת וְלַנּוּ בַגִּבְעָה אוֹ בָרָמָה׃

יד וַיַּעַבְרוּ וַיֵּלֵכוּ וַתָּבֹא לָהֶם הַשֶּׁמֶשׁ אֵצֶל הַגִּבְעָה אֲשֶׁר לְבִנְיָמִן׃

טו וַיָּסֻרוּ שָׁם לָבוֹא לָלוּן בַּגִּבְעָה וַיָּבֹא וַיֵּשֶׁב בִּרְחוֹב הָעִיר וְאֵין אִישׁ מְאַסֵּף־אוֹתָם הַבַּיְתָה לָלוּן׃

טז וְהִנֵּה ׀ אִישׁ זָקֵן בָּא מִן־מַעֲשֵׂהוּ מִן־הַשָּׂדֶה בָּעֶרֶב וְהָאִישׁ מֵהַר אֶפְרַיִם וְהוּא־גָר בַּגִּבְעָה וְאַנְשֵׁי הַמָּקוֹם בְּנֵי יְמִינִי׃

יז וַיִּשָּׂא עֵינָיו וַיַּרְא אֶת־הָאִישׁ הָאֹרֵחַ בִּרְחֹב הָעִיר וַיֹּאמֶר הָאִישׁ הַזָּקֵן אָנָה תֵלֵךְ וּמֵאַיִן תָּבוֹא׃

יח וַיֹּאמֶר אֵלָיו עֹבְרִים אֲנַחְנוּ מִבֵּית־לֶחֶם יְהוּדָה עַד־יַרְכְּתֵי הַר־אֶפְרַיִם מִשָּׁם אָנֹכִי וָאֵלֵךְ עַד־בֵּית לֶחֶם יְהוּדָה וְאֶת־בֵּית יְהֹוָה אֲנִי הֹלֵךְ וְאֵין אִישׁ מְאַסֵּף אוֹתִי הַבָּיְתָה׃

יט וְגַם־תֶּבֶן גַּם־מִסְפּוֹא יֵשׁ לַחֲמוֹרֵינוּ וְגַם לֶחֶם וָיַיִן יֶשׁ־לִי וְלַאֲמָתֶךָ וְלַנַּעַר עִם־עֲבָדֶיךָ אֵין מַחְסוֹר כָּל־דָּבָר׃

כ וַיֹּאמֶר הָאִישׁ הַזָּקֵן שָׁלוֹם לָךְ רַק כָּל־מַחְסוֹרְךָ עָלָי רַק בָּרְחוֹב אַל־תָּלַן׃

כא וַיְבִיאֵהוּ לְבֵיתוֹ וַיָּבָל לַחֲמוֹרִים וַיִּרְחֲצוּ רַגְלֵיהֶם וַיֹּאכְלוּ וַיִּשְׁתּוּ׃

כב הֵמָּה מֵיטִיבִים אֶת־לִבָּם וְהִנֵּה אַנְשֵׁי הָעִיר אַנְשֵׁי בְנֵי־בְלִיַּעַל נָסַבּוּ אֶת־הַבַּיִת מִתְדַּפְּקִים עַל־הַדָּלֶת וַיֹּאמְרוּ אֶל־

Shoftim/Judges
Chapter 19

שופטים
פרק יט

to the aged owner of the house, "Bring out the man who has come into your house, so that we can be intimate with him."

הָאִישׁ בַּעַל הַבַּיִת הַזָּקֵן לֵאמֹר הוֹצֵא אֶת־הָאִישׁ אֲשֶׁר־בָּא אֶל־בֵּיתְךָ וְנֵדָעֶנּוּ׃

23 The owner of the house went out and said to them, "Please, my friends, do not commit such a wrong. Since this man has entered my house, do not perpetrate this outrage.

כג וַיֵּצֵא אֲלֵיהֶם הָאִישׁ בַּעַל הַבַּיִת וַיֹּאמֶר אֲלֵהֶם אַל־אַחַי אַל־תָּרֵעוּ נָא אַחֲרֵי אֲשֶׁר־בָּא הָאִישׁ הַזֶּה אֶל־בֵּיתִי אַל־תַּעֲשׂוּ אֶת־הַנְּבָלָה הַזֹּאת׃

24 Look, here is my virgin daughter, and his concubine. Let me bring them out to you. Have your pleasure of them, do what you like with them; but don't do that outrageous thing to this man."

כד הִנֵּה בִתִּי הַבְּתוּלָה וּפִילַגְשֵׁהוּ אוֹצִיאָה־נָּא אוֹתָם וְעַנּוּ אוֹתָם וַעֲשׂוּ לָהֶם הַטּוֹב בְּעֵינֵיכֶם וְלָאִישׁ הַזֶּה לֹא תַעֲשׂוּ דְּבַר הַנְּבָלָה הַזֹּאת׃

25 But the men would not listen to him, so the man seized his concubine and pushed her out to them. They raped her and abused her all night long until morning; and they let her go when dawn broke.

כה וְלֹא־אָבוּ הָאֲנָשִׁים לִשְׁמֹעַ לוֹ וַיַּחֲזֵק הָאִישׁ בְּפִילַגְשׁוֹ וַיֹּצֵא אֲלֵיהֶם הַחוּץ וַיֵּדְעוּ אוֹתָהּ וַיִּתְעַלְּלוּ־בָהּ כָּל־הַלַּיְלָה עַד־הַבֹּקֶר וַיְשַׁלְּחוּהָ בעלות [כַּעֲלוֹת] הַשָּׁחַר׃

26 Toward morning the woman came back; and as it was growing light, she collapsed at the entrance of the man's house where her husband was.

כו וַתָּבֹא הָאִשָּׁה לִפְנוֹת הַבֹּקֶר וַתִּפֹּל פֶּתַח בֵּית־הָאִישׁ אֲשֶׁר־אֲדוֹנֶיהָ שָּׁם עַד־הָאוֹר׃

27 When her husband arose in the morning, he opened the doors of the house and went out to continue his journey; and there was the woman, his concubine, lying at the entrance of the house, with her hands on the threshold.

כז וַיָּקָם אֲדֹנֶיהָ בַּבֹּקֶר וַיִּפְתַּח דַּלְתוֹת הַבַּיִת וַיֵּצֵא לָלֶכֶת לְדַרְכּוֹ וְהִנֵּה הָאִשָּׁה פִילַגְשׁוֹ נֹפֶלֶת פֶּתַח הַבַּיִת וְיָדֶיהָ עַל־הַסַּף׃

28 "Get up," he said to her, "let us go." But there was no reply. So the man placed her on the donkey and set out for home.

כח וַיֹּאמֶר אֵלֶיהָ קוּמִי וְנֵלֵכָה וְאֵין עֹנֶה וַיִּקָּחֶהָ עַל־הַחֲמוֹר וַיָּקָם הָאִישׁ וַיֵּלֶךְ לִמְקֹמוֹ׃

29 When he came home, he picked up a knife, and took hold of his concubine and cut her up limb by limb into twelve parts. He sent them throughout the territory of *Yisrael*.

כט וַיָּבֹא אֶל־בֵּיתוֹ וַיִּקַּח אֶת־הַמַּאֲכֶלֶת וַיַּחֲזֵק בְּפִילַגְשׁוֹ וַיְנַתְּחֶהָ לַעֲצָמֶיהָ לִשְׁנֵים עָשָׂר נְתָחִים וַיְשַׁלְּחֶהָ בְּכֹל גְּבוּל יִשְׂרָאֵל׃

30 And everyone who saw it cried out, "Never has such a thing happened or been seen from the day the Israelites came out of the land of Egypt to this day! Put your mind to this; take counsel and decide."

ל וְהָיָה כָל־הָרֹאֶה וְאָמַר לֹא־נִהְיְתָה וְלֹא־נִרְאֲתָה כָּזֹאת לְמִיּוֹם עֲלוֹת בְּנֵי־יִשְׂרָאֵל מֵאֶרֶץ מִצְרַיִם עַד הַיּוֹם הַזֶּה שִׂימוּ־לָכֶם עָלֶיהָ עֻצוּ וְדַבֵּרוּ׃

v'-ha-YAH khol ha-ro-EH v'-a-MAR lo nih-y'-TAH v'-lo nir-a-TAH ka-ZOT l'-mi-YOM a-LOT b'-nay yis-ra-AYL may-E-retz mitz-RA-yim AD ha-YOM ha-ZEH see-mu la-KHEM a-LE-ha U-tzu v'-da-BAY-ru

Inside the Knesset

19:30 Never has such a thing happened or been seen Jewish tradition understands that the passages of the *Tanakh* are not always presented in chronological order. According to *Rashi*, this story, along with the narrative of *Micha*'s idol, occurred at the beginning of the era of the Judges. Rabbi Shlomo Aviner suggests that these narratives were placed here, at the end of the book, as another reminder of the sad results

Shoftim/Judges
Chapter 20

שופטים
פרק כ

20 1 Thereupon all the Israelites – from *Dan* to *Be'er Sheva* and [from] the land of *Gilad* – marched forth, and the community assembled to a man before Hashem at *Mitzpa*.

א וַיֵּצְאוּ כָּל־בְּנֵי יִשְׂרָאֵל וַתִּקָּהֵל הָעֵדָה כְּאִישׁ אֶחָד לְמִדָּן וְעַד־בְּאֵר שֶׁבַע וְאֶרֶץ הַגִּלְעָד אֶל־יְהֹוָה הַמִּצְפָּה:

va-yay-tz'-U kol b'-NAY yis-ra-AYL va-ti-ka-HAYL ha-ay-DAH k'-EESH e-KHAD l'-mi-DAN v'-ad b'-AYR SHE-va v'-E-retz ha-gil-AD el a-do-NAI ha-mitz-PAH

2 All the leaders of the people [and] all the tribes of *Yisrael* presented themselves in the assembly of Hashem's people, 400,000 fighting men on foot.

ב וַיִּתְיַצְּבוּ פִּנּוֹת כָּל־הָעָם כֹּל שִׁבְטֵי יִשְׂרָאֵל בִּקְהַל עַם הָאֱלֹהִים אַרְבַּע מֵאוֹת אֶלֶף אִישׁ רַגְלִי שֹׁלֵף חָרֶב:

3 The Benjaminites heard that the Israelites had come up to *Mitzpa*. – The Israelites said, "Tell us, how did this evil thing happen?"

ג וַיִּשְׁמְעוּ בְּנֵי בִנְיָמִן כִּי־עָלוּ בְנֵי־יִשְׂרָאֵל הַמִּצְפָּה וַיֹּאמְרוּ בְּנֵי יִשְׂרָאֵל דַּבְּרוּ אֵיכָה נִהְיְתָה הָרָעָה הַזֹּאת:

4 And the Levite, the husband of the murdered woman, replied, "My concubine and I came to *Giva* of *Binyamin* to spend the night.

ד וַיַּעַן הָאִישׁ הַלֵּוִי אִישׁ הָאִשָּׁה הַנִּרְצָחָה וַיֹּאמַר הַגִּבְעָתָה אֲשֶׁר לְבִנְיָמִן בָּאתִי אֲנִי וּפִילַגְשִׁי לָלוּן:

5 The citizens of *Giva* set out to harm me. They gathered against me around the house in the night; they meant to kill me, and they ravished my concubine until she died.

ה וַיָּקֻמוּ עָלַי בַּעֲלֵי הַגִּבְעָה וַיָּסֹבּוּ עָלַי אֶת־הַבַּיִת לָיְלָה אוֹתִי דִּמּוּ לַהֲרֹג וְאֶת־פִּילַגְשִׁי עִנּוּ וַתָּמֹת:

6 So I took hold of my concubine and I cut her in pieces and sent them through every part of *Yisrael*'s territory. For an outrageous act of depravity had been committed in *Yisrael*.

ו וָאֹחֵז בְּפִילַגְשִׁי וָאֲנַתְּחֶהָ וָאֲשַׁלְּחֶהָ בְּכָל־שְׂדֵה נַחֲלַת יִשְׂרָאֵל כִּי עָשׂוּ זִמָּה וּנְבָלָה בְּיִשְׂרָאֵל:

---

of having no king: disunity, disorder and violence. Seeing these repeated tragedies at the end of the book of *Shoftim* highlights the importance of the rise of the monarchy, described in the next book, *Shmuel*. Though the contemporary State of Israel has no king, Rabbi Abraham Isaac Kook says that a democratically elected Jewish government has a status similar to that of a monarchy. The Jewish people are fortunate that the State of Israel has a set and ordered government to protect society and to care for the nation.

20:1 From *Dan* to *Be'er Sheva* *Be'er Sheva*, mentioned in this verse as the southern boundary of Jewish settlement in *Eretz Yisrael*, was a vital city in biblical times. *Be'er Sheva* is one of the primary places where *Avraham* lives and digs a well, *be'er* (באר) in Hebrew. *Yitzchak* builds an altar there, and *Yaakov* passes through on the way to *Beit El* and later stops to bring sacrifices there on his way down to Egypt. In contemporary Israel, *Be'er Sheva* is known as "the capital of the *Negev* Desert." It is a thriving, multicultural city with a population including many Jews from Ethiopia and the former Soviet Union, a major hospital and a large university. The city is one of the many ancient cities in the Land of Israel that the Children of Israel have revived and developed.

Modern Court House in Beer Sheva

Shoftim/Judges
Chapter 20

שׁוֹפְטִים
פרק כ

7 Now you are all Israelites; produce a plan of action here and now!"

ז הִנֵּה כֻלְּכֶם בְּנֵי יִשְׂרָאֵל הָבוּ לָכֶם דָּבָר וְעֵצָה הֲלֹם׃

8 Then all the people rose, as one man, and declared, "We will not go back to our homes, we will not enter our houses!

ח וַיָּקׇם כׇּל־הָעָם כְּאִישׁ אֶחָד לֵאמֹר לֹא נֵלֵךְ אִישׁ לְאׇהֳלוֹ וְלֹא נָסוּר אִישׁ לְבֵיתוֹ׃

9 But this is what we will do to *Giva*: [we will wage war] against it according to lot.

ט וְעַתָּה זֶה הַדָּבָר אֲשֶׁר נַעֲשֶׂה לַגִּבְעָה עָלֶיהָ בְּגוֹרָל׃

10 We will take from all the tribes of *Yisrael* ten men to the hundred, a hundred to the thousand, and a thousand to the ten thousand to supply provisions for the troops – to prepare for their going to Geba in *Binyamin* for all the outrage it has committed in *Yisrael*."

י וְלָקַחְנוּ עֲשָׂרָה אֲנָשִׁים לַמֵּאָה לְכֹל שִׁבְטֵי יִשְׂרָאֵל וּמֵאָה לָאֶלֶף וְאֶלֶף לָרְבָבָה לָקַחַת צֵדָה לָעָם לַעֲשׂוֹת לְבוֹאָם לְגֶבַע בִּנְיָמִן כְּכׇל־הַנְּבָלָה אֲשֶׁר עָשָׂה בְּיִשְׂרָאֵל׃

11 So all the men of *Yisrael*, united as one man, massed against the town.

יא וַיֵּאָסֵף כׇּל־אִישׁ יִשְׂרָאֵל אֶל־הָעִיר כְּאִישׁ אֶחָד חֲבֵרִים׃

12 And the tribes of *Yisrael* sent men through the whole tribe of *Binyamin*, saying, "What is this evil thing that has happened among you?

יב וַיִּשְׁלְחוּ שִׁבְטֵי יִשְׂרָאֵל אֲנָשִׁים בְּכׇל־שִׁבְטֵי בִנְיָמִן לֵאמֹר מָה הָרָעָה הַזֹּאת אֲשֶׁר נִהְיְתָה בָּכֶם׃

13 Come, hand over those scoundrels in *Giva* so that we may put them to death and stamp out the evil from *Yisrael*." But the Benjaminites would not yield to the demand of their fellow Israelites.

יג וְעַתָּה תְּנוּ אֶת־הָאֲנָשִׁים בְּנֵי־בְלִיַּעַל אֲשֶׁר בַּגִּבְעָה וּנְמִיתֵם וּנְבַעֲרָה רָעָה מִיִּשְׂרָאֵל וְלֹא אָבוּ [בְּנֵי] בִּנְיָמִן לִשְׁמֹעַ בְּקוֹל אֲחֵיהֶם בְּנֵי־יִשְׂרָאֵל׃

14 So the Benjaminites gathered from their towns to *Giva* in order to take the field against the Israelites.

יד וַיֵּאָסְפוּ בְנֵי־בִנְיָמִן מִן־הֶעָרִים הַגִּבְעָתָה לָצֵאת לַמִּלְחָמָה עִם־בְּנֵי יִשְׂרָאֵל׃

15 On that day the Benjaminites mustered from the towns 26,000 fighting men, mustered apart from the inhabitants of *Giva*; 700 picked men

טו וַיִּתְפָּקְדוּ בְנֵי בִנְיָמִן בַּיּוֹם הַהוּא מֵהֶעָרִים עֶשְׂרִים וְשִׁשָּׁה אֶלֶף אִישׁ שֹׁלֵף חָרֶב לְבַד מִיֹּשְׁבֵי הַגִּבְעָה הִתְפָּקְדוּ שְׁבַע מֵאוֹת אִישׁ בָּחוּר׃

16 of all this force – 700 picked men – were left-handed. Every one of them could sling a stone at a hair and not miss.

טז מִכֹּל הָעָם הַזֶּה שְׁבַע מֵאוֹת אִישׁ בָּחוּר אִטֵּר יַד־יְמִינוֹ כׇּל־זֶה קֹלֵעַ בָּאֶבֶן אֶל־הַשַּׂעֲרָה וְלֹא יַחֲטִא׃

17 The men of *Yisrael* other than *Binyamin* mustered 400,000 fighting men, warriors to a man.

יז וְאִישׁ יִשְׂרָאֵל הִתְפָּקְדוּ לְבַד מִבִּנְיָמִן אַרְבַּע מֵאוֹת אֶלֶף אִישׁ שֹׁלֵף חָרֶב כׇּל־זֶה אִישׁ מִלְחָמָה׃

Shoftim/Judges
Chapter 20

18 They proceeded to *Beit El* and inquired of *Hashem*; the Israelites asked, "Who of us shall advance first to fight the Benjaminites?" And *Hashem* replied, "*Yehuda* first."

19 So the Israelites arose in the morning and encamped against *Giva*.

20 The men of *Yisrael* took the field against the Benjaminites; the men of *Yisrael* drew up in battle order against them at *Giva*.

21 But the Benjaminites issued from *Giva*, and that day they struck down 22,000 men of *Yisrael*.

22 Now the army – the men of *Yisrael* – rallied and again drew up in battle order at the same place as they had on the first day.

23 For the Israelites had gone up and wept before *Hashem* until evening. They had inquired of *Hashem*, "Shall we again join battle with our kinsmen the Benjaminites?" And *Hashem* had replied, "March against them."

24 The Israelites advanced against the *Binyamin*ites on the second day.

25 But the Benjaminites came out from *Giva* against them on the second day and struck down 18,000 more of the Israelites, all of them fighting men.

26 Then all the Israelites, all the army, went up and came to *Beit El* and they sat there, weeping before *Hashem*. They fasted that day until evening, and presented burnt offerings and offerings of well-being to *Hashem*.

27 The Israelites inquired of *Hashem* (for the *Aron Brit Hashem* was there in those days,

28 and *Pinchas* son of *Elazar* son of *Aharon* the *Kohen* ministered before Him in those days), "Shall we again take the field against our kinsmen the Benjaminites, or shall we not?" *Hashem* answered, "Go up, for tomorrow I will deliver them into your hands."

29 *Yisrael* put men in ambush against *Giva* on all sides.

650

Shoftim/Judges
Chapter 20

30 And on the third day, the Israelites went up against the Benjaminites, as before, and engaged them in battle at *Giva*.

31 The Benjaminites dashed out to meet the army and were drawn away from the town onto the roads, of which one runs to *Beit El* and the other to *Giva*. As before, they started out by striking some of the men dead in the open field, about 30 men of *Yisrael*.

32 The Benjaminites thought, "They are being routed before us as previously." But the Israelites had planned: "We will take to flight and draw them away from the town to the roads."

33 And while the main body of the Israelites had moved away from their positions and had drawn up in battle order at Baal-tamar, the Israelite ambush was rushing out from its position at Maareh-geba.

34 Thus 10,000 picked men of all *Yisrael* came to a point south of *Giva*, and the battle was furious. Before they realized that disaster was approaching,

35 *Hashem* routed the Benjaminites before *Yisrael*. That day the Israelites slew 25,100 men of *Binyamin*, all of them fighting men.

36 Then the Benjaminites realized that they were routed. Now the Israelites had yielded ground to the Benjaminites, for they relied on the ambush which they had laid against *Giva*.

37 One ambush quickly deployed against *Giva*, and the other ambush advanced and put the whole town to the sword.

38 A time had been agreed upon by the Israelite men with those in ambush: When a huge column of smoke was sent up from the town,

39 the Israelite men were to turn about in battle. *Binyamin* had begun by striking dead about 30 Israelite men, and they thought, "They are being routed before us as in the previous fighting."

40 But when the column, the pillar of smoke, began to rise from the city, the Benjaminites looked behind them, and there was the whole town going up in smoke to the sky!

שופטים
פרק כ

ל וַיַּעֲלוּ בְנֵי־יִשְׂרָאֵל אֶל־בְּנֵי בִנְיָמִן בַּיּוֹם הַשְּׁלִישִׁי וַיַּעַרְכוּ אֶל־הַגִּבְעָה כְּפַעַם בְּפָעַם:

לא וַיֵּצְאוּ בְנֵי־בִנְיָמִן לִקְרַאת הָעָם הָנְתְּקוּ מִן־הָעִיר וַיָּחֵלּוּ לְהַכּוֹת מֵהָעָם חֲלָלִים כְּפַעַם בְּפַעַם בַּמְסִלּוֹת אֲשֶׁר אַחַת עֹלָה בֵית־אֵל וְאַחַת גִּבְעָתָה בַּשָּׂדֶה כִּשְׁלֹשִׁים אִישׁ בְּיִשְׂרָאֵל:

לב וַיֹּאמְרוּ בְּנֵי בִנְיָמִן נִגָּפִים הֵם לְפָנֵינוּ כְּבָרִאשֹׁנָה וּבְנֵי יִשְׂרָאֵל אָמְרוּ נָנוּסָה וּנְתַקְנֻהוּ מִן־הָעִיר אֶל־הַמְסִלּוֹת:

לג וְכֹל אִישׁ יִשְׂרָאֵל קָמוּ מִמְּקוֹמוֹ וַיַּעַרְכוּ בְּבַעַל תָּמָר וְאֹרֵב יִשְׂרָאֵל מֵגִיחַ מִמְּקֹמוֹ מִמַּעֲרֵה־גָבַע:

לד וַיָּבֹאוּ מִנֶּגֶד לַגִּבְעָה עֲשֶׂרֶת אֲלָפִים אִישׁ בָּחוּר מִכָּל־יִשְׂרָאֵל וְהַמִּלְחָמָה כָּבֵדָה וְהֵם לֹא יָדְעוּ כִּי־נֹגַעַת עֲלֵיהֶם הָרָעָה:

לה וַיִּגֹּף יְהֹוָה אֶת־בִּנְיָמִן לִפְנֵי יִשְׂרָאֵל וַיַּשְׁחִיתוּ בְנֵי יִשְׂרָאֵל בְּבִנְיָמִן בַּיּוֹם הַהוּא עֶשְׂרִים וַחֲמִשָּׁה אֶלֶף וּמֵאָה אִישׁ כָּל־אֵלֶּה שֹׁלֵף חָרֶב:

לו וַיִּרְאוּ בְנֵי־בִנְיָמִן כִּי נִגָּפוּ וַיִּתְּנוּ אִישׁ־יִשְׂרָאֵל מָקוֹם לְבִנְיָמִן כִּי בָטְחוּ אֶל־הָאֹרֵב אֲשֶׁר שָׂמוּ אֶל־הַגִּבְעָה:

לז וְהָאֹרֵב הֵחִישׁוּ וַיִּפְשְׁטוּ אֶל־הַגִּבְעָה וַיִּמְשֹׁךְ הָאֹרֵב וַיַּךְ אֶת־כָּל־הָעִיר לְפִי־חָרֶב:

לח וְהַמּוֹעֵד הָיָה לְאִישׁ יִשְׂרָאֵל עִם־הָאֹרֵב הֶרֶב לְהַעֲלוֹתָם מַשְׂאַת הֶעָשָׁן מִן־הָעִיר:

לט וַיַּהֲפֹךְ אִישׁ־יִשְׂרָאֵל בַּמִּלְחָמָה וּבִנְיָמִן הֵחֵל לְהַכּוֹת חֲלָלִים בְּאִישׁ־יִשְׂרָאֵל כִּשְׁלֹשִׁים אִישׁ כִּי אָמְרוּ אַךְ נִגּוֹף נִגָּף הוּא לְפָנֵינוּ כַּמִּלְחָמָה הָרִאשֹׁנָה:

מ וְהַמַּשְׂאֵת הֵחֵלָּה לַעֲלוֹת מִן־הָעִיר עַמּוּד עָשָׁן וַיִּפֶן בִּנְיָמִן אַחֲרָיו וְהִנֵּה עָלָה כְלִיל־הָעִיר הַשָּׁמָיְמָה:

Shoftim/Judges
Chapter 21

שופטים
פרק כא

41 And now the Israelites turned about, and the men of *Binyamin* were thrown into panic, for they realized that disaster had overtaken them.

מא וְאִישׁ יִשְׂרָאֵל הָפַךְ וַיִּבָּהֵל אִישׁ בִּנְיָמִן כִּי רָאָה כִּי־נָגְעָה עָלָיו הָרָעָה׃

42 They retreated before the men of *Yisrael* along the road to the wilderness, where the fighting caught up with them; meanwhile those from the towns were massacring them in it.

מב וַיִּפְנוּ לִפְנֵי אִישׁ יִשְׂרָאֵל אֶל־דֶּרֶךְ הַמִּדְבָּר וְהַמִּלְחָמָה הִדְבִּיקָתְהוּ וַאֲשֶׁר מֵהֶעָרִים מַשְׁחִיתִים אוֹתוֹ בְּתוֹכוֹ׃

43 They encircled the Benjaminites, pursued them, and trod them down [from] Menuhah to a point opposite *Giva* on the east.

מג כִּתְּרוּ אֶת־בִּנְיָמִן הִרְדִיפֻהוּ מְנוּחָה הִדְרִיכֻהוּ עַד נֹכַח הַגִּבְעָה מִמִּזְרַח־שָׁמֶשׁ׃

44 That day 18,000 men of *Binyamin* fell, all of them brave men.

מד וַיִּפְּלוּ מִבִּנְיָמִן שְׁמֹנָה־עָשָׂר אֶלֶף אִישׁ אֶת־כָּל־אֵלֶּה אַנְשֵׁי־חָיִל׃

45 They turned and fled to the wilderness, to the Rock of Rimmon; but [the Israelites] picked off another 5,000 on the roads and, continuing in hot pursuit of them up to Gidom, they slew 2,000 more.

מה וַיִּפְנוּ וַיָּנֻסוּ הַמִּדְבָּרָה אֶל־סֶלַע הָרִמּוֹן וַיְעֹלְלֻהוּ בַּמְסִלּוֹת חֲמֵשֶׁת אֲלָפִים אִישׁ וַיַּדְבִּיקוּ אַחֲרָיו עַד־גִּדְעֹם וַיַּכּוּ מִמֶּנּוּ אַלְפַּיִם אִישׁ׃

46 Thus the total number of Benjaminites who fell that day came to 25,000 fighting men, all of them brave.

מו וַיְהִי כָל־הַנֹּפְלִים מִבִּנְיָמִן עֶשְׂרִים וַחֲמִשָּׁה אֶלֶף אִישׁ שֹׁלֵף חֶרֶב בַּיּוֹם הַהוּא אֶת־כָּל־אֵלֶּה אַנְשֵׁי־חָיִל׃

47 But 600 men turned and fled to the wilderness, to the Rock of Rimmon; they remained at the Rock of Rimmon four months.

מז וַיִּפְנוּ וַיָּנֻסוּ הַמִּדְבָּרָה אֶל־סֶלַע הָרִמּוֹן שֵׁשׁ מֵאוֹת אִישׁ וַיֵּשְׁבוּ בְּסֶלַע רִמּוֹן אַרְבָּעָה חֳדָשִׁים׃

48 The men of *Yisrael*, meanwhile, turned back to the rest of the Benjaminites and put them to the sword – towns, people, cattle – everything that remained. Finally, they set fire to all the towns that were left.

מח וְאִישׁ יִשְׂרָאֵל שָׁבוּ אֶל־בְּנֵי בִנְיָמִן וַיַּכּוּם לְפִי־חֶרֶב מֵעִיר מְתֹם עַד־בְּהֵמָה עַד כָּל־הַנִּמְצָא גַּם כָּל־הֶעָרִים הַנִּמְצָאוֹת שִׁלְּחוּ בָאֵשׁ׃

21

1 Now the men of *Yisrael* had taken an oath at *Mitzpa*: "None of us will give his daughter in marriage to a Benjaminite."

כא א וְאִישׁ יִשְׂרָאֵל נִשְׁבַּע בַּמִּצְפָּה לֵאמֹר אִישׁ מִמֶּנּוּ לֹא־יִתֵּן בִּתּוֹ לְבִנְיָמִן לְאִשָּׁה׃

2 The people came to *Beit El* and sat there before *Hashem* until evening. They wailed and wept bitterly,

ב וַיָּבֹא הָעָם בֵּית־אֵל וַיֵּשְׁבוּ שָׁם עַד־הָעֶרֶב לִפְנֵי הָאֱלֹהִים וַיִּשְׂאוּ קוֹלָם וַיִּבְכּוּ בְּכִי גָדוֹל׃

3 and they said, "O God of *Yisrael*, why has this happened in *Yisrael*, that one tribe must now be missing from *Yisrael*?"

ג וַיֹּאמְרוּ לָמָה יְהֹוָה אֱלֹהֵי יִשְׂרָאֵל הָיְתָה זֹּאת בְּיִשְׂרָאֵל לְהִפָּקֵד הַיּוֹם מִיִּשְׂרָאֵל שֵׁבֶט אֶחָד׃

4 Early the next day, the people built a *Mizbayach* there, and they brought burnt offerings and offerings of well-being.

ד וַיְהִי מִמָּחֳרָת וַיַּשְׁכִּימוּ הָעָם וַיִּבְנוּ־שָׁם מִזְבֵּחַ וַיַּעֲלוּ עֹלוֹת וּשְׁלָמִים׃

Shoftim/Judges
Chapter 21

5 The Israelites asked, "Is there anyone from all the tribes of *Yisrael* who failed to come up to the assembly before *Hashem*?" For a solemn oath had been taken concerning anyone who did not go up to *Hashem* at *Mitzpa*: "He shall be put to death."

6 The Israelites now relented toward their kinsmen the Benjaminites, and they said, "This day one tribe has been cut off from *Yisrael*!

7 What can we do to provide wives for those who are left, seeing that we have sworn by *Hashem* not to give any of our daughters to them in marriage?"

8 They inquired, "Is there anyone from the tribes of *Yisrael* who did not go up to *Hashem* at *Mitzpa*?" Now no one from Jabesh-gilead had come to the camp, to the assembly.

9 For, when the roll of the troops was taken, not one of the inhabitants of Jabesh-gilead was present.

10 So the assemblage dispatched 12,000 of the warriors, instructing them as follows: "Go and put the inhabitants of Jabesh-gilead to the sword, women and children included.

11 This is what you are to do: Proscribe every man, and every woman who has known a man carnally."

12 They found among the inhabitants of Jabesh-gilead 400 maidens who had not known a man carnally; and they brought them to the camp at *Shilo*, which is in the land of Canaan.

13 Then the whole community sent word to the Benjaminites who were at the Rock of Rimmon, and offered them terms of peace.

14 Thereupon the Benjaminites returned, and they gave them the girls who had been spared from the women of Jabesh-gilead. But there were not enough of them.

15 Now the people had relented toward *Binyamin*, for *Hashem* had made a breach in the tribes of *Yisrael*.

16 So the elders of the community asked, "What can we do about wives for those who are left, since the women of *Binyamin* have been killed off?"

שופטים
פרק כא

ה וַיֹּאמְרוּ בְּנֵי יִשְׂרָאֵל מִי אֲשֶׁר לֹא־עָלָה בַקָּהָל מִכָּל־שִׁבְטֵי יִשְׂרָאֵל אֶל־יְהֹוָה כִּי הַשְּׁבוּעָה הַגְּדוֹלָה הָיְתָה לַאֲשֶׁר לֹא־עָלָה אֶל־יְהֹוָה הַמִּצְפָּה לֵאמֹר מוֹת יוּמָת:

ו וַיִּנָּחֲמוּ בְּנֵי יִשְׂרָאֵל אֶל־בִּנְיָמִן אָחִיו וַיֹּאמְרוּ נִגְדַּע הַיּוֹם שֵׁבֶט אֶחָד מִיִּשְׂרָאֵל:

ז מַה־נַּעֲשֶׂה לָהֶם לַנּוֹתָרִים לְנָשִׁים וַאֲנַחְנוּ נִשְׁבַּעְנוּ בַיהֹוָה לְבִלְתִּי תֵּת־לָהֶם מִבְּנוֹתֵינוּ לְנָשִׁים:

ח וַיֹּאמְרוּ מִי אֶחָד מִשִּׁבְטֵי יִשְׂרָאֵל אֲשֶׁר לֹא־עָלָה אֶל־יְהֹוָה הַמִּצְפָּה וְהִנֵּה לֹא בָא־אִישׁ אֶל־הַמַּחֲנֶה מִיָּבֵישׁ גִּלְעָד אֶל־הַקָּהָל:

ט וַיִּתְפָּקֵד הָעָם וְהִנֵּה אֵין־שָׁם אִישׁ מִיּוֹשְׁבֵי יָבֵשׁ גִּלְעָד:

י וַיִּשְׁלְחוּ־שָׁם הָעֵדָה שְׁנֵים־עָשָׂר אֶלֶף אִישׁ מִבְּנֵי הֶחָיִל וַיְצַוּוּ אוֹתָם לֵאמֹר לְכוּ וְהִכִּיתֶם אֶת־יוֹשְׁבֵי יָבֵשׁ גִּלְעָד לְפִי־חֶרֶב וְהַנָּשִׁים וְהַטָּף:

יא וְזֶה הַדָּבָר אֲשֶׁר תַּעֲשׂוּ כָּל־זָכָר וְכָל־אִשָּׁה יֹדַעַת מִשְׁכַּב־זָכָר תַּחֲרִימוּ:

יב וַיִּמְצְאוּ מִיּוֹשְׁבֵי יָבֵישׁ גִּלְעָד אַרְבַּע מֵאוֹת נַעֲרָה בְתוּלָה אֲשֶׁר לֹא־יָדְעָה אִישׁ לְמִשְׁכַּב זָכָר וַיָּבִיאוּ אוֹתָם אֶל־הַמַּחֲנֶה שִׁלֹה אֲשֶׁר בְּאֶרֶץ כְּנָעַן:

יג וַיִּשְׁלְחוּ כָּל־הָעֵדָה וַיְדַבְּרוּ אֶל־בְּנֵי בִנְיָמִן אֲשֶׁר בְּסֶלַע רִמּוֹן וַיִּקְרְאוּ לָהֶם שָׁלוֹם:

יד וַיָּשָׁב בִּנְיָמִן בָּעֵת הַהִיא וַיִּתְּנוּ לָהֶם הַנָּשִׁים אֲשֶׁר חִיּוּ מִנְּשֵׁי יָבֵשׁ גִּלְעָד וְלֹא־מָצְאוּ לָהֶם כֵּן:

טו וְהָעָם נִחָם לְבִנְיָמִן כִּי־עָשָׂה יְהֹוָה פֶּרֶץ בְּשִׁבְטֵי יִשְׂרָאֵל:

טז וַיֹּאמְרוּ זִקְנֵי הָעֵדָה מַה־נַּעֲשֶׂה לַנּוֹתָרִים לְנָשִׁים כִּי־נִשְׁמְדָה מִבִּנְיָמִן אִשָּׁה:

Shoftim/Judges
Chapter 21

שופטים
פרק כא

17 For they said, "There must be a saving remnant for *Binyamin*, that a tribe may not be blotted out of *Yisrael*;

יז וַיֹּאמְרוּ יְרֻשַּׁת פְּלֵיטָה לְבִנְיָמִן וְלֹא־יִמָּחֶה שֵׁבֶט מִיִּשְׂרָאֵל׃

18 yet we cannot give them any of our daughters as wives," since the Israelites had taken an oath: "Cursed be anyone who gives a wife to *Binyamin*!"

יח וַאֲנַחְנוּ לֹא נוּכַל לָתֵת־לָהֶם נָשִׁים מִבְּנוֹתֵינוּ כִּי־נִשְׁבְּעוּ בְנֵי־יִשְׂרָאֵל לֵאמֹר אָרוּר נֹתֵן אִשָּׁה לְבִנְיָמִן׃

19 They said, "The annual feast of *Hashem* is now being held at *Shilo*." (It lies north of *Beit El*, east of the highway that runs from *Beit El* to *Shechem*, and south of Lebonah.)

יט וַיֹּאמְרוּ הִנֵּה חַג־יְהֹוָה בְּשִׁלוֹ מִיָּמִים יָמִימָה אֲשֶׁר מִצְּפוֹנָה לְבֵית־אֵל מִזְרְחָה הַשֶּׁמֶשׁ לִמְסִלָּה הָעֹלָה מִבֵּית־אֵל שְׁכֶמָה וּמִנֶּגֶב לִלְבוֹנָה׃

20 So they instructed the Benjaminites as follows: "Go and lie in wait in the vineyards.

כ וַיְצַוּוּ [וַיְצַוּוּ] אֶת־בְּנֵי בִנְיָמִן לֵאמֹר לְכוּ וַאֲרַבְתֶּם בַּכְּרָמִים׃

21 As soon as you see the girls of *Shilo* coming out to join in the dances, come out from the vineyards; let each of you seize a wife from among the girls of *Shilo*, and be off for the land of *Binyamin*.

כא וּרְאִיתֶם וְהִנֵּה אִם־יֵצְאוּ בְנוֹת־שִׁילוֹ לָחוּל בַּמְּחֹלוֹת וִיצָאתֶם מִן־הַכְּרָמִים וַחֲטַפְתֶּם לָכֶם אִישׁ אִשְׁתּוֹ מִבְּנוֹת שִׁילוֹ וַהֲלַכְתֶּם אֶרֶץ בִּנְיָמִן׃

22 And if their fathers or brothers come to us to complain, we shall say to them, 'Be generous to them for our sake! We could not provide any of them with a wife on account of the war, and you would have incurred guilt if you yourselves had given them [wives].'"

כב וְהָיָה כִּי־יָבֹאוּ אֲבוֹתָם אוֹ אֲחֵיהֶם לָרוֹב [לָרִיב] אֵלֵינוּ וְאָמַרְנוּ אֲלֵיהֶם חָנּוּנוּ אוֹתָם כִּי לֹא לָקַחְנוּ אִישׁ אִשְׁתּוֹ בַּמִּלְחָמָה כִּי לֹא אַתֶּם נְתַתֶּם לָהֶם כָּעֵת תֶּאְשָׁמוּ׃

23 The Benjaminites did so. They took to wife, from the dancers whom they carried off, as many as they themselves numbered. Then they went back to their own territory, and rebuilt their towns and settled in them.

כג וַיַּעֲשׂוּ־כֵן בְּנֵי בִנְיָמִן וַיִּשְׂאוּ נָשִׁים לְמִסְפָּרָם מִן־הַמְּחֹלְלוֹת אֲשֶׁר גָּזָלוּ וַיֵּלְכוּ וַיָּשׁוּבוּ אֶל־נַחֲלָתָם וַיִּבְנוּ אֶת־הֶעָרִים וַיֵּשְׁבוּ בָּהֶם׃

va-ya-a-su KHAYN b'-NAY vin-ya-MIN va-yis-U na-SHEEM l'-mis-pa-RAM min ha-m'-kho-l'-LOT a-SHER ga-ZA-lu va-yay-l'-KHU va-ya-SHU-vu el na-kha-la-TAM va-yiv-NU et he-a-REEM va-yay-sh'-VU ba-HEM

24 Thereupon the Israelites dispersed, each to his own tribe and clan; everyone departed for his own territory.

כד וַיִּתְהַלְּכוּ מִשָּׁם בְּנֵי־יִשְׂרָאֵל בָּעֵת הַהִיא אִישׁ לְשִׁבְטוֹ וּלְמִשְׁפַּחְתּוֹ וַיֵּצְאוּ מִשָּׁם אִישׁ לְנַחֲלָתוֹ׃

25 In those days there was no king in *Yisrael*; everyone did as he pleased.

כה בַּיָּמִים הָהֵם אֵין מֶלֶךְ בְּיִשְׂרָאֵל אִישׁ הַיָּשָׁר בְּעֵינָיו יַעֲשֶׂה׃

21:23 The Benjaminites did so The men of the tribe of *Binyamin* are now allowed to marry women from other tribes, overturning the oath those tribes made to prevent their daughters from marrying men from *Binyamin* (verse 1). This event brought about the reunification of the twelve tribes of Israel. The Talmud (*Taanit* 30b) records that this happened on the fifteenth day of the Hebrew month of *Av*, which helped turn that day into one of perpetual joy. The fact that the Children of Israel are once again united in the Land of Israel is indeed a cause for celebration.

Sefer Shmuel
The Book of Samuel

Introduction and commentary by Rabbi Shmuel Jablon

Before the prophet *Shmuel* (Samuel) became the judge of Israel, the nation was in dire straits. The previous book of *Shoftim* (Judges) describes many instances of the Children of Israel violating God's will by engaging in idolatry and immorality, and then being punished with subjugation to other nations. Though there were great heroes and times of triumph during the period of the judges, much of it was bleak. The Nation of Israel often failed to live up to the challenge of living as a holy and free people in its land.

As the Bible transitions into *Sefer Shmuel*, we learn that even the *Mishkan* at *Shilo* is not free of transgressions. The sons of *Eli* the *Kohen Gadol* (High Priest) are sinning, thereby discouraging the people from making pilgrimages to this holy place. It is against this backdrop that *Shmuel* is born to *Elkana* and *Chana*. While still barren, *Chana* prays for a child at *Shilo* and vows that if her request is granted, her son will be totally sanctified to *Hashem*. The miraculous child fulfills her vow. *Shmuel* grows up under *Eli*'s tutelage in *Shilo*, and later replaces him as Israel's primary leader.

As a prophet and a leader, *Shmuel* faces a daunting task. As Rabbi Shlomo Aviner notes in his book "Heroes of the *Tanakh*", "The prophet *Shmuel* purified the People of Israel…But he also dealt with the nation's national and military sides; not only the spiritual." Thus, in this book we learn of his struggles against the Philistines, the primary enemy of the Children of Israel at this time, and of his strengthening the Israelites' service of God. We also learn of his anointing *Shaul* as the first king of Israel. When *Shaul* fails to fulfill the command to completely eradicate Amalek, it is *Shmuel* who tells him that he has lost the kingdom, and who anoints his successor *David*.

Unlike *Shaul*, *David* will not rule in accordance with the people's initial request for a king "like all the other nations" (I Samuel 8:5), who leads the nation by simply maintaining order and commanding the military. Rather, he will be a king who will combine his extraordinary spiritual and physical gifts to lead the nation to new heights in its service of *Hashem*, and its strengthening of the Land of Israel. Young *David*'s miraculous defeat of the giant Philistine Goliath foreshadows his later achievements as king. While his victory is undoubtedly a military achievement, it is also spiritual. *David* faces an enemy who fights not only against the People of Israel, but also against God Himself. *David* recognizes this, and acts to save his people, returning honor to them and to *Hashem*.

King *David* is the epitome of the bright and shining monarch of Israel. He represents both physical and spiritual strength. He is a great military figure who vanquishes the enemies of Israel. As king, he rules first in *Chevron*, unites the entire Nation of Israel and then succeeds in conquering the holy city of *Yerushalayim*. He is responsible for bringing the Holy Ark to *Yerushalayim* and acquiring the future site of the Holy Temple. He is also known as *n'eem z'mirot yisrael* (נעים זמירות ישראל) (II Samuel 23:1), often translated as 'the sweet singer of Israel,' who writes songs of praise to *Hashem*, including most of the Book of *Tehillim*, and is proud to dance before God's Holy Ark. He is an example of a true "master of repentance," one who takes responsibility for his sins and atones for them with a broken heart.

By the time King *David* passes the reign over the Kingdom of Israel to his son *Shlomo,* as described in the beginning of *Sefer Melachim*, he has established and stabilized the kingdom, and its people live as a vibrant, free and holy nation in the entire Land of Israel. They are united both physically and spiritually, and are on the cusp of achieving their greatest triumph – the building of the *Beit Hamikdash* in *Yerushalayim*. In addition, they are finally at peace with their enemies. It is not surprising that the dynasty of *David* is eternal. Nor is it surprising that Jewish tradition teaches that the future King *Mashiach*, who will once again unite the Children of Israel in *Eretz Yisrael* in peace, will be one of *David*'s descendants. May our study of *Sefer Shmuel* hasten the *Mashiach*'s arrival, speedily and in our days.

Map of the Journey of the *Aron* (Ark)

This map traces the journey of the *Aron* (Ark of the Covenant) from the *Mishkan* (Tabernacle) in *Shilo* (Shiloh) to *Ir David* (the City of David) in *Yerushalayim* (Jerusalem), as described in *Sefer Shmuel* I (4:1–7:2) and *Sefer Shmuel* II (6:2–17).

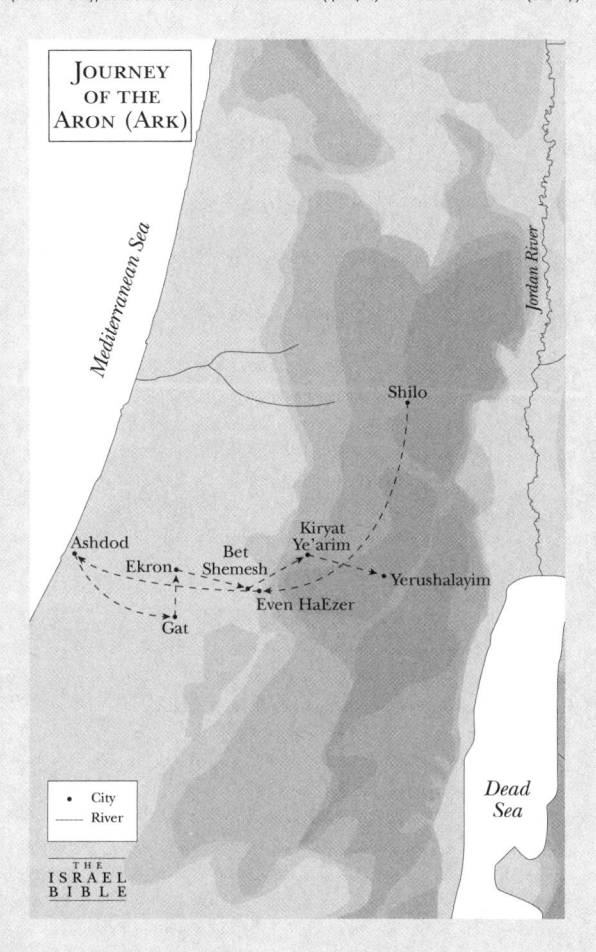

1. **Shilo** was the home of the *Mishkan* (Tabernacle) for 369 years. It was from here that the *Aron* was taken and brought to the battlefield (I Samuel 4:3–4).
2. **Even Ha-Ezer** was where the Israelites set up camp for their battle against the Philistines. It was from here that the Aron was captured (I Samuel 4:1, 11).
3. The Philistines brought the *Aron* to the Philistine city of **Ashdod,** where they placed it in the temple of their god, Dagon (I Samuel 5:1–2).
4. The *Aron* is moved from *Ashdod* to the Philistine city of **Gat** (I Samuel 5:8).
5. From Gat, the Ark was brought to the Philistine city of **Ekron** (I Samuel 5:10).
6. Fearing death, the Philistines sent the *Aron* back to Israelite city of **Bet Shemesh** (I Samuel 6:11–12).
7. The *Aron* is then brought to the house of *Avinadav* in **Kiryat Ye'arim** where it remains for 20 years (I Samuel 6:21–7:2).
8. After capturing **Yerushalayim** from the Jebusites, King *David* sent for the *Aron*. After a brief stay at the home of *Oved Edom* the Gittite, it finally reaches its ultimate destination (II Samuel 6:2–17).

Shmuel I / I Samuel
Chapter 1

שמואל א
פרק א

1 1 There was a man from Ramathaim of the Zuphites, in the hill country of *Efraim*, whose name was *Elkana* son of Jeroham son of Elihu son of Tohu son of Zuph, an Ephraimite.

א וַיְהִי אִישׁ אֶחָד מִן־הָרָמָתַיִם צוֹפִים מֵהַר אֶפְרָיִם וּשְׁמוֹ אֶלְקָנָה בֶּן־יְרֹחָם בֶּן־אֱלִיהוּא בֶּן־תֹּחוּ בֶן־צוּף אֶפְרָתִי:

2 He had two wives, one named *Chana* and the other *Penina*; *Penina* had children, but *Chana* was childless.

ב וְלוֹ שְׁתֵּי נָשִׁים שֵׁם אַחַת חַנָּה וְשֵׁם הַשֵּׁנִית פְּנִנָּה וַיְהִי לִפְנִנָּה יְלָדִים וּלְחַנָּה אֵין יְלָדִים:

3 This man used to go up from his town every year to worship and to offer sacrifice to the Lord of Hosts at *Shilo*. – *Chofni* and *Pinchas*, the two sons of *Eli*, were *Kohanim* of *Hashem* there.

ג וְעָלָה הָאִישׁ הַהוּא מֵעִירוֹ מִיָּמִים יָמִימָה לְהִשְׁתַּחֲוֺת וְלִזְבֹּחַ לַיהוָה צְבָאוֹת בְּשִׁלֹה וְשָׁם שְׁנֵי בְנֵי־עֵלִי חָפְנִי וּפִנְחָס כֹּהֲנִים לַיהוָה:

4 One such day, *Elkana* offered a sacrifice. He used to give portions to his wife *Penina* and to all her sons and daughters;

ד וַיְהִי הַיּוֹם וַיִּזְבַּח אֶלְקָנָה וְנָתַן לִפְנִנָּה אִשְׁתּוֹ וּלְכָל־בָּנֶיהָ וּבְנוֹתֶיהָ מָנוֹת:

5 but to *Chana* he would give one portion only – though *Chana* was his favorite – for *Hashem* had closed her womb.

ה וּלְחַנָּה יִתֵּן מָנָה אַחַת אַפָּיִם כִּי אֶת־חַנָּה אָהֵב וַיהוָה סָגַר רַחְמָהּ:

6 Moreover, her rival, to make her miserable, would taunt her that *Hashem* had closed her womb.

ו וְכִעֲסַתָּה צָרָתָהּ גַּם־כַּעַס בַּעֲבוּר הַרְּעִמָהּ כִּי־סָגַר יְהוָה בְּעַד רַחְמָהּ:

7 This happened year after year: Every time she went up to the House of *Hashem*, the other would taunt her, so that she wept and would not eat.

ז וְכֵן יַעֲשֶׂה שָׁנָה בְשָׁנָה מִדֵּי עֲלֹתָהּ בְּבֵית יְהוָה כֵּן תַּכְעִסֶנָּה וַתִּבְכֶּה וְלֹא תֹאכַל:

8 Her husband *Elkana* said to her, "*Chana*, why are you crying and why aren't you eating? Why are you so sad? Am I not more devoted to you than ten sons?"

ח וַיֹּאמֶר לָהּ אֶלְקָנָה אִישָׁהּ חַנָּה לָמֶה תִבְכִּי וְלָמֶה לֹא תֹאכְלִי וְלָמֶה יֵרַע לְבָבֵךְ הֲלוֹא אָנֹכִי טוֹב לָךְ מֵעֲשָׂרָה בָּנִים:

9 After they had eaten and drunk at *Shilo*, *Chana* rose. – The *Kohen Eli* was sitting on the seat near the doorpost of the temple of *Hashem*. –

ט וַתָּקָם חַנָּה אַחֲרֵי אָכְלָה בְשִׁלֹה וְאַחֲרֵי שָׁתֹה וְעֵלִי הַכֹּהֵן יֹשֵׁב עַל־הַכִּסֵּא עַל־מְזוּזַת הֵיכַל יְהוָה:

10 In her wretchedness, she prayed to *Hashem*, weeping all the while.

י וְהִיא מָרַת נָפֶשׁ וַתִּתְפַּלֵּל עַל־יְהוָה וּבָכֹה תִבְכֶּה:

v'-HEE ma-RAT NA-fesh va-tit-pa-LAYL al a-do-NAI u-va-KHOH tiv-KEH

1:10 In her wretchedness, she prayed to *Hashem* *Chana* is heartbroken because she has no children, and goes to pray at the *Mishkan* in *Shilo*. The *Mishkan* stands in *Shilo* for three hundred sixty-nine years before the building of the *Beit Hamikdash* in *Yerushalayim*. During that time, it serves as the central focal point of the national service of *Hashem*. Unfortunately, many of the Israelites ignore the *Mishkan*, and refrain from visiting it for the pilgrimage festivals. Therefore, according to the Sages when *Elkana* and *Chana*, who were prophets, make their pilgrimages, they travel along different routes each time, in order to encourage others to join them and to serve *Hashem* properly. Established in 1978, contemporary *Shilo* is a thriving Jewish community built adjacent to the ancient site where the *Mishkan* stood and *Chana* prayed for a child. In addition to the fascinating archaeological site excavated by the Israel Antiquities Authority, modern *Shilo* contains several synagogues, one of which is built as a replica of the *Mishkan*. God continues to hear the prayers of His children in *Shilo*, the very same location where *Chana* taught her people how to pray.

Archaeological site of biblical Shilo

Shmuel I/I Samuel
Chapter 1

שמואל א
פרק א

11 And she made this vow: "Lord of Hosts, if You will look upon the suffering of Your maidservant and will remember me and not forget Your maidservant, and if You will grant Your maidservant a male child, I will dedicate him to *Hashem* for all the days of his life; and no razor shall ever touch his head."

יא וַתִּדֹּר נֶדֶר וַתֹּאמַר יְהֹוָה צְבָאוֹת אִם־רָאֹה תִרְאֶה ׀ בָּעֳנִי אֲמָתֶךָ וּזְכַרְתַּנִי וְלֹא־תִשְׁכַּח אֶת־אֲמָתֶךָ וְנָתַתָּה לַאֲמָתְךָ זֶרַע אֲנָשִׁים וּנְתַתִּיו לַיהֹוָה כָּל־יְמֵי חַיָּיו וּמוֹרָה לֹא־יַעֲלֶה עַל־רֹאשׁוֹ:

12 As she kept on praying before *Hashem*, *Eli* watched her mouth.

יב וְהָיָה כִּי הִרְבְּתָה לְהִתְפַּלֵּל לִפְנֵי יְהֹוָה וְעֵלִי שֹׁמֵר אֶת־פִּיהָ:

13 Now *Chana* was praying in her heart; only her lips moved, but her voice could not be heard. So *Eli* thought she was drunk.

יג וְחַנָּה הִיא מְדַבֶּרֶת עַל־לִבָּהּ רַק שְׂפָתֶיהָ נָּעוֹת וְקוֹלָהּ לֹא יִשָּׁמֵעַ וַיַּחְשְׁבֶהָ עֵלִי לְשִׁכֹּרָה:

14 *Eli* said to her, "How long will you make a drunken spectacle of yourself? Sober up!"

יד וַיֹּאמֶר אֵלֶיהָ עֵלִי עַד־מָתַי תִּשְׁתַּכָּרִין הָסִירִי אֶת־יֵינֵךְ מֵעָלָיִךְ:

15 And *Chana* replied, "Oh no, my lord! I am a very unhappy woman. I have drunk no wine or other strong drink, but I have been pouring out my heart to *Hashem*.

טו וַתַּעַן חַנָּה וַתֹּאמֶר לֹא אֲדֹנִי אִשָּׁה קְשַׁת־רוּחַ אָנֹכִי וְיַיִן וְשֵׁכָר לֹא שָׁתִיתִי וָאֶשְׁפֹּךְ אֶת־נַפְשִׁי לִפְנֵי יְהֹוָה:

16 Do not take your maidservant for a worthless woman; I have only been speaking all this time out of my great anguish and distress."

טז אַל־תִּתֵּן אֶת־אֲמָתְךָ לִפְנֵי בַּת־בְּלִיָּעַל כִּי־מֵרֹב שִׂיחִי וְכַעְסִי דִּבַּרְתִּי עַד־הֵנָּה:

17 "Then go in peace," said *Eli*, "and may the God of *Yisrael* grant you what you have asked of Him."

יז וַיַּעַן עֵלִי וַיֹּאמֶר לְכִי לְשָׁלוֹם וֵאלֹהֵי יִשְׂרָאֵל יִתֵּן אֶת־שֵׁלָתֵךְ אֲשֶׁר שָׁאַלְתְּ מֵעִמּוֹ:

18 She answered, "You are most kind to your handmaid." So the woman left, and she ate, and was no longer downcast.

יח וַתֹּאמֶר תִּמְצָא שִׁפְחָתְךָ חֵן בְּעֵינֶיךָ וַתֵּלֶךְ הָאִשָּׁה לְדַרְכָּהּ וַתֹּאכַל וּפָנֶיהָ לֹא־הָיוּ־לָהּ עוֹד:

19 Early next morning they bowed low before *Hashem*, and they went back home to *Rama*. *Elkana* knew his wife *Chana* and *Hashem* remembered her.

יט וַיַּשְׁכִּמוּ בַבֹּקֶר וַיִּשְׁתַּחֲווּ לִפְנֵי יְהֹוָה וַיָּשֻׁבוּ וַיָּבֹאוּ אֶל־בֵּיתָם הָרָמָתָה וַיֵּדַע אֶלְקָנָה אֶת־חַנָּה אִשְׁתּוֹ וַיִּזְכְּרֶהָ יְהֹוָה:

20 *Chana* conceived, and at the turn of the year bore a son. She named him *Shmuel*, meaning, "I asked *Hashem* for him."

כ וַיְהִי לִתְקֻפוֹת הַיָּמִים וַתַּהַר חַנָּה וַתֵּלֶד בֵּן וַתִּקְרָא אֶת־שְׁמוֹ שְׁמוּאֵל כִּי מֵיְהֹוָה שְׁאִלְתִּיו:

21 And when the man *Elkana* and all his household were going up to offer to *Hashem* the annual sacrifice and his votive sacrifice,

כא וַיַּעַל הָאִישׁ אֶלְקָנָה וְכָל־בֵּיתוֹ לִזְבֹּחַ לַיהֹוָה אֶת־זֶבַח הַיָּמִים וְאֶת־נִדְרוֹ:

22 *Chana* did not go up. She said to her husband, "When the child is weaned, I will bring him. For when he has appeared before *Hashem*, he must remain there for good."

כב וְחַנָּה לֹא עָלָתָה כִּי־אָמְרָה לְאִישָׁהּ עַד יִגָּמֵל הַנַּעַר וַהֲבִאֹתִיו וְנִרְאָה אֶת־פְּנֵי יְהֹוָה וְיָשַׁב שָׁם עַד־עוֹלָם:

Shmuel I / I Samuel
Chapter 2

23 Her husband *Elkana* said to her, "Do as you think best. Stay home until you have weaned him. May *Hashem* fulfill His word." So the woman stayed home and nursed her son until she weaned him.

כג וַיֹּאמֶר לָהּ אֶלְקָנָה אִישָׁהּ עֲשִׂי הַטּוֹב בְּעֵינַיִךְ שְׁבִי עַד־גָּמְלֵךְ אֹתוֹ אַךְ יָקֵם יְהֹוָה אֶת־דְּבָרוֹ וַתֵּשֶׁב הָאִשָּׁה וַתֵּינֶק אֶת־בְּנָהּ עַד־גָּמְלָהּ אֹתוֹ:

24 When she had weaned him, she took him up with her, along with three bulls, one *efah* of flour, and a jar of wine. And though the boy was still very young, she brought him to the House of *Hashem* at *Shilo.*

כד וַתַּעֲלֵהוּ עִמָּהּ כַּאֲשֶׁר גְּמָלַתּוּ בְּפָרִים שְׁלֹשָׁה וְאֵיפָה אַחַת קֶמַח וְנֵבֶל יַיִן וַתְּבִאֵהוּ בֵית־יְהֹוָה שִׁלוֹ וְהַנַּעַר נָעַר:

25 After slaughtering the bull, they brought the boy to *Eli.*

כה וַיִּשְׁחֲטוּ אֶת־הַפָּר וַיָּבִיאוּ אֶת־הַנַּעַר אֶל־עֵלִי:

26 She said, "Please, my lord! As you live, my lord, I am the woman who stood here beside you and prayed to *Hashem.*

כו וַתֹּאמֶר בִּי אֲדֹנִי חֵי נַפְשְׁךָ אֲדֹנִי אֲנִי הָאִשָּׁה הַנִּצֶּבֶת עִמְּכָה בָּזֶה לְהִתְפַּלֵּל אֶל־יְהֹוָה:

27 It was this boy I prayed for; and *Hashem* has granted me what I asked of Him.

כז אֶל־הַנַּעַר הַזֶּה הִתְפַּלָּלְתִּי וַיִּתֵּן יְהֹוָה לִי אֶת־שְׁאֵלָתִי אֲשֶׁר שָׁאַלְתִּי מֵעִמּוֹ:

28 I, in turn, hereby lend him to *Hashem.* For as long as he lives he is lent to *Hashem.*" And they bowed low there before *Hashem.*

כח וְגַם אָנֹכִי הִשְׁאִלְתִּהוּ לַיהֹוָה כָּל־הַיָּמִים אֲשֶׁר הָיָה הוּא שָׁאוּל לַיהֹוָה וַיִּשְׁתַּחוּ שָׁם לַיהֹוָה:

2

1 And *Chana* prayed: My heart exults in *Hashem*; I have triumphed through *Hashem.* I gloat over my enemies; I rejoice in Your deliverance.

א וַתִּתְפַּלֵּל חַנָּה וַתֹּאמַר עָלַץ לִבִּי בַּיהֹוָה רָמָה קַרְנִי בַּיהֹוָה רָחַב פִּי עַל־אוֹיְבַי כִּי שָׂמַחְתִּי בִּישׁוּעָתֶךָ:

va-tit-pa-LAYL kha-NAH va-to-MAR a-LATZ li-BEE ba-do-NAI RA-mah kar-NEE ba-do-NAI RA-khav pee al o-y'-VAI kee sa-MAKH-tee bee-shu-a-TE-kha

2 There is no holy one like *Hashem,* Truly, there is none beside You; There is no rock like our God.

ב אֵין־קָדוֹשׁ כַּיהֹוָה כִּי אֵין בִּלְתֶּךָ וְאֵין צוּר כֵּאלֹהֵינוּ:

3 Talk no more with lofty pride, Let no arrogance cross your lips! For *Hashem* is an all-knowing *Hashem*; By Him actions are measured.

ג אַל־תַּרְבּוּ תְדַבְּרוּ גְּבֹהָה גְבֹהָה יֵצֵא עָתָק מִפִּיכֶם כִּי אֵל דֵּעוֹת יְהֹוָה וְלֹא [וְלוֹ] נִתְכְּנוּ עֲלִלוֹת:

Chana Senesh (1921–1944)

2:1 And *Chana* prayed *Chana*'s prayer of thanksgiving, recorded in this chapter, is considered a model prayer. In her time, there was still no established liturgy, and there was not yet any concept of organized prayer among the Israelites. *Chana*'s prayer was a spontaneous expression of her deep spirit, after finally being blessed with the child for whom she had desperately longed. Over 3,000 years later, another Jewish heroine with the same first name would be born – Chana Senesh. Born in Hungary in 1921, she fulfilled her Zionist dream and immigrated to the Land of Israel. During World War II, she daringly volunteered to parachute into Nazi-occupied Europe to assist the British army and the Hungarian Jewish community. Tragically, she was caught, tortured and executed. Throughout her life, Senesh composed beautiful poetry; the most prominent one for which she is remembered is *Eli* (אלי) – 'My God', which she wrote on the shores of Caesarea. Like her biblical namesake *Chana,* the deepest expression of Senesh's soul is her prayer: "My God, My God, may these things never end, the sand and the sea, the rustle of the waters, the lightning of the heavens, the prayer of Man."

Shmuel I / I Samuel
Chapter 2

שמואל א
פרק ב

4 The bows of the mighty are broken, And the faltering are girded with strength.

ד קֶשֶׁת גִּבֹּרִים חַתִּים וְנִכְשָׁלִים אָזְרוּ חָיִל:

5 Men once sated must hire out for bread; Men once hungry hunger no more. While the barren woman bears seven, The mother of many is forlorn.

ה שְׂבֵעִים בַּלֶּחֶם נִשְׂכָּרוּ וּרְעֵבִים חָדֵלּוּ עַד־עֲקָרָה יָלְדָה שִׁבְעָה וְרַבַּת בָּנִים אֻמְלָלָה:

6 Hashem deals death and gives life, Casts down into Sheol and raises up.

ו יְהֹוָה מֵמִית וּמְחַיֶּה מוֹרִיד שְׁאוֹל וַיָּעַל:

7 Hashem makes poor and makes rich; He casts down, He also lifts high.

ז יְהֹוָה מוֹרִישׁ וּמַעֲשִׁיר מַשְׁפִּיל אַף־מְרוֹמֵם:

8 He raises the poor from the dust, Lifts up the needy from the dunghill, Setting them with nobles, Granting them seats of honor. For the pillars of the earth are Hashem's; He has set the world upon them.

ח מֵקִים מֵעָפָר דָּל מֵאַשְׁפֹּת יָרִים אֶבְיוֹן לְהוֹשִׁיב עִם־נְדִיבִים וְכִסֵּא כָבוֹד יַנְחִלֵם כִּי לַיהֹוָה מְצֻקֵי אֶרֶץ וַיָּשֶׁת עֲלֵיהֶם תֵּבֵל:

9 He guards the steps of His faithful, But the wicked perish in darkness – For not by strength shall man prevail.

ט רַגְלֵי חֲסִידָו [חֲסִידָיו] יִשְׁמֹר וּרְשָׁעִים בַּחֹשֶׁךְ יִדָּמּוּ כִּי־לֹא בְכֹחַ יִגְבַּר־אִישׁ:

10 The foes of Hashem shall be shattered; He will thunder against them in the heavens. Hashem will judge the ends of the earth. He will give power to His king, And triumph to His anointed one.

י יְהֹוָה יֵחַתּוּ מְרִיבוֹ [מְרִיבָיו] עָלוֹ [עָלָיו] בַּשָּׁמַיִם יַרְעֵם יְהֹוָה יָדִין אַפְסֵי־אָרֶץ וְיִתֶּן־עֹז לְמַלְכּוֹ וְיָרֵם קֶרֶן מְשִׁיחוֹ:

a-do-NAI yay-KHA-tu m'-ree-VAV a-LAV ba-sha-MA-yim yar-AYM a-do-NAI ya-DEEN af-say A-retz v'-yi-ten OZ l'-mal-KO v'-ya-RAYM KE-ren m'-shee-KHO

11 Then Elkana [and Chana] went home to Rama; and the boy entered the service of Hashem under the Kohen Eli.

יא וַיֵּלֶךְ אֶלְקָנָה הָרָמָתָה עַל־בֵּיתוֹ וְהַנַּעַר הָיָה מְשָׁרֵת אֶת־יְהֹוָה אֶת־פְּנֵי עֵלִי הַכֹּהֵן:

12 Now Eli's sons were scoundrels; they paid no heed to Hashem.

יב וּבְנֵי עֵלִי בְּנֵי בְלִיָּעַל לֹא יָדְעוּ אֶת־יְהֹוָה:

13 This is how the Kohanim used to deal with the people: When anyone brought a sacrifice, the Kohen's boy would come along with a three-pronged fork while the meat was boiling,

יג וּמִשְׁפַּט הַכֹּהֲנִים אֶת־הָעָם כָּל־אִישׁ זֹבֵחַ זֶבַח וּבָא נַעַר הַכֹּהֵן כְּבַשֵּׁל הַבָּשָׂר וְהַמַּזְלֵג שְׁלֹשׁ־הַשִּׁנַּיִם בְּיָדוֹ:

2:10 He will give power to His king, and triumph to His anointed one *Chana* is a prophetess, and so she prays not only for herself, but for the entire Nation of Israel. While thanking *Hashem* for her own child, she also prays for two separate leaders who will shape the nation: "His king" and "His anointed one." The famed commentator *Radak* notes that *Chana* knew that her son would be responsible for establishing the monarchy over the People of Israel. Thus, "His king" refers to *Shaul*, who would be the only king from his tribe of *Binyamin*, and "His anointed one" refers to *David*, from the tribe of *Yehuda*, who would establish the eternal monarchy that would span the generations. *Chana* is thus a role model, teaching us to look beyond our individual needs when we pray, and also to long for the reestablishment of the kingdom of *David* at the hands of his descendant, the *Mashiach*.

Shmuel I / I Samuel

Chapter 2

שמואל א — פרק ב

14 and he would thrust it into the cauldron, or the kettle, or the great pot, or the small cooking-pot; and whatever the fork brought up, the *Kohen* would take away on it. This was the practice at *Shilo* with all the Israelites who came there.

יד וְהִכָּה בַכִּיּוֹר אוֹ בַדּוּד אוֹ בַקַּלַּחַת אוֹ בַפָּרוּר כֹּל אֲשֶׁר יַעֲלֶה הַמַּזְלֵג יִקַּח הַכֹּהֵן בּוֹ כָּכָה יַעֲשׂוּ לְכָל־יִשְׂרָאֵל הַבָּאִים שָׁם בְּשִׁלֹה:

15 [But now] even before the suet was turned into smoke, the *Kohen*'s boy would come and say to the man who was sacrificing, "Hand over some meat to roast for the *Kohen*; for he won't accept boiled meat from you, only raw."

טו גַּם בְּטֶרֶם יַקְטִרוּן אֶת־הַחֵלֶב וּבָא נַעַר הַכֹּהֵן וְאָמַר לָאִישׁ הַזֹּבֵחַ תְּנָה בָשָׂר לִצְלוֹת לַכֹּהֵן וְלֹא־יִקַּח מִמְּךָ בָּשָׂר מְבֻשָּׁל כִּי אִם־חָי:

16 And if the man said to him, "Let them first turn the suet into smoke, and then take as much as you want," he would reply, "No, hand it over at once or I'll take it by force."

טז וַיֹּאמֶר אֵלָיו הָאִישׁ קַטֵּר יַקְטִירוּן כַּיּוֹם הַחֵלֶב וְקַח־לְךָ כַּאֲשֶׁר תְּאַוֶּה נַפְשֶׁךָ וְאָמַר לוֹ [לֹא] כִּי עַתָּה תִתֵּן וְאִם־לֹא לָקַחְתִּי בְחָזְקָה:

17 The sin of the young men against *Hashem* was very great, for the men treated *Hashem*'s offerings impiously.

יז וַתְּהִי חַטַּאת הַנְּעָרִים גְּדוֹלָה מְאֹד אֶת־פְּנֵי יְהוָה כִּי נִאֲצוּ הָאֲנָשִׁים אֵת מִנְחַת יְהוָה:

18 *Shmuel* was engaged in the service of *Hashem* as an attendant, girded with a linen ephod.

יח וּשְׁמוּאֵל מְשָׁרֵת אֶת־פְּנֵי יְהוָה נַעַר חָגוּר אֵפוֹד בָּד:

19 His mother would also make a little robe for him and bring it up to him every year, when she made the pilgrimage with her husband to offer the annual sacrifice.

יט וּמְעִיל קָטֹן תַּעֲשֶׂה־לּוֹ אִמּוֹ וְהַעַלְתָה לוֹ מִיָּמִים יָמִימָה בַּעֲלוֹתָהּ אֶת־אִישָׁהּ לִזְבֹּחַ אֶת־זֶבַח הַיָּמִים:

20 *Eli* would bless *Elkana* and his wife, and say, "May *Hashem* grant you offspring by this woman in place of the loan she made to *Hashem*." Then they would return home.

כ וּבֵרַךְ עֵלִי אֶת־אֶלְקָנָה וְאֶת־אִשְׁתּוֹ וְאָמַר יָשֵׂם יְהוָה לְךָ זֶרַע מִן־הָאִשָּׁה הַזֹּאת תַּחַת הַשְּׁאֵלָה אֲשֶׁר שָׁאַל לַיהוָה וְהָלְכוּ לִמְקֹמוֹ:

21 For *Hashem* took note of *Chana*; she conceived and bore three sons and two daughters. Young *Shmuel* meanwhile grew up in the service of *Hashem*.

כא כִּי־פָקַד יְהוָה אֶת־חַנָּה וַתַּהַר וַתֵּלֶד שְׁלֹשָׁה־בָנִים וּשְׁתֵּי בָנוֹת וַיִּגְדַּל הַנַּעַר שְׁמוּאֵל עִם־יְהוָה:

22 Now *Eli* was very old. When he heard all that his sons were doing to all *Yisrael*, and how they lay with the women who performed tasks at the entrance of the Tent of Meeting,

כב וְעֵלִי זָקֵן מְאֹד וְשָׁמַע אֵת כָּל־אֲשֶׁר יַעֲשׂוּן בָּנָיו לְכָל־יִשְׂרָאֵל וְאֵת אֲשֶׁר־יִשְׁכְּבוּן אֶת־הַנָּשִׁים הַצֹּבְאוֹת פֶּתַח אֹהֶל מוֹעֵד:

23 he said to them, "Why do you do such things? I get evil reports about you from the people on all hands.

כג וַיֹּאמֶר לָהֶם לָמָּה תַעֲשׂוּן כַּדְּבָרִים הָאֵלֶּה אֲשֶׁר אָנֹכִי שֹׁמֵעַ אֶת־דִּבְרֵיכֶם רָעִים מֵאֵת כָּל־הָעָם אֵלֶּה:

24 Don't, my sons! It is no favorable report I hear the people of *Hashem* spreading about.

כד אַל בָּנַי כִּי לוֹא־טוֹבָה הַשְּׁמֻעָה אֲשֶׁר אָנֹכִי שֹׁמֵעַ מַעֲבִרִים עַם־יְהוָה:

25 If a man sins against a man, *Hashem* may pardon him; but if a man offends against *Hashem*, who can obtain pardon for him?" But they ignored their father's plea; for *Hashem* was resolved that they should die.

כה אִם־יֶחֱטָא אִישׁ לְאִישׁ וּפִלְלוֹ אֱלֹהִים וְאִם לַיהוָה יֶחֱטָא־אִישׁ מִי יִתְפַּלֶּל־לוֹ וְלֹא יִשְׁמְעוּ לְקוֹל אֲבִיהֶם כִּי־חָפֵץ יְהוָה לַהֲמִיתָם:

Shmuel I/I Samuel
Chapter 2

שמואל א
פרק ב

26 Young *Shmuel*, meanwhile, grew in esteem and favor both with *Hashem* and with men.

כו וְהַנַּעַר שְׁמוּאֵל הֹלֵךְ וְגָדֵל וָטוֹב גַּם עִם־יְהוָה וְגַם עִם־אֲנָשִׁים׃

27 A man of *Hashem* came to *Eli* and said to him, "Thus said *Hashem*: Lo, I revealed Myself to your father's house in Egypt when they were subject to the House of Pharaoh,

כז וַיָּבֹא אִישׁ־אֱלֹהִים אֶל־עֵלִי וַיֹּאמֶר אֵלָיו כֹּה אָמַר יְהוָה הֲנִגְלֹה נִגְלֵיתִי אֶל־בֵּית אָבִיךָ בִּהְיוֹתָם בְּמִצְרַיִם לְבֵית פַּרְעֹה׃

28 and I chose them from among all the tribes of *Yisrael* to be My *Kohanim* – to ascend My *Mizbayach*, to burn incense, [and] to carry an ephod before Me – and I assigned to your father's house all offerings by fire of the Israelites.

כח וּבָחֹר אֹתוֹ מִכָּל־שִׁבְטֵי יִשְׂרָאֵל לִי לְכֹהֵן לַעֲלוֹת עַל־מִזְבְּחִי לְהַקְטִיר קְטֹרֶת לָשֵׂאת אֵפוֹד לְפָנָי וָאֶתְּנָה לְבֵית אָבִיךָ אֶת־כָּל־אִשֵּׁי בְּנֵי יִשְׂרָאֵל׃

29 Why, then, do you maliciously trample upon the sacrifices and offerings that I have commanded? You have honored your sons more than Me, feeding on the first portions of every offering of My people *Yisrael*.

כט לָמָּה תִבְעֲטוּ בְּזִבְחִי וּבְמִנְחָתִי אֲשֶׁר צִוִּיתִי מָעוֹן וַתְּכַבֵּד אֶת־בָּנֶיךָ מִמֶּנִּי לְהַבְרִיאֲכֶם מֵרֵאשִׁית כָּל־מִנְחַת יִשְׂרָאֵל לְעַמִּי׃

30 Assuredly – declares *Hashem*, the God of *Yisrael* – I intended for you and your father's house to remain in My service forever. But now – declares *Hashem* – far be it from Me! For I honor those who honor Me, but those who spurn Me shall be dishonored.

ל לָכֵן נְאֻם־יְהוָה אֱלֹהֵי יִשְׂרָאֵל אָמוֹר אָמַרְתִּי בֵּיתְךָ וּבֵית אָבִיךָ יִתְהַלְּכוּ לְפָנַי עַד־עוֹלָם וְעַתָּה נְאֻם־יְהוָה חָלִילָה לִּי כִּי־מְכַבְּדַי אֲכַבֵּד וּבֹזַי יֵקָלּוּ׃

31 A time is coming when I will break your power and that of your father's house, and there shall be no elder in your house.

לא הִנֵּה יָמִים בָּאִים וְגָדַעְתִּי אֶת־זְרֹעֲךָ וְאֶת־זְרֹעַ בֵּית אָבִיךָ מִהְיוֹת זָקֵן בְּבֵיתֶךָ׃

32 You will gaze grudgingly at all the bounty that will be bestowed on *Yisrael*, but there shall never be an elder in your house.

לב וְהִבַּטְתָּ צַר מָעוֹן בְּכֹל אֲשֶׁר־יֵיטִיב אֶת־יִשְׂרָאֵל וְלֹא־יִהְיֶה זָקֵן בְּבֵיתְךָ כָּל־הַיָּמִים׃

33 I shall not cut off all your offspring from My *Mizbayach*; [but,] to make your eyes pine and your spirit languish, all the increase in your house shall die as [ordinary] men.

לג וְאִישׁ לֹא־אַכְרִית לְךָ מֵעִם מִזְבְּחִי לְכַלּוֹת אֶת־עֵינֶיךָ וְלַאֲדִיב אֶת־נַפְשֶׁךָ וְכָל־מַרְבִּית בֵּיתְךָ יָמוּתוּ אֲנָשִׁים׃

34 And this shall be a sign for you: The fate of your two sons *Chofni* and *Pinchas* – they shall both die on the same day.

לד וְזֶה־לְּךָ הָאוֹת אֲשֶׁר יָבֹא אֶל־שְׁנֵי בָנֶיךָ אֶל־חָפְנִי וּפִינְחָס בְּיוֹם אֶחָד יָמוּתוּ שְׁנֵיהֶם׃

35 And I will raise up for Myself a faithful *Kohen*, who will act in accordance with My wishes and My purposes. I will build for him an enduring house, and he shall walk before My anointed evermore.

לה וַהֲקִימֹתִי לִי כֹּהֵן נֶאֱמָן כַּאֲשֶׁר בִּלְבָבִי וּבְנַפְשִׁי יַעֲשֶׂה וּבָנִיתִי לוֹ בַּיִת נֶאֱמָן וְהִתְהַלֵּךְ לִפְנֵי־מְשִׁיחִי כָּל־הַיָּמִים׃

36 And all the survivors of your house shall come and bow low to him for the sake of a money fee and a loaf of bread, and shall say, 'Please, assign me to one of the priestly duties, that I may have a morsel of bread to eat.'"

לו וְהָיָה כָּל־הַנּוֹתָר בְּבֵיתְךָ יָבוֹא לְהִשְׁתַּחֲוֺת לוֹ לַאֲגוֹרַת כֶּסֶף וְכִכַּר־לָחֶם וְאָמַר סְפָחֵנִי נָא אֶל־אַחַת הַכְּהֻנּוֹת לֶאֱכֹל פַּת־לָחֶם׃

664

Shmuel I / I Samuel

Chapter 3

1 Young *Shmuel* was in the service of *Hashem* under *Eli*. In those days the word of *Hashem* was rare; prophecy was not widespread.

2 One day, *Eli* was asleep in his usual place; his eyes had begun to fail and he could barely see.

3 The lamp of *Hashem* had not yet gone out, and *Shmuel* was sleeping in the temple of *Hashem* where the *Aron* of *Hashem* was.

4 *Hashem* called out to *Shmuel*, and he answered, "I'm coming."

5 He ran to *Eli* and said, "Here I am; you called me." But he replied, "I didn't call you; go back to sleep." So he went back and lay down.

6 Again *Hashem* called, "*Shmuel*!" *Shmuel* rose and went to *Eli* and said, "Here I am; you called me." But he replied, "I didn't call, my son; go back to sleep." –

7 Now *Shmuel* had not yet experienced *Hashem*; the word of *Hashem* had not yet been revealed to him. –

8 *Hashem* called *Shmuel* again, a third time, and he rose and went to *Eli* and said, "Here I am; you called me." Then *Eli* understood that *Hashem* was calling the boy.

9 And *Eli* said to *Shmuel*, "Go lie down. If you are called again, say, 'Speak, *Hashem*, for Your servant is listening.'" And *Shmuel* went to his place and lay down.

10 *Hashem* came, and stood there, and He called as before: "*Shmuel*! *Shmuel*!" And *Shmuel* answered, "Speak, for Your servant is listening."

11 *Hashem* said to *Shmuel*: "I am going to do in *Yisrael* such a thing that both ears of anyone who hears about it will tingle.

12 In that day I will fulfill against *Eli* all that I spoke concerning his house, from beginning to end.

שמואל א
פרק ג

א וְהַנַּעַר שְׁמוּאֵל מְשָׁרֵת אֶת־יְהֹוָה לִפְנֵי עֵלִי וּדְבַר־יְהֹוָה הָיָה יָקָר בַּיָּמִים הָהֵם אֵין חָזוֹן נִפְרָץ:

ב וַיְהִי בַּיּוֹם הַהוּא וְעֵלִי שֹׁכֵב בִּמְקֹמוֹ וְעֵינָו [וְעֵינָיו] הֵחֵלּוּ כֵהוֹת לֹא יוּכַל לִרְאוֹת:

ג וְנֵר אֱלֹהִים טֶרֶם יִכְבֶּה וּשְׁמוּאֵל שֹׁכֵב בְּהֵיכַל יְהֹוָה אֲשֶׁר־שָׁם אֲרוֹן אֱלֹהִים:

ד וַיִּקְרָא יְהֹוָה אֶל־שְׁמוּאֵל וַיֹּאמֶר הִנֵּנִי:

ה וַיָּרָץ אֶל־עֵלִי וַיֹּאמֶר הִנְנִי כִּי־קָרָאתָ לִּי וַיֹּאמֶר לֹא־קָרָאתִי שׁוּב שְׁכָב וַיֵּלֶךְ וַיִּשְׁכָּב:

ו וַיֹּסֶף יְהֹוָה קְרֹא עוֹד שְׁמוּאֵל וַיָּקָם שְׁמוּאֵל וַיֵּלֶךְ אֶל־עֵלִי וַיֹּאמֶר הִנְנִי כִּי קָרָאתָ לִי וַיֹּאמֶר לֹא־קָרָאתִי בְנִי שׁוּב שְׁכָב:

ז וּשְׁמוּאֵל טֶרֶם יָדַע אֶת־יְהֹוָה וְטֶרֶם יִגָּלֶה אֵלָיו דְּבַר־יְהֹוָה:

ח וַיֹּסֶף יְהֹוָה קְרֹא־שְׁמוּאֵל בַּשְּׁלִשִׁית וַיָּקָם וַיֵּלֶךְ אֶל־עֵלִי וַיֹּאמֶר הִנְנִי כִּי קָרָאתָ לִי וַיָּבֶן עֵלִי כִּי יְהֹוָה קֹרֵא לַנָּעַר:

ט וַיֹּאמֶר עֵלִי לִשְׁמוּאֵל לֵךְ שְׁכָב וְהָיָה אִם־יִקְרָא אֵלֶיךָ וְאָמַרְתָּ דַּבֵּר יְהֹוָה כִּי שֹׁמֵעַ עַבְדֶּךָ וַיֵּלֶךְ שְׁמוּאֵל וַיִּשְׁכַּב בִּמְקוֹמוֹ:

י וַיָּבֹא יְהֹוָה וַיִּתְיַצַּב וַיִּקְרָא כְפַעַם־בְּפַעַם שְׁמוּאֵל שְׁמוּאֵל וַיֹּאמֶר שְׁמוּאֵל דַּבֵּר כִּי שֹׁמֵעַ עַבְדֶּךָ:

יא וַיֹּאמֶר יְהֹוָה אֶל־שְׁמוּאֵל הִנֵּה אָנֹכִי עֹשֶׂה דָבָר בְּיִשְׂרָאֵל אֲשֶׁר כָּל־שֹׁמְעוֹ תְּצִלֶּינָה שְׁתֵּי אָזְנָיו:

יב בַּיּוֹם הַהוּא אָקִים אֶל־עֵלִי אֵת כָּל־אֲשֶׁר דִּבַּרְתִּי אֶל־בֵּיתוֹ הָחֵל וְכַלֵּה:

Shmuel I/I Samuel

Chapter 4

שמואל א

פרק ד

13 And I declare to him that I sentence his house to endless punishment for the iniquity he knew about – how his sons committed sacrilege at will – and he did not rebuke them.

יג וְהִגַּדְתִּי לוֹ כִּי־שֹׁפֵט אֲנִי אֶת־בֵּיתוֹ עַד־עוֹלָם בַּעֲוֺן אֲשֶׁר־יָדַע כִּי־מְקַלְלִים לָהֶם בָּנָיו וְלֹא כִהָה בָּם׃

v'-hi-GAD-tee LO kee sho-FAYT a-NEE et bay-TO ad o-LAM ba-a-VON a-sher ya-DA kee m'-ka-l'-LEEM la-HEM ba-NAV v'-LO khi-HAH BAM

14 Assuredly, I swear concerning the house of *Eli* that the iniquity of the house of *Eli* will never be expiated by sacrifice or offering."

יד וְלָכֵן נִשְׁבַּעְתִּי לְבֵית עֵלִי אִם־יִתְכַּפֵּר עֲוֺן בֵּית־עֵלִי בְּזֶבַח וּבְמִנְחָה עַד־עוֹלָם׃

15 *Shmuel* lay there until morning; and then he opened the doors of the House of *Hashem*. *Shmuel* was afraid to report the vision to *Eli*,

טו וַיִּשְׁכַּב שְׁמוּאֵל עַד־הַבֹּקֶר וַיִּפְתַּח אֶת־דַּלְתוֹת בֵּית־יְהוָה וּשְׁמוּאֵל יָרֵא מֵהַגִּיד אֶת־הַמַּרְאָה אֶל־עֵלִי׃

16 but *Eli* summoned *Shmuel* and said, "*Shmuel*, my son"; and he answered, "Here."

טז וַיִּקְרָא עֵלִי אֶת־שְׁמוּאֵל וַיֹּאמֶר שְׁמוּאֵל בְּנִי וַיֹּאמֶר הִנֵּנִי׃

17 And [*Eli*] asked, "What did He say to you? Keep nothing from me. Thus and more may *Hashem* do to you if you keep from me a single word of all that He said to you!"

יז וַיֹּאמֶר מָה הַדָּבָר אֲשֶׁר דִּבֶּר אֵלֶיךָ אַל־נָא תְכַחֵד מִמֶּנִּי כֹּה יַעֲשֶׂה־לְּךָ אֱלֹהִים וְכֹה יוֹסִיף אִם־תְּכַחֵד מִמֶּנִּי דָּבָר מִכָּל־הַדָּבָר אֲשֶׁר־דִּבֶּר אֵלֶיךָ׃

18 *Shmuel* then told him everything, withholding nothing from him. And [*Eli*] said, "He is *Hashem*; He will do what He deems right."

יח וַיַּגֶּד־לוֹ שְׁמוּאֵל אֶת־כָּל־הַדְּבָרִים וְלֹא כִחֵד מִמֶּנּוּ וַיֹּאמַר יְהוָה הוּא הַטּוֹב בְּעֵינָו יַעֲשֶׂה׃

19 *Shmuel* grew up and *Hashem* was with him: He did not leave any of *Shmuel*'s predictions unfulfilled.

יט וַיִּגְדַּל שְׁמוּאֵל וַיהוָה הָיָה עִמּוֹ וְלֹא־הִפִּיל מִכָּל־דְּבָרָיו אָרְצָה׃

20 All *Yisrael*, from *Dan* to *Be'er Sheva*, knew that *Shmuel* was trustworthy as a *Navi* of *Hashem*.

כ וַיֵּדַע כָּל־יִשְׂרָאֵל מִדָּן וְעַד־בְּאֵר שָׁבַע כִּי נֶאֱמָן שְׁמוּאֵל לְנָבִיא לַיהוָה׃

21 And *Hashem* continued to appear at *Shilo*: *Hashem* revealed Himself to *Shmuel* at *Shilo* with the word of *Hashem*;

כא וַיֹּסֶף יְהוָה לְהֵרָאֹה בְשִׁלֹה כִּי־נִגְלָה יְהוָה אֶל־שְׁמוּאֵל בְּשִׁלוֹ בִּדְבַר יְהוָה׃

4:1 and *Shmuel*'s word went forth to all *Yisrael*. *Yisrael* marched out to engage the Philistines in battle; they encamped near *Even Ha-Ezer*, while the Philistines encamped at Aphek.

ד א וַיְהִי דְבַר־שְׁמוּאֵל לְכָל־יִשְׂרָאֵל וַיֵּצֵא יִשְׂרָאֵל לִקְרַאת פְּלִשְׁתִּים לַמִּלְחָמָה וַיַּחֲנוּ עַל־הָאֶבֶן הָעֵזֶר וּפְלִשְׁתִּים חָנוּ בַאֲפֵק׃

3:13 I sentence his house to endless punishment God tells *Shmuel* that He will punish *Eli* for failing to rebuke his sons, *Chofni* and *Pinchas*, for their immoral behavior while serving in their leadership roles at the *Mishkan* in *Shilo*. Through their actions, they profane the *Mishkan* and discourage people from making pilgrimages there. Consequently, *Eli*'s sons will be killed and there will be no one left to continue his family's mantle of leadership. Instead, *Shmuel* will become the new prophet and leader of the people. He will act the way a true leader should, travelling among the people as an inspiring role model, bringing them closer to *Hashem*.

Shmuel I/I Samuel
Chapter 4

שמואל א
פרק ד

2 The Philistines arrayed themselves against *Yisrael*; and when the battle was fought, *Yisrael* was routed by the Philistines, who slew about four thousand men on the field of battle.

ב וַיַּעַרְכוּ פְלִשְׁתִּים לִקְרַאת יִשְׂרָאֵל וַתִּטֹּשׁ הַמִּלְחָמָה וַיִּנָּגֶף יִשְׂרָאֵל לִפְנֵי פְלִשְׁתִּים וַיַּכּוּ בַמַּעֲרָכָה בַּשָּׂדֶה כְּאַרְבַּעַת אֲלָפִים אִישׁ:

3 When the [Israelite] troops returned to the camp, the elders of *Yisrael* asked, "Why did *Hashem* put us to rout today before the Philistines? Let us fetch the *Aron Brit Hashem* from *Shilo*; thus He will be present among us and will deliver us from the hands of our enemies."

ג וַיָּבֹא הָעָם אֶל־הַמַּחֲנֶה וַיֹּאמְרוּ זִקְנֵי יִשְׂרָאֵל לָמָּה נְגָפָנוּ יְהוָה הַיּוֹם לִפְנֵי פְלִשְׁתִּים נִקְחָה אֵלֵינוּ מִשִּׁלֹה אֶת־אֲרוֹן בְּרִית יְהוָה וְיָבֹא בְקִרְבֵּנוּ וְיֹשִׁעֵנוּ מִכַּף אֹיְבֵינוּ:

4 So the troops sent men to *Shilo*; there *Eli's* two sons, *Chofni* and *Pinchas*, were in charge of the *Aron Brit Hashem*, and they brought down from there the *Aron Habrit* of the Lord of Hosts Enthroned on the *Keruvim*.

ד וַיִּשְׁלַח הָעָם שִׁלֹה וַיִּשְׂאוּ מִשָּׁם אֵת אֲרוֹן בְּרִית־יְהוָה צְבָאוֹת יֹשֵׁב הַכְּרֻבִים וְשָׁם שְׁנֵי בְנֵי־עֵלִי עִם־אֲרוֹן בְּרִית הָאֱלֹהִים חָפְנִי וּפִינְחָס:

5 When the *Aron Brit Hashem* entered the camp, all *Yisrael* burst into a great shout, so that the earth resounded.

ה וַיְהִי כְּבוֹא אֲרוֹן בְּרִית־יְהוָה אֶל־הַמַּחֲנֶה וַיָּרִעוּ כָל־יִשְׂרָאֵל תְּרוּעָה גְדוֹלָה וַתֵּהֹם הָאָרֶץ:

6 The Philistines heard the noise of the shouting and they wondered, "Why is there such a loud shouting in the camp of the Hebrews?" And when they learned that the *Aron* of *Hashem* had come to the camp,

ו וַיִּשְׁמְעוּ פְלִשְׁתִּים אֶת־קוֹל הַתְּרוּעָה וַיֹּאמְרוּ מֶה קוֹל הַתְּרוּעָה הַגְּדוֹלָה הַזֹּאת בְּמַחֲנֵה הָעִבְרִים וַיֵּדְעוּ כִּי אֲרוֹן יְהוָה בָּא אֶל־הַמַּחֲנֶה:

7 the Philistines were frightened; for they said, "*Hashem* has come to the camp." And they cried, "Woe to us! Nothing like this has ever happened before.

ז וַיִּרְאוּ הַפְּלִשְׁתִּים כִּי אָמְרוּ בָּא אֱלֹהִים אֶל־הַמַּחֲנֶה וַיֹּאמְרוּ אוֹי לָנוּ כִּי לֹא הָיְתָה כָּזֹאת אֶתְמוֹל שִׁלְשֹׁם:

8 Woe to us! Who will save us from the power of this mighty *Hashem*? He is the same *Hashem* who struck the Egyptians with every kind of plague in the wilderness!

ח אוֹי לָנוּ מִי יַצִּילֵנוּ מִיַּד הָאֱלֹהִים הָאַדִּירִים הָאֵלֶּה אֵלֶּה הֵם הָאֱלֹהִים הַמַּכִּים אֶת־מִצְרַיִם בְּכָל־מַכָּה בַּמִּדְבָּר:

9 Brace yourselves and be men, O Philistines! Or you will become slaves to the Hebrews as they were slaves to you. Be men and fight!"

ט הִתְחַזְּקוּ וִהְיוּ לַאֲנָשִׁים פְּלִשְׁתִּים פֶּן תַּעַבְדוּ לָעִבְרִים כַּאֲשֶׁר עָבְדוּ לָכֶם וִהְיִיתֶם לַאֲנָשִׁים וְנִלְחַמְתֶּם:

10 The Philistines fought; *Yisrael* was routed, and they all fled to their homes. The defeat was very great, thirty thousand foot soldiers of *Yisrael* fell there.

י וַיִּלָּחֲמוּ פְלִשְׁתִּים וַיִּנָּגֶף יִשְׂרָאֵל וַיָּנֻסוּ אִישׁ לְאֹהָלָיו וַתְּהִי הַמַּכָּה גְּדוֹלָה מְאֹד וַיִּפֹּל מִיִּשְׂרָאֵל שְׁלֹשִׁים אֶלֶף רַגְלִי:

11 The *Aron* of *Hashem* was captured, and *Eli's* two sons, *Chofni* and *Pinchas*, were slain.

יא וַאֲרוֹן אֱלֹהִים נִלְקָח וּשְׁנֵי בְנֵי־עֵלִי מֵתוּ חָפְנִי וּפִינְחָס:

12 A *Binyaminite* ran from the battlefield and reached *Shilo* the same day; his clothes were rent and there was earth on his head.

יב וַיָּרָץ אִישׁ־בִּנְיָמִן מֵהַמַּעֲרָכָה וַיָּבֹא שִׁלֹה בַּיּוֹם הַהוּא וּמַדָּיו קְרֻעִים וַאֲדָמָה עַל־רֹאשׁוֹ:

Shmuel I / I Samuel
Chapter 4

שמואל א
פרק ד

13 When he arrived, he found *Eli* sitting on a seat, waiting beside the road – his heart trembling for the *Aron* of *Hashem*. The man entered the city to spread the news, and the whole city broke out in a cry.

יג וַיָּבוֹא וְהִנֵּה עֵלִי יֹשֵׁב עַל־הַכִּסֵּא יָ[ד] דֶּרֶךְ מְצַפֶּה כִּי־הָיָה לִבּוֹ חָרֵד עַל אֲרוֹן הָאֱלֹהִים וְהָאִישׁ בָּא לְהַגִּיד בָּעִיר וַתִּזְעַק כָּל־הָעִיר:

va-ya-VO v'-hi-NAY ay-LEE yo-SHAYV al ha-ki-SAY YAD DE-rekh m'-tza-PEH kee ha-YAH li-BO kha-RAYD AL a-RON ha-e-lo-HEEM v'-ha-EESH BA l'-ha-GEED ba-EER va-tiz-AK kol ha-EER

14 And when *Eli* heard the sound of the outcry and asked, "What is the meaning of this uproar?" the man rushed over to tell *Eli*.

יד וַיִּשְׁמַע עֵלִי אֶת־קוֹל הַצְּעָקָה וַיֹּאמֶר מֶה קוֹל הֶהָמוֹן הַזֶּה וְהָאִישׁ מִהַר וַיָּבֹא וַיַּגֵּד לְעֵלִי:

15 Now *Eli* was ninety-eight years old; his eyes were fixed in a blind stare.

טו וְעֵלִי בֶּן־תִּשְׁעִים וּשְׁמֹנֶה שָׁנָה וְעֵינָיו קָמָה וְלֹא יָכוֹל לִרְאוֹת:

16 The man said to *Eli*, "I am the one who came from the battlefield; I have just fled from the battlefield." [*Eli*] asked, "What happened, my son?"

טז וַיֹּאמֶר הָאִישׁ אֶל־עֵלִי אָנֹכִי הַבָּא מִן־הַמַּעֲרָכָה וַאֲנִי מִן־הַמַּעֲרָכָה נַסְתִּי הַיּוֹם וַיֹּאמֶר מֶה־הָיָה הַדָּבָר בְּנִי:

17 The bearer of the news replied, "*Yisrael* fled before the Philistines and the troops also suffered a great slaughter. Your two sons, *Chofni* and *Pinchas*, are dead, and the *Aron* of *Hashem* has been captured."

יז וַיַּעַן הַמְבַשֵּׂר וַיֹּאמֶר נָס יִשְׂרָאֵל לִפְנֵי פְלִשְׁתִּים וְגַם מַגֵּפָה גְדוֹלָה הָיְתָה בָעָם וְגַם־שְׁנֵי בָנֶיךָ מֵתוּ חָפְנִי וּפִינְחָס וַאֲרוֹן הָאֱלֹהִים נִלְקָחָה:

18 When he mentioned the *Aron* of *Hashem*, [*Eli*] fell backward off the seat beside the gate, broke his neck and died; for he was an old man and heavy. He had been a chieftain of *Yisrael* for forty years.

יח וַיְהִי כְּהַזְכִּירוֹ אֶת־אֲרוֹן הָאֱלֹהִים וַיִּפֹּל מֵעַל־הַכִּסֵּא אֲחֹרַנִּית בְּעַד יַד הַשַּׁעַר וַתִּשָּׁבֵר מַפְרַקְתּוֹ וַיָּמֹת כִּי־זָקֵן הָאִישׁ וְכָבֵד וְהוּא שָׁפַט אֶת־יִשְׂרָאֵל אַרְבָּעִים שָׁנָה:

19 His daughter-in-law, the wife of *Pinchas*, was with child, about to give birth. When she heard the report that the *Aron* of *Hashem* was captured and that her father-in-law and her husband were dead, she was seized with labor pains, and she crouched down and gave birth.

יט וְכַלָּתוֹ אֵשֶׁת־פִּינְחָס הָרָה לָלַת וַתִּשְׁמַע אֶת־הַשְּׁמֻעָה אֶל־הִלָּקַח אֲרוֹן הָאֱלֹהִים וּמֵת חָמִיהָ וְאִישָׁהּ וַתִּכְרַע וַתֵּלֶד כִּי־נֶהֶפְכוּ עָלֶיהָ צִרֶיהָ:

20 As she lay dying, the women attending her said, "Do not be afraid, for you have borne a son." But she did not respond or pay heed.

כ וּכְעֵת מוּתָהּ וַתְּדַבֵּרְנָה הַנִּצָּבוֹת עָלֶיהָ אַל־תִּירְאִי כִּי בֵן יָלָדְתְּ וְלֹא עָנְתָה וְלֹא־שָׁתָה לִבָּהּ:

4:13 The whole city broke out in a cry After the terrible battlefield loss to the Philistines, a man from the tribe of *Binyamin* runs to *Shilo* to deliver the news to *Eli*. *Rashi* reports a tradition that this man was none other than *Shaul*, who would later be selected as the first king of Israel. This is significant, as leaders of Israel are often military men. For example, *Avraham* (see Genesis 14, which describes the war he fought to save his nephew Lot), *Moshe* (see Numbers 21, where he leads Israel in battle against *Sihon* and Og) and *Yehoshua* were all spiritual and military figures. Fighting just wars is an imperative, and it is the responsibility of the Israelite leader to lead his troops into battle. Therefore, it's not surprising that the first king of Israel is also a soldier.

Shmuel I / I Samuel
Chapter 5

שמואל א
פרק ה

21 She named the boy Ichabod, meaning, "The glory has departed from *Yisrael*" – referring to the capture of the *Aron* of *Hashem* and to [the death of] her father-in-law and her husband.

כא וַתִּקְרָא לַנַּעַר אִי־כָבוֹד לֵאמֹר גָּלָה כָבוֹד מִיִּשְׂרָאֵל אֶל־הִלָּקַח אֲרוֹן הָאֱלֹהִים וְאֶל־חָמִיהָ וְאִישָׁהּ:

22 "The glory is gone from *Yisrael*," she said, "for the *Aron* of *Hashem* has been captured."

כב וַתֹּאמֶר גָּלָה כָבוֹד מִיִּשְׂרָאֵל כִּי נִלְקַח אֲרוֹן הָאֱלֹהִים:

5 1 When the Philistines captured the *Aron* of *Hashem*, they brought it from *Even Ha-Ezer* to *Ashdod*.

ה א וּפְלִשְׁתִּים לָקְחוּ אֵת אֲרוֹן הָאֱלֹהִים וַיְבִאֻהוּ מֵאֶבֶן הָעֵזֶר אַשְׁדּוֹדָה:

uf-lish-TEEM la-k'-KHU AYT a-RON ha-e-lo-HEEM vai-vi-U-hu may-E-ven ha-E-zer ash-DO-dah

2 The Philistines took the *Aron* of *Hashem* and brought it into the temple of Dagon and they set it up beside Dagon.

ב וַיִּקְחוּ פְלִשְׁתִּים אֶת־אֲרוֹן הָאֱלֹהִים וַיָּבִיאוּ אֹתוֹ בֵּית דָּגוֹן וַיַּצִּיגוּ אֹתוֹ אֵצֶל דָּגוֹן:

3 Early the next day, the Ashdodites found Dagon lying face down on the ground in front of the *Aron* of *Hashem*. They picked Dagon up and put him back in his place;

ג וַיַּשְׁכִּמוּ אַשְׁדּוֹדִים מִמָּחֳרָת וְהִנֵּה דָגוֹן נֹפֵל לְפָנָיו אַרְצָה לִפְנֵי אֲרוֹן יְהוָה וַיִּקְחוּ אֶת־דָּגוֹן וַיָּשִׁבוּ אֹתוֹ לִמְקוֹמוֹ:

4 but early the next morning, Dagon was again lying prone on the ground in front of the *Aron* of *Hashem*. The head and both hands of Dagon were cut off, lying on the threshold; only Dagon's trunk was left intact.

ד וַיַּשְׁכִּמוּ בַבֹּקֶר מִמָּחֳרָת וְהִנֵּה דָגוֹן נֹפֵל לְפָנָיו אַרְצָה לִפְנֵי אֲרוֹן יְהוָה וְרֹאשׁ דָּגוֹן וּשְׁתֵּי כַּפּוֹת יָדָיו כְּרֻתוֹת אֶל־הַמִּפְתָּן רַק דָּגוֹן נִשְׁאַר עָלָיו:

5 That is why, to this day, the priests of Dagon and all who enter the temple of Dagon do not tread on the threshold of Dagon in *Ashdod*.

ה עַל־כֵּן לֹא־יִדְרְכוּ כֹהֲנֵי דָגוֹן וְכָל־הַבָּאִים בֵּית־דָּגוֹן עַל־מִפְתַּן דָּגוֹן בְּאַשְׁדּוֹד עַד הַיּוֹם הַזֶּה:

6 The hand of *Hashem* lay heavy upon the Ashdodites, and He wrought havoc among them: He struck *Ashdod* and its territory with hemorrhoids.

ו וַתִּכְבַּד יַד־יְהוָה אֶל־הָאַשְׁדּוֹדִים וַיְשִׁמֵּם וַיַּךְ אֹתָם בָּעֳפָלִים [בַּטְּחֹרִים] אֶת־אַשְׁדּוֹד וְאֶת־גְּבוּלֶיהָ:

7 When the men of *Ashdod* saw how matters stood, they said, "The *Aron* of the God of *Yisrael* must not remain with us, for His hand has dealt harshly with us and with our god Dagon."

ז וַיִּרְאוּ אַנְשֵׁי־אַשְׁדּוֹד כִּי־כֵן וְאָמְרוּ לֹא־יֵשֵׁב אֲרוֹן אֱלֹהֵי יִשְׂרָאֵל עִמָּנוּ כִּי־קָשְׁתָה יָדוֹ עָלֵינוּ וְעַל דָּגוֹן אֱלֹהֵינוּ:

5:1 To *Ashdod* The coastal city of *Ashdod* is located in the land allocated to the tribe of *Yehuda*. However, it is conquered by the invading Philistines, and becomes one of their strongholds. Modern *Ashdod* was built on the same site in 1956. One of the largest cities in Israel, it welcomes tourists from around the world who come both for its commerce and its beaches. It is truly a miracle that the city once conquered by Philistines in ships now hosts the largest port of the State of Israel, thus providing tremendous economic support to the entire nation.

Coastal city of Ashdod

Shmuel I/I Samuel
Chapter 6

8 They sent messengers and assembled all the lords of the Philistines and asked, "What shall we do with the *Aron* of the God of *Yisrael*?" They answered, "Let the *Aron* of the God of *Yisrael* be removed to Gath." So they moved the *Aron* of the God of *Yisrael* [to Gath].

9 And after they had moved it, the hand of *Hashem* came against the city, causing great panic; He struck the people of the city, young and old, so that hemorrhoids broke out among them.

10 Then they sent the *Aron* of *Hashem* to Ekron. But when the *Aron* of *Hashem* came to Ekron, the Ekronites cried out, "They have moved the *Aron* of the God of *Yisrael* to us to slay us and our kindred."

11 They too sent messengers and assembled all the lords of the Philistines and said, "Send the *Aron* of the God of *Yisrael* away, and let it return to its own place, that it may not slay us and our kindred." For the panic of death pervaded the whole city, so heavily had the hand of *Hashem* fallen there;

12 and the men who did not die were stricken with hemorrhoids. The outcry of the city went up to heaven.

6

1 The *Aron* of *Hashem* remained in the territory of the Philistines seven months.

2 Then the Philistines summoned the priests and the diviners and asked, "What shall we do about the *Aron* of *Hashem*? Tell us with what we shall send it off to its own place."

3 They answered, "If you are going to send the *Aron* of the God of *Yisrael* away, do not send it away without anything; you must also pay an indemnity to Him. Then you will be healed, and He will make Himself known to you; otherwise His hand will not turn away from you."

4 They asked, "What is the indemnity that we should pay to Him?" They answered, "Five golden hemorrhoids and five golden mice, corresponding to the number of lords of the Philistines; for the same plague struck all of you and your lords.

5 You shall make figures of your hemorrhoids and of the mice that are ravaging your land; thus you shall honor the God of *Yisrael*, and perhaps He will lighten the weight of His hand upon you and your gods and your land.

שמואל א
פרק ו

ח וַיִּשְׁלְחוּ וַיַּאַסְפוּ אֶת־כָּל־סַרְנֵי פְלִשְׁתִּים אֲלֵיהֶם וַיֹּאמְרוּ מַה־נַּעֲשֶׂה לַאֲרוֹן אֱלֹהֵי יִשְׂרָאֵל וַיֹּאמְרוּ גַּת יִסֹּב אֲרוֹן אֱלֹהֵי יִשְׂרָאֵל וַיַּסֵּבּוּ אֶת־אֲרוֹן אֱלֹהֵי יִשְׂרָאֵל:

ט וַיְהִי אַחֲרֵי הֵסַבּוּ אֹתוֹ וַתְּהִי יַד־יְהֹוָה בָּעִיר מְהוּמָה גְּדוֹלָה מְאֹד וַיַּךְ אֶת־אַנְשֵׁי הָעִיר מִקָּטֹן וְעַד־גָּדוֹל וַיִּשָּׂתְרוּ לָהֶם עפלים [טְחֹרִים]:

י וַיְשַׁלְּחוּ אֶת־אֲרוֹן הָאֱלֹהִים עֶקְרוֹן וַיְהִי כְּבוֹא אֲרוֹן הָאֱלֹהִים עֶקְרוֹן וַיִּזְעֲקוּ הָעֶקְרֹנִים לֵאמֹר הֵסַבּוּ אֵלַי אֶת־אֲרוֹן אֱלֹהֵי יִשְׂרָאֵל לַהֲמִיתֵנִי וְאֶת־עַמִּי:

יא וַיִּשְׁלְחוּ וַיַּאַסְפוּ אֶת־כָּל־סַרְנֵי פְלִשְׁתִּים וַיֹּאמְרוּ שַׁלְּחוּ אֶת־אֲרוֹן אֱלֹהֵי יִשְׂרָאֵל וְיָשֹׁב לִמְקֹמוֹ וְלֹא־יָמִית אֹתִי וְאֶת־עַמִּי כִּי־הָיְתָה מְהוּמַת־מָוֶת בְּכָל־הָעִיר כָּבְדָה מְאֹד יַד הָאֱלֹהִים שָׁם:

יב וְהָאֲנָשִׁים אֲשֶׁר לֹא־מֵתוּ הֻכּוּ בעפלים [בַּטְּחֹרִים] וַתַּעַל שַׁוְעַת הָעִיר הַשָּׁמָיִם:

ו א וַיְהִי אֲרוֹן־יְהֹוָה בִּשְׂדֵה פְלִשְׁתִּים שִׁבְעָה חֳדָשִׁים:

ב וַיִּקְרְאוּ פְלִשְׁתִּים לַכֹּהֲנִים וְלַקֹּסְמִים לֵאמֹר מַה־נַּעֲשֶׂה לַאֲרוֹן יְהֹוָה הוֹדִעֻנוּ בַּמֶּה נְשַׁלְּחֶנּוּ לִמְקוֹמוֹ:

ג וַיֹּאמְרוּ אִם־מְשַׁלְּחִים אֶת־אֲרוֹן אֱלֹהֵי יִשְׂרָאֵל אַל־תְּשַׁלְּחוּ אֹתוֹ רֵיקָם כִּי־הָשֵׁב תָּשִׁיבוּ לוֹ אָשָׁם אָז תֵּרָפְאוּ וְנוֹדַע לָכֶם לָמָּה לֹא־תָסוּר יָדוֹ מִכֶּם:

ד וַיֹּאמְרוּ מָה הָאָשָׁם אֲשֶׁר נָשִׁיב לוֹ וַיֹּאמְרוּ מִסְפַּר סַרְנֵי פְלִשְׁתִּים חֲמִשָּׁה עפלי [טְחֹרֵי] זָהָב וַחֲמִשָּׁה עַכְבְּרֵי זָהָב כִּי־מַגֵּפָה אַחַת לְכֻלָּם וּלְסַרְנֵיכֶם:

ה וַעֲשִׂיתֶם צַלְמֵי עפליכם [טְחֹרֵיכֶם] וְצַלְמֵי עַכְבְּרֵיכֶם הַמַּשְׁחִיתִם אֶת־הָאָרֶץ וּנְתַתֶּם לֵאלֹהֵי יִשְׂרָאֵל כָּבוֹד אוּלַי יָקֵל אֶת־יָדוֹ מֵעֲלֵיכֶם וּמֵעַל אֱלֹהֵיכֶם וּמֵעַל אַרְצְכֶם:

670

Shmuel I/I Samuel
Chapter 6

שמואל א
פרק ו

6 Don't harden your hearts as the Egyptians and Pharaoh hardened their hearts. As you know, when He made a mockery of them, they had to let *Yisrael* go, and they departed.

וְלָמָּה תְכַבְּדוּ אֶת־לְבַבְכֶם כַּאֲשֶׁר כִּבְּדוּ מִצְרַיִם וּפַרְעֹה אֶת־לִבָּם הֲלוֹא כַּאֲשֶׁר הִתְעַלֵּל בָּהֶם וַיְשַׁלְּחוּם וַיֵּלֵכוּ׃

7 Therefore, get a new cart ready and two milch cows that have not borne a yoke; harness the cows to the cart, but take back indoors the calves that follow them.

וְעַתָּה קְחוּ וַעֲשׂוּ עֲגָלָה חֲדָשָׁה אֶחָת וּשְׁתֵּי פָרוֹת עָלוֹת אֲשֶׁר לֹא־עָלָה עֲלֵיהֶם עֹל וַאֲסַרְתֶּם אֶת־הַפָּרוֹת בָּעֲגָלָה וַהֲשֵׁיבֹתֶם בְּנֵיהֶם מֵאַחֲרֵיהֶם הַבָּיְתָה׃

8 Take the *Aron* of *Hashem* and place it on the cart; and put next to it in a chest the gold objects you are paying Him as indemnity. Send it off, and let it go its own way.

וּלְקַחְתֶּם אֶת־אֲרוֹן יְהוָה וּנְתַתֶּם אֹתוֹ אֶל־הָעֲגָלָה וְאֵת ׀ כְּלֵי הַזָּהָב אֲשֶׁר הֲשֵׁבֹתֶם לוֹ אָשָׁם תָּשִׂימוּ בָאַרְגַּז מִצִּדּוֹ וְשִׁלַּחְתֶּם אֹתוֹ וְהָלָךְ׃

9 Then watch: If it goes up the road to *Beit Shemesh*, to His own territory, it was He who has inflicted this great harm on us. But if not, we shall know that it was not His hand that struck us; it just happened to us by chance."

וּרְאִיתֶם אִם־דֶּרֶךְ גְּבוּלוֹ יַעֲלֶה בֵּית שֶׁמֶשׁ הוּא עָשָׂה לָנוּ אֶת־הָרָעָה הַגְּדוֹלָה הַזֹּאת וְאִם־לֹא וְיָדַעְנוּ כִּי לֹא יָדוֹ נָגְעָה בָּנוּ מִקְרֶה הוּא הָיָה לָנוּ׃

ur-ee-TEM im DE-rekh g'-vu-LO ya-a-LEH BAYT SHE-mesh HU A-sah LA-nu et ha-ra-AH ha-g'-do-LAH ha-ZOT v'-im LO v'-ya-DA-nu KEE LO ya-DO na-g'-AH BA-nu mik-REH HU HA-yah LA-nu

10 The men did so. They took two milch cows and harnessed them to the cart, and shut up their calves indoors.

וַיַּעֲשׂוּ הָאֲנָשִׁים כֵּן וַיִּקְחוּ שְׁתֵּי פָרוֹת עָלוֹת וַיַּאַסְרוּם בָּעֲגָלָה וְאֶת־בְּנֵיהֶם כָּלוּ בַבָּיִת׃

11 They placed the *Aron* of *Hashem* on the cart together with the chest, the golden mice, and the figures of their hemorrhoids.

וַיָּשִׂמוּ אֶת־אֲרוֹן יְהוָה אֶל־הָעֲגָלָה וְאֵת הָאַרְגַּז וְאֵת עַכְבְּרֵי הַזָּהָב וְאֵת צַלְמֵי טְחֹרֵיהֶם׃

12 The cows went straight ahead along the road to *Beit Shemesh*. They went along a single highroad, lowing as they went, and turning off neither to the right nor to the left; and the lords of the Philistines walked behind them as far as the border of *Beit Shemesh*.

וַיִּשַּׁרְנָה הַפָּרוֹת בַּדֶּרֶךְ עַל־דֶּרֶךְ בֵּית שֶׁמֶשׁ בִּמְסִלָּה אַחַת הָלְכוּ הָלֹךְ וְגָעוֹ וְלֹא־סָרוּ יָמִין וּשְׂמֹאול וְסַרְנֵי פְלִשְׁתִּים הֹלְכִים אַחֲרֵיהֶם עַד־גְּבוּל בֵּית שָׁמֶשׁ׃

13 The people of *Beit Shemesh* were reaping their wheat harvest in the valley. They looked up and saw the *Aron*, and they rejoiced when they saw [it].

וּבֵית שֶׁמֶשׁ קֹצְרִים קְצִיר־חִטִּים בָּעֵמֶק וַיִּשְׂאוּ אֶת־עֵינֵיהֶם וַיִּרְאוּ אֶת־הָאָרוֹן וַיִּשְׂמְחוּ לִרְאוֹת׃

Beit Shemesh

6:9 To *Beit Shemesh* *Beit Shemesh*, west of *Yerushalayim*, is in the territory of *Yehuda* (Joshua 15) and is one of the cities set aside for the *Leviim*. In 1948, the area was significant in the fighting between Arabs and Jews. It was from this area that thirty-five fighters set off to try to rescue the besieged Jewish communities in *Gush Etzion*. They were discovered and massacred by Arabs before completing their mission. Shortly after the War of Independence, a new Jewish community was built in *Beit Shemesh*. It was first settled by immigrants from Iran, Iraq and Morocco, and later by a large Russian and Ethiopian population. In more recent years, many North American Jews have made their home in the biblical city of *Beit Shemesh*.

Shmuel I/I Samuel
Chapter 7

14 The cart came into the field of *Yehoshua* of *Beit Shemesh* and it stopped there. They split up the wood of the cart and presented the cows as a burnt offering to *Hashem*. A large stone was there;

15 and the *Leviim* took down the *Aron* of *Hashem* and the chest beside it containing the gold objects and placed them on the large stone. Then the men of *Beit Shemesh* presented burnt offerings and other sacrifices to *Hashem* that day.

16 The five lords of the Philistines saw this and returned the same day to Ekron.

17 The following were the golden hemorrhoids that the Philistines paid as an indemnity to *Hashem*: For *Ashdod*, one; for *Azza*, one; for *Ashkelon*, one; for Gath, one; for Ekron, one.

18 As for the golden mice, their number accorded with all the Philistine towns that belonged to the five lords – both fortified towns and unwalled villages, as far as the great stone on which the *Aron* of *Hashem* was set down, to this day, in the field of *Yehoshua* of *Beit Shemesh*.

19 [*Hashem*] struck at the men of *Beit Shemesh* because they looked into the *Aron* of *Hashem*; He struck down seventy men among the people [and] fifty thousand men. The people mourned, for He had inflicted a great slaughter upon the population.

20 And the men of *Beit Shemesh* asked, "Who can stand in attendance on *Hashem*, this holy *Hashem*? And to whom shall He go up from us?"

21 They sent messengers to the inhabitants of *Kiryat Ye'arim* to say, "The Philistines have sent back the *Aron* of *Hashem*. Come down and take it into your keeping."

7 1 The men of *Kiryat Ye'arim* came and took up the *Aron* of *Hashem* and brought it into the house of *Avinadav* on the hill; and they consecrated his son *Elazar* to have charge of the *Aron* of *Hashem*.

2 A long time elapsed from the day that the *Aron* was housed in *Kiryat Ye'arim*, twenty years in all; and all the House of *Yisrael* yearned after *Hashem*.

שמואל א
פרק ז

יד וְהָעֲגָלָה בָּאָה אֶל־שְׂדֵה יְהוֹשֻׁעַ בֵּית־הַשִּׁמְשִׁי וַתַּעֲמֹד שָׁם וְשָׁם אֶבֶן גְּדוֹלָה וַיְבַקְּעוּ אֶת־עֲצֵי הָעֲגָלָה וְאֶת־הַפָּרוֹת הֶעֱלוּ עֹלָה לַיהוָה:

טו וְהַלְוִיִּם הוֹרִידוּ אֶת־אֲרוֹן יְהוָה וְאֶת־הָאַרְגַּז אֲשֶׁר־אִתּוֹ אֲשֶׁר־בּוֹ כְלֵי־זָהָב וַיָּשִׂמוּ אֶל־הָאֶבֶן הַגְּדוֹלָה וְאַנְשֵׁי בֵית־שֶׁמֶשׁ הֶעֱלוּ עֹלוֹת וַיִּזְבְּחוּ זְבָחִים בַּיּוֹם הַהוּא לַיהוָה:

טז וַחֲמִשָּׁה סַרְנֵי־פְלִשְׁתִּים רָאוּ וַיָּשֻׁבוּ עֶקְרוֹן בַּיּוֹם הַהוּא:

יז וְאֵלֶּה טְחֹרֵי הַזָּהָב אֲשֶׁר הֵשִׁיבוּ פְלִשְׁתִּים אָשָׁם לַיהוָה לְאַשְׁדּוֹד אֶחָד לְעַזָּה אֶחָד לְאַשְׁקְלוֹן אֶחָד לְגַת אֶחָד לְעֶקְרוֹן אֶחָד:

יח וְעַכְבְּרֵי הַזָּהָב מִסְפַּר כָּל־עָרֵי פְלִשְׁתִּים לַחֲמֵשֶׁת הַסְּרָנִים מֵעִיר מִבְצָר וְעַד כֹּפֶר הַפְּרָזִי וְעַד אָבֵל הַגְּדוֹלָה אֲשֶׁר הִנִּיחוּ עָלֶיהָ אֵת אֲרוֹן יְהוָה עַד הַיּוֹם הַזֶּה בִּשְׂדֵה יְהוֹשֻׁעַ בֵּית־הַשִּׁמְשִׁי:

יט וַיַּךְ בְּאַנְשֵׁי בֵית־שֶׁמֶשׁ כִּי רָאוּ בַּאֲרוֹן יְהוָה וַיַּךְ בָּעָם שִׁבְעִים אִישׁ חֲמִשִּׁים אֶלֶף אִישׁ וַיִּתְאַבְּלוּ הָעָם כִּי־הִכָּה יְהוָה בָּעָם מַכָּה גְדוֹלָה:

כ וַיֹּאמְרוּ אַנְשֵׁי בֵית־שֶׁמֶשׁ מִי יוּכַל לַעֲמֹד לִפְנֵי יְהוָה הָאֱלֹהִים הַקָּדוֹשׁ הַזֶּה וְאֶל־מִי יַעֲלֶה מֵעָלֵינוּ:

כא וַיִּשְׁלְחוּ מַלְאָכִים אֶל־יוֹשְׁבֵי קִרְיַת־יְעָרִים לֵאמֹר הֵשִׁבוּ פְלִשְׁתִּים אֶת־אֲרוֹן יְהוָה רְדוּ הַעֲלוּ אֹתוֹ אֲלֵיכֶם:

ז א וַיָּבֹאוּ אַנְשֵׁי קִרְיַת יְעָרִים וַיַּעֲלוּ אֶת־אֲרוֹן יְהוָה וַיָּבִאוּ אֹתוֹ אֶל־בֵּית אֲבִינָדָב בַּגִּבְעָה וְאֶת־אֶלְעָזָר בְּנוֹ קִדְּשׁוּ לִשְׁמֹר אֶת־אֲרוֹן יְהוָה:

ב וַיְהִי מִיּוֹם שֶׁבֶת הָאָרוֹן בְּקִרְיַת יְעָרִים וַיִּרְבּוּ הַיָּמִים וַיִּהְיוּ עֶשְׂרִים שָׁנָה וַיִּנָּהוּ כָּל־בֵּית יִשְׂרָאֵל אַחֲרֵי יְהוָה:

Shmuel I / I Samuel

Chapter 7

3 And *Shmuel* said to all the House of *Yisrael*, "If you mean to return to *Hashem* with all your heart, you must remove the alien gods and the Ashtaroth from your midst and direct your heart to *Hashem* and serve Him alone. Then He will deliver you from the hands of the Philistines."

4 And the Israelites removed the Baalim and Ashtaroth and they served *Hashem* alone.

5 *Shmuel* said, "Assemble all *Yisrael* at *Mitzpa*, and I will pray to *Hashem* for you."

6 They assembled at *Mitzpa*, and they drew water and poured it out before *Hashem*; they fasted that day, and there they confessed that they had sinned against *Hashem*. And *Shmuel* acted as chieftain of the Israelites at *Mitzpa*.

7 When the Philistines heard that the Israelites had assembled at *Mitzpa*, the lords of the Philistines marched out against *Yisrael*. Hearing of this, the Israelites were terrified of the Philistines

8 and they implored *Shmuel*, "Do not neglect us and do not refrain from crying out to *Hashem* our God to save us from the hands of the Philistines."

9 Thereupon *Shmuel* took a suckling lamb and sacrificed it as a whole burnt offering to *Hashem*; and *Shmuel* cried out to *Hashem* in behalf of *Yisrael*, and *Hashem* responded to him.

10 For as *Shmuel* was presenting the burnt offering and the Philistines advanced to attack *Yisrael*, *Hashem* thundered mightily against the Philistines that day. He threw them into confusion, and they were routed by *Yisrael*.

11 The men of *Yisrael* sallied out of *Mitzpa* and pursued the Philistines, striking them down to a point below Beth-car.

12 *Shmuel* took a stone and set it up between *Mitzpa* and Shen, and named it *Even Ha-Ezer*: "For up to now," he said, "*Hashem* has helped us."

13 The Philistines were humbled and did not invade the territory of *Yisrael* again; and the hand of *Hashem* was set against the Philistines as long as *Shmuel* lived.

ג וַיֹּאמֶר שְׁמוּאֵל אֶל־כָּל־בֵּית יִשְׂרָאֵל לֵאמֹר אִם־בְּכָל־לְבַבְכֶם אַתֶּם שָׁבִים אֶל־יְהֹוָה הָסִירוּ אֶת־אֱלֹהֵי הַנֵּכָר מִתּוֹכְכֶם וְהָעַשְׁתָּרוֹת וְהָכִינוּ לְבַבְכֶם אֶל־יְהֹוָה וְעִבְדֻהוּ לְבַדּוֹ וְיַצֵּל אֶתְכֶם מִיַּד פְּלִשְׁתִּים:

ד וַיָּסִירוּ בְּנֵי יִשְׂרָאֵל אֶת־הַבְּעָלִים וְאֶת־הָעַשְׁתָּרֹת וַיַּעַבְדוּ אֶת־יְהֹוָה לְבַדּוֹ:

ה וַיֹּאמֶר שְׁמוּאֵל קִבְצוּ אֶת־כָּל־יִשְׂרָאֵל הַמִּצְפָּתָה וְאֶתְפַּלֵּל בַּעַדְכֶם אֶל־יְהֹוָה:

ו וַיִּקָּבְצוּ הַמִּצְפָּתָה וַיִּשְׁאֲבוּ־מַיִם וַיִּשְׁפְּכוּ לִפְנֵי יְהֹוָה וַיָּצוּמוּ בַּיּוֹם הַהוּא וַיֹּאמְרוּ שָׁם חָטָאנוּ לַיהֹוָה וַיִּשְׁפֹּט שְׁמוּאֵל אֶת־בְּנֵי יִשְׂרָאֵל בַּמִּצְפָּה:

ז וַיִּשְׁמְעוּ פְלִשְׁתִּים כִּי־הִתְקַבְּצוּ בְנֵי־יִשְׂרָאֵל הַמִּצְפָּתָה וַיַּעֲלוּ סַרְנֵי־פְלִשְׁתִּים אֶל־יִשְׂרָאֵל וַיִּשְׁמְעוּ בְּנֵי יִשְׂרָאֵל וַיִּרְאוּ מִפְּנֵי פְלִשְׁתִּים:

ח וַיֹּאמְרוּ בְנֵי־יִשְׂרָאֵל אֶל־שְׁמוּאֵל אַל־תַּחֲרֵשׁ מִמֶּנּוּ מִזְּעֹק אֶל־יְהֹוָה אֱלֹהֵינוּ וְיֹשִׁעֵנוּ מִיַּד פְּלִשְׁתִּים:

ט וַיִּקַּח שְׁמוּאֵל טְלֵה חָלָב אֶחָד וַיַּעֲלֵהוּ [וַיַּעֲלֶהוּ] עוֹלָה כָּלִיל לַיהֹוָה וַיִּזְעַק שְׁמוּאֵל אֶל־יְהֹוָה בְּעַד יִשְׂרָאֵל וַיַּעֲנֵהוּ יְהֹוָה:

י וַיְהִי שְׁמוּאֵל מַעֲלֶה הָעוֹלָה וּפְלִשְׁתִּים נִגְּשׁוּ לַמִּלְחָמָה בְּיִשְׂרָאֵל וַיַּרְעֵם יְהֹוָה בְּקוֹל־גָּדוֹל בַּיּוֹם הַהוּא עַל־פְּלִשְׁתִּים וַיְהֻמֵּם וַיִּנָּגְפוּ לִפְנֵי יִשְׂרָאֵל:

יא וַיֵּצְאוּ אַנְשֵׁי יִשְׂרָאֵל מִן־הַמִּצְפָּה וַיִּרְדְּפוּ אֶת־פְּלִשְׁתִּים וַיַּכּוּם עַד־מִתַּחַת לְבֵית כָּר:

יב וַיִּקַּח שְׁמוּאֵל אֶבֶן אַחַת וַיָּשֶׂם בֵּין־הַמִּצְפָּה וּבֵין הַשֵּׁן וַיִּקְרָא אֶת־שְׁמָהּ אֶבֶן הָעָזֶר וַיֹּאמַר עַד־הֵנָּה עֲזָרָנוּ יְהֹוָה:

יג וַיִּכָּנְעוּ הַפְּלִשְׁתִּים וְלֹא־יָסְפוּ עוֹד לָבוֹא בִּגְבוּל יִשְׂרָאֵל וַתְּהִי יַד־יְהֹוָה בַּפְּלִשְׁתִּים כֹּל יְמֵי שְׁמוּאֵל:

Shmuel I/I Samuel
Chapter 8

שמואל א
פרק ח

14 The towns which the Philistines had taken from *Yisrael*, from Ekron to Gath, were restored to *Yisrael*; *Yisrael* recovered all her territory from the Philistines. There was also peace between *Yisrael* and the Amorites.

יד וַתָּשֹׁבְנָה הֶעָרִים אֲשֶׁר לָקְחוּ־פְלִשְׁתִּים מֵאֵת יִשְׂרָאֵל לְיִשְׂרָאֵל מֵעֶקְרוֹן וְעַד־גַּת וְאֶת־גְּבוּלָן הִצִּיל יִשְׂרָאֵל מִיַּד פְּלִשְׁתִּים וַיְהִי שָׁלוֹם בֵּין יִשְׂרָאֵל וּבֵין הָאֱמֹרִי׃

15 *Shmuel* judged *Yisrael* as long as he lived.

טו וַיִּשְׁפֹּט שְׁמוּאֵל אֶת־יִשְׂרָאֵל כֹּל יְמֵי חַיָּיו׃

16 Each year he made the rounds of *Beit El*, *Gilgal*, and *Mitzpa*, and acted as judge over *Yisrael* at all those places.

טז וְהָלַךְ מִדֵּי שָׁנָה בְּשָׁנָה וְסָבַב בֵּית־אֵל וְהַגִּלְגָּל וְהַמִּצְפָּה וְשָׁפַט אֶת־יִשְׂרָאֵל אֵת כָּל־הַמְּקוֹמוֹת הָאֵלֶּה׃

v'-ha-LAKH mi-DAY sha-NAH b'-sha-NAH v'-sa-VAV bayt AYL v'-ha-gil-GAL v'-ha-mitz-PAH v'-sha-FAT et yis-ra-AYL AYT kol ha-m'-ko-MOT ha-AY-leh

17 Then he would return to *Rama*, for his home was there, and there too he would judge *Yisrael*. He built a *Mizbayach* there to *Hashem*.

יז וּתְשֻׁבָתוֹ הָרָמָתָה כִּי־שָׁם בֵּיתוֹ וְשָׁם שָׁפָט אֶת־יִשְׂרָאֵל וַיִּבֶן־שָׁם מִזְבֵּחַ לַיהוָה׃

8

1 When *Shmuel* grew old, he appointed his sons judges over *Yisrael*.

א וַיְהִי כַּאֲשֶׁר זָקֵן שְׁמוּאֵל וַיָּשֶׂם אֶת־בָּנָיו שֹׁפְטִים לְיִשְׂרָאֵל׃

2 The name of his first-born son was *Yoel*, and his second son's name was *Aviya*; they sat as judges in *Be'er Sheva*.

ב וַיְהִי שֶׁם־בְּנוֹ הַבְּכוֹר יוֹאֵל וְשֵׁם מִשְׁנֵהוּ אֲבִיָּה שֹׁפְטִים בִּבְאֵר שָׁבַע׃

3 But his sons did not follow in his ways; they were bent on gain, they accepted bribes, and they subverted justice.

ג וְלֹא־הָלְכוּ בָנָיו בדרכו [בִּדְרָכָיו] וַיִּטּוּ אַחֲרֵי הַבָּצַע וַיִּקְחוּ־שֹׁחַד וַיַּטּוּ מִשְׁפָּט׃

4 All the elders of *Yisrael* assembled and came to *Shmuel* at *Rama*,

ד וַיִּתְקַבְּצוּ כֹּל זִקְנֵי יִשְׂרָאֵל וַיָּבֹאוּ אֶל־שְׁמוּאֵל הָרָמָתָה׃

5 and they said to him, "You have grown old, and your sons have not followed your ways. Therefore appoint a king for us, to govern us like all other nations."

ה וַיֹּאמְרוּ אֵלָיו הִנֵּה אַתָּה זָקַנְתָּ וּבָנֶיךָ לֹא הָלְכוּ בִּדְרָכֶיךָ עַתָּה שִׂימָה־לָּנוּ מֶלֶךְ לְשָׁפְטֵנוּ כְּכָל־הַגּוֹיִם׃

7:16 Each year he made the rounds As the prophet and judge of the People of Israel, *Shmuel* could follow *Eli*'s example and require that the people come to him. However, he does not wish to live in an ivory tower. *Shmuel* becomes a different type of leader, who goes to the people in order to meet with them, inspire and serve them. Thus, he travels to the major cities of Israel on an annual basis. He serves as a role model for future leaders who would travel throughout the land to the homes and communities of their followers to offer inspiration. This has long been the practice of Israel's chief rabbis, whose mission includes traveling throughout Israel to reach and teach the people they serve. One of the most famous examples was when Rabbi Abraham Isaac Kook and nine other prominent rabbis visited early Jewish agricultural settlements in the Galilee region in 1913–14. Many of the residents of these settlements were not religiously observant, but Rabbi Kook and his colleagues felt obligated to teach them, and show their love to them all.

Rabbi Abraham Isaac Kook (1865–1935)

Shmuel I / I Samuel
Chapter 8

שמואל א
פרק ח

6 *Shmuel* was displeased that they said "Give us a king to govern us." *Shmuel* prayed to *Hashem*,

וַיֵּרַע הַדָּבָר בְּעֵינֵי שְׁמוּאֵל כַּאֲשֶׁר אָמְרוּ תְּנָה־לָּנוּ מֶלֶךְ לְשָׁפְטֵנוּ וַיִּתְפַּלֵּל שְׁמוּאֵל אֶל־יְהוָה:

va-YAY-ra ha-da-VAR b'-ay-NAY sh'-mu-AYL ka-a-SHER a-m'-RU t'-nah LA-nu ME-lekh l'-shof-TAY-nu va-yit-pa-LAYL sh'-mu-AYL el a-do-NAI

7 and *Hashem* replied to *Shmuel*, "Heed the demand of the people in everything they say to you. For it is not you that they have rejected; it is Me they have rejected as their king.

8 Like everything else they have done ever since I brought them out of Egypt to this day – forsaking Me and worshiping other gods – so they are doing to you.

9 Heed their demand; but warn them solemnly, and tell them about the practices of any king who will rule over them."

10 *Shmuel* reported all the words of *Hashem* to the people, who were asking him for a king.

11 He said, "This will be the practice of the king who will rule over you: He will take your sons and appoint them as his charioteers and horsemen, and they will serve as outrunners for his chariots.

12 He will appoint them as his chiefs of thousands and of fifties; or they will have to plow his fields, reap his harvest, and make his weapons and the equipment for his chariots.

13 He will take your daughters as perfumers, cooks, and bakers.

8:6 Shmuel was displeased While *Shmuel* expressed his displeasure with the people's request, it was not their actual request for a king that troubled him. In fact, the *Torah* includes a commandment requiring the people to appoint a king (Deuteronomy 17:15). The problem, *Rashi* notes, was that they wanted a king "like all the other nations" (verse 5). This request ignores the uniqueness of the People of Israel, and the unusual type of leader their king should be, a very different model than that followed by "all the other nations." Rabbi Shlomo Aviner notes that because of their request, this is exactly the kind of king they receive. King *Shaul* is a righteous individual who is very successful in uniting and organizing the people. But a king of Israel is required to be even more than that. He is to meant lift the people spiritually, to bring them closer to *Hashem* so that they can serve as a "light unto the nations" (Isaiah 42:6). King *Shaul* is unable to do this. For example, as detailed in Chapter 15, he does not completely destroy Amalek and their animals, thereby defying God's will in order to please the people. By contrast, King *David* constantly seeks to elevate the nation, even at the expense of his own honor. For example, he dances before the Holy Ark when it was brought to *Yerushalayim*, even though this conduct could be deemed unseemly for a king. Therefore, *Shaul*'s kingship is of a temporary nature, while *David*'s dynasty becomes the eternal monarchy of the Jewish People.

Shmuel I / I Samuel
Chapter 9

שמואל א
פרק ט

14 He will seize your choice fields, vineyards, and olive groves, and give them to his courtiers.

יד וְאֶת־שְׂדוֹתֵיכֶם וְאֶת־כַּרְמֵיכֶם וְזֵיתֵיכֶם הַטּוֹבִים יִקָּח וְנָתַן לַעֲבָדָיו:

15 He will take a tenth part of your grain and vintage and give it to his eunuchs and courtiers.

טו וְזַרְעֵיכֶם וְכַרְמֵיכֶם יַעְשֹׂר וְנָתַן לְסָרִיסָיו וְלַעֲבָדָיו:

16 He will take your male and female slaves, your choice young men, and your asses, and put them to work for him.

טז וְאֶת־עַבְדֵיכֶם וְאֶת־שִׁפְחוֹתֵיכֶם וְאֶת־בַּחוּרֵיכֶם הַטּוֹבִים וְאֶת־חֲמוֹרֵיכֶם יִקָּח וְעָשָׂה לִמְלַאכְתּוֹ:

17 He will take a tenth part of your flocks, and you shall become his slaves.

יז צֹאנְכֶם יַעְשֹׂר וְאַתֶּם תִּהְיוּ־לוֹ לַעֲבָדִים:

18 The day will come when you cry out because of the king whom you yourselves have chosen; and *Hashem* will not answer you on that day."

יח וּזְעַקְתֶּם בַּיּוֹם הַהוּא מִלִּפְנֵי מַלְכְּכֶם אֲשֶׁר בְּחַרְתֶּם לָכֶם וְלֹא־יַעֲנֶה יְהֹוָה אֶתְכֶם בַּיּוֹם הַהוּא:

19 But the people would not listen to *Shmuel's* warning. "No," they said. "We must have a king over us,

יט וַיְמָאֲנוּ הָעָם לִשְׁמֹעַ בְּקוֹל שְׁמוּאֵל וַיֹּאמְרוּ לֹּא כִּי אִם־מֶלֶךְ יִהְיֶה עָלֵינוּ:

20 that we may be like all the other nations: Let our king rule over us and go out at our head and fight our battles."

כ וְהָיִינוּ גַם־אֲנַחְנוּ כְּכָל־הַגּוֹיִם וּשְׁפָטָנוּ מַלְכֵּנוּ וְיָצָא לְפָנֵינוּ וְנִלְחַם אֶת־מִלְחֲמֹתֵנוּ:

21 When *Shmuel* heard all that the people said, he reported it to *Hashem*.

כא וַיִּשְׁמַע שְׁמוּאֵל אֵת כָּל־דִּבְרֵי הָעָם וַיְדַבְּרֵם בְּאָזְנֵי יְהֹוָה:

22 And *Hashem* said to *Shmuel*, "Heed their demands and appoint a king for them." *Shmuel* then said to the men of *Yisrael*, "All of you go home."

כב וַיֹּאמֶר יְהֹוָה אֶל־שְׁמוּאֵל שְׁמַע בְּקוֹלָם וְהִמְלַכְתָּ לָהֶם מֶלֶךְ וַיֹּאמֶר שְׁמוּאֵל אֶל־אַנְשֵׁי יִשְׂרָאֵל לְכוּ אִישׁ לְעִירוֹ:

9 1 There was a man of *Binyamin* whose name was *Keesh* son of Abiel son of Zeror son of Becorath son of Aphiah, a *Binyamin*ite, a man of substance.

ט א וַיְהִי־אִישׁ מִבֶּן־יָמִין [מִבִּנְיָמִין] וּשְׁמוֹ קִישׁ בֶּן־אֲבִיאֵל בֶּן־צְרוֹר בֶּן־בְּכוֹרַת בֶּן־אֲפִיחַ בֶּן־אִישׁ יְמִינִי גִּבּוֹר חָיִל:

2 He had a son whose name was *Shaul*, an excellent young man; no one among the Israelites was handsomer than he; he was a head taller than any of the people.

ב וְלוֹ־הָיָה בֵן וּשְׁמוֹ שָׁאוּל בָּחוּר וָטוֹב וְאֵין אִישׁ מִבְּנֵי יִשְׂרָאֵל טוֹב מִמֶּנּוּ מִשִּׁכְמוֹ וָמַעְלָה גָּבֹהַּ מִכָּל־הָעָם:

3 Once the asses of *Shaul's* father *Keesh* went astray, and *Keesh* said to his son *Shaul*, "Take along one of the servants and go out and look for the asses."

ג וַתֹּאבַדְנָה הָאֲתֹנוֹת לְקִישׁ אֲבִי שָׁאוּל וַיֹּאמֶר קִישׁ אֶל־שָׁאוּל בְּנוֹ קַח־נָא אִתְּךָ אֶת־אַחַד מֵהַנְּעָרִים וְקוּם לֵךְ בַּקֵּשׁ אֶת־הָאֲתֹנֹת:

4 He passed into the hill country of *Efraim*. He crossed the district of Shalishah, but they did not find them. They passed through the district of Shaalim, but they were not there. They traversed the [entire] territory of *Binyamin*, and still they did not find them.

ד וַיַּעֲבֹר בְּהַר־אֶפְרַיִם וַיַּעֲבֹר בְּאֶרֶץ־שָׁלִשָׁה וְלֹא מָצָאוּ וַיַּעַבְרוּ בְאֶרֶץ־שַׁעֲלִים וָאַיִן וַיַּעֲבֹר בְּאֶרֶץ־יְמִינִי וְלֹא מָצָאוּ:

676

Shmuel I / I Samuel
Chapter 9

שמואל א
פרק ט

5 When they reached the district of Zuph, *Shaul* said to the servant who was with him, "Let us turn back, or my father will stop worrying about the asses and begin to worry about us."

ה הֵמָּה בָּאוּ בְּאֶרֶץ צוּף וְשָׁאוּל אָמַר לְנַעֲרוֹ אֲשֶׁר־עִמּוֹ לְכָה וְנָשׁוּבָה פֶּן־יֶחְדַּל אָבִי מִן־הָאֲתֹנוֹת וְדָאַג לָנוּ:

6 But he replied, "There is a man of *Hashem* in that town, and the man is highly esteemed; everything that he says comes true. Let us go there; perhaps he will tell us about the errand on which we set out."

ו וַיֹּאמֶר לוֹ הִנֵּה־נָא אִישׁ־אֱלֹהִים בָּעִיר הַזֹּאת וְהָאִישׁ נִכְבָּד כֹּל אֲשֶׁר־יְדַבֵּר בּוֹא יָבוֹא עַתָּה נֵלֲכָה שָּׁם אוּלַי יַגִּיד לָנוּ אֶת־דַּרְכֵּנוּ אֲשֶׁר־הָלַכְנוּ עָלֶיהָ:

7 "But if we go," *Shaul* said to his servant, "what can we bring the man? For the food in our bags is all gone, and there is nothing we can bring to the man of *Hashem* as a present. What have we got?"

ז וַיֹּאמֶר שָׁאוּל לְנַעֲרוֹ וְהִנֵּה נֵלֵךְ וּמַה־נָּבִיא לָאִישׁ כִּי הַלֶּחֶם אָזַל מִכֵּלֵינוּ וּתְשׁוּרָה אֵין־לְהָבִיא לְאִישׁ הָאֱלֹהִים מָה אִתָּנוּ:

8 The servant answered *Shaul* again, "I happen to have a quarter-*shekel* of silver. I can give that to the man of *Hashem* and he will tell us about our errand." –

ח וַיֹּסֶף הַנַּעַר לַעֲנוֹת אֶת־שָׁאוּל וַיֹּאמֶר הִנֵּה נִמְצָא בְיָדִי רֶבַע שֶׁקֶל כָּסֶף וְנָתַתִּי לְאִישׁ הָאֱלֹהִים וְהִגִּיד לָנוּ אֶת־דַּרְכֵּנוּ:

9 Formerly in *Yisrael*, when a man went to inquire of *Hashem*, he would say, "Come, let us go to the seer," for the *Navi* of today was formerly called a seer. –

ט לְפָנִים בְּיִשְׂרָאֵל כֹּה־אָמַר הָאִישׁ בְּלֶכְתּוֹ לִדְרוֹשׁ אֱלֹהִים לְכוּ וְנֵלְכָה עַד־הָרֹאֶה כִּי לַנָּבִיא הַיּוֹם יִקָּרֵא לְפָנִים הָרֹאֶה:

10 *Shaul* said to his servant, "A good idea; let us go." And they went to the town where the man of *Hashem* lived.

י וַיֹּאמֶר שָׁאוּל לְנַעֲרוֹ טוֹב דְּבָרְךָ לְכָה נֵלֵכָה וַיֵּלְכוּ אֶל־הָעִיר אֲשֶׁר־שָׁם אִישׁ הָאֱלֹהִים:

11 As they were climbing the ascent to the town, they met some girls coming out to draw water, and they asked them, "Is the seer in town?"

יא הֵמָּה עֹלִים בְּמַעֲלֵה הָעִיר וְהֵמָּה מָצְאוּ נְעָרוֹת יֹצְאוֹת לִשְׁאֹב מָיִם וַיֹּאמְרוּ לָהֶן הֲיֵשׁ בָּזֶה הָרֹאֶה:

12 "Yes," they replied. "He is up there ahead of you. Hurry, for he has just come to the town because the people have a sacrifice at the shrine today.

יב וַתַּעֲנֶינָה אוֹתָם וַתֹּאמַרְנָה יֵשׁ הִנֵּה לְפָנֶיךָ מַהֵר עַתָּה כִּי הַיּוֹם בָּא לָעִיר כִּי זֶבַח הַיּוֹם לָעָם בַּבָּמָה:

13 As soon as you enter the town, you will find him before he goes up to the shrine to eat; the people will not eat until he comes; for he must first bless the sacrifice and only then will the guests eat. Go up at once, for you will find him right away."

יג כְּבֹאֲכֶם הָעִיר כֵּן תִּמְצְאוּן אֹתוֹ בְּטֶרֶם יַעֲלֶה הַבָּמָתָה לֶאֱכֹל כִּי לֹא־יֹאכַל הָעָם עַד־בֹּאוֹ כִּי־הוּא יְבָרֵךְ הַזֶּבַח אַחֲרֵי־כֵן יֹאכְלוּ הַקְּרֻאִים וְעַתָּה עֲלוּ כִּי־אֹתוֹ כְהַיּוֹם תִּמְצְאוּן אֹתוֹ:

k'-vo-a-KHEM ha-EER KAYN tim-tz'-UN o-TO b'-TE-rem ya-a-LEH ha-ba-MA-tah le-e-KHOL KEE lo yo-KHAL ha-AM ad bo-O kee HU y'-va-RAYKH ha-ZE-vakh a-kha-ray KHAYN yo-kh'-LU ha-k'-ru-EEM v'-a-TAH a-LU kee o-TO kh'-ha-YOM tim-tz'-UN o-TO

9:13 for he must first bless the sacrifice *Rashi* notes that since the *Mishkan* at *Shilo* lies in ruins, the People of Israel are allowed to offer sacrifices to *Hashem* in other places. However, once the *Beit Hamikdash* would be established in *Yerushalayim*, no further sacrifices would ever again be permitted in any other location, even after the *Beit Hamikdash* is destroyed. This law is a reminder of the eternal sanctity of *Yerushalayim* and *Har Habayit*. The holiness of *Har Habayit* is everlasting, and one day, the third Temple will be built there.

Shmuel I/I Samuel

Chapter 9

14 So they went up to the town; and as they were entering the town, *Shmuel* came out toward them, on his way up to the shrine.

15 Now the day before *Shaul* came, *Hashem* had revealed the following to *Shmuel*:

16 "At this time tomorrow, I will send a man to you from the territory of *Binyamin*, and you shall anoint him ruler of My people *Yisrael*. He will deliver My people from the hands of the Philistines; for I have taken note of My people, their outcry has come to Me."

17 As soon as *Shmuel* saw *Shaul*, *Hashem* declared to him, "This is the man that I told you would govern My people."

18 *Shaul* approached *Shmuel* inside the gate and said to him, "Tell me, please, where is the house of the seer?"

19 And *Shmuel* answered *Shaul*, "I am the seer. Go up ahead of me to the shrine, for you shall eat with me today; and in the morning I will let you go, after telling you whatever may be on your mind.

20 As for your asses that strayed three days ago, do not concern yourself about them, for they have been found. And for whom is all *Yisrael* yearning, if not for you and all your ancestral house?"

21 *Shaul* replied, "But I am only a *Binyamin*ite, from the smallest of the tribes of *Yisrael*, and my clan is the least of all the clans of the tribe of *Binyamin*! Why do you say such things to me?"

22 *Shmuel* took *Shaul* and his servant and brought them into the hall, and gave them a place at the head of the guests, who numbered about thirty.

23 And *Shmuel* said to the cook, "Bring the portion which I gave you and told you to set aside."

24 The cook lifted up the thigh and what was on it, and set it before *Shaul*. And [*Shmuel*] said, "What has been reserved is set before you. Eat; it has been kept for you for this occasion, when I said I was inviting the people." So *Shaul* ate with *Shmuel* that day.

25 They then descended from the shrine to the town, and [*Shmuel*] talked with *Shaul* on the roof.

שמואל א

פרק ט

יד וַיַּעֲלוּ הָעִיר הֵמָּה בָּאִים בְּתוֹךְ הָעִיר וְהִנֵּה שְׁמוּאֵל יֹצֵא לִקְרָאתָם לַעֲלוֹת הַבָּמָה:

טו וַיהוָה גָּלָה אֶת־אֹזֶן שְׁמוּאֵל יוֹם אֶחָד לִפְנֵי בוֹא־שָׁאוּל לֵאמֹר:

טז כָּעֵת מָחָר אֶשְׁלַח אֵלֶיךָ אִישׁ מֵאֶרֶץ בִּנְיָמִן וּמְשַׁחְתּוֹ לְנָגִיד עַל־עַמִּי יִשְׂרָאֵל וְהוֹשִׁיעַ אֶת־עַמִּי מִיַּד פְּלִשְׁתִּים כִּי רָאִיתִי אֶת־עַמִּי כִּי בָּאָה צַעֲקָתוֹ אֵלָי:

יז וּשְׁמוּאֵל רָאָה אֶת־שָׁאוּל וַיהוָה עָנָהוּ הִנֵּה הָאִישׁ אֲשֶׁר אָמַרְתִּי אֵלֶיךָ זֶה יַעְצֹר בְּעַמִּי:

יח וַיִּגַּשׁ שָׁאוּל אֶת־שְׁמוּאֵל בְּתוֹךְ הַשָּׁעַר וַיֹּאמֶר הַגִּידָה־נָּא לִי אֵי־זֶה בֵּית הָרֹאֶה:

יט וַיַּעַן שְׁמוּאֵל אֶת־שָׁאוּל וַיֹּאמֶר אָנֹכִי הָרֹאֶה עֲלֵה לְפָנַי הַבָּמָה וַאֲכַלְתֶּם עִמִּי הַיּוֹם וְשִׁלַּחְתִּיךָ בַבֹּקֶר וְכֹל אֲשֶׁר בִּלְבָבְךָ אַגִּיד לָךְ:

כ וְלָאֲתֹנוֹת הָאֹבְדוֹת לְךָ הַיּוֹם שְׁלֹשֶׁת הַיָּמִים אַל־תָּשֶׂם אֶת־לִבְּךָ לָהֶם כִּי נִמְצָאוּ וּלְמִי כָּל־חֶמְדַּת יִשְׂרָאֵל הֲלוֹא לְךָ וּלְכֹל בֵּית אָבִיךָ:

כא וַיַּעַן שָׁאוּל וַיֹּאמֶר הֲלוֹא בֶן־יְמִינִי אָנֹכִי מִקַּטַנֵּי שִׁבְטֵי יִשְׂרָאֵל וּמִשְׁפַּחְתִּי הַצְּעִרָה מִכָּל־מִשְׁפְּחוֹת שִׁבְטֵי בִנְיָמִן וְלָמָּה דִּבַּרְתָּ אֵלַי כַּדָּבָר הַזֶּה:

כב וַיִּקַּח שְׁמוּאֵל אֶת־שָׁאוּל וְאֶת־נַעֲרוֹ וַיְבִיאֵם לִשְׁכָּתָה וַיִּתֵּן לָהֶם מָקוֹם בְּרֹאשׁ הַקְּרוּאִים וְהֵמָּה כִּשְׁלֹשִׁים אִישׁ:

כג וַיֹּאמֶר שְׁמוּאֵל לַטַּבָּח תְּנָה אֶת־הַמָּנָה אֲשֶׁר נָתַתִּי לָךְ אֲשֶׁר אָמַרְתִּי אֵלֶיךָ שִׂים אֹתָהּ עִמָּךְ:

כד וַיָּרֶם הַטַּבָּח אֶת־הַשּׁוֹק וְהֶעָלֶיהָ וַיָּשֶׂם לִפְנֵי שָׁאוּל וַיֹּאמֶר הִנֵּה הַנִּשְׁאָר שִׂים־לְפָנֶיךָ אֱכֹל כִּי לַמּוֹעֵד שָׁמוּר־לְךָ לֵאמֹר הָעָם קָרָאתִי וַיֹּאכַל שָׁאוּל עִם־שְׁמוּאֵל בַּיּוֹם הַהוּא:

כה וַיֵּרְדוּ מֵהַבָּמָה הָעִיר וַיְדַבֵּר עִם־שָׁאוּל עַל־הַגָּג:

Shmuel I / I Samuel
Chapter 10

שמואל א
פרק י

26 Early, at the break of day, *Shmuel* called to *Shaul* on the roof. He said, "Get up, and I will send you off." *Shaul* arose, and the two of them, *Shmuel* and he, went outside.

כו וַיַּשְׁכִּמוּ וַיְהִי כַּעֲלוֹת הַשַּׁחַר וַיִּקְרָא שְׁמוּאֵל אֶל־שָׁאוּל הַגָג [הַגָּגָה] לֵאמֹר קוּמָה וַאֲשַׁלְּחֶךָּ וַיָּקָם שָׁאוּל וַיֵּצְאוּ שְׁנֵיהֶם הוּא וּשְׁמוּאֵל הַחוּצָה:

27 As they were walking toward the end of the town, *Shmuel* said to *Shaul*, "Tell the servant to walk ahead of us" – and he walked ahead – "but you stop here a moment and I will make known to you the word of *Hashem*."

כז הֵמָּה יוֹרְדִים בִּקְצֵה הָעִיר וּשְׁמוּאֵל אָמַר אֶל־שָׁאוּל אֱמֹר לַנַּעַר וְיַעֲבֹר לְפָנֵינוּ וַיַּעֲבֹר וְאַתָּה עֲמֹד כַּיּוֹם וְאַשְׁמִיעֲךָ אֶת־דְּבַר אֱלֹהִים:

10

1 *Shmuel* took a flask of oil and poured some on *Shaul*'s head and kissed him, and said, "*Hashem* herewith anoints you ruler over His own people.

א וַיִּקַּח שְׁמוּאֵל אֶת־פַּךְ הַשֶּׁמֶן וַיִּצֹק עַל־רֹאשׁוֹ וַיִּשָּׁקֵהוּ וַיֹּאמֶר הֲלוֹא כִּי־מְשָׁחֲךָ יְהוָה עַל־נַחֲלָתוֹ לְנָגִיד:

2 When you leave me today, you will meet two men near the tomb of *Rachel* in the territory of *Binyamin*, at Zelzah, and they will tell you that the asses you set out to look for have been found, and that your father has stopped being concerned about the asses and is worrying about you, saying: 'What shall I do about my son?'

ב בְּלֶכְתְּךָ הַיּוֹם מֵעִמָּדִי וּמָצָאתָ שְׁנֵי אֲנָשִׁים עִם־קְבֻרַת רָחֵל בִּגְבוּל בִּנְיָמִן בְּצֶלְצַח וְאָמְרוּ אֵלֶיךָ נִמְצְאוּ הָאֲתֹנוֹת אֲשֶׁר הָלַכְתָּ לְבַקֵּשׁ וְהִנֵּה נָטַשׁ אָבִיךָ אֶת־דִּבְרֵי הָאֲתֹנוֹת וְדָאַג לָכֶם לֵאמֹר מָה אֶעֱשֶׂה לִבְנִי:

b'-lekh-t'-KHA ha-YOM may-i-ma-DEE u-ma-TZA-ta sh'-NAY a-na-SHEEM im k'-vu-RAT ra-KHAYL big-VUL bin-ya-MIN b'-tzel-TZAKH v'-a-m'-RU ay-LE-kha nim-tz'-U ha-a-to-NOT a-SHER ha-LAKH-ta l'-va-KAYSH v'-hi-NAY na-TASH a-VEE-kha et div-RAY ha-a-to-NOT v'-da-AG la-KHEM lay-MOR MAH e-e-SEH liv-NEE

3 You shall pass on from there until you come to the terebinth of *Tavor*. There you will be met by three men making a pilgrimage to *Hashem* at *Beit El*. One will be carrying three kids, another will be carrying three loaves of bread, and the third will be carrying a jar of wine.

ג וְחָלַפְתָּ מִשָּׁם וָהָלְאָה וּבָאתָ עַד־אֵלוֹן תָּבוֹר וּמְצָאוּךָ שָּׁם שְׁלֹשָׁה אֲנָשִׁים עֹלִים אֶל־הָאֱלֹהִים בֵּית־אֵל אֶחָד נֹשֵׂא שְׁלֹשָׁה גְדָיִים וְאֶחָד נֹשֵׂא שְׁלֹשֶׁת כִּכְּרוֹת לֶחֶם וְאֶחָד נֹשֵׂא נֵבֶל־יָיִן:

4 They will greet you and offer you two loaves of bread, which you shall accept.

ד וְשָׁאֲלוּ לְךָ לְשָׁלוֹם וְנָתְנוּ לְךָ שְׁתֵּי־לֶחֶם וְלָקַחְתָּ מִיָּדָם:

Rachel's Tomb in Beit Lechem

10:2 You will meet two men near the tomb of Rachel Already in biblical times, the tomb of *Rachel* was a well-known landmark for the Israelites. Ever since *Yaakov* buried his beloved wife *Rachel* (Genesis 35:19), the Children of Israel have prayed at this holy site. According to the Sages, *Yosef* stopped to pray at his mother's grave on his way down to Egypt, and when the Children of Israel were exiled from the land, they also passed by *Rachel*'s tomb and she cried to God on their behalf, saving them from complete destruction. During the period of Turkish rule over the Land of Israel, Sir Moses Montefiore renovated the tomb and constructed the domed building that covers the site in Bethlehem until today. *Rachel*'s Tomb was one of the holy places liberated by Israel in the Six Day War, and is again a site of prayer for the Jewish people.

Shmuel I/I Samuel
Chapter 10

5 After that, you are to go on to the Hill of *Hashem*, where the Philistine prefects reside. There, as you enter the town, you will encounter a band of *Neviim* coming down from the shrine, preceded by lyres, timbrels, flutes, and harps, and they will be speaking in ecstasy.

6 The spirit of *Hashem* will grip you, and you will speak in ecstasy along with them; you will become another man.

7 And once these signs have happened to you, act when the occasion arises, for *Hashem* is with you.

8 After that, you are to go down to *Gilgal* ahead of me, and I will come down to you to present burnt offerings and offer sacrifices of well-being. Wait seven days until I come to you and instruct you what you are to do next."

9 As [*Shaul*] turned around to leave *Shmuel*, *Hashem* gave him another heart; and all those signs were fulfilled that same day.

10 And when they came there, to the Hill, he saw a band of *Neviim* coming toward him. Thereupon the spirit of *Hashem* gripped him, and he spoke in ecstasy among them.

11 When all who knew him previously saw him speaking in ecstasy together with the *Neviim*, the people said to one another, "What's happened to the son of *Keesh*? Is *Shaul* too among the *Neviim*?"

12 But another person there spoke up and said, "And who are their fathers?" Thus the proverb arose: "Is *Shaul* too among the *Neviim*?"

13 And when he stopped speaking in ecstasy, he entered the shrine.

14 *Shaul*'s uncle asked him and his servant, "Where did you go?" "To look for the asses," he replied. "And when we saw that they were not to be found, we went to *Shmuel*."

15 "Tell me," said *Shaul*'s uncle, "what did *Shmuel* say to you?"

16 *Shaul* answered his uncle, "He just told us that the asses had been found." But he did not tell him anything of what *Shmuel* had said about the kingship.

שמואל א
פרק י

ה אַחַר כֵּן תָּבוֹא גִּבְעַת הָאֱלֹהִים אֲשֶׁר־שָׁם נְצִבֵי פְלִשְׁתִּים וִיהִי כְבֹאֲךָ שָׁם הָעִיר וּפָגַעְתָּ חֶבֶל נְבִיאִים יֹרְדִים מֵהַבָּמָה וְלִפְנֵיהֶם נֵבֶל וְתֹף וְחָלִיל וְכִנּוֹר וְהֵמָּה מִתְנַבְּאִים:

ו וְצָלְחָה עָלֶיךָ רוּחַ יְהוָה וְהִתְנַבִּיתָ עִמָּם וְנֶהְפַּכְתָּ לְאִישׁ אַחֵר:

ז וְהָיָה כִּי תבאינה [תָבֹאנָה] הָאֹתוֹת הָאֵלֶּה לָךְ עֲשֵׂה לְךָ אֲשֶׁר תִּמְצָא יָדֶךָ כִּי הָאֱלֹהִים עִמָּךְ:

ח וְיָרַדְתָּ לְפָנַי הַגִּלְגָּל וְהִנֵּה אָנֹכִי יֹרֵד אֵלֶיךָ לְהַעֲלוֹת עֹלוֹת לִזְבֹּחַ זִבְחֵי שְׁלָמִים שִׁבְעַת יָמִים תּוֹחֵל עַד־בּוֹאִי אֵלֶיךָ וְהוֹדַעְתִּי לְךָ אֵת אֲשֶׁר תַּעֲשֶׂה:

ט וְהָיָה כְּהַפְנֹתוֹ שִׁכְמוֹ לָלֶכֶת מֵעִם שְׁמוּאֵל וַיַּהֲפָךְ־לוֹ אֱלֹהִים לֵב אַחֵר וַיָּבֹאוּ כָּל־הָאֹתוֹת הָאֵלֶּה בַּיּוֹם הַהוּא:

י וַיָּבֹאוּ שָׁם הַגִּבְעָתָה וְהִנֵּה חֶבֶל־נְבִאִים לִקְרָאתוֹ וַתִּצְלַח עָלָיו רוּחַ אֱלֹהִים וַיִּתְנַבֵּא בְּתוֹכָם:

יא וַיְהִי כָּל־יוֹדְעוֹ מֵאִתְּמוֹל שִׁלְשׁוֹם וַיִּרְאוּ וְהִנֵּה עִם־נְבִאִים נִבָּא וַיֹּאמֶר הָעָם אִישׁ אֶל־רֵעֵהוּ מַה־זֶּה הָיָה לְבֶן־קִישׁ הֲגַם שָׁאוּל בַּנְּבִיאִים:

יב וַיַּעַן אִישׁ מִשָּׁם וַיֹּאמֶר וּמִי אֲבִיהֶם עַל־כֵּן הָיְתָה לְמָשָׁל הֲגַם שָׁאוּל בַּנְּבִאִים:

יג וַיְכַל מֵהִתְנַבּוֹת וַיָּבֹא הַבָּמָה:

יד וַיֹּאמֶר דּוֹד שָׁאוּל אֵלָיו וְאֶל־נַעֲרוֹ אָן הֲלַכְתֶּם וַיֹּאמֶר לְבַקֵּשׁ אֶת־הָאֲתֹנוֹת וַנִּרְאֶה כִי־אַיִן וַנָּבוֹא אֶל־שְׁמוּאֵל:

טו וַיֹּאמֶר דּוֹד שָׁאוּל הַגִּידָה־נָּא לִי מָה־אָמַר לָכֶם שְׁמוּאֵל:

טז וַיֹּאמֶר שָׁאוּל אֶל־דּוֹדוֹ הַגֵּד הִגִּיד לָנוּ כִּי נִמְצְאוּ הָאֲתֹנוֹת וְאֶת־דְּבַר הַמְּלוּכָה לֹא־הִגִּיד לוֹ אֲשֶׁר אָמַר שְׁמוּאֵל:

Shmuel I/I Samuel

Chapter 11

שמואל א

פרק יא

17 *Shmuel* summoned the people to *Hashem* at *Mitzpa*

יז וַיַּצְעֵ֧ק שְׁמוּאֵ֛ל אֶת־הָעָ֖ם אֶל־יְהֹוָ֑ה הַמִּצְפָּֽה׃

18 and said to them, "Thus said *Hashem*, the God of *Yisrael*: 'I brought *Yisrael* out of Egypt, and I delivered you from the hands of the Egyptians and of all the kingdoms that oppressed you.'

יח וַיֹּ֣אמֶר ׀ אֶל־בְּנֵ֣י יִשְׂרָאֵ֗ל כֹּֽה־אָמַ֤ר יְהֹוָה֙ אֱלֹהֵ֣י יִשְׂרָאֵ֔ל אָנֹכִ֛י הֶעֱלֵ֥יתִי אֶת־יִשְׂרָאֵ֖ל מִמִּצְרָ֑יִם וָאַצִּ֤יל אֶתְכֶם֙ מִיַּ֣ד מִצְרַ֔יִם וּמִיַּ֖ד כׇּל־הַמַּמְלָכ֥וֹת הַלֹּחֲצִ֥ים אֶתְכֶֽם׃

19 But today you have rejected your God who delivered you from all your troubles and calamities. For you said, 'No, set up a king over us!' Now station yourselves before *Hashem*, by your tribes and clans."

יט וְאַתֶּ֨ם הַיּ֜וֹם מְאַסְתֶּ֣ם אֶת־אֱלֹהֵיכֶ֗ם אֲשֶׁר־ה֣וּא מוֹשִׁ֣יעַ לָכֶם֮ מִכׇּל־רָעֽוֹתֵיכֶ֣ם וְצָרֹֽתֵיכֶם֒ וַתֹּ֣אמְרוּ ל֔וֹ כִּי־מֶ֖לֶךְ תָּשִׂ֣ים עָלֵ֑ינוּ וְעַתָּ֗ה הִֽתְיַצְּבוּ֙ לִפְנֵ֣י יְהֹוָ֔ה לְשִׁבְטֵיכֶ֖ם וּלְאַלְפֵיכֶֽם׃

20 *Shmuel* brought forward each of the tribes of *Yisrael*, and the lot indicated the tribe of *Binyamin*.

כ וַיַּקְרֵ֣ב שְׁמוּאֵ֔ל אֵ֖ת כׇּל־שִׁבְטֵ֣י יִשְׂרָאֵ֑ל וַיִּלָּכֵ֖ד שֵׁ֥בֶט בִּנְיָמִֽן׃

21 Then *Shmuel* brought forward the tribe of *Binyamin* by its clans, and the clan of the Matrites was indicated; and then *Shaul* son of *Keesh* was indicated. But when they looked for him, he was not to be found.

כא וַיַּקְרֵ֞ב אֶת־שֵׁ֤בֶט בִּנְיָמִן֙ לְמִשְׁפְּחֹתָ֔ו [לְמִשְׁפְּחֹתָֽיו] וַתִּלָּכֵ֖ד מִשְׁפַּ֣חַת הַמַּטְרִ֑י וַיִּלָּכֵד֙ שָׁא֣וּל בֶּן־קִ֔ישׁ וַיְבַקְשֻׁ֖הוּ וְלֹ֥א נִמְצָֽא׃

22 They inquired of *Hashem* again, "Has anyone else come here?" And *Hashem* replied, "Yes; he is hiding among the baggage."

כב וַיִּשְׁאֲלוּ־עוֹד֙ בַּיהֹוָ֔ה הֲבָ֥א ע֖וֹד הֲלֹ֣ם אִ֑ישׁ וַיֹּ֣אמֶר יְהֹוָ֔ה הִנֵּה־ה֥וּא נֶחְבָּ֖א אֶל־הַכֵּלִֽים׃

23 So they ran over and brought him from there; and when he took his place among the people, he stood a head taller than all the people.

כג וַיָּרֻ֙צוּ֙ וַיִּקָּחֻ֣הוּ מִשָּׁ֔ם וַיִּתְיַצֵּ֖ב בְּת֣וֹךְ הָעָ֑ם וַיִּגְבַּהּ֙ מִכׇּל־הָעָ֔ם מִשִּׁכְמ֖וֹ וָמָֽעְלָה׃

24 And *Shmuel* said to the people, "Do you see the one whom *Hashem* has chosen? There is none like him among all the people." And all the people acclaimed him, shouting, "Long live the king!"

כד וַיֹּ֤אמֶר שְׁמוּאֵל֙ אֶל־כׇּל־הָעָ֔ם הַרְּאִיתֶם֙ אֲשֶׁ֣ר בָּחַר־בּ֣וֹ יְהֹוָ֔ה כִּ֛י אֵ֥ין כָּמֹ֖הוּ בְּכׇל־הָעָ֑ם וַיָּרִ֧עוּ כׇל־הָעָ֛ם וַיֹּאמְר֖וּ יְחִ֥י הַמֶּֽלֶךְ׃

25 *Shmuel* expounded to the people the rules of the monarchy, and recorded them in a document which he deposited before *Hashem*. *Shmuel* then sent the people back to their homes.

כה וַיְדַבֵּ֨ר שְׁמוּאֵ֜ל אֶל־הָעָ֗ם אֵ֚ת מִשְׁפַּ֣ט הַמְּלֻכָ֔ה וַיִּכְתֹּ֣ב בַּסֵּ֔פֶר וַיַּנַּ֖ח לִפְנֵ֣י יְהֹוָ֑ה וַיְשַׁלַּ֧ח שְׁמוּאֵ֛ל אֶת־כׇּל־הָעָ֖ם אִ֥ישׁ לְבֵיתֽוֹ׃

26 *Shaul* also went home to *Giva*, accompanied by upstanding men whose hearts *Hashem* had touched.

כו וְגַ֨ם־שָׁא֔וּל הָלַ֥ךְ לְבֵית֖וֹ גִּבְעָ֑תָה וַיֵּלְכ֣וּ עִמּ֔וֹ הַחַ֕יִל אֲשֶׁר־נָגַ֥ע אֱלֹהִ֖ים בְּלִבָּֽם׃

27 But some scoundrels said, "How can this fellow save us?" So they scorned him and brought him no gift. But he pretended not to mind.

כז וּבְנֵ֧י בְלִיַּ֣עַל אָמְר֗וּ מַה־יֹּשִׁעֵ֙נוּ֙ זֶ֔ה וַיִּבְזֻ֕הוּ וְלֹא־הֵבִ֥יאוּ ל֖וֹ מִנְחָ֑ה וַיְהִ֖י כְּמַחֲרִֽישׁ׃

11 1 Nahash the Ammonite marched up and besieged Jabesh-gilead. All the men of Jabesh-gilead said to Nahash, "Make a pact with us, and we will serve you."

יא א וַיַּ֗עַל נָחָשׁ֙ הָעַמּוֹנִ֔י וַיִּ֖חַן עַל־יָבֵ֣שׁ גִּלְעָ֑ד וַיֹּ֨אמְר֜וּ כׇּל־אַנְשֵׁ֤י יָבֵישׁ֙ אֶל־נָחָ֔שׁ כְּרׇת־לָ֥נוּ בְרִ֖ית וְנַעַבְדֶֽךָּ׃

Shmuel I / I Samuel
Chapter 11

2 But Nahash the Ammonite answered them, "I will make a pact with you on this condition, that everyone's right eye be gouged out; I will make this a humiliation for all *Yisrael*."

3 The elders of Jabesh said to him, "Give us seven days' respite, so that we may send messengers throughout the territory of *Yisrael*; if no one comes to our aid, we will surrender to you."

4 When the messengers came to *Giva* of *Shaul* and gave this report in the hearing of the people, all the people broke into weeping.

5 *Shaul* was just coming from the field driving the cattle; and *Shaul* asked, "Why are the people crying?" And they told him about the situation of the men of Jabesh.

6 When he heard these things, the spirit of *Hashem* gripped *Shaul* and his anger blazed up.

7 He took a yoke of oxen and cut them into pieces, which he sent by messengers throughout the territory of *Yisrael*, with the warning, "Thus shall be done to the cattle of anyone who does not follow *Shaul* and *Shmuel* into battle!" Terror from *Hashem* fell upon the people, and they came out as one man.

8 [*Shaul*] mustered them in Bezek, and the Israelites numbered 300,000, the men of *Yehuda* 30,000.

9 The messengers who had come were told, "Thus shall you speak to the men of Jabesh-gilead: Tomorrow, when the sun grows hot, you shall be saved." When the messengers came and told this to the men of Jabesh-gilead, they rejoiced.

10 The men of Jabesh then told [the Ammonites], "Tomorrow we will surrender to you, and you can do to us whatever you please."

11 The next day, *Shaul* divided the troops into three columns; at the morning watch they entered the camp and struck down the Ammonites until the day grew hot. The survivors scattered; no two were left together.

12 The people then said to *Shmuel*, "Who was it said, 'Shall *Shaul* be king over us?' Hand the men over and we will put them to death!"

שמואל א

פרק יא

ב וַיֹּאמֶר אֲלֵיהֶם נָחָשׁ הָעַמּוֹנִי בְּזֹאת אֶכְרֹת לָכֶם בִּנְקוֹר לָכֶם כָּל־עֵין יָמִין וְשַׂמְתִּיהָ חֶרְפָּה עַל־כָּל־יִשְׂרָאֵל:

ג וַיֹּאמְרוּ אֵלָיו זִקְנֵי יָבֵישׁ הֶרֶף לָנוּ שִׁבְעַת יָמִים וְנִשְׁלְחָה מַלְאָכִים בְּכֹל גְּבוּל יִשְׂרָאֵל וְאִם־אֵין מוֹשִׁיעַ אֹתָנוּ וְיָצָאנוּ אֵלֶיךָ:

ד וַיָּבֹאוּ הַמַּלְאָכִים גִּבְעַת שָׁאוּל וַיְדַבְּרוּ הַדְּבָרִים בְּאָזְנֵי הָעָם וַיִּשְׂאוּ כָל־הָעָם אֶת־קוֹלָם וַיִּבְכּוּ:

ה וְהִנֵּה שָׁאוּל בָּא אַחֲרֵי הַבָּקָר מִן־הַשָּׂדֶה וַיֹּאמֶר שָׁאוּל מַה־לָּעָם כִּי יִבְכּוּ וַיְסַפְּרוּ־לוֹ אֶת־דִּבְרֵי אַנְשֵׁי יָבֵישׁ:

ו וַתִּצְלַח רוּחַ־אֱלֹהִים עַל־שָׁאוּל בְּשָׁמְעוֹ [כְּשָׁמְעוֹ] אֶת־הַדְּבָרִים הָאֵלֶּה וַיִּחַר אַפּוֹ מְאֹד:

ז וַיִּקַּח צֶמֶד בָּקָר וַיְנַתְּחֵהוּ וַיְשַׁלַּח בְּכָל־גְּבוּל יִשְׂרָאֵל בְּיַד הַמַּלְאָכִים לֵאמֹר אֲשֶׁר אֵינֶנּוּ יֹצֵא אַחֲרֵי שָׁאוּל וְאַחַר שְׁמוּאֵל כֹּה יֵעָשֶׂה לִבְקָרוֹ וַיִּפֹּל פַּחַד־יְהוָה עַל־הָעָם וַיֵּצְאוּ כְּאִישׁ אֶחָד:

ח וַיִּפְקְדֵם בְּבָזֶק וַיִּהְיוּ בְנֵי־יִשְׂרָאֵל שְׁלֹשׁ מֵאוֹת אֶלֶף וְאִישׁ יְהוּדָה שְׁלֹשִׁים אָלֶף:

ט וַיֹּאמְרוּ לַמַּלְאָכִים הַבָּאִים כֹּה תֹאמְרוּן לְאִישׁ יָבֵישׁ גִּלְעָד מָחָר תִּהְיֶה־לָכֶם תְּשׁוּעָה בחם [כְּחֹם] הַשָּׁמֶשׁ וַיָּבֹאוּ הַמַּלְאָכִים וַיַּגִּידוּ לְאַנְשֵׁי יָבֵישׁ וַיִּשְׂמָחוּ:

י וַיֹּאמְרוּ אַנְשֵׁי יָבֵישׁ מָחָר נֵצֵא אֲלֵיכֶם וַעֲשִׂיתֶם לָנוּ כְּכָל־הַטּוֹב בְּעֵינֵיכֶם:

יא וַיְהִי מִמָּחֳרָת וַיָּשֶׂם שָׁאוּל אֶת־הָעָם שְׁלֹשָׁה רָאשִׁים וַיָּבֹאוּ בְתוֹךְ־הַמַּחֲנֶה בְּאַשְׁמֹרֶת הַבֹּקֶר וַיַּכּוּ אֶת־עַמּוֹן עַד־חֹם הַיּוֹם וַיְהִי הַנִּשְׁאָרִים וַיָּפֻצוּ וְלֹא נִשְׁאֲרוּ־בָם שְׁנַיִם יָחַד:

יב וַיֹּאמֶר הָעָם אֶל־שְׁמוּאֵל מִי הָאֹמֵר שָׁאוּל יִמְלֹךְ עָלֵינוּ תְּנוּ הָאֲנָשִׁים וּנְמִיתֵם:

682

Shmuel I / I Samuel
Chapter 12

שמואל א
פרק יב

13 But *Shaul* replied, "No man shall be put to death this day! For this day *Hashem* has brought victory to *Yisrael*."

יג וַיֹּאמֶר שָׁאוּל לֹא־יוּמַת אִישׁ בַּיּוֹם הַזֶּה כִּי הַיּוֹם עָשָׂה־יְהֹוָה תְּשׁוּעָה בְּיִשְׂרָאֵל:

14 *Shmuel* said to the people, "Come, let us go to *Gilgal* and there inaugurate the monarchy."

יד וַיֹּאמֶר שְׁמוּאֵל אֶל־הָעָם לְכוּ וְנֵלְכָה הַגִּלְגָּל וּנְחַדֵּשׁ שָׁם הַמְּלוּכָה:

va-YO-mer sh'-mu-AYL el ha-AM l'-KHU v'-nay-l'-KHAH ha-gil-GAL un-kha-DAYSH SHAM ha-m'-lu-KHAH

15 So all the people went to *Gilgal*, and there at *Gilgal* they declared *Shaul* king before *Hashem*. They offered sacrifices of well-being there before *Hashem*; and *Shaul* and all the men of *Yisrael* held a great celebration there.

טו וַיֵּלְכוּ כָל־הָעָם הַגִּלְגָּל וַיַּמְלִכוּ שָׁם אֶת־שָׁאוּל לִפְנֵי יְהֹוָה בַּגִּלְגָּל וַיִּזְבְּחוּ־שָׁם זְבָחִים שְׁלָמִים לִפְנֵי יְהֹוָה וַיִּשְׂמַח שָׁם שָׁאוּל וְכָל־אַנְשֵׁי יִשְׂרָאֵל עַד־מְאֹד:

12

1 Then *Shmuel* said to all *Yisrael*, "I have yielded to you in all you have asked of me and have set a king over you.

א וַיֹּאמֶר שְׁמוּאֵל אֶל־כָּל־יִשְׂרָאֵל הִנֵּה שָׁמַעְתִּי בְקֹלְכֶם לְכֹל אֲשֶׁר־אֲמַרְתֶּם לִי וָאַמְלִיךְ עֲלֵיכֶם מֶלֶךְ:

2 Henceforth the king will be your leader. "As for me, I have grown old and gray – but my sons are still with you – and I have been your leader from my youth to this day.

ב וְעַתָּה הִנֵּה הַמֶּלֶךְ מִתְהַלֵּךְ לִפְנֵיכֶם וַאֲנִי זָקַנְתִּי וָשַׂבְתִּי וּבָנַי הִנָּם אִתְּכֶם וַאֲנִי הִתְהַלַּכְתִּי לִפְנֵיכֶם מִנְּעֻרַי עַד־הַיּוֹם הַזֶּה:

3 Here I am! Testify against me, in the presence of *Hashem* and in the presence of His anointed one: Whose ox have I taken, or whose ass have I taken? Whom have I defrauded or whom have I robbed? From whom have I taken a bribe to look the other way? I will return it to you."

ג הִנְנִי עֲנוּ בִי נֶגֶד יְהֹוָה וְנֶגֶד מְשִׁיחוֹ אֶת־שׁוֹר מִי לָקַחְתִּי וַחֲמוֹר מִי לָקַחְתִּי וְאֶת־מִי עָשַׁקְתִּי אֶת־מִי רַצּוֹתִי וּמִיַּד־מִי לָקַחְתִּי כֹפֶר וְאַעְלִים עֵינַי בּוֹ וְאָשִׁיב לָכֶם:

4 They responded, "You have not defrauded us, and you have not robbed us, and you have taken nothing from anyone."

ד וַיֹּאמְרוּ לֹא עֲשַׁקְתָּנוּ וְלֹא רַצּוֹתָנוּ וְלֹא־לָקַחְתָּ מִיַּד־אִישׁ מְאוּמָה:

5 He said to them, "*Hashem* then is witness, and His anointed is witness, to your admission this day that you have found nothing in my possession." They responded, "He is!"

ה וַיֹּאמֶר אֲלֵיהֶם עֵד יְהֹוָה בָּכֶם וְעֵד מְשִׁיחוֹ הַיּוֹם הַזֶּה כִּי לֹא מְצָאתֶם בְּיָדִי מְאוּמָה וַיֹּאמֶר עֵד:

6 *Shmuel* said to the people, "*Hashem* [is witness], He who appointed *Moshe* and *Aharon* and who brought your fathers out of the land of Egypt.

ו וַיֹּאמֶר שְׁמוּאֵל אֶל־הָעָם יְהֹוָה אֲשֶׁר עָשָׂה אֶת־מֹשֶׁה וְאֶת־אַהֲרֹן וַאֲשֶׁר הֶעֱלָה אֶת־אֲבֹתֵיכֶם מֵאֶרֶץ מִצְרָיִם:

Rashi (1040–1105)

11:14 *Shmuel* said to the people *Shmuel* tells the people it is time to renew the monarchy, which leads to a second coronation of King *Shaul* and great rejoicing. *Rashi* explains the need for this renewal: Previously, not everyone had acquiesced to *Shaul*'s appointment. At this point, though, the entire nation willingly agrees. Monarchy, like all just forms of governments, requires the consent of the governed. Therefore, it is not surprising that Israel's government in the contemporary pre-messianic era is a democracy. In fact, it is the only democracy in a region of autocracies and theocracies.

Shmuel I/I Samuel
Chapter 12

שמואל א
פרק יב

7 Come, stand before *Hashem* while I cite against you all the kindnesses that *Hashem* has done to you and your fathers.

ז וְעַתָּה הִתְיַצְּבוּ וְאִשָּׁפְטָה אִתְּכֶם לִפְנֵי יְהוָה אֵת כָּל־צִדְקוֹת יְהוָה אֲשֶׁר־עָשָׂה אִתְּכֶם וְאֶת־אֲבוֹתֵיכֶם:

8 "When *Yaakov* came to Egypt, your fathers cried out to *Hashem*, and *Hashem* sent *Moshe* and *Aharon*, who brought your fathers out of Egypt and settled them in this place.

ח כַּאֲשֶׁר־בָּא יַעֲקֹב מִצְרָיִם וַיִּזְעֲקוּ אֲבוֹתֵיכֶם אֶל־יְהוָה וַיִּשְׁלַח יְהוָה אֶת־מֹשֶׁה וְאֶת־אַהֲרֹן וַיּוֹצִיאוּ אֶת־אֲבֹתֵיכֶם מִמִּצְרַיִם וַיֹּשִׁבוּם בַּמָּקוֹם הַזֶּה:

9 But they forgot *Hashem* their God; so He delivered them into the hands of Sisera the military commander of Hazor, into the hands of the Philistines, and into the hands of the kind of Moab; and these made war upon them.

ט וַיִּשְׁכְּחוּ אֶת־יְהוָה אֱלֹהֵיהֶם וַיִּמְכֹּר אֹתָם בְּיַד סִיסְרָא שַׂר־צְבָא חָצוֹר וּבְיַד־פְּלִשְׁתִּים וּבְיַד מֶלֶךְ מוֹאָב וַיִּלָּחֲמוּ בָּם:

10 They cried to *Hashem*, 'We are guilty, for we have forsaken *Hashem* and worshiped the Baalim and Ashtaroth. Oh, deliver us from our enemies and we will serve You.'

י וַיִּזְעֲקוּ אֶל־יְהוָה וַיֹּאמֶר [וַיֹּאמְרוּ] חָטָאנוּ כִּי עָזַבְנוּ אֶת־יְהוָה וַנַּעֲבֹד אֶת־הַבְּעָלִים וְאֶת־הָעַשְׁתָּרוֹת וְעַתָּה הַצִּילֵנוּ מִיַּד אֹיְבֵינוּ וְנַעַבְדֶךָּ:

11 And *Hashem* sent *Yerubaal* and Bedan and *Yiftach* and *Shmuel*, and delivered you from the enemies around you; and you dwelt in security.

יא וַיִּשְׁלַח יְהוָה אֶת־יְרֻבַּעַל וְאֶת־בְּדָן וְאֶת־יִפְתָּח וְאֶת־שְׁמוּאֵל וַיַּצֵּל אֶתְכֶם מִיַּד אֹיְבֵיכֶם מִסָּבִיב וַתֵּשְׁבוּ בֶּטַח:

12 But when you saw that Nahash king of the Ammonites was advancing against you, you said to me, 'No, we must have a king reigning over us' – though *Hashem* your God is your King.

יב וַתִּרְאוּ כִּי־נָחָשׁ מֶלֶךְ בְּנֵי־עַמּוֹן בָּא עֲלֵיכֶם וַתֹּאמְרוּ לִי לֹא כִּי־מֶלֶךְ יִמְלֹךְ עָלֵינוּ וַיהוָה אֱלֹהֵיכֶם מַלְכְּכֶם:

13 "Well, *Hashem* has set a king over you! Here is the king that you have chosen, that you have asked for.

יג וְעַתָּה הִנֵּה הַמֶּלֶךְ אֲשֶׁר בְּחַרְתֶּם אֲשֶׁר שְׁאֶלְתֶּם וְהִנֵּה נָתַן יְהוָה עֲלֵיכֶם מֶלֶךְ:

14 "If you will revere *Hashem*, worship Him, and obey Him, and will not flout *Hashem*'s command, if both you and the king who reigns over you will follow *Hashem* your God, [well and good].

יד אִם־תִּירְאוּ אֶת־יְהוָה וַעֲבַדְתֶּם אֹתוֹ וּשְׁמַעְתֶּם בְּקֹלוֹ וְלֹא תַמְרוּ אֶת־פִּי יְהוָה וִהְיִתֶם גַּם־אַתֶּם וְגַם־הַמֶּלֶךְ אֲשֶׁר מָלַךְ עֲלֵיכֶם אַחַר יְהוָה אֱלֹהֵיכֶם:

im tee-r'-U et a-do-NAI va-a-vad-TEM o-TO u-sh'-ma-TEM b'-ko-LO v'-LO tam-RU et PEE a-do-NAI vih-yi-TEM gam a-TEM v'-GAM ha-ME-lekh a-sher ma-LAKH a-lay-KHEM a-KHAR a-do-NAI e-lo-hay-KHEM

12:14 If you will revere *Hashem*, worship Him, and obey Him The prophet *Shmuel* clarifies to the people that the key to their success will not be their king, but rather their observance of *Hashem*'s commandments. As *Rashi* explains, observance of the laws will mean that the People of Israel and its king all live to ripe, old ages. This theme is repeated frequently in the *Tanakh*. In order for the Children of Israel to be able to live as a free nation in the Land of Israel, they must observe God's *Torah*. This is a reminder that their goal is not merely to be free, but rather to be a holy and free nation in *Eretz Yisrael*. If they do not aspire to this objective, the land will not tolerate their sins and will eventually spit them out (Leviticus 18:26–30).

Shmuel I / I Samuel
Chapter 13

15 But if you do not obey *Hashem* and you flout *Hashem*'s command, the hand of *Hashem* will strike you as it did your fathers.

16 "Now stand by and see the marvelous thing that *Hashem* will do before your eyes.

17 It is the season of the wheat harvest. I will pray to *Hashem* and He will send thunder and rain; then you will take thought and realize what a wicked thing you did in the sight of *Hashem* when you asked for a king."

18 *Shmuel* prayed to *Hashem*, and *Hashem* sent thunder and rain that day, and the people stood in awe of *Hashem* and of *Shmuel*.

19 The people all said to *Shmuel*, "Intercede for your servants with *Hashem* your God that we may not die, for we have added to all our sins the wickedness of asking for a king."

20 But *Shmuel* said to the people, "Have no fear. You have, indeed, done all those wicked things. Do not, however, turn away from *Hashem*, but serve *Hashem* with all your heart.

21 Do not turn away to follow worthless things, which can neither profit nor save but are worthless.

22 For the sake of His great name, *Hashem* will never abandon His people, seeing that *Hashem* undertook to make you His people.

23 "As for me, far be it from me to sin against *Hashem* and refrain from praying for you; and I will continue to instruct you in the practice of what is good and right.

24 Above all, you must revere *Hashem* and serve Him faithfully with all your heart; and consider how grandly He has dealt with you.

25 For if you persist in your wrongdoing, both you and your king shall be swept away."

13 1 *Shaul* was … years old when he became king, and he reigned over *Yisrael* two years.

2 *Shaul* picked 3,000 Israelites, of whom 2,000 were with *Shaul* in Michmas and in the hill country of *Beit El*, and 1,000 with *Yonatan* in *Giva* of *Binyamin*; the rest of the troops he sent back to their homes.

שמואל א
פרק יג

טו וְאִם־לֹא תִשְׁמְעוּ בְּקוֹל יְהֹוָה וּמְרִיתֶם אֶת־פִּי יְהֹוָה וְהָיְתָה יַד־יְהֹוָה בָּכֶם וּבַאֲבֹתֵיכֶם:

טז גַּם־עַתָּה הִתְיַצְּבוּ וּרְאוּ אֶת־הַדָּבָר הַגָּדוֹל הַזֶּה אֲשֶׁר יְהֹוָה עֹשֶׂה לְעֵינֵיכֶם:

יז הֲלוֹא קְצִיר־חִטִּים הַיּוֹם אֶקְרָא אֶל־יְהֹוָה וְיִתֵּן קֹלוֹת וּמָטָר וּדְעוּ וּרְאוּ כִּי־רָעַתְכֶם רַבָּה אֲשֶׁר עֲשִׂיתֶם בְּעֵינֵי יְהֹוָה לִשְׁאוֹל לָכֶם מֶלֶךְ:

יח וַיִּקְרָא שְׁמוּאֵל אֶל־יְהֹוָה וַיִּתֵּן יְהֹוָה קֹלֹת וּמָטָר בַּיּוֹם הַהוּא וַיִּירָא כָל־הָעָם מְאֹד אֶת־יְהֹוָה וְאֶת־שְׁמוּאֵל:

יט וַיֹּאמְרוּ כָל־הָעָם אֶל־שְׁמוּאֵל הִתְפַּלֵּל בְּעַד־עֲבָדֶיךָ אֶל־יְהֹוָה אֱלֹהֶיךָ וְאַל־נָמוּת כִּי־יָסַפְנוּ עַל־כָּל־חַטֹּאתֵינוּ רָעָה לִשְׁאֹל לָנוּ מֶלֶךְ:

כ וַיֹּאמֶר שְׁמוּאֵל אֶל־הָעָם אַל־תִּירָאוּ אַתֶּם עֲשִׂיתֶם אֵת כָּל־הָרָעָה הַזֹּאת אַךְ אַל־תָּסוּרוּ מֵאַחֲרֵי יְהֹוָה וַעֲבַדְתֶּם אֶת־יְהֹוָה בְּכָל־לְבַבְכֶם:

כא וְלֹא תָּסוּרוּ כִּי אַחֲרֵי הַתֹּהוּ אֲשֶׁר לֹא־יוֹעִילוּ וְלֹא יַצִּילוּ כִּי־תֹהוּ הֵמָּה:

כב כִּי לֹא־יִטֹּשׁ יְהֹוָה אֶת־עַמּוֹ בַּעֲבוּר שְׁמוֹ הַגָּדוֹל כִּי הוֹאִיל יְהֹוָה לַעֲשׂוֹת אֶתְכֶם לוֹ לְעָם:

כג גַּם אָנֹכִי חָלִילָה לִּי מֵחֲטֹא לַיהֹוָה מֵחֲדֹל לְהִתְפַּלֵּל בַּעַדְכֶם וְהוֹרֵיתִי אֶתְכֶם בְּדֶרֶךְ הַטּוֹבָה וְהַיְשָׁרָה:

כד אַךְ יְראוּ אֶת־יְהֹוָה וַעֲבַדְתֶּם אֹתוֹ בֶּאֱמֶת בְּכָל־לְבַבְכֶם כִּי רְאוּ אֵת אֲשֶׁר־הִגְדִּל עִמָּכֶם:

כה וְאִם־הָרֵעַ תָּרֵעוּ גַּם־אַתֶּם גַּם־מַלְכְּכֶם תִּסָּפוּ:

יג א בֶּן־שָׁנָה שָׁאוּל בְּמָלְכוֹ וּשְׁתֵּי שָׁנִים מָלַךְ עַל־יִשְׂרָאֵל:

ב וַיִּבְחַר־לוֹ שָׁאוּל שְׁלֹשֶׁת אֲלָפִים מִיִּשְׂרָאֵל וַיִּהְיוּ עִם־שָׁאוּל אַלְפַּיִם בְּמִכְמָשׂ וּבְהַר בֵּית־אֵל וְאֶלֶף הָיוּ עִם־יוֹנָתָן בְּגִבְעַת בִּנְיָמִין וְיֶתֶר הָעָם שִׁלַּח אִישׁ לְאֹהָלָיו:

Shmuel I / I Samuel
Chapter 13

שמואל א
פרק יג

3 *Yonatan* struck down the Philistine prefect in Geba; and the Philistines heard about it. *Shaul* had the *shofar* sounded throughout the land, saying, "Let the Hebrews hear."

ג וַיַּךְ יוֹנָתָן אֵת נְצִיב פְּלִשְׁתִּים אֲשֶׁר בְּגֶבַע וַיִּשְׁמְעוּ פְּלִשְׁתִּים וְשָׁאוּל תָּקַע בַּשּׁוֹפָר בְּכָל־הָאָרֶץ לֵאמֹר יִשְׁמְעוּ הָעִבְרִים׃

4 When all *Yisrael* heard that *Shaul* had struck down the Philistine prefect, and that *Yisrael* had incurred the wrath of the Philistines, all the people rallied to *Shaul* at *Gilgal*.

ד וְכָל־יִשְׂרָאֵל שָׁמְעוּ לֵאמֹר הִכָּה שָׁאוּל אֶת־נְצִיב פְּלִשְׁתִּים וְגַם־נִבְאַשׁ יִשְׂרָאֵל בַּפְּלִשְׁתִּים וַיִּצָּעֲקוּ הָעָם אַחֲרֵי שָׁאוּל הַגִּלְגָּל׃

5 The Philistines, in turn, gathered to attack *Yisrael*: 30,000 chariots and 6,000 horsemen, and troops as numerous as the sands of the seashore. They marched up and encamped at Michmas, east of *Beit Aven*.

ה וּפְלִשְׁתִּים נֶאֶסְפוּ לְהִלָּחֵם עִם־יִשְׂרָאֵל שְׁלֹשִׁים אֶלֶף רֶכֶב וְשֵׁשֶׁת אֲלָפִים פָּרָשִׁים וְעָם כַּחוֹל אֲשֶׁר עַל־שְׂפַת־הַיָּם לָרֹב וַיַּעֲלוּ וַיַּחֲנוּ בְמִכְמָשׂ קִדְמַת בֵּית אָוֶן׃

6 When the men of *Yisrael* saw that they were in trouble – for the troops were hard pressed – the people hid in caves, among thorns, among rocks, in tunnels, and in cisterns.

ו וְאִישׁ יִשְׂרָאֵל רָאוּ כִּי צַר־לוֹ כִּי נִגַּשׂ הָעָם וַיִּתְחַבְּאוּ הָעָם בַּמְּעָרוֹת וּבַחֲוָחִים וּבַסְּלָעִים וּבַצְּרִחִים וּבַבֹּרוֹת׃

7 Some Hebrews crossed the *Yarden*, [to] the territory of *Gad* and *Gilad*. *Shaul* was still at *Gilgal*, and the rest of the people rallied to him in alarm.

ז וְעִבְרִים עָבְרוּ אֶת־הַיַּרְדֵּן אֶרֶץ גָּד וְגִלְעָד וְשָׁאוּל עוֹדֶנּוּ בַגִּלְגָּל וְכָל־הָעָם חָרְדוּ אַחֲרָיו׃

8 He waited seven days, the time that *Shmuel* [had set]. But when *Shmuel* failed to come to *Gilgal*, and the people began to scatter,

ח וַיּוֹחֶל [וַיּוֹחֶל] שִׁבְעַת יָמִים לַמּוֹעֵד אֲשֶׁר שְׁמוּאֵל וְלֹא־בָא שְׁמוּאֵל הַגִּלְגָּל וַיָּפֶץ הָעָם מֵעָלָיו׃

9 *Shaul* said, "Bring me the burnt offering and the sacrifice of well-being"; and he presented the burnt offering.

ט וַיֹּאמֶר שָׁאוּל הַגִּשׁוּ אֵלַי הָעֹלָה וְהַשְּׁלָמִים וַיַּעַל הָעֹלָה׃

10 He had just finished presenting the burnt offering when *Shmuel* arrived; and *Shaul* went out to meet him and welcome him.

י וַיְהִי כְּכַלֹּתוֹ לְהַעֲלוֹת הָעֹלָה וְהִנֵּה שְׁמוּאֵל בָּא וַיֵּצֵא שָׁאוּל לִקְרָאתוֹ לְבָרֲכוֹ׃

11 But *Shmuel* said, "What have you done?" *Shaul* replied, "I saw the people leaving me and scattering; you had not come at the appointed time, and the Philistines had gathered at Michmas.

יא וַיֹּאמֶר שְׁמוּאֵל מֶה עָשִׂיתָ וַיֹּאמֶר שָׁאוּל כִּי־רָאִיתִי כִי־נָפַץ הָעָם מֵעָלַי וְאַתָּה לֹא־בָאתָ לְמוֹעֵד הַיָּמִים וּפְלִשְׁתִּים נֶאֱסָפִים מִכְמָשׂ׃

12 I thought the Philistines would march down against me at *Gilgal* before I had entreated *Hashem*, so I forced myself to present the burnt offering."

יב וָאֹמַר עַתָּה יֵרְדוּ פְלִשְׁתִּים אֵלַי הַגִּלְגָּל וּפְנֵי יְהוָה לֹא חִלִּיתִי וָאֶתְאַפַּק וָאַעֲלֶה הָעֹלָה׃

13 *Shmuel* answered *Shaul*, "You acted foolishly in not keeping the commandments that *Hashem* your God laid upon you! Otherwise *Hashem* would have established your dynasty over *Yisrael* forever.

יג וַיֹּאמֶר שְׁמוּאֵל אֶל־שָׁאוּל נִסְכָּלְתָּ לֹא שָׁמַרְתָּ אֶת־מִצְוַת יְהוָה אֱלֹהֶיךָ אֲשֶׁר צִוָּךְ כִּי עַתָּה הֵכִין יְהוָה אֶת־מַמְלַכְתְּךָ אֶל־יִשְׂרָאֵל עַד־עוֹלָם׃

Shmuel I / I Samuel
Chapter 13

שמואל א
פרק יג

14 But now your dynasty will not endure. *Hashem* will seek out a man after His own heart, and *Hashem* will appoint him ruler over His people, because you did not abide by what *Hashem* had commanded you."

יד וְעַתָּה מַמְלַכְתְּךָ לֹא־תָקוּם בִּקֵּשׁ יְהֹוָה לוֹ אִישׁ כִּלְבָבוֹ וַיְצַוֵּהוּ יְהֹוָה לְנָגִיד עַל־עַמּוֹ כִּי לֹא שָׁמַרְתָּ אֵת אֲשֶׁר־צִוְּךָ יְהֹוָה:

15 *Shmuel* arose and went up from *Gilgal* to *Giva* of *Binyamin*. *Shaul* numbered the troops who remained with him – about 600 strong.

טו וַיָּקָם שְׁמוּאֵל וַיַּעַל מִן־הַגִּלְגָּל גִּבְעַת בִּנְיָמִן וַיִּפְקֹד שָׁאוּל אֶת־הָעָם הַנִּמְצְאִים עִמּוֹ כְּשֵׁשׁ מֵאוֹת אִישׁ:

16 *Shaul* and his son *Yonatan*, and the troops who remained with them, stayed in Geba of *Binyamin*, while the Philistines were encamped at Michmas.

טז וְשָׁאוּל וְיוֹנָתָן בְּנוֹ וְהָעָם הַנִּמְצָא עִמָּם יֹשְׁבִים בְּגֶבַע בִּנְיָמִן וּפְלִשְׁתִּים חָנוּ בְמִכְמָשׂ:

17 The raiders came out of the Philistine camp in three columns: One column headed for the Ophrah road that leads to the district of Shual,

יז וַיֵּצֵא הַמַּשְׁחִית מִמַּחֲנֵה פְלִשְׁתִּים שְׁלֹשָׁה רָאשִׁים הָרֹאשׁ אֶחָד יִפְנֶה אֶל־דֶּרֶךְ עָפְרָה אֶל־אֶרֶץ שׁוּעָל:

18 another column headed for the Beth-horon road, and the third column headed for the border road that overlooks the valley of Zeboim toward the desert.

יח וְהָרֹאשׁ אֶחָד יִפְנֶה דֶּרֶךְ בֵּית חֹרוֹן וְהָרֹאשׁ אֶחָד יִפְנֶה דֶּרֶךְ הַגְּבוּל הַנִּשְׁקָף עַל־גֵּי הַצְּבֹעִים הַמִּדְבָּרָה:

19 No smith was to be found in all the land of *Yisrael*, for the Philistines were afraid that the Hebrews would make swords or spears.

יט וְחָרָשׁ לֹא יִמָּצֵא בְּכֹל אֶרֶץ יִשְׂרָאֵל כִּי־אָמַר [אָמְרוּ] פְלִשְׁתִּים פֶּן יַעֲשׂוּ הָעִבְרִים חֶרֶב אוֹ חֲנִית:

v'- kha-RASH LO yi-ma-TZAY b'-KHOL E-retz yis-ra-AYL kee a-m'-RU f'-lish-TEEM PEN ya-a-SU ha-iv-REEM KHE-rev O kha-NEET

20 So all the Israelites had to go down to the Philistines to have their plowshares, their mattocks, axes, and colters sharpened.

כ וַיֵּרְדוּ כָל־יִשְׂרָאֵל הַפְּלִשְׁתִּים לִלְטוֹשׁ אִישׁ אֶת־מַחֲרַשְׁתּוֹ וְאֶת־אֵתוֹ וְאֶת־קַרְדֻּמּוֹ וְאֵת מַחֲרֵשָׁתוֹ:

21 The charge for sharpening was a *pim* for plowshares, mattocks, three-pronged forks, and axes, and for setting the goads.

כא וְהָיְתָה הַפְּצִירָה פִים לַמַּחֲרֵשֹׁת וְלָאֵתִים וְלִשְׁלֹשׁ קִלְּשׁוֹן וּלְהַקַּרְדֻּמִּים וּלְהַצִּיב הַדָּרְבָן:

13:19 No smith was to be found in all the land of *Yisrael* Under Philistine rule, the People of Israel are not allowed to engage in metal work, as the Philistines are afraid they will use these workshops to make weapons. Therefore, any time the Israelites need metal work, such as for sharpening plows, they have to travel and pay exorbitant prices to have the work done by Philistine craftsmen. Later, this becomes a model for oppressors of the Jews, who would control access to weapons and minimize economic opportunities. During British rule over the Land of Israel, Jews were similarly not allowed to maintain weapons. Like *Shaul* and *Yonatan* who made secret weapons to defend their people, there were brave Jews who secretly imported weapons and made bullets that later became critical in the War of Independence. For example, the Ayalon Institute near Rehovot was the site of a secret bullet factory, hidden under what was officially a *kibbutz* training center. Despite harsh conditions and life-threatening risks in the pre-State days, young Jews worked underground making bullets that would later be used to defend the newborn State of Israel against its enemies.

Ayalon Institute underground bullet factory

Shmuel I / I Samuel
Chapter 14

22 Thus on the day of the battle, no sword or spear was to be found in the possession of any of the troops with *Shaul* and *Yonatan*; only *Shaul* and *Yonatan* had them.

23 Now the Philistine garrison had marched out to the pass of Michmas.

14 1 One day, *Yonatan* son of *Shaul* said to the attendant who carried his arms, "Come, let us cross over to the Philistine garrison on the other side"; but he did not tell his father.

2 Now *Shaul* was staying on the outskirts of *Giva*, under the pomegranate tree at Migron, and the troops with him numbered about 600.

3 *Achiya* son of *Achituv* brother of Ichabod son of *Pinchas* son of *Eli*, the *Kohen* of *Hashem* at *Shilo*, was there bearing an ephod. – The troops did not know that *Yonatan* had gone.

4 At the crossing by which *Yonatan* sought to reach the Philistine garrison, there was a rocky crag on one side, and another rocky crag on the other, the one called Bozez and the other Seneh.

5 One crag was located on the north, near Michmas, and the other on the south, near Geba.

6 *Yehonatan* said to the attendant who carried his arms, "Come, let us cross over to the outpost of those uncircumcised fellows. Perhaps *Hashem* will act in our behalf, for nothing prevents *Hashem* from winning a victory by many or by few."

7 His arms-bearer answered him, "Do whatever you like. You go first, I am with you, whatever you decide."

8 *Yehonatan* said, "We'll cross over to those men and let them see us.

9 If they say to us, 'Wait until we get to you,' then we'll stay where we are, and not go up to them.

10 But if they say, 'Come up to us,' then we will go up, for *Hashem* is delivering them into our hands. That shall be our sign."

11 They both showed themselves to the Philistine outpost and the Philistines said, "Look, some Hebrews are coming out of the holes where they have been hiding."

שמואל א
פרק יד

כב וְהָיָה בְּיוֹם מִלְחֶמֶת וְלֹא נִמְצָא חֶרֶב וַחֲנִית בְּיַד כָּל־הָעָם אֲשֶׁר אֶת־שָׁאוּל וְאֶת־יוֹנָתָן וַתִּמָּצֵא לְשָׁאוּל וּלְיוֹנָתָן בְּנוֹ:

כג וַיֵּצֵא מַצַּב פְּלִשְׁתִּים אֶל־מַעֲבַר מִכְמָשׂ:

יד א וַיְהִי הַיּוֹם וַיֹּאמֶר יוֹנָתָן בֶּן־שָׁאוּל אֶל־הַנַּעַר נֹשֵׂא כֵלָיו לְכָה וְנַעְבְּרָה אֶל־מַצַּב פְּלִשְׁתִּים אֲשֶׁר מֵעֵבֶר הַלָּז וּלְאָבִיו לֹא הִגִּיד:

ב וְשָׁאוּל יוֹשֵׁב בִּקְצֵה הַגִּבְעָה תַּחַת הָרִמּוֹן אֲשֶׁר בְּמִגְרוֹן וְהָעָם אֲשֶׁר עִמּוֹ כְּשֵׁשׁ מֵאוֹת אִישׁ:

ג וַאֲחִיָּה בֶן־אֲחִטוּב אֲחִי אִיכָבוֹד בֶּן־פִּינְחָס בֶּן־עֵלִי כֹּהֵן יְהוָה בְּשִׁלוֹ נֹשֵׂא אֵפוֹד וְהָעָם לֹא יָדַע כִּי הָלַךְ יוֹנָתָן:

ד וּבֵין הַמַּעְבְּרוֹת אֲשֶׁר בִּקֵּשׁ יוֹנָתָן לַעֲבֹר עַל־מַצַּב פְּלִשְׁתִּים שֵׁן־הַסֶּלַע מֵהָעֵבֶר מִזֶּה וְשֵׁן־הַסֶּלַע מֵהָעֵבֶר מִזֶּה וְשֵׁם הָאֶחָד בּוֹצֵץ וְשֵׁם הָאֶחָד סֶנֶּה:

ה הַשֵּׁן הָאֶחָד מָצוּק מִצָּפוֹן מוּל מִכְמָשׂ וְהָאֶחָד מִנֶּגֶב מוּל גָּבַע:

ו וַיֹּאמֶר יְהוֹנָתָן אֶל־הַנַּעַר נֹשֵׂא כֵלָיו לְכָה וְנַעְבְּרָה אֶל־מַצַּב הָעֲרֵלִים הָאֵלֶּה אוּלַי יַעֲשֶׂה יְהוָה לָנוּ כִּי אֵין לַיהוָה מַעְצוֹר לְהוֹשִׁיעַ בְּרַב אוֹ בִמְעָט:

ז וַיֹּאמֶר לוֹ נֹשֵׂא כֵלָיו עֲשֵׂה כָּל־אֲשֶׁר בִּלְבָבֶךָ נְטֵה לָךְ הִנְנִי עִמְּךָ כִּלְבָבֶךָ:

ח וַיֹּאמֶר יְהוֹנָתָן הִנֵּה אֲנַחְנוּ עֹבְרִים אֶל־הָאֲנָשִׁים וְנִגְלִינוּ אֲלֵיהֶם:

ט אִם־כֹּה יֹאמְרוּ אֵלֵינוּ דֹּמּוּ עַד־הַגִּיעֵנוּ אֲלֵיכֶם וְעָמַדְנוּ תַחְתֵּינוּ וְלֹא נַעֲלֶה אֲלֵיהֶם:

י וְאִם־כֹּה יֹאמְרוּ עֲלוּ עָלֵינוּ וְעָלִינוּ כִּי־נְתָנָם יְהוָה בְּיָדֵנוּ וְזֶה־לָּנוּ הָאוֹת:

יא וַיִּגָּלוּ שְׁנֵיהֶם אֶל־מַצַּב פְּלִשְׁתִּים וַיֹּאמְרוּ פְלִשְׁתִּים הִנֵּה עִבְרִים יֹצְאִים מִן־הַחֹרִים אֲשֶׁר הִתְחַבְּאוּ־שָׁם:

Shmuel I / I Samuel
Chapter 14

12 The men of the outpost shouted to *Yonatan* and his arms-bearer, "Come up to us, and we'll teach you a lesson." Then *Yonatan* said to his arms-bearer, "Follow me, for *Hashem* will deliver them into the hands of *Yisrael*."

13 And *Yonatan* clambered up on his hands and feet, his arms-bearer behind him; [the Philistines] fell before *Yonatan*, and his arms-bearer finished them off behind him.

14 The initial attack that *Yonatan* and his arms-bearer made accounted for some twenty men, within a space about half a furrow long [in] an acre of land.

15 Terror broke out among all the troops both in the camp [and] in the field; the outposts and the raiders were also terrified. The very earth quaked, and a terror from *Hashem* ensued.

16 *Shaul*'s scouts in *Giva* of *Binyamin* saw that the multitude was scattering in all directions.

17 And *Shaul* said to the troops with him, "Take a count and see who has left us." They took a count and found that *Yonatan* and his arms-bearer were missing.

18 Thereupon *Shaul* said to *Achiya*, "Bring the *Aron* of *Hashem* here"; for the *Aron* of *Hashem* was at the time among the Israelites.

19 But while *Shaul* was speaking to the *Kohen*, the confusion in the Philistine camp kept increasing; and *Shaul* said to the *Kohen*, "Withdraw your hand."

20 *Shaul* and the troops with him assembled and rushed into battle; they found [the Philistines] in very great confusion, every man's sword turned against his fellow.

21 And the Hebrews who had previously sided with the Philistines, who had come up with them in the army [from] round about – they too joined the Israelites who were with *Shaul* and *Yonatan*.

22 When all the men of *Yisrael* who were hiding in the hill country of *Efraim* heard that the Philistines were fleeing, they too pursued them in battle.

23 Thus *Hashem* brought victory to *Yisrael* that day. The fighting passed beyond *Beit Aven*.

שמואל א
פרק יד

יב וַיַּעֲנוּ אַנְשֵׁי הַמַּצָּבָה אֶת־יוֹנָתָן וְאֶת־נֹשֵׂא כֵלָיו וַיֹּאמְרוּ עֲלוּ אֵלֵינוּ וְנוֹדִיעָה אֶתְכֶם דָּבָר וַיֹּאמֶר יוֹנָתָן אֶל־נֹשֵׂא כֵלָיו עֲלֵה אַחֲרַי כִּי־נְתָנָם יְהוָה בְּיַד יִשְׂרָאֵל:

יג וַיַּעַל יוֹנָתָן עַל־יָדָיו וְעַל־רַגְלָיו וְנֹשֵׂא כֵלָיו אַחֲרָיו וַיִּפְּלוּ לִפְנֵי יוֹנָתָן וְנֹשֵׂא כֵלָיו מְמוֹתֵת אַחֲרָיו:

יד וַתְּהִי הַמַּכָּה הָרִאשֹׁנָה אֲשֶׁר הִכָּה יוֹנָתָן וְנֹשֵׂא כֵלָיו כְּעֶשְׂרִים אִישׁ כְּבַחֲצִי מַעֲנָה צֶמֶד שָׂדֶה:

טו וַתְּהִי חֲרָדָה בַמַּחֲנֶה בַשָּׂדֶה וּבְכָל־הָעָם הַמַּצָּב וְהַמַּשְׁחִית חָרְדוּ גַם־הֵמָּה וַתִּרְגַּז הָאָרֶץ וַתְּהִי לְחֶרְדַּת אֱלֹהִים:

טז וַיִּרְאוּ הַצֹּפִים לְשָׁאוּל בְּגִבְעַת בִּנְיָמִן וְהִנֵּה הֶהָמוֹן נָמוֹג וַיֵּלֶךְ וַהֲלֹם:

יז וַיֹּאמֶר שָׁאוּל לָעָם אֲשֶׁר אִתּוֹ פִּקְדוּ־נָא וּרְאוּ מִי הָלַךְ מֵעִמָּנוּ וַיִּפְקְדוּ וְהִנֵּה אֵין יוֹנָתָן וְנֹשֵׂא כֵלָיו:

יח וַיֹּאמֶר שָׁאוּל לַאֲחִיָּה הַגִּישָׁה אֲרוֹן הָאֱלֹהִים כִּי־הָיָה אֲרוֹן הָאֱלֹהִים בַּיּוֹם הַהוּא וּבְנֵי יִשְׂרָאֵל:

יט וַיְהִי עַד דִּבֶּר שָׁאוּל אֶל־הַכֹּהֵן וְהֶהָמוֹן אֲשֶׁר בְּמַחֲנֵה פְלִשְׁתִּים וַיֵּלֶךְ הָלוֹךְ וָרָב וַיֹּאמֶר שָׁאוּל אֶל־הַכֹּהֵן אֱסֹף יָדֶךָ:

כ וַיִּזָּעֵק שָׁאוּל וְכָל־הָעָם אֲשֶׁר אִתּוֹ וַיָּבֹאוּ עַד־הַמִּלְחָמָה וְהִנֵּה הָיְתָה חֶרֶב אִישׁ בְּרֵעֵהוּ מְהוּמָה גְּדוֹלָה מְאֹד:

כא וְהָעִבְרִים הָיוּ לַפְּלִשְׁתִּים כְּאֶתְמוֹל שִׁלְשׁוֹם אֲשֶׁר עָלוּ עִמָּם בַּמַּחֲנֶה סָבִיב וְגַם־הֵמָּה לִהְיוֹת עִם־יִשְׂרָאֵל אֲשֶׁר עִם־שָׁאוּל וְיוֹנָתָן:

כב וְכֹל אִישׁ יִשְׂרָאֵל הַמִּתְחַבְּאִים בְּהַר־אֶפְרַיִם שָׁמְעוּ כִּי־נָסוּ פְלִשְׁתִּים וַיַּדְבְּקוּ גַם־הֵמָּה אַחֲרֵיהֶם בַּמִּלְחָמָה:

כג וַיּוֹשַׁע יְהוָה בַּיּוֹם הַהוּא אֶת־יִשְׂרָאֵל וְהַמִּלְחָמָה עָבְרָה אֶת־בֵּית אָוֶן:

Shmuel I / I Samuel
Chapter 14

שמואל א
פרק יד

24 The men of *Yisrael* were distressed that day. For *Shaul* had laid an oath upon the troops: "Cursed be the man who eats any food before night falls and I take revenge on my enemies." So none of the troops ate anything.

כד וְאִישׁ־יִשְׂרָאֵל נִגַּשׂ בַּיּוֹם הַהוּא וַיֹּאֶל שָׁאוּל אֶת־הָעָם לֵאמֹר אָרוּר הָאִישׁ אֲשֶׁר־יֹאכַל לֶחֶם עַד־הָעֶרֶב וְנִקַּמְתִּי מֵאֹיְבַי וְלֹא טָעַם כָּל־הָעָם לָחֶם׃

25 Everybody came to a stack of beehives where some honey had spilled on the ground.

כה וְכָל־הָאָרֶץ בָּאוּ בַיָּעַר וַיְהִי דְבַשׁ עַל־פְּנֵי הַשָּׂדֶה׃

26 When the troops came to the beehives and found the flow of honey there, no one put his hand to his mouth, for the troops feared the oath.

כו וַיָּבֹא הָעָם אֶל־הַיַּעַר וְהִנֵּה הֵלֶךְ דְּבָשׁ וְאֵין־מַשִּׂיג יָדוֹ אֶל־פִּיו כִּי־יָרֵא הָעָם אֶת־הַשְּׁבֻעָה׃

27 *Yonatan*, however, had not heard his father adjure the troops. So he put out the stick he had with him, dipped it into the beehive of honey, and brought his hand back to his mouth; and his eyes lit up.

כז וְיוֹנָתָן לֹא־שָׁמַע בְּהַשְׁבִּיעַ אָבִיו אֶת־הָעָם וַיִּשְׁלַח אֶת־קְצֵה הַמַּטֶּה אֲשֶׁר בְּיָדוֹ וַיִּטְבֹּל אוֹתָהּ בְּיַעְרַת הַדְּבָשׁ וַיָּשֶׁב יָדוֹ אֶל־פִּיו וַתָּאֹרְנָה [וַתָּאַרְנָה] עֵינָיו׃

28 At this one of the soldiers spoke up, "Your father adjured the troops: 'Cursed be the man who eats anything this day.' And so the troops are faint."

כח וַיַּעַן אִישׁ מֵהָעָם וַיֹּאמֶר הַשְׁבֵּעַ הִשְׁבִּיעַ אָבִיךָ אֶת־הָעָם לֵאמֹר אָרוּר הָאִישׁ אֲשֶׁר־יֹאכַל לֶחֶם הַיּוֹם וַיָּעַף הָעָם׃

29 *Yonatan* answered, "My father has brought trouble on the people. See for yourselves how my eyes lit up when I tasted that bit of honey.

כט וַיֹּאמֶר יוֹנָתָן עָכַר אָבִי אֶת־הָאָרֶץ רְאוּ־נָא כִּי־אֹרוּ עֵינַי כִּי טָעַמְתִּי מְעַט דְּבַשׁ הַזֶּה׃

va-YO-mer yo-na-TAN a-KHAR a-VEE et ha-A-retz r'-u NA kee O-ru ay-NAI KEE ta-AM-tee m'-AT d'-VASH ha-ZEH

30 If only the troops had eaten today of spoil captured from the enemy, the defeat of the Philistines would have been greater still!"

ל אַף כִּי לוּא אָכֹל אָכַל הַיּוֹם הָעָם מִשְּׁלַל אֹיְבָיו אֲשֶׁר מָצָא כִּי עַתָּה לֹא־רָבְתָה מַכָּה בַּפְּלִשְׁתִּים׃

31 They struck down the Philistines that day from Michmas to Aijalon, and the troops were famished.

לא וַיַּכּוּ בַיּוֹם הַהוּא בַּפְּלִשְׁתִּים מִמִּכְמָשׂ אַיָּלֹנָה וַיָּעַף הָעָם מְאֹד׃

32 The troops pounced on the spoil; they took the sheep and cows and calves and slaughtered them on the ground, and the troops ate with the blood.

לב ויעש [וַיַּעַט] הָעָם אֶל־שָׁלָל [הַשָּׁלָל] וַיִּקְחוּ צֹאן וּבָקָר וּבְנֵי בָקָר וַיִּשְׁחֲטוּ־אָרְצָה וַיֹּאכַל הָעָם עַל־הַדָּם׃

14:29 *Yonatan* answered, "My father has brought trouble on the people Though King *Shaul* had instructed the soldiers of Israel not to eat, his son *Yehonatan* eats honey, and declares that his father erred by issuing such an order. Rabbi Shlomo Aviner notes that although righteous individuals like King *Shaul* may be able to fast in battle, soldiers need to eat and drink in order to maintain their physical and emotional strength. Armies need to make sure that their soldiers have high morale so that they can succeed. Today, there are organizations that assist the Israeli Defense Forces by providing soldiers not only with essential items they need for battle, but also with extra amenities, to demonstrate that the IDF has many supporters from around the world who pray and work for their success. This raises the morale of Israel's soldiers and contributes to the success of their holy mission.

Shmuel I / I Samuel
Chapter 14

33 When it was reported to *Shaul* that the troops were sinning against *Hashem*, eating with the blood, he said, "You have acted faithlessly. Roll a large stone over to me today."

34 And *Shaul* ordered, "Spread out among the troops and tell them that everyone must bring me his ox or his sheep and slaughter it here, and then eat. You must not sin against *Hashem* and eat with the blood." Every one of the troops brought his own ox with him that night and slaughtered it there.

35 Thus *Shaul* set up a *Mizbayach* to *Hashem*; it was the first *Mizbayach* he erected to *Hashem*.

36 *Shaul* said, "Let us go down after the Philistines by night and plunder among them until the light of morning; and let us not leave a single survivor among them." "Do whatever you please," they replied. But the *Kohen* said, "Let us approach *Hashem* here."

37 So *Shaul* inquired of *Hashem*, "Shall I go down after the Philistines? Will You deliver them into the hands of *Yisrael*?" But this time He did not respond to him.

38 Then *Shaul* said, "Come forward, all chief officers of the troops, and find out how this guilt was incurred today.

39 For as *Hashem* lives who brings victory to *Yisrael*, even if it was through my son *Yonatan*, he shall be put to death!" Not one soldier answered him.

40 And he said to all the Israelites, "You stand on one side, and my son *Yonatan* and I shall stand on the other." The troops said to *Shaul*, "Do as you please."

41 *Shaul* then said to *Hashem*, the God of *Yisrael*, "Show Thammim." *Yonatan* and *Shaul* were indicated by lot, and the troops were cleared.

42 And *Shaul* said, "Cast the lots between my son and me"; and *Yonatan* was indicated.

43 *Shaul* said to *Yonatan*, "Tell me, what have you done?" And *Yonatan* told him, "I only tasted a bit of honey with the tip of the stick in my hand. I am ready to die."

44 *Shaul* said, "Thus and more may *Hashem* do: You shall be put to death, *Yonatan*!"

שמואל א
פרק יד

לג וַיַּגִּ֤ידוּ לְשָׁאוּל֙ לֵאמֹ֔ר הִנֵּ֥ה הָעָ֛ם חֹטִ֖אים לַֽיהוָ֑ה לֶאֱכֹ֣ל עַל־הַדָּ֑ם וַיֹּ֨אמֶר֙ בְּגַדְתֶּ֔ם גֹּֽלּוּ־אֵלַ֥י הַיּ֖וֹם אֶ֥בֶן גְּדוֹלָֽה׃

לד וַיֹּ֣אמֶר שָׁא֡וּל פֻּ֣צוּ בָעָם֩ וַאֲמַרְתֶּ֨ם לָהֶ֜ם הַגִּ֧ישׁוּ אֵלַ֣י אִ֣ישׁ שׁוֹר֗וֹ וְאִ֣ישׁ שְׂיֵ֡הוּ וּשְׁחַטְתֶּ֤ם בָּזֶה֙ וַאֲכַלְתֶּ֔ם וְלֹא־תֶחֶטְא֥וּ לַֽיהוָ֖ה לֶאֱכֹ֣ל אֶל־הַדָּ֑ם וַיַּגִּ֣שׁוּ כָל־הָ֠עָם אִ֣ישׁ שׁוֹר֧וֹ בְיָד֛וֹ הַלַּ֖יְלָה וַיִּשְׁחֲטוּ־שָֽׁם׃

לה וַיִּ֧בֶן שָׁא֛וּל מִזְבֵּ֖חַ לַֽיהוָ֑ה אֹת֣וֹ הֵחֵ֔ל לִבְנ֥וֹת מִזְבֵּ֖חַ לַֽיהוָֽה׃

לו וַיֹּ֣אמֶר שָׁא֡וּל נֵרְדָ֣ה אַחֲרֵי֩ פְלִשְׁתִּ֨ים לַ֜יְלָה וְֽנָבֹ֣זָה בָהֶ֣ם עַד־א֣וֹר הַבֹּ֗קֶר וְלֹֽא־נַשְׁאֵ֤ר בָּהֶם֙ אִ֔ישׁ וַיֹּ֣אמְר֔וּ כָּל־הַטּ֥וֹב בְּעֵינֶ֖יךָ עֲשֵׂ֑ה וַיֹּ֣אמֶר הַכֹּהֵ֔ן נִקְרְבָ֥ה הֲלֹ֖ם אֶל־הָאֱלֹהִֽים׃

לז וַיִּשְׁאַ֤ל שָׁאוּל֙ בֵּֽאלֹהִ֔ים הַֽאֵרֵד֙ אַחֲרֵ֣י פְלִשְׁתִּ֔ים הֲתִתְּנֵ֖ם בְּיַ֣ד יִשְׂרָאֵ֑ל וְלֹ֥א עָנָ֖הוּ בַּיּ֥וֹם הַהֽוּא׃

לח וַיֹּ֣אמֶר שָׁא֔וּל גֹּ֣שֽׁוּ הֲלֹ֔ם כֹּ֖ל פִּנּ֣וֹת הָעָ֑ם וּדְע֣וּ וּרְא֔וּ בַּמָּ֗ה הָיְתָ֛ה הַחַטָּ֥את הַזֹּ֖את הַיּֽוֹם׃

לט כִּ֣י חַי־יְהוָ֗ה הַמּוֹשִׁ֙יעַ֙ אֶת־יִשְׂרָאֵ֔ל כִּ֧י אִם־יֶשְׁנ֛וֹ בְּיוֹנָתָ֥ן בְּנִ֖י כִּ֣י מ֣וֹת יָמ֑וּת וְאֵ֥ין עֹנֵ֖הוּ מִכָּל־הָעָֽם׃

מ וַיֹּ֣אמֶר אֶל־כָּל־יִשְׂרָאֵ֗ל אַתֶּם֙ תִּהְי֣וּ לְעֵ֣בֶר אֶחָ֔ד וַֽאֲנִי֙ וְיוֹנָתָ֣ן בְּנִ֔י נִֽהְיֶ֖ה לְעֵ֣בֶר אֶחָ֑ד וַיֹּ֤אמְרוּ הָעָם֙ אֶל־שָׁא֔וּל הַטּ֥וֹב בְּעֵינֶ֖יךָ עֲשֵֽׂה׃

מא וַיֹּ֣אמֶר שָׁא֗וּל אֶל־יְהוָ֛ה אֱלֹהֵ֥י יִשְׂרָאֵ֖ל הָ֣בָה תָמִ֑ים וַיִּלָּכֵ֧ד יוֹנָתָ֛ן וְשָׁא֖וּל וְהָעָ֥ם יָצָֽאוּ׃

מב וַיֹּ֣אמֶר שָׁא֔וּל הַפִּ֕ילוּ בֵּינִ֕י וּבֵ֖ין יוֹנָתָ֣ן בְּנִ֑י וַיִּלָּכֵ֖ד יוֹנָתָֽן׃

מג וַיֹּ֤אמֶר שָׁאוּל֙ אֶל־י֣וֹנָתָ֔ן הַגִּ֥ידָה לִּ֖י מֶ֣ה עָשִׂ֑יתָה וַיַּגֶּד־ל֣וֹ יוֹנָתָ֗ן וַיֹּאמֶר֩ טָעֹ֨ם טָעַ֜מְתִּי בִּקְצֵ֨ה הַמַּטֶּ֧ה אֲשֶׁר־בְּיָדִ֛י מְעַ֥ט דְּבַ֖שׁ הִנְנִ֥י אָמֽוּת׃

מד וַיֹּ֣אמֶר שָׁא֔וּל כֹּֽה־יַעֲשֶׂ֥ה אֱלֹהִ֖ים וְכֹ֣ה יוֹסִ֑ף כִּי־מ֥וֹת תָּמ֖וּת יוֹנָתָֽן׃

Shmuel I / I Samuel
Chapter 15

45 But the troops said to *Shaul*, "Shall *Yonatan* die, after bringing this great victory to *Yisrael*? Never! As *Hashem* lives, not a hair of his head shall fall to the ground! For he brought this day to pass with the help of *Hashem*." Thus the troops saved *Yonatan* and he did not die.

46 *Shaul* broke off his pursuit of the Philistines, and the Philistines returned to their homes.

47 After *Shaul* had secured his kingship over *Yisrael*, he waged war on every side against all his enemies: against the Moabites, Ammonites, Edomites, the Philistines, and the kings of Zobah; and wherever he turned he worsted [them].

48 He was triumphant, defeating the Amalekites and saving *Yisrael* from those who plundered it.

49 *Shaul*'s sons were: *Yonatan*, Ishvi, and Malchishua; and the names of his two daughters were Merab, the older, and *Michal*, the younger.

50 The name of *Shaul*'s wife was Ahinoam daughter of Ahimaaz; and the name of his army commander was Abiner son of *Shaul*'s uncle Ner.

51 Keesh, *Shaul*'s father, and Ner, *Avner*'s father, were sons of Abiel.

52 There was bitter war against the Philistines all the days of *Shaul*; and whenever *Shaul* noticed any stalwart man or warrior, he would take him into his service.

15 1 *Shmuel* said to *Shaul*, "I am the one *Hashem* sent to anoint you king over His people *Yisrael*. Therefore, listen to *Hashem*'s command!

2 "Thus said the Lord of Hosts: I am exacting the penalty for what Amalek did to *Yisrael*, for the assault he made upon them on the road, on their way up from Egypt.

3 Now go, attack Amalek, and proscribe all that belongs to him. Spare no one, but kill alike men and women, infants and sucklings, oxen and sheep, camels and asses!"

4 *Shaul* mustered the troops and enrolled them at Telaim: 200,000 men on foot, and 10,000 men of *Yehuda*.

Shmuel I / I Samuel
Chapter 15

שמואל א
פרק טו

5 Then *Shaul* advanced as far as the city of Amalek and lay in wait in the wadi.

ה וַיָּבֹא שָׁאוּל עַד־עִיר עֲמָלֵק וַיָּרֶב בַּנָּחַל׃

6 *Shaul* said to the Kenites, "Come, withdraw at once from among the Amalekites, that I may not destroy you along with them; for you showed kindness to all the Israelites when they left Egypt." So the Kenites withdrew from among the Amalekites.

ו וַיֹּאמֶר שָׁאוּל אֶל־הַקֵּינִי לְכוּ סֻּרוּ רְדוּ מִתּוֹךְ עֲמָלֵקִי פֶּן־אֹסִפְךָ עִמּוֹ וְאַתָּה עָשִׂיתָה חֶסֶד עִם־כָּל־בְּנֵי יִשְׂרָאֵל בַּעֲלוֹתָם מִמִּצְרָיִם וַיָּסַר קֵינִי מִתּוֹךְ עֲמָלֵק׃

7 *Shaul* destroyed Amalek from Havilah all the way to Shur, which is close to Egypt,

ז וַיַּךְ שָׁאוּל אֶת־עֲמָלֵק מֵחֲוִילָה בּוֹאֲךָ שׁוּר אֲשֶׁר עַל־פְּנֵי מִצְרָיִם׃

8 and he captured King Agag of Amalek alive. He proscribed all the people, putting them to the sword;

ח וַיִּתְפֹּשׂ אֶת־אֲגַג מֶלֶךְ־עֲמָלֵק חָי וְאֶת־כָּל־הָעָם הֶחֱרִים לְפִי־חָרֶב׃

9 but *Shaul* and the troops spared Agag and the best of the sheep, the oxen, the second-born, the lambs, and all else that was of value. They would not proscribe them; they proscribed only what was cheap and worthless.

ט וַיַּחְמֹל שָׁאוּל וְהָעָם עַל־אֲגָג וְעַל־מֵיטַב הַצֹּאן וְהַבָּקָר וְהַמִּשְׁנִים וְעַל־הַכָּרִים וְעַל־כָּל־הַטּוֹב וְלֹא אָבוּ הַחֲרִימָם וְכָל־הַמְּלָאכָה נְמִבְזָה וְנָמֵס אֹתָהּ הֶחֱרִימוּ׃

10 The word of *Hashem* then came to *Shmuel*:

י וַיְהִי דְּבַר־יְהֹוָה אֶל־שְׁמוּאֵל לֵאמֹר׃

11 "I regret that I made *Shaul* king, for he has turned away from Me and has not carried out My commands." *Shmuel* was distressed and he entreated *Hashem* all night long.

יא נִחַמְתִּי כִּי־הִמְלַכְתִּי אֶת־שָׁאוּל לְמֶלֶךְ כִּי־שָׁב מֵאַחֲרַי וְאֶת־דְּבָרַי לֹא הֵקִים וַיִּחַר לִשְׁמוּאֵל וַיִּזְעַק אֶל־יְהֹוָה כָּל־הַלָּיְלָה׃

ni-KHAM-tee kee him-LAKH-tee et sha-UL l'-ME-lekh kee SHAV may-a-kha-RAI v'-et d'-va-RAI lo hay-KEEM va-YI-khar lish-mu-AYL va-yiz-AK el a-do-NAI kol ha-LAI-la

12 Early in the morning *Shmuel* went to meet *Shaul*. *Shmuel* was told, "*Shaul* went to *Carmel*, where he erected a monument for himself; then he left and went on down to *Gilgal*."

יב וַיַּשְׁכֵּם שְׁמוּאֵל לִקְרַאת שָׁאוּל בַּבֹּקֶר וַיֻּגַּד לִשְׁמוּאֵל לֵאמֹר בָּא־שָׁאוּל הַכַּרְמֶלָה וְהִנֵּה מַצִּיב לוֹ יָד וַיִּסֹּב וַיַּעֲבֹר וַיֵּרֶד הַגִּלְגָּל׃

13 When *Shmuel* came to *Shaul*, *Shaul* said to him, "Blessed are you of *Hashem*! I have fulfilled *Hashem*'s command."

יג וַיָּבֹא שְׁמוּאֵל אֶל־שָׁאוּל וַיֹּאמֶר לוֹ שָׁאוּל בָּרוּךְ אַתָּה לַיהֹוָה הֲקִימֹתִי אֶת־דְּבַר יְהֹוָה׃

14 "Then what," demanded *Shmuel*, "is this bleating of sheep in my ears, and the lowing of oxen that I hear?"

יד וַיֹּאמֶר שְׁמוּאֵל וּמֶה קוֹל־הַצֹּאן הַזֶּה בְּאָזְנָי וְקוֹל הַבָּקָר אֲשֶׁר אָנֹכִי שֹׁמֵעַ׃

15:11 I regret that I made Shaul king *Shaul*'s error of not completely eradicating the evil Amalek costs him his kingdom. Yet, King *David*'s sin with *Batsheva* (II Samuel 11–12) does not have a similar result. In his *Book of the Principles*, Rabbi Yosef Albo, a philosopher in fifteenth century Spain, notes that King *David*'s sin, though grave, is a personal one. Therefore, his punishment only impacts him and his family. However, King *Shaul*'s transgression was of a national scope, impacting the future of the nation. In fact, the Rabbis of the *Midrash* teach that the evil Haman mentioned in *Megillat Esther* descends from Amalek's King *Agag*, whom *Shaul* kept alive long enough to father a child. Thus, the punishment has to be one that impacts his rule over the whole nation.

Shmuel I/I Samuel
Chapter 15

15	*Shaul* answered, "They were brought from the Amalekites, for the troops spared the choicest of the sheep and oxen for sacrificing to *Hashem* your God. And we proscribed the rest."
16	*Shmuel* said to *Shaul*, "Stop! Let me tell you what *Hashem* said to me last night!" "Speak," he replied.
17	And *Shmuel* said, "You may look small to yourself, but you are the head of the tribes of *Yisrael*. *Hashem* anointed you king over *Yisrael*,
18	and *Hashem* sent you on a mission, saying, 'Go and proscribe the sinful Amalekites; make war on them until you have exterminated them.'
19	Why did you disobey *Hashem* and swoop down on the spoil in defiance of *Hashem*'s will?"
20	*Shaul* said to *Shmuel*, "But I did obey *Hashem*! I performed the mission on which *Hashem* sent me: I captured King Agag of Amalek, and I proscribed Amalek,
21	and the troops took from the spoil some sheep and oxen – the best of what had been proscribed – to sacrifice to *Hashem* your God at *Gilgal*."
22	But *Shmuel* said: "Does *Hashem* delight in burnt offerings and sacrifices As much as in obedience to *Hashem*'s command? Surely, obedience is better than sacrifice, Compliance than the fat of rams.
23	For rebellion is like the sin of divination, Defiance, like the iniquity of teraphim. Because you rejected *Hashem*'s command, He has rejected you as king."
24	*Shaul* said to *Shmuel*, "I did wrong to transgress *Hashem*'s command and your instructions; but I was afraid of the troops and I yielded to them.
25	Please, forgive my offense and come back with me, and I will bow low to *Hashem*."
26	But *Shmuel* said to *Shaul*, "I will not go back with you; for you have rejected *Hashem*'s command, and *Hashem* has rejected you as king over *Yisrael*."
27	As *Shmuel* turned to leave, *Shaul* seized the corner of his robe, and it tore.

טו וַיֹּאמֶר שָׁאוּל מֵעֲמָלֵקִי הֱבִיאוּם אֲשֶׁר חָמַל הָעָם עַל־מֵיטַב הַצֹּאן וְהַבָּקָר לְמַעַן זְבֹחַ לַיהֹוָה אֱלֹהֶיךָ וְאֶת־הַיּוֹתֵר הֶחֱרַמְנוּ:

טז וַיֹּאמֶר שְׁמוּאֵל אֶל־שָׁאוּל הֶרֶף וְאַגִּידָה לְּךָ אֵת אֲשֶׁר דִּבֶּר יְהֹוָה אֵלַי הַלָּיְלָה וַיֹּאמְרוּ [וַיֹּאמֶר] לוֹ דַּבֵּר:

יז וַיֹּאמֶר שְׁמוּאֵל הֲלוֹא אִם־קָטֹן אַתָּה בְּעֵינֶיךָ רֹאשׁ שִׁבְטֵי יִשְׂרָאֵל אָתָּה וַיִּמְשָׁחֲךָ יְהֹוָה לְמֶלֶךְ עַל־יִשְׂרָאֵל:

יח וַיִּשְׁלָחֲךָ יְהֹוָה בְּדָרֶךְ וַיֹּאמֶר לֵךְ וְהַחֲרַמְתָּה אֶת־הַחַטָּאִים אֶת־עֲמָלֵק וְנִלְחַמְתָּ בוֹ עַד כַּלּוֹתָם אֹתָם:

יט וְלָמָּה לֹא־שָׁמַעְתָּ בְּקוֹל יְהֹוָה וַתַּעַט אֶל־הַשָּׁלָל וַתַּעַשׂ הָרַע בְּעֵינֵי יְהֹוָה:

כ וַיֹּאמֶר שָׁאוּל אֶל־שְׁמוּאֵל אֲשֶׁר שָׁמַעְתִּי בְּקוֹל יְהֹוָה וָאֵלֵךְ בַּדֶּרֶךְ אֲשֶׁר־שְׁלָחַנִי יְהֹוָה וָאָבִיא אֶת־אֲגַג מֶלֶךְ עֲמָלֵק וְאֶת־עֲמָלֵק הֶחֱרַמְתִּי:

כא וַיִּקַּח הָעָם מֵהַשָּׁלָל צֹאן וּבָקָר רֵאשִׁית הַחֵרֶם לִזְבֹּחַ לַיהֹוָה אֱלֹהֶיךָ בַּגִּלְגָּל:

כב וַיֹּאמֶר שְׁמוּאֵל הַחֵפֶץ לַיהֹוָה בְּעֹלוֹת וּזְבָחִים כִּשְׁמֹעַ בְּקוֹל יְהֹוָה הִנֵּה שְׁמֹעַ מִזֶּבַח טוֹב לְהַקְשִׁיב מֵחֵלֶב אֵילִים:

כג כִּי חַטַּאת־קֶסֶם מֶרִי וְאָוֶן וּתְרָפִים הַפְצַר יַעַן מָאַסְתָּ אֶת־דְּבַר יְהֹוָה וַיִּמְאָסְךָ מִמֶּלֶךְ:

כד וַיֹּאמֶר שָׁאוּל אֶל־שְׁמוּאֵל חָטָאתִי כִּי־עָבַרְתִּי אֶת־פִּי־יְהֹוָה וְאֶת־דְּבָרֶיךָ כִּי יָרֵאתִי אֶת־הָעָם וָאֶשְׁמַע בְּקוֹלָם:

כה וְעַתָּה שָׂא נָא אֶת־חַטָּאתִי וְשׁוּב עִמִּי וְאֶשְׁתַּחֲוֶה לַיהֹוָה:

כו וַיֹּאמֶר שְׁמוּאֵל אֶל־שָׁאוּל לֹא אָשׁוּב עִמָּךְ כִּי מָאַסְתָּה אֶת־דְּבַר יְהֹוָה וַיִּמְאָסְךָ יְהֹוָה מִהְיוֹת מֶלֶךְ עַל־יִשְׂרָאֵל:

כז וַיִּסֹּב שְׁמוּאֵל לָלֶכֶת וַיַּחֲזֵק בִּכְנַף־מְעִילוֹ וַיִּקָּרַע:

Shmuel I/I Samuel
Chapter 15

שמואל א
פרק טו

28 And *Shmuel* said to him, "*Hashem* has this day torn the kingship over *Yisrael* away from you and has given it to another who is worthier than you.

כח וַיֹּאמֶר אֵלָיו שְׁמוּאֵל קָרַע יְהֹוָה אֶת־מַמְלְכוּת יִשְׂרָאֵל מֵעָלֶיךָ הַיּוֹם וּנְתָנָהּ לְרֵעֲךָ הַטּוֹב מִמֶּךָּ:

va-YO-mer ay-LAV sh'-mu-EL ka-RA a-do-NAI et mam-l'-KHUT yis-ra-AYL may-a-LE-kha ha-YOM un-ta-NAH l'-ray-a-KHA ha-TOV mi-ME-ka

29 Moreover, the Glory of *Yisrael* does not deceive or change His mind, for He is not human that He should change His mind."

כט וְגַם נֵצַח יִשְׂרָאֵל לֹא יְשַׁקֵּר וְלֹא יִנָּחֵם כִּי לֹא אָדָם הוּא לְהִנָּחֵם:

v'-GAM NAY-tzakh yis-ra-AYL LO y'-sha-KAYR v'-LO y'-na-KHAYM KEE LO a-DAM hu l'-hi-na-KHAYM

30 But [*Shaul*] pleaded, "I did wrong. Please, honor me in the presence of the elders of my people and in the presence of *Yisrael*, and come back with me until I have bowed low to *Hashem* your God."

ל וַיֹּאמֶר חָטָאתִי עַתָּה כַּבְּדֵנִי נָא נֶגֶד זִקְנֵי־עַמִּי וְנֶגֶד יִשְׂרָאֵל וְשׁוּב עִמִּי וְהִשְׁתַּחֲוֵיתִי לַיהֹוָה אֱלֹהֶיךָ:

31 So *Shmuel* followed *Shaul* back, and *Shaul* bowed low to *Hashem*.

לא וַיָּשׇׁב שְׁמוּאֵל אַחֲרֵי שָׁאוּל וַיִּשְׁתַּחוּ שָׁאוּל לַיהֹוָה:

32 *Shmuel* said, "Bring forward to me King Agag of Amalek." Agag approached him with faltering steps; and Agag said, "Ah, bitter death is at hand!"

לב וַיֹּאמֶר שְׁמוּאֵל הַגִּישׁוּ אֵלַי אֶת־אֲגַג מֶלֶךְ עֲמָלֵק וַיֵּלֶךְ אֵלָיו אֲגַג מַעֲדַנֹּת וַיֹּאמֶר אֲגָג אָכֵן סָר מַר־הַמָּוֶת:

33 *Shmuel* said: "As your sword has bereaved women, So shall your mother be bereaved among women." And *Shmuel* cut Agag down before *Hashem* at Gilgal.

לג וַיֹּאמֶר שְׁמוּאֵל כַּאֲשֶׁר שִׁכְּלָה נָשִׁים חַרְבֶּךָ כֵּן־תִּשְׁכַּל מִנָּשִׁים אִמֶּךָ וַיְשַׁסֵּף שְׁמוּאֵל אֶת־אֲגָג לִפְנֵי יְהֹוָה בַּגִּלְגָּל:

34 *Shmuel* then departed for *Rama*, and *Shaul* went up to his home at *Giva* of *Shaul*.

לד וַיֵּלֶךְ שְׁמוּאֵל הָרָמָתָה וְשָׁאוּל עָלָה אֶל־בֵּיתוֹ גִּבְעַת שָׁאוּל:

35 *Shmuel* never saw *Shaul* again to the day of his death. But *Shmuel* grieved over *Shaul*, because *Hashem* regretted that He had made *Shaul* king over *Yisrael*.

לה וְלֹא־יָסַף שְׁמוּאֵל לִרְאוֹת אֶת־שָׁאוּל עַד־יוֹם מוֹתוֹ כִּי־הִתְאַבֵּל שְׁמוּאֵל אֶל־שָׁאוּל וַיהֹוָה נִחָם כִּי־הִמְלִיךְ אֶת־שָׁאוּל עַל־יִשְׂרָאֵל:

Sarah Aaronsohn
(1890–1917)

15:29 The Glory of *Yisrael* does not deceive When World War I broke out in 1914, many young Zionists perceived the crisis as an opportunity through which the political landscape of Palestine could be transformed to advance the dream of Jewish self-determination in their homeland. Sarah Aaronsohn, one of the first generation of native-born Zionists, was born in 1890 in Zichron Yaakov. With Aaronsohn at the helm, a young group of idealists formed a clandestine organization they called "NILI," which was a Hebrew acronym based on the phrase in this verse verse, *Netzach Yisrael Lo Yishaker* (נצח ישראל לא ישקר), 'The Glory of Israel does not deceive.' NILI conducted espionage against the Ottoman authorities on behalf of the Allies. They hoped that with their assistance, the British would come to power and reward the Jews with an independent state in Palestine. In 1917, however, the Turks discovered Sarah Aaronsohn's espionage and arrested her. Despite interrogations and torture, she refused to disclose any information about NILI's efforts, taking her own life instead. She sacrificed her life for the millenia-old dream to promote the independence of the Jewish people. Sarah Aaronsohn is remembered to this day as a national hero of Israel.

Shmuel I / I Samuel
Chapter 16

16 ¹ And *Hashem* said to *Shmuel*, "How long will you grieve over *Shaul*, since I have rejected him as king over *Yisrael*? Fill your horn with oil and set out; I am sending you to *Yishai* the Bethlehemite, for I have decided on one of his sons to be king."

² *Shmuel* replied, "How can I go? If *Shaul* hears of it, he will kill me." *Hashem* answered, "Take a heifer with you, and say, 'I have come to sacrifice to *Hashem*.'

³ Invite *Yishai* to the sacrificial feast, and then I will make known to you what you shall do; you shall anoint for Me the one I point out to you."

⁴ *Shmuel* did what *Hashem* commanded. When he came to *Beit Lechem*, the elders of the city went out in alarm to meet him and said, "Do you come on a peaceful errand?"

⁵ "Yes," he replied, "I have come to sacrifice to *Hashem*. Purify yourselves and join me in the sacrificial feast." He also instructed *Yishai* and his sons to purify themselves and invited them to the sacrificial feast.

⁶ When they arrived and he saw *Eliav*, he thought: "Surely *Hashem*'s anointed stands before Him."

⁷ But *Hashem* said to *Shmuel*, "Pay no attention to his appearance or his stature, for I have rejected him. For not as man sees [does *Hashem* see]; man sees only what is visible, but *Hashem* sees into the heart."

⁸ Then *Yishai* called *Avinadav* and had him pass before *Shmuel*; but he said, "*Hashem* has not chosen this one either."

⁹ Next *Yishai* presented Shammah; and again he said, "*Hashem* has not chosen this one either."

¹⁰ Thus *Yishai* presented seven of his sons before *Shmuel*, and *Shmuel* said to *Yishai*, "*Hashem* has not chosen any of these."

¹¹ Then *Shmuel* asked *Yishai*, "Are these all the boys you have?" He replied, "There is still the youngest; he is tending the flock." And *Shmuel* said to *Yishai*, "Send someone to bring him, for we will not sit down to eat until he gets here."

שמואל א
פרק טז

א וַיֹּאמֶר יְהֹוָה אֶל־שְׁמוּאֵל עַד־מָתַי אַתָּה מִתְאַבֵּל אֶל־שָׁאוּל וַאֲנִי מְאַסְתִּיו מִמְּלֹךְ עַל־יִשְׂרָאֵל מַלֵּא קַרְנְךָ שֶׁמֶן וְלֵךְ אֶשְׁלָחֲךָ אֶל־יִשַׁי בֵּית־הַלַּחְמִי כִּי־רָאִיתִי בְּבָנָיו לִי מֶלֶךְ:

ב וַיֹּאמֶר שְׁמוּאֵל אֵיךְ אֵלֵךְ וְשָׁמַע שָׁאוּל וַהֲרָגָנִי וַיֹּאמֶר יְהֹוָה עֶגְלַת בָּקָר תִּקַּח בְּיָדֶךָ וְאָמַרְתָּ לִזְבֹּחַ לַיהֹוָה בָּאתִי:

ג וְקָרָאתָ לְיִשַׁי בַּזָּבַח וְאָנֹכִי אוֹדִיעֲךָ אֵת אֲשֶׁר־תַּעֲשֶׂה וּמָשַׁחְתָּ לִי אֵת אֲשֶׁר־אֹמַר אֵלֶיךָ:

ד וַיַּעַשׂ שְׁמוּאֵל אֵת אֲשֶׁר דִּבֶּר יְהֹוָה וַיָּבֹא בֵּית לָחֶם וַיֶּחֶרְדוּ זִקְנֵי הָעִיר לִקְרָאתוֹ וַיֹּאמֶר שָׁלֹם בּוֹאֶךָ:

ה וַיֹּאמֶר שָׁלוֹם לִזְבֹּחַ לַיהֹוָה בָּאתִי הִתְקַדְּשׁוּ וּבָאתֶם אִתִּי בַּזָּבַח וַיְקַדֵּשׁ אֶת־יִשַׁי וְאֶת־בָּנָיו וַיִּקְרָא לָהֶם לַזָּבַח:

ו וַיְהִי בְּבוֹאָם וַיַּרְא אֶת־אֱלִיאָב וַיֹּאמֶר אַךְ נֶגֶד יְהֹוָה מְשִׁיחוֹ:

ז וַיֹּאמֶר יְהֹוָה אֶל־שְׁמוּאֵל אַל־תַּבֵּט אֶל־מַרְאֵהוּ וְאֶל־גְּבֹהַּ קוֹמָתוֹ כִּי מְאַסְתִּיהוּ כִּי לֹא אֲשֶׁר יִרְאֶה הָאָדָם כִּי הָאָדָם יִרְאֶה לַעֵינַיִם וַיהֹוָה יִרְאֶה לַלֵּבָב:

ח וַיִּקְרָא יִשַׁי אֶל־אֲבִינָדָב וַיַּעֲבִרֵהוּ לִפְנֵי שְׁמוּאֵל וַיֹּאמֶר גַּם־בָּזֶה לֹא־בָחַר יְהֹוָה:

ט וַיַּעֲבֵר יִשַׁי שַׁמָּה וַיֹּאמֶר גַּם־בָּזֶה לֹא־בָחַר יְהֹוָה:

י וַיַּעֲבֵר יִשַׁי שִׁבְעַת בָּנָיו לִפְנֵי שְׁמוּאֵל וַיֹּאמֶר שְׁמוּאֵל אֶל־יִשַׁי לֹא־בָחַר יְהֹוָה בָּאֵלֶּה:

יא וַיֹּאמֶר שְׁמוּאֵל אֶל־יִשַׁי הֲתַמּוּ הַנְּעָרִים וַיֹּאמֶר עוֹד שָׁאַר הַקָּטָן וְהִנֵּה רֹעֶה בַּצֹּאן וַיֹּאמֶר שְׁמוּאֵל אֶל־יִשַׁי שִׁלְחָה וְקָחֶנּוּ כִּי לֹא־נָסֹב עַד־בֹּאוֹ פֹה:

Shmuel I / I Samuel
Chapter 16

שמואל א
פרק טז

va-YO-mer sh'-mu-AYL el yi-SHAI ha-TA-mu ha-n'-a-REEM va-YO-mer OD sha-AR ha-ka-TAN v'-hi-NAY ro-EH ba-TZON va-YO-mer sh'-mu-EL el yi-SHAI shil-KHAH v'-ka-KHE-nu kee LO na-SOV ad bo-O FOH

12 So they sent and brought him. He was ruddy-cheeked, bright-eyed, and handsome. And *Hashem* said, "Rise and anoint him, for this is the one."

יב וַיִּשְׁלַח וַיְבִיאֵהוּ וְהוּא אַדְמוֹנִי עִם־יְפֵה עֵינַיִם וְטוֹב רֹאִי וַיֹּאמֶר יְהֹוָה קוּם מְשָׁחֵהוּ כִּי־זֶה הוּא:

13 *Shmuel* took the horn of oil and anointed him in the presence of his brothers; and the spirit of *Hashem* gripped *David* from that day on. *Shmuel* then set out for *Rama*.

יג וַיִּקַּח שְׁמוּאֵל אֶת־קֶרֶן הַשֶּׁמֶן וַיִּמְשַׁח אֹתוֹ בְּקֶרֶב אֶחָיו וַתִּצְלַח רוּחַ־יְהֹוָה אֶל־דָּוִד מֵהַיּוֹם הַהוּא וָמָעְלָה וַיָּקָם שְׁמוּאֵל וַיֵּלֶךְ הָרָמָתָה:

14 Now the spirit of *Hashem* had departed from *Shaul*, and an evil spirit from *Hashem* began to terrify him.

יד וְרוּחַ יְהֹוָה סָרָה מֵעִם שָׁאוּל וּבִעֲתַתּוּ רוּחַ־רָעָה מֵאֵת יְהֹוָה:

15 *Shaul*'s courtiers said to him, "An evil spirit of *Hashem* is terrifying you.

טו וַיֹּאמְרוּ עַבְדֵי־שָׁאוּל אֵלָיו הִנֵּה־נָא רוּחַ־אֱלֹהִים רָעָה מְבַעִתֶּךָ:

16 Let our lord give the order [and] the courtiers in attendance on you will look for someone who is skilled at playing the lyre; whenever the evil spirit of *Hashem* comes over you, he will play it and you will feel better."

טז יֹאמַר־נָא אֲדֹנֵנוּ עֲבָדֶיךָ לְפָנֶיךָ יְבַקְשׁוּ אִישׁ יֹדֵעַ מְנַגֵּן בַּכִּנּוֹר וְהָיָה בִּהְיוֹת עָלֶיךָ רוּחַ־אֱלֹהִים רָעָה וְנִגֵּן בְּיָדוֹ וְטוֹב לָךְ:

17 So *Shaul* said to his courtiers, "Find me someone who can play well and bring him to me."

יז וַיֹּאמֶר שָׁאוּל אֶל־עֲבָדָיו רְאוּ־נָא לִי אִישׁ מֵיטִיב לְנַגֵּן וַהֲבִיאוֹתֶם אֵלָי:

18 One of the attendants spoke up, "I have observed a son of *Yishai* the Bethlehemite who is skilled in music; he is a stalwart fellow and a warrior, sensible in speech, and handsome in appearance, and *Hashem* is with him."

יח וַיַּעַן אֶחָד מֵהַנְּעָרִים וַיֹּאמֶר הִנֵּה רָאִיתִי בֵּן לְיִשַׁי בֵּית הַלַּחְמִי יֹדֵעַ נַגֵּן וְגִבּוֹר חַיִל וְאִישׁ מִלְחָמָה וּנְבוֹן דָּבָר וְאִישׁ תֹּאַר וַיהֹוָה עִמּוֹ:

19 Whereupon *Shaul* sent messengers to *Yishai* to say, "Send me your son *David*, who is with the flock."

יט וַיִּשְׁלַח שָׁאוּל מַלְאָכִים אֶל־יִשָׁי וַיֹּאמֶר שִׁלְחָה אֵלַי אֶת־דָּוִד בִּנְךָ אֲשֶׁר בַּצֹּאן:

20 *Yishai* took an ass [laden with] bread, a skin of wine, and a kid, and sent them to *Shaul* by his son *David*.

כ וַיִּקַּח יִשַׁי חֲמוֹר לֶחֶם וְנֹאד יַיִן וּגְדִי עִזִּים אֶחָד וַיִּשְׁלַח בְּיַד־דָּוִד בְּנוֹ אֶל־שָׁאוּל:

21 So *David* came to *Shaul* and entered his service; [*Shaul*] took a strong liking to him and made him one of his arms-bearers.

כא וַיָּבֹא דָוִד אֶל־שָׁאוּל וַיַּעֲמֹד לְפָנָיו וַיֶּאֱהָבֵהוּ מְאֹד וַיְהִי־לוֹ נֹשֵׂא כֵלִים:

22 *Shaul* sent word to *Yishai*, "Let *David* remain in my service, for I am pleased with him."

כב וַיִּשְׁלַח שָׁאוּל אֶל־יִשַׁי לֵאמֹר יַעֲמָד־נָא דָוִד לְפָנַי כִּי־מָצָא חֵן בְּעֵינָי:

Shepherd in the Kidron Valley

16:11 There is still the youngest; he is tending the flock Young *David* is not the only great leader of the Children of Israel who was a shepherd before *Hashem* called him to a leadership role. For example, *Moshe* was also a shepherd. Shepherds bear great responsibility for the flock as a whole, and also for each individual sheep. Each one must be cared for, and must be counted as part of the flock for tithing. This is perfect training for leaders, who must lead the nation as a whole, and also maintain concern and compassion for each individual.

Shmuel I/I Samuel
Chapter 17

23 Whenever the [evil] spirit of *Hashem* came upon *Shaul*, *David* would take the lyre and play it; *Shaul* would find relief and feel better, and the evil spirit would leave him.

17

1 The Philistines assembled their forces for battle; they massed at Socoh of *Yehuda*, and encamped at Ephes-dammim, between Socoh and *Azeika*.

2 *Shaul* and the men of *Yisrael* massed and encamped in the valley of Elah. They drew up their line of battle against the Philistines,

3 with the Philistines stationed on one hill and *Yisrael* stationed on the opposite hill; the ravine was between them.

4 A champion of the Philistine forces stepped forward; his name was Goliath of Gath, and he was six *amot* and a *zeret* tall.

5 He had a bronze helmet on his head, and wore a breastplate of scale armor, a bronze breastplate weighing five thousand *shekalim*.

6 He had bronze greaves on his legs, and a bronze javelin [slung] from his shoulders.

7 The shaft of his spear was like a weaver's bar, and the iron head of his spear weighed six hundred *shekalim*; and the shield-bearer marched in front of him.

8 He stopped and called out to the ranks of *Yisrael* and he said to them, "Why should you come out to engage in battle? I am the Philistine [champion], and you are *Shaul*'s servants. Choose one of your men and let him come down against me.

9 If he bests me in combat and kills me, we will become your slaves; but if I best him and kill him, you shall be our slaves and serve us."

10 And the Philistine ended, "I herewith defy the ranks of *Yisrael*. Get me a man and let's fight it out!"

11 When *Shaul* and all *Yisrael* heard these words of the Philistine, they were dismayed and terror-stricken.

שמואל א
פרק יז

כג וְהָיָה בִּהְיוֹת רוּחַ־אֱלֹהִים אֶל־שָׁאוּל וְלָקַח דָּוִד אֶת־הַכִּנּוֹר וְנִגֵּן בְּיָדוֹ וְרָוַח לְשָׁאוּל וְטוֹב לוֹ וְסָרָה מֵעָלָיו רוּחַ הָרָעָה:

יז א וַיַּאַסְפוּ פְלִשְׁתִּים אֶת־מַחֲנֵיהֶם לַמִּלְחָמָה וַיֵּאָסְפוּ שֹׂכֹה אֲשֶׁר לִיהוּדָה וַיַּחֲנוּ בֵּין־שׂוֹכֹה וּבֵין־עֲזֵקָה בְּאֶפֶס דַּמִּים:

ב וְשָׁאוּל וְאִישׁ־יִשְׂרָאֵל נֶאֶסְפוּ וַיַּחֲנוּ בְּעֵמֶק הָאֵלָה וַיַּעַרְכוּ מִלְחָמָה לִקְרַאת פְּלִשְׁתִּים:

ג וּפְלִשְׁתִּים עֹמְדִים אֶל־הָהָר מִזֶּה וְיִשְׂרָאֵל עֹמְדִים אֶל־הָהָר מִזֶּה וְהַגַּיְא בֵּינֵיהֶם:

ד וַיֵּצֵא אִישׁ־הַבֵּנַיִם מִמַּחֲנוֹת פְּלִשְׁתִּים גָּלְיָת שְׁמוֹ מִגַּת גָּבְהוֹ שֵׁשׁ אַמּוֹת וָזָרֶת:

ה וְכוֹבַע נְחֹשֶׁת עַל־רֹאשׁוֹ וְשִׁרְיוֹן קַשְׂקַשִּׂים הוּא לָבוּשׁ וּמִשְׁקַל הַשִּׁרְיוֹן חֲמֵשֶׁת־אֲלָפִים שְׁקָלִים נְחֹשֶׁת:

ו וּמִצְחַת נְחֹשֶׁת עַל־רַגְלָיו וְכִידוֹן נְחֹשֶׁת בֵּין כְּתֵפָיו:

ז וְחֵץ [וְעֵץ] חֲנִיתוֹ כִּמְנוֹר אֹרְגִים וְלַהֶבֶת חֲנִיתוֹ שֵׁשׁ־מֵאוֹת שְׁקָלִים בַּרְזֶל וְנֹשֵׂא הַצִּנָּה הֹלֵךְ לְפָנָיו:

ח וַיַּעֲמֹד וַיִּקְרָא אֶל־מַעַרְכֹת יִשְׂרָאֵל וַיֹּאמֶר לָהֶם לָמָּה תֵצְאוּ לַעֲרֹךְ מִלְחָמָה הֲלוֹא אָנֹכִי הַפְּלִשְׁתִּי וְאַתֶּם עֲבָדִים לְשָׁאוּל בְּרוּ־לָכֶם אִישׁ וְיֵרֵד אֵלָי:

ט אִם־יוּכַל לְהִלָּחֵם אִתִּי וְהִכָּנִי וְהָיִינוּ לָכֶם לַעֲבָדִים וְאִם־אֲנִי אוּכַל־לוֹ וְהִכִּיתִיו וִהְיִיתֶם לָנוּ לַעֲבָדִים וַעֲבַדְתֶּם אֹתָנוּ:

י וַיֹּאמֶר הַפְּלִשְׁתִּי אֲנִי חֵרַפְתִּי אֶת־מַעַרְכוֹת יִשְׂרָאֵל הַיּוֹם הַזֶּה תְּנוּ־לִי אִישׁ וְנִלָּחֲמָה יָחַד:

יא וַיִּשְׁמַע שָׁאוּל וְכָל־יִשְׂרָאֵל אֶת־דִּבְרֵי הַפְּלִשְׁתִּי הָאֵלֶּה וַיֵּחַתּוּ וַיִּרְאוּ מְאֹד:

Shmuel I / I Samuel

Chapter 17

12 *David* was the son of a certain Ephrathite of *Beit Lechem* in *Yehuda* whose name was *Yishai*. He had eight sons, and in the days of *Shaul* the man was already old, advanced in years.

13 The three oldest sons of *Yishai* had left and gone with *Shaul* to the war. The names of his three sons who had gone to the war were *Eliav* the first-born, the next *Avinadav*, and the third Shammah;

14 and *David* was the youngest. The three oldest had followed *Shaul*,

15 and *David* would go back and forth from attending on *Shaul* to shepherd his father's flock at *Beit Lechem*.

16 The Philistine stepped forward morning and evening and took his stand for forty days.

17 *Yishai* said to his son *David*, "Take an *efah* of this parched corn and these ten loaves of bread for your brothers, and carry them quickly to your brothers in camp.

18 Take these ten cheeses to the captain of their thousand. Find out how your brothers are and bring some token from them."

19 *Shaul* and the brothers and all the men of *Yisrael* were in the valley of Elah, in the war against the Philistines.

20 Early next morning, *David* left someone in charge of the flock, took [the provisions], and set out, as his father *Yishai* had instructed him. He reached the barricade as the army was going out to the battle lines shouting the war cry.

21 *Yisrael* and the Philistines drew up their battle lines opposite each other.

22 *David* left his baggage with the man in charge of the baggage and ran toward the battle line and went to greet his brothers.

23 While he was talking to them, the champion, whose name was Goliath, the Philistine of Gath, stepped forward from the Philistine ranks and spoke the same words as before; and *David* heard him.

24 When the men of *Yisrael* saw the man, they fled in terror.

שמואל א

פרק יז

יב וְדָוִד בֶּן־אִישׁ אֶפְרָתִי הַזֶּה מִבֵּית לֶחֶם יְהוּדָה וּשְׁמוֹ יִשַׁי וְלוֹ שְׁמֹנָה בָנִים וְהָאִישׁ בִּימֵי שָׁאוּל זָקֵן בָּא בַאֲנָשִׁים:

יג וַיֵּלְכוּ שְׁלֹשֶׁת בְּנֵי־יִשַׁי הַגְּדֹלִים הָלְכוּ אַחֲרֵי־שָׁאוּל לַמִּלְחָמָה וְשֵׁם שְׁלֹשֶׁת בָּנָיו אֲשֶׁר הָלְכוּ בַּמִּלְחָמָה אֱלִיאָב הַבְּכוֹר וּמִשְׁנֵהוּ אֲבִינָדָב וְהַשְּׁלִשִׁי שַׁמָּה:

יד וְדָוִד הוּא הַקָּטָן וּשְׁלֹשָׁה הַגְּדֹלִים הָלְכוּ אַחֲרֵי שָׁאוּל:

טו וְדָוִד הֹלֵךְ וָשָׁב מֵעַל שָׁאוּל לִרְעוֹת אֶת־צֹאן אָבִיו בֵּית־לָחֶם:

טז וַיִּגַּשׁ הַפְּלִשְׁתִּי הַשְׁכֵּם וְהַעֲרֵב וַיִּתְיַצֵּב אַרְבָּעִים יוֹם:

יז וַיֹּאמֶר יִשַׁי לְדָוִד בְּנוֹ קַח־נָא לְאַחֶיךָ אֵיפַת הַקָּלִיא הַזֶּה וַעֲשָׂרָה לֶחֶם הַזֶּה וְהָרֵץ הַמַּחֲנֶה לְאַחֶיךָ:

יח וְאֵת עֲשֶׂרֶת חֲרִצֵי הֶחָלָב הָאֵלֶּה תָּבִיא לְשַׂר־הָאָלֶף וְאֶת־אַחֶיךָ תִּפְקֹד לְשָׁלוֹם וְאֶת־עֲרֻבָּתָם תִּקָּח:

יט וְשָׁאוּל וְהֵמָּה וְכָל־אִישׁ יִשְׂרָאֵל בְּעֵמֶק הָאֵלָה נִלְחָמִים עִם־פְּלִשְׁתִּים:

כ וַיַּשְׁכֵּם דָּוִד בַּבֹּקֶר וַיִּטֹּשׁ אֶת־הַצֹּאן עַל־שֹׁמֵר וַיִּשָּׂא וַיֵּלֶךְ כַּאֲשֶׁר צִוָּהוּ יִשָׁי וַיָּבֹא הַמַּעְגָּלָה וְהַחַיִל הַיֹּצֵא אֶל־הַמַּעֲרָכָה וְהֵרֵעוּ בַּמִּלְחָמָה:

כא וַתַּעֲרֹךְ יִשְׂרָאֵל וּפְלִשְׁתִּים מַעֲרָכָה לִקְרַאת מַעֲרָכָה:

כב וַיִּטֹּשׁ דָּוִד אֶת־הַכֵּלִים מֵעָלָיו עַל־יַד שׁוֹמֵר הַכֵּלִים וַיָּרָץ הַמַּעֲרָכָה וַיָּבֹא וַיִּשְׁאַל לְאֶחָיו לְשָׁלוֹם:

כג וְהוּא מְדַבֵּר עִמָּם וְהִנֵּה אִישׁ הַבֵּנַיִם עוֹלֶה גָּלְיָת הַפְּלִשְׁתִּי שְׁמוֹ מִגַּת ממערות [מִמַּעַרְכוֹת] פְּלִשְׁתִּים וַיְדַבֵּר כַּדְּבָרִים הָאֵלֶּה וַיִּשְׁמַע דָּוִד:

כד וְכֹל אִישׁ יִשְׂרָאֵל בִּרְאוֹתָם אֶת־הָאִישׁ וַיָּנֻסוּ מִפָּנָיו וַיִּירְאוּ מְאֹד:

Shmuel I/I Samuel
Chapter 17

25 And the men of *Yisrael* were saying [among themselves], "Do you see that man coming out? He comes out to defy *Yisrael*! The man who kills him will be rewarded by the king with great riches; he will also give him his daughter in marriage and grant exemption to his father's house in *Yisrael*."

וַיֹּאמֶר אִישׁ יִשְׂרָאֵל הַרְאִיתֶם הָאִישׁ הָעֹלֶה הַזֶּה כִּי לְחָרֵף אֶת־יִשְׂרָאֵל עֹלֶה וְהָיָה הָאִישׁ אֲשֶׁר־יַכֶּנּוּ יַעְשְׁרֶנּוּ הַמֶּלֶךְ עֹשֶׁר גָּדוֹל וְאֶת־בִּתּוֹ יִתֶּן־לוֹ וְאֵת בֵּית אָבִיו יַעֲשֶׂה חָפְשִׁי בְּיִשְׂרָאֵל: כה

26 *David* asked the men standing near him, "What will be done for the man who kills that Philistine and removes the disgrace from *Yisrael*? Who is that uncircumcised Philistine that he dares defy the ranks of the living God?"

וַיֹּאמֶר דָּוִד אֶל־הָאֲנָשִׁים הָעֹמְדִים עִמּוֹ לֵאמֹר מַה־יֵּעָשֶׂה לָאִישׁ אֲשֶׁר יַכֶּה אֶת־הַפְּלִשְׁתִּי הַלָּז וְהֵסִיר חֶרְפָּה מֵעַל יִשְׂרָאֵל כִּי מִי הַפְּלִשְׁתִּי הֶעָרֵל הַזֶּה כִּי חֵרֵף מַעַרְכוֹת אֱלֹהִים חַיִּים: כו

va-YO-mer da-VID el ha-a-na-SHEEM ha-o-m'-DEEM i-MO lay-MOR mah yay-a-SEH la-EESH a-SHER ya-KEH et ha-p'-lish-TEE ha-LAZ v'-hay-SEER kher-PAH may-AL yis-ra-AYL KEE MEE ha-p'-lish-TEE he-a-RAYL ha-ZEH KEE khay-RAYF ma-ar-KHOT e-lo-HEEM kha-YEEM

27 The troops told him in the same words what would be done for the man who killed him.

וַיֹּאמֶר לוֹ הָעָם כַּדָּבָר הַזֶּה לֵאמֹר כֹּה יֵעָשֶׂה לָאִישׁ אֲשֶׁר יַכֶּנּוּ: כז

28 When *Eliav*, his oldest brother, heard him speaking to the men, *Eliav* became angry with *David* and said, "Why did you come down here, and with whom did you leave those few sheep in the wilderness? I know your impudence and your impertinence: you came down to watch the fighting!"

וַיִּשְׁמַע אֱלִיאָב אָחִיו הַגָּדוֹל בְּדַבְּרוֹ אֶל־הָאֲנָשִׁים וַיִּחַר־אַף אֱלִיאָב בְּדָוִד וַיֹּאמֶר לָמָּה־זֶּה יָרַדְתָּ וְעַל־מִי נָטַשְׁתָּ מְעַט הַצֹּאן הָהֵנָּה בַּמִּדְבָּר אֲנִי יָדַעְתִּי אֶת־זְדֹנְךָ וְאֵת רֹעַ לְבָבֶךָ כִּי לְמַעַן רְאוֹת הַמִּלְחָמָה יָרָדְתָּ: כח

29 But *David* replied, "What have I done now? I was only asking!"

וַיֹּאמֶר דָּוִד מֶה עָשִׂיתִי עָתָּה הֲלוֹא דָּבָר הוּא: כט

30 And he turned away from him toward someone else; he asked the same question, and the troops gave him the same answer as before.

וַיִּסֹּב מֵאֶצְלוֹ אֶל־מוּל אַחֵר וַיֹּאמֶר כַּדָּבָר הַזֶּה וַיְשִׁבֻהוּ הָעָם דָּבָר כַּדָּבָר הָרִאשׁוֹן: ל

31 The things *David* said were overheard and were reported to *Shaul*, who had him brought over.

וַיִּשָּׁמְעוּ הַדְּבָרִים אֲשֶׁר דִּבֶּר דָּוִד וַיַּגִּדוּ לִפְנֵי־שָׁאוּל וַיִּקָּחֵהוּ: לא

32 *David* said to *Shaul*, "Let no man's courage fail him. Your servant will go and fight that Philistine!"

וַיֹּאמֶר דָּוִד אֶל־שָׁאוּל אַל־יִפֹּל לֵב־אָדָם עָלָיו עַבְדְּךָ יֵלֵךְ וְנִלְחַם עִם־הַפְּלִשְׁתִּי הַזֶּה: לב

17:26 That he dares defy the ranks of the living God? *David* expresses his conviction that the battle against Goliath and the Philistines is far more than an ordinary military affair. Goliath taunts the entire Nation of Israel, and thus by extension, the God of Israel. Defeating him is therefore not only a military necessity, but also a spiritual imperative. *David* understands that an attack on the People of Israel is always an attack on God Himself, and is prepared to risk his life to defeat Goliath in order to defend the nation and God's honor. *Hashem* responds by granting the nation a miraculous victory at the hands of the young *David*. We see similar stories in our own generation, when the small Nation of Israel has miraculously defeated armies far larger than their own, and whose citizens have frequently seen the hand of God intervening to save Jews from peril.

Valley of Elah where David fought Goliath

Shmuel I / I Samuel
Chapter 17

שמואל א
פרק יז

33 But *Shaul* said to *David*, "You cannot go to that Philistine and fight him; you are only a boy, and he has been a warrior from his youth!"

לג וַיֹּאמֶר שָׁאוּל אֶל־דָּוִד לֹא תוּכַל לָלֶכֶת אֶל־הַפְּלִשְׁתִּי הַזֶּה לְהִלָּחֵם עִמּוֹ כִּי־נַעַר אַתָּה וְהוּא אִישׁ מִלְחָמָה מִנְּעֻרָיו:

34 *David* replied to *Shaul*, "Your servant has been tending his father's sheep, and if a lion or a bear came and carried off an animal from the flock,

לד וַיֹּאמֶר דָּוִד אֶל־שָׁאוּל רֹעֶה הָיָה עַבְדְּךָ לְאָבִיו בַּצֹּאן וּבָא הָאֲרִי וְאֶת־הַדּוֹב וְנָשָׂא שֶׂה מֵהָעֵדֶר:

35 I would go after it and fight it and rescue it from its mouth. And if it attacked me, I would seize it by the beard and strike it down and kill it.

לה וְיָצָאתִי אַחֲרָיו וְהִכִּתִיו וְהִצַּלְתִּי מִפִּיו וַיָּקָם עָלַי וְהֶחֱזַקְתִּי בִּזְקָנוֹ וְהִכִּתִיו וַהֲמִיתִּיו:

36 Your servant has killed both lion and bear; and that uncircumcised Philistine shall end up like one of them, for he has defied the ranks of the living *Hashem*.

לו גַּם אֶת־הָאֲרִי גַּם־הַדּוֹב הִכָּה עַבְדֶּךָ וְהָיָה הַפְּלִשְׁתִּי הֶעָרֵל הַזֶּה כְּאַחַד מֵהֶם כִּי חֵרֵף מַעַרְכֹת אֱלֹהִים חַיִּים:

37 *Hashem*," *David* went on, "who saved me from lion and bear will also save me from that Philistine." "Then go," *Shaul* said to *David*, "and may *Hashem* be with you!"

לז וַיֹּאמֶר דָּוִד יְהֹוָה אֲשֶׁר הִצִּלַנִי מִיַּד הָאֲרִי וּמִיַּד הַדֹּב הוּא יַצִּילֵנִי מִיַּד הַפְּלִשְׁתִּי הַזֶּה וַיֹּאמֶר שָׁאוּל אֶל־דָּוִד לֵךְ וַיהֹוָה יִהְיֶה עִמָּךְ:

38 *Shaul* clothed *David* in his own garment; he placed a bronze helmet on his head and fastened a breastplate on him.

לח וַיַּלְבֵּשׁ שָׁאוּל אֶת־דָּוִד מַדָּיו וְנָתַן קוֹבַע נְחֹשֶׁת עַל־רֹאשׁוֹ וַיַּלְבֵּשׁ אֹתוֹ שִׁרְיוֹן:

39 *David* girded his sword over his garment. Then he tried to walk; but he was not used to it. And *David* said to *Shaul*, "I cannot walk in these, for I am not used to them." So *David* took them off.

לט וַיַּחְגֹּר דָּוִד אֶת־חַרְבּוֹ מֵעַל לְמַדָּיו וַיֹּאֶל לָלֶכֶת כִּי לֹא־נִסָּה וַיֹּאמֶר דָּוִד אֶל־שָׁאוּל לֹא אוּכַל לָלֶכֶת בָּאֵלֶּה כִּי לֹא נִסִּיתִי וַיְסִרֵם דָּוִד מֵעָלָיו:

40 He took his stick, picked a few smooth stones from the wadi, put them in the pocket of his shepherd's bag and, sling in hand, he went toward the Philistine.

מ וַיִּקַּח מַקְלוֹ בְּיָדוֹ וַיִּבְחַר־לוֹ חֲמִשָּׁה חַלֻּקֵי־אֲבָנִים מִן־הַנַּחַל וַיָּשֶׂם אֹתָם בִּכְלִי הָרֹעִים אֲשֶׁר־לוֹ וּבַיַּלְקוּט וְקַלְעוֹ בְיָדוֹ וַיִּגַּשׁ אֶל־הַפְּלִשְׁתִּי:

41 The Philistine, meanwhile, was coming closer to *David*, preceded by his shield-bearer.

מא וַיֵּלֶךְ הַפְּלִשְׁתִּי הֹלֵךְ וְקָרֵב אֶל־דָּוִד וְהָאִישׁ נֹשֵׂא הַצִּנָּה לְפָנָיו:

42 When the Philistine caught sight of *David*, he scorned him, for he was but a boy, ruddy and handsome.

מב וַיַּבֵּט הַפְּלִשְׁתִּי וַיִּרְאֶה אֶת־דָּוִד וַיִּבְזֵהוּ כִּי־הָיָה נַעַר וְאַדְמֹנִי עִם־יְפֵה מַרְאֶה:

43 And the Philistine called out to *David*, "Am I a dog that you come against me with sticks?" The Philistine cursed *David* by his gods;

מג וַיֹּאמֶר הַפְּלִשְׁתִּי אֶל־דָּוִד הֲכֶלֶב אָנֹכִי כִּי־אַתָּה בָא־אֵלַי בַּמַּקְלוֹת וַיְקַלֵּל הַפְּלִשְׁתִּי אֶת־דָּוִד בֵּאלֹהָיו:

44 and the Philistine said to *David*, "Come here, and I will give your flesh to the birds of the sky and the beasts of the field."

מד וַיֹּאמֶר הַפְּלִשְׁתִּי אֶל־דָּוִד לְכָה אֵלַי וְאֶתְּנָה אֶת־בְּשָׂרְךָ לְעוֹף הַשָּׁמַיִם וּלְבֶהֱמַת הַשָּׂדֶה:

45 *David* replied to the Philistine, "You come against me with sword and spear and javelin; but I come against you in the name of the Lord of Hosts, the God of the ranks of *Yisrael*, whom you have defied.

מה וַיֹּאמֶר דָּוִד אֶל־הַפְּלִשְׁתִּי אַתָּה בָּא אֵלַי בְּחֶרֶב וּבַחֲנִית וּבְכִידוֹן וְאָנֹכִי בָא־אֵלֶיךָ בְּשֵׁם יְהֹוָה צְבָאוֹת אֱלֹהֵי מַעַרְכוֹת יִשְׂרָאֵל אֲשֶׁר חֵרַפְתָּ:

Shmuel I / I Samuel
Chapter 17

שמואל א
פרק יז

46 This very day *Hashem* will deliver you into my hands. I will kill you and cut off your head; and I will give the carcasses of the Philistine camp to the birds of the sky and the beasts of the earth. All the earth shall know that there is a *Hashem* in *Yisrael*.

מו הַיּוֹם הַזֶּה יְסַגֶּרְךָ יְהֹוָה בְּיָדִי וְהִכִּיתִךָ וַהֲסִרֹתִי אֶת־רֹאשְׁךָ מֵעָלֶיךָ וְנָתַתִּי פֶּגֶר מַחֲנֵה פְלִשְׁתִּים הַיּוֹם הַזֶּה לְעוֹף הַשָּׁמַיִם וּלְחַיַּת הָאָרֶץ וְיֵדְעוּ כָּל־הָאָרֶץ כִּי יֵשׁ אֱלֹהִים לְיִשְׂרָאֵל:

47 And this whole assembly shall know that *Hashem* can give victory without sword or spear. For the battle is *Hashem*'s, and He will deliver you into our hands."

מז וְיֵדְעוּ כָּל־הַקָּהָל הַזֶּה כִּי־לֹא בְּחֶרֶב וּבַחֲנִית יְהוֹשִׁיעַ יְהֹוָה כִּי לַיהֹוָה הַמִּלְחָמָה וְנָתַן אֶתְכֶם בְּיָדֵנוּ:

48 When the Philistine began to advance toward him again, *David* quickly ran up to the battle line to face the Philistine.

מח וְהָיָה כִּי־קָם הַפְּלִשְׁתִּי וַיֵּלֶךְ וַיִּקְרַב לִקְרַאת דָּוִד וַיְמַהֵר דָּוִד וַיָּרָץ הַמַּעֲרָכָה לִקְרַאת הַפְּלִשְׁתִּי:

49 *David* put his hand into the bag; he took out a stone and slung it. It struck the Philistine in the forehead; the stone sank into his forehead, and he fell face down on the ground.

מט וַיִּשְׁלַח דָּוִד אֶת־יָדוֹ אֶל־הַכֶּלִי וַיִּקַּח מִשָּׁם אֶבֶן וַיְקַלַּע וַיַּךְ אֶת־הַפְּלִשְׁתִּי אֶל־מִצְחוֹ וַתִּטְבַּע הָאֶבֶן בְּמִצְחוֹ וַיִּפֹּל עַל־פָּנָיו אָרְצָה:

50 Thus *David* bested the Philistine with sling and stone; he struck him down and killed him. *David* had no sword;

נ וַיֶּחֱזַק דָּוִד מִן־הַפְּלִשְׁתִּי בַּקֶּלַע וּבָאֶבֶן וַיַּךְ אֶת־הַפְּלִשְׁתִּי וַיְמִיתֵהוּ וְחֶרֶב אֵין בְּיַד־דָּוִד:

51 so *David* ran up and stood over the Philistine, grasped his sword and pulled it from its sheath; and with it he dispatched him and cut off his head. When the Philistines saw that their warrior was dead, they ran.

נא וַיָּרָץ דָּוִד וַיַּעֲמֹד אֶל־הַפְּלִשְׁתִּי וַיִּקַּח אֶת־חַרְבּוֹ וַיִּשְׁלְפָהּ מִתַּעְרָהּ וַיְמֹתְתֵהוּ וַיִּכְרָת־בָּהּ אֶת־רֹאשׁוֹ וַיִּרְאוּ הַפְּלִשְׁתִּים כִּי־מֵת גִּבּוֹרָם וַיָּנֻסוּ:

52 The men of *Yisrael* and *Yehuda* rose up with a war cry and they pursued the Philistines all the way to Gai and up to the gates of Ekron; the Philistines fell mortally wounded along the road to Shaarim up to Gath and Ekron.

נב וַיָּקֻמוּ אַנְשֵׁי יִשְׂרָאֵל וִיהוּדָה וַיָּרִעוּ וַיִּרְדְּפוּ אֶת־הַפְּלִשְׁתִּים עַד־בּוֹאֲךָ גַיְא וְעַד שַׁעֲרֵי עֶקְרוֹן וַיִּפְּלוּ חַלְלֵי פְלִשְׁתִּים בְּדֶרֶךְ שַׁעֲרַיִם וְעַד־גַּת וְעַד־עֶקְרוֹן:

53 Then the Israelites returned from chasing the Philistines and looted their camp.

נג וַיָּשֻׁבוּ בְּנֵי יִשְׂרָאֵל מִדְּלֹק אַחֲרֵי פְלִשְׁתִּים וַיָּשֹׁסּוּ אֶת־מַחֲנֵיהֶם:

54 *David* took the head of the Philistine and brought it to *Yerushalayim*; and he put his weapons in his own tent.

נד וַיִּקַּח דָּוִד אֶת־רֹאשׁ הַפְּלִשְׁתִּי וַיְבִאֵהוּ יְרוּשָׁלָ͏ִם וְאֶת־כֵּלָיו שָׂם בְּאָהֳלוֹ:

55 When *Shaul* saw *David* going out to assault the Philistine, he asked his army commander *Avner*, "Whose son is that boy, *Avner*?" And *Avner* replied, "By your life, Your Majesty, I do not know."

נה וְכִרְאוֹת שָׁאוּל אֶת־דָּוִד יֹצֵא לִקְרַאת הַפְּלִשְׁתִּי אָמַר אֶל־אַבְנֵר שַׂר הַצָּבָא בֶּן־מִי־זֶה הַנַּעַר אַבְנֵר וַיֹּאמֶר אַבְנֵר חֵי־נַפְשְׁךָ הַמֶּלֶךְ אִם־יָדָעְתִּי:

56 "Then find out whose son that young fellow is," the king ordered.

נו וַיֹּאמֶר הַמֶּלֶךְ שְׁאַל אַתָּה בֶּן־מִי־זֶה הָעָלֶם:

57 So when *David* returned after killing the Philistine, *Avner* took him and brought him to *Shaul*, with the head of the Philistine still in his hand.

נז וּכְשׁוּב דָּוִד מֵהַכּוֹת אֶת־הַפְּלִשְׁתִּי וַיִּקַּח אֹתוֹ אַבְנֵר וַיְבִאֵהוּ לִפְנֵי שָׁאוּל וְרֹאשׁ הַפְּלִשְׁתִּי בְּיָדוֹ:

Shmuel I / I Samuel
Chapter 18

שמואל א
פרק יח

58 *Shaul* said to him, "Whose son are you, my boy?" And *David* answered, "The son of your servant *Yishai* the Bethlehemite."

נח וַיֹּאמֶר אֵלָיו שָׁאוּל בֶּן־מִי אַתָּה הַנָּעַר וַיֹּאמֶר דָּוִד בֶּן־עַבְדְּךָ יִשַׁי בֵּית הַלַּחְמִי:

18 1 When [*David*] finished speaking with *Shaul*, *Yehonatan*'s soul became bound up with the soul of *David*; *Yehonatan* loved *David* as himself.

יח א וַיְהִי כְּכַלֹּתוֹ לְדַבֵּר אֶל־שָׁאוּל וְנֶפֶשׁ יְהוֹנָתָן נִקְשְׁרָה בְּנֶפֶשׁ דָּוִד וַיֶּאֱהָבֵהוּ [וַיֶּאֱהָבֵהוּ] יְהוֹנָתָן כְּנַפְשׁוֹ:

2 *Shaul* took him [into his service] that day and would not let him return to his father's house. –

ב וַיִּקָּחֵהוּ שָׁאוּל בַּיּוֹם הַהוּא וְלֹא נְתָנוֹ לָשׁוּב בֵּית אָבִיו:

3 *Yehonatan* and *David* made a pact, because [*Yehonatan*] loved him as himself.

ג וַיִּכְרֹת יְהוֹנָתָן וְדָוִד בְּרִית בְּאַהֲבָתוֹ אֹתוֹ כְּנַפְשׁוֹ:

4 *Yehonatan* took off the cloak and tunic he was wearing and gave them to *David*, together with his sword, bow, and belt.

ד וַיִּתְפַּשֵּׁט יְהוֹנָתָן אֶת־הַמְּעִיל אֲשֶׁר עָלָיו וַיִּתְּנֵהוּ לְדָוִד וּמַדָּיו וְעַד־חַרְבּוֹ וְעַד־קַשְׁתּוֹ וְעַד־חֲגֹרוֹ:

va-yit-pa-SHAYT y'-ho-na-TAN et ha-m'-EEL a-SHER a-LAV va-yi-t'-NAY-hu l'-da-VID u-ma-DAV v'-ad khar-BO v'-ad kash-TO v'-ad kha-go-RO

5 *David* went out [with the troops], and he was successful in every mission on which *Shaul* sent him, and *Shaul* put him in command of all the soldiers; this pleased all the troops and *Shaul*'s courtiers as well.

ה וַיֵּצֵא דָוִד בְּכֹל אֲשֶׁר יִשְׁלָחֶנּוּ שָׁאוּל יַשְׂכִּיל וַיְשִׂמֵהוּ שָׁאוּל עַל אַנְשֵׁי הַמִּלְחָמָה וַיִּיטַב בְּעֵינֵי כָל־הָעָם וְגַם בְּעֵינֵי עַבְדֵי שָׁאוּל:

6 When the [troops] came home [and] *David* returned from killing the Philistine, the women of all the towns of *Yisrael* came out singing and dancing to greet King *Shaul* with timbrels, shouting, and sistrums.

ו וַיְהִי בְּבוֹאָם בְּשׁוּב דָּוִד מֵהַכּוֹת אֶת־הַפְּלִשְׁתִּי וַתֵּצֶאנָה הַנָּשִׁים מִכָּל־עָרֵי יִשְׂרָאֵל לָשׁוֹר [לָשִׁיר] וְהַמְּחֹלוֹת לִקְרַאת שָׁאוּל הַמֶּלֶךְ בְּתֻפִּים בְּשִׂמְחָה וּבְשָׁלִשִׁים:

7 The women sang as they danced, and they chanted: *Shaul* has slain his thousands; *David*, his tens of thousands!

ז וַתַּעֲנֶינָה הַנָּשִׁים הַמְשַׂחֲקוֹת וַתֹּאמַרְןָ הִכָּה שָׁאוּל בַּאֲלָפוֹ [בַּאֲלָפָיו] וְדָוִד בְּרִבְבֹתָיו:

8 *Shaul* was much distressed and greatly vexed about the matter. For he said, "To *David* they have given tens of thousands, and to me they have given thousands. All that he lacks is the kingship!"

ח וַיִּחַר לְשָׁאוּל מְאֹד וַיֵּרַע בְּעֵינָיו הַדָּבָר הַזֶּה וַיֹּאמֶר נָתְנוּ לְדָוִד רְבָבוֹת וְלִי נָתְנוּ הָאֲלָפִים וְעוֹד לוֹ אַךְ הַמְּלוּכָה:

9 From that day on *Shaul* kept a jealous eye on *David*.

ט וַיְהִי שָׁאוּל עוֹיֵן [עוֹיֵן] אֶת־דָּוִד מֵהַיּוֹם הַהוּא וָהָלְאָה:

18:4 *Yehonatan* took off the cloak and tunic he was wearing and gave them to *David* The Sages view the mutual affection shared by *Yehonatan* and *David* as the epitome of true love between friends, as neither has any ulterior motives (*Ethics of the Fathers* 5:16). Indeed, as the heir apparent, *Yehonatan* has every reason to be jealous of *David* who was destined to be the new king of Israel. But instead, *Yehonatan* accepts the decree. He not only protects *David* from his father, King *Shaul*, but also gives him the symbol of his position as heir to the throne. *Yehonatan* recognizes that *David* is to be the founder of the eternal dynasty of Israel.

Shmuel I / I Samuel
Chapter 18

10 The next day an evil spirit of *Hashem* gripped *Shaul* and he began to rave in the house, while *David* was playing [the lyre], as he did daily. *Shaul* had a spear in his hand,

11 and *Shaul* threw the spear, thinking to pin *David* to the wall. But *David* eluded him twice.

12 *Shaul* was afraid of *David*, for *Hashem* was with him and had turned away from *Shaul*.

13 So *Shaul* removed him from his presence and appointed him chief of a thousand, to march at the head of the troops.

14 *David* was successful in all his undertakings, for *Hashem* was with him;

15 and when *Shaul* saw that he was successful, he dreaded him.

16 All *Yisrael* and *Yehuda* loved *David*, for he marched at their head.

17 *Shaul* said to *David*, "Here is my older daughter, Merab; I will give her to you in marriage; in return, you be my warrior and fight the battles of *Hashem*." *Shaul* thought: "Let not my hand strike him; let the hand of the Philistines strike him."

18 *David* replied to *Shaul*, "Who am I and what is my life – my father's family in *Yisrael* – that I should become Your Majesty's son-in-law?"

19 But at the time that Merab, daughter of *Shaul*, should have been given to *David*, she was given in marriage to Adriel the Meholathite.

20 Now *Michal* daughter of *Shaul* had fallen in love with *David*; and when this was reported to *Shaul*, he was pleased.

21 *Shaul* thought: "I will give her to him, and she can serve as a snare for him, so that the Philistines may kill him." So *Shaul* said to *David*, "You can become my son-in-law even now through the second one."

22 And *Shaul* instructed his courtiers to say to *David* privately, "The king is fond of you and all his courtiers like you. So why not become the king's son-in-law?"

שמואל א
פרק יח

י וַיְהִי מִמָּחֳרָת וַתִּצְלַח רוּחַ אֱלֹהִים רָעָה אֶל־שָׁאוּל וַיִּתְנַבֵּא בְתוֹךְ־הַבַּיִת וְדָוִד מְנַגֵּן בְּיָדוֹ כְּיוֹם בְּיוֹם וְהַחֲנִית בְּיַד־שָׁאוּל:

יא וַיָּטֶל שָׁאוּל אֶת־הַחֲנִית וַיֹּאמֶר אַכֶּה בְדָוִד וּבַקִּיר וַיִּסֹּב דָּוִד מִפָּנָיו פַּעֲמָיִם:

יב וַיִּרָא שָׁאוּל מִלִּפְנֵי דָוִד כִּי־הָיָה יְהֹוָה עִמּוֹ וּמֵעִם שָׁאוּל סָר:

יג וַיְסִרֵהוּ שָׁאוּל מֵעִמּוֹ וַיְשִׂמֵהוּ לוֹ שַׂר־אָלֶף וַיֵּצֵא וַיָּבֹא לִפְנֵי הָעָם:

יד וַיְהִי דָוִד לְכָל־דְּרָכָו מַשְׂכִּיל וַיהֹוָה עִמּוֹ:

טו וַיַּרְא שָׁאוּל אֲשֶׁר־הוּא מַשְׂכִּיל מְאֹד וַיָּגָר מִפָּנָיו:

טז וְכָל־יִשְׂרָאֵל וִיהוּדָה אֹהֵב אֶת־דָּוִד כִּי־הוּא יוֹצֵא וָבָא לִפְנֵיהֶם:

יז וַיֹּאמֶר שָׁאוּל אֶל־דָּוִד הִנֵּה בִתִּי הַגְּדוֹלָה מֵרַב אֹתָהּ אֶתֶּן־לְךָ לְאִשָּׁה אַךְ הֱיֵה־לִּי לְבֶן־חַיִל וְהִלָּחֵם מִלְחֲמוֹת יְהֹוָה וְשָׁאוּל אָמַר אַל־תְּהִי יָדִי בּוֹ וּתְהִי־בוֹ יַד־פְּלִשְׁתִּים:

יח וַיֹּאמֶר דָּוִד אֶל־שָׁאוּל מִי אָנֹכִי וּמִי חַיַּי מִשְׁפַּחַת אָבִי בְּיִשְׂרָאֵל כִּי־אֶהְיֶה חָתָן לַמֶּלֶךְ:

יט וַיְהִי בְּעֵת תֵּת אֶת־מֵרַב בַּת־שָׁאוּל לְדָוִד וְהִיא נִתְּנָה לְעַדְרִיאֵל הַמְּחֹלָתִי לְאִשָּׁה:

כ וַתֶּאֱהַב מִיכַל בַּת־שָׁאוּל אֶת־דָּוִד וַיַּגִּדוּ לְשָׁאוּל וַיִּשַׁר הַדָּבָר בְּעֵינָיו:

כא וַיֹּאמֶר שָׁאוּל אֶתְּנֶנָּה לוֹ וּתְהִי־לוֹ לְמוֹקֵשׁ וּתְהִי־בוֹ יַד־פְּלִשְׁתִּים וַיֹּאמֶר שָׁאוּל אֶל־דָּוִד בִּשְׁתַּיִם תִּתְחַתֵּן בִּי הַיּוֹם:

כב וַיְצַו שָׁאוּל אֶת־עֲבָדָו דַּבְּרוּ אֶל־דָּוִד בַּלָּט לֵאמֹר הִנֵּה חָפֵץ בְּךָ הַמֶּלֶךְ וְכָל־עֲבָדָיו אֲהֵבוּךָ וְעַתָּה הִתְחַתֵּן בַּמֶּלֶךְ:

Shmuel I/I Samuel
Chapter 19

שמואל א
פרק יט

23 When the king's courtiers repeated these words to *David*, *David* replied, "Do you think that becoming the son-in-law of a king is a small matter, when I am but a poor man of no consequence?"

כג וַיְדַבְּרוּ עַבְדֵי שָׁאוּל בְּאׇזְנֵי דָוִד אֶת־הַדְּבָרִים הָאֵלֶּה וַיֹּאמֶר דָּוִד הַנְקַלָּה בְעֵינֵיכֶם הִתְחַתֵּן בַּמֶּלֶךְ וְאָנֹכִי אִישׁ־רָשׁ וְנִקְלֶה׃

24 *Shaul*'s courtiers reported to him, "This is what *David* answered."

כד וַיַּגִּדוּ עַבְדֵי שָׁאוּל לוֹ לֵאמֹר כַּדְּבָרִים הָאֵלֶּה דִּבֶּר דָּוִד׃

25 And *Shaul* said, "Say this to *David*: 'The king desires no other bride-price than the foreskins of a hundred Philistines, as vengeance on the king's enemies.'" – *Shaul* intended to bring about *David*'s death at the hands of the Philistines. –

כה וַיֹּאמֶר שָׁאוּל כֹּה־תֹאמְרוּ לְדָוִד אֵין־חֵפֶץ לַמֶּלֶךְ בְּמֹהַר כִּי בְּמֵאָה עׇרְלוֹת פְּלִשְׁתִּים לְהִנָּקֵם בְּאֹיְבֵי הַמֶּלֶךְ וְשָׁאוּל חָשַׁב לְהַפִּיל אֶת־דָּוִד בְּיַד־פְּלִשְׁתִּים׃

26 When his courtiers told this to *David*, *David* was pleased with the idea of becoming the king's son-in-law. Before the time had expired,

כו וַיַּגִּדוּ עֲבָדָיו לְדָוִד אֶת־הַדְּבָרִים הָאֵלֶּה וַיִּשַׁר הַדָּבָר בְּעֵינֵי דָוִד לְהִתְחַתֵּן בַּמֶּלֶךְ וְלֹא מָלְאוּ הַיָּמִים׃

27 *David* went out with his men and killed two hundred Philistines; *David* brought their foreskins and they were counted out for the king, that he might become the king's son-in-law. *Shaul* then gave him his daughter *Michal* in marriage.

כז וַיָּקׇם דָּוִד וַיֵּלֶךְ הוּא וַאֲנָשָׁיו וַיַּךְ בַּפְּלִשְׁתִּים מָאתַיִם אִישׁ וַיָּבֵא דָוִד אֶת־עׇרְלֹתֵיהֶם וַיְמַלְאוּם לַמֶּלֶךְ לְהִתְחַתֵּן בַּמֶּלֶךְ וַיִּתֶּן־לוֹ שָׁאוּל אֶת־מִיכַל בִּתּוֹ לְאִשָּׁה׃

28 When *Shaul* realized that *Hashem* was with *David* and that *Michal* daughter of *Shaul* loved him,

כח וַיַּרְא שָׁאוּל וַיֵּדַע כִּי יְהֹוָה עִם־דָּוִד וּמִיכַל בַּת־שָׁאוּל אֲהֵבַתְהוּ׃

29 *Shaul* grew still more afraid of *David*; and *Shaul* was *David*'s enemy ever after.

כט וַיֹּסֶף שָׁאוּל לֵרֹא מִפְּנֵי דָוִד עוֹד וַיְהִי שָׁאוּל אֹיֵב אֶת־דָּוִד כׇּל־הַיָּמִים׃

30 The Philistine chiefs marched out [to battle]; and every time they marched out, *David* was more successful than all the other officers of *Shaul*. His reputation soared.

ל וַיֵּצְאוּ שָׂרֵי פְלִשְׁתִּים וַיְהִי מִדֵּי צֵאתָם שָׂכַל דָּוִד מִכֹּל עַבְדֵי שָׁאוּל וַיִּיקַר שְׁמוֹ מְאֹד׃

19

1 *Shaul* urged his son *Yonatan* and all his courtiers to kill *David*. But *Shaul*'s son *Yehonatan* was very fond of *David*,

יט א וַיְדַבֵּר שָׁאוּל אֶל־יוֹנָתָן בְּנוֹ וְאֶל־כׇּל־עֲבָדָיו לְהָמִית אֶת־דָּוִד וִיהוֹנָתָן בֶּן־שָׁאוּל חָפֵץ בְּדָוִד מְאֹד׃

2 and *Yehonatan* told *David*, "My father *Shaul* is bent on killing you. Be on your guard tomorrow morning; get to a secret place and remain in hiding.

ב וַיַּגֵּד יְהוֹנָתָן לְדָוִד לֵאמֹר מְבַקֵּשׁ שָׁאוּל אָבִי לַהֲמִיתֶךָ וְעַתָּה הִשָּׁמֶר־נָא בַבֹּקֶר וְיָשַׁבְתָּ בַסֵּתֶר וְנַחְבֵּאתָ׃

3 I will go out and stand next to my father in the field where you will be, and I will speak to my father about you. If I learn anything, I will tell you."

ג וַאֲנִי אֵצֵא וְעָמַדְתִּי לְיַד־אָבִי בַּשָּׂדֶה אֲשֶׁר אַתָּה שָׁם וַאֲנִי אֲדַבֵּר בְּךָ אֶל־אָבִי וְרָאִיתִי מָה וְהִגַּדְתִּי לָךְ׃

4 So *Yehonatan* spoke well of *David* to his father *Shaul*. He said to him, "Let not Your Majesty wrong his servant *David*, for he has not wronged you; indeed, all his actions have been very much to your advantage.

ד וַיְדַבֵּר יְהוֹנָתָן בְּדָוִד טוֹב אֶל־שָׁאוּל אָבִיו וַיֹּאמֶר אֵלָיו אַל־יֶחֱטָא הַמֶּלֶךְ בְּעַבְדּוֹ בְדָוִד כִּי לוֹא חָטָא לָךְ וְכִי מַעֲשָׂיו טוֹב־לְךָ מְאֹד׃

Shmuel I / I Samuel
Chapter 19

5 He took his life in his hands and killed the Philistine, and *Hashem* wrought a great victory for all *Yisrael*. You saw it and rejoiced. Why then should you incur the guilt of shedding the blood of an innocent man, killing *David* without cause?"

6 *Shaul* heeded *Yehonatan*'s plea, and *Shaul* swore, "As *Hashem* lives, he shall not be put to death!"

7 *Yehonatan* called *David*, and *Yehonatan* told him all this. Then *Yehonatan* brought *David* to *Shaul*, and he served him as before.

8 Fighting broke out again. *David* went out and fought the Philistines. He inflicted a great defeat upon them and they fled before him.

9 Then an evil spirit of *Hashem* came upon *Shaul* while he was sitting in his house with his spear in his hand, and *David* was playing [the lyre].

10 *Shaul* tried to pin *David* to the wall with the spear, but he eluded *Shaul*, so that he drove the spear into the wall. *David* fled and got away. That night

11 *Shaul* sent messengers to *David*'s home to keep watch on him and to kill him in the morning. But *David*'s wife *Michal* told him, "Unless you run for your life tonight, you will be killed tomorrow."

12 *Michal* let *David* down from the window and he escaped and fled.

> va-TO-red mi-KHAL et da-VID b'-AD ha-kha-LON va-YAY-lekh va-yiv-RAKH va-yi-ma-LAYT

13 *Michal* then took the household idol, laid it on the bed, and covered it with a cloth; and at its head she put a net of goat's hair.

14 *Shaul* sent messengers to seize *David*; but she said, "He is sick."

19:12 *Michal* let *David* down from the window
Michal, daughter of King *Shaul*, is *David*'s wife. *Shaul* had thought that she would be loyal to her father and surrender *David* to him. However, like her brother *Yehonatan*, *Michal* recognizes that *David* and his descendants are destined to be the eternal kings of Israel. She risks her life to help her beloved husband escape. According to the Sages (*Sanhedrin* 19b), when *Shaul* later gives her as a wife to another man (25:44), they heroically refrain from all contact with each other, as they both understand that she is still married to *David*. Her loyalty to *Hashem*'s will, despite the risks involved, forever serves as an inspiration to those who seek to overcome all challenges to do the will of God.

Shmuel I / I Samuel
Chapter 20

15 Shaul, however, sent back the messengers to see David for themselves. "Bring him up to me in the bed," he ordered, "that he may be put to death."

16 When the messengers came, they found the household idol in the bed, with the net of goat's hair at its head.

17 Shaul said to Michal, "Why did you play that trick on me and let my enemy get away safely?" "Because," Michal answered Shaul, "he said to me: 'Help me get away or I'll kill you.'"

18 David made good his escape, and he came to Shmuel at Rama and told him all that Shaul had done to him. He and Shmuel went and stayed at Naioth.

19 Shaul was told that David was at Naioth in Rama,

20 and Shaul sent messengers to seize David. They saw a band of Neviim speaking in ecstasy, with Shmuel standing by as their leader; and the spirit of Hashem came upon Shaul's messengers and they too began to speak in ecstasy.

21 When Shaul was told about this, he sent other messengers; but they too spoke in ecstasy. Shaul sent a third group of messengers; and they also spoke in ecstasy.

22 So he himself went to Rama. When he came to the great cistern at Secu, he asked, "Where are Shmuel and David?" and was told that they were at Naioth in Rama.

23 He was on his way there, to Naioth in Rama, when the spirit of Hashem came upon him too; and he walked on, speaking in ecstasy, until he reached Naioth in Rama.

24 Then he too stripped off his clothes and he too spoke in ecstasy before Shmuel; and he lay naked all that day and all night. That is why people say, "Is Shaul too among the Neviim?"

20

1 David fled from Naioth in Rama; he came to Yehonatan and said, "What have I done, what is my crime and my guilt against your father, that he seeks my life?"

שמואל א
פרק כ

טו וַיִּשְׁלַח שָׁאוּל אֶת־הַמַּלְאָכִים לִרְאוֹת אֶת־דָּוִד לֵאמֹר הַעֲלוּ אֹתוֹ בַמִּטָּה אֵלַי לַהֲמִתוֹ:

טז וַיָּבֹאוּ הַמַּלְאָכִים וְהִנֵּה הַתְּרָפִים אֶל־הַמִּטָּה וּכְבִיר הָעִזִּים מְרַאֲשֹׁתָיו:

יז וַיֹּאמֶר שָׁאוּל אֶל־מִיכַל לָמָּה כָּכָה רִמִּיתִנִי וַתְּשַׁלְּחִי אֶת־אֹיְבִי וַיִּמָּלֵט וַתֹּאמֶר מִיכַל אֶל־שָׁאוּל הוּא־אָמַר אֵלַי שַׁלְּחִנִי לָמָה אֲמִיתֵךְ:

יח וְדָוִד בָּרַח וַיִּמָּלֵט וַיָּבֹא אֶל־שְׁמוּאֵל הָרָמָתָה וַיַּגֶּד־לוֹ אֵת כָּל־אֲשֶׁר עָשָׂה־לוֹ שָׁאוּל וַיֵּלֶךְ הוּא וּשְׁמוּאֵל וַיֵּשְׁבוּ בנוית [בְּנָיוֹת]:

יט וַיֻּגַּד לְשָׁאוּל לֵאמֹר הִנֵּה דָוִד בנוית [בְּנָיוֹת] בָּרָמָה:

כ וַיִּשְׁלַח שָׁאוּל מַלְאָכִים לָקַחַת אֶת־דָּוִד וַיַּרְא אֶת־לַהֲקַת הַנְּבִיאִים נִבְּאִים וּשְׁמוּאֵל עֹמֵד נִצָּב עֲלֵיהֶם וַתְּהִי עַל־מַלְאֲכֵי שָׁאוּל רוּחַ אֱלֹהִים וַיִּתְנַבְּאוּ גַּם־הֵמָּה:

כא וַיַּגִּדוּ לְשָׁאוּל וַיִּשְׁלַח מַלְאָכִים אֲחֵרִים וַיִּתְנַבְּאוּ גַּם־הֵמָּה וַיֹּסֶף שָׁאוּל וַיִּשְׁלַח מַלְאָכִים שְׁלִשִׁים וַיִּתְנַבְּאוּ גַם־הֵמָּה:

כב וַיֵּלֶךְ גַּם־הוּא הָרָמָתָה וַיָּבֹא עַד־בּוֹר הַגָּדוֹל אֲשֶׁר בַּשֶּׂכוּ וַיִּשְׁאַל וַיֹּאמֶר אֵיפֹה שְׁמוּאֵל וְדָוִד וַיֹּאמֶר הִנֵּה בנוית [בְּנָיוֹת] בָּרָמָה:

כג וַיֵּלֶךְ שָׁם אֶל־נוית [נָיוֹת] בָּרָמָה וַתְּהִי עָלָיו גַּם־הוּא רוּחַ אֱלֹהִים וַיֵּלֶךְ הָלוֹךְ וַיִּתְנַבֵּא עַד־בֹּאוֹ בנוית [בְּנָיוֹת] בָּרָמָה:

כד וַיִּפְשַׁט גַּם־הוּא בְּגָדָיו וַיִּתְנַבֵּא גַם־הוּא לִפְנֵי שְׁמוּאֵל וַיִּפֹּל עָרֹם כָּל־הַיּוֹם הַהוּא וְכָל־הַלָּיְלָה עַל־כֵּן יֹאמְרוּ הֲגַם שָׁאוּל בַּנְּבִיאִם:

כ א וַיִּבְרַח דָּוִד מנוות [מִנָּיוֹת] בְּרָמָה וַיָּבֹא וַיֹּאמֶר לִפְנֵי יְהוֹנָתָן מֶה עָשִׂיתִי מֶה־עֲוֹנִי וּמֶה־חַטָּאתִי לִפְנֵי אָבִיךָ כִּי מְבַקֵּשׁ אֶת־נַפְשִׁי:

Shmuel I / I Samuel
Chapter 20

שמואל א
פרק כ

2 He replied, "Heaven forbid! You shall not die. My father does not do anything, great or small, without disclosing it to me; why should my father conceal this matter from me? It cannot be!"

ב וַיֹּאמֶר לוֹ חָלִילָה לֹא תָמוּת הִנֵּה לו־עשה [לֹא־] [יַעֲשֶׂה] אָבִי דָּבָר גָּדוֹל אוֹ דָבָר קָטֹן וְלֹא יִגְלֶה אֶת־אָזְנִי וּמַדּוּעַ יַסְתִּיר אָבִי מִמֶּנִּי אֶת־הַדָּבָר הַזֶּה אֵין זֹאת:

3 David swore further, "Your father knows well that you are fond of me and has decided: *Yehonatan* must not learn of this or he will be grieved. But, as *Hashem* lives and as you live, there is only a step between me and death."

ג וַיִּשָּׁבַע עוֹד דָּוִד וַיֹּאמֶר יָדֹעַ יָדַע אָבִיךָ כִּי־מָצָאתִי חֵן בְּעֵינֶיךָ וַיֹּאמֶר אַל־יֵדַע־זֹאת יְהוֹנָתָן פֶּן־יֵעָצֵב וְאוּלָם חַי־יְהוָה וְחֵי נַפְשֶׁךָ כִּי כְפֶשַׂע בֵּינִי וּבֵין הַמָּוֶת:

4 *Yehonatan* said to *David*, "Whatever you want, I will do it for you."

ד וַיֹּאמֶר יְהוֹנָתָן אֶל־דָּוִד מַה־תֹּאמַר נַפְשְׁךָ וְאֶעֱשֶׂה־לָּךְ:

5 *David* said to *Yehonatan*, "Tomorrow is the new moon, and I am to sit with the king at the meal. Instead, let me go and I will hide in the countryside until the third evening.

ה וַיֹּאמֶר דָּוִד אֶל־יְהוֹנָתָן הִנֵּה־חֹדֶשׁ מָחָר וְאָנֹכִי יָשֹׁב־אֵשֵׁב עִם־הַמֶּלֶךְ לֶאֱכוֹל וְשִׁלַּחְתַּנִי וְנִסְתַּרְתִּי בַשָּׂדֶה עַד הָעֶרֶב הַשְּׁלִשִׁית:

6 If your father notes my absence, you say, '*David* asked my permission to run down to his home town, *Beit Lechem*, for the whole family has its annual sacrifice there.'

ו אִם־פָּקֹד יִפְקְדֵנִי אָבִיךָ וְאָמַרְתָּ נִשְׁאֹל נִשְׁאַל מִמֶּנִּי דָוִד לָרוּץ בֵּית־לֶחֶם עִירוֹ כִּי זֶבַח הַיָּמִים שָׁם לְכָל־הַמִּשְׁפָּחָה:

7 If he says 'Good,' your servant is safe; but if his anger flares up, know that he is resolved to do [me] harm.

ז אִם־כֹּה יֹאמַר טוֹב שָׁלוֹם לְעַבְדֶּךָ וְאִם־חָרֹה יֶחֱרֶה לוֹ דַּע כִּי־כָלְתָה הָרָעָה מֵעִמּוֹ:

8 Deal faithfully with your servant, since you have taken your servant into a covenant of *Hashem* with you. And if I am guilty, kill me yourself, but don't make me go back to your father."

ח וְעָשִׂיתָ חֶסֶד עַל־עַבְדֶּךָ כִּי בִּבְרִית יְהוָה הֵבֵאתָ אֶת־עַבְדְּךָ עִמָּךְ וְאִם־יֶשׁ־בִּי עָוֹן הֲמִיתֵנִי אַתָּה וְעַד־אָבִיךָ לָמָּה־זֶּה תְבִיאֵנִי:

9 *Yehonatan* replied, "Don't talk like that! If I learn that my father has resolved to kill you, I will surely tell you about it."

ט וַיֹּאמֶר יְהוֹנָתָן חָלִילָה לָּךְ כִּי אִם־יָדֹעַ אֵדַע כִּי־כָלְתָה הָרָעָה מֵעִם אָבִי לָבוֹא עָלֶיךָ וְלֹא אֹתָהּ אַגִּיד לָךְ:

10 *David* said to *Yehonatan*, "Who will tell me if your father answers you harshly?"

י וַיֹּאמֶר דָּוִד אֶל־יְהוֹנָתָן מִי יַגִּיד לִי אוֹ מַה־יַּעַנְךָ אָבִיךָ קָשָׁה:

11 *Yehonatan* said to *David*, "Let us go into the open"; and they both went out into the open.

יא וַיֹּאמֶר יְהוֹנָתָן אֶל־דָּוִד לְכָה וְנֵצֵא הַשָּׂדֶה וַיֵּצְאוּ שְׁנֵיהֶם הַשָּׂדֶה:

12 Then *Yehonatan* said to *David*, "By *Hashem*, the God of *Yisrael*! I will sound out my father at this time tomorrow, [or] on the third day; and if [his response] is favorable for *David*, I will send a message to you at once and disclose it to you.

יב וַיֹּאמֶר יְהוֹנָתָן אֶל־דָּוִד יְהוָה אֱלֹהֵי יִשְׂרָאֵל כִּי־אֶחְקֹר אֶת־אָבִי כָּעֵת מָחָר הַשְּׁלִשִׁית וְהִנֵּה־טוֹב אֶל־דָּוִד וְלֹא־אָז אֶשְׁלַח אֵלֶיךָ וְגָלִיתִי אֶת־אָזְנֶךָ:

13 But if my father intends to do you harm, may *Hashem* do thus to *Yehonatan* and more if I do [not] disclose it to you and send you off to escape unharmed. May *Hashem* be with you, as He used to be with my father.

יג כֹּה־יַעֲשֶׂה יְהוָה לִיהוֹנָתָן וְכֹה יֹסִיף כִּי־יֵיטִב אֶל־אָבִי אֶת־הָרָעָה עָלֶיךָ וְגָלִיתִי אֶת־אָזְנֶךָ וְשִׁלַּחְתִּיךָ וְהָלַכְתָּ לְשָׁלוֹם וִיהִי יְהוָה עִמָּךְ כַּאֲשֶׁר הָיָה עִם־אָבִי:

Shmuel I / I Samuel
Chapter 20

שמואל א
פרק כ

14 Nor shall you fail to show me *Hashem*'s faithfulness, while I am alive; nor, when I am dead,

יד וְלֹא אִם־עוֹדֶנִּי חָי וְלֹא־תַעֲשֶׂה עִמָּדִי חֶסֶד יְהוָה וְלֹא אָמוּת:

15 shall you ever discontinue your faithfulness to my house – not even after *Hashem* has wiped out every one of *David*'s enemies from the face of the earth.

טו וְלֹא־תַכְרִת אֶת־חַסְדְּךָ מֵעִם בֵּיתִי עַד־עוֹלָם וְלֹא בְּהַכְרִת יְהוָה אֶת־אֹיְבֵי דָוִד אִישׁ מֵעַל פְּנֵי הָאֲדָמָה:

16 Thus has *Yehonatan* covenanted with the house of *David*; and may *Hashem* requite the enemies of *David*!"

טז וַיִּכְרֹת יְהוֹנָתָן עִם־בֵּית דָּוִד וּבִקֵּשׁ יְהוָה מִיַּד אֹיְבֵי דָוִד:

17 *Yehonatan*, out of his love for *David*, adjured him again, for he loved him as himself.

יז וַיּוֹסֶף יְהוֹנָתָן לְהַשְׁבִּיעַ אֶת־דָּוִד בְּאַהֲבָתוֹ אֹתוֹ כִּי־אַהֲבַת נַפְשׁוֹ אֲהֵבוֹ:

18 *Yehonatan* said to him, "Tomorrow will be the new moon; and you will be missed when your seat remains vacant.

va-yo-mer LO y'-ho-na-TAN ma-KHAR KHO-desh v'-NIF-kad-TA KEE yi-pa-KAYD mo-sha-VE-kha

יח וַיֹּאמֶר־לוֹ יְהוֹנָתָן מָחָר חֹדֶשׁ וְנִפְקַדְתָּ כִּי יִפָּקֵד מוֹשָׁבֶךָ:

19 So the day after tomorrow, go down all the way to the place where you hid the other time, and stay close to the Ezel stone.

יט וְשִׁלַּשְׁתָּ תֵּרֵד מְאֹד וּבָאתָ אֶל־הַמָּקוֹם אֲשֶׁר־נִסְתַּרְתָּ שָּׁם בְּיוֹם הַמַּעֲשֶׂה וְיָשַׁבְתָּ אֵצֶל הָאֶבֶן הָאָזֶל:

20 Now I will shoot three arrows to one side of it, as though I were shooting at a mark,

כ וַאֲנִי שְׁלֹשֶׁת הַחִצִּים צִדָּה אוֹרֶה לְשַׁלַּח־לִי לְמַטָּרָה:

21 and I will order the boy to go and find the arrows. If I call to the boy, 'Hey! the arrows are on this side of you,' be reassured and come, for you are safe and there is no danger – as *Hashem* lives!

כא וְהִנֵּה אֶשְׁלַח אֶת־הַנַּעַר לֵךְ מְצָא אֶת־הַחִצִּים אִם־אָמֹר אֹמַר לַנַּעַר הִנֵּה הַחִצִּים מִמְּךָ וָהֵנָּה קָחֶנּוּ וָבֹאָה כִּי־שָׁלוֹם לְךָ וְאֵין דָּבָר חַי־יְהוָה:

22 But if, instead, I call to the lad, 'Hey! the arrows are beyond you,' then leave, for *Hashem* has sent you away.

כב וְאִם־כֹּה אֹמַר לָעֶלֶם הִנֵּה הַחִצִּים מִמְּךָ וָהָלְאָה לֵךְ כִּי שִׁלֵּחֲךָ יְהוָה:

23 As for the promise we made to each other, may *Hashem* be [witness] between you and me forever."

כג וְהַדָּבָר אֲשֶׁר דִּבַּרְנוּ אֲנִי וָאָתָּה הִנֵּה יְהוָה בֵּינִי וּבֵינְךָ עַד־עוֹלָם:

24 *David* hid in the field. The new moon came, and the king sat down to partake of the meal.

כד וַיִּסָּתֵר דָּוִד בַּשָּׂדֶה וַיְהִי הַחֹדֶשׁ וַיֵּשֶׁב הַמֶּלֶךְ עַל־[אֶל־] הַלֶּחֶם לֶאֱכוֹל:

25 When the king took his usual place on the seat by the wall, *Yehonatan* rose and *Avner* sat down at *Shaul*'s side; but *David*'s place remained vacant.

כה וַיֵּשֶׁב הַמֶּלֶךְ עַל־מוֹשָׁבוֹ כְּפַעַם בְּפַעַם אֶל־מוֹשַׁב הַקִּיר וַיָּקָם יְהוֹנָתָן וַיֵּשֶׁב אַבְנֵר מִצַּד שָׁאוּל וַיִּפָּקֵד מְקוֹם דָּוִד:

Full moon over the walls of Jerusalem

20:18 Tomorrow will be the new moon The Sages teach that the moon is a symbol of the People of Israel. Just as the moon waxes and wanes, appearing tiny when it is new but large by the middle of the month, the Children of Israel follow a similar cycle. Though at times they are a small and downtrodden nation, they will again become great in the eyes of all. In our era, with the establishment of the State of Israel, we are beginning to see the truth of this statement. When the world is ultimately blessed with the *Mashiach*, from the house of *David*, the light from the People of Israel will shine its brightest, originating in the Land of Israel and illuminating the entire world.

Shmuel I / I Samuel
Chapter 20

שמואל א
פרק כ

26 That day, however, *Shaul* said nothing. "It's accidental," he thought. "He must be unclean and not yet cleansed."

כו וְלֹא־דִבֶּר שָׁאוּל מְאוּמָה בַּיּוֹם הַהוּא כִּי אָמַר מִקְרֶה הוּא בִּלְתִּי טָהוֹר הוּא כִּי־לֹא טָהוֹר׃

27 But on the day after the new moon, the second day, *David*'s place was vacant again. So *Shaul* said to his son *Yehonatan*, "Why didn't the son of *Yishai* come to the meal yesterday or today?"

כז וַיְהִי מִמָּחֳרַת הַחֹדֶשׁ הַשֵּׁנִי וַיִּפָּקֵד מְקוֹם דָּוִד וַיֹּאמֶר שָׁאוּל אֶל־יְהוֹנָתָן בְּנוֹ מַדּוּעַ לֹא־בָא בֶן־יִשַׁי גַּם־תְּמוֹל גַּם־הַיּוֹם אֶל־הַלָּחֶם׃

28 *Yehonatan* answered *Shaul*, "*David* begged leave of me to go to *Beit Lechem*.

כח וַיַּעַן יְהוֹנָתָן אֶת־שָׁאוּל נִשְׁאֹל נִשְׁאַל דָּוִד מֵעִמָּדִי עַד־בֵּית לָחֶם׃

29 He said, 'Please let me go, for we are going to have a family feast in our town and my brother has summoned me to it. Do me a favor, let me slip away to see my kinsmen.' That is why he has not come to the king's table."

כט וַיֹּאמֶר שַׁלְּחֵנִי נָא כִּי זֶבַח מִשְׁפָּחָה לָנוּ בָּעִיר וְהוּא צִוָּה־לִי אָחִי וְעַתָּה אִם־מָצָאתִי חֵן בְּעֵינֶיךָ אִמָּלְטָה נָּא וְאֶרְאֶה אֶת־אֶחָי עַל־כֵּן לֹא־בָא אֶל־שֻׁלְחַן הַמֶּלֶךְ׃

30 *Shaul* flew into a rage against *Yehonatan*. "You son of a perverse, rebellious woman!" he shouted. "I know that you side with the son of *Yishai* – to your shame, and to the shame of your mother's nakedness!

ל וַיִּחַר־אַף שָׁאוּל בִּיהוֹנָתָן וַיֹּאמֶר לוֹ בֶּן־נַעֲוַת הַמַּרְדּוּת הֲלוֹא יָדַעְתִּי כִּי־בֹחֵר אַתָּה לְבֶן־יִשַׁי לְבָשְׁתְּךָ וּלְבֹשֶׁת עֶרְוַת אִמֶּךָ׃

31 For as long as the son of *Yishai* lives on earth, neither you nor your kingship will be secure. Now then, have him brought to me, for he is marked for death."

לא כִּי כָל־הַיָּמִים אֲשֶׁר בֶּן־יִשַׁי חַי עַל־הָאֲדָמָה לֹא תִכּוֹן אַתָּה וּמַלְכוּתֶךָ וְעַתָּה שְׁלַח וְקַח אֹתוֹ אֵלַי כִּי בֶן־מָוֶת הוּא׃

32 But *Yehonatan* spoke up and said to his father, "Why should he be put to death? What has he done?"

לב וַיַּעַן יְהוֹנָתָן אֶת־שָׁאוּל אָבִיו וַיֹּאמֶר אֵלָיו לָמָּה יוּמַת מֶה עָשָׂה׃

33 At that, *Shaul* threw his spear at him to strike him down; and *Yehonatan* realized that his father was determined to do away with *David*.

לג וַיָּטֶל שָׁאוּל אֶת־הַחֲנִית עָלָיו לְהַכֹּתוֹ וַיֵּדַע יְהוֹנָתָן כִּי־כָלָה הִיא מֵעִם אָבִיו לְהָמִית אֶת־דָּוִד׃

34 *Yehonatan* rose from the table in a rage. He ate no food on the second day of the new moon, because he was grieved about *David*, and because his father had humiliated him.

לד וַיָּקָם יְהוֹנָתָן מֵעִם הַשֻּׁלְחָן בָּחֳרִי־אָף וְלֹא־אָכַל בְּיוֹם־הַחֹדֶשׁ הַשֵּׁנִי לֶחֶם כִּי נֶעֱצַב אֶל־דָּוִד כִּי הִכְלִמוֹ אָבִיו׃

35 In the morning, *Yehonatan* went out into the open for the meeting with *David*, accompanied by a young boy.

לה וַיְהִי בַבֹּקֶר וַיֵּצֵא יְהוֹנָתָן הַשָּׂדֶה לְמוֹעֵד דָּוִד וְנַעַר קָטֹן עִמּוֹ׃

36 He said to the boy, "Run ahead and find the arrows that I shoot." And as the boy ran, he shot the arrows past him.

לו וַיֹּאמֶר לְנַעֲרוֹ רֻץ מְצָא נָא אֶת־הַחִצִּים אֲשֶׁר אָנֹכִי מוֹרֶה הַנַּעַר רָץ וְהוּא־יָרָה הַחֵצִי לְהַעֲבִרוֹ׃

37 When the boy came to the place where the arrows shot by *Yehonatan* had fallen, *Yehonatan* called out to the boy, "Hey, the arrows are beyond you!"

לז וַיָּבֹא הַנַּעַר עַד־מְקוֹם הַחֵצִי אֲשֶׁר יָרָה יְהוֹנָתָן וַיִּקְרָא יְהוֹנָתָן אַחֲרֵי הַנַּעַר וַיֹּאמֶר הֲלוֹא הַחֵצִי מִמְּךָ וָהָלְאָה׃

Shmuel I / I Samuel
Chapter 21

שמואל א
פרק כא

38 And *Yehonatan* called after the boy, "Quick, hurry up. Don't stop!" So *Yehonatan*'s boy gathered the arrows and came back to his master. –

לח וַיִּקְרָא יְהוֹנָתָן אַחֲרֵי הַנַּעַר מְהֵרָה חוּשָׁה אַל־תַּעֲמֹד וַיְלַקֵּט נַעַר יְהוֹנָתָן אֶת־הַחֵצִי [הַחִצִּים] וַיָּבֹא אֶל־אֲדֹנָיו׃

39 The boy suspected nothing; only *Yehonatan* and *David* knew the arrangement. –

לט וְהַנַּעַר לֹא־יָדַע מְאוּמָה אַךְ יְהוֹנָתָן וְדָוִד יָדְעוּ אֶת־הַדָּבָר׃

40 *Yehonatan* handed the gear to his boy and told him, "Take these back to the town."

מ וַיִּתֵּן יְהוֹנָתָן אֶת־כֵּלָיו אֶל־הַנַּעַר אֲשֶׁר־לוֹ וַיֹּאמֶר לוֹ לֵךְ הָבֵיא הָעִיר׃

41 When the boy got there, *David* emerged from his concealment at the *Negev*. He flung himself face down on the ground and bowed low three times. They kissed each other and wept together; *David* wept the longer.

מא הַנַּעַר בָּא וְדָוִד קָם מֵאֵצֶל הַנֶּגֶב וַיִּפֹּל לְאַפָּיו אַרְצָה וַיִּשְׁתַּחוּ שָׁלֹשׁ פְּעָמִים וַיִּשְּׁקוּ אִישׁ אֶת־רֵעֵהוּ וַיִּבְכּוּ אִישׁ אֶת־רֵעֵהוּ עַד־דָּוִד הִגְדִּיל׃

42 *Yehonatan* said to *David*, "Go in peace! For we two have sworn to each other in the name of *Hashem*: 'May *Hashem* be [witness] between you and me, and between your offspring and mine, forever!'"

מב וַיֹּאמֶר יְהוֹנָתָן לְדָוִד לֵךְ לְשָׁלוֹם אֲשֶׁר נִשְׁבַּעְנוּ שְׁנֵינוּ אֲנַחְנוּ בְּשֵׁם יְהוָה לֵאמֹר יְהוָה יִהְיֶה בֵּינִי וּבֵינֶךָ וּבֵין זַרְעִי וּבֵין זַרְעֲךָ עַד־עוֹלָם׃

21

1 *David* then went his way, and *Yehonatan* returned to the town.

כא א וַיָּקָם וַיֵּלַךְ וִיהוֹנָתָן בָּא הָעִיר׃

2 *David* went to the *Kohen Achimelech* at *Nov*. *Achimelech* came out in alarm to meet *David*, and he said to him, "Why are you alone, and no one with you?"

ב וַיָּבֹא דָוִד נֹבֶה אֶל־אֲחִימֶלֶךְ הַכֹּהֵן וַיֶּחֱרַד אֲחִימֶלֶךְ לִקְרַאת דָּוִד וַיֹּאמֶר לוֹ מַדּוּעַ אַתָּה לְבַדֶּךָ וְאִישׁ אֵין אִתָּךְ׃

3 *David* answered the *Kohen Achimelech*, "The king has ordered me on a mission, and he said to me, 'No one must know anything about the mission on which I am sending you and for which I have given you orders.' So I have directed [my] young men to such and such a place.

ג וַיֹּאמֶר דָּוִד לַאֲחִימֶלֶךְ הַכֹּהֵן הַמֶּלֶךְ צִוַּנִי דָבָר וַיֹּאמֶר אֵלַי אִישׁ אַל־יֵדַע מְאוּמָה אֶת־הַדָּבָר אֲשֶׁר־אָנֹכִי שֹׁלֵחֲךָ וַאֲשֶׁר צִוִּיתִךָ וְאֶת־הַנְּעָרִים יוֹדַעְתִּי אֶל־מְקוֹם פְּלֹנִי אַלְמוֹנִי׃

4 Now then, what have you got on hand? Any loaves of bread? Let me have them – or whatever is available."

ד וְעַתָּה מַה־יֵּשׁ תַּחַת־יָדְךָ חֲמִשָּׁה־לֶחֶם תְּנָה בְיָדִי אוֹ הַנִּמְצָא׃

5 The *Kohen* answered *David*, "I have no ordinary bread on hand; there is only consecrated bread – provided the young men have kept away from women."

ה וַיַּעַן הַכֹּהֵן אֶת־דָּוִד וַיֹּאמֶר אֵין־לֶחֶם חֹל אֶל־תַּחַת יָדִי כִּי־אִם־לֶחֶם קֹדֶשׁ יֵשׁ אִם־נִשְׁמְרוּ הַנְּעָרִים אַךְ מֵאִשָּׁה׃

6 In reply to the *Kohen*, *David* said, "I assure you that women have been kept from us, as always. Whenever I went on a mission, even if the journey was a common one, the vessels of the young men were consecrated; all the more then may consecrated food be put into their vessels today."

ו וַיַּעַן דָּוִד אֶת־הַכֹּהֵן וַיֹּאמֶר לוֹ כִּי אִם־אִשָּׁה עֲצֻרָה־לָנוּ כִּתְמוֹל שִׁלְשֹׁם בְּצֵאתִי וַיִּהְיוּ כְלֵי־הַנְּעָרִים קֹדֶשׁ וְהוּא דֶּרֶךְ חֹל וְאַף כִּי הַיּוֹם יִקְדַּשׁ בַּכֶּלִי׃

Shmuel I/I Samuel
Chapter 21

שמואל א
פרק כא

7 So the *Kohen* gave him consecrated bread, because there was none there except the bread of display, which had been removed from the presence of *Hashem*, to be replaced by warm bread as soon as it was taken away. –

ז וַיִּתֶּן־לוֹ הַכֹּהֵן קֹדֶשׁ כִּי לֹא־הָיָה שָׁם לֶחֶם כִּי־אִם־לֶחֶם הַפָּנִים הַמּוּסָרִים מִלִּפְנֵי יְהוָה לָשׂוּם לֶחֶם חֹם בְּיוֹם הִלָּקְחוֹ:

va-yi-ten LO ha-ko-HAYN KO-desh KEE lo ha-YAH SHAM LE-khem kee im LE-khem ha-pa-NEEM ha-mu-sa-REEM mi-lif-NAY a-do-NAI la-SUM LE-khem KHOM b'-YOM hi-la-k'-KHO

8 Now one of *Shaul*'s officials was there that day, detained before *Hashem*; his name was *Doeg Ha'adomi*, *Shaul*'s chief herdsman.

ח וְשָׁם אִישׁ מֵעַבְדֵי שָׁאוּל בַּיּוֹם הַהוּא נֶעְצָר לִפְנֵי יְהוָה וּשְׁמוֹ דֹּאֵג הָאֲדֹמִי אַבִּיר הָרֹעִים אֲשֶׁר לְשָׁאוּל:

9 *David* said to *Achimelech*, "Haven't you got a spear or sword on hand? I didn't take my sword or any of my weapons with me, because the king's mission was urgent."

ט וַיֹּאמֶר דָּוִד לַאֲחִימֶלֶךְ וְאִין יֶשׁ־פֹּה תַחַת־יָדְךָ חֲנִית אוֹ־חָרֶב כִּי גַם־חַרְבִּי וְגַם־כֵּלַי לֹא־לָקַחְתִּי בְיָדִי כִּי־הָיָה דְבַר־הַמֶּלֶךְ נָחוּץ:

10 The *Kohen* said, "There is the sword of Goliath the Philistine whom you slew in the valley of Elah; it is over there, wrapped in a cloth, behind the ephod. If you want to take that one, take it, for there is none here but that one." *David* replied, "There is none like it; give it to me."

י וַיֹּאמֶר הַכֹּהֵן חֶרֶב גָּלְיָת הַפְּלִשְׁתִּי אֲשֶׁר־הִכִּיתָ בְּעֵמֶק הָאֵלָה הִנֵּה־הִיא לוּטָה בַשִּׂמְלָה אַחֲרֵי הָאֵפוֹד אִם־אֹתָהּ תִּקַּח־לְךָ קָח כִּי אֵין אַחֶרֶת זוּלָתָהּ בָּזֶה וַיֹּאמֶר דָּוִד אֵין כָּמוֹהָ תְּנֶנָּה לִּי:

11 That day *David* continued on his flight from *Shaul* and he came to King Achish of Gath.

יא וַיָּקָם דָּוִד וַיִּבְרַח בַּיּוֹם־הַהוּא מִפְּנֵי שָׁאוּל וַיָּבֹא אֶל־אָכִישׁ מֶלֶךְ גַּת:

12 The courtiers of Achish said to him, "Why, that's *David*, king of the land! That's the one of whom they sing as they dance: *Shaul* has slain his thousands; *David*, his tens of thousands."

יב וַיֹּאמְרוּ עַבְדֵי אָכִישׁ אֵלָיו הֲלוֹא־זֶה דָוִד מֶלֶךְ הָאָרֶץ הֲלוֹא לָזֶה יַעֲנוּ בַמְּחֹלוֹת לֵאמֹר הִכָּה שָׁאוּל באלפו [בַּאֲלָפָיו] וְדָוִד ברבבתו [בְּרִבְבֹתָיו]:

13 These words worried *David* and he became very much afraid of King Achish of Gath.

יג וַיָּשֶׂם דָּוִד אֶת־הַדְּבָרִים הָאֵלֶּה בִּלְבָבוֹ וַיִּרָא מְאֹד מִפְּנֵי אָכִישׁ מֶלֶךְ־גַּת:

14 So he concealed his good sense from them; he feigned madness for their benefit. He scratched marks on the doors of the gate and let his saliva run down his beard.

יד וַיְשַׁנּוֹ אֶת־טַעְמוֹ בְּעֵינֵיהֶם וַיִּתְהֹלֵל בְּיָדָם וַיְתָו ויתיו [וַיְתָיו] עַל־דַּלְתוֹת הַשַּׁעַר וַיּוֹרֶד רִירוֹ אֶל־זְקָנוֹ:

15 And Achish said to his courtiers, "You see the man is raving; why bring him to me?

טו וַיֹּאמֶר אָכִישׁ אֶל־עֲבָדָיו הִנֵּה תִרְאוּ אִישׁ מִשְׁתַּגֵּעַ לָמָּה תָּבִיאוּ אֹתוֹ אֵלָי:

21:7 Bread of display The term 'bread of display,' or 'shewbread,' refers to twelve special loaves that were placed on the Table, one of the vessels in the sanctuary of the *Mishkan*, and later in the *Beit Hamikdash*. Each loaf represents one tribe of Israel. Each week, the loaves are replaced and the old ones are then eaten by the *Kohanim*, priests. As *Rashi* notes, Jewish tradition teaches that a miracle surrounded the bread of display. When the priests received them a full week after being placed on the Table, the loaves were still as warm and fresh as they were when they were first baked. This was a reminder of *Hashem*'s constant watch over His sanctuary and His people.

Shmuel I / I Samuel
Chapter 22

שמואל א
פרק כב

16 Do I lack madmen that you have brought this fellow to rave for me? Should this fellow enter my house?"

טז חֲסַר מְשֻׁגָּעִים אָנִי כִּי־הֲבֵאתֶם אֶת־זֶה לְהִשְׁתַּגֵּעַ עָלָי הֲזֶה יָבוֹא אֶל־בֵּיתִי׃

22 1 *David* departed from there and escaped to the cave of *Adulam*; and when his brothers and all his father's house heard, they joined him down there.

כב א וַיֵּלֶךְ דָּוִד מִשָּׁם וַיִּמָּלֵט אֶל־מְעָרַת עֲדֻלָּם וַיִּשְׁמְעוּ אֶחָיו וְכָל־בֵּית אָבִיו וַיֵּרְדוּ אֵלָיו שָׁמָּה׃

2 Everyone who was in straits and everyone who was in debt and everyone who was desperate joined him, and he became their leader; there were about four hundred men with him.

ב וַיִּתְקַבְּצוּ אֵלָיו כָּל־אִישׁ מָצוֹק וְכָל־אִישׁ אֲשֶׁר־לוֹ נֹשֶׁא וְכָל־אִישׁ מַר־נֶפֶשׁ וַיְהִי עֲלֵיהֶם לְשָׂר וַיִּהְיוּ עִמּוֹ כְּאַרְבַּע מֵאוֹת אִישׁ׃

3 *David* went from there to Mizpeh of Moab, and he said to the king of Moab, "Let my father and mother come [and stay] with you, until I know what *Hashem* will do for me."

ג וַיֵּלֶךְ דָּוִד מִשָּׁם מִצְפֵּה מוֹאָב וַיֹּאמֶר אֶל־מֶלֶךְ מוֹאָב יֵצֵא־נָא אָבִי וְאִמִּי אִתְּכֶם עַד אֲשֶׁר אֵדַע מַה־יַּעֲשֶׂה־לִּי אֱלֹהִים׃

4 So he led them to the king of Moab, and they stayed with him as long as *David* remained in the stronghold.

ד וַיַּנְחֵם אֶת־פְּנֵי מֶלֶךְ מוֹאָב וַיֵּשְׁבוּ עִמּוֹ כָּל־יְמֵי הֱיוֹת־דָּוִד בַּמְּצוּדָה׃

5 But the *Navi Gad* said to *David*, "Do not stay in the stronghold; go at once to the territory of *Yehuda*." So *David* left and went to the forest of Hereth.

ה וַיֹּאמֶר גָּד הַנָּבִיא אֶל־דָּוִד לֹא תֵשֵׁב בַּמְּצוּדָה לֵךְ וּבָאתָ־לְּךָ אֶרֶץ יְהוּדָה וַיֵּלֶךְ דָּוִד וַיָּבֹא יַעַר חָרֶת׃

6 When *Shaul* heard that *David* and the men with him had been located – *Shaul* was then in *Giva*, sitting under the tamarisk tree on the height, spear in hand, with all his courtiers in attendance upon him –

ו וַיִּשְׁמַע שָׁאוּל כִּי נוֹדַע דָּוִד וַאֲנָשִׁים אֲשֶׁר אִתּוֹ וְשָׁאוּל יוֹשֵׁב בַּגִּבְעָה תַּחַת־הָאֶשֶׁל בָּרָמָה וַחֲנִיתוֹ בְיָדוֹ וְכָל־עֲבָדָיו נִצָּבִים עָלָיו׃

7 *Shaul* said to the courtiers standing about him, "Listen, men of *Binyamin*! Will the son of *Yishai* give fields and vineyards to every one of you? And will he make all of you captains of thousands or captains of hundreds?

ז וַיֹּאמֶר שָׁאוּל לַעֲבָדָיו הַנִּצָּבִים עָלָיו שִׁמְעוּ־נָא בְּנֵי יְמִינִי גַּם־לְכֻלְּכֶם יִתֵּן בֶּן־יִשַׁי שָׂדוֹת וּכְרָמִים לְכֻלְּכֶם יָשִׂים שָׂרֵי אֲלָפִים וְשָׂרֵי מֵאוֹת׃

8 Is that why all of you have conspired against me? For no one informs me when my own son makes a pact with the son of *Yishai*; no one is concerned for me and no one informs me when my own son has set my servant in ambush against me, as is now the case."

ח כִּי קְשַׁרְתֶּם כֻּלְּכֶם עָלַי וְאֵין־גֹּלֶה אֶת־אָזְנִי בִּכְרָת־בְּנִי עִם־בֶּן־יִשַׁי וְאֵין־חֹלֶה מִכֶּם עָלַי וְגֹלֶה אֶת־אָזְנִי כִּי הֵקִים בְּנִי אֶת־עַבְדִּי עָלַי לְאֹרֵב כַּיּוֹם הַזֶּה׃

9 *Doeg Ha'adomi*, who was standing among the courtiers of *Shaul*, spoke up: "I saw the son of *Yishai* come to *Achimelech* son of *Achituv* at Nov.

ט וַיַּעַן דֹּאֵג הָאֲדֹמִי וְהוּא נִצָּב עַל־עַבְדֵי־שָׁאוּל וַיֹּאמַר רָאִיתִי אֶת־בֶּן־יִשַׁי בָּא נֹבֶה אֶל־אֲחִימֶלֶךְ בֶּן־אֲחִטוּב׃

10 He inquired of *Hashem* on his behalf and gave him provisions; he also gave him the sword of Goliath the Philistine."

י וַיִּשְׁאַל־לוֹ בַּיהוָה וְצֵידָה נָתַן לוֹ וְאֵת חֶרֶב גָּלְיָת הַפְּלִשְׁתִּי נָתַן לוֹ׃

Shmuel I / I Samuel
Chapter 22

11 Thereupon the king sent for the *Kohen Achimelech* son of *Achituv* and for all the *Kohanim* belonging to his father's house at *Nov*. They all came to the king,

יא וַיִּשְׁלַח הַמֶּלֶךְ לִקְרֹא אֶת־אֲחִימֶלֶךְ בֶּן־אֲחִיטוּב הַכֹּהֵן וְאֵת כָּל־בֵּית אָבִיו הַכֹּהֲנִים אֲשֶׁר בְּנֹב וַיָּבֹאוּ כֻלָּם אֶל־הַמֶּלֶךְ׃

12 and *Shaul* said, "Listen to me, son of *Achituv*." "Yes, my lord," he replied.

יב וַיֹּאמֶר שָׁאוּל שְׁמַע־נָא בֶּן־אֲחִיטוּב וַיֹּאמֶר הִנְנִי אֲדֹנִי׃

13 And *Shaul* said to him, "Why have you and the son of *Yishai* conspired against me? You gave him food and a sword, and inquired of *Hashem* for him — that he may rise in ambush against me, as is now the case."

יג וַיֹּאמֶר אלו [אֵלָיו] שָׁאוּל לָמָּה קְשַׁרְתֶּם עָלַי אַתָּה וּבֶן־יִשָׁי בְּתִתְּךָ לוֹ לֶחֶם וְחֶרֶב וְשָׁאוֹל לוֹ בֵּאלֹהִים לָקוּם אֵלַי לְאֹרֵב כַּיּוֹם הַזֶּה׃

va-YO-mer ay-LAV sha-UL LA-mah k'-shar-TEM a-LAI a-TAH u-ven yi-SHAI b'-ti-t'-KHA LO LE-khem v'-KHE-rev v'-sha-OL LO bay-lo-HEEM la-KUM ay-LAI l'-o-RAYV ka-YOM ha-ZEH

14 *Achimelech* replied to the king, "But who is there among all your courtiers as trusted as *David*, son-in-law of Your Majesty and obedient to your bidding, and esteemed in your household?

יד וַיַּעַן אֲחִימֶלֶךְ אֶת־הַמֶּלֶךְ וַיֹּאמַר וּמִי בְכָל־עֲבָדֶיךָ כְּדָוִד נֶאֱמָן וַחֲתַן הַמֶּלֶךְ וְסָר אֶל־מִשְׁמַעְתֶּךָ וְנִכְבָּד בְּבֵיתֶךָ׃

15 This is the first time that I inquired of *Hashem* for him; I have done no wrong. Let not Your Majesty find fault with his servant [or] with any of my father's house; for your servant knew nothing whatever about all this."

טו הַיּוֹם הַחִלֹּתִי לשאול־[לִשְׁאָל־] לוֹ בֵאלֹהִים חָלִילָה לִּי אַל־יָשֵׂם הַמֶּלֶךְ בְּעַבְדּוֹ דָבָר בְּכָל־בֵּית אָבִי כִּי לֹא־יָדַע עַבְדְּךָ בְּכָל־זֹאת דָּבָר קָטֹן אוֹ גָדוֹל׃

16 But the king said, "You shall die, *Achimelech*, you and all your father's house."

טז וַיֹּאמֶר הַמֶּלֶךְ מוֹת תָּמוּת אֲחִימֶלֶךְ אַתָּה וְכָל־בֵּית אָבִיךָ׃

17 And the king commanded the guards standing by, "Turn about and kill the *Kohanim* of *Hashem*, for they are in league with *David*; they knew he was running away and they did not inform me." But the king's servants would not raise a hand to strike down the *Kohanim* of *Hashem*.

יז וַיֹּאמֶר הַמֶּלֶךְ לָרָצִים הַנִּצָּבִים עָלָיו סֹבּוּ וְהָמִיתוּ כֹהֲנֵי יְהֹוָה כִּי גַם־יָדָם עִם־דָּוִד וְכִי יָדְעוּ כִּי־בֹרֵחַ הוּא וְלֹא גָלוּ אֶת־אָזְנוֹ [אָזְנִי] וְלֹא־אָבוּ עַבְדֵי הַמֶּלֶךְ לִשְׁלֹחַ אֶת־יָדָם לִפְגֹעַ בְּכֹהֲנֵי יְהֹוָה׃

18 Thereupon the king said to Doeg, "You, Doeg, go and strike down the *Kohanim*." And *Doeg Ha'adomi* went and struck down the *Kohanim* himself; that day, he killed eighty-five men who wore the linen ephod.

יח וַיֹּאמֶר הַמֶּלֶךְ לדויג [לְדוֹאֵג] סֹב אַתָּה וּפְגַע בַּכֹּהֲנִים וַיִּסֹּב דויג [דּוֹאֵג] הָאֲדֹמִי וַיִּפְגַּע־הוּא בַּכֹּהֲנִים וַיָּמָת ׀ בַּיּוֹם הַהוּא שְׁמֹנִים וַחֲמִשָּׁה אִישׁ נֹשֵׂא אֵפוֹד בָּד׃

22:13 And inquired of *Hashem* for him The *Urim Ve'Tumim*, mystical objects in the *Kohen Gadol's* breastplate, were used to receive communication from *Hashem*. Divine messages were transmitted through the illumination of the twelve stones on the breastplate, which represented the twelve tribes of Israel. *Rashi* explains that by using the *Urim Ve'Tumim* to ask *Hashem* to provide instruction to *David*, the *Kohanim* treated *David* as a king, since they are not allowed to inquire of the *Urim Ve'Tumim* for a regular citizen. Thus, King *Shaul* was angry not only that *Achimelech* had assisted *David*, but that he related to him as the king. The use of the *Urim Ve'Tumim* is another example of the high level of God's direct involvement in the lives of the Children of Israel, felt most acutely in *Eretz Yisrael*.

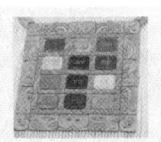

Replica of the breastplate, central Sephardic synagogue, Ramat Gan

Shmuel I / I Samuel
Chapter 23

19 He put *Nov*, the town of the *Kohanim*, to the sword: men and women, children and infants, oxen, asses, and sheep – [all] to the sword.

20 But one son of *Achimelech* son of *Achituv* escaped – his name was *Evyatar* – and he fled to *David*.

21 When *Evyatar* told *David* that *Shaul* had killed the *Kohanim* of *Hashem*,

22 *David* said to *Evyatar*, "I knew that day, when *Doeg Ha'adomi* was there, that he would tell *Shaul*. I am to blame for all the deaths in your father's house.

23 Stay with me; do not be afraid; for whoever seeks your life must seek my life also. It will be my care to guard you."

23 1 *David* was told: "The Philistines are raiding Keilah and plundering the threshing floors."

2 *David* consulted *Hashem*, "Shall I go and attack those Philistines?" And *Hashem* said to *David*, "Go; attack the Philistines and you will save Keilah."

3 But *David*'s men said to him, "Look, we are afraid here in *Yehuda*, how much more if we go to Keilah against the forces of the Philistines!"

4 So *David* consulted *Hashem* again, and *Hashem* answered him, "March down at once to Keilah, for I am going to deliver the Philistines into your hands."

5 *David* and his men went to Keilah and fought against the Philistines; he drove off their cattle and inflicted a severe defeat on them. Thus *David* saved the inhabitants of Keilah.

6 When *Evyatar* son of *Achimelech* fled to *David* at Keilah, he brought down an ephod with him.

7 *Shaul* was told that *David* had come to Keilah, and *Shaul* thought, "*Hashem* has delivered him into my hands, for he has shut himself in by entering a town with gates and bars."

8 *Shaul* summoned all the troops for war, to go down to Keilah and besiege *David* and his men.

שמואל א
פרק כג

יט וְאֵת נֹב עִיר־הַכֹּהֲנִים הִכָּה לְפִי־חֶרֶב מֵאִישׁ וְעַד־אִשָּׁה מֵעוֹלֵל וְעַד־יוֹנֵק וְשׁוֹר וַחֲמוֹר וָשֶׂה לְפִי־חָרֶב:

כ וַיִּמָּלֵט בֵּן־אֶחָד לַאֲחִימֶלֶךְ בֶּן־אֲחִטוּב וּשְׁמוֹ אֶבְיָתָר וַיִּבְרַח אַחֲרֵי דָוִד:

כא וַיַּגֵּד אֶבְיָתָר לְדָוִד כִּי הָרַג שָׁאוּל אֵת כֹּהֲנֵי יְהוָה:

כב וַיֹּאמֶר דָּוִד לְאֶבְיָתָר יָדַעְתִּי בַּיּוֹם הַהוּא כִּי־שָׁם דּוֹיֵג [דּוֹאֵג] הָאֲדֹמִי כִּי־הַגֵּד יַגִּיד לְשָׁאוּל אָנֹכִי סַבֹּתִי בְּכָל־נֶפֶשׁ בֵּית אָבִיךָ:

כג שְׁבָה אִתִּי אַל־תִּירָא כִּי אֲשֶׁר־יְבַקֵּשׁ אֶת־נַפְשִׁי יְבַקֵּשׁ אֶת־נַפְשֶׁךָ כִּי־מִשְׁמֶרֶת אַתָּה עִמָּדִי:

כג א וַיַּגִּדוּ לְדָוִד לֵאמֹר הִנֵּה פְלִשְׁתִּים נִלְחָמִים בִּקְעִילָה וְהֵמָּה שֹׁסִים אֶת־הַגֳּרָנוֹת:

ב וַיִּשְׁאַל דָּוִד בַּיהוָה לֵאמֹר הַאֵלֵךְ וְהִכֵּיתִי בַּפְּלִשְׁתִּים הָאֵלֶּה וַיֹּאמֶר יְהוָה אֶל־דָּוִד לֵךְ וְהִכִּיתָ בַפְּלִשְׁתִּים וְהוֹשַׁעְתָּ אֶת־קְעִילָה:

ג וַיֹּאמְרוּ אַנְשֵׁי דָוִד אֵלָיו הִנֵּה אֲנַחְנוּ פֹה בִיהוּדָה יְרֵאִים וְאַף כִּי־נֵלֵךְ קְעִלָה אֶל־מַעַרְכוֹת פְּלִשְׁתִּים:

ד וַיּוֹסֶף עוֹד דָּוִד לִשְׁאֹל בַּיהוָה וַיַּעֲנֵהוּ יְהוָה וַיֹּאמֶר קוּם רֵד קְעִילָה כִּי־אֲנִי נֹתֵן אֶת־פְּלִשְׁתִּים בְּיָדֶךָ:

ה וַיֵּלֶךְ דָּוִד ואנשו [וַאֲנָשָׁיו] קְעִילָה וַיִּלָּחֶם בַּפְּלִשְׁתִּים וַיִּנְהַג אֶת־מִקְנֵיהֶם וַיַּךְ בָּהֶם מַכָּה גְדוֹלָה וַיֹּשַׁע דָּוִד אֵת יֹשְׁבֵי קְעִילָה:

ו וַיְהִי בִּבְרֹחַ אֶבְיָתָר בֶּן־אֲחִימֶלֶךְ אֶל־דָּוִד קְעִילָה אֵפוֹד יָרַד בְּיָדוֹ:

ז וַיֻּגַּד לְשָׁאוּל כִּי־בָא דָוִד קְעִילָה וַיֹּאמֶר שָׁאוּל נִכַּר אֹתוֹ אֱלֹהִים בְּיָדִי כִּי נִסְגַּר לָבוֹא בְּעִיר דְּלָתַיִם וּבְרִיחַ:

ח וַיְשַׁמַּע שָׁאוּל אֶת־כָּל־הָעָם לַמִּלְחָמָה לָרֶדֶת קְעִילָה לָצוּר אֶל־דָּוִד וְאֶל־אֲנָשָׁיו:

Shmuel I/I Samuel
Chapter 23

שמואל א
פרק כג

9 When *David* learned that *Shaul* was planning to harm him, he told the *Kohen Evyatar* to bring the ephod forward.

ט וַיֵּדַע דָּוִד כִּי עָלָיו שָׁאוּל מַחֲרִישׁ הָרָעָה וַיֹּאמֶר אֶל־אֶבְיָתָר הַכֹּהֵן הַגִּישָׁה הָאֵפוֹד׃

10 And *David* said, "*Hashem*, God of *Yisrael*, Your servant has heard that *Shaul* intends to come to Keilah and destroy the town because of me.

י וַיֹּאמֶר דָּוִד יְהֹוָה אֱלֹהֵי יִשְׂרָאֵל שָׁמֹעַ שָׁמַע עַבְדְּךָ כִּי־מְבַקֵּשׁ שָׁאוּל לָבוֹא אֶל־קְעִילָה לְשַׁחֵת לָעִיר בַּעֲבוּרִי׃

11 Will the citizens of Keilah deliver me into his hands? Will *Shaul* come down, as Your servant has heard? *Hashem*, God of *Yisrael*, tell Your servant!" And *Hashem* said, "He will."

יא הֲיַסְגִּרֻנִי בַעֲלֵי קְעִילָה בְיָדוֹ הֲיֵרֵד שָׁאוּל כַּאֲשֶׁר שָׁמַע עַבְדֶּךָ יְהֹוָה אֱלֹהֵי יִשְׂרָאֵל הַגֶּד־נָא לְעַבְדֶּךָ וַיֹּאמֶר יְהֹוָה יֵרֵד׃

12 *David* continued, "Will the citizens of Keilah deliver me and my men into *Shaul*'s hands?" And *Hashem* answered, "They will."

יב וַיֹּאמֶר דָּוִד הֲיַסְגִּרוּ בַּעֲלֵי קְעִילָה אֹתִי וְאֶת־אֲנָשַׁי בְּיַד־שָׁאוּל וַיֹּאמֶר יְהֹוָה יַסְגִּירוּ׃

13 So *David* and his men, about six hundred in number, left Keilah at once and moved about wherever they could. And when *Shaul* was told that *David* had got away from Keilah, he did not set out.

יג וַיָּקָם דָּוִד וַאֲנָשָׁיו כְּשֵׁשׁ־מֵאוֹת אִישׁ וַיֵּצְאוּ מִקְּעִלָה וַיִּתְהַלְּכוּ בַּאֲשֶׁר יִתְהַלָּכוּ וּלְשָׁאוּל הֻגַּד כִּי־נִמְלַט דָּוִד מִקְּעִילָה וַיֶּחְדַּל לָצֵאת׃

14 *David* was staying in the strongholds of the wilderness [of *Yehuda*]; he stayed in the hill country, in the wilderness of Ziph. *Shaul* searched for him constantly, but *Hashem* did not deliver him into his hands.

יד וַיֵּשֶׁב דָּוִד בַּמִּדְבָּר בַּמְּצָדוֹת וַיֵּשֶׁב בָּהָר בְּמִדְבַּר־זִיף וַיְבַקְשֵׁהוּ שָׁאוּל כָּל־הַיָּמִים וְלֹא־נְתָנוֹ אֱלֹהִים בְּיָדוֹ׃

15 *David* was once at Horesh in the wilderness of Ziph, when *David* learned that *Shaul* had come out to seek his life.

טו וַיַּרְא דָוִד כִּי־יָצָא שָׁאוּל לְבַקֵּשׁ אֶת־נַפְשׁוֹ וְדָוִד בְּמִדְבַּר־זִיף בַּחֹרְשָׁה׃

16 And *Shaul*'s son *Yehonatan* came to *David* at Horesh and encouraged him in [the name of] *Hashem*.

טז וַיָּקָם יְהוֹנָתָן בֶּן־שָׁאוּל וַיֵּלֶךְ אֶל־דָּוִד חֹרְשָׁה וַיְחַזֵּק אֶת־יָדוֹ בֵּאלֹהִים׃

17 He said to him, "Do not be afraid: the hand of my father *Shaul* will never touch you. You are going to be king over *Yisrael* and I shall be second to you; and even my father *Shaul* knows this is so."

יז וַיֹּאמֶר אֵלָיו אַל־תִּירָא כִּי לֹא תִמְצָאֲךָ יַד שָׁאוּל אָבִי וְאַתָּה תִּמְלֹךְ עַל־יִשְׂרָאֵל וְאָנֹכִי אֶהְיֶה־לְּךָ לְמִשְׁנֶה וְגַם־שָׁאוּל אָבִי יֹדֵעַ כֵּן׃

va-YO-mer ay-LAV al tee-RA KEE LO tim-tza-a-KHA yad sha-UL a-VEE v'-a-TAH tim-LOKH al yis-ra-AYL v'-a-no-KHEE eh-yeh l'-KHA l'-mish-NEH v'-GAM sha-UL a-VEE yo-DAY-a KAYN

23:17 Do not be afraid: the hand of my father *Shaul* will never touch you This verse again demonstrates *Yehonatan*'s selflessness and love for *David*. Despite his awareness that the consequence of *David* becoming king is that he will not succeed his father on the throne, *Yehonatan* recognizes that *Hashem* has designated his beloved friend *David* as the next king of Israel. Displaying great admiration for his friend and sacrifice for the sake of the nation as well as for *David*, *Yehonatan* expresses his desire to serve under *David*. *Yehonatan* is a powerful and inspiring model, not only of an elevated level of friendship, but also of an individual willing to make any sacrifice necessary to advance the will of God and the wellbeing of Israel.

Shmuel I / I Samuel
Chapter 24

18 And the two of them entered into a pact before *Hashem*. *David* remained in Horesh, and *Yehonatan* went home.

19 Some Ziphites went up to *Shaul* in *Giva* and said, "*David* is hiding among us in the strongholds of Horesh, at the hill of Hachilah south of Jeshimon.

20 So if Your Majesty has the desire to come down, come down, and it will be our task to deliver him into Your Majesty's hands."

21 And *Shaul* replied, "May you be blessed of *Hashem* for the compassion you have shown me!

22 Go now and prepare further. Look around and learn what places he sets foot on [and] who has seen him there, for I have been told he is a very cunning fellow.

23 Look around and learn in which of all his hiding places he has been hiding, and return to me when you are certain. I will then go with you, and if he is in the region, I will search him out among all the clans of *Yehuda*."

24 They left at once for Ziph, ahead of *Shaul*; *David* and his men were then in the wilderness of Maon, in the Arabah, to the south of Jeshimon.

25 When *Shaul* and his men came to search, *David* was told about it; and he went down to the rocky region and stayed in the wilderness of Maon. On hearing this, *Shaul* pursued *David* in the wilderness of Maon.

26 *Shaul* was making his way along one side of a hill, and *David* and his men were on the other side of the hill. *David* was trying hard to elude *Shaul*, and *Shaul* and his men were trying to encircle *David* and his men and capture them,

27 when a messenger came and told *Shaul*, "Come quickly, for the Philistines have invaded the land."

28 *Shaul* gave up his pursuit of *David* and went to meet the Philistines. That is why that place came to be called the Rock of Separation.

24

1 *David* went from there and stayed in the wildernesses of *Ein Gedi*.

2 When *Shaul* returned from pursuing the Philistines, he was told that *David* was in the wilderness of *Ein Gedi*.

שמואל א
פרק כד

יח וַיִּכְרְתוּ שְׁנֵיהֶם בְּרִית לִפְנֵי יְהוָה וַיֵּשֶׁב דָּוִד בַּחֹרְשָׁה וִיהוֹנָתָן הָלַךְ לְבֵיתוֹ:

יט וַיַּעֲלוּ זִפִים אֶל־שָׁאוּל הַגִּבְעָתָה לֵאמֹר הֲלוֹא דָוִד מִסְתַּתֵּר עִמָּנוּ בַמְּצָדוֹת בַּחֹרְשָׁה בְּגִבְעַת הַחֲכִילָה אֲשֶׁר מִימִין הַיְשִׁימוֹן:

כ וְעַתָּה לְכָל־אַוַּת נַפְשְׁךָ הַמֶּלֶךְ לָרֶדֶת רֵד וְלָנוּ הַסְגִּירוֹ בְּיַד הַמֶּלֶךְ:

כא וַיֹּאמֶר שָׁאוּל בְּרוּכִים אַתֶּם לַיהוָה כִּי חֲמַלְתֶּם עָלָי:

כב לְכוּ־נָא הָכִינוּ עוֹד וּדְעוּ וּרְאוּ אֶת־מְקוֹמוֹ אֲשֶׁר תִּהְיֶה רַגְלוֹ מִי רָאָהוּ שָׁם כִּי אָמַר אֵלַי עָרוֹם יַעְרִם הוּא:

כג וּרְאוּ וּדְעוּ מִכֹּל הַמַּחֲבֹאִים אֲשֶׁר יִתְחַבֵּא שָׁם וְשַׁבְתֶּם אֵלַי אֶל־נָכוֹן וְהָלַכְתִּי אִתְּכֶם וְהָיָה אִם־יֶשְׁנוֹ בָאָרֶץ וְחִפַּשְׂתִּי אֹתוֹ בְּכֹל אַלְפֵי יְהוּדָה:

כד וַיָּקוּמוּ וַיֵּלְכוּ זִיפָה לִפְנֵי שָׁאוּל וְדָוִד וַאֲנָשָׁיו בְּמִדְבַּר מָעוֹן בָּעֲרָבָה אֶל יְמִין הַיְשִׁימוֹן:

כה וַיֵּלֶךְ שָׁאוּל וַאֲנָשָׁיו לְבַקֵּשׁ וַיַּגִּדוּ לְדָוִד וַיֵּרֶד הַסֶּלַע וַיֵּשֶׁב בְּמִדְבַּר מָעוֹן וַיִּשְׁמַע שָׁאוּל וַיִּרְדֹּף אַחֲרֵי־דָוִד מִדְבַּר מָעוֹן:

כו וַיֵּלֶךְ שָׁאוּל מִצַּד הָהָר מִזֶּה וְדָוִד וַאֲנָשָׁיו מִצַּד הָהָר מִזֶּה וַיְהִי דָוִד נֶחְפָּז לָלֶכֶת מִפְּנֵי שָׁאוּל וְשָׁאוּל וַאֲנָשָׁיו עֹטְרִים אֶל־דָּוִד וְאֶל־אֲנָשָׁיו לְתָפְשָׂם:

כז וּמַלְאָךְ בָּא אֶל־שָׁאוּל לֵאמֹר מַהֲרָה וְלֵכָה כִּי־פָשְׁטוּ פְלִשְׁתִּים עַל־הָאָרֶץ:

כח וַיָּשָׁב שָׁאוּל מִרְדֹף אַחֲרֵי דָוִד וַיֵּלֶךְ לִקְרַאת פְּלִשְׁתִּים עַל־כֵּן קָרְאוּ לַמָּקוֹם הַהוּא סֶלַע הַמַּחְלְקוֹת:

כד

א וַיַּעַל דָּוִד מִשָּׁם וַיֵּשֶׁב בִּמְצָדוֹת עֵין־גֶּדִי:

ב וַיְהִי כַּאֲשֶׁר שָׁב שָׁאוּל מֵאַחֲרֵי פְּלִשְׁתִּים וַיַּגִּדוּ לוֹ לֵאמֹר הִנֵּה דָוִד בְּמִדְבַּר עֵין גֶּדִי:

Shmuel I / I Samuel
Chapter 24

שמואל א
פרק כד

3 So *Shaul* took three thousand picked men from all *Yisrael* and went in search of *David* and his men in the direction of the rocks of the wild goats;

ג וַיִּקַּח שָׁאוּל שְׁלֹשֶׁת אֲלָפִים אִישׁ בָּחוּר מִכָּל־יִשְׂרָאֵל וַיֵּלֶךְ לְבַקֵּשׁ אֶת־דָּוִד וַאֲנָשָׁיו עַל־פְּנֵי צוּרֵי הַיְּעֵלִים:

4 and he came to the sheepfolds along the way. There was a cave there, and *Shaul* went in to relieve himself. Now *David* and his men were sitting in the back of the cave.

ד וַיָּבֹא אֶל־גִּדְרוֹת הַצֹּאן עַל־הַדֶּרֶךְ וְשָׁם מְעָרָה וַיָּבֹא שָׁאוּל לְהָסֵךְ אֶת־רַגְלָיו וְדָוִד וַאֲנָשָׁיו בְּיַרְכְּתֵי הַמְּעָרָה יֹשְׁבִים:

5 *David*'s men said to him, "This is the day of which *Hashem* said to you, 'I will deliver your enemy into your hands; you can do with him as you please.'" *David* went and stealthily cut off the corner of *Shaul*'s cloak.

ה וַיֹּאמְרוּ אַנְשֵׁי דָוִד אֵלָיו הִנֵּה הַיּוֹם אֲשֶׁר־אָמַר יְהֹוָה אֵלֶיךָ הִנֵּה אָנֹכִי נֹתֵן אֶת־אֹיִבְךָ [אֹיִבְךָ] בְּיָדֶךָ וְעָשִׂיתָ לּוֹ כַּאֲשֶׁר יִטַב בְּעֵינֶיךָ וַיָּקָם דָּוִד וַיִּכְרֹת אֶת־כְּנַף־הַמְּעִיל אֲשֶׁר־לְשָׁאוּל בַּלָּט:

6 But afterward *David* reproached himself for cutting off the corner of *Shaul*'s cloak.

ו וַיְהִי אַחֲרֵי־כֵן וַיַּךְ לֵב־דָּוִד אֹתוֹ עַל אֲשֶׁר כָּרַת אֶת־כָּנָף אֲשֶׁר לְשָׁאוּל:

7 He said to his men, "*Hashem* forbid that I should do such a thing to my lord – *Hashem*'s anointed – that I should raise my hand against him; for he is *Hashem*'s anointed."

ז וַיֹּאמֶר לַאֲנָשָׁיו חָלִילָה לִּי מֵיהֹוָה אִם־אֶעֱשֶׂה אֶת־הַדָּבָר הַזֶּה לַאדֹנִי לִמְשִׁיחַ יְהֹוָה לִשְׁלֹחַ יָדִי בּוֹ כִּי־מְשִׁיחַ יְהֹוָה הוּא:

va-YO-mer l'-a-na-SHAV kha-LEE-lah LEE may-a-do-NAI im e-e-SEH et ha-da-VAR ha-ZEH la-do-NEE lim-SHEE-akh a-do-NAI lish-LO-akh ya-DEE BO kee m'-SHEE-akh a-do-NAI HU

8 *David* rebuked his men and did not permit them to attack *Shaul*. *Shaul* left the cave and started on his way.

ח וַיְשַׁסַּע דָּוִד אֶת־אֲנָשָׁיו בַּדְּבָרִים וְלֹא נְתָנָם לָקוּם אֶל־שָׁאוּל וְשָׁאוּל קָם מֵהַמְּעָרָה וַיֵּלֶךְ בַּדָּרֶךְ:

9 Then *David* also went out of the cave and called after *Shaul*, "My lord king!" *Shaul* looked around and *David* bowed low in homage, with his face to the ground.

ט וַיָּקָם דָּוִד אַחֲרֵי־כֵן וַיֵּצֵא מִן־הַמְּעָרָה [מֵהַמְּעָרָה] וַיִּקְרָא אַחֲרֵי־שָׁאוּל לֵאמֹר אֲדֹנִי הַמֶּלֶךְ וַיַּבֵּט שָׁאוּל אַחֲרָיו וַיִּקֹּד דָּוִד אַפַּיִם אַרְצָה וַיִּשְׁתָּחוּ:

10 And *David* said to *Shaul*, "Why do you listen to the people who say, '*David* is out to do you harm?'

י וַיֹּאמֶר דָּוִד לְשָׁאוּל לָמָּה תִשְׁמַע אֶת־דִּבְרֵי אָדָם לֵאמֹר הִנֵּה דָוִד מְבַקֵּשׁ רָעָתֶךָ:

24:7 *Hashem* forbid that I Though *David* could have legitimately killed King *Shaul* in self-defense, he merely cuts his royal cloak, and refrains from harming him physically. However, despite this extreme restraint, after the fact *David* greatly regrets his act, feeling that he has shown disrespect to the king of Israel. Despite everything *Shaul* had done to him, *David* honors King *Shaul* and his position as the anointed king of Israel. This esteem continues until the very end, expressed in the beautiful eulogy he delivers for *Shaul* after his death (see II Samuel 1:17–27). The leaders of the nation must be respected by all, as they are chosen by *Hashem* and charged with the responsibility of leading His people and guiding them in their holy mission. *David* has the strength and wisdom to understand this, even while being pursued by the king whose throne he would later inherit.

Shmuel I / I Samuel
Chapter 24

שמואל א
פרק כד

11	You can see for yourself now that *Hashem* delivered you into my hands in the cave today. And though I was urged to kill you, I showed you pity; for I said, 'I will not raise a hand against my lord, since he is *Hashem*'s anointed.'
12	Please, sir, take a close look at the corner of your cloak in my hand; for when I cut off the corner of your cloak, I did not kill you. You must see plainly that I have done nothing evil or rebellious, and I have never wronged you. Yet you are bent on taking my life.
13	May *Hashem* judge between you and me! And may He take vengeance upon you for me, but my hand will never touch you.
14	As the ancient proverb has it: 'Wicked deeds come from wicked men!' My hand will never touch you.
15	Against whom has the king of *Yisrael* come out? Whom are you pursuing? A dead dog? A single flea?
16	May *Hashem* be arbiter and may He judge between you and me! May He take note and uphold my cause, and vindicate me against you."
17	When *David* finished saying these things to *Shaul*, *Shaul* said, "Is that your voice, my son *David*?" And *Shaul* broke down and wept.
18	He said to *David*, "You are right, not I; for you have treated me generously, but I have treated you badly.
19	Yes, you have just revealed how generously you treated me, for *Hashem* delivered me into your hands and you did not kill me.
20	If a man meets his enemy, does he let him go his way unharmed? Surely, *Hashem* will reward you generously for what you have done for me this day.
21	I know now that you will become king, and that the kingship over *Yisrael* will remain in your hands.
22	So swear to me by *Hashem* that you will not destroy my descendants or wipe out my name from my father's house."
23	*David* swore to *Shaul*, *Shaul* went home, and *David* and his men went up to the strongholds.

יא הִנֵּה֩ הַיּ֨וֹם הַזֶּ֜ה רָא֣וּ עֵינֶ֗יךָ אֵת֩ אֲשֶׁר־נְתָנְךָ֨ יְהֹוָ֤ה ׀ הַיּוֹם֙ בְּיָדִי֙ בַּמְּעָרָ֔ה וְאָמַ֥ר לַהֲרָגְךָ֖ וַתָּ֣חׇס עָלֶ֑יךָ וָאֹמַ֗ר לֹא־אֶשְׁלַ֤ח יָדִי֙ בַּאדֹנִ֔י כִּי־מְשִׁ֥יחַ יְהֹוָ֖ה הֽוּא׃

יב וְאָבִ֣י רְאֵ֔ה גַּ֗ם רְאֵ֛ה אֶת־כְּנַ֥ף מְעִילְךָ֖ בְּיָדִ֑י כִּ֡י בְּכׇרְתִי֩ אֶת־כְּנַ֨ף מְעִילְךָ֜ וְלֹ֣א הֲרַגְתִּ֗יךָ דַּ֤ע וּרְאֵה֙ כִּי֩ אֵ֨ין בְּיָדִ֜י רָעָ֤ה וָפֶ֙שַׁע֙ וְלֹא־חָטָ֣אתִי לָ֔ךְ וְאַתָּ֛ה צֹדֶ֥ה אֶת־נַפְשִׁ֖י לְקַחְתָּֽהּ׃

יג יִשְׁפֹּ֤ט יְהֹוָה֙ בֵּינִ֣י וּבֵינֶ֔ךָ וּנְקָמַ֥נִי יְהֹוָ֖ה מִמֶּ֑ךָּ וְיָדִ֖י לֹ֥א תִֽהְיֶה־בָּֽךְ׃

יד כַּאֲשֶׁ֣ר יֹאמַ֗ר מְשַׁל֙ הַקַּדְמֹנִ֔י מֵרְשָׁעִ֖ים יֵ֣צֵא רֶ֑שַׁע וְיָדִ֖י לֹ֥א תִהְיֶה־בָּֽךְ׃

טו אַחֲרֵ֨י מִ֤י יָצָא֙ מֶ֣לֶךְ יִשְׂרָאֵ֔ל אַחֲרֵ֥י מִ֖י אַתָּ֣ה רֹדֵ֑ף אַחֲרֵי֙ כֶּ֣לֶב מֵ֔ת אַחֲרֵ֖י פַּרְעֹ֥שׁ אֶחָֽד׃

טז וְהָיָ֤ה יְהֹוָה֙ לְדַיָּ֔ן וְשָׁפַ֖ט בֵּינִ֣י וּבֵינֶ֑ךָ וְיֵ֙רֶא֙ וְיָרֵ֣ב אֶת־רִיבִ֔י וְיִשְׁפְּטֵ֖נִי מִיָּדֶֽךָ׃

יז וַיְהִ֣י ׀ כְּכַלּ֣וֹת דָּוִ֗ד לְדַבֵּ֞ר אֶת־הַדְּבָרִ֤ים הָאֵ֙לֶּה֙ אֶל־שָׁא֔וּל וַיֹּ֣אמֶר שָׁא֔וּל הֲקֹלְךָ֥ זֶ֖ה בְּנִ֣י דָוִ֑ד וַיִּשָּׂ֥א שָׁא֛וּל קֹל֖וֹ וַיֵּֽבְךְּ׃

יח וַיֹּ֙אמֶר֙ אֶל־דָּוִ֔ד צַדִּ֥יק אַתָּ֖ה מִמֶּ֑נִּי כִּ֤י אַתָּה֙ גְּמַלְתַּ֣נִי הַטּוֹבָ֔ה וַאֲנִ֖י גְּמַלְתִּ֥יךָ הָרָעָֽה׃

יט וְאַתָּה֙ [וְאַתָּ֣ה] הִגַּ֣דְתָּ הַיּ֔וֹם אֵ֛ת אֲשֶׁר־עָשִׂ֥יתָה אִתִּ֖י טוֹבָ֑ה אֵת֩ אֲשֶׁ֨ר סִגְּרַ֧נִי יְהֹוָ֛ה בְּיָדְךָ֖ וְלֹ֥א הֲרַגְתָּֽנִי׃

כ וְכִי־יִמְצָ֥א אִישׁ֙ אֶת־אֹ֣יְב֔וֹ וְשִׁלְּח֖וֹ בְּדֶ֣רֶךְ טוֹבָ֑ה וַֽיהֹוָה֙ יְשַׁלֶּמְךָ֣ טוֹבָ֔ה תַּ֚חַת הַיּ֣וֹם הַזֶּ֔ה אֲשֶׁ֥ר עָשִׂ֖יתָה לִֽי׃

כא וְעַתָּה֙ הִנֵּ֣ה יָדַ֔עְתִּי כִּ֥י מָלֹ֖ךְ תִּמְל֑וֹךְ וְקָ֙מָה֙ בְּיָ֣דְךָ֔ מַמְלֶ֖כֶת יִשְׂרָאֵֽל׃

כב וְעַתָּ֗ה הִשָּׁ֤בְעָה לִּי֙ בַּיהֹוָ֔ה אִם־תַּכְרִ֥ית אֶת־זַרְעִ֖י אַֽחֲרָ֑י וְאִם־תַּשְׁמִ֥יד אֶת־שְׁמִ֖י מִבֵּ֥ית אָבִֽי׃

כג וַיִּשָּׁבַ֥ע דָּוִ֖ד לְשָׁא֑וּל וַיֵּ֤לֶךְ שָׁאוּל֙ אֶל־בֵּית֔וֹ וְדָוִד֙ וַאֲנָשָׁ֔יו עָל֖וּ עַל־הַמְּצוּדָֽה׃

Shmuel I / I Samuel
Chapter 25

25 1 Shmuel died, and all Yisrael gathered and made lament for him; and they buried him in Rama, his home. David went down to the wilderness of Paran.

2 There was a man in Maon whose possessions were in Carmel. The man was very wealthy; he owned three thousand sheep and a thousand goats. At the time, he was shearing his sheep in Carmel.

3 The man's name was Naval, and his wife's name was Avigail. The woman was intelligent and beautiful, but the man, a Calebite, was a hard man and an evildoer.

4 David was in the wilderness when he heard that Naval was shearing his sheep.

5 David dispatched ten young men, and David instructed the young men, "Go up to Carmel. When you come to Naval, greet him in my name.

6 Say as follows: 'To life! Greetings to you and to your household and to all that is yours!

7 I hear that you are now doing your shearing. As you know, your shepherds have been with us; we did not harm them, and nothing of theirs was missing all the time they were in Carmel.

8 Ask your young men and they will tell you. So receive these young men graciously, for we have come on a festive occasion. Please give your servants and your son David whatever you can.'"

9 David's young men went and delivered this message to Naval in the name of David. When they stopped speaking,

10 Naval answered David's servants, "Who is David? Who is the son of Yishai? There are many slaves nowadays who run away from their masters.

11 Should I then take my bread and my water, and the meat that I slaughtered for my own shearers, and give them to men who come from I don't know where?"

12 Thereupon David's young men retraced their steps; and when they got back, they told him all this.

13 And David said to his men, "Gird on your swords." Each girded on his sword; David too girded on his sword. About four hundred men went up after David, while two hundred remained with the baggage.

Shmuel I/I Samuel
Chapter 25

שמואל א
פרק כה

14 One of [Naval's] young men told *Avigail*, *Naval's* wife, that *David* had sent messengers from the wilderness to greet their master, and that he had spurned them.	וְלַאֲבִיגַיִל אֵשֶׁת נָבָל הִגִּיד נַעַר־אֶחָד מֵהַנְּעָרִים לֵאמֹר הִנֵּה שָׁלַח דָּוִד מַלְאָכִים מֵהַמִּדְבָּר לְבָרֵךְ אֶת־אֲדֹנֵינוּ וַיָּעַט בָּהֶם: יד
15 "But the men had been very friendly to us; we were not harmed, nor did we miss anything all the time that we went about with them while we were in the open.	וְהָאֲנָשִׁים טֹבִים לָנוּ מְאֹד וְלֹא הָכְלַמְנוּ וְלֹא־פָקַדְנוּ מְאוּמָה כָּל־יְמֵי הִתְהַלַּכְנוּ אִתָּם בִּהְיוֹתֵנוּ בַּשָּׂדֶה: טו
16 They were a wall about us both by night and by day all the time that we were with them tending the flocks.	חוֹמָה הָיוּ עָלֵינוּ גַּם־לַיְלָה גַּם־יוֹמָם כָּל־יְמֵי הֱיוֹתֵנוּ עִמָּם רֹעִים הַצֹּאן: טז
17 So consider carefully what you should do, for harm threatens our master and all his household; he is such a nasty fellow that no one can speak to him."	וְעַתָּה דְּעִי וּרְאִי מַה־תַּעֲשִׂי כִּי־כָלְתָה הָרָעָה אֶל־אֲדֹנֵינוּ וְעַל כָּל־בֵּיתוֹ וְהוּא בֶּן־בְּלִיַּעַל מִדַּבֵּר אֵלָיו: יז
18 *Avigail* quickly got together two hundred loaves of bread, two jars of wine, five dressed sheep, five *se'eem* of parched corn, one hundred cakes of raisin, and two hundred cakes of pressed figs. She loaded them on asses,	וַתְּמַהֵר אבוגיל [אֲבִיגַיִל] וַתִּקַּח מָאתַיִם לֶחֶם וּשְׁנַיִם נִבְלֵי־יַיִן וְחָמֵשׁ צֹאן עשוות [עֲשׂוּיוֹת] וְחָמֵשׁ סְאִים קָלִי וּמֵאָה צִמֻּקִים וּמָאתַיִם דְּבֵלִים וַתָּשֶׂם עַל־הַחֲמֹרִים: יח
19 and she told her young men, "Go on ahead of me, and I'll follow you"; but she did not tell her husband *Naval*.	וַתֹּאמֶר לִנְעָרֶיהָ עִבְרוּ לְפָנַי הִנְנִי אַחֲרֵיכֶם בָּאָה וּלְאִישָׁהּ נָבָל לֹא הִגִּידָה: יט
20 She was riding on the ass and going down a trail on the hill, when *David* and his men appeared, coming down toward her; and she met them. –	וְהָיָה הִיא רֹכֶבֶת עַל־הַחֲמוֹר וְיֹרֶדֶת בְּסֵתֶר הָהָר וְהִנֵּה דָוִד וַאֲנָשָׁיו יֹרְדִים לִקְרָאתָהּ וַתִּפְגֹּשׁ אֹתָם: כ
21 Now *David* had been saying, "It was all for nothing that I protected that fellow's possessions in the wilderness, and that nothing he owned is missing. He has paid me back evil for good.	וְדָוִד אָמַר אַךְ לַשֶּׁקֶר שָׁמַרְתִּי אֶת־כָּל־אֲשֶׁר לָזֶה בַּמִּדְבָּר וְלֹא־נִפְקַד מִכָּל־אֲשֶׁר־לוֹ מְאוּמָה וַיָּשֶׁב־לִי רָעָה תַּחַת טוֹבָה: כא
22 May *Hashem* do thus and more to the enemies of *David* if, by the light of morning, I leave a single male of his." –	כֹּה־יַעֲשֶׂה אֱלֹהִים לְאֹיְבֵי דָוִד וְכֹה יֹסִיף אִם־אַשְׁאִיר מִכָּל־אֲשֶׁר־לוֹ עַד־הַבֹּקֶר מַשְׁתִּין בְּקִיר: כב
23 When *Avigail* saw *David*, she quickly dismounted from the ass and threw herself face down before *David*, bowing to the ground.	וַתֵּרֶא אֲבִיגַיִל אֶת־דָּוִד וַתְּמַהֵר וַתֵּרֶד מֵעַל הַחֲמוֹר וַתִּפֹּל לְאַפֵּי דָוִד עַל־פָּנֶיהָ וַתִּשְׁתַּחוּ אָרֶץ: כג
24 Prostrate at his feet, she pleaded, "Let the blame be mine, my lord, but let your handmaid speak to you; hear your maid's plea.	וַתִּפֹּל עַל־רַגְלָיו וַתֹּאמֶר בִּי־אֲנִי אֲדֹנִי הֶעָוֹן וּתְדַבֶּר־נָא אֲמָתְךָ בְּאָזְנֶיךָ וּשְׁמַע אֵת דִּבְרֵי אֲמָתֶךָ: כד
25 Please, my lord, pay no attention to that wretched fellow *Naval*. For he is just what his name says: His name means 'boor' and he is a boor. "Your handmaid did not see the young men whom my lord sent.	אַל־נָא יָשִׂים אֲדֹנִי אֶת־לִבּוֹ אֶל־אִישׁ הַבְּלִיַּעַל הַזֶּה עַל־נָבָל כִּי כִשְׁמוֹ כֶּן־הוּא נָבָל שְׁמוֹ וּנְבָלָה עִמּוֹ וַאֲנִי אֲמָתְךָ לֹא רָאִיתִי אֶת־נַעֲרֵי אֲדֹנִי אֲשֶׁר שָׁלָחְתָּ: כה

Shmuel I/I Samuel
Chapter 25

שמואל א
פרק כה

26 I swear, my lord, as *Hashem* lives and as you live – *Hashem* who has kept you from seeking redress by blood with your own hands – let your enemies and all who would harm my lord fare like *Naval*!

כו וְעַתָּה אֲדֹנִי חַי־יְהֹוָה וְחֵי־נַפְשְׁךָ אֲשֶׁר מְנָעֲךָ יְהֹוָה מִבּוֹא בְדָמִים וְהוֹשֵׁעַ יָדְךָ לָךְ וְעַתָּה יִהְיוּ כְנָבָל אֹיְבֶיךָ וְהַמְבַקְשִׁים אֶל־אֲדֹנִי רָעָה:

27 Here is the present which your maidservant has brought to my lord; let it be given to the young men who are the followers of my lord.

כז וְעַתָּה הַבְּרָכָה הַזֹּאת אֲשֶׁר־הֵבִיא שִׁפְחָתְךָ לַאדֹנִי וְנִתְּנָה לַנְּעָרִים הַמִּתְהַלְּכִים בְּרַגְלֵי אֲדֹנִי:

28 Please pardon your maid's boldness. For *Hashem* will grant my lord an enduring house, because my lord is fighting the battles of *Hashem*, and no wrong is ever to be found in you.

כח שָׂא נָא לְפֶשַׁע אֲמָתֶךָ כִּי עָשֹׂה־יַעֲשֶׂה יְהֹוָה לַאדֹנִי בַּיִת נֶאֱמָן כִּי־מִלְחֲמוֹת יְהֹוָה אֲדֹנִי נִלְחָם וְרָעָה לֹא־תִמָּצֵא בְךָ מִיָּמֶיךָ:

SA NA l'-FE-sha a-ma-TE-kha KEE a-soh ya-a-SEH a-do-NAI la-do-NEE BA-yit ne-e-MAN kee mil-kha-MOT a-do-NAI a-do-NEE nil-KHAM v'-ra-AH lo ti-ma-TZAY v'-KHA mi-ya-ME-kha

29 And if anyone sets out to pursue you and seek your life, the life of my lord will be bound up in the bundle of life in the care of *Hashem*; but He will fling away the lives of your enemies as from the hollow of a sling.

כט וַיָּקָם אָדָם לִרְדָפְךָ וּלְבַקֵּשׁ אֶת־נַפְשֶׁךָ וְהָיְתָה נֶפֶשׁ אֲדֹנִי צְרוּרָה בִּצְרוֹר הַחַיִּים אֵת יְהֹוָה אֱלֹהֶיךָ וְאֵת נֶפֶשׁ אֹיְבֶיךָ יְקַלְּעֶנָּה בְּתוֹךְ כַּף הַקָּלַע:

30 And when *Hashem* has accomplished for my lord all the good He has promised you, and has appointed you ruler of *Yisrael*,

ל וְהָיָה כִּי־יַעֲשֶׂה יְהֹוָה לַאדֹנִי כְּכֹל אֲשֶׁר־דִּבֶּר אֶת־הַטּוֹבָה עָלֶיךָ וְצִוְּךָ לְנָגִיד עַל־יִשְׂרָאֵל:

31 do not let this be a cause of stumbling and of faltering courage to my lord that you have shed blood needlessly and that my lord sought redress with his own hands. And when *Hashem* has prospered my lord, remember your maid."

לא וְלֹא תִהְיֶה זֹאת לְךָ לְפוּקָה וּלְמִכְשׁוֹל לֵב לַאדֹנִי וְלִשְׁפָּךְ־דָּם חִנָּם וּלְהוֹשִׁיעַ אֲדֹנִי לוֹ וְהֵיטִב יְהֹוָה לַאדֹנִי וְזָכַרְתָּ אֶת־אֲמָתֶךָ:

32 *David* said to *Avigail*, "Praised be *Hashem*, the God of *Yisrael*, who sent you this day to meet me!

לב וַיֹּאמֶר דָּוִד לַאֲבִיגַל בָּרוּךְ יְהֹוָה אֱלֹהֵי יִשְׂרָאֵל אֲשֶׁר שְׁלָחֵךְ הַיּוֹם הַזֶּה לִקְרָאתִי:

33 And blessed be your prudence, and blessed be you yourself for restraining me from seeking redress in blood by my own hands.

לג וּבָרוּךְ טַעְמֵךְ וּבְרוּכָה אָתְּ אֲשֶׁר כְּלִתִנִי הַיּוֹם הַזֶּה מִבּוֹא בְדָמִים וְהֹשֵׁעַ יָדִי לִי:

34 For as sure as *Hashem*, the God of *Yisrael*, lives – who has kept me from harming you – had you not come quickly to meet me, not a single male of *Naval*'s line would have been left by daybreak."

לד וְאוּלָם חַי־יְהֹוָה אֱלֹהֵי יִשְׂרָאֵל אֲשֶׁר מְנָעַנִי מֵהָרַע אֹתָךְ כִּי לוּלֵי מִהַרְתְּ וַתָּבֹאתִ [וַתָּבֹאת] לִקְרָאתִי כִּי אִם־נוֹתַר לְנָבָל עַד־אוֹר הַבֹּקֶר מַשְׁתִּין בְּקִיר:

25:28 Because my lord is fighting the battles of Hashem *Metzudat David* explains that the prophetess *Avigail* is warning *David* that he should kill only if necessary as part of *Hashem*'s wars against enemies such as the Philistines, but not in order to exact revenge. This is one of the foundations of Jewish military ethics: The People of Israel are required to fight wars only to defend themselves and to strengthen the Promised Land. The State of Israel follows this biblical mandate, as can be seen even in the name given to the Israeli army: The Israel Defense Forces, or in Hebrew, *Tz'va HaHaganah L'Yisrael* (צבא ההגנה לישראל).

Israel Defense Forces insignia

722

Shmuel I/I Samuel
Chapter 26

שמואל א
פרק כו

לה וַיִּקַּח דָּוִד מִיָּדָהּ אֵת אֲשֶׁר־הֵבִיאָה לּוֹ וְלָהּ אָמַר עֲלִי לְשָׁלוֹם לְבֵיתֵךְ רְאִי שָׁמַעְתִּי בְקוֹלֵךְ וָאֶשָּׂא פָּנָיִךְ:

35 David then accepted from her what she had brought him, and he said to her, "Go up to your home safely. See, I have heeded your plea and respected your wish."

לו וַתָּבֹא אֲבִיגַיִל אֶל־נָבָל וְהִנֵּה־לוֹ מִשְׁתֶּה בְּבֵיתוֹ כְּמִשְׁתֵּה הַמֶּלֶךְ וְלֵב נָבָל טוֹב עָלָיו וְהוּא שִׁכֹּר עַד־מְאֹד וְלֹא־הִגִּידָה לּוֹ דָּבָר קָטֹן וְגָדוֹל עַד־אוֹר הַבֹּקֶר:

36 When *Avigail* came home to *Naval*, he was having a feast in his house, a feast fit for a king; *Naval* was in a merry mood and very drunk, so she did not tell him anything at all until daybreak.

לז וַיְהִי בַבֹּקֶר בְּצֵאת הַיַּיִן מִנָּבָל וַתַּגֶּד־לוֹ אִשְׁתּוֹ אֶת־הַדְּבָרִים הָאֵלֶּה וַיָּמָת לִבּוֹ בְּקִרְבּוֹ וְהוּא הָיָה לְאָבֶן:

37 The next morning, when *Naval* had slept off the wine, his wife told him everything that had happened; and his courage died within him, and he became like a stone.

לח וַיְהִי כַּעֲשֶׂרֶת הַיָּמִים וַיִּגֹּף יְהוָה אֶת־נָבָל וַיָּמֹת:

38 About ten days later *Hashem* struck *Naval* and he died.

לט וַיִּשְׁמַע דָּוִד כִּי מֵת נָבָל וַיֹּאמֶר בָּרוּךְ יְהוָה אֲשֶׁר רָב אֶת־רִיב חֶרְפָּתִי מִיַּד נָבָל וְאֶת־עַבְדּוֹ חָשַׂךְ מֵרָעָה וְאֵת רָעַת נָבָל הֵשִׁיב יְהוָה בְּרֹאשׁוֹ וַיִּשְׁלַח דָּוִד וַיְדַבֵּר בַּאֲבִיגַיִל לְקַחְתָּהּ לוֹ לְאִשָּׁה:

39 When *David* heard that *Naval* was dead, he said, "Praised be *Hashem* who championed my cause against the insults of *Naval* and held back His servant from wrongdoing; *Hashem* has brought *Naval*'s wrongdoing down on his own head." *David* sent messengers to propose marriage to *Avigail*, to take her as his wife.

מ וַיָּבֹאוּ עַבְדֵי דָוִד אֶל־אֲבִיגַיִל הַכַּרְמֶלָה וַיְדַבְּרוּ אֵלֶיהָ לֵאמֹר דָּוִד שְׁלָחָנוּ אֵלַיִךְ לְקַחְתֵּךְ לוֹ לְאִשָּׁה:

40 When *David*'s servants came to *Avigail* at *Carmel* and told her that *David* had sent them to her to make her his wife,

מא וַתָּקָם וַתִּשְׁתַּחוּ אַפַּיִם אָרְצָה וַתֹּאמֶר הִנֵּה אֲמָתְךָ לְשִׁפְחָה לִרְחֹץ רַגְלֵי עַבְדֵי אֲדֹנִי:

41 she immediately bowed low with her face to the ground and said, "Your handmaid is ready to be your maidservant, to wash the feet of my lord's servants."

מב וַתְּמַהֵר וַתָּקָם אֲבִיגַיִל וַתִּרְכַּב עַל־הַחֲמוֹר וְחָמֵשׁ נַעֲרֹתֶיהָ הַהֹלְכוֹת לְרַגְלָהּ וַתֵּלֶךְ אַחֲרֵי מַלְאֲכֵי דָוִד וַתְּהִי־לוֹ לְאִשָּׁה:

42 Then *Avigail* rose quickly and mounted an ass, and with five of her maids in attendance she followed *David*'s messengers; and she became his wife.

מג וְאֶת־אֲחִינֹעַם לָקַח דָּוִד מִיִּזְרְעֶאל וַתִּהְיֶיןָ גַּם־שְׁתֵּיהֶן לוֹ לְנָשִׁים:

43 Now *David* had taken Ahinoam of *Yizrael*; so both of them became his wives.

מד וְשָׁאוּל נָתַן אֶת־מִיכַל בִּתּוֹ אֵשֶׁת דָּוִד לְפַלְטִי בֶן־לַיִשׁ אֲשֶׁר מִגַּלִּים:

44 *Shaul* had given his daughter *Michal*, *David*'s wife, to Palti son of Laish from Gallim.

כו א וַיָּבֹאוּ הַזִּפִים אֶל־שָׁאוּל הַגִּבְעָתָה לֵאמֹר הֲלוֹא דָוִד מִסְתַּתֵּר בְּגִבְעַת הַחֲכִילָה עַל פְּנֵי הַיְשִׁימֹן:

26 1 The Ziphites came to *Shaul* at *Giva* and said, "*David* is hiding in the hill of Hachilah facing Jeshimon."

ב וַיָּקָם שָׁאוּל וַיֵּרֶד אֶל־מִדְבַּר־זִיף וְאִתּוֹ שְׁלֹשֶׁת־אֲלָפִים אִישׁ בְּחוּרֵי יִשְׂרָאֵל לְבַקֵּשׁ אֶת־דָּוִד בְּמִדְבַּר־זִיף:

2 *Shaul* went down at once to the wilderness of Ziph, together with three thousand picked men of *Yisrael*, to search for *David* in the wilderness of Ziph,

Shmuel I / I Samuel
Chapter 26

3 and *Shaul* encamped on the hill of Hachilah which faces Jeshimon, by the road. When *David*, who was then living in the wilderness, learned that *Shaul* had come after him into the wilderness,

4 *David* sent out scouts and made sure that *Shaul* had come.

5 *David* went at once to the place where *Shaul* had encamped, and *David* saw the spot where *Shaul* and his army commander, *Avner* son of Ner, lay asleep. *Shaul* lay asleep inside the barricade and the troops were posted around him.

6 *David* spoke up and asked *Achimelech* the Hittite and *Avishai* son of *Tzeruya*, *Yoav*'s brother, "Who will go down with me into the camp to *Shaul*?" And *Avishai* answered, "I will go down with you."

7 So *David* and *Avishai* approached the troops by night, and found *Shaul* fast asleep inside the barricade, his spear stuck in the ground at his head, and *Avner* and the troops sleeping around him.

8 And *Avishai* said to *David*, "*Hashem* has delivered your enemy into your hands today. Let me pin him to the ground with a single thrust of the spear. I will not have to strike him twice."

9 But *David* said to *Avishai*, "Don't do him violence! No one can lay hands on *Hashem*'s anointed with impunity."

10 And *David* went on, "As *Hashem* lives, *Hashem* Himself will strike him down, or his time will come and he will die, or he will go down to battle and perish.

11 But *Hashem* forbid that I should lay a hand on *Hashem*'s anointed! Just take the spear and the water jar at his head and let's be off."

12 So *David* took away the spear and the water jar at *Shaul*'s head, and they left. No one saw or knew or woke up; all remained asleep; a deep sleep from *Hashem* had fallen upon them.

13 *David* crossed over to the other side and stood afar on top of a hill; there was considerable distance between them.

Shmuel I/I Samuel
Chapter 26

שמואל א
פרק כו

14 And *David* shouted to the troops and to *Avner* son of Ner, "*Avner*, aren't you going to answer?" And *Avner* shouted back, "Who are you to shout at the king?"

יד וַיִּקְרָא דָוִד אֶל־הָעָם וְאֶל־אַבְנֵר בֶּן־נֵר לֵאמֹר הֲלוֹא תַעֲנֶה אַבְנֵר וַיַּעַן אַבְנֵר וַיֹּאמֶר מִי אַתָּה קָרָאתָ אֶל־הַמֶּלֶךְ׃

15 And *David* answered *Avner*, "You are a man, aren't you? And there is no one like you in *Yisrael*! So why didn't you keep watch over your lord the king? For one of [our] troops came to do violence to your lord the king.

טו וַיֹּאמֶר דָּוִד אֶל־אַבְנֵר הֲלוֹא־אִישׁ אַתָּה וּמִי כָמוֹךָ בְּיִשְׂרָאֵל וְלָמָּה לֹא שָׁמַרְתָּ אֶל־אֲדֹנֶיךָ הַמֶּלֶךְ כִּי־בָא אַחַד הָעָם לְהַשְׁחִית אֶת־הַמֶּלֶךְ אֲדֹנֶיךָ׃

16 You have not given a good account of yourself! As *Hashem* lives, [all of] you deserve to die, because you did not keep watch over your lord, *Hashem*'s anointed. Look around, where are the king's spear and the water jar that were at his head?"

טז לֹא־טוֹב הַדָּבָר הַזֶּה אֲשֶׁר עָשִׂיתָ חַי־יְהֹוָה כִּי בְנֵי־מָוֶת אַתֶּם אֲשֶׁר לֹא־שְׁמַרְתֶּם עַל־אֲדֹנֵיכֶם עַל־מְשִׁיחַ יְהֹוָה וְעַתָּה רְאֵה אֵי־חֲנִית הַמֶּלֶךְ וְאֶת־צַפַּחַת הַמַּיִם אֲשֶׁר מראשתו [מְרַאֲשֹׁתָיו]׃

17 *Shaul* recognized *David*'s voice, and he asked, "Is that your voice, my son *David*?" And *David* replied, "It is, my lord king."

יז וַיַּכֵּר שָׁאוּל אֶת־קוֹל דָּוִד וַיֹּאמֶר הֲקוֹלְךָ זֶה בְּנִי דָוִד וַיֹּאמֶר דָּוִד קוֹלִי אֲדֹנִי הַמֶּלֶךְ׃

18 And he went on, "But why does my lord continue to pursue his servant? What have I done, and what wrong am I guilty of?

יח וַיֹּאמֶר לָמָּה זֶּה אֲדֹנִי רֹדֵף אַחֲרֵי עַבְדּוֹ כִּי מֶה עָשִׂיתִי וּמַה־בְּיָדִי רָעָה׃

19 Now let my lord the king hear his servant out. If *Hashem* has incited you against me, let Him be appeased by an offering; but if it is men, may they be accursed of *Hashem*! For they have driven me out today, so that I cannot have a share in *Hashem*'s possession, but am told, 'Go and worship other gods.'

יט וְעַתָּה יִשְׁמַע־נָא אֲדֹנִי הַמֶּלֶךְ אֵת דִּבְרֵי עַבְדּוֹ אִם־יְהֹוָה הֱסִיתְךָ בִי יָרַח מִנְחָה וְאִם בְּנֵי הָאָדָם אֲרוּרִים הֵם לִפְנֵי יְהֹוָה כִּי־גֵרְשׁוּנִי הַיּוֹם מֵהִסְתַּפֵּחַ בְּנַחֲלַת יְהֹוָה לֵאמֹר לֵךְ עֲבֹד אֱלֹהִים אֲחֵרִים׃

v'-a-TAH yish-ma NA a-do-NEE ha-ME-lekh AYT div-RAY av-DO im a-do-NAI he-see-t'-KHA VEE ya-RAKH min-KHAH v'-IM b'-NAY ha-a-DAM a-ru-REEM HAYM lif-NAY a-do-NAI kee gay-r'-SHU-nee ha-YOM may-his-ta-PAY-akh b'-na-kha-LAT a-do-NAI lay-MOR LAYKH a-VOD e-lo-HEEM a-khay-REEM

20 Oh, let my blood not fall to the ground, away from the presence of *Hashem*! For the king of *Yisrael* has come out to seek a single flea – as if he were hunting a partridge in the hills."

כ וְעַתָּה אַל־יִפֹּל דָּמִי אַרְצָה מִנֶּגֶד פְּנֵי יְהֹוָה כִּי־יָצָא מֶלֶךְ יִשְׂרָאֵל לְבַקֵּשׁ אֶת־פַּרְעֹשׁ אֶחָד כַּאֲשֶׁר יִרְדֹּף הַקֹּרֵא בֶּהָרִים׃

26:19 Go and worship other gods As *Rashi* explains, *David* makes the surprising claim that God told him to go and worship other gods, because he was compelled to run away to the land of the Philistines, and in a certain sense, leaving the Land of Israel is tantamount to worshipping idols. This is reflected in the Talmudic statement (*Ketubot* 110a), "one who lives outside of *Eretz Yisrael* is like one who has no God." The Rabbis make this dramatic statement because the People of Israel are commanded to live in *Eretz Yisrael*, and it is the only place in the world where one can fulfill all of the commandments. It is also the place that *Hashem* has chosen to reveal Himself through awe inspiring miracles, from biblical through modern times. Hence, leaving the Land of Israel greatly reduces a person's relationship with God, and is somewhat similar to idolatry.

Shmuel I / I Samuel
Chapter 27

שמואל א
פרק כז

21 And *Shaul* answered, "I am in the wrong. Come back, my son *David*, for I will never harm you again, seeing how you have held my life precious this day. Yes, I have been a fool, and I have erred so very much."

כא וַיֹּאמֶר שָׁאוּל חָטָאתִי שׁוּב בְּנִי־דָוִד כִּי לֹא־אָרַע לְךָ עוֹד תַּחַת אֲשֶׁר יָקְרָה נַפְשִׁי בְּעֵינֶיךָ הַיּוֹם הַזֶּה הִנֵּה הִסְכַּלְתִּי וָאֶשְׁגֶּה הַרְבֵּה מְאֹד:

22 *David* replied, "Here is Your Majesty's spear. Let one of the young men come over and get it.

כב וַיַּעַן דָּוִד וַיֹּאמֶר הִנֵּה הַחֲנִית [הַחֲנִית] הַמֶּלֶךְ וְיַעֲבֹר אֶחָד מֵהַנְּעָרִים וְיִקָּחֶהָ:

23 And *Hashem* will requite every man for his right conduct and loyalty – for this day *Hashem* delivered you into my hands and I would not raise a hand against *Hashem*'s anointed.

כג וַיהוָה יָשִׁיב לָאִישׁ אֶת־צִדְקָתוֹ וְאֶת־אֱמֻנָתוֹ אֲשֶׁר נְתָנְךָ יְהוָה הַיּוֹם בְּיָד וְלֹא אָבִיתִי לִשְׁלֹחַ יָדִי בִּמְשִׁיחַ יְהוָה:

24 And just as I valued your life highly this day, so may *Hashem* value my life and may He rescue me from all trouble."

כד וְהִנֵּה כַּאֲשֶׁר גָּדְלָה נַפְשְׁךָ הַיּוֹם הַזֶּה בְּעֵינָי כֵּן תִּגְדַּל נַפְשִׁי בְּעֵינֵי יְהוָה וְיַצִּלֵנִי מִכָּל־צָרָה:

25 *Shaul* answered *David*, "May you be blessed, my son *David*. You shall achieve, and you shall prevail." *David* then went his way, and *Shaul* returned home.

כה וַיֹּאמֶר שָׁאוּל אֶל־דָּוִד בָּרוּךְ אַתָּה בְּנִי דָוִד גַּם עָשֹׂה תַעֲשֶׂה וְגַם יָכֹל תּוּכָל וַיֵּלֶךְ דָּוִד לְדַרְכּוֹ וְשָׁאוּל שָׁב לִמְקוֹמוֹ:

27 1 *David* said to himself, "Some day I shall certainly perish at the hands of *Shaul*. The best thing for me is to flee to the land of the Philistines; *Shaul* will then give up hunting me throughout the territory of *Yisrael*, and I will escape him."

כז א וַיֹּאמֶר דָּוִד אֶל־לִבּוֹ עַתָּה אֶסָּפֶה יוֹם־אֶחָד בְּיַד־שָׁאוּל אֵין־לִי טוֹב כִּי הִמָּלֵט אִמָּלֵט אֶל־אֶרֶץ פְּלִשְׁתִּים וְנוֹאַשׁ מִמֶּנִּי שָׁאוּל לְבַקְשֵׁנִי עוֹד בְּכָל־גְּבוּל יִשְׂרָאֵל וְנִמְלַטְתִּי מִיָּדוֹ:

2 So *David* and the six hundred men with him went and crossed over to King Achish son of Maoch of Gath.

ב וַיָּקָם דָּוִד וַיַּעֲבֹר הוּא וְשֵׁשׁ־מֵאוֹת אִישׁ אֲשֶׁר עִמּוֹ אֶל־אָכִישׁ בֶּן־מָעוֹךְ מֶלֶךְ גַּת:

3 *David* and his men stayed with Achish in Gath, each man with his family, and *David* with his two wives, Ahinoam the Yizraelite and *Avigail* wife of *Naval* the Carmelite.

ג וַיֵּשֶׁב דָּוִד עִם־אָכִישׁ בְּגַת הוּא וַאֲנָשָׁיו אִישׁ וּבֵיתוֹ דָּוִד וּשְׁתֵּי נָשָׁיו אֲחִינֹעַם הַיִּזְרְעֵאלִת וַאֲבִיגַיִל אֵשֶׁת־נָבָל הַכַּרְמְלִית:

4 And when *Shaul* was told that *David* had fled to Gath, he did not pursue him any more.

ד וַיֻּגַּד לְשָׁאוּל כִּי־בָרַח דָּוִד גַּת וְלֹא־יוֹסַף [יָסַף] עוֹד לְבַקְשׁוֹ:

5 *David* said to Achish, "If you please, let a place be granted me in one of the country towns where I can live; why should your servant remain with you in the royal city?"

ה וַיֹּאמֶר דָּוִד אֶל־אָכִישׁ אִם־נָא מָצָאתִי חֵן בְּעֵינֶיךָ יִתְּנוּ־לִי מָקוֹם בְּאַחַת עָרֵי הַשָּׂדֶה וְאֵשְׁבָה שָּׁם וְלָמָּה יֵשֵׁב עַבְדְּךָ בְּעִיר הַמַּמְלָכָה עִמָּךְ:

6 At that time Achish granted him *Tziklag*; that is how *Tziklag* came to belong to the kings of *Yehuda*, as is still the case.

ו וַיִּתֶּן־לוֹ אָכִישׁ בַּיּוֹם הַהוּא אֶת־צִקְלָג לָכֵן הָיְתָה צִקְלַג לְמַלְכֵי יְהוּדָה עַד הַיּוֹם הַזֶּה:

va-yi-ten LO a-KHEESH ba-YOM ha-HU et tzik-LAG la-KHAYN ha-y'-TAH tzik-LAG l'-mal-KHAY y'-hu-DAH AD ha-YOM ha-ZEH

27:6 That is how *Tziklag* came to belong to the kings of *Yehuda* Achish gives *David* the city of *Tziklag* as a place for him to dwell. *Metzudat David* points out that *Tziklag* was actually part of the designated in-

Shmuel I / I Samuel
Chapter 28

שמואל א
פרק כח

7 The length of time that *David* lived in Philistine territory was a year and four months.

ז וַיְהִי מִסְפַּר הַיָּמִים אֲשֶׁר־יָשַׁב דָּוִד בִּשְׂדֵה פְלִשְׁתִּים יָמִים וְאַרְבָּעָה חֳדָשִׁים:

8 *David* and his men went up and raided the Geshurites, the Gizrites, and the Amalekites – who were the inhabitants of the region of Olam, all the way to Shur and to the land of Egypt. –

ח וַיַּעַל דָּוִד וַאֲנָשָׁיו וַיִּפְשְׁטוּ אֶל־הַגְּשׁוּרִי והגרזי [וְהַגִּזְרִי] וְהָעֲמָלֵקִי כִּי הֵנָּה יֹשְׁבוֹת הָאָרֶץ אֲשֶׁר מֵעוֹלָם בּוֹאֲךָ שׁוּרָה וְעַד־אֶרֶץ מִצְרָיִם:

9 When *David* attacked a region, he would leave no man or woman alive; he would take flocks, herds, asses, camels, and clothing. When he returned and came to Achish,

ט וְהִכָּה דָוִד אֶת־הָאָרֶץ וְלֹא יְחַיֶּה אִישׁ וְאִשָּׁה וְלָקַח צֹאן וּבָקָר וַחֲמֹרִים וּגְמַלִּים וּבְגָדִים וַיָּשָׁב וַיָּבֹא אֶל־אָכִישׁ:

10 Achish would ask, "Where did you raid today?" and *David* would reply, "The *Negev* of *Yehuda*," or "the *Negev* of the Jerahmeelites," or "the *Negev* of the Kenites."

י וַיֹּאמֶר אָכִישׁ אַל־פְּשַׁטְתֶּם הַיּוֹם וַיֹּאמֶר דָּוִד עַל־נֶגֶב יְהוּדָה וְעַל־נֶגֶב הַיְּרַחְמְאֵלִי וְאֶל־נֶגֶב הַקֵּינִי:

11 *David* would leave no man or woman alive to be brought to Gath; for he thought, "They might tell about us: *David* did this." Such was his practice as long as he stayed in the territory of the Philistines.

יא וְאִישׁ וְאִשָּׁה לֹא־יְחַיֶּה דָוִד לְהָבִיא גַת לֵאמֹר פֶּן־יַגִּדוּ עָלֵינוּ לֵאמֹר כֹּה־עָשָׂה דָוִד וְכֹה מִשְׁפָּטוֹ כָּל־הַיָּמִים אֲשֶׁר יָשַׁב בִּשְׂדֵה פְלִשְׁתִּים:

12 Achish trusted *David*. He thought: "He has aroused the wrath of his own people *Yisrael*, and so he will be my vassal forever."

יב וַיַּאֲמֵן אָכִישׁ בְּדָוִד לֵאמֹר הַבְאֵשׁ הִבְאִישׁ בְּעַמּוֹ בְיִשְׂרָאֵל וְהָיָה לִי לְעֶבֶד עוֹלָם:

28
1 At that time the Philistines mustered their forces for war, to take the field against *Yisrael*. Achish said to *David*, "You know, of course, that you and your men must march out with my forces."

כח א וַיְהִי בַּיָּמִים הָהֵם וַיִּקְבְּצוּ פְלִשְׁתִּים אֶת־מַחֲנֵיהֶם לַצָּבָא לְהִלָּחֵם בְּיִשְׂרָאֵל וַיֹּאמֶר אָכִישׁ אֶל־דָּוִד יָדֹעַ תֵּדַע כִּי אִתִּי תֵּצֵא בַמַּחֲנֶה אַתָּה וַאֲנָשֶׁיךָ:

2 *David* answered Achish, "You surely know what your servant will do." "In that case," Achish replied to *David*, "I will appoint you my bodyguard for life."

ב וַיֹּאמֶר דָּוִד אֶל־אָכִישׁ לָכֵן אַתָּה תֵדַע אֵת אֲשֶׁר־יַעֲשֶׂה עַבְדֶּךָ וַיֹּאמֶר אָכִישׁ אֶל־דָּוִד לָכֵן שֹׁמֵר לְרֹאשִׁי אֲשִׂימְךָ כָּל־הַיָּמִים:

3 Now *Shmuel* had died and all *Yisrael* made lament for him; and he was buried in his own town of *Rama*. And *Shaul* had forbidden [recourse to] ghosts and familiar spirits in the land.

ג וּשְׁמוּאֵל מֵת וַיִּסְפְּדוּ־לוֹ כָּל־יִשְׂרָאֵל וַיִּקְבְּרֻהוּ בָרָמָה וּבְעִירוֹ וְשָׁאוּל הֵסִיר הָאֹבוֹת וְאֶת־הַיִּדְּעֹנִים מֵהָאָרֶץ:

ush-mu-AYL MAYT va-yis-p'-du LO kol yis-ra-AYL va-yik-b'-RU-hu va-ra-MAH uv-ee-RO v'-sha-UL hay-SEER ha-o-VOT v'-et ha-yi-d'-o-NEEM may-ha-A-retz

Tomb of Shmuel the Prophet

heritance of *David*'s tribe *Yehuda*, but it had been taken by the Philistines. At various times, many areas of *Eretz Yisrael* have been conquered by different invaders. Yet, this does not detract from the rights of the People of Israel. Just as Achish enables *David* to reclaim *Tziklag*, in 1967 divine Providence allowed the Jewish people to reclaim much of Judea, Samaria, the Golan Heights and the Gaza Strip during the Six Day War, tripling the size of Israel in less than a week.

28:3 And he was buried in his own town of *Rama* When the prophet *Shmuel* dies on the

Shmuel I/I Samuel
Chapter 28

שמואל א
פרק כח

4 The Philistines mustered and they marched to Shunem and encamped; and *Shaul* gathered all *Yisrael*, and they encamped at Gilboa.

ד וַיִּקָּבְצוּ פְלִשְׁתִּים וַיָּבֹאוּ וַיַּחֲנוּ בְשׁוּנֵם וַיִּקְבֹּץ שָׁאוּל אֶת־כָּל־יִשְׂרָאֵל וַיַּחֲנוּ בַּגִּלְבֹּעַ:

5 When *Shaul* saw the Philistine force, his heart trembled with fear.

ה וַיַּרְא שָׁאוּל אֶת־מַחֲנֵה פְלִשְׁתִּים וַיִּרָא וַיֶּחֱרַד לִבּוֹ מְאֹד:

6 And *Shaul* inquired of *Hashem*, but *Hashem* did not answer him, either by dreams or by Urim or by *Neviim*.

ו וַיִּשְׁאַל שָׁאוּל בַּיהוָה וְלֹא עָנָהוּ יְהוָה גַּם בַּחֲלֹמוֹת גַּם בָּאוּרִים גַּם בַּנְּבִיאִם:

7 Then *Shaul* said to his courtiers, "Find me a woman who consults ghosts, so that I can go to her and inquire through her." And his courtiers told him that there was a woman in En-dor who consulted ghosts.

ז וַיֹּאמֶר שָׁאוּל לַעֲבָדָיו בַּקְּשׁוּ־לִי אֵשֶׁת בַּעֲלַת־אוֹב וְאֵלְכָה אֵלֶיהָ וְאֶדְרְשָׁה־בָּהּ וַיֹּאמְרוּ עֲבָדָיו אֵלָיו הִנֵּה אֵשֶׁת בַּעֲלַת־אוֹב בְּעֵין דּוֹר:

8 *Shaul* disguised himself; he put on different clothes and set out with two men. They came to the woman by night, and he said, "Please divine for me by a ghost. Bring up for me the one I shall name to you."

ח וַיִּתְחַפֵּשׂ שָׁאוּל וַיִּלְבַּשׁ בְּגָדִים אֲחֵרִים וַיֵּלֶךְ הוּא וּשְׁנֵי אֲנָשִׁים עִמּוֹ וַיָּבֹאוּ אֶל־הָאִשָּׁה לָיְלָה וַיֹּאמֶר קסומי־[קָסֳמִי־] נָא לִי בָּאוֹב וְהַעֲלִי לִי אֵת אֲשֶׁר־אֹמַר אֵלָיִךְ:

9 But the woman answered him, "You know what *Shaul* has done, how he has banned [the use of] ghosts and familiar spirits in the land. So why are you laying a trap for me, to get me killed?"

ט וַתֹּאמֶר הָאִשָּׁה אֵלָיו הִנֵּה אַתָּה יָדַעְתָּ אֵת אֲשֶׁר־עָשָׂה שָׁאוּל אֲשֶׁר הִכְרִית אֶת־הָאֹבוֹת וְאֶת־הַיִּדְּעֹנִי מִן־הָאָרֶץ וְלָמָה אַתָּה מִתְנַקֵּשׁ בְּנַפְשִׁי לַהֲמִיתֵנִי:

10 *Shaul* swore to her by *Hashem*: "As *Hashem* lives, you won't get into trouble over this."

י וַיִּשָּׁבַע לָהּ שָׁאוּל בַּיהוָה לֵאמֹר חַי־יְהוָה אִם־יִקְּרֵךְ עָוֹן בַּדָּבָר הַזֶּה:

11 At that, the woman asked, "Whom shall I bring up for you?" He answered, "Bring up *Shmuel* for me."

יא וַתֹּאמֶר הָאִשָּׁה אֶת־מִי אַעֲלֶה־לָּךְ וַיֹּאמֶר אֶת־שְׁמוּאֵל הַעֲלִי־לִי:

12 Then the woman recognized *Shmuel*, and she shrieked loudly, and said to *Shaul*, "Why have you deceived me? You are *Shaul*!"

יב וַתֵּרֶא הָאִשָּׁה אֶת־שְׁמוּאֵל וַתִּזְעַק בְּקוֹל גָּדוֹל וַתֹּאמֶר הָאִשָּׁה אֶל־שָׁאוּל לֵאמֹר לָמָּה רִמִּיתָנִי וְאַתָּה שָׁאוּל:

13 The king answered her, "Don't be afraid. What do you see?" And the woman said to *Shaul*, "I see a divine being coming up from the earth."

יג וַיֹּאמֶר לָהּ הַמֶּלֶךְ אַל־תִּירְאִי כִּי מָה רָאִית וַתֹּאמֶר הָאִשָּׁה אֶל־שָׁאוּל אֱלֹהִים רָאִיתִי עֹלִים מִן־הָאָרֶץ:

---

twenty-eighth day of the Hebrew month of *Iyar*, he is buried in *Rama*. According to tradition, *Shmuel*'s burial site is in the northwest outskirts of modern Jerusalem, near the neighborhood of *Ramot*. It has long been a place of prayer and study for the Jewish people. Given its strategic location along the road between *Yerushalayim* and *Tel Aviv*, the Arabs used it during the War of Independence and the Six Day War as a base from which to fire at Israeli soldiers. This holy site was liberated by the Israeli Army during the Six Day War.

Shmuel I/I Samuel
Chapter 28

שמואל א
פרק כח

14 "What does he look like?" he asked her. "It is an old man coming up," she said, "and he is wrapped in a robe." Then *Shaul* knew that it was *Shmuel*; and he bowed low in homage with his face to the ground.

יד וַיֹּ֤אמֶר לָהּ֙ מַֽה־תָּאֳר֔וֹ וַתֹּ֕אמֶר אִ֥ישׁ זָקֵ֖ן עֹלֶ֑ה וְה֣וּא עֹטֶ֣ה מְעִ֔יל וַיֵּ֤דַע שָׁאוּל֙ כִּֽי־שְׁמוּאֵ֣ל ה֔וּא וַיִּקֹּ֥ד אַפַּ֛יִם אַ֖רְצָה וַיִּשְׁתָּֽחוּ:

15 *Shmuel* said to *Shaul*, "Why have you disturbed me and brought me up?" And *Shaul* answered, "I am in great trouble. The Philistines are attacking me and *Hashem* has turned away from me; He no longer answers me, either by *Neviim* or in dreams. So I have called you to tell me what I am to do."

טו וַיֹּ֤אמֶר שְׁמוּאֵל֙ אֶל־שָׁא֔וּל לָ֥מָּה הִרְגַּזְתַּ֖נִי לְהַעֲל֣וֹת אֹתִ֑י וַיֹּ֣אמֶר שָׁא֡וּל צַר־לִ֣י מְאֹד֩ וּפְלִשְׁתִּ֨ים ׀ נִלְחָמִ֜ים בִּ֗י וֵֽאלֹהִ֞ים סָ֤ר מֵֽעָלַי֙ וְלֹֽא־עָנָ֣נִי ע֗וֹד גַּ֤ם בְּיַֽד־הַנְּבִיאִם֙ גַּם־בַּ֣חֲלֹמ֔וֹת וָאֶקְרָאֶ֣ה לְךָ֔ לְהוֹדִיעֵ֖נִי מָ֥ה אֶעֱשֶֽׂה:

16 *Shmuel* said, "Why do you ask me, seeing that *Hashem* has turned away from you and has become your adversary?

טז וַיֹּ֣אמֶר שְׁמוּאֵ֔ל וְלָ֖מָּה תִּשְׁאָלֵ֑נִי וַיהֹוָ֛ה סָ֥ר מֵעָלֶ֖יךָ וַיְהִ֥י עָרֶֽךָ:

17 *Hashem* has done for Himself as He foretold through me: *Hashem* has torn the kingship out of your hands and has given it to your fellow, to *David*,

יז וַיַּ֤עַשׂ יְהֹוָה֙ ל֔וֹ כַּאֲשֶׁ֖ר דִּבֶּ֣ר בְּיָדִ֑י וַיִּקְרַ֨ע יְהֹוָ֤ה אֶת־הַמַּמְלָכָה֙ מִיָּדֶ֔ךָ וַֽיִּתְּנָ֖הּ לְרֵעֲךָ֥ לְדָוִֽד:

18 because you did not obey *Hashem* and did not execute His wrath upon the Amalekites. That is why *Hashem* has done this to you today.

יח כַּאֲשֶׁ֤ר לֹֽא־שָׁמַ֙עְתָּ֙ בְּק֣וֹל יְהֹוָ֔ה וְלֹֽא־עָשִׂ֥יתָ חֲרוֹן־אַפּ֖וֹ בַּעֲמָלֵ֑ק עַל־כֵּן֙ הַדָּבָ֣ר הַזֶּ֔ה עָשָֽׂה־לְךָ֥ יְהֹוָ֖ה הַיּ֥וֹם הַזֶּֽה:

19 Further, *Hashem* will deliver the Israelites who are with you into the hands of the Philistines. Tomorrow your sons and you will be with me; and *Hashem* will also deliver the Israelite forces into the hands of the Philistines."

יט וְיִתֵּ֣ן יְ֠הֹוָה גַּ֣ם אֶת־יִשְׂרָאֵ֤ל עִמְּךָ֙ בְּיַד־פְּלִשְׁתִּ֔ים וּמָחָ֕ר אַתָּ֥ה וּבָנֶ֖יךָ עִמִּ֑י גַּ֚ם אֶת־מַחֲנֵ֣ה יִשְׂרָאֵ֔ל יִתֵּ֥ן יְהֹוָ֖ה בְּיַד־פְּלִשְׁתִּֽים:

20 At once *Shaul* flung himself prone on the ground, terrified by *Shmuel*'s words. Besides, there was no strength in him, for he had not eaten anything all day and all night.

כ וַיְמַהֵ֣ר שָׁא֗וּל וַיִּפֹּ֤ל מְלֹא־קֽוֹמָתוֹ֙ אַ֔רְצָה וַיִּרָ֥א מְאֹ֖ד מִדִּבְרֵ֣י שְׁמוּאֵ֑ל גַּם־כֹּ֙חַ֙ לֹא־הָ֣יָה ב֔וֹ כִּ֣י לֹ֤א אָכַל֙ לֶ֔חֶם כָּל־הַיּ֖וֹם וְכָל־הַלָּֽיְלָה:

21 The woman went up to *Shaul* and, seeing how greatly disturbed he was, she said to him, "Your handmaid listened to you; I took my life in my hands and heeded the request you made of me.

כא וַתָּב֤וֹא הָֽאִשָּׁה֙ אֶל־שָׁא֔וּל וַתֵּ֖רֶא כִּֽי־נִבְהַ֣ל מְאֹ֑ד וַתֹּ֣אמֶר אֵלָ֗יו הִנֵּ֨ה שָׁמְעָ֤ה שִׁפְחָֽתְךָ֙ בְּקוֹלֶ֔ךָ וָאָשִׂ֥ים נַפְשִׁ֖י בְּכַפִּ֑י וָֽאֶשְׁמַע֙ אֶת־דְּבָרֶ֔יךָ אֲשֶׁ֥ר דִּבַּ֖רְתָּ אֵלָֽי:

22 So now you listen to me: Let me set before you a bit of food. Eat, and then you will have the strength to go on your way."

כב וְעַתָּ֗ה שְׁמַֽע־נָ֤א גַם־אַתָּה֙ בְּק֣וֹל שִׁפְחָתֶ֔ךָ וְאָשִׂ֧מָה לְפָנֶ֛יךָ פַּת־לֶ֖חֶם וֶאֱכ֑וֹל וִיהִ֤י בְךָ֙ כֹּ֔חַ כִּ֥י תֵלֵ֖ךְ בַּדָּֽרֶךְ:

23 He refused, saying, "I will not eat." But when his courtiers as well as the woman urged him, he listened to them; he got up from the ground and sat on the bed.

כג וַיְמָאֵ֗ן וַיֹּ֙אמֶר֙ לֹ֣א אֹכַ֔ל וַיִּפְרְצוּ־ב֤וֹ עֲבָדָיו֙ וְגַם־הָ֣אִשָּׁ֔ה וַיִּשְׁמַ֖ע לְקֹלָ֑ם וַיָּ֙קָם֙ מֵהָאָ֔רֶץ וַיֵּ֖שֶׁב אֶל־הַמִּטָּֽה:

24 The woman had a stall-fed calf in the house; she hastily slaughtered it, and took flour and kneaded it, and baked some unleavened cakes.

כד וְלָאִשָּׁ֤ה עֵֽגֶל־מַרְבֵּק֙ בַּבַּ֔יִת וַתְּמַהֵ֖ר וַתִּזְבָּחֵ֑הוּ וַתִּקַּ֥ח קֶ֛מַח וַתָּ֖לָשׁ וַתֹּפֵ֥הוּ מַצּֽוֹת:

Shmuel I/I Samuel
Chapter 29

שמואל א
פרק כט

25 She set this before *Shaul* and his courtiers, and they ate. Then they rose and left the same night.

כה וַתַּגֵּשׁ לִפְנֵי־שָׁאוּל וְלִפְנֵי עֲבָדָיו וַיֹּאכֵלוּ וַיָּקֻמוּ וַיֵּלְכוּ בַּלַּיְלָה הַהוּא׃

29 1 The Philistines mustered all their forces at Aphek, while *Yisrael* was encamping at the spring in *Yizrael*.

כט א וַיִּקְבְּצוּ פְלִשְׁתִּים אֶת־כָּל־מַחֲנֵיהֶם אֲפֵקָה וְיִשְׂרָאֵל חֹנִים בַּעַיִן אֲשֶׁר בְּיִזְרְעֶאל׃

2 The Philistine lords came marching, each with his units of hundreds and of thousands; and *David* and his men came marching last, with Achish.

ב וְסַרְנֵי פְלִשְׁתִּים עֹבְרִים לְמֵאוֹת וְלַאֲלָפִים וְדָוִד וַאֲנָשָׁיו עֹבְרִים בָּאַחֲרֹנָה עִם־אָכִישׁ׃

v'-sar-NAY f'-lish-TEEM o-v'-REEM l'-may-OT v'-la-a-la-FEEM v'-da-VID va-a-na-SHAV o-v'-REEM ba-a-kha-ro-NAH im a-KHEESH

3 The Philistine officers asked, "Who are those Hebrews?" "Why, that's *David*, the servant of King *Shaul* of *Yisrael*," Achish answered the Philistine officers. "He has been with me for a year or more, and I have found no fault in him from the day he defected until now."

ג וַיֹּאמְרוּ שָׂרֵי פְלִשְׁתִּים מָה הָעִבְרִים הָאֵלֶּה וַיֹּאמֶר אָכִישׁ אֶל־שָׂרֵי פְלִשְׁתִּים הֲלוֹא־זֶה דָוִד עֶבֶד שָׁאוּל מֶלֶךְ־יִשְׂרָאֵל אֲשֶׁר הָיָה אִתִּי זֶה יָמִים אוֹ־זֶה שָׁנִים וְלֹא־מָצָאתִי בוֹ מְאוּמָה מִיּוֹם נָפְלוֹ עַד־הַיּוֹם הַזֶּה׃

4 But the Philistine officers were angry with him; and the Philistine officers said to him, "Send the man back; let him go back to the place you assigned him. He shall not march down with us to the battle, or else he may become our adversary in battle. For with what could that fellow appease his master if not with the heads of these men?

ד וַיִּקְצְפוּ עָלָיו שָׂרֵי פְלִשְׁתִּים וַיֹּאמְרוּ לוֹ שָׂרֵי פְלִשְׁתִּים הָשֵׁב אֶת־הָאִישׁ וְיָשֹׁב אֶל־מְקוֹמוֹ אֲשֶׁר הִפְקַדְתּוֹ שָׁם וְלֹא־יֵרֵד עִמָּנוּ בַּמִּלְחָמָה וְלֹא־יִהְיֶה־לָּנוּ לְשָׂטָן בַּמִּלְחָמָה וּבַמָּה יִתְרַצֶּה זֶה אֶל־אֲדֹנָיו הֲלוֹא בְּרָאשֵׁי הָאֲנָשִׁים הָהֵם׃

5 Remember, he is the *David* of whom they sang as they danced: *Shaul* has slain his thousands; *David*, his tens of thousands."

ה הֲלוֹא־זֶה דָוִד אֲשֶׁר יַעֲנוּ־לוֹ בַּמְּחֹלוֹת לֵאמֹר הִכָּה שָׁאוּל בַּאֲלָפָיו וְדָוִד ברבבתו [בְּרִבְבֹתָיו]׃

6 Achish summoned *David* and said to him, "As *Hashem* lives, you are an honest man, and I would like to have you serve in my forces; for I have found no fault with you from the day you joined me until now. But you are not acceptable to the other lords.

ו וַיִּקְרָא אָכִישׁ אֶל־דָּוִד וַיֹּאמֶר אֵלָיו חַי־יְהוָה כִּי־יָשָׁר אַתָּה וְטוֹב בְּעֵינַי צֵאתְךָ וּבֹאֲךָ אִתִּי בַּמַּחֲנֶה כִּי לֹא־מָצָאתִי בְךָ רָעָה מִיּוֹם בֹּאֲךָ אֵלַי עַד־הַיּוֹם הַזֶּה וּבְעֵינֵי הַסְּרָנִים לֹא־טוֹב אָתָּה׃

29:2 ***David* and his men came marching last, with Achish** It is certainly impossible that *David* would have been willing, as this verse implies, to wage war against Israel. Though he was fleeing from King *Shaul*, *David* remains completely loyal to his people throughout his travails. In this instance, he feigns loyalty to Achish and uses the advantage gained by his trust to spy against the Philistines, gaining information which will later helps him defeat this enemy. This is reminiscent of a more recent Israeli spy, Eli Cohen. During the 1960s Cohen managed to infiltrate the highest echelons of the Syrian army, to spy on Israel's behalf. He provided the IDF with critical information that would assist Israel in the Six Day War and enable it to liberate the Golan Heights. Though Cohen was captured and executed by the Syrians, the State and People of Israel continue to benefit from his sacrifice to this very day. The Golan Heights is home to flourishing communities, and provides great strategic value to Israel.

"Martyrs of the struggle for Israeli independence." Eli Cohen (1924–1965), bottom left

Shmuel I / I Samuel
Chapter 30

7 So go back in peace, and do nothing to displease the Philistine lords."

8 *David*, however, said to Achish, "But what have I done, what fault have you found in your servant from the day I appeared before you to this day, that I should not go and fight against the enemies of my lord the king?"

9 Achish replied to *David*, "I know; you are as acceptable to me as an angel of *Hashem*. But the Philistine officers have decided that you must not march out with us to the battle.

10 So rise early in the morning, you and your lord's servants who came with you – rise early in the morning, and leave as soon as it is light."

11 Accordingly, *David* and his men rose early in the morning to leave, to return to the land of the Philistines, while the Philistines marched up to *Yizrael*.

Chapter 30

1 By the time *David* and his men arrived in *Tziklag*, on the third day, the Amalekites had made a raid into the *Negev* and against *Tziklag*; they had stormed *Tziklag* and burned it down.

2 They had taken the women in it captive, low-born and high-born alike; they did not kill any, but carried them off and went their way.

3 When *David* and his men came to the town and found it burned down, and their wives and sons and daughters taken captive,

4 *David* and the troops with him broke into tears, until they had no strength left for weeping.

5 *David*'s two wives had been taken captive, Ahinoam of *Yizrael* and *Avigail* wife of *Naval* from Carmel.

6 *David* was in great danger, for the troops threatened to stone him; for all the troops were embittered on account of their sons and daughters. But *David* sought strength in *Hashem* his God.

7 *David* said to the *Kohen Evyatar* son of *Achimelech*, "Bring the ephod up to me." When *Evyatar* brought up the ephod to *David*,

8 *David* inquired of *Hashem*, "Shall I pursue those raiders? Will I overtake them?" And He answered him, "Pursue, for you shall overtake and you shall rescue."

Shmuel I / I Samuel
Chapter 30

שמואל א
פרק ל

9 So *David* and the six hundred men with him set out, and they came to the Wadi Besor, where a halt was made by those who were to be left behind.

ט וַיֵּ֣לֶךְ דָּוִ֗ד ה֚וּא וְשֵׁשׁ־מֵא֥וֹת אִישׁ֙ אֲשֶׁ֣ר אִתּ֔וֹ וַיָּבֹ֖אוּ עַד־נַ֣חַל הַבְּשׂ֑וֹר וְהַנּֽוֹתָרִ֖ים עָמָֽדוּ׃

10 *David* continued the pursuit with four hundred men; two hundred men had halted, too faint to cross the Wadi Besor.

י וַיִּרְדֹּ֣ף דָּוִ֔ד ה֖וּא וְאַרְבַּע־מֵא֣וֹת אִ֑ישׁ וַיַּעַמְדוּ֙ מָאתַ֣יִם אִ֔ישׁ אֲשֶׁ֣ר פִּגְּר֔וּ מֵעֲבֹ֖ר אֶת־נַ֥חַל הַבְּשֽׂוֹר׃

11 They came upon an Egyptian in the open country and brought him to *David*. They gave him food to eat and water to drink;

יא וַֽיִּמְצְא֤וּ אִישׁ־מִצְרִי֙ בַּשָּׂדֶ֔ה וַיִּקְח֥וּ אֹת֖וֹ אֶל־דָּוִ֑ד וַיִּתְּנוּ־ל֥וֹ לֶ֙חֶם֙ וַיֹּאכַ֔ל וַיַּשְׁקֻ֖הוּ מָֽיִם׃

12 he was also given a piece of pressed fig cake and two cakes of raisins. He ate and regained his strength, for he had eaten no food and drunk no water for three days and three nights.

יב וַיִּתְּנוּ־לוֹ֩ פֶ֨לַח דְּבֵלָ֜ה וּשְׁנֵ֣י צִמֻּקִ֗ים וַיֹּ֙אכַל֙ וַתָּ֣שָׁב רוּח֣וֹ אֵלָ֔יו כִּ֠י לֹֽא־אָ֤כַל לֶ֙חֶם֙ וְלֹא־שָׁ֣תָה מַ֔יִם שְׁלֹשָׁ֥ה יָמִ֖ים וּשְׁלֹשָׁ֥ה לֵילֽוֹת׃

13 Then *David* asked him, "To whom do you belong and where are you from?" "I am an Egyptian boy," he answered, "the slave of an Amalekite. My master abandoned me when I fell ill three days ago.

יג וַיֹּ֧אמֶר ל֣וֹ דָוִ֗ד לְמִי־אַ֙תָּה֙ וְאֵ֣י מִזֶּ֣ה אָ֔תָּה וַיֹּ֗אמֶר נַ֧עַר מִצְרִ֛י אָנֹ֖כִי עֶ֣בֶד לְאִ֣ישׁ עֲמָלֵקִ֑י וַיַּעַזְבֵ֣נִי אֲדֹנִ֔י כִּ֥י חָלִ֖יתִי הַיּ֥וֹם שְׁלֹשָֽׁה׃

14 We had raided the *Negev* of the Cherethites, and [the *Negev*] of *Yehuda*, and the *Negev* of *Kalev*; we also burned down *Tziklag*."

יד אֲנַ֡חְנוּ פָּשַׁ֜טְנוּ נֶ֧גֶב הַכְּרֵתִ֛י וְעַל־אֲשֶׁ֥ר לִֽיהוּדָ֖ה וְעַל־נֶ֣גֶב כָּלֵ֑ב וְאֶת־צִֽקְלַ֖ג שָׂרַ֥פְנוּ בָאֵֽשׁ׃

15 And *David* said to him, "Can you lead me down to that band?" He replied, "Swear to me by *Hashem* that you will not kill me or deliver me into my master's hands, and I will lead you down to that band."

טו וַיֹּ֤אמֶר אֵלָיו֙ דָּוִ֔ד הֲתוֹרִדֵ֖נִי אֶל־הַגְּד֣וּד הַזֶּ֑ה וַיֹּ֡אמֶר הִשָּׁבְעָה֩ לִּ֨י בֵֽאלֹהִ֜ים אִם־תְּמִיתֵ֗נִי וְאִם־תַּסְגִּרֵ֙נִי֙ בְּיַד־אֲדֹנִ֔י וְאוֹרִֽדְךָ֖ אֶל־הַגְּד֥וּד הַזֶּֽה׃

16 So he led him down, and there they were, scattered all over the ground, eating and drinking and making merry because of all the vast spoil they had taken from the land of the Philistines and from the land of *Yehuda*.

טז וַיֹּ֣רִדֵ֔הוּ וְהִנֵּ֥ה נְטֻשִׁ֖ים עַל־פְּנֵ֣י כָל־הָאָ֑רֶץ אֹכְלִ֤ים וְשֹׁתִים֙ וְחֹ֣גְגִ֔ים בְּכֹל֙ הַשָּׁלָ֣ל הַגָּד֔וֹל אֲשֶׁ֥ר לָקְח֛וּ מֵאֶ֥רֶץ פְּלִשְׁתִּ֖ים וּמֵאֶ֥רֶץ יְהוּדָֽה׃

17 *David* attacked them from before dawn until the evening of the next day; none of them escaped, except four hundred young men who mounted camels and got away.

יז וַיַּכֵּ֥ם דָּוִ֛ד מֵהַנֶּ֖שֶׁף וְעַד־הָעֶ֣רֶב לְמׇֽחֳרָתָ֑ם וְלֹֽא־נִמְלַ֤ט מֵהֶם֙ אִ֔ישׁ כִּי֩ אִם־אַרְבַּ֨ע מֵא֧וֹת אִישׁ־נַ֛עַר אֲשֶׁר־רָכְב֥וּ עַל־הַגְּמַלִּ֖ים וַיָּנֻֽסוּ׃

va-ya-KAYM da-VID may-ha-NE-shef v'-ad ha-E-rev l'-ma-kho-ra-TAM v'-lo nim-LAT may-HEM EESH KEE im ar-BA may-OT eesh NA-ar a-sher ra-kh'-VU al ha-g'-ma-LEEM va-ya-NU-su

---

30:17 *David* attacked them from before dawn until the evening of the next day *David* successfully defeats the Amalekites and recovers everything they had taken. Amalek represents the epitome of evil, as they sought to destroy the People of Israel for no particular reason. In the *Torah*, *Hashem* commands the Children of Israel to wipe out this evil tribe (Exodus 17:14–16; Deuteronomy 25:19). Throughout history, there have been continual

Shmuel I / I Samuel
Chapter 30

שמואל א
פרק ל

18 *David* rescued everything the Amalekites had taken; *David* also rescued his two wives.

וַיַּצֵּל דָּוִד אֵת כָּל־אֲשֶׁר לָקְחוּ עֲמָלֵק וְאֶת־שְׁתֵּי נָשָׁיו הִצִּיל דָּוִד:

19 Nothing of theirs was missing – young or old, sons or daughters, spoil or anything else that had been carried off – *David* recovered everything.

וְלֹא נֶעְדַּר־לָהֶם מִן־הַקָּטֹן וְעַד־הַגָּדוֹל וְעַד־בָּנִים וּבָנוֹת וּמִשָּׁלָל וְעַד כָּל־אֲשֶׁר לָקְחוּ לָהֶם הַכֹּל הֵשִׁיב דָּוִד:

20 *David* took all the flocks and herds, which [the troops] drove ahead of the other livestock; and they declared, "This is *David*'s spoil."

וַיִּקַּח דָּוִד אֶת־כָּל־הַצֹּאן וְהַבָּקָר נָהֲגוּ לִפְנֵי הַמִּקְנֶה הַהוּא וַיֹּאמְרוּ זֶה שְׁלַל דָּוִד:

21 When *David* reached the two hundred men who were too faint to follow *David* and who had been left at the Wadi Besor, they came out to welcome *David* and the troops with him; *David* came forward with the troops and greeted them.

וַיָּבֹא דָוִד אֶל־מָאתַיִם הָאֲנָשִׁים אֲשֶׁר־פִּגְּרוּ מִלֶּכֶת אַחֲרֵי דָוִד וַיֹּשִׁיבֻם בְּנַחַל הַבְּשׂוֹר וַיֵּצְאוּ לִקְרַאת דָּוִד וְלִקְרַאת הָעָם אֲשֶׁר־אִתּוֹ וַיִּגַּשׁ דָּוִד אֶת־הָעָם וַיִּשְׁאַל לָהֶם לְשָׁלוֹם:

22 But all the mean and churlish fellows among the men who had accompanied *David* spoke up, "Since they did not accompany us, we will not give them any of the spoil that we seized – except that each may take his wife and children and go."

וַיַּעַן כָּל־אִישׁ־רָע וּבְלִיַּעַל מֵהָאֲנָשִׁים אֲשֶׁר הָלְכוּ עִם־דָּוִד וַיֹּאמְרוּ יַעַן אֲשֶׁר לֹא־הָלְכוּ עִמִּי לֹא־נִתֵּן לָהֶם מֵהַשָּׁלָל אֲשֶׁר הִצַּלְנוּ כִּי־אִם־אִישׁ אֶת־אִשְׁתּוֹ וְאֶת־בָּנָיו וְיִנְהֲגוּ וְיֵלֵכוּ:

23 *David*, however, spoke up, "You must not do that, my brothers, in view of what *Hashem* has granted us, guarding us and delivering into our hands the band that attacked us.

וַיֹּאמֶר דָּוִד לֹא־תַעֲשׂוּ כֵן אֶחָי אֵת אֲשֶׁר־נָתַן יְהוָה לָנוּ וַיִּשְׁמֹר אֹתָנוּ וַיִּתֵּן אֶת־הַגְּדוּד הַבָּא עָלֵינוּ בְּיָדֵנוּ:

24 How could anyone agree with you in this matter? The share of those who remain with the baggage shall be the same as the share of those who go down to battle; they shall share alike."

וּמִי יִשְׁמַע לָכֶם לַדָּבָר הַזֶּה כִּי כְּחֵלֶק הַיֹּרֵד בַּמִּלְחָמָה וּכְחֵלֶק הַיֹּשֵׁב עַל־הַכֵּלִים יַחְדָּו יַחֲלֹקוּ:

25 So from that day on it was made a fixed rule for *Yisrael*, continuing to the present day.

וַיְהִי מֵהַיּוֹם הַהוּא וָמָעְלָה וַיְשִׂמֶהָ לְחֹק וּלְמִשְׁפָּט לְיִשְׂרָאֵל עַד הַיּוֹם הַזֶּה:

26 When *David* reached *Tziklag*, he sent some of the spoil to the elders of *Yehuda* [and] to his friends, saying, "This is a present for you from our spoil of the enemies of *Hashem*."

וַיָּבֹא דָוִד אֶל־צִקְלַג וַיְשַׁלַּח מֵהַשָּׁלָל לְזִקְנֵי יְהוּדָה לְרֵעֵהוּ לֵאמֹר הִנֵּה לָכֶם בְּרָכָה מִשְּׁלַל אֹיְבֵי יְהוָה:

27 [He sent the spoil to the elders] in *Beit El*, Ramoth-negeb, and Jattir;

לַאֲשֶׁר בְּבֵית־אֵל וְלַאֲשֶׁר בְּרָמוֹת־נֶגֶב וְלַאֲשֶׁר בְּיַתִּר:

28 in Aroer, Siphmoth, and Eshtemoa;

וְלַאֲשֶׁר בַּעֲרֹעֵר וְלַאֲשֶׁר בְּשִׂפְמוֹת וְלַאֲשֶׁר בְּאֶשְׁתְּמֹעַ:

battles against Amalek. Often it looks like Amalek, or their successors, might be victorious. However, in the end, God's people always succeed. This is one of the great lessons of Jewish history. Though it may take many years, the Jewish people always overcome their enemies.

Shmuel I/I Samuel
Chapter 31

שמואל א
פרק לא

29 in Racal, in the towns of the Jerahmeelites, and in the towns of the Kenites;

כט וְלַאֲשֶׁר בְּרָכָל וְלַאֲשֶׁר בְּעָרֵי הַיְּרַחְמְאֵלִי וְלַאֲשֶׁר בְּעָרֵי הַקֵּינִי׃

30 in Hormah, Bor-ashan, and Athach;

ל וְלַאֲשֶׁר בְּחָרְמָה וְלַאֲשֶׁר בְּבוֹר־עָשָׁן וְלַאֲשֶׁר בַּעֲתָךְ׃

31 and to those in *Chevron* – all the places where *David* and his men had roamed.

לא וְלַאֲשֶׁר בְּחֶבְרוֹן וּלְכָל־הַמְּקֹמוֹת אֲשֶׁר־הִתְהַלֶּךְ־שָׁם דָּוִד הוּא וַאֲנָשָׁיו׃

31

1 The Philistines attacked *Yisrael*, and the men of *Yisrael* fled before the Philistines and [many] fell on Mount Gilboa.

א וּפְלִשְׁתִּים נִלְחָמִים בְּיִשְׂרָאֵל וַיָּנֻסוּ אַנְשֵׁי יִשְׂרָאֵל מִפְּנֵי פְלִשְׁתִּים וַיִּפְּלוּ חֲלָלִים בְּהַר הַגִּלְבֹּעַ׃

2 The Philistines pursued *Shaul* and his sons, and the Philistines struck down *Yehonatan*, *Avinadav*, and Malchishua, sons of *Shaul*.

ב וַיַּדְבְּקוּ פְלִשְׁתִּים אֶת־שָׁאוּל וְאֶת־בָּנָיו וַיַּכּוּ פְלִשְׁתִּים אֶת־יְהוֹנָתָן וְאֶת־אֲבִינָדָב וְאֶת־מַלְכִּי־שׁוּעַ בְּנֵי שָׁאוּל׃

3 The battle raged around *Shaul*, and some of the archers hit him, and he was severely wounded by the archers.

ג וַתִּכְבַּד הַמִּלְחָמָה אֶל־שָׁאוּל וַיִּמְצָאֻהוּ הַמּוֹרִים אֲנָשִׁים בַּקָּשֶׁת וַיָּחֶל מְאֹד מֵהַמּוֹרִים׃

4 *Shaul* said to his arms-bearer, "Draw your sword and run me through, so that the uncircumcised may not run me through and make sport of me." But his arms-bearer, in his great awe, refused; whereupon *Shaul* grasped the sword and fell upon it.

ד וַיֹּאמֶר שָׁאוּל לְנֹשֵׂא כֵלָיו שְׁלֹף חַרְבְּךָ וְדָקְרֵנִי בָהּ פֶּן־יָבוֹאוּ הָעֲרֵלִים הָאֵלֶּה וּדְקָרֻנִי וְהִתְעַלְּלוּ־בִי וְלֹא אָבָה נֹשֵׂא כֵלָיו כִּי יָרֵא מְאֹד וַיִּקַּח שָׁאוּל אֶת־הַחֶרֶב וַיִּפֹּל עָלֶיהָ׃

va-YO-mer sha-UL l'-no-SAY khay-LAV sh'-LOF khar-b'-KHA v'-dok-RAY-nee VAH pen ya-VO-u ha-a-ray-LEEM ha-AY-leh u-d'-ka-RU-nee v'-hit-a-l'-lu VEE v'-LO a-VAH no-SAY khay-LAV KEE ya-RAY m'-OD va-yi-KAKH sha-UL et ha-KHE-rev va-yi-POL a-LE-ha

5 When his arms-bearer saw that *Shaul* was dead, he too fell on his sword and died with him.

ה וַיַּרְא נֹשֵׂא־כֵלָיו כִּי מֵת שָׁאוּל וַיִּפֹּל גַּם־הוּא עַל־חַרְבּוֹ וַיָּמָת עִמּוֹ׃

6 Thus *Shaul* and his three sons and his arms-bearer, as well as all his men, died together on that day.

ו וַיָּמָת שָׁאוּל וּשְׁלֹשֶׁת בָּנָיו וְנֹשֵׂא כֵלָיו גַּם כָּל־אֲנָשָׁיו בַּיּוֹם הַהוּא יַחְדָּו׃

31:4 Whereupon *Shaul* grasped the sword and fell upon it Normally, suicide is absolutely forbidden in Jewish law. However, there are rare exceptions. The Sages teach that King *Shaul*'s death is even greater than his life. Though he knows it will lead to his death, he and *Yehonatan* lead the army into battle. Rather than allow himself to be captured and killed, he falls on his sword, as he is well aware that the capture of a king of Israel would bring despair to the entire nation. Thus, Jewish law views King *Shaul* as a prime example of self-sacrifice, as he sanctifies the name of *Hashem* and the People of Israel through his death. True leaders know that they don't represent themselves alone; they represent the entire nation, and are therefore willing to make the necessary sacrifices. While *Shaul*'s death serves in Jewish law as the model of a rare acceptable form of suicide, the most famous such act in Jewish history took place on the mountain of Masada. According to Josephus Flavius in *The Jewish War*, the 960 Jewish inhabitants of the fortress on Masada, the last Jewish stronghold against the Romans after the destruction of the second Temple, killed themselves rather than surrender to the Roman soldiers.

Masada fortress in the Judean Desert

Shmuel I / I Samuel
Chapter 31

7 And when the men of *Yisrael* on the other side of the valley and on the other side of the *Yarden* saw that the men of *Yisrael* had fled and that *Shaul* and his sons were dead, they abandoned the towns and fled; the Philistines then came and occupied them.

8 The next day the Philistines came to strip the slain, and they found *Shaul* and his three sons lying on Mount Gilboa.

9 They cut off his head and stripped him of his armor, and they sent them throughout the land of the Philistines, to spread the news in the temples of their idols and among the people.

10 They placed his armor in the temple of Ashtaroth, and they impaled his body on the wall of Beth-shan.

11 When the inhabitants of Jabesh-gilead heard about it – what the Philistines had done to *Shaul* –

12 all their stalwart men set out and marched all night; they removed the bodies of *Shaul* and his sons from the wall of Beth-shan and came to Jabesh and burned them there.

13 Then they took the bones and buried them under the tamarisk tree in Jabesh, and they fasted for seven days.

Shmuel II / II Samuel
Chapter 1

שמואל ב
פרק א

1 ¹ After the death of *Shaul* – *David* had already returned from defeating the Amalekites – *David* stayed two days in *Tziklag*.

² On the third day, a man came from *Shaul*'s camp, with his clothes rent and earth on his head; and as he approached *David*, he flung himself to the ground and bowed low.

³ *David* said to him, "Where are you coming from?" He answered, "I have just escaped from the camp of *Yisrael*."

⁴ "What happened?" asked *David*. "Tell me!" And he told him how the troops had fled the battlefield, and that, moreover, many of the troops had fallen and died; also that *Shaul* and his son *Yehonatan* were dead.

⁵ "How do you know," *David* asked the young man who brought him the news, "that *Shaul* and his son *Yehonatan* are dead?"

⁶ The young man who brought him the news answered, "I happened to be at Mount Gilboa, and I saw *Shaul* leaning on his spear, and the chariots and horsemen closing in on him.

⁷ He looked around and saw me, and he called to me. When I responded, 'At your service,'

⁸ he asked me, 'Who are you?' And I told him that I was an Amalekite.

⁹ Then he said to me, 'Stand over me, and finish me off, for I am in agony and am barely alive.'

¹⁰ So I stood over him and finished him off, for I knew that he would never rise from where he was lying. Then I took the crown from his head and the armlet from his arm, and I have brought them here to my lord."

¹¹ *David* took hold of his clothes and rent them, and so did all the men with him.

¹² They lamented and wept, and they fasted until evening for *Shaul* and his son *Yehonatan*, and for the soldiers of *Hashem* and the House of *Yisrael* who had fallen by the sword.

¹³ *David* said to the young man who had brought him the news, "Where are you from?" He replied, "I am the son of a resident alien, an Amalekite."

א וַיְהִ֗י אַֽחֲרֵי֙ מ֣וֹת שָׁא֔וּל וְדָוִ֣ד שָׁ֔ב מֵהַכּ֖וֹת אֶת־הָעֲמָלֵ֑ק וַיֵּ֧שֶׁב דָּוִ֛ד בְּצִֽקְלָ֖ג יָמִ֥ים שְׁנָֽיִם׃

ב וַיְהִ֣י ׀ בַּיּ֣וֹם הַשְּׁלִישִׁ֗י וְהִנֵּה֩ אִ֨ישׁ בָּ֤א מִן־הַֽמַּחֲנֶה֙ מֵעִ֣ם שָׁא֔וּל וּבְגָדָ֣יו קְרֻעִ֔ים וַאֲדָמָ֖ה עַל־רֹאשׁ֑וֹ וַיְהִי֙ בְּבֹא֣וֹ אֶל־דָּוִ֔ד וַיִּפֹּ֥ל אַ֖רְצָה וַיִּשְׁתָּֽחוּ׃

ג וַיֹּ֤אמֶר לוֹ֙ דָּוִ֔ד אֵ֥י מִזֶּ֖ה תָּב֑וֹא וַיֹּ֣אמֶר אֵלָ֔יו מִמַּחֲנֵ֥ה יִשְׂרָאֵ֖ל נִמְלָֽטְתִּי׃

ד וַיֹּ֨אמֶר אֵלָ֥יו דָּוִ֛ד מֶה־הָיָ֥ה הַדָּבָ֖ר הַגֶּד־נָ֣א לִ֑י וַ֠יֹּ֠אמֶר אֲשֶׁר־נָ֨ס הָעָ֜ם מִן־הַמִּלְחָמָ֗ה וְגַם־הַרְבֵּ֞ה נָפַ֤ל מִן־הָעָם֙ וַיָּמֻ֔תוּ וְגַ֗ם שָׁא֛וּל וִיהֽוֹנָתָ֥ן בְּנ֖וֹ מֵֽתוּ׃

ה וַיֹּ֣אמֶר דָּוִ֔ד אֶל־הַנַּ֖עַר הַמַּגִּ֣יד ל֑וֹ אֵ֣יךְ יָדַ֔עְתָּ כִּי־מֵ֥ת שָׁא֖וּל וִיהֽוֹנָתָ֥ן בְּנֽוֹ׃

ו וַיֹּ֜אמֶר הַנַּ֣עַר ׀ הַמַּגִּ֣יד ל֗וֹ נִקְרֹ֤א נִקְרֵ֨יתִי֙ בְּהַ֣ר הַגִּלְבֹּ֔עַ וְהִנֵּ֥ה שָׁא֖וּל נִשְׁעָ֣ן עַל־חֲנִית֑וֹ וְהִנֵּ֥ה הָרֶ֛כֶב וּבַעֲלֵ֥י הַפָּרָשִׁ֖ים הִדְבִּקֻֽהוּ׃

ז וַיִּ֥פֶן אַחֲרָ֖יו וַיִּרְאֵ֑נִי וַיִּקְרָ֣א אֵלָ֔י וָאֹמַ֖ר הִנֵּֽנִי׃

ח וַיֹּ֥אמֶר לִ֖י מִי־אָ֑תָּה ויאמר [וָאֹמַ֣ר] אֵלָ֔יו עֲמָלֵקִ֖י אָנֹֽכִי׃

ט וַיֹּ֣אמֶר אֵלַ֗י עֲמָד־נָ֤א עָלַי֙ וּמֹ֣תְתֵ֔נִי כִּ֥י אֲחָזַ֖נִי הַשָּׁבָ֑ץ כִּֽי־כָל־ע֥וֹד נַפְשִׁ֖י בִּֽי׃

י וָאֶעֱמֹ֤ד עָלָיו֙ וַאֲמֹ֣תְתֵ֔הוּ כִּ֣י יָדַ֔עְתִּי כִּ֛י לֹ֥א יִֽחְיֶ֖ה אַחֲרֵ֣י נִפְל֑וֹ וָאֶקַּ֞ח הַנֵּ֣זֶר ׀ אֲשֶׁ֣ר עַל־רֹאשׁ֗וֹ וְאֶצְעָדָה֙ אֲשֶׁ֣ר עַל־זְרֹע֔וֹ וָאֲבִיאֵ֥ם אֶל־אֲדֹנִ֖י הֵֽנָּה׃

יא וַיַּחֲזֵ֥ק דָּוִ֛ד בבגדו [בִּבְגָדָ֖יו] וַיִּקְרָעֵ֑ם וְגַ֥ם כָּל־הָאֲנָשִׁ֖ים אֲשֶׁ֥ר אִתּֽוֹ׃

יב וַֽיִּסְפְּדוּ֙ וַיִּבְכּ֔וּ וַיָּצֻ֖מוּ עַד־הָעָ֑רֶב עַל־שָׁא֞וּל וְעַל־יְהוֹנָתָ֣ן בְּנ֗וֹ וְעַל־עַ֤ם יְהוָה֙ וְעַל־בֵּ֣ית יִשְׂרָאֵ֔ל כִּ֥י נָפְל֖וּ בֶּחָֽרֶב׃

יג וַיֹּ֣אמֶר דָּוִ֗ד אֶל־הַנַּ֙עַר֙ הַמַּגִּ֣יד ל֔וֹ אֵ֥י מִזֶּ֖ה אָ֑תָּה וַיֹּ֕אמֶר בֶּן־אִ֛ישׁ גֵּ֥ר עֲמָלֵקִ֖י אָנֹֽכִי׃

Shmuel II/II Samuel
Chapter 1

שמואל ב
פרק א

14 "How did you dare," *David* said to him, "to lift your hand and kill *Hashem*'s anointed?"

יד וַיֹּאמֶר אֵלָיו דָּוִד אֵיךְ לֹא יָרֵאתָ לִשְׁלֹחַ יָדְךָ לְשַׁחֵת אֶת־מְשִׁיחַ יְהֹוָה׃

15 Thereupon *David* called one of the attendants and said to him, "Come over and strike him!" He struck him down and he died.

טו וַיִּקְרָא דָוִד לְאַחַד מֵהַנְּעָרִים וַיֹּאמֶר גַּשׁ פְּגַע־בּוֹ וַיַּכֵּהוּ וַיָּמֹת׃

16 And *David* said to him, "Your blood be on your own head! Your own mouth testified against you when you said, 'I put *Hashem*'s anointed to death.'"

טז וַיֹּאמֶר אֵלָיו דָּוִד דמיך [דָּמְךָ] עַל־רֹאשֶׁךָ כִּי פִיךָ עָנָה בְךָ לֵאמֹר אָנֹכִי מֹתַתִּי אֶת־מְשִׁיחַ יְהֹוָה׃

17 And *David* intoned this dirge over *Shaul* and his son *Yehonatan* –

יז וַיְקֹנֵן דָּוִד אֶת־הַקִּינָה הַזֹּאת עַל־שָׁאוּל וְעַל־יְהוֹנָתָן בְּנוֹ׃

18 He ordered the Judites to be taught [The Song of the] Bow. It is recorded in the Book of Jashar.

יח וַיֹּאמֶר לְלַמֵּד בְּנֵי־יְהוּדָה קָשֶׁת הִנֵּה כְתוּבָה עַל־סֵפֶר הַיָּשָׁר׃

19 Your glory, O *Yisrael*, Lies slain on your heights; How have the mighty fallen!

יט הַצְּבִי יִשְׂרָאֵל עַל־בָּמוֹתֶיךָ חָלָל אֵיךְ נָפְלוּ גִבּוֹרִים׃

20 Tell it not in Gath, Do not proclaim it in the streets of *Ashkelon*, Lest the daughters of the Philistine rejoice, Lest the daughters of the uncircumcised exult.

כ אַל־תַּגִּידוּ בְגַת אַל־תְּבַשְּׂרוּ בְּחוּצֹת אַשְׁקְלוֹן פֶּן־תִּשְׂמַחְנָה בְּנוֹת פְּלִשְׁתִּים פֶּן־תַּעֲלֹזְנָה בְּנוֹת הָעֲרֵלִים׃

21 O hills of Gilboa – Let there be no dew or rain on you, Or bountiful fields, For there the shield of warriors lay rejected, The shield of *Shaul*, Polished with oil no more.

כא הָרֵי בַגִּלְבֹּעַ אַל־טַל וְאַל־מָטָר עֲלֵיכֶם וּשְׂדֵי תְרוּמֹת כִּי שָׁם נִגְעַל מָגֵן גִּבּוֹרִים מָגֵן שָׁאוּל בְּלִי מָשִׁיחַ בַּשָּׁמֶן׃

22 From the blood of slain, From the fat of warriors – The bow of *Yehonatan* Never turned back; The sword of *Shaul* Never withdrew empty.

כב מִדַּם חֲלָלִים מֵחֵלֶב גִּבּוֹרִים קֶשֶׁת יְהוֹנָתָן לֹא נָשׂוֹג אָחוֹר וְחֶרֶב שָׁאוּל לֹא תָשׁוּב רֵיקָם׃

23 *Shaul* and *Yehonatan*, Beloved and cherished, Never parted In life or in death! They were swifter than eagles, They were stronger than lions!

כג שָׁאוּל וִיהוֹנָתָן הַנֶּאֱהָבִים וְהַנְּעִימִם בְּחַיֵּיהֶם וּבְמוֹתָם לֹא נִפְרָדוּ מִנְּשָׁרִים קַלּוּ מֵאֲרָיוֹת גָּבֵרוּ׃

sha-UL vee-ho-na-TAN ha-ne-e-ha-VEEM v'-ha-n'-ee-MIM b'-kha-yay-HEM uv-mo-TAM LO nif-RA-du mi-n'-sha-REEM KA-lu may-a-ra-YOT ga-VAY-ru

24 Daughters of *Yisrael*, Weep over *Shaul*, Who clothed you in crimson and finery, Who decked your robes with jewels of gold.

כד בְּנוֹת יִשְׂרָאֵל אֶל־שָׁאוּל בְּכֶינָה הַמַּלְבִּשְׁכֶם שָׁנִי עִם־עֲדָנִים הַמַּעֲלֶה עֲדִי זָהָב עַל לְבוּשְׁכֶן׃

1:23 *Shaul* and *Yehonatan*, beloved and cherished, never parted in life or in death Though King *Shaul* had tried to kill *David*, *David* deeply mourns his death and that of his close friend *Yehonatan*, *Shaul*'s son. In his powerful eulogy, *David* says that *Shaul* and *Yehonatan* are not separated in death. *Radak* explains that this means that although they knew they would die in battle, King *Shaul* and *Yehonatan* would not separate from the People of Israel. They do not flee, but rather lead the nation into battle, and they heroically fall together. They serve as powerful role models for the soldiers of the Israeli Defense Forces, who willingly risk their lives every day for the People and State of Israel.

President Reuven Rivlin visiting IDF soldiers

Shmuel II/II Samuel
Chapter 2

שמואל ב
פרק ב

25 How have the mighty fallen In the thick of battle – *Yehonatan*, slain on your heights!

אֵיךְ נָפְלוּ גִבֹּרִים בְּתוֹךְ הַמִּלְחָמָה יְהוֹנָתָן עַל־בָּמוֹתֶיךָ חָלָל:

26 I grieve for you, My brother *Yehonatan*, You were most dear to me. Your love was wonderful to me More than the love of women.

צַר־לִי עָלֶיךָ אָחִי יְהוֹנָתָן נָעַמְתָּ לִּי מְאֹד נִפְלְאַתָה אַהֲבָתְךָ לִי מֵאַהֲבַת נָשִׁים:

27 How have the mighty fallen, The weapons of war perished!

אֵיךְ נָפְלוּ גִבּוֹרִים וַיֹּאבְדוּ כְּלֵי מִלְחָמָה:

2 1 Sometime afterward, *David* inquired of *Hashem*, "Shall I go up to one of the towns of *Yehuda*?" *Hashem* answered, "Yes." *David* further asked, "Which one shall I go up to?" And *Hashem* replied, "To *Chevron*."

א וַיְהִי אַחֲרֵי־כֵן וַיִּשְׁאַל דָּוִד בַּיהוָֹה לֵאמֹר הַאֶעֱלֶה בְּאַחַת עָרֵי יְהוּדָה וַיֹּאמֶר יְהוָֹה אֵלָיו עֲלֵה וַיֹּאמֶר דָּוִד אָנָה אֶעֱלֶה וַיֹּאמֶר חֶבְרֹנָה:

2 So *David* went up there, along with his two wives, Ahinoam of *Yizrael* and *Avigail* wife of *Naval* the Carmelite.

ב וַיַּעַל שָׁם דָּוִד וְגַם שְׁתֵּי נָשָׁיו אֲחִינֹעַם הַיִּזְרְעֵלִית וַאֲבִיגַיִל אֵשֶׁת נָבָל הַכַּרְמְלִי:

3 *David* also took the men who were with him, each with his family, and they settled in the towns about *Chevron*.

ג וַאֲנָשָׁיו אֲשֶׁר־עִמּוֹ הֶעֱלָה דָוִד אִישׁ וּבֵיתוֹ וַיֵּשְׁבוּ בְּעָרֵי חֶבְרוֹן:

4 The men of *Yehuda* came and there they anointed *David* king over the House of *Yehuda*. *David* was told about the men of Jabesh-gilead who buried *Shaul*.

ד וַיָּבֹאוּ אַנְשֵׁי יְהוּדָה וַיִּמְשְׁחוּ־שָׁם אֶת־דָּוִד לְמֶלֶךְ עַל־בֵּית יְהוּדָה וַיַּגִּדוּ לְדָוִד לֵאמֹר אַנְשֵׁי יָבֵישׁ גִּלְעָד אֲשֶׁר קָבְרוּ אֶת־שָׁאוּל:

va-ya-VO-u an-SHAY y'-hu-DAH va-yim-sh'-khu SHAM et da-VID l'-ME-lekh al BAYT y'-hu-DAH va-ya-GI-du l'-da-VID lay-MOR an-SHAY ya-VAYSH gil-AD a-SHER ka-v'-RU at sha-UL

5 So *David* sent messengers to the men of Jabesh-gilead and said to them, "May you be blessed of *Hashem* because you performed this act of faithfulness to your lord *Shaul* and buried him.

ה וַיִּשְׁלַח דָּוִד מַלְאָכִים אֶל־אַנְשֵׁי יָבֵישׁ גִּלְעָד וַיֹּאמֶר אֲלֵיהֶם בְּרֻכִים אַתֶּם לַיהוָֹה אֲשֶׁר עֲשִׂיתֶם הַחֶסֶד הַזֶּה עִם־אֲדֹנֵיכֶם עִם־שָׁאוּל וַתִּקְבְּרוּ אֹתוֹ:

6 May *Hashem* in turn show you true faithfulness; and I too will reward you generously because you performed this act.

ו וְעַתָּה יַעַשׂ־יְהוָֹה עִמָּכֶם חֶסֶד וֶאֱמֶת וְגַם אָנֹכִי אֶעֱשֶׂה אִתְּכֶם הַטּוֹבָה הַזֹּאת אֲשֶׁר עֲשִׂיתֶם הַדָּבָר הַזֶּה:

2:4 The men of *Yehuda* came and there they anointed *David* king over the House of *Yehuda* At God's instruction, following the death of King *Shaul*, *David* goes to the holy city of *Chevron*. There, he is anointed king by the people of *Yehuda*. Though the prophet *Shmuel* had already anointed him, his anointment by the people demonstrates their acceptance of his reign. King *David* rules from *Chevron* for seven and one half years (see verse 11). This shows that *Chevron* is not only the burial site of the Patriarchs and Matriarchs *Avraham* and *Sara*, *Yitzchak* and *Rivka* and *Yaakov* and *Leah*; it is also the cradle of Israel's monarchy. Today's Jewish community of *Chevron* serves a critical function by preserving Jewish sovereignty over this ancient and historic city, and the right of all to pray at the Cave of the Patriarchs.

Ariel view of the Cave of Machpela and the city of Chevron

Shmuel II / II Samuel
Chapter 2

7 Now take courage and be brave men; for your lord *Shaul* is dead and the House of *Yehuda* have already anointed me king over them."

8 But *Avner* son of Ner, *Shaul*'s army commander, had taken *Ish-boshet* son of *Shaul* and brought him across to Mahanaim

9 and made him king over *Gilad*, the Assyriaites, *Yizrael*, *Efraim*, and *Binyamin* – over all *Yisrael*.

10 *Ish-boshet* son of *Shaul* was forty years old when he became king of *Yisrael*, and he reigned two years. But the House of *Yehuda* supported *David*.

11 The length of time that *David* reigned in *Chevron* over the House of *Yehuda* was seven years and six months.

12 Once *Avner* son of Ner and the soldiers of *Ish-boshet* son of *Shaul* marched out from Mahanaim to *Givon*,

13 and *Yoav* son of *Tzeruya* and the soldiers of *David* [also] came out. They confronted one another at the pool of *Givon*: one group sat on one side of the pool, and the other group on the other side of the pool.

14 *Avner* said to *Yoav*, "Let the young men come forward and sport before us." "Yes, let them," *Yoav* answered.

15 They came forward and were counted off, twelve for *Binyamin* and *Ish-boshet* son of *Shaul*, and twelve of *David*'s soldiers.

16 Each one grasped his opponent's head [and thrust] his dagger into his opponent's side; thus they fell together. That place, which is in *Givon*, was called Helkath-hazzurim.

17 A fierce battle ensued that day, and *Avner* and the men of *Yisrael* were routed by *David*'s soldiers.

18 The three sons of *Tzeruya* were there – *Yoav*, *Avishai*, and *Asael*. *Asael* was swift of foot, like a gazelle in the open field.

19 And *Asael* ran after *Avner*, swerving neither right nor left in his pursuit of *Avner*.

Shmuel II / II Samuel
Chapter 2

שמואל ב
פרק ב

20 *Avner* looked back and shouted, "Is that you, *Asael*?" "Yes, it is," he called back.

כ וַיִּפֶן אַבְנֵר אַחֲרָיו וַיֹּאמֶר הַאַתָּה זֶה עֲשָׂהאֵל וַיֹּאמֶר אָנֹכִי׃

21 *Avner* said to him, "Turn to the right or to the left, and seize one of our boys and strip off his tunic." But *Asael* would not leave off.

כא וַיֹּאמֶר לוֹ אַבְנֵר נְטֵה לְךָ עַל־יְמִינְךָ אוֹ עַל־שְׂמֹאלֶךָ וֶאֱחֹז לְךָ אֶחָד מֵהַנְּעָרִים וְקַח־לְךָ אֶת־חֲלִצָתוֹ וְלֹא־אָבָה עֲשָׂהאֵל לָסוּר מֵאַחֲרָיו׃

22 *Avner* again begged *Asael*, "Stop pursuing me, or I'll have to strike you down. How will I look your brother *Yoav* in the face?"

כב וַיֹּסֶף עוֹד אַבְנֵר לֵאמֹר אֶל־עֲשָׂהאֵל סוּר לְךָ מֵאַחֲרָי לָמָּה אַכֶּכָּה אַרְצָה וְאֵיךְ אֶשָּׂא פָנַי אֶל־יוֹאָב אָחִיךָ׃

23 When he refused to desist, *Avner* struck him in the belly with a backward thrust of his spear and the spear protruded from his back. He fell there and died on the spot. And all who came to the place where *Asael* fell and died halted;

כג וַיְמָאֵן לָסוּר וַיַּכֵּהוּ אַבְנֵר בְּאַחֲרֵי הַחֲנִית אֶל־הַחֹמֶשׁ וַתֵּצֵא הַחֲנִית מֵאַחֲרָיו וַיִּפָּל־שָׁם וַיָּמָת תַּחְתָּו [תַּחְתָּיו] וַיְהִי כָּל־הַבָּא אֶל־הַמָּקוֹם אֲשֶׁר־נָפַל שָׁם עֲשָׂהאֵל וַיָּמֹת וַיַּעֲמֹדוּ׃

24 but *Yoav* and *Avishai* continued to pursue *Avner*. And the sun was setting as they reached the hill of Ammah, which faces Giah on the road to the wilderness of *Givon*.

כד וַיִּרְדְּפוּ יוֹאָב וַאֲבִישַׁי אַחֲרֵי אַבְנֵר וְהַשֶּׁמֶשׁ בָּאָה וְהֵמָּה בָּאוּ עַד־גִּבְעַת אַמָּה אֲשֶׁר עַל־פְּנֵי־גִיחַ דֶּרֶךְ מִדְבַּר גִּבְעוֹן׃

25 The Benjaminites rallied behind *Avner*, forming a single company; and they took up a position on the top of a hill.

כה וַיִּתְקַבְּצוּ בְנֵי־בִנְיָמִן אַחֲרֵי אַבְנֵר וַיִּהְיוּ לַאֲגֻדָּה אֶחָת וַיַּעַמְדוּ עַל רֹאשׁ־גִּבְעָה אֶחָת׃

26 *Avner* then called out to *Yoav*, "Must the sword devour forever? You know how bitterly it's going to end! How long will you delay ordering your troops to stop the pursuit of their kinsmen?"

כו וַיִּקְרָא אַבְנֵר אֶל־יוֹאָב וַיֹּאמֶר הֲלָנֶצַח תֹּאכַל חֶרֶב הֲלוֹא יָדַעְתָּה כִּי־מָרָה תִהְיֶה בָּאַחֲרוֹנָה וְעַד־מָתַי לֹא־תֹאמַר לָעָם לָשׁוּב מֵאַחֲרֵי אֲחֵיהֶם׃

27 And *Yoav* replied, "As *Hashem* lives, if you hadn't spoken up, the troops would have given up the pursuit of their kinsmen only the next morning."

כז וַיֹּאמֶר יוֹאָב חַי הָאֱלֹהִים כִּי לוּלֵא דִּבַּרְתָּ כִּי אָז מֵהַבֹּקֶר נַעֲלָה הָעָם אִישׁ מֵאַחֲרֵי אָחִיו׃

28 *Yoav* then sounded the *shofar*, and all the troops halted; they ceased their pursuit of *Yisrael* and stopped the fighting.

כח וַיִּתְקַע יוֹאָב בַּשּׁוֹפָר וַיַּעַמְדוּ כָּל־הָעָם וְלֹא־יִרְדְּפוּ עוֹד אַחֲרֵי יִשְׂרָאֵל וְלֹא־יָסְפוּ עוֹד לְהִלָּחֵם׃

29 *Avner* and his men marched through the Arabah all that night and, after crossing the *Yarden*, they marched through all of Bithron until they came to Mahanaim.

כט וְאַבְנֵר וַאֲנָשָׁיו הָלְכוּ בָּעֲרָבָה כֹּל הַלַּיְלָה הַהוּא וַיַּעַבְרוּ אֶת־הַיַּרְדֵּן וַיֵּלְכוּ כָּל־הַבִּתְרוֹן וַיָּבֹאוּ מַחֲנָיִם׃

30 After *Yoav* gave up the pursuit of *Avner*, he assembled all the troops and found nineteen of *David*'s soldiers missing, besides *Asael*.

ל וְיוֹאָב שָׁב מֵאַחֲרֵי אַבְנֵר וַיִּקְבֹּץ אֶת־כָּל־הָעָם וַיִּפָּקְדוּ מֵעַבְדֵי דָוִד תִּשְׁעָה־עָשָׂר אִישׁ וַעֲשָׂהאֵל׃

31 *David*'s soldiers, on the other hand, defeated the Benjaminites and the men under *Avner* and killed three hundred and sixty men.

לא וְעַבְדֵי דָוִד הִכּוּ מִבִּנְיָמִן וּבְאַנְשֵׁי אַבְנֵר שְׁלֹשׁ־מֵאוֹת וְשִׁשִּׁים אִישׁ מֵתוּ׃

32 They bore *Asael* away and buried him in his father's tomb in *Beit Lechem*. Then *Yoav* and his men marched all night; day broke upon them in *Chevron*.

לב וַיִּשְׂאוּ אֶת־עֲשָׂהאֵל וַיִּקְבְּרֻהוּ בְּקֶבֶר אָבִיו אֲשֶׁר בֵּית לָחֶם וַיֵּלְכוּ כָל־הַלַּיְלָה יוֹאָב וַאֲנָשָׁיו וַיֵּאֹר לָהֶם בְּחֶבְרוֹן׃

Shmuel II / II Samuel
Chapter 3

3 1 The war between the House of *Shaul* and the House of *David* was long-drawn-out; but *David* kept growing stronger, while the House of *Shaul* grew weaker.

2 Sons were born to *David* in *Chevron*: His first-born was *Amnon*, by Ahinoam of *Yizrael*;

3 his second was Chileab, by *Avigail* wife of *Naval* the Carmelite; the third was *Avshalom* son of Maacah, daughter of King Talmai of Geshur;

4 the fourth was *Adoniyahu* son of Haggith; the fifth was Shephatiah son of Abital;

5 and the sixth was Ithream, by *David*'s wife Eglah. These were born to *David* in *Chevron*.

6 During the war between the House of *Shaul* and the House of *David*, *Avner* supported the House of *Shaul*.

7 Now *Shaul* had a concubine named Rizpah, daughter of Aiah; and [*Ish-boshet*] said to *Avner*, "Why have you lain with my father's concubine?"

8 *Avner* was very upset by what *Ish-boshet* said, and he replied, "Am I a dog's head from *Yehuda*? Here I have been loyally serving the House of your father *Shaul* and his kinsfolk and friends, and I have not betrayed you into the hands of *David*; yet this day you reproach me over a woman!

9 May *Hashem* do thus and more to *Avner* if I do not do for *David* as *Hashem* swore to him –

10 to transfer the kingship from the House of *Shaul*, and to establish the throne of *David* over *Yisrael* and *Yehuda* from *Dan* to *Be'er Sheva*."

l'-ha-a-VEER ha-mam-la-KHAH mi-BAYT sha-UL ul-ha-KEEM et ki-SAY da-VID al yis-ra-AYL v'-al y'-hu-DAH mi-DAN v'-ad b'-AYR SHA-va

> **3:10 From *Dan* to *Be'er Sheva*** Because the city of *Dan* was in the north and *Be'er Sheva* was in the south, the expression "from *Dan* to *Be'er Sheva*" is used to symbolize the expansiveness of the Promised Land. It is this critical unity of the entire nation throughout the land that will allow for a strong and vibrant Kingdom of Israel. Indeed, the reigns of *David* and *Shlomo* over the united Kingdom of Israel are considered the best of times for the Jewish monarchy. With the division of the kingdom, however, things begin to deteriorate, with both military defeats and regression to idolatry, until ultimately both the kingdom of *Yisrael* and the kingdom of *Yehuda* are destroyed and their inhabitants exiled. This highlights how essential unity is for the people and the Land of Israel.

Shmuel II/II Samuel
Chapter 3

שמואל ב
פרק ג

11 [*Ish-boshet*] could say nothing more in reply to *Avner*, because he was afraid of him.

יא וְלֹא־יָכֹל עוֹד לְהָשִׁיב אֶת־אַבְנֵר דָּבָר מִיִּרְאָתוֹ אֹתוֹ׃

12 *Avner* immediately sent messengers to *David*, saying, "To whom shall the land belong?" and to say [further], "Make a pact with me, and I will help you and bring all *Yisrael* over to your side."

יב וַיִּשְׁלַח אַבְנֵר מַלְאָכִים ׀ אֶל־דָּוִד תַּחְתָּו [תַּחְתָּיו] לֵאמֹר לְמִי־אָרֶץ לֵאמֹר כָּרְתָה בְרִיתְךָ אִתִּי וְהִנֵּה יָדִי עִמָּךְ לְהָסֵב אֵלֶיךָ אֶת־כָּל־יִשְׂרָאֵל׃

13 He replied, "Good; I will make a pact with you. But I make one demand upon you: Do not appear before me unless you bring *Michal* daughter of *Shaul* when you come before me."

יג וַיֹּאמֶר טוֹב אֲנִי אֶכְרֹת אִתְּךָ בְּרִית אַךְ דָּבָר אֶחָד אָנֹכִי שֹׁאֵל מֵאִתְּךָ לֵאמֹר לֹא־תִרְאֶה אֶת־פָּנַי כִּי ׀ אִם־לִפְנֵי הֱבִיאֲךָ אֵת מִיכַל בַּת־שָׁאוּל בְּבֹאֲךָ לִרְאוֹת אֶת־פָּנָי׃

14 *David* also sent messengers to *Ish-boshet* son of *Shaul*, to say, "Give me my wife *Michal*, for whom I paid the bride-price of one hundred Philistine foreskins."

יד וַיִּשְׁלַח דָּוִד מַלְאָכִים אֶל־אִישׁ־בֹּשֶׁת בֶּן־שָׁאוּל לֵאמֹר תְּנָה אֶת־אִשְׁתִּי אֶת־מִיכַל אֲשֶׁר אֵרַשְׂתִּי לִי בְּמֵאָה עָרְלוֹת פְּלִשְׁתִּים׃

15 So *Ish-boshet* sent and had her taken away from [her] husband, Paltiel son of Laish.

טו וַיִּשְׁלַח אִישׁ בֹּשֶׁת וַיִּקָּחֶהָ מֵעִם אִישׁ מֵעִם פַּלְטִיאֵל בֶּן־לוש [לָיִשׁ]׃

16 Her husband walked with her as far as Bahurim, weeping as he followed her; then *Avner* ordered him to turn back, and he went back.

טז וַיֵּלֶךְ אִתָּהּ אִישָׁהּ הָלוֹךְ וּבָכֹה אַחֲרֶיהָ עַד־בַּחֻרִים וַיֹּאמֶר אֵלָיו אַבְנֵר לֵךְ שׁוּב וַיָּשֹׁב׃

17 *Avner* had conferred with the elders of *Yisrael*, saying, "You have wanted *David* to be king over you all along.

יז וּדְבַר־אַבְנֵר הָיָה עִם־זִקְנֵי יִשְׂרָאֵל לֵאמֹר גַּם־תְּמוֹל גַּם־שִׁלְשֹׁם הֱיִיתֶם מְבַקְשִׁים אֶת־דָּוִד לְמֶלֶךְ עֲלֵיכֶם׃

18 Now act! For *Hashem* has said concerning *David*: I will deliver My people *Yisrael* from the hands of the Philistines and all its other enemies through My servant *David*."

יח וְעַתָּה עֲשׂוּ כִּי יְהֹוָה אָמַר אֶל־דָּוִד לֵאמֹר בְּיַד ׀ דָּוִד עַבְדִּי הוֹשִׁיעַ אֶת־עַמִּי יִשְׂרָאֵל מִיַּד פְּלִשְׁתִּים וּמִיַּד כָּל־אֹיְבֵיהֶם׃

19 *Avner* also talked with the Benjaminites; then *Avner* went and informed *David* in *Chevron* of all the wishes of *Yisrael* and of the whole House of *Binyamin*.

יט וַיְדַבֵּר גַּם־אַבְנֵר בְּאׇזְנֵי בִנְיָמִין וַיֵּלֶךְ גַּם־אַבְנֵר לְדַבֵּר בְּאׇזְנֵי דָוִד בְּחֶבְרוֹן אֵת כָּל־אֲשֶׁר־טוֹב בְּעֵינֵי יִשְׂרָאֵל וּבְעֵינֵי כָּל־בֵּית בִּנְיָמִן׃

20 When *Avner* came to *David* in *Chevron*, accompanied by twenty men, *David* made a feast for *Avner* and the men with him.

כ וַיָּבֹא אַבְנֵר אֶל־דָּוִד חֶבְרוֹן וְאִתּוֹ עֶשְׂרִים אֲנָשִׁים וַיַּעַשׂ דָּוִד לְאַבְנֵר וְלַאֲנָשִׁים אֲשֶׁר־אִתּוֹ מִשְׁתֶּה׃

21 *Avner* said to *David*, "Now I will go and rally all *Yisrael* to Your Majesty. They will make a pact with you, and you can reign over all that your heart desires." And *David* dismissed *Avner*, who went away unharmed.

כא וַיֹּאמֶר אַבְנֵר אֶל־דָּוִד אָקוּמָה ׀ וְאֵלֵכָה וְאֶקְבְּצָה אֶל־אֲדֹנִי הַמֶּלֶךְ אֶת־כָּל־יִשְׂרָאֵל וְיִכְרְתוּ אִתְּךָ בְּרִית וּמָלַכְתָּ בְּכֹל אֲשֶׁר־תְּאַוֶּה נַפְשֶׁךָ וַיְשַׁלַּח דָּוִד אֶת־אַבְנֵר וַיֵּלֶךְ בְּשָׁלוֹם׃

22 Just then *David's* soldiers and *Yoav* returned from a raid, bringing much plunder with them; *Avner* was no longer with *David* in *Chevron*, for he had been dismissed and had gone away unharmed.

כב וְהִנֵּה עַבְדֵי דָוִד וְיוֹאָב בָּא מֵהַגְּדוּד וְשָׁלָל רָב עִמָּם הֵבִיאוּ וְאַבְנֵר אֵינֶנּוּ עִם־דָּוִד בְּחֶבְרוֹן כִּי שִׁלְּחוֹ וַיֵּלֶךְ בְּשָׁלוֹם׃

Shmuel II/II Samuel
Chapter 3

שמואל ב
פרק ג

23 When *Yoav* and the whole force with him arrived, *Yoav* was told that *Avner* son of Ner had come to the king, had been dismissed by him, and had gone away unharmed.

כג וְיוֹאָב וְכָל־הַצָּבָא אֲשֶׁר־אִתּוֹ בָּאוּ וַיַּגִּדוּ לְיוֹאָב לֵאמֹר בָּא־אַבְנֵר בֶּן־נֵר אֶל־הַמֶּלֶךְ וַיְשַׁלְּחֵהוּ וַיֵּלֶךְ בְּשָׁלוֹם:

24 *Yoav* went to the king and said, "What have you done? Here *Avner* came to you; why did you let him go? Now he has gotten away!

כד וַיָּבֹא יוֹאָב אֶל־הַמֶּלֶךְ וַיֹּאמֶר מֶה עָשִׂיתָה הִנֵּה־בָא אַבְנֵר אֵלֶיךָ לָמָּה־זֶּה שִׁלַּחְתּוֹ וַיֵּלֶךְ הָלוֹךְ:

25 Don't you know that *Avner* son of Ner came only to deceive you, to learn your comings and goings and to find out all that you are planning?"

כה יָדַעְתָּ אֶת־אַבְנֵר בֶּן־נֵר כִּי לְפַתֹּתְךָ בָּא וְלָדַעַת אֶת־מוֹצָאֲךָ וְאֶת־מבואך [מוֹבָאֶךָ] וְלָדַעַת אֵת כָּל־אֲשֶׁר אַתָּה עֹשֶׂה:

26 *Yoav* left *David* and sent messengers after *Avner*, and they brought him back from the cistern of Sirah; but *David* knew nothing about it.

כו וַיֵּצֵא יוֹאָב מֵעִם דָּוִד וַיִּשְׁלַח מַלְאָכִים אַחֲרֵי אַבְנֵר וַיָּשִׁבוּ אֹתוֹ מִבּוֹר הַסִּרָה וְדָוִד לֹא יָדָע:

27 When *Avner* returned to *Chevron*, *Yoav* took him aside within the gate to talk to him privately; there he struck him in the belly. Thus [*Avner*] died for shedding the blood of *Asael*, *Yoav*'s brother.

כז וַיָּשָׁב אַבְנֵר חֶבְרוֹן וַיַּטֵּהוּ יוֹאָב אֶל־תּוֹךְ הַשַּׁעַר לְדַבֵּר אִתּוֹ בַּשֶּׁלִי וַיַּכֵּהוּ שָׁם הַחֹמֶשׁ וַיָּמָת בְּדַם עֲשָׂה־אֵל אָחִיו:

28 Afterward, when *David* heard of it, he said, "Both I and my kingdom are forever innocent before God of shedding the blood of *Avner* son of Ner.

כח וַיִּשְׁמַע דָּוִד מֵאַחֲרֵי כֵן וַיֹּאמֶר נָקִי אָנֹכִי וּמַמְלַכְתִּי מֵעִם יְהוָה עַד־עוֹלָם מִדְּמֵי אַבְנֵר בֶּן־נֵר:

29 May [the guilt] fall upon the head of *Yoav* and all his father's house. May the house of *Yoav* never be without someone suffering from a discharge or an eruption, or a male who handles the spindle, or one slain by the sword, or one lacking bread." –

כט יָחֻלוּ עַל־רֹאשׁ יוֹאָב וְאֶל כָּל־בֵּית אָבִיו וְאַל־יִכָּרֵת מִבֵּית יוֹאָב זָב וּמְצֹרָע וּמַחֲזִיק בַּפֶּלֶךְ וְנֹפֵל בַּחֶרֶב וַחֲסַר־לָחֶם:

30 Now *Yoav* and his brother *Avishai* had killed *Avner* because he had killed their brother *Asael* during the battle at *Givon*. –

ל וְיוֹאָב וַאֲבִישַׁי אָחִיו הָרְגוּ לְאַבְנֵר עַל אֲשֶׁר הֵמִית אֶת־עֲשָׂהאֵל אֲחִיהֶם בְּגִבְעוֹן בַּמִּלְחָמָה:

31 *David* then ordered *Yoav* and all the troops with him to rend their clothes, gird on sackcloth, and make lament before *Avner*; and King *David* himself walked behind the bier.

לא וַיֹּאמֶר דָּוִד אֶל־יוֹאָב וְאֶל־כָּל־הָעָם אֲשֶׁר־אִתּוֹ קִרְעוּ בִגְדֵיכֶם וְחִגְרוּ שַׂקִּים וְסִפְדוּ לִפְנֵי אַבְנֵר וְהַמֶּלֶךְ דָּוִד הֹלֵךְ אַחֲרֵי הַמִּטָּה:

32 And so they buried *Avner* at *Chevron*; the king wept aloud by *Avner*'s grave, and all the troops wept.

לב וַיִּקְבְּרוּ אֶת־אַבְנֵר בְּחֶבְרוֹן וַיִּשָּׂא הַמֶּלֶךְ אֶת־קוֹלוֹ וַיֵּבְךְּ אֶל־קֶבֶר אַבְנֵר וַיִּבְכּוּ כָּל־הָעָם:

33 And the king intoned this dirge over *Avner*, "Should *Avner* have died the death of a churl?

לג וַיְקֹנֵן הַמֶּלֶךְ אֶל־אַבְנֵר וַיֹּאמַר הַכְּמוֹת נָבָל יָמוּת אַבְנֵר:

34 Your hands were not bound, Your feet were not put in fetters; But you fell as one falls Before treacherous men!" And all the troops continued to weep over him.

לד יָדֶךָ לֹא־אֲסֻרוֹת וְרַגְלֶיךָ לֹא־לִנְחֻשְׁתַּיִם הֻגָּשׁוּ כִּנְפוֹל לִפְנֵי בְנֵי־עַוְלָה נָפָלְתָּ וַיֹּסִפוּ כָל־הָעָם לִבְכּוֹת עָלָיו:

Shmuel II/II Samuel
Chapter 4

שמואל ב
פרק ד

35 All the troops came to urge *David* to eat something while it was still day; but *David* swore, "May *Hashem* do thus to me and more if I eat bread or anything else before sundown."

לה וַיָּבֹא כָל־הָעָם לְהַבְרוֹת אֶת־דָּוִד לֶחֶם בְּעוֹד הַיּוֹם וַיִּשָּׁבַע דָּוִד לֵאמֹר כֹּה יַעֲשֶׂה־לִּי אֱלֹהִים וְכֹה יֹסִיף כִּי אִם־לִפְנֵי בוֹא־הַשֶּׁמֶשׁ אֶטְעַם־לֶחֶם אוֹ כָל־מְאוּמָה:

36 All the troops took note of it and approved, just as all the troops approved everything else the king did.

לו וְכָל־הָעָם הִכִּירוּ וַיִּיטַב בְּעֵינֵיהֶם כְּכֹל אֲשֶׁר עָשָׂה הַמֶּלֶךְ בְּעֵינֵי כָל־הָעָם טוֹב:

37 That day all the troops and all *Yisrael* knew that it was not by the king's will that *Avner* son of Ner was killed.

לז וַיֵּדְעוּ כָל־הָעָם וְכָל־יִשְׂרָאֵל בַּיּוֹם הַהוּא כִּי לֹא הָיְתָה מֵהַמֶּלֶךְ לְהָמִית אֶת־אַבְנֵר בֶּן־נֵר:

38 And the king said to his soldiers, "You well know that a prince, a great man in *Yisrael*, has fallen this day.

לח וַיֹּאמֶר הַמֶּלֶךְ אֶל־עֲבָדָיו הֲלוֹא תֵדְעוּ כִּי־שַׂר וְגָדוֹל נָפַל הַיּוֹם הַזֶּה בְּיִשְׂרָאֵל:

39 And today I am weak, even though anointed king; those men, the sons of *Tzeruya*, are too savage for me. May *Hashem* requite the wicked for their wickedness!"

לט וְאָנֹכִי הַיּוֹם רַךְ וּמָשׁוּחַ מֶלֶךְ וְהָאֲנָשִׁים הָאֵלֶּה בְּנֵי צְרוּיָה קָשִׁים מִמֶּנִּי יְשַׁלֵּם יְהוָה לְעֹשֵׂה הָרָעָה כְּרָעָתוֹ:

4 1 When [*Ish-boshet*] son of *Shaul* heard that *Avner* had died in *Chevron*, he lost heart and all *Yisrael* was alarmed.

ד א וַיִּשְׁמַע בֶּן־שָׁאוּל כִּי מֵת אַבְנֵר בְּחֶבְרוֹן וַיִּרְפּוּ יָדָיו וְכָל־יִשְׂרָאֵל נִבְהָלוּ:

2 The son of *Shaul* [had] two company commanders, one named Baanah and the other Rechab, sons of Rimmon the Beerothite – Benjaminites, since Beeroth too was considered part of *Binyamin*.

ב וּשְׁנֵי אֲנָשִׁים שָׂרֵי־גְדוּדִים הָיוּ בֶן־שָׁאוּל שֵׁם הָאֶחָד בַּעֲנָה וְשֵׁם הַשֵּׁנִי רֵכָב בְּנֵי רִמּוֹן הַבְּאֵרֹתִי מִבְּנֵי בִנְיָמִן כִּי גַּם־בְּאֵרוֹת תֵּחָשֵׁב עַל־בִּנְיָמִן:

3 The Beerothites had fled to Gittaim, where they have sojourned to this day.

ג וַיִּבְרְחוּ הַבְּאֵרֹתִים גִּתָּיְמָה וַיִּהְיוּ־שָׁם גָּרִים עַד הַיּוֹם הַזֶּה:

4 *Yehonatan* son of *Shaul* had a son whose feet were crippled. He was five years old when the news about *Shaul* and *Yehonatan* came from *Yizrael*, and his nurse picked him up and fled; but as she was fleeing in haste, he fell and was lamed. His name was *Mefiboshet*.

ד וְלִיהוֹנָתָן בֶּן־שָׁאוּל בֵּן נְכֵה רַגְלָיִם בֶּן־חָמֵשׁ שָׁנִים הָיָה בְּבֹא שְׁמֻעַת שָׁאוּל וִיהוֹנָתָן מִיִּזְרְעֶאל וַתִּשָּׂאֵהוּ אֹמַנְתּוֹ וַתָּנֹס וַיְהִי בְּחָפְזָהּ לָנוּס וַיִּפֹּל וַיִּפָּסֵחַ וּשְׁמוֹ מְפִיבֹשֶׁת:

5 Rechab and Baanah, sons of Rimmon the Beerothite, started out, and they reached the home of *Ish-boshet* at the heat of the day, when he was taking his midday rest.

ה וַיֵּלְכוּ בְּנֵי רִמּוֹן הַבְּאֵרֹתִי רֵכָב וּבַעֲנָה וַיָּבֹאוּ כְּחֹם הַיּוֹם אֶל־בֵּית אִישׁ בֹּשֶׁת וְהוּא שֹׁכֵב אֵת מִשְׁכַּב הַצָּהֳרָיִם:

6 So they went inside the house, as though fetching wheat, and struck him in the belly. Rechab and his brother Baanah slipped by,

ו וְהֵנָּה בָּאוּ עַד־תּוֹךְ הַבַּיִת לֹקְחֵי חִטִּים וַיַּכֻּהוּ אֶל־הַחֹמֶשׁ וְרֵכָב וּבַעֲנָה אָחִיו נִמְלָטוּ:

744

Shmuel II/II Samuel
Chapter 5

שמואל ב
פרק ה

7 and entered the house while he was asleep on his bed in his bed chamber; and they stabbed him to death. They cut off his head and took his head and made their way all night through the Arabah.

ז וַיָּבֹאוּ הַבַּיִת וְהוּא־שֹׁכֵב עַל־מִטָּתוֹ בַּחֲדַר מִשְׁכָּבוֹ וַיַּכֻּהוּ וַיְמִתֻהוּ וַיָּסִירוּ אֶת־רֹאשׁוֹ וַיִּקְחוּ אֶת־רֹאשׁוֹ וַיֵּלְכוּ דֶרֶךְ הָעֲרָבָה כָּל־הַלָּיְלָה:

8 They brought the head of *Ish-boshet* to *David* in *Chevron*. "Here," they said to the king, "is the head of your enemy, *Ish-boshet* son of *Shaul*, who sought your life. This day *Hashem* has avenged my lord the king upon *Shaul* and his offspring."

ח וַיָּבִאוּ אֶת־רֹאשׁ אִישׁ־בֹּשֶׁת אֶל־דָּוִד חֶבְרוֹן וַיֹּאמְרוּ אֶל־הַמֶּלֶךְ הִנֵּה־רֹאשׁ אִישׁ־בֹּשֶׁת בֶּן־שָׁאוּל אֹיִבְךָ אֲשֶׁר בִּקֵּשׁ אֶת־נַפְשֶׁךָ וַיִּתֵּן יְהֹוָה לַאדֹנִי הַמֶּלֶךְ נְקָמוֹת הַיּוֹם הַזֶּה מִשָּׁאוּל וּמִזַּרְעוֹ:

9 But *David* answered Rechab and his brother Baanah, the sons of Rimmon the Beerothite, and said to them, "As *Hashem* lives, who has rescued me from every trouble:

ט וַיַּעַן דָּוִד אֶת־רֵכָב וְאֶת־בַּעֲנָה אָחִיו בְּנֵי רִמּוֹן הַבְּאֵרֹתִי וַיֹּאמֶר לָהֶם חַי־יְהֹוָה אֲשֶׁר־פָּדָה אֶת־נַפְשִׁי מִכָּל־צָרָה:

10 The man who told me in *Tziklag* that *Shaul* was dead thought he was bringing good news. But instead of rewarding him for the news, I seized and killed him.

י כִּי הַמַּגִּיד לִי לֵאמֹר הִנֵּה־מֵת שָׁאוּל וְהוּא־הָיָה כִמְבַשֵּׂר בְּעֵינָיו וָאֹחֲזָה בוֹ וָאֶהְרְגֵהוּ בְּצִקְלָג אֲשֶׁר לְתִתִּי־לוֹ בְּשֹׂרָה:

11 How much more, then, when wicked men have killed a blameless man in bed in his own house! I will certainly avenge his blood on you, and I will rid the earth of you."

יא אַף כִּי־אֲנָשִׁים רְשָׁעִים הָרְגוּ אֶת־אִישׁ־צַדִּיק בְּבֵיתוֹ עַל־מִשְׁכָּבוֹ וְעַתָּה הֲלוֹא אֲבַקֵּשׁ אֶת־דָּמוֹ מִיֶּדְכֶם וּבִעַרְתִּי אֶתְכֶם מִן־הָאָרֶץ:

AF kee a-na-SHEEM r'-sha-EEM ha-r'-GU et eesh tza-DEEK b'-vay-TO al mish-ka-VO v'-a-TAH ha-LO a-va-KAYSH et da-MO mi-yed-KHEM u-vi-ar-TEE et-KHEM min ha-A-retz

12 *David* gave orders to the young men, who killed them; they cut off their hands and feet and hung them up by the pool in *Chevron*. And they took the head of *Ish-boshet* and buried it in the grave of *Avner* at *Chevron*.

יב וַיְצַו דָּוִד אֶת־הַנְּעָרִים וַיַּהַרְגוּם וַיְקַצְּצוּ אֶת־יְדֵיהֶם וְאֶת־רַגְלֵיהֶם וַיִּתְלוּ עַל־הַבְּרֵכָה בְּחֶבְרוֹן וְאֵת רֹאשׁ אִישׁ־בֹּשֶׁת לָקָחוּ וַיִּקְבְּרוּ בְקֶבֶר־אַבְנֵר בְּחֶבְרוֹן:

5 1 All the tribes of *Yisrael* came to *David* at *Chevron* and said, "We are your own flesh and blood.

ה א וַיָּבֹאוּ כָּל־שִׁבְטֵי יִשְׂרָאֵל אֶל־דָּוִד חֶבְרוֹנָה וַיֹּאמְרוּ לֵאמֹר הִנְנוּ עַצְמְךָ וּבְשָׂרְךָ אֲנָחְנוּ:

4:11 I will certainly avenge his blood on you King *David* helps establish an important principle of military ethics: One may not wantonly kill, even to advance a just cause. While one must kill in self-defense, the murder of innocents is a crime. This truth is taken to heart by the Israel Defense Forces, whose soldiers often risk their lives to avoid unintentionally killing civilians. Often, dangerous house-to-house combat is chosen over safer aerial bombings, in order to minimize the number of civilian casualties. The enemies of Israel are aware of this, and have been known to take advantage of the kindness and morality of the IDF by positioning their weapons and fighters near schools, homes and hospitals. But this has not deterred the Israeli army from being the world's most moral military forces.

Shmuel II/II Samuel
Chapter 5

שמואל ב
פרק ה

2 Long before now, when *Shaul* was king over us, it was you who led *Yisrael* in war; and *Hashem* said to you: You shall shepherd My people *Yisrael*; you shall be ruler of *Yisrael*."

ב גַּם־אֶתְמוֹל גַּם־שִׁלְשׁוֹם בִּהְיוֹת שָׁאוּל מֶלֶךְ עָלֵינוּ אַתָּה הָיִיתָה [הָיִיתָ] מוֹצִיא [הַמּוֹצִיא] וְהַמֵּבִי [וְהַמֵּבִיא] אֶת־יִשְׂרָאֵל וַיֹּאמֶר יְהֹוָה לְךָ אַתָּה תִרְעֶה אֶת־עַמִּי אֶת־יִשְׂרָאֵל וְאַתָּה תִּהְיֶה לְנָגִיד עַל־יִשְׂרָאֵל:

3 All the elders of *Yisrael* came to the king at *Chevron*, and King *David* made a pact with them in *Chevron* before *Hashem*. And they anointed *David* king over *Yisrael*.

ג וַיָּבֹאוּ כָּל־זִקְנֵי יִשְׂרָאֵל אֶל־הַמֶּלֶךְ חֶבְרוֹנָה וַיִּכְרֹת לָהֶם הַמֶּלֶךְ דָּוִד בְּרִית בְּחֶבְרוֹן לִפְנֵי יְהֹוָה וַיִּמְשְׁחוּ אֶת־דָּוִד לְמֶלֶךְ עַל־יִשְׂרָאֵל:

4 *David* was thirty years old when he became king, and he reigned forty years.

ד בֶּן־שְׁלֹשִׁים שָׁנָה דָּוִד בְּמָלְכוֹ אַרְבָּעִים שָׁנָה מָלָךְ:

5 In *Chevron* he reigned over *Yehuda* seven years and six months, and in *Yerushalayim* he reigned over all *Yisrael* and *Yehuda* thirty-three years.

ה בְּחֶבְרוֹן מָלַךְ עַל־יְהוּדָה שֶׁבַע שָׁנִים וְשִׁשָּׁה חֳדָשִׁים וּבִירוּשָׁלַ͏ִם מָלַךְ שְׁלֹשִׁים וְשָׁלֹשׁ שָׁנָה עַל כָּל־יִשְׂרָאֵל וִיהוּדָה:

6 The king and his men set out for *Yerushalayim* against the Jebusites who inhabited the region. *David* was told, "You will never get in here! Even the blind and the lame will turn you back." (They meant: *David* will never enter here.)

ו וַיֵּלֶךְ הַמֶּלֶךְ וַאֲנָשָׁיו יְרוּשָׁלַ͏ִם אֶל־הַיְבֻסִי יוֹשֵׁב הָאָרֶץ וַיֹּאמֶר לְדָוִד לֵאמֹר לֹא־תָבוֹא הֵנָּה כִּי אִם־הֱסִירְךָ הַעִוְרִים וְהַפִּסְחִים לֵאמֹר לֹא־יָבוֹא דָוִד הֵנָּה:

7 But *David* captured the stronghold of *Tzion*; it is now the City of *David*.

ז וַיִּלְכֹּד דָּוִד אֵת מְצֻדַת צִיּוֹן הִיא עִיר דָּוִד:

va-yil-KOD da-VID AYT m'-tzu-DAT tzi-YON HEE EER da-VID

8 On that occasion *David* said, "Those who attack the Jebusites shall reach the water channel and [strike down] the lame and the blind, who are hateful to *David*." That is why they say: "No one who is blind or lame may enter the House."

ח וַיֹּאמֶר דָּוִד בַּיּוֹם הַהוּא כָּל־מַכֵּה יְבֻסִי וְיִגַּע בַּצִּנּוֹר וְאֶת־הַפִּסְחִים וְאֶת־הַעִוְרִים שנאו [שְׂנֻאֵי] נֶפֶשׁ דָּוִד עַל־כֵּן יֹאמְרוּ עִוֵּר וּפִסֵּחַ לֹא יָבוֹא אֶל־הַבָּיִת:

9 *David* occupied the stronghold and renamed it the City of *David*; *David* also fortified the surrounding area, from the Millo inward.

ט וַיֵּשֶׁב דָּוִד בַּמְּצֻדָה וַיִּקְרָא־לָהּ עִיר דָּוִד וַיִּבֶן דָּוִד סָבִיב מִן־הַמִּלּוֹא וָבָיְתָה:

5:7 *David* captured the stronghold of *Tzion* Once the entire Nation of Israel unites behind King *David*, he is able to conquer the holy city of *Yerushalayim* from the pagan Jebusites, and to rule there for thirty-three years. His palace is located in the City of David, just outside the present walls of the Old City of *Yerushalayim*. After fifteen years of archaeological excavations at this site, a Canaanite fortress dating back to the eighteenth century BCE was uncovered. This impressive structure is the largest fortress to have been discovered in Israel from before the time of King Herod. It protects the *Gichon* spring where *Shlomo* is anointed king (I Kings 1:38), making it possible to access the spring only from within the city of *Yerushalayim*. As this verse describes, when King *David* enters the city he conquers the "stronghold of *Tzion*" from the Jebusites, quite possibly referring to this very fortress discovered thousands of years later. Visitors to modern day *Yerushalayim* can visit this site and be inspired by seeing firsthand evidence of the truth of the Bible.

Archeological excavations in the City of David

746

Shmuel II / II Samuel
Chapter 5

שמואל ב
פרק ה

10 *David* kept growing stronger, for *Hashem*, the God of Hosts, was with him.

יַוַיֵּלֶךְ דָּוִד הָלוֹךְ וְגָדוֹל וַיהוָה אֱלֹהֵי צְבָאוֹת עִמּוֹ:

11 King Hiram of Tyre sent envoys to *David* with cedar logs, carpenters, and stonemasons; and they built a palace for *David*.

יאוַיִּשְׁלַח חִירָם מֶלֶךְ־צֹר מַלְאָכִים אֶל־דָּוִד וַעֲצֵי אֲרָזִים וְחָרָשֵׁי עֵץ וְחָרָשֵׁי אֶבֶן קִיר וַיִּבְנוּ־בַיִת לְדָוִד:

12 Thus *David* knew that *Hashem* had established him as king over *Yisrael* and had exalted his kingship for the sake of His people *Yisrael*.

יבוַיֵּדַע דָּוִד כִּי־הֱכִינוֹ יְהוָה לְמֶלֶךְ עַל־יִשְׂרָאֵל וְכִי נִשֵּׂא מַמְלַכְתּוֹ בַּעֲבוּר עַמּוֹ יִשְׂרָאֵל:

13 After he left *Chevron*, *David* took more concubines and wives in *Yerushalayim*, and more sons and daughters were born to *David*.

יגוַיִּקַּח דָּוִד עוֹד פִּלַגְשִׁים וְנָשִׁים מִירוּשָׁלַיִם אַחֲרֵי בֹּאוֹ מֵחֶבְרוֹן וַיִּוָּלְדוּ עוֹד לְדָוִד בָּנִים וּבָנוֹת:

14 These are the names of the children born to him in *Yerushalayim*: Shammua, Shobab, *Natan*, and *Shlomo*;

ידוְאֵלֶּה שְׁמוֹת הַיִּלֹּדִים לוֹ בִּירוּשָׁלָ͏ִם שַׁמּוּעַ וְשׁוֹבָב וְנָתָן וּשְׁלֹמֹה:

15 Ibhar, Elishua, Nepheg, and Japhia;

טווְיִבְחָר וֶאֱלִישׁוּעַ וְנֶפֶג וְיָפִיעַ:

16 Elishama, Eliada, and Eliphelet.

טזוֶאֱלִישָׁמָע וְאֶלְיָדָע וֶאֱלִיפָלֶט:

17 When the Philistines heard that *David* had been anointed king over *Yisrael*, the Philistines marched up in search of *David*; but *David* heard of it, and he went down to the fastness.

יזוַיִּשְׁמְעוּ פְלִשְׁתִּים כִּי־מָשְׁחוּ אֶת־דָּוִד לְמֶלֶךְ עַל־יִשְׂרָאֵל וַיַּעֲלוּ כָל־פְּלִשְׁתִּים לְבַקֵּשׁ אֶת־דָּוִד וַיִּשְׁמַע דָּוִד וַיֵּרֶד אֶל־הַמְּצוּדָה:

18 The Philistines came and spread out over the Valley of Rephaim.

יחוּפְלִשְׁתִּים בָּאוּ וַיִּנָּטְשׁוּ בְּעֵמֶק רְפָאִים:

19 *David* inquired of *Hashem*, "Shall I go up against the Philistines? Will You deliver them into my hands?" And *Hashem* answered *David*, "Go up, and I will deliver the Philistines into your hands."

יטוַיִּשְׁאַל דָּוִד בַּיהוָה לֵאמֹר הַאֶעֱלֶה אֶל־פְּלִשְׁתִּים הֲתִתְּנֵם בְּיָדִי וַיֹּאמֶר יְהוָה אֶל־דָּוִד עֲלֵה כִּי־נָתֹן אֶתֵּן אֶת־הַפְּלִשְׁתִּים בְּיָדֶךָ:

20 Thereupon *David* marched to Baal-perazim, and *David* defeated them there. And he said, "*Hashem* has broken through my enemies before me as waters break through [a dam]." That is why that place was named Baal-perazim.

כוַיָּבֹא דָוִד בְּבַעַל־פְּרָצִים וַיַּכֵּם שָׁם דָּוִד וַיֹּאמֶר פָּרַץ יְהוָה אֶת־אֹיְבַי לְפָנַי כְּפֶרֶץ מָיִם עַל־כֵּן קָרָא שֵׁם־הַמָּקוֹם הַהוּא בַּעַל פְּרָצִים:

21 The Philistines abandoned their idols there, and *David* and his men carried them off.

כאוַיַּעַזְבוּ־שָׁם אֶת־עֲצַבֵּיהֶם וַיִּשָּׂאֵם דָּוִד וַאֲנָשָׁיו:

22 Once again the Philistines marched up and spread out over the Valley of Rephaim.

כבוַיֹּסִפוּ עוֹד פְּלִשְׁתִּים לַעֲלוֹת וַיִּנָּטְשׁוּ בְּעֵמֶק רְפָאִים:

23 *David* inquired of *Hashem*, and He answered, "Do not go up, but circle around behind them and confront them at the baca trees.

כגוַיִּשְׁאַל דָּוִד בַּיהוָה וַיֹּאמֶר לֹא תַעֲלֶה הָסֵב אֶל־אַחֲרֵיהֶם וּבָאתָ לָהֶם מִמּוּל בְּכָאִים:

24 And when you hear the sound of marching in the tops of the baca trees, then go into action, for *Hashem* will be going in front of you to attack the Philistine forces."

כדוִיהִי בשמעך [כְּשָׁמְעֲךָ] אֶת־קוֹל צְעָדָה בְּרָאשֵׁי הַבְּכָאִים אָז תֶּחֱרָץ כִּי אָז יָצָא יְהוָה לְפָנֶיךָ לְהַכּוֹת בְּמַחֲנֵה פְלִשְׁתִּים:

Shmuel II/II Samuel
Chapter 6

25 *David* did as *Hashem* had commanded him; and he routed the Philistines from Geba all the way to Gezer.

6

1 *David* again assembled all the picked men of *Yisrael*, thirty thousand strong.

2 Then *David* and all the troops that were with him set out from Baalim of *Yehuda* to bring up from there the *Aron* of *Hashem* to which the Name was attached, the name Lord of Hosts Enthroned on the *Keruvim*.

3 They loaded the *Aron* of *Hashem* onto a new cart and conveyed it from the house of *Avinadav*, which was on the hill; and *Avinadav*'s sons, Uzza and Ahio, guided the new cart.

4 They conveyed it from *Avinadav*'s house on the hill, [Uzzah walking] alongside the *Aron* of *Hashem* and Ahio walking in front of the *Aron*.

5 Meanwhile, *David* and all the House of *Yisrael* danced before *Hashem* to [the sound of] all kinds of cypress wood [instruments], with lyres, harps, timbrels, sistrums, and cymbals.

6 But when they came to the threshing floor of Nacon, Uzzah reached out for the *Aron* of *Hashem* and grasped it, for the oxen had stumbled.

7 *Hashem* was incensed at Uzzah. And *Hashem* struck him down on the spot for his indiscretion, and he died there beside the *Aron* of *Hashem*.

8 *David* was distressed because *Hashem* had inflicted a breach upon Uzzah; and that place was named Peretz-uzzah, as it is still called.

9 *David* was afraid of *Hashem* that day; he said, "How can I let the *Aron* of *Hashem* come to me?"

10 So *David* would not bring the *Aron* of *Hashem* to his place in the City of *David*; instead, *David* diverted it to the house of *Oved Edom* the Gittite.

11 The *Aron* of *Hashem* remained in the house of *Oved Edom* the Gittite three months, and *Hashem* blessed *Oved Edom* and his whole household.

שמואל ב
פרק ו

כה וַיַּ֤עַשׂ דָּוִד֙ כֵּ֔ן כַּאֲשֶׁ֥ר צִוָּ֖הוּ יְהוָ֑ה וַיַּךְ֙ אֶת־פְּלִשְׁתִּ֔ים מִגֶּ֖בַע עַד־בֹּאֲךָ֥ גָֽזֶר׃

ו א וַיֹּ֨סֶף ע֥וֹד דָּוִ֛ד אֶת־כָּל־בָּח֥וּר בְּיִשְׂרָאֵ֖ל שְׁלֹשִׁ֥ים אָֽלֶף׃

ב וַיָּ֣קָם ׀ וַיֵּ֣לֶךְ דָּוִ֗ד וְכָל־הָעָם֙ אֲשֶׁ֣ר אִתּ֔וֹ מִֽבַּעֲלֵ֖י יְהוּדָ֑ה לְהַעֲל֣וֹת מִשָּׁ֗ם אֵ֚ת אֲר֣וֹן הָאֱלֹהִ֔ים אֲשֶׁר־נִקְרָ֣א שֵׁ֗ם שֵׁ֣ם יְהוָ֧ה צְבָא֛וֹת יֹשֵׁ֥ב הַכְּרֻבִ֖ים עָלָֽיו׃

ג וַיַּרְכִּ֜בוּ אֶת־אֲר֤וֹן הָֽאֱלֹהִים֙ אֶל־עֲגָלָ֣ה חֲדָשָׁ֔ה וַיִּשָּׂאֻ֔הוּ מִבֵּ֥ית אֲבִינָדָ֖ב אֲשֶׁ֣ר בַּגִּבְעָ֑ה וְעֻזָּ֣א וְאַחְי֗וֹ בְּנֵי֙ אֲבִ֣ינָדָ֔ב נֹהֲגִ֖ים אֶת־הָעֲגָלָ֥ה חֲדָשָֽׁה׃

ד וַיִּשָּׂאֻ֗הוּ מִבֵּ֤ית אֲבִֽינָדָב֙ אֲשֶׁ֣ר בַּגִּבְעָ֔ה עִ֖ם אֲר֣וֹן הָאֱלֹהִ֑ים וְאַחְי֕וֹ הֹלֵ֖ךְ לִפְנֵ֥י הָאָרֽוֹן׃

ה וְדָוִ֣ד ׀ וְכָל־בֵּ֣ית יִשְׂרָאֵ֗ל מְשַׂחֲקִים֙ לִפְנֵ֣י יְהוָ֔ה בְּכֹ֖ל עֲצֵ֣י בְרוֹשִׁ֑ים וּבְכִנֹּר֤וֹת וּבִנְבָלִים֙ וּבְתֻפִּ֔ים וּבִמְנַֽעַנְעִ֖ים וּֽבְצֶלְצֶלִֽים׃

ו וַיָּבֹ֖אוּ עַד־גֹּ֣רֶן נָכ֑וֹן וַיִּשְׁלַ֤ח עֻזָּא֙ אֶל־אֲר֣וֹן הָאֱלֹהִ֔ים וַיֹּ֣אחֶז בּ֔וֹ כִּ֥י שָׁמְט֖וּ הַבָּקָֽר׃

ז וַיִּֽחַר־אַ֤ף יְהוָה֙ בְּעֻזָּ֔ה וַיַּכֵּ֥הוּ שָׁ֛ם הָאֱלֹהִ֖ים עַל־הַשַּׁ֑ל וַיָּ֣מָת שָׁ֔ם עִ֖ם אֲר֥וֹן הָאֱלֹהִֽים׃

ח וַיִּ֣חַר לְדָוִ֔ד עַל֩ אֲשֶׁ֨ר פָּרַ֧ץ יְהוָ֛ה פֶּ֖רֶץ בְּעֻזָּ֑ה וַיִּקְרָ֞א לַמָּק֤וֹם הַהוּא֙ פֶּ֣רֶץ עֻזָּ֔ה עַ֖ד הַיּ֥וֹם הַזֶּֽה׃

ט וַיִּרָ֥א דָוִ֛ד אֶת־יְהוָ֖ה בַּיּ֣וֹם הַה֑וּא וַיֹּ֕אמֶר אֵ֛יךְ יָב֥וֹא אֵלַ֖י אֲר֥וֹן יְהוָֽה׃

י וְלֹֽא־אָבָ֣ה דָוִ֗ד לְהָסִ֥יר אֵלָ֛יו אֶת־אֲר֥וֹן יְהוָ֖ה עַל־עִ֣יר דָּוִ֑ד וַיַּטֵּ֣הוּ דָוִ֔ד בֵּ֖ית עֹבֵֽד־אֱד֥וֹם הַגִּתִּֽי׃

יא וַיֵּשֶׁב֩ אֲר֨וֹן יְהוָ֜ה בֵּ֣ית עֹבֵ֥ד אֱדֹ֛ם הַגִּתִּ֖י שְׁלֹשָׁ֣ה חֳדָשִׁ֑ים וַיְבָ֧רֶךְ יְהוָ֛ה אֶת־עֹבֵ֥ד אֱדֹ֖ם וְאֶת־כָּל־בֵּיתֽוֹ׃

Shmuel II / II Samuel
Chapter 6

שמואל ב / פרק ו

12 It was reported to King *David*: "*Hashem* has blessed *Oved Edom*'s house and all that belongs to him because of the *Aron* of *Hashem*." Thereupon *David* went and brought up the *Aron* of *Hashem* from the house of *Oved Edom* to the City of *David*, amid rejoicing.

יב וַיֻּגַּד לַמֶּלֶךְ דָּוִד לֵאמֹר בֵּרַךְ יְהֹוָה אֶת־בֵּית עֹבֵד אֱדֹם וְאֶת־כָּל־אֲשֶׁר־לוֹ בַּעֲבוּר אֲרוֹן הָאֱלֹהִים וַיֵּלֶךְ דָּוִד וַיַּעַל אֶת־אֲרוֹן הָאֱלֹהִים מִבֵּית עֹבֵד אֱדֹם עִיר דָּוִד בְּשִׂמְחָה:

> va-yu-GAD la-ME-lekh da-VID lay-MOR bay-RAKH a-do-NAI et BAYT o-VAYD e-DOM v'-et kol a-sher LO ba-a-VUR a-RON ha-e-lo-HEEM va-YAY-lekh da-VID va-YA-al et a-RON ha-e-lo-HEEM mi-BAYT o-VAYD e-DOM EER da-VID b'-sim-KHAH

13 When the bearers of the *Aron* of *Hashem* had moved forward six paces, he sacrificed an ox and a fatling.

יג וַיְהִי כִּי צָעֲדוּ נֹשְׂאֵי אֲרוֹן־יְהֹוָה שִׁשָּׁה צְעָדִים וַיִּזְבַּח שׁוֹר וּמְרִיא:

14 *David* whirled with all his might before *Hashem*; *David* was girt with a linen ephod.

יד וְדָוִד מְכַרְכֵּר בְּכָל־עֹז לִפְנֵי יְהֹוָה וְדָוִד חָגוּר אֵפוֹד בָּד:

15 Thus *David* and all the House of *Yisrael* brought up the *Aron* of *Hashem* with shouts and with blasts of the *shofar*.

טו וְדָוִד וְכָל־בֵּית יִשְׂרָאֵל מַעֲלִים אֶת־אֲרוֹן יְהֹוָה בִּתְרוּעָה וּבְקוֹל שׁוֹפָר:

16 As the *Aron* of *Hashem* entered the City of *David*, *Michal* daughter of *Shaul* looked out of the window and saw King *David* leaping and whirling before *Hashem*; and she despised him for it.

טז וְהָיָה אֲרוֹן יְהֹוָה בָּא עִיר דָּוִד וּמִיכַל בַּת־שָׁאוּל נִשְׁקְפָה בְּעַד הַחַלּוֹן וַתֵּרֶא אֶת־הַמֶּלֶךְ דָּוִד מְפַזֵּז וּמְכַרְכֵּר לִפְנֵי יְהֹוָה וַתִּבֶז לוֹ בְּלִבָּהּ:

17 They brought in the *Aron* of *Hashem* and set it up in its place inside the tent which *David* had pitched for it, and *David* sacrificed burnt offerings and offerings of well-being before *Hashem*.

יז וַיָּבִאוּ אֶת־אֲרוֹן יְהֹוָה וַיַּצִּגוּ אֹתוֹ בִּמְקוֹמוֹ בְּתוֹךְ הָאֹהֶל אֲשֶׁר נָטָה־לוֹ דָּוִד וַיַּעַל דָּוִד עֹלוֹת לִפְנֵי יְהֹוָה וּשְׁלָמִים:

18 When *David* finished sacrificing the burnt offerings and the offerings of well-being, he blessed the people in the name of the Lord of Hosts.

יח וַיְכַל דָּוִד מֵהַעֲלוֹת הָעוֹלָה וְהַשְּׁלָמִים וַיְבָרֶךְ אֶת־הָעָם בְּשֵׁם יְהֹוָה צְבָאוֹת:

19 And he distributed among all the people – the entire multitude of *Yisrael*, man and woman alike – to each a loaf of bread, a cake made in a pan, and a raisin cake. Then all the people left for their homes.

יט וַיְחַלֵּק לְכָל־הָעָם לְכָל־הֲמוֹן יִשְׂרָאֵל לְמֵאִישׁ וְעַד־אִשָּׁה לְאִישׁ חַלַּת לֶחֶם אַחַת וְאֶשְׁפָּר אֶחָד וַאֲשִׁישָׁה אֶחָת וַיֵּלֶךְ כָּל־הָעָם אִישׁ לְבֵיתוֹ:

6:12 Thereupon *David* went and brought up the *Aron* of *Hashem* King *David* is ready to bring the Holy Ark to the City of David, also known as *Tzion* and *Yerushalayim*. He does this with great joy, participating personally in the festive dancing. Bringing the Holy Ark to *Yerushalayim* transforms the city, making it the spiritual, in addition to political, capital of the nation. Once the *Beit Hamikdash* is built, the people will bring their sacrifices to *Yerushalayim* and be inspired by the Divine Presence that rests there. *Yerushalayim* then becomes the eternal focal point of the Jewish people, and all who seek closeness with the Almighty.

749

Shmuel II/II Samuel
Chapter 7

20 *David* went home to greet his household. And *Michal* daughter of *Shaul* came out to meet *David* and said, "Didn't the king of *Yisrael* do himself honor today – exposing himself today in the sight of the slavegirls of his subjects, as one of the riffraff might expose himself!"

21 *David* answered *Michal*, "It was before *Hashem* who chose me instead of your father and all his family and appointed me ruler over *Hashem*'s people *Yisrael*! I will dance before *Hashem*

22 and dishonor myself even more, and be low in my own esteem; but among the slavegirls that you speak of I will be honored."

23 So to her dying day *Michal* daughter of *Shaul* had no children.

7 1 When the king was settled in his palace and *Hashem* had granted him safety from all the enemies around him,

2 the king said to the *Navi Natan*: "Here I am dwelling in a house of cedar, while the *Aron* of *Hashem* abides in a tent!"

3 *Natan* said to the king, "Go and do whatever you have in mind, for *Hashem* is with you."

4 But that same night the word of *Hashem* came to *Natan*:

5 "Go and say to My servant *David*: Thus said *Hashem*: Are you the one to build a house for Me to dwell in?

6 From the day that I brought the people of *Yisrael* out of Egypt to this day I have not dwelt in a house, but have moved about in Tent and *Mishkan*.

7 As I moved about wherever the Israelites went, did I ever reproach any of the tribal leaders whom I appointed to care for My people *Yisrael*: Why have you not built Me a house of cedar?

8 "Further, say thus to My servant *David*: Thus said the LORD of Hosts: I took you from the pasture, from following the flock, to be ruler of My people *Yisrael*,

שמואל ב
פרק ז

כ וַיָּשָׁב דָּוִד לְבָרֵךְ אֶת־בֵּיתוֹ וַתֵּצֵא מִיכַל בַּת־שָׁאוּל לִקְרַאת דָּוִד וַתֹּאמֶר מַה־נִּכְבַּד הַיּוֹם מֶלֶךְ יִשְׂרָאֵל אֲשֶׁר נִגְלָה הַיּוֹם לְעֵינֵי אַמְהוֹת עֲבָדָיו כְּהִגָּלוֹת נִגְלוֹת אַחַד הָרֵקִים:

כא וַיֹּאמֶר דָּוִד אֶל־מִיכַל לִפְנֵי יְהֹוָה אֲשֶׁר בָּחַר־בִּי מֵאָבִיךְ וּמִכָּל־בֵּיתוֹ לְצַוֹּת אֹתִי נָגִיד עַל־עַם יְהֹוָה עַל־יִשְׂרָאֵל וְשִׂחַקְתִּי לִפְנֵי יְהֹוָה:

כב וּנְקַלֹּתִי עוֹד מִזֹּאת וְהָיִיתִי שָׁפָל בְּעֵינָי וְעִם־הָאֲמָהוֹת אֲשֶׁר אָמַרְתְּ עִמָּם אִכָּבֵדָה:

כג וּלְמִיכַל בַּת־שָׁאוּל לֹא־הָיָה לָהּ יָלֶד עַד יוֹם מוֹתָהּ:

ז א וַיְהִי כִּי־יָשַׁב הַמֶּלֶךְ בְּבֵיתוֹ וַיהֹוָה הֵנִיחַ־לוֹ מִסָּבִיב מִכָּל־אֹיְבָיו:

ב וַיֹּאמֶר הַמֶּלֶךְ אֶל־נָתָן הַנָּבִיא רְאֵה נָא אָנֹכִי יוֹשֵׁב בְּבֵית אֲרָזִים וַאֲרוֹן הָאֱלֹהִים יֹשֵׁב בְּתוֹךְ הַיְרִיעָה:

ג וַיֹּאמֶר נָתָן אֶל־הַמֶּלֶךְ כֹּל אֲשֶׁר בִּלְבָבְךָ לֵךְ עֲשֵׂה כִּי יְהֹוָה עִמָּךְ:

ד וַיְהִי בַּלַּיְלָה הַהוּא וַיְהִי דְּבַר־יְהֹוָה אֶל־נָתָן לֵאמֹר:

ה לֵךְ וְאָמַרְתָּ אֶל־עַבְדִּי אֶל־דָּוִד כֹּה אָמַר יְהֹוָה הַאַתָּה תִּבְנֶה־לִּי בַיִת לְשִׁבְתִּי:

ו כִּי לֹא יָשַׁבְתִּי בְּבַיִת לְמִיּוֹם הַעֲלֹתִי אֶת־בְּנֵי יִשְׂרָאֵל מִמִּצְרַיִם וְעַד הַיּוֹם הַזֶּה וָאֶהְיֶה מִתְהַלֵּךְ בְּאֹהֶל וּבְמִשְׁכָּן:

ז בְּכֹל אֲשֶׁר־הִתְהַלַּכְתִּי בְּכָל־בְּנֵי יִשְׂרָאֵל הֲדָבָר דִּבַּרְתִּי אֶת־אַחַד שִׁבְטֵי יִשְׂרָאֵל אֲשֶׁר צִוִּיתִי לִרְעוֹת אֶת־עַמִּי אֶת־יִשְׂרָאֵל לֵאמֹר לָמָּה לֹא־בְנִיתֶם לִי בֵּית אֲרָזִים:

ח וְעַתָּה כֹּה־תֹאמַר לְעַבְדִּי לְדָוִד כֹּה אָמַר יְהֹוָה צְבָאוֹת אֲנִי לְקַחְתִּיךָ מִן־הַנָּוֶה מֵאַחַר הַצֹּאן לִהְיוֹת נָגִיד עַל־עַמִּי עַל־יִשְׂרָאֵל:

Shmuel II/II Samuel
Chapter 7

שְׁמוּאֵל ב
פרק ז

9 and I have been with you wherever you went, and have cut down all your enemies before you. Moreover, I will give you great renown like that of the greatest men on earth.

ט וָאֶהְיֶה עִמְּךָ בְּכֹל אֲשֶׁר הָלַכְתָּ וָאַכְרִתָה אֶת־כָּל־אֹיְבֶיךָ מִפָּנֶיךָ וְעָשִׂתִי לְךָ שֵׁם גָּדוֹל כְּשֵׁם הַגְּדֹלִים אֲשֶׁר בָּאָרֶץ׃

10 I will establish a home for My people *Yisrael* and will plant them firm, so that they shall dwell secure and shall tremble no more. Evil men shall not oppress them any more as in the past,

י וְשַׂמְתִּי מָקוֹם לְעַמִּי לְיִשְׂרָאֵל וּנְטַעְתִּיו וְשָׁכַן תַּחְתָּיו וְלֹא יִרְגַּז עוֹד וְלֹא־יֹסִיפוּ בְנֵי־עַוְלָה לְעַנּוֹתוֹ כַּאֲשֶׁר בָּרִאשׁוֹנָה׃

11 ever since I appointed chieftains over My people *Yisrael*. I will give you safety from all your enemies. "*Hashem* declares to you that He, *Hashem*, will establish a house for you.

יא וּלְמִן־הַיּוֹם אֲשֶׁר צִוִּיתִי שֹׁפְטִים עַל־עַמִּי יִשְׂרָאֵל וַהֲנִיחֹתִי לְךָ מִכָּל־אֹיְבֶיךָ וְהִגִּיד לְךָ יְהֹוָה כִּי־בַיִת יַעֲשֶׂה־לְּךָ יְהֹוָה׃

12 When your days are done and you lie with your fathers, I will raise up your offspring after you, one of your own issue, and I will establish his kingship.

יב כִּי יִמְלְאוּ יָמֶיךָ וְשָׁכַבְתָּ אֶת־אֲבֹתֶיךָ וַהֲקִימֹתִי אֶת־זַרְעֲךָ אַחֲרֶיךָ אֲשֶׁר יֵצֵא מִמֵּעֶיךָ וַהֲכִינֹתִי אֶת־מַמְלַכְתּוֹ׃

13 He shall build a house for My name, and I will establish his royal throne forever.

יג הוּא יִבְנֶה־בַּיִת לִשְׁמִי וְכֹנַנְתִּי אֶת־כִּסֵּא מַמְלַכְתּוֹ עַד־עוֹלָם׃

HU yiv-neh BA-yit lish-MEE v'-kho-nan-TEE et ki-SAY mam-lakh-TO ad o-LAM

14 I will be a father to him, and he shall be a son to Me. When he does wrong, I will chastise him with the rod of men and the affliction of mortals;

יד אֲנִי אֶהְיֶה־לּוֹ לְאָב וְהוּא יִהְיֶה־לִּי לְבֵן אֲשֶׁר בְּהַעֲוֺתוֹ וְהֹכַחְתִּיו בְּשֵׁבֶט אֲנָשִׁים וּבְנִגְעֵי בְּנֵי אָדָם׃

15 but I will never withdraw My favor from him as I withdrew it from *Shaul*, whom I removed to make room for you.

טו וְחַסְדִּי לֹא־יָסוּר מִמֶּנּוּ כַּאֲשֶׁר הֲסִרֹתִי מֵעִם שָׁאוּל אֲשֶׁר הֲסִרֹתִי מִלְּפָנֶיךָ׃

16 Your house and your kingship shall ever be secure before you; your throne shall be established forever."

טז וְנֶאְמַן בֵּיתְךָ וּמַמְלַכְתְּךָ עַד־עוֹלָם לְפָנֶיךָ כִּסְאֲךָ יִהְיֶה נָכוֹן עַד־עוֹלָם׃

17 *Natan* spoke to *David* in accordance with all these words and all this prophecy.

יז כְּכֹל הַדְּבָרִים הָאֵלֶּה וּכְכֹל הַחִזָּיוֹן הַזֶּה כֵּן דִּבֶּר נָתָן אֶל־דָּוִד׃

18 Then King *David* came and sat before *Hashem*, and he said, "What am I, O *Hashem*, and what is my family, that You have brought me thus far?

יח וַיָּבֹא הַמֶּלֶךְ דָּוִד וַיֵּשֶׁב לִפְנֵי יְהֹוָה וַיֹּאמֶר מִי אָנֹכִי אֲדֹנָי יְהֹוִה וּמִי בֵיתִי כִּי הֲבִיאֹתַנִי עַד־הֲלֹם׃

7:13 He shall build a house for My name King *David* wants to build the *Beit Hamikdash* for *Hashem*. However, *Hashem* tells him that his son, not he, will build it. As the king who helps conquer the Land of Israel, fights Amalek and solidifies the monarchy, King *David* plays an important part in the process of establishing the Israelites in their land. He is even able to make preparations for the building of the *Beit Hamikdash*. However, as a warrior, he cannot be the one to build the Holy Temple, which is intended to promote peace and harmony among Israel and all the nations of the world. Additionally, as the service in the *Beit Hamikdash* brings people closer to God and helps atone for their sins and prolongs life, it cannot be built by a warrior, who shortens the lives of others. Therefore, *David*'s role ends after defeating Amalek, and his son *Shlomo*, a man of peace, becomes God's choice to build of the world's holiest site, the *Beit Hamikdash* in *Yerushalayim*.

Shmuel II/II Samuel

Chapter 8

שמואל ב

פרק ח

19 Yet even this, O *Hashem*, has seemed too little to You; for You have spoken of Your servant's house also for the future. May that be the law for the people, O *Hashem*.

יט וַתִּקְטַן עוֹד זֹאת בְּעֵינֶיךָ אֲדֹנָי יֱהֹוִה וַתְּדַבֵּר גַּם אֶל־בֵּית־עַבְדְּךָ לְמֵרָחוֹק וְזֹאת תּוֹרַת הָאָדָם אֲדֹנָי יֱהֹוִה:

20 What more can *David* say to You? You know Your servant, O *Hashem*.

כ וּמַה־יּוֹסִיף דָּוִד עוֹד לְדַבֵּר אֵלֶיךָ וְאַתָּה יָדַעְתָּ אֶת־עַבְדְּךָ אֲדֹנָי יֱהֹוִה:

21 For Your word's sake and of Your own accord You have wrought this great thing, and made it known to Your servant.

כא בַּעֲבוּר דְּבָרְךָ וּכְלִבְּךָ עָשִׂיתָ אֵת כָּל־הַגְּדוּלָּה הַזֹּאת לְהוֹדִיעַ אֶת־עַבְדֶּךָ:

22 You are great indeed, O *Hashem*! There is none like You and there is no other God but You, as we have always heard.

כב עַל־כֵּן גָּדַלְתָּ אֲדֹנָי יֱהֹוִה כִּי־אֵין כָּמוֹךָ וְאֵין אֱלֹהִים זוּלָתֶךָ בְּכֹל אֲשֶׁר־שָׁמַעְנוּ בְּאָזְנֵינוּ:

23 And who is like Your people *Yisrael*, a unique nation on earth, whom *Hashem* went and redeemed as His people, winning renown for Himself and doing great and marvelous deeds for them [and] for Your land — [driving out] nations and their gods before Your people, whom You redeemed for Yourself from Egypt.

כג וּמִי כְעַמְּךָ כְּיִשְׂרָאֵל גּוֹי אֶחָד בָּאָרֶץ אֲשֶׁר הָלְכוּ־אֱלֹהִים לִפְדּוֹת־לוֹ לְעָם וְלָשׂוּם לוֹ שֵׁם וְלַעֲשׂוֹת לָכֶם הַגְּדוּלָּה וְנֹרָאוֹת לְאַרְצֶךָ מִפְּנֵי עַמְּךָ אֲשֶׁר פָּדִיתָ לְּךָ מִמִּצְרַיִם גּוֹיִם וֵאלֹהָיו:

24 You have established Your people *Yisrael* as Your very own people forever; and You, *Hashem*, have become their God.

כד וַתְּכוֹנֵן לְךָ אֶת־עַמְּךָ יִשְׂרָאֵל לְךָ לְעָם עַד־עוֹלָם וְאַתָּה יְהֹוָה הָיִיתָ לָהֶם לֵאלֹהִים:

25 "And now, O *Hashem*, fulfill Your promise to Your servant and his house forever; and do as You have promised.

כה וְעַתָּה יְהֹוָה אֱלֹהִים הַדָּבָר אֲשֶׁר דִּבַּרְתָּ עַל־עַבְדְּךָ וְעַל־בֵּיתוֹ הָקֵם עַד־עוֹלָם וַעֲשֵׂה כַּאֲשֶׁר דִּבַּרְתָּ:

26 And may Your name be glorified forever, in that men will say, 'the LORD of Hosts is God over *Yisrael*'; and may the house of Your servant *David* be established before You.

כו וְיִגְדַּל שִׁמְךָ עַד־עוֹלָם לֵאמֹר יְהֹוָה צְבָאוֹת אֱלֹהִים עַל־יִשְׂרָאֵל וּבֵית עַבְדְּךָ דָוִד יִהְיֶה נָכוֹן לְפָנֶיךָ:

27 Because You, LORD of Hosts, the God of *Yisrael*, have revealed to Your servant that You will build a house for him, Your servant has ventured to offer this prayer to You.

כז כִּי־אַתָּה יְהֹוָה צְבָאוֹת אֱלֹהֵי יִשְׂרָאֵל גָּלִיתָה אֶת־אֹזֶן עַבְדְּךָ לֵאמֹר בַּיִת אֶבְנֶה־לָּךְ עַל־כֵּן מָצָא עַבְדְּךָ אֶת־לִבּוֹ לְהִתְפַּלֵּל אֵלֶיךָ אֶת־הַתְּפִלָּה הַזֹּאת:

28 And now, O *Hashem*, You are *Hashem* and Your words will surely come true, and You have made this gracious promise to Your servant.

כח וְעַתָּה אֲדֹנָי יֱהֹוִה אַתָּה־הוּא הָאֱלֹהִים וּדְבָרֶיךָ יִהְיוּ אֱמֶת וַתְּדַבֵּר אֶל־עַבְדְּךָ אֶת־הַטּוֹבָה הַזֹּאת:

29 Be pleased, therefore, to bless Your servant's house, that it abide before You forever; for You, O *Hashem*, have spoken. May Your servant's house be blessed forever by Your blessing."

כט וְעַתָּה הוֹאֵל וּבָרֵךְ אֶת־בֵּית עַבְדְּךָ לִהְיוֹת לְעוֹלָם לְפָנֶיךָ כִּי־אַתָּה אֲדֹנָי יֱהֹוִה דִּבַּרְתָּ וּמִבִּרְכָתְךָ יְבֹרַךְ בֵּית־עַבְדְּךָ לְעוֹלָם:

8 1 Some time afterward, *David* attacked the Philistines and subdued them; and *David* took Metheg-ammah from the Philistines.

ח א וַיְהִי אַחֲרֵי־כֵן וַיַּךְ דָּוִד אֶת־פְּלִשְׁתִּים וַיַּכְנִיעֵם וַיִּקַּח דָּוִד אֶת־מֶתֶג הָאַמָּה מִיַּד פְּלִשְׁתִּים:

752

Shmuel II / II Samuel
Chapter 8

שמואל ב
פרק ח

2 He also defeated the Moabites. He made them lie down on the ground and he measured them off with a cord; he measured out two lengths of cord for those who were to be put to death, and one length for those to be spared. And the Moabites became tributary vassals of *David*.

ב וַיַּ֣ךְ אֶת־מוֹאָ֗ב וַיְמַדְּדֵ֤ם בַּחֶ֙בֶל֙ הַשְׁכֵּ֣ב אוֹתָ֣ם אַ֔רְצָה וַיְמַדֵּ֤ד שְׁנֵֽי־חֲבָלִים֙ לְהָמִ֔ית וּמְלֹ֥א הַחֶ֖בֶל לְהַחֲי֑וֹת וַתְּהִ֤י מוֹאָב֙ לְדָוִ֣ד לַעֲבָדִ֔ים נֹשְׂאֵ֖י מִנְחָֽה׃

3 *David* defeated Hadadezer son of Rehob, king of Zobah, who was then on his way to restore his monument at the Euphrates River.

ג וַיַּ֣ךְ דָּוִ֔ד אֶת־הֲדַדְעֶ֥זֶר בֶּן־רְחֹ֖ב מֶ֣לֶךְ צוֹבָ֑ה בְּלֶכְתּ֕וֹ לְהָשִׁ֥יב יָד֖וֹ בִּנְהַר־[פְּרָֽת׃]

4 *David* captured 1,700 horsemen and 20,000 foot soldiers of his force; and *David* hamstrung all the chariot horses, except for 100 which he retained.

ד וַיִּלְכֹּ֨ד דָּוִ֜ד מִמֶּ֗נּוּ וּשְׁבַע־מֵא֤וֹת פָּרָשִׁים֙ וְעֶשְׂרִ֣ים אֶ֔לֶף אִ֖ישׁ רַגְלִ֑י וַיְעַקֵּ֤ר דָּוִד֙ אֶת־כָּל־הָרֶ֔כֶב וַיּוֹתֵ֥ר מִמֶּ֖נּוּ מֵ֥אָה רָֽכֶב׃

5 And when the Arameans of Damascus came to the aid of King Hadadezer of Zobah, *David* struck down 22,000 of the Arameans.

ה וַתָּבֹא֙ אֲרַ֣ם דַּמֶּ֔שֶׂק לַעְזֹ֕ר לַהֲדַדְעֶ֖זֶר מֶ֣לֶךְ צוֹבָ֑ה וַיַּ֤ךְ דָּוִד֙ בַּאֲרָ֔ם עֶשְׂרִֽים־וּשְׁנַ֥יִם אֶ֖לֶף אִֽישׁ׃

6 *David* stationed garrisons in Aram of Damascus, and the Arameans became tributary vassals of *David*. *Hashem* gave *David* victory wherever he went.

ו וַיָּ֨שֶׂם דָּוִ֤ד נְצִבִים֙ בַּאֲרַ֣ם דַּמֶּ֔שֶׂק וַתְּהִ֤י אֲרָם֙ לְדָוִ֣ד לַעֲבָדִ֔ים נוֹשְׂאֵ֖י מִנְחָ֑ה וַיֹּ֤שַׁע יְהוָה֙ אֶת־דָּוִ֔ד בְּכֹ֖ל אֲשֶׁ֥ר הָלָֽךְ׃

7 *David* took the gold shields carried by Hadadezer's retinue and brought them to *Yerushalayim*;

ז וַיִּקַּ֣ח דָּוִ֗ד אֵ֚ת שִׁלְטֵ֣י הַזָּהָ֔ב אֲשֶׁ֣ר הָי֔וּ אֶ֖ל עַבְדֵ֣י הֲדַדְעָ֑זֶר וַיְבִיאֵ֖ם יְרוּשָׁלָֽם׃

8 and from Betah and Berothai, towns of Hadadezer, King *David* took a vast amount of copper.

ח וּמִבֶּ֥טַח וּמִבֵּרֹתַ֖י עָרֵ֣י הֲדַדְעָ֑זֶר לָקַ֞ח הַמֶּ֧לֶךְ דָּוִ֛ד נְחֹ֖שֶׁת הַרְבֵּ֥ה מְאֹֽד׃

9 When King Toi of Hamath heard that *David* had defeated the entire army of Hadadezer,

ט וַיִּשְׁמַ֕ע תֹּ֖עִי מֶ֣לֶךְ חֲמָ֑ת כִּ֚י הִכָּ֣ה דָוִ֔ד אֵ֖ת כָּל־חֵ֥יל הֲדַדְעָֽזֶר׃

10 Toi sent his son Joram to King *David* to greet him and to congratulate him on his military victory over Hadadezer – for Hadadezer had been at war with Toi. [*Yoram*] brought with him objects of silver, gold, and copper.

י וַיִּשְׁלַ֣ח תֹּ֣עִי אֶת־יֽוֹרָם־בְּנ֣וֹ אֶל־הַמֶּֽלֶךְ־דָּ֠וִד לִשְׁאָל־ל֨וֹ לְשָׁל֜וֹם וּֽלְבָרֲכ֗וֹ עַל֩ אֲשֶׁ֨ר נִלְחַ֤ם בַּהֲדַדְעֶ֙זֶר֙ וַיַּכֵּ֔הוּ כִּי־אִ֛ישׁ מִלְחֲמ֥וֹת תֹּ֖עִי הָיָ֣ה הֲדַדְעָ֑זֶר וּבְיָד֗וֹ הָי֛וּ כְּלֵי־כֶ֥סֶף וּכְלֵי־זָהָ֖ב וּכְלֵ֥י נְחֹֽשֶׁת׃

11 King *David* dedicated these to *Hashem*, along with the other silver and gold that he dedicated, [taken] from all the nations he had conquered:

יא גַּם־אֹתָ֕ם הִקְדִּ֛ישׁ הַמֶּ֥לֶךְ דָּוִ֖ד לַיהוָ֑ה עִם־הַכֶּ֣סֶף וְהַזָּהָ֗ב אֲשֶׁ֤ר הִקְדִּישׁ֙ מִכָּל־הַגּוֹיִ֔ם אֲשֶׁ֖ר כִּבֵּֽשׁ׃

12 from Edom, Moab, and Ammon; from the Philistines and the Amalekites, and from the plunder of Hadadezer son of Rehob, king of Zobah.

יב מֵאֲרָ֤ם וּמִמּוֹאָב֙ וּמִבְּנֵ֣י עַמּ֔וֹן וּמִפְּלִשְׁתִּ֖ים וּמֵֽעֲמָלֵ֑ק וּמִשְּׁלַ֛ל הֲדַדְעֶ֥זֶר בֶּן־רְחֹ֖ב מֶ֥לֶךְ צוֹבָֽה׃

13 *David* gained fame when he returned from defeating Edom in the Valley of Salt, 18,000 in all.

יג וַיַּ֤עַשׂ דָּוִד֙ שֵׁ֔ם בְּשֻׁב֕וֹ מֵהַכּוֹת֥וֹ אֶת־אֲרָ֖ם בְּגֵיא־מֶ֑לַח שְׁמוֹנָ֥ה עָשָׂ֖ר אָֽלֶף׃

14 He stationed garrisons in Edom – he stationed garrisons in all of Edom – and all the Edomites became vassals of *David*. *Hashem* gave *David* victory wherever he went.

יד וַיָּ֨שֶׂם בֶּאֱד֜וֹם נְצִבִ֗ים בְּכָל־אֱדוֹם֙ שָׂ֣ם נְצִבִ֔ים וַיְהִ֥י כָל־אֱד֖וֹם עֲבָדִ֣ים לְדָוִ֑ד וַיּ֤וֹשַׁע יְהוָה֙ אֶת־דָּוִ֔ד בְּכֹ֖ל אֲשֶׁ֥ר הָלָֽךְ׃

Shmuel II / II Samuel
Chapter 9

שמואל ב
פרק ט

15 *David* reigned over all *Yisrael*, and *David* executed true justice among all his people.

וַיִּמְלֹךְ דָּוִד עַל־כָּל־יִשְׂרָאֵל וַיְהִי דָוִד עֹשֶׂה מִשְׁפָּט וּצְדָקָה לְכָל־עַמּוֹ:

va-yim-LOKH da-VID al kol yis-ra-AYL vai-HEE da-VID o-SEH mish-PAT utz-da-KAH l'-khol a-MO

16 *Yoav* son of *Tzeruya* was commander of the army; *Yehoshafat* son of *Achilud* was recorder;

וְיוֹאָב בֶּן־צְרוּיָה עַל־הַצָּבָא וִיהוֹשָׁפָט בֶּן־אֲחִילוּד מַזְכִּיר:

17 *Tzadok* son of *Achituv* and *Achimelech* son of *Evyatar* were *Kohanim*; *Seraya* was scribe;

וְצָדוֹק בֶּן־אֲחִיטוּב וַאֲחִימֶלֶךְ בֶּן־אֶבְיָתָר כֹּהֲנִים וּשְׂרָיָה סוֹפֵר:

18 Benaiah son of *Yehoyada* was commander of the Cherethites and the Pelethites; and *David's* sons were *Kohanim*.

וּבְנָיָהוּ בֶּן־יְהוֹיָדָע וְהַכְּרֵתִי וְהַפְּלֵתִי וּבְנֵי דָוִד כֹּהֲנִים הָיוּ:

9 1 *David* inquired, "Is there anyone still left of the House of *Shaul* with whom I can keep faith for the sake of *Yehonatan*?"

וַיֹּאמֶר דָּוִד הֲכִי יֶשׁ־עוֹד אֲשֶׁר נוֹתַר לְבֵית שָׁאוּל וְאֶעֱשֶׂה עִמּוֹ חֶסֶד בַּעֲבוּר יְהוֹנָתָן:

2 There was a servant of the House of *Shaul* named Ziba, and they summoned him to *David*. "Are you Ziba?" the king asked him. "Yes, sir," he replied.

וּלְבֵית שָׁאוּל עֶבֶד וּשְׁמוֹ צִיבָא וַיִּקְרְאוּ־לוֹ אֶל־דָּוִד וַיֹּאמֶר הַמֶּלֶךְ אֵלָיו הַאַתָּה צִיבָא וַיֹּאמֶר עַבְדֶּךָ:

3 The king continued, "Is there anyone at all left of the House of *Shaul* with whom I can keep faith as pledged before *Hashem*?" Ziba answered the king, "Yes, there is still a son of *Yehonatan* whose feet are crippled."

וַיֹּאמֶר הַמֶּלֶךְ הַאֶפֶס עוֹד אִישׁ לְבֵית שָׁאוּל וְאֶעֱשֶׂה עִמּוֹ חֶסֶד אֱלֹהִים וַיֹּאמֶר צִיבָא אֶל־הַמֶּלֶךְ עוֹד בֵּן לִיהוֹנָתָן נְכֵה רַגְלָיִם:

4 "Where is he?" the king asked, and Ziba said to the king, "He is in the house of Machir son of Ammiel, in Lo-debar."

וַיֹּאמֶר־לוֹ הַמֶּלֶךְ אֵיפֹה הוּא וַיֹּאמֶר צִיבָא אֶל־הַמֶּלֶךְ הִנֵּה־הוּא בֵּית מָכִיר בֶּן־עַמִּיאֵל בְּלוֹ דְבָר:

5 King *David* had him brought from the house of Machir son of Ammiel, at Lo-debar;

וַיִּשְׁלַח הַמֶּלֶךְ דָּוִד וַיִּקָּחֵהוּ מִבֵּית מָכִיר בֶּן־עַמִּיאֵל מִלּוֹ דְבָר:

6 and when *Mefiboshet* son of *Yehonatan* son of *Shaul* came to *David*, he flung himself on his face and prostrated himself. *David* said, "*Mefiboshet*!" and he replied, "At your service, sir."

וַיָּבֹא מְפִיבֹשֶׁת בֶּן־יְהוֹנָתָן בֶּן־שָׁאוּל אֶל־דָּוִד וַיִּפֹּל עַל־פָּנָיו וַיִּשְׁתָּחוּ וַיֹּאמֶר דָּוִד מְפִיבֹשֶׁת וַיֹּאמֶר הִנֵּה עַבְדֶּךָ:

8:15 *David* **executed true justice among all his people** King *David* was an ideal king, not only because of his military prowess, and not even because of the beautiful Psalms he wrote, but because he ruled the nation with "true justice among all his people." The medieval commentator *Ralbag*, also known as Gersonides, notes that the emphasis on "true justice" indicates that King *David* does not rule only with pure justice, which always follows the "letter of the law." He goes beyond that, practicing righteousness to make sure that everyone gets not only that to which they are legally entitled, but whatever they need. This commitment to the highest level of ethics epitomizes the righteous reign of King *David* in the eyes of God.

Shmuel II / II Samuel
Chapter 9

שמואל ב
פרק ט

7 *David* said to him, "Don't be afraid, for I will keep faith with you for the sake of your father *Yehonatan*. I will give you back all the land of your grandfather *Shaul*; moreover, you shall always eat at my table."

ז וַיֹּאמֶר לוֹ דָוִד אַל־תִּירָא כִּי עָשֹׂה אֶעֱשֶׂה עִמְּךָ חֶסֶד בַּעֲבוּר יְהוֹנָתָן אָבִיךָ וַהֲשִׁבֹתִי לְךָ אֶת־כָּל־שְׂדֵה שָׁאוּל אָבִיךָ וְאַתָּה תֹּאכַל לֶחֶם עַל־שֻׁלְחָנִי תָּמִיד:

8 [*Mefiboshet*] prostrated himself again, and said, "What is your servant, that you should show regard for a dead dog like me?"

ח וַיִּשְׁתַּחוּ וַיֹּאמֶר מֶה עַבְדֶּךָ כִּי פָנִיתָ אֶל־הַכֶּלֶב הַמֵּת אֲשֶׁר כָּמוֹנִי:

9 The king summoned Ziba, *Shaul*'s steward, and said to him, "I give to your master's grandson everything that belonged to *Shaul* and to his entire family.

ט וַיִּקְרָא הַמֶּלֶךְ אֶל־צִיבָא נַעַר שָׁאוּל וַיֹּאמֶר אֵלָיו כֹּל אֲשֶׁר הָיָה לְשָׁאוּל וּלְכָל־בֵּיתוֹ נָתַתִּי לְבֶן־אֲדֹנֶיךָ:

10 You and your sons and your slaves shall farm the land for him and shall bring in [its yield] to provide food for your master's grandson to live on; but *Mefiboshet*, your master's grandson, shall always eat at my table." – Ziba had fifteen sons and twenty slaves. –

י וְעָבַדְתָּ לּוֹ אֶת־הָאֲדָמָה אַתָּה וּבָנֶיךָ וַעֲבָדֶיךָ וְהֵבֵאתָ וְהָיָה לְבֶן־אֲדֹנֶיךָ לֶּחֶם וַאֲכָלוֹ וּמְפִיבֹשֶׁת בֶּן־אֲדֹנֶיךָ יֹאכַל תָּמִיד לֶחֶם עַל־שֻׁלְחָנִי וּלְצִיבָא חֲמִשָּׁה עָשָׂר בָּנִים וְעֶשְׂרִים עֲבָדִים:

11 Ziba said to the king, "Your servant will do just as my lord the king has commanded him." "*Mefiboshet* shall eat at my table like one of the king's sons."

יא וַיֹּאמֶר צִיבָא אֶל־הַמֶּלֶךְ כְּכֹל אֲשֶׁר יְצַוֶּה אֲדֹנִי הַמֶּלֶךְ אֶת־עַבְדּוֹ כֵּן יַעֲשֶׂה עַבְדֶּךָ וּמְפִיבֹשֶׁת אֹכֵל עַל־שֻׁלְחָנִי כְּאַחַד מִבְּנֵי הַמֶּלֶךְ:

12 *Mefiboshet* had a young son named Mica; and all the members of Ziba's household worked for *Mefiboshet*.

יב וְלִמְפִיבֹשֶׁת בֵּן־קָטָן וּשְׁמוֹ מִיכָא וְכֹל מוֹשַׁב בֵּית־צִיבָא עֲבָדִים לִמְפִיבֹשֶׁת:

13 *Mefiboshet* lived in *Yerushalayim*, for he ate regularly at the king's table. He was lame in both feet.

יג וּמְפִיבֹשֶׁת יֹשֵׁב בִּירוּשָׁלַםִ כִּי עַל־שֻׁלְחַן הַמֶּלֶךְ תָּמִיד הוּא אֹכֵל וְהוּא פִּסֵּחַ שְׁתֵּי רַגְלָיו:

um-fee-VO-shet yo-SHAYV bee-ru-sha-LA-yim KEE al shul-KHAN ha-ME-lekh ta-MEED HU o-KHAYL v'-HU fi-SAY-akh sh'-TAY rag-LAV

9:13 Mefiboshet lived in Yerushalayim For the sake of his beloved friend *Yehonatan*, King *David* gives *Mefiboshet* a place at his table in the royal palace in *Yerushalayim*. As *Yerushalayim* is the city of peace, it stands to reason that this is the place where King *David* made such a peaceful gesture. Hashem intends for *Yerushalayim* to be a place where all of Israel will be content with one another. To that end, the holy capital city is not the property of any one tribe. Rather, it belongs to the entire nation, and is the eternal religious and political center of the entire Jewish people. Nir Barkat, mayor of Jerusalem, emphasized this idea in an article he published in honor of Jerusalem Day. He wrote, "My vision for the future of the city of Jerusalem is rooted in the past. Three thousand years ago, the Land of Israel was divided into allotments for each of the twelve tribes – except for the city of Jerusalem. Instead, Jerusalem was designated as a city for all; it was to remain an open, uniting and united capital. Jerusalem became the center of the world, with leadership, innovation and inspiration emanating from the city.... Forty-nine years ago, the capital of the Jewish people and the State of Israel were reunited, allowing the city to live up to its promise as a center for all people, with respect toward all religions.... A united Jerusalem is the only viable option for a vibrant and thriving Jerusalem. This is our future. This is Jerusalem."

Jerusalem Mayor Nir Barkat (b. 1959)

Shmuel II / II Samuel
Chapter 10

שמואל ב
פרק י

10 ¹ Some time afterward, the king of Ammon died, and his son Hanun succeeded him as king.

² *David* said, "I will keep faith with Hanun son of Nahash, just as his father kept faith with me." He sent his courtiers with a message of condolence to him over his father. But when *David*'s courtiers came to the land of Ammon,

³ the Ammonite officials said to their lord Hanun, "Do you think *David* is really honoring your father just because he sent you men with condolences? Why, *David* has sent his courtiers to you to explore and spy out the city, and to overthrow it."

⁴ So Hanun seized *David*'s courtiers, clipped off one side of their beards and cut away half of their garments at the buttocks, and sent them off.

⁵ When *David* was told of it, he dispatched men to meet them, for the men were greatly embarrassed. And the king gave orders: "Stop in *Yericho* until your beards grow back; then you can return."

⁶ The Ammonites realized that they had incurred the wrath of *David*; so the Ammonites sent agents and hired Arameans of Bethrehob and Arameans of Zobah – 20,000 foot soldiers – the king of Maacah [with] 1,000 men, and 12,000 men from Tob.

⁷ On learning this, *David* sent out *Yoav* and the whole army – [including] the professional fighters.

⁸ The Ammonites marched out and took up their battle position at the entrance of the gate, while the Arameans of Zobah and Rehob and the men of Tob and Maacah took their stand separately in the open.

⁹ *Yoav* saw that there was a battle line against him both front and rear. So he made a selection from all the picked men of *Yisrael* and arrayed them against the Arameans,

¹⁰ and the rest of the troops he put under the command of his brother *Avishai* and arrayed them against the Ammonites.

¹¹ [*Yoav*] said, "If the Arameans prove too strong for me, you come to my aid; and if the Ammonites prove too strong for you, I will come to your aid.

Shmuel II/II Samuel
Chapter 11

שמואל ב
פרק יא

12 Let us be strong and resolute for the sake of our people and the land of our God; and *Hashem* will do what He deems right."

חֲזַק וְנִתְחַזַּק בְּעַד־עַמֵּנוּ וּבְעַד עָרֵי אֱלֹהֵינוּ וַיהֹוָה יַעֲשֶׂה הַטּוֹב בְּעֵינָיו:

kha-ZAK v'-nit-kha-ZAK b'-AD a-MAY-nu uv-AD a-RAY e-lo-HAY-nu va-do-NAI ya-a-SEH ha-TOV b'-ay-NAV

13 *Yoav* and the troops with him marched into battle against the Arameans, who fled before him.

וַיִּגַּשׁ יוֹאָב וְהָעָם אֲשֶׁר עִמּוֹ לַמִּלְחָמָה בַּאֲרָם וַיָּנֻסוּ מִפָּנָיו:

14 And when the Ammonites saw that the Arameans had fled, they fled before *Avishai* and withdrew into the city. So *Yoav* broke off the attack against the Ammonites, and went to *Yerushalayim*.

וּבְנֵי עַמּוֹן רָאוּ כִּי־נָס אֲרָם וַיָּנֻסוּ מִפְּנֵי אֲבִישַׁי וַיָּבֹאוּ הָעִיר וַיָּשָׁב יוֹאָב מֵעַל בְּנֵי עַמּוֹן וַיָּבֹא יְרוּשָׁלָם:

15 When the Arameans saw that they had been routed by *Yisrael*, they regrouped their forces.

וַיַּרְא אֲרָם כִּי נִגַּף לִפְנֵי יִשְׂרָאֵל וַיֵּאָסְפוּ יָחַד:

16 Hadadezer sent for and brought out the Arameans from across the Euphrates; they came to Helam, led by Shobach, Hadadezer's army commander.

וַיִּשְׁלַח הֲדַדְעֶזֶר וַיֹּצֵא אֶת־אֲרָם אֲשֶׁר מֵעֵבֶר הַנָּהָר וַיָּבֹאוּ חֵילָם וְשׁוֹבַךְ שַׂר־צְבָא הֲדַדְעֶזֶר לִפְנֵיהֶם:

17 *David* was informed of it; he assembled all *Yisrael*, crossed the *Yarden*, and came to Helam. The Arameans drew up their forces against *David* and attacked him;

וַיֻּגַּד לְדָוִד וַיֶּאֱסֹף אֶת־כָּל־יִשְׂרָאֵל וַיַּעֲבֹר אֶת־הַיַּרְדֵּן וַיָּבֹא חֵלָאמָה וַיַּעַרְכוּ אֲרָם לִקְרַאת דָּוִד וַיִּלָּחֲמוּ עִמּוֹ:

18 but the Arameans were put to flight by *Yisrael*. *David* killed 700 Aramean charioteers and 40,000 horsemen; he also struck down Shobach, Hadadezer's army commander, who died there.

וַיָּנָס אֲרָם מִפְּנֵי יִשְׂרָאֵל וַיַּהֲרֹג דָּוִד מֵאֲרָם שְׁבַע מֵאוֹת רֶכֶב וְאַרְבָּעִים אֶלֶף פָּרָשִׁים וְאֵת שׁוֹבַךְ שַׂר־צְבָאוֹ הִכָּה וַיָּמָת שָׁם:

19 And when all the vassal kings of Hadadezer saw that they had been routed by *Yisrael*, they submitted to *Yisrael* and became their vassals. And the Arameans were afraid to help the Ammonites any more.

וַיִּרְאוּ כָל־הַמְּלָכִים עַבְדֵי הֲדַדְעֶזֶר כִּי נִגְּפוּ לִפְנֵי יִשְׂרָאֵל וַיַּשְׁלִמוּ אֶת־יִשְׂרָאֵל וַיַּעַבְדוּם וַיִּרְאוּ אֲרָם לְהוֹשִׁיעַ עוֹד אֶת־בְּנֵי עַמּוֹן:

11 1 At the turn of the year, the season when kings go out [to battle], *David* sent *Yoav* with his officers and all *Yisrael* with him, and they devastated Ammon and besieged Rabbah; *David* remained in *Yerushalayim*.

יא א וַיְהִי לִתְשׁוּבַת הַשָּׁנָה לְעֵת צֵאת הַמַּלְאכִים וַיִּשְׁלַח דָּוִד אֶת־יוֹאָב וְאֶת־עֲבָדָיו עִמּוֹ וְאֶת־כָּל־יִשְׂרָאֵל וַיַּשְׁחִתוּ אֶת־בְּנֵי עַמּוֹן וַיָּצֻרוּ עַל־רַבָּה וְדָוִד יוֹשֵׁב בִּירוּשָׁלָם:

10:12 Let us be strong and resolute for the sake of our people and the land of our God *Yoav* instructs his soldiers in much the same way as today's soldiers of Israel are instructed. The soldiers must strengthen themselves to go into battle, fighting to protect the People of Israel and the cities of God. *Hashem* will respond by doing what is right in His eyes. *Ralbag* notes that in most cases, God expects of humans to do their part and not to rely on a miracle. Once people do what is expected, *Hashem* may choose to provide miracles and redemption. Nowadays, this is a daily occurrence for the soldiers of the Israeli Defense Forces, who strengthen themselves for battle and have often been rewarded by God with miracles.

Shmuel II/II Samuel

Chapter 11

שמואל ב
פרק יא

2 Late one afternoon, *David* rose from his couch and strolled on the roof of the royal palace; and from the roof he saw a woman bathing. The woman was very beautiful,

ב וַיְהִ֣י לְעֵ֣ת הָעֶ֗רֶב וַיָּ֨קׇם דָּוִ֜ד מֵעַ֤ל מִשְׁכָּבוֹ֙ וַיִּתְהַלֵּךְ֙ עַל־גַּ֣ג בֵּית־הַמֶּ֔לֶךְ וַיַּ֥רְא אִשָּׁ֛ה רֹחֶ֖צֶת מֵעַ֣ל הַגָּ֑ג וְהָ֣אִשָּׁ֔ה טוֹבַ֥ת מַרְאֶ֖ה מְאֹֽד׃

3 and the king sent someone to make inquiries about the woman. He reported, "She is *Batsheva* daughter of Eliam [and] wife of *Uriya* the Hittite."

ג וַיִּשְׁלַ֣ח דָּוִ֔ד וַיִּדְרֹ֖שׁ לָאִשָּׁ֑ה וַיֹּ֗אמֶר הֲלוֹא־זֹאת֙ בַּת־שֶׁ֣בַע בַּת־אֱלִיעָ֔ם אֵ֖שֶׁת אוּרִיָּ֥ה הַחִתִּֽי׃

4 *David* sent messengers to fetch her; she came to him and he lay with her – she had just purified herself after her period – and she went back home.

ד וַיִּשְׁלַח֩ דָּוִ֨ד מַלְאָכִ֜ים וַיִּקָּחֶ֗הָ וַתָּב֤וֹא אֵלָיו֙ וַיִּשְׁכַּ֣ב עִמָּ֔הּ וְהִ֥יא מִתְקַדֶּ֖שֶׁת מִטֻּמְאָתָ֑הּ וַתָּ֖שׇׁב אֶל־בֵּיתָֽהּ׃

va-yish-LAKH da-VID mal-a-KHEEM va-yi-ka-KHE-ha va-ta-VO ay-LAV va-yish-KAV i-MAH v'-HEE mit-ka-DE-shet mi-tum-a-TAH va-TA-shov el bay-TAH

5 The woman conceived, and she sent word to *David*, "I am pregnant."

ה וַתַּ֖הַר הָאִשָּׁ֑ה וַתִּשְׁלַח֙ וַתַּגֵּ֣ד לְדָוִ֔ד וַתֹּ֖אמֶר הָרָ֥ה אָנֹֽכִי׃

6 Thereupon *David* sent a message to *Yoav*, "Send *Uriya* the Hittite to me"; and *Yoav* sent *Uriya* to *David*.

ו וַיִּשְׁלַ֤ח דָּוִד֙ אֶל־יוֹאָ֔ב שְׁלַ֣ח אֵלַ֔י אֶת־אֽוּרִיָּ֖ה הַחִתִּ֑י וַיִּשְׁלַ֥ח יוֹאָ֛ב אֶת־אֽוּרִיָּ֖ה אֶל־דָּוִֽד׃

7 When *Uriya* came to him, *David* asked him how *Yoav* and the troops were faring and how the war was going.

ז וַיָּבֹ֥א אוּרִיָּ֖ה אֵלָ֑יו וַיִּשְׁאַ֣ל דָּוִ֗ד לִשְׁל֤וֹם יוֹאָב֙ וְלִשְׁל֣וֹם הָעָ֔ם וְלִשְׁל֖וֹם הַמִּלְחָמָֽה׃

8 Then *David* said to *Uriya*, "Go down to your house and bathe your feet." When *Uriya* left the royal palace, a present from the king followed him.

ח וַיֹּ֤אמֶר דָּוִד֙ לְא֣וּרִיָּ֔ה רֵ֥ד לְבֵיתְךָ֖ וּרְחַ֣ץ רַגְלֶ֑יךָ וַיֵּצֵ֤א אֽוּרִיָּה֙ מִבֵּ֣ית הַמֶּ֔לֶךְ וַתֵּצֵ֥א אַחֲרָ֖יו מַשְׂאַ֥ת הַמֶּֽלֶךְ׃

9 But *Uriya* slept at the entrance of the royal palace, along with the other officers of his lord, and did not go down to his house.

ט וַיִּשְׁכַּ֣ב אוּרִיָּ֗ה פֶּ֚תַח בֵּ֣ית הַמֶּ֔לֶךְ אֵ֖ת כׇּל־עַבְדֵ֣י אֲדֹנָ֑יו וְלֹ֥א יָרַ֖ד אֶל־בֵּיתֽוֹ׃

10 When *David* was told that *Uriya* had not gone down to his house, he said to *Uriya*, "You just came from a journey; why didn't you go down to your house?"

י וַיַּגִּ֤דוּ לְדָוִד֙ לֵאמֹ֔ר לֹא־יָרַ֥ד אוּרִיָּ֖ה אֶל־בֵּית֑וֹ וַיֹּ֨אמֶר דָּוִ֜ד אֶל־אוּרִיָּ֗ה הֲל֤וֹא מִדֶּ֙רֶךְ֙ אַתָּ֣ה בָ֔א מַדּ֖וּעַ לֹא־יָרַ֥דְתָּ אֶל־בֵּיתֶֽךָ׃

11:4 *David* sent messengers to fetch her The incident of *David* and *Batsheva* is quite difficult to understand. How could such a righteous king seemingly succumb to such behavior? The Sages of the Talmud (*Shabbat* 56a) teach that while his actions were wrong, technically speaking, King *David* did not commit adultery. The soldiers of ancient Israel's army were accustomed to grant their wives a conditional bill of divorce prior to going to battle, so that if they were captured or went missing, their wives could remarry. Therefore, at the time of the sin, *Batsheva* was technically not married. Yet, despite this technicality, the prophet *Natan* tells King *David* he has sinned, and King *David* indeed repents. We are all expected to rise above what may be technically permitted, and live completely moral lives.

Shmuel II/II Samuel
Chapter 11

שמואל ב
פרק יא

11 *Uriya* answered *David*, "The *Aron* and *Yisrael* and *Yehuda* are located at Succoth, and my master *Yoav* and Your Majesty's men are camped in the open; how can I go home and eat and drink and sleep with my wife? As you live, by your very life, I will not do this!"

יא וַיֹּ֨אמֶר אוּרִיָּ֜ה אֶל־דָּוִ֗ד הָ֠אָרוֹן וְיִשְׂרָאֵ֨ל וִֽיהוּדָ֜ה יֹשְׁבִ֣ים בַּסֻּכּ֗וֹת וַאדֹנִ֨י יוֹאָ֜ב וְעַבְדֵ֤י אֲדֹנִי֙ עַל־פְּנֵ֤י הַשָּׂדֶה֙ חֹנִ֔ים וַאֲנִ֞י אָב֧וֹא אֶל־בֵּיתִ֛י לֶאֱכֹ֥ל וְלִשְׁתּ֖וֹת וְלִשְׁכַּ֣ב עִם־אִשְׁתִּ֑י חַיֶּ֙ךָ֙ וְחֵ֣י נַפְשֶׁ֔ךָ אִֽם־אֶעֱשֶׂ֖ה אֶת־הַדָּבָ֥ר הַזֶּֽה:

12 *David* said to *Uriya*, "Stay here today also, and tomorrow I will send you off." So *Uriya* remained in *Yerushalayim* that day. The next day,

יב וַיֹּ֨אמֶר דָּוִ֜ד אֶל־אוּרִיָּ֗ה שֵׁ֥ב בָּזֶ֛ה גַּם־הַיּ֖וֹם וּמָחָ֣ר אֲשַׁלְּחֶ֑ךָּ וַיֵּ֨שֶׁב אוּרִיָּ֧ה בִירוּשָׁלַ֛͏ִם בַּיּ֥וֹם הַה֖וּא וּמִֽמָּחֳרָֽת:

13 *David* summoned him, and he ate and drank with him until he got him drunk; but in the evening, [*Uriya*] went out to sleep in the same place, with his lord's officers; he did not go down to his home.

יג וַיִּקְרָא־ל֣וֹ דָוִ֗ד וַיֹּ֧אכַל לְפָנָ֛יו וַיֵּ֖שְׁתְּ וַֽיְשַׁכְּרֵ֑הוּ וַיֵּצֵ֣א בָעֶ֗רֶב לִשְׁכַּ֤ב בְּמִשְׁכָּבוֹ֙ עִם־עַבְדֵ֣י אֲדֹנָ֔יו וְאֶל־בֵּית֖וֹ לֹ֥א יָרָֽד:

14 In the morning, *David* wrote a letter to *Yoav*, which he sent with *Uriya*.

יד וַיְהִ֣י בַבֹּ֔קֶר וַיִּכְתֹּ֥ב דָּוִ֛ד סֵ֖פֶר אֶל־יוֹאָ֑ב וַיִּשְׁלַ֖ח בְּיַ֥ד אוּרִיָּֽה:

15 He wrote in the letter as follows: "Place *Uriya* in the front line where the fighting is fiercest; then fall back so that he may be killed."

טו וַיִּכְתֹּ֥ב בַּסֵּ֖פֶר לֵאמֹ֑ר הָב֣וּ אֶת־אֽוּרִיָּ֗ה אֶל־מוּל֙ פְּנֵ֤י הַמִּלְחָמָה֙ הַֽחֲזָקָ֔ה וְשַׁבְתֶּ֥ם מֵאַחֲרָ֖יו וְנִכָּ֥ה וָמֵֽת:

16 So when *Yoav* was besieging the city, he stationed *Uriya* at the point where he knew that there were able warriors.

טז וַיְהִ֕י בִּשְׁמ֥וֹר יוֹאָ֖ב אֶל־הָעִ֑יר וַיִּתֵּן֙ אֶת־א֣וּרִיָּ֔ה אֶל־הַמָּקוֹם֙ אֲשֶׁ֣ר יָדַ֔ע כִּ֥י אַנְשֵׁי־חַ֖יִל שָֽׁם:

17 The men of the city sallied out and attacked *Yoav*, and some of *David*'s officers among the troops fell; *Uriya* the Hittite was among those who died.

יז וַיֵּ֨צְא֜וּ אַנְשֵׁ֤י הָעִיר֙ וַיִּלָּחֲמ֣וּ אֶת־יוֹאָ֔ב וַיִּפֹּ֥ל מִן־הָעָ֖ם מֵעַבְדֵ֣י דָוִ֑ד וַיָּ֕מָת גַּ֖ם אוּרִיָּ֥ה הַחִתִּֽי:

18 *Yoav* sent a full report of the battle to *David*.

יח וַיִּשְׁלַ֖ח יוֹאָ֑ב וַיַּגֵּ֣ד לְדָוִ֔ד אֶת־כָּל־דִּבְרֵ֖י הַמִּלְחָמָֽה:

19 He instructed the messenger as follows: "When you finish reporting to the king all about the battle,

יט וַיְצַ֥ו אֶת־הַמַּלְאָ֖ךְ לֵאמֹ֑ר כְּכַלּוֹתְךָ֗ אֵ֛ת כָּל־דִּבְרֵ֥י הַמִּלְחָמָ֖ה לְדַבֵּ֥ר אֶל־הַמֶּֽלֶךְ:

20 the king may get angry and say to you, 'Why did you come so close to the city to attack it? Didn't you know that they would shoot from the wall?

כ וְהָיָ֗ה אִֽם־תַּעֲלֶה֙ חֲמַ֣ת הַמֶּ֔לֶךְ וְאָמַ֣ר לְךָ֔ מַדּ֛וּעַ נִגַּשְׁתֶּ֥ם אֶל־הָעִ֖יר לְהִלָּחֵ֑ם הֲל֣וֹא יְדַעְתֶּ֔ם אֵ֥ת אֲשֶׁר־יֹר֖וּ מֵעַ֥ל הַחוֹמָֽה:

21 Who struck down *Avimelech* son of Jerubbesheth? Was it not a woman who dropped an upper millstone on him from the wall at Thebez, from which he died? Why did you come so close to the wall?' Then say: 'Your servant *Uriya* the Hittite was among those killed.'"

כא מִֽי־הִכָּ֞ה אֶת־אֲבִימֶ֣לֶךְ בֶּן־יְרֻבֶּ֗שֶׁת הֲלוֹא־אִשָּׁ֡ה הִשְׁלִ֣יכָה עָלָיו֩ פֶּ֨לַח רֶ֜כֶב מֵעַ֤ל הַֽחוֹמָה֙ וַיָּ֣מָת בְּתֵבֵ֔ץ לָ֥מָּה נִגַּשְׁתֶּ֖ם אֶל־הַֽחוֹמָ֑ה וְאָ֣מַרְתָּ֔ גַּ֗ם עַבְדְּךָ֛ אוּרִיָּ֥ה הַחִתִּ֖י מֵֽת:

22 The messenger set out; he came and told *David* all that *Yoav* had sent him to say.

כב וַיֵּ֖לֶךְ הַמַּלְאָ֑ךְ וַיָּבֹא֙ וַיַּגֵּ֣ד לְדָוִ֔ד אֵ֛ת כָּל־אֲשֶׁ֥ר שְׁלָח֖וֹ יוֹאָֽב:

23 The messenger said to *David*, "First the men prevailed against us and sallied out against us into the open; then we drove them back up to the entrance to the gate.

כג וַיֹּ֤אמֶר הַמַּלְאָךְ֙ אֶל־דָּוִ֔ד כִּֽי־גָבְר֤וּ עָלֵ֙ינוּ֙ הָ֣אֲנָשִׁ֔ים וַיֵּצְא֥וּ אֵלֵ֖ינוּ הַשָּׂדֶ֑ה וַנִּהְיֶ֥ה עֲלֵיהֶ֖ם עַד־פֶּ֥תַח הַשָּֽׁעַר:

Shmuel II/II Samuel
Chapter 12

24 But the archers shot at your men from the wall and some of Your Majesty's men fell; your servant *Uriya* the Hittite also fell."

25 Whereupon *David* said to the messenger, "Give *Yoav* this message: 'Do not be distressed about the matter. The sword always takes its toll. Press your attack on the city and destroy it!' Encourage him!"

26 When *Uriya*'s wife heard that her husband *Uriya* was dead, she lamented over her husband.

27 After the period of mourning was over, *David* sent and had her brought into his palace; she became his wife and she bore him a son. But *Hashem* was displeased with what *David* had done,

12 1 and *Hashem* sent *Natan* to *David*. He came to him and said, "There were two men in the same city, one rich and one poor.

2 The rich man had very large flocks and herds,

3 but the poor man had only one little ewe lamb that he had bought. He tended it and it grew up together with him and his children: it used to share his morsel of bread, drink from his cup, and nestle in his bosom; it was like a daughter to him.

4 One day, a traveler came to the rich man, but he was loath to take anything from his own flocks or herds to prepare a meal for the guest who had come to him; so he took the poor man's lamb and prepared it for the man who had come to him."

5 *David* flew into a rage against the man, and said to *Natan*, "As *Hashem* lives, the man who did this deserves to die!

6 He shall pay for the lamb four times over, because he did such a thing and showed no pity."

7 And *Natan* said to *David*, "That man is you! Thus said *Hashem*, the God of *Yisrael*: 'It was I who anointed you king over *Yisrael* and it was I who rescued you from the hand of *Shaul*.

8 I gave you your master's house and possession of your master's wives; and I gave you the House of *Yisrael* and *Yehuda*; and if that were not enough, I would give you twice as much more.

שמואל ב
פרק יב

כד וַיֹּראוּ [וַיֹּרוּ] הַמּוֹראִים [הַמּוֹרִים] אֶל־עֲבָדֶךָ מֵעַל הַחוֹמָה וַיָּמוּתוּ מֵעַבְדֵי הַמֶּלֶךְ וְגַם עַבְדְּךָ אוּרִיָּה הַחִתִּי מֵת:

כה וַיֹּאמֶר דָּוִד אֶל־הַמַּלְאָךְ כֹּה־תֹאמַר אֶל־יוֹאָב אַל־יֵרַע בְּעֵינֶיךָ אֶת־הַדָּבָר הַזֶּה כִּי־כָזֹה וְכָזֶה תֹּאכַל הֶחָרֶב הַחֲזֵק מִלְחַמְתְּךָ אֶל־הָעִיר וְהָרְסָהּ וְחַזְּקֵהוּ:

כו וַתִּשְׁמַע אֵשֶׁת אוּרִיָּה כִּי־מֵת אוּרִיָּה אִישָׁהּ וַתִּסְפֹּד עַל־בַּעְלָהּ:

כז וַיַּעֲבֹר הָאֵבֶל וַיִּשְׁלַח דָּוִד וַיַּאַסְפָהּ אֶל־בֵּיתוֹ וַתְּהִי־לוֹ לְאִשָּׁה וַתֵּלֶד לוֹ בֵּן וַיֵּרַע הַדָּבָר אֲשֶׁר־עָשָׂה דָוִד בְּעֵינֵי יְהוָה:

יב א וַיִּשְׁלַח יְהוָה אֶת־נָתָן אֶל־דָּוִד וַיָּבֹא אֵלָיו וַיֹּאמֶר לוֹ שְׁנֵי אֲנָשִׁים הָיוּ בְּעִיר אֶחָת אֶחָד עָשִׁיר וְאֶחָד רָאשׁ:

ב לְעָשִׁיר הָיָה צֹאן וּבָקָר הַרְבֵּה מְאֹד:

ג וְלָרָשׁ אֵין־כֹּל כִּי אִם־כִּבְשָׂה אַחַת קְטַנָּה אֲשֶׁר קָנָה וַיְחַיֶּהָ וַתִּגְדַּל עִמּוֹ וְעִם־בָּנָיו יַחְדָּו מִפִּתּוֹ תֹאכַל וּמִכֹּסוֹ תִשְׁתֶּה וּבְחֵיקוֹ תִשְׁכָּב וַתְּהִי־לוֹ כְּבַת:

ד וַיָּבֹא הֵלֶךְ לְאִישׁ הֶעָשִׁיר וַיַּחְמֹל לָקַחַת מִצֹּאנוֹ וּמִבְּקָרוֹ לַעֲשׂוֹת לָאֹרֵחַ הַבָּא־לוֹ וַיִּקַּח אֶת־כִּבְשַׂת הָאִישׁ הָרָאשׁ וַיַּעֲשֶׂהָ לָאִישׁ הַבָּא אֵלָיו:

ה וַיִּחַר־אַף דָּוִד בָּאִישׁ מְאֹד וַיֹּאמֶר אֶל־נָתָן חַי־יְהוָה כִּי בֶן־מָוֶת הָאִישׁ הָעֹשֶׂה זֹאת:

ו וְאֶת־הַכִּבְשָׂה יְשַׁלֵּם אַרְבַּעְתָּיִם עֵקֶב אֲשֶׁר עָשָׂה אֶת־הַדָּבָר הַזֶּה וְעַל אֲשֶׁר לֹא־חָמָל:

ז וַיֹּאמֶר נָתָן אֶל־דָּוִד אַתָּה הָאִישׁ כֹּה־אָמַר יְהוָה אֱלֹהֵי יִשְׂרָאֵל אָנֹכִי מְשַׁחְתִּיךָ לְמֶלֶךְ עַל־יִשְׂרָאֵל וְאָנֹכִי הִצַּלְתִּיךָ מִיַּד שָׁאוּל:

ח וָאֶתְּנָה לְךָ אֶת־בֵּית אֲדֹנֶיךָ וְאֶת־נְשֵׁי אֲדֹנֶיךָ בְּחֵיקֶךָ וָאֶתְּנָה לְךָ אֶת־בֵּית יִשְׂרָאֵל וִיהוּדָה וְאִם־מְעָט וְאֹסִפָה לְּךָ כָּהֵנָּה וְכָהֵנָּה:

Shmuel II/II Samuel
Chapter 12

9 Why then have you flouted the command of *Hashem* and done what displeases Him? You have put *Uriya* the Hittite to the sword; you took his wife and made her your wife and had him killed by the sword of the Ammonites.

10 Therefore the sword shall never depart from your House – because you spurned Me by taking the wife of *Uriya* the Hittite and making her your wife.'

11 Thus said *Hashem*: 'I will make a calamity rise against you from within your own house; I will take your wives and give them to another man before your very eyes and he shall sleep with your wives under this very sun.

12 You acted in secret, but I will make this happen in the sight of all *Yisrael* and in broad daylight.'"

13 *David* said to *Natan*, "I stand guilty before *Hashem*!" And *Natan* replied to *David*, "*Hashem* has remitted your sin; you shall not die.

14 However, since you have spurned the enemies of *Hashem* by this deed, even the child about to be born to you shall die."

15 *Natan* went home, and *Hashem* afflicted the child that *Uriya*'s wife had borne to *David*, and it became critically ill.

16 *David* entreated *Hashem* for the boy; *David* fasted, and he went in and spent the night lying on the ground.

17 The senior servants of his household tried to induce him to get up from the ground; but he refused, nor would he partake of food with them.

18 On the seventh day the child died. *David*'s servants were afraid to tell *David* that the child was dead; for they said, "We spoke to him when the child was alive and he wouldn't listen to us; how can we tell him that the child is dead? He might do something terrible."

19 When *David* saw his servants talking in whispers, *David* understood that the child was dead; *David* asked his servants, "Is the child dead?" "Yes," they replied.

Shmuel II / II Samuel
Chapter 12

שמואל ב
פרק יב

20 Thereupon *David* rose from the ground; he bathed and anointed himself, and he changed his clothes. He went into the House of *Hashem* and prostrated himself. Then he went home and asked for food, which they set before him, and he ate.

כ וַיָּקָם דָּוִד מֵהָאָרֶץ וַיִּרְחַץ וַיָּסֶךְ וַיְחַלֵּף שמלתו [שִׂמְלֹתָיו] וַיָּבֹא בֵית־יְהֹוָה וַיִּשְׁתָּחוּ וַיָּבֹא אֶל־בֵּיתוֹ וַיִּשְׁאַל וַיָּשִׂימוּ לוֹ לֶחֶם וַיֹּאכַל:

21 His courtiers asked him, "Why have you acted in this manner? While the child was alive, you fasted and wept; but now that the child is dead, you rise and take food!"

כא וַיֹּאמְרוּ עֲבָדָיו אֵלָיו מָה־הַדָּבָר הַזֶּה אֲשֶׁר עָשִׂיתָה בַּעֲבוּר הַיֶּלֶד חַי צַמְתָּ וַתֵּבְךְּ וְכַאֲשֶׁר מֵת הַיֶּלֶד קַמְתָּ וַתֹּאכַל לָחֶם:

22 He replied, "While the child was still alive, I fasted and wept because I thought: 'Who knows? *Hashem* may have pity on me, and the child may live.'

כב וַיֹּאמֶר בְּעוֹד הַיֶּלֶד חַי צַמְתִּי וָאֶבְכֶּה כִּי אָמַרְתִּי מִי יוֹדֵעַ יחנני [וְחַנַּנִי] יְהֹוָה וְחַי הַיָּלֶד:

23 But now that he is dead, why should I fast? Can I bring him back again? I shall go to him, but he will never come back to me."

כג וְעַתָּה מֵת לָמָּה זֶּה אֲנִי צָם הַאוּכַל לַהֲשִׁיבוֹ עוֹד אֲנִי הֹלֵךְ אֵלָיו וְהוּא לֹא־יָשׁוּב אֵלָי:

24 *David* consoled his wife *Batsheva*; he went to her and lay with her. She bore a son and she named him *Shlomo*. *Hashem* favored him,

כד וַיְנַחֵם דָּוִד אֵת בַּת־שֶׁבַע אִשְׁתּוֹ וַיָּבֹא אֵלֶיהָ וַיִּשְׁכַּב עִמָּהּ וַתֵּלֶד בֵּן ויקרא [וַתִּקְרָא] אֶת־שְׁמוֹ שְׁלֹמֹה וַיהֹוָה אֲהֵבוֹ:

vai-na-KHAYM da-VID AYT bat SHE-va ish-TO va-ya-VO ay-LE-ha va-yish-KAV i-MAH va-TAY-led BAYN va-tik-RA et sh'-MO sh'-lo-MOH va-do-NAI a-hay-VO

25 and He sent a message through the *Navi Natan*; and he was named Jedidiah at the instance of *Hashem*.

כה וַיִּשְׁלַח בְּיַד נָתָן הַנָּבִיא וַיִּקְרָא אֶת־שְׁמוֹ יְדִידְיָהּ בַּעֲבוּר יְהֹוָה:

26 *Yoav* attacked Rabbah of Ammon and captured the royal city.

כו וַיִּלָּחֶם יוֹאָב בְּרַבַּת בְּנֵי עַמּוֹן וַיִּלְכֹּד אֶת־עִיר הַמְּלוּכָה:

27 *Yoav* sent messengers to *David* and said, "I have attacked Rabbah and I have already captured the water city.

כז וַיִּשְׁלַח יוֹאָב מַלְאָכִים אֶל־דָּוִד וַיֹּאמֶר נִלְחַמְתִּי בְרַבָּה גַּם־לָכַדְתִּי אֶת־עִיר הַמָּיִם:

28 Now muster the rest of the troops and besiege the city and capture it; otherwise I will capture the city myself, and my name will be connected with it."

כח וְעַתָּה אֱסֹף אֶת־יֶתֶר הָעָם וַחֲנֵה עַל־הָעִיר וְלָכְדָהּ פֶּן־אֶלְכֹּד אֲנִי אֶת־הָעִיר וְנִקְרָא שְׁמִי עָלֶיהָ:

29 *David* mustered all the troops and marched on Rabbah, and he attacked it and captured it.

כט וַיֶּאֱסֹף דָּוִד אֶת־כָּל־הָעָם וַיֵּלֶךְ רַבָּתָה וַיִּלָּחֶם בָּהּ וַיִּלְכְּדָהּ:

12:24 She bore a son and she named him *Shlomo* King *David* repents for what he did, and he and *Batsheva* are blessed with a son. The son is known as Solomon, or in Hebrew, *Shlomo* (שלמה), which comes from the word *shalom* (שלום), 'peace.' Additionally, he is also called by the name Jedidiah, in Hebrew, *Yedidya* (ידידיה), meaning 'beloved of God.' *Radak* suggests that *Hashem* wants his name to be *Shlomo*, as he would be the next king of Israel, and during his rule God would bless him and the People of Israel with peace. But *Shlomo* is also called *Yedidya*, as he is truly the beloved of God. During his reign, the Nation of Israel achieves the greatest heights of peace in the Land of Israel, peace among the People of Israel, and service to *Hashem* in the *Beit Hamikdash*.

שלמה
שלום

Shmuel II / II Samuel — Chapter 13

30 The crown was taken from the head of their king and it was placed on *David*'s head – it weighed a *kikar* of gold, and [on it] were precious stones. He also carried off a vast amount of booty from the city.

31 He led out the people who lived there and set them to work with saws, iron threshing boards, and iron axes, or assigned them to brickmaking; *David* did this to all the towns of Ammon. Then *David* and all the troops returned to *Yerushalayim*.

13 1 This happened sometime afterward: *Avshalom* son of *David* had a beautiful sister named *Tamar*, and *Amnon* son of *David* became infatuated with her.

2 *Amnon* was so distraught because of his [half-]sister *Tamar* that he became sick; for she was a virgin, and it seemed impossible to *Amnon* to do anything to her.

3 *Amnon* had a friend named *Yonadav*, the son of *David*'s brother Shimah; *Yonadav* was a very clever man.

4 He asked him, "Why are you so dejected, O prince, morning after morning? Tell me!" *Amnon* replied, "I am in love with *Tamar*, the sister of my brother *Avshalom*!"

5 *Yonadav* said to him, "Lie down in your bed and pretend you are sick. When your father comes to see you, say to him, 'Let my sister *Tamar* come and give me something to eat. Let her prepare the food in front of me, so that I may look on, and let her serve it to me.'"

6 *Amnon* lay down and pretended to be sick. The king came to see him, and *Amnon* said to the king, "Let my sister *Tamar* come and prepare a couple of cakes in front of me, and let her bring them to me."

7 *David* sent a message to *Tamar* in the palace, "Please go to the house of your brother *Amnon* and prepare some food for him."

8 *Tamar* went to the house of her brother *Amnon*, who was in bed. She took dough and kneaded it into cakes in front of him, and cooked the cakes.

9 She took the pan and set out [the cakes], but *Amnon* refused to eat and ordered everyone to withdraw. After everyone had withdrawn,

ל וַיִּקַּח אֶת־עֲטֶרֶת־מַלְכָּם מֵעַל רֹאשׁוֹ וּמִשְׁקָלָהּ כִּכַּר זָהָב וְאֶבֶן יְקָרָה וַתְּהִי עַל־רֹאשׁ דָּוִד וּשְׁלַל הָעִיר הוֹצִיא הַרְבֵּה מְאֹד:

לא וְאֶת־הָעָם אֲשֶׁר־בָּהּ הוֹצִיא וַיָּשֶׂם בַּמְּגֵרָה וּבַחֲרִצֵי הַבַּרְזֶל וּבְמַגְזְרֹת הַבַּרְזֶל וְהֶעֱבִיר אוֹתָם במלכן [בַּמַּלְבֵּן] וְכֵן יַעֲשֶׂה לְכֹל עָרֵי בְנֵי־עַמּוֹן וַיָּשָׁב דָּוִד וְכָל־הָעָם יְרוּשָׁלָ͏ִם:

יג א וַיְהִי אַחֲרֵי־כֵן וּלְאַבְשָׁלוֹם בֶּן־דָּוִד אָחוֹת יָפָה וּשְׁמָהּ תָּמָר וַיֶּאֱהָבֶהָ אַמְנוֹן בֶּן־דָּוִד:

ב וַיֵּצֶר לְאַמְנוֹן לְהִתְחַלּוֹת בַּעֲבוּר תָּמָר אֲחֹתוֹ כִּי בְתוּלָה הִיא וַיִּפָּלֵא בְּעֵינֵי אַמְנוֹן לַעֲשׂוֹת לָהּ מְאוּמָה:

ג וּלְאַמְנוֹן רֵעַ וּשְׁמוֹ יוֹנָדָב בֶּן־שִׁמְעָה אֲחִי דָוִד וְיוֹנָדָב אִישׁ חָכָם מְאֹד:

ד וַיֹּאמֶר לוֹ מַדּוּעַ אַתָּה כָּכָה דַּל בֶּן־הַמֶּלֶךְ בַּבֹּקֶר בַּבֹּקֶר הֲלוֹא תַּגִּיד לִי וַיֹּאמֶר לוֹ אַמְנוֹן אֶת־תָּמָר אֲחוֹת אַבְשָׁלֹם אָחִי אֲנִי אֹהֵב:

ה וַיֹּאמֶר לוֹ יְהוֹנָדָב שְׁכַב עַל־מִשְׁכָּבְךָ וְהִתְחָל וּבָא אָבִיךָ לִרְאוֹתֶךָ וְאָמַרְתָּ אֵלָיו תָּבֹא נָא תָמָר אֲחוֹתִי וְתַבְרֵנִי לֶחֶם וְעָשְׂתָה לְעֵינַי אֶת־הַבִּרְיָה לְמַעַן אֲשֶׁר אֶרְאֶה וְאָכַלְתִּי מִיָּדָהּ:

ו וַיִּשְׁכַּב אַמְנוֹן וַיִּתְחָל וַיָּבֹא הַמֶּלֶךְ לִרְאֹתוֹ וַיֹּאמֶר אַמְנוֹן אֶל־הַמֶּלֶךְ תָּבוֹא־נָא תָּמָר אֲחֹתִי וּתְלַבֵּב לְעֵינַי שְׁתֵּי לְבִבוֹת וְאֶבְרֶה מִיָּדָהּ:

ז וַיִּשְׁלַח דָּוִד אֶל־תָּמָר הַבַּיְתָה לֵאמֹר לְכִי נָא בֵּית אַמְנוֹן אָחִיךְ וַעֲשִׂי־לוֹ הַבִּרְיָה:

ח וַתֵּלֶךְ תָּמָר בֵּית אַמְנוֹן אָחִיהָ וְהוּא שֹׁכֵב וַתִּקַּח אֶת־הַבָּצֵק ותלוש [וַתָּלָשׁ] וַתְּלַבֵּב לְעֵינָיו וַתְּבַשֵּׁל אֶת־הַלְּבִבוֹת:

ט וַתִּקַּח אֶת־הַמַּשְׂרֵת וַתִּצֹק לְפָנָיו וַיְמָאֵן לֶאֱכוֹל וַיֹּאמֶר אַמְנוֹן הוֹצִיאוּ כָל־אִישׁ מֵעָלַי וַיֵּצְאוּ כָל־אִישׁ מֵעָלָיו:

Shmuel II / II Samuel
Chapter 13

10 *Amnon* said to *Tamar*, "Bring the food inside and feed me." *Tamar* took the cakes she had made and brought them to her brother inside.

11 But when she served them to him, he caught hold of her and said to her, "Come lie with me, sister."

12 But she said to him, "Don't, brother. Don't force me. Such things are not done in *Yisrael*! Don't do such a vile thing!

13 Where will I carry my shame? And you, you will be like any of the scoundrels in *Yisrael*! Please, speak to the king; he will not refuse me to you."

14 But he would not listen to her; he overpowered her and lay with her by force.

15 Then *Amnon* felt a very great loathing for her; indeed, his loathing for her was greater than the passion he had felt for her. And *Amnon* said to her, "Get out!"

16 She pleaded with him, "Please don't commit this wrong; to send me away would be even worse than the first wrong you committed against me." But he would not listen to her.

17 He summoned his young attendant and said, "Get that woman out of my presence, and bar the door behind her." –

18 She was wearing an ornamented tunic, for maiden princesses were customarily dressed in such garments. – His attendant took her outside and barred the door after her.

19 *Tamar* put dust on her head and rent the ornamented tunic she was wearing; she put her hands on her head, and walked away, screaming loudly as she went.

20 Her brother *Avshalom* said to her, "Was it your brother *Amnon* who did this to you? For the present, sister, keep quiet about it; he is your brother. Don't brood over the matter." And *Tamar* remained in her brother *Avshalom*'s house, forlorn.

שמואל ב
פרק יג

י וַיֹּאמֶר אַמְנוֹן אֶל־תָּמָר הָבִיאִי הַבִּרְיָה הַחֶדֶר וְאֶבְרֶה מִיָּדֵךְ וַתִּקַּח תָּמָר אֶת־הַלְּבִבוֹת אֲשֶׁר עָשָׂתָה וַתָּבֵא לְאַמְנוֹן אָחִיהָ הֶחָדְרָה׃

יא וַתַּגֵּשׁ אֵלָיו לֶאֱכֹל וַיַּחֲזֶק־בָּהּ וַיֹּאמֶר לָהּ בּוֹאִי שִׁכְבִי עִמִּי אֲחוֹתִי׃

יב וַתֹּאמֶר לוֹ אַל־אָחִי אַל־תְּעַנֵּנִי כִּי לֹא־יֵעָשֶׂה כֵן בְּיִשְׂרָאֵל אַל־תַּעֲשֵׂה אֶת־הַנְּבָלָה הַזֹּאת׃

יג וַאֲנִי אָנָה אוֹלִיךְ אֶת־חֶרְפָּתִי וְאַתָּה תִּהְיֶה כְּאַחַד הַנְּבָלִים בְּיִשְׂרָאֵל וְעַתָּה דַּבֶּר־נָא אֶל־הַמֶּלֶךְ כִּי לֹא יִמְנָעֵנִי מִמֶּךָּ׃

יד וְלֹא אָבָה לִשְׁמֹעַ בְּקוֹלָהּ וַיֶּחֱזַק מִמֶּנָּה וַיְעַנֶּהָ וַיִּשְׁכַּב אֹתָהּ׃

טו וַיִּשְׂנָאֶהָ אַמְנוֹן שִׂנְאָה גְּדוֹלָה מְאֹד כִּי גְדוֹלָה הַשִּׂנְאָה אֲשֶׁר שְׂנֵאָהּ מֵאַהֲבָה אֲשֶׁר אֲהֵבָהּ וַיֹּאמֶר־לָהּ אַמְנוֹן קוּמִי לֵכִי׃

טז וַתֹּאמֶר לוֹ אַל־אוֹדֹת הָרָעָה הַגְּדוֹלָה הַזֹּאת מֵאַחֶרֶת אֲשֶׁר־עָשִׂיתָ עִמִּי לְשַׁלְּחֵנִי וְלֹא אָבָה לִשְׁמֹעַ לָהּ׃

יז וַיִּקְרָא אֶת־נַעֲרוֹ מְשָׁרְתוֹ וַיֹּאמֶר שִׁלְחוּ־נָא אֶת־זֹאת מֵעָלַי הַחוּצָה וּנְעֹל הַדֶּלֶת אַחֲרֶיהָ׃

יח וְעָלֶיהָ כְּתֹנֶת פַּסִּים כִּי כֵן תִּלְבַּשְׁןָ בְנוֹת־הַמֶּלֶךְ הַבְּתוּלֹת מְעִילִים וַיֹּצֵא אוֹתָהּ מְשָׁרְתוֹ הַחוּץ וְנָעַל הַדֶּלֶת אַחֲרֶיהָ׃

יט וַתִּקַּח תָּמָר אֵפֶר עַל־רֹאשָׁהּ וּכְתֹנֶת הַפַּסִּים אֲשֶׁר עָלֶיהָ קָרָעָה וַתָּשֶׂם יָדָהּ עַל־רֹאשָׁהּ וַתֵּלֶךְ הָלוֹךְ וְזָעָקָה׃

כ וַיֹּאמֶר אֵלֶיהָ אַבְשָׁלוֹם אָחִיהָ הַאֲמִינוֹן אָחִיךְ הָיָה עִמָּךְ וְעַתָּה אֲחוֹתִי הַחֲרִישִׁי אָחִיךְ הוּא אַל־תָּשִׁיתִי אֶת־לִבֵּךְ לַדָּבָר הַזֶּה וַתֵּשֶׁב תָּמָר וְשֹׁמֵמָה בֵּית אַבְשָׁלוֹם אָחִיהָ׃

Shmuel II / II Samuel
Chapter 13

שמואל ב
פרק יג

21 When King *David* heard about all this, he was greatly upset.

וְהַמֶּ֣לֶךְ דָּוִ֗ד שָׁמַ֕ע אֵ֥ת כָּל־הַדְּבָרִ֖ים הָאֵ֑לֶּה וַיִּ֥חַר ל֖וֹ מְאֹֽד׃ כא

v'-ha-ME-lekh da-VID sha-MA AYT kol ha-d'-va-REEM ha-AY-leh va-yi-KHAR LO m'-OD

22 *Avshalom* didn't utter a word to *Amnon*, good or bad; but *Avshalom* hated *Amnon* because he had violated his sister *Tamar*.

וְלֹֽא־דִבֶּ֧ר אַבְשָׁל֛וֹם עִם־אַמְנ֖וֹן לְמֵרָ֣ע וְעַד־ט֑וֹב כִּֽי־שָׂנֵ֤א אַבְשָׁלוֹם֙ אֶת־אַמְנ֔וֹן עַל־דְּבַר֙ אֲשֶׁ֣ר עִנָּ֔ה אֵ֖ת תָּמָ֥ר אֲחֹתֽוֹ׃ כב

23 Two years later, when *Avshalom* was having his flocks sheared at Baal-hazor near *Efraim*, *Avshalom* invited all the king's sons.

וַֽיְהִי֙ לִשְׁנָתַ֣יִם יָמִ֔ים וַיִּהְי֤וּ גֹֽזְזִים֙ לְאַבְשָׁל֔וֹם בְּבַ֥עַל חָצ֖וֹר אֲשֶׁ֣ר עִם־אֶפְרָ֑יִם וַיִּקְרָ֥א אַבְשָׁל֖וֹם לְכָל־בְּנֵ֥י הַמֶּֽלֶךְ׃ כג

24 And *Avshalom* came to the king and said, "Your servant is having his flocks sheared. Would Your Majesty and your retinue accompany your servant?"

וַיָּבֹ֤א אַבְשָׁלוֹם֙ אֶל־הַמֶּ֔לֶךְ וַיֹּ֕אמֶר הִנֵּה־נָ֥א גֹזְזִ֖ים לְעַבְדֶּ֑ךָ יֵֽלֶךְ־נָ֥א הַמֶּ֛לֶךְ וַעֲבָדָ֖יו עִם־עַבְדֶּֽךָ׃ כד

25 But the king answered *Avshalom*, "No, my son. We must not all come, or we'll be a burden to you." He urged him, but he would not go, and he said goodbye to him.

וַיֹּ֨אמֶר הַמֶּ֜לֶךְ אֶל־אַבְשָׁל֗וֹם אַל־בְּנִי֙ אַל־נָ֣א נֵלֵ֣ךְ כֻּלָּ֔נוּ וְלֹ֥א נִכְבַּ֖ד עָלֶ֑יךָ וַיִּפְרָץ־בּ֛וֹ וְלֹא־אָבָ֥ה לָלֶ֖כֶת וַֽיְבָרְכֵֽהוּ׃ כה

26 Thereupon *Avshalom* said, "In that case, let my brother *Amnon* come with us," to which the king replied, "He shall not go with you."

וַיֹּ֙אמֶר֙ אַבְשָׁל֔וֹם וָלֹ֕א יֵֽלֶךְ־נָ֥א אִתָּ֖נוּ אַמְנ֣וֹן אָחִ֑י וַיֹּ֤אמֶר לוֹ֙ הַמֶּ֔לֶךְ לָ֥מָּה יֵלֵ֖ךְ עִמָּֽךְ׃ כו

27 But *Avshalom* urged him, and he sent with him *Amnon* and all the other princes.

וַיִּפְרָץ־בּ֖וֹ אַבְשָׁל֑וֹם וַיִּשְׁלַ֤ח אִתּוֹ֙ אֶת־אַמְנ֔וֹן וְאֵ֖ת כָּל־בְּנֵ֥י הַמֶּֽלֶךְ׃ כז

28 Now *Avshalom* gave his attendants these orders: "Watch, and when *Amnon* is merry with wine and I tell you to strike down *Amnon*, kill him! Don't be afraid, for it is I who give you the order. Act with determination, like brave men!"

וַיְצַו֩ אַבְשָׁל֨וֹם אֶת־נְעָרָ֜יו לֵאמֹ֗ר רְא֣וּ נָ֠א כְּט֨וֹב לֵב־אַמְנ֤וֹן בַּיַּ֙יִן֙ וְאָמַרְתִּ֣י אֲלֵיכֶ֔ם הַכּ֧וּ אֶת־אַמְנ֛וֹן וַהֲמִתֶּ֥ם אֹת֖וֹ אַל־תִּירָ֑אוּ הֲל֗וֹא כִּ֤י אָֽנֹכִי֙ צִוִּ֣יתִי אֶתְכֶ֔ם חִזְק֖וּ וִהְי֥וּ לִבְנֵי־חָֽיִל׃ כח

29 *Avshalom*'s attendants did to *Amnon* as *Avshalom* had ordered; whereupon all the other princes mounted their mules and fled.

וַֽיַּעֲשׂ֞וּ נַעֲרֵ֤י אַבְשָׁלוֹם֙ לְאַמְנ֔וֹן כַּאֲשֶׁ֥ר צִוָּ֖ה אַבְשָׁל֑וֹם וַיָּקֻ֣מוּ ׀ כָּל־בְּנֵ֣י הַמֶּ֗לֶךְ וַֽיִּרְכְּב֛וּ אִ֥ישׁ עַל־פִּרְדּ֖וֹ וַיָּנֻֽסוּ׃ כט

13:21 When King *David* heard about all this, he was greatly upset One of the Bible's many gifts to the world is its emphasis on sexual morality. *Hashem* commands the observance of strict standards that elevate sexuality from mere physicality to the realm of holiness (see Leviticus, chapters 18 and 20). In addition to the spiritual benefits of these laws, they serve to protect women from physical and sexual abuse. Therefore, the debased actions of *Amnon* are a violation of every biblical norm and greatly anger his father, King *David*.

Shmuel II/II Samuel
Chapter 14

שמואל ב
פרק יד

30 They were still on the road when a rumor reached *David* that *Avshalom* had killed all the princes, and that not one of them had survived.

לוַיְהִי הֵמָּה בַדֶּרֶךְ וְהַשְּׁמֻעָה בָאָה אֶל־דָּוִד לֵאמֹר הִכָּה אַבְשָׁלוֹם אֶת־כָּל־בְּנֵי הַמֶּלֶךְ וְלֹא־נוֹתַר מֵהֶם אֶחָד:

31 At this, *David* rent his garment and lay down on the ground, and all his courtiers stood by with their clothes rent.

לאוַיָּקָם הַמֶּלֶךְ וַיִּקְרַע אֶת־בְּגָדָיו וַיִּשְׁכַּב אָרְצָה וְכָל־עֲבָדָיו נִצָּבִים קְרֻעֵי בְגָדִים:

32 But *Yonadav*, the son of *David*'s brother Shimah, said, "My lord must not think that all the young princes have been killed. Only *Amnon* is dead; for this has been decided by *Avshalom* ever since his sister *Tamar* was violated.

לבוַיַּעַן יוֹנָדָב בֶּן־שִׁמְעָה אֲחִי־דָוִד וַיֹּאמֶר אַל־יֹאמַר אֲדֹנִי אֵת כָּל־הַנְּעָרִים בְּנֵי־הַמֶּלֶךְ הֵמִיתוּ כִּי־אַמְנוֹן לְבַדּוֹ מֵת כִּי־עַל־פִּי אַבְשָׁלוֹם הָיְתָה שׂוּמָה מִיּוֹם עַנֹּתוֹ אֵת תָּמָר אֲחֹתוֹ:

33 So my lord the king must not think for a moment that all the princes are dead; *Amnon* alone is dead."

לגוְעַתָּה אַל־יָשֵׂם אֲדֹנִי הַמֶּלֶךְ אֶל־לִבּוֹ דָּבָר לֵאמֹר כָּל־בְּנֵי הַמֶּלֶךְ מֵתוּ כִּי־אִם־אַמְנוֹן לְבַדּוֹ מֵת:

34 Meanwhile *Avshalom* had fled. The watchman on duty looked up and saw a large crowd coming from the road to his rear, from the side of the hill.

לדוַיִּבְרַח אַבְשָׁלוֹם וַיִּשָּׂא הַנַּעַר הַצֹּפֶה אֶת־עֵינָו [עֵינָיו] וַיַּרְא וְהִנֵּה עַם־רַב הֹלְכִים מִדֶּרֶךְ אַחֲרָיו מִצַּד הָהָר:

35 *Yonadav* said to the king, "See, the princes have come! It is just as your servant said."

להוַיֹּאמֶר יוֹנָדָב אֶל־הַמֶּלֶךְ הִנֵּה בְנֵי־הַמֶּלֶךְ בָּאוּ כִּדְבַר עַבְדְּךָ כֵּן הָיָה:

36 As he finished speaking, the princes came in and broke into weeping; and *David* and all his courtiers wept bitterly, too.

לווַיְהִי כְּכַלֹּתוֹ לְדַבֵּר וְהִנֵּה בְנֵי־הַמֶּלֶךְ בָּאוּ וַיִּשְׂאוּ קוֹלָם וַיִּבְכּוּ וְגַם־הַמֶּלֶךְ וְכָל־עֲבָדָיו בָּכוּ בְּכִי גָּדוֹל מְאֹד:

37 *Avshalom* had fled, and he came to Talmai son of Ammihud, king of Geshur. And [King *David*] mourned over his son a long time.

לזוְאַבְשָׁלוֹם בָּרַח וַיֵּלֶךְ אֶל־תַּלְמַי בֶּן־עַמִּיחוּר [עַמִּיהוּד] מֶלֶךְ גְּשׁוּר וַיִּתְאַבֵּל עַל־בְּנוֹ כָּל־הַיָּמִים:

38 *Avshalom*, who had fled to Geshur, remained there three years.

לחוְאַבְשָׁלוֹם בָּרַח וַיֵּלֶךְ גְּשׁוּר וַיְהִי־שָׁם שָׁלֹשׁ שָׁנִים:

39 And King *David* was pining away for *Avshalom*, for [the king] had gotten over *Amnon*'s death.

לטוַתְּכַל דָּוִד הַמֶּלֶךְ לָצֵאת אֶל־אַבְשָׁלוֹם כִּי־נִחַם עַל־אַמְנוֹן כִּי־מֵת:

14 1 *Yoav* son of *Tzeruya* could see that the king's mind was on *Avshalom*;

יד אוַיֵּדַע יוֹאָב בֶּן־צְרֻיָה כִּי־לֵב הַמֶּלֶךְ עַל־אַבְשָׁלוֹם:

2 so *Yoav* sent to *Tekoa* and brought a clever woman from there. He said to her, "Pretend you are in mourning; put on mourning clothes and don't anoint yourself with oil; and act like a woman who has grieved a long time over a departed one.

בוַיִּשְׁלַח יוֹאָב תְּקוֹעָה וַיִּקַּח מִשָּׁם אִשָּׁה חֲכָמָה וַיֹּאמֶר אֵלֶיהָ הִתְאַבְּלִי־נָא וְלִבְשִׁי־נָא בִגְדֵי־אֵבֶל וְאַל־תָּסוּכִי שֶׁמֶן וְהָיִית כְּאִשָּׁה זֶה יָמִים רַבִּים מִתְאַבֶּלֶת עַל־מֵת:

va-yish-LAKH yo-AV t'-KO-ah va-yi-KAKH mi-SHAM i-SHAH kha-kha-MAH va-YO-mer ay-LE-ha hit-a-b'-lee NA v'-liv-shee NA vig-day AY-vel v'-al ta-SU-khee SHE-men v'-ha-YEET k'-i-SHAH ZEH ya-MEEM ra-BEEM mit-a-BE-let al MAYT

14:2 So *Yoav* sent to *Tekoa* According to *Rashi*, the biblical town of *Tekoa*, located near both *Yerushalayim* and *Chevron*, was well known for its abundance of both olive oil and wisdom. Today, the modern community of *Tekoa* is an important part of the *Gush Etzion* region of Judea. It is home to over 750 Jewish

Ariel view of Tekoa

Shmuel II / II Samuel
Chapter 14

שמואל ב
פרק יד

3 Go to the king and say to him thus and thus." And Yoav told her what to say.	ג וּבָאת אֶל־הַמֶּלֶךְ וְדִבַּרְתְּ אֵלָיו כַּדָּבָר הַזֶּה וַיָּשֶׂם יוֹאָב אֶת־הַדְּבָרִים בְּפִיהָ:
4 The woman of *Tekoa* came to the king, flung herself face down to the ground, and prostrated herself. She cried out, "Help, O king!"	ד וַתֹּאמֶר הָאִשָּׁה הַתְּקֹעִית אֶל־הַמֶּלֶךְ וַתִּפֹּל עַל־אַפֶּיהָ אַרְצָה וַתִּשְׁתָּחוּ וַתֹּאמֶר הוֹשִׁעָה הַמֶּלֶךְ:
5 The king asked her, "What troubles you?" And she answered, "Alas, I am a widow, my husband is dead.	ה וַיֹּאמֶר־לָהּ הַמֶּלֶךְ מַה־לָּךְ וַתֹּאמֶר אֲבָל אִשָּׁה־אַלְמָנָה אָנִי וַיָּמָת אִישִׁי:
6 Your maidservant had two sons. The two of them came to blows out in the fields where there was no one to stop them, and one of them struck the other and killed him.	ו וּלְשִׁפְחָתְךָ שְׁנֵי בָנִים וַיִּנָּצוּ שְׁנֵיהֶם בַּשָּׂדֶה וְאֵין מַצִּיל בֵּינֵיהֶם וַיַּכּוֹ הָאֶחָד אֶת־הָאֶחָד וַיָּמֶת אֹתוֹ:
7 Then the whole clan confronted your maidservant and said, 'Hand over the one who killed his brother, that we may put him to death for the slaying of his brother, even though we wipe out the heir.' Thus they would quench the last ember remaining to me, and leave my husband without name or remnant upon the earth."	ז וְהִנֵּה קָמָה כָל־הַמִּשְׁפָּחָה עַל־שִׁפְחָתֶךָ וַיֹּאמְרוּ תְּנִי אֶת־מַכֵּה אָחִיו וּנְמִתֵהוּ בְּנֶפֶשׁ אָחִיו אֲשֶׁר הָרָג וְנַשְׁמִידָה גַּם אֶת־הַיּוֹרֵשׁ וְכִבּוּ אֶת־גַּחַלְתִּי אֲשֶׁר נִשְׁאָרָה לְבִלְתִּי שום־[שִׂים־] לְאִישִׁי שֵׁם וּשְׁאֵרִית עַל־פְּנֵי הָאֲדָמָה:
8 The king said to the woman, "Go home. I will issue an order in your behalf."	ח וַיֹּאמֶר הַמֶּלֶךְ אֶל־הָאִשָּׁה לְכִי לְבֵיתֵךְ וַאֲנִי אֲצַוֶּה עָלָיִךְ:
9 And the woman of *Tekoa* said to the king, "My lord king, may the guilt be on me and on my ancestral house; Your Majesty and his throne are guiltless."	ט וַתֹּאמֶר הָאִשָּׁה הַתְּקוֹעִית אֶל־הַמֶּלֶךְ עָלַי אֲדֹנִי הַמֶּלֶךְ הֶעָוֹן וְעַל־בֵּית אָבִי וְהַמֶּלֶךְ וְכִסְאוֹ נָקִי:
10 The king said, "If anyone says anything more to you, have him brought to me, and he will never trouble you again."	י וַיֹּאמֶר הַמֶּלֶךְ הַמְדַבֵּר אֵלַיִךְ וַהֲבֵאתוֹ אֵלַי וְלֹא־יֹסִיף עוֹד לָגַעַת בָּךְ:
11 She replied, "Let Your Majesty be mindful of *Hashem* your God and restrain the blood avenger bent on destruction, so that my son may not be killed." And he said, "As *Hashem* lives, not a hair of your son shall fall to the ground."	יא וַתֹּאמֶר יִזְכָּר־נָא הַמֶּלֶךְ אֶת־יְהוָה אֱלֹהֶיךָ מהרבית [מֵהַרְבַּת] גֹּאֵל הַדָּם לְשַׁחֵת וְלֹא יַשְׁמִידוּ אֶת־בְּנִי וַיֹּאמֶר חַי־יְהוָה אִם־יִפֹּל מִשַּׂעֲרַת בְּנֵךְ אָרְצָה:
12 Then the woman said, "Please let your maidservant say another word to my lord the king." "Speak on," said the king.	יב וַתֹּאמֶר הָאִשָּׁה תְּדַבֶּר־נָא שִׁפְחָתְךָ אֶל־אֲדֹנִי הַמֶּלֶךְ דָּבָר וַיֹּאמֶר דַּבֵּרִי:

families, and is known throughout Israel as a community where Orthodox and secular Jews live together in mutual respect and harmony. It is also known for its efforts to forge peaceful ties with neighboring Arab villages.

Shmuel II/II Samuel
Chapter 14

13 And the woman said, "Why then have you planned the like against *Hashem*'s people? In making this pronouncement, Your Majesty condemns himself in that Your Majesty does not bring back his own banished one.

14 We must all die; we are like water that is poured out on the ground and cannot be gathered up. *Hashem* will not take away the life of one who makes plans so that no one may be kept banished.

15 And the reason I have come to say these things to the king, my lord, is that the people have frightened me. Your maidservant thought I would speak to Your Majesty; perhaps Your Majesty would act on his handmaid's plea.

16 For Your Majesty would surely agree to deliver his handmaid from the hands of anyone [who would seek to] cut off both me and my son from the heritage of *Hashem*.

17 Your maidservant thought, 'Let the word of my lord the king provide comfort; for my lord the king is like an angel of *Hashem*, understanding everything, good and bad.' May *Hashem* your God be with you."

18 In reply, the king said to the woman, "Do not withhold from me anything I ask you!" The woman answered, "Let my lord the king speak."

19 The king asked, "Is *Yoav* in league with you in all this?" The woman replied, "As you live, my lord the king, it is just as my lord the king says. Yes, your servant *Yoav* was the one who instructed me, and it was he who told your maidservant everything she was to say.

20 It was to conceal the real purpose of the matter that your servant *Yoav* did this thing. My lord is as wise as an angel of *Hashem*, and he knows all that goes on in the land."

21 Then the king said to *Yoav*, "I will do this thing. Go and bring back my boy *Avshalom*."

שמואל ב
פרק יד

יג וַתֹּאמֶר הָאִשָּׁה וְלָמָּה חָשַׁבְתָּה כָּזֹאת עַל־עַם אֱלֹהִים וּמִדַּבֵּר הַמֶּלֶךְ הַדָּבָר הַזֶּה כְּאָשֵׁם לְבִלְתִּי הָשִׁיב הַמֶּלֶךְ אֶת־נִדְּחוֹ׃

יד כִּי־מוֹת נָמוּת וְכַמַּיִם הַנִּגָּרִים אַרְצָה אֲשֶׁר לֹא יֵאָסֵפוּ וְלֹא־יִשָּׂא אֱלֹהִים נֶפֶשׁ וְחָשַׁב מַחֲשָׁבוֹת לְבִלְתִּי יִדַּח מִמֶּנּוּ נִדָּח׃

טו וְעַתָּה אֲשֶׁר־בָּאתִי לְדַבֵּר אֶל־הַמֶּלֶךְ אֲדֹנִי אֶת־הַדָּבָר הַזֶּה כִּי יֵרְאֻנִי הָעָם וַתֹּאמֶר שִׁפְחָתְךָ אֲדַבְּרָה־נָּא אֶל־הַמֶּלֶךְ אוּלַי יַעֲשֶׂה הַמֶּלֶךְ אֶת־דְּבַר אֲמָתוֹ׃

טז כִּי יִשְׁמַע הַמֶּלֶךְ לְהַצִּיל אֶת־אֲמָתוֹ מִכַּף הָאִישׁ לְהַשְׁמִיד אֹתִי וְאֶת־בְּנִי יַחַד מִנַּחֲלַת אֱלֹהִים׃

יז וַתֹּאמֶר שִׁפְחָתְךָ יִהְיֶה־נָּא דְבַר־אֲדֹנִי הַמֶּלֶךְ לִמְנוּחָה כִּי כְּמַלְאַךְ הָאֱלֹהִים כֵּן אֲדֹנִי הַמֶּלֶךְ לִשְׁמֹעַ הַטּוֹב וְהָרָע וַיהֹוָה אֱלֹהֶיךָ יְהִי עִמָּךְ׃

יח וַיַּעַן הַמֶּלֶךְ וַיֹּאמֶר אֶל־הָאִשָּׁה אַל־נָא תְכַחֲדִי מִמֶּנִּי דָּבָר אֲשֶׁר אָנֹכִי שֹׁאֵל אֹתָךְ וַתֹּאמֶר הָאִשָּׁה יְדַבֶּר־נָא אֲדֹנִי הַמֶּלֶךְ׃

יט וַיֹּאמֶר הַמֶּלֶךְ הֲיַד יוֹאָב אִתָּךְ בְּכָל־זֹאת וַתַּעַן הָאִשָּׁה וַתֹּאמֶר חֵי־נַפְשְׁךָ אֲדֹנִי הַמֶּלֶךְ אִם־אִשׁ לְהֵמִין וּלְהַשְׂמִיל מִכֹּל אֲשֶׁר־דִּבֶּר אֲדֹנִי הַמֶּלֶךְ כִּי־עַבְדְּךָ יוֹאָב הוּא צִוָּנִי וְהוּא שָׂם בְּפִי שִׁפְחָתְךָ אֵת כָּל־הַדְּבָרִים הָאֵלֶּה׃

כ לְבַעֲבוּר סַבֵּב אֶת־פְּנֵי הַדָּבָר עָשָׂה עַבְדְּךָ יוֹאָב אֶת־הַדָּבָר הַזֶּה וַאדֹנִי חָכָם כְּחָכְמַת מַלְאַךְ הָאֱלֹהִים לָדַעַת אֶת־כָּל־אֲשֶׁר בָּאָרֶץ׃

כא וַיֹּאמֶר הַמֶּלֶךְ אֶל־יוֹאָב הִנֵּה־נָא עָשִׂיתִי אֶת־הַדָּבָר הַזֶּה וְלֵךְ הָשֵׁב אֶת־הַנַּעַר אֶת־אַבְשָׁלוֹם׃

Shmuel II / II Samuel
Chapter 14

22 *Yoav* flung himself face down on the ground and prostrated himself. *Yoav* blessed the king and said, "Today your servant knows that he has found favor with you, my lord king, for Your Majesty has granted his servant's request."

23 And *Yoav* went at once to Geshur and brought *Avshalom* to *Yerushalayim*.

24 But the king said, "Let him go directly to his house and not present himself to me." So *Avshalom* went directly to his house and did not present himself to the king.

25 No one in all *Yisrael* was so admired for his beauty as *Avshalom*; from the sole of his foot to the crown of his head he was without blemish.

26 When he cut his hair – he had to have it cut every year, for it grew too heavy for him – the hair of his head weighed two hundred *shekalim* by the royal weight.

27 *Avshalom* had three sons and a daughter whose name was *Tamar*; she was a beautiful woman.

28 *Avshalom* lived in *Yerushalayim* two years without appearing before the king.

29 Then *Avshalom* sent for *Yoav*, in order to send him to the king; but *Yoav* would not come to him. He sent for him a second time, but he would not come.

30 So [*Avshalom*] said to his servants, "Look, *Yoav*'s field is next to mine, and he has barley there. Go and set it on fire." And *Avshalom*'s servants set the field on fire.

31 *Yoav* came at once to *Avshalom*'s house and said to him, "Why did your servants set fire to my field?"

32 *Avshalom* replied to *Yoav*, "I sent for you to come here; I wanted to send you to the king to say [on my behalf]: 'Why did I leave Geshur? I would be better off if I were still there. Now let me appear before the king; and if I am guilty of anything, let him put me to death!'"

33 *Yoav* went to the king and reported to him; whereupon he summoned *Avshalom*. He came to the king and flung himself face down to the ground before the king. And the king kissed *Avshalom*.

Shmuel II / II Samuel
Chapter 15

15 **1** Sometime afterward, *Avshalom* provided himself with a chariot, horses, and fifty outrunners.

2 *Avshalom* used to rise early and stand by the road to the city gates; and whenever a man had a case that was to come before the king for judgment, *Avshalom* would call out to him, "What town are you from?" And when he answered, "Your servant is from such and such a tribe in *Yisrael*,"

3 *Avshalom* would say to him, "It is clear that your claim is right and just, but there is no one assigned to you by the king to hear it."

4 And *Avshalom* went on, "If only I were appointed judge in the land and everyone with a legal dispute came before me, I would see that he got his rights."

5 And if a man approached to bow to him, [*Avshalom*] would extend his hand and take hold of him and kiss him.

6 *Avshalom* did this to every Israelite who came to the king for judgment. Thus *Avshalom* won away the hearts of the men of *Yisrael*.

7 After a period of forty years had gone by, *Avshalom* said to the king, "Let me go to *Chevron* and fulfill a vow that I made to *Hashem*.

8 For your servant made a vow when I lived in Geshur of Aram: If *Hashem* ever brings me back to *Yerushalayim*, I will worship *Hashem*."

9 The king said to him, "Go in peace"; and so he set out for *Chevron*.

10 But *Avshalom* sent agents to all the tribes of *Yisrael* to say, "When you hear the blast of the horn, announce that *Avshalom* has become king in *Chevron*."

11 Two hundred men of *Yerushalayim* accompanied *Avshalom*; they were invited and went in good faith, suspecting nothing.

12 *Avshalom* also sent [to fetch] *Achitofel* the Gilonite, *David*'s counselor, from his town, Giloh, when the sacrifices were to be offered. The conspiracy gained strength, and the people supported *Avshalom* in increasing numbers.

שמואל ב
פרק טו

טו **א** וַיְהִי מֵאַחֲרֵי כֵן וַיַּעַשׂ לוֹ אַבְשָׁלוֹם מֶרְכָּבָה וְסֻסִים וַחֲמִשִּׁים אִישׁ רָצִים לְפָנָיו:

ב וְהִשְׁכִּים אַבְשָׁלוֹם וְעָמַד עַל־יַד דֶּרֶךְ הַשָּׁעַר וַיְהִי כָּל־הָאִישׁ אֲשֶׁר־יִהְיֶה־לּוֹ־רִיב לָבוֹא אֶל־הַמֶּלֶךְ לַמִּשְׁפָּט וַיִּקְרָא אַבְשָׁלוֹם אֵלָיו וַיֹּאמֶר אֵי־מִזֶּה עִיר אַתָּה וַיֹּאמֶר מֵאַחַד שִׁבְטֵי־יִשְׂרָאֵל עַבְדֶּךָ:

ג וַיֹּאמֶר אֵלָיו אַבְשָׁלוֹם רְאֵה דְבָרֶךָ טוֹבִים וּנְכֹחִים וְשֹׁמֵעַ אֵין־לְךָ מֵאֵת הַמֶּלֶךְ:

ד וַיֹּאמֶר אַבְשָׁלוֹם מִי־יְשִׂמֵנִי שֹׁפֵט בָּאָרֶץ וְעָלַי יָבוֹא כָּל־אִישׁ אֲשֶׁר־יִהְיֶה־לּוֹ־רִיב וּמִשְׁפָּט וְהִצְדַּקְתִּיו:

ה וְהָיָה בִּקְרָב־אִישׁ לְהִשְׁתַּחֲוֹת לוֹ וְשָׁלַח אֶת־יָדוֹ וְהֶחֱזִיק לוֹ וְנָשַׁק לוֹ:

ו וַיַּעַשׂ אַבְשָׁלוֹם כַּדָּבָר הַזֶּה לְכָל־יִשְׂרָאֵל אֲשֶׁר־יָבֹאוּ לַמִּשְׁפָּט אֶל־הַמֶּלֶךְ וַיְגַנֵּב אַבְשָׁלוֹם אֶת־לֵב אַנְשֵׁי יִשְׂרָאֵל:

ז וַיְהִי מִקֵּץ אַרְבָּעִים שָׁנָה וַיֹּאמֶר אַבְשָׁלוֹם אֶל־הַמֶּלֶךְ אֵלֲכָה נָּא וַאֲשַׁלֵּם אֶת־נִדְרִי אֲשֶׁר־נָדַרְתִּי לַיהוָה בְּחֶבְרוֹן:

ח כִּי־נֵדֶר נָדַר עַבְדְּךָ בְּשִׁבְתִּי בִגְשׁוּר בַּאֲרָם לֵאמֹר אִם־יָשִׁיב [יָשׁוֹב] יְשִׁיבֵנִי יְהוָה יְרוּשָׁלִַם וְעָבַדְתִּי אֶת־יְהוָה:

ט וַיֹּאמֶר־לוֹ הַמֶּלֶךְ לֵךְ בְּשָׁלוֹם וַיָּקָם וַיֵּלֶךְ חֶבְרוֹנָה:

י וַיִּשְׁלַח אַבְשָׁלוֹם מְרַגְּלִים בְּכָל־שִׁבְטֵי יִשְׂרָאֵל לֵאמֹר כְּשָׁמְעֲכֶם אֶת־קוֹל הַשֹּׁפָר וַאֲמַרְתֶּם מָלַךְ אַבְשָׁלוֹם בְּחֶבְרוֹן:

יא וְאֶת־אַבְשָׁלוֹם הָלְכוּ מָאתַיִם אִישׁ מִירוּשָׁלִַם קְרֻאִים וְהֹלְכִים לְתֻמָּם וְלֹא יָדְעוּ כָּל־דָּבָר:

יב וַיִּשְׁלַח אַבְשָׁלוֹם אֶת־אֲחִיתֹפֶל הַגִּילֹנִי יוֹעֵץ דָּוִד מֵעִירוֹ מִגִּלֹה בְּזָבְחוֹ אֶת־הַזְּבָחִים וַיְהִי הַקֶּשֶׁר אַמִּץ וְהָעָם הוֹלֵךְ וָרָב אֶת־אַבְשָׁלוֹם:

Shmuel II / II Samuel
Chapter 15

13 Someone came and told *David*, "The loyalty of the men of *Yisrael* has veered toward *Avshalom*."

14 Whereupon *David* said to all the courtiers who were with him in *Yerushalayim*, "Let us flee at once, or none of us will escape from *Avshalom*. We must get away quickly, or he will soon overtake us and bring down disaster upon us and put the city to the sword."

15 The king's courtiers said to the king, "Whatever our lord the king decides, your servants are ready."

16 So the king left, followed by his entire household, except for ten concubines whom the king left to mind the palace.

17 The king left, followed by all the people, and they stopped at the last house.

18 All his followers marched past him, including all the Cherethites and all the Pelethites; and all the Gittites, six hundred men who had accompanied him from Gath, also marched by the king.

19 And the king said to Ittai the Gittite, "Why should you too go with us? Go back and stay with the [new] king, for you are a foreigner and you are also an exile from your country.

20 You came only yesterday; should I make you wander about with us today, when I myself must go wherever I can? Go back, and take your kinsmen with you, [in] true faithfulness."

21 Ittai replied to the king, "As *Hashem* lives and as my lord the king lives, wherever my lord the king may be, there your servant will be, whether for death or for life!"

22 And *David* said to Ittai, "Then march by." And Ittai the Gittite and all his men and all the children who were with him marched by.

23 The whole countryside wept aloud as the troops marched by. The king crossed the Kidron Valley, and all the troops crossed by the road to the wilderness.

24 Then *Tzadok* appeared, with all the *Leviim* carrying the *Aron Brit Hashem*; and they set down the *Aron* of *Hashem* until all the people had finished marching out of the city. *Evyatar* also came up.

Shmuel II/II Samuel
Chapter 15

שמואל ב
פרק טו

25 But the king said to *Tzadok*, "Take the *Aron* of *Hashem* back to the city. If I find favor with *Hashem*, He will bring me back and let me see it and its abode.

כה וַיֹּאמֶר הַמֶּלֶךְ לְצָדוֹק הָשֵׁב אֶת־אֲרוֹן הָאֱלֹהִים הָעִיר אִם־אֶמְצָא חֵן בְּעֵינֵי יְהֹוָה וֶהֱשִׁבַנִי וְהִרְאַנִי אֹתוֹ וְאֶת־נָוֵהוּ:

26 And if He should say, 'I do not want you,' I am ready; let Him do with me as He pleases."

כו וְאִם כֹּה יֹאמַר לֹא חָפַצְתִּי בָּךְ הִנְנִי יַעֲשֶׂה־לִּי כַּאֲשֶׁר טוֹב בְּעֵינָיו:

27 And the king said to the *Kohen Tzadok*, "Do you understand? You return to the safety of the city with your two sons, your own son Ahimaaz and *Evyatar*'s son *Yehonatan*.

כז וַיֹּאמֶר הַמֶּלֶךְ אֶל־צָדוֹק הַכֹּהֵן הֲרוֹאֶה אַתָּה שֻׁבָה הָעִיר בְּשָׁלוֹם וַאֲחִימַעַץ בִּנְךָ וִיהוֹנָתָן בֶּן־אֶבְיָתָר שְׁנֵי בְנֵיכֶם אִתְּכֶם:

28 Look, I shall linger in the steppes of the wilderness until word comes from you to inform me."

כח רְאוּ אָנֹכִי מִתְמַהְמֵהַּ בְּעַבְרוֹת [בְּעַרְבוֹת] הַמִּדְבָּר עַד בּוֹא דָבָר מֵעִמָּכֶם לְהַגִּיד לִי:

29 *Tzadok* and *Evyatar* brought the *Aron* of *Hashem* back to *Yerushalayim*, and they stayed there.

כט וַיָּשֶׁב צָדוֹק וְאֶבְיָתָר אֶת־אֲרוֹן הָאֱלֹהִים יְרוּשָׁלָ͏ִם וַיֵּשְׁבוּ שָׁם:

30 *David* meanwhile went up the slope of the [Mount of] Olives, weeping as he went; his head was covered and he walked barefoot. And all the people who were with him covered their heads and wept as they went up.

ל וְדָוִד עֹלֶה בְמַעֲלֵה הַזֵּיתִים עֹלֶה וּבוֹכֶה וְרֹאשׁ לוֹ חָפוּי וְהוּא הֹלֵךְ יָחֵף וְכָל־הָעָם אֲשֶׁר־אִתּוֹ חָפוּ אִישׁ רֹאשׁוֹ וְעָלוּ עָלֹה וּבָכֹה:

v'-da-VID o-LEH v'-ma-a-LAY ha-zay-TEEM o-LEH u-vo-KHEH v'-ROSH LO kha-FUY v'-HU ho-LAYKH ya-KHAYF v'-khol ha-AM a-sher i-TO kha-FU EESH ro-SHO v'-a-LU a-LOH u-va-KHOH

31 *David* [was] told that *Achitofel* was among the conspirators with *Avshalom*, and he prayed, "Please, *Hashem*, frustrate *Achitofel*'s counsel!"

לא וְדָוִד הִגִּיד לֵאמֹר אֲחִיתֹפֶל בַּקֹּשְׁרִים עִם־אַבְשָׁלוֹם וַיֹּאמֶר דָּוִד סַכֶּל־נָא אֶת־עֲצַת אֲחִיתֹפֶל יְהֹוָה:

32 When *David* reached the top, where people would prostrate themselves to *Hashem*, Hushai the Archite was there to meet him, with his robe torn and with earth on his head.

לב וַיְהִי דָוִד בָּא עַד־הָרֹאשׁ אֲשֶׁר־יִשְׁתַּחֲוֶה שָׁם לֵאלֹהִים וְהִנֵּה לִקְרָאתוֹ חוּשַׁי הָאַרְכִּי קָרוּעַ כֻּתָּנְתּוֹ וַאֲדָמָה עַל־רֹאשׁוֹ:

33 *David* said to him, "If you march on with me, you will be a burden to me.

לג וַיֹּאמֶר לוֹ דָּוִד אִם עָבַרְתָּ אִתִּי וְהָיִתָ עָלַי לְמַשָּׂא:

15:30 *David* meanwhile went up the slope of the [Mount of] Olives In distress, King *David* ascends the Mount of Olives, *Har HaZeitim* (הר הזיתים), the mountain just east of the Temple Mount that later becomes a very significant location for the Jewish people. During the time of the *Beit Hamikdash*, the red heifer, whose ashes are needed for complete ritual purification, is to be slaughtered on *Har HaZeitim*, in view of the Temple. *Har HaZeitim* is also home to the most important Jewish cemetery in Israel, due to its proximity to the Temple Mount. In fact, there is a tradition, based on a verse in *Zecharya* (14:4), that those who are buried on *Har HaZeitim* will be the first to be resurrected in the times of *Mashiach*. *Har HaZeitim* gets its name from the many olive trees that once grew there. According the Sages, the olive branch brought back to *Noach* in the mouth of the dove was taken from an olive tree on *Har HaZeitim*.

Mount of Olives

Shmuel II / II Samuel
Chapter 16

שמואל ב
פרק טז

34 But if you go back to the city and say to *Avshalom*, 'I will be your servant, O king; I was your father's servant formerly, and now I will be yours,' then you can nullify *Achitofel*'s counsel for me.

לד וְאִם־הָעִיר תָּשׁוּב וְאָמַרְתָּ לְאַבְשָׁלוֹם עַבְדְּךָ אֲנִי הַמֶּלֶךְ אֶהְיֶה עֶבֶד אָבִיךָ וַאֲנִי מֵאָז וְעַתָּה וַאֲנִי עַבְדֶּךָ וְהֵפַרְתָּה לִי אֵת עֲצַת אֲחִיתֹפֶל:

35 You will have the *Kohanim Tzadok* and *Evyatar* there, and you can report everything that you hear in the king's palace to the *Kohanim Tzadok* and *Evyatar*.

לה וַהֲלוֹא עִמְּךָ שָׁם צָדוֹק וְאֶבְיָתָר הַכֹּהֲנִים וְהָיָה כָּל־הַדָּבָר אֲשֶׁר תִּשְׁמַע מִבֵּית הַמֶּלֶךְ תַּגִּיד לְצָדוֹק וּלְאֶבְיָתָר הַכֹּהֲנִים:

36 Also, their two sons are there with them, *Tzadok*'s son Ahimaaz and *Evyatar*'s son Yehonatan; and through them you can report to me everything you hear."

לו הִנֵּה־שָׁם עִמָּם שְׁנֵי בְנֵיהֶם אֲחִימַעַץ לְצָדוֹק וִיהוֹנָתָן לְאֶבְיָתָר וּשְׁלַחְתֶּם בְּיָדָם אֵלַי כָּל־דָּבָר אֲשֶׁר תִּשְׁמָעוּ:

37 And so Hushai, the friend of *David*, reached the city as *Avshalom* was entering *Yerushalayim*.

לז וַיָּבֹא חוּשַׁי רֵעֶה דָוִד הָעִיר וְאַבְשָׁלֹם יָבֹא יְרוּשָׁלָ͏ִם:

16 1 *David* had passed a little beyond the summit when Ziba the servant of *Mefiboshet* came toward him with a pair of saddled asses carrying two hundred loaves of bread, one hundred cakes of raisin, one hundred cakes of figs, and a jar of wine.

טז א וְדָוִד עָבַר מְעַט מֵהָרֹאשׁ וְהִנֵּה צִיבָא נַעַר מְפִי־בֹשֶׁת לִקְרָאתוֹ וְצֶמֶד חֲמֹרִים חֲבֻשִׁים וַעֲלֵיהֶם מָאתַיִם לֶחֶם וּמֵאָה צִמּוּקִים וּמֵאָה קַיִץ וְנֵבֶל יָיִן:

2 The king asked Ziba, "What are you doing with these?" Ziba answered, "The asses are for Your Majesty's family to ride on, the bread and figs are for the attendants to eat, and the wine is to be drunk by any who are exhausted in the wilderness."

ב וַיֹּאמֶר הַמֶּלֶךְ אֶל־צִיבָא מָה־אֵלֶּה לָּךְ וַיֹּאמֶר צִיבָא הַחֲמוֹרִים לְבֵית־הַמֶּלֶךְ לִרְכֹּב וְלַלֶּחֶם [וְהַלֶּחֶם] וְהַקַּיִץ לֶאֱכוֹל הַנְּעָרִים וְהַיַּיִן לִשְׁתּוֹת הַיָּעֵף בַּמִּדְבָּר:

3 "And where is your master's son?" the king asked. "He is staying in *Yerushalayim*," Ziba replied to the king, "for he thinks that the House of *Yisrael* will now give him back the throne of his grandfather."

ג וַיֹּאמֶר הַמֶּלֶךְ וְאַיֵּה בֶּן־אֲדֹנֶיךָ וַיֹּאמֶר צִיבָא אֶל־הַמֶּלֶךְ הִנֵּה יוֹשֵׁב בִּירוּשָׁלַ͏ִם כִּי אָמַר הַיּוֹם יָשִׁיבוּ לִי בֵּית יִשְׂרָאֵל אֵת מַמְלְכוּת אָבִי:

va-YO-mer ha-ME-lekh v'-a-YAY ben a-do-NE-kha va-YO-mer tzee-VA el ha-ME-lekh hi-NAY yo-SHAYV bee-ru-sha-LA-yim KEE a-MAR ha-YOM ya-SHEE-vu LEE BAYT yis-ra-AYL AYT mam-l'-KHUT a-VEE

4 The king said to Ziba, "Then all that belongs to *Mefiboshet* is now yours!" And Ziba replied, "I bow low. Your Majesty is most gracious to me."

ד וַיֹּאמֶר הַמֶּלֶךְ לְצִבָא הִנֵּה לְךָ כֹּל אֲשֶׁר לִמְפִי־בֹשֶׁת וַיֹּאמֶר צִיבָא הִשְׁתַּחֲוֵיתִי אֶמְצָא־חֵן בְּעֵינֶיךָ אֲדֹנִי הַמֶּלֶךְ:

16:3 He is staying in *Yerushalayim* *Yerushalayim* is to be both the political and spiritual capital of Israel. It is to be the seat of the monarchy, from where the king and his officers will rule the nation. But it is also to be the location of the Holy Temple and the Supreme Court known as the *Sanhedrin* (סנהדרין). Thus, *Yerushalayim* serves a double function, which allows the People of Israel to be a free and holy nation in the Land of Israel. The prophet *Yeshayahu* (2:3) expresses this when he says, "For instruction shall come forth from *Tzion*, the word of *Hashem* from *Yerushalayim*." Rabbi Abraham Isaac Kook explained that the name *Tzion* refers to the political and national aspects of the city, while *Yerushalayim* refers to its spiritual aspects. Both are essential elements of *Yerushalayim*; together, they allow the Jewish people to fulfill its holy mission.

Shmuel II / II Samuel
Chapter 16

5 As King *David* was approaching Bahurim, a member of *Shaul*'s clan – a man named *Shim'i* son of Gera – came out from there, hurling insults as he came.

6 He threw stones at *David* and all King *David*'s courtiers, while all the troops and all the warriors were at his right and his left.

7 And these are the insults that *Shim'i* hurled: "Get out, get out, you criminal, you villain!

8 *Hashem* is paying you back for all your crimes against the family of *Shaul*, whose throne you seized. *Hashem* is handing over the throne to your son *Avshalom*; you are in trouble because you are a criminal!"

9 *Avishai* son of *Tzeruya* said to the king, "Why let that dead dog abuse my lord the king? Let me go over and cut off his head!"

10 But the king said, "What has this to do with you, you sons of *Tzeruya*? He is abusing [me] only because *Hashem* told him to abuse *David*; and who is to say, 'Why did You do that?'"

11 *David* said further to *Avishai* and all the courtiers, "If my son, my own issue, seeks to kill me, how much more the Benjaminite! Let him go on hurling abuse, for *Hashem* has told him to.

12 Perhaps *Hashem* will look upon my punishment and recompense me for the abuse [*Shim'i*] has uttered today."

13 *David* and his men continued on their way, while *Shim'i* walked alongside on the slope of the hill, insulting him as he walked, and throwing stones at him and flinging dirt.

14 The king and all who accompanied him arrived exhausted, and he rested there.

15 Meanwhile *Avshalom* and all the people, the men of *Yisrael*, arrived in *Yerushalayim*, together with *Achitofel*.

16 When Hushai the Archite, *David*'s friend, came before *Avshalom*, Hushai said to *Avshalom*, "Long live the king! Long live the king!"

17 But *Avshalom* said to Hushai, "Is this your loyalty to your friend? Why didn't you go with your friend?"

Shmuel II / II Samuel

Chapter 17

18 "Not at all!" Hushai replied. "I am for the one whom *Hashem* and this people and all the men of *Yisrael* have chosen, and I will stay with him.

19 Furthermore, whom should I serve, if not *David's* son? As I was in your father's service, so I will be in yours."

20 *Avshalom* then said to *Achitofel*, "What do you advise us to do?"

21 And *Achitofel* said to *Avshalom*, "Have intercourse with your father's concubines, whom he left to mind the palace; and when all *Yisrael* hears that you have dared the wrath of your father, all who support you will be encouraged."

22 So they pitched a tent for *Avshalom* on the roof, and *Avshalom* lay with his father's concubines with the full knowledge of all *Yisrael*. –

23 In those days, the advice which *Achitofel* gave was accepted like an oracle sought from *Hashem*; that is how all the advice of *Achitofel* was esteemed both by *David* and by *Avshalom*.

17 1 And *Achitofel* said to *Avshalom*, "Let me pick twelve thousand men and set out tonight in pursuit of *David*.

2 I will come upon him when he is weary and disheartened, and I will throw him into a panic; and when all the troops with him flee, I will kill the king alone.

3 And I will bring back all the people to you; when all have come back [except] the man you are after, all the people will be at peace."

4 The advice pleased *Avshalom* and all the elders of *Yisrael*.

5 But *Avshalom* said, "Summon Hushai the Archite as well, so we can hear what he too has to say."

6 Hushai came to *Avshalom*, and *Avshalom* said to him, "This is what *Achitofel* has advised. Shall we follow his advice? If not, what do you say?"

7 Hushai said to *Avshalom*, "This time the advice that *Achitofel* has given is not good.

שמואל ב

פרק יז

יח וַיֹּאמֶר חוּשַׁי אֶל־אַבְשָׁלֹם לֹא כִּי אֲשֶׁר בָּחַר יְהֹוָה וְהָעָם הַזֶּה וְכָל־אִישׁ יִשְׂרָאֵל לֹא [לוֹ] אֶהְיֶה וְאִתּוֹ אֵשֵׁב:

יט וְהַשֵּׁנִית לְמִי אֲנִי אֶעֱבֹד הֲלוֹא לִפְנֵי בְנוֹ כַּאֲשֶׁר עָבַדְתִּי לִפְנֵי אָבִיךָ כֵּן אֶהְיֶה לְפָנֶיךָ:

כ וַיֹּאמֶר אַבְשָׁלוֹם אֶל־אֲחִיתֹפֶל הָבוּ לָכֶם עֵצָה מַה־נַּעֲשֶׂה:

כא וַיֹּאמֶר אֲחִיתֹפֶל אֶל־אַבְשָׁלֹם בּוֹא אֶל־פִּלַגְשֵׁי אָבִיךָ אֲשֶׁר הִנִּיחַ לִשְׁמוֹר הַבָּיִת וְשָׁמַע כָּל־יִשְׂרָאֵל כִּי־נִבְאַשְׁתָּ אֶת־אָבִיךָ וְחָזְקוּ יְדֵי כָּל־אֲשֶׁר אִתָּךְ:

כב וַיַּטּוּ לְאַבְשָׁלוֹם הָאֹהֶל עַל־הַגָּג וַיָּבֹא אַבְשָׁלוֹם אֶל־פִּלַגְשֵׁי אָבִיו לְעֵינֵי כָּל־יִשְׂרָאֵל:

כג וַעֲצַת אֲחִיתֹפֶל אֲשֶׁר יָעַץ בַּיָּמִים הָהֵם כַּאֲשֶׁר יִשְׁאַל־[אִישׁ] בִּדְבַר הָאֱלֹהִים כֵּן כָּל־עֲצַת אֲחִיתֹפֶל גַּם־לְדָוִד גַּם לְאַבְשָׁלֹם:

יז א וַיֹּאמֶר אֲחִיתֹפֶל אֶל־אַבְשָׁלֹם אֶבְחֲרָה נָּא שְׁנֵים־עָשָׂר אֶלֶף אִישׁ וְאָקוּמָה וְאֶרְדְּפָה אַחֲרֵי־דָוִד הַלָּיְלָה:

ב וְאָבוֹא עָלָיו וְהוּא יָגֵעַ וּרְפֵה יָדַיִם וְהַחֲרַדְתִּי אֹתוֹ וְנָס כָּל־הָעָם אֲשֶׁר־אִתּוֹ וְהִכֵּיתִי אֶת־הַמֶּלֶךְ לְבַדּוֹ:

ג וְאָשִׁיבָה כָל־הָעָם אֵלֶיךָ כְּשׁוּב הַכֹּל הָאִישׁ אֲשֶׁר אַתָּה מְבַקֵּשׁ כָּל־הָעָם יִהְיֶה שָׁלוֹם:

ד וַיִּישַׁר הַדָּבָר בְּעֵינֵי אַבְשָׁלֹם וּבְעֵינֵי כָּל־זִקְנֵי יִשְׂרָאֵל:

ה וַיֹּאמֶר אַבְשָׁלוֹם קְרָא נָא גַּם לְחוּשַׁי הָאַרְכִּי וְנִשְׁמְעָה מַה־בְּפִיו גַּם־הוּא:

ו וַיָּבֹא חוּשַׁי אֶל־אַבְשָׁלוֹם וַיֹּאמֶר אַבְשָׁלוֹם אֵלָיו לֵאמֹר כַּדָּבָר הַזֶּה דִּבֶּר אֲחִיתֹפֶל הֲנַעֲשֶׂה אֶת־דְּבָרוֹ אִם־אַיִן אַתָּה דַבֵּר:

ז וַיֹּאמֶר חוּשַׁי אֶל־אַבְשָׁלוֹם לֹא־טוֹבָה הָעֵצָה אֲשֶׁר־יָעַץ אֲחִיתֹפֶל בַּפַּעַם הַזֹּאת:

Shmuel II / II Samuel
Chapter 17

8 You know," Hushai continued, "that your father and his men are courageous fighters, and they are as desperate as a bear in the wild robbed of her whelps. Your father is an experienced soldier, and he will not spend the night with the troops;

9 even now he must be hiding in one of the pits or in some other place. And if any of them fall at the first attack, whoever hears of it will say, 'A disaster has struck the troops that follow *Avshalom*';

10 and even if he is a brave man with the heart of a lion, he will be shaken – for all *Yisrael* knows that your father and the soldiers with him are courageous fighters.

11 So I advise that all *Yisrael* from *Dan* to *Be'er Sheva* – as numerous as the sands of the sea – be called up to join you, and that you yourself march into battle.

12 When we come upon him in whatever place he may be, we'll descend on him [as thick] as dew falling on the ground; and no one will survive, neither he nor any of the men with him.

13 And if he withdraws into a city, all *Yisrael* will bring ropes to that city and drag its stones as far as the riverbed, until not even a pebble of it is left."

14 *Avshalom* and all *Yisrael* agreed that the advice of Hushai the Archite was better than that of *Achitofel*. – Hashem had decreed that *Achitofel*'s sound advice be nullified, in order that Hashem might bring ruin upon *Avshalom*.

15 Then Hushai told the *Kohanim Tzadok* and *Evyatar*, "This is what *Achitofel* advised *Avshalom* and the elders of *Yisrael*; this is what I advised.

16 Now send at once and tell *David*, 'Do not spend the night at the fords of the wilderness, but cross over at once; otherwise the king and all the troops with him will be annihilated.'"

17 *Yehonatan* and Ahimaaz were staying at Enrogel, and a slave girl would go and bring them word and they in turn would go and inform King *David*. For they themselves dared not be seen entering the city.

Shmuel II / II Samuel
Chapter 17

שמואל ב
פרק יז

18 But a boy saw them and informed *Avshalom*. They left at once and came to the house of a man in Bahurim who had a well in his courtyard. They got down into it,

יח וַיַּרְא אֹתָם נַעַר וַיַּגֵּד לְאַבְשָׁלֹם וַיֵּלְכוּ שְׁנֵיהֶם מְהֵרָה וַיָּבֹאוּ אֶל־בֵּית־אִישׁ בְּבַחוּרִים וְלוֹ בְאֵר בַּחֲצֵרוֹ וַיֵּרְדוּ שָׁם:

19 and the wife took a cloth, spread it over the mouth of the well, and scattered groats on top of it, so that nothing would be noticed.

יט וַתִּקַּח הָאִשָּׁה וַתִּפְרֹשׂ אֶת־הַמָּסָךְ עַל־פְּנֵי הַבְּאֵר וַתִּשְׁטַח עָלָיו הָרִפוֹת וְלֹא נוֹדַע דָּבָר:

20 When *Avshalom*'s servants came to the woman at the house and asked where Ahimaaz and *Yehonatan* were, the woman told them that they had crossed a bit beyond the water. They searched, but found nothing; and they returned to *Yerushalayim*.

כ וַיָּבֹאוּ עַבְדֵי אַבְשָׁלוֹם אֶל־הָאִשָּׁה הַבַּיְתָה וַיֹּאמְרוּ אַיֵּה אֲחִימַעַץ וִיהוֹנָתָן וַתֹּאמֶר לָהֶם הָאִשָּׁה עָבְרוּ מִיכַל הַמָּיִם וַיְבַקְשׁוּ וְלֹא מָצָאוּ וַיָּשֻׁבוּ יְרוּשָׁלָם:

21 After they were gone, [Ahimaaz and *Yehonatan*] came up from the well and went and informed King *David*. They said to *David*, "Go and cross the water quickly, for *Achitofel* has advised thus and thus concerning you."

כא וַיְהִי אַחֲרֵי לֶכְתָּם וַיַּעֲלוּ מֵהַבְּאֵר וַיֵּלְכוּ וַיַּגִּדוּ לַמֶּלֶךְ דָּוִד וַיֹּאמְרוּ אֶל־דָּוִד קוּמוּ וְעִבְרוּ מְהֵרָה אֶת־הַמַּיִם כִּי־כָכָה יָעַץ עֲלֵיכֶם אֲחִיתֹפֶל:

22 *David* and all the troops with him promptly crossed the *Yarden*, and by daybreak not one was left who had not crossed the *Yarden*.

כב וַיָּקָם דָּוִד וְכָל־הָעָם אֲשֶׁר אִתּוֹ וַיַּעַבְרוּ אֶת־הַיַּרְדֵּן עַד־אוֹר הַבֹּקֶר עַד־אַחַד לֹא נֶעְדָּר אֲשֶׁר לֹא־עָבַר אֶת־הַיַּרְדֵּן:

va-ya-KOM da-VID v'-khol ha-AM a-SHER i-TO va-ya-av-RU et ha-yar-DAYN ad OR ha-BO-ker ad a-KHAD LO ne-DAR a-SHER lo a-VAR et ha-yar-DAYN

23 When *Achitofel* saw that his advice had not been followed, he saddled his ass and went home to his native town. He set his affairs in order, and then he hanged himself. He was buried in his ancestral tomb.

כג וַאֲחִיתֹפֶל רָאָה כִּי לֹא נֶעֶשְׂתָה עֲצָתוֹ וַיַּחֲבֹשׁ אֶת־הַחֲמוֹר וַיָּקָם וַיֵּלֶךְ אֶל־בֵּיתוֹ אֶל־עִירוֹ וַיְצַו אֶל־בֵּיתוֹ וַיֵּחָנַק וַיָּמָת וַיִּקָּבֵר בְּקֶבֶר אָבִיו:

24 *David* had reached Mahanaim when *Avshalom* and all the men of *Yisrael* with him crossed the *Yarden*.

כד וְדָוִד בָּא מַחֲנָיְמָה וְאַבְשָׁלֹם עָבַר אֶת־הַיַּרְדֵּן הוּא וְכָל־אִישׁ יִשְׂרָאֵל עִמּוֹ:

25 *Avshalom* had appointed *Amasa* army commander in place of *Yoav*; *Amasa* was the son of a man named Ithra the Israelite, who had married Abigal, daughter of Nahash and sister of *Yoav*'s mother *Tzeruya*.

כה וְאֶת־עֲמָשָׂא שָׂם אַבְשָׁלֹם תַּחַת יוֹאָב עַל־הַצָּבָא וַעֲמָשָׂא בֶן־אִישׁ וּשְׁמוֹ יִתְרָא הַיִּשְׂרְאֵלִי אֲשֶׁר־בָּא אֶל־אֲבִיגַל בַּת־נָחָשׁ אֲחוֹת צְרוּיָה אֵם יוֹאָב:

26 The Israelites and *Avshalom* encamped in the district of *Gilad*.

כו וַיִּחַן יִשְׂרָאֵל וְאַבְשָׁלֹם אֶרֶץ הַגִּלְעָד:

Jordan River

17:22 *David* and all the troops with him promptly crossed the *Yarden* The Hebrew name for the Jordan river is *Yarden* (ירדן), a word formed from the Hebrew words *yorayd Dan* (יורד דן), which means 'descends [from] Dan.' The territory of Dan is the northernmost part of *Eretz Yisrael*. The Jordan river flows the length of the country from north to south, starting near Dan at the foot of Mount *Chermon*, and ending at the Dead Sea. In its 250 km course, the *Yarden* descends from a height of over 2800 km above sea level to more than 350 km below, making it the river with the lowest elevation in the world.

ירדן

Shmuel II / II Samuel
Chapter 18

שמואל ב
פרק יח

27 When *David* reached Mahanaim, Shobi son of Nahash from Rabbath-ammon, Machir son of Ammiel from Lo-debar, and *Barzilai* the Giladite from Rogelim

כז וַיְהִי כְּבוֹא דָוִד מַחֲנָיְמָה וְשֹׁבִי בֶן־נָחָשׁ מֵרַבַּת בְּנֵי־עַמּוֹן וּמָכִיר בֶּן־עַמִּיאֵל מִלֹּא דְבָר וּבַרְזִלַּי הַגִּלְעָדִי מֵרֹגְלִים:

28 presented* couches, basins, and earthenware; also wheat, barley, flour, parched grain, beans, lentils, parched grain,

כח מִשְׁכָּב וְסַפּוֹת וּכְלִי יוֹצֵר וְחִטִּים וּשְׂעֹרִים וְקֶמַח וְקָלִי וּפוֹל וַעֲדָשִׁים וְקָלִי:

29 honey, curds, a flock, and cheese from the herd for *David* and the troops with him to eat. For they knew that the troops must have grown hungry, faint, and thirsty in the wilderness.

כט וּדְבַשׁ וְחֶמְאָה וְצֹאן וּשְׁפוֹת בָּקָר הִגִּישׁוּ לְדָוִד וְלָעָם אֲשֶׁר־אִתּוֹ לֶאֱכוֹל כִּי אָמְרוּ הָעָם רָעֵב וְעָיֵף וְצָמֵא בַּמִּדְבָּר:

18 1 *David* mustered the troops who were with him and set over them captains of thousands and captains of hundreds.

יח א וַיִּפְקֹד דָּוִד אֶת־הָעָם אֲשֶׁר אִתּוֹ וַיָּשֶׂם עֲלֵיהֶם שָׂרֵי אֲלָפִים וְשָׂרֵי מֵאוֹת:

2 *David* sent out the troops, one-third under the command of *Yoav*, one-third under the command of *Yoav*'s brother *Avishai* son of *Tzeruya*, and one-third under the command of Ittai the Gittite. And *David* said to the troops, "I myself will march out with you."

ב וַיְשַׁלַּח דָּוִד אֶת־הָעָם הַשְּׁלִשִׁית בְּיַד־יוֹאָב וְהַשְּׁלִשִׁית בְּיַד אֲבִישַׁי בֶּן־צְרוּיָה אֲחִי יוֹאָב וְהַשְּׁלִשִׁית בְּיַד אִתַּי הַגִּתִּי וַיֹּאמֶר הַמֶּלֶךְ אֶל־הָעָם יָצֹא אֵצֵא גַם־אֲנִי עִמָּכֶם:

3 But the troops replied, "No! For if some of us flee, the rest will not be concerned about us; even if half of us should die, the others will not be concerned about us. But you are worth ten thousand of us. Therefore, it is better for you to support us from the town."

ג וַיֹּאמֶר הָעָם לֹא תֵצֵא כִּי אִם־נֹס נָנוּס לֹא־יָשִׂימוּ אֵלֵינוּ לֵב וְאִם־יָמֻתוּ חֶצְיֵנוּ לֹא־יָשִׂימוּ אֵלֵינוּ לֵב כִּי־עַתָּה כָמֹנוּ עֲשָׂרָה אֲלָפִים וְעַתָּה טוֹב כִּי־תִהְיֶה־לָּנוּ מֵעִיר לַעְזִיר [לַעְזוֹר]:

4 And the king said to them, "I will do whatever you think best." So the king stood beside the gate as all the troops marched out by their hundreds and thousands.

ד וַיֹּאמֶר אֲלֵיהֶם הַמֶּלֶךְ אֲשֶׁר־יִיטַב בְּעֵינֵיכֶם אֶעֱשֶׂה וַיַּעֲמֹד הַמֶּלֶךְ אֶל־יַד הַשַּׁעַר וְכָל־הָעָם יָצְאוּ לְמֵאוֹת וְלַאֲלָפִים:

5 The king gave orders to *Yoav, Avishai,* and Ittai: "Deal gently with my boy *Avshalom,* for my sake." All the troops heard the king give the order about *Avshalom* to all the officers.

ה וַיְצַו הַמֶּלֶךְ אֶת־יוֹאָב וְאֶת־אֲבִישַׁי וְאֶת־אִתַּי לֵאמֹר לְאַט־לִי לַנַּעַר לְאַבְשָׁלוֹם וְכָל־הָעָם שָׁמְעוּ בְּצַוֹּת הַמֶּלֶךְ אֶת־כָּל־הַשָּׂרִים עַל־דְּבַר אַבְשָׁלוֹם:

vai-TZAV ha-ME-lekh et yo-AV v'-et a-vee-SHAI v'-et i-TAI lay-MOR l'-at LEE la-NA-ar l'-av-sha-LOM v'-khol ha-AM sha-m'-U b'-tza-VOT ha-ME-lekh et kol ha-sa-REEM al d'-VAR av-sha-LOM

---

* "presented" brought up from verse 29 for clarity

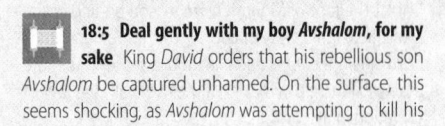

18:5 Deal gently with my boy *Avshalom,* for my sake King *David* orders that his rebellious son *Avshalom* be captured unharmed. On the surface, this seems shocking, as *Avshalom* was attempting to kill his father. Rabbi Shlomo Aviner notes that throughout *David*'s struggles, he retains his attribute of mercy. Thus, though he has no intention of surrendering to King *Shaul* who wants to kill him, *David* nevertheless respects him

Rabbi Shlomo Aviner (b. 1943)

778

Shmuel II / II Samuel
Chapter 18

שְׁמוּאֵל ב
פרק יח

6 The troops marched out into the open to confront the Israelites, and the battle was fought in the forest of *Efraim*.

וַיֵּצֵא הָעָם הַשָּׂדֶה לִקְרַאת יִשְׂרָאֵל וַתְּהִי הַמִּלְחָמָה בְּיַעַר אֶפְרָיִם:

7 The Israelite troops were routed by *David*'s followers, and a great slaughter took place there that day – twenty thousand men.

וַיִּנָּגְפוּ שָׁם עַם יִשְׂרָאֵל לִפְנֵי עַבְדֵי דָוִד וַתְּהִי־שָׁם הַמַּגֵּפָה גְדוֹלָה בַּיּוֹם הַהוּא עֶשְׂרִים אָלֶף:

8 The battle spread out over that whole region, and the forest devoured more troops that day than the sword.

וַתְּהִי־שָׁם הַמִּלְחָמָה נפצית [נָפֹצֶת] עַל־פְּנֵי כָל־הָאָרֶץ וַיֶּרֶב הַיַּעַר לֶאֱכֹל בָּעָם מֵאֲשֶׁר אָכְלָה הַחֶרֶב בַּיּוֹם הַהוּא:

9 *Avshalom* encountered some of *David*'s followers. *Avshalom* was riding on a mule, and as the mule passed under the tangled branches of a great terebinth, his hair got caught in the terebinth; he was held between heaven and earth as the mule under him kept going.

וַיִּקָּרֵא אַבְשָׁלוֹם לִפְנֵי עַבְדֵי דָוִד וְאַבְשָׁלוֹם רֹכֵב עַל־הַפֶּרֶד וַיָּבֹא הַפֶּרֶד תַּחַת שׂוֹבֶךְ הָאֵלָה הַגְּדוֹלָה וַיֶּחֱזַק רֹאשׁוֹ בָאֵלָה וַיֻּתַּן בֵּין הַשָּׁמַיִם וּבֵין הָאָרֶץ וְהַפֶּרֶד אֲשֶׁר־תַּחְתָּיו עָבָר:

10 One of the men saw it and told *Yoav*, "I have just seen *Avshalom* hanging from a terebinth."

וַיַּרְא אִישׁ אֶחָד וַיַּגֵּד לְיוֹאָב וַיֹּאמֶר הִנֵּה רָאִיתִי אֶת־אַבְשָׁלֹם תָּלוּי בָּאֵלָה:

11 *Yoav* said to the man who told him, "You saw it! Why didn't you kill him then and there? I would have owed you ten *shekalim* of silver and a belt."

וַיֹּאמֶר יוֹאָב לָאִישׁ הַמַּגִּיד לוֹ וְהִנֵּה רָאִיתָ וּמַדּוּעַ לֹא־הִכִּיתוֹ שָׁם אָרְצָה וְעָלַי לָתֶת לְךָ עֲשָׂרָה כֶסֶף וַחֲגֹרָה אֶחָת:

12 But the man answered *Yoav*, "Even if I had a thousand *shekalim* of silver in my hands, I would not raise a hand against the king's son. For the king charged you and *Avishai* and Ittai in our hearing, 'Watch over my boy *Avshalom*, for my sake.'

וַיֹּאמֶר הָאִישׁ אֶל־יוֹאָב ולא [וְלוּא] אָנֹכִי שֹׁקֵל עַל־כַּפַּי אֶלֶף כֶּסֶף לֹא־אֶשְׁלַח יָדִי אֶל־בֶּן־הַמֶּלֶךְ כִּי בְאָזְנֵינוּ צִוָּה הַמֶּלֶךְ אֹתְךָ וְאֶת־אֲבִישַׁי וְאֶת־אִתַּי לֵאמֹר שִׁמְרוּ־מִי בַנַּעַר בְּאַבְשָׁלוֹם:

13 If I betrayed myself – and nothing is hidden from the king – you would have stood aloof."

אוֹ־עָשִׂיתִי בנפשו [בְנַפְשִׁי] שֶׁקֶר וְכָל־דָּבָר לֹא־יִכָּחֵד מִן־הַמֶּלֶךְ וְאַתָּה תִּתְיַצֵּב מִנֶּגֶד:

14 *Yoav* replied, "Then I will not wait for you." He took three darts in his hand and drove them into *Avshalom*'s chest. [*Avshalom*] was still alive in the thick growth of the terebinth,

וַיֹּאמֶר יוֹאָב לֹא־כֵן אֹחִילָה לְפָנֶיךָ וַיִּקַּח שְׁלֹשָׁה שְׁבָטִים בְּכַפּוֹ וַיִּתְקָעֵם בְּלֵב אַבְשָׁלוֹם עוֹדֶנּוּ חַי בְּלֵב הָאֵלָה:

15 when ten of *Yoav*'s young arms-bearers closed in and struck at *Avshalom* until he died.

וַיָּסֹבּוּ עֲשָׂרָה נְעָרִים נֹשְׂאֵי כְּלֵי יוֹאָב וַיַּכּוּ אֶת־אַבְשָׁלוֹם וַיְמִיתֻהוּ:

(see I Samuel 24). Similarly, he also still loves his son *Avshalom*, though *Avshalom* wants to murder him. The Sages (*Yevamot* 79a) consider the attribute of mercy to be one of the hallmarks of the Children of Israel. Failing to act with mercy is cause for punishment and even exile from the Land of Israel, as it says in *Hoshea* (4:1–3), "Because there is no honesty and no goodness and no obedience to *Hashem* in the land…For that, the earth is withered…"

Shmuel II/II Samuel
Chapter 18

16	Then *Yoav* sounded the horn, and the troops gave up their pursuit of the Israelites; for *Yoav* held the troops in check.
17	They took *Avshalom* and flung him into a large pit in the forest, and they piled up a very great heap of stones over it. Then all the Israelites fled to their homes. –
18	Now *Avshalom*, in his lifetime, had taken the pillar which is in the Valley of the King and set it up for himself; for he said, "I have no son to keep my name alive." He had named the pillar after himself, and it has been called *Avshalom*'s Monument to this day.
19	Ahimaaz son of *Tzadok* said, "Let me run and report to the king that *Hashem* has vindicated him against his enemies."
20	But *Yoav* said to him, "You shall not be the one to bring tidings today. You may bring tidings some other day, but you'll not bring any today; for the king's son is dead!"
21	And *Yoav* said to a Cushite, "Go tell the king what you have seen." The Cushite bowed to *Yoav* and ran off.
22	But Ahimaaz son of *Tzadok* again said to *Yoav*, "No matter what, let me run, too, behind the Cushite." *Yoav* asked, "Why should you run, my boy, when you have no news worth telling?"
23	"I am going to run anyway." "Then run," he said. So Ahimaaz ran by way of the Plain, and he passed the Cushite.
24	*David* was sitting between the two gates. The watchman on the roof of the gate walked over to the city wall. He looked up and saw a man running alone.
25	The watchman called down and told the king; and the king said, "If he is alone, he has news to report." As he was coming nearer,
26	the watchman saw another man running; and he called out to the gatekeeper, "There is another man running alone." And the king said, "That one, too, brings news."

שמואל ב
פרק יח

טז וַיִּתְקַע יוֹאָב בַּשֹּׁפָר וַיָּשָׁב הָעָם מִרְדֹף אַחֲרֵי יִשְׂרָאֵל כִּי־חָשַׂךְ יוֹאָב אֶת־הָעָם:

יז וַיִּקְחוּ אֶת־אַבְשָׁלוֹם וַיַּשְׁלִיכוּ אֹתוֹ בַיַּעַר אֶל־הַפַּחַת הַגָּדוֹל וַיַּצִּבוּ עָלָיו גַּל־אֲבָנִים גָּדוֹל מְאֹד וְכָל־יִשְׂרָאֵל נָסוּ אִישׁ לאהלו [לְאֹהָלָיו]:

יח וְאַבְשָׁלֹם לָקַח וַיַּצֶּב־לוֹ בחיו [בְחַיָּיו] אֶת־מַצֶּבֶת אֲשֶׁר בְּעֵמֶק־הַמֶּלֶךְ כִּי אָמַר אֵין־לִי בֵן בַּעֲבוּר הַזְכִּיר שְׁמִי וַיִּקְרָא לַמַּצֶּבֶת עַל־שְׁמוֹ וַיִּקָּרֵא לָהּ יַד אַבְשָׁלֹם עַד הַיּוֹם הַזֶּה:

יט וַאֲחִימַעַץ בֶּן־צָדוֹק אָמַר אָרוּצָה נָּא וַאֲבַשְּׂרָה אֶת־הַמֶּלֶךְ כִּי־שְׁפָטוֹ יְהוָה מִיַּד אֹיְבָיו:

כ וַיֹּאמֶר לוֹ יוֹאָב לֹא אִישׁ בְּשֹׂרָה אַתָּה הַיּוֹם הַזֶּה וּבִשַּׂרְתָּ בְּיוֹם אַחֵר וְהַיּוֹם הַזֶּה לֹא תְבַשֵּׂר כִּי־על [כֵּן] בֶּן־הַמֶּלֶךְ מֵת:

כא וַיֹּאמֶר יוֹאָב לַכּוּשִׁי לֵךְ הַגֵּד לַמֶּלֶךְ אֲשֶׁר רָאִיתָה וַיִּשְׁתַּחוּ כוּשִׁי לְיוֹאָב וַיָּרֹץ:

כב וַיֹּסֶף עוֹד אֲחִימַעַץ בֶּן־צָדוֹק וַיֹּאמֶר אֶל־יוֹאָב וִיהִי מָה אָרֻצָה־נָּא גַם־אָנִי אַחֲרֵי הַכּוּשִׁי וַיֹּאמֶר יוֹאָב לָמָּה־זֶּה אַתָּה רָץ בְּנִי וּלְכָה אֵין־בְּשׂוֹרָה מֹצֵאת:

כג וִיהִי־מָה אָרוּץ וַיֹּאמֶר לוֹ רוּץ וַיָּרָץ אֲחִימַעַץ דֶּרֶךְ הַכִּכָּר וַיַּעֲבֹר אֶת־הַכּוּשִׁי:

כד וְדָוִד יוֹשֵׁב בֵּין־שְׁנֵי הַשְּׁעָרִים וַיֵּלֶךְ הַצֹּפֶה אֶל־גַּג הַשַּׁעַר אֶל־הַחוֹמָה וַיִּשָּׂא אֶת־עֵינָיו וַיַּרְא וְהִנֵּה־אִישׁ רָץ לְבַדּוֹ:

כה וַיִּקְרָא הַצֹּפֶה וַיַּגֵּד לַמֶּלֶךְ וַיֹּאמֶר הַמֶּלֶךְ אִם־לְבַדּוֹ בְּשׂוֹרָה בְּפִיו וַיֵּלֶךְ הָלוֹךְ וְקָרֵב:

כו וַיַּרְא הַצֹּפֶה אִישׁ־אַחֵר רָץ וַיִּקְרָא הַצֹּפֶה אֶל־הַשֹּׁעֵר וַיֹּאמֶר הִנֵּה־אִישׁ רָץ לְבַדּוֹ וַיֹּאמֶר הַמֶּלֶךְ גַּם־זֶה מְבַשֵּׂר:

Shmuel II / II Samuel
Chapter 19

27 The watchman said, "I can see that the first one runs like Ahimaaz son of *Tzadok*"; to which the king replied, "He is a good man, and he comes with good news."

28 Ahimaaz called out and said to the king, "All is well!" He bowed low with his face to the ground and said, "Praised be *Hashem* your God, who has delivered up the men who raised their hand against my lord the king."

29 The king asked, "Is my boy *Avshalom* safe?" And Ahimaaz answered, "I saw a large crowd when Your Majesty's servant *Yoav* was sending your servant off, but I don't know what it was about."

30 The king said, "Step aside and stand over there"; he stepped aside and waited.

31 Just then the Cushite came up; and the Cushite said, "Let my lord the king be informed that *Hashem* has vindicated you today against all who rebelled against you!"

32 The king asked the Cushite, "Is my boy *Avshalom* safe?" And the Cushite replied, "May the enemies of my lord the king and all who rose against you to do you harm fare like that young man!"

19

1 The king was shaken. He went up to the upper chamber of the gateway and wept, moaning these words as he went, "My son *Avshalom*! O my son, my son *Avshalom*! If only I had died instead of you! O *Avshalom*, my son, my son!"

2 *Yoav* was told that the king was weeping and mourning over *Avshalom*.

3 And the victory that day was turned into mourning for all the troops, for that day the troops heard that the king was grieving over his son.

4 The troops stole into town that day like troops ashamed after running away in battle.

5 The king covered his face and the king kept crying aloud, "O my son *Avshalom*! O *Avshalom*, my son, my son!"

שמואל ב
פרק יט

כז וַיֹּאמֶר הַצֹּפֶה אֲנִי רֹאֶה אֶת־מְרוּצַת הָרִאשׁוֹן כִּמְרֻצַת אֲחִימַעַץ בֶּן־צָדוֹק וַיֹּאמֶר הַמֶּלֶךְ אִישׁ־טוֹב זֶה וְאֶל־בְּשׂוֹרָה טוֹבָה יָבוֹא׃

כח וַיִּקְרָא אֲחִימַעַץ וַיֹּאמֶר אֶל־הַמֶּלֶךְ שָׁלוֹם וַיִּשְׁתַּחוּ לַמֶּלֶךְ לְאַפָּיו אָרְצָה וַיֹּאמֶר בָּרוּךְ יְהֹוָה אֱלֹהֶיךָ אֲשֶׁר סִגַּר אֶת־הָאֲנָשִׁים אֲשֶׁר־נָשְׂאוּ אֶת־יָדָם בַּאדֹנִי הַמֶּלֶךְ׃

כט וַיֹּאמֶר הַמֶּלֶךְ שָׁלוֹם לַנַּעַר לְאַבְשָׁלוֹם וַיֹּאמֶר אֲחִימַעַץ רָאִיתִי הֶהָמוֹן הַגָּדוֹל לִשְׁלֹחַ אֶת־עֶבֶד הַמֶּלֶךְ יוֹאָב וְאֶת־עַבְדֶּךָ וְלֹא יָדַעְתִּי מָה׃

ל וַיֹּאמֶר הַמֶּלֶךְ סֹב הִתְיַצֵּב כֹּה וַיִּסֹּב וַיַּעֲמֹד׃

לא וְהִנֵּה הַכּוּשִׁי בָּא וַיֹּאמֶר הַכּוּשִׁי יִתְבַּשֵּׂר אֲדֹנִי הַמֶּלֶךְ כִּי־שְׁפָטְךָ יְהֹוָה הַיּוֹם מִיַּד כָּל־הַקָּמִים עָלֶיךָ׃

לב וַיֹּאמֶר הַמֶּלֶךְ אֶל־הַכּוּשִׁי הֲשָׁלוֹם לַנַּעַר לְאַבְשָׁלוֹם וַיֹּאמֶר הַכּוּשִׁי יִהְיוּ כַנַּעַר אֹיְבֵי אֲדֹנִי הַמֶּלֶךְ וְכֹל אֲשֶׁר־קָמוּ עָלֶיךָ לְרָעָה׃

יט א וַיִּרְגַּז הַמֶּלֶךְ וַיַּעַל עַל־עֲלִיַּת הַשַּׁעַר וַיֵּבְךְּ וְכֹה אָמַר בְּלֶכְתּוֹ בְּנִי אַבְשָׁלוֹם בְּנִי בְנִי אַבְשָׁלוֹם מִי־יִתֵּן מוּתִי אֲנִי תַחְתֶּיךָ אַבְשָׁלוֹם בְּנִי בְנִי׃

ב וַיֻּגַּד לְיוֹאָב הִנֵּה הַמֶּלֶךְ בֹּכֶה וַיִּתְאַבֵּל עַל־אַבְשָׁלֹם׃

ג וַתְּהִי הַתְּשֻׁעָה בַּיּוֹם הַהוּא לְאֵבֶל לְכָל־הָעָם כִּי־שָׁמַע הָעָם בַּיּוֹם הַהוּא לֵאמֹר נֶעֱצַב הַמֶּלֶךְ עַל־בְּנוֹ׃

ד וַיִּתְגַּנֵּב הָעָם בַּיּוֹם הַהוּא לָבוֹא הָעִיר כַּאֲשֶׁר יִתְגַּנֵּב הָעָם הַנִּכְלָמִים בְּנוּסָם בַּמִּלְחָמָה׃

ה וְהַמֶּלֶךְ לָאַט אֶת־פָּנָיו וַיִּזְעַק הַמֶּלֶךְ קוֹל גָּדוֹל בְּנִי אַבְשָׁלוֹם אַבְשָׁלוֹם בְּנִי בְנִי׃

Shmuel II / II Samuel
Chapter 19

6 *Yoav* came to the king in his quarters and said, "Today you have humiliated all your followers, who this day saved your life, and the lives of your sons and daughters, and the lives of your wives and concubines,

וַיָּבֹא יוֹאָב אֶל־הַמֶּלֶךְ הַבָּיִת וַיֹּאמֶר הֹבַשְׁתָּ הַיּוֹם אֶת־פְּנֵי כָל־עֲבָדֶיךָ הַמְמַלְּטִים אֶת־נַפְשְׁךָ הַיּוֹם וְאֵת נֶפֶשׁ בָּנֶיךָ וּבְנֹתֶיךָ וְנֶפֶשׁ נָשֶׁיךָ וְנֶפֶשׁ פִּלַגְשֶׁיךָ:

va-ya-VO yo-AV el ha-ME-lekh ha-BA-yit va-YO-mer ho-VASH-ta ha-YOM et p'-NAY khol a-va-DE-kha ha-m'-ma-l'-TEEM et naf-sh'-KHA ha-YOM v'-AYT NE-fesh ba-NE-kha u-v'-no-TE-kha v'-NE-fesh na-SHE-kha v'-NE-fesh pi-lag-SHE-kha

7 by showing love for those who hate you and hate for those who love you. For you have made clear today that the officers and men mean nothing to you. I am sure that if *Avshalom* were alive today and the rest of us dead, you would have preferred it.

לְאַהֲבָה אֶת־שֹׂנְאֶיךָ וְלִשְׂנֹא אֶת־אֹהֲבֶיךָ כִּי הִגַּדְתָּ הַיּוֹם כִּי אֵין לְךָ שָׂרִים וַעֲבָדִים כִּי יָדַעְתִּי הַיּוֹם כִּי לֻא [לוּ] אַבְשָׁלוֹם חַי וְכֻלָּנוּ הַיּוֹם מֵתִים כִּי־אָז יָשָׁר בְּעֵינֶיךָ:

8 Now arise, come out and placate your followers! For I swear by *Hashem* that if you do not come out, not a single man will remain with you overnight; and that would be a greater disaster for you than any disaster that has befallen you from your youth until now."

וְעַתָּה קוּם צֵא וְדַבֵּר עַל־לֵב עֲבָדֶיךָ כִּי בַיהֹוָה נִשְׁבַּעְתִּי כִּי־אֵינְךָ יוֹצֵא אִם־יָלִין אִישׁ אִתְּךָ הַלַּיְלָה וְרָעָה לְךָ זֹאת מִכָּל־הָרָעָה אֲשֶׁר־בָּאָה עָלֶיךָ מִנְּעֻרֶיךָ עַד־עָתָּה:

9 So the king arose and sat down in the gateway; and when all the troops were told that the king was sitting in the gateway, all the troops presented themselves to the king. Now the Israelites had fled to their homes.

וַיָּקָם הַמֶּלֶךְ וַיֵּשֶׁב בַּשָּׁעַר וּלְכָל־הָעָם הִגִּידוּ לֵאמֹר הִנֵּה הַמֶּלֶךְ יוֹשֵׁב בַּשַּׁעַר וַיָּבֹא כָל־הָעָם לִפְנֵי הַמֶּלֶךְ וְיִשְׂרָאֵל נָס אִישׁ לְאֹהָלָיו:

10 All the people throughout the tribes of *Yisrael* were arguing: Some said, "The king saved us from the hands of our enemies, and he delivered us from the hands of the Philistines; and just now he had to flee the country because of *Avshalom*.

וַיְהִי כָל־הָעָם נָדוֹן בְּכָל־שִׁבְטֵי יִשְׂרָאֵל לֵאמֹר הַמֶּלֶךְ הִצִּילָנוּ מִכַּף אֹיְבֵינוּ וְהוּא מִלְּטָנוּ מִכַּף פְּלִשְׁתִּים וְעַתָּה בָּרַח מִן־הָאָרֶץ מֵעַל אַבְשָׁלוֹם:

11 But *Avshalom*, whom we anointed over us, has died in battle; why then do you sit idle instead of escorting the king back?"

וְאַבְשָׁלוֹם אֲשֶׁר מָשַׁחְנוּ עָלֵינוּ מֵת בַּמִּלְחָמָה וְעַתָּה לָמָה אַתֶּם מַחֲרִשִׁים לְהָשִׁיב אֶת־הַמֶּלֶךְ:

19:6 Today you have humiliated all your followers *Yoav* is upset that King *David* mourned his rebellious son *Avshalom*. *Yoav* had killed *Avshalom*, though King *David* had commanded that he be captured unharmed. King *David* is extremely angry that *Yoav* has disobeyed him. Rabbi Shlomo Aviner points out that in Jewish Law, any act of disobedience to the king can be punished by death. However, King *David* is more concerned with ensuring that the Kingdom of Israel remains secure and strong, and thus needs *Yoav* to remain as his leading general. However, before his death, King *David* instructs his son *Shlomo* to punish *Yoav* for having killed *Avner, Amasa* (II Kings 2:5) and, according to *Radak, Avshalom*. *Shlomo* tries *Yoav* for the murders and convicts him of violating the will of the king (*Sanhedrin* 49a), an act which itself is a danger to the People of Israel. Obeying the dictates of just rulers and governments is itself a religious act, as it allows for a strong, cohesive and just nation.

Shmuel II/II Samuel
Chapter 19

שמואל ב
פרק יט

12 The talk of all *Yisrael* reached the king in his quarters. So King *David* sent this message to the *Kohanim Tzadok* and *Evyatar*: "Speak to the elders of *Yehuda* and say, 'Why should you be the last to bring the king back to his palace?

יב וְהַמֶּלֶךְ דָּוִד שָׁלַח אֶל־צָדוֹק וְאֶל־אֶבְיָתָר הַכֹּהֲנִים לֵאמֹר דַּבְּרוּ אֶל־זִקְנֵי יְהוּדָה לֵאמֹר לָמָּה תִהְיוּ אַחֲרֹנִים לְהָשִׁיב אֶת־הַמֶּלֶךְ אֶל־בֵּיתוֹ וּדְבַר כָּל־יִשְׂרָאֵל בָּא אֶל־הַמֶּלֶךְ אֶל־בֵּיתוֹ:

13 You are my kinsmen, my own flesh and blood! Why should you be the last to escort the king back?'

יג אַחַי אַתֶּם עַצְמִי וּבְשָׂרִי אַתֶּם וְלָמָּה תִהְיוּ אַחֲרֹנִים לְהָשִׁיב אֶת־הַמֶּלֶךְ:

14 And to *Amasa* say this, 'You are my own flesh and blood. May *Hashem* do thus and more to me if you do not become my army commander permanently in place of *Yoav*!'"

יד וְלַעֲמָשָׂא תֹּמְרוּ הֲלוֹא עַצְמִי וּבְשָׂרִי אָתָּה כֹּה יַעֲשֶׂה־לִּי אֱלֹהִים וְכֹה יוֹסִיף אִם־לֹא שַׂר־צָבָא תִּהְיֶה לְפָנַי כָּל־הַיָּמִים תַּחַת יוֹאָב:

15 So [*Amasa*] swayed the hearts of all the Judites as one man; and they sent a message to the king: "Come back with all your followers."

טו וַיַּט אֶת־לְבַב כָּל־אִישׁ־יְהוּדָה כְּאִישׁ אֶחָד וַיִּשְׁלְחוּ אֶל־הַמֶּלֶךְ שׁוּב אַתָּה וְכָל־עֲבָדֶיךָ:

16 The king started back and arrived at the *Yarden*; and the Judites went to *Gilgal* to meet the king and to conduct the king across the *Yarden*.

טז וַיָּשָׁב הַמֶּלֶךְ וַיָּבֹא עַד־הַיַּרְדֵּן וִיהוּדָה בָּא הַגִּלְגָּלָה לָלֶכֶת לִקְרַאת הַמֶּלֶךְ לְהַעֲבִיר אֶת־הַמֶּלֶךְ אֶת־הַיַּרְדֵּן:

17 *Shim'i* son of Gera, the Benjaminite from Bahurim, hurried down with the Judites to meet King *David*,

יז וַיְמַהֵר שִׁמְעִי בֶן־גֵּרָא בֶּן־הַיְמִינִי אֲשֶׁר מִבַּחוּרִים וַיֵּרֶד עִם־אִישׁ יְהוּדָה לִקְרַאת הַמֶּלֶךְ דָּוִד:

18 accompanied by a thousand Benjaminites. And Ziba, the servant of the House of *Shaul*, together with his fifteen sons and twenty slaves, rushed down to the *Yarden* ahead of the king

יח וְאֶלֶף אִישׁ עִמּוֹ מִבִּנְיָמִן וְצִיבָא נַעַר בֵּית שָׁאוּל וַחֲמֵשֶׁת עָשָׂר בָּנָיו וְעֶשְׂרִים עֲבָדָיו אִתּוֹ וְצָלְחוּ הַיַּרְדֵּן לִפְנֵי הַמֶּלֶךְ:

19 while the crossing was being made, to escort the king's family over, and to do whatever he wished. *Shim'i* son of Gera flung himself before the king as he was about to cross the *Yarden*.

יט וְעָבְרָה הָעֲבָרָה לַעֲבִיר אֶת־בֵּית הַמֶּלֶךְ וְלַעֲשׂוֹת הַטּוֹב בְּעֵינָו [בְּעֵינָיו] וְשִׁמְעִי בֶן־גֵּרָא נָפַל לִפְנֵי הַמֶּלֶךְ בְּעָבְרוֹ בַּיַּרְדֵּן:

20 He said to the king, "Let not my lord hold me guilty, and do not remember the wrong your servant committed on the day my lord the king left *Yerushalayim*; let Your Majesty give it no thought.

כ וַיֹּאמֶר אֶל־הַמֶּלֶךְ אַל־יַחֲשָׁב־לִי אֲדֹנִי עָוֹן וְאַל־תִּזְכֹּר אֵת אֲשֶׁר הֶעֱוָה עַבְדְּךָ בַּיּוֹם אֲשֶׁר־יָצָא אֲדֹנִי־הַמֶּלֶךְ מִירוּשָׁלָ͏ִם לָשׂוּם הַמֶּלֶךְ אֶל־לִבּוֹ:

21 For your servant knows that he has sinned; so here I have come down today, the first of all the House of *Yosef*, to meet my lord the king."

כא כִּי יָדַע עַבְדְּךָ כִּי אֲנִי חָטָאתִי וְהִנֵּה־בָאתִי הַיּוֹם רִאשׁוֹן לְכָל־בֵּית יוֹסֵף לָרֶדֶת לִקְרַאת אֲדֹנִי הַמֶּלֶךְ:

22 Thereupon *Avishai* son of *Tzeruya* spoke up, "Shouldn't *Shim'i* be put to death for that – insulting *Hashem*'s anointed?"

כב וַיַּעַן אֲבִישַׁי בֶּן־צְרוּיָה וַיֹּאמֶר הֲתַחַת זֹאת לֹא יוּמַת שִׁמְעִי כִּי קִלֵּל אֶת־מְשִׁיחַ יְהוָה:

23 But *David* said, "What has this to do with you, you sons of *Tzeruya*, that you should cross me today? Should a single Israelite be put to death today? Don't I know that today I am again king over *Yisrael*?"

כג וַיֹּאמֶר דָּוִד מַה־לִּי וְלָכֶם בְּנֵי צְרוּיָה כִּי־תִהְיוּ־לִי הַיּוֹם לְשָׂטָן הַיּוֹם יוּמַת אִישׁ בְּיִשְׂרָאֵל כִּי הֲלוֹא יָדַעְתִּי כִּי הַיּוֹם אֲנִי־מֶלֶךְ עַל־יִשְׂרָאֵל:

Shmuel II / II Samuel
Chapter 19

24 Then the king said to *Shim'i*, "You shall not die"; and the king gave him his oath.

25 *Mefiboshet*, the grandson of *Shaul*, also came down to meet the king. He had not pared his toenails, or trimmed his mustache, or washed his clothes from the day that the king left until the day he returned safe.

26 When he came [from] *Yerushalayim* to meet the king, the king asked him, "Why didn't you come with me, *Mefiboshet*?"

27 He replied, "My lord the king, my own servant deceived me. Your servant planned to saddle his ass and ride on it and go with Your Majesty – for your servant is lame.

28 [Ziba] has slandered your servant to my lord the king. But my lord the king is like an angel of *Hashem*; do as you see fit.

29 For all the members of my father's family deserved only death from my lord the king; yet you set your servant among those who ate at your table. What right have I to appeal further to Your Majesty?"

30 The king said to him, "You need not speak further. I decree that you and Ziba shall divide the property."

31 And *Mefiboshet* said to the king, "Let him take it all, as long as my lord the king has come home safe."

32 *Barzilai* the Giladite had come down from Rogelin and passed on to the *Yarden* with the king, to see him off at the *Yarden*.

33 *Barzilai* was very old, eighty years of age; and he had provided the king with food during his stay at Mahanaim, for he was a very wealthy man.

34 The king said to *Barzilai*, "Cross over with me, and I will provide for you in *Yerushalayim* at my side."

35 But *Barzilai* said to the king, "How many years are left to me that I should go up with Your Majesty to *Yerushalayim*?

36 I am now eighty years old. Can I tell the difference between good and bad? Can your servant taste what he eats and drinks? Can I still listen to the singing of men and women? Why then should your servant continue to be a burden to my lord the king?

שמואל ב
פרק יט

כד וַיֹּאמֶר הַמֶּלֶךְ אֶל־שִׁמְעִי לֹא תָמוּת וַיִּשָּׁבַע לוֹ הַמֶּלֶךְ:

כה וּמְפִבֹשֶׁת בֶּן־שָׁאוּל יָרַד לִקְרַאת הַמֶּלֶךְ וְלֹא־עָשָׂה רַגְלָיו וְלֹא־עָשָׂה שְׂפָמוֹ וְאֶת־בְּגָדָיו לֹא כִבֵּס לְמִן־הַיּוֹם לֶכֶת הַמֶּלֶךְ עַד־הַיּוֹם אֲשֶׁר־בָּא בְשָׁלוֹם:

כו וַיְהִי כִּי־בָא יְרוּשָׁלַם לִקְרַאת הַמֶּלֶךְ וַיֹּאמֶר לוֹ הַמֶּלֶךְ לָמָּה לֹא־הָלַכְתָּ עִמִּי מְפִיבֹשֶׁת:

כז וַיֹּאמַר אֲדֹנִי הַמֶּלֶךְ עַבְדִּי רִמָּנִי כִּי־אָמַר עַבְדְּךָ אֶחְבְּשָׁה־לִּי הַחֲמוֹר וְאֶרְכַּב עָלֶיהָ וְאֵלֵךְ אֶת־הַמֶּלֶךְ כִּי פִסֵּחַ עַבְדֶּךָ:

כח וַיְרַגֵּל בְּעַבְדְּךָ אֶל־אֲדֹנִי הַמֶּלֶךְ וַאדֹנִי הַמֶּלֶךְ כְּמַלְאַךְ הָאֱלֹהִים וַעֲשֵׂה הַטּוֹב בְּעֵינֶיךָ:

כט כִּי לֹא הָיָה כָּל־בֵּית אָבִי כִּי אִם־אַנְשֵׁי־מָוֶת לַאדֹנִי הַמֶּלֶךְ וַתָּשֶׁת אֶת־עַבְדְּךָ בְּאֹכְלֵי שֻׁלְחָנֶךָ וּמַה־יֶּשׁ־לִי עוֹד צְדָקָה וְלִזְעֹק עוֹד אֶל־הַמֶּלֶךְ:

ל וַיֹּאמֶר לוֹ הַמֶּלֶךְ לָמָּה תְּדַבֵּר עוֹד דְּבָרֶיךָ אָמַרְתִּי אַתָּה וְצִיבָא תַּחְלְקוּ אֶת־הַשָּׂדֶה:

לא וַיֹּאמֶר מְפִיבֹשֶׁת אֶל־הַמֶּלֶךְ גַּם אֶת־הַכֹּל יִקָּח אַחֲרֵי אֲשֶׁר־בָּא אֲדֹנִי הַמֶּלֶךְ בְּשָׁלוֹם אֶל־בֵּיתוֹ:

לב וּבַרְזִלַּי הַגִּלְעָדִי יָרַד מֵרֹגְלִים וַיַּעֲבֹר אֶת־הַמֶּלֶךְ הַיַּרְדֵּן לְשַׁלְּחוֹ אֶת־בירדן [הַיַּרְדֵּן]:

לג וּבַרְזִלַּי זָקֵן מְאֹד בֶּן־שְׁמֹנִים שָׁנָה וְהוּא־כִלְכַּל אֶת־הַמֶּלֶךְ בְשִׁיבָתוֹ בְמַחֲנַיִם כִּי־אִישׁ גָּדוֹל הוּא מְאֹד:

לד וַיֹּאמֶר הַמֶּלֶךְ אֶל־בַּרְזִלָּי אַתָּה עֲבֹר אִתִּי וְכִלְכַּלְתִּי אֹתְךָ עִמָּדִי בִּירוּשָׁלָם:

לה וַיֹּאמֶר בַּרְזִלַּי אֶל־הַמֶּלֶךְ כַּמָּה יְמֵי שְׁנֵי חַיַּי כִּי־אֶעֱלֶה אֶת־הַמֶּלֶךְ יְרוּשָׁלָם:

לו בֶּן־שְׁמֹנִים שָׁנָה אָנֹכִי הַיּוֹם הַאֵדַע בֵּין־טוֹב לְרָע אִם־יִטְעַם עַבְדְּךָ אֶת־אֲשֶׁר אֹכַל וְאֶת־אֲשֶׁר אֶשְׁתֶּה אִם־אֶשְׁמַע עוֹד בְּקוֹל שָׁרִים וְשָׁרוֹת וְלָמָּה יִהְיֶה עַבְדְּךָ עוֹד לְמַשָּׂא אֶל־אֲדֹנִי הַמֶּלֶךְ:

Shmuel II / II Samuel — Chapter 20

שמואל ב
פרק כ

37 Your servant could barely cross the *Yarden* with your Majesty! Why should Your Majesty reward me so generously?

לו כִּמְעַט יַעֲבֹר עַבְדְּךָ אֶת־הַיַּרְדֵּן אֶת־הַמֶּלֶךְ וְלָמָּה יִגְמְלֵנִי הַמֶּלֶךְ הַגְּמוּלָה הַזֹּאת:

38 Let your servant go back, and let me die in my own town, near the graves of my father and mother. But here is your servant Chimham; let him cross with my lord the king, and do for him as you see fit."

לח יָשָׁב־נָא עַבְדְּךָ וְאָמֻת בְּעִירִי עִם קֶבֶר אָבִי וְאִמִּי וְהִנֵּה עַבְדְּךָ כִמְהָם יַעֲבֹר עִם־אֲדֹנִי הַמֶּלֶךְ וַעֲשֵׂה־לוֹ אֵת אֲשֶׁר־טוֹב בְּעֵינֶיךָ:

39 And the king said, "Chimham shall cross with me, and I will do for him as you see fit; and anything you want me to do, I will do for you."

לט וַיֹּאמֶר הַמֶּלֶךְ אִתִּי יַעֲבֹר כִּמְהָם וַאֲנִי אֶעֱשֶׂה־לּוֹ אֶת־הַטּוֹב בְּעֵינֶיךָ וְכֹל אֲשֶׁר־תִּבְחַר עָלַי אֶעֱשֶׂה־לָּךְ:

40 All the troops crossed the *Yarden*; and when the king was ready to cross, the king kissed *Barzilai* and bade him farewell; and [*Barzilai*] returned to his home.

מ וַיַּעֲבֹר כָּל־הָעָם אֶת־הַיַּרְדֵּן וְהַמֶּלֶךְ עָבָר וַיִּשַּׁק הַמֶּלֶךְ לְבַרְזִלַּי וַיְבָרֲכֵהוּ וַיָּשָׁב לִמְקֹמוֹ:

41 The king passed on to *Gilgal*, with Chimham accompanying him; and all the Judite soldiers and part of the Israelite army escorted the king across.

מא וַיַּעֲבֹר הַמֶּלֶךְ הַגִּלְגָּלָה וְכִמְהָן עָבַר עִמּוֹ וְכָל־עַם יְהוּדָה וַיְעֱבִרוּ [הֶעֱבִירוּ] אֶת־הַמֶּלֶךְ וְגַם חֲצִי עַם יִשְׂרָאֵל:

42 Then all the men of *Yisrael* came to the king and said to the king, "Why did our kinsmen, the men of *Yehuda*, steal you away and escort the king and his family across the *Yarden*, along with all *David*'s men?"

מב וְהִנֵּה כָּל־אִישׁ יִשְׂרָאֵל בָּאִים אֶל־הַמֶּלֶךְ וַיֹּאמְרוּ אֶל־הַמֶּלֶךְ מַדּוּעַ גְּנָבוּךָ אַחֵינוּ אִישׁ יְהוּדָה וַיַּעֲבִרוּ אֶת־הַמֶּלֶךְ וְאֶת־בֵּיתוֹ אֶת־הַיַּרְדֵּן וְכָל־אַנְשֵׁי דָוִד עִמּוֹ:

43 All the men of *Yehuda* replied to the men of *Yisrael*, "Because the king is our relative! Why should this upset you? Have we consumed anything that belongs to the king? Has he given us any gifts?"

מג וַיַּעַן כָּל־אִישׁ יְהוּדָה עַל־אִישׁ יִשְׂרָאֵל כִּי־קָרוֹב הַמֶּלֶךְ אֵלַי וְלָמָּה זֶּה חָרָה לְךָ עַל־הַדָּבָר הַזֶּה הֶאָכוֹל אָכַלְנוּ מִן־הַמֶּלֶךְ אִם־נִשֵּׂאת נִשָּׂא לָנוּ:

44 But the men of *Yisrael* answered the men of *Yehuda*, "We have ten shares in the king, and in *David*, too, we have more than you. Why then have you slighted us? Were we not the first to propose that our king be brought back?" However, the men of *Yehuda* prevailed over the men of *Yisrael*.

מד וַיַּעַן אִישׁ־יִשְׂרָאֵל אֶת־אִישׁ יְהוּדָה וַיֹּאמֶר עֶשֶׂר־יָדוֹת לִי בַמֶּלֶךְ וְגַם־בְּדָוִד אֲנִי מִמְּךָ וּמַדּוּעַ הֱקִלֹּתַנִי וְלֹא־הָיָה דְבָרִי רִאשׁוֹן לִי לְהָשִׁיב אֶת־מַלְכִּי וַיִּקֶשׁ דְּבַר־אִישׁ יְהוּדָה מִדְּבַר אִישׁ יִשְׂרָאֵל:

20

1 A scoundrel named Sheba son of Bichri, a Benjaminite, happened to be there. He sounded the *shofar* and proclaimed: "We have no portion in *David*, No share in *Yishai*'s son! Every man to his tent, O *Yisrael*!"

כ א וְשָׁם נִקְרָא אִישׁ בְּלִיַּעַל וּשְׁמוֹ שֶׁבַע בֶּן־בִּכְרִי אִישׁ יְמִינִי וַיִּתְקַע בַּשֹּׁפָר וַיֹּאמֶר אֵין־לָנוּ חֵלֶק בְּדָוִד וְלֹא נַחֲלָה־לָנוּ בְּבֶן־יִשַׁי אִישׁ לְאֹהָלָיו יִשְׂרָאֵל:

v'-SHAM nik-RA EESH b'-li-YA-al u-sh'-MO SHE-va ben bikh-REE EESH y'-mee-NEE va-yit-KA ba-sho-FAR va-YO-mer ayn LA-nu KHAY-lek b'-da-VID v'-LO na-kha-lah LA-nu b'-ven yi-SHAI EESH l'-o-ha-LAV yis-ra-AYL

20:1 He sounded the *shofar* The ram's horn, *shofar* (שופר), has a critical place in Judaism. *Hashem* commands the Jewish people to listen to the sounds of the *shofar* on *Rosh Hashana*, and there are

Shmuel II/II Samuel
Chapter 20

שמואל ב
פרק כ

2 All the men of *Yisrael* left *David* and followed Sheba son of Bichri; but the men of *Yehuda* accompanied their king from the *Yarden* to *Yerushalayim*.

ב וַיַּעַל כָּל־אִישׁ יִשְׂרָאֵל מֵאַחֲרֵי דָוִד אַחֲרֵי שֶׁבַע בֶּן־בִּכְרִי וְאִישׁ יְהוּדָה דָּבְקוּ בְמַלְכָּם מִן־הַיַּרְדֵּן וְעַד־יְרוּשָׁלָ͏ִם׃

3 *David* went to his palace in *Yerushalayim*, and the king took the ten concubines he had left to mind the palace and put them in a guarded place; he provided for them, but he did not cohabit with them. They remained in seclusion until the day they died, in living widowhood.

ג וַיָּבֹא דָוִד אֶל־בֵּיתוֹ יְרוּשָׁלַ͏ִם וַיִּקַּח הַמֶּלֶךְ אֵת עֶשֶׂר־נָשִׁים פִּלַגְשִׁים אֲשֶׁר הִנִּיחַ לִשְׁמֹר הַבַּיִת וַיִּתְּנֵם בֵּית־מִשְׁמֶרֶת וַיְכַלְכְּלֵם וַאֲלֵיהֶם לֹא־בָא וַתִּהְיֶינָה צְרֻרוֹת עַד־יוֹם מֻתָן אַלְמְנוּת חַיּוּת׃

4 The king said to *Amasa*, "Call up the men of *Yehuda* to my standard, and report here three days from now."

ד וַיֹּאמֶר הַמֶּלֶךְ אֶל־עֲמָשָׂא הַזְעֶק־לִי אֶת־אִישׁ־יְהוּדָה שְׁלֹשֶׁת יָמִים וְאַתָּה פֹּה עֲמֹד׃

5 *Amasa* went to call up *Yehuda*, but he took longer than the time set for him.

ה וַיֵּלֶךְ עֲמָשָׂא לְהַזְעִיק אֶת־יְהוּדָה וַיִּיחֶר [וַיּוֹחֶר] מִן־הַמּוֹעֵד אֲשֶׁר יְעָדוֹ׃

6 And *David* said to *Avishai*, "Now Sheba son of Bichri will cause us more trouble than *Avshalom*. So take your lord's servants and pursue him, before he finds fortified towns and eludes us."

ו וַיֹּאמֶר דָּוִד אֶל־אֲבִישַׁי עַתָּה יֵרַע לָנוּ שֶׁבַע בֶּן־בִּכְרִי מִן־אַבְשָׁלוֹם אַתָּה קַח אֶת־עַבְדֵי אֲדֹנֶיךָ וּרְדֹף אַחֲרָיו פֶּן־מָצָא לוֹ עָרִים בְּצֻרוֹת וְהִצִּיל עֵינֵנוּ׃

7 *Yoav*'s men, the Cherethites and Pelethites, and all the warriors, marched out behind him. They left *Yerushalayim* in pursuit of Sheba son of Bichri.

ז וַיֵּצְאוּ אַחֲרָיו אַנְשֵׁי יוֹאָב וְהַכְּרֵתִי וְהַפְּלֵתִי וְכָל־הַגִּבֹּרִים וַיֵּצְאוּ מִירוּשָׁלָ͏ִם לִרְדֹּף אַחֲרֵי שֶׁבַע בֶּן־בִּכְרִי׃

8 They were near the great stone in *Givon* when *Amasa* appeared before them. *Yoav* was wearing his military dress, with his sword girded over it and fastened around his waist in its sheath; and, as he stepped forward, it fell out.

ח הֵם עִם־הָאֶבֶן הַגְּדוֹלָה אֲשֶׁר בְּגִבְעוֹן וַעֲמָשָׂא בָּא לִפְנֵיהֶם וְיוֹאָב חָגוּר מִדּוֹ לְבֻשׁוּ וְעָלָו [וְעָלָיו] חֲגוֹר חֶרֶב מְצֻמֶּדֶת עַל־מָתְנָיו בְּתַעְרָהּ וְהוּא יָצָא וַתִּפֹּל׃

9 *Yoav* said to *Amasa*, "How are you, brother?" and with his right hand *Yoav* took hold of *Amasa*'s beard as if to kiss him.

ט וַיֹּאמֶר יוֹאָב לַעֲמָשָׂא הֲשָׁלוֹם אַתָּה אָחִי וַתֹּחֶז יַד־יְמִין יוֹאָב בִּזְקַן עֲמָשָׂא לִנְשָׁק־לוֹ׃

10 *Amasa* was not on his guard against the sword in *Yoav*'s [left] hand, and [*Yoav*] drove it into his belly so that his entrails poured out on the ground and he died; he did not need to strike him a second time. *Yoav* and his brother *Avishai* then set off in pursuit of Sheba son of Bichri,

י וַעֲמָשָׂא לֹא־נִשְׁמַר בַּחֶרֶב אֲשֶׁר בְּיַד־יוֹאָב וַיַּכֵּהוּ בָהּ אֶל־הַחֹמֶשׁ וַיִּשְׁפֹּךְ מֵעָיו אַרְצָה וְלֹא־שָׁנָה לוֹ וַיָּמֹת וְיוֹאָב וַאֲבִישַׁי אָחִיו רָדַף אַחֲרֵי שֶׁבַע בֶּן־בִּכְרִי׃

---

times that it is to be blown in the *Beit Hamikdash*, such as on public fasts. It is also to be sounded at the end of the *yovel*, the Jubilee year. But in addition to these spiritual functions, it also has military usages. The *shofar* serves as the method of assembling soldiers and of sounding a warning call. The common feature is that in all these cases, the *shofar* is sounded to get everyone's attention to fulfill their particular mission. It serves to awaken those who are slumbering, either physically or spiritually.

Blowing the shofar at the Western Wall

Shmuel II / II Samuel
Chapter 20

11 while one of *Yoav*'s henchmen stood by the corpse and called out, "Whoever favors *Yoav*, and whoever is on *David*'s side, follow *Yoav*!"

12 *Amasa* lay in the middle of the road, drenched in his blood; and the man saw that everyone stopped. And when he saw that all the people were stopping, he dragged *Amasa* from the road into the field and covered him with a garment.

13 Once he was removed from the road, everybody continued to follow *Yoav* in pursuit of Sheba son of Bichri.

14 [Sheba] had passed through all the tribes of *Yisrael* up to Abel of Beth-maacah; and all the *B'erites* assembled and followed him inside.

15 [*Yoav*'s men] came and besieged him in Abel of Beth-maacah; they threw up a siegemound against the city and it stood against the rampart. All the troops with *Yoav* were engaged in battering the wall,

16 when a clever woman shouted from the city, "Listen! Listen! Tell *Yoav* to come over here so I can talk to him."

17 He approached her, and the woman asked, "Are you *Yoav*?" "Yes," he answered; and she said to him, "Listen to what your handmaid has to say." "I'm listening," he replied.

18 And she continued, "In olden times people used to say, 'Let them inquire of Abel,' and that was the end of the matter.

19 I am one of those who seek the welfare of the faithful in *Yisrael*. But you seek to bring death upon a mother city in *Yisrael*! Why should you destroy *Hashem*'s possession?"

20 *Yoav* replied, "Far be it, far be it from me to destroy or to ruin!

21 Not at all! But a certain man from the hill country of *Efraim*, named Sheba son of Bichri, has rebelled against King *David*. Just hand him alone over to us, and I will withdraw from the city." The woman assured *Yoav*, "His head shall be thrown over the wall to you."

שמואל ב
פרק כ

יא וְאִישׁ עָמַד עָלָיו מִנַּעֲרֵי יוֹאָב וַיֹּאמֶר מִי אֲשֶׁר חָפֵץ בְּיוֹאָב וּמִי אֲשֶׁר־לְדָוִד אַחֲרֵי יוֹאָב:

יב וַעֲמָשָׂא מִתְגֹּלֵל בַּדָּם בְּתוֹךְ הַמְסִלָּה וַיַּרְא הָאִישׁ כִּי־עָמַד כָּל־הָעָם וַיַּסֵּב אֶת־עֲמָשָׂא מִן־הַמְסִלָּה הַשָּׂדֶה וַיַּשְׁלֵךְ עָלָיו בֶּגֶד כַּאֲשֶׁר רָאָה כָּל־הַבָּא עָלָיו וְעָמָד:

יג כַּאֲשֶׁר הֹגָה מִן־הַמְסִלָּה עָבַר כָּל־אִישׁ אַחֲרֵי יוֹאָב לִרְדֹּף אַחֲרֵי שֶׁבַע בֶּן־בִּכְרִי:

יד וַיַּעֲבֹר בְּכָל־שִׁבְטֵי יִשְׂרָאֵל אָבֵלָה וּבֵית מַעֲכָה וְכָל־הַבֵּרִים וַיִּקְלֻהוּ [וַיִּקָּהֲלוּ] וַיָּבֹאוּ אַף־אַחֲרָיו:

טו וַיָּבֹאוּ וַיָּצֻרוּ עָלָיו בְּאָבֵלָה בֵּית הַמַּעֲכָה וַיִּשְׁפְּכוּ סֹלְלָה אֶל־הָעִיר וַתַּעֲמֹד בַּחֵל וְכָל־הָעָם אֲשֶׁר אֶת־יוֹאָב מַשְׁחִיתִם לְהַפִּיל הַחוֹמָה:

טז וַתִּקְרָא אִשָּׁה חֲכָמָה מִן־הָעִיר שִׁמְעוּ שִׁמְעוּ אִמְרוּ־נָא אֶל־יוֹאָב קְרַב עַד־הֵנָּה וַאֲדַבְּרָה אֵלֶיךָ:

יז וַיִּקְרַב אֵלֶיהָ וַתֹּאמֶר הָאִשָּׁה הַאַתָּה יוֹאָב וַיֹּאמֶר אָנִי וַתֹּאמֶר לוֹ שְׁמַע דִּבְרֵי אֲמָתֶךָ וַיֹּאמֶר שֹׁמֵעַ אָנֹכִי:

יח וַתֹּאמֶר לֵאמֹר דַּבֵּר יְדַבְּרוּ בָרִאשֹׁנָה לֵאמֹר שָׁאֹל יְשָׁאֲלוּ בְּאָבֵל וְכֵן הֵתַמּוּ:

יט אָנֹכִי שְׁלֻמֵי אֱמוּנֵי יִשְׂרָאֵל אַתָּה מְבַקֵּשׁ לְהָמִית עִיר וְאֵם בְּיִשְׂרָאֵל לָמָּה תְבַלַּע נַחֲלַת יְהֹוָה:

כ וַיַּעַן יוֹאָב וַיֹּאמַר חָלִילָה חָלִילָה לִי אִם־אֲבַלַּע וְאִם־אַשְׁחִית:

כא לֹא־כֵן הַדָּבָר כִּי אִישׁ מֵהַר אֶפְרַיִם שֶׁבַע בֶּן־בִּכְרִי שְׁמוֹ נָשָׂא יָדוֹ בַּמֶּלֶךְ בְּדָוִד תְּנוּ־אֹתוֹ לְבַדּוֹ וְאֵלְכָה מֵעַל הָעִיר וַתֹּאמֶר הָאִשָּׁה אֶל־יוֹאָב הִנֵּה רֹאשׁוֹ מֻשְׁלָךְ אֵלֶיךָ בְּעַד הַחוֹמָה:

Shmuel II / II Samuel
Chapter 21

22 The woman came to all the people with her clever plan; and they cut off the head of Sheba son of Bichri and threw it down to *Yoav*. He then sounded the *shofar*; all the men dispersed to their homes, and *Yoav* returned to the king in *Yerushalayim*.

23 *Yoav* was commander of the whole army [of] *Yisrael*; Benaiah son of *Yehoyada* was commander of the Cherethites and the Pelethites;

24 Adoram was in charge of forced labor; *Yehoshafat* son of *Achilud* was recorder;

25 Sheva was scribe; and *Tzadok* and *Evyatar* were *Kohanim*.

26 Ira the Yairite also served *David* as *Kohen*.

21 1 There was a famine during the reign of *David*, year after year for three years. *David* inquired of *Hashem*, and *Hashem* replied, "It is because of the bloodguilt of *Shaul* and [his] house, for he put some Givonites to death."

2 The king summoned the Givonites and spoke to them. – Now the Givonites were not of Israelite stock, but a remnant of the Amorites, to whom the Israelites had given an oath; and *Shaul* had tried to wipe them out in his zeal for the people of *Yisrael* and *Yehuda*.

3 *David* asked the Givonites, "What shall I do for you? How shall I make expiation, so that you may bless *Hashem*'s own people?"

4 The Givonites answered him, "We have no claim for silver or gold against *Shaul* and his household; and we have no claim on the life of any other man in *Yisrael*." And [*David*] responded, "Whatever you say I will do for you."

5 Thereupon they said to the king, "The man who massacred us and planned to exterminate us, so that we should not survive in all the territory of *Yisrael*

6 let seven of his male issue be handed over to us, and we will impale them before *Hashem* in *Giva* of *Shaul*, the chosen of *Hashem*." And the king replied, "I will do so."

7 The king spared *Mefiboshet* son of *Yehonatan* son of *Shaul*, because of the oath before *Hashem* between the two, between *David* and *Yehonatan* son of *Shaul*.

שמואל ב
פרק כא

כב וַתָּבוֹא הָאִשָּׁה אֶל־כָּל־הָעָם בְּחָכְמָתָהּ וַיִּכְרְתוּ אֶת־רֹאשׁ שֶׁבַע בֶּן־בִּכְרִי וַיַּשְׁלִכוּ אֶל־יוֹאָב וַיִּתְקַע בַּשּׁוֹפָר וַיָּפֻצוּ מֵעַל־הָעִיר אִישׁ לְאֹהָלָיו וְיוֹאָב שָׁב יְרוּשָׁלִַם אֶל־הַמֶּלֶךְ׃

כג וְיוֹאָב אֶל כָּל־הַצָּבָא יִשְׂרָאֵל וּבְנָיָה בֶּן־יְהוֹיָדָע עַל־הכרי [הַכְּרֵתִי] וְעַל־הַפְּלֵתִי׃

כד וַאֲדֹרָם עַל־הַמַּס וִיהוֹשָׁפָט בֶּן־אֲחִילוּד הַמַּזְכִּיר׃

כה ושיא [וּשְׁוָא] סֹפֵר וְצָדוֹק וְאֶבְיָתָר כֹּהֲנִים׃

כו וְגַם עִירָא הַיָּאִרִי הָיָה כֹהֵן לְדָוִד׃

כא א וַיְהִי רָעָב בִּימֵי דָוִד שָׁלֹשׁ שָׁנִים שָׁנָה אַחֲרֵי שָׁנָה וַיְבַקֵּשׁ דָּוִד אֶת־פְּנֵי יְהֹוָה וַיֹּאמֶר יְהֹוָה אֶל־שָׁאוּל וְאֶל־בֵּית הַדָּמִים עַל־אֲשֶׁר־הֵמִית אֶת־הַגִּבְעֹנִים׃

ב וַיִּקְרָא הַמֶּלֶךְ לַגִּבְעֹנִים וַיֹּאמֶר אֲלֵיהֶם וְהַגִּבְעֹנִים לֹא מִבְּנֵי יִשְׂרָאֵל הֵמָּה כִּי אִם־מִיֶּתֶר הָאֱמֹרִי וּבְנֵי יִשְׂרָאֵל נִשְׁבְּעוּ לָהֶם וַיְבַקֵּשׁ שָׁאוּל לְהַכֹּתָם בְּקַנֹּאתוֹ לִבְנֵי־יִשְׂרָאֵל וִיהוּדָה׃

ג וַיֹּאמֶר דָּוִד אֶל־הַגִּבְעֹנִים מָה אֶעֱשֶׂה לָכֶם וּבַמָּה אֲכַפֵּר וּבָרְכוּ אֶת־נַחֲלַת יְהֹוָה׃

ד וַיֹּאמְרוּ לוֹ הַגִּבְעֹנִים אֵין־לי [לָנוּ] כֶּסֶף וְזָהָב עִם־שָׁאוּל וְעִם־בֵּיתוֹ וְאֵין־לָנוּ אִישׁ לְהָמִית בְּיִשְׂרָאֵל וַיֹּאמֶר מָה־אַתֶּם אֹמְרִים אֶעֱשֶׂה לָכֶם׃

ה וַיֹּאמְרוּ אֶל־הַמֶּלֶךְ הָאִישׁ אֲשֶׁר כִּלָּנוּ וַאֲשֶׁר דִּמָּה־לָנוּ נִשְׁמַדְנוּ מֵהִתְיַצֵּב בְּכָל־גְּבֻל יִשְׂרָאֵל׃

ו ינתן [יֻתַּן־] לָנוּ שִׁבְעָה אֲנָשִׁים מִבָּנָיו וְהוֹקַעֲנוּם לַיהֹוָה בְּגִבְעַת שָׁאוּל בְּחִיר יְהֹוָה וַיֹּאמֶר הַמֶּלֶךְ אֲנִי אֶתֵּן׃

ז וַיַּחְמֹל הַמֶּלֶךְ עַל־מְפִי־בֹשֶׁת בֶּן־יְהוֹנָתָן בֶּן־שָׁאוּל עַל־שְׁבֻעַת יְהֹוָה אֲשֶׁר בֵּינֹתָם בֵּין דָּוִד וּבֵין יְהוֹנָתָן בֶּן־שָׁאוּל׃

Shmuel II / II Samuel
Chapter 21

שמואל ב
פרק כא

8 Instead, the king took Armoni and *Mefiboshet*, the two sons that Rizpah daughter of Aiah bore to *Shaul*, and the five sons that Merab daughter of *Shaul* bore to Adriel son of *Barzilai* the Meholathite,

ח וַיִּקַּח הַמֶּלֶךְ אֶת־שְׁנֵי בְּנֵי רִצְפָּה בַת־אַיָּה אֲשֶׁר יָלְדָה לְשָׁאוּל אֶת־אַרְמֹנִי וְאֶת־מְפִבֹשֶׁת וְאֶת־חֲמֵשֶׁת בְּנֵי מִיכַל בַּת־שָׁאוּל אֲשֶׁר יָלְדָה לְעַדְרִיאֵל בֶּן־בַּרְזִלַּי הַמְּחֹלָתִי:

9 and he handed them over to the Givonites. They impaled them on the mountain before *Hashem*; all seven of them perished at the same time. They were put to death in the first days of the harvest, the beginning of the barley harvest.

ט וַיִּתְּנֵם בְּיַד הַגִּבְעֹנִים וַיֹּקִיעֻם בָּהָר לִפְנֵי יְהֹוָה וַיִּפְּלוּ שְׁבַעְתָּם [שְׁבַעְתָּיִם] יָחַד וְהֵם [וְהֵמָּה] הֻמְתוּ בִּימֵי קָצִיר בָּרִאשֹׁנִים תְּחִלַּת [בִּתְחִלַּת] קְצִיר שְׂעֹרִים:

10 Then Rizpah daughter of Aiah took sackcloth and spread it on a rock for herself, and she stayed there from the beginning of the harvest until rain from the sky fell on the bodies; she did not let the birds of the sky settle on them by day or the wild beasts [approach] by night.

י וַתִּקַּח רִצְפָּה בַת־אַיָּה אֶת־הַשַּׂק וַתַּטֵּהוּ לָהּ אֶל־הַצּוּר מִתְּחִלַּת קָצִיר עַד נִתַּךְ־מַיִם עֲלֵיהֶם מִן־הַשָּׁמָיִם וְלֹא־נָתְנָה עוֹף הַשָּׁמַיִם לָנוּחַ עֲלֵיהֶם יוֹמָם וְאֶת־חַיַּת הַשָּׂדֶה לָיְלָה:

11 *David* was told what *Shaul*'s concubine Rizpah daughter of Aiah had done.

יא וַיֻּגַּד לְדָוִד אֵת אֲשֶׁר־עָשְׂתָה רִצְפָּה בַת־אַיָּה פִּלֶגֶשׁ שָׁאוּל:

12 And *David* went and took the bones of *Shaul* and of his son *Yehonatan* from the citizens of Jabesh-gilead, who had made off with them from the public square of Beth-shan, where the Philistines had hung them up on the day the Philistines killed *Shaul* at Gilboa.

יב וַיֵּלֶךְ דָּוִד וַיִּקַּח אֶת־עַצְמוֹת שָׁאוּל וְאֶת־עַצְמוֹת יְהוֹנָתָן בְּנוֹ מֵאֵת בַּעֲלֵי יָבֵישׁ גִּלְעָד אֲשֶׁר גָּנְבוּ אֹתָם מֵרְחֹב בֵּית־שַׁן אֲשֶׁר תְּלָאוּם [תְּלָאוּם] שָׁם הַפְּלִשְׁתִּים [שָׁמָּה] [פְּלִשְׁתִּים] בְּיוֹם הַכּוֹת פְּלִשְׁתִּים אֶת־שָׁאוּל בַּגִּלְבֹּעַ:

13 He brought up the bones of *Shaul* and of his son *Yehonatan* from there; and he gathered the bones of those who had been impaled.

יג וַיַּעַל מִשָּׁם אֶת־עַצְמוֹת שָׁאוּל וְאֶת־עַצְמוֹת יְהוֹנָתָן בְּנוֹ וַיַּאַסְפוּ אֶת־עַצְמוֹת הַמּוּקָעִים:

14 And they buried the bones of *Shaul* and of his son *Yehonatan* in Zela, in the territory of *Binyamin*, in the tomb of his father *Keesh*. And when all that the king had commanded was done, *Hashem* responded to the plea of the land thereafter.

יד וַיִּקְבְּרוּ אֶת־עַצְמוֹת־שָׁאוּל וִיהוֹנָתָן־בְּנוֹ בְּאֶרֶץ בִּנְיָמִן בְּצֵלָע בְּקֶבֶר קִישׁ אָבִיו וַיַּעֲשׂוּ כֹּל אֲשֶׁר־צִוָּה הַמֶּלֶךְ וַיֵּעָתֵר אֱלֹהִים לָאָרֶץ אַחֲרֵי־כֵן:

va-yik-b'-RU et atz-MOT sha-UL vee-ho-na-tan b'-NO b'-E-retz bin-ya-MIN b'-tzay-LA b'-KE-ver KEESH a-VEEV va-ya-a-SU KOL a-sher tzi-VAH ha-ME-lekh va-yay-a-TAYR e-lo-HEEM la-A-retz a-kha-ray KHAYN

21:14 And they buried the bones of *Shaul* King David buries the remains of King *Shaul* and Yonatan in their ancestral burial area within the territory of the tribe of *Binyamin*. Metzudat David adds that David also makes sure that they are properly eulogized throughout the land, with King *David* himself giving one of the eulogies. Though this was particularly important due to the honor given to a king, the concern that everyone be provided a proper burial has been a core value from antiquity until today. For example, following Israel's War for Independence, the army's Chief Rabbi, Shlomo Goren, worked day and night to bring the remains of fallen Israeli fighters to proper burial. He risked his life by walking through minefields, and often dug through the earth with his own hands, to ensure that every soldier killed in action would receive a proper burial.

Shmuel II / II Samuel
Chapter 22

15 Again war broke out between the Philistines and *Yisrael*, and *David* and the men with him went down and fought the Philistines; *David* grew weary,

16 and Ishbi-benob tried to kill *David*. – He was a descendant of the Raphah; his bronze spear weighed three hundred *shekalim* and he wore new armor.

17 But *Avishai* son of *Tzeruya* came to his aid; he attacked the Philistine and killed him. It was then that *David*'s men declared to him on oath, "You shall not go with us into battle any more, lest you extinguish the lamp of *Yisrael*!"

18 After this, fighting broke out again with the Philistines, at Gob; that was when Sibbecai the Hushathite killed Saph, a descendant of the Raphah.

19 Again there was fighting with the Philistines at Gob; and *Elchanan* son of Jaareoregim the Bethlehemite killed Goliath the Gittite, whose spear had a shaft like a weaver's bar.

20 Once again there was fighting, at Gath. There was a giant of a man, who had six fingers on each hand and six toes on each foot, twenty-four in all; he too was descended from the Raphah.

21 When he taunted *Yisrael*, *Yehonatan*, the son of *David*'s brother *Shim'i*, killed him.

22 Those four were descended from the Raphah in Gath, and they fell by the hands of *David* and his men.

22

1 *David* addressed the words of this song to *Hashem*, after *Hashem* had saved him from the hands of all his enemies and from the hands of *Shaul*.

2 He said: *Hashem*, my crag, my fastness, my deliverer!

3 O *Hashem*, the rock wherein I take shelter: My shield, my mighty champion, my fortress and refuge! My savior, You who rescue me from violence!

e-lo-HAY tzu-REE e-khe-seh BO ma-gi-NEE v'-KE-ren yish-EE mis-ga-BEE um-nu-SEE mo-shi-EE may-kha-MAS to-shi-AY-nee

---

22:3 O Hashem, the rock wherein I take shelter At various points in this chapter, King *David* refers to *Hashem* as "my rock." *Rashi* notes that a rock represents both strength and protection, as rocks can protect travelers from the wind and rain. It is interesting to note that the State of Israel's Declaration of Independence invokes divine protection by use of the phrase, "placing our trust in the Rock of Israel." *Hashem*'s help would in-

Signing the Declaration of Independence

Shmuel II / II Samuel
Chapter 22

4 All praise! I called on *Hashem*, And I was delivered from my enemies.

5 For the breakers of Death encompassed me, The torrents of Belial terrified me;

6 The snares of Sheol encircled me, The coils of Death engulfed me.

7 In my anguish I called on *Hashem*, Cried out to my God; In His Abode He heard my voice, My cry entered His ears.

8 Then the earth rocked and quaked, The foundations of heaven shook Rocked by His indignation.

9 Smoke went up from His nostrils, From His mouth came devouring fire; Live coals blazed forth from Him.

10 He bent the sky and came down, Thick cloud beneath His feet.

11 He mounted a cherub and flew; He was seen on the wings of the wind.

12 He made pavilions of darkness about Him, Dripping clouds, huge thunderheads;

13 In the brilliance before Him Blazed fiery coals.

14 *Hashem* thundered forth from heaven, The Most High sent forth His voice;

15 He let loose bolts, and scattered them; Lightning, and put them to rout.

16 The bed of the sea was exposed, The foundations of the world were laid bare By the mighty roaring of *Hashem*, At the blast of the breath of His nostrils.

17 He reached down from on high, He took me, Drew me out of the mighty waters;

18 He rescued me from my enemy so strong, From foes too mighty for me.

שמואל ב
פרק כב

ד מְהֻלָּל אֶקְרָא יְהֹוָה וּמֵאֹיְבַי אִוָּשֵׁעַ:

ה כִּי אֲפָפֻנִי מִשְׁבְּרֵי־מָוֶת נַחֲלֵי בְלִיַּעַל יְבַעֲתֻנִי:

ו חֶבְלֵי שְׁאוֹל סַבֻּנִי קִדְּמֻנִי מֹקְשֵׁי־מָוֶת:

ז בַּצַּר־לִי אֶקְרָא יְהֹוָה וְאֶל־אֱלֹהַי אֶקְרָא וַיִּשְׁמַע מֵהֵיכָלוֹ קוֹלִי וְשַׁוְעָתִי בְּאָזְנָיו:

ח ותגעש [וַיִּתְגָּעַשׁ] וַתִּרְעַשׁ הָאָרֶץ מוֹסְדוֹת הַשָּׁמַיִם יִרְגָּזוּ וַיִּתְגָּעֲשׁוּ כִּי־חָרָה לוֹ:

ט עָלָה עָשָׁן בְּאַפּוֹ וְאֵשׁ מִפִּיו תֹּאכֵל גֶּחָלִים בָּעֲרוּ מִמֶּנּוּ:

י וַיֵּט שָׁמַיִם וַיֵּרַד וַעֲרָפֶל תַּחַת רַגְלָיו:

יא וַיִּרְכַּב עַל־כְּרוּב וַיָּעֹף וַיֵּרָא עַל־כַּנְפֵי־רוּחַ:

יב וַיָּשֶׁת חֹשֶׁךְ סְבִיבֹתָיו סֻכּוֹת חַשְׁרַת־מַיִם עָבֵי שְׁחָקִים:

יג מִנֹּגַהּ נֶגְדּוֹ בָּעֲרוּ גַּחֲלֵי־אֵשׁ:

יד יַרְעֵם מִן־שָׁמַיִם יְהֹוָה וְעֶלְיוֹן יִתֵּן קוֹלוֹ:

טו וַיִּשְׁלַח חִצִּים וַיְפִיצֵם בָּרָק ויהמם [וַיָּהֹם]:

טז וַיֵּרָאוּ אֲפִקֵי יָם יִגָּלוּ מֹסְדוֹת תֵּבֵל בְּגַעֲרַת יְהֹוָה מִנִּשְׁמַת רוּחַ אַפּוֹ:

יז יִשְׁלַח מִמָּרוֹם יִקָּחֵנִי יַמְשֵׁנִי מִמַּיִם רַבִּים:

יח יַצִּילֵנִי מֵאֹיְבִי עָז מִשֹּׂנְאַי כִּי אָמְצוּ מִמֶּנִּי:

---

deed be necessary to establish an independent, free, democratic Jewish State in the Land of Israel that would be able to absorb Jews from around the world. Thankfully, the Rock of Israel continues to strengthen and protect the State of Israel.

Shmuel II / II Samuel
Chapter 22

שמואל ב
פרק כב

19	They attacked me on my day of calamity, But *Hashem* was my stay.	יְקַדְּמֻנִי בְּיוֹם אֵידִי וַיְהִי יְהֹוָה מִשְׁעָן לִי: יט
20	He brought me out to freedom, He rescued me because He was pleased with me.	וַיֹּצֵא לַמֶּרְחָב אֹתִי יְחַלְּצֵנִי כִּי־חָפֵץ בִּי: כ
21	*Hashem* rewarded me according to my merit, He requited the cleanness of my hands.	יִגְמְלֵנִי יְהֹוָה כְּצִדְקָתִי כְּבֹר יָדַי יָשִׁיב לִי: כא
22	For I have kept the ways of *Hashem* And have not been guilty before my God;	כִּי שָׁמַרְתִּי דַּרְכֵי יְהֹוָה וְלֹא רָשַׁעְתִּי מֵאֱלֹהָי: כב
23	I am mindful of all His rules And have not departed from His laws.	כִּי כָל־מִשְׁפָּטוֹ [מִשְׁפָּטָיו] לְנֶגְדִּי וְחֻקֹּתָיו לֹא־אָסוּר מִמֶּנָּה: כג
24	I have been blameless before Him, And have guarded myself against sinning –	וָאֶהְיֶה תָמִים לוֹ וָאֶשְׁתַּמְּרָה מֵעֲוֹנִי: כד
25	And *Hashem* has requited my merit, According to my purity in His sight.	וַיָּשֶׁב יְהֹוָה לִי כְּצִדְקָתִי כְּבֹרִי לְנֶגֶד עֵינָיו: כה
26	With the loyal You deal loyally; With the blameless hero, blamelessly.	עִם־חָסִיד תִּתְחַסָּד עִם־גִּבּוֹר תָּמִים תִּתַּמָּם: כו
27	With the pure You act in purity, And with the perverse You are wily.	עִם־נָבָר תִּתָּבָר וְעִם־עִקֵּשׁ תִּתַּפָּל: כז
28	To humble folk You give victory, And You look with scorn on the haughty.	וְאֶת־עַם עָנִי תּוֹשִׁיעַ וְעֵינֶיךָ עַל־רָמִים תַּשְׁפִּיל: כח
29	You, *Hashem*, are my lamp; *Hashem* lights up my darkness.	כִּי־אַתָּה נֵירִי יְהֹוָה וַיהֹוָה יַגִּיהַּ חָשְׁכִּי: כט
30	With You, I can rush a barrier, With my God, I can scale a wall.	כִּי בְכָה אָרוּץ גְּדוּד בֵּאלֹהַי אֲדַלֶּג־שׁוּר: ל
31	The way of *Hashem* is perfect, The word of *Hashem* is pure. He is a shield to all who take refuge in Him.	הָאֵל תָּמִים דַּרְכּוֹ אִמְרַת יְהֹוָה צְרוּפָה מָגֵן הוּא לְכֹל הַחֹסִים בּוֹ: לא
32	Yea, who is a god except *Hashem*, Who is a rock except *Hashem* –	כִּי מִי־אֵל מִבַּלְעֲדֵי יְהֹוָה וּמִי צוּר מִבַּלְעֲדֵי אֱלֹהֵינוּ: לב
33	The *Hashem*, my mighty stronghold, Who kept my path secure;	הָאֵל מָעוּזִּי חָיִל וַיַּתֵּר תָּמִים דרכו [דַּרְכִּי]: לג
34	Who made my legs like a deer's, And set me firm on the heights;	מְשַׁוֶּה רגליו [רַגְלַי] כָּאַיָּלוֹת וְעַל בָּמוֹתַי יַעֲמִדֵנִי: לד
35	Who trained my hands for battle, So that my arms can bend a bow of bronze!	מְלַמֵּד יָדַי לַמִּלְחָמָה וְנִחַת קֶשֶׁת־נְחוּשָׁה זְרֹעֹתָי: לה
36	You have granted me the shield of Your protection And Your providence has made me great.	וַתִּתֶּן־לִי מָגֵן יִשְׁעֶךָ וַעֲנֹתְךָ תַּרְבֵּנִי: לו
37	You have let me stride on freely, And my feet have not slipped.	תַּרְחִיב צַעֲדִי תַּחְתֵּנִי וְלֹא מָעֲדוּ קַרְסֻלָּי: לז
38	I pursued my enemies and wiped them out, I did not turn back till I destroyed them.	אֶרְדְּפָה אֹיְבַי וָאַשְׁמִידֵם וְלֹא אָשׁוּב עַד־כַּלּוֹתָם: לח

Shmuel II / II Samuel
Chapter 23

שמואל ב
פרק כג

39 I destroyed them, I struck them down; They rose no more, they lay at my feet.

לט וָאֲכַלֵּם וָאֶמְחָצֵם וְלֹא יְקוּמוּן וַיִּפְּלוּ תַּחַת רַגְלָי׃

40 You have girt me with strength for battle, Brought low my foes before me,

מ וַתַּזְרֵנִי חַיִל לַמִּלְחָמָה תַּכְרִיעַ קָמַי תַּחְתֵּנִי׃

41 Made my enemies turn tail before me, My foes – and I wiped them out.

מא וְאֹיְבַי תַּתָּה לִּי עֹרֶף מְשַׂנְאַי וָאַצְמִיתֵם׃

42 They looked, but there was none to deliver; To *Hashem*, but He answered them not.

מב יִשְׁעוּ וְאֵין מֹשִׁיעַ אֶל־יְהֹוָה וְלֹא עָנָם׃

43 I pounded them like dust of the earth, Stamped, crushed them like dirt of the streets.

מג וְאֶשְׁחָקֵם כַּעֲפַר־אָרֶץ כְּטִיט־חוּצוֹת אֲדִקֵּם אֶרְקָעֵם׃

44 You have rescued me from the strife of peoples, Kept me to be a ruler of nations; Peoples I knew not must serve me.

מד וַתְּפַלְּטֵנִי מֵרִיבֵי עַמִּי תִּשְׁמְרֵנִי לְרֹאשׁ גּוֹיִם עַם לֹא־יָדַעְתִּי יַעַבְדֻנִי׃

45 Aliens have cringed before me, Paid me homage at the mere report of me.

מה בְּנֵי נֵכָר יִתְכַּחֲשׁוּ־לִי לִשְׁמוֹעַ אֹזֶן יִשָּׁמְעוּ לִי׃

46 Aliens have lost courage And come trembling out of their fastnesses.

מו בְּנֵי נֵכָר יִבֹּלוּ וְיַחְגְּרוּ מִמִּסְגְּרוֹתָם׃

47 *Hashem* lives! Blessed is my rock! Exalted be *Hashem*, the rock Who gives me victory;

מז חַי־יְהֹוָה וּבָרוּךְ צוּרִי וְיָרֻם אֱלֹהֵי צוּר יִשְׁעִי׃

48 The *Hashem* who has vindicated me And made peoples subject to me,

מח הָאֵל הַנֹּתֵן נְקָמֹת לִי וּמוֹרִיד עַמִּים תַּחְתֵּנִי׃

49 Rescued me from my enemies, Raised me clear of my foes, Saved me from lawless men!

מט וּמוֹצִיאִי מֵאֹיְבָי וּמִקָּמַי תְּרוֹמְמֵנִי מֵאִישׁ חֲמָסִים תַּצִּילֵנִי׃

50 For this I sing Your praise among the nations And hymn Your name:

נ עַל־כֵּן אוֹדְךָ יְהֹוָה בַּגּוֹיִם וּלְשִׁמְךָ אֲזַמֵּר׃

51 Tower of victory to His king, Who deals graciously with His anointed, With *David* and his offspring evermore.

נא מִגְדִּיל [מִגְדּוֹל] יְשׁוּעוֹת מַלְכּוֹ וְעֹשֶׂה־חֶסֶד לִמְשִׁיחוֹ לְדָוִד וּלְזַרְעוֹ עַד־עוֹלָם׃

23
1 These are the last words of *David*: The utterance of *David* son of *Yishai*, The utterance of the man set on high, The anointed of the God of *Yaakov*, The favorite of the songs of *Yisrael*:

כג א וְאֵלֶּה דִּבְרֵי דָוִד הָאַחֲרֹנִים נְאֻם דָּוִד בֶּן־יִשַׁי וּנְאֻם הַגֶּבֶר הֻקַם עָל מְשִׁיחַ אֱלֹהֵי יַעֲקֹב וּנְעִים זְמִרוֹת יִשְׂרָאֵל׃

> v'-AY-leh div-RAY da-VID ha-a-kha-ro-NEEM n'-UM da-VID ben yi-SHAI un-UM ha-GE-ver hu-KAM AL m'-SHEE-akh e-lo-HAY ya-a-KOV u-n'-EEM z'-mi-ROT yis-ra-AYL

23:1 The favorite of the songs of *Yisrael* The Hebrew words *n'eem zemirot yisrael* (נעים זמרות ישראל), 'the favorite of the songs of *Yisrael*' or 'the sweet singer of Israel,' are a reference to King *David*. Though much of this chapter focuses on his worldly accomplishments, King *David* is an intensely spiritual person who strives with every ounce of his being to serve *Hashem*. According to the Sages (*Sanhedrin* 16b), King *David* had a harp hanging by his bed which would wake him when the wind blew its strings in the middle

Shmuel II / II Samuel
Chapter 23

שמואל ב
פרק כג

2 The spirit of *Hashem* has spoken through me, His message is on my tongue;

ב רוּחַ יְהֹוָה דִּבֶּר־בִּי וּמִלָּתוֹ עַל־לְשׁוֹנִי:

3 The God of *Yisrael* has spoken, The Rock of *Yisrael* said concerning me: "He who rules men justly, He who rules in awe of *Hashem*

ג אָמַר אֱלֹהֵי יִשְׂרָאֵל לִי דִבֶּר צוּר יִשְׂרָאֵל מוֹשֵׁל בָּאָדָם צַדִּיק מוֹשֵׁל יִרְאַת אֱלֹהִים:

4 Is like the light of morning at sunrise, A morning without clouds – Through sunshine and rain [Bringing] vegetation out of the earth."

ד וּכְאוֹר בֹּקֶר יִזְרַח־שָׁמֶשׁ בֹּקֶר לֹא עָבוֹת מִנֹּגַהּ מִמָּטָר דֶּשֶׁא מֵאָרֶץ:

5 Is not my House established before *Hashem*? For He has granted me an eternal pact, Drawn up in full and secured. Will He not cause all my success And [my] every desire to blossom?

ה כִּי־לֹא־כֵן בֵּיתִי עִם־אֵל כִּי בְרִית עוֹלָם שָׂם לִי עֲרוּכָה בַכֹּל וּשְׁמֻרָה כִּי־כָל־יִשְׁעִי וְכָל־חֵפֶץ כִּי־לֹא יַצְמִיחַ:

6 But the wicked shall all Be raked aside like thorns; For no one will take them in his hand.

ו וּבְלִיַּעַל כְּקוֹץ מֻנָד כֻּלָּהַם כִּי־לֹא בְיָד יִקָּחוּ:

7 Whoever touches them Must arm himself with iron And the shaft of a spear; And they must be burned up on the spot.

ז וְאִישׁ יִגַּע בָּהֶם יִמָּלֵא בַרְזֶל וְעֵץ חֲנִית וּבָאֵשׁ שָׂרוֹף יִשָּׂרְפוּ בַּשָּׁבֶת:

8 These are the names of *David*'s warriors: Josheb-basshebeth, a Tahchemonite, the chief officer – he is Adino the Eznite; [he wielded his spear] against eight hundred and slew them on one occasion.

ח אֵלֶּה שְׁמוֹת הַגִּבֹּרִים אֲשֶׁר לְדָוִד יֹשֵׁב בַּשֶּׁבֶת תַּחְכְּמֹנִי רֹאשׁ הַשָּׁלִשִׁי הוּא עֲדִינוֹ הָעֶצְנוֹ [הָעֶצְנִי] עַל־שְׁמֹנֶה מֵאוֹת חָלָל בְּפַעַם אֶחָד [אֶחָת:]

9 Next to him was *Elazar* son of Dodo son of Ahohi. He was one of the three warriors with *David* when they defied the Philistines gathered there for battle. The Israelite soldiers retreated,

ט וְאַחֲרוֹ [וְאַחֲרָיו] אֶלְעָזָר בֶּן־דֹּדִי [דֹּדוֹ] בֶּן־אֲחֹחִי בִּשְׁלֹשָׁה גִּבֹּרִים [הַגִּבֹּרִים] עִם־דָּוִד בְּחָרְפָם בַּפְּלִשְׁתִּים נֶאֶסְפוּ־שָׁם לַמִּלְחָמָה וַיַּעֲלוּ אִישׁ יִשְׂרָאֵל:

10 but he held his ground. He struck down Philistines until his arm grew tired and his hand stuck to his sword; and *Hashem* wrought a great victory that day. Then the troops came back to him – but only to strip [the slain].

י הוּא קָם וַיַּךְ בַּפְּלִשְׁתִּים עַד כִּי־יָגְעָה יָדוֹ וַתִּדְבַּק יָדוֹ אֶל־הַחֶרֶב וַיַּעַשׂ יְהֹוָה תְּשׁוּעָה גְדוֹלָה בַּיּוֹם הַהוּא וְהָעָם יָשֻׁבוּ אַחֲרָיו אַךְ־לְפַשֵּׁט:

11 Next to him was Shammah son of Age the Ararite. The Philistines had gathered in force where there was a plot of ground full of lentils; and the troops fled from the Philistines.

יא וְאַחֲרָיו שַׁמָּא בֶן־אָגֵא הָרָרִי וַיֵּאָסְפוּ פְלִשְׁתִּים לַחַיָּה וַתְּהִי־שָׁם חֶלְקַת הַשָּׂדֶה מְלֵאָה עֲדָשִׁים וְהָעָם נָס מִפְּנֵי פְלִשְׁתִּים:

12 But [Shammah] took his stand in the middle of the plot and defended it, and he routed the Philistines. Thus *Hashem* wrought a great victory.

יב וַיִּתְיַצֵּב בְּתוֹךְ־הַחֶלְקָה וַיַּצִּילֶהָ וַיַּךְ אֶת־פְּלִשְׁתִּים וַיַּעַשׂ יְהֹוָה תְּשׁוּעָה גְדוֹלָה:

---

of the night. He would then arise and spend the rest of the night in study and praying. In addition to being a scholar, King *David* is the author of most of *Sefer Tehillim*, the Book of Psalms, excelling not only in *Torah* study but also in prayer. And when he sins, he repents with a broken heart. Though his wish to build God's Holy Temple is not granted, he is able to make many of its preparations. King *David* serves as the quintessential leader who uses all of his talents, and all aspects of his personality, to serve *Hashem* and His people.

Shmuel II/II Samuel
Chapter 23

13 Once, during the harvest, three of the thirty chiefs went down to *David* at the cave of *Adulam*, while a force of Philistines was encamped in the Valley of Rephaim.

14 *David* was then in the stronghold, and a Philistine garrison was then at *Beit Lechem*.

15 *David* felt a craving and said, "If only I could get a drink of water from the cistern which is by the gate of *Beit Lechem*!"

16 So the three warriors got through the Philistine camp and drew water from the cistern which is by the gate of *Beit Lechem*, and they carried it back. But when they brought it to *David* he would not drink it, and he poured it out as a libation to *Hashem*.

17 For he said, "*Hashem* forbid that I should do this! Can [I drink] the blood of the men who went at the risk of their lives?" So he would not drink it. Such were the exploits of the three warriors.

18 *Avishai*, the brother of *Yoav* son of *Tzeruya*, was head of another three. He once wielded his spear against three hundred and slew them.

19 He won a name among the three; since he was the most highly regarded among the three, he became their leader. However, he did not attain to the three.

20 Benaiah son of *Yehoyada*, from Kabzeel, was a brave soldier who performed great deeds. He killed the two [sons] of Ariel of Moab. Once, on a snowy day, he went down into a pit and killed a lion.

21 He also killed an Egyptian, a huge man. The Egyptian had a spear in his hand, yet [Benaiah] went down against him with a club, wrenched the spear out of the Egyptian's hand, and killed him with his own spear.

22 Such were the exploits of Benaiah son of *Yehoyada*; and he won a name among the three warriors.

23 He was highly regarded among the thirty, but he did not attain to the three. *David* put him in charge of his bodyguard.

24 Among the thirty were *Asael*, the brother of *Yoav*; *Elhacnan* son of Dodo [from] *Beit Lechem*,

שמואל ב
פרק כג

יג וַיֵּרְדוּ שְׁלֹשִׁים [שְׁלֹשָׁה] מֵהַשְּׁלֹשִׁים רֹאשׁ וַיָּבֹאוּ אֶל־קָצִיר אֶל־דָּוִד אֶל־מְעָרַת עֲדֻלָּם וְחַיַּת פְּלִשְׁתִּים חֹנָה בְּעֵמֶק רְפָאִים:

יד וְדָוִד אָז בַּמְּצוּדָה וּמַצַּב פְּלִשְׁתִּים אָז בֵּית לָחֶם:

טו וַיִּתְאַוֶּה דָוִד וַיֹּאמַר מִי יַשְׁקֵנִי מַיִם מִבֹּאר בֵּית־לֶחֶם אֲשֶׁר בַּשָּׁעַר:

טז וַיִּבְקְעוּ שְׁלֹשֶׁת הַגִּבֹּרִים בְּמַחֲנֵה פְלִשְׁתִּים וַיִּשְׁאֲבוּ־מַיִם מִבֹּאר בֵּית־לֶחֶם אֲשֶׁר בַּשַּׁעַר וַיִּשְׂאוּ וַיָּבִאוּ אֶל־דָּוִד וְלֹא אָבָה לִשְׁתּוֹתָם וַיַּסֵּךְ אֹתָם לַיהוָה:

יז וַיֹּאמֶר חָלִילָה לִּי יְהוָה מֵעֲשֹׂתִי זֹאת הֲדַם הָאֲנָשִׁים הַהֹלְכִים בְּנַפְשׁוֹתָם וְלֹא אָבָה לִשְׁתּוֹתָם אֵלֶּה עָשׂוּ שְׁלֹשֶׁת הַגִּבֹּרִים:

יח וַאֲבִישַׁי אֲחִי יוֹאָב בֶּן־צְרוּיָה הוּא רֹאשׁ הַשְּׁלִשִׁי [הַשְּׁלֹשָׁה] וְהוּא עוֹרֵר אֶת־חֲנִיתוֹ עַל־שְׁלֹשׁ מֵאוֹת חָלָל וְלוֹ־שֵׁם בַּשְּׁלֹשָׁה:

יט מִן־הַשְּׁלֹשָׁה הֲכִי נִכְבָּד וַיְהִי לָהֶם לְשָׂר וְעַד־הַשְּׁלֹשָׁה לֹא־בָא:

כ וּבְנָיָהוּ בֶן־יְהוֹיָדָע בֶּן־אִישׁ־חַי [חַיִל] רַב־פְּעָלִים מִקַּבְצְאֵל הוּא הִכָּה אֵת שְׁנֵי אֲרִאֵל מוֹאָב וְהוּא יָרַד וְהִכָּה אֶת־הָאֲרִיָּה [הָאֲרִי] בְּתוֹךְ הַבֹּאר בְּיוֹם הַשָּׁלֶג:

כא וְהוּא־הִכָּה אֶת־אִישׁ מִצְרִי אשר [אִישׁ] מַרְאֶה וּבְיַד הַמִּצְרִי חֲנִית וַיֵּרֶד אֵלָיו בַּשָּׁבֶט וַיִּגְזֹל אֶת־הַחֲנִית מִיַּד הַמִּצְרִי וַיַּהַרְגֵהוּ בַּחֲנִיתוֹ:

כב אֵלֶּה עָשָׂה בְּנָיָהוּ בֶּן־יְהוֹיָדָע וְלוֹ־שֵׁם בִּשְׁלֹשָׁה הַגִּבֹּרִים:

כג מִן־הַשְּׁלֹשִׁים נִכְבָּד וְאֶל־הַשְּׁלֹשָׁה לֹא־בָא וַיְשִׂמֵהוּ דָוִד אֶל־מִשְׁמַעְתּוֹ:

כד עֲשָׂה־אֵל אֲחִי־יוֹאָב בַּשְּׁלֹשִׁים אֶלְחָנָן בֶּן־דֹּדוֹ בֵּית לָחֶם:

Shmuel II / II Samuel
Chapter 24

שְׁמוּאֵל ב
פרק כד

25 Shammah the Harodite, *Elika* the Harodite,

כה שַׁמָּה הַחֲרֹדִי אֱלִיקָא הַחֲרֹדִי:

26 Helez the Paltite, Ira son of Ikkesh from *Tekoa*,

כו חֶלֶץ הַפַּלְטִי עִירָא בֶן־עִקֵּשׁ הַתְּקוֹעִי:

27 Abiezer of *Anatot*, Mebunnai the Hushathite,

כז אֲבִיעֶזֶר הָעַנְּתֹתִי מְבֻנַּי הַחֻשָׁתִי:

28 Zalmon the Ahohite, Maharai the Netophathite,

כח צַלְמוֹן הָאֲחֹחִי מַהְרַי הַנְּטֹפָתִי:

29 Heleb son of Baanah the Netophathite, Ittai son of Ribai from *Giva* of the Benjaminites,

כט חֵלֶב בֶּן־בַּעֲנָה הַנְּטֹפָתִי אִתַּי בֶּן־רִיבַי מִגִּבְעַת בְּנֵי בִנְיָמִן:

30 Benaiah of Pirathon, Hiddai of Nahale-gaash,

ל בְּנָיָהוּ פִּרְעָתֹנִי הִדַּי מִנַּחֲלֵי גָעַשׁ:

31 Abi-albon the Arbathite, Azmaveth the Barhumite,

לא אֲבִי־עַלְבוֹן הָעַרְבָתִי עַזְמָוֶת הַבַּרְחֻמִי:

32 Eliahba of Shaalbon, sons of Jashen, *Yehonatan*,

לב אֶלְיַחְבָּא הַשַּׁעַלְבֹנִי בְּנֵי יָשֵׁן יְהוֹנָתָן:

33 Shammah the Ararite, Ahiam son of Sharar the Ararite,

לג שַׁמָּה הַהֲרָרִי אֲחִיאָם בֶּן־שָׁרָר הָאֲרָרִי:

34 Eliphelet son of Ahasbai son of the Maacathite, Eliam son of *Achitofel* the Gilonite,

לד אֱלִיפֶלֶט בֶּן־אֲחַסְבַּי בֶּן־הַמַּעֲכָתִי אֱלִיעָם בֶּן־אֲחִיתֹפֶל הַגִּלֹנִי:

35 Hezrai the Carmelite, Paarai the Arbite,

לה חֶצְרַי [חֶצְרוֹ] הַכַּרְמְלִי פַּעֲרַי הָאַרְבִּי:

36 Igal son of *Natan* from Zobah, Bani the Gadite,

לו יִגְאָל בֶּן־נָתָן מִצֹּבָה בָּנִי הַגָּדִי:

37 Zelek the Ammonite, Naharai the Beerothite – the arms-bearer of *Yoav* son of *Tzeruya*

לז צֶלֶק הָעַמֹּנִי נַחְרַי הַבְּאֵרֹתִי נֹשֵׂא [נֹשְׂאֵי] כְּלֵי יוֹאָב בֶּן־צְרֻיָה:

38 Ira the Ithrite, Gareb the Ithrite,

לח עִירָא הַיִּתְרִי גָּרֵב הַיִּתְרִי:

39 *Uriya* the Hittite: thirty-seven in all.

לט אוּרִיָּה הַחִתִּי כֹּל שְׁלֹשִׁים וְשִׁבְעָה:

24 1 The anger of *Hashem* again flared up against *Yisrael*; and He incited *David* against them, saying, "Go and number *Yisrael* and *Yehuda*."

כד א וַיֹּסֶף אַף־יְהוָה לַחֲרוֹת בְּיִשְׂרָאֵל וַיָּסֶת אֶת־דָּוִד בָּהֶם לֵאמֹר לֵךְ מְנֵה אֶת־יִשְׂרָאֵל וְאֶת־יְהוּדָה:

2 The king said to *Yoav*, his army commander, "Make the rounds of all the tribes of *Yisrael*, from *Dan* to *Be'er Sheva*, and take a census of the people, so that I may know the size of the population."

ב וַיֹּאמֶר הַמֶּלֶךְ אֶל־יוֹאָב שַׂר־הַחַיִל אֲשֶׁר־אִתּוֹ שׁוּט־נָא בְּכָל־שִׁבְטֵי יִשְׂרָאֵל מִדָּן וְעַד־בְּאֵר שֶׁבַע וּפִקְדוּ אֶת־הָעָם וְיָדַעְתִּי אֵת מִסְפַּר הָעָם:

3 *Yoav* answered the king, "May *Hashem* your God increase the number of the people a hundredfold, while your own eyes see it! But why should my lord king want this?"

ג וַיֹּאמֶר יוֹאָב אֶל־הַמֶּלֶךְ וְיוֹסֵף יְהוָה אֱלֹהֶיךָ אֶל־הָעָם כָּהֵם וְכָהֵם מֵאָה פְעָמִים וְעֵינֵי אֲדֹנִי־הַמֶּלֶךְ רֹאוֹת וַאדֹנִי הַמֶּלֶךְ לָמָּה חָפֵץ בַּדָּבָר הַזֶּה:

4 However, the king's command to *Yoav* and to the officers of the army remained firm; and *Yoav* and the officers of the army set out, at the instance of the king, to take a census of the people of *Yisrael*.

ד וַיֶּחֱזַק דְּבַר־הַמֶּלֶךְ אֶל־יוֹאָב וְעַל שָׂרֵי הֶחָיִל וַיֵּצֵא יוֹאָב וְשָׂרֵי הַחַיִל לִפְנֵי הַמֶּלֶךְ לִפְקֹד אֶת־הָעָם אֶת־יִשְׂרָאֵל:

5 They crossed the *Yarden* and encamped at Aroer, on the right side of the town, which is in the middle of the wadi of *Gad*, and [went on] to Jazer.

ה וַיַּעַבְרוּ אֶת־הַיַּרְדֵּן וַיַּחֲנוּ בַעֲרוֹעֵר יְמִין הָעִיר אֲשֶׁר בְּתוֹךְ־הַנַּחַל הַגָּד וְאֶל־יַעְזֵר:

796

Shmuel II/II Samuel
Chapter 24

שמואל ב
פרק כד

6 They continued to *Gilad* and to the region of Tahtim-hodshi, and they came to Dan-jaan and around to Sidon.

ו וַיָּבֹאוּ הַגִּלְעָדָה וְאֶל־אֶרֶץ תַּחְתִּים חָדְשִׁי וַיָּבֹאוּ דָּנָה יַּעַן וְסָבִיב אֶל־צִידוֹן:

7 They went onto the fortress of Tyre and all the towns of the Hivites and Canaanites, and finished at *Be'er Sheva* in southern *Yehuda*.

ז וַיָּבֹאוּ מִבְצַר־צֹר וְכָל־עָרֵי הַחִוִּי וְהַכְּנַעֲנִי וַיֵּצְאוּ אֶל־נֶגֶב יְהוּדָה בְּאֵר שָׁבַע:

8 They traversed the whole country, and then they came back to *Yerushalayim* at the end of nine months and twenty days.

ח וַיָּשֻׁטוּ בְּכָל־הָאָרֶץ וַיָּבֹאוּ מִקְצֵה תִשְׁעָה חֳדָשִׁים וְעֶשְׂרִים יוֹם יְרוּשָׁלָ͏ִם:

9 *Yoav* reported to the king the number of the people that had been recorded: in *Yisrael* there were 800,000 soldiers ready to draw the sword, and the men of *Yehuda* numbered 500,000.

ט וַיִּתֵּן יוֹאָב אֶת־מִסְפַּר מִפְקַד־הָעָם אֶל־הַמֶּלֶךְ וַתְּהִי יִשְׂרָאֵל שְׁמֹנֶה מֵאוֹת אֶלֶף אִישׁ־חַיִל שֹׁלֵף חֶרֶב וְאִישׁ יְהוּדָה חֲמֵשׁ־מֵאוֹת אֶלֶף אִישׁ:

10 But afterward *David* reproached himself for having numbered the people. And *David* said to *Hashem*, "I have sinned grievously in what I have done. Please, *Hashem*, remit the guilt of Your servant, for I have acted foolishly."

י וַיַּךְ לֵב־דָּוִד אֹתוֹ אַחֲרֵי־כֵן סָפַר אֶת־הָעָם וַיֹּאמֶר דָּוִד אֶל־יְהֹוָה חָטָאתִי מְאֹד אֲשֶׁר עָשִׂיתִי וְעַתָּה יְהֹוָה הַעֲבֶר־נָא אֶת־עֲוֹן עַבְדְּךָ כִּי נִסְכַּלְתִּי מְאֹד:

11 When *David* rose in the morning, the word of *Hashem* had come to the *Navi Gad*, *David's* seer:

יא וַיָּקָם דָּוִד בַּבֹּקֶר וּדְבַר־יְהֹוָה הָיָה אֶל־גָּד הַנָּבִיא חֹזֵה דָוִד לֵאמֹר:

12 "Go and tell *David*, 'Thus said *Hashem*: I hold three things over you; choose one of them, and I will bring it upon you.'"

יב הָלוֹךְ וְדִבַּרְתָּ אֶל־דָּוִד כֹּה אָמַר יְהֹוָה שָׁלֹשׁ אָנֹכִי נוֹטֵל עָלֶיךָ בְּחַר־לְךָ אַחַת־מֵהֶם וְאֶעֱשֶׂה־לָּךְ:

13 *Gad* came to *David* and told him; he asked, "Shall a seven-year famine come upon you in the land, or shall you be in flight from your adversaries for three months while they pursue you, or shall there be three days of pestilence in your land? Now consider carefully what reply I shall take back to Him who sent me."

יג וַיָּבֹא־גָד אֶל־דָּוִד וַיַּגֶּד־לוֹ וַיֹּאמֶר לוֹ הֲתָבוֹא לְךָ שֶׁבַע שָׁנִים רָעָב בְּאַרְצֶךָ אִם־שְׁלֹשָׁה חֳדָשִׁים נֻסְךָ לִפְנֵי־צָרֶיךָ וְהוּא רֹדְפֶךָ וְאִם־הֱיוֹת שְׁלֹשֶׁת יָמִים דֶּבֶר בְּאַרְצֶךָ עַתָּה דַּע וּרְאֵה מָה־אָשִׁיב שֹׁלְחִי דָּבָר:

14 *David* said to *Gad*, "I am in great distress. Let us fall into the hands of *Hashem*, for His compassion is great; and let me not fall into the hands of men."

יד וַיֹּאמֶר דָּוִד אֶל־גָּד צַר־לִי מְאֹד נִפְּלָה־נָּא בְיַד־יְהֹוָה כִּי־רַבִּים רחמו [רַחֲמָיו] וּבְיַד־אָדָם אַל־אֶפֹּלָה:

15 *Hashem* sent a pestilence upon *Yisrael* from morning until the set time; and 70,000 of the people died, from *Dan* to *Be'er Sheva*.

טו וַיִּתֵּן יְהֹוָה דֶּבֶר בְּיִשְׂרָאֵל מֵהַבֹּקֶר וְעַד־עֵת מוֹעֵד וַיָּמָת מִן־הָעָם מִדָּן וְעַד־בְּאֵר שֶׁבַע שִׁבְעִים אֶלֶף אִישׁ:

16 But when the angel extended his hand against *Yerushalayim* to destroy it, *Hashem* renounced further punishment and said to the angel who was destroying the people, "Enough! Stay your hand!" The angel of *Hashem* was then by the threshing floor of Araunah the Jebusite.

טז וַיִּשְׁלַח יָדוֹ הַמַּלְאָךְ יְרוּשָׁלַ͏ִם לְשַׁחֲתָהּ וַיִּנָּחֶם יְהֹוָה אֶל־הָרָעָה וַיֹּאמֶר לַמַּלְאָךְ הַמַּשְׁחִית בָּעָם רַב עַתָּה הֶרֶף יָדֶךָ וּמַלְאַךְ יְהֹוָה הָיָה עִם־גֹּרֶן האורנה [הָאֲרַוְנָה] הַיְבֻסִי:

Shmuel II / II Samuel
Chapter 24

שמואל ב
פרק כד

17 When *David* saw the angel who was striking down the people, he said to *Hashem*, "I alone am guilty, I alone have done wrong; but these poor sheep, what have they done? Let Your hand fall upon me and my father's house!"

יז וַיֹּאמֶר דָּוִד אֶל־יְהֹוָה בִּרְאֹתוֹ אֶת־הַמַּלְאָךְ הַמַּכֶּה בָעָם וַיֹּאמֶר הִנֵּה אָנֹכִי חָטָאתִי וְאָנֹכִי הֶעֱוֵיתִי וְאֵלֶּה הַצֹּאן מֶה עָשׂוּ תְּהִי נָא יָדְךָ בִּי וּבְבֵית אָבִי׃

18 *Gad* came to *David* the same day and said to him, "Go and set up a *Mizbayach* to *Hashem* on the threshing floor of Araunah the Jebusite."

יח וַיָּבֹא־גָד אֶל־דָּוִד בַּיּוֹם הַהוּא וַיֹּאמֶר לוֹ עֲלֵה הָקֵם לַיהֹוָה מִזְבֵּחַ בְּגֹרֶן אֲרַנְיָה [אֲרַוְנָה] הַיְבֻסִי׃

19 *David* went up, following *Gad*'s instructions, as *Hashem* had commanded.

יט וַיַּעַל דָּוִד כִּדְבַר־גָּד כַּאֲשֶׁר צִוָּה יְהֹוָה׃

20 Araunah looked out and saw the king and his courtiers approaching him. So Araunah went out and bowed low to the king, with his face to the ground.

כ וַיַּשְׁקֵף אֲרַוְנָה וַיַּרְא אֶת־הַמֶּלֶךְ וְאֶת־עֲבָדָיו עֹבְרִים עָלָיו וַיֵּצֵא אֲרַוְנָה וַיִּשְׁתַּחוּ לַמֶּלֶךְ אַפָּיו אָרְצָה׃

21 And Araunah asked, "Why has my lord the king come to his servant?" *David* replied, "To buy the threshing floor from you, that I may build a *Mizbayach* to *Hashem* and that the plague against the people may be checked."

כא וַיֹּאמֶר אֲרַוְנָה מַדּוּעַ בָּא אֲדֹנִי־הַמֶּלֶךְ אֶל־עַבְדּוֹ וַיֹּאמֶר דָּוִד לִקְנוֹת מֵעִמְּךָ אֶת־הַגֹּרֶן לִבְנוֹת מִזְבֵּחַ לַיהֹוָה וְתֵעָצַר הַמַּגֵּפָה מֵעַל הָעָם׃

22 And Araunah said to *David*, "Let my lord the king take it and offer up whatever he sees fit. Here are oxen for a burnt offering, and the threshing boards and the gear of the oxen for wood.

כב וַיֹּאמֶר אֲרַוְנָה אֶל־דָּוִד יִקַּח וְיַעַל אֲדֹנִי הַמֶּלֶךְ הַטּוֹב בְּעֵינָו [בְּעֵינָיו] רְאֵה הַבָּקָר לָעֹלָה וְהַמֹּרִגִּים וּכְלֵי הַבָּקָר לָעֵצִים׃

23 All this, O king, Araunah gives to Your Majesty. And may *Hashem* your God," Araunah added, "respond to you with favor!"

כג הַכֹּל נָתַן אֲרַוְנָה הַמֶּלֶךְ לַמֶּלֶךְ וַיֹּאמֶר אֲרַוְנָה אֶל־הַמֶּלֶךְ יְהֹוָה אֱלֹהֶיךָ יִרְצֶךָ׃

24 But the king replied to Araunah, "No, I will buy them from you at a price. I cannot sacrifice to *Hashem* my God burnt offerings that have cost me nothing." So *David* bought the threshing floor and the oxen for fifty *shekalim* of silver.

כד וַיֹּאמֶר הַמֶּלֶךְ אֶל־אֲרַוְנָה לֹא כִּי־קָנוֹ אֶקְנֶה מֵאוֹתְךָ בִּמְחִיר וְלֹא אַעֲלֶה לַיהֹוָה אֱלֹהַי עֹלוֹת חִנָּם וַיִּקֶן דָּוִד אֶת־הַגֹּרֶן וְאֶת־הַבָּקָר בְּכֶסֶף שְׁקָלִים חֲמִשִּׁים׃

va-YO-mer ha-ME-lekh el a-RAV-nah LO kee ka-NO ek-NEH may-o-t'-KHA bim-KHEER v'-LO a-a-LEH la-do-NAI e-lo-HAI o-LOT KHI-nam va-YI-ken da-VID et ha-GO-ren v'-et ha-ba-KAR b'-KHE-sef sh'-ka-LEEM kha-mi-SHEEM

24:24 But the king replied to Araunah, "No, I will buy them from you at a price" King *David* purchases the threshing floor of Araunah the Jebusite and, according to one classic rabbinic opinion, the entire city of *Yerushalayim*. That threshing floor, the place where he intends to offer sacrifices, is now called the Temple Mount in *Yerushalayim*. As this site would later become the location of the *Beit Hamikdash*, *David* purchases the land publicly, just as *Avraham* did when he purchased the cave of Machpelah in *Chevron* for a great sum of money and in front of witnesses (Genesis 23). Although, like *Avraham*, *David* was offered the site as a gift, he does not want any future generations to claim that it was stolen by the Children of Israel. Since the sale of each is recorded in the Bible, the Sages of the *Midrash* teach that *Yerushalayim*, *Chevron* and *Shechem* (which was similarly purchased by Jacob, see Genesis 33:19) are the three places that indisputably belong to the Jewish people.

Ancient Israelite coin from approximately 68 CE

798

Shmuel II/II Samuel
Chapter 24

25 And *David* built there a *Mizbayach* to *Hashem* and sacrificed burnt offerings and offerings of well-being. *Hashem* responded to the plea for the land, and the plague against *Yisrael* was checked.

שמואל ב
פרק כד

כה וַיִּבֶן שָׁם דָּוִד מִזְבֵּחַ לַיהֹוָה וַיַּעַל עֹלוֹת וּשְׁלָמִים וַיֵּעָתֵר יְהֹוָה לָאָרֶץ וַתֵּעָצַר הַמַּגֵּפָה מֵעַל יִשְׂרָאֵל׃

Sefer Melachim
The Book of Kings

Introduction and commentary by Rabbi Shmuel Jablon

Though *Sefer Melachim* (Book of Kings) is divided into two parts, Jewish tradition considers it a single book of 47 chapters. As we study these chapters, we experience both the highest points of the history of the Children of Israel, and the lowest. Despite the tragic ending, the high points of the book allow us to maintain hope for future.

The book begins with King *Shlomo* ascending the throne of his father, King *David*, as the first heir to the Davidic dynasty. Unlike his father, King *Shlomo* rules over a kingdom that is united, strong and at peace. He is well-known for his wisdom and for his righteousness as a judge. He is also blessed with the opportunity to build the *Beit Hamikdash* in *Yerushalayim*. The *Beit Hamikdash* becomes the focal point of prayers and of the service of *Hashem*, for the People of Israel and all those who believe in the One true God. It is an awe-inspiring structure that serves to honor and glorify the Almighty, and to bring His children closer to Him. This is one of the highest points in the history of Israel – the people live as a secure, prosperous and free nation in the Land of Israel, they are able to serve *Hashem* in the most meaningful of ways, and to serve as a light to the other nations.

Unfortunately, the People of Israel are unable to maintain the heights of spiritual and political achievement attained during the times of King *Shlomo*. After his death, the kingdom is divided into two parts: the northern kingdom of *Yisrael* and the southern kingdom of *Yehuda*. Accounts of the sins of the nation and its leaders dominate the second half of *Sefer Melachim*. Idol worship becomes rampant, and even reaches the Holy Temple.

To be sure, there are important kings and righteous leaders who offer hope. For example, we learn of King *Chizkiyahu*, who serves *Hashem* and merits a miraculous rescue of the city of *Yerushalayim*, and of King *Yoshiyahu*, who, after discovering a *Torah* scroll hidden away by his predecessors, leads the people in nationwide repentance. However, such heartening events are overshadowed by the eventual destruction of both kingdoms and exile of their inhabitants. *Sefer Melachim* ends with the exile of the people of the kingdom of *Yehuda* to Babylonia and the burning of the *Beit Hamikdash* in *Yerushalayim*.

It would be tempting to close the book with feelings of despair. But, Jewish tradition teaches that just as the *Beit Hamikdash* was destroyed on the ninth day of the Hebrew month of *Av*, the *Mashiach*, a future king from the House of *David*, will be born on that same date. Thus, at the very depths of our grief, we find hope for the future. We know that the People of Israel will yet reach incredible heights, just as they did in the days of King *Shlomo*. This is hinted at in the story of *Eliyahu* the prophet, who does not die but rather ascends to the next world in a fiery chariot. *Eliyahu*, who is said to be the prophet who will announce the arrival of the *Mashiach*, is thus our link to both the past and the future.

We live in times of redemption. The Children of Israel have come home from the four corners of the earth to *Eretz Yisrael*, and have achieved sovereignty for the first time in millennia. As in the days of King *Shlomo*, the righteous among the nations admire the Jewish State for its wisdom, justice and concern for all mankind. *Yerushalayim* is again the center of prayer to *Hashem*. All of this, coming so soon after the Holocaust and generations of persecution, is clearly a miracle from God.

There is still a long way to go until the complete redemption. However, *Sefer Melachim* reminds us of the heights the People of Israel can reach, and the profound impact this can have on the entire world. We pray that the State and People of Israel reach these heights, and that our generation will be blessed with complete redemption.

Chart of the Kings of Israel

Relevant Verses	Years of Reign	Kings of Yehuda (Judah)	Years from Creation*	Secular date**	Kings of Yisrael (Israel)	Years of Reign	Relevant Verses
I Samuel 9–31	2	**Shaul**	2882	1012 BCE	Shaul	2	I Samuel 9–31
II Samuel 2– I Kings 2	40	**David**	2884	1010 BCE	David	40	II Samuel 2– I Kings 2
I Kings 2–11	40	**Shlomo**	2924	970 BCE	Shlomo	40	I Kings 2–11
I Kings 12:1–19, 14:21–31	17	**Rechovam**	2964	931 BCE	Yerovam son of Nevat	22	I Kings 12:20–14:20
I Kings 15:1–8	3	**Aviyam**	2981	914 BCE			
I Kings 15:9–24	41	**Asa**	2983	911 BCE			
			2985	909 BCE	Nadav	2	I Kings 15:25–32
			2986	908 BCE	Basha	24	I Kings 15:33–16:7
			3009	885 BCE	Eila	2	I Kings 16:8–14
			3010	884 BCE	Zimri	7 days	I Kings 16:15–20
			3010	884 BCE	Omri	12	I Kings 16:21–28
			3021	873 BCE	Achav	22	I Kings 16:29–22:40
I Kings 22:41–51	25	**Yehoshafat**	3024	870 BCE			
			3042	852 BCE	Achazyahu	2	I Kings 22:52– II Kings 1:18
			3043	851 BCE	Yehoram	12	II Kings 3:1–9:26
II Kings 8:16–24	8	**Yehoram**	3047	851 BCE			
II Kings 8:25–9:29	1	**Achazyahu**	3055	842 BCE	Yehu	28	II Kings 9:1–10:36
II Kings 11:1–20	6	**Atalya**	3056	842 BCE			
II Kings 11:2–12:22	40	**Yehoash**	3062	842 BCE			
			3083	819 BCE	Yehoachaz	17	II Kings 13:1–9
			3099	805 BCE	Yoash	16	II Kings 13:10–25
II Kings 14:1–22	29	**Amatzya**	3100	805 BCE			
			3115	790 BCE	Yeravam son of Yoash	41	II Kings 14:23–29
II Kings 15:1–7	52	**Uzziyahu**	3115	788 BCE			
			3153	750 BCE	Zecharya	6 months	II Kings 15:8–12
			3153	749 BCE	Shalum	1 month	II Kings 15:13–16
			3153	749 BCE	Menachem son of Gadi	10	II Kings 15:17–22
			3163	738 BCE	Pekachya	2	II Kings 15:23–26

Relevant Verses	Years of Reign	Kings of Yehuda (Judah)	Years from Creation*	Secular date**	Kings of Yisrael (Israel)	Years of Reign	Relevant Verses
			3165	736 BCE	*Pekach* son of *Remalya*	20	II Kings 15:27–31
II Kings 15:32–38	16	**Yotam**	3167	758 BCE			
II Kings 16:1–20	16	**Achaz**	3183	742 BCE			
			3185	732 BCE	*Hoshea* son of *Eila*	9	II Kings 17:1–6
II Kings 18:1–20:21	29	**Chizkiyahu**	3198	726 BCE			
			3205	722 BCE	Exile of Ten Tribes – end of the Kingdom of *Yisrael*		II Kings 17:5–41
II Kings 21:1–18	55	**Menashe**	3228	697 BCE			
II Kings 21:19–26	2	**Amon**	3283	642 BCE			
II Kings 22:1–23:30	31	**Yoshiyahu**	3285	640 BCE			
II Kings 23:31–35	3 months	**Yehoachaz**	3316	609 BCE			
II Kings 23:34–24:7	11	**Yehoyakim**	3316	609 BCE			
II Kings 24:8–17	3 months	**Yehoyachin**	3327	598 BCE			
II Kings 24:17–25:7	11	**Tzidkiyahu**	3327	597 BCE			
II Kings 25:8–21		**Destruction of the *Beit Hamikdash* and exile of Yehuda**	3338	586 BCE			

* The Hebrew dates for this chart, which are counted from creation, were taken from "The Sequence of Events in the Old Testament," by Eliezer Shulman. The secular dates are based on "The Chronology of the Kings of Israel and Judah" by Gershon Galil.

** There is about a 165 year discrepancy between the traditional Jewish dates, which are based on the second-century rabbinic work *Seder Olam,* and the accepted historical dates. Thus, while secular historians date the destruction of the first *Beit Hamikdash* as having occurred in 586 BCE, the traditional Jewish dating of the same event is 422 BCE. The gap in the chronology narrows over time and eventually disappears around the time of the destruction of the second *Beit Hamikdash.*

Melachim I / I Kings
Chapter 1

מלכים א
פרק א

1 **1** King *David* was now old, advanced in years; and though they covered him with bedclothes, he never felt warm.

א וְהַמֶּ֤לֶךְ דָּוִד֙ זָקֵ֔ן בָּ֖א בַּיָּמִ֑ים וַיְכַסֻּ֙הוּ֙ בַּבְּגָדִ֔ים וְלֹ֥א יִחַ֖ם לֽוֹ׃

2 His courtiers said to him, "Let a young virgin be sought for my lord the king, to wait upon Your Majesty and be his attendant; and let her lie in your bosom, and my lord the king will be warm."

ב וַיֹּ֧אמְרוּ ל֣וֹ עֲבָדָ֗יו יְבַקְשׁ֞וּ לַאדֹנִ֤י הַמֶּ֙לֶךְ֙ נַעֲרָ֣ה בְתוּלָ֔ה וְעָֽמְדָה֙ לִפְנֵ֣י הַמֶּ֔לֶךְ וּתְהִי־ל֖וֹ סֹכֶ֑נֶת וְשָׁכְבָ֣ה בְחֵיקֶ֔ךָ וְחַ֖ם לַאדֹנִ֥י הַמֶּֽלֶךְ׃

3 So they looked for a beautiful girl throughout the territory of *Yisrael*. They found Abishag the Shunammite and brought her to the king.

ג וַיְבַקְשׁוּ֙ נַעֲרָ֣ה יָפָ֔ה בְּכֹ֖ל גְּב֣וּל יִשְׂרָאֵ֑ל וַֽיִּמְצְא֗וּ אֶת־אֲבִישַׁג֙ הַשּׁ֣וּנַמִּ֔ית וַיָּבִ֥אוּ אֹתָ֖הּ לַמֶּֽלֶךְ׃

4 The girl was exceedingly beautiful. She became the king's attendant and waited upon him; but the king was not intimate with her.

ד וְהַֽנַּעֲרָ֖ה יָפָ֣ה עַד־מְאֹ֑ד וַתְּהִ֨י לַמֶּ֤לֶךְ סֹכֶ֙נֶת֙ וַתְּשָׁ֣רְתֵ֔הוּ וְהַמֶּ֖לֶךְ לֹ֥א יְדָעָֽהּ׃

5 Now *Adoniyahu* son of Haggith went about boasting, "I will be king!" He provided himself with chariots and horses, and an escort of fifty outrunners.

ה וַאֲדֹנִיָּ֧ה בֶן־חַגִּ֛ית מִתְנַשֵּׂ֥א לֵאמֹ֖ר אֲנִ֣י אֶמְלֹ֑ךְ וַיַּ֣עַשׂ ל֗וֹ רֶ֚כֶב וּפָ֣רָשִׁ֔ים וַחֲמִשִּׁ֥ים אִ֖ישׁ רָצִ֥ים לְפָנָֽיו׃

6 His father had never scolded him: "Why did you do that?" He was the one born after *Avshalom* and, like him, was very handsome.

ו וְלֹֽא־עֲצָב֨וֹ אָבִ֤יו מִיָּמָיו֙ לֵאמֹ֔ר מַדּ֖וּעַ כָּ֣כָה עָשִׂ֑יתָ וְגַם־ה֤וּא טֽוֹב־תֹּ֙אַר֙ מְאֹ֔ד וְאֹת֥וֹ יָלְדָ֖ה אַחֲרֵ֥י אַבְשָׁלֽוֹם׃

7 He conferred with *Yoav* son of *Tzeruya* and with the *Kohen Evyatar*, and they supported *Adoniyahu*;

ז וַיִּהְי֣וּ דְבָרָ֔יו עִ֚ם יוֹאָ֣ב בֶּן־צְרוּיָ֔ה וְעִ֖ם אֶבְיָתָ֣ר הַכֹּהֵ֑ן וַֽיַּעְזְר֔וּ אַחֲרֵ֖י אֲדֹנִיָּֽה׃

8 but the *Kohen Tzadok*, Benaiah son of *Yehoyada*, the *Navi Natan*, *Shim'i* and Rei, and *David*'s own fighting men did not side with *Adoniyahu*.

ח וְצָד֣וֹק הַ֠כֹּהֵ֠ן וּבְנָיָ֨הוּ בֶן־יְהוֹיָדָ֜ע וְנָתָ֤ן הַנָּבִיא֙ וְשִׁמְעִ֣י וְרֵעִ֔י וְהַגִּבּוֹרִ֖ים אֲשֶׁ֣ר לְדָוִ֑ד לֹ֥א הָי֖וּ עִם־אֲדֹנִיָּֽהוּ׃

9 *Adoniyahu* made a sacrificial feast of sheep, oxen, and fatlings at the Zoheleth stone which is near En-rogel; he invited all his brother princes and all the king's courtiers of the tribe of *Yehuda*;

ט וַיִּזְבַּ֣ח אֲדֹנִיָּ֗הוּ צֹ֤אן וּבָקָר֙ וּמְרִ֔יא עִם־אֶ֣בֶן הַזֹּחֶ֔לֶת אֲשֶׁר־אֵ֖צֶל עֵ֣ין רֹגֵ֑ל וַיִּקְרָ֗א אֶת־כָּל־אֶחָיו֙ בְּנֵ֣י הַמֶּ֔לֶךְ וּלְכָל־אַנְשֵׁ֥י יְהוּדָ֖ה עַבְדֵ֥י הַמֶּֽלֶךְ׃

10 but he did not invite the *Navi Natan*, or Benaiah, or the fighting men, or his brother *Shlomo*.

י וְֽאֶת־נָתָן֩ הַנָּבִ֨יא וּבְנָיָ֜הוּ וְאֶת־הַגִּבּוֹרִ֛ים וְאֶת־שְׁלֹמֹ֥ה אָחִ֖יו לֹ֥א קָרָֽא׃

11 Then *Natan* said to *Batsheva*, *Shlomo*'s mother, "You must have heard that *Adoniyahu* son of Haggith has assumed the kingship without the knowledge of our lord *David*.

יא וַיֹּ֣אמֶר נָתָ֗ן אֶל־בַּת־שֶׁ֤בַע אֵם־שְׁלֹמֹה֙ לֵאמֹ֔ר הֲל֣וֹא שָׁמַ֔עַתְּ כִּ֥י מָלַ֖ךְ אֲדֹנִיָּ֣הוּ בֶן־חַגִּ֑ית וַאֲדֹנֵ֖ינוּ דָוִ֥ד לֹ֥א יָדָֽע׃

12 Now take my advice, so that you may save your life and the life of your son *Shlomo*.

יב וְעַתָּ֕ה לְכִ֛י אִיעָצֵ֥ךְ נָ֖א עֵצָ֑ה וּמַלְּטִי֙ אֶת־נַפְשֵׁ֔ךְ וְאֶת־נֶ֥פֶשׁ בְּנֵ֖ךְ שְׁלֹמֹֽה׃

13 Go immediately to King *David* and say to him, 'Did not you, O lord king, swear to your maidservant: "Your son *Shlomo* shall succeed me as king, and he shall sit upon my throne"? Then why has *Adoniyahu* become king?'

יג לְכִ֞י וּבֹ֣אִי ׀ אֶל־הַמֶּ֣לֶךְ דָּוִ֗ד וְאָמַ֤רְתְּ אֵלָיו֙ הֲלֹֽא־אַתָּ֞ה אֲדֹנִ֣י הַמֶּ֗לֶךְ נִשְׁבַּ֤עְתָּ לַאֲמָֽתְךָ֙ לֵאמֹ֔ר כִּֽי־שְׁלֹמֹ֤ה בְנֵךְ֙ יִמְלֹ֣ךְ אַחֲרַ֔י וְה֖וּא יֵשֵׁ֣ב עַל־כִּסְאִ֑י וּמַדּ֖וּעַ מָלַ֥ךְ אֲדֹנִיָּֽהוּ׃

Melachim I / I Kings
Chapter 1

מלכים א
פרק א

14 While you are still there talking with the king, I will come in after you and confirm your words."

יד הִנֵּה עוֹדָךְ מְדַבֶּרֶת שָׁם עִם־הַמֶּלֶךְ וַאֲנִי אָבוֹא אַחֲרַיִךְ וּמִלֵּאתִי אֶת־דְּבָרָיִךְ:

15 So *Batsheva* went to the king in his chamber. – The king was very old, and Abishag the Shunammite was waiting on the king.

טו וַתָּבֹא בַת־שֶׁבַע אֶל־הַמֶּלֶךְ הַחַדְרָה וְהַמֶּלֶךְ זָקֵן מְאֹד וַאֲבִישַׁג הַשּׁוּנַמִּית מְשָׁרַת אֶת־הַמֶּלֶךְ:

16 *Batsheva* bowed low in homage to the king; and the king asked, "What troubles you?"

טז וַתִּקֹּד בַּת־שֶׁבַע וַתִּשְׁתַּחוּ לַמֶּלֶךְ וַיֹּאמֶר הַמֶּלֶךְ מַה־לָּךְ:

17 She answered him, "My lord, you yourself swore to your maidservant by *Hashem* your God: 'Your son *Shlomo* shall succeed me as king, and he shall sit upon my throne.'

יז וַתֹּאמֶר לוֹ אֲדֹנִי אַתָּה נִשְׁבַּעְתָּ בַּיהוָה אֱלֹהֶיךָ לַאֲמָתֶךָ כִּי־שְׁלֹמֹה בְנֵךְ יִמְלֹךְ אַחֲרָי וְהוּא יֵשֵׁב עַל־כִּסְאִי:

18 Yet now *Adoniyahu* has become king, and you, my lord the king, know nothing about it.

יח וְעַתָּה הִנֵּה אֲדֹנִיָּה מָלָךְ וְעַתָּה אֲדֹנִי הַמֶּלֶךְ לֹא יָדָעְתָּ:

19 He has prepared a sacrificial feast of a great many oxen, fatlings, and sheep, and he has invited all the king's sons and *Evyatar* the *Kohen* and *Yoav* commander of the army; but he has not invited your servant *Shlomo*.

יט וַיִּזְבַּח שׁוֹר וּמְרִיא־וְצֹאן לָרֹב וַיִּקְרָא לְכָל־בְּנֵי הַמֶּלֶךְ וּלְאֶבְיָתָר הַכֹּהֵן וּלְיֹאָב שַׂר הַצָּבָא וְלִשְׁלֹמֹה עַבְדְּךָ לֹא קָרָא:

20 And so the eyes of all *Yisrael* are upon you, O lord king, to tell them who shall succeed my lord the king on the throne.

כ וְאַתָּה אֲדֹנִי הַמֶּלֶךְ עֵינֵי כָל־יִשְׂרָאֵל עָלֶיךָ לְהַגִּיד לָהֶם מִי יֵשֵׁב עַל־כִּסֵּא אֲדֹנִי־הַמֶּלֶךְ אַחֲרָיו:

21 Otherwise, when my lord the king lies down with his fathers, my son *Shlomo* and I will be regarded as traitors."

כא וְהָיָה כִּשְׁכַב אֲדֹנִי־הַמֶּלֶךְ עִם־אֲבֹתָיו וְהָיִיתִי אֲנִי וּבְנִי שְׁלֹמֹה חַטָּאִים:

22 She was still talking to the king when the *Navi Natan* arrived.

כב וְהִנֵּה עוֹדֶנָּה מְדַבֶּרֶת עִם־הַמֶּלֶךְ וְנָתָן הַנָּבִיא בָּא:

23 They announced to the king, "The *Navi Natan* is here," and he entered the king's presence. Bowing low to the king with his face to the ground,

כג וַיַּגִּידוּ לַמֶּלֶךְ לֵאמֹר הִנֵּה נָתָן הַנָּבִיא וַיָּבֹא לִפְנֵי הַמֶּלֶךְ וַיִּשְׁתַּחוּ לַמֶּלֶךְ עַל־אַפָּיו אָרְצָה:

24 *Natan* said, "O lord king, you must have said, '*Adoniyahu* shall succeed me as king and he shall sit upon my throne.'

כד וַיֹּאמֶר נָתָן אֲדֹנִי הַמֶּלֶךְ אַתָּה אָמַרְתָּ אֲדֹנִיָּהוּ יִמְלֹךְ אַחֲרָי וְהוּא יֵשֵׁב עַל־כִּסְאִי:

25 For he has gone down today and prepared a sacrificial feast of a great many oxen, fatlings, and sheep. He invited all the king's sons and the army officers and *Evyatar* the *Kohen*. At this very moment they are eating and drinking with him, and they are shouting, 'Long live King *Adoniyahu*!'

כה כִּי יָרַד הַיּוֹם וַיִּזְבַּח שׁוֹר וּמְרִיא־וְצֹאן לָרֹב וַיִּקְרָא לְכָל־בְּנֵי הַמֶּלֶךְ וּלְשָׂרֵי הַצָּבָא וּלְאֶבְיָתָר הַכֹּהֵן וְהִנָּם אֹכְלִים וְשֹׁתִים לְפָנָיו וַיֹּאמְרוּ יְחִי הַמֶּלֶךְ אֲדֹנִיָּהוּ:

26 But he did not invite me your servant, or the *Kohen Tzadok*, or Benaiah son of *Yehoyada*, or your servant *Shlomo*.

כו וְלִי אֲנִי־עַבְדֶּךָ וּלְצָדֹק הַכֹּהֵן וְלִבְנָיָהוּ בֶן־יְהוֹיָדָע וְלִשְׁלֹמֹה עַבְדְּךָ לֹא קָרָא:

Melachim I/I Kings
Chapter 1

מלכים א
פרק א

27 Can this decision have come from my lord the king, without your telling your servant who is to succeed to the throne of my lord the king?"

כז אִם מֵאֵת אֲדֹנִי הַמֶּלֶךְ נִהְיָה הַדָּבָר הַזֶּה וְלֹא הוֹדַעְתָּ אֶת־עבדיך [עַבְדְּךָ] מִי יֵשֵׁב עַל־כִּסֵּא אֲדֹנִי־הַמֶּלֶךְ אַחֲרָיו׃

28 King *David*'s response was: "Summon *Batsheva*!" She entered the king's presence and stood before the king.

כח וַיַּעַן הַמֶּלֶךְ דָּוִד וַיֹּאמֶר קִרְאוּ־לִי לְבַת־שָׁבַע וַתָּבֹא לִפְנֵי הַמֶּלֶךְ וַתַּעֲמֹד לִפְנֵי הַמֶּלֶךְ׃

29 And the king took an oath, saying, "As *Hashem* lives, who has rescued me from every trouble:

כט וַיִּשָּׁבַע הַמֶּלֶךְ וַיֹּאמַר חַי־יְהוָה אֲשֶׁר־פָּדָה אֶת־נַפְשִׁי מִכָּל־צָרָה׃

30 The oath I swore to you by *Hashem*, the God of *Yisrael*, that your son *Shlomo* should succeed me as king and that he should sit upon my throne in my stead, I will fulfill this very day!"

ל כִּי כַּאֲשֶׁר נִשְׁבַּעְתִּי לָךְ בַּיהוָה אֱלֹהֵי יִשְׂרָאֵל לֵאמֹר כִּי־שְׁלֹמֹה בְנֵךְ יִמְלֹךְ אַחֲרַי וְהוּא יֵשֵׁב עַל־כִּסְאִי תַּחְתָּי כִּי כֵּן אֶעֱשֶׂה הַיּוֹם הַזֶּה׃

31 *Batsheva* bowed low in homage to the king with her face to the ground, and she said, "May my lord King *David* live forever!"

לא וַתִּקֹּד בַּת־שֶׁבַע אַפַּיִם אֶרֶץ וַתִּשְׁתַּחוּ לַמֶּלֶךְ וַתֹּאמֶר יְחִי אֲדֹנִי הַמֶּלֶךְ דָּוִד לְעֹלָם׃

va-ti-KOD bat SHE-va a-PA-yim E-retz va-tish-TA-khu la-ME-lekh va-TO-mer y'-KHEE a-do-NEE ha-ME-lekh da-VID l'-o-LAM

32 Then King *David* said, "Summon to me the *Kohen Tzadok*, the *Navi Natan*, and Benaiah son of *Yehoyada*." When they came before the king,

לב וַיֹּאמֶר הַמֶּלֶךְ דָּוִד קִרְאוּ־לִי לְצָדוֹק הַכֹּהֵן וּלְנָתָן הַנָּבִיא וְלִבְנָיָהוּ בֶּן־יְהוֹיָדָע וַיָּבֹאוּ לִפְנֵי הַמֶּלֶךְ׃

33 the king said to them, "Take my loyal soldiers, and have my son *Shlomo* ride on my mule and bring him down to *Gichon*.

לג וַיֹּאמֶר הַמֶּלֶךְ לָהֶם קְחוּ עִמָּכֶם אֶת־עַבְדֵי אֲדֹנֵיכֶם וְהִרְכַּבְתֶּם אֶת־שְׁלֹמֹה בְנִי עַל־הַפִּרְדָּה אֲשֶׁר־לִי וְהוֹרַדְתֶּם אֹתוֹ אֶל־גִּחוֹן׃

34 Let the *Kohen Tzadok* and the *Navi Natan* anoint him there king over *Yisrael*, whereupon you shall sound the *shofar* and shout, 'Long live King *Shlomo*!'

לד וּמָשַׁח אֹתוֹ שָׁם צָדוֹק הַכֹּהֵן וְנָתָן הַנָּבִיא לְמֶלֶךְ עַל־יִשְׂרָאֵל וּתְקַעְתֶּם בַּשּׁוֹפָר וַאֲמַרְתֶּם יְחִי הַמֶּלֶךְ שְׁלֹמֹה׃

35 Then march up after him, and let him come in and sit on my throne. For he shall succeed me as king; him I designate to be ruler of *Yisrael* and *Yehuda*."

לה וַעֲלִיתֶם אַחֲרָיו וּבָא וְיָשַׁב עַל־כִּסְאִי וְהוּא יִמְלֹךְ תַּחְתָּי וְאֹתוֹ צִוִּיתִי לִהְיוֹת נָגִיד עַל־יִשְׂרָאֵל וְעַל־יְהוּדָה׃

36 Benaiah son of *Yehoyada* spoke up and said to the king, "*Amen*! And may *Hashem*, the God of my lord the king, so ordain.

לו וַיַּעַן בְּנָיָהוּ בֶן־יְהוֹיָדָע אֶת־הַמֶּלֶךְ וַיֹּאמֶר אָמֵן כֵּן יֹאמַר יְהוָה אֱלֹהֵי אֲדֹנִי הַמֶּלֶךְ׃

1:31 May my lord King *David* live forever While on his sickbed, King *David* promises *Batsheva* that their son *Shlomo* will follow him to the throne. *Batsheva* then bows and says "May my lord King *David* live forever." As all people must one day die, her words are somewhat puzzling. However, her statement must be understood on a deeper level. King *David* represents the eternal monarchy over the Nation of Israel in the Land of Israel. By praying for him to "live forever" *Batsheva* is actually praying for the eternity of the people, the land and the sovereign monarchy of Israel. Her prayers are answered with the anointing of King *Shlomo*, who solidifies the kingdom and helps it attain the heights of holiness with the building of the *Beit Hamikdash* in *Yerushalayim*.

Melachim I / I Kings
Chapter 1

מלכים א
פרק א

37 As *Hashem* was with my lord the king, so may He be with *Shlomo*; and may He exalt his throne even higher than the throne of my lord King *David*."

לז כַּאֲשֶׁר הָיָה יְהוָה עִם־אֲדֹנִי הַמֶּלֶךְ כֵּן יְהִי [יִהְיֶה] עִם־שְׁלֹמֹה וִיגַדֵּל אֶת־כִּסְאוֹ מִכִּסֵּא אֲדֹנִי הַמֶּלֶךְ דָּוִד׃

38 Then the *Kohen Tzadok*, and the *Navi Natan*, and Benaiah son of *Yehoyada* went down with the Cherethites and the Pelethites. They had *Shlomo* ride on King *David*'s mule and they led him to *Gichon*.

לח וַיֵּרֶד צָדוֹק הַכֹּהֵן וְנָתָן הַנָּבִיא וּבְנָיָהוּ בֶן־יְהוֹיָדָע וְהַכְּרֵתִי וְהַפְּלֵתִי וַיַּרְכִּבוּ אֶת־שְׁלֹמֹה עַל־פִּרְדַּת הַמֶּלֶךְ דָּוִד וַיֹּלִכוּ אֹתוֹ עַל־גִּחוֹן׃

39 The *Kohen Tzadok* took the horn of oil from the Tent and anointed *Shlomo*. They sounded the *shofar* and all the people shouted, "Long live King *Shlomo*!"

לט וַיִּקַּח צָדוֹק הַכֹּהֵן אֶת־קֶרֶן הַשֶּׁמֶן מִן־הָאֹהֶל וַיִּמְשַׁח אֶת־שְׁלֹמֹה וַיִּתְקְעוּ בַּשּׁוֹפָר וַיֹּאמְרוּ כָּל־הָעָם יְחִי הַמֶּלֶךְ שְׁלֹמֹה׃

40 All the people then marched up behind him, playing on flutes and making merry till the earth was split open by the uproar.

מ וַיַּעֲלוּ כָל־הָעָם אַחֲרָיו וְהָעָם מְחַלְּלִים בַּחֲלִלִים וּשְׂמֵחִים שִׂמְחָה גְדוֹלָה וַתִּבָּקַע הָאָרֶץ בְּקוֹלָם׃

41 *Adoniyahu* and all the guests who were with him, who had just finished eating, heard it. When *Yoav* heard the sound of the *shofar*, he said, "Why is the city in such an uproar?"

מא וַיִּשְׁמַע אֲדֹנִיָּהוּ וְכָל־הַקְּרֻאִים אֲשֶׁר אִתּוֹ וְהֵם כִּלּוּ לֶאֱכֹל וַיִּשְׁמַע יוֹאָב אֶת־קוֹל הַשּׁוֹפָר וַיֹּאמֶר מַדּוּעַ קוֹל־הַקִּרְיָה הוֹמָה׃

42 He was still speaking when the *Kohen Yonatan* son of *Evyatar* arrived. "Come in," said *Adoniyahu*. "You are a worthy man, and you surely bring good news."

מב עוֹדֶנּוּ מְדַבֵּר וְהִנֵּה יוֹנָתָן בֶּן־אֶבְיָתָר הַכֹּהֵן בָּא וַיֹּאמֶר אֲדֹנִיָּהוּ בֹּא כִּי אִישׁ חַיִל אַתָּה וְטוֹב תְּבַשֵּׂר׃

43 But *Yonatan* replied to *Adoniyahu*, "Alas, our lord King *David* has made *Shlomo* king!

מג וַיַּעַן יוֹנָתָן וַיֹּאמֶר לַאֲדֹנִיָּהוּ אֲבָל אֲדֹנֵינוּ הַמֶּלֶךְ־דָּוִד הִמְלִיךְ אֶת־שְׁלֹמֹה׃

44 The king sent with him the *Kohen Tzadok* and the *Navi Natan* and Benaiah son of *Yehoyada*, and the Cherethites and Pelethites. They had him ride on the king's mule,

מד וַיִּשְׁלַח אִתּוֹ־הַמֶּלֶךְ אֶת־צָדוֹק הַכֹּהֵן וְאֶת־נָתָן הַנָּבִיא וּבְנָיָהוּ בֶּן־יְהוֹיָדָע וְהַכְּרֵתִי וְהַפְּלֵתִי וַיַּרְכִּבוּ אֹתוֹ עַל פִּרְדַּת הַמֶּלֶךְ׃

45 and the *Kohen Tzadok* and the *Navi Natan* anointed him king at *Gichon*. Then they came up from there making merry, and the city went into an uproar. That's the noise you heard.

מה וַיִּמְשְׁחוּ אֹתוֹ צָדוֹק הַכֹּהֵן וְנָתָן הַנָּבִיא לְמֶלֶךְ בְּגִחוֹן וַיַּעֲלוּ מִשָּׁם שְׂמֵחִים וַתֵּהֹם הַקִּרְיָה הוּא הַקּוֹל אֲשֶׁר שְׁמַעְתֶּם׃

46 Further, *Shlomo* seated himself on the royal throne;

מו וְגַם יָשַׁב שְׁלֹמֹה עַל כִּסֵּא הַמְּלוּכָה׃

47 further, the king's courtiers came to congratulate our lord King *David*, saying, 'May *Hashem* make the renown of *Shlomo* even greater than yours, and may He exalt his throne even higher than yours!' And the king bowed low on his couch.

מז וְגַם־בָּאוּ עַבְדֵי הַמֶּלֶךְ לְבָרֵךְ אֶת־אֲדֹנֵינוּ הַמֶּלֶךְ דָּוִד לֵאמֹר יֵיטֵב אֱלֹהֶיךָ [אֱלֹהִים] אֶת־שֵׁם שְׁלֹמֹה מִשְּׁמֶךָ וִיגַדֵּל אֶת־כִּסְאוֹ מִכִּסְאֶךָ וַיִּשְׁתַּחוּ הַמֶּלֶךְ עַל־הַמִּשְׁכָּב׃

48 And further, this is what the king said, 'Praised be *Hashem*, the God of *Yisrael* who has this day provided a successor to my throne, while my own eyes can see it.'"

מח וְגַם־כָּכָה אָמַר הַמֶּלֶךְ בָּרוּךְ יְהוָה אֱלֹהֵי יִשְׂרָאֵל אֲשֶׁר נָתַן הַיּוֹם יֹשֵׁב עַל־כִּסְאִי וְעֵינַי רֹאוֹת׃

Melachim I/I Kings
Chapter 2

49 Thereupon, all of *Adoniyahu*'s guests rose in alarm and each went his own way.

50 *Adoniyahu*, in fear of *Shlomo*, went at once [to the Tent] and grasped the horns of the *Mizbayach*.

51 It was reported to *Shlomo*: "*Adoniyahu* is in fear of King *Shlomo* and has grasped the horns of the *Mizbayach*, saying, 'Let King *Shlomo* first swear to me that he will not put his servant to the sword.'"

52 *Shlomo* said, "If he behaves worthily, not a hair of his head shall fall to the ground; but if he is caught in any offense, he shall die."

53 So King *Shlomo* sent and had him taken down from the *Mizbayach*. He came and bowed before King *Shlomo*, and *Shlomo* said to him, "Go home."

2 1 When *David*'s life was drawing to a close, he instructed his son *Shlomo* as follows:

2 "I am going the way of all the earth; be strong and show yourself a man.

3 Keep the charge of *Hashem* your God, walking in His ways and following His laws, His commandments, His rules, and His admonitions as recorded in the Teaching of *Moshe*, in order that you may succeed in whatever you undertake and wherever you turn.

4 Then *Hashem* will fulfill the promise that He made concerning me: 'If your descendants are scrupulous in their conduct, and walk before Me faithfully, with all their heart and soul, your line on the throne of *Yisrael* shall never end!'

5 "Further, you know what *Yoav* son of *Tzeruya* did to me, what he did to the two commanders of *Yisrael*'s forces, *Avner* son of Ner and *Amasa* son of Jether: he killed them, shedding blood of war in peacetime, staining the girdle of his loins and the sandals on his feet with blood of war.

6 So act in accordance with your wisdom, and see that his white hair does not go down to Sheol in peace.

7 "But deal graciously with the sons of *Barzilai* the Giladite, for they befriended me when I fled from your brother *Avshalom*; let them be among those that eat at your table.

מלכים א
פרק ב

מט וַיֶּחֶרְדוּ וַיָּקֻמוּ כָּל־הַקְּרֻאִים אֲשֶׁר לַאֲדֹנִיָּהוּ וַיֵּלְכוּ אִישׁ לְדַרְכּוֹ׃

נ וַאֲדֹנִיָּהוּ יָרֵא מִפְּנֵי שְׁלֹמֹה וַיָּקָם וַיֵּלֶךְ וַיַּחֲזֵק בְּקַרְנוֹת הַמִּזְבֵּחַ׃

נא וַיֻּגַּד לִשְׁלֹמֹה לֵאמֹר הִנֵּה אֲדֹנִיָּהוּ יָרֵא אֶת־הַמֶּלֶךְ שְׁלֹמֹה וְהִנֵּה אָחַז בְּקַרְנוֹת הַמִּזְבֵּחַ לֵאמֹר יִשָּׁבַע־לִי כַיּוֹם הַמֶּלֶךְ שְׁלֹמֹה אִם־יָמִית אֶת־עַבְדּוֹ בֶּחָרֶב׃

נב וַיֹּאמֶר שְׁלֹמֹה אִם יִהְיֶה לְבֶן־חַיִל לֹא־יִפֹּל מִשַּׂעֲרָתוֹ אָרְצָה וְאִם־רָעָה תִמָּצֵא־בוֹ וָמֵת׃

נג וַיִּשְׁלַח הַמֶּלֶךְ שְׁלֹמֹה וַיֹּרִדֻהוּ מֵעַל הַמִּזְבֵּחַ וַיָּבֹא וַיִּשְׁתַּחוּ לַמֶּלֶךְ שְׁלֹמֹה וַיֹּאמֶר־לוֹ שְׁלֹמֹה לֵךְ לְבֵיתֶךָ׃

ב א וַיִּקְרְבוּ יְמֵי־דָוִד לָמוּת וַיְצַו אֶת־שְׁלֹמֹה בְנוֹ לֵאמֹר׃

ב אָנֹכִי הֹלֵךְ בְּדֶרֶךְ כָּל־הָאָרֶץ וְחָזַקְתָּ וְהָיִיתָ לְאִישׁ׃

ג וְשָׁמַרְתָּ אֶת־מִשְׁמֶרֶת יְהֹוָה אֱלֹהֶיךָ לָלֶכֶת בִּדְרָכָיו לִשְׁמֹר חֻקֹּתָיו מִצְוֺתָיו וּמִשְׁפָּטָיו וְעֵדְוֺתָיו כַּכָּתוּב בְּתוֹרַת מֹשֶׁה לְמַעַן תַּשְׂכִּיל אֵת כָּל־אֲשֶׁר תַּעֲשֶׂה וְאֵת כָּל־אֲשֶׁר תִּפְנֶה שָׁם׃

ד לְמַעַן יָקִים יְהֹוָה אֶת־דְּבָרוֹ אֲשֶׁר דִּבֶּר עָלַי לֵאמֹר אִם־יִשְׁמְרוּ בָנֶיךָ אֶת־דַּרְכָּם לָלֶכֶת לְפָנַי בֶּאֱמֶת בְּכָל־לְבָבָם וּבְכָל־נַפְשָׁם לֵאמֹר לֹא־יִכָּרֵת לְךָ אִישׁ מֵעַל כִּסֵּא יִשְׂרָאֵל׃

ה וְגַם אַתָּה יָדַעְתָּ אֵת אֲשֶׁר־עָשָׂה לִי יוֹאָב בֶּן־צְרוּיָה אֲשֶׁר עָשָׂה לִשְׁנֵי־שָׂרֵי צִבְאוֹת יִשְׂרָאֵל לְאַבְנֵר בֶּן־נֵר וְלַעֲמָשָׂא בֶן־יֶתֶר וַיַּהַרְגֵם וַיָּשֶׂם דְּמֵי־מִלְחָמָה בְּשָׁלֹם וַיִּתֵּן דְּמֵי מִלְחָמָה בַּחֲגֹרָתוֹ אֲשֶׁר בְּמָתְנָיו וּבְנַעֲלוֹ אֲשֶׁר בְּרַגְלָיו׃

ו וְעָשִׂיתָ כְּחָכְמָתֶךָ וְלֹא־תוֹרֵד שֵׂיבָתוֹ בְּשָׁלֹם שְׁאֹל׃

ז וְלִבְנֵי בַרְזִלַּי הַגִּלְעָדִי תַּעֲשֶׂה־חֶסֶד וְהָיוּ בְּאֹכְלֵי שֻׁלְחָנֶךָ כִּי־כֵן קָרְבוּ אֵלַי בְּבָרְחִי מִפְּנֵי אַבְשָׁלוֹם אָחִיךָ׃

Melachim I / I Kings
Chapter 2

מלכים א
פרק ב

8 "You must also deal with *Shim'i* son of Gera, the *Binyamin*ite from Bahurim. He insulted me outrageously when I was on my way to Mahanaim; but he came down to meet me at the *Yarden*, and I swore to him by *Hashem*: 'I will not put you to the sword.'

ח וְהִנֵּה עִמְּךָ שִׁמְעִי בֶן־גֵּרָא בֶן־הַיְמִינִי מִבַּחֻרִים וְהוּא קִלְלַנִי קְלָלָה נִמְרֶצֶת בְּיוֹם לֶכְתִּי מַחֲנָיִם וְהוּא־יָרַד לִקְרָאתִי הַיַּרְדֵּן וָאֶשָּׁבַע לוֹ בַיהֹוָה לֵאמֹר אִם־אֲמִיתְךָ בֶּחָרֶב:

9 So do not let him go unpunished; for you are a wise man and you will know how to deal with him and send his gray hair down to Sheol in blood."

ט וְעַתָּה אַל־תְּנַקֵּהוּ כִּי אִישׁ חָכָם אָתָּה וְיָדַעְתָּ אֵת אֲשֶׁר תַּעֲשֶׂה־לּוֹ וְהוֹרַדְתָּ אֶת־שֵׂיבָתוֹ בְּדָם שְׁאוֹל:

10 So *David* slept with his fathers, and he was buried in the City of *David*.

י וַיִּשְׁכַּב דָּוִד עִם־אֲבֹתָיו וַיִּקָּבֵר בְּעִיר דָּוִד:

11 The length of *David*'s reign over *Yisrael* was forty years: he reigned seven years in *Chevron*, and he reigned thirty-three years in *Yerushalayim*.

יא וְהַיָּמִים אֲשֶׁר מָלַךְ דָּוִד עַל־יִשְׂרָאֵל אַרְבָּעִים שָׁנָה בְּחֶבְרוֹן מָלַךְ שֶׁבַע שָׁנִים וּבִירוּשָׁלַיִם מָלַךְ שְׁלֹשִׁים וְשָׁלֹשׁ שָׁנִים:

12 And *Shlomo* sat upon the throne of his father *David*, and his rule was firmly established.

יב וּשְׁלֹמֹה יָשַׁב עַל־כִּסֵּא דָּוִד אָבִיו וַתִּכֹּן מַלְכֻתוֹ מְאֹד:

ush-lo-MO ya-SHAV al ki-SAY da-VID a-VEEV va-ti-KON mal-khu-TO m'-OD

13 *Adoniyahu* son of Haggith came to see *Batsheva*, *Shlomo*'s mother. She said, "Do you come with friendly intent?" "Yes," he replied;

יג וַיָּבֹא אֲדֹנִיָּהוּ בֶן־חַגֵּית אֶל־בַּת־שֶׁבַע אֵם־שְׁלֹמֹה וַתֹּאמֶר הֲשָׁלוֹם בֹּאֶךָ וַיֹּאמֶר שָׁלוֹם:

14 and he continued, "I would like to have a word with you." "Speak up," she said.

יד וַיֹּאמֶר דָּבָר לִי אֵלָיִךְ וַתֹּאמֶר דַּבֵּר:

15 Then he said, "You know that the kingship was rightly mine and that all *Yisrael* wanted me to reign. But the kingship passed on to my brother; it came to him by the will of *Hashem*.

טו וַיֹּאמֶר אַתְּ יָדַעַתְּ כִּי־לִי הָיְתָה הַמְּלוּכָה וְעָלַי שָׂמוּ כָל־יִשְׂרָאֵל פְּנֵיהֶם לִמְלֹךְ וַתִּסֹּב הַמְּלוּכָה וַתְּהִי לְאָחִי כִּי מֵיְהֹוָה הָיְתָה לּוֹ:

16 And now I have one request to make of you; do not refuse me." She said, "Speak up."

טז וְעַתָּה שְׁאֵלָה אַחַת אָנֹכִי שֹׁאֵל מֵאִתָּךְ אַל־תָּשִׁבִי אֶת־פָּנָי וַתֹּאמֶר אֵלָיו דַּבֵּר:

17 He replied, "Please ask King *Shlomo* – for he won't refuse you – to give me Abishag the Shunammite as wife."

יז וַיֹּאמֶר אִמְרִי־נָא לִשְׁלֹמֹה הַמֶּלֶךְ כִּי לֹא־יָשִׁיב אֶת־פָּנָיִךְ וְיִתֶּן־לִי אֶת־אֲבִישַׁג הַשּׁוּנַמִּית לְאִשָּׁה:

18 "Very well," said *Batsheva*, "I will speak to the king in your behalf."

יח וַתֹּאמֶר בַּת־שֶׁבַע טוֹב אָנֹכִי אֲדַבֵּר עָלֶיךָ אֶל־הַמֶּלֶךְ:

2:12 His rule was firmly established King *Shlomo*'s throne is "firmly established." Unlike his father *David*, *Shlomo* rules a kingdom that is consistently strong and at peace. Under his rule, the Kingdom of Israel grows into a world power, with the ability to spread monotheism throughout the world, and becomes a shining example of a just society. The knowledge of the One true God and His insistence on justice and righteousness is key to building a just society, as this keeps people from oppressing others and encourages them to make the world a better place. Today's State of Israel embraces this same opportunity on a daily basis, shining as a moral light in a world all too often darkened by hate, poverty and injustice.

An IDF doctor in Japan following an earthquake and tsunami, 2011

Melachim I / I Kings
Chapter 2

מלכים א
פרק ב

19 So *Batsheva* went to King *Shlomo* to speak to him about *Adoniyahu*. The king rose to greet her and bowed down to her. He sat on his throne; and he had a throne placed for the queen mother, and she sat on his right.

יט וַתָּבֹא בַת־שֶׁבַע אֶל־הַמֶּלֶךְ שְׁלֹמֹה לְדַבֶּר־לוֹ עַל־אֲדֹנִיָּהוּ וַיָּקָם הַמֶּלֶךְ לִקְרָאתָהּ וַיִּשְׁתַּחוּ לָהּ וַיֵּשֶׁב עַל־כִּסְאוֹ וַיָּשֶׂם כִּסֵּא לְאֵם הַמֶּלֶךְ וַתֵּשֶׁב לִימִינוֹ:

20 She said, "I have one small request to make of you, do not refuse me." He responded, "Ask, Mother; I shall not refuse you."

כ וַתֹּאמֶר שְׁאֵלָה אַחַת קְטַנָּה אָנֹכִי שֹׁאֶלֶת מֵאִתָּךְ אַל־תָּשֶׁב אֶת־פָּנָי וַיֹּאמֶר־לָהּ הַמֶּלֶךְ שַׁאֲלִי אִמִּי כִּי לֹא־אָשִׁיב אֶת־פָּנָיִךְ:

21 Then she said, "Let *Abishag* the Shunammite be given to your brother *Adoniyahu* as wife."

כא וַתֹּאמֶר יֻתַּן אֶת־אֲבִישַׁג הַשֻּׁנַמִּית לַאֲדֹנִיָּהוּ אָחִיךָ לְאִשָּׁה:

22 The king replied to his mother, "Why request *Abishag* the Shunammite for *Adoniyahu*? Request the kingship for him! For he is my older brother, and the *Kohen Evyatar* and *Yoav* son of *Tzeruya* are on his side."

כב וַיַּעַן הַמֶּלֶךְ שְׁלֹמֹה וַיֹּאמֶר לְאִמּוֹ וְלָמָה אַתְּ שֹׁאֶלֶת אֶת־אֲבִישַׁג הַשֻּׁנַמִּית לַאֲדֹנִיָּהוּ וְשַׁאֲלִי־לוֹ אֶת־הַמְּלוּכָה כִּי הוּא אָחִי הַגָּדוֹל מִמֶּנִּי וְלוֹ וּלְאֶבְיָתָר הַכֹּהֵן וּלְיוֹאָב בֶּן־צְרוּיָה:

23 Thereupon, King *Shlomo* swore by *Hashem*, saying, "So may *Hashem* do to me and even more, if broaching this matter does not cost *Adoniyahu* his life!

כג וַיִּשָּׁבַע הַמֶּלֶךְ שְׁלֹמֹה בַּיהוָה לֵאמֹר כֹּה יַעֲשֶׂה־לִּי אֱלֹהִים וְכֹה יוֹסִיף כִּי בְנַפְשׁוֹ דִּבֶּר אֲדֹנִיָּהוּ אֶת־הַדָּבָר הַזֶּה:

24 Now, as *Hashem* lives, who has established me and set me on the throne of my father *David* and who has provided him with a house, as he promised, *Adoniyahu* shall be put to death this very day!"

כד וְעַתָּה חַי־יְהוָה אֲשֶׁר הֱכִינַנִי וַיּוֹשִׁיבִינִי [וַיּוֹשִׁיבַנִי] עַל־כִּסֵּא דָּוִד אָבִי וַאֲשֶׁר עָשָׂה־לִי בַּיִת כַּאֲשֶׁר דִּבֵּר כִּי הַיּוֹם יוּמַת אֲדֹנִיָּהוּ:

25 And *Shlomo* instructed Benaiah son of *Yehoyada*, who struck *Adoniyahu* down; and so he died.

כה וַיִּשְׁלַח הַמֶּלֶךְ שְׁלֹמֹה בְּיַד בְּנָיָהוּ בֶן־יְהוֹיָדָע וַיִּפְגַּע־בּוֹ וַיָּמֹת:

26 To the *Kohen Evyatar*, the king said, "Go to your estate at *Anatot*! You deserve to die, but I shall not put you to death at this time, because you carried the *Aron* of my God before my father *David* and because you shared all the hardships that my father endured."

כו וּלְאֶבְיָתָר הַכֹּהֵן אָמַר הַמֶּלֶךְ עֲנָתֹת לֵךְ עַל־שָׂדֶיךָ כִּי אִישׁ מָוֶת אָתָּה וּבַיּוֹם הַזֶּה לֹא אֲמִיתֶךָ כִּי־נָשָׂאתָ אֶת־אֲרוֹן אֲדֹנָי יְהוִֹה לִפְנֵי דָּוִד אָבִי וְכִי הִתְעַנִּיתָ בְּכֹל אֲשֶׁר־הִתְעַנָּה אָבִי:

27 So *Shlomo* dismissed *Evyatar* from his office of *Kohen* of *Hashem* – thus fulfilling what *Hashem* had spoken at *Shilo* regarding the house of *Eli*.

כז וַיְגָרֶשׁ שְׁלֹמֹה אֶת־אֶבְיָתָר מִהְיוֹת כֹּהֵן לַיהוָה לְמַלֵּא אֶת־דְּבַר יְהוָה אֲשֶׁר דִּבֶּר עַל־בֵּית עֵלִי בְּשִׁלֹה:

28 When the news reached *Yoav*, he fled to the Tent of *Hashem* and grasped the horns of the *Mizbayach* – for *Yoav* had sided with *Adoniyahu*, though he had not sided with *Avshalom*.

כח וְהַשְּׁמֻעָה בָּאָה עַד־יוֹאָב כִּי יוֹאָב נָטָה אַחֲרֵי אֲדֹנִיָּה וְאַחֲרֵי אַבְשָׁלוֹם לֹא נָטָה וַיָּנָס יוֹאָב אֶל־אֹהֶל יְהוָה וַיַּחֲזֵק בְּקַרְנוֹת הַמִּזְבֵּחַ:

29 King *Shlomo* was told that *Yoav* had fled to the Tent of *Hashem* and that he was there by the *Mizbayach*; so *Shlomo* sent Benaiah son of *Yehoyada*, saying, "Go and strike him down."

כט וַיֻּגַּד לַמֶּלֶךְ שְׁלֹמֹה כִּי נָס יוֹאָב אֶל־אֹהֶל יְהוָה וְהִנֵּה אֵצֶל הַמִּזְבֵּחַ וַיִּשְׁלַח שְׁלֹמֹה אֶת־בְּנָיָהוּ בֶן־יְהוֹיָדָע לֵאמֹר לֵךְ פְּגַע־בּוֹ:

Melachim I / I Kings
Chapter 2

30 Benaiah went to the Tent of *Hashem* and said to him, "Thus said the king: Come out!" "No!" he replied; "I will die here." Benaiah reported back to the king that *Yoav* had answered thus and thus,

31 and the king said, "Do just as he said; strike him down and bury him, and remove guilt from me and my father's house for the blood of the innocent that *Yoav* has shed.

32 Thus *Hashem* will bring his blood guilt down upon his own head, because, unbeknown to my father, he struck down with the sword two men more righteous and honorable than he – *Avner* son of Ner, the army commander of *Yisrael*, and *Amasa* son of Jether, the army commander of *Yehuda*.

33 May the guilt for their blood come down upon the head of *Yoav* and his descendants forever, and may good fortune from *Hashem* be granted forever to *David* and his descendants, his house and his throne."

34 So Benaiah son of *Yehoyada* went up and struck him down. And he was buried at his home in the wilderness.

35 In his place, the king appointed Benaiah son of *Yehoyada* over the army, and in place of *Evyatar*, the king appointed the *Kohen Tzadok*.

36 Then the king summoned *Shim'i* and said to him, "Build yourself a house in *Yerushalayim* and stay there – do not ever go out from there anywhere else.

37 On the very day that you go out and cross the Wadi Kidron, you can be sure that you will die; your blood shall be on your own head."

38 "That is fair," said *Shim'i* to the king, "your servant will do just as my lord the king has spoken." And for a long time, *Shim'i* remained in *Yerushalayim*.

39 Three years later, two slaves of *Shim'i* ran away to King Achish son of Maacah of Gath. *Shim'i* was told, "Your slaves are in Gath."

40 *Shim'i* thereupon saddled his ass and went to Achish in Gath to claim his slaves; and *Shim'i* returned from Gath with his slaves.

מלכים א
פרק ב

ל וַיָּבֹא בְנָיָהוּ אֶל־אֹהֶל יְהֹוָה וַיֹּאמֶר אֵלָיו כֹּה־אָמַר הַמֶּלֶךְ צֵא וַיֹּאמֶר לֹא כִּי פֹה אָמוּת וַיָּשֶׁב בְּנָיָהוּ אֶת־הַמֶּלֶךְ דָּבָר לֵאמֹר כֹּה־דִבֶּר יוֹאָב וְכֹה עָנָנִי:

לא וַיֹּאמֶר לוֹ הַמֶּלֶךְ עֲשֵׂה כַּאֲשֶׁר דִּבֶּר וּפְגַע־בּוֹ וּקְבַרְתּוֹ וַהֲסִירֹתָ דְּמֵי חִנָּם אֲשֶׁר שָׁפַךְ יוֹאָב מֵעָלַי וּמֵעַל בֵּית אָבִי:

לב וְהֵשִׁיב יְהֹוָה אֶת־דָּמוֹ עַל־רֹאשׁוֹ אֲשֶׁר פָּגַע בִּשְׁנֵי־אֲנָשִׁים צַדִּקִים וְטֹבִים מִמֶּנּוּ וַיַּהַרְגֵם בַּחֶרֶב וְאָבִי דָוִד לֹא יָדָע אֶת־אַבְנֵר בֶּן־נֵר שַׂר־צְבָא יִשְׂרָאֵל וְאֶת־עֲמָשָׂא בֶן־יֶתֶר שַׂר־צְבָא יְהוּדָה:

לג וְשָׁבוּ דְמֵיהֶם בְּרֹאשׁ יוֹאָב וּבְרֹאשׁ זַרְעוֹ לְעֹלָם וּלְדָוִד וּלְזַרְעוֹ וּלְבֵיתוֹ וּלְכִסְאוֹ יִהְיֶה שָׁלוֹם עַד־עוֹלָם מֵעִם יְהֹוָה:

לד וַיַּעַל בְּנָיָהוּ בֶּן־יְהוֹיָדָע וַיִּפְגַּע־בּוֹ וַיְמִתֵהוּ וַיִּקָּבֵר בְּבֵיתוֹ בַּמִּדְבָּר:

לה וַיִּתֵּן הַמֶּלֶךְ אֶת־בְּנָיָהוּ בֶן־יְהוֹיָדָע תַּחְתָּיו עַל־הַצָּבָא וְאֶת־צָדוֹק הַכֹּהֵן נָתַן הַמֶּלֶךְ תַּחַת אֶבְיָתָר:

לו וַיִּשְׁלַח הַמֶּלֶךְ וַיִּקְרָא לְשִׁמְעִי וַיֹּאמֶר לוֹ בְּנֵה־לְךָ בַיִת בִּירוּשָׁלַםִ וְיָשַׁבְתָּ שָׁם וְלֹא־תֵצֵא מִשָּׁם אָנֶה וָאָנָה:

לז וְהָיָה בְּיוֹם צֵאתְךָ וְעָבַרְתָּ אֶת־נַחַל קִדְרוֹן יָדֹעַ תֵּדַע כִּי מוֹת תָּמוּת דָּמְךָ יִהְיֶה בְרֹאשֶׁךָ:

לח וַיֹּאמֶר שִׁמְעִי לַמֶּלֶךְ טוֹב הַדָּבָר כַּאֲשֶׁר דִּבֶּר אֲדֹנִי הַמֶּלֶךְ כֵּן יַעֲשֶׂה עַבְדֶּךָ וַיֵּשֶׁב שִׁמְעִי בִּירוּשָׁלַםִ יָמִים רַבִּים:

לט וַיְהִי מִקֵּץ שָׁלֹשׁ שָׁנִים וַיִּבְרְחוּ שְׁנֵי־עֲבָדִים לְשִׁמְעִי אֶל־אָכִישׁ בֶּן־מַעֲכָה מֶלֶךְ גַּת וַיַּגִּידוּ לְשִׁמְעִי לֵאמֹר הִנֵּה עֲבָדֶיךָ בְּגַת:

מ וַיָּקָם שִׁמְעִי וַיַּחֲבֹשׁ אֶת־חֲמֹרוֹ וַיֵּלֶךְ גַּתָה אֶל־אָכִישׁ לְבַקֵּשׁ אֶת־עֲבָדָיו וַיֵּלֶךְ שִׁמְעִי וַיָּבֵא אֶת־עֲבָדָיו מִגַּת:

Melachim I/I Kings
Chapter 3

מלכים א
פרק ג

מא וַיֻּגַּד לִשְׁלֹמֹה כִּי־הָלַךְ שִׁמְעִי מִירוּשָׁלַ͏ִם גַּת וַיָּשֹׁב:

41 *Shlomo* was told that *Shim'i* had gone from *Yerushalayim* to Gath and back,

מב וַיִּשְׁלַח הַמֶּלֶךְ וַיִּקְרָא לְשִׁמְעִי וַיֹּאמֶר אֵלָיו הֲלוֹא הִשְׁבַּעְתִּיךָ בַיהוָה וָאָעִד בְּךָ לֵאמֹר בְּיוֹם צֵאתְךָ וְהָלַכְתָּ אָנֶה וָאָנָה יָדֹעַ תֵּדַע כִּי מוֹת תָּמוּת וַתֹּאמֶר אֵלַי טוֹב הַדָּבָר שָׁמָעְתִּי:

42 and the king summoned *Shim'i* and said to him, "Did I not adjure you by *Hashem* and warn you, 'On the very day that you leave and go anywhere else, you can be sure that you will die,' and did you not say to me, 'It is fair; I accept'?

מג וּמַדּוּעַ לֹא שָׁמַרְתָּ אֵת שְׁבֻעַת יְהוָה וְאֶת־הַמִּצְוָה אֲשֶׁר־צִוִּיתִי עָלֶיךָ:

43 Why did you not abide by the oath before *Hashem* and by the orders which I gave you?"

מד וַיֹּאמֶר הַמֶּלֶךְ אֶל־שִׁמְעִי אַתָּה יָדַעְתָּ אֵת כָּל־הָרָעָה אֲשֶׁר יָדַע לְבָבְךָ אֲשֶׁר עָשִׂיתָ לְדָוִד אָבִי וְהֵשִׁיב יְהוָה אֶת־רָעָתְךָ בְּרֹאשֶׁךָ:

44 The king said further to *Shim'i*, "You know all the wrong, which you remember very well, that you did to my father *David*. Now *Hashem* brings down your wrongdoing upon your own head.

מה וְהַמֶּלֶךְ שְׁלֹמֹה בָּרוּךְ וְכִסֵּא דָוִד יִהְיֶה נָכוֹן לִפְנֵי יְהוָה עַד־עוֹלָם:

45 But King *Shlomo* shall be blessed, and the throne of *David* shall be established before *Hashem* forever."

מו וַיְצַו הַמֶּלֶךְ אֶת־בְּנָיָהוּ בֶּן־יְהוֹיָדָע וַיֵּצֵא וַיִּפְגַּע־בּוֹ וַיָּמֹת וְהַמַּמְלָכָה נָכוֹנָה בְּיַד־שְׁלֹמֹה:

46 The king gave orders to Benaiah son of *Yehoyada* and he went out and struck *Shim'i* down; and so he died. Thus the kingdom was secured in *Shlomo*'s hands.

3

ג א וַיִּתְחַתֵּן שְׁלֹמֹה אֶת־פַּרְעֹה מֶלֶךְ מִצְרָיִם וַיִּקַּח אֶת־בַּת־פַּרְעֹה וַיְבִיאֶהָ אֶל־עִיר דָּוִד עַד כַּלֹּתוֹ לִבְנוֹת אֶת־בֵּיתוֹ וְאֶת־בֵּית יְהוָה וְאֶת־חוֹמַת יְרוּשָׁלַ͏ִם סָבִיב:

1 *Shlomo* allied himself by marriage with Pharaoh king of Egypt. He married Pharaoh's daughter and brought her to the City of *David* [to live there] until he had finished building his palace, and the House of *Hashem*, and the walls around *Yerushalayim*.

ב רַק הָעָם מְזַבְּחִים בַּבָּמוֹת כִּי לֹא־נִבְנָה בַיִת לְשֵׁם יְהוָה עַד הַיָּמִים הָהֵם:

2 The people, however, continued to offer sacrifices at the open shrines, because up to that time no house had been built for the name of *Hashem*.

ג וַיֶּאֱהַב שְׁלֹמֹה אֶת־יְהוָה לָלֶכֶת בְּחֻקּוֹת דָּוִד אָבִיו רַק בַּבָּמוֹת הוּא מְזַבֵּחַ וּמַקְטִיר:

3 And *Shlomo*, though he loved *Hashem* and followed the practices of his father *David*, also sacrificed and offered at the shrines.

ד וַיֵּלֶךְ הַמֶּלֶךְ גִּבְעֹנָה לִזְבֹּחַ שָׁם כִּי הִיא הַבָּמָה הַגְּדוֹלָה אֶלֶף עֹלוֹת יַעֲלֶה שְׁלֹמֹה עַל הַמִּזְבֵּחַ הַהוּא:

4 The king went to *Givon* to sacrifice there, for that was the largest shrine; on that altar *Shlomo* presented a thousand burnt offerings.

ה בְּגִבְעוֹן נִרְאָה יְהוָֹה אֶל־שְׁלֹמֹה בַּחֲלוֹם הַלָּיְלָה וַיֹּאמֶר אֱלֹהִים שְׁאַל מָה אֶתֶּן־לָךְ:

5 At *Givon Hashem* appeared to *Shlomo* in a dream by night; and *Hashem* said, "Ask, what shall I grant you?"

ו וַיֹּאמֶר שְׁלֹמֹה אַתָּה עָשִׂיתָ עִם־עַבְדְּךָ דָוִד אָבִי חֶסֶד גָּדוֹל כַּאֲשֶׁר הָלַךְ לְפָנֶיךָ בֶּאֱמֶת וּבִצְדָקָה וּבְיִשְׁרַת לֵבָב עִמָּךְ וַתִּשְׁמָר־לוֹ אֶת־הַחֶסֶד הַגָּדוֹל הַזֶּה וַתִּתֶּן־לוֹ בֵן יֹשֵׁב עַל־כִּסְאוֹ כַּיּוֹם הַזֶּה:

6 *Shlomo* said, "You dealt most graciously with Your servant my father *David*, because he walked before You in faithfulness and righteousness and in integrity of heart. You have continued this great kindness to him by giving him a son to occupy his throne, as is now the case.

Melachim I / I Kings

Chapter 3

מלכים א

פרק ג

7 And now, *Hashem* my God, You have made Your servant king in place of my father *David*; but I am a young lad, with no experience in leadership.

ז וְעַתָּה יְהֹוָה אֱלֹהָי אַתָּה הִמְלַכְתָּ אֶת־עַבְדְּךָ תַּחַת דָּוִד אָבִי וְאָנֹכִי נַעַר קָטֹן לֹא אֵדַע צֵאת וָבֹא׃

8 Your servant finds himself in the midst of the people You have chosen, a people too numerous to be numbered or counted.

ח וְעַבְדְּךָ בְּתוֹךְ עַמְּךָ אֲשֶׁר בָּחָרְתָּ עַם־רָב אֲשֶׁר לֹא־יִמָּנֶה וְלֹא יִסָּפֵר מֵרֹב׃

9 Grant, then, Your servant an understanding mind to judge Your people, to distinguish between good and bad; for who can judge this vast people of Yours?"

ט וְנָתַתָּ לְעַבְדְּךָ לֵב שֹׁמֵעַ לִשְׁפֹּט אֶת־עַמְּךָ לְהָבִין בֵּין־טוֹב לְרָע כִּי מִי יוּכַל לִשְׁפֹּט אֶת־עַמְּךָ הַכָּבֵד הַזֶּה׃

v'-na-ta-TA l'-av-d'-KHA LAYV sho-MAY-a lish-POT et a-m'-KHA l'-ha-VEEN bayn TOV l'-RA KEE MEE yu-KHAL lish-POT et a-m'-KHA ha-ka-VAYD ha-ZEH

10 *Hashem* was pleased that *Shlomo* had asked for this.

י וַיִּיטַב הַדָּבָר בְּעֵינֵי אֲדֹנָי כִּי שָׁאַל שְׁלֹמֹה אֶת־הַדָּבָר הַזֶּה׃

11 And *Hashem* said to him, "Because you asked for this – you did not ask for long life, you did not ask for riches, you did not ask for the life of your enemies, but you asked for discernment in dispensing justice

יא וַיֹּאמֶר אֱלֹהִים אֵלָיו יַעַן אֲשֶׁר שָׁאַלְתָּ אֶת־הַדָּבָר הַזֶּה וְלֹא־שָׁאַלְתָּ לְּךָ יָמִים רַבִּים וְלֹא־שָׁאַלְתָּ לְּךָ עֹשֶׁר וְלֹא שָׁאַלְתָּ נֶפֶשׁ אֹיְבֶיךָ וְשָׁאַלְתָּ לְּךָ הָבִין לִשְׁמֹעַ מִשְׁפָּט׃

12 I now do as you have spoken. I grant you a wise and discerning mind; there has never been anyone like you before, nor will anyone like you arise again.

יב הִנֵּה עָשִׂיתִי כִּדְבָרֶיךָ הִנֵּה נָתַתִּי לְךָ לֵב חָכָם וְנָבוֹן אֲשֶׁר כָּמוֹךָ לֹא־הָיָה לְפָנֶיךָ וְאַחֲרֶיךָ לֹא־יָקוּם כָּמוֹךָ׃

13 And I also grant you what you did not ask for – both riches and glory all your life – the like of which no king has ever had.

יג וְגַם אֲשֶׁר לֹא־שָׁאַלְתָּ נָתַתִּי לָךְ גַּם־עֹשֶׁר גַּם־כָּבוֹד אֲשֶׁר לֹא־הָיָה כָמוֹךָ אִישׁ בַּמְּלָכִים כָּל־יָמֶיךָ׃

14 And I will further grant you long life, if you will walk in My ways and observe My laws and commandments, as did your father *David*."

יד וְאִם תֵּלֵךְ בִּדְרָכַי לִשְׁמֹר חֻקַּי וּמִצְוֹתַי כַּאֲשֶׁר הָלַךְ דָּוִיד אָבִיךָ וְהַאֲרַכְתִּי אֶת־יָמֶיךָ׃

15 Then *Shlomo* awoke: it was a dream! He went to *Yerushalayim*, stood before the *Aron Brit Hashem*, and sacrificed burnt offerings and presented offerings of well-being; and he made a banquet for all his courtiers.

טו וַיִּקַץ שְׁלֹמֹה וְהִנֵּה חֲלוֹם וַיָּבוֹא יְרוּשָׁלַםִ וַיַּעֲמֹד לִפְנֵי אֲרוֹן בְּרִית־אֲדֹנָי וַיַּעַל עֹלוֹת וַיַּעַשׂ שְׁלָמִים וַיַּעַשׂ מִשְׁתֶּה לְכָל־עֲבָדָיו׃

3:9 Grant, then, Your servant an understanding mind to judge Your people King *Shlomo* attains prophecy and *Hashem* asks him what he desires. Though he could have sought riches or long life, he asks for "an understanding mind" so that he can properly judge the Children of Israel. According to Jewish tradition, King *Shlomo* becomes the wisest of all men and masters all subjects and languages, even those of the animals (I Kings 5:9–14). He also demonstrates deep understanding of human beings, as demonstrated by the well-known case, described in this chapter, where he correctly discerns who is the true mother of a disputed baby. The People of Israel rejoice in their king's wisdom, and thus unite behind him (see 4:1). This is King *Shlomo*'s reward for asking *Hashem* for something that would not only help him, but would bring benefit to the nation and the entire world. Going beyond one's individual needs to serve the nation is one of the signs of a true leader.

Melachim I / I Kings
Chapter 3

16 Later two prostitutes came to the king and stood before him.

17 The first woman said, "Please, my lord! This woman and I live in the same house; and I gave birth to a child while she was in the house.

18 On the third day after I was delivered, this woman also gave birth to a child. We were alone; there was no one else with us in the house, just the two of us in the house.

19 During the night this woman's child died, because she lay on it.

20 She arose in the night and took my son from my side while your maidservant was asleep, and laid him in her bosom; and she laid her dead son in my bosom.

21 When I arose in the morning to nurse my son, there he was, dead; but when I looked at him closely in the morning, it was not the son I had borne."

22 The other woman spoke up, "No, the live one is my son, and the dead one is yours!" But the first insisted, "No, the dead boy is yours; mine is the live one!" And they went on arguing before the king.

23 The king said, "One says, 'This is my son, the live one, and the dead one is yours'; and the other says, 'No, the dead boy is yours, mine is the live one.'

24 So the king gave the order, "Fetch me a sword." A sword was brought before the king,

25 and the king said, "Cut the live child in two, and give half to one and half to the other."

26 But the woman whose son was the live one pleaded with the king, for she was overcome with compassion for her son. "Please, my lord," she cried, "give her the live child; only don't kill it!" The other insisted, "It shall be neither yours nor mine; cut it in two!"

27 Then the king spoke up. "Give the live child to her," he said, "and do not put it to death; she is its mother."

מלכים א
פרק ג

טז אָז תָּבֹאנָה שְׁתַּיִם נָשִׁים זֹנוֹת אֶל־הַמֶּלֶךְ וַתַּעֲמֹדְנָה לְפָנָיו:

יז וַתֹּאמֶר הָאִשָּׁה הָאַחַת בִּי אֲדֹנִי אֲנִי וְהָאִשָּׁה הַזֹּאת יֹשְׁבֹת בְּבַיִת אֶחָד וָאֵלֵד עִמָּהּ בַּבָּיִת:

יח וַיְהִי בַּיּוֹם הַשְּׁלִישִׁי לְלִדְתִּי וַתֵּלֶד גַּם־הָאִשָּׁה הַזֹּאת וַאֲנַחְנוּ יַחְדָּו אֵין־זָר אִתָּנוּ בַּבַּיִת זוּלָתִי שְׁתַּיִם־אֲנַחְנוּ בַּבָּיִת:

יט וַיָּמָת בֶּן־הָאִשָּׁה הַזֹּאת לָיְלָה אֲשֶׁר שָׁכְבָה עָלָיו:

כ וַתָּקָם בְּתוֹךְ הַלַּיְלָה וַתִּקַּח אֶת־בְּנִי מֵאֶצְלִי וַאֲמָתְךָ יְשֵׁנָה וַתַּשְׁכִּיבֵהוּ בְּחֵיקָהּ וְאֶת־בְּנָהּ הַמֵּת הִשְׁכִּיבָה בְחֵיקִי:

כא וָאָקֻם בַּבֹּקֶר לְהֵינִיק אֶת־בְּנִי וְהִנֵּה־מֵת וָאֶתְבּוֹנֵן אֵלָיו בַּבֹּקֶר וְהִנֵּה לֹא־הָיָה בְנִי אֲשֶׁר יָלָדְתִּי:

כב וַתֹּאמֶר הָאִשָּׁה הָאַחֶרֶת לֹא כִי בְּנִי הַחַי וּבְנֵךְ הַמֵּת וְזֹאת אֹמֶרֶת לֹא כִי בְּנֵךְ הַמֵּת וּבְנִי הֶחָי וַתְּדַבֵּרְנָה לִפְנֵי הַמֶּלֶךְ:

כג וַיֹּאמֶר הַמֶּלֶךְ זֹאת אֹמֶרֶת זֶה־בְּנִי הַחַי וּבְנֵךְ הַמֵּת וְזֹאת אֹמֶרֶת לֹא כִי בְּנֵךְ הַמֵּת וּבְנִי הֶחָי:

כד וַיֹּאמֶר הַמֶּלֶךְ קְחוּ לִי־חָרֶב וַיָּבִאוּ הַחֶרֶב לִפְנֵי הַמֶּלֶךְ:

כה וַיֹּאמֶר הַמֶּלֶךְ גִּזְרוּ אֶת־הַיֶּלֶד הַחַי לִשְׁנָיִם וּתְנוּ אֶת־הַחֲצִי לְאַחַת וְאֶת־הַחֲצִי לְאֶחָת:

כו וַתֹּאמֶר הָאִשָּׁה אֲשֶׁר־בְּנָהּ הַחַי אֶל־הַמֶּלֶךְ כִּי־נִכְמְרוּ רַחֲמֶיהָ עַל־בְּנָהּ וַתֹּאמֶר בִּי אֲדֹנִי תְּנוּ־לָהּ אֶת־הַיָּלוּד הַחַי וְהָמֵת אַל־תְּמִיתֻהוּ וְזֹאת אֹמֶרֶת גַּם־לִי גַם־לָךְ לֹא יִהְיֶה גְּזֹרוּ:

כז וַיַּעַן הַמֶּלֶךְ וַיֹּאמֶר תְּנוּ־לָהּ אֶת־הַיָּלוּד הַחַי וְהָמֵת לֹא תְמִיתֻהוּ הִיא אִמּוֹ:

Melachim I/I Kings
Chapter 4

מלכים א
פרק ד

28 When all *Yisrael* heard the decision that the king had rendered, they stood in awe of the king; for they saw that he possessed divine wisdom to execute justice.

כח וַיִּשְׁמְעוּ כָל־יִשְׂרָאֵל אֶת־הַמִּשְׁפָּט אֲשֶׁר שָׁפַט הַמֶּלֶךְ וַיִּרְאוּ מִפְּנֵי הַמֶּלֶךְ כִּי רָאוּ כִּי־חָכְמַת אֱלֹהִים בְּקִרְבּוֹ לַעֲשׂוֹת מִשְׁפָּט׃

4

1 King *Shlomo* was now king over all *Yisrael*.

א וַיְהִי הַמֶּלֶךְ שְׁלֹמֹה מֶלֶךְ עַל־כָּל־יִשְׂרָאֵל׃

2 These were his officials: *Azarya* son of *Tzadok* – the *Kohen*;

ב וְאֵלֶּה הַשָּׂרִים אֲשֶׁר־לוֹ עֲזַרְיָהוּ בֶן־צָדוֹק הַכֹּהֵן׃

3 Elihoreph and *Achiya* sons of Shisha – scribes; *Yehoshafat* son of *Achilud* – recorder;

ג אֱלִיחֹרֶף וַאֲחִיָּה בְּנֵי שִׁישָׁא סֹפְרִים יְהוֹשָׁפָט בֶּן־אֲחִילוּד הַמַּזְכִּיר׃

4 Benaiah son of *Yehoyada* – over the army; *Tzadok* and *Evyatar* – *Kohanim*;

ד וּבְנָיָהוּ בֶן־יְהוֹיָדָע עַל־הַצָּבָא וְצָדוֹק וְאֶבְיָתָר כֹּהֲנִים׃

5 *Azarya* son of *Natan* – in charge of the prefects; Zabud son of *Natan* the *Kohen* – companion of the king;

ה וַעֲזַרְיָהוּ בֶן־נָתָן עַל־הַנִּצָּבִים וְזָבוּד בֶּן־נָתָן כֹּהֵן רֵעֶה הַמֶּלֶךְ׃

6 Ahishar – in charge of the palace; and Adoniram son of Abda – in charge of the forced labor.

ו וַאֲחִישָׁר עַל־הַבָּיִת וַאֲדֹנִירָם בֶּן־עַבְדָּא עַל־הַמַּס׃

7 *Shlomo* had twelve prefects governing all *Yisrael*, who provided food for the king and his household; each had to provide food for one month in the year.

ז וְלִשְׁלֹמֹה שְׁנֵים־עָשָׂר נִצָּבִים עַל־כָּל־יִשְׂרָאֵל וְכִלְכְּלוּ אֶת־הַמֶּלֶךְ וְאֶת־בֵּיתוֹ חֹדֶשׁ בַּשָּׁנָה יִהְיֶה עַל־אֶחָד [הָאֶחָד] לְכַלְכֵּל׃

8 And these were their names: Ben-hur, in the hill country of *Efraim*;

ח וְאֵלֶּה שְׁמוֹתָם בֶּן־חוּר בְּהַר אֶפְרָיִם׃

9 Bendeker, in Makaz, Shaalbim, *Beit Shemesh*, and Elon-beth-hanan;

ט בֶּן־דֶּקֶר בְּמָקַץ וּבְשַׁעַלְבִים וּבֵית שָׁמֶשׁ וְאֵילוֹן בֵּית חָנָן׃

10 Ben-hesed in Arubboth – he governed Socho and all the Hepher area;

י בֶּן־חֶסֶד בָּאֲרֻבּוֹת לוֹ שֹׂכֹה וְכָל־אֶרֶץ חֵפֶר׃

11 Ben-abinadab, [in] all of Naphath-dor (*Shlomo's* daughter Taphath was his wife);

יא בֶּן־אֲבִינָדָב כָּל־נָפַת דֹּאר טָפַת בַּת־שְׁלֹמֹה הָיְתָה לּוֹ לְאִשָּׁה׃

12 Baana son of *Achilud* [in] Taanach and Megiddo and all *Beit-Shean*, which is beside Zarethan, below *Yizrael* – from *Beit-Shean* to Abel-meholah as far as the other side of Jokmeam;

יב בַּעֲנָא בֶּן־אֲחִילוּד תַּעְנַךְ וּמְגִדּוֹ וְכָל־בֵּית שְׁאָן אֲשֶׁר אֵצֶל צָרְתַנָה מִתַּחַת לְיִזְרְעֶאל מִבֵּית שְׁאָן עַד אָבֵל מְחוֹלָה עַד מֵעֵבֶר לְיָקְמֳעָם׃

13 Ben-geber, in Ramoth-gilead – he governed the villages of *Yair* son of *Menashe* which are in *Gilad*, and he also governed the district of Argob which is in Bashan, sixty large towns with walls and bronze bars;

יג בֶּן־גֶּבֶר בְּרָמֹת גִּלְעָד לוֹ חַוֺּת יָאִיר בֶּן־מְנַשֶּׁה אֲשֶׁר בַּגִּלְעָד לוֹ חֶבֶל אַרְגֹּב אֲשֶׁר בַּבָּשָׁן שִׁשִּׁים עָרִים גְּדֹלוֹת חוֹמָה וּבְרִיחַ נְחֹשֶׁת׃

14 Ahinadab son of *Ido*, in Mahanaim;

יד אֲחִינָדָב בֶּן־עִדֹּא מַחֲנָיְמָה׃

15 Ahimaaz, in *Naftali* (he too took a daughter of *Shlomo* – Basemath – to wife);

טו אֲחִימַעַץ בְּנַפְתָּלִי גַּם־הוּא לָקַח אֶת־בָּשְׂמַת בַּת־שְׁלֹמֹה לְאִשָּׁה׃

16 Baanah son of Hushi, in *Asher* and Bealoth;

טז בַּעֲנָא בֶּן־חוּשָׁי בְּאָשֵׁר וּבְעָלוֹת׃

Melachim I / I Kings
Chapter 5

מלכים א
פרק ה

17 *Yehoshafat* son of Paruah, in *Yissachar*;

יְהוֹשָׁפָט בֶּן־פָּרוּחַ בְּיִשָּׂשכָר:

18 *Shim'i* son of Ela, in *Binyamin*;

שִׁמְעִי בֶן־אֵלָא בְּבִנְיָמִן:

19 Geber son of *Uri*, in the region of *Gilad*, the country of Sihon, king of the Amorites, and Og, king of Bashan; and one prefect who was in the land.

גֶּבֶר בֶּן־אֻרִי בְּאֶרֶץ גִּלְעָד אֶרֶץ סִיחוֹן מֶלֶךְ הָאֱמֹרִי וְעֹג מֶלֶךְ הַבָּשָׁן וּנְצִיב אֶחָד אֲשֶׁר בָּאָרֶץ:

20 *Yehuda* and *Yisrael* were as numerous as the sands of the sea; they ate and drank and were content.

יְהוּדָה וְיִשְׂרָאֵל רַבִּים כַּחוֹל אֲשֶׁר־עַל־הַיָּם לָרֹב אֹכְלִים וְשֹׁתִים וּשְׂמֵחִים:

y'-hu-DAH v'-yis-ra-AYL ra-BEEM ka-KHOL a-asher al ha-YAM la-ROV o-kh'-LEEM v'-sho-TEEM us-may-KHEEM

5 1 *Shlomo*'s rule extended over all the kingdoms from the Euphrates to the land of the Philistines and the boundary of Egypt. They brought *Shlomo* tribute and were subject to him all his life.

וּשְׁלֹמֹה הָיָה מוֹשֵׁל בְּכָל־הַמַּמְלָכוֹת מִן־הַנָּהָר אֶרֶץ פְּלִשְׁתִּים וְעַד גְּבוּל מִצְרָיִם מַגִּשִׁים מִנְחָה וְעֹבְדִים אֶת־שְׁלֹמֹה כָּל־יְמֵי חַיָּיו:

2 *Shlomo*'s daily provisions consisted of 30 *kors* of semolina, and 60 *kors* of [ordinary] flour,

וַיְהִי לֶחֶם־שְׁלֹמֹה לְיוֹם אֶחָד שְׁלֹשִׁים כֹּר סֹלֶת וְשִׁשִּׁים כֹּר קָמַח:

3 10 fattened oxen, 20 pasture-fed oxen, and 100 sheep and goats, besides deer and gazelles, roebucks and fatted geese.

עֲשָׂרָה בָקָר בְּרִאִים וְעֶשְׂרִים בָּקָר רְעִי וּמֵאָה צֹאן לְבַד מֵאַיָּל וּצְבִי וְיַחְמוּר וּבַרְבֻּרִים אֲבוּסִים:

4 For he controlled the whole region west of the Euphrates – all the kings west of the Euphrates, from Tiphsah to *Azza* – and he had peace on all his borders roundabout.

כִּי־הוּא רֹדֶה בְּכָל־עֵבֶר הַנָּהָר מִתִּפְסַח וְעַד־עַזָּה בְּכָל־מַלְכֵי עֵבֶר הַנָּהָר וְשָׁלוֹם הָיָה לוֹ מִכָּל־עֲבָרָיו מִסָּבִיב:

5 All the days of *Shlomo*, *Yehuda* and *Yisrael* from *Dan* to *Be'er Sheva* dwelt in safety, everyone under his own vine and under his own fig tree.

וַיֵּשֶׁב יְהוּדָה וְיִשְׂרָאֵל לָבֶטַח אִישׁ תַּחַת גַּפְנוֹ וְתַחַת תְּאֵנָתוֹ מִדָּן וְעַד־בְּאֵר שָׁבַע כֹּל יְמֵי שְׁלֹמֹה:

6 *Shlomo* had 40,000 stalls of horses for his chariotry and 12,000 horsemen.

וַיְהִי לִשְׁלֹמֹה אַרְבָּעִים אֶלֶף אֻרְוֹת סוּסִים לְמֶרְכָּבוֹ וּשְׁנֵים־עָשָׂר אֶלֶף פָּרָשִׁים:

7 All those prefects, each during his month, would furnish provisions for King *Shlomo* and for all who were admitted to King *Shlomo*'s table; they did not fall short in anything.

וְכִלְכְּלוּ הַנִּצָּבִים הָאֵלֶּה אֶת־הַמֶּלֶךְ שְׁלֹמֹה וְאֵת כָּל־הַקָּרֵב אֶל־שֻׁלְחַן הַמֶּלֶךְ־שְׁלֹמֹה אִישׁ חָדְשׁוֹ לֹא יְעַדְּרוּ דָּבָר:

8 They would also, each in his turn, deliver barley and straw for the horses and the swift steeds to the places where they were stationed.

וְהַשְּׂעֹרִים וְהַתֶּבֶן לַסּוּסִים וְלָרָכֶשׁ יָבִאוּ אֶל־הַמָּקוֹם אֲשֶׁר יִהְיֶה־שָּׁם אִישׁ כְּמִשְׁפָּטוֹ:

4:20 *Yehuda* and *Yisrael* were as numerous as the sands of the sea Unlike King *David* who began his rule only over *Yehuda*, King *Shlomo* rises to power over a united kingdom comprising all of *Yehuda* and *Yisrael*. As *Radak* notes, everyone in the kingdom recognizes King *Shlomo*'s rule, due to the universal recognition of his God-given wisdom. The chapter ends with the reward for unity among the People of Israel: they become as numerous as the sand on the sea shore and successful in the Land of Israel, thereby seeing the fulfillment of the blessing *Hashem* gave to *Avraham* (Genesis 22:17).

Melachim I/I Kings
Chapter 5

מלכים א
פרק ה

9 *Hashem* endowed *Shlomo* with wisdom and discernment in great measure, with understanding as vast as the sands on the seashore.

ט וַיִּתֵּן אֱלֹהִים חָכְמָה לִשְׁלֹמֹה וּתְבוּנָה הַרְבֵּה מְאֹד וְרֹחַב לֵב כַּחוֹל אֲשֶׁר עַל־שְׂפַת הַיָּם:

10 *Shlomo*'s wisdom was greater than the wisdom of all the Kedemites and than all the wisdom of the Egyptians.

י וַתֵּרֶב חָכְמַת שְׁלֹמֹה מֵחָכְמַת כָּל־בְּנֵי־קֶדֶם וּמִכֹּל חָכְמַת מִצְרָיִם:

11 He was the wisest of all men: [wiser] than Ethan the Ezrahite, and *Hayman*, Chalkol, and Darda the sons of Mahol. His fame spread among all the surrounding nations.

יא וַיֶּחְכַּם מִכָּל־הָאָדָם מֵאֵיתָן הָאֶזְרָחִי וְהֵימָן וְכַלְכֹּל וְדַרְדַּע בְּנֵי מָחוֹל וַיְהִי־שְׁמוֹ בְכָל־הַגּוֹיִם סָבִיב:

12 He composed three thousand proverbs, and his songs numbered one thousand and five.

יב וַיְדַבֵּר שְׁלֹשֶׁת אֲלָפִים מָשָׁל וַיְהִי שִׁירוֹ חֲמִשָּׁה וָאָלֶף:

13 He discoursed about trees, from the cedar in Lebanon to the hyssop that grows out of the wall; and he discoursed about beasts, birds, creeping things, and fishes.

יג וַיְדַבֵּר עַל־הָעֵצִים מִן־הָאֶרֶז אֲשֶׁר בַּלְּבָנוֹן וְעַד הָאֵזוֹב אֲשֶׁר יֹצֵא בַּקִּיר וַיְדַבֵּר עַל־הַבְּהֵמָה וְעַל־הָעוֹף וְעַל־הָרֶמֶשׂ וְעַל־הַדָּגִים:

14 Men of all peoples came to hear *Shlomo*'s wisdom, [sent] by all the kings of the earth who had heard of his wisdom.

יד וַיָּבֹאוּ מִכָּל־הָעַמִּים לִשְׁמֹעַ אֵת חָכְמַת שְׁלֹמֹה מֵאֵת כָּל־מַלְכֵי הָאָרֶץ אֲשֶׁר שָׁמְעוּ אֶת־חָכְמָתוֹ:

15 King Hiram of Tyre sent his officials to *Shlomo* when he heard that he had been anointed king in place of his father; for Hiram had always been a friend of *David*.

טו וַיִּשְׁלַח חִירָם מֶלֶךְ־צוֹר אֶת־עֲבָדָיו אֶל־שְׁלֹמֹה כִּי שָׁמַע כִּי אֹתוֹ מָשְׁחוּ לְמֶלֶךְ תַּחַת אָבִיהוּ כִּי אֹהֵב הָיָה חִירָם לְדָוִד כָּל־הַיָּמִים:

16 *Shlomo* sent this message to Hiram:

טז וַיִּשְׁלַח שְׁלֹמֹה אֶל־חִירָם לֵאמֹר:

17 "You know that my father *David* could not build a house for the name of *Hashem* his God because of the enemies that encompassed him, until *Hashem* had placed them under the soles of his feet.

יז אַתָּה יָדַעְתָּ אֶת־דָּוִד אָבִי כִּי לֹא יָכֹל לִבְנוֹת בַּיִת לְשֵׁם יְהוָה אֱלֹהָיו מִפְּנֵי הַמִּלְחָמָה אֲשֶׁר סְבָבֻהוּ עַד תֵּת־יְהוָה אֹתָם תַּחַת כַּפּוֹת רגלו [רַגְלָי]:

18 But now *Hashem* my God has given me respite all around; there is no adversary and no mischance.

יח וְעַתָּה הֵנִיחַ יְהוָה אֱלֹהַי לִי מִסָּבִיב אֵין שָׂטָן וְאֵין פֶּגַע רָע:

19 And so I propose to build a house for the name of *Hashem* my God, as *Hashem* promised my father *David*, saying, 'Your son, whom I will set on your throne in your place, shall build the house for My name.'

יט וְהִנְנִי אֹמֵר לִבְנוֹת בַּיִת לְשֵׁם יְהוָה אֱלֹהָי כַּאֲשֶׁר דִּבֶּר יְהוָה אֶל־דָּוִד אָבִי לֵאמֹר בִּנְךָ אֲשֶׁר אֶתֵּן תַּחְתֶּיךָ עַל־כִּסְאֶךָ הוּא־יִבְנֶה הַבַּיִת לִשְׁמִי:

v'-hi-n'-NEE o-MAYR liv-NOT BA-yit l'-SHAYM a-do-NAI e-lo-HAI ka-a-SHER di-BER a-do-NAI el da-VID a-VEE lay-MOR bin-KHA a-SHER e-TAYN takh-TE-kha al kis-E-kha hu yiv-NEH ha-BA-yit lish-MEE

5:19 I propose to build a house for the name of *Hashem* my God Because King *Shlomo* reigns over a united and strong kingdom living at peace, he is able to embark upon the building of the *Beit Hamikdash* in *Yerushalayim*. The Talmud (*Zevachim* 118) relates that the *Mishkan* stood in *Gilgal* for 14 years, in *Shilo* for 369 years,

Melachim I / I Kings
Chapter 5

מלכים א
פרק ה

20 Please, then, give orders for cedars to be cut for me in the Lebanon. My servants will work with yours, and I will pay you any wages you may ask for your servants; for as you know, there is none among us who knows how to cut timber like the Sidonians."

כ וְעַתָּה צַוֵּה וְיִכְרְתוּ־לִי אֲרָזִים מִן־הַלְּבָנוֹן וַעֲבָדַי יִהְיוּ עִם־עֲבָדֶיךָ וּשְׂכַר עֲבָדֶיךָ אֶתֵּן לְךָ כְּכֹל אֲשֶׁר תֹּאמֵר כִּי אַתָּה יָדַעְתָּ כִּי אֵין בָּנוּ אִישׁ יֹדֵעַ לִכְרָת־עֵצִים כַּצִּדֹנִים:

21 When Hiram heard *Shlomo*'s message, he was overjoyed. "Praised be *Hashem* this day," he said, "for granting *David* a wise son to govern this great people."

כא וַיְהִי כִּשְׁמֹעַ חִירָם אֶת־דִּבְרֵי שְׁלֹמֹה וַיִּשְׂמַח מְאֹד וַיֹּאמֶר בָּרוּךְ יְהֹוָה הַיּוֹם אֲשֶׁר נָתַן לְדָוִד בֵּן חָכָם עַל־הָעָם הָרָב הַזֶּה:

22 So Hiram sent word to *Shlomo*: "I have your message; I will supply all the cedar and cypress logs you require.

כב וַיִּשְׁלַח חִירָם אֶל־שְׁלֹמֹה לֵאמֹר שָׁמַעְתִּי אֵת אֲשֶׁר־שָׁלַחְתָּ אֵלָי אֲנִי אֶעֱשֶׂה אֶת־כָּל־חֶפְצְךָ בַּעֲצֵי אֲרָזִים וּבַעֲצֵי בְרוֹשִׁים:

23 My servants will bring them down to the sea from the Lebanon; and at the sea I will make them into floats and [deliver them] to any place that you designate to me. There I shall break them up for you to carry away. You, in turn, will supply the food I require for my household."

כג עֲבָדַי יֹרִדוּ מִן־הַלְּבָנוֹן יָמָּה וַאֲנִי אֲשִׂימֵם דֹּבְרוֹת בַּיָּם עַד־הַמָּקוֹם אֲשֶׁר־תִּשְׁלַח אֵלַי וְנִפַּצְתִּים שָׁם וְאַתָּה תִשָּׂא וְאַתָּה תַּעֲשֶׂה אֶת־חֶפְצִי לָתֵת לֶחֶם בֵּיתִי:

24 So Hiram kept *Shlomo* provided with all the cedar and cypress wood he required,

כד וַיְהִי חִירוֹם נֹתֵן לִשְׁלֹמֹה עֲצֵי אֲרָזִים וַעֲצֵי בְרוֹשִׁים כָּל־חֶפְצוֹ:

25 and *Shlomo* delivered to Hiram 20,000 *kors* of wheat as provisions for his household and 20 *kors* of beaten oil. Such was *Shlomo*'s annual payment to Hiram.

כה וּשְׁלֹמֹה נָתַן לְחִירָם עֶשְׂרִים אֶלֶף כֹּר חִטִּים מַכֹּלֶת לְבֵיתוֹ וְעֶשְׂרִים כֹּר שֶׁמֶן כָּתִית כֹּה־יִתֵּן שְׁלֹמֹה לְחִירָם שָׁנָה בְשָׁנָה:

26 *Hashem* had given *Shlomo* wisdom, as He had promised him. There was friendship between Hiram and *Shlomo*, and the two of them made a treaty.

כו וַיהֹוָה נָתַן חָכְמָה לִשְׁלֹמֹה כַּאֲשֶׁר דִּבֶּר־לוֹ וַיְהִי שָׁלֹם בֵּין חִירָם וּבֵין שְׁלֹמֹה וַיִּכְרְתוּ בְרִית שְׁנֵיהֶם:

27 King *Shlomo* imposed forced labor on all *Yisrael*; the levy came to 30,000 men.

כז וַיַּעַל הַמֶּלֶךְ שְׁלֹמֹה מַס מִכָּל־יִשְׂרָאֵל וַיְהִי הַמַּס שְׁלֹשִׁים אֶלֶף אִישׁ:

---

and in *Nov* and *Givon* together for another 57 years, equaling a total of 440 years. After this period, work on a permanent House of God can finally begin. This monumental project is the high point of the history of the People of Israel. The purpose of the exodus from Egypt was to receive the *Torah* and to observe it in *Eretz Yisrael*, which includes serving *Hashem* in the place He chose – the *Beit Hamikdash* in *Yerushalayim* (see Exodus 6:6–8). This Temple would serve as a focal point for worship of God, by the Children of Israel and the rest of the world.

Melachim I / I Kings
Chapter 6

28 He sent them to the Lebanon in shifts of 10,000 a month: they would spend one month in the Lebanon and two months at home. Adoniram was in charge of the forced labor.

29 *Shlomo* also had 70,000 porters and 80,000 quarriers in the hills,

30 apart from *Shlomo's* 3,300 officials who were in charge of the work and supervised the gangs doing the work.

31 The king ordered huge blocks of choice stone to be quarried, so that the foundations of the house might be laid with hewn stones.

32 *Shlomo's* masons, Hiram's masons, and the men of Gebal shaped them. Thus the timber and the stones for building the house were made ready.

6

1 In the four hundred and eightieth year after the Israelites left the land of Egypt, in the month of Ziv – that is, the second month – in the fourth year of his reign over *Yisrael, Shlomo* began to build the House of *Hashem*.

2 The House which King *Shlomo* built for *Hashem* was 60 *amot* long, 20 *amot* wide, and 30 *amot* high.

3 The portico in front of the Great Hall of the House was 20 *amot* long – along the width of the House – and 10 *amot* deep to the front of the House.

4 He made windows for the House, recessed and latticed.

5 Against the outside wall of the House – the outside walls of the House enclosing the Great Hall and the Shrine – he built a storied structure; and he made side chambers all around.

6 The lowest story was 5 *amot* wide, the middle one 6 *amot* wide, and the third 7 *amot* wide; for he had provided recesses around the outside of the House so as not to penetrate the walls of the House.

7 When the House was built, only finished stones cut at the quarry were used, so that no hammer or ax or any iron tool was heard in the House while it was being built.

מלכים א
פרק ו

כח וַיִּשְׁלָחֵם לְבָנוֹנָה עֲשֶׂרֶת אֲלָפִים בַּחֹדֶשׁ חֲלִיפוֹת חֹדֶשׁ יִהְיוּ בַלְּבָנוֹן שְׁנַיִם חֳדָשִׁים בְּבֵיתוֹ וַאֲדֹנִירָם עַל־הַמַּס:

כט וַיְהִי לִשְׁלֹמֹה שִׁבְעִים אֶלֶף נֹשֵׂא סַבָּל וּשְׁמֹנִים אֶלֶף חֹצֵב בָּהָר:

ל לְבַד מִשָּׂרֵי הַנִּצָּבִים לִשְׁלֹמֹה אֲשֶׁר עַל־הַמְּלָאכָה שְׁלֹשֶׁת אֲלָפִים וּשְׁלֹשׁ מֵאוֹת הָרֹדִים בָּעָם הָעֹשִׂים בַּמְּלָאכָה:

לא וַיְצַו הַמֶּלֶךְ וַיַּסִּעוּ אֲבָנִים גְּדֹלוֹת אֲבָנִים יְקָרוֹת לְיַסֵּד הַבָּיִת אַבְנֵי גָזִית:

לב וַיִּפְסְלוּ בֹּנֵי שְׁלֹמֹה וּבֹנֵי חִירוֹם וְהַגִּבְלִים וַיָּכִינוּ הָעֵצִים וְהָאֲבָנִים לִבְנוֹת הַבָּיִת:

א וַיְהִי בִשְׁמוֹנִים שָׁנָה וְאַרְבַּע מֵאוֹת שָׁנָה לְצֵאת בְּנֵי־יִשְׂרָאֵל מֵאֶרֶץ־מִצְרַיִם בַּשָּׁנָה הָרְבִיעִית בְּחֹדֶשׁ זִו הוּא הַחֹדֶשׁ הַשֵּׁנִי לִמְלֹךְ שְׁלֹמֹה עַל־יִשְׂרָאֵל וַיִּבֶן הַבַּיִת לַיהוָה:

ב וְהַבַּיִת אֲשֶׁר בָּנָה הַמֶּלֶךְ שְׁלֹמֹה לַיהוָה שִׁשִּׁים־אַמָּה אָרְכּוֹ וְעֶשְׂרִים רָחְבּוֹ וּשְׁלֹשִׁים אַמָּה קוֹמָתוֹ:

ג וְהָאוּלָם עַל־פְּנֵי הֵיכַל הַבַּיִת עֶשְׂרִים אַמָּה אָרְכּוֹ עַל־פְּנֵי רֹחַב הַבָּיִת עֶשֶׂר בָּאַמָּה רָחְבּוֹ עַל־פְּנֵי הַבָּיִת:

ד וַיַּעַשׂ לַבָּיִת חַלּוֹנֵי שְׁקֻפִים אֲטֻמִים:

ה וַיִּבֶן עַל־קִיר הַבַּיִת יצוע [יָצִיעַ] סָבִיב אֶת־קִירוֹת הַבַּיִת סָבִיב לַהֵיכָל וְלַדְּבִיר וַיַּעַשׂ צְלָעוֹת סָבִיב:

ו הַיָּצוּעַ [הַיָּצִיעַ] הַתַּחְתֹּנָה חָמֵשׁ בָּאַמָּה רָחְבָּהּ וְהַתִּיכֹנָה שֵׁשׁ בָּאַמָּה רָחְבָּהּ וְהַשְּׁלִישִׁית שֶׁבַע בָּאַמָּה רָחְבָּהּ כִּי מִגְרָעוֹת נָתַן לַבַּיִת סָבִיב חוּצָה לְבִלְתִּי אֲחֹז בְּקִירוֹת־הַבָּיִת:

ז וְהַבַּיִת בְּהִבָּנֹתוֹ אֶבֶן־שְׁלֵמָה מַסָּע נִבְנָה וּמַקָּבוֹת וְהַגַּרְזֶן כָּל־כְּלִי בַרְזֶל לֹא־נִשְׁמַע בַּבַּיִת בְּהִבָּנֹתוֹ:

Melachim I / I Kings
Chapter 6

מלכים א
פרק ו

8 The entrance to the middle [story of] the side chambers was on the right side of the House; and winding stairs led up to the middle chambers, and from the middle chambers to the third story.

ח פֶּתַח הַצֵּלָע הַתִּיכֹנָה אֶל־כֶּתֶף הַבַּיִת הַיְמָנִית וּבְלוּלִּים יַעֲלוּ עַל־הַתִּיכֹנָה וּמִן־הַתִּיכֹנָה אֶל־הַשְּׁלִשִׁים׃

9 When he finished building the House, he paneled the House with beams and planks of cedar.

ט וַיִּבֶן אֶת־הַבַּיִת וַיְכַלֵּהוּ וַיִּסְפֹּן אֶת־הַבַּיִת גֵּבִים וּשְׂדֵרֹת בָּאֲרָזִים׃

10 He built the storied structure against the entire House – each story 5 *amot* high, so that it encased the House with timbers of cedar.

י וַיִּבֶן אֶת־הַיָּצוּעַ [הַיָּצִיעַ] עַל־כָּל־הַבַּיִת חָמֵשׁ אַמּוֹת קוֹמָתוֹ וַיֶּאֱחֹז אֶת־הַבַּיִת בַּעֲצֵי אֲרָזִים׃

11 Then the word of *Hashem* came to *Shlomo*,

יא וַיְהִי דְּבַר־יְהוָה אֶל־שְׁלֹמֹה לֵאמֹר׃

12 "With regard to this House you are building – if you follow My laws and observe My rules and faithfully keep My commandments, I will fulfill for you the promise that I gave to your father *David*:

יב הַבַּיִת הַזֶּה אֲשֶׁר־אַתָּה בֹנֶה אִם־תֵּלֵךְ בְּחֻקֹּתַי וְאֶת־מִשְׁפָּטַי תַּעֲשֶׂה וְשָׁמַרְתָּ אֶת־כָּל־מִצְוֺתַי לָלֶכֶת בָּהֶם וַהֲקִמֹתִי אֶת־דְּבָרִי אִתָּךְ אֲשֶׁר דִּבַּרְתִּי אֶל־דָּוִד אָבִיךָ׃

13 I will abide among the children of *Yisrael*, and I will never forsake My people *Yisrael*."

יג וְשָׁכַנְתִּי בְּתוֹךְ בְּנֵי יִשְׂרָאֵל וְלֹא אֶעֱזֹב אֶת־עַמִּי יִשְׂרָאֵל׃

v'-SHA-khan-TEE b'-TOKH b'-NAY yis-ra-AYL v'-LO e-e-ZOV et a-MEE yis-ra-AYL

14 When *Shlomo* had completed the construction of the House,

יד וַיִּבֶן שְׁלֹמֹה אֶת־הַבַּיִת וַיְכַלֵּהוּ׃

15 he paneled the walls of the House on the inside with planks of cedar. He also overlaid the walls on the inside with wood, from the floor of the House to the ceiling. And he overlaid the floor of the House with planks of cypress.

טו וַיִּבֶן אֶת־קִירוֹת הַבַּיִת מִבַּיְתָה בְּצַלְעוֹת אֲרָזִים מִקַּרְקַע הַבַּיִת עַד־קִירוֹת הַסִּפֻּן צִפָּה עֵץ מִבָּיִת וַיְצַף אֶת־קַרְקַע הַבַּיִת בְּצַלְעוֹת בְּרוֹשִׁים׃

16 Twenty *amot* from the rear of the House, he built [a partition] of cedar planks from the floor to the walls; he furnished its interior to serve as a shrine, as the Holy of Holies.

טז וַיִּבֶן אֶת־עֶשְׂרִים אַמָּה מִיַּרְכְּתֵי [מִיַּרְכְּתֵי] הַבַּיִת בְּצַלְעוֹת אֲרָזִים מִן־הַקַּרְקַע עַד־הַקִּירוֹת וַיִּבֶן לוֹ מִבַּיִת לִדְבִיר לְקֹדֶשׁ הַקֳּדָשִׁים׃

17 The front part of the House, that is, the Great Hall, measured 40 *amot*.

יז וְאַרְבָּעִים בָּאַמָּה הָיָה הַבָּיִת הוּא הַהֵיכָל לִפְנָי׃

6:13 I will never forsake My people *Yisrael* King *Shlomo* concludes the building of the *Beit Hamikdash* in *Yerushalayim*. This holiest place on earth is a massive and awe-inspiring complex that brings the entire world closer to God. Though *Hashem* will allow it to stand only if the Children of Israel serve Him properly (see 9:8), Rabbi Shlomo Aviner points out that God's commitment in this verse is not conditional. *Hashem*'s covenant with His people is eternal. Though He may "hide His face" at certain points in history, He will never leave His people or allow other nations to flourish in the Promised Land. Despite the many years of exile and suffering that the Jewish people have experienced, *Hashem*'s covenant remains, as does the promise of a return to *Eretz Yisrael*. He has begun to fulfill that promise in our era, before our very eyes.

Melachim I / I Kings
Chapter 6

מלכים א
פרק ו

18 The cedar of the interior of the House had carvings of gourds and calyxes; it was all cedar, no stone was exposed.

יח וְאֶ֨רֶז אֶל־הַבַּ֤יִת פְּנִ֙ימָה֙ מִקְלַ֣עַת פְּקָעִ֔ים וּפְטוּרֵ֖י צִצִּ֑ים הַכֹּ֣ל אֶ֔רֶז אֵ֥ין אֶ֖בֶן נִרְאָֽה׃

19 In the innermost part of the House, he fixed a Shrine in which to place the *Aron Brit Hashem*.

יט וּדְבִ֧יר בְּתוֹךְ־הַבַּ֛יִת מִפְּנִ֖ימָה הֵכִ֑ין לְתִתֵּ֣ן שָׁ֔ם אֶת־אֲר֖וֹן בְּרִ֥ית יְהֹוָֽה׃

20 The interior of the Shrine was 20 *amot* long, 20 *amot* wide, and 20 *amot* high. He overlaid it with solid gold; he similarly overlaid [its] cedar *Mizbayach*.

כ וְלִפְנֵ֣י הַדְּבִ֡יר עֶשְׂרִים֩ אַמָּ֨ה אֹ֜רֶךְ וְעֶשְׂרִ֧ים אַמָּ֣ה רֹ֗חַב וְעֶשְׂרִ֤ים אַמָּה֙ קוֹמָת֔וֹ וַיְצַפֵּ֖הוּ זָהָ֣ב סָג֑וּר וַיְצַ֥ף מִזְבֵּ֖חַ אָֽרֶז׃

21 *Shlomo* overlaid the interior of the House with solid gold; and he inserted golden chains into the door of the Shrine. He overlaid [the Shrine] with gold,

כא וַיְצַ֨ף שְׁלֹמֹ֧ה אֶת־הַבַּ֛יִת מִפְּנִ֖ימָה זָהָ֣ב סָג֑וּר וַיְעַבֵּ֞ר בְּרַתִּיק֤וֹת [בְּרַתּוּקוֹת] זָהָב֙ לִפְנֵ֣י הַדְּבִ֔יר וַיְצַפֵּ֖הוּ זָהָֽב׃

22 so that the entire House was overlaid with gold; he even overlaid with gold the entire *Mizbayach* of the Shrine. And so the entire House was completed.

כב וְאֶת־כָּל־הַבַּ֛יִת צִפָּ֥ה זָהָ֖ב עַד־תֹּ֣ם כָּל־הַבָּ֑יִת וְכָל־הַמִּזְבֵּ֥חַ אֲשֶׁר־לַדְּבִ֖יר צִפָּ֥ה זָהָֽב׃

23 In the Shrine he made two cherubim of olive wood, each 10 *amot* high.

כג וַיַּ֥עַשׂ בַּדְּבִ֖יר שְׁנֵ֣י כְרוּבִ֑ים עֲצֵי־שָׁ֔מֶן עֶ֥שֶׂר אַמּ֖וֹת קוֹמָתֽוֹ׃

24 [One] had a wing measuring 5 *amot* and another wing measuring 5 *amot*, so that the spread from wingtip to wingtip was 10 *amot*;

כד וְחָמֵ֣שׁ אַמּ֗וֹת כְּנַ֤ף הַכְּרוּב֙ הָֽאֶחָ֔ת וְחָמֵ֣שׁ אַמּ֔וֹת כְּנַ֥ף הַכְּר֖וּב הַשֵּׁנִ֑ית עֶ֣שֶׂר אַמּ֔וֹת מִקְצ֥וֹת כְּנָפָ֖יו וְעַד־קְצ֥וֹת כְּנָפָֽיו׃

25 and the wingspread of the other cherub was also 10 *amot*. The two cherubim had the same measurements and proportions:

כה וְעֶ֙שֶׂר֙ בָּאַמָּ֔ה הַכְּר֖וּב הַשֵּׁנִ֑י מִדָּ֥ה אַחַ֛ת וְקֶ֥צֶב אֶחָ֖ד לִשְׁנֵ֥י הַכְּרֻבִֽים׃

26 the height of the one cherub was 10 *amot*, and so was that of the other cherub.

כו קוֹמַת֙ הַכְּר֣וּב הָֽאֶחָ֔ד עֶ֖שֶׂר בָּאַמָּ֑ה וְכֵ֖ן הַכְּר֥וּב הַשֵּׁנִֽי׃

27 He placed the cherubim inside the inner chamber. Since the wings of the cherubim were extended, a wing of the one touched one wall and a wing of the other touched the other wall, while their wings in the center of the chamber touched each other.

כז וַיִּתֵּ֨ן אֶת־הַכְּרוּבִ֜ים בְּת֣וֹךְ ׀ הַבַּ֣יִת הַפְּנִימִ֗י וַֽיִּפְרְשׂוּ֘ אֶת־כַּנְפֵ֣י הַכְּרֻבִים֒ וַתִּגַּ֤ע כְּנַף־הָֽאֶחָד֙ בַּקִּ֔יר וּכְנַף֙ הַכְּר֣וּב הַשֵּׁנִ֔י נֹגַ֖עַת בַּקִּ֣יר הַשֵּׁנִ֑י וְכַנְפֵיהֶם֙ אֶל־תּ֣וֹךְ הַבַּ֔יִת נֹגְעֹ֖ת כָּנָ֥ף אֶל־כָּנָֽף׃

28 He overlaid the cherubim with gold.

כח וַיְצַ֥ף אֶת־הַכְּרוּבִ֖ים זָהָֽב׃

29 All over the walls of the House, of both the inner area and the outer area, he carved reliefs of cherubim, palms, and calyxes,

כט וְאֵת֩ כָּל־קִיר֨וֹת הַבַּ֜יִת מֵסַ֣ב ׀ קָלַ֗ע פִּתּוּחֵי֙ מִקְלְעוֹת֙ כְּרוּבִ֣ים וְתִמֹרֹ֔ת וּפְטוּרֵ֖י צִצִּ֑ים מִלִּפְנִ֖ים וְלַחִיצֽוֹן׃

30 and he overlaid the floor of the House with gold, both the inner and the outer areas.

ל וְאֶת־קַרְקַ֥ע הַבַּ֖יִת צִפָּ֣ה זָהָ֑ב לִפְנִ֖ימָה וְלַחִיצֽוֹן׃

31 For the entrance of the Shrine he made doors of olive wood, the pilasters and the doorposts having five sides.

לא וְאֵת֙ פֶּ֣תַח הַדְּבִ֔יר עָשָׂ֖ה דַּלְת֣וֹת עֲצֵי־שָׁ֑מֶן הָאַ֥יִל מְזוּז֖וֹת חֲמִשִֽׁית׃

Melachim I / I Kings
Chapter 7

מלכים א
פרק ז

32 The double doors were of olive wood, and on them he carved reliefs of cherubim, palms, and calyxes. He overlaid them with gold, hammering the gold onto the cherubim and the palms.

לב וּשְׁתֵּי דַּלְתוֹת עֲצֵי־שֶׁמֶן וְקָלַע עֲלֵיהֶם מִקְלְעוֹת כְּרוּבִים וְתִמֹרוֹת וּפְטוּרֵי צִצִּים וְצִפָּה זָהָב וַיָּרֶד עַל־הַכְּרוּבִים וְעַל־הַתִּמֹרוֹת אֶת־הַזָּהָב:

33 For the entrance of the Great Hall, too, he made doorposts of oleaster wood, having four sides,

לג וְכֵן עָשָׂה לְפֶתַח הַהֵיכָל מְזוּזוֹת עֲצֵי־שָׁמֶן מֵאֵת רְבִעִית:

34 and the double doors of cypress wood, each door consisting of two rounded planks.

לד וּשְׁתֵּי דַלְתוֹת עֲצֵי בְרוֹשִׁים שְׁנֵי צְלָעִים הַדֶּלֶת הָאַחַת גְּלִילִים וּשְׁנֵי קְלָעִים הַדֶּלֶת הַשֵּׁנִית גְּלִילִים:

35 On them he carved cherubim, palms, and calyxes, overlaying them with gold applied evenly over the carvings.

לה וְקָלַע כְּרוּבִים וְתִמֹרוֹת וּפְטֻרֵי צִצִּים וְצִפָּה זָהָב מְיֻשָּׁר עַל־הַמְּחֻקֶּה:

36 He built the inner enclosure of three courses of hewn stones and one course of cedar beams.

לו וַיִּבֶן אֶת־הֶחָצֵר הַפְּנִימִית שְׁלֹשָׁה טוּרֵי גָזִית וְטוּר כְּרֻתֹת אֲרָזִים:

37 In the fourth year, in the month of Ziv, the foundations of the House were laid;

לז בַּשָּׁנָה הָרְבִיעִית יֻסַּד בֵּית יְהֹוָה בְּיֶרַח זִו:

38 and in the eleventh year, in the month of Bul – that is, the eighth month – the House was completed according to all its details and all its specifications. It took him seven years to build it.

לח וּבַשָּׁנָה הָאַחַת עֶשְׂרֵה בְּיֶרַח בּוּל הוּא הַחֹדֶשׁ הַשְּׁמִינִי כָּלָה הַבַּיִת לְכָל־דְּבָרָיו וּלְכָל־מִשְׁפָּטוֹ [מִשְׁפָּטָיו] וַיִּבְנֵהוּ שֶׁבַע שָׁנִים:

7

1 And it took *Shlomo* thirteen years to build his palace, until his whole palace was completed.

א וְאֶת־בֵּיתוֹ בָּנָה שְׁלֹמֹה שְׁלֹשׁ עֶשְׂרֵה שָׁנָה וַיְכַל אֶת־כָּל־בֵּיתוֹ:

v'-et bay-TO ba-NAH sh'-lo-MO sh'-LOSH es-RAY sha-NAH vai-KHAL et kol bay-TO

2 He built the Lebanon Forest House with four rows of cedar columns, and with hewn cedar beams above the columns. Its length was 100 *amot*, its breadth 50 *amot*, and its height 30 *amot*.

ב וַיִּבֶן אֶת־בֵּית יַעַר הַלְּבָנוֹן מֵאָה אַמָּה אָרְכּוֹ וַחֲמִשִּׁים אַמָּה רָחְבּוֹ וּשְׁלֹשִׁים אַמָּה קוֹמָתוֹ עַל אַרְבָּעָה טוּרֵי עַמּוּדֵי אֲרָזִים וּכְרֻתוֹת אֲרָזִים עַל־הָעַמּוּדִים:

3 It was paneled above with cedar, with the planks that were above on the 45 columns – 15 in each row.

ג וְסָפֻן בָּאֶרֶז מִמַּעַל עַל־הַצְּלָעוֹת אֲשֶׁר עַל־הָעַמּוּדִים אַרְבָּעִים וַחֲמִשָּׁה חֲמִשָּׁה עָשָׂר הַטּוּר:

Rabbi Abraham Issac Kook (1865–1935)

7:1 And it took *Shlomo* thirteen years to build his palace *Rashi* notes that King *Shlomo* is praised for working much quicker to build the *Beit Hamikdash* than his own palace. Yet, on the surface, the descriptions of the opulence of his palace seem far from spiritual and out of place. In truth, however, this description communicates an eternal religious value. Rabbi Abraham Isaac Kook teaches that just as a poor, depressed person often has a difficult time serving *Hashem* due to his need to focus on daily survival, an impoverished nation will also have a difficult time serving God. King *Shlomo*, who dwelled in a magnificent palace, represents the nation he rules; under his reign, Israel attains the highest levels of physical and financial power, and is thus also able to attain the highest spiritual levels. We are fortunate to see a glimpse of this today, as the modern State of Israel has miraculously grown from a poor nation to a country with a strong, vibrant economy that can sustain its people both physically and spiritually.

Melachim I/I Kings
Chapter 7

4 And there were three rows of window frames, with three tiers of windows facing each other.

5 All the doorways and doorposts had square frames – with three tiers of windows facing each other.

6 He made the portico of columns 50 *amot* long and 30 *amot* wide; the portico was in front of [the columns], and there were columns with a canopy in front of them.

7 He made the throne portico, where he was to pronounce judgment – the Hall of Judgment. It was paneled with cedar from floor to floor.

8 The house that he used as a residence, in the rear courtyard, back of the portico, was of the same construction. *Shlomo* also constructed a palace like that portico for the daughter of Pharaoh, whom he had married.

9 All these buildings, from foundation to coping and all the way out to the great courtyard, were of choice stones, hewn according to measure, smooth on all sides.

10 The foundations were huge blocks of choice stone, stones of 10 *amot* and stones of 8 *amot*;

11 and above were choice stones, hewn according to measure, and cedar wood.

12 The large surrounding courtyard had three tiers of hewn stone and a row of cedar beams, the same as for the inner court of the House of *Hashem*, and for the portico of the House.

13 King *Shlomo* sent for Hiram and brought him down from Tyre.

14 He was the son of a widow of the tribe of *Naftali*, and his father had been a Tyrian, a coppersmith. He was endowed with skill, ability, and talent for executing all work in bronze. He came to King *Shlomo* and executed all his work.

15 He cast two columns of bronze; one column was 18 *amot* high and measured 12 *amot* in circumference, [and similarly] the other column.

מלכים א
פרק ז

ד וּשְׁקֻפִים שְׁלֹשָׁה טוּרִים וּמֶחֱזָה אֶל־מֶחֱזָה שָׁלֹשׁ פְּעָמִים׃

ה וְכָל־הַפְּתָחִים וְהַמְּזוּזוֹת רְבֻעִים שָׁקֶף וּמוּל מֶחֱזָה אֶל־מֶחֱזָה שָׁלֹשׁ פְּעָמִים׃

ו וְאֵת אוּלָם הָעַמּוּדִים עָשָׂה חֲמִשִּׁים אַמָּה אָרְכּוֹ וּשְׁלֹשִׁים אַמָּה רָחְבּוֹ וְאוּלָם עַל־פְּנֵיהֶם וְעַמֻּדִים וְעָב עַל־פְּנֵיהֶם׃

ז וְאוּלָם הַכִּסֵּא אֲשֶׁר יִשְׁפָּט־שָׁם אֻלָם הַמִּשְׁפָּט עָשָׂה וְסָפוּן בָּאֶרֶז מֵהַקַּרְקַע עַד־הַקַּרְקָע׃

ח וּבֵיתוֹ אֲשֶׁר־יֵשֶׁב שָׁם חָצֵר הָאַחֶרֶת מִבֵּית לָאוּלָם כַּמַּעֲשֶׂה הַזֶּה הָיָה וּבַיִת יַעֲשֶׂה לְבַת־פַּרְעֹה אֲשֶׁר לָקַח שְׁלֹמֹה כָּאוּלָם הַזֶּה׃

ט כָּל־אֵלֶּה אֲבָנִים יְקָרֹת כְּמִדֹּת גָּזִית מְגֹרָרוֹת בַּמְּגֵרָה מִבַּיִת וּמִחוּץ וּמִמַּסָּד עַד־הַטְּפָחוֹת וּמִחוּץ עַד־הֶחָצֵר הַגְּדוֹלָה׃

י וּמְיֻסָּד אֲבָנִים יְקָרוֹת אֲבָנִים גְּדֹלוֹת אַבְנֵי עֶשֶׂר אַמּוֹת וְאַבְנֵי שְׁמֹנֶה אַמּוֹת׃

יא וּמִלְמַעְלָה אֲבָנִים יְקָרוֹת כְּמִדּוֹת גָּזִית וָאָרֶז׃

יב וְהֶחָצֵר הַגְּדוֹלָה סָבִיב שְׁלֹשָׁה טוּרִים גָּזִית וְטוּר כְּרֻתֹת אֲרָזִים וְלַחֲצַר בֵּית־יְהֹוָה הַפְּנִימִית וּלְאֻלָם הַבָּיִת׃

יג וַיִּשְׁלַח הַמֶּלֶךְ שְׁלֹמֹה וַיִּקַּח אֶת־חִירָם מִצֹּר׃

יד בֶּן־אִשָּׁה אַלְמָנָה הוּא מִמַּטֵּה נַפְתָּלִי וְאָבִיו אִישׁ־צֹרִי חֹרֵשׁ נְחֹשֶׁת וַיִּמָּלֵא אֶת־הַחָכְמָה וְאֶת־הַתְּבוּנָה וְאֶת־הַדַּעַת לַעֲשׂוֹת כָּל־מְלָאכָה בַּנְּחֹשֶׁת וַיָּבוֹא אֶל־הַמֶּלֶךְ שְׁלֹמֹה וַיַּעַשׂ אֶת־כָּל־מְלַאכְתּוֹ׃

טו וַיָּצַר אֶת־שְׁנֵי הָעַמּוּדִים נְחֹשֶׁת שְׁמֹנֶה עֶשְׂרֵה אַמָּה קוֹמַת הָעַמּוּד הָאֶחָד וְחוּט שְׁתֵּים־עֶשְׂרֵה אַמָּה יָסֹב אֶת־הָעַמּוּד הַשֵּׁנִי׃

Melachim I / I Kings
Chapter 7

16 He made two capitals, cast in bronze, to be set upon the two columns, the height of each of the two capitals being 5 *amot*;

17 also nets of meshwork with festoons of chainwork for the capitals that were on the top of the columns, seven for each of the two capitals.

18 He made the columns so that there were two rows [of pomegranates] encircling the top of the one network, to cover the capitals that were on the top of the pomegranates; and he did the same for [the network on] the second capital.

19 The capitals upon the columns of the portico were of lily design, 4 *amot* high;

20 so also the capitals upon the two columns extended above and next to the bulge that was beside the network. There were 200 pomegranates in rows around the top of the second capital.

21 He set up the columns at the portico of the Great Hall; he set up one column on the right and named it Jachin, and he set up the other column on the left and named it *Boaz*.

22 Upon the top of the columns there was a lily design. Thus the work of the columns was completed.

23 Then he made the tank of cast metal, 10 *amot* across from brim to brim, completely round; it was 5 *amot* high, and it measured 30 *amot* in circumference.

24 There were gourds below the brim completely encircling it – ten to an *amah*, encircling the tank; the gourds were in two rows, cast in one piece with it.

25 It stood upon twelve oxen: three facing north, three facing west, three facing south, and three facing east, with the tank resting upon them; their haunches were all turned inward.

26 It was a *tefach* thick, and its brim was made like that of a cup, like the petals of a lily. Its capacity was 2,000 *bat*.

מלכים א
פרק ז

טז וּשְׁתֵּי כֹתָרֹת עָשָׂה לָתֵת עַל־רָאשֵׁי הָעַמּוּדִים מֻצַק נְחֹשֶׁת חָמֵשׁ אַמּוֹת קוֹמַת הַכֹּתֶרֶת הָאֶחָת וְחָמֵשׁ אַמּוֹת קוֹמַת הַכֹּתֶרֶת הַשֵּׁנִית:

יז שְׂבָכִים מַעֲשֵׂה שְׂבָכָה גְּדִלִים מַעֲשֵׂה שַׁרְשְׁרוֹת לַכֹּתָרֹת אֲשֶׁר עַל־רֹאשׁ הָעַמּוּדִים שִׁבְעָה לַכֹּתֶרֶת הָאֶחָת וְשִׁבְעָה לַכֹּתֶרֶת הַשֵּׁנִית:

יח וַיַּעַשׂ אֶת־הָעַמּוּדִים וּשְׁנֵי טוּרִים סָבִיב עַל־הַשְּׂבָכָה הָאֶחָת לְכַסּוֹת אֶת־הַכֹּתָרֹת אֲשֶׁר עַל־רֹאשׁ הָרִמֹּנִים וְכֵן עָשָׂה לַכֹּתֶרֶת הַשֵּׁנִית:

יט וְכֹתָרֹת אֲשֶׁר עַל־רֹאשׁ הָעַמּוּדִים מַעֲשֵׂה שׁוּשַׁן בָּאוּלָם אַרְבַּע אַמּוֹת:

כ וְכֹתָרֹת עַל־שְׁנֵי הָעַמּוּדִים גַּם־מִמַּעַל מִלְּעֻמַּת הַבֶּטֶן אֲשֶׁר לְעֵבֶר שבכה [הַשְּׂבָכָה] וְהָרִמּוֹנִים מָאתַיִם טֻרִים סָבִיב עַל הַכֹּתֶרֶת הַשֵּׁנִית:

כא וַיָּקֶם אֶת־הָעַמֻּדִים לְאֻלָם הַהֵיכָל וַיָּקֶם אֶת־הָעַמּוּד הַיְמָנִי וַיִּקְרָא אֶת־שְׁמוֹ יָכִין וַיָּקֶם אֶת־הָעַמּוּד הַשְּׂמָאלִי וַיִּקְרָא אֶת־שְׁמוֹ בֹּעַז:

כב וְעַל רֹאשׁ הָעַמּוּדִים מַעֲשֵׂה שׁוֹשָׁן וַתִּתֹּם מְלֶאכֶת הָעַמּוּדִים:

כג וַיַּעַשׂ אֶת־הַיָּם מוּצָק עֶשֶׂר בָּאַמָּה מִשְּׂפָתוֹ עַד־שְׂפָתוֹ עָגֹל סָבִיב וְחָמֵשׁ בָּאַמָּה קוֹמָתוֹ וקוה [וְקָו] שְׁלֹשִׁים בָּאַמָּה יָסֹב אֹתוֹ סָבִיב:

כד וּפְקָעִים מִתַּחַת לִשְׂפָתוֹ סָבִיב סֹבְבִים אֹתוֹ עֶשֶׂר בָּאַמָּה מַקִּפִים אֶת־הַיָּם סָבִיב שְׁנֵי טוּרִים הַפְּקָעִים יְצֻקִים בִּיצֻקָתוֹ:

כה עֹמֵד עַל־שְׁנֵי עָשָׂר בָּקָר שְׁלֹשָׁה פֹנִים צָפוֹנָה וּשְׁלֹשָׁה פֹנִים יָמָּה וּשְׁלֹשָׁה פֹּנִים נֶגְבָּה וּשְׁלֹשָׁה פֹּנִים מִזְרָחָה וְהַיָּם עֲלֵיהֶם מִלְמָעְלָה וְכָל־אֲחֹרֵיהֶם בָּיְתָה:

כו וְעָבְיוֹ טֶפַח וּשְׂפָתוֹ כְּמַעֲשֵׂה שְׂפַת־כּוֹס פֶּרַח שׁוֹשָׁן אַלְפַּיִם בַּת יָכִיל:

Melachim I / I Kings
Chapter 7

מלכים א
פרק ז

#	English	#	Hebrew

27 He made the ten laver stands of bronze. The length of each laver stand was 4 *amot* and the width 4 *amot*, and the height was 3 *amot*.

כז וַיַּעַשׂ אֶת־הַמְּכֹנוֹת עֶשֶׂר נְחֹשֶׁת אַרְבַּע בָּאַמָּה אֹרֶךְ הַמְּכוֹנָה הָאֶחָת וְאַרְבַּע בָּאַמָּה רָחְבָּהּ וְשָׁלֹשׁ בָּאַמָּה קוֹמָתָהּ:

28 The structure of the laver stands was as follows: They had insets, and there were insets within the frames;

כח וְזֶה מַעֲשֵׂה הַמְּכוֹנָה מִסְגְּרֹת לָהֶם וּמִסְגְּרֹת בֵּין הַשְׁלַבִּים:

29 and on the insets within the frames were lions, oxen, and cherubim. Above the frames was a stand; and both above and below the lions and the oxen were spirals of hammered metal.

כט וְעַל־הַמִּסְגְּרוֹת אֲשֶׁר בֵּין הַשְׁלַבִּים אֲרָיוֹת בָּקָר וּכְרוּבִים וְעַל־הַשְׁלַבִּים כֵּן מִמָּעַל וּמִתַּחַת לַאֲרָיוֹת וְלַבָּקָר לֹיוֹת מַעֲשֵׂה מוֹרָד:

30 Each laver stand had four bronze wheels and [two] bronze axletrees. Its four legs had brackets; the brackets were under the laver, cast with spirals beyond each.

ל וְאַרְבָּעָה אוֹפַנֵּי נְחֹשֶׁת לַמְּכוֹנָה הָאַחַת וְסַרְנֵי נְחֹשֶׁת וְאַרְבָּעָה פַעֲמֹתָיו כְּתֵפֹת לָהֶם מִתַּחַת לַכִּיֹּר הַכְּתֵפֹת יְצֻקוֹת מֵעֵבֶר אִישׁ לֹיוֹת:

31 Its funnel, within the crown, rose an *amah* above it; this funnel was round, in the fashion of a stand, an *amah* and a half in diameter. On the funnel too there were carvings. But the insets were square, not round.

לא וּפִיהוּ מִבֵּית לַכֹּתֶרֶת וָמַעְלָה בָּאַמָּה וּפִיהָ עָגֹל מַעֲשֵׂה־כֵן אַמָּה וַחֲצִי הָאַמָּה וְגַם־עַל־פִּיהָ מִקְלָעוֹת וּמִסְגְּרֹתֵיהֶם מְרֻבָּעוֹת לֹא עֲגֻלּוֹת:

32 And below the insets were the four wheels. The axletrees of the wheels were [fixed] in the laver stand, and the height of each wheel was an *amah* and a half.

לב וְאַרְבַּעַת הָאוֹפַנִּים לְמִתַּחַת לַמִּסְגְּרוֹת וִידוֹת הָאוֹפַנִּים בַּמְּכוֹנָה וְקוֹמַת הָאוֹפַן הָאֶחָד אַמָּה וַחֲצִי הָאַמָּה:

33 The structure of the wheels was like the structure of chariot wheels; and their axletrees, their rims, their spokes, and their hubs were all of cast metal.

לג וּמַעֲשֵׂה הָאוֹפַנִּים כְּמַעֲשֵׂה אוֹפַן הַמֶּרְכָּבָה יְדוֹתָם וְגַבֵּיהֶם וְחִשֻּׁקֵיהֶם וְחִשֻּׁרֵיהֶם הַכֹּל מוּצָק:

34 Four brackets ran to the four corners of each laver stand; the brackets were of a piece with the laver stand.

לד וְאַרְבַּע כְּתֵפוֹת אֶל אַרְבַּע פִּנּוֹת הַמְּכֹנָה הָאֶחָת מִן־הַמְּכֹנָה כְּתֵפֶיהָ:

35 At the top of the laver stand was a round band half an *amah* high, and together with the top of the laver stand; its sides and its insets were of one piece with it.

לה וּבְרֹאשׁ הַמְּכוֹנָה חֲצִי הָאַמָּה קוֹמָה עָגֹל סָבִיב וְעַל רֹאשׁ הַמְּכֹנָה יְדֹתֶיהָ וּמִסְגְּרֹתֶיהָ מִמֶּנָּה:

36 On its surface – on its sides – and on its insets [Hiram] engraved cherubim, lions, and palms, as the clear space on each allowed, with spirals roundabout.

לו וַיְפַתַּח עַל־הַלֻּחֹת יְדֹתֶיהָ וְעַל ומסגרתיה [מִסְגְּרֹתֶיהָ] כְּרוּבִים אֲרָיוֹת וְתִמֹרֹת כְּמַעַר־אִישׁ וְלֹיוֹת סָבִיב:

37 It was after this manner that he made the ten laver stands, all of them cast alike, of the same measure and the same form.

לז כָּזֹאת עָשָׂה אֵת עֶשֶׂר הַמְּכֹנוֹת מוּצָק אֶחָד מִדָּה אַחַת קֶצֶב אֶחָד לְכֻלָּהְנָה:

38 Then he made ten bronze lavers, one laver on each of the ten laver stands, each laver measuring 4 *amot* and each laver containing forty *bat*.

לח וַיַּעַשׂ עֲשָׂרָה כִיֹּרוֹת נְחֹשֶׁת אַרְבָּעִים בַּת יָכִיל הַכִּיּוֹר הָאֶחָד אַרְבַּע בָּאַמָּה הַכִּיּוֹר הָאֶחָד כִּיּוֹר אֶחָד עַל־הַמְּכוֹנָה הָאַחַת לְעֶשֶׂר הַמְּכֹנוֹת:

826

Melachim I / I Kings
Chapter 7

39 He disposed the laver stands, five at the right side of the House and five at its left side; and the tank he placed on the right side of the House, at the southeast [corner].

40 Hiram also made the lavers, the scrapers, and the sprinkling bowls. So Hiram finished all the work that he had been doing for King *Shlomo* on the House of *Hashem*:

41 the two columns, the two globes of the capitals upon the columns; and the two pieces of network to cover the two globes of the capitals upon the columns;

42 the four hundred pomegranates for the two pieces of network, two rows of pomegranates for each network, to cover the two globes of the capitals upon the columns;

43 the ten stands and the ten lavers upon the stands;

44 the one tank with the twelve oxen underneath the tank;

45 the pails, the scrapers, and the sprinkling bowls. All those vessels in the House of *Hashem* that Hiram made for King *Shlomo* were of burnished bronze.

46 The king had them cast in earthen molds, in the plain of the *Yarden* between Succoth and Zarethan.

47 *Shlomo* left all the vessels [unweighed] because of their very great quantity; the weight of the bronze was not reckoned.

48 And *Shlomo* made all the furnishings that were in the House of *Hashem*: the *Mizbayach*, of gold; the table for the bread of display, of gold;

49 the *menorahs* – five on the right side and five on the left – in front of the Shrine, of solid gold; and the petals, lamps, and tongs, of gold;

50 the basins, snuffers, sprinkling bowls, ladles, and fire pans, of solid gold; and the hinge sockets for the doors of the innermost part of the House, the Holy of Holies, and for the doors of the Great Hall of the House, of gold.

מלכים א

פרק ז

לט וַיִּתֵּן אֶת־הַמְּכֹנוֹת חָמֵשׁ עַל־כֶּתֶף הַבַּיִת מִיָּמִין וְחָמֵשׁ עַל־כֶּתֶף הַבַּיִת מִשְּׂמֹאלוֹ וְאֶת־הַיָּם נָתַן מִכֶּתֶף הַבַּיִת הַיְמָנִית קֵדְמָה מִמּוּל נֶגֶב:

מ וַיַּעַשׂ חִירוֹם אֶת־הַכִּיֹּרוֹת וְאֶת־הַיָּעִים וְאֶת־הַמִּזְרָקוֹת וַיְכַל חִירָם לַעֲשׂוֹת אֶת־כָּל־הַמְּלָאכָה אֲשֶׁר עָשָׂה לַמֶּלֶךְ שְׁלֹמֹה בֵּית יְהֹוָה:

מא עַמֻּדִים שְׁנַיִם וְגֻלֹּת הַכֹּתָרֹת אֲשֶׁר־עַל־רֹאשׁ הָעַמֻּדִים שְׁתָּיִם וְהַשְּׂבָכוֹת שְׁתַּיִם לְכַסּוֹת אֶת־שְׁתֵּי גֻּלֹּת הַכֹּתָרֹת אֲשֶׁר עַל־רֹאשׁ הָעַמּוּדִים:

מב וְאֶת־הָרִמֹּנִים אַרְבַּע מֵאוֹת לִשְׁתֵּי הַשְּׂבָכוֹת שְׁנֵי־טוּרִים רִמֹּנִים לַשְּׂבָכָה הָאֶחָת לְכַסּוֹת אֶת־שְׁתֵּי גֻּלֹּת הַכֹּתָרֹת אֲשֶׁר עַל־פְּנֵי הָעַמּוּדִים:

מג וְאֶת־הַמְּכֹנוֹת עָשֶׂר וְאֶת־הַכִּיֹּרֹת עֲשָׂרָה עַל־הַמְּכֹנוֹת:

מד וְאֶת־הַיָּם הָאֶחָד וְאֶת־הַבָּקָר שְׁנֵים־עָשָׂר תַּחַת הַיָּם:

מה וְאֶת־הַסִּירוֹת וְאֶת־הַיָּעִים וְאֶת־הַמִּזְרָקוֹת וְאֵת כָּל־הַכֵּלִים הָאֹהֶל [הָאֵלֶּה] אֲשֶׁר עָשָׂה חִירָם לַמֶּלֶךְ שְׁלֹמֹה בֵּית יְהֹוָה נְחֹשֶׁת מְמֹרָט:

מו בְּכִכַּר הַיַּרְדֵּן יְצָקָם הַמֶּלֶךְ בְּמַעֲבֵה הָאֲדָמָה בֵּין סֻכּוֹת וּבֵין צָרְתָן:

מז וַיַּנַּח שְׁלֹמֹה אֶת־כָּל־הַכֵּלִים מֵרֹב מְאֹד מְאֹד לֹא נֶחְקַר מִשְׁקַל הַנְּחֹשֶׁת:

מח וַיַּעַשׂ שְׁלֹמֹה אֵת כָּל־הַכֵּלִים אֲשֶׁר בֵּית יְהֹוָה אֵת מִזְבַּח הַזָּהָב וְאֶת־הַשֻּׁלְחָן אֲשֶׁר עָלָיו לֶחֶם הַפָּנִים זָהָב:

מט וְאֶת־הַמְּנֹרוֹת חָמֵשׁ מִיָּמִין וְחָמֵשׁ מִשְּׂמֹאול לִפְנֵי הַדְּבִיר זָהָב סָגוּר וְהַפֶּרַח וְהַנֵּרֹת וְהַמֶּלְקָחַיִם זָהָב:

נ וְהַסִּפּוֹת וְהַמְזַמְּרוֹת וְהַמִּזְרָקוֹת וְהַכַּפּוֹת וְהַמַּחְתּוֹת זָהָב סָגוּר וְהַפֹּתוֹת לְדַלְתוֹת הַבַּיִת הַפְּנִימִי לְקֹדֶשׁ הַקֳּדָשִׁים לְדַלְתֵי הַבַּיִת לַהֵיכָל זָהָב:

Melachim I / I Kings
Chapter 8

51 When all the work that King *Shlomo* had done in the House of *Hashem* was completed, *Shlomo* brought in the sacred donations of his father *David* – the silver, the gold, and the vessels – and deposited them in the treasury of the House of *Hashem*.

נא וַתִּשְׁלַם כָּל־הַמְּלָאכָה אֲשֶׁר עָשָׂה הַמֶּלֶךְ שְׁלֹמֹה בֵּית יְהֹוָה וַיָּבֵא שְׁלֹמֹה אֶת־קָדְשֵׁי ׀ דָּוִד אָבִיו אֶת־הַכֶּסֶף וְאֶת־הַזָּהָב וְאֶת־הַכֵּלִים נָתַן בְּאֹצְרוֹת בֵּית יְהֹוָה:

8

1 Then *Shlomo* convoked the elders of *Yisrael* – all the heads of the tribes and the ancestral chieftains of the Israelites – before King *Shlomo* in *Yerushalayim*, to bring up the *Aron Brit Hashem* from the City of *David*, that is, *Tzion*.

א אָז יַקְהֵל שְׁלֹמֹה אֶת־זִקְנֵי יִשְׂרָאֵל אֶת־כָּל־רָאשֵׁי הַמַּטּוֹת נְשִׂיאֵי הָאָבוֹת לִבְנֵי יִשְׂרָאֵל אֶל־הַמֶּלֶךְ שְׁלֹמֹה יְרוּשָׁלָ‍ִם לְהַעֲלוֹת אֶת־אֲרוֹן בְּרִית־יְהֹוָה מֵעִיר דָּוִד הִיא צִיּוֹן:

az yak-HAYL sh'-lo-MOH et zik-NAY yis-ra-AYL et kol ra-SHAY ha-ma-TOT n'-see-AY ha-a-VOT liv-NAY yis-ra-AYL el ha-ME-lekh sh'-lo-MOH y'-ru-sha-la-IM l'-ha-a-LOT et a-RON b'-REET a-do-NAI may-EER da-VID HEE tzi-YON

2 All the men of *Yisrael* gathered before King *Shlomo* at the Feast, in the month of Ethanim – that is, the seventh month.

ב וַיִּקָּהֲלוּ אֶל־הַמֶּלֶךְ שְׁלֹמֹה כָּל־אִישׁ יִשְׂרָאֵל בְּיֶרַח הָאֵתָנִים בֶּחָג הוּא הַחֹדֶשׁ הַשְּׁבִיעִי:

3 When all the elders of *Yisrael* had come, the *Kohanim* lifted the *Aron*

ג וַיָּבֹאוּ כֹּל זִקְנֵי יִשְׂרָאֵל וַיִּשְׂאוּ הַכֹּהֲנִים אֶת־הָאָרוֹן:

4 and carried up the *Aron* of *Hashem*. Then the *Kohanim* and the *Leviim* brought the Tent of Meeting and all the holy vessels that were in the Tent.

ד וַיַּעֲלוּ אֶת־אֲרוֹן יְהֹוָה וְאֶת־אֹהֶל מוֹעֵד וְאֶת־כָּל־כְּלֵי הַקֹּדֶשׁ אֲשֶׁר בָּאֹהֶל וַיַּעֲלוּ אֹתָם הַכֹּהֲנִים וְהַלְוִיִּם:

5 Meanwhile, King *Shlomo* and the whole community of *Yisrael*, who were assembled with him before the *Aron*, were sacrificing sheep and oxen in such abundance that they could not be numbered or counted.

ה וְהַמֶּלֶךְ שְׁלֹמֹה וְכָל־עֲדַת יִשְׂרָאֵל הַנּוֹעָדִים עָלָיו אִתּוֹ לִפְנֵי הָאָרוֹן מְזַבְּחִים צֹאן וּבָקָר אֲשֶׁר לֹא־יִסָּפְרוּ וְלֹא יִמָּנוּ מֵרֹב:

8:1 And the ancestral chieftains of the Israelites The Hebrew term for 'ancestral chieftains' is *n'see-ay ha'avot* (נשיאי האבות). *N'see-ay* is a plural form of the word *nasi* (נשיא), which literally means 'elevated,' but is commonly used to mean 'prince' as a title of leadership. In modern Hebrew, it is translated as 'president.' In 1960, the famed IDF General and biblical archaeologist Yigael Yadin was called to present his archaeological findings to Israeli President Yitzchak Ben-Zvi in the presence of Prime Minister Ben Gurion and other members of Knesset. He writes about the phenomenal presentation, "When my time came to report, I projected a slide of a document and read aloud the first line: 'Shimon Bar Kosiba, Nasi of Israel.' And turning the our Head of State, I said, 'Your Excellency, I am honored to be able to tell you that we have discovered fifteen dispatches by the last President of ancient Israel, 1,800 years ago.' For a moment the audience seemed struck dumb. Then the silence was shattered with cries of astonishment and joy." Not only was he a *Nasi*, 'president,' Bar Kosiba (Kokhba) was also the last military leader of ancient Israel. In essence, he "sent" his dispatches to his successor, Yigael Yadin, one of the first generation of Israeli generals in 1,800 years, so that he could turn them over to another *Nasi*, the modern President of Israel.

President Yitzchak Ben-Zvi (1884–1963)

Melachim I / I Kings
Chapter 8

מלכים א
פרק ח

6 The *Kohanim* brought the *Aron Brit Hashem* to its place underneath the wings of the cherubim, in the Shrine of the House, in the Holy of Holies;	ו וַיָּבִאוּ הַכֹּהֲנִים אֶת־אֲרוֹן בְּרִית־יְהֹוָה אֶל־מְקוֹמוֹ אֶל־דְּבִיר הַבַּיִת אֶל־קֹדֶשׁ הַקֳּדָשִׁים אֶל־תַּחַת כַּנְפֵי הַכְּרוּבִים:

va-ya-VEE-u ha-ko-ha-NEEM et a-RON b'-reet a-do-NAI el m'-ko-MO el d'-VEER ha-BA-yit el KO-desh ha-ko-da-SHEEM el TA-khat kan-FAY ha-k'-ru-VEEM

7 for the cherubim had their wings spread out over the place of the *Aron*, so that the cherubim shielded the *Aron* and its poles from above.	ז כִּי הַכְּרוּבִים פֹּרְשִׂים כְּנָפַיִם אֶל־מְקוֹם הָאָרוֹן וַיָּסֹכּוּ הַכְּרֻבִים עַל־הָאָרוֹן וְעַל־בַּדָּיו מִלְמָעְלָה:
8 The poles projected so that the ends of the poles were visible in the sanctuary in front of the Shrine, but they could not be seen outside; and there they remain to this day.	ח וַיַּאֲרִכוּ הַבַּדִּים וַיֵּרָאוּ רָאשֵׁי הַבַּדִּים מִן־הַקֹּדֶשׁ עַל־פְּנֵי הַדְּבִיר וְלֹא יֵרָאוּ הַחוּצָה וַיִּהְיוּ שָׁם עַד הַיּוֹם הַזֶּה:
9 There was nothing inside the *Aron* but the two tablets of stone which *Moshe* placed there at Horeb, when *Hashem* made [a covenant] with the Israelites after their departure from the land of Egypt.	ט אֵין בָּאָרוֹן רַק שְׁנֵי לֻחוֹת הָאֲבָנִים אֲשֶׁר הִנִּחַ שָׁם מֹשֶׁה בְּחֹרֵב אֲשֶׁר כָּרַת יְהֹוָה עִם־בְּנֵי יִשְׂרָאֵל בְּצֵאתָם מֵאֶרֶץ מִצְרָיִם:
10 When the *Kohanim* came out of the sanctuary – for the cloud had filled the House of *Hashem*	י וַיְהִי בְּצֵאת הַכֹּהֲנִים מִן־הַקֹּדֶשׁ וְהֶעָנָן מָלֵא אֶת־בֵּית יְהֹוָה:
11 and the *Kohanim* were not able to remain and perform the service because of the cloud, for the Presence of *Hashem* filled the House of *Hashem*	יא וְלֹא־יָכְלוּ הַכֹּהֲנִים לַעֲמֹד לְשָׁרֵת מִפְּנֵי הֶעָנָן כִּי־מָלֵא כְבוֹד־יְהֹוָה אֶת־בֵּית יְהֹוָה:
12 then *Shlomo* declared: "*Hashem* has chosen To abide in a thick cloud:	יב אָז אָמַר שְׁלֹמֹה יְהֹוָה אָמַר לִשְׁכֹּן בָּעֲרָפֶל:
13 I have now built for You A stately House, A place where You May dwell forever."	יג בָּנֹה בָנִיתִי בֵּית זְבֻל לָךְ מָכוֹן לְשִׁבְתְּךָ עוֹלָמִים:
14 Then, with the whole congregation of *Yisrael* standing, the king faced about and blessed the whole congregation of *Yisrael*.	יד וַיַּסֵּב הַמֶּלֶךְ אֶת־פָּנָיו וַיְבָרֶךְ אֵת כָּל־קְהַל יִשְׂרָאֵל וְכָל־קְהַל יִשְׂרָאֵל עֹמֵד:
15 He said: "Praised be *Hashem*, the God of *Yisrael*, who has fulfilled with deeds the promise He made to my father *David*. For He said,	טו וַיֹּאמֶר בָּרוּךְ יְהֹוָה אֱלֹהֵי יִשְׂרָאֵל אֲשֶׁר דִּבֶּר בְּפִיו אֵת דָּוִד אָבִי וּבְיָדוֹ מִלֵּא לֵאמֹר:

8:6 The *Kohanim* brought the *Aron Brit Hashem* The Holy Ark is brought from the City of David to the holiest place on earth: the Holy of Holies in the *Beit Hamikdash*. While the entire *Har Habayit* is endowed with a high degree of spirituality, the Temple's courtyard is infused with a higher level, and the interior of the *Beit Hamikdash* itself with an even higher one. But the highest level of sanctity is found inside the Holy of Holies, the innermost room of Temple. The only person ever allowed to enter this chamber is the Kohen *Gadol* (כהן גדול), 'High Priest,' and only on *Yom Kippur*, the holiest day of the year, as part of the special service of the day. The Ark of the Covenant, which contains the Tablets of the Law, is placed there upon the "Foundation Stone," which is, according to the Sages of the Talmud (*Yoma* 54b), where the creation of the world began. It is the same location where *Avraham* was willing to sacrifice *Yitzchak* (Genesis 22), and the site where the Ark will again rest in the Third *Beit Hamikdash*.

Melachim I / I Kings
Chapter 8

16 'Ever since I brought My people *Yisrael* out of Egypt, I have not chosen a city among all the tribes of *Yisrael* for building a House where My name might abide; but I have chosen *David* to rule My people *Yisrael*.'

17 "Now my father *David* had intended to build a House for the name of *Hashem*, the God of *Yisrael*.

18 But *Hashem* said to my father *David*, 'As regards your intention to build a House for My name, you did right to have that intention.

19 However, you shall not build the House yourself; instead, your son, the issue of your loins, shall build the House for My name.'

20 "And *Hashem* has fulfilled the promise that He made: I have succeeded my father *David* and have ascended the throne of *Yisrael*, as *Hashem* promised. I have built the House for the name of *Hashem*, the God of *Yisrael*;

21 and I have set a place there for the *Aron*, containing the covenant which *Hashem* made with our fathers when He brought them out from the land of Egypt."

22 Then *Shlomo* stood before the *Mizbayach* of *Hashem* in the presence of the whole community of *Yisrael*; he spread the palms of his hands toward heaven

23 and said, "O God of *Yisrael*, in the heavens above and on the earth below there is no god like You, who keep Your gracious covenant with Your servants when they walk before You in wholehearted devotion;

24 You who have kept the promises You made to Your servant, my father *David*, fulfilling with deeds the promise You made – as is now the case.

25 And now, O God of *Yisrael*, keep the further promise that You made to Your servant, my father *David*: 'Your line on the throne of *Yisrael* shall never end, if only your descendants will look to their way and walk before Me as you have walked before Me.'

26 Now, therefore, O God of *Yisrael*, let the promise that You made to Your servant my father *David* be fulfilled.

מלכים א
פרק ח

טז מִן־הַיּוֹם אֲשֶׁר הוֹצֵאתִי אֶת־עַמִּי אֶת־יִשְׂרָאֵל מִמִּצְרַיִם לֹא־בָחַרְתִּי בְעִיר מִכֹּל שִׁבְטֵי יִשְׂרָאֵל לִבְנוֹת בַּיִת לִהְיוֹת שְׁמִי שָׁם וָאֶבְחַר בְּדָוִד לִהְיוֹת עַל־עַמִּי יִשְׂרָאֵל׃

יז וַיְהִי עִם־לְבַב דָּוִד אָבִי לִבְנוֹת בַּיִת לְשֵׁם יְהוָה אֱלֹהֵי יִשְׂרָאֵל׃

יח וַיֹּאמֶר יְהוָה אֶל־דָּוִד אָבִי יַעַן אֲשֶׁר הָיָה עִם־לְבָבְךָ לִבְנוֹת בַּיִת לִשְׁמִי הֱטִיבֹתָ כִּי הָיָה עִם־לְבָבֶךָ׃

יט רַק אַתָּה לֹא תִבְנֶה הַבָּיִת כִּי אִם־בִּנְךָ הַיֹּצֵא מֵחֲלָצֶיךָ הוּא־יִבְנֶה הַבַּיִת לִשְׁמִי׃

כ וַיָּקֶם יְהוָה אֶת־דְּבָרוֹ אֲשֶׁר דִּבֵּר וָאָקֻם תַּחַת דָּוִד אָבִי וָאֵשֵׁב עַל־כִּסֵּא יִשְׂרָאֵל כַּאֲשֶׁר דִּבֶּר יְהוָה וָאֶבְנֶה הַבַּיִת לְשֵׁם יְהוָה אֱלֹהֵי יִשְׂרָאֵל׃

כא וָאָשִׂם שָׁם מָקוֹם לָאָרוֹן אֲשֶׁר־שָׁם בְּרִית יְהוָה אֲשֶׁר כָּרַת עִם־אֲבֹתֵינוּ בְּהוֹצִיאוֹ אֹתָם מֵאֶרֶץ מִצְרָיִם׃

כב וַיַּעֲמֹד שְׁלֹמֹה לִפְנֵי מִזְבַּח יְהוָה נֶגֶד כָּל־קְהַל יִשְׂרָאֵל וַיִּפְרֹשׂ כַּפָּיו הַשָּׁמָיִם׃

כג וַיֹּאמַר יְהוָה אֱלֹהֵי יִשְׂרָאֵל אֵין־כָּמוֹךָ אֱלֹהִים בַּשָּׁמַיִם מִמַּעַל וְעַל־הָאָרֶץ מִתָּחַת שֹׁמֵר הַבְּרִית וְהַחֶסֶד לַעֲבָדֶיךָ הַהֹלְכִים לְפָנֶיךָ בְּכָל־לִבָּם׃

כד אֲשֶׁר שָׁמַרְתָּ לְעַבְדְּךָ דָּוִד אָבִי אֵת אֲשֶׁר־דִּבַּרְתָּ לּוֹ וַתְּדַבֵּר בְּפִיךָ וּבְיָדְךָ מִלֵּאתָ כַּיּוֹם הַזֶּה׃

כה וְעַתָּה יְהוָה אֱלֹהֵי יִשְׂרָאֵל שְׁמֹר לְעַבְדְּךָ דָוִד אָבִי אֵת אֲשֶׁר דִּבַּרְתָּ לּוֹ לֵאמֹר לֹא־יִכָּרֵת לְךָ אִישׁ מִלְּפָנַי יֹשֵׁב עַל־כִּסֵּא יִשְׂרָאֵל רַק אִם־יִשְׁמְרוּ בָנֶיךָ אֶת־דַּרְכָּם לָלֶכֶת לְפָנַי כַּאֲשֶׁר הָלַכְתָּ לְפָנָי׃

כו וְעַתָּה אֱלֹהֵי יִשְׂרָאֵל יֵאָמֶן נָא דבריך [דְּבָרְךָ] אֲשֶׁר דִּבַּרְתָּ לְעַבְדְּךָ דָּוִד אָבִי׃

Melachim I / I Kings
Chapter 8

27 "But will *Hashem* really dwell on earth? Even the heavens to their uttermost reaches cannot contain You, how much less this House that I have built!

28 Yet turn, *Hashem* my God, to the prayer and supplication of Your servant, and hear the cry and prayer which Your servant offers before You this day.

29 May Your eyes be open day and night toward this House, toward the place of which You have said, 'My name shall abide there'; may You heed the prayers which Your servant will offer toward this place.

30 And when You hear the supplications which Your servant and Your people *Yisrael* offer toward this place, give heed in Your heavenly abode – give heed and pardon.

31 "Whenever one man commits an offense against another, and the latter utters an imprecation to bring a curse upon him, and comes with his imprecation before Your *Mizbayach* in this House,

32 oh, hear in heaven and take action to judge Your servants, condemning him who is in the wrong and bringing down the punishment of his conduct on his head, vindicating him who is in the right by rewarding him according to his righteousness.

33 "Should Your people *Yisrael* be routed by an enemy because they have sinned against You, and then turn back to You and acknowledge Your name, and they offer prayer and supplication to You in this House,

34 oh, hear in heaven and pardon the sin of Your people *Yisrael*, and restore them to the land that You gave to their fathers.

35 "Should the heavens be shut up and there be no rain, because they have sinned against You, and then they pray toward this place and acknowledge Your name and repent of their sins, when You answer them,

36 oh, hear in heaven and pardon the sin of Your servants, Your people *Yisrael*, after You have shown them the proper way in which they are to walk; and send down rain upon the land which You gave to Your people as their heritage.

מלכים א
פרק ח

כז כִּי הַאֻמְנָם יֵשֵׁב אֱלֹהִים עַל־הָאָרֶץ הִנֵּה הַשָּׁמַיִם וּשְׁמֵי הַשָּׁמַיִם לֹא יְכַלְכְּלוּךָ אַף כִּי־הַבַּיִת הַזֶּה אֲשֶׁר בָּנִיתִי:

כח וּפָנִיתָ אֶל־תְּפִלַּת עַבְדְּךָ וְאֶל־תְּחִנָּתוֹ יְהֹוָה אֱלֹהָי לִשְׁמֹעַ אֶל־הָרִנָּה וְאֶל־הַתְּפִלָּה אֲשֶׁר עַבְדְּךָ מִתְפַּלֵּל לְפָנֶיךָ הַיּוֹם:

כט לִהְיוֹת עֵינֶךָ פְתֻחוֹת אֶל־הַבַּיִת הַזֶּה לַיְלָה וָיוֹם אֶל־הַמָּקוֹם אֲשֶׁר אָמַרְתָּ יִהְיֶה שְׁמִי שָׁם לִשְׁמֹעַ אֶל־הַתְּפִלָּה אֲשֶׁר יִתְפַּלֵּל עַבְדְּךָ אֶל־הַמָּקוֹם הַזֶּה:

ל וְשָׁמַעְתָּ אֶל־תְּחִנַּת עַבְדְּךָ וְעַמְּךָ יִשְׂרָאֵל אֲשֶׁר יִתְפַּלְלוּ אֶל־הַמָּקוֹם הַזֶּה וְאַתָּה תִּשְׁמַע אֶל־מְקוֹם שִׁבְתְּךָ אֶל־הַשָּׁמַיִם וְשָׁמַעְתָּ וְסָלָחְתָּ:

לא אֵת אֲשֶׁר יֶחֱטָא אִישׁ לְרֵעֵהוּ וְנָשָׁא־בוֹ אָלָה לְהַאֲלֹתוֹ וּבָא אָלָה לִפְנֵי מִזְבַּחֲךָ בַּבַּיִת הַזֶּה:

לב וְאַתָּה תִּשְׁמַע הַשָּׁמַיִם וְעָשִׂיתָ וְשָׁפַטְתָּ אֶת־עֲבָדֶיךָ לְהַרְשִׁיעַ רָשָׁע לָתֵת דַּרְכּוֹ בְּרֹאשׁוֹ וּלְהַצְדִּיק צַדִּיק לָתֶת לוֹ כְּצִדְקָתוֹ:

לג בְּהִנָּגֵף עַמְּךָ יִשְׂרָאֵל לִפְנֵי אוֹיֵב אֲשֶׁר יֶחֶטְאוּ־לָךְ וְשָׁבוּ אֵלֶיךָ וְהוֹדוּ אֶת־שְׁמֶךָ וְהִתְפַּלְלוּ וְהִתְחַנְנוּ אֵלֶיךָ בַּבַּיִת הַזֶּה:

לד וְאַתָּה תִּשְׁמַע הַשָּׁמַיִם וְסָלַחְתָּ לְחַטַּאת עַמְּךָ יִשְׂרָאֵל וַהֲשֵׁבֹתָם אֶל־הָאֲדָמָה אֲשֶׁר נָתַתָּ לַאֲבוֹתָם:

לה בְּהֵעָצֵר שָׁמַיִם וְלֹא־יִהְיֶה מָטָר כִּי יֶחֶטְאוּ־לָךְ וְהִתְפַּלְלוּ אֶל־הַמָּקוֹם הַזֶּה וְהוֹדוּ אֶת־שְׁמֶךָ וּמֵחַטָּאתָם יְשׁוּבוּן כִּי תַעֲנֵם:

לו וְאַתָּה תִּשְׁמַע הַשָּׁמַיִם וְסָלַחְתָּ לְחַטַּאת עֲבָדֶיךָ וְעַמְּךָ יִשְׂרָאֵל כִּי תוֹרֵם אֶת־הַדֶּרֶךְ הַטּוֹבָה אֲשֶׁר יֵלְכוּ־בָהּ וְנָתַתָּה מָטָר עַל־אַרְצְךָ אֲשֶׁר־נָתַתָּה לְעַמְּךָ לְנַחֲלָה:

Melachim I/I Kings
Chapter 8

מלכים א
פרק ח

37 So, too, if there is a famine in the land, if there is pestilence, blight, mildew, locusts or caterpillars, or if an enemy oppresses them in any of the settlements of the land.

לז רָעָב כִּי־יִהְיֶה בָאָרֶץ דֶּבֶר כִּי־יִהְיֶה שִׁדָּפוֹן יֵרָקוֹן אַרְבֶּה חָסִיל כִּי יִהְיֶה כִּי יָצַר־לוֹ אֹיְבוֹ בְּאֶרֶץ שְׁעָרָיו כָּל־נֶגַע כָּל־מַחֲלָה׃

38 "In any plague and in any disease, in any prayer or supplication offered by any person among all Your people *Yisrael* – each of whom knows his own affliction – when he spreads his palms toward this House,

לח כָּל־תְּפִלָּה כָל־תְּחִנָּה אֲשֶׁר תִהְיֶה לְכָל־הָאָדָם לְכֹל עַמְּךָ יִשְׂרָאֵל אֲשֶׁר יֵדְעוּן אִישׁ נֶגַע לְבָבוֹ וּפָרַשׂ כַּפָּיו אֶל־הַבַּיִת הַזֶּה׃

39 oh, hear in Your heavenly abode, and pardon and take action! Render to each man according to his ways as You know his heart to be – for You alone know the hearts of all men

לט וְאַתָּה תִּשְׁמַע הַשָּׁמַיִם מְכוֹן שִׁבְתֶּךָ וְסָלַחְתָּ וְעָשִׂיתָ וְנָתַתָּ לָאִישׁ כְּכָל־דְּרָכָיו אֲשֶׁר תֵּדַע אֶת־לְבָבוֹ כִּי־אַתָּה יָדַעְתָּ לְבַדְּךָ אֶת־לְבַב כָּל־בְּנֵי הָאָדָם׃

40 so that they may revere You all the days that they live on the land that You gave to our fathers.

מ לְמַעַן יִרָאוּךָ כָּל־הַיָּמִים אֲשֶׁר־הֵם חַיִּים עַל־פְּנֵי הָאֲדָמָה אֲשֶׁר נָתַתָּה לַאֲבֹתֵינוּ׃

41 "Or if a foreigner who is not of Your people *Yisrael* comes from a distant land for the sake of Your name

מא וְגַם אֶל־הַנָּכְרִי אֲשֶׁר לֹא־מֵעַמְּךָ יִשְׂרָאֵל הוּא וּבָא מֵאֶרֶץ רְחוֹקָה לְמַעַן שְׁמֶךָ׃

v'-GAM el ha-nokh-REE a-SHER lo may-a-m'-KHA yis-ra-AYL HU u-VA may-E-retz r'-kho-KAH l'-MA-an sh'-ME-kha

42 for they shall hear about Your great name and Your mighty hand and Your outstretched arm – when he comes to pray toward this House,

מב כִּי יִשְׁמְעוּן אֶת־שִׁמְךָ הַגָּדוֹל וְאֶת־יָדְךָ הַחֲזָקָה וּזְרֹעֲךָ הַנְּטוּיָה וּבָא וְהִתְפַּלֵּל אֶל־הַבַּיִת הַזֶּה׃

43 oh, hear in Your heavenly abode and grant all that the foreigner asks You for. Thus all the peoples of the earth will know Your name and revere You, as does Your people *Yisrael*; and they will recognize that Your name is attached to this House that I have built.

מג אַתָּה תִּשְׁמַע הַשָּׁמַיִם מְכוֹן שִׁבְתֶּךָ וְעָשִׂיתָ כְּכֹל אֲשֶׁר־יִקְרָא אֵלֶיךָ הַנָּכְרִי לְמַעַן יֵדְעוּן כָּל־עַמֵּי הָאָרֶץ אֶת־שְׁמֶךָ לְיִרְאָה אֹתְךָ כְּעַמְּךָ יִשְׂרָאֵל וְלָדַעַת כִּי־שִׁמְךָ נִקְרָא עַל־הַבַּיִת הַזֶּה אֲשֶׁר בָּנִיתִי׃

44 "When Your people take the field against their enemy by whatever way You send them, and they pray to *Hashem* in the direction of the city which You have chosen, and of the House which I have built to Your name,

מד כִּי־יֵצֵא עַמְּךָ לַמִּלְחָמָה עַל־אֹיְבוֹ בַּדֶּרֶךְ אֲשֶׁר תִּשְׁלָחֵם וְהִתְפַּלְלוּ אֶל־יְהוָה דֶּרֶךְ הָעִיר אֲשֶׁר בָּחַרְתָּ בָּהּ וְהַבַּיִת אֲשֶׁר־בָּנִתִי לִשְׁמֶךָ׃

8:41 A foreigner who is not of Your people Israel King *Shlomo* dedicated the first *Beit Hamikdash* on the festival of *Sukkot* and, in his inaugural address, asked *Hashem* to hear the prayers of foreigners who would "come to pray towards this house" (verse 42). The first Temple was constructed with the assistance of members of gentile nations, under the leadership of Hiram of Tyre. Similarly, the second Temple was built thanks to the permission and encouragement of Cyrus of Persia, and the third Temple will one day also be built with the participation of righteous non-Jews (see commentary to Isaiah 2:3). This international participation is necessary, as the the *Beit Hamikdash* is meant to be a "house of prayer for all nations" (Isaiah 56:7). King *Shlomo's* dedication speech has been memorialized on an imposing glass monument standing tall at the Western Wall today, etched with his universal message to inspire visitors and worshippers from all countries, nationalities and backgrounds.

Melachim I/I Kings
Chapter 8

מלכים א
פרק ח

45	oh, hear in heaven their prayer and supplication and uphold their cause.	וְשָׁמַעְתָּ הַשָּׁמַיִם אֶת־תְּפִלָּתָם וְאֶת־תְּחִנָּתָם וְעָשִׂיתָ מִשְׁפָּטָם:	מה
46	"When they sin against You – for there is no man who does not sin – and You are angry with them and deliver them to the enemy, and their captors carry them off to an enemy land, near or far;	כִּי יֶחֶטְאוּ־לָךְ כִּי אֵין אָדָם אֲשֶׁר לֹא־יֶחֱטָא וְאָנַפְתָּ בָם וּנְתַתָּם לִפְנֵי אוֹיֵב וְשָׁבוּם שֹׁבֵיהֶם אֶל־אֶרֶץ הָאוֹיֵב רְחוֹקָה אוֹ קְרוֹבָה:	מו
47	and then they take it to heart in the land to which they have been carried off, and they repent and make supplication to You in the land of their captors, saying: 'We have sinned, we have acted perversely, we have acted wickedly,'	וְהֵשִׁיבוּ אֶל־לִבָּם בָּאָרֶץ אֲשֶׁר נִשְׁבּוּ־שָׁם וְשָׁבוּ וְהִתְחַנְּנוּ אֵלֶיךָ בְּאֶרֶץ שֹׁבֵיהֶם לֵאמֹר חָטָאנוּ וְהֶעֱוִינוּ רָשָׁעְנוּ:	מז
48	and they turn back to You with all their heart and soul, in the land of the enemies who have carried them off, and they pray to You in the direction of their land which You gave to their fathers, of the city which You have chosen, and of the House which I have built to Your name	וְשָׁבוּ אֵלֶיךָ בְּכָל־לְבָבָם וּבְכָל־נַפְשָׁם בְּאֶרֶץ אֹיְבֵיהֶם אֲשֶׁר־שָׁבוּ אֹתָם וְהִתְפַּלְלוּ אֵלֶיךָ דֶּרֶךְ אַרְצָם אֲשֶׁר נָתַתָּה לַאֲבוֹתָם הָעִיר אֲשֶׁר בָּחַרְתָּ וְהַבַּיִת אֲשֶׁר־בנית [בָּנִיתִי] לִשְׁמֶךָ:	מח
49	oh, give heed in Your heavenly abode to their prayer and supplication, uphold their cause,	וְשָׁמַעְתָּ הַשָּׁמַיִם מְכוֹן שִׁבְתְּךָ אֶת־תְּפִלָּתָם וְאֶת־תְּחִנָּתָם וְעָשִׂיתָ מִשְׁפָּטָם:	מט
50	and pardon Your people who have sinned against You for all the transgressions that they have committed against You. Grant them mercy in the sight of their captors that they may be merciful to them.	וְסָלַחְתָּ לְעַמְּךָ אֲשֶׁר חָטְאוּ־לָךְ וּלְכָל־פִּשְׁעֵיהֶם אֲשֶׁר פָּשְׁעוּ־בָךְ וּנְתַתָּם לְרַחֲמִים לִפְנֵי שֹׁבֵיהֶם וְרִחֲמוּם:	נ
51	For they are Your very own people that You freed from Egypt, from the midst of the iron furnace.	כִּי־עַמְּךָ וְנַחֲלָתְךָ הֵם אֲשֶׁר הוֹצֵאתָ מִמִּצְרַיִם מִתּוֹךְ כּוּר הַבַּרְזֶל:	נא
52	May Your eyes be open to the supplication of Your servant and the supplication of Your people *Yisrael*, and may You heed them whenever they call upon You.	לִהְיוֹת עֵינֶיךָ פְתֻחֹת אֶל־תְּחִנַּת עַבְדְּךָ וְאֶל־תְּחִנַּת עַמְּךָ יִשְׂרָאֵל לִשְׁמֹעַ אֲלֵיהֶם בְּכֹל קָרְאָם אֵלֶיךָ:	נב
53	For You, O *Hashem*, have set them apart for Yourself from all the peoples of the earth as Your very own, as You promised through *Moshe* Your servant when You freed our fathers from Egypt."	כִּי־אַתָּה הִבְדַּלְתָּם לְךָ לְנַחֲלָה מִכֹּל עַמֵּי הָאָרֶץ כַּאֲשֶׁר דִּבַּרְתָּ בְּיַד מֹשֶׁה עַבְדֶּךָ בְּהוֹצִיאֲךָ אֶת־אֲבֹתֵינוּ מִמִּצְרַיִם אֲדֹנָי יֱהֹוִה:	נג
54	When *Shlomo* finished offering to *Hashem* all this prayer and supplication, he rose from where he had been kneeling, in front of the *Mizbayach* of *Hashem*, his hands spread out toward heaven.	וַיְהִי כְּכַלּוֹת שְׁלֹמֹה לְהִתְפַּלֵּל אֶל־יְהֹוָה אֵת כָּל־הַתְּפִלָּה וְהַתְּחִנָּה הַזֹּאת קָם מִלִּפְנֵי מִזְבַּח יְהֹוָה מִכְּרֹעַ עַל־בִּרְכָּיו וְכַפָּיו פְּרֻשׂוֹת הַשָּׁמָיִם:	נד
55	He stood, and in a loud voice blessed the whole congregation of *Yisrael*:	וַיַּעֲמֹד וַיְבָרֶךְ אֵת כָּל־קְהַל יִשְׂרָאֵל קוֹל גָּדוֹל לֵאמֹר:	נה
56	"Praised be *Hashem* who has granted a haven to His people *Yisrael*, just as He promised; not a single word has failed of all the gracious promises that He made through His servant *Moshe*.	בָּרוּךְ יְהֹוָה אֲשֶׁר נָתַן מְנוּחָה לְעַמּוֹ יִשְׂרָאֵל כְּכֹל אֲשֶׁר דִּבֵּר לֹא־נָפַל דָּבָר אֶחָד מִכֹּל דְּבָרוֹ הַטּוֹב אֲשֶׁר דִּבֶּר בְּיַד מֹשֶׁה עַבְדּוֹ:	נו

Melachim I/I Kings
Chapter 8

מלכים א
פרק ח

57 May *Hashem* our God be with us, as He was with our fathers. May He never abandon or forsake us.

נז יְהִי יְהֹוָה אֱלֹהֵינוּ עִמָּנוּ כַּאֲשֶׁר הָיָה עִם־אֲבֹתֵינוּ אַל־יַעַזְבֵנוּ וְאַל־יִטְּשֵׁנוּ׃

58 May He incline our hearts to Him, that we may walk in all His ways and keep the commandments, the laws, and the rules, which He enjoined upon our fathers.

נח לְהַטּוֹת לְבָבֵנוּ אֵלָיו לָלֶכֶת בְּכָל־דְּרָכָיו וְלִשְׁמֹר מִצְוֹתָיו וְחֻקָּיו וּמִשְׁפָּטָיו אֲשֶׁר צִוָּה אֶת־אֲבֹתֵינוּ׃

59 And may these words of mine, which I have offered in supplication before *Hashem*, be close to *Hashem* our God day and night, that He may provide for His servant and for His people *Yisrael*, according to each day's needs

נט וְיִהְיוּ דְבָרַי אֵלֶּה אֲשֶׁר הִתְחַנַּנְתִּי לִפְנֵי יְהֹוָה קְרֹבִים אֶל־יְהֹוָה אֱלֹהֵינוּ יוֹמָם וָלָיְלָה לַעֲשׂוֹת מִשְׁפַּט עַבְדּוֹ וּמִשְׁפַּט עַמּוֹ יִשְׂרָאֵל דְּבַר־יוֹם בְּיוֹמוֹ׃

60 to the end that all the peoples of the earth may know that *Hashem* alone is *Hashem*, there is no other.

ס לְמַעַן דַּעַת כָּל־עַמֵּי הָאָרֶץ כִּי יְהֹוָה הוּא הָאֱלֹהִים אֵין עוֹד׃

61 And may you be wholehearted with *Hashem* our God, to walk in His ways and keep His commandments, even as now."

סא וְהָיָה לְבַבְכֶם שָׁלֵם עִם יְהֹוָה אֱלֹהֵינוּ לָלֶכֶת בְּחֻקָּיו וְלִשְׁמֹר מִצְוֺתָיו כַּיּוֹם הַזֶּה׃

62 The king and all *Yisrael* with him offered sacrifices before *Hashem*.

סב וְהַמֶּלֶךְ וְכָל־יִשְׂרָאֵל עִמּוֹ זֹבְחִים זֶבַח לִפְנֵי יְהֹוָה׃

63 *Shlomo* offered 22,000 oxen and 120,000 sheep as sacrifices of well-being to *Hashem*. Thus the king and all the Israelites dedicated the House of *Hashem*.

סג וַיִּזְבַּח שְׁלֹמֹה אֵת זֶבַח הַשְּׁלָמִים אֲשֶׁר זָבַח לַיהֹוָה בָּקָר עֶשְׂרִים וּשְׁנַיִם אֶלֶף וְצֹאן מֵאָה וְעֶשְׂרִים אָלֶף וַיַּחְנְכוּ אֶת־בֵּית יְהֹוָה הַמֶּלֶךְ וְכָל־בְּנֵי יִשְׂרָאֵל׃

64 That day the king consecrated the center of the court that was in front of the House of *Hashem*. For it was there that he presented the burnt offerings, the meal offerings, and the fat parts of the offerings of well-being, because the bronze *Mizbayach* that was before *Hashem* was too small to hold the burnt offerings, the meal offerings, and the fat parts of the offerings of well-being.

סד בַּיּוֹם הַהוּא קִדַּשׁ הַמֶּלֶךְ אֶת־תּוֹךְ הֶחָצֵר אֲשֶׁר לִפְנֵי בֵית־יְהֹוָה כִּי־עָשָׂה שָׁם אֶת־הָעֹלָה וְאֶת־הַמִּנְחָה וְאֵת חֶלְבֵי הַשְּׁלָמִים כִּי־מִזְבַּח הַנְּחֹשֶׁת אֲשֶׁר לִפְנֵי יְהֹוָה קָטֹן מֵהָכִיל אֶת־הָעֹלָה וְאֶת־הַמִּנְחָה וְאֵת חֶלְבֵי הַשְּׁלָמִים׃

65 So *Shlomo* and all *Yisrael* with him – a great assemblage, [coming] from Lebo-hamath to the Wadi of Egypt – observed the Feast at that time before *Hashem* our God, seven days and again seven days, fourteen days in all.

סה וַיַּעַשׂ שְׁלֹמֹה בָעֵת־הַהִיא אֶת־הֶחָג וְכָל־יִשְׂרָאֵל עִמּוֹ קָהָל גָּדוֹל מִלְּבוֹא חֲמָת עַד־נַחַל מִצְרַיִם לִפְנֵי יְהֹוָה אֱלֹהֵינוּ שִׁבְעַת יָמִים וְשִׁבְעַת יָמִים אַרְבָּעָה עָשָׂר יוֹם׃

66 On the eighth day he let the people go. They bade the king good-bye and went to their homes, joyful and glad of heart over all the goodness that *Hashem* had shown to His servant *David* and His people *Yisrael*.

סו בַּיּוֹם הַשְּׁמִינִי שִׁלַּח אֶת־הָעָם וַיְבָרְכוּ אֶת־הַמֶּלֶךְ וַיֵּלְכוּ לְאָהֳלֵיהֶם שְׂמֵחִים וְטוֹבֵי לֵב עַל כָּל־הַטּוֹבָה אֲשֶׁר עָשָׂה יְהֹוָה לְדָוִד עַבְדּוֹ וּלְיִשְׂרָאֵל עַמּוֹ׃

Melachim I / I Kings
Chapter 9

9 1 When *Shlomo* had finished building the House of *Hashem* and the royal palace and everything that *Shlomo* had set his heart on constructing,

2 *Hashem* appeared to *Shlomo* a second time, as He had appeared to him at *Givon*.

3 *Hashem* said to him, "I have heard the prayer and the supplication which you have offered to Me. I consecrate this House which you have built and I set My name there forever. My eyes and My heart shall ever be there.

4 As for you, if you walk before Me as your father *David* walked before Me, wholeheartedly and with uprightness, doing all that I have commanded you [and] keeping My laws and My rules,

5 then I will establish your throne of kingship over *Yisrael* forever, as I promised your father *David*, saying, 'Your line on the throne of *Yisrael* shall never end.'

6 [But] if you and your descendants turn away from Me and do not keep the commandments [and] the laws which I have set before you, and go and serve other gods and worship them,

7 then I will sweep *Yisrael* off the land which I gave them; I will reject the House which I have consecrated to My name; and *Yisrael* shall become a proverb and a byword among all peoples.

8 And as for this House, once so exalted, everyone passing by it shall be appalled and shall hiss. And when they ask, 'Why did *Hashem* do thus to the land and to this House?'

9 they shall be told, 'It is because they forsook *Hashem* their God who freed them from the land of Egypt, and they embraced other gods and worshiped them and served them; therefore *Hashem* has brought all this calamity upon them.'"

10 At the end of the twenty years during which *Shlomo* constructed the two buildings, *Hashem*'s House and the royal palace

11 since King Hiram of Tyre had supplied *Shlomo* with all the cedar and cypress timber and gold that he required – King *Shlomo* in turn gave Hiram twenty towns in the region of Galilee.

מלכים א
פרק ט

א וַיְהִי כְּכַלּוֹת שְׁלֹמֹה לִבְנוֹת אֶת־בֵּית־יְהֹוָה וְאֶת־בֵּית הַמֶּלֶךְ וְאֵת כָּל־חֵשֶׁק שְׁלֹמֹה אֲשֶׁר חָפֵץ לַעֲשׂוֹת:

ב וַיֵּרָא יְהֹוָה אֶל־שְׁלֹמֹה שֵׁנִית כַּאֲשֶׁר נִרְאָה אֵלָיו בְּגִבְעוֹן:

ג וַיֹּאמֶר יְהֹוָה אֵלָיו שָׁמַעְתִּי אֶת־תְּפִלָּתְךָ וְאֶת־תְּחִנָּתְךָ אֲשֶׁר הִתְחַנַּנְתָּה לְפָנַי הִקְדַּשְׁתִּי אֶת־הַבַּיִת הַזֶּה אֲשֶׁר בָּנִתָה לָשׂוּם־שְׁמִי שָׁם עַד־עוֹלָם וְהָיוּ עֵינַי וְלִבִּי שָׁם כָּל־הַיָּמִים:

ד וְאַתָּה אִם־תֵּלֵךְ לְפָנַי כַּאֲשֶׁר הָלַךְ דָּוִד אָבִיךָ בְּתָם־לֵבָב וּבְיֹשֶׁר לַעֲשׂוֹת כְּכֹל אֲשֶׁר צִוִּיתִיךָ חֻקַּי וּמִשְׁפָּטַי תִּשְׁמֹר:

ה וַהֲקִמֹתִי אֶת־כִּסֵּא מַמְלַכְתְּךָ עַל־יִשְׂרָאֵל לְעֹלָם כַּאֲשֶׁר דִּבַּרְתִּי עַל־דָּוִד אָבִיךָ לֵאמֹר לֹא־יִכָּרֵת לְךָ אִישׁ מֵעַל כִּסֵּא יִשְׂרָאֵל:

ו אִם־שׁוֹב תְּשֻׁבוּן אַתֶּם וּבְנֵיכֶם מֵאַחֲרַי וְלֹא תִשְׁמְרוּ מִצְוֹתַי חֻקֹּתַי אֲשֶׁר נָתַתִּי לִפְנֵיכֶם וַהֲלַכְתֶּם וַעֲבַדְתֶּם אֱלֹהִים אֲחֵרִים וְהִשְׁתַּחֲוִיתֶם לָהֶם:

ז וְהִכְרַתִּי אֶת־יִשְׂרָאֵל מֵעַל פְּנֵי הָאֲדָמָה אֲשֶׁר נָתַתִּי לָהֶם וְאֶת־הַבַּיִת אֲשֶׁר הִקְדַּשְׁתִּי לִשְׁמִי אֲשַׁלַּח מֵעַל פָּנָי וְהָיָה יִשְׂרָאֵל לְמָשָׁל וְלִשְׁנִינָה בְּכָל־הָעַמִּים:

ח וְהַבַּיִת הַזֶּה יִהְיֶה עֶלְיוֹן כָּל־עֹבֵר עָלָיו יִשֹּׁם וְשָׁרָק וְאָמְרוּ עַל־מֶה עָשָׂה יְהֹוָה כָּכָה לָאָרֶץ הַזֹּאת וְלַבַּיִת הַזֶּה:

ט וְאָמְרוּ עַל אֲשֶׁר עָזְבוּ אֶת־יְהֹוָה אֱלֹהֵיהֶם אֲשֶׁר הוֹצִיא אֶת־אֲבֹתָם מֵאֶרֶץ מִצְרַיִם וַיַּחֲזִקוּ בֵּאלֹהִים אֲחֵרִים וַיִּשְׁתַּחֲווּ [וַיִּשְׁתַּחֲווּ] לָהֶם וַיַּעַבְדֻם עַל־כֵּן הֵבִיא יְהֹוָה עֲלֵיהֶם אֵת כָּל־הָרָעָה הַזֹּאת:

י וַיְהִי מִקְצֵה עֶשְׂרִים שָׁנָה אֲשֶׁר־בָּנָה שְׁלֹמֹה אֶת־שְׁנֵי הַבָּתִּים אֶת־בֵּית יְהֹוָה וְאֶת־בֵּית הַמֶּלֶךְ:

יא חִירָם מֶלֶךְ־צֹר נִשָּׂא אֶת־שְׁלֹמֹה בַּעֲצֵי אֲרָזִים וּבַעֲצֵי בְרוֹשִׁים וּבַזָּהָב לְכָל־חֶפְצוֹ אָז יִתֵּן הַמֶּלֶךְ שְׁלֹמֹה לְחִירָם עֶשְׂרִים עִיר בְּאֶרֶץ הַגָּלִיל:

Melachim I / I Kings
Chapter 9

12 But when Hiram came from Tyre to inspect the towns that *Shlomo* had given him, he was not pleased with them.

יב וַיֵּצֵ֤א חִירָם֙ מִצֹּ֔ר לִרְא֖וֹת אֶת־הֶעָרִ֑ים אֲשֶׁ֥ר נָתַן־ל֖וֹ שְׁלֹמֹ֑ה וְלֹ֥א יָשְׁר֖וּ בְּעֵינָֽיו׃

13 "My brother," he said, "what sort of towns are these you have given me?" So they were named the land of Cabul, as is still the case.

יג וַיֹּ֕אמֶר מָ֚ה הֶעָרִ֣ים הָאֵ֔לֶּה אֲשֶׁר־נָתַ֖תָּה לִ֣י אָחִ֑י וַיִּקְרָ֤א לָהֶם֙ אֶ֣רֶץ כָּב֔וּל עַ֖ד הַיּ֥וֹם הַזֶּֽה׃

14 However, Hiram sent the king one hundred and twenty *kikarim* of gold.

יד וַיִּשְׁלַ֥ח חִירָ֖ם לַמֶּ֑לֶךְ מֵאָ֥ה וְעֶשְׂרִ֖ים כִּכַּ֥ר זָהָֽב׃

15 This was the purpose of the forced labor which *Shlomo* imposed: It was to build the House of *Hashem*, his own palace, the Millo, and the wall of *Yerushalayim*, and [to fortify] Hazor, Megiddo, and Gezer.

טו וְזֶ֨ה דְבַר־הַמַּ֜ס אֲשֶׁר־הֶעֱלָ֣ה ׀ הַמֶּ֣לֶךְ שְׁלֹמֹ֗ה לִבְנוֹת֙ אֶת־בֵּ֣ית יְהֹוָ֔ה וְאֶת־בֵּית֖וֹ וְאֶת־הַמִּלּ֑וֹא וְאֵ֖ת חוֹמַ֣ת יְרוּשָׁלָ֑͏ִם וְאֶת־חָצֹ֥ר וְאֶת־מְגִדּ֖וֹ וְאֶת־גָּֽזֶר׃

v'-ZEH d'-var ha-MAS a-sher he-e-LAH ha-ME-lekh sh'-lo-MO liv-NOT et BAYT a-do-NAI v'-et bay-TO v'-et ha-mi-LO v'-AYT kho-MAT y'-ru-sha-LA-im v'-et kha-TZOR v'-et m'-gi-DO v'-et GA-zer

16 Pharaoh king of Egypt had come up and captured Gezer; he destroyed it by fire, killed the Canaanites who dwelt in the town, and gave it as dowry to his daughter, *Shlomo*'s wife.

טז פַּרְעֹ֨ה מֶלֶךְ־מִצְרַ֜יִם עָלָ֗ה וַיִּלְכֹּ֤ד אֶת־גֶּ֙זֶר֙ וַיִּשְׂרְפָ֣הּ בָּאֵ֔שׁ וְאֶת־הַֽכְּנַעֲנִ֛י הַיֹּשֵׁ֥ב בָּעִ֖יר הָרָ֑ג וַֽיִּתְּנָהּ֙ שִׁלֻּחִ֔ים לְבִתּ֖וֹ אֵ֥שֶׁת שְׁלֹמֹֽה׃

17 So *Shlomo* fortified Gezer, lower Beth-horon,

יז וַיִּ֣בֶן שְׁלֹמֹ֔ה אֶת־גָּ֖זֶר וְאֶת־בֵּ֥ית חֹרֹ֖ן תַּחְתּֽוֹן׃

18 Baalith, and *Tamar* in the wilderness, in the land [of *Yehuda*],

יח וְאֶֽת־בַּעֲלָ֛ת וְאֶת־תמר [תַּדְמֹ֥ר] בַּמִּדְבָּ֖ר בָּאָֽרֶץ׃

19 and all of *Shlomo*'s garrison towns, chariot towns, and cavalry towns – everything that *Shlomo* set his heart on building in *Yerushalayim* and in the Lebanon, and throughout the territory that he ruled.

יט וְאֵ֣ת כׇּל־עָרֵ֣י הַֽמִּסְכְּנוֹת֮ אֲשֶׁ֣ר הָי֣וּ לִשְׁלֹמֹה֒ וְאֵת֙ עָרֵ֣י הָרֶ֔כֶב וְאֵ֖ת עָרֵ֣י הַפָּרָשִׁ֑ים וְאֵ֣ת ׀ חֵ֣שֶׁק שְׁלֹמֹ֗ה אֲשֶׁ֤ר חָשַׁק֙ לִבְנ֤וֹת בִּירוּשָׁלַ֙͏ִם֙ וּבַלְּבָנ֔וֹן וּבְכֹ֖ל אֶ֥רֶץ מֶמְשַׁלְתּֽוֹ׃

20 All the people that were left of the Amorites, Hittites, Perizzites, Hivites, and Jebusites who were not of the Israelite stock

כ כׇּל־הָ֠עָ֠ם הַנּוֹתָ֨ר מִן־הָאֱמֹרִ֜י הַחִתִּ֧י הַפְּרִזִּ֛י הַחִוִּ֥י וְהַיְבוּסִ֖י אֲשֶׁ֥ר לֹֽא־מִבְּנֵ֥י יִשְׂרָאֵ֖ל הֵֽמָּה׃

9:15 The wall of *Yerushalayim* The walls of *Yerushalayim*, like those of all ancient cities, have great importance; they are designed to provide physical protection from invaders. In *Yerushalayim*'s case, however, they also have spiritual significance, as certain commandments, like the eating of the Passover sacrifice, must be performed only within the city's walls. The current Old City of *Yerushalayim*, in which the Western Wall and the Temple Mount are located, is still surrounded by walls. These walls are much newer, having been built by the Turkish ruler of the city almost 500 years ago. Yet, they too have spiritual significance as the boundary of the heart of the holiest city on earth.

Walls of the Old City of Jerusalem

Melachim I / I Kings
Chapter 10

21 those of their descendants who remained in the land and whom the Israelites were not able to annihilate – of these *Shlomo* made a slave force, as is still the case.

כא בְּנֵיהֶם אֲשֶׁר נֹתְרוּ אַחֲרֵיהֶם בָּאָרֶץ אֲשֶׁר לֹא־יָכְלוּ בְּנֵי יִשְׂרָאֵל לְהַחֲרִימָם וַיַּעֲלֵם שְׁלֹמֹה לְמַס־עֹבֵד עַד הַיּוֹם הַזֶּה׃

22 But he did not reduce any Israelites to slavery; they served, rather, as warriors and as his attendants, officials, and officers, and as commanders of his chariotry and cavalry.

כב וּמִבְּנֵי יִשְׂרָאֵל לֹא־נָתַן שְׁלֹמֹה עָבֶד כִּי־הֵם אַנְשֵׁי הַמִּלְחָמָה וַעֲבָדָיו וְשָׂרָיו וְשָׁלִשָׁיו וְשָׂרֵי רִכְבּוֹ וּפָרָשָׁיו׃

23 These were the prefects that were in charge of *Shlomo*'s works and were foremen over the people engaged in the work, who numbered 550.

כג אֵלֶּה שָׂרֵי הַנִּצָּבִים אֲשֶׁר עַל־הַמְּלָאכָה לִשְׁלֹמֹה חֲמִשִּׁים וַחֲמֵשׁ מֵאוֹת הָרֹדִים בָּעָם הָעֹשִׂים בַּמְּלָאכָה׃

24 As soon as Pharaoh's daughter went up from the City of *David* to the palace that he had built for her, he built the Millo.

כד אַךְ בַּת־פַּרְעֹה עָלְתָה מֵעִיר דָּוִד אֶל־בֵּיתָהּ אֲשֶׁר בָּנָה־לָהּ אָז בָּנָה אֶת־הַמִּלּוֹא׃

25 *Shlomo* used to offer burnt offerings and sacrifices of well-being three times a year on the *Mizbayach* that he had built for *Hashem*, and he used to offer incense on the one that was before *Hashem*. And he kept the House in repair.

כה וְהֶעֱלָה שְׁלֹמֹה שָׁלֹשׁ פְּעָמִים בַּשָּׁנָה עֹלוֹת וּשְׁלָמִים עַל־הַמִּזְבֵּחַ אֲשֶׁר בָּנָה לַיהוָה וְהַקְטֵיר אִתּוֹ אֲשֶׁר לִפְנֵי יְהוָה וְשִׁלַּם אֶת־הַבָּיִת׃

26 King *Shlomo* also built a fleet of ships at Eziongeber, which is near Eloth on the shore of the Sea of Reeds in the land of Edom.

כו וָאֳנִי עָשָׂה הַמֶּלֶךְ שְׁלֹמֹה בְּעֶצְיוֹן־גֶּבֶר אֲשֶׁר אֶת־אֵלוֹת עַל־שְׂפַת יַם־סוּף בְּאֶרֶץ אֱדוֹם׃

27 Hiram sent servants of his with the fleet, mariners who were experienced on the sea, to serve with *Shlomo*'s men.

כז וַיִּשְׁלַח חִירָם בָּאֳנִי אֶת־עֲבָדָיו אַנְשֵׁי אֳנִיּוֹת יֹדְעֵי הַיָּם עִם עַבְדֵי שְׁלֹמֹה׃

28 They came to Ophir; there they obtained gold in the amount of four hundred and twenty *kikarim*, which they delivered to King *Shlomo*.

כח וַיָּבֹאוּ אוֹפִירָה וַיִּקְחוּ מִשָּׁם זָהָב אַרְבַּע־מֵאוֹת וְעֶשְׂרִים כִּכָּר וַיָּבִאוּ אֶל־הַמֶּלֶךְ שְׁלֹמֹה׃

10 1 The queen of Sheba heard of *Shlomo*'s fame, through the name of *Hashem*, and she came to test him with hard questions.

י א וּמַלְכַּת־שְׁבָא שֹׁמַעַת אֶת־שֵׁמַע שְׁלֹמֹה לְשֵׁם יְהוָה וַתָּבֹא לְנַסֹּתוֹ בְּחִידוֹת׃

2 She arrived in *Yerushalayim* with a very large retinue, with camels bearing spices, a great quantity of gold, and precious stones. When she came to *Shlomo*, she asked him all that she had in mind.

ב וַתָּבֹא יְרוּשָׁלְַמָה בְּחַיִל כָּבֵד מְאֹד גְּמַלִּים נֹשְׂאִים בְּשָׂמִים וְזָהָב רַב־מְאֹד וְאֶבֶן יְקָרָה וַתָּבֹא אֶל־שְׁלֹמֹה וַתְּדַבֵּר אֵלָיו אֵת כָּל־אֲשֶׁר הָיָה עִם־לְבָבָהּ׃

3 *Shlomo* had answers for all her questions; there was nothing that the king did not know, [nothing] to which he could not give her an answer.

ג וַיַּגֶּד־לָהּ שְׁלֹמֹה אֶת־כָּל־דְּבָרֶיהָ לֹא־הָיָה דָּבָר נֶעְלָם מִן־הַמֶּלֶךְ אֲשֶׁר לֹא הִגִּיד לָהּ׃

4 When the queen of Sheba observed all of *Shlomo*'s wisdom, and the palace he had built,

ד וַתֵּרֶא מַלְכַּת־שְׁבָא אֵת כָּל־חָכְמַת שְׁלֹמֹה וְהַבַּיִת אֲשֶׁר בָּנָה׃

Melachim I / I Kings
Chapter 10

5 the fare of his table, the seating of his courtiers, the service and attire of his attendants, and his wine service, and the burnt offerings that he offered at the House of *Hashem*, she was left breathless.

6 She said to the king, "The report I heard in my own land about you and your wisdom was true.

7 But I did not believe the reports until I came and saw with my own eyes that not even the half had been told me; your wisdom and wealth surpass the reports that I heard.

8 How fortunate are your men and how fortunate are these your courtiers, who are always in attendance on you and can hear your wisdom!

9 Praised be *Hashem* your God, who delighted in you and set you on the throne of *Yisrael*. It is because of *Hashem*'s everlasting love for *Yisrael* that He made you king to administer justice and righteousness."

10 She presented the king with one hundred and twenty *kikarim* of gold, and a large quantity of spices, and precious stones. Never again did such a vast quantity of spices arrive as that which the queen of Sheba gave to King *Shlomo*.

11 Moreover, Hiram's fleet, which carried gold from Ophir, brought in from Ophir a huge quantity of almug wood and precious stones.

12 The king used the almug wood for decorations in the House of *Hashem* and in the royal palace, and for harps and lyres for the musicians. Such a quantity of almug wood has never arrived or been seen to this day.

13 King *Shlomo*, in turn, gave the queen of Sheba everything she wanted and asked for, in addition to what King *Shlomo* gave her out of his royal bounty. Then she and her attendants left and returned to her own land.

14 The weight of the gold which *Shlomo* received every year was 666 *kikarim* of gold,

15 besides what came from tradesmen, from the traffic of the merchants, and from all the kings of Arabia and the governors of the regions.

מלכים א
פרק י

ה וּמַאֲכַל שֻׁלְחָנוֹ וּמוֹשַׁב עֲבָדָיו וּמַעֲמַד מְשָׁרְתוֹ [מְשָׁרְתָיו] וּמַלְבֻּשֵׁיהֶם וּמַשְׁקָיו וְעֹלָתוֹ אֲשֶׁר יַעֲלֶה בֵּית יְהוָה וְלֹא־הָיָה בָהּ עוֹד רוּחַ׃

ו וַתֹּאמֶר אֶל־הַמֶּלֶךְ אֱמֶת הָיָה הַדָּבָר אֲשֶׁר שָׁמַעְתִּי בְּאַרְצִי עַל־דְּבָרֶיךָ וְעַל־חָכְמָתֶךָ׃

ז וְלֹא־הֶאֱמַנְתִּי לַדְּבָרִים עַד אֲשֶׁר־בָּאתִי וַתִּרְאֶינָה עֵינַי וְהִנֵּה לֹא־הֻגַּד־לִי הַחֵצִי הוֹסַפְתָּ חָכְמָה וָטוֹב אֶל־הַשְּׁמוּעָה אֲשֶׁר שָׁמָעְתִּי׃

ח אַשְׁרֵי אֲנָשֶׁיךָ אַשְׁרֵי עֲבָדֶיךָ אֵלֶּה הָעֹמְדִים לְפָנֶיךָ תָּמִיד הַשֹּׁמְעִים אֶת־חָכְמָתֶךָ׃

ט יְהִי יְהוָה אֱלֹהֶיךָ בָּרוּךְ אֲשֶׁר חָפֵץ בְּךָ לְתִתְּךָ עַל־כִּסֵּא יִשְׂרָאֵל בְּאַהֲבַת יְהוָה אֶת־יִשְׂרָאֵל לְעֹלָם וַיְשִׂימְךָ לְמֶלֶךְ לַעֲשׂוֹת מִשְׁפָּט וּצְדָקָה׃

י וַתִּתֵּן לַמֶּלֶךְ מֵאָה וְעֶשְׂרִים כִּכַּר זָהָב וּבְשָׂמִים הַרְבֵּה מְאֹד וְאֶבֶן יְקָרָה לֹא־בָא כַבֹּשֶׂם הַהוּא עוֹד לָרֹב אֲשֶׁר־נָתְנָה מַלְכַּת־שְׁבָא לַמֶּלֶךְ שְׁלֹמֹה׃

יא וְגַם אֳנִי חִירָם אֲשֶׁר־נָשָׂא זָהָב מֵאוֹפִיר הֵבִיא מֵאֹפִיר עֲצֵי אַלְמֻגִּים הַרְבֵּה מְאֹד וְאֶבֶן יְקָרָה׃

יב וַיַּעַשׂ הַמֶּלֶךְ אֶת־עֲצֵי הָאַלְמֻגִּים מִסְעָד לְבֵית־יְהוָה וּלְבֵית הַמֶּלֶךְ וְכִנֹּרוֹת וּנְבָלִים לַשָּׁרִים לֹא בָא־כֵן עֲצֵי אַלְמֻגִּים וְלֹא נִרְאָה עַד הַיּוֹם הַזֶּה׃

יג וְהַמֶּלֶךְ שְׁלֹמֹה נָתַן לְמַלְכַּת־שְׁבָא אֶת־כָּל־חֶפְצָהּ אֲשֶׁר שָׁאָלָה מִלְּבַד אֲשֶׁר נָתַן־לָהּ כְּיַד הַמֶּלֶךְ שְׁלֹמֹה וַתֵּפֶן וַתֵּלֶךְ לְאַרְצָהּ הִיא וַעֲבָדֶיהָ׃

יד וַיְהִי מִשְׁקַל הַזָּהָב אֲשֶׁר־בָּא לִשְׁלֹמֹה בְּשָׁנָה אֶחָת שֵׁשׁ מֵאוֹת שִׁשִּׁים וָשֵׁשׁ כִּכַּר זָהָב׃

טו לְבַד מֵאַנְשֵׁי הַתָּרִים וּמִסְחַר הָרֹכְלִים וְכָל־מַלְכֵי הָעֶרֶב וּפַחוֹת הָאָרֶץ׃

Melachim I / I Kings
Chapter 10

מלכים א
פרק י

טז וַיַּעַשׂ הַמֶּלֶךְ שְׁלֹמֹה מָאתַיִם צִנָּה זָהָב שָׁחוּט שֵׁשׁ־מֵאוֹת זָהָב יַעֲלֶה עַל־הַצִּנָּה הָאֶחָת׃

16 King *Shlomo* made 200 shields of beaten gold – 600 *shekalim* of gold to each shield –

יז וּשְׁלֹשׁ־מֵאוֹת מָגִנִּים זָהָב שָׁחוּט שְׁלֹשֶׁת מָנִים זָהָב יַעֲלֶה עַל־הַמָּגֵן הָאֶחָת וַיִּתְּנֵם הַמֶּלֶךְ בֵּית יַעַר הַלְּבָנוֹן׃

17 and 300 bucklers of beaten gold – three *manim* of gold to each buckler. The king placed them in the Lebanon Forest House.

יח וַיַּעַשׂ הַמֶּלֶךְ כִּסֵּא־שֵׁן גָּדוֹל וַיְצַפֵּהוּ זָהָב מוּפָז׃

18 The king also made a large throne of ivory, and he overlaid it with refined gold.

יט שֵׁשׁ מַעֲלוֹת לַכִּסֵּה וְרֹאשׁ־עָגֹל לַכִּסֵּה מֵאַחֲרָיו וְיָדֹת מִזֶּה וּמִזֶּה אֶל־מְקוֹם הַשָּׁבֶת וּשְׁנַיִם אֲרָיוֹת עֹמְדִים אֵצֶל הַיָּדוֹת׃

19 Six steps led up to the throne, and the throne had a back with a rounded top, and arms on either side of the seat. Two lions stood beside the arms,

כ וּשְׁנֵים עָשָׂר אֲרָיִים עֹמְדִים שָׁם עַל־שֵׁשׁ הַמַּעֲלוֹת מִזֶּה וּמִזֶּה לֹא־נַעֲשָׂה כֵן לְכָל־מַמְלָכוֹת׃

20 and twelve lions stood on the six steps, six on either side. No such throne was ever made for any other kingdom.

כא וְכֹל כְּלֵי מַשְׁקֵה הַמֶּלֶךְ שְׁלֹמֹה זָהָב וְכֹל כְּלֵי בֵּית־יַעַר הַלְּבָנוֹן זָהָב סָגוּר אֵין כֶּסֶף לֹא נֶחְשָׁב בִּימֵי שְׁלֹמֹה לִמְאוּמָה׃

21 All King *Shlomo*'s drinking cups were of gold, and all the utensils of the Lebanon Forest House were of pure gold: silver did not count for anything in *Shlomo*'s days.

כב כִּי אֳנִי תַרְשִׁישׁ לַמֶּלֶךְ בַּיָּם עִם אֳנִי חִירָם אַחַת לְשָׁלֹשׁ שָׁנִים תָּבוֹא אֳנִי תַרְשִׁישׁ נֹשְׂאֵת זָהָב וָכֶסֶף שֶׁנְהַבִּים וְקֹפִים וְתֻכִּיִּים׃

22 For the king had a Tarshish fleet on the sea, along with Hiram's fleet. Once every three years, the Tarshish fleet came in, bearing gold and silver, ivory, apes, and peacocks.

כג וַיִּגְדַּל הַמֶּלֶךְ שְׁלֹמֹה מִכֹּל מַלְכֵי הָאָרֶץ לְעֹשֶׁר וּלְחָכְמָה׃

23 King *Shlomo* excelled all the kings on earth in wealth and in wisdom.

כד וְכָל־הָאָרֶץ מְבַקְשִׁים אֶת־פְּנֵי שְׁלֹמֹה לִשְׁמֹעַ אֶת־חָכְמָתוֹ אֲשֶׁר־נָתַן אֱלֹהִים בְּלִבּוֹ׃

24 All the world came to pay homage to *Shlomo* and to listen to the wisdom with which *Hashem* had endowed him;

v'-KHOL ha-A-retz m'-vak-SHEEM et p'-NAY sh'-lo-MOH lish-MO-a et khokh-ma-TO a-sher na-TAN e-lo-HEEM b'-li-BO

כה וְהֵמָּה מְבִאִים אִישׁ מִנְחָתוֹ כְּלֵי כֶסֶף וּכְלֵי זָהָב וּשְׂלָמוֹת וְנֵשֶׁק וּבְשָׂמִים סוּסִים וּפְרָדִים דְּבַר־שָׁנָה בְּשָׁנָה׃

25 and each one would bring his tribute – silver and gold objects, robes, weapons and spices, horses and mules – in the amount due each year.

10:24 All the world came to pay homage to Shlomo Rabbi Shlomo Aviner points out that this verse represents a great sanctification of *Hashem*'s name. Though King *Shlomo* is the wealthiest, most powerful king of the time, this is not the reason why he is sought out by the entire world. Rather, everyone wishes to be in his presence because of the great wisdom *Hashem* has given him. This demonstrates that Israel is unlike all other kingdoms; it is a holy nation. When Jewish leaders represent the highest levels of ethics and wisdom, they sanctify God's name among all the people of the world.

Melachim I/I Kings
Chapter 11

מלכים א
פרק יא

26 *Shlomo* assembled chariots and horses. He had 1,400 chariots and 12,000 horses, which he stationed in the chariot towns and with the king in *Yerushalayim*.

כו וַיֶּאֱסֹף שְׁלֹמֹה רֶכֶב וּפָרָשִׁים וַיְהִי־לוֹ אֶלֶף וְאַרְבַּע־מֵאוֹת רֶכֶב וּשְׁנֵים־עָשָׂר אֶלֶף פָּרָשִׁים וַיַּנְחֵם בְּעָרֵי הָרֶכֶב וְעִם־הַמֶּלֶךְ בִּירוּשָׁלָ͏ִם׃

27 The king made silver as plentiful in *Yerushalayim* as stones, and cedars as plentiful as sycamores in the Shephelah.

כז וַיִּתֵּן הַמֶּלֶךְ אֶת־הַכֶּסֶף בִּירוּשָׁלַ͏ִם כָּאֲבָנִים וְאֵת הָאֲרָזִים נָתַן כַּשִּׁקְמִים אֲשֶׁר־בַּשְּׁפֵלָה לָרֹב׃

28 *Shlomo*'s horses were procured from *Mizraim* and Kue. The king's dealers would buy them from Kue at a fixed price.

כח וּמוֹצָא הַסּוּסִים אֲשֶׁר לִשְׁלֹמֹה מִמִּצְרָיִם וּמִקְוֵה סֹחֲרֵי הַמֶּלֶךְ יִקְחוּ מִקְוֵה בִּמְחִיר׃

29 A chariot imported from *Mizraim* cost 600 *shekalim* of silver, and a horse 150; these in turn were exported by them to all the kings of the Hittites and the kings of the Arameans.

כט וַתַּעֲלֶה וַתֵּצֵא מֶרְכָּבָה מִמִּצְרַיִם בְּשֵׁשׁ מֵאוֹת כֶּסֶף וְסוּס בַּחֲמִשִּׁים וּמֵאָה וְכֵן לְכָל־מַלְכֵי הַחִתִּים וּלְמַלְכֵי אֲרָם בְּיָדָם יֹצִאוּ׃

11

1 King *Shlomo* loved many foreign women in addition to Pharaoh's daughter – Moabite, Amonite, Edomite, Phoenician, and Hittite women,

יא א וְהַמֶּלֶךְ שְׁלֹמֹה אָהַב נָשִׁים נָכְרִיּוֹת רַבּוֹת וְאֶת־בַּת־פַּרְעֹה מוֹאֲבִיּוֹת עַמֳּנִיּוֹת אֲדֹמִיֹּת צֵדְנִיֹּת חִתִּיֹּת׃

v'-ha-ME-lekh sh'-lo-MOH a-HAV na-SHEEM nokh-ri-YOT ra-BOT v'-et bat par-OH mo-a-vee-YOT a-mo-nee-YOT a-do-mee-YOT tzay-d'-nee-YOT khi-tee-YOT

2 from the nations of which *Hashem* had said to the Israelites, "None of you shall join them and none of them shall join you, lest they turn your heart away to follow their gods." Such *Shlomo* clung to and loved.

ב מִן־הַגּוֹיִם אֲשֶׁר אָמַר־יְהֹוָה אֶל־בְּנֵי יִשְׂרָאֵל לֹא־תָבֹאוּ בָהֶם וְהֵם לֹא־יָבֹאוּ בָכֶם אָכֵן יַטּוּ אֶת־לְבַבְכֶם אַחֲרֵי אֱלֹהֵיהֶם בָּהֶם דָּבַק שְׁלֹמֹה לְאַהֲבָה׃

3 He had seven hundred royal wives and three hundred concubines; and his wives turned his heart away.

ג וַיְהִי־לוֹ נָשִׁים שָׂרוֹת שְׁבַע מֵאוֹת וּפִלַגְשִׁים שְׁלֹשׁ מֵאוֹת וַיַּטּוּ נָשָׁיו אֶת־לִבּוֹ׃

4 In his old age, his wives turned away *Shlomo*'s heart after other gods, and he was not as wholeheartedly devoted to *Hashem* his God as his father *David* had been.

ד וַיְהִי לְעֵת זִקְנַת שְׁלֹמֹה נָשָׁיו הִטּוּ אֶת־לְבָבוֹ אַחֲרֵי אֱלֹהִים אֲחֵרִים וְלֹא־הָיָה לְבָבוֹ שָׁלֵם עִם־יְהֹוָה אֱלֹהָיו כִּלְבַב דָּוִיד אָבִיו׃

5 *Shlomo* followed Ashtoreth the goddess of the Phoenicians, and Milcom the abomination of the Amonites.

ה וַיֵּלֶךְ שְׁלֹמֹה אַחֲרֵי עַשְׁתֹּרֶת אֱלֹהֵי צִדֹנִים וְאַחֲרֵי מִלְכֹּם שִׁקֻּץ עַמֹּנִים׃

11:1 King *Shlomo* loved many foreign women It seems shocking that the wise and righteous King *Shlomo* loves and marries foreign women. *Rambam* notes that he certainly does not marry these women without them first converting to Judaism. Yet, they clearly do not convert with a full heart, as evidenced by their continuing idolatrous practices. How, then, can King *Shlomo* make such a mistake? Rabbi Aviner suggests that *Shlomo* thought he could spread belief in *Hashem* throughout the world, and that in order to do that he would need to incorporate representatives of other nations into the People of Israel. Though he has noble intentions, he makes a mistake in not sufficiently protecting himself and the People of Israel from the dangers of foreign influence and idol worship.

Melachim I / I Kings
Chapter 11

6 *Shlomo* did what was displeasing to *Hashem* and did not remain loyal to *Hashem* like his father *David*.

7 At that time, *Shlomo* built a shrine for Chemosh the abomination of Moab on the hill near *Yerushalayim*, and one for Molech the abomination of the Amonites.

8 And he did the same for all his foreign wives who offered and sacrificed to their gods.

9 *Hashem* was angry with *Shlomo*, because his heart turned away from *Hashem*, the God of *Yisrael*, who had appeared to him twice

10 and had commanded him about this matter, not to follow other gods; he did not obey what *Hashem* had commanded.

11 And *Hashem* said to *Shlomo*, "Because you are guilty of this – you have not kept My covenant and the laws which I enjoined upon you – I will tear the kingdom away from you and give it to one of your servants.

12 But, for the sake of your father *David*, I will not do it in your lifetime; I will tear it away from your son.

13 However, I will not tear away the whole kingdom; I will give your son one tribe, for the sake of My servant *David* and for the sake of *Yerushalayim* which I have chosen."

14 So *Hashem* raised up an adversary against *Shlomo*, the Edomite Hadad, who was of the royal family of Edom.

15 When *David* was in Edom, *Yoav* the army commander went up to bury the slain, and he killed every male in Edom;

16 for *Yoav* and all *Yisrael* stayed there for six months until he had killed off every male in Edom.

17 But Hadad, together with some Edomite men, servants of his father, escaped and headed for Egypt; Hadad was then a young boy.

18 Setting out from Midian, they came to Paran and took along with them men from Paran. Thus they came to Egypt, to Pharaoh king of Egypt, who gave him a house, assigned a food allowance to him, and granted him an estate.

Melachim I / I Kings
Chapter 11

19 Pharaoh took a great liking to Hadad and gave him his sister-in-law, the sister of Queen Tahpenes, as wife.

20 The sister of Tahpenes bore him a son, Genubath. Tahpenes weaned him in Pharaoh's palace, and Genubath remained in Pharaoh's palace among the sons of Pharaoh.

21 When Hadad heard in Egypt that *David* had been laid to rest with his fathers and that *Yoav* the army commander was dead, Hadad said to Pharaoh, "Give me leave to go to my own country."

22 Pharaoh replied, "What do you lack with me, that you want to go to your own country?" But he said, "Nevertheless, give me leave to go."

23 Another adversary that *Hashem* raised up against *Shlomo* was Rezon son of Eliada, who had fled from his lord, King Hadadezer of Zobah,

24 when *David* was slaughtering them. He gathered men about him and became captain over a troop; they went to Damascus and settled there, and they established a kingdom in Damascus.

25 He was an adversary of *Yisrael* all the days of *Shlomo*, adding to the trouble [caused by] Hadad; he repudiated [the authority of] *Yisrael* and reigned over Aram.

26 *Yerovam* son of Nebat, an Ephraimite of Zeredah, the son of a widow whose name was Zeruah, was in *Shlomo*'s service; he raised his hand against the king.

27 The circumstances under which he raised his hand against the king were as follows: *Shlomo* built the Millo and repaired the breach of the city of his father, *David*.

28 This *Yerovam* was an able man, and when *Shlomo* saw that the young man was a capable worker, he appointed him over all the forced labor of the House of *Yosef*.

29 During that time *Yerovam* went out of *Yerushalayim* and the *Navi Achiya* of *Shilo* met him on the way. He had put on a new robe; and when the two were alone in the open country,

30 *Achiya* took hold of the new robe he was wearing and tore it into twelve pieces.

מלכים א
פרק יא

יט וַיִּמְצָא הֲדַד חֵן בְּעֵינֵי פַרְעֹה מְאֹד וַיִּתֶּן־לוֹ אִשָּׁה אֶת־אֲחוֹת אִשְׁתּוֹ אֲחוֹת תַּחְפְּנֵיס הַגְּבִירָה׃

כ וַתֵּלֶד לוֹ אֲחוֹת תַּחְפְּנֵיס אֵת גְּנֻבַת בְּנוֹ וַתִּגְמְלֵהוּ תַחְפְּנֵס בְּתוֹךְ בֵּית פַּרְעֹה וַיְהִי גְנֻבַת בֵּית פַּרְעֹה בְּתוֹךְ בְּנֵי פַרְעֹה׃

כא וַהֲדַד שָׁמַע בְּמִצְרַיִם כִּי־שָׁכַב דָּוִד עִם־אֲבֹתָיו וְכִי־מֵת יוֹאָב שַׂר־הַצָּבָא וַיֹּאמֶר הֲדַד אֶל־פַּרְעֹה שַׁלְּחֵנִי וְאֵלֵךְ אֶל־אַרְצִי׃

כב וַיֹּאמֶר לוֹ פַרְעֹה כִּי מָה־אַתָּה חָסֵר עִמִּי וְהִנְּךָ מְבַקֵּשׁ לָלֶכֶת אֶל־אַרְצֶךָ וַיֹּאמֶר לֹא כִּי שַׁלֵּחַ תְּשַׁלְּחֵנִי׃

כג וַיָּקֶם אֱלֹהִים לוֹ שָׂטָן אֶת־רְזוֹן בֶּן־אֶלְיָדָע אֲשֶׁר בָּרַח מֵאֵת הֲדַדְעֶזֶר מֶלֶךְ־צוֹבָה אֲדֹנָיו׃

כד וַיִּקְבֹּץ עָלָיו אֲנָשִׁים וַיְהִי שַׂר־גְּדוּד בַּהֲרֹג דָּוִד אֹתָם וַיֵּלְכוּ דַמֶּשֶׂק וַיֵּשְׁבוּ בָהּ וַיִּמְלְכוּ בְּדַמָּשֶׂק׃

כה וַיְהִי שָׂטָן לְיִשְׂרָאֵל כָּל־יְמֵי שְׁלֹמֹה וְאֶת־הָרָעָה אֲשֶׁר הֲדָד וַיָּקָץ בְּיִשְׂרָאֵל וַיִּמְלֹךְ עַל־אֲרָם׃

כו וְיָרָבְעָם בֶּן־נְבָט אֶפְרָתִי מִן־הַצְּרֵדָה וְשֵׁם אִמּוֹ צְרוּעָה אִשָּׁה אַלְמָנָה עֶבֶד לִשְׁלֹמֹה וַיָּרֶם יָד בַּמֶּלֶךְ׃

כז וְזֶה הַדָּבָר אֲשֶׁר־הֵרִים יָד בַּמֶּלֶךְ שְׁלֹמֹה בָּנָה אֶת־הַמִּלּוֹא סָגַר אֶת־פֶּרֶץ עִיר דָּוִד אָבִיו׃

כח וְהָאִישׁ יָרָבְעָם גִּבּוֹר חָיִל וַיַּרְא שְׁלֹמֹה אֶת־הַנַּעַר כִּי־עֹשֵׂה מְלָאכָה הוּא וַיַּפְקֵד אֹתוֹ לְכָל־סֵבֶל בֵּית יוֹסֵף׃

כט וַיְהִי בָּעֵת הַהִיא וְיָרָבְעָם יָצָא מִירוּשָׁלָםִ וַיִּמְצָא אֹתוֹ אֲחִיָּה הַשִּׁילֹנִי הַנָּבִיא בַּדֶּרֶךְ וְהוּא מִתְכַּסֶּה בְּשַׂלְמָה חֲדָשָׁה וּשְׁנֵיהֶם לְבַדָּם בַּשָּׂדֶה׃

ל וַיִּתְפֹּשׂ אֲחִיָּה בַּשַּׂלְמָה הַחֲדָשָׁה אֲשֶׁר עָלָיו וַיִּקְרָעֶהָ שְׁנֵים עָשָׂר קְרָעִים׃

Melachim I / I Kings
Chapter 11

מלכים א
פרק יא

31	"Take ten pieces," he said to *Yerovam*. "For thus said *Hashem*, the God of *Yisrael*: I am about to tear the kingdom out of *Shlomo*'s hands, and I will give you ten tribes.	לא וַיֹּאמֶר לְיָרָבְעָם קַח־לְךָ עֲשָׂרָה קְרָעִים כִּי כֹה אָמַר יְהֹוָה אֱלֹהֵי יִשְׂרָאֵל הִנְנִי קֹרֵעַ אֶת־הַמַּמְלָכָה מִיַּד שְׁלֹמֹה וְנָתַתִּי לְךָ אֵת עֲשָׂרָה הַשְּׁבָטִים:
32	But one tribe shall remain his – for the sake of My servant *David* and for the sake of *Yerushalayim*, the city that I have chosen out of all the tribes of *Yisrael*.	לב וְהַשֵּׁבֶט הָאֶחָד יִהְיֶה־לּוֹ לְמַעַן עַבְדִּי דָוִד וּלְמַעַן יְרוּשָׁלִַם הָעִיר אֲשֶׁר בָּחַרְתִּי בָהּ מִכֹּל שִׁבְטֵי יִשְׂרָאֵל:
33	For they have forsaken Me; they have worshiped Ashtoreth the goddess of the Phoenicians, Chemosh the god of Moab, and Milcom the god of the Amonites; they have not walked in My ways, or done what is pleasing to Me, or [kept] My laws and rules, as his father *David* did.	לג יַעַן אֲשֶׁר עֲזָבוּנִי וַיִּשְׁתַּחֲווּ לְעַשְׁתֹּרֶת אֱלֹהֵי צִדֹנִין לִכְמוֹשׁ אֱלֹהֵי מוֹאָב וּלְמִלְכֹּם אֱלֹהֵי בְנֵי־עַמּוֹן וְלֹא־הָלְכוּ בִדְרָכַי לַעֲשׂוֹת הַיָּשָׁר בְּעֵינַי וְחֻקֹּתַי וּמִשְׁפָּטַי כְּדָוִד אָבִיו:
34	However, I will not take the entire kingdom away from him, but will keep him as ruler as long as he lives for the sake of My servant *David* whom I chose, and who kept My commandments and My laws.	לד וְלֹא־אֶקַּח אֶת־כָּל־הַמַּמְלָכָה מִיָּדוֹ כִּי נָשִׂיא אֲשִׁתֶנּוּ כֹּל יְמֵי חַיָּיו לְמַעַן דָּוִד עַבְדִּי אֲשֶׁר בָּחַרְתִּי אֹתוֹ אֲשֶׁר שָׁמַר מִצְוֺתַי וְחֻקֹּתָי:
35	But I will take the kingship out of the hands of his son and give it to you – the ten tribes.	לה וְלָקַחְתִּי הַמְּלוּכָה מִיַּד בְּנוֹ וּנְתַתִּיהָ לְּךָ אֵת עֲשֶׂרֶת הַשְּׁבָטִים:
36	To his son I will give one tribe, so that there may be a lamp for My servant *David* forever before Me in *Yerushalayim* – the city where I have chosen to establish My name.	לו וְלִבְנוֹ אֶתֵּן שֵׁבֶט־אֶחָד לְמַעַן הֱיוֹת־נִיר לְדָוִיד־עַבְדִּי כָּל־הַיָּמִים לְפָנַי בִּירוּשָׁלִָם הָעִיר אֲשֶׁר בָּחַרְתִּי לִי לָשׂוּם שְׁמִי שָׁם:
37	But you have been chosen by Me; reign wherever you wish, and you shall be king over *Yisrael*.	לז וְאֹתְךָ אֶקַּח וּמָלַכְתָּ בְּכֹל אֲשֶׁר־תְּאַוֶּה נַפְשֶׁךָ וְהָיִיתָ מֶּלֶךְ עַל־יִשְׂרָאֵל:
38	If you heed all that I command you, and walk in My ways, and do what is right in My sight, keeping My laws and commandments as My servant *David* did, then I will be with you and I will build for you a lasting dynasty as I did for *David*. I hereby give *Yisrael* to you;	לח וְהָיָה אִם־תִּשְׁמַע אֶת־כָּל־אֲשֶׁר אֲצַוֶּךָ וְהָלַכְתָּ בִדְרָכַי וְעָשִׂיתָ הַיָּשָׁר בְּעֵינַי לִשְׁמוֹר חֻקּוֹתַי וּמִצְוֺתַי כַּאֲשֶׁר עָשָׂה דָּוִד עַבְדִּי וְהָיִיתִי עִמָּךְ וּבָנִיתִי לְךָ בַיִת־נֶאֱמָן כַּאֲשֶׁר בָּנִיתִי לְדָוִד וְנָתַתִּי לְךָ אֶת־יִשְׂרָאֵל:
39	and I will chastise *David*'s descendants for that [sin], though not forever."	לט וַאעַנֶּה אֶת־זֶרַע דָּוִד לְמַעַן זֹאת אַךְ לֹא כָל־הַיָּמִים:
40	*Shlomo* sought to put *Yerovam* to death, but *Yerovam* promptly fled to King Shishak of Egypt; and he remained in Egypt till the death of *Shlomo*.	מ וַיְבַקֵּשׁ שְׁלֹמֹה לְהָמִית אֶת־יָרָבְעָם וַיָּקָם יָרָבְעָם וַיִּבְרַח מִצְרַיִם אֶל־שִׁישַׁק מֶלֶךְ־מִצְרַיִם וַיְהִי בְמִצְרַיִם עַד־מוֹת שְׁלֹמֹה:
41	The other events of *Shlomo*'s reign, and all his actions and his wisdom, are recorded in the book of the Annals of *Shlomo*.	מא וְיֶתֶר דִּבְרֵי שְׁלֹמֹה וְכָל־אֲשֶׁר עָשָׂה וְחָכְמָתוֹ הֲלוֹא־הֵם כְּתֻבִים עַל־סֵפֶר דִּבְרֵי שְׁלֹמֹה:

Melachim I/I Kings
Chapter 12

42 The length of *Shlomo*'s reign in *Yerushalayim*, over all *Yisrael*, was forty years.

43 *Shlomo* slept with his fathers and was buried in the city of his father *David*; and his son *Rechovam* succeeded him as king.

12

1 *Rechovam* went to *Shechem*, for all *Yisrael* had come to *Shechem* to acclaim him as king.

2 *Yerovam* son of Nebat learned of it while he was still in Egypt; for *Yerovam* had fled from King *Shlomo*, and had settled in Egypt.

3 They sent for him; and *Yerovam* and all the assembly of *Yisrael* came and spoke to *Rechovam* as follows:

4 "Your father made our yoke heavy. Now lighten the harsh labor and the heavy yoke which your father laid on us, and we will serve you."

5 He answered them, "Go away for three days and then come back to me." So the people went away.

6 King *Rechovam* took counsel with the elders who had served his father *Shlomo* during his lifetime. He said, "What answer do you advise [me] to give to this people?"

7 They answered him, "If you will be a servant to those people today and serve them, and if you respond to them with kind words, they will be your servants always."

8 But he ignored the advice that the elders gave him, and took counsel with the young men who had grown up with him and were serving him.

9 "What," he asked, "do you advise that we reply to the people who said to me, 'Lighten the yoke that your father placed upon us'?"

10 And the young men who had grown up with him answered, "Speak thus to the people who said to you, 'Your father made our yoke heavy, now you make it lighter for us.' Say to them, 'My little finger is thicker than my father's loins.

11 My father imposed a heavy yoke on you, and I will add to your yoke; my father flogged you with whips, but I will flog you with scorpions.'"

מלכים א
פרק יב

מב וְהַיָּמִים אֲשֶׁר מָלַךְ שְׁלֹמֹה בִירוּשָׁלַם עַל־כָּל־יִשְׂרָאֵל אַרְבָּעִים שָׁנָה:

מג וַיִּשְׁכַּב שְׁלֹמֹה עִם־אֲבֹתָיו וַיִּקָּבֵר בְּעִיר דָּוִד אָבִיו וַיִּמְלֹךְ רְחַבְעָם בְּנוֹ תַּחְתָּיו:

יב א וַיֵּלֶךְ רְחַבְעָם שְׁכֶם כִּי שְׁכֶם בָּא כָל־יִשְׂרָאֵל לְהַמְלִיךְ אֹתוֹ:

ב וַיְהִי כִּשְׁמֹעַ יָרָבְעָם בֶּן־נְבָט וְהוּא עוֹדֶנּוּ בְמִצְרַיִם אֲשֶׁר בָּרַח מִפְּנֵי הַמֶּלֶךְ שְׁלֹמֹה וַיֵּשֶׁב יָרָבְעָם בְּמִצְרָיִם:

ג וַיִּשְׁלְחוּ וַיִּקְרְאוּ־לוֹ ויבאו [וַיָּבֹא] יָרָבְעָם וְכָל־קְהַל יִשְׂרָאֵל וַיְדַבְּרוּ אֶל־רְחַבְעָם לֵאמֹר:

ד אָבִיךָ הִקְשָׁה אֶת־עֻלֵּנוּ וְאַתָּה עַתָּה הָקֵל מֵעֲבֹדַת אָבִיךָ הַקָּשָׁה וּמֵעֻלּוֹ הַכָּבֵד אֲשֶׁר־נָתַן עָלֵינוּ וְנַעַבְדֶךָּ:

ה וַיֹּאמֶר אֲלֵיהֶם לְכוּ עֹד שְׁלֹשָׁה יָמִים וְשׁוּבוּ אֵלָי וַיֵּלְכוּ הָעָם:

ו וַיִּוָּעַץ הַמֶּלֶךְ רְחַבְעָם אֶת־הַזְּקֵנִים אֲשֶׁר־הָיוּ עֹמְדִים אֶת־פְּנֵי שְׁלֹמֹה אָבִיו בִּהְיֹתוֹ חַי לֵאמֹר אֵיךְ אַתֶּם נוֹעָצִים לְהָשִׁיב אֶת־הָעָם־הַזֶּה דָּבָר:

ז וידבר [וַיְדַבְּרוּ] אֵלָיו לֵאמֹר אִם־הַיּוֹם תִּהְיֶה־עֶבֶד לָעָם הַזֶּה וַעֲבַדְתָּם וַעֲנִיתָם וְדִבַּרְתָּ אֲלֵיהֶם דְּבָרִים טוֹבִים וְהָיוּ לְךָ עֲבָדִים כָּל־הַיָּמִים:

ח וַיַּעֲזֹב אֶת־עֲצַת הַזְּקֵנִים אֲשֶׁר יְעָצֻהוּ וַיִּוָּעַץ אֶת־הַיְלָדִים אֲשֶׁר גָּדְלוּ אִתּוֹ אֲשֶׁר הָעֹמְדִים לְפָנָיו:

ט וַיֹּאמֶר אֲלֵיהֶם מָה אַתֶּם נוֹעָצִים וְנָשִׁיב דָּבָר אֶת־הָעָם הַזֶּה אֲשֶׁר דִּבְּרוּ אֵלַי לֵאמֹר הָקֵל מִן־הָעֹל אֲשֶׁר־נָתַן אָבִיךָ עָלֵינוּ:

י וַיְדַבְּרוּ אֵלָיו הַיְלָדִים אֲשֶׁר גָּדְלוּ אִתּוֹ לֵאמֹר כֹּה־תֹאמַר לָעָם הַזֶּה אֲשֶׁר דִּבְּרוּ אֵלֶיךָ לֵאמֹר אָבִיךָ הִכְבִּיד אֶת־עֻלֵּנוּ וְאַתָּה הָקֵל מֵעָלֵינוּ כֹּה תְּדַבֵּר אֲלֵיהֶם קָטָנִּי עָבָה מִמָּתְנֵי אָבִי:

יא וְעַתָּה אָבִי הֶעְמִיס עֲלֵיכֶם עֹל כָּבֵד וַאֲנִי אוֹסִיף עַל־עֻלְּכֶם אָבִי יִסַּר אֶתְכֶם בַּשּׁוֹטִים וַאֲנִי אֲיַסֵּר אֶתְכֶם בָּעַקְרַבִּים:

Melachim I / I Kings
Chapter 12

12 *Yerovam* and all the people came to *Rechovam* on the third day, since the king had told them: "Come back on the third day."

13 The king answered the people harshly, ignoring the advice that the elders had given him.

14 He spoke to them in accordance with the advice of the young men, and said, "My father made your yoke heavy, but I will add to your yoke; my father flogged you with whips, but I will flog you with scorpions."

15 (The king did not listen to the people; for *Hashem* had brought it about in order to fulfill the promise that *Hashem* had made through *Achiya* the Shilonite to *Yerovam* son of Nebat.)

16 When all *Yisrael* saw that the king had not listened to them, the people answered the king: "We have no portion in *David*, No share in *Yishai*'s son! To your tents, O *Yisrael*! Now look to your own House, O *David*." So the Israelites returned to their homes.

17 But *Rechovam* continued to reign over the Israelites who lived in the towns of *Yehuda*.

18 King *Rechovam* sent Adoram, who was in charge of the forced labor, but all *Yisrael* pelted him to death with stones. Thereupon King *Rechovam* hurriedly mounted his chariot and fled to *Yerushalayim*.

19 Thus *Yisrael* revolted against the House of *David*, as is still the case.

20 When all *Yisrael* heard that *Yerovam* had returned, they sent messengers and summoned him to the assembly and made him king over all *Yisrael*. Only the tribe of *Yehuda* remained loyal to the House of *David*.

21 On his return to *Yerushalayim*, *Rechovam* mustered all the House of *Yehuda* and the tribe of *Binyamin*, 180,000 picked warriors, to fight against the House of *Yisrael*, in order to restore the kingship to *Rechovam* son of *Shlomo*.

22 But the word of *Hashem* came to *Shemaya*, the man of *Hashem*:

23 "Say to King *Rechovam* son of *Shlomo* of *Yehuda*, and to all the House of *Yehuda* and *Binyamin* and the rest of the people:

מלכים א
פרק יב

יב וַיָּבוֹ [וַיָּבוֹא] יָרָבְעָם וְכָל־הָעָם אֶל־רְחַבְעָם בַּיּוֹם הַשְּׁלִישִׁי כַּאֲשֶׁר דִּבֶּר הַמֶּלֶךְ לֵאמֹר שׁוּבוּ אֵלַי בַּיּוֹם הַשְּׁלִישִׁי:

יג וַיַּעַן הַמֶּלֶךְ אֶת־הָעָם קָשָׁה וַיַּעֲזֹב אֶת־עֲצַת הַזְּקֵנִים אֲשֶׁר יְעָצֻהוּ:

יד וַיְדַבֵּר אֲלֵיהֶם כַּעֲצַת הַיְלָדִים לֵאמֹר אָבִי הִכְבִּיד אֶת־עֻלְּכֶם וַאֲנִי אֹסִיף עַל־עֻלְּכֶם אָבִי יִסַּר אֶתְכֶם בַּשּׁוֹטִים וַאֲנִי אֲיַסֵּר אֶתְכֶם בָּעַקְרַבִּים:

טו וְלֹא־שָׁמַע הַמֶּלֶךְ אֶל־הָעָם כִּי־הָיְתָה סִבָּה מֵעִם יְהֹוָה לְמַעַן הָקִים אֶת־דְּבָרוֹ אֲשֶׁר דִּבֶּר יְהֹוָה בְּיַד אֲחִיָּה הַשִּׁילֹנִי אֶל־יָרָבְעָם בֶּן־נְבָט:

טז וַיַּרְא כָּל־יִשְׂרָאֵל כִּי לֹא־שָׁמַע הַמֶּלֶךְ אֲלֵיהֶם וַיָּשִׁבוּ הָעָם אֶת־הַמֶּלֶךְ דָּבָר לֵאמֹר מַה־לָּנוּ חֵלֶק בְּדָוִד וְלֹא־נַחֲלָה בְּבֶן־יִשַׁי לְאֹהָלֶיךָ יִשְׂרָאֵל עַתָּה רְאֵה בֵיתְךָ דָּוִד וַיֵּלֶךְ יִשְׂרָאֵל לְאֹהָלָיו:

יז וּבְנֵי יִשְׂרָאֵל הַיֹּשְׁבִים בְּעָרֵי יְהוּדָה וַיִּמְלֹךְ עֲלֵיהֶם רְחַבְעָם:

יח וַיִּשְׁלַח הַמֶּלֶךְ רְחַבְעָם אֶת־אֲדֹרָם אֲשֶׁר עַל־הַמַּס וַיִּרְגְּמוּ כָל־יִשְׂרָאֵל בּוֹ אֶבֶן וַיָּמֹת וְהַמֶּלֶךְ רְחַבְעָם הִתְאַמֵּץ לַעֲלוֹת בַּמֶּרְכָּבָה לָנוּס יְרוּשָׁלָם:

יט וַיִּפְשְׁעוּ יִשְׂרָאֵל בְּבֵית דָּוִד עַד הַיּוֹם הַזֶּה:

כ וַיְהִי כִּשְׁמֹעַ כָּל־יִשְׂרָאֵל כִּי־שָׁב יָרָבְעָם וַיִּשְׁלְחוּ וַיִּקְרְאוּ אֹתוֹ אֶל־הָעֵדָה וַיַּמְלִיכוּ אֹתוֹ עַל־כָּל־יִשְׂרָאֵל לֹא הָיָה אַחֲרֵי בֵית־דָּוִד זוּלָתִי שֵׁבֶט־יְהוּדָה לְבַדּוֹ:

כא ויבאו [וַיָּבֹא] רְחַבְעָם יְרוּשָׁלַם וַיַּקְהֵל אֶת־כָּל־בֵּית יְהוּדָה וְאֶת־שֵׁבֶט בִּנְיָמִן מֵאָה וּשְׁמֹנִים אֶלֶף בָּחוּר עֹשֵׂה מִלְחָמָה לְהִלָּחֵם עִם־בֵּית יִשְׂרָאֵל לְהָשִׁיב אֶת־הַמְּלוּכָה לִרְחַבְעָם בֶּן־שְׁלֹמֹה:

כב וַיְהִי דְּבַר הָאֱלֹהִים אֶל־שְׁמַעְיָה אִישׁ־הָאֱלֹהִים לֵאמֹר:

כג אֱמֹר אֶל־רְחַבְעָם בֶּן־שְׁלֹמֹה מֶלֶךְ יְהוּדָה וְאֶל־כָּל־בֵּית יְהוּדָה וּבִנְיָמִין וְיֶתֶר הָעָם לֵאמֹר:

Melachim I / I Kings
Chapter 12
מלכים א
פרק יב

24 Thus said *Hashem*: You shall not set out to make war on your kinsmen the Israelites. Let every man return to his home, for this thing has been brought about by Me." They heeded the word of *Hashem* and turned back, in accordance with the word of *Hashem*.

כד כֹּה אָמַר יְהֹוָה לֹא־תַעֲלוּ וְלֹא־תִלָּחֲמוּן עִם־אֲחֵיכֶם בְּנֵי־יִשְׂרָאֵל שׁוּבוּ אִישׁ לְבֵיתוֹ כִּי מֵאִתִּי נִהְיָה הַדָּבָר הַזֶּה וַיִּשְׁמְעוּ אֶת־דְּבַר יְהֹוָה וַיָּשֻׁבוּ לָלֶכֶת כִּדְבַר יְהֹוָה׃

25 *Yerovam* fortified *Shechem* in the hill country of *Efraim* and resided there; he moved out from there and fortified Penuel.

כה וַיִּבֶן יָרָבְעָם אֶת־שְׁכֶם בְּהַר אֶפְרַיִם וַיֵּשֶׁב בָּהּ וַיֵּצֵא מִשָּׁם וַיִּבֶן אֶת־פְּנוּאֵל׃

26 *Yerovam* said to himself, "Now the kingdom may well return to the House of *David*.

כו וַיֹּאמֶר יָרָבְעָם בְּלִבּוֹ עַתָּה תָּשׁוּב הַמַּמְלָכָה לְבֵית דָּוִד׃

27 If these people still go up to offer sacrifices at the House of *Hashem* in *Yerushalayim*, the heart of these people will turn back to their master, King *Rechovam* of *Yehuda*; they will kill me and go back to King *Rechovam* of *Yehuda*."

כז אִם־יַעֲלֶה הָעָם הַזֶּה לַעֲשׂוֹת זְבָחִים בְּבֵית־יְהֹוָה בִּירוּשָׁלִַם וְשָׁב לֵב הָעָם הַזֶּה אֶל־אֲדֹנֵיהֶם אֶל־רְחַבְעָם מֶלֶךְ יְהוּדָה וַהֲרָגֻנִי וְשָׁבוּ אֶל־רְחַבְעָם מֶלֶךְ־יְהוּדָה׃

28 So the king took counsel and made two golden calves. He said to the people, "You have been going up to *Yerushalayim* long enough. This is your god, O *Yisrael*, who brought you up from the land of Egypt!"

כח וַיִּוָּעַץ הַמֶּלֶךְ וַיַּעַשׂ שְׁנֵי עֶגְלֵי זָהָב וַיֹּאמֶר אֲלֵהֶם רַב־לָכֶם מֵעֲלוֹת יְרוּשָׁלִַם הִנֵּה אֱלֹהֶיךָ יִשְׂרָאֵל אֲשֶׁר הֶעֱלוּךָ מֵאֶרֶץ מִצְרָיִם׃

va-yi-va-ATZ ha-ME-lekh va-YA-as sh'-NAY eg-LAY za-HAV va-YO-mer a-lay-HEM rav la-KHEM may-a-LOT y'-ru-sha-LA-im hi-NAY e-lo-HE-kha yis-ra-AYL a-SHER he-e-LU-kha may-E-retz mizt-RA-yim

29 He set up one in *Beit El* and placed the other in *Dan*.

כט וַיָּשֶׂם אֶת־הָאֶחָד בְּבֵית־אֵל וְאֶת־הָאֶחָד נָתַן בְּדָן׃

30 That proved to be a cause of guilt, for the people went to worship [the calf at *Beit El* and] the one at *Dan*.

ל וַיְהִי הַדָּבָר הַזֶּה לְחַטָּאת וַיֵּלְכוּ הָעָם לִפְנֵי הָאֶחָד עַד־דָּן׃

31 He also made cult places and appointed *Kohanim* from the ranks of the people who were not of Levite descent.

לא וַיַּעַשׂ אֶת־בֵּית בָּמוֹת וַיַּעַשׂ כֹּהֲנִים מִקְצוֹת הָעָם אֲשֶׁר לֹא־הָיוּ מִבְּנֵי לֵוִי׃

12:28 You have been going up to *Yerushalayim* long enough The division of the People of Israel into two kingdoms – *Yisrael* in the north and *Yehuda* in the south – is a tragedy. *Yerovam*, the king of Israel, wants to prevent the people under his control from making pilgrimages to the *Beit Hamikdash* in *Yerushalayim*, which is located in the rival kingdom of *Yehuda*. *Yerovam* is afraid that his people will kill him if they decide that the king of Judah, *Rechovam*, son of King *Shlomo*, is the true king. Therefore, *Yerovam* tells his subjects not to travel to *Yerushalayim*. He erects idolatrous golden calves, and establishes his own festivals within the northern kingdom. This leads the people to idolatry and hastens the end of his kingdom. It is easy to see that severing the connection to *Yerushalayim* is both spiritually and physically dangerous. It results both in distance from *Hashem* and lack of unity among the people, ultimately leading to destruction and exile.

Melachim I/I Kings
Chapter 13

מלכים א
פרק יג

32 He stationed at *Beit El* the *Kohanim* of the shrines that he had appointed to sacrifice to the calves that he had made. And *Yerovam* established a festival on the fifteenth day of the eighth month; in imitation of the festival in *Yehuda*, he established one at *Beit El*, and he ascended the altar [there].

וַיַּעַשׂ יָרָבְעָם חָג בַּחֹדֶשׁ הַשְּׁמִינִי בַּחֲמִשָּׁה־עָשָׂר יוֹם לַחֹדֶשׁ כֶּחָג אֲשֶׁר בִּיהוּדָה וַיַּעַל עַל־הַמִּזְבֵּחַ כֵּן עָשָׂה בְּבֵית־אֵל לְזַבֵּחַ לָעֲגָלִים אֲשֶׁר־עָשָׂה וְהֶעֱמִיד בְּבֵית אֵל אֶת־כֹּהֲנֵי הַבָּמוֹת אֲשֶׁר עָשָׂה:

33 On the fifteenth day of the eighth month – the month in which he had contrived of his own mind to establish a festival for the Israelites – *Yerovam* ascended the *Mizbayach* that he had made in *Beit El*. As he ascended the altar to present an offering,

וַיַּעַל עַל־הַמִּזְבֵּחַ אֲשֶׁר־עָשָׂה בְּבֵית־אֵל בַּחֲמִשָּׁה עָשָׂר יוֹם בַּחֹדֶשׁ הַשְּׁמִינִי בַּחֹדֶשׁ אֲשֶׁר־בָּדָא מִלִּבַּד [מִלִּבּוֹ] וַיַּעַשׂ חָג לִבְנֵי יִשְׂרָאֵל וַיַּעַל עַל־הַמִּזְבֵּחַ לְהַקְטִיר:

13 1 a man of *Hashem* arrived at *Beit El* from *Yehuda* at the command of *Hashem*. While *Yerovam* was standing on the altar to present the offering, the man of *Hashem*, at the command of *Hashem*, cried out against the altar:

וְהִנֵּה אִישׁ אֱלֹהִים בָּא מִיהוּדָה בִּדְבַר יְהֹוָה אֶל־בֵּית־אֵל וְיָרָבְעָם עֹמֵד עַל־הַמִּזְבֵּחַ לְהַקְטִיר:

v'-hi-NAY eesh e-lo-HEEM ba mee-hu-DAH bid-VAR a-do-NAI el bayt ayl v'-ya-rov-AM o-MAYD al ha-miz-BAY-akh l'-hak-TEER

2 "O altar, altar! Thus said *Hashem*: A son shall be born to the House of *David*, *Yoshiyahu* by name; and he shall slaughter upon you the *Kohanim* of the shrines who bring offerings upon you. And human bones shall be burned upon you."

וַיִּקְרָא עַל־הַמִּזְבֵּחַ בִּדְבַר יְהֹוָה וַיֹּאמֶר מִזְבֵּחַ מִזְבֵּחַ כֹּה אָמַר יְהֹוָה הִנֵּה־בֵן נוֹלָד לְבֵית־דָּוִד יֹאשִׁיָּהוּ שְׁמוֹ וְזָבַח עָלֶיךָ אֶת־כֹּהֲנֵי הַבָּמוֹת הַמַּקְטִרִים עָלֶיךָ וְעַצְמוֹת אָדָם יִשְׂרְפוּ עָלֶיךָ:

3 He gave a portent on that day, saying, "Here is the portent that *Hashem* has decreed: This altar shall break apart, and the ashes on it shall be spilled."

וְנָתַן בַּיּוֹם הַהוּא מוֹפֵת לֵאמֹר זֶה הַמּוֹפֵת אֲשֶׁר דִּבֶּר יְהֹוָה הִנֵּה הַמִּזְבֵּחַ נִקְרָע וְנִשְׁפַּךְ הַדֶּשֶׁן אֲשֶׁר־עָלָיו:

4 When the king heard what the man of *Hashem* had proclaimed against the altar in *Beit El*, *Yerovam* stretched out his arm above the altar and cried, "Seize him!" But the arm that he stretched out against him became rigid, and he could not draw it back.

וַיְהִי כִשְׁמֹעַ הַמֶּלֶךְ אֶת־דְּבַר אִישׁ־הָאֱלֹהִים אֲשֶׁר קָרָא עַל־הַמִּזְבֵּחַ בְּבֵית־אֵל וַיִּשְׁלַח יָרָבְעָם אֶת־יָדוֹ מֵעַל הַמִּזְבֵּחַ לֵאמֹר תִּפְשֻׂהוּ וַתִּיבַשׁ יָדוֹ אֲשֶׁר שָׁלַח עָלָיו וְלֹא יָכֹל לַהֲשִׁיבָהּ אֵלָיו:

Ariel view of Beit El

13:1 A man of *Hashem* arrived at *Beit El* from *Yehuda* *Beit El* is a spiritually significant location mentioned several times in the Bible. *Avraham* first calls out in the name of Hashem to the east of *Beit El* (Genesis 12:8), and this is also where *Yaakov* awakes from his dream and declares "How awesome is this place! This is none other than the abode of God, and that is the gateway to heaven" (Genesis 28:17). *Beit El* is also chosen as a place of worship and prayer during the era of the judges (Judges 20:26). Therefore, it is not surprising that King *Yerovam* chooses *Beit El* as the location in which to erect his alternate altar to God. In spite of *Beit El*'s holiness, though, the *Beit Hamikdash* in *Yerushalayim* is the only place where the Children of Israel are permitted to offer sacrifices. Though *Hashem* had ordained that *Shlomo*'s kingdom would be split, He did not intend to diminish the centrality of *Yerushalayim* and the Temple. Therefore, what *Yerovam* does is a grave sin which causes others to sin as well. *Hashem* sends a prophet to proclaim that *Yerovam* will lose the kingdom and his altar will be destroyed. As recorded in *Sefer Melachim* II 23, the righteous King of the house of *David*, *Yoshiyahu*, destroys the altar in fulfilment of this prophecy.

Melachim I / I Kings
Chapter 13

5 The altar broke apart and its ashes were spilled – the very portent that the man of *Hashem* had announced at *Hashem*'s command.

6 Then the king spoke up and said to the man of *Hashem*, "Please entreat *Hashem* your God and pray for me that I may be able to draw back my arm." The man of *Hashem* entreated *Hashem* and the king was able to draw his arm back; it became as it was before.

7 The king said to the man of *Hashem*, "Come with me to my house and have some refreshment; and I shall give you a gift."

8 But the man of *Hashem* replied to the king, "Even if you give me half your wealth, I will not go in with you, nor will I eat bread or drink water in this place;

9 for so I was commanded by the word of *Hashem*: You shall eat no bread and drink no water, nor shall you go back by the road by which you came."

10 So he left by another road and did not go back by the road on which he had come to *Beit El*.

11 There was an old *Navi* living in *Beit El*; and his sons came and told him all the things that the man of *Hashem* had done that day in *Beit El* [and] the words that he had spoken to the king. When they told it to their father,

12 their father said to them, "Which road did he leave by?" His sons had seen the road taken by the man of *Hashem* who had come from *Yehuda*.

13 "Saddle the ass for me," he said to his sons. They saddled the ass for him, and he mounted it

14 and rode after the man of *Hashem*. He came upon him sitting under a terebinth and said to him, "Are you the man of *Hashem* who came from *Yehuda*?" "Yes, I am," he answered.

15 "Come home with me," he said, "and have something to eat."

16 He replied, "I may not go back with you and enter your home; and I may not eat bread or drink water in this place;

848

Melachim I / I Kings
Chapter 13

17 the order I received by the word of *Hashem* was: You shall not eat bread or drink water there; nor shall you return by the road on which you came."

18 "I am a *Navi*, too," said the other, "and an angel said to me by command of *Hashem*: Bring him back with you to your house, that he may eat bread and drink water." He was lying to him.

19 So he went back with him, and he ate bread and drank water in his house.

20 While they were sitting at the table, the word of *Hashem* came to the *Navi* who had brought him back.

21 He cried out to the man of *Hashem* who had come from *Yehuda*: "Thus said *Hashem*: Because you have flouted the word of *Hashem* and have not observed what *Hashem* your God commanded you,

22 but have gone back and eaten bread and drunk water in the place of which He said to you, 'Do not eat bread or drink water [there],' your corpse shall not come to the grave of your fathers."

23 After he had eaten bread and had drunk, he saddled the ass for him – for the *Navi* whom he had brought back.

24 He set out, and a lion came upon him on the road and killed him. His corpse lay on the road, with the ass standing beside it, and the lion also standing beside the corpse.

25 Some men who passed by saw the corpse lying on the road and the lion standing beside the corpse; they went and told it in the town where the old *Navi* lived.

26 And when the *Navi* who had brought him back from the road heard it, he said, "That is the man of *Hashem* who flouted *Hashem*'s command; *Hashem* gave him over to the lion, which mauled him and killed him in accordance with the word that *Hashem* had spoken to him."

27 He said to his sons, "Saddle the ass for me," and they did so.

28 He set out and found the corpse lying on the road, with the ass and the lion standing beside the corpse; the lion had not eaten the corpse nor had it mauled the ass.

מלכים א
פרק יג

יז כִּי־דָבָר אֵלַי בִּדְבַר יְהֹוָה לֹא־תֹאכַל לֶחֶם וְלֹא־תִשְׁתֶּה שָׁם מָיִם לֹא־תָשׁוּב לָלֶכֶת בַּדֶּרֶךְ אֲשֶׁר־הָלַכְתָּ בָּהּ׃

יח וַיֹּאמֶר לוֹ גַּם־אֲנִי נָבִיא כָּמוֹךָ וּמַלְאָךְ דִּבֶּר אֵלַי בִּדְבַר יְהֹוָה לֵאמֹר הֲשִׁבֵהוּ אִתְּךָ אֶל־בֵּיתֶךָ וְיֹאכַל לֶחֶם וְיֵשְׁתְּ מָיִם כִּחֵשׁ לוֹ׃

יט וַיָּשָׁב אִתּוֹ וַיֹּאכַל לֶחֶם בְּבֵיתוֹ וַיֵּשְׁתְּ מָיִם׃

כ וַיְהִי הֵם יֹשְׁבִים אֶל־הַשֻּׁלְחָן וַיְהִי דְבַר־יְהֹוָה אֶל־הַנָּבִיא אֲשֶׁר הֱשִׁיבוֹ׃

כא וַיִּקְרָא אֶל־אִישׁ הָאֱלֹהִים אֲשֶׁר־בָּא מִיהוּדָה לֵאמֹר כֹּה אָמַר יְהֹוָה יַעַן כִּי מָרִיתָ פִּי יְהֹוָה וְלֹא שָׁמַרְתָּ אֶת־הַמִּצְוָה אֲשֶׁר צִוְּךָ יְהֹוָה אֱלֹהֶיךָ׃

כב וַתָּשָׁב וַתֹּאכַל לֶחֶם וַתֵּשְׁתְּ מַיִם בַּמָּקוֹם אֲשֶׁר דִּבֶּר אֵלֶיךָ אַל־תֹּאכַל לֶחֶם וְאַל־תֵּשְׁתְּ מָיִם לֹא־תָבוֹא נִבְלָתְךָ אֶל־קֶבֶר אֲבֹתֶיךָ׃

כג וַיְהִי אַחֲרֵי אָכְלוֹ לֶחֶם וְאַחֲרֵי שְׁתוֹתוֹ וַיַּחֲבָשׁ־לוֹ הַחֲמוֹר לַנָּבִיא אֲשֶׁר הֱשִׁיבוֹ׃

כד וַיֵּלֶךְ וַיִּמְצָאֵהוּ אַרְיֵה בַּדֶּרֶךְ וַיְמִיתֵהוּ וַתְּהִי נִבְלָתוֹ מֻשְׁלֶכֶת בַּדֶּרֶךְ וְהַחֲמוֹר עֹמֵד אֶצְלָהּ וְהָאַרְיֵה עֹמֵד אֵצֶל הַנְּבֵלָה׃

כה וְהִנֵּה אֲנָשִׁים עֹבְרִים וַיִּרְאוּ אֶת־הַנְּבֵלָה מֻשְׁלֶכֶת בַּדֶּרֶךְ וְאֶת־הָאַרְיֵה עֹמֵד אֵצֶל הַנְּבֵלָה וַיָּבֹאוּ וַיְדַבְּרוּ בָעִיר אֲשֶׁר הַנָּבִיא הַזָּקֵן יֹשֵׁב בָּהּ׃

כו וַיִּשְׁמַע הַנָּבִיא אֲשֶׁר הֱשִׁיבוֹ מִן־הַדֶּרֶךְ וַיֹּאמֶר אִישׁ הָאֱלֹהִים הוּא אֲשֶׁר מָרָה אֶת־פִּי יְהֹוָה וַיִּתְּנֵהוּ יְהֹוָה לָאַרְיֵה וַיִּשְׁבְּרֵהוּ וַיְמִתֵהוּ כִּדְבַר יְהֹוָה אֲשֶׁר דִּבֶּר־לוֹ׃

כז וַיְדַבֵּר אֶל־בָּנָיו לֵאמֹר חִבְשׁוּ־לִי אֶת־הַחֲמוֹר וַיַּחֲבֹשׁוּ׃

כח וַיֵּלֶךְ וַיִּמְצָא אֶת־נִבְלָתוֹ מֻשְׁלֶכֶת בַּדֶּרֶךְ וַחֲמוֹר וְהָאַרְיֵה עֹמְדִים אֵצֶל הַנְּבֵלָה לֹא־אָכַל הָאַרְיֵה אֶת־הַנְּבֵלָה וְלֹא שָׁבַר אֶת־הַחֲמוֹר׃

Melachim I/I Kings
Chapter 14

29 The *Navi* lifted up the corpse of the man of *Hashem*, laid it on the ass, and brought it back; it was brought to the town of the old *Navi* for lamentation and burial.

30 He laid the corpse in his own burial place; and they lamented over it, "Alas, my brother!"

31 After burying him, he said to his sons, "When I die, bury me in the grave where the man of *Hashem* lies buried; lay my bones beside his.

32 For what he announced by the word of *Hashem* against the altar in *Beit El*, and against all the cult places in the towns of *Shomron*, shall surely come true."

33 Even after this incident, *Yerovam* did not turn back from his evil way, but kept on appointing *Kohanim* for the shrines from the ranks of the people. He ordained as *Kohanim* of the shrines any who so desired.

34 Thereby the House of *Yerovam* incurred guilt – to their utter annihilation from the face of the earth.

14

1 At that time, *Aviya*, a son of *Yerovam*, fell sick.

2 *Yerovam* said to his wife, "Go and disguise yourself, so that you will not be recognized as *Yerovam*'s wife, and go to *Shilo*. The *Navi Achiya* lives there, the one who predicted that I would be king over this people.

3 Take with you ten loaves, some wafers, and a jug of honey, and go to him; he will tell you what will happen to the boy."

4 *Yerovam*'s wife did so; she left and went to *Shilo* and came to the house of *Achiya*. Now *Achiya* could not see, for his eyes had become sightless with age;

5 but *Hashem* had said to *Achiya*, "*Yerovam*'s wife is coming to inquire of you concerning her son, who is sick. Speak to her thus and thus. When she arrives, she will be in disguise."

6 *Achiya* heard the sound of her feet as she came through the door, and he said, "Come in, wife of *Yerovam*. Why are you disguised? I have a harsh message for you.

מלכים א
פרק יד

כט וַיִּשָּׂא הַנָּבִיא אֶת־נִבְלַת אִישׁ־הָאֱלֹהִים וַיַּנִּחֵהוּ אֶל־הַחֲמוֹר וַיְשִׁיבֵהוּ וַיָּבֹא אֶל־עִיר הַנָּבִיא הַזָּקֵן לִסְפֹּד וּלְקָבְרוֹ:

ל וַיַּנַּח אֶת־נִבְלָתוֹ בְּקִבְרוֹ וַיִּסְפְּדוּ עָלָיו הוֹי אָחִי:

לא וַיְהִי אַחֲרֵי קָבְרוֹ אֹתוֹ וַיֹּאמֶר אֶל־בָּנָיו לֵאמֹר בְּמוֹתִי וּקְבַרְתֶּם אֹתִי בַּקֶּבֶר אֲשֶׁר אִישׁ הָאֱלֹהִים קָבוּר בּוֹ אֵצֶל עַצְמֹתָיו הַנִּיחוּ אֶת־עַצְמֹתָי:

לב כִּי הָיֹה יִהְיֶה הַדָּבָר אֲשֶׁר קָרָא בִּדְבַר יְהֹוָה עַל־הַמִּזְבֵּחַ אֲשֶׁר בְּבֵית־אֵל וְעַל כָּל־בָּתֵּי הַבָּמוֹת אֲשֶׁר בְּעָרֵי שֹׁמְרוֹן:

לג אַחַר הַדָּבָר הַזֶּה לֹא־שָׁב יָרָבְעָם מִדַּרְכּוֹ הָרָעָה וַיָּשָׁב וַיַּעַשׂ מִקְצוֹת הָעָם כֹּהֲנֵי בָמוֹת הֶחָפֵץ יְמַלֵּא אֶת־יָדוֹ וִיהִי כֹּהֲנֵי בָמוֹת:

לד וַיְהִי בַּדָּבָר הַזֶּה לְחַטַּאת בֵּית יָרָבְעָם וּלְהַכְחִיד וּלְהַשְׁמִיד מֵעַל פְּנֵי הָאֲדָמָה:

יד א בָּעֵת הַהִיא חָלָה אֲבִיָּה בֶן־יָרָבְעָם:

ב וַיֹּאמֶר יָרָבְעָם לְאִשְׁתּוֹ קוּמִי נָא וְהִשְׁתַּנִּית וְלֹא יֵדְעוּ כִּי־אתי [אַתְּ] אֵשֶׁת יָרָבְעָם וְהָלַכְתְּ שִׁלֹה הִנֵּה־שָׁם אֲחִיָּה הַנָּבִיא הוּא־דִבֶּר עָלַי לְמֶלֶךְ עַל־הָעָם הַזֶּה:

ג וְלָקַחַתְּ בְּיָדֵךְ עֲשָׂרָה לֶחֶם וְנִקֻּדִים וּבַקְבֻּק דְּבַשׁ וּבָאת אֵלָיו הוּא יַגִּיד לָךְ מַה־יִּהְיֶה לַנָּעַר:

ד וַתַּעַשׂ כֵּן אֵשֶׁת יָרָבְעָם וַתָּקָם וַתֵּלֶךְ שִׁלֹה וַתָּבֹא בֵּית אֲחִיָּה וַאֲחִיָּהוּ לֹא־יָכֹל לִרְאוֹת כִּי קָמוּ עֵינָיו מִשֵּׂיבוֹ:

ה וַיהוָה אָמַר אֶל־אֲחִיָּהוּ הִנֵּה אֵשֶׁת יָרָבְעָם בָּאָה לִדְרֹשׁ דָּבָר מֵעִמְּךָ אֶל־בְּנָהּ כִּי־חֹלֶה הוּא כָּזֹה וְכָזֶה תְּדַבֵּר אֵלֶיהָ וִיהִי כְבֹאָהּ וְהִיא מִתְנַכֵּרָה:

ו וַיְהִי כִשְׁמֹעַ אֲחִיָּהוּ אֶת־קוֹל רַגְלֶיהָ בָּאָה בַפֶּתַח וַיֹּאמֶר בֹּאִי אֵשֶׁת יָרָבְעָם לָמָּה זֶּה אַתְּ מִתְנַכֵּרָה וְאָנֹכִי שָׁלוּחַ אֵלַיִךְ קָשָׁה:

Melachim I / I Kings
Chapter 14

מלכים א
פרק יד

7 Go tell *Yerovam*: Thus said *Hashem*, the God of *Yisrael*: I raised you up from among the people and made you a ruler over My people *Yisrael*;

ז לְכִי אִמְרִי לְיָרָבְעָם כֹּה־אָמַר יְהֹוָה אֱלֹהֵי יִשְׂרָאֵל יַעַן אֲשֶׁר הֲרִימֹתִיךָ מִתּוֹךְ הָעָם וָאֶתֶּנְךָ נָגִיד עַל עַמִּי יִשְׂרָאֵל:

8 I tore away the kingdom from the House of *David* and gave it to you. But you have not been like My servant *David*, who kept My commandments and followed Me with all his heart, doing only what was right in My sight.

ח וָאֶקְרַע אֶת־הַמַּמְלָכָה מִבֵּית דָּוִד וָאֶתְּנֶהָ לָךְ וְלֹא־הָיִיתָ כְּעַבְדִּי דָוִד אֲשֶׁר שָׁמַר מִצְוֺתַי וַאֲשֶׁר־הָלַךְ אַחֲרַי בְּכָל־לְבָבוֹ לַעֲשׂוֹת רַק הַיָּשָׁר בְּעֵינָי:

9 You have acted worse than all those who preceded you; you have gone and made for yourself other gods and molten images to vex Me; and Me you have cast behind your back.

ט וַתָּרַע לַעֲשׂוֹת מִכֹּל אֲשֶׁר־הָיוּ לְפָנֶיךָ וַתֵּלֶךְ וַתַּעֲשֶׂה־לְּךָ אֱלֹהִים אֲחֵרִים וּמַסֵּכוֹת לְהַכְעִיסֵנִי וְאֹתִי הִשְׁלַכְתָּ אַחֲרֵי גַוֶּךָ:

10 Therefore I will bring disaster upon the House of *Yerovam* and will cut off from *Yerovam* every male, bond and free, in *Yisrael*. I will sweep away the House of *Yerovam* utterly, as dung is swept away.

י לָכֵן הִנְנִי מֵבִיא רָעָה אֶל־בֵּית יָרָבְעָם וְהִכְרַתִּי לְיָרָבְעָם מַשְׁתִּין בְּקִיר עָצוּר וְעָזוּב בְּיִשְׂרָאֵל וּבִעַרְתִּי אַחֲרֵי בֵית־יָרָבְעָם כַּאֲשֶׁר יְבַעֵר הַגָּלָל עַד־תֻּמּוֹ:

11 Anyone belonging to *Yerovam* who dies in the town shall be devoured by dogs; and anyone who dies in the open country shall be eaten by the birds of the air; for *Hashem* has spoken.

יא הַמֵּת לְיָרָבְעָם בָּעִיר יֹאכְלוּ הַכְּלָבִים וְהַמֵּת בַּשָּׂדֶה יֹאכְלוּ עוֹף הַשָּׁמָיִם כִּי יְהֹוָה דִּבֵּר:

12 As for you, go back home; as soon as you set foot in the town, the child will die.

יב וְאַתְּ קוּמִי לְכִי לְבֵיתֵךְ בְּבֹאָה רַגְלַיִךְ הָעִירָה וּמֵת הַיָּלֶד:

13 And all *Yisrael* shall lament over him and bury him; he alone of *Yerovam*'s family shall be brought to burial, for in him alone of the House of *Yerovam* has some devotion been found to *Hashem*, the God of *Yisrael*.

יג וְסָפְדוּ־לוֹ כָל־יִשְׂרָאֵל וְקָבְרוּ אֹתוֹ כִּי־זֶה לְבַדּוֹ יָבֹא לְיָרָבְעָם אֶל־קָבֶר יַעַן נִמְצָא־בוֹ דָּבָר טוֹב אֶל־יְהֹוָה אֱלֹהֵי יִשְׂרָאֵל בְּבֵית יָרָבְעָם:

v'-sa-f'-du LO khol yis-ra-AYL v'-ka-v'-RU o-TO kee ZEH l'-va-DO ya-VO l'-ya-rov-AM el KA-ver YA-an nim-tza VO da-VAR TOV el a-do-NAI e-lo-HAY yis-ra-AYL b'-VAYT ya-rov-AM

14 Moreover, *Hashem* will raise up a king over *Yisrael* who will destroy the House of *Yerovam*, this day and even now.

יד וְהֵקִים יְהֹוָה לוֹ מֶלֶךְ עַל־יִשְׂרָאֵל אֲשֶׁר יַכְרִית אֶת־בֵּית יָרָבְעָם זֶה הַיּוֹם וּמֶה גַּם־עָתָּה:

14:13 He alone of *Yerovam*'s family shall be brought to burial King *Yerovam*'s wife is told that *Yerovam* and his house have been so evil that not only will their son *Aviya* die, but the entire family line will be destroyed. However, *Aviya* will be granted a proper burial as he had "some devotion" towards *Hashem*. Rashi says that the good deed referenced here occurred when his father placed *Aviya* as a guard to prevent the people of the kingdom from making pilgrimages to *Yerushalayim*. *Aviya* not only abandoned his post so that they would be able to go, but he went on a pilgrimage to the holy city himself. This demonstrates both the gravity of the sin of attempting to sever the people's tie to *Yerushalayim*, and also the merit that one can acquire by strengthening this eternal bond.

Melachim I / I Kings
Chapter 14

15 "*Hashem* will strike *Yisrael* until it sways like a reed in water. He will uproot *Yisrael* from this good land that He gave to their fathers, and will scatter them beyond the Euphrates, because they have provoked *Hashem* by the sacred posts that they have made for themselves.

16 He will forsake *Yisrael* because of the sins that *Yerovam* committed and led *Yisrael* to commit."

17 *Yerovam*'s wife got up and left, and she went to *Tirtza*. As soon as she stepped over the threshold of her house, the child died.

18 They buried him and all *Yisrael* lamented over him, in accordance with the word that *Hashem* had spoken through His servant the *Navi Achiya*.

19 The other events of *Yerovam*'s reign, how he fought and how he ruled, are recorded in the Annals of the Kings of *Yisrael*.

20 *Yerovam* reigned twenty-two years; then he slept with his fathers, and his son *Nadav* succeeded him as king.

21 Meanwhile, *Rechovam* son of *Shlomo* had become king in *Yehuda*. *Rechovam* was forty-one years old when he became king, and he reigned seventeen years in *Yerushalayim* – the city *Hashem* had chosen out of all the tribes of *Yisrael* to establish His name there. His mother's name was Naamah the Amonitess.

22 *Yehuda* did what was displeasing to *Hashem*, and angered Him more than their fathers had done by the sins that they committed.

23 They too built for themselves shrines, pillars, and sacred posts on every high hill and under every leafy tree;

24 there were also male prostitutes in the land. [*Yehuda*] imitated all the abhorrent practices of the nations that *Hashem* had dispossessed before the Israelites.

25 In the fifth year of King *Rechovam*, King Shishak of Egypt marched against *Yerushalayim*

טו וְהִכָּה יְהוָה אֶת־יִשְׂרָאֵל כַּאֲשֶׁר יָנוּד הַקָּנֶה בַּמַּיִם וְנָתַשׁ אֶת־יִשְׂרָאֵל מֵעַל הָאֲדָמָה הַטּוֹבָה הַזֹּאת אֲשֶׁר נָתַן לַאֲבוֹתֵיהֶם וְזֵרָם מֵעֵבֶר לַנָּהָר יַעַן אֲשֶׁר עָשׂוּ אֶת־אֲשֵׁרֵיהֶם מַכְעִיסִים אֶת־יְהוָה׃

טז וְיִתֵּן אֶת־יִשְׂרָאֵל בִּגְלַל חַטֹּאות יָרָבְעָם אֲשֶׁר חָטָא וַאֲשֶׁר הֶחֱטִיא אֶת־יִשְׂרָאֵל׃

יז וַתָּקָם אֵשֶׁת יָרָבְעָם וַתֵּלֶךְ וַתָּבֹא תִרְצָתָה הִיא בָּאָה בְסַף־הַבַּיִת וְהַנַּעַר מֵת׃

יח וַיִּקְבְּרוּ אֹתוֹ וַיִּסְפְּדוּ־לוֹ כָּל־יִשְׂרָאֵל כִּדְבַר יְהוָה אֲשֶׁר דִּבֶּר בְּיַד־עַבְדּוֹ אֲחִיָּהוּ הַנָּבִיא׃

יט וְיֶתֶר דִּבְרֵי יָרָבְעָם אֲשֶׁר נִלְחַם וַאֲשֶׁר מָלָךְ הִנָּם כְּתוּבִים עַל־סֵפֶר דִּבְרֵי הַיָּמִים לְמַלְכֵי יִשְׂרָאֵל׃

כ וְהַיָּמִים אֲשֶׁר מָלַךְ יָרָבְעָם עֶשְׂרִים וּשְׁתַּיִם שָׁנָה וַיִּשְׁכַּב עִם־אֲבֹתָיו וַיִּמְלֹךְ נָדָב בְּנוֹ תַּחְתָּיו׃

כא וּרְחַבְעָם בֶּן־שְׁלֹמֹה מָלַךְ בִּיהוּדָה בֶּן־אַרְבָּעִים וְאַחַת שָׁנָה רְחַבְעָם בְּמָלְכוֹ וּשְׁבַע עֶשְׂרֵה שָׁנָה מָלַךְ בִּירוּשָׁלַם הָעִיר אֲשֶׁר־בָּחַר יְהוָה לָשׂוּם אֶת־שְׁמוֹ שָׁם מִכֹּל שִׁבְטֵי יִשְׂרָאֵל וְשֵׁם אִמּוֹ נַעֲמָה הָעַמֹּנִית׃

כב וַיַּעַשׂ יְהוּדָה הָרַע בְּעֵינֵי יְהוָה וַיְקַנְאוּ אֹתוֹ מִכֹּל אֲשֶׁר עָשׂוּ אֲבֹתָם בְּחַטֹּאתָם אֲשֶׁר חָטָאוּ׃

כג וַיִּבְנוּ גַם־הֵמָּה לָהֶם בָּמוֹת וּמַצֵּבוֹת וַאֲשֵׁרִים עַל כָּל־גִּבְעָה גְבֹהָה וְתַחַת כָּל־עֵץ רַעֲנָן׃

כד וְגַם־קָדֵשׁ הָיָה בָאָרֶץ עָשׂוּ כְּכֹל הַתּוֹעֲבֹת הַגּוֹיִם אֲשֶׁר הוֹרִישׁ יְהוָה מִפְּנֵי בְּנֵי יִשְׂרָאֵל׃

כה וַיְהִי בַּשָּׁנָה הַחֲמִישִׁית לַמֶּלֶךְ רְחַבְעָם עָלָה שׁוֹשַׁק [שִׁישַׁק] מֶלֶךְ־מִצְרַיִם עַל־יְרוּשָׁלָ͏ִם׃

Melachim I / I Kings
Chapter 15

מלכים א
פרק טו

26 and carried off the treasures of the House of *Hashem* and the treasures of the royal palace. He carried off everything; he even carried off all the golden shields that *Shlomo* had made.

כו וַיִּקַּח אֶת־אֹצְרוֹת בֵּית־יְהֹוָה וְאֶת־אוֹצְרוֹת בֵּית הַמֶּלֶךְ וְאֶת־הַכֹּל לָקָח וַיִּקַּח אֶת־כָּל־מָגִנֵּי הַזָּהָב אֲשֶׁר עָשָׂה שְׁלֹמֹה:

27 King *Rechovam* had bronze shields made instead, and he entrusted them to the officers of the guard who guarded the entrance to the royal palace.

כז וַיַּעַשׂ הַמֶּלֶךְ רְחַבְעָם תַּחְתָּם מָגִנֵּי נְחֹשֶׁת וְהִפְקִיד עַל־יַד שָׂרֵי הָרָצִים הַשֹּׁמְרִים פֶּתַח בֵּית הַמֶּלֶךְ:

28 Whenever the king went into the House of *Hashem*, the guards would carry them and then bring them back to the armory of the guards.

כח וַיְהִי מִדֵּי־בֹא הַמֶּלֶךְ בֵּית יְהֹוָה יִשָּׂאוּם הָרָצִים וֶהֱשִׁיבוּם אֶל־תָּא הָרָצִים:

29 The other events of *Rechovam*'s reign, and all his actions, are recorded in the Annals of the Kings of *Yehuda*.

כט וְיֶתֶר דִּבְרֵי רְחַבְעָם וְכָל־אֲשֶׁר עָשָׂה הֲלֹא־הֵמָּה כְתוּבִים עַל־סֵפֶר דִּבְרֵי הַיָּמִים לְמַלְכֵי יְהוּדָה:

30 There was continual war between *Rechovam* and *Yerovam*.

ל וּמִלְחָמָה הָיְתָה בֵין־רְחַבְעָם וּבֵין יָרָבְעָם כָּל־הַיָּמִים:

31 *Rechovam* slept with his fathers and was buried with his fathers in the City of *David*; his mother's name was Naamah the Amonitess. His son *Aviyam* succeeded him as king.

לא וַיִּשְׁכַּב רְחַבְעָם עִם־אֲבֹתָיו וַיִּקָּבֵר עִם־אֲבֹתָיו בְּעִיר דָּוִד וְשֵׁם אִמּוֹ נַעֲמָה הָעַמֹּנִית וַיִּמְלֹךְ אֲבִיָּם בְּנוֹ תַּחְתָּיו:

15
1 In the eighteenth year of King *Yerovam* son of Nebat, *Aviyam* became king over *Yehuda*.

טו א וּבִשְׁנַת שְׁמֹנֶה עֶשְׂרֵה לַמֶּלֶךְ יָרָבְעָם בֶּן־נְבָט מָלַךְ אֲבִיָּם עַל־יְהוּדָה:

2 He reigned three years in *Yerushalayim*; his mother's name was Maacah daughter of Abishalom.

sha-LOSH sha-NEEM ma-LAKH bee-ru-sha-LA-im v'-SHAYM i-MO ma-a-KHAH bat a-vee-sha-LOM

ב שָׁלֹשׁ שָׁנִים מָלַךְ בִּירוּשָׁלָ‍ִם וְשֵׁם אִמּוֹ מַעֲכָה בַּת־אֲבִישָׁלוֹם:

3 He continued in all the sins that his father before him had committed; he was not wholehearted with *Hashem* his God, like his father *David*.

ג וַיֵּלֶךְ בְּכָל־חַטֹּאות אָבִיו אֲשֶׁר־עָשָׂה לְפָנָיו וְלֹא־הָיָה לְבָבוֹ שָׁלֵם עִם־יְהֹוָה אֱלֹהָיו כִּלְבַב דָּוִד אָבִיו:

4 Yet, for the sake of *David*, *Hashem* his God gave him a lamp in *Yerushalayim*, by raising up his descendant after him and by preserving *Yerushalayim*.

ד כִּי לְמַעַן דָּוִד נָתַן יְהֹוָה אֱלֹהָיו לוֹ נִיר בִּירוּשָׁלָ‍ִם לְהָקִים אֶת־בְּנוֹ אַחֲרָיו וּלְהַעֲמִיד אֶת־יְרוּשָׁלָ‍ִם:

View of Yerushalayim

15:2 He reigned three years in *Yerushalayim* The Hebrew name of the Holy City of Jerusalem is *Yerushalayim* (ירושלים). This name consists of two important words that capture the essence of the city: *Yira* (יראה), 'fear,' refers to the awe and reverence that everyone is supposed to have for the Almighty God. Indeed, one is able to feel a special connection to *Hashem* in this holy city, which can fill a person with both awe and fear. The second word is *shalom* (שלום), 'peace.' The prayer of all who serve *Hashem* is that He will bless the entire world with peace. This peace emanates from *Yerushalayim*, where everyone comes together in the worship of the Almighty. The best place to establish an awe-inspired connection with *Hashem* and to pray for peace is in His holy city, *Yerushalayim*.

Melachim I / I Kings

Chapter 15

5 For *David* had done what was pleasing to *Hashem* and never turned throughout his life from all that He had commanded him, except in the matter of *Uriya* the Hittite.

6 There was war between *Aviyam* and *Yerovam* all the days of his life.

7 The other events of *Aviyam*'s reign and all his actions are recorded in the Annals of the Kings of *Yehuda*; there was war between *Aviyam* and *Yerovam*.

8 *Aviyam* slept with his fathers; he was buried in the City of *David*, and his son *Asa* succeeded him as king.

9 In the twentieth year of King *Yerovam* of *Yisrael*, *Asa* became king over *Yehuda*.

10 He reigned forty-one years in *Yerushalayim*; his mother's name was Maacah daughter of Abishalom.

11 *Asa* did what was pleasing to *Hashem*, as his father *David* had done.

12 He expelled the male prostitutes from the land, and he removed all the idols that his ancestors had made.

13 He also deposed his mother Maacah from the rank of queen mother, because she had made an abominable thing for [the goddess] Asherah. *Asa* cut down her abominable thing and burnt it in the Wadi Kidron.

14 The shrines, indeed, were not abolished; however, *Asa* was wholehearted with *Hashem* his God all his life.

15 He brought into the House of *Hashem* all the consecrated things of his father and his own consecrated things – silver, gold, and utensils.

16 There was war between *Asa* and King *Basha* of *Yisrael* all their days.

17 King *Basha* of *Yisrael* advanced against *Yehuda*, and he fortified *Rama* to prevent anyone belonging to King *Asa* from going out or coming in.

מלכים א

פרק טו

ה אֲשֶׁר־עָשָׂה דָוִד אֶת־הַיָּשָׁר בְּעֵינֵי יְהֹוָה וְלֹא־סָר מִכֹּל אֲשֶׁר־צִוָּהוּ כֹּל יְמֵי חַיָּיו רַק בִּדְבַר אוּרִיָּה הַחִתִּי:

ו וּמִלְחָמָה הָיְתָה בֵין־רְחַבְעָם וּבֵין יָרָבְעָם כָּל־יְמֵי חַיָּיו:

ז וְיֶתֶר דִּבְרֵי אֲבִיָּם וְכָל־אֲשֶׁר עָשָׂה הֲלֹוא־הֵם כְּתוּבִים עַל־סֵפֶר דִּבְרֵי הַיָּמִים לְמַלְכֵי יְהוּדָה וּמִלְחָמָה הָיְתָה בֵּין אֲבִיָּם וּבֵין יָרָבְעָם:

ח וַיִּשְׁכַּב אֲבִיָּם עִם־אֲבֹתָיו וַיִּקְבְּרוּ אֹתוֹ בְּעִיר דָּוִד וַיִּמְלֹךְ אָסָא בְנוֹ תַּחְתָּיו:

ט וּבִשְׁנַת עֶשְׂרִים לְיָרָבְעָם מֶלֶךְ יִשְׂרָאֵל מָלַךְ אָסָא מֶלֶךְ יְהוּדָה:

י וְאַרְבָּעִים וְאַחַת שָׁנָה מָלַךְ בִּירוּשָׁלָ͏ִם וְשֵׁם אִמּוֹ מַעֲכָה בַּת־אֲבִישָׁלוֹם:

יא וַיַּעַשׂ אָסָא הַיָּשָׁר בְּעֵינֵי יְהֹוָה כְּדָוִד אָבִיו:

יב וַיַּעֲבֵר הַקְּדֵשִׁים מִן־הָאָרֶץ וַיָּסַר אֶת־כָּל־הַגִּלֻּלִים אֲשֶׁר עָשׂוּ אֲבֹתָיו:

יג וְגַם אֶת־מַעֲכָה אִמּוֹ וַיְסִרֶהָ מִגְּבִירָה אֲשֶׁר־עָשְׂתָה מִפְלֶצֶת לָאֲשֵׁרָה וַיִּכְרֹת אָסָא אֶת־מִפְלַצְתָּהּ וַיִּשְׂרֹף בְּנַחַל קִדְרוֹן:

יד וְהַבָּמוֹת לֹא־סָרוּ רַק לְבַב־אָסָא הָיָה שָׁלֵם עִם־יְהֹוָה כָּל־יָמָיו:

טו וַיָּבֵא אֶת־קָדְשֵׁי אָבִיו וקדשו [וְקָדְשֵׁי] בֵּית יְהֹוָה כֶּסֶף וְזָהָב וְכֵלִים:

טז וּמִלְחָמָה הָיְתָה בֵּין אָסָא וּבֵין בַּעְשָׁא מֶלֶךְ־יִשְׂרָאֵל כָּל־יְמֵיהֶם:

יז וַיַּעַל בַּעְשָׁא מֶלֶךְ־יִשְׂרָאֵל עַל־יְהוּדָה וַיִּבֶן אֶת־הָרָמָה לְבִלְתִּי תֵּת יֹצֵא וָבָא לְאָסָא מֶלֶךְ יְהוּדָה:

Melachim I/I Kings
Chapter 15

18 So *Asa* took all the silver and gold that remained in the treasuries of the House of *Hashem* as well as the treasuries of the royal palace, and he entrusted them to his officials. King *Asa* sent them to King Ben-hadad son of Tabrimmon son of Hezion of Aram, who resided in Damascus, with this message:

19 "There is a pact between you and me, and between your father and my father. I herewith send you a gift of silver and gold: Go and break your pact with King *Basha* of *Yisrael*, so that he may withdraw from me."

20 Ben-hadad responded to King *Asa*'s request; he sent his army commanders against the towns of *Yisrael* and captured Ijon, *Dan*, Abel-beth-maacah, and all Chinneroth, as well as all the land of *Naftali*.

21 When *Basha* heard about it, he stopped fortifying *Rama* and remained in *Tirtza*.

22 Then King *Asa* mustered all *Yehuda*, with no exemptions; and they carried away the stones and timber with which *Basha* had fortified *Rama*. With these King *Asa* fortified Geba of *Binyamin*, and *Mitzpa*.

23 All the other events of *Asa*'s reign, and all his exploits, and all his actions, and the towns that he fortified, are recorded in the Annals of the Kings of *Yehuda*. However, in his old age he suffered from a foot ailment.

24 *Asa* slept with his fathers and was buried with his fathers in the city of his father *David*. His son *Yehoshafat* succeeded him as king.

25 *Nadav* son of *Yerovam* had become king over *Yisrael* in the second year of King *Asa* of *Yehuda*, and he reigned over *Yisrael* for two years.

26 He did what was displeasing to *Hashem*; he continued in the ways of his father, in the sins which he caused *Yisrael* to commit.

27 Then *Basha* son of *Achiya*, of the House of *Yissachar*, conspired against him; and *Basha* struck him down at Gibbethon of the Philistines, while *Nadav* and all *Yisrael* were laying siege to Gibbethon.

מלכים א
פרק טו

יח וַיִּקַּח אָסָא אֶת־כָּל־הַכֶּסֶף וְהַזָּהָב הַנּוֹתָרִים בְּאוֹצְרוֹת בֵּית־יְהֹוָה וְאֶת־אוֹצְרוֹת בֵּית מֶלֶךְ [הַמֶּלֶךְ] וַיִּתְּנֵם בְּיַד־עֲבָדָיו וַיִּשְׁלָחֵם הַמֶּלֶךְ אָסָא אֶל־בֶּן־הֲדַד בֶּן־טַבְרִמֹּן בֶּן־חֶזְיוֹן מֶלֶךְ אֲרָם הַיֹּשֵׁב בְּדַמֶּשֶׂק לֵאמֹר:

יט בְּרִית בֵּינִי וּבֵינֶךָ בֵּין אָבִי וּבֵין אָבִיךָ הִנֵּה שָׁלַחְתִּי לְךָ שֹׁחַד כֶּסֶף וְזָהָב לֵךְ הָפֵרָה אֶת־בְּרִיתְךָ אֶת־בַּעְשָׁא מֶלֶךְ־יִשְׂרָאֵל וְיַעֲלֶה מֵעָלָי:

כ וַיִּשְׁמַע בֶּן־הֲדַד אֶל־הַמֶּלֶךְ אָסָא וַיִּשְׁלַח אֶת־שָׂרֵי הַחֲיָלִים אֲשֶׁר־לוֹ עַל־עָרֵי יִשְׂרָאֵל וַיַּךְ אֶת־עִיּוֹן וְאֶת־דָּן וְאֵת אָבֵל בֵּית־מַעֲכָה וְאֵת כָּל־כִּנְרוֹת עַל כָּל־אֶרֶץ נַפְתָּלִי:

כא וַיְהִי כִּשְׁמֹעַ בַּעְשָׁא וַיֶּחְדַּל מִבְּנוֹת אֶת־הָרָמָה וַיֵּשֶׁב בְּתִרְצָה:

כב וְהַמֶּלֶךְ אָסָא הִשְׁמִיעַ אֶת־כָּל־יְהוּדָה אֵין נָקִי וַיִּשְׂאוּ אֶת־אַבְנֵי הָרָמָה וְאֶת־עֵצֶיהָ אֲשֶׁר בָּנָה בַּעְשָׁא וַיִּבֶן בָּם הַמֶּלֶךְ אָסָא אֶת־גֶּבַע בִּנְיָמִן וְאֶת־הַמִּצְפָּה:

כג וְיֶתֶר כָּל־דִּבְרֵי־אָסָא וְכָל־גְּבוּרָתוֹ וְכָל־אֲשֶׁר עָשָׂה וְהֶעָרִים אֲשֶׁר בָּנָה הֲלֹא־הֵמָּה כְתוּבִים עַל־סֵפֶר דִּבְרֵי הַיָּמִים לְמַלְכֵי יְהוּדָה רַק לְעֵת זִקְנָתוֹ חָלָה אֶת־רַגְלָיו:

כד וַיִּשְׁכַּב אָסָא עִם־אֲבֹתָיו וַיִּקָּבֵר עִם־אֲבֹתָיו בְּעִיר דָּוִד אָבִיו וַיִּמְלֹךְ יְהוֹשָׁפָט בְּנוֹ תַּחְתָּיו:

כה וְנָדָב בֶּן־יָרָבְעָם מָלַךְ עַל־יִשְׂרָאֵל בִּשְׁנַת שְׁתַּיִם לְאָסָא מֶלֶךְ יְהוּדָה וַיִּמְלֹךְ עַל־יִשְׂרָאֵל שְׁנָתָיִם:

כו וַיַּעַשׂ הָרַע בְּעֵינֵי יְהֹוָה וַיֵּלֶךְ בְּדֶרֶךְ אָבִיו וּבְחַטָּאתוֹ אֲשֶׁר הֶחֱטִיא אֶת־יִשְׂרָאֵל:

כז וַיִּקְשֹׁר עָלָיו בַּעְשָׁא בֶן־אֲחִיָּה לְבֵית יִשָּׂשכָר וַיַּכֵּהוּ בַעְשָׁא בְּגִבְּתוֹן אֲשֶׁר לַפְּלִשְׁתִּים וְנָדָב וְכָל־יִשְׂרָאֵל צָרִים עַל־גִּבְּתוֹן:

Melachim I / I Kings
Chapter 16

28 *Basha* killed him in the third year of King *Asa* of *Yehuda* and became king in his stead.

29 As soon as he became king, he struck down all the House of *Yerovam*; he did not spare a single soul belonging to *Yerovam* until he destroyed it – in accordance with the word that *Hashem* had spoken through His servant, the *Navi Achiya* the Shilonite

30 because of the sins which *Yerovam* committed and which he caused *Yisrael* to commit thereby vexing *Hashem*, the God of *Yisrael*.

31 The other events of *Nadav*'s reign and all his actions are recorded in the Annals of the Kings of *Yisrael*.

32 There was war between *Asa* and King *Basha* of *Yisrael* all their days.

33 In the third year of King *Asa* of *Yehuda*, *Basha* son of *Achiya* became king in *Tirtza* over all *Yisrael* – for twenty-four years.

34 He did what was displeasing to *Hashem*; he followed the ways of *Yerovam* and the sins which he caused *Yisrael* to commit.

16

1 The word of *Hashem* came to *Yehu* son of *Chanani* against *Basha*:

2 "Because I lifted you up from the dust and made you a ruler over My people *Yisrael*, but you followed the way of *Yerovam* and caused My people *Yisrael* to sin, vexing Me with their sins

3 I am going to sweep away *Basha* and his house. I will make your house like the House of *Yerovam* son of Nebat.

4 Anyone belonging to *Basha* who dies in the town shall be devoured by dogs, and anyone belonging to him who dies in the open country shall be devoured by the birds of the sky."

5 The other events of *Basha*'s reign and his actions and his exploits are recorded in the Annals of the Kings of *Yisrael*.

6 *Basha* slept with his fathers and was buried in *Tirtza*. His son *Eila* succeeded him as king.

מלכים א
פרק טז

כח וַיְמִתֵהוּ בַעְשָׁא בִּשְׁנַת שָׁלֹשׁ לְאָסָא מֶלֶךְ יְהוּדָה וַיִּמְלֹךְ תַּחְתָּיו:

כט וַיְהִי כְמָלְכוֹ הִכָּה אֶת־כָּל־בֵּית יָרָבְעָם לֹא־הִשְׁאִיר כָּל־נְשָׁמָה לְיָרָבְעָם עַד־הִשְׁמִדוֹ כִּדְבַר יְהֹוָה אֲשֶׁר דִּבֶּר בְּיַד־עַבְדּוֹ אֲחִיָּה הַשִּׁילֹנִי:

ל עַל־חַטֹּאות יָרָבְעָם אֲשֶׁר חָטָא וַאֲשֶׁר הֶחֱטִיא אֶת־יִשְׂרָאֵל בְּכַעְסוֹ אֲשֶׁר הִכְעִיס אֶת־יְהֹוָה אֱלֹהֵי יִשְׂרָאֵל:

לא וְיֶתֶר דִּבְרֵי נָדָב וְכָל־אֲשֶׁר עָשָׂה הֲלֹא־הֵם כְּתוּבִים עַל־סֵפֶר דִּבְרֵי הַיָּמִים לְמַלְכֵי יִשְׂרָאֵל:

לב וּמִלְחָמָה הָיְתָה בֵּין אָסָא וּבֵין בַּעְשָׁא מֶלֶךְ־יִשְׂרָאֵל כָּל־יְמֵיהֶם:

לג בִּשְׁנַת שָׁלֹשׁ לְאָסָא מֶלֶךְ יְהוּדָה מָלַךְ בַּעְשָׁא בֶן־אֲחִיָּה עַל־כָּל־יִשְׂרָאֵל בְּתִרְצָה עֶשְׂרִים וְאַרְבַּע שָׁנָה:

לד וַיַּעַשׂ הָרַע בְּעֵינֵי יְהֹוָה וַיֵּלֶךְ בְּדֶרֶךְ יָרָבְעָם וּבְחַטָּאתוֹ אֲשֶׁר הֶחֱטִיא אֶת־יִשְׂרָאֵל:

טז א וַיְהִי דְבַר־יְהֹוָה אֶל־יֵהוּא בֶן־חֲנָנִי עַל־בַּעְשָׁא לֵאמֹר:

ב יַעַן אֲשֶׁר הֲרִימֹתִיךָ מִן־הֶעָפָר וָאֶתֶּנְךָ נָגִיד עַל עַמִּי יִשְׂרָאֵל וַתֵּלֶךְ בְּדֶרֶךְ יָרָבְעָם וַתַּחֲטִא אֶת־עַמִּי יִשְׂרָאֵל לְהַכְעִיסֵנִי בְּחַטֹּאתָם:

ג הִנְנִי מַבְעִיר אַחֲרֵי בַעְשָׁא וְאַחֲרֵי בֵיתוֹ וְנָתַתִּי אֶת־בֵּיתְךָ כְּבֵית יָרָבְעָם בֶּן־נְבָט:

ד הַמֵּת לְבַעְשָׁא בָּעִיר יֹאכְלוּ הַכְּלָבִים וְהַמֵּת לוֹ בַּשָּׂדֶה יֹאכְלוּ עוֹף הַשָּׁמָיִם:

ה וְיֶתֶר דִּבְרֵי בַעְשָׁא וַאֲשֶׁר עָשָׂה וּגְבוּרָתוֹ הֲלֹא־הֵם כְּתוּבִים עַל־סֵפֶר דִּבְרֵי הַיָּמִים לְמַלְכֵי יִשְׂרָאֵל:

ו וַיִּשְׁכַּב בַּעְשָׁא עִם־אֲבֹתָיו וַיִּקָּבֵר בְּתִרְצָה וַיִּמְלֹךְ אֵלָה בְנוֹ תַּחְתָּיו:

856

Melachim I / I Kings
Chapter 16

מלכים א
פרק טז

7 But the word of *Hashem* had come through the *Navi Yehu* son of *Chanani* against *Basha* and against his house, that it would fare like the House of *Yerovam*, which he himself had struck down, because of all the evil he did which was displeasing to *Hashem*, vexing him with his deeds.

ז וְגַם בְּיַד־יֵהוּא בֶן־חֲנָנִי הַנָּבִיא דְּבַר־יְהֹוָה הָיָה אֶל־בַּעְשָׁא וְאֶל־בֵּיתוֹ וְעַל כָּל־הָרָעָה ׀ אֲשֶׁר־עָשָׂה ׀ בְּעֵינֵי יְהֹוָה לְהַכְעִיסוֹ בְּמַעֲשֵׂה יָדָיו לִהְיוֹת כְּבֵית יָרָבְעָם וְעַל אֲשֶׁר־הִכָּה אֹתוֹ:

8 In the twenty-sixth year of King *Asa* of *Yehuda*, *Eila* son of *Basha* became king over *Yisrael*, at *Tirtza* — for two years.

ח בִּשְׁנַת עֶשְׂרִים וָשֵׁשׁ שָׁנָה לְאָסָא מֶלֶךְ יְהוּדָה מָלַךְ אֵלָה בֶן־בַּעְשָׁא עַל־יִשְׂרָאֵל בְּתִרְצָה שְׁנָתָיִם:

9 His officer *Zimri*, commander of half the chariotry, committed treason against him while he was at *Tirtza* drinking himself drunk in the house of Arza, who was in charge of the palace at *Tirtza*.

ט וַיִּקְשֹׁר עָלָיו עַבְדּוֹ זִמְרִי שַׂר מַחֲצִית הָרָכֶב וְהוּא בְתִרְצָה שֹׁתֶה שִׁכּוֹר בֵּית אַרְצָא אֲשֶׁר עַל־הַבַּיִת בְּתִרְצָה:

10 *Zimri* entered, struck him down, and killed him; he succeeded him as king in the twenty-seventh year of King *Asa* of *Yehuda*.

י וַיָּבֹא זִמְרִי וַיַּכֵּהוּ וַיְמִיתֵהוּ בִּשְׁנַת עֶשְׂרִים וָשֶׁבַע לְאָסָא מֶלֶךְ יְהוּדָה וַיִּמְלֹךְ תַּחְתָּיו:

11 No sooner had he become king and ascended the throne than he struck down all the House of *Basha*; he did not leave a single male of his, nor any kinsman or friend.

יא וַיְהִי בְמָלְכוֹ כְּשִׁבְתּוֹ עַל־כִּסְאוֹ הִכָּה אֶת־כָּל־בֵּית בַּעְשָׁא לֹא־הִשְׁאִיר לוֹ מַשְׁתִּין בְּקִיר וְגֹאֲלָיו וְרֵעֵהוּ:

12 Thus *Zimri* destroyed all the House of *Basha*, in accordance with the word that *Hashem* had spoken through the *Navi Yehu*

יב וַיַּשְׁמֵד זִמְרִי אֵת כָּל־בֵּית בַּעְשָׁא כִּדְבַר יְהֹוָה אֲשֶׁר דִּבֶּר אֶל־בַּעְשָׁא בְּיַד יֵהוּא הַנָּבִיא:

13 because of the sinful acts which *Basha* and his son *Eila* committed, and which they caused *Yisrael* to commit, vexing *Hashem*, the God of *Yisrael*, with their false gods.

יג אֶל כָּל־חַטֹּאות בַּעְשָׁא וְחַטֹּאות אֵלָה בְנוֹ אֲשֶׁר חָטְאוּ וַאֲשֶׁר הֶחֱטִיאוּ אֶת־יִשְׂרָאֵל לְהַכְעִיס אֶת־יְהֹוָה אֱלֹהֵי יִשְׂרָאֵל בְּהַבְלֵיהֶם:

14 The other events of *Eila*'s reign and all his actions are recorded in the Annals of the Kings of *Yisrael*.

יד וְיֶתֶר דִּבְרֵי אֵלָה וְכָל־אֲשֶׁר עָשָׂה הֲלוֹא־הֵם כְּתוּבִים עַל־סֵפֶר דִּבְרֵי הַיָּמִים לְמַלְכֵי יִשְׂרָאֵל:

15 During the twenty-seventh year of King *Asa* of *Yehuda*, *Zimri* reigned in *Tirtza* for seven days. At the time, the troops were encamped at Gibbethon of the Philistines.

טו בִּשְׁנַת עֶשְׂרִים וָשֶׁבַע שָׁנָה לְאָסָא מֶלֶךְ יְהוּדָה מָלַךְ זִמְרִי שִׁבְעַת יָמִים בְּתִרְצָה וְהָעָם חֹנִים עַל־גִּבְּתוֹן אֲשֶׁר לַפְּלִשְׁתִּים:

16 When the troops who were encamped there learned that *Zimri* had committed treason and had struck down the king, that very day, in the camp, all *Yisrael* acclaimed the army commander *Omri* king over *Yisrael*.

טז וַיִּשְׁמַע הָעָם הַחֹנִים לֵאמֹר קָשַׁר זִמְרִי וְגַם הִכָּה אֶת־הַמֶּלֶךְ וַיַּמְלִכוּ כָל־יִשְׂרָאֵל אֶת־עָמְרִי שַׂר־צָבָא עַל־יִשְׂרָאֵל בַּיּוֹם הַהוּא בַּמַּחֲנֶה:

17 *Omri* and all *Yisrael* then withdrew from Gibbethon and laid siege to *Tirtza*.

יז וַיַּעֲלֶה עָמְרִי וְכָל־יִשְׂרָאֵל עִמּוֹ מִגִּבְּתוֹן וַיָּצֻרוּ עַל־תִּרְצָה:

Melachim I/I Kings
Chapter 16

מלכים א
פרק טז

18 When *Zimri* saw that the town was taken, he went into the citadel of the royal palace and burned down the royal palace over himself. And so he died

יח וַיְהִי כִּרְאוֹת זִמְרִי כִּי־נִלְכְּדָה הָעִיר וַיָּבֹא אֶל־אַרְמוֹן בֵּית־הַמֶּלֶךְ וַיִּשְׂרֹף עָלָיו אֶת־בֵּית־מֶלֶךְ בָּאֵשׁ וַיָּמֹת:

19 because of the sins which he committed and caused *Yisrael* to commit, doing what was displeasing to *Hashem* and following the ways of *Yerovam*.

יט עַל־חַטֹּאתָו [חַטֹּאתָיו] אֲשֶׁר חָטָא לַעֲשׂוֹת הָרַע בְּעֵינֵי יְהוָה לָלֶכֶת בְּדֶרֶךְ יָרָבְעָם וּבְחַטָּאתוֹ אֲשֶׁר עָשָׂה לְהַחֲטִיא אֶת־יִשְׂרָאֵל:

20 The other events of *Zimri*'s reign, and the treason which he committed, are recorded in the Annals of the Kings of *Yisrael*.

כ וְיֶתֶר דִּבְרֵי זִמְרִי וְקִשְׁרוֹ אֲשֶׁר קָשָׁר הֲלֹא־הֵם כְּתוּבִים עַל־סֵפֶר דִּבְרֵי הַיָּמִים לְמַלְכֵי יִשְׂרָאֵל:

21 Then the people of *Yisrael* split into two factions: a part of the people followed Tibni son of Ginath to make him king, and the other part followed *Omri*.

כא אָז יֵחָלֵק הָעָם יִשְׂרָאֵל לַחֵצִי חֲצִי הָעָם הָיָה אַחֲרֵי תִבְנִי בֶן־גִּינַת לְהַמְלִיכוֹ וְהַחֲצִי אַחֲרֵי עָמְרִי:

22 Those who followed *Omri* proved stronger than those who followed Tibni son of Ginath; Tibni died and *Omri* became king.

כב וַיֶּחֱזַק הָעָם אֲשֶׁר אַחֲרֵי עָמְרִי אֶת־הָעָם אֲשֶׁר אַחֲרֵי תִּבְנִי בֶן־גִּינַת וַיָּמָת תִּבְנִי וַיִּמְלֹךְ עָמְרִי:

23 In the thirty-first year of King *Asa* of *Yehuda*, *Omri* became king over *Yisrael* – for twelve years. He reigned in *Tirtza* six years.

כג בִּשְׁנַת שְׁלֹשִׁים וְאַחַת שָׁנָה לְאָסָא מֶלֶךְ יְהוּדָה מָלַךְ עָמְרִי עַל־יִשְׂרָאֵל שְׁתֵּים עֶשְׂרֵה שָׁנָה בְּתִרְצָה מָלַךְ שֵׁשׁ־שָׁנִים:

24 Then he bought the hill of *Shomron* from Shemer for two *kikarim* of silver; he built [a town] on the hill and named the town which he built *Shomron*, after Shemer, the owner of the hill.

כד וַיִּקֶן אֶת־הָהָר שֹׁמְרוֹן מֵאֵת שֶׁמֶר בְּכִכְּרַיִם כָּסֶף וַיִּבֶן אֶת־הָהָר וַיִּקְרָא אֶת־שֵׁם הָעִיר אֲשֶׁר בָּנָה עַל שֶׁם־שֶׁמֶר אֲדֹנֵי הָהָר שֹׁמְרוֹן:

va-YI-ken et ha-HAR sho-m'-RON MAY-et SHE-mer b'-khi-k'-RA-yim KA-sef va-YI-ven et ha-HAR va-yik-RA et SHAYM ha-EER a-SHER ba-NAH AL shem SHE-mer a-do-NAY ha-HAR sho-m'-RON

25 *Omri* did what was displeasing to *Hashem*; he was worse than all who preceded him.

כה וַיַּעֲשֶׂה עָמְרִי הָרַע בְּעֵינֵי יְהוָה וַיָּרַע מִכֹּל אֲשֶׁר לְפָנָיו:

16:24 Then he bought the hill of *Shomron* from Shemer for two talents of silver Samaria, known in Hebrew as *Shomron*, is an important part of both the biblical heartland and the modern State of Israel. Omri purchases this land to be the capital of the kingdom of Yisrael. The area of *Shomron*, which comprises over eleven percent of the modern State of Israel, was liberated during the Six Day War and is home to many vibrant communities; some of the more well-known ones include Ariel, Karnei Shomron, Elon Moreh and Itamar. As it is located in the middle of Israel it plays a vital role in the spirituality, economics and security of the country. Ruling in a period of much upheaval, when assassinations of the kings of the northern Kingdom prevented any dynasty from lasting very long, *Omri* is notable as the first monarch in a family that ruled for four generations. The Talmudic sages (*Sanhedrin* 102b) ask why Omri deserved this privilege, despite the fact that he was worse than the kings who preceded him (verse 25) as he had seen their punishment and yet continued their evil practices. They answer that *Omri*'s one redeeming merit was that he purchased the city of *Shomron*. Because he added this important city to the Land of Israel, he deserved the merit of having his family rule over Israel for 48 years.

View of Shomron

Melachim I / I Kings
Chapter 17

26 He followed all the ways of *Yerovam* son of Nebat and the sins which he committed and caused *Yisrael* to commit, vexing *Hashem*, the God of *Yisrael*, with their futilities.

כו וַיֵּ֗לֶךְ בְּכׇל־דֶּ֙רֶךְ֙ יָרׇבְעָ֣ם בֶּן־נְבָ֔ט וּבְחַטֹּאתָ֖יו [וּבְחַטֹּאתוֹ֙] אֲשֶׁ֣ר הֶחֱטִ֔יא אֶת־יִשְׂרָאֵ֑ל לְהַכְעִ֗יס אֶת־יְהֹוָ֛ה אֱלֹהֵ֥י יִשְׂרָאֵ֖ל בְּהַבְלֵיהֶֽם׃

27 The other events of *Omri's* reign, [and] his actions, and the exploits he performed, are recorded in the Annals of the Kings of *Yisrael*.

כז וְיֶ֨תֶר דִּבְרֵ֤י עׇמְרִי֙ אֲשֶׁ֣ר עָשָׂ֔ה וּגְבוּרָת֖וֹ אֲשֶׁ֣ר עָשָׂ֑ה הֲלֹא־הֵ֣ם כְּתוּבִ֗ים עַל־סֵ֛פֶר דִּבְרֵ֥י הַיָּמִ֖ים לְמַלְכֵ֥י יִשְׂרָאֵֽל׃

28 *Omri* slept with his fathers and was buried in *Shomron*; and his son *Achav* succeeded him as king.

כח וַיִּשְׁכַּ֤ב עׇמְרִי֙ עִם־אֲבֹתָ֔יו וַיִּקָּבֵ֖ר בְּשֹׁמְר֑וֹן וַיִּמְלֹ֛ךְ אַחְאָ֥ב בְּנ֖וֹ תַּחְתָּֽיו׃

29 *Achav* son of *Omri* became king over *Yisrael* in the thirty-eighth year of King *Asa* of *Yehuda*, and *Achav* son of *Omri* reigned over *Yisrael* in *Shomron* for twenty-two years.

כט וְאַחְאָ֣ב בֶּן־עׇמְרִ֗י מָלַךְ֙ עַל־יִשְׂרָאֵ֔ל בִּשְׁנַ֨ת שְׁלֹשִׁ֤ים וּשְׁמֹנֶה֙ שָׁנָ֔ה לְאָסָ֖א מֶ֣לֶךְ יְהוּדָ֑ה וַ֠יִּמְלֹ֠ךְ אַחְאָ֨ב בֶּן־עׇמְרִ֤י עַל־יִשְׂרָאֵל֙ בְּשֹׁ֣מְר֔וֹן עֶשְׂרִ֥ים וּשְׁתַּ֖יִם שָׁנָֽה׃

30 *Achav* son of *Omri* did what was displeasing to *Hashem*, more than all who preceded him.

ל וַיַּ֨עַשׂ אַחְאָ֧ב בֶּן־עׇמְרִ֛י הָרַ֖ע בְּעֵינֵ֣י יְהֹוָ֑ה מִכֹּ֖ל אֲשֶׁ֥ר לְפָנָֽיו׃

31 Not content to follow the sins of *Yerovam* son of Nebat, he took as wife Jezebel daughter of King Ethbaal of the Phoenicians, and he went and served Baal and worshiped him.

לא וַיְהִי֙ הֲנָקֵ֣ל לֶכְתּ֔וֹ בְּחַטֹּ֖אות יָרׇבְעָ֣ם בֶּן־נְבָ֑ט וַיִּקַּ֨ח אִשָּׁ֜ה אֶת־אִיזֶ֗בֶל בַּת־אֶתְבַּ֙עַל֙ מֶ֣לֶךְ צִידֹנִ֔ים וַיֵּ֙לֶךְ֙ וַֽיַּעֲבֹ֣ד אֶת־הַבַּ֔עַל וַיִּשְׁתַּ֖חוּ לֽוֹ׃

32 He erected a altar to Baal in the temple of Baal which he built in *Shomron*.

לב וַיָּ֥קֶם מִזְבֵּ֖חַ לַבָּ֑עַל בֵּ֣ית הַבַּ֔עַל אֲשֶׁ֥ר בָּנָ֖ה בְּשֹׁמְרֽוֹן׃

33 *Achav* also made a sacred post. *Achav* did more to vex *Hashem*, the God of *Yisrael*, than all the kings of *Yisrael* who preceded him.

לג וַיַּ֥עַשׂ אַחְאָ֖ב אֶת־הָאֲשֵׁרָ֑ה וַיּ֨וֹסֶף אַחְאָ֜ב לַעֲשׂ֗וֹת לְהַכְעִיס֙ אֶת־יְהֹוָ֣ה אֱלֹהֵ֣י יִשְׂרָאֵ֔ל מִכֹּ֗ל מַלְכֵ֣י יִשְׂרָאֵ֔ל אֲשֶׁ֥ר הָי֖וּ לְפָנָֽיו׃

34 During his reign, Hiel the Beit Elite fortified *Yericho*. He laid its foundations at the cost of *Aviram* his first-born, and set its gates in place at the cost of Segub his youngest, in accordance with the words that *Hashem* had spoken through *Yehoshua* son of *Nun*.

לד בְּיָמָ֞יו בָּנָ֥ה חִיאֵ֛ל בֵּ֥ית הָאֱלִ֖י אֶת־יְרִיח֑וֹ בַּאֲבִירָ֤ם בְּכֹרוֹ֙ יִסְּדָ֔הּ וּבִשְׂגִ֥יב [וּבִשְׂג֛וּב] צְעִיר֖וֹ הִצִּ֣יב דְּלָתֶ֑יהָ כִּדְבַ֣ר יְהֹוָ֔ה אֲשֶׁ֣ר דִּבֶּ֔ר בְּיַ֖ד יְהוֹשֻׁ֥עַ בִּן־נֽוּן׃

17

1 *Eliyahu* the Tishbite, an inhabitant of *Gilad*, said to *Achav*, "As *Hashem* lives, the God of *Yisrael* whom I serve, there will be no dew or rain except at my bidding."

יז א וַיֹּ֩אמֶר֩ אֵלִיָּ֨הוּ הַתִּשְׁבִּ֜י מִתֹּשָׁבֵ֣י גִלְעָד֮ אֶל־אַחְאָב֒ חַי־יְהֹוָ֞ה אֱלֹהֵ֤י יִשְׂרָאֵל֙ אֲשֶׁ֣ר עָמַ֣דְתִּי לְפָנָ֔יו אִם־יִהְיֶ֛ה הַשָּׁנִ֥ים הָאֵ֖לֶּה טַ֣ל וּמָטָ֑ר כִּ֖י אִם־לְפִ֥י דְבָרִֽי׃

2 The word of *Hashem* came to him:

ב וַיְהִ֥י דְבַר־יְהֹוָ֖ה אֵלָ֥יו לֵאמֹֽר׃

3 "Leave this place; turn eastward and go into hiding by the Wadi Cherith, which is east of the *Yarden*.

ג לֵ֣ךְ מִזֶּ֔ה וּפָנִ֥יתָ לְּךָ֖ קֵ֑דְמָה וְנִסְתַּרְתָּ֙ בְּנַ֣חַל כְּרִ֔ית אֲשֶׁ֖ר עַל־פְּנֵ֥י הַיַּרְדֵּֽן׃

4 You will drink from the wadi, and I have commanded the ravens to feed you there."

ד וְהָיָ֖ה מֵהַנַּ֣חַל תִּשְׁתֶּ֑ה וְאֶת־הָעֹרְבִ֣ים צִוִּ֔יתִי לְכַלְכֶּלְךָ֖ שָֽׁם׃

Melachim I / I Kings
Chapter 17

מלכים א
פרק יז

5 He proceeded to do as *Hashem* had bidden: he went, and he stayed by the Wadi Cherith, which is east of the *Yarden*.

ה וַיֵּלֶךְ וַיַּעַשׂ כִּדְבַר יְהֹוָה וַיֵּלֶךְ וַיֵּשֶׁב בְּנַחַל כְּרִית אֲשֶׁר עַל־פְּנֵי הַיַּרְדֵּן:

6 The ravens brought him bread and meat every morning and every evening, and he drank from the wadi.

ו וְהָעֹרְבִים מְבִיאִים לוֹ לֶחֶם וּבָשָׂר בַּבֹּקֶר וְלֶחֶם וּבָשָׂר בָּעָרֶב וּמִן־הַנַּחַל יִשְׁתֶּה:

7 After some time the wadi dried up, because there was no rain in the land.

ז וַיְהִי מִקֵּץ יָמִים וַיִּיבַשׁ הַנָּחַל כִּי לֹא־הָיָה גֶשֶׁם בָּאָרֶץ:

8 And the word of *Hashem* came to him:

ח וַיְהִי דְבַר־יְהֹוָה אֵלָיו לֵאמֹר:

9 "Go at once to Zarephath of Sidon, and stay there; I have designated a widow there to feed you."

ט קוּם לֵךְ צָרְפַתָה אֲשֶׁר לְצִידוֹן וְיָשַׁבְתָּ שָׁם הִנֵּה צִוִּיתִי שָׁם אִשָּׁה אַלְמָנָה לְכַלְכְּלֶךָ:

10 So he went at once to Zarephath. When he came to the entrance of the town, a widow was there gathering wood. He called out to her, "Please bring me a little water in your pitcher, and let me drink."

י וַיָּקָם וַיֵּלֶךְ צָרְפַתָה וַיָּבֹא אֶל־פֶּתַח הָעִיר וְהִנֵּה־שָׁם אִשָּׁה אַלְמָנָה מְקֹשֶׁשֶׁת עֵצִים וַיִּקְרָא אֵלֶיהָ וַיֹּאמַר קְחִי־נָא לִי מְעַט־מַיִם בַּכְּלִי וְאֶשְׁתֶּה:

11 As she went to fetch it, he called out to her, "Please bring along a piece of bread for me."

יא וַתֵּלֶךְ לָקַחַת וַיִּקְרָא אֵלֶיהָ וַיֹּאמַר לִקְחִי־נָא לִי פַּת־לֶחֶם בְּיָדֵךְ:

12 "As *Hashem* your God lives," she replied, "I have nothing baked, nothing but a handful of flour in a jar and a little oil in a jug. I am just gathering a couple of sticks, so that I can go home and prepare it for me and my son; we shall eat it and then we shall die."

יב וַתֹּאמֶר חַי־יְהֹוָה אֱלֹהֶיךָ אִם־יֶשׁ־לִי מָעוֹג כִּי אִם־מְלֹא כַף־קֶמַח בַּכַּד וּמְעַט־שֶׁמֶן בַּצַּפָּחַת וְהִנְנִי מְקֹשֶׁשֶׁת שְׁנַיִם עֵצִים וּבָאתִי וַעֲשִׂיתִיהוּ לִי וְלִבְנִי וַאֲכַלְנֻהוּ וָמָתְנוּ:

13 "Don't be afraid," said *Eliyahu* to her. "Go and do as you have said; but first make me a small cake from what you have there, and bring it out to me; then make some for yourself and your son.

יג וַיֹּאמֶר אֵלֶיהָ אֵלִיָּהוּ אַל־תִּירְאִי בֹּאִי עֲשִׂי כִדְבָרֵךְ אַךְ עֲשִׂי־לִי מִשָּׁם עֻגָה קְטַנָּה בָרִאשֹׁנָה וְהוֹצֵאת לִי וְלָךְ וְלִבְנֵךְ תַּעֲשִׂי בָּאַחֲרֹנָה:

14 For thus said *Hashem*, the God of *Yisrael*: The jar of flour shall not give out and the jug of oil shall not fail until the day that *Hashem* sends rain upon the ground."

יד כִּי כֹה אָמַר יְהֹוָה אֱלֹהֵי יִשְׂרָאֵל כַּד הַקֶּמַח לֹא תִכְלָה וְצַפַּחַת הַשֶּׁמֶן לֹא תֶחְסָר עַד יוֹם תתן [תֵּת־] יְהֹוָה גֶּשֶׁם עַל־פְּנֵי הָאֲדָמָה:

KEE KHO a-MAR a-do-NAI e-lo-HAY yis-ra-AYL KAD ha-KE-makh LO tikh-LAH v'-tza-PA-khat ha-SHE-men LO tekh-SAR AD YOM tayt a-do-NAI GE-shem al p'-NAY ha-a-da-MAH

17:14 The jar of flour shall not give out and the jug of oil shall not fail The contents of the widow's jug of oil and jar of flour, both of which are close to empty, do not diminish during the entire period of drought. This miracle follows a familiar pattern. In general, when *Hashem* performs miracles, He does so by using that which is already in existence. Thus, He does not create flour or oil where there is nothing, but rather extends the supply of the quantity that is already present. This is similar to the miracles performed in the establishment and subsequent flourishing of the State of Israel. The People of Israel had to do real work, and

An Earthenware pot from King David era

Melachim I / I Kings
Chapter 18

15 She went and did as *Eliyahu* had spoken, and she and he and her household had food for a long time.

16 The jar of flour did not give out, nor did the jug of oil fail, just as *Hashem* had spoken through *Eliyahu*.

17 After a while, the son of the mistress of the house fell sick, and his illness grew worse, until he had no breath left in him.

18 She said to *Eliyahu*, "What harm have I done you, O man of *Hashem*, that you should come here to recall my sin and cause the death of my son?"

19 "Give me the boy," he said to her; and taking him from her arms, he carried him to the upper chamber where he was staying, and laid him down on his own bed.

20 He cried out to *Hashem* and said, "*Hashem* my God, will You bring calamity upon this widow whose guest I am, and let her son die?"

21 Then he stretched out over the child three times, and cried out to *Hashem*, saying, "*Hashem* my God, let this child's life return to his body!"

22 *Hashem* heard *Eliyahu*'s plea; the child's life returned to his body, and he revived.

23 *Eliyahu* picked up the child and brought him down from the upper room into the main room, and gave him to his mother. "See," said *Eliyahu*, "your son is alive."

24 And the woman answered *Eliyahu*, "Now I know that you are a man of *Hashem* and that the word of *Hashem* is truly in your mouth."

18 1 Much later, in the third year, the word of *Hashem* came to *Eliyahu*: "Go, appear before *Achav*; then I will send rain upon the earth."

2 Thereupon *Eliyahu* set out to appear before *Achav*. The famine was severe in *Shomron*.

---

to be willing to give up their lives for a Jewish State in the Land of Israel. After they had done so, God then met the people more than halfway by performing miracles of truly biblical proportions. For example, though the Jewish people have always been vastly outnumbered by their enemies, *Hashem* continually grants victory to the Israel Defense Forces. Similarly, the massive ingathering of the exiles from all corners of the Earth is a miraculous fulfillment of the biblical prophecy, "Your children shall return to their country" (Jeremiah 31:16).

Melachim I / I Kings
Chapter 18

3 Achav had summoned *Ovadya*, the steward of the palace. *Ovadya* revered *Hashem* greatly.

4 When Jezebel was killing off the *Neviim* of *Hashem*, *Ovadya* had taken a hundred *Neviim* and hidden them, fifty to a cave, and provided them with food and drink.

5 And *Achav* had said to *Ovadya*, "Go through the land, to all the springs of water and to all the wadis. Perhaps we shall find some grass to keep horses and mules alive, so that we are not left without beasts."

6 They divided the country between them to explore it, *Achav* going alone in one direction and *Ovadya* going alone in another direction.

7 *Ovadya* was on the road, when *Eliyahu* suddenly confronted him. [*Ovadya*] recognized him and flung himself on his face, saying, "Is that you, my lord *Eliyahu*?"

8 "Yes, it is I," he answered. "Go tell your lord: *Eliyahu* is here!"

9 But he said, "What wrong have I done, that you should hand your servant over to *Achav* to be killed?

10 As *Hashem* your God lives, there is no nation or kingdom to which my lord has not sent to look for you; and when they said, 'He is not here,' he made that kingdom or nation swear that you could not be found.

11 And now you say, 'Go tell your lord: *Eliyahu* is here!'

12 When I leave you, the spirit of *Hashem* will carry you off I don't know where; and when I come and tell *Achav* and he does not find you, he will kill me. Yet your servant has revered *Hashem* from my youth.

13 My lord has surely been told what I did when Jezebel was killing the *Neviim* of *Hashem*, how I hid a hundred of the *Neviim* of *Hashem*, fifty men to a cave, and provided them with food and drink.

מלכים א
פרק יח

ג וַיִּקְרָא אַחְאָב אֶל־עֹבַדְיָהוּ אֲשֶׁר עַל־הַבָּיִת וְעֹבַדְיָהוּ הָיָה יָרֵא אֶת־יְהֹוָה מְאֹד:

ד וַיְהִי בְּהַכְרִית אִיזֶבֶל אֵת נְבִיאֵי יְהֹוָה וַיִּקַּח עֹבַדְיָהוּ מֵאָה נְבִאִים וַיַּחְבִּיאֵם חֲמִשִּׁים אִישׁ בַּמְּעָרָה וְכִלְכְּלָם לֶחֶם וָמָיִם:

ה וַיֹּאמֶר אַחְאָב אֶל־עֹבַדְיָהוּ לֵךְ בָּאָרֶץ אֶל־כָּל־מַעְיְנֵי הַמַּיִם וְאֶל כָּל־הַנְּחָלִים אוּלַי נִמְצָא חָצִיר וּנְחַיֶּה סוּס וָפֶרֶד וְלוֹא נַכְרִית מֵהַבְּהֵמָה:

ו וַיְחַלְּקוּ לָהֶם אֶת־הָאָרֶץ לַעֲבָר־בָּהּ אַחְאָב הָלַךְ בְּדֶרֶךְ אֶחָד לְבַדּוֹ וְעֹבַדְיָהוּ הָלַךְ בְּדֶרֶךְ־אֶחָד לְבַדּוֹ:

ז וַיְהִי עֹבַדְיָהוּ בַּדֶּרֶךְ וְהִנֵּה אֵלִיָּהוּ לִקְרָאתוֹ וַיַּכִּרֵהוּ וַיִּפֹּל עַל־פָּנָיו וַיֹּאמֶר הַאַתָּה זֶה אֲדֹנִי אֵלִיָּהוּ:

ח וַיֹּאמֶר לוֹ אָנִי לֵךְ אֱמֹר לַאדֹנֶיךָ הִנֵּה אֵלִיָּהוּ:

ט וַיֹּאמֶר מֶה חָטָאתִי כִּי־אַתָּה נֹתֵן אֶת־עַבְדְּךָ בְּיַד־אַחְאָב לַהֲמִיתֵנִי:

י חַי יְהֹוָה אֱלֹהֶיךָ אִם־יֶשׁ־גּוֹי וּמַמְלָכָה אֲשֶׁר לֹא־שָׁלַח אֲדֹנִי שָׁם לְבַקֶּשְׁךָ וְאָמְרוּ אָיִן וְהִשְׁבִּיעַ אֶת־הַמַּמְלָכָה וְאֶת־הַגּוֹי כִּי לֹא יִמְצָאֶכָּה:

יא וְעַתָּה אַתָּה אֹמֵר לֵךְ אֱמֹר לַאדֹנֶיךָ הִנֵּה אֵלִיָּהוּ:

יב וְהָיָה אֲנִי ׀ אֵלֵךְ מֵאִתָּךְ וְרוּחַ יְהֹוָה ׀ יִשָּׂאֲךָ עַל אֲשֶׁר לֹא־אֵדָע וּבָאתִי לְהַגִּיד לְאַחְאָב וְלֹא יִמְצָאֲךָ וַהֲרָגָנִי וְעַבְדְּךָ יָרֵא אֶת־יְהֹוָה מִנְּעֻרָי:

יג הֲלֹא־הֻגַּד לַאדֹנִי אֵת אֲשֶׁר־עָשִׂיתִי בַּהֲרֹג אִיזֶבֶל אֵת נְבִיאֵי יְהֹוָה וָאַחְבִּא מִנְּבִיאֵי יְהֹוָה מֵאָה אִישׁ חֲמִשִּׁים חֲמִשִּׁים אִישׁ בַּמְּעָרָה וָאֲכַלְכְּלֵם לֶחֶם וָמָיִם:

Melachim I / I Kings
Chapter 18

14 And now you say, 'Go tell your lord: *Eliyahu* is here.' Why, he will kill me!"

15 *Eliyahu* replied, "As the Lord of Hosts lives, whom I serve, I will appear before him this very day."

16 *Ovadya* went to find *Achav*, and informed him; and *Achav* went to meet *Eliyahu*.

17 When *Achav* caught sight of *Eliyahu*, *Achav* said to him, "Is that you, you troubler of *Yisrael*?"

18 He retorted, "It is not I who have brought trouble on *Yisrael*, but you and your father's House, by forsaking the commandments of *Hashem* and going after the Baalim.

19 Now summon all *Yisrael* to join me at Mount *Carmel*, together with the four hundred and fifty *Neviim* of Baal and the four hundred *Neviim* of Asherah, who eat at Jezebel's table."

20 *Achav* sent orders to all the Israelites and gathered the *Neviim* at Mount *Carmel*.

21 *Eliyahu* approached all the people and said, "How long will you keep hopping between two opinions? If *Hashem* is *Hashem*, follow Him; and if Baal, follow him!" But the people answered him not a word.

22 Then *Eliyahu* said to the people, "I am the only *Navi* of *Hashem* left, while the *Neviim* of Baal are four hundred and fifty men.

23 Let two young bulls be given to us. Let them choose one bull, cut it up, and lay it on the wood, but let them not apply fire; I will prepare the other bull, and lay it on the wood, and will not apply fire.

24 You will then invoke your god by name, and I will invoke *Hashem* by name; and let us agree: the god who responds with fire, that one is *Hashem*." And all the people answered, "Very good!"

25 *Eliyahu* said to the *Neviim* of Baal, "Choose one bull and prepare it first, for you are the majority; invoke your god by name, but apply no fire."

מלכים א
פרק יח

יד וְעַתָּה אַתָּה אֹמֵר לֵךְ אֱמֹר לַאדֹנֶיךָ הִנֵּה אֵלִיָּהוּ וַהֲרָגָנִי׃

טו וַיֹּאמֶר אֵלִיָּהוּ חַי יְהוָה צְבָאוֹת אֲשֶׁר עָמַדְתִּי לְפָנָיו כִּי הַיּוֹם אֵרָאֶה אֵלָיו׃

טז וַיֵּלֶךְ עֹבַדְיָהוּ לִקְרַאת אַחְאָב וַיַּגֶּד־לוֹ וַיֵּלֶךְ אַחְאָב לִקְרַאת אֵלִיָּהוּ׃

יז וַיְהִי כִּרְאוֹת אַחְאָב אֶת־אֵלִיָּהוּ וַיֹּאמֶר אַחְאָב אֵלָיו הַאַתָּה זֶה עֹכֵר יִשְׂרָאֵל׃

יח וַיֹּאמֶר לֹא עָכַרְתִּי אֶת־יִשְׂרָאֵל כִּי אִם־אַתָּה וּבֵית אָבִיךָ בַּעֲזָבְכֶם אֶת־מִצְוֺת יְהוָה וַתֵּלֶךְ אַחֲרֵי הַבְּעָלִים׃

יט וְעַתָּה שְׁלַח קְבֹץ אֵלַי אֶת־כָּל־יִשְׂרָאֵל אֶל־הַר הַכַּרְמֶל וְאֶת־נְבִיאֵי הַבַּעַל אַרְבַּע מֵאוֹת וַחֲמִשִּׁים וּנְבִיאֵי הָאֲשֵׁרָה אַרְבַּע מֵאוֹת אֹכְלֵי שֻׁלְחַן אִיזָבֶל׃

כ וַיִּשְׁלַח אַחְאָב בְּכָל־בְּנֵי יִשְׂרָאֵל וַיִּקְבֹּץ אֶת־הַנְּבִיאִים אֶל־הַר הַכַּרְמֶל׃

כא וַיִּגַּשׁ אֵלִיָּהוּ אֶל־כָּל־הָעָם וַיֹּאמֶר עַד־מָתַי אַתֶּם פֹּסְחִים עַל־שְׁתֵּי הַסְּעִפִּים אִם־יְהוָה הָאֱלֹהִים לְכוּ אַחֲרָיו וְאִם־הַבַּעַל לְכוּ אַחֲרָיו וְלֹא־עָנוּ הָעָם אֹתוֹ דָּבָר׃

כב וַיֹּאמֶר אֵלִיָּהוּ אֶל־הָעָם אֲנִי נוֹתַרְתִּי נָבִיא לַיהוָה לְבַדִּי וּנְבִיאֵי הַבַּעַל אַרְבַּע־מֵאוֹת וַחֲמִשִּׁים אִישׁ׃

כג וְיִתְּנוּ־לָנוּ שְׁנַיִם פָּרִים וְיִבְחֲרוּ לָהֶם הַפָּר הָאֶחָד וִינַתְּחֻהוּ וְיָשִׂימוּ עַל־הָעֵצִים וְאֵשׁ לֹא יָשִׂימוּ וַאֲנִי אֶעֱשֶׂה אֶת־הַפָּר הָאֶחָד וְנָתַתִּי עַל־הָעֵצִים וְאֵשׁ לֹא אָשִׂים׃

כד וּקְרָאתֶם בְּשֵׁם אֱלֹהֵיכֶם וַאֲנִי אֶקְרָא בְשֵׁם־יְהוָה וְהָיָה הָאֱלֹהִים אֲשֶׁר־יַעֲנֶה בָאֵשׁ הוּא הָאֱלֹהִים וַיַּעַן כָּל־הָעָם וַיֹּאמְרוּ טוֹב הַדָּבָר׃

כה וַיֹּאמֶר אֵלִיָּהוּ לִנְבִיאֵי הַבַּעַל בַּחֲרוּ לָכֶם הַפָּר הָאֶחָד וַעֲשׂוּ רִאשֹׁנָה כִּי אַתֶּם הָרַבִּים וְקִרְאוּ בְּשֵׁם אֱלֹהֵיכֶם וְאֵשׁ לֹא תָשִׂימוּ׃

Melachim I / I Kings
Chapter 18

מלכים א
פרק יח

26 They took the bull that was given them; they prepared it, and invoked Baal by name from morning until noon, shouting, "O Baal, answer us!" But there was no sound, and none who responded; so they performed a hopping dance about the *altar* that had been set up.

כו וַיִּקְחוּ אֶת־הַפָּר אֲשֶׁר־נָתַן לָהֶם וַיַּעֲשׂוּ וַיִּקְרְאוּ בְשֵׁם־הַבַּעַל מֵהַבֹּקֶר וְעַד־הַצָּהֳרַיִם לֵאמֹר הַבַּעַל עֲנֵנוּ וְאֵין קוֹל וְאֵין עֹנֶה וַיְפַסְּחוּ עַל־הַמִּזְבֵּחַ אֲשֶׁר עָשָׂה:

27 When noon came, *Eliyahu* mocked them, saying, "Shout louder! After all, he is a god. But he may be in conversation, he may be detained, or he may be on a journey, or perhaps he is asleep and will wake up."

כז וַיְהִי בַצָּהֳרַיִם וַיְהַתֵּל בָּהֶם אֵלִיָּהוּ וַיֹּאמֶר קִרְאוּ בְקוֹל־גָּדוֹל כִּי־אֱלֹהִים הוּא כִּי שִׂיחַ וְכִי־שִׂיג לוֹ וְכִי־דֶרֶךְ לוֹ אוּלַי יָשֵׁן הוּא וְיִקָץ:

28 So they shouted louder, and gashed themselves with knives and spears, according to their practice, until the blood streamed over them.

כח וַיִּקְרְאוּ בְּקוֹל גָּדוֹל וַיִּתְגֹּדְדוּ כְּמִשְׁפָּטָם בַּחֲרָבוֹת וּבָרְמָחִים עַד־שְׁפָךְ־דָּם עֲלֵיהֶם:

29 When noon passed, they kept raving until the hour of presenting the meal offering. Still there was no sound, and none who responded or heeded.

כט וַיְהִי כַּעֲבֹר הַצָּהֳרַיִם וַיִּתְנַבְּאוּ עַד לַעֲלוֹת הַמִּנְחָה וְאֵין־קוֹל וְאֵין־עֹנֶה וְאֵין קָשֶׁב:

30 Then *Eliyahu* said to all the people, "Come closer to me"; and all the people came closer to him. He repaired the damaged *Mizbayach* of *Hashem*.

ל וַיֹּאמֶר אֵלִיָּהוּ לְכָל־הָעָם גְּשׁוּ אֵלַי וַיִּגְּשׁוּ כָל־הָעָם אֵלָיו וַיְרַפֵּא אֶת־מִזְבַּח יְהוָה הֶהָרוּס:

31 Then *Eliyahu* took twelve stones, corresponding to the number of the tribes of the sons of *Yaakov* — to whom the word of *Hashem* had come: "*Yisrael* shall be your name"

לא וַיִּקַּח אֵלִיָּהוּ שְׁתֵּים עֶשְׂרֵה אֲבָנִים כְּמִסְפַּר שִׁבְטֵי בְנֵי־יַעֲקֹב אֲשֶׁר הָיָה דְבַר־יְהוָה אֵלָיו לֵאמֹר יִשְׂרָאֵל יִהְיֶה שְׁמֶךָ:

32 and with the stones he built a *Mizbayach* in the name of *Hashem*. Around the *Mizbayach* he made a trench large enough for two *se'eem* of seed.

לב וַיִּבְנֶה אֶת־הָאֲבָנִים מִזְבֵּחַ בְּשֵׁם יְהוָה וַיַּעַשׂ תְּעָלָה כְּבֵית סָאתַיִם זֶרַע סָבִיב לַמִּזְבֵּחַ:

33 He laid out the wood, and he cut up the bull and laid it on the wood.

לג וַיַּעֲרֹךְ אֶת־הָעֵצִים וַיְנַתַּח אֶת־הַפָּר וַיָּשֶׂם עַל־הָעֵצִים:

34 And he said, "Fill four jars with water and pour it over the burnt offering and the wood." Then he said, "Do it a second time"; and they did it a second time. "Do it a third time," he said; and they did it a third time.

לד וַיֹּאמֶר מִלְאוּ אַרְבָּעָה כַדִּים מַיִם וְיִצְקוּ עַל־הָעֹלָה וְעַל־הָעֵצִים וַיֹּאמֶר שְׁנוּ וַיִּשְׁנוּ וַיֹּאמֶר שַׁלֵּשׁוּ וַיְשַׁלֵּשׁוּ:

35 The water ran down around the *Mizbayach*, and even the trench was filled with water.

לה וַיֵּלְכוּ הַמַּיִם סָבִיב לַמִּזְבֵּחַ וְגַם אֶת־הַתְּעָלָה מִלֵּא־מָיִם:

36 When it was time to present the meal offering, the *Navi Eliyahu* came forward and said, "*Hashem*, God of *Avraham*, *Yitzchak*, and *Yisrael*! Let it be known today that You are *Hashem* in *Yisrael* and that I am Your servant, and that I have done all these things at Your bidding.

לו וַיְהִי בַּעֲלוֹת הַמִּנְחָה וַיִּגַּשׁ אֵלִיָּהוּ הַנָּבִיא וַיֹּאמַר יְהוָה אֱלֹהֵי אַבְרָהָם יִצְחָק וְיִשְׂרָאֵל הַיּוֹם יִוָּדַע כִּי־אַתָּה אֱלֹהִים בְּיִשְׂרָאֵל וַאֲנִי עַבְדֶּךָ וּבִדְבָרֶיךָ [וּבִדְבָרְךָ] עָשִׂיתִי אֵת כָּל־הַדְּבָרִים הָאֵלֶּה:

Melachim I/I Kings
Chapter 18

מלכים א
פרק יח

37 Answer me, *Hashem*, answer me, that this people may know that You, *Hashem*, are *Hashem*; for You have turned their hearts backward."

לו עֲנֵנִי יְהֹוָה עֲנֵנִי וְיֵדְעוּ הָעָם הַזֶּה כִּי־אַתָּה יְהֹוָה הָאֱלֹהִים וְאַתָּה הֲסִבֹּתָ אֶת־לִבָּם אֲחֹרַנִּית:

38 Then fire from *Hashem* descended and consumed the burnt offering, the wood, the stones, and the earth; and it licked up the water that was in the trench.

לח וַתִּפֹּל אֵשׁ־יְהֹוָה וַתֹּאכַל אֶת־הָעֹלָה וְאֶת־הָעֵצִים וְאֶת־הָאֲבָנִים וְאֶת־הֶעָפָר וְאֶת־הַמַּיִם אֲשֶׁר־בַּתְּעָלָה לִחֵכָה:

va-ti-POL aysh a-do-NAI va-TO-khal et ha-o-LAH v'-et ha-ay-TZEEM v'-et ha-a-va-NEEM v'-et he-a-FAR v'-et ha-MA-yim a-sher ba-t'-a-LAH li-KHAY-khah

39 When they saw this, all the people flung themselves on their faces and cried out: "*Hashem* alone is *Hashem*, *Hashem* alone is *Hashem*!"

לט וַיַּרְא כָּל־הָעָם וַיִּפְּלוּ עַל־פְּנֵיהֶם וַיֹּאמְרוּ יְהֹוָה הוּא הָאֱלֹהִים יְהֹוָה הוּא הָאֱלֹהִים:

40 Then *Eliyahu* said to them, "Seize the *Neviim* of Baal, let not a single one of them get away." They seized them, and *Eliyahu* took them down to the Wadi Kishon and slaughtered them there.

מ וַיֹּאמֶר אֵלִיָּהוּ לָהֶם תִּפְשׂוּ אֶת־נְבִיאֵי הַבַּעַל אִישׁ אַל־יִמָּלֵט מֵהֶם וַיִּתְפְּשׂוּם וַיּוֹרִדֵם אֵלִיָּהוּ אֶל־נַחַל קִישׁוֹן וַיִּשְׁחָטֵם שָׁם:

41 *Eliyahu* said to *Achav*, "Go up, eat and drink, for there is a rumbling of [approaching] rain,"

מא וַיֹּאמֶר אֵלִיָּהוּ לְאַחְאָב עֲלֵה אֱכֹל וּשְׁתֵה כִּי־קוֹל הֲמוֹן הַגָּשֶׁם:

42 and *Achav* went up to eat and drink. *Eliyahu* meanwhile climbed to the top of Mount *Carmel*, crouched on the ground, and put his face between his knees.

מב וַיַּעֲלֶה אַחְאָב לֶאֱכֹל וְלִשְׁתּוֹת וְאֵלִיָּהוּ עָלָה אֶל־רֹאשׁ הַכַּרְמֶל וַיִּגְהַר אַרְצָה וַיָּשֶׂם פָּנָיו בֵּין ברכו [בִּרְכָּיו:]

43 And he said to his servant, "Go up and look toward the Sea." He went up and looked and reported, "There is nothing." Seven times [*Eliyahu*] said, "Go back,"

מג וַיֹּאמֶר אֶל־נַעֲרוֹ עֲלֵה־נָא הַבֵּט דֶּרֶךְ־יָם וַיַּעַל וַיַּבֵּט וַיֹּאמֶר אֵין מְאוּמָה וַיֹּאמֶר שֻׁב שֶׁבַע פְּעָמִים:

44 and the seventh time, [the servant] reported, "A cloud as small as a man's hand is rising in the west." Then [*Eliyahu*] said, "Go say to *Achav*, 'Hitch up [your chariot] and go down before the rain stops you.'"

מד וַיְהִי בַּשְּׁבִעִית וַיֹּאמֶר הִנֵּה־עָב קְטַנָּה כְּכַף־אִישׁ עֹלָה מִיָּם וַיֹּאמֶר עֲלֵה אֱמֹר אֶל־אַחְאָב אֱסֹר וָרֵד וְלֹא יַעֲצָרְכָה הַגָּשֶׁם:

45 Meanwhile the sky grew black with clouds; there was wind, and a heavy downpour fell; *Achav* mounted his chariot and drove off to *Yizrael*.

מה וַיְהִי עַד־כֹּה וְעַד־כֹּה וְהַשָּׁמַיִם הִתְקַדְּרוּ עָבִים וְרוּחַ וַיְהִי גֶּשֶׁם גָּדוֹל וַיִּרְכַּב אַחְאָב וַיֵּלֶךְ יִזְרְעֶאלָה:

Mount Carmel

18:38 Then fire from *Hashem* descended In miraculous fashion, *Hashem* accepts the prophet *Eliyahu*'s offerings. This may be surprising, as *Eliyahu* did not offer these sacrifices in the *Beit Hamikdash* in *Yerushalayim*, the only place Israelite sacrifice is allowed. His battle with the prophets of the Baal and his offerings to *Hashem* take place on Mount *Carmel* in northern Israel, near the Mediterranean coast and the modern city of Haifa. The Sages (*Yevamot* 90b) teach that this was an extraordinary case where, because of the danger of the People of Israel being lost to idolatry, *Eliyahu* the prophet was permitted to temporarily suspend the law and offer a sacrifice outside of the *Beit Hamikdash*. As the offering is received and the Israelites accept *Hashem*'s rule, it becomes clear to see that he was right to do so. Sometimes, prophets demonstrate that extraordinary circumstances require extraordinary actions.

Melachim I / I Kings
Chapter 19

מלכים א
פרק יט

46 The hand of *Hashem* had come upon *Eliyahu*. He tied up his skirts and ran in front of *Achav* all the way to *Yizrael*.

19 1 When *Achav* told Jezebel all that *Eliyahu* had done and how he had put all the *Neviim* to the sword,

2 Jezebel sent a messenger to *Eliyahu*, saying, "Thus and more may the gods do if by this time tomorrow I have not made you like one of them."

3 Frightened, he fled at once for his life. He came to *Be'er Sheva*, which is in *Yehuda*, and left his servant there;

4 he himself went a day's journey into the wilderness. He came to a broom bush and sat down under it, and prayed that he might die. "Enough!" he cried. "Now, *Hashem*, take my life, for I am no better than my fathers."

5 He lay down and fell asleep under a broom bush. Suddenly an angel touched him and said to him, "Arise and eat."

6 He looked about; and there, beside his head, was a cake baked on hot stones and a jar of water! He ate and drank, and lay down again.

7 The angel of *Hashem* came a second time and touched him and said, "Arise and eat, or the journey will be too much for you."

8 He arose and ate and drank; and with the strength from that meal he walked forty days and forty nights as far as the mountain of *Hashem* at Horeb.

9 There he went into a cave, and there he spent the night. Then the word of *Hashem* came to him. He said to him, "Why are you here, *Eliyahu*?"

10 He replied, "I am moved by zeal for *Hashem*, the God of Hosts, for the Israelites have forsaken Your covenant, torn down Your *mizbachot*, and put Your *Neviim* to the sword. I alone am left, and they are out to take my life."

11 "Come out," He called, "and stand on the mountain before *Hashem*." And lo, *Hashem* passed by. There was a great and mighty wind, splitting mountains and shattering rocks by the power of *Hashem*; but *Hashem* was not in the wind. After the wind – an earthquake; but *Hashem* was not in the earthquake.

מה וְיַד־יְהוָה הָיְתָה אֶל־אֵלִיָּהוּ וַיְשַׁנֵּס מָתְנָיו וַיָּרָץ לִפְנֵי אַחְאָב עַד־בֹּאֲכָה יִזְרְעֶאלָה׃

א וַיַּגֵּד אַחְאָב לְאִיזֶבֶל אֵת כָּל־אֲשֶׁר עָשָׂה אֵלִיָּהוּ וְאֵת כָּל־אֲשֶׁר הָרַג אֶת־כָּל־הַנְּבִיאִים בֶּחָרֶב׃

ב וַתִּשְׁלַח אִיזֶבֶל מַלְאָךְ אֶל־אֵלִיָּהוּ לֵאמֹר כֹּה־יַעֲשׂוּן אֱלֹהִים וְכֹה יוֹסִפוּן כִּי־כָעֵת מָחָר אָשִׂים אֶת־נַפְשְׁךָ כְּנֶפֶשׁ אַחַד מֵהֶם׃

ג וַיַּרְא וַיָּקָם וַיֵּלֶךְ אֶל־נַפְשׁוֹ וַיָּבֹא בְּאֵר שֶׁבַע אֲשֶׁר לִיהוּדָה וַיַּנַּח אֶת־נַעֲרוֹ שָׁם׃

ד וְהוּא־הָלַךְ בַּמִּדְבָּר דֶּרֶךְ יוֹם וַיָּבֹא וַיֵּשֶׁב תַּחַת רֹתֶם אַחַת [אֶחָד] וַיִּשְׁאַל אֶת־נַפְשׁוֹ לָמוּת וַיֹּאמֶר ׀ רַב עַתָּה יְהוָה קַח נַפְשִׁי כִּי־לֹא־טוֹב אָנֹכִי מֵאֲבֹתָי׃

ה וַיִּשְׁכַּב וַיִּישַׁן תַּחַת רֹתֶם אֶחָד וְהִנֵּה־זֶה מַלְאָךְ נֹגֵעַ בּוֹ וַיֹּאמֶר לוֹ קוּם אֱכוֹל׃

ו וַיַּבֵּט וְהִנֵּה מְרַאֲשֹׁתָיו עֻגַת רְצָפִים וְצַפַּחַת מָיִם וַיֹּאכַל וַיֵּשְׁתְּ וַיָּשָׁב וַיִּשְׁכָּב׃

ז וַיָּשָׁב מַלְאַךְ יְהוָה ׀ שֵׁנִית וַיִּגַּע־בּוֹ וַיֹּאמֶר קוּם אֱכֹל כִּי רַב מִמְּךָ הַדָּרֶךְ׃

ח וַיָּקָם וַיֹּאכַל וַיִּשְׁתֶּה וַיֵּלֶךְ בְּכֹחַ ׀ הָאֲכִילָה הַהִיא אַרְבָּעִים יוֹם וְאַרְבָּעִים לַיְלָה עַד הַר הָאֱלֹהִים חֹרֵב׃

ט וַיָּבֹא־שָׁם אֶל־הַמְּעָרָה וַיָּלֶן שָׁם וְהִנֵּה דְבַר־יְהוָה אֵלָיו וַיֹּאמֶר לוֹ מַה־לְּךָ פֹה אֵלִיָּהוּ׃

י וַיֹּאמֶר קַנֹּא קִנֵּאתִי לַיהוָה ׀ אֱלֹהֵי צְבָאוֹת כִּי־עָזְבוּ בְרִיתְךָ בְּנֵי יִשְׂרָאֵל אֶת־מִזְבְּחֹתֶיךָ הָרָסוּ וְאֶת־נְבִיאֶיךָ הָרְגוּ בֶחָרֶב וָאִוָּתֵר אֲנִי לְבַדִּי וַיְבַקְשׁוּ אֶת־נַפְשִׁי לְקַחְתָּהּ׃

יא וַיֹּאמֶר צֵא וְעָמַדְתָּ בָהָר לִפְנֵי יְהוָה וְהִנֵּה יְהוָה עֹבֵר וְרוּחַ גְּדוֹלָה וְחָזָק מְפָרֵק הָרִים וּמְשַׁבֵּר סְלָעִים לִפְנֵי יְהוָה לֹא בָרוּחַ יְהוָה וְאַחַר הָרוּחַ רַעַשׁ לֹא בָרַעַשׁ יְהוָה׃

Melachim I/I Kings
Chapter 19

מלכים א
פרק יט

12 After the earthquake – fire; but *Hashem* was not in the fire. And after the fire – a soft murmuring sound.

יב וְאַחַר הָרַעַשׁ אֵשׁ לֹא בָאֵשׁ יְהֹוָה וְאַחַר הָאֵשׁ קוֹל דְּמָמָה דַקָּה:

13 When *Eliyahu* heard it, he wrapped his mantle about his face and went out and stood at the entrance of the cave. Then a voice addressed him: "Why are you here, *Eliyahu*?"

יג וַיְהִי כִּשְׁמֹעַ אֵלִיָּהוּ וַיָּלֶט פָּנָיו בְּאַדַּרְתּוֹ וַיֵּצֵא וַיַּעֲמֹד פֶּתַח הַמְּעָרָה וְהִנֵּה אֵלָיו קוֹל וַיֹּאמֶר מַה־לְּךָ פֹה אֵלִיָּהוּ:

14 He answered, "I am moved by zeal for *Hashem*, the God of Hosts; for the Israelites have forsaken Your covenant, torn down Your *mizbachot*, and have put Your *Neviim* to the sword. I alone am left, and they are out to take my life."

יד וַיֹּאמֶר קַנֹּא קִנֵּאתִי לַיהֹוָה אֱלֹהֵי צְבָאוֹת כִּי־עָזְבוּ בְרִיתְךָ בְּנֵי יִשְׂרָאֵל אֶת־מִזְבְּחֹתֶיךָ הָרָסוּ וְאֶת־נְבִיאֶיךָ הָרְגוּ בֶחָרֶב וָאִוָּתֵר אֲנִי לְבַדִּי וַיְבַקְשׁוּ אֶת־נַפְשִׁי לְקַחְתָּהּ:

15 *Hashem* said to him, "Go back by the way you came, [and] on to the wilderness of Damascus. When you get there, anoint Hazael as king of Aram.

טו וַיֹּאמֶר יְהֹוָה אֵלָיו לֵךְ שׁוּב לְדַרְכְּךָ מִדְבַּרָה דַמָּשֶׂק וּבָאתָ וּמָשַׁחְתָּ אֶת־חֲזָאֵל לְמֶלֶךְ עַל־אֲרָם:

16 Also anoint *Yehu* son of Nimshi as king of *Yisrael*, and anoint *Elisha* son of *Shafat* of Abel-meholah to succeed you as *Navi*.

טז וְאֵת יֵהוּא בֶן־נִמְשִׁי תִּמְשַׁח לְמֶלֶךְ עַל־יִשְׂרָאֵל וְאֶת־אֱלִישָׁע בֶּן־שָׁפָט מֵאָבֵל מְחוֹלָה תִּמְשַׁח לְנָבִיא תַּחְתֶּיךָ:

v'-AYT YAY-hu ven nim-SHEE tim-SHAKH l'-ME-lekh al yis-ra-AYL v'-et e-lee-SHA ben sha-FAT may-a-VAYL m'-kho-LAH tim-SHAKH l'-na-VEE takh-TE-kha

17 Whoever escapes the sword of Hazael shall be slain by *Yehu*, and whoever escapes the sword of *Yehu* shall be slain by *Elisha*.

יז וְהָיָה הַנִּמְלָט מֵחֶרֶב חֲזָאֵל יָמִית יֵהוּא וְהַנִּמְלָט מֵחֶרֶב יֵהוּא יָמִית אֱלִישָׁע:

18 I will leave in *Yisrael* only seven thousand – every knee that has not knelt to Baal and every mouth that has not kissed him."

יח וְהִשְׁאַרְתִּי בְיִשְׂרָאֵל שִׁבְעַת אֲלָפִים כָּל־הַבִּרְכַּיִם אֲשֶׁר לֹא־כָרְעוּ לַבַּעַל וְכָל־הַפֶּה אֲשֶׁר לֹא־נָשַׁק לוֹ:

19 He set out from there and came upon *Elisha* son of *Shafat* as he was plowing. There were twelve yoke of oxen ahead of him, and he was with the twelfth. *Eliyahu* came over to him and threw his mantle over him.

יט וַיֵּלֶךְ מִשָּׁם וַיִּמְצָא אֶת־אֱלִישָׁע בֶּן־שָׁפָט וְהוּא חֹרֵשׁ שְׁנֵים־עָשָׂר צְמָדִים לְפָנָיו וְהוּא בִּשְׁנֵים הֶעָשָׂר וַיַּעֲבֹר אֵלִיָּהוּ אֵלָיו וַיַּשְׁלֵךְ אַדַּרְתּוֹ אֵלָיו:

20 He left the oxen and ran after *Eliyahu*, saying: "Let me kiss my father and mother good-by, and I will follow you." And he answered him, "Go back. What have I done to you?"

כ וַיַּעֲזֹב אֶת־הַבָּקָר וַיָּרָץ אַחֲרֵי אֵלִיָּהוּ וַיֹּאמֶר אֶשְּׁקָה־נָּא לְאָבִי וּלְאִמִּי וְאֵלְכָה אַחֲרֶיךָ וַיֹּאמֶר לוֹ לֵךְ שׁוּב כִּי מֶה־עָשִׂיתִי לָךְ:

19:16 *Elisha* son of Shaphat of Abel-meholah to succeed you as *Navi* *Eliyahu* is such a central prophet in Jewish history that the Sages (*Sanhedrin* 98a, based on Malachi 2:23–24) teach that he will be the one to usher in the righteous *Mashiach* when *Hashem* so decrees. Yet, *Hashem* instructs *Eliyahu* that he must anoint *Elisha* to replace him as prophet. Though his strengths no longer fit the needs of his generation, we await the day when *Eliyahu* will once again rise up to herald the coming of the *Mashiach*.

Melachim I/I Kings
Chapter 20

מלכים א
פרק כ

21 He turned back from him and took the yoke of oxen and slaughtered them; he boiled their meat with the gear of the oxen and gave it to the people, and they ate. Then he arose and followed *Eliyahu* and became his attendant.

כא וַיָּשָׁב מֵאַחֲרָיו וַיִּקַּח אֶת־צֶמֶד הַבָּקָר וַיִּזְבָּחֵהוּ וּבִכְלִי הַבָּקָר בִּשְּׁלָם הַבָּשָׂר וַיִּתֵּן לָעָם וַיֹּאכֵלוּ וַיָּקָם וַיֵּלֶךְ אַחֲרֵי אֵלִיָּהוּ וַיְשָׁרְתֵהוּ׃

20

1 King Ben-hadad of Aram gathered his whole army; thirty-two kings accompanied him with horses and chariots. He advanced against *Shomron*, laid siege to it, and attacked it.

א וּבֶן־הֲדַד מֶלֶךְ־אֲרָם קָבַץ אֶת־כָּל־חֵילוֹ וּשְׁלֹשִׁים וּשְׁנַיִם מֶלֶךְ אִתּוֹ וְסוּס וָרָכֶב וַיַּעַל וַיָּצַר עַל־שֹׁמְרוֹן וַיִּלָּחֶם בָּהּ׃

2 And he sent messengers to *Achav* inside the city

ב וַיִּשְׁלַח מַלְאָכִים אֶל־אַחְאָב מֶלֶךְ־יִשְׂרָאֵל הָעִירָה׃

3 to say to him, "Thus said Ben-hadad: Your silver and gold are mine, and your beautiful wives and children are mine."

ג וַיֹּאמֶר לוֹ כֹּה אָמַר בֶּן־הֲדַד כַּסְפְּךָ וּזְהָבְךָ לִי־הוּא וְנָשֶׁיךָ וּבָנֶיךָ הַטּוֹבִים לִי־הֵם׃

4 The king of *Yisrael* replied, "As you say, my lord king: I and all I have are yours."

ד וַיַּעַן מֶלֶךְ־יִשְׂרָאֵל וַיֹּאמֶר כִּדְבָרְךָ אֲדֹנִי הַמֶּלֶךְ לְךָ אֲנִי וְכָל־אֲשֶׁר־לִי׃

5 Then the messengers came again and said, "Thus said Ben-hadad: When I sent you the order to give me your silver and gold, and your wives and children,

ה וַיָּשֻׁבוּ הַמַּלְאָכִים וַיֹּאמְרוּ כֹּה־אָמַר בֶּן־הֲדַד לֵאמֹר כִּי־שָׁלַחְתִּי אֵלֶיךָ לֵאמֹר כַּסְפְּךָ וּזְהָבְךָ וְנָשֶׁיךָ וּבָנֶיךָ לִי תִתֵּן׃

6 I meant that tomorrow at this time I will send my servants to you and they will search your house and the houses of your courtiers and seize everything you prize and take it away."

ו כִּי אִם־כָּעֵת מָחָר אֶשְׁלַח אֶת־עֲבָדַי אֵלֶיךָ וְחִפְּשׂוּ אֶת־בֵּיתְךָ וְאֵת בָּתֵּי עֲבָדֶיךָ וְהָיָה כָּל־מַחְמַד עֵינֶיךָ יָשִׂימוּ בְיָדָם וְלָקָחוּ׃

KEE im ka-AYT ma-KHAR esh-LAKH et a-va-DAI ay-LE-kha v'-khi-p'-SU et BAY-t'-KHA v'-AYT ba-TAY a-va-DE-kha v'-ha-YAH kol makh-MAD ay-NE-kha ya-SEE-mu v'-ya-DAM v'-la-KA-khu

7 Then the king of *Yisrael* summoned all the elders of the land, and he said, "See for yourselves how that man is bent on evil! For when he demanded my wives and my children, my silver and my gold, I did not refuse him."

ז וַיִּקְרָא מֶלֶךְ־יִשְׂרָאֵל לְכָל־זִקְנֵי הָאָרֶץ וַיֹּאמֶר דְּעוּ־נָא וּרְאוּ כִּי רָעָה זֶה מְבַקֵּשׁ כִּי־שָׁלַח אֵלַי לְנָשַׁי וּלְבָנַי וּלְכַסְפִּי וְלִזְהָבִי וְלֹא מָנַעְתִּי מִמֶּנּוּ׃

8 All the elders and all the people said, "Do not obey and do not submit!"

ח וַיֹּאמְרוּ אֵלָיו כָּל־הַזְּקֵנִים וְכָל־הָעָם אַל־תִּשְׁמַע וְלוֹא תֹאבֶה׃

20:6 And seize everything you prize and take it away According to *Rashi*, Ben-Hadad is demanding that the People of Israel turn over their *Torah* scrolls to him. *Rashi* notes that *Achav* understands that the *Torah* is not his private possession, but rather a national treasure. Thus, he asks the elders of the kingdom what to do. Though the elders have sinned through idolatry, they still have honor for the *Torah* and refuse to permit turning over the precious scrolls to the enemy. Even one who is almost totally disconnected spiritually still maintains a small connection to *Hashem*, and that connection often emerges in times of crisis.

Rashi
(1040–1105)

Melachim I / I Kings
Chapter 20

מלכים א
פרק כ

9 So he said to Ben-hadad's messengers, "Tell my lord the king: All that you first demanded of your servant I shall do, but this thing I cannot do." The messengers went and reported this to him.

ט וַיֹּאמֶר לְמַלְאֲכֵי בֶן־הֲדַד אִמְרוּ לַאדֹנִי הַמֶּלֶךְ כֹּל אֲשֶׁר־שָׁלַחְתָּ אֶל־עַבְדְּךָ בָרִאשֹׁנָה אֶעֱשֶׂה וְהַדָּבָר הַזֶּה לֹא אוּכַל לַעֲשׂוֹת וַיֵּלְכוּ הַמַּלְאָכִים וַיְשִׁבֻהוּ דָּבָר:

10 Thereupon Ben-hadad sent him this message: "May the gods do thus to me and even more, if the dust of *Shomron* will provide even a handful for each of the men who follow me!"

י וַיִּשְׁלַח אֵלָיו בֶּן־הֲדַד וַיֹּאמֶר כֹּה־יַעֲשׂוּן לִי אֱלֹהִים וְכֹה יוֹסִפוּ אִם־יִשְׂפֹּק עֲפַר שֹׁמְרוֹן לִשְׁעָלִים לְכָל־הָעָם אֲשֶׁר בְּרַגְלָי:

11 The king of *Yisrael* replied, "Tell him: Let not him who girds on his sword boast like him who ungirds it!"

יא וַיַּעַן מֶלֶךְ־יִשְׂרָאֵל וַיֹּאמֶר דַּבְּרוּ אַל־יִתְהַלֵּל חֹגֵר כִּמְפַתֵּחַ:

12 On hearing this reply – while he and the other kings were drinking together at Succoth – he commanded his followers, "Advance!" And they advanced against the city.

יב וַיְהִי כִּשְׁמֹעַ אֶת־הַדָּבָר הַזֶּה וְהוּא שֹׁתֶה הוּא וְהַמְּלָכִים בַּסֻּכּוֹת וַיֹּאמֶר אֶל־עֲבָדָיו שִׂימוּ וַיָּשִׂימוּ עַל־הָעִיר:

13 Then a certain *Navi* went up to King *Achav* of *Yisrael* and said, "Thus said *Hashem*: Do you see that great host? I will deliver it into your hands today, and you shall know that I am *Hashem*."

יג וְהִנֵּה נָבִיא אֶחָד נִגַּשׁ אֶל־אַחְאָב מֶלֶךְ־יִשְׂרָאֵל וַיֹּאמֶר כֹּה אָמַר יְהֹוָה הֲרָאִיתָ אֵת כָּל־הֶהָמוֹן הַגָּדוֹל הַזֶּה הִנְנִי נֹתְנוֹ בְיָדְךָ הַיּוֹם וְיָדַעְתָּ כִּי־אֲנִי יְהֹוָה:

14 "Through whom?" asked *Achav*. He answered, "Thus said *Hashem*: Through the aides of the provincial governors." He asked, "Who shall begin the battle?" And he answered, "You."

יד וַיֹּאמֶר אַחְאָב בְּמִי וַיֹּאמֶר כֹּה־אָמַר יְהֹוָה בְּנַעֲרֵי שָׂרֵי הַמְּדִינוֹת וַיֹּאמֶר מִי־יֶאְסֹר הַמִּלְחָמָה וַיֹּאמֶר אָתָּה:

15 So he mustered the aides of the provincial governors, 232 strong, and then he mustered all the troops – all the Israelites – 7,000 strong.

טו וַיִּפְקֹד אֶת־נַעֲרֵי שָׂרֵי הַמְּדִינוֹת וַיִּהְיוּ מָאתַיִם שְׁנַיִם וּשְׁלֹשִׁים וְאַחֲרֵיהֶם פָּקַד אֶת־כָּל־הָעָם כָּל־בְּנֵי יִשְׂרָאֵל שִׁבְעַת אֲלָפִים:

16 They marched out at noon, while Ben-hadad was drinking himself drunk at Succoth together with the thirty-two kings allied with him.

טז וַיֵּצְאוּ בַּצָּהֳרָיִם וּבֶן־הֲדַד שֹׁתֶה שִׁכּוֹר בַּסֻּכּוֹת הוּא וְהַמְּלָכִים שְׁלֹשִׁים־וּשְׁנַיִם מֶלֶךְ עֹזֵר אֹתוֹ:

17 The aides of the provincial governors rushed out first. Ben-hadad sent [scouts], who told him, "Some men have come out from *Shomron*."

יז וַיֵּצְאוּ נַעֲרֵי שָׂרֵי הַמְּדִינוֹת בָּרִאשֹׁנָה וַיִּשְׁלַח בֶּן־הֲדַד וַיַּגִּידוּ לוֹ לֵאמֹר אֲנָשִׁים יָצְאוּ מִשֹּׁמְרוֹן:

18 He said, "If they have come out to surrender, take them alive; and if they have come out for battle, take them alive anyhow."

יח וַיֹּאמֶר אִם־לְשָׁלוֹם יָצָאוּ תִּפְשׂוּם חַיִּים וְאִם לְמִלְחָמָה יָצָאוּ חַיִּים תִּפְשׂוּם:

19 But the others – the aides of the provincial governors, with the army behind them – had already rushed out of the city,

יט וְאֵלֶּה יָצְאוּ מִן־הָעִיר נַעֲרֵי שָׂרֵי הַמְּדִינוֹת וְהַחַיִל אֲשֶׁר אַחֲרֵיהֶם:

20 and each of them struck down his opponent. The Arameans fled, and *Yisrael* pursued them; but King Ben-hadad of Aram escaped on a horse with other horsemen.

כ וַיַּכּוּ אִישׁ אִישׁוֹ וַיָּנֻסוּ אֲרָם וַיִּרְדְּפֵם יִשְׂרָאֵל וַיִּמָּלֵט בֶּן־הֲדַד מֶלֶךְ אֲרָם עַל־סוּס וּפָרָשִׁים:

Melachim I / I Kings
Chapter 20

21 The king of *Yisrael* came out and attacked the horses and chariots, and inflicted a great defeat on the Arameans.

22 Then the *Navi* approached the king of *Yisrael* and said to him, "Go, keep up your efforts, and consider well what you must do; for the king of Aram will attack you at the turn of the year."

23 Now the ministers of the king of Aram said to him, "Their *Hashem* is a God of mountains; that is why they got the better of us. But if we fight them in the plain, we will surely get the better of them.

24 Do this: Remove all the kings from their posts and appoint governors in their place.

25 Then muster for yourself an army equal to the army you lost, horse for horse and chariot for chariot. And let us fight them in the plain, and we will surely get the better of them." He took their advice and acted accordingly.

26 At the turn of the year, Ben-hadad mustered the Arameans and advanced on Aphek to fight *Yisrael*.

27 Now the Israelites had been mustered and provisioned, and they went out against them; but when the Israelites encamped against them, they looked like two flocks of goats, while the Arameans covered the land.

28 Then the man of *Hashem* approached and spoke to the king of *Yisrael*, "Thus said *Hashem*: Because the Arameans have said, '*Hashem* is a God of mountains, but He is not a God of lowlands,' I will deliver that great host into your hands; and you shall know that I am *Hashem*."

29 For seven days they were encamped opposite each other. On the seventh day, the battle was joined and the Israelites struck down 100,000 Aramean foot soldiers in one day.

30 The survivors fled to Aphek, inside the town, and the wall fell on the 27,000 survivors. Ben-hadad also fled and took refuge inside the town, in an inner chamber.

מלכים א
פרק כ

כא וַיֵּצֵא מֶלֶךְ יִשְׂרָאֵל וַיַּךְ אֶת־הַסּוּס וְאֶת־הָרָכֶב וְהִכָּה בַאֲרָם מַכָּה גְדוֹלָה׃

כב וַיִּגַּשׁ הַנָּבִיא אֶל־מֶלֶךְ יִשְׂרָאֵל וַיֹּאמֶר לוֹ לֵךְ הִתְחַזַּק וְדַע וּרְאֵה אֵת אֲשֶׁר־תַּעֲשֶׂה כִּי לִתְשׁוּבַת הַשָּׁנָה מֶלֶךְ אֲרָם עֹלֶה עָלֶיךָ׃

כג וְעַבְדֵי מֶלֶךְ־אֲרָם אָמְרוּ אֵלָיו אֱלֹהֵי הָרִים אֱלֹהֵיהֶם עַל־כֵּן חָזְקוּ מִמֶּנּוּ וְאוּלָם נִלָּחֵם אִתָּם בַּמִּישׁוֹר אִם־לֹא נֶחֱזַק מֵהֶם׃

כד וְאֶת־הַדָּבָר הַזֶּה עֲשֵׂה הָסֵר הַמְּלָכִים אִישׁ מִמְּקֹמוֹ וְשִׂים פַּחוֹת תַּחְתֵּיהֶם׃

כה וְאַתָּה תִמְנֶה־לְךָ חַיִל כַּחַיִל הַנֹּפֵל מֵאוֹתָךְ וְסוּס כַּסּוּס וְרֶכֶב כָּרֶכֶב וְנִלָּחֲמָה אוֹתָם בַּמִּישׁוֹר אִם־לֹא נֶחֱזַק מֵהֶם וַיִּשְׁמַע לְקֹלָם וַיַּעַשׂ כֵּן׃

כו וַיְהִי לִתְשׁוּבַת הַשָּׁנָה וַיִּפְקֹד בֶּן־הֲדַד אֶת־אֲרָם וַיַּעַל אֲפֵקָה לַמִּלְחָמָה עִם־יִשְׂרָאֵל׃

כז וּבְנֵי יִשְׂרָאֵל הָתְפָּקְדוּ וְכָלְכְּלוּ וַיֵּלְכוּ לִקְרָאתָם וַיַּחֲנוּ בְנֵי־יִשְׂרָאֵל נֶגְדָּם כִּשְׁנֵי חֲשִׂפֵי עִזִּים וַאֲרָם מִלְאוּ אֶת־הָאָרֶץ׃

כח וַיִּגַּשׁ אִישׁ הָאֱלֹהִים וַיֹּאמֶר אֶל־מֶלֶךְ יִשְׂרָאֵל וַיֹּאמֶר כֹּה־אָמַר יְהֹוָה יַעַן אֲשֶׁר אָמְרוּ אֲרָם אֱלֹהֵי הָרִים יְהֹוָה וְלֹא־אֱלֹהֵי עֲמָקִים הוּא וְנָתַתִּי אֶת־כָּל־הֶהָמוֹן הַגָּדוֹל הַזֶּה בְּיָדֶךָ וִידַעְתֶּם כִּי־אֲנִי יְהֹוָה׃

כט וַיַּחֲנוּ אֵלֶּה נֹכַח אֵלֶּה שִׁבְעַת יָמִים וַיְהִי בַּיּוֹם הַשְּׁבִיעִי וַתִּקְרַב הַמִּלְחָמָה וַיַּכּוּ בְנֵי־יִשְׂרָאֵל אֶת־אֲרָם מֵאָה־אֶלֶף רַגְלִי בְּיוֹם אֶחָד׃

ל וַיָּנֻסוּ הַנּוֹתָרִים אֲפֵקָה אֶל־הָעִיר וַתִּפֹּל הַחוֹמָה עַל־עֶשְׂרִים וְשִׁבְעָה אֶלֶף אִישׁ הַנּוֹתָרִים וּבֶן־הֲדַד נָס וַיָּבֹא אֶל־הָעִיר חֶדֶר בְּחָדֶר׃

Melachim I / I Kings
Chapter 20

מלכים א
פרק כ

31 His ministers said to him, "We have heard that the kings of the House of *Yisrael* are magnanimous kings. Let us put sackcloth on our loins and ropes on our heads, and surrender to the king of *Yisrael*; perhaps he will spare your life."

לא וַיֹּאמְרוּ אֵלָיו עֲבָדָיו הִנֵּה־נָא שָׁמַעְנוּ כִּי מַלְכֵי בֵּית יִשְׂרָאֵל כִּי־מַלְכֵי חֶסֶד הֵם נָשִׂימָה נָּא שַׂקִּים בְּמָתְנֵינוּ וַחֲבָלִים בְּרֹאשֵׁנוּ וְנֵצֵא אֶל־מֶלֶךְ יִשְׂרָאֵל אוּלַי יְחַיֶּה אֶת־נַפְשֶׁךָ:

32 So they girded sackcloth on their loins and wound ropes around their heads, and came to the king of *Yisrael* and said, "Your servant Ben-hadad says, 'I beg you, spare my life.'" He replied, "Is he still alive? He is my brother."

לב וַיַּחְגְּרוּ שַׂקִּים בְּמָתְנֵיהֶם וַחֲבָלִים בְּרָאשֵׁיהֶם וַיָּבֹאוּ אֶל־מֶלֶךְ יִשְׂרָאֵל וַיֹּאמְרוּ עַבְדְּךָ בֶן־הֲדַד אָמַר תְּחִי־נָא נַפְשִׁי וַיֹּאמֶר הַעוֹדֶנּוּ חַי אָחִי הוּא:

33 The men divined his meaning and quickly caught the word from him, saying, "Yes, Ben-hadad is your brother." "Go, bring him," he said. Ben-hadad came out to him, and he invited him into his chariot.

לג וְהָאֲנָשִׁים יְנַחֲשׁוּ וַיְמַהֲרוּ וַיַּחְלְטוּ הֲמִמֶּנּוּ וַיֹּאמְרוּ אָחִיךָ בֶן־הֲדַד וַיֹּאמֶר בֹּאוּ קָחֻהוּ וַיֵּצֵא אֵלָיו בֶּן־הֲדַד וַיַּעֲלֵהוּ עַל־הַמֶּרְכָּבָה:

34 Ben-hadad said to him, "I will give back the towns that my father took from your father, and you may set up bazaars for yourself in Damascus as my father did in *Shomron*." "And I, for my part," [said *Achav*,] "will let you go home under these terms." So he made a treaty with him and dismissed him.

לד וַיֹּאמֶר אֵלָיו הֶעָרִים אֲשֶׁר־לָקַח־אָבִי מֵאֵת אָבִיךָ אָשִׁיב וְחוּצוֹת תָּשִׂים לְךָ בְדַמֶּשֶׂק כַּאֲשֶׁר־שָׂם אָבִי בְּשֹׁמְרוֹן וַאֲנִי בַּבְּרִית אֲשַׁלְּחֶךָּ וַיִּכְרָת־לוֹ בְרִית וַיְשַׁלְּחֵהוּ:

35 A certain man, a disciple of the *Neviim*, said to another, at the word of *Hashem*, "Strike me"; but the man refused to strike him.

לה וְאִישׁ אֶחָד מִבְּנֵי הַנְּבִיאִים אָמַר אֶל־רֵעֵהוּ בִּדְבַר יְהוָה הַכֵּינִי נָא וַיְמָאֵן הָאִישׁ לְהַכֹּתוֹ:

36 He said to him, "Because you have not obeyed *Hashem*, a lion will strike you dead as soon as you leave me." And when he left, a lion came upon him and killed him.

לו וַיֹּאמֶר לוֹ יַעַן אֲשֶׁר לֹא־שָׁמַעְתָּ בְּקוֹל יְהוָה הִנְּךָ הוֹלֵךְ מֵאִתִּי וְהִכְּךָ הָאַרְיֵה וַיֵּלֶךְ מֵאֶצְלוֹ וַיִּמְצָאֵהוּ הָאַרְיֵה וַיַּכֵּהוּ:

37 Then he met another man and said, "Come, strike me." So the man struck him and wounded him.

לז וַיִּמְצָא אִישׁ אַחֵר וַיֹּאמֶר הַכֵּינִי נָא וַיַּכֵּהוּ הָאִישׁ הַכֵּה וּפָצֹעַ:

38 Then the *Navi*, disguised by a cloth over his eyes, went and waited for the king by the road.

לח וַיֵּלֶךְ הַנָּבִיא וַיַּעֲמֹד לַמֶּלֶךְ עַל־הַדָּרֶךְ וַיִּתְחַפֵּשׂ בָּאֲפֵר עַל־עֵינָיו:

39 As the king passed by, he cried out to the king and said, "Your servant went out into the thick of the battle. Suddenly a man came over and brought a man to me, saying, 'Guard this man! If he is missing, it will be your life for his, or you will have to pay a *kikar* of silver.'

לט וַיְהִי הַמֶּלֶךְ עֹבֵר וְהוּא צָעַק אֶל־הַמֶּלֶךְ וַיֹּאמֶר עַבְדְּךָ יָצָא בְקֶרֶב־הַמִּלְחָמָה וְהִנֵּה־אִישׁ סָר וַיָּבֵא אֵלַי אִישׁ וַיֹּאמֶר שְׁמֹר אֶת־הָאִישׁ הַזֶּה אִם־הִפָּקֵד יִפָּקֵד וְהָיְתָה נַפְשְׁךָ תַּחַת נַפְשׁוֹ אוֹ כִכַּר־כֶּסֶף תִּשְׁקוֹל:

40 While your servant was busy here and there, [the man] got away." The king of *Yisrael* responded, "You have your verdict; you pronounced it yourself."

מ וַיְהִי עַבְדְּךָ עֹשֵׂה הֵנָּה וָהֵנָּה וְהוּא אֵינֶנּוּ וַיֹּאמֶר אֵלָיו מֶלֶךְ־יִשְׂרָאֵל כֵּן מִשְׁפָּטֶךָ אַתָּה חָרָצְתָּ:

41 Quickly he removed the cloth from his eyes, and the king recognized him as one of the *Neviim*.

מא וַיְמַהֵר וַיָּסַר אֶת־הָאֲפֵר מֵעַל [מֵעֲלֵי] עֵינָיו וַיַּכֵּר אֹתוֹ מֶלֶךְ יִשְׂרָאֵל כִּי מֵהַנְּבִאִים הוּא:

Melachim I / I Kings — Chapter 21

מלכים א
פרק כא

42 He said to him, "Thus said *Hashem*: Because you have set free the man whom I doomed, your life shall be forfeit for his life and your people for his people."

מב וַיֹּאמֶר אֵלָיו כֹּה אָמַר יְהֹוָה יַעַן שִׁלַּחְתָּ אֶת־אִישׁ־חֶרְמִי מִיָּד וְהָיְתָה נַפְשְׁךָ תַּחַת נַפְשׁוֹ וְעַמְּךָ תַּחַת עַמּוֹ׃

43 Dispirited and sullen, the king left for home and came to *Shomron*.

מג וַיֵּלֶךְ מֶלֶךְ־יִשְׂרָאֵל עַל־בֵּיתוֹ סַר וְזָעֵף וַיָּבֹא שֹׁמְרוֹנָה׃

כא

1 [The following events] occurred sometime afterward: *Navot* the Yizraelite owned a vineyard in *Yizrael*, adjoining the palace of King *Achav* of *Shomron*.

א וַיְהִי אַחַר הַדְּבָרִים הָאֵלֶּה כֶּרֶם הָיָה לְנָבוֹת הַיִּזְרְעֵאלִי אֲשֶׁר בְּיִזְרְעֶאל אֵצֶל הֵיכַל אַחְאָב מֶלֶךְ שֹׁמְרוֹן׃

2 *Achav* said to *Navot*, "Give me your vineyard, so that I may have it as a vegetable garden, since it is right next to my palace. I will give you a better vineyard in exchange; or, if you prefer, I will pay you the price in money."

ב וַיְדַבֵּר אַחְאָב אֶל־נָבוֹת לֵאמֹר תְּנָה־לִּי אֶת־כַּרְמְךָ וִיהִי־לִי לְגַן־יָרָק כִּי הוּא קָרוֹב אֵצֶל בֵּיתִי וְאֶתְּנָה לְךָ תַּחְתָּיו כֶּרֶם טוֹב מִמֶּנּוּ אִם טוֹב בְּעֵינֶיךָ אֶתְּנָה־לְךָ כֶסֶף מְחִיר זֶה׃

3 But *Navot* replied, "*Hashem* forbid that I should give up to you what I have inherited from my fathers!"

ג וַיֹּאמֶר נָבוֹת אֶל־אַחְאָב חָלִילָה לִּי מֵיהֹוָה מִתִּתִּי אֶת־נַחֲלַת אֲבֹתַי לָךְ׃

4 *Achav* went home dispirited and sullen because of the answer that *Navot* the Yizraelite had given him: "I will not give up to you what I have inherited from my fathers!" He lay down on his bed and turned away his face, and he would not eat.

ד וַיָּבֹא אַחְאָב אֶל־בֵּיתוֹ סַר וְזָעֵף עַל־הַדָּבָר אֲשֶׁר־דִּבֶּר אֵלָיו נָבוֹת הַיִּזְרְעֵאלִי וַיֹּאמֶר לֹא־אֶתֵּן לְךָ אֶת־נַחֲלַת אֲבוֹתָי וַיִּשְׁכַּב עַל־מִטָּתוֹ וַיַּסֵּב אֶת־פָּנָיו וְלֹא־אָכַל לָחֶם׃

5 His wife Jezebel came to him and asked him, "Why are you so dispirited that you won't eat?"

ה וַתָּבֹא אֵלָיו אִיזֶבֶל אִשְׁתּוֹ וַתְּדַבֵּר אֵלָיו מַה־זֶּה רוּחֲךָ סָרָה וְאֵינְךָ אֹכֵל לָחֶם׃

6 So he told her, "I spoke to *Navot* the Yizraelite and proposed to him, 'Sell me your vineyard for money, or if you prefer, I'll give you another vineyard in exchange'; but he answered, 'I will not give my vineyard to you.'"

ו וַיְדַבֵּר אֵלֶיהָ כִּי־אֲדַבֵּר אֶל־נָבוֹת הַיִּזְרְעֵאלִי וָאֹמַר לוֹ תְּנָה־לִּי אֶת־כַּרְמְךָ בְּכֶסֶף אוֹ אִם־חָפֵץ אַתָּה אֶתְּנָה־לְךָ כֶרֶם תַּחְתָּיו וַיֹּאמֶר לֹא־אֶתֵּן לְךָ אֶת־כַּרְמִי׃

7 His wife Jezebel said to him, "Now is the time to show yourself king over *Yisrael*. Rise and eat something, and be cheerful; I will get the vineyard of *Navot* the Yizraelite for you."

ז וַתֹּאמֶר אֵלָיו אִיזֶבֶל אִשְׁתּוֹ אַתָּה עַתָּה תַּעֲשֶׂה מְלוּכָה עַל־יִשְׂרָאֵל קוּם אֱכָל־לֶחֶם וְיִטַב לִבֶּךָ אֲנִי אֶתֵּן לְךָ אֶת־כֶּרֶם נָבוֹת הַיִּזְרְעֵאלִי׃

8 So she wrote letters in *Achav*'s name and sealed them with his seal, and sent the letters to the elders and the nobles who lived in the same town with *Navot*.

ח וַתִּכְתֹּב סְפָרִים בְּשֵׁם אַחְאָב וַתַּחְתֹּם בְּחֹתָמוֹ וַתִּשְׁלַח הספרים [סְפָרִים] אֶל־הַזְּקֵנִים וְאֶל־הַחֹרִים אֲשֶׁר בְּעִירוֹ הַיֹּשְׁבִים אֶת־נָבוֹת׃

9 In the letters she wrote as follows: "Proclaim a fast and seat *Navot* at the front of the assembly.

ט וַתִּכְתֹּב בַּסְּפָרִים לֵאמֹר קִרְאוּ־צוֹם וְהוֹשִׁיבוּ אֶת־נָבוֹת בְּרֹאשׁ הָעָם׃

10 And seat two scoundrels opposite him, and let them testify against him: 'You have reviled *Hashem* and king!' Then take him out and stone him to death."

י וְהוֹשִׁיבוּ שְׁנַיִם אֲנָשִׁים בְּנֵי־בְלִיַּעַל נֶגְדּוֹ וִיעִדֻהוּ לֵאמֹר בֵּרַכְתָּ אֱלֹהִים וָמֶלֶךְ וְהוֹצִיאֻהוּ וְסִקְלֻהוּ וְיָמֹת׃

Melachim I / I Kings
Chapter 21

מלכים א
פרק כא

11 His townsmen – the elders and nobles who lived in his town – did as Jezebel had instructed them, just as was written in the letters she had sent them:

יא וַיַּעֲשׂוּ אַנְשֵׁי עִירוֹ הַזְּקֵנִים וְהַחֹרִים אֲשֶׁר הַיֹּשְׁבִים בְּעִירוֹ כַּאֲשֶׁר שָׁלְחָה אֲלֵיהֶם אִיזָבֶל כַּאֲשֶׁר כָּתוּב בַּסְּפָרִים אֲשֶׁר שָׁלְחָה אֲלֵיהֶם:

12 They proclaimed a fast and seated *Navot* at the front of the assembly.

יב קָרְאוּ צוֹם וְהֹשִׁיבוּ אֶת־נָבוֹת בְּרֹאשׁ הָעָם:

13 Then the two scoundrels came and sat down opposite him; and the scoundrels testified against *Navot* publicly as follows: "*Navot* has reviled *Hashem* and king." Then they took him outside the town and stoned him to death.

יג וַיָּבֹאוּ שְׁנֵי הָאֲנָשִׁים בְּנֵי־בְלִיַּעַל וַיֵּשְׁבוּ נֶגְדּוֹ וַיְעִדֻהוּ אַנְשֵׁי הַבְּלִיַּעַל אֶת־נָבוֹת נֶגֶד הָעָם לֵאמֹר בֵּרַךְ נָבוֹת אֱלֹהִים וָמֶלֶךְ וַיֹּצִאֻהוּ מִחוּץ לָעִיר וַיִּסְקְלֻהוּ בָאֲבָנִים וַיָּמֹת:

14 Word was sent to Jezebel: "*Navot* has been stoned to death."

יד וַיִּשְׁלְחוּ אֶל־אִיזֶבֶל לֵאמֹר סֻקַּל נָבוֹת וַיָּמֹת:

15 As soon as Jezebel heard that *Navot* had been stoned to death, she said to *Achav*, "Go and take possession of the vineyard which *Navot* the Yizraelite refused to sell you for money; for *Navot* is no longer alive, he is dead."

טו וַיְהִי כִּשְׁמֹעַ אִיזֶבֶל כִּי־סֻקַּל נָבוֹת וַיָּמֹת וַתֹּאמֶר אִיזֶבֶל אֶל־אַחְאָב קוּם רֵשׁ אֶת־כֶּרֶם נָבוֹת הַיִּזְרְעֵאלִי אֲשֶׁר מֵאֵן לָתֶת־לְךָ בְכֶסֶף כִּי אֵין נָבוֹת חַי כִּי־מֵת:

16 When *Achav* heard that *Navot* was dead, *Achav* set out for the vineyard of *Navot* the Yizraelite to take possession of it.

טז וַיְהִי כִּשְׁמֹעַ אַחְאָב כִּי מֵת נָבוֹת וַיָּקָם אַחְאָב לָרֶדֶת אֶל־כֶּרֶם נָבוֹת הַיִּזְרְעֵאלִי לְרִשְׁתּוֹ:

17 Then the word of *Hashem* came to *Eliyahu* the Tishbite:

יז וַיְהִי דְּבַר־יְהֹוָה אֶל־אֵלִיָּהוּ הַתִּשְׁבִּי לֵאמֹר:

18 "Go down and confront King *Achav* of *Yisrael* who [resides] in *Shomron*. He is now in *Navot*'s vineyard; he has gone down there to take possession of it.

יח קוּם רֵד לִקְרַאת אַחְאָב מֶלֶךְ־יִשְׂרָאֵל אֲשֶׁר בְּשֹׁמְרוֹן הִנֵּה בְּכֶרֶם נָבוֹת אֲשֶׁר־יָרַד שָׁם לְרִשְׁתּוֹ:

19 Say to him, 'Thus said *Hashem*: Would you murder and take possession? Thus said *Hashem*: In the very place where the dogs lapped up *Navot*'s blood, the dogs will lap up your blood too.'"

יט וְדִבַּרְתָּ אֵלָיו לֵאמֹר כֹּה אָמַר יְהֹוָה הֲרָצַחְתָּ וְגַם־יָרָשְׁתָּ וְדִבַּרְתָּ אֵלָיו לֵאמֹר כֹּה אָמַר יְהֹוָה בִּמְקוֹם אֲשֶׁר לָקְקוּ הַכְּלָבִים אֶת־דַּם נָבוֹת יָלֹקּוּ הַכְּלָבִים אֶת־דָּמְךָ גַּם־אָתָּה:

v'-di-bar-TA ay-LAV lay-MOR KOH a-MAR a-do-NAI ha-ra-TZAKH-ta v'-gam ya-RASH-ta v'-di-bar-TA ay-LAV lay-MOR KOH a-MAR a-do-NAI bim-KOM a-SHER la-k'-KU ha-k'-la-VEEM et DAM na-VOT ya-LO-ku ha-k'-la-VEEM et da-m'-KHA gam A-tah

21:19 Would you murder and take possession? Selling ancestral land is considered inappropriate in all but the most extreme circumstances. Thus, it is not surprising that *Navot* does not want to sell his portion. When he is cruelly murdered and his land seized, *Eliyahu* confronts *Achav* with harsh criticism. The phenomenon of land being wrongfully seized from its rightful owners is a theme that has repeated itself many times in *Eretz Yisrael*. Today, despite centuries of persecution and forcible exile from the land, the Children of Israel have returned home. Israel wants to live in peace with its neighbors and to preserve the rights of mi-

Melachim I/I Kings
Chapter 22

מלכים א
פרק כב

20 *Achav* said to *Eliyahu*, "So you have found me, my enemy?" "Yes, I have found you," he replied. "Because you have committed yourself to doing what is evil in the sight of *Hashem*,

כ וַיֹּאמֶר אַחְאָב אֶל־אֵלִיָּהוּ הַמְצָאתַנִי אֹיְבִי וַיֹּאמֶר מָצָאתִי יַעַן הִתְמַכֶּרְךָ לַעֲשׂוֹת הָרַע בְּעֵינֵי יְהוָה:

21 I will bring disaster upon you. I will make a clean sweep of you, I will cut off from *Yisrael* every male belonging to *Achav*, bond and free.

כא הִנְנִי מֵבִי [מֵבִיא] אֵלֶיךָ רָעָה וּבִעַרְתִּי אַחֲרֶיךָ וְהִכְרַתִּי לְאַחְאָב מַשְׁתִּין בְּקִיר וְעָצוּר וְעָזוּב בְּיִשְׂרָאֵל:

22 And I will make your house like the House of *Yerovam* son of Nebat and like the House of *Basha* son of *Achiya*, because of the provocation you have caused by leading *Yisrael* to sin.

כב וְנָתַתִּי אֶת־בֵּיתְךָ כְּבֵית יָרָבְעָם בֶּן־נְבָט וּכְבֵית בַּעְשָׁא בֶן־אֲחִיָּה אֶל־הַכַּעַס אֲשֶׁר הִכְעַסְתָּ וַתַּחֲטִא אֶת־יִשְׂרָאֵל:

23 And *Hashem* has also spoken concerning Jezebel: 'The dogs shall devour Jezebel in the field of *Yizrael*.

כג וְגַם־לְאִיזֶבֶל דִּבֶּר יְהוָה לֵאמֹר הַכְּלָבִים יֹאכְלוּ אֶת־אִיזֶבֶל בְּחֵל יִזְרְעֶאל:

24 All of *Achav*'s line who die in the town shall be devoured by dogs, and all who die in the open country shall be devoured by the birds of the sky.'"

כד הַמֵּת לְאַחְאָב בָּעִיר יֹאכְלוּ הַכְּלָבִים וְהַמֵּת בַּשָּׂדֶה יֹאכְלוּ עוֹף הַשָּׁמָיִם:

25 Indeed, there never was anyone like *Achav*, who committed himself to doing what was displeasing to *Hashem*, at the instigation of his wife Jezebel.

כה רַק לֹא־הָיָה כְאַחְאָב אֲשֶׁר הִתְמַכֵּר לַעֲשׂוֹת הָרַע בְּעֵינֵי יְהוָה אֲשֶׁר־הֵסַתָּה אֹתוֹ אִיזֶבֶל אִשְׁתּוֹ:

26 He acted most abominably, straying after the fetishes just like the Amorites, whom *Hashem* had dispossessed before the Israelites.

כו וַיַּתְעֵב מְאֹד לָלֶכֶת אַחֲרֵי הַגִּלֻּלִים כְּכֹל אֲשֶׁר עָשׂוּ הָאֱמֹרִי אֲשֶׁר הוֹרִישׁ יְהוָה מִפְּנֵי בְּנֵי יִשְׂרָאֵל:

27 When *Achav* heard these words, he rent his clothes and put sackcloth on his body. He fasted and lay in sackcloth and walked about subdued.

כז וַיְהִי כִשְׁמֹעַ אַחְאָב אֶת־הַדְּבָרִים הָאֵלֶּה וַיִּקְרַע בְּגָדָיו וַיָּשֶׂם־שַׂק עַל־בְּשָׂרוֹ וַיָּצוֹם וַיִּשְׁכַּב בַּשָּׂק וַיְהַלֵּךְ אַט:

28 Then the word of *Hashem* came to *Eliyahu* the Tishbite:

כח וַיְהִי דְּבַר־יְהוָה אֶל־אֵלִיָּהוּ הַתִּשְׁבִּי לֵאמֹר:

29 "Have you seen how *Achav* has humbled himself before Me? Because he has humbled himself before Me, I will not bring the disaster in his lifetime; I will bring the disaster upon his house in his son's time."

כט הֲרָאִיתָ כִּי־נִכְנַע אַחְאָב מִלְּפָנָי יַעַן כִּי־נִכְנַע מִפָּנַי לֹא־אָבִי [אָבִיא] הָרָעָה בְּיָמָיו בִּימֵי בְנוֹ אָבִיא הָרָעָה עַל־בֵּיתוֹ:

22 1 There was a lull of three years, with no war between *Aram* and *Yisrael*.

כב א וַיֵּשְׁבוּ שָׁלֹשׁ שָׁנִים אֵין מִלְחָמָה בֵּין אֲרָם וּבֵין יִשְׂרָאֵל:

---

norities within its borders. But it also wants to make sure that the Children of Israel are in possession of their rightful homeland. Now that the State of Israel is in possession of much of the biblical Land of Israel, the Jewish people have begun to return to the land that is rightfully theirs.

Melachim I/I Kings
Chapter 22

מלכים א
פרק כב

2 In the third year, King *Yehoshafat* of *Yehuda* came to visit the king of *Yisrael*.

ב וַיְהִי בַּשָּׁנָה הַשְּׁלִישִׁית וַיֵּרֶד יְהוֹשָׁפָט מֶלֶךְ־יְהוּדָה אֶל־מֶלֶךְ יִשְׂרָאֵל׃

vai-HEE ba-sha-NAH ha-sh'-lee-SHEET va-YAY-red y'-ho-sha-FAT me-lekh y'-hu-DAH el ME-lekh yis-ra-AYL

3 The king of *Yisrael* said to his courtiers, "You know that Ramoth-gilead belongs to us, and yet we do nothing to recover it from the hands of the king of Aram."

ג וַיֹּאמֶר מֶלֶךְ־יִשְׂרָאֵל אֶל־עֲבָדָיו הַיְדַעְתֶּם כִּי־לָנוּ רָמֹת גִּלְעָד וַאֲנַחְנוּ מַחְשִׁים מִקַּחַת אֹתָהּ מִיַּד מֶלֶךְ אֲרָם׃

4 And he said to *Yehoshafat*, "Will you come with me to battle at Ramoth-gilead?" *Yehoshafat* answered the king of *Yisrael*, "I will do what you do; my troops shall be your troops, my horses shall be your horses."

ד וַיֹּאמֶר אֶל־יְהוֹשָׁפָט הֲתֵלֵךְ אִתִּי לַמִּלְחָמָה רָמֹת גִּלְעָד וַיֹּאמֶר יְהוֹשָׁפָט אֶל־מֶלֶךְ יִשְׂרָאֵל כָּמוֹנִי כָמוֹךָ כְּעַמִּי כְעַמֶּךָ כְּסוּסַי כְּסוּסֶיךָ׃

5 But *Yehoshafat* said further to the king of *Yisrael*, "Please, first inquire of *Hashem*."

ה וַיֹּאמֶר יְהוֹשָׁפָט אֶל־מֶלֶךְ יִשְׂרָאֵל דְּרָשׁ־נָא כַיּוֹם אֶת־דְּבַר יְהוָה׃

6 So the king of *Yisrael* gathered the *Neviim*, about four hundred men, and asked them, "Shall I march upon Ramoth-gilead for battle, or shall I not?" "March," they said, "and *Hashem* will deliver [it] into Your Majesty's hands."

ו וַיִּקְבֹּץ מֶלֶךְ־יִשְׂרָאֵל אֶת־הַנְּבִיאִים כְּאַרְבַּע מֵאוֹת אִישׁ וַיֹּאמֶר אֲלֵהֶם הַאֵלֵךְ עַל־רָמֹת גִּלְעָד לַמִּלְחָמָה אִם־אֶחְדָּל וַיֹּאמְרוּ עֲלֵה וְיִתֵּן אֲדֹנָי בְּיַד הַמֶּלֶךְ׃

7 Then *Yehoshafat* asked, "Isn't there another *Navi* of *Hashem* here through whom we can inquire?"

ז וַיֹּאמֶר יְהוֹשָׁפָט הַאֵין פֹּה נָבִיא לַיהוָה עוֹד וְנִדְרְשָׁה מֵאוֹתוֹ׃

8 And the king of *Yisrael* answered *Yehoshafat*, "There is one more man through whom we can inquire of *Hashem*; but I hate him, because he never prophesies anything good for me, but only misfortune – *Michaihu* son of Imlah." But King *Yehoshafat* said, "Don't say that, Your Majesty."

ח וַיֹּאמֶר מֶלֶךְ־יִשְׂרָאֵל אֶל־יְהוֹשָׁפָט עוֹד אִישׁ־אֶחָד לִדְרֹשׁ אֶת־יְהוָה מֵאֹתוֹ וַאֲנִי שְׂנֵאתִיו כִּי לֹא־יִתְנַבֵּא עָלַי טוֹב כִּי אִם־רָע מִיכָיְהוּ בֶּן־יִמְלָה וַיֹּאמֶר יְהוֹשָׁפָט אַל־יֹאמַר הַמֶּלֶךְ כֵּן׃

9 So the king of *Yisrael* summoned an officer and said, "Bring *Michaihu* son of Imlah at once."

ט וַיִּקְרָא מֶלֶךְ יִשְׂרָאֵל אֶל־סָרִיס אֶחָד וַיֹּאמֶר מַהֲרָה מִיכָיְהוּ בֶן־יִמְלָה׃

ירד

22:2 King *Yehoshafat* of *Yehuda* came to visit the king of *Yisrael* In describing *Yehoshafat*'s visit to the king of *Yisrael*, the verse uses the Hebrew word *yarad* (ירד), which literally means 'he came down.' When the Bible makes references to 'going up' or 'going down,' these terms often have spiritual, rather than physical, meaning. Therefore, going to *Yerushalayim*, or immigrating to *Eretz Yisrael*, is always referred to as "going up," while leaving *Yerushalayim* or the Land of Israel is always called "going down." Since *Yehoshafat* is going from *Yerushalayim* in *Yehuda* to the less holy northern kingdom of Israel, the Bible says he "came (down) to visit." In Modern Hebrew, the same expressions are used. Immigrating to Israel is known as *aliyah*, 'ascent,' while leaving is known as *yerida*, 'descent.'

Melachim I / I Kings
Chapter 22

10 The king of *Yisrael* and King *Yehoshafat* of *Yehuda* were seated on their thrones, arrayed in their robes, on the threshing floor at the entrance of the gate of *Shomron*; and all the *Neviim* were prophesying before them.

11 *Tzidkiyahu* son of *Chenaanah* had provided himself with iron horns; and he said, "Thus said *Hashem*: With these you shall gore the Arameans till you make an end of them."

12 And all the other *Neviim* were prophesying similarly, "March upon Ramoth-gilead and triumph! *Hashem* will deliver it into Your Majesty's hands."

13 The messenger who had gone to summon *Michaihu* said to him: "Look, the words of the *Neviim* are with one accord favorable to the king. Let your word be like that of the rest of them; speak a favorable word."

14 "As *Hashem* lives," *Michaihu* answered, "I will speak only what *Hashem* tells me."

15 When he came before the king, the king said to him, "*Michaihu*, shall we march upon Ramoth-gilead for battle, or shall we not?" He answered him, "March and triumph! *Hashem* will deliver [it] into Your Majesty's hands."

16 The king said to him, "How many times must I adjure you to tell me nothing but the truth in the name of *Hashem*?"

17 Then he said, "I saw all *Yisrael* scattered over the hills like sheep without a shepherd; and *Hashem* said, 'These have no master; let everyone return to his home in safety.'"

18 "Didn't I tell you," said the king of *Yisrael* to *Yehoshafat*, "that he would not prophesy good fortune for me, but only misfortune?"

19 But [*Michaihu*] said, "I call upon you to hear the word of *Hashem*! I saw *Hashem* seated upon His throne, with all the host of heaven standing in attendance to the right and to the left of Him.

20 *Hashem* asked, 'Who will entice *Achav* so that he will march and fall at Ramoth-gilead?' Then one said thus and another said thus,

מלכים א
פרק כב

י וּמֶ֤לֶךְ יִשְׂרָאֵל֙ וִיהוֹשָׁפָ֣ט מֶלֶךְ־יְהוּדָ֔ה יֹשְׁבִ֤ים אִישׁ֙ עַל־כִּסְא֔וֹ מְלֻבָּשִׁ֖ים בְּגָדִ֑ים בְּגֹ֗רֶן פֶּ֚תַח שַׁ֣עַר שֹׁמְר֔וֹן וְכָ֨ל־הַנְּבִיאִ֔ים מִֽתְנַבְּאִ֖ים לִפְנֵיהֶֽם:

יא וַיַּ֥עַשׂ ל֛וֹ צִדְקִיָּ֥ה בֶֽן־כְּנַעֲנָ֖ה קַרְנֵ֣י בַרְזֶ֑ל וַיֹּ֙אמֶר֙ כֹּֽה־אָמַ֣ר יְהֹוָ֔ה בְּאֵ֛לֶּה תְּנַגַּ֥ח אֶת־אֲרָ֖ם עַד־כַּלֹּתָֽם:

יב וְכָל־הַנְּבִאִ֔ים נִבְּאִ֥ים כֵּ֖ן לֵאמֹ֑ר עֲלֵ֞ה רָמֹ֤ת גִּלְעָד֙ וְהַצְלַ֔ח וְנָתַ֥ן יְהֹוָ֖ה בְּיַ֥ד הַמֶּֽלֶךְ:

יג וְהַמַּלְאָ֞ךְ אֲשֶׁר־הָלַ֣ךְ ׀ לִקְרֹ֣א מִיכָ֗יְהוּ דִּבֶּ֤ר אֵלָיו֙ לֵאמֹ֔ר הִנֵּה־נָ֞א דִּבְרֵ֧י הַנְּבִיאִ֛ים פֶּה־אֶחָ֥ד ט֖וֹב אֶל־הַמֶּ֑לֶךְ יְהִי־נָ֣א דברי [דְבָרְךָ֗] כִּדְבַ֛ר אַחַ֥ד מֵהֶ֖ם וְדִבַּ֥רְתָּ טּֽוֹב:

יד וַיֹּ֖אמֶר מִיכָ֑יְהוּ חַי־יְהֹוָ֕ה כִּ֠י אֶת־אֲשֶׁ֨ר יֹאמַ֧ר יְהֹוָ֛ה אֵלַ֖י אֹת֥וֹ אֲדַבֵּֽר:

טו וַיָּבוֹא֮ אֶל־הַמֶּלֶךְ֒ וַיֹּ֨אמֶר הַמֶּ֜לֶךְ אֵלָ֗יו מִיכָ֙יְהוּ֙ הֲנֵלֵ֞ךְ אֶל־רָמֹ֥ת גִּלְעָ֛ד לַמִּלְחָמָ֖ה אִם־נֶחְדָּ֑ל וַיֹּ֤אמֶר אֵלָיו֙ עֲלֵ֣ה וְהַצְלַ֔ח וְנָתַ֥ן יְהֹוָ֖ה בְּיַ֥ד הַמֶּֽלֶךְ:

טז וַיֹּ֤אמֶר אֵלָיו֙ הַמֶּ֔לֶךְ עַד־כַּמֶּ֥ה פְעָמִ֖ים אֲנִ֣י מַשְׁבִּעֶ֑ךָ אֲ֠שֶׁ֠ר לֹֽא־תְדַבֵּ֥ר אֵלַ֛י רַק־אֱמֶ֖ת בְּשֵׁ֥ם יְהֹוָֽה:

יז וַיֹּ֗אמֶר רָאִ֤יתִי אֶת־כָּל־יִשְׂרָאֵל֙ נְפֹצִ֣ים אֶל־הֶֽהָרִ֔ים כַּצֹּ֕אן אֲשֶׁ֥ר אֵין־לָהֶ֖ם רֹעֶ֑ה וַיֹּ֤אמֶר יְהֹוָה֙ לֹֽא־אֲדֹנִ֣ים לָאֵ֔לֶּה יָשׁ֥וּבוּ אִישׁ־לְבֵית֖וֹ בְּשָׁלֽוֹם:

יח וַיֹּ֥אמֶר מֶלֶךְ־יִשְׂרָאֵ֖ל אֶל־יְהוֹשָׁפָ֑ט הֲל֙וֹא֙ אָמַ֣רְתִּי אֵלֶ֔יךָ ל֥וֹא־יִתְנַבֵּ֛א עָלַ֥י ט֖וֹב כִּ֥י אִם־רָֽע:

יט וַיֹּ֕אמֶר לָכֵ֖ן שְׁמַ֣ע דְּבַר־יְהֹוָ֑ה רָאִ֤יתִי אֶת־יְהֹוָה֙ יֹשֵׁ֣ב עַל־כִּסְא֔וֹ וְכָל־צְבָ֤א הַשָּׁמַ֙יִם֙ עֹמֵ֣ד עָלָ֔יו מִימִינ֖וֹ וּמִשְּׂמֹאלֽוֹ:

כ וַיֹּ֣אמֶר יְהֹוָ֗ה מִ֤י יְפַתֶּה֙ אֶת־אַחְאָ֔ב וְיַ֕עַל וְיִפֹּ֖ל בְּרָמֹ֣ת גִּלְעָ֑ד וַיֹּ֤אמֶר זֶה֙ בְּכֹ֔ה וְזֶ֥ה אֹמֵ֖ר בְּכֹֽה:

Melachim I / I Kings
Chapter 22

מלכים א
פרק כב

כא וַיֵּצֵא הָרוּחַ וַיַּעֲמֹד לִפְנֵי יְהֹוָה וַיֹּאמֶר אֲנִי אֲפַתֶּנּוּ וַיֹּאמֶר יְהֹוָה אֵלָיו בַּמָּה:

21 until a certain spirit came forward and stood before *Hashem* and said, 'I will entice him.' 'How?' *Hashem* asked him.

כב וַיֹּאמֶר אֵצֵא וְהָיִיתִי רוּחַ שֶׁקֶר בְּפִי כָּל־נְבִיאָיו וַיֹּאמֶר תְּפַתֶּה וְגַם־תּוּכָל צֵא וַעֲשֵׂה־כֵן:

22 And he replied, 'I will go out and be a lying spirit in the mouth of all his *Neviim*.' Then He said, 'You will entice and you will prevail. Go out and do it.'

כג וְעַתָּה הִנֵּה נָתַן יְהֹוָה רוּחַ שֶׁקֶר בְּפִי כָּל־נְבִיאֶיךָ אֵלֶּה וַיהֹוָה דִּבֶּר עָלֶיךָ רָעָה:

23 So *Hashem* has put a lying spirit in the mouth of all these *Neviim* of yours; for *Hashem* has decreed disaster upon you."

כד וַיִּגַּשׁ צִדְקִיָּהוּ בֶן־כְּנַעֲנָה וַיַּכֶּה אֶת־מִיכָיְהוּ עַל־הַלֶּחִי וַיֹּאמֶר אֵי־זֶה עָבַר רוּחַ־יְהֹוָה מֵאִתִּי לְדַבֵּר אוֹתָךְ:

24 Thereupon *Tzidkiyahu* son of Chenaanah stepped up and struck *Michaihu* on the cheek, and demanded, "Which way did the spirit of *Hashem* pass from me to speak with you?"

כה וַיֹּאמֶר מִיכָיְהוּ הִנְּךָ רֹאֶה בַּיּוֹם הַהוּא אֲשֶׁר תָּבֹא חֶדֶר בְּחֶדֶר לְהֵחָבֵה:

25 And *Michaihu* replied, "You'll find out on the day when you try to hide in the innermost room."

כו וַיֹּאמֶר מֶלֶךְ יִשְׂרָאֵל קַח אֶת־מִיכָיְהוּ וַהֲשִׁיבֵהוּ אֶל־אָמֹן שַׂר־הָעִיר וְאֶל־יוֹאָשׁ בֶּן־הַמֶּלֶךְ:

26 Then the king of *Yisrael* said, "Take *Michaihu* and turn him over to Ammon, the city's governor, and to Prince *Yoash*,

כז וְאָמַרְתָּ כֹּה אָמַר הַמֶּלֶךְ שִׂימוּ אֶת־זֶה בֵּית הַכֶּלֶא וְהַאֲכִילֻהוּ לֶחֶם לַחַץ וּמַיִם לַחַץ עַד בֹּאִי בְשָׁלוֹם:

27 and say, 'The king's orders are: Put this fellow in prison, and let his fare be scant bread and scant water until I come home safe.'"

כח וַיֹּאמֶר מִיכָיְהוּ אִם־שׁוֹב תָּשׁוּב בְּשָׁלוֹם לֹא־דִבֶּר יְהֹוָה בִּי וַיֹּאמֶר שִׁמְעוּ עַמִּים כֻּלָּם:

28 To which *Michaihu* retorted, "If you ever come home safe, *Hashem* has not spoken through me." He said further, "Listen, all you peoples!"

כט וַיַּעַל מֶלֶךְ־יִשְׂרָאֵל וִיהוֹשָׁפָט מֶלֶךְ־יְהוּדָה רָמֹת גִּלְעָד:

29 So the king of *Yisrael* and King *Yehoshafat* of *Yehuda* marched upon Ramoth-gilead.

ל וַיֹּאמֶר מֶלֶךְ יִשְׂרָאֵל אֶל־יְהוֹשָׁפָט הִתְחַפֵּשׂ וָבֹא בַמִּלְחָמָה וְאַתָּה לְבַשׁ בְּגָדֶיךָ וַיִּתְחַפֵּשׂ מֶלֶךְ יִשְׂרָאֵל וַיָּבוֹא בַּמִּלְחָמָה:

30 The king of *Yisrael* said to *Yehoshafat*, "Disguise yourself and go into the battle; but you, wear your robes." So the king of *Yisrael* went into the battle disguised.

לא וּמֶלֶךְ אֲרָם צִוָּה אֶת־שָׂרֵי הָרֶכֶב אֲשֶׁר־לוֹ שְׁלֹשִׁים וּשְׁנַיִם לֵאמֹר לֹא תִּלָּחֲמוּ אֶת־קָטֹן וְאֶת־גָּדוֹל כִּי אִם־אֶת־מֶלֶךְ יִשְׂרָאֵל לְבַדּוֹ:

31 Now the king of Aram had instructed his thirty-two chariot officers: "Don't attack anyone, small or great, except the king of *Yisrael*."

לב וַיְהִי כִּרְאוֹת שָׂרֵי הָרֶכֶב אֶת־יְהוֹשָׁפָט וְהֵמָּה אָמְרוּ אַךְ מֶלֶךְ־יִשְׂרָאֵל הוּא וַיָּסֻרוּ עָלָיו לְהִלָּחֵם וַיִּזְעַק יְהוֹשָׁפָט:

32 So when the chariot officers saw *Yehoshafat*, whom they took for the king of *Yisrael*, they turned upon him to attack him, and *Yehoshafat* cried out.

לג וַיְהִי כִּרְאוֹת שָׂרֵי הָרֶכֶב כִּי־לֹא־מֶלֶךְ יִשְׂרָאֵל הוּא וַיָּשׁוּבוּ מֵאַחֲרָיו:

33 And when the chariot officers became aware that he was not the king of *Yisrael*, they turned back from pursuing him.

Melachim I / I Kings
Chapter 22

34 Then a man drew his bow at random and he hit the king of *Yisrael* between the plates of the armor; and he said to his charioteer, "Turn the horses around and get me behind the lines; I'm wounded."

35 The battle raged all day long, and the king remained propped up in the chariot facing Aram; the blood from the wound ran down into the hollow of the chariot, and at dusk he died.

36 As the sun was going down, a shout went through the army: "Every man to his own town! Every man to his own district."

37 So the king died and was brought to *Shomron*. They buried the king in *Shomron*,

38 and they flushed out the chariot at the pool of *Shomron*. Thus the dogs lapped up his blood and the whores bathed [in it], in accordance with the word that *Hashem* had spoken.

39 The other events of *Achav*'s reign, and all his actions – the ivory palace that he built and all the towns that he fortified – are all recorded in the Annals of the Kings of *Yisrael*.

40 *Achav* slept with his fathers, and his son *Achazyahu* succeeded him as king.

41 *Yehoshafat* son of *Asa* had become king of *Yehuda* in the fourth year of King *Achav* of *Yisrael*.

42 *Yehoshafat* was thirty-five years old when he became king, and he reigned in *Yerushalayim* for twenty-five years. His mother's name was Azubah daughter of Shilhi.

43 He followed closely the course of his father *Asa* and did not deviate from it, doing what was pleasing to *Hashem*.

44 However, the shrines did not cease to function; the people still sacrificed and offered at the shrines.

45 And further, *Yehoshafat* submitted to the king of *Yisrael*.

46 As for the other events of *Yehoshafat*'s reign and the valor he displayed in battle, they are recorded in the Annals of the Kings of *Yehuda*.

47 He also stamped out the remaining male prostitutes who had survived in the land from the time of his father *Asa*.

מלכים א
פרק כב

לד וְאִישׁ מָשַׁךְ בַּקֶּשֶׁת לְתֻמּוֹ וַיַּכֶּה אֶת־מֶלֶךְ יִשְׂרָאֵל בֵּין הַדְּבָקִים וּבֵין הַשִּׁרְיָן וַיֹּאמֶר לְרַכָּבוֹ הֲפֹךְ יָדְךָ וְהוֹצִיאֵנִי מִן־הַמַּחֲנֶה כִּי הָחֳלֵיתִי׃

לה וַתַּעֲלֶה הַמִּלְחָמָה בַּיּוֹם הַהוּא וְהַמֶּלֶךְ הָיָה מָעֳמָד בַּמֶּרְכָּבָה נֹכַח אֲרָם וַיָּמָת בָּעֶרֶב וַיִּצֶק דַּם־הַמַּכָּה אֶל־חֵיק הָרָכֶב׃

לו וַיַּעֲבֹר הָרִנָּה בַּמַּחֲנֶה כְּבֹא הַשֶּׁמֶשׁ לֵאמֹר אִישׁ אֶל־עִירוֹ וְאִישׁ אֶל־אַרְצוֹ׃

לז וַיָּמָת הַמֶּלֶךְ וַיָּבוֹא שֹׁמְרוֹן וַיִּקְבְּרוּ אֶת־הַמֶּלֶךְ בְּשֹׁמְרוֹן׃

לח וַיִּשְׁטֹף אֶת־הָרֶכֶב עַל בְּרֵכַת שֹׁמְרוֹן וַיָּלֹקּוּ הַכְּלָבִים אֶת־דָּמוֹ וְהַזֹּנוֹת רָחָצוּ כִּדְבַר יְהֹוָה אֲשֶׁר דִּבֵּר׃

לט וְיֶתֶר דִּבְרֵי אַחְאָב וְכָל־אֲשֶׁר עָשָׂה וּבֵית הַשֵּׁן אֲשֶׁר בָּנָה וְכָל־הֶעָרִים אֲשֶׁר בָּנָה הֲלוֹא־הֵם כְּתוּבִים עַל־סֵפֶר דִּבְרֵי הַיָּמִים לְמַלְכֵי יִשְׂרָאֵל׃

מ וַיִּשְׁכַּב אַחְאָב עִם־אֲבֹתָיו וַיִּמְלֹךְ אֲחַזְיָהוּ בְנוֹ תַּחְתָּיו׃

מא וִיהוֹשָׁפָט בֶּן־אָסָא מָלַךְ עַל־יְהוּדָה בִּשְׁנַת אַרְבַּע לְאַחְאָב מֶלֶךְ יִשְׂרָאֵל׃

מב יְהוֹשָׁפָט בֶּן־שְׁלֹשִׁים וְחָמֵשׁ שָׁנָה בְּמָלְכוֹ וְעֶשְׂרִים וְחָמֵשׁ שָׁנָה מָלַךְ בִּירוּשָׁלָ͏ִם וְשֵׁם אִמּוֹ עֲזוּבָה בַּת־שִׁלְחִי׃

מג וַיֵּלֶךְ בְּכָל־דֶּרֶךְ אָסָא אָבִיו לֹא־סָר מִמֶּנּוּ לַעֲשׂוֹת הַיָּשָׁר בְּעֵינֵי יְהֹוָה׃

מד אַךְ הַבָּמוֹת לֹא־סָרוּ עוֹד הָעָם מְזַבְּחִים וּמְקַטְּרִים בַּבָּמוֹת׃

מה וַיַּשְׁלֵם יְהוֹשָׁפָט עִם־מֶלֶךְ יִשְׂרָאֵל׃

מו וְיֶתֶר דִּבְרֵי יְהוֹשָׁפָט וּגְבוּרָתוֹ אֲשֶׁר־עָשָׂה וַאֲשֶׁר נִלְחָם הֲלֹא־הֵם כְּתוּבִים עַל־סֵפֶר דִּבְרֵי הַיָּמִים לְמַלְכֵי יְהוּדָה׃

מז וְיֶתֶר הַקָּדֵשׁ אֲשֶׁר נִשְׁאַר בִּימֵי אָסָא אָבִיו בִּעֵר מִן־הָאָרֶץ׃

Melachim I / I Kings
Chapter 22

מלכים א
פרק כב

48 There was no king in Edom; a viceroy acted as king.

מח וּמֶ֖לֶךְ אֵ֣ין בֶּאֱד֑וֹם נִצָּ֖ב מֶֽלֶךְ׃

49 *Yehoshafat* constructed Tarshish ships to sail to Ophir for gold. But he did not sail because the ships were wrecked at Ezion-geber.

מט יְהוֹשָׁפָ֡ט עשר [עָשָׂה֩] אֳנִיּ֨וֹת תַּרְשִׁ֜ישׁ לָלֶ֧כֶת אוֹפִ֛ירָה לַזָּהָ֖ב וְלֹ֣א הָלָ֑ךְ כִּֽי־נשברה [נִשְׁבְּר֥וּ] אֳנִיּ֖וֹת בְּעֶצְי֥וֹן גָּֽבֶר׃

50 Then *Achazyahu* son of *Achav* proposed to *Yehoshafat*, "Let my servants sail on the ships with your servants"; but *Yehoshafat* would not agree.

נ אָ֠ז אָמַ֞ר אֲחַזְיָ֤הוּ בֶן־אַחְאָב֙ אֶל־יְה֣וֹשָׁפָ֔ט יֵלְכ֧וּ עֲבָדַ֛י עִם־עֲבָדֶ֖יךָ בָּאֳנִיּ֑וֹת וְלֹ֥א אָבָ֖ה יְהוֹשָׁפָֽט׃

51 *Yehoshafat* slept with his fathers and was buried with his fathers in the city of his father *David*, and his son *Yehoram* succeeded him as king.

נא וַיִּשְׁכַּ֤ב יְהֽוֹשָׁפָט֙ עִם־אֲבֹתָ֔יו וַיִּקָּבֵר֙ עִם־אֲבֹתָ֔יו בְּעִ֖יר דָּוִ֣ד אָבִ֑יו וַיִּמְלֹ֛ךְ יְהוֹרָ֥ם בְּנ֖וֹ תַּחְתָּֽיו׃

52 [Meanwhile,] *Achazyahu* son of *Achav* had become king of *Yisrael*, in *Shomron*, in the seventeenth year of King *Yehoshafat* of *Yehuda*; he reigned over *Yisrael* two years.

נב אֲחַזְיָ֣הוּ בֶן־אַחְאָ֗ב מָלַ֤ךְ עַל־יִשְׂרָאֵל֙ בְּשֹׁ֣מְר֔וֹן בִּשְׁנַת֙ שְׁבַ֣ע עֶשְׂרֵ֔ה לִיהוֹשָׁפָ֖ט מֶ֣לֶךְ יְהוּדָ֑ה וַיִּמְלֹ֥ךְ עַל־יִשְׂרָאֵ֖ל שְׁנָתָֽיִם׃

53 He did what was displeasing to *Hashem*, following in the footsteps of his father and his mother, and in those of *Yerovam* son of Nebat who had caused *Yisrael* to sin.

נג וַיַּ֥עַשׂ הָרַ֖ע בְּעֵינֵ֣י יְהֹוָ֑ה וַיֵּ֗לֶךְ בְּדֶ֤רֶךְ אָבִיו֙ וּבְדֶ֣רֶךְ אִמּ֔וֹ וּבְדֶ֙רֶךְ֙ יָרָבְעָ֣ם בֶּן־נְבָ֔ט אֲשֶׁ֥ר הֶחֱטִ֖יא אֶת־יִשְׂרָאֵֽל׃

54 He worshiped Baal and bowed down to him; he vexed *Hashem*, the God of *Yisrael*, just as his father had done.

נד וַֽיַּעֲבֹד֙ אֶת־הַבַּ֔עַל וַיִּֽשְׁתַּחֲוֶ֖ה ל֑וֹ וַיַּכְעֵ֗ס אֶת־יְהֹוָה֙ אֱלֹהֵ֣י יִשְׂרָאֵ֔ל כְּכֹ֥ל אֲשֶׁר־עָשָׂ֖ה אָבִֽיו׃

Melachim II / II Kings
Chapter 1

מלכים ב
פרק א

1 ¹ After *Achav*'s death, Moab rebelled against *Yisrael*.

א וַיִּפְשַׁע מוֹאָב בְּיִשְׂרָאֵל אַחֲרֵי מוֹת אַחְאָב:

² *Achazyahu* fell through the lattice in his upper chamber at *Shomron* and was injured. So he sent messengers, whom he instructed: "Go inquire of Baal-zebub, the god of Ekron, whether I shall recover from this injury."

ב וַיִּפֹּל אֲחַזְיָה בְּעַד הַשְּׂבָכָה בַּעֲלִיָּתוֹ אֲשֶׁר בְּשֹׁמְרוֹן וַיָּחַל וַיִּשְׁלַח מַלְאָכִים וַיֹּאמֶר אֲלֵהֶם לְכוּ דִרְשׁוּ בְּבַעַל זְבוּב אֱלֹהֵי עֶקְרוֹן אִם־אֶחְיֶה מֵחֳלִי זֶה:

va-yi-POL a-khaz-YAH b'-AD ha-s'-va-KHAH ba-a-li-ya-TO a-SHER b'-sho-m'-RON va-YA-khal va-yish-LAKH mal-a-KHEEM va-YO-mer a-lay-HEM l'-KHU dir-SHU b'-VA-al z'-VUV e-lo-HAY ek-RON im ekh-YEH may-kho-LEE ZEH

³ But an angel of *Hashem* said to *Eliyahu* the Tishbite, "Go and confront the messengers of the king of *Shomron* and say to them, 'Is there no *Hashem* in *Yisrael* that you go to inquire of Baal-zebub, the god of Ekron?

ג וּמַלְאַךְ יְהֹוָה דִּבֶּר אֶל־אֵלִיָּה הַתִּשְׁבִּי קוּם עֲלֵה לִקְרַאת מַלְאֲכֵי מֶלֶךְ־שֹׁמְרוֹן וְדַבֵּר אֲלֵהֶם הַמִבְּלִי אֵין־אֱלֹהִים בְּיִשְׂרָאֵל אַתֶּם הֹלְכִים לִדְרֹשׁ בְּבַעַל זְבוּב אֱלֹהֵי עֶקְרוֹן:

⁴ Assuredly, thus said *Hashem*: You shall not rise from the bed you are lying on, but you shall die.'" And *Eliyahu* went.

ד וְלָכֵן כֹּה־אָמַר יְהֹוָה הַמִּטָּה אֲשֶׁר־עָלִיתָ שָּׁם לֹא־תֵרֵד מִמֶּנָּה כִּי מוֹת תָּמוּת וַיֵּלֶךְ אֵלִיָּה:

⁵ The messengers returned to *Achazyahu*; and he asked, "Why have you come back?"

ה וַיָּשׁוּבוּ הַמַּלְאָכִים אֵלָיו וַיֹּאמֶר אֲלֵהֶם מַה־זֶּה שַׁבְתֶּם:

⁶ They answered him, "A man came toward us and said to us, 'Go back to the king who sent you, and say to him: Thus said *Hashem*: Is there no *Hashem* in *Yisrael* that you must send to inquire of Baal-zebub, the god of Ekron? Assuredly, you shall not rise from the bed you are lying on, but shall die.'"

ו וַיֹּאמְרוּ אֵלָיו אִישׁ עָלָה לִקְרָאתֵנוּ וַיֹּאמֶר אֵלֵינוּ לְכוּ שׁוּבוּ אֶל־הַמֶּלֶךְ אֲשֶׁר־שָׁלַח אֶתְכֶם וְדִבַּרְתֶּם אֵלָיו כֹּה אָמַר יְהֹוָה הַמִבְּלִי אֵין־אֱלֹהִים בְּיִשְׂרָאֵל אַתָּה שֹׁלֵחַ לִדְרֹשׁ בְּבַעַל זְבוּב אֱלֹהֵי עֶקְרוֹן לָכֵן הַמִּטָּה אֲשֶׁר־עָלִיתָ שָּׁם לֹא־תֵרֵד מִמֶּנָּה כִּי־מוֹת תָּמוּת:

⁷ "What sort of man was it," he asked them, "who came toward you and said these things to you?"

ז וַיְדַבֵּר אֲלֵהֶם מֶה מִשְׁפַּט הָאִישׁ אֲשֶׁר עָלָה לִקְרַאתְכֶם וַיְדַבֵּר אֲלֵיכֶם אֶת־הַדְּבָרִים הָאֵלֶּה:

⁸ "A hairy man," they replied, "with a leather belt tied around his waist." "That's *Eliyahu* the Tishbite!" he said.

ח וַיֹּאמְרוּ אֵלָיו אִישׁ בַּעַל שֵׂעָר וְאֵזוֹר עוֹר אָזוּר בְּמָתְנָיו וַיֹּאמַר אֵלִיָּה הַתִּשְׁבִּי הוּא:

א **1:2 He sent messengers** In biblical Hebrew, the word *malach* (מלאך) means 'messenger.' There are two kinds of messengers. One is a human messenger, and the other is an angel, a messenger of God. According to Jewish belief, angels do not have independent free will. Rather, they are *Hashem*'s messengers who are able to fulfill only the specific mission He gives them. When human beings use their free will to do the Lord's bidding, they can become even greater than angels, as they are choosing on their own to obey God. And when they show their loyalty to *Hashem* by doing His bidding and improving His world, they become like angels, His messengers to the rest of the world.

מלאך

Melachim II / II Kings

Chapter 1

מלכים ב

פרק א

ט וַיִּשְׁלַח אֵלָיו שַׂר־חֲמִשִּׁים וַחֲמִשָּׁיו וַיַּעַל אֵלָיו וְהִנֵּה יֹשֵׁב עַל־רֹאשׁ הָהָר וַיְדַבֵּר אֵלָיו אִישׁ הָאֱלֹהִים הַמֶּלֶךְ דִּבֶּר רֵדָה:

י וַיַּעֲנֶה אֵלִיָּהוּ וַיְדַבֵּר אֶל־שַׂר הַחֲמִשִּׁים וְאִם־אִישׁ אֱלֹהִים אָנִי תֵּרֶד אֵשׁ מִן־הַשָּׁמַיִם וְתֹאכַל אֹתְךָ וְאֶת־חֲמִשֶּׁיךָ וַתֵּרֶד אֵשׁ מִן־הַשָּׁמַיִם וַתֹּאכַל אֹתוֹ וְאֶת־חֲמִשָּׁיו:

יא וַיָּשָׁב וַיִּשְׁלַח אֵלָיו שַׂר־חֲמִשִּׁים אַחֵר וַחֲמִשָּׁיו וַיַּעַן וַיְדַבֵּר אֵלָיו אִישׁ הָאֱלֹהִים כֹּה־אָמַר הַמֶּלֶךְ מְהֵרָה רֵדָה:

יב וַיַּעַן אֵלִיָּה וַיְדַבֵּר אֲלֵיהֶם אִם־אִישׁ הָאֱלֹהִים אָנִי תֵּרֶד אֵשׁ מִן־הַשָּׁמַיִם וְתֹאכַל אֹתְךָ וְאֶת־חֲמִשֶּׁיךָ וַתֵּרֶד אֵשׁ־אֱלֹהִים מִן־הַשָּׁמַיִם וַתֹּאכַל אֹתוֹ וְאֶת־חֲמִשָּׁיו:

יג וַיָּשָׁב וַיִּשְׁלַח שַׂר־חֲמִשִּׁים שְׁלִשִׁים וַחֲמִשָּׁיו וַיַּעַל וַיָּבֹא שַׂר־הַחֲמִשִּׁים הַשְּׁלִישִׁי וַיִּכְרַע עַל־בִּרְכָּיו לְנֶגֶד אֵלִיָּהוּ וַיִּתְחַנֵּן אֵלָיו וַיְדַבֵּר אֵלָיו אִישׁ הָאֱלֹהִים תִּיקַר־נָא נַפְשִׁי וְנֶפֶשׁ עֲבָדֶיךָ אֵלֶּה חֲמִשִּׁים בְּעֵינֶיךָ:

יד הִנֵּה יָרְדָה אֵשׁ מִן־הַשָּׁמַיִם וַתֹּאכַל אֶת־שְׁנֵי שָׂרֵי הַחֲמִשִּׁים הָרִאשֹׁנִים וְאֶת־חֲמִשֵּׁיהֶם וְעַתָּה תִּיקַר נַפְשִׁי בְּעֵינֶיךָ:

טו וַיְדַבֵּר מַלְאַךְ יְהוָה אֶל־אֵלִיָּהוּ רֵד אוֹתוֹ אַל־תִּירָא מִפָּנָיו וַיָּקָם וַיֵּרֶד אוֹתוֹ אֶל־הַמֶּלֶךְ:

טז וַיְדַבֵּר אֵלָיו כֹּה־אָמַר יְהוָה יַעַן אֲשֶׁר־שָׁלַחְתָּ מַלְאָכִים לִדְרֹשׁ בְּבַעַל זְבוּב אֱלֹהֵי עֶקְרוֹן הַמִבְּלִי אֵין־אֱלֹהִים בְּיִשְׂרָאֵל לִדְרֹשׁ בִּדְבָרוֹ לָכֵן הַמִּטָּה אֲשֶׁר־עָלִיתָ שָּׁם לֹא־תֵרֵד מִמֶּנָּה כִּי־מוֹת תָּמוּת:

יז וַיָּמָת כִּדְבַר יְהוָה אֲשֶׁר־דִּבֶּר אֵלִיָּהוּ וַיִּמְלֹךְ יְהוֹרָם תַּחְתָּיו בִּשְׁנַת שְׁתַּיִם לִיהוֹרָם בֶּן־יְהוֹשָׁפָט מֶלֶךְ יְהוּדָה כִּי לֹא־הָיָה לוֹ בֵּן:

יח וְיֶתֶר דִּבְרֵי אֲחַזְיָהוּ אֲשֶׁר עָשָׂה הֲלוֹא־הֵמָּה כְתוּבִים עַל־סֵפֶר דִּבְרֵי הַיָּמִים לְמַלְכֵי יִשְׂרָאֵל:

9 Then he sent to him a captain of fifty with his fifty men. He climbed up to him, and found him sitting at the top of a hill. "Man of *Hashem*," he said to him, "by order of the king, come down!"

10 *Eliyahu* replied to the captain of the fifty, "If I am a man of *Hashem*, let fire come down from heaven and consume you with your fifty men!" And fire came down from heaven and consumed him and his fifty men.

11 The king then sent to him another captain with his fifty men; and he addressed him as follows: "Man of *Hashem*, by order of the king, come down at once!"

12 But *Eliyahu* answered him, "If I am a man of *Hashem*, let fire come down from heaven and consume you with your fifty men!" And fire of *Hashem* came down from heaven and consumed him and his fifty men.

13 Then he sent a third captain of fifty with his fifty men. The third captain of fifty climbed to the top, knelt before *Eliyahu*, and implored him, saying, "Oh, man of *Hashem*, please have regard for my life and the lives of these fifty servants of yours!

14 Already fire has come from heaven and consumed the first two captains of fifty and their men; I beg you, have regard for my life!"

15 Then the angel of *Hashem* said to *Eliyahu*, "Go down with him, do not be afraid of him." So he rose and went down with him to the king.

16 He said to him, "Because you sent messengers to inquire of Baal-zebub the god of Ekron – as if there were no *Hashem* in *Yisrael* whose word you could seek – assuredly, you shall not rise from the bed which you are lying on; but you shall die."

17 And [*Achazyahu*] died, according to the word of *Hashem* that *Eliyahu* had spoken. *Yehoram* succeeded him as king, in the second year of King *Yehoram* son of *Yehoshafat* of *Yehuda*, for he had no son.

18 The other events of *Achazyahu*'s reign [and] his actions are recorded in the Annals of the Kings of *Yisrael*.

Melachim II / II Kings
Chapter 2

2 1 When *Hashem* was about to take *Eliyahu* up to heaven in a whirlwind, *Eliyahu* and *Elisha* had set out from *Gilgal*.

2 *Eliyahu* said to *Elisha*, "Stay here, for *Hashem* has sent me on to *Beit El*." "As *Hashem* lives and as you live," said *Elisha*, "I will not leave you." So they went down to *Beit El*.

3 Disciples of the *Neviim* at *Beit El* came out to *Elisha* and said to him, "Do you know that *Hashem* will take your master away from you today?" He replied, "I know it, too; be silent."

4 Then *Eliyahu* said to him, "*Elisha*, stay here, for *Hashem* has sent me on to *Yericho*." "As *Hashem* lives and as you live," said *Elisha*, "I will not leave you." So they went on to *Yericho*.

5 The disciples of the *Neviim* who were at *Yericho* came over to *Elisha* and said to him, "Do you know that *Hashem* will take your master away from you today?" He replied, "I know it, too; be silent."

6 *Eliyahu* said to him, "Stay here, for *Hashem* has sent me on to the *Yarden*." "As *Hashem* lives and as you live, I will not leave you," he said, and the two of them went on.

7 Fifty men of the disciples of the *Neviim* followed and stood by at a distance from them as the two of them stopped at the *Yarden*.

8 Thereupon *Eliyahu* took his mantle and, rolling it up, he struck the water; it divided to the right and left, so that the two of them crossed over on dry land.

9 As they were crossing, *Eliyahu* said to *Elisha*, "Tell me, what can I do for you before I am taken from you?" *Elisha* answered, "Let a double portion of your spirit pass on to me."

10 "You have asked a difficult thing," he said. "If you see me as I am being taken from you, this will be granted to you; if not, it will not."

מלכים ב
פרק ב

ב א וַיְהִ֗י בְּהַעֲל֤וֹת יְהֹוָה֙ אֶת־אֵ֣לִיָּ֔הוּ בַּֽסְעָרָ֖ה הַשָּׁמָ֑יִם וַיֵּ֧לֶךְ אֵלִיָּ֛הוּ וֶאֱלִישָׁ֖ע מִן־הַגִּלְגָּֽל׃

ב וַיֹּ֩אמֶר֩ אֵלִיָּ֨הוּ אֶל־אֱלִישָׁ֜ע שֵֽׁב־נָ֣א פֹ֗ה כִּ֤י יְהֹוָה֙ שְׁלָחַ֣נִי עַד־בֵּֽית־אֵ֔ל וַיֹּ֣אמֶר אֱלִישָׁ֔ע חַי־יְהֹוָ֥ה וְחֵֽי־נַפְשְׁךָ֖ אִם־אֶעֶזְבֶ֑ךָּ וַיֵּרְד֖וּ בֵּֽית־אֵֽל׃

ג וַיֵּצְא֨וּ בְנֵֽי־הַנְּבִיאִ֥ים אֲשֶׁר־בֵּֽית־אֵ֛ל אֶל־אֱלִישָׁ֖ע וַיֹּאמְר֣וּ אֵלָ֗יו הֲיָדַ֨עְתָּ֙ כִּ֣י הַיּ֗וֹם יְהֹוָ֛ה לֹקֵ֥חַ אֶת־אֲדֹנֶ֖יךָ מֵעַ֣ל רֹאשֶׁ֑ךָ וַיֹּ֛אמֶר גַּם־אֲנִ֥י יָדַ֖עְתִּי הֶחֱשֽׁוּ׃

ד וַיֹּ֩אמֶר֩ ל֨וֹ אֵלִיָּ֜הוּ אֱלִישָׁ֣ע ׀ שֵֽׁב־נָ֣א פֹ֗ה כִּ֤י יְהֹוָה֙ שְׁלָחַ֣נִי יְרִיח֔וֹ וַיֹּ֕אמֶר חַי־יְהֹוָ֥ה וְחֵֽי־נַפְשְׁךָ֖ אִם־אֶעֶזְבֶ֑ךָּ וַיָּבֹ֖אוּ יְרִיחֽוֹ׃

ה וַיִּגְּשׁ֨וּ בְנֵֽי־הַנְּבִיאִ֥ים אֲשֶׁר־בִּירִיחוֹ֮ אֶל־אֱלִישָׁע֒ וַיֹּאמְר֣וּ אֵלָ֗יו הֲיָדַ֨עְתָּ֙ כִּ֣י הַיּ֗וֹם יְהֹוָ֛ה לֹקֵ֥חַ אֶת־אֲדֹנֶ֖יךָ מֵעַ֣ל רֹאשֶׁ֑ךָ וַיֹּ֛אמֶר גַּם־אֲנִ֥י יָדַ֖עְתִּי הֶחֱשֽׁוּ׃

ו וַיֹּאמֶר֩ ל֨וֹ אֵלִיָּ֜הוּ שֵֽׁב־נָ֣א פֹ֗ה כִּ֤י יְהֹוָה֙ שְׁלָחַ֣נִי הַיַּרְדֵּ֔נָה וַיֹּ֕אמֶר חַי־יְהֹוָ֥ה וְחֵֽי־נַפְשְׁךָ֖ אִם־אֶעֶזְבֶ֑ךָּ וַיֵּלְכ֖וּ שְׁנֵיהֶֽם׃

ז וַחֲמִשִּׁ֨ים אִ֜ישׁ מִבְּנֵ֤י הַנְּבִיאִים֙ הָֽלְכ֔וּ וַיַּעַמְד֥וּ מִנֶּ֖גֶד מֵרָח֑וֹק וּשְׁנֵיהֶ֖ם עָמְד֥וּ עַל־הַיַּרְדֵּֽן׃

ח וַיִּקַּח֩ אֵלִיָּ֨הוּ אֶת־אַדַּרְתּ֤וֹ וַיִּגְלֹם֙ וַיַּכֶּ֣ה אֶת־הַמַּ֔יִם וַיֵּחָצ֖וּ הֵ֣נָּה וָהֵ֑נָּה וַיַּעַבְר֥וּ שְׁנֵיהֶ֖ם בֶּחָרָבָֽה׃

ט וַיְהִ֣י כְעָבְרָ֗ם וְאֵ֨לִיָּ֜הוּ אָמַ֤ר אֶל־אֱלִישָׁע֙ שְׁאַל֙ מָ֣ה אֶעֱשֶׂה־לָּ֔ךְ בְּטֶ֖רֶם אֶלָּקַ֣ח מֵעִמָּ֑ךְ וַיֹּ֣אמֶר אֱלִישָׁ֔ע וִיהִי־נָ֛א פִּי־שְׁנַ֥יִם בְּרוּחֲךָ֖ אֵלָֽי׃

י וַיֹּ֖אמֶר הִקְשִׁ֣יתָ לִשְׁא֑וֹל אִם־תִּרְאֶ֨ה אֹתִ֜י לֻקָּ֤ח מֵֽאִתָּךְ֙ יְהִי־לְךָ֣ כֵ֔ן וְאִם־אַ֖יִן לֹ֥א יִֽהְיֶֽה׃

Melachim II / II Kings
Chapter 2

11 As they kept on walking and talking, a fiery chariot with fiery horses suddenly appeared and separated one from the other; and *Eliyahu* went up to heaven in a whirlwind.

יא וַיְהִי הֵמָּה הֹלְכִים הָלוֹךְ וְדַבֵּר וְהִנֵּה רֶכֶב־אֵשׁ וְסוּסֵי אֵשׁ וַיַּפְרִדוּ בֵּין שְׁנֵיהֶם וַיַּעַל אֵלִיָּהוּ בַּסְעָרָה הַשָּׁמָיִם:

> vai-HEE HAY-mah ho-l'-KHEEM ha-LOKH v'-da-BAYR v'-hi-NAY re-khev AYSH v'-SU-say AYSH va-yaf-RI-du BAYN sh'-nay-HEM va-YA-al AY-li-YA-hu bas-a-RAH ha-sha-MA-yim

12 *Elisha* saw it, and he cried out, "Oh, father, father! *Yisrael*'s chariots and horsemen!" When he could no longer see him, he grasped his garments and rent them in two.

יב וֶאֱלִישָׁע רֹאֶה וְהוּא מְצַעֵק אָבִי אָבִי רֶכֶב יִשְׂרָאֵל וּפָרָשָׁיו וְלֹא רָאָהוּ עוֹד וַיַּחֲזֵק בִּבְגָדָיו וַיִּקְרָעֵם לִשְׁנַיִם קְרָעִים:

13 He picked up *Eliyahu*'s mantle, which had dropped from him; and he went back and stood on the bank of the *Yarden*.

יג וַיָּרֶם אֶת־אַדֶּרֶת אֵלִיָּהוּ אֲשֶׁר נָפְלָה מֵעָלָיו וַיָּשָׁב וַיַּעֲמֹד עַל־שְׂפַת הַיַּרְדֵּן:

14 Taking the mantle which had dropped from *Eliyahu*, he struck the water and said, "Where is *Hashem*, the God of *Eliyahu*?" As he too struck the water, it parted to the right and to the left, and *Elisha* crossed over.

יד וַיִּקַּח אֶת־אַדֶּרֶת אֵלִיָּהוּ אֲשֶׁר־נָפְלָה מֵעָלָיו וַיַּכֶּה אֶת־הַמַּיִם וַיֹּאמַר אַיֵּה יְהֹוָה אֱלֹהֵי אֵלִיָּהוּ אַף־הוּא וַיַּכֶּה אֶת־הַמַּיִם וַיֵּחָצוּ הֵנָּה וָהֵנָּה וַיַּעֲבֹר אֱלִישָׁע:

15 When the disciples of the *Neviim* at *Yericho* saw him from a distance, they exclaimed, "The spirit of *Eliyahu* has settled on *Elisha*!" And they went to meet him and bowed low before him to the ground.

טו וַיִּרְאֻהוּ בְנֵי־הַנְּבִיאִים אֲשֶׁר־בִּירִיחוֹ מִנֶּגֶד וַיֹּאמְרוּ נָחָה רוּחַ אֵלִיָּהוּ עַל־אֱלִישָׁע וַיָּבֹאוּ לִקְרָאתוֹ וַיִּשְׁתַּחֲווּ־לוֹ אָרְצָה:

16 They said to him, "Your servants have fifty able men with them. Let them go and look for your master; perhaps the spirit of *Hashem* has carried him off and cast him upon some mountain or into some valley." "Do not send them," he replied.

טז וַיֹּאמְרוּ אֵלָיו הִנֵּה־נָא יֵשׁ־אֶת־עֲבָדֶיךָ חֲמִשִּׁים אֲנָשִׁים בְּנֵי־חַיִל יֵלְכוּ נָא וִיבַקְשׁוּ אֶת־אֲדֹנֶיךָ פֶּן־נְשָׂאוֹ רוּחַ יְהֹוָה וַיַּשְׁלִכֵהוּ בְּאַחַד הֶהָרִים אוֹ בְּאַחַת הגיאות [הַגֵּאָיוֹת] וַיֹּאמֶר לֹא תִשְׁלָחוּ:

17 But they kept pressing him for a long time, until he said, "Send them." So they sent out fifty men, who searched for three days but did not find him.

יז וַיִּפְצְרוּ־בוֹ עַד־בֹּשׁ וַיֹּאמֶר שְׁלָחוּ וַיִּשְׁלְחוּ חֲמִשִּׁים אִישׁ וַיְבַקְשׁוּ שְׁלֹשָׁה־יָמִים וְלֹא מְצָאֻהוּ:

18 They came back to him while he was still in *Yericho*; and he said to them, "I told you not to go."

יח וַיָּשֻׁבוּ אֵלָיו וְהוּא יֹשֵׁב בִּירִיחוֹ וַיֹּאמֶר אֲלֵהֶם הֲלוֹא־אָמַרְתִּי אֲלֵיכֶם אַל־תֵּלֵכוּ:

2:11 *Eliyahu* went up to heaven in a whirlwind In one of the Bible's most powerful images, *Eliyahu* the Prophet leaves this world and ascends to the heavens in a fiery chariot. The Sages teach (*Bava Batra* 121b) that *Eliyahu* did not die, but left this world while still alive. Because he remains alive, he maintains contact with the world below. He is therefore able to understand the needs of every generation. This constant connection is part of what makes him one of history's most beloved prophets. Tradition teaches that when God decides it is time to reveal the *Mashiach*, *Eliyahu* will return to proclaim his arrival to the world. According to the prophet *Malachi*, after he returns "He shall reconcile parents with children and children with their parents" (3:24). *Eliyahu* will bring peace to the world, creating the right environment for the arrival of the *Mashiach*.

Melachim II/II Kings
Chapter 3

מלכים ב
פרק ג

19 The men of the town said to *Elisha*, "Look, the town is a pleasant place to live in, as my lord can see; but the water is bad and the land causes bereavement."

יט וַיֹּאמְרוּ אַנְשֵׁי הָעִיר אֶל־אֱלִישָׁע הִנֵּה־נָא מוֹשַׁב הָעִיר טוֹב כַּאֲשֶׁר אֲדֹנִי רֹאֶה וְהַמַּיִם רָעִים וְהָאָרֶץ מְשַׁכָּלֶת:

20 He responded, "Bring me a new dish and put salt in it." They brought it to him;

כ וַיֹּאמֶר קְחוּ־לִי צְלֹחִית חֲדָשָׁה וְשִׂימוּ שָׁם מֶלַח וַיִּקְחוּ אֵלָיו:

21 he went to the spring and threw salt into it. And he said, "Thus said *Hashem*: I heal this water; no longer shall death and bereavement come from it!"

כא וַיֵּצֵא אֶל־מוֹצָא הַמַּיִם וַיַּשְׁלֶךְ־שָׁם מֶלַח וַיֹּאמֶר כֹּה־אָמַר יְהוָה רִפִּאתִי לַמַּיִם הָאֵלֶּה לֹא־יִהְיֶה מִשָּׁם עוֹד מָוֶת וּמְשַׁכָּלֶת:

22 The water has remained wholesome to this day, in accordance with the word spoken by *Elisha*.

כב וַיֵּרָפוּ הַמַּיִם עַד הַיּוֹם הַזֶּה כִּדְבַר אֱלִישָׁע אֲשֶׁר דִּבֵּר:

23 From there he went up to *Beit El*. As he was going up the road, some little boys came out of the town and jeered at him, saying, "Go away, baldhead! Go away, baldhead!"

כג וַיַּעַל מִשָּׁם בֵּית־אֵל וְהוּא עֹלֶה בַדֶּרֶךְ וּנְעָרִים קְטַנִּים יָצְאוּ מִן־הָעִיר וַיִּתְקַלְּסוּ־בוֹ וַיֹּאמְרוּ לוֹ עֲלֵה קֵרֵחַ עֲלֵה קֵרֵחַ:

24 He turned around and looked at them and cursed them in the name of *Hashem*. Thereupon, two she-bears came out of the woods and mangled forty-two of the children.

כד וַיִּפֶן אַחֲרָיו וַיִּרְאֵם וַיְקַלְלֵם בְּשֵׁם יְהוָה וַתֵּצֶאנָה שְׁתַּיִם דֻּבִּים מִן־הַיַּעַר וַתְּבַקַּעְנָה מֵהֶם אַרְבָּעִים וּשְׁנֵי יְלָדִים:

25 He went on from there to Mount *Carmel*, and from there he returned to *Shomron*.

כה וַיֵּלֶךְ מִשָּׁם אֶל־הַר הַכַּרְמֶל וּמִשָּׁם שָׁב שֹׁמְרוֹן:

3 1 *Yehoram* son of *Achav* became king of *Yisrael* in *Shomron* in the eighteenth year of King *Yehoshafat* of *Yehuda*; and he reigned twelve years.

ג א וִיהוֹרָם בֶּן־אַחְאָב מָלַךְ עַל־יִשְׂרָאֵל בְּשֹׁמְרוֹן בִּשְׁנַת שְׁמֹנֶה עֶשְׂרֵה לִיהוֹשָׁפָט מֶלֶךְ יְהוּדָה וַיִּמְלֹךְ שְׁתֵּים־עֶשְׂרֵה שָׁנָה:

2 He did what was displeasing to *Hashem*, yet not like his father and mother, for he removed the pillars of Baal that his father had made.

ב וַיַּעֲשֶׂה הָרַע בְּעֵינֵי יְהוָה רַק לֹא כְאָבִיו וּכְאִמּוֹ וַיָּסַר אֶת־מַצְּבַת הַבַּעַל אֲשֶׁר עָשָׂה אָבִיו:

3 However, he clung to the sins which *Yerovam* son of Nebat caused *Yisrael* to commit; he did not depart from them.

ג רַק בְּחַטֹּאות יָרָבְעָם בֶּן־נְבָט אֲשֶׁר־הֶחֱטִיא אֶת־יִשְׂרָאֵל דָּבֵק לֹא־סָר מִמֶּנָּה:

4 Now King Mesha of Moab was a sheep breeder; and he used to pay as tribute to the king of *Yisrael* a hundred thousand lambs and the wool of a hundred thousand rams.

ד וּמֵישַׁע מֶלֶךְ־מוֹאָב הָיָה נֹקֵד וְהֵשִׁיב לְמֶלֶךְ־יִשְׂרָאֵל מֵאָה־אֶלֶף כָּרִים וּמֵאָה אֶלֶף אֵילִים צָמֶר:

5 But when *Achav* died, the king of Moab rebelled against the king of *Yisrael*.

ה וַיְהִי כְּמוֹת אַחְאָב וַיִּפְשַׁע מֶלֶךְ־מוֹאָב בְּמֶלֶךְ יִשְׂרָאֵל:

Melachim II / II Kings
Chapter 3

מלכים ב
פרק ג

6 So King *Yehoram* promptly set out from *Shomron* and mustered all *Yisrael*.

א וַיֵּצֵא הַמֶּלֶךְ יְהוֹרָם בַּיּוֹם הַהוּא מִשֹּׁמְרוֹן וַיִּפְקֹד אֶת־כָּל־יִשְׂרָאֵל׃

7 At the same time, he sent this message to King *Yehoshafat* of *Yehuda*: "The king of Moab has rebelled against me; will you come with me to make war on Moab?" He replied, "I will go. I will do what you do: my troops shall be your troops, my horses shall be your horses."

ז וַיֵּלֶךְ וַיִּשְׁלַח אֶל־יְהוֹשָׁפָט מֶלֶךְ־יְהוּדָה לֵאמֹר מֶלֶךְ מוֹאָב פָּשַׁע בִּי הֲתֵלֵךְ אִתִּי אֶל־מוֹאָב לַמִּלְחָמָה וַיֹּאמֶר אֶעֱלֶה כָּמוֹנִי כָמוֹךָ כְּעַמִּי כְעַמֶּךָ כְּסוּסַי כְּסוּסֶיךָ׃

8 And he asked, "Which route shall we take?" [*Yehoram*] replied, "The road through the wilderness of Edom."

ח וַיֹּאמֶר אֵי־זֶה הַדֶּרֶךְ נַעֲלֶה וַיֹּאמֶר דֶּרֶךְ מִדְבַּר אֱדוֹם׃

9 So the king of *Yisrael*, the king of *Yehuda*, and the king of Edom set out, and they marched for seven days until they rounded [the tip of the Dead Sea]; and there was no water left for the army or for the animals that were with them.

ט וַיֵּלֶךְ מֶלֶךְ יִשְׂרָאֵל וּמֶלֶךְ־יְהוּדָה וּמֶלֶךְ אֱדוֹם וַיָּסֹבּוּ דֶּרֶךְ שִׁבְעַת יָמִים וְלֹא־הָיָה מַיִם לַמַּחֲנֶה וְלַבְּהֵמָה אֲשֶׁר בְּרַגְלֵיהֶם׃

10 "Alas!" cried the king of *Yisrael*. "*Hashem* has brought these three kings together only to deliver them into the hands of Moab."

י וַיֹּאמֶר מֶלֶךְ יִשְׂרָאֵל אֲהָהּ כִּי־קָרָא יְהוָה לִשְׁלֹשֶׁת הַמְּלָכִים הָאֵלֶּה לָתֵת אוֹתָם בְּיַד־מוֹאָב׃

11 But *Yehoshafat* said, "Isn't there a *Navi* of *Hashem* here, through whom we may inquire of *Hashem*?" One of the courtiers of the king of *Yisrael* spoke up and said, "*Elisha* son of *Shafat*, who poured water on the hands of *Eliyahu*, is here."

יא וַיֹּאמֶר יְהוֹשָׁפָט הַאֵין פֹּה נָבִיא לַיהוָה וְנִדְרְשָׁה אֶת־יְהוָה מֵאוֹתוֹ וַיַּעַן אֶחָד מֵעַבְדֵי מֶלֶךְ־יִשְׂרָאֵל וַיֹּאמֶר פֹּה אֱלִישָׁע בֶּן־שָׁפָט אֲשֶׁר־יָצַק מַיִם עַל־יְדֵי אֵלִיָּהוּ׃

12 "The word of *Hashem* is with him," said *Yehoshafat*. So the king of *Yisrael* and *Yehoshafat* and the king of Edom went down to him.

יב וַיֹּאמֶר יְהוֹשָׁפָט יֵשׁ אוֹתוֹ דְּבַר־יְהוָה וַיֵּרְדוּ אֵלָיו מֶלֶךְ יִשְׂרָאֵל וִיהוֹשָׁפָט וּמֶלֶךְ אֱדוֹם׃

13 *Elisha* said to the king of *Yisrael*, "What have you to do with me? Go to your father's *Neviim* or your mother's *Neviim*." But the king of *Yisrael* said, "Don't [say that], for *Hashem* has brought these three kings together only to deliver them into the hands of Moab."

יג וַיֹּאמֶר אֱלִישָׁע אֶל־מֶלֶךְ יִשְׂרָאֵל מַה־לִּי וָלָךְ לֵךְ אֶל־נְבִיאֵי אָבִיךָ וְאֶל־נְבִיאֵי אִמֶּךָ וַיֹּאמֶר לוֹ מֶלֶךְ יִשְׂרָאֵל אַל כִּי־קָרָא יְהוָה לִשְׁלֹשֶׁת הַמְּלָכִים הָאֵלֶּה לָתֵת אוֹתָם בְּיַד־מוֹאָב׃

14 "As the Lord of Hosts lives, whom I serve," *Elisha* answered, "were it not that I respect King *Yehoshafat* of *Yehuda*, I wouldn't look at you or notice you.

יד וַיֹּאמֶר אֱלִישָׁע חַי־יְהוָה צְבָאוֹת אֲשֶׁר עָמַדְתִּי לְפָנָיו כִּי לוּלֵי פְּנֵי יְהוֹשָׁפָט מֶלֶךְ־יְהוּדָה אֲנִי נֹשֵׂא אִם־אַבִּיט אֵלֶיךָ וְאִם־אֶרְאֶךָּ׃

15 Now then, get me a musician." As the musician played, the hand of *Hashem* came upon him,

טו וְעַתָּה קְחוּ־לִי מְנַגֵּן וְהָיָה כְּנַגֵּן הַמְנַגֵּן וַתְּהִי עָלָיו יַד־יְהוָה׃

Melachim II / II Kings
Chapter 3

16 and he said, "Thus said *Hashem*: This wadi shall be full of pools.

va-YO-mer KOH a-MAR a-do-NAI a-SOH ha-NA-khal ha-ZEH gay-VEEM gay-VEEM

טז וַיֹּאמֶר כֹּה אָמַר יְהוָה עָשֹׂה הַנַּחַל הַזֶּה גֵּבִים גֵּבִים׃

17 For thus said *Hashem*: You shall see no wind, you shall see no rain, and yet the wadi shall be filled with water; and you and your cattle and your pack animals shall drink.

יז כִּי־כֹה אָמַר יְהוָה לֹא־תִרְאוּ רוּחַ וְלֹא־תִרְאוּ גֶשֶׁם וְהַנַּחַל הַהוּא יִמָּלֵא מָיִם וּשְׁתִיתֶם אַתֶּם וּמִקְנֵיכֶם וּבְהֶמְתְּכֶם׃

18 And this is but a slight thing in the sight of *Hashem*, for He will also deliver Moab into your hands.

יח וְנָקַל זֹאת בְּעֵינֵי יְהוָה וְנָתַן אֶת־מוֹאָב בְּיֶדְכֶם׃

19 You shall conquer every fortified town and every splendid city; you shall fell every good tree and stop up all wells of water; and every fertile field you shall ruin with stones."

יט וְהִכִּיתֶם כָּל־עִיר מִבְצָר וְכָל־עִיר מִבְחוֹר וְכָל־עֵץ טוֹב תַּפִּילוּ וְכָל־מַעְיְנֵי־מַיִם תִּסְתֹּמוּ וְכֹל הַחֶלְקָה הַטּוֹבָה תַּכְאִבוּ בָּאֲבָנִים׃

20 And in the morning, when it was time to present the meal offering, water suddenly came from the direction of Edom and the land was covered by the water.

כ וַיְהִי בַבֹּקֶר כַּעֲלוֹת הַמִּנְחָה וְהִנֵּה־מַיִם בָּאִים מִדֶּרֶךְ אֱדוֹם וַתִּמָּלֵא הָאָרֶץ אֶת־הַמָּיִם׃

21 Meanwhile, all the Moabites had heard that the kings were advancing to make war on them; every man old enough to bear arms rallied, and they stationed themselves at the border.

כא וְכָל־מוֹאָב שָׁמְעוּ כִּי־עָלוּ הַמְּלָכִים לְהִלָּחֶם בָּם וַיִּצָּעֲקוּ מִכֹּל חֹגֵר חֲגֹרָה וָמָעְלָה וַיַּעַמְדוּ עַל־הַגְּבוּל׃

22 Next morning, when they rose, the sun was shining over the water, and from the distance the water appeared to the Moabites as red as blood.

כב וַיַּשְׁכִּימוּ בַבֹּקֶר וְהַשֶּׁמֶשׁ זָרְחָה עַל־הַמָּיִם וַיִּרְאוּ מוֹאָב מִנֶּגֶד אֶת־הַמַּיִם אֲדֻמִּים כַּדָּם׃

23 "That's blood!" they said. "The kings must have fought among themselves and killed each other. Now to the spoil, Moab!"

כג וַיֹּאמְרוּ דָּם זֶה הָחֳרֵב נֶחֶרְבוּ הַמְּלָכִים וַיַּכּוּ אִישׁ אֶת־רֵעֵהוּ וְעַתָּה לַשָּׁלָל מוֹאָב׃

24 They entered the Israelite camp, and the Israelites arose and attacked the Moabites, who fled before them. They advanced, constantly attacking the Moabites,

כד וַיָּבֹאוּ אֶל־מַחֲנֵה יִשְׂרָאֵל וַיָּקֻמוּ יִשְׂרָאֵל וַיַּכּוּ אֶת־מוֹאָב וַיָּנֻסוּ מִפְּנֵיהֶם וַיָּבוֹ [וַיַּכּוּ־] בָהּ וְהַכּוֹת אֶת־מוֹאָב׃

3:16 This wadi shall be full of pools When the kings and their armies face death due to lack of water, *Elisha* prophesies that the valley will be filled with pools of water. Thus, they will be saved from death, and will be able to quench their thirst. There have been many times in history, from biblical through modern times, when the People of Israel needed miracles in order to have sufficient water. The most famous biblical example is the rock that provided water for the Israelites in the desert. In modern times, one of the many miracles in the creation and prospering of the State of Israel has been the ability to find sufficient water to literally make the desert bloom. For example, Israeli farmers have pioneered innovative drip irrigation methods that have allowed Israel to become leaders in agriculture. Though Israel must conserve water, *Hashem* has provided it with a sufficient amount to meet all of its needs, and the wisdom to use it efficiently.

Drip irrigation in Hatzerim, Israel

Melachim II / II Kings
Chapter 4

25 and they destroyed the towns. Every man threw a stone into each fertile field, so that it was covered over; and they stopped up every spring and felled every fruit tree. Only the walls of Kir-hareseth were left, and then the slingers surrounded it and attacked it.

26 Seeing that the battle was going against him, the king of Moab led an attempt of seven hundred swordsmen to break a way through to the king of Edom; but they failed.

27 So he took his first-born son, who was to succeed him as king, and offered him up on the wall as a burnt offering. A great wrath came upon *Yisrael*, so they withdrew from him and went back to [their own] land.

4 1 A certain woman, the wife of one of the disciples of the *Neviim*, cried out to *Elisha*: "Your servant my husband is dead, and you know how your servant revered *Hashem*. And now a creditor is coming to seize my two children as slaves."

2 *Elisha* said to her, "What can I do for you? Tell me, what have you in the house?" She replied, "Your maidservant has nothing at all in the house, except a jug of oil."

3 "Go," he said, "and borrow vessels outside, from all your neighbors, empty vessels, as many as you can.

va-YO-mer l'-KHEE sha-a-lee LAKH kay-LEEM min ha-KHUTZ may-AYT kol sh'-khay-NA-yikh kay-LEEM ray-KEEM al tam-EE-tee

4 Then go in and shut the door behind you and your children, and pour [oil] into all those vessels, removing each one as it is filled."

5 She went away and shut the door behind her and her children. They kept bringing [vessels] to her and she kept pouring.

4:3 Borrow vessels God again performs a miracle with human partnership, utilizing items that already exists in nature. Thus, this miracle emanates from existing oil, and continues only as long as additional jugs are brought. David Ben Gurion, the first Prime Minister of Israel, famously said "in Israel, in order to be a realist, one must believe in miracles." Indeed, surrounded by enemies and lacking natural resources, there is no logical reason that the State of Israel exists at all, let alone as a strong and vibrant nation. It is only due to *Hashem*'s miracles, which He attaches to the great efforts of many human beings, that Israel is here to bring blessing to the world.

Prime Minister David Ben Gurion (1886–1973)

Melachim II / II Kings
Chapter 4

	English	Hebrew
6	When the vessels were full, she said to her son, "Bring me another vessel." He answered her, "There are no more vessels"; and the oil stopped.	ו וַיְהִי כִּמְלֹאת הַכֵּלִים וַתֹּאמֶר אֶל־בְּנָהּ הַגִּישָׁה אֵלַי עוֹד כֶּלִי וַיֹּאמֶר אֵלֶיהָ אֵין עוֹד כֶּלִי וַיַּעֲמֹד הַשָּׁמֶן:
7	She came and told the man of *Hashem*, and he said, "Go sell the oil and pay your debt, and you and your children can live on the rest."	ז וַתָּבֹא וַתַּגֵּד לְאִישׁ הָאֱלֹהִים וַיֹּאמֶר לְכִי מִכְרִי אֶת־הַשֶּׁמֶן וְשַׁלְּמִי אֶת־נִשְׁיֵכִי [נִשְׁיֵךְ] וְאַתְּ בניכי [וּבָנַיִךְ] תִּחְיִי בַּנּוֹתָר:
8	One day *Elisha* visited Shunem. A wealthy woman lived there, and she urged him to have a meal; and whenever he passed by, he would stop there for a meal.	ח וַיְהִי הַיּוֹם וַיַּעֲבֹר אֱלִישָׁע אֶל־שׁוּנֵם וְשָׁם אִשָּׁה גְדוֹלָה וַתַּחֲזֶק־בּוֹ לֶאֱכָל־לָחֶם וַיְהִי מִדֵּי עָבְרוֹ יָסֻר שָׁמָּה לֶאֱכָל־לָחֶם:
9	Once she said to her husband, "I am sure it is a holy man of *Hashem* who comes this way regularly.	ט וַתֹּאמֶר אֶל־אִישָׁהּ הִנֵּה־נָא יָדַעְתִּי כִּי אִישׁ אֱלֹהִים קָדוֹשׁ הוּא עֹבֵר עָלֵינוּ תָּמִיד:
10	Let us make a small enclosed upper chamber and place a bed, a table, a chair, and a *menorah* there for him, so that he can stop there whenever he comes to us."	י נַעֲשֶׂה־נָּא עֲלִיַּת־קִיר קְטַנָּה וְנָשִׂים לוֹ שָׁם מִטָּה וְשֻׁלְחָן וְכִסֵּא וּמְנוֹרָה וְהָיָה בְּבֹאוֹ אֵלֵינוּ יָסוּר שָׁמָּה:
11	One day he came there; he retired to the upper chamber and lay down there.	יא וַיְהִי הַיּוֹם וַיָּבֹא שָׁמָּה וַיָּסַר אֶל־הָעֲלִיָּה וַיִּשְׁכַּב־שָׁמָּה:
12	He said to his servant Gehazi, "Call that Shunammite woman." He called her, and she stood before him.	יב וַיֹּאמֶר אֶל־גֵּחֲזִי נַעֲרוֹ קְרָא לַשּׁוּנַמִּית הַזֹּאת וַיִּקְרָא־לָהּ וַתַּעֲמֹד לְפָנָיו:
13	He said to him, "Tell her, 'You have gone to all this trouble for us. What can we do for you? Can we speak in your behalf to the king or to the army commander?'" She replied, "I live among my own people."	יג וַיֹּאמֶר לוֹ אֱמָר־נָא אֵלֶיהָ הִנֵּה חָרַדְתְּ אֵלֵינוּ אֶת־כָּל־הַחֲרָדָה הַזֹּאת מֶה לַעֲשׂוֹת לָךְ הֲיֵשׁ לְדַבֶּר־לָךְ אֶל־הַמֶּלֶךְ אוֹ אֶל־שַׂר הַצָּבָא וַתֹּאמֶר בְּתוֹךְ עַמִּי אָנֹכִי יֹשָׁבֶת:
14	"What then can be done for her?" he asked. "The fact is," said Gehazi, "she has no son, and her husband is old."	יד וַיֹּאמֶר וּמֶה לַעֲשׂוֹת לָהּ וַיֹּאמֶר גֵּיחֲזִי אֲבָל בֵּן אֵין־לָהּ וְאִישָׁהּ זָקֵן:
15	"Call her," he said. He called her, and she stood in the doorway.	טו וַיֹּאמֶר קְרָא־לָהּ וַיִּקְרָא־לָהּ וַתַּעֲמֹד בַּפָּתַח:
16	And *Elisha* said, "At this season next year, you will be embracing a son." She replied, "Please, my lord, man of *Hashem*, do not delude your maidservant."	טז וַיֹּאמֶר לַמּוֹעֵד הַזֶּה כָּעֵת חַיָּה אתי [אַתְּ] חֹבֶקֶת בֵּן וַתֹּאמֶר אַל־אֲדֹנִי אִישׁ הָאֱלֹהִים אַל־תְּכַזֵּב בְּשִׁפְחָתֶךָ:
17	The woman conceived and bore a son at the same season the following year, as *Elisha* had assured her.	יז וַתַּהַר הָאִשָּׁה וַתֵּלֶד בֵּן לַמּוֹעֵד הַזֶּה כָּעֵת חַיָּה אֲשֶׁר־דִּבֶּר אֵלֶיהָ אֱלִישָׁע:
18	The child grew up. One day, he went out to his father among the reapers.	יח וַיִּגְדַּל הַיָּלֶד וַיְהִי הַיּוֹם וַיֵּצֵא אֶל־אָבִיו אֶל־הַקֹּצְרִים:
19	[Suddenly] he cried to his father, "Oh, my head, my head!" He said to a servant, "Carry him to his mother."	יט וַיֹּאמֶר אֶל־אָבִיו רֹאשִׁי רֹאשִׁי וַיֹּאמֶר אֶל־הַנַּעַר שָׂאֵהוּ אֶל־אִמּוֹ:

Melachim II / II Kings — Chapter 4 / מלכים ב פרק ד

#	English	Hebrew
20	He picked him up and brought him to his mother. And the child sat on her lap until noon; and he died.	וַיִּשָּׂאֵהוּ וַיְבִיאֵהוּ אֶל־אִמּוֹ וַיֵּשֶׁב עַל־בִּרְכֶּיהָ עַד־הַצָּהֳרַיִם וַיָּמֹת:
21	She took him up and laid him on the bed of the man of *Hashem*, and left him and closed the door.	וַתַּעַל וַתַּשְׁכִּבֵהוּ עַל־מִטַּת אִישׁ הָאֱלֹהִים וַתִּסְגֹּר בַּעֲדוֹ וַתֵּצֵא:
22	Then she called to her husband: "Please, send me one of the servants and one of the she-asses, so I can hurry to the man of *Hashem* and back."	וַתִּקְרָא אֶל־אִישָׁהּ וַתֹּאמֶר שִׁלְחָה נָא לִי אֶחָד מִן־הַנְּעָרִים וְאַחַת הָאֲתֹנוֹת וְאָרוּצָה עַד־אִישׁ הָאֱלֹהִים וְאָשׁוּבָה:
23	But he said, "Why are you going to him today? It is neither new moon nor *Shabbat*." She answered, "It's all right."	וַיֹּאמֶר מַדּוּעַ אתי [אַתְּ] הלכתי [הֹלֶכֶת] אֵלָיו הַיּוֹם לֹא־חֹדֶשׁ וְלֹא שַׁבָּת וַתֹּאמֶר שָׁלוֹם:
24	She had the ass saddled, and said to her servant, "Urge [the beast] on; see that I don't slow down unless I tell you."	וַתַּחֲבֹשׁ הָאָתוֹן וַתֹּאמֶר אֶל־נַעֲרָהּ נְהַג וָלֵךְ אַל־תַּעֲצָר־לִי לִרְכֹּב כִּי אִם־אָמַרְתִּי לָךְ:
25	She went on until she came to the man of *Hashem* on Mount *Carmel*. When the man of *Hashem* saw her from afar, he said to his servant Gehazi, "There is that Shunammite woman.	וַתֵּלֶךְ וַתָּבוֹא אֶל־אִישׁ הָאֱלֹהִים אֶל־הַר הַכַּרְמֶל וַיְהִי כִּרְאוֹת אִישׁ־הָאֱלֹהִים אֹתָהּ מִנֶּגֶד וַיֹּאמֶר אֶל־גֵּיחֲזִי נַעֲרוֹ הִנֵּה הַשּׁוּנַמִּית הַלָּז:
26	Go, hurry toward her and ask her, 'How are you? How is your husband? How is the child?'" "We are well," she replied.	עַתָּה רוּץ־נָא לִקְרָאתָהּ וֶאֱמָר־לָהּ הֲשָׁלוֹם לָךְ הֲשָׁלוֹם לְאִישֵׁךְ הֲשָׁלוֹם לַיָּלֶד וַתֹּאמֶר שָׁלוֹם:
27	But when she came up to the man of *Hashem* on the mountain, she clasped his feet. Gehazi stepped forward to push her away; but the man of *Hashem* said, "Let her alone, for she is in bitter distress; and *Hashem* has hidden it from me and has not told me."	וַתָּבֹא אֶל־אִישׁ הָאֱלֹהִים אֶל־הָהָר וַתַּחֲזֵק בְּרַגְלָיו וַיִּגַּשׁ גֵּיחֲזִי לְהָדְפָהּ וַיֹּאמֶר אִישׁ הָאֱלֹהִים הַרְפֵּה־לָהּ כִּי־נַפְשָׁהּ מָרָה־לָהּ וַיהוָה הֶעְלִים מִמֶּנִּי וְלֹא הִגִּיד לִי:
28	Then she said, "Did I ask my lord for a son? Didn't I say: 'Don't mislead me'?"	וַתֹּאמֶר הֲשָׁאַלְתִּי בֵן מֵאֵת אֲדֹנִי הֲלֹא אָמַרְתִּי לֹא תַשְׁלֶה אֹתִי:
29	He said to Gehazi, "Tie up your skirts, take my staff in your hand, and go. If you meet anyone, do not greet him; and if anyone greets you, do not answer him. And place my staff on the face of the boy."	וַיֹּאמֶר לְגֵיחֲזִי חֲגֹר מָתְנֶיךָ וְקַח מִשְׁעַנְתִּי בְיָדְךָ וָלֵךְ כִּי־תִמְצָא אִישׁ לֹא תְבָרְכֶנּוּ וְכִי־יְבָרֶכְךָ אִישׁ לֹא תַעֲנֶנּוּ וְשַׂמְתָּ מִשְׁעַנְתִּי עַל־פְּנֵי הַנָּעַר:
30	But the boy's mother said, "As *Hashem* lives and as you live, I will not leave you!" So he arose and followed her.	וַתֹּאמֶר אֵם הַנַּעַר חַי־יְהוָה וְחֵי־נַפְשְׁךָ אִם־אֶעֶזְבֶךָּ וַיָּקָם וַיֵּלֶךְ אַחֲרֶיהָ:
31	Gehazi had gone on before them and had placed the staff on the boy's face; but there was no sound or response. He turned back to meet him and told him, "The boy has not awakened."	וְגֵחֲזִי עָבַר לִפְנֵיהֶם וַיָּשֶׂם אֶת־הַמִּשְׁעֶנֶת עַל־פְּנֵי הַנַּעַר וְאֵין קוֹל וְאֵין קָשֶׁב וַיָּשָׁב לִקְרָאתוֹ וַיַּגֶּד־לוֹ לֵאמֹר לֹא הֵקִיץ הַנָּעַר:
32	*Elisha* came into the house, and there was the boy, laid out dead on his couch.	וַיָּבֹא אֱלִישָׁע הַבָּיְתָה וְהִנֵּה הַנַּעַר מֵת מֻשְׁכָּב עַל־מִטָּתוֹ:

Melachim II/II Kings
Chapter 4

מלכים ב
פרק ד

33	He went in, shut the door behind the two of them, and prayed to *Hashem*.
34	Then he mounted [the bed] and placed himself over the child. He put his mouth on its mouth, his eyes on its eyes, and his hands on its hands, as he bent over it. And the body of the child became warm.
35	He stepped down, walked once up and down the room, then mounted and bent over him. Thereupon, the boy sneezed seven times, and the boy opened his eyes.
36	[*Elisha*] called Gehazi and said, "Call the Shunammite woman," and he called her. When she came to him, he said, "Pick up your son."
37	She came and fell at his feet and bowed low to the ground; then she picked up her son and left.
38	*Elisha* returned to *Gilgal*. There was a famine in the land, and the disciples of the *Neviim* were sitting before him. He said to his servant, "Set the large pot [on the fire] and cook a stew for the disciples of the *Neviim*."
39	So one of them went out into the fields to gather sprouts. He came across a wild vine and picked from it wild gourds, as many as his garment would hold. Then he came back and sliced them into the pot of stew, for they did not know [what they were];
40	and they served it for the men to eat. While they were still eating of the stew, they began to cry out: "O man of *Hashem*, there is death in the pot!" And they could not eat it.
41	"Fetch some flour," [*Elisha*] said. He threw it into the pot and said, "Serve it to the people and let them eat." And there was no longer anything harmful in the pot.
42	A man came from Baal-shalishah and he brought the man of *Hashem* some bread of the first reaping – twenty loaves of barley bread, and some fresh grain in his sack. And [*Elisha*] said, "Give it to the people and let them eat."
43	His attendant replied, "How can I set this before a hundred men?" But he said, "Give it to the people and let them eat. For thus said *Hashem*: They shall eat and have some left over."

לג וַיָּבֹא וַיִּסְגֹּר הַדֶּלֶת בְּעַד שְׁנֵיהֶם וַיִּתְפַּלֵּל אֶל־יְהֹוָה:

לד וַיַּעַל וַיִּשְׁכַּב עַל־הַיֶּלֶד וַיָּשֶׂם פִּיו עַל־פִּיו וְעֵינָיו עַל־עֵינָיו וְכַפָּיו עַל־כַּפּוֹ [כַּפָּיו] וַיִּגְהַר עָלָיו וַיָּחָם בְּשַׂר הַיָּלֶד:

לה וַיָּשָׁב וַיֵּלֶךְ בַּבַּיִת אַחַת הֵנָּה וְאַחַת הֵנָּה וַיַּעַל וַיִּגְהַר עָלָיו וַיְזוֹרֵר הַנַּעַר עַד־שֶׁבַע פְּעָמִים וַיִּפְקַח הַנַּעַר אֶת־עֵינָיו:

לו וַיִּקְרָא אֶל־גֵּחֲזִי וַיֹּאמֶר קְרָא אֶל־הַשֻּׁנַמִּית הַזֹּאת וַיִּקְרָאֶהָ וַתָּבוֹא אֵלָיו וַיֹּאמֶר שְׂאִי בְנֵךְ:

לז וַתָּבֹא וַתִּפֹּל עַל־רַגְלָיו וַתִּשְׁתַּחוּ אָרְצָה וַתִּשָּׂא אֶת־בְּנָהּ וַתֵּצֵא:

לח וֶאֱלִישָׁע שָׁב הַגִּלְגָּלָה וְהָרָעָב בָּאָרֶץ וּבְנֵי הַנְּבִיאִים יֹשְׁבִים לְפָנָיו וַיֹּאמֶר לְנַעֲרוֹ שְׁפֹת הַסִּיר הַגְּדוֹלָה וּבַשֵּׁל נָזִיד לִבְנֵי הַנְּבִיאִים:

לט וַיֵּצֵא אֶחָד אֶל־הַשָּׂדֶה לְלַקֵּט אֹרֹת וַיִּמְצָא גֶּפֶן שָׂדֶה וַיְלַקֵּט מִמֶּנּוּ פַּקֻּעֹת שָׂדֶה מְלֹא בִגְדוֹ וַיָּבֹא וַיְפַלַּח אֶל־סִיר הַנָּזִיד כִּי־לֹא יָדָעוּ:

מ וַיִּצְקוּ לַאֲנָשִׁים לֶאֱכוֹל וַיְהִי כְּאָכְלָם מֵהַנָּזִיד וְהֵמָּה צָעָקוּ וַיֹּאמְרוּ מָוֶת בַּסִּיר אִישׁ הָאֱלֹהִים וְלֹא יָכְלוּ לֶאֱכֹל:

מא וַיֹּאמֶר וּקְחוּ־קֶמַח וַיַּשְׁלֵךְ אֶל־הַסִּיר וַיֹּאמֶר צַק לָעָם וְיֹאכֵלוּ וְלֹא הָיָה דָּבָר רָע בַּסִּיר:

מב וְאִישׁ בָּא מִבַּעַל שָׁלִשָׁה וַיָּבֵא לְאִישׁ הָאֱלֹהִים לֶחֶם בִּכּוּרִים עֶשְׂרִים־לֶחֶם שְׂעֹרִים וְכַרְמֶל בְּצִקְלֹנוֹ וַיֹּאמֶר תֵּן לָעָם וְיֹאכֵלוּ:

מג וַיֹּאמֶר מְשָׁרְתוֹ מָה אֶתֵּן זֶה לִפְנֵי מֵאָה אִישׁ וַיֹּאמֶר תֵּן לָעָם וְיֹאכֵלוּ כִּי כֹה אָמַר יְהֹוָה אָכֹל וְהוֹתֵר:

Melachim II/II Kings
Chapter 5

44 So he set it before them; and when they had eaten, they had some left over, as *Hashem* had said.

וַיִּתֵּ֧ן לִפְנֵיהֶ֛ם וַיֹּאכְל֥וּ וַיּוֹתִ֖רוּ כִּדְבַ֥ר יְהוָֽה׃

5 1 Naaman, commander of the army of the king of Aram, was important to his lord and high in his favor, for through him *Hashem* had granted victory to Aram. But the man, though a great warrior, was a leper.

וְ֠נַעֲמָן שַׂר־צְבָ֨א מֶֽלֶךְ־אֲרָ֜ם הָיָ֣ה אִישׁ֩ גָּד֨וֹל לִפְנֵ֤י אֲדֹנָיו֙ וּנְשֻׂ֣א פָנִ֔ים כִּי־ב֛וֹ נָֽתַן־יְהוָ֥ה תְּשׁוּעָ֖ה לַאֲרָ֑ם וְהָאִ֗ישׁ הָיָ֛ה גִּבּ֥וֹר חַ֖יִל מְצֹרָֽע׃

2 Once, when the Arameans were out raiding, they carried off a young girl from the land of *Yisrael*, and she became an attendant to Naaman's wife.

וַאֲרָם֙ יָצְא֣וּ גְדוּדִ֔ים וַיִּשְׁבּ֛וּ מֵאֶ֥רֶץ יִשְׂרָאֵ֖ל נַעֲרָ֣ה קְטַנָּ֑ה וַתְּהִ֕י לִפְנֵ֖י אֵ֥שֶׁת נַעֲמָֽן׃

3 She said to her mistress, "I wish Master could come before the *Navi* in *Shomron*; he would cure him of his leprosy."

וַתֹּ֙אמֶר֙ אֶל־גְּבִרְתָּ֔הּ אַחֲלֵ֣י אֲדֹנִ֔י לִפְנֵ֥י הַנָּבִ֖יא אֲשֶׁ֣ר בְּשֹׁמְר֑וֹן אָ֛ז יֶאֱסֹ֥ף אֹת֖וֹ מִצָּרַעְתּֽוֹ׃

4 [Naaman] went and told his lord just what the girl from the land of *Yisrael* had said.

וַיָּבֹ֕א וַיַּגֵּ֥ד לַאדֹנָ֖יו לֵאמֹ֑ר כָּזֹ֤את וְכָזֹאת֙ דִּבְּרָ֣ה הַֽנַּעֲרָ֔ה אֲשֶׁ֖ר מֵאֶ֥רֶץ יִשְׂרָאֵֽל׃

5 And the king of Aram said, "Go to the king of *Yisrael*, and I will send along a letter." He set out, taking with him ten *kikarim* of silver, six thousand *shekalim* of gold, and ten changes of clothing.

וַיֹּ֤אמֶר מֶֽלֶךְ־אֲרָם֙ לֶךְ־בֹּ֔א וְאֶשְׁלְחָ֥ה סֵ֖פֶר אֶל־מֶ֣לֶךְ יִשְׂרָאֵ֑ל וַיֵּלֶךְ֩ וַיִּקַּ֨ח בְּיָד֜וֹ עֶ֣שֶׂר כִּכְּרֵי־כֶ֗סֶף וְשֵׁ֤שֶׁת אֲלָפִים֙ זָהָ֔ב וְעֶ֖שֶׂר חֲלִיפ֥וֹת בְּגָדִֽים׃

6 He brought the letter to the king of *Yisrael*. It read: "Now, when this letter reaches you, know that I have sent my courtier Naaman to you, that you may cure him of his leprosy."

וַיָּבֵ֣א הַסֵּ֔פֶר אֶל־מֶ֥לֶךְ יִשְׂרָאֵ֖ל לֵאמֹ֑ר וְעַתָּ֗ה כְּב֨וֹא הַסֵּ֤פֶר הַזֶּה֙ אֵלֶ֔יךָ הִנֵּ֨ה שָׁלַ֤חְתִּי אֵלֶ֙יךָ֙ אֶת־נַעֲמָ֣ן עַבְדִּ֔י וַאֲסַפְתּ֖וֹ מִצָּרַעְתּֽוֹ׃

7 When the king of *Yisrael* read the letter, he rent his clothes and cried, "Am I *Hashem*, to deal death or give life, that this fellow writes to me to cure a man of leprosy? Just see for yourselves that he is seeking a pretext against me!"

וַיְהִ֡י כִּקְרֹא֩ מֶֽלֶךְ־יִשְׂרָאֵ֨ל אֶת־הַסֵּ֜פֶר וַיִּקְרַ֣ע בְּגָדָ֗יו וַיֹּ֙אמֶר֙ הַאֱלֹהִ֥ים אָ֙נִי֙ לְהָמִ֣ית וּֽלְהַחֲי֔וֹת כִּֽי־זֶה֙ שֹׁלֵ֣חַ אֵלַ֔י לֶאֱסֹ֥ף אִ֖ישׁ מִצָּֽרַעְתּ֑וֹ כִּ֤י אַךְ־דְּעֽוּ־נָא֙ וּרְא֔וּ כִּֽי־מִתְאַנֶּ֥ה ה֖וּא לִֽי׃

8 When *Elisha*, the man of *Hashem*, heard that the king of *Yisrael* had rent his clothes, he sent a message to the king: "Why have you rent your clothes? Let him come to me, and he will learn that there is a *Navi* in *Yisrael*."

וַיְהִ֞י כִּשְׁמֹ֣עַ ׀ אֱלִישָׁ֣ע אִישׁ־הָאֱלֹהִ֗ים כִּֽי־קָרַ֤ע מֶֽלֶךְ־יִשְׂרָאֵל֙ אֶת־בְּגָדָ֔יו וַיִּשְׁלַ֥ח אֶל־הַמֶּ֖לֶךְ לֵאמֹ֑ר לָ֤מָּה קָרַ֙עְתָּ֙ בְּגָדֶ֔יךָ יָבֹֽא־נָ֣א אֵלַ֔י וְיֵדַ֕ע כִּ֛י יֵ֥שׁ נָבִ֖יא בְּיִשְׂרָאֵֽל׃

9 So Naaman came with his horses and chariots and halted at the door of *Elisha*'s house.

וַיָּבֹ֥א נַעֲמָ֖ן בְּסוּסָ֣ו [בְּסוּסָ֖יו] וּבְרִכְבּ֑וֹ וַיַּעֲמֹ֥ד פֶּֽתַח־הַבַּ֖יִת לֶאֱלִישָֽׁע׃

10 *Elisha* sent a messenger to say to him, "Go and bathe seven times in the *Yarden*, and your flesh shall be restored and you shall be clean."

וַיִּשְׁלַ֥ח אֵלָ֛יו אֱלִישָׁ֖ע מַלְאָ֣ךְ לֵאמֹ֑ר הָל֗וֹךְ וְרָחַצְתָּ֤ שֶֽׁבַע־פְּעָמִים֙ בַּיַּרְדֵּ֔ן וְיָשֹׁ֧ב בְּשָׂרְךָ֛ לְךָ֖ וּטְהָֽר׃

va-yish-LAKH ay-LAV e-lee-SHA mal-AKH lay-MOR ha-LOKH v'-ra-khatz-TA she-va p'-a-MEEM ba-yar-DAYN v'-ya-SHOV b'-sa-r'-KHA l'-KHA ut-HAR

5:10 Go and bathe seven times in the *Yarden* Previously (Joshua 3), the *Yarden* river split to allow the Children of Israel to cross into *Eretz Yisrael*. Now, the *Yarden* is again part of a miracle, as it cures *Naaman* of his affliction. The Land of Israel has amazing powers to provide spiritual, emotional and physical

Jordan River

Melachim II/II Kings
Chapter 5

מלכים ב
פרק ה

11 But Naaman was angered and walked away. "I thought," he said, "he would surely come out to me, and would stand and invoke *Hashem* his God by name, and would wave his hand toward the spot, and cure the affected part.

יא וַיִּקְצֹף נַעֲמָן וַיֵּלַךְ וַיֹּאמֶר הִנֵּה אָמַרְתִּי אֵלַי יֵצֵא יָצוֹא וְעָמַד וְקָרָא בְשֵׁם־יְהוָה אֱלֹהָיו וְהֵנִיף יָדוֹ אֶל־הַמָּקוֹם וְאָסַף הַמְּצֹרָע:

12 Are not the Amanah and the Pharpar, the rivers of Damascus, better than all the waters of *Yisrael*? I could bathe in them and be clean!" And he stalked off in a rage.

יב הֲלֹא טוֹב אבנה [אֲמָנָה] וּפַרְפַּר נַהֲרוֹת דַּמֶּשֶׂק מִכֹּל מֵימֵי יִשְׂרָאֵל הֲלֹא־אֶרְחַץ בָּהֶם וְטָהָרְתִּי וַיִּפֶן וַיֵּלֶךְ בְּחֵמָה:

13 But his servants came forward and spoke to him. "Sir," they said, "if the *Navi* told you to do something difficult, would you not do it? How much more when he has only said to you, 'Bathe and be clean.'"

יג וַיִּגְּשׁוּ עֲבָדָיו וַיְדַבְּרוּ אֵלָיו וַיֹּאמְרוּ אָבִי דָּבָר גָּדוֹל הַנָּבִיא דִּבֶּר אֵלֶיךָ הֲלוֹא תַעֲשֶׂה וְאַף כִּי־אָמַר אֵלֶיךָ רְחַץ וּטְהָר:

14 So he went down and immersed himself in the *Yarden* seven times, as the man of *Hashem* had bidden; and his flesh became like a little boy's, and he was clean.

יד וַיֵּרֶד וַיִּטְבֹּל בַּיַּרְדֵּן שֶׁבַע פְּעָמִים כִּדְבַר אִישׁ הָאֱלֹהִים וַיָּשָׁב בְּשָׂרוֹ כִּבְשַׂר נַעַר קָטֹן וַיִּטְהָר:

15 Returning with his entire retinue to the man of *Hashem*, he stood before him and exclaimed, "Now I know that there is no *Hashem* in the whole world except in *Yisrael*! So please accept a gift from your servant."

טו וַיָּשָׁב אֶל־אִישׁ הָאֱלֹהִים הוּא וְכָל־מַחֲנֵהוּ וַיָּבֹא וַיַּעֲמֹד לְפָנָיו וַיֹּאמֶר הִנֵּה־נָא יָדַעְתִּי כִּי אֵין אֱלֹהִים בְּכָל־הָאָרֶץ כִּי אִם־בְּיִשְׂרָאֵל וְעַתָּה קַח־נָא בְרָכָה מֵאֵת עַבְדֶּךָ:

16 But he replied, "As *Hashem* lives, whom I serve, I will not accept anything." He pressed him to accept, but he refused.

טז וַיֹּאמֶר חַי־יְהוָה אֲשֶׁר־עָמַדְתִּי לְפָנָיו אִם־אֶקָּח וַיִּפְצַר־בּוֹ לָקַחַת וַיְמָאֵן:

17 And Naaman said, "Then at least let your servant be given two mule-loads of earth; for your servant will never again offer up burnt offering or sacrifice to any god, except *Hashem*.

יז וַיֹּאמֶר נַעֲמָן וָלֹא יֻתַּן־נָא לְעַבְדְּךָ מַשָּׂא צֶמֶד־פְּרָדִים אֲדָמָה כִּי לוֹא־יַעֲשֶׂה עוֹד עַבְדְּךָ עֹלָה וָזֶבַח לֵאלֹהִים אֲחֵרִים כִּי אִם־לַיהוָה:

18 But may *Hashem* pardon your servant for this: When my master enters the temple of Rimmon to bow low in worship there, and he is leaning on my arm so that I must bow low in the temple of Rimmon – when I bow low in the temple of Rimmon, may *Hashem* pardon your servant in this."

יח לַדָּבָר הַזֶּה יִסְלַח יְהוָה לְעַבְדֶּךָ בְּבוֹא אֲדֹנִי בֵית־רִמּוֹן לְהִשְׁתַּחֲוֺת שָׁמָּה וְהוּא נִשְׁעָן עַל־יָדִי וְהִשְׁתַּחֲוֵיתִי בֵּית רִמֹּן בְּהִשְׁתַּחֲוָיָתִי בֵּית רִמֹּן יִסְלַח־נָא יְהוָה לְעַבְדְּךָ בַּדָּבָר הַזֶּה:

19 And he said to him, "Go in peace." When he had gone some distance from him,

יט וַיֹּאמֶר לוֹ לֵךְ לְשָׁלוֹם וַיֵּלֶךְ מֵאִתּוֹ כִּבְרַת־אָרֶץ:

---

healing. The Sages teach (*Bava Batra* 158b) that Israel's very air makes one wise, and the sprouting of its fruits heralds redemption. The miracles of Israel are all-encompassing. Sometimes we do not perceive them, or perhaps do not merit an individual miracle. But if one is spiritually attuned, it is possible to appreciate the many miracles God performs in the Promised Land each and every day.

Melachim II / II Kings
Chapter 6

מלכים ב
פרק ו

20 Gehazi, the attendant of *Elisha* the man of *Hashem*, thought: "My master has let that Aramean Naaman off without accepting what he brought! As *Hashem* lives, I will run after him and get something from him."

כ וַיֹּאמֶר גֵּיחֲזִי נַעַר אֱלִישָׁע אִישׁ־הָאֱלֹהִים הִנֵּה ׀ חָשַׂךְ אֲדֹנִי אֶת־נַעֲמָן הָאֲרַמִּי הַזֶּה מִקַּחַת מִיָּדוֹ אֵת אֲשֶׁר־הֵבִיא חַי־יְהֹוָה כִּי־אִם־רַצְתִּי אַחֲרָיו וְלָקַחְתִּי מֵאִתּוֹ מְאוּמָה:

21 So Gehazi hurried after Naaman. When Naaman saw someone running after him, he alighted from his chariot to meet him and said, "Is all well?"

כא וַיִּרְדֹּף גֵּחֲזִי אַחֲרֵי נַעֲמָן וַיִּרְאֶה נַעֲמָן רָץ אַחֲרָיו וַיִּפֹּל מֵעַל הַמֶּרְכָּבָה לִקְרָאתוֹ וַיֹּאמֶר הֲשָׁלוֹם:

22 "All is well," he replied. "My master has sent me to say: Two youths, disciples of the *Neviim*, have just come to me from the hill country of *Efraim*. Please give them a *kikar* of silver and two changes of clothing."

כב וַיֹּאמֶר ׀ שָׁלוֹם אֲדֹנִי שְׁלָחַנִי לֵאמֹר הִנֵּה עַתָּה זֶה בָּאוּ אֵלַי שְׁנֵי־נְעָרִים מֵהַר אֶפְרַיִם מִבְּנֵי הַנְּבִיאִים תְּנָה־נָּא לָהֶם כִּכַּר־כֶּסֶף וּשְׁתֵּי חֲלִפוֹת בְּגָדִים:

23 Naaman said, "Please take two *kikarim*." He urged him, and he wrapped the two *kikarim* of silver in two bags and gave them, along with two changes of clothes, to two of his servants, who carried them ahead of him.

כג וַיֹּאמֶר נַעֲמָן הוֹאֵל קַח כִּכָּרָיִם וַיִּפְרָץ־בּוֹ וַיָּצַר כִּכְּרַיִם כֶּסֶף בִּשְׁנֵי חֲרִטִים וּשְׁתֵּי חֲלִפוֹת בְּגָדִים וַיִּתֵּן אֶל־שְׁנֵי נְעָרָיו וַיִּשְׂאוּ לְפָנָיו:

24 When [Gehazi] arrived at the citadel, he took [the things] from them and deposited them in the house. Then he dismissed the men and they went their way.

כד וַיָּבֹא אֶל־הָעֹפֶל וַיִּקַּח מִיָּדָם וַיִּפְקֹד בַּבָּיִת וַיְשַׁלַּח אֶת־הָאֲנָשִׁים וַיֵּלֵכוּ:

25 He entered and stood before his master; and *Elisha* said to him, "Where have you been, Gehazi?" He replied, "Your servant has not gone anywhere."

כה וְהוּא־בָא וַיַּעֲמֹד אֶל־אֲדֹנָיו וַיֹּאמֶר אֵלָיו אֱלִישָׁע מֵאָן [מֵאַיִן] גֵּחֲזִי וַיֹּאמֶר לֹא־הָלַךְ עַבְדְּךָ אָנֶה וָאָנָה:

26 Then [*Elisha*] said to him, "Did not my spirit go along when a man got down from his chariot to meet you? Is this a time to take money in order to buy clothing and olive groves and vineyards, sheep and oxen, and male and female slaves?

כו וַיֹּאמֶר אֵלָיו לֹא־לִבִּי הָלַךְ כַּאֲשֶׁר הָפַךְ־אִישׁ מֵעַל מֶרְכַּבְתּוֹ לִקְרָאתֶךָ הַעֵת לָקַחַת אֶת־הַכֶּסֶף וְלָקַחַת בְּגָדִים וְזֵיתִים וּכְרָמִים וְצֹאן וּבָקָר וַעֲבָדִים וּשְׁפָחוֹת:

27 Surely, the leprosy of Naaman shall cling to you and to your descendants forever." And as [Gehazi] left his presence, he was snow-white with leprosy.

כז וְצָרַעַת נַעֲמָן תִּדְבַּק־בְּךָ וּבְזַרְעֲךָ לְעוֹלָם וַיֵּצֵא מִלְּפָנָיו מְצֹרָע כַּשָּׁלֶג:

6

1 The disciples of the *Neviim* said to *Elisha*, "See, the place where we live under your direction is too cramped for us.

א וַיֹּאמְרוּ בְנֵי־הַנְּבִיאִים אֶל־אֱלִישָׁע הִנֵּה־נָא הַמָּקוֹם אֲשֶׁר אֲנַחְנוּ יֹשְׁבִים שָׁם לְפָנֶיךָ צַר מִמֶּנּוּ:

va-yo-m'-RU v'nay ha-n'-vee-EEM el e-lee-SHA hi-nay NA ha-ma-KOM a-SHER a-NAKH-nu yo-sh'-VEEM SHAM l'-fa-NE-kha TZAR mi-ME-nu

---

צר

6:1 Too cramped for us *Elisha's* disciples complain that their living quarters are too cramped, *tzar* (צר). In Hebrew, *tzar* means 'narrow,' and is often used metaphorically to describe a place of trouble. For example, in *Tehillim* (118:5) King *David* proclaims that he is calling out to *Hashem* from a place of trouble and

Melachim II/II Kings
Chapter 6

מלכים ב
פרק ו

2 Let us go to the *Yarden*, and let us each get a log there and build quarters there for ourselves to live in." "Do so," he replied.

ב נֵלְכָה־נָּא עַד־הַיַּרְדֵּן וְנִקְחָה מִשָּׁם אִישׁ קוֹרָה אֶחָת וְנַעֲשֶׂה־לָּנוּ שָׁם מָקוֹם לָשֶׁבֶת שָׁם וַיֹּאמֶר לֵכוּ׃

3 Then one of them said, "Will you please come along with your servants?" "Yes, I will come," he said;

ג וַיֹּאמֶר הָאֶחָד הוֹאֶל נָא וְלֵךְ אֶת־עֲבָדֶיךָ וַיֹּאמֶר אֲנִי אֵלֵךְ׃

4 and he accompanied them. So they went to the *Yarden* and cut timber.

ד וַיֵּלֶךְ אִתָּם וַיָּבֹאוּ הַיַּרְדֵּנָה וַיִּגְזְרוּ הָעֵצִים׃

5 As one of them was felling a trunk, the iron ax head fell into the water. And he cried aloud, "Alas, master, it was a borrowed one!"

ה וַיְהִי הָאֶחָד מַפִּיל הַקּוֹרָה וְאֶת־הַבַּרְזֶל נָפַל אֶל־הַמָּיִם וַיִּצְעַק וַיֹּאמֶר אֲהָהּ אֲדֹנִי וְהוּא שָׁאוּל׃

6 "Where did it fall?" asked the man of *Hashem*. He showed him the spot; and he cut off a stick and threw it in, and he made the ax head float.

ו וַיֹּאמֶר אִישׁ־הָאֱלֹהִים אָנָה נָפָל וַיַּרְאֵהוּ אֶת־הַמָּקוֹם וַיִּקְצָב־עֵץ וַיַּשְׁלֶךְ־שָׁמָּה וַיָּצֶף הַבַּרְזֶל׃

7 "Pick it up," he said; so he reached out and took it.

ז וַיֹּאמֶר הָרֶם לָךְ וַיִּשְׁלַח יָדוֹ וַיִּקָּחֵהוּ׃

8 While the king of Aram was waging war against *Yisrael*, he took counsel with his officers and said, "I will encamp in such and such a place."

ח וּמֶלֶךְ אֲרָם הָיָה נִלְחָם בְּיִשְׂרָאֵל וַיִּוָּעַץ אֶל־עֲבָדָיו לֵאמֹר אֶל־מְקוֹם פְּלֹנִי אַלְמֹנִי תַּחֲנֹתִי׃

9 But the man of *Hashem* sent word to the king of *Yisrael*, "Take care not to pass through that place, for the Arameans are encamped there."

ט וַיִּשְׁלַח אִישׁ הָאֱלֹהִים אֶל־מֶלֶךְ יִשְׂרָאֵל לֵאמֹר הִשָּׁמֶר מֵעֲבֹר הַמָּקוֹם הַזֶּה כִּי־שָׁם אֲרָם נְחִתִּים׃

10 So the king of *Yisrael* sent word to the place of which the man of *Hashem* had told him. Time and again he alerted such a place and took precautions there.

י וַיִּשְׁלַח מֶלֶךְ יִשְׂרָאֵל אֶל־הַמָּקוֹם אֲשֶׁר אָמַר־לוֹ אִישׁ־הָאֱלֹהִים והזהירה [וְהִזְהִירוֹ] וְנִשְׁמַר שָׁם לֹא אַחַת וְלֹא שְׁתָּיִם׃

11 Greatly agitated about this matter, the king of Aram summoned his officers and said to them, "Tell me! Who of us is on the side of the king of *Yisrael*?"

יא וַיִּסָּעֵר לֵב מֶלֶךְ־אֲרָם עַל־הַדָּבָר הַזֶּה וַיִּקְרָא אֶל־עֲבָדָיו וַיֹּאמֶר אֲלֵיהֶם הֲלוֹא תַּגִּידוּ לִי מִי מִשֶּׁלָּנוּ אֶל־מֶלֶךְ יִשְׂרָאֵל׃

12 "No one, my lord king," said one of the officers. "*Elisha*, that *Navi* in *Yisrael*, tells the king of *Yisrael* the very words you speak in your bedroom."

יב וַיֹּאמֶר אַחַד מֵעֲבָדָיו לוֹא אֲדֹנִי הַמֶּלֶךְ כִּי־אֱלִישָׁע הַנָּבִיא אֲשֶׁר בְּיִשְׂרָאֵל יַגִּיד לְמֶלֶךְ יִשְׂרָאֵל אֶת־הַדְּבָרִים אֲשֶׁר תְּדַבֵּר בַּחֲדַר מִשְׁכָּבֶךָ׃

---

pain, "*min hamaytzar*" (מן המצר). In this verse, it can have both the literal and the metaphoric meanings, as there is insufficient space and also troubles from enemies. For both types of difficulty, divine assistance is needed.

Melachim II/II Kings
Chapter 6

מלכים ב
פרק ו

13 "Go find out where he is," he said, "so that I can have him seized." It was reported to him that [*Elisha*] was in Dothan;

יג וַיֹּאמֶר לְכוּ וּרְאוּ אֵיכֹה הוּא וְאֶשְׁלַח וְאֶקָּחֵהוּ וַיֻּגַּד־לוֹ לֵאמֹר הִנֵּה בְדֹתָן׃

14 so he sent horses and chariots there and a strong force. They arrived at night and encircled the town.

יד וַיִּשְׁלַח־שָׁמָּה סוּסִים וְרֶכֶב וְחַיִל כָּבֵד וַיָּבֹאוּ לַיְלָה וַיַּקִּפוּ עַל־הָעִיר׃

15 When the attendant of the man of *Hashem* rose early and went outside, he saw a force, with horses and chariots, surrounding the town. "Alas, master, what shall we do?" his servant asked him.

טו וַיַּשְׁכֵּם מְשָׁרֵת אִישׁ הָאֱלֹהִים לָקוּם וַיֵּצֵא וְהִנֵּה־חַיִל סוֹבֵב אֶת־הָעִיר וְסוּס וָרָכֶב וַיֹּאמֶר נַעֲרוֹ אֵלָיו אֲהָהּ אֲדֹנִי אֵיכָה נַעֲשֶׂה׃

16 "Have no fear," he replied. "There are more on our side than on theirs."

טז וַיֹּאמֶר אַל־תִּירָא כִּי רַבִּים אֲשֶׁר אִתָּנוּ מֵאֲשֶׁר אוֹתָם׃

17 Then *Elisha* prayed: "*Hashem*, open his eyes and let him see." And *Hashem* opened the servant's eyes and he saw the hills all around *Elisha* covered with horses and chariots of fire.

יז וַיִּתְפַּלֵּל אֱלִישָׁע וַיֹּאמַר יְהוָה פְּקַח־נָא אֶת־עֵינָיו וְיִרְאֶה וַיִּפְקַח יְהוָה אֶת־עֵינֵי הַנַּעַר וַיַּרְא וְהִנֵּה הָהָר מָלֵא סוּסִים וְרֶכֶב אֵשׁ סְבִיבֹת אֱלִישָׁע׃

18 [The Arameans] came down against him, and *Elisha* prayed to *Hashem*: "Please strike this people with a blinding light." And He struck them with a blinding light, as *Elisha* had asked.

יח וַיֵּרְדוּ אֵלָיו וַיִּתְפַּלֵּל אֱלִישָׁע אֶל־יְהוָה וַיֹּאמַר הַךְ־נָא אֶת־הַגּוֹי־הַזֶּה בַּסַּנְוֵרִים וַיַּכֵּם בַּסַּנְוֵרִים כִּדְבַר אֱלִישָׁע׃

19 *Elisha* said to them, "This is not the road, and that is not the town; follow me, and I will lead you to the man you want." And he led them to *Shomron*.

יט וַיֹּאמֶר אֲלֵהֶם אֱלִישָׁע לֹא זֶה הַדֶּרֶךְ וְלֹא זֹה הָעִיר לְכוּ אַחֲרַי וְאוֹלִיכָה אֶתְכֶם אֶל־הָאִישׁ אֲשֶׁר תְּבַקֵּשׁוּן וַיֹּלֶךְ אוֹתָם שֹׁמְרוֹנָה׃

20 When they entered *Shomron*, *Elisha* said, "*Hashem*, open the eyes of these men so that they may see." *Hashem* opened their eyes and they saw that they were inside *Shomron*.

כ וַיְהִי כְּבֹאָם שֹׁמְרוֹן וַיֹּאמֶר אֱלִישָׁע יְהוָה פְּקַח אֶת־עֵינֵי־אֵלֶּה וְיִרְאוּ וַיִּפְקַח יְהוָה אֶת־עֵינֵיהֶם וַיִּרְאוּ וְהִנֵּה בְּתוֹךְ שֹׁמְרוֹן׃

21 When the king of *Yisrael* saw them, he said to *Elisha*, "Father, shall I strike them down?"

כא וַיֹּאמֶר מֶלֶךְ־יִשְׂרָאֵל אֶל־אֱלִישָׁע כִּרְאֹתוֹ אוֹתָם הַאַכֶּה אַכֶּה אָבִי׃

22 "No, do not," he replied. "Did you take them captive with your sword and bow that you would strike them down? Rather, set food and drink before them, and let them eat and drink and return to their master."

כב וַיֹּאמֶר לֹא תַכֶּה הַאֲשֶׁר שָׁבִיתָ בְּחַרְבְּךָ וּבְקַשְׁתְּךָ אַתָּה מַכֶּה שִׂים לֶחֶם וָמַיִם לִפְנֵיהֶם וְיֹאכְלוּ וְיִשְׁתּוּ וְיֵלְכוּ אֶל־אֲדֹנֵיהֶם׃

23 So he prepared a lavish feast for them and, after they had eaten and drunk, he let them go, and they returned to their master. And the Aramean bands stopped invading the land of *Yisrael*.

כג וַיִּכְרֶה לָהֶם כֵּרָה גְדוֹלָה וַיֹּאכְלוּ וַיִּשְׁתּוּ וַיְשַׁלְּחֵם וַיֵּלְכוּ אֶל־אֲדֹנֵיהֶם וְלֹא־יָסְפוּ עוֹד גְּדוּדֵי אֲרָם לָבוֹא בְּאֶרֶץ יִשְׂרָאֵל׃

Melachim II / II Kings
Chapter 7

מלכים ב
פרק ז

24 Sometime later, King Ben-hadad of Aram mustered his entire army and marched upon *Shomron* and besieged it.

כד וַיְהִי אַחֲרֵי־כֵן וַיִּקְבֹּץ בֶּן־הֲדַד מֶלֶךְ־אֲרָם אֶת־כָּל־מַחֲנֵהוּ וַיַּעַל וַיָּצַר עַל־שֹׁמְרוֹן:

25 There was a great famine in *Shomron*, and the siege continued until a donkey's head sold for eighty [*shekalim*] of silver and a quarter of a *kav* of doves' dung for five *shekalim*.

כה וַיְהִי רָעָב גָּדוֹל בְּשֹׁמְרוֹן וְהִנֵּה צָרִים עָלֶיהָ עַד הֱיוֹת רֹאשׁ־חֲמוֹר בִּשְׁמֹנִים כֶּסֶף וְרֹבַע הַקַּב חרייונים [דִּבְיוֹנִים] בַּחֲמִשָּׁה־כָסֶף:

26 Once, when the king of *Yisrael* was walking on the city wall, a woman cried out to him: "Help me, Your Majesty!"

כו וַיְהִי מֶלֶךְ יִשְׂרָאֵל עֹבֵר עַל־הַחֹמָה וְאִשָּׁה צָעֲקָה אֵלָיו לֵאמֹר הוֹשִׁיעָה אֲדֹנִי הַמֶּלֶךְ:

27 "Don't [ask me]," he replied. "Let *Hashem* help you! Where could I get help for you, from the threshing floor or from the winepress?

כז וַיֹּאמֶר אַל־יוֹשִׁעֵךְ יְהוָה מֵאַיִן אוֹשִׁיעֵךְ הֲמִן־הַגֹּרֶן אוֹ מִן־הַיָּקֶב:

28 But what troubles you?" the king asked her. The woman answered, "That woman said to me, 'Give up your son and we will eat him today; and tomorrow we'll eat my son.'

כח וַיֹּאמֶר־לָהּ הַמֶּלֶךְ מַה־לָּךְ וַתֹּאמֶר הָאִשָּׁה הַזֹּאת אָמְרָה אֵלַי תְּנִי אֶת־בְּנֵךְ וְנֹאכְלֶנּוּ הַיּוֹם וְאֶת־בְּנִי נֹאכַל מָחָר:

29 So we cooked my son and we ate him. The next day I said to her, 'Give up your son and let's eat him'; but she hid her son."

כט וַנְּבַשֵּׁל אֶת־בְּנִי וַנֹּאכְלֵהוּ וָאֹמַר אֵלֶיהָ בַּיּוֹם הָאַחֵר תְּנִי אֶת־בְּנֵךְ וְנֹאכְלֶנּוּ וַתַּחְבִּא אֶת־בְּנָהּ:

30 When the king heard what the woman said, he rent his clothes; and as he walked along the wall, the people could see that he was wearing sackcloth underneath.

ל וַיְהִי כִשְׁמֹעַ הַמֶּלֶךְ אֶת־דִּבְרֵי הָאִשָּׁה וַיִּקְרַע אֶת־בְּגָדָיו וְהוּא עֹבֵר עַל־הַחֹמָה וַיַּרְא הָעָם וְהִנֵּה הַשַּׂק עַל־בְּשָׂרוֹ מִבָּיִת:

31 He said, "Thus and more may *Hashem* do to me if the head of *Elisha* son of *Shafat* remains on his shoulders today."

לא וַיֹּאמֶר כֹּה־יַעֲשֶׂה־לִּי אֱלֹהִים וְכֹה יוֹסִף אִם־יַעֲמֹד רֹאשׁ אֱלִישָׁע בֶּן־שָׁפָט עָלָיו הַיּוֹם:

32 Now *Elisha* was sitting at home and the elders were sitting with him. The king had sent ahead one of his men; but before the messenger arrived, [*Elisha*] said to the elders, "Do you see – that murderer has sent someone to cut off my head! Watch when the messenger comes, and shut the door and hold the door fast against him. No doubt the sound of his master's footsteps will follow."

לב וֶאֱלִישָׁע יֹשֵׁב בְּבֵיתוֹ וְהַזְּקֵנִים יֹשְׁבִים אִתּוֹ וַיִּשְׁלַח אִישׁ מִלְּפָנָיו בְּטֶרֶם יָבֹא הַמַּלְאָךְ אֵלָיו וְהוּא אָמַר אֶל־הַזְּקֵנִים הַרְּאִיתֶם כִּי־שָׁלַח בֶּן־הַמְרַצֵּחַ הַזֶּה לְהָסִיר אֶת־רֹאשִׁי רְאוּ כְּבֹא הַמַּלְאָךְ סִגְרוּ הַדֶּלֶת וּלְחַצְתֶּם אֹתוֹ בַּדָּלֶת הֲלוֹא קוֹל רַגְלֵי אֲדֹנָיו אַחֲרָיו:

33 While he was still talking to them, the messenger came to him and said, "This calamity is from *Hashem*. What more can I hope for from *Hashem*?"

לג עוֹדֶנּוּ מְדַבֵּר עִמָּם וְהִנֵּה הַמַּלְאָךְ יֹרֵד אֵלָיו וַיֹּאמֶר הִנֵּה־זֹאת הָרָעָה מֵאֵת יְהוָה מָה־אוֹחִיל לַיהוָה עוֹד:

7

1 And *Elisha* replied, "Hear the word of *Hashem*. Thus said *Hashem*: This time tomorrow, a *se'ah* of choice flour shall sell for a *shekel* at the gate of *Shomron*, and two *se'eem* of barley for a *shekel*."

ז א וַיֹּאמֶר אֱלִישָׁע שִׁמְעוּ דְּבַר־יְהוָה כֹּה אָמַר יְהוָה כָּעֵת מָחָר סְאָה־סֹלֶת בְּשֶׁקֶל וְסָאתַיִם שְׂעֹרִים בְּשֶׁקֶל בְּשַׁעַר שֹׁמְרוֹן:

Melachim II / II Kings
Chapter 7

מלכים ב
פרק ז

2 The aide on whose arm the king was leaning spoke up and said to the man of *Hashem*, "Even if *Hashem* were to make windows in the sky, could this come to pass?" And he retorted, "You shall see it with your own eyes, but you shall not eat of it."

ב וַיַּעַן הַשָּׁלִישׁ אֲשֶׁר־לַמֶּלֶךְ נִשְׁעָן עַל־יָדוֹ אֶת־אִישׁ הָאֱלֹהִים וַיֹּאמַר הִנֵּה יְהֹוָה עֹשֶׂה אֲרֻבּוֹת בַּשָּׁמַיִם הֲיִהְיֶה הַדָּבָר הַזֶּה וַיֹּאמֶר הִנְּכָה רֹאֶה בְּעֵינֶיךָ וּמִשָּׁם לֹא תֹאכֵל׃

3 There were four men, lepers, outside the gate. They said to one another, "Why should we sit here waiting for death?"

ג וְאַרְבָּעָה אֲנָשִׁים הָיוּ מְצֹרָעִים פֶּתַח הַשָּׁעַר וַיֹּאמְרוּ אִישׁ אֶל־רֵעֵהוּ מָה אֲנַחְנוּ יֹשְׁבִים פֹּה עַד־מָתְנוּ׃

v'-ar-ba-AH a-na-SHEEM ha-YU m'-tzo-ra-EEM PE-takh ha-SHA-ar va-yo-m'-RU EESH el ray-AY-hu MAH a-NAKH-nu yo-sh'-VEEM POH ad MAT-nu

4 If we decide to go into the town, what with the famine in the town, we shall die there; and if we just sit here, still we die. Come, let us desert to the Aramean camp. If they let us live, we shall live; and if they put us to death, we shall but die."

ד אִם־אָמַרְנוּ נָבוֹא הָעִיר וְהָרָעָב בָּעִיר וָמַתְנוּ שָׁם וְאִם־יָשַׁבְנוּ פֹה וָמָתְנוּ וְעַתָּה לְכוּ וְנִפְּלָה אֶל־מַחֲנֵה אֲרָם אִם־יְחַיֻּנוּ נִחְיֶה וְאִם־יְמִיתֻנוּ וָמָתְנוּ׃

5 They set out at twilight for the Aramean camp; but when they came to the edge of the Aramean camp, there was no one there.

ה וַיָּקוּמוּ בַנֶּשֶׁף לָבוֹא אֶל־מַחֲנֵה אֲרָם וַיָּבֹאוּ עַד־קְצֵה מַחֲנֵה אֲרָם וְהִנֵּה אֵין־שָׁם אִישׁ׃

6 For *Hashem* had caused the Aramean camp to hear a sound of chariots, a sound of horses – the din of a huge army. They said to one another, "The king of *Yisrael* must have hired the kings of the Hittites and the kings of Mizraim to attack us!"

ו וַאדֹנָי הִשְׁמִיעַ אֶת־מַחֲנֵה אֲרָם קוֹל רֶכֶב קוֹל סוּס קוֹל חַיִל גָּדוֹל וַיֹּאמְרוּ אִישׁ אֶל־אָחִיו הִנֵּה שָׂכַר־עָלֵינוּ מֶלֶךְ יִשְׂרָאֵל אֶת־מַלְכֵי הַחִתִּים וְאֶת־מַלְכֵי מִצְרַיִם לָבוֹא עָלֵינוּ׃

7 And they fled headlong in the twilight, abandoning their tents and horses and asses – the [entire] camp just as it was – as they fled for their lives.

ז וַיָּקוּמוּ וַיָּנוּסוּ בַנֶּשֶׁף וַיַּעַזְבוּ אֶת־אָהֳלֵיהֶם וְאֶת־סוּסֵיהֶם וְאֶת־חֲמֹרֵיהֶם הַמַּחֲנֶה כַּאֲשֶׁר־הִיא וַיָּנֻסוּ אֶל־נַפְשָׁם׃

va-ya-ku-MU va-ya-NU-su va-NE-shef va-ya-az-VU et o-ha-lay-HEM v'-ET su-say-HEM v'-et kha-MO-ray-HEM ha-ma-kha-NEH ka-a-SHER HEE va-ya-NU-su el naf-SHAM

Israeli postage stamp honoring Rabbi Aryeh Levin circa 1982

7:3 There were four men, lepers, outside the gate. One of the most righteous and pious Jerusalemites of the 20th century, Rabbi Aryeh Levin (1885–1969), was beloved for his visits to the sick. Rabbi Levin would go to the hospitals of Jerusalem every Friday and speak with the nurses to find out which patients received no visitors. At the beds of these forgotten souls whom no relatives came to see, he would sit for hours, caressing each one's hand and offering words of encouragement and cheer. He was also a frequent visitor at hospitals for lepers, including a hospital in Bethlehem where most of the patients were Arabs. Rabbi Levin began this practice after he had found a woman weeping bitterly by the Western Wall. He asked her, "what makes you cry so intensely?" She explained that her child had no cure, and was locked up in the leper hospital. Rabbi Levin immediately decided to visit the young child, and when he arrived, all the patients burst into tears. It had been years since they had the privilege of seeing a visitor from the outside world.

7:7 And they fled headlong in the twilight The enemies of Israel miraculously flee, abandoning their entire camp. Similarly, there have been times in the State of Israel's history where the enemy fled before engaging the Israel Defense Forces. A famous example occurred during the Six Day War, when IDF Chief

Melachim II / II Kings
Chapter 7

8 When those lepers came to the edge of the camp, they went into one of the tents and ate and drank; then they carried off silver and gold and clothing from there and buried it. They came back and went into another tent, and they carried off what was there and buried it.

9 Then they said to one another, "We are not doing right. This is a day of good news, and we are keeping silent! If we wait until the light of morning, we shall incur guilt. Come, let us go and inform the king's palace."

10 They went and called out to the gatekeepers of the city and told them, "We have been to the Aramean camp. There is not a soul there, nor any human sound; but the horses are tethered and the asses are tethered and the tents are undisturbed."

11 The gatekeepers called out, and the news was passed on into the king's palace.

12 The king rose in the night and said to his courtiers, "I will tell you what the Arameans have done to us. They know that we are starving, so they have gone out of camp and hidden in the fields, thinking: When they come out of the town, we will take them alive and get into the town."

13 But one of the courtiers spoke up, "Let a few of the remaining horses that are still here be taken – they are like those that are left here of the whole multitude of *Yisrael*, out of the whole multitude of *Yisrael* that have perished – and let us send and find out."

14 They took two teams of horses and the king sent them after the Aramean army, saying, "Go and find out."

15 They followed them as far as the *Yarden*, and found the entire road full of clothing and gear which the Arameans had thrown away in their haste; and the messengers returned and told the king.

מלכים ב
פרק ז

ח וַיָּבֹאוּ הַמְצֹרָעִים הָאֵלֶּה עַד־קְצֵה הַמַּחֲנֶה וַיָּבֹאוּ אֶל־אֹהֶל אֶחָד וַיֹּאכְלוּ וַיִּשְׁתּוּ וַיִּשְׂאוּ מִשָּׁם כֶּסֶף וְזָהָב וּבְגָדִים וַיֵּלְכוּ וַיַּטְמִנוּ וַיָּשֻׁבוּ וַיָּבֹאוּ אֶל־אֹהֶל אַחֵר וַיִּשְׂאוּ מִשָּׁם וַיֵּלְכוּ וַיַּטְמִנוּ:

ט וַיֹּאמְרוּ אִישׁ אֶל־רֵעֵהוּ לֹא־כֵן אֲנַחְנוּ עֹשִׂים הַיּוֹם הַזֶּה יוֹם־בְּשֹׂרָה הוּא וַאֲנַחְנוּ מַחְשִׁים וְחִכִּינוּ עַד־אוֹר הַבֹּקֶר וּמְצָאָנוּ עָווֹן וְעַתָּה לְכוּ וְנָבֹאָה וְנַגִּידָה בֵּית הַמֶּלֶךְ:

י וַיָּבֹאוּ וַיִּקְרְאוּ אֶל־שֹׁעֵר הָעִיר וַיַּגִּידוּ לָהֶם לֵאמֹר בָּאנוּ אֶל־מַחֲנֵה אֲרָם וְהִנֵּה אֵין־שָׁם אִישׁ וְקוֹל אָדָם כִּי אִם־הַסּוּס אָסוּר וְהַחֲמוֹר אָסוּר וְאֹהָלִים כַּאֲשֶׁר־הֵמָּה:

יא וַיִּקְרָא הַשֹּׁעֲרִים וַיַּגִּידוּ בֵּית הַמֶּלֶךְ פְּנִימָה:

יב וַיָּקָם הַמֶּלֶךְ לַיְלָה וַיֹּאמֶר אֶל־עֲבָדָיו אַגִּידָה־נָּא לָכֶם אֵת אֲשֶׁר־עָשׂוּ לָנוּ אֲרָם יָדְעוּ כִּי־רְעֵבִים אֲנַחְנוּ וַיֵּצְאוּ מִן־הַמַּחֲנֶה לְהֵחָבֵה בהשדה [בַשָּׂדֶה] לֵאמֹר כִּי־יֵצְאוּ מִן־הָעִיר וְנִתְפְּשֵׂם חַיִּים וְאֶל־הָעִיר נָבֹא:

יג וַיַּעַן אֶחָד מֵעֲבָדָיו וַיֹּאמֶר וְיִקְחוּ־נָא חֲמִשָּׁה מִן־הַסּוּסִים הַנִּשְׁאָרִים אֲשֶׁר נִשְׁאֲרוּ־בָהּ הִנָּם כְּכָל־ההמון [הֲמוֹן] יִשְׂרָאֵל אֲשֶׁר נִשְׁאֲרוּ־בָהּ הִנָּם כְּכָל־הֲמוֹן יִשְׂרָאֵל אֲשֶׁר־תָּמּוּ וְנִשְׁלְחָה וְנִרְאֶה:

יד וַיִּקְחוּ שְׁנֵי רֶכֶב סוּסִים וַיִּשְׁלַח הַמֶּלֶךְ אַחֲרֵי מַחֲנֵה־אֲרָם לֵאמֹר לְכוּ וּרְאוּ:

טו וַיֵּלְכוּ אַחֲרֵיהֶם עַד־הַיַּרְדֵּן וְהִנֵּה כָל־הַדֶּרֶךְ מְלֵאָה בְגָדִים וְכֵלִים אֲשֶׁר־הִשְׁלִיכוּ אֲרָם בהחפזם [בְּחָפְזָם] וַיָּשֻׁבוּ הַמַּלְאָכִים וַיַּגִּדוּ לַמֶּלֶךְ:

Rabbi Shlomo Goren and his driver single-handedly captured the holy city of *Chevron*. When they drove into *Chevron*, mistakenly thinking IDF soldiers were already there, they were greeted with a city full of white flags and empty of soldiers. *Hashem*'s miracles are always in evidence among the soldiers of Israel.

Rabbi Shlomo Goren
(1917–1994)

Melachim II/II Kings
Chapter 8

מלכים ב
פרק ח

16 The people then went out and plundered the Aramean camp. So a *se'ah* of choice flour sold for a *shekel*, and two *se'eem* of barley for a *shekel* – as *Hashem* had spoken.

טז וַיֵּצֵא הָעָם וַיָּבֹזּוּ אֵת מַחֲנֵה אֲרָם וַיְהִי סְאָה־סֹלֶת בְּשֶׁקֶל וְסָאתַיִם שְׂעֹרִים בְּשֶׁקֶל כִּדְבַר יְהֹוָה:

17 Now the king had put the aide on whose arm he leaned in charge of the gate; and he was trampled to death in the gate by the people – just as the man of *Hashem* had spoken, as he had spoken when the king came down to him.

יז וְהַמֶּלֶךְ הִפְקִיד אֶת־הַשָּׁלִישׁ אֲשֶׁר־נִשְׁעָן עַל־יָדוֹ עַל־הַשַּׁעַר וַיִּרְמְסֻהוּ הָעָם בַּשַּׁעַר וַיָּמֹת כַּאֲשֶׁר דִּבֶּר אִישׁ הָאֱלֹהִים אֲשֶׁר דִּבֶּר בְּרֶדֶת הַמֶּלֶךְ אֵלָיו:

18 For when the man of *Hashem* said to the king, "This time tomorrow two *se'eem* of barley shall sell at the gate of *Shomron* for a *shekel*, and a *se'ah* of choice flour for a *shekel*,"

יח וַיְהִי כְּדַבֵּר אִישׁ הָאֱלֹהִים אֶל־הַמֶּלֶךְ לֵאמֹר סָאתַיִם שְׂעֹרִים בְּשֶׁקֶל וּסְאָה־סֹלֶת בְּשֶׁקֶל יִהְיֶה כָּעֵת מָחָר בְּשַׁעַר שֹׁמְרוֹן:

19 the aide answered the man of *Hashem* and said, "Even if *Hashem* made windows in the sky, could this come to pass?" And he retorted, "You shall see it with your own eyes, but you shall not eat of it."

יט וַיַּעַן הַשָּׁלִישׁ אֶת־אִישׁ הָאֱלֹהִים וַיֹּאמַר וְהִנֵּה יְהֹוָה עֹשֶׂה אֲרֻבּוֹת בַּשָּׁמַיִם הֲיִהְיֶה כַּדָּבָר הַזֶּה וַיֹּאמֶר הִנְּךָ רֹאֶה בְּעֵינֶיךָ וּמִשָּׁם לֹא תֹאכֵל:

20 That is exactly what happened to him: The people trampled him to death in the gate.

כ וַיְהִי־לוֹ כֵּן וַיִּרְמְסוּ אֹתוֹ הָעָם בַּשַּׁעַר וַיָּמֹת:

8

1 *Elisha* had said to the woman whose son he revived, "Leave immediately with your family and go sojourn somewhere else; for *Hashem* has decreed a seven-year famine upon the land, and it has already begun."

א וֶאֱלִישָׁע דִּבֶּר אֶל־הָאִשָּׁה אֲשֶׁר־הֶחֱיָה אֶת־בְּנָהּ לֵאמֹר קוּמִי וּלְכִי אַתִּי [אַתְּ] וּבֵיתֵךְ וְגוּרִי בַּאֲשֶׁר תָּגוּרִי כִּי־קָרָא יְהֹוָה לָרָעָב וְגַם־בָּא אֶל־הָאָרֶץ שֶׁבַע שָׁנִים:

2 The woman had done as the man of *Hashem* had spoken; she left with her family and sojourned in the land of the Philistines for seven years.

ב וַתָּקָם הָאִשָּׁה וַתַּעַשׂ כִּדְבַר אִישׁ הָאֱלֹהִים וַתֵּלֶךְ הִיא וּבֵיתָהּ וַתָּגָר בְּאֶרֶץ־פְּלִשְׁתִּים שֶׁבַע שָׁנִים:

3 At the end of the seven years, the woman returned from the land of the Philistines and went to the king to complain about her house and farm.

ג וַיְהִי מִקְצֵה שֶׁבַע שָׁנִים וַתָּשָׁב הָאִשָּׁה מֵאֶרֶץ פְּלִשְׁתִּים וַתֵּצֵא לִצְעֹק אֶל־הַמֶּלֶךְ אֶל־בֵּיתָהּ וְאֶל־שָׂדָהּ:

4 Now the king was talking to Gehazi, the servant of the man of *Hashem*, and he said, "Tell me all the wonderful things that *Elisha* has done."

ד וְהַמֶּלֶךְ מְדַבֵּר אֶל־גֵּחֲזִי נַעַר אִישׁ־הָאֱלֹהִים לֵאמֹר סַפְּרָה־נָּא לִי אֵת כָּל־הַגְּדֹלוֹת אֲשֶׁר־עָשָׂה אֱלִישָׁע:

5 While he was telling the king how [*Elisha*] had revived a dead person, in came the woman whose son he had revived, complaining to the king about her house and farm. "My lord king," said Gehazi, "this is the woman and this is her son whom *Elisha* revived."

ה וַיְהִי הוּא מְסַפֵּר לַמֶּלֶךְ אֵת אֲשֶׁר־הֶחֱיָה אֶת־הַמֵּת וְהִנֵּה הָאִשָּׁה אֲשֶׁר־הֶחֱיָה אֶת־בְּנָהּ צֹעֶקֶת אֶל־הַמֶּלֶךְ עַל־בֵּיתָהּ וְעַל־שָׂדָהּ וַיֹּאמֶר גֵּחֲזִי אֲדֹנִי הַמֶּלֶךְ זֹאת הָאִשָּׁה וְזֶה־בְּנָהּ אֲשֶׁר־הֶחֱיָה אֱלִישָׁע:

6 The king questioned the woman, and she told him [the story]; so the king assigned a eunuch to her and instructed him: "Restore all her property, and all the revenue from her farm from the time she left the country until now."

ו וַיִּשְׁאַל הַמֶּלֶךְ לָאִשָּׁה וַתְּסַפֶּר־לוֹ וַיִּתֶּן־לָהּ הַמֶּלֶךְ סָרִיס אֶחָד לֵאמֹר הָשֵׁיב אֶת־כָּל־אֲשֶׁר־לָהּ וְאֵת כָּל־תְּבוּאֹת הַשָּׂדֶה מִיּוֹם עָזְבָה אֶת־הָאָרֶץ וְעַד־עָתָּה:

Melachim II / II Kings
Chapter 8

מלכים ב
פרק ח

7 *Elisha* arrived in Damascus at a time when King Ben-hadad of Aram was ill. The king* was told, "The man of *Hashem* is on his way here,"

ז וַיָּבֹא אֱלִישָׁע דַּמֶּשֶׂק וּבֶן־הֲדַד מֶלֶךְ־אֲרָם חֹלֶה וַיֻּגַּד־לוֹ לֵאמֹר בָּא אִישׁ הָאֱלֹהִים עַד־הֵנָּה׃

8 and he said to Hazael, "Take a gift with you and go meet the man of *Hashem*, and through him inquire of *Hashem*: Will I recover from this illness?"

ח וַיֹּאמֶר הַמֶּלֶךְ אֶל־חֲזָהאֵל קַח בְּיָדְךָ מִנְחָה וְלֵךְ לִקְרַאת אִישׁ הָאֱלֹהִים וְדָרַשְׁתָּ אֶת־יְהוָה מֵאוֹתוֹ לֵאמֹר הַאֶחְיֶה מֵחֳלִי זֶה׃

9 Hazael went to meet him, taking with him as a gift forty camel-loads of all the bounty of Damascus. He came and stood before him and said, "Your son, King Ben-hadad of Aram, has sent me to you to ask: Will I recover from this illness?"

ט וַיֵּלֶךְ חֲזָהאֵל לִקְרָאתוֹ וַיִּקַּח מִנְחָה בְיָדוֹ וְכָל־טוּב דַּמֶּשֶׂק מַשָּׂא אַרְבָּעִים גָּמָל וַיָּבֹא וַיַּעֲמֹד לְפָנָיו וַיֹּאמֶר בִּנְךָ בֶן־הֲדַד מֶלֶךְ־אֲרָם שְׁלָחַנִי אֵלֶיךָ לֵאמֹר הַאֶחְיֶה מֵחֳלִי זֶה׃

10 *Elisha* said to him, "Go and say to him, 'You will recover.' However, *Hashem* has revealed to me that he will die."

י וַיֹּאמֶר אֵלָיו אֱלִישָׁע לֵךְ אֱמָר־לֹא [לוֹ] חָיֹה תִחְיֶה וְהִרְאַנִי יְהוָה כִּי־מוֹת יָמוּת׃

11 The man of *Hashem* kept his face expressionless for a long time; and then he wept.

יא וַיַּעֲמֵד אֶת־פָּנָיו וַיָּשֶׂם עַד־בֹּשׁ וַיֵּבְךְּ אִישׁ הָאֱלֹהִים׃

12 "Why does my lord weep?" asked Hazael. "Because I know," he replied, "what harm you will do to *B'nei Yisrael*: you will set their fortresses on fire, put their young men to the sword, dash their little ones in pieces, and rip open their pregnant women."

יב וַיֹּאמֶר חֲזָהאֵל מַדּוּעַ אֲדֹנִי בֹכֶה וַיֹּאמֶר כִּי־יָדַעְתִּי אֵת אֲשֶׁר־תַּעֲשֶׂה לִבְנֵי יִשְׂרָאֵל רָעָה מִבְצְרֵיהֶם תְּשַׁלַּח בָּאֵשׁ וּבַחֻרֵיהֶם בַּחֶרֶב תַּהֲרֹג וְעֹלְלֵיהֶם תְּרַטֵּשׁ וְהָרֹתֵיהֶם תְּבַקֵּעַ׃

13 "But how," asked Hazael, "can your servant, who is a mere dog, perform such a mighty deed?" *Elisha* replied, "*Hashem* has shown me a vision of you as king of Aram."

יג וַיֹּאמֶר חֲזָהאֵל כִּי מָה עַבְדְּךָ הַכֶּלֶב כִּי יַעֲשֶׂה הַדָּבָר הַגָּדוֹל הַזֶּה וַיֹּאמֶר אֱלִישָׁע הִרְאַנִי יְהוָה אֹתְךָ מֶלֶךְ עַל־אֲרָם׃

14 He left *Elisha* and returned to his master, who asked him, "What did *Elisha* say to you?" He replied, "He told me that you would recover."

יד וַיֵּלֶךְ מֵאֵת אֱלִישָׁע וַיָּבֹא אֶל־אֲדֹנָיו וַיֹּאמֶר לוֹ מָה־אָמַר לְךָ אֱלִישָׁע וַיֹּאמֶר אָמַר לִי חָיֹה תִחְיֶה׃

15 The next day, [Hazael] took a piece of netting, dipped it in water, and spread it over his face. So [Ben-hadad] died, and Hazael succeeded him as king.

טו וַיְהִי מִמָּחֳרָת וַיִּקַּח הַמַּכְבֵּר וַיִּטְבֹּל בַּמַּיִם וַיִּפְרֹשׂ עַל־פָּנָיו וַיָּמֹת וַיִּמְלֹךְ חֲזָהאֵל תַּחְתָּיו׃

16 In the fifth year of King *Yoram* son of *Achav* of *Yisrael* – Yehoshafat had been king of Yehuda – *Yoram* son of King *Yehoshafat* of *Yehuda* became king.

טז וּבִשְׁנַת חָמֵשׁ לְיוֹרָם בֶּן־אַחְאָב מֶלֶךְ יִשְׂרָאֵל וִיהוֹשָׁפָט מֶלֶךְ יְהוּדָה מָלַךְ יְהוֹרָם בֶּן־יְהוֹשָׁפָט מֶלֶךְ יְהוּדָה׃

17 He was thirty-two years old when he became king, and he reigned in *Yerushalayim* eight years.

יז בֶּן־שְׁלֹשִׁים וּשְׁתַּיִם שָׁנָה הָיָה בְמָלְכוֹ וּשְׁמֹנֶה שנה [שָׁנִים] מָלַךְ בִּירוּשָׁלָםִ׃

18 He followed the practices of the kings of *Yisrael* – whatever the House of *Achav* did, for he had married a daughter of *Achav* – and he did what was displeasing to *Hashem*.

יח וַיֵּלֶךְ בְּדֶרֶךְ מַלְכֵי יִשְׂרָאֵל כַּאֲשֶׁר עָשׂוּ בֵּית אַחְאָב כִּי בַּת־אַחְאָב הָיְתָה־לּוֹ לְאִשָּׁה וַיַּעַשׂ הָרַע בְּעֵינֵי יְהוָה׃

---
* "The king" brought up from verse 8 for clarity

Melachim II / II Kings
Chapter 8

מלכים ב
פרק ח

19 However, *Hashem* refrained from destroying *Yehuda*, for the sake of His servant *David*, in accordance with His promise to maintain a lamp for his descendants for all time.

יט וְלֹא־אָבָה יְהֹוָה לְהַשְׁחִית אֶת־יְהוּדָה לְמַעַן דָּוִד עַבְדּוֹ כַּאֲשֶׁר אָמַר־לוֹ לָתֵת לוֹ נִיר לְבָנָיו כָּל־הַיָּמִים׃

v'-lo a-VAH a-do-NAI l'-hash-KHEET et y'-hu-DAH l-MA-an da-VID av-DO ka-a-SHER a-mar LO la-TAYT LO NEER l'-va-NAV kol ha-ya-MEEM

20 During his reign, the Edomites rebelled against *Yehuda*'s rule and set up a king of their own.

כ בְּיָמָיו פָּשַׁע אֱדוֹם מִתַּחַת יַד־יְהוּדָה וַיַּמְלִכוּ עֲלֵיהֶם מֶלֶךְ׃

21 *Yoram* crossed over to Zair with all his chariotry. He arose by night and attacked the Edomites, who were surrounding him and the chariot commanders; but his troops fled to their homes.

כא וַיַּעֲבֹר יוֹרָם צָעִירָה וְכָל־הָרֶכֶב עִמּוֹ וַיְהִי־הוּא קָם לַיְלָה וַיַּכֶּה אֶת־אֱדוֹם הַסֹּבֵיב אֵלָיו וְאֵת שָׂרֵי הָרֶכֶב וַיָּנָס הָעָם לְאֹהָלָיו׃

22 Thus Edom fell away from *Yehuda*, as is still the case. Libnah likewise fell away at that time.

כב וַיִּפְשַׁע אֱדוֹם מִתַּחַת יַד־יְהוּדָה עַד הַיּוֹם הַזֶּה אָז תִּפְשַׁע לִבְנָה בָּעֵת הַהִיא׃

23 The other events of *Yoram*'s reign, and all his actions, are recorded in the Annals of the Kings of *Yehuda*.

כג וְיֶתֶר דִּבְרֵי יוֹרָם וְכָל־אֲשֶׁר עָשָׂה הֲלוֹא־הֵם כְּתוּבִים עַל־סֵפֶר דִּבְרֵי הַיָּמִים לְמַלְכֵי יְהוּדָה׃

24 *Yoram* slept with his fathers and was buried with his fathers in the City of *David*; his son *Achazyahu* succeeded him as king.

כד וַיִּשְׁכַּב יוֹרָם עִם־אֲבֹתָיו וַיִּקָּבֵר עִם־אֲבֹתָיו בְּעִיר דָּוִד וַיִּמְלֹךְ אֲחַזְיָהוּ בְנוֹ תַּחְתָּיו׃

25 In the twelfth year of King *Yoram* son of *Achav* of *Yisrael*, *Achazyahu* son of *Yoram* became king of *Yehuda*.

כה בִּשְׁנַת שְׁתֵּים־עֶשְׂרֵה שָׁנָה לְיוֹרָם בֶּן־אַחְאָב מֶלֶךְ יִשְׂרָאֵל מָלַךְ אֲחַזְיָהוּ בֶן־יְהוֹרָם מֶלֶךְ יְהוּדָה׃

26 *Achazyahu* was twenty-two years old when he became king, and he reigned in *Yerushalayim* one year; his mother's name was *Atalya* daughter of King *Omri* of *Yisrael*.

כו בֶּן־עֶשְׂרִים וּשְׁתַּיִם שָׁנָה אֲחַזְיָהוּ בְמָלְכוֹ וְשָׁנָה אַחַת מָלַךְ בִּירוּשָׁלִָם וְשֵׁם אִמּוֹ עֲתַלְיָהוּ בַּת־עָמְרִי מֶלֶךְ יִשְׂרָאֵל׃

27 He walked in the ways of the House of *Achav* and did what was displeasing to *Hashem*, like the House of *Achav*, for he was related by marriage to the House of *Achav*.

כז וַיֵּלֶךְ בְּדֶרֶךְ בֵּית אַחְאָב וַיַּעַשׂ הָרַע בְּעֵינֵי יְהֹוָה כְּבֵית אַחְאָב כִּי חֲתַן בֵּית־אַחְאָב הוּא׃

28 He marched with *Yoram* son of *Achav* to battle against King Hazael of Aram at Ramoth-gilead, but the Arameans wounded *Yoram*.

כח וַיֵּלֶךְ אֶת־יוֹרָם בֶּן־אַחְאָב לַמִּלְחָמָה עִם־חֲזָהאֵל מֶלֶךְ־אֲרָם בְּרָמֹת גִּלְעָד וַיַּכּוּ אֲרַמִּים אֶת־יוֹרָם׃

נֵר
נִיר

8:19 To maintain a lamp for his descendants for all time *Hashem* is not yet ready to destroy *Yehuda*, due to the promise that He had made to King *David* to give him an eternal kingdom. The Hebrew word used for 'kingdom' in this verse is *nir* (נִיר), which can also mean a 'light' or a 'lamp,' from the word *ner* (נֵר), which means 'candle.' The kingdom of *David* is intended to give eternal light to the entire Nation of Israel, and by extension the entire world. Even in the absence of a kingdom, the knowledge that *Hashem* will eventually return the monarchy to *David* through the *Mashiach* is a source of light and hope to all.

Melachim II / II Kings
Chapter 9

29 King *Yoram* retired to *Yizrael* to recover from the wounds which the Arameans had inflicted upon him at *Rama*, when he fought against King Hazael of Aram. And King *Achazyahu* son of *Yoram* of *Yehuda* went down to *Yizrael* to visit *Yoram* son of *Achav* while he was ill.

9

1 Then the *Navi* Elisha summoned one of the disciples of the *Neviim* and said to him, "Tie up your skirts, and take along this flask of oil, and go to Ramoth-gilead.

2 When you arrive there, go and see *Yehu* son of *Yehoshafat* son of Nimshi; get him to leave his comrades, and take him into an inner room.

3 Then take the flask of oil and pour some on his head, and say, 'Thus said *Hashem*: I anoint you king over *Yisrael*.' Then open the door and flee without delay."

4 The young man, the servant of the *Navi*, went to Ramoth-gilead.

5 When he arrived, the army commanders were sitting together. He said, "Commander, I have a message for you." "For which one of us?" *Yehu* asked. He answered, "For you, commander."

6 So [*Yehu*] arose and went inside; and [the disciple] poured the oil on his head, and said to him, "Thus said *Hashem*, the God of *Yisrael*: I anoint you king over the people of *Hashem*, over *Yisrael*.

va-YA-kom va-ya-VO ha-BAItah va-yi-TZOK ha-SHE-men el ro-SHO va-YO-mer LO koh a-MAR a-do-NAI e-lo-HAY yis-ra-AYL m'-shakh-TEE-kha l'-ME-lekh el AM a-do-NAI el yis-ra-AYL

7 You shall strike down the House of *Achav* your master; thus will I avenge on Jezebel the blood of My servants the *Neviim*, and the blood of the other servants of *Hashem*.

8 The whole House of *Achav* shall perish, and I will cut off every male belonging to *Achav*, bond and free in *Yisrael*.

א 9:6 I anoint you king over the people of *Hashem*
The Hebrew word *mashiach* (משיח) means 'anointed one.' According to biblical law, kings and high priests are to be anointed with oil, which symbolizes their designation for their holy positions. In Hebrew, the Messiah is referred to as the *Mashiach*, as he will be a king who is anointed for this holiest of roles. He will lead the Jewish people and bring peace and justice to the entire world. We pray for, and eagerly await, his coming each and every day.

משיח

Melachim II / II Kings
Chapter 9

מלכים ב
פרק ט

ט וְנָתַתִּי אֶת־בֵּית אַחְאָב כְּבֵית יָרָבְעָם בֶּן־נְבָט וּכְבֵית בַּעְשָׁא בֶן־אֲחִיָּה:

9 I will make the House of *Achav* like the House of *Yerovam* son of Nebat, and like the House of *Basha* son of *Achiya*.

י וְאֶת־אִיזֶבֶל יֹאכְלוּ הַכְּלָבִים בְּחֵלֶק יִזְרְעֶאל וְאֵין קֹבֵר וַיִּפְתַּח הַדֶּלֶת וַיָּנֹס:

10 The dogs shall devour Jezebel in the field of *Yizrael*, with none to bury her." Then he opened the door and fled.

יא וְיֵהוּא יָצָא אֶל־עַבְדֵי אֲדֹנָיו וַיֹּאמֶר לוֹ הֲשָׁלוֹם מַדּוּעַ בָּא־הַמְשֻׁגָּע הַזֶּה אֵלֶיךָ וַיֹּאמֶר אֲלֵיהֶם אַתֶּם יְדַעְתֶּם אֶת־הָאִישׁ וְאֶת־שִׂיחוֹ:

11 *Yehu* went out to the other officers of his master, and they asked him, "Is all well? What did that madman come to you for?" He said to them, "You know the man and his ranting!"

יב וַיֹּאמְרוּ שֶׁקֶר הַגֶּד־נָא לָנוּ וַיֹּאמֶר כָּזֹאת וְכָזֹאת אָמַר אֵלַי לֵאמֹר כֹּה אָמַר יְהֹוָה מְשַׁחְתִּיךָ לְמֶלֶךְ אֶל־יִשְׂרָאֵל:

12 "You're lying," they said. "Tell us [the truth]." Then he replied, "Thus and thus he said: Thus said *Hashem*: I anoint you king over *Yisrael*!"

יג וַיְמַהֲרוּ וַיִּקְחוּ אִישׁ בִּגְדוֹ וַיָּשִׂימוּ תַחְתָּיו אֶל־גֶּרֶם הַמַּעֲלוֹת וַיִּתְקְעוּ בַּשּׁוֹפָר וַיֹּאמְרוּ מָלַךְ יֵהוּא:

13 Quickly each man took his cloak and placed it under him, on the top step. They sounded the *shofar* and proclaimed, "*Yehu* is king!"

יד וַיִּתְקַשֵּׁר יֵהוּא בֶּן־יְהוֹשָׁפָט בֶּן־נִמְשִׁי אֶל־יוֹרָם וְיוֹרָם הָיָה שֹׁמֵר בְּרָמֹת גִּלְעָד הוּא וְכָל־יִשְׂרָאֵל מִפְּנֵי חֲזָאֵל מֶלֶךְ־אֲרָם:

14 Thus *Yehu* son of *Yehoshafat* son of Nimshi conspired against *Yoram*. *Yoram* and all *Yisrael* had been defending Ramoth-gilead against King Hazael of Aram,

טו וַיָּשָׁב יְהוֹרָם הַמֶּלֶךְ לְהִתְרַפֵּא בְיִזְרְעֶאל מִן־הַמַּכִּים אֲשֶׁר יַכֻּהוּ אֲרַמִּים בְּהִלָּחֲמוֹ אֶת־חֲזָאֵל מֶלֶךְ אֲרָם וַיֹּאמֶר יֵהוּא אִם־יֵשׁ נַפְשְׁכֶם אַל־יֵצֵא פָלִיט מִן־הָעִיר לָלֶכֶת לגיד [לְהַגִּיד] בְּיִזְרְעֶאל:

15 but King *Yoram* had gone back to *Yizrael* to recover from the wounds which the Arameans had inflicted on him in his battle with King Hazael of Aram. *Yehu* said, "If such is your wish, allow no one to slip out of the town to go and report this in *Yizrael*."

טז וַיִּרְכַּב יֵהוּא וַיֵּלֶךְ יִזְרְעֶאלָה כִּי יוֹרָם שֹׁכֵב שָׁמָּה וַאֲחַזְיָה מֶלֶךְ יְהוּדָה יָרַד לִרְאוֹת אֶת־יוֹרָם:

16 Then *Yehu* mounted his chariot and drove to *Yizrael*; for *Yoram* was lying ill there, and King *Achazyahu* of *Yehuda* had gone down to visit *Yoram*.

יז וְהַצֹּפֶה עֹמֵד עַל־הַמִּגְדָּל בְּיִזְרְעֶאל וַיַּרְא אֶת־שִׁפְעַת יֵהוּא בְּבֹאוֹ וַיֹּאמֶר שִׁפְעַת אֲנִי רֹאֶה וַיֹּאמֶר יְהוֹרָם קַח רַכָּב וּשְׁלַח לִקְרָאתָם וְיֹאמַר הֲשָׁלוֹם:

17 The lookout was stationed on the tower in *Yizrael*, and he saw the troop of *Yehu* as he approached. He called out, "I see a troop!" *Yoram* said, "Dispatch a horseman to meet them and let him ask: Is all well?"

יח וַיֵּלֶךְ רֹכֵב הַסּוּס לִקְרָאתוֹ וַיֹּאמֶר כֹּה־אָמַר הַמֶּלֶךְ הֲשָׁלוֹם וַיֹּאמֶר יֵהוּא מַה־לְּךָ וּלְשָׁלוֹם סֹב אֶל־אַחֲרָי וַיַּגֵּד הַצֹּפֶה לֵאמֹר בָּא הַמַּלְאָךְ עַד־הֵם וְלֹא־שָׁב:

18 The horseman went to meet him, and he said, "The king inquires: Is all well?" *Yehu* replied, "What concern of yours is it whether all is well? Fall in behind me." The lookout reported: "The messenger has reached them, but has not turned back."

יט וַיִּשְׁלַח רֹכֵב סוּס שֵׁנִי וַיָּבֹא אֲלֵהֶם וַיֹּאמֶר כֹּה־אָמַר הַמֶּלֶךְ שָׁלוֹם וַיֹּאמֶר יֵהוּא מַה־לְּךָ וּלְשָׁלוֹם סֹב אֶל־אַחֲרָי:

19 So he sent out a second horseman. He came to them and said, "Thus says the king: Is all well?" *Yehu* answered, "What concern of yours is it whether all is well? Fall in behind me."

Melachim II / II Kings
Chapter 9

מלכים ב
פרק ט

20 And the lookout reported, "The messenger has reached them, but has not turned back. And it looks like the driving of *Yehu* son of Nimshi, who drives wildly."

כ וַיַּגֵּ֤ד הַצֹּפֶה֙ לֵאמֹ֔ר בָּ֥א עַד־אֲלֵיהֶ֖ם וְלֹא־שָׁ֑ב וְהַמִּנְהָ֗ג כְּמִנְהַג֙ יֵה֣וּא בֶן־נִמְשִׁ֔י כִּ֥י בְשִׁגָּע֖וֹן יִנְהָֽג׃

21 *Yoram* ordered, "Hitch up [the chariot]!" They hitched up his chariot; and King *Yoram* of *Yisrael* and King *Achazyahu* of *Yehuda* went out, each in his own chariot, to meet *Yehu*. They met him at the field of *Navot* the Yizraelite.

כא וַיֹּ֤אמֶר יְהוֹרָם֙ אֱסֹ֔ר וַיֶּאְסֹ֖ר רִכְבּ֑וֹ וַיֵּצֵ֣א יְהוֹרָ֣ם מֶֽלֶךְ־יִ֠שְׂרָאֵ֠ל וַאֲחַזְיָ֨הוּ מֶֽלֶךְ־יְהוּדָ֜ה אִ֣ישׁ בְּרִכְבּ֗וֹ וַיֵּֽצְאוּ֙ לִקְרַ֣את יֵה֔וּא וַיִּמְצָאֻ֔הוּ בְּחֶלְקַ֖ת נָב֥וֹת הַיִּזְרְעֵאלִֽי׃

22 When *Yoram* saw *Yehu*, he asked, "Is all well, *Yehu*?" But *Yehu* replied, "How can all be well as long as your mother Jezebel carries on her countless harlotries and sorceries?"

כב וַיְהִ֗י כִּרְא֤וֹת יְהוֹרָם֙ אֶת־יֵה֔וּא וַיֹּ֖אמֶר הֲשָׁל֣וֹם יֵה֑וּא וַיֹּ֨אמֶר֙ מָ֣ה הַשָּׁל֔וֹם עַד־זְנוּנֵ֞י אִיזֶ֧בֶל אִמְּךָ֛ וּכְשָׁפֶ֖יהָ הָרַבִּֽים׃

23 Thereupon *Yoram* turned his horses around and fled, crying out to *Achazyahu*, "Treason, *Achazyahu*!"

כג וַיַּהֲפֹ֧ךְ יְהוֹרָ֛ם יָדָ֖יו וַיָּנֹ֑ס וַיֹּ֥אמֶר אֶל־אֲחַזְיָ֖הוּ מִרְמָ֥ה אֲחַזְיָֽה׃

24 But *Yehu* drew his bow and hit *Yoram* between the shoulders, so that the arrow pierced his heart; and he collapsed in his chariot.

כד וְיֵה֞וּא מִלֵּ֧א יָד֣וֹ בַקֶּ֗שֶׁת וַיַּ֤ךְ אֶת־יְהוֹרָם֙ בֵּ֣ין זְרֹעָ֔יו וַיֵּצֵ֥א הַחֵ֖צִי מִלִּבּ֑וֹ וַיִּכְרַ֖ע בְּרִכְבּֽוֹ׃

25 *Yehu* thereupon ordered his officer Bidkar, "Pick him up and throw him into the field of *Navot* the Yizraelite. Remember how you and I were riding side by side behind his father *Achav*, when *Hashem* made this pronouncement about him:

כה וַיֹּ֗אמֶר אֶל־בִּדְקַר֙ שלשה [שָֽׁלִשׁ֔וֹ] שָׂ֚א הַשְׁלִכֵ֔הוּ בְּחֶלְקַ֕ת שְׂדֵ֖ה נָב֣וֹת הַיִּזְרְעֵאלִ֑י כִּֽי־זְכֹ֞ר אֲנִ֣י וָאַ֗תָּה אֵ֣ת רֹכְבִ֤ים צְמָדִים֙ אַחֲרֵי֙ אַחְאָ֣ב אָבִ֔יו וַֽיהוָה֙ נָשָׂ֣א עָלָ֔יו אֶת־הַמַּשָּׂ֖א הַזֶּֽה׃

26 'I swear, I have taken note of the blood of *Navot* and the blood of his sons yesterday – declares *Hashem*. And I will requite you in this plot – declares *Hashem*.' So pick him up and throw him unto the plot in accordance with the word of *Hashem*."

כו אִם־לֹ֡א אֶת־דְּמֵ֣י נָבוֹת֩ וְאֶת־דְּמֵ֨י בָנָ֜יו רָאִ֤יתִי אֶ֙מֶשׁ֙ נְאֻם־יְהוָ֔ה וְשִׁלַּמְתִּ֥י לְךָ֖ בַּחֶלְקָ֣ה הַזֹּ֑את נְאֻם־יְהוָ֑ה וְעַתָּ֗ה שָׂ֧א הַשְׁלִכֵ֛הוּ בַּחֶלְקָ֖ה כִּדְבַ֥ר יְהוָֽה׃

27 On seeing this, King *Achazyahu* of *Yehuda* fled along the road to Beth-haggan. *Yehu* pursued him and said, "Shoot him down too!" [And they shot him] in his chariot at the ascent of Gur, which is near Ibleam. He fled to Megiddo and died there.

כז וַאֲחַזְיָ֤ה מֶֽלֶךְ־יְהוּדָה֙ רָאָ֔ה וַיָּ֕נָס דֶּ֖רֶךְ בֵּ֣ית הַגָּ֑ן וַיִּרְדֹּ֨ף אַחֲרָ֜יו יֵה֗וּא וַ֠יֹּ֠אמֶר גַּם־אֹת֞וֹ הַכֻּ֣הוּ אֶל־הַמֶּרְכָּבָ֗ה בְּמַעֲלֵה־גוּר֙ אֲשֶׁ֣ר אֶֽת־יִבְלְעָ֔ם וַיָּ֥נָס מְגִדּ֖וֹ וַיָּ֥מָת שָֽׁם׃

28 His servants conveyed him in a chariot to *Yerushalayim*, and they buried him in his grave with his fathers, in the City of *David*.

כח וַיַּרְכִּ֧בוּ אֹת֛וֹ עֲבָדָ֖יו יְרוּשָׁלָ֑יְמָה וַיִּקְבְּר֨וּ אֹת֧וֹ בִקְבֻרָת֛וֹ עִם־אֲבֹתָ֖יו בְּעִ֥יר דָּוִֽד׃

29 *Achazyahu* had become king over *Yehuda* in the eleventh year of *Yoram* son of *Achav*.)

כט וּבִשְׁנַת֙ אַחַ֣ת עֶשְׂרֵ֣ה שָׁנָ֔ה לְיוֹרָ֖ם בֶּן־אַחְאָ֑ב מָלַ֥ךְ אֲחַזְיָ֖ה עַל־יְהוּדָֽה׃

30 *Yehu* went on to *Yizrael*. When Jezebel heard of it, she painted her eyes with kohl and dressed her hair, and she looked out of the window.

ל וַיָּב֥וֹא יֵה֖וּא יִזְרְעֶ֑אלָה וְאִיזֶ֣בֶל שָׁמְעָ֗ה וַתָּ֨שֶׂם בַּפּ֤וּךְ עֵינֶ֙יהָ֙ וַתֵּ֣יטֶב אֶת־רֹאשָׁ֔הּ וַתַּשְׁקֵ֖ף בְּעַ֥ד הַחַלּֽוֹן׃

Melachim II/II Kings
Chapter 10

31 As *Yehu* entered the gate, she called out, "Is all well, *Zimri*, murderer of your master?"

32 He looked up toward the window and said, "Who is on my side, who?" And two or three eunuchs leaned out toward him.

33 "Throw her down," he said. They threw her down; and her blood spattered on the wall and on the horses, and they trampled her.

34 Then he went inside and ate and drank. And he said, "Attend to that cursed woman and bury her, for she was a king's daughter."

35 So they went to bury her; but all they found of her were the skull, the feet, and the hands.

36 They came back and reported to him; and he said, "It is just as *Hashem* spoke through His servant *Eliyahu* the Tishbite: The dogs shall devour the flesh of Jezebel in the field of *Yizrael*;

37 and the carcass of Jezebel shall be like dung on the ground, in the field of *Yizrael*, so that none will be able to say: 'This was Jezebel.'"

10 1 *Achav* had seventy descendants in *Shomron*. *Yehu* wrote letters and sent them to *Shomron*, to the elders and officials of *Yizrael* and to the guardians of [the children] of *Achav*, as follows:

2 "Now, when this letter reaches you – since your master's sons are with you and you also have chariots and horses, and a fortified city and weapons

3 select the best and the most suitable of your master's sons and set him on his father's throne, and fight for your master's house."

4 But they were overcome by fear, for they thought, "If the two kings could not stand up to him, how can we?"

5 The steward of the palace and the governor of the city and the elders and the guardians sent this message to *Yehu*: "We are your subjects, and we shall do whatever you tell us to. We shall not proclaim anyone king; do whatever you like."

Melachim II / II Kings
Chapter 10

6 He wrote them a second time: "If you are on my side and are ready to obey me, take the heads of the attendants of your master's sons and come to me in *Yizrael* tomorrow at this time." Now the princes, seventy in number, were with the notables of the town, who were rearing them.

7 But when the letter reached them, they took the princes and slaughtered all seventy of them; they put their heads in baskets and sent them to him in *Yizrael*.

8 A messenger came and reported to him: "They have brought the heads of the princes." He said, "Pile them up in two heaps at the entrance of the gate before morning."

9 In the morning he went out and stood there; and he said to all the people, "Are you blameless? True, I conspired against my master and killed him; but who struck down all of these?

10 Know, then, that nothing that *Hashem* has spoken concerning the House of *Achav* shall remain unfulfilled, for *Hashem* has done what he announced through His servant *Eliyahu*."

11 And *Yehu* struck down all that were left of the House of *Achav* in *Yizrael* – and all his notables, intimates, and *Kohanim* – till he left him no survivor.

12 He then set out for *Shomron*. On the way, when he was at Beth-eked of the shepherds,

13 *Yehu* came upon the kinsmen of King *Achazyahu* of *Yehuda*. "Who are you?" he asked. They replied, "We are the kinsmen of *Achazyahu*, and we have come to pay our respects to the sons of the king and the sons of the queen mother."

14 "Take them alive!" he said. They took them alive and then slaughtered them at the pit of Beth-eked, forty-two of them; he did not spare a single one.

15 He went on from there, and he met Jehonadab son of Rechab coming toward him. He greeted him and said to him, "Are you as wholehearted with me as I am with you?" "I am," Jehonadab replied. "If so, [said *Yehu*,] "give me your hand." He gave him his hand and [*Yehu*] helped him into the chariot.

Melachim II / II Kings
Chapter 10

16 "Come with me," he said, "and see my zeal for *Hashem*." And he was taken along in the chariot.	טז וַיֹּאמֶר לְכָה אִתִּי וּרְאֵה בְּקִנְאָתִי לַיהֹוָה וַיַּרְכִּבוּ אֹתוֹ בְּרִכְבּוֹ:
17 Arriving in *Shomron*, [*Yehu*] struck down all the survivors of [the House of] *Achav* in *Shomron*, until he wiped it out, fulfilling the word that *Hashem* had spoken to *Eliyahu*.	יז וַיָּבֹא שֹׁמְרוֹן וַיַּךְ אֶת־כָּל־הַנִּשְׁאָרִים לְאַחְאָב בְּשֹׁמְרוֹן עַד־הִשְׁמִדוֹ כִּדְבַר יְהֹוָה אֲשֶׁר דִּבֶּר אֶל־אֵלִיָּהוּ:
18 *Yehu* assembled all the people and said to them, "*Achav* served Baal little; *Yehu* shall serve him much!	יח וַיִּקְבֹּץ יֵהוּא אֶת־כָּל־הָעָם וַיֹּאמֶר אֲלֵהֶם אַחְאָב עָבַד אֶת־הַבַּעַל מְעָט יֵהוּא יַעַבְדֶנּוּ הַרְבֵּה:
19 Therefore, summon to me all the *Neviim* of Baal, all his worshipers, and all his *Kohanim*: let no one fail to come, for I am going to hold a great sacrifice for Baal. Whoever fails to come shall forfeit his life." *Yehu* was acting with guile in order to exterminate the worshipers of Baal.	יט וְעַתָּה כָל־נְבִיאֵי הַבַּעַל כָּל־עֹבְדָיו וְכָל־כֹּהֲנָיו קִרְאוּ אֵלַי אִישׁ אַל־יִפָּקֵד כִּי זֶבַח גָּדוֹל לִי לַבַּעַל כֹּל אֲשֶׁר־יִפָּקֵד לֹא יִחְיֶה וְיֵהוּא עָשָׂה בְעָקְבָּה לְמַעַן הַאֲבִיד אֶת־עֹבְדֵי הַבָּעַל:
20 *Yehu* gave orders to convoke a solemn assembly for Baal, and one was proclaimed.	כ וַיֹּאמֶר יֵהוּא קַדְּשׁוּ עֲצָרָה לַבָּעַל וַיִּקְרָאוּ:
21 *Yehu* sent word throughout *Yisrael*, and all the worshipers of Baal came, not a single one remained behind. They came into the temple of Baal, and the temple of Baal was filled from end to end.	כא וַיִּשְׁלַח יֵהוּא בְּכָל־יִשְׂרָאֵל וַיָּבֹאוּ כָּל־עֹבְדֵי הַבַּעַל וְלֹא־נִשְׁאַר אִישׁ אֲשֶׁר לֹא־בָא וַיָּבֹאוּ בֵּית הַבָּעַל וַיִּמָּלֵא בֵית־הַבַּעַל פֶּה לָפֶה:
22 He said to the man in charge of the wardrobe, "Bring out the vestments for all the worshipers of Baal"; and he brought vestments out for them.	כב וַיֹּאמֶר לַאֲשֶׁר עַל־הַמֶּלְתָּחָה הוֹצֵא לְבוּשׁ לְכֹל עֹבְדֵי הַבָּעַל וַיֹּצֵא לָהֶם הַמַּלְבּוּשׁ:
23 Then *Yehu* and Jehonadab son of Rechab came into the temple of Baal, and they said to the worshipers of Baal, "Search and make sure that there are no worshipers of *Hashem* among you, but only worshipers of Baal."	כג וַיָּבֹא יֵהוּא וִיהוֹנָדָב בֶּן־רֵכָב בֵּית הַבָּעַל וַיֹּאמֶר לְעֹבְדֵי הַבַּעַל חַפְּשׂוּ וּרְאוּ פֶּן־יֶשׁ־פֹּה עִמָּכֶם מֵעַבְדֵי יְהֹוָה כִּי אִם־עֹבְדֵי הַבַּעַל לְבַדָּם:
24 So they went in to offer sacrifices and burnt offerings. But *Yehu* had stationed eighty of his men outside and had said, "Whoever permits the escape of a single one of the men I commit to your charge shall forfeit life for life."	כד וַיָּבֹאוּ לַעֲשׂוֹת זְבָחִים וְעֹלוֹת וְיֵהוּא שָׂם־לוֹ בַחוּץ שְׁמֹנִים אִישׁ וַיֹּאמֶר הָאִישׁ אֲשֶׁר־יִמָּלֵט מִן־הָאֲנָשִׁים אֲשֶׁר אֲנִי מֵבִיא עַל־יְדֵיכֶם נַפְשׁוֹ תַּחַת נַפְשׁוֹ:
25 When *Yehu* had finished presenting the burnt offering, he said to the guards and to the officers, "Come in and strike them down; let no man get away!" The guards and the officers struck them down with the sword and left them lying where they were; then they proceeded to the interior of the temple of Baal.	כה וַיְהִי כְּכַלֹּתוֹ לַעֲשׂוֹת הָעֹלָה וַיֹּאמֶר יֵהוּא לָרָצִים וְלַשָּׁלִשִׁים בֹּאוּ הַכּוּם אִישׁ אַל־יֵצֵא וַיַּכּוּם לְפִי־חָרֶב וַיַּשְׁלִכוּ הָרָצִים וְהַשָּׁלִשִׁים וַיֵּלְכוּ עַד־עִיר בֵּית־הַבָּעַל:
26 They brought out the pillars of the temple of Baal and burned them.	כו וַיֹּצִאוּ אֶת־מַצְּבוֹת בֵּית־הַבַּעַל וַיִּשְׂרְפוּהָ:

Melachim II / II Kings
Chapter 10

מלכים ב
פרק י

27 They destroyed the pillar of Baal, and they tore down the temple of Baal and turned it into latrines, as is still the case.

כז וַיִּתְּצוּ אֵת מַצְּבַת הַבָּעַל וַיִּתְּצוּ אֶת־בֵּית הַבַּעַל וַיְשִׂמֻהוּ למחראות [לְמוֹצָאוֹת] עַד־הַיּוֹם:

va-yi-t'-TZU AYT ma-tz'-VAT ha-BA-al va-yi-t'-TZU et BAYT ha-BA-al vai-si-MU-hu l'-mo-tza-OT ad ha-YOM

28 Thus *Yehu* eradicated the Baal from *Yisrael*.

כח וַיַּשְׁמֵד יֵהוּא אֶת־הַבַּעַל מִיִּשְׂרָאֵל:

29 However, *Yehu* did not turn away from the sinful objects by which *Yerovam* son of Nebat had caused *Yisrael* to sin, namely, the golden calves at *Beit El* and at *Dan*.

כט רַק חֲטָאֵי יָרָבְעָם בֶּן־נְבָט אֲשֶׁר הֶחֱטִיא אֶת־יִשְׂרָאֵל לֹא־סָר יֵהוּא מֵאַחֲרֵיהֶם עֶגְלֵי הַזָּהָב אֲשֶׁר בֵּית־אֵל וַאֲשֶׁר בְּדָן:

30 *Hashem* said to *Yehu*, "Because you have acted well and done what was pleasing to Me, having carried out all that I desired upon the House of *Achav*, four generations of your descendants shall occupy the throne of *Yisrael*."

ל וַיֹּאמֶר יְהֹוָה אֶל־יֵהוּא יַעַן אֲשֶׁר־הֱטִיבֹתָ לַעֲשׂוֹת הַיָּשָׁר בְּעֵינַי כְּכֹל אֲשֶׁר בִּלְבָבִי עָשִׂיתָ לְבֵית אַחְאָב בְּנֵי רְבִעִים יֵשְׁבוּ לְךָ עַל־כִּסֵּא יִשְׂרָאֵל:

31 But *Yehu* was not careful to follow the Teaching of *Hashem*, the God of *Yisrael*, with all his heart; he did not turn away from the sins that *Yerovam* had caused *Yisrael* to commit.

לא וְיֵהוּא לֹא שָׁמַר לָלֶכֶת בְּתוֹרַת־יְהֹוָה אֱלֹהֵי־יִשְׂרָאֵל בְּכָל־לְבָבוֹ לֹא סָר מֵעַל חַטֹּאות יָרָבְעָם אֲשֶׁר הֶחֱטִיא אֶת־יִשְׂרָאֵל:

32 In those days *Hashem* began to reduce *Yisrael*; and Hazael harassed them throughout the territory of *Yisrael*

לב בַּיָּמִים הָהֵם הֵחֵל יְהֹוָה לְקַצּוֹת בְּיִשְׂרָאֵל וַיַּכֵּם חֲזָאֵל בְּכָל־גְּבוּל יִשְׂרָאֵל:

33 east of the *Yarden*, all the land of *Gilad* – the Gadites, the Reubenites, and the Manassites – from Aroer, by the Wadi Arnon, up to *Gilad* and Bashan.

לג מִן־הַיַּרְדֵּן מִזְרַח הַשֶּׁמֶשׁ אֵת כָּל־אֶרֶץ הַגִּלְעָד הַגָּדִי וְהָרֻאוּבֵנִי וְהַמְנַשִּׁי מֵעֲרֹעֵר אֲשֶׁר עַל־נַחַל אַרְנֹן וְהַגִּלְעָד וְהַבָּשָׁן:

10:27 They destroyed the pillar of Baal While *Hashem* requires only the Jewish people to keep the *Torah*'s many commandments, there are seven laws that, according to Jewish tradition, are universal and incumbent upon all of mankind (*Sanhedrin* 56a). These seven "Noahide laws" ensure that society functions with a basic level of morality and religious values. Maimonides writes that anyone who keeps these laws properly is considered "righteous among the nations" and earns a share in the world to come. These seven universal commandments are:

1. Establish courts of justice
2. Do not curse God
3. Do not engage in idol worship
4. Do not engage in acts of sexual immorality such as adultery and incest
5. Do not murder
6. Do not steal
7. Do not eat the limb of a live animal

The requirement to renounce idolatry and serve the Lord exclusively is included in these laws. *Hashem* has no tolerance for idolatry, which brings with it sins such as human sacrifice, especially in the Land of Israel. In fact, engaging in idol worship results in exile from the land (see Deuteronomy 29:23–27). Furthermore, there is a commandment to destroy places of idol worship found in the Holy Land. God has made clear that there can be no tolerance for idolatry in the "palace of the King," particularly when it ensnares the hearts of the Children of Israel.

Melachim II / II Kings
Chapter 11

34 The other events of *Yehu*'s reign, and all his actions, and all his exploits, are recorded in the Annals of the Kings of *Yisrael*.

35 *Yehu* slept with his fathers and he was buried in *Shomron*; he was succeeded as king by his son *Yehoachaz*.

36 *Yehu* reigned over *Yisrael* for twenty-eight years in *Shomron*.

11 1 When *Atalya*, the mother of *Achazyahu*, learned that her son was dead, she promptly killed off all who were of royal stock.

2 But *Yehosheva*, daughter of King *Yoram* and sister of *Achazyahu*, secretly took *Achazyahu*'s son *Yoash* away from among the princes who were being slain, and [put] him and his nurse in a bedroom. And they kept him hidden from *Atalya* so that he was not put to death.

3 He stayed with her for six years, hidden in the House of *Hashem*, while *Atalya* reigned over the land.

4 In the seventh year, *Yehoyada* sent for the chiefs of the hundreds of the Carites and of the guards, and had them come to him in the House of *Hashem*. He made a pact with them, exacting an oath from them in the House of *Hashem*, and he showed them the king's son.

5 He instructed them: "This is what you must do: One-third of those who are on duty for the week shall maintain guard over the royal palace;

6 another third shall be [stationed] at the Sur Gate; and the other third shall be at the gate behind the guards; you shall keep guard over the House on every side.

7 The two divisions of yours who are off duty this week shall keep guard over the House of *Hashem* for the protection of the king.

8 You shall surround the king on every side, every man with his weapons at the ready; and whoever breaks through the ranks shall be killed. Stay close to the king in his comings and goings."

9 The chiefs of hundreds did just as *Yehoyada* ordered: Each took his men – those who were on duty that week and those who were off duty that week – and they presented themselves to *Yehoyada* the Kohen.

Melachim II/II Kings
Chapter 11

מלכים ב
פרק יא

10 The *Kohen* gave the chiefs of hundreds King David's spears and quivers that were kept in the House of *Hashem*.

י וַיִּתֵּן הַכֹּהֵן לְשָׂרֵי הַמֵּאיוֹת [הַמֵּאוֹת] אֶת־הַחֲנִית וְאֶת־הַשְּׁלָטִים אֲשֶׁר לַמֶּלֶךְ דָּוִד אֲשֶׁר בְּבֵית יְהֹוָה:

11 The guards, each with his weapons at the ready, stationed themselves – from the south end of the House to the north end of the House, at the *Mizbayach* and the House – to guard the king on every side.

יא וַיַּעַמְדוּ הָרָצִים אִישׁ וְכֵלָיו בְּיָדוֹ מִכֶּתֶף הַבַּיִת הַיְמָנִית עַד־כֶּתֶף הַבַּיִת הַשְּׂמָאלִית לַמִּזְבֵּחַ וְלַבָּיִת עַל־הַמֶּלֶךְ סָבִיב:

12 [*Yehoyada*] then brought out the king's son, and placed upon him the crown and the insignia. They anointed him and proclaimed him king; they clapped their hands and shouted, "Long live the king!"

יב וַיּוֹצִא אֶת־בֶּן־הַמֶּלֶךְ וַיִּתֵּן עָלָיו אֶת־הַנֵּזֶר וְאֶת־הָעֵדוּת וַיַּמְלִכוּ אֹתוֹ וַיִּמְשָׁחֻהוּ וַיַּכּוּ־כָף וַיֹּאמְרוּ יְחִי הַמֶּלֶךְ:

va-yo-TZI et ben ha-ME-lekh va-yi-TAYN a-LAV et ha-NAY-zer v'-et HA-ay-DUT va-yam-LI-khu o-TO va-yim-sha-KHU-hu va-YA-ku KHAF va-yo-m'-RU y'-KHEE ha-ME-lekh

13 When *Atalya* heard the shouting of the guards [and] the people, she came out to the people in the House of *Hashem*.

יג וַתִּשְׁמַע עֲתַלְיָה אֶת־קוֹל הָרָצִין הָעָם וַתָּבֹא אֶל־הָעָם בֵּית יְהֹוָה:

14 She looked about and saw the king standing by the pillar, as was the custom, the chiefs with their trumpets beside the king, and all the people of the land rejoicing and blowing trumpets. *Atalya* rent her garments and cried out, "Treason, treason!"

יד וַתֵּרֶא וְהִנֵּה הַמֶּלֶךְ עֹמֵד עַל־הָעַמּוּד כַּמִּשְׁפָּט וְהַשָּׂרִים וְהַחֲצֹצְרוֹת אֶל־הַמֶּלֶךְ וְכָל־עַם הָאָרֶץ שָׂמֵחַ וְתֹקֵעַ בַּחֲצֹצְרוֹת וַתִּקְרַע עֲתַלְיָה אֶת־בְּגָדֶיהָ וַתִּקְרָא קֶשֶׁר קָשֶׁר:

15 Then the *Kohen Yehoyada* gave the command to the army officers, the chiefs of hundreds, and said to them, "Take her out between the ranks and, if anyone follows her, put him to the sword." For the *Kohen* thought: "Let her not be put to death in the House of *Hashem*."

טו וַיְצַו יְהוֹיָדָע הַכֹּהֵן אֶת־שָׂרֵי הַמֵּאיוֹת [הַמֵּאוֹת] פְּקֻדֵי הַחַיִל וַיֹּאמֶר אֲלֵיהֶם הוֹצִיאוּ אֹתָהּ אֶל־מִבֵּית לַשְּׂדֵרֹת וְהַבָּא אַחֲרֶיהָ הָמֵת בֶּחָרֶב כִּי אָמַר הַכֹּהֵן אַל־תּוּמַת בֵּית יְהֹוָה:

16 They cleared a passageway for her and she entered the royal palace through the horses' entrance: there she was put to death.

טז וַיָּשִׂמוּ לָהּ יָדַיִם וַתָּבוֹא דֶּרֶךְ־מְבוֹא הַסּוּסִים בֵּית הַמֶּלֶךְ וַתּוּמַת שָׁם:

11:12 And placed upon him the crown and the insignia. The Hebrew word used for 'insignia' in the verse is *aydut* (עדות). This term, usually translated as 'testimony,' is often used to refer to the tablets on which the Ten Commandments were written and the ark that contained them (see Exodus 32:15 and 26:33). As the Ten Commandments are representative of the entire *Torah*, *Rashi* explains that in this verse, the term *aydut* hints to the fact that the new king is not only given a crown, but also a *Torah* scroll. This practice is based on the command for a king to write a *Torah* scroll and have it in his presence at all times (Deuteronomy 17:19). The king must always remember that he is subservient to God, Who is the King of Kings, and is expected to follow His *Torah*. The *Torah* is the testimony and insignia of the People of Israel. When they properly observe its laws they are then deserving of *Hashem*'s promise to possess the Land of Israel.

An open Torah scroll

Melachim II/II Kings
Chapter 12

17 And *Yehoyada* solemnized the covenant between *Hashem*, on the one hand, and the king and the people, on the other – as well as between the king and the people – that they should be the people of *Hashem*.

18 Thereupon all the people of the land went to the temple of Baal. They tore it down and smashed its altars and images to bits, and they slew Mattan, the priest of Baal, in front of the altars. [*Yehoyada*] the *Kohen* then placed guards over the House of *Hashem*.

19 He took the chiefs of hundreds, the Carites, the guards, and all the people of the land, and they escorted the king from the House of *Hashem* into the royal palace by the gate of the guards. And he ascended the royal throne.

20 All the people of the land rejoiced, and the city was quiet. As for *Atalya*, she had been put to the sword in the royal palace.

12 1 *Yehoash* was seven years old when he became king.

2 *Yehoash* began his reign in the seventh year of *Yehu*, and he reigned in *Yerushalayim* forty years. His mother's name was Zibiah of *Be'er Sheva*.

3 All his days *Yehoash* did what was pleasing to *Hashem*, as the *Kohen Yehoyada* instructed him.

4 The shrines, however, were not removed; the people continued to sacrifice and offer at the shrines.

5 *Yehoash* said to the *Kohanim*, "All the money, current money, brought into the House of *Hashem* as sacred donations – any money a man may pay as the money equivalent of persons, or any other money that a man may be minded to bring to the House of *Hashem* –

6 let the *Kohanim* receive it, each from his benefactor; they, in turn, shall make repairs on the House, wherever damage may be found."

7 But in the twenty-third year of King *Yehoash*, [it was found that] the *Kohanim* had not made the repairs on the House.

מלכים ב
פרק יב

יז וַיִּכְרֹת יְהוֹיָדָע אֶת־הַבְּרִית בֵּין יְהוָֹה וּבֵין הַמֶּלֶךְ וּבֵין הָעָם לִהְיוֹת לְעָם לַיהוָֹה וּבֵין הַמֶּלֶךְ וּבֵין הָעָם:

יח וַיָּבֹאוּ כָל־עַם הָאָרֶץ בֵּית־הַבַּעַל וַיִּתְּצֻהוּ אֶת־מִזְבְּחֹתָו [מִזְבְּחֹתָיו] וְאֶת־צְלָמָיו שִׁבְּרוּ הֵיטֵב וְאֵת מַתָּן כֹּהֵן הַבַּעַל הָרְגוּ לִפְנֵי הַמִּזְבְּחוֹת וַיָּשֶׂם הַכֹּהֵן פְּקֻדֹּת עַל־בֵּית יְהוָֹה:

יט וַיִּקַּח אֶת־שָׂרֵי הַמֵּאוֹת וְאֶת־הַכָּרִי וְאֶת־הָרָצִים וְאֵת כָּל־עַם הָאָרֶץ וַיֹּרִידוּ אֶת־הַמֶּלֶךְ מִבֵּית יְהוָֹה וַיָּבוֹאוּ דֶּרֶךְ־שַׁעַר הָרָצִים בֵּית הַמֶּלֶךְ וַיֵּשֶׁב עַל־כִּסֵּא הַמְּלָכִים:

כ וַיִּשְׂמַח כָּל־עַם־הָאָרֶץ וְהָעִיר שָׁקָטָה וְאֶת־עֲתַלְיָהוּ הֵמִיתוּ בַחֶרֶב בֵּית מֶלֶךְ [הַמֶּלֶךְ]:

יב א בֶּן־שֶׁבַע שָׁנִים יְהוֹאָשׁ בְּמָלְכוֹ:

ב בִּשְׁנַת־שֶׁבַע לְיֵהוּא מָלַךְ יְהוֹאָשׁ וְאַרְבָּעִים שָׁנָה מָלַךְ בִּירוּשָׁלָם וְשֵׁם אִמּוֹ צִבְיָה מִבְּאֵר שָׁבַע:

ג וַיַּעַשׂ יְהוֹאָשׁ הַיָּשָׁר בְּעֵינֵי יְהוָֹה כָּל־יָמָיו אֲשֶׁר הוֹרָהוּ יְהוֹיָדָע הַכֹּהֵן:

ד רַק הַבָּמוֹת לֹא־סָרוּ עוֹד הָעָם מְזַבְּחִים וּמְקַטְּרִים בַּבָּמוֹת:

ה וַיֹּאמֶר יְהוֹאָשׁ אֶל־הַכֹּהֲנִים כֹּל כֶּסֶף הַקֳּדָשִׁים אֲשֶׁר־יוּבָא בֵית־יְהוָֹה כֶּסֶף עוֹבֵר אִישׁ כֶּסֶף נַפְשׁוֹת עֶרְכּוֹ כָּל־כֶּסֶף אֲשֶׁר יַעֲלֶה עַל לֶב־אִישׁ לְהָבִיא בֵּית יְהוָֹה:

ו יִקְחוּ לָהֶם הַכֹּהֲנִים אִישׁ מֵאֵת מַכָּרוֹ וְהֵם יְחַזְּקוּ אֶת־בֶּדֶק הַבַּיִת לְכֹל אֲשֶׁר־יִמָּצֵא שָׁם בָּדֶק:

ז וַיְהִי בִּשְׁנַת עֶשְׂרִים וְשָׁלֹשׁ שָׁנָה לַמֶּלֶךְ יְהוֹאָשׁ לֹא־חִזְּקוּ הַכֹּהֲנִים אֶת־בֶּדֶק הַבָּיִת:

Melachim II / II Kings
Chapter 12

8 So King *Yehoash* summoned the *Kohen Yehoyada* and the other *Kohanim* and said to them, "Why have you not kept the House in repair? Now do not accept money from your benefactors any more, but have it donated for the repair of the House."

ח וַיִּקְרָא הַמֶּלֶךְ יְהוֹאָשׁ לִיהוֹיָדָע הַכֹּהֵן וְלַכֹּהֲנִים וַיֹּאמֶר אֲלֵהֶם מַדּוּעַ אֵינְכֶם מְחַזְּקִים אֶת־בֶּדֶק הַבָּיִת וְעַתָּה אַל־תִּקְחוּ־כֶסֶף מֵאֵת מַכָּרֵיכֶם כִּי־לְבֶדֶק הַבַּיִת תִּתְּנֻהוּ:

9 The *Kohanim* agreed that they would neither accept money from the people nor make repairs on the House.

ט וַיֵּאֹתוּ הַכֹּהֲנִים לְבִלְתִּי קְחַת־כֶּסֶף מֵאֵת הָעָם וּלְבִלְתִּי חַזֵּק אֶת־בֶּדֶק הַבָּיִת:

10 And the *Kohen Yehoyada* took a chest and bored a hole in its lid. He placed it at the right side of the *Mizbayach* as one entered the House of *Hashem*, and the priestly guards of the threshold deposited there all the money that was brought into the House of *Hashem*.

י וַיִּקַּח יְהוֹיָדָע הַכֹּהֵן אֲרוֹן אֶחָד וַיִּקֹּב חֹר בְּדַלְתּוֹ וַיִּתֵּן אֹתוֹ אֵצֶל הַמִּזְבֵּחַ בְּיָמִין [מִיָּמִין] בְּבוֹא־אִישׁ בֵּית יְהוָה וְנָתְנוּ־שָׁמָּה הַכֹּהֲנִים שֹׁמְרֵי הַסַּף אֶת־כָּל־הַכֶּסֶף הַמּוּבָא בֵית־יְהוָה:

va-yi-KAKH y'-ho-ya-DA ha-ko-HAYN a-RON e-KHAD va-yi-KOV KHOR b'-dal-TO va-yi-TAYN ot-TO AY-tzel ha-miz-BAY-akh mi-ya-MIN b'vo EESH BAYT a-do-NAI v'-na-t'-nu SHA-mah ha-ko-ha-NEEM sho-m'-RAY ha-SAF et kol ha-KE-sef ha-mu-VA vayt a-do-NAI

11 Whenever they saw that there was much money in the chest, the royal scribe and the *Kohen Gadol* would come up and put the money accumulated in the House of *Hashem* into bags, and they would count it.

יא וַיְהִי כִּרְאוֹתָם כִּי־רַב הַכֶּסֶף בָּאָרוֹן וַיַּעַל סֹפֵר הַמֶּלֶךְ וְהַכֹּהֵן הַגָּדוֹל וַיָּצֻרוּ וַיִּמְנוּ אֶת־הַכֶּסֶף הַנִּמְצָא בֵית־יְהוָה:

12 Then they would deliver the money that was weighed out to the overseers of the work, who were in charge of the House of *Hashem*. These, in turn, used to pay the carpenters and the laborers who worked on the House of *Hashem*,

יב וְנָתְנוּ אֶת־הַכֶּסֶף הַמְתֻכָּן עַל־יד [יְדֵי] עֹשֵׂי הַמְּלָאכָה הפקדים [הַמֻּפְקָדִים] בֵּית יְהוָה וַיּוֹצִיאֻהוּ לְחָרָשֵׁי הָעֵץ וְלַבֹּנִים הָעֹשִׂים בֵּית יְהוָה:

13 and the masons and the stonecutters. They also paid for wood and for quarried stone with which to make the repairs on the House of *Hashem*, and for every other expenditure that had to be made in repairing the House.

יג וְלַגֹּדְרִים וּלְחֹצְבֵי הָאֶבֶן וְלִקְנוֹת עֵצִים וְאַבְנֵי מַחְצֵב לְחַזֵּק אֶת־בֶּדֶק בֵּית־יְהוָה וּלְכֹל אֲשֶׁר־יֵצֵא עַל־הַבַּיִת לְחָזְקָה:

14 However, no silver bowls and no snuffers, basins, or trumpets – no vessels of gold or silver – were made at the House of *Hashem* from the money brought into the House of *Hashem*;

יד אַךְ לֹא יֵעָשֶׂה בֵּית יְהוָה סִפּוֹת כֶּסֶף מְזַמְּרוֹת מִזְרָקוֹת חֲצֹצְרוֹת כָּל־כְּלִי זָהָב וּכְלִי־כָסֶף מִן־הַכֶּסֶף הַמּוּבָא בֵית־יְהוָה:

12:10 Deposited there all the money that was brought into the House of Hashem According to Jewish law, money that is designated for use in the *Beit Hamikdash* is endowed with a special status and must be used only for its intended purpose. In the Holy Temple, it is therefore necessary to ensure that donated funds are properly secured and then distributed for care of the *Beit Hamikdash* and communal offerings. Today, without a *Beit Hamikdash*, we are likewise required to make sure that we are completely honest in our financial dealings, and that money is used for its intended purpose.

Melachim II / II Kings
Chapter 13

מלכים ב
פרק יג

15 this was given only to the overseers of the work for the repair of the House of *Hashem*.

טו כִּי־לְעֹשֵׂ֧י הַמְּלָאכָ֛ה יִתְּנֻ֖הוּ וְחִזְּקוּ־ב֑וֹ אֶת־בֵּ֥ית יְהוָֽה׃

16 No check was kept on the men to whom the money was delivered to pay the workers; for they dealt honestly.

טז וְלֹ֧א יְחַשְּׁב֣וּ אֶת־הָאֲנָשִׁ֗ים אֲשֶׁ֨ר יִתְּנ֤וּ אֶת־הַכֶּ֙סֶף֙ עַל־יָדָ֔ם לָתֵ֖ת לְעֹשֵׂ֣י הַמְּלָאכָ֑ה כִּ֥י בֶאֱמֻנָ֖ה הֵ֥ם עֹשִֽׂים׃

17 Money brought as a guilt offering or as a sin offering was not deposited in the House of *Hashem*; it went to the *Kohanim*.

יז כֶּ֤סֶף אָשָׁם֙ וְכֶ֣סֶף חַטָּא֔וֹת לֹ֥א יוּבָ֖א בֵּ֣ית יְהוָ֑ה לַכֹּהֲנִ֖ים יִהְיֽוּ׃

18 At that time, King Hazael of Aram came up and attacked Gath and captured it; and Hazael proceeded to march on *Yerushalayim*.

יח אָ֣ז יַעֲלֶ֗ה חֲזָאֵל֙ מֶ֣לֶךְ אֲרָ֔ם וַיִּלָּ֖חֶם עַל־גַּ֑ת וַֽיִּלְכְּדָ֑הּ וַיָּ֤שֶׂם חֲזָאֵל֙ פָּנָ֔יו לַעֲל֖וֹת עַל־יְרוּשָׁלָֽ͏ִם׃

19 Thereupon King *Yoash* of *Yehuda* took all the objects that had been consecrated by his fathers, Kings *Yehoshafat*, *Yehoram*, and *Achazyahu* of *Yehuda*, and by himself, and all the gold that there was in the treasuries of the Temple of *Hashem* and in the royal palace, and he sent them to King Hazael of Aram, who then turned back from his march on *Yerushalayim*.

יט וַיִּקַּ֞ח יְהוֹאָ֣שׁ מֶֽלֶךְ־יְהוּדָ֗ה אֵ֣ת כָּל־הַקֳּדָשִׁ֡ים אֲשֶׁר־הִקְדִּ֣ישׁוּ יְהוֹשָׁפָ֣ט וִיהוֹרָם֩ וַאֲחַזְיָ֨הוּ אֲבֹתָ֜יו מַלְכֵ֤י יְהוּדָה֙ וְאֶת־קֳדָשָׁ֔יו וְאֵ֣ת כָּל־הַזָּהָ֗ב הַנִּמְצָ֛א בְּאֹצְר֥וֹת בֵּית־יְהוָ֖ה וּבֵ֣ית הַמֶּ֑לֶךְ וַיִּשְׁלַ֗ח לַחֲזָאֵל֙ מֶ֣לֶךְ אֲרָ֔ם וַיַּ֖עַל מֵעַ֥ל יְרוּשָׁלָֽ͏ִם׃

20 The other events of *Yoash*'s reign, and all his actions, are recorded in the Annals of the Kings of *Yehuda*.

כ וְיֶ֛תֶר דִּבְרֵ֥י יוֹאָ֖שׁ וְכָל־אֲשֶׁ֣ר עָשָׂ֑ה הֲלוֹא־הֵ֣ם כְּתוּבִ֗ים עַל־סֵ֛פֶר דִּבְרֵ֥י הַיָּמִ֖ים לְמַלְכֵ֥י יְהוּדָֽה׃

21 His courtiers formed a conspiracy against *Yoash* and assassinated him at Beth-millo that leads down to Silla.

כא וַיָּקֻ֥מוּ עֲבָדָ֖יו וַיִּקְשְׁרוּ־קָ֑שֶׁר וַיַּכּ֤וּ אֶת־יוֹאָשׁ֙ בֵּ֣ית מִלֹּ֔א הַיּוֹרֵ֖ד סִלָּֽא׃

22 The courtiers who assassinated him were Jozacar son of Shimeath and Jehozabad son of Shomer. He died and was buried with his fathers in the City of *David*; and his son *Amatzya* succeeded him as king.

כב וְיוֹזָבָ֣ד בֶּן־שִׁמְעָ֗ת וִיהוֹזָבָד֙ בֶּן־שֹׁמֵ֔ר עֲבָדָ֥יו הִכֻּ֖הוּ וַיָּמֹ֑ת וַיִּקְבְּר֤וּ אֹתוֹ֙ עִם־אֲבֹתָ֔יו בְּעִ֖יר דָּוִ֑ד וַיִּמְלֹ֛ךְ אֲמַצְיָ֥ה בְנ֖וֹ תַּחְתָּֽיו׃

13 1 In the twenty-third year of King *Yoash* son of *Achazyahu* of *Yehuda*, *Yehoachaz* son of *Yehu* became king over *Yisrael* in *Shomron* – for seventeen years.

יג א בִּשְׁנַ֨ת עֶשְׂרִ֤ים וְשָׁלֹשׁ֙ שָׁנָ֔ה לְיוֹאָ֥שׁ בֶּן־אֲחַזְיָ֖הוּ מֶ֣לֶךְ יְהוּדָ֑ה מָלַ֡ךְ יְהוֹאָחָ֣ז בֶּן־יֵהוּא֩ עַל־יִשְׂרָאֵ֜ל בְּשֹׁמְר֗וֹן שְׁבַ֥ע עֶשְׂרֵ֖ה שָׁנָֽה׃

2 He did what was displeasing to *Hashem*. He persisted in the sins which *Yerovam* son of Nebat had caused *Yisrael* to commit; he did not depart from them.

ב וַיַּ֥עַשׂ הָרַ֖ע בְּעֵינֵ֣י יְהוָ֑ה וַיֵּ֡לֶךְ אַחַ֣ר חַטֹּ֩את֩ יָרָבְעָ֨ם בֶּן־נְבָ֜ט אֲשֶׁר־הֶחֱטִ֥יא אֶת־יִשְׂרָאֵ֖ל לֹא־סָ֥ר מִמֶּֽנָּה׃

3 *Hashem* was angry with *Yisrael* and He repeatedly delivered them into the hands of King Hazael of Aram and into the hands of Ben-hadad son of Hazael.

ג וַיִּֽחַר־אַ֤ף יְהוָה֙ בְּיִשְׂרָאֵ֔ל וַֽיִּתְּנֵ֛ם בְּיַ֥ד ׀ חֲזָאֵ֥ל מֶֽלֶךְ־אֲרָ֖ם וּבְיַ֣ד בֶּן־הֲדַ֣ד בֶּן־חֲזָאֵ֑ל כָּל־הַיָּמִֽים׃

Melachim II / II Kings
Chapter 13

4 But *Yehoachaz* pleaded with *Hashem*; and *Hashem* listened to him, for He saw the suffering that the king of Aram inflicted upon *Yisrael*.

5 So *Hashem* granted *Yisrael* a deliverer, and they gained their freedom from Aram; and *Yisrael* dwelt in its homes as before.

6 However, they did not depart from the sins which the House of *Yerovam* had caused *Yisrael* to commit; they persisted in them. Even the sacred post stood in *Shomron*.

7 In fact, *Yehoachaz* was left with a force of only fifty horsemen, ten chariots, and ten thousand foot soldiers; for the king of Aram had decimated them and trampled them like the dust under his feet.

8 The other events of *Yehoachaz*'s reign, and all his actions and his exploits, are recorded in the Annals of the Kings of *Yisrael*.

9 *Yehoachaz* slept with his fathers and he was buried in *Shomron*; his son *Yoash* succeeded him as king.

10 In the thirty-seventh year of King *Yoash* of *Yehuda*, *Yehoash* son of *Yehoachaz* became king of *Yisrael* in *Shomron* – for sixteen years.

11 He did what was displeasing to *Hashem*; he did not depart from any of the sins which *Yerovam* son of Nebat had caused *Yisrael* to commit; he persisted in them.

12 The other events of *Yoash*'s reign, and all his actions, and his exploits in his war with King *Amatzya* of *Yehuda*, are recorded in the Annals of the Kings of *Yisrael*.

13 *Yoash* slept with his fathers and *Yerovam* occupied his throne; *Yoash* was buried in *Shomron* with the kings of *Yisrael*.

14 *Elisha* had been stricken with the illness of which he was to die, and King *Yoash* of *Yisrael* went down to see him. He wept over him and cried, "Father, father! *Yisrael*'s chariots and horsemen!"

15 *Elisha* said to him, "Get a bow and arrows"; and he brought him a bow and arrows.

16 Then he said to the king of *Yisrael*, "Grasp the bow!" And when he had grasped it, *Elisha* put his hands over the king's hands.

מלכים ב
פרק יג

ד וַיְחַל יְהוֹאָחָז אֶת־פְּנֵי יְהוָה וַיִּשְׁמַע אֵלָיו יְהוָה כִּי רָאָה אֶת־לַחַץ יִשְׂרָאֵל כִּי־לָחַץ אֹתָם מֶלֶךְ אֲרָם׃

ה וַיִּתֵּן יְהוָה לְיִשְׂרָאֵל מוֹשִׁיעַ וַיֵּצְאוּ מִתַּחַת יַד־אֲרָם וַיֵּשְׁבוּ בְנֵי־יִשְׂרָאֵל בְּאָהֳלֵיהֶם כִּתְמוֹל שִׁלְשׁוֹם׃

ו אַךְ לֹא־סָרוּ מֵחַטֹּאות בֵּית־יָרָבְעָם אֲשֶׁר־הֶחֱטִיא [הֶחֱטִיא] אֶת־יִשְׂרָאֵל בָּהּ הָלָךְ וְגַם הָאֲשֵׁרָה עָמְדָה בְּשֹׁמְרוֹן׃

ז כִּי לֹא הִשְׁאִיר לִיהוֹאָחָז עָם כִּי אִם־חֲמִשִּׁים פָּרָשִׁים וַעֲשָׂרָה רֶכֶב וַעֲשֶׂרֶת אֲלָפִים רַגְלִי כִּי אִבְּדָם מֶלֶךְ אֲרָם וַיְשִׂמֵם כֶּעָפָר לָדֻשׁ׃

ח וְיֶתֶר דִּבְרֵי יְהוֹאָחָז וְכָל־אֲשֶׁר עָשָׂה וּגְבוּרָתוֹ הֲלוֹא־הֵם כְּתוּבִים עַל־סֵפֶר דִּבְרֵי הַיָּמִים לְמַלְכֵי יִשְׂרָאֵל׃

ט וַיִּשְׁכַּב יְהוֹאָחָז עִם־אֲבֹתָיו וַיִּקְבְּרֻהוּ בְּשֹׁמְרוֹן וַיִּמְלֹךְ יוֹאָשׁ בְּנוֹ תַּחְתָּיו׃

י בִּשְׁנַת שְׁלֹשִׁים וָשֶׁבַע שָׁנָה לְיוֹאָשׁ מֶלֶךְ יְהוּדָה מָלַךְ יְהוֹאָשׁ בֶּן־יְהוֹאָחָז עַל־יִשְׂרָאֵל בְּשֹׁמְרוֹן שֵׁשׁ עֶשְׂרֵה שָׁנָה׃

יא וַיַּעֲשֶׂה הָרַע בְּעֵינֵי יְהוָה לֹא סָר מִכָּל־חַטֹּאות יָרָבְעָם בֶּן־נְבָט אֲשֶׁר־הֶחֱטִיא אֶת־יִשְׂרָאֵל בָּהּ הָלָךְ׃

יב וְיֶתֶר דִּבְרֵי יוֹאָשׁ וְכָל־אֲשֶׁר עָשָׂה וּגְבוּרָתוֹ אֲשֶׁר נִלְחַם עִם אֲמַצְיָה מֶלֶךְ־יְהוּדָה הֲלוֹא־הֵם כְּתוּבִים עַל־סֵפֶר דִּבְרֵי הַיָּמִים לְמַלְכֵי יִשְׂרָאֵל׃

יג וַיִּשְׁכַּב יוֹאָשׁ עִם־אֲבֹתָיו וְיָרָבְעָם יָשַׁב עַל־כִּסְאוֹ וַיִּקָּבֵר יוֹאָשׁ בְּשֹׁמְרוֹן עִם מַלְכֵי יִשְׂרָאֵל׃

יד וֶאֱלִישָׁע חָלָה אֶת־חָלְיוֹ אֲשֶׁר יָמוּת בּוֹ וַיֵּרֶד אֵלָיו יוֹאָשׁ מֶלֶךְ־יִשְׂרָאֵל וַיֵּבְךְּ עַל־פָּנָיו וַיֹּאמַר אָבִי אָבִי רֶכֶב יִשְׂרָאֵל וּפָרָשָׁיו׃

טו וַיֹּאמֶר לוֹ אֱלִישָׁע קַח קֶשֶׁת וְחִצִּים וַיִּקַּח אֵלָיו קֶשֶׁת וְחִצִּים׃

טז וַיֹּאמֶר לְמֶלֶךְ יִשְׂרָאֵל הַרְכֵּב יָדְךָ עַל־הַקֶּשֶׁת וַיַּרְכֵּב יָדוֹ וַיָּשֶׂם אֱלִישָׁע יָדָיו עַל־יְדֵי הַמֶּלֶךְ׃

Melachim II / II Kings
Chapter 13

מלכים ב
פרק יג

17 "Open the window toward the east," he said; and he opened it. *Elisha* said, "Shoot!" and he shot. Then he said, "An arrow of victory for *Hashem*! An arrow of victory over Aram! You shall rout Aram completely at Aphek."

יז וַיֹּאמֶר פְּתַח הַחַלּוֹן קֵדְמָה וַיִּפְתָּח וַיֹּאמֶר אֱלִישָׁע יְרֵה וַיּוֹר וַיֹּאמֶר חֵץ־תְּשׁוּעָה לַיהֹוָה וְחֵץ תְּשׁוּעָה בַאֲרָם וְהִכִּיתָ אֶת־אֲרָם בַּאֲפֵק עַד־כַּלֵּה:

18 He said, "Now pick up the arrows." And he picked them up. "Strike the ground!" he said to the king of *Yisrael*; and he struck three times and stopped.

יח וַיֹּאמֶר קַח הַחִצִּים וַיִּקָּח וַיֹּאמֶר לְמֶלֶךְ־יִשְׂרָאֵל הַךְ־אַרְצָה וַיַּךְ שָׁלֹשׁ־פְּעָמִים וַיַּעֲמֹד:

19 The man of *Hashem* was angry with him and said to him, "If only you had struck five or six times! Then you would have annihilated Aram; as it is, you shall defeat Aram only three times."

יט וַיִּקְצֹף עָלָיו אִישׁ הָאֱלֹהִים וַיֹּאמֶר לְהַכּוֹת חָמֵשׁ אוֹ־שֵׁשׁ פְּעָמִים אָז הִכִּיתָ אֶת־אֲרָם עַד־כַּלֵּה וְעַתָּה שָׁלֹשׁ פְּעָמִים תַּכֶּה אֶת־אֲרָם:

20 *Elisha* died and he was buried. Now bands of Moabites used to invade the land at the coming of every year.

כ וַיָּמָת אֱלִישָׁע וַיִּקְבְּרֻהוּ וּגְדוּדֵי מוֹאָב יָבֹאוּ בָאָרֶץ בָּא שָׁנָה:

21 Once a man was being buried, when the people caught sight of such a band; so they threw the corpse into *Elisha*'s grave and made off. When the [dead] man came in contact with *Elisha*'s bones, he came to life and stood up.

כא וַיְהִי הֵם קֹבְרִים אִישׁ וְהִנֵּה רָאוּ אֶת־הַגְּדוּד וַיַּשְׁלִיכוּ אֶת־הָאִישׁ בְּקֶבֶר אֱלִישָׁע וַיֵּלֶךְ וַיִּגַּע הָאִישׁ בְּעַצְמוֹת אֱלִישָׁע וַיְחִי וַיָּקָם עַל־רַגְלָיו:

22 King Hazael of Aram had oppressed the Israelites throughout the reign of *Yehoachaz*.

כב וַחֲזָאֵל מֶלֶךְ אֲרָם לָחַץ אֶת־יִשְׂרָאֵל כֹּל יְמֵי יְהוֹאָחָז:

23 But *Hashem* was gracious and merciful to them, and He turned back to them for the sake of His covenant with *Avraham*, *Yitzchak*, and *Yaakov*. He refrained from destroying them, and He still did not cast them out from His presence.

va-ya-KHON a-do-NAI o-TAM va-ra-kha-MAYM vai-YI-fen a-lay-HEM l'-MA-an b'-ree-TO et av-ra-HAM yitz-KHAK v'-ya-a-KOV v'-LO a-VAH hash-khee-TAM v'-lo hish-lee-KHAM may-al pa-NAV ad A-tah

כג וַיָּחָן יְהֹוָה אֹתָם וַיְרַחֲמֵם וַיִּפֶן אֲלֵיהֶם לְמַעַן בְּרִיתוֹ אֶת־אַבְרָהָם יִצְחָק וְיַעֲקֹב וְלֹא אָבָה הַשְׁחִיתָם וְלֹא־הִשְׁלִיכָם מֵעַל־פָּנָיו עַד־עָתָּה:

24 When King Hazael of Aram died, his son Ben-hadad succeeded him as king;

כד וַיָּמָת חֲזָאֵל מֶלֶךְ אֲרָם וַיִּמְלֹךְ בֶּן־הֲדַד בְּנוֹ תַּחְתָּיו:

25 and then *Yehoash* son of *Yehoachaz* recovered from Ben-hadad son of Hazael the towns which had been taken from his father *Yehoachaz* in war. Three times *Yoash* defeated him, and he recovered the towns of *Yisrael*.

כה וַיָּשָׁב יְהוֹאָשׁ בֶּן־יְהוֹאָחָז וַיִּקַּח אֶת־הֶעָרִים מִיַּד בֶּן־הֲדַד בֶּן־חֲזָאֵל אֲשֶׁר לָקַח מִיַּד יְהוֹאָחָז אָבִיו בַּמִּלְחָמָה שָׁלֹשׁ פְּעָמִים הִכָּהוּ יוֹאָשׁ וַיָּשֶׁב אֶת־עָרֵי יִשְׂרָאֵל:

רחמים

13:23 Gracious and merciful to them Because of His everlasting covenant with the People of Israel, *Hashem* has compassion for them. In Hebrew, the word for 'compassion,' *rachamim* (רחמים), comes from the word that means 'womb,' *rechem* (רחם). A mother always feels compassion for the child she lovingly carried in her womb for nine months. We pray for *Hashem* to have the same compassion upon His children, whom He has lovingly carried for millennia, and when we show compassion to others, we emulate one of God's attributes.

Melachim II / II Kings
Chapter 14

1 In the second year of King *Yoash* son of Joahaz of *Yisrael*, *Amatzya* son of King *Yoash* of *Yehuda* became king.

2 He was twenty-five years old when he became king, and he reigned twenty-nine years in *Yerushalayim*; his mother's name was Jehoaddan of *Yerushalayim*.

3 He did what was pleasing to *Hashem*, but not like his ancestor *David*; he did just as his father *Yoash* had done.

4 However, the shrines were not removed; the people continued to sacrifice and make offerings at the shrines.

5 Once he had the kingdom firmly in his grasp, he put to death the courtiers who had assassinated his father the king.

6 But he did not put to death the children of the assassins, in accordance with what is written in the Book of the Teaching of *Moshe*, where *Hashem* commanded, "Parents shall not be put to death for children, nor children be put to death for parents; a person shall be put to death only for his own crime."

7 He defeated ten thousand Edomites in the Valley of Salt, and he captured Sela in battle and renamed it Joktheel, as is still the case.

8 Then *Amatzya* sent envoys to King *Yehoash* son of *Yehoachaz* son of *Yehu* of *Yisrael*, with this message: "Come, let us confront each other."

9 King *Yehoash* of *Yisrael* sent back this message to King *Amatzya* of *Yehuda*: "The thistle in Lebanon sent this message to the cedar in Lebanon, 'Give your daughter to my son in marriage.' But a wild beast in Lebanon went by and trampled down the thistle.

10 Because you have defeated Edom, you have become arrogant. Stay home and enjoy your glory, rather than provoke disaster and fall, dragging *Yehuda* down with you."

11 But *Amatzya* paid no heed; so King *Yehoash* of *Yisrael* advanced, and he and King *Amatzya* of *Yehuda* confronted each other at *Beit Shemesh* in *Yehuda*.

מלכים ב
פרק יד

א בִּשְׁנַת שְׁתַּיִם לְיוֹאָשׁ בֶּן־יוֹאָחָז מֶלֶךְ יִשְׂרָאֵל מָלַךְ אֲמַצְיָהוּ בֶן־יוֹאָשׁ מֶלֶךְ יְהוּדָה:

ב בֶּן־עֶשְׂרִים וְחָמֵשׁ שָׁנָה הָיָה בְמָלְכוֹ וְעֶשְׂרִים וָתֵשַׁע שָׁנָה מָלַךְ בִּירוּשָׁלָ͏ִם וְשֵׁם אִמּוֹ יהועדין [יְהוֹעַדָּן] מִן־יְרוּשָׁלָ͏ִם:

ג וַיַּעַשׂ הַיָּשָׁר בְּעֵינֵי יְהֹוָה רַק לֹא כְּדָוִד אָבִיו כְּכֹל אֲשֶׁר־עָשָׂה יוֹאָשׁ אָבִיו עָשָׂה:

ד רַק הַבָּמוֹת לֹא־סָרוּ עוֹד הָעָם מְזַבְּחִים וּמְקַטְּרִים בַּבָּמוֹת:

ה וַיְהִי כַּאֲשֶׁר חָזְקָה הַמַּמְלָכָה בְּיָדוֹ וַיַּךְ אֶת־עֲבָדָיו הַמַּכִּים אֶת־הַמֶּלֶךְ אָבִיו:

ו וְאֶת־בְּנֵי הַמַּכִּים לֹא הֵמִית כַּכָּתוּב בְּסֵפֶר תּוֹרַת־מֹשֶׁה אֲשֶׁר־צִוָּה יְהֹוָה לֵאמֹר לֹא־יוּמְתוּ אָבוֹת עַל־בָּנִים וּבָנִים לֹא־יוּמְתוּ עַל־אָבוֹת כִּי אִם־אִישׁ בְּחֶטְאוֹ ימות [יוּמָת]:

ז הוּא־הִכָּה אֶת־אֱדוֹם בְּגֵיא־המלח [מֶלַח] עֲשֶׂרֶת אֲלָפִים וְתָפַשׂ אֶת־הַסֶּלַע בַּמִּלְחָמָה וַיִּקְרָא אֶת־שְׁמָהּ יָקְתְאֵל עַד הַיּוֹם הַזֶּה:

ח אָז שָׁלַח אֲמַצְיָה מַלְאָכִים אֶל־יְהוֹאָשׁ בֶּן־יְהוֹאָחָז בֶּן־יֵהוּא מֶלֶךְ יִשְׂרָאֵל לֵאמֹר לְכָה נִתְרָאֶה פָנִים:

ט וַיִּשְׁלַח יְהוֹאָשׁ מֶלֶךְ־יִשְׂרָאֵל אֶל־אֲמַצְיָהוּ מֶלֶךְ־יְהוּדָה לֵאמֹר הַחוֹחַ אֲשֶׁר בַּלְּבָנוֹן שָׁלַח אֶל־הָאֶרֶז אֲשֶׁר בַּלְּבָנוֹן לֵאמֹר תְּנָה־אֶת־בִּתְּךָ לִבְנִי לְאִשָּׁה וַתַּעֲבֹר חַיַּת הַשָּׂדֶה אֲשֶׁר בַּלְּבָנוֹן וַתִּרְמֹס אֶת־הַחוֹחַ:

י הַכֵּה הִכִּיתָ אֶת־אֱדוֹם וּנְשָׂאֲךָ לִבֶּךָ הִכָּבֵד וְשֵׁב בְּבֵיתֶךָ וְלָמָּה תִתְגָּרֶה בְּרָעָה וְנָפַלְתָּה אַתָּה וִיהוּדָה עִמָּךְ:

יא וְלֹא־שָׁמַע אֲמַצְיָהוּ וַיַּעַל יְהוֹאָשׁ מֶלֶךְ־יִשְׂרָאֵל וַיִּתְרָאוּ פָנִים הוּא וַאֲמַצְיָהוּ מֶלֶךְ־יְהוּדָה בְּבֵית שֶׁמֶשׁ אֲשֶׁר לִיהוּדָה:

Melachim II / II Kings
Chapter 14

מלכים ב
פרק יד

12 The Judites were routed by *Yisrael*, and they all fled to their homes.

יב וַיִּנָּגֶף יְהוּדָה לִפְנֵי יִשְׂרָאֵל וַיָּנֻסוּ אִישׁ לְאֹהָלוֹ [לְאֹהָלָיו]:

13 King *Yehoash* of *Yisrael* captured King *Amatzya* son of *Yehoash* son of *Achazyahu* of *Yehuda* at *Beit Shemesh*. He marched on *Yerushalayim*, and he made a breach of four hundred *amot* in the wall of *Yerushalayim*, from the *Efraim* Gate to the Corner Gate.

יג וְאֵת אֲמַצְיָהוּ מֶלֶךְ־יְהוּדָה בֶן־יְהוֹאָשׁ בֶּן־אֲחַזְיָהוּ תָּפַשׂ יְהוֹאָשׁ מֶלֶךְ־יִשְׂרָאֵל בְּבֵית שָׁמֶשׁ וַיָּבֹאוּ [וַיָּבֹא] יְרוּשָׁלִַם וַיִּפְרֹץ בְּחוֹמַת יְרוּשָׁלִַם בְּשַׁעַר אֶפְרַיִם עַד־שַׁעַר הַפִּנָּה אַרְבַּע מֵאוֹת אַמָּה:

14 He carried off all the gold and silver and all the vessels that there were in the House of *Hashem* and in the treasuries of the royal palace, as well as hostages; and he returned to *Shomron*.

יד וְלָקַח אֶת־כָּל־הַזָּהָב־וְהַכֶּסֶף וְאֵת כָּל־הַכֵּלִים הַנִּמְצְאִים בֵּית־יְהֹוָה וּבְאֹצְרוֹת בֵּית הַמֶּלֶךְ וְאֵת בְּנֵי הַתַּעֲרֻבוֹת וַיָּשָׁב שֹׁמְרוֹנָה:

15 The other events of *Yehoash*'s reign, and all his actions and exploits, and his war with King *Amatzya* of *Yehuda*, are recorded in the Annals of the Kings of *Yisrael*.

טו וְיֶתֶר דִּבְרֵי יְהוֹאָשׁ אֲשֶׁר עָשָׂה וּגְבוּרָתוֹ וַאֲשֶׁר נִלְחַם עִם אֲמַצְיָהוּ מֶלֶךְ־יְהוּדָה הֲלֹא־הֵם כְּתוּבִים עַל־סֵפֶר דִּבְרֵי הַיָּמִים לְמַלְכֵי יִשְׂרָאֵל:

16 *Yehoash* slept with his fathers, and was buried in *Shomron* with the kings of *Yisrael*; his son *Yerovam* succeeded him as king.

טז וַיִּשְׁכַּב יְהוֹאָשׁ עִם־אֲבֹתָיו וַיִּקָּבֵר בְּשֹׁמְרוֹן עִם מַלְכֵי יִשְׂרָאֵל וַיִּמְלֹךְ יָרָבְעָם בְּנוֹ תַּחְתָּיו:

17 King *Amatzya* son of *Yoash* of *Yehuda* lived fifteen years after the death of King *Yehoash* son of *Yehoachaz* of *Yisrael*.

יז וַיְחִי אֲמַצְיָהוּ בֶן־יוֹאָשׁ מֶלֶךְ יְהוּדָה אַחֲרֵי מוֹת יְהוֹאָשׁ בֶּן־יְהוֹאָחָז מֶלֶךְ יִשְׂרָאֵל חֲמֵשׁ עֶשְׂרֵה שָׁנָה:

18 The other events of *Amatzya*'s reign are recorded in the Annals of the Kings of *Yehuda*.

יח וְיֶתֶר דִּבְרֵי אֲמַצְיָהוּ הֲלֹא־הֵם כְּתוּבִים עַל־סֵפֶר דִּבְרֵי הַיָּמִים לְמַלְכֵי יְהוּדָה:

19 A conspiracy was formed against him in *Yerushalayim* and he fled to *Lachish*; but they sent men after him to *Lachish*, and they killed him there.

יט וַיִּקְשְׁרוּ עָלָיו קֶשֶׁר בִּירוּשָׁלִַם וַיָּנָס לָכִישָׁה וַיִּשְׁלְחוּ אַחֲרָיו לָכִישָׁה וַיְמִתֻהוּ שָׁם:

20 They brought back his body on horses, and he was buried with his fathers in *Yerushalayim*, in the City of *David*.

כ וַיִּשְׂאוּ אֹתוֹ עַל־הַסּוּסִים וַיִּקָּבֵר בִּירוּשָׁלִַם עִם־אֲבֹתָיו בְּעִיר דָּוִד:

21 Then all the people of *Yehuda* took *Azarya*, who was sixteen years old, and proclaimed him king to succeed his father *Amatzya*.

כא וַיִּקְחוּ כָּל־עַם יְהוּדָה אֶת־עֲזַרְיָה וְהוּא בֶּן־שֵׁשׁ עֶשְׂרֵה שָׁנָה וַיַּמְלִכוּ אֹתוֹ תַּחַת אָבִיו אֲמַצְיָהוּ:

22 It was he who rebuilt *Eilat* and restored it to *Yehuda*, after King [*Amatzya*] slept with his fathers.

כב הוּא בָּנָה אֶת־אֵילַת וַיְשִׁבֶהָ לִיהוּדָה אַחֲרֵי שְׁכַב־הַמֶּלֶךְ עִם־אֲבֹתָיו:

23 In the fifteenth year of King *Amatzya* son of *Yoash* of *Yehuda*, King *Yerovam* son of *Yoash* of *Yisrael* became king in *Shomron* – for forty-one years.

כג בִּשְׁנַת חֲמֵשׁ־עֶשְׂרֵה שָׁנָה לַאֲמַצְיָהוּ בֶן־יוֹאָשׁ מֶלֶךְ יְהוּדָה מָלַךְ יָרָבְעָם בֶּן־יוֹאָשׁ מֶלֶךְ־יִשְׂרָאֵל בְּשֹׁמְרוֹן אַרְבָּעִים וְאַחַת שָׁנָה:

24 He did what was displeasing to *Hashem*; he did not depart from all the sins that *Yerovam* son of Nebat had caused *Yisrael* to commit.

כד וַיַּעַשׂ הָרַע בְּעֵינֵי יְהֹוָה לֹא סָר מִכָּל־חַטֹּאות יָרָבְעָם בֶּן־נְבָט אֲשֶׁר הֶחֱטִיא אֶת־יִשְׂרָאֵל:

Melachim II/II Kings
Chapter 15

מלכים ב
פרק טו

25 It was he who restored the territory of *Yisrael* from Lebo-hamath to the sea of the Arabah, in accordance with the promise that *Hashem*, the God of *Yisrael*, had made through His servant, the *Navi Yona* son of *Amitai* from Gath-hepher.

כה הוּא הֵשִׁיב אֶת־גְּבוּל יִשְׂרָאֵל מִלְּבוֹא חֲמָת עַד־יָם הָעֲרָבָה כִּדְבַר יְהֹוָה אֱלֹהֵי יִשְׂרָאֵל אֲשֶׁר דִּבֶּר בְּיַד־עַבְדּוֹ יוֹנָה בֶן־אֲמִתַּי הַנָּבִיא אֲשֶׁר מִגַּת הַחֵפֶר:

HU hay-SHEEV et g'-VUL yis-ra-AYL mi-l'-VO kha-MAT ad YAM ha-a-ra-VAH kid-VAR a-do-NAI e-lo-HAY yis-ra-AYL a-SHER di-BER b'-yad av-DO yo-NAH ven a-mi-TAI ha-na-VEE a-SHER mi-GAT ha-KHAY-fer

26 For *Hashem* saw the very bitter plight of *Yisrael*, with neither bond nor free left, and with none to help *Yisrael*.

כו כִּי־רָאָה יְהֹוָה אֶת־עֳנִי יִשְׂרָאֵל מֹרֶה מְאֹד וְאֶפֶס עָצוּר וְאֶפֶס עָזוּב וְאֵין עֹזֵר לְיִשְׂרָאֵל:

27 And *Hashem* resolved not to blot out the name of *Yisrael* from under heaven; and he delivered them through *Yerovam* son of *Yoash*.

כז וְלֹא־דִבֶּר יְהֹוָה לִמְחוֹת אֶת־שֵׁם יִשְׂרָאֵל מִתַּחַת הַשָּׁמָיִם וַיּוֹשִׁיעֵם בְּיַד יָרָבְעָם בֶּן־יוֹאָשׁ:

28 The other events of *Yerovam*'s reign, and all his actions and exploits, how he fought and recovered Damascus and Hamath for *Yehuda* in *Yisrael*, are recorded in the Annals of the Kings of *Yisrael*.

כח וְיֶתֶר דִּבְרֵי יָרָבְעָם וְכָל־אֲשֶׁר עָשָׂה וּגְבוּרָתוֹ אֲשֶׁר־נִלְחָם וַאֲשֶׁר הֵשִׁיב אֶת־דַּמֶּשֶׂק וְאֶת־חֲמָת לִיהוּדָה בְּיִשְׂרָאֵל הֲלֹא־הֵם כְּתוּבִים עַל־סֵפֶר דִּבְרֵי הַיָּמִים לְמַלְכֵי יִשְׂרָאֵל:

29 *Yerovam* slept with his fathers, the kings of *Yisrael*, and his son *Zecharya* succeeded him as king.

כט וַיִּשְׁכַּב יָרָבְעָם עִם־אֲבֹתָיו עִם מַלְכֵי יִשְׂרָאֵל וַיִּמְלֹךְ זְכַרְיָה בְנוֹ תַּחְתָּיו:

15

1 In the twenty-seventh year of King *Yerovam* of *Yisrael*, *Azarya* son of King *Amatzya* of *Yehuda* became king.

טו א בִּשְׁנַת עֶשְׂרִים וָשֶׁבַע שָׁנָה לְיָרָבְעָם מֶלֶךְ יִשְׂרָאֵל מָלַךְ עֲזַרְיָה בֶן־אֲמַצְיָה מֶלֶךְ יְהוּדָה:

2 He was sixteen years old when he became king, and he reigned fifty-two years in *Yerushalayim*; his mother's name was Jecoliah of *Yerushalayim*.

ב בֶּן־שֵׁשׁ עֶשְׂרֵה שָׁנָה הָיָה בְמָלְכוֹ וַחֲמִשִּׁים וּשְׁתַּיִם שָׁנָה מָלַךְ בִּירוּשָׁלָ͏ִם וְשֵׁם אִמּוֹ יְכָלְיָהוּ מִירוּשָׁלָ͏ִם:

3 He did what was pleasing to *Hashem*, just as his father *Amatzya* had done.

ג וַיַּעַשׂ הַיָּשָׁר בְּעֵינֵי יְהֹוָה כְּכֹל אֲשֶׁר־עָשָׂה אֲמַצְיָהוּ אָבִיו:

4 However, the shrines were not removed; the people continued to sacrifice and make offerings at the shrines.

ד רַק הַבָּמוֹת לֹא־סָרוּ עוֹד הָעָם מְזַבְּחִים וּמְקַטְּרִים בַּבָּמוֹת:

14:25 Had made through His servant, the *Navi Yona* son of *Amittai* The prophet *Yona* mentioned here is the same prophet we learn about in *Sefer Yona*, who runs away to avoid traveling to the large Assyrian city Nineveh to deliver *Hashem*'s word. *Rashi* suggests that *Yona* is afraid that Nineveh will obey God's word, in contrast to the People of Israel who had not done so. This would look bad for the Children of Israel and give God even more reason to punish them. Therefore, *Yona* decides the only way to protect the Israelites is to flee by boat from the Land of Israel, so that he would no longer have to deliver the prophecy to Nineveh. But he ultimately learns that one can flee neither *Hashem* nor His commandments, and returns to fulfill his mission.

Rashi
(1040–1105)

Melachim II / II Kings
Chapter 15

5 *Hashem* struck the king with a plague, and he was a leper until the day of his death; he lived in isolated quarters, while *Yotam*, the king's son, was in charge of the palace and governed the people of the land.

6 The other events of *Azarya*'s reign, and all his actions, are recorded in the Annals of the Kings of *Yehuda*.

7 *Azarya* slept with his fathers, and he was buried with his fathers in the City of *David*; his son *Yotam* succeeded him as king.

8 In the thirty-eighth year of King *Azarya* of *Yehuda*, *Zecharya* son of *Yerovam* became king over *Yisrael* in *Shomron* – for six months.

9 He did what was displeasing to *Hashem*, as his fathers had done; he did not depart from the sins which *Yerovam* son of Nebat had caused *Yisrael* to commit.

10 *Shalum* son of Jabesh conspired against him and struck him down before the people and killed him, and succeeded him as king.

11 The other events of *Zecharya*'s reign are recorded in the Annals of the Kings of *Yisrael*.

12 This was in accord with the word that *Hashem* had spoken to *Yehu*: "Four generations of your descendants shall occupy the throne of *Yisrael*." And so it came about.

13 *Shalum* son of Jabesh became king in the thirty-ninth year of King *Uzziyahu* of *Yehuda*, and he reigned in *Shomron* one month.

14 Then *Menachem* son of Gadi set out from *Tirtza* and came to *Shomron*; he attacked *Shalum* son of Jabesh in *Shomron* and killed him, and he succeeded him as king.

va-YA-al m'-na-KHAYM ben ga-DEE mi-tir-TZAH va-ya-VO sho-m'-RON va-YAKH et sha-LUM ben ya-VAYSH b'-sho-m'-RON vai-mee-TAY-hu va-yim-LOKH takh-TAV

ה וַיְנַגַּע יְהֹוָה אֶת־הַמֶּלֶךְ וַיְהִי מְצֹרָע עַד־יוֹם מֹתוֹ וַיֵּשֶׁב בְּבֵית הַחָפְשִׁית וְיוֹתָם בֶּן־הַמֶּלֶךְ עַל־הַבַּיִת שֹׁפֵט אֶת־עַם הָאָרֶץ:

ו וְיֶתֶר דִּבְרֵי עֲזַרְיָהוּ וְכָל־אֲשֶׁר עָשָׂה הֲלֹא־הֵם כְּתוּבִים עַל־סֵפֶר דִּבְרֵי הַיָּמִים לְמַלְכֵי יְהוּדָה:

ז וַיִּשְׁכַּב עֲזַרְיָה עִם־אֲבֹתָיו וַיִּקְבְּרוּ אֹתוֹ עִם־אֲבֹתָיו בְּעִיר דָּוִד וַיִּמְלֹךְ יוֹתָם בְּנוֹ תַּחְתָּיו:

ח בִּשְׁנַת שְׁלֹשִׁים וּשְׁמֹנֶה שָׁנָה לַעֲזַרְיָהוּ מֶלֶךְ יְהוּדָה מָלַךְ זְכַרְיָהוּ בֶן־יָרָבְעָם עַל־יִשְׂרָאֵל בְּשֹׁמְרוֹן שִׁשָּׁה חֳדָשִׁים:

ט וַיַּעַשׂ הָרַע בְּעֵינֵי יְהֹוָה כַּאֲשֶׁר עָשׂוּ אֲבֹתָיו לֹא סָר מֵחַטֹּאות יָרָבְעָם בֶּן־נְבָט אֲשֶׁר הֶחֱטִיא אֶת־יִשְׂרָאֵל:

י וַיִּקְשֹׁר עָלָיו שַׁלֻּם בֶּן־יָבֵשׁ וַיַּכֵּהוּ קָבָל־עָם וַיְמִיתֵהוּ וַיִּמְלֹךְ תַּחְתָּיו:

יא וְיֶתֶר דִּבְרֵי זְכַרְיָה הִנָּם כְּתוּבִים עַל־סֵפֶר דִּבְרֵי הַיָּמִים לְמַלְכֵי יִשְׂרָאֵל:

יב הוּא דְבַר־יְהֹוָה אֲשֶׁר דִּבֶּר אֶל־יֵהוּא לֵאמֹר בְּנֵי רְבִיעִים יֵשְׁבוּ לְךָ עַל־כִּסֵּא יִשְׂרָאֵל וַיְהִי־כֵן:

יג שַׁלּוּם בֶּן־יָבֵישׁ מָלַךְ בִּשְׁנַת שְׁלֹשִׁים וָתֵשַׁע שָׁנָה לְעֻזִּיָּה מֶלֶךְ יְהוּדָה וַיִּמְלֹךְ יֶרַח־יָמִים בְּשֹׁמְרוֹן:

יד וַיַּעַל מְנַחֵם בֶּן־גָּדִי מִתִּרְצָה וַיָּבֹא שֹׁמְרוֹן וַיַּךְ אֶת־שַׁלּוּם בֶּן־יָבֵישׁ בְּשֹׁמְרוֹן וַיְמִיתֵהוּ וַיִּמְלֹךְ תַּחְתָּיו:

15:14 Then *Menachem* son of Gadi The name Menacham, meaning 'he brings comfort,' is a very special one in Jewish tradition. There is an opinion in the Talmud (*Sanhedrin* 98b) that the *Mashiach* will have this name, as his role will be to bring comfort to the Children of Israel and the entire world. The potential for greatness in the name *Menachem* makes it all the more tragic that this *Menachem* is so evil.

Melachim II / II Kings
Chapter 15

15 The other events of *Shalum*'s reign, and the conspiracy that he formed, are recorded in the Annals of the Kings of *Yisrael*.

16 At that time, [marching] from *Tirtza*, *Menachem* subdued Tiphsah and all who were in it, and its territory; and because it did not surrender, he massacred [its people] and ripped open all its pregnant women.

17 In the thirty-ninth year of King *Azarya* of *Yehuda*, *Menachem* son of *Gadi* became king over *Yisrael* in *Shomron* – for ten years.

18 He did what was displeasing to *Hashem*; throughout his days he did not depart from the sins which *Yerovam* son of Nebat had caused *Yisrael* to commit.

19 King Pul of Assyria invaded the land, and *Menachem* gave Pul a thousand *kikarim* of silver that he might support him and strengthen his hold on the kingdom.

20 *Menachem* exacted the money from *Yisrael*: every man of means had to pay fifty *shekalim* of silver for the king of Assyria. The king of Assyria withdrew and did not remain in the land.

21 The other events of *Menachem*'s reign, and all his actions, are recorded in the Annals of the Kings of *Yisrael*.

22 *Menachem* slept with his fathers, and his son *Pekachya* succeeded him as king.

23 In the fiftieth year of King *Azarya* of *Yehuda*, *Pekachya* son of *Menachem* became king over *Yisrael* in *Shomron* – for two years.

24 He did what was displeasing to *Hashem*; he did not depart from the sins which *Yerovam* son of Nebat had caused *Yisrael* to commit.

25 His aide, *Pekach* son of Remaliah, conspired against him and struck him down in the royal palace in *Shomron*; with him were fifty Giladites, with men from Argob and Arieh; and he killed him and succeeded him as king.

26 The other events of *Pekachya*'s reign, and all his actions, are recorded in the Annals of the Kings of *Yisrael*.

מלכים ב
פרק טו

טו וְיֶ֨תֶר דִּבְרֵ֤י שַׁלּוּם֙ וְקִשְׁר֣וֹ אֲשֶׁ֣ר קָשָׁ֔ר הִנָּ֣ם כְּתֻבִ֗ים עַל־סֵ֛פֶר דִּבְרֵ֥י הַיָּמִ֖ים לְמַלְכֵ֥י יִשְׂרָאֵֽל׃

טז אָ֣ז יַכֶּֽה־מְ֠נַחֵם אֶת־תִּפְסַ֨ח וְאֶת־כָּל־אֲשֶׁר־בָּ֤הּ וְאֶת־גְּבוּלֶ֙יהָ֙ מִתִּרְצָ֔ה כִּ֛י לֹ֥א פָתַ֖ח וַיַּ֑ךְ אֵ֛ת כָּל־הֶהָרוֹתֶ֖יהָ בִּקֵּֽעַ׃

יז בִּשְׁנַ֨ת שְׁלֹשִׁ֤ים וָתֵ֙שַׁע֙ שָׁנָ֔ה לַעֲזַרְיָ֖ה מֶ֣לֶךְ יְהוּדָ֑ה מָ֠לַךְ מְנַחֵ֨ם בֶּן־גָּדִ֧י עַל־יִשְׂרָאֵ֛ל עֶ֥שֶׂר שָׁנִ֖ים בְּשֹׁמְרֽוֹן׃

יח וַיַּ֥עַשׂ הָרַ֖ע בְּעֵינֵ֣י יְהוָ֑ה לֹ֣א סָ֗ר מֵעַ֞ל חַטֹּ֛אות יָרָבְעָ֥ם בֶּן־נְבָ֖ט אֲשֶׁר־הֶחֱטִ֣יא אֶת־יִשְׂרָאֵ֖ל כָּל־יָמָֽיו׃

יט בָּ֣א פ֤וּל מֶֽלֶךְ־אַשּׁוּר֙ עַל־הָאָ֔רֶץ וַיִּתֵּ֤ן מְנַחֵם֙ לְפ֔וּל אֶ֖לֶף כִּכַּר־כָּ֑סֶף לִהְי֤וֹת יָדָיו֙ אִתּ֔וֹ לְהַחֲזִ֥יק הַמַּמְלָכָ֖ה בְּיָדֽוֹ׃

כ וַיֹּצֵא֩ מְנַחֵ֨ם אֶת־הַכֶּ֜סֶף עַל־יִשְׂרָאֵ֗ל עַ֚ל כָּל־גִּבּוֹרֵ֣י הַחַ֔יִל לָתֵת֙ לְמֶ֣לֶךְ אַשּׁ֔וּר חֲמִשִּׁ֧ים שְׁקָלִ֛ים כֶּ֖סֶף לְאִ֣ישׁ אֶחָ֑ד וַיָּ֙שָׁב֙ מֶ֣לֶךְ אַשּׁ֔וּר וְלֹא־עָ֥מַד שָׁ֖ם בָּאָֽרֶץ׃

כא וְיֶ֛תֶר דִּבְרֵ֥י מְנַחֵ֖ם וְכָל־אֲשֶׁ֣ר עָשָׂ֑ה הֲלוֹא־הֵ֣ם כְּתוּבִ֗ים עַל־סֵ֛פֶר דִּבְרֵ֥י הַיָּמִ֖ים לְמַלְכֵ֥י יִשְׂרָאֵֽל׃

כב וַיִּשְׁכַּ֤ב מְנַחֵם֙ עִם־אֲבֹתָ֔יו וַיִּמְלֹ֛ךְ פְּקַחְיָ֥ה בְנ֖וֹ תַּחְתָּֽיו׃

כג בִּשְׁנַ֨ת חֲמִשִּׁ֤ים שָׁנָה֙ לַעֲזַרְיָ֣ה מֶ֣לֶךְ יְהוּדָ֑ה מָ֠לַךְ פְּקַחְיָ֨ה בֶן־מְנַחֵ֧ם עַל־יִשְׂרָאֵ֛ל בְּשֹׁמְר֖וֹן שְׁנָתָֽיִם׃

כד וַיַּ֥עַשׂ הָרַ֖ע בְּעֵינֵ֣י יְהוָ֑ה לֹ֣א סָ֗ר מֵֽחַטֹּאות֙ יָרָבְעָ֣ם בֶּן־נְבָ֔ט אֲשֶׁ֥ר הֶחֱטִ֖יא אֶת־יִשְׂרָאֵֽל׃

כה וַיִּקְשֹׁ֣ר עָלָיו֩ פֶּ֨קַח בֶּן־רְמַלְיָ֜הוּ שָׁלִישׁ֗וֹ וַיַּכֵּ֨הוּ בְשֹׁמְר֜וֹן בְּאַרְמ֤וֹן בֵּית־מֶ֙לֶךְ֙ [הַמֶּ֔לֶךְ] אֶת־אַרְגֹּ֖ב וְאֶת־הָאַרְיֵ֑ה וְעִמּ֛וֹ חֲמִשִּׁ֥ים אִ֖ישׁ מִבְּנֵ֣י גִלְעָדִ֑ים וַיְמִתֵ֖הוּ וַיִּמְלֹ֥ךְ תַּחְתָּֽיו׃

כו וְיֶ֛תֶר דִּבְרֵ֥י פְקַחְיָ֖ה וְכָל־אֲשֶׁ֣ר עָשָׂ֑ה הִנָּ֣ם כְּתוּבִ֗ים עַל־סֵ֛פֶר דִּבְרֵ֥י הַיָּמִ֖ים לְמַלְכֵ֥י יִשְׂרָאֵֽל׃

Melachim II / II Kings
Chapter 16

27 In the fifty-second year of King *Azarya* of *Yehuda*, *Pekach* son of Remaliah became king over *Yisrael* and *Shomron* – for twenty years.

28 He did what was displeasing to *Hashem*; he did not depart from the sins which *Yerovam* son of Nebat had caused *Yisrael* to commit.

29 In the days of King *Pekach* of *Yisrael*, King Tiglath-Pileser of Assyria came and captured Ijon, Abel-bethmaacah, Janoah, Kedesh, Hazor – *Gilad*, Galilee, the entire region of *Naftali*; and he deported the inhabitants to Assyria.

30 *Hoshea* son of *Eila* conspired against *Pekach* son of Remaliah, attacked him, and killed him. He succeeded him as king in the twentieth year of *Yotam* son of *Uzziyahu*.

31 The other events of *Pekach*'s reign, and all his actions, are recorded in the Annals of the Kings of *Yisrael*.

32 In the second year of King *Pekach* son of Remaliah of *Yisrael*, *Yotam* son of King *Uzziyahu* of *Yehuda* became king.

33 He was twenty-five years old when he became king, and he reigned sixteen years in *Yerushalayim*; his mother's name was Jerusha daughter of *Tzadok*.

34 He did what was pleasing to *Hashem*, just as his father *Uzziyahu* had done.

35 However, the shrines were not removed; the people continued to sacrifice and make offerings at the shrines. It was he who built the Upper Gate of the House of *Hashem*.

36 The other events of *Yotam*'s reign, and all his actions, are recorded in the Annals of the Kings of *Yehuda*.

37 In those days, *Hashem* began to incite King Rezin of Aram and *Pekach* son of Remaliah against *Yehuda*.

38 *Yotam* slept with his fathers, and he was buried with his fathers in the city of his ancestor *David*; his son *Achaz* succeeded him as king.

16 1 In the seventeenth year of *Pekach* son of Remaliah, *Achaz* son of King *Yotam* of *Yehuda* became king.

Melachim II / II Kings
Chapter 16

מלכים ב
פרק טז

2 Achaz was twenty years old when he became king, and he reigned sixteen years in *Yerushalayim*. He did not do what was pleasing to *Hashem* his God, as his ancestor *David* had done,

ב בֶּן־עֶשְׂרִים שָׁנָה אָחָז בְּמָלְכוֹ וְשֵׁשׁ־עֶשְׂרֵה שָׁנָה מָלַךְ בִּירוּשָׁלָם וְלֹא־עָשָׂה הַיָּשָׁר בְּעֵינֵי יְהֹוָה אֱלֹהָיו כְּדָוִד אָבִיו:

3 but followed the ways of the kings of *Yisrael*. He even consigned his son to the fire, in the abhorrent fashion of the nations which *Hashem* had dispossessed before the Israelites.

ג וַיֵּלֶךְ בְּדֶרֶךְ מַלְכֵי יִשְׂרָאֵל וְגַם אֶת־בְּנוֹ הֶעֱבִיר בָּאֵשׁ כְּתֹעֲבוֹת הַגּוֹיִם אֲשֶׁר הוֹרִישׁ יְהֹוָה אֹתָם מִפְּנֵי בְּנֵי יִשְׂרָאֵל:

4 He sacrificed and made offerings at the shrines, on the hills, and under every leafy tree.

ד וַיְזַבֵּחַ וַיְקַטֵּר בַּבָּמוֹת וְעַל־הַגְּבָעוֹת וְתַחַת כָּל־עֵץ רַעֲנָן:

5 Then King Rezin of Aram and King *Pekach* son of Remaliah of *Yisrael* advanced on *Yerushalayim* for battle. They besieged *Achaz*, but could not overcome [him].

ה אָז יַעֲלֶה רְצִין מֶלֶךְ־אֲרָם וּפֶקַח בֶּן־רְמַלְיָהוּ מֶלֶךְ־יִשְׂרָאֵל יְרוּשָׁלַם לַמִּלְחָמָה וַיָּצֻרוּ עַל־אָחָז וְלֹא יָכְלוּ לְהִלָּחֵם:

6 At that time King Rezin of Aram recovered *Eilat* for Aram; he drove out the Judites from *Eilat*, and Edomites came to *Eilat* and settled there, as is still the case.

ו בָּעֵת הַהִיא הֵשִׁיב רְצִין מֶלֶךְ־אֲרָם אֶת־אֵילַת לַאֲרָם וַיְנַשֵּׁל אֶת־הַיְהוּדִים מֵאֵילוֹת וַאֲרַמִּים [וַאֲדוֹמִים] בָּאוּ אֵילַת וַיֵּשְׁבוּ שָׁם עַד הַיּוֹם הַזֶּה:

ba-AYT ha-HEE hay-SHEEV r'-TZEEN me-lekh a-RAM et ay-LAT la-a-RAM vai-na-SHAYL et ha-y'-hu-DEEM may-ay-LOT va-a-do-MEEM BA-u ay-LAT va-yay-sh'-VU SHAM AD ha-YOM ha-ZEH

7 *Achaz* sent messengers to King Tiglath-Pileser of Assyria to say, "I am your servant and your son; come and deliver me from the hands of the king of Aram and from the hands of the king of *Yisrael*, who are attacking me."

ז וַיִּשְׁלַח אָחָז מַלְאָכִים אֶל־תִּגְלַת פְּלֶסֶר מֶלֶךְ־אַשּׁוּר לֵאמֹר עַבְדְּךָ וּבִנְךָ אָנִי עֲלֵה וְהוֹשִׁעֵנִי מִכַּף מֶלֶךְ־אֲרָם וּמִכַּף מֶלֶךְ יִשְׂרָאֵל הַקּוֹמִים עָלָי:

8 *Achaz* took the gold and silver that were on hand in the House of *Hashem* and in the treasuries of the royal palace and sent them as a gift to the king of Assyria.

ח וַיִּקַּח אָחָז אֶת־הַכֶּסֶף וְאֶת־הַזָּהָב הַנִּמְצָא בֵּית יְהֹוָה וּבְאֹצְרוֹת בֵּית הַמֶּלֶךְ וַיִּשְׁלַח לְמֶלֶךְ־אַשּׁוּר שֹׁחַד:

9 The king of Assyria responded to his request; the king of Assyria marched against Damascus and captured it. He deported its inhabitants to Kir and put Rezin to death.

ט וַיִּשְׁמַע אֵלָיו מֶלֶךְ אַשּׁוּר וַיַּעַל מֶלֶךְ אַשּׁוּר אֶל־דַּמֶּשֶׂק וַיִּתְפְּשֶׂהָ וַיַּגְלֶהָ קִירָה וְאֶת־רְצִין הֵמִית:

16:6 And Edomites came to *Eilat* The city of *Eilat*, located on the shores of the Red Sea, had been conquered by King *David* and built as an important port by King *Shlomo*. Here it is reconquered by Edom, the descendants of Esau. But foreign rule over any part of *Eretz Yisrael* is only temporary. During Israel's War of Independence in 1949, the Israel Defense Forces were able to reclaim *Eilat*. Today, this city serves as an important port city, naval base, and a popular destination for tourists. Just as in the time of King *Shlomo*, it plays a critical role in Israel's economy and defense.

Aeriel view of Eilat

Melachim II / II Kings
Chapter 16

10 When King *Achaz* went to Damascus to greet King Tiglath-Pileser of Assyria, he saw the altar in Damascus. King *Achaz* sent the *Kohen Uriya* a sketch of the altar and a detailed plan of its construction.

11 The *Kohen Uriya* did just as King *Achaz* had instructed him from Damascus; the *Kohen Uriya* built the altar before King *Achaz* returned from Damascus.

12 When the king returned from Damascus, and when the king saw the altar, the king drew near the altar, ascended it,

13 and offered his burnt offering and meal offering; he poured his libation, and he dashed the blood of his offering of well-being against the altar.

14 As for the bronze *Mizbayach* which had been before *Hashem*, he moved it from its place in front of the Temple, between the [new] altar and the House of *Hashem*, and placed it on the north side of the [new] altar.

15 And King *Achaz* commanded the *Kohen Uriya*: "On the great altar you shall offer the morning burnt offering and the evening meal offering and the king's burnt offering and his meal offering, with the burnt offerings of all the people of the land, their meal offerings and their libations. And against it you shall dash the blood of all the burnt offerings and all the blood of the sacrifices. And I will decide about the bronze *Mizbayach*."

16 *Uriya* did just as King *Achaz* commanded.

17 King *Achaz* cut off the insets – the laver stands – and removed the lavers from them. He also removed the tank from the bronze oxen that supported it and set it on a stone pavement

18 on account of the king of Assyria. He also extended to the House of *Hashem* the *Shabbat* passage that had been built in the palace and the king's outer entrance.

19 The other events of *Achaz*'s reign, and his actions, are recorded in the Annals of the Kings of *Yehuda*.

מלכים ב
פרק טז

י וַיֵּלֶךְ הַמֶּלֶךְ אָחָז לִקְרַאת תִּגְלַת פִּלְאֶסֶר מֶלֶךְ־אַשּׁוּר דּוּמֶּשֶׂק וַיַּרְא אֶת־הַמִּזְבֵּחַ אֲשֶׁר בְּדַמָּשֶׂק וַיִּשְׁלַח הַמֶּלֶךְ אָחָז אֶל־אוּרִיָּה הַכֹּהֵן אֶת־דְּמוּת הַמִּזְבֵּחַ וְאֶת־תַּבְנִיתוֹ לְכָל־מַעֲשֵׂהוּ:

יא וַיִּבֶן אוּרִיָּה הַכֹּהֵן אֶת־הַמִּזְבֵּחַ כְּכֹל אֲשֶׁר־שָׁלַח הַמֶּלֶךְ אָחָז מִדַּמֶּשֶׂק כֵּן עָשָׂה אוּרִיָּה הַכֹּהֵן עַד־בּוֹא הַמֶּלֶךְ־אָחָז מִדַּמָּשֶׂק:

יב וַיָּבֹא הַמֶּלֶךְ מִדַּמֶּשֶׂק וַיַּרְא הַמֶּלֶךְ אֶת־הַמִּזְבֵּחַ וַיִּקְרַב הַמֶּלֶךְ עַל־הַמִּזְבֵּחַ וַיַּעַל עָלָיו:

יג וַיַּקְטֵר אֶת־עֹלָתוֹ וְאֶת־מִנְחָתוֹ וַיַּסֵּךְ אֶת־נִסְכּוֹ וַיִּזְרֹק אֶת־דַּם־הַשְּׁלָמִים אֲשֶׁר־לוֹ עַל־הַמִּזְבֵּחַ:

יד וְאֵת הַמִּזְבַּח הַנְּחֹשֶׁת אֲשֶׁר לִפְנֵי יְהוָה וַיַּקְרֵב מֵאֵת פְּנֵי הַבַּיִת מִבֵּין הַמִּזְבֵּחַ וּמִבֵּין בֵּית יְהוָה וַיִּתֵּן אֹתוֹ עַל־יֶרֶךְ הַמִּזְבֵּחַ צָפוֹנָה:

טו ויצוהו [וַיְצַוֶּה] הַמֶּלֶךְ־אָחָז אֶת־אוּרִיָּה הַכֹּהֵן לֵאמֹר עַל הַמִּזְבֵּחַ הַגָּדוֹל הַקְטֵר אֶת־עֹלַת־הַבֹּקֶר וְאֶת־מִנְחַת הָעֶרֶב וְאֶת־עֹלַת הַמֶּלֶךְ וְאֶת־מִנְחָתוֹ וְאֵת עֹלַת כָּל־עַם הָאָרֶץ וּמִנְחָתָם וְנִסְכֵּיהֶם וְכָל־דַּם עֹלָה וְכָל־דַּם־זֶבַח עָלָיו תִּזְרֹק וּמִזְבַּח הַנְּחֹשֶׁת יִהְיֶה־לִּי לְבַקֵּר:

טז וַיַּעַשׂ אוּרִיָּה הַכֹּהֵן כְּכֹל אֲשֶׁר־צִוָּה הַמֶּלֶךְ אָחָז:

יז וַיְקַצֵּץ הַמֶּלֶךְ אָחָז אֶת־הַמִּסְגְּרוֹת הַמְּכֹנוֹת וַיָּסַר מֵעֲלֵיהֶם ואת־[אֶת־]הַכִּיֹּר וְאֶת־הַיָּם הוֹרִד מֵעַל הַבָּקָר הַנְּחֹשֶׁת אֲשֶׁר תַּחְתֶּיהָ וַיִּתֵּן אֹתוֹ עַל מַרְצֶפֶת אֲבָנִים:

יח וְאֶת־מיסך [מוּסַךְ] הַשַּׁבָּת אֲשֶׁר־בָּנוּ בַבַּיִת וְאֶת־מְבוֹא הַמֶּלֶךְ הַחִיצוֹנָה הֵסֵב בֵּית יְהוָה מִפְּנֵי מֶלֶךְ אַשּׁוּר:

יט וְיֶתֶר דִּבְרֵי אָחָז אֲשֶׁר עָשָׂה הֲלֹא־הֵם כְּתוּבִים עַל־סֵפֶר דִּבְרֵי הַיָּמִים לְמַלְכֵי יְהוּדָה:

Melachim II / II Kings
Chapter 17

20 *Achaz* slept with his fathers and was buried with his fathers in the City of *David*; his son *Chizkiyahu* succeeded him as king.

17 1 In the twelfth year of King *Achaz* of *Yehuda*, *Hoshea* son of *Eila* became king over *Yisrael* in *Shomron* – for nine years.

2 He did what was displeasing to *Hashem*, though not as much as the kings of *Yisrael* who preceded him.

3 King Shalmaneser marched against him, and *Hoshea* became his vassal and paid him tribute.

4 But the king of Assyria caught *Hoshea* in an act of treachery: he had sent envoys to King So of Egypt, and he had not paid the tribute to the king of Assyria, as in previous years. And the king of Assyria arrested him and put him in prison.

5 Then the king of Assyria marched against the whole land; he came to *Shomron* and besieged it for three years.

6 In the ninth year of *Hoshea*, the king of Assyria captured *Shomron*. He deported the Israelites to Assyria and settled them in Halah, at the [River] Habor, at the River Gozan, and in the towns of Media.

7 This happened because the Israelites sinned against *Hashem* their God, who had freed them from the land of Egypt, from the hand of Pharaoh king of Egypt. They worshiped other gods

8 and followed the customs of the nations which *Hashem* had dispossessed before the Israelites and the customs which the kings of *Yisrael* had practiced.

9 The Israelites committed against *Hashem* their God acts which were not right: They built for themselves shrines in all their settlements, from watchtowers to fortified cities;

10 they set up pillars and sacred posts for themselves on every lofty hill and under every leafy tree;

11 and they offered sacrifices there, at all the shrines, like the nations whom *Hashem* had driven into exile before them. They committed wicked acts to vex *Hashem*,

---

מלכים ב
פרק יז

כ וַיִּשְׁכַּב אָחָז עִם־אֲבֹתָיו וַיִּקָּבֵר עִם־אֲבֹתָיו בְּעִיר דָּוִד וַיִּמְלֹךְ חִזְקִיָּהוּ בְנוֹ תַּחְתָּיו׃

יז א בִּשְׁנַת שְׁתֵּים עֶשְׂרֵה לְאָחָז מֶלֶךְ יְהוּדָה מָלַךְ הוֹשֵׁעַ בֶּן־אֵלָה בְשֹׁמְרוֹן עַל־יִשְׂרָאֵל תֵּשַׁע שָׁנִים׃

ב וַיַּעַשׂ הָרַע בְּעֵינֵי יְהֹוָה רַק לֹא כְּמַלְכֵי יִשְׂרָאֵל אֲשֶׁר הָיוּ לְפָנָיו׃

ג עָלָיו עָלָה שַׁלְמַנְאֶסֶר מֶלֶךְ אַשּׁוּר וַיְהִי־לוֹ הוֹשֵׁעַ עֶבֶד וַיָּשֶׁב לוֹ מִנְחָה׃

ד וַיִּמְצָא מֶלֶךְ־אַשּׁוּר בְּהוֹשֵׁעַ קֶשֶׁר אֲשֶׁר שָׁלַח מַלְאָכִים אֶל־סוֹא מֶלֶךְ־מִצְרַיִם וְלֹא־הֶעֱלָה מִנְחָה לְמֶלֶךְ אַשּׁוּר כְּשָׁנָה בְשָׁנָה וַיַּעַצְרֵהוּ מֶלֶךְ אַשּׁוּר וַיַּאַסְרֵהוּ בֵּית כֶּלֶא׃

ה וַיַּעַל מֶלֶךְ־אַשּׁוּר בְּכָל־הָאָרֶץ וַיַּעַל שֹׁמְרוֹן וַיָּצַר עָלֶיהָ שָׁלֹשׁ שָׁנִים׃

ו בִּשְׁנַת הַתְּשִׁיעִית לְהוֹשֵׁעַ לָכַד מֶלֶךְ־אַשּׁוּר אֶת־שֹׁמְרוֹן וַיֶּגֶל אֶת־יִשְׂרָאֵל אַשּׁוּרָה וַיֹּשֶׁב אֹתָם בַּחְלַח וּבְחָבוֹר נְהַר גּוֹזָן וְעָרֵי מָדָי׃

ז וַיְהִי כִּי־חָטְאוּ בְנֵי־יִשְׂרָאֵל לַיהֹוָה אֱלֹהֵיהֶם הַמַּעֲלֶה אֹתָם מֵאֶרֶץ מִצְרַיִם מִתַּחַת יַד פַּרְעֹה מֶלֶךְ־מִצְרָיִם וַיִּירְאוּ אֱלֹהִים אֲחֵרִים׃

ח וַיֵּלְכוּ בְּחֻקּוֹת הַגּוֹיִם אֲשֶׁר הוֹרִישׁ יְהֹוָה מִפְּנֵי בְּנֵי יִשְׂרָאֵל וּמַלְכֵי יִשְׂרָאֵל אֲשֶׁר עָשׂוּ׃

ט וַיְחַפְּאוּ בְנֵי־יִשְׂרָאֵל דְּבָרִים אֲשֶׁר לֹא־כֵן עַל־יְהֹוָה אֱלֹהֵיהֶם וַיִּבְנוּ לָהֶם בָּמוֹת בְּכָל־עָרֵיהֶם מִמִּגְדַּל נוֹצְרִים עַד־עִיר מִבְצָר׃

י וַיַּצִּבוּ לָהֶם מַצֵּבוֹת וַאֲשֵׁרִים עַל כָּל־גִּבְעָה גְבֹהָה וְתַחַת כָּל־עֵץ רַעֲנָן׃

יא וַיְקַטְּרוּ־שָׁם בְּכָל־בָּמוֹת כַּגּוֹיִם אֲשֶׁר־הֶגְלָה יְהֹוָה מִפְּנֵיהֶם וַיַּעֲשׂוּ דְּבָרִים רָעִים לְהַכְעִיס אֶת־יְהֹוָה׃

Melachim II / II Kings
Chapter 17

12 and they worshiped fetishes concerning which *Hashem* had said to them, "You must not do this thing."

13 *Hashem* warned *Yisrael* and *Yehuda* by every *Navi* [and] every seer, saying: "Turn back from your wicked ways, and observe My commandments and My laws, according to all the Teaching that I commanded your fathers and that I transmitted to you through My servants the *Neviim*."

14 But they did not obey; they stiffened their necks, like their fathers who did not have faith in *Hashem* their God;

15 they spurned His laws and the covenant that He had made with their fathers, and the warnings He had given them. They went after delusion and were deluded; [they imitated] the nations that were about them, which *Hashem* had forbidden them to emulate.

16 They rejected all the commandments of *Hashem* their God; they made molten idols for themselves – two calves – and they made a sacred post and they bowed down to all the host of heaven, and they worshiped Baal.

17 They consigned their sons and daughters to the fire; they practiced augury and divination, and gave themselves over to what was displeasing to *Hashem* and vexed Him.

18 *Hashem* was incensed at *Yisrael* and He banished them from His presence; none was left but the tribe of *Yehuda* alone.

19 Nor did *Yehuda* keep the commandments of *Hashem* their God; they followed the customs that *Yisrael* had practiced.

20 So *Hashem* spurned all the offspring of *Yisrael*, and He afflicted them and delivered them into the hands of plunderers, and finally He cast them out from His presence.

21 For *Yisrael* broke away from the House of *David*, and they made *Yerovam* son of Nebat king. *Yerovam* caused *Yisrael* to stray from *Hashem* and to commit great sin,

22 and the Israelites persisted in all the sins which *Yerovam* had committed; they did not depart from them.

מלכים ב
פרק יז

יב וַיַּעַבְדוּ הַגִּלֻּלִים אֲשֶׁר אָמַר יְהֹוָה לָהֶם לֹא תַעֲשׂוּ אֶת־הַדָּבָר הַזֶּה:

יג וַיָּעַד יְהֹוָה בְּיִשְׂרָאֵל וּבִיהוּדָה בְּיַד כָּל־נְבִיאוֹ [נְבִיאֵי] כָל־חֹזֶה לֵאמֹר שֻׁבוּ מִדַּרְכֵיכֶם הָרָעִים וְשִׁמְרוּ מִצְוֹתַי חֻקּוֹתַי כְּכָל־הַתּוֹרָה אֲשֶׁר צִוִּיתִי אֶת־אֲבוֹתֵיכֶם וַאֲשֶׁר שָׁלַחְתִּי אֲלֵיכֶם בְּיַד עֲבָדַי הַנְּבִיאִים:

יד וְלֹא שָׁמֵעוּ וַיַּקְשׁוּ אֶת־עָרְפָּם כְּעֹרֶף אֲבוֹתָם אֲשֶׁר לֹא הֶאֱמִינוּ בַּיהֹוָה אֱלֹהֵיהֶם:

טו וַיִּמְאֲסוּ אֶת־חֻקָּיו וְאֶת־בְּרִיתוֹ אֲשֶׁר כָּרַת אֶת־אֲבוֹתָם וְאֵת עֵדְוֹתָיו אֲשֶׁר הֵעִיד בָּם וַיֵּלְכוּ אַחֲרֵי הַהֶבֶל וַיֶּהְבָּלוּ וְאַחֲרֵי הַגּוֹיִם אֲשֶׁר סְבִיבֹתָם אֲשֶׁר צִוָּה יְהֹוָה אֹתָם לְבִלְתִּי עֲשׂוֹת כָּהֶם:

טז וַיַּעַזְבוּ אֶת־כָּל־מִצְוֹת יְהֹוָה אֱלֹהֵיהֶם וַיַּעֲשׂוּ לָהֶם מַסֵּכָה שְׁנֵים [שְׁנֵי] עֲגָלִים וַיַּעֲשׂוּ אֲשֵׁירָה וַיִּשְׁתַּחֲווּ לְכָל־צְבָא הַשָּׁמַיִם וַיַּעַבְדוּ אֶת־הַבָּעַל:

יז וַיַּעֲבִירוּ אֶת־בְּנֵיהֶם וְאֶת־בְּנוֹתֵיהֶם בָּאֵשׁ וַיִּקְסְמוּ קְסָמִים וַיְנַחֵשׁוּ וַיִּתְמַכְּרוּ לַעֲשׂוֹת הָרַע בְּעֵינֵי יְהֹוָה לְהַכְעִיסוֹ:

יח וַיִּתְאַנַּף יְהֹוָה מְאֹד בְּיִשְׂרָאֵל וַיְסִרֵם מֵעַל פָּנָיו לֹא נִשְׁאַר רַק שֵׁבֶט יְהוּדָה לְבַדּוֹ:

יט גַּם־יְהוּדָה לֹא שָׁמַר אֶת־מִצְוֹת יְהֹוָה אֱלֹהֵיהֶם וַיֵּלְכוּ בְּחֻקּוֹת יִשְׂרָאֵל אֲשֶׁר עָשׂוּ:

כ וַיִּמְאַס יְהֹוָה בְּכָל־זֶרַע יִשְׂרָאֵל וַיְעַנֵּם וַיִּתְּנֵם בְּיַד־שֹׁסִים עַד אֲשֶׁר הִשְׁלִיכָם מִפָּנָיו:

כא כִּי־קָרַע יִשְׂרָאֵל מֵעַל בֵּית דָּוִד וַיַּמְלִיכוּ אֶת־יָרָבְעָם בֶּן־נְבָט וַיַּדֵּא [וַיַּדַּח] יָרָבְעָם אֶת־יִשְׂרָאֵל מֵאַחֲרֵי יְהֹוָה וְהֶחֱטִיאָם חֲטָאָה גְדוֹלָה:

כב וַיֵּלְכוּ בְּנֵי יִשְׂרָאֵל בְּכָל־חַטֹּאות יָרָבְעָם אֲשֶׁר עָשָׂה לֹא־סָרוּ מִמֶּנָּה:

Melachim II / II Kings
Chapter 17

23 In the end, *Hashem* removed *Yisrael* from His presence, as He had warned them through all His servants the *Neviim*. So the Israelites were deported from their land to Assyria, as is still the case.

AD a-sher hay-SEER a-do-NAI et yis-ra-AYL may-AL pa-NAV ka-a-SHER di-BER b'-YAD kol a-va-DAV ha-n'-vee-EEM va-YI-gel yis-ra-AYL may-AL ad-ma-TO a-SHU-rah AD ha-YOM ha-ZEH

24 The king of Assyria brought [people] from Babylon, Cuthah, Avva, Hamath, and Sephar-vaim, and he settled them in the towns of *Shomron* in place of the Israelites; they took possession of *Shomron* and dwelt in its towns.

25 When they first settled there, they did not worship *Hashem*; so *Hashem* sent lions against them which killed some of them.

26 They said to the king of Assyria: "The nations which you deported and resettled in the towns of *Shomron* do not know the rules of the God of the land; therefore He has let lions loose against them which are killing them – for they do not know the rules of the God of the land."

27 The king of Assyria gave an order: "Send there one of the *Kohanim* whom you have deported; let him go and dwell there, and let him teach them the practices of the God of the land."

28 So one of the *Kohanim* whom they had exiled from *Shomron* came and settled in *Beit El*; he taught them how to worship *Hashem*.

29 However, each nation continued to make its own gods and to set them up in the cult places which had been made by the people of *Shomron*; each nation [set them up] in the towns in which it lived.

17:23 So the Israelites were deported from their land to Assyria The northern kingdom of Israel is destroyed, and its ten tribes are exiled to Assyria. Unlike the exiles of *Yehuda*, who return from Babylonia after seventy years, the ten tribes remain in exile. These tribes are known as "the lost tribes of Israel," as they disappeared due to persecution and assimilation. However, according to Jewish tradition (*Sanhedrin* 110b), these tribes will return to Israel in the era of the *Mashiach*. The *Bnei Menashe*, 'children of *Menashe*,' are members of a tribe from northeast India who claim descent from the lost tribe of *Menashe*. For thousands of years they have continued the Jewish practices of their ancestors, including observing the *Shabbat* and Jewish dietary laws, celebrating the festivals and following the laws of family purity. And, throughout that time they dreamed of returning to the Land of Israel. In recent years, thousands of *Bnei Menashe* have been brought back home to the loving embrace of their brothers and sisters in Israel. The return of the lost tribes to *Eretz Yisrael* is additional proof that we are living through the dawn of the era of redemption.

Members of the Bnei Menashe arrive at Ben Gurion airport

Melachim II / II Kings
Chapter 17

30 The Babylonians made Succoth-benoth, and the men of Cuth made Nergal, and the men of Hamath made Ashima,

31 and the Avvites made Nibhaz and Tartak; and the Sepharvites burned their children [as offerings] to Adrammelech and Anamelech, the gods of Sepharvaim.

32 They worshiped *Hashem*, but they also appointed from their own ranks *Kohanim* of the shrines, who officiated for them in the cult places.

33 They worshiped *Hashem*, while serving their own gods according to the practices of the nations from which they had been deported.

34 To this day, they follow their former practices. They do not worship *Hashem* [properly]. They do not follow the laws and practices, the Teaching and Instruction that *Hashem* enjoined upon the descendants of *Yaakov* – who was given the name *Yisrael*

35 with whom He made a covenant and whom He commanded: "You shall worship no other gods; you shall not bow down to them nor serve them nor sacrifice to them.

36 You must worship only *Hashem* your God, who brought you out of the land of Egypt with great might and with an outstretched arm: to Him alone shall you bow down and to Him alone shall you sacrifice.

37 You shall observe faithfully, all your days, the laws and the practices; the Teaching and Instruction that I wrote down for you; do not worship other gods.

38 Do not forget the covenant that I made with you; do not worship other gods.

39 Worship only *Hashem* your God, and He will save you from the hands of all your enemies."

40 But they did not obey; they continued their former practices.

41 Those nations worshiped *Hashem*, but they also served their idols. To this day their children and their children's children do as their ancestors did.

מלכים ב
פרק יז

ל וְאַנְשֵׁי בָבֶל עָשׂוּ אֶת־סֻכּוֹת בְּנוֹת וְאַנְשֵׁי־כוּת עָשׂוּ אֶת־נֵרְגַל וְאַנְשֵׁי חֲמָת עָשׂוּ אֶת־אֲשִׁימָא:

לא וְהָעַוִּים עָשׂוּ נִבְחַז וְאֶת־תַּרְתָּק וְהַסְפַרְוִים שֹׂרְפִים אֶת־בְּנֵיהֶם בָּאֵשׁ לְאַדְרַמֶּלֶךְ וַעֲנַמֶּלֶךְ אלה [אֱלֹהֵי] ספרים [סְפַרְוָיִם]:

לב וַיִּהְיוּ יְרֵאִים אֶת־יְהֹוָה וַיַּעֲשׂוּ לָהֶם מִקְצוֹתָם כֹּהֲנֵי בָמוֹת וַיִּהְיוּ עֹשִׂים לָהֶם בְּבֵית הַבָּמוֹת:

לג אֶת־יְהֹוָה הָיוּ יְרֵאִים וְאֶת־אֱלֹהֵיהֶם הָיוּ עֹבְדִים כְּמִשְׁפַּט הַגּוֹיִם אֲשֶׁר־הִגְלוּ אֹתָם מִשָּׁם:

לד עַד הַיּוֹם הַזֶּה הֵם עֹשִׂים כַּמִּשְׁפָּטִים הָרִאשֹׁנִים אֵינָם יְרֵאִים אֶת־יְהֹוָה וְאֵינָם עֹשִׂים כְּחֻקֹּתָם וּכְמִשְׁפָּטָם וְכַתּוֹרָה וְכַמִּצְוָה אֲשֶׁר צִוָּה יְהֹוָה אֶת־בְּנֵי יַעֲקֹב אֲשֶׁר־שָׂם שְׁמוֹ יִשְׂרָאֵל:

לה וַיִּכְרֹת יְהֹוָה אִתָּם בְּרִית וַיְצַוֵּם לֵאמֹר לֹא תִירְאוּ אֱלֹהִים אֲחֵרִים וְלֹא־תִשְׁתַּחֲווּ לָהֶם וְלֹא תַעַבְדוּם וְלֹא תִזְבְּחוּ לָהֶם:

לו כִּי אִם־אֶת־יְהֹוָה אֲשֶׁר הֶעֱלָה אֶתְכֶם מֵאֶרֶץ מִצְרַיִם בְּכֹחַ גָּדוֹל וּבִזְרוֹעַ נְטוּיָה אֹתוֹ תִירָאוּ וְלוֹ תִשְׁתַּחֲווּ וְלוֹ תִזְבָּחוּ:

לז וְאֶת־הַחֻקִּים וְאֶת־הַמִּשְׁפָּטִים וְהַתּוֹרָה וְהַמִּצְוָה אֲשֶׁר כָּתַב לָכֶם תִּשְׁמְרוּן לַעֲשׂוֹת כָּל־הַיָּמִים וְלֹא תִירְאוּ אֱלֹהִים אֲחֵרִים:

לח וְהַבְּרִית אֲשֶׁר־כָּרַתִּי אִתְּכֶם לֹא תִשְׁכָּחוּ וְלֹא תִירְאוּ אֱלֹהִים אֲחֵרִים:

לט כִּי אִם־אֶת־יְהֹוָה אֱלֹהֵיכֶם תִּירָאוּ וְהוּא יַצִּיל אֶתְכֶם מִיַּד כָּל־אֹיְבֵיכֶם:

מ וְלֹא שָׁמֵעוּ כִּי אִם־כְּמִשְׁפָּטָם הָרִאשׁוֹן הֵם עֹשִׂים:

מא וַיִּהְיוּ הַגּוֹיִם הָאֵלֶּה יְרֵאִים אֶת־יְהֹוָה וְאֶת־פְּסִילֵיהֶם הָיוּ עֹבְדִים גַּם־בְּנֵיהֶם וּבְנֵי בְנֵיהֶם כַּאֲשֶׁר עָשׂוּ אֲבֹתָם הֵם עֹשִׂים עַד הַיּוֹם הַזֶּה:

Melachim II / II Kings
Chapter 18

18 ¹ In the third year of King *Hoshea* son of *Eila* of *Yisrael*, *Chizkiyahu* son of King *Achaz* of *Yehuda* became king.

² He was twenty-five years old when he became king, and he reigned in *Yerushalayim* twenty-nine years; his mother's name was Abi daughter of *Zecharya*.

³ He did what was pleasing to *Hashem*, just as his father *David* had done.

⁴ He abolished the shrines and smashed the pillars and cut down the sacred post. He also broke into pieces the bronze serpent that *Moshe* had made, for until that time the Israelites had been offering sacrifices to it; it was called Nehushtan.

⁵ He trusted only in *Hashem* the God of *Yisrael*; there was none like him among all the kings of *Yehuda* after him, nor among those before him.

⁶ He clung to *Hashem*; he did not turn away from following Him, but kept the commandments that *Hashem* had given to *Moshe*.

⁷ And *Hashem* was always with him; he was successful wherever he turned. He rebelled against the king of Assyria and would not serve him.

v'-ha-YAH a-do-NAI i-MO b'-KHOL a-sher yay-TZAY yas-KEEL va-yim-ROD b'-ME-lekh a-SHUR v'-LO a-va-DO

⁸ He overran Philistia as far as *Azza* and its border areas, from watchtower to fortified town.

⁹ In the fourth year of King *Chizkiyahu*, which was the seventh year of King *Hoshea* son of *Eila* of *Yisrael*, King Shalmaneser of Assyria marched against *Shomron* and besieged it,

¹⁰ and he captured it at the end of three years. In the sixth year of *Chizkiyahu*, which was the ninth year of King *Hoshea* of *Yisrael*, *Shomron* was captured;

מלכים ב
פרק יח

יח א וַיְהִי בִּשְׁנַת שָׁלֹשׁ לְהוֹשֵׁעַ בֶּן־אֵלָה מֶלֶךְ יִשְׂרָאֵל מָלַךְ חִזְקִיָּה בֶן־אָחָז מֶלֶךְ יְהוּדָה:

ב בֶּן־עֶשְׂרִים וְחָמֵשׁ שָׁנָה הָיָה בְמָלְכוֹ וְעֶשְׂרִים וָתֵשַׁע שָׁנָה מָלַךְ בִּירוּשָׁלָ͏ִם וְשֵׁם אִמּוֹ אֲבִי בַּת־זְכַרְיָה:

ג וַיַּעַשׂ הַיָּשָׁר בְּעֵינֵי יְהוָה כְּכֹל אֲשֶׁר־עָשָׂה דָּוִד אָבִיו:

ד הוּא הֵסִיר אֶת־הַבָּמוֹת וְשִׁבַּר אֶת־הַמַּצֵּבֹת וְכָרַת אֶת־הָאֲשֵׁרָה וְכִתַּת נְחַשׁ הַנְּחֹשֶׁת אֲשֶׁר־עָשָׂה מֹשֶׁה כִּי עַד־הַיָּמִים הָהֵמָּה הָיוּ בְנֵי־יִשְׂרָאֵל מְקַטְּרִים לוֹ וַיִּקְרָא־לוֹ נְחֻשְׁתָּן:

ה בַּיהוָה אֱלֹהֵי־יִשְׂרָאֵל בָּטָח וְאַחֲרָיו לֹא־הָיָה כָמֹהוּ בְּכֹל מַלְכֵי יְהוּדָה וַאֲשֶׁר הָיוּ לְפָנָיו:

ו וַיִּדְבַּק בַּיהוָה לֹא־סָר מֵאַחֲרָיו וַיִּשְׁמֹר מִצְוֺתָיו אֲשֶׁר־צִוָּה יְהוָה אֶת־מֹשֶׁה:

ז וְהָיָה יְהוָה עִמּוֹ בְּכֹל אֲשֶׁר־יֵצֵא יַשְׂכִּיל וַיִּמְרֹד בְּמֶלֶךְ־אַשּׁוּר וְלֹא עֲבָדוֹ:

ח הוּא־הִכָּה אֶת־פְּלִשְׁתִּים עַד־עַזָּה וְאֶת־גְּבוּלֶיהָ מִמִּגְדַּל נוֹצְרִים עַד־עִיר מִבְצָר:

ט וַיְהִי בַּשָּׁנָה הָרְבִיעִית לַמֶּלֶךְ חִזְקִיָּהוּ הִיא הַשָּׁנָה הַשְּׁבִיעִית לְהוֹשֵׁעַ בֶּן־אֵלָה מֶלֶךְ יִשְׂרָאֵל עָלָה שַׁלְמַנְאֶסֶר מֶלֶךְ־אַשּׁוּר עַל־שֹׁמְרוֹן וַיָּצַר עָלֶיהָ:

י וַיִּלְכְּדֻהָ מִקְצֵה שָׁלֹשׁ שָׁנִים בִּשְׁנַת־שֵׁשׁ לְחִזְקִיָּה הִיא שְׁנַת־תֵּשַׁע לְהוֹשֵׁעַ מֶלֶךְ יִשְׂרָאֵל נִלְכְּדָה שֹׁמְרוֹן:

18:7 He rebelled against the king of Assyria King *Chizkiyahu* rebels against Sennacherib, king of Assyria, by refusing to pay tribute. He wants the kingdom of *Yehuda* to be completely independent. *Ramban* writes that since the Land of Israel is the inheritance of the People of Israel, the Jewish people are required not only to reside in *Eretz Yisrael*, but also to be the sovereign rulers of the land, with their own government, military and political structure. The State of Israel is thus a miraculous fulfillment of the centuries-old words of *Ramban*.

Ramban (1194–1270)

Melachim II / II Kings
Chapter 18

11 and the king of Assyria deported the Israelites to Assyria. He settled them in Halah, along the Habor [and] the River Gozan, and in the towns of Media.

12 [This happened] because they did not obey *Hashem* their God; they transgressed His covenant – all that *Moshe* the servant of *Hashem* had commanded. They did not obey and they did not fulfill it.

13 In the fourteenth year of King *Chizkiyahu*, King Sennacherib of Assyria marched against all the fortified towns of *Yehuda* and seized them.

14 King *Chizkiyahu* sent this message to the king of Assyria at Lachish: "I have done wrong; withdraw from me; and I shall bear whatever you impose on me." So the king of Assyria imposed upon King *Chizkiyahu* of *Yehuda* a payment of three hundred *kikarim* of silver and thirty *kikarim* of gold.

15 *Chizkiyahu* gave him all the silver that was on hand in the House of *Hashem* and in the treasuries of the palace.

16 At that time *Chizkiyahu* cut down the doors and the doorposts of the Temple of *Hashem*, which King *Chizkiyahu* had overlaid [with gold], and gave them to the king of Assyria.

17 But the king of Assyria sent the Tartan, the Rabsaris, and the Rabshakeh from Lachish with a large force to King *Chizkiyahu* in *Yerushalayim*. They marched up to *Yerushalayim*; and when they arrived, they took up a position near the conduit of the Upper Pool, by the road of the Fuller's Field.

18 They summoned the king; and Eliakim son of *Chilkiyahu*, who was in charge of the palace, Shebna the scribe, and Joah son of *Asaf* the recorder went out to them.

19 The Rabshakeh said to them, "You tell *Chizkiyahu*: Thus said the Great King, the King of Assyria: What makes you so confident?

20 You must think that mere talk is counsel and valor for war! Look, on whom are you relying, that you have rebelled against me?

21 You rely, of all things, on Egypt, that splintered reed of a staff, which enters and punctures the palm of anyone who leans on it! That's what Pharaoh king of Egypt is like to all who rely on him.

מלכים ב
פרק יח

יא וַיֶּגֶל מֶלֶךְ־אַשּׁוּר אֶת־יִשְׂרָאֵל אַשּׁוּרָה וַיַּנְחֵם בַּחְלַח וּבְחָבוֹר נְהַר גּוֹזָן וְעָרֵי מָדָי:

יב עַל אֲשֶׁר לֹא־שָׁמְעוּ בְּקוֹל יְהוָה אֱלֹהֵיהֶם וַיַּעַבְרוּ אֶת־בְּרִיתוֹ אֵת כָּל־אֲשֶׁר צִוָּה מֹשֶׁה עֶבֶד יְהוָה וְלֹא שָׁמְעוּ וְלֹא עָשׂוּ:

יג וּבְאַרְבַּע עֶשְׂרֵה שָׁנָה לַמֶּלֶךְ חִזְקִיָּה עָלָה סַנְחֵרִיב מֶלֶךְ־אַשּׁוּר עַל כָּל־עָרֵי יְהוּדָה הַבְּצֻרוֹת וַיִּתְפְּשֵׂם:

יד וַיִּשְׁלַח חִזְקִיָּה מֶלֶךְ־יְהוּדָה אֶל־מֶלֶךְ־אַשּׁוּר לָכִישָׁה לֵאמֹר חָטָאתִי שׁוּב מֵעָלַי אֵת אֲשֶׁר־תִּתֵּן עָלַי אֶשָּׂא וַיָּשֶׂם מֶלֶךְ־אַשּׁוּר עַל־חִזְקִיָּה מֶלֶךְ־יְהוּדָה שְׁלֹשׁ מֵאוֹת כִּכַּר־כֶּסֶף וּשְׁלֹשִׁים כִּכַּר זָהָב:

טו וַיִּתֵּן חִזְקִיָּה אֶת־כָּל־הַכֶּסֶף הַנִּמְצָא בֵית־יְהוָה וּבְאֹצְרוֹת בֵּית הַמֶּלֶךְ:

טז בָּעֵת הַהִיא קִצַּץ חִזְקִיָּה אֶת־דַּלְתוֹת הֵיכַל יְהוָה וְאֶת־הָאֹמְנוֹת אֲשֶׁר צִפָּה חִזְקִיָּה מֶלֶךְ יְהוּדָה וַיִּתְּנֵם לְמֶלֶךְ אַשּׁוּר:

יז וַיִּשְׁלַח מֶלֶךְ־אַשּׁוּר אֶת־תַּרְתָּן וְאֶת־רַב־סָרִיס וְאֶת־רַב־שָׁקֵה מִן־לָכִישׁ אֶל־הַמֶּלֶךְ חִזְקִיָּהוּ בְּחֵיל כָּבֵד יְרוּשָׁלָ͏ִם וַיַּעֲלוּ וַיָּבֹאוּ יְרוּשָׁלַ͏ִם וַיַּעֲלוּ וַיָּבֹאוּ וַיַּעַמְדוּ בִּתְעָלַת הַבְּרֵכָה הָעֶלְיוֹנָה אֲשֶׁר בִּמְסִלַּת שְׂדֵה כוֹבֵס:

יח וַיִּקְרְאוּ אֶל־הַמֶּלֶךְ וַיֵּצֵא אֲלֵהֶם אֶלְיָקִים בֶּן־חִלְקִיָּהוּ אֲשֶׁר עַל־הַבַּיִת וְשֶׁבְנָה הַסֹּפֵר וְיוֹאָח בֶּן־אָסָף הַמַּזְכִּיר:

יט וַיֹּאמֶר אֲלֵהֶם רַב־שָׁקֵה אִמְרוּ־נָא אֶל־חִזְקִיָּהוּ כֹּה־אָמַר הַמֶּלֶךְ הַגָּדוֹל מֶלֶךְ אַשּׁוּר מָה הַבִּטָּחוֹן הַזֶּה אֲשֶׁר בָּטָחְתָּ:

כ אָמַרְתָּ אַךְ־דְּבַר־שְׂפָתַיִם עֵצָה וּגְבוּרָה לַמִּלְחָמָה עַתָּה עַל־מִי בָטַחְתָּ כִּי מָרַדְתָּ בִּי:

כא עַתָּה הִנֵּה בָטַחְתָּ לְּךָ עַל־מִשְׁעֶנֶת הַקָּנֶה הָרָצוּץ הַזֶּה עַל־מִצְרַיִם אֲשֶׁר יִסָּמֵךְ אִישׁ עָלָיו וּבָא בְכַפּוֹ וּנְקָבָהּ כֵּן פַּרְעֹה מֶלֶךְ־מִצְרַיִם לְכָל־הַבֹּטְחִים עָלָיו:

Melachim II / II Kings
Chapter 18

22 And if you tell me that you are relying on *Hashem* your God, He is the very one whose shrines and altars *Chizkiyahu* did away with, telling *Yehuda* and *Yerushalayim*, 'You must worship only at this *Mizbayach* in *Yerushalayim*.'

23 Come now, make this wager with my master, the king of Assyria: I'll give you two thousand horses if you can produce riders to mount them.

24 So how could you refuse anything even to the deputy of one of my master's lesser servants, relying on Egypt for chariots and horsemen?

25 And do you think I have marched against this land to destroy it without *Hashem*? *Hashem* Himself told me: Go up against that land and destroy it."

26 Eliakim son of *Chilkiyahu*, Shebna, and Joah replied to the Rabshakeh, "Please, speak to your servants in Aramaic, for we understand it; do not speak to us in Judean in the hearing of the people on the wall."

27 But the Rabshakeh answered them, "Was it to your master and to you that my master sent me to speak those words? It was precisely to the men who are sitting on the wall – who will have to eat their dung and drink their urine with you."

28 And the Rabshakeh stood and called out in a loud voice in Judean: "Hear the words of the Great King, the King of Assyria.

29 Thus said the king: Don't let *Chizkiyahu* deceive you, for he will not be able to deliver you from my hands.

30 Don't let *Chizkiyahu* make you rely on *Hashem*, saying: *Hashem* will surely save us: this city will not fall into the hands of the king of Assyria.

31 Don't listen to *Chizkiyahu*. For thus said the king of Assyria: Make your peace with me and come out to me, so that you may all eat from your vines and your fig trees and drink water from your cisterns,

32 until I come and take you away to a land like your own, a land of grain [fields] and vineyards, of bread and wine, of olive oil and honey, so that you may live and not die. Don't listen to *Chizkiyahu*, who misleads you by saying, '*Hashem* will save us.'

מלכים ב
פרק יח

כב וְכִי־תֹאמְרוּן אֵלַי אֶל־יְהֹוָה אֱלֹהֵינוּ בָּטָחְנוּ הֲלוֹא־הוּא אֲשֶׁר הֵסִיר חִזְקִיָּהוּ אֶת־בָּמֹתָיו וְאֶת־מִזְבְּחֹתָיו וַיֹּאמֶר לִיהוּדָה וְלִירוּשָׁלַם לִפְנֵי הַמִּזְבֵּחַ הַזֶּה תִּשְׁתַּחֲווּ בִּירוּשָׁלָם:

כג וְעַתָּה הִתְעָרֶב נָא אֶת־אֲדֹנִי אֶת־מֶלֶךְ אַשּׁוּר וְאֶתְּנָה לְךָ אַלְפַּיִם סוּסִים אִם־תּוּכַל לָתֶת לְךָ רֹכְבִים עֲלֵיהֶם:

כד וְאֵיךְ תָּשִׁיב אֵת פְּנֵי פַחַת אַחַד עַבְדֵי אֲדֹנִי הַקְּטַנִּים וַתִּבְטַח לְךָ עַל־מִצְרַיִם לְרֶכֶב וּלְפָרָשִׁים:

כה עַתָּה הֲמִבַּלְעֲדֵי יְהֹוָה עָלִיתִי עַל־הַמָּקוֹם הַזֶּה לְהַשְׁחִתוֹ יְהֹוָה אָמַר אֵלַי עֲלֵה עַל־הָאָרֶץ הַזֹּאת וְהַשְׁחִיתָהּ:

כו וַיֹּאמֶר אֶלְיָקִים בֶּן־חִלְקִיָּהוּ וְשֶׁבְנָה וְיוֹאָח אֶל־רַב־שָׁקֵה דַּבֶּר־נָא אֶל־עֲבָדֶיךָ אֲרָמִית כִּי שֹׁמְעִים אֲנָחְנוּ וְאַל־תְּדַבֵּר עִמָּנוּ יְהוּדִית בְּאָזְנֵי הָעָם אֲשֶׁר עַל־הַחֹמָה:

כז וַיֹּאמֶר אֲלֵיהֶם רַב־שָׁקֵה הַעַל אֲדֹנֶיךָ וְאֵלֶיךָ שְׁלָחַנִי אֲדֹנִי לְדַבֵּר אֶת־הַדְּבָרִים הָאֵלֶּה הֲלֹא עַל־הָאֲנָשִׁים הַיֹּשְׁבִים עַל־הַחֹמָה לֶאֱכֹל אֶת־חֲרֵיהֶם [צוֹאָתָם] וְלִשְׁתּוֹת אֶת־שֵׁינֵיהֶם [מֵימֵי רַגְלֵיהֶם] עִמָּכֶם:

כח וַיַּעֲמֹד רַב־שָׁקֵה וַיִּקְרָא בְקוֹל־גָּדוֹל יְהוּדִית וַיְדַבֵּר וַיֹּאמֶר שִׁמְעוּ דְּבַר־הַמֶּלֶךְ הַגָּדוֹל מֶלֶךְ אַשּׁוּר:

כט כֹּה אָמַר הַמֶּלֶךְ אַל־יַשִּׁיא לָכֶם חִזְקִיָּהוּ כִּי־לֹא יוּכַל לְהַצִּיל אֶתְכֶם מִיָּדוֹ:

ל וְאַל־יַבְטַח אֶתְכֶם חִזְקִיָּהוּ אֶל־יְהֹוָה לֵאמֹר הַצֵּל יַצִּילֵנוּ יְהֹוָה וְלֹא תִנָּתֵן אֶת־הָעִיר הַזֹּאת בְּיַד מֶלֶךְ אַשּׁוּר:

לא אַל־תִּשְׁמְעוּ אֶל־חִזְקִיָּהוּ כִּי כֹה אָמַר מֶלֶךְ אַשּׁוּר עֲשׂוּ־אִתִּי בְרָכָה וּצְאוּ אֵלַי וְאִכְלוּ אִישׁ־גַּפְנוֹ וְאִישׁ תְּאֵנָתוֹ וּשְׁתוּ אִישׁ מֵי־בוֹרוֹ:

לב עַד־בֹּאִי וְלָקַחְתִּי אֶתְכֶם אֶל־אֶרֶץ כְּאַרְצְכֶם אֶרֶץ דָּגָן וְתִירוֹשׁ אֶרֶץ לֶחֶם וּכְרָמִים אֶרֶץ זֵית יִצְהָר וּדְבַשׁ וִחְיוּ וְלֹא תָמֻתוּ וְאַל־תִּשְׁמְעוּ אֶל־חִזְקִיָּהוּ כִּי־יַסִּית אֶתְכֶם לֵאמֹר יְהֹוָה יַצִּילֵנוּ:

Melachim II / II Kings
Chapter 19

33 Did any of the gods of other nations save his land from the king of Assyria?

34 Where were the gods of Hamath and Arpad? Where were the gods of Sepharvaim, Hena, and Ivvah? [And] did they save *Shomron* from me?

35 Which among all the gods of [those] countries saved their countries from me, that *Hashem* should save *Yerushalayim* from me?"

36 But the people were silent and did not say a word in reply; for the king's order was: "Do not answer him."

37 And so Eliakim son of *Chilkiyahu*, who was in charge of the palace, Shebna the scribe, and Joah son of *Asaf* the recorder came to *Chizkiyahu* with their clothes rent, and they reported to him what the Rabshakeh had said.

19 1 When King *Chizkiyahu* heard this, he rent his clothes, and covered himself with sackcloth, and went into the House of *Hashem*.

2 He also sent Eliakim, who was in charge of the palace, Shebna the scribe, and the senior *Kohanim*, covered with sackcloth, to the *Navi Yeshayahu* son of *Amotz*.

3 They said to him, "Thus said *Chizkiyahu*: This day is a day of distress, of chastisement, and of disgrace. The babes have reached the birthstool, but the strength to give birth is lacking.

4 Perhaps *Hashem* your God will take note of all the words of the Rabshakeh, whom his master the king of Assyria has sent to blaspheme the living *Hashem*, and will mete out judgment for the words that *Hashem* your God has heard – if you will offer up prayer for the surviving remnant."

5 When King *Chizkiyahu*'s ministers came to *Yeshayahu*,

6 *Yeshayahu* said to them, "Tell your master as follows: Thus said *Hashem*: Do not be frightened by the words of blasphemy against Me that you have heard from the minions of the king of Assyria.

7 I will delude him; he will hear a rumor and return to his land, and I will make him fall by the sword in his land."

מלכים ב
פרק יט

לג הַהַצֵּל הִצִּילוּ אֱלֹהֵי הַגּוֹיִם אִישׁ אֶת־אַרְצוֹ מִיַּד מֶלֶךְ אַשּׁוּר:

לד אַיֵּה אֱלֹהֵי חֲמָת וְאַרְפָּד אַיֵּה אֱלֹהֵי סְפַרְוַיִם הֵנַע וְעִוָּה כִּי־הִצִּילוּ אֶת־שֹׁמְרוֹן מִיָּדִי:

לה מִי בְּכָל־אֱלֹהֵי הָאֲרָצוֹת אֲשֶׁר־הִצִּילוּ אֶת־אַרְצָם מִיָּדִי כִּי־יַצִּיל יְהוָה אֶת־יְרוּשָׁלַיִם מִיָּדִי:

לו וְהֶחֱרִישׁוּ הָעָם וְלֹא־עָנוּ אֹתוֹ דָּבָר כִּי־מִצְוַת הַמֶּלֶךְ הִיא לֵאמֹר לֹא תַעֲנֻהוּ:

לז וַיָּבֹא אֶלְיָקִים בֶּן־חִלְקִיָּה אֲשֶׁר־עַל־הַבַּיִת וְשֶׁבְנָא הַסֹּפֵר וְיוֹאָח בֶּן־אָסָף הַמַּזְכִּיר אֶל־חִזְקִיָּהוּ קְרוּעֵי בְגָדִים וַיַּגִּדוּ לוֹ דִּבְרֵי רַב־שָׁקֵה:

יט א וַיְהִי כִּשְׁמֹעַ הַמֶּלֶךְ חִזְקִיָּהוּ וַיִּקְרַע אֶת־בְּגָדָיו וַיִּתְכַּס בַּשָּׂק וַיָּבֹא בֵּית יְהוָה:

ב וַיִּשְׁלַח אֶת־אֶלְיָקִים אֲשֶׁר־עַל־הַבַּיִת וְשֶׁבְנָא הַסֹּפֵר וְאֵת זִקְנֵי הַכֹּהֲנִים מִתְכַּסִּים בַּשַּׂקִּים אֶל־יְשַׁעְיָהוּ הַנָּבִיא בֶּן־אָמוֹץ:

ג וַיֹּאמְרוּ אֵלָיו כֹּה אָמַר חִזְקִיָּהוּ יוֹם־צָרָה וְתוֹכֵחָה וּנְאָצָה הַיּוֹם הַזֶּה כִּי בָאוּ בָנִים עַד־מַשְׁבֵּר וְכֹחַ אַיִן לְלֵדָה:

ד אוּלַי יִשְׁמַע יְהוָה אֱלֹהֶיךָ אֵת כָּל־דִּבְרֵי רַב־שָׁקֵה אֲשֶׁר שְׁלָחוֹ מֶלֶךְ־אַשּׁוּר אֲדֹנָיו לְחָרֵף אֱלֹהִים חַי וְהוֹכִיחַ בַּדְּבָרִים אֲשֶׁר שָׁמַע יְהוָה אֱלֹהֶיךָ וְנָשָׂאתָ תְפִלָּה בְּעַד הַשְּׁאֵרִית הַנִּמְצָאָה:

ה וַיָּבֹאוּ עַבְדֵי הַמֶּלֶךְ חִזְקִיָּהוּ אֶל־יְשַׁעְיָהוּ:

ו וַיֹּאמֶר לָהֶם יְשַׁעְיָהוּ כֹּה תֹאמְרוּן אֶל־אֲדֹנֵיכֶם כֹּה אָמַר יְהוָה אַל־תִּירָא מִפְּנֵי הַדְּבָרִים אֲשֶׁר שָׁמַעְתָּ אֲשֶׁר גִּדְּפוּ נַעֲרֵי מֶלֶךְ־אַשּׁוּר אֹתִי:

ז הִנְנִי נֹתֵן בּוֹ רוּחַ וְשָׁמַע שְׁמוּעָה וְשָׁב לְאַרְצוֹ וְהִפַּלְתִּיו בַּחֶרֶב בְּאַרְצוֹ:

Melachim II / II Kings
Chapter 19

מלכים ב
פרק יט

8 The Rabshakeh, meanwhile, heard that [the king] had left Lachish; he turned back and found the king of Assyria attacking Libnah.

ח וַיָּשָׁב רַב־שָׁקֵה וַיִּמְצָא אֶת־מֶלֶךְ אַשּׁוּר נִלְחָם עַל־לִבְנָה כִּי שָׁמַע כִּי נָסַע מִלָּכִישׁ:

9 But [the king of Assyria] learned that King Tirhakah of Nubia had come out to fight him; so he again sent messengers to *Chizkiyahu*, saying,

ט וַיִּשְׁמַע אֶל־תִּרְהָקָה מֶלֶךְ־כּוּשׁ לֵאמֹר הִנֵּה יָצָא לְהִלָּחֵם אִתָּךְ וַיָּשָׁב וַיִּשְׁלַח מַלְאָכִים אֶל־חִזְקִיָּהוּ לֵאמֹר:

10 "Tell this to King *Chizkiyahu* of *Yehuda*: Do not let your God, on whom you are relying, mislead you into thinking that *Yerushalayim* will not be delivered into the hands of the king of Assyria.

י כֹּה תֹאמְרוּן אֶל־חִזְקִיָּהוּ מֶלֶךְ־יְהוּדָה לֵאמֹר אַל־יַשִּׁאֲךָ אֱלֹהֶיךָ אֲשֶׁר אַתָּה בֹּטֵחַ בּוֹ לֵאמֹר לֹא תִנָּתֵן יְרוּשָׁלַם בְּיַד מֶלֶךְ אַשּׁוּר:

11 You yourself have heard what the kings of Assyria have done to all the lands, how they have annihilated them; and can you escape?

יא הִנֵּה אַתָּה שָׁמַעְתָּ אֵת אֲשֶׁר עָשׂוּ מַלְכֵי אַשּׁוּר לְכָל־הָאֲרָצוֹת לְהַחֲרִימָם וְאַתָּה תִּנָּצֵל:

12 Were the nations that my predecessors destroyed – Gozan, Haran, Rezeph, and the Beth-edenites in Telassar – saved by their gods?

יב הַהִצִּילוּ אֹתָם אֱלֹהֵי הַגּוֹיִם אֲשֶׁר שִׁחֲתוּ אֲבוֹתַי אֶת־גּוֹזָן וְאֶת־חָרָן וְרֶצֶף וּבְנֵי־עֶדֶן אֲשֶׁר בִּתְלַאשָּׂר:

13 Where is the king of Hamath? And the king of Arpad? And the kings of Lair, Sepharvaim, Hena, and Ivvah?"

יג אַיּוֹ מֶלֶךְ־חֲמָת וּמֶלֶךְ אַרְפָּד וּמֶלֶךְ לָעִיר סְפַרְוָיִם הֵנַע וְעִוָּה:

14 *Chizkiyahu* took the letter from the messengers and read it. *Chizkiyahu* then went up to the House of *Hashem* and spread it out before *Hashem*.

יד וַיִּקַּח חִזְקִיָּהוּ אֶת־הַסְּפָרִים מִיַּד הַמַּלְאָכִים וַיִּקְרָאֵם וַיַּעַל בֵּית יְהֹוָה וַיִּפְרְשֵׂהוּ חִזְקִיָּהוּ לִפְנֵי יְהֹוָה:

15 And *Chizkiyahu* prayed to *Hashem* and said, "Lord of Hosts, Enthroned on the *Keruvim*! You alone are God of all the kingdoms of the earth. You made the heavens and the earth.

טו וַיִּתְפַּלֵּל חִזְקִיָּהוּ לִפְנֵי יְהֹוָה וַיֹּאמַר יְהֹוָה אֱלֹהֵי יִשְׂרָאֵל יֹשֵׁב הַכְּרֻבִים אַתָּה־הוּא הָאֱלֹהִים לְבַדְּךָ לְכֹל מַמְלְכוֹת הָאָרֶץ אַתָּה עָשִׂיתָ אֶת־הַשָּׁמַיִם וְאֶת־הָאָרֶץ:

16 *Hashem*, incline Your ear and hear; open Your eyes and see. Hear the words that Sennacherib has sent to blaspheme the living *Hashem*!

טז הַטֵּה יְהֹוָה אָזְנְךָ וּשֲׁמָע פְּקַח יְהֹוָה עֵינֶיךָ וּרְאֵה וּשְׁמַע אֵת דִּבְרֵי סַנְחֵרִיב אֲשֶׁר שְׁלָחוֹ לְחָרֵף אֱלֹהִים חָי:

17 True, *Hashem*, the kings of Assyria have annihilated the nations and their lands,

יז אָמְנָם יְהֹוָה הֶחֱרִיבוּ מַלְכֵי אַשּׁוּר אֶת־הַגּוֹיִם וְאֶת־אַרְצָם:

18 and have committed their gods to the flames and have destroyed them; for they are not gods, but man's handiwork of wood and stone.

יח וְנָתְנוּ אֶת־אֱלֹהֵיהֶם בָּאֵשׁ כִּי לֹא אֱלֹהִים הֵמָּה כִּי אִם־מַעֲשֵׂה יְדֵי־אָדָם עֵץ וָאֶבֶן וַיְאַבְּדוּם:

19 But now, *Hashem* our God, deliver us from his hands, and let all the kingdoms of the earth know that You alone, *Hashem*, are *Hashem*."

יט וְעַתָּה יְהֹוָה אֱלֹהֵינוּ הוֹשִׁיעֵנוּ נָא מִיָּדוֹ וְיֵדְעוּ כָּל־מַמְלְכוֹת הָאָרֶץ כִּי אַתָּה יְהֹוָה אֱלֹהִים לְבַדֶּךָ:

20 Then *Yeshayahu* son of *Amotz* sent this message to *Chizkiyahu*: "Thus said *Hashem*, the God of *Yisrael*: I have heard the prayer you have offered to Me concerning King Sennacherib of Assyria.

כ וַיִּשְׁלַח יְשַׁעְיָהוּ בֶן־אָמוֹץ אֶל־חִזְקִיָּהוּ לֵאמֹר כֹּה־אָמַר יְהֹוָה אֱלֹהֵי יִשְׂרָאֵל אֲשֶׁר הִתְפַּלַּלְתָּ אֵלַי אֶל־סַנְחֵרִב מֶלֶךְ־אַשּׁוּר שָׁמָעְתִּי:

Melachim II / II Kings
Chapter 19

21 This is the word that *Hashem* has spoken concerning him: "Fair Maiden *Tzion* despises you, She mocks at you; Fair *Yerushalayim* shakes Her head at you.

22 Whom have you blasphemed and reviled? Against whom made loud your voice And haughtily raised your eyes? Against the Holy One of *Yisrael*!

23 Through your envoys you have blasphemed my Lord. Because you thought, 'Thanks to my vast chariotry, It is I who have climbed the highest mountains, To the remotest parts of the Lebanon, And have cut down its loftiest cedars, Its choicest cypresses, And have reached its remotest lodge, Its densest forest.

24 It is I who have drawn and drunk the waters of strangers; I have dried up with the soles of my feet All the streams of Egypt.'

25 Have you not heard? Of old I planned that very thing, I designed it long ago, And now have fulfilled it. And it has come to pass, Laying waste fortified towns In desolate heaps.

26 Their inhabitants are helpless, Dismayed and shamed. They were but grass of the field And green herbage, Grass of the roofs that is blasted Before the standing grain.

27 I know your stayings And your goings and comings, And how you have raged against Me.

28 Because you have raged against Me, And your tumult has reached My ears, I will place My hook in your nose And My bit between your jaws; And I will make you go back by the road By which you came.

29 "And this is the sign for you: This year you eat what grows of itself, and the next year what springs from that; and in the third year, sow and reap, and plant vineyards and eat their fruit.

30 And the survivors of the House of *Yehuda* that have escaped shall regenerate its stock below and produce boughs above.

31 For a remnant shall come forth from *Yerushalayim*, Survivors from Mount *Tzion*. The zeal of the Lord of Hosts Shall bring this to pass.

מלכים ב
פרק יט

כא זֶ֣ה הַדָּבָ֔ר אֲשֶׁר־דִּבֶּ֥ר יְהֹוָ֖ה עָלָ֑יו בָּזָ֨ה לְךָ֜ לָעֲגָ֣ה לְךָ֗ בְּתוּלַת֙ בַּת־צִיּ֔וֹן אַחֲרֶ֙יךָ֙ רֹ֣אשׁ הֵנִ֔יעָה בַּ֖ת יְרוּשָׁלָֽםִ׃

כב אֶת־מִ֤י חֵרַ֙פְתָּ֙ וְגִדַּ֔פְתָּ וְעַל־מִ֖י הֲרִימ֣וֹתָ קּ֑וֹל וַתִּשָּׂ֥א מָר֛וֹם עֵינֶ֖יךָ עַל־קְד֥וֹשׁ יִשְׂרָאֵֽל׃

כג בְּיַ֣ד מַלְאָכֶ֘יךָ֮ חֵרַ֣פְתָּ ׀ אֲדֹנָי֒ וַתֹּ֗אמֶר בְּרֹ֥ב [בְּרֶ֣כֶב] רִכְבִּ֗י אֲנִ֥י עָלִ֛יתִי מְר֥וֹם הָרִ֖ים יַרְכְּתֵ֣י לְבָנ֑וֹן וְאֶכְרֹ֞ת קוֹמַ֤ת אֲרָזָיו֙ מִבְח֣וֹר בְּרֹשָׁ֔יו וְאָב֛וֹאָה מְל֥וֹן קִצֹּ֖ה יַ֥עַר כַּרְמִלּֽוֹ׃

כד אֲנִ֣י קַ֔רְתִּי וְשָׁתִ֖יתִי מַ֣יִם זָרִ֑ים וְאַחְרִב֙ בְּכַף־פְּעָמַ֔י כֹּ֖ל יְאֹרֵ֥י מָצֽוֹר׃

כה הֲלֹֽא־שָׁמַ֤עְתָּ לְמֵ֣רָחוֹק֙ אֹתָ֣הּ עָשִׂ֔יתִי לְמִ֥ימֵי קֶ֖דֶם וִיצַרְתִּ֑יהָ עַתָּ֣ה הֲבֵיאתִ֔יהָ וּתְהִ֗י לַהְשׁ֛וֹת גַּלִּ֥ים נִצִּ֖ים עָרִ֥ים בְּצֻרֽוֹת׃

כו וְיֹֽשְׁבֵיהֶן֙ קִצְרֵי־יָ֔ד חַ֖תּוּ וַיֵּבֹ֑שׁוּ הָי֞וּ עֵ֤שֶׂב שָׂדֶה֙ וִ֣ירַק דֶּ֔שֶׁא חֲצִ֣יר גַּגּ֔וֹת וּשְׁדֵפָ֖ה לִפְנֵ֥י קָמָֽה׃

כז וְשִׁבְתְּךָ֛ וְצֵאתְךָ֥ וּבֹאֲךָ֖ יָדָ֑עְתִּי וְאֵ֖ת הִתְרַגֶּזְךָ֥ אֵלָֽי׃

כח יַ֚עַן הִתְרַגֶּזְךָ֣ אֵלַ֔י וְשַׁאֲנַנְךָ֖ עָלָ֣ה בְאׇזְנָ֑י וְשַׂמְתִּ֨י חַחִ֜י בְּאַפֶּ֗ךָ וּמִתְגִּי֙ בִּשְׂפָתֶ֔יךָ וַהֲשִׁ֣בֹתִ֔יךָ בַּדֶּ֖רֶךְ אֲשֶׁר־בָּ֥אתָ בָּֽהּ׃

כט וְזֶה־לְּךָ֣ הָא֔וֹת אָכ֤וֹל הַשָּׁנָה֙ סָפִ֔יחַ וּבַשָּׁנָ֥ה הַשֵּׁנִ֖ית סָחִ֑ישׁ וּבַשָּׁנָ֣ה הַשְּׁלִישִׁ֗ית זִרְע֧וּ וְקִצְר֛וּ וְנִטְע֥וּ כְרָמִ֖ים וְאִכְל֥וּ פִרְיָֽם׃

ל וְיָ֨סְפָ֜ה פְּלֵיטַ֧ת בֵּית־יְהוּדָ֛ה הַנִּשְׁאָרָ֖ה שֹׁ֣רֶשׁ לְמָ֑טָּה וְעָשָׂ֥ה פְרִ֖י לְמָֽעְלָה׃

לא כִּ֤י מִירוּשָׁלַ֙͏ִם֙ תֵּצֵ֣א שְׁאֵרִ֔ית וּפְלֵיטָ֖ה מֵהַ֣ר צִיּ֑וֹן קִנְאַ֛ת יְהֹוָ֥ה [צְבָא֖וֹת] תַּעֲשֶׂה־זֹּֽאת׃

Melachim II / II Kings
Chapter 20

32 Assuredly, thus said *Hashem* concerning the king of Assyria: He shall not enter this city: He shall not shoot an arrow at it, Or advance upon it with a shield, Or pile up a siege mound against it.

33 He shall go back By the way he came; He shall not enter this city – declares *Hashem*.

34 I will protect and save this city for My sake, And for the sake of My servant *David*."

35 That night an angel of *Hashem* went out and struck down one hundred and eighty-five thousand in the Assyrian camp, and the following morning they were all dead corpses.

vai-HEE ba-LAI-lah ha-HU va-yay-TZAY mal-AKH a-do-NAI va-YAKH b'-ma-kha-NAY a-SHUR may-AH sh'-mo-NEEM va-kha-mi-SHAH A-lef va-yash-KEE-mu va-BO-ker v'-hi-NAY khu-LAM p'-ga-REEM may-TEEM

36 So King Sennacherib of Assyria broke camp and retreated, and stayed in Nineveh.

37 While he was worshiping in the temple of his god Nisroch, his sons Adrammelech and Sarezer struck him down with the sword. They fled to the land of Ararat, and his son Esarhaddon succeeded him as king.

20
1 In those days *Chizkiyahu* fell dangerously ill. The *Navi Yeshayahu* son of *Amotz* came and said to him, "Thus said *Hashem*: Set your affairs in order, for you are going to die; you will not get well."

ba-ya-MEEM ha-HAYM kha-LAH khiz-ki-YA-hu la-MUT va-ya-VO ay-LAV y'-sha-YA-hu ven a-MOTZ ha-na-VEE va-YO-mer ay-LAV koh a-MAR a-do-NAI TZAV l'-vay-TE-kha KEE MAYT a-TAH v'-LO tikh-YEH

19:35 An angel of *Hashem* went out and struck down After the threats of the Assyrians and the supplications of King *Chizkiyahu*, *Hashem* performs a wondrous miracle. The Assyrian soldiers besieging *Yerushalayim* are struck down in one night, thereby saving the city and its inhabitants. This miracle was repeated in the twentieth century, during the Six Day War. The surrounding Arab nations had threatened to "throw the Jews into the sea." Many felt all was lost, and tens of thousands of graves were dug throughout Israel to prepare for the mass casualties many thought were impending. Yet in only six days, God struck down Israel's enemies in the most miraculous of fashions. The Egyptian air force was destroyed while still on the ground. The Jordanians then entered the war, leading to Israel's liberation of *Yerushalayim*, Judea and Samaria. And Syria, despite having the advantage of the high ground from which it had terrorized Israeli farmers for decades, was driven from the Golan Heights. The entire world stood in awe of Israel's miraculous victory, reminiscent of *Hashem's* sudden defeat of the Assyrian army long ago.

Egyptian war planes destroyed on the ground, 1967

20:1 For you are going to die; you will not get well King *Chizkiyahu* is told that he is going to be punished by losing his life in this world and, as *Rashi* explains, the next world as well. The reason for the punishment is that until now he has refrained from getting married and having children. *Chizkiyahu's* intentions are pure, since he has received a prophetic revela-

Melachim II/II Kings
Chapter 20

2 Thereupon *Chizkiyahu* turned his face to the wall and prayed to *Hashem*. He said,

3 "Please, *Hashem*, remember how I have walked before You sincerely and wholeheartedly, and have done what is pleasing to You." And *Chizkiyahu* wept profusely.

4 Before *Yeshayahu* had gone out of the middle court, the word of *Hashem* came to him:

5 "Go back and say to *Chizkiyahu*, the ruler of My people: Thus said *Hashem*, the God of your father *David*: I have heard your prayer, I have seen your tears. I am going to heal you; on the third day you shall go up to the House of *Hashem*.

6 And I will add fifteen years to your life. I will also rescue you and this city from the hands of the king of Assyria. I will protect this city for My sake and for the sake of My servant *David*."

7 Then *Yeshayahu* said, "Get a cake of figs." And they got one, and they applied it to the rash, and he recovered.

8 *Chizkiyahu* asked *Yeshayahu*, "What is the sign that *Hashem* will heal me and that I shall go up to the House of *Hashem* on the third day?"

9 *Yeshayahu* replied, "This is the sign for you from *Hashem* that *Hashem* will do the thing that He has promised: Shall the shadow advance ten steps or recede ten steps?"

10 *Chizkiyahu* said, "It is easy for the shadow to lengthen ten steps, but not for the shadow to recede ten steps."

---

tion that his son will be evil. As a result, he wishes to refrain from having children, in order to avoid bringing such a person into the world. However, *Chizkiyahu* is told that his responsibility is to follow *Hashem*'s commandment to have children, regardless of the consequences. Rabbi Shlomo Aviner notes that *Chizkiyahu*'s decision to avoid having children could be particularly devastating, because his descendants represent the continuation of the Davidic dynasty. After hearing the rebuke, *Chizkiyahu* understands that he has erred, prays to God for forgiveness and corrects his mistake. Though his son *Menashe* is indeed evil, his great-grandson is the righteous King *Yoshiyahu*, who is responsible for creating a religious renaissance in the kingdom. *Yoshiyahu* gets rid of all forms of idolatry, including the altar erected by *Yerovam* (thus fulfilling the prophecy stated in I Kings 13:2), and renews the people's covenant with *Hashem*.

Melachim II / II Kings — Chapter 20

11 So the *Navi Yeshayahu* called to *Hashem*, and He made the shadow which had descended on the dial of *Achaz* recede ten steps.

12 At that time, King Berodach-baladan son of Baladan of Babylon sent [envoys with] a letter and a gift to *Chizkiyahu*, for he had heard about *Chizkiyahu*'s illness.

13 *Chizkiyahu* heard about them and he showed them all his treasure-house – the silver, the gold, the spices, and the fragrant oil – and his armory, and everything that was to be found in his storehouses. There was nothing in his palace or in all his realm that *Chizkiyahu* did not show them.

14 Then the *Navi Yeshayahu* came to King *Chizkiyahu*. "What," he demanded of him, "did those men say to you? Where have they come to you from?" "They have come," *Chizkiyahu* replied, "from a far country, from Babylon."

15 Next he asked, "What have they seen in your palace?" And *Chizkiyahu* replied, "They have seen everything that is in my palace. There was nothing in my storehouses that I did not show them."

16 Then *Yeshayahu* said to *Chizkiyahu*, "Hear the word of *Hashem*:

17 A time is coming when everything in your palace which your ancestors have stored up to this day will be carried off to Babylon; nothing will remain behind, said *Hashem*.

18 And some of your sons, your own issue, whom you will have fathered, will be taken to serve as eunuchs in the palace of the king of Babylon."

19 *Chizkiyahu* declared to *Yeshayahu*, "The word of *Hashem* that you have spoken is good." For he thought, "It means that safety is assured for my time."

20 The other events of *Chizkiyahu*'s reign, and all his exploits, and how he made the pool and the conduit and brought the water into the city, are recorded in the Annals of the Kings of *Yehuda*.

21 *Chizkiyahu* slept with his fathers, and his son *Menashe* succeeded him as king.

מלכים ב · פרק כ

יא וַיִּקְרָא יְשַׁעְיָהוּ הַנָּבִיא אֶל־יְהֹוָה וַיָּשֶׁב אֶת־הַצֵּל בַּמַּעֲלוֹת אֲשֶׁר יָרְדָה בְּמַעֲלוֹת אָחָז אֲחֹרַנִּית עֶשֶׂר מַעֲלוֹת׃

יב בָּעֵת הַהִיא שָׁלַח בְּרֹאדַךְ בַּלְאֲדָן בֶּן־בַּלְאֲדָן מֶלֶךְ־בָּבֶל סְפָרִים וּמִנְחָה אֶל־חִזְקִיָּהוּ כִּי שָׁמַע כִּי חָלָה חִזְקִיָּהוּ׃

יג וַיִּשְׁמַע עֲלֵיהֶם חִזְקִיָּהוּ וַיַּרְאֵם אֶת־כָּל־בֵּית נְכֹתֹה אֶת־הַכֶּסֶף וְאֶת־הַזָּהָב וְאֶת־הַבְּשָׂמִים וְאֵת שֶׁמֶן הַטּוֹב וְאֵת בֵּית כֵּלָיו וְאֵת כָּל־אֲשֶׁר נִמְצָא בְּאֹצְרֹתָיו לֹא־הָיָה דָבָר אֲשֶׁר לֹא־הֶרְאָם חִזְקִיָּהוּ בְּבֵיתוֹ וּבְכָל־מֶמְשַׁלְתּוֹ׃

יד וַיָּבֹא יְשַׁעְיָהוּ הַנָּבִיא אֶל־הַמֶּלֶךְ חִזְקִיָּהוּ וַיֹּאמֶר אֵלָיו מָה אָמְרוּ הָאֲנָשִׁים הָאֵלֶּה וּמֵאַיִן יָבֹאוּ אֵלֶיךָ וַיֹּאמֶר חִזְקִיָּהוּ מֵאֶרֶץ רְחוֹקָה בָּאוּ מִבָּבֶל׃

טו וַיֹּאמֶר מָה רָאוּ בְּבֵיתֶךָ וַיֹּאמֶר חִזְקִיָּהוּ אֵת כָּל־אֲשֶׁר בְּבֵיתִי רָאוּ לֹא־הָיָה דָבָר אֲשֶׁר לֹא־הִרְאִיתִם בְּאֹצְרֹתָי׃

טז וַיֹּאמֶר יְשַׁעְיָהוּ אֶל־חִזְקִיָּהוּ שְׁמַע דְּבַר־יְהֹוָה׃

יז הִנֵּה יָמִים בָּאִים וְנִשָּׂא כָּל־אֲשֶׁר בְּבֵיתֶךָ וַאֲשֶׁר אָצְרוּ אֲבֹתֶיךָ עַד־הַיּוֹם הַזֶּה בָּבֶלָה לֹא־יִוָּתֵר דָּבָר אָמַר יְהֹוָה׃

יח וּמִבָּנֶיךָ אֲשֶׁר יֵצְאוּ מִמְּךָ אֲשֶׁר תּוֹלִיד יקח [יִקָּחוּ] וְהָיוּ סָרִיסִים בְּהֵיכַל מֶלֶךְ בָּבֶל׃

יט וַיֹּאמֶר חִזְקִיָּהוּ אֶל־יְשַׁעְיָהוּ טוֹב דְּבַר־יְהֹוָה אֲשֶׁר דִּבַּרְתָּ וַיֹּאמֶר הֲלוֹא אִם־שָׁלוֹם וֶאֱמֶת יִהְיֶה בְיָמָי׃

כ וְיֶתֶר דִּבְרֵי חִזְקִיָּהוּ וְכָל־גְּבוּרָתוֹ וַאֲשֶׁר עָשָׂה אֶת־הַבְּרֵכָה וְאֶת־הַתְּעָלָה וַיָּבֵא אֶת־הַמַּיִם הָעִירָה הֲלֹא־הֵם כְּתוּבִים עַל־סֵפֶר דִּבְרֵי הַיָּמִים לְמַלְכֵי יְהוּדָה׃

כא וַיִּשְׁכַּב חִזְקִיָּהוּ עִם־אֲבֹתָיו וַיִּמְלֹךְ מְנַשֶּׁה בְנוֹ תַּחְתָּיו׃

Melachim II / II Kings
Chapter 21

21 1 *Menashe* was twelve years old when he became king, and he reigned fifty-five years in *Yerushalayim*; his mother's name was Hephzibah.

2 He did what was displeasing to *Hashem*, following the abhorrent practices of the nations that *Hashem* had dispossessed before the Israelites.

3 He rebuilt the shrines that his father *Chizkiyahu* had destroyed; he erected altars for Baal and made a sacred post, as King *Achav* of *Yisrael* had done. He bowed down to all the host of heaven and worshiped them,

4 and he built altars for them in the House of *Hashem*, of which *Hashem* had said, "I will establish My name in *Yerushalayim*."

5 He built altars for all the hosts of heaven in the two courts of the House of *Hashem*.

6 He consigned his son to the fire; he practiced soothsaying and divination, and consulted ghosts and familiar spirits; he did much that was displeasing to *Hashem*, to vex Him.

7 The sculptured image of Asherah that he made he placed in the House concerning which *Hashem* had said to *David* and to his son *Shlomo*, "In this House and in *Yerushalayim*, which I chose out of all the tribes of *Yisrael*, I will establish My name forever.

8 And I will not again cause the feet of *Yisrael* to wander from the land that I gave to their fathers, if they will but faithfully observe all that I have commanded them – all the Teachings with which My servant *Moshe* charged them."

v'-LO o-SEEF l'-ha-NEED RE-gel yis-ra-AYL min ha-a-da-MAH a-SHER na-TA-tee la-a-vo-TAM RAK im yish-m'-RU la-a-SOT k'-KHOL a-SHER tzi-vee-TEEM UL-khol ha-to-RAH a-sher tzi-VAH o-TAM av-DEE mo-SHEH

21:8 If they will but faithfully observe all that I have commanded them *Menashe* is the epitome of an evil king. He engages in the worst kinds of idolatry and commits countless acts of murder, influencing the rest of the nation to follow his evil ways. As a result of *Menashe*'s sins, *Hashem* determines that He will exile the Children of Israel. Though *Eretz Yisrael* is an eternal inheritance of the Children of Israel, living in the land depends upon the observance of God's commandments. The Land of Israel is considered to be "the Palace of the King," and the laws of the King of Kings must be followed. Today's State of Israel invests tremendous resources in order to fully facilitate religious life. The Israeli government spends great sums on religious services, such as synagogues and schools, so that the Children of Israel can obey all of *Hashem*'s commandments. This has resulted in the flourishing of religious life throughout *Eretz Yisrael* at levels not seen in millennia.

Melachim II / II Kings
Chapter 21

מלכים ב
פרק כא

9 But they did not obey, and *Menashe* led them astray to do greater evil than the nations that *Hashem* had destroyed before the Israelites.

ט וְלֹא שָׁמֵעוּ וַיַּתְעֵם מְנַשֶּׁה לַעֲשׂוֹת אֶת־הָרָע מִן־הַגּוֹיִם אֲשֶׁר הִשְׁמִיד יְהֹוָה מִפְּנֵי בְּנֵי יִשְׂרָאֵל:

10 Therefore *Hashem* spoke through His servants the *Neviim*:

י וַיְדַבֵּר יְהֹוָה בְּיַד־עֲבָדָיו הַנְּבִיאִים לֵאמֹר:

11 "Because King *Menashe* of *Yehuda* has done these abhorrent things – he has outdone in wickedness all that the Amorites did before his time – and because he led *Yehuda* to sin with his fetishes,

יא יַעַן אֲשֶׁר עָשָׂה מְנַשֶּׁה מֶלֶךְ־יְהוּדָה הַתֹּעֵבוֹת הָאֵלֶּה הֵרַע מִכֹּל אֲשֶׁר־עָשׂוּ הָאֱמֹרִי אֲשֶׁר לְפָנָיו וַיַּחֲטִא גַם־אֶת־יְהוּדָה בְּגִלּוּלָיו:

12 assuredly, thus said *Hashem*, the God of *Yisrael*: I am going to bring such a disaster on *Yerushalayim* and *Yehuda* that both ears of everyone who hears about it will tingle.

יב לָכֵן כֹּה־אָמַר יְהֹוָה אֱלֹהֵי יִשְׂרָאֵל הִנְנִי מֵבִיא רָעָה עַל־יְרוּשָׁלַם וִיהוּדָה אֲשֶׁר כָּל־שֹׁמְעָיו [שֹׁמְעָהּ] תִּצַּלְנָה שְׁתֵּי אָזְנָיו:

13 I will apply to *Yerushalayim* the measuring line of *Shomron* and the weights of the House of *Achav*; I will wipe *Yerushalayim* clean as one wipes a dish and turns it upside down.

יג וְנָטִיתִי עַל־יְרוּשָׁלַם אֵת קָו שֹׁמְרוֹן וְאֶת־מִשְׁקֹלֶת בֵּית אַחְאָב וּמָחִיתִי אֶת־יְרוּשָׁלַם כַּאֲשֶׁר־יִמְחֶה אֶת־הַצַּלַּחַת מָחָה וְהָפַךְ עַל־פָּנֶיהָ:

14 And I will cast off the remnant of My own people and deliver them into the hands of their enemies. They shall be plunder and prey to all their enemies

יד וְנָטַשְׁתִּי אֵת שְׁאֵרִית נַחֲלָתִי וּנְתַתִּים בְּיַד אֹיְבֵיהֶם וְהָיוּ לְבַז וְלִמְשִׁסָּה לְכָל־אֹיְבֵיהֶם:

15 because they have done what is displeasing to Me and have been vexing Me from the day that their fathers came out of Egypt to this day."

טו יַעַן אֲשֶׁר עָשׂוּ אֶת־הָרַע בְּעֵינַי וַיִּהְיוּ מַכְעִסִים אֹתִי מִן־הַיּוֹם אֲשֶׁר יָצְאוּ אֲבוֹתָם מִמִּצְרַיִם וְעַד הַיּוֹם הַזֶּה:

16 Moreover, *Menashe* put so many innocent persons to death that he filled *Yerushalayim* [with blood] from end to end – besides the sin he committed in causing *Yehuda* to do what was displeasing to *Hashem*.

טז וְגַם דָּם נָקִי שָׁפַךְ מְנַשֶּׁה הַרְבֵּה מְאֹד עַד אֲשֶׁר־מִלֵּא אֶת־יְרוּשָׁלַם פֶּה לָפֶה לְבַד מֵחַטָּאתוֹ אֲשֶׁר הֶחֱטִיא אֶת־יְהוּדָה לַעֲשׂוֹת הָרַע בְּעֵינֵי יְהֹוָה:

17 The other events of *Menashe*'s reign, and all his actions, and the sins he committed, are recorded in the Annals of the Kings of *Yehuda*.

יז וְיֶתֶר דִּבְרֵי מְנַשֶּׁה וְכָל־אֲשֶׁר עָשָׂה וְחַטָּאתוֹ אֲשֶׁר חָטָא הֲלֹא־הֵם כְּתוּבִים עַל־סֵפֶר דִּבְרֵי הַיָּמִים לְמַלְכֵי יְהוּדָה:

18 *Menashe* slept with his fathers and was buried in the garden of his palace, in the garden of Uzza; and his son *Amon* succeeded him as king.

יח וַיִּשְׁכַּב מְנַשֶּׁה עִם־אֲבֹתָיו וַיִּקָּבֵר בְּגַן־בֵּיתוֹ בְּגַן־עֻזָּא וַיִּמְלֹךְ אָמוֹן בְּנוֹ תַּחְתָּיו:

19 *Amon* was twenty-two years old when he became king, and he reigned two years in *Yerushalayim*; his mother's name was Meshullemeth daughter of Haruz of Jotbah.

יט בֶּן־עֶשְׂרִים וּשְׁתַּיִם שָׁנָה אָמוֹן בְּמָלְכוֹ וּשְׁתַּיִם שָׁנִים מָלַךְ בִּירוּשָׁלָם וְשֵׁם אִמּוֹ מְשֻׁלֶּמֶת בַּת־חָרוּץ מִן־יָטְבָה:

20 He did what was displeasing to *Hashem*, as his father *Menashe* had done.

כ וַיַּעַשׂ הָרַע בְּעֵינֵי יְהֹוָה כַּאֲשֶׁר עָשָׂה מְנַשֶּׁה אָבִיו:

Melachim II / II Kings
Chapter 22

21 He walked in all the ways of his father, worshiping the fetishes which his father had worshiped and bowing down to them.

22 He forsook *Hashem*, the God of his fathers, and did not follow the way of *Hashem*.

23 *Amon*'s courtiers conspired against him; and they killed the king in his palace.

24 But the people of the land put to death all who had conspired against King *Amon*, and the people of the land made his son *Yoshiyahu* king in his stead.

25 The other events of *Amon*'s reign [and] his actions are recorded in the Annals of the Kings of *Yehuda*.

26 He was buried in his tomb in the garden of Uzza; and his son *Yoshiyahu* succeeded him as king.

22 1 *Yoshiyahu* was eight years old when he became king, and he reigned thirty-one years in *Yerushalayim*. His mother's name was Jedidah daughter of Adaiah of Bozkath.

2 He did what was pleasing to *Hashem* and he followed all the ways of his ancestor *David*; he did not deviate to the right or to the left.

3 In the eighteenth year of King *Yoshiyahu*, the king sent the scribe *Shafan* son of Azaliah son of Meshullam to the House of *Hashem*, saying,

4 "Go to the *Kohen Gadol Chilkiyahu* and let him weigh the silver that has been deposited in the House of *Hashem*, which the guards of the threshold have collected from the people.

5 And let it be delivered to the overseers of the work who are in charge at the House of *Hashem*, that they in turn may pay it out to the workmen that are in the House of *Hashem*, for the repair of the House:

6 to the carpenters, the laborers, and the masons, and for the purchase of wood and quarried stones for repairing the House.

7 However, no check is to be kept on them for the silver that is delivered to them, for they deal honestly."

מלכים ב
פרק כב

כא וַיֵּלֶךְ בְּכָל־הַדֶּרֶךְ אֲשֶׁר הָלַךְ אָבִיו וַיַּעֲבֹד אֶת־הַגִּלֻּלִים אֲשֶׁר עָבַד אָבִיו וַיִּשְׁתַּחוּ לָהֶם:

כב וַיַּעֲזֹב אֶת־יְהֹוָה אֱלֹהֵי אֲבֹתָיו וְלֹא הָלַךְ בְּדֶרֶךְ יְהֹוָה:

כג וַיִּקְשְׁרוּ עַבְדֵי־אָמוֹן עָלָיו וַיָּמִיתוּ אֶת־הַמֶּלֶךְ בְּבֵיתוֹ:

כד וַיַּךְ עַם־הָאָרֶץ אֵת כָּל־הַקֹּשְׁרִים עַל־הַמֶּלֶךְ אָמוֹן וַיַּמְלִיכוּ עַם־הָאָרֶץ אֶת־יֹאשִׁיָּהוּ בְנוֹ תַּחְתָּיו:

כה וְיֶתֶר דִּבְרֵי אָמוֹן אֲשֶׁר עָשָׂה הֲלֹא־הֵם כְּתוּבִים עַל־סֵפֶר דִּבְרֵי הַיָּמִים לְמַלְכֵי יְהוּדָה:

כו וַיִּקְבֹּר אֹתוֹ בִּקְבֻרָתוֹ בְּגַן־עֻזָּא וַיִּמְלֹךְ יֹאשִׁיָּהוּ בְנוֹ תַּחְתָּיו:

כב א בֶּן־שְׁמֹנֶה שָׁנָה יֹאשִׁיָּהוּ בְמָלְכוֹ וּשְׁלֹשִׁים וְאַחַת שָׁנָה מָלַךְ בִּירוּשָׁלָ͏ִם וְשֵׁם אִמּוֹ יְדִידָה בַת־עֲדָיָה מִבָּצְקַת:

ב וַיַּעַשׂ הַיָּשָׁר בְּעֵינֵי יְהֹוָה וַיֵּלֶךְ בְּכָל־דֶּרֶךְ דָּוִד אָבִיו וְלֹא־סָר יָמִין וּשְׂמֹאול:

ג וַיְהִי בִּשְׁמֹנֶה עֶשְׂרֵה שָׁנָה לַמֶּלֶךְ יֹאשִׁיָּהוּ שָׁלַח הַמֶּלֶךְ אֶת־שָׁפָן בֶּן־אֲצַלְיָהוּ בֶן־מְשֻׁלָּם הַסֹּפֵר בֵּית יְהֹוָה לֵאמֹר:

ד עֲלֵה אֶל־חִלְקִיָּהוּ הַכֹּהֵן הַגָּדוֹל וְיַתֵּם אֶת־הַכֶּסֶף הַמּוּבָא בֵּית יְהֹוָה אֲשֶׁר אָסְפוּ שֹׁמְרֵי הַסַּף מֵאֵת הָעָם:

ה ויתנה [וְיִתְּנֻהוּ] עַל־יַד עֹשֵׂי הַמְּלָאכָה הַמֻּפְקָדִים בבית [בְּבֵית] יְהֹוָה וְיִתְּנוּ אֹתוֹ לְעֹשֵׂי הַמְּלָאכָה אֲשֶׁר בְּבֵית יְהֹוָה לְחַזֵּק בֶּדֶק הַבָּיִת:

ו לֶחָרָשִׁים וְלַבֹּנִים וְלַגֹּדְרִים וְלִקְנוֹת עֵצִים וְאַבְנֵי מַחְצֵב לְחַזֵּק אֶת־הַבָּיִת:

ז אַךְ לֹא־יֵחָשֵׁב אִתָּם הַכֶּסֶף הַנִּתָּן עַל־יָדָם כִּי בֶאֱמוּנָה הֵם עֹשִׂים:

Melachim II / II Kings
Chapter 22

מלכים ב
פרק כב

8 Then the *Kohen Gadol Chilkiyahu* said to the scribe *Shafan*, "I have found a scroll of the Teaching in the House of *Hashem*." And *Chilkiyahu* gave the scroll to *Shafan*, who read it.

ח וַיֹּאמֶר חִלְקִיָּהוּ הַכֹּהֵן הַגָּדוֹל עַל־שָׁפָן הַסֹּפֵר סֵפֶר הַתּוֹרָה מָצָאתִי בְּבֵית יְהֹוָה וַיִּתֵּן חִלְקִיָּה אֶת־הַסֵּפֶר אֶל־שָׁפָן וַיִּקְרָאֵהוּ:

9 The scribe *Shafan* then went to the king and reported to the king: "Your servants have melted down the silver that was deposited in the House, and they have delivered it to the overseers of the work who are in charge at the House of *Hashem*."

ט וַיָּבֹא שָׁפָן הַסֹּפֵר אֶל־הַמֶּלֶךְ וַיָּשֶׁב אֶת־הַמֶּלֶךְ דָּבָר וַיֹּאמֶר הִתִּיכוּ עֲבָדֶיךָ אֶת־הַכֶּסֶף הַנִּמְצָא בַבַּיִת וַיִּתְּנֻהוּ עַל־יַד עֹשֵׂי הַמְּלָאכָה הַמֻּפְקָדִים בֵּית יְהֹוָה:

10 The scribe *Shafan* also told the king, "The *Kohen Gadol Chilkiyahu* has given me a scroll"; and *Shafan* read it to the king.

י וַיַּגֵּד שָׁפָן הַסֹּפֵר לַמֶּלֶךְ לֵאמֹר סֵפֶר נָתַן לִי חִלְקִיָּה הַכֹּהֵן וַיִּקְרָאֵהוּ שָׁפָן לִפְנֵי הַמֶּלֶךְ:

11 When the king heard the words of the scroll of the Teaching, he rent his clothes.

vai-HEE kish-MO-a ha-ME-lekh et div-RAY SAY-fer ha-to-RAH va-yik-RA et b'-ga-DAV

יא וַיְהִי כִּשְׁמֹעַ הַמֶּלֶךְ אֶת־דִּבְרֵי סֵפֶר הַתּוֹרָה וַיִּקְרַע אֶת־בְּגָדָיו:

12 And the king gave orders to the *Kohen Chilkiyahu*, and to *Achikam* son of *Shafan*, Achbor son of Michaiah, the scribe *Shafan*, and Asaiah the king's minister:

יב וַיְצַו הַמֶּלֶךְ אֶת־חִלְקִיָּה הַכֹּהֵן וְאֶת־אֲחִיקָם בֶּן־שָׁפָן וְאֶת־עַכְבּוֹר בֶּן־מִיכָיָה וְאֵת שָׁפָן הַסֹּפֵר וְאֵת עֲשָׂיָה עֶבֶד־הַמֶּלֶךְ לֵאמֹר:

13 "Go, inquire of *Hashem* on my behalf, and on behalf of the people, and on behalf of all *Yehuda*, concerning the words of this scroll that has been found. For great indeed must be the wrath of *Hashem* that has been kindled against us, because our fathers did not obey the words of this scroll to do all that has been prescribed for us."

יג לְכוּ דִרְשׁוּ אֶת־יְהֹוָה בַּעֲדִי וּבְעַד־הָעָם וּבְעַד כָּל־יְהוּדָה עַל־דִּבְרֵי הַסֵּפֶר הַנִּמְצָא הַזֶּה כִּי־גְדוֹלָה חֲמַת יְהֹוָה אֲשֶׁר־הִיא נִצְּתָה בָנוּ עַל אֲשֶׁר לֹא־שָׁמְעוּ אֲבֹתֵינוּ עַל־דִּבְרֵי הַסֵּפֶר הַזֶּה לַעֲשׂוֹת כְּכָל־הַכָּתוּב עָלֵינוּ:

14 So the *Kohen Chilkiyahu*, and *Achikam*, Achbor, *Shafan*, and Asaiah went to the *Neviah Chulda* – the wife of *Shalum* son of *Tikvah* son of Harhas, the keeper of the wardrobe – who was living in *Yerushalayim* in the Mishneh, and they spoke to her.

יד וַיֵּלֶךְ חִלְקִיָּהוּ הַכֹּהֵן וַאֲחִיקָם וְעַכְבּוֹר וְשָׁפָן וַעֲשָׂיָה אֶל־חֻלְדָּה הַנְּבִיאָה אֵשֶׁת שַׁלֻּם בֶּן־תִּקְוָה בֶּן־חַרְחַס שֹׁמֵר הַבְּגָדִים וְהִיא יֹשֶׁבֶת בִּירוּשָׁלַםִ בַּמִּשְׁנֶה וַיְדַבְּרוּ אֵלֶיהָ:

22:11 He rent his clothes In Jewish tradition, tearing one's garment is a symbol of intense mourning. For the first time, King *Yoshiyahu* hears the words of God's *Torah*, which has been hidden away for many years. He becomes aware of how low the People of Israel have sunk. This is the beginning of his resolve to lead a campaign of repentance and bring the nation back to God. Though *Hashem* has already declared that, due to *Menashe*'s sins, He was going to exile the nation (II Kings 21:10–15), He resolves to gives them another chance. Through the uncovered *Torah* scroll, He sends them the message that even though they have turned their backs on Him, He has not given up on His people. Instead of sending them away, He wants them to repent, and to remain with Him in the Holy Land.

IDF soldiers reading from the Torah near Gaza

Melachim II / II Kings
Chapter 23

מלכים ב
פרק כג

15 She responded: "Thus said *Hashem*, the God of *Yisrael*: Say to the man who sent you to me:

טו וַתֹּאמֶר אֲלֵיהֶם כֹּה־אָמַר יְהֹוָה אֱלֹהֵי יִשְׂרָאֵל אִמְרוּ לָאִישׁ אֲשֶׁר־שָׁלַח אֶתְכֶם אֵלָי:

16 Thus said *Hashem*: I am going to bring disaster upon this place and its inhabitants, in accordance with all the words of the scroll which the king of *Yehuda* has read.

טז כֹּה אָמַר יְהֹוָה הִנְנִי מֵבִיא רָעָה אֶל־הַמָּקוֹם הַזֶּה וְעַל־יֹשְׁבָיו אֵת כָּל־דִּבְרֵי הַסֵּפֶר אֲשֶׁר קָרָא מֶלֶךְ יְהוּדָה:

17 Because they have forsaken Me and have made offerings to other gods and vexed Me with all their deeds, My wrath is kindled against this place and it shall not be quenched.

יז תַּחַת אֲשֶׁר עֲזָבוּנִי וַיְקַטְּרוּ לֵאלֹהִים אֲחֵרִים לְמַעַן הַכְעִיסֵנִי בְּכֹל מַעֲשֵׂה יְדֵיהֶם וְנִצְּתָה חֲמָתִי בַּמָּקוֹם הַזֶּה וְלֹא תִכְבֶּה:

18 But say this to the king of *Yehuda*, who sent you to inquire of *Hashem*: Thus said *Hashem*, the God of *Yisrael*: As for the words which you have heard

יח וְאֶל־מֶלֶךְ יְהוּדָה הַשֹּׁלֵחַ אֶתְכֶם לִדְרֹשׁ אֶת־יְהֹוָה כֹּה תֹאמְרוּ אֵלָיו כֹּה־אָמַר יְהֹוָה אֱלֹהֵי יִשְׂרָאֵל הַדְּבָרִים אֲשֶׁר שָׁמָעְתָּ:

19 because your heart was softened and you humbled yourself before *Hashem* when you heard what I decreed against this place and its inhabitants – that it will become a desolation and a curse – and because you rent your clothes and wept before Me, I for My part have listened – declares *Hashem*.

יט יַעַן רַךְ־לְבָבְךָ וַתִּכָּנַע מִפְּנֵי יְהֹוָה בְּשָׁמְעֲךָ אֲשֶׁר דִּבַּרְתִּי עַל־הַמָּקוֹם הַזֶּה וְעַל־יֹשְׁבָיו לִהְיוֹת לְשַׁמָּה וְלִקְלָלָה וַתִּקְרַע אֶת־בְּגָדֶיךָ וַתִּבְכֶּה לְפָנָי וְגַם אָנֹכִי שָׁמַעְתִּי נְאֻם־יְהֹוָה:

20 Assuredly, I will gather you to your fathers and you will be laid in your tomb in peace. Your eyes shall not see all the disaster which I will bring upon this place." So they brought back the reply to the king.

כ לָכֵן הִנְנִי אֹסִפְךָ עַל־אֲבֹתֶיךָ וְנֶאֱסַפְתָּ אֶל־קִבְרֹתֶיךָ בְּשָׁלוֹם וְלֹא־תִרְאֶינָה עֵינֶיךָ בְּכֹל הָרָעָה אֲשֶׁר־אֲנִי מֵבִיא עַל־הַמָּקוֹם הַזֶּה וַיָּשִׁיבוּ אֶת־הַמֶּלֶךְ דָּבָר:

23

1 At the king's summons, all the elders of *Yehuda* and *Yerushalayim* assembled before him.

כג א וַיִּשְׁלַח הַמֶּלֶךְ וַיַּאַסְפוּ אֵלָיו כָּל־זִקְנֵי יְהוּדָה וִירוּשָׁלָ͏ִם:

2 The king went up to the House of *Hashem*, together with all the men of *Yehuda* and all the inhabitants of *Yerushalayim*, and the *Kohanim* and *Neviim* – all the people, young and old. And he read to them the entire text of the covenant scroll which had been found in the House of *Hashem*.

ב וַיַּעַל הַמֶּלֶךְ בֵּית־יְהֹוָה וְכָל־אִישׁ יְהוּדָה וְכָל־יֹשְׁבֵי יְרוּשָׁלַ͏ִם אִתּוֹ וְהַכֹּהֲנִים וְהַנְּבִיאִים וְכָל־הָעָם לְמִקָּטֹן וְעַד־גָּדוֹל וַיִּקְרָא בְאָזְנֵיהֶם אֶת־כָּל־דִּבְרֵי סֵפֶר הַבְּרִית הַנִּמְצָא בְּבֵית יְהֹוָה:

3 The king stood by the pillar and solemnized the covenant before *Hashem*: that they would follow *Hashem* and observe His commandments, His injunctions, and His laws with all their heart and soul; that they would fulfill all the terms of this covenant as inscribed upon the scroll. And all the people entered into the covenant.

ג וַיַּעֲמֹד הַמֶּלֶךְ עַל־הָעַמּוּד וַיִּכְרֹת אֶת־הַבְּרִית לִפְנֵי יְהֹוָה לָלֶכֶת אַחַר יְהֹוָה וְלִשְׁמֹר מִצְוֺתָיו וְאֶת־עֵדְוֺתָיו וְאֶת־חֻקֹּתָיו בְּכָל־לֵב וּבְכָל־נֶפֶשׁ לְהָקִים אֶת־דִּבְרֵי הַבְּרִית הַזֹּאת הַכְּתֻבִים עַל־הַסֵּפֶר הַזֶּה וַיַּעֲמֹד כָּל־הָעָם בַּבְּרִית:

Melachim II / II Kings
Chapter 23

4 Then the king ordered the *Kohen Gadol Chilkiyahu*, the *Kohanim* of the second rank, and the guards of the threshold to bring out of the Temple of *Hashem* all the objects made for Baal and Asherah and all the host of heaven. He burned them outside *Yerushalayim* in the fields of Kidron, and he removed the ashes to *Beit El*.

5 He suppressed the idolatrous priests whom the kings of *Yehuda* had appointed to make offerings at the shrines in the towns of *Yehuda* and in the environs of *Yerushalayim*, and those who made offerings to Baal, to the sun and moon and constellations – all the host of heaven.

6 He brought out the [image of] Asherah from the House of *Hashem* to the Kidron Valley outside *Yerushalayim*, and burned it in the Kidron Valley; he beat it to dust and scattered its dust over the burial ground of the common people.

7 He tore down the cubicles of the male prostitutes in the House of *Hashem*, at the place where the women wove coverings for Asherah.

8 He brought all the *Kohanim* from the towns of *Yehuda* [to *Yerushalayim*] and defiled the shrines where the *Kohanim* had been making offerings – from Geba to *Be'er Sheva*. He also demolished the shrines of the gates, which were at the entrance of the gate of *Yehoshua*, the city prefect – which were on a person's left [as he entered] the city gate.

9 The *Kohanim* of the shrines, however, did not ascend the *Mizbayach* of *Hashem* in *Yerushalayim*, but they ate unleavened bread along with their kinsmen.

10 He also defiled Topheth, which is in the Valley of Ben-hinnom, so that no one might consign his son or daughter to the fire of Molech.

11 He did away with the horses that the kings of *Yehuda* had dedicated to the sun, at the entrance of the House of *Hashem*, near the chamber of the eunuch Nathan-melech, which was in the precincts. He burned the chariots of the sun.

מלכים ב
פרק כג

ד וַיְצַו הַמֶּלֶךְ אֶת־חִלְקִיָּהוּ הַכֹּהֵן הַגָּדוֹל וְאֶת־כֹּהֲנֵי הַמִּשְׁנֶה וְאֶת־שֹׁמְרֵי הַסַּף לְהוֹצִיא מֵהֵיכַל יְהֹוָה אֵת כָּל־הַכֵּלִים הָעֲשׂוּיִם לַבַּעַל וְלָאֲשֵׁרָה וּלְכֹל צְבָא הַשָּׁמָיִם וַיִּשְׂרְפֵם מִחוּץ לִירוּשָׁלַיִם בְּשַׁדְמוֹת קִדְרוֹן וְנָשָׂא אֶת־עֲפָרָם בֵּית־אֵל:

ה וְהִשְׁבִּית אֶת־הַכְּמָרִים אֲשֶׁר נָתְנוּ מַלְכֵי יְהוּדָה וַיְקַטֵּר בַּבָּמוֹת בְּעָרֵי יְהוּדָה וּמְסִבֵּי יְרוּשָׁלָ͏ִם וְאֶת־הַמְקַטְּרִים לַבַּעַל לַשֶּׁמֶשׁ וְלַיָּרֵחַ וְלַמַּזָּלוֹת וּלְכֹל צְבָא הַשָּׁמָיִם:

ו וַיֹּצֵא אֶת־הָאֲשֵׁרָה מִבֵּית יְהֹוָה מִחוּץ לִירוּשָׁלַיִם אֶל־נַחַל קִדְרוֹן וַיִּשְׂרֹף אֹתָהּ בְּנַחַל קִדְרוֹן וַיָּדֶק לְעָפָר וַיַּשְׁלֵךְ אֶת־עֲפָרָהּ עַל־קֶבֶר בְּנֵי הָעָם:

ז וַיִּתֹּץ אֶת־בָּתֵּי הַקְּדֵשִׁים אֲשֶׁר בְּבֵית יְהֹוָה אֲשֶׁר הַנָּשִׁים אֹרְגוֹת שָׁם בָּתִּים לָאֲשֵׁרָה:

ח וַיָּבֵא אֶת־כָּל־הַכֹּהֲנִים מֵעָרֵי יְהוּדָה וַיְטַמֵּא אֶת־הַבָּמוֹת אֲשֶׁר קִטְּרוּ־שָׁמָּה הַכֹּהֲנִים מִגֶּבַע עַד־בְּאֵר שָׁבַע וְנָתַץ אֶת־בָּמוֹת הַשְּׁעָרִים אֲשֶׁר־פֶּתַח שַׁעַר יְהוֹשֻׁעַ שַׂר־הָעִיר אֲשֶׁר־עַל־שְׂמֹאול אִישׁ בְּשַׁעַר הָעִיר:

ט אַךְ לֹא יַעֲלוּ כֹּהֲנֵי הַבָּמוֹת אֶל־מִזְבַּח יְהֹוָה בִּירוּשָׁלָ͏ִם כִּי אִם־אָכְלוּ מַצּוֹת בְּתוֹךְ אֲחֵיהֶם:

י וְטִמֵּא אֶת־הַתֹּפֶת אֲשֶׁר בְּגֵי [בֶן־] הִנֹּם לְבִלְתִּי לְהַעֲבִיר אִישׁ אֶת־בְּנוֹ וְאֶת־בִּתּוֹ בָּאֵשׁ לַמֹּלֶךְ:

יא וַיַּשְׁבֵּת אֶת־הַסּוּסִים אֲשֶׁר נָתְנוּ מַלְכֵי יְהוּדָה לַשֶּׁמֶשׁ מִבֹּא בֵית־יְהֹוָה אֶל־לִשְׁכַּת נְתַן־מֶלֶךְ הַסָּרִיס אֲשֶׁר בַּפַּרְוָרִים וְאֶת־מַרְכְּבוֹת הַשֶּׁמֶשׁ שָׂרַף בָּאֵשׁ:

Melachim II / II Kings
Chapter 23

מלכים ב
פרק כג

12 And the king tore down the altars made by the kings of *Yehuda* on the roof by the upper chamber of *Achaz*, and the altars made by *Menashe* in the two courts of the House of *Hashem*. He removed them quickly from there and scattered their rubble in the Kidron Valley.

יב וְאֶת־הַֽמִּזְבְּח֡וֹת אֲשֶׁ֣ר עַל־הַגָּג֩ עֲלִיַּ֨ת אָחָ֜ז אֲשֶׁר־עָשׂ֣וּ ׀ מַלְכֵ֣י יְהוּדָ֗ה וְאֶת־הַֽמִּזְבְּחוֹת֙ אֲשֶׁר־עָשָׂ֣ה מְנַשֶּׁ֔ה בִּשְׁתֵּ֛י חַצְר֥וֹת בֵּית־יְהוָ֖ה נָתַ֣ץ הַמֶּ֑לֶךְ וַיָּ֣רָץ מִשָּׁ֔ם וְהִשְׁלִ֥יךְ אֶת־עֲפָרָ֖ם אֶל־נַ֥חַל קִדְרֽוֹן:

13 The king also defiled the shrines facing *Yerushalayim*, to the south of the Mount of the Destroyer, which King *Shlomo* of *Yisrael* had built for Ashtoreth, the abomination of the Sidonians, for Chemosh, the abomination of Moab, and for Milcom, the detestable thing of the Amonites.

יג וְֽאֶת־הַבָּמ֞וֹת אֲשֶׁ֣ר ׀ עַל־פְּנֵ֣י יְרוּשָׁלַ֗͏ִם אֲשֶׁר֙ מִימִ֣ין לְהַר־הַמַּשְׁחִ֔ית אֲשֶׁ֣ר בָּנָ֞ה שְׁלֹמֹ֤ה מֶֽלֶךְ־יִשְׂרָאֵל֙ לְעַשְׁתֹּ֣רֶת ׀ שִׁקֻּ֣ץ צִידֹנִ֗ים וְלִכְמוֹשׁ֙ שִׁקֻּ֣ץ מוֹאָ֔ב וּלְמִלְכֹּ֖ם תּוֹעֲבַ֣ת בְּנֵֽי־עַמּ֑וֹן טִמֵּ֖א הַמֶּֽלֶךְ:

14 He shattered their pillars and cut down their sacred posts and covered their sites with human bones.

יד וְשִׁבַּר֙ אֶת־הַמַּצֵּב֔וֹת וַיִּכְרֹ֖ת אֶת־הָאֲשֵׁרִ֑ים וַיְמַלֵּ֥א אֶת־מְקוֹמָ֖ם עַצְמ֥וֹת אָדָֽם:

15 As for the altar in *Beit El* [and] the shrine made by *Yerovam* son of Nebat who caused *Yisrael* to sin – that altar, too, and the shrine as well, he tore down. He burned down the shrine and beat it to dust, and he burned the sacred post.

טו וְגַ֨ם אֶת־הַמִּזְבֵּ֜חַ אֲשֶׁ֣ר בְּבֵֽית־אֵ֗ל הַבָּמָה֙ אֲשֶׁ֨ר עָשָׂ֜ה יָרָבְעָ֤ם בֶּן־נְבָט֙ אֲשֶׁ֤ר הֶחֱטִיא֙ אֶת־יִשְׂרָאֵ֔ל גַּ֣ם אֶת־הַמִּזְבֵּ֧חַ הַה֛וּא וְאֶת־הַבָּמָ֖ה נָתָ֑ץ וַיִּשְׂרֹ֧ף אֶת־הַבָּמָ֛ה הֵדַ֥ק לְעָפָ֖ר וְשָׂרַ֥ף אֲשֵׁרָֽה:

16 *Yoshiyahu* turned and saw the graves that were there on the hill; and he had the bones taken out of the graves and burned on the altar. Thus he defiled it, in fulfillment of the word of *Hashem* foretold by the man of *Hashem* who foretold these happenings.

טז וַיִּ֣פֶן יֹאשִׁיָּ֗הוּ וַיַּ֨רְא אֶת־הַקְּבָרִ֤ים אֲשֶׁר־שָׁם֙ בָּהָ֔ר וַיִּשְׁלַ֗ח וַיִּקַּ֤ח אֶת־הָֽעֲצָמוֹת֙ מִן־הַקְּבָרִ֔ים וַיִּשְׂרֹ֖ף עַל־הַמִּזְבֵּ֑חַ וַיְטַמְּאֵ֗הוּ כִּדְבַ֤ר יְהוָה֙ אֲשֶׁ֣ר קָרָ֔א אִ֣ישׁ הָאֱלֹהִ֔ים אֲשֶׁ֣ר קָרָ֔א אֶת־הַדְּבָרִ֖ים הָאֵֽלֶּה:

17 He asked, "What is the marker I see there?" And the men of the town replied, "That is the grave of the man of *Hashem* who came from *Yehuda* and foretold these things that you have done to the altar of *Beit El*."

יז וַיֹּ֕אמֶר מָ֚ה הַצִּיּ֣וּן הַלָּ֔ז אֲשֶׁ֖ר אֲנִ֣י רֹאֶ֑ה וַיֹּאמְר֨וּ אֵלָ֜יו אַנְשֵׁ֣י הָעִ֗יר הַקֶּ֤בֶר אִישׁ־הָֽאֱלֹהִים֙ אֲשֶׁר־בָּ֣א מִֽיהוּדָ֔ה וַיִּקְרָ֗א אֶת־הַדְּבָרִ֤ים הָאֵ֙לֶּה֙ אֲשֶׁ֣ר עָשִׂ֔יתָ עַ֖ל הַמִּזְבַּ֥ח בֵּֽית־אֵֽל:

18 "Let him be," he said, "let no one disturb his bones." So they left his bones undisturbed together with the bones of the *Navi* who came from *Shomron*.

יח וַיֹּ֙אמֶר֙ הַנִּ֣יחוּ ל֔וֹ אִ֖ישׁ אַל־יָנַ֣ע עַצְמֹתָ֑יו וַֽיְמַלְּטוּ֙ עַצְמֹתָ֔יו אֵ֖ת עַצְמ֥וֹת הַנָּבִ֖יא אֲשֶׁר־בָּ֥א מִשֹּׁמְרֽוֹן:

19 *Yoshiyahu* also abolished all the cult places in the towns of *Shomron*, which the kings of *Yisrael* had built, vexing [*Hashem*]. He dealt with them just as he had done to *Beit El*:

יט וְגַם֩ אֶת־כָּל־בָּתֵּ֨י הַבָּמ֜וֹת אֲשֶׁ֣ר ׀ בְּעָרֵ֣י שֹׁמְר֗וֹן אֲשֶׁ֤ר עָשׂוּ֙ מַלְכֵ֣י יִשְׂרָאֵ֔ל לְהַכְעִ֖יס הֵסִ֣יר יֹאשִׁיָּ֑הוּ וַיַּ֣עַשׂ לָהֶ֔ם כְּכָל־הַֽמַּעֲשִׂ֔ים אֲשֶׁ֥ר עָשָׂ֖ה בְּבֵֽית־אֵֽל:

20 He slew on the altars all the priests of the shrines who were there, and he burned human bones on them. Then he returned to *Yerushalayim*.

כ וַ֠יִּזְבַּח אֶת־כָּל־כֹּהֲנֵ֨י הַבָּמ֤וֹת אֲשֶׁר־שָׁם֙ עַל־הַֽמִּזְבְּח֔וֹת וַיִּשְׂרֹ֛ף אֶת־עַצְמ֥וֹת אָדָ֖ם עֲלֵיהֶ֑ם וַיָּ֖שָׁב יְרוּשָׁלָֽ͏ִם:

Melachim II / II Kings
Chapter 23

מלכים ב
פרק כג

21 The king commanded all the people, "Offer the *Pesach* sacrifice to *Hashem* your God as prescribed in this scroll of the covenant."

כא וַיְצַו הַמֶּלֶךְ אֶת־כָּל־הָעָם לֵאמֹר עֲשׂוּ פֶסַח לַיהֹוָה אֱלֹהֵיכֶם כַּכָּתוּב עַל סֵפֶר הַבְּרִית הַזֶּה׃

22 Now the *Pesach* sacrifice had not been offered in that manner in the days of the chieftains who ruled *Yisrael*, or during the days of the kings of *Yisrael* and the kings of *Yehuda*.

כב כִּי לֹא נַעֲשָׂה כַּפֶּסַח הַזֶּה מִימֵי הַשֹּׁפְטִים אֲשֶׁר שָׁפְטוּ אֶת־יִשְׂרָאֵל וְכֹל יְמֵי מַלְכֵי יִשְׂרָאֵל וּמַלְכֵי יְהוּדָה׃

KEE LO na-a-SAH ka-PE-sakh ha-ZEH mee-MAY ha-SHO-f'-TEEM a-SHER sha-f'-TU et yis-ra-AYL v'-KHOL y'-MAY mal-KHAY yis-ra-AYL u-mal-KHAY y'-hu-DAH

23 Only in the eighteenth year of King *Yoshiyahu* was such a *Pesach* sacrifice offered in that manner to *Hashem* in *Yerushalayim*.

כג כִּי אִם־בִּשְׁמֹנֶה עֶשְׂרֵה שָׁנָה לַמֶּלֶךְ יֹאשִׁיָּהוּ נַעֲשָׂה הַפֶּסַח הַזֶּה לַיהֹוָה בִּירוּשָׁלָםִ׃

24 *Yoshiyahu* also did away with the necromancers and the mediums, the idols and the fetishes – all the detestable things that were to be seen in the land of *Yehuda* and *Yerushalayim*. Thus he fulfilled the terms of the Teaching recorded in the scroll that the *Kohen Chilkiyahu* had found in the House of *Hashem*.

כד וְגַם אֶת־הָאֹבוֹת וְאֶת־הַיִּדְּעֹנִים וְאֶת־הַתְּרָפִים וְאֶת־הַגִּלֻּלִים וְאֵת כָּל־הַשִּׁקֻּצִים אֲשֶׁר נִרְאוּ בְּאֶרֶץ יְהוּדָה וּבִירוּשָׁלַםִ בִּעֵר יֹאשִׁיָּהוּ לְמַעַן הָקִים אֶת־דִּבְרֵי הַתּוֹרָה הַכְּתֻבִים עַל־הַסֵּפֶר אֲשֶׁר מָצָא חִלְקִיָּהוּ הַכֹּהֵן בֵּית יְהֹוָה׃

25 There was no king like him before who turned back to *Hashem* with all his heart and soul and might, in full accord with the Teaching of *Moshe*; nor did any like him arise after him.

כה וְכָמֹהוּ לֹא־הָיָה לְפָנָיו מֶלֶךְ אֲשֶׁר־שָׁב אֶל־יְהֹוָה בְּכָל־לְבָבוֹ וּבְכָל־נַפְשׁוֹ וּבְכָל־מְאֹדוֹ כְּכֹל תּוֹרַת מֹשֶׁה וְאַחֲרָיו לֹא־קָם כָּמֹהוּ׃

26 However, *Hashem* did not turn away from His awesome wrath which had blazed up against *Yehuda* because of all the things *Menashe* did to vex Him.

כו אַךְ לֹא־שָׁב יְהֹוָה מֵחֲרוֹן אַפּוֹ הַגָּדוֹל אֲשֶׁר־חָרָה אַפּוֹ בִּיהוּדָה עַל כָּל־הַכְּעָסִים אֲשֶׁר הִכְעִיסוֹ מְנַשֶּׁה׃

27 *Hashem* said, "I will also banish *Yehuda* from My presence as I banished *Yisrael*; and I will reject the city of *Yerushalayim* which I chose and the House where I said My name would abide."

כז וַיֹּאמֶר יְהֹוָה גַּם אֶת־יְהוּדָה אָסִיר מֵעַל פָּנַי כַּאֲשֶׁר הֲסִרֹתִי אֶת־יִשְׂרָאֵל וּמָאַסְתִּי אֶת־הָעִיר הַזֹּאת אֲשֶׁר־בָּחַרְתִּי אֶת־יְרוּשָׁלַםִ וְאֶת־הַבַּיִת אֲשֶׁר אָמַרְתִּי יִהְיֶה שְׁמִי שָׁם׃

23:22 Now the *Pesach* sacrifice had not been offered in that manner *Yoshiyahu* is a righteous king who restores service of *Hashem* and observance of His *Torah* among the Children of Israel. His unique ability and success is symbolized by the massive observance of the *Pesach* sacrifice. Rashi notes that there had never been as many people observing this commandment. The *Pesach* sacrifice is a central commandment, as it proclaims *Hashem*'s active involvement in history and His selection of the Children of Israel as His holy nation. It also shows that though God may punish the Children of Israel, His bond with them is eternal. This message will take on special significance during the long and arduous exile from the Land of Israel.

944

Melachim II / II Kings
Chapter 24

28 The other events of *Yoshiyahu*'s reign, and all his actions, are recorded in the Annals of the Kings of *Yehuda*.

29 In his days, Pharaoh Neco, king of Egypt, marched against the king of Assyria to the River Euphrates; King *Yoshiyahu* marched toward him, but when he confronted him at Megiddo, [Pharaoh Neco] slew him.

30 His servants conveyed his body in a chariot from Megiddo to *Yerushalayim*, and they buried him in his tomb. Then the people of the land took *Yehoachaz*; they anointed him and made him king in place of his father.

31 *Yehoachaz* was twenty-three years old when he became king, and he reigned three months in *Yerushalayim*; his mother's name was Hamutal daughter of *Yirmiyahu* of Libnah.

32 He did what was displeasing to *Hashem*, just as his fathers had done.

33 Pharaoh Neco imprisoned him in Riblah in the region of Hamath, to keep him from reigning in *Yerushalayim*. And he imposed on the land an indemnity of one hundred *kikarim* of silver and a *kikar* of gold.

34 Then Pharaoh Neco appointed Eliakim son of *Yoshiyahu* king in place of his father *Yoshiyahu*, changing his name to *Yehoyakim*. He took *Yehoachaz* and brought him to Egypt, where he died.

35 *Yehoyakim* gave Pharaoh the silver and the gold, and he made an assessment on the land to pay the money demanded by Pharaoh. He exacted from the people of the land the silver and gold to be paid Pharaoh Neco, according to each man's assessment.

36 *Yehoyakim* was twenty-five years old when he became king, and he reigned eleven years in *Yerushalayim*; his mother's name was Zebudah daughter of Pedaiah of Rumah.

37 He did what was displeasing to *Hashem*, just as his ancestors had done.

24 1 In his days, King Nebuchadnezzar of Babylon came up, and *Yehoyakim* became his vassal for three years. Then he turned and rebelled against him.

מלכים ב
פרק כד

כח וְיֶ֨תֶר דִּבְרֵ֤י יֹאשִׁיָּ֙הוּ֙ וְכׇל־אֲשֶׁ֣ר עָשָׂ֔ה הֲלֹא־הֵ֣ם כְּתוּבִ֗ים עַל־סֵ֛פֶר דִּבְרֵ֥י הַיָּמִ֖ים לְמַלְכֵ֥י יְהוּדָֽה׃

כט בְּיָמָ֡יו עָלָה֩ פַרְעֹ֨ה נְכֹ֧ה מֶלֶךְ־מִצְרַ֛יִם עַל־מֶ֥לֶךְ אַשּׁ֖וּר עַל־נְהַר־פְּרָ֑ת וַיֵּ֨לֶךְ הַמֶּ֤לֶךְ יֹאשִׁיָּ֙הוּ֙ לִקְרָאת֔וֹ וַיְמִיתֵ֙הוּ֙ בִּמְגִדּ֔וֹ כִּרְאֹת֖וֹ אֹתֽוֹ׃

ל וַיַּרְכִּבֻ֨הוּ עֲבָדָ֥יו מֵת֙ מִמְּגִדּ֔וֹ וַיְבִאֻ֙הוּ֙ יְר֣וּשָׁלַ֔͏ִם וַיִּקְבְּרֻ֖הוּ בִּקְבֻרָת֑וֹ וַיִּקַּ֣ח עַם־הָאָ֗רֶץ אֶת־יְהֽוֹאָחָז֙ בֶּן־יֹ֣אשִׁיָּ֔הוּ וַיִּמְשְׁח֥וּ אֹת֛וֹ וַיַּמְלִ֥יכוּ אֹת֖וֹ תַּ֥חַת אָבִֽיו׃

לא בֶּן־עֶשְׂרִ֨ים וְשָׁלֹ֤שׁ שָׁנָה֙ יְהוֹאָחָ֣ז בְּמׇלְכ֔וֹ וּשְׁלֹשָׁ֣ה חֳדָשִׁ֔ים מָלַ֖ךְ בִּירוּשָׁלָ֑͏ִם וְשֵׁ֣ם אִמּ֔וֹ חֲמוּטַ֥ל בַּֽת־יִרְמְיָ֖הוּ מִלִּבְנָֽה׃

לב וַיַּ֥עַשׂ הָרַ֖ע בְּעֵינֵ֣י יְהֹוָ֑ה כְּכֹ֥ל אֲשֶׁר־עָשׂ֖וּ אֲבֹתָֽיו׃

לג וַיַּאַסְרֵ֣הוּ פַרְעֹ֣ה נְכֹה֩ בְרִבְלָ֨ה בְּאֶ֤רֶץ חֲמָת֙ [מִמְּלֹ֣ךְ] בִּירוּשָׁלָ֔͏ִם וַיִּתֶּן־עֹ֙נֶשׁ֙ עַל־הָאָ֔רֶץ מֵאָ֥ה כִכַּר־כֶּ֖סֶף וְכִכַּ֥ר זָהָֽב׃

לד וַיַּמְלֵךְ֩ פַּרְעֹ֨ה נְכֹ֜ה אֶת־אֶלְיָקִ֣ים בֶּן־יֹאשִׁיָּ֗הוּ תַּ֚חַת יֹאשִׁיָּ֣הוּ אָבִ֔יו וַיַּסֵּ֥ב אֶת־שְׁמ֖וֹ יְהוֹיָקִ֑ים וְאֶת־יְהוֹאָחָ֣ז לָקָ֔ח וַיָּבֹ֥א מִצְרַ֖יִם וַיָּ֥מׇת שָֽׁם׃

לה וְהַכֶּ֣סֶף וְהַזָּהָ֗ב נָתַ֤ן יְהוֹיָקִים֙ לְפַרְעֹ֔ה אַ֚ךְ הֶעֱרִ֣יךְ אֶת־הָאָ֔רֶץ לָתֵ֥ת אֶת־הַכֶּ֖סֶף עַל־פִּ֣י פַרְעֹ֑ה אִ֣ישׁ כְּעֶרְכּ֗וֹ נָגַ֤שׂ אֶת־הַכֶּ֙סֶף֙ וְאֶת־הַזָּהָ֔ב אֶת־עַם֙ הָאָ֔רֶץ לָתֵ֖ת לְפַרְעֹ֥ה נְכֹֽה׃

לו בֶּן־עֶשְׂרִ֨ים וְחָמֵ֤שׁ שָׁנָה֙ יְהוֹיָקִ֣ים בְּמׇלְכ֔וֹ וְאַחַ֤ת עֶשְׂרֵה֙ שָׁנָ֔ה מָלַ֖ךְ בִּירוּשָׁלָ֑͏ִם וְשֵׁ֣ם אִמּ֔וֹ [זְבִידָּ֛ה] בַת־פְּדָיָ֖ה מִן־רוּמָֽה׃

לז וַיַּ֥עַשׂ הָרַ֖ע בְּעֵינֵ֣י יְהֹוָ֑ה כְּכֹ֥ל אֲשֶׁר־עָשׂ֖וּ אֲבֹתָֽיו׃

כד א בְּיָמָ֣יו עָלָ֔ה נְבֻכַדְנֶאצַּ֖ר מֶ֣לֶךְ בָּבֶ֑ל וַיְהִי־ל֨וֹ יְהוֹיָקִ֥ים עֶ֙בֶד֙ שָׁלֹ֣שׁ שָׁנִ֔ים וַיָּ֖שׇׁב וַיִּמְרׇד־בּֽוֹ׃

Melachim II / II Kings
Chapter 24

מלכים ב
פרק כד

2 *Hashem* let loose against him the raiding bands of the Chaldeans, Arameans, Moabites, and Amonites; He let them loose against *Yehuda* to destroy it, in accordance with the word that *Hashem* had spoken through His servants the *Neviim*.

ב וַיְשַׁלַּח יְהֹוָה בּוֹ אֶת־גְּדוּדֵי כַשְׂדִּים וְאֶת־גְּדוּדֵי אֲרָם וְאֵת גְּדוּדֵי מוֹאָב וְאֵת גְּדוּדֵי בְנֵי־עַמּוֹן וַיְשַׁלְּחֵם בִּיהוּדָה לְהַאֲבִידוֹ כִּדְבַר יְהֹוָה אֲשֶׁר דִּבֶּר בְּיַד עֲבָדָיו הַנְּבִיאִים:

3 All this befell *Yehuda* at the command of *Hashem*, who banished [them] from His presence because of all the sins that *Menashe* had committed,

ג אַךְ עַל־פִּי יְהֹוָה הָיְתָה בִּיהוּדָה לְהָסִיר מֵעַל פָּנָיו בְּחַטֹּאת מְנַשֶּׁה כְּכֹל אֲשֶׁר עָשָׂה:

4 and also because of the blood of the innocent that he shed. For he filled *Yerushalayim* with the blood of the innocent, and *Hashem* would not forgive.

ד וְגַם דַּם־הַנָּקִי אֲשֶׁר שָׁפָךְ וַיְמַלֵּא אֶת־יְרוּשָׁלִַם דָּם נָקִי וְלֹא־אָבָה יְהֹוָה לִסְלֹחַ:

5 The other events of *Yehoyakim*'s reign, and all of his actions, are recorded in the Annals of the Kings of *Yehuda*.

ה וְיֶתֶר דִּבְרֵי יְהוֹיָקִים וְכָל־אֲשֶׁר עָשָׂה הֲלֹא־הֵם כְּתוּבִים עַל־סֵפֶר דִּבְרֵי הַיָּמִים לְמַלְכֵי יְהוּדָה:

6 *Yehoyakim* slept with his fathers, and his son *Yehoyachin* succeeded him as king.

ו וַיִּשְׁכַּב יְהוֹיָקִים עִם־אֲבֹתָיו וַיִּמְלֹךְ יְהוֹיָכִין בְּנוֹ תַּחְתָּיו:

7 The king of Egypt did not venture out of his country again, for the king of Babylon had seized all the land that had belonged to the king of Egypt, from the Wadi of Egypt to the River Euphrates.

ז וְלֹא־הֹסִיף עוֹד מֶלֶךְ מִצְרַיִם לָצֵאת מֵאַרְצוֹ כִּי־לָקַח מֶלֶךְ בָּבֶל מִנַּחַל מִצְרַיִם עַד־נְהַר־פְּרָת כֹּל אֲשֶׁר הָיְתָה לְמֶלֶךְ מִצְרָיִם:

8 *Yehoyachin* was eighteen years old when he became king, and he reigned three months in *Yerushalayim*; his mother's name was Nehushta daughter of Elnathan of *Yerushalayim*.

ח בֶּן־שְׁמֹנֶה עֶשְׂרֵה שָׁנָה יְהוֹיָכִין בְּמָלְכוֹ וּשְׁלֹשָׁה חֳדָשִׁים מָלַךְ בִּירוּשָׁלִָם וְשֵׁם אִמּוֹ נְחֻשְׁתָּא בַת־אֶלְנָתָן מִירוּשָׁלָיִם:

9 He did what was displeasing to *Hashem*, just as his father had done.

ט וַיַּעַשׂ הָרַע בְּעֵינֵי יְהֹוָה כְּכֹל אֲשֶׁר־עָשָׂה אָבִיו:

10 At that time, the troops of King Nebuchadnezzar of Babylon marched against *Yerushalayim*, and the city came under siege.

י בָּעֵת הַהִיא עָלָה [עָלוּ] עַבְדֵי נְבֻכַדְנֶאצַּר מֶלֶךְ־בָּבֶל יְרוּשָׁלִָם וַתָּבֹא הָעִיר בַּמָּצוֹר:

11 King Nebuchadnezzar of Babylon advanced against the city while his troops were besieging it.

יא וַיָּבֹא נְבוּכַדְנֶאצַּר מֶלֶךְ־בָּבֶל עַל־הָעִיר וַעֲבָדָיו צָרִים עָלֶיהָ:

12 Thereupon King *Yehoyachin* of *Yehuda*, along with his mother, and his courtiers, commanders, and officers, surrendered to the king of Babylon. The king of Babylon took him captive in the eighth year of his reign.

יב וַיֵּצֵא יְהוֹיָכִין מֶלֶךְ־יְהוּדָה עַל־מֶלֶךְ בָּבֶל הוּא וְאִמּוֹ וַעֲבָדָיו וְשָׂרָיו וְסָרִיסָיו וַיִּקַּח אֹתוֹ מֶלֶךְ בָּבֶל בִּשְׁנַת שְׁמֹנֶה לְמָלְכוֹ:

13 He carried off from *Yerushalayim* all the treasures of the House of *Hashem* and the treasures of the royal palace; he stripped off all the golden decorations in the Temple of *Hashem* – which King *Shlomo* of *Yisrael* had made – as *Hashem* had warned.

יג וַיּוֹצֵא מִשָּׁם אֶת־כָּל־אוֹצְרוֹת בֵּית יְהֹוָה וְאוֹצְרוֹת בֵּית הַמֶּלֶךְ וַיְקַצֵּץ אֶת־כָּל־כְּלֵי הַזָּהָב אֲשֶׁר עָשָׂה שְׁלֹמֹה מֶלֶךְ־יִשְׂרָאֵל בְּהֵיכַל יְהֹוָה כַּאֲשֶׁר דִּבֶּר יְהֹוָה:

Melachim II / II Kings
Chapter 25

14 He exiled all of *Yerushalayim*: all the commanders and all the warriors – ten thousand exiles – as well as all the craftsmen and smiths; only the poorest people in the land were left.

יד וְהִגְלָה אֶת־כָּל־יְרוּשָׁלַם וְאֶת־כָּל־הַשָּׂרִים וְאֵת כָּל־גִּבּוֹרֵי הַחַיִל עֲשֶׂרֶת [עֲשָׂרָה] אֲלָפִים גּוֹלֶה וְכָל־הֶחָרָשׁ וְהַמַּסְגֵּר לֹא נִשְׁאַר זוּלַת דַּלַּת עַם־הָאָרֶץ:

v'-hig-LAH et kol y'-ru-sha-LA-im v'-et kol ha-sa-REEM v'-AYT kol gi-bo-RAY ha-KHA-yil a-SE-ret a-la-FEEM go-LEH v'-khol he-kha-RASH v'-ha-mas-GAYR lo nish-AR zu-LAT da-LAT am ha-A-retz

15 He deported *Yehoyachin* to Babylon; and the king's wives and officers and the notables of the land were brought as exiles from *Yerushalayim* to Babylon.

טו וַיֶּגֶל אֶת־יְהוֹיָכִין בָּבֶלָה וְאֶת־אֵם הַמֶּלֶךְ וְאֶת־נְשֵׁי הַמֶּלֶךְ וְאֶת־סָרִיסָיו וְאֵת אוּלֵי [אֵילֵי] הָאָרֶץ הוֹלִיךְ גּוֹלָה מִירוּשָׁלַם בָּבֶלָה:

16 All the able men, to the number of seven thousand – all of them warriors, trained for battle – and a thousand craftsmen and smiths were brought to Babylon as exiles by the king of Babylon.

טז וְאֵת כָּל־אַנְשֵׁי הַחַיִל שִׁבְעַת אֲלָפִים וְהֶחָרָשׁ וְהַמַּסְגֵּר אֶלֶף הַכֹּל גִּבּוֹרִים עֹשֵׂי מִלְחָמָה וַיְבִיאֵם מֶלֶךְ־בָּבֶל גּוֹלָה בָּבֶלָה:

17 And the king of Babylon appointed Mattaniah, *Yehoyachin*'s uncle, king in his place, changing his name to *Tzidkiyahu*.

יז וַיַּמְלֵךְ מֶלֶךְ־בָּבֶל אֶת־מַתַּנְיָה דֹדוֹ תַּחְתָּיו וַיַּסֵּב אֶת־שְׁמוֹ צִדְקִיָּהוּ:

18 *Tzidkiyahu* was twenty-one years old when he became king, and he reigned eleven years in *Yerushalayim*; his mother's name was Hamutal daughter of *Yirmiyahu* of Libnah.

יח בֶּן־עֶשְׂרִים וְאַחַת שָׁנָה צִדְקִיָּהוּ בְמָלְכוֹ וְאַחַת עֶשְׂרֵה שָׁנָה מָלַךְ בִּירוּשָׁלָם וְשֵׁם אִמּוֹ חֲמִיטַל [חֲמוּטַל] בַּת־יִרְמְיָהוּ מִלִּבְנָה:

19 He did what was displeasing to *Hashem*, just as *Yehoyakim* had done.

יט וַיַּעַשׂ הָרַע בְּעֵינֵי יְהוָה כְּכֹל אֲשֶׁר־עָשָׂה יְהוֹיָקִים:

20 Indeed, *Yerushalayim* and *Yehuda* were a cause of anger for *Hashem*, so that He cast them out of His presence. *Tzidkiyahu* rebelled against the king of Babylon.

כ כִּי עַל־אַף יְהוָה הָיְתָה בִירוּשָׁלַם וּבִיהוּדָה עַד־הִשְׁלִכוֹ אֹתָם מֵעַל פָּנָיו וַיִּמְרֹד צִדְקִיָּהוּ בְּמֶלֶךְ בָּבֶל:

25 **1** And in the ninth year of his reign, on the tenth day of the tenth month, Nebuchadnezzar moved against *Yerushalayim* with his whole army. He besieged it; and they built towers against it all around.

כה א וַיְהִי בִשְׁנַת הַתְּשִׁיעִית לְמָלְכוֹ בַּחֹדֶשׁ הָעֲשִׂירִי בֶּעָשׂוֹר לַחֹדֶשׁ בָּא נְבֻכַדְנֶאצַּר מֶלֶךְ־בָּבֶל הוּא וְכָל־חֵילוֹ עַל־יְרוּשָׁלַם וַיִּחַן עָלֶיהָ וַיִּבְנוּ עָלֶיהָ דָּיֵק סָבִיב:

24:14 All the craftsmen and smiths During the first stage of the exile to Babylon, Nebuchadnezzar carried away all the leaders of the Children of Israel, in the stage of exile known as *galut cheresh umasger* (גלות חרש ומסגר), 'the exile of the craftsmen and smiths.' During this exile, the royalty, military elite, Torah scholars and all the dignitaries were taken away from *Yerushalayim*. Nebuchadnezzar left behind only the poor people, ruled by a government under his control. By depriving the people of their leadership, Nebuchadnezzar believed that he would end all possibility of revolt against his rule. Yet, due to *Hashem*'s intention to destroy the city, a rebellion leading to the ultimate destruction will take place. Despite the plans of even the most powerful human beings, God's plans can never be thwarted.

Melachim II / II Kings
Chapter 25

מלכים ב
פרק כה

2 The city continued in a state of siege until the eleventh year of King *Tzidkiyahu*.

ב וַתָּבֹא הָעִיר בַּמָּצוֹר עַד עַשְׁתֵּי עֶשְׂרֵה שָׁנָה לַמֶּלֶךְ צִדְקִיָּהוּ:

3 By the ninth day [of the fourth month] the famine had become acute in the city; there was no food left for the common people.

ג בְּתִשְׁעָה לַחֹדֶשׁ וַיֶּחֱזַק הָרָעָב בָּעִיר וְלֹא־הָיָה לֶחֶם לְעַם הָאָרֶץ:

4 Then [the wall of] the city was breached. All the soldiers [left the city] by night through the gate between the double walls, which is near the king's garden – the Chaldeans were all around the city; and [the king] set out for the Arabah.

ד וַתִּבָּקַע הָעִיר וְכָל־אַנְשֵׁי הַמִּלְחָמָה הַלַּיְלָה דֶּרֶךְ שַׁעַר בֵּין הַחֹמֹתַיִם אֲשֶׁר עַל־גַּן הַמֶּלֶךְ וְכַשְׂדִּים עַל־הָעִיר סָבִיב וַיֵּלֶךְ דֶּרֶךְ הָעֲרָבָה:

5 But the Chaldean troops pursued the king, and they overtook him in the steppes of *Yericho* as his entire force left him and scattered.

ה וַיִּרְדְּפוּ חֵיל־כַּשְׂדִּים אַחַר הַמֶּלֶךְ וַיַּשִּׂגוּ אֹתוֹ בְּעַרְבוֹת יְרֵחוֹ וְכָל־חֵילוֹ נָפֹצוּ מֵעָלָיו:

6 They captured the king and brought him before the king of Babylon at Riblah; and they put him on trial.

ו וַיִּתְפְּשׂוּ אֶת־הַמֶּלֶךְ וַיַּעֲלוּ אֹתוֹ אֶל־מֶלֶךְ בָּבֶל רִבְלָתָה וַיְדַבְּרוּ אִתּוֹ מִשְׁפָּט:

7 They slaughtered *Tzidkiyahu*'s sons before his eyes; then *Tzidkiyahu*'s eyes were put out. He was chained in bronze fetters and he was brought to Babylon.

ז וְאֶת־בְּנֵי צִדְקִיָּהוּ שָׁחֲטוּ לְעֵינָיו וְאֶת־עֵינֵי צִדְקִיָּהוּ עִוֵּר וַיַּאַסְרֵהוּ בַנְחֻשְׁתַּיִם וַיְבִאֵהוּ בָּבֶל:

8 On the seventh day of the fifth month – that was the nineteenth year of King Nebuchadnezzar of Babylon – Nebuzaradan, the chief of the guards, an officer of the king of Babylon, came to *Yerushalayim*.

ח וּבַחֹדֶשׁ הַחֲמִישִׁי בְּשִׁבְעָה לַחֹדֶשׁ הִיא שְׁנַת תְּשַׁע־עֶשְׂרֵה שָׁנָה לַמֶּלֶךְ נְבֻכַדְנֶאצַּר מֶלֶךְ־בָּבֶל בָּא נְבוּזַרְאֲדָן רַב־טַבָּחִים עֶבֶד מֶלֶךְ־בָּבֶל יְרוּשָׁלָ͏ִם:

9 He burned the House of *Hashem*, the king's palace, and all the houses of *Yerushalayim*; he burned down the house of every notable person.

va-yis-ROF et bayt a-do-NAI v'-et BAYT ha-ME-lekh v'-ayt kol ba-TAY y'-ru-sha-LA-im v'-et kol BAYT ga-DOL sa-RAF ba-AYSH

ט וַיִּשְׂרֹף אֶת־בֵּית־יְהֹוָה וְאֶת־בֵּית הַמֶּלֶךְ וְאֵת כָּל־בָּתֵּי יְרוּשָׁלַ͏ִם וְאֶת־כָּל־בֵּית גָּדוֹל שָׂרַף בָּאֵשׁ:

10 The entire Chaldean force that was with the chief of the guard tore down the walls of *Yerushalayim* on every side.

י וְאֶת־חוֹמֹת יְרוּשָׁלַ͏ִם סָבִיב נָתְצוּ כָּל־חֵיל כַּשְׂדִּים אֲשֶׁר רַב־טַבָּחִים:

25:9 He burned the House of *Hashem* At the time, this is the greatest calamity to have ever occurred to the Children of Israel. *Hashem* permits Nebuchadnezzar to destroy His *Beit Hamikdash*, the spiritual center of the universe. He also allows the burning of the king's house, which represents the monarchy, and the houses of prayer and study in *Yerushalayim*. The nation is exiled, and only a small group of poor people remains in the land under the leadership of *Gedalya* the son of *Achikam*. When *Gedalya* is killed and the rest of the people flee to Egypt, it seems that all ties between the Children of Israel and their land have been lost, as there isn't even a small Jewish presence left in *Eretz Yisrael*. However, despite the utter desecration, destruction and despair, the People of Israel will again rise and the *Beit Hamikdash* will be rebuilt. *Sefer Melachim* hints to this renewal as it ends on a somewhat positive note with the release of King *Yehoyachin* from prison and his rise in stature.

Melachim II/II Kings

Chapter 25

11 The remnant of the people that was left in the city, the defectors who had gone over to the king of Babylon – and the remnant of the population – were taken into exile by Nebuzaradan, the chief of the guards.

12 But some of the poorest in the land were left by the chief of the guards, to be vinedressers and field hands.

13 The Chaldeans broke up the bronze columns of the House of *Hashem*, the stands, and the bronze tank that was in the House of *Hashem*; and they carried the bronze away to Babylon.

14 They also took all the pails, scrapers, snuffers, ladles, and all the other bronze vessels used in the service.

15 The chief of the guards took whatever was of gold and whatever was of silver: firepans and sprinkling bowls.

16 The two columns, the one tank, and the stands that *Shlomo* provided for the House of *Hashem* – all these objects contained bronze beyond weighing.

17 The one column was eighteen *amot* high. It had a bronze capital above it; the height of the capital was three *amot*, and there was a meshwork [decorated] with pomegranates about the capital, all made of bronze. And the like was true of the other column with its meshwork.

18 The chief of the guards also took *Seraya*, the chief *Kohen*, *Tzefanya*, the deputy *Kohen*, and the three guardians of the threshold.

19 And from the city he took a eunuch who was in command of the soldiers; five royal privy councillors who were present in the city; the scribe of the army commander, who was in charge of mustering the people of the land; and sixty of the common people who were inside the city.

20 Nebuzaradan, the chief of the guards, took them and brought them to the king of Babylon at Riblah.

21 The king of Babylon had them struck down and put to death at Riblah, in the region of Hamath. Thus *Yehuda* was exiled from its land.

מלכים ב

פרק כה

יא וְאֵת יֶתֶר הָעָם הַנִּשְׁאָרִים בָּעִיר וְאֶת־הַנֹּפְלִים אֲשֶׁר נָפְלוּ עַל־הַמֶּלֶךְ בָּבֶל וְאֵת יֶתֶר הֶהָמוֹן הֶגְלָה נְבוּזַרְאֲדָן רַב־טַבָּחִים:

יב וּמִדַּלַּת הָאָרֶץ הִשְׁאִיר רַב־טַבָּחִים לְכֹרְמִים וּלְיֹגְבִים:

יג וְאֶת־עַמּוּדֵי הַנְּחֹשֶׁת אֲשֶׁר בֵּית־יְהוָה וְאֶת־הַמְּכֹנוֹת וְאֶת־יָם הַנְּחֹשֶׁת אֲשֶׁר בְּבֵית־יְהוָה שִׁבְּרוּ כַשְׂדִּים וַיִּשְׂאוּ אֶת־נְחֻשְׁתָּם בָּבֶלָה:

יד וְאֶת־הַסִּירֹת וְאֶת־הַיָּעִים וְאֶת־הַמְזַמְּרוֹת וְאֶת־הַכַּפּוֹת וְאֵת כָּל־כְּלֵי הַנְּחֹשֶׁת אֲשֶׁר יְשָׁרְתוּ־בָם לָקָחוּ:

טו וְאֶת־הַמַּחְתּוֹת וְאֶת־הַמִּזְרָקוֹת אֲשֶׁר זָהָב זָהָב וַאֲשֶׁר־כֶּסֶף כָּסֶף לָקַח רַב־טַבָּחִים:

טז הָעַמּוּדִים שְׁנַיִם הַיָּם הָאֶחָד וְהַמְּכֹנוֹת אֲשֶׁר־עָשָׂה שְׁלֹמֹה לְבֵית יְהוָה לֹא־הָיָה מִשְׁקָל לִנְחֹשֶׁת כָּל־הַכֵּלִים הָאֵלֶּה:

יז שְׁמֹנֶה עֶשְׂרֵה אַמָּה קוֹמַת הָעַמּוּד הָאֶחָד וְכֹתֶרֶת עָלָיו נְחֹשֶׁת וְקוֹמַת הַכֹּתֶרֶת שָׁלֹשׁ אמה [אַמּוֹת] וּשְׂבָכָה וְרִמֹּנִים עַל־הַכֹּתֶרֶת סָבִיב הַכֹּל נְחֹשֶׁת וְכָאֵלֶּה לַעַמּוּד הַשֵּׁנִי עַל־הַשְּׂבָכָה:

יח וַיִּקַּח רַב־טַבָּחִים אֶת־שְׂרָיָה כֹּהֵן הָרֹאשׁ וְאֶת־צְפַנְיָהוּ כֹּהֵן מִשְׁנֶה וְאֶת־שְׁלֹשֶׁת שֹׁמְרֵי הַסַּף:

יט וּמִן־הָעִיר לָקַח סָרִיס אֶחָד אֲשֶׁר־הוּא פָקִיד עַל־אַנְשֵׁי הַמִּלְחָמָה וַחֲמִשָּׁה אֲנָשִׁים מֵרֹאֵי פְנֵי־הַמֶּלֶךְ אֲשֶׁר נִמְצְאוּ בָעִיר וְאֵת הַסֹּפֵר שַׂר הַצָּבָא הַמַּצְבִּא אֶת־עַם הָאָרֶץ וְשִׁשִּׁים אִישׁ מֵעַם הָאָרֶץ הַנִּמְצְאִים בָּעִיר:

כ וַיִּקַּח אֹתָם נְבוּזַרְאֲדָן רַב־טַבָּחִים וַיֹּלֶךְ אֹתָם עַל־מֶלֶךְ בָּבֶל רִבְלָתָה:

כא וַיַּךְ אֹתָם מֶלֶךְ בָּבֶל וַיְמִיתֵם בְּרִבְלָה בְּאֶרֶץ חֲמָת וַיִּגֶל יְהוּדָה מֵעַל אַדְמָתוֹ:

Melachim II/II Kings
Chapter 25

22 King Nebuchadnezzar of Babylon put *Gedalya* son of *Achikam* son of *Shafan* in charge of the people whom he left in the land of *Yehuda*.

23 When the officers of the troops and their men heard that the king of Babylon had put *Gedalya* in charge, they came to *Gedalya* at *Mitzpa* with Ishmael son of Nethaniah, *Yochanan* son of Kareah, *Seraya* son of Tanhumeth the Netophathite, and Jaazaniah son of the Maachite, together with their men.

24 *Gedalya* reassured them and their men, saying, "Do not be afraid of the servants of the Chaldeans. Stay in the land and serve the king of Babylon, and it will go well with you."

25 In the seventh month, Ishmael son of Nethaniah son of Elishama, who was of royal descent, came with ten men, and they struck down *Gedalya* and he died; [they also killed] the Judeans and the Chaldeans who were present with him at *Mitzpa*.

26 And all the people, young and old, and the officers of the troops set out and went to Egypt because they were afraid of the Chaldeans.

27 In the thirty-seventh year of the exile of King *Yehoyachin* of *Yehuda*, on the twenty-seventh day of the twelfth month, King Evilmerodach of Babylon, in the year he became king, took note of King *Yehoyachin* of *Yehuda* and released him from prison.

28 He spoke kindly to him, and gave him a throne above those of other kings who were with him in Babylon.

29 His prison garments were removed, and [*Yehoyachin*] received regular rations by his favor for the rest of his life.

30 A regular allotment of food was given him at the instance of the king – an allotment for each day – all the days of his life.

מלכים ב
פרק כה

כב וְהָעָם הַנִּשְׁאָר בְּאֶרֶץ יְהוּדָה אֲשֶׁר הִשְׁאִיר נְבוּכַדְנֶאצַּר מֶלֶךְ בָּבֶל וַיַּפְקֵד עֲלֵיהֶם אֶת־גְּדַלְיָהוּ בֶּן־אֲחִיקָם בֶּן־שָׁפָן:

כג וַיִּשְׁמְעוּ כָל־שָׂרֵי הַחֲיָלִים הֵמָּה וְהָאֲנָשִׁים כִּי־הִפְקִיד מֶלֶךְ־בָּבֶל אֶת־גְּדַלְיָהוּ וַיָּבֹאוּ אֶל־גְּדַלְיָהוּ הַמִּצְפָּה וְיִשְׁמָעֵאל בֶּן־נְתַנְיָה וְיוֹחָנָן בֶּן־קָרֵחַ וּשְׂרָיָה בֶן־תַּנְחֻמֶת הַנְּטֹפָתִי וְיַאֲזַנְיָהוּ בֶּן־הַמַּעֲכָתִי הֵמָּה וְאַנְשֵׁיהֶם:

כד וַיִּשָּׁבַע לָהֶם גְּדַלְיָהוּ וּלְאַנְשֵׁיהֶם וַיֹּאמֶר לָהֶם אַל־תִּירְאוּ מֵעַבְדֵי הַכַּשְׂדִּים שְׁבוּ בָאָרֶץ וְעִבְדוּ אֶת־מֶלֶךְ בָּבֶל וְיִטַב לָכֶם:

כה וַיְהִי בַּחֹדֶשׁ הַשְּׁבִיעִי בָּא יִשְׁמָעֵאל בֶּן־נְתַנְיָה בֶן־אֱלִישָׁמָע מִזֶּרַע הַמְּלוּכָה וַעֲשָׂרָה אֲנָשִׁים אִתּוֹ וַיַּכּוּ אֶת־גְּדַלְיָהוּ וַיָּמֹת וְאֶת־הַיְּהוּדִים וְאֶת־הַכַּשְׂדִּים אֲשֶׁר־הָיוּ אִתּוֹ בַּמִּצְפָּה:

כו וַיָּקֻמוּ כָל־הָעָם מִקָּטֹן וְעַד־גָּדוֹל וְשָׂרֵי הַחֲיָלִים וַיָּבֹאוּ מִצְרָיִם כִּי יָרְאוּ מִפְּנֵי כַשְׂדִּים:

כז וַיְהִי בִשְׁלֹשִׁים וָשֶׁבַע שָׁנָה לְגָלוּת יְהוֹיָכִין מֶלֶךְ־יְהוּדָה בִּשְׁנֵים עָשָׂר חֹדֶשׁ בְּעֶשְׂרִים וְשִׁבְעָה לַחֹדֶשׁ נָשָׂא אֱוִיל מְרֹדַךְ מֶלֶךְ בָּבֶל בִּשְׁנַת מָלְכוֹ אֶת־רֹאשׁ יְהוֹיָכִין מֶלֶךְ־יְהוּדָה מִבֵּית כֶּלֶא:

כח וַיְדַבֵּר אִתּוֹ טֹבוֹת וַיִּתֵּן אֶת־כִּסְאוֹ מֵעַל כִּסֵּא הַמְּלָכִים אֲשֶׁר אִתּוֹ בְּבָבֶל:

כט וְשִׁנָּא אֵת בִּגְדֵי כִלְאוֹ וְאָכַל לֶחֶם תָּמִיד לְפָנָיו כָּל־יְמֵי חַיָּיו:

ל וַאֲרֻחָתוֹ אֲרֻחַת תָּמִיד נִתְּנָה־לּוֹ מֵאֵת הַמֶּלֶךְ דְּבַר־יוֹם בְּיוֹמוֹ כֹּל יְמֵי חַיָּו:

Sefer Yeshayahu
The Book of Isaiah

Introduction and commentary by Rabbi Yaakov Beasley

Sefer Yeshayahu (Isaiah) is the first and the longest of the books of the Latter Prophets. *Yeshayahu's* prophecies are recorded in both prose and poetry, and his imagery is considered among the most beautiful in the Bible.

Yeshayahu prophesies during the reigns of at least four kings of *Yehuda* in the second half of the eighth century BCE: *Uzziyahu* (769–733), *Yotam* (758–743 as regent), *Achaz* (743–733 as regent; 733–727), and *Chizkiyahu* (727–698). It appears that his prophecies also continue into the reign of the next king, *Menashe*.

During his lifetime, *Yeshayahu* sees the fortunes of the two kingdoms in Israel, *Shomron* in the north and *Yehuda* in the south, decline dramatically. When he begins his prophetic career, the two kingdoms live in prosperity, harmony, and stability. Within fifty years, the ten tribes of the northern kingdom are a distant memory, exiled to the edges of the Assyrian Empire in 722 BCE. The fortunes of southern kingdom of *Yehuda* are only slightly better; most of its cities are destroyed in the Assyrian invasion of 701 BCE.

Yeshayahu is given the task of explaining why the tragedies are occurring and advising what changes need to be made. Although he uttered many pronouncements of rebuke, *Yeshayahu* is most well-known for his prophecies of consolation and hope. Despite the bleak circumstances of the present, *Yeshayahu* is always able to describe a brighter future which features return and redemption, with the Jewish people living peacefully in their land. These images remain an integral part of Israel's consciousness until today.

The political quiet that exists at the beginning of his life is disturbed with the emergence of the rapacious Assyrian Empire in the east. The kings of the region face two options – either submit to the might of the Assyrians, or attempt to form alliances to oppose the behemoth rising against them. In fact, the kings of Aram and *Yisrael* invade *Yehuda* in 733, in an attempt to pressure King *Achaz* into joining their coalition against Assyria. Instead of supporting them, *Achaz* chooses to ask the Assyrian king *Tiglat-Pileser* for assistance, a decision that would prove nearly fatal for the Jewish people. *Yeshayahu* condemns this decision.

More important to *Yeshayahu*, however, is his attempt to change the people's focus from politics to morality. While they are engaged in political intrigue, the people perform their ritual obligations almost robotically, without passion, and they fail to maintain a just and moral society. Indeed, other prophets among *Yeshayahu*'s contemporaries (*Micha, Hoshea,* and *Amos*) also rail against these failures. Their message is clear: If the people can improve their personal lives, live in justice and peace with each other and serve *Hashem* with sincerity, then the political turmoil will disappear.

The structure of the book reflects these messages. The first section (chapters 1–6) serves as an introduction to the entire book, contrasting the present sinful state of the people with the wonderful potential future that awaits them. The next section (chapters 7–12) describes the immediate threat of the Assyrian invasion, and then its ultimate defeat by a son of *David* who will bring peace and righteousness to Israel. Chapters 13–23 describe a series of judgments against the nations, and chapters 24–27 describe judgments against *Yehuda*. After eight more chapters discussing the woes of Israel and other nations, there is a four-chapter historical summary of the events of *Yeshayahu*'s time (chapters 36–39). Finally, there is a long section of prophecies of consolation that spans from the relief of immediate troubles into the future beyond the horizon, when the People of Israel will return from exile and dwell again in the Land of Israel.

Chart of the Empires that Ruled the Land of Israel

Yeshayahu lived during the period when the Assyrian Empire controlled the region. At this time, the Assyrians captured the Kingdom of *Yisrael* and exiled its inhabitants, causing the ten tribes of Israel to be "lost." *Yeshayahu* also witnessed the capture of some of the cities of the Kingdom of *Yehuda* and the attempt by the Assyrian army to capture *Yerushalayim*. If not for God's intervention, the Kingdom of *Yehuda* would also have fallen to the Assyrians. The Assyrian Empire was just one of many empires that controlled all or parts of the Holy Land over the ages. The following is a list of the major empires that controlled the Land of Israel throughout history, and some of the significant events that occurred during their reigns.

Empire	Years	Significant Events in the Land of Israel	Relevant Verses
Canaanite	c. 15th century BCE–1273 BCE	*Avraham* arrives in the land of Canaan. *Hashem* promises that his descendants, through *Yitzchak*, will inherit the land.	Genesis 12:1–9, 13:14–17, 15:18–21, 17:8, 21:12
Israelite	1273–586 BCE	*Yehoshua* conquers the Land of Israel from the Canaanites, fulfilling *Hashem*'s promise to give it to *Avraham*'s descendants. The Children of Israel live and rule in the Land of Israel until the Babylonian exile.	The events of this time are described throughout the books of the Prophets.
Assyrian	740–c. 625 BCE	Assyrian captivity of parts of the kingdom of *Yisrael* begins in approximately 740 BCE. In 721 BCE, the entire kingdom of *Yisrael* is captured by the Assyrians. The ten tribes that belonged to the kingdom are exiled and "lost." Sennacherib captures some cities belonging to the kingdom *Yehuda* and lays siege around *Yerushalayim* in approximately 701 BCE, but is not successful in conquering the capital city.	II Kings 15:29, I Chronicles 5:26, II Kings 17:1–6, II Kings 18:9–12, II Kings 18:13–19:37, Isaiah 36–37
Egyptian	609–605 BCE	King *Yoshiyahu* of the kingdom of *Yehuda* refuses to let Pharaoh Neco pass through his land on his way to fight with the Assyrians against the Babylonians at Carchemish. Instead, the Judeans fight against the Egyptians at *Megiddo* and *Yoshiyahu* is killed in 609 BCE. The kingdom of *Yehuda* becomes subordinate to the Egyptians.	II Kings 23:29–30, II Chronicles 35:20–25
Babylonian	605–538 BCE	The Babylonian Empire takes control of the kingdom of *Yehuda*. Ignoring *Yirmiyahu*'s call to accept the reign of the Babylonians, the people of *Yehuda* try to free themselves of Babylonian rule. This angers Nebuchadnezzar and leads to the exile. The exile of the artisans and craftsmen takes place in 597 BCE, followed by the destruction of the first *Beit Hamikdash* and the exile of the rest of the people in 586 BCE.	II Kings 24–25
Persian	538–333 BCE	Cyrus of Persia defeats the Babylonians and declares that the Jews can return to the Land of Israel and rebuild the *Beit Hamikdash* in 538 BCE. Construction of the Second Temple is completed in the 6th year of King Darius.	Ezra 1:-3, 6:13–15
Seleucid	333–142 BCE	Alexander the Great conquers the region in 333 BCE. During the reign of King Antiochus IV, the *Beit Hamikdash* is desecrated, leading to the Maccabean revolt. As a result, the Second Temple is cleansed and re-dedicated, and the Maccabees establish semi-autonomy in 142 BCE.	
Hasmonean	142–63 BCE	The Hasmonean dynasty, established by the Maccabees, becomes semi-autonomous in 142 BCE, and eventually gains independence from the disintegrating Seleucid empire. The Jews thus regain full control of the Land of Israel for the first time since the Babylonian exile.	

Empire	Years	Significant Events in the Land of Israel	Relevant Verses
Roman	63 BCE–313 CE	The Land of Israel came under Roman rule in 63 BCE. The second *Beit Hamikdash* is destroyed by the Romans in 70 CE, and the *Bar Kochba* revolt takes place in 132 CE.	
Byzantine	313–637	In response to religious persecution, a fixed Hebrew calendar is established in approximately 360 CE. The Jerusalem Talmud is completed in approximately 400 CE.	
Muslim	638–1099	The Dome of the Rock is built on the site of the Holy Temple in 688–691 CE. Jewish scribes, known as the Masorites, create the Masoretic text of the Bible working mainly in *Tiveria* (Tiberias) and *Yerushalayim*.	
Crusaders	1099–1291	The Crusaders come from Europe to capture the Holy Land, following an appeal by Pope Urban II. On their way, they massacre those who are not Christian. Thousands of Jews are killed.	
Mamluk	1291–1517	In the 1400s, the Sephardic community established by the Ramban (Nachmanides) moves inside the city walls of *Yerushalayim* and establishes the Ramban Synagogue, which still exists today. After the expulsion from Spain in 1492, more Jews begin migrating to the Land of Israel. Many settle the city of *Tzfat*, which eventually becomes the center of *Kabbalah* (Jewish mysticism).	
Ottoman	1517–1917	Under Sultan Suleiman the Magnificent, the walls of Jerusalem are rebuilt in 1535–1538. These are the current walls of Jerusalem's Old City. Also during Ottoman rule, the First *Aliyah* (wave of immigration to Israel) and Second *Aliyah* both take place, in 1882–1903 and 1904–1914 respectively.	
British	1917–1948	While the Land of Israel is under British control, the world experiences World War II and the Holocaust. In addition, more waves of immigration to the Land of Israel take place, namely the Third *Aliyah* in 1919–1923, the Fourth *Aliyah* in 1924–1928, the Fifth *Aliyah* in 1929–1939 and *Aliyah Bet*, in 1934–1948.	
Jewish	1948-Present	The declaration of the State of Israel on May 14, 1948 (the 5th of *Iyar* 5708) begins the return of Jewish sovereignty to the Land of Israel for the first time in approximately 2,000 years.	

Yeshayahu/Isaiah
Chapter 1

ישעיהו
פרק א

1 1 The prophecies of *Yeshayahu* son of *Amotz*, who prophesied concerning *Yehuda* and *Yerushalayim* in the reigns of *Uzziyahu*, *Yotam*, *Achaz*, and *Chizkiyahu*, kings of *Yehuda*.

א חֲזוֹן יְשַׁעְיָהוּ בֶן־אָמוֹץ אֲשֶׁר חָזָה עַל־יְהוּדָה וִירוּשָׁלָ͏ִם בִּימֵי עֻזִּיָּהוּ יוֹתָם אָחָז יְחִזְקִיָּהוּ מַלְכֵי יְהוּדָה׃

2 Hear, O heavens, and give ear, O earth, For *Hashem* has spoken: "I reared children and brought them up – And they have rebelled against Me!

ב שִׁמְעוּ שָׁמַיִם וְהַאֲזִינִי אֶרֶץ כִּי יְהֹוָה דִּבֵּר בָּנִים גִּדַּלְתִּי וְרוֹמַמְתִּי וְהֵם פָּשְׁעוּ בִי׃

3 An ox knows its owner, An ass its master's crib: *Yisrael* does not know, My people takes no thought."

ג יָדַע שׁוֹר קֹנֵהוּ וַחֲמוֹר אֵבוּס בְּעָלָיו יִשְׂרָאֵל לֹא יָדַע עַמִּי לֹא הִתְבּוֹנָן׃

4 Ah, sinful nation! People laden with iniquity! Brood of evildoers! Depraved children! They have forsaken *Hashem*, Spurned the Holy One of *Yisrael*, Turned their backs [on Him].

ד הוֹי גּוֹי חֹטֵא עַם כֶּבֶד עָוֹן זֶרַע מְרֵעִים בָּנִים מַשְׁחִיתִים עָזְבוּ אֶת־יְהֹוָה נִאֲצוּ אֶת־קְדוֹשׁ יִשְׂרָאֵל נָזֹרוּ אָחוֹר׃

5 Why do you seek further beatings, That you continue to offend? Every head is ailing, And every heart is sick.

ה עַל מֶה תֻכּוּ עוֹד תּוֹסִיפוּ סָרָה כָּל־רֹאשׁ לָחֳלִי וְכָל־לֵבָב דַּוָּי׃

6 From head to foot No spot is sound: All bruises, and welts, And festering sores – Not pressed out, not bound up, Not softened with oil.

ו מִכַּף־רֶגֶל וְעַד־רֹאשׁ אֵין־בּוֹ מְתֹם פֶּצַע וְחַבּוּרָה וּמַכָּה טְרִיָּה לֹא־זֹרוּ וְלֹא חֻבָּשׁוּ וְלֹא רֻכְּכָה בַּשָּׁמֶן׃

7 Your land is a waste, Your cities burnt down; Before your eyes, the yield of your soil Is consumed by strangers – A wasteland as overthrown by strangers!

ז אַרְצְכֶם שְׁמָמָה עָרֵיכֶם שְׂרֻפוֹת אֵשׁ אַדְמַתְכֶם לְנֶגְדְּכֶם זָרִים אֹכְלִים אֹתָהּ וּשְׁמָמָה כְּמַהְפֵּכַת זָרִים׃

8 Fair *Tzion* is left Like a booth in a vineyard, Like a hut in a cucumber field, Like a city beleaguered.

ח וְנוֹתְרָה בַת־צִיּוֹן כְּסֻכָּה בְכָרֶם כִּמְלוּנָה בְמִקְשָׁה כְּעִיר נְצוּרָה׃

9 Had not the Lord of Hosts Left us some survivors, We should be like Sodom, Another Gomorrah.

ט לוּלֵי יְהֹוָה צְבָאוֹת הוֹתִיר לָנוּ שָׂרִיד כִּמְעָט כִּסְדֹם הָיִינוּ לַעֲמֹרָה דָּמִינוּ׃

lu-LAY a-do-NAI tz'-va-OT ho-TEER LA-nu sa-REED kim-AT kis-DOM ha-YEE-nu la-a-mo-RAH da-MEE-nu

10 Hear the word of *Hashem*, You chieftains of Sodom; Give ear to our God's instruction, You folk of Gomorrah!

י שִׁמְעוּ דְבַר־יְהֹוָה קְצִינֵי סְדֹם הַאֲזִינוּ תּוֹרַת אֱלֹהֵינוּ עַם עֲמֹרָה׃

1:9 We should be like Sodom, another Gomorrah The first chapter of *Sefer Yeshayahu* begins with a description of the devastation caused to *Yehuda* during the Assyrian invasion of 701 BCE. Only through *Hashem*'s kindness and mercy, and not through their own merit and strength, do the Jewish people merit to remain in the land. The people remark that they were nearly wiped out, as were Sodom and Gomorrah in times of old. By way of allusion, in verse 10 the prophet begins to convey the message that the reason for this was because they had adopted the ways of Sodom and Gomorrah, oppressing the poor while feigning piety. In order to remain in the Land of Israel, they must learn to behave towards everyone with genuine piety.

Yeshayahu/Isaiah

Chapter 1

11 "What need have I of all your sacrifices?" Says *Hashem*. "I am sated with burnt offerings of rams, And suet of fatlings, And blood of bulls; And I have no delight In lambs and he-goats.

12 That you come to appear before Me – Who asked that of you? Trample My courts

13 no more; Bringing oblations is futile, Incense is offensive to Me. New moon and *Shabbat*, Proclaiming of solemnities, Assemblies with iniquity, I cannot abide.

14 Your new moons and fixed seasons Fill Me with loathing; They are become a burden to Me, I cannot endure them.

15 And when you lift up your hands, I will turn My eyes away from you; Though you pray at length, I will not listen. Your hands are stained with crime –

16 Wash yourselves clean; Put your evil doings Away from My sight. Cease to do evil;

17 Learn to do good. Devote yourselves to justice; Aid the wronged. Uphold the rights of the orphan; Defend the cause of the widow.

18 "Come, let us reach an understanding, – says *Hashem*. Be your sins like crimson, They can turn snow-white; Be they red as dyed wool, They can become like fleece."

19 If, then, you agree and give heed, You will eat the good things of the earth;

20 But if you refuse and disobey, You will be devoured [by] the sword. – For it was *Hashem* who spoke.

21 Alas, she has become a harlot, The faithful city That was filled with justice, Where righteousness dwelt – But now murderers.

22 Your silver has turned to dross; Your wine is cut with water.

23 Your rulers are rogues And cronies of thieves, Every one avid for presents And greedy for gifts; They do not judge the case of the orphan, And the widow's cause never reaches them.

24 Assuredly, this is the declaration Of the Sovereign, the Lord of Hosts, The Mighty One of *Yisrael*: "Ah, I will get satisfaction from My foes; I will wreak vengeance on My enemies!

Yeshayahu/Isaiah
Chapter 2

ישעיהו
פרק ב

25 I will turn My hand against you, And smelt out your dross as with lye, And remove all your slag:

כה וְאָשִׁיבָה יָדִי עָלַיִךְ וְאֶצְרֹף כַּבֹּר סִיגָיִךְ וְאָסִירָה כָּל־בְּדִילָיִךְ:

26 I will restore your magistrates as of old, And your counselors as of yore. After that you shall be called City of Righteousness, Faithful City."

כו וְאָשִׁיבָה שֹׁפְטַיִךְ כְּבָרִאשֹׁנָה וְיֹעֲצַיִךְ כְּבַתְּחִלָּה אַחֲרֵי־כֵן יִקָּרֵא לָךְ עִיר הַצֶּדֶק קִרְיָה נֶאֱמָנָה:

27 *Tzion* shall be saved in the judgment; Her repentant ones, in the retribution.

כז צִיּוֹן בְּמִשְׁפָּט תִּפָּדֶה וְשָׁבֶיהָ בִּצְדָקָה:

28 But rebels and sinners shall all be crushed, And those who forsake *Hashem* shall perish.

כח וְשֶׁבֶר פֹּשְׁעִים וְחַטָּאִים יַחְדָּו וְעֹזְבֵי יְהוָה יִכְלוּ:

29 Truly, you shall be shamed Because of the terebinths you desired, And you shall be confounded Because of the gardens you coveted.

כט כִּי יֵבֹשׁוּ מֵאֵילִים אֲשֶׁר חֲמַדְתֶּם וְתַחְפְּרוּ מֵהַגַּנּוֹת אֲשֶׁר בְּחַרְתֶּם:

30 For you shall be like a terebinth Wilted of leaf, And like a garden That has no water,

ל כִּי תִהְיוּ כְּאֵלָה נֹבֶלֶת עָלֶהָ וּכְגַנָּה אֲשֶׁר־מַיִם אֵין לָהּ:

31 Stored wealth shall become as tow, And he who amassed it a spark; And the two shall burn together, With none to quench.

לא וְהָיָה הֶחָסֹן לִנְעֹרֶת וּפֹעֲלוֹ לְנִיצוֹץ וּבָעֲרוּ שְׁנֵיהֶם יַחְדָּו וְאֵין מְכַבֶּה:

2 1 The word that *Yeshayahu* son of *Amotz* prophesied concerning *Yehuda* and *Yerushalayim*.

ב א הַדָּבָר אֲשֶׁר חָזָה יְשַׁעְיָהוּ בֶּן־אָמוֹץ עַל־יְהוּדָה וִירוּשָׁלָ‍ִם:

2 In the days to come, The Mount of *Hashem*'s House Shall stand firm above the mountains And tower above the hills; And all the nations Shall gaze on it with joy.

ב וְהָיָה בְּאַחֲרִית הַיָּמִים נָכוֹן יִהְיֶה הַר בֵּית־יְהוָה בְּרֹאשׁ הֶהָרִים וְנִשָּׂא מִגְּבָעוֹת וְנָהֲרוּ אֵלָיו כָּל־הַגּוֹיִם:

3 And the many peoples shall go and say: "Come, Let us go up to the Mount of *Hashem*, To the House of the God of *Yaakov*; That He may instruct us in His ways, And that we may walk in His paths." For instruction shall come forth from *Tzion*, The word of *Hashem* from *Yerushalayim*.

ג וְהָלְכוּ עַמִּים רַבִּים וְאָמְרוּ לְכוּ וְנַעֲלֶה אֶל־הַר־יְהוָה אֶל־בֵּית אֱלֹהֵי יַעֲקֹב וְיֹרֵנוּ מִדְּרָכָיו וְנֵלְכָה בְּאֹרְחֹתָיו כִּי מִצִּיּוֹן תֵּצֵא תוֹרָה וּדְבַר־יְהוָה מִירוּשָׁלָ‍ִם:

v'-ha-l'-KHU a-MEEM ra-BEEM v'-a-m'-RU l'-KHU v'-na-a-LEH el har a-do-NAI el BAYT e-lo-HAY ya-a-KOV v'-yo-RAY-nu mi-d'-ra-KHAV v'-nay-l'-KHAH b'-o-r'-kho-TAV KEE mi-tzi-YON tay-TZAY to-RAH ud-var a-do-NAI mee-ru-sha-LA-im

Rabbi Joseph Rosen
(1858–1936)

2:3 And the many peoples shall go and say According to Rabbi Joseph Rosen, a great nineteenth-century *Torah* scholar, the job of awakening the will of *Hashem* to rebuild the *Beit Hamikdash* is not limited to the Jewish people. Rather, the third Temple will be built by all of mankind. And if the *Beit Hamikdash* is to be built through prayers and good deeds, as Jewish tradition teaches, it is the prayers and good deeds of all of humanity that will rouse *Hashem* to build it. Once built, it will be a house of God for all nations. People of all backgrounds will visit there in order to learn God's *Torah* and walk in His ways. Our generation is blessed to see this promise being fulfilled, with millions of non-Jews realizing that "from *Tzion* shall come forth the *Torah* and the word of *Hashem* from *Yerushalayim*."

Yeshayahu/Isaiah
Chapter 2

4 Thus He will judge among the nations And arbitrate for the many peoples, And they shall beat their swords into plowshares And their spears into pruning hooks: Nation shall not take up Sword against nation; They shall never again know war.

5 O House of *Yaakov*! Come, let us walk By the light of *Hashem*.

6 For you have forsaken [the ways of] your people, O House of *Yaakov*! For they are full [of practices] from the East, And of soothsaying like the Philistines; They abound in customs of the aliens.

7 Their land is full of silver and gold, There is no limit to their treasures; Their land is full of horses, There is no limit to their chariots.

8 And their land is full of idols; They bow down to the work of their hands, To what their own fingers have wrought.

9 But man shall be humbled, And mortal brought low – Oh, do not forgive them!

10 Go deep into the rock, Bury yourselves in the ground, Before the terror of *Hashem* And His dread majesty!

11 Man's haughty look shall be brought low, And the pride of mortals shall be humbled. None but *Hashem* shall be Exalted in that day.

12 For the Lord of Hosts has ready a day Against all that is proud and arrogant, Against all that is lofty – so that it is brought low:

13 Against all the cedars of Lebanon, Tall and stately, And all the oaks of Bashan;

14 Against all the high mountains And all the lofty hills;

15 Against every soaring tower And every mighty wall;

16 Against all the ships of Tarshish And all the gallant barks.

17 Then man's haughtiness shall be humbled And the pride of man brought low. None but *Hashem* shall be Exalted in that day.

18 As for idols, they shall vanish completely.

Yeshayahu/Isaiah
Chapter 3

19 And men shall enter caverns in the rock And hollows in the ground – Before the terror of *Hashem* And His dread majesty, When He comes forth to overawe the earth.

יט וּבָ֙אוּ֙ בִּמְעָר֣וֹת צֻרִ֔ים וּבִמְחִלּ֖וֹת עָפָ֑ר מִפְּנֵ֞י פַּ֤חַד יְהֹוָה֙ וּמֵהֲדַ֣ר גְּאוֹנ֔וֹ בְּקוּמ֖וֹ לַעֲרֹ֥ץ הָאָֽרֶץ׃

20 On that day, men shall fling away, To the flying foxes and the bats, The idols of silver And the idols of gold Which they made for worshiping.

כ בַּיּ֤וֹם הַהוּא֙ יַשְׁלִ֣יךְ הָאָדָ֔ם אֵ֚ת אֱלִילֵ֣י כַסְפּ֔וֹ וְאֵ֖ת אֱלִילֵ֣י זְהָב֑וֹ אֲשֶׁ֤ר עָֽשׂוּ־לוֹ֙ לְהִֽשְׁתַּחֲוֺ֔ת לַחְפֹּ֥ר פֵּר֖וֹת וְלָעֲטַלֵּפִֽים׃

21 And they shall enter the clefts in the rocks And the crevices in the cliffs, Before the terror of *Hashem* And His dread majesty, When He comes forth to overawe the earth.

כא לָבוֹא֙ בְּנִקְר֣וֹת הַצֻּרִ֔ים וּבִסְעִפֵ֖י הַסְּלָעִ֑ים מִפְּנֵ֞י פַּ֤חַד יְהֹוָה֙ וּמֵהֲדַ֣ר גְּאוֹנ֔וֹ בְּקוּמ֖וֹ לַעֲרֹ֥ץ הָאָֽרֶץ׃

22 Oh, cease to glorify man, Who has only a breath in his nostrils! For by what does he merit esteem?

כב חִדְל֣וּ לָכֶ֗ם מִן־הָֽאָדָם֙ אֲשֶׁ֤ר נְשָׁמָה֙ בְּאַפּ֔וֹ כִּֽי־בַמֶּ֥ה נֶחְשָׁ֖ב הֽוּא׃

3

1 For lo! The Sovereign LORD of Hosts Will remove from *Yerushalayim* and from *Yehuda* Prop and stay, Every prop of food And every prop of water:

א כִּי֩ הִנֵּ֨ה הָאָד֜וֹן יְהֹוָ֣ה צְבָא֗וֹת מֵסִ֤יר מִירוּשָׁלַ֙͏ִם֙ וּמִ֣יהוּדָ֔ה מַשְׁעֵ֖ן וּמַשְׁעֵנָ֑ה כֹּ֚ל מִשְׁעַן־לֶ֔חֶם וְכֹ֖ל מִשְׁעַן־מָֽיִם׃

2 Soldier and warrior, Magistrate and *Navi*, Augur and elder;

ב גִּבּ֖וֹר וְאִ֣ישׁ מִלְחָמָ֑ה שׁוֹפֵ֥ט וְנָבִ֖יא וְקֹסֵ֥ם וְזָקֵֽן׃

3 Captain of fifty, Magnate and counselor, Skilled artisan and expert enchanter;

ג שַׂר־חֲמִשִּׁ֖ים וּנְשׂ֣וּא פָנִ֑ים וְיוֹעֵ֛ץ וַחֲכַ֥ם חֲרָשִׁ֖ים וּנְב֥וֹן לָֽחַשׁ׃

4 **And He will make boys their rulers, And babes shall govern them.**

v'-na-ta-TEE n'-a-REEM sa-ray-HEM v'-ta-a-lu-LEEM yim-sh'-lu VAM

ד וְנָתַתִּ֥י נְעָרִ֖ים שָׂרֵיהֶ֑ם וְתַעֲלוּלִ֖ים יִמְשְׁלוּ־בָֽם׃

5 So the people shall oppress one another – Each oppressing his fellow: The young shall bully the old; And the despised [shall bully] the honored.

ה וְנִגַּ֣שׂ הָעָ֔ם אִ֥ישׁ בְּאִ֖ישׁ וְאִ֣ישׁ בְּרֵעֵ֑הוּ יִרְהֲב֗וּ הַנַּ֙עַר֙ בַּזָּקֵ֔ן וְהַנִּקְלֶ֖ה בַּנִּכְבָּֽד׃

6 For should a man seize his brother, In whose father's house there is clothing: "Come, be a chief over us, And let this ruin be under your care,"

ו כִּֽי־יִתְפֹּ֨שׂ אִ֤ישׁ בְּאָחִיו֙ בֵּ֣ית אָבִ֔יו שִׂמְלָ֣ה לְכָ֔ה קָצִ֖ין תִּֽהְיֶה־לָּ֑נוּ וְהַמַּכְשֵׁלָ֥ה הַזֹּ֖את תַּ֥חַת יָדֶֽךָ׃

3:4 And He will make boys their rulers After the removal of the competent and qualified leadership of *Yehuda* (verses 1–3), young and inexperienced leaders will rule in their place. These rulers will lead the people even further astray from *Hashem*. The chapter describes a collapse of social order under their governance; the people oppress one another, there is a lack of respect between friends and the young behave with arrogance towards their elders, as the nation continues on its path of Sodom-like behavior (verse 9). In verses 10–11, *Yeshayahu* promises that *Hashem* will reward the righteous and punish the wicked. Leadership carries with it tremendous responsibility: A leader has the potential to carry his nation to great heights or to lead it to its downfall. Jewish leadership in the Land of Israel is charged with the responsibility to lead the nation in justice and morality. Anything less than that is intolerable in *Hashem*'s eyes, and will be punished.

Yeshayahu/Isaiah
Chapter 3

7 The other will thereupon protest, "I will not be a dresser of wounds, With no food or clothing in my own house. You shall not make me chief of a people!"

8 Ah, *Yerushalayim* has stumbled, And *Yehuda* has fallen, Because by word and deed They insult *Hashem*, Defying His majestic glance.

9 Their partiality in judgment accuses them; They avow their sins like Sodom, They do not conceal them. Woe to them! For ill Have they served themselves.

10 (Hail the just man, for he shall fare well; He shall eat the fruit of his works.

11 Woe to the wicked man, for he shall fare ill; As his hands have dealt, so shall it be done to him.)

12 My people's rulers are babes, It is governed by women. O my people! Your leaders are misleaders; They have confused the course of your paths.

13 *Hashem* stands up to plead a cause, He rises to champion peoples.

14 *Hashem* will bring this charge Against the elders and officers of His people: "It is you who have ravaged the vineyard; That which was robbed from the poor is in your houses.

15 How dare you crush My people And grind the faces of the poor?" – says *Hashem* my God of Hosts.

16 *Hashem* said: "Because the daughters of *Tzion* Are so vain And walk with heads thrown back, With roving eyes, And with mincing gait, Making a tinkling with their feet" –

17 My Lord will bare the pates Of the daughters of *Tzion*, *Hashem* will uncover their heads.

18 In that day, *Hashem* will strip off the finery of the anklets, the fillets, and the crescents;

19 of the eardrops, the bracelets, and the veils;

20 the turbans, the armlets, and the sashes; of the talismans and the amulets;

21 the signet rings and the nose rings;

22 of the festive robes, the mantles, and the shawls; the purses,

ישעיהו
פרק ג

ז יִשָּׂ֣א בַיּוֹם֩ הַה֨וּא ׀ לֵאמֹ֜ר לֹא־אֶהְיֶ֣ה חֹבֵ֗שׁ וּבְבֵיתִי֙ אֵ֣ין לֶ֣חֶם וְאֵ֣ין שִׂמְלָ֔ה לֹ֥א תְשִׂימֻ֖נִי קְצִ֥ין עָֽם׃

ח כִּ֤י כָֽשְׁלָה֙ יְר֣וּשָׁלַ֔͏ִם וִֽיהוּדָ֖ה נָפָ֑ל כִּֽי־לְשׁוֹנָ֤ם וּמַֽעַלְלֵיהֶם֙ אֶל־יְהוָ֔ה לַמְר֖וֹת עֵנֵ֥י כְבוֹדֽוֹ׃

ט הַכָּרַ֤ת פְּנֵיהֶם֙ עָ֣נְתָה בָּ֔ם וְחַטָּאתָ֛ם כִּסְדֹ֥ם הִגִּ֖ידוּ לֹ֣א כִחֵ֑דוּ א֣וֹי לְנַפְשָׁ֔ם כִּֽי־גָמְל֥וּ לָהֶ֖ם רָעָֽה׃

י אִמְר֥וּ צַדִּ֖יק כִּי־ט֑וֹב כִּֽי־פְרִ֥י מַעַלְלֵיהֶ֖ם יֹאכֵֽלוּ׃

יא א֖וֹי לְרָשָׁ֣ע רָ֑ע כִּֽי־גְמ֥וּל יָדָ֖יו יֵעָ֥שֶׂה לּֽוֹ׃

יב עַמִּי֙ נֹגְשָׂ֣יו מְעוֹלֵ֔ל וְנָשִׁ֖ים מָ֣שְׁלוּ ב֑וֹ עַמִּי֙ מְאַשְּׁרֶ֣יךָ מַתְעִ֔ים וְדֶ֥רֶךְ אֹרְחֹתֶ֖יךָ בִּלֵּֽעוּ׃

יג נִצָּ֥ב לָרִ֖יב יְהוָ֑ה וְעֹמֵ֖ד לָדִ֥ין עַמִּֽים׃

יד יְהוָה֙ בְּמִשְׁפָּ֣ט יָב֔וֹא עִם־זִקְנֵ֥י עַמּ֖וֹ וְשָׂרָ֑יו וְאַתֶּם֙ בִּֽעַרְתֶּ֣ם הַכֶּ֔רֶם גְּזֵלַ֥ת הֶֽעָנִ֖י בְּבָתֵּיכֶֽם׃

טו מַלָּכֶ֣ם [מַה־] [לָּכֶ֔ם] תְּדַכְּא֣וּ עַמִּ֔י וּפְנֵ֥י עֲנִיִּ֖ים תִּטְחָ֑נוּ נְאֻם־אֲדֹנָ֥י יְהוִ֖ה צְבָאֽוֹת׃

טז וַיֹּ֣אמֶר יְהוָ֗ה יַ֚עַן כִּ֤י גָֽבְהוּ֙ בְּנ֣וֹת צִיּ֔וֹן וַתֵּלַ֙כְנָה֙ נְטוּי֣וֹת [נְטוּוֹת] גָּר֔וֹן וּֽמְשַׂקְּר֖וֹת עֵינָ֑יִם הָל֤וֹךְ וְטָפֹף֙ תֵּלַ֔כְנָה וּבְרַגְלֵיהֶ֖ם תְּעַכַּֽסְנָה׃

יז וְשִׂפַּ֣ח אֲדֹנָ֔י קָדְקֹ֖ד בְּנ֣וֹת צִיּ֑וֹן וַיהוָ֖ה פָּתְהֵ֥ן יְעָרֶֽה׃

יח בַּיּ֨וֹם הַה֜וּא יָסִ֣יר אֲדֹנָ֗י אֵ֣ת תִּפְאֶ֧רֶת הָעֲכָסִ֛ים וְהַשְּׁבִיסִ֖ים וְהַשַּׂהֲרֹנִֽים׃

יט הַנְּטִיפ֥וֹת וְהַשֵּׁיר֖וֹת וְהָֽרְעָלֽוֹת׃

כ הַפְּאֵרִ֤ים וְהַצְּעָדוֹת֙ וְהַקִּשֻּׁרִ֔ים וּבָתֵּ֥י הַנֶּ֖פֶשׁ וְהַלְּחָשִֽׁים׃

כא הַטַּבָּע֖וֹת וְנִזְמֵ֥י הָאָֽף׃

כב הַמַּֽחֲלָצוֹת֙ וְהַמַּ֣עֲטָפ֔וֹת וְהַמִּטְפָּח֖וֹת וְהָחֲרִיטִֽים׃

Yeshayahu/Isaiah
Chapter 4

ישעיהו
פרק ד

23 the lace gowns, and the linen vests; and the kerchiefs and the capes.

וְהַגִּלְיֹנִים וְהַסְּדִינִים וְהַצְּנִיפוֹת וְהָרְדִידִים:

24 And then – Instead of perfume, there shall be rot; And instead of an apron, a rope; Instead of a diadem of beaten-work, A shorn head; Instead of a rich robe, A girding of sackcloth; A burn instead of beauty.

וְהָיָה תַחַת בֹּשֶׂם מַק יִהְיֶה וְתַחַת חֲגוֹרָה נִקְפָּה וְתַחַת מַעֲשֵׂה מִקְשֶׁה קָרְחָה וְתַחַת פְּתִיגִיל מַחֲגֹרֶת שָׂק כִּי־תַחַת יֹפִי:

25 Her men shall fall by the sword, Her fighting manhood in battle;

מְתַיִךְ בַּחֶרֶב יִפֹּלוּ וּגְבוּרָתֵךְ בַּמִּלְחָמָה:

26 And her gates shall lament and mourn, And she shall be emptied, Shall sit on the ground.

וְאָנוּ וְאָבְלוּ פְּתָחֶיהָ וְנִקָּתָה לָאָרֶץ תֵּשֵׁב:

4 1 In that day, seven women shall take hold of one man, saying, "We will eat our own food And wear our own clothes; Only let us be called by your name – Take away our disgrace!"

ד א וְהֶחֱזִיקוּ שֶׁבַע נָשִׁים בְּאִישׁ אֶחָד בַּיּוֹם הַהוּא לֵאמֹר לַחְמֵנוּ נֹאכֵל וְשִׂמְלָתֵנוּ נִלְבָּשׁ רַק יִקָּרֵא שִׁמְךָ עָלֵינוּ אֱסֹף חֶרְפָּתֵנוּ:

2 In that day, The radiance of *Hashem* Will lend beauty and glory, And the splendor of the land [Will give] dignity and majesty, To the survivors of *Yisrael*.

ב בַּיּוֹם הַהוּא יִהְיֶה צֶמַח יְהֹוָה לִצְבִי וּלְכָבוֹד וּפְרִי הָאָרֶץ לְגָאוֹן וּלְתִפְאֶרֶת לִפְלֵיטַת יִשְׂרָאֵל:

ba-YOM ha-HU yih-YEH TZE-makh a-do-NAI litz-VEE ul-kha-VOD uf-REE ha-A-retz l'-ga-ON ul-tif-E-ret lif-lay-TAT yis-ra-AYL

3 And those who remain in *Tzion* And are left in *Yerushalayim* – All who are inscribed for life in *Yerushalayim* – Shall be called holy.

ג וְהָיָה הַנִּשְׁאָר בְּצִיּוֹן וְהַנּוֹתָר בִּירוּשָׁלַיִם קָדוֹשׁ יֵאָמֶר לוֹ כָּל־הַכָּתוּב לַחַיִּים בִּירוּשָׁלָיִם:

4 When my Lord has washed away The filth of the daughters of *Tzion*, And from *Yerushalayim*'s midst Has rinsed out her infamy – In a spirit of judgment And in a spirit of purging –

ד אִם רָחַץ אֲדֹנָי אֵת צֹאַת בְּנוֹת־צִיּוֹן וְאֶת־דְּמֵי יְרוּשָׁלַיִם יָדִיחַ מִקִּרְבָּהּ בְּרוּחַ מִשְׁפָּט וּבְרוּחַ בָּעֵר:

5 *Hashem* will create over the whole shrine and meeting place of Mount *Tzion* cloud by day and smoke with a glow of flaming fire by night. Indeed, over all the glory shall hang a canopy,

ה וּבָרָא יְהֹוָה עַל כָּל־מְכוֹן הַר־צִיּוֹן וְעַל־מִקְרָאֶהָ עָנָן יוֹמָם וְעָשָׁן וְנֹגַהּ אֵשׁ לֶהָבָה לָיְלָה כִּי עַל־כָּל־כָּבוֹד חֻפָּה:

6 which shall serve as a pavilion for shade from heat by day and as a shelter for protection against drenching rain.

ו וְסֻכָּה תִּהְיֶה לְצֵל־יוֹמָם מֵחֹרֶב וּלְמַחְסֶה וּלְמִסְתּוֹר מִזֶּרֶם וּמִמָּטָר:

Ramban (1194–1270)

4:2 Dignity and majesty to the survivors of *Yisrael* *Ramban* writes that nowhere in the world would one find a land which is good and bountiful when settled by its people, but desolate when ruled by foreigners. However, this is exactly what *Hashem* promises regarding the Land of Israel, as it says in *Vayikra* (26:32), "I will make the land desolate, so that your enemies who settle in it shall be appalled by it." This guarantees that throughout the ages, *Eretz Yisrael* will not accept its enemies; it will prosper only for the Children of Israel. Today, one can see this blessing fulfilled, as her children have returned home. The land which lay desolate for centuries under foreign rule again flourishes and blooms, giving dignity and majesty to her people.

Yeshayahu/Isaiah
Chapter 5

ישעיהו
פרק ה

5 **1** Let me sing for my beloved A song of my lover about his vineyard. My beloved had a vineyard On a fruitful hill.

א אָשִׁירָה נָּא לִידִידִי שִׁירַת דּוֹדִי לְכַרְמוֹ כֶּרֶם הָיָה לִידִידִי בְּקֶרֶן בֶּן־שָׁמֶן׃

a-SHEE-ra NA lee-dee-DEE shee-RAT do-DEE l'-khar-MO KE-rem ha-YAH lee-dee-DEE b'-KE-ren ben SHA-men

2 He broke the ground, cleared it of stones, And planted it with choice vines. He built a watchtower inside it, He even hewed a wine press in it; For he hoped it would yield grapes. Instead, it yielded wild grapes.

ב וַיְעַזְּקֵהוּ וַיְסַקְּלֵהוּ וַיִּטָּעֵהוּ שֹׂרֵק וַיִּבֶן מִגְדָּל בְּתוֹכוֹ וְגַם־יֶקֶב חָצֵב בּוֹ וַיְקַו לַעֲשׂוֹת עֲנָבִים וַיַּעַשׂ בְּאֻשִׁים׃

3 "Now, then, Dwellers of *Yerushalayim* And men of *Yehuda*, You be the judges Between Me and My vineyard:

ג וְעַתָּה יוֹשֵׁב יְרוּשָׁלַםִ וְאִישׁ יְהוּדָה שִׁפְטוּ־נָא בֵּינִי וּבֵין כַּרְמִי׃

4 What more could have been done for My vineyard That I failed to do in it? Why, when I hoped it would yield grapes, Did it yield wild grapes?

ד מַה־לַּעֲשׂוֹת עוֹד לְכַרְמִי וְלֹא עָשִׂיתִי בּוֹ מַדּוּעַ קִוֵּיתִי לַעֲשׂוֹת עֲנָבִים וַיַּעַשׂ בְּאֻשִׁים׃

5 "Now I am going to tell you What I will do to My vineyard: I will remove its hedge, That it may be ravaged; I will break down its wall, That it may be trampled.

ה וְעַתָּה אוֹדִיעָה־נָּא אֶתְכֶם אֵת אֲשֶׁר־אֲנִי עֹשֶׂה לְכַרְמִי הָסֵר מְשׂוּכָּתוֹ וְהָיָה לְבָעֵר פָּרֹץ גְּדֵרוֹ וְהָיָה לְמִרְמָס׃

6 And I will make it a desolation; It shall not be pruned or hoed, And it shall be overgrown with briers and thistles. And I will command the clouds To drop no rain on it."

ו וַאֲשִׁיתֵהוּ בָתָה לֹא יִזָּמֵר וְלֹא יֵעָדֵר וְעָלָה שָׁמִיר וָשָׁיִת וְעַל הֶעָבִים אֲצַוֶּה מֵהַמְטִיר עָלָיו מָטָר׃

7 For the vineyard of the Lord of Hosts Is the House of *Yisrael*, And the seedlings he lovingly tended Are the men of *Yehuda*. And He hoped for justice, But behold, injustice; For equity, But behold, iniquity!

ז כִּי כֶרֶם יְהוָה צְבָאוֹת בֵּית יִשְׂרָאֵל וְאִישׁ יְהוּדָה נְטַע שַׁעֲשׁוּעָיו וַיְקַו לְמִשְׁפָּט וְהִנֵּה מִשְׂפָּח לִצְדָקָה וְהִנֵּה צְעָקָה׃

8 Ah, Those who add house to house And join field to field, Till there is room for none but you To dwell in the land!

ח הוֹי מַגִּיעֵי בַיִת בְּבַיִת שָׂדֶה בְשָׂדֶה יַקְרִיבוּ עַד אֶפֶס מָקוֹם וְהוּשַׁבְתֶּם לְבַדְּכֶם בְּקֶרֶב הָאָרֶץ׃

א **5:1 A song of my lover about his vineyard** This chapter presents one of the most famous parables in the Bible, known as the song of the vineyard. *Yeshayahu* gathers the people together to pass judgment on a disobedient vineyard. Despite the owner's efforts to care for the vineyard that he loves (a metaphor for God's care for the Children of Israel), it produces unripe grapes. Therefore, the owner announces that he will tear down the walls that protect the vineyard from thorns and other dangers of the forest. With beautiful word-play, *Yeshayahu* states, though the men of *Yehuda* are "the seedlings He lovingly tended," instead of 'justice,' in Hebrew *mishpat* (משפט), they caused 'injustice,' *mispach* (משפח). Instead of 'equity,' *tzedaka* (צדקה), they caused 'iniquity,' *tza'aka* (צעקה) (verse 7). *Hashem* will therefore remove His protection from Israel and allow for its enemies to enter. The theme of injustice and oppression leading to destruction plays a prominent role in *Yeshayahu's* prophecies. Ultimately, *Tzion* will be redeemed through justice and righteousness (Isaiah 1:27).

צדקה
משפט

Yeshayahu/Isaiah
Chapter 5

9 In my hearing [said] the Lord of Hosts: Surely, great houses Shall lie forlorn, Spacious and splendid ones Without occupants.

10 For ten acres of vineyard Shall yield just one *bat*, And a field sown with a *chomer* of seed Shall yield a mere *efah*.

11 Ah, Those who chase liquor From early in the morning, And till late in the evening Are inflamed by wine!

12 Who, at their banquets, Have lyre and lute, Timbrel, flute, and wine; But who never give a thought To the plan of *Hashem*, And take no note Of what He is designing.

13 Assuredly, My people will suffer exile For not giving heed, Its multitude victims of hunger And its masses parched with thirst.

14 Assuredly, Sheol has opened wide its gullet And parted its jaws in a measureless gape; And down into it shall go, That splendor and tumult, That din and revelry.

15 Yea, man is bowed, And mortal brought low; Brought low is the pride of the haughty.

16 And the Lord of Hosts is exalted by judgment, The Holy *Hashem* proved holy by retribution.

17 Then lambs shall graze As in their meadows, And strangers shall feed On the ruins of the stout.

18 Ah, Those who haul sin with cords of falsehood And iniquity as with cart ropes!

19 Who say, "Let Him speed, let Him hasten His purpose, If we are to give thought; Let the plans of the Holy One of *Yisrael* Be quickly fulfilled, If we are to give heed."

20 Ah, Those who call evil good And good evil; Who present darkness as light And light as darkness; Who present bitter as sweet And sweet as bitter!

21 Ah, Those who are so wise – In their own opinion; So clever – In their own judgment!

22 Ah, Those who are so doughty – As drinkers of wine, And so valiant – As mixers of drink!

23 Who vindicate him who is in the wrong In return for a bribe, And withhold vindication From him who is in the right.

ישעיהו
פרק ה

ט בְּאָזְנַי יְהוָה צְבָאוֹת אִם־לֹא בָּתִּים רַבִּים לְשַׁמָּה יִהְיוּ גְּדֹלִים וְטוֹבִים מֵאֵין יוֹשֵׁב:

י כִּי עֲשֶׂרֶת צִמְדֵּי־כֶרֶם יַעֲשׂוּ בַּת אֶחָת וְזֶרַע חֹמֶר יַעֲשֶׂה אֵיפָה:

יא הוֹי מַשְׁכִּימֵי בַבֹּקֶר שֵׁכָר יִרְדֹּפוּ מְאַחֲרֵי בַנֶּשֶׁף יַיִן יַדְלִיקֵם:

יב וְהָיָה כִנּוֹר וָנֶבֶל תֹּף וְחָלִיל וָיַיִן מִשְׁתֵּיהֶם וְאֵת פֹּעַל יְהוָה לֹא יַבִּיטוּ וּמַעֲשֵׂה יָדָיו לֹא רָאוּ:

יג לָכֵן גָּלָה עַמִּי מִבְּלִי־דָעַת וּכְבוֹדוֹ מְתֵי רָעָב וַהֲמוֹנוֹ צִחֵה צָמָא:

יד לָכֵן הִרְחִיבָה שְּׁאוֹל נַפְשָׁהּ וּפָעֲרָה פִיהָ לִבְלִי־חֹק וְיָרַד הֲדָרָהּ וַהֲמוֹנָהּ וּשְׁאוֹנָהּ וְעָלֵז בָּהּ:

טו וַיִּשַּׁח אָדָם וַיִּשְׁפַּל־אִישׁ וְעֵינֵי גְבֹהִים תִּשְׁפַּלְנָה:

טז וַיִּגְבַּהּ יְהוָה צְבָאוֹת בַּמִּשְׁפָּט וְהָאֵל הַקָּדוֹשׁ נִקְדָּשׁ בִּצְדָקָה:

יז וְרָעוּ כְבָשִׂים כְּדָבְרָם וְחָרְבוֹת מֵחִים גָּרִים יֹאכֵלוּ:

יח הוֹי מֹשְׁכֵי הֶעָוֺן בְּחַבְלֵי הַשָּׁוְא וְכַעֲבוֹת הָעֲגָלָה חַטָּאָה:

יט הָאֹמְרִים יְמַהֵר יָחִישָׁה מַעֲשֵׂהוּ לְמַעַן נִרְאֶה וְתִקְרַב וְתָבוֹאָה עֲצַת קְדוֹשׁ יִשְׂרָאֵל וְנֵדָעָה:

כ הוֹי הָאֹמְרִים לָרַע טוֹב וְלַטּוֹב רָע שָׂמִים חֹשֶׁךְ לְאוֹר וְאוֹר לְחֹשֶׁךְ שָׂמִים מַר לְמָתוֹק וּמָתוֹק לְמָר:

כא הוֹי חֲכָמִים בְּעֵינֵיהֶם וְנֶגֶד פְּנֵיהֶם נְבֹנִים:

כב הוֹי גִּבּוֹרִים לִשְׁתּוֹת יָיִן וְאַנְשֵׁי־חַיִל לִמְסֹךְ שֵׁכָר:

כג מַצְדִּיקֵי רָשָׁע עֵקֶב שֹׁחַד וְצִדְקַת צַדִּיקִים יָסִירוּ מִמֶּנּוּ:

Yeshayahu/Isaiah
Chapter 6

ישעיהו
פרק ו

24 Assuredly, As straw is consumed by a tongue of fire And hay shrivels as it burns, Their stock shall become like rot, And their buds shall blow away like dust. For they have rejected the instruction of the Lord of Hosts, Spurned the word of the Holy One of *Yisrael*.

לָכֵן כֶּאֱכֹל קַשׁ לְשׁוֹן אֵשׁ וַחֲשַׁשׁ לֶהָבָה יִרְפֶּה שָׁרְשָׁם כַּמָּק יִהְיֶה וּפִרְחָם כָּאָבָק יַעֲלֶה כִּי מָאֲסוּ אֵת תּוֹרַת יְהֹוָה צְבָאוֹת וְאֵת אִמְרַת קְדוֹשׁ־יִשְׂרָאֵל נִאֵצוּ:

25 That is why *Hashem*'s anger was roused Against His people, Why He stretched out His arm against it And struck it, So that the mountains quaked, And its corpses lay Like refuse in the streets. Yet his anger has not turned back, And His arm is outstretched still.

עַל־כֵּן חָרָה אַף־יְהֹוָה בְּעַמּוֹ וַיֵּט יָדוֹ עָלָיו וַיַּכֵּהוּ וַיִּרְגְּזוּ הֶהָרִים וַתְּהִי נִבְלָתָם כַּסּוּחָה בְּקֶרֶב חוּצוֹת בְּכָל־זֹאת לֹא־שָׁב אַפּוֹ וְעוֹד יָדוֹ נְטוּיָה:

26 He will raise an ensign to a nation afar, Whistle to one at the end of the earth. There it comes with lightning speed!

וְנָשָׂא־נֵס לַגּוֹיִם מֵרָחוֹק וְשָׁרַק לוֹ מִקְצֵה הָאָרֶץ וְהִנֵּה מְהֵרָה קַל יָבוֹא:

27 In its ranks, none is weary or stumbles, They never sleep or slumber; The belts on their waists do not come loose, Nor do the thongs of their sandals break.

אֵין־עָיֵף וְאֵין־כּוֹשֵׁל בּוֹ לֹא יָנוּם וְלֹא יִישָׁן וְלֹא נִפְתַּח אֵזוֹר חֲלָצָיו וְלֹא נִתַּק שְׂרוֹךְ נְעָלָיו:

28 Their arrows are sharpened, And all their bows are drawn. Their horses' hoofs are like flint, Their chariot wheels like the whirlwind.

אֲשֶׁר חִצָּיו שְׁנוּנִים וְכָל־קַשְּׁתֹתָיו דְּרֻכוֹת פַּרְסוֹת סוּסָיו כַּצַּר נֶחְשָׁבוּ וְגַלְגִּלָּיו כַּסּוּפָה:

29 Their roaring is like a lion's, They roar like the great beasts; When they growl and seize a prey, They carry it off and none can recover it.

שְׁאָגָה לוֹ כַּלָּבִיא ושאג [יִשְׁאַג] כַּכְּפִירִים וְיִנְהֹם וְיֹאחֵז טֶרֶף וְיַפְלִיט וְאֵין מַצִּיל:

30 But in that day, a roaring shall resound over him like that of the sea; and then he shall look below and, behold, Distressing darkness, with light; Darkness, in its lowering clouds.

וְיִנְהֹם עָלָיו בַּיּוֹם הַהוּא כְּנַהֲמַת־יָם וְנִבַּט לָאָרֶץ וְהִנֵּה־חֹשֶׁךְ צַר וָאוֹר חָשַׁךְ בַּעֲרִיפֶיהָ:

6

1 In the year that King *Uzziyahu* died, I beheld my Lord seated on a high and lofty throne; and the skirts of His robe filled the Temple.

בִּשְׁנַת־מוֹת הַמֶּלֶךְ עֻזִּיָּהוּ וָאֶרְאֶה אֶת־אֲדֹנָי יֹשֵׁב עַל־כִּסֵּא רָם וְנִשָּׂא וְשׁוּלָיו מְלֵאִים אֶת־הַהֵיכָל:

bish-nat MOT ha-ME-lekh u-zi-YA-hu va-er-EH et a-do-NAI yo-SHAYV al ki-SAY RAM v'-ni-SA v'-shu-LAV m'-lay-EEM et ha-hay-KHAL

6:1 I beheld my Lord seated on a high and lofty throne *Yeshayahu* sees *Hashem* sitting on His heavenly throne, with the base of the throne filling the Temple. Though He dwells on high, God is still intimately involved in this world, the manifestation of his presence emanating from the *Beit Hamikdash*. Rabbi Abraham Isaac Kook expressed a similar idea in the 1920's, when he wrote that the State of Israel will be an ideal state which will be "the pedestal of God's throne in this world, whose aim is that the Lord be acknowledged as one and His name as one."

Rabbi Abraham Issac Kook (1865–1935)

Yeshayahu/Isaiah
Chapter 7

2 Seraphs stood in attendance on Him. Each of them had six wings: with two he covered his face, with two he covered his legs, and with two he would fly.

3 And one would call to the other, "Holy, holy, holy! the Lord of Hosts! His presence fills all the earth!"

4 The doorposts would shake at the sound of the one who called, and the House kept filling with smoke.

5 I cried, "Woe is me; I am lost! For I am a man of unclean lips And I live among a people Of unclean lips; Yet my own eyes have beheld The King Lord of Hosts."

6 Then one of the seraphs flew over to me with a live coal, which he had taken from the *Mizbayach* with a pair of tongs.

7 He touched it to my lips and declared, "Now that this has touched your lips, Your guilt shall depart And your sin be purged away."

8 Then I heard the voice of my Lord saying, "Whom shall I send? Who will go for us?" And I said, "Here am I; send me."

9 And He said, "Go, say to that people: 'Hear, indeed, but do not understand; See, indeed, but do not grasp.'

10 Dull that people's mind, Stop its ears, And seal its eyes – Lest, seeing with its eyes And hearing with its ears, It also grasp with its mind, And repent and save itself."

11 I asked, "How long, my Lord?" And He replied: "Till towns lie waste without inhabitants And houses without people, And the ground lies waste and desolate –

12 For *Hashem* will banish the population – And deserted sites are many In the midst of the land.

13 "But while a tenth part yet remains in it, it shall repent. It shall be ravaged like the terebinth and the oak, of which stumps are left even when they are felled: its stump shall be a holy seed."

7

1 In the reign of *Achaz* son of *Yotam* son of *Uzziyahu*, king of *Yehuda*, King Rezin of Aram and King *Pekach* son of Remaliah of *Yisrael* marched upon *Yerushalayim* to attack it; but they were not able to attack it.

Yeshayahu/Isaiah
Chapter 7

ישעיהו
פרק ז

2 Now, when it was reported to the House of *David* that Aram had allied itself with *Efraim*, their hearts and the hearts of their people trembled as trees of the forest sway before a wind.

ב וַיֻּגַּד לְבֵית דָּוִד לֵאמֹר נָחָה אֲרָם עַל־אֶפְרָיִם וַיָּנַע לְבָבוֹ וּלְבַב עַמּוֹ כְּנוֹעַ עֲצֵי־יַעַר מִפְּנֵי־רוּחַ:

3 But *Hashem* said to *Yeshayahu*, "Go out with your son *Shear Yashuv* to meet *Achaz* at the end of the conduit of the Upper Pool, by the road of the Fuller's Field.

ג וַיֹּאמֶר יְהוָה אֶל־יְשַׁעְיָהוּ צֵא־נָא לִקְרַאת אָחָז אַתָּה וּשְׁאָר יָשׁוּב בְּנֶךָ אֶל־קְצֵה תְּעָלַת הַבְּרֵכָה הָעֶלְיוֹנָה אֶל־מְסִלַּת שְׂדֵה כוֹבֵס:

va-YO-mer a-do-NAI el y'-sha-YA-hu tzay NA lik-RAT a-KHAZ a-TAH ush-AR ya-SHUV b'-NE-kha el k'-TZAY t'-a-LAT ha-b'-ray-KHAH ha-el-yo-NAH el m'-si-LAT s'-DAY kho-VAYS

4 And say to him: Be firm and be calm. Do not be afraid and do not lose heart on account of those two smoking stubs of firebrands, on account of the raging of Rezin and his Arameans and the son of Remaliah.

ד וְאָמַרְתָּ אֵלָיו הִשָּׁמֵר וְהַשְׁקֵט אַל־תִּירָא וּלְבָבְךָ אַל־יֵרַךְ מִשְּׁנֵי זַנְבוֹת הָאוּדִים הָעֲשֵׁנִים הָאֵלֶּה בָּחֳרִי־אַף רְצִין וַאֲרָם וּבֶן־רְמַלְיָהוּ:

5 Because the Arameans – with *Efraim* and the son of Remaliah – have plotted against you, saying,

ה יַעַן כִּי־יָעַץ עָלֶיךָ אֲרָם רָעָה אֶפְרַיִם וּבֶן־רְמַלְיָהוּ לֵאמֹר:

6 'We will march against *Yehuda* and invade and conquer it, and we will set up as king in it the son of Tabeel,'

ו נַעֲלֶה בִיהוּדָה וּנְקִיצֶנָּה וְנַבְקִעֶנָּה אֵלֵינוּ וְנַמְלִיךְ מֶלֶךְ בְּתוֹכָהּ אֵת בֶּן־טָבְאַל:

7 thus said my God: It shall not succeed, It shall not come to pass.

ז כֹּה אָמַר אֲדֹנָי יְהוִה לֹא תָקוּם וְלֹא תִהְיֶה:

8 For the chief city of Aram is Damascus, And the chief of Damascus is Rezin;

ח כִּי רֹאשׁ אֲרָם דַּמֶּשֶׂק וְרֹאשׁ דַּמֶּשֶׂק רְצִין וּבְעוֹד שִׁשִּׁים וְחָמֵשׁ שָׁנָה יֵחַת אֶפְרַיִם מֵעָם:

9 The chief city of *Efraim* is *Shomron*, And the chief of *Shomron* is the son of Remaliah. And in another sixty-five years, *Efraim* shall be shattered as a people.* If you will not believe, for you cannot be trusted…"

ט וְרֹאשׁ אֶפְרַיִם שֹׁמְרוֹן וְרֹאשׁ שֹׁמְרוֹן בֶּן־רְמַלְיָהוּ אִם לֹא תַאֲמִינוּ כִּי לֹא תֵאָמֵנוּ:

---

* "And in another sixty-five years, *Efraim* shall be shattered as a people" brought down from verse 8 for clarity

---

7:3 At the end of the conduit of the Upper Pool *Yeshayahu* and his son *Shear-Yashuv* confront *Achaz*, then king of *Yehuda*, who was facing an invasion from Aram (Syria) and the northern kingdom of Israel. While *Achaz* fearfully refers to them as two powerful princes, *Yeshayahu* tries to assure him that they are only tails of smoking firebrands, meaning two kingdoms on their deathbeds. Therefore, says *Yeshayahu*, *Yehuda* has only to trust in *Hashem*, and nothing to fear. This meeting – a paradigmatic demonstration of faith in God – occurred at the Launderer's Pool. This pool of water is mentioned two other times in the Bible, and there are various opinions with regard to its exact location. One opinion is a location in the northeast of *Yerushalayim*, close to today's Lions' Gate, where a dam forms a pool carved into a riverbed. Another opinion suggests the pool was in the northwest of the city, where a channel of a riverbed was discovered. While it is unclear if one of these is the pool referred to in this verse, we do know that both of these pools were within the city limits during the time of the Second Temple, and were used by tens of thousands of pilgrims each year for drinking, cleaning and purification in preparation for their visit to the nearby *Beit Hamikdash*.

Yeshayahu/Isaiah
Chapter 7

10 *Hashem* spoke further to *Achaz*:

11 "Ask for a sign from *Hashem* your God, anywhere down to Sheol or up to the sky."

12 But *Achaz* replied, "I will not ask, and I will not test *Hashem*."

13 "Listen, House of *David*," [*Yeshayahu*] retorted, "is it not enough for you to treat men as helpless that you also treat my God as helpless?

14 Assuredly, my Lord will give you a sign of His own accord! Look, the young woman is with child and about to give birth to a son. Let her name him *Imanu-El*.

15 (By the time he learns to reject the bad and choose the good, people will be feeding on curds and honey.)

16 For before the lad knows to reject the bad and choose the good, the ground whose two kings you dread shall be abandoned.

17 *Hashem* will cause to come upon you and your people and your ancestral house such days as never have come since *Efraim* turned away from *Yehuda* – that selfsame king of Assyria!

18 "In that day, *Hashem* will whistle to the flies at the ends of the water channels of Egypt and to the bees in the land of Assyria;

19 and they shall all come and alight in the rugged wadis, and in the clefts of the rocks, and in all the thornbrakes, and in all the watering places.

20 "In that day, my Lord will cut away with the razor that is hired beyond the Euphrates – with the king of Assyria – the hair of the head and the hair of the legs, and it shall clip off the beard as well.

21 And in that day, each man shall save alive a heifer of the herd and two animals of the flock.

22 (And he shall obtain so much milk that he shall eat curds.) Thus everyone who is left in the land shall feed on curds and honey.

23 "For in that day, every spot where there could stand a thousand vines worth a thousand *shekalim* of silver shall become a wilderness of thornbush and thistle.

Yeshayahu/Isaiah
Chapter 8

24 One will have to go there with bow and arrows, for the country shall be all thornbushes and thistles.

25 But the perils of thornbush and thistle shall not spread to any of the hills that could only be tilled with a hoe; and here cattle shall be let loose, and sheep and goats shall tramp about."

8

1 *Hashem* said to me, "Get yourself a large sheet and write on it in common script 'For Maher-shalal-hash-baz';

2 and call reliable witnesses, the *kohen Uriya* and *Zecharya* son of JeBerechiah, to witness for Me."

3 I was intimate with the *Neviah*, and she conceived and bore a son; and *Hashem* said to me, "Name him Maher-shalal-hash-baz.

4 For before the boy learns to call 'Father' and 'Mother,' the wealth of Damascus and the spoils of *Shomron*, and the delights of Rezin and of the son of Remaliah,* shall be carried off before the king of Assyria."

5 Again *Hashem* spoke to me, thus:

6 "Because that people has spurned The gently flowing waters of Siloam" –

7 Assuredly, My Lord will bring up against them The mighty, massive waters of the Euphrates, The king of Assyria and all his multitude. It shall rise above all its channels, And flow over all its beds,

8 And swirl through *Yehuda* like a flash flood Reaching up to the neck. But with us is *Hashem*, Whose wings are spread As wide as your land is broad!

9 Band together, O peoples – you shall be broken! Listen to this, you remotest parts of the earth: Gird yourselves – you shall be broken; Gird yourselves – you shall be broken!

10 Hatch a plot – it shall be foiled; Agree on action – it shall not succeed. For with us is *Hashem*!

11 For this is what *Hashem* said to me, when He took me by the hand and charged me not to walk in the path of that people:

---

* "and the delights of Rezin and of the son of Remaliah" brought up from verse 6 for clarity

Yeshayahu/Isaiah
Chapter 8

ישעיהו
פרק ח

12 "You must not call conspiracy All that that people calls conspiracy, Nor revere what it reveres, Nor hold it in awe.

יב לֹא־תֹאמְר֣וּן קֶ֔שֶׁר לְכֹ֛ל אֲשֶׁר־יֹאמַ֥ר הָעָ֥ם הַזֶּ֖ה קָ֑שֶׁר וְאֶת־מוֹרָא֥וֹ לֹֽא־תִֽירְא֖וּ וְלֹ֥א תַעֲרִֽיצוּ׃

13 None but the Lord of Hosts Shall you account holy; Give reverence to Him alone, Hold Him alone in awe.

יג אֶת־יְהֹוָ֥ה צְבָא֖וֹת אֹת֣וֹ תַקְדִּ֑ישׁוּ וְה֥וּא מוֹרַאֲכֶ֖ם וְה֥וּא מַֽעֲרִֽצְכֶֽם׃

14 He shall be for a sanctuary, A stone men strike against: A rock men stumble over For the two Houses of *Yisrael*, And a trap and a snare for those Who dwell in *Yerushalayim*.

יד וְהָיָ֖ה לְמִקְדָּ֑שׁ וּלְאֶ֣בֶן נֶ֠גֶף וּלְצ֨וּר מִכְשׁ֜וֹל לִשְׁנֵ֣י בָתֵּ֣י יִשְׂרָאֵ֗ל לְפַ֥ח וּלְמוֹקֵ֖שׁ לְיוֹשֵׁ֥ב יְרוּשָׁלָֽ͏ִם׃

15 The masses shall trip over these And shall fall and be injured, Shall be snared and be caught.

טו וְכָ֧שְׁלוּ בָ֛ם רַבִּ֖ים וְנָפְל֣וּ וְנִשְׁבָּ֑רוּ וְנוֹקְשׁ֖וּ וְנִלְכָּֽדוּ׃

16 Bind up the message, Seal the instruction with My disciples."

טז צ֖וֹר תְּעוּדָ֑ה חֲת֥וֹם תּוֹרָ֖ה בְּלִמֻּדָֽי׃

17 So I will wait for *Hashem*, who is hiding His face from the House of *Yaakov*, and I will trust in Him.

יז וְחִכִּיתִי֙ לַיהֹוָ֔ה הַמַּסְתִּ֥יר פָּנָ֖יו מִבֵּ֣ית יַעֲקֹ֑ב וְקִוֵּ֖יתִי־לֽוֹ׃

18 Here stand I and the children *Hashem* has given me as signs and portents in *Yisrael* from the Lord of Hosts, who dwells on Mount *Tzion*.

יח הִנֵּ֣ה אָנֹכִ֗י וְהַיְלָדִים֙ אֲשֶׁ֣ר נָֽתַן־לִ֣י יְהֹוָ֔ה לְאֹת֥וֹת וּלְמוֹפְתִ֖ים בְּיִשְׂרָאֵ֑ל מֵעִם֙ יְהֹוָ֣ה צְבָא֔וֹת הַשֹּׁכֵ֖ן בְּהַ֥ר צִיּֽוֹן׃

hi-NAY a-no-KHEE v'-hai-la-DEEM a-SHER na-tan LEE a-do-NAI l'-o-TOT ul-mof-TEEM b'-yis-ra-AYL may-IM a-do-NAI tz'-va-OT ha-sho-KHAYN b'-HAR tzi-YON

19 Now, should people say to you, "Inquire of the ghosts and familiar spirits that chirp and moan; for a people may inquire of its divine beings – of the dead on behalf of the living –

יט וְכִֽי־יֹאמְר֣וּ אֲלֵיכֶ֗ם דִּרְשׁ֤וּ אֶל־הָֽאֹבוֹת֙ וְאֶל־הַיִּדְּעֹנִ֔ים הַֽמְצַפְצְפִ֖ים וְהַמַּהְגִּ֑ים הֲלוֹא־עַם֙ אֶל־אֱלֹהָ֣יו יִדְרֹ֔שׁ בְּעַ֥ד הַחַיִּ֖ים אֶל־הַמֵּתִֽים׃

20 for instruction and message," surely, for one who speaks thus there shall be no dawn.

כ לְתוֹרָ֖ה וְלִתְעוּדָ֑ה אִם־לֹ֤א יֹֽאמְרוּ֙ כַּדָּבָ֣ר הַזֶּ֔ה אֲשֶׁ֥ר אֵֽין־ל֖וֹ שָֽׁחַר׃

21 And he shall go about in it wretched and hungry; and when he is hungry, he shall rage and revolt against his king and his divine beings. He may turn his face upward

כא וְעָ֥בַר בָּ֖הּ נִקְשֶׁ֣ה וְרָעֵ֑ב וְהָיָ֨ה כִֽי־יִרְעַ֜ב וְהִתְקַצַּ֗ף וְקִלֵּ֧ל בְּמַלְכּ֛וֹ וּבֵֽאלֹהָ֖יו וּפָנָ֥ה לְמָֽעְלָה׃

22 or he may look below, but behold, Distress and darkness, with no daybreak; Straitness and gloom, with no dawn.

כב וְאֶל־אֶ֖רֶץ יַבִּ֑יט וְהִנֵּ֨ה צָרָ֤ה וַחֲשֵׁכָה֙ מְע֣וּף צוּקָ֔ה וַאֲפֵלָ֖ה מְנֻדָּֽח׃

The Temple Mount, Mount Tzion

8:18 the LORD of Hosts, who dwells on Mount Tzion After describing the upcoming Assyrian invasion, the prophet takes steps to ensure that a small remnant of believers in *Hashem*'s salvation will remain. He goes so far as to name his children with names of hope and promise, as signs that the redemption will come. *Yeshayahu* points to the fact that God's presence continues to reside on Mount *Tzion*. Regarding the *Beit Hamikdash* and *Yerushalayim*, the *Rambam* states, "even though it is destroyed, it still possesses its holiness." This means that *Hashem* will never abandon His land or His people. Instead, He remains with His children even while they are in exile, and guarantees that He will redeem them at the right time (Deuteronomy 30:3–5).

Yeshayahu/Isaiah
Chapter 9

ישעיהו
פרק ט

23 For if there were to be any break of day for that [land] which is in straits, only the former [king] would have brought abasement to the land of *Zevulun* and the land of *Naftali* – while the later one would have brought honor to the Way of the Sea, the other side of the *Yarden*, and Galilee of the Nations.

כג כִּי לֹא מוּעָף לַאֲשֶׁר מוּצָק לָהּ כָּעֵת הָרִאשׁוֹן הֵקַל אַרְצָה זְבֻלוּן וְאַרְצָה נַפְתָּלִי וְהָאַחֲרוֹן הִכְבִּיד דֶּרֶךְ הַיָּם עֵבֶר הַיַּרְדֵּן גְּלִיל הַגּוֹיִם׃

9:1 The people that walked in darkness have seen a brilliant light; On those who dwelt in a land of gloom Light has dawned.

ט א הָעָם הַהֹלְכִים בַּחֹשֶׁךְ רָאוּ אוֹר גָּדוֹל יֹשְׁבֵי בְּאֶרֶץ צַלְמָוֶת אוֹר נָגַהּ עֲלֵיהֶם׃

2 You have magnified that nation, Have given it great joy; They have rejoiced before You As they rejoice at reaping time, As they exult When dividing spoil.

ב הִרְבִּיתָ הַגּוֹי לֹא [לוֹ] הִגְדַּלְתָּ הַשִּׂמְחָה שָׂמְחוּ לְפָנֶיךָ כְּשִׂמְחַת בַּקָּצִיר כַּאֲשֶׁר יָגִילוּ בְּחַלְּקָם שָׁלָל׃

3 For the yoke that they bore And the stick on their back – The rod of their taskmaster – You have broken as on the day of Midian.

ג כִּי אֶת־עֹל סֻבֳּלוֹ וְאֵת מַטֵּה שִׁכְמוֹ שֵׁבֶט הַנֹּגֵשׂ בּוֹ הַחִתֹּתָ כְּיוֹם מִדְיָן׃

4 Truly, all the boots put on to stamp with And all the garments donned in infamy Have been fed to the flames, Devoured by fire.

ד כִּי כָל־סְאוֹן סֹאֵן בְּרַעַשׁ וְשִׂמְלָה מְגוֹלָלָה בְדָמִים וְהָיְתָה לִשְׂרֵפָה מַאֲכֹלֶת אֵשׁ׃

5 For a child has been born to us, A son has been given us. And authority has settled on his shoulders. He has been named "The Mighty *Hashem* is planning grace; The Eternal Father, a peaceable ruler" –

ה כִּי־יֶלֶד יֻלַּד־לָנוּ בֵּן נִתַּן־לָנוּ וַתְּהִי הַמִּשְׂרָה עַל־שִׁכְמוֹ וַיִּקְרָא שְׁמוֹ פֶּלֶא יוֹעֵץ אֵל גִּבּוֹר אֲבִיעַד שַׂר־שָׁלוֹם׃

kee YE-led yu-lad LA-nu BEN ni-tan LA-nu va-t'-HEE ha-mis-RAH al shikh-MO va-yik-RA sh'-MO PE-le yo-AYTZ AYL gi-BOR a-vee AD sar sha-LOM

6 In token of abundant authority And of peace without limit Upon *David*'s throne and kingdom, That it may be firmly established In justice and in equity Now and evermore. The zeal of the Lord of Hosts Shall bring this to pass.

ו לְמַרְבֵּה [לְמַרְבֵּה] הַמִּשְׂרָה וּלְשָׁלוֹם אֵין־קֵץ עַל־כִּסֵּא דָוִד וְעַל־מַמְלַכְתּוֹ לְהָכִין אֹתָהּ וּלְסַעֲדָהּ בְּמִשְׁפָּט וּבִצְדָקָה מֵעַתָּה וְעַד־עוֹלָם קִנְאַת יְהוָה צְבָאוֹת תַּעֲשֶׂה־זֹּאת׃

7 My Lord Let loose a word against *Yaakov* And it fell upon *Yisrael*.

ז דָּבָר שָׁלַח אֲדֹנָי בְּיַעֲקֹב וְנָפַל בְּיִשְׂרָאֵל׃

8 But all the people noted – *Efraim* and the inhabitants of *Shomron* – In arrogance and haughtiness:

ח וְיָדְעוּ הָעָם כֻּלּוֹ אֶפְרַיִם וְיוֹשֵׁב שֹׁמְרוֹן בְּגַאֲוָה וּבְגֹדֶל לֵבָב לֵאמֹר׃

9:5 For a child has been born to us *Yeshayahu*'s prophecy of the upcoming salvation of the people is combined with a vision regarding the birth of a child. Judging from the context of the prophecy, *Yeshayahu* appears to be referring to the righteous King *Chizkiyahu*, whom tradition credits with educating all the Children of Israel about the intricacies of *Hashem*'s laws. Over the last three chapters, *Yeshayahu* has combined prophecies of redemption with announcements of upcoming births. This signifies that even if the present may seem difficult, the future will always be brighter.

970

Yeshayahu/Isaiah
Chapter 10

9 "Bricks have fallen – We'll rebuild with dressed stone; Sycamores have been felled – We'll grow cedars instead!"

10 So *Hashem* let the enemies of Rezin Triumph over it And stirred up its foes –

11 Aram from the east And Philistia from the west – Who devoured *Yisrael* With greedy mouths. Yet His anger has not turned back, And His arm is outstretched still.

12 For the people has not turned back To Him who struck it And has not sought the Lord of Hosts.

13 So *Hashem* will cut off from *Yisrael* Head and tail, Palm branch and reed, In a single day.

14 Elders and magnates – Such are the heads; *Neviim* who give false instruction, Such are the tails

15 That people's leaders have been misleaders, So they that are led have been confused.

16 That is why my Lord Will not spare their youths, Nor show compassion To their orphans and widows; For all are ungodly and wicked, And every mouth speaks impiety.

17 Already wickedness has blazed forth like a fire Devouring thorn and thistle. It has kindled the thickets of the wood, Which have turned into billowing smoke. Yet His anger has not turned back, And His arm is outstretched still.*

18 By the fury of the Lord of Hosts, The earth was shaken. Next, the people became like devouring fire: No man spared his countryman.

19 They snatched on the right, but remained hungry, And consumed on the left without being sated. Each devoured the flesh of his own kindred –

20 *Menashe Efraim*'s, and *Efraim Menashe*'s, And both of them against *Yehuda*! Yet His anger has not turned back, And His arm is outstretched still.

10

1 Ha! Those who write out evil writs And compose iniquitous documents,

2 To subvert the cause of the poor, To rob of their rights the needy of My people; That widows may be their spoil, And fatherless children their booty!

---

* "Yet His anger has not turned back, And His arm is outstretched still" brought down from verse 16 for clarity

ישעיהו
פרק י

ט לְבֵנִים נָפָלוּ וְגָזִית נִבְנֶה שִׁקְמִים גֻּדָּעוּ וַאֲרָזִים נַחֲלִיף׃

י וַיְשַׂגֵּב יְהֹוָה אֶת־צָרֵי רְצִין עָלָיו וְאֶת־אֹיְבָיו יְסַכְסֵךְ׃

יא אֲרָם מִקֶּדֶם וּפְלִשְׁתִּים מֵאָחוֹר וַיֹּאכְלוּ אֶת־יִשְׂרָאֵל בְּכָל־פֶּה בְּכָל־זֹאת לֹא־שָׁב אַפּוֹ וְעוֹד יָדוֹ נְטוּיָה׃

יב וְהָעָם לֹא־שָׁב עַד־הַמַּכֵּהוּ וְאֶת־יְהֹוָה צְבָאוֹת לֹא דָרָשׁוּ׃

יג וַיַּכְרֵת יְהֹוָה מִיִּשְׂרָאֵל רֹאשׁ וְזָנָב כִּפָּה וְאַגְמוֹן יוֹם אֶחָד׃

יד זָקֵן וּנְשׂוּא־פָנִים הוּא הָרֹאשׁ וְנָבִיא מוֹרֶה־שֶּׁקֶר הוּא הַזָּנָב׃

טו וַיִּהְיוּ מְאַשְּׁרֵי הָעָם־הַזֶּה מַתְעִים וּמְאֻשָּׁרָיו מְבֻלָּעִים׃

טז עַל־כֵּן עַל־בַּחוּרָיו לֹא־יִשְׂמַח אֲדֹנָי וְאֶת־יְתֹמָיו וְאֶת־אַלְמְנֹתָיו לֹא יְרַחֵם כִּי כֻלּוֹ חָנֵף וּמֵרַע וְכָל־פֶּה דֹּבֵר נְבָלָה בְּכָל־זֹאת לֹא־שָׁב אַפּוֹ וְעוֹד יָדוֹ נְטוּיָה׃

יז כִּי־בָעֲרָה כָאֵשׁ רִשְׁעָה שָׁמִיר וָשַׁיִת תֹּאכֵל וַתִּצַּת בְּסִבְכֵי הַיַּעַר וַיִּתְאַבְּכוּ גֵּאוּת עָשָׁן׃

יח בְּעֶבְרַת יְהֹוָה צְבָאוֹת נֶעְתַּם אָרֶץ וַיְהִי הָעָם כְּמַאֲכֹלֶת אֵשׁ אִישׁ אֶל־אָחִיו לֹא יַחְמֹלוּ׃

יט וַיִּגְזֹר עַל־יָמִין וְרָעֵב וַיֹּאכַל עַל־שְׂמֹאול וְלֹא שָׂבֵעוּ אִישׁ בְּשַׂר־זְרֹעוֹ יֹאכֵלוּ׃

כ מְנַשֶּׁה אֶת־אֶפְרַיִם וְאֶפְרַיִם אֶת־מְנַשֶּׁה יַחְדָּו הֵמָּה עַל־יְהוּדָה בְּכָל־זֹאת לֹא־שָׁב אַפּוֹ וְעוֹד יָדוֹ נְטוּיָה׃

י א הוֹי הַחֹקְקִים חִקְקֵי־אָוֶן וּמְכַתְּבִים עָמָל כִּתֵּבוּ׃

ב לְהַטּוֹת מִדִּין דַּלִּים וְלִגְזֹל מִשְׁפַּט עֲנִיֵּי עַמִּי לִהְיוֹת אַלְמָנוֹת שְׁלָלָם וְאֶת־יְתוֹמִים יָבֹזּוּ׃

Yeshayahu/Isaiah
Chapter 10

ישעיהו
פרק י

3 What will you do on the day of punishment, When the calamity comes from afar? To whom will you flee for help, And how will you save your carcasses

ג וּמַה־תַּעֲשׂוּ לְיוֹם פְּקֻדָּה וּלְשׁוֹאָה מִמֶּרְחָק תָּבוֹא עַל־מִי תָּנוּסוּ לְעֶזְרָה וְאָנָה תַעַזְבוּ כְּבוֹדְכֶם׃

4 From collapsing under [fellow] prisoners, From falling beneath the slain? Yet His anger has not turned back, And his arm is outstretched still.

ד בִּלְתִּי כָרַע תַּחַת אַסִּיר וְתַחַת הֲרוּגִים יִפֹּלוּ בְּכָל־זֹאת לֹא־שָׁב אַפּוֹ וְעוֹד יָדוֹ נְטוּיָה׃

5 Ha! Assyria, rod of My anger, In whose hand, as a staff, is My fury!

ה הוֹי אַשּׁוּר שֵׁבֶט אַפִּי וּמַטֶּה־הוּא בְיָדָם זַעְמִי׃

HOY a-SHUR SHAY-vet a-PEE u-ma-teh HU v'-ya-DAM za-MEE

6 I send him against an ungodly nation, I charge him against a people that provokes Me, To take its spoil and to seize its booty And to make it a thing trampled Like the mire of the streets.

ו בְּגוֹי חָנֵף אֲשַׁלְּחֶנּוּ וְעַל־עַם עֶבְרָתִי אֲצַוֶּנּוּ לִשְׁלֹל שָׁלָל וְלָבֹז בַּז וּלְשִׂימוֹ [וּלְשׂוּמוֹ] מִרְמָס כְּחֹמֶר חוּצוֹת׃

7 But he has evil plans, His mind harbors evil designs; For he means to destroy, To wipe out nations, not a few.

ז וְהוּא לֹא־כֵן יְדַמֶּה וּלְבָבוֹ לֹא־כֵן יַחְשֹׁב כִּי לְהַשְׁמִיד בִּלְבָבוֹ וּלְהַכְרִית גּוֹיִם לֹא מְעָט׃

8 For he thinks, "After all, I have kings as my captains!

ח כִּי יֹאמַר הֲלֹא שָׂרַי יַחְדָּו מְלָכִים׃

9 Was Calno any different from Carchemish? Or Hamath from Arpad? Or *Shomron* from Damascus?

ט הֲלֹא כְּכַרְכְּמִישׁ כַּלְנוֹ אִם־לֹא כְאַרְפַּד חֲמָת אִם־לֹא כְדַמֶּשֶׂק שֹׁמְרוֹן׃

10 Since I was able to seize The insignificant kingdoms, Whose images exceeded *Yerushalayim*'s and *Shomron*'s,

י כַּאֲשֶׁר מָצְאָה יָדִי לְמַמְלְכֹת הָאֱלִיל וּפְסִילֵיהֶם מִירוּשָׁלַםִ וּמִשֹּׁמְרוֹן׃

11 Shall I not do to *Yerushalayim* and her images What I did to *Shomron* and her idols?"

יא הֲלֹא כַּאֲשֶׁר עָשִׂיתִי לְשֹׁמְרוֹן וְלֶאֱלִילֶיהָ כֵּן אֶעֱשֶׂה לִירוּשָׁלַםִ וְלַעֲצַבֶּיהָ׃

12 But when my Lord has carried out all his purpose on Mount *Tzion* and in *Yerushalayim*, He will punish the majestic pride and overbearing arrogance of the king of Assyria.

יב וְהָיָה כִּי־יְבַצַּע אֲדֹנָי אֶת־כָּל־מַעֲשֵׂהוּ בְּהַר צִיּוֹן וּבִירוּשָׁלָםִ אֶפְקֹד עַל־פְּרִי־גֹדֶל לְבַב מֶלֶךְ־אַשּׁוּר וְעַל־תִּפְאֶרֶת רוּם עֵינָיו׃

10:5 Assyria, rod of My anger Ancient idol-worshippers believed that the fortunes of their countries were directly tied to the strength of their gods. Therefore, if another country was to conquer theirs, they would have no problem transferring their worship and loyalty to the invaders' gods, as these were clearly stronger. Against that background, what *Yeshayahu* says to the people in this verse is quite revolutionary: Not only are the Assyrian gods non-existent, but *Hashem* Himself controls the Assyrians, and is using them as an instrument to punish Israel. Should the People of Israel return to God and practice justice and righteousness, however, *Hashem* will break the Assyrian yoke of oppression and punish the Assyrians for their arrogance. *Yeshayahu*'s eternal message to the Children of Israel is that God is always the cause of everything that occurs to them, and the nature of their fortune will be determined only on the basis of their record of adherence to His laws.

Yeshayahu/Isaiah
Chapter 10

13 For he thought, "By the might of my hand have I wrought it, By my skill, for I am clever: I have erased the borders of peoples; I have plundered their treasures, And exiled their vast populations.

14 I was able to seize, like a nest, The wealth of peoples; As one gathers abandoned eggs, So I gathered all the earth: Nothing so much as flapped a wing Or opened a mouth to peep."

15 Does an ax boast over him who hews with it, Or a saw magnify itself above him who wields it? As though the rod raised him who lifts it, As though the staff lifted the man!

16 Assuredly, The Sovereign Lord of Hosts will send A wasting away in its fatness; And under its body shall burn A burning like that of fire, Destroying frame and flesh. It shall be like a sick man who pines away.*

17 The Light of *Yisrael* will be fire And its Holy One flame. It will burn and consume its thorns And its thistles in a single day,

18 And the mass of its scrub and its farm land.

19 What trees remain of its scrub Shall be so few that a boy may record them.

20 And in that day, The remnant of *Yisrael* And the escaped of the House of *Yaakov* Shall lean no more upon him that beats it, But shall lean sincerely On *Hashem*, the Holy One of *Yisrael*.

21 Only a remnant shall return, Only a remnant of *Yaakov*, To Mighty *Hashem*.

22 Even if your people, O *Yisrael*, Should be as the sands of the sea, Only a remnant of it shall return. Destruction is decreed; Retribution comes like a flood!

23 For my Lord God of Hosts is carrying out A decree of destruction upon all the land.

24 Assuredly, thus said my Lord God of Hosts: "O My people that dwells in *Tzion*, have no fear of Assyria, who beats you with a rod and wields his staff over you as did the Egyptians.

---

* "Destroying frame and flesh. It shall be like a sick man who pines away" brought up from verse 18 for clarity

Yeshayahu/Isaiah

Chapter 11

25 For very soon My wrath will have spent itself, and My anger that was bent on wasting them."

26 The Lord of Hosts will brandish a scourge over him as when He beat Midian at the Rock of Oreb, and will wield His staff as He did over the Egyptians by the sea.

27 And in that day, His burden shall drop from your back, And his yoke from your neck; The yoke shall be destroyed because of fatness.

28 He advanced upon Aiath, He proceeded to Migron, At Michmas he deposited his baggage.

29 They made the crossing; "Geba is to be our night quarters!" *Rama* was alarmed; *Giva* of *Shaul* took to flight.

30 "Give a shrill cry, O Bath-gallim! Hearken, Laishah! Take up the cry, *Anatot*!"

31 Madmenah ran away; The dwellers of Gebim sought refuge.

32 This same day at *Nov* He shall stand and wave his hand. O mount of Fair *Tzion*! O hill of *Yerushalayim*!

33 Lo! The Sovereign Lord of Hosts Will hew off the tree-crowns with an ax: The tall ones shall be felled, The lofty ones cut down:

34 The thickets of the forest shall be hacked away with iron, And the Lebanon trees shall fall in their majesty.

11

1 But a shoot shall grow out of the stump of *Yishai*, A twig shall sprout from his stock.

2 The spirit of *Hashem* shall alight upon him: A spirit of wisdom and insight, A spirit of counsel and valor, A spirit of devotion and reverence for *Hashem*.

3 He shall sense the truth by his reverence for *Hashem*: He shall not judge by what his eyes behold, Nor decide by what his ears perceive.

4 Thus he shall judge the poor with equity And decide with justice for the lowly of the land. He shall strike down a land with the rod of his mouth And slay the wicked with the breath of his lips.

5 Justice shall be the girdle of his loins, And faithfulness the girdle of his waist.

ישעיהו

פרק יא

כה כִּי־עוֹד מְעַט מִזְעָר וְכָלָה זַעַם וְאַפִּי עַל־תַּבְלִיתָם:

כו וְעוֹרֵר עָלָיו יְהֹוָה צְבָאוֹת שׁוֹט כְּמַכַּת מִדְיָן בְּצוּר עוֹרֵב וּמַטֵּהוּ עַל־הַיָּם וּנְשָׂאוֹ בְּדֶרֶךְ מִצְרָיִם:

כז וְהָיָה בַּיּוֹם הַהוּא יָסוּר סֻבֳּלוֹ מֵעַל שִׁכְמֶךָ וְעֻלּוֹ מֵעַל צַוָּארֶךָ וְחֻבַּל עֹל מִפְּנֵי־שָׁמֶן:

כח בָּא עַל־עַיַּת עָבַר בְּמִגְרוֹן לְמִכְמָשׂ יַפְקִיד כֵּלָיו:

כט עָבְרוּ מַעְבָּרָה גֶּבַע מָלוֹן לָנוּ חָרְדָה הָרָמָה גִּבְעַת שָׁאוּל נָסָה:

ל צַהֲלִי קוֹלֵךְ בַּת־גַּלִּים הַקְשִׁיבִי לַיְשָׁה עֲנִיָּה עֲנָתוֹת:

לא נָדְדָה מַדְמֵנָה יֹשְׁבֵי הַגֵּבִים הֵעִיזוּ:

לב עוֹד הַיּוֹם בְּנֹב לַעֲמֹד יְנֹפֵף יָדוֹ הַר בֵּית־[בַּת־] צִיּוֹן גִּבְעַת יְרוּשָׁלָםִ:

לג הִנֵּה הָאָדוֹן יְהֹוָה צְבָאוֹת מְסָעֵף פֻּארָה בְּמַעֲרָצָה וְרָמֵי הַקּוֹמָה גְּדֻעִים וְהַגְּבֹהִים יִשְׁפָּלוּ:

לד וְנִקַּף סִבְכֵי הַיַּעַר בַּבַּרְזֶל וְהַלְּבָנוֹן בְּאַדִּיר יִפּוֹל:

פרק יא

א וְיָצָא חֹטֶר מִגֵּזַע יִשָׁי וְנֵצֶר מִשָּׁרָשָׁיו יִפְרֶה:

ב וְנָחָה עָלָיו רוּחַ יְהֹוָה רוּחַ חָכְמָה וּבִינָה רוּחַ עֵצָה וּגְבוּרָה רוּחַ דַּעַת וְיִרְאַת יְהֹוָה:

ג וַהֲרִיחוֹ בְּיִרְאַת יְהֹוָה וְלֹא־לְמַרְאֵה עֵינָיו יִשְׁפּוֹט וְלֹא־לְמִשְׁמַע אָזְנָיו יוֹכִיחַ:

ד וְשָׁפַט בְּצֶדֶק דַּלִּים וְהוֹכִיחַ בְּמִישׁוֹר לְעַנְוֵי־אָרֶץ וְהִכָּה־אֶרֶץ בְּשֵׁבֶט פִּיו וּבְרוּחַ שְׂפָתָיו יָמִית רָשָׁע:

ה וְהָיָה צֶדֶק אֵזוֹר מָתְנָיו וְהָאֱמוּנָה אֵזוֹר חֲלָצָיו:

Yeshayahu/Isaiah
Chapter 11

ישעיהו
פרק יא

6 The wolf shall dwell with the lamb, The leopard lie down with the kid; The calf, the beast of prey, and the fatling together, With a little boy to herd them.

ו וְגָר זְאֵב עִם־כֶּבֶשׂ וְנָמֵר עִם־גְּדִי יִרְבָּץ וְעֵגֶל וּכְפִיר וּמְרִיא יַחְדָּו וְנַעַר קָטֹן נֹהֵג בָּם׃

7 The cow and the bear shall graze, Their young shall lie down together; And the lion, like the ox, shall eat straw.

ז וּפָרָה וָדֹב תִּרְעֶינָה יַחְדָּו יִרְבְּצוּ יַלְדֵיהֶן וְאַרְיֵה כַּבָּקָר יֹאכַל־תֶּבֶן׃

8 A babe shall play Over a viper's hole, And an infant pass his hand Over an adder's den.

ח וְשִׁעֲשַׁע יוֹנֵק עַל־חֻר פָּתֶן וְעַל מְאוּרַת צִפְעוֹנִי גָּמוּל יָדוֹ הָדָה׃

9 In all of My sacred mount Nothing evil or vile shall be done; For the land shall be filled with devotion to *Hashem* As water covers the sea.

ט לֹא־יָרֵעוּ וְלֹא־יַשְׁחִיתוּ בְּכָל־הַר קָדְשִׁי כִּי־מָלְאָה הָאָרֶץ דֵּעָה אֶת־יְהוָה כַּמַּיִם לַיָּם מְכַסִּים׃

10 In that day, The stock of *Yishai* that has remained standing Shall become a standard to peoples – Nations shall seek his counsel And his abode shall be honored.

י וְהָיָה בַּיּוֹם הַהוּא שֹׁרֶשׁ יִשַׁי אֲשֶׁר עֹמֵד לְנֵס עַמִּים אֵלָיו גּוֹיִם יִדְרֹשׁוּ וְהָיְתָה מְנֻחָתוֹ כָּבוֹד׃

11 In that day, my Lord will apply His hand again to redeeming the other part of His people from Assyria – as also from Egypt, Pathros, Nubia, Elam, Shinar, Hamath, and the coastlands.

יא וְהָיָה בַּיּוֹם הַהוּא יוֹסִיף אֲדֹנָי שֵׁנִית יָדוֹ לִקְנוֹת אֶת־שְׁאָר עַמּוֹ אֲשֶׁר יִשָּׁאֵר מֵאַשּׁוּר וּמִמִּצְרַיִם וּמִפַּתְרוֹס וּמִכּוּשׁ וּמֵעֵילָם וּמִשִּׁנְעָר וּמֵחֲמָת וּמֵאִיֵּי הַיָּם׃

12 He will hold up a signal to the nations And assemble the banished of *Yisrael*, And gather the dispersed of *Yehuda* From the four corners of the earth.

יב וְנָשָׂא נֵס לַגּוֹיִם וְאָסַף נִדְחֵי יִשְׂרָאֵל וּנְפֻצוֹת יְהוּדָה יְקַבֵּץ מֵאַרְבַּע כַּנְפוֹת הָאָרֶץ׃

v'-na-SA NAYS la-go-YIM v'-a-SAF nid-KHAY yis-ra-AYL un-fu-TZOT y'-hu-DAH y'-ka-BAYTZ may-ar-BA kan-FOT ha-A-retz

13 Then *Efraim*'s envy shall cease And *Yehuda*'s harassment shall end; *Efraim* shall not envy *Yehuda*, And *Yehuda* shall not harass *Efraim*.

יג וְסָרָה קִנְאַת אֶפְרַיִם וְצֹרְרֵי יְהוּדָה יִכָּרֵתוּ אֶפְרַיִם לֹא־יְקַנֵּא אֶת־יְהוּדָה וִיהוּדָה לֹא־יָצֹר אֶת־אֶפְרָיִם׃

14 They shall pounce on the back of Philistia to the west, And together plunder the peoples of the east; Edom and Moab shall be subject to them And the children of Ammon shall obey them.

יד וְעָפוּ בְכָתֵף פְּלִשְׁתִּים יָמָּה יַחְדָּו יָבֹזּוּ אֶת־בְּנֵי־קֶדֶם אֱדוֹם וּמוֹאָב מִשְׁלוֹח יָדָם וּבְנֵי עַמּוֹן מִשְׁמַעְתָּם׃

15 *Hashem* will dry up the tongue of the Egyptian sea. – He will raise His hand over the Euphrates with the might of His wind and break it into seven wadis, so that it can be trodden dry-shod.

טו וְהֶחֱרִים יְהוָה אֵת לְשׁוֹן יָם־מִצְרַיִם וְהֵנִיף יָדוֹ עַל־הַנָּהָר בַּעְיָם רוּחוֹ וְהִכָּהוּ לְשִׁבְעָה נְחָלִים וְהִדְרִיךְ בַּנְּעָלִים׃

New immigrants from France arrive at Ben Gurion airport

11:12 And assemble the banished of *Yisrael* For thousands of years, Jews read these prophecies and believed them, yet wondered how and when they would actually take place. During the past century, Jews have returned to the Land of Israel from literally all parts of the earth: from Asia and Russia, Europe, North and South America, Australia and New Zealand. This section was chosen as the *Haftarah* portion to be read on Israel's Independence Day, expressing the hope and belief that the founding of the State of Israel is the beginning of the fulfillment of these prophecies.

Yeshayahu/Isaiah
Chapter 12

16 Thus there shall be a highway for the other part of His people out of Assyria, such as there was for *Yisrael* when it left the land of Egypt.

טז וְהָיְתָה מְסִלָּה לִשְׁאָר עַמּוֹ אֲשֶׁר יִשָּׁאֵר מֵאַשּׁוּר כַּאֲשֶׁר הָיְתָה לְיִשְׂרָאֵל בְּיוֹם עֲלֹתוֹ מֵאֶרֶץ מִצְרָיִם:

12

1 In that day, you shall say: "I give thanks to You, *Hashem*! Although You were wroth with me, Your wrath has turned back and You comfort me,

א וְאָמַרְתָּ בַּיּוֹם הַהוּא אוֹדְךָ יְהֹוָה כִּי אָנַפְתָּ בִּי יָשֹׁב אַפְּךָ וּתְנַחֲמֵנִי:

2 Behold the God who gives me triumph! I am confident, unafraid; For Yah *Hashem* is my strength and might, And He has been my deliverance."

ב הִנֵּה אֵל יְשׁוּעָתִי אֶבְטַח וְלֹא אֶפְחָד כִּי־עָזִּי וְזִמְרָת יָהּ יְהֹוָה וַיְהִי־לִי לִישׁוּעָה:

3 Joyfully shall you draw water From the fountains of triumph,

ג וּשְׁאַבְתֶּם־מַיִם בְּשָׂשׂוֹן מִמַּעַיְנֵי הַיְשׁוּעָה:

4 And you shall say on that day: "Praise *Hashem*, proclaim His name. Make His deeds known among the peoples; Declare that His name is exalted.

ד וַאֲמַרְתֶּם בַּיּוֹם הַהוּא הוֹדוּ לַיהֹוָה קִרְאוּ בִשְׁמוֹ הוֹדִיעוּ בָעַמִּים עֲלִילֹתָיו הַזְכִּירוּ כִּי נִשְׂגָּב שְׁמוֹ:

5 Hymn *Hashem*, For He has done gloriously; Let this be made known In all the world!

ה זַמְּרוּ יְהֹוָה כִּי גֵאוּת עָשָׂה מידעת [מוּדַעַת] זֹאת בְּכָל־הָאָרֶץ:

za-m'-RU a-do-NAI KEE gay-UT a-SAH mu-DA-at ZOT b'-khol ha-A-retz

6 Oh, shout for joy, You who dwell in *Tzion*! For great in your midst Is the Holy One of *Yisrael*."

ו צַהֲלִי וָרֹנִּי יוֹשֶׁבֶת צִיּוֹן כִּי־גָדוֹל בְּקִרְבֵּךְ קְדוֹשׁ יִשְׂרָאֵל:

13

1 The "Babylon" Pronouncement, a prophecy of *Yeshayahu* son of *Amotz*.

א מַשָּׂא בָּבֶל אֲשֶׁר חָזָה יְשַׁעְיָהוּ בֶּן־אָמוֹץ:

2 "Raise a standard upon a bare hill, Cry aloud to them; Wave a hand, and let them enter The gates of the nobles!

ב עַל הַר־נִשְׁפֶּה שְׂאוּ־נֵס הָרִימוּ קוֹל לָהֶם הָנִיפוּ יָד וְיָבֹאוּ פִּתְחֵי נְדִיבִים:

AL har nish-PEH s'-u NAYS ha-REE-mu KOL la-HEM ha-NEE-fu YAD v'-ya-VO-u pit-KHAY n'-dee-VEEM

12:5 Hymn *Hashem*, for He has done gloriously The Talmud (*Sanhedrin* 94a) states that after *Yehuda*'s miraculous deliverance from the Assyrian invasion, *Hashem* desired to crown the righteous king *Chizkiyahu* as the *Mashiach*. Only one thing was required – that *Chizkiyahu* sing a song of praise before Him. Instead, though, *Chizkiyahu* arose that morning, and continued with his regular daily routine, the study of the *Torah*, until *Yeshayahu* instructed him to sing. Unfortunately, as the song was not spontaneous but rather came as a response to a command, the opportunity was lost. In this verse, *Yeshayahu* teaches the importance of appreciating everything that occurs for us, and being able to sing praise for it before *Hashem*.

13:2 Raise a standard upon a bare hill *Yeshayahu* begins a series of prophecies against the nations (chapters 13–23) with a message to Babylon. He calls on *Hashem*'s army to assemble on a mountaintop against the Babylonians. The word that describes the mountain is *nishpeh* (נשפה), which means 'bare.' The selected mountaintop is bare and empty of trees – most likely so that the *nays* (נס), the 'standard' or signal for the warriors to gather, might be better seen from it. *Yeshayahu* contrasts the barren mountain of Babylon (which means 'gates of gods' in Ugaritic) with the genuine mountain of *Hashem* in *Yerushalayim* described in chapter 2, which is the source of knowledge and righteousness for the world.

Yeshayahu/Isaiah

Chapter 13

3 I have summoned My purified guests To execute My wrath; Behold, I have called My stalwarts, My proudly exultant ones."

ג אֲנִי צִוֵּיתִי לִמְקֻדָּשָׁי גַּם קָרָאתִי גִבּוֹרַי לְאַפִּי עַלִּיזֵי גַּאֲוָתִי׃

4 Hark! a tumult on the mountains – As of a mighty force; Hark! an uproar of kingdoms, Nations assembling! the Lord of Hosts is mustering A host for war.

ד קוֹל הָמוֹן בֶּהָרִים דְּמוּת עַם־רָב קוֹל שְׁאוֹן מַמְלְכוֹת גּוֹיִם נֶאֱסָפִים יְהוָה צְבָאוֹת מְפַקֵּד צְבָא מִלְחָמָה׃

5 They come from a distant land, From the end of the sky – *Hashem* with the weapons of His wrath – To ravage all the earth!

ה בָּאִים מֵאֶרֶץ מֶרְחָק מִקְצֵה הַשָּׁמָיִם יְהוָה וּכְלֵי זַעְמוֹ לְחַבֵּל כָּל־הָאָרֶץ׃

6 Howl! For the day of *Hashem* is near; It shall come like havoc from *Shaddai*.

ו הֵילִילוּ כִּי קָרוֹב יוֹם יְהוָה כְּשֹׁד מִשַּׁדַּי יָבוֹא׃

7 Therefore all hands shall grow limp, And all men's hearts shall sink;

ז עַל־כֵּן כָּל־יָדַיִם תִּרְפֶּינָה וְכָל־לְבַב אֱנוֹשׁ יִמָּס׃

8 And, overcome by terror, They shall be seized by pangs and throes, Writhe like a woman in travail. They shall gaze at each other in horror, Their faces livid with fright.

ח וְנִבְהָלוּ צִירִים וַחֲבָלִים יֹאחֵזוּן כַּיּוֹלֵדָה יְחִילוּן אִישׁ אֶל־רֵעֵהוּ יִתְמָהוּ פְּנֵי לְהָבִים פְּנֵיהֶם׃

9 Lo! The day of *Hashem* is coming With pitiless fury and wrath, To make the earth a desolation, To wipe out the sinners upon it.

ט הִנֵּה יוֹם־יְהוָה בָּא אַכְזָרִי וְעֶבְרָה וַחֲרוֹן אָף לָשׂוּם הָאָרֶץ לְשַׁמָּה וְחַטָּאֶיהָ יַשְׁמִיד מִמֶּנָּה׃

10 The stars and constellations of heaven Shall not give off their light; The sun shall be dark when it rises, And the moon shall diffuse no glow.

י כִּי־כוֹכְבֵי הַשָּׁמַיִם וּכְסִילֵיהֶם לֹא יָהֵלּוּ אוֹרָם חָשַׁךְ הַשֶּׁמֶשׁ בְּצֵאתוֹ וְיָרֵחַ לֹא־יַגִּיהַּ אוֹרוֹ׃

11 "And I will requite to the world its evil, And to the wicked their iniquity; I will put an end to the pride of the arrogant And humble the haughtiness of tyrants.

יא וּפָקַדְתִּי עַל־תֵּבֵל רָעָה וְעַל־רְשָׁעִים עֲוֺנָם וְהִשְׁבַּתִּי גְּאוֹן זֵדִים וְגַאֲוַת עָרִיצִים אַשְׁפִּיל׃

12 I will make people scarcer than fine gold, And men than gold of Ophir."

יב אוֹקִיר אֱנוֹשׁ מִפָּז וְאָדָם מִכֶּתֶם אוֹפִיר׃

13 Therefore shall heaven be shaken, And earth leap out of its place, At the fury of the Lord of Hosts On the day of His burning wrath.

יג עַל־כֵּן שָׁמַיִם אַרְגִּיז וְתִרְעַשׁ הָאָרֶץ מִמְּקוֹמָהּ בְּעֶבְרַת יְהוָה צְבָאוֹת וּבְיוֹם חֲרוֹן אַפּוֹ׃

14 Then like gazelles that are chased, And like sheep that no man gathers, Each man shall turn back to his people, They shall flee every one to his land.

יד וְהָיָה כִּצְבִי מֻדָּח וּכְצֹאן וְאֵין מְקַבֵּץ אִישׁ אֶל־עַמּוֹ יִפְנוּ וְאִישׁ אֶל־אַרְצוֹ יָנוּסוּ׃

15 All who remain shall be pierced through, All who are caught Shall fall by the sword.

טו כָּל־הַנִּמְצָא יִדָּקֵר וְכָל־הַנִּסְפֶּה יִפּוֹל בֶּחָרֶב׃

16 And their babes shall be dashed to pieces in their sight, Their homes shall be plundered, And their wives shall be raped.

טז וְעֹלְלֵיהֶם יְרֻטְּשׁוּ לְעֵינֵיהֶם יִשַּׁסּוּ בָּתֵּיהֶם וּנְשֵׁיהֶם תשגלנה [תִּשָּׁכַבְנָה]׃

Yeshayahu/Isaiah
Chapter 14

ישעיהו
פרק יד

17 "Behold, I stir up the Medes against them, Who do not value silver Or delight in gold.

יז הִנְנִי מֵעִיר עֲלֵיהֶם אֶת־מָדָי אֲשֶׁר־כֶּסֶף לֹא יַחְשֹׁבוּ וְזָהָב לֹא יַחְפְּצוּ־בוֹ׃

18 Their bows shall shatter the young; They shall show no pity to infants, They shall not spare the children."

יח וּקְשָׁתוֹת נְעָרִים תְּרַטַּשְׁנָה וּפְרִי־בֶטֶן לֹא יְרַחֵמוּ עַל־בָּנִים לֹא־תָחוּס עֵינָם׃

19 And Babylon, glory of kingdoms, Proud splendor of the Chaldeans, Shall become like Sodom and Gomorrah Overturned by *Hashem*.

יט וְהָיְתָה בָבֶל צְבִי מַמְלָכוֹת תִּפְאֶרֶת גְּאוֹן כַּשְׂדִּים כְּמַהְפֵּכַת אֱלֹהִים אֶת־סְדֹם וְאֶת־עֲמֹרָה׃

20 Nevermore shall it be settled Nor dwelt in through all the ages. No Arab shall pitch his tent there, No shepherds make flocks lie down there.

כ לֹא־תֵשֵׁב לָנֶצַח וְלֹא תִשְׁכֹּן עַד־דּוֹר וָדוֹר וְלֹא־יַהֵל שָׁם עֲרָבִי וְרֹעִים לֹא־יַרְבִּצוּ שָׁם׃

21 But beasts shall lie down there, And the houses be filled with owls; There shall ostriches make their home, And there shall satyrs dance.

כא וְרָבְצוּ־שָׁם צִיִּים וּמָלְאוּ בָתֵּיהֶם אֹחִים וְשָׁכְנוּ שָׁם בְּנוֹת יַעֲנָה וּשְׂעִירִים יְרַקְּדוּ־שָׁם׃

22 And jackals shall abide in its castles And dragons in the palaces of pleasure. Her hour is close at hand; Her days will not be long.

כב וְעָנָה אִיִּים בְּאַלְמְנוֹתָיו וְתַנִּים בְּהֵיכְלֵי עֹנֶג וְקָרוֹב לָבוֹא עִתָּהּ וְיָמֶיהָ לֹא יִמָּשֵׁכוּ׃

14 1 But *Hashem* will pardon *Yaakov*, and will again choose *Yisrael*, and will settle them on their own soil. And strangers shall join them and shall cleave to the House of *Yaakov*.

KEE y'-ra-KHAYM a-do-NAI et ya-a-KOV u-va-KHAR OD b'-yis-ra-AYL v'-hi-nee-KHAM al ad-ma-TAM v'-nil-VAH ha-GAYR a-lay-HEM v'-nis-p'-KHU al BAYT ya-a-KOV

יד א כִּי יְרַחֵם יְהוָה אֶת־יַעֲקֹב וּבָחַר עוֹד בְּיִשְׂרָאֵל וְהִנִּיחָם עַל־אַדְמָתָם וְנִלְוָה הַגֵּר עֲלֵיהֶם וְנִסְפְּחוּ עַל־בֵּית יַעֲקֹב׃

2 For peoples shall take them and bring them to their homeland; and the House of *Yisrael* shall possess them as slaves and handmaids on the soil of *Hashem*. They shall be captors of their captors and masters to their taskmasters.

ב וּלְקָחוּם עַמִּים וֶהֱבִיאוּם אֶל־מְקוֹמָם וְהִתְנַחֲלוּם בֵּית־יִשְׂרָאֵל עַל אַדְמַת יְהוָה לַעֲבָדִים וְלִשְׁפָחוֹת וְהָיוּ שֹׁבִים לְשֹׁבֵיהֶם וְרָדוּ בְּנֹגְשֵׂיהֶם׃

3 And when *Hashem* has given you rest from your sorrow and trouble, and from the hard service that you were made to serve,

ג וְהָיָה בְּיוֹם הָנִיחַ יְהוָה לְךָ מֵעָצְבְּךָ וּמֵרָגְזֶךָ וּמִן־הָעֲבֹדָה הַקָּשָׁה אֲשֶׁר עֻבַּד־בָּךְ׃

4 you shall recite this song of scorn over the king of Babylon: How is the taskmaster vanished, How is oppression ended!

ד וְנָשָׂאתָ הַמָּשָׁל הַזֶּה עַל־מֶלֶךְ בָּבֶל וְאָמָרְתָּ אֵיךְ שָׁבַת נֹגֵשׂ שָׁבְתָה מַדְהֵבָה׃

5 *Hashem* has broken the staff of the wicked, The rod of tyrants,

ה שָׁבַר יְהוָה מַטֵּה רְשָׁעִים שֵׁבֶט מֹשְׁלִים׃

6 That smote peoples in wrath With stroke unceasing, That belabored nations in fury In relentless pursuit.

ו מַכֶּה עַמִּים בְּעֶבְרָה מַכַּת בִּלְתִּי סָרָה רֹדֶה בָאַף גּוֹיִם מֻרְדָּף בְּלִי חָשָׂךְ׃

7 All the earth is calm, untroubled; Loudly it cheers.

ז נָחָה שָׁקְטָה כָּל־הָאָרֶץ פָּצְחוּ רִנָּה׃

Yeshayahu/Isaiah
Chapter 14

8 Even pines rejoice at your fate, And cedars of Lebanon: "Now that you have lain down, None shall come up to fell us."

9 Sheol below was astir To greet your coming – Rousing for you the shades Of all earth's chieftains, Raising from their thrones All the kings of nations.

10 All speak up and say to you, "So you have been stricken as we were, You have become like us!

11 Your pomp is brought down to Sheol, And the strains of your lutes! Worms are to be your bed, Maggots your blanket!"

12 How are you fallen from heaven, O Shining One, son of Dawn! How are you felled to earth, O vanquisher of nations!

13 Once you thought in your heart, "I will climb to the sky; Higher than the stars of *Hashem* I will set my throne. I will sit in the mount of assembly, On the summit of Zaphon:

14 I will mount the back of a cloud – I will match the Most High."

e-e-LEH al BA-mo-tay av e-da-MEH l'-el-YON

15 Instead, you are brought down to Sheol, To the bottom of the Pit.

16 They who behold you stare; They peer at you closely: "Is this the man Who shook the earth, Who made realms tremble,

17 Who made the world like a waste And wrecked its towns, Who never released his prisoners to their homes?"

18 All the kings of nations Were laid, every one, in honor Each in his tomb;

19 While you were left lying unburied, Like loathsome carrion, Like a trampled corpse [In] the clothing of slain gashed by the sword Who sink to the very stones of the Pit.

אדם
אדמה

14:14 I will match the Most High The Hebrew word for 'man' is *adam* (אדם). Rabbi Yeshaya Horowitz, who lived in Prague in the sixteenth and seventeenth centuries and is better known by the acronym of his important work as "the Shelah", points out that the word *adam* may originate from the word *edameh* (אֲדַמֶּה), 'I will match,' in this verse – indicating that man's mission in this world is *imitatio dei*, the imperative to imitate God by emulating His actions. At the same time, man should not become haughty due to his lofty task. This too is hinted at by the word *adam*, which may also be derived from the word *adama* (אֲדָמָה) 'earth,' reminding man of his lowly origins, as he was fashioned from the earth (Genesis 2:7).

Yeshayahu/Isaiah

Chapter 15

ישעיהו
פרק יד

20 You shall not have a burial like them; Because you destroyed your country, Murdered your people. Let the breed of evildoers Nevermore be named!

כ לֹא־תֵחַד אִתָּם בִּקְבוּרָה כִּי־אַרְצְךָ שִׁחַתָּ עַמְּךָ הָרָגְתָּ לֹא־יִקָּרֵא לְעוֹלָם זֶרַע מְרֵעִים׃

21 Prepare a slaughtering block for his sons Because of the guilt of their father. Let them not arise to possess the earth! Then the world's face shall be covered with towns.

כא הָכִינוּ לְבָנָיו מַטְבֵּחַ בַּעֲוֺן אֲבוֹתָם בַּל־יָקֻמוּ וְיָרְשׁוּ אָרֶץ וּמָלְאוּ פְנֵי־תֵבֵל עָרִים׃

22 I will rise up against them – declares the Lord of Hosts – and will wipe out from Babylon name and remnant, kith and kin – declares *Hashem*

כב וְקַמְתִּי עֲלֵיהֶם נְאֻם יְהוָה צְבָאוֹת וְהִכְרַתִּי לְבָבֶל שֵׁם וּשְׁאָר וְנִין וָנֶכֶד נְאֻם־יְהוָה׃

23 and I will make it a home of bitterns, pools of water. I will sweep it with a broom of extermination – declares the Lord of Hosts.

כג וְשַׂמְתִּיהָ לְמוֹרַשׁ קִפֹּד וְאַגְמֵי־מָיִם וְטֵאטֵאתִיהָ בְּמַטְאֲטֵא הַשְׁמֵד נְאֻם יְהוָה צְבָאוֹת׃

24 the Lord of Hosts has sworn this oath: "As I have designed, so shall it happen; What I have planned, that shall come to pass:

כד נִשְׁבַּע יְהוָה צְבָאוֹת לֵאמֹר אִם־לֹא כַּאֲשֶׁר דִּמִּיתִי כֵּן הָיָתָה וְכַאֲשֶׁר יָעַצְתִּי הִיא תָקוּם׃

25 To break Assyria in My land, To crush him on My mountain." And his yoke shall drop off them, And his burden shall drop from their backs.

כה לִשְׁבֹּר אַשּׁוּר בְּאַרְצִי וְעַל־הָרַי אֲבוּסֶנּוּ וְסָר מֵעֲלֵיהֶם עֻלּוֹ וְסֻבֳּלוֹ מֵעַל שִׁכְמוֹ יָסוּר׃

26 That is the plan that is planned For all the earth; That is why an arm is poised Over all the nations.

כו זֹאת הָעֵצָה הַיְּעוּצָה עַל־כָּל־הָאָרֶץ וְזֹאת הַיָּד הַנְּטוּיָה עַל־כָּל־הַגּוֹיִם׃

27 For the Lord of Hosts has planned, Who then can foil it? It is His arm that is poised, And who can stay it?

כז כִּי־יְהוָה צְבָאוֹת יָעָץ וּמִי יָפֵר וְיָדוֹ הַנְּטוּיָה וּמִי יְשִׁיבֶנָּה׃

28 This pronouncement was made in the year that King *Achaz* died:

כח בִּשְׁנַת־מוֹת הַמֶּלֶךְ אָחָז הָיָה הַמַּשָּׂא הַזֶּה׃

29 Rejoice not, all Philistia, Because the staff of him that beat you is broken. For from the stock of a snake there sprouts an asp, A flying seraph branches out from it.

כט אַל־תִּשְׂמְחִי פְלֶשֶׁת כֻּלֵּךְ כִּי נִשְׁבַּר שֵׁבֶט מַכֵּךְ כִּי־מִשֹּׁרֶשׁ נָחָשׁ יֵצֵא צֶפַע וּפִרְיוֹ שָׂרָף מְעוֹפֵף׃

30 The first-born of the poor shall graze And the destitute lie down secure. I will kill your stock by famine, And it shall slay the very last of you.

ל וְרָעוּ בְּכוֹרֵי דַלִּים וְאֶבְיוֹנִים לָבֶטַח יִרְבָּצוּ וְהֵמַתִּי בָרָעָב שָׁרְשֵׁךְ וּשְׁאֵרִיתֵךְ יַהֲרֹג׃

31 Howl, O gate; cry out, O city; Quake, all Philistia! For a stout one is coming from the north And there is no straggler in his ranks.

לא הֵילִילִי שַׁעַר זַעֲקִי־עִיר נָמוֹג פְּלֶשֶׁת כֻּלֵּךְ כִּי מִצָּפוֹן עָשָׁן בָּא וְאֵין בּוֹדֵד בְּמוֹעָדָיו׃

32 And what will he answer the messengers of any nation? That *Tzion* has been established by *Hashem*: In it, the needy of His people shall find shelter.

לב וּמַה־יַּעֲנֶה מַלְאֲכֵי־גוֹי כִּי יְהוָה יִסַּד צִיּוֹן וּבָהּ יֶחֱסוּ עֲנִיֵּי עַמּוֹ׃

15 1 The "Moab" Pronouncement. Ah, in the night Ar was sacked, Moab was ruined; Ah, in the night Kir was sacked, Moab was ruined.

טו א מַשָּׂא מוֹאָב כִּי בְּלֵיל שֻׁדַּד עָר מוֹאָב נִדְמָה כִּי בְּלֵיל שֻׁדַּד קִיר־מוֹאָב נִדְמָה׃

Yeshayahu/Isaiah
Chapter 16

ישעיהו
פרק טז

2 He went up to the temple to weep, Dibon [went] to the outdoor shrines. Over Nebo and Medeba Moab is wailing; On every head is baldness, Every beard is shorn.

ב עָלָה הַבַּיִת וְדִיבֹן הַבָּמוֹת לְבֶכִי עַל־נְבוֹ וְעַל מֵידְבָא מוֹאָב יְיֵלִיל בְּכָל־רֹאשָׁיו קׇרְחָה כׇּל־זָקָן גְּרוּעָה׃

3 In its streets, they are girt with sackcloth; On its roofs, in its squares, Everyone is wailing, Streaming with tears.

ג בְּחוּצֹתָיו חָגְרוּ שָׂק עַל גַּגּוֹתֶיהָ וּבִרְחֹבֹתֶיהָ כֻּלֹּה יְיֵלִיל יֹרֵד בַּבֶּכִי׃

4 Heshbon and Elealeh cry out, Their voice carries to Jahaz. Therefore, The shock troops of Moab shout, His body is convulsed.

ד וַתִּזְעַק חֶשְׁבּוֹן וְאֶלְעָלֵה עַד־יַהַץ נִשְׁמַע קוֹלָם עַל־כֵּן חֲלֻצֵי מוֹאָב יָרִיעוּ נַפְשׁוֹ יָרְעָה לּוֹ׃

5 **My heart cries out for Moab** – His fugitives flee down to Zoar, To Eglath-shelishiyah. For the ascent of Luhith They ascend with weeping; On the road to Horonaim They raise a cry of anguish.

ה לִבִּי לְמוֹאָב יִזְעָק בְּרִיחֶהָ עַד־צֹעַר עֶגְלַת שְׁלִשִׁיָּה כִּי מַעֲלֵה הַלּוּחִית בִּבְכִי יַעֲלֶה־בּוֹ כִּי דֶּרֶךְ חוֹרֹנַיִם זַעֲקַת־שֶׁבֶר יְעֹעֵרוּ׃

li-BEE l'-mo-AV yiz-AK b'-ree-KHE-ha ad TZO-ar eg-LAT sh'-li-shi-YAH KEE ma-a-LAY ha-lu-KHEET biv-KHEE ya-a-leh BO KEE DE-rekh kho-ro-NA-yim za-a-kat SHE-ver y'-o-AY-ru

6 Ah, the waters of Nimrim Are become a desolation; The grass is sear, The herbage is gone, Vegetation is vanished.

ו כִּי־מֵי נִמְרִים מְשַׁמּוֹת יִהְיוּ כִּי־יָבֵשׁ חָצִיר כָּלָה דֶשֶׁא יֶרֶק לֹא הָיָה׃

7 Therefore, The gains they have made, and their stores, They carry to the Wadi of Willows.

ז עַל־כֵּן יִתְרָה עָשָׂה וּפְקֻדָּתָם עַל נַחַל הָעֲרָבִים יִשָּׂאוּם׃

8 Ah, the cry has compassed The country of Moab: All the way to Eglaim her wailing, Even at Beer-elim her wailing!

ח כִּי־הִקִּיפָה הַזְּעָקָה אֶת־גְּבוּל מוֹאָב עַד־אֶגְלַיִם יִלְלָתָהּ וּבְאֵר אֵילִים יִלְלָתָהּ׃

9 Ah, the waters of Dimon are full of blood For I pour added [water] on Dimon; I drench it – for Moab's refugees – With soil for its remnant.

ט כִּי מֵי דִימוֹן מָלְאוּ דָם כִּי־אָשִׁית עַל־דִּימוֹן נוֹסָפוֹת לִפְלֵיטַת מוֹאָב אַרְיֵה וְלִשְׁאֵרִית אֲדָמָה׃

16

1 Dispatch as messenger The ruler of the land, From Sela in the wilderness To the mount of Fair *Tzion*:

א שִׁלְחוּ־כַר מֹשֵׁל־אֶרֶץ מִסֶּלַע מִדְבָּרָה אֶל־הַר בַּת־צִיּוֹן׃

2 "Like fugitive birds, Like nestlings driven away, Moab's villagers linger By the fords of the Arnon.

ב וְהָיָה כְעוֹף־נוֹדֵד קֵן מְשֻׁלָּח תִּהְיֶינָה בְּנוֹת מוֹאָב מַעְבָּרֹת לְאַרְנוֹן׃

3 Give advice, Offer counsel. At high noon make Your shadow like night: Conceal the outcasts, Betray not the fugitives.

ג הָבִיאוּ [הָבִיאִי] עֵצָה עֲשׂוּ פְלִילָה שִׁיתִי כַלַּיִל צִלֵּךְ בְּתוֹךְ צָהֳרָיִם סַתְּרִי נִדָּחִים נֹדֵד אַל־תְּגַלִּי׃

15:5 My heart cries out for Moab Having taunted Babylon, Assyria, and the Philistines, *Yeshayahu* now turns to *Yehuda*'s southeastern neighbor, Moab. As the previous prophecies describe, the upcoming destruction and desolation of Moab will be total. What is noteworthy, however, is the prophet's refusal to rejoice over Moab's downfall. Though Moab is one of Israel's ancient enemies, *Yeshayahu* cannot restrain himself from sympathizing over their plight. This is reminiscent of the verse in Proverbs (24:17) "If your enemy falls, do not exult; If he trips, let your heart not rejoice."

Yeshayahu/Isaiah
Chapter 16

4 Let Moab's outcasts Find asylum in you; Be a shelter for them Against the despoiler." For violence has vanished, Rapine is ended, And marauders have perished from this land.

יָגוּרוּ בָךְ נִדָּחַי מוֹאָב הֱוִי־סֵתֶר לָמוֹ מִפְּנֵי שׁוֹדֵד כִּי־אָפֵס הַמֵּץ כָּלָה שֹׁד תַּמּוּ רֹמֵס מִן־הָאָרֶץ:

5 And a throne shall be established in goodness In the tent of *David*, And on it shall sit in faithfulness A ruler devoted to justice And zealous for equity.

וְהוּכַן בַּחֶסֶד כִּסֵּא וְיָשַׁב עָלָיו בֶּאֱמֶת בְּאֹהֶל דָּוִד שֹׁפֵט וְדֹרֵשׁ מִשְׁפָּט וּמְהִר צֶדֶק:

v'-hu-KHAN ba-KHE-sed ki-SAY v'-ya-SHAV a-LAV be-e-MET b'-O-hel da-VID sho-FAYT v'-do-RAYSH mish-PAT um-HEER TZE-dek

6 "We have heard of Moab's pride – Most haughty is he – Of his pride and haughtiness and arrogance, And of the iniquity in him."

שָׁמַעְנוּ גְאוֹן־מוֹאָב גֵּא מְאֹד גַּאֲוָתוֹ וּגְאוֹנוֹ וְעֶבְרָתוֹ לֹא־כֵן בַּדָּיו:

7 Ah, let Moab howl; Let all in Moab howl! For the raisin-cakes of Kir-hareseth You shall moan most pitifully.

לָכֵן יְיֵלִיל מוֹאָב לְמוֹאָב כֻּלֹּה יְיֵלִיל לַאֲשִׁישֵׁי קִיר־חֲרֶשֶׂת תֶּהְגּוּ אַךְ־נְכָאִים:

8 The vineyards of Heshbon are withered, And the vines of Sibmah; Their tendrils spread To Baale-goiim, And reached to Jazer, And strayed to the desert; Their shoots spread out And crossed the sea.

כִּי שַׁדְמוֹת חֶשְׁבּוֹן אֻמְלָל גֶּפֶן שִׂבְמָה בַּעֲלֵי גוֹיִם הָלְמוּ שְׂרוּקֶּיהָ עַד־יַעְזֵר נָגָעוּ תָּעוּ מִדְבָּר שְׁלֻחוֹתֶיהָ נִטְּשׁוּ עָבְרוּ יָם:

9 Therefore, As I weep for Jazer, So I weep for Sibmah's vines; O Heshbon and Elealeh, I drench you with my tears. Ended are the shouts Over your fig and grain harvests.

עַל־כֵּן אֶבְכֶּה בִּבְכִי יַעְזֵר גֶּפֶן שִׂבְמָה אֲרַיָּוֶךְ דִּמְעָתִי חֶשְׁבּוֹן וְאֶלְעָלֵה כִּי עַל־קֵיצֵךְ וְעַל־קְצִירֵךְ הֵידָד נָפָל:

10 Rejoicing and gladness Are gone from the farm land; In the vineyards no shouting Or cheering is heard. No more does the treader Tread wine in the presses – The shouts have been silenced.

וְנֶאֱסַף שִׂמְחָה וָגִיל מִן־הַכַּרְמֶל וּבַכְּרָמִים לֹא־יְרֻנָּן לֹא יְרֹעָע יַיִן בַּיְקָבִים לֹא־יִדְרֹךְ הַדֹּרֵךְ הֵידָד הִשְׁבַּתִּי:

11 Therefore, Like a lyre my heart moans for Moab, And my very soul for Kir-heres.

עַל־כֵּן מֵעַי לְמוֹאָב כַּכִּנּוֹר יֶהֱמוּ וְקִרְבִּי לְקִיר חָרֶשׂ:

12 And when it has become apparent that Moab has gained nothing in the outdoor shrine, he shall come to pray in his temple – but to no avail.

וְהָיָה כִי־נִרְאָה כִּי־נִלְאָה מוֹאָב עַל־הַבָּמָה וּבָא אֶל־מִקְדָּשׁוֹ לְהִתְפַּלֵּל וְלֹא יוּכָל:

13 That is the word that *Hashem* spoke concerning Moab long ago.

זֶה הַדָּבָר אֲשֶׁר דִּבֶּר יְהוָה אֶל־מוֹאָב מֵאָז:

16:5 A ruler devoted to justice, and zealous for equity In the time of King *David*, Moab paid tribute to *Yisrael* and *Yehuda* (II Samuel 8:2). *Yeshayahu* foresees a time when the remnant of Moab that survives the calamities will once again send tribute to *Yehuda* and live with Israel in friendship and brotherhood. However, for that to happen, the king that sits on *David*'s throne will have to be a worthy one, who promotes justice for the poor and needy; instead of delaying justice, he hastens to execute it quickly throughout *Eretz Yisrael*.

Yeshayahu/Isaiah

Chapter 17

ישעיהו

פרק יז

14 And now *Hashem* has spoken: In three years, fixed like the years of a hired laborer, Moab's population, with all its huge multitude, shall shrink. Only a remnant shall be left, of no consequence.

וְעַתָּה דִּבֶּר יְהֹוָה לֵאמֹר בְּשָׁלֹשׁ שָׁנִים כִּשְׁנֵי שָׂכִיר וְנִקְלָה כְּבוֹד מוֹאָב בְּכֹל הֶהָמוֹן הָרָב וּשְׁאָר מְעַט מִזְעָר לוֹא כַבִּיר׃

17

1 The "Damascus" Pronouncement. Behold, Damascus shall cease to be a city; It shall become a heap of ruins.

מַשָּׂא דַּמָּשֶׂק הִנֵּה דַמֶּשֶׂק מוּסָר מֵעִיר וְהָיְתָה מְעִי מַפָּלָה׃

2 The towns of Aroer shall be deserted; They shall be a place for flocks To lie down, with none disturbing.

עֲזֻבוֹת עָרֵי עֲרֹעֵר לַעֲדָרִים תִּהְיֶינָה וְרָבְצוּ וְאֵין מַחֲרִיד׃

3 Fortresses shall cease from *Efraim*, And sovereignty from Damascus; The remnant of Aram shall become Like the mass of Israelites – declares the Lord of Hosts.

וְנִשְׁבַּת מִבְצָר מֵאֶפְרַיִם וּמַמְלָכָה מִדַּמֶּשֶׂק וּשְׁאָר אֲרָם כִּכְבוֹד בְּנֵי־יִשְׂרָאֵל יִהְיוּ נְאֻם יְהֹוָה צְבָאוֹת׃

4 In that day, The mass of *Yaakov* shall dwindle, And the fatness of his body become lean:

וְהָיָה בַּיּוֹם הַהוּא יִדַּל כְּבוֹד יַעֲקֹב וּמִשְׁמַן בְּשָׂרוֹ יֵרָזֶה׃

5 After being like the standing grain Harvested by the reaper – Who reaps ears by the armful – He shall be like the ears that are gleaned In the Valley of Rephaim.

וְהָיָה כֶּאֱסֹף קָצִיר קָמָה וּזְרֹעוֹ שִׁבֳּלִים יִקְצוֹר וְהָיָה כִּמְלַקֵּט שִׁבֳּלִים בְּעֵמֶק רְפָאִים׃

6 Only gleanings shall be left of him, As when one beats an olive tree: Two berries or three on the topmost branch, Four or five on the boughs of the crown – declares *Hashem*, the God of *Yisrael*.

וְנִשְׁאַר־בּוֹ עוֹלֵלֹת כְּנֹקֶף זַיִת שְׁנַיִם שְׁלֹשָׁה גַּרְגְּרִים בְּרֹאשׁ אָמִיר אַרְבָּעָה חֲמִשָּׁה בִּסְעִפֶיהָ פֹּרִיָּה נְאֻם־יְהֹוָה אֱלֹהֵי יִשְׂרָאֵל׃

7 In that day, men shall turn to their Maker, their eyes look to the Holy One of *Yisrael*;

בַּיּוֹם הַהוּא יִשְׁעֶה הָאָדָם עַל־עֹשֵׂהוּ וְעֵינָיו אֶל־קְדוֹשׁ יִשְׂרָאֵל תִּרְאֶינָה׃

ba-YOM ha-HU yish-EH ha-a-DAM al o-SAY-hu v'-ay-NAV el k'-DOSH yis-ra-AYL tir-E-nah

8 they shall not turn to the altars that their own hands made, or look to the sacred posts and incense stands that their own fingers wrought.

וְלֹא יִשְׁעֶה אֶל־הַמִּזְבְּחוֹת מַעֲשֵׂה יָדָיו וַאֲשֶׁר עָשׂוּ אֶצְבְּעֹתָיו לֹא יִרְאֶה וְהָאֲשֵׁרִים וְהָחַמָּנִים׃

17:7 In that day, men shall turn to their Maker *Yeshayahu* prophesies about Damascus, the capital city of Aram. Once Israel's vicious enemy to the north, Aram had allied itself with Israel in a futile attempt to stave off destruction at the hands of the invading Assyrians. *Yeshayahu* describes the totality of the destruction of both Aram and *Yisrael*, but then notes that a few of the Israelites are to be saved, as a remnant made holy, awakened to return to God. This remnant appears in the time of King *Yoshiyahu*, about whom the Bible recounts that offerings of money were made for the Temple service by men of "*Menashe* and *Ephraim*, and from all the remnant of *Yisrael*," which the *Leviim* collected and brought to *Yerushalayim* (II Chronicles 34:9). Similarly, in the times of *Mashiach*, the entire kingdom of *Yisrael*, the remnants of all ten of its "lost tribes," will return to the Lord and their land.

Yeshayahu/Isaiah
Chapter 18

ישעיהו
פרק יח

9 In that day, their fortress cities shall be like the deserted sites which the Horesh and the Amir abandoned because of the Israelites; and there shall be desolation.

ט בַּיּוֹם הַהוּא יִהְיוּ עָרֵי מָעֻזּוֹ כַּעֲזוּבַת הַחֹרֶשׁ וְהָאָמִיר אֲשֶׁר עָזְבוּ מִפְּנֵי בְּנֵי יִשְׂרָאֵל וְהָיְתָה שְׁמָמָה:

10 Truly, you have forgotten the God who saves you And have not remembered the Rock who shelters you; That is why, though you plant a delightful sapling, What you sow proves a disappointing slip.

י כִּי שָׁכַחַתְּ אֱלֹהֵי יִשְׁעֵךְ וְצוּר מָעֻזֵּךְ לֹא זָכָרְתְּ עַל־כֵּן תִּטְּעִי נִטְעֵי נַעֲמָנִים וּזְמֹרַת זָר תִּזְרָעֶנּוּ:

11 On the day that you plant, you see it grow; On the morning you sow, you see it bud – But the branches wither away On a day of sickness and mortal agony.

יא בְּיוֹם נִטְעֵךְ תְּשַׂגְשֵׂגִי וּבַבֹּקֶר זַרְעֵךְ תַּפְרִיחִי נֵד קָצִיר בְּיוֹם נַחֲלָה וּכְאֵב אָנוּשׁ:

12 Ah, the roar of many peoples That roar as roars the sea, The rage of nations that rage As rage the mighty waters –

יב הוֹי הֲמוֹן עַמִּים רַבִּים כַּהֲמוֹת יַמִּים יֶהֱמָיוּן וּשְׁאוֹן לְאֻמִּים כִּשְׁאוֹן מַיִם כַּבִּירִים יִשָּׁאוּן:

13 Nations raging like massive waters! But He shouts at them, and they flee far away, Driven like chaff before winds in the hills, And like tumbleweed before a gale.

יג לְאֻמִּים כִּשְׁאוֹן מַיִם רַבִּים יִשָּׁאוּן וְגָעַר בּוֹ וְנָס מִמֶּרְחָק וְרֻדַּף כְּמֹץ הָרִים לִפְנֵי־רוּחַ וּכְגַלְגַּל לִפְנֵי סוּפָה:

14 At eventide, lo, terror! By morning, it is no more. Such is the lot of our despoilers, The portion of them that plunder us.

יד לְעֵת עֶרֶב וְהִנֵּה בַלָּהָה בְּטֶרֶם בֹּקֶר אֵינֶנּוּ זֶה חֵלֶק שׁוֹסֵינוּ וְגוֹרָל לְבֹזְזֵינוּ:

18

1 Ah, land in the deep shadow of wings, Beyond the rivers of Nubia!

יח א הוֹי אֶרֶץ צִלְצַל כְּנָפָיִם אֲשֶׁר מֵעֵבֶר לְנַהֲרֵי־כוּשׁ:

2 Go, swift messengers, To a nation far and remote, To a people thrust forth and away – A nation of gibber and chatter – Whose land is cut off by streams; Which sends out envoys by sea, In papyrus vessels upon the water!*

ב הַשֹּׁלֵחַ בַּיָּם צִירִים וּבִכְלֵי־גֹמֶא עַל־פְּנֵי־מַיִם לְכוּ מַלְאָכִים קַלִּים אֶל־גּוֹי מְמֻשָּׁךְ וּמוֹרָט אֶל־עַם נוֹרָא מִן־הוּא וָהָלְאָה גּוֹי קַו־קָו וּמְבוּסָה אֲשֶׁר־בָּזְאוּ נְהָרִים אַרְצוֹ:

3 [Say this:] "All you who live in the world And inhabit the earth, When a flag is raised in the hills, take note! When a *shofar* is blown, give heed!"

ג כָּל־יֹשְׁבֵי תֵבֵל וְשֹׁכְנֵי אָרֶץ כִּנְשֹׂא־נֵס הָרִים תִּרְאוּ וְכִתְקֹעַ שׁוֹפָר תִּשְׁמָעוּ:

kol yo-sh'-VAY tay-VAYL v'-sho-kh'-NAY A-retz kin-so NAYS ha-REEM tir-U v'-khit-KO-a sho-FAR tish-MA-u

4 For thus *Hashem* said to me: "I rest calm and confident in My habitation – Like a scorching heat upon sprouts, Like a rain-cloud in the heat of reaping time."

ד כִּי כֹה אָמַר יְהֹוָה אֵלַי אשקוטה [אֶשְׁקֳטָה] וְאַבִּיטָה בִמְכוֹנִי כְּחֹם צַח עֲלֵי־אוֹר כְּעָב טַל בְּחֹם קָצִיר:

---

* "Which sends out envoys by sea, In papyrus vessels upon the water!" brought down from the beginning of the verse for clarity

---

18:3 When a flag is raised in the hills, take note The word *nays* (נס) in this verse means 'flag' or 'banner,' but the same word also means 'miracle.' Just as a banner serves as a reminder to onlookers, a miracle is also meant to remind "all inhabitants of the world" that *Hashem* directs all events from behind the scenes.

נס

984

Yeshayahu/Isaiah
Chapter 19

5 For before the harvest, yet after the budding, When the blossom has hardened into berries, He will trim away the twigs with pruning hooks, And lop off the trailing branches.

6 They shall all be left To the kites of the hills And to the beasts of the earth; The kites shall summer on them And all the beasts of the earth shall winter on them.

7 In that time, Tribute shall be brought to the Lord of Hosts [From] a people far and remote, From a people thrust forth and away – A nation of gibber and chatter, Whose land is cut off by streams – At the place where the name of the Lord of Hosts abides, At Mount *Tzion*.

19

1 The "Egypt" Pronouncement. Mounted on a swift cloud, *Hashem* will come to Egypt; Egypt's idols shall tremble before Him, And the heart of the Egyptians shall sink within them.

2 "I will incite Egyptian against Egyptian: They shall war with each other, Every man with his fellow, City with city And kingdom with kingdom.

3 Egypt shall be drained of spirit, And I will confound its plans; So they will consult the idols and the shades And the ghosts and the familiar spirits.

4 And I will place the Egyptians At the mercy of a harsh master, And a ruthless king shall rule them" – declares the Sovereign, the Lord of Hosts.

5 Water shall fail from the seas, Rivers dry up and be parched,

6 Channels turn foul as they ebb, And Egypt's canals run dry. Reed and rush shall decay,

7 And the Nile papyrus by the Nile-side And everything sown by the Nile Shall wither, blow away, and vanish.

8 The fishermen shall lament; All who cast lines in the Nile shall mourn, And those who spread nets on the water shall languish.

9 The flax workers, too, shall be dismayed, Both carders and weavers chagrined.

10 Her foundations shall be crushed, And all who make dams shall be despondent.

ישעיהו
פרק יט

ה כִּי־לִפְנֵי קָצִיר כְּתָם־פֶּרַח וּבֹסֶר גֹּמֵל יִהְיֶה נִצָּה וְכָרַת הַזַּלְזַלִּים בַּמַּזְמֵרוֹת וְאֶת־הַנְּטִישׁוֹת הֵסִיר הֵתַז׃

ו יֵעָזְבוּ יַחְדָּו לְעֵיט הָרִים וּלְבֶהֱמַת הָאָרֶץ וְקָץ עָלָיו הָעַיִט וְכָל־בֶּהֱמַת הָאָרֶץ עָלָיו תֶּחֱרָף׃

ז בָּעֵת הַהִיא יוּבַל־שַׁי לַיהוָה צְבָאוֹת עַם מְמֻשָּׁךְ וּמוֹרָט וּמֵעַם נוֹרָא מִן־הוּא וָהָלְאָה גּוֹי קַו־קָו וּמְבוּסָה אֲשֶׁר בָּזְאוּ נְהָרִים אַרְצוֹ אֶל־מְקוֹם שֵׁם־יְהוָה צְבָאוֹת הַר־צִיּוֹן׃

יט א מַשָּׂא מִצְרָיִם הִנֵּה יְהוָה רֹכֵב עַל־עָב קַל וּבָא מִצְרַיִם וְנָעוּ אֱלִילֵי מִצְרַיִם מִפָּנָיו וּלְבַב מִצְרַיִם יִמַּס בְּקִרְבּוֹ׃

ב וְסִכְסַכְתִּי מִצְרַיִם בְּמִצְרַיִם וְנִלְחֲמוּ אִישׁ־בְּאָחִיו וְאִישׁ בְּרֵעֵהוּ עִיר בְּעִיר מַמְלָכָה בְּמַמְלָכָה׃

ג וְנָבְקָה רוּחַ־מִצְרַיִם בְּקִרְבּוֹ וַעֲצָתוֹ אֲבַלֵּעַ וְדָרְשׁוּ אֶל־הָאֱלִילִים וְאֶל־הָאִטִּים וְאֶל־הָאֹבוֹת וְאֶל־הַיִּדְּעֹנִים׃

ד וְסִכַּרְתִּי אֶת־מִצְרַיִם בְּיַד אֲדֹנִים קָשֶׁה וּמֶלֶךְ עַז יִמְשָׁל־בָּם נְאֻם הָאָדוֹן יְהוָה צְבָאוֹת׃

ה וְנִשְּׁתוּ־מַיִם מֵהַיָּם וְנָהָר יֶחֱרַב וְיָבֵשׁ׃

ו וְהֶאֶזְנִיחוּ נְהָרוֹת דָּלֲלוּ וְחָרְבוּ יְאֹרֵי מָצוֹר קָנֶה וָסוּף קָמֵלוּ׃

ז עָרוֹת עַל־יְאוֹר עַל־פִּי יְאוֹר וְכֹל מִזְרַע יְאוֹר יִיבַשׁ נִדַּף וְאֵינֶנּוּ׃

ח וְאָנוּ הַדַּיָּגִים וְאָבְלוּ כָּל־מַשְׁלִיכֵי בַיְאוֹר חַכָּה וּפֹרְשֵׂי מִכְמֹרֶת עַל־פְּנֵי־מַיִם אֻמְלָלוּ׃

ט וּבֹשׁוּ עֹבְדֵי פִשְׁתִּים שְׂרִיקוֹת וְאֹרְגִים חוֹרָי׃

י וְהָיוּ שָׁתֹתֶיהָ מְדֻכָּאִים כָּל־עֹשֵׂי שֶׂכֶר אַגְמֵי־נָפֶשׁ׃

Yeshayahu/Isaiah
Chapter 19

11 Utter fools are the nobles of Tanis; The sagest of Pharaoh's advisers [Have made] absurd predictions. How can you say to Pharaoh, "I am a scion of sages, A scion of Kedemite kings"?

12 Where, indeed, are your sages? Let them tell you, let them discover What the LORD of Hosts has planned against Egypt.

13 The nobles of Tanis have been fools, The nobles of Memphis deluded; Egypt has been led astray By the chiefs of her tribes.

14 *Hashem* has mixed within her A spirit of distortion, Which shall lead Egypt astray I all her undertakings As a vomiting drunkard goes astray;

15 Nothing shall be achieved in Egypt By either head or tail, Palm branch or reed.

16 In that day, the Egyptians shall be like women, trembling and terrified because the LORD of Hosts will raise His hand against them.

17 And the land of *Yehuda* shall also be the dread of the Egyptians; they shall quake whenever anybody mentions it to them, because of what the LORD of Hosts is planning against them.

18 In that day, there shall be several towns in the land of Egypt speaking the language of Canaan and swearing loyalty to the LORD of Hosts; one shall be called Town of Heres.

ba-YOM ha-HU yih-YU kha-MAYSH a-REEM b'-E-retz mitz-RA-yim m'-da-b'-ROT s'-FAT k'-NA-an v'-nish-ba-OT la-do-NAI tz'-va-OT eer ha-HE-res yay-a-MAYR l'-e-KHAT

19 In that day, there shall be a altar to *Hashem* inside the land of Egypt and a pillar to *Hashem* at its border.

19:18 Speaking the language of Canaan *Yeshayahu* prophesies that there will be five Egyptian cities that speak the language of Canaan and swear by *Hashem*'s name. According to *Ramban* (Exodus 30:13), the term "language of Canaan" refers to the Hebrew language, known in Jewish literature as *Lashon HaKodesh* (לשון הקודש), 'the Holy Tongue,' because it is the language with which God speaks to His prophets and His nation. After the Egyptians in these cities experience *Hashem*'s strength, they will be so moved to worship Him that they will learn the holy language and erect an altar on which to serve God. This will also represent a partial fulfillment of another of *Yeshayahu*'s prophecies, that in the future the whole world will be filled with knowledge of God (11:9).

986

Yeshayahu/Isaiah
Chapter 20

ישעיהו
פרק כ

20 They shall serve as a symbol and reminder of the Lord of Hosts in the land of Egypt, so that when [the Egyptians] cry out to *Hashem* against oppressors, He will send them a savior and champion to deliver them.

כ וְהָיָה לְאוֹת וּלְעֵד לַיהוָה צְבָאוֹת בְּאֶרֶץ מִצְרָיִם כִּי־יִצְעֲקוּ אֶל־יְהוָה מִפְּנֵי לֹחֲצִים וְיִשְׁלַח לָהֶם מוֹשִׁיעַ וָרָב וְהִצִּילָם׃

21 For *Hashem* will make Himself known to the Egyptians, and the Egyptians shall acknowledge *Hashem* in that day, and they shall serve [Him] with sacrifice and oblation and shall make vows to *Hashem* and fulfill them.

כא וְנוֹדַע יְהוָה לְמִצְרַיִם וְיָדְעוּ מִצְרַיִם אֶת־יְהוָה בַּיּוֹם הַהוּא וְעָבְדוּ זֶבַח וּמִנְחָה וְנָדְרוּ־נֶדֶר לַיהוָה וְשִׁלֵּמוּ׃

22 *Hashem* will first afflict and then heal the Egyptians; when they turn back to *Hashem*, He will respond to their entreaties and heal them.

כב וְנָגַף יְהוָה אֶת־מִצְרַיִם נָגֹף וְרָפוֹא וְשָׁבוּ עַד־יְהוָה וְנֶעְתַּר לָהֶם וּרְפָאָם׃

23 In that day, there shall be a highway from Egypt to Assyria. The Assyrians shall join with the Egyptians and Egyptians with the Assyrians, and then the Egyptians together with the Assyrians shall serve [*Hashem*].

כג בַּיּוֹם הַהוּא תִּהְיֶה מְסִלָּה מִמִּצְרַיִם אַשּׁוּרָה וּבָא־אַשּׁוּר בְּמִצְרַיִם וּמִצְרַיִם בְּאַשּׁוּר וְעָבְדוּ מִצְרַיִם אֶת־אַשּׁוּר׃

24 In that day, *Yisrael* shall be a third partner with Egypt and Assyria as a blessing on earth;

כד בַּיּוֹם הַהוּא יִהְיֶה יִשְׂרָאֵל שְׁלִישִׁיָּה לְמִצְרַיִם וּלְאַשּׁוּר בְּרָכָה בְּקֶרֶב הָאָרֶץ׃

25 for the Lord of Hosts will bless them, saying, "Blessed be My people Egypt, My handiwork Assyria, and My very own *Yisrael*."

כה אֲשֶׁר בֵּרֲכוֹ יְהוָה צְבָאוֹת לֵאמֹר בָּרוּךְ עַמִּי מִצְרַיִם וּמַעֲשֵׂה יָדַי אַשּׁוּר וְנַחֲלָתִי יִשְׂרָאֵל׃

20

1 It was the year that the Tartan came to *Ashdod* – being sent by King Sargon of Assyria – and attacked *Ashdod* and took it.

כ א בִּשְׁנַת בֹּא תַרְתָּן אַשְׁדּוֹדָה בִּשְׁלֹחַ אֹתוֹ סַרְגוֹן מֶלֶךְ אַשּׁוּר וַיִּלָּחֶם בְּאַשְׁדּוֹד וַיִּלְכְּדָהּ׃

2 Previously, *Hashem* had spoken to *Yeshayahu* son of *Amotz*, saying, "Go, untie the sackcloth from your loins and take your sandals off your feet," which he had done, going naked and barefoot.

ב בָּעֵת הַהִיא דִּבֶּר יְהוָה בְּיַד יְשַׁעְיָהוּ בֶן־אָמוֹץ לֵאמֹר לֵךְ וּפִתַּחְתָּ הַשַּׂק מֵעַל מָתְנֶיךָ וְנַעַלְךָ תַחֲלֹץ מֵעַל רַגְלֶיךָ וַיַּעַשׂ כֵּן הָלֹךְ עָרוֹם וְיָחֵף׃

> ba-AYT ha-HEE di-BER a-do-NAI b'-YAD y'-sha-YA-hu ven a-MOTZ lay-MOR LAYKH u-fi-takh-TA ha-SAK may-AL mot-NE-kha v'-na-al-KHA ta-kha-LOTZ may-AL rag-LE-kha va-YA-as KAYN ha-LOKH a-ROM v'-ya-KHAYF

20:2 Go, untie the sackcloth from your loins Egypt encouraged the Philistines to revolt against Assyria, and supported the rebellion for three years (713–711 BCE), only to then cowardly hand the Philistine king of *Ashdod* over to the Assyrians. In an attempt to dissuade *Yehuda* from similarly relying on Egypt for protection against the Assyrian army, *Yeshayahu* becomes a living sign to the people. He is to loosen his clothes at his loins, wear no upper garments, and go barefoot. This behavior is designed to signify that the Egyptians and Ethiopians will be led away as captives by the king of Assyria, and to remind the people not to rebel against *Hashem*'s message or try to rely on Egypt for salvation. Though it is tempting to rely on people or material wealth for success, *Yeshayahu*'s message is that God is the only true source of success and salvation.

Yeshayahu/Isaiah
Chapter 21

3 And now *Hashem* said, "It is a sign and a portent for Egypt and Nubia. Just as My servant *Yeshayahu* has gone naked and barefoot for three years,

4 so shall the king of Assyria drive off the captives of Egypt and the exiles of Nubia, young and old, naked and barefoot and with bared buttocks – to the shame of Egypt!

5 And they shall be dismayed and chagrined because of Nubia their hope and Egypt their boast.

6 In that day, the dwellers of this coastland shall say, 'If this could happen to those we looked to, to whom we fled for help and rescue from the king of Assyria, how can we ourselves escape?'"

21

1 The "Desert of the Sea" Pronouncement. Like the gales That race through the *Negev*, It comes from the desert, The terrible land.

2 A harsh prophecy Has been announced to me: "The betrayer is betraying, The ravager ravaging. Advance, Elam! Lay siege, Media! I have put an end To all her sighing."

3 Therefore my loins Are seized with trembling; I am gripped by pangs Like a woman in travail, Too anguished to hear, Too frightened to see.

4 My mind is confused, I shudder in panic. My night of pleasure He has turned to terror:

5 "Set the table!" To "Let the watchman watch!" "Eat and drink!" To "Up, officers! Grease the shields!"

> a-ROKH ha-shul-KHAN tza-FOH ha-tza-FEET a-KHOL sha-TOH KU-mu ha-sa-REEM mish-KHU ma-GAYN

6 For thus my Lord said to me: "Go, set up a sentry; Let him announce what he sees.

7 He will see mounted men, Horsemen in pairs – Riders on asses, Riders on camels – And he will listen closely, Most attentively."

21:5 Eat and drink *Yeshayahu* relays another prophecy directed towards Babylon. Since their country is protected by watchmen, its nobles eat, oblivious to the danger that approaches. Their dining, however, is interrupted with the call to battle. The fulfillment of *Yeshayahu*'s prophecy is described in *Sefer Daniel* 5, which depicts the capture of Babylon as its inhabitants are engaged in revelry at Belshazzar's feast. To *Yehuda*, which looks for allies against the Assyrian threat, *Yeshayahu* reiterates that Babylon's time is also limited. The surest guarantee of safety is trust in *Hashem* alone.

Yeshayahu/Isaiah

Chapter 22

8 And [like] a lion he called out: "On my Lord's lookout I stand Ever by day, And at my post I watch Every night.

9 And there they come, mounted men – Horsemen in pairs!" Then he spoke up and said, "Fallen, fallen is Babylon, And all the images of her gods Have crashed to the ground!"

10 My threshing, the product of my threshing floor: What I have heard from the LORD of Hosts, The God of *Yisrael* – That I have told to you.

11 The "Dumah" Pronouncement. A call comes to me from Seir: "Watchman, what of the night? Watchman, what of the night?"

12 The watchman replied, "Morning came, and so did night. If you would inquire, inquire. Come back again."

13 The "In the Steppe" Pronouncement. In the scrub, in the steppe, you will lodge, O caravans of the Dedanites!

14 Meet the thirsty with water, You who dwell in the land of Tema; Greet the fugitive with bread.

15 For they have fled before swords: Before the whetted sword, Before the bow that was drawn, Before the stress of war.

16 For thus my Lord has said to me: "In another year, fixed like the years of a hired laborer, all the multitude of Kedar shall vanish;

17 the remaining bows of Kedar's warriors shall be few in number; for *Hashem*, the God of *Yisrael*, has spoken.

22

1 The "Valley of Vision" Pronouncement. What can have happened to you That you have gone, all of you, up on the roofs,

2 O you who were full of tumult, You clamorous town, You city so gay? Your slain are not the slain of the sword Nor the dead of battle.

3 Your officers have all departed, They fled far away; Your survivors were all taken captive, Taken captive without their bows.

4 That is why I say, "Let me be, I will weep bitterly. Press not to comfort me For the ruin of my poor people."

Yeshayahu/Isaiah — Chapter 22

ישעיהו
פרק כב

5 For my Lord God of Hosts had a day Of tumult and din and confusion – Kir raged in the Valley of Vision, And Shoa on the hill;

ה כִּי יוֹם מְהוּמָה וּמְבוּסָה וּמְבוּכָה לַאדֹנָי יְהוִה צְבָאוֹת בְּגֵיא חִזָּיוֹן מְקַרְקַר קִר וְשׁוֹעַ אֶל־הָהָר:

6 While Elam bore the quiver In troops of mounted men, And Kir bared the shield –

ו וְעֵילָם נָשָׂא אַשְׁפָּה בְּרֶכֶב אָדָם פָּרָשִׁים וְקִיר עֵרָה מָגֵן:

7 And your choicest lowlands Were filled with chariots and horsemen: They stormed at *Yehuda*'s* gateway

ז וַיְהִי מִבְחַר־עֲמָקַיִךְ מָלְאוּ רָכֶב וְהַפָּרָשִׁים שֹׁת שָׁתוּ הַשָּׁעְרָה:

8 And pressed beyond its screen. You gave thought on that day To the arms in the Forest House,

ח וַיְגַל אֵת מָסַךְ יְהוּדָה וַתַּבֵּט בַּיּוֹם הַהוּא אֶל־נֶשֶׁק בֵּית הַיָּעַר:

9 And you took note of the many breaches In the City of *David*. And you collected the water of the Lower Pool;

ט וְאֵת בְּקִיעֵי עִיר־דָּוִד רְאִיתֶם כִּי־רָבּוּ וַתְּקַבְּצוּ אֶת־מֵי הַבְּרֵכָה הַתַּחְתּוֹנָה:

10 and you counted the houses of *Yerushalayim* and pulled houses down to fortify the wall;

י וְאֶת־בָּתֵּי יְרוּשָׁלַם סְפַרְתֶּם וַתִּתְּצוּ הַבָּתִּים לְבַצֵּר הַחוֹמָה:

11 and you constructed a basin between the two walls for the water of the old pool. But you gave no thought to Him who planned it, You took no note of Him who designed it long before.

יא וּמִקְוָה ׀ עֲשִׂיתֶם בֵּין הַחֹמֹתַיִם לְמֵי הַבְּרֵכָה הַיְשָׁנָה וְלֹא הִבַּטְתֶּם אֶל־עֹשֶׂיהָ וְיֹצְרָהּ מֵרָחוֹק לֹא רְאִיתֶם:

u-mik-VAH a-see-TEM BAYN ha-kho-mo-TA-yim l'-MAY ha-b'-ray-KHAH hai-sha-NAH v'-LO hi-bat-TEM el o-SE-ha v'-yo-tz'-RAH may-ra-KHOK LO r'-ee-TEM

12 My Lord God of Hosts summoned on that day To weeping and lamenting, To tonsuring and girding with sackcloth.

יב וַיִּקְרָא אֲדֹנָי יְהוִה צְבָאוֹת בַּיּוֹם הַהוּא לִבְכִי וּלְמִסְפֵּד וּלְקָרְחָה וְלַחֲגֹר שָׂק:

13 Instead, there was rejoicing and merriment, Killing of cattle and slaughtering of sheep, Eating of meat and drinking of wine: "Eat and drink, for tomorrow we die!"

יג וְהִנֵּה ׀ שָׂשׂוֹן וְשִׂמְחָה הָרֹג ׀ בָּקָר וְשָׁחֹט צֹאן אָכֹל בָּשָׂר וְשָׁתוֹת יָיִן אָכוֹל וְשָׁתוֹ כִּי מָחָר נָמוּת:

14 Then the LORD of Hosts revealed Himself to my ears: "This iniquity shall never be forgiven you Until you die," said my Lord God of Hosts.

יד וְנִגְלָה בְאָזְנָי יְהוִה צְבָאוֹת אִם־יְכֻפַּר הֶעָוֹן הַזֶּה לָכֶם עַד־תְּמֻתוּן אָמַר אֲדֹנָי יְהוִה צְבָאוֹת:

---

* The word "Yehuda" brought up from verse 8 for clarity

22:11 And you constructed a basin between the two walls Verses 8–11 describe the serious military preparations made to fend off the upcoming Assyrian assault. *Yeshayahu* does not oppose this *per se* – he simply asks that they combine their trust in themselves with faith in *Hashem*. The "basin between the two walls" refers to *Chizkiyahu's* tunnel, which he dug in order to provide a source of water for the besieged city of *Yerushalayim* (II Chronicles 32). The tunnel was re-discovered in 1867 by the British explorer Captain Charles Warren. Near the exit from the tunnel, an ancient Hebrew inscription describing its amazing construction was discovered. A team of diggers started at each end of the 1,500 foot-long tunnel. They eventually met in the middle by listening for the sounds of each other's pickaxes. The marks of the ancient pickaxes are visible on the walls of the tunnel, going first in one direction and switching in the middle to go in the other direction. Today, wading through the water of *Chizkiyahu's* tunnel is a popular attraction among visitors to the city of *Yerushalayim*.

The ancient inscription outside *Chizkiyahu's* water tunnel

Yeshayahu/Isaiah
Chapter 23

15 Thus said my Lord God of Hosts: Go in to see that steward, that Shebna, in charge of the palace:

16 What have you here, and whom have you here, That you have hewn out a tomb for yourself here? – O you who have hewn your tomb on high; O you who have hollowed out for yourself an abode in the cliff!

17 *Hashem* is about to shake you Severely, fellow, and then wrap you around Himself.

18 Indeed, He will wind you about Him as a headdress, a turban. Off to a broad land! There shall you die, and there shall be the chariots bearing your body, O shame of your master's house!

19 For I will hurl you from your station And you shall be torn down from your stand.

20 And in that day, I will summon My servant Eliakim son of *Chilkiyahu*,

21 and I will invest him with your tunic, gird him with your sash, and deliver your authority into his hand; and he shall be a father to the inhabitants of *Yerushalayim* and the men of *Yehuda*.

22 I will place the keys of *David*'s palace on his shoulders; and what he unlocks none may shut, and what he locks none may open.

23 He shall be a seat of honor to his father's household. I will fix him as a peg in a firm place,

24 on which all the substance of his father's household shall be hung: the sprouts and the leaves – all the small vessels, from bowls to all sorts of jars.

25 In that day – declares the LORD of Hosts – the peg fixed in a firm place shall give way: it shall be cut down and shall fall, and the weight it supports shall be destroyed. For it is *Hashem* who has spoken.

23 1 The "Tyre" Pronouncement. Howl, you ships of Tarshish! For havoc has been wrought, not a house is left; As they came from the land of Kittim, This was revealed to them.

2 Moan, you coastland dwellers, You traders of Sidon, Once thronged by seafarers,

3 Over many waters Your revenue came: From the trade of nations, From the grain of Shihor, The harvest of the Nile.

Yeshayahu/Isaiah
Chapter 23

4 Be ashamed, O Sidon! For the sea – this stronghold of the sea – declares, "I am as one who has never labored, Never given birth, Never raised youths Or reared maidens!"

5 When the Egyptians heard it, they quailed As when they heard about Tyre.

6 Pass on to Tarshish – Howl, you coastland dwellers!

7 Was such your merry city In former times, of yore? Did her feet carry her off To sojourn far away?

8 Who was it that planned this For crown-wearing Tyre, Whose merchants were nobles, Whose traders the world honored?

9 The Lord of Hosts planned it – To defile all glorious beauty, To shame all the honored of the world.

a-do-NAI tz'-va-OT y'-a-TZAH l'-kha-LAYL g'-ON kol tz'-VEE l'-ha-KAYL kol nikh-ba-day A-retz

10 Traverse your land like the Nile, Fair Tarshish; This is a harbor no more.

11 *Hashem* poised His arm o'er the sea And made kingdoms quake; It was He decreed destruction For Phoenicia's strongholds,

12 And said, "You shall be gay no more, O plundered one, Fair Maiden Sidon. Up, cross over to Kittim – Even there you shall have no rest."

13 Behold the land of Chaldea – This is the people that has ceased to be. Assyria, which founded it for ships, Which raised its watchtowers, Erected its ramparts, Has turned it into a ruin.

14 Howl, O ships of Tarshish, For your stronghold is destroyed!

23:9 To defile all glorious beauty *Yeshayahu* concludes his prophecies against the nations with a description of the impending downfall of Tyre. Just as Babylon and Assyria represented the pinnacle of military might in the ancient world, Tyre represented the height of commercial power and riches. Based on the coast of what is today Lebanon, Tyre established trading colonies throughout the Mediterranean Sea, as far away as Spain. Verses 1–7 describe how the shocking news of Tyre's downfall would reverberate throughout the ancient world. *Yeshayahu* places the blame for the downfall on Tyre's sense of pride; rather than being thankful to *Hashem* who granted them riches, they viewed themselves as a great power. This idea of pride is a common theme throughout the prophecies of *Yeshayahu*. In chapter 2, he describes the pride of Israel as being the source of their sins which ultimately lead to their exile. When humanity abandons its arrogance and recognizes God's goodness, He will again reveal Himself to the world.

Yeshayahu/Isaiah
Chapter 24

15 In that day, Tyre shall remain forgotten for seventy years, equaling the lifetime of one king. After a lapse of seventy years, it shall go with Tyre as with the harlot in the ditty:

טו וְהָיָה בַּיּוֹם הַהוּא וְנִשְׁכַּחַת צֹר שִׁבְעִים שָׁנָה כִּימֵי מֶלֶךְ אֶחָד מִקֵּץ שִׁבְעִים שָׁנָה יִהְיֶה לְצֹר כְּשִׁירַת הַזּוֹנָה׃

16 Take a lyre, go about the town, Harlot long forgotten; Sweetly play, make much music, To bring you back to mind.

טז קְחִי כִנּוֹר סֹבִּי עִיר זוֹנָה נִשְׁכָּחָה הֵיטִיבִי נַגֵּן הַרְבִּי־שִׁיר לְמַעַן תִּזָּכֵרִי׃

17 For after a lapse of seventy years, *Hashem* will take note of Tyre, and she shall resume her "fee-taking" and "play the harlot" with all the kingdoms of the world, on the face of the earth.

יז וְהָיָה מִקֵּץ שִׁבְעִים שָׁנָה יִפְקֹד יְהֹוָה אֶת־צֹר וְשָׁבָה לְאֶתְנַנָּה וְזָנְתָה אֶת־כָּל־מַמְלְכוֹת הָאָרֶץ עַל־פְּנֵי הָאֲדָמָה׃

18 But her profits and "hire" shall be consecrated to *Hashem*. They shall not be treasured or stored; rather shall her profits go to those who abide before *Hashem*, that they may eat their fill and clothe themselves elegantly.

יח וְהָיָה סַחְרָהּ וְאֶתְנַנָּהּ קֹדֶשׁ לַיהֹוָה לֹא יֵאָצֵר וְלֹא יֵחָסֵן כִּי לַיֹּשְׁבִים לִפְנֵי יְהֹוָה יִהְיֶה סַחְרָהּ לֶאֱכֹל לְשָׂבְעָה וְלִמְכַסֶּה עָתִיק׃

24

1 Behold, *Hashem* will strip the earth bare, And lay it waste, And twist its surface, And scatter its inhabitants.

א הִנֵּה יְהֹוָה בּוֹקֵק הָאָרֶץ וּבוֹלְקָהּ וְעִוָּה פָנֶיהָ וְהֵפִיץ יֹשְׁבֶיהָ׃

2 Layman and *Kohen* shall fare alike, Slave and master, Handmaid and mistress, Buyer and seller, Lender and borrower, Creditor and debtor.

ב וְהָיָה כָעָם כַּכֹּהֵן כַּעֶבֶד כַּאדֹנָיו כַּשִּׁפְחָה כַּגְּבִרְתָּהּ כַּקּוֹנֶה כַּמּוֹכֵר כַּמַּלְוֶה כַּלֹּוֶה כַּנֹּשֶׁה כַּאֲשֶׁר נֹשֶׁא בוֹ׃

3 The earth shall be bare, bare; It shall be plundered, plundered; For it is *Hashem* who spoke this word.

ג הִבּוֹק תִּבּוֹק הָאָרֶץ וְהִבּוֹז תִּבּוֹז כִּי יְהֹוָה דִּבֶּר אֶת־הַדָּבָר הַזֶּה׃

4 The earth is withered, sear; The world languishes, it is sear; The most exalted people of the earth languish.

ד אָבְלָה נָבְלָה הָאָרֶץ אֻמְלְלָה נָבְלָה תֵבֵל אֻמְלָלוּ מְרוֹם עַם־הָאָרֶץ׃

5 For the earth was defiled Under its inhabitants; Because they transgressed teachings, Violated laws, Broke the ancient covenant.

ה וְהָאָרֶץ חָנְפָה תַּחַת יֹשְׁבֶיהָ כִּי־עָבְרוּ תוֹרֹת חָלְפוּ חֹק הֵפֵרוּ בְּרִית עוֹלָם׃

v'-ha-A-retz kha-n'-FAH TA-khat yo-sh'-VE-ha kee a-v'-RU to-ROT kha-l'-FU KHOK hay-FAY-ru b'-REET o-LAM

24:5 For the earth was defiled under its inhabitants Chapter 24 begins four chapters which describe the total destruction of the earth, for it to then be replaced by a more righteous and just world. *Yeshayahu* explains why this will occur – it is the same reason that led God to bring about the flood in the times of *Noach*. Due to man's wicked behavior, the earth is "defiled" or "polluted" by sin (see Leviticus 18:25, Numbers 35:33), and must be purged. The eternal covenant between *Hashem* and man was made after the flood between God and *Noach* (Genesis 9:16). According to Jewish tradition, the Seven Noahide Laws, universal laws applying to all of mankind, were given by God at that time. These laws serve as the foundation of all ethics and morality, and, if followed appropriately, will ensure that the world is filled with justice and righteousness. (For a list of the seven laws, see the commentary to II Kings 10:27).

Yeshayahu/Isaiah
Chapter 24

6 That is why a curse consumes the earth, And its inhabitants pay the penalty; That is why earth's dwellers have dwindled, And but few men are left.

7 The new wine fails, The vine languishes; And all the merry-hearted sigh.

8 Stilled is the merriment of timbrels, Ended the clamor of revelers, Stilled the merriment of lyres.

9 They drink their wine without song; Liquor tastes bitter to the drinker.

10 Towns are broken, empty; Every house is shut, none enters;

11 Even over wine, a cry goes up in the streets: The sun has set on all joy, The gladness of the earth is banished.

12 Desolation is left in the town And the gate is battered to ruins.

13 For thus shall it be among the peoples In the midst of the earth: As when the olive tree is beaten out, Like gleanings when the vintage is over.

14 These shall lift up their voices, Exult in the majesty of *Hashem*. They shall shout from the sea:

15 Therefore, honor *Hashem* with lights In the coastlands of the sea – The name of *Hashem*, the God of *Yisrael*.

16 From the end of the earth We hear singing: Glory to the righteous! And I said: I waste away! I waste away! Woe is me! The faithless have acted faithlessly; The faithless have broken faith!

17 Terror, and pit, and trap Upon you who dwell on earth!

18 He who flees at the report of the terror Shall fall into the pit; And he who climbs out of the pit Shall be caught in the trap. For sluices are opened on high, And earth's foundations tremble.

19 The earth is breaking, breaking; The earth is crumbling, crumbling. The earth is tottering, tottering;

20 The earth is swaying like a drunkard; It is rocking to and fro like a hut. Its iniquity shall weigh it down, And it shall fall, to rise no more.

21 In that day, *Hashem* will punish The host of heaven in heaven And the kings of the earth on earth.

Yeshayahu/Isaiah
Chapter 25

ישעיהו
פרק כה

22 They shall be gathered in a dungeon As captives are gathered; And shall be locked up in a prison. But after many days they shall be remembered.

כב וְאֻסְּפוּ אֲסֻפָּה אַסִּיר עַל־בּוֹר וְסֻגְּרוּ עַל־מַסְגֵּר וּמֵרֹב יָמִים יִפָּקֵדוּ׃

23 Then the moon shall be ashamed, And the sun shall be abashed. For the Lord of Hosts will reign On Mount *Tzion* and in *Yerushalayim*, And the Presence will be revealed to His elders.

כג וְחָפְרָה הַלְּבָנָה וּבוֹשָׁה הַחַמָּה כִּי־מָלַךְ יְהֹוָה צְבָאוֹת בְּהַר צִיּוֹן וּבִירוּשָׁלַ͏ִם וְנֶגֶד זְקֵנָיו כָּבוֹד׃

25 1 *Hashem*, You are my God; I will extol You, I will praise Your name. For You planned graciousness of old, Counsels of steadfast faithfulness.

כה א יְהֹוָה אֱלֹהַי אַתָּה אֲרוֹמִמְךָ אוֹדֶה שִׁמְךָ כִּי עָשִׂיתָ פֶּלֶא עֵצוֹת מֵרָחוֹק אֱמוּנָה אֹמֶן׃

2 For You have turned a city into a stone heap, A walled town into a ruin, The citadel of strangers into rubble, Never to be rebuilt.

ב כִּי שַׂמְתָּ מֵעִיר לַגָּל קִרְיָה בְצוּרָה לְמַפֵּלָה אַרְמוֹן זָרִים מֵעִיר לְעוֹלָם לֹא יִבָּנֶה׃

3 Therefore a fierce people must honor You, A city of cruel nations must fear You.

ג עַל־כֵּן יְכַבְּדוּךָ עַם־עָז קִרְיַת גּוֹיִם עָרִיצִים יִירָאוּךָ׃

4 For You have been a refuge for the poor man, A shelter for the needy man in his distress – Shelter from rainstorm, shade from heat. When the fury of tyrants was like a winter rainstorm,

ד כִּי־הָיִיתָ מָעוֹז לַדָּל מָעוֹז לָאֶבְיוֹן בַּצַּר־לוֹ מַחְסֶה מִזֶּרֶם צֵל מֵחֹרֶב כִּי רוּחַ עָרִיצִים כְּזֶרֶם קִיר׃

5 The rage of strangers like heat in the desert, You subdued the heat with the shade of clouds, The singing of the tyrants was vanquished.

ה כְּחֹרֶב בְּצָיוֹן שְׁאוֹן זָרִים תַּכְנִיעַ חֹרֶב בְּצֵל עָב זְמִיר עָרִיצִים יַעֲנֶה׃

6 The Lord of Hosts will make on this mount For all the peoples A banquet of rich viands, A banquet of choice wines – Of rich viands seasoned with marrow, Of choice wines well refined.

ו וְעָשָׂה יְהֹוָה צְבָאוֹת לְכָל־הָעַמִּים בָּהָר הַזֶּה מִשְׁתֵּה שְׁמָנִים מִשְׁתֵּה שְׁמָרִים שְׁמָנִים מְמֻחָיִם שְׁמָרִים מְזֻקָּקִים׃

7 And He will destroy on this mount the shroud That is drawn over the faces of all the peoples And the covering that is spread Over all the nations:

ז וּבִלַּע בָּהָר הַזֶּה פְּנֵי־הַלּוֹט הַלּוֹט עַל־כָּל־הָעַמִּים וְהַמַּסֵּכָה הַנְּסוּכָה עַל־כָּל־הַגּוֹיִם׃

8 He will destroy death forever. My *Hashem* will wipe the tears away From all faces And will put an end to the reproach of His people Over all the earth – For it is *Hashem* who has spoken.

ח בִּלַּע הַמָּוֶת לָנֶצַח וּמָחָה אֲדֹנָי יְהֹוִה דִּמְעָה מֵעַל כָּל־פָּנִים וְחֶרְפַּת עַמּוֹ יָסִיר מֵעַל כָּל־הָאָרֶץ כִּי יְהֹוָה דִּבֵּר׃

bi-LA ha-MA-vet la-NE-tzakh u-ma-KHAH a-do-NAI e-lo-HEEM dim-AH may-AL kol pa-NEEM v'-kher-PAT a-MO ya-SEER may-AL kol ha-A-retz KEE a-do-NAI di-BAYR

25:8 He will destroy death forever Celebrating the ultimate defeat of evil, *Hashem* will hold a banquet at His mountain (*Tzion*), and all those who celebrate will witness the undoing of *Adam*'s punishment; the removal of death from the world. This idea also appears in the prophecies of *Hoshea* – "From Sheol itself I will save them, Redeem them from very Death. Where, O Death, are your plagues? Your pestilence where, O Sheol?" (Hosea 13:14). The wiping away of tears in this verse refers to *Rachel*'s tears in *Yirmiyahu*'s prophecy of the ingathering of the exiles (31:15), as the verse states, "Restrain your voice from weeping, your eyes from shedding tears; for there is a reward for your labor, declares *Hashem*. They shall return from the enemy's land." God's

Yeshayahu/Isaiah
Chapter 26

ישעיהו
פרק כו

9 In that day they shall say: This is our God; We trusted in Him, and He delivered us. This is *Hashem*, in whom we trusted; Let us rejoice and exult in His deliverance!

ט וְאָמַר בַּיּוֹם הַהוּא הִנֵּה אֱלֹהֵינוּ זֶה קִוִּינוּ לוֹ וְיוֹשִׁיעֵנוּ זֶה יְהֹוָה קִוִּינוּ לוֹ נָגִילָה וְנִשְׂמְחָה בִּישׁוּעָתוֹ:

10 For the hand of *Hashem* shall descend Upon this mount, And Moab shall be trampled under Him As straw is threshed to bits at Madmenah.

י כִּי־תָנוּחַ יַד־יְהֹוָה בָּהָר הַזֶּה וְנָדוֹשׁ מוֹאָב תַּחְתָּיו כְּהִדּוּשׁ מַתְבֵּן במי [בְּמוֹ] מַדְמֵנָה:

11 Then He will spread out His hands in their homeland, As a swimmer spreads his hands out to swim, And He will humble their pride Along with the emblems of their power.

יא וּפֵרַשׂ יָדָיו בְּקִרְבּוֹ כַּאֲשֶׁר יְפָרֵשׂ הַשֹּׂחֶה לִשְׂחוֹת וְהִשְׁפִּיל גַּאֲוָתוֹ עִם אָרְבּוֹת יָדָיו:

12 Yea, the secure fortification of their walls He will lay low and humble, Will raze to the ground, to the very dust.

יב וּמִבְצַר מִשְׂגַּב חוֹמֹתֶיךָ הֵשַׁח הִשְׁפִּיל הִגִּיעַ לָאָרֶץ עַד־עָפָר:

26

1 In that day, this song shall be sung In the land of *Yehuda*: Ours is a mighty city; He makes victory our inner and outer wall.

כו א בַּיּוֹם הַהוּא יוּשַׁר הַשִּׁיר־הַזֶּה בְּאֶרֶץ יְהוּדָה עִיר עָז־לָנוּ יְשׁוּעָה יָשִׁית חוֹמוֹת וָחֵל:

2 Open the gates, and let A righteous nation enter, [A nation] that keeps faith.

ב פִּתְחוּ שְׁעָרִים וְיָבֹא גוֹי־צַדִּיק שֹׁמֵר אֱמֻנִים:

pit-KHU sh'-a-REEM v'-ya-VO goy tza-DEEK sho-MAYR e-mu-NEEM

3 The confident mind You guard in safety, In safety because it trusts in You.

ג יֵצֶר סָמוּךְ תִּצֹּר שָׁלוֹם שָׁלוֹם כִּי בְךָ בָּטוּחַ:

4 Trust in *Hashem* for ever and ever, For in Yah *Hashem* you have an everlasting Rock.

ד בִּטְחוּ בַיהֹוָה עֲדֵי־עַד כִּי בְּיָהּ יְהֹוָה צוּר עוֹלָמִים:

5 For He has brought low those who dwelt high up, Has humbled the secure city, Humbled it to the ground, Leveled it with the dust –

ה כִּי הֵשַׁח יֹשְׁבֵי מָרוֹם קִרְיָה נִשְׂגָּבָה יַשְׁפִּילֶנָּה יַשְׁפִּילָהּ עַד־אֶרֶץ יַגִּיעֶנָּה עַד־עָפָר:

6 To be trampled underfoot, By the feet of the needy, By the soles of the poor.

ו תִּרְמְסֶנָּה רָגֶל רַגְלֵי עָנִי פַּעֲמֵי דַלִּים:

7 The path is level for the righteous man; O Just One, You make smooth the course of the righteous.

ז אֹרַח לַצַּדִּיק מֵישָׁרִים יָשָׁר מַעְגַּל צַדִּיק תְּפַלֵּס:

26:2 A righteous nation Israel's first Chief Rabbi, Abraham Isaac Kook, expounds upon the nature of righteousness, described in beautiful poetry in this verse. "The purely righteous do not complain about evil, but increase justice. They do not complain about godlessness, but increase faith. They do not complain about ignorance, but increase wisdom." Let us strive to become "purely righteous" by increasing justice, faith and wisdom in this world.

consolation from the pains of death and exile will be an important part of the redemption and complete return to Israel, for which His nation prays every day.

Rabbi Abraham Issac Kook (1865–1935)

Yeshayahu/Isaiah
Chapter 26

8 For Your just ways, *Hashem*, we look to You; We long for the name by which You are called.

9 At night I yearn for You with all my being, I seek You with all the spirit within me. For when Your judgments are wrought on earth, The inhabitants of the world learn righteousness.

10 But when the scoundrel is spared, he learns not righteousness; In a place of integrity, he does wrong – He ignores the majesty of *Hashem*.

11 *Hashem*! They see not Your hand exalted. Let them be shamed as they behold Your zeal for Your people And fire consuming Your adversaries.

12 *Hashem*! May You appoint well-being for us, Since You have also requited all our misdeeds.

13 *Hashem* our God! Lords other than You possessed us, But only Your name shall we utter.

14 They are dead, they can never live; Shades, they can never rise; Of a truth, You have dealt with them and wiped them out, Have put an end to all mention of them.

15 When You added to the nation, *Hashem*, When You added to the nation, Extending all the boundaries of the land, You were honored.

16 *Hashem*! In their distress, they sought You; Your chastisement reduced them To anguished whispered prayer.

17 Like a woman with child Approaching childbirth, Writhing and screaming in her pangs, So are we become because of You, *Hashem*.

18 We were with child, we writhed – It is as though we had given birth to wind; We have won no victory on earth; The inhabitants of the world have not come to life!

19 Oh, let Your dead revive! Let corpses arise! Awake and shout for joy, You who dwell in the dust! – For Your dew is like the dew on fresh growth; You make the land of the shades come to life.

20 Go, my people, enter your chambers, And lock your doors behind you. Hide but a little moment, Until the indignation passes.

ישעיהו
פרק כו

ח אַף אֹרַח מִשְׁפָּטֶיךָ יְהֹוָה קִוִּינוּךָ לְשִׁמְךָ וּלְזִכְרְךָ תַּאֲוַת־נָפֶשׁ:

ט נַפְשִׁי אִוִּיתִיךָ בַּלַּיְלָה אַף־רוּחִי בְקִרְבִּי אֲשַׁחֲרֶךָּ כִּי כַּאֲשֶׁר מִשְׁפָּטֶיךָ לָאָרֶץ צֶדֶק לָמְדוּ יֹשְׁבֵי תֵבֵל:

י יֻחַן רָשָׁע בַּל־לָמַד צֶדֶק בְּאֶרֶץ נְכֹחוֹת יְעַוֵּל וּבַל־יִרְאֶה גֵּאוּת יְהֹוָה:

יא יְהֹוָה רָמָה יָדְךָ בַּל־יֶחֱזָיוּן יֶחֱזוּ וְיֵבֹשׁוּ קִנְאַת־עָם אַף־אֵשׁ צָרֶיךָ תֹאכְלֵם:

יב יְהֹוָה תִּשְׁפֹּת שָׁלוֹם לָנוּ כִּי גַּם כָּל־מַעֲשֵׂינוּ פָּעַלְתָּ לָּנוּ:

יג יְהֹוָה אֱלֹהֵינוּ בְּעָלוּנוּ אֲדֹנִים זוּלָתֶךָ לְבַד־בְּךָ נַזְכִּיר שְׁמֶךָ:

יד מֵתִים בַּל־יִחְיוּ רְפָאִים בַּל־יָקֻמוּ לָכֵן פָּקַדְתָּ וַתַּשְׁמִידֵם וַתְּאַבֵּד כָּל־זֵכֶר לָמוֹ:

טו יָסַפְתָּ לַגּוֹי יְהֹוָה יָסַפְתָּ לַגּוֹי נִכְבָּדְתָּ רִחַקְתָּ כָּל־קַצְוֵי־אָרֶץ:

טז יְהֹוָה בַּצַּר פְּקָדוּךָ צָקוּן לַחַשׁ מוּסָרְךָ לָמוֹ:

יז כְּמוֹ הָרָה תַּקְרִיב לָלֶדֶת תָּחִיל תִּזְעַק בַּחֲבָלֶיהָ כֵּן הָיִינוּ מִפָּנֶיךָ יְהֹוָה:

יח הָרִינוּ חַלְנוּ כְּמוֹ יָלַדְנוּ רוּחַ יְשׁוּעֹת בַּל־נַעֲשֶׂה אֶרֶץ וּבַל־יִפְּלוּ יֹשְׁבֵי תֵבֵל:

יט יִחְיוּ מֵתֶיךָ נְבֵלָתִי יְקוּמוּן הָקִיצוּ וְרַנְּנוּ שֹׁכְנֵי עָפָר כִּי טַל אוֹרֹת טַלֶּךָ וָאָרֶץ רְפָאִים תַּפִּיל:

כ לֵךְ עַמִּי בֹּא בַחֲדָרֶיךָ וּסְגֹר דְּלָתֶיךָ [דְּלָתְךָ] בַּעֲדֶךָ חֲבִי כִמְעַט־רֶגַע עַד־יַעֲבָר [יַעֲבוֹר] זָעַם:

Yeshayahu/Isaiah
Chapter 27

ישעיהו
פרק כז

21 For lo! *Hashem* shall come forth from His place To punish the dwellers of the earth For their iniquity; And the earth shall disclose its bloodshed And shall no longer conceal its slain.

כא כִּי־הִנֵּה יְהֹוָה יֹצֵא מִמְּקוֹמוֹ לִפְקֹד עֲוֹן יֹשֵׁב־הָאָרֶץ עָלָיו וְגִלְּתָה הָאָרֶץ אֶת־דָּמֶיהָ וְלֹא־תְכַסֶּה עוֹד עַל־הֲרוּגֶיהָ:

27 1 In that day *Hashem* will punish, With His great, cruel, mighty sword Leviathan the Elusive Serpent – Leviathan the Twisting Serpent; He will slay the Dragon of the sea.

כז א בַּיּוֹם הַהוּא יִפְקֹד יְהֹוָה בְּחַרְבּוֹ הַקָּשָׁה וְהַגְּדוֹלָה וְהַחֲזָקָה עַל לִוְיָתָן נָחָשׁ בָּרִחַ וְעַל לִוְיָתָן נָחָשׁ עֲקַלָּתוֹן וְהָרַג אֶת־הַתַּנִּין אֲשֶׁר בַּיָּם:

2 In that day, They shall sing of it: "Vineyard of Delight."

ב בַּיּוֹם הַהוּא כֶּרֶם חֶמֶד עַנּוּ־לָהּ:

3 I *Hashem* keep watch over it, I water it every moment; That no harm may befall it, I watch it night and day.

ג אֲנִי יְהֹוָה נֹצְרָהּ לִרְגָעִים אַשְׁקֶנָּה פֶּן יִפְקֹד עָלֶיהָ לַיְלָה וָיוֹם אֶצֳּרֶנָּה:

4 There is no anger in Me: If one offers Me thorns and thistles, I will march to battle against him, And set all of them on fire.

ד חֵמָה אֵין לִי מִי־יִתְּנֵנִי שָׁמִיר שַׁיִת בַּמִּלְחָמָה אֶפְשְׂעָה בָהּ אֲצִיתֶנָּה יָּחַד:

5 But if he holds fast to My refuge, He makes Me his friend; He makes Me his friend.

ה אוֹ יַחֲזֵק בְּמָעוּזִּי יַעֲשֶׂה שָׁלוֹם לִי שָׁלוֹם יַעֲשֶׂה־לִּי:

6 [In days] to come *Yaakov* shall strike root, *Yisrael* shall sprout and blossom, And the face of the world Shall be covered with fruit.

ו הַבָּאִים יַשְׁרֵשׁ יַעֲקֹב יָצִיץ וּפָרַח יִשְׂרָאֵל וּמָלְאוּ פְנֵי־תֵבֵל תְּנוּבָה:

ha-ba-EEM yash-RAYSH ya-a-KOV ya-TZEETZ u-fa-RAKH yis-ra-AYL u-ma-l'-U f'-nay tay-VAYL t'-nu-VAH

7 Was he beaten as his beater has been? Did he suffer such slaughter as his slayers?

ז הַכְּמַכַּת מַכֵּהוּ הִכָּהוּ אִם־כְּהֶרֶג הֲרֻגָיו הֹרָג:

8 Assailing them with fury unchained, His pitiless blast bore them off On a day of gale.

ח בְּסַאסְּאָה בְּשַׁלְּחָהּ תְּרִיבֶנָּה הָגָה בְּרוּחוֹ הַקָּשָׁה בְּיוֹם קָדִים:

9 Assuredly, by this alone Shall *Yaakov*'s sin be purged away; This is the only price For removing his guilt: That he make all the altar-stones Like shattered blocks of chalk – With no sacred post left standing, Nor any incense *Mizbayach*.

ט לָכֵן בְּזֹאת יְכֻפַּר עֲוֹן־יַעֲקֹב וְזֶה כָּל־פְּרִי הָסִר חַטָּאתוֹ בְּשׂוּמוֹ כָּל־אַבְנֵי מִזְבֵּחַ כְּאַבְנֵי־גִר מְנֻפָּצוֹת לֹא־יָקֻמוּ אֲשֵׁרִים וְחַמָּנִים:

27:6 *Yaakov* shall strike root In chapter 5, Yeshayahu describes Israel as a rebellious vine that produces inferior fruits. Here is the happy conclusion to *Hashem*'s song to His vineyard. While God may punish, it is not out of anger or fury (verse 4), but the hope that it will lead to harmony between Israel and *Hashem*. In this chapter, Israel is attached to its land with an unbreakable connection, like a deeply rooted vineyard. As a result, "*Yaakov* shall strike root, *Yisrael* shall sprout and blossom, and the face of the world shall be covered with fruit." Indeed, with the contemporary return of the Jews to *Eretz Yisrael*, the former desert land has begun to blossom and bud, a sure sign of divine favor.

A vineyard on the Judean hills

Yeshayahu/Isaiah
Chapter 28

10 Thus fortified cities lie desolate, Homesteads deserted, forsaken like a wilderness; There calves graze, there they lie down And consume its boughs.

11 When its crown is withered, they break; Women come and make fires with them. For they are a people without understanding; That is why Their Maker will show them no mercy, Their Creator will deny them grace.

12 And in that day, *Hashem* will beat out [the peoples like grain] from the channel of the Euphrates to the Wadi of Egypt; and you shall be picked up one by one, O children of *Yisrael*!

13 And in that day, a great *shofar* shall be sounded; and the strayed who are in the land of Assyria and the expelled who are in the land of Egypt shall come and worship *Hashem* on the holy mount, in *Yerushalayim*.

28

1 Ah, the proud crowns of the drunkards of *Efraim*, Whose glorious beauty is but wilted flowers On the heads of men bloated with rich food, Who are overcome by wine!

2 Lo, my Lord has something strong and mighty, Like a storm of hail, A shower of pestilence. Something like a storm of massive, torrential rain Shall be hurled with force to the ground.

3 Trampled underfoot shall be The proud crowns of the drunkards of *Efraim*,

4 The wilted flowers – On the heads of men bloated with rich food – That are his glorious beauty. They shall be like an early fig Before the fruit harvest; Whoever sees it devours it While it is still in his hand.

5 In that day, the Lord of Hosts shall become a crown of beauty and a diadem of glory for the remnant of His people,

6 and a spirit of judgment for him who sits in judgment and of valor for those who repel attacks at the gate.

7 But these are also muddled by wine And dazed by liquor: *Kohen* and *Navi* Are muddled by liquor; They are confused by wine, They are dazed by liquor; They are muddled in their visions, They stumble in judgment.

Yeshayahu/Isaiah
Chapter 28

ישעיהו
פרק כח

8 Yea, all tables are covered With vomit and filth, So that no space is left.

כִּי כָּל־שֻׁלְחָנוֹת מָלְאוּ קִיא צֹאָה בְּלִי מָקוֹם:

9 "To whom would he give instruction? To whom expound a message? To those newly weaned from milk, Just taken away from the breast?

אֶת־מִי יוֹרֶה דֵעָה וְאֶת־מִי יָבִין שְׁמוּעָה גְּמוּלֵי מֵחָלָב עַתִּיקֵי מִשָּׁדָיִם:

10 That same mutter upon mutter, Murmur upon murmur, Now here, now there!"

כִּי צַו לָצָו צַו לָצָו קַו לָקָו קַו לָקָו זְעֵיר שָׁם זְעֵיר שָׁם:

11 Truly, as one who speaks to that people in a stammering jargon and an alien tongue

כִּי בְּלַעֲגֵי שָׂפָה וּבְלָשׁוֹן אַחֶרֶת יְדַבֵּר אֶל־הָעָם הַזֶּה:

12 is he who declares to them, "This is the resting place, let the weary rest; this is the place of repose." They refuse to listen.

אֲשֶׁר אָמַר אֲלֵיהֶם זֹאת הַמְּנוּחָה הָנִיחוּ לֶעָיֵף וְזֹאת הַמַּרְגֵּעָה וְלֹא אָבוּא שְׁמוֹעַ:

13 To them the word of *Hashem* is: "Mutter upon mutter, Murmur upon murmur, Now here, now there." And so they will march, But they shall fall backward, And be injured and snared and captured.

וְהָיָה לָהֶם דְּבַר־יְהֹוָה צַו לָצָו צַו לָצָו קַו לָקָו קַו לָקָו זְעֵיר שָׁם זְעֵיר שָׁם לְמַעַן יֵלְכוּ וְכָשְׁלוּ אָחוֹר וְנִשְׁבָּרוּ וְנוֹקְשׁוּ וְנִלְכָּדוּ:

14 Hear now the word of *Hashem*, You men of mockery, Who govern that people In *Yerushalayim*!

לָכֵן שִׁמְעוּ דְבַר־יְהֹוָה אַנְשֵׁי לָצוֹן מֹשְׁלֵי הָעָם הַזֶּה אֲשֶׁר בִּירוּשָׁלָיִם:

15 For you have said, "We have made a covenant with Death, Concluded a pact with Sheol. When the sweeping flood passes through, It shall not reach us; For we have made falsehood our refuge, Taken shelter in treachery."

כִּי אֲמַרְתֶּם כָּרַתְנוּ בְרִית אֶת־מָוֶת וְעִם־שְׁאוֹל עָשִׂינוּ חֹזֶה שִׁיט [שׁוֹט] שׁוֹטֵף כִּי־עָבַר [יַעֲבֹר] לֹא יְבוֹאֵנוּ כִּי שַׂמְנוּ כָזָב מַחְסֵנוּ וּבַשֶּׁקֶר נִסְתָּרְנוּ:

16 Assuredly, Thus said *Hashem*: "Behold, I will found in *Tzion*, Stone by stone, A tower of precious cornerstones, Exceedingly firm; He who trusts need not fear.

לָכֵן כֹּה אָמַר אֲדֹנָי יְהֹוִה הִנְנִי יִסַּד בְּצִיּוֹן אָבֶן אֶבֶן בֹּחַן פִּנַּת יִקְרַת מוּסָד מוּסָד הַמַּאֲמִין לֹא יָחִישׁ:

la-KHAYN KO a-MAR a-do-NAI e-lo-HEEM hi-n'-NEE yi-SAD b'-tzi-YON A-ven E-ven BO-khan pi-NAT yik-RAT mu-SAD mu-SAD ha-ma-a-MEEN LO ya-KHEESH

17 But I will apply judgment as a measuring line And retribution as weights; Hail shall sweep away the refuge of falsehood, And flood-waters engulf your shelter.

וְשַׂמְתִּי מִשְׁפָּט לְקָו וּצְדָקָה לְמִשְׁקָלֶת וְיָעָה בָרָד מַחְסֵה כָזָב וְסֵתֶר מַיִם יִשְׁטֹפוּ:

18 Your covenant with Death shall be annulled, Your pact with Sheol shall not endure; When the sweeping flood passes through, You shall be its victims.

וְכֻפַּר בְּרִיתְכֶם אֶת־מָוֶת וְחָזוּתְכֶם אֶת־שְׁאוֹל לֹא תָקוּם שׁוֹט שׁוֹטֵף כִּי יַעֲבֹר וִהְיִיתֶם לוֹ לְמִרְמָס:

28:16 I will found in *Tzion*, stone by stone The Hebrew word for 'stone' is *even* (אבן). What is interesting about this word is that it contains within it the Hebrew words for 'father,' *av* (אב), and 'son,' *ben* (בן). Once again, the Hebrew root of a simple word teaches a profound lesson, by alluding to the fact that the bond between a father and his son is as strong as a rock, and as precious as a fine stone.

אבן

Yeshayahu/Isaiah
Chapter 28

ישעיהו
פרק כח

19 It shall catch you Every time it passes through; It shall pass through every morning, Every day and every night. And it shall be sheer horror To grasp the message."

יט מִדֵּי עׇבְרוֹ יִקַּח אֶתְכֶם כִּי־בַבֹּקֶר בַּבֹּקֶר יַעֲבֹר בַּיּוֹם וּבַלָּיְלָה וְהָיָה רַק־זְוָעָה הָבִין שְׁמוּעָה׃

20 The couch is too short for stretching out, And the cover too narrow for curling up!

כ כִּי־קָצַר הַמַּצָּע מֵהִשְׂתָּרֵעַ וְהַמַּסֵּכָה צָרָה כְּהִתְכַּנֵּס׃

21 For *Hashem* will arise As on the hill of *Perazim*, He will rouse Himself As in the vale of *Givon*, To do His work – Strange is His work! And to perform His task – Astounding is His task!

כא כִּי כְהַר־פְּרָצִים יָקוּם יְהֹוָה כְּעֵמֶק בְּגִבְעוֹן יִרְגָּז לַעֲשׂוֹת מַעֲשֵׂהוּ זָר מַעֲשֵׂהוּ וְלַעֲבֹד עֲבֹדָתוֹ נׇכְרִיָּה עֲבֹדָתוֹ׃

22 Therefore, refrain from mockery, Lest your bonds be tightened. For I have heard a decree of destruction From my Lord God of Hosts Against all the land.

כב וְעַתָּה אַל־תִּתְלוֹצָצוּ פֶּן־יֶחְזְקוּ מוֹסְרֵיכֶם כִּי־כָלָה וְנֶחֱרָצָה שָׁמַעְתִּי מֵאֵת אֲדֹנָי יֱהֹוִה צְבָאוֹת עַל־כׇּל־הָאָרֶץ׃

23 Give diligent ear to my words, Attend carefully to what I say.

כג הַאֲזִינוּ וְשִׁמְעוּ קוֹלִי הַקְשִׁיבוּ וְשִׁמְעוּ אִמְרָתִי׃

24 Does he who plows to sow Plow all the time, Breaking up and furrowing his land?

כד הֲכֹל הַיּוֹם יַחֲרֹשׁ הַחֹרֵשׁ לִזְרֹעַ יְפַתַּח וִישַׂדֵּד אַדְמָתוֹ׃

25 When he has smoothed its surface, Does he not rather broadcast black cumin And scatter cumin, Or set wheat in a row, Barley in a strip, And emmer in a patch?

כה הֲלוֹא אִם־שִׁוָּה פָנֶיהָ וְהֵפִיץ קֶצַח וְכַמֹּן יִזְרֹק וְשָׂם חִטָּה שׂוֹרָה וּשְׂעֹרָה נִסְמָן וְכֻסֶּמֶת גְּבֻלָתוֹ׃

ha-LO im shi-VAH fa-NE-ha v'-hay-FEETZ KE-tzakh v'-kha-MON yiz-ROK v'-SAM khi-TAH so-RAH us-o-RAH nis-MAN v'-khu-SE-met g'-vu-la-TO

26 For He teaches him the right manner, His *Hashem* instructs him.

כו וְיִסְּרוֹ לַמִּשְׁפָּט אֱלֹהָיו יוֹרֶנּוּ׃

27 So, too, black cumin is not threshed with a threshing board, Nor is the wheel of a threshing sledge rolled over cumin; But black cumin is beaten out with a stick And cumin with a rod.

כז כִּי לֹא בֶחָרוּץ יוּדַשׁ קֶצַח וְאוֹפַן עֲגָלָה עַל־כַּמֹּן יוּסָּב כִּי בַמַּטֶּה יֵחָבֶט קֶצַח וְכַמֹּן בַּשָּׁבֶט׃

28 It is cereal that is crushed. For even if he threshes it thoroughly, And the wheel of his sledge and his horses overwhelm it, He does not crush it.

כח לֶחֶם יוּדָק כִּי לֹא לָנֶצַח אָדוֹשׁ יְדוּשֶׁנּוּ וְהָמַם גִּלְגַּל עֶגְלָתוֹ וּפָרָשָׁיו לֹא־יְדֻקֶּנּוּ׃

A wheat field in the Elah Valleh

28:25 Or set wheat in a row Wheat, the first of the seven special agricultural products of *Eretz Yisrael* (Deuteronomy 8:8), has been one of the world's major crops since biblical times. The first mention of wheat in the Bible is found in *Sefer Bereishit* (30:14): "Once, at the time of the wheat harvest, *Reuven* came upon some mandrakes in the field…" So important is wheat flour that the Rabbis taught: "Where there is no flour, there is no *Torah*; and where there is no *Torah*, there is no flour" (*Ethics of the Fathers*), emphasizing the mutual dependency of the physical world and spiritual pursuits.

Yeshayahu/Isaiah
Chapter 29

29 That, too, is ordered by the Lord of Hosts; His counsel is unfathomable, His wisdom marvelous.

29 1 "Ah, Ariel, Ariel, City where *David* camped! Add year to year, Let festivals come in their cycles!

2 And I will harass Ariel, And there shall be sorrow and sighing. She shall be to Me like Ariel.

3 And I will camp against you round about; I will lay siege to you with a mound, And I will set up siegeworks against you.

4 And you shall speak from lower than the ground, Your speech shall be humbler than the sod; Your speech shall sound like a ghost's from the ground, Your voice shall chirp from the sod.

5 And like fine dust shall be The multitude of your strangers; And like flying chaff, The multitude of tyrants." And suddenly, in an instant,

6 She shall be remembered of the Lord of Hosts With roaring, and shaking, and deafening noise, Storm, and tempest, and blaze of consuming fire.

7 Then, like a dream, a vision of the night, Shall be the multitude of nations That war upon Ariel, And all her besiegers, and the siegeworks against her, And those who harass her.

8 Like one who is hungry And dreams he is eating, But wakes to find himself empty; And like one who is thirsty And dreams he is drinking, But wakes to find himself faint And utterly parched – So shall be all the multitude of nations That war upon Mount *Tzion*.

9 Act stupid and be stupefied! Act blind and be blinded! (They are drunk, but not from wine, They stagger, but not from liquor.)

10 For *Hashem* has spread over you A spirit of deep sleep, And has shut your eyes, the *Neviim*, And covered your heads, the seers;

11 So that all prophecy has been to you Like the words of a sealed document. If it is handed to one who can read and he is asked to read it, he will say, "I can't, because it is sealed";

12 and if the document is handed to one who cannot read and he is asked to read it, he will say, "I can't read."

ישעיהו
פרק כט

כט גַּם־זֹאת מֵעִם יְהֹוָה צְבָאוֹת יָצָאָה הִפְלִיא עֵצָה הִגְדִּיל תּוּשִׁיָּה:

כט א הוֹי אֲרִיאֵל אֲרִיאֵל קִרְיַת חָנָה דָוִד סְפוּ שָׁנָה עַל־שָׁנָה חַגִּים יִנְקֹפוּ:

ב וַהֲצִיקוֹתִי לַאֲרִיאֵל וְהָיְתָה תַאֲנִיָּה וַאֲנִיָּה וְהָיְתָה לִּי כַּאֲרִיאֵל:

ג וְחָנִיתִי כַדּוּר עָלָיִךְ וְצַרְתִּי עָלַיִךְ מֻצָּב וַהֲקִימֹתִי עָלַיִךְ מְצֻרֹת:

ד וְשָׁפַלְתְּ מֵאֶרֶץ תְּדַבֵּרִי וּמֵעָפָר תִּשַּׁח אִמְרָתֵךְ וְהָיָה כְּאוֹב מֵאֶרֶץ קוֹלֵךְ וּמֵעָפָר אִמְרָתֵךְ תְּצַפְצֵף:

ה וְהָיָה כְּאָבָק דַּק הֲמוֹן זָרָיִךְ וּכְמֹץ עֹבֵר הֲמוֹן עָרִיצִים וְהָיָה לְפֶתַע פִּתְאֹם:

ו מֵעִם יְהֹוָה צְבָאוֹת תִּפָּקֵד בְּרַעַם וּבְרַעַשׁ וְקוֹל גָּדוֹל סוּפָה וּסְעָרָה וְלַהַב אֵשׁ אוֹכֵלָה:

ז וְהָיָה כַּחֲלוֹם חֲזוֹן לַיְלָה הֲמוֹן כָּל־הַגּוֹיִם הַצֹּבְאִים עַל־אֲרִיאֵל וְכָל־צֹבֶיהָ וּמְצֹדָתָהּ וְהַמְּצִיקִים לָהּ:

ח וְהָיָה כַּאֲשֶׁר יַחֲלֹם הָרָעֵב וְהִנֵּה אוֹכֵל וְהֵקִיץ וְרֵיקָה נַפְשׁוֹ וְכַאֲשֶׁר יַחֲלֹם הַצָּמֵא וְהִנֵּה שֹׁתֶה וְהֵקִיץ וְהִנֵּה עָיֵף וְנַפְשׁוֹ שׁוֹקֵקָה כֵּן יִהְיֶה הֲמוֹן כָּל־הַגּוֹיִם הַצֹּבְאִים עַל־הַר צִיּוֹן:

ט הִתְמַהְמְהוּ וּתְמָהוּ הִשְׁתַּעַשְׁעוּ וָשֹׁעוּ שָׁכְרוּ וְלֹא־יַיִן נָעוּ וְלֹא שֵׁכָר:

י כִּי־נָסַךְ עֲלֵיכֶם יְהֹוָה רוּחַ תַּרְדֵּמָה וַיְעַצֵּם אֶת־עֵינֵיכֶם אֶת־הַנְּבִיאִים וְאֶת־רָאשֵׁיכֶם הַחֹזִים כִּסָּה:

יא וַתְּהִי לָכֶם חָזוּת הַכֹּל כְּדִבְרֵי הַסֵּפֶר הֶחָתוּם אֲשֶׁר־יִתְּנוּ אֹתוֹ אֶל־יוֹדֵעַ הַסֵּפֶר [סֵפֶר] לֵאמֹר קְרָא נָא־זֶה וְאָמַר לֹא אוּכַל כִּי חָתוּם הוּא:

יב וְנִתַּן הַסֵּפֶר עַל אֲשֶׁר לֹא־יָדַע סֵפֶר לֵאמֹר קְרָא נָא־זֶה וְאָמַר לֹא יָדַעְתִּי סֵפֶר:

Yeshayahu/Isaiah
Chapter 29

13 My Lord said: Because that people has approached [Me] with its mouth And honored Me with its lips, But has kept its heart far from Me, And its worship of Me has been A commandment of men, learned by rote –

va-YO-mer a-do-NAI YA-an KEE ni-GASH ha-AM ha-ZEH b'-FEEV u-vis-fa-TAV ki-b'-DU-nee v'-li-BO ri-KHAK mi-ME-nee va-t'-HEE yir-a-TAM o-TEE mitz-VAT a-na-SHEEM m'-lu-ma-DAH

14 Truly, I shall further baffle that people With bafflement upon bafflement; And the wisdom of its wise shall fail, And the prudence of its prudent shall vanish.

15 Ha! Those who would hide their plans Deep from *Hashem*! Who do their work in dark places And say, "Who sees us, who takes note of us?"

16 How perverse of you! Should the potter be accounted as the clay? Should what is made say of its Maker, "He did not make me," And what is formed say of Him who formed it, "He did not understand"?

17 Surely, in a little while, Lebanon will be transformed into farm land, And farm land accounted as mere brush.

18 In that day, the deaf shall hear even written words, And the eyes of the blind shall see Even in darkness and obscurity.

19 Then the humble shall have increasing joy through *Hashem*, And the neediest of men shall exult In the Holy One of *Yisrael*.

20 For the tyrant shall be no more, The scoffer shall cease to be; And those diligent for evil shall be wiped out,

21 Who cause men to lose their lawsuits, Laying a snare for the arbiter at the gate, And wronging by falsehood Him who was in the right.

29:13 And its worship of Me has been a commandment of men, learned by rote For what sin did God punish *Yehuda*? Compared to *Shomron*, the northern kingdom, with all its idolatries and immoralities, *Yehuda* seemed positively pious. In fact, they had purified their country under *Chizkiyahu*. *Yeshayahu* answers with one sentence. Though the people prayed and performed the ritual commandments, their service was not genuine, but only lip-service. Some commentators understood this as hypocrisy; however others interpret *Yeshayahu's* description in a more literal sense – unfeeling, robotic observance that has no value. *Hashem* wants both our consistent external actions with corresponding internal feelings united in His service.

Yeshayahu/Isaiah
Chapter 30

22 Assuredly, thus said *Hashem* to the House of *Yaakov*, Who redeemed *Avraham*: No more shall *Yaakov* be shamed, No longer his face grow pale.

23 For when he – that is, his children – behold what My hands have wrought in his midst, they will hallow My name. Men will hallow the Holy One of *Yaakov* And stand in awe of the God of *Yisrael*.

24 And the confused shall acquire insight And grumblers accept instruction.

30 1 Oh, disloyal sons! – declares *Hashem* – Making plans Against My wishes, Weaving schemes Against My will, Thereby piling Guilt on guilt –

2 Who set out to go down to Egypt Without asking Me, To seek refuge with Pharaoh, To seek shelter under the protection of Egypt.

3 The refuge with Pharaoh shall result in your shame; The shelter under Egypt's protection, in your chagrin.

4 Though his officers are present in Zoan, And his messengers reach as far as Hanes,

5 They all shall come to shame Because of a people that does not avail them, That is of no help or avail, But [brings] only chagrin and disgrace.

6 The "Beasts of the *Negev*" Pronouncement. Through a land of distress and hardship, Of lion and roaring king-beast, Of viper and flying seraph, They convey their wealth on the backs of asses, Their treasures on camels' humps, To a people of no avail.

7 For the help of Egypt Shall be vain and empty. Truly, I call this, "They are a threat that has ceased."

8 Now, Go, write it down on a tablet And inscribe it in a record, That it may be with them for future days, A witness forever.

9 For it is a rebellious people, Faithless children, Children who refused to heed The instruction of *Hashem*;

10 Who said to the seers, "Do not see," To the *Neviim*, "Do not prophesy truth to us; Speak to us falsehoods, Prophesy delusions.

11 Leave the way! Get off the path! Let us hear no more About the Holy One of *Yisrael*!"

Yeshayahu/Isaiah
Chapter 30

12 Assuredly, Thus said the Holy One of *Yisrael*: Because you have rejected this word, And have put your trust and reliance In that which is fraudulent and tortuous –

13 Of a surety, This iniquity shall work on you Like a spreading breach that occurs in a lofty wall, Whose crash comes sudden and swift.

14 It is smashed as one smashes an earthen jug, Ruthlessly shattered So that no shard is left in its breakage To scoop coals from a brazier, Or ladle water from a puddle.

15 For thus said my God, The Holy One of *Yisrael*, "You shall triumph by stillness and quiet; Your victory shall come about Through calm and confidence." But you refused.

16 "No," you declared. "We shall flee on steeds" – Therefore you shall flee! "We shall ride on swift mounts" – Therefore your pursuers shall prove swift!

17 One thousand before the shout of one – You shall flee at the shout of five; Till what is left of you Is like a mast on a hilltop, Like a pole upon a mountain.

18 Truly, *Hashem* is waiting to show you grace, Truly, He will arise to pardon you. For *Hashem* is a God of justice; Happy are all who wait for Him.

v'-la-KHAYN y'-kha-KEH a-do-NAI la-kha-nan-KHEM v'-la-KHAYN ya-RUM l'-ra-khem-KHEM kee e-lo-HAY mish-PAT a-do-NAI ash-RAY kol kho-KHAY LO

19 Indeed, O people in *Tzion*, dwellers of *Yerushalayim*, you shall not have cause to weep. He will grant you His favor at the sound of your cry; He will respond as soon as He hears it.

30:18 Truly, *Hashem* is waiting Despite the fate of *Ashdod* ten years earlier, abandoned by Egypt to destruction by Assyria, there were still those in *Yehuda* who felt that an alliance with Pharaoh would be the best defense against the Assyrians. *Yeshayahu* describes a delegation that traveled southwards through the *Negev* desert with donkeys bearing treasures, in hopes of buying Egyptian loyalty. *Hashem* expresses His frustration with Israel for continuing their rebellious practices, placing their trust in others and not in Him. However, *Yeshayahu* states, divine patience was not yet exhausted. If they would cry out to *Hashem* (verse 19) and abolish idolatry entirely (verse 22), He would be gracious to his people. This is an important message for mankind. *Hashem* is a God of patience and forgiveness. Though people sin and turn their backs on Him, He is always waiting for them to correct their ways, so that He can be gracious to them and have compassion on them.

Yeshayahu/Isaiah
Chapter 30

ישעיהו
פרק ל

20 My Lord will provide for you meager bread and scant water. Then your Guide will no more be ignored, but your eyes will watch your Guide;

כ וְנָתַן לָכֶם אֲדֹנָי לֶחֶם צָר וּמַיִם לָחַץ וְלֹא־יִכָּנֵף עוֹד מוֹרֶיךָ וְהָיוּ עֵינֶיךָ רֹאוֹת אֶת־מוֹרֶיךָ׃

21 and, whenever you deviate to the right or to the left, your ears will heed the command from behind you: "This is the road; follow it!"

כא וְאָזְנֶיךָ תִּשְׁמַעְנָה דָבָר מֵאַחֲרֶיךָ לֵאמֹר זֶה הַדֶּרֶךְ לְכוּ בוֹ כִּי תַאֲמִינוּ וְכִי תַשְׂמְאִילוּ׃

22 And you will treat as unclean the silver overlay of your images and the golden plating of your idols. You will cast them away like a menstruous woman. "Out!" you will call to them.

כב וְטִמֵּאתֶם אֶת־צִפּוּי פְּסִילֵי כַסְפֶּךָ וְאֶת־אֲפֻדַּת מַסֵּכַת זְהָבֶךָ תִּזְרֵם כְּמוֹ דָוָה צֵא תֹּאמַר לוֹ׃

23 So rain shall be provided for the seed with which you sow the ground, and the bread that the ground brings forth shall be rich and fat. Your livestock, in that day, shall graze in broad pastures;

כג וְנָתַן מְטַר זַרְעֲךָ אֲשֶׁר־תִּזְרַע אֶת־הָאֲדָמָה וְלֶחֶם תְּבוּאַת הָאֲדָמָה וְהָיָה דָשֵׁן וְשָׁמֵן יִרְעֶה מִקְנֶיךָ בַּיּוֹם הַהוּא כַּר נִרְחָב׃

24 as for the cattle and the asses that till the soil, they shall partake of salted fodder that has been winnowed with shovel and fan.

כד וְהָאֲלָפִים וְהָעֲיָרִים עֹבְדֵי הָאֲדָמָה בְּלִיל חָמִיץ יֹאכֵלוּ אֲשֶׁר־זֹרֶה בָרַחַת וּבַמִּזְרֶה׃

25 And on every high mountain and on every lofty hill, there shall appear brooks and watercourses – on a day of heavy slaughter, when towers topple.

כה וְהָיָה עַל־כָּל־הַר גָּבֹהַּ וְעַל כָּל־גִּבְעָה נִשָּׂאָה פְּלָגִים יִבְלֵי־מָיִם בְּיוֹם הֶרֶג רָב בִּנְפֹל מִגְדָּלִים׃

26 And the light of the moon shall become like the light of the sun, and the light of the sun shall become sevenfold, like the light of the seven days, when *Hashem* binds up His people's wounds and heals the injuries it has suffered.

כו וְהָיָה אוֹר־הַלְּבָנָה כְּאוֹר הַחַמָּה וְאוֹר הַחַמָּה יִהְיֶה שִׁבְעָתַיִם כְּאוֹר שִׁבְעַת הַיָּמִים בְּיוֹם חֲבֹשׁ יְהֹוָה אֶת־שֶׁבֶר עַמּוֹ וּמַחַץ מַכָּתוֹ יִרְפָּא׃

27 Behold *Hashem* Himself Comes from afar In blazing wrath, With a heavy burden – His lips full of fury, His tongue like devouring fire,

כז הִנֵּה שֵׁם־יְהֹוָה בָּא מִמֶּרְחָק בֹּעֵר אַפּוֹ וְכֹבֶד מַשָּׂאָה שְׂפָתָיו מָלְאוּ זַעַם וּלְשׁוֹנוֹ כְּאֵשׁ אֹכָלֶת׃

28 And his breath like a raging torrent Reaching halfway up the neck – To set a misguiding yoke upon nations And a misleading bridle upon the jaws of peoples,

כח וְרוּחוֹ כְּנַחַל שׁוֹטֵף עַד־צַוָּאר יֶחֱצֶה לַהֲנָפָה גוֹיִם בְּנָפַת שָׁוְא וְרֶסֶן מַתְעֶה עַל לְחָיֵי עַמִּים׃

29 For you, there shall be singing As on a night when a festival is hallowed; There shall be rejoicing as when they march With flute, with timbrels, and with lyres* To the Rock of *Yisrael* on the Mount of *Hashem*.

כט הַשִּׁיר יִהְיֶה לָכֶם כְּלֵיל הִתְקַדֶּשׁ־חָג וְשִׂמְחַת לֵבָב כַּהוֹלֵךְ בֶּחָלִיל לָבוֹא בְהַר־יְהֹוָה אֶל־צוּר יִשְׂרָאֵל׃

30 For *Hashem* will make His majestic voice heard And display the sweep of His arm In raging wrath, In a devouring blaze of fire, In tempest, and rainstorm, and hailstones.

ל וְהִשְׁמִיעַ יְהֹוָה אֶת־הוֹד קוֹלוֹ וְנַחַת זְרוֹעוֹ יַרְאֶה בְּזַעַף אָף וְלַהַב אֵשׁ אוֹכֵלָה נֶפֶץ וָזֶרֶם וְאֶבֶן בָּרָד׃

---

* "with timbrels, and with lyres" brought up from verse 32 for clarity

Yeshayahu/Isaiah
Chapter 31

31 Truly, Assyria, who beats with the rod, Shall be cowed by the voice of *Hashem*;

32 And each time the appointed staff passes by, *Hashem* will bring down [His arm] upon him And will do battle with him as he waves it.

33 The Topheth has long been ready for him; He too is destined for Melech – His firepit has been made both wide and deep, With plenty of fire and firewood, And with the breath of *Hashem* Burning in it like a stream of sulfur.

31

1 Ha! Those who go down to Egypt for help And rely upon horses! They have put their trust in abundance of chariots, In vast numbers of riders, And they have not turned to the Holy One of *Yisrael*, They have not sought *Hashem*.

2 But He too is wise! He has brought on misfortune, And has not canceled His word. So He shall rise against the house of evildoers, And the allies of the workers of iniquity.

3 For the Egyptians are man, not *Hashem*, And their horses are flesh, not spirit; And when *Hashem* stretches out His arm, The helper shall trip And the helped one shall fall, And both shall perish together.

4 For thus *Hashem* has said to me: As a lion – a great beast – Growls over its prey And, when the shepherds gather In force against him, Is not dismayed by their cries Nor cowed by their noise – So the Lord of Hosts will descend to make war Against the mount and the hill of *Tzion*.

5 Like the birds that fly, even so will the Lord of Hosts shield *Yerushalayim*, shielding and saving, protecting and rescuing.

6 Return, O children of *Yisrael*, to Him to whom they have been so shamefully false;

7 for in that day everyone will reject his idols of silver and idols of gold, which your hands have made for your guilt.

8 Then Assyria shall fall, Not by the sword of man; A sword not of humans shall devour him. He shall shrivel before the sword, And his young men pine away.

Yeshayahu/Isaiah
Chapter 32

ישעיהו
פרק לב

9 His rock shall melt with terror, And his officers shall collapse from weakness – Declares *Hashem*, who has a fire in *Tzion*, Who has an oven in *Yerushalayim*.

וְסַלְעוֹ מִמָּגוֹר יַעֲבוֹר וְחַתּוּ מִנֵּס שָׂרָיו נְאֻם־יְהוָה אֲשֶׁר־אוּר לוֹ בְּצִיּוֹן וְתַנּוּר לוֹ בִּירוּשָׁלָ͏ִם:

v'-sal-O mi-ma-GOR ya-a-VOR v'-kha-TU mi-NAYS sa-RAV n'-um a-do-NAI a-sher UR LO b'-tzi-YON v'-ta-NUR LO bee-ru-sha-LA-im

32

1 Behold, a king shall reign in righteousness, And ministers shall govern with justice;

הֵן לְצֶדֶק יִמְלָךְ־מֶלֶךְ וּלְשָׂרִים לְמִשְׁפָּט יָשֹׂרוּ:

2 Every one of them shall be Like a refuge from gales, A shelter from rainstorms; Like brooks of water in a desert, Like the shade of a massive rock In a languishing land.

וְהָיָה־אִישׁ כְּמַחֲבֵא־רוּחַ וְסֵתֶר זָרֶם כְּפַלְגֵי־מַיִם בְּצָיוֹן כְּצֵל סֶלַע־כָּבֵד בְּאֶרֶץ עֲיֵפָה:

3 Then the eyes of those who have sight shall not be sealed, And the ears of those who have hearing shall listen;

וְלֹא תִשְׁעֶינָה עֵינֵי רֹאִים וְאָזְנֵי שֹׁמְעִים תִּקְשַׁבְנָה:

4 And the minds of the thoughtless shall attend and note, And the tongues of mumblers shall speak with fluent eloquence.

וּלְבַב נִמְהָרִים יָבִין לָדָעַת וּלְשׁוֹן עִלְּגִים תְּמַהֵר לְדַבֵּר צָחוֹת:

5 No more shall a villain be called noble, Nor shall "gentleman" be said of a knave.

לֹא־יִקָּרֵא עוֹד לְנָבָל נָדִיב וּלְכִילַי לֹא יֵאָמֵר שׁוֹעַ:

6 For the villain speaks villainy And plots treachery; To act impiously And to preach disloyalty against *Hashem*; To leave the hungry unsatisfied And deprive the thirsty of drink.

כִּי נָבָל נְבָלָה יְדַבֵּר וְלִבּוֹ יַעֲשֶׂה־אָוֶן לַעֲשׂוֹת חֹנֶף וּלְדַבֵּר אֶל־יְהוָה תּוֹעָה לְהָרִיק נֶפֶשׁ רָעֵב וּמַשְׁקֶה צָמֵא יַחְסִיר:

7 As for the knave, his tools are knavish. He forges plots To destroy the poor with falsehoods And the needy when they plead their cause.

וְכֵלַי כֵּלָיו רָעִים הוּא זִמּוֹת יָעָץ לְחַבֵּל ענוים [עֲנִיִּים] בְּאִמְרֵי־שֶׁקֶר וּבְדַבֵּר אֶבְיוֹן מִשְׁפָּט:

8 But the noble has noble intentions And is constant in noble acts.

וְנָדִיב נְדִיבוֹת יָעָץ וְהוּא עַל־נְדִיבוֹת יָקוּם:

9 You carefree women, Attend, hear my words! You confident ladies, Give ear to my speech!

נָשִׁים שַׁאֲנַנּוֹת קֹמְנָה שְׁמַעְנָה קוֹלִי בָּנוֹת בֹּטְחוֹת הַאְזֵנָּה אִמְרָתִי:

10 In little more than a year, You shall be troubled, O confident ones, When the vintage is over And no ingathering takes place.

יָמִים עַל־שָׁנָה תִּרְגַּזְנָה בֹּטְחוֹת כִּי כָּלָה בָצִיר אֹסֶף בְּלִי יָבוֹא:

31:9 Who has a fire in *Tzion*, who has an oven in *Yerushalayim* In Hebrew, the word *shuv* (שוב) means both 'repent,' and 'return.' *Yeshayahu* begs the people to repent and return to *Hashem*. If they do so, he promises, Assyria will fall before God, whom the prophet describes as both a 'fire,' in Hebrew *ur* (אור), and an 'oven,' *tanur* (תנור). While both metaphors involve fire, there is an importance difference between a fire and an oven. The metaphor of fire describes *Hashem* burning and destroying the Assyrian enemy. But in the metaphor of the oven, the same fire is a source of heat and comfort, thus reminding us that our actions determine whether *Hashem* relates to us as fire of destruction or a helpful oven.

אור
תנור

Yeshayahu/Isaiah
Chapter 33

11 Tremble, you carefree ones! Quake, O confident ones! Strip yourselves naked, Put the cloth about your loins!

יא חִרְדוּ שַׁאֲנַנּוֹת רְגָזָה בֹּטְחוֹת פְּשֹׁטָה וְעֹרָה וַחֲגוֹרָה עַל־חֲלָצָיִם׃

12 Lament upon the breasts, For the pleasant fields, For the spreading grapevines,

יב עַל־שָׁדַיִם סֹפְדִים עַל־שְׂדֵי־חֶמֶד עַל־גֶּפֶן פֹּרִיָּה׃

13 For my people's soil – It shall be overgrown with briers and thistles – Aye, and for all the houses of delight, For the city of mirth.

יג עַל אַדְמַת עַמִּי קוֹץ שָׁמִיר תַּעֲלֶה כִּי עַל־כָּל־בָּתֵּי מָשׂוֹשׂ קִרְיָה עַלִּיזָה׃

14 For the castle shall be abandoned, The noisy city forsaken; Citadel and tower shall become Bare places forever, A stamping ground for wild asses, A pasture for flocks –

יד כִּי־אַרְמוֹן נֻטָּשׁ הֲמוֹן עִיר עֻזָּב עֹפֶל וָבַחַן הָיָה בְעַד מְעָרוֹת עַד־עוֹלָם מְשׂוֹשׂ פְּרָאִים מִרְעֵה עֲדָרִים׃

15 Till a spirit from on high is poured out on us, And wilderness is transformed into farm land, While farm land rates as mere brush.

טו עַד־יֵעָרֶה עָלֵינוּ רוּחַ מִמָּרוֹם וְהָיָה מִדְבָּר לַכַּרְמֶל וכרמל [וְהַכַּרְמֶל] לַיַּעַר יֵחָשֵׁב׃

16 Then justice shall abide in the wilderness And righteousness shall dwell on the farm land.

טז וְשָׁכַן בַּמִּדְבָּר מִשְׁפָּט וּצְדָקָה בַּכַּרְמֶל תֵּשֵׁב׃

17 For the work of righteousness shall be peace, And the effect of righteousness, calm and confidence forever.

יז וְהָיָה מַעֲשֵׂה הַצְּדָקָה שָׁלוֹם וַעֲבֹדַת הַצְּדָקָה הַשְׁקֵט וָבֶטַח עַד־עוֹלָם׃

18 Then my people shall dwell in peaceful homes, In secure dwellings, In untroubled places of rest.

יח וְיָשַׁב עַמִּי בִּנְוֵה שָׁלוֹם וּבְמִשְׁכְּנוֹת מִבְטַחִים וּבִמְנוּחֹת שַׁאֲנַנּוֹת׃

v'-ya-SHAV a-MEE bin-VAY sha-LOM uv-mish-k'-NOT miv-ta-KHEEM u-vim-nu-KHOT sha-a-na-NOT

19 And the brush shall sink and vanish, Even as the city is laid low.

יט וּבָרַד בְּרֶדֶת הַיָּעַר וּבַשִּׁפְלָה תִּשְׁפַּל הָעִיר׃

20 Happy shall you be who sow by all waters, Who send out cattle and asses to pasture.

כ אַשְׁרֵיכֶם זֹרְעֵי עַל־כָּל־מָיִם מְשַׁלְּחֵי רֶגֶל־הַשּׁוֹר וְהַחֲמוֹר׃

33

1 Ha, you ravager who are not ravaged, You betrayer who have not been betrayed! When you have done ravaging, you shall be ravaged; When you have finished betraying, you shall be betrayed.

לג א הוֹי שׁוֹדֵד וְאַתָּה לֹא שָׁדוּד וּבוֹגֵד וְלֹא־בָגְדוּ בוֹ כַּהֲתִמְךָ שׁוֹדֵד תּוּשַּׁד כַּנְּלֹתְךָ לִבְגֹּד יִבְגְּדוּ־בָךְ׃

Rambam (1135–1204)

32:18 Then my people shall dwell in peaceful homes The ultimate hope that *Yeshayahu* holds for his people is that they can dwell calmly in the Land of Israel. His supplications are the prayers of all the prophets. For example, *Hoshea* writes, "In that day I will make a covenant for them with the beasts of the field; the birds of the air and the creeping things of the ground; I will also banish bow, sword and war from the land. Thus I will let them lie down in safety" (2:20). Rambam similarly concludes the *Mishneh Torah*, his monumental work summarizing Jewish law, with the declaration that the reason the Jewish people want the *Mashiach* to come is not because they want to rule over other nations, but rather out of desire to dwell in quiet and peace in their land so they can pursue righteousness. This remains the hope and dream of the Jewish people today: that the *Mashiach* will come quickly and bring peace to the entire world.

Yeshayahu/Isaiah
Chapter 33

ישעיהו
פרק לג

2 *Hashem*, be gracious to us! It is to You we have looked; Be their arm every morning, Also our deliverance in time of stress.

ב יְהֹוָה חָנֵּנוּ לְךָ קִוִּינוּ הֱיֵה זְרֹעָם לַבְּקָרִים אַף־יְשׁוּעָתֵנוּ בְּעֵת צָרָה׃

3 At [Your] roaring, peoples have fled, Before Your majesty nations have scattered;

ג מִקּוֹל הָמוֹן נָדְדוּ עַמִּים מֵרוֹמְמֻתֶךָ נָפְצוּ גּוֹיִם׃

4 And spoil was gathered as locusts are gathered, It was amassed as grasshoppers are amassed.

ד וְאֻסַּף שְׁלַלְכֶם אֹסֶף הֶחָסִיל כְּמַשַּׁק גֵּבִים שׁוֹקֵק בּוֹ׃

5 *Hashem* is exalted, He dwells on high! [Of old] He filled *Tzion* With justice and righteousness.

ה נִשְׂגָּב יְהֹוָה כִּי שֹׁכֵן מָרוֹם מִלֵּא צִיּוֹן מִשְׁפָּט וּצְדָקָה׃

nis-GAV a-do-NAI KEE sho-KHAYN ma-ROM mi-LAY tzi-YON mish-PAT utz-da-KAH

6 Faithfulness to Your charge was [her] wealth, Wisdom and devotion [her] triumph, Reverence for *Hashem* – that was her treasure.

ו וְהָיָה אֱמוּנַת עִתֶּיךָ חֹסֶן יְשׁוּעֹת חָכְמַת וָדָעַת יִרְאַת יְהֹוָה הִיא אוֹצָרוֹ׃

7 Hark! The Arielites cry aloud; Shalom's messengers weep bitterly.

ז הֵן אֶרְאֶלָּם צָעֲקוּ חֻצָה מַלְאֲכֵי שָׁלוֹם מַר יִבְכָּיוּן׃

8 Highways are desolate, Wayfarers have ceased. A covenant has been renounced, Cities rejected Mortal man despised.

ח נָשַׁמּוּ מְסִלּוֹת שָׁבַת עֹבֵר אֹרַח הֵפֵר בְּרִית מָאַס עָרִים לֹא חָשַׁב אֱנוֹשׁ׃

9 The land is wilted and withered; Lebanon disgraced and moldering, *Sharon* is become like a desert, And Bashan and *Carmel* are stripped bare.

ט אָבַל אֻמְלְלָה אָרֶץ הֶחְפִּיר לְבָנוֹן קָמַל הָיָה הַשָּׁרוֹן כָּעֲרָבָה וְנֹעֵר בָּשָׁן וְכַרְמֶל׃

10 "Now I will arise," says *Hashem*, "Now I will exalt Myself, now raise Myself high.

י עַתָּה אָקוּם יֹאמַר יְהֹוָה עַתָּה אֵרוֹמָם עַתָּה אֶנָּשֵׂא׃

11 You shall conceive hay, Give birth to straw; My breath will devour you like fire.

יא תַּהֲרוּ חֲשַׁשׁ תֵּלְדוּ קַשׁ רוּחֲכֶם אֵשׁ תֹּאכַלְכֶם׃

12 Peoples shall be burnings of lime, Thorns cut down that are set on fire.

יב וְהָיוּ עַמִּים מִשְׂרְפוֹת שִׂיד קוֹצִים כְּסוּחִים בָּאֵשׁ יִצַּתּוּ׃

13 Hear, you who are far, what I have done; You who are near, note My might."

יג שִׁמְעוּ רְחוֹקִים אֲשֶׁר עָשִׂיתִי וּדְעוּ קְרוֹבִים גְּבֻרָתִי׃

14 Sinners in *Tzion* are frightened, The godless are seized with trembling: "Who of us can dwell with the devouring fire: Who of us can dwell with the never-dying blaze?"

יד פָּחֲדוּ בְצִיּוֹן חַטָּאִים אָחֲזָה רְעָדָה חֲנֵפִים מִי יָגוּר לָנוּ אֵשׁ אוֹכֵלָה מִי־יָגוּר לָנוּ מוֹקְדֵי עוֹלָם׃

33:5 he filled *tzion* with justice and righteousness the last word of this verse is *tzedaka* (צדקה). in hebrew, this word is used to mean both 'charity' and 'justice.' while in english these concepts are very different, the hebrew word teaches that the act of giving to those who are less fortunate is not to be seen primarily as benevolence or kindness. rather, it is an act of justice and righteousness, which fulfills a duty expected of everyone, both rich and poor.

צדקה

Yeshayahu/Isaiah
Chapter 34

ישעיהו
פרק לד

15 He who walks in righteousness, Speaks uprightly, Spurns profit from fraudulent dealings, Waves away a bribe instead of grasping it, Stops his ears against listening to infamy, Shuts his eyes against looking at evil –

טו הֹלֵךְ צְדָקוֹת וְדֹבֵר מֵישָׁרִים מֹאֵס בְּבֶצַע מַעֲשַׁקּוֹת נֹעֵר כַּפָּיו מִתְּמֹךְ בַּשֹּׁחַד אֹטֵם אָזְנוֹ מִשְּׁמֹעַ דָּמִים וְעֹצֵם עֵינָיו מֵרְאוֹת בְּרָע:

16 Such a one shall dwell in lofty security, With inaccessible cliffs for his stronghold, With his food supplied And his drink assured.

טז הוּא מְרוֹמִים יִשְׁכֹּן מְצָדוֹת סְלָעִים מִשְׂגַּבּוֹ לַחְמוֹ נִתָּן מֵימָיו נֶאֱמָנִים:

17 When your eyes behold a king in his beauty, When they contemplate the land round about,

יז מֶלֶךְ בְּיָפְיוֹ תֶּחֱזֶינָה עֵינֶיךָ תִּרְאֶינָה אֶרֶץ מַרְחַקִּים:

18 Your throat shall murmur in awe, "Where is one who could count? Where is one who could weigh? Where is one who could count [all these] towers?"

יח לִבְּךָ יֶהְגֶּה אֵימָה אַיֵּה סֹפֵר אַיֵּה שֹׁקֵל אַיֵּה סֹפֵר אֶת־הַמִּגְדָּלִים:

19 No more shall you see the barbarian folk, The people of speech too obscure to comprehend, So stammering of tongue that they are not understood.

יט אֶת־עַם נוֹעָז לֹא תִרְאֶה עַם עִמְקֵי שָׂפָה מִשְּׁמוֹעַ נִלְעַג לָשׁוֹן אֵין בִּינָה:

20 When you gaze upon *Tzion*, our city of assembly, Your eyes shall behold *Yerushalayim* As a secure homestead, A tent not to be transported, Whose pegs shall never be pulled up, And none of whose ropes shall break.

כ חֲזֵה צִיּוֹן קִרְיַת מוֹעֲדֵנוּ עֵינֶיךָ תִרְאֶינָה יְרוּשָׁלַ͏ִם נָוֶה שַׁאֲנָן אֹהֶל בַּל־יִצְעָן בַּל־יִסַּע יְתֵדֹתָיו לָנֶצַח וְכָל־חֲבָלָיו בַּל־יִנָּתֵקוּ:

21 For there *Hashem* in His greatness shall be for us Like a region of rivers, of broad streams, Where no floating vessels can sail And no mighty craft can travel – Their ropes are slack, They cannot steady the sockets of their masts, They cannot spread a sail.*

כא כִּי אִם־שָׁם אַדִּיר יְהֹוָה לָנוּ מְקוֹם־נְהָרִים יְאֹרִים רַחֲבֵי יָדָיִם בַּל־תֵּלֶךְ בּוֹ אֳנִי־שַׁיִט וְצִי אַדִּיר לֹא יַעַבְרֶנּוּ:

22 For *Hashem* shall be our ruler, *Hashem* shall be our prince, *Hashem* shall be our king: He shall deliver us.

כב כִּי יְהֹוָה שֹׁפְטֵנוּ יְהֹוָה מְחֹקְקֵנוּ יְהֹוָה מַלְכֵּנוּ הוּא יוֹשִׁיעֵנוּ:

23 Then shall indeed much spoil be divided, Even the lame shall seize booty.

כג נִטְּשׁוּ חֲבָלָיִךְ בַּל־יְחַזְּקוּ כֵן־תָּרְנָם בַּל־פָּרְשׂוּ נֵס אָז חֻלַּק עַד־שָׁלָל מַרְבֶּה פִּסְחִים בָּזְזוּ בַז:

24 And none who lives there shall say, "I am sick"; It shall be inhabited by folk whose sin has been forgiven.

כד וּבַל־יֹאמַר שָׁכֵן חָלִיתִי הָעָם הַיֹּשֵׁב בָּהּ נְשֻׂא עָוֺן:

34 1 Approach, O nations, and listen, Give heed, O peoples! Let the earth and those in it hear; The world, and what it brings forth.

לד א קִרְבוּ גוֹיִם לִשְׁמֹעַ וּלְאֻמִּים הַקְשִׁיבוּ תִּשְׁמַע הָאָרֶץ וּמְלֹאָהּ תֵּבֵל וְכָל־צֶאֱצָאֶיהָ:

2 For *Hashem* is angry at all the nations, Furious at all their host; He has doomed them, consigned them to slaughter.

ב כִּי קֶצֶף לַיהֹוָה עַל־כָּל־הַגּוֹיִם וְחֵמָה עַל־כָּל־צְבָאָם הֶחֱרִימָם נְתָנָם לַטָּבַח:

---

* "Their ropes are slack, They cannot steady the sockets of their masts, They cannot spread a sail" brought up from verse 23 for clarity

Yeshayahu/Isaiah
Chapter 34

3 Their slain shall be left lying, And the stench of their corpses shall mount; And the hills shall be drenched with their blood,

4 All the host of heaven shall molder. The heavens shall be rolled up like a scroll, And all their host shall wither Like a leaf withering on the vine, Or shriveled fruit on a fig tree.

5 For My sword shall be drunk in the sky; Lo, it shall come down upon Edom, Upon the people I have doomed, To wreak judgment.

6 *Hashem* has a sword; it is sated with blood, It is gorged with fat – The blood of lambs and he-goats, The kidney fat of rams. For *Hashem* holds a sacrifice in Bozrah, A great slaughter in the land of Edom.

7 Wild oxen shall fall with them, Young bulls with mighty steers; And their land shall be drunk with blood, Their soil shall be saturated with fat.

8 For it is *Hashem*'s day of retribution, The year of vindication for *Tzion*'s cause.

9 Its streams shall be turned to pitch And its soil to sulfur. Its land shall become burning pitch,

10 Night and day it shall never go out; Its smoke shall rise for all time. Through the ages it shall lie in ruins; Through the aeons none shall traverse it.

11 Jackdaws and owls shall possess it; Great owls and ravens shall dwell there. He shall measure it with a line of chaos And with weights of emptiness.

12 It shall be called, "No kingdom is there," Its nobles and all its lords shall be nothing.

13 Thorns shall grow up in its palaces, Nettles and briers in its strongholds. It shall be a home of jackals, An abode of ostriches.

14 Wildcats shall meet hyenas, Goat-demons shall greet each other; There too the lilith shall repose And find herself a resting place.

15 There the arrow-snake shall nest and lay eggs, And shall brood and hatch in its shade. There too the buzzards shall gather With one another.

ישעיהו
פרק לד

ג וְחַלְלֵיהֶם יֻשְׁלָכוּ וּפִגְרֵיהֶם יַעֲלֶה בׇאְשָׁם וְנָמַסּוּ הָרִים מִדָּמָם:

ד וְנָמַקּוּ כׇּל־צְבָא הַשָּׁמַיִם וְנָגֹלּוּ כַסֵּפֶר הַשָּׁמָיִם וְכׇל־צְבָאָם יִבּוֹל כִּנְבֹל עָלֶה מִגֶּפֶן וּכְנֹבֶלֶת מִתְּאֵנָה:

ה כִּי־רִוְּתָה בַשָּׁמַיִם חַרְבִּי הִנֵּה עַל־אֱדוֹם תֵּרֵד וְעַל־עַם חֶרְמִי לְמִשְׁפָּט:

ו חֶרֶב לַיהֹוָה מָלְאָה דָם הֻדַּשְׁנָה מֵחֵלֶב מִדַּם כָּרִים וְעַתּוּדִים מֵחֵלֶב כִּלְיוֹת אֵילִים כִּי זֶבַח לַיהֹוָה בְּבׇצְרָה וְטֶבַח גָּדוֹל בְּאֶרֶץ אֱדוֹם:

ז וְיָרְדוּ רְאֵמִים עִמָּם וּפָרִים עִם־אַבִּירִים וְרִוְּתָה אַרְצָם מִדָּם וַעֲפָרָם מֵחֵלֶב יְדֻשָּׁן:

ח כִּי יוֹם נָקָם לַיהֹוָה שְׁנַת שִׁלּוּמִים לְרִיב צִיּוֹן:

ט וְנֶהֶפְכוּ נְחָלֶיהָ לְזֶפֶת וַעֲפָרָהּ לְגׇפְרִית וְהָיְתָה אַרְצָהּ לְזֶפֶת בֹּעֵרָה:

י לַיְלָה וְיוֹמָם לֹא תִכְבֶּה לְעוֹלָם יַעֲלֶה עֲשָׁנָהּ מִדּוֹר לָדוֹר תֶּחֱרָב לְנֵצַח נְצָחִים אֵין עֹבֵר בָּהּ:

יא וִירֵשׁוּהָ קָאַת וְקִפּוֹד וְיַנְשׁוֹף וְעֹרֵב יִשְׁכְּנוּ־בָהּ וְנָטָה עָלֶיהָ קַו־תֹהוּ וְאַבְנֵי־בֹהוּ:

יב חֹרֶיהָ וְאֵין־שָׁם מְלוּכָה יִקְרָאוּ וְכׇל־שָׂרֶיהָ יִהְיוּ אָפֶס:

יג וְעָלְתָה אַרְמְנֹתֶיהָ סִירִים קִמּוֹשׂ וָחוֹחַ בְּמִבְצָרֶיהָ וְהָיְתָה נְוֵה תַנִּים חָצִיר לִבְנוֹת יַעֲנָה:

יד וּפָגְשׁוּ צִיִּים אֶת־אִיִּים וְשָׂעִיר עַל־רֵעֵהוּ יִקְרָא אַךְ־שָׁם הִרְגִּיעָה לִּילִית וּמָצְאָה לָהּ מָנוֹחַ:

טו שָׁמָּה קִנְּנָה קִפּוֹז וַתְּמַלֵּט וּבָקְעָה וְדָגְרָה בְצִלָּהּ אַךְ־שָׁם נִקְבְּצוּ דַיּוֹת אִשָּׁה רְעוּתָהּ:

Yeshayahu/Isaiah
Chapter 35

ישעיהו
פרק לה

16 Search and read it in the scroll of *Hashem*: Not one of these shall be absent, Not one shall miss its fellow. For His mouth has spoken, It is His spirit that has assembled them,

טז דִּרְשׁוּ מֵעַל־סֵפֶר יְהֹוָה וּקְרָאוּ אַחַת מֵהֵנָּה לֹא נֶעְדָּרָה אִשָּׁה רְעוּתָהּ לֹא פָקָדוּ כִּי־פִי הוּא צִוָּה וְרוּחוֹ הוּא קִבְּצָן׃

dir-SHU may-al SAY-fer a-do-NAI uk-RA-u a-KHAT may-HAY-nah LO ne-DA-rah i-SHAH r'-u-TAH LO fa-KA-du kee FEE HU tzi-VAH v'-ru-KHO HU ki-b'-TZAN

17 And it is He who apportioned it to them by lot, Whose hand divided it for them with the line. They shall possess it for all time, They shall dwell there through the ages.

יז וְהוּא־הִפִּיל לָהֶן גּוֹרָל וְיָדוֹ חִלְּקַתָּה לָהֶם בַּקָּו עַד־עוֹלָם יִירָשׁוּהָ לְדוֹר וָדוֹר יִשְׁכְּנוּ־בָהּ׃

35 1 The arid desert shall be glad, The wilderness shall rejoice And shall blossom like a rose.

לה א יְשֻׂשׂוּם מִדְבָּר וְצִיָּה וְתָגֵל עֲרָבָה וְתִפְרַח כַּחֲבַצָּלֶת׃

2 It shall blossom abundantly, It shall also exult and shout. It shall receive the glory of Lebanon, The splendor of *Carmel* and *Sharon*. They shall behold the glory of *Hashem*, The splendor of our God.

ב פָּרֹחַ תִּפְרַח וְתָגֵל אַף גִּילַת וְרַנֵּן כְּבוֹד הַלְּבָנוֹן נִתַּן־לָהּ הֲדַר הַכַּרְמֶל וְהַשָּׁרוֹן הֵמָּה יִרְאוּ כְבוֹד־יְהֹוָה הֲדַר אֱלֹהֵינוּ׃

3 Strengthen the hands that are slack; Make firm the tottering knees!

ג חַזְּקוּ יָדַיִם רָפוֹת וּבִרְכַּיִם כֹּשְׁלוֹת אַמֵּצוּ׃

4 Say to the anxious of heart, "Be strong, fear not; Behold your God! Requital is coming, The recompense of *Hashem* – He Himself is coming to give you triumph."

ד אִמְרוּ לְנִמְהֲרֵי־לֵב חִזְקוּ אַל־תִּירָאוּ הִנֵּה אֱלֹהֵיכֶם נָקָם יָבוֹא גְּמוּל אֱלֹהִים הוּא יָבוֹא וְיֹשַׁעֲכֶם׃

5 Then the eyes of the blind shall be opened, And the ears of the deaf shall be unstopped.

ה אָז תִּפָּקַחְנָה עֵינֵי עִוְרִים וְאָזְנֵי חֵרְשִׁים תִּפָּתַחְנָה׃

6 Then the lame shall leap like a deer, And the tongue of the dumb shall shout aloud; For waters shall burst forth in the desert, Streams in the wilderness.

ו אָז יְדַלֵּג כָּאַיָּל פִּסֵּחַ וְתָרֹן לְשׁוֹן אִלֵּם כִּי־נִבְקְעוּ בַמִּדְבָּר מַיִם וּנְחָלִים בָּעֲרָבָה׃

7 Torrid earth shall become a pool; Parched land, fountains of water; The home of jackals, a pasture; The abode [of ostriches], reeds and rushes.

ז וְהָיָה הַשָּׁרָב לַאֲגַם וְצִמָּאוֹן לְמַבּוּעֵי מָיִם בִּנְוֵה תַנִּים רִבְצָהּ חָצִיר לְקָנֶה וָגֹמֶא׃

8 And a highway shall appear there, Which shall be called the Sacred Way. No one unclean shall pass along it, But it shall be for them. No traveler, not even fools, shall go astray.

ח וְהָיָה־שָׁם מַסְלוּל וָדֶרֶךְ וְדֶרֶךְ הַקֹּדֶשׁ יִקָּרֵא לָהּ לֹא־יַעַבְרֶנּוּ טָמֵא וְהוּא־לָמוֹ הֹלֵךְ דֶּרֶךְ וֶאֱוִילִים לֹא יִתְעוּ׃

Rashi (1040–1105)

34:16 Search and read it in the scroll of *Hashem* *Yeshayahu* states that a reading of "the scroll of *Hashem*" will reveal that none of the animals "shall be absent." *Rashi* suggests that this "scroll of *Hashem*" refers to *Sefer Bereishit*, which describes how every creature and its mate was gathered to *Noach* in the ark at the time of the flood. Since these animals heeded *Hashem*'s command to come to the ark, not one of them went missing. The message, then, is clear. If even animals are capable of obeying divine decrees and thereby rewarded with protection, then how much more so should humanity be willing to listen to *Hashem*'s word.

Yeshayahu/Isaiah
Chapter 36

ישעיהו
פרק לו

9 No lion shall be there, No ferocious beast shall set foot on it – These shall not be found there. But the redeemed shall walk it;

ט לֹא־יִהְיֶה שָׁם אַרְיֵה וּפְרִיץ חַיּוֹת בַּל־יַעֲלֶנָּה לֹא תִמָּצֵא שָׁם וְהָלְכוּ גְּאוּלִים:

10 And the ransomed of *Hashem* shall return, And come with shouting to *Tzion*, Crowned with joy everlasting. They shall attain joy and gladness, While sorrow and sighing flee.

י וּפְדוּיֵי יְהֹוָה יְשֻׁבוּן וּבָאוּ צִיּוֹן בְּרִנָּה וְשִׂמְחַת עוֹלָם עַל־רֹאשָׁם שָׂשׂוֹן וְשִׂמְחָה יַשִּׂיגוּ וְנָסוּ יָגוֹן וַאֲנָחָה:

uf-du-YAY a-do-NAI y'-shu-VUN u-VA-u tzi-YON b'-ri-NAH v'-sim-KHAT o-LAM al ro-SHAM sa-SON v'-sim-KHAH ya-SEE-gu v'-NA-su ya-GON va-a-na-KHAH

36 1 In the fourteenth year of King *Chizkiyahu*, King Sennacherib of Assyria marched against all the fortified towns of *Yehuda* and seized them.

לו א וַיְהִי בְּאַרְבַּע עֶשְׂרֵה שָׁנָה לַמֶּלֶךְ חִזְקִיָּהוּ עָלָה סַנְחֵרִיב מֶלֶךְ־אַשּׁוּר עַל כָּל־עָרֵי יְהוּדָה הַבְּצֻרוֹת וַיִּתְפְּשֵׂם:

2 From Lachish, the king of Assyria sent the Rabshakeh, with a large force, to King *Chizkiyahu* in *Yerushalayim*. [The Rabshakeh] took up a position near the conduit of the Upper Pool, by the road of the Fuller's Field;

ב וַיִּשְׁלַח מֶלֶךְ־אַשּׁוּר אֶת־רַב־שָׁקֵה מִלָּכִישׁ יְרוּשָׁלְַמָה אֶל־הַמֶּלֶךְ חִזְקִיָּהוּ בְּחֵיל כָּבֵד וַיַּעֲמֹד בִּתְעָלַת הַבְּרֵכָה הָעֶלְיוֹנָה בִּמְסִלַּת שְׂדֵה כוֹבֵס:

3 and Eliakim son of *Chilkiyahu* who was in charge of the palace, Shebna the scribe, and Joah son of *Asaf* the recorder went out to him.

ג וַיֵּצֵא אֵלָיו אֶלְיָקִים בֶּן־חִלְקִיָּהוּ אֲשֶׁר עַל־הַבָּיִת וְשֶׁבְנָא הַסֹּפֵר וְיוֹאָח בֶּן־אָסָף הַמַּזְכִּיר:

4 The Rabshakeh said to them, "You tell *Chizkiyahu*: Thus said the Great King, the king of Assyria: What makes you so confident?

ד וַיֹּאמֶר אֲלֵיהֶם רַב־שָׁקֵה אִמְרוּ־נָא אֶל־חִזְקִיָּהוּ כֹּה־אָמַר הַמֶּלֶךְ הַגָּדוֹל מֶלֶךְ אַשּׁוּר מָה הַבִּטָּחוֹן הַזֶּה אֲשֶׁר בָּטָחְתָּ:

5 I suppose mere talk makes counsel and valor for war! Look, on whom are you relying, that you have rebelled against me?

ה אָמַרְתִּי אַךְ־דְּבַר־שְׂפָתַיִם עֵצָה וּגְבוּרָה לַמִּלְחָמָה עַתָּה עַל־מִי בָטַחְתָּ כִּי מָרַדְתָּ בִּי:

6 You are relying on Egypt, that splintered reed of a staff, which enters and punctures the palm of anyone who leans on it. That's what Pharaoh king of Egypt is like to all who rely on him.

ו הִנֵּה בָטַחְתָּ עַל־מִשְׁעֶנֶת הַקָּנֶה הָרָצוּץ הַזֶּה עַל־מִצְרַיִם אֲשֶׁר יִסָּמֵךְ אִישׁ עָלָיו וּבָא בְכַפּוֹ וּנְקָבָהּ כֵּן פַּרְעֹה מֶלֶךְ־מִצְרַיִם לְכָל־הַבֹּטְחִים עָלָיו:

אושר
שמחה

35:10 Crowned with joy everlasting The Hebrew language includes many words used to describe various forms of happiness. According to former British Chief Rabbi Jonathan Sacks, the term *osher* (אושר) refers to a type of personal happiness that one experiences when engaging in an activity such as listening to music or observing something spectacular in nature. *Simcha* (שמחה), on the other hand, is a type of happiness that is created in the company of others, such as when celebrating a wedding or laughing as a family. In this verse, *Yeshayahu* promises that the ransomed of *Hashem* will return with 'everlasting joy,' *simchat olam* (שמחת עולם), upon their heads. The *simcha*, the shared joy of the redemption of the nation returning to *Hashem* and to the Holy Land, will last forever.

Rabbi Lord Jonathan Sacks (1948–2020)

1014

Yeshayahu/Isaiah
Chapter 36

7 And if you tell me that you are relying on *Hashem* your God, He is the very one whose shrines and altars *Chizkiyahu* did away with, telling *Yehuda* and *Yerushalayim*, 'You must worship only at this *Mizbayach*!'

> v'-khee to-MAR ay-LAI el a-do-NAI e-lo-HAY-nu ba-TAKH-nu ha-LO HU a-SHER hay-SEER khiz-ki-YA-hu et ba-mo-TAV v'-et miz-b'-kho-TAV va-YO-mer lee-hu-DAH v'-lee-ru-sha-LA-im lif-NAY ha-miz-BAY-akh ha-ZEH tish-ta-kha-VU

ז וְכִי־תֹאמַ֣ר אֵלַ֔י אֶל־יְהֹוָ֥ה אֱלֹהֵ֖ינוּ בָּטָ֑חְנוּ הֲלוֹא־ה֗וּא אֲשֶׁ֨ר הֵסִ֤יר חִזְקִיָּ֙הוּ֙ אֶת־בָּמֹתָ֣יו וְאֶת־מִזְבְּחֹתָ֔יו וַיֹּ֤אמֶר לִֽיהוּדָה֙ וְלִיר֣וּשָׁלַ֔͏ִם לִפְנֵ֛י הַמִּזְבֵּ֥חַ הַזֶּ֖ה תִּֽשְׁתַּחֲו֑וּ׃

8 Come now, make this wager with my master, the king of Assyria: I'll give you two thousand horses, if you can produce riders to mount them.

ח וְעַתָּה֙ הִתְעָ֣רֶב נָ֔א אֶת־אֲדֹנִ֖י הַמֶּ֣לֶךְ אַשּׁ֑וּר וְאֶתְּנָ֤ה לְךָ֙ אַלְפַּ֣יִם סוּסִ֔ים אִם־תּוּכַ֕ל לָ֥תֶת לְךָ֖ רֹכְבִ֥ים עֲלֵיהֶֽם׃

9 So how could you refuse anything, even to the deputy of one of my master's lesser servants, relying on Egypt for chariots and horsemen?

ט וְאֵ֣יךְ תָּשִׁ֗יב אֵ֠ת פְּנֵ֨י פַחַ֥ת אַחַ֛ד עַבְדֵ֥י אֲדֹנִ֖י הַקְּטַנִּ֑ים וַתִּבְטַ֤ח לְךָ֙ עַל־מִצְרַ֔יִם לְרֶ֖כֶב וּלְפָרָשִֽׁים׃

10 And do you think I have marched against this land to destroy it without *Hashem*? *Hashem* Himself told me: Go up against that land and destroy it."

י וְעַתָּה֙ הֲמִבַּלְעֲדֵ֣י יְהֹוָ֔ה עָלִ֛יתִי עַל־הָאָ֥רֶץ הַזֹּ֖את לְהַשְׁחִיתָ֑הּ יְהֹוָה֙ אָמַ֣ר אֵלַ֔י עֲלֵ֛ה אֶל־הָאָ֥רֶץ הַזֹּ֖את וְהַשְׁחִיתָֽהּ׃

11 *Eliakim*, *Shebna*, and *Joah* replied to the *Rabshakeh*, "Please, speak to your servants in Aramaic, since we understand it; do not speak to us in Judean in the hearing of the people on the wall."

יא וַיֹּ֣אמֶר אֶלְיָקִ֣ים וְשֶׁבְנָ֣א וְיוֹאָח֮ אֶל־רַב־שָׁקֵה֒ דַּבֶּר־נָ֤א אֶל־עֲבָדֶ֙יךָ֙ אֲרָמִ֔ית כִּ֥י שֹׁמְעִ֖ים אֲנָ֑חְנוּ וְאַל־תְּדַבֵּ֤ר אֵלֵ֙ינוּ֙ יְהוּדִ֔ית בְּאׇזְנֵ֣י הָעָ֔ם אֲשֶׁ֖ר עַל־הַחוֹמָֽה׃

12 But the *Rabshakeh* replied, "Was it to your master and to you that my master sent me to speak those words? It was precisely to the men who are sitting on the wall – who will have to eat their dung and drink their urine with you."

יב וַיֹּ֣אמֶר רַב־שָׁקֵ֗ה הַאֶ֨ל אֲדֹנֶ֤יךָ וְאֵלֶ֙יךָ֙ שְׁלָחַ֣נִי אֲדֹנִ֔י לְדַבֵּ֖ר אֶת־הַדְּבָרִ֣ים הָאֵ֑לֶּה הֲלֹ֣א עַל־הָאֲנָשִׁ֗ים הַיֹּֽשְׁבִים֙ עַל־הַ֣חוֹמָ֔ה לֶאֱכֹ֣ל אֶת־חראיהם [צוֹאָתָ֗ם] וְלִשְׁתּ֛וֹת אֶת־שֵׁינֵיהֶ֖ם [מֵֽימֵי] [רַגְלֵיהֶ֑ם] עִמָּכֶֽם׃

13 And the *Rabshakeh* stood and called out in a loud voice in Judean:

יג וַֽיַּעֲמֹד֙ רַב־שָׁקֵ֔ה וַיִּקְרָ֥א בְקוֹל־גָּד֖וֹל יְהוּדִ֑ית וַיֹּ֕אמֶר שִׁמְע֗וּ אֶת־דִּבְרֵ֛י הַמֶּ֥לֶךְ הַגָּד֖וֹל מֶ֥לֶךְ אַשּֽׁוּר׃

14 "Hear the words of the Great King, the king of Assyria! Thus said the king: Don't let *Chizkiyahu* deceive you, for he will not be able to save you.

יד כֹּ֚ה אָמַ֣ר הַמֶּ֔לֶךְ אַל־יַשִּׁ֥יא לָכֶ֖ם חִזְקִיָּ֑הוּ כִּ֥י לֹא־יוּכַ֖ל לְהַצִּ֥יל אֶתְכֶֽם׃

36:7 Whose shrines and altars *Chizkiyahu* did away with Chapters 36–39 describe the most important event of *Yeshayahu's* career – the Assyrian invasion of *Yehuda* and siege on *Yerushalayim* in 701 BCE. Chapter 36 describes how the Assyrian envoy *Rabshakeh* taunts the trust that *Chizkiyahu* and the people place in *Hashem*. He points to the seeming contradiction between their trust in God and *Chizkiyahu's* recent religious reforms, in which the king had removed the shrines and broken down the altars outside the *Beit Hamikdash*, at which the people had improperly worshipped *Hashem* for centuries. What he did not understand, though, is that God does not require a multitude of sacrifices to please Him. Instead, He desires a just and righteous society centered around the Temple.

Yeshayahu/Isaiah
Chapter 37

15 Don't let *Chizkiyahu* make you rely on *Hashem*, saying, '*Hashem* will surely save us; this city will not fall into the hands of Assyria!'

16 Don't listen to *Chizkiyahu*. For thus said the king of Assyria: Make your peace with me and come out to me, so that you may all eat from your vines and your fig trees and drink water from your cisterns,

17 until I come and take you away to a land like your own, a land of bread and wine, of grain [fields] and vineyards.

18 Beware of letting *Chizkiyahu* mislead you by saying, '*Hashem* will save us.' Did any of the gods of the other nations save his land from the king of Assyria?

19 Where were the gods of Hamath and Arpad? Where were the gods of Sepharvaim? And did they save *Shomron* from me?

20 Which among all the gods of those countries saved their countries from me, that *Hashem* should save *Yerushalayim* from me?"

21 But they were silent and did not answer him with a single word; for the king's order was: "Do not answer him."

22 And so Eliakim son of *Chilkiyahu* who was in charge of the palace, Shebna the scribe, and Joah son of *Asaf* the recorder came to *Chizkiyahu* with their clothes rent, and they reported to him what the Rabshakeh had said.

37 1 When King *Chizkiyahu* heard this, he rent his clothes and covered himself with sackcloth and went into the House of *Hashem*.

2 He also sent Eliakim, who was in charge of the palace, Shebna, the scribe, and the senior *Kohanim*, covered with sackcloth, to the *Navi Yeshayahu* son of *Amotz*.

3 They said to him, "Thus said *Chizkiyahu*: This day is a day of distress, of chastisement, and of disgrace. The babes have reached the birthstool, but the strength to give birth is lacking.

Yeshayahu/Isaiah
Chapter 37

4 Perhaps *Hashem* your God will take note of the words of the Rabshakeh, whom his master the king of Assyria has sent to blaspheme the living *Hashem*, and will mete out judgment for the words that *Hashem* your God has heard – if you will offer up prayer for the surviving remnant."

5 When King *Chizkiyahu*'s ministers came to *Yeshayahu*,

6 *Yeshayahu* said to them, "Tell your master as follows: Thus said *Hashem*: Do not be frightened by the words of blasphemy against Me that you have heard from the minions of the king of Assyria.

7 I will delude him: He will hear a rumor and return to his land, and I will make him fall by the sword in his land."

8 The Rabshakeh, meanwhile, heard that [the King] had left Lachish; he turned back and found the king of Assyria attacking Libnah.

9 But [the king of Assyria] learned that King Tirhakah of Nubia had come out to fight him; and when he heard it, he sent messengers to *Chizkiyahu*, saying,

10 "Tell this to King *Chizkiyahu* of *Yehuda*: Do not let your God, on whom you are relying, mislead you into thinking that *Yerushalayim* will not be delivered into the hands of the king of Assyria.

11 You yourself have heard what the kings of Assyria have done to all the lands, how they have annihilated them; and can you escape?

12 Were the nations that my predecessors destroyed – Gozan, Haran, Rezeph, and the Bethedenites in Telassar – saved by their gods?

13 Where is the king of Hamath? and the king of Arpad? and the kings of Lair, Sepharvaim, Hena, and Ivvah?"

14 *Chizkiyahu* received the letter from the messengers and read it. *Chizkiyahu* then went up to the House of *Hashem* and spread it out before *Hashem*.

15 And *Chizkiyahu* prayed to *Hashem*:

16 "O Lord of Hosts, enthroned on the *Keruvim*! You alone are God of all the kingdoms of the earth. You made the heavens and the earth.

ישעיהו
פרק לז

ד אוּלַ֡י יִשְׁמַע֩ יְהֹוָ֨ה אֱלֹהֶ֜יךָ אֵ֣ת ׀ דִּבְרֵ֣י רַב־שָׁקֵ֗ה אֲשֶׁר֩ שְׁלָח֨וֹ מֶֽלֶךְ־אַשּׁ֤וּר ׀ אֲדֹנָיו֙ לְחָרֵף֙ אֱלֹהִ֣ים חַ֔י וְהוֹכִ֙יחַ֙ בַּדְּבָרִ֔ים אֲשֶׁ֥ר שָׁמַ֖ע יְהֹוָ֣ה אֱלֹהֶ֑יךָ וְנָשָׂ֣אתָ תְפִלָּ֔ה בְּעַ֖ד הַשְּׁאֵרִ֥ית הַנִּמְצָאָֽה׃

ה וַיָּבֹ֗אוּ עַבְדֵ֛י הַמֶּ֥לֶךְ חִזְקִיָּ֖הוּ אֶל־יְשַֽׁעְיָֽהוּ׃

ו וַיֹּ֤אמֶר אֲלֵיהֶם֙ יְשַֽׁעְיָ֔הוּ כֹּ֥ה תֹאמְר֖וּן אֶל־אֲדֹנֵיכֶ֑ם כֹּ֣ה ׀ אָמַ֣ר יְהֹוָ֗ה אַל־תִּירָא֙ מִפְּנֵ֤י הַדְּבָרִים֙ אֲשֶׁ֣ר שָׁמַ֔עְתָּ אֲשֶׁ֧ר גִּדְּפ֛וּ נַעֲרֵ֥י מֶֽלֶךְ־אַשּׁ֖וּר אוֹתִֽי׃

ז הִנְנִ֨י נוֹתֵ֥ן בּוֹ֙ ר֔וּחַ וְשָׁמַ֥ע שְׁמוּעָ֖ה וְשָׁ֣ב אֶל־אַרְצ֑וֹ וְהִפַּלְתִּ֥יו בַּחֶ֖רֶב בְּאַרְצֽוֹ׃

ח וַיָּ֙שׇׁב֙ רַב־שָׁקֵ֔ה וַיִּמְצָא֙ אֶת־מֶ֣לֶךְ אַשּׁ֔וּר נִלְחָ֖ם עַל־לִבְנָ֑ה כִּ֣י שָׁמַ֔ע כִּ֥י נָסַ֖ע מִלָּכִֽישׁ׃

ט וַיִּשְׁמַ֗ע עַל־תִּרְהָ֤קָה מֶֽלֶךְ־כּוּשׁ֙ לֵאמֹ֔ר יָצָ֖א לְהִלָּחֵ֣ם אִתָּ֑ךְ וַיִּשְׁמַע֙ וַיִּשְׁלַ֣ח מַלְאָכִ֔ים אֶל־חִזְקִיָּ֖הוּ לֵאמֹֽר׃

י כֹּ֣ה תֹאמְר֗וּן אֶל־חִזְקִיָּ֤הוּ מֶֽלֶךְ־יְהוּדָה֙ לֵאמֹ֔ר אַל־יַשִּׁאֲךָ֣ אֱלֹהֶ֔יךָ אֲשֶׁ֥ר אַתָּ֛ה בּוֹטֵ֥חַ בּ֖וֹ לֵאמֹ֑ר לֹ֤א תִנָּתֵן֙ יְר֣וּשָׁלַ֔͏ִם בְּיַ֖ד מֶ֥לֶךְ אַשּֽׁוּר׃

יא הִנֵּ֣ה ׀ אַתָּ֣ה שָׁמַ֗עְתָּ אֲשֶׁ֨ר עָשׂ֜וּ מַלְכֵ֥י אַשּׁ֛וּר לְכׇל־הָאֲרָצ֖וֹת לְהַחֲרִימָ֑ם וְאַתָּ֖ה תִּנָּצֵֽל׃

יב הַהִצִּ֨ילוּ אוֹתָ֜ם אֱלֹהֵ֣י הַגּוֹיִ֗ם אֲשֶׁ֣ר הִשְׁחִ֣יתוּ אֲבוֹתַ֔י אֶת־גּוֹזָ֖ן וְאֶת־חָרָ֑ן וְרֶ֥צֶף וּבְנֵי־עֶ֖דֶן אֲשֶׁ֥ר בִּתְלַשָּֽׂר׃

יג אַיֵּ֤ה מֶֽלֶךְ־חֲמָת֙ וּמֶ֣לֶךְ אַרְפָּ֔ד וּמֶ֖לֶךְ לָעִ֣יר סְפַרְוָ֑יִם הֵנַ֖ע וְעִוָּֽה׃

יד וַיִּקַּ֨ח חִזְקִיָּ֧הוּ אֶת־הַסְּפָרִ֛ים מִיַּ֥ד הַמַּלְאָכִ֖ים וַיִּקְרָאֵ֑הוּ וַיַּ֙עַל֙ בֵּ֣ית יְהֹוָ֔ה וַיִּפְרְשֵׂ֥הוּ חִזְקִיָּ֖הוּ לִפְנֵ֥י יְהֹוָֽה׃

טו וַיִּתְפַּלֵּ֙ל חִזְקִיָּ֧הוּ אֶל־יְהֹוָ֖ה לֵאמֹֽר׃

טז יְהֹוָ֨ה צְבָא֜וֹת אֱלֹהֵ֤י יִשְׂרָאֵל֙ יֹשֵׁ֣ב הַכְּרֻבִ֔ים אַתָּה־ה֤וּא הָֽאֱלֹהִים֙ לְבַדְּךָ֔ לְכֹ֖ל מַמְלְכ֣וֹת הָאָ֑רֶץ אַתָּ֣ה עָשִׂ֔יתָ אֶת־הַשָּׁמַ֖יִם וְאֶת־הָאָֽרֶץ׃

Yeshayahu/Isaiah
Chapter 37

17 *Hashem*, incline Your ear and hear, open Your eye and see. Hear all the words that Sennacherib has sent to blaspheme the living *Hashem*!

18 True, *Hashem*, the kings of Assyria have annihilated all the nations and their lands

19 and have committed their gods to the flames and have destroyed them; for they are not gods, but man's handwork of wood and stone.

20 But now, *Hashem* our God, deliver us from his hands, and let all the kingdoms of the earth know that You, *Hashem*, alone [are *Hashem*]."

v'-a-TAH a-do-NAI e-lo-HAY-nu ho-shee-AY-nu mi-ya-DO v'-yay-d'-U kol mam-l'-KHOT ha-A-retz kee a-TAH a-do-NAI l'-va-DE-kha

21 Then *Yeshayahu* son of *Amotz* sent this message to *Chizkiyahu*: "Thus said *Hashem*, the God of *Yisrael*, to whom you have prayed, concerning King Sennacherib of Assyria

22 this is the word that *Hashem* has spoken concerning him: Fair Maiden *Tzion* despises you, She mocks at you; Fair *Yerushalayim* shakes Her head at you.

23 Whom have you blasphemed and reviled? Against whom made loud your voice And haughtily raised your eyes? Against the Holy One of *Yisrael*!

24 Through your servants you have blasphemed my Lord. Because you thought, 'Thanks to my vast chariotry, It is I who have climbed the highest mountains, To the remotest parts of the Lebanon, And have cut down its loftiest cedars, Its choicest cypresses, And have reached its highest peak, Its densest forest.

ישעיהו
פרק לז

יז הַטֵּה יְהוָה אָזְנְךָ וּשְׁמָע פְּקַח יְהוָה עֵינֶךָ וּרְאֵה וּשְׁמַע אֵת כָּל־דִּבְרֵי סַנְחֵרִיב אֲשֶׁר שָׁלַח לְחָרֵף אֱלֹהִים חָי׃

יח אָמְנָם יְהוָה הֶחֱרִיבוּ מַלְכֵי אַשּׁוּר אֶת־כָּל־הָאֲרָצוֹת וְאֶת־אַרְצָם׃

יט וְנָתֹן אֶת־אֱלֹהֵיהֶם בָּאֵשׁ כִּי לֹא אֱלֹהִים הֵמָּה כִּי אִם־מַעֲשֵׂה יְדֵי־אָדָם עֵץ וָאֶבֶן וַיְאַבְּדוּם׃

כ וְעַתָּה יְהוָה אֱלֹהֵינוּ הוֹשִׁיעֵנוּ מִיָּדוֹ וְיֵדְעוּ כָּל־מַמְלְכוֹת הָאָרֶץ כִּי־אַתָּה יְהוָה לְבַדֶּךָ׃

כא וַיִּשְׁלַח יְשַׁעְיָהוּ בֶן־אָמוֹץ אֶל־חִזְקִיָּהוּ לֵאמֹר כֹּה־אָמַר יְהוָה אֱלֹהֵי יִשְׂרָאֵל אֲשֶׁר הִתְפַּלַּלְתָּ אֵלַי אֶל־סַנְחֵרִיב מֶלֶךְ אַשּׁוּר׃

כב זֶה הַדָּבָר אֲשֶׁר־דִּבֶּר יְהוָה עָלָיו בָּזָה לְךָ לָעֲגָה לְךָ בְּתוּלַת בַּת־צִיּוֹן אַחֲרֶיךָ רֹאשׁ הֵנִיעָה בַּת יְרוּשָׁלָ͏ִם׃

כג אֶת־מִי חֵרַפְתָּ וְגִדַּפְתָּ וְעַל־מִי הֲרִימוֹתָה קּוֹל וַתִּשָּׂא מָרוֹם עֵינֶיךָ אֶל־קְדוֹשׁ יִשְׂרָאֵל׃

כד בְּיַד עֲבָדֶיךָ חֵרַפְתָּ ׀ אֲדֹנָי וַתֹּאמֶר בְּרֹב רִכְבִּי אֲנִי עָלִיתִי מְרוֹם הָרִים יַרְכְּתֵי לְבָנוֹן וְאֶכְרֹת קוֹמַת אֲרָזָיו מִבְחַר בְּרֹשָׁיו וְאָבוֹא מְרוֹם קִצּוֹ יַעַר כַּרְמִלּוֹ׃

37:20 Let all the kingdoms of the earth know that You, *Hashem*, alone [are *Hashem*] In his prayer at *Yerushalayim*'s most dire hour, *Chizkiyahu* reveals himself to be a true *eved Hashem* (עבד השם), 'servant of God.' He prays not for the sake of his own honor, nor even for his country or his people, whose fate is bound up with his own, but for *Hashem*'s glory in front of the world at large. This is similar to *Moshe*'s song, sung after the Jews crossed the Sea of Reeds, joyfully declaring, "The peoples hear, they tremble; agony grips the dwellers in Philistia. Now are the clans of Edom dismayed; the tribes of Moab – trembling grips them…*Hashem* will reign for ever and ever!" (Exodus 15:14–15, 18). *David* expressed this best – "May they know that Your name, Yours alone, is *Hashem*, supreme over all the earth" (Psalm 83:19). A true servant of God and leader of Israel recognizes that his ultimate purpose in this world is to spread knowledge of *Hashem* and His glory throughout the world.

Yeshayahu/Isaiah

Chapter 37

ישעיהו

פרק לז

25 It is I who have drawn And drunk water. I have dried up with the soles of my feet All the streams of Egypt.'

כה אֲנִי קַרְתִּי וְשָׁתִיתִי מָיִם וְאַחְרִב בְּכַף־פְּעָמַי כֹּל יְאֹרֵי מָצוֹר׃

26 Have you not heard? Of old I planned that very thing, I designed it long ago, And now have fulfilled it. And it has come to pass, Laying fortified towns waste in desolate heaps.

כו הֲלוֹא־שָׁמַעְתָּ לְמֵרָחוֹק אוֹתָהּ עָשִׂיתִי מִימֵי קֶדֶם וִיצַרְתִּיהָ עַתָּה הֲבֵאתִיהָ וּתְהִי לְהַשְׁאוֹת גַּלִּים נִצִּים עָרִים בְּצֻרוֹת׃

27 Their inhabitants are helpless, Dismayed and shamed. They were but grass of the field And green herbage, Grass of the roofs that is blasted Before the east wind.

כז וְיֹשְׁבֵיהֶן קִצְרֵי־יָד חַתּוּ וָבֹשׁוּ הָיוּ עֵשֶׂב שָׂדֶה וִירַק דֶּשֶׁא חֲצִיר גַּגּוֹת וּשְׁדֵמָה לִפְנֵי קָמָה׃

28 I know your stayings And your goings and comings, And how you have raged against Me,

כח וְשִׁבְתְּךָ וְצֵאתְךָ וּבוֹאֲךָ יָדָעְתִּי וְאֵת הִתְרַגֶּזְךָ אֵלָי׃

29 Because you have raged against Me, And your tumult has reached My ears, I will place My hook in your nose And My bit between your jaws; And I will make you go back by the road By which you came.

כט יַעַן הִתְרַגֶּזְךָ אֵלַי וְשַׁאֲנַנְךָ עָלָה בְאָזְנָי וְשַׂמְתִּי חַחִי בְּאַפֶּךָ וּמִתְגִּי בִּשְׂפָתֶיךָ וַהֲשִׁיבֹתִיךָ בַּדֶּרֶךְ אֲשֶׁר־בָּאתָ בָּהּ׃

30 "And this is the sign for you: This year you eat what grows of itself, and the next year what springs from that, and in the third year sow and reap and plant vineyards and eat their fruit.

ל וְזֶה־לְּךָ הָאוֹת אָכוֹל הַשָּׁנָה סָפִיחַ וּבַשָּׁנָה הַשֵּׁנִית שָׁחִיס וּבַשָּׁנָה הַשְּׁלִישִׁית זִרְעוּ וְקִצְרוּ וְנִטְעוּ כְרָמִים וְאִכוֹל [וְאִכְלוּ] פִרְיָם׃

31 And the survivors of the House of *Yehuda* that have escaped shall renew its trunk below and produce boughs above.

לא וְיָסְפָה פְּלֵיטַת בֵּית־יְהוּדָה הַנִּשְׁאָרָה שֹׁרֶשׁ לְמָטָּה וְעָשָׂה פְרִי לְמָעְלָה׃

32 For a remnant shall come forth from *Yerushalayim*, Survivors from Mount *Tzion*. The zeal of the Lord of Hosts Shall bring this to pass.

לב כִּי מִירוּשָׁלַםִ תֵּצֵא שְׁאֵרִית וּפְלֵיטָה מֵהַר צִיּוֹן קִנְאַת יְהוָה צְבָאוֹת תַּעֲשֶׂה־זֹּאת׃

33 "Assuredly, thus said *Hashem* concerning the king of Assyria: He shall not enter this city; He shall not shoot an arrow at it, Or advance upon it with a shield, Or pile up a siegemound against it.

לג לָכֵן כֹּה־אָמַר יְהוָה אֶל־מֶלֶךְ אַשּׁוּר לֹא יָבוֹא אֶל־הָעִיר הַזֹּאת וְלֹא־יוֹרֶה שָׁם חֵץ וְלֹא־יְקַדְּמֶנָּה מָגֵן וְלֹא־יִשְׁפֹּךְ עָלֶיהָ סֹלְלָה׃

34 He shall go back By the way he came, He shall not enter this city – declares *Hashem*;

לד בַּדֶּרֶךְ אֲשֶׁר־בָּא בָּהּ יָשׁוּב וְאֶל־הָעִיר הַזֹּאת לֹא יָבוֹא נְאֻם־יְהוָה׃

35 I will protect and save this city for My sake And for the sake of My servant *David*."

לה וְגַנּוֹתִי עַל־הָעִיר הַזֹּאת לְהוֹשִׁיעָהּ לְמַעֲנִי וּלְמַעַן דָּוִד עַבְדִּי׃

36 [That night] an angel of *Hashem* went out and struck down one hundred and eighty-five thousand in the Assyrian camp, and the following morning they were all dead corpses.

לו וַיֵּצֵא מַלְאַךְ יְהוָה וַיַּכֶּה בְּמַחֲנֵה אַשּׁוּר מֵאָה וּשְׁמֹנִים וַחֲמִשָּׁה אָלֶף וַיַּשְׁכִּימוּ בַבֹּקֶר וְהִנֵּה כֻלָּם פְּגָרִים מֵתִים׃

37 So King Sennacherib of Assyria broke camp and retreated, and stayed in Nineveh.

לז וַיִּסַּע וַיֵּלֶךְ וַיָּשָׁב סַנְחֵרִיב מֶלֶךְ־אַשּׁוּר וַיֵּשֶׁב בְּנִינְוֵה׃

Yeshayahu/Isaiah
Chapter 38

ישעיהו
פרק לח

38 While he was worshiping in the temple of his god Nisroch, he was struck down with the sword by his sons Adrammelech and Sarezer. They fled to the land of Ararat, and his son Esarhaddon succeeded him as king.

לח וַיְהִי הוּא מִשְׁתַּחֲוֶה בֵּית נִסְרֹךְ אֱלֹהָיו וְאַדְרַמֶּלֶךְ וְשַׂרְאֶצֶר בָּנָיו הִכֻּהוּ בַחֶרֶב וְהֵמָּה נִמְלְטוּ אֶרֶץ אֲרָרָט וַיִּמְלֹךְ אֵסַר־חַדֹּן בְּנוֹ תַּחְתָּיו׃

38

1 In those days *Chizkiyahu* fell dangerously ill. The *Navi Yeshayahu* son of *Amotz* came and said to him, "Thus said *Hashem*: Set your affairs in order, for you are going to die; you will not get well."

א בַּיָּמִים הָהֵם חָלָה חִזְקִיָּהוּ לָמוּת וַיָּבוֹא אֵלָיו יְשַׁעְיָהוּ בֶן־אָמוֹץ הַנָּבִיא וַיֹּאמֶר אֵלָיו כֹּה־אָמַר יְהוָה צַו לְבֵיתֶךָ כִּי מֵת אַתָּה וְלֹא תִחְיֶה׃

ba-ya-MEEM ha-HAYM kha-LAH khiz-ki-YA-hu la-MUT va-ya-VO ay-LAV y'-sha-ya-HU ven a-MOTZ ha-na-VEE va-YO-mer ay-LAV koh a-MAR a-do-NAI TZAV l'-vay-TE-kha KEE MAYT a-TAH v'-LO tikh-YEH

2 Thereupon *Chizkiyahu* turned his face to the wall and prayed to *Hashem*.

ב וַיַּסֵּב חִזְקִיָּהוּ פָּנָיו אֶל־הַקִּיר וַיִּתְפַּלֵּל אֶל־יְהוָה׃

3 "Please, *Hashem*," he said, "remember how I have walked before You sincerely and wholeheartedly, and have done what is pleasing to You." And *Chizkiyahu* wept profusely.

ג וַיֹּאמַר אָנָּה יְהוָה זְכָר־נָא אֵת אֲשֶׁר הִתְהַלַּכְתִּי לְפָנֶיךָ בֶּאֱמֶת וּבְלֵב שָׁלֵם וְהַטּוֹב בְּעֵינֶיךָ עָשִׂיתִי וַיֵּבְךְּ חִזְקִיָּהוּ בְּכִי גָדוֹל׃

4 Then the word of *Hashem* came to *Yeshayahu*:

ד וַיְהִי דְּבַר־יְהוָה אֶל־יְשַׁעְיָהוּ לֵאמֹר׃

5 "Go and tell *Chizkiyahu*: Thus said *Hashem*, the God of your father *David*: I have heard your prayer, I have seen your tears. I hereby add fifteen years to your life.

ה הָלוֹךְ וְאָמַרְתָּ אֶל־חִזְקִיָּהוּ כֹּה־אָמַר יְהוָה אֱלֹהֵי דָּוִד אָבִיךָ שָׁמַעְתִּי אֶת־תְּפִלָּתֶךָ רָאִיתִי אֶת־דִּמְעָתֶךָ הִנְנִי יוֹסִף עַל־יָמֶיךָ חֲמֵשׁ עֶשְׂרֵה שָׁנָה׃

6 I will also rescue you and this city from the hands of the king of Assyria. I will protect this city.

ו וּמִכַּף מֶלֶךְ־אַשּׁוּר אַצִּילְךָ וְאֵת הָעִיר הַזֹּאת וְגַנּוֹתִי עַל־הָעִיר הַזֹּאת׃

7 And this is the sign for you from *Hashem* that *Hashem* will do the thing that He has promised:

ז וְזֶה־לְּךָ הָאוֹת מֵאֵת יְהוָה אֲשֶׁר יַעֲשֶׂה יְהוָה אֶת־הַדָּבָר הַזֶּה אֲשֶׁר דִּבֵּר׃

8 I am going to make the shadow on the steps, which has descended on the dial of *Achaz* because of the sun, recede ten steps." And the sun['s shadow] receded ten steps, the same steps as it had descended.

ח הִנְנִי מֵשִׁיב אֶת־צֵל הַמַּעֲלוֹת אֲשֶׁר יָרְדָה בְמַעֲלוֹת אָחָז בַּשֶּׁמֶשׁ אֲחֹרַנִּית עֶשֶׂר מַעֲלוֹת וַתָּשָׁב הַשֶּׁמֶשׁ עֶשֶׂר מַעֲלוֹת בַּמַּעֲלוֹת אֲשֶׁר יָרָדָה׃

38:1 For you are going to die; you will not get well The Talmud (*Berachot* 10a) relates an ancient tradition regarding this exchange between *Yeshayahu* the prophet and King *Chizkiyahu*. When *Chizkiyahu* became sick, *Yeshayahu* came and said "You shall die and not live," meaning you shall die in this world and not live in the world to come either, because you did not try to have children. *Chizkiyahu* responded that he acted this way because he saw through prophecy that his children would be evil (referring to his son and successor, *Menashe*). *Yeshayahu* said: "Why did you meddle with God's secrets? You should have done as you were commanded!" *Chizkiyahu* repented, and was granted additional years of life. The Talmud concludes with an important lesson: Even if a sharp sword rests upon a man's neck, he should not desist from prayer. It is never too late to return to *Hashem* and call out to Him in sincere prayer.

Yeshayahu/Isaiah
Chapter 38

9 A poem by King *Chizkiyahu* of *Yehuda* when he recovered from the illness he had suffered:

10 I had thought: I must depart in the middle of my days; I have been consigned to the gates of Sheol For the rest of my years.

11 I thought, I shall never see Yah, Yah in the land of the living, Or ever behold men again Among those who inhabit the earth.

12 My dwelling is pulled up and removed from me Like a tent of shepherds; My life is rolled up like a web And cut from the thrum. Only from daybreak to nightfall Was I kept whole,

13 Then it was as though a lion Were breaking all my bones; I cried out until morning. (Only from daybreak to nightfall Was I kept whole.)

14 I piped like a swift or a swallow, I moaned like a dove, As my eyes, all worn, looked to heaven: "My Lord, I am in straits; Be my surety!"

15 What can I say? He promised me, And He it is who has wrought it. All my sleep had fled Because of the bitterness of my soul.

16 My Lord, for all that and despite it My life-breath is revived; You have restored me to health and revived me.

17 Truly, it was for my own good That I had such great bitterness: You saved my life From the pit of destruction, For You have cast behind Your back All my offenses.

18 For it is not Sheol that praises You, Not [the Land of] Death that extols You; Nor do they who descend into the Pit Hope for Your grace.

19 The living, only the living Can give thanks to You As I do this day; Fathers relate to children Your acts of grace:

20 "[It has pleased] *Hashem* to deliver us, That is why we offer up music All the days of our lives At the House of *Hashem*."

21 When *Yeshayahu* said, "Let them take a cake of figs and apply it to the rash, and he will recover,"

22 *Chizkiyahu* asked, "What will be the sign that I shall go up to the House of *Hashem*?"

ט מִכְתָּב לְחִזְקִיָּהוּ מֶלֶךְ־יְהוּדָה בַּחֲלֹתוֹ וַיְחִי מֵחָלְיוֹ:

י אֲנִי אָמַרְתִּי בִּדְמִי יָמַי אֵלֵכָה בְּשַׁעֲרֵי שְׁאוֹל פֻּקַּדְתִּי יֶתֶר שְׁנוֹתָי:

יא אָמַרְתִּי לֹא־אֶרְאֶה יָהּ יָהּ בְּאֶרֶץ הַחַיִּים לֹא־אַבִּיט אָדָם עוֹד עִם־יוֹשְׁבֵי חָדֶל:

יב דּוֹרִי נִסַּע וְנִגְלָה מִנִּי כְּאֹהֶל רֹעִי קִפַּדְתִּי כָאֹרֵג חַיַּי מִדַּלָּה יְבַצְּעֵנִי מִיּוֹם עַד־לַיְלָה תַּשְׁלִימֵנִי:

יג שִׁוִּיתִי עַד־בֹּקֶר כָּאֲרִי כֵּן יְשַׁבֵּר כָּל־עַצְמוֹתָי מִיּוֹם עַד־לַיְלָה תַּשְׁלִימֵנִי:

יד כְּסוּס עָגוּר כֵּן אֲצַפְצֵף אֶהְגֶּה כַּיּוֹנָה דַּלּוּ עֵינַי לַמָּרוֹם אֲדֹנָי עָשְׁקָה־לִּי עָרְבֵנִי:

טו מָה־אֲדַבֵּר וְאָמַר־לִי וְהוּא עָשָׂה אֶדַּדֶּה כָל־שְׁנוֹתַי עַל־מַר נַפְשִׁי:

טז אֲדֹנָי עֲלֵיהֶם יִחְיוּ וּלְכָל־בָּהֶן חַיֵּי רוּחִי וְתַחֲלִימֵנִי וְהַחֲיֵנִי:

יז הִנֵּה לְשָׁלוֹם מַר־לִי מָר וְאַתָּה חָשַׁקְתָּ נַפְשִׁי מִשַּׁחַת בְּלִי כִּי הִשְׁלַכְתָּ אַחֲרֵי גֵוְךָ כָּל־חֲטָאָי:

יח כִּי לֹא שְׁאוֹל תּוֹדֶךָּ מָוֶת יְהַלְלֶךָּ לֹא־יְשַׂבְּרוּ יוֹרְדֵי־בוֹר אֶל־אֲמִתֶּךָ:

יט חַי חַי הוּא יוֹדֶךָ כָּמוֹנִי הַיּוֹם אָב לְבָנִים יוֹדִיעַ אֶל־אֲמִתֶּךָ:

כ יְהוָה לְהוֹשִׁיעֵנִי וּנְגִנוֹתַי נְנַגֵּן כָּל־יְמֵי חַיֵּינוּ עַל־בֵּית יְהוָה:

כא וַיֹּאמֶר יְשַׁעְיָהוּ יִשְׂאוּ דְּבֶלֶת תְּאֵנִים וְיִמְרְחוּ עַל־הַשְּׁחִין וְיֶחִי:

כב וַיֹּאמֶר חִזְקִיָּהוּ מָה אוֹת כִּי אֶעֱלֶה בֵּית יְהוָה:

Yeshayahu/Isaiah
Chapter 39

ישעיהו
פרק לט

39 ¹ At that time, Merodach-baladan son of Baladan, the king of Babylon, sent [envoys with] a letter and a gift to *Chizkiyahu*, for he had heard about his illness and recovery.

א בָּעֵת הַהִוא שָׁלַח מְרֹדַךְ בַּלְאֲדָן בֶּן־בַּלְאֲדָן מֶלֶךְ־בָּבֶל סְפָרִים וּמִנְחָה אֶל־חִזְקִיָּהוּ וַיִּשְׁמַע כִּי חָלָה וַיֶּחֱזָק׃

² *Chizkiyahu* was pleased by their coming, and he showed them his treasure house – the silver, the gold, the spices, and the fragrant oil – and all his armory, and everything that was to be found in his storehouses. There was nothing in his palace or in all his realm that *Chizkiyahu* did not show them.

ב וַיִּשְׂמַח עֲלֵיהֶם חִזְקִיָּהוּ וַיַּרְאֵם אֶת־בֵּית נְכֹתֹה [נְכֹתוֹ] אֶת־הַכֶּסֶף וְאֶת־הַזָּהָב וְאֶת־הַבְּשָׂמִים וְאֵת הַשֶּׁמֶן הַטּוֹב וְאֵת כָּל־בֵּית כֵּלָיו וְאֵת כָּל־אֲשֶׁר נִמְצָא בְּאֹצְרֹתָיו לֹא־הָיָה דָבָר אֲשֶׁר לֹא־הֶרְאָם חִזְקִיָּהוּ בְּבֵיתוֹ וּבְכָל־מֶמְשַׁלְתּוֹ׃

³ Then the *Navi Yeshayahu* came to King *Chizkiyahu*. "What," he demanded of him, "did those men say to you? Where have they come to you from?" "They have come to me," replied *Chizkiyahu*, "from a far country, from Babylon."

ג וַיָּבֹא יְשַׁעְיָהוּ הַנָּבִיא אֶל־הַמֶּלֶךְ חִזְקִיָּהוּ וַיֹּאמֶר אֵלָיו מָה אָמְרוּ הָאֲנָשִׁים הָאֵלֶּה וּמֵאַיִן יָבֹאוּ אֵלֶיךָ וַיֹּאמֶר חִזְקִיָּהוּ מֵאֶרֶץ רְחוֹקָה בָּאוּ אֵלַי מִבָּבֶל׃

⁴ Next he asked, "What have they seen in your palace?" And *Chizkiyahu* replied, "They have seen everything there is in my palace. There was nothing in my storehouses that I did not show them."

ד וַיֹּאמֶר מָה רָאוּ בְּבֵיתֶךָ וַיֹּאמֶר חִזְקִיָּהוּ אֵת כָּל־אֲשֶׁר בְּבֵיתִי רָאוּ לֹא־הָיָה דָבָר אֲשֶׁר לֹא־הִרְאִיתִים בְּאוֹצְרֹתָי׃

⁵ Then *Yeshayahu* said to *Chizkiyahu*, "Hear the word of the Lord of Hosts:

ה וַיֹּאמֶר יְשַׁעְיָהוּ אֶל־חִזְקִיָּהוּ שְׁמַע דְּבַר־יְהֹוָה צְבָאוֹת׃

⁶ A time is coming when everything in your palace, which your ancestors have stored up to this day, will be carried off to Babylon; nothing will be left behind, said *Hashem*.

ו הִנֵּה יָמִים בָּאִים וְנִשָּׂא כָּל־אֲשֶׁר בְּבֵיתֶךָ וַאֲשֶׁר אָצְרוּ אֲבֹתֶיךָ עַד־הַיּוֹם הַזֶּה בָּבֶלָה לֹא־יִוָּתֵר דָּבָר אָמַר יְהֹוָה׃

⁷ And some of your sons, your own issue, whom you will have fathered, will be taken to serve as eunuchs in the palace of the king of Babylon."

ז וּמִבָּנֶיךָ אֲשֶׁר יֵצְאוּ מִמְּךָ אֲשֶׁר תּוֹלִיד יִקָּחוּ וְהָיוּ סָרִיסִים בְּהֵיכַל מֶלֶךְ בָּבֶל׃

⁸ *Chizkiyahu* declared to *Yeshayahu*, "The word of *Hashem* that you have spoken is good." For he thought, "It means that safety is assured for my time."

ח וַיֹּאמֶר חִזְקִיָּהוּ אֶל־יְשַׁעְיָהוּ טוֹב דְּבַר־יְהֹוָה אֲשֶׁר דִּבַּרְתָּ וַיֹּאמֶר כִּי יִהְיֶה שָׁלוֹם וֶאֱמֶת בְּיָמָי׃

va-YO-mer khiz-ki-YA-hu el y'-sha-YA-hu TOV d'-var a-do-NAI a-SHER di-BAR-ta va-YO-mer KEE yih-YEH sha-LOM ve-e-MET b'-ya-MAI

39:8 The word of *Hashem* that you have spoken is good. King *Chizkiyahu*'s response to *Yeshayahu*'s prophecy, that future calamities that would befall his people do not matter as long as "safety is assured for my time," appears callous and out of character for the righteous king. However, it actually reflects *Chizkiyahu*'s ability to see the good within the message delivered to him by *Yeshayahu*. It assured him of offspring, sons to sit upon his throne, and respite for his people. Most importantly, he understood that the period of peace would give the Children of Israel another chance to repent and erase the decree against them entirely. One should never underestimate the opportunity to make meaningful changes when given a second chance.

Yeshayahu/Isaiah
Chapter 40

ישעיהו
פרק מ

40 1 Comfort, oh comfort My people, Says your God.

נַחֲמוּ נַחֲמוּ עַמִּי יֹאמַר אֱלֹהֵיכֶם׃

na-kha-MU na-kha-MU a-MEE yo-MAR e-lo-hay-KHEM

2 Speak tenderly to *Yerushalayim*, And declare to her That her term of service is over, That her iniquity is expiated; For she has received at the hand of *Hashem* Double for all her sins.

דַּבְּרוּ עַל־לֵב יְרוּשָׁלַ͏ִם וְקִרְאוּ אֵלֶיהָ כִּי מָלְאָה צְבָאָהּ כִּי נִרְצָה עֲוֺנָהּ כִּי לָקְחָה מִיַּד יְהֹוָה כִּפְלַיִם בְּכׇל־חַטֹּאתֶיהָ׃

3 A voice rings out: "Clear in the desert A road for *Hashem*! Level in the wilderness A highway for our God!

קוֹל קוֹרֵא בַּמִּדְבָּר פַּנּוּ דֶּרֶךְ יְהֹוָה יַשְּׁרוּ בָּעֲרָבָה מְסִלָּה לֵאלֹהֵינוּ׃

4 Let every valley be raised, Every hill and mount made low. Let the rugged ground become level And the ridges become a plain.

כׇּל־גֶּיא יִנָּשֵׂא וְכׇל־הַר וְגִבְעָה יִשְׁפָּלוּ וְהָיָה הֶעָקֹב לְמִישׁוֹר וְהָרְכָסִים לְבִקְעָה׃

5 The Presence of *Hashem* shall appear And all flesh, as one, shall behold – For *Hashem* Himself has spoken."

וְנִגְלָה כְּבוֹד יְהֹוָה וְרָאוּ כׇל־בָּשָׂר יַחְדָּו כִּי פִּי יְהֹוָה דִּבֵּר׃

6 A voice rings out: "Proclaim!" Another asks, "What shall I proclaim?" "All flesh is grass, All its goodness like flowers of the field:

קוֹל אֹמֵר קְרָא וְאָמַר מָה אֶקְרָא כׇּל־הַבָּשָׂר חָצִיר וְכׇל־חַסְדּוֹ כְּצִיץ הַשָּׂדֶה׃

7 Grass withers, flowers fade When the breath of *Hashem* blows on them. Indeed, man is but grass:

יָבֵשׁ חָצִיר נָבֵל צִיץ כִּי רוּחַ יְהֹוָה נָשְׁבָה בּוֹ אָכֵן חָצִיר הָעָם׃

8 Grass withers, flowers fade – But the word of our God is always fulfilled!"

יָבֵשׁ חָצִיר נָבֵל צִיץ וּדְבַר־אֱלֹהֵינוּ יָקוּם לְעוֹלָם׃

9 Ascend a lofty mountain, O herald of joy to *Tzion*; Raise your voice with power, O herald of joy to *Yerushalayim* – Raise it, have no fear; Announce to the cities of *Yehuda*: Behold your God!

עַל הַר־גָּבֹהַּ עֲלִי־לָךְ מְבַשֶּׂרֶת צִיּוֹן הָרִימִי בַכֹּחַ קוֹלֵךְ מְבַשֶּׂרֶת יְרוּשָׁלָ͏ִם הָרִימִי אַל־תִּירָאִי אִמְרִי לְעָרֵי יְהוּדָה הִנֵּה אֱלֹהֵיכֶם׃

10 Behold, *Hashem* comes in might, And His arm wins triumph for Him; See, His reward is with Him, His recompense before Him.

הִנֵּה אֲדֹנָי יֱהֹוִה בְּחָזָק יָבוֹא וּזְרֹעוֹ מֹשְׁלָה לוֹ הִנֵּה שְׂכָרוֹ אִתּוֹ וּפְעֻלָּתוֹ לְפָנָיו׃

11 Like a shepherd He pastures His flock: He gathers the lambs in His arms And carries them in His bosom; Gently He drives the mother sheep.

כְּרֹעֶה עֶדְרוֹ יִרְעֶה בִּזְרֹעוֹ יְקַבֵּץ טְלָאִים וּבְחֵיקוֹ יִשָּׂא עָלוֹת יְנַהֵל׃

40:1 Comfort, oh comfort My people The *Torah* is always very careful to use words sparingly and not to repeat even a single word unnecessarily. If so, why is the word "comfort" repeated twice in this verse? The prophecy considers the future destructions of both the first and the second *Beit Hamikdash*. The loss of both Temples would constitute a double calamity for the Jewish people, and *Hashem* consequently promises that His consolation will also be double. This chapter is read annually on the *Shabbat* following the ninth day of the Hebrew month of *Av*, the national day of mourning for the destruction of the Temples. Each year, these words bring renewed hope that we will witness the double consolation promised in these verses, speedily in our days. May His comforting blessings be showered upon us all.

Yeshayahu/Isaiah
Chapter 40

12 Who measured the waters with the hollow of His hand, And gauged the skies with a *zeret*, And meted earth's dust with a measure, And weighed the mountains with a scale And the hills with a balance?

13 Who has plumbed the mind of *Hashem*, What man could tell Him His plan?

14 Whom did He consult, and who taught Him, Guided Him in the way of right? Who guided Him in knowledge And showed Him the path of wisdom?

15 The nations are but a drop in a bucket, Reckoned as dust on a balance; The very coastlands He lifts like motes.

16 Lebanon is not fuel enough, Nor its beasts enough for sacrifice.

17 All nations are as naught in His sight; He accounts them as less than nothing.

18 To whom, then, can you liken *Hashem*, What form compare to Him?

19 The idol? A woodworker shaped it, And a smith overlaid it with gold, Forging links of silver.

20 As a gift, he chooses the mulberry – A wood that does not rot – Then seeks a skillful woodworker To make a firm idol, That will not topple.

21 Do you not know? Have you not heard? Have you not been told From the very first? Have you not discerned How the earth was founded?

22 It is He who is enthroned above the vault of the earth, So that its inhabitants seem as grasshoppers; Who spread out the skies like gauze, Stretched them out like a tent to dwell in.

23 He brings potentates to naught, Makes rulers of the earth as nothing.

24 Hardly are they planted, Hardly are they sown, Hardly has their stem Taken root in earth, When He blows upon them and they dry up, And the storm bears them off like straw.

25 To whom, then, can you liken Me, To whom can I be compared? – says the Holy One.

ישעיהו
פרק מ

יב מִֽי־מָדַ֨ד בְּשָׁעֳל֜וֹ מַ֗יִם וְשָׁמַ֨יִם֙ בַּזֶּ֣רֶת תִּכֵּ֔ן וְכָ֥ל בַּשָּׁלִ֖שׁ עֲפַ֣ר הָאָ֑רֶץ וְשָׁקַ֤ל בַּפֶּ֙לֶס֙ הָרִ֔ים וּגְבָע֖וֹת בְּמֹאזְנָֽיִם׃

יג מִֽי־תִכֵּ֥ן אֶת־ר֖וּחַ יְהֹוָ֑ה וְאִ֥ישׁ עֲצָת֖וֹ יוֹדִיעֶֽנּוּ׃

יד אֶת־מִ֤י נוֹעָץ֙ וַיְבִינֵ֔הוּ וַֽיְלַמְּדֵ֖הוּ בְּאֹ֣רַח מִשְׁפָּ֑ט וַיְלַמְּדֵ֣הוּ דַ֔עַת וְדֶ֥רֶךְ תְּבוּנ֖וֹת יוֹדִיעֶֽנּוּ׃

טו הֵ֤ן גּוֹיִם֙ כְּמַ֣ר מִדְּלִ֔י וּכְשַׁ֥חַק מֹאזְנַ֖יִם נֶחְשָׁ֑בוּ הֵ֥ן אִיִּ֖ים כַּדַּ֥ק יִטּֽוֹל׃

טז וּלְבָנ֕וֹן אֵ֥ין דֵּ֖י בָּעֵ֑ר וְחַ֨יָּת֔וֹ אֵ֥ין דֵּ֖י עוֹלָֽה׃

יז כׇּל־הַגּוֹיִ֖ם כְּאַ֣יִן נֶגְדּ֑וֹ מֵאֶ֥פֶס וָתֹ֖הוּ נֶחְשְׁבוּ־לֽוֹ׃

יח וְאֶל־מִ֖י תְּדַמְּי֣וּן אֵ֑ל וּמַה־דְּמ֖וּת תַּ֥עַרְכוּ לֽוֹ׃

יט הַפֶּ֙סֶל֙ נָסַ֣ךְ חָרָ֔שׁ וְצֹרֵ֖ף בַּזָּהָ֣ב יְרַקְּעֶ֑נּוּ וּרְתֻק֥וֹת כֶּ֖סֶף צוֹרֵֽף׃

כ הַֽמְסֻכָּ֣ן תְּרוּמָ֔ה עֵ֥ץ לֹא־יִרְקַ֖ב יִבְחָ֑ר חָרָ֤שׁ חָכָם֙ יְבַקֶּשׁ־ל֔וֹ לְהָכִ֥ין פֶּ֖סֶל לֹ֥א יִמּֽוֹט׃

כא הֲל֤וֹא תֵֽדְעוּ֙ הֲל֣וֹא תִשְׁמָ֔עוּ הֲל֛וֹא הֻגַּ֥ד מֵרֹ֖אשׁ לָכֶ֑ם הֲלוֹא֙ הֲבִ֣ינֹתֶ֔ם מוֹסְד֖וֹת הָאָֽרֶץ׃

כב הַיֹּשֵׁב֙ עַל־ח֣וּג הָאָ֔רֶץ וְיֹשְׁבֶ֖יהָ כַּחֲגָבִ֑ים הַנּוֹטֶ֤ה כַדֹּק֙ שָׁמַ֔יִם וַיִּמְתָּחֵ֥ם כָּאֹ֖הֶל לָשָֽׁבֶת׃

כג הַנּוֹתֵ֥ן רוֹזְנִ֖ים לְאָ֑יִן שֹׁ֥פְטֵי אֶ֖רֶץ כַּתֹּ֥הוּ עָשָֽׂה׃

כד אַ֣ף בַּל־נִטָּ֗עוּ אַ֚ף בַּל־זֹרָ֔עוּ אַ֥ף בַּל־שֹׁרֵ֖שׁ בָּאָ֣רֶץ גִּזְעָ֑ם וְגַם־נָשַׁ֤ף בָּהֶם֙ וַיִּבָ֔שׁוּ וּסְעָרָ֖ה כַּקַּ֥שׁ תִּשָּׂאֵֽם׃

כה וְאֶל־מִ֥י תְדַמְּי֖וּנִי וְאֶשְׁוֶ֑ה יֹאמַ֖ר קָדֽוֹשׁ׃

Yeshayahu/Isaiah

Chapter 41

ישעיהו

פרק מא

26 Lift high your eyes and see: Who created these? He who sends out their host by count, Who calls them each by name: Because of His great might and vast power, Not one fails to appear.

כו שְׂאוּ־מָרוֹם עֵינֵיכֶם וּרְאוּ מִי־בָרָא אֵלֶּה הַמּוֹצִיא בְמִסְפָּר צְבָאָם לְכֻלָּם בְּשֵׁם יִקְרָא מֵרֹב אוֹנִים וְאַמִּיץ כֹּחַ אִישׁ לֹא נֶעְדָּר׃

27 Why do you say, O *Yaakov*, Why declare, O *Yisrael*, "My way is hid from *Hashem*, My cause is ignored by my God"?

כז לָמָּה תֹאמַר יַעֲקֹב וּתְדַבֵּר יִשְׂרָאֵל נִסְתְּרָה דַרְכִּי מֵיהוָה וּמֵאֱלֹהַי מִשְׁפָּטִי יַעֲבוֹר׃

28 Do you not know? Have you not heard? *Hashem* is God from of old, Creator of the earth from end to end He never grows faint or weary, His wisdom cannot be fathomed.

כח הֲלוֹא יָדַעְתָּ אִם־לֹא שָׁמַעְתָּ אֱלֹהֵי עוֹלָם יְהוָה בּוֹרֵא קְצוֹת הָאָרֶץ לֹא יִיעַף וְלֹא יִיגָע אֵין חֵקֶר לִתְבוּנָתוֹ׃

29 He gives strength to the weary, Fresh vigor to the spent.

כט נֹתֵן לַיָּעֵף כֹּחַ וּלְאֵין אוֹנִים עָצְמָה יַרְבֶּה׃

30 Youths may grow faint and weary, And young men stumble and fall;

ל וְיִעֲפוּ נְעָרִים וְיִגָעוּ וּבַחוּרִים כָּשׁוֹל יִכָּשֵׁלוּ׃

31 But they who trust in *Hashem* shall renew their strength As eagles grow new plumes: They shall run and not grow weary, They shall march and not grow faint.

לא וְקוֵֹי יְהוָה יַחֲלִיפוּ כֹחַ יַעֲלוּ אֵבֶר כַּנְּשָׁרִים יָרוּצוּ וְלֹא יִיגָעוּ יֵלְכוּ וְלֹא יִיעָפוּ׃

41 1 Stand silent before Me, coastlands, And let nations renew their strength. Let them approach to state their case; Let us come forward together for argument.

מא א הַחֲרִישׁוּ אֵלַי אִיִּים וּלְאֻמִּים יַחֲלִיפוּ כֹחַ יִגְּשׁוּ אָז יְדַבֵּרוּ יַחְדָּו לַמִּשְׁפָּט נִקְרָבָה׃

2 Who has roused a victor from the East, Summoned him to His service? Has delivered up nations to him, And trodden sovereigns down? Has rendered their swords like dust, Their bows like wind-blown straw?

ב מִי הֵעִיר מִמִּזְרָח צֶדֶק יִקְרָאֵהוּ לְרַגְלוֹ יִתֵּן לְפָנָיו גּוֹיִם וּמְלָכִים יַרְדְּ יִתֵּן כֶּעָפָר חַרְבּוֹ כְּקַשׁ נִדָּף קַשְׁתּוֹ׃

3 He pursues them, he goes on unscathed; No shackle is placed on his feet.

ג יִרְדְּפֵם יַעֲבוֹר שָׁלוֹם אֹרַח בְּרַגְלָיו לֹא יָבוֹא׃

4 Who has wrought and achieved this? He who announced the generations from the start – I, *Hashem*, who was first And will be with the last as well.

ד מִי־פָעַל וְעָשָׂה קֹרֵא הַדֹּרוֹת מֵרֹאשׁ אֲנִי יְהוָה רִאשׁוֹן וְאֶת־אַחֲרֹנִים אֲנִי־הוּא׃

5 The coastlands look on in fear, The ends of earth tremble. They draw near and come;

ה רָאוּ אִיִּים וְיִירָאוּ קְצוֹת הָאָרֶץ יֶחֱרָדוּ קָרְבוּ וַיֶּאֱתָיוּן׃

6 Each one helps the other Saying to his fellow, "Take courage!"

ו אִישׁ אֶת־רֵעֵהוּ יַעְזֹרוּ וּלְאָחִיו יֹאמַר חֲזָק׃

7 The woodworker encourages the smith; He who flattens with the hammer [Encourages] him who pounds the anvil. He says of the riveting, "It is good!" And he fixes it with nails, That it may not topple.

ז וַיְחַזֵּק חָרָשׁ אֶת־צֹרֵף מַחֲלִיק פַּטִּישׁ אֶת־הוֹלֶם פָּעַם אֹמֵר לַדֶּבֶק טוֹב הוּא וַיְחַזְּקֵהוּ בְמַסְמְרִים לֹא יִמּוֹט׃

Yeshayahu/Isaiah
Chapter 41

ישעיהו
פרק מא

8 But you, *Yisrael*, My servant, *Yaakov*, whom I have chosen, Seed of *Avraham* My friend –

ח וְאַתָּה יִשְׂרָאֵל עַבְדִּי יַעֲקֹב אֲשֶׁר בְּחַרְתִּיךָ זֶרַע אַבְרָהָם אֹהֲבִי:

v'-a-TAH yis-ra-AYL av-DEE ya-a-KOV a-SHER b'-khar-TEE-kha ZE-ra av-ra-HAM o-ha-VEE

9 You whom I drew from the ends of the earth And called from its far corners, To whom I said: You are My servant; I chose you, I have not rejected you –

ט אֲשֶׁר הֶחֱזַקְתִּיךָ מִקְצוֹת הָאָרֶץ וּמֵאֲצִילֶיהָ קְרָאתִיךָ וָאֹמַר לְךָ עַבְדִּי־אַתָּה בְּחַרְתִּיךָ וְלֹא מְאַסְתִּיךָ:

10 Fear not, for I am with you, Be not frightened, for I am your God; I strengthen you and I help you, I uphold you with My victorious right hand.

י אַל־תִּירָא כִּי עִמְּךָ־אָנִי אַל־תִּשְׁתָּע כִּי־אֲנִי אֱלֹהֶיךָ אִמַּצְתִּיךָ אַף־עֲזַרְתִּיךָ אַף־תְּמַכְתִּיךָ בִּימִין צִדְקִי:

11 Shamed and chagrined shall be All who contend with you; They who strive with you Shall become as naught and shall perish.

יא הֵן יֵבֹשׁוּ וְיִכָּלְמוּ כֹּל הַנֶּחֱרִים בָּךְ יִהְיוּ כְאַיִן וְיֹאבְדוּ אַנְשֵׁי רִיבֶךָ:

12 You may seek, but shall not find Those who struggle with you; Less than nothing shall be The men who battle against you.

יב תְּבַקְשֵׁם וְלֹא תִמְצָאֵם אַנְשֵׁי מַצֻּתֶךָ יִהְיוּ כְאַיִן וּכְאֶפֶס אַנְשֵׁי מִלְחַמְתֶּךָ:

13 For I *Hashem* am your God, Who grasped your right hand, Who say to you: Have no fear; I will be your help.

יג כִּי אֲנִי יְהוָה אֱלֹהֶיךָ מַחֲזִיק יְמִינֶךָ הָאֹמֵר לְךָ אַל־תִּירָא אֲנִי עֲזַרְתִּיךָ:

14 Fear not, O worm *Yaakov*, O men of *Yisrael*: I will help you – declares *Hashem* – I your Redeemer, the Holy One of *Yisrael*.

יד אַל־תִּירְאִי תּוֹלַעַת יַעֲקֹב מְתֵי יִשְׂרָאֵל אֲנִי עֲזַרְתִּיךְ נְאֻם־יְהוָה וְגֹאֲלֵךְ קְדוֹשׁ יִשְׂרָאֵל:

15 I will make of you a threshing board, A new thresher, with many spikes; You shall thresh mountains to dust, And make hills like chaff.

טו הִנֵּה שַׂמְתִּיךְ לְמוֹרַג חָרוּץ חָדָשׁ בַּעַל פִּיפִיּוֹת תָּדוּשׁ הָרִים וְתָדֹק וּגְבָעוֹת כַּמֹּץ תָּשִׂים:

16 You shall winnow them And the wind shall carry them off; The whirlwind shall scatter them. But you shall rejoice in *Hashem*, And glory in the Holy One of *Yisrael*.

טז תִּזְרֵם וְרוּחַ תִּשָּׂאֵם וּסְעָרָה תָּפִיץ אוֹתָם וְאַתָּה תָּגִיל בַּיהוָה בִּקְדוֹשׁ יִשְׂרָאֵל תִּתְהַלָּל:

17 The poor and the needy Seek water, and there is none; Their tongue is parched with thirst. I *Hashem* will respond to them. I, the God of *Yisrael*, will not forsake them.

יז הָעֲנִיִּים וְהָאֶבְיוֹנִים מְבַקְשִׁים מַיִם וָאַיִן לְשׁוֹנָם בַּצָּמָא נָשָׁתָּה אֲנִי יְהוָה אֶעֱנֵם אֱלֹהֵי יִשְׂרָאֵל לֹא אֶעֶזְבֵם:

18 I will open up streams on the bare hills And fountains amid the valleys; I will turn the desert into ponds, The arid land into springs of water.

יח אֶפְתַּח עַל־שְׁפָיִים נְהָרוֹת וּבְתוֹךְ בְּקָעוֹת מַעְיָנוֹת אָשִׂים מִדְבָּר לַאֲגַם־מַיִם וְאֶרֶץ צִיָּה לְמוֹצָאֵי מָיִם:

41:8 Seed of *Avraham* My friend Out of all of Israel's ancestors, *Avraham* is singled out as *ohavee* (אהבי), which means 'my friend,' or more literally, 'my lover.' Rashi explains that unlike everyone else who followed *Hashem*, *Avraham* did not serve God out of familial obligation or fear, but sought after Him like a lover searches for his beloved. We, too, should strive to emulate *Avraham*, to serve *Hashem* out of love and not fear.

אהבי

Yeshayahu/Isaiah

Chapter 42

ישעיהו

פרק מב

19 I will plant cedars in the wilderness, Acacias and myrtles and oleasters; I will set cypresses in the desert, Box trees and elms as well –

יט אֶתֵּן בַּמִּדְבָּר אֶרֶז שִׁטָּה וַהֲדַס וְעֵץ שָׁמֶן אָשִׂים בָּעֲרָבָה בְּרוֹשׁ תִּדְהָר וּתְאַשּׁוּר יַחְדָּו׃

20 That men may see and know, Consider and comprehend That *Hashem*'s hand has done this, That the Holy One of *Yisrael* has wrought it.

כ לְמַעַן יִרְאוּ וְיֵדְעוּ וְיָשִׂימוּ וְיַשְׂכִּילוּ יַחְדָּו כִּי יַד־יְהֹוָה עָשְׂתָה זֹּאת וּקְדוֹשׁ יִשְׂרָאֵל בְּרָאָהּ׃

21 Submit your case, says *Hashem*; Offer your pleas, says the King of *Yaakov*.

כא קָרְבוּ רִיבְכֶם יֹאמַר יְהֹוָה הַגִּישׁוּ עֲצֻמוֹתֵיכֶם יֹאמַר מֶלֶךְ יַעֲקֹב׃

22 Let them approach and tell us what will happen. Tell us what has occurred, And we will take note of it; Or announce to us what will occur, That we may know the outcome.

כב יַגִּישׁוּ וְיַגִּידוּ לָנוּ אֵת אֲשֶׁר תִּקְרֶינָה הָרִאשֹׁנוֹת מָה הֵנָּה הַגִּידוּ וְנָשִׂימָה לִבֵּנוּ וְנֵדְעָה אַחֲרִיתָן אוֹ הַבָּאוֹת הַשְׁמִיעֻנוּ׃

23 Foretell what is yet to happen, That we may know that you are gods! Do anything, good or bad, That we may be awed and see.

כג הַגִּידוּ הָאֹתִיּוֹת לְאָחוֹר וְנֵדְעָה כִּי אֱלֹהִים אַתֶּם אַף־תֵּיטִיבוּ וְתָרֵעוּ וְנִשְׁתָּעָה וְנֵרֶא [וְנִרְאֶה] יַחְדָּו׃

24 Why, you are less than nothing, Your effect is less than nullity; One who chooses you is an abomination.

כד הֵן־אַתֶּם מֵאַיִן וּפָעָלְכֶם מֵאָפַע תּוֹעֵבָה יִבְחַר בָּכֶם׃

25 I have roused him from the north, and he has come, From the sunrise, one who invokes My name; And he has trampled rulers like mud, Like a potter treading clay.

כה הַעִירוֹתִי מִצָּפוֹן וַיַּאת מִמִּזְרַח־שֶׁמֶשׁ יִקְרָא בִשְׁמִי וְיָבֹא סְגָנִים כְּמוֹ־חֹמֶר וּכְמוֹ יוֹצֵר יִרְמָס־טִיט׃

26 Who foretold this from the start, that we may note it; From aforetime, that we might say, "He is right"? Not one foretold, not one announced; No one has heard your utterance!

כו מִי־הִגִּיד מֵרֹאשׁ וְנֵדָעָה וּמִלְּפָנִים וְנֹאמַר צַדִּיק אַף אֵין־מַגִּיד אַף אֵין מַשְׁמִיעַ אַף אֵין־שֹׁמֵעַ אִמְרֵיכֶם׃

27 The things once predicted to *Tzion* – Behold, here they are! And again I send a herald to *Yerushalayim*.

כז רִאשׁוֹן לְצִיּוֹן הִנֵּה הִנָּם וְלִירוּשָׁלַ͏ִם מְבַשֵּׂר אֶתֵּן׃

28 But I look and there is not a man; Not one of them can predict Or can respond when I question him.

כח וְאֵרֶא וְאֵין אִישׁ וּמֵאֵלֶּה וְאֵין יוֹעֵץ וְאֶשְׁאָלֵם וְיָשִׁיבוּ דָבָר׃

29 See, they are all nothingness, Their works are nullity, Their statues are naught and nil.

כט הֵן כֻּלָּם אָוֶן אֶפֶס מַעֲשֵׂיהֶם רוּחַ וָתֹהוּ נִסְכֵּיהֶם׃

42 1 This is My servant, whom I uphold, My chosen one, in whom I delight. I have put My spirit upon him, He shall teach the true way to the nations.

מב א הֵן עַבְדִּי אֶתְמָךְ־בּוֹ בְּחִירִי רָצְתָה נַפְשִׁי נָתַתִּי רוּחִי עָלָיו מִשְׁפָּט לַגּוֹיִם יוֹצִיא׃

2 He shall not cry out or shout aloud, Or make his voice heard in the streets.

ב לֹא יִצְעַק וְלֹא יִשָּׂא וְלֹא־יַשְׁמִיעַ בַּחוּץ קוֹלוֹ׃

3 He shall not break even a bruised reed, Or snuff out even a dim wick. He shall bring forth the true way.

ג קָנֶה רָצוּץ לֹא יִשְׁבּוֹר וּפִשְׁתָּה כֵהָה לֹא יְכַבֶּנָּה לֶאֱמֶת יוֹצִיא מִשְׁפָּט׃

Yeshayahu/Isaiah
Chapter 42

ישעיהו
פרק מב

4 He shall not grow dim or be bruised Till he has established the true way on earth; And the coastlands shall await his teaching.

ד לֹא יִכְהֶה וְלֹא יָרוּץ עַד־יָשִׂים בָּאָרֶץ מִשְׁפָּט וּלְתוֹרָתוֹ אִיִּים יְיַחֵילוּ׃

5 Thus said *Hashem* the LORD, Who created the heavens and stretched them out, Who spread out the earth and what it brings forth, Who gave breath to the people upon it And life to those who walk thereon:

ה כֹּה־אָמַר הָאֵל ׀ יְהֹוָה בּוֹרֵא הַשָּׁמַיִם וְנוֹטֵיהֶם רֹקַע הָאָרֶץ וְצֶאֱצָאֶיהָ נֹתֵן נְשָׁמָה לָעָם עָלֶיהָ וְרוּחַ לַהֹלְכִים בָּהּ׃

6 I *Hashem*, in My grace, have summoned you, And I have grasped you by the hand. I created you, and appointed you A covenant people, a light of nations –

ו אֲנִי יְהֹוָה קְרָאתִיךָ בְצֶדֶק וְאַחְזֵק בְּיָדֶךָ וְאֶצָּרְךָ וְאֶתֶּנְךָ לִבְרִית עָם לְאוֹר גּוֹיִם׃

a-NEE a-do-NAI k'-ra-TEE-kha v'-TZE-dek v'-akh-ZAYK b'-ya-DE-kha v'-e-tzor-KHA v'-e-ten-KHA liv-REET AM l'-OR go-YIM

7 Opening eyes deprived of light, Rescuing prisoners from confinement, From the dungeon those who sit in darkness.

ז לִפְקֹחַ עֵינַיִם עִוְרוֹת לְהוֹצִיא מִמַּסְגֵּר אַסִּיר מִבֵּית כֶּלֶא יֹשְׁבֵי חֹשֶׁךְ׃

8 I am *Hashem*, that is My name; I will not yield My glory to another, Nor My renown to idols.

ח אֲנִי יְהֹוָה הוּא שְׁמִי וּכְבוֹדִי לְאַחֵר לֹא־אֶתֵּן וּתְהִלָּתִי לַפְּסִילִים׃

9 See, the things once predicted have come, And now I foretell new things, Announce to you ere they sprout up.

ט הָרִאשֹׁנוֹת הִנֵּה־בָאוּ וַחֲדָשׁוֹת אֲנִי מַגִּיד בְּטֶרֶם תִּצְמַחְנָה אַשְׁמִיע אֶתְכֶם׃

10 Sing to *Hashem* a new song, His praise from the ends of the earth – You who sail the sea and you creatures in it, You coastlands and their inhabitants!

י שִׁירוּ לַיהֹוָה שִׁיר חָדָשׁ תְּהִלָּתוֹ מִקְצֵה הָאָרֶץ יוֹרְדֵי הַיָּם וּמְלֹאוֹ אִיִּים וְיֹשְׁבֵיהֶם׃

11 Let the desert and its towns cry aloud, The villages where Kedar dwells; Let Sela's inhabitants shout, Call out from the peaks of the mountains.

יא יִשְׂאוּ מִדְבָּר וְעָרָיו חֲצֵרִים תֵּשֵׁב קֵדָר יָרֹנּוּ יֹשְׁבֵי סֶלַע מֵרֹאשׁ הָרִים יִצְוָחוּ׃

12 Let them do honor to *Hashem*, And tell His glory in the coastlands.

יב יָשִׂימוּ לַיהֹוָה כָּבוֹד וּתְהִלָּתוֹ בָּאִיִּים יַגִּידוּ׃

42:6 A light of nations This famous phrase captures the mission statement of the People of Israel. For most of Jewish history, the role of "light unto the nations" has been understood primarily as a private call to have a positive influence on the world by living an ethical life and setting a personal example of righteous behavior. Rarely was anyone on the outside ever interested in what the Jews as a nation had to say, and so the concept of '*ohr goyim*' was an ideal that individual Jews strived for. However, *Yeshayahu* is calling for so much more. The "light" in his stirring description is capable of opening the eyes of the blind and leading the imprisoned out of darkness. The establishment of the State of Israel and its role on the international stage calls for a transformation of the "light unto the nations" metaphor from a passive, individual candle, to a powerful blaze, firing up the nations and igniting the world with righteousness. The State of Israel represents the historic opportunity for the People of Israel to fulfil their religious destiny as a nation.

Emblem of the State of Israel

Yeshayahu/Isaiah
Chapter 42

13 *Hashem* goes forth like a warrior, Like a fighter He whips up His rage. He yells, He roars aloud, He charges upon His enemies.

14 "I have kept silent far too long, Kept still and restrained Myself; Now I will scream like a woman in labor, I will pant and I will gasp.

15 Hills and heights will I scorch, Cause all their green to wither; I will turn rivers into isles, And dry the marshes up.

16 I will lead the blind By a road they did not know, And I will make them walk By paths they never knew. I will turn darkness before them to light, Rough places into level ground. These are the promises – I will keep them without fail.

17 Driven back and utterly shamed Shall be those who trust in an image, Those who say to idols, 'You are our gods!'"

18 Listen, you who are deaf; You blind ones, look up and see!

19 Who is so blind as My servant, So deaf as the messenger I send? Who is so blind as the chosen one, So blind as the servant of *Hashem*?

20 Seeing many things, he gives no heed; With ears open, he hears nothing.

21 *Hashem* desires His [servant's] vindication, That he may magnify and glorify [His] Teaching.

22 Yet it is a people plundered and despoiled: All of them are trapped in holes, Imprisoned in dungeons. They are given over to plunder, with none to rescue them; To despoilment, with none to say "Give back!"

23 If only you would listen to this, Attend and give heed from now on!

24 Who was it gave *Yaakov* over to despoilment And *Yisrael* to plunderers? Surely, *Hashem* against whom they sinned In whose ways they would not walk And whose Teaching they would not obey.

25 So He poured out wrath upon them, His anger and the fury of war. It blazed upon them all about, but they heeded not; It burned among them, but they gave it no thought.

Yeshayahu/Isaiah
Chapter 43

ישעיהו
פרק מג

43 1 But now thus said *Hashem* – Who created you, O *Yaakov*, Who formed you, O *Yisrael*: Fear not, for I will redeem you; I have singled you out by name, You are Mine.

א וְעַתָּה כֹּה־אָמַר יְהֹוָה בֹּרַאֲךָ יַעֲקֹב וְיֹצֶרְךָ יִשְׂרָאֵל אַל־תִּירָא כִּי גְאַלְתִּיךָ קָרָאתִי בְשִׁמְךָ לִי־אָתָּה׃

v'-a-TAH koh a-MAR a-do-NAI bo-ra-a-KHA ya-a-KOV v'-yo-tzer-KHA yis-ra-AYL al tee-RA KEE g'-al-TEE-kha ka-RA-tee v'-shim-KHA lee A-tah

2 When you pass through water, I will be with you; Through streams, They shall not overwhelm you. When you walk through fire, You shall not be scorched; Through flame, It shall not burn you.

ב כִּי־תַעֲבֹר בַּמַּיִם אִתְּךָ־אָנִי וּבַנְּהָרוֹת לֹא יִשְׁטְפוּךָ כִּי־תֵלֵךְ בְּמוֹ־אֵשׁ לֹא תִכָּוֶה וְלֶהָבָה לֹא תִבְעַר־בָּךְ׃

3 For I *Hashem* am your God, The Holy One of *Yisrael*, your Savior. I give Egypt as a ransom for you, Ethiopia and Saba in exchange for you.

ג כִּי אֲנִי יְהֹוָה אֱלֹהֶיךָ קְדוֹשׁ יִשְׂרָאֵל מוֹשִׁיעֶךָ נָתַתִּי כׇפְרְךָ מִצְרַיִם כּוּשׁ וּסְבָא תַּחְתֶּיךָ׃

4 Because you are precious to Me, And honored, and I love you, I give men in exchange for you And peoples in your stead.

ד מֵאֲשֶׁר יָקַרְתָּ בְעֵינַי נִכְבַּדְתָּ וַאֲנִי אֲהַבְתִּיךָ וְאֶתֵּן אָדָם תַּחְתֶּיךָ וּלְאֻמִּים תַּחַת נַפְשֶׁךָ׃

5 Fear not, for I am with you: I will bring your folk from the East, Will gather you out of the West;

ה אַל־תִּירָא כִּי אִתְּךָ־אָנִי מִמִּזְרָח אָבִיא זַרְעֶךָ וּמִמַּעֲרָב אֲקַבְּצֶךָּ׃

6 I will say to the North, "Give back!" And to the South, "Do not withhold! Bring My sons from afar, And My daughters from the end of the earth –

ו אֹמַר לַצָּפוֹן תֵּנִי וּלְתֵימָן אַל־תִּכְלָאִי הָבִיאִי בָנַי מֵרָחוֹק וּבְנוֹתַי מִקְצֵה הָאָרֶץ׃

7 All who are linked to My name, Whom I have created, Formed, and made for My glory –

ז כֹּל הַנִּקְרָא בִשְׁמִי וְלִכְבוֹדִי בְּרָאתִיו יְצַרְתִּיו אַף־עֲשִׂיתִיו׃

8 Setting free that people, Blind though it has eyes And deaf though it has ears."

ח הוֹצִיא עַם־עִוֵּר וְעֵינַיִם יֵשׁ וְחֵרְשִׁים וְאׇזְנַיִם לָמוֹ׃

9 All the nations assemble as one, The peoples gather. Who among them declared this, Foretold to us the things that have happened? Let them produce their witnesses and be vindicated, That men, hearing them, may say, "It is true!"

ט כׇּל־הַגּוֹיִם נִקְבְּצוּ יַחְדָּו וְיֵאָסְפוּ לְאֻמִּים מִי בָהֶם יַגִּיד זֹאת וְרִאשֹׁנוֹת יַשְׁמִיעֻנוּ יִתְּנוּ עֵדֵיהֶם וְיִצְדָּקוּ וְיִשְׁמְעוּ וְיֹאמְרוּ אֱמֶת׃

10 My witnesses are you – declares *Hashem* – My servant, whom I have chosen. To the end that you may take thought, And believe in Me, And understand that I am He: Before Me no god was formed, And after Me none shall exist –

י אַתֶּם עֵדַי נְאֻם־יְהֹוָה וְעַבְדִּי אֲשֶׁר בָּחָרְתִּי לְמַעַן תֵּדְעוּ וְתַאֲמִינוּ לִי וְתָבִינוּ כִּי־אֲנִי הוּא לְפָנַי לֹא־נוֹצַר אֵל וְאַחֲרַי לֹא יִהְיֶה׃

43:1 But now As he often does, *Yeshayahu* delivers severe rebuke (42:18–25) followed by comfort and consolation. He tells the people that *Hashem* has not cast Israel off. Rather, He will be present during the difficulties and will even bring a speedy return and restoration to Israel (verses 3–7). The opening words, "but now," mark the sharp contrast between the closing of chapter 42 and the opening of chapter 43. The prophet reassures that although Israel has undergone severe punishment and is still suffering, a dramatic change is approaching. The nation will return to its land in a remarkable expression of *Hashem*'s declaration, "You are Mine."

Yeshayahu/Isaiah
Chapter 43

11 None but me, *Hashem*; Beside Me, none can grant triumph.

12 I alone foretold the triumph And I brought it to pass; I announced it, And no strange god was among you. So you are My witnesses – declares *Hashem* – And I am *Hashem*.

13 Ever since day was, I am He; None can deliver from My hand. When I act, who can reverse it?

14 Thus said *Hashem*, Your Redeemer, the Holy One of *Yisrael*: For your sake I send to Babylon; I will bring down all [her] bars, And the Chaldeans shall raise their voice in lamentation.

15 I am your Holy One, *Hashem*, Your King, the Creator of *Yisrael*.

16 Thus said *Hashem*, Who made a road through the sea And a path through mighty waters,

17 Who destroyed chariots and horses, And all the mighty host – They lay down to rise no more, They were extinguished, quenched like a wick:

18 Do not recall what happened of old, Or ponder what happened of yore!

19 I am about to do something new; Even now it shall come to pass, Suddenly you shall perceive it: I will make a road through the wilderness And rivers in the desert.

20 The wild beasts shall honor Me, Jackals and ostriches, For I provide water in the wilderness, Rivers in the desert, To give drink to My chosen people,

21 The people I formed for Myself That they might declare My praise.

22 But you have not worshiped Me, O *Yaakov*, That you should be weary of Me, O *Yisrael*.

23 You have not brought Me your sheep for burnt offerings, Nor honored Me with your sacrifices. I have not burdened you with meal offerings, Nor wearied you about frankincense.

24 You have not bought Me fragrant reed with money, Nor sated Me with the fat of your sacrifices. Instead, you have burdened Me with your sins, You have wearied Me with your iniquities.

Yeshayahu/Isaiah
Chapter 44

25 It is I, I who – for My own sake – Wipe your transgressions away And remember your sins no more.

26 Help me remember! Let us join in argument, Tell your version, That you may be vindicated.

27 Your earliest ancestor sinned, And your spokesmen transgressed against Me.

28 So I profaned the holy princes; I abandoned *Yaakov* to proscription And *Yisrael* to mockery.

44 1 But hear, now, O *Yaakov* My servant, *Yisrael* whom I have chosen!

2 Thus said *Hashem*, your Maker, Your Creator who has helped you since birth: Fear not, My servant *Yaakov*, Jeshurun whom I have chosen,

3 Even as I pour water on thirsty soil, And rain upon dry ground, So will I pour My spirit on your offspring, My blessing upon your posterity.

> KEE e-tzak MA-yim al tza-MAY v'-no-z'-LEEM al ya-ba-SHAH e-TZOK ru-KHEE al zar-E-kha u-vir-kha-TEE al tze-e-tza-E-kha

4 And they shall sprout like grass, Like willows by watercourses.

5 One shall say, "I am *Hashem*'s," Another shall use the name of "*Yaakov*," Another shall mark his arm "of *Hashem*" And adopt the name of "*Yisrael*."

6 Thus said *Hashem*, the King of *Yisrael*, Their Redeemer, the Lord of Hosts: I am the first and I am the last, And there is no god but Me.

7 Who like Me can announce, Can foretell it – and match Me thereby? Even as I told the future to an ancient people, So let him foretell coming events to them.

8 Do not be frightened, do not be shaken! Have I not from of old predicted to you? I foretold, and you are My witnesses. Is there any god, then, but Me? "There is no other rock; I know none!"

44:3 Even as I pour water on thirsty soil... So will I pour My spirit on your offspring Water is often used as a metaphor for *Torah*. The Talmud (*Taanit* 7a) explains that "just as water leaves a high place and flows downward to a low place, so does *Torah* knowledge flow away from those who are arrogant and toward those who are humble." Furthermore, just as water nourishes and sustains the "thirsty soil" and "dry ground," the Bible is the source of our spiritual nourishment.

Yeshayahu/Isaiah
Chapter 44

9 The makers of idols All work to no purpose; And the things they treasure Can do no good, As they themselves can testify. They neither look nor think, And so they shall be shamed.

10 Who would fashion a god Or cast a statue That can do no good?

11 Lo, all its adherents shall be shamed; They are craftsmen, are merely human. Let them all assemble and stand up! They shall be cowed, and they shall be shamed.

12 The craftsman in iron, with his tools, Works it over charcoal And fashions it by hammering, Working with the strength of his arm. Should he go hungry, his strength would ebb; Should he drink no water, he would grow faint.

13 The craftsman in wood measures with a line And marks out a shape with a stylus; He forms it with scraping tools, Marking it out with a compass. He gives it a human form, The beauty of a man, to dwell in a shrine.

14 For his use he cuts down cedars; He chooses plane trees and oaks. He sets aside trees of the forest; Or plants firs, and the rain makes them grow.

15 All this serves man for fuel: He takes some to warm himself, And he builds a fire and bakes bread. He also makes a god of it and worships it, Fashions an idol and bows down to it!

16 Part of it he burns in a fire: On that part he roasts* meat, He eats* the roast and is sated; He also warms himself and cries, "Ah, I am warm! I can feel the heat!"

17 Of the rest he makes a god – his own carving! He bows down to it, worships it; He prays to it and cries, "Save me, for you are my god!"

18 They have no wit or judgment: Their eyes are besmeared, and they see not; Their minds, and they cannot think.

19 They do not give thought, They lack the wit and judgment to say: "Part of it I burned in a fire; I also baked bread on the coals, I roasted meat and ate it – Should I make the rest an abhorrence? Should I bow to a block of wood?"

---

* The words "roasts" and "eats" transposed for clarity

Yeshayahu/Isaiah
Chapter 45

20 He pursues ashes! A deluded mind has led him astray, And he cannot save himself; He never says to himself, "The thing in my hand is a fraud!"

21 Remember these things, O *Yaakov* For you, O *Yisrael*, are My servant: I fashioned you, you are My servant – O *Yisrael*, never forget Me.

22 I wipe away your sins like a cloud, Your transgressions like mist – Come back to Me, for I redeem you.

23 Shout, O heavens, for *Hashem* has acted; Shout aloud, O depths of the earth! Shout for joy, O mountains, O forests with all your trees! For *Hashem* has redeemed *Yaakov*, Has glorified Himself through *Yisrael*.

24 Thus said *Hashem*, your Redeemer, Who formed you in the womb: It is I, *Hashem*, who made everything, Who alone stretched out the heavens And unaided spread out the earth;

25 Who annul the omens of diviners, And make fools of the augurs; Who turn sages back And make nonsense of their knowledge;

26 But confirm the word of My servant And fulfill the prediction of My messengers. It is I who say of *Yerushalayim*, "It shall be inhabited," And of the towns of *Yehuda*, "They shall be rebuilt; And I will restore their ruined places."

27 [I,] who said to the deep, "Be dry; I will dry up your floods,"

28 Am the same who says of Cyrus, "He is My shepherd; He shall fulfill all My purposes! He shall say of *Yerushalayim*, 'She shall be rebuilt,' And to the Temple: 'You shall be founded again.'"

45

1 Thus said *Hashem* to Cyrus, His anointed one – Whose right hand He has grasped, Treading down nations before him, Ungirding the loins of kings, Opening doors before him And letting no gate stay shut:

2 I will march before you And level the hills that loom up; I will shatter doors of bronze And cut down iron bars.

3 I will give you treasures concealed in the dark And secret hoards – So that you may know that it is I *Hashem*, The God of *Yisrael*, who call you by name.

ישעיהו
פרק מה

כ רֹעֶה אֵפֶר לֵב הוּתַל הִטָּהוּ וְלֹא־יַצִּיל אֶת־נַפְשׁוֹ וְלֹא יֹאמַר הֲלוֹא שֶׁקֶר בִּימִינִי׃

כא זְכָר־אֵלֶּה יַעֲקֹב וְיִשְׂרָאֵל כִּי עַבְדִּי־אָתָּה יְצַרְתִּיךָ עֶבֶד־לִי אַתָּה יִשְׂרָאֵל לֹא תִנָּשֵׁנִי׃

כב מָחִיתִי כָעָב פְּשָׁעֶיךָ וְכֶעָנָן חַטֹּאותֶיךָ שׁוּבָה אֵלַי כִּי גְאַלְתִּיךָ׃

כג רָנּוּ שָׁמַיִם כִּי־עָשָׂה יְהֹוָה הָרִיעוּ תַּחְתִּיּוֹת אָרֶץ פִּצְחוּ הָרִים רִנָּה יַעַר וְכָל־עֵץ בּוֹ כִּי־גָאַל יְהֹוָה יַעֲקֹב וּבְיִשְׂרָאֵל יִתְפָּאָר׃

כד כֹּה־אָמַר יְהֹוָה גֹּאֲלֶךָ וְיֹצֶרְךָ מִבָּטֶן אָנֹכִי יְהֹוָה עֹשֶׂה כֹּל נֹטֶה שָׁמַיִם לְבַדִּי רֹקַע הָאָרֶץ מִי אִתִּי [מֵאִתִּי]׃

כה מֵפֵר אֹתוֹת בַּדִּים וְקֹסְמִים יְהוֹלֵל מֵשִׁיב חֲכָמִים אָחוֹר וְדַעְתָּם יְשַׂכֵּל׃

כו מֵקִים דְּבַר עַבְדּוֹ וַעֲצַת מַלְאָכָיו יַשְׁלִים הָאֹמֵר לִירוּשָׁלַ͏ִם תּוּשָׁב וּלְעָרֵי יְהוּדָה תִּבָּנֶינָה וְחָרְבוֹתֶיהָ אֲקוֹמֵם׃

כז הָאֹמֵר לַצּוּלָה חֳרָבִי וְנַהֲרֹתַיִךְ אוֹבִישׁ׃

כח הָאֹמֵר לְכוֹרֶשׁ רֹעִי וְכָל־חֶפְצִי יַשְׁלִם וְלֵאמֹר לִירוּשָׁלַ͏ִם תִּבָּנֶה וְהֵיכָל תִּוָּסֵד׃

מה א כֹּה־אָמַר יְהֹוָה לִמְשִׁיחוֹ לְכוֹרֶשׁ אֲשֶׁר־הֶחֱזַקְתִּי בִימִינוֹ לְרַד־לְפָנָיו גּוֹיִם וּמָתְנֵי מְלָכִים אֲפַתֵּחַ לִפְתֹּחַ לְפָנָיו דְּלָתַיִם וּשְׁעָרִים לֹא יִסָּגֵרוּ׃

ב אֲנִי לְפָנֶיךָ אֵלֵךְ וַהֲדוּרִים אוֹשִׁר [אֲיַשֵּׁר] דַּלְתוֹת נְחוּשָׁה אֲשַׁבֵּר וּבְרִיחֵי בַרְזֶל אֲגַדֵּעַ׃

ג וְנָתַתִּי לְךָ אוֹצְרוֹת חֹשֶׁךְ וּמַטְמֻנֵי מִסְתָּרִים לְמַעַן תֵּדַע כִּי־אֲנִי יְהֹוָה הַקּוֹרֵא בְשִׁמְךָ אֱלֹהֵי יִשְׂרָאֵל׃

Yeshayahu/Isaiah
Chapter 45

ישעיהו
פרק מה

4 For the sake of My servant *Yaakov*, *Yisrael* My chosen one, I call you by name, I hail you by title, though you have not known Me.

לְמַעַן עַבְדִּי יַעֲקֹב וְיִשְׂרָאֵל בְּחִירִי וָאֶקְרָא לְךָ בִּשְׁמֶךָ אֲכַנְּךָ וְלֹא יְדַעְתָּנִי׃

l'-MA-an av-DEE ya-a-KOV v'-yis-ra-AYL b'-khee-REE va-ek-RA l'-KHA bish-ME-kha a-kha-n'-KHA v'-LO y'-da-TA-nee

5 I am *Hashem* and there is none else; Beside Me, there is no god. I engird you, though you have not known Me,

אֲנִי יְהֹוָה וְאֵין עוֹד זוּלָתִי אֵין אֱלֹהִים אֲאַזֶּרְךָ וְלֹא יְדַעְתָּנִי׃

6 So that they may know, from east to west, That there is none but Me. I am *Hashem* and there is none else,

לְמַעַן יֵדְעוּ מִמִּזְרַח־שֶׁמֶשׁ וּמִמַּעֲרָבָה כִּי־אֶפֶס בִּלְעָדָי אֲנִי יְהֹוָה וְאֵין עוֹד׃

7 I form light and create darkness, I make weal and create woe – I *Hashem* do all these things.

יוֹצֵר אוֹר וּבוֹרֵא חֹשֶׁךְ עֹשֶׂה שָׁלוֹם וּבוֹרֵא רָע אֲנִי יְהֹוָה עֹשֶׂה כָל־אֵלֶּה׃

8 Pour down, O skies, from above! Let the heavens rain down victory! Let the earth open up and triumph sprout Yes, let vindication spring up: I *Hashem* have created it.

הַרְעִיפוּ שָׁמַיִם מִמַּעַל וּשְׁחָקִים יִזְּלוּ־צֶדֶק תִּפְתַּח־אֶרֶץ וְיִפְרוּ־יֶשַׁע וּצְדָקָה תַצְמִיחַ יַחַד אֲנִי יְהֹוָה בְּרָאתִיו׃

9 Shame on him who argues with his Maker, Though naught but a potsherd of earth! Shall the clay say to the potter, "What are you doing? Your work has no handles"?

הוֹי רָב אֶת־יֹצְרוֹ חֶרֶשׂ אֶת־חַרְשֵׂי אֲדָמָה הֲיֹאמַר חֹמֶר לְיֹצְרוֹ מַה־תַּעֲשֶׂה וּפָעָלְךָ אֵין־יָדַיִם לוֹ׃

10 Shame on him who asks his father, "What are you begetting?" Or a woman, "What are you bearing?"

הוֹי אֹמֵר לְאָב מַה־תּוֹלִיד וּלְאִשָּׁה מַה־תְּחִילִין׃

11 Thus said *Hashem*, *Yisrael*'s Holy One and Maker: Will you question Me on the destiny of My children, Will you instruct Me about the work of My hands?

כֹּה־אָמַר יְהֹוָה קְדוֹשׁ יִשְׂרָאֵל וְיֹצְרוֹ הָאֹתִיּוֹת שְׁאָלוּנִי עַל־בָּנַי וְעַל־פֹּעַל יָדַי תְּצַוֻּנִי׃

12 It was I who made the earth And created man upon it; My own hands stretched out the heavens, And I marshaled all their host.

אָנֹכִי עָשִׂיתִי אֶרֶץ וְאָדָם עָלֶיהָ בָרָאתִי אֲנִי יָדַי נָטוּ שָׁמַיִם וְכָל־צְבָאָם צִוֵּיתִי׃

13 It was I who roused him for victory And who level all roads for him. He shall rebuild My city And let My exiled people go Without price and without payment – said the Lord of Hosts.

אָנֹכִי הַעִירֹתִהוּ בְצֶדֶק וְכָל־דְּרָכָיו אֲיַשֵּׁר הוּא־יִבְנֶה עִירִי וְגָלוּתִי יְשַׁלֵּחַ לֹא בִמְחִיר וְלֹא בְשֹׁחַד אָמַר יְהֹוָה צְבָאוֹת׃

45:4 For the sake of My servant *Yaakov*, *Yisrael* My chosen one The speed with which Cyrus rose to world dominion was nothing short of miraculous. At the beginning of the chapter, *Yeshayahu* predicts that on the night Cyrus will march his army into Babylonia, the gates of the city will be left open. In Cyrus's own chronicle of his conquest, he describes in amazement how the gates of the cities opened before his armies. According to the prophet, this will be a sign to the new king Cyrus that he was chosen for a larger, divine purpose – restoring the People of Israel to their natural home. Indeed, one of the first things Cyrus does as king is grant permission to the Jews to return to Israel and to rebuild the *Beit Hamikdash* (see Ezra 1), as predicted above (44:26–28).

Yeshayahu/Isaiah
Chapter 45

יד כֹּה ׀ אָמַר יְהֹוָה יְגִיעַ מִצְרַיִם וּסְחַר־כּוּשׁ וּסְבָאִים אַנְשֵׁי מִדָּה עָלַיִךְ יַעֲבֹרוּ וְלָךְ יִהְיוּ אַחֲרַיִךְ יֵלֵכוּ בַּזִּקִּים יַעֲבֹרוּ וְאֵלַיִךְ יִשְׁתַּחֲווּ אֵלַיִךְ יִתְפַּלָּלוּ אַךְ בָּךְ אֵל וְאֵין עוֹד אֶפֶס אֱלֹהִים:

טו אָכֵן אַתָּה אֵל מִסְתַּתֵּר אֱלֹהֵי יִשְׂרָאֵל מוֹשִׁיעַ:

טז בּוֹשׁוּ וְגַם־נִכְלְמוּ כֻּלָּם יַחְדָּו הָלְכוּ בַכְּלִמָּה חָרָשֵׁי צִירִים:

יז יִשְׂרָאֵל נוֹשַׁע בַּיהֹוָה תְּשׁוּעַת עוֹלָמִים לֹא־תֵבֹשׁוּ וְלֹא־תִכָּלְמוּ עַד־עוֹלְמֵי עַד:

יח כִּי כֹה אָמַר־יְהֹוָה בּוֹרֵא הַשָּׁמַיִם הוּא הָאֱלֹהִים יֹצֵר הָאָרֶץ וְעֹשָׂהּ הוּא כוֹנְנָהּ לֹא־תֹהוּ בְרָאָהּ לָשֶׁבֶת יְצָרָהּ אֲנִי יְהֹוָה וְאֵין עוֹד:

יט לֹא בַסֵּתֶר דִּבַּרְתִּי בִּמְקוֹם אֶרֶץ חֹשֶׁךְ לֹא אָמַרְתִּי לְזֶרַע יַעֲקֹב תֹּהוּ בַקְּשׁוּנִי אֲנִי יְהֹוָה דֹּבֵר צֶדֶק מַגִּיד מֵישָׁרִים:

כ הִקָּבְצוּ וָבֹאוּ הִתְנַגְּשׁוּ יַחְדָּו פְּלִיטֵי הַגּוֹיִם לֹא יָדְעוּ הַנֹּשְׂאִים אֶת־עֵץ פִּסְלָם וּמִתְפַּלְלִים אֶל־אֵל לֹא יוֹשִׁיעַ:

כא הַגִּידוּ וְהַגִּישׁוּ אַף יִוָּעֲצוּ יַחְדָּו מִי הִשְׁמִיעַ זֹאת מִקֶּדֶם מֵאָז הִגִּידָהּ הֲלוֹא אֲנִי יְהֹוָה וְאֵין־עוֹד אֱלֹהִים מִבַּלְעָדַי אֵל־צַדִּיק וּמוֹשִׁיעַ אַיִן זוּלָתִי:

כב פְּנוּ־אֵלַי וְהִוָּשְׁעוּ כׇּל־אַפְסֵי־אָרֶץ כִּי אֲנִי־אֵל וְאֵין עוֹד:

כג בִּי נִשְׁבַּעְתִּי יָצָא מִפִּי צְדָקָה דָּבָר וְלֹא יָשׁוּב כִּי־לִי תִּכְרַע כׇּל־בֶּרֶךְ תִּשָּׁבַע כׇּל־לָשׁוֹן:

כד אַךְ בַּיהֹוָה לִי אָמַר צְדָקוֹת וָעֹז עָדָיו יָבוֹא וְיֵבֹשׁוּ כֹּל הַנֶּחֱרִים בּוֹ:

כה בַּיהֹוָה יִצְדְּקוּ וְיִתְהַלְלוּ כׇּל־זֶרַע יִשְׂרָאֵל:

14 Thus said *Hashem*: Egypt's wealth and Nubia's gains And Sabaites, long of limb, Shall pass over to you and be yours, Pass over and follow you in fetters, Bow low to you And reverently address you: "Only among you is *Hashem*, There is no other god at all!

15 You are indeed a *Hashem* who concealed Himself, O God of *Yisrael*, who bring victory!

16 Those who fabricate idols, All are shamed and disgraced; To a man, they slink away in disgrace.

17 But *Yisrael* has won through *Hashem* Triumph everlasting. You shall not be shamed or disgraced In all the ages to come!"

18 For thus said *Hashem*, The Creator of heaven who alone is *Hashem*, Who formed the earth and made it, Who alone established it – He did not create it a waste, But formed it for habitation: I am *Hashem*, and there is none else.

19 I did not speak in secret, At a site in a land of darkness; I did not say to the stock of *Yaakov*, "Seek Me out in a wasteland" – I *Hashem*, who foretell reliably, Who announce what is true.

20 Come, gather together, Draw nigh, you remnants of the nations! No foreknowledge had they who carry their wooden images And pray to a god who cannot give success.

21 Speak up, compare testimony – Let them even take counsel together! Who announced this aforetime, Foretold it of old? Was it not I *Hashem*? Then there is no god beside Me, No *Hashem* exists beside Me Who foretells truly and grants success.

22 Turn to Me and gain success, All the ends of earth! For I am *Hashem*, and there is none else.

23 By Myself have I sworn, From My mouth has issued truth, A word that shall not turn back: To Me every knee shall bend, Every tongue swear loyalty.

24 They shall say: "Only through *Hashem* Can I find victory and might. When people trust in Him, All their adversaries are put to shame.

25 It is through *Hashem* that all the offspring of *Yisrael* Have vindication and glory."

Yeshayahu/Isaiah
Chapter 46

א כָּרַע בֵּל קֹרֵס נְבוֹ הָיוּ עֲצַבֵּיהֶם לַחַיָּה וְלַבְּהֵמָה נְשֻׂאֹתֵיכֶם עֲמוּסוֹת מַשָּׂא לַעֲיֵפָה:

1 Bel is bowed, Nebo is cowering, Their images are a burden for beasts and cattle; The things you would carry [in procession] Are now piled as a burden On tired [beasts].

ב קָרְסוּ כָרְעוּ יַחְדָּו לֹא יָכְלוּ מַלֵּט מַשָּׂא וְנַפְשָׁם בַּשְּׁבִי הָלָכָה:

2 They cowered, they bowed as well, They could not rescue the burden, And they themselves went into captivity.

ג שִׁמְעוּ אֵלַי בֵּית יַעֲקֹב וְכָל־שְׁאֵרִית בֵּית יִשְׂרָאֵל הַעֲמֻסִים מִנִּי־בֶטֶן הַנְּשֻׂאִים מִנִּי־רָחַם:

3 Listen to Me, O House of *Yaakov*, All that are left of the House of *Yisrael*, Who have been carried since birth, Supported since leaving the womb:

ד וְעַד־זִקְנָה אֲנִי הוּא וְעַד־שֵׂיבָה אֲנִי אֶסְבֹּל אֲנִי עָשִׂיתִי וַאֲנִי אֶשָּׂא וַאֲנִי אֶסְבֹּל וַאֲמַלֵּט:

4 Till you grow old, I will still be the same; When you turn gray, it is I who will carry; I was the Maker, and I will be the Bearer; And I will carry and rescue [you].

ה לְמִי תְדַמְיוּנִי וְתַשְׁווּ וְתַמְשִׁלוּנִי וְנִדְמֶה:

5 To whom can you compare Me Or declare Me similar? To whom can you liken Me, So that we seem comparable?

ו הַזָּלִים זָהָב מִכִּיס וְכֶסֶף בַּקָּנֶה יִשְׁקֹלוּ יִשְׂכְּרוּ צוֹרֵף וְיַעֲשֵׂהוּ אֵל יִסְגְּדוּ אַף־יִשְׁתַּחֲווּ:

6 Those who squander gold from the purse And weigh out silver on the balance, They hire a metal worker to make it into a god, To which they bow down and prostrate themselves.

ז יִשָּׂאֻהוּ עַל־כָּתֵף יִסְבְּלֻהוּ וְיַנִּיחֻהוּ תַחְתָּיו וְיַעֲמֹד מִמְּקוֹמוֹ לֹא יָמִישׁ אַף־יִצְעַק אֵלָיו וְלֹא יַעֲנֶה מִצָּרָתוֹ לֹא יוֹשִׁיעֶנּוּ:

7 They must carry it on their backs and transport it; When they put it down, it stands, It does not budge from its place. If they cry out to it, it does not answer; It cannot save them from their distress.

ח זִכְרוּ־זֹאת וְהִתְאֹשָׁשׁוּ הָשִׁיבוּ פוֹשְׁעִים עַל־לֵב:

8 Keep this in mind, and stand firm! Take this to heart, you sinners!

ט זִכְרוּ רִאשֹׁנוֹת מֵעוֹלָם כִּי אָנֹכִי אֵל וְאֵין עוֹד אֱלֹהִים וְאֶפֶס כָּמוֹנִי:

9 Bear in mind what happened of old; For I am *Hashem*, and there is none else, I am divine, and there is none like Me.

י מַגִּיד מֵרֵאשִׁית אַחֲרִית וּמִקֶּדֶם אֲשֶׁר לֹא־נַעֲשׂוּ אֹמֵר עֲצָתִי תָקוּם וְכָל־חֶפְצִי אֶעֱשֶׂה:

10 I foretell the end from the beginning, And from the start, things that had not occurred. I say: My plan shall be fulfilled; I will do all I have purposed.

יא קֹרֵא מִמִּזְרָח עַיִט מֵאֶרֶץ מֶרְחָק אִישׁ עֲצָתוֹ [עֲצָתִי] אַף־דִּבַּרְתִּי אַף־אֲבִיאֶנָּה יָצַרְתִּי אַף־אֶעֱשֶׂנָּה:

11 I summoned that swooping bird from the East; From a distant land, the man for My purpose. I have spoken, so I will bring it to pass; I have designed it, so I will complete it.

יב שִׁמְעוּ אֵלַי אַבִּירֵי לֵב הָרְחוֹקִים מִצְּדָקָה:

12 Listen to Me, you stubborn of heart, Who are far from victory:

Yeshayahu/Isaiah
Chapter 47

ישעיהו
פרק מז

13 I am bringing My victory close; It shall not be far, And My triumph shall not be delayed. I will grant triumph in *Tzion* To *Yisrael*, in whom I glory.

יג קֵרַבְתִּי צִדְקָתִי לֹא תִרְחָק וּתְשׁוּעָתִי לֹא תְאַחֵר וְנָתַתִּי בְצִיּוֹן תְּשׁוּעָה לְיִשְׂרָאֵל תִּפְאַרְתִּי׃

kay-RAV-tee tzid-ka-TEE LO tir-KHAK ut-shu-a-TEE LO t'-a-KHAYR v'-na-ta-TEE v'-tzi-YON t'-shu-AH l'-yis-ra-AYL tif-ar-TEE

47 1 Get down, sit in the dust, Fair Maiden Babylon; Sit, dethroned, on the ground, O Fair Chaldea; Nevermore shall they call you The tender and dainty one.

מז א רְדִי וּשְׁבִי עַל־עָפָר בְּתוּלַת בַּת־בָּבֶל שְׁבִי־לָאָרֶץ אֵין־כִּסֵּא בַּת־כַּשְׂדִּים כִּי לֹא תוֹסִיפִי יִקְרְאוּ־לָךְ רַכָּה וַעֲנֻגָּה׃

2 Grasp the handmill and grind meal. Remove your veil, Strip off your train, bare your leg, Wade through the rivers.

ב קְחִי רֵחַיִם וְטַחֲנִי קָמַח גַּלִּי צַמָּתֵךְ חֶשְׂפִּי־שֹׁבֶל גַּלִּי־שׁוֹק עִבְרִי נְהָרוֹת׃

3 Your nakedness shall be uncovered, And your shame shall be exposed. I will take vengeance, And let no man intercede.

ג תִּגָּל עֶרְוָתֵךְ גַּם תֵּרָאֶה חֶרְפָּתֵךְ נָקָם אֶקָּח וְלֹא אֶפְגַּע אָדָם׃

4 Our Redeemer – Lord of Hosts is His name – Is the Holy One of *Yisrael*.

ד גֹּאֲלֵנוּ יְהֹוָה צְבָאוֹת שְׁמוֹ קְדוֹשׁ יִשְׂרָאֵל׃

go-a-LAY-nu a-do-NAI tz'-va-OT sh'-MO k'-DOSH yis-ra-AYL

5 Sit silent; retire into darkness, O Fair Chaldea; Nevermore shall they call you Mistress of Kingdoms.

ה שְׁבִי דוּמָם וּבֹאִי בַחֹשֶׁךְ בַּת־כַּשְׂדִּים כִּי לֹא תוֹסִיפִי יִקְרְאוּ־לָךְ גְּבֶרֶת מַמְלָכוֹת׃

6 I was angry at My people, I defiled My heritage; I put them into your hands, But you showed them no mercy. Even upon the aged you made Your yoke exceedingly heavy.

ו קָצַפְתִּי עַל־עַמִּי חִלַּלְתִּי נַחֲלָתִי וָאֶתְּנֵם בְּיָדֵךְ לֹא־שַׂמְתְּ לָהֶם רַחֲמִים עַל־זָקֵן הִכְבַּדְתְּ עֻלֵּךְ מְאֹד׃

7 You thought, "I shall always be The mistress still." You did not take these things to heart, You gave no thought to the end of it.

ז וַתֹּאמְרִי לְעוֹלָם אֶהְיֶה גְבָרֶת עַד לֹא־שַׂמְתְּ אֵלֶּה עַל־לִבֵּךְ לֹא זָכַרְתְּ אַחֲרִיתָהּ׃

46:13 I will grant triumph in *Tzion* to *Yisrael*, in whom I glory In the Bible, the word *Tzion* often refers to *Yerushalayim*. Reflecting upon the significance of the holy city, Holocaust survivor and Nobel prize winner Elie Wiesel said, "Jerusalem must remain the world's Jewish spiritual capital, not a symbol of anguish and bitterness, but a symbol of trust and hope. As the Hasidic master Rebbe Nahman of Bratslav said, 'Everything in this world has a heart; the heart itself has its own heart.' Jerusalem is the heart of our heart, the soul of our soul."

47:4 Our Redeemer – Lord of Hosts is His name *Yeshayahu* portrays Babylon in its humiliation as a female in deep distress, working at a wheel, exposed in the marketplace. Suddenly, Israel (or *Yeshayahu* himself) exclaims, "Our Redeemer – Lord of hosts is His name, the Holy One of *Yisrael*." This highlights the difference between Israel and Babylon. Though punished and exiled, *Hashem* is always present for the Israelites, offering hope and encouragement that they will be redeemed and returned to their land. Babylon, on the other hand, remains friendless and alone.

Elie Wiesel (1928–2016)

Yeshayahu/Isaiah

Chapter 48

8 And now hear this, O pampered one – Who dwell in security, Who think to yourself, "I am, and there is none but me; I shall not become a widow Or know loss of children" –

9 These two things shall come upon you, Suddenly, in one day: Loss of children and widowhood Shall come upon you in full measure, Despite your many enchantments And all your countless spells.

10 You were secure in your wickedness; You thought, "No one can see me." It was your skill and your science That led you astray. And you thought to yourself, "I am, and there is none but me."

11 Evil is coming upon you Which you will not know how to charm away; Disaster is falling upon you Which you will not be able to appease; Coming upon you suddenly Is ruin of which you know nothing.

12 Stand up, with your spells and your many enchantments On which you labored since youth! Perhaps you'll be able to profit, Perhaps you will find strength.

13 You are helpless, despite all your art. Let them stand up and help you now, Th scanners of heaven, the star-gazers, Who announce, month by month, Whatever will come upon you.

14 See, they are become like straw, Fire consumes them; They cannot save themselves From the power of the flame; This is no coal for warming oneself, No fire to sit by!

15 This is what they have profited you – The traders you dealt with since youth – Each has wandered off his own way, There is none to save you. 1

48 1 Listen to this, O House of *Yaakov*, Who bear the name *Yisrael* And have issued from the waters of *Yehuda*, Who swear by the name of *Hashem* And invoke the God of *Yisrael* – Though not in truth and sincerity –

2 For you are called after the Holy City And you do lean on the God of *Yisrael*, Whose name is Lord of Hosts:

3 Long ago, I foretold things that happened, From My mouth they issued, and I announced them; Suddenly I acted, and they came to pass.

ישעיהו

פרק מח

ח וְעַתָּה שִׁמְעִי־זֹאת עֲדִינָה הַיּוֹשֶׁבֶת לָבֶטַח הָאֹמְרָה בִּלְבָבָהּ אֲנִי וְאַפְסִי עוֹד לֹא אֵשֵׁב אַלְמָנָה וְלֹא אֵדַע שְׁכוֹל:

ט וְתָבֹאנָה לָּךְ שְׁתֵּי־אֵלֶּה רֶגַע בְּיוֹם אֶחָד שְׁכוֹל וְאַלְמֹן כְּתֻמָּם בָּאוּ עָלַיִךְ בְּרֹב כְּשָׁפַיִךְ בְּעָצְמַת חֲבָרַיִךְ מְאֹד:

י וַתִּבְטְחִי בְרָעָתֵךְ אָמַרְתְּ אֵין רֹאָנִי חָכְמָתֵךְ וְדַעְתֵּךְ הִיא שׁוֹבְבָתֶךְ וַתֹּאמְרִי בְלִבֵּךְ אֲנִי וְאַפְסִי עוֹד:

יא וּבָא עָלַיִךְ רָעָה לֹא תֵדְעִי שַׁחְרָהּ וְתִפֹּל עָלַיִךְ הֹוָה לֹא תוּכְלִי כַּפְּרָהּ וְתָבֹא עָלַיִךְ פִּתְאֹם שׁוֹאָה לֹא תֵדָעִי:

יב עִמְדִי־נָא בַחֲבָרַיִךְ וּבְרֹב כְּשָׁפַיִךְ בַּאֲשֶׁר יָגַעַתְּ מִנְּעוּרָיִךְ אוּלַי תּוּכְלִי הוֹעִיל אוּלַי תַּעֲרוֹצִי:

יג נִלְאֵית בְּרֹב עֲצָתָיִךְ יַעַמְדוּ־נָא וְיוֹשִׁיעֻךְ הברו [הֹבְרֵי] שָׁמַיִם הַחֹזִים בַּכּוֹכָבִים מוֹדִיעִם לֶחֳדָשִׁים מֵאֲשֶׁר יָבֹאוּ עָלָיִךְ:

יד הִנֵּה הָיוּ כְקַשׁ אֵשׁ שְׂרָפָתַם לֹא־יַצִּילוּ אֶת־נַפְשָׁם מִיַּד לֶהָבָה אֵין־גַּחֶלֶת לַחְמָם אוּר לָשֶׁבֶת נֶגְדּוֹ:

טו כֵּן הָיוּ־לָךְ אֲשֶׁר יָגָעַתְּ סֹחֲרַיִךְ מִנְּעוּרַיִךְ אִישׁ לְעֶבְרוֹ תָּעוּ אֵין מוֹשִׁיעֵךְ:

מח א שִׁמְעוּ־זֹאת בֵּית־יַעֲקֹב הַנִּקְרָאִים בְּשֵׁם יִשְׂרָאֵל וּמִמֵּי יְהוּדָה יָצָאוּ הַנִּשְׁבָּעִים בְּשֵׁם יְהֹוָה וּבֵאלֹהֵי יִשְׂרָאֵל יַזְכִּירוּ לֹא בֶאֱמֶת וְלֹא בִצְדָקָה:

ב כִּי־מֵעִיר הַקֹּדֶשׁ נִקְרָאוּ וְעַל־אֱלֹהֵי יִשְׂרָאֵל נִסְמָכוּ יְהֹוָה צְבָאוֹת שְׁמוֹ:

ג הָרִאשֹׁנוֹת מֵאָז הִגַּדְתִּי וּמִפִּי יָצְאוּ וְאַשְׁמִיעֵם פִּתְאֹם עָשִׂיתִי וַתָּבֹאנָה:

Yeshayahu/Isaiah
Chapter 48

ישעיהו

פרק מח

4 Because I know how stubborn you are (Your neck is like an iron sinew And your forehead bronze),

ד מִדַּעְתִּי כִּי קָשֶׁה אָתָּה וְגִיד בַּרְזֶל עָרְפֶּךָ וּמִצְחֲךָ נְחוּשָׁה:

5 Therefore I told you long beforehand, Announced things to you ere they happened – That you might not say, "My idol caused them, My carved and molten images ordained them."

ה וָאַגִּיד לְךָ מֵאָז בְּטֶרֶם תָּבוֹא הִשְׁמַעְתִּיךָ פֶּן־תֹּאמַר עָצְבִּי עָשָׂם וּפִסְלִי וְנִסְכִּי צִוָּם:

6 You have heard all this; look, must you not acknowledge it? As of now, I announce to you new things, Well-guarded secrets you did not know.

ו שָׁמַעְתָּ חֲזֵה כֻּלָּהּ וְאַתֶּם הֲלוֹא תַגִּידוּ הִשְׁמַעְתִּיךָ חֲדָשׁוֹת מֵעַתָּה וּנְצֻרוֹת וְלֹא יְדַעְתָּם:

7 Only now are they created, and not of old; Before today you had not heard them; You cannot say, "I knew them already."

ז עַתָּה נִבְרְאוּ וְלֹא מֵאָז וְלִפְנֵי־יוֹם וְלֹא שְׁמַעְתָּם פֶּן־תֹּאמַר הִנֵּה יְדַעְתִּין:

8 You had never heard, you had never known, Your ears were not opened of old. Though I know that you are treacherous, That you were called a rebel from birth,

ח גַּם לֹא־שָׁמַעְתָּ גַּם לֹא יָדַעְתָּ גַּם מֵאָז לֹא־פִתְּחָה אָזְנֶךָ כִּי יָדַעְתִּי בָּגוֹד תִּבְגּוֹד וּפֹשֵׁעַ מִבֶּטֶן קֹרָא לָךְ:

9 For the sake of My name I control My wrath; To My own glory, I am patient with you, And I will not destroy you.

ט לְמַעַן שְׁמִי אַאֲרִיךְ אַפִּי וּתְהִלָּתִי אֶחֱטָם־לָךְ לְבִלְתִּי הַכְרִיתֶךָ:

10 See, I refine you, but not as silver; I test you in the furnace of affliction.

י הִנֵּה צְרַפְתִּיךָ וְלֹא בְכָסֶף בְּחַרְתִּיךָ בְּכוּר עֹנִי:

11 For My sake, My own sake, do I act – Lest [My name] be dishonored! I will not give My glory to another.

יא לְמַעֲנִי לְמַעֲנִי אֶעֱשֶׂה כִּי אֵיךְ יֵחָל וּכְבוֹדִי לְאַחֵר לֹא־אֶתֵּן:

12 Listen to Me, O *Yaakov, Yisrael*, whom I have called: I am He – I am the first, And I am the last as well.

יב שְׁמַע אֵלַי יַעֲקֹב וְיִשְׂרָאֵל מְקֹרָאִי אֲנִי־הוּא אֲנִי רִאשׁוֹן אַף אֲנִי אַחֲרוֹן:

13 My own hand founded the earth, My right hand spread out the skies. I call unto them, let them stand up.

יג אַף־יָדִי יָסְדָה אֶרֶץ וִימִינִי טִפְּחָה שָׁמָיִם קֹרֵא אֲנִי אֲלֵיהֶם יַעַמְדוּ יַחְדָּו:

14 Assemble, all of you, and listen! Who among you foretold these things: "He whom *Hashem* loves Shall work His will against Babylon, And, with His might, against Chaldea"?

יד הִקָּבְצוּ כֻלְּכֶם וּשְׁמָעוּ מִי בָהֶם הִגִּיד אֶת־אֵלֶּה יְהוָה אֲהֵבוֹ יַעֲשֶׂה חֶפְצוֹ בְּבָבֶל וּזְרֹעוֹ כַּשְׂדִּים:

15 I, I predicted, and I called him; I have brought him and he shall succeed in his mission.

טו אֲנִי אֲנִי דִּבַּרְתִּי אַף־קְרָאתִיו הֲבִיאֹתִיו וְהִצְלִיחַ דַּרְכּוֹ:

16 Draw near to Me and hear this: From the beginning, I did not speak in secret; From the time anything existed, I was there. "And now *Hashem* has sent me, endowed with His spirit."

טז קִרְבוּ אֵלַי שִׁמְעוּ־זֹאת לֹא מֵרֹאשׁ בַּסֵּתֶר דִּבַּרְתִּי מֵעֵת הֱיוֹתָהּ שָׁם אָנִי וְעַתָּה אֲדֹנָי יְהוִה שְׁלָחַנִי וְרוּחוֹ:

17 Thus said *Hashem* your Redeemer, The Holy One of *Yisrael*: I *Hashem* am your God, Instructing you for your own benefit, Guiding you in the way you should go.

יז כֹּה־אָמַר יְהוָה גֹּאֲלְךָ קְדוֹשׁ יִשְׂרָאֵל אֲנִי יְהוָה אֱלֹהֶיךָ מְלַמֶּדְךָ לְהוֹעִיל מַדְרִיכֲךָ בְּדֶרֶךְ תֵּלֵךְ:

Yeshayahu/Isaiah
Chapter 49

יח לוּא הִקְשַׁבְתָּ לְמִצְוֹתָי וַיְהִי כַנָּהָר שְׁלוֹמֶךָ וְצִדְקָתְךָ כְּגַלֵּי הַיָּם:

18 If only you would heed My commands! Then your prosperity would be like a river, Your triumph like the waves of the sea.

יט וַיְהִי כַחוֹל זַרְעֶךָ וְצֶאֱצָאֵי מֵעֶיךָ כִּמְעֹתָיו לֹא־יִכָּרֵת וְלֹא־יִשָּׁמֵד שְׁמוֹ מִלְּפָנָי:

19 Your offspring would be as many as the sand, Their issue as many as its grains. Their name would never be cut off Or obliterated from before Me.

כ צְאוּ מִבָּבֶל בִּרְחוּ מִכַּשְׂדִּים בְּקוֹל רִנָּה הַגִּידוּ הַשְׁמִיעוּ זֹאת הוֹצִיאוּהָ עַד־קְצֵה הָאָרֶץ אִמְרוּ גָּאַל יְהוָה עַבְדּוֹ יַעֲקֹב:

20 Go forth from Babylon, Flee from Chaldea! Declare this with loud shouting, Announce this, Bring out the word to the ends of the earth! Say: "*Hashem* has redeemed His servant *Yaakov*!"

כא וְלֹא צָמְאוּ בָּחֳרָבוֹת הוֹלִיכָם מַיִם מִצּוּר הִזִּיל לָמוֹ וַיִּבְקַע־צוּר וַיָּזֻבוּ מָיִם:

21 They have known no thirst, Though He led them through parched places; He made water flow for them from the rock; He cleaved the rock and water gushed forth.

כב אֵין שָׁלוֹם אָמַר יְהוָה לָרְשָׁעִים:

22 There is no safety – said *Hashem* – for the wicked.

AYN sha-LOM a-MAR a-do-NAI la-r'-sha-EEM

49

מט א שִׁמְעוּ אִיִּים אֵלַי וְהַקְשִׁיבוּ לְאֻמִּים מֵרָחוֹק יְהוָה מִבֶּטֶן קְרָאָנִי מִמְּעֵי אִמִּי הִזְכִּיר שְׁמִי:

1 Listen, O coastlands, to me, And give heed, O nations afar: *Hashem* appointed me before I was born, He named me while I was in my mother's womb.

ב וַיָּשֶׂם פִּי כְּחֶרֶב חַדָּה בְּצֵל יָדוֹ הֶחְבִּיאָנִי וַיְשִׂימֵנִי לְחֵץ בָּרוּר בְּאַשְׁפָּתוֹ הִסְתִּירָנִי:

2 He made my mouth like a sharpened blade, He hid me in the shadow of His hand, And He made me like a polished arrow; He concealed me in His quiver.

ג וַיֹּאמֶר לִי עַבְדִּי־אָתָּה יִשְׂרָאֵל אֲשֶׁר־בְּךָ אֶתְפָּאָר:

3 And He said to me, "You are My servant, *Yisrael* in whom I glory."

ד וַאֲנִי אָמַרְתִּי לְרִיק יָגַעְתִּי לְתֹהוּ וְהֶבֶל כֹּחִי כִלֵּיתִי אָכֵן מִשְׁפָּטִי אֶת־יְהוָה וּפְעֻלָּתִי אֶת־אֱלֹהָי:

4 I thought, "I have labored in vain, I have spent my strength for empty breath." But my case rested with *Hashem*, My recompense was in the hands of my God.

ה וְעַתָּה אָמַר יְהוָה יֹצְרִי מִבֶּטֶן לְעֶבֶד לוֹ לְשׁוֹבֵב יַעֲקֹב אֵלָיו וְיִשְׂרָאֵל לֹא [לוֹ] יֵאָסֵף וְאֶכָּבֵד בְּעֵינֵי יְהוָה וֵאלֹהַי הָיָה עֻזִּי:

5 And now *Hashem* has resolved – He who formed me in the womb to be His servant – To bring back *Yaakov* to Himself, That *Yisrael* may be restored to Him. ,And I have been honored in the sight of *Hashem*, My *Hashem* has been my strength.

Rabbi Abraham Ibn Ezra (1089–1167)

48:22 There is no safety *Yeshayahu* provides a triumphant account of the future journey out of Babylon and the return to Israel. In verse 21, he even includes allusions to the original journey through the desert to the Land of Israel. He concludes the section with the brief statement, "There is no safety – said *Hashem* – for the wicked." Most commentators suggest that this is a continuation of the above contrast between Israel and Babylon; while Israel is redeemed, the wicked Babylon will find no peace. The commentator *Ibn Ezra*, however, suggests that "the wicked" refers to the Jews who refuse to leave Babylon when they have the opportunity, choosing to live among an idolatrous people rather than return to the Holy Land.

Yeshayahu/Isaiah
Chapter 49

ישעיהו
פרק מט

6 For He has said: "It is too little that you should be My servant In that I raise up the tribes of *Yaakov* And restore the survivors of *Yisrael*: I will also make you a light of nations, That My salvation may reach the ends of the earth."

ו וַיֹּאמֶר נָקֵל מִהְיוֹתְךָ לִי עֶבֶד לְהָקִים אֶת־שִׁבְטֵי יַעֲקֹב וּנְצִירֵי [וּנְצוּרֵי] יִשְׂרָאֵל לְהָשִׁיב וּנְתַתִּיךָ לְאוֹר גּוֹיִם לִהְיוֹת יְשׁוּעָתִי עַד־קְצֵה הָאָרֶץ׃

7 Thus said *Hashem*, The Redeemer of *Yisrael*, his Holy One, To the despised one, To the abhorred nations, To the slave of rulers: Kings shall see and stand up; Nobles, and they shall prostrate themselves – To the honor of *Hashem*, who is faithful, To the Holy One of *Yisrael* who chose you.

ז כֹּה אָמַר־יְהֹוָה גֹּאֵל יִשְׂרָאֵל קְדוֹשׁוֹ לִבְזֹה־נֶפֶשׁ לִמְתָעֵב גּוֹי לְעֶבֶד מֹשְׁלִים מְלָכִים יִרְאוּ וָקָמוּ שָׂרִים וְיִשְׁתַּחֲווּ לְמַעַן יְהֹוָה אֲשֶׁר נֶאֱמָן קְדֹשׁ יִשְׂרָאֵל וַיִּבְחָרֶךָּ׃

8 Thus said *Hashem*: In an hour of favor I answer you, And on a day of salvation I help you – I created you and appointed you a covenant people – Restoring the land, Allotting anew the desolate holdings,

ח כֹּה אָמַר יְהֹוָה בְּעֵת רָצוֹן עֲנִיתִיךָ וּבְיוֹם יְשׁוּעָה עֲזַרְתִּיךָ וְאֶצָּרְךָ וְאֶתֶּנְךָ לִבְרִית עָם לְהָקִים אֶרֶץ לְהַנְחִיל נְחָלוֹת שֹׁמֵמוֹת׃

9 Saying to the prisoners, "Go free," To those who are in darkness, "Show yourselves." They shall pasture along the roads, On every bare height shall be their pasture.

ט לֵאמֹר לַאֲסוּרִים צֵאוּ לַאֲשֶׁר בַּחֹשֶׁךְ הִגָּלוּ עַל־דְּרָכִים יִרְעוּ וּבְכׇל־שְׁפָיִים מַרְעִיתָם׃

10 They shall not hunger or thirst, Hot wind and sun shall not strike them; For He who loves them will lead them, He will guide them to springs of water.

י לֹא יִרְעָבוּ וְלֹא יִצְמָאוּ וְלֹא־יַכֵּם שָׁרָב וָשָׁמֶשׁ כִּי־מְרַחֲמָם יְנַהֲגֵם וְעַל־מַבּוּעֵי מַיִם יְנַהֲלֵם׃

11 I will make all My mountains a road, And My highways shall be built up.

יא וְשַׂמְתִּי כׇל־הָרַי לַדָּרֶךְ וּמְסִלֹּתַי יְרֻמוּן׃

12 Look! These are coming from afar, These from the north and the west, And these from the land of Sinim.

יב הִנֵּה־אֵלֶּה מֵרָחוֹק יָבֹאוּ וְהִנֵּה־אֵלֶּה מִצָּפוֹן וּמִיָּם וְאֵלֶּה מֵאֶרֶץ סִינִים׃

13 Shout, O heavens, and rejoice, O earth! Break into shouting, O hills! For *Hashem* has comforted His people, And has taken back His afflicted ones in love.

יג רׇנּוּ שָׁמַיִם וְגִילִי אָרֶץ יפצחו [וּפִצְחוּ] הָרִים רִנָּה כִּי־נִחַם יְהֹוָה עַמּוֹ וַעֲנִיָּו יְרַחֵם׃

14 *Tzion* says, "*Hashem* has forsaken me, My Lord has forgotten me."

יד וַתֹּאמֶר צִיּוֹן עֲזָבַנִי יְהֹוָה וַאדֹנָי שְׁכֵחָנִי׃

15 Can a woman forget her baby, Or disown the child of her womb? Though she might forget, I never could forget you.

טו הֲתִשְׁכַּח אִשָּׁה עוּלָהּ מֵרַחֵם בֶּן־בִּטְנָהּ גַּם־אֵלֶּה תִשְׁכַּחְנָה וְאָנֹכִי לֹא אֶשְׁכָּחֵךְ׃

ha-tish-KAKH i-SHAH u-LAH may-ra-KHAYM ben bit-NAH gam AY-leh tish-KAKH-nah v'-a-no-KHEE lo esh-ka-KHAYKH

49:15 I never could forget you The relationship between *Hashem* and the Children of Israel is often compared to that of a husband and wife. There is, however, an additional element to the relationship; that of a parent and a child. While husbands and wives can fall out of love and the relationship can be formally ended, the mother who carries and gives birth to a child will always be that child's mother. In verse 14, Israel expresses its feelings of being abandoned and forgotten by *Hashem*. God responds in this verse by saying that His love for

Yeshayahu/Isaiah
Chapter 49

ישעיהו
פרק מט

16 See, I have engraved you On the palms of My hands, Your walls are ever before Me.

טז הֵן עַל־כַּפַּיִם חַקֹּתִיךְ חוֹמֹתַיִךְ נֶגְדִּי תָּמִיד:

17 Swiftly your children are coming; Those who ravaged and ruined you shall leave you.

יז מִהֲרוּ בָּנָיִךְ מְהָרְסַיִךְ וּמַחֲרִבַיִךְ מִמֵּךְ יֵצֵאוּ:

18 Look up all around you and see: They are all assembled, are come to you! As I live – declares *Hashem* – You shall don them all like jewels, Deck yourself with them like a bride.

יח שְׂאִי־סָבִיב עֵינַיִךְ וּרְאִי כֻּלָּם נִקְבְּצוּ בָאוּ־לָךְ חַי־אָנִי נְאֻם־יְהֹוָה כִּי כֻלָּם כָּעֲדִי תִלְבָּשִׁי וּתְקַשְּׁרִים כַּכַּלָּה:

19 As for your ruins and desolate places And your land laid waste – You shall soon be crowded with settlers, While destroyers stay far from you.

יט כִּי חָרְבֹתַיִךְ וְשֹׁמְמֹתַיִךְ וְאֶרֶץ הֲרִסֻתֵיךְ כִּי עַתָּה תֵּצְרִי מִיּוֹשֵׁב וְרָחֲקוּ מְבַלְּעָיִךְ:

20 The children you thought you had lost Shall yet say in your hearing, "The place is too crowded for me; Make room for me to settle."

כ עוֹד יֹאמְרוּ בְאָזְנַיִךְ בְּנֵי שִׁכֻּלָיִךְ צַר־לִי הַמָּקוֹם גְּשָׁה־לִּי וְאֵשֵׁבָה:

21 And you will say to yourself, "Who bore these for me When I was bereaved and barren, Exiled and disdained – By whom, then, were these reared? I was left all alone – And where have these been?"

כא וְאָמַרְתְּ בִּלְבָבֵךְ מִי יָלַד־לִי אֶת־אֵלֶּה וַאֲנִי שְׁכוּלָה וְגַלְמוּדָה גֹּלָה וְסוּרָה וְאֵלֶּה מִי גִדֵּל הֵן אֲנִי נִשְׁאַרְתִּי לְבַדִּי אֵלֶּה אֵיפֹה הֵם:

22 Thus said *Hashem*: I will raise My hand to nations And lift up My ensign to peoples; And they shall bring your sons in their bosoms, And carry your daughters on their backs.

כב כֹּה־אָמַר אֲדֹנָי יְהֹוִה הִנֵּה אֶשָּׂא אֶל־גּוֹיִם יָדִי וְאֶל־עַמִּים אָרִים נִסִּי וְהֵבִיאוּ בָנַיִךְ בְּחֹצֶן וּבְנֹתַיִךְ עַל־כָּתֵף תִּנָּשֶׂאנָה:

koh a-MAR a-do-NAI e-lo-HEEM hi-NAY e-SA el go-YIM ya-DEE v'-el a-MEEM a-REEM ni-SEE v'-hay-VEE-u va-NA-yikh b'-KHO-tzen uv-no-TA-yikh al ka-TAYF ti-na-SE-na

23 Kings shall tend your children, Their queens shall serve you as nurses. They shall bow to you, face to the ground, And lick the dust of your feet. And you shall know that I am *Hashem* – Those who trust in Me shall not be shamed.

כג וְהָיוּ מְלָכִים אֹמְנַיִךְ וְשָׂרוֹתֵיהֶם מֵינִיקֹתַיִךְ אַפַּיִם אֶרֶץ יִשְׁתַּחֲווּ לָךְ וַעֲפַר רַגְלַיִךְ יְלַחֵכוּ וְיָדַעַתְּ כִּי־אֲנִי יְהֹוָה אֲשֶׁר לֹא־יֵבֹשׁוּ קֹוָי:

24 Can spoil be taken from a warrior, Or captives retrieved from a victor?

כד הֲיֻקַּח מִגִּבּוֹר מַלְקוֹחַ וְאִם־שְׁבִי צַדִּיק יִמָּלֵט:

Major-General Orde Charles Wingate (1903–1944)

the Children of Israel is even deeper than a mother's love for her child, and promises that He could never forget His people.

49:22 And they shall bring your sons in their bosoms *Yeshayahu* describes the great contributions that the nations and individual non-Jews will play in the resettlement of *Eretz Yisrael*. In modern times, this prophecy is being fulfilled by the unprecedented number of non-Jews who visit, support and pray for Israel. Great individual Christian warriors for *Tzion* have also emerged to fulfill *Yeshayahu's* prophecy. For example, Major-General Orde Charles Wingate (1903–1944) was a British officer in Palestine during the Mandate, and trained many of the future leaders of the Israeli army. He drew on his love and knowledge of the Bible, and distilled strategies from the battles of *Yehoshua*, *Gidon* and King *David*. Known throughout Israel as "*ha-yedid*" (הידיד) or, 'the friend,' the Jewish people remember Orde Wingate and all the righteous non-Jews whose love for the Bible drove them to stand with Israel in her moment of need.

Yeshayahu/Isaiah
Chapter 50

ישעיהו
פרק נ

25 Yet thus said *Hashem*: Captives shall be taken from a warrior And spoil shall be retrieved from a tyrant; For I will contend with your adversaries, And I will deliver your children.

כה כִּי־כֹה אָמַר יְהֹוָה גַּם־שְׁבִי גִבּוֹר יֻקָּח וּמַלְקוֹחַ עָרִיץ יִמָּלֵט וְאֶת־יְרִיבֵךְ אָנֹכִי אָרִיב וְאֶת־בָּנַיִךְ אָנֹכִי אוֹשִׁיעַ׃

26 I will make your oppressors eat their own flesh, They shall be drunk with their own blood as with wine. And all mankind shall know That I *Hashem* am your Savior, The Mighty One of *Yaakov*, your Redeemer.

כו וְהַאֲכַלְתִּי אֶת־מוֹנַיִךְ אֶת־בְּשָׂרָם וְכֶעָסִיס דָּמָם יִשְׁכָּרוּן וְיָדְעוּ כָל־בָּשָׂר כִּי אֲנִי יְהֹוָה מוֹשִׁיעֵךְ וְגֹאֲלֵךְ אֲבִיר יַעֲקֹב׃

50 1 Thus said *Hashem*: Where is the bill of divorce Of your mother whom I dismissed? And which of My creditors was it To whom I sold you off? You were only sold off for your sins, And your mother dismissed for your crimes.

א כֹּה אָמַר יְהֹוָה אֵי זֶה סֵפֶר כְּרִיתוּת אִמְּכֶם אֲשֶׁר שִׁלַּחְתִּיהָ אוֹ מִי מִנּוֹשַׁי אֲשֶׁר־מָכַרְתִּי אֶתְכֶם לוֹ הֵן בַּעֲוֺנֹתֵיכֶם נִמְכַּרְתֶּם וּבְפִשְׁעֵיכֶם שֻׁלְּחָה אִמְּכֶם׃

KOH a-MAR a-do-NAI AY ZEH SAY-fer k'-ree-TUT i-m'-KHEM a-SHER shi-lakh-TEE-ha O MEE mi-no-SHAI a-sher ma-KHAR-tee et-KHEM LO HAYN ba-a-vo-no-tay-KHEM nim-kar-TEM uv-fish-ay-KHEM shu-l'-KHAH i-m'-KHEM

2 Why, when I came, was no one there, Why, when I called, would none respond? Is my arm, then, too short to rescue, Have I not the power to save? With a mere rebuke I dry up the sea, And turn rivers into desert. Their fish stink from lack of water; They lie dead of thirst.

ב מַדּוּעַ בָּאתִי וְאֵין אִישׁ קָרָאתִי וְאֵין עוֹנֶה הֲקָצוֹר קָצְרָה יָדִי מִפְּדוּת וְאִם־אֵין־בִּי כֹחַ לְהַצִּיל הֵן בְּגַעֲרָתִי אַחֲרִיב יָם אָשִׂים נְהָרוֹת מִדְבָּר תִּבְאַשׁ דְּגָתָם מֵאֵין מַיִם וְתָמֹת בַּצָּמָא׃

3 I clothe the skies in blackness And make their raiment sackcloth.

ג אַלְבִּישׁ שָׁמַיִם קַדְרוּת וְשַׂק אָשִׂים כְּסוּתָם׃

4 *Hashem* gave me a skilled tongue, To know how to speak timely words to the weary. Morning by morning, He rouses, He rouses my ear To give heed like disciples.

ד אֲדֹנָי יֱהֹוִה נָתַן לִי לְשׁוֹן לִמּוּדִים לָדַעַת לָעוּת אֶת־יָעֵף דָּבָר יָעִיר בַּבֹּקֶר בַּבֹּקֶר יָעִיר לִי אֹזֶן לִשְׁמֹעַ כַּלִּמּוּדִים׃

5 *Hashem* opened my ears And I did not disobey, I did not run away.

ה אֲדֹנָי יֱהֹוִה פָּתַח־לִי אֹזֶן וְאָנֹכִי לֹא מָרִיתִי אָחוֹר לֹא נְסוּגֹתִי׃

6 I offered my back to the floggers, And my cheeks to those who tore out my hair. I did not hide my face From insult and spittle.

ו גֵּוִי נָתַתִּי לְמַכִּים וּלְחָיַי לְמֹרְטִים פָּנַי לֹא הִסְתַּרְתִּי מִכְּלִמּוֹת וָרֹק׃

50:1 Where is the bill of divorce of your mother whom I dismissed? The prophets traditionally compare the relationship between *Hashem* and the Jewish people to that of a marriage, and to that of a parent and child. Having been exiled, Israel has good reason to fear that they have been divorced from God, or sold (see Psalms 44:13). However, *Hashem* assures His people that he has not written them a bill of divorce, nor has He sold them for any price. Despite everything, the People of Israel are still *Hashem*'s children and the objects of His affection. The bond between God and Israel is eternal, and their claim to *Eretz Yisrael*, which He gave them, will never be uprooted.

Yeshayahu/Isaiah
Chapter 51

ישעיהו
פרק נא

7 But *Hashem* will help me – Therefore I feel no disgrace; Therefore I have set my face like flint, And I know I shall not be shamed.

ז וַאדֹנָי יְהוִה יַעֲזָר־לִי עַל־כֵּן לֹא נִכְלָמְתִּי עַל־כֵּן שַׂמְתִּי פָנַי כַּחַלָּמִישׁ וָאֵדַע כִּי־לֹא אֵבוֹשׁ:

8 My Vindicator is at hand – Who dares contend with me? Let us stand up together! Who would be my opponent? Let him approach me!

ח קָרוֹב מַצְדִּיקִי מִי־יָרִיב אִתִּי נַעַמְדָה יָּחַד מִי־בַעַל מִשְׁפָּטִי יִגַּשׁ אֵלָי:

9 Lo, *Hashem* will help me – Who can get a verdict against me? They shall all wear out like a garment, The moth shall consume them.

ט הֵן אֲדֹנָי יְהוִה יַעֲזָר־לִי מִי־הוּא יַרְשִׁיעֵנִי הֵן כֻּלָּם כַּבֶּגֶד יִבְלוּ עָשׁ יֹאכְלֵם:

10 Who among you reveres *Hashem* And heeds the voice of His servant? – Though he walk in darkness And have no light, Let him trust in the name of *Hashem* And rely upon his God.

י מִי בָכֶם יְרֵא יְהוָה שֹׁמֵעַ בְּקוֹל עַבְדּוֹ אֲשֶׁר הָלַךְ חֲשֵׁכִים וְאֵין נֹגַהּ לוֹ יִבְטַח בְּשֵׁם יְהוָה וְיִשָּׁעֵן בֵּאלֹהָיו:

11 But you are all kindlers of fire, Girding on firebrands. Walk by the blaze of your fire, By the brands that you have lit! This has come to you from My hand: You shall lie down in pain.

יא הֵן כֻּלְּכֶם קֹדְחֵי אֵשׁ מְאַזְּרֵי זִיקוֹת לְכוּ בְּאוּר אֶשְׁכֶם וּבְזִיקוֹת בִּעַרְתֶּם מִיָּדִי הָיְתָה־זֹּאת לָכֶם לְמַעֲצֵבָה תִּשְׁכָּבוּן:

51 1 Listen to Me, you who pursue justice, You who seek *Hashem*: Look to the rock you were hewn from, To the quarry you were dug from.

נא א שִׁמְעוּ אֵלַי רֹדְפֵי צֶדֶק מְבַקְשֵׁי יְהוָה הַבִּיטוּ אֶל־צוּר חֻצַּבְתֶּם וְאֶל־מַקֶּבֶת בּוֹר נֻקַּרְתֶּם:

2 Look back to *Avraham* your father And to *Sara* who brought you forth. For he was only one when I called him, But I blessed him and made him many.

ב הַבִּיטוּ אֶל־אַבְרָהָם אֲבִיכֶם וְאֶל־שָׂרָה תְּחוֹלֶלְכֶם כִּי־אֶחָד קְרָאתִיו וַאֲבָרְכֵהוּ וְאַרְבֵּהוּ:

3 Truly *Hashem* has comforted *Tzion*, Comforted all her ruins; He has made her wilderness like Eden, Her desert like the Garden of *Hashem*. Gladness and joy shall abide there, Thanksgiving and the sound of music.

ג כִּי־נִחַם יְהוָה צִיּוֹן נִחַם כָּל־חָרְבֹתֶיהָ וַיָּשֶׂם מִדְבָּרָהּ כְּעֵדֶן וְעַרְבָתָהּ כְּגַן־יְהוָה שָׂשׂוֹן וְשִׂמְחָה יִמָּצֵא בָהּ תּוֹדָה וְקוֹל זִמְרָה:

kee ni-KHAM a-do-NAI tzi-YON ni-KHAM kol kho-r'-vo-TE-ha va-YA-sem mid-ba-RAH k'-AY-den v'-ar-va-TAH k'-gan a-do-NAI sa-SON v'-sim-KHA yi-ma-TZAY VAH to-DA v'-KOL zim-RAH

4 Hearken to Me, My people, And give ear to Me, O My nation, For teaching shall go forth from Me, My way for the light of peoples. In a moment I will bring it:

ד הַקְשִׁיבוּ אֵלַי עַמִּי וּלְאוּמִּי אֵלַי הַאֲזִינוּ כִּי תוֹרָה מֵאִתִּי תֵצֵא וּמִשְׁפָּטִי לְאוֹר עַמִּים אַרְגִּיעַ:

51:3 Comforted all her ruins; he has made her wilderness like Eden The Land of Israel has a supernatural quality to it. While under foreign occupation, it resembles an arid desert. However, under Jewish sovereignty, it comes to life, flourishes, and yields great produce. Indeed, for nearly two millennia, as the land switched hands numerous times between various foreign powers, including the Romans, the Arabs and the Turks, the land lay utterly desolate. Amazingly, the modern rebirth of the Jewish state in 1948 has brought with it an astounding development of the land, to the point where once again the Jewish people can claim a flourishing country all their own. In agriculture, technology, and culture, Israel ranks among the most advanced countries of the world. Indeed, we are witnessing the Lord comfort "all her ruins."

The blooming Israeli desert

Yeshayahu/Isaiah
Chapter 51

5 The triumph I grant is near, The success I give has gone forth. My arms shall provide for the peoples; The coastlands shall trust in Me, They shall look to My arm.

6 Raise your eyes to the heavens, And look upon the earth beneath: Though the heavens should melt away like smoke, And the earth wear out like a garment, And its inhabitants die out as well, My victory shall stand forever, My triumph shall remain unbroken.

7 Listen to Me, you who care for the right, O people who lay My instruction to heart! Fear not the insults of men, And be not dismayed at their jeers;

8 For the moth shall eat them up like a garment, The worm shall eat them up like wool. But My triumph shall endure forever, My salvation through all the ages.

9 Awake, awake, clothe yourself with splendor. O arm of *Hashem*! Awake as in days of old, As in former ages! It was you that hacked Rahab in pieces, That pierced the Dragon.

10 It was you that dried up the Sea, The waters of the great deep; That made the abysses of the Sea A road the redeemed might walk.

11 So let the ransomed of *Hashem* return, And come with shouting to *Tzion*, Crowned with joy everlasting. Let them attain joy and gladness, While sorrow and sighing flee.

12 I, I am He who comforts you! What ails you that you fear Man who must die, Mortals who fare like grass?

13 You have forgotten *Hashem* your Maker, Who stretched out the skies and made firm the earth! And you live all day in constant dread Because of the rage of an oppressor Who is aiming to cut [you] down. Yet of what account is the rage of an oppressor?

14 Quickly the crouching one is freed; He is not cut down and slain, And he shall not want for food.

15 For I *Hashem* your God – Who stir up the sea into roaring waves, Whose name is Lord of Hosts –

ישעיהו
פרק נא

ה קָר֤וֹב צִדְקִי֙ יָצָ֣א יִשְׁעִ֔י וּזְרֹעַ֖י עַמִּ֣ים יִשְׁפֹּ֑טוּ אֵלַי֙ אִיִּ֣ים יְקַוּ֔וּ וְאֶל־זְרֹעִ֖י יְיַחֵלֽוּן׃

ו שְׂאוּ֩ לַשָּׁמַ֨יִם עֵינֵיכֶ֜ם וְֽהַבִּ֧יטוּ אֶל־הָאָ֣רֶץ מִתַּ֗חַת כִּֽי־שָׁמַ֜יִם כֶּעָשָׁ֣ן נִמְלָ֗חוּ וְהָאָ֙רֶץ֙ כַּבֶּ֣גֶד תִּבְלֶ֔ה וְיֹשְׁבֶ֖יהָ כְּמוֹ־כֵ֣ן יְמוּת֑וּן וִישׁוּעָתִי֙ לְעוֹלָ֣ם תִּֽהְיֶ֔ה וְצִדְקָתִ֖י לֹ֥א תֵחָֽת׃

ז שִׁמְע֤וּ אֵלַי֙ יֹ֣דְעֵי צֶ֔דֶק עַ֖ם תּוֹרָתִ֣י בְלִבָּ֑ם אַל־תִּֽירְאוּ֙ חֶרְפַּ֣ת אֱנ֔וֹשׁ וּמִגִּדֻּפֹתָ֖ם אַל־תֵּחָֽתּוּ׃

ח כִּ֤י כַבֶּ֙גֶד֙ יֹאכְלֵ֣ם עָ֔שׁ וְכַצֶּ֖מֶר יֹאכְלֵ֣ם סָ֑ס וְצִדְקָתִי֙ לְעוֹלָ֣ם תִּֽהְיֶ֔ה וִישׁוּעָתִ֖י לְד֥וֹר דּוֹרִֽים׃

ט עוּרִ֥י עוּרִ֛י לִבְשִׁי־עֹ֖ז זְר֣וֹעַ יְהֹוָ֑ה ע֚וּרִי כִּ֣ימֵי קֶ֔דֶם דֹּר֖וֹת עוֹלָמִ֑ים הֲל֥וֹא אַתְּ־הִ֛יא הַמַּחְצֶ֥בֶת רַ֖הַב מְחוֹלֶ֥לֶת תַּנִּֽין׃

י הֲל֤וֹא אַתְּ־הִיא֙ הַמַּֽחֲרֶ֣בֶת יָ֔ם מֵ֖י תְּה֣וֹם רַבָּ֑ה הַשָּׂ֙מָה֙ מַֽעֲמַקֵּי־יָ֔ם דֶּ֖רֶךְ לַֽעֲבֹ֥ר גְּאוּלִֽים׃

יא וּפְדוּיֵ֨י יְהֹוָ֜ה יְשׁוּב֗וּן וּבָ֤אוּ צִיּוֹן֙ בְּרִנָּ֔ה וְשִׂמְחַ֥ת עוֹלָ֖ם עַל־רֹאשָׁ֑ם שָׂשׂ֤וֹן וְשִׂמְחָה֙ יַשִּׂ֔יגוּן נָ֖סוּ יָג֥וֹן וַאֲנָחָֽה׃

יב אָנֹכִ֧י אָנֹכִ֛י ה֖וּא מְנַחֶמְכֶ֑ם מִי־אַ֤תְּ וַתִּֽירְאִי֙ מֵאֱנ֣וֹשׁ יָמ֔וּת וּמִבֶּן־אָדָ֖ם חָצִ֥יר יִנָּתֵֽן׃

יג וַתִּשְׁכַּ֞ח יְהֹוָ֣ה עֹשֶׂ֗ךָ נוֹטֶ֣ה שָׁמַ֘יִם֮ וְיֹסֵ֣ד אָ֒רֶץ֒ וַתְּפַחֵ֨ד תָּמִ֜יד כָּל־הַיּ֗וֹם מִפְּנֵי֙ חֲמַ֣ת הַמֵּצִ֔יק כַּאֲשֶׁ֥ר כּוֹנֵ֖ן לְהַשְׁחִ֑ית וְאַיֵּ֖ה חֲמַ֥ת הַמֵּצִֽיק׃

יד מִהַ֥ר צֹעֶ֖ה לְהִפָּתֵ֑חַ וְלֹא־יָמ֣וּת לַשַּׁ֔חַת וְלֹ֥א יֶחְסַ֖ר לַחְמֽוֹ׃

טו וְאָֽנֹכִי֙ יְהֹוָ֣ה אֱלֹהֶ֔יךָ רֹגַ֣ע הַיָּ֔ם וַיֶּהֱמ֖וּ גַּלָּ֑יו יְהֹוָ֥ה צְבָא֖וֹת שְׁמֽוֹ׃

Yeshayahu/Isaiah
Chapter 52

16 Have put My words in your mouth And sheltered you with My hand; I, who planted the skies and made firm the earth, Have said to *Tzion*: You are My people!

17 Rouse, rouse yourself! Arise, O *Yerushalayim*, You who from *Hashem*'s hand Have drunk the cup of His wrath, You who have drained to the dregs The bowl, the cup of reeling!

18 She has none to guide her Of all the sons she bore; None takes her by the hand, Of all the sons she reared.

19 These two things have befallen you: Wrack and ruin – who can console you? Famine and sword – how shall I comfort you?

20 Your sons lie in a swoon At the corner of every street – Like an antelope caught in a net – Drunk with the wrath of *Hashem*, With the rebuke of your God.

21 Therefore, Listen to this, unhappy one, Who are drunk, but not with wine!

22 Thus said *Hashem*, your Lord, Your God who champions His people: Herewith I take from your hand The cup of reeling, The bowl, the cup of My wrath; You shall never drink it again.

23 I will put it in the hands of your tormentors, Who have commanded you, "Get down, that we may walk over you" – So that you made your back like the ground, Like a street for passersby.

52 1 Awake, awake, O *Tzion*! Clothe yourself in splendor; Put on your robes of majesty, *Yerushalayim*, holy city! For the uncircumcised and the unclean Shall never enter you again.

2 Arise, shake off the dust, Sit [on your throne], *Yerushalayim*! Loose the bonds from your neck, O captive one, Fair *Tzion*!

3 For thus said *Hashem*: You were sold for no price, And shall be redeemed without money.

4 For thus said *Hashem*: Of old, My people went down To Egypt to sojourn there; But Assyria has robbed them, Giving nothing in return.

ישעיהו
פרק נב

טז וָאָשִׂים דְּבָרַי בְּפִיךָ וּבְצֵל יָדִי כִּסִּיתִיךָ לִנְטֹעַ שָׁמַיִם וְלִיסֹד אָרֶץ וְלֵאמֹר לְצִיּוֹן עַמִּי־אָתָּה:

יז הִתְעוֹרְרִי הִתְעוֹרְרִי קוּמִי יְרוּשָׁלַ͏ִם אֲשֶׁר שָׁתִית מִיַּד יְהוָה אֶת־כּוֹס חֲמָתוֹ אֶת־קֻבַּעַת כּוֹס הַתַּרְעֵלָה שָׁתִית מָצִית:

יח אֵין־מְנַהֵל לָהּ מִכָּל־בָּנִים יָלָדָה וְאֵין מַחֲזִיק בְּיָדָהּ מִכָּל־בָּנִים גִּדֵּלָה:

יט שְׁתַּיִם הֵנָּה קֹרְאֹתַיִךְ מִי יָנוּד לָךְ הַשֹּׁד וְהַשֶּׁבֶר וְהָרָעָב וְהַחֶרֶב מִי אֲנַחֲמֵךְ:

כ בָּנַיִךְ עֻלְּפוּ שָׁכְבוּ בְּרֹאשׁ כָּל־חוּצוֹת כְּתוֹא מִכְמָר הַמְלֵאִים חֲמַת־יְהוָה גַּעֲרַת אֱלֹהָיִךְ:

כא לָכֵן שִׁמְעִי־נָא זֹאת עֲנִיָּה וּשְׁכֻרַת וְלֹא מִיָּיִן:

כב כֹּה־אָמַר אֲדֹנַיִךְ יְהוָה וֵאלֹהַיִךְ יָרִיב עַמּוֹ הִנֵּה לָקַחְתִּי מִיָּדֵךְ אֶת־כּוֹס הַתַּרְעֵלָה אֶת־קֻבַּעַת כּוֹס חֲמָתִי לֹא־תוֹסִיפִי לִשְׁתּוֹתָהּ עוֹד:

כג וְשַׂמְתִּיהָ בְּיַד־מוֹגַיִךְ אֲשֶׁר־אָמְרוּ לְנַפְשֵׁךְ שְׁחִי וְנַעֲבֹרָה וַתָּשִׂימִי כָאָרֶץ גֵּוֵךְ וְכַחוּץ לַעֹבְרִים:

נב א עוּרִי עוּרִי לִבְשִׁי עֻזֵּךְ צִיּוֹן לִבְשִׁי בִּגְדֵי תִפְאַרְתֵּךְ יְרוּשָׁלַ͏ִם עִיר הַקֹּדֶשׁ כִּי לֹא יוֹסִיף יָבֹא־בָךְ עוֹד עָרֵל וְטָמֵא:

ב הִתְנַעֲרִי מֵעָפָר קוּמִי שְּׁבִי יְרוּשָׁלָ͏ִם התפתחו [הִתְפַּתְּחִי] מוֹסְרֵי צַוָּארֵךְ שְׁבִיָּה בַּת־צִיּוֹן:

ג כִּי־כֹה אָמַר יְהוָה חִנָּם נִמְכַּרְתֶּם וְלֹא בְכֶסֶף תִּגָּאֵלוּ:

ד כִּי כֹה אָמַר אֲדֹנָי יְהוִה מִצְרַיִם יָרַד־עַמִּי בָרִאשֹׁנָה לָגוּר שָׁם וְאַשּׁוּר בְּאֶפֶס עֲשָׁקוֹ:

Yeshayahu/Isaiah
Chapter 52

5 What therefore do I gain here? – declares *Hashem* – For My people has been carried off for nothing, Their mockers howl – declares *Hashem* – And constantly, unceasingly, My name is reviled.

ה וְעַתָּה מי־לי־[מַה־] [לִי־] פֹה נְאֻם־יְהֹוָה כִּי־לֻקַּח עַמִּי חִנָּם משלו [מֹשְׁלָיו] יְהֵילִילוּ נְאֻם־יְהֹוָה וְתָמִיד כׇּל־הַיּוֹם שְׁמִי מִנֹּאָץ׃

6 Assuredly, My people shall learn My name, Assuredly [they shall learn] on that day That I, the One who promised, Am now at hand.

ו לָכֵן יֵדַע עַמִּי שְׁמִי לָכֵן בַּיּוֹם הַהוּא כִּי־אֲנִי־הוּא הַמְדַבֵּר הִנֵּנִי׃

7 How welcome on the mountain Are the footsteps of the herald Announcing happiness, Heralding good fortune, Announcing victory, Telling *Tzion*, "Your God is King!"

ז מַה־נָּאווּ עַל־הֶהָרִים רַגְלֵי מְבַשֵּׂר מַשְׁמִיעַ שָׁלוֹם מְבַשֵּׂר טוֹב מַשְׁמִיעַ יְשׁוּעָה אֹמֵר לְצִיּוֹן מָלַךְ אֱלֹהָיִךְ׃

8 Hark! Your watchmen raise their voices, As one they shout for joy; For every eye shall behold *Hashem*'s return to *Tzion*.

ח קוֹל צֹפַיִךְ נָשְׂאוּ קוֹל יַחְדָּו יְרַנֵּנוּ כִּי עַיִן בְּעַיִן יִרְאוּ בְּשׁוּב יְהֹוָה צִיּוֹן׃

9 Raise a shout together, O ruins of *Yerushalayim*! For *Hashem* will comfort His people, Will redeem *Yerushalayim*.

ט פִּצְחוּ רַנְּנוּ יַחְדָּו חׇרְבוֹת יְרוּשָׁלָ͏ִם כִּי־נִחַם יְהֹוָה עַמּוֹ גָּאַל יְרוּשָׁלָ͏ִם׃

pitz-KHU ra-n'-NU yakh-DAV kho-r'-VOT y'-ru-sha-LA-im kee ni-KHAM a-do-NAI a-MO ga-AL y'-ru-sha-LA-im

10 *Hashem* will bare His holy arm In the sight of all the nations, And the very ends of earth shall see The victory of our God.

י חָשַׂף יְהֹוָה אֶת־זְרוֹעַ קׇדְשׁוֹ לְעֵינֵי כׇּל־הַגּוֹיִם וְרָאוּ כׇּל־אַפְסֵי־אָרֶץ אֵת יְשׁוּעַת אֱלֹהֵינוּ׃

11 Turn, turn away, touch naught unclean As you depart from there; Keep pure, as you go forth from there, You who bear the vessels of *Hashem*!

יא סוּרוּ סוּרוּ צְאוּ מִשָּׁם טָמֵא אַל־תִּגָּעוּ צְאוּ מִתּוֹכָהּ הִבָּרוּ נֹשְׂאֵי כְּלֵי יְהֹוָה׃

12 For you will not depart in haste, Nor will you leave in flight; For *Hashem* is marching before you, The God of *Yisrael* is your rear guard.

יב כִּי לֹא בְחִפָּזוֹן תֵּצֵאוּ וּבִמְנוּסָה לֹא תֵלֵכוּן כִּי־הֹלֵךְ לִפְנֵיכֶם יְהֹוָה וּמְאַסִּפְכֶם אֱלֹהֵי יִשְׂרָאֵל׃

13 "Indeed, My servant shall prosper, Be exalted and raised to great heights.

יג הִנֵּה יַשְׂכִּיל עַבְדִּי יָרוּם וְנִשָּׂא וְגָבַהּ מְאֹד׃

14 Just as the many were appalled at him – So marred was his appearance, unlike that of man, form, beyond human semblance –

יד כַּאֲשֶׁר שָׁמְמוּ עָלֶיךָ רַבִּים כֵּן־מִשְׁחַת מֵאִישׁ מַרְאֵהוּ וְתֹאֲרוֹ מִבְּנֵי אָדָם׃

52:9 Will redeem *Yerushalayim* *Hashem* has many titles in the Bible, one of which is *go-ayl* (גואל), 'redeemer.' In Isaiah 49:7, He is referred to as the "Redeemer of Israel," and here He will "redeem *Yerushalayim*." The same word is used in the Bible in another context. *Sefer Vayikra* (25:25) states "his nearest redeemer shall come," referring to someone so deeply in debt that he is forced to sell his property until his closest relative comes to his aid. The *go-ayl* in this context is the person's closest relative. By referring to *Hashem* as the Redeemer of Israel, the prophet is expressing the idea that He is closer to them than any of their other close relations.

גואל

Yeshayahu/Isaiah
Chapter 53

15 Just so he shall startle many nations. Kings shall be silenced because of him, For they shall see what has not been told them, Shall behold what they never have heard."

53 1 "Who can believe what we have heard? Upon whom has the arm of *Hashem*- been revealed?

2 For he has grown, by His favor, like a tree crown, Like a tree trunk out of arid ground. He had no form or beauty, that we should look at him: No charm, that we should find him pleasing.

3 He was despised, shunned by men, A man of suffering, familiar with disease. As one who hid his face from us, He was despised, we held him of no account.

4 Yet it was our sickness that he was bearing, Our suffering that he endured. We accounted him plagued, Smitten and afflicted by *Hashem*;

5 But he was wounded because of our sins, Crushed because of our iniquities. He bore the chastisement that made us whole, And by his bruises we were healed.

6 We all went astray like sheep, Each going his own way; And *Hashem* visited upon him The guilt of all of us."

7 He was maltreated, yet he was submissive, He did not open his mouth; Like a sheep being led to slaughter, Like a ewe, dumb before those who shear her, He did not open his mouth.

8 By oppressive judgment he was taken away, Who could describe his abode? For he was cut off from the land of the living Through the sin of my people, who deserved the punishment.

9 And his grave was set among the wicked, And with the rich, in his death – Though he had done no injustice And had spoken no falsehood.

10 But *Hashem* chose to crush him by disease, That, if he made himself an offering for guilt, He might see offspring and have long life, And that through him *Hashem*'s purpose might prosper.

11 Out of his anguish he shall see it; He shall enjoy it to the full through his devotion. "My righteous servant makes the many righteous, It is their punishment that he bears;

ישעיהו
פרק נג

טו כֵּן יַזֶּה גּוֹיִם רַבִּים עָלָיו יִקְפְּצוּ מְלָכִים פִּיהֶם כִּי אֲשֶׁר לֹא־סֻפַּר לָהֶם רָאוּ וַאֲשֶׁר לֹא־שָׁמְעוּ הִתְבּוֹנָנוּ:

נג א מִי הֶאֱמִין לִשְׁמֻעָתֵנוּ וּזְרוֹעַ יְהוָה עַל־מִי נִגְלָתָה:

ב וַיַּעַל כַּיּוֹנֵק לְפָנָיו וְכַשֹּׁרֶשׁ מֵאֶרֶץ צִיָּה לֹא־תֹאַר לוֹ וְלֹא הָדָר וְנִרְאֵהוּ וְלֹא־מַרְאֶה וְנֶחְמְדֵהוּ:

ג נִבְזֶה וַחֲדַל אִישִׁים אִישׁ מַכְאֹבוֹת וִידוּעַ חֹלִי וּכְמַסְתֵּר פָּנִים מִמֶּנּוּ נִבְזֶה וְלֹא חֲשַׁבְנֻהוּ:

ד אָכֵן חֳלָיֵנוּ הוּא נָשָׂא וּמַכְאֹבֵינוּ סְבָלָם וַאֲנַחְנוּ חֲשַׁבְנֻהוּ נָגוּעַ מֻכֵּה אֱלֹהִים וּמְעֻנֶּה:

ה וְהוּא מְחֹלָל מִפְּשָׁעֵנוּ מְדֻכָּא מֵעֲוֺנֹתֵינוּ מוּסַר שְׁלוֹמֵנוּ עָלָיו וּבַחֲבֻרָתוֹ נִרְפָּא־לָנוּ:

ו כֻּלָּנוּ כַּצֹּאן תָּעִינוּ אִישׁ לְדַרְכּוֹ פָּנִינוּ וַיהוָה הִפְגִּיעַ בּוֹ אֵת עֲוֺן כֻּלָּנוּ:

ז נִגַּשׂ וְהוּא נַעֲנֶה וְלֹא יִפְתַּח־פִּיו כַּשֶּׂה לַטֶּבַח יוּבָל וּכְרָחֵל לִפְנֵי גֹזְזֶיהָ נֶאֱלָמָה וְלֹא יִפְתַּח פִּיו:

ח מֵעֹצֶר וּמִמִּשְׁפָּט לֻקָּח וְאֶת־דּוֹרוֹ מִי יְשׂוֹחֵחַ כִּי נִגְזַר מֵאֶרֶץ חַיִּים מִפֶּשַׁע עַמִּי נֶגַע לָמוֹ:

ט וַיִּתֵּן אֶת־רְשָׁעִים קִבְרוֹ וְאֶת־עָשִׁיר בְּמֹתָיו עַל לֹא־חָמָס עָשָׂה וְלֹא מִרְמָה בְּפִיו:

י וַיהוָה חָפֵץ דַּכְּאוֹ הֶחֱלִי אִם־תָּשִׂים אָשָׁם נַפְשׁוֹ יִרְאֶה זֶרַע יַאֲרִיךְ יָמִים וְחֵפֶץ יְהוָה בְּיָדוֹ יִצְלָח:

יא מֵעֲמַל נַפְשׁוֹ יִרְאֶה יִשְׂבָּע בְּדַעְתּוֹ יַצְדִּיק צַדִּיק עַבְדִּי לָרַבִּים וַעֲוֺנֹתָם הוּא יִסְבֹּל:

Yeshayahu/Isaiah
Chapter 54

ישעיהו
פרק נד

12 Assuredly, I will give him the many as his portion, He shall receive the multitude as his spoil. For he exposed himself to death And was numbered among the sinners, Whereas he bore the guilt of the many And made intercession for sinners."

לָכֵן אֲחַלֶּק־לוֹ בָרַבִּים וְאֶת־עֲצוּמִים יְחַלֵּק שָׁלָל תַּחַת אֲשֶׁר הֶעֱרָה לַמָּוֶת נַפְשׁוֹ וְאֶת־פֹּשְׁעִים נִמְנָה וְהוּא חֵטְא־רַבִּים נָשָׂא וְלַפֹּשְׁעִים יַפְגִּיעַ:

la-KHAYN a-kha-lek LO va-ra-BEEM v'-et a-tzu-MEEM y'-kha-LAYK sha-LAL TA-khat a-SHER he-e-RAH la-MA-vet naf-SHO v'-et po-sh'-EEM nim-NAH v'-HU khayt ra-BEEM na-SA v'-la-po-sh'-EEM yaf-GEE-a

54 1 Shout, O barren one, You who bore no child! Shout aloud for joy, You who did not travail! For the children of the wife forlorn Shall outnumber those of the espoused – said *Hashem*.

נד א רָנִּי עֲקָרָה לֹא יָלָדָה פִּצְחִי רִנָּה וְצַהֲלִי לֹא־חָלָה כִּי־רַבִּים בְּנֵי־שׁוֹמֵמָה מִבְּנֵי בְעוּלָה אָמַר יְהוָה:

2 Enlarge the site of your tent, Extend the size of your dwelling, Do not stint! Lengthen the ropes, and drive the pegs firm.

ב הַרְחִיבִי ׀ מְקוֹם אָהֳלֵךְ וִירִיעוֹת מִשְׁכְּנוֹתַיִךְ יַטּוּ אַל־תַּחְשֹׂכִי הַאֲרִיכִי מֵיתָרַיִךְ וִיתֵדֹתַיִךְ חַזֵּקִי:

har-KHEE-vee m'-KOM a-ho-LAYKH vee-ree-OT mish-k'-no-TA-yikh ya-TU al takh-SO-khee ha-a-REE-khee may-ta-RA-yikh vee-tay-do-TA-yikh kha-ZAY-kee

3 For you shall spread out to the right and the left; Your offspring shall dispossess nations And shall people the desolate towns.

ג כִּי־יָמִין וּשְׂמֹאול תִּפְרֹצִי וְזַרְעֵךְ גּוֹיִם יִירָשׁ וְעָרִים נְשַׁמּוֹת יוֹשִׁיבוּ:

4 Fear not, you shall not be shamed; Do not cringe, you shall not be disgraced. For you shall forget The reproach of your youth, And remember no more The shame of your widowhood.

ד אַל־תִּירְאִי כִּי־לֹא תֵבוֹשִׁי וְאַל־תִּכָּלְמִי כִּי לֹא תַחְפִּירִי כִּי בֹשֶׁת עֲלוּמַיִךְ תִּשְׁכָּחִי וְחֶרְפַּת אַלְמְנוּתַיִךְ לֹא תִזְכְּרִי־עוֹד:

5 For He who made you will espouse you – His name is "Lord of Hosts." The Holy One of *Yisrael* will redeem you – He is called "God of all the Earth."

ה כִּי בֹעֲלַיִךְ עֹשַׂיִךְ יְהוָה צְבָאוֹת שְׁמוֹ וְגֹאֲלֵךְ קְדוֹשׁ יִשְׂרָאֵל אֱלֹהֵי כָל־הָאָרֶץ יִקָּרֵא:

53:12 Assuredly, I will give him the many as his portion Chapter 53 begins with a description of the suffering that Israel experiences. In this verse, however, *Yeshayahu* articulates the reward that awaits the nation. Because Israel, despite its suffering, placed the welfare of others above its own, it is promised that one day it too will be counted among the mighty, and that its portion, *Eretz Yisrael*, will be considered great. Today, the State of Israel is among the world's leaders in science, technology and medicine, and stands out in the region. In 2015, for example, the U.S. Patent Office reported 3,804 patents from Israel, as compared with 364 from Saudi Arabia, 56 from the United Arab Emirates, and 30 from Egypt. Truly, *Yeshayahu's* blessing is being realized and Israel's "portion" is growing.

54:2 Enlarge the site of your tent This verse contains a call to action for Jews everywhere to settle every corner of *Eretz Yisrael* and "enlarge" their presence in the land. Based on this verse, the *Vilna Gaon* urged his students in the eighteenth century to move to Israel. "All the precious treasures included in the blessing of *harchava* ('enlargement') will come only when action is first taken by the People of Israel themselves in an awakening from below" said the *Vilna Gaon*. "Our task is to not sit passively and wait for redemption from exile, but rather to take action and bring it about." The Jewish people are not prisoners of fate, but partners with God in shaping their destiny. When they take action and settle the land, He will respond in kind and hasten the ingathering of the exiles.

Rabbi Elijah Kremer, the Vilna Gaon (1720–1797)

Yeshayahu/Isaiah
Chapter 55

6 *Hashem* has called you back As a wife forlorn and forsaken. Can one cast off the wife of his youth? – said your God.

7 For a little while I forsook you, But with vast love I will bring you back.

8 In slight anger, for a moment, I hid My face from you; But with kindness everlasting I will take you back in love – said *Hashem* your Redeemer.

9 For this to Me is like the waters of *Noach*: As I swore that the waters of *Noach* Nevermore would flood the earth, So I swear that I will not Be angry with you or rebuke you.

10 For the mountains may move And the hills be shaken, But my loyalty shall never move from you, Nor My covenant of friendship be shaken – said *Hashem*, who takes you back in love.

11 Unhappy, storm-tossed one, uncomforted! I will lay carbuncles as your building stones And make your foundations of sapphires.

12 I will make your battlements of rubies, Your gates of precious stones, The whole encircling wall of gems.

13 And all your children shall be disciples of *Hashem*, And great shall be the happiness of your children;

14 You shall be established through righteousness. You shall be safe from oppression, And shall have no fear; From ruin, and it shall not come near you.

15 Surely no harm can be done Without My consent: Whoever would harm you Shall fall because of you.

16 It is I who created the smith To fan the charcoal fire And produce the tools for his work; So it is I who create The instruments of havoc.

17 No weapon formed against you Shall succeed, And every tongue that contends with you at law You shall defeat. Such is the lot of the servants of *Hashem*, Such their triumph through Me – declares *Hashem*.

55 1 Ho, all who are thirsty, Come for water, Even if you have no money; Come, buy food and eat: Buy food without money, Wine and milk without cost.

Yeshayahu/Isaiah
Chapter 55

ישעיהו
פרק נה

2 Why do you spend money for what is not bread, Your earnings for what does not satisfy? Give heed to Me, And you shall eat choice food And enjoy the richest viands.

ב לָמָּה תִשְׁקְלוּ־כֶסֶף בְּלוֹא־לֶחֶם וִיגִיעֲכֶם בְּלוֹא לְשָׂבְעָה שִׁמְעוּ שָׁמוֹעַ אֵלַי וְאִכְלוּ־טוֹב וְתִתְעַנַּג בַּדֶּשֶׁן נַפְשְׁכֶם׃

3 Incline your ear and come to Me; Hearken, and you shall be revived. And I will make with you an everlasting covenant, The enduring loyalty promised to *David*.

ג הַטּוּ אָזְנְכֶם וּלְכוּ אֵלַי שִׁמְעוּ וּתְחִי נַפְשְׁכֶם וְאֶכְרְתָה לָכֶם בְּרִית עוֹלָם חַסְדֵי דָוִד הַנֶּאֱמָנִים׃

4 As I made him a leader of peoples, A prince and commander of peoples,

ד הֵן עֵד לְאוּמִּים נְתַתִּיו נָגִיד וּמְצַוֵּה לְאֻמִּים׃

5 So you shall summon a nation you did not know, And a nation that did not know you Shall come running to you – For the sake of *Hashem* your God, The Holy One of *Yisrael* who has glorified you.

ה הֵן גּוֹי לֹא־תֵדַע תִּקְרָא וְגוֹי לֹא־יְדָעוּךָ אֵלֶיךָ יָרוּצוּ לְמַעַן יְהוָֹה אֱלֹהֶיךָ וְלִקְדוֹשׁ יִשְׂרָאֵל כִּי פֵאֲרָךְ׃

6 Seek *Hashem* while He can be found, Call to Him while He is near.

dir-SHU a-do-NAI b'-hi-ma-tz'-O k'-ra-U-hu bih-yo-TO ka-ROV

ו דִּרְשׁוּ יְהוָֹה בְּהִמָּצְאוֹ קְרָאֻהוּ בִּהְיוֹתוֹ קָרוֹב׃

7 Let the wicked give up his ways, The sinful man his plans; Let him turn back to *Hashem*, And He will pardon him; To our God, For he freely forgives.

ז יַעֲזֹב רָשָׁע דַּרְכּוֹ וְאִישׁ אָוֶן מַחְשְׁבֹתָיו וְיָשֹׁב אֶל־יְהוָֹה וִירַחֲמֵהוּ וְאֶל־אֱלֹהֵינוּ כִּי־יַרְבֶּה לִסְלוֹחַ׃

8 For My plans are not your plans, Nor are My ways your ways – declares *Hashem*.

ח כִּי לֹא מַחְשְׁבוֹתַי מַחְשְׁבוֹתֵיכֶם וְלֹא דַרְכֵיכֶם דְּרָכָי נְאֻם יְהוָֹה׃

9 But as the heavens are high above the earth, So are My ways high above your ways And My plans above your plans.

ט כִּי־גָבְהוּ שָׁמַיִם מֵאָרֶץ כֵּן גָּבְהוּ דְרָכַי מִדַּרְכֵיכֶם וּמַחְשְׁבֹתַי מִמַּחְשְׁבֹתֵיכֶם׃

10 For as the rain or snow drops from heaven And returns not there, But soaks the earth And makes it bring forth vegetation, Yielding seed for sowing and bread for eating,

י כִּי כַּאֲשֶׁר יֵרֵד הַגֶּשֶׁם וְהַשֶּׁלֶג מִן־הַשָּׁמַיִם וְשָׁמָּה לֹא יָשׁוּב כִּי אִם־הִרְוָה אֶת־הָאָרֶץ וְהוֹלִידָהּ וְהִצְמִיחָהּ וְנָתַן זֶרַע לַזֹּרֵעַ וְלֶחֶם לָאֹכֵל׃

11 So is the word that issues from My mouth: It does not come back to Me unfulfilled, But performs what I purpose, Achieves what I sent it to do.

יא כֵּן יִהְיֶה דְבָרִי אֲשֶׁר יֵצֵא מִפִּי לֹא־יָשׁוּב אֵלַי רֵיקָם כִּי אִם־עָשָׂה אֶת־אֲשֶׁר חָפַצְתִּי וְהִצְלִיחַ אֲשֶׁר שְׁלַחְתִּיו׃

55:6 Seek *Hashem* while He can be found The prophetic counsel "seek *Hashem* while He can be found; call to him while He is near" introduces a section offering hope and reward for those who sincerely desire to repent. This chapter is traditionally read publicly on fast days, days meant for introspection and inner reflection, and commentators provide many interpretations to its meaning. Some understand the phrase "seek *Hashem* while He can be found" as referring to the month before the Jewish New Year, *Rosh Hashana*, when prayer is especially desirable. The Jerusalem Talmud understands it in terms of location, "seek *Hashem* where He is found – in the synagogues, and in the study halls." The underlying message is the same: If you seek *Hashem* out in the right way, you will be able to find Him, and He is always there awaiting your return.

Yeshayahu/Isaiah
Chapter 56

12 Yea, you shall leave in joy and be led home secure. Before you, mount and hill shall shout aloud, And all the trees of the field shall clap their hands.

13 Instead of the brier, a cypress shall rise Instead of the nettle, a myrtle shall rise. These shall stand as a testimony to *Hashem*, As an everlasting sign that shall not perish.

56 1 Thus said *Hashem*: Observe what is right and do what is just; For soon My salvation shall come, And my deliverance be revealed.

2 Happy is the man who does this, The man who holds fast to it: Who keeps the *Shabbat* and does not profane it, And stays his hand from doing any evil.

3 Let not the foreigner say, Who has attached himself to *Hashem*, "*Hashem* will keep me apart from His people"; And let not the eunuch say, "I am a withered tree."

4 For thus said *Hashem*: "As for the eunuchs who keep My *Shabbatot*, Who have chosen what I desire And hold fast to My covenant –

5 I will give them, in My House And within My walls, A monument and a name Better than sons or daughters. I will give them an everlasting name Which shall not perish.

v'-na-ta-TEE la-HEM b'-vay-TEE uv-kho-mo-TAI YAD va-SHAYM TOV mi-ba-NEEM u-mi-ba-NOT SHAYM o-LAM e-ten LO a-SHER LO y'-ka-RAYT

6 As for the foreigners Who attach themselves to *Hashem*, To minister to Him, And to love the name of *Hashem*, To be His servants – All who keep the *Shabbat* and do not profane it, And who hold fast to My covenant –

56:5 A monument and a name Jerusalem's famous Holocaust museum, *Yad Vashem* ('a monument and a name'), takes its name from this biblical verse. *Yeshayahu* articulates *Hashem*'s promise that even those who are unable to have sons and daughters will be memorialized in *Yerushalayim* by their "everlasting name." According to its mission statement, the museum "safeguards the memory of the past and imparts its meaning for future generations." *Yad Vashem* has already collected and memorialized the names of over four million Jewish victims of Nazi persecution, and aims to persist until all 6,000,0000 names are recovered. The museum is often a first stop for visitors to the Jewish State, because in order to appreciate the State of Israel, one must understand the tragedy of the Holocaust.

Hall of Names at Yad Vashem

1053

Yeshayahu/Isaiah
Chapter 57

7 I will bring them to My sacred mount And let them rejoice in My house of prayer. Their burnt offerings and sacrifices Shall be welcome on My *Mizbayach*; For My House shall be called A house of prayer for all peoples."

8 Thus declares *Hashem*, Who gathers the dispersed of *Yisrael*: "I will gather still more to those already gathered."

9 All you wild beasts, come and devour, All you beasts of the forest!

10 The watchmen are blind, all of them, They perceive nothing. They are all dumb dogs That cannot bark; They lie sprawling, They love to drowse.

11 Moreover, the dogs are greedy; They never know satiety. As for the shepherds, they know not What it is to give heed. Everyone has turned his own way, Every last one seeks his own advantage.

12 "Come, I'll get some wine Let us swill liquor. And tomorrow will be just the same, Or even much grander!"

57

1 The righteous man perishes, And no one considers; Pious men are taken away, And no one gives thought That because of evil The righteous was taken away.

2 Yet he shall come to peace, He shall have rest on his couch Who walked straightforward.

3 But as for you, come closer, You sons of a sorceress, You offspring of an adulterer and a harlot!

4 With whom do you act so familiarly? At whom do you open your mouth And stick out your tongue? Why, you are children of iniquity, Offspring of treachery –

5 You who inflame yourselves Among the terebinths, Under every verdant tree; Who slaughter children in the wadis, Among the clefts of the rocks.

6 With such are your share and portion, They, they are your allotment; To them you have poured out libations, Presented offerings. Should I relent in the face of this?

ישעיהו
פרק נז

ז וַהֲבִיאוֹתִים אֶל־הַר קָדְשִׁי וְשִׂמַּחְתִּים בְּבֵית תְּפִלָּתִי עוֹלֹתֵיהֶם וְזִבְחֵיהֶם לְרָצוֹן עַל־מִזְבְּחִי כִּי בֵיתִי בֵּית־תְּפִלָּה יִקָּרֵא לְכָל־הָעַמִּים:

ח נְאֻם אֲדֹנָי יֱהֹוִה מְקַבֵּץ נִדְחֵי יִשְׂרָאֵל עוֹד אֲקַבֵּץ עָלָיו לְנִקְבָּצָיו:

ט כֹּל חַיְתוֹ שָׂדָי אֵתָיוּ לֶאֱכֹל כָּל־חַיְתוֹ בַּיָּעַר:

י צפו [צֹפָיו] עִוְרִים כֻּלָּם לֹא יָדָעוּ כֻּלָּם כְּלָבִים אִלְּמִים לֹא יוּכְלוּ לִנְבֹּחַ הֹזִים שֹׁכְבִים אֹהֲבֵי לָנוּם:

יא וְהַכְּלָבִים עַזֵּי־נֶפֶשׁ לֹא יָדְעוּ שָׂבְעָה וְהֵמָּה רֹעִים לֹא יָדְעוּ הָבִין כֻּלָּם לְדַרְכָּם פָּנוּ אִישׁ לְבִצְעוֹ מִקָּצֵהוּ:

יב אֵתָיוּ אֶקְחָה־יַיִן וְנִסְבְּאָה שֵׁכָר וְהָיָה כָזֶה יוֹם מָחָר גָּדוֹל יֶתֶר מְאֹד:

נז

א הַצַּדִּיק אָבָד וְאֵין אִישׁ שָׂם עַל־לֵב וְאַנְשֵׁי־חֶסֶד נֶאֱסָפִים בְּאֵין מֵבִין כִּי־מִפְּנֵי הָרָעָה נֶאֱסַף הַצַּדִּיק:

ב יָבוֹא שָׁלוֹם יָנוּחוּ עַל־מִשְׁכְּבוֹתָם הֹלֵךְ נְכֹחוֹ:

ג וְאַתֶּם קִרְבוּ־הֵנָּה בְּנֵי עֹנְנָה זֶרַע מְנָאֵף וַתִּזְנֶה:

ד עַל־מִי תִּתְעַנָּגוּ עַל־מִי תַּרְחִיבוּ פֶה תַּאֲרִיכוּ לָשׁוֹן הֲלוֹא־אַתֶּם יִלְדֵי־פֶשַׁע זֶרַע שָׁקֶר:

ה הַנֵּחָמִים בָּאֵלִים תַּחַת כָּל־עֵץ רַעֲנָן שֹׁחֲטֵי הַיְלָדִים בַּנְּחָלִים תַּחַת סְעִפֵי הַסְּלָעִים:

ו בְּחַלְּקֵי־נַחַל חֶלְקֵךְ הֵם הֵם גּוֹרָלֵךְ גַּם־לָהֶם שָׁפַכְתְּ נֶסֶךְ הֶעֱלִית מִנְחָה הַעַל אֵלֶּה אֶנָּחֵם:

Yeshayahu/Isaiah
Chapter 57

ישעיהו
פרק נז

7 On a high and lofty hill You have set your couch; There, too, you have gone up To perform sacrifices.

ז עַל הַר־גָּבֹהַּ וְנִשָּׂא שַׂמְתְּ מִשְׁכָּבֵךְ גַּם־שָׁם עָלִית לִזְבֹּחַ זָבַח׃

8 Behind the door and doorpost You have directed your thoughts; Abandoning Me, you have gone up On the couch you made so wide. You have made a covenant with them, You have loved bedding with them; You have chosen lust.

ח וְאַחַר הַדֶּלֶת וְהַמְּזוּזָה שַׂמְתְּ זִכְרוֹנֵךְ כִּי מֵאִתִּי גִּלִּית וַתַּעֲלִי הִרְחַבְתְּ מִשְׁכָּבֵךְ וַתִּכְרָת־לָךְ מֵהֶם אָהַבְתְּ מִשְׁכָּבָם יָד חָזִית׃

9 You have approached the king with oil, You have provided many perfumes. And you have sent your envoys afar, Even down to the netherworld.

ט וַתָּשֻׁרִי לַמֶּלֶךְ בַּשֶּׁמֶן וַתַּרְבִּי רִקֻּחָיִךְ וַתְּשַׁלְּחִי צִירַיִךְ עַד־מֵרָחֹק וַתַּשְׁפִּילִי עַד־שְׁאוֹל׃

10 Though wearied by much travel, You never said, "I give up!" You found gratification for your lust, And so you never cared.

י בְּרֹב דַּרְכֵּךְ יָגַעַתְּ לֹא אָמַרְתְּ נוֹאָשׁ חַיַּת יָדֵךְ מָצָאת עַל־כֵּן לֹא חָלִית׃

11 Whom do you dread and fear, That you tell lies? But you gave no thought to Me, You paid no heed. It is because I have stood idly by so long That you have no fear of Me.

יא וְאֶת־מִי דָּאַגְתְּ וַתִּירְאִי כִּי תְכַזֵּבִי וְאוֹתִי לֹא זָכַרְתְּ לֹא־שַׂמְתְּ עַל־לִבֵּךְ הֲלֹא אֲנִי מַחְשֶׁה וּמֵעֹלָם וְאוֹתִי לֹא תִירָאִי׃

12 I hereby pronounce judgment upon your deeds: Your assorted [idols]* shall not avail you,

יב אֲנִי אַגִּיד צִדְקָתֵךְ וְאֶת־מַעֲשַׂיִךְ וְלֹא יוֹעִילוּךְ׃

13 Shall not save you when you cry out. They shall all be borne off by the wind, Snatched away by a breeze. But those who trust in Me shall inherit the land And possess My sacred mount.

יג בְּזַעֲקֵךְ יַצִּילֻךְ קִבּוּצַיִךְ וְאֶת־כֻּלָּם יִשָּׂא־רוּחַ יִקַּח־הָבֶל וְהַחוֹסֶה בִי יִנְחַל־אֶרֶץ וְיִירַשׁ הַר־קָדְשִׁי׃

14 [The Lord] says: Build up, build up a highway! Clear a road! Remove all obstacles From the road of My people!

יד וְאָמַר סֹלּוּ־סֹלּוּ פַּנּוּ־דָרֶךְ הָרִימוּ מִכְשׁוֹל מִדֶּרֶךְ עַמִּי׃

15 For thus said He who high aloft Forever dwells, whose name is holy: I dwell on high, in holiness; Yet with the contrite and the lowly in spirit – Reviving the spirits of the lowly, Reviving the hearts of the contrite.

טו כִּי כֹה אָמַר רָם וְנִשָּׂא שֹׁכֵן עַד וְקָדוֹשׁ שְׁמוֹ מָרוֹם וְקָדוֹשׁ אֶשְׁכּוֹן וְאֶת־דַּכָּא וּשְׁפַל־רוּחַ לְהַחֲיוֹת רוּחַ שְׁפָלִים וּלְהַחֲיוֹת לֵב נִדְכָּאִים׃

16 For I will not always contend, I will not be angry forever: Nay, I who make spirits flag, Also create the breath of life.

טז כִּי לֹא לְעוֹלָם אָרִיב וְלֹא לָנֶצַח אֶקְצוֹף כִּי־רוּחַ מִלְּפָנַי יַעֲטוֹף וּנְשָׁמוֹת אֲנִי עָשִׂיתִי׃

17 For their sinful greed I was angry; I struck them and turned away in My wrath. Though stubborn, they follow the way of their hearts,

יז בַּעֲוֺן בִּצְעוֹ קָצַפְתִּי וְאַכֵּהוּ הַסְתֵּר וְאֶקְצֹף וַיֵּלֶךְ שׁוֹבָב בְּדֶרֶךְ לִבּוֹ׃

18 I note how they fare and will heal them: I will guide them and mete out solace to them, And to the mourners among them

יח דְּרָכָיו רָאִיתִי וְאֶרְפָּאֵהוּ וְאַנְחֵהוּ וַאֲשַׁלֵּם נִחֻמִים לוֹ וְלַאֲבֵלָיו׃

---

* "Your assorted [idols]" brought up from verse 13 for clarity

Yeshayahu/Isaiah
Chapter 58

ישעיהו
פרק נח

19 heartening, comforting words It shall be well, Well with the far and the near – said *Hashem* – And I will heal them.

בּוֹרֵא נוּב [נִיב] שְׂפָתָיִם שָׁלוֹם שָׁלוֹם לָרָחוֹק וְלַקָּרוֹב אָמַר יְהֹוָה וּרְפָאתִיו:

bo-RAY NEEV s'-fa-TA-yim sha-LOM sha-LOM la-ra-KHOK v'-la-ka-ROV a-MAR a-do-NAI ur-fa-TEEV

20 But the wicked are like the troubled sea Which cannot rest, Whose waters toss up mire and mud.

וְהָרְשָׁעִים כַּיָּם נִגְרָשׁ כִּי הַשְׁקֵט לֹא יוּכָל וַיִּגְרְשׁוּ מֵימָיו רֶפֶשׁ וָטִיט:

21 There is no safety – said my God – For the wicked.

אֵין שָׁלוֹם אָמַר אֱלֹהַי לָרְשָׁעִים:

58 1 Cry with full throat, without restraint; Raise your voice like a *shofar*! Declare to My people their transgression, To the House of *Yaakov* their sin.

קְרָא בְגָרוֹן אַל־תַּחְשֹׂךְ כַּשּׁוֹפָר הָרֵם קוֹלֶךָ וְהַגֵּד לְעַמִּי פִּשְׁעָם וּלְבֵית יַעֲקֹב חַטֹּאתָם:

2 To be sure, they seek Me daily, Eager to learn My ways. Like a nation that does what is right, That has not abandoned the laws of its *Hashem*, They ask Me for the right way, They are eager for the nearness of *Hashem*:

וְאוֹתִי יוֹם יוֹם יִדְרֹשׁוּן וְדַעַת דְּרָכַי יֶחְפָּצוּן כְּגוֹי אֲשֶׁר־צְדָקָה עָשָׂה וּמִשְׁפַּט אֱלֹהָיו לֹא עָזָב יִשְׁאָלוּנִי מִשְׁפְּטֵי־צֶדֶק קִרְבַת אֱלֹהִים יֶחְפָּצוּן:

3 "Why, when we fasted, did You not see? When we starved our bodies, did You pay no heed?" Because on your fast day You see to your business And oppress all your laborers!

לָמָּה צַּמְנוּ וְלֹא רָאִיתָ עִנִּינוּ נַפְשֵׁנוּ וְלֹא תֵדָע הֵן בְּיוֹם צֹמְכֶם תִּמְצְאוּ־חֵפֶץ וְכָל־עַצְּבֵיכֶם תִּנְגֹּשׂוּ:

4 Because you fast in strife and contention, And you strike with a wicked fist! Your fasting today is not such As to make your voice heard on high.

הֵן לְרִיב וּמַצָּה תָּצוּמוּ וּלְהַכּוֹת בְּאֶגְרֹף רֶשַׁע לֹא־תָצוּמוּ כַיּוֹם לְהַשְׁמִיעַ בַּמָּרוֹם קוֹלְכֶם:

5 Is such the fast I desire, A day for men to starve their bodies? Is it bowing the head like a bulrush And lying in sackcloth and ashes? Do you call that a fast, A day when *Hashem* is favorable?

הֲכָזֶה יִהְיֶה צוֹם אֶבְחָרֵהוּ יוֹם עַנּוֹת אָדָם נַפְשׁוֹ הֲלָכֹף כְּאַגְמֹן רֹאשׁוֹ וְשַׂק וָאֵפֶר יַצִּיעַ הֲלָזֶה תִּקְרָא־צוֹם וְיוֹם רָצוֹן לַיהֹוָה:

6 No, this is the fast I desire: To unlock fetters of wickedness, And untie the cords of the yoke To let the oppressed go free; To break off every yoke.

הֲלוֹא זֶה צוֹם אֶבְחָרֵהוּ פַּתֵּחַ חַרְצֻבּוֹת רֶשַׁע הַתֵּר אֲגֻדּוֹת מוֹטָה וְשַׁלַּח רְצוּצִים חָפְשִׁים וְכָל־מוֹטָה תְּנַתֵּקוּ:

7 It is to share your bread with the hungry, And to take the wretched poor into your home; When you see the naked, to clothe him, And not to ignore your own kin.

הֲלוֹא פָרֹס לָרָעֵב לַחְמֶךָ וַעֲנִיִּים מְרוּדִים תָּבִיא בָיִת כִּי־תִרְאֶה עָרֹם וְכִסִּיתוֹ וּמִבְּשָׂרְךָ לֹא תִתְעַלָּם:

57:19 It shall be well, well with the far and the near *Yeshayahu* concludes the chapter with a promise that *Hashem* will provide the exiles who return with healing and comfort. The blessing of peace is proffered both to the far (those still in exile) and to the near (the exiles who already arrived in the Land of Israel). *Rashi* interprets the terms "far" and "near" as spiritual markers – whether one has engaged in righteous behavior from birth, or only recently returned wholeheartedly to the right path, *Hashem*'s blessing of peace is upon them.

Yeshayahu/Isaiah
Chapter 58

ישעיהו
פרק נח

8 Then shall your light burst through like the dawn And your healing spring up quickly; Your Vindicator shall march before you, The Presence of *Hashem* shall be your rear guard.

ח אָז יִבָּקַע כַּשַּׁחַר אוֹרֶךָ וַאֲרֻכָתְךָ מְהֵרָה תִצְמָח וְהָלַךְ לְפָנֶיךָ צִדְקֶךָ כְּבוֹד יְהֹוָה יַאַסְפֶךָ׃

9 Then, when you call, *Hashem* will answer; When you cry, He will say: Here I am. If you banish the yoke from your midst, The menacing hand, and evil speech,

ט אָז תִּקְרָא וַיהֹוָה יַעֲנֶה תְּשַׁוַּע וְיֹאמַר הִנֵּנִי אִם־תָּסִיר מִתּוֹכְךָ מוֹטָה שְׁלַח אֶצְבַּע וְדַבֶּר־אָוֶן׃

10 And you offer your compassion to the hungry And satisfy the famished creature – Then shall your light shine in darkness, And your gloom shall be like noonday.

י וְתָפֵק לָרָעֵב נַפְשֶׁךָ וְנֶפֶשׁ נַעֲנָה תַּשְׂבִּיעַ וְזָרַח בַּחֹשֶׁךְ אוֹרֶךָ וַאֲפֵלָתְךָ כַּצָּהֳרָיִם׃

11 *Hashem* will guide you always; He will slake your thirst in parched places And give strength to your bones. You shall be like a watered garden, Like a spring whose waters do not fail.

יא וְנָחֲךָ יְהֹוָה תָּמִיד וְהִשְׂבִּיעַ בְּצַחְצָחוֹת נַפְשֶׁךָ וְעַצְמֹתֶיךָ יַחֲלִיץ וְהָיִיתָ כְּגַן רָוֶה וּכְמוֹצָא מַיִם אֲשֶׁר לֹא־יְכַזְּבוּ מֵימָיו׃

12 Men from your midst shall rebuild ancient ruins, You shall restore foundations laid long ago. And you shall be called "Repairer of fallen walls, Restorer of lanes for habitation."

יב וּבָנוּ מִמְּךָ חָרְבוֹת עוֹלָם מוֹסְדֵי דוֹר־וָדוֹר תְּקוֹמֵם וְקֹרָא לְךָ גֹּדֵר פֶּרֶץ מְשֹׁבֵב נְתִיבוֹת לָשָׁבֶת׃

u-va-NU mi-m'-KHA khor-VOT o-LAM mo-s'-DAY dor va-DOR t'-ko-MAYM v'-ko-RA l'-KHA go-DAYR PE-retz m'-sho-VAYV n'-tee-VOT la-SHA-vet

13 If you refrain from trampling the *Shabbat*, From pursuing your affairs on My holy day; If you call the *Shabbat* "delight," *Hashem*'s holy day "honored"; And if you honor it and go not your ways Nor look to your affairs, nor strike bargains –

יג אִם־תָּשִׁיב מִשַּׁבָּת רַגְלֶךָ עֲשׂוֹת חֲפָצֶיךָ בְּיוֹם קָדְשִׁי וְקָרָאתָ לַשַּׁבָּת עֹנֶג לִקְדוֹשׁ יְהֹוָה מְכֻבָּד וְכִבַּדְתּוֹ מֵעֲשׂוֹת דְּרָכֶיךָ מִמְּצוֹא חֶפְצְךָ וְדַבֵּר דָּבָר׃

14 Then you can seek the favor of *Hashem*. I will set you astride the heights of the earth, And let you enjoy the heritage of your father *Yaakov* – For the mouth of *Hashem* has spoken.

יד אָז תִּתְעַנַּג עַל־יְהֹוָה וְהִרְכַּבְתִּיךָ עַל־בָּמֳתֵי אָרֶץ וְהַאֲכַלְתִּיךָ נַחֲלַת יַעֲקֹב אָבִיךָ כִּי פִּי יְהֹוָה דִּבֵּר׃

AZ tit-a-NAG al a-do-NAI v'-hir-kav-TEE-kha al BA-mo-tay A-retz v'-ha-a-khal-TEE-kha na-kha-LAT ya-a-KOV a-VEE-kha KEE PEE a-do-NAI di-BAYR

Naomi Shemer (1930–2004)

58:12 You shall restore foundations laid long ago Although the Old City was lost in the 1948 War of Independence, it was liberated in the June 1967 Six-Day War. In May of 1967, Israeli songwriter, Naomi Shemer (1930–2004), composed the song *Yerushalayim Shel Zahav* (ירושלים של זהב), 'Jerusalem of Gold,' for the Israeli Song Festival. In it, she poetically describes the people's 2,000 year long, ongoing yearning for the city, "How the cisterns have dried, the market-place is empty, and no one frequents the Temple Mount, in the Old City. Jerusalem of gold, and of bronze, and of light, behold I am a lyre for all your songs." Not only an instant national hit, when war broke out a month later its lyrics and melody expressed the longing for ancient Jerusalem, which would be liberated in that war, in a way that mere words could not. Just after the war, Shemer added another stanza, "The cisterns are filled again with water, the square with joyous crowd, on the Temple Mount within the Old City, the *shofar* rings out loud." The ancient ruins were rebuilt and the foundations laid long ago restored. Fittingly, "*Yerushalayim Shel Zahav*" has become Israel's unofficial national anthem.

58:14 The heritage of your father *Yaakov* *Yeshayahu* describes the beautiful rewards for

Yeshayahu/Isaiah
Chapter 59

נט א הֵן לֹא־קָצְרָה יַד־יְהֹוָה מֵהוֹשִׁיעַ וְלֹא־כָבְדָה אָזְנוֹ מִשְּׁמוֹעַ:

ב כִּי אִם־עֲוֺנֹתֵיכֶם הָיוּ מַבְדִּלִים בֵּינֵכֶם לְבֵין אֱלֹהֵיכֶם וְחַטֹּאותֵיכֶם הִסְתִּירוּ פָנִים מִכֶּם מִשְּׁמוֹעַ:

ג כִּי כַפֵּיכֶם נְגֹאֲלוּ בַדָּם וְאֶצְבְּעוֹתֵיכֶם בֶּעָוֺן שִׂפְתוֹתֵיכֶם דִּבְּרוּ־שֶׁקֶר לְשׁוֹנְכֶם עַוְלָה תֶהְגֶּה:

ד אֵין־קֹרֵא בְצֶדֶק וְאֵין נִשְׁפָּט בֶּאֱמוּנָה בָּטוֹחַ עַל־תֹּהוּ וְדַבֶּר־שָׁוְא הָרוֹ עָמָל וְהוֹלֵיד אָוֶן:

ה בֵּיצֵי צִפְעוֹנִי בִּקֵּעוּ וְקוּרֵי עַכָּבִישׁ יֶאֱרֹגוּ הָאֹכֵל מִבֵּיצֵיהֶם יָמוּת וְהַזּוּרֶה תִּבָּקַע אֶפְעֶה:

ו קוּרֵיהֶם לֹא־יִהְיוּ לְבֶגֶד וְלֹא יִתְכַּסּוּ בְּמַעֲשֵׂיהֶם מַעֲשֵׂיהֶם מַעֲשֵׂי־אָוֶן וּפֹעַל חָמָס בְּכַפֵּיהֶם:

ז רַגְלֵיהֶם לָרַע יָרֻצוּ וִימַהֲרוּ לִשְׁפֹּךְ דָּם נָקִי מַחְשְׁבוֹתֵיהֶם מַחְשְׁבוֹת אָוֶן שֹׁד וָשֶׁבֶר בִּמְסִלּוֹתָם:

ח דֶּרֶךְ שָׁלוֹם לֹא יָדָעוּ וְאֵין מִשְׁפָּט בְּמַעְגְּלוֹתָם נְתִיבוֹתֵיהֶם עִקְּשׁוּ לָהֶם כֹּל דֹּרֵךְ בָּהּ לֹא יָדַע שָׁלוֹם:

ט עַל־כֵּן רָחַק מִשְׁפָּט מִמֶּנּוּ וְלֹא תַשִּׂיגֵנוּ צְדָקָה נְקַוֶּה לָאוֹר וְהִנֵּה־חֹשֶׁךְ לִנְגֹהוֹת בָּאֲפֵלוֹת נְהַלֵּךְ:

י נְגַשְׁשָׁה כַעִוְרִים קִיר וּכְאֵין עֵינַיִם נְגַשֵּׁשָׁה כָּשַׁלְנוּ בַצָּהֳרַיִם כַּנֶּשֶׁף בָּאַשְׁמַנִּים כַּמֵּתִים:

יא נֶהֱמֶה כַדֻּבִּים כֻּלָּנוּ וְכַיּוֹנִים הָגֹה נֶהְגֶּה נְקַוֶּה לַמִּשְׁפָּט וָאַיִן לִישׁוּעָה רָחֲקָה מִמֶּנּוּ:

יב כִּי־רַבּוּ פְשָׁעֵינוּ נֶגְדֶּךָ וְחַטֹּאותֵינוּ עָנְתָה בָּנוּ כִּי־פְשָׁעֵינוּ אִתָּנוּ וַעֲוֺנֹתֵינוּ יְדַעֲנוּם:

59 1 No, *Hashem*'s arm is not too short to save, Or His ear too dull to hear;

2 But your iniquities have been a barrier Between you and your God, Your sins have made Him turn His face away And refuse to hear you.

3 For your hands are defiled with crime And your fingers with iniquity. Your lips speak falsehood, Your tongue utters treachery.

4 No one sues justly Or pleads honestly; They rely on emptiness and speak falsehood, Conceiving wrong and begetting evil.

5 They hatch adder's eggs And weave spider webs; He who eats of those eggs will die, And if one is crushed, it hatches out a viper.

6 Their webs will not serve as a garment, What they make cannot serve as clothing; Their deeds are deeds of mischief, Their hands commit lawless acts,

7 Their feet run after evil, They hasten to shed the blood of the innocent. Their plans are plans of mischief, Destructiveness and injury are on their roads.

8 They do not care for the way of integrity, There is no justice on their paths. They make their courses crooked, No one who walks in them cares for integrity.

9 "That is why redress is far from us, And vindication does not reach us. We hope for light, and lo! there is darkness; For a gleam, and we must walk in gloom.

10 We grope, like blind men along a wall; Like those without eyes we grope. We stumble at noon, as if in darkness; Among the sturdy, we are like the dead.

11 We all growl like bears And moan like doves. We hope for redress, and there is none; For victory, and it is far from us.

12 For our many sins are before You, Our guilt testifies against us. We are aware of our sins, And we know well our iniquities:

following *Hashem*'s commandments. Those who do so will delight in the heritage of *Yaakov*. And what is heritage of *Yaakov*? As it says in *Sefer Bereishit*, *Hashem* promised *Yaakov* that the "the ground upon which you are lying (i.e. the Land of Israel) I will assign to you and to your offspring" (Geneis 28:13).

1058

Yeshayahu/Isaiah
Chapter 59

13 Rebellion, faithlessness to *Hashem*, And turning away from our God, Planning fraud and treachery, Conceiving lies and uttering them with the throat.

יג פָּשֹׁעַ וְכַחֵשׁ בַּיהוָה וְנָסוֹג מֵאַחַר אֱלֹהֵינוּ דַּבֶּר־עֹשֶׁק וְסָרָה הֹרוֹ וְהֹגוֹ מִלֵּב דִּבְרֵי־שָׁקֶר:

14 And so redress is turned back And vindication stays afar, Because honesty stumbles in the public square And uprightness cannot enter.

יד וְהֻסַּג אָחוֹר מִשְׁפָּט וּצְדָקָה מֵרָחוֹק תַּעֲמֹד כִּי־כָשְׁלָה בָרְחוֹב אֱמֶת וּנְכֹחָה לֹא־תוּכַל לָבוֹא:

15 Honesty has been lacking, He who turns away from evil is despoiled." *Hashem* saw and was displeased That there was no redress.

טו וַתְּהִי הָאֱמֶת נֶעְדֶּרֶת וְסָר מֵרָע מִשְׁתּוֹלֵל וַיַּרְא יְהוָה וַיֵּרַע בְּעֵינָיו כִּי־אֵין מִשְׁפָּט:

16 He saw that there was no man, He gazed long, but no one intervened. Then His own arm won Him triumph, His victorious right hand supported Him.

טז וַיַּרְא כִּי־אֵין אִישׁ וַיִּשְׁתּוֹמֵם כִּי אֵין מַפְגִּיעַ וַתּוֹשַׁע לוֹ זְרֹעוֹ וְצִדְקָתוֹ הִיא סְמָכָתְהוּ:

17 He donned victory like a coat of mail, With a helmet of triumph on His head; He clothed Himself with garments of retribution, Wrapped himself in zeal as in a robe.

יז וַיִּלְבַּשׁ צְדָקָה כַּשִּׁרְיָן וְכוֹבַע יְשׁוּעָה בְּרֹאשׁוֹ וַיִּלְבַּשׁ בִּגְדֵי נָקָם תִּלְבֹּשֶׁת וַיַּעַט כַּמְעִיל קִנְאָה:

18 According to their deserts, So shall He repay fury to His foes; He shall make requital to His enemies, Requital to the distant lands.

יח כְּעַל גְּמֻלוֹת כְּעַל יְשַׁלֵּם חֵמָה לְצָרָיו גְּמוּל לְאֹיְבָיו לָאִיִּים גְּמוּל יְשַׁלֵּם:

19 From the west, they shall revere the name of *Hashem*, And from the east, His Presence. For He shall come like a hemmed-in stream Which the wind of *Hashem* drives on;

יט וְיִירְאוּ מִמַּעֲרָב אֶת־שֵׁם יְהוָה וּמִמִּזְרַח־שֶׁמֶשׁ אֶת־כְּבוֹדוֹ כִּי־יָבוֹא כַנָּהָר צָר רוּחַ יְהוָה נֹסְסָה בוֹ:

20 He shall come as redeemer to *Tzion*, To those in *Yaakov* who turn back from sin – declares *Hashem*.

כ וּבָא לְצִיּוֹן גּוֹאֵל וּלְשָׁבֵי פֶשַׁע בְּיַעֲקֹב נְאֻם יְהוָה:

u-VA l'-tzi-YON go-AYL ul-sha-VAY FE-sha b'-ya-a-KOV n'-UM a-do-NAI

21 And this shall be My covenant with them, said *Hashem*: My spirit which is upon you, and the words which I have placed in your mouth, shall not be absent from your mouth, nor from the mouth of your children, nor from the mouth of your children's children – said *Hashem* – from now on, for all time.

כא וַאֲנִי זֹאת בְּרִיתִי אוֹתָם אָמַר יְהוָה רוּחִי אֲשֶׁר עָלֶיךָ וּדְבָרַי אֲשֶׁר־שַׂמְתִּי בְּפִיךָ לֹא־יָמוּשׁוּ מִפִּיךָ וּמִפִּי זַרְעֲךָ וּמִפִּי זֶרַע זַרְעֲךָ אָמַר יְהוָה מֵעַתָּה וְעַד־עוֹלָם:

59:20 He shall come as redeemer to *Tzion* After the climactic battle described above, *Yeshayahu* promises that a redeemer will come to *Tzion*. Rashi observes, "As long as *Tzion* is in ruins, the redeemer has not yet come." On a simple level, Rashi is saying that once the redeemer comes, *Tzion* will be rebuilt. Hence, if *Tzion* remains in ruins then surely he has not yet come. On a deeper level, perhaps he is implying that for the redeemer to come, *Tzion* cannot be in a state of disrepair; instead, the city of *Yerushalayim* and the Land of Israel must first be built by the returnees to the land. Only then will God's spirit enter the people. Indeed, as the returnees of modern times have begun to rebuild and *Eretz Yisrael* flourishes, our generation eagerly awaits the redeemer to come.

Yeshayahu/Isaiah
Chapter 60

ישעיהו
פרק ס

60

ס **1** Arise, shine, for your light has dawned; The Presence of *Hashem* has shone upon you!

קוּמִי אוֹרִי כִּי בָא אוֹרֵךְ וּכְבוֹד יְהֹוָה עָלַיִךְ זָרָח:

KU-mee O-ree KEE VA o-RAYKH ukh-VOD a-do-NAI a-LA-yikh za-RAKH

2 Behold! Darkness shall cover the earth, And thick clouds the peoples; But upon you *Hashem* will shine, And His Presence be seen over you.

כִּי־הִנֵּה הַחֹשֶׁךְ יְכַסֶּה־אֶרֶץ וַעֲרָפֶל לְאֻמִּים וְעָלַיִךְ יִזְרַח יְהֹוָה וּכְבוֹדוֹ עָלַיִךְ יֵרָאֶה:

3 And nations shall walk by your light, Kings, by your shining radiance.

וְהָלְכוּ גוֹיִם לְאוֹרֵךְ וּמְלָכִים לְנֹגַהּ זַרְחֵךְ:

4 Raise your eyes and look about: They have all gathered and come to you. Your sons shall be brought from afar, Your daughters like babes on shoulders.

שְׂאִי־סָבִיב עֵינַיִךְ וּרְאִי כֻּלָּם נִקְבְּצוּ בָאוּ־לָךְ בָּנַיִךְ מֵרָחוֹק יָבֹאוּ וּבְנֹתַיִךְ עַל־צַד תֵּאָמַנָה:

5 As you behold, you will glow; Your heart will throb and thrill – For the wealth of the sea shall pass on to you, The riches of nations shall flow to you.

אָז תִּרְאִי וְנָהַרְתְּ וּפָחַד וְרָחַב לְבָבֵךְ כִּי־יֵהָפֵךְ עָלַיִךְ הֲמוֹן יָם חֵיל גּוֹיִם יָבֹאוּ לָךְ:

6 Dust clouds of camels shall cover you, Dromedaries of Midian and Ephah. They all shall come from Sheba; They shall bear gold and frankincense, And shall herald the glories of *Hashem*.

שִׁפְעַת גְּמַלִּים תְּכַסֵּךְ בִּכְרֵי מִדְיָן וְעֵיפָה כֻּלָּם מִשְּׁבָא יָבֹאוּ זָהָב וּלְבוֹנָה יִשָּׂאוּ וּתְהִלֹּת יְהֹוָה יְבַשֵּׂרוּ:

7 All the flocks of Kedar shall be assembled for you, The rams of Nebaioth shall serve your needs; They shall be welcome offerings on My *Mizbayach*, And I will add glory to My glorious House.

כָּל־צֹאן קֵדָר יִקָּבְצוּ לָךְ אֵילֵי נְבָיוֹת יְשָׁרְתוּנֶךְ יַעֲלוּ עַל־רָצוֹן מִזְבְּחִי וּבֵית תִּפְאַרְתִּי אֲפָאֵר:

8 Who are these that float like a cloud, Like doves to their cotes?

מִי־אֵלֶּה כָּעָב תְּעוּפֶינָה וְכַיּוֹנִים אֶל־אֲרֻבֹּתֵיהֶם:

60:1 Arise, shine The prophet addresses *Yerushalayim*, calling upon the city to awaken and shine its light upon the world. Chaim Weizman (1874–1952) was a prominent scientist and Zionist leader who would have the honor of becoming the first President of the State of Israel. In 1948, Weizman eloquently explained the illumination that Jerusalem would provide the world as the new capital of the Jewish State: "Jerusalem holds a unique place in the heart of every Jew. Its restoration symbolizes the redemption of Israel. Rome was to the Italians the emblem of their military conquests and political organization. Athens embodies for the Greeks the noblest their genius had wrought in art and thought. To us Jerusalem has both a spiritual and a temporal significance. It is the City of God… it is also the capital of David and Solomon.… To the followers of the two other great monotheistic religions, Jerusalem is a site of sacred associations and holy memories. To us it is that and more than that. It is the centre of our ancient national glory. It was our lodestar in all our wanderings. It embodies all that is noblest in our hopes for the future. Jerusalem is the eternal mother of the Jewish people, precious and beloved even in its desolation. When David made Jerusalem the capital of Judea, on that day there began the Jewish Commonwealth. When Titus destroyed it on the 9th of Av, on that day there ended the Jewish Commonwealth. Nevertheless, even though our Commonwealth was destroyed, we never gave up Jerusalem.… It seems inconceivable that the establishment of a Jewish State should be accompanied by the detachment from it of its spiritual centre and historical capital."

Chaim Weizman (1874–1952)

Yeshayahu/Isaiah
Chapter 60

ישעיהו
פרק ס

9 Behold, the coastlands await me, With ships of Tarshish in the lead, To bring your sons from afar, And their silver and gold as well – For the name of *Hashem* your God, For the Holy One of *Yisrael*, who has glorified you.

ט כִּי־לִי ׀ אִיִּים יְקַוּוּ וָאֳנִיּוֹת תַּרְשִׁישׁ בָּרִאשֹׁנָה לְהָבִיא בָנַיִךְ מֵרָחוֹק כַּסְפָּם וּזְהָבָם אִתָּם לְשֵׁם יְהֹוָה אֱלֹהַיִךְ וְלִקְדוֹשׁ יִשְׂרָאֵל כִּי פֵאֲרָךְ:

10 Aliens shall rebuild your walls, Their kings shall wait upon you – For in anger I struck you down, But in favor I take you back.

י וּבָנוּ בְנֵי־נֵכָר חֹמֹתַיִךְ וּמַלְכֵיהֶם יְשָׁרְתוּנֶךְ כִּי בְקִצְפִּי הִכִּיתִיךְ וּבִרְצוֹנִי רִחַמְתִּיךְ:

11 Your gates shall always stay open – Day and night they shall never be shut – To let in the wealth of the nations, With their kings in procession.

יא וּפִתְּחוּ שְׁעָרַיִךְ תָּמִיד יוֹמָם וָלַיְלָה לֹא יִסָּגֵרוּ לְהָבִיא אֵלַיִךְ חֵיל גּוֹיִם וּמַלְכֵיהֶם נְהוּגִים:

12 For the nation or the kingdom That does not serve you shall perish; Such nations shall be destroyed.

יב כִּי־הַגּוֹי וְהַמַּמְלָכָה אֲשֶׁר לֹא־יַעַבְדוּךְ יֹאבֵדוּ וְהַגּוֹיִם חָרֹב יֶחֱרָבוּ:

13 The majesty of Lebanon shall come to you – Cypress and pine and box – To adorn the site of My Sanctuary, To glorify the place where My feet rest.

יג כְּבוֹד הַלְּבָנוֹן אֵלַיִךְ יָבוֹא בְּרוֹשׁ תִּדְהָר וּתְאַשּׁוּר יַחְדָּו לְפָאֵר מְקוֹם מִקְדָּשִׁי וּמְקוֹם רַגְלַי אֲכַבֵּד:

14 Bowing before you, shall come The children of those who tormented you; Prostrate at the soles of your feet Shall be all those who reviled you; And you shall be called "City of *Hashem*, *Tzion* of the Holy One of *Yisrael*."

יד וְהָלְכוּ אֵלַיִךְ שְׁחוֹחַ בְּנֵי מְעַנַּיִךְ וְהִשְׁתַּחֲווּ עַל־כַּפּוֹת רַגְלַיִךְ כָּל־מְנַאֲצָיִךְ וְקָרְאוּ לָךְ עִיר יְהֹוָה צִיּוֹן קְדוֹשׁ יִשְׂרָאֵל:

15 Whereas you have been forsaken, Rejected, with none passing through, I will mak you a pride everlasting, A joy for age after age.

טו תַּחַת הֱיוֹתֵךְ עֲזוּבָה וּשְׂנוּאָה וְאֵין עוֹבֵר וְשַׂמְתִּיךְ לִגְאוֹן עוֹלָם מְשׂוֹשׂ דּוֹר וָדוֹר:

16 You shall suck the milk of the nations, Suckle at royal breasts. And you shall know That I *Hashem* am your Savior, I, The Mighty One of *Yaakov*, am your Redeemer.

טז וְיָנַקְתְּ חֲלֵב גּוֹיִם וְשֹׁד מְלָכִים תִּינָקִי וְיָדַעַתְּ כִּי אֲנִי יְהֹוָה מוֹשִׁיעֵךְ וְגֹאֲלֵךְ אֲבִיר יַעֲקֹב:

17 Instead of copper I will bring gold, Instead of iron I will bring silver; Instead of wood, copper; And instead of stone, iron. And I will appoint Well-being as your government, Prosperity as your officials.

יז תַּחַת הַנְּחֹשֶׁת אָבִיא זָהָב וְתַחַת הַבַּרְזֶל אָבִיא כֶסֶף וְתַחַת הָעֵצִים נְחֹשֶׁת וְתַחַת הָאֲבָנִים בַּרְזֶל וְשַׂמְתִּי פְקֻדָּתֵךְ שָׁלוֹם וְנֹגְשַׂיִךְ צְדָקָה:

18 The cry "Violence!" Shall no more be heard in your land, Nor "Wrack and ruin!" Within your borders. And you shall name your walls "Victory" And your gates "Renown."

יח לֹא־יִשָּׁמַע עוֹד חָמָס בְּאַרְצֵךְ שֹׁד וָשֶׁבֶר בִּגְבוּלָיִךְ וְקָרָאת יְשׁוּעָה חוֹמֹתַיִךְ וּשְׁעָרַיִךְ תְּהִלָּה:

19 No longer shall you need the sun For light by day, Nor the shining of the moon For radiance [by night]; For *Hashem* shall be your light everlasting, Your God shall be your glory.

יט לֹא־יִהְיֶה־לָּךְ עוֹד הַשֶּׁמֶשׁ לְאוֹר יוֹמָם וּלְנֹגַהּ הַיָּרֵחַ לֹא־יָאִיר לָךְ וְהָיָה־לָךְ יְהֹוָה לְאוֹר עוֹלָם וֵאלֹהַיִךְ לְתִפְאַרְתֵּךְ:

Yeshayahu/Isaiah Chapter 61

20 Your sun shall set no more, Your moon no more withdraw; For *Hashem* shall be a light to you forever, And your days of mourning shall be ended.

כ לֹא־יָבוֹא עוֹד שִׁמְשֵׁךְ וִירֵחֵךְ לֹא יֵאָסֵף כִּי יְהֹוָה יִהְיֶה־לָּךְ לְאוֹר עוֹלָם וְשָׁלְמוּ יְמֵי אֶבְלֵךְ:

21 And your people, all of them righteous, Shall possess the land for all time; They are the shoot that I planted, My handiwork in which I glory.

כא וְעַמֵּךְ כֻּלָּם צַדִּיקִים לְעוֹלָם יִירְשׁוּ אָרֶץ נֵצֶר מטעו [מַטָּעַי] מַעֲשֵׂה יָדַי לְהִתְפָּאֵר:

22 The smallest shall become a clan; The least, a mighty nation. I *Hashem* will speed it in due time.

כב הַקָּטֹן יִהְיֶה לָאֶלֶף וְהַצָּעִיר לְגוֹי עָצוּם אֲנִי יְהֹוָה בְּעִתָּהּ אֲחִישֶׁנָּה:

61

1 The spirit of *Hashem* is upon me, Because *Hashem* has anointed me; He has sent me as a herald of joy to the humble, To bind up the wounded of heart, To proclaim release to the captives, Liberation to the imprisoned;

א רוּחַ אֲדֹנָי יֱהֹוִה עָלָי יַעַן מָשַׁח יְהֹוָה אֹתִי לְבַשֵּׂר עֲנָוִים שְׁלָחַנִי לַחֲבֹשׁ לְנִשְׁבְּרֵי־לֵב לִקְרֹא לִשְׁבוּיִם דְּרוֹר וְלַאֲסוּרִים פְּקַח־קוֹחַ:

2 To proclaim a year of *Hashem*'s favor And a day of vindication by our God; To comfort all who mourn –

ב לִקְרֹא שְׁנַת־רָצוֹן לַיהֹוָה וְיוֹם נָקָם לֵאלֹהֵינוּ לְנַחֵם כָּל־אֲבֵלִים:

3 To provide for the mourners in *Tzion* – To give them a turban instead of ashes, The festive ointment instead of mourning, A garment of splendor instead of a drooping spirit. They shall be called terebinths of victory, Planted by *Hashem* for His glory.

ג לָשׂוּם לַאֲבֵלֵי צִיּוֹן לָתֵת לָהֶם פְּאֵר תַּחַת אֵפֶר שֶׁמֶן שָׂשׂוֹן תַּחַת אֵבֶל מַעֲטֵה תְהִלָּה תַּחַת רוּחַ כֵּהָה וְקֹרָא לָהֶם אֵילֵי הַצֶּדֶק מַטַּע יְהֹוָה לְהִתְפָּאֵר:

4 And they shall build the ancient ruins, Raise up the desolations of old, And renew the ruined cities, The desolations of many ages.

ד וּבָנוּ חָרְבוֹת עוֹלָם שֹׁמְמוֹת רִאשֹׁנִים יְקוֹמֵמוּ וְחִדְּשׁוּ עָרֵי חֹרֶב שֹׁמְמוֹת דּוֹר וָדוֹר:

5 Strangers shall stand and pasture your flocks, Aliens shall be your plowmen and vine-trimmers;

ה וְעָמְדוּ זָרִים וְרָעוּ צֹאנְכֶם וּבְנֵי נֵכָר אִכָּרֵיכֶם וְכֹרְמֵיכֶם:

v'-a-m'-DU za-REEM v'-ra-U tzo-n'-KHEM uv-NAY nay-KHAR i-ka-ray-HEM v'-kho-r'-may-KHEM

6 While you shall be called "*Kohanim* of *Hashem*," And termed "Servants of our God." You shall enjoy the wealth of nations And revel in their riches.

ו וְאַתֶּם כֹּהֲנֵי יְהֹוָה תִּקָּרֵאוּ מְשָׁרְתֵי אֱלֹהֵינוּ יֵאָמֵר לָכֶם חֵיל גּוֹיִם תֹּאכֵלוּ וּבִכְבוֹדָם תִּתְיַמָּרוּ:

61:5 Strangers shall stand and pasture your flocks During the Messianic age, non-Jews will play an essential role in helping the Jewish people settle the Land of Israel through agriculture, as this verse states, and they will also partner with the Jews in spiritual pursuits. Rabbi Israel Lipschitz (1782–1860), in his commentary *Tiferet Yisrael*, quotes this verse to prove that non-Jews will participate in the actual construction of the Holy Temple, similar to the assistance King *Shlomo* sought from King Hiram of Tyre who sent builders and artisans to help build the first *Beit Hamikdash*. In modern times, this verse serves as the inspiration for the hundreds of Christian volunteers who travel each year during the harvest season to assist Jewish farmers in Israel.

Rabbi Israel Lipschitz (1782–1860)

Yeshayahu/Isaiah
Chapter 62

ישעיהו
פרק סב

7 Because your shame was double – Men cried, "Disgrace is their portion" – Assuredly, They shall have a double share in their land, Joy shall be theirs for all time.

ז תַּחַת בָּשְׁתְּכֶם מִשְׁנֶה וּכְלִמָּה יָרֹנּוּ חֶלְקָם לָכֵן בְּאַרְצָם מִשְׁנֶה יִירָשׁוּ שִׂמְחַת עוֹלָם תִּהְיֶה לָהֶם:

8 For I *Hashem* love justice, I hate robbery with a burnt offering. I will pay them their wages faithfully, And make a covenant with them for all time.

ח כִּי אֲנִי יְהוָה אֹהֵב מִשְׁפָּט שֹׂנֵא גָזֵל בְּעוֹלָה וְנָתַתִּי פְעֻלָּתָם בֶּאֱמֶת וּבְרִית עוֹלָם אֶכְרוֹת לָהֶם:

9 Their offspring shall be known among the nations, Their descendants in the midst of the peoples. All who see them shall recognize That they are a stock *Hashem* has blessed.

ט וְנוֹדַע בַּגּוֹיִם זַרְעָם וְצֶאֱצָאֵיהֶם בְּתוֹךְ הָעַמִּים כָּל־רֹאֵיהֶם יַכִּירוּם כִּי הֵם זֶרַע בֵּרַךְ יְהוָה:

10 I greatly rejoice in *Hashem*, My whole being exults in my God. For He has clothed me with garments of triumph, Wrapped me in a robe of victory, Like a bridegroom adorned with a turban, Like a bride bedecked with her finery.

י שׂוֹשׂ אָשִׂישׂ בַּיהוָה תָּגֵל נַפְשִׁי בֵּאלֹהַי כִּי הִלְבִּישַׁנִי בִּגְדֵי־יֶשַׁע מְעִיל צְדָקָה יְעָטָנִי כֶּחָתָן יְכַהֵן פְּאֵר וְכַכַּלָּה תַּעְדֶּה כֵלֶיהָ:

SOS a-SEES ba-do-NAI ta-GAYL naf-SHEE bay-lo-HAI KEE hil-bee-SHA-nee big-day YE-sha m'-EEL tz'-da-KAH y'-a-TA-nee ke-kha-TAN y'-kha-HAYN p'-AYR v'-kha-ka-LAH ta-DEH khay-LE-ha

11 For as the earth brings forth her growth And a garden makes the seed shoot up, So *Hashem* will make Victory and renown shoot up In the presence of all the nations.

יא כִּי כָאָרֶץ תּוֹצִיא צִמְחָהּ וּכְגַנָּה זֵרוּעֶיהָ תַצְמִיחַ כֵּן אֲדֹנָי יְהוִה יַצְמִיחַ צְדָקָה וּתְהִלָּה נֶגֶד כָּל־הַגּוֹיִם:

62 1 For the sake of *Tzion* I will not be silent, For the sake of *Yerushalayim* I will not be still, Till her victory emerge resplendent And her triumph like a flaming torch.

סב א לְמַעַן צִיּוֹן לֹא אֶחֱשֶׁה וּלְמַעַן יְרוּשָׁלַ͏ִם לֹא אֶשְׁקוֹט עַד־יֵצֵא כַנֹּגַהּ צִדְקָהּ וִישׁוּעָתָהּ כְּלַפִּיד יִבְעָר:

2 Nations shall see your victory, And every king your majesty; And you shall be called by a new name Which *Hashem* Himself shall bestow.

ב וְרָאוּ גוֹיִם צִדְקֵךְ וְכָל־מְלָכִים כְּבוֹדֵךְ וְקֹרָא לָךְ שֵׁם חָדָשׁ אֲשֶׁר פִּי יְהוָה יִקֳּבֶנּוּ:

3 You shall be a glorious crown In the hand of *Hashem*, And a royal diadem In the palm of your God.

ג וְהָיִיתְ עֲטֶרֶת תִּפְאֶרֶת בְּיַד־יְהוָה וּצְנִיף [וּצְנוּף] מְלוּכָה בְּכַף־אֱלֹהָיִךְ:

61:10 I greatly rejoice in *Hashem* *Yeshayahu* speaks in his own voice, rejoicing in *Hashem*'s goodness to His people. The salvation of the Jewish people, returned and dwelling safely in their own land, will be as visible as the fine jewels worn by a bridegroom and bride on their wedding day. In the meantime, while *Har Habayit* lies in ruin, the Jewish people observe a number of customs mourning the loss of the *Beit Hamikdash*. These include not wearing excessive amounts of jewelry and smashing a glass at Jewish wedding ceremonies, both as a reminder that the complete rebuilding of *Yerushalayim* and the *Beit Hamikdash* has yet to come.

Yeshayahu/Isaiah
Chapter 62

ישעיהו
פרק סב

4 Nevermore shall you be called "Forsaken," Nor shall your land be called "Desolate"; But you shall be called "I delight in her," And your land "Espoused." For *Hashem* takes delight in you, And your land shall be espoused.

לֹא־יֵאָמֵר לָךְ עוֹד עֲזוּבָה וּלְאַרְצֵךְ לֹא־יֵאָמֵר עוֹד שְׁמָמָה כִּי לָךְ יִקָּרֵא חֶפְצִי־בָהּ וּלְאַרְצֵךְ בְּעוּלָה כִּי־חָפֵץ יְהֹוָה בָּךְ וְאַרְצֵךְ תִּבָּעֵל׃

5 As a youth espouses a maiden, Your sons shall espouse you; And as a bridegroom rejoices over his bride, So will your God rejoice over you.

כִּי־יִבְעַל בָּחוּר בְּתוּלָה יִבְעָלוּךְ בָּנָיִךְ וּמְשׂוֹשׂ חָתָן עַל־כַּלָּה יָשִׂישׂ עָלַיִךְ אֱלֹהָיִךְ׃

6 Upon your walls, O *Yerushalayim*, I have set watchmen, Who shall never be silent By day or by night. O you, *Hashem*'s remembrancers Take no rest

עַל־חוֹמֹתַיִךְ יְרוּשָׁלַ͏ִם הִפְקַדְתִּי שֹׁמְרִים כָּל־הַיּוֹם וְכָל־הַלַּיְלָה תָּמִיד לֹא יֶחֱשׁוּ הַמַּזְכִּרִים אֶת־יְהֹוָה אַל־דֳּמִי לָכֶם׃

al kho-mo-TA-yikh y'-ru-sha-LA-im hif-KAD-tee sho-m'-REEM kol ha-YOM v'-khol ha-LAI-lah ta-MEED lo ye-khe-SHU ha-maz-ki-REEM et a-do-NAI al do-MEE la-KHEM

7 And give no rest to Him, Until He establish *Yerushalayim* And make her renowned on earth.

וְאַל־תִּתְּנוּ דֳמִי לוֹ עַד־יְכוֹנֵן וְעַד־יָשִׂים אֶת־יְרוּשָׁלַ͏ִם תְּהִלָּה בָּאָרֶץ׃

v'-al ti-t'-NU da-MEE LO ad y'-kho-NAYN v'-ad ya-SEEM et y'-ru-sha-LA-im t'-hi-LAH ba-A-retz

8 *Hashem* has sworn by His right hand, By His mighty arm: Nevermore will I give your new grain To your enemies for food, Nor shall foreigners drink the new wine For which you have labored.

נִשְׁבַּע יְהֹוָה בִּימִינוֹ וּבִזְרוֹעַ עֻזּוֹ אִם־אֶתֵּן אֶת־דְּגָנֵךְ עוֹד מַאֲכָל לְאֹיְבַיִךְ וְאִם־יִשְׁתּוּ בְנֵי־נֵכָר תִּירוֹשֵׁךְ אֲשֶׁר יָגַעַתְּ בּוֹ׃

9 But those who harvest it shall eat it And give praise to *Hashem*; And those who gather it shall drink it In My sacred courts.

כִּי מְאַסְפָיו יֹאכְלֻהוּ וְהִלְלוּ אֶת־יְהֹוָה וּמְקַבְּצָיו יִשְׁתֻּהוּ בְּחַצְרוֹת קָדְשִׁי׃

10 Pass through, pass through the gates! Clear the road for the people; Build up, build up the highway, Remove the rocks! Raise an ensign over the peoples!

עִבְרוּ עִבְרוּ בַּשְּׁעָרִים פַּנּוּ דֶּרֶךְ הָעָם סֹלּוּ סֹלּוּ הַמְסִלָּה סַקְּלוּ מֵאֶבֶן הָרִימוּ נֵס עַל־הָעַמִּים׃

62:6 Who shall never be silent by day or by night If the watchmen are upon the walls all day and all night, then why is the superfluous word *tamid* (תמיד) 'always,' included in this verse? 20th century American Rabbi David Stavsky explains in his book of sermons: "*Tamid*, 'always,' refers to speaking up about *Yerushalayim*. Never should we remain silent when *Yerushalayim* is threatened. We are not to remain quiet and passive. We are the guardians…. Therefore, *Yerushalayim* never can become a bargaining chip in achieving peace. Not the Vatican, not Washington, not Hamas, not Hezbollah, not any Arab fundamentalist or terrorist can dictate terms. Threats of Jihad should not make us waiver. *Yerushalayim* is finally ours, and we are the watchmen *tamid*, always."

62:7 And give no rest to Him The Hebrew word for rest in this verse is *damee* (דמי), which also means 'silence.' Interestingly, the same Hebrew word, *dam* (דם), means 'blood.' Commentators explain the connection in light of Ezekiel 16:6, "Live in spite of your blood." The hidden meaning behind the verse is, 'by your silence you shall live.' In relationships, the truism "silence is golden" can protect against an insensitive remark. So too when it comes to our relationship with *Hashem*. Oftentimes we cannot comprehend His ways, and we become frustrated and even angry with the suffering we see in this world. Nevertheless, we must try to emulate *Aharon*'s example after losing two of his sons: *Vayidom Aharon* (וידם אהרן), '*Aharon* was silent' (Leviticus 10:3).

Rabbi David Stavsky (1930–2004)

Yeshayahu/Isaiah
Chapter 63

11 See, *Hashem* has proclaimed To the end of the earth: Announce to Fair *Tzion*, Your Deliverer is coming! See, his reward is with Him, His recompense before Him.

12 And they shall be called, "The Holy People, The Redeemed of *Hashem*," And you shall be called, "Sought Out, A City Not Forsaken."

63 1 Who is this coming from Edom, In crimsoned garments from Bozrah – Who is this, majestic in attire, Pressing forward in His great might? "It is I, who contend victoriously, Powerful to give triumph."

2 Why is your clothing so red, Your garments like his who treads grapes?

3 "I trod out a vintage alone; Of the peoples no man was with Me. I trod them down in My anger, Trampled them in My rage; Their life-blood bespattered My garments, And all My clothing was stained.

4 For I had planned a day of vengeance, And My year of redemption arrived.

5 Then I looked, but there was none to help; I stared, but there was none to aid – So My own arm wrought the triumph, And My own rage was My aid.

6 I trampled peoples in My anger, I made them drunk with My rage, And I hurled their glory to the ground."

7 I will recount the kind acts of *Hashem*, The praises of *Hashem* – For all that *Hashem* has wrought for us, The vast bounty to the House of *Yisrael* That He bestowed upon them According to His mercy and His great kindness.

8 He thought: Surely they are My people, Children who will not play false. So He was their Deliverer.

9 In all their troubles He was troubled, And the angel of His Presence delivered them. In His love and pity He Himself redeemed them, Raised them, and exalted them All the days of old.

10 But they rebelled, and grieved His holy spirit; Then He became their enemy, And Himself made war against them.

יא הִנֵּה יְהוָה הִשְׁמִיעַ אֶל־קְצֵה הָאָרֶץ אִמְרוּ לְבַת־צִיּוֹן הִנֵּה יִשְׁעֵךְ בָּא הִנֵּה שְׂכָרוֹ אִתּוֹ וּפְעֻלָּתוֹ לְפָנָיו:

יב וְקָרְאוּ לָהֶם עַם־הַקֹּדֶשׁ גְּאוּלֵי יְהוָה וְלָךְ יִקָּרֵא דְרוּשָׁה עִיר לֹא נֶעֱזָבָה:

סג א מִי־זֶה ׀ בָּא מֵאֱדוֹם חֲמוּץ בְּגָדִים מִבָּצְרָה זֶה הָדוּר בִּלְבוּשׁוֹ צֹעֶה בְּרֹב כֹּחוֹ אֲנִי מְדַבֵּר בִּצְדָקָה רַב לְהוֹשִׁיעַ:

ב מַדּוּעַ אָדֹם לִלְבוּשֶׁךָ וּבְגָדֶיךָ כְּדֹרֵךְ בְּגַת:

ג פּוּרָה ׀ דָּרַכְתִּי לְבַדִּי וּמֵעַמִּים אֵין־אִישׁ אִתִּי וְאֶדְרְכֵם בְּאַפִּי וְאֶרְמְסֵם בַּחֲמָתִי וְיֵז נִצְחָם עַל־בְּגָדַי וְכָל־מַלְבּוּשַׁי אֶגְאָלְתִּי:

ד כִּי יוֹם נָקָם בְּלִבִּי וּשְׁנַת גְּאוּלַי בָּאָה:

ה וְאַבִּיט וְאֵין עֹזֵר וְאֶשְׁתּוֹמֵם וְאֵין סוֹמֵךְ וַתּוֹשַׁע לִי זְרֹעִי וַחֲמָתִי הִיא סְמָכָתְנִי:

ו וְאָבוּס עַמִּים בְּאַפִּי וַאֲשַׁכְּרֵם בַּחֲמָתִי וְאוֹרִיד לָאָרֶץ נִצְחָם:

ז חַסְדֵי יְהוָה ׀ אַזְכִּיר תְּהִלֹּת יְהוָה כְּעַל כֹּל אֲשֶׁר־גְּמָלָנוּ יְהוָה וְרַב־טוּב לְבֵית יִשְׂרָאֵל אֲשֶׁר־גְּמָלָם כְּרַחֲמָיו וּכְרֹב חֲסָדָיו:

ח וַיֹּאמֶר אַךְ־עַמִּי הֵמָּה בָּנִים לֹא יְשַׁקֵּרוּ וַיְהִי לָהֶם לְמוֹשִׁיעַ:

ט בְּכָל־צָרָתָם ׀ לֹא [לוֹ] צָר וּמַלְאַךְ פָּנָיו הוֹשִׁיעָם בְּאַהֲבָתוֹ וּבְחֶמְלָתוֹ הוּא גְאָלָם וַיְנַטְּלֵם וַיְנַשְּׂאֵם כָּל־יְמֵי עוֹלָם:

י וְהֵמָּה מָרוּ וְעִצְּבוּ אֶת־רוּחַ קָדְשׁוֹ וַיֵּהָפֵךְ לָהֶם לְאוֹיֵב הוּא נִלְחַם־בָּם:

Yeshayahu/Isaiah
Chapter 63

11 Then they remembered the ancient days, Him, who pulled His people out [of the water]: "Where is He who brought them up from the Sea Along with the shepherd of His flock? Where is He who put In their midst His holy spirit,

יא וַיִּזְכֹּר יְמֵי־עוֹלָם מֹשֶׁה עַמּוֹ אַיֵּה הַמַּעֲלֵם מִיָּם אֵת רֹעֵי צֹאנוֹ אַיֵּה הַשָּׂם בְּקִרְבּוֹ אֶת־רוּחַ קָדְשׁוֹ׃

12 Who made His glorious arm March at the right hand of *Moshe*, Who divided the waters before them To make Himself a name for all time,

יב מוֹלִיךְ לִימִין מֹשֶׁה זְרוֹעַ תִּפְאַרְתּוֹ בּוֹקֵעַ מַיִם מִפְּנֵיהֶם לַעֲשׂוֹת לוֹ שֵׁם עוֹלָם׃

13 Who led them through the deeps So that they did not stumble – As a horse in a desert,

יג מוֹלִיכָם בַּתְּהֹמוֹת כַּסּוּס בַּמִּדְבָּר לֹא יִכָּשֵׁלוּ׃

14 Like a beast descending to the plain?" 'Twas the spirit of *Hashem* gave them rest; Thus did You shepherd Your people To win for Yourself a glorious name.

יד כַּבְּהֵמָה בַּבִּקְעָה תֵרֵד רוּחַ יְהוָה תְּנִיחֶנּוּ כֵּן נִהַגְתָּ עַמְּךָ לַעֲשׂוֹת לְךָ שֵׁם תִּפְאָרֶת׃

15 Look down from heaven and see, From Your holy and glorious height! Where is Your zeal, Your power? Your yearning and Your love Are being withheld from us!

טו הַבֵּט מִשָּׁמַיִם וּרְאֵה מִזְּבֻל קָדְשְׁךָ וְתִפְאַרְתֶּךָ אַיֵּה קִנְאָתְךָ וּגְבוּרֹתֶךָ הֲמוֹן מֵעֶיךָ וְרַחֲמֶיךָ אֵלַי הִתְאַפָּקוּ׃

16 Surely You are our Father: Though *Avraham* regard us not, And *Yisrael* recognize us not, You, *Hashem*, are our Father; From of old, Your name is "Our Redeemer."

טז כִּי־אַתָּה אָבִינוּ כִּי אַבְרָהָם לֹא יְדָעָנוּ וְיִשְׂרָאֵל לֹא יַכִּירָנוּ אַתָּה יְהוָה אָבִינוּ גֹּאֲלֵנוּ מֵעוֹלָם שְׁמֶךָ׃

kee a-TAH a-VEE-nu KEE av-ra-HAM LO y'-da-A-nu v'-yis-ra-AYL LO ya-kee-RA-nu a-TAH a-do-NAI a-VEE-nu go-a-LAY-nu may-o-LAM sh'-ME-kha

17 Why, *Hashem*, do You make us stray from Your ways, And turn our hearts away from revering You? Relent for the sake of Your servants, The tribes that are Your very own!

יז לָמָּה תַתְעֵנוּ יְהוָה מִדְּרָכֶיךָ תַּקְשִׁיחַ לִבֵּנוּ מִיִּרְאָתֶךָ שׁוּב לְמַעַן עֲבָדֶיךָ שִׁבְטֵי נַחֲלָתֶךָ׃

18 Our foes have trampled Your Sanctuary, Which Your holy people possessed but a little while.

יח לַמִּצְעָר יָרְשׁוּ עַם־קָדְשֶׁךָ צָרֵינוּ בּוֹסְסוּ מִקְדָּשֶׁךָ׃

19 We have become as a people You never ruled, To which Your name was never attached. If You would but tear open the heavens and come down, So that mountains would quake before

יט הָיִינוּ מֵעוֹלָם לֹא־מָשַׁלְתָּ בָּם לֹא־נִקְרָא שִׁמְךָ עֲלֵיהֶם לוּא־קָרַעְתָּ שָׁמַיִם יָרַדְתָּ מִפָּנֶיךָ הָרִים נָזֹלּוּ׃

63:16 Though *Avraham* regard us not, and *Yisrael* recognize us not In this verse, the Jewish people turn to *Hashem* as their redeemer. At times, they feel that they are entitled to divine privilege on the mere basis of their descent from *Avraham* and *Yaakov*. However, they now renounce this with the realization that their forefathers, however righteous they were and through whom they were privileged to dwell in the land, could not intercede with *Hashem* when they sinned and were punished. They had to personally learn to trust in God alone as their Father. With this new understanding and trust in *Hashem*, they will merit to return to the land.

Yeshayahu/Isaiah
Chapter 64

64

1 You – As when fire kindles brushwood, And fire makes water boil – To make Your name known to Your adversaries So that nations will tremble at Your Presence,

2 When You did wonders we dared not hope for, You came down And mountains quaked before You.

3 Such things had never been heard or noted. No eye has seen [them], O *Hashem*, but You, Who act for those who trust in You.

4 Yet you have struck him who would gladly do justice, And remember You in Your ways. It is because You are angry that we have sinned; We have been steeped in them from of old, And can we be saved?

5 We have all become like an unclean thing, And all our virtues like a filthy rag. We are all withering like leaves, And our iniquities, like a wind, carry us off.

6 Yet no one invokes Your name, Rouses himself to cling to You. For You have hidden Your face from us, MAnd made us melt because of our iniquities.

7 But now, *Hashem*, You are our Father; We are the clay, and You are the Potter, We are all the work of Your hands.

v'-a-TAH a-do-NAI a-VEE-nu A-tah a-NAKH-nu ha-KHO-mer v'-a-TAH yo-tz'-RAY-nu u-ma-a-SAY ya-d'-KHA ku-LA-nu

8 Be not implacably angry, *Hashem*, Do not remember iniquity forever. Oh, look down to Your people, to us all!

9 Your holy cities have become a desert: *Tzion* has become a desert, *Yerushalayim* a desolation.

10 Our holy Temple, our pride, Where our fathers praised You, Has been consumed by fire: And all that was dear to us is ruined.

ישעיהו
פרק סד

א כְּקְדֹחַ אֵשׁ הֲמָסִים מַיִם תִּבְעֶה־אֵשׁ לְהוֹדִיעַ שִׁמְךָ לְצָרֶיךָ מִפָּנֶיךָ גּוֹיִם יִרְגָּזוּ:

ב בַּעֲשׂוֹתְךָ נוֹרָאוֹת לֹא נְקַוֶּה יָרַדְתָּ מִפָּנֶיךָ הָרִים נָזֹלּוּ:

ג וּמֵעוֹלָם לֹא־שָׁמְעוּ לֹא הֶאֱזִינוּ עַיִן לֹא־רָאָתָה אֱלֹהִים זוּלָתְךָ יַעֲשֶׂה לִמְחַכֵּה־לוֹ:

ד פָּגַעְתָּ אֶת־שָׂשׂ וְעֹשֵׂה צֶדֶק בִּדְרָכֶיךָ יִזְכְּרוּךָ הֵן־אַתָּה קָצַפְתָּ וַנֶּחֱטָא בָּהֶם עוֹלָם וְנִוָּשֵׁעַ:

ה וַנְּהִי כַטָּמֵא כֻּלָּנוּ וּכְבֶגֶד עִדִּים כָּל־צִדְקֹתֵינוּ וַנָּבֶל כֶּעָלֶה כֻּלָּנוּ וַעֲוֺנֵנוּ כָּרוּחַ יִשָּׂאֻנוּ:

ו וְאֵין־קוֹרֵא בְשִׁמְךָ מִתְעוֹרֵר לְהַחֲזִיק בָּךְ כִּי־הִסְתַּרְתָּ פָּנֶיךָ מִמֶּנּוּ וַתְּמוּגֵנוּ בְּיַד־עֲוֺנֵנוּ:

ז וְעַתָּה יְהֹוָה אָבִינוּ אָתָּה אֲנַחְנוּ הַחֹמֶר וְאַתָּה יֹצְרֵנוּ וּמַעֲשֵׂה יָדְךָ כֻּלָּנוּ:

ח אַל־תִּקְצֹף יְהֹוָה עַד־מְאֹד וְאַל־לָעַד תִּזְכֹּר עָוֺן הֵן הַבֶּט־נָא עַמְּךָ כֻלָּנוּ:

ט עָרֵי קָדְשְׁךָ הָיוּ מִדְבָּר צִיּוֹן מִדְבָּר הָיָתָה יְרוּשָׁלַ͏ִם שְׁמָמָה:

י בֵּית קָדְשֵׁנוּ וְתִפְאַרְתֵּנוּ אֲשֶׁר הִלְלוּךָ אֲבֹתֵינוּ הָיָה לִשְׂרֵפַת אֵשׁ וְכָל־מַחֲמַדֵּינוּ הָיָה לְחָרְבָּה:

64:7 We are the clay, and You are the Potter *Yeshayahu* presents the people's confession, that they are impure and unworthy of divine assistance, to *Hashem*. He then prays to God in their name not to be angry forever with them. They humbly acknowledge that they are like clay, and that *Hashem* is their potter. The people hope that since God formed Israel, He will not forsake the work of His hands (see Psalms 138:8). Rather, they hope for complete forgiveness, a return to their land and the rebuilding of the holy cities and the *Beit Hamikdash* which had become desolate (verses 9–10). This appeal was echoed throughout the generations, and has begun to be answered in our times.

Yeshayahu/Isaiah
Chapter 65

11 At such things will You restrain Yourself, *Hashem*, Will You stand idly by and let us suffer so heavily?

65 1 I responded to those who did not ask, I was at hand to those who did not seek Me; I said, "Here I am, here I am," To a nation that did not invoke My name.

2 I constantly spread out My hands To a disloyal people, Who walk the way that is not good, Following their own designs;

3 The people who provoke My anger, Who continually, to My very face, Sacrifice in gardens and burn incense on tiles;

4 Who sit inside tombs And pass the night in secret places; Who eat the flesh of swine, With broth of unclean things in their bowls;

5 Who say, "Keep your distance! Don't come closer! For I would render you consecrated." Such things make My anger rage, Like fire blazing all day long.

6 See, this is recorded before Me; I will not stand idly by, but will repay, Deliver their sins* into their bosom,

7 And the sins of their fathers as well – said *Hashem* – For they made offerings upon the mountains And affronted Me upon the hills. I will count out their recompense in full, Into their bosoms.

8 Thus said *Hashem*: As, when new wine is present in the cluster, One says, "Don't destroy it; there's good in it," So will I do for the sake of My servants, And not destroy everything.

9 I will bring forth offspring from *Yaakov*, From *Yehuda* heirs to My mountains; My chosen ones shall take possession, My servants shall dwell thereon.

10 *Sharon* shall become a pasture for flocks, And the Valley of Achor a place for cattle to lie down, For My people who seek Me.

11 But as for you who forsake *Hashem*, Who ignore My holy mountain, Who set a table for Luck And fill a mixing bowl for Destiny:

---
* "their sins" brought up from verse 7 for clarity

Yeshayahu/Isaiah
Chapter 65

ישעיהו
פרק סה

12 I will destine you for the sword, You will all kneel down, to be slaughtered – Because, when I called, you did not answer, When I spoke, you would not listen. You did what I hold evil, And chose what I do not want.

יב וּמָנִיתִי אֶתְכֶם לַחֶרֶב וְכֻלְּכֶם לַטֶּבַח תִּכְרָעוּ יַעַן קָרָאתִי וְלֹא עֲנִיתֶם דִּבַּרְתִּי וְלֹא שְׁמַעְתֶּם וַתַּעֲשׂוּ הָרַע בְּעֵינַי וּבַאֲשֶׁר לֹא־חָפַצְתִּי בְּחַרְתֶּם:

13 Assuredly, thus said *Hashem*: My servants shall eat, and you shall hunger; My servants shall drink, and you shall thirst; My servants shall rejoice, and you shall be shamed;

יג לָכֵן כֹּה־אָמַר אֲדֹנָי יֱהֹוִה הִנֵּה עֲבָדַי יֹאכֵלוּ וְאַתֶּם תִּרְעָבוּ הִנֵּה עֲבָדַי יִשְׁתּוּ וְאַתֶּם תִּצְמָאוּ הִנֵּה עֲבָדַי יִשְׂמָחוּ וְאַתֶּם תֵּבֹשׁוּ:

14 My servants shall shout in gladness, And you shall cry out in anguish, Howling in heartbreak.

יד הִנֵּה עֲבָדַי יָרֹנּוּ מִטּוּב לֵב וְאַתֶּם תִּצְעֲקוּ מִכְּאֵב לֵב וּמִשֵּׁבֶר רוּחַ תְּיֵלִילוּ:

15 You shall leave behind a name By which My chosen ones shall curse: "So may *Hashem* slay you!" But His servants shall be given a different name.

טו וְהִנַּחְתֶּם שִׁמְכֶם לִשְׁבוּעָה לִבְחִירַי וֶהֱמִיתְךָ אֲדֹנָי יֱהֹוִה וְלַעֲבָדָיו יִקְרָא שֵׁם אַחֵר:

16 For whoever blesses himself in the land Shall bless himself by the true *Hashem*; And whoever swears in the land Shall swear by the true *Hashem*. The former troubles shall be forgotten, Shall be hidden from My eyes.

טז אֲשֶׁר הַמִּתְבָּרֵךְ בָּאָרֶץ יִתְבָּרֵךְ בֵּאלֹהֵי אָמֵן וְהַנִּשְׁבָּע בָּאָרֶץ יִשָּׁבַע בֵּאלֹהֵי אָמֵן כִּי נִשְׁכְּחוּ הַצָּרוֹת הָרִאשֹׁנוֹת וְכִי נִסְתְּרוּ מֵעֵינָי:

17 For behold! I am creating A new heaven and a new earth; The former things shall not be remembered, They shall never come to mind.

יז כִּי־הִנְנִי בוֹרֵא שָׁמַיִם חֲדָשִׁים וָאָרֶץ חֲדָשָׁה וְלֹא תִזָּכַרְנָה הָרִאשֹׁנוֹת וְלֹא תַעֲלֶינָה עַל־לֵב:

18 Be glad, then, and rejoice forever In what I am creating. For I shall create *Yerushalayim* as a joy, And her people as a delight;

יח כִּי־אִם־שִׂישׂוּ וְגִילוּ עֲדֵי־עַד אֲשֶׁר אֲנִי בוֹרֵא כִּי הִנְנִי בוֹרֵא אֶת־יְרוּשָׁלַם גִּילָה וְעַמָּהּ מָשׂוֹשׂ:

19 And I will rejoice in *Yerushalayim* And delight in her people. Never again shall be heard there The sounds of weeping and wailing.

יט וְגַלְתִּי בִירוּשָׁלַם וְשַׂשְׂתִּי בְעַמִּי וְלֹא־יִשָּׁמַע בָּהּ עוֹד קוֹל בְּכִי וְקוֹל זְעָקָה:

v'-gal-TEE vee-ru-sha-LA-im v'-sas-TEE v'-a-MEE v'-lo yi-sha-MA BAH OD KOL b'-KHEE v'-KOL z'-a-KAH

20 No more shall there be an infant or graybeard Who does not live out his days. He who dies at a hundred years Shall be reckoned a youth, And he who fails to reach a hundred Shall be reckoned accursed.

כ לֹא־יִהְיֶה מִשָּׁם עוֹד עוּל יָמִים וְזָקֵן אֲשֶׁר לֹא־יְמַלֵּא אֶת־יָמָיו כִּי הַנַּעַר בֶּן־מֵאָה שָׁנָה יָמוּת וְהַחוֹטֶא בֶּן־מֵאָה שָׁנָה יְקֻלָּל:

65:19 And I will rejoice in *Yerushalayim*, and delight in her people *Yeshayahu's* vision of the redemption is a natural one. As the next verse states, there will be death, and people will still sin. However, the people will dwell safely in their land. They will live for an entire lifespan (verse 20), build houses and plant fields and vineyards (verse 21), and live without fear of invasion and exile. For this alone, *Hashem* rejoices with *Yerushalayim* and the People of Israel.

Yeshayahu/Isaiah
Chapter 66

21 They shall build houses and dwell in them, They shall plant vineyards and enjoy their fruit.

22 They shall not build for others to dwell in, Or plant for others to enjoy. For the days of My people shall be As long as the days of a tree, My chosen ones shall outlive The work of their hands.

23 They shall not toil to no purpose; They shall not bear children for terror, But they shall be a people blessed by *Hashem*, And their offspring shall remain with them.

24 Before they pray, I will answer; While they are still speaking, I will respond.

25 The wolf and the lamb shall graze together, And the lion shall eat straw like the ox, And the serpent's food shall be earth. In all My sacred mount Nothing evil or vile shall be done – said *Hashem*.

66 1 Thus said *Hashem*: The heaven is My throne And the earth is My footstool: Where could you build a house for Me, What place could serve as My abode?

2 All this was made by My hand, And thus it all came into being – declares *Hashem*. Yet to such a one I look: To the poor and brokenhearted, Who is concerned about My word.

3 As for those who slaughter oxen and slay humans, Who sacrifice sheep and immolate dogs, Who present as oblation the blood of swine, Who offer incense and worship false gods – Just as they have chosen their ways And take pleasure in their abominations,

4 So will I choose to mock them, To bring on them the very thing they dread. For I called and none responded, I spoke and none paid heed. They did what I deem evil And chose what I do not want.

5 Hear the word of *Hashem*, You who are concerned about His word! Your kinsmen who hate you, Who spurn you because of Me, are saying, "Let *Hashem* manifest His Presence, So that we may look upon your joy." But theirs shall be the shame.

6 Hark, tumult from the city, Thunder from the Temple! It is the thunder of *Hashem* As He deals retribution to His foes.

ישעיהו
פרק סו

כא וּבָנוּ בָתִּים וְיָשָׁבוּ וְנָטְעוּ כְרָמִים וְאָכְלוּ פִּרְיָם:

כב לֹא יִבְנוּ וְאַחֵר יֵשֵׁב לֹא יִטְּעוּ וְאַחֵר יֹאכֵל כִּי־כִימֵי הָעֵץ יְמֵי עַמִּי וּמַעֲשֵׂה יְדֵיהֶם יְבַלּוּ בְחִירָי:

כג לֹא יִיגְעוּ לָרִיק וְלֹא יֵלְדוּ לַבֶּהָלָה כִּי זֶרַע בְּרוּכֵי יְהֹוָה הֵמָּה וְצֶאֱצָאֵיהֶם אִתָּם:

כד וְהָיָה טֶרֶם־יִקְרָאוּ וַאֲנִי אֶעֱנֶה עוֹד הֵם מְדַבְּרִים וַאֲנִי אֶשְׁמָע:

כה זְאֵב וְטָלֶה יִרְעוּ כְאֶחָד וְאַרְיֵה כַּבָּקָר יֹאכַל־תֶּבֶן וְנָחָשׁ עָפָר לַחְמוֹ לֹא־יָרֵעוּ וְלֹא־יַשְׁחִיתוּ בְּכָל־הַר קָדְשִׁי אָמַר יְהֹוָה:

סו א כֹּה אָמַר יְהֹוָה הַשָּׁמַיִם כִּסְאִי וְהָאָרֶץ הֲדֹם רַגְלָי אֵי־זֶה בַיִת אֲשֶׁר תִּבְנוּ־לִי וְאֵי־זֶה מָקוֹם מְנוּחָתִי:

ב וְאֶת־כָּל־אֵלֶּה יָדִי עָשָׂתָה וַיִּהְיוּ כָל־אֵלֶּה נְאֻם־יְהֹוָה וְאֶל־זֶה אַבִּיט אֶל־עָנִי וּנְכֵה־רוּחַ וְחָרֵד עַל־דְּבָרִי:

ג שׁוֹחֵט הַשּׁוֹר מַכֵּה־אִישׁ זוֹבֵחַ הַשֶּׂה עֹרֵף כֶּלֶב מַעֲלֵה מִנְחָה דַּם־חֲזִיר מַזְכִּיר לְבֹנָה מְבָרֵךְ אָוֶן גַּם־הֵמָּה בָּחֲרוּ בְּדַרְכֵיהֶם וּבְשִׁקּוּצֵיהֶם נַפְשָׁם חָפֵצָה:

ד גַּם־אֲנִי אֶבְחַר בְּתַעֲלֻלֵיהֶם וּמְגוּרֹתָם אָבִיא לָהֶם יַעַן קָרָאתִי וְאֵין עוֹנֶה דִּבַּרְתִּי וְלֹא שָׁמֵעוּ וַיַּעֲשׂוּ הָרַע בְּעֵינַי וּבַאֲשֶׁר לֹא־חָפַצְתִּי בָּחָרוּ:

ה שִׁמְעוּ דְּבַר־יְהֹוָה הַחֲרֵדִים אֶל־דְּבָרוֹ אָמְרוּ אֲחֵיכֶם שֹׂנְאֵיכֶם מְנַדֵּיכֶם לְמַעַן שְׁמִי יִכְבַּד יְהֹוָה וְנִרְאֶה בְשִׂמְחַתְכֶם וְהֵם יֵבֹשׁוּ:

ו קוֹל שָׁאוֹן מֵעִיר קוֹל מֵהֵיכָל קוֹל יְהֹוָה מְשַׁלֵּם גְּמוּל לְאֹיְבָיו:

Yeshayahu/Isaiah
Chapter 66

ישעיהו
פרק סו

7 Before she labored, she was delivered; Before her pangs came, she bore a son.

בְּטֶרֶם תָּחִיל יָלָדָה בְּטֶרֶם יָבוֹא חֵבֶל לָהּ וְהִמְלִיטָה זָכָר: ז

8 Who ever heard the like? Who ever witnessed such events? Can a land pass through travail In a single day? Or is a nation born All at once? Yet *Tzion* travailed And at once bore her children!

מִי־שָׁמַע כָּזֹאת מִי רָאָה כָּאֵלֶּה הֲיוּחַל אֶרֶץ בְּיוֹם אֶחָד אִם־יִוָּלֵד גּוֹי פַּעַם אֶחָת כִּי־חָלָה גַּם־יָלְדָה צִיּוֹן אֶת־בָּנֶיהָ: ח

9 Shall I who bring on labor not bring about birth? – says *Hashem*. Shall I who cause birth shut the womb? – said your God.

הַאֲנִי אַשְׁבִּיר וְלֹא אוֹלִיד יֹאמַר יְהֹוָה אִם־אֲנִי הַמּוֹלִיד וְעָצַרְתִּי אָמַר אֱלֹהָיִךְ: ט

10 Rejoice with *Yerushalayim* and be glad for her, All you who love her! Join in her jubilation, All you who mourned over her –

שִׂמְחוּ אֶת־יְרוּשָׁלַ͏ִם וְגִילוּ בָהּ כָּל־אֹהֲבֶיהָ שִׂישׂוּ אִתָּהּ מָשׂוֹשׂ כָּל־הַמִּתְאַבְּלִים עָלֶיהָ: י

11 That you may suck from her breast Consolation to the full, That you may draw from her bosom Glory to your delight.

לְמַעַן תִּינְקוּ וּשְׂבַעְתֶּם מִשֹּׁד תַּנְחֻמֶיהָ לְמַעַן תָּמֹצּוּ וְהִתְעַנַּגְתֶּם מִזִּיז כְּבוֹדָהּ: יא

12 For thus said *Hashem*: I will extend to her Prosperity like a stream, The wealth of nations Like a wadi in flood; And you shall drink of it. You shall be carried on shoulders And dandled upon knees.

כִּי־כֹה ׀ אָמַר יְהֹוָה הִנְנִי נֹטֶה־אֵלֶיהָ כְּנָהָר שָׁלוֹם וּכְנַחַל שׁוֹטֵף כְּבוֹד גּוֹיִם וִינַקְתֶּם עַל־צַד תִּנָּשֵׂאוּ וְעַל־בִּרְכַּיִם תְּשָׁעֳשָׁעוּ: יב

kee KHOH a-MAR a-do-NAI hi-n'-NEE no-teh ay-LE-ha k'-na-HAR sha-LOM ukh-NA-khal sho-TAYF k'-VOD go-YIM vee-nak-TEM al TZAD ti-na-SAY-u v'-al bir-KA-yim t'-sha-o-SHA-u

13 As a mother comforts her son So I will comfort you; You shall find comfort in *Yerushalayim*.

כְּאִישׁ אֲשֶׁר אִמּוֹ תְּנַחֲמֶנּוּ כֵּן אָנֹכִי אֲנַחֶמְכֶם וּבִירוּשָׁלַ͏ִם תְּנֻחָמוּ: יג

14 You shall see and your heart shall rejoice, Your limbs shall flourish like grass. The power of *Hashem* shall be revealed In behalf of His servants; But He shall rage against His foes.

וּרְאִיתֶם וְשָׂשׂ לִבְּכֶם וְעַצְמוֹתֵיכֶם כַּדֶּשֶׁא תִפְרַחְנָה וְנוֹדְעָה יַד־יְהֹוָה אֶת־עֲבָדָיו וְזָעַם אֶת־אֹיְבָיו: יד

15 See, *Hashem* is coming with fire – His chariots are like a whirlwind – To vent His anger in fury, His rebuke in flaming fire.

כִּי־הִנֵּה יְהֹוָה בָּאֵשׁ יָבוֹא וְכַסּוּפָה מַרְכְּבֹתָיו לְהָשִׁיב בְּחֵמָה אַפּוֹ וְגַעֲרָתוֹ בְּלַהֲבֵי־אֵשׁ: טו

16 For with fire will *Hashem* contend, With His sword, against all flesh; And many shall be the slain of *Hashem*.

כִּי בָאֵשׁ יְהֹוָה נִשְׁפָּט וּבְחַרְבּוֹ אֶת־כָּל־בָּשָׂר וְרַבּוּ חַלְלֵי יְהֹוָה: טז

66:12 I will extend to her prosperity like a stream
In this final chapter of *Yeshayahu*, the prophet assures the Jewish people that *Hashem* will extend *shalom* (שלום) upon them, and that all the nations will come forth with blessings like a torrent or river sweeping effortlessly along. The Hebrew word *shalom* is usually understood to mean 'peace,' but it is translated here as 'prosperity.' Jewish tradition (*Mishna Uktzin*) teaches that peace is like a vessel that holds all of the other precious blessings in our lives. The blessing of peace is the ultimate blessing, since all the other blessings of the world are contained within it.

Yeshayahu/Isaiah
Chapter 66

17 Those who sanctify and purify themselves to enter the groves, imitating one in the center, eating the flesh of the swine, the reptile, and the mouse, shall one and all come to an end – declares *Hashem*.

18 For I [know] their deeds and purposes. [The time] has come to gather all the nations and tongues; they shall come and behold My glory.

19 I will set a sign among them, and send from them survivors to the nations: to Tarshish, Pul, and Lud – that draw the bow – to Tubal, Javan, and the distant coasts, that have never heard My fame nor beheld My glory. They shall declare My glory among these nations.

20 And out of all the nations, said *Hashem*, they shall bring all your brothers on horses, in chariots and drays, on mules and dromedaries, to *Yerushalayim* My holy mountain as an offering to *Hashem* – just as the Israelites bring an offering in a pure vessel to the House of *Hashem*.

21 And from them likewise I will take some to be levitical *Kohanim*, said *Hashem*.

22 For as the new heaven and the new earth Which I will make Shall endure by My will – declares *Hashem* – So shall your seed and your name endure.

23 And new moon after new moon, And *Shabbat* after *Shabbat*, All flesh shall come to worship Me – said *Hashem*.

24 They shall go out and gaze On the corpses of the men who rebelled against Me: Their worms shall not die, Nor their fire be quenched; They shall be a horror To all flesh. And new moon after new moon, And *Shabbat* after *Shabbat*, All flesh shall come to worship Me – said *Hashem*.

ישעיהו
פרק סו

יז הַמִּתְקַדְּשִׁים וְהַמִּטַּהֲרִים אֶל־הַגַּנּוֹת אַחַר אֶחָד [אַחַת] בַּתָּוֶךְ אֹכְלֵי בְּשַׂר הַחֲזִיר וְהַשֶּׁקֶץ וְהָעַכְבָּר יַחְדָּו יָסֻפוּ נְאֻם־יְהֹוָה:

יח וְאָנֹכִי מַעֲשֵׂיהֶם וּמַחְשְׁבֹתֵיהֶם בָּאָה לְקַבֵּץ אֶת־כָּל־הַגּוֹיִם וְהַלְּשֹׁנוֹת וּבָאוּ וְרָאוּ אֶת־כְּבוֹדִי:

יט וְשַׂמְתִּי בָהֶם אוֹת וְשִׁלַּחְתִּי מֵהֶם פְּלֵיטִים אֶל־הַגּוֹיִם תַּרְשִׁישׁ פּוּל וְלוּד מֹשְׁכֵי קֶשֶׁת תֻּבַל וְיָוָן הָאִיִּים הָרְחֹקִים אֲשֶׁר לֹא־שָׁמְעוּ אֶת־שִׁמְעִי וְלֹא־רָאוּ אֶת־כְּבוֹדִי וְהִגִּידוּ אֶת־כְּבוֹדִי בַּגּוֹיִם:

כ וְהֵבִיאוּ אֶת־כָּל־אֲחֵיכֶם מִכָּל־הַגּוֹיִם מִנְחָה לַיהֹוָה בַּסּוּסִים וּבָרֶכֶב וּבַצַּבִּים וּבַפְּרָדִים וּבַכִּרְכָּרוֹת עַל הַר קָדְשִׁי יְרוּשָׁלַםִ אָמַר יְהֹוָה כַּאֲשֶׁר יָבִיאוּ בְנֵי יִשְׂרָאֵל אֶת־הַמִּנְחָה בִּכְלִי טָהוֹר בֵּית יְהֹוָה:

כא וְגַם־מֵהֶם אֶקַּח לַכֹּהֲנִים לַלְוִיִּם אָמַר יְהֹוָה:

כב כִּי כַאֲשֶׁר הַשָּׁמַיִם הַחֳדָשִׁים וְהָאָרֶץ הַחֲדָשָׁה אֲשֶׁר אֲנִי עֹשֶׂה עֹמְדִים לְפָנַי נְאֻם־יְהֹוָה כֵּן יַעֲמֹד זַרְעֲכֶם וְשִׁמְכֶם:

כג וְהָיָה מִדֵּי־חֹדֶשׁ בְּחָדְשׁוֹ וּמִדֵּי שַׁבָּת בְּשַׁבַּתּוֹ יָבוֹא כָל־בָּשָׂר לְהִשְׁתַּחֲוֺת לְפָנַי אָמַר יְהֹוָה:

כד וְיָצְאוּ וְרָאוּ בְּפִגְרֵי הָאֲנָשִׁים הַפֹּשְׁעִים בִּי כִּי תוֹלַעְתָּם לֹא תָמוּת וְאִשָּׁם לֹא תִכְבֶּה וְהָיוּ דֵרָאוֹן לְכָל־בָּשָׂר:

Sefer Yirmiyahu
The Book of Jeremiah

Introduction and commentary by Rabbi Yaakov Beasley

Yirmiyahu (Jeremiah) lives during the tragic final years of Israel's southern kingdom, *Yehuda*, just before its destruction in 586 BCE at the hands of Babylonia. He prophesies for forty years, beginning during the reign of King *Yoshiyahu*, a strong point in the history of the kingdom of *Yehuda*, and ending after the small remnant of Jews left in *Yerushalayim* following the Temple's destruction flees to Egypt.

Yirmiyhau's prophecy is intensely personal; we know much more about his personal life than we know of the life of any other prophet. Born to a priestly family in *Anatot* (1:1), he becomes a prophet at a very young age. He is commanded by God not to marry or raise children, to symbolize His plan to destroy the next generation (16:1–4). His prophecies contain many predictions of doom and a desperate cry to Israel to accept the upcoming upheaval and submit to Babylonian rule – a demand that earns him the title of traitor among his own people.

In truth, *Yirmiyahu* loves his people too much to stand by while they commit national suicide. As such, he never ceases to speak to them, and even when his prophecies are proven true, his only response to the destruction and exile is devastation. This response finds its eloquent and heartbreaking voice in *Megillat Eicha*, which, according to tradition, was also authored by *Yirmiyahu*. *Sefer Yirmiyahu* also includes several sections which describe the emotional price of being the lone voice of a painful truth.

Sefer Yirmiyhau is not structured chronologically. The first 35 chapters are a collection of prophecies directed to the kingdom of *Yehuda* about the upcoming destruction. They describe the sins which are the cause of the impending devastation, and include the ultimately futile request for the people not to rebel against Babylonian dominion. *Yirmiyhau* also intersperses promises that *Hashem* will return His scattered people to live in

Israel in peace. Of specific interest is a prophecy to the Jews who are exiled, that their exile will last for seventy years. After this, however, the prophet states that the Babylonian empire will fall, and their descendants will have the opportunity to return to *Eretz Yisrael* (29:5–14). Chapters 36–38 include *Yirmiyhau*'s personal sufferings and 39–44 describe the downfall of *Yerushalayim*. In the final chapters of the book, *Yirmiyhau* prophesies against the nations that participated in, or cheered at, Israel's downfall, for the Lord does not forgive the insult against His people.

While *Yirmiyhau* is known as the prophet of doom, his prophecies also contain much promise. By the time he becomes a prophet, the destruction of *Yehuda* and the *Beit Hamikdash* is almost inevitable. *Yirmiyhau* tries one last time to awaken the Israelite nation to return to *Hashem*, but they refuse to listen and are exiled from their land. However, even in exile, far from their land, the Jewish people are not to abandon hope. As *Hashem* promises through *Yirmiyhau*, "I will delight in treating them graciously, and I will plant them in this land faithfully, with all My heart and soul" (32:41).

Map of the Two Kingdoms of Israel

After King *Shlomo*'s death, the united Kingdom of Israel splits into two: the northern kingdom of *Yisrael* under the leadership of *Yerovam*, and the southern kingdom of *Yehuda* under the leadership of *Rechovam* son of *Shlomo*. The kingdom of *Yehuda* was made up primarily of the tribes of *Yehuda* and *Binyamin*, and the kingdom of *Yisrael* was made up of the other ten tribes. By *Yirmiyahu*'s time, *Yisrael* had already been exiled by the Assyrians and "lost," and *Yehuda* was on the verge of being exiled as well. As a prophet, *Yirmiyahu*'s job was to speak to the people of *Yehuda* and try to urge them to repent in order to prevent the final exile and destruction of the kingdom. The following is a map delineating the boundaries of the two kingdoms of Israel, *Yehuda* and *Yisrael*, at the time that the kingdom split.

Yirmiyahu/Jeremiah
Chapter 1

ירמיהו
פרק א

1 ¹ The words of *Yirmiyahu* son of *Chilkiyahu*, one of the *Kohanim* at *Anatot* in the territory of *Binyamin*.

א דִּבְרֵי יִרְמְיָהוּ בֶּן־חִלְקִיָּהוּ מִן־הַכֹּהֲנִים אֲשֶׁר בַּעֲנָתוֹת בְּאֶרֶץ בִּנְיָמִן׃

² The word of *Hashem* came to him in the days of King *Yoshiyahu* son of *Amon* of *Yehuda*, in the thirteenth year of his reign,

ב אֲשֶׁר הָיָה דְבַר־יְהֹוָה אֵלָיו בִּימֵי יֹאשִׁיָּהוּ בֶן־אָמוֹן מֶלֶךְ יְהוּדָה בִּשְׁלֹשׁ־עֶשְׂרֵה שָׁנָה לְמָלְכוֹ׃

³ and throughout the days of King *Yehoyakim* son of *Yoshiyahu* of *Yehuda*, and until the end of the eleventh year of King *Tzidkiyahu* son of *Yoshiyahu* of *Yehuda*, when *Yerushalayim* went into exile in the fifth month.

ג וַיְהִי בִּימֵי יְהוֹיָקִים בֶּן־יֹאשִׁיָּהוּ מֶלֶךְ יְהוּדָה עַד־תֹּם עַשְׁתֵּי עֶשְׂרֵה שָׁנָה לְצִדְקִיָּהוּ בֶן־יֹאשִׁיָּהוּ מֶלֶךְ יְהוּדָה עַד־גְּלוֹת יְרוּשָׁלַםִ בַּחֹדֶשׁ הַחֲמִישִׁי׃

⁴ The word of *Hashem* came to me:

ד וַיְהִי דְבַר־יְהֹוָה אֵלַי לֵאמֹר׃

⁵ Before I created you in the womb, I selected you; Before you were born, I consecrated you; I appointed you a *Navi* concerning the nations.

ה בְּטֶרֶם אֶצָּרְךָ [אֶצָּרְךָ] בַבֶּטֶן יְדַעְתִּיךָ וּבְטֶרֶם תֵּצֵא מֵרֶחֶם הִקְדַּשְׁתִּיךָ נָבִיא לַגּוֹיִם נְתַתִּיךָ׃

⁶ I replied: Ah, *Hashem*! I don't know how to speak, For I am still a boy.

ו וָאֹמַר אֲהָהּ אֲדֹנָי יְהֹוִה הִנֵּה לֹא־יָדַעְתִּי דַּבֵּר כִּי־נַעַר אָנֹכִי׃

⁷ And *Hashem* said to me: Do not say, "I am still a boy," But go wherever I send you And speak whatever I command you.

ז וַיֹּאמֶר יְהֹוָה אֵלַי אַל־תֹּאמַר נַעַר אָנֹכִי כִּי עַל־כָּל־אֲשֶׁר אֶשְׁלָחֲךָ תֵּלֵךְ וְאֵת כָּל־אֲשֶׁר אֲצַוְּךָ תְּדַבֵּר׃

⁸ Have no fear of them, For I am with you to deliver you – declares *Hashem*.

ח אַל־תִּירָא מִפְּנֵיהֶם כִּי־אִתְּךָ אֲנִי לְהַצִּלֶךָ נְאֻם־יְהֹוָה׃

⁹ *Hashem* put out His hand and touched my mouth, and *Hashem* said to me: Herewith I put My words into your mouth.

ט וַיִּשְׁלַח יְהֹוָה אֶת־יָדוֹ וַיַּגַּע עַל־פִּי וַיֹּאמֶר יְהֹוָה אֵלַי הִנֵּה נָתַתִּי דְבָרַי בְּפִיךָ׃

¹⁰ See, I appoint you this day Over nations and kingdoms: To uproot and to pull down, To destroy and to overthrow, To build and to plant.

י רְאֵה הִפְקַדְתִּיךָ הַיּוֹם הַזֶּה עַל־הַגּוֹיִם וְעַל־הַמַּמְלָכוֹת לִנְתוֹשׁ וְלִנְתוֹץ וּלְהַאֲבִיד וְלַהֲרוֹס לִבְנוֹת וְלִנְטוֹעַ׃

¹¹ The word of *Hashem* came to me: What do you see, *Yirmiyahu*? I replied: I see a branch of an almond tree.

יא וַיְהִי דְבַר־יְהֹוָה אֵלַי לֵאמֹר מָה־אַתָּה רֹאֶה יִרְמְיָהוּ וָאֹמַר מַקֵּל שָׁקֵד אֲנִי רֹאֶה׃

vai-HEE d'-var a-do-NAI ay-LAI lay-MOR mah a-TAH ro-EH yir-m'-YA-hu va-o-MAR ma-KAYL sha-KAYD a-NEE ro-EH

Blossoming almond tree in Jerusalem

1:11 I see a branch of an almond-tree In his first vision, *Yirmiyahu* is shown an almond branch, *makel shaked* (מקל שקד) in Hebrew. *Hashem* explains that the branch symbolizes His watching over His word to perform it. The Hebrew word he chooses for 'watch,' *shoked* (שקד), also means 'to hasten.' *Yirmiyahu* deliberately chose this word since it is similar to the word for 'almond,' *shaked* (שקד). Commentators give two explanations for this wordplay. First, just as the almond tree blossoms quickly, so too *Hashem* will hasten to punish Israel. Furthermore, the almond tree is the first to blossom in *Eretz Yisrael*. When all else is dead, the almond trees awaken the countryside from its winter slumber. So too, although the people are spiritually dead, God's word, like the almond blossoms, will awaken the nation.

שקד

Yirmiyahu/Jeremiah
Chapter 2

12 *Hashem* said to me: You have seen right, For I am watchful to bring My word to pass.

13 And the word of *Hashem* came to me a second time: What do you see? I replied: I see a steaming pot, Tipped away from the north.

14 And *Hashem* said to me: From the north shall disaster break loose Upon all the inhabitants of the land!

15 For I am summoning all the peoples Of the kingdoms of the north – declares *Hashem*. They shall come, and shall each set up a throne Before the gates of *Yerushalayim*, Against its walls roundabout, And against all the towns of *Yehuda*.

16 And I will argue My case against them For all their wickedness: They have forsaken Me And sacrificed to other gods And worshiped the works of their hands.

17 So you, gird up your loins, Arise and speak to them All that I command you. Do not break down before them, Lest I break you before them.

18 I make you this day A fortified city, And an iron pillar, And bronze walls Against the whole land – Against *Yehuda*'s kings and officers, And against its *Kohanim* and citizens.

19 They will attack you, But they shall not overcome you; For I am with you – declares *Hashem* – to save you.

2 1 The word of *Hashem* came to me, saying,

2 Go proclaim to *Yerushalayim*: Thus said *Hashem*: I accounted to your favor The devotion of your youth, Your love as a bride – How you followed Me in the wilderness, In a land not sown.

3 *Yisrael* was holy to *Hashem*, The first fruits of His harvest. All who ate of it were held guilty; Disaster befell them – declares *Hashem*.

4 Hear the word of *Hashem*, O House of *Yaakov*, Every clan of the House of *Yisrael*!

5 Thus said *Hashem*: What wrong did your fathers find in Me That they abandoned Me And went after delusion and were deluded?

Yirmiyahu/Jeremiah
Chapter 2

ירמיהו
פרק ב

6 They never asked themselves, "Where is *Hashem*, Who brought us up from the land of Egypt, Who led us through the wilderness, A land of deserts and pits, A land of drought and darkness, A land no man had traversed, Where no human being had dwelt?"

ו וְלֹא אָמְרוּ אַיֵּה יְהֹוָה הַמַּעֲלֶה אֹתָנוּ מֵאֶרֶץ מִצְרָיִם הַמּוֹלִיךְ אֹתָנוּ בַּמִּדְבָּר בְּאֶרֶץ עֲרָבָה וְשׁוּחָה בְּאֶרֶץ צִיָּה וְצַלְמָוֶת בְּאֶרֶץ לֹא־עָבַר בָּהּ אִישׁ וְלֹא־יָשַׁב אָדָם שָׁם׃

7 I brought you to this country of farm land To enjoy its fruit and its bounty; But you came and defiled My land, You made My possession abhorrent.

ז וָאָבִיא אֶתְכֶם אֶל־אֶרֶץ הַכַּרְמֶל לֶאֱכֹל פִּרְיָהּ וְטוּבָהּ וַתָּבֹאוּ וַתְּטַמְּאוּ אֶת־אַרְצִי וְנַחֲלָתִי שַׂמְתֶּם לְתוֹעֵבָה׃

8 The *Kohanim* never asked themselves, "Where is *Hashem*?" The guardians of the Teaching ignored Me; The rulers rebelled against Me, And the *Neviim* prophesied by Baal And followed what can do no good.

ח הַכֹּהֲנִים לֹא אָמְרוּ אַיֵּה יְהֹוָה וְתֹפְשֵׂי הַתּוֹרָה לֹא יְדָעוּנִי וְהָרֹעִים פָּשְׁעוּ בִי וְהַנְּבִיאִים נִבְּאוּ בַבַּעַל וְאַחֲרֵי לֹא־יוֹעִלוּ הָלָכוּ׃

9 Oh, I will go on accusing you – declares *Hashem* – And I will accuse your children's children!

ט לָכֵן עֹד אָרִיב אִתְּכֶם נְאֻם־יְהֹוָה וְאֶת־בְּנֵי בְנֵיכֶם אָרִיב׃

10 Just cross over to the isles of the Kittim and look, Send to Kedar and observe carefully; See if aught like this has ever happened:

י כִּי עִבְרוּ אִיֵּי כִתִּיִּים וּרְאוּ וְקֵדָר שִׁלְחוּ וְהִתְבּוֹנְנוּ מְאֹד וּרְאוּ הֵן הָיְתָה כָּזֹאת׃

11 Has any nation changed its gods Even though they are no-gods? But My people has exchanged its glory For what can do no good.

יא הַהֵימִיר גּוֹי אֱלֹהִים וְהֵמָּה לֹא אֱלֹהִים וְעַמִּי הֵמִיר כְּבוֹדוֹ בְּלוֹא יוֹעִיל׃

12 Be appalled, O heavens, at this; Be horrified, utterly dazed! – says *Hashem*.

יב שֹׁמּוּ שָׁמַיִם עַל־זֹאת וְשַׂעֲרוּ חָרְבוּ מְאֹד נְאֻם־יְהֹוָה׃

13 For My people have done a twofold wrong: They have forsaken Me, the Fount of living waters, And hewed them out cisterns, broken cisterns, Which cannot even hold water.

יג כִּי־שְׁתַּיִם רָעוֹת עָשָׂה עַמִּי אֹתִי עָזְבוּ מְקוֹר מַיִם חַיִּים לַחְצֹב לָהֶם בֹּארוֹת בֹּארֹת נִשְׁבָּרִים אֲשֶׁר לֹא־יָכִלוּ הַמָּיִם׃

kee sh'-TA-yim ra-OT a-SAH a-MEE o-TEE a-z'-VU m'-KOR MA-yim kha-YEEM lakh-TZOV la-HEM bo-ROT bo-ROT nish-ba-REEM a-SHER lo ya-KHI-lu ha-MA-yim

14 Is *Yisrael* a bondman? Is he a home-born slave? Then why is he given over to plunder?

יד הַעֶבֶד יִשְׂרָאֵל אִם־יְלִיד בַּיִת הוּא מַדּוּעַ הָיָה לָבַז׃

2:13 They have forsaken Me, the Fount of living waters Water is a precious resource. While in some locations there were natural springs that provided water for the ancient Israelites, the people also carved out many cisterns in which to store rain water, to ensure they would have enough to drink. Although ancient workers developed a special kind of plaster that was used to line the inside of the cisterns to prevent the water from seeping out, cracks would often develop, causing the water to be lost. *Yirmiyahu* compares *Hashem* to a fountain of natural spring water, while the false gods are likened to cracked and broken cisterns. Though the fountains provide life-giving waters, the people foolishly choose to drink from cisterns which cannot contain their water, relying on meaningless idols rather than God, the true source of life.

Plastered water cistern found at Qumran

Yirmiyahu/Jeremiah
Chapter 2

15 Lions have roared over him, Have raised their cries. They have made his land a waste, His cities desolate, without inhabitants.

16 Those, too, in Noph and Tahpanhes Will lay bare your head.

17 See, that is the price you have paid For forsaking *Hashem* your God While He led you in the way.

18 What, then, is the good of your going to Egypt To drink the waters of the Nile? And what is the good of your going to Assyria To drink the waters of the Euphrates?

19 Let your misfortune reprove you, Let your afflictions rebuke you; Mark well how bad and bitter it is That you forsake *Hashem* your God, That awe for Me is not in you – declares the lord God of Hosts.

20 For long ago you broke your yoke, Tore off your yoke-bands, And said, "I will not work!" On every high hill and under every verdant tree, You recline as a whore.

21 I planted you with noble vines, All with choicest seed; Alas, I find you changed Into a base, an alien vine!

22 Though you wash with natron And use much lye, Your guilt is ingrained before Me – declares *Hashem*.

23 How can you say, "I am not defiled, I have not gone after the Baalim"? Look at your deeds in the Valley, Consider what you have done! Like a lustful she-camel, Restlessly running about,

24 Or like a wild ass used to the desert, Snuffing the wind in her eagerness, Whose passion none can restrain, None that seek her need grow weary – In her season, they'll find her!

25 Save your foot from going bare, And your throat from thirst. But you say, "It is no use. No, I love the strangers, And after them I must go."

26 Like a thief chagrined when he is caught, So is the House of *Yisrael* chagrined – They, their kings, their officers, And their *Kohanim* and *Neviim*.

27 They said to wood, "You are my father," To stone, "You gave birth to me," While to Me they turned their backs And not their faces. But in their hour of calamity they cry, "Arise and save us!"

ירמיהו
פרק ב

טו עָלָיו יִשְׁאֲגוּ כְפִרִים נָתְנוּ קוֹלָם וַיָּשִׁיתוּ אַרְצוֹ לְשַׁמָּה עָרָיו נצתה [נִצְּתוּ] מִבְּלִי יֹשֵׁב׃

טז גַּם־בְּנֵי־נֹף ותחפנס [וְתַחְפַּנְחֵס] יִרְעוּךְ קָדְקֹד׃

יז הֲלוֹא־זֹאת תַּעֲשֶׂה־לָּךְ עׇזְבֵךְ אֶת־יְהֹוָה אֱלֹהַיִךְ בְּעֵת מוֹלִיכֵךְ בַּדָּרֶךְ׃

יח וְעַתָּה מַה־לָּךְ לְדֶרֶךְ מִצְרַיִם לִשְׁתּוֹת מֵי שִׁחוֹר וּמַה־לָּךְ לְדֶרֶךְ אַשּׁוּר לִשְׁתּוֹת מֵי נָהָר׃

יט תְּיַסְּרֵךְ רָעָתֵךְ וּמְשֻׁבוֹתַיִךְ תּוֹכִחֻךְ וּדְעִי וּרְאִי כִּי־רַע וָמָר עׇזְבֵךְ אֶת־יְהֹוָה אֱלֹהָיִךְ וְלֹא פַחְדָּתִי אֵלַיִךְ נְאֻם־אֲדֹנָי יֱהֹוִה צְבָאוֹת׃

כ כִּי מֵעוֹלָם שָׁבַרְתִּי עֻלֵּךְ נִתַּקְתִּי מוֹסְרוֹתַיִךְ וַתֹּאמְרִי לֹא אעבד [אֶעֱבוֹר] כִּי עַל־כׇּל־גִּבְעָה גְבֹהָה וְתַחַת כׇּל־עֵץ רַעֲנָן אַתְּ צֹעָה זֹנָה׃

כא וְאָנֹכִי נְטַעְתִּיךְ שׂוֹרֵק כֻּלֹּה זֶרַע אֱמֶת וְאֵיךְ נֶהְפַּכְתְּ לִי סוּרֵי הַגֶּפֶן נׇכְרִיָּה׃

כב כִּי אִם־תְּכַבְּסִי בַּנֶּתֶר וְתַרְבִּי־לָךְ בֹּרִית נִכְתָּם עֲוֺנֵךְ לְפָנַי נְאֻם אֲדֹנָי יֱהֹוִה׃

כג אֵיךְ תֹּאמְרִי לֹא נִטְמֵאתִי אַחֲרֵי הַבְּעָלִים לֹא הָלַכְתִּי רְאִי דַרְכֵּךְ בַּגַּיְא דְּעִי מֶה עָשִׂית בִּכְרָה קַלָּה מְשָׂרֶכֶת דְּרָכֶיהָ׃

כד פֶּרֶה לִמֻּד מִדְבָּר בְּאַוַּת נפשו [נַפְשָׁהּ] שָׁאֲפָה רוּחַ תַּאֲנָתָהּ מִי יְשִׁיבֶנָּה כׇּל־מְבַקְשֶׁיהָ לֹא יִיעָפוּ בְּחׇדְשָׁהּ יִמְצָאוּנְהָ׃

כה מִנְעִי רַגְלֵךְ מִיָּחֵף וגורנך [וּגְרוֹנֵךְ] מִצִּמְאָה וַתֹּאמְרִי נוֹאָשׁ לוֹא כִּי־אָהַבְתִּי זָרִים וְאַחֲרֵיהֶם אֵלֵךְ׃

כו כְּבֹשֶׁת גַּנָּב כִּי יִמָּצֵא כֵּן הֹבִישׁוּ בֵּית יִשְׂרָאֵל הֵמָּה מַלְכֵיהֶם שָׂרֵיהֶם וְכֹהֲנֵיהֶם וּנְבִיאֵיהֶם׃

כז אֹמְרִים לָעֵץ אָבִי אַתָּה וְלָאֶבֶן אַתְּ ילדתני [יְלִדְתָּנוּ] כִּי־פָנוּ אֵלַי עֹרֶף וְלֹא פָנִים וּבְעֵת רָעָתָם יֹאמְרוּ קוּמָה וְהוֹשִׁיעֵנוּ׃

Yirmiyahu/Jeremiah
Chapter 3

28 And where are those gods You made for yourself? Let them arise and save you, if they can, In your hour of calamity. For your gods have become, O *Yehuda*, As many as your towns!

29 Why do you call Me to account? You have all rebelled against Me – declares *Hashem*.

30 To no purpose did I smite your children; They would not accept correction. Your sword has devoured your *Neviim* Like a ravening lion.

31 O generation, behold the word of *Hashem*! Have I been like a desert to *Yisrael*, Or like a land of deep gloom? Then why do My people say, "We have broken loose, We will not come to You any more?"

32 Can a maiden forget her jewels, A bride her adornments? Yet My people have forgotten Me – Days without number.

33 How skillfully you plan your way To seek out love! Why, you have even taught The worst of women your ways.

34 Moreover, on your garments is found The lifeblood of the innocent poor – You did not catch them breaking in. Yet, despite all these things,

35 You say, "I have been acquitted; Surely, His anger has turned away from me." Lo, I will bring you to judgment For saying, "I have not sinned."

36 How you cheapen yourself, By changing your course! You shall be put to shame through Egypt, Just as you were put to shame through Assyria.

37 From this way, too, you will come out With your hands on your head; For *Hashem* has rejected those you trust, You will not prosper with them.1

3 1 [The word of *Hashem* came to me] as follows: If a man divorces his wife, and she leaves him and marries another man, can he ever go back to her? Would not such a land be defiled? Now you have whored with many lovers: can you return to Me? – says *Hashem*.

2 Look up to the bare heights, and see: Where have they not lain with you? You waited for them on the roadside Like a bandit in the wilderness. And you defiled the land With your whoring and your debauchery.

Yirmiyahu/Jeremiah
Chapter 3

3 And when showers were withheld And the late rains did not come, You had the brazenness of a street woman, You refused to be ashamed.

4 Just now you called to Me, "Father! You are the Companion of my youth.

5 Does one hate for all time? Does one rage forever?" That is how you spoke; You did wrong, and had your way.

6 *Hashem* said to me in the days of King *Yoshiyahu*: Have you seen what Rebel *Yisrael* did, going to every high mountain and under every leafy tree, and whoring there?

7 I thought: After she has done all these things, she will come back to Me. But she did not come back; and her sister, Faithless *Yehuda*, saw it.

8 I noted: Because Rebel *Yisrael* had committed adultery, I cast her off and handed her a bill of divorce; yet her sister, Faithless *Yehuda*, was not afraid – she too went and whored.

9 Indeed, the land was defiled by her casual immorality, as she committed adultery with stone and with wood.

10 And after all that, her sister, Faithless *Yehuda*, did not return to Me wholeheartedly, but insincerely – declares *Hashem*.

11 And *Hashem* said to me: Rebel *Yisrael* has shown herself more in the right than Faithless *Yehuda*.

12 Go, make this proclamation toward the north, and say: Turn back, O Rebel *Yisrael* – declares *Hashem*. I will not look on you in anger, for I am compassionate – declares *Hashem*; I do not bear a grudge for all time.

13 Only recognize your sin; for you have transgressed against *Hashem* your God, and scattered your favors among strangers under every leafy tree, and you have not heeded Me – declares *Hashem*.

14 Turn back, rebellious children – declares *Hashem*. Since I have espoused you, I will take you, one from a town and two from a clan, and bring you to *Tzion*.

15 And I will give you shepherds after My own heart, who will pasture you with knowledge and skill.

ירמיהו
פרק ג

ג וַיִּמָּנְעוּ רְבִבִים וּמַלְקוֹשׁ לוֹא הָיָה וּמֵצַח אִשָּׁה זוֹנָה הָיָה לָךְ מֵאַנְתְּ הִכָּלֵם:

ד הֲלוֹא מֵעַתָּה קראתי [קָרָאת] לִי אָבִי אַלּוּף נְעֻרַי אָתָּה:

ה הֲיִנְטֹר לְעוֹלָם אִם־יִשְׁמֹר לָנֶצַח הִנֵּה דברתי [דִבַּרְתְּ] וַתַּעֲשִׂי הָרָעוֹת וַתּוּכָל:

ו וַיֹּאמֶר יְהוָה אֵלַי בִּימֵי יֹאשִׁיָּהוּ הַמֶּלֶךְ הֲרָאִיתָ אֲשֶׁר עָשְׂתָה מְשֻׁבָה יִשְׂרָאֵל הֹלְכָה הִיא עַל־כָּל־הַר גָּבֹהַּ וְאֶל־תַּחַת כָּל־עֵץ רַעֲנָן וַתִּזְנִי־שָׁם:

ז וָאֹמַר אַחֲרֵי עֲשׂוֹתָהּ אֶת־כָּל־אֵלֶּה אֵלַי תָּשׁוּב וְלֹא־שָׁבָה ותראה [וַתֵּרֶא] בָּגוֹדָה אֲחוֹתָהּ יְהוּדָה:

ח וָאֵרֶא כִּי עַל־כָּל־אֹדוֹת אֲשֶׁר נִאֲפָה מְשֻׁבָה יִשְׂרָאֵל שִׁלַּחְתִּיהָ וָאֶתֵּן אֶת־סֵפֶר כְּרִיתֻתֶיהָ אֵלֶיהָ וְלֹא יָרְאָה בֹּגֵדָה יְהוּדָה אֲחוֹתָהּ וַתֵּלֶךְ וַתִּזֶן גַּם־הִיא:

ט וְהָיָה מִקֹּל זְנוּתָהּ וַתֶּחֱנַף אֶת־הָאָרֶץ וַתִּנְאַף אֶת־הָאֶבֶן וְאֶת־הָעֵץ:

י וְגַם־בְּכָל־זֹאת לֹא־שָׁבָה אֵלַי בָּגוֹדָה אֲחוֹתָהּ יְהוּדָה בְּכָל־לִבָּהּ כִּי אִם־בְּשֶׁקֶר נְאֻם־יְהוָה:

יא וַיֹּאמֶר יְהוָה אֵלַי צִדְּקָה נַפְשָׁהּ מְשֻׁבָה יִשְׂרָאֵל מִבֹּגֵדָה יְהוּדָה:

יב הָלֹךְ וְקָרָאתָ אֶת־הַדְּבָרִים הָאֵלֶּה צָפוֹנָה וְאָמַרְתָּ שׁוּבָה מְשֻׁבָה יִשְׂרָאֵל נְאֻם־יְהוָה לוֹא־אַפִּיל פָּנַי בָּכֶם כִּי־חָסִיד אֲנִי נְאֻם־יְהוָה לֹא אֶטּוֹר לְעוֹלָם:

יג אַךְ דְּעִי עֲוֺנֵךְ כִּי בַּיהוָה אֱלֹהַיִךְ פָּשָׁעַתְּ וַתְּפַזְּרִי אֶת־דְּרָכַיִךְ לַזָּרִים תַּחַת כָּל־עֵץ רַעֲנָן וּבְקוֹלִי לֹא־שְׁמַעְתֶּם נְאֻם־יְהוָה:

יד שׁוּבוּ בָנִים שׁוֹבָבִים נְאֻם־יְהוָה כִּי אָנֹכִי בָּעַלְתִּי בָכֶם וְלָקַחְתִּי אֶתְכֶם אֶחָד מֵעִיר וּשְׁנַיִם מִמִּשְׁפָּחָה וְהֵבֵאתִי אֶתְכֶם צִיּוֹן:

טו וְנָתַתִּי לָכֶם רֹעִים כְּלִבִּי וְרָעוּ אֶתְכֶם דֵּעָה וְהַשְׂכֵּיל:

Yirmiyahu/Jeremiah
Chapter 3

ירמיהו
פרק ג

16 And when you increase and are fertile in the land, in those days – declares *Hashem* – men shall no longer speak of the *Aron Brit Hashem*, nor shall it come to mind. They shall not mention it, or miss it, or make another.

טז וְהָיָה כִּי תִרְבּוּ וּפְרִיתֶם בָּאָרֶץ בַּיָּמִים הָהֵמָּה נְאֻם־יְהֹוָה לֹא־יֹאמְרוּ עוֹד אֲרוֹן בְּרִית־יְהֹוָה וְלֹא יַעֲלֶה עַל־לֵב וְלֹא יִזְכְּרוּ־בוֹ וְלֹא יִפְקֹדוּ וְלֹא יֵעָשֶׂה עוֹד:

17 At that time, they shall call *Yerushalayim* "Throne of *Hashem*," and all nations shall assemble there, in the name of *Hashem*, at *Yerushalayim*. They shall no longer follow the willfulness of their evil hearts.

יז בָּעֵת הַהִיא יִקְרְאוּ לִירוּשָׁלַם כִּסֵּא יְהֹוָה וְנִקְווּ אֵלֶיהָ כָל־הַגּוֹיִם לְשֵׁם יְהֹוָה לִירוּשָׁלָם וְלֹא־יֵלְכוּ עוֹד אַחֲרֵי שְׁרִרוּת לִבָּם הָרָע:

18 In those days, the House of *Yehuda* shall go with the House of *Yisrael*; they shall come together from the land of the north to the land I gave your fathers as a possession.

יח בַּיָּמִים הָהֵמָּה יֵלְכוּ בֵית־יְהוּדָה עַל־בֵּית יִשְׂרָאֵל וְיָבֹאוּ יַחְדָּו מֵאֶרֶץ צָפוֹן עַל־הָאָרֶץ אֲשֶׁר הִנְחַלְתִּי אֶת־אֲבוֹתֵיכֶם:

19 I had resolved to adopt you as My child, and I gave you a desirable land – the fairest heritage of all the nations; and I thought you would surely call Me "Father," and never cease to be loyal to Me.

יט וְאָנֹכִי אָמַרְתִּי אֵיךְ אֲשִׁיתֵךְ בַּבָּנִים וְאֶתֶּן־לָךְ אֶרֶץ חֶמְדָּה נַחֲלַת צְבִי צִבְאוֹת גּוֹיִם וָאֹמַר אָבִי תִּקְרְאוּ־[תִּקְרְאִי־] לִי וּמֵאַחֲרַי לֹא תָשׁוּבוּ [תָשׁוּבִי]:

v'-a-no-KHEE a-MAR-tee AYKH a-shee-TAYKH ba-ba-NEEM v'-e-ten LAKH E-retz khem-DAH na-kha-LAT tz'-VEE tziv-OT go-YIM va-o-MAR a-VEE tik-r'-ee LEE u-may-a-kha-RAI LO ta-SHU-vee

20 Instead, you have broken faith with Me, as a woman breaks faith with a paramour, O House of *Yisrael* – declares *Hashem*.

כ אָכֵן בָּגְדָה אִשָּׁה מֵרֵעָהּ כֵּן בְּגַדְתֶּם בִּי בֵּית יִשְׂרָאֵל נְאֻם־יְהֹוָה:

21 Hark! On the bare heights is heard The suppliant weeping of the people of *Yisrael*, For they have gone a crooked way, Ignoring *Hashem* their God.

כא קוֹל עַל־שְׁפָיִים נִשְׁמָע בְּכִי תַחֲנוּנֵי בְּנֵי יִשְׂרָאֵל כִּי הֶעֱווּ אֶת־דַּרְכָּם שָׁכְחוּ אֶת־יְהֹוָה אֱלֹהֵיהֶם:

22 Turn back, O rebellious children, I will heal your afflictions! "Here we are, we come to You, For You, *Hashem*, are our God!

כב שׁוּבוּ בָּנִים שׁוֹבָבִים אֶרְפָּה מְשׁוּבֹתֵיכֶם הִנְנוּ אָתָנוּ לָךְ כִּי אַתָּה יְהֹוָה אֱלֹהֵינוּ:

23 Surely, futility comes from the hills, Confusion from the mountains. Only through *Hashem* our God Is there deliverance for *Yisrael*.

כג אָכֵן לַשֶּׁקֶר מִגְּבָעוֹת הָמוֹן הָרִים אָכֵן בַּיהֹוָה אֱלֹהֵינוּ תְּשׁוּעַת יִשְׂרָאֵל:

24 But the Shameful Thing has consumed The possessions of our fathers ever since our youth – Their flocks and herds, Their sons and daughters.

כד וְהַבֹּשֶׁת אָכְלָה אֶת־יְגִיעַ אֲבוֹתֵינוּ מִנְּעוּרֵינוּ אֶת־צֹאנָם וְאֶת־בְּקָרָם אֶת־בְּנֵיהֶם וְאֶת־בְּנוֹתֵיהֶם:

ארץ חמדה

3:19 A desirable land – the fairest heritage of all the nations *Yirmiyahu* describes the Land of Israel as *eretz chemda* (ארץ חמדה), 'a desirable land.' The commentator *Radak* explains that *Yirmiyahu* uses this description since *Eretz Yisrael* is desired by all the nations. *Hashem*'s holy presence is so palpable there, that everyone senses its holiness and wants it. One needs to look no further than the morning newspapers or the nightly news to appreciate the accuracy of the *Radak*'s words. Despite its small size, Israel is a "desired land" sought after by "all the nations."

Yirmiyahu/Jeremiah
Chapter 4

ירמיהו
פרק ד

25 Let us lie down in our shame, Let our disgrace cover us; For we have sinned against *Hashem* our God, We and our fathers from our youth to this day, And we have not heeded *Hashem* our God."

כה נִשְׁכְּבָה בְּבָשְׁתֵּנוּ וּתְכַסֵּנוּ כְּלִמָּתֵנוּ כִּי לַיהוָה אֱלֹהֵינוּ חָטָאנוּ אֲנַחְנוּ וַאֲבוֹתֵינוּ מִנְּעוּרֵינוּ וְעַד־הַיּוֹם הַזֶּה וְלֹא שָׁמַעְנוּ בְּקוֹל יְהוָה אֱלֹהֵינוּ׃

4 1 If you return, O *Yisrael* – declares *Hashem* – If you return to Me, If you remove your abominations from My presence And do not waver,

ד א אִם־תָּשׁוּב יִשְׂרָאֵל נְאֻם־יְהוָה אֵלַי תָּשׁוּב וְאִם־תָּסִיר שִׁקּוּצֶיךָ מִפָּנַי וְלֹא תָנוּד׃

2 And swear, "As *Hashem* lives," In sincerity, justice, and righteousness – Nations shall bless themselves by you And praise themselves by you.

ב וְנִשְׁבַּעְתָּ חַי־יְהוָה בֶּאֱמֶת בְּמִשְׁפָּט וּבִצְדָקָה וְהִתְבָּרְכוּ בוֹ גּוֹיִם וּבוֹ יִתְהַלָּלוּ׃

3 For thus said *Hashem* to the men of *Yehuda* and to *Yerushalayim*: Break up the untilled ground, And do not sow among thorns.

ג כִּי־כֹה ׀ אָמַר יְהוָה לְאִישׁ יְהוּדָה וְלִירוּשָׁלִַם נִירוּ לָכֶם נִיר וְאַל־תִּזְרְעוּ אֶל־קוֹצִים׃

4 Open your hearts to *Hashem*, Remove the thickening about your hearts – O men of *Yehuda* and inhabitants of *Yerushalayim* – Lest My wrath break forth like fire, And burn, with none to quench it, Because of your wicked acts.

ד הִמֹּלוּ לַיהוָה וְהָסִרוּ עָרְלוֹת לְבַבְכֶם אִישׁ יְהוּדָה וְיֹשְׁבֵי יְרוּשָׁלִָם פֶּן־תֵּצֵא כָאֵשׁ חֲמָתִי וּבָעֲרָה וְאֵין מְכַבֶּה מִפְּנֵי רֹעַ מַעַלְלֵיכֶם׃

5 Proclaim in *Yehuda*, Announce in *Yerushalayim*, And say: "Blow the *shofar* in the land!" Shout aloud and say: "Assemble, and let us go Into the fortified cities!"

ה הַגִּידוּ בִיהוּדָה וּבִירוּשָׁלִַם הַשְׁמִיעוּ וְאִמְרוּ וְתִקְעוּ [תִּקְעוּ] שׁוֹפָר בָּאָרֶץ קִרְאוּ מַלְאוּ וְאִמְרוּ הֵאָסְפוּ וְנָבוֹאָה אֶל־עָרֵי הַמִּבְצָר׃

6 Set up a signpost: To *Tzion*. Take refuge, do not delay! For I bring evil from the north, And great disaster.

ו שְׂאוּ־נֵס צִיּוֹנָה הָעִיזוּ אַל־תַּעֲמֹדוּ כִּי רָעָה אָנֹכִי מֵבִיא מִצָּפוֹן וְשֶׁבֶר גָּדוֹל׃

s'-u NAYS tzi-YO-nah ha-EE-zu al ta-a-MO-du KEE ra-AH a-no-KHEE may-VEE mi-tza-FON v'-SHE-ver ga-DOL

7 The lion has come up from his thicket: The destroyer of nations has set out, Has departed from his place, To make your land a desolation; Your cities shall be ruined, Without inhabitants.

ז עָלָה אַרְיֵה מִסֻּבְּכוֹ וּמַשְׁחִית גּוֹיִם נָסַע יָצָא מִמְּקֹמוֹ לָשׂוּם אַרְצֵךְ לְשַׁמָּה עָרַיִךְ תִּצֶּינָה מֵאֵין יוֹשֵׁב׃

8 For this, put on sackcloth, Mourn and wail; For the blazing anger of *Hashem* Has not turned away from us.

ח עַל־זֹאת חִגְרוּ שַׂקִּים סִפְדוּ וְהֵילִילוּ כִּי לֹא־שָׁב חֲרוֹן אַף־יְהוָֹה מִמֶּנּוּ׃

4:6 Set up a signpost: To *Tzion* After the sentry alerts the nation to the invaders from the north, the people flock to *Yerushalayim* for protection. To guide and direct them, signposts will be established on the roadways. The Hebrew term *nes tziona* (נס ציונה), 'a signpost: To *Tzion*,' became the name of one of the first towns established in Israel by returning Jews at the end of the nineteenth century. In 1891, a man by the name of Michael Halperin gathered a group of people in Central Israel and unfurled a blue and white flag emblazoned with the words *nes tziona* written in gold. This location became the modern-day city of *Nes Tziona*, and Halperin's banner became the model for the future Israeli flag.

Nes Tziona

Yirmiyahu/Jeremiah
Chapter 4

9 And in that day – declares *Hashem* – The mind of the king And the mind of the nobles shall fail, The *Kohanim* shall be appalled, And the *Neviim* shall stand aghast.

10 And I said: Ah, *Hashem*! Surely You have deceived this people and *Yerushalayim* saying: It shall be well with you – Yet the sword threatens the very life!

11 At that time, it shall be said concerning this people and *Yerushalayim*: The conduct of My poor people is like searing wind From the bare heights of the desert – It will not serve to winnow or to fan.

12 A full blast from them comes against Me: Now I in turn will bring charges against them.

13 Lo, he ascends like clouds, His chariots are like a whirlwind, His horses are swifter than eagles. Woe to us, we are ruined!

14 Wash your heart clean of wickedness, O *Yerushalayim*, that you may be rescued. How long will you harbor within you Your evil designs?

15 Hark, one proclaims from *Dan* And announces calamity from Mount *Efraim*!

16 Tell the nations: Here they are! Announce concerning *Yerushalayim*: Watchers are coming from a distant land, They raise their voices against the towns of *Yehuda*.

17 Like guards of fields, they surround her on every side. For she has rebelled against Me – declares *Hashem*.

18 Your conduct and your acts Have brought this upon you; This is your bitter punishment; It pierces your very heart.

19 Oh, my suffering, my suffering! How I writhe! Oh, the walls of my heart! My heart moans within me, I cannot be silent; For I hear the blare of *shofarot*, Alarms of war.

20 Disaster overtakes disaster, For all the land has been ravaged. Suddenly my tents have been ravaged, In a moment, my tent cloths.

21 How long must I see standards And hear the blare of *shofarot*?

ירמיהו
פרק ד

ט וְהָיָה בַיּוֹם־הַהוּא נְאֻם־יְהֹוָה יֹאבַד לֵב־הַמֶּלֶךְ וְלֵב הַשָּׂרִים וְנָשַׁמּוּ הַכֹּהֲנִים וְהַנְּבִיאִים יִתְמָהוּ:

י וָאֹמַר אֲהָהּ אֲדֹנָי יְהֹוִה אָכֵן הַשֵּׁא הִשֵּׁאתָ לָעָם הַזֶּה וְלִירוּשָׁלַ͏ִם לֵאמֹר שָׁלוֹם יִהְיֶה לָכֶם וְנָגְעָה חֶרֶב עַד־הַנָּפֶשׁ:

יא בָּעֵת הַהִיא יֵאָמֵר לָעָם־הַזֶּה וְלִירוּשָׁלַ͏ִם רוּחַ צַח שְׁפָיִים בַּמִּדְבָּר דֶּרֶךְ בַּת־עַמִּי לוֹא לִזְרוֹת וְלוֹא לְהָבַר:

יב רוּחַ מָלֵא מֵאֵלֶּה יָבוֹא לִי עַתָּה גַּם־אֲנִי אֲדַבֵּר מִשְׁפָּטִים אוֹתָם:

יג הִנֵּה כַּעֲנָנִים יַעֲלֶה וְכַסּוּפָה מַרְכְּבוֹתָיו קַלּוּ מִנְּשָׁרִים סוּסָיו אוֹי לָנוּ כִּי שֻׁדָּדְנוּ:

יד כַּבְּסִי מֵרָעָה לִבֵּךְ יְרוּשָׁלַ͏ִם לְמַעַן תִּוָּשֵׁעִי עַד־מָתַי תָּלִין בְּקִרְבֵּךְ מַחְשְׁבוֹת אוֹנֵךְ:

טו כִּי קוֹל מַגִּיד מִדָּן וּמַשְׁמִיעַ אָוֶן מֵהַר אֶפְרָיִם:

טז הַזְכִּירוּ לַגּוֹיִם הִנֵּה הַשְׁמִיעוּ עַל־יְרוּשָׁלַ͏ִם נֹצְרִים בָּאִים מֵאֶרֶץ הַמֶּרְחָק וַיִּתְּנוּ עַל־עָרֵי יְהוּדָה קוֹלָם:

יז כְּשֹׁמְרֵי שָׂדַי הָיוּ עָלֶיהָ מִסָּבִיב כִּי־אֹתִי מָרָתָה נְאֻם־יְהֹוָה:

יח דַּרְכֵּךְ וּמַעֲלָלַיִךְ עָשׂוֹ אֵלֶּה לָךְ זֹאת רָעָתֵךְ כִּי מָר כִּי נָגַע עַד־לִבֵּךְ:

יט מֵעַי מֵעַי אחולה [אוֹחִילָה] קִירוֹת לִבִּי הֹמֶה־לִּי לִבִּי לֹא אַחֲרִישׁ כִּי קוֹל שׁוֹפָר שמעתי [שָׁמַעַתְּ] נַפְשִׁי תְּרוּעַת מִלְחָמָה:

כ שֶׁבֶר עַל־שֶׁבֶר נִקְרָא כִּי שֻׁדְּדָה כָּל־הָאָרֶץ פִּתְאֹם שֻׁדְּדוּ אֹהָלַי רֶגַע יְרִיעֹתָי:

כא עַד־מָתַי אֶרְאֶה־נֵּס אֶשְׁמְעָה קוֹל שׁוֹפָר:

Yirmiyahu/Jeremiah
Chapter 5

22 For My people are stupid, They give Me no heed; They are foolish children, They are not intelligent. They are clever at doing wrong, But unable to do right.

23 I look at the earth, It is unformed and void; At the skies, And their light is gone.

24 I look at the mountains, They are quaking; And all the hills are rocking.

25 I look: no man is left, And all the birds of the sky have fled.

26 I look: the farm land is desert, And all its towns are in ruin – Because of *Hashem*, Because of His blazing anger.

27 For thus said *Hashem*: The whole land shall be desolate, But I will not make an end of it.)

28 For this the earth mourns, And skies are dark above – Because I have spoken, I have planned, And I will not relent or turn back from it.

29 At the shout of horseman and bowman The whole city flees. They enter the thickets, They clamber up the rocks. The whole city is deserted, Not a man remains there.

30 And you, who are doomed to ruin, What do you accomplish by wearing crimson, By decking yourself in jewels of gold, By enlarging your eyes with kohl? You beautify yourself in vain: Lovers despise you, They seek your life!

31 I hear a voice as of one in travail, Anguish as of a woman bearing her first child, The voice of Fair *Tzion* Panting, stretching out her hands: "Alas for me! I faint Before the killers!"

5

1 Roam the streets of *Yerushalayim*, Search its squares, Look about and take note: You will not find a man, There is none who acts justly, Who seeks integrity – That I should pardon her.

2 Even when they say, "As *Hashem* lives," They are sure to be swearing falsely.

3 *Hashem*, Your eyes look for integrity. You have struck them, but they sensed no pain; You have consumed them, but they would accept no discipline. They made their faces harder than rock, They refused to turn back.

Yirmiyahu/Jeremiah
Chapter 5

ירמיהו
פרק ה

4 Then I thought: These are just poor folk; They act foolishly; For they do not know the way of *Hashem*, The rules of their God.

ד וַאֲנִי אָמַרְתִּי אַךְ־דַּלִּים הֵם נוֹאֲלוּ כִּי לֹא יָדְעוּ דֶּרֶךְ יְהֹוָה מִשְׁפַּט אֱלֹהֵיהֶם:

5 So I will go to the wealthy And speak with them: Surely they know the way of *Hashem*, The rules of their God. But they as well had broken the yoke, Had snapped the bonds.

ה אֵלֲכָה־לִּי אֶל־הַגְּדֹלִים וַאֲדַבְּרָה אוֹתָם כִּי הֵמָּה יָדְעוּ דֶּרֶךְ יְהֹוָה מִשְׁפַּט אֱלֹהֵיהֶם אַךְ הֵמָּה יַחְדָּו שָׁבְרוּ עֹל נִתְּקוּ מוֹסֵרוֹת:

6 Therefore, The lion of the forest strikes them down, The wolf of the desert ravages them. A leopard lies in wait by their towns; Whoever leaves them will be torn in pieces. For their transgressions are many, Their rebellious acts unnumbered.

ו עַל־כֵּן הִכָּם אַרְיֵה מִיַּעַר זְאֵב עֲרָבוֹת יְשָׁדְדֵם נָמֵר שֹׁקֵד עַל־עָרֵיהֶם כָּל־הַיּוֹצֵא מֵהֵנָּה יִטָּרֵף כִּי רַבּוּ פִּשְׁעֵיהֶם עָצְמוּ משבותיהם [מְשׁוּבוֹתֵיהֶם]:

al KAYN hi-KAM ar-YAY mi-YA-ar z'-AYV a-ra-VOT y'-sho-d'-DAYM na-MAYR sho-KAYD al a-ray-HEM kol ha-yo-TZAY may-HAY-nah yi-ta-RAYF KEE ra-BU pish-ay-HEM a-tz'-MU m'-shu-vo-tay-HEM

7 Why should I forgive you? Your children have forsaken Me And sworn by no-gods. When I fed them their fill, They committed adultery And went trooping to the harlot's house.

ז אֵי לָזֹאת אסלוח־[אֶסְלַח־] לָךְ בָּנַיִךְ עֲזָבוּנִי וַיִּשָּׁבְעוּ בְּלֹא אֱלֹהִים וָאַשְׂבִּעַ אוֹתָם וַיִּנְאָפוּ וּבֵית זוֹנָה יִתְגֹּדָדוּ:

8 They were well-fed, lusty stallions, Each neighing at another's wife.

ח סוּסִים מְיֻזָּנִים מַשְׁכִּים הָיוּ אִישׁ אֶל־אֵשֶׁת רֵעֵהוּ יִצְהָלוּ:

9 Shall I not punish such deeds? – says *Hashem* – Shall I not bring retribution On a nation such as this?

ט הַעַל־אֵלֶּה לוֹא־אֶפְקֹד נְאֻם־יְהֹוָה וְאִם בְּגוֹי אֲשֶׁר־כָּזֶה לֹא תִתְנַקֵּם נַפְשִׁי:

10 Go up among her vines and destroy; Lop off her trailing branches, For they are not of *Hashem*. (But do not make an end.)

י עֲלוּ בְשָׁרוֹתֶיהָ וְשַׁחֵתוּ וְכָלָה אַל־תַּעֲשׂוּ הָסִירוּ נְטִישׁוֹתֶיהָ כִּי לוֹא לַיהֹוָה הֵמָּה:

11 For the House of *Yisrael* and the House of *Yehuda* Have betrayed Me – declares *Hashem*.

יא כִּי בָגוֹד בָּגְדוּ בִּי בֵּית יִשְׂרָאֵל וּבֵית יְהוּדָה נְאֻם־יְהֹוָה:

12 They have been false to *Hashem* And said: "It is not so! No trouble shall come upon us, We shall not see sword or famine.

יב כִּחֲשׁוּ בַּיהֹוָה וַיֹּאמְרוּ לֹא־הוּא וְלֹא־תָבוֹא עָלֵינוּ רָעָה וְחֶרֶב וְרָעָב לוֹא נִרְאֶה:

13 The *Neviim* shall prove mere wind For the Word is not in them; Thus-and-thus shall be done to them!"

יג וְהַנְּבִיאִים יִהְיוּ לְרוּחַ וְהַדִּבֵּר אֵין בָּהֶם כֹּה יֵעָשֶׂה לָהֶם:

A lion at the Ramat Gan safari

5:6 The lion of the forest strikes them down In ancient times, the Land of Israel was filled with a variety of animal species, including lions, wolves and leopards, some of which are still found in Israel today. When the Jewish people were obedient to *Hashem*, these animals would not pose a threat, as it says in *Sefer Vayikra* (26:6), "I will grant peace in the land… I will give the land respite from vicious beasts." Should the people sin, however, the animals would become their enemy (Leviticus 26:22). Reflecting these verses, *Yirmiyahu* describes the dangers that await the besieged Israelites by comparing them to wild animals preparing to attack.

Yirmiyahu/Jeremiah
Chapter 5

ירמיהו
פרק ה

14 Assuredly, thus said *Hashem*, The God of Hosts: Because they said that, I am putting My words into your mouth as fire, And this people shall be firewood, Which it will consume.

יד לָכֵן כֹּה־אָמַר יְהֹוָה אֱלֹהֵי צְבָאוֹת יַעַן דַּבֶּרְכֶם אֶת־הַדָּבָר הַזֶּה הִנְנִי נֹתֵן דְּבָרַי בְּפִיךָ לְאֵשׁ וְהָעָם הַזֶּה עֵצִים וַאֲכָלָתַם:

15 Lo, I am bringing against you, O House of *Yisrael*, A nation from afar – declares *Hashem*; It is an enduring nation, It is an ancient nation; A nation whose language you do not know – You will not understand what they say.

טו הִנְנִי מֵבִיא עֲלֵיכֶם גּוֹי מִמֶּרְחָק בֵּית יִשְׂרָאֵל נְאֻם־יְהֹוָה גּוֹי ׀ אֵיתָן הוּא גּוֹי מֵעוֹלָם הוּא גּוֹי לֹא־תֵדַע לְשֹׁנוֹ וְלֹא תִשְׁמַע מַה־יְדַבֵּר:

16 Their quivers are like a yawning grave – They are all mighty men.

טז אַשְׁפָּתוֹ כְּקֶבֶר פָּתוּחַ כֻּלָּם גִּבּוֹרִים:

17 They will devour your harvest and food, They will devour your sons and daughters, They will devour your flocks and herds, They will devour your vines and fig trees. They will batter down with the sword The fortified towns on which you rely.

יז וְאָכַל קְצִירְךָ וְלַחְמֶךָ יֹאכְלוּ בָּנֶיךָ וּבְנוֹתֶיךָ יֹאכַל צֹאנְךָ וּבְקָרֶךָ יֹאכַל גַּפְנְךָ וּתְאֵנָתֶךָ יְרֹשֵׁשׁ עָרֵי מִבְצָרֶיךָ אֲשֶׁר אַתָּה בּוֹטֵחַ בָּהֵנָּה בֶּחָרֶב:

18 But even in those days – declares *Hashem* – I will not make an end of you.

יח וְגַם בַּיָּמִים הָהֵמָּה נְאֻם־יְהֹוָה לֹא־אֶעֱשֶׂה אִתְּכֶם כָּלָה:

19 And when they ask, "Because of what did *Hashem* our God do all these things?" you shall answer them, "Because you forsook Me and served alien gods on your own land, you will have to serve foreigners in a land not your own."

יט וְהָיָה כִּי תֹאמְרוּ תַּחַת מֶה עָשָׂה יְהֹוָה אֱלֹהֵינוּ לָנוּ אֶת־כָּל־אֵלֶּה וְאָמַרְתָּ אֲלֵיהֶם כַּאֲשֶׁר עֲזַבְתֶּם אוֹתִי וַתַּעַבְדוּ אֱלֹהֵי נֵכָר בְּאַרְצְכֶם כֵּן תַּעַבְדוּ זָרִים בְּאֶרֶץ לֹא לָכֶם:

20 Proclaim this to the House of *Yaakov* And announce it in *Yehuda*:

כ הַגִּידוּ זֹאת בְּבֵית יַעֲקֹב וְהַשְׁמִיעוּהָ בִיהוּדָה לֵאמֹר:

21 Hear this, O foolish people, Devoid of intelligence, That have eyes but can't see, That have ears but can't hear!

כא שִׁמְעוּ־נָא זֹאת עַם סָכָל וְאֵין לֵב עֵינַיִם לָהֶם וְלֹא יִרְאוּ אָזְנַיִם לָהֶם וְלֹא יִשְׁמָעוּ:

22 Should you not revere Me – says *Hashem* – Should you not tremble before Me, Who set the sand as a boundary to the sea, As a limit for all time, not to be transgressed? Though its waves toss, they cannot prevail; Though they roar, they cannot pass it.

כב הַאוֹתִי לֹא־תִירָאוּ נְאֻם־יְהֹוָה אִם מִפָּנַי לֹא תָחִילוּ אֲשֶׁר־שַׂמְתִּי חוֹל גְּבוּל לַיָּם חָק־עוֹלָם וְלֹא יַעַבְרֶנְהוּ וַיִּתְגָּעֲשׁוּ וְלֹא יוּכָלוּ וְהָמוּ גַלָּיו וְלֹא יַעַבְרֻנְהוּ:

23 Yet this people has a wayward and defiant heart; They have turned aside and gone their way.

כג וְלָעָם הַזֶּה הָיָה לֵב סוֹרֵר וּמוֹרֶה סָרוּ וַיֵּלֵכוּ:

24 They have not said to themselves, "Let us revere *Hashem* our God, Who gives the rain, The early and late rain in season, Who keeps for our benefit The weeks appointed for harvest."

כד וְלֹא־אָמְרוּ בִלְבָבָם נִירָא נָא אֶת־יְהֹוָה אֱלֹהֵינוּ הַנֹּתֵן גֶּשֶׁם וירה [יוֹרֶה] וּמַלְקוֹשׁ בְּעִתּוֹ שְׁבֻעוֹת חֻקּוֹת קָצִיר יִשְׁמָר־לָנוּ:

25 It is your iniquities that have diverted these things, Your sins that have withheld the bounty from you.

כה עֲוֺנוֹתֵיכֶם הִטּוּ־אֵלֶּה וְחַטֹּאותֵיכֶם מָנְעוּ הַטּוֹב מִכֶּם:

Yirmiyahu/Jeremiah
Chapter 6

ירמיהו
פרק ו

26 For among My people are found wicked men, Who lurk, like fowlers lying in wait; They set up a trap to catch men.

כו כִּי־נִמְצְא֥וּ בְעַמִּ֖י רְשָׁעִ֑ים יָשׁוּר֙ כְּשַׁ֣ךְ יְקוּשִׁ֔ים הִצִּ֖יבוּ מַשְׁחִ֥ית אֲנָשִׁ֥ים יִלְכֹּֽדוּ׃

27 As a cage is full of birds, So their houses are full of guile; That is why they have grown so wealthy.

כז כִּכְל֣וּב מָלֵ֣א ע֔וֹף כֵּ֥ן בָּתֵּיהֶ֖ם מְלֵאִ֣ים מִרְמָ֑ה עַל־כֵּ֥ן גָּדְל֖וּ וַֽיַּעֲשִֽׁירוּ׃

28 They have become fat and sleek; They pass beyond the bounds of wickedness, And they prosper. They will not judge the case of the orphan, Nor give a hearing to the plea of the needy.

כח שָׁמְנ֣וּ עָשְׁת֔וּ גַּ֥ם עָבְר֖וּ דִבְרֵי־רָ֑ע דִּ֣ין לֹא־דָ֗נוּ דִּ֤ין יָתוֹם֙ וְיַצְלִ֔יחוּ וּמִשְׁפַּ֥ט אֶבְיוֹנִ֖ים לֹ֥א שָׁפָֽטוּ׃

29 Shall I not punish such deeds — says *Hashem* — Shall I not bring retribution On a nation such as this?

כט הַֽעַל־אֵ֥לֶּה לֹֽא־אֶפְקֹ֖ד נְאֻם־יְהֹוָ֑ה אִ֚ם בְּג֣וֹי אֲשֶׁר־כָּזֶ֔ה לֹ֥א תִתְנַקֵּ֖ם נַפְשִֽׁי׃

30 An appalling, horrible thing Has happened in the land:

ל שַׁמָּה֙ וְשַׁ֣עֲרוּרָ֔ה נִהְיְתָ֖ה בָּאָֽרֶץ׃

31 The *Neviim* prophesy falsely, And the *Kohanim* rule accordingly; And My people like it so. But what will you do at the end of it?

לא הַנְּבִיאִ֞ים נִבְּא֣וּ בַשֶּׁ֗קֶר וְהַכֹּֽהֲנִים֙ יִרְדּ֣וּ עַל־יְדֵיהֶ֔ם וְעַמִּ֖י אָ֣הֲבוּ כֵ֑ן וּמַֽה־תַּעֲשׂ֖וּ לְאַחֲרִיתָֽהּ׃

6

1 Flee for refuge, O people of *Binyamin*, Out of the midst of *Yerushalayim*! Blow the *shofar* in *Tekoa*, Set up a signal at Beth-haccerem! For evil is appearing from the north, And great disaster.

א הָעִ֣זוּ ׀ בְּנֵ֣י בִנְיָמִ֗ן מִקֶּ֙רֶב֙ יְר֣וּשָׁלִַ֔ם וּבִתְק֙וֹעַ֙ תִּקְע֣וּ שׁוֹפָ֔ר וְעַל־בֵּ֥ית הַכֶּ֖רֶם שְׂא֣וּ מַשְׂאֵ֑ת כִּ֥י רָעָ֛ה נִשְׁקְפָ֥ה מִצָּפ֖וֹן וְשֶׁ֥בֶר גָּדֽוֹל׃

2 Fair *Tzion*, the lovely and delicate, I will destroy.

ha-na-VAH v'-ha-m'-u-na-GAH da-MEE-tee bat tzi-YON

ב הַנָּוָה֙ וְהַמְּעֻנָּגָ֔ה דָּמִ֖יתִי בַּת־צִיּֽוֹן׃

3 Against her come shepherds with their flocks, They pitch tents all around her; Each grazes the sheep under his care.

ג אֵלֶ֛יהָ יָבֹ֥אוּ רֹעִ֖ים וְעֶדְרֵיהֶ֑ם תָּקְע֨וּ עָלֶ֤יהָ אֹהָלִים֙ סָבִ֔יב רָע֖וּ אִ֥ישׁ אֶת־יָדֽוֹ׃

4 Prepare for battle against her: "Up! we will attack at noon." "Alas for us! for day is declining, The shadows of evening grow long."

ד קַדְּשׁ֤וּ עָלֶ֙יהָ֙ מִלְחָמָ֔ה ק֖וּמוּ וְנַעֲלֶ֣ה בַֽצָּהֳרָ֑יִם א֥וֹי לָ֙נוּ֙ כִּי־פָנָ֣ה הַיּ֔וֹם כִּ֥י יִנָּט֖וּ צִלְלֵי־עָֽרֶב׃

5 "Up! let us attack by night, And wreck her fortresses."

ה ק֖וּמוּ וְנַעֲלֶ֣ה בַלָּ֑יְלָה וְנַשְׁחִ֖יתָה אַרְמְנוֹתֶֽיהָ׃

6 For thus said the Lord of Hosts: Hew down her trees, And raise a siegemound against *Yerushalayim*. She is the city destined for punishment; Only fraud is found in her midst.

ו כִּ֣י כֹ֤ה אָמַר֙ יְהֹוָ֣ה צְבָא֔וֹת כִּרְת֣וּ עֵצָ֔ה וְשִׁפְכ֥וּ עַל־יְרוּשָׁלִַ֖ם סֹלְלָ֑ה הִ֤יא הָעִיר֙ הׇפְקַ֔ד כֻּלָּ֖הּ עֹ֥שֶׁק בְּקִרְבָּֽהּ׃

Rashi (1040–1105)

6:2 The lovely and delicate In describing the coming invasion, *Yirmiyahu* describes *Tzion* as "lovely and delicate." Some commentators suggest that this is a mocking reference to the women of *Yerushalayim*, whose extravagant tastes and styles contrast with the simple and honest manners of the country dwellers. *Rashi*, however, understands the phrase "lovely and delicate" as a description of the Land of Israel itself. Her gentle green hills and rolling pastures provided perfect grounds for shepherds to graze their flocks, as described in the next verse.

Yirmiyahu/Jeremiah
Chapter 6

7 As a well flows with water, So she flows with wickedness. Lawlessness and rapine are heard in her; Before Me constantly are sickness and wounds.

8 Accept rebuke, O *Yerushalayim*, Lest I come to loathe you, Lest I make you a desolation, An uninhabited land.

9 Thus said the Lord of Hosts: Let them glean over and over, as a vine, The remnant of *Yisrael*. Pass your hand again, Like a vintager, Over its branches.

10 To whom shall I speak, Give warning that they may hear? Their ears are blocked And they cannot listen. See, the word of *Hashem* has become for them An object of scorn; they will have none of it.

11 But I am filled with the wrath of *Hashem*, I cannot hold it in. Pour it on the infant in the street, And on the company of youths gathered together! Yes, men and women alike shall be captured, Elders and those of advanced years.

12 Their houses shall pass to others, Fields and wives as well, For I will stretch out My arm Against the inhabitants of the country – declares *Hashem*.

13 For from the smallest to the greatest, They are all greedy for gain; *Kohen* and *Navi* alike, They all act falsely.

14 They offer healing offhand For the wounds of My people, Saying, "All is well, all is well," When nothing is well.

15 They have acted shamefully; They have done abhorrent things – Yet they do not feel shame, And they cannot be made to blush. Assuredly, they shall fall among the falling, They shall stumble at the time when I punish them – said *Hashem*.

16 Thus said *Hashem*: Stand by the roads and consider, Inquire about ancient paths: Which is the road to happiness? Travel it, and find tranquillity for yourselves. But they said, "We will not."

17 And I raised up watchmen for you: "Hearken to the sound of the *shofar*!" But they said, "We will not."

18 Hear well, O nations, And know, O community, what is in store for them.

Yirmiyahu/Jeremiah

Chapter 7

19 Hear, O earth! I am going to bring disaster upon this people, The outcome of their own schemes; For they would not hearken to My words, And they rejected My Instruction.

20 What need have I of frankincense That comes from Sheba, Or fragrant cane from a distant land? Your burnt offerings are not acceptable And your sacrifices are not pleasing to Me.

21 Assuredly, thus said *Hashem*: I shall put before this people stumbling blocks Over which they shall stumble – Fathers and children alike, Neighbor and friend shall perish.

22 Thus said *Hashem*: See, a people comes from the northland, A great nation is roused From the remotest parts of the earth.

23 They grasp the bow and javelin; They are cruel, they show no mercy; The sound of them is like the roaring sea. They ride upon horses, Accoutered like a man for battle, Against you, O Fair *Tzion*!

24 "We have heard the report of them, Our hands fail; Pain seizes us, Agony like a woman in childbirth.

25 Do not go out into the country, Do not walk the roads! For the sword of the enemy is there, Terror on every side."

26 My poor people, Put on sackcloth And strew dust on yourselves! Mourn, as for an only child; Wail bitterly, For suddenly the destroyer Is coming upon us.

27 I have made you an assayer of My people – A refiner – You are to note and assay their ways.

28 They are copper and iron: They are all stubbornly defiant; They deal basely All of them act corruptly.

29 The bellows puff; The lead is consumed by fire. Yet the smelter smelts to no purpose – The dross is not separated out.

30 They are called "rejected silver," For *Hashem* has rejected them.

7 1 The word which came to *Yirmiyahu* from *Hashem*:

2 Stand at the gate of the House of *Hashem*, and there proclaim this word: Hear the word of *Hashem*, all you of *Yehuda* who enter these gates to worship *Hashem*!

1091

Yirmiyahu/Jeremiah
Chapter 7

3 Thus said the Lord of Hosts, the God of *Yisrael*: Mend your ways and your actions, and I will let you dwell in this place.

כֹּה־אָמַר יְהֹוָה צְבָאוֹת אֱלֹהֵי יִשְׂרָאֵל הֵיטִיבוּ דַרְכֵיכֶם וּמַעַלְלֵיכֶם וַאֲשַׁכְּנָה אֶתְכֶם בַּמָּקוֹם הַזֶּה׃

4 Don't put your trust in illusions and say, "The Temple of *Hashem*, the Temple of *Hashem*, the Temple of *Hashem* are these [buildings]."

אַל־תִּבְטְחוּ לָכֶם אֶל־דִּבְרֵי הַשֶּׁקֶר לֵאמֹר הֵיכַל יְהֹוָה הֵיכַל יְהֹוָה הֵיכַל יְהֹוָה הֵמָּה׃

al tiv-t'-KHU la-KHEM el div-RAY ha-SHE-ker lay-MOR hay-KHAL a-do-NAI hay-KHAL a-do-NAI hay-KHAL a-do-NAI HAY-mah

5 No, if you really mend your ways and your actions; if you execute justice between one man and another;

כִּי אִם־הֵיטֵיב תֵּיטִיבוּ אֶת־דַּרְכֵיכֶם וְאֶת־מַעַלְלֵיכֶם אִם־עָשׂוֹ תַעֲשׂוּ מִשְׁפָּט בֵּין אִישׁ וּבֵין רֵעֵהוּ׃

6 if you do not oppress the stranger, the orphan, and the widow; if you do not shed the blood of the innocent in this place; if you do not follow other gods, to your own hurt –

גֵּר יָתוֹם וְאַלְמָנָה לֹא תַעֲשֹׁקוּ וְדָם נָקִי אַל־תִּשְׁפְּכוּ בַּמָּקוֹם הַזֶּה וְאַחֲרֵי אֱלֹהִים אֲחֵרִים לֹא תֵלְכוּ לְרַע לָכֶם׃

7 then only will I let you dwell in this place, in the land that I gave to your fathers for all time.

וְשִׁכַּנְתִּי אֶתְכֶם בַּמָּקוֹם הַזֶּה בָּאָרֶץ אֲשֶׁר נָתַתִּי לַאֲבוֹתֵיכֶם לְמִן־עוֹלָם וְעַד־עוֹלָם׃

8 See, you are relying on illusions that are of no avail.

הִנֵּה אַתֶּם בֹּטְחִים לָכֶם עַל־דִּבְרֵי הַשָּׁקֶר לְבִלְתִּי הוֹעִיל׃

9 Will you steal and murder and commit adultery and swear falsely, and sacrifice to Baal, and follow other gods whom you have not experienced,

הֲגָנֹב רָצֹחַ וְנָאֹף וְהִשָּׁבֵעַ לַשֶּׁקֶר וְקַטֵּר לַבָּעַל וְהָלֹךְ אַחֲרֵי אֱלֹהִים אֲחֵרִים אֲשֶׁר לֹא־יְדַעְתֶּם׃

10 and then come and stand before Me in this House which bears My name and say, "We are safe"? – [Safe] to do all these abhorrent things!

וּבָאתֶם וַעֲמַדְתֶּם לְפָנַי בַּבַּיִת הַזֶּה אֲשֶׁר נִקְרָא־שְׁמִי עָלָיו וַאֲמַרְתֶּם נִצַּלְנוּ לְמַעַן עֲשׂוֹת אֵת כָּל־הַתּוֹעֵבוֹת הָאֵלֶּה׃

11 Do you consider this House, which bears My name, to be a den of thieves? As for Me, I have been watching – declares *Hashem*.

הַמְעָרַת פָּרִצִים הָיָה הַבַּיִת הַזֶּה אֲשֶׁר נִקְרָא־שְׁמִי עָלָיו בְּעֵינֵיכֶם גַּם אָנֹכִי הִנֵּה רָאִיתִי נְאֻם־יְהֹוָה׃

12 Just go to My place at *Shilo*, where I had established My name formerly, and see what I did to it because of the wickedness of My people *Yisrael*.

כִּי לְכוּ־נָא אֶל־מְקוֹמִי אֲשֶׁר בְּשִׁילוֹ אֲשֶׁר שִׁכַּנְתִּי שְׁמִי שָׁם בָּרִאשׁוֹנָה וּרְאוּ אֵת אֲשֶׁר־עָשִׂיתִי לוֹ מִפְּנֵי רָעַת עַמִּי יִשְׂרָאֵל׃

7:4 The Temple of *Hashem* One of *Yirmiyahu's* most famous outcries is uttered in the Temple courtyard. Surrounded by people who came to offer sacrifices, he assails their false sense of security and their belief that as long as the *Beit Hamikdash* stands, *Yerushalayim* can never be overrun. *Yirmiyahu* criticizes their false piety and emphasis on ritual matters while ignoring the needs of others, crying out "the Temple of *Hashem*" three times. Rabbi Samson Raphael Hirsch suggests that the following verses are a continuation of this one, and the meaning is: What is the real "Temple of *Hashem*"? Repentance, justice and charity.

Rabbi Samson R. Hirsch (1808–1888)

Yirmiyahu/Jeremiah
Chapter 7

יג וְעַתָּה יַעַן עֲשׂוֹתְכֶם אֶת־כָּל־הַמַּעֲשִׂים הָאֵלֶּה נְאֻם־יְהֹוָה וָאֲדַבֵּר אֲלֵיכֶם הַשְׁכֵּם וְדַבֵּר וְלֹא שְׁמַעְתֶּם וָאֶקְרָא אֶתְכֶם וְלֹא עֲנִיתֶם׃

13 And now, because you do all these things – declares *Hashem* – and though I spoke to you persistently, you would not listen; and though I called to you, you would not respond –

יד וְעָשִׂיתִי לַבַּיִת אֲשֶׁר נִקְרָא־שְׁמִי עָלָיו אֲשֶׁר אַתֶּם בֹּטְחִים בּוֹ וְלַמָּקוֹם אֲשֶׁר־נָתַתִּי לָכֶם וְלַאֲבוֹתֵיכֶם כַּאֲשֶׁר עָשִׂיתִי לְשִׁלוֹ׃

14 therefore I will do to the House which bears My name, on which you rely, and to the place which I gave you and your fathers, just what I did to *Shilo*.

טו וְהִשְׁלַכְתִּי אֶתְכֶם מֵעַל פָּנָי כַּאֲשֶׁר הִשְׁלַכְתִּי אֶת־כָּל־אֲחֵיכֶם אֵת כָּל־זֶרַע אֶפְרָיִם׃

15 And I will cast you out of My presence as I cast out your brothers, the whole brood of *Efraim*.

טז וְאַתָּה אַל־תִּתְפַּלֵּל בְּעַד־הָעָם הַזֶּה וְאַל־תִּשָּׂא בַעֲדָם רִנָּה וּתְפִלָּה וְאַל־תִּפְגַּע־בִּי כִּי־אֵינֶנִּי שֹׁמֵעַ אֹתָךְ׃

16 As for you, do not pray for this people, do not raise a cry of prayer on their behalf, do not plead with Me; for I will not listen to you.

יז הַאֵינְךָ רֹאֶה מָה הֵמָּה עֹשִׂים בְּעָרֵי יְהוּדָה וּבְחֻצוֹת יְרוּשָׁלָם׃

17 Don't you see what they are doing in the towns of *Yehuda* and in the streets of *Yerushalayim*?

יח הַבָּנִים מְלַקְּטִים עֵצִים וְהָאָבוֹת מְבַעֲרִים אֶת־הָאֵשׁ וְהַנָּשִׁים לָשׁוֹת בָּצֵק לַעֲשׂוֹת כַּוָּנִים לִמְלֶכֶת הַשָּׁמַיִם וְהַסֵּךְ נְסָכִים לֵאלֹהִים אֲחֵרִים לְמַעַן הַכְעִסֵנִי׃

18 The children gather sticks, the fathers build the fire, and the mothers knead dough, to make cakes for the Queen of Heaven, and they pour libations to other gods, to vex Me.

יט הַאֹתִי הֵם מַכְעִסִים נְאֻם־יְהֹוָה הֲלוֹא אֹתָם לְמַעַן בֹּשֶׁת פְּנֵיהֶם׃

19 Is it Me they are vexing? – says *Hashem*. It is rather themselves, to their own disgrace.

כ לָכֵן כֹּה־אָמַר ׀ אֲדֹנָי יְהֹוִה הִנֵּה אַפִּי וַחֲמָתִי נִתֶּכֶת אֶל־הַמָּקוֹם הַזֶּה עַל־הָאָדָם וְעַל־הַבְּהֵמָה וְעַל־עֵץ הַשָּׂדֶה וְעַל־פְּרִי הָאֲדָמָה וּבָעֲרָה וְלֹא תִכְבֶּה׃

20 Assuredly, thus said *Hashem*: My wrath and My fury will be poured out upon this place, on man and on beast, on the trees of the field and the fruit of the soil. It shall burn, with none to quench it.

כא כֹּה אָמַר יְהֹוָה צְבָאוֹת אֱלֹהֵי יִשְׂרָאֵל עֹלוֹתֵיכֶם סְפוּ עַל־זִבְחֵיכֶם וְאִכְלוּ בָשָׂר׃

21 Thus said the LORD of Hosts, the God of *Yisrael*: Add your burnt offerings to your other sacrifices and eat the meat!

כב כִּי לֹא־דִבַּרְתִּי אֶת־אֲבוֹתֵיכֶם וְלֹא צִוִּיתִים בְּיוֹם הוֹצִיא [הוֹצִיאִי] אוֹתָם מֵאֶרֶץ מִצְרָיִם עַל־דִּבְרֵי עוֹלָה וָזָבַח׃

22 For when I freed your fathers from the land of Egypt, I did not speak with them or command them concerning burnt offerings or sacrifice.

כג כִּי אִם־אֶת־הַדָּבָר הַזֶּה צִוִּיתִי אוֹתָם לֵאמֹר שִׁמְעוּ בְקוֹלִי וְהָיִיתִי לָכֶם לֵאלֹהִים וְאַתֶּם תִּהְיוּ־לִי לְעָם וַהֲלַכְתֶּם בְּכָל־הַדֶּרֶךְ אֲשֶׁר אֲצַוֶּה אֶתְכֶם לְמַעַן יִיטַב לָכֶם׃

23 But this is what I commanded them: Do My bidding, that I may be your God and you may be My people; walk only in the way that I enjoin upon you, that it may go well with you.

כד וְלֹא שָׁמְעוּ וְלֹא־הִטּוּ אֶת־אָזְנָם וַיֵּלְכוּ בְּמֹעֵצוֹת בִּשְׁרִרוּת לִבָּם הָרָע וַיִּהְיוּ לְאָחוֹר וְלֹא לְפָנִים׃

24 Yet they did not listen or give ear; they followed their own counsels, the willfulness of their evil hearts. They have gone backward, not forward,

Yirmiyahu/Jeremiah
Chapter 8

25 from the day your fathers left the land of Egypt until today. And though I kept sending all My servants, the *Neviim*, to them daily and persistently,

26 they would not listen to Me or give ear. They stiffened their necks, they acted worse than their fathers.

27 You shall say all these things to them, but they will not listen to you; you shall call to them, but they will not respond to you.

28 Then say to them: This is the nation that would not obey *Hashem* their God, that would not accept rebuke. Faithfulness has perished, vanished from their mouths.

29 Shear your locks and cast them away, Take up a lament on the heights, For *Hashem* has spurned and cast off The brood that provoked His wrath.

30 For the people of *Yehuda* have done what displeases Me – declares *Hashem*. They have set up their abominations in the House which is called by My name, and they have defiled it.

31 And they have built the shrines of Topheth in the Valley of Ben-hinnom to burn their sons and daughters in fire – which I never commanded, which never came to My mind.

32 Assuredly, a time is coming – declares *Hashem* – when men shall no longer speak of Topheth or the Valley of Ben-hinnom, but of the Valley of Slaughter; and they shall bury in Topheth until no room is left.

33 The carcasses of this people shall be food for the birds of the sky and the beasts of the earth, with none to frighten them off.

34 And I will silence in the towns of *Yehuda* and the streets of *Yerushalayim* the sound of mirth and gladness, the voice of bridegroom and bride. For the whole land shall fall to ruin.

8

1 At that time – declares *Hashem* – the bones of the kings of *Yehuda*, of its officers, of the *Kohanim*, of the *Neviim*, and of the inhabitants of *Yerushalayim* shall be taken out of their graves

Yirmiyahu/Jeremiah
Chapter 8

2 and exposed to the sun, the moon, and all the host of heaven which they loved and served and followed, to which they turned and bowed down. They shall not be gathered for reburial; they shall become dung upon the face of the earth.

3 And death shall be preferable to life for all that are left of this wicked folk, in all the other places to which I shall banish them – declares the Lord of Hosts.

4 Say to them: Thus said *Hashem*: When men fall, do they not get up again? If they turn aside, do they not turn back?

5 Why is this people – *Yerushalayim* – rebellious With a persistent rebellion? They cling to deceit, They refuse to return.

6 I have listened and heard: They do not speak honestly. No one regrets his wickedness And says, "What have I done!" They all persist in their wayward course Like a steed dashing forward in the fray.

7 Even the stork in the sky knows her seasons, And the turtledove, swift, and crane Keep the time of their coming; But My people pay no heed To the law of *Hashem*.

8 How can you say, "We are wise, And we possess the Instruction of *Hashem*"? Assuredly, for naught has the pen labored, For naught the scribes!

9 The wise shall be put to shame, Shall be dismayed and caught; See, they reject the word of *Hashem*, So their wisdom amounts to nothing.

10 Assuredly, I will give their wives to others, And their fields to dispossessors; For from the smallest to the greatest, They are all greedy for gain; *Kohen* and *Navi* alike, They all act falsely.

11 They offer healing offhand For the wounds of My poor people, Saying, "All is well, all is well," When nothing is well.

12 They have acted shamefully; They have done abhorrent things – Yet they do not feel shame, They cannot be made to blush. Assuredly, they shall fall among the falling, They shall stumble at the time of their doom – said *Hashem*.

Yirmiyahu / Jeremiah
Chapter 8

13 I will make an end of them – declares *Hashem*: No grapes left on the vine, No figs on the fig tree, The leaves all withered; Whatever I have given them is gone.

יג אָסֹף אֲסִיפֵם נְאֻם־יְהֹוָה אֵין עֲנָבִים בַּגֶּפֶן וְאֵין תְּאֵנִים בַּתְּאֵנָה וְהֶעָלֶה נָבֵל וָאֶתֵּן לָהֶם יַעַבְרוּם׃

14 Why are we sitting by? Let us gather into the fortified cities And meet our doom there. For *Hashem* our God has doomed us, He has made us drink a bitter draft, Because we sinned against *Hashem*.

יד עַל־מָה אֲנַחְנוּ יֹשְׁבִים הֵאָסְפוּ וְנָבוֹא אֶל־עָרֵי הַמִּבְצָר וְנִדְּמָה־שָּׁם כִּי יְהֹוָה אֱלֹהֵינוּ הֲדִמָּנוּ וַיַּשְׁקֵנוּ מֵי־רֹאשׁ כִּי חָטָאנוּ לַיהֹוָה׃

15 We hoped for good fortune, but no happiness came; For a time of relief – instead there is terror!

טו קַוֵּה לְשָׁלוֹם וְאֵין טוֹב לְעֵת מַרְפֵּה וְהִנֵּה בְעָתָה׃

16 The snorting of their horses was heard from *Dan*; At the loud neighing of their steeds The whole land quaked. They came and devoured the land and what was in it, The towns and those who dwelt in them.

טז מִדָּן נִשְׁמַע נַחְרַת סוּסָיו מִקּוֹל מִצְהֲלוֹת אַבִּירָיו רָעֲשָׁה כָּל־הָאָרֶץ וַיָּבוֹאוּ וַיֹּאכְלוּ אֶרֶץ וּמְלוֹאָהּ עִיר וְיֹשְׁבֵי בָהּ׃

17 Lo, I will send serpents against you, Adders that cannot be charmed, And they shall bite you – declares *Hashem*.

יז כִּי הִנְנִי מְשַׁלֵּחַ בָּכֶם נְחָשִׁים צִפְעֹנִים אֲשֶׁר אֵין־לָהֶם לָחַשׁ וְנִשְּׁכוּ אֶתְכֶם נְאֻם־יְהֹוָה׃

18 When in grief I would seek comfort, My heart is sick within me.

יח מַבְלִיגִיתִי עֲלֵי יָגוֹן עָלַי לִבִּי דַוָּי׃

19 "Is not *Hashem* in *Tzion*? Is not her King within her? Why then did they anger Me with their images, With alien futilities?" Hark! The outcry of my poor people From the land far and wide:

יט הִנֵּה־קוֹל שַׁוְעַת בַּת־עַמִּי מֵאֶרֶץ מַרְחַקִּים הַיהֹוָה אֵין בְּצִיּוֹן אִם־מַלְכָּהּ אֵין בָּהּ מַדּוּעַ הִכְעִסוּנִי בִּפְסִלֵיהֶם בְּהַבְלֵי נֵכָר׃

20 "Harvest is past, Summer is gone, But we have not been saved."

כ עָבַר קָצִיר כָּלָה קָיִץ וַאֲנַחְנוּ לוֹא נוֹשָׁעְנוּ׃

21 Because my people is shattered I am shattered; I am dejected, seized by desolation.

כא עַל־שֶׁבֶר בַּת־עַמִּי הָשְׁבָּרְתִּי קָדַרְתִּי שַׁמָּה הֶחֱזִקָתְנִי׃

22 Is there no balm in *Gilad*? Can no physician be found? Why has healing not yet Come to my poor people?

ha-tzo-REE AYN b'-gil-AD im ro-FAY AYN SHAM KEE ma-DU-a LO a-l'-TAH a-ru-KHAT bat a-MEE

כב הַצֳרִי אֵין בְּגִלְעָד אִם־רֹפֵא אֵין שָׁם כִּי מַדּוּעַ לֹא עָלְתָה אֲרֻכַת בַּת־עַמִּי׃

8:22 Is there no balm in *Gilad* *Yirmiyahu* laments the people's suffering. Despite condemning their immorality, impudence and hypocrisy, he nevertheless identifies with their pain. Wistfully, he calls out, "Is there no balm in *Gilad*?" *Gilad* is located on the plains of Jordan, across the river from *Yerushalayim*, and was famous for its medicines. The commentators understand this balm as a metaphor – righteousness and good deeds could have healed the people, but they were too distant.

Yirmiyahu/Jeremiah
Chapter 9

23 Oh, that my head were water, My eyes a fount of tears! Then would I weep day and night For the slain of my poor people.

9 1 Oh, to be in the desert, At an encampment for wayfarers! Oh, to leave my people, To go away from them – For they are all adulterers, A band of rogues.

2 They bend their tongues like bows; They are valorous in the land For treachery, not for honesty; They advance from evil to evil. And they do not heed Me – declares *Hashem*.

3 Beware, every man of his friend! Trust not even a brother! For every brother takes advantage, Every friend is base in his dealings.

4 One man cheats the other, They will not speak truth; They have trained their tongues to speak falsely; They wear themselves out working iniquity.

5 You dwell in the midst of deceit. In their deceit, they refuse to heed Me – declares *Hashem*.

6 Assuredly, thus said the Lord of Hosts: Lo, I shall smelt and assay them – For what else can I do because of My poor people?

7 Their tongue is a sharpened arrow, They use their mouths to deceive. One speaks to his fellow in friendship, But lays an ambush for him in his heart.

8 Shall I not punish them for such deeds? – says *Hashem* – Shall I not bring retribution On such a nation as this?

9 For the mountains I take up weeping and wailing, For the pastures in the wilderness, a dirge. They are laid waste; no man passes through, And no sound of cattle is heard. Birds of the sky and beasts as well Have fled and are gone.

10 I will turn *Yerushalayim* into rubble, Into dens for jackals; And I will make the towns of *Yehuda* A desolation without inhabitants.

11 What man is so wise That he understands this? To whom has *Hashem*'s mouth spoken, So that he can explain it: Why is the land in ruins, Laid waste like a wilderness, With none passing through?

12 *Hashem* replied: Because they forsook the Teaching I had set before them. They did not obey Me and they did not follow it,

ירמיהו
פרק ט

כג מִי־יִתֵּן רֹאשִׁי מַיִם וְעֵינִי מְקוֹר דִּמְעָה וְאֶבְכֶּה יוֹמָם וָלַיְלָה אֵת חַלְלֵי בַת־עַמִּי:

ט א מִי־יִתְּנֵנִי בַמִּדְבָּר מְלוֹן אֹרְחִים וְאֶעֶזְבָה אֶת־עַמִּי וְאֵלְכָה מֵאִתָּם כִּי כֻלָּם מְנָאֲפִים עֲצֶרֶת בֹּגְדִים:

ב וַיַּדְרְכוּ אֶת־לְשׁוֹנָם קַשְׁתָּם שֶׁקֶר וְלֹא לֶאֱמוּנָה גָּבְרוּ בָאָרֶץ כִּי מֵרָעָה אֶל־רָעָה יָצָאוּ וְאֹתִי לֹא־יָדָעוּ נְאֻם־יְהוָה:

ג אִישׁ מֵרֵעֵהוּ הִשָּׁמֵרוּ וְעַל־כָּל־אָח אַל־תִּבְטָחוּ כִּי כָל־אָח עָקוֹב יַעְקֹב וְכָל־רֵעַ רָכִיל יַהֲלֹךְ:

ד וְאִישׁ בְּרֵעֵהוּ יְהָתֵלּוּ וֶאֱמֶת לֹא יְדַבֵּרוּ לִמְּדוּ לְשׁוֹנָם דַּבֶּר־שֶׁקֶר הַעֲוֵה נִלְאוּ:

ה שִׁבְתְּךָ בְּתוֹךְ מִרְמָה בְּמִרְמָה מֵאֲנוּ דַעַת־אוֹתִי נְאֻם־יְהוָה:

ו לָכֵן כֹּה אָמַר יְהוָה צְבָאוֹת הִנְנִי צוֹרְפָם וּבְחַנְתִּים כִּי־אֵיךְ אֶעֱשֶׂה מִפְּנֵי בַּת־עַמִּי:

ז חֵץ שׁוֹחֵט [שָׁחוּט] לְשׁוֹנָם מִרְמָה דִבֵּר בְּפִיו שָׁלוֹם אֶת־רֵעֵהוּ יְדַבֵּר וּבְקִרְבּוֹ יָשִׂים אָרְבּוֹ:

ח הַעַל־אֵלֶּה לֹא־אֶפְקָד־בָּם נְאֻם־יְהוָה אִם בְּגוֹי אֲשֶׁר־כָּזֶה לֹא תִתְנַקֵּם נַפְשִׁי:

ט עַל־הֶהָרִים אֶשָּׂא בְכִי וָנֶהִי וְעַל־נְאוֹת מִדְבָּר קִינָה כִּי נִצְּתוּ מִבְּלִי־אִישׁ עֹבֵר וְלֹא שָׁמְעוּ קוֹל מִקְנֶה מֵעוֹף הַשָּׁמַיִם וְעַד־בְּהֵמָה נָדְדוּ הָלָכוּ:

י וְנָתַתִּי אֶת־יְרוּשָׁלַ͏ִם לְגַלִּים מְעוֹן תַּנִּים וְאֶת־עָרֵי יְהוּדָה אֶתֵּן שְׁמָמָה מִבְּלִי יוֹשֵׁב:

יא מִי־הָאִישׁ הֶחָכָם וְיָבֵן אֶת־זֹאת וַאֲשֶׁר דִּבֶּר פִּי־יְהוָה אֵלָיו וְיַגִּדָהּ עַל־מָה אָבְדָה הָאָרֶץ נִצְּתָה כַמִּדְבָּר מִבְּלִי עֹבֵר:

יב וַיֹּאמֶר יְהוָה עַל־עָזְבָם אֶת־תּוֹרָתִי אֲשֶׁר נָתַתִּי לִפְנֵיהֶם וְלֹא־שָׁמְעוּ בְקוֹלִי וְלֹא־הָלְכוּ בָהּ:

Yirmiyahu/Jeremiah
Chapter 9

ירמיהו
פרק ט

13 but followed their own willful heart and followed the Baalim, as their fathers had taught them.

יג וַיֵּלְכוּ אַחֲרֵי שְׁרִרוּת לִבָּם וְאַחֲרֵי הַבְּעָלִים אֲשֶׁר לִמְּדוּם אֲבוֹתָם׃

14 Assuredly, thus said the Lord of Hosts, the God of *Yisrael*: I am going to feed that people wormwood and make them drink a bitter draft.

יד לָכֵן כֹּה־אָמַר יְהֹוָה צְבָאוֹת אֱלֹהֵי יִשְׂרָאֵל הִנְנִי מַאֲכִילָם אֶת־הָעָם הַזֶּה לַעֲנָה וְהִשְׁקִיתִים מֵי־רֹאשׁ׃

15 I will scatter them among nations which they and their fathers never knew; and I will dispatch the sword after them until I have consumed them.

טו וַהֲפִצוֹתִים בַּגּוֹיִם אֲשֶׁר לֹא יָדְעוּ הֵמָּה וַאֲבוֹתָם וְשִׁלַּחְתִּי אַחֲרֵיהֶם אֶת־הַחֶרֶב עַד כַּלּוֹתִי אוֹתָם׃

16 Thus said the Lord of Hosts: Listen! Summon the dirge-singers, let them come; Send for the skilled women, let them come.

טז כֹּה אָמַר יְהֹוָה צְבָאוֹת הִתְבּוֹנְנוּ וְקִרְאוּ לַמְקוֹנְנוֹת וּתְבוֹאֶינָה וְאֶל־הַחֲכָמוֹת שִׁלְחוּ וְתָבוֹאנָה׃

17 Let them quickly start a wailing for us, That our eyes may run with tears, Our pupils flow with water.

יז וּתְמַהֵרְנָה וְתִשֶּׂנָה עָלֵינוּ נֶהִי וְתֵרַדְנָה עֵינֵינוּ דִּמְעָה וְעַפְעַפֵּינוּ יִזְּלוּ־מָיִם׃

18 For the sound of wailing Is heard from *Tzion*: How we are despoiled! How greatly we are shamed! Ah, we must leave our land, Abandon our dwellings!

יח כִּי קוֹל נְהִי נִשְׁמַע מִצִּיּוֹן אֵיךְ שֻׁדָּדְנוּ בֹּשְׁנוּ מְאֹד כִּי־עָזַבְנוּ אָרֶץ כִּי הִשְׁלִיכוּ מִשְׁכְּנוֹתֵינוּ׃

19 Hear, O women, the word of *Hashem*, Let your ears receive the word of His mouth, And teach your daughters wailing, And one another lamentation.

יט כִּי־שְׁמַעְנָה נָשִׁים דְּבַר־יְהֹוָה וְתִקַּח אָזְנְכֶם דְּבַר־פִּיו וְלַמֵּדְנָה בְנוֹתֵיכֶם נֶהִי וְאִשָּׁה רְעוּתָהּ קִינָה׃

20 For death has climbed through our windows, Has entered our fortresses, To cut off babes from the streets, Young men from the squares.

כ כִּי־עָלָה מָוֶת בְּחַלּוֹנֵינוּ בָּא בְּאַרְמְנוֹתֵינוּ לְהַכְרִית עוֹלָל מִחוּץ בַּחוּרִים מֵרְחֹבוֹת׃

21 Speak thus – says *Hashem*: The carcasses of men shall lie Like dung upon the fields, Like sheaves behind the reaper, With none to pick them up.

כא דַּבֵּר כֹּה נְאֻם־יְהֹוָה וְנָפְלָה נִבְלַת הָאָדָם כְּדֹמֶן עַל־פְּנֵי הַשָּׂדֶה וּכְעָמִיר מֵאַחֲרֵי הַקֹּצֵר וְאֵין מְאַסֵּף׃

22 Thus said *Hashem*: Let not the wise man glory in his wisdom; Let not the strong man glory in his strength; Let not the rich man glory in his riches.

כב כֹּה אָמַר יְהֹוָה אַל־יִתְהַלֵּל חָכָם בְּחָכְמָתוֹ וְאַל־יִתְהַלֵּל הַגִּבּוֹר בִּגְבוּרָתוֹ אַל־יִתְהַלֵּל עָשִׁיר בְּעָשְׁרוֹ׃

23 But only in this should one glory: In his earnest devotion to Me. For I *Hashem* act with kindness, Justice, and equity in the world; For in these I delight – declares *Hashem*.

כג כִּי אִם־בְּזֹאת יִתְהַלֵּל הַמִּתְהַלֵּל הַשְׂכֵּל וְיָדֹעַ אוֹתִי כִּי אֲנִי יְהֹוָה עֹשֶׂה חֶסֶד מִשְׁפָּט וּצְדָקָה בָּאָרֶץ כִּי־בְאֵלֶּה חָפַצְתִּי נְאֻם־יְהֹוָה׃

KEE im b'-ZOT yit-ha-LAYL ha-mit-ha-LAYL has-KAYL v'-ya-DO-a o-TEE KEE a-NEE a-do-NAI O-seh KHE-sed mish-PAT utz-da-KAH ba-A-retz kee v'-AY-leh kha-FATZ-tee n'-um a-do-NAI

9:23 For in these I delight *Yirmiyahu* contrasts two separate ways of living. Some people strive for wisdom, power, and riches, through which they can take pride in themselves. But all this is foolish when compared to *Hashem*, Who has infinite wisdom, power and riches. On the other hand, righteous people strive

Rambam (1135–1204)

Yirmiyahu/Jeremiah
Chapter 10

24 Lo, days are coming – declares *Hashem* – when I will take note of everyone circumcised in the foreskin:

25 of Egypt, *Yehuda*, Edom, the Amonites, Moab, and all the desert dwellers who have the hair of their temples clipped. For all these nations are uncircumcised, but all the House of *Yisrael* are uncircumcised of heart.

10 1 Hear the word which *Hashem* has spoken to you, O House of *Yisrael*!

2 Thus said *Hashem*: Do not learn to go the way of the nations, And do not be dismayed by portents in the sky; Let the nations be dismayed by them!

3 For the laws of the nations are delusions: For it is the work of a craftsman's hands. He cuts down a tree in the forest with an ax,

4 He adorns it with silver and gold, He fastens it with nails and hammer, So that it does not totter.

5 They are like a scarecrow in a cucumber patch, They cannot speak. They have to be carried, For they cannot walk. Be not afraid of them, for they can do no harm; Nor is it in them to do any good.

6 *Hashem*, there is none like You! You are great and Your name is great in power.

7 Who would not revere You, O King of the nations? For that is Your due, Since among all the wise of the nations And among all their royalty, There is none like You.

8 But they are both dull and foolish; [Their] doctrine is but delusion; It is a piece of wood,

9 Silver beaten flat, that is brought from Tarshish, And gold from Uphaz, The work of a craftsman and the goldsmith's hands; Their clothing is blue and purple, All of them are the work of skilled men.

ירמיהו
פרק י

כד הִנֵּה יָמִים בָּאִים נְאֻם־יְהֹוָה וּפָקַדְתִּי עַל־כָּל־מוּל בְּעָרְלָה:

כה עַל־מִצְרַיִם וְעַל־יְהוּדָה וְעַל־אֱדוֹם וְעַל־בְּנֵי עַמּוֹן וְעַל־מוֹאָב וְעַל כָּל־קְצוּצֵי פֵאָה הַיֹּשְׁבִים בַּמִּדְבָּר כִּי כָל־הַגּוֹיִם עֲרֵלִים וְכָל־בֵּית יִשְׂרָאֵל עַרְלֵי־לֵב:

א שִׁמְעוּ אֶת־הַדָּבָר אֲשֶׁר דִּבֶּר יְהֹוָה עֲלֵיכֶם בֵּית יִשְׂרָאֵל:

ב כֹּה ׀ אָמַר יְהֹוָה אֶל־דֶּרֶךְ הַגּוֹיִם אַל־תִּלְמָדוּ וּמֵאֹתוֹת הַשָּׁמַיִם אַל־תֵּחָתּוּ כִּי־יֵחַתּוּ הַגּוֹיִם מֵהֵמָּה:

ג כִּי־חֻקּוֹת הָעַמִּים הֶבֶל הוּא כִּי־עֵץ מִיַּעַר כְּרָתוֹ מַעֲשֵׂה יְדֵי־חָרָשׁ בַּמַּעֲצָד:

ד בְּכֶסֶף וּבְזָהָב יְיַפֵּהוּ בְּמַסְמְרוֹת וּבְמַקָּבוֹת יְחַזְּקוּם וְלוֹא יָפִיק:

ה כְּתֹמֶר מִקְשָׁה הֵמָּה וְלֹא יְדַבֵּרוּ נָשׂוֹא יִנָּשׂוּא כִּי לֹא יִצְעָדוּ אַל־תִּירְאוּ מֵהֶם כִּי־לֹא יָרֵעוּ וְגַם־הֵיטֵיב אֵין אוֹתָם:

ו מֵאֵין כָּמוֹךָ יְהֹוָה גָּדוֹל אַתָּה וְגָדוֹל שִׁמְךָ בִּגְבוּרָה:

ז מִי לֹא יִרָאֲךָ מֶלֶךְ הַגּוֹיִם כִּי לְךָ יָאָתָה כִּי בְכָל־חַכְמֵי הַגּוֹיִם וּבְכָל־מַלְכוּתָם מֵאֵין כָּמוֹךָ:

ח וּבְאַחַת יִבְעֲרוּ וְיִכְסָלוּ מוּסַר הֲבָלִים עֵץ הוּא:

ט כֶּסֶף מְרֻקָּע מִתַּרְשִׁישׁ יוּבָא וְזָהָב מֵאוּפָז מַעֲשֵׂה חָרָשׁ וִידֵי צוֹרֵף תְּכֵלֶת וְאַרְגָּמָן לְבוּשָׁם מַעֲשֵׂה חֲכָמִים כֻּלָּם:

---

to know and understand God's ways. As *Rambam* writes, this knowledge will motivate the person to seek God's true delights: Loving-kindness, justice, and right- eousness. In this way, righteous people will imitate *Hashem*'s ways.

Yirmiyahu/Jeremiah
Chapter 10

ירמיהו
פרק י

10 But *Hashem* is truly God: He is a living God, The everlasting King. At His wrath, the earth quakes, And nations cannot endure His rage.

וַיהוָה אֱלֹהִים אֱמֶת הוּא־אֱלֹהִים חַיִּים וּמֶלֶךְ עוֹלָם מִקִּצְפּוֹ תִּרְעַשׁ הָאָרֶץ וְלֹא־יָכִלוּ גוֹיִם זַעְמוֹ:

va-do-NAI e-lo-HEEM e-MET hu e-lo-HEEM kha-YEEM u-ME-lekh o-LAM mi-kitz-PO tir-ASH ha-A-retz v'-lo ya-KHI-lu go-YIM za-MO

11 Thus shall you say to them: Let the gods, who did not make heaven and earth, perish from the earth and from under these heavens.

כִּדְנָה תֵּאמְרוּן לְהוֹם אֱלָהַיָּא דִּי־שְׁמַיָּא וְאַרְקָא לָא עֲבַדוּ יֵאבַדוּ מֵאַרְעָא וּמִן־תְּחוֹת שְׁמַיָּא אֵלֶּה:

12 He made the earth by His might, Established the world by His wisdom, And by His understanding stretched out the skies.

עֹשֵׂה אֶרֶץ בְּכֹחוֹ מֵכִין תֵּבֵל בְּחָכְמָתוֹ וּבִתְבוּנָתוֹ נָטָה שָׁמָיִם:

13 When He makes His voice heard, There is a rumbling of water in the skies; He makes vapors rise from the end of the earth, He makes lightning for the rain, And brings forth wind from His treasuries.

לְקוֹל תִּתּוֹ הֲמוֹן מַיִם בַּשָּׁמַיִם וַיַּעֲלֶה נְשִׂאִים מִקְצֵה ארץ [הָאָרֶץ] בְּרָקִים לַמָּטָר עָשָׂה וַיּוֹצֵא רוּחַ מֵאֹצְרֹתָיו:

14 Every man is proved dull, without knowledge; Every goldsmith is put to shame because of the idol For his molten image is a deceit – There is no breath in them.

נִבְעַר כָּל־אָדָם מִדַּעַת הֹבִישׁ כָּל־צוֹרֵף מִפָּסֶל כִּי שֶׁקֶר נִסְכּוֹ וְלֹא־רוּחַ בָּם:

15 They are delusion, a work of mockery; In their hour of doom, they shall perish.

הֶבֶל הֵמָּה מַעֲשֵׂה תַּעְתֻּעִים בְּעֵת פְּקֻדָּתָם יֹאבֵדוּ:

16 Not like these is the Portion of *Yaakov*; For it is He who formed all things, And *Yisrael* is His very own tribe: Lord of Hosts is His name.

לֹא־כְאֵלֶּה חֵלֶק יַעֲקֹב כִּי־יוֹצֵר הַכֹּל הוּא וְיִשְׂרָאֵל שֵׁבֶט נַחֲלָתוֹ יְהוָה צְבָאוֹת שְׁמוֹ:

17 Gather up your bundle from the ground, You who dwell under siege!

אִסְפִּי מֵאֶרֶץ כִּנְעָתֵךְ ישבתי [יֹשֶׁבֶת] בַּמָּצוֹר:

18 For thus said *Hashem*: I will fling away the inhabitants of the land this time: I will harass them so that they shall feel it.

כִּי־כֹה אָמַר יְהוָה הִנְנִי קוֹלֵעַ אֶת־יוֹשְׁבֵי הָאָרֶץ בַּפַּעַם הַזֹּאת וַהֲצֵרוֹתִי לָהֶם לְמַעַן יִמְצָאוּ:

19 Woe unto me for my hurt, My wound is severe! I thought, "This is but a sickness And I must bear it."

אוֹי לִי עַל־שִׁבְרִי נַחְלָה מַכָּתִי וַאֲנִי אָמַרְתִּי אַךְ זֶה חֳלִי וְאֶשָּׂאֶנּוּ:

ה׳
אלוי

10:10 But *Hashem* is truly God *Hashem* has many names in the Bible, each representing a distinct divine attribute. In his book of sermons, *I Submit*, Rabbi David Stavsky explains the difference between the two divine names mentioned in this verse. Commenting on the words *Hashem Hu Ha-Elokim* (ה׳ הוא האלהים) (I Kings 18:39), 'But *Hashem* is truly God,' Rabbi Stavsky uncovers a deeper lesson behind the use of these two names together. "The word *Hashem* (Lord) means *rachamim*, 'mercy,' 'kindness,' 'forgiveness.' The word *Elokim* (God) means *midat hadin*, 'the God of judgement.' At first, judgment seems harsh, cruel, punishing. But, no, we say they are together '*Hashem Hu Ha-Elokim*.' In the *Elokim*, in the judgment, there is, was, and always will be *Hashem*. He is not just a God of judgment – for in His judgment is compassion and kindness – may we merit to understand it."

Rabbi David Stavsky (1930–2004)

Yirmiyahu/Jeremiah
Chapter 11

20 My tents are ravaged, All my tent cords are broken. My children have gone forth from me And are no more; No one is left to stretch out my tent And hang my tent cloths.

21 For the shepherds are dull And did not seek *Hashem*; Therefore they have not prospered And all their flock is scattered.

22 Hark, a noise! It is coming, A great commotion out of the north, That the towns of *Yehuda* may be made a desolation, A haunt of jackals.

23 I know, *Hashem*, that man's road is not his [to choose], That man, as he walks, cannot direct his own steps.

24 Chastise me, *Hashem*, but in measure; Not in Your wrath, lest You reduce me to naught.

25 Pour out Your wrath on the nations who have not heeded You, Upon the clans that have not invoked Your name. For they have devoured *Yaakov*, Have devoured and consumed him, And have laid desolate his homesteads.

sh'-FOKH kha-ma-t'-KHA al ha-go-YIM a-SHER lo y'-da-U-kha v'-AL mish-pa-KHOT a-SHER b'-shim-KHA LO ka-RA-u kee a-kh'-LU et ya-a-KOV va-a-kha-LU-hu vai-kha-LU-hu v'-et na-VAY-hu hay-SHA-mu

11

1 The word which came to *Yirmiyahu* from *Hashem*:

2 "Hear the terms of this covenant, and recite them to the men of *Yehuda* and the inhabitants of *Yerushalayim*!

3 And say to them, Thus said *Hashem*, the God of *Yisrael*: Cursed be the man who will not obey the terms of this covenant,

---

10:25 Pour out Your wrath on the nations who have not heeded You In chapter 10, *Yirmiyahu* mocks the futility of idolatry, and describes how the northern country, Babylonia, would turn the land of *Yehuda* into a desolate place that would be home for jackals. He concludes, however, with a plea for justice. If Israel is to be destroyed, then other nations who engaged in evil and violence should also be punished. Their attacks on Israel were motivated by hatred and vindictiveness, and they too should face *Hashem*'s anger. This verse is recited on *Pesach* night during the *Seder* meal, when Jews remember the deliverance from Egypt and pray for the final redemption.

Yirmiyahu/Jeremiah
Chapter 11

4 which I enjoined upon your fathers when I freed them from the land of Egypt, the iron crucible, saying, 'Obey Me and observe them, just as I command you, that you may be My people and I may be your God' –

5 in order to fulfill the oath which I swore to your fathers, to give them a land flowing with milk and honey, as is now the case." And I responded, "*Amen, Hashem*."

6 And *Hashem* said to me, "Proclaim all these things through the towns of *Yehuda* and the streets of *Yerushalayim*: Hear the terms of this covenant, and perform them.

7 For I have repeatedly and persistently warned your fathers from the time I brought them out of Egypt to this day, saying: Obey My commands.

8 But they would not listen or give ear; they all followed the willfulness of their evil hearts. So I have brought upon them all the terms of this covenant, because they did not do what I commanded them to do."

9 *Hashem* said to me, "A conspiracy exists among the men of *Yehuda* and the inhabitants of *Yerushalayim*.

10 They have returned to the iniquities of their fathers of old, who refused to heed My words. They, too, have followed other gods and served them. The House of *Yisrael* and the House of *Yehuda* have broken the covenant that I made with their fathers."

11 Assuredly, thus said *Hashem*: I am going to bring upon them disaster from which they will not be able to escape. Then they will cry out to me, but I will not listen to them.

12 And the townsmen of *Yehuda* and the inhabitants of *Yerushalayim* will go and cry out to the gods to which they sacrifice; but they will not be able to rescue them in their time of disaster.

13 For your gods have become as many as your towns, O *Yehuda*, and you have set up as many altars to Shame as there are streets in *Yerushalayim* – altars for sacrifice to Baal.

14 As for you, do not pray for this people, do not raise a cry of prayer on their behalf; for I will not listen when they call to Me on account of their disaster.

ירמיהו
פרק יא

ד אֲשֶׁר צִוִּיתִי אֶת־אֲבוֹתֵיכֶם בְּיוֹם הוֹצִיאִי־אוֹתָם מֵאֶרֶץ־מִצְרַיִם מִכּוּר הַבַּרְזֶל לֵאמֹר שִׁמְעוּ בְקוֹלִי וַעֲשִׂיתֶם אוֹתָם כְּכֹל אֲשֶׁר־אֲצַוֶּה אֶתְכֶם וִהְיִיתֶם לִי לְעָם וְאָנֹכִי אֶהְיֶה לָכֶם לֵאלֹהִים:

ה לְמַעַן הָקִים אֶת־הַשְּׁבוּעָה אֲשֶׁר־ נִשְׁבַּעְתִּי לַאֲבוֹתֵיכֶם לָתֵת לָהֶם אֶרֶץ זָבַת חָלָב וּדְבַשׁ כַּיּוֹם הַזֶּה וָאַעַן וָאֹמַר אָמֵן יְהוָה:

ו וַיֹּאמֶר יְהוָה אֵלַי קְרָא אֶת־כָּל־הַדְּבָרִים הָאֵלֶּה בְּעָרֵי יְהוּדָה וּבְחֻצוֹת יְרוּשָׁלָ͏ִם לֵאמֹר שִׁמְעוּ אֶת־דִּבְרֵי הַבְּרִית הַזֹּאת וַעֲשִׂיתֶם אוֹתָם:

ז כִּי הָעֵד הַעִדֹתִי בַּאֲבוֹתֵיכֶם בְּיוֹם הַעֲלוֹתִי אוֹתָם מֵאֶרֶץ מִצְרַיִם וְעַד־ הַיּוֹם הַזֶּה הַשְׁכֵּם וְהָעֵד לֵאמֹר שִׁמְעוּ בְּקוֹלִי:

ח וְלֹא שָׁמְעוּ וְלֹא־הִטּוּ אֶת־אָזְנָם וַיֵּלְכוּ אִישׁ בִּשְׁרִירוּת לִבָּם הָרָע וָאָבִיא עֲלֵיהֶם אֶת־כָּל־דִּבְרֵי הַבְּרִית־הַזֹּאת אֲשֶׁר־צִוִּיתִי לַעֲשׂוֹת וְלֹא עָשׂוּ:

ט וַיֹּאמֶר יְהוָה אֵלָי נִמְצָא־קֶשֶׁר בְּאִישׁ יְהוּדָה וּבְיֹשְׁבֵי יְרוּשָׁלָ͏ִם:

י שָׁבוּ עַל־עֲוֺנֹת אֲבוֹתָם הָרִאשֹׁנִים אֲשֶׁר מֵאֲנוּ לִשְׁמוֹעַ אֶת־דְּבָרַי וְהֵמָּה הָלְכוּ אַחֲרֵי אֱלֹהִים אֲחֵרִים לְעָבְדָם הֵפֵרוּ בֵית־יִשְׂרָאֵל וּבֵית יְהוּדָה אֶת־בְּרִיתִי אֲשֶׁר כָּרַתִּי אֶת־אֲבוֹתָם:

יא לָכֵן כֹּה אָמַר יְהוָה הִנְנִי מֵבִיא אֲלֵיהֶם רָעָה אֲשֶׁר לֹא־יוּכְלוּ לָצֵאת מִמֶּנָּה וְזָעֲקוּ אֵלַי וְלֹא אֶשְׁמַע אֲלֵיהֶם:

יב וְהָלְכוּ עָרֵי יְהוּדָה וְיֹשְׁבֵי יְרוּשָׁלָ͏ִם וְזָעֲקוּ אֶל־הָאֱלֹהִים אֲשֶׁר הֵם מְקַטְּרִים לָהֶם וְהוֹשֵׁעַ לֹא־יוֹשִׁיעוּ לָהֶם בְּעֵת רָעָתָם:

יג כִּי מִסְפַּר עָרֶיךָ הָיוּ אֱלֹהֶיךָ יְהוּדָה וּמִסְפַּר חֻצוֹת יְרוּשָׁלַ͏ִם שַׂמְתֶּם מִזְבְּחוֹת לַבֹּשֶׁת מִזְבְּחוֹת לְקַטֵּר לַבָּעַל:

יד וְאַתָּה אַל־תִּתְפַּלֵּל בְּעַד־הָעָם הַזֶּה וְאַל־תִּשָּׂא בַעֲדָם רִנָּה וּתְפִלָּה כִּי אֵינֶנִּי שֹׁמֵעַ בְּעֵת קָרְאָם אֵלַי בְּעַד רָעָתָם:

Yirmiyahu/Jeremiah
Chapter 11

ירמיהו
פרק יא

15 Why should My beloved be in My House, Who executes so many vile designs? The sacral flesh will pass away from you, For you exult while performing your evil deeds.

טו מֶה לִידִידִי בְּבֵיתִי עֲשׂוֹתָהּ הַמְזִמָּתָה הָרַבִּים וּבְשַׂר־קֹדֶשׁ יַעַבְרוּ מֵעָלָיִךְ כִּי רָעָתֵכִי אָז תַּעֲלֹזִי:

16 *Hashem* named you "Verdant olive tree, Fair, with choice fruit." But with a great roaring sound He has set it on fire, And its boughs are broken.

טז זַיִת רַעֲנָן יְפֵה פְרִי־תֹאַר קָרָא יְהֹוָה שְׁמֵךְ לְקוֹל ׀ הֲמוּלָּה גְדֹלָה הִצִּית אֵשׁ עָלֶיהָ וְרָעוּ דָּלִיּוֹתָיו:

ZA-yit ra-a-NAN y'-FAY f'-ree TO-ar ka-RA a-do-NAI sh'-MAYKH l'-KOL ha-mu-LAH g'-do-LAH hi-TZEET AYSH a-LE-ha v'-ra-U da-li-yo-TAV

17 The Lord of Hosts, who planted you, has decreed disaster for you, because of the evil wrought by the House of *Yisrael* and the House of *Yehuda*, who angered Me by sacrificing to Baal.

יז וַיהֹוָה צְבָאוֹת הַנּוֹטֵעַ אוֹתָךְ דִּבֶּר עָלַיִךְ רָעָה בִּגְלַל רָעַת בֵּית־יִשְׂרָאֵל וּבֵית יְהוּדָה אֲשֶׁר עָשׂוּ לָהֶם לְהַכְעִסֵנִי לְקַטֵּר לַבָּעַל:

18 *Hashem* informed me, and I knew – Then You let me see their deeds.

יח וַיהֹוָה הוֹדִיעַנִי וָאֵדָעָה אָז הִרְאִיתַנִי מַעַלְלֵיהֶם:

19 For I was like a docile lamb Led to the slaughter; I did not realize That it was against me They fashioned their plots: "Let us destroy the tree with its fruit, Let us cut him off from the land of the living. That his name be remembered no more!"

יט וַאֲנִי כְּכֶבֶשׂ אַלּוּף יוּבַל לִטְבוֹחַ וְלֹא־יָדַעְתִּי כִּי־עָלַי ׀ חָשְׁבוּ מַחֲשָׁבוֹת נַשְׁחִיתָה עֵץ בְּלַחְמוֹ וְנִכְרְתֶנּוּ מֵאֶרֶץ חַיִּים וּשְׁמוֹ לֹא־יִזָּכֵר עוֹד:

20 O Lord of Hosts, O just Judge, Who test the thoughts and the mind, Let me see Your retribution upon them, For I lay my case before You.

כ וַיהֹוָה צְבָאוֹת שֹׁפֵט צֶדֶק בֹּחֵן כְּלָיוֹת וָלֵב אֶרְאֶה נִקְמָתְךָ מֵהֶם כִּי אֵלֶיךָ גִּלִּיתִי אֶת־רִיבִי:

21 Assuredly, thus said the Lord of Hosts concerning the men of *Anatot* who seek your life and say, "You must not prophesy any more in the name of *Hashem*, or you will die by our hand" –

כא לָכֵן כֹּה־אָמַר יְהֹוָה עַל־אַנְשֵׁי עֲנָתוֹת הַמְבַקְשִׁים אֶת־נַפְשְׁךָ לֵאמֹר לֹא תִנָּבֵא בְּשֵׁם יְהֹוָה וְלֹא תָמוּת בְּיָדֵנוּ:

22 Assuredly, thus said the Lord of Hosts: "I am going to deal with them: the young men shall die by the sword, their boys and girls shall die by famine.

כב לָכֵן כֹּה אָמַר יְהֹוָה צְבָאוֹת הִנְנִי פֹקֵד עֲלֵיהֶם הַבַּחוּרִים יָמֻתוּ בַחֶרֶב בְּנֵיהֶם וּבְנוֹתֵיהֶם יָמֻתוּ בָּרָעָב:

23 No remnant shall be left of them, for I will bring disaster on the men of *Anatot*, the year of their doom."

כג וּשְׁאֵרִית לֹא תִהְיֶה לָהֶם כִּי־אָבִיא רָעָה אֶל־אַנְשֵׁי עֲנָתוֹת שְׁנַת פְּקֻדָּתָם:

Olive tree on Mount Tavor

11:16 Verdant olive tree The first time the olive tree is mentioned in the Bible is when *Noach* checks to see if the flood waters have receded. When the dove returns with an olive branch in its mouth, *Noach* knows that the water has receded sufficiently and life has begun anew (Genesis 8:11, 21). Pure olive oil was also used for the lighting of the golden *menorah* lamp in the *Beit Hamikdash*, as well as to anoint priests and kings as part of their initiation. One lesson we can take from the olive is that just like an olive yields oil only when pressed, so too, as human beings, when we are pressed between the millstones of life, our best selves emerge. Often, we rise to the occasion to meet life's tests only when challenged.

Yirmiyahu/Jeremiah
Chapter 12

ירמיהו
פרק יב

יב 1 You will win, *Hashem*, if I make claim against You, Yet I shall present charges against You: Why does the way of the wicked prosper? Why are the workers of treachery at ease?

א צַדִּיק אַתָּה יְהֹוָה כִּי אָרִיב אֵלֶיךָ אַךְ מִשְׁפָּטִים אֲדַבֵּר אוֹתָךְ מַדּוּעַ דֶּרֶךְ רְשָׁעִים צָלֵחָה שָׁלוּ כָּל־בֹּגְדֵי בָגֶד:

2 You have planted them, and they have taken root, They spread, they even bear fruit. You are present in their mouths, But far from their thoughts.

ב נְטַעְתָּם גַּם־שֹׁרָשׁוּ יֵלְכוּ גַּם־עָשׂוּ פֶרִי קָרוֹב אַתָּה בְּפִיהֶם וְרָחוֹק מִכִּלְיוֹתֵיהֶם:

3 Yet You, *Hashem*, have noted and observed me; You have tested my heart, and found it with You. Drive them out like sheep to the slaughter, Prepare them for the day of slaying!

ג וְאַתָּה יְהֹוָה יְדַעְתָּנִי תִּרְאֵנִי וּבָחַנְתָּ לִבִּי אִתָּךְ הַתִּקֵם כְּצֹאן לְטִבְחָה וְהַקְדִּשֵׁם לְיוֹם הֲרֵגָה:

4 How long must the land languish, And the grass of all the countryside dry up? Must beasts and birds perish, Because of the evil of its inhabitants, Who say, "He will not look upon our future"?

ד עַד־מָתַי תֶּאֱבַל הָאָרֶץ וְעֵשֶׂב כָּל־הַשָּׂדֶה יִיבָשׁ מֵרָעַת יֹשְׁבֵי־בָהּ סָפְתָה בְהֵמוֹת וָעוֹף כִּי אָמְרוּ לֹא יִרְאֶה אֶת־אַחֲרִיתֵנוּ:

5 If you race with the foot-runners and they exhaust you, How then can you compete with horses? If you are secure only in a tranquil land, How will you fare in the jungle of the *Yarden*?

ה כִּי אֶת־רַגְלִים רַצְתָּה וַיַּלְאוּךָ וְאֵיךְ תְּתַחֲרֶה אֶת־הַסּוּסִים וּבְאֶרֶץ שָׁלוֹם אַתָּה בוֹטֵחַ וְאֵיךְ תַּעֲשֶׂה בִּגְאוֹן הַיַּרְדֵּן:

6 For even your kinsmen and your father's house, Even they are treacherous toward you, They cry after you as a mob. Do not believe them When they speak cordially to you.

ו כִּי גַם־אַחֶיךָ וּבֵית־אָבִיךָ גַּם־הֵמָּה בָּגְדוּ בָךְ גַּם־הֵמָּה קָרְאוּ אַחֲרֶיךָ מָלֵא אַל־תַּאֲמֵן בָּם כִּי־יְדַבְּרוּ אֵלֶיךָ טוֹבוֹת:

7 I have abandoned My House, I have deserted My possession, I have given over My dearly beloved Into the hands of her enemies.

ז עָזַבְתִּי אֶת־בֵּיתִי נָטַשְׁתִּי אֶת־נַחֲלָתִי נָתַתִּי אֶת־יְדִדוּת נַפְשִׁי בְּכַף אֹיְבֶיהָ:

8 My own people acted toward Me Like a lion in the forest; She raised her voice against Me – Therefore I have rejected her.

ח הָיְתָה־לִּי נַחֲלָתִי כְּאַרְיֵה בַיָּעַר נָתְנָה עָלַי בְּקוֹלָהּ עַל־כֵּן שְׂנֵאתִיהָ:

9 My own people acts toward Me Like a bird of prey [or] a hyena; Let the birds of prey surround her! Go, gather all the wild beasts, Bring them to devour!

ט הַעַיִט צָבוּעַ נַחֲלָתִי לִי הַעַיִט סָבִיב עָלֶיהָ לְכוּ אִסְפוּ כָּל־חַיַּת הַשָּׂדֶה הֵתָיוּ לְאָכְלָה:

10 Many shepherds have destroyed My vineyard, Have trampled My field, Have made My delightful field A desolate wilderness.

י רֹעִים רַבִּים שִׁחֲתוּ כַרְמִי בֹּסְסוּ אֶת־חֶלְקָתִי נָתְנוּ אֶת־חֶלְקַת חֶמְדָּתִי לְמִדְבַּר שְׁמָמָה:

11 They have made her a desolation; Desolate, she pours out grief to Me. The whole land is laid desolate, But no man gives it thought.

יא שָׂמָהּ לִשְׁמָמָה אָבְלָה עָלַי שְׁמֵמָה נָשַׁמָּה כָּל־הָאָרֶץ כִּי אֵין אִישׁ שָׂם עַל־לֵב:

12 Spoilers have come Upon all the bare heights of the wilderness. For a sword of *Hashem* devours From one end of the land to the other; No flesh is safe.

יב עַל־כָּל־שְׁפָיִם בַּמִּדְבָּר בָּאוּ שֹׁדְדִים כִּי חֶרֶב לַיהֹוָה אֹכְלָה מִקְצֵה־אֶרֶץ וְעַד־קְצֵה הָאָרֶץ אֵין שָׁלוֹם לְכָל־בָּשָׂר:

Yirmiyahu/Jeremiah
Chapter 13

13 They have sown wheat and reaped thorns, They have endured pain to no avail. Be shamed, then, by your harvest – By the blazing wrath of *Hashem*!

14 Thus said *Hashem*: As for My wicked neighbors who encroach on the heritage that I gave to My people *Yisrael* – I am going to uproot them from their soil, and I will uproot the House of *Yehuda* out of the midst of them.

> KOH a-MAR a-do-NAI al kol sh'-khay-NAI ha-ra-EEM ha-no-g'-EEM ba-na-kha-LAH a-sher hin-KHAL-tee et a-MEE et yis-ra-AYL hi-n'-NEE no-t'-SHAM may-AL ad-ma-TAM v'-et BAYT y'-hu-DAH e-TOSH mi-to-KHAM

15 Then, after I have uprooted them, I will take them back into favor, and restore them each to his own inheritance and his own land.

16 And if they learn the ways of My people, to swear by My name – "As *Hashem* lives" – just as they once taught My people to swear by Baal, then they shall be built up in the midst of My people.

17 But if they do not give heed, I will tear out that nation, tear it out and destroy it – declares *Hashem*.

13

1 Thus *Hashem* said to me: "Go buy yourself a loincloth of linen, and put it around your loins, but do not dip it into water."

2 So I bought the loincloth in accordance with *Hashem*'s command, and put it about my loins.

3 And the word of *Hashem* came to me a second time:

4 "Take the loincloth which you bought, which is about your loins, and go at once to Perath and cover it up there in a cleft of the rock."

5 I went and buried it at Perath, as *Hashem* had commanded me.

6 Then, after a long time, *Hashem* said to me, "Go at once to Perath and take there the loincloth which I commanded you to bury there."

12:14 As for My wicked neighbors Through their actions, the nations have violated the heritage which *Hashem* designated for His people, namely, *Eretz Yisrael*. These evil nations will therefore be uprooted from their land and sent into exile. God will then uproot *Yehuda* from among them, and replant them in safety and security in the Land of Israel. By calling Ammon and Moab "My wicked neighbors," *Hashem* explicitly identifies Himself as one with the People of Israel – their enemies are His enemies.

Yirmiyahu/Jeremiah
Chapter 13

ירמיהו
פרק יג

7 So I went to Perath and dug up the loincloth from the place where I had buried it; and found the loincloth ruined; it was not good for anything.

ז וָאֵלֵךְ פְּרָתָה וָאֶחְפֹּר וָאֶקַּח אֶת־הָאֵזוֹר מִן־הַמָּקוֹם אֲשֶׁר־טְמַנְתִּיו שָׁמָּה וְהִנֵּה נִשְׁחַת הָאֵזוֹר לֹא יִצְלַח לַכֹּל׃

8 The word of *Hashem* came to me:

ח וַיְהִי דְבַר־יְהֹוָה אֵלַי לֵאמֹר׃

9 Thus said *Hashem*: Even so will I ruin the overweening pride of *Yehuda* and *Yerushalayim*.

ט כֹּה אָמַר יְהֹוָה כָּכָה אַשְׁחִית אֶת־גְּאוֹן יְהוּדָה וְאֶת־גְּאוֹן יְרוּשָׁלַםִ הָרָב׃

10 This wicked people who refuse to heed My bidding, who follow the willfulness of their own hearts, who follow other gods and serve them and worship them, shall become like that loincloth, which is not good for anything.

י הָעָם הַזֶּה הָרָע הַמֵּאֲנִים לִשְׁמוֹעַ אֶת־דְּבָרַי הַהֹלְכִים בִּשְׁרִרוּת לִבָּם וַיֵּלְכוּ אַחֲרֵי אֱלֹהִים אֲחֵרִים לְעָבְדָם וּלְהִשְׁתַּחֲוֺת לָהֶם וִיהִי כָּאֵזוֹר הַזֶּה אֲשֶׁר לֹא־יִצְלַח לַכֹּל׃

11 For as the loincloth clings close to the loins of a man, so I brought close to Me the whole House of *Yisrael* and the whole House of *Yehuda* – declares *Hashem* – that they might be My people, for fame, and praise, and splendor. But they would not obey.

יא כִּי כַּאֲשֶׁר יִדְבַּק הָאֵזוֹר אֶל־מָתְנֵי־אִישׁ כֵּן הִדְבַּקְתִּי אֵלַי אֶת־כָּל־בֵּית יִשְׂרָאֵל וְאֶת־כָּל־בֵּית יְהוּדָה נְאֻם־יְהֹוָה לִהְיוֹת לִי לְעָם וּלְשֵׁם וְלִתְהִלָּה וּלְתִפְאָרֶת וְלֹא שָׁמֵעוּ׃

12 And speak this word to them: Thus said *Hashem*, the God of *Yisrael*: "Every jar should be filled with wine." And when they say to you, "Don't we know that every jar should be filled with wine?"

יב וְאָמַרְתָּ אֲלֵיהֶם אֶת־הַדָּבָר הַזֶּה כֹּה־אָמַר יְהֹוָה אֱלֹהֵי יִשְׂרָאֵל כָּל־נֵבֶל יִמָּלֵא יָיִן וְאָמְרוּ אֵלֶיךָ הֲיָדֹעַ לֹא נֵדַע כִּי כָל־נֵבֶל יִמָּלֵא יָיִן׃

v'-a-mar-TA a-lay-HEM et ha-da-VAR ha-ZEH koh a-MAR a-do-NAI e-lo-HAY yis-ra-AYL kol NAY-vel yi-MA-lay YA-yin va'-a-m'-RU ay-LE-kha ha-ya-DO-a LO nay-DA kee khol NAY-vel yi-MA-lay YA-yin

13 say to them, "Thus said *Hashem*: I am going to fill with drunkenness all the inhabitants of this land, and the kings who sit on the throne of *David*, and the *Kohanim* and the *Neviim*, and all the inhabitants of *Yerushalayim*.

יג וְאָמַרְתָּ אֲלֵיהֶם כֹּה־אָמַר יְהֹוָה הִנְנִי מְמַלֵּא אֶת־כָּל־יֹשְׁבֵי הָאָרֶץ הַזֹּאת וְאֶת־הַמְּלָכִים הַיֹּשְׁבִים לְדָוִד עַל־כִּסְאוֹ וְאֶת־הַכֹּהֲנִים וְאֶת־הַנְּבִיאִים וְאֵת כָּל־יֹשְׁבֵי יְרוּשָׁלָםִ שִׁכָּרוֹן׃

14 And I will smash them one against the other, parents and children alike – declares *Hashem*; no pity, compassion, or mercy will stop Me from destroying them."

יד וְנִפַּצְתִּים אִישׁ אֶל־אָחִיו וְהָאָבוֹת וְהַבָּנִים יַחְדָּו נְאֻם־יְהֹוָה לֹא־אֶחְמוֹל וְלֹא־אָחוּס וְלֹא אֲרַחֵם מֵהַשְׁחִיתָם׃

15 Attend and give ear; be not haughty, For *Hashem* has spoken.

טו שִׁמְעוּ וְהַאֲזִינוּ אַל־תִּגְבָּהוּ כִּי יְהֹוָה דִּבֵּר׃

13:12 Every jar should be filled with wine According to *Radak*, the metaphor of the jars filled with wine symbolizes the Israelites whose minds will be so preoccupied with the afflictions that will befall them, it will be as if they are intoxicated. In verse 13, *Yirmiyahu* clarifies that no one will be immune from punishment, and even the leadership of the people – the kings, princes, and prophets – will be punished. The wine imagery is particularly poignant, since *Yehuda* is associated with wine; *Yaakov* blessed his son *Yehuda* that he should be so rich that he will wash his garments in wine (Genesis 49:11). To this day, the hilly area of *Yehuda* south of *Yerushalayim* is internationally renowned for its bountiful vineyards.

Vineyard in Yehuda

Yirmiyahu/Jeremiah
Chapter 14

16 Give honor to *Hashem* your God Before He brings darkness, Before your feet stumble On the mountains in shadow – When you hope for light, And it is turned to darkness And becomes deep gloom.

17 For if you will not give heed, My inmost self must weep, Because of your arrogance; My eye must stream and flow With copious tears, Because the flock of *Hashem* Is taken captive.

18 Say to the king and the queen mother, "Sit in a lowly spot; For your diadems are abased, Your glorious crowns."

19 The cities of the *Negev* are shut, There is no one to open them; *Yehuda* is exiled completely, All of it exiled.

20 Raise your eyes and behold Those who come from the north: Where are the sheep entrusted to you, The flock you took pride in?

21 What will you say when they appoint as your heads Those among you whom you trained to be tame? Shall not pangs seize you Like a woman in childbirth?

22 And when you ask yourself, "Why have these things befallen me?" It is because of your great iniquity That your skirts are lifted up, Your limbs exposed.

23 Can the Cushite change his skin, Or the leopard his spots? Just as much can you do good, Who are practiced in doing evil!

24 So I will scatter you like straw that flies Before the desert wind.

25 This shall be your lot, Your measured portion from Me – declares *Hashem*. Because you forgot Me And trusted in falsehood,

26 I in turn will lift your skirts over your face And your shame shall be seen.

27 I behold your adulteries, Your lustful neighing, Your unbridled depravity, your vile acts On the hills of the countryside. Woe to you, O *Yerushalayim*, Who will not be clean! How much longer shall it be?

14 1 The word of *Hashem* which came to *Yirmiyahu* concerning the droughts.

Yirmiyahu/Jeremiah
Chapter 14

ירמיהו
פרק יד

2 *Yehuda* is in mourning, Her settlements languish. Men are bowed to the ground, And the outcry of *Yerushalayim* rises.

ב אָבְלָה יְהוּדָה וּשְׁעָרֶיהָ אֻמְלְלוּ קָדְרוּ לָאָרֶץ וְצִוְחַת יְרוּשָׁלַ͏ִם עָלָתָה׃

3 Their nobles sent their servants for water; They came to the cisterns, they found no water. They returned, their vessels empty. They are shamed and humiliated, They cover their heads.

ג וְאַדִּרֵיהֶם שָׁלְחוּ צעוריהם [צְעִירֵיהֶם] לַמָּיִם בָּאוּ עַל־גֵּבִים לֹא־מָצְאוּ מַיִם שָׁבוּ כְלֵיהֶם רֵיקָם בֹּשׁוּ וְהָכְלְמוּ וְחָפוּ רֹאשָׁם׃

4 Because of the ground there is dismay, For there has been no rain on the earth. The plowmen are shamed, They cover their heads.

ד בַּעֲבוּר הָאֲדָמָה חַתָּה כִּי לֹא־הָיָה גֶשֶׁם בָּאָרֶץ בֹּשׁוּ אִכָּרִים חָפוּ רֹאשָׁם׃

5 Even the hind in the field Forsakes her new-born fawn, Because there is no grass.

ה כִּי גַם־אַיֶּלֶת בַּשָּׂדֶה יָלְדָה וְעָזוֹב כִּי לֹא־הָיָה דֶּשֶׁא׃

6 And the wild asses stand on the bare heights, Snuffing the air like jackals; Their eyes pine, Because there is no herbage.

ו וּפְרָאִים עָמְדוּ עַל־שְׁפָיִם שָׁאֲפוּ רוּחַ כַּתַּנִּים כָּלוּ עֵינֵיהֶם כִּי־אֵין עֵשֶׂב׃

7 Though our iniquities testify against us, Act, *Hashem*, for the sake of Your name; Though our rebellions are many And we have sinned against You.

ז אִם־עֲוֺנֵינוּ עָנוּ בָנוּ יְהֹוָה עֲשֵׂה לְמַעַן שְׁמֶךָ כִּי־רַבּוּ מְשׁוּבֹתֵינוּ לְךָ חָטָאנוּ׃

im a-vo-NAY-nu A-nu VA-nu a-do-NAI a-SAY l'-MA-an sh'-ME-kha kee ra-BU m'-shu-vo-TAY-nu l'-KHA kha-TA-nu

8 O Hope of *Yisrael*, Its deliverer in time of trouble, Why are You like a stranger in the land, Like a traveler who stops only for the night?

ח מִקְוֵה יִשְׂרָאֵל מוֹשִׁיעוֹ בְּעֵת צָרָה לָמָּה תִהְיֶה כְּגֵר בָּאָרֶץ וּכְאֹרֵחַ נָטָה לָלוּן׃

9 Why are You like a man who is stunned, Like a warrior who cannot give victory? Yet You are in our midst, *Hashem*, And Your name is attached to us – Do not forsake us!

ט לָמָּה תִהְיֶה כְּאִישׁ נִדְהָם כְּגִבּוֹר לֹא־יוּכַל לְהוֹשִׁיעַ וְאַתָּה בְקִרְבֵּנוּ יְהֹוָה וְשִׁמְךָ עָלֵינוּ נִקְרָא אַל־תַּנִּחֵנוּ׃

10 Thus said *Hashem* concerning this people: "Truly, they love to stray, they have not restrained their feet; so *Hashem* has no pleasure in them. Now He will recall their iniquity and punish their sin."

י כֹּה־אָמַר יְהֹוָה לָעָם הַזֶּה כֵּן אָהֲבוּ לָנוּעַ רַגְלֵיהֶם לֹא חָשָׂכוּ וַיהֹוָה לֹא רָצָם עַתָּה יִזְכֹּר עֲוֺנָם וְיִפְקֹד חַטֹּאתָם׃

11 And *Hashem* said to me, "Do not pray for the benefit of this people.

יא וַיֹּאמֶר יְהֹוָה אֵלָי אַל־תִּתְפַּלֵּל בְּעַד־הָעָם הַזֶּה לְטוֹבָה׃

14:7 We have sinned against You This chapter contains a prophecy to *Yirmiyahu* "concerning the droughts" (verse 1). Due to lack of water, neither people nor animals have enough to eat or drink, and therefore *Yehuda* is in a state of mourning. Since Israel is a land with few rivers and lakes, it is dependent on rain from Heaven for its subsistence. As such, *Sefer Devarim* (11:11–12) states that *Eretz Yisrael* "soaks up its water from the rains of heaven. It is a land which *Hashem* your God looks after, on which *Hashem* your God always keeps His eye." Because the Israelites are dependent on *Hashem* for their water, the amount of rain that falls is reflective of the relationship between the people and their Creator. Droughts are sent to encourage Israel to repent and to reevaluate their relationship with God. The lack of water at this time is indicative of the fact that the people have sinned against *Hashem*.

Yirmiyahu/Jeremiah
Chapter 14

12 When they fast, I will not listen to their outcry; and when they present burnt offering and meal offering, I will not accept them. I will exterminate them by war, famine, and disease."

13 I said, "Ah, *Hashem*! The *Neviim* are saying to them, 'You shall not see the sword, famine shall not come upon you, but I will give you unfailing security in this place.'"

14 *Hashem* replied: It is a lie that the *Neviim* utter in My name. I have not sent them or commanded them. I have not spoken to them. A lying vision, an empty divination, the deceit of their own contriving – that is what they prophesy to you!

15 Assuredly, thus said *Hashem* concerning the *Neviim* who prophesy in My name though I have not sent them, and who say, "Sword and famine shall not befall this land"; those very *Neviim* shall perish by sword and famine.

16 And the people to whom they prophesy shall be left lying in the streets of *Yerushalayim* because of the famine and the sword, with none to bury them – they, their wives, their sons, and their daughters. I will pour out upon them [the requital of] their wickedness.

17 And do you speak to them thus: Let my eyes run with tears, Day and night let them not cease, For my hapless people has suffered A grievous injury, a very painful wound.

18 If I go out to the country – Lo, the slain of the sword. If I enter the city – Lo, those who are sick with famine. Both *Kohen* and *Navi* roam the land, They know not where.

19 Have You, then, rejected *Yehuda*? Have You spurned *Tzion*? Why have You smitten us So that there is no cure? Why do we hope for happiness, But find no good; For a time of healing, And meet terror instead?

20 We acknowledge our wickedness, *Hashem* – The iniquity of our fathers – For we have sinned against You.

21 For Your name's sake, do not disown us; Do not dishonor Your glorious throne. Remember, do not annul Your covenant with us.

Yirmiyahu/Jeremiah
Chapter 15

22 Can any of the false gods of the nations give rain? Can the skies of themselves give showers? Only You can, *Hashem* our God! So we hope in You, For only You made all these things.

הֲיֵשׁ בְּהַבְלֵי הַגּוֹיִם מַגְשִׁמִים וְאִם־הַשָּׁמַיִם יִתְּנוּ רְבִבִים הֲלֹא אַתָּה־הוּא יְהֹוָה אֱלֹהֵינוּ וּנְקַוֶּה־לָּךְ כִּי־אַתָּה עָשִׂיתָ אֶת־כָּל־אֵלֶּה׃

15 1 *Hashem* said to me, "Even if *Moshe* and *Shmuel* were to intercede with Me, I would not be won over to that people. Dismiss them from My presence, and let them go forth!

וַיֹּאמֶר יְהֹוָה אֵלַי אִם־יַעֲמֹד מֹשֶׁה וּשְׁמוּאֵל לְפָנַי אֵין נַפְשִׁי אֶל־הָעָם הַזֶּה שַׁלַּח מֵעַל־פָּנַי וְיֵצֵאוּ׃

va-YO-mer a-do-NAI ay-LAI im ya-a-MOD mo-SHEH ush-mu-AYL l'-fa-NAI AYN naf-SHEE el ha-AM ha-ZEH sha-LAKH may-al pa-NAI v'-yay-TZAY-u

2 And if they ask you, 'To what shall we go forth?' answer them, 'Thus said *Hashem*: Those destined for the plague, to the plague; Those destined for the sword, to the sword; Those destined for famine, to famine; Those destined for captivity, to captivity.

3 And I will appoint over them four kinds [of punishment] – declares *Hashem* – the sword to slay, the dogs to drag, the birds of the sky, and the beasts of the earth to devour and destroy.

4 I will make them a horror to all the kingdoms of the earth, on account of King *Menashe* son of *Chizkiyahu* of *Yehuda*, and of what he did in *Yerushalayim*.'"

5 But who will pity you, O *Yerushalayim*, Who will console you? Who will turn aside to inquire About your welfare?

6 You cast Me off – declares *Hashem* – You go ever backward. So I have stretched out My hand to destroy you; I cannot relent.

7 I will scatter them as with a winnowing fork Through the settlements of the earth. I will bereave, I will destroy My people, For they would not turn back from their ways.

15:1 Even if *Moshe* and *Shmuel* were to intercede with Me Announcing four causes of destruction that await Israel (death, sword, famine and captivity), *Yirmiyahu* declares that even the prayers of *Moshe* and *Shmuel* would not be able to save the people. Rashi explains that both *Moshe* and *Shmuel* were able to induce Israel to repent, before they stood in front of *Hashem* to intercede on the people's behalf and ask for mercy. However, God declares, since *Yirmiyahu* was not successful in influencing the people to change their ways, his prayers are ineffective. Without repentance, even the prayers of *Moshe* and *Shmuel*, which had been accepted in the past, would not be successful at this time.

Yirmiyahu/Jeremiah
Chapter 15

ירמיהו
פרק טו

8 Their widows shall be more numerous Than the sands of the seas. I will bring against them – Young men and mothers together – A destroyer at noonday. I will bring down suddenly upon them Alarm and terror.

ח עָצְמוּ־לִי אַלְמְנֹתָו מֵחוֹל יַמִּים הֵבֵאתִי לָהֶם עַל־אֵם בָּחוּר שֹׁדֵד בַּצׇּהֳרָיִם הִפַּלְתִּי עָלֶיהָ פִּתְאֹם עִיר וּבֶהָלוֹת:

9 She who bore seven is forlorn, Utterly disconsolate; Her sun has set while it is still day, She is shamed and humiliated. The remnant of them I will deliver to the sword, To the power of their enemies – declares *Hashem*.

ט אֻמְלְלָה יֹלֶדֶת הַשִּׁבְעָה נָפְחָה נַפְשָׁהּ בָּאה [בָּא] שִׁמְשָׁהּ בְּעֹד יוֹמָם בּוֹשָׁה וְחָפֵרָה וּשְׁאֵרִיתָם לַחֶרֶב אֶתֵּן לִפְנֵי אֹיְבֵיהֶם נְאֻם־יְהֹוָה:

10 Woe is me, my mother, that you ever bore me – A man of conflict and strife with all the land! I have not lent, And I have not borrowed; Yet everyone curses me.

י אוֹי־לִי אִמִּי כִּי יְלִדְתִּנִי אִישׁ רִיב וְאִישׁ מָדוֹן לְכׇל־הָאָרֶץ לֹא־נָשִׁיתִי וְלֹא־נָשׁוּ־בִי כֻּלֹּה מְקַלְלַוְנִי:

11 *Hashem* said: Surely, a mere remnant of you Will I spare for a better fate! By the enemy from the north* In a time of distress and a time of disaster, Surely, I will have you struck down!

יא אָמַר יְהֹוָה אִם־לֹא שרותך [שֵׁרִיתִיךָ] לְטוֹב אִם־לוֹא ׀ הִפְגַּעְתִּי בְךָ בְּעֵת־רָעָה וּבְעֵת צָרָה אֶת־הָאֹיֵב:

12 Can iron break iron and bronze?

יב הֲיָרֹעַ בַּרְזֶל ׀ בַּרְזֶל מִצָּפוֹן וּנְחֹשֶׁת:

13 I will hand over your wealth and your treasures As a spoil, free of charge, Because of all your sins throughout your territory.

יג חֵילְךָ וְאוֹצְרוֹתֶיךָ לָבַז אֶתֵּן לֹא בִמְחִיר וּבְכׇל־חַטֹּאותֶיךָ וּבְכׇל־גְּבוּלֶיךָ:

14 And I will bring your enemies By way of a land you have not known. For a fire has flared in My wrath, It blazes against you.

יד וְהַעֲבַרְתִּי אֶת־אֹיְבֶיךָ בְּאֶרֶץ לֹא יָדָעְתָּ כִּי־אֵשׁ קָדְחָה בְאַפִּי עֲלֵיכֶם תּוּקָד:

15 *Hashem*, you know – Remember me and take thought of me, Avenge me on those who persecute me; Do not yield to Your patience, Do not let me perish! Consider how I have borne insult On Your account.

טו אַתָּה יָדַעְתָּ יְהֹוָה זׇכְרֵנִי וּפׇקְדֵנִי וְהִנָּקֶם לִי מֵרֹדְפַי אַל־לְאֶרֶךְ אַפְּךָ תִּקָּחֵנִי דַּע שְׂאֵתִי עָלֶיךָ חֶרְפָּה:

16 When Your words were offered, I devoured them; Your word brought me the delight and joy Of knowing that Your name is attached to me, *Hashem*, the L<small>ORD</small> of Hosts.

טז נִמְצְאוּ דְבָרֶיךָ וָאֹכְלֵם וַיְהִי דבריך [דְבָרְךָ] לִי לְשָׂשׂוֹן וּלְשִׂמְחַת לְבָבִי כִּי־נִקְרָא שִׁמְךָ עָלַי יְהֹוָה אֱלֹהֵי צְבָאוֹת:

17 I have not sat in the company of revelers And made merry! I have sat lonely because of Your hand upon me, For You have filled me with gloom.

יז לֹא־יָשַׁבְתִּי בְסוֹד־מְשַׂחֲקִים וָאֶעְלֹז מִפְּנֵי יָדְךָ בָּדָד יָשַׁבְתִּי כִּי־זַעַם מִלֵּאתָנִי:

18 Why must my pain be endless, My wound incurable, Resistant to healing? You have been to me like a spring that fails, Like waters that cannot be relied on.

יח לָמָּה הָיָה כְאֵבִי נֶצַח וּמַכָּתִי אֲנוּשָׁה מֵאֲנָה הֵרָפֵא הָיוֹ תִהְיֶה לִי כְּמוֹ אַכְזָב מַיִם לֹא נֶאֱמָנוּ:

---

* "from the north" brought up from verse 12 for clarity

Yirmiyahu/Jeremiah
Chapter 16

19 Assuredly, thus said *Hashem*: If you turn back, I shall take you back And you shall stand before Me; If you produce what is noble Out of the worthless, You shall be My spokesman. They shall come back to you, Not you to them.

20 Against this people I will make you As a fortified wall of bronze: They will attack you But they shall not overcome you, For I am with you to deliver and save you – declares *Hashem*.

21 I will save you from the hands of the wicked And rescue you from the clutches of the violent.

16

1 The word of *Hashem* came to me:

2 You are not to marry and not to have sons and daughters in this place.

3 For thus said *Hashem* concerning any sons and daughters that may be born in this place, and concerning the mothers who bear them, and concerning the fathers who beget them in this land:

4 They shall die gruesome deaths. They shall not be lamented or buried; they shall be like dung on the surface of the ground. They shall be consumed by the sword and by famine, and their corpses shall be food for the birds of the sky and the beasts of the earth.

5 For thus said *Hashem*: Do not enter a house of mourning, Do not go to lament and to condole with them; For I have withdrawn My favor from that people – declares *Hashem* – My kindness and compassion.

6 Great and small alike shall die in this land, They shall not be buried; men shall not lament them, Nor gash and tonsure themselves for them.

7 They shall not break bread for a mourner To comfort him for a bereavement, Nor offer one a cup of consolation For the loss of his father or mother.

8 Nor shall you enter a house of feasting, To sit down with them to eat and drink.

9 For thus said the Lord of Hosts, the God of *Yisrael*: I am going to banish from this place, in your days and before your eyes, the sound of mirth and gladness, the voice of bridegroom and bride.

ירמיהו
פרק טז

יט לָכֵן כֹּה־אָמַר יְהוָה אִם־תָּשׁוּב וַאֲשִׁיבְךָ לְפָנַי תַּעֲמֹד וְאִם־תּוֹצִיא יָקָר מִזּוֹלֵל כְּפִי תִהְיֶה יָשֻׁבוּ הֵמָּה אֵלֶיךָ וְאַתָּה לֹא־תָשׁוּב אֲלֵיהֶם:

כ וּנְתַתִּיךָ לָעָם הַזֶּה לְחוֹמַת נְחֹשֶׁת בְּצוּרָה וְנִלְחֲמוּ אֵלֶיךָ וְלֹא־יוּכְלוּ לָךְ כִּי־אִתְּךָ אֲנִי לְהוֹשִׁיעֲךָ וּלְהַצִּילֶךָ נְאֻם־יְהוָה:

כא וְהִצַּלְתִּיךָ מִיַּד רָעִים וּפְדִתִיךָ מִכַּף עָרִצִים:

טז א וַיְהִי דְבַר־יְהוָה אֵלַי לֵאמֹר:

ב לֹא־תִקַּח לְךָ אִשָּׁה וְלֹא־יִהְיוּ לְךָ בָּנִים וּבָנוֹת בַּמָּקוֹם הַזֶּה:

ג כִּי־כֹה ׀ אָמַר יְהוָה עַל־הַבָּנִים וְעַל־הַבָּנוֹת הַיִּלּוֹדִים בַּמָּקוֹם הַזֶּה וְעַל־אִמֹּתָם הַיֹּלְדוֹת אוֹתָם וְעַל־אֲבוֹתָם הַמּוֹלִדִים אוֹתָם בָּאָרֶץ הַזֹּאת:

ד מְמוֹתֵי תַחֲלֻאִים יָמֻתוּ לֹא יִסָּפְדוּ וְלֹא יִקָּבֵרוּ לְדֹמֶן עַל־פְּנֵי הָאֲדָמָה יִהְיוּ וּבַחֶרֶב וּבָרָעָב יִכְלוּ וְהָיְתָה נִבְלָתָם לְמַאֲכָל לְעוֹף הַשָּׁמַיִם וּלְבֶהֱמַת הָאָרֶץ:

ה כִּי־כֹה ׀ אָמַר יְהוָה אַל־תָּבוֹא בֵּית מַרְזֵחַ וְאַל־תֵּלֵךְ לִסְפּוֹד וְאַל־תָּנֹד לָהֶם כִּי־אָסַפְתִּי אֶת־שְׁלוֹמִי מֵאֵת הָעָם־הַזֶּה נְאֻם־יְהוָה אֶת־הַחֶסֶד וְאֶת־הָרַחֲמִים:

ו וּמֵתוּ גְדֹלִים וּקְטַנִּים בָּאָרֶץ הַזֹּאת לֹא יִקָּבֵרוּ וְלֹא־יִסְפְּדוּ לָהֶם וְלֹא יִתְגֹּדַד וְלֹא יִקָּרֵחַ לָהֶם:

ז וְלֹא־יִפְרְסוּ לָהֶם עַל־אֵבֶל לְנַחֲמוֹ עַל־מֵת וְלֹא־יַשְׁקוּ אוֹתָם כּוֹס תַּנְחוּמִים עַל־אָבִיו וְעַל־אִמּוֹ:

ח וּבֵית־מִשְׁתֶּה לֹא־תָבוֹא לָשֶׁבֶת אוֹתָם לֶאֱכֹל וְלִשְׁתּוֹת:

ט כִּי כֹה אָמַר יְהוָה צְבָאוֹת אֱלֹהֵי יִשְׂרָאֵל הִנְנִי מַשְׁבִּית מִן־הַמָּקוֹם הַזֶּה לְעֵינֵיכֶם וּבִימֵיכֶם קוֹל שָׂשׂוֹן וְקוֹל שִׂמְחָה קוֹל חָתָן וְקוֹל כַּלָּה:

1112

Yirmiyahu/Jeremiah
Chapter 16

ירמיהו
פרק טז

10 And when you announce all these things to that people, and they ask you, "Why has *Hashem* decreed upon us all this fearful evil? What is the iniquity and what the sin that we have committed against *Hashem* our God?"

י וְהָיָה כִּי תַגִּיד לָעָם הַזֶּה אֵת כָּל־הַדְּבָרִים הָאֵלֶּה וְאָמְרוּ אֵלֶיךָ עַל־מֶה דִבֶּר יְהֹוָה עָלֵינוּ אֵת כָּל־הָרָעָה הַגְּדוֹלָה הַזֹּאת וּמֶה עֲוֺנֵנוּ וּמֶה חַטָּאתֵנוּ אֲשֶׁר חָטָאנוּ לַיהֹוָה אֱלֹהֵינוּ׃

11 say to them, "Because your fathers deserted Me – declares *Hashem* – and followed other gods and served them and worshiped them; they deserted Me and did not keep My Instruction.

יא וְאָמַרְתָּ אֲלֵיהֶם עַל אֲשֶׁר־עָזְבוּ אֲבוֹתֵיכֶם אוֹתִי נְאֻם־יְהֹוָה וַיֵּלְכוּ אַחֲרֵי אֱלֹהִים אֲחֵרִים וַיַּעַבְדוּם וַיִּשְׁתַּחֲווּ לָהֶם וְאֹתִי עָזָבוּ וְאֶת־תּוֹרָתִי לֹא שָׁמָרוּ׃

12 And you have acted worse than your fathers, every one of you following the willfulness of his evil heart and paying no heed to Me.

יב וְאַתֶּם הֲרֵעֹתֶם לַעֲשׂוֹת מֵאֲבוֹתֵיכֶם וְהִנְּכֶם הֹלְכִים אִישׁ אַחֲרֵי שְׁרִרוּת לִבּוֹ־הָרָע לְבִלְתִּי שְׁמֹעַ אֵלָי׃

13 Therefore I will hurl you out of this land to a land that neither you nor your fathers have known, and there you will serve other gods, day and night; for I will show you no mercy."

יג וְהֵטַלְתִּי אֶתְכֶם מֵעַל הָאָרֶץ הַזֹּאת עַל־הָאָרֶץ אֲשֶׁר לֹא יְדַעְתֶּם אַתֶּם וַאֲבוֹתֵיכֶם וַעֲבַדְתֶּם־שָׁם אֶת־אֱלֹהִים אֲחֵרִים יוֹמָם וָלַיְלָה אֲשֶׁר לֹא־אֶתֵּן לָכֶם חֲנִינָה׃

14 Assuredly, a time is coming – declares *Hashem* – when it shall no more be said, "As *Hashem* lives who brought the Israelites out of the land of Egypt,"

יד לָכֵן הִנֵּה־יָמִים בָּאִים נְאֻם־יְהֹוָה וְלֹא־יֵאָמֵר עוֹד חַי־יְהֹוָה אֲשֶׁר הֶעֱלָה אֶת־בְּנֵי יִשְׂרָאֵל מֵאֶרֶץ מִצְרָיִם׃

15 but rather, "As *Hashem* lives who brought the Israelites out of the northland, and out of all the lands to which He had banished them." For I will bring them back to their land, which I gave to their fathers.

טו כִּי אִם־חַי־יְהֹוָה אֲשֶׁר הֶעֱלָה אֶת־בְּנֵי יִשְׂרָאֵל מֵאֶרֶץ צָפוֹן וּמִכֹּל הָאֲרָצוֹת אֲשֶׁר הִדִּיחָם שָׁמָּה וַהֲשִׁבֹתִים עַל־אַדְמָתָם אֲשֶׁר נָתַתִּי לַאֲבוֹתָם׃

KEE im khai a-do-NAI a-SHER he-e-LAH et b'-NAY yis-ra-AYL may-E-retz tza-FON u-mi-KOL ha-a-ra-TZOT a-SHER hi-dee-KHAM SHA-mah va-ha-shi-vo-TEEM al ad-ma-TAM a-SHER na-TA-tee la-a-vo-TAM

16 Lo, I am sending for many fishermen – declares *Hashem* – And they shall haul them out; And after that I will send for many hunters, And they shall hunt them Out of every mountain and out of every hill And out of the clefts of the rocks.

טז הִנְנִי שֹׁלֵחַ לְדַוָּגִים [לְדַיָּגִים] רַבִּים נְאֻם־יְהֹוָה וְדִיגוּם וְאַחֲרֵי־כֵן אֶשְׁלַח לְרַבִּים צַיָּדִים וְצָדוּם מֵעַל כָּל־הַר וּמֵעַל כָּל־גִּבְעָה וּמִנְּקִיקֵי הַסְּלָעִים׃

Malbim (1809–1879)

16:15 For I will bring them back to their land Yirmiyahu interrupts a description of death and exile with an uplifting message of consolation, declaring that *Hashem* will bring the Children of Israel back from captivity to their land. He declares that the salvation from the future exile will be so great that it will overshadow the past miracles of the exodus from Egypt. According to *Malbim*, the future redemption will stand out from the first, since it will return the Nation of Israel to the land they had already inherited, occupied and enjoyed. The joy of returning to their land will be even greater in their eyes than the miracles of the redemption from Egypt. This is a powerful message with great relevance in our generation: The miracle of the State of Israel and the extraordinary events we experience today are in fact greater than the exodus.

Yirmiyahu/Jeremiah
Chapter 17

17 For My eyes are on all their ways, They are not hidden from My presence, Their iniquity is not concealed from My sight.

18 I will pay them in full – Nay, doubly for their iniquity and their sins – Because they have defiled My land With the corpses of their abominations, And have filled My own possession With their abhorrent things.

19 *Hashem*, my strength and my stronghold, My refuge in a day of trouble, To You nations shall come From the ends of the earth and say: Our fathers inherited utter delusions, Things that are futile and worthless.

20 Can a man make gods for himself? No-gods are they!

21 Assuredly, I will teach them, Once and for all I will teach them My power and My might. And they shall learn that My name is *Hashem*.

17

1 The guilt of *Yehuda* is inscribed with a stylus of iron, Engraved with an adamant point On the tablet of their hearts, And on the horns of their altars,

2 While their children remember Their altars and sacred posts, By verdant trees, Upon lofty hills.

3 Because of the sin of your shrines Throughout your borders, I will make your rampart a heap in the field, And all your treasures a spoil.

4 You will forfeit, by your own act, The inheritance I have given you; I will make you a slave to your enemies In a land you have never known. For you have kindled the flame of My wrath Which shall burn for all time.

5 Thus said *Hashem*: Cursed is he who trusts in man, Who makes mere flesh his strength, And turns his thoughts from *Hashem*.

6 He shall be like a bush in the desert, Which does not sense the coming of good: It is set in the scorched places of the wilderness, In a barren land without inhabitant.

v'-ha-YAH k'-ar-AR ba-a-ra-VAH v'-LO yir-EH kee ya-VO TOV v'-sha-KHAN kha-ray-REEM ba-mid-BAR E-retz m'-lay-KHAH v'-LO tay-SHAYV

17:6 He shall be like a bush in the desert To illustrate the difference between trusting in *Hashem* and trusting in man, *Yirmiyahu* paints a strong contrast between two vivid images. One who relies on

Yirmiyahu/Jeremiah
Chapter 17

7 Blessed is he who trusts in *Hashem*, Whose trust is *Hashem* alone.

8 He shall be like a tree planted by waters, Sending forth its roots by a stream: It does not sense the coming of heat, Its leaves are ever fresh; It has no care in a year of drought, It does not cease to yield fruit.

9 Most devious is the heart; It is perverse – who can fathom it?

10 I *Hashem* probe the heart, Search the mind – To repay every man according to his ways, With the proper fruit of his deeds.

11 Like a partridge hatching what she did not lay, So is one who amasses wealth by unjust means; In the middle of his life it will leave him, And in the end he will be proved a fool.

12 O Throne of Glory exalted from of old, Our Sacred Shrine!

13 O Hope of *Yisrael*! *Hashem*! All who forsake You shall be put to shame, Those in the land who turn from You Shall be doomed men, For they have forsaken *Hashem*, The Fount of living waters.

14 Heal me, *Hashem*, and let me be healed; Save me, and let me be saved; For You are my glory.

15 See, they say to me: "Where is the prediction of *Hashem*? Let it come to pass!"

16 But I have not evaded Being a shepherd in your service, Nor have I longed for the fatal day. You know the utterances of my lips, They were ever before You.

17 Do not be a cause of dismay to me; You are my refuge in a day of calamity.

ירמיהו
פרק יז

ז בָּרוּךְ הַגֶּבֶר אֲשֶׁר יִבְטַח בַּיהֹוָה וְהָיָה יְהֹוָה מִבְטַחוֹ:

ח וְהָיָה כְּעֵץ ׀ שָׁתוּל עַל־מַיִם וְעַל־יוּבַל יְשַׁלַּח שָׁרָשָׁיו וְלֹא יִרָא [יִרְאֶה] כִּי־יָבֹא חֹם וְהָיָה עָלֵהוּ רַעֲנָן וּבִשְׁנַת בַּצֹּרֶת לֹא יִדְאָג וְלֹא יָמִישׁ מֵעֲשׂוֹת פֶּרִי:

ט עָקֹב הַלֵּב מִכֹּל וְאָנֻשׁ הוּא מִי יֵדָעֶנּוּ:

י אֲנִי יְהֹוָה חֹקֵר לֵב בֹּחֵן כְּלָיוֹת וְלָתֵת לְאִישׁ כדרכו [כִּדְרָכָיו] כִּפְרִי מַעֲלָלָיו:

יא קֹרֵא דָגַר וְלֹא יָלָד עֹשֶׂה עֹשֶׁר וְלֹא בְמִשְׁפָּט בַּחֲצִי יָמָו [יָמָיו] יַעַזְבֶנּוּ וּבְאַחֲרִיתוֹ יִהְיֶה נָבָל:

יב כִּסֵּא כָבוֹד מָרוֹם מֵרִאשׁוֹן מְקוֹם מִקְדָּשֵׁנוּ:

יג מִקְוֵה יִשְׂרָאֵל יְהֹוָה כָּל־עֹזְבֶיךָ יֵבֹשׁוּ יסורי [וְסוּרַי] בָּאָרֶץ יִכָּתֵבוּ כִּי עָזְבוּ מְקוֹר מַיִם־חַיִּים אֶת־יְהֹוָה:

יד רְפָאֵנִי יְהֹוָה וְאֵרָפֵא הוֹשִׁיעֵנִי וְאִוָּשֵׁעָה כִּי תְהִלָּתִי אָתָּה:

טו הִנֵּה־הֵמָּה אֹמְרִים אֵלָי אַיֵּה דְבַר־יְהֹוָה יָבוֹא נָא:

טז וַאֲנִי לֹא־אַצְתִּי ׀ מֵרֹעֶה אַחֲרֶיךָ וְיוֹם אָנוּשׁ לֹא הִתְאַוֵּיתִי אַתָּה יָדָעְתָּ מוֹצָא שְׂפָתַי נֹכַח פָּנֶיךָ הָיָה:

יז אַל־תִּהְיֵה־לִי לִמְחִתָּה מַחֲסִי־אַתָּה בְּיוֹם רָעָה:

ערער
ערירי

man is compared to a small shrub in the barren and rocky desert. The Hebrew name for this plant is *arar* (ערער), similar to the Hebrew word for 'childless,' *areeree* (ערירי), invoking feelings of lifelessness and emptiness. Someone who relies on *Hashem*, however, is likened to a majestic tree with deep roots beside an ever-flowing river, growing tall and whose branches provide shelter from the heat (verse 8). Israel has two choices: They can trust in God and remain secure in their land, flourishing like the tree by the river, or they can cut themselves off from the Divine Presence and choose to be exiled to the wilderness of the *arar*.

Yirmiyahu/Jeremiah
Chapter 17

18 Let my persecutors be shamed, And let not me be shamed; Let them be dismayed, And let not me be dismayed. Bring on them the day of disaster, And shatter them with double destruction.

19 Thus said *Hashem* to me: Go and stand in the People's Gate, by which the kings of *Yehuda* enter and by which they go forth, and in all the gates of *Yerushalayim*,

20 and say to them: Hear the word of *Hashem*, O kings of *Yehuda*, and all *Yehuda*, and all the inhabitants of *Yerushalayim* who enter by these gates!

21 Thus said *Hashem*: Guard yourselves for your own sake against carrying burdens on the *Shabbat* day, and bringing them through the gates of *Yerushalayim*.

22 Nor shall you carry out burdens from your houses on the *Shabbat* day, or do any work, but you shall hallow the *Shabbat* day, as I commanded your fathers.

23 But they would not listen or turn their ear; they stiffened their necks and would not pay heed or accept discipline.

24 If you obey Me – declares *Hashem* – and do not bring in burdens through the gates of this city on the *Shabbat* day, but hallow the *Shabbat* day and do no work on it,

25 then through the gates of this city shall enter kings who sit upon the throne of *David*, with their officers – riding on chariots and horses, they and their officers – and the men of *Yehuda* and the inhabitants of *Yerushalayim*. And this city shall be inhabited for all time.

26 And people shall come from the towns of *Yehuda* and from the environs of *Yerushalayim*, and from the land of *Binyamin*, and from the Shephelah, and from the hill country, and from the *Negev*, bringing burnt offerings and sacrifices, meal offerings and frankincense, and bringing offerings of thanksgiving to the House of *Hashem*.

Yirmiyahu/Jeremiah
Chapter 18

27 But if you do not obey My command to hallow the *Shabbat* day and to carry in no burdens through the gates of *Yerushalayim* on the *Shabbat* day, then I will set fire to its gates; it shall consume the fortresses of *Yerushalayim* and it shall not be extinguished.

18 1 The word which came to *Yirmiyahu* from *Hashem*:

2 "Go down to the house of a potter, and there I will impart My words to you."

3 So I went down to the house of a potter, and found him working at the wheel.

4 And if the vessel he was making was spoiled, as happens to clay in the potter's hands, he would make it into another vessel, such as the potter saw fit to make.

5 Then the word of *Hashem* came to me:

6 O House of *Yisrael*, can I not deal with you like this potter? – says *Hashem*. Just like clay in the hands of the potter, so are you in My hands, O House of *Yisrael*!

7 At one moment I may decree that a nation or a kingdom shall be uprooted and pulled down and destroyed;

8 but if that nation against which I made the decree turns back from its wickedness, I change My mind concerning the punishment I planned to bring on it.

9 At another moment I may decree that a nation or a kingdom shall be built and planted;

10 but if it does what is displeasing to Me and does not obey Me, then I change My mind concerning the good I planned to bestow upon it.

11 And now, say to the men of *Yehuda* and the inhabitants of *Yerushalayim*: Thus said *Hashem*: I am devising disaster for you and laying plans against you. Turn back, each of you, from your wicked ways, and mend your ways and your actions!

12 But they will say, "It is no use. We will keep on following our own plans; each of us will act in the willfulness of his evil heart."

ירמיהו
פרק יח

כז וְאִם־לֹא תִשְׁמְעוּ אֵלַי לְקַדֵּשׁ אֶת־יוֹם הַשַּׁבָּת וּלְבִלְתִּי שְׂאֵת מַשָּׂא וּבֹא בְּשַׁעֲרֵי יְרוּשָׁלַםִ בְּיוֹם הַשַּׁבָּת וְהִצַּתִּי אֵשׁ בִּשְׁעָרֶיהָ וְאָכְלָה אַרְמְנוֹת יְרוּשָׁלָםִ וְלֹא תִכְבֶּה׃

יח א הַדָּבָר אֲשֶׁר הָיָה אֶל־יִרְמְיָהוּ מֵאֵת יְהוָה לֵאמֹר׃

ב קוּם וְיָרַדְתָּ בֵּית הַיּוֹצֵר וְשָׁמָּה אַשְׁמִיעֲךָ אֶת־דְּבָרָי׃

ג וָאֵרֵד בֵּית הַיּוֹצֵר והנהו [וְהִנֵּה־] [הוּא] עֹשֶׂה מְלָאכָה עַל־הָאָבְנָיִם׃

ד וְנִשְׁחַת הַכְּלִי אֲשֶׁר הוּא עֹשֶׂה בַּחֹמֶר בְּיַד הַיּוֹצֵר וְשָׁב וַיַּעֲשֵׂהוּ כְּלִי אַחֵר כַּאֲשֶׁר יָשַׁר בְּעֵינֵי הַיּוֹצֵר לַעֲשׂוֹת׃

ה וַיְהִי דְבַר־יְהוָה אֵלַי לֵאמוֹר׃

ו הֲכַיּוֹצֵר הַזֶּה לֹא־אוּכַל לַעֲשׂוֹת לָכֶם בֵּית יִשְׂרָאֵל נְאֻם־יְהוָה הִנֵּה כַחֹמֶר בְּיַד הַיּוֹצֵר כֵּן־אַתֶּם בְּיָדִי בֵּית יִשְׂרָאֵל׃

ז רֶגַע אֲדַבֵּר עַל־גּוֹי וְעַל־מַמְלָכָה לִנְתוֹשׁ וְלִנְתוֹץ וּלְהַאֲבִיד׃

ח וְשָׁב הַגּוֹי הַהוּא מֵרָעָתוֹ אֲשֶׁר דִּבַּרְתִּי עָלָיו וְנִחַמְתִּי עַל־הָרָעָה אֲשֶׁר חָשַׁבְתִּי לַעֲשׂוֹת לוֹ׃

ט וְרֶגַע אֲדַבֵּר עַל־גּוֹי וְעַל־מַמְלָכָה לִבְנוֹת וְלִנְטֹעַ׃

י וְעָשָׂה הרעה [הָרַע] בְּעֵינַי לְבִלְתִּי שְׁמֹעַ בְּקוֹלִי וְנִחַמְתִּי עַל־הַטּוֹבָה אֲשֶׁר אָמַרְתִּי לְהֵיטִיב אוֹתוֹ׃

יא וְעַתָּה אֱמָר־נָא אֶל־אִישׁ־יְהוּדָה וְעַל־יוֹשְׁבֵי יְרוּשָׁלַםִ לֵאמֹר כֹּה אָמַר יְהוָה הִנֵּה אָנֹכִי יוֹצֵר עֲלֵיכֶם רָעָה וְחֹשֵׁב עֲלֵיכֶם מַחֲשָׁבָה שׁוּבוּ נָא אִישׁ מִדַּרְכּוֹ הָרָעָה וְהֵיטִיבוּ דַרְכֵיכֶם וּמַעַלְלֵיכֶם׃

יב וְאָמְרוּ נוֹאָשׁ כִּי־אַחֲרֵי מַחְשְׁבוֹתֵינוּ נֵלֵךְ וְאִישׁ שְׁרִרוּת לִבּוֹ־הָרָע נַעֲשֶׂה׃

Yirmiyahu/Jeremiah
Chapter 18

ירמיהו
פרק יח

13 Assuredly, thus said *Hashem*: Inquire among the nations: Who has heard anything like this? Maiden *Yisrael* has done A most horrible thing.

לָכֵן כֹּה אָמַר יְהֹוָה שַׁאֲלוּ־נָא בַּגּוֹיִם מִי שָׁמַע כָּאֵלֶּה שַׁעֲרֻרִת עָשְׂתָה מְאֹד בְּתוּלַת יִשְׂרָאֵל׃

14 Does one forsake Lebanon snow From the mountainous rocks? Does one abandon cool water Flowing from afar?

הֲיַעֲזֹב מִצּוּר שָׂדַי שֶׁלֶג לְבָנוֹן אִם־יִנָּתְשׁוּ מַיִם זָרִים קָרִים נוֹזְלִים׃

ha-ya-a-ZOV mi-TZUR sha-DAI SHE-leg l'-va-NON im yi-na-t'-SHU MA-yim za-REEM ka-REEM no-z'-LEEM

15 Yet My people have forgotten Me: They sacrifice to a delusion: They are made to stumble in their ways – The ancient paths – And to walk instead on byways, On a road not built up.

כִּי־שְׁכֵחֻנִי עַמִּי לַשָּׁוְא יְקַטֵּרוּ וַיַּכְשִׁלוּם בְּדַרְכֵיהֶם שְׁבִילֵי עוֹלָם לָלֶכֶת נְתִיבוֹת דֶּרֶךְ לֹא סְלוּלָה׃

16 So their land will become a desolation, An object of hissing for all time. Every passerby will be appalled And will shake his head.

לָשׂוּם אַרְצָם לְשַׁמָּה שְׁרוּקֹת [שְׁרִיקוֹת] עוֹלָם כֹּל עוֹבֵר עָלֶיהָ יִשֹּׁם וְיָנִיד בְּרֹאשׁוֹ׃

17 Like the east wind, I will scatter them Before the enemy. I will look upon their back, not their face, In their day of disaster.

כְּרוּחַ־קָדִים אֲפִיצֵם לִפְנֵי אוֹיֵב עֹרֶף וְלֹא־פָנִים אֶרְאֵם בְּיוֹם אֵידָם׃

18 They said, "Come let us devise a plot against *Yirmiyahu* – for instruction shall not fail from the *Kohen*, nor counsel from the wise, nor oracle from the *Navi*. Come, let us strike him with the tongue, and we shall no longer have to listen to all those words of his."

וַיֹּאמְרוּ לְכוּ וְנַחְשְׁבָה עַל־יִרְמְיָהוּ מַחֲשָׁבוֹת כִּי לֹא־תֹאבַד תּוֹרָה מִכֹּהֵן וְעֵצָה מֵחָכָם וְדָבָר מִנָּבִיא לְכוּ וְנַכֵּהוּ בַלָּשׁוֹן וְאַל־נַקְשִׁיבָה אֶל־כָּל־דְּבָרָיו׃

19 Listen to me, *Hashem* – And take note of what my enemies say!

הַקְשִׁיבָה יְהֹוָה אֵלָי וּשְׁמַע לְקוֹל יְרִיבָי׃

20 Should good be repaid with evil? Yet they have dug a pit for me. Remember how I stood before You To plead in their behalf, To turn Your anger away from them!

הַיְשֻׁלַּם תַּחַת־טוֹבָה רָעָה כִּי־כָרוּ שׁוּחָה לְנַפְשִׁי זְכֹר עָמְדִי לְפָנֶיךָ לְדַבֵּר עֲלֵיהֶם טוֹבָה לְהָשִׁיב אֶת־חֲמָתְךָ מֵהֶם׃

21 Oh, give their children over to famine, Mow them down by the sword. Let their wives be bereaved Of children and husbands, Let their men be struck down by the plague, And their young men be slain in battle by the sword.

לָכֵן תֵּן אֶת־בְּנֵיהֶם לָרָעָב וְהַגִּרֵם עַל־יְדֵי־חֶרֶב וְתִהְיֶנָה נְשֵׁיהֶם שַׁכֻּלוֹת וְאַלְמָנוֹת וְאַנְשֵׁיהֶם יִהְיוּ הֲרֻגֵי מָוֶת בַּחוּרֵיהֶם מֻכֵּי־חֶרֶב בַּמִּלְחָמָה׃

18:14 Does one forsake Lebanon snow from the mountainous rocks? The prophet contrasts the steadfastness of nature with the inconsistency of the Israelites, who change their ways and stumble from one failure to another, astonishing everyone who sees them. This is unlike the snows in Lebanon to Israel's north. There, the summits consistently remain white. Indeed, the snow would disappear if found anywhere else. So too, the natural place of the Jewish people is with *Hashem* in the Land of Israel, but they refuse to remain with Him, and will therefore be scattered.

Yirmiyahu/Jeremiah
Chapter 19

ירמיהו
פרק יט

22 Let an outcry be heard from their houses When You bring sudden marauders against them; For they have dug a pit to trap me, And laid snares for my feet.

כב תִּשָּׁמַע זְעָקָה מִבָּתֵּיהֶם כִּי־תָבִיא עֲלֵיהֶם גְּדוּד פִּתְאֹם כִּי־כָרוּ שִׁיחָה [שׁוּחָה] לְלָכְדֵנִי וּפַחִים טָמְנוּ לְרַגְלָי׃

23 *Hashem*, You know All their plots to kill me. Do not pardon their iniquity, Do not blot out their guilt from Your presence. Let them be made to stumble before You – Act against them in Your hour of wrath!

כג וְאַתָּה יְהֹוָה יָדַעְתָּ אֶת־כָּל־עֲצָתָם עָלַי לַמָּוֶת אַל־תְּכַפֵּר עַל־עֲוֺנָם וְחַטָּאתָם מִלְּפָנֶיךָ אַל־תֶּמְחִי וְהָיוּ [וְיִהְיוּ] מֻכְשָׁלִים לְפָנֶיךָ בְּעֵת אַפְּךָ עֲשֵׂה בָהֶם׃

19

1 Thus said *Hashem*: Go buy a jug of potter's ware. And [take] some of the elders of the people and the *Kohanim*,

יט א כֹּה אָמַר יְהֹוָה הָלוֹךְ וְקָנִיתָ בַקְבֻּק יוֹצֵר חָרֶשׂ וּמִזִּקְנֵי הָעָם וּמִזִּקְנֵי הַכֹּהֲנִים׃

2 and go out to the Valley of Ben-hinnom – at the entrance of the Harsith Gate – and proclaim there the words which I will speak to you.

ב וְיָצָאתָ אֶל־גֵּיא בֶן־הִנֹּם אֲשֶׁר פֶּתַח שַׁעַר הַחַרְסוּת [הַחַרְסִית] וְקָרָאתָ שָּׁם אֶת־הַדְּבָרִים אֲשֶׁר־אֲדַבֵּר אֵלֶיךָ׃

v'-ya-TZA-ta el GAY ven hi-NOM a-SHER PE-takh SHA-ar ha-khar-SEET v'-ka-RA-ta SHAM et ha-d'-va-REEM a-SHER a-da-BAYR ay-LE-kha

3 Say: "Hear the word of *Hashem*, O kings of *Yehuda* and inhabitants of *Yerushalayim*! Thus said the Lord of Hosts, the God of *Yisrael*: I am going to bring such disaster upon this place that the ears of all who hear about it will tingle.

ג וְאָמַרְתָּ שִׁמְעוּ דְבַר־יְהֹוָה מַלְכֵי יְהוּדָה וְיֹשְׁבֵי יְרוּשָׁלָ͏ִם כֹּה־אָמַר יְהֹוָה צְבָאוֹת אֱלֹהֵי יִשְׂרָאֵל הִנְנִי מֵבִיא רָעָה עַל־הַמָּקוֹם הַזֶּה אֲשֶׁר כָּל־שֹׁמְעָהּ תִּצַּלְנָה אָזְנָיו׃

4 For they and their fathers and the kings of *Yehuda* have forsaken Me, and have made this place alien [to Me]; they have sacrificed in it to other gods whom they have not experienced, and they have filled this place with the blood of the innocent.

ד יַעַן אֲשֶׁר עֲזָבֻנִי וַיְנַכְּרוּ אֶת־הַמָּקוֹם הַזֶּה וַיְקַטְּרוּ־בוֹ לֵאלֹהִים אֲחֵרִים אֲשֶׁר לֹא־יְדָעוּם הֵמָּה וַאֲבוֹתֵיהֶם וּמַלְכֵי יְהוּדָה וּמָלְאוּ אֶת־הַמָּקוֹם הַזֶּה דַּם נְקִיִּם׃

5 They have built shrines to Baal, to put their children to the fire as burnt offerings to Baal – which I never commanded, never decreed, and which never came to My mind.

ה וּבָנוּ אֶת־בָּמוֹת הַבַּעַל לִשְׂרֹף אֶת־בְּנֵיהֶם בָּאֵשׁ עֹלוֹת לַבָּעַל אֲשֶׁר לֹא־צִוִּיתִי וְלֹא דִבַּרְתִּי וְלֹא עָלְתָה עַל־לִבִּי׃

6 Assuredly, a time is coming – declares *Hashem* – when this place shall no longer be called Topheth or Valley of Ben-hinnom, but Valley of Slaughter.

ו לָכֵן הִנֵּה־יָמִים בָּאִים נְאֻם־יְהֹוָה וְלֹא־יִקָּרֵא לַמָּקוֹם הַזֶּה עוֹד הַתֹּפֶת וְגֵיא בֶן־הִנֹּם כִּי אִם־גֵּיא הַהֲרֵגָה׃

Valley of Hinnom

19:2 Go out to the Valley of Ben-hinnom *Yirmiyahu* is told to rebuke the people for abandoning *Hashem* and worshipping idols, and to warn them of the harsh punishments that they will suffer as a result. In order to demonstrate to the Israelites the severity of the retribution awaiting them, he is to break a clay flask in front of the elders, their leaders (verse 10).

This display was to take place in the valley of Ben-hinnom, outside the gate of Harsith. Since this valley is where the sinful Israelites worship the false god Baal and offer their children to the fire god Molech (see also Jeremiah 7:31 and 32:35), it is an appropriate place for *Yirmiyahu* to deliver this message. The valley is located just below the walls of Jerusalem's Old City.

Yirmiyahu/Jeremiah
Chapter 20

ירמיהו
פרק כ

7 "And I will frustrate the plans of *Yehuda* and *Yerushalayim* in this place. I will cause them to fall by the sword before their enemies, by the hand of those who seek their lives; and I will give their carcasses as food to the birds of the sky and the beasts of the earth.

ז וּבַקֹּתִי אֶת־עֲצַת יְהוּדָה וִירוּשָׁלַ͏ִם בַּמָּקוֹם הַזֶּה וְהִפַּלְתִּים בַּחֶרֶב לִפְנֵי אֹיְבֵיהֶם וּבְיַד מְבַקְשֵׁי נַפְשָׁם וְנָתַתִּי אֶת־נִבְלָתָם לְמַאֲכָל לְעוֹף הַשָּׁמַיִם וּלְבֶהֱמַת הָאָרֶץ׃

8 And I will make this city an object of horror and hissing; everyone who passes by it will be appalled and will hiss over all its wounds.

ח וְשַׂמְתִּי אֶת־הָעִיר הַזֹּאת לְשַׁמָּה וְלִשְׁרֵקָה כֹּל עֹבֵר עָלֶיהָ יִשֹּׁם וְיִשְׁרֹק עַל־כָּל־מַכֹּתֶהָ׃

9 And I will cause them to eat the flesh of their sons and the flesh of their daughters, and they shall devour one another's flesh – because of the desperate straits to which they will be reduced by their enemies, who seek their life."

ט וְהַאֲכַלְתִּים אֶת־בְּשַׂר בְּנֵיהֶם וְאֵת בְּשַׂר בְּנֹתֵיהֶם וְאִישׁ בְּשַׂר־רֵעֵהוּ יֹאכֵלוּ בְּמָצוֹר וּבְמָצוֹק אֲשֶׁר יָצִיקוּ לָהֶם אֹיְבֵיהֶם וּמְבַקְשֵׁי נַפְשָׁם׃

10 Then you shall smash the jug in the sight of the men who go with you,

י וְשָׁבַרְתָּ הַבַּקְבֻּק לְעֵינֵי הָאֲנָשִׁים הַהֹלְכִים אוֹתָךְ׃

11 and say to them: "Thus said the Lord of Hosts: So will I smash this people and this city, as one smashes a potter's vessel, which can never be mended. And they shall bury in Topheth until no room is left for burying.

יא וְאָמַרְתָּ אֲלֵיהֶם כֹּה־אָמַר יְהֹוָה צְבָאוֹת כָּכָה אֶשְׁבֹּר אֶת־הָעָם הַזֶּה וְאֶת־הָעִיר הַזֹּאת כַּאֲשֶׁר יִשְׁבֹּר אֶת־כְּלִי הַיּוֹצֵר אֲשֶׁר לֹא־יוּכַל לְהֵרָפֵה עוֹד וּבְתֹפֶת יִקְבְּרוּ מֵאֵין מָקוֹם לִקְבּוֹר׃

12 That is what I will do to this place and its inhabitants – declares *Hashem*. I will make this city like Topheth:

יב כֵּן־אֶעֱשֶׂה לַמָּקוֹם הַזֶּה נְאֻם־יְהֹוָה וּלְיוֹשְׁבָיו וְלָתֵת אֶת־הָעִיר הַזֹּאת כְּתֹפֶת׃

13 the houses of *Yerushalayim* and the houses of the kings of *Yehuda* shall be unclean, like that place Topheth – all the houses on the roofs of which offerings were made to the whole host of heaven and libations were poured out to other gods."

יג וְהָיוּ בָּתֵּי יְרוּשָׁלַ͏ִם וּבָתֵּי מַלְכֵי יְהוּדָה כִּמְקוֹם הַתֹּפֶת הַטְּמֵאִים לְכֹל הַבָּתִּים אֲשֶׁר קִטְּרוּ עַל־גַּגֹּתֵיהֶם לְכֹל צְבָא הַשָּׁמַיִם וְהַסֵּךְ נְסָכִים לֵאלֹהִים אֲחֵרִים׃

14 When *Yirmiyahu* returned from Topheth, where *Hashem* had sent him to prophesy, he stood in the court of the House of *Hashem* and said to all the people:

יד וַיָּבֹא יִרְמְיָהוּ מֵהַתֹּפֶת אֲשֶׁר שְׁלָחוֹ יְהֹוָה שָׁם לְהִנָּבֵא וַיַּעֲמֹד בַּחֲצַר בֵּית־יְהֹוָה וַיֹּאמֶר אֶל־כָּל־הָעָם׃

15 "Thus said the Lord of Hosts, the God of *Yisrael*: I am going to bring upon this city and upon all its villages all the disaster which I have decreed against it, for they have stiffened their necks and refused to heed My words."

טו כֹּה־אָמַר יְהֹוָה צְבָאוֹת אֱלֹהֵי יִשְׂרָאֵל הִנְנִי מבי [מֵבִיא] אֶל־הָעִיר הַזֹּאת וְעַל־כָּל־עָרֶיהָ אֵת כָּל־הָרָעָה אֲשֶׁר דִּבַּרְתִּי עָלֶיהָ כִּי הִקְשׁוּ אֶת־עָרְפָּם לְבִלְתִּי שְׁמוֹעַ אֶת־דְּבָרָי׃

20

1 *Pashḥur* son of *Immer*, the *Kohen* who was chief officer of the House of *Hashem*, heard *Yirmiyahu* prophesy these things.

כ א וַיִּשְׁמַע פַּשְׁחוּר בֶּן־אִמֵּר הַכֹּהֵן וְהוּא־פָקִיד נָגִיד בְּבֵית יְהֹוָה אֶת־יִרְמְיָהוּ נִבָּא אֶת־הַדְּבָרִים הָאֵלֶּה׃

2 *Pashḥur* thereupon had *Yirmiyahu* flogged and put in the cell at the Upper *Binyamin* Gate in the House of *Hashem*.

ב וַיַּכֶּה פַשְׁחוּר אֵת יִרְמְיָהוּ הַנָּבִיא וַיִּתֵּן אֹתוֹ עַל־הַמַּהְפֶּכֶת אֲשֶׁר בְּשַׁעַר בִּנְיָמִן הָעֶלְיוֹן אֲשֶׁר בְּבֵית יְהֹוָה׃

Yirmiyahu/Jeremiah
Chapter 20

ירמיהו
פרק כ

3 The next day, Pashhur released *Yirmiyahu* from the cell. But *Yirmiyahu* said to him, "*Hashem* has named you not Pashhur, but Magor-missabib.

ג וַיְהִי מִמׇּחֳרָת וַיֹּצֵא פַשְׁחוּר אֶת־יִרְמְיָהוּ מִן־הַמַּהְפָּכֶת וַיֹּאמֶר אֵלָיו יִרְמְיָהוּ לֹא פַשְׁחוּר קָרָא יְהֹוָה שְׁמֶךָ כִּי אִם־מָגוֹר מִסָּבִיב׃

vai-HEE mi-ma-kho-RAT va-yo-TZAY fash-KHUR et yir-m'-YA-hu min ha-mah-PA-khet va-YO-mer ay-LAV yir-m'-YA-hu LO fash-KHUR ka-RA a-do-NAI sh'-ME-kha KEE im ma-GOR mi-sa-VEEV

4 For thus said *Hashem*: I am going to deliver you and all your friends over to terror: they will fall by the sword of their enemies while you look on. I will deliver all *Yehuda* into the hands of the king of Babylon; he will exile them to Babylon or put them to the sword.

ד כִּי כֹה אָמַר יְהֹוָה הִנְנִי נֹתֶנְךָ לְמָגוֹר לְךָ וּלְכׇל־אֹהֲבֶיךָ וְנָפְלוּ בְּחֶרֶב אֹיְבֵיהֶם וְעֵינֶיךָ רֹאוֹת וְאֶת־כׇּל־יְהוּדָה אֶתֵּן בְּיַד מֶלֶךְ־בָּבֶל וְהִגְלָם בָּבֶלָה וְהִכָּם בֶּחָרֶב׃

5 And I will deliver all the wealth, all the riches, and all the prized possessions of this city, and I will also deliver all the treasures of the kings of *Yehuda* into the hands of their enemies: they shall seize them as plunder and carry them off to Babylon.

ה וְנָתַתִּי אֶת־כׇּל־חֹסֶן הָעִיר הַזֹּאת וְאֶת־כׇּל־יְגִיעָהּ וְאֶת־כׇּל־יְקָרָהּ וְאֵת כׇּל־אוֹצְרוֹת מַלְכֵי יְהוּדָה אֶתֵּן בְּיַד אֹיְבֵיהֶם וּבְזָזוּם וּלְקָחוּם וֶהֱבִיאוּם בָּבֶלָה׃

6 As for you, Pashhur, and all who live in your house, you shall go into captivity. You shall come to Babylon; there you shall die and there you shall be buried, and so shall all your friends to whom you prophesied falsely."

ו וְאַתָּה פַשְׁחוּר וְכֹל יֹשְׁבֵי בֵיתֶךָ תֵּלְכוּ בַּשֶּׁבִי וּבָבֶל תָּבוֹא וְשָׁם תָּמוּת וְשָׁם תִּקָּבֵר אַתָּה וְכׇל־אֹהֲבֶיךָ אֲשֶׁר־נִבֵּאתָ לָהֶם בַּשָּׁקֶר׃

7 You enticed me, *Hashem*, and I was enticed; You overpowered me and You prevailed. I have become a constant laughingstock, Everyone jeers at me.

ז פִּתִּיתַנִי יְהֹוָה וָאֶפָּת חֲזַקְתַּנִי וַתּוּכָל הָיִיתִי לִשְׂחוֹק כׇּל־הַיּוֹם כֻּלֹּה לֹעֵג לִי׃

8 For every time I speak, I must cry out, Must shout, "Lawlessness and rapine!" For the word of *Hashem* causes me Constant disgrace and contempt.

ח כִּי־מִדֵּי אֲדַבֵּר אֶזְעָק חָמָס וָשֹׁד אֶקְרָא כִּי־הָיָה דְבַר־יְהֹוָה לִי לְחֶרְפָּה וּלְקֶלֶס כׇּל־הַיּוֹם׃

9 I thought, "I will not mention Him, No more will I speak in His name" — But [His word] was like a raging fire in my heart, Shut up in my bones; I could not hold it in, I was helpless.

ט וְאָמַרְתִּי לֹא־אֶזְכְּרֶנּוּ וְלֹא־אֲדַבֵּר עוֹד בִּשְׁמוֹ וְהָיָה בְלִבִּי כְּאֵשׁ בֹּעֶרֶת עָצֻר בְּעַצְמֹתָי וְנִלְאֵיתִי כַּלְכֵל וְלֹא אוּכָל׃

20:3 ***Hashem* has named you not Pashhur, but Magor-missabib** In a failed attempt to silence *Yirmiyahu*, Pashhur, an official in the *Beit Hamikdash*, places the prophet in jail. *Yirmiyahu* is not deterred, and defiantly tells Pashhur that his name is *magor-misaviv* (מגור מסביב), 'terror from all sides' (verse 3). This insult has two layers of meaning. It describes the fate that awaits Pashhur, his family and the entire corrupt bureaucracy as described in this verse. But it also describes the tragedy of the situation. The *Beit Hamikdash* is *Hashem*'s home, where peace and tranquility are to dwell. Yet they have turned it into a place of terror, where disagreement is stifled and people live in fear of offending the authorities.

Yirmiyahu/Jeremiah
Chapter 21

ירמיהו
פרק כא

10 I heard the whispers of the crowd – Terror all around: "Inform! Let us inform against him!" All my [supposed] friends Are waiting for me to stumble: "Perhaps he can be entrapped, And we can prevail against him And take our vengeance on him."

י כִּי שָׁמַעְתִּי דִּבַּת רַבִּים מָגוֹר מִסָּבִיב הַגִּידוּ וְנַגִּידֶנּוּ כֹּל אֱנוֹשׁ שְׁלוֹמִי שֹׁמְרֵי צַלְעִי אוּלַי יְפֻתֶּה וְנוּכְלָה לוֹ וְנִקְחָה נִקְמָתֵנוּ מִמֶּנּוּ׃

11 But *Hashem* is with me like a mighty warrior; Therefore my persecutors shall stumble; They shall not prevail and shall not succeed. They shall be utterly shamed With a humiliation for all time, Which shall not be forgotten.

יא וַיהוָה אוֹתִי כְּגִבּוֹר עָרִיץ עַל־כֵּן רֹדְפַי יִכָּשְׁלוּ וְלֹא יֻכָלוּ בֹּשׁוּ מְאֹד כִּי־לֹא הִשְׂכִּילוּ כְּלִמַּת עוֹלָם לֹא תִשָּׁכֵחַ׃

12 O Lord of Hosts, You who test the righteous, Who examine the heart and the mind, Let me see Your retribution upon them, For I lay my case before You.

יב וַיהוָה צְבָאוֹת בֹּחֵן צַדִּיק רֹאֶה כְלָיוֹת וָלֵב אֶרְאֶה נִקְמָתְךָ מֵהֶם כִּי אֵלֶיךָ גִּלִּיתִי אֶת־רִיבִי׃

13 Sing unto *Hashem*, Praise *Hashem*, For He has rescued the needy From the hands of evildoers!

יג שִׁירוּ לַיהוָה הַלְלוּ אֶת־יְהוָה כִּי הִצִּיל אֶת־נֶפֶשׁ אֶבְיוֹן מִיַּד מְרֵעִים׃

14 Accursed be the day That I was born! Let not the day be blessed When my mother bore me!

יד אָרוּר הַיּוֹם אֲשֶׁר יֻלַּדְתִּי בּוֹ יוֹם אֲשֶׁר־יְלָדַתְנִי אִמִּי אַל־יְהִי בָרוּךְ׃

15 Accursed be the man Who brought my father the news And said, "A boy Is born to you," And gave him such joy!

טו אָרוּר הָאִישׁ אֲשֶׁר בִּשַּׂר אֶת־אָבִי לֵאמֹר יֻלַּד־לְךָ בֵּן זָכָר שַׂמֵּחַ שִׂמֳּחָהוּ׃

16 Let that man become like the cities Which *Hashem* overthrew without relenting! Let him hear shrieks in the morning And battle shouts at noontide –

טז וְהָיָה הָאִישׁ הַהוּא כֶּעָרִים אֲשֶׁר־הָפַךְ יְהוָה וְלֹא נִחָם וְשָׁמַע זְעָקָה בַּבֹּקֶר וּתְרוּעָה בְּעֵת צָהֳרָיִם׃

17 Because he did not kill me before birth So that my mother might be my grave, And her womb big [with me] for all time.

יז אֲשֶׁר לֹא־מוֹתְתַנִי מֵרָחֶם וַתְּהִי־לִי אִמִּי קִבְרִי וְרַחְמָה הֲרַת עוֹלָם׃

18 Why did I ever issue from the womb, To see misery and woe, To spend all my days in shame!

יח לָמָּה זֶּה מֵרֶחֶם יָצָאתִי לִרְאוֹת עָמָל וְיָגוֹן וַיִּכְלוּ בְּבֹשֶׁת יָמָי׃

21 1 The word which came to *Yirmiyahu* from *Hashem*, when King *Tzidkiyahu* sent to him Pashhur son of Malchiah and the *Kohen Tzefanya*, son of Maaseiah, to say,

כא א הַדָּבָר אֲשֶׁר־הָיָה אֶל־יִרְמְיָהוּ מֵאֵת יְהוָה בִּשְׁלֹחַ אֵלָיו הַמֶּלֶךְ צִדְקִיָּהוּ אֶת־פַּשְׁחוּר בֶּן־מַלְכִּיָּה וְאֶת־צְפַנְיָה בֶן־מַעֲשֵׂיָה הַכֹּהֵן לֵאמֹר׃

2 "Please inquire of *Hashem* on our behalf, for King Nebuchadrezzar of Babylon is attacking us. Perhaps *Hashem* will act for our sake in accordance with all His wonders, so that [Nebuchadrezzar] will withdraw from us."

ב דְּרָשׁ־נָא בַעֲדֵנוּ אֶת־יְהוָה כִּי נְבוּכַדְרֶאצַּר מֶלֶךְ־בָּבֶל נִלְחָם עָלֵינוּ אוּלַי יַעֲשֶׂה יְהוָה אוֹתָנוּ כְּכָל־נִפְלְאֹתָיו וְיַעֲלֶה מֵעָלֵינוּ׃

3 *Yirmiyahu* answered them, "Thus shall you say to *Tzidkiyahu*:

ג וַיֹּאמֶר יִרְמְיָהוּ אֲלֵיהֶם כֹּה תֹאמְרֻן אֶל־צִדְקִיָּהוּ׃

Yirmiyahu / Jeremiah
Chapter 21

ירמיהו
פרק כא

4 Thus said *Hashem*, the God of *Yisrael*: I am going to turn around the weapons in your hands with which you are battling outside the wall against those who are besieging you – the king of Babylon and the Chaldeans – and I will take them into the midst of this city;

ד כֹּה־אָמַר יְהֹוָה אֱלֹהֵי יִשְׂרָאֵל הִנְנִי מֵסֵב אֶת־כְּלֵי הַמִּלְחָמָה אֲשֶׁר בְּיֶדְכֶם אֲשֶׁר אַתֶּם נִלְחָמִים בָּם אֶת־מֶלֶךְ בָּבֶל וְאֶת־הַכַּשְׂדִּים הַצָּרִים עֲלֵיכֶם מִחוּץ לַחוֹמָה וְאָסַפְתִּי אוֹתָם אֶל־תּוֹךְ הָעִיר הַזֹּאת׃

5 and I Myself will battle against you with an outstretched mighty arm, with anger and rage and great wrath.

ה וְנִלְחַמְתִּי אֲנִי אִתְּכֶם בְּיָד נְטוּיָה וּבִזְרוֹעַ חֲזָקָה וּבְאַף וּבְחֵמָה וּבְקֶצֶף גָּדוֹל׃

6 I will strike the inhabitants of this city, man and beast: they shall die by a terrible pestilence.

ו וְהִכֵּיתִי אֶת־יוֹשְׁבֵי הָעִיר הַזֹּאת וְאֶת־הָאָדָם וְאֶת־הַבְּהֵמָה בְּדֶבֶר גָּדוֹל יָמֻתוּ׃

7 And then – declares *Hashem* – I will deliver King *Tzidkiyahu* of *Yehuda* and his courtiers and the people – those in this city who survive the pestilence, the sword, and the famine – into the hands of King Nebuchadrezzar of Babylon, into the hands of their enemies, into the hands of those who seek their lives. He will put them to the sword without pity, without compassion, without mercy.

ז וְאַחֲרֵי־כֵן נְאֻם־יְהֹוָה אֶתֵּן אֶת־צִדְקִיָּהוּ מֶלֶךְ־יְהוּדָה וְאֶת־עֲבָדָיו וְאֶת־הָעָם וְאֶת־הַנִּשְׁאָרִים בָּעִיר הַזֹּאת מִן־הַדֶּבֶר מִן־הַחֶרֶב וּמִן־הָרָעָב בְּיַד נְבוּכַדְרֶאצַּר מֶלֶךְ־בָּבֶל וּבְיַד אֹיְבֵיהֶם וּבְיַד מְבַקְשֵׁי נַפְשָׁם וְהִכָּם לְפִי־חֶרֶב לֹא־יָחוּס עֲלֵיהֶם וְלֹא יַחְמֹל וְלֹא יְרַחֵם׃

8 "And to this people you shall say: Thus said *Hashem*: I set before you the way of life and the way of death.

ח וְאֶל־הָעָם הַזֶּה תֹּאמַר כֹּה אָמַר יְהֹוָה הִנְנִי נֹתֵן לִפְנֵיכֶם אֶת־דֶּרֶךְ הַחַיִּים וְאֶת־דֶּרֶךְ הַמָּוֶת׃

9 Whoever remains in this city shall die by the sword, by famine, and by pestilence; but whoever leaves and goes over to the Chaldeans who are besieging you shall live; he shall at least gain his life.

ט הַיֹּשֵׁב בָּעִיר הַזֹּאת יָמוּת בַּחֶרֶב וּבָרָעָב וּבַדָּבֶר וְהַיּוֹצֵא וְנָפַל עַל־הַכַּשְׂדִּים הַצָּרִים עֲלֵיכֶם [וְחָיָה] יִחְיֶה וְהָיְתָה־לּוֹ נַפְשׁוֹ לְשָׁלָל׃

10 For I have set My face against this city for evil and not for good – declares *Hashem*. It shall be delivered into the hands of the king of Babylon, who will destroy it by fire."

י כִּי שַׂמְתִּי פָנַי בָּעִיר הַזֹּאת לְרָעָה וְלֹא לְטוֹבָה נְאֻם־יְהֹוָה בְּיַד־מֶלֶךְ בָּבֶל תִּנָּתֵן וּשְׂרָפָהּ בָּאֵשׁ׃

11 To the House of the king of *Yehuda*: Hear the word of *Hashem*!

יא וּלְבֵית מֶלֶךְ יְהוּדָה שִׁמְעוּ דְּבַר־יְהֹוָה׃

12 O House of *David*, thus said *Hashem*: Render just verdicts Morning by morning; Rescue him who is robbed From him who defrauded him. Else My wrath will break forth like fire And burn, with none to quench it, Because of your wicked acts.

יב בֵּית דָּוִד כֹּה אָמַר יְהֹוָה דִּינוּ לַבֹּקֶר מִשְׁפָּט וְהַצִּילוּ גָזוּל מִיַּד עוֹשֵׁק פֶּן־תֵּצֵא כָאֵשׁ חֲמָתִי וּבָעֲרָה וְאֵין מְכַבֶּה מִפְּנֵי רֹעַ מַעַלְלֵיהֶם [מַעַלְלֵיכֶם]׃

BAYT da-VID KOH a-MAR a-do-NAI DEE-nu la-BO-ker mish-PAT v'-ha-TZEE-lu ga-ZUL mi-YAD o-SHAYK pen tay-TZAY kha-AYSH kha-ma-TEE u-va-a-RAH v'-AYN m'-kha-BEH mi-p'-NAY RO-a ma-a-l'-lay-KHEM

21:12 Render just verdicts morning by morning In 598 BCE, the new puppet king of *Yehuda*, *Tzidkiyahu*, asks *Yirmiyahu* if the upcoming destruction can be avoided. *Yirmiyahu's* answer, after threatening destruction, reflects the answer of all the prophets. If there is justice and righteousness in *Eretz Yisrael*, it will be safe from

Yirmiyahu/Jeremiah
Chapter 22

ירמיהו
פרק כב

13 I will deal with you, O inhabitants of the valley, O rock of the plain – declares *Hashem* – You who say, "Who can come down against us? Who can get into our lairs?"

יג הִנְנִי אֵלַיִךְ יֹשֶׁבֶת הָעֵמֶק צוּר הַמִּישֹׁר נְאֻם־יְהֹוָה הָאֹמְרִים מִי־יֵחַת עָלֵינוּ וּמִי יָבוֹא בִּמְעוֹנוֹתֵינוּ׃

14 I will punish you according to your deeds – declares *Hashem*. I will set fire to its forest; It shall consume all that is around it.

יד וּפָקַדְתִּי עֲלֵיכֶם כִּפְרִי מַעַלְלֵיכֶם נְאֻם־יְהֹוָה וְהִצַּתִּי אֵשׁ בְּיַעְרָהּ וְאָכְלָה כָּל־סְבִיבֶיהָ׃

22

1 Thus said *Hashem*: Go down to the palace of the king of *Yehuda*, where you shall utter this word.

כב א כֹּה אָמַר יְהֹוָה רֵד בֵּית־מֶלֶךְ יְהוּדָה וְדִבַּרְתָּ שָׁם אֶת־הַדָּבָר הַזֶּה׃

2 Say: "Hear the word of *Hashem*: O king of *Yehuda*, you who sit on the throne of *David*, and your courtiers and your subjects who enter these gates!

ב וְאָמַרְתָּ שְׁמַע דְּבַר־יְהֹוָה מֶלֶךְ יְהוּדָה הַיֹּשֵׁב עַל־כִּסֵּא דָוִד אַתָּה וַעֲבָדֶיךָ וְעַמְּךָ הַבָּאִים בַּשְּׁעָרִים הָאֵלֶּה׃

3 Thus said *Hashem*: Do what is just and right; rescue from the defrauder him who is robbed; do not wrong the stranger, the fatherless, and the widow; commit no lawless act, and do not shed the blood of the innocent in this place.

ג כֹּה ׀ אָמַר יְהֹוָה עֲשׂוּ מִשְׁפָּט וּצְדָקָה וְהַצִּילוּ גָזוּל מִיַּד עָשׁוֹק וְגֵר יָתוֹם וְאַלְמָנָה אַל־תֹּנוּ אַל־תַּחְמֹסוּ וְדָם נָקִי אַל־תִּשְׁפְּכוּ בַּמָּקוֹם הַזֶּה׃

4 For if you fulfill this command, then through the gates of this palace shall enter kings of *David*'s line who sit upon his throne, riding horse-drawn chariots, with their courtiers and their subjects.

ד כִּי אִם־עָשׂוֹ תַּעֲשׂוּ אֶת־הַדָּבָר הַזֶּה וּבָאוּ בְשַׁעֲרֵי הַבַּיִת הַזֶּה מְלָכִים יֹשְׁבִים לְדָוִד עַל־כִּסְאוֹ רֹכְבִים בָּרֶכֶב וּבַסּוּסִים הוּא וַעֲבָדָו [וַעֲבָדָיו] וְעַמּוֹ׃

5 But if you do not heed these commands, I swear by Myself – declares *Hashem* – that this palace shall become a ruin."

ה וְאִם לֹא תִשְׁמְעוּ אֶת־הַדְּבָרִים הָאֵלֶּה בִּי נִשְׁבַּעְתִּי נְאֻם־יְהֹוָה כִּי־לְחׇרְבָּה יִהְיֶה הַבַּיִת הַזֶּה׃

6 For thus said *Hashem* concerning the royal palace of *Yehuda*: You are as *Gilad* to Me, As the summit of Lebanon; But I will make you a desert, Uninhabited towns.

ו כִּי־כֹה ׀ אָמַר יְהֹוָה עַל־בֵּית מֶלֶךְ יְהוּדָה גִּלְעָד אַתָּה לִי רֹאשׁ הַלְּבָנוֹן אִם־לֹא אֲשִׁיתְךָ מִדְבָּר עָרִים לֹא נושבה [נוֹשָׁבוּ]׃

7 I will appoint destroyers against you, Each with his tools; They shall cut down your choicest cedars And make them fall into the fire.

ז וְקִדַּשְׁתִּי עָלֶיךָ מַשְׁחִתִים אִישׁ וְכֵלָיו וְכָרְתוּ מִבְחַר אֲרָזֶיךָ וְהִפִּילוּ עַל־הָאֵשׁ׃

8 And when many nations pass by this city and one man asks another, "Why did *Hashem* do thus to that great city?"

ח וְעָבְרוּ גּוֹיִם רַבִּים עַל הָעִיר הַזֹּאת וְאָמְרוּ אִישׁ אֶל־רֵעֵהוּ עַל־מֶה עָשָׂה יְהֹוָה כָּכָה לָעִיר הַגְּדוֹלָה הַזֹּאת׃

all threats. *Yirmiyahu* emphasizes that this must occur in the morning, since in the ancient world, courts opened at dawn, before the daytime heat became too unbearable. The idea of promoting justice in the land is a theme that appears throughout the Bible. *Hashem* is described as one who "He loves what is right and just" (Psalms 33:5), and it is what He demands of His children as well. It is only through justice and righteousness, therefore, that the People of Israel will merit to remain in the Land of Israel.

Yirmiyahu/Jeremiah
Chapter 22

9 the reply will be, "Because they forsook the covenant with *Hashem* their God and bowed down to other gods and served them."

ט וְאָמְרוּ עַל אֲשֶׁר עָזְבוּ אֶת־בְּרִית יְהֹוָה אֱלֹהֵיהֶם וַיִּשְׁתַּחֲווּ לֵאלֹהִים אֲחֵרִים וַיַּעַבְדוּם׃

10 Do not weep for the dead And do not lament for him; Weep rather for him who is leaving, For he shall never come back To see the land of his birth!

י אַל־תִּבְכּוּ לְמֵת וְאַל־תָּנֻדוּ לוֹ בְּכוּ בָכוֹ לַהֹלֵךְ כִּי לֹא יָשׁוּב עוֹד וְרָאָה אֶת־אֶרֶץ מוֹלַדְתּוֹ׃

11 For thus said *Hashem* concerning *Shalum* son of King *Yoshiyahu* of *Yehuda*, who succeeded his father *Yoshiyahu* as king, but who has gone forth from this place: He shall never come back.

יא כִּי כֹה אָמַר־יְהֹוָה אֶל־שַׁלֻּם בֶּן־יֹאשִׁיָּהוּ מֶלֶךְ יְהוּדָה הַמֹּלֵךְ תַּחַת יֹאשִׁיָּהוּ אָבִיו אֲשֶׁר יָצָא מִן־הַמָּקוֹם הַזֶּה לֹא־יָשׁוּב שָׁם עוֹד׃

12 He shall die in the place to which he was exiled, and he shall not see this land again.

יב כִּי בִּמְקוֹם אֲשֶׁר־הִגְלוּ אֹתוֹ שָׁם יָמוּת וְאֶת־הָאָרֶץ הַזֹּאת לֹא־יִרְאֶה עוֹד׃

13 Ha! he who builds his house with unfairness And his upper chambers with injustice, Who makes his fellow man work without pay And does not give him his wages,

יג הוֹי בֹּנֶה בֵיתוֹ בְּלֹא־צֶדֶק וַעֲלִיּוֹתָיו בְּלֹא מִשְׁפָּט בְּרֵעֵהוּ יַעֲבֹד חִנָּם וּפֹעֲלוֹ לֹא יִתֶּן־לוֹ׃

14 Who thinks: I will build me a vast palace With spacious upper chambers, Provided with windows, Paneled in cedar, Painted with vermilion!

יד הָאֹמֵר אֶבְנֶה־לִּי בֵּית מִדּוֹת וַעֲלִיּוֹת מְרֻוָּחִים וְקָרַע לוֹ חַלּוֹנָי וְסָפוּן בָּאָרֶז וּמָשׁוֹחַ בַּשָּׁשַׁר׃

15 Do you think you are more a king Because you compete in cedar? Your father ate and drank And dispensed justice and equity – Then all went well with him.

טו הֲתִמְלֹךְ כִּי אַתָּה מְתַחֲרֶה בָאָרֶז אָבִיךָ הֲלוֹא אָכַל וְשָׁתָה וְעָשָׂה מִשְׁפָּט וּצְדָקָה אָז טוֹב לוֹ׃

ha-tim-LOKH KEE a-TAH m'-ta-kha-REH va-A-rez a-VEE-kha ha-LO a-KHAL v'-sha-TAH v'-a-SAH mish-PAT utz-da-KAH AZ TOV LO

16 He upheld the rights of the poor and needy – Then all was well. That is truly heeding Me – declares *Hashem*.

טז דָּן דִּין־עָנִי וְאֶבְיוֹן אָז טוֹב הֲלוֹא־הִיא הַדַּעַת אֹתִי נְאֻם־יְהֹוָה׃

17 But your eyes and your mind are only On ill-gotten gains, On shedding the blood of the innocent, On committing fraud and violence.

יז כִּי אֵין עֵינֶיךָ וְלִבְּךָ כִּי אִם־עַל־בִּצְעֶךָ וְעַל דַּם־הַנָּקִי לִשְׁפּוֹךְ וְעַל־הָעֹשֶׁק וְעַל־הַמְּרוּצָה לַעֲשׂוֹת׃

18 Assuredly, thus said *Hashem* concerning *Yehoyakim* son of *Yoshiyahu*, king of *Yehuda*: They shall not mourn for him, "Ah, brother! Ah, sister!" They shall not mourn for him, "Ah, lord! Ah, his majesty!"

יח לָכֵן כֹּה־אָמַר יְהֹוָה אֶל־יְהוֹיָקִים בֶּן־יֹאשִׁיָּהוּ מֶלֶךְ יְהוּדָה לֹא־יִסְפְּדוּ לוֹ הוֹי אָחִי וְהוֹי אָחוֹת לֹא־יִסְפְּדוּ לוֹ הוֹי אָדוֹן וְהוֹי הֹדֹה׃

22:15 Your father ate and drank and dispensed justice and equity *Yirmiyahu* wistfully compares the evil king of *Yehuda*, *Yehoyakim*, with his righteous predecessor, his father King *Yoshiyahu*. *Yehoyakim* misused the throne for his personal benefit at the expense of the poor, building himself new mansions of cedar. *Yoshiyahu* also enjoyed the material comforts of the king's palace, but understood his primary duties, to care for and protect the poor and the needy. *Yirmiyahu* emphasizes that it was precisely because the righteous King *Yoshiyahu* cared for others that he was blessed with success.

Yirmiyahu/Jeremiah
Chapter 23

19 He shall have the burial of an ass, Dragged out and left lying Outside the gates of *Yerushalayim*.

20 Climb Lebanon and cry out, Raise your voice in Bashan, Cry out from Abarim, For all your lovers are crushed.

21 I spoke to you when you were prosperous; You said, "I will not listen." That was your way ever since your youth, You would not heed Me.

22 All your shepherds shall be devoured by the wind, And your lovers shall go into captivity. Then you shall be shamed and humiliated Because of all your depravity.

23 You who dwell in Lebanon, Nestled among the cedars, How much grace will you have When pains come upon you, Travail as in childbirth!

24 As I live – declares *Hashem* – if you, O King Coniah, son of *Yehoyakim*, of *Yehuda*, were a signet on my right hand, I would tear you off even from there.

25 I will deliver you into the hands of those who seek your life, into the hands of those you dread, into the hands of King Nebuchadrezzar of Babylon and into the hands of the Chaldeans.

26 I will hurl you and the mother who bore you into another land, where you were not born; there you shall both die.

27 They shall not return to the land that they yearn to come back to.

28 Is this man Coniah A wretched broken pot, A vessel no one wants? Why are he and his offspring hurled out, And cast away in a land they knew not?

29 O land, land, land, Hear the word of *Hashem*!

30 Thus said *Hashem*: Record this man as without succession, One who shall never be found acceptable; For no man of his offspring shall be accepted To sit on the throne of *David* And to rule again in *Yehuda*.

23

1 Ah, shepherds who let the flock of My pasture stray and scatter! – declares *Hashem*.

Yirmiyahu/Jeremiah
Chapter 23

ירמיהו
פרק כג

2 Assuredly, thus said *Hashem*, the God of *Yisrael*, concerning the shepherds who should tend My people: It is you who let My flock scatter and go astray. You gave no thought to them, but I am going to give thought to you, for your wicked acts – declares *Hashem*.

ב לָכֵן כֹּה־אָמַר יְהֹוָה אֱלֹהֵי יִשְׂרָאֵל עַל־הָרֹעִים הָרֹעִים אֶת־עַמִּי אַתֶּם הֲפִצֹתֶם אֶת־צֹאנִי וַתַּדִּחוּם וְלֹא פְקַדְתֶּם אֹתָם הִנְנִי פֹקֵד עֲלֵיכֶם אֶת־רֹעַ מַעַלְלֵיכֶם נְאֻם־יְהֹוָה:

3 And I Myself will gather the remnant of My flock from all the lands to which I have banished them, and I will bring them back to their pasture, where they shall be fertile and increase.

ג וַאֲנִי אֲקַבֵּץ אֶת־שְׁאֵרִית צֹאנִי מִכֹּל הָאֲרָצוֹת אֲשֶׁר־הִדַּחְתִּי אֹתָם שָׁם וַהֲשִׁבֹתִי אֶתְהֶן עַל־נְוֵהֶן וּפָרוּ וְרָבוּ:

4 And I will appoint over them shepherds who will tend them; they shall no longer fear or be dismayed, and none of them shall be missing – declares *Hashem*.

ד וַהֲקִמֹתִי עֲלֵיהֶם רֹעִים וְרָעוּם וְלֹא־יִירְאוּ עוֹד וְלֹא־יֵחַתּוּ וְלֹא יִפָּקֵדוּ נְאֻם־יְהֹוָה:

5 See, a time is coming – declares *Hashem* – when I will raise up a true branch of *David*'s line. He shall reign as king and shall prosper, and he shall do what is just and right in the land.

ה הִנֵּה יָמִים בָּאִים נְאֻם־יְהֹוָה וַהֲקִמֹתִי לְדָוִד צֶמַח צַדִּיק וּמָלַךְ מֶלֶךְ וְהִשְׂכִּיל וְעָשָׂה מִשְׁפָּט וּצְדָקָה בָּאָרֶץ:

6 In his days *Yehuda* shall be delivered and *Yisrael* shall dwell secure. And this is the name by which he shall be called: "*Hashem* is our Vindicator."

ו בְּיָמָיו תִּוָּשַׁע יְהוּדָה וְיִשְׂרָאֵל יִשְׁכֹּן לָבֶטַח וְזֶה־שְּׁמוֹ אֲשֶׁר־יִקְרְאוֹ יְהֹוָה צִדְקֵנוּ:

b'-ya-MAV ti-va-SHA y'-hu-DAH v'-yis-ra-AYL yish-KON la-VE-takh v'-zeh sh'-MO a-sher yik-r'-U a-do-NAI tzid-KAY-nu

7 Assuredly, a time is coming – declares *Hashem* – when it shall no more be said, "As *Hashem* lives, who brought the Israelites out of the land of Egypt,"

ז לָכֵן הִנֵּה־יָמִים בָּאִים נְאֻם־יְהֹוָה וְלֹא־יֹאמְרוּ עוֹד חַי־יְהֹוָה אֲשֶׁר הֶעֱלָה אֶת־בְּנֵי יִשְׂרָאֵל מֵאֶרֶץ מִצְרָיִם:

8 but rather, "As *Hashem* lives, who brought out and led the offspring of the House of *Yisrael* from the northland and from all the lands to which I have banished them." And they shall dwell upon their own soil.

ח כִּי אִם־חַי־יְהֹוָה אֲשֶׁר הֶעֱלָה וַאֲשֶׁר הֵבִיא אֶת־זֶרַע בֵּית יִשְׂרָאֵל מֵאֶרֶץ צָפוֹנָה וּמִכֹּל הָאֲרָצוֹת אֲשֶׁר הִדַּחְתִּים שָׁם וְיָשְׁבוּ עַל־אַדְמָתָם:

9 Concerning the *Neviim*. My heart is crushed within me, All my bones are trembling; I have become like a drunken man, Like one overcome by wine – Because of *Hashem* and His holy word.

ט לַנְּבִאִים נִשְׁבַּר לִבִּי בְקִרְבִּי רָחֲפוּ כָּל־עַצְמוֹתַי הָיִיתִי כְּאִישׁ שִׁכּוֹר וּכְגֶבֶר עֲבָרוֹ יָיִן מִפְּנֵי יְהֹוָה וּמִפְּנֵי דִּבְרֵי קָדְשׁוֹ:

השם צדקנו

23:6 He shall be called: "*Hashem* is our Vindicator" After comparing the evil leadership of the people to wicked shepherds that cause the sheep to scatter, *Yirmiyahu* describes the ideal leader, a descendant of *David*. In his days, the exiled northern tribes of the kingdom of *Yisrael* will reunite with the kingdom of *Yehuda* and together they will dwell safely in the Land of Israel. The leader will be given the name *Hashem tzidkaynu* (השם צדקנו), '*Hashem* is our Vindicator.' The root of the word *tzidkaynu* is *tzedek* (צדק), 'righteousness,' indicating the ideals through which he will lead the nation. *Yirmiyahu* gives the same name to *Yerushalayim* (33:16), representing the values for which the rebuilt city will be known around the world.

1127

Yirmiyahu/Jeremiah
Chapter 23

10 For the land is full of adulterers, The land mourns because of a curse; The pastures of the wilderness are dried up. For they run to do evil, They strain to do wrong.

11 For both *Navi* and *Kohen* are godless; Even in My House I find their wickedness – declares *Hashem*.

12 Assuredly, Their path shall become Like slippery ground; They shall be thrust into darkness And there they shall fall; For I will bring disaster upon them, The year of their doom – declares *Hashem*.

13 In the *Neviim* of *Shomron* I saw a repulsive thing: They prophesied by Baal And led My people *Yisrael* astray.

14 But what I see in the *Neviim* of *Yerushalayim* Is something horrifying: Adultery and false dealing. They encourage evildoers, So that no one turns back from his wickedness. To Me they are all like Sodom, And [all] its inhabitants like Gomorrah.

15 Assuredly, thus said the Lord of Hosts concerning the *Neviim*: I am going to make them eat wormwood And drink a bitter draft; For from the *Neviim* of *Yerushalayim* Godlessness has gone forth to the whole land.

16 Thus said the Lord of Hosts: Do not listen to the words of the *Neviim* Who prophesy to you. They are deluding you, The prophecies they speak are from their own minds, Not from the mouth of *Hashem*.

17 They declare to men who despise Me: *Hashem* has said: "All shall be well with you"; And to all who follow their willful hearts they say: "No evil shall befall you."

18 But he who has stood in the council of *Hashem*, And seen, and heard His word – He who has listened to His word must obey.

19 Lo, the storm of *Hashem* goes forth in fury, A whirling storm, It shall whirl down upon the heads of the wicked.

20 The anger of *Hashem* shall not turn back Till it has fulfilled and completed His purposes. In the days to come You shall clearly perceive it.

21 I did not send those *Neviim*, But they rushed in; I did not speak to them, Yet they prophesied.

Yirmiyahu/Jeremiah
Chapter 23

22 If they have stood in My council, Let them announce My words to My people And make them turn back From their evil ways and wicked acts.

23 Am I only a *Hashem* near at hand – says *Hashem* – And not a *Hashem* far away?

24 If a man enters a hiding place, Do I not see him? – says *Hashem*. For I fill both heaven and earth – declares *Hashem*.

25 I have heard what the *Neviim* say, who prophesy falsely in My name: "I had a dream, I had a dream."

26 How long will there be in the minds of the *Neviim* who prophesy falsehood – the *Neviim* of their own deceitful minds –

27 the plan to make My people forget My name, by means of the dreams which they tell each other, just as their fathers forgot My name because of Baal?

28 Let the *Navi* who has a dream tell the dream; and let him who has received My word report My word faithfully! How can straw be compared to grain? – says *Hashem*.

29 Behold, My word is like fire – declares *Hashem* – and like a hammer that shatters rock!

30 Assuredly, I am going to deal with the *Neviim* – declares *Hashem* – who steal My words from one another.

31 I am going to deal with the *Neviim* – declares *Hashem* – who wag their tongues and make oracular utterances.

32 I am going to deal with those who prophesy lying dreams – declares *Hashem* – who relate them to lead My people astray with their reckless lies, when I did not send them or command them. They do this people no good – declares *Hashem*.

33 And when this people – or a *Navi* or a *Kohen* – asks you, "What is the burden of *Hashem*?" you shall answer them, "What is the burden? I will cast you oV" – declares *Hashem*.

34 As for the *Navi* or *Kohen* or layman who shall say "the burden of *Hashem*," I will punish that person and his house.

Yirmiyahu/Jeremiah
Chapter 24

35 Thus you shall speak to each other, every one to his fellow, "What has *Hashem* answered?" or "What has *Hashem* spoken?"

36 But do not mention "the burden of *Hashem*" any more. Does a man regard his own word as a "burden," that you pervert the words of the living *Hashem*, the Lord of Hosts, our God?

37 Thus you shall speak to the *Navi*: "What did *Hashem* answer you?" or "What did *Hashem* speak?"

38 But if you say "the burden of *Hashem*" – assuredly, thus said *Hashem*: Because you said this thing, "the burden of *Hashem*," whereas I sent word to you not to say "the burden of *Hashem*,"

39 I will utterly forget you and I will cast you away from My presence, together with the city that I gave to you and your fathers.

40 And I will lay upon you a disgrace for all time, shame for all time, which shall never be forgotten.

24

1 *Hashem* showed me two baskets of figs, placed in front of the Temple of *Hashem*. This was after King Nebuchadrezzar of Babylon had exiled King *Yechonya* son of *Yehoyakim* of *Yehuda*, and the officials of *Yehuda*, and the craftsmen and smiths, from *Yerushalayim*, and had brought them to Babylon.

2 One basket contained very good figs, like first-ripened figs, and the other basket contained very bad figs, so bad that they could not be eaten.

ha-DUD e-KHAD t'-ay-NEEM to-VOT m'-OD kit-ay-NAY ha-ba-ku-ROT v'-ha-DUD e-KHAD t'-ay-NEEM ra-OT m'-OD a-SHER lo tay-a-KHAL-nah may-RO-a

---

24:2 One basket contained very good figs After the captivity of the ruling classes in 597 BCE, *Yirmiyahu* is shown a vision of two baskets of figs: one basket has good, ripe figs, the other has rotten figs that cannot be eaten. Until this time, exile from the Land of Israel, the source of all goodness and blessing, was considered the worst possible punishment. Those who remained thought they had been spared, while those who were exiled thought that *Hashem* had abandoned them. *Yirmiyahu* explains that in reality, the opposite is true; those in exile will rediscover the ways of God and return (represented in the image by the ripe figs), while those who remain in the land (the bad figs) will eventually be destroyed. The use of the fig, one of the seven agricultural species unique to *Eretz Yisrael*, is significant in this metaphor, as the Bible also uses the image of a fig tree to denote peace and prosperity in the land (see I Kings 5:5).

Ripe figs in a Tel Aviv market

Yirmiyahu/Jeremiah
Chapter 25

ירמיהו
פרק כה

3 And *Hashem* said to me, "What do you see, *Yirmiyahu*?" I answered, "Figs – the good ones are very good, and the bad ones very bad, so bad that they cannot be eaten."

ג וַיֹּאמֶר יְהוָה אֵלַי מָה־אַתָּה רֹאֶה יִרְמְיָהוּ וָאֹמַר תְּאֵנִים הַתְּאֵנִים הַטֹּבוֹת טֹבוֹת מְאֹד וְהָרָעוֹת רָעוֹת מְאֹד אֲשֶׁר לֹא־תֵאָכַלְנָה מֵרֹעַ:

4 Then the word of *Hashem* came to me:

ד וַיְהִי דְבַר־יְהוָה אֵלַי לֵאמֹר:

5 Thus said *Hashem*, the God of *Yisrael*: As with these good figs, so will I single out for good the Judean exiles whom I have driven out from this place to the land of the Chaldeans.

ה כֹּה־אָמַר יְהוָה אֱלֹהֵי יִשְׂרָאֵל כַּתְּאֵנִים הַטֹּבוֹת הָאֵלֶּה כֵּן־אַכִּיר אֶת־גָּלוּת יְהוּדָה אֲשֶׁר שִׁלַּחְתִּי מִן־הַמָּקוֹם הַזֶּה אֶרֶץ כַּשְׂדִּים לְטוֹבָה:

6 I will look upon them favorably, and I will bring them back to this land; I will build them and not overthrow them; I will plant them and not uproot them.

ו וְשַׂמְתִּי עֵינִי עֲלֵיהֶם לְטוֹבָה וַהֲשִׁבֹתִים עַל־הָאָרֶץ הַזֹּאת וּבְנִיתִים וְלֹא אֶהֱרֹס וּנְטַעְתִּים וְלֹא אֶתּוֹשׁ:

7 And I will give them the understanding to acknowledge Me, for I am *Hashem*. And they shall be My people and I will be their God, when they turn back to Me with all their heart.

ז וְנָתַתִּי לָהֶם לֵב לָדַעַת אֹתִי כִּי אֲנִי יְהוָה וְהָיוּ־לִי לְעָם וְאָנֹכִי אֶהְיֶה לָהֶם לֵאלֹהִים כִּי־יָשֻׁבוּ אֵלַי בְּכָל־לִבָּם:

8 And like the bad figs, which are so bad that they cannot be eaten – thus said *Hashem* – so will I treat King *Tzidkiyahu* of *Yehuda* and his officials and the remnant of *Yerushalayim* that is left in this land, and those who are living in the land of Egypt:

ח וְכַתְּאֵנִים הָרָעוֹת אֲשֶׁר לֹא־תֵאָכַלְנָה מֵרֹעַ כִּי־כֹה אָמַר יְהוָה כֵּן אֶתֵּן אֶת־צִדְקִיָּהוּ מֶלֶךְ־יְהוּדָה וְאֶת־שָׂרָיו וְאֵת שְׁאֵרִית יְרוּשָׁלַםִ הַנִּשְׁאָרִים בָּאָרֶץ הַזֹּאת וְהַיֹּשְׁבִים בְּאֶרֶץ מִצְרָיִם:

9 I will make them a horror – an evil – to all the kingdoms of the earth, a disgrace and a proverb, a byword and a curse in all the places to which I banish them.

ט וּנְתַתִּים לְזַעֲוָה [לְזַוָעָה] לְרָעָה לְכֹל מַמְלְכוֹת הָאָרֶץ לְחֶרְפָּה וּלְמָשָׁל לִשְׁנִינָה וְלִקְלָלָה בְּכָל־הַמְּקֹמוֹת אֲשֶׁר־אַדִּיחֵם שָׁם:

10 I will send the sword, famine, and pestilence against them until they are exterminated from the land that I gave to them and their fathers.

י וְשִׁלַּחְתִּי בָם אֶת־הַחֶרֶב אֶת־הָרָעָב וְאֶת־הַדָּבֶר עַד־תֻּמָּם מֵעַל הָאֲדָמָה אֲשֶׁר־נָתַתִּי לָהֶם וְלַאֲבוֹתֵיהֶם:

25

1 The word which came to *Yirmiyahu* concerning all the people of *Yehuda*, in the fourth year of King *Yehoyakim* son of *Yoshiyahu* of *Yehuda*, which was the first year of King Nebuchadrezzar of Babylon.

כה א הַדָּבָר אֲשֶׁר־הָיָה עַל־יִרְמְיָהוּ עַל־כָּל־עַם יְהוּדָה בַּשָּׁנָה הָרְבִעִית לִיהוֹיָקִים בֶּן־יֹאשִׁיָּהוּ מֶלֶךְ יְהוּדָה הִיא הַשָּׁנָה הָרִאשֹׁנִית לִנְבוּכַדְרֶאצַּר מֶלֶךְ בָּבֶל:

2 This is what the *Navi Yirmiyahu* said to all the people of *Yehuda* and to all the inhabitants of *Yerushalayim*:

ב אֲשֶׁר דִּבֶּר יִרְמְיָהוּ הַנָּבִיא עַל־כָּל־עַם יְהוּדָה וְאֶל כָּל־יֹשְׁבֵי יְרוּשָׁלַםִ לֵאמֹר:

3 From the thirteenth year of King *Yoshiyahu* son of *Amon* of *Yehuda*, to this day – these twenty-three years – the word of *Hashem* has come to me. I have spoken to you persistently, but you would not listen.

ג מִן־שְׁלֹשׁ עֶשְׂרֵה שָׁנָה לְיֹאשִׁיָּהוּ בֶן־אָמוֹן מֶלֶךְ יְהוּדָה וְעַד הַיּוֹם הַזֶּה זֶה שָׁלֹשׁ וְעֶשְׂרִים שָׁנָה הָיָה דְבַר־יְהוָה אֵלָי וָאֲדַבֵּר אֲלֵיכֶם אַשְׁכֵּים וְדַבֵּר וְלֹא שְׁמַעְתֶּם:

Yirmiyahu/Jeremiah
Chapter 25

4 Moreover, *Hashem* constantly sent all his servants the *Neviim* to you, but you would not listen or incline your ears to hear

5 when they said, "Turn back, every one, from your evil ways and your wicked acts, that you may remain throughout the ages on the soil which *Hashem* gave to you and your fathers.

6 Do not follow other gods, to serve them and worship them. Do not vex Me with what your own hands have made, and I will not bring disaster upon you."

7 But you would not listen to Me – declares *Hashem* – but vexed Me with what your hands made, to your own hurt.

8 Assuredly, thus said the Lord of Hosts: Because you would not listen to My words,

9 I am going to send for all the peoples of the north – declares *Hashem* – and for My servant, King Nebuchadrezzar of Babylon, and bring them against this land and its inhabitants, and against all those nations roundabout. I will exterminate them and make them a desolation, an object of hissing – ruins for all time.

10 And I will banish from them the sound of mirth and gladness, the voice of bridegroom and bride, and the sound of the mill and the light of the lamp.

11 This whole land shall be a desolate ruin. And those nations shall serve the king of Babylon seventy years.

12 When the seventy years are over, I will punish the king of Babylon and that nation and the land of the Chaldeans for their sins – declares *Hashem* – and I will make it a desolation for all time.

13 And I will bring upon that land all that I have decreed against it, all that is recorded in this book – that which *Yirmiyahu* prophesied against all the nations.

14 For they too shall be enslaved by many nations and great kings; and I will requite them according to their acts and according to their conduct.

ירמיהו
פרק כה

ד וְשָׁלַח יְהֹוָה אֲלֵיכֶם אֶת־כָּל־עֲבָדָיו הַנְּבִאִים הַשְׁכֵּם וְשָׁלֹחַ וְלֹא שְׁמַעְתֶּם וְלֹא־הִטִּיתֶם אֶת־אָזְנְכֶם לִשְׁמֹעַ׃

ה לֵאמֹר שׁוּבוּ־נָא אִישׁ מִדַּרְכּוֹ הָרָעָה וּמֵרֹעַ מַעַלְלֵיכֶם וּשְׁבוּ עַל־הָאֲדָמָה אֲשֶׁר נָתַן יְהֹוָה לָכֶם וְלַאֲבוֹתֵיכֶם לְמִן־עוֹלָם וְעַד־עוֹלָם׃

ו וְאַל־תֵּלְכוּ אַחֲרֵי אֱלֹהִים אֲחֵרִים לְעָבְדָם וּלְהִשְׁתַּחֲוֹת לָהֶם וְלֹא־תַכְעִיסוּ אוֹתִי בְּמַעֲשֵׂה יְדֵיכֶם וְלֹא אָרַע לָכֶם׃

ז וְלֹא־שְׁמַעְתֶּם אֵלַי נְאֻם־יְהֹוָה לְמַעַן הכעסוני [הַכְעִיסֵנִי] בְּמַעֲשֵׂה יְדֵיכֶם לְרַע לָכֶם׃

ח לָכֵן כֹּה אָמַר יְהֹוָה צְבָאוֹת יַעַן אֲשֶׁר לֹא־שְׁמַעְתֶּם אֶת־דְּבָרָי׃

ט הִנְנִי שֹׁלֵחַ וְלָקַחְתִּי אֶת־כָּל־מִשְׁפְּחוֹת צָפוֹן נְאֻם־יְהֹוָה וְאֶל־נְבוּכַדְרֶאצַּר מֶלֶךְ־בָּבֶל עַבְדִּי וַהֲבִאֹתִים עַל־הָאָרֶץ הַזֹּאת וְעַל־יֹשְׁבֶיהָ וְעַל כָּל־הַגּוֹיִם הָאֵלֶּה סָבִיב וְהַחֲרַמְתִּים וְשַׂמְתִּים לְשַׁמָּה וְלִשְׁרֵקָה וּלְחָרְבוֹת עוֹלָם׃

י וְהַאֲבַדְתִּי מֵהֶם קוֹל שָׂשׂוֹן וְקוֹל שִׂמְחָה קוֹל חָתָן וְקוֹל כַּלָּה קוֹל רֵחַיִם וְאוֹר נֵר׃

יא וְהָיְתָה כָּל־הָאָרֶץ הַזֹּאת לְחָרְבָּה לְשַׁמָּה וְעָבְדוּ הַגּוֹיִם הָאֵלֶּה אֶת־מֶלֶךְ בָּבֶל שִׁבְעִים שָׁנָה׃

יב וְהָיָה כִמְלֹאות שִׁבְעִים שָׁנָה אֶפְקֹד עַל־מֶלֶךְ־בָּבֶל וְעַל־הַגּוֹי הַהוּא נְאֻם־יְהֹוָה אֶת־עֲוֺנָם וְעַל־אֶרֶץ כַּשְׂדִּים וְשַׂמְתִּי אֹתוֹ לְשִׁמְמוֹת עוֹלָם׃

יג והבאתי [וְהֵבֵאתִי] עַל־הָאָרֶץ הַהִיא אֶת־כָּל־דְּבָרַי אֲשֶׁר־דִּבַּרְתִּי עָלֶיהָ אֵת כָּל־הַכָּתוּב בַּסֵּפֶר הַזֶּה אֲשֶׁר־נִבָּא יִרְמְיָהוּ עַל־כָּל־הַגּוֹיִם׃

יד כִּי עָבְדוּ־בָם גַּם־הֵמָּה גּוֹיִם רַבִּים וּמְלָכִים גְּדוֹלִים וְשִׁלַּמְתִּי לָהֶם כְּפָעֳלָם וּכְמַעֲשֵׂה יְדֵיהֶם׃

Yirmiyahu/Jeremiah
Chapter 25

15 For thus said *Hashem*, the God of *Yisrael*, to me: "Take from My hand this cup of wine – of wrath – and make all the nations to whom I send you drink of it.

16 Let them drink and retch and act crazy, because of the sword that I am sending among them."

17 So I took the cup from the hand of *Hashem* and gave drink to all the nations to whom *Hashem* had sent me:

18 *Yerushalayim* and the towns of *Yehuda*, and its kings and officials, to make them a desolate ruin, an object of hissing and a curse – as is now the case;

19 Pharaoh king of Egypt, his courtiers, his officials, and all his people;

20 all the mixed peoples; all the kings of the land of *Utz*; all the kings of the land of the Philistines – *Ashkelon*, *Azza*, Ekron, and what is left of *Ashdod*;

21 Edom, Moab, and Ammon;

22 all the kings of Tyre and all the kings of Sidon, and all the kings of the coastland across the sea;

23 Dedan, Tema, and Buz, and all those who have their hair clipped;

24 all the kings of Arabia, and all the kings of the mixed peoples who live in the desert;

25 all the kings of Zimri and all the kings of Elam and all the kings of Media;

26 all the kings of the north, whether far from or close to each other – all the royal lands which are on the earth. And last of all, the king of Sheshach shall drink.

27 Say to them: "Thus said the Lord of Hosts, the God of *Yisrael*: Drink and get drunk and vomit; fall and never rise again, because of the sword that I send among you."

28 And if they refuse to take the cup from your hand and drink, say to them, "Thus said the Lord of Hosts: You must drink!

Yirmiyahu/Jeremiah
Chapter 25

ירמיהו
פרק כה

29 If I am bringing the punishment first on the city that bears My name, do you expect to go unpunished? You will not go unpunished, for I am summoning the sword against all the inhabitants of the earth – declares the Lord of Hosts."

כט כִּי הִנֵּה בָעִיר אֲשֶׁר נִקְרָא־שְׁמִי עָלֶיהָ אָנֹכִי מֵחֵל לְהָרַע וְאַתֶּם הִנָּקֵה תִנָּקוּ לֹא תִנָּקוּ כִּי חֶרֶב אֲנִי קֹרֵא עַל־כָּל־יֹשְׁבֵי הָאָרֶץ נְאֻם יְהֹוָה צְבָאוֹת׃

30 You are to prophesy all those things to them, and then say to them: *Hashem* roars from on high, He makes His voice heard from His holy dwelling; He roars aloud over His [earthly] abode; He utters shouts like the grape-treaders, Against all the dwellers on earth.

ל וְאַתָּה תִּנָּבֵא אֲלֵיהֶם אֵת כָּל־הַדְּבָרִים הָאֵלֶּה וְאָמַרְתָּ אֲלֵיהֶם יְהֹוָה מִמָּרוֹם יִשְׁאָג וּמִמְּעוֹן קָדְשׁוֹ יִתֵּן קוֹלוֹ שָׁאֹג יִשְׁאַג עַל־נָוֵהוּ הֵידָד כְּדֹרְכִים יַעֲנֶה אֶל כָּל־יֹשְׁבֵי הָאָרֶץ׃

v'-a-TAH ti-na-VAY a-lay-HEM AYT kol ha-d'-va-REEM ha-AY-leh v'-a-mar-TA a-lay-HEM a-do-NAI mi-ma-ROM yish-AG u-mi-m'-ON kod-SHO yi-TAYN ko-LO sha-OG yish-AG al na-VAY-hu hay-DAD k'-do-r'-KHEEM ya-a-NEH EL kol yo-sh'-VAY ha-A-retz

31 Tumult has reached the ends of the earth, For *Hashem* has a case against the nations, He contends with all flesh. He delivers the wicked to the sword – declares *Hashem*.

לא בָּא שָׁאוֹן עַד־קְצֵה הָאָרֶץ כִּי רִיב לַיהֹוָה בַּגּוֹיִם נִשְׁפָּט הוּא לְכָל־בָּשָׂר הָרְשָׁעִים נְתָנָם לַחֶרֶב נְאֻם־יְהֹוָה׃

32 Thus said the Lord of Hosts: Disaster goes forth From nation to nation; A great storm is unleashed From the remotest parts of earth.

לב כֹּה אָמַר יְהֹוָה צְבָאוֹת הִנֵּה רָעָה יֹצֵאת מִגּוֹי אֶל־גּוֹי וְסַעַר גָּדוֹל יֵעוֹר מִיַּרְכְּתֵי־אָרֶץ׃

33 In that day, the earth shall be strewn with the slain of *Hashem* from one end to the other. They shall not be mourned, or gathered and buried; they shall become dung upon the face of the earth.

לג וְהָיוּ חַלְלֵי יְהֹוָה בַּיּוֹם הַהוּא מִקְצֵה הָאָרֶץ וְעַד־קְצֵה הָאָרֶץ לֹא יִסָּפְדוּ וְלֹא יֵאָסְפוּ וְלֹא יִקָּבֵרוּ לְדֹמֶן עַל־פְּנֵי הָאֲדָמָה יִהְיוּ׃

34 Howl, you shepherds, and yell, Strew [dust] on yourselves, you lords of the flock! For the day of your slaughter draws near. I will break you in pieces, And you shall fall like a precious vessel.

לד הֵילִילוּ הָרֹעִים וְזַעֲקוּ וְהִתְפַּלְּשׁוּ אַדִּירֵי הַצֹּאן כִּי־מָלְאוּ יְמֵיכֶם לִטְבוֹחַ וּתְפוֹצוֹתִיכֶם וּנְפַלְתֶּם כִּכְלִי חֶמְדָּה׃

35 Flight shall fail the shepherds, And escape, the lords of the flock.

לה וְאָבַד מָנוֹס מִן־הָרֹעִים וּפְלֵיטָה מֵאַדִּירֵי הַצֹּאן׃

36 Hark, the outcry of the shepherds, And the howls of the lords of the flock! For *Hashem* is ravaging their pasture.

לו קוֹל צַעֲקַת הָרֹעִים וִילְלַת אַדִּירֵי הַצֹּאן כִּי־שֹׁדֵד יְהֹוָה אֶת־מַרְעִיתָם׃

25:30 *Hashem* **roars from on high** The prophecy in this chapter was uttered in the year 605 BCE, a pivotal time for *Yirmiyahu*. At the great battle of Carchemish, Babylonia decisively defeated Assyria and Egypt, becoming the sole dominant power in the ancient world. Those nations, like *Yehuda*, who had sided with the losers would soon face Babylonia's wrath. *Yirmiyahu* assures the people that this dark period is temporary; the Babylonians will fall to the Persians seventy years later. And though the *Beit Hamikdash* will be destroyed, ultimately *Hashem* will hold all the nations accountable for this outrage. Roaring like a lion, His wrath will go forth and exact retribution for the violence done to the Children of Israel and to His land.

Yirmiyahu/Jeremiah
Chapter 26

37 The peaceful meadows shall be wiped out By the fierce wrath of *Hashem*.

38 Like a lion, He has gone forth from His lair; The land has become a desolation, Because of the oppressive wrath, Because of His fierce anger.

26 1 At the beginning of the reign of King *Yehoyakim* son of *Yoshiyahu* of *Yehuda*, this word came from *Hashem*:

2 "Thus said *Hashem*: Stand in the court of the House of *Hashem*, and speak to [the men of] all the towns of *Yehuda*, who are coming to worship in the House of *Hashem*, all the words which I command you to speak to them. Do not omit anything.

3 Perhaps they will listen and turn back, each from his evil way, that I may renounce the punishment I am planning to bring upon them for their wicked acts.

4 "Say to them: Thus said *Hashem*: If you do not obey Me, abiding by the Teaching that I have set before you,

5 heeding the words of My servants the *Neviim* whom I have been sending to you persistently – but you have not heeded –

6 then I will make this House like *Shilo*, and I will make this city a curse for all the nations of earth."

7 The *Kohanim* and *Neviim* and all the people heard *Yirmiyahu* speaking these words in the House of *Hashem*.

8 And when *Yirmiyahu* finished speaking all that *Hashem* had commanded him to speak to all the people, the *Kohanim* and the *Neviim* and all the people seized him, shouting, "You shall die!

9 How dare you prophesy in the name of *Hashem* that this House shall become like *Shilo* and this city be made desolate, without inhabitants?" And all the people crowded about *Yirmiyahu* in the House of *Hashem*.

10 When the officials of *Yehuda* heard about this, they went up from the king's palace to the House of *Hashem* and held a session at the entrance of the New Gate of the House of *Hashem*.

לז וְנָדַמּוּ נְאוֹת הַשָּׁלוֹם מִפְּנֵי חֲרוֹן אַף־יְהֹוָה:

לח עָזַב כַּכְּפִיר סֻכּוֹ כִּי־הָיְתָה אַרְצָם לְשַׁמָּה מִפְּנֵי חֲרוֹן הַיּוֹנָה וּמִפְּנֵי חֲרוֹן אַפּוֹ:

כו א בְּרֵאשִׁית מַמְלְכוּת יְהוֹיָקִים בֶּן־יֹאשִׁיָּהוּ מֶלֶךְ יְהוּדָה הָיָה הַדָּבָר הַזֶּה מֵאֵת יְהֹוָה לֵאמֹר:

ב כֹּה אָמַר יְהֹוָה עֲמֹד בַּחֲצַר בֵּית־יְהֹוָה וְדִבַּרְתָּ עַל־כָּל־עָרֵי יְהוּדָה הַבָּאִים לְהִשְׁתַּחֲוֹת בֵּית־יְהֹוָה אֵת כָּל־הַדְּבָרִים אֲשֶׁר צִוִּיתִיךָ לְדַבֵּר אֲלֵיהֶם אַל־תִּגְרַע דָּבָר:

ג אוּלַי יִשְׁמְעוּ וְיָשֻׁבוּ אִישׁ מִדַּרְכּוֹ הָרָעָה וְנִחַמְתִּי אֶל־הָרָעָה אֲשֶׁר אָנֹכִי חֹשֵׁב לַעֲשׂוֹת לָהֶם מִפְּנֵי רֹעַ מַעַלְלֵיהֶם:

ד וְאָמַרְתָּ אֲלֵיהֶם כֹּה אָמַר יְהֹוָה אִם־לֹא תִשְׁמְעוּ אֵלַי לָלֶכֶת בְּתוֹרָתִי אֲשֶׁר נָתַתִּי לִפְנֵיכֶם:

ה לִשְׁמֹעַ עַל־דִּבְרֵי עֲבָדַי הַנְּבִאִים אֲשֶׁר אָנֹכִי שֹׁלֵחַ אֲלֵיכֶם וְהַשְׁכֵּם וְשָׁלֹחַ וְלֹא שְׁמַעְתֶּם:

ו וְנָתַתִּי אֶת־הַבַּיִת הַזֶּה כְּשִׁלֹה וְאֶת־הָעִיר הַזֹּאתָה [הַזֹּאת] אֶתֵּן לִקְלָלָה לְכֹל גּוֹיֵי הָאָרֶץ:

ז וַיִּשְׁמְעוּ הַכֹּהֲנִים וְהַנְּבִאִים וְכָל־הָעָם אֶת־יִרְמְיָהוּ מְדַבֵּר אֶת־הַדְּבָרִים הָאֵלֶּה בְּבֵית יְהֹוָה:

ח וַיְהִי כְּכַלּוֹת יִרְמְיָהוּ לְדַבֵּר אֵת כָּל־אֲשֶׁר־צִוָּה יְהֹוָה לְדַבֵּר אֶל־כָּל־הָעָם וַיִּתְפְּשׂוּ אֹתוֹ הַכֹּהֲנִים וְהַנְּבִאִים וְכָל־הָעָם לֵאמֹר מוֹת תָּמוּת:

ט מַדּוּעַ נִבֵּיתָ בְשֵׁם־יְהֹוָה לֵאמֹר כְּשִׁלוֹ יִהְיֶה הַבַּיִת הַזֶּה וְהָעִיר הַזֹּאת תֶּחֱרַב מֵאֵין יוֹשֵׁב וַיִּקָּהֵל כָּל־הָעָם אֶל־יִרְמְיָהוּ בְּבֵית יְהֹוָה:

י וַיִּשְׁמְעוּ שָׂרֵי יְהוּדָה אֵת הַדְּבָרִים הָאֵלֶּה וַיַּעֲלוּ מִבֵּית־הַמֶּלֶךְ בֵּית יְהֹוָה וַיֵּשְׁבוּ בְּפֶתַח שַׁעַר־יְהֹוָה הֶחָדָשׁ:

Yirmiyahu/Jeremiah
Chapter 26

11 The *Kohanim* and *Neviim* said to the officials and to all the people, "This man deserves the death penalty, for he has prophesied against this city, as you yourselves have heard."

12 *Yirmiyahu* said to the officials and to all the people, "It was *Hashem* who sent me to prophesy against this House and this city all the words you heard.

13 Therefore mend your ways and your acts, and heed *Hashem* your God, that *Hashem* may renounce the punishment He has decreed for you.

14 As for me, I am in your hands: do to me what seems good and right to you.

15 But know that if you put me to death, you and this city and its inhabitants will be guilty of shedding the blood of an innocent man. For in truth *Hashem* has sent me to you, to speak all these words to you."

16 Then the officials and all the people said to the *Kohanim* and *Neviim*, "This man does not deserve the death penalty, for he spoke to us in the name of *Hashem* our God."

17 And some of the elders of the land arose and said to the entire assemblage of the people,

18 "*Micha* the Morashtite, who prophesied in the days of King *Chizkiyahu* of *Yehuda*, said to all the people of *Yehuda*: 'Thus said the Lord of Hosts: *Tzion* shall be plowed as a field, *Yerushalayim* shall become heaps of ruins And the *Har Habayit* a shrine in the woods.'

19 "Did King *Chizkiyahu* of *Yehuda*, and all *Yehuda*, put him to death? Did he not rather fear *Hashem* and implore *Hashem*, so that *Hashem* renounced the punishment He had decreed against them? We are about to do great injury to ourselves!"

*he-ha-MAYT he-mi-TU-hu khiz-ki-YA-hu me-lekh y'-hu-DAH v'-khol y'-hu-DAH
ha-LO ya-RAY et a-do-NAI vai-KHAL et p'-NAY a-do-NAI va-yi-na-KHEM
a-do-NAI el ha-ra-AH a-sher di-BER a-lay-HEM va-a-NAKH-nu o-SEEM ra-AH
g'-do-LAH al naf-sho-TAY-nu*

ירמיהו
פרק כו

יא וַיֹּאמְרוּ הַכֹּהֲנִים וְהַנְּבִיאִים אֶל־הַשָּׂרִים וְאֶל־כָּל־הָעָם לֵאמֹר מִשְׁפַּט־מָוֶת לָאִישׁ הַזֶּה כִּי נִבָּא אֶל־הָעִיר הַזֹּאת כַּאֲשֶׁר שְׁמַעְתֶּם בְּאָזְנֵיכֶם:

יב וַיֹּאמֶר יִרְמְיָהוּ אֶל־כָּל־הַשָּׂרִים וְאֶל־כָּל־הָעָם לֵאמֹר יְהוָה שְׁלָחַנִי לְהִנָּבֵא אֶל־הַבַּיִת הַזֶּה וְאֶל־הָעִיר הַזֹּאת אֵת כָּל־הַדְּבָרִים אֲשֶׁר שְׁמַעְתֶּם:

יג וְעַתָּה הֵיטִיבוּ דַרְכֵיכֶם וּמַעַלְלֵיכֶם וְשִׁמְעוּ בְּקוֹל יְהוָה אֱלֹהֵיכֶם וְיִנָּחֵם יְהוָה אֶל־הָרָעָה אֲשֶׁר דִּבֶּר עֲלֵיכֶם:

יד וַאֲנִי הִנְנִי בְיֶדְכֶם עֲשׂוּ־לִי כַּטּוֹב וְכַיָּשָׁר בְּעֵינֵיכֶם:

טו אַךְ יָדֹעַ תֵּדְעוּ כִּי אִם־מְמִתִים אַתֶּם אֹתִי כִּי־דָם נָקִי אַתֶּם נֹתְנִים עֲלֵיכֶם וְאֶל־הָעִיר הַזֹּאת וְאֶל־יֹשְׁבֶיהָ כִּי בֶאֱמֶת שְׁלָחַנִי יְהוָה עֲלֵיכֶם לְדַבֵּר בְּאָזְנֵיכֶם אֵת כָּל־הַדְּבָרִים הָאֵלֶּה:

טז וַיֹּאמְרוּ הַשָּׂרִים וְכָל־הָעָם אֶל־הַכֹּהֲנִים וְאֶל־הַנְּבִיאִים אֵין־לָאִישׁ הַזֶּה מִשְׁפַּט־מָוֶת כִּי בְּשֵׁם יְהוָה אֱלֹהֵינוּ דִּבֶּר אֵלֵינוּ:

יז וַיָּקֻמוּ אֲנָשִׁים מִזִּקְנֵי הָאָרֶץ וַיֹּאמְרוּ אֶל־כָּל־קְהַל הָעָם לֵאמֹר:

יח מִיכָיָה [מִיכָה] הַמּוֹרַשְׁתִּי הָיָה נִבָּא בִּימֵי חִזְקִיָּהוּ מֶלֶךְ־יְהוּדָה וַיֹּאמֶר אֶל־כָּל־עַם יְהוּדָה לֵאמֹר כֹּה־אָמַר יְהוָה צְבָאוֹת צִיּוֹן שָׂדֶה תֵחָרֵשׁ וִירוּשָׁלַיִם עִיִּים תִּהְיֶה וְהַר הַבַּיִת לְבָמוֹת יָעַר:

יט הֶהָמֵת הֱמִתֻהוּ חִזְקִיָּהוּ מֶלֶךְ־יְהוּדָה וְכָל־יְהוּדָה הֲלֹא יָרֵא אֶת־יְהוָה וַיְחַל אֶת־פְּנֵי יְהוָה וַיִּנָּחֶם יְהוָה אֶל־הָרָעָה אֲשֶׁר־דִּבֶּר עֲלֵיהֶם וַאֲנַחְנוּ עֹשִׂים רָעָה גְדוֹלָה עַל־נַפְשׁוֹתֵינוּ:

26:19 Did King *Chizkiyahu* of *Yehuda*, and all *Yehuda*, put him to death? *Yirmiyahu* is arrested by the officers and placed on trial as a false prophet. They claim that *Yirmi-* *yahu*'s prophecies of destruction and exile contradict the eternal bond between *Hashem* and His people. However, the elders of Israel come to *Yirmiyahu*'s

Yirmiyahu/Jeremiah
Chapter 27

20 There was also a man prophesying in the name of *Hashem*, *Uriya* son of *Shemaya* from *Kiryat Ye'arim*, who prophesied against this city and this land the same things as *Yirmiyahu*.

21 King *Yehoyakim* and all his warriors and all the officials heard about his address, and the king wanted to put him to death. *Uriya* heard of this and fled in fear, and came to Egypt.

22 But King *Yehoyakim* sent men to Egypt, Elnathan son of Achbor and men with him to Egypt.

23 They took *Uriya* out of Egypt and brought him to King *Yehoyakim*, who had him put to the sword and his body thrown into the burial place of the common people.

24 However, *Achikam* son of *Shafan* protected *Yirmiyahu*, so that he was not handed over to the people for execution.

27

1 At the beginning of the reign of King *Yehoyakim* son of *Yoshiyahu* of *Yehuda*, this word came to *Yirmiyahu* from *Hashem*:

2 Thus said *Hashem* to me: Make for yourself thongs and bars of a yoke, and put them on your neck.

koh a-MAR a-do-NAI ay-LAI a-SAY l'-KHA mo-say-ROT u-mo-TOT un-ta-TAM al tza-va-RE-kha

3 And send them to the king of Edom, the king of Moab, the king of the Amonites, the king of Tyre, and the king of Sidon, by envoys who have come to King *Tzidkiyahu* of *Yehuda* in *Yerushalayim*;

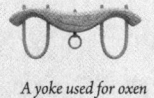

A yoke used for oxen

defense. A century earlier, at the time of the Assyrian invasion, the prophet *Micha* had also spoken against the city. Rather than feeling threatened, the righteous king *Chizkiyahu* had led the people in repentance, and God saved the people. *Yirmiyahu* is hoping that the people of his generation will have a similar response to his prophecies, that they will return to *Hashem* and be spared. The message is true for all time, as it says in *Yechezkel* 33:11: "As I live – declares *Hashem* – it is not My desire that the wicked shall die, but that the wicked [one] turn from his [evil] ways and live."

27:2 Put them on your neck In the year 593 BCE, *Tzidkiyahu* leads a confederation of neighboring states in planning a rebellion against Babylonia. *Yirmiyahu* warns them against this folly by means of a highly visual symbol. He walks through the streets wearing a yoke, normally used to harness oxen while plowing, on his neck. When onlookers ask him about his strange behavior, he answers that this was the divine message: Accept the yoke of Babylonia and submit peacefully in order to live. Had the people listened, they would have avoided the destruction of the *Beit Hamikdash* and exile from their land.

Yirmiyahu/Jeremiah
Chapter 27

4 and give them this charge to their masters: Thus said the Lord of Hosts, the God of *Yisrael*: Say this to your masters:

5 "It is I who made the earth, and the men and beasts who are on the earth, by My great might and My outstretched arm; and I give it to whomever I deem proper.

6 I herewith deliver all these lands to My servant, King Nebuchadnezzar of Babylon; I even give him the wild beasts to serve him.

7 All nations shall serve him, his son and his grandson – until the turn of his own land comes, when many nations and great kings shall subjugate him.

8 The nation or kingdom that does not serve him – King Nebuchadnezzar of Babylon – and does not put its neck under the yoke of the king of Babylon, that nation I will visit – declares *Hashem* – with sword, famine, and pestilence, until I have destroyed it by his hands.

9 As for you, give no heed to your *Neviim*, augurs, dreamers, diviners, and sorcerers, who say to you, 'Do not serve the king of Babylon.'

10 For they prophesy falsely to you – with the result that you shall be banished from your land; I will drive you out and you shall perish.

11 But the nation that puts its neck under the yoke of the king of Babylon, and serves him, will be left by Me on its own soil – declares *Hashem* – to till it and dwell on it."

12 I also spoke to King *Tzidkiyahu* of *Yehuda* in just the same way: "Put your necks under the yoke of the king of Babylon; serve him and his people, and live!

13 Otherwise you will die together with your people, by sword, famine, and pestilence, as *Hashem* has decreed against any nation that does not serve the king of Babylon.

14 Give no heed to the words of the *Neviim* who say to you, 'Do not serve the king of Babylon,' for they prophesy falsely to you.

Yirmiyahu/Jeremiah
Chapter 28

ירמיהו
פרק כח

15 I have not sent them – declares *Hashem* – and they prophesy falsely in My name, with the result that I will drive you out and you shall perish, together with the *Neviim* who prophesy to you."

16 And to the *Kohanim* and to all that people I said: "Thus said *Hashem*: Give no heed to the words of the *Neviim* who prophesy to you, 'The vessels of the House of *Hashem* shall shortly be brought back from Babylon,' for they prophesy falsely to you.

17 Give them no heed. Serve the king of Babylon, and live! Otherwise this city shall become a ruin.

18 If they are really *Neviim* and the word of *Hashem* is with them, let them intercede with the Lord of Hosts not to let the vessels remaining in the House of *Hashem*, in the royal palace of *Yehuda*, and in *Yerushalayim*, go to Babylon!

19 "For thus said the Lord of Hosts concerning the columns, the tank, the stands, and the rest of the vessels remaining in this city,

20 which King Nebuchadnezzar of Babylon did not take when he exiled King *Yechonya* son of *Yehoyakim* of *Yehuda*, from *Yerushalayim* to Babylon, with all the nobles of *Yehuda* and *Yerushalayim*;

21 for thus said the Lord of Hosts, the God of *Yisrael*, concerning the vessels remaining in the House of *Hashem*, in the royal palace of *Yehuda*, and in *Yerushalayim*:

22 They shall be brought to Babylon, and there they shall remain, until I take note of them – declares the Lord of Hosts – and bring them up and restore them to this place."

28 1 That year, early in the reign of King *Tzidkiyahu* of *Yehuda*, in the fifth month of the fourth year, the *Navi Chananya* son of Azzur, who was from *Givon*, spoke to me in the House of *Hashem*, in the presence of the *Kohanim* and all the people. He said:

2 "Thus said the Lord of Hosts, the God of *Yisrael*: I hereby break the yoke of the king of Babylon.

טו כִּי לֹא שְׁלַחְתִּים נְאֻם־יְהֹוָה וְהֵם נִבְּאִים בִּשְׁמִי לַשָּׁקֶר לְמַעַן הַדִּיחִי אֶתְכֶם וַאֲבַדְתֶּם אַתֶּם וְהַנְּבִאִים הַנִּבְּאִים לָכֶם:

טז וְאֶל־הַכֹּהֲנִים וְאֶל־כָּל־הָעָם הַזֶּה דִּבַּרְתִּי לֵאמֹר כֹּה אָמַר יְהֹוָה אַל־תִּשְׁמְעוּ אֶל־דִּבְרֵי נְבִיאֵיכֶם הַנִּבְּאִים לָכֶם לֵאמֹר הִנֵּה כְלֵי בֵית־יְהֹוָה מוּשָׁבִים מִבָּבֶלָה עַתָּה מְהֵרָה כִּי שֶׁקֶר הֵמָּה נִבְּאִים לָכֶם:

יז אַל־תִּשְׁמְעוּ אֲלֵיהֶם עִבְדוּ אֶת־מֶלֶךְ־בָּבֶל וִחְיוּ לָמָּה תִהְיֶה הָעִיר הַזֹּאת חָרְבָּה:

יח וְאִם־נְבִאִים הֵם וְאִם־יֵשׁ דְּבַר־יְהֹוָה אִתָּם יִפְגְּעוּ־נָא בַּיהֹוָה צְבָאוֹת לְבִלְתִּי־בֹאוּ הַכֵּלִים הַנּוֹתָרִים בְּבֵית־יְהֹוָה וּבֵית מֶלֶךְ יְהוּדָה וּבִירוּשָׁלַ͏ִם בָּבֶלָה:

יט כִּי כֹה אָמַר יְהֹוָה צְבָאוֹת אֶל־הָעַמֻּדִים וְעַל־הַיָּם וְעַל־הַמְּכֹנוֹת וְעַל יֶתֶר הַכֵּלִים הַנּוֹתָרִים בָּעִיר הַזֹּאת:

כ אֲשֶׁר לֹא־לְקָחָם נְבוּכַדְנֶאצַּר מֶלֶךְ בָּבֶל בַּגְלוֹתוֹ אֶת־יְכׇנְיָה בֶן־יְהוֹיָקִים מֶלֶךְ־יְהוּדָה מִירוּשָׁלַ͏ִם בָּבֶלָה וְאֵת כָּל־חֹרֵי יְהוּדָה וִירוּשָׁלָ͏ִם:

כא כִּי כֹה אָמַר יְהֹוָה צְבָאוֹת אֱלֹהֵי יִשְׂרָאֵל עַל־הַכֵּלִים הַנּוֹתָרִים בֵּית יְהֹוָה וּבֵית מֶלֶךְ־יְהוּדָה וִירוּשָׁלָ͏ִם:

כב בָּבֶלָה יוּבָאוּ וְשָׁמָּה יִהְיוּ עַד יוֹם פׇּקְדִי אֹתָם נְאֻם־יְהֹוָה וְהַעֲלִיתִים וַהֲשִׁיבֹתִים אֶל־הַמָּקוֹם הַזֶּה:

כח א וַיְהִי בַּשָּׁנָה הַהִיא בְּרֵאשִׁית מַמְלֶכֶת צִדְקִיָּה מֶלֶךְ־יְהוּדָה בשנת [בַּשָּׁנָה] הָרְבִעִית בַּחֹדֶשׁ הַחֲמִישִׁי אָמַר אֵלַי חֲנַנְיָה בֶן־עַזּוּר הַנָּבִיא אֲשֶׁר מִגִּבְעוֹן בְּבֵית יְהֹוָה לְעֵינֵי הַכֹּהֲנִים וְכׇל־הָעָם לֵאמֹר:

ב כֹּה־אָמַר יְהֹוָה צְבָאוֹת אֱלֹהֵי יִשְׂרָאֵל לֵאמֹר שָׁבַרְתִּי אֶת־עֹל מֶלֶךְ בָּבֶל:

Yirmiyahu/Jeremiah
Chapter 28

ירמיהו
פרק כח

3 In two years, I will restore to this place all the vessels of the House of *Hashem* which King Nebuchadnezzar of Babylon took from this place and brought to Babylon.

ג בְּעוֹד ׀ שְׁנָתַיִם יָמִים אֲנִי מֵשִׁיב אֶל־הַמָּקוֹם הַזֶּה אֶת־כָּל־כְּלֵי בֵּית יְהֹוָה אֲשֶׁר לָקַח נְבוּכַדְנֶאצַּר מֶלֶךְ־בָּבֶל מִן־הַמָּקוֹם הַזֶּה וַיְבִיאֵם בָּבֶל׃

4 And I will bring back to this place King *Yechonya* son of *Yehoyakim* of *Yehuda*, and all the Judean exiles who went to Babylon – declares *Hashem*. Yes, I will break the yoke of the king of Babylon."

ד וְאֶת־יְכָנְיָה בֶן־יְהוֹיָקִים מֶלֶךְ־יְהוּדָה וְאֶת־כָּל־גָּלוּת יְהוּדָה הַבָּאִים בָּבֶלָה אֲנִי מֵשִׁיב אֶל־הַמָּקוֹם הַזֶּה נְאֻם־יְהֹוָה כִּי אֶשְׁבֹּר אֶת־עֹל מֶלֶךְ בָּבֶל׃

5 Then the *Navi Yirmiyahu* answered the *Navi Chananya* in the presence of the *Kohanim* and of all the people who were standing in the House of *Hashem*.

ה וַיֹּאמֶר יִרְמְיָה הַנָּבִיא אֶל־חֲנַנְיָה הַנָּבִיא לְעֵינֵי הַכֹּהֲנִים וּלְעֵינֵי כָּל־הָעָם הָעֹמְדִים בְּבֵית יְהֹוָה׃

6 The *Navi Yirmiyahu* said: "Amen! May *Hashem* do so! May *Hashem* fulfill what you have prophesied and bring back from Babylon to this place the vessels of the House of *Hashem* and all the exiles!

ו וַיֹּאמֶר יִרְמְיָה הַנָּבִיא אָמֵן כֵּן יַעֲשֶׂה יְהֹוָה יָקֵם יְהֹוָה אֶת־דְּבָרֶיךָ אֲשֶׁר נִבֵּאתָ לְהָשִׁיב כְּלֵי בֵית־יְהֹוָה וְכָל־הַגּוֹלָה מִבָּבֶל אֶל־הַמָּקוֹם הַזֶּה׃

7 But just listen to this word which I address to you and to all the people:

ז אַךְ־שְׁמַע־נָא הַדָּבָר הַזֶּה אֲשֶׁר אָנֹכִי דֹּבֵר בְּאָזְנֶיךָ וּבְאָזְנֵי כָּל־הָעָם׃

8 The *Neviim* who lived before you and me from ancient times prophesied war, disaster, and pestilence against many lands and great kingdoms.

ח הַנְּבִיאִים אֲשֶׁר הָיוּ לְפָנַי וּלְפָנֶיךָ מִן־הָעוֹלָם וַיִּנָּבְאוּ אֶל־אֲרָצוֹת רַבּוֹת וְעַל־מַמְלָכוֹת גְּדֹלוֹת לְמִלְחָמָה וּלְרָעָה וּלְדָבֶר׃

ha-n'-vee-EEM a-SHER ha-YU l'-fa-NAI ul-fa-NE-kha min ha-o-LAM va-yi-na-v'-U el a-ra-TZOT ra-BOT v'-al mam-la-KHOT g'-do-LOT l'-mil-kha-MAH ul-ra-AH ul-DA-ver

9 So if a *Navi* prophesies good fortune, then only when the word of the *Navi* comes true can it be known that *Hashem* really sent him."

ט הַנָּבִיא אֲשֶׁר יִנָּבֵא לְשָׁלוֹם בְּבֹא דְּבַר הַנָּבִיא יִוָּדַע הַנָּבִיא אֲשֶׁר־שְׁלָחוֹ יְהֹוָה בֶּאֱמֶת׃

10 But the *Navi Chananya* removed the bar from the neck of the *Navi Yirmiyahu*, and broke it;

י וַיִּקַּח חֲנַנְיָה הַנָּבִיא אֶת־הַמּוֹטָה מֵעַל צַוַּאר יִרְמְיָה הַנָּבִיא וַיִּשְׁבְּרֵהוּ׃

11 and *Chananya* said in the presence of all the people, "Thus said *Hashem*: So will I break the yoke of King Nebuchadnezzar of Babylon from off the necks of all the nations, in two years." And the *Navi Yirmiyahu* went on his way.

יא וַיֹּאמֶר חֲנַנְיָה לְעֵינֵי כָל־הָעָם לֵאמֹר כֹּה אָמַר יְהֹוָה כָּכָה אֶשְׁבֹּר אֶת־עֹל ׀ נְבֻכַדְנֶאצַּר מֶלֶךְ־בָּבֶל בְּעוֹד שְׁנָתַיִם יָמִים מֵעַל צַוַּאר כָּל־הַגּוֹיִם וַיֵּלֶךְ יִרְמְיָה הַנָּבִיא לְדַרְכּוֹ׃

28:8 Prophesied war, disaster, and pestilence against many lands *Chananya* dramatically breaks *Yirmiyahu's* symbolic yoke, claiming that the Babylonian empire will be overthrown in two years. *Yirmiyahu* argues that while this is a more reassuring message, it is false. It is easy to ingratiate oneself with the masses by telling them what they want to hear, but telling them the truth requires courage and the willingness to speak out and become unpopular. The great prophets of Israel uttered their prophecies fearlessly, conveying the divine message without hesitation or fear. Everyone is a messenger of God in this world. One must never hesitate to stand up for God, His people and His land, *Eretz Yisrael*, even when it seems like an unpopular message.

Yirmiyahu/Jeremiah
Chapter 29

12 After the *Navi Chananya* had broken the bar from off the neck of the *Navi Yirmiyahu*, the word of *Hashem* came to *Yirmiyahu*:

13 "Go say to *Chananya*: Thus said *Hashem*: You broke bars of wood, but you shall make bars of iron instead.

14 For thus said the Lord of Hosts, the God of *Yisrael*: I have put an iron yoke upon the necks of all those nations, that they may serve King Nebuchadnezzar of Babylon – and serve him they shall! I have even given the wild beasts to him."

15 And the *Navi Yirmiyahu* said to the *Navi Chananya*, "Listen, *Chananya*! *Hashem* did not send you, and you have given this people lying assurances.

16 Assuredly, thus said *Hashem*: I am going to banish you from off the earth. This year you shall die, for you have urged disloyalty to *Hashem*."

17 And the *Navi Chananya* died that year, in the seventh month.

29

1 This is the text of the letter which the *Navi Yirmiyahu* sent from *Yerushalayim* to the *Kohanim*, the *Neviim*, the rest of the elders of the exile community, and to all the people whom Nebuchadnezzar had exiled from *Yerushalayim* to Babylon –

2 after King *Yechonya*, the queen mother, the eunuchs, the officials of *Yehuda* and *Yerushalayim*, and the craftsmen and smiths had left *Yerushalayim*.

3 [The letter was sent] through Elasah son of *Shafan* and Gemariah son of *Chilkiyahu*, whom King *Tzidkiyahu* of *Yehuda* had dispatched to Babylon, to King Nebuchadnezzar of Babylon.

4 Thus said the Lord of Hosts, the God of *Yisrael*, to the whole community which I exiled from *Yerushalayim* to Babylon:

5 Build houses and live in them, plant gardens and eat their fruit.

6 Take wives and beget sons and daughters; and take wives for your sons, and give your daughters to husbands, that they may bear sons and daughters. Multiply there, do not decrease.

Yirmiyahu/Jeremiah
Chapter 29

ירמיהו
פרק כט

7 And seek the welfare of the city to which I have exiled you and pray to *Hashem* in its behalf; for in its prosperity you shall prosper.

ז וְדִרְשׁוּ אֶת־שְׁלוֹם הָעִיר אֲשֶׁר הִגְלֵיתִי אֶתְכֶם שָׁמָּה וְהִתְפַּלְלוּ בַעֲדָהּ אֶל־יְהֹוָה כִּי בִשְׁלוֹמָהּ יִהְיֶה לָכֶם שָׁלוֹם:

8 For thus said the Lord of Hosts, the God of *Yisrael*: Let not the *Neviim* and diviners in your midst deceive you, and pay no heed to the dreams they dream.

ח כִּי כֹה אָמַר יְהֹוָה צְבָאוֹת אֱלֹהֵי יִשְׂרָאֵל אַל־יַשִּׁיאוּ לָכֶם נְבִיאֵיכֶם אֲשֶׁר־בְּקִרְבְּכֶם וְקֹסְמֵיכֶם וְאַל־תִּשְׁמְעוּ אֶל־חֲלֹמֹתֵיכֶם אֲשֶׁר אַתֶּם מַחְלְמִים:

9 For they prophesy to you in My name falsely; I did not send them – declares *Hashem*.

ט כִּי בְשֶׁקֶר הֵם נִבְּאִים לָכֶם בִּשְׁמִי לֹא שְׁלַחְתִּים נְאֻם־יְהֹוָה:

10 For thus said *Hashem*: When Babylon's seventy years are over, I will take note of you, and I will fulfill to you My promise of favor – to bring you back to this place.

י כִּי־כֹה אָמַר יְהֹוָה כִּי לְפִי מְלֹאת לְבָבֶל שִׁבְעִים שָׁנָה אֶפְקֹד אֶתְכֶם וַהֲקִמֹתִי עֲלֵיכֶם אֶת־דְּבָרִי הַטּוֹב לְהָשִׁיב אֶתְכֶם אֶל־הַמָּקוֹם הַזֶּה:

11 For I am mindful of the plans I have made concerning you – declares *Hashem* – plans for your welfare, not for disaster, to give you a hopeful future.

יא כִּי אָנֹכִי יָדַעְתִּי אֶת־הַמַּחֲשָׁבֹת אֲשֶׁר אָנֹכִי חֹשֵׁב עֲלֵיכֶם נְאֻם־יְהֹוָה מַחְשְׁבוֹת שָׁלוֹם וְלֹא לְרָעָה לָתֵת לָכֶם אַחֲרִית וְתִקְוָה:

12 When you call Me, and come and pray to Me, I will give heed to you.

יב וּקְרָאתֶם אֹתִי וַהֲלַכְתֶּם וְהִתְפַּלַּלְתֶּם אֵלָי וְשָׁמַעְתִּי אֲלֵיכֶם:

13 You will search for Me and find Me, if only you seek Me wholeheartedly.

יג וּבִקַּשְׁתֶּם אֹתִי וּמְצָאתֶם כִּי תִדְרְשֻׁנִי בְּכָל־לְבַבְכֶם:

u-vi-kash-TEM o-TEE um-tza-TEM KEE tid-r'-SHU-nee b'-khol l'-vav-KHEM

14 I will be at hand for you – declares *Hashem* – and I will restore your fortunes. And I will gather you from all the nations and from all the places to which I have banished you – declares *Hashem* – and I will bring you back to the place from which I have exiled you.

יד וְנִמְצֵאתִי לָכֶם נְאֻם־יְהֹוָה וְשַׁבְתִּי אֶת־שְׁבִיתְכֶם [שְׁבוּתְכֶם] וְקִבַּצְתִּי אֶתְכֶם מִכָּל־הַגּוֹיִם וּמִכָּל־הַמְּקוֹמוֹת אֲשֶׁר הִדַּחְתִּי אֶתְכֶם שָׁם נְאֻם־יְהֹוָה וַהֲשִׁבֹתִי אֶתְכֶם אֶל־הַמָּקוֹם אֲשֶׁר־הִגְלֵיתִי אֶתְכֶם מִשָּׁם:

15 But you say, "*Hashem* has raised up *Neviim* for us in Babylon."

טו כִּי אֲמַרְתֶּם הֵקִים לָנוּ יְהֹוָה נְבִאִים בָּבֶלָה:

16 Thus said *Hashem* concerning the king who sits on the throne of *David*, and concerning all the people who dwell in this city, your brothers who did not go out with you into exile –

טז כִּי־כֹה אָמַר יְהֹוָה אֶל־הַמֶּלֶךְ הַיּוֹשֵׁב אֶל־כִּסֵּא דָוִד וְאֶל־כָּל־הָעָם הַיּוֹשֵׁב בָּעִיר הַזֹּאת אֲחֵיכֶם אֲשֶׁר לֹא־יָצְאוּ אִתְּכֶם בַּגּוֹלָה:

29:13 You will search for Me and find Me *Yirmiyahu* pens a letter to the exiles in Babylonia. He tells them to disregard the false prophecies, according to which they will return to Israel soon. Instead, they are to settle in Babylonia and raise families there, as they will remain there for seventy years, and only after that will they be permitted to return to Israel. However, only those who truly desire to return to their homeland will be given divine assistance to do so. In his work, *The Kuzari*, medieval philosopher Rabbi Yehuda Halevi lists the people's lack of desire to return to their homeland as Israel's greatest historic failing. This serves as a reminder to Jews in today's generation not to take Israel for granted.

Rabbi Judah Halevi (1075–1141)

Yirmiyahu/Jeremiah
Chapter 29

17 thus said the LORD of Hosts: I am going to let loose sword, famine, and pestilence against them and I will treat them as loathsome figs, so bad that they cannot be eaten.

18 I will pursue them with the sword, with famine, and with pestilence; and I will make them a horror to all the kingdoms of the earth, a curse and an object of horror and hissing and scorn among all the nations to which I shall banish them,

19 because they did not heed My words – declares *Hashem* – when I persistently sent to them My servants, the *Neviim*, and they did not heed – declares *Hashem*.

20 But you, the whole exile community which I banished from *Yerushalayim* to Babylon, hear the word of *Hashem*!

21 Thus said the LORD of Hosts, the God of *Yisrael*, concerning *Achav* son of Kolaiah and *Tzidkiyahu* son of Maaseiah, who prophesy falsely to you in My name: I am going to deliver them into the hands of King Nebuchadrezzar of Babylon, and he shall put them to death before your eyes.

22 And the whole community of *Yehuda* in Babylonia shall use a curse derived from their fate: "May *Hashem* make you like *Tzidkiyahu* and *Achav*, whom the king of Babylon consigned to the flames!" –

23 because they did vile things in *Yisrael*, committing adultery with the wives of their fellows and speaking in My name false words which I had not commanded them. I am He who knows and bears witness – declares *Hashem*.

24 Concerning *Shemaya* the Nehelamite you shall say:

25 Thus said the LORD of Hosts, the God of *Yisrael*: Because you sent letters in your own name to all the people in *Yerushalayim*, to *Tzefanya* son of Maaseiah and to the rest of the *Kohanim*, as follows,

26 "*Hashem* appointed you *Kohen* in place of the *Kohen Yehoyada*, to exercise authority in the House of *Hashem* over every madman who wants to play the *Navi*, to put him into the stocks and into the pillory.

ירמיהו
פרק כט

יז כֹּה אָמַר יְהֹוָה צְבָאוֹת הִנְנִי מְשַׁלֵּחַ בָּם אֶת־הַחֶרֶב אֶת־הָרָעָב וְאֶת־הַדָּבֶר וְנָתַתִּי אוֹתָם כַּתְּאֵנִים הַשֹּׁעָרִים אֲשֶׁר לֹא־תֵאָכַלְנָה מֵרֹעַ:

יח וְרָדַפְתִּי אַחֲרֵיהֶם בַּחֶרֶב בָּרָעָב וּבַדָּבֶר וּנְתַתִּים [לְזַעֲוָה] לְכֹל מַמְלְכוֹת הָאָרֶץ לְאָלָה וּלְשַׁמָּה וְלִשְׁרֵקָה וּלְחֶרְפָּה בְּכָל־הַגּוֹיִם אֲשֶׁר־הִדַּחְתִּים שָׁם:

יט תַּחַת אֲשֶׁר־לֹא־שָׁמְעוּ אֶל־דְּבָרַי נְאֻם־יְהֹוָה אֲשֶׁר שָׁלַחְתִּי אֲלֵיהֶם אֶת־עֲבָדַי הַנְּבִאִים הַשְׁכֵּם וְשָׁלֹחַ וְלֹא שְׁמַעְתֶּם נְאֻם־יְהֹוָה:

כ וְאַתֶּם שִׁמְעוּ דְבַר־יְהֹוָה כָּל־הַגּוֹלָה אֲשֶׁר־שִׁלַּחְתִּי מִירוּשָׁלִַם בָּבֶלָה:

כא כֹּה־אָמַר יְהֹוָה צְבָאוֹת אֱלֹהֵי יִשְׂרָאֵל אֶל־אַחְאָב בֶּן־קוֹלָיָה וְאֶל־צִדְקִיָּהוּ בֶן־מַעֲשֵׂיָה הַנִּבְּאִים לָכֶם בִּשְׁמִי שָׁקֶר הִנְנִי נֹתֵן אֹתָם בְּיַד נְבוּכַדְרֶאצַּר מֶלֶךְ־בָּבֶל וְהִכָּם לְעֵינֵיכֶם:

כב וְלֻקַּח מֵהֶם קְלָלָה לְכֹל גָּלוּת יְהוּדָה אֲשֶׁר בְּבָבֶל לֵאמֹר יְשִׂמְךָ יְהֹוָה כְּצִדְקִיָּהוּ וּכְאֶחָב אֲשֶׁר־קָלָם מֶלֶךְ־בָּבֶל בָּאֵשׁ:

כג יַעַן אֲשֶׁר עָשׂוּ נְבָלָה בְּיִשְׂרָאֵל וַיְנַאֲפוּ אֶת־נְשֵׁי רֵעֵיהֶם וַיְדַבְּרוּ דָבָר בִּשְׁמִי שֶׁקֶר אֲשֶׁר לוֹא צִוִּיתִם וְאָנֹכִי הוידע [הַיּוֹדֵעַ] וָעֵד נְאֻם־יְהֹוָה:

כד וְאֶל־שְׁמַעְיָהוּ הַנֶּחֱלָמִי תֹּאמַר לֵאמֹר:

כה כֹּה־אָמַר יְהֹוָה צְבָאוֹת אֱלֹהֵי יִשְׂרָאֵל לֵאמֹר יַעַן אֲשֶׁר אַתָּה שָׁלַחְתָּ בְשִׁמְכָה סְפָרִים אֶל־כָּל־הָעָם אֲשֶׁר בִּירוּשָׁלִַם וְאֶל־צְפַנְיָה בֶן־מַעֲשֵׂיָה הַכֹּהֵן וְאֶל כָּל־הַכֹּהֲנִים לֵאמֹר:

כו יְהֹוָה נְתָנְךָ כֹהֵן תַּחַת יְהוֹיָדָע הַכֹּהֵן לִהְיוֹת פְּקִדִים בֵּית יְהֹוָה לְכָל־אִישׁ מְשֻׁגָּע וּמִתְנַבֵּא וְנָתַתָּה אֹתוֹ אֶל־הַמַּהְפֶּכֶת וְאֶל־הַצִּינֹק:

Yirmiyahu/Jeremiah
Chapter 30

ירמיהו
פרק ל

27 Now why have you not rebuked *Yirmiyahu* the Anatotite, who plays the *Navi* among you?

כז וְעַתָּה לָמָּה לֹא גָעַרְתָּ בְּיִרְמְיָהוּ הָעֲנְתֹתִי הַמִּתְנַבֵּא לָכֶם׃

28 For he has actually sent a message to us in Babylon to this effect: It will be a long time. Build houses and live in them, plant gardens and enjoy their fruit." –

כח כִּי עַל־כֵּן שָׁלַח אֵלֵינוּ בָּבֶל לֵאמֹר אֲרֻכָּה הִיא בְּנוּ בָתִּים וְשֵׁבוּ וְנִטְעוּ גַנּוֹת וְאִכְלוּ אֶת־פְּרִיהֶן׃

29 When the *Kohen Tzefanya* read this letter in the hearing of the *Navi Yirmiyahu*,

כט וַיִּקְרָא צְפַנְיָה הַכֹּהֵן אֶת־הַסֵּפֶר הַזֶּה בְּאָזְנֵי יִרְמְיָהוּ הַנָּבִיא׃

30 the word of *Hashem* came to *Yirmiyahu*:

ל וַיְהִי דְּבַר־יְהֹוָה אֶל־יִרְמְיָהוּ לֵאמֹר׃

31 Send a message to the entire exile community: "Thus said *Hashem* concerning *Shemaya* the Nehelamite: Because *Shemaya* prophesied to you, though I did not send him, and made you false promises,

לא שְׁלַח עַל־כָּל־הַגּוֹלָה לֵאמֹר כֹּה אָמַר יְהֹוָה אֶל־שְׁמַעְיָה הַנֶּחֱלָמִי יַעַן אֲשֶׁר נִבָּא לָכֶם שְׁמַעְיָה וַאֲנִי לֹא שְׁלַחְתִּיו וַיַּבְטַח אֶתְכֶם עַל־שָׁקֶר׃

32 assuredly, thus said *Hashem*: I am going to punish *Shemaya* the Nehelamite and his offspring. There shall be no man of his line dwelling among this people or seeing the good things I am going to do for My people – declares *Hashem* – for he has urged disloyalty toward *Hashem*."

לב לָכֵן כֹּה־אָמַר יְהֹוָה הִנְנִי פֹקֵד עַל־שְׁמַעְיָה הַנֶּחֱלָמִי וְעַל־זַרְעוֹ לֹא־יִהְיֶה לוֹ אִישׁ יוֹשֵׁב בְּתוֹךְ־הָעָם הַזֶּה וְלֹא־יִרְאֶה בַטּוֹב אֲשֶׁר־אֲנִי עֹשֶׂה לְעַמִּי נְאֻם־יְהֹוָה כִּי־סָרָה דִבֶּר עַל־יְהֹוָה׃

30

1 The word which came to *Yirmiyahu* from *Hashem*:

א הַדָּבָר אֲשֶׁר הָיָה אֶל־יִרְמְיָהוּ מֵאֵת יְהֹוָה לֵאמֹר׃

2 Thus said *Hashem*, the God of *Yisrael*: Write down in a scroll all the words that I have spoken to you.

ב כֹּה־אָמַר יְהֹוָה אֱלֹהֵי יִשְׂרָאֵל לֵאמֹר כְּתָב־לְךָ אֵת כָּל־הַדְּבָרִים אֲשֶׁר־דִּבַּרְתִּי אֵלֶיךָ אֶל־סֵפֶר׃

3 For days are coming – declares *Hashem* – when I will restore the fortunes of My people *Yisrael* and *Yehuda*, said *Hashem*; and I will bring them back to the land that I gave their fathers, and they shall possess it.

ג כִּי הִנֵּה יָמִים בָּאִים נְאֻם־יְהֹוָה וְשַׁבְתִּי אֶת־שְׁבוּת עַמִּי יִשְׂרָאֵל וִיהוּדָה אָמַר יְהֹוָה וַהֲשִׁבֹתִים אֶל־הָאָרֶץ אֲשֶׁר־נָתַתִּי לַאֲבוֹתָם וִירֵשׁוּהָ׃

KEE hi-NAY ya-MEEM ba-EEM n'-um a-do-NAI v'-shav-TEE et sh'-VUT a-MEE yis-ra-AYL vee-hu-DAH a-MAR a-do-NAI va-ha-shi-vo-TEEM el ha-A-retz a-sher na-TA-tee la-a-vo-TAM vee-ray-SHU-ha

4 And these are the words that *Hashem* spoke concerning *Yisrael* and *Yehuda*:

ד וְאֵלֶּה הַדְּבָרִים אֲשֶׁר דִּבֶּר יְהֹוָה אֶל־יִשְׂרָאֵל וְאֶל־יְהוּדָה׃

30:3 I will bring them back to the land that I gave their fathers The return of the Jewish People to the Land of Israel has great significance to all. The legendary first Chief Rabbi of Israel, Abraham Isaac Kook, wrote that "The building of the Israeli nation means the building of the land, the government, the army, the people and the spirit together... the rebirth of the nation is the foundation of the 'Great *Teshuva*' ('Return') – the 'Great *Teshuva*' of the Jewish nation and the *teshuva* of the entire world which comes in its wake."

Rabbi Abraham Isaac Kook (1865–1935)

1144

Yirmiyahu/Jeremiah
Chapter 30

5 Thus said *Hashem*: We have heard cries of panic, Terror without relief.

6 Ask and see: Surely males do not bear young! Why then do I see every man With his hands on his loins Like a woman in labor? Why have all faces turned pale?

7 Ah, that day is awesome; There is none like it! It is a time of trouble for *Yaakov*, But he shall be delivered from it.

8 In that day – declares the Lord of Hosts – I will break the yoke from off your neck and I will rip off your bonds. Strangers shall no longer make slaves of them;

9 instead, they shall serve *Hashem* their God and *David*, the king whom I will raise up for them.

10 But you, Have no fear, My servant *Yaakov* – declares *Hashem* – Be not dismayed, O *Yisrael*! I will deliver you from far away, Your folk from their land of captivity. And *Yaakov* shall again have calm And quiet with none to trouble him;

11 For I am with you to deliver you – declares *Hashem*. I will make an end of all the nations Among which I have dispersed you; But I will not make an end of you! I will not leave you unpunished, But will chastise you in measure.

12 For thus said *Hashem*: Your injury is incurable, Your wound severe;

13 No one pleads for the healing of your sickness, There is no remedy, no recovery for you.

14 All your lovers have forgotten you, They do not seek you out; For I have struck you as an enemy strikes, With cruel chastisement, Because your iniquity was so great And your sins so many.

15 Why cry out over your injury, That your wound is incurable? I did these things to you Because your iniquity was so great And your sins so many.

16 Assuredly, All who wanted to devour you shall be devoured, And every one of your foes shall go into captivity; Those who despoiled you shall be despoiled, And all who pillaged you I will give up to pillage.

Yirmiyahu/Jeremiah
Chapter 31

17 But I will bring healing to you And cure you of your wounds – declares *Hashem*. Though they called you "Outcast, That *Tzion* whom no one seeks out,"

18 Thus said *Hashem*: I will restore the fortunes of *Yaakov*'s tents And have compassion upon his dwellings. The city shall be rebuilt on its mound, And the fortress in its proper place.

19 From them shall issue thanksgiving And the sound of dancers. I will multiply them, And they shall not be few; I will make them honored, And they shall not be humbled.

20 His children shall be as of old, And his community shall be established by My grace; And I will deal with all his oppressors.

21 His chieftain shall be one of his own, His ruler shall come from his midst; I will bring him near, that he may approach Me – declares *Hashem* – For who would otherwise dare approach Me?

22 You shall be My people, And I will be your God.

23 Lo, the storm of *Hashem* goes forth in fury, A raging tempest; It shall whirl down upon the head of the wicked.

24 The anger of *Hashem* shall not turn back Till it has fulfilled and completed His purposes. In the days to come You shall perceive it.

25 At that time – declares *Hashem* – I will be God to all the clans of *Yisrael*, and they shall be My people.

31

1 Thus said *Hashem*: The people escaped from the sword, Found favor in the wilderness; When *Yisrael* was marching homeward

2 *Hashem* revealed Himself to me of old. Eternal love I conceived for you then; Therefore I continue My grace to you.

3 I will build you firmly again, O Maiden *Yisrael*! Again you shall take up your timbrels And go forth to the rhythm of the dancers.

Yirmiyahu/Jeremiah
Chapter 31

ירמיהו
פרק לא

4 Again you shall plant vineyards On the hills of *Shomron*; Men shall plant and live to enjoy them.

OD ti-t'-EE kh'-ra-MEEM b'-ha-RAY sho-m'-RON na-t'-U no-t'-EEM v'-khi-LAY-lu

ד עוֹד תִּטְּעִי כְרָמִים בְּהָרֵי שֹׁמְרוֹן נָטְעוּ נֹטְעִים וְחִלֵּלוּ׃

5 For the day is coming when watchmen Shall proclaim on the heights of *Efraim*: Come, let us go up to *Tzion*, To *Hashem* our God!

ה כִּי יֶשׁ־יוֹם קָרְאוּ נֹצְרִים בְּהַר אֶפְרָיִם קוּמוּ וְנַעֲלֶה צִיּוֹן אֶל־יְהֹוָה אֱלֹהֵינוּ׃

6 For thus said *Hashem*: Cry out in joy for *Yaakov*, Shout at the crossroads of the nations! Sing aloud in praise, and say: Save, *Hashem*, Your people, The remnant of *Yisrael*.

ו כִּי־כֹה ׀ אָמַר יְהֹוָה רָנּוּ לְיַעֲקֹב שִׂמְחָה וְצַהֲלוּ בְּרֹאשׁ הַגּוֹיִם הַשְׁמִיעוּ הַלְלוּ וְאִמְרוּ הוֹשַׁע יְהֹוָה אֶת־עַמְּךָ אֵת שְׁאֵרִית יִשְׂרָאֵל׃

7 I will bring them in from the northland, Gather them from the ends of the earth – The blind and the lame among them, Those with child and those in labor – In a vast throng they shall return here.

ז הִנְנִי מֵבִיא אוֹתָם מֵאֶרֶץ צָפוֹן וְקִבַּצְתִּים מִיַּרְכְּתֵי־אָרֶץ בָּם עִוֵּר וּפִסֵּחַ הָרָה וְיֹלֶדֶת יַחְדָּו קָהָל גָּדוֹל יָשׁוּבוּ הֵנָּה׃

8 They shall come with weeping, And with compassion will I guide them. I will lead them to streams of water, By a level road where they will not stumble. For I am ever a Father to *Yisrael*, *Efraim* is My first-born.

ח בִּבְכִי יָבֹאוּ וּבְתַחֲנוּנִים אוֹבִילֵם אוֹלִיכֵם אֶל־נַחֲלֵי מַיִם בְּדֶרֶךְ יָשָׁר לֹא יִכָּשְׁלוּ בָּהּ כִּי־הָיִיתִי לְיִשְׂרָאֵל לְאָב וְאֶפְרַיִם בְּכוֹרִי הוּא׃

9 Hear the word of *Hashem*, O nations, And tell it in the isles afar. Say: He who scattered *Yisrael* will gather them, And will guard them as a shepherd his flock.

ט שִׁמְעוּ דְבַר־יְהֹוָה גּוֹיִם וְהַגִּידוּ בָאִיִּים מִמֶּרְחָק וְאִמְרוּ מְזָרֵה יִשְׂרָאֵל יְקַבְּצֶנּוּ וּשְׁמָרוֹ כְּרֹעֶה עֶדְרוֹ׃

10 For *Hashem* will ransom *Yaakov*, Redeem him from one too strong for him.

י כִּי־פָדָה יְהֹוָה אֶת־יַעֲקֹב וּגְאָלוֹ מִיַּד חָזָק מִמֶּנּוּ׃

11 They shall come and shout on the heights of *Tzion*, Radiant over the bounty of *Hashem* – Over new grain and wine and oil, And over sheep and cattle. They shall fare like a watered garden, They shall never languish again.

יא וּבָאוּ וְרִנְּנוּ בִמְרוֹם־צִיּוֹן וְנָהֲרוּ אֶל־טוּב יְהֹוָה עַל־דָּגָן וְעַל־תִּירֹשׁ וְעַל־יִצְהָר וְעַל־בְּנֵי־צֹאן וּבָקָר וְהָיְתָה נַפְשָׁם כְּגַן רָוֶה וְלֹא־יוֹסִיפוּ לְדַאֲבָה עוֹד׃

12 Then shall maidens dance gaily, Young men and old alike. I will turn their mourning to joy, I will comfort them and cheer them in their grief.

יב אָז תִּשְׂמַח בְּתוּלָה בְּמָחוֹל וּבַחֻרִים וּזְקֵנִים יַחְדָּו וְהָפַכְתִּי אֶבְלָם לְשָׂשׂוֹן וְנִחַמְתִּים וְשִׂמַּחְתִּים מִיגוֹנָם׃

Logo for Israel's Ministry of Tourism

31:4 Again you shall plant vineyards on the hills of *Shomron* Return of life to the Holy Land is symbolized by the rejuvenation of vineyards in Samaria, a miracle taking place today. Grapes and vineyards play a prominent role throughout *Tanakh*. The first cultivated plants mentioned in the Bible were grapevines: "*Noach*, the tiller of soil, was the first to plant a vineyard" (Genesis 9:20). Grapes are mentioned more than any other fruit in the entire *Tanakh*. When *Moshe* sent the 12 spies to scout out *Eretz Yisrael*, the book of *Bamidbar* (13:23) records that they returned with a sample of grapes that was so large it had to be carried on poles by strong men, an image used as the logo of Israel's Ministry of Tourism. This honored fruit aslo plays a prominent role in Judaism, as *Shabbat* and Holiday meals begin with a blessing over a cup of wine.

Yirmiyahu/Jeremiah
Chapter 31

ירמיהו
פרק לא

13 I will give the *Kohanim* their fill of fatness, And My people shall enjoy My full bounty – declares *Hashem*.

יג וְרִוֵּיתִי נֶפֶשׁ הַכֹּהֲנִים דָּשֶׁן וְעַמִּי אֶת־טוּבִי יִשְׂבָּעוּ נְאֻם־יְהֹוָה:

14 Thus said *Hashem*: A cry is heard in *Rama* – Wailing, bitter weeping – *Rachel* weeping for her children. She refuses to be comforted For her children, who are gone.

יד כֹּה ׀ אָמַר יְהֹוָה קוֹל בְּרָמָה נִשְׁמָע נְהִי בְּכִי תַמְרוּרִים רָחֵל מְבַכָּה עַל־בָּנֶיהָ מֵאֲנָה לְהִנָּחֵם עַל־בָּנֶיהָ כִּי אֵינֶנּוּ:

15 Thus said *Hashem*: Restrain your voice from weeping, Your eyes from shedding tears; For there is a reward for your labor – declares *Hashem*: They shall return from the enemy's land.

טו כֹּה ׀ אָמַר יְהֹוָה מִנְעִי קוֹלֵךְ מִבֶּכִי וְעֵינַיִךְ מִדִּמְעָה כִּי יֵשׁ שָׂכָר לִפְעֻלָּתֵךְ נְאֻם־יְהֹוָה וְשָׁבוּ מֵאֶרֶץ אוֹיֵב:

16 And there is hope for your future – declares *Hashem*: Your children shall return to their country.

טז וְיֵשׁ־תִּקְוָה לְאַחֲרִיתֵךְ נְאֻם־יְהֹוָה וְשָׁבוּ בָנִים לִגְבוּלָם:

v'-yaysh tik-VAH l'-a-kha-ree-TAYKH n'-um a-do-NAI v'-SHA-vu va-NEEM lig-vu-LAM

17 I can hear *Efraim* lamenting: You have chastised me, and I am chastised Like a calf that has not been broken. Receive me back, let me return, For You, *Hashem*, are my God.

יז שָׁמוֹעַ שָׁמַעְתִּי אֶפְרַיִם מִתְנוֹדֵד יִסַּרְתַּנִי וָאִוָּסֵר כְּעֵגֶל לֹא לֻמָּד הֲשִׁיבֵנִי וְאָשׁוּבָה כִּי אַתָּה יְהֹוָה אֱלֹהָי:

18 Now that I have turned back, I am filled with remorse; Now that I am made aware, I strike my thigh. I am ashamed and humiliated, For I bear the disgrace of my youth.

יח כִּי־אַחֲרֵי שׁוּבִי נִחַמְתִּי וְאַחֲרֵי הִוָּדְעִי סָפַקְתִּי עַל־יָרֵךְ בֹּשְׁתִּי וְגַם־נִכְלַמְתִּי כִּי נָשָׂאתִי חֶרְפַּת נְעוּרָי:

19 Truly, *Efraim* is a dear son to Me, A child that is dandled! Whenever I have turned against him, My thoughts would dwell on him still. That is why My heart yearns for him; I will receive him back in love – declares *Hashem*.

יט הֲבֵן יַקִּיר לִי אֶפְרַיִם אִם יֶלֶד שַׁעֲשֻׁעִים כִּי־מִדֵּי דַבְּרִי בּוֹ זָכֹר אֶזְכְּרֶנּוּ עוֹד עַל־כֵּן הָמוּ מֵעַי לוֹ רַחֵם אֲרַחֲמֶנּוּ נְאֻם־יְהֹוָה:

20 Erect markers, Set up signposts; Keep in mind the highway, The road that you traveled. Return, Maiden *Yisrael*! Return to these towns of yours!

כ הַצִּיבִי לָךְ צִיֻּנִים שִׂמִי לָךְ תַּמְרוּרִים שִׁתִי לִבֵּךְ לַמְסִלָּה דֶּרֶךְ הָלָכְתְּ [הָלָכְתִּי] שׁוּבִי בְּתוּלַת יִשְׂרָאֵל שֻׁבִי אֶל־עָרַיִךְ אֵלֶּה:

21 How long will you waver, O rebellious daughter? (For *Hashem* has created something new on earth: A woman courts a man.)

כא עַד־מָתַי תִּתְחַמָּקִין הַבַּת הַשּׁוֹבֵבָה כִּי־בָרָא יְהֹוָה חֲדָשָׁה בָּאָרֶץ נְקֵבָה תְּסוֹבֵב גָּבֶר:

31:16 Your children shall return to their country
In this moving passage, God speaks directly to the matriarch *Rachel*, who is known in Jewish tradition as having a special role in the redemption of her children, the Jewish people, and their return to Israel. According to Jewish tradition, when her father Laban gave her sister *Leah* to *Yaakov* in marriage in her stead, *Rachel* revealed to *Leah* a secret sign she had made with *Yaakov* in order to spare *Leah* from embarrassment. Because of *Rachel's* unparalleled selflessness and love for her sister, it is *Rachel's* prayers, tears and cries for compassion to her children that are heard by God more than any other biblical figure. God promises *Rachel* that those tears are not for naught, but rather "There is a reward for your labor" (verse 16) and "your children shall return to their country." In a moving example of symbolism, this verse is often sung with emotion at Ben Gurion Airport as new Jewish immigrants arrive in Israel.

Greeting new immigrants with "your children shall return to their country"

Yirmiyahu/Jeremiah
Chapter 31

22 Thus said the Lord of Hosts, the God of *Yisrael*: They shall again say this in the land of *Yehuda* and in its towns, when I restore their fortunes: "*Hashem* bless you, Abode of righteousness, O holy mountain!"

כב כֹּה־אָמַר יְהֹוָה צְבָאוֹת אֱלֹהֵי יִשְׂרָאֵל עוֹד יֹאמְרוּ אֶת־הַדָּבָר הַזֶּה בְּאֶרֶץ יְהוּדָה וּבְעָרָיו בְּשׁוּבִי אֶת־שְׁבוּתָם יְבָרֶכְךָ יְהֹוָה נְוֵה־צֶדֶק הַר הַקֹּדֶשׁ:

23 *Yehuda* and all its towns alike shall be inhabited by the farmers and such as move about with the flocks.

כג וְיָשְׁבוּ בָהּ יְהוּדָה וְכָל־עָרָיו יַחְדָּו אִכָּרִים וְנָסְעוּ בַּעֵדֶר:

24 For I will give the thirsty abundant drink, and satisfy all who languish.

כד כִּי הִרְוֵיתִי נֶפֶשׁ עֲיֵפָה וְכָל־נֶפֶשׁ דָּאֲבָה מִלֵּאתִי:

25 At this I awoke and looked about, and my sleep had been pleasant to me.

כה עַל־זֹאת הֱקִיצֹתִי וָאֶרְאֶה וּשְׁנָתִי עָרְבָה לִי:

26 See, a time is coming – declares *Hashem* – when I will sow the House of *Yisrael* and the House of *Yehuda* with seed of men and seed of cattle;

כו הִנֵּה יָמִים בָּאִים נְאֻם־יְהֹוָה וְזָרַעְתִּי אֶת־בֵּית יִשְׂרָאֵל וְאֶת־בֵּית יְהוּדָה זֶרַע אָדָם וְזֶרַע בְּהֵמָה:

27 and just as I was watchful over them to uproot and to pull down, to overthrow and to destroy and to bring disaster, so I will be watchful over them to build and to plant – declares *Hashem*.

כז וְהָיָה כַּאֲשֶׁר שָׁקַדְתִּי עֲלֵיהֶם לִנְתוֹשׁ וְלִנְתוֹץ וְלַהֲרֹס וּלְהַאֲבִיד וּלְהָרֵעַ כֵּן אֶשְׁקֹד עֲלֵיהֶם לִבְנוֹת וְלִנְטוֹעַ נְאֻם־יְהֹוָה:

28 In those days, they shall no longer say, "Parents have eaten sour grapes and children's teeth are blunted."

כח בַּיָּמִים הָהֵם לֹא־יֹאמְרוּ עוֹד אָבוֹת אָכְלוּ בֹסֶר וְשִׁנֵּי בָנִים תִּקְהֶינָה:

29 But every one shall die for his own sins: whosoever eats sour grapes, his teeth shall be blunted.

כט כִּי אִם־אִישׁ בַּעֲוֹנוֹ יָמוּת כָּל־הָאָדָם הָאֹכֵל הַבֹּסֶר תִּקְהֶינָה שִׁנָּיו:

30 See, a time is coming – declares *Hashem* – when I will make a new covenant with the House of *Yisrael* and the House of *Yehuda*.

ל הִנֵּה יָמִים בָּאִים נְאֻם־יְהֹוָה וְכָרַתִּי אֶת־בֵּית יִשְׂרָאֵל וְאֶת־בֵּית יְהוּדָה בְּרִית חֲדָשָׁה:

hi-NAY ya-MEEM ba-EEM n'-UM a-do-NAI v'-kha-ra-TEE et BAYT yis-ra-AYL v'-et BAYT y'-du-DAH b'-REET kha-da-SHAH

31 It will not be like the covenant I made with their fathers, when I took them by the hand to lead them out of the land of Egypt, a covenant which they broke, though I espoused them – declares *Hashem*.

לא לֹא כַבְּרִית אֲשֶׁר כָּרַתִּי אֶת־אֲבוֹתָם בְּיוֹם הֶחֱזִיקִי בְיָדָם לְהוֹצִיאָם מֵאֶרֶץ מִצְרָיִם אֲשֶׁר־הֵמָּה הֵפֵרוּ אֶת־בְּרִיתִי וְאָנֹכִי בָּעַלְתִּי בָם נְאֻם־יְהֹוָה:

32 But such is the covenant I will make with the House of *Yisrael* after these days – declares *Hashem*: I will put My Teaching into their inmost being and inscribe it upon their hearts. Then I will be their God, and they shall be My people.

לב כִּי זֹאת הַבְּרִית אֲשֶׁר אֶכְרֹת אֶת־בֵּית יִשְׂרָאֵל אַחֲרֵי הַיָּמִים הָהֵם נְאֻם־יְהֹוָה נָתַתִּי אֶת־תּוֹרָתִי בְּקִרְבָּם וְעַל־לִבָּם אֶכְתֳּבֶנָּה וְהָיִיתִי לָהֶם לֵאלֹהִים וְהֵמָּה יִהְיוּ־לִי לְעָם:

31:30 I will make a new covenant The Children of Israel were unfaithful to *Hashem* and were twice exiled from their land. Throughout the ages, they have experienced oppression and persecution. Yet, God promises that as long as the celestial bodies of heaven continue to function according to the divinely ordained laws of nature, Israel will continue to be His chosen people (verses 34–35). This verse confirms that God has not abandoned or replaced His people; the Nation of Israel will never be cast away from *Hashem*.

Yirmiyahu/Jeremiah
Chapter 32

33 No longer will they need to teach one another and say to one another, "Heed *Hashem*"; for all of them, from the least of them to the greatest, shall heed Me – declares *Hashem*. For I will forgive their iniquities, And remember their sins no more.

34 Thus said *Hashem*, Who established the sun for light by day, The laws of moon and stars for light by night, Who stirs up the sea into roaring waves, Whose name is LORD of Hosts:

35 If these laws should ever be annulled by Me – declares *Hashem* – Only then would the offspring of *Yisrael* cease To be a nation before Me for all time.

36 Thus said *Hashem*: If the heavens above could be measured, and the foundations of the earth below could be fathomed, only then would I reject all the offspring of *Yisrael* for all that they have done – declares *Hashem*.

37 See, a time is coming – declares *Hashem* – when the city shall be rebuilt for *Hashem* from the Tower of Hananel to the Corner Gate;

38 and the measuring line shall go straight out to the Gareb Hill, and then turn toward Goah.

39 And the entire Valley of the Corpses and Ashes, and all the fields as far as the Wadi Kidron, and the corner of the Horse Gate on the east, shall be holy to *Hashem*. They shall never again be uprooted or overthrown.

32

1 The word which came to *Yirmiyahu* from *Hashem* in the tenth year of King *Tzidkiyahu* of *Yehuda*, which was the eighteenth year of Nebuchadrezzar.

2 At that time the army of the king of Babylon was besieging *Yerushalayim*, and the *Navi Yirmiyahu* was confined in the prison compound attached to the palace of the king of *Yehuda*.

3 For King *Tzidkiyahu* of *Yehuda* had confined him, saying, "How dare you prophesy: 'Thus said *Hashem*: I am delivering this city into the hands of the king of Babylon, and he shall capture it.

4 And King *Tzidkiyahu* of *Yehuda* shall not escape from the Chaldeans; he shall be delivered into the hands of the king of Babylon, and he shall speak to him face to face and see him in person.

Yirmiyahu/Jeremiah
Chapter 32

ירמיהו
פרק לב

5 And *Tzidkiyahu* shall be brought to Babylon, there to remain until I take note of him – declares *Hashem*. When you wage war against the Chaldeans, you shall not be successful.'"

ה וּבָבֶל יוֹלִךְ אֶת־צִדְקִיָּהוּ וְשָׁם יִהְיֶה עַד־פָּקְדִי אֹתוֹ נְאֻם־יְהֹוָה כִּי תִלָּחֲמוּ אֶת־הַכַּשְׂדִּים לֹא תַצְלִיחוּ:

6 *Yirmiyahu* said: The word of *Hashem* came to me:

ו וַיֹּאמֶר יִרְמְיָהוּ הָיָה דְּבַר־יְהֹוָה אֵלַי לֵאמֹר:

7 *Chanamel*, the son of your uncle *Shalum*, will come to you and say, "Buy my land in *Anatot*, for you are next in succession to redeem it by purchase."

ז הִנֵּה חֲנַמְאֵל בֶּן־שַׁלֻּם דֹּדְךָ בָּא אֵלֶיךָ לֵאמֹר קְנֵה לְךָ אֶת־שָׂדִי אֲשֶׁר בַּעֲנָתוֹת כִּי לְךָ מִשְׁפַּט הַגְּאֻלָּה לִקְנוֹת:

hi-NAY kha-nam-AYL ben sha-LUM do-d'-KHA BA ay-LE-kha lay-MOR k'-NAY l'-KHA et sa-DEE a-SHER ba-a-na-TOT KEE l'-KHA mish-PAT ha-g'-u-LAH lik-NOT

8 And just as *Hashem* had said, my cousin *Chanamel* came to me in the prison compound and said to me, "Please buy my land in *Anatot*, in the territory of *Binyamin*; for the right of succession is yours, and you have the duty of redemption. Buy it." Then I knew that it was indeed the word of *Hashem*.

ח וַיָּבֹא אֵלַי חֲנַמְאֵל בֶּן־דֹּדִי כִּדְבַר יְהֹוָה אֶל־חֲצַר הַמַּטָּרָה וַיֹּאמֶר אֵלַי קְנֵה נָא אֶת־שָׂדִי אֲשֶׁר־בַּעֲנָתוֹת אֲשֶׁר בְּאֶרֶץ בִּנְיָמִין כִּי־לְךָ מִשְׁפַּט הַיְרֻשָּׁה וּלְךָ הַגְּאֻלָּה קְנֵה־לָךְ וָאֵדַע כִּי דְבַר־יְהֹוָה הוּא:

9 So I bought the land in *Anatot* from my cousin *Chanamel*. I weighed out the money to him, seventeen *shekalim* of silver.

ט וָאֶקְנֶה אֶת־הַשָּׂדֶה מֵאֵת חֲנַמְאֵל בֶּן־דֹּדִי אֲשֶׁר בַּעֲנָתוֹת וָאֶשְׁקֳלָה־לּוֹ אֶת־הַכֶּסֶף שִׁבְעָה שְׁקָלִים וַעֲשָׂרָה הַכָּסֶף:

10 I wrote a deed, sealed it, and had it witnessed; and I weighed out the silver on a balance.

י וָאֶכְתֹּב בַּסֵּפֶר וָאֶחְתֹּם וָאָעֵד עֵדִים וָאֶשְׁקֹל הַכֶּסֶף בְּמֹאזְנָיִם:

11 I took the deed of purchase, the sealed text and the open one according to rule and law,

יא וָאֶקַּח אֶת־סֵפֶר הַמִּקְנָה אֶת־הֶחָתוּם הַמִּצְוָה וְהַחֻקִּים וְאֶת־הַגָּלוּי:

12 and gave the deed to *Baruch* son of *Nerya* son of *Machseya* in the presence of my kinsman *Chanamel*, of the witnesses who were named in the deed, and all the Judeans who were sitting in the prison compound.

יב וָאֶתֵּן אֶת־הַסֵּפֶר הַמִּקְנָה אֶל־בָּרוּךְ בֶּן־נֵרִיָּה בֶּן־מַחְסֵיָה לְעֵינֵי חֲנַמְאֵל דֹּדִי וּלְעֵינֵי הָעֵדִים הַכֹּתְבִים בְּסֵפֶר הַמִּקְנָה לְעֵינֵי כָּל־הַיְּהוּדִים הַיֹּשְׁבִים בַּחֲצַר הַמַּטָּרָה:

13 In their presence I charged *Baruch* as follows:

יג וָאֲצַוֶּה אֶת־בָּרוּךְ לְעֵינֵיהֶם לֵאמֹר:

14 Thus said the Lord of Hosts, the God of *Yisrael*: "Take these documents, this deed of purchase, the sealed text and the open one, and put them into an earthen jar, so that they may last a long time."

יד כֹּה־אָמַר יְהֹוָה צְבָאוֹת אֱלֹהֵי יִשְׂרָאֵל לָקוֹחַ אֶת־הַסְּפָרִים הָאֵלֶּה אֵת סֵפֶר הַמִּקְנָה הַזֶּה וְאֵת הֶחָתוּם וְאֵת סֵפֶר הַגָּלוּי הַזֶּה וּנְתַתָּם בִּכְלִי־חָרֶשׂ לְמַעַן יַעַמְדוּ יָמִים רַבִּים:

The modern town of Anatot

32:7 Buy my land in *Anatot* At a time of impending destruction, *Yirmiyahu* is told to redeem his family's property. This symbolic purchase reflects not only the biblical law that land could be redeemed by relatives (see Leviticus 25, Ruth 4), but it also demonstrates *Yirmiyahu's* total faith that even though the exile to Babylonia is quickly approaching, it will in fact be only temporary. The sale also demonstrates, with poetic words and symbolic action, the eternal connection between the Jewish people and the land. Though currently on the brink of exile, they remain attached to their land, with the deed preserved in an earthenware vessel.

Yirmiyahu/Jeremiah
Chapter 32

ירמיהו
פרק לב

15 For thus said the Lord of Hosts, the God of *Yisrael*: "Houses, fields, and vineyards shall again be purchased in this land."

טו כִּי כֹה אָמַר יְהֹוָה צְבָאוֹת אֱלֹהֵי יִשְׂרָאֵל עוֹד יִקָּנוּ בָתִּים וְשָׂדוֹת וּכְרָמִים בָּאָרֶץ הַזֹּאת׃

16 But after I had given the deed to *Baruch* son of *Nerya*, I prayed to *Hashem*:

טז וָאֶתְפַּלֵּל אֶל־יְהֹוָה אַחֲרֵי תִתִּי אֶת־סֵפֶר הַמִּקְנָה אֶל־בָּרוּךְ בֶּן־נֵרִיָּה לֵאמֹר׃

17 "Ah, *Hashem*! You made heaven and earth with Your great might and outstretched arm. Nothing is too wondrous for You!

יז אֲהָהּ אֲדֹנָי יֱהֹוִה הִנֵּה אַתָּה עָשִׂיתָ אֶת־הַשָּׁמַיִם וְאֶת־הָאָרֶץ בְּכֹחֲךָ הַגָּדוֹל וּבִזְרֹעֲךָ הַנְּטוּיָה לֹא־יִפָּלֵא מִמְּךָ כָּל־דָּבָר׃

18 You show kindness to the thousandth generation, but visit the guilt of the fathers upon their children after them. O great and mighty *Hashem* whose name is Lord of Hosts,

יח עֹשֶׂה חֶסֶד לַאֲלָפִים וּמְשַׁלֵּם עֲוֺן אָבוֹת אֶל־חֵיק בְּנֵיהֶם אַחֲרֵיהֶם הָאֵל הַגָּדוֹל הַגִּבּוֹר יְהֹוָה צְבָאוֹת שְׁמוֹ׃

19 wondrous in purpose and mighty in deed, whose eyes observe all the ways of men, so as to repay every man according to his ways, and with the proper fruit of his deeds!

יט גְּדֹל הָעֵצָה וְרַב הָעֲלִילִיָּה אֲשֶׁר־עֵינֶיךָ פְקֻחוֹת עַל־כָּל־דַּרְכֵי בְּנֵי אָדָם לָתֵת לְאִישׁ כִּדְרָכָיו וְכִפְרִי מַעֲלָלָיו׃

20 You displayed signs and marvels in the land of Egypt with lasting effect, and won renown in *Yisrael* and among mankind to this very day.

כ אֲשֶׁר־שַׂמְתָּ אֹתוֹת וּמֹפְתִים בְּאֶרֶץ־מִצְרַיִם עַד־הַיּוֹם הַזֶּה וּבְיִשְׂרָאֵל וּבָאָדָם וַתַּעֲשֶׂה־לְּךָ שֵׁם כַּיּוֹם הַזֶּה׃

21 You freed Your people *Yisrael* from the land of Egypt with signs and marvels, with a strong hand and an outstretched arm, and with great terror.

כא וַתֹּצֵא אֶת־עַמְּךָ אֶת־יִשְׂרָאֵל מֵאֶרֶץ מִצְרָיִם בְּאֹתוֹת וּבְמוֹפְתִים וּבְיָד חֲזָקָה וּבְאֶזְרוֹעַ נְטוּיָה וּבְמוֹרָא גָּדוֹל׃

22 You gave them this land that You had sworn to their fathers to give them, a land flowing with milk and honey,

כב וַתִּתֵּן לָהֶם אֶת־הָאָרֶץ הַזֹּאת אֲשֶׁר־נִשְׁבַּעְתָּ לַאֲבוֹתָם לָתֵת לָהֶם אֶרֶץ זָבַת חָלָב וּדְבָשׁ׃

23 and they came and took possession of it. But they did not listen to You or follow Your Teaching; they did nothing of what You commanded them to do. Therefore you have caused all this misfortune to befall them.

כג וַיָּבֹאוּ וַיִּרְשׁוּ אֹתָהּ וְלֹא־שָׁמְעוּ בְקוֹלֶךָ וּבְתֹרוֹתְךָ [וּבְתוֹרָתְךָ] לֹא־הָלָכוּ אֵת כָּל־אֲשֶׁר צִוִּיתָה לָהֶם לַעֲשׂוֹת לֹא עָשׂוּ וַתַּקְרֵא אֹתָם אֵת כָּל־הָרָעָה הַזֹּאת׃

24 Here are the siegemounds, raised against the city to storm it; and the city, because of sword and famine and pestilence, is at the mercy of the Chaldeans who are attacking it. What You threatened has come to pass – as You see.

כד הִנֵּה הַסֹּלְלוֹת בָּאוּ הָעִיר לְלָכְדָהּ וְהָעִיר נִתְּנָה בְּיַד הַכַּשְׂדִּים הַנִּלְחָמִים עָלֶיהָ מִפְּנֵי הַחֶרֶב וְהָרָעָב וְהַדָּבֶר וַאֲשֶׁר דִּבַּרְתָּ הָיָה וְהִנְּךָ רֹאֶה׃

25 Yet You, *Hashem*, said to me: Buy the land for money and call in witnesses – when the city is at the mercy of the Chaldeans!"

כה וְאַתָּה אָמַרְתָּ אֵלַי אֲדֹנָי יֱהֹוִה קְנֵה־לְךָ הַשָּׂדֶה בַּכֶּסֶף וְהָעֵד עֵדִים וְהָעִיר נִתְּנָה בְּיַד הַכַּשְׂדִּים׃

26 Then the word of *Hashem* came to *Yirmiyahu*:

כו וַיְהִי דְּבַר־יְהֹוָה אֶל־יִרְמְיָהוּ לֵאמֹר׃

27 "Behold I am *Hashem*, the God of all flesh. Is anything too wondrous for Me?

כז הִנֵּה אֲנִי יְהֹוָה אֱלֹהֵי כָּל־בָּשָׂר הֲמִמֶּנִּי יִפָּלֵא כָּל־דָּבָר׃

1152

Yirmiyahu/Jeremiah
Chapter 32

28 Assuredly, thus said *Hashem*: I am delivering this city into the hands of the Chaldeans and of King Nebuchadrezzar of Babylon, and he shall capture it.

29 And the Chaldeans who have been attacking this city shall come and set this city on fire and burn it down – with the houses on whose roofs they made offerings to Baal and poured out libations to other gods, so as to vex Me.

30 For the people of *Yisrael* and *Yehuda* have done nothing but evil in My sight since their youth; the people of *Yisrael* have done nothing but vex Me by their conduct – declares *Hashem*.

31 This city has aroused My anger and My wrath from the day it was built until this day; so that it must be removed from My sight

32 because of all the wickedness of the people of *Yisrael* and *Yehuda* who have so acted as to vex Me – they, their kings, their officials, their *Kohanim* and *Neviim*, and the men of *Yehuda* and the inhabitants of *Yerushalayim*.

33 They turned their backs to Me, not their faces; though I have taught them persistently, they do not give heed or accept rebuke.

34 They placed their abominations in the House which bears My name and defiled it;

35 and they built the shrines of Baal which are in the Valley of Ben-hinnom, where they offered up their sons and daughters to Molech – when I had never commanded, or even thought [of commanding], that they should do such an abominable thing, and so bring guilt on *Yehuda*.

36 But now, assuredly, thus said *Hashem*, the God of *Yisrael*, concerning this city of which you say, "It is being delivered into the hands of the king of Babylon through the sword, through famine, and through pestilence":

37 See, I will gather them from all the lands to which I have banished them in My anger and wrath, and in great rage; and I will bring them back to this place and let them dwell secure.

38 They shall be My people, and I will be their God.

ירמיהו
פרק לב

כח לָכֵן כֹּה אָמַר יְהֹוָה הִנְנִי נֹתֵן אֶת־הָעִיר הַזֹּאת בְּיַד הַכַּשְׂדִּים וּבְיַד נְבוּכַדְרֶאצַּר מֶלֶךְ־בָּבֶל וּלְכָדָהּ:

כט וּבָאוּ הַכַּשְׂדִּים הַנִּלְחָמִים עַל־הָעִיר הַזֹּאת וְהִצִּיתוּ אֶת־הָעִיר הַזֹּאת בָּאֵשׁ וּשְׂרָפוּהָ וְאֵת הַבָּתִּים אֲשֶׁר קִטְּרוּ עַל־גַּגּוֹתֵיהֶם לַבַּעַל וְהִסִּכוּ נְסָכִים לֵאלֹהִים אֲחֵרִים לְמַעַן הַכְעִסֵנִי:

ל כִּי־הָיוּ בְנֵי־יִשְׂרָאֵל וּבְנֵי יְהוּדָה אַךְ עֹשִׂים הָרַע בְּעֵינַי מִנְּעֻרֹתֵיהֶם כִּי בְנֵי־יִשְׂרָאֵל אַךְ מַכְעִסִים אֹתִי בְּמַעֲשֵׂה יְדֵיהֶם נְאֻם־יְהֹוָה:

לא כִּי עַל־אַפִּי וְעַל־חֲמָתִי הָיְתָה לִּי הָעִיר הַזֹּאת לְמִן־הַיּוֹם אֲשֶׁר בָּנוּ אוֹתָהּ וְעַד הַיּוֹם הַזֶּה לַהֲסִירָהּ מֵעַל פָּנָי:

לב עַל כָּל־רָעַת בְּנֵי־יִשְׂרָאֵל וּבְנֵי יְהוּדָה אֲשֶׁר עָשׂוּ לְהַכְעִסֵנִי הֵמָּה מַלְכֵיהֶם שָׂרֵיהֶם כֹּהֲנֵיהֶם וּנְבִיאֵיהֶם וְאִישׁ יְהוּדָה וְיֹשְׁבֵי יְרוּשָׁלָיִם:

לג וַיִּפְנוּ אֵלַי עֹרֶף וְלֹא פָנִים וְלַמֵּד אֹתָם הַשְׁכֵּם וְלַמֵּד וְאֵינָם שֹׁמְעִים לָקַחַת מוּסָר:

לד וַיָּשִׂימוּ שִׁקּוּצֵיהֶם בַּבַּיִת אֲשֶׁר־נִקְרָא־שְׁמִי עָלָיו לְטַמְּאוֹ:

לה וַיִּבְנוּ אֶת־בָּמוֹת הַבַּעַל אֲשֶׁר בְּגֵיא בֶן־הִנֹּם לְהַעֲבִיר אֶת־בְּנֵיהֶם וְאֶת־בְּנוֹתֵיהֶם לַמֹּלֶךְ אֲשֶׁר לֹא־צִוִּיתִים וְלֹא עָלְתָה עַל־לִבִּי לַעֲשׂוֹת הַתּוֹעֵבָה הַזֹּאת לְמַעַן החטי [הַחֲטִיא] אֶת־יְהוּדָה:

לו וְעַתָּה לָכֵן כֹּה־אָמַר יְהֹוָה אֱלֹהֵי יִשְׂרָאֵל אֶל־הָעִיר הַזֹּאת אֲשֶׁר אַתֶּם אֹמְרִים נִתְּנָה בְּיַד מֶלֶךְ־בָּבֶל בַּחֶרֶב וּבָרָעָב וּבַדָּבֶר:

לז הִנְנִי מְקַבְּצָם מִכָּל־הָאֲרָצוֹת אֲשֶׁר הִדַּחְתִּים שָׁם בְּאַפִּי וּבַחֲמָתִי וּבְקֶצֶף גָּדוֹל וַהֲשִׁבֹתִים אֶל־הַמָּקוֹם הַזֶּה וְהֹשַׁבְתִּים לָבֶטַח:

לח וְהָיוּ לִי לְעָם וַאֲנִי אֶהְיֶה לָהֶם לֵאלֹהִים:

Yirmiyahu/Jeremiah
Chapter 33

39 I will give them a single heart and a single nature to revere Me for all time, and it shall be well with them and their children after them.

40 And I will make an everlasting covenant with them that I will not turn away from them and that I will treat them graciously; and I will put into their hearts reverence for Me, so that they do not turn away from Me.

41 I will delight in treating them graciously, and I will plant them in this land faithfully, with all My heart and soul.

42 For thus said *Hashem*: As I have brought this terrible disaster upon this people, so I am going to bring upon them the vast good fortune which I have promised for them.

43 And fields shall again be purchased in this land of which you say, "It is a desolation, without man or beast; it is delivered into the hands of the Chaldeans."

44 Fields shall be purchased, and deeds written and sealed, and witnesses called in the land of *Binyamin* and in the environs of *Yerushalayim*, and in the towns of *Yehuda*; the towns of the hill country, the towns of the Shephelah, and the towns of the *Negev*. For I will restore their fortunes – declares *Hashem*.

33

1 The word of *Hashem* came to *Yirmiyahu* a second time, while he was still confined in the prison compound, as follows:

2 Thus said *Hashem* who is planning it, *Hashem* who is shaping it to bring it about, Whose name is *Hashem*:

3 Call to Me, and I will answer you, And I will tell you wondrous things, Secrets you have not known.

4 For thus said *Hashem*, the God of *Yisrael*, concerning the houses of this city and the palaces of the kings of *Yehuda* that were torn down for [defense] against the siegemounds and against the sword,

5 and were filled by those who went to fight the Chaldeans, – with the corpses of the men whom I struck down in My anger and rage, hiding My face from this city because of all their wickedness:

ירמיהו
פרק לג

לט וְנָתַתִּי לָהֶם לֵב אֶחָד וְדֶרֶךְ אֶחָד לְיִרְאָה אוֹתִי כָּל־הַיָּמִים לְטוֹב לָהֶם וְלִבְנֵיהֶם אַחֲרֵיהֶם:

מ וְכָרַתִּי לָהֶם בְּרִית עוֹלָם אֲשֶׁר לֹא־אָשׁוּב מֵאַחֲרֵיהֶם לְהֵיטִיבִי אוֹתָם וְאֶת־יִרְאָתִי אֶתֵּן בִּלְבָבָם לְבִלְתִּי סוּר מֵעָלָי:

מא וְשַׂשְׂתִּי עֲלֵיהֶם לְהֵטִיב אוֹתָם וּנְטַעְתִּים בָּאָרֶץ הַזֹּאת בֶּאֱמֶת בְּכָל־לִבִּי וּבְכָל־נַפְשִׁי:

מב כִּי־כֹה אָמַר יְהֹוָה כַּאֲשֶׁר הֵבֵאתִי אֶל־הָעָם הַזֶּה אֵת כָּל־הָרָעָה הַגְּדוֹלָה הַזֹּאת כֵּן אָנֹכִי מֵבִיא עֲלֵיהֶם אֶת־כָּל־הַטּוֹבָה אֲשֶׁר אָנֹכִי דֹּבֵר עֲלֵיהֶם:

מג וְנִקְנָה הַשָּׂדֶה בָּאָרֶץ הַזֹּאת אֲשֶׁר אַתֶּם אֹמְרִים שְׁמָמָה הִיא מֵאֵין אָדָם וּבְהֵמָה נִתְּנָה בְּיַד הַכַּשְׂדִּים:

מד שָׂדוֹת בַּכֶּסֶף יִקְנוּ וְכָתוֹב בַּסֵּפֶר וְחָתוֹם וְהָעֵד עֵדִים בְּאֶרֶץ בִּנְיָמִן וּבִסְבִיבֵי יְרוּשָׁלַיִם וּבְעָרֵי יְהוּדָה וּבְעָרֵי הָהָר וּבְעָרֵי הַשְּׁפֵלָה וּבְעָרֵי הַנֶּגֶב כִּי־אָשִׁיב אֶת־שְׁבוּתָם נְאֻם־יְהֹוָה:

לג א וַיְהִי דְבַר־יְהֹוָה אֶל־יִרְמְיָהוּ שֵׁנִית וְהוּא עוֹדֶנּוּ עָצוּר בַּחֲצַר הַמַּטָּרָה לֵאמֹר:

ב כֹּה־אָמַר יְהֹוָה עֹשָׂהּ יְהֹוָה יוֹצֵר אוֹתָהּ לַהֲכִינָהּ יְהֹוָה שְׁמוֹ:

ג קְרָא אֵלַי וְאֶעֱנֶךָּ וְאַגִּידָה לְּךָ גְּדֹלוֹת וּבְצֻרוֹת לֹא יְדַעְתָּם:

ד כִּי כֹה אָמַר יְהֹוָה אֱלֹהֵי יִשְׂרָאֵל עַל־בָּתֵּי הָעִיר הַזֹּאת וְעַל־בָּתֵּי מַלְכֵי יְהוּדָה הַנְּתֻצִים אֶל־הַסֹּלְלוֹת וְאֶל־הֶחָרֶב:

ה בָּאִים לְהִלָּחֵם אֶת־הַכַּשְׂדִּים וּלְמַלְאָם אֶת־פִּגְרֵי הָאָדָם אֲשֶׁר־הִכֵּיתִי בְאַפִּי וּבַחֲמָתִי וַאֲשֶׁר הִסְתַּרְתִּי פָנַי מֵהָעִיר הַזֹּאת עַל כָּל־רָעָתָם:

Yirmiyahu/Jeremiah
Chapter 33

6 I am going to bring her relief and healing. I will heal them and reveal to them abundance of true favor.

7 And I will restore the fortunes of *Yehuda* and *Yisrael*, and I will rebuild them as of old.

8 And I will purge them of all the sins which they committed against Me, and I will pardon all the sins which they committed against Me, by which they rebelled against Me.

9 And she shall gain through Me renown, joy, fame, and glory above all the nations on earth, when they hear of all the good fortune I provide for them. They will thrill and quiver because of all the good fortune and all the prosperity that I provide for her.

10 Thus said *Hashem*: Again there shall be heard in this place, which you say is ruined, without man or beast – in the towns of *Yehuda* and the streets of *Yerushalayim* that are desolate, without man, without inhabitants, without beast –

11 the sound of mirth and gladness, the voice of bridegroom and bride, the voice of those who cry, "Give thanks to the Lord of Hosts, for *Hashem* is good, for His kindness is everlasting!" as they bring thanksgiving offerings to the House of *Hashem*. For I will restore the fortunes of the land as of old – said *Hashem*.

> KOL sa-SON v'-KOL sim-KHAH KOL kha-TAN v'-KOL ka-LAH KOL o-m'-REEM ho-DU et a-do-NAI tz'-va-OT kee TOV a-do-NAI kee l'-o-LAM khas-DO m'-vee-EEM to-DAH BAYT a-do-NAI kee a-SHEEV et sh'-vut ha-A-retz k'-va-ree-sho-NAH a-MAR a-do-NAI

12 Thus said the Lord of Hosts: In this ruined place, without man and beast, and in all its towns, there shall again be a pasture for shepherds, where they can rest their flocks.

ששון
שמחה

33:11 The sound of mirth and gladness The *Torah* never uses extraneous words and every Hebrew letter of the *Tanakh* has infinite meaning. If so, why does this verse use two different expressions to connote happiness: *Sasson* (ששון), 'mirth,' and *simcha* (שמחה), 'gladness'? According to Rabbi Mordechai Willig, *sasson* is the enduring happy feeling of satisfaction and fulfillment. *Simcha*, on the other hand, refers to an exuberant but temporary experience of joy, felt on special occasions. The feeling of *simcha* is more intense but short lived, while *sasson* is less powerful but persists endlessly. Yirmiyahu promises that one day the Land of Israel will be filled with the sweet sounds of both *sasson* and *simcha*. Not only will there be intense gladness over the redemption, but the people will experience the long-lasting joy of dwelling permanently in *Eretz Yisrael* in the presence of God.

Yirmiyahu/Jeremiah
Chapter 33

יג בְּעָרֵי הָהָר בְּעָרֵי הַשְּׁפֵלָה וּבְעָרֵי הַנֶּגֶב וּבְאֶרֶץ בִּנְיָמִן וּבִסְבִיבֵי יְרוּשָׁלַם וּבְעָרֵי יְהוּדָה עֹד תַּעֲבֹרְנָה הַצֹּאן עַל־יְדֵי מוֹנֶה אָמַר יְהֹוָה׃

13 In the towns of the hill country, in the towns of the Shephelah, and in the towns of the *Negev*, in the land of *Binyamin* and in the environs of *Yerushalayim* and in the towns of *Yehuda*, sheep shall pass again under the hands of one who counts them – said *Hashem*.

יד הִנֵּה יָמִים בָּאִים נְאֻם־יְהֹוָה וַהֲקִמֹתִי אֶת־הַדָּבָר הַטּוֹב אֲשֶׁר דִּבַּרְתִּי אֶל־בֵּית יִשְׂרָאֵל וְעַל־בֵּית יְהוּדָה׃

14 See, days are coming – declares *Hashem* – when I will fulfill the promise that I made concerning the House of *Yisrael* and the House of *Yehuda*.

טו בַּיָּמִים הָהֵם וּבָעֵת הַהִיא אַצְמִיחַ לְדָוִד צֶמַח צְדָקָה וְעָשָׂה מִשְׁפָּט וּצְדָקָה בָּאָרֶץ׃

15 In those days and at that time, I will raise up a true branch of *David*'s line, and he shall do what is just and right in the land.

טז בַּיָּמִים הָהֵם תִּוָּשַׁע יְהוּדָה וִירוּשָׁלַם תִּשְׁכּוֹן לָבֶטַח וְזֶה אֲשֶׁר־יִקְרָא־לָהּ יְהֹוָה צִדְקֵנוּ׃

16 In those days *Yehuda* shall be delivered and *Yisrael* shall dwell secure. And this is what she shall be called: "*Hashem* is our Vindicator."

יז כִּי־כֹה אָמַר יְהֹוָה לֹא־יִכָּרֵת לְדָוִד אִישׁ יֹשֵׁב עַל־כִּסֵּא בֵית־יִשְׂרָאֵל׃

17 For thus said *Hashem*: There shall never be an end to men of *David*'s line who sit upon the throne of the House of *Yisrael*.

יח וְלַכֹּהֲנִים הַלְוִיִּם לֹא־יִכָּרֵת אִישׁ מִלְּפָנָי מַעֲלֶה עוֹלָה וּמַקְטִיר מִנְחָה וְעֹשֶׂה־זֶּבַח כָּל־הַיָּמִים׃

18 Nor shall there ever be an end to the line of the levitical *Kohanim* before Me, of those who present burnt offerings and turn the meal offering to smoke and perform sacrifices.

יט וַיְהִי דְּבַר־יְהֹוָה אֶל־יִרְמְיָהוּ לֵאמוֹר׃

19 The word of *Hashem* came to *Yirmiyahu*:

כ כֹּה אָמַר יְהֹוָה אִם־תָּפֵרוּ אֶת־בְּרִיתִי הַיּוֹם וְאֶת־בְּרִיתִי הַלָּיְלָה וּלְבִלְתִּי הֱיוֹת יוֹמָם־וָלַיְלָה בְּעִתָּם׃

20 Thus said *Hashem*: If you could break My covenant with the day and My covenant with the night, so that day and night should not come at their proper time,

כא גַּם־בְּרִיתִי תֻפַר אֶת־דָּוִד עַבְדִּי מִהְיוֹת־לוֹ בֵן מֹלֵךְ עַל־כִּסְאוֹ וְאֶת־הַלְוִיִּם הַכֹּהֲנִים מְשָׁרְתָי׃

21 only then could My covenant with My servant *David* be broken – so that he would not have a descendant reigning upon his throne – or with My ministrants, the levitical *Kohanim*.

כב אֲשֶׁר לֹא־יִסָּפֵר צְבָא הַשָּׁמַיִם וְלֹא יִמַּד חוֹל הַיָּם כֵּן אַרְבֶּה אֶת־זֶרַע דָּוִד עַבְדִּי וְאֶת־הַלְוִיִּם מְשָׁרְתֵי אֹתִי׃

22 Like the host of heaven which cannot be counted, and the sand of the sea which cannot be measured, so will I multiply the offspring of My servant *David*, and of the *Leviim* who minister to Me.

כג וַיְהִי דְּבַר־יְהֹוָה אֶל־יִרְמְיָהוּ לֵאמֹר׃

23 The word of *Hashem* came to *Yirmiyahu*:

כד הֲלוֹא רָאִיתָ מָה־הָעָם הַזֶּה דִּבְּרוּ לֵאמֹר שְׁתֵּי הַמִּשְׁפָּחוֹת אֲשֶׁר בָּחַר יְהֹוָה בָּהֶם וַיִּמְאָסֵם וְאֶת־עַמִּי יִנְאָצוּן מִהְיוֹת עוֹד גּוֹי לִפְנֵיהֶם׃

24 You see what this people said: "The two families which *Hashem* chose have now been rejected by Him." Thus they despise My people, and regard them as no longer a nation.

כה כֹּה אָמַר יְהֹוָה אִם־לֹא בְרִיתִי יוֹמָם וָלָיְלָה חֻקּוֹת שָׁמַיִם וָאָרֶץ לֹא־שָׂמְתִּי׃

25 Thus said *Hashem*: As surely as I have established My covenant with day and night – the laws of heaven and earth –

Yirmiyahu/Jeremiah
Chapter 34

26 so I will never reject the offspring of *Yaakov* and My servant *David*; I will never fail to take from his offspring rulers for the descendants of *Avraham*, *Yitzchak*, and *Yaakov*. Indeed, I will restore their fortunes and take them back in love.

34 1 The word which came to *Yirmiyahu* from *Hashem*, when King Nebuchadrezzar of Babylon and all his army, and all the kingdoms of the earth and all the peoples under his sway, were waging war against *Yerushalayim* and all its towns:

2 Thus said *Hashem*, the God of *Yisrael*: Go speak to King *Tzidkiyahu* of *Yehuda*, and say to him: "Thus said *Hashem*: I am going to deliver this city into the hands of the king of Babylon, and he will destroy it by fire.

3 And you will not escape from him; you will be captured and handed over to him. And you will see the king of Babylon face to face and speak to him in person; and you will be brought to Babylon.

4 But hear the word of *Hashem*, O King *Tzidkiyahu* of *Yehuda*! Thus said *Hashem* concerning you: You will not die by the sword.

5 You will die a peaceful death; and as incense was burned for your ancestors, the earlier kings who preceded you, so they will burn incense for you, and they will lament for you 'Ah, lord!' For I Myself have made the promise – declares *Hashem*."

6 The *Navi Yirmiyahu* spoke all these words to King *Tzidkiyahu* of *Yehuda* in *Yerushalayim*,

7 when the army of the king of Babylon was waging war against *Yerushalayim* and against the remaining towns of *Yehuda* – against *Lachish* and *Azeika*, for they were the only fortified towns of *Yehuda* that were left.

8 The word which came to *Yirmiyahu* from *Hashem* after King *Tzidkiyahu* had made a covenant with all the people in *Yerushalayim* to proclaim a release among them –

9 that everyone should set free his Hebrew slaves, both male and female, and that no one should keep his fellow Judean enslaved.

Yirmiyahu/Jeremiah
Chapter 34

10 Everyone, officials and people, who had entered into the covenant agreed to set their male and female slaves free and not keep them enslaved any longer; they complied and let them go.

י וַיִּשְׁמְעוּ כָל־הַשָּׂרִים וְכָל־הָעָם אֲשֶׁר־בָּאוּ בַבְּרִית לְשַׁלַּח אִישׁ אֶת־עַבְדּוֹ וְאִישׁ אֶת־שִׁפְחָתוֹ חָפְשִׁים לְבִלְתִּי עֲבָד־בָּם עוֹד וַיִּשְׁמְעוּ וַיְשַׁלֵּחוּ:

11 But afterward they turned about and brought back the men and women they had set free, and forced them into slavery again.

יא וַיָּשׁוּבוּ אַחֲרֵי־כֵן וַיָּשִׁבוּ אֶת־הָעֲבָדִים וְאֶת־הַשְּׁפָחוֹת אֲשֶׁר שִׁלְּחוּ חָפְשִׁים וַיִּכְבְּשׁוּם [וַיִּכְבְּשׁוּם] לַעֲבָדִים וְלִשְׁפָחוֹת:

12 Then it was that the word of *Hashem* came to Yirmiyahu from *Hashem*:

יב וַיְהִי דְבַר־יְהֹוָה אֶל־יִרְמְיָהוּ מֵאֵת יְהֹוָה לֵאמֹר:

13 Thus said *Hashem*, the God of *Yisrael*: I made a covenant with your fathers when I brought them out of the land of Egypt, the house of bondage, saying:

יג כֹּה־אָמַר יְהֹוָה אֱלֹהֵי יִשְׂרָאֵל אָנֹכִי כָּרַתִּי בְרִית אֶת־אֲבוֹתֵיכֶם בְּיוֹם הוֹצִאִי אוֹתָם מֵאֶרֶץ מִצְרַיִם מִבֵּית עֲבָדִים לֵאמֹר:

14 "In the seventh year each of you must let go any fellow Hebrew who may be sold to you; when he has served you six years, you must set him free." But your fathers would not obey Me or give ear.

יד מִקֵּץ שֶׁבַע שָׁנִים תְּשַׁלְּחוּ אִישׁ אֶת־אָחִיו הָעִבְרִי אֲשֶׁר־יִמָּכֵר לְךָ וַעֲבָדְךָ שֵׁשׁ שָׁנִים וְשִׁלַּחְתּוֹ חָפְשִׁי מֵעִמָּךְ וְלֹא־שָׁמְעוּ אֲבוֹתֵיכֶם אֵלַי וְלֹא הִטּוּ אֶת־אָזְנָם:

15 Lately you turned about and did what is proper in My sight, and each of you proclaimed a release to his countrymen; and you made a covenant accordingly before Me in the House which bears My name.

טו וַתָּשֻׁבוּ אַתֶּם הַיּוֹם וַתַּעֲשׂוּ אֶת־הַיָּשָׁר בְּעֵינַי לִקְרֹא דְרוֹר אִישׁ לְרֵעֵהוּ וַתִּכְרְתוּ בְרִית לְפָנַי בַּבַּיִת אֲשֶׁר־נִקְרָא שְׁמִי עָלָיו:

16 But now you have turned back and have profaned My name; each of you has brought back the men and women whom you had given their freedom, and forced them to be your slaves again.

טז וַתָּשֻׁבוּ וַתְּחַלְּלוּ אֶת־שְׁמִי וַתָּשִׁבוּ אִישׁ אֶת־עַבְדּוֹ וְאִישׁ אֶת־שִׁפְחָתוֹ אֲשֶׁר־שִׁלַּחְתֶּם חָפְשִׁים לְנַפְשָׁם וַתִּכְבְּשׁוּ אֹתָם לִהְיוֹת לָכֶם לַעֲבָדִים וְלִשְׁפָחוֹת:

17 Assuredly, thus said *Hashem*: You would not obey Me and proclaim a release, each to his kinsman and countryman. Lo! I proclaim your release — declares *Hashem* — to the sword, to pestilence, and to famine; and I will make you a horror to all the kingdoms of the earth.

יז לָכֵן כֹּה־אָמַר יְהֹוָה אַתֶּם לֹא־שְׁמַעְתֶּם אֵלַי לִקְרֹא דְרוֹר אִישׁ לְאָחִיו וְאִישׁ לְרֵעֵהוּ הִנְנִי קֹרֵא לָכֶם דְּרוֹר נְאֻם־יְהֹוָה אֶל־הַחֶרֶב אֶל־הַדֶּבֶר וְאֶל־הָרָעָב וְנָתַתִּי אֶתְכֶם לְזַעֲוָה [לְזַעֲוָה] לְכֹל מַמְלְכוֹת הָאָרֶץ:

la-KHAYN koh a-MAR a-do-NAI a-TEM lo sh'-ma-TEM ay-LAI lik-RO d'-ROR EESH l'-a-KHEEV v'-EESH l'-ray-AY-hu hi-n'-NEE ko-RAY la-KHEM d'-ROR n'-um a-do-NAI el ha-KHE-rev el ha-DE-ver v'-el ha-ra-AV v'-na-ta-TEE et-KHEM l'-za-a-VAH l'-KHOL mam-l'-KHOT ha-A-retz

---

34:17 You would not obey Me and proclaim a release
With the Babylonian onslaught, the nobility and landowners made a covenant with the people to release all the slaves and workers from their servitude. Once the threat receded temporarily, they reneged on their promise and re-enslaved the poor workers. God de-

Yirmiyahu/Jeremiah
Chapter 35

18 I will make the men who violated My covenant, who did not fulfill the terms of the covenant which they made before Me, [like] the calf which they cut in two so as to pass between the halves:

יח וְנָתַתִּי אֶת־הָאֲנָשִׁים הָעֹבְרִים אֶת־בְּרִתִי אֲשֶׁר לֹא־הֵקִימוּ אֶת־דִּבְרֵי הַבְּרִית אֲשֶׁר כָּרְתוּ לְפָנָי הָעֵגֶל אֲשֶׁר כָּרְתוּ לִשְׁנַיִם וַיַּעַבְרוּ בֵּין בְּתָרָיו׃

19 The officers of *Yehuda* and *Yerushalayim*, the officials, the *Kohanim*, and all the people of the land who passed between the halves of the calf

יט שָׂרֵי יְהוּדָה וְשָׂרֵי יְרוּשָׁלַםִ הַסָּרִסִים וְהַכֹּהֲנִים וְכֹל עַם הָאָרֶץ הָעֹבְרִים בֵּין בִּתְרֵי הָעֵגֶל׃

20 shall be handed over to their enemies, to those who seek to kill them. Their carcasses shall become food for the birds of the sky and the beasts of the earth.

כ וְנָתַתִּי אוֹתָם בְּיַד אֹיְבֵיהֶם וּבְיַד מְבַקְשֵׁי נַפְשָׁם וְהָיְתָה נִבְלָתָם לְמַאֲכָל לְעוֹף הַשָּׁמַיִם וּלְבֶהֱמַת הָאָרֶץ׃

21 I will hand over King *Tzidkiyahu* of *Yehuda* and his officers to their enemies, who seek to kill them – to the army of the king of Babylon which has withdrawn from you.

כא וְאֶת־צִדְקִיָּהוּ מֶלֶךְ־יְהוּדָה וְאֶת־שָׂרָיו אֶתֵּן בְּיַד אֹיְבֵיהֶם וּבְיַד מְבַקְשֵׁי נַפְשָׁם וּבְיַד חֵיל מֶלֶךְ בָּבֶל הָעֹלִים מֵעֲלֵיכֶם׃

22 I hereby give the command – declares *Hashem* – by which I will bring them back against this city. They shall attack it and capture it, and burn it down. I will make the towns of *Yehuda* a desolation, without inhabitant.

כב הִנְנִי מְצַוֶּה נְאֻם־יְהוָה וַהֲשִׁבֹתִים אֶל־הָעִיר הַזֹּאת וְנִלְחֲמוּ עָלֶיהָ וּלְכָדוּהָ וּשְׂרָפֻהָ בָאֵשׁ וְאֶת־עָרֵי יְהוּדָה אֶתֵּן שְׁמָמָה מֵאֵין יֹשֵׁב׃

35

1 The word which came to *Yirmiyahu* from *Hashem* in the days of King *Yehoyakim* son of *Yoshiyahu* of *Yehuda*:

לה א הַדָּבָר אֲשֶׁר־הָיָה אֶל־יִרְמְיָהוּ מֵאֵת יְהוָה בִּימֵי יְהוֹיָקִים בֶּן־יֹאשִׁיָּהוּ מֶלֶךְ יְהוּדָה לֵאמֹר׃

2 Go to the house of the Rechabites and speak to them, and bring them to the House of *Hashem*, to one of the chambers, and give them wine to drink.

ב הָלוֹךְ אֶל־בֵּית הָרֵכָבִים וְדִבַּרְתָּ אוֹתָם וַהֲבִאוֹתָם בֵּית יְהוָה אֶל־אַחַת הַלְּשָׁכוֹת וְהִשְׁקִיתָ אוֹתָם יָיִן׃

ha-LOKH el BAYT ha-ray-kha-VEEM v'-di-bar-TA o-TAM va-ha-vi-o-TAM BAYT a-do-NAI el a-KHAT ha-l'-sha-KHOT v'-hish-kee-TA o-TAM YA-yin

3 So I took Jaazaniah son of *Yirmiyahu* son of Habazziniah, and his brothers, all his sons, and the whole household of the Rechabites;

ג וָאֶקַּח אֶת־יַאֲזַנְיָה בֶן־יִרְמְיָהוּ בֶּן־חֲבַצִּנְיָה וְאֶת־אֶחָיו וְאֶת־כָּל־בָּנָיו וְאֵת כָּל־בֵּית הָרֵכָבִים׃

---

clares this injustice intolerable. He freed the Jewish people from Egyptian servitude so that they would dwell as a free nation in the Land of Israel, living up to the highest standards of ethics and morality. However, should they begin to enslave others or engage in other unscrupulous or deceptive behavior, *Hashem* will give the nations of the world the freedom to strike, and they will once again become slaves to foreigners.

35:2 Go to the house of the Rechabites *Yirmiyahu* wishes to demonstrate the meaning of true fidelity and loyalty. He brings the tribe of the Rechabites, descendants of Jethro, into the *Beit Hamikdash* and offers them wine. They refuse, explaining that they live by a set of laws passed down from generation to generation, including prohibitions against planting vineyards or drinking wine. Their loyal behavior offers a subtle rebuke to the wayward People of Israel.

Yirmiyahu/Jeremiah
Chapter 35

4 and I brought them to the House of *Hashem*, to the chamber of the sons of Hanan son of Igdaliah, the man of *Hashem*, which is next to the chamber of the officials and above the chamber of Maaseiah son of *Shalum*, the guardian of the threshold.

5 I set bowls full of wine and cups before the men of the house of the Rechabites, and said to them, "Have some wine."

6 They replied, "We will not drink wine, for our ancestor, Yonadav son of Rechab, commanded us: 'You shall never drink wine, either you or your children.

7 Nor shall you build houses or sow fields or plant vineyards, nor shall you own such things; but you shall live in tents all your days, so that you may live long upon the land where you sojourn.'

8 And we have obeyed our ancestor Yonadav son of Rechab in all that he commanded us: we never drink wine, neither we nor our wives nor our sons and daughters.

9 Nor do we build houses to live in, and we do not own vineyards or fields for sowing;

10 but we live in tents. We have obeyed and done all that our ancestor *Yonadav* commanded us.

11 But when King Nebuchadrezzar of Babylon invaded the country, we said, 'Come, let us go into *Yerushalayim* because of the army of the Chaldeans and the army of Aram.' And so we are living in *Yerushalayim*."

12 Then the word of *Hashem* came to *Yirmiyahu*:

13 Thus said the Lord of Hosts, the God of *Yisrael*: Go say to the men of *Yehuda* and the inhabitants of *Yerushalayim*: "You can learn a lesson [here] about obeying My commands – declares *Hashem*.

14 The commands of *Yonadav* son of Rechab have been fulfilled: he charged his children not to drink wine, and to this day they have not drunk, in obedience to the charge of their ancestor. But I spoke to you persistently, and you did not listen to Me.

Yirmiyahu/Jeremiah
Chapter 36

ירמיהו
פרק לו

15 I persistently sent you all My servants, the *Neviim*, to say: 'Turn back, every one of you, from your wicked ways and mend your deeds; do not follow other gods or serve them. Then you may remain on the land that I gave to you and your fathers.' But you did not give ear or listen to Me.

טו וָאֶשְׁלַח אֲלֵיכֶם אֶת־כָּל־עֲבָדַי הַנְּבִאִים הַשְׁכֵּים וְשָׁלֹחַ לֵאמֹר שֻׁבוּ־נָא אִישׁ מִדַּרְכּוֹ הָרָעָה וְהֵיטִיבוּ מַעַלְלֵיכֶם וְאַל־תֵּלְכוּ אַחֲרֵי אֱלֹהִים אֲחֵרִים לְעָבְדָם וּשְׁבוּ אֶל־הָאֲדָמָה אֲשֶׁר־נָתַתִּי לָכֶם וְלַאֲבֹתֵיכֶם וְלֹא הִטִּיתֶם אֶת־אָזְנְכֶם וְלֹא שְׁמַעְתֶּם אֵלָי׃

16 The family of *Yonadav* son of Rechab have indeed fulfilled the charge which their ancestor gave them; but this people has not listened to Me.

טז כִּי הֵקִימוּ בְּנֵי יְהוֹנָדָב בֶּן־רֵכָב אֶת־מִצְוַת אֲבִיהֶם אֲשֶׁר צִוָּם וְהָעָם הַזֶּה לֹא שָׁמְעוּ אֵלָי׃

17 Assuredly, thus said *Hashem*, the the Lord of Hosts, the God of *Yisrael*: I am going to bring upon *Yehuda* and upon all the inhabitants of *Yerushalayim* all the disaster with which I have threatened them; for I spoke to them, but they would not listen; I called to them, but they would not respond."

יז לָכֵן כֹּה־אָמַר יְהוָה אֱלֹהֵי צְבָאוֹת אֱלֹהֵי יִשְׂרָאֵל הִנְנִי מֵבִיא אֶל־יְהוּדָה וְאֶל כָּל־יוֹשְׁבֵי יְרוּשָׁלַםִ אֵת כָּל־הָרָעָה אֲשֶׁר דִּבַּרְתִּי עֲלֵיהֶם יַעַן דִּבַּרְתִּי אֲלֵיהֶם וְלֹא שָׁמֵעוּ וָאֶקְרָא לָהֶם וְלֹא עָנוּ׃

18 And to the family of the Rechabites *Yirmiyahu* said: "Thus said the Lord of Hosts, the God of *Yisrael*: Because you have obeyed the charge of your ancestor *Yonadav* and kept all his commandments, and done all that he enjoined upon you,

יח וּלְבֵית הָרֵכָבִים אָמַר יִרְמְיָהוּ כֹּה־אָמַר יְהוָה צְבָאוֹת אֱלֹהֵי יִשְׂרָאֵל יַעַן אֲשֶׁר שְׁמַעְתֶּם עַל־מִצְוַת יְהוֹנָדָב אֲבִיכֶם וַתִּשְׁמְרוּ אֶת־כָּל־מִצְוֹתָיו וַתַּעֲשׂוּ כְּכֹל אֲשֶׁר־צִוָּה אֶתְכֶם׃

19 assuredly, thus said the Lord of Hosts, the God of *Yisrael*: There shall never cease to be a man of the line of *Yonadav* son of Rechab standing before Me."

יט לָכֵן כֹּה אָמַר יְהוָה צְבָאוֹת אֱלֹהֵי יִשְׂרָאֵל לֹא־יִכָּרֵת אִישׁ לְיוֹנָדָב בֶּן־רֵכָב עֹמֵד לְפָנַי כָּל־הַיָּמִים׃

36

1 In the fourth year of King *Yehoyakim* son of *Yoshiyahu* of *Yehuda*, this word came to *Yirmiyahu* from *Hashem*:

לו א וַיְהִי בַּשָּׁנָה הָרְבִיעִת לִיהוֹיָקִים בֶּן־יֹאשִׁיָּהוּ מֶלֶךְ יְהוּדָה הָיָה הַדָּבָר הַזֶּה אֶל־יִרְמְיָהוּ מֵאֵת יְהוָה לֵאמֹר׃

2 Get a scroll and write upon it all the words that I have spoken to you – concerning *Yisrael* and *Yehuda* and all the nations – from the time I first spoke to you in the days of *Yoshiyahu* to this day.

ב קַח־לְךָ מְגִלַּת־סֵפֶר וְכָתַבְתָּ אֵלֶיהָ אֵת כָּל־הַדְּבָרִים אֲשֶׁר־דִּבַּרְתִּי אֵלֶיךָ עַל־יִשְׂרָאֵל וְעַל־יְהוּדָה וְעַל־כָּל־הַגּוֹיִם מִיּוֹם דִּבַּרְתִּי אֵלֶיךָ מִימֵי יֹאשִׁיָּהוּ וְעַד הַיּוֹם הַזֶּה׃

3 Perhaps when the House of *Yehuda* hear of all the disasters I intend to bring upon them, they will turn back from their wicked ways, and I will pardon their iniquity and their sin.

ג אוּלַי יִשְׁמְעוּ בֵּית יְהוּדָה אֵת כָּל־הָרָעָה אֲשֶׁר אָנֹכִי חֹשֵׁב לַעֲשׂוֹת לָהֶם לְמַעַן יָשׁוּבוּ אִישׁ מִדַּרְכּוֹ הָרָעָה וְסָלַחְתִּי לַעֲוֹנָם וּלְחַטָּאתָם׃

4 So *Yirmiyahu* called *Baruch* son of *Nerya*; and *Baruch* wrote down in the scroll, at *Yirmiyahu*'s dictation, all the words which *Hashem* had spoken to him.

ד וַיִּקְרָא יִרְמְיָהוּ אֶת־בָּרוּךְ בֶּן־נֵרִיָּה וַיִּכְתֹּב בָּרוּךְ מִפִּי יִרְמְיָהוּ אֵת כָּל־דִּבְרֵי יְהוָה אֲשֶׁר־דִּבֶּר אֵלָיו עַל־מְגִלַּת־סֵפֶר׃

5 *Yirmiyahu* instructed *Baruch*, "I am in hiding; I cannot go to the House of *Hashem*.

ה וַיְצַוֶּה יִרְמְיָהוּ אֶת־בָּרוּךְ לֵאמֹר אֲנִי עָצוּר לֹא אוּכַל לָבוֹא בֵּית יְהוָה׃

Yirmiyahu/Jeremiah
Chapter 36

6 But you go and read aloud the words of *Hashem* from the scroll which you wrote at my dictation, to all the people in the House of *Hashem* on a fast day; thus you will also be reading them to all the Judeans who come in from the towns.

7 Perhaps their entreaty will be accepted by *Hashem*, if they turn back from their wicked ways. For great is the anger and wrath with which *Hashem* has threatened this people."

8 *Baruch* son of *Nerya* did just as the *Navi Yirmiyahu* had instructed him, about reading the words of *Hashem* from the scroll in the House of *Hashem*.

9 In the ninth month of the fifth year of King *Yehoyakim* son of *Yoshiyahu* of *Yehuda*, all the people in *Yerushalayim* and all the people coming from *Yehuda* proclaimed a fast before *Hashem* in *Yerushalayim*.

10 It was then that *Baruch* – in the chamber of Gemariah son of *Shafan* the scribe, in the upper court, near the new gateway of the House of *Hashem* – read the words of *Yirmiyahu* from the scroll to all the people in the House of *Hashem*.

11 *Michaihu* son of Gemariah son of *Shafan* heard all the words of *Hashem* [read] from the scroll,

12 and he went down to the king's palace, to the chamber of the scribe. There he found all the officials in session: Elishama the scribe, Delaiah son of *Shemaya*, Elnathan son of Achbor, Gemariah son of *Shafan*, *Tzidkiyahu* son of *Chananya*, and all the other officials.

13 And *Michaihu* told them all that he had heard as *Baruch* read from the scroll in the hearing of the people.

14 Then all the officials sent Jehudi son of Nethaniah son of Shelemiah son of *Kushi* to say to *Baruch*, "Take that scroll from which you read to the people, and come along!" And *Baruch* took the scroll and came to them.

15 They said, "Sit down and read it to us." And *Baruch* read it to them.

16 When they heard all these words, they turned to each other in fear; and they said to *Baruch*, "We must report all this to the king."

ירמיהו
פרק לו

ו וּבָאתָ אַתָּה וְקָרָאתָ בַמְּגִלָּה אֲשֶׁר־כָּתַבְתָּ־מִפִּי אֶת־דִּבְרֵי יְהֹוָה בְּאׇזְנֵי הָעָם בֵּית יְהֹוָה בְּיוֹם צוֹם וְגַם בְּאׇזְנֵי כׇל־יְהוּדָה הַבָּאִים מֵעָרֵיהֶם תִּקְרָאֵם׃

ז אוּלַי תִּפֹּל תְּחִנָּתָם לִפְנֵי יְהֹוָה וְיָשֻׁבוּ אִישׁ מִדַּרְכּוֹ הָרָעָה כִּי־גָדוֹל הָאַף וְהַחֵמָה אֲשֶׁר־דִּבֶּר יְהֹוָה אֶל־הָעָם הַזֶּה׃

ח וַיַּעַשׂ בָּרוּךְ בֶּן־נֵרִיָּה כְּכֹל אֲשֶׁר־צִוָּהוּ יִרְמְיָהוּ הַנָּבִיא לִקְרֹא בַסֵּפֶר דִּבְרֵי יְהֹוָה בֵּית יְהֹוָה׃

ט וַיְהִי בַשָּׁנָה הַחֲמִשִׁית לִיהוֹיָקִים בֶּן־יֹאשִׁיָּהוּ מֶלֶךְ־יְהוּדָה בַּחֹדֶשׁ הַתְּשִׁעִי קָרְאוּ צוֹם לִפְנֵי יְהֹוָה כׇּל־הָעָם בִּירוּשָׁלָ͏ִם וְכׇל־הָעָם הַבָּאִים מֵעָרֵי יְהוּדָה בִּירוּשָׁלָ͏ִם׃

י וַיִּקְרָא בָרוּךְ בַּסֵּפֶר אֶת־דִּבְרֵי יִרְמְיָהוּ בֵּית יְהֹוָה בְּלִשְׁכַּת גְּמַרְיָהוּ בֶן־שָׁפָן הַסֹּפֵר בֶּחָצֵר הָעֶלְיוֹן פֶּתַח שַׁעַר בֵּית־יְהֹוָה הֶחָדָשׁ בְּאׇזְנֵי כׇּל־הָעָם׃

יא וַיִּשְׁמַע מִכָיְהוּ בֶן־גְּמַרְיָהוּ בֶן־שָׁפָן אֶת־כׇּל־דִּבְרֵי יְהֹוָה מֵעַל הַסֵּפֶר׃

יב וַיֵּרֶד בֵּית־הַמֶּלֶךְ עַל־לִשְׁכַּת הַסֹּפֵר וְהִנֵּה־שָׁם כׇּל־הַשָּׂרִים יוֹשְׁבִים אֱלִישָׁמָע הַסֹּפֵר וּדְלָיָהוּ בֶן־שְׁמַעְיָהוּ וְאֶלְנָתָן בֶּן־עַכְבּוֹר וּגְמַרְיָהוּ בֶן־שָׁפָן וְצִדְקִיָּהוּ בֶן־חֲנַנְיָהוּ וְכׇל־הַשָּׂרִים׃

יג וַיַּגֵּד לָהֶם מִכָיְהוּ אֵת כׇּל־הַדְּבָרִים אֲשֶׁר שָׁמֵעַ בִּקְרֹא בָרוּךְ בַּסֵּפֶר בְּאׇזְנֵי הָעָם׃

יד וַיִּשְׁלְחוּ כׇל־הַשָּׂרִים אֶל־בָּרוּךְ אֶת־יְהוּדִי בֶּן־נְתַנְיָהוּ בֶּן־שֶׁלֶמְיָהוּ בֶן־כּוּשִׁי לֵאמֹר הַמְּגִלָּה אֲשֶׁר קָרָאתָ בָּהּ בְּאׇזְנֵי הָעָם קָחֶנָּה בְיָדְךָ וָלֵךְ וַיִּקַּח בָּרוּךְ בֶּן־נֵרִיָּהוּ אֶת־הַמְּגִלָּה בְּיָדוֹ וַיָּבֹא אֲלֵיהֶם׃

טו וַיֹּאמְרוּ אֵלָיו שֵׁב נָא וּקְרָאֶנָּה בְּאׇזְנֵינוּ וַיִּקְרָא בָרוּךְ בְּאׇזְנֵיהֶם׃

טז וַיְהִי כְּשׇׁמְעָם אֶת־כׇּל־הַדְּבָרִים פָּחֲדוּ אִישׁ אֶל־רֵעֵהוּ וַיֹּאמְרוּ אֶל־בָּרוּךְ הַגֵּיד נַגִּיד לַמֶּלֶךְ אֵת כׇּל־הַדְּבָרִים הָאֵלֶּה׃

Yirmiyahu/Jeremiah
Chapter 36

ירמיהו
פרק לו

17 And they questioned *Baruch* further, "Tell us how you wrote down all these words that he spoke."

יז וְאֶת־בָּרוּךְ שָׁאֲלוּ לֵאמֹר הַגֶּד־נָא לָנוּ אֵיךְ כָּתַבְתָּ אֶת־כָּל־הַדְּבָרִים הָאֵלֶּה מִפִּיו:

18 He answered them, "He himself recited all those words to me, and I would write them down in the scroll in ink."

יח וַיֹּאמֶר לָהֶם בָּרוּךְ מִפִּיו יִקְרָא אֵלַי אֵת כָּל־הַדְּבָרִים הָאֵלֶּה וַאֲנִי כֹּתֵב עַל־הַסֵּפֶר בַּדְּיוֹ:

19 The officials said to *Baruch*, "Go into hiding, you and *Yirmiyahu*. Let no man know where you are!"

יט וַיֹּאמְרוּ הַשָּׂרִים אֶל־בָּרוּךְ לֵךְ הִסָּתֵר אַתָּה וְיִרְמְיָהוּ וְאִישׁ אַל־יֵדַע אֵיפֹה אַתֶּם:

20 And they went to the king in the court, after leaving the scroll in the chamber of the scribe Elishama. And they reported all these matters to the king.

כ וַיָּבֹאוּ אֶל־הַמֶּלֶךְ חָצֵרָה וְאֶת־הַמְּגִלָּה הִפְקִדוּ בְּלִשְׁכַּת אֱלִישָׁמָע הַסֹּפֵר וַיַּגִּידוּ בְּאָזְנֵי הַמֶּלֶךְ אֵת כָּל־הַדְּבָרִים:

21 The king sent Jehudi to get the scroll and he fetched it from the chamber of the scribe Elishama. Jehudi read it to the king and to all the officials who were in attendance on the king.

כא וַיִּשְׁלַח הַמֶּלֶךְ אֶת־יְהוּדִי לָקַחַת אֶת־הַמְּגִלָּה וַיִּקָּחֶהָ מִלִּשְׁכַּת אֱלִישָׁמָע הַסֹּפֵר וַיִּקְרָאֶהָ יְהוּדִי בְּאָזְנֵי הַמֶּלֶךְ וּבְאָזְנֵי כָּל־הַשָּׂרִים הָעֹמְדִים מֵעַל הַמֶּלֶךְ:

22 Since it was the ninth month, the king was sitting in the winter house, with a fire burning in the brazier before him.

כב וְהַמֶּלֶךְ יוֹשֵׁב בֵּית הַחֹרֶף בַּחֹדֶשׁ הַתְּשִׁיעִי וְאֶת־הָאָח לְפָנָיו מְבֹעָרֶת:

v'-ha-ME-lekh yo-SHAYV BAYT ha-KHO-ref ba-KHO-desh ha-t'-shee-EE v'-et ha-AKH l'-fa-NAV m'-vo-A-ret

23 And every time Jehudi read three or four columns, [the king] would cut it up with a scribe's knife and throw it into the fire in the brazier, until the entire scroll was consumed by the fire in the brazier.

כג וַיְהִי כִּקְרוֹא יְהוּדִי שָׁלֹשׁ דְּלָתוֹת וְאַרְבָּעָה יִקְרָעֶהָ בְּתַעַר הַסֹּפֵר וְהַשְׁלֵךְ אֶל־הָאֵשׁ אֲשֶׁר אֶל־הָאָח עַד־תֹּם כָּל־הַמְּגִלָּה עַל־הָאֵשׁ אֲשֶׁר עַל־הָאָח:

24 Yet the king and all his courtiers who heard all these words showed no fear and did not tear their garments;

כד וְלֹא פָחֲדוּ וְלֹא קָרְעוּ אֶת־בִּגְדֵיהֶם הַמֶּלֶךְ וְכָל־עֲבָדָיו הַשֹּׁמְעִים אֵת כָּל־הַדְּבָרִים הָאֵלֶּה:

25 moreover, Elnathan, Delaiah, and Gemariah begged the king not to burn the scroll, but he would not listen to them.

כה וְגַם אֶלְנָתָן וּדְלָיָהוּ וּגְמַרְיָהוּ הִפְגִּעוּ בַמֶּלֶךְ לְבִלְתִּי שְׂרֹף אֶת־הַמְּגִלָּה וְלֹא שָׁמַע אֲלֵיהֶם:

36:22 The king was sitting in the winter house The dramatic showdown between the word of God, as dictated to *Baruch* by *Yirmiyahu*, and the unrepentant *Yehoyakim*, takes place in the king's winter palace. The ninth month on the Hebrew calendar, the month of *Kislev*, occurs in the dead of winter. *Kislev* can be a cold, bitter month, with fierce rains and snow. The aristocracy and the wealthy class could afford to build winter homes heated by coal stoves. In this fire *Yehoyakim* mockingly burns *Yirmiyahu's* scroll, sealing his own fate. Ruins of a palace found in *Ramat Rachel*, in southeast Jerusalem, have been identified as the winter palace of *Yehoyakim*.

Palace in Ramat Rachel

Yirmiyahu/Jeremiah
Chapter 37

26 The king ordered Jerahmeel, the king's son, and *Seraya* son of Azriel, and Shelemiah son of Abdeel to arrest the scribe *Baruch* and the *Navi Yirmiyahu*. But *Hashem* hid them.

27 The word of *Hashem* came to *Yirmiyahu* after the king had burned the scroll containing the words that *Baruch* had written at *Yirmiyahu*'s dictation:

28 Get yourself another scroll, and write upon it the same words that were in the first scroll that was burned by King *Yehoyakim* of *Yehuda*.

29 And concerning King *Yehoyakim* of *Yehuda* you shall say: Thus said *Hashem*: You burned that scroll, saying, "How dare you write in it that the king of Babylon will come and destroy this land and cause man and beast to cease from it?"

30 Assuredly, thus said *Hashem* concerning King *Yehoyakim* of *Yehuda*: He shall not have any of his line sitting on the throne of *David*; and his own corpse shall be left exposed to the heat by day and the cold by night.

31 And I will punish him and his offspring and his courtiers for their iniquity; I will bring on them and on the inhabitants of *Yerushalayim* and on all the men of *Yehuda* all the disasters of which I have warned them – but they would not listen.

32 So *Yirmiyahu* got another scroll and gave it to the scribe *Baruch* son of *Nerya*. And at *Yirmiyahu*'s dictation, he wrote in it the whole text of the scroll that King *Yehoyakim* of *Yehuda* had burned; and more of the like was added.

37

1 *Tzidkiyahu* son of *Yoshiyahu* became king instead of Coniah son of *Yehoyakim*, for King Nebuchadrezzar of Babylon set him up as king over the land of *Yehuda*.

2 Neither he nor his courtiers nor the people of the land gave heed to the words which *Hashem* spoke through the *Navi Yirmiyahu*.

3 Yet King *Tzidkiyahu* sent Jehucal son of Shelemiah and *Tzefanya* son of the *Kohen* Maaseiah to the *Navi Yirmiyahu*, to say, "Please pray on our behalf to *Hashem* our God."

Yirmiyahu/Jeremiah
Chapter 37

4 (*Yirmiyahu* could still go in and out among the people, for they had not yet put him in prison.

5 The army of Pharaoh had set out from Egypt; and when the Chaldeans who were besieging *Yerushalayim* heard the report, they raised the siege of *Yerushalayim*.)

6 Then the word of *Hashem* came to the *Navi Yirmiyahu*:

7 Thus said *Hashem*, the God of *Yisrael*: Thus shall you say to the king of *Yehuda* who sent you to Me to inquire of Me: "The army of Pharaoh, which set out to help you, will return to its own land, to Egypt.

8 And the Chaldeans will come back and attack this city and they will capture it and destroy it by fire."

9 Thus said *Hashem*: Do not delude yourselves into thinking, "The Chaldeans will go away from us." They will not.

10 Even if you defeated the whole army of the Chaldeans that are fighting against you, and only wounded men were left lying in their tents, they would get up and burn this city down!

11 When the army of the Chaldeans raised the siege of *Yerushalayim* on account of the army of Pharaoh,

12 *Yirmiyahu* was going to leave *Yerushalayim* and go to the territory of *Binyamin* to share in some property there among the people.

> va-yay-TZAY yir-m'-YA-hu mee-ru-sha-LA-im la-LE-khet E-retz bin-ya-MIN la-kha-LIK mi-SHAM b'-TOKH ha-AM

13 When he got to the *Binyamin* Gate, there was a guard officer there named Irijah son of Shelemiah son of *Chananya*; and he arrested the *Navi Yirmiyahu*, saying, "You are defecting to the Chaldeans!"

ירמיהו
פרק לז

ד וְיִרְמְיָהוּ בָּא וְיֹצֵא בְּתוֹךְ הָעָם וְלֹא־נָתְנוּ אֹתוֹ בֵּית הַכְּלִיא [הַכְּלוּא]:

ה וְחֵיל פַּרְעֹה יָצָא מִמִּצְרָיִם וַיִּשְׁמְעוּ הַכַּשְׂדִּים הַצָּרִים עַל־יְרוּשָׁלִַם אֶת־שִׁמְעָם וַיֵּעָלוּ מֵעַל יְרוּשָׁלִָם:

ו וַיְהִי דְּבַר־יְהֹוָה אֶל־יִרְמְיָהוּ הַנָּבִיא לֵאמֹר:

ז כֹּה־אָמַר יְהֹוָה אֱלֹהֵי יִשְׂרָאֵל כֹּה תֹאמְרוּ אֶל־מֶלֶךְ יְהוּדָה הַשֹּׁלֵחַ אֶתְכֶם אֵלַי לְדָרְשֵׁנִי הִנֵּה חֵיל פַּרְעֹה הַיֹּצֵא לָכֶם לְעֶזְרָה שָׁב לְאַרְצוֹ מִצְרָיִם:

ח וְשָׁבוּ הַכַּשְׂדִּים וְנִלְחֲמוּ עַל־הָעִיר הַזֹּאת וּלְכָדֻהָ וּשְׂרָפֻהָ בָאֵשׁ:

ט כֹּה אָמַר יְהֹוָה אַל־תַּשִּׁאוּ נַפְשֹׁתֵיכֶם לֵאמֹר הָלֹךְ יֵלְכוּ מֵעָלֵינוּ הַכַּשְׂדִּים כִּי־לֹא יֵלֵכוּ:

י כִּי אִם־הִכִּיתֶם כָּל־חֵיל כַּשְׂדִּים הַנִּלְחָמִים אִתְּכֶם וְנִשְׁאֲרוּ בָם אֲנָשִׁים מְדֻקָּרִים אִישׁ בְּאָהֳלוֹ יָקוּמוּ וְשָׂרְפוּ אֶת־הָעִיר הַזֹּאת בָּאֵשׁ:

יא וְהָיָה בְּהֵעָלוֹת חֵיל הַכַּשְׂדִּים מֵעַל יְרוּשָׁלִָם מִפְּנֵי חֵיל פַּרְעֹה:

יב וַיֵּצֵא יִרְמְיָהוּ מִירוּשָׁלִַם לָלֶכֶת אֶרֶץ בִּנְיָמִן לַחֲלִק מִשָּׁם בְּתוֹךְ הָעָם:

יג וַיְהִי־הוּא בְּשַׁעַר בִּנְיָמִן וְשָׁם בַּעַל פְּקִדֻת וּשְׁמוֹ יִרְאִיָּיה בֶּן־שֶׁלֶמְיָה בֶּן־חֲנַנְיָה וַיִּתְפֹּשׂ אֶת־יִרְמְיָהוּ הַנָּבִיא לֵאמֹר אֶל־הַכַּשְׂדִּים אַתָּה נֹפֵל:

37:12 And go to the territory of *Binyamin* The Egyptians manage to temporarily repulse the Babylonian invaders, thus ending the siege of *Yerushalayim*. With the siege lifted, *Yirmiyahu* leaves the capital for the tribal land of *Binyamin*, to inherit a portion of land. The area of *Binyamin* encompasses the mountain ridges found to the immediate north of *Yerushalayim*, and included *Yirmiyahu*'s hometown, the priestly city *Anatot*. This has been identified with the contemporary Arab village of Anata, which is now a neighborhood of Jerusalem.

Yirmiyahu/Jeremiah
Chapter 38

14 *Yirmiyahu* answered, "That's a lie! I'm not defecting to the Chaldeans!" But Irijah would not listen to him; he arrested *Yirmiyahu* and brought him to the officials.

15 The officials were furious with *Yirmiyahu*; they beat him and put him into prison, in the house of the scribe *Yehonatan* – for it had been made into a jail.

16 Thus *Yirmiyahu* came to the pit and the cells, and *Yirmiyahu* remained there a long time.

17 Then King *Tzidkiyahu* sent for him, and the king questioned him secretly in his palace. He asked, "Is there any word from *Hashem*?" "There is!" *Yirmiyahu* answered, and he continued, "You will be delivered into the hands of the king of Babylon."

18 And *Yirmiyahu* said to King *Tzidkiyahu*, "What wrong have I done to you, to your courtiers, and to this people, that you have put me in jail?

19 And where are those *Neviim* of yours who prophesied to you that the king of Babylon would never move against you and against this land?

20 Now, please hear me, O lord king, and grant my plea: Don't send me back to the house of the scribe *Yehonatan* to die there."

21 So King *Tzidkiyahu* gave instructions to lodge *Yirmiyahu* in the prison compound and to supply him daily with a loaf of bread from the Bakers' Street – until all the bread in the city was gone. *Yirmiyahu* remained in the prison compound.

38 1 Shephatiah son of Mattan, Gedaliah son of Pashhur, Jucal son of Shelemiah, and Pashhur son of Malchiah heard what *Yirmiyahu* was saying to all the people:

2 "Thus said *Hashem*: Whoever remains in this city shall die by the sword, by famine, and by pestilence; but whoever surrenders to the Chaldeans shall live; he shall at least gain his life and shall live.

3 Thus said *Hashem*: This city shall be delivered into the hands of the king of Babylon's army, and he shall capture it."

Yirmiyahu/Jeremiah
Chapter 38

4 Then the officials said to the king, "Let that man be put to death, for he disheartens the soldiers, and all the people who are left in this city, by speaking such things to them. That man is not seeking the welfare of this people, but their harm!"

ד וַיֹּאמְרוּ הַשָּׂרִים אֶל־הַמֶּלֶךְ יוּמַת נָא אֶת־הָאִישׁ הַזֶּה כִּי־עַל־כֵּן הוּא־מְרַפֵּא אֶת־יְדֵי אַנְשֵׁי הַמִּלְחָמָה הַנִּשְׁאָרִים בָּעִיר הַזֹּאת וְאֵת יְדֵי כָל־הָעָם לְדַבֵּר אֲלֵיהֶם כַּדְּבָרִים הָאֵלֶּה כִּי הָאִישׁ הַזֶּה אֵינֶנּוּ דֹרֵשׁ לְשָׁלוֹם לָעָם הַזֶּה כִּי אִם־לְרָעָה:

5 King *Tzidkiyahu* replied, "He is in your hands; the king cannot oppose you in anything!"

ה וַיֹּאמֶר הַמֶּלֶךְ צִדְקִיָּהוּ הִנֵּה־הוּא בְּיֶדְכֶם כִּי־אֵין הַמֶּלֶךְ יוּכַל אֶתְכֶם דָּבָר:

va-YO-mer ha-ME-lekh tzid-ki-YA-hu hi-nay HU b'-yed-KHEM kee AYN ha-ME-lekh yu-KHAL et-KHEM da-VAR

6 So they took *Yirmiyahu* and put him down in the pit of Malchiah, the king's son, which was in the prison compound; they let *Yirmiyahu* down by ropes. There was no water in the pit, only mud, and *Yirmiyahu* sank into the mud.

ו וַיִּקְחוּ אֶת־יִרְמְיָהוּ וַיַּשְׁלִכוּ אֹתוֹ אֶל־הַבּוֹר מַלְכִּיָּהוּ בֶן־הַמֶּלֶךְ אֲשֶׁר בַּחֲצַר הַמַּטָּרָה וַיְשַׁלְּחוּ אֶת־יִרְמְיָהוּ בַחֲבָלִים וּבַבּוֹר אֵין־מַיִם כִּי אִם־טִיט וַיִּטְבַּע יִרְמְיָהוּ בַּטִּיט:

7 *Eved Melech* the Cushite, a eunuch who was in the king's palace, heard that they had put *Yirmiyahu* in the pit. The king was then sitting at the *Binyamin* Gate;

ז וַיִּשְׁמַע עֶבֶד־מֶלֶךְ הַכּוּשִׁי אִישׁ סָרִיס וְהוּא בְּבֵית הַמֶּלֶךְ כִּי־נָתְנוּ אֶת־יִרְמְיָהוּ אֶל־הַבּוֹר וְהַמֶּלֶךְ יוֹשֵׁב בְּשַׁעַר בִּנְיָמִן:

8 so *Eved Melech* left the king's palace, and spoke to the king:

ח וַיֵּצֵא עֶבֶד־מֶלֶךְ מִבֵּית הַמֶּלֶךְ וַיְדַבֵּר אֶל־הַמֶּלֶךְ לֵאמֹר:

9 "O lord king, those men have acted wickedly in all they did to the *Navi Yirmiyahu*; they have put him down in the pit, to die there of hunger." For there was no more bread in the city.

ט אֲדֹנִי הַמֶּלֶךְ הֵרֵעוּ הָאֲנָשִׁים הָאֵלֶּה אֵת כָּל־אֲשֶׁר עָשׂוּ לְיִרְמְיָהוּ הַנָּבִיא אֵת אֲשֶׁר־הִשְׁלִיכוּ אֶל־הַבּוֹר וַיָּמָת תַּחְתָּיו מִפְּנֵי הָרָעָב כִּי אֵין הַלֶּחֶם עוֹד בָּעִיר:

10 Then the king instructed *Eved Melech* the Cushite, "Take with you thirty men from here, and pull the *Navi Yirmiyahu* up from the pit before he dies."

י וַיְצַוֶּה הַמֶּלֶךְ אֵת עֶבֶד־מֶלֶךְ הַכּוּשִׁי לֵאמֹר קַח בְּיָדְךָ מִזֶּה שְׁלֹשִׁים אֲנָשִׁים וְהַעֲלִיתָ אֶת־יִרְמְיָהוּ הַנָּבִיא מִן־הַבּוֹר בְּטֶרֶם יָמוּת:

11 So *Eved Melech* took the men with him, and went to the king's palace, to a place below the treasury. There they got worn cloths and rags, which they let down to *Yirmiyahu* in the pit by ropes.

יא וַיִּקַּח עֶבֶד־מֶלֶךְ אֶת־הָאֲנָשִׁים בְּיָדוֹ וַיָּבֹא בֵית־הַמֶּלֶךְ אֶל־תַּחַת הָאוֹצָר וַיִּקַּח מִשָּׁם בְּלוֹיֵ הַסְּחָבוֹת [סְחָבוֹת] וּבְלוֹיֵ מְלָחִים וַיְשַׁלְּחֵם אֶל־יִרְמְיָהוּ אֶל־הַבּוֹר בַּחֲבָלִים:

צדק

38:5 The king cannot oppose you in anything
Among the tragedies of Israel's downfall is the reign of the final king of *David's* dynasty, *Tzidkiyahu*. Unlike his predecessors who were genuinely wicked, *Tzidkiyahu* is good at heart, as suggested by his name *Tzidkiyahu*, which comes from the word *tzedek* (צדק), 'righteousness.' He secretly tries to support *Yirmiyahu* (see Jeremiah 37:21) and repeatedly inquires of the word of *Hashem* (21:2; 37:17; 38:14). However, *Tzidkiyahu* does not heed *Yirmiyahu's* plea to submit to Babylonia, as he is weak and unable to oppose his officers. They desire to kill *Yirmiyahu* for preaching against Israel, and argue that his words weaken the resolve of the people to keep fighting. By listening to his officers instead of the prophet, his fate and that of the people are sealed. Had *Tzidkiyahu* repented and led the people to follow God's word, they would have been able to avert the disaster and remain in Israel, God's Land.

Yirmiyahu/Jeremiah
Chapter 38

12 And *Eved Melech* the Cushite called to *Yirmiyahu*, "Put the worn cloths and rags under your armpits, inside the ropes." *Yirmiyahu* did so,

יב וַיֹּאמֶר עֶבֶד־מֶלֶךְ הַכּוּשִׁי אֶל־יִרְמְיָהוּ שִׂים נָא בְּלוֹאֵי הַסְּחָבוֹת וְהַמְּלָחִים תַּחַת אַצִּלוֹת יָדֶיךָ מִתַּחַת לַחֲבָלִים וַיַּעַשׂ יִרְמְיָהוּ כֵּן:

13 and they pulled *Yirmiyahu* up by the ropes and got him out of the pit. And *Yirmiyahu* remained in the prison compound.

יג וַיִּמְשְׁכוּ אֶת־יִרְמְיָהוּ בַּחֲבָלִים וַיַּעֲלוּ אֹתוֹ מִן־הַבּוֹר וַיֵּשֶׁב יִרְמְיָהוּ בַּחֲצַר הַמַּטָּרָה:

14 King *Tzidkiyahu* sent for the *Navi Yirmiyahu*, and had him brought to him at the third entrance of the House of *Hashem*. And the king said to *Yirmiyahu*, "I want to ask you something; don't conceal anything from me."

יד וַיִּשְׁלַח הַמֶּלֶךְ צִדְקִיָּהוּ וַיִּקַּח אֶת־יִרְמְיָהוּ הַנָּבִיא אֵלָיו אֶל־מָבוֹא הַשְּׁלִישִׁי אֲשֶׁר בְּבֵית יְהֹוָה וַיֹּאמֶר הַמֶּלֶךְ אֶל־יִרְמְיָהוּ שֹׁאֵל אֲנִי אֹתְךָ דָּבָר אַל־תְּכַחֵד מִמֶּנִּי דָּבָר:

15 *Yirmiyahu* answered the king, "If I tell you, you'll surely kill me; and if I give you advice, you won't listen to me."

טו וַיֹּאמֶר יִרְמְיָהוּ אֶל־צִדְקִיָּהוּ כִּי אַגִּיד לְךָ הֲלוֹא הָמֵת תְּמִיתֵנִי וְכִי אִיעָצְךָ לֹא תִשְׁמַע אֵלָי:

16 Thereupon King *Tzidkiyahu* secretly promised *Yirmiyahu* on oath: "As *Hashem* lives who has given us this life, I will not put you to death or leave you in the hands of those men who seek your life."

טז וַיִּשָּׁבַע הַמֶּלֶךְ צִדְקִיָּהוּ אֶל־יִרְמְיָהוּ בַּסֵּתֶר לֵאמֹר חַי־יְהֹוָה אֵת אֲשֶׁר עָשָׂה־לָנוּ אֶת־הַנֶּפֶשׁ הַזֹּאת אִם־אֲמִיתֶךָ וְאִם־אֶתֶּנְךָ בְּיַד הָאֲנָשִׁים הָאֵלֶּה אֲשֶׁר מְבַקְשִׁים אֶת־נַפְשֶׁךָ:

17 Then *Yirmiyahu* said to *Tzidkiyahu*, "Thus said *Hashem*, the the LORD of Hosts, the God of *Yisrael*: If you surrender to the officers of the king of Babylon, your life will be spared and this city will not be burned down. You and your household will live.

יז וַיֹּאמֶר יִרְמְיָהוּ אֶל־צִדְקִיָּהוּ כֹּה־אָמַר יְהֹוָה אֱלֹהֵי צְבָאוֹת אֱלֹהֵי יִשְׂרָאֵל אִם־יָצֹא תֵצֵא אֶל־שָׂרֵי מֶלֶךְ־בָּבֶל וְחָיְתָה נַפְשֶׁךָ וְהָעִיר הַזֹּאת לֹא תִשָּׂרֵף בָּאֵשׁ וְחָיִתָה אַתָּה וּבֵיתֶךָ:

18 But if you do not surrender to the officers of the king of Babylon, this city will be delivered into the hands of the Chaldeans, who will burn it down; and you will not escape from them."

יח וְאִם לֹא־תֵצֵא אֶל־שָׂרֵי מֶלֶךְ בָּבֶל וְנִתְּנָה הָעִיר הַזֹּאת בְּיַד הַכַּשְׂדִּים וּשְׂרָפוּהָ בָּאֵשׁ וְאַתָּה לֹא־תִמָּלֵט מִיָּדָם:

19 King *Tzidkiyahu* said to *Yirmiyahu*, "I am worried about the Judeans who have defected to the Chaldeans; that they [the Chaldeans] might hand me over to them to abuse me."

יט וַיֹּאמֶר הַמֶּלֶךְ צִדְקִיָּהוּ אֶל־יִרְמְיָהוּ אֲנִי דֹאֵג אֶת־הַיְּהוּדִים אֲשֶׁר נָפְלוּ אֶל־הַכַּשְׂדִּים פֶּן־יִתְּנוּ אֹתִי בְּיָדָם וְהִתְעַלְּלוּ־בִי:

20 "They will not hand you over," *Yirmiyahu* replied. "Listen to the voice of *Hashem*, to what I tell you, that it may go well with you and your life be spared.

כ וַיֹּאמֶר יִרְמְיָהוּ לֹא יִתֵּנוּ שְׁמַע־נָא בְּקוֹל יְהֹוָה לַאֲשֶׁר אֲנִי דֹּבֵר אֵלֶיךָ וְיִיטַב לְךָ וּתְחִי נַפְשֶׁךָ:

21 For this is what *Hashem* has shown me if you refuse to surrender:

כא וְאִם־מָאֵן אַתָּה לָצֵאת זֶה הַדָּבָר אֲשֶׁר הִרְאַנִי יְהֹוָה:

Yirmiyahu/Jeremiah
Chapter 39

22 All the women who are left in the palace of the king of *Yehuda* shall be brought out to the officers of the king of Babylon; and they shall say: The men who were your friends Have seduced you and vanquished you. Now that your feet are sunk in the mire, They have turned their backs [on you].

23 They will bring out all your wives and children to the Chaldeans, and you yourself will not escape from them. You will be captured by the king of Babylon, and this city shall be burned down."

24 *Tzidkiyahu* said to *Yirmiyahu*, "Don't let anyone know about this conversation, or you will die.

25 If the officials should hear that I have spoken with you, and they should come and say to you, 'Tell us what you said to the king; hide nothing from us, or we'll kill you. And what did the king say to you?'

26 say to them, 'I was presenting my petition to the king not to send me back to the house of *Yehonatan* to die there.'"

27 All the officials did come to *Yirmiyahu* to question him; and he replied to them just as the king had instructed him. So they stopped questioning him, for the conversation had not been overheard.

28 *Yirmiyahu* remained in the prison compound until the day *Yerushalayim* was captured. When *Yerushalayim* was captured…

39 1 In the ninth year of King *Tzidkiyahu* of *Yehuda*, in the tenth month, King Nebuchadrezzar of Babylon moved against *Yerushalayim* with his whole army, and they laid siege to it.

2 And in the eleventh year of *Tzidkiyahu*, on the ninth day of the fourth month, the [walls of] the city were breached.

3 All the officers of the king of Babylon entered, and took up quarters at the middle gate – Nergal-sarezer, Samgar-nebo, Sarsechim the Rab-saris, Nergal-sarezer the Rab-mag, and all the rest of the officers of the king of Babylon.

4 When King *Tzidkiyahu* of *Yehuda* saw them, he and all the soldiers fled. They left the city at night, by way of the king's garden, through the gate between the double walls; and he set out toward the Arabah.

ירמיהו
פרק לט

כב וְהִנֵּה כָל־הַנָּשִׁים אֲשֶׁר נִשְׁאֲרוּ בְּבֵית מֶלֶךְ־יְהוּדָה מוּצָאוֹת אֶל־שָׂרֵי מֶלֶךְ בָּבֶל וְהֵנָּה אֹמְרוֹת הִסִּיתוּךָ וְיָכְלוּ לְךָ אַנְשֵׁי שְׁלֹמֶךָ הָטְבְּעוּ בַבֹּץ רַגְלֶךָ נָסֹגוּ אָחוֹר:

כג וְאֶת־כָּל־נָשֶׁיךָ וְאֶת־בָּנֶיךָ מוֹצִאִים אֶל־הַכַּשְׂדִּים וְאַתָּה לֹא־תִמָּלֵט מִיָּדָם כִּי בְיַד מֶלֶךְ־בָּבֶל תִּתָּפֵשׂ וְאֶת־הָעִיר הַזֹּאת תִּשְׂרֹף בָּאֵשׁ:

כד וַיֹּאמֶר צִדְקִיָּהוּ אֶל־יִרְמְיָהוּ אִישׁ אַל־יֵדַע בַּדְּבָרִים־הָאֵלֶּה וְלֹא תָמוּת:

כה וְכִי־יִשְׁמְעוּ הַשָּׂרִים כִּי־דִבַּרְתִּי אִתָּךְ וּבָאוּ אֵלֶיךָ וְאָמְרוּ אֵלֶיךָ הַגִּידָה־נָּא לָנוּ מַה־דִּבַּרְתָּ אֶל־הַמֶּלֶךְ אַל־תְּכַחֵד מִמֶּנּוּ וְלֹא נְמִיתֶךָ וּמַה־דִּבֶּר אֵלֶיךָ הַמֶּלֶךְ:

כו וְאָמַרְתָּ אֲלֵיהֶם מַפִּיל־אֲנִי תְחִנָּתִי לִפְנֵי הַמֶּלֶךְ לְבִלְתִּי הֲשִׁיבֵנִי בֵּית יְהוֹנָתָן לָמוּת שָׁם:

כז וַיָּבֹאוּ כָל־הַשָּׂרִים אֶל־יִרְמְיָהוּ וַיִּשְׁאֲלוּ אֹתוֹ וַיַּגֵּד לָהֶם כְּכָל־הַדְּבָרִים הָאֵלֶּה אֲשֶׁר צִוָּה הַמֶּלֶךְ וַיַּחֲרִשׁוּ מִמֶּנּוּ כִּי לֹא־נִשְׁמַע הַדָּבָר:

כח וַיֵּשֶׁב יִרְמְיָהוּ בַּחֲצַר הַמַּטָּרָה עַד־יוֹם אֲשֶׁר־נִלְכְּדָה יְרוּשָׁלָ͏ִם וְהָיָה כַּאֲשֶׁר נִלְכְּדָה יְרוּשָׁלָ͏ִם:

לט א בַּשָּׁנָה הַתְּשִׁעִית לְצִדְקִיָּהוּ מֶלֶךְ־יְהוּדָה בַּחֹדֶשׁ הָעֲשִׂרִי בָּא נְבוּכַדְרֶאצַּר מֶלֶךְ־בָּבֶל וְכָל־חֵילוֹ אֶל־יְרוּשָׁלַ͏ִם וַיָּצֻרוּ עָלֶיהָ:

ב בְּעַשְׁתֵּי־עֶשְׂרֵה שָׁנָה לְצִדְקִיָּהוּ בַּחֹדֶשׁ הָרְבִיעִי בְּתִשְׁעָה לַחֹדֶשׁ הָבְקְעָה הָעִיר:

ג וַיָּבֹאוּ כֹּל שָׂרֵי מֶלֶךְ־בָּבֶל וַיֵּשְׁבוּ בְּשַׁעַר הַתָּוֶךְ נֵרְגַל שַׂר־אֶצֶר סַמְגַּר־נְבוּ שַׂר־סְכִים רַב־סָרִיס נֵרְגַל שַׂר־אֶצֶר רַב־מָג וְכָל־שְׁאֵרִית שָׂרֵי מֶלֶךְ בָּבֶל:

ד וַיְהִי כַּאֲשֶׁר רָאָם צִדְקִיָּהוּ מֶלֶךְ־יְהוּדָה וְכֹל אַנְשֵׁי הַמִּלְחָמָה וַיִּבְרְחוּ וַיֵּצְאוּ לַיְלָה מִן־הָעִיר דֶּרֶךְ גַּן הַמֶּלֶךְ בְּשַׁעַר בֵּין הַחֹמֹתָיִם וַיֵּצֵא דֶּרֶךְ הָעֲרָבָה:

Yirmiyahu/Jeremiah
Chapter 39

ירמיהו
פרק לט

5 But the Chaldean troops pursued them, and they overtook *Tzidkiyahu* in the steppes of *Yericho*. They captured him and brought him before King Nebuchadrezzar of Babylon at Riblah in the region of Hamath; and he put him on trial.

ה וַיִּרְדְּפוּ חֵיל־כַּשְׂדִּים אַחֲרֵיהֶם וַיַּשִּׂגוּ אֶת־צִדְקִיָּהוּ בְּעַרְבוֹת יְרֵחוֹ וַיִּקְחוּ אֹתוֹ וַיַּעֲלֻהוּ אֶל־נְבוּכַדְרֶאצַּר מֶלֶךְ־בָּבֶל רִבְלָתָה בְּאֶרֶץ חֲמָת וַיְדַבֵּר אִתּוֹ מִשְׁפָּטִים:

va-yir-d'-FU khayl kas-DEEM a-kha-ray-HEM va-ya-SEE-gu et tzid-ki-YA-hu b'ar-VOT y'-ray-KHO va-yik-KHU o-TO va-ya-a-LU-hu el n'-vu-khad-RE-tzar me-lekh ba-VEL riv-LA-tah b'-E-retz kha-MAT vai-da-BAYR i-TO mish-pa-TEEM

6 The king of Babylon had *Tzidkiyahu*'s children slaughtered at Riblah before his eyes; the king of Babylon had all the nobles of *Yehuda* slaughtered.

ו וַיִּשְׁחַט מֶלֶךְ בָּבֶל אֶת־בְּנֵי צִדְקִיָּהוּ בְּרִבְלָה לְעֵינָיו וְאֵת כָּל־חֹרֵי יְהוּדָה שָׁחַט מֶלֶךְ בָּבֶל:

7 Then the eyes of *Tzidkiyahu* were put out and he was chained in bronze fetters, that he might be brought to Babylon.

ז וְאֶת־עֵינֵי צִדְקִיָּהוּ עִוֵּר וַיַּאַסְרֵהוּ בַּנְחֻשְׁתַּיִם לָבִיא אֹתוֹ בָּבֶלָה:

8 The Chaldeans burned down the king's palace and the houses of the people by fire, and they tore down the walls of *Yerushalayim*.

ח וְאֶת־בֵּית הַמֶּלֶךְ וְאֶת־בֵּית הָעָם שָׂרְפוּ הַכַּשְׂדִּים בָּאֵשׁ וְאֶת־חֹמוֹת יְרוּשָׁלַ͏ִם נָתָצוּ:

9 The remnant of the people that was left in the city, and the defectors who had gone over to him – the remnant of the people that was left – were exiled by Nebuzaradan, the chief of the guards, to Babylon.

ט וְאֵת יֶתֶר הָעָם הַנִּשְׁאָרִים בָּעִיר וְאֶת־הַנֹּפְלִים אֲשֶׁר נָפְלוּ עָלָיו וְאֵת יֶתֶר הָעָם הַנִּשְׁאָרִים הֶגְלָה נְבוּזַרְאֲדָן רַב־טַבָּחִים בָּבֶל:

10 But some of the poorest people who owned nothing were left in the land of *Yehuda* by Nebuzaradan, the chief of the guards, and he gave them vineyards and fields at that time.

י וּמִן־הָעָם הַדַּלִּים אֲשֶׁר אֵין־לָהֶם מְאוּמָה הִשְׁאִיר נְבוּזַרְאֲדָן רַב־טַבָּחִים בְּאֶרֶץ יְהוּדָה וַיִּתֵּן לָהֶם כְּרָמִים וִיגֵבִים בַּיּוֹם הַהוּא:

11 King Nebuchadrezzar of Babylon had given orders to Nebuzaradan, the chief of the guards, concerning *Yirmiyahu*:

יא וַיְצַו נְבוּכַדְרֶאצַּר מֶלֶךְ־בָּבֶל עַל־יִרְמְיָהוּ בְּיַד נְבוּזַרְאֲדָן רַב־טַבָּחִים לֵאמֹר:

12 "Take him and look after him; do him no harm, but grant whatever he asks of you."

יב קָחֶנּוּ וְעֵינֶיךָ שִׂים עָלָיו וְאַל־תַּעַשׂ לוֹ מְאוּמָה רָּע כִּי אִם כַּאֲשֶׁר יְדַבֵּר אֵלֶיךָ כֵּן עֲשֵׂה עִמּוֹ:

13 So Nebuzaradan, the chief of the guards, and Nebushazban the Rab-saris, and Nergal-sarezer the Rab-mag, and all the commanders of the king of Babylon sent

יג וַיִּשְׁלַח נְבוּזַרְאֲדָן רַב־טַבָּחִים וּנְבוּשַׁזְבָּן רַב־סָרִיס וְנֵרְגַל שַׂר־אֶצֶר רַב־מָג וְכֹל רַבֵּי מֶלֶךְ־בָּבֶל:

39:5 And they overtook *Tzidkiyahu* in the steppes of *Yericho* Chapter 39 describes the tragic, final downfall of *Yerushalayim*. *Tzidkiyahu* attempts to flee, but is caught just miles away from the *Yarden* river, in *Yericho*. Rashi elaborates that "a cave went from his house until the plains of *Yericho*, and he fled through the cave. The Holy One, Blessed be He, ordained a deer walking on the roof of the cave. The Chaldeans pursued the deer, and when they reached the entrance of the cave in the plains of *Yericho*, they saw him and captured him." This is what *Yechezkel* said about him, (12:13) "I will spread My net over him, and he shall be caught in My snare." No matter what plans a person makes, God's plan prevails.

The plains of Yericho

Yirmiyahu/Jeremiah
Chapter 40

ירמיהו
פרק מ

14 and had *Yirmiyahu* brought from the prison compound. They committed him to the care of *Gedalya* son of *Achikam* son of *Shafan*, that he might be left at liberty in a house. So he dwelt among the people.

וַיִּשְׁלְחוּ וַיִּקְחוּ אֶת־יִרְמְיָהוּ מֵחֲצַר הַמַּטָּרָה וַיִּתְּנוּ אֹתוֹ אֶל־גְּדַלְיָהוּ בֶן־אֲחִיקָם בֶּן־שָׁפָן לְהוֹצִאֵהוּ אֶל־הַבָּיִת וַיֵּשֶׁב בְּתוֹךְ הָעָם:

15 The word of *Hashem* had come to *Yirmiyahu* while he was still confined in the prison compound:

וְאֶל־יִרְמְיָהוּ הָיָה דְבַר־יְהֹוָה בִּהְיֹתוֹ עָצוּר בַּחֲצַר הַמַּטָּרָה לֵאמֹר:

16 Go and say to *Eved Melech* the Ethiopian: "Thus said the LORD of Hosts, the God of *Yisrael*: I am going to fulfill My words concerning this city – for disaster, not for good – and they shall come true on that day in your presence.

הָלוֹךְ וְאָמַרְתָּ לְעֶבֶד־מֶלֶךְ הַכּוּשִׁי לֵאמֹר כֹּה־אָמַר יְהֹוָה צְבָאוֹת אֱלֹהֵי יִשְׂרָאֵל הִנְנִי מבי [מֵבִיא] אֶת־דְּבָרַי אֶל־הָעִיר הַזֹּאת לְרָעָה וְלֹא לְטוֹבָה וְהָיוּ לְפָנֶיךָ בַּיּוֹם הַהוּא:

17 But I will save you on that day – declares *Hashem*; you shall not be delivered into the hands of the men you dread.

וְהִצַּלְתִּיךָ בַּיּוֹם־הַהוּא נְאֻם־יְהֹוָה וְלֹא תִנָּתֵן בְּיַד הָאֲנָשִׁים אֲשֶׁר־אַתָּה יָגוֹר מִפְּנֵיהֶם:

18 I will rescue you, and you shall not fall by the sword. You shall escape with your life, because you trusted Me – declares *Hashem*."

כִּי מַלֵּט אֲמַלֶּטְךָ וּבַחֶרֶב לֹא תִפֹּל וְהָיְתָה לְךָ נַפְשְׁךָ לְשָׁלָל כִּי־בָטַחְתָּ בִּי נְאֻם־יְהֹוָה:

40 1 The word that came to *Yirmiyahu* from *Hashem*, after Nebuzaradan, the chief of the guards, set him free at *Rama*, to which he had taken him, chained in fetters, among those from *Yerushalayim* and *Yehuda* who were being exiled to Babylon.

מ א הַדָּבָר אֲשֶׁר־הָיָה אֶל־יִרְמְיָהוּ מֵאֵת יְהֹוָה אַחַר שַׁלַּח אֹתוֹ נְבוּזַרְאֲדָן רַב־טַבָּחִים מִן־הָרָמָה בְּקַחְתּוֹ אֹתוֹ וְהוּא־אָסוּר בָּאזִקִּים בְּתוֹךְ כׇּל־גָּלוּת יְרוּשָׁלַ͏ִם וִיהוּדָה הַמֻּגְלִים בָּבֶלָה:

ha-da-VAR a-SHER ha-YAH el yir-m'-YA-hu may-AYT a-do-NAI a-KHAR sha-LAKH o-TO n'-vu-zar-a-DAN rav ta-ba-KHEEM min ha-ra-MAH b'kakh-TO o-TO v'hu a-SUR ba-zi-KEEM b'TOKH kol ga-LUT y'-ru-sha-LA-im vee-hu-DAH ha-mug-LEEM ba-VE-lah

2 The chief of the guards took charge of *Yirmiyahu*, and he said to him, "*Hashem* your God threatened this place with this disaster;

ב וַיִּקַּח רַב־טַבָּחִים לְיִרְמְיָהוּ וַיֹּאמֶר אֵלָיו יְהֹוָה אֱלֹהֶיךָ דִּבֶּר אֶת־הָרָעָה הַזֹּאת אֶל־הַמָּקוֹם הַזֶּה:

3 and now *Hashem* has brought it about. He has acted as He threatened, because you sinned against *Hashem* and did not obey Him. That is why this has happened to you.

ג וַיָּבֵא וַיַּעַשׂ יְהֹוָה כַּאֲשֶׁר דִּבֵּר כִּי־חֲטָאתֶם לַיהֹוָה וְלֹא־שְׁמַעְתֶּם בְּקוֹלוֹ וְהָיָה לָכֶם דבר [הַדָּבָר] הַזֶּה:

40:1 Set him free at *Rama* Although King Nebuchadnezzar of Babylon orders his soldiers to treat *Yirmiyahu* with respect and consideration, only when the convoy reaches *Rama*, about nine kilometers north of *Yerushalayim*, does the Babylonian captain release him from his chains. According to *Rashi*, *Yirmiyahu* voluntarily fettered himself to the chains leading the exiles away from Israel in order to demonstrate his complete identification with his people and their suffering. Such is the characteristic of a true leader. Though mistreated and abused by them, *Yirmiyahu* still identifies with, and cares for, his people.

Yirmiyahu/Jeremiah
Chapter 40

ירמיהו
פרק מ

4 Now, I release you this day from the fetters which were on your hands. If you would like to go with me to Babylon, come, and I will look after you. And if you don't want to come with me to Babylon, you need not. See, the whole land is before you: go wherever seems good and right to you." –

ד וְעַתָּה הִנֵּה פִתַּחְתִּיךָ הַיּוֹם מִן־הָאזִקִּים אֲשֶׁר עַל־יָדֶךָ אִם־טוֹב בְּעֵינֶיךָ לָבוֹא אִתִּי בָבֶל בֹּא וְאָשִׂים אֶת־עֵינִי עָלֶיךָ וְאִם־רַע בְּעֵינֶיךָ לָבוֹא־אִתִּי בָבֶל חֲדָל רְאֵה כָּל־הָאָרֶץ לְפָנֶיךָ אֶל־טוֹב וְאֶל־הַיָּשָׁר בְּעֵינֶיךָ לָלֶכֶת שָׁמָּה לֵךְ:

5 But [Yirmiyahu] still did not turn back. – "Or go to Gedalya son of Achikam son of Shafan, whom the king of Babylon has put in charge of the towns of Yehuda, and stay with him among the people, or go wherever you want to go." The chief of the guards gave him an allowance of food, and dismissed him.

ה וְעוֹדֶנּוּ לֹא־יָשׁוּב וְשֻׁבָה אֶל־גְּדַלְיָה בֶן־אֲחִיקָם בֶּן־שָׁפָן אֲשֶׁר הִפְקִיד מֶלֶךְ־בָּבֶל בְּעָרֵי יְהוּדָה וְשֵׁב אִתּוֹ בְּתוֹךְ הָעָם אוֹ אֶל־כָּל־הַיָּשָׁר בְּעֵינֶיךָ לָלֶכֶת לֵךְ וַיִּתֶּן־לוֹ רַב־טַבָּחִים אֲרֻחָה וּמַשְׂאֵת וַיְשַׁלְּחֵהוּ:

6 So Yirmiyahu came to Gedalya son of Achikam at Mitzpa, and stayed with him among the people who were left in the land.

ו וַיָּבֹא יִרְמְיָהוּ אֶל־גְּדַלְיָה בֶן־אֲחִיקָם הַמִּצְפָּתָה וַיֵּשֶׁב אִתּוֹ בְּתוֹךְ הָעָם הַנִּשְׁאָרִים בָּאָרֶץ:

7 The officers of the troops in the open country, and their men with them, heard that the king of Babylon had put Gedalya son of Achikam in charge of the region, and that he had put in his charge the men, women, and children – of the poorest in the land – those who had not been exiled to Babylon.

ז וַיִּשְׁמְעוּ כָל־שָׂרֵי הַחֲיָלִים אֲשֶׁר בַּשָּׂדֶה הֵמָּה וְאַנְשֵׁיהֶם כִּי־הִפְקִיד מֶלֶךְ־בָּבֶל אֶת־גְּדַלְיָהוּ בֶן־אֲחִיקָם בָּאָרֶץ וְכִי הִפְקִיד אִתּוֹ אֲנָשִׁים וְנָשִׁים וָטָף וּמִדַּלַּת הָאָרֶץ מֵאֲשֶׁר לֹא־הָגְלוּ בָּבֶלָה:

8 So they with their men came to Gedalya at Mitzpa – Ishmael son of Nethaniah; Yochanan and Yonatan the sons of Kareah; Seraya son of Tanhumeth; the sons of Ephai the Netophathite; and Jezaniah son of the Maacathite.

ח וַיָּבֹאוּ אֶל־גְּדַלְיָה הַמִּצְפָּתָה וְיִשְׁמָעֵאל בֶּן־נְתַנְיָהוּ וְיוֹחָנָן וְיוֹנָתָן בְּנֵי־קָרֵחַ וּשְׂרָיָה בֶן־תַּנְחֻמֶת וּבְנֵי עופי [עֵיפַי] הַנְּטֹפָתִי וִיזַנְיָהוּ בֶּן־הַמַּעֲכָתִי הֵמָּה וְאַנְשֵׁיהֶם:

9 Gedalya son of Achikam son of Shafan reassured them and their men, saying, "Do not be afraid to serve the Chaldeans. Stay in the land and serve the king of Babylon, and it will go well with you.

ט וַיִּשָּׁבַע לָהֶם גְּדַלְיָהוּ בֶן־אֲחִיקָם בֶּן־שָׁפָן וּלְאַנְשֵׁיהֶם לֵאמֹר אַל־תִּירְאוּ מֵעֲבוֹד הַכַּשְׂדִּים שְׁבוּ בָאָרֶץ וְעִבְדוּ אֶת־מֶלֶךְ בָּבֶל וְיִיטַב לָכֶם:

10 I am going to stay in Mitzpa to attend upon the Chaldeans who will come to us. But you may gather wine and figs and oil and put them in your own vessels, and settle in the towns you have occupied."

י וַאֲנִי הִנְנִי יֹשֵׁב בַּמִּצְפָּה לַעֲמֹד לִפְנֵי הַכַּשְׂדִּים אֲשֶׁר יָבֹאוּ אֵלֵינוּ וְאַתֶּם אִסְפוּ יַיִן וְקַיִץ וְשֶׁמֶן וְשִׂמוּ בִּכְלֵיכֶם וּשְׁבוּ בְּעָרֵיכֶם אֲשֶׁר־תְּפַשְׂתֶּם:

11 Likewise, all the Judeans who were in Moab, Ammon, and Edom, or who were in other lands, heard that the king of Babylon had let a remnant stay in Yehuda, and that he had put Gedalya son of Achikam son of Shafan in charge of them.

יא וְגַם כָּל־הַיְּהוּדִים אֲשֶׁר־בְּמוֹאָב וּבִבְנֵי־עַמּוֹן וּבֶאֱדוֹם וַאֲשֶׁר בְּכָל־הָאֲרָצוֹת שָׁמְעוּ כִּי־נָתַן מֶלֶךְ־בָּבֶל שְׁאֵרִית לִיהוּדָה וְכִי הִפְקִיד עֲלֵיהֶם אֶת־גְּדַלְיָהוּ בֶן־אֲחִיקָם בֶּן־שָׁפָן:

12 All these Judeans returned from all the places to which they had scattered. They came to the land of Yehuda, to Gedalya at Mitzpa, and they gathered large quantities of wine and figs.

יב וַיָּשֻׁבוּ כָל־הַיְּהוּדִים מִכָּל־הַמְּקֹמוֹת אֲשֶׁר נִדְּחוּ־שָׁם וַיָּבֹאוּ אֶרֶץ־יְהוּדָה אֶל־גְּדַלְיָהוּ הַמִּצְפָּתָה וַיַּאַסְפוּ יַיִן וָקַיִץ הַרְבֵּה מְאֹד:

Yirmiyahu/Jeremiah
Chapter 41

ירמיהו
פרק מא

13 *Yochanan* son of Kareah, and all the officers of the troops in the open country, came to *Gedalya* at *Mitzpa*

יג וְיוֹחָנָן בֶּן־קָרֵחַ וְכָל־שָׂרֵי הַחֲיָלִים אֲשֶׁר בַּשָּׂדֶה בָּאוּ אֶל־גְּדַלְיָהוּ הַמִּצְפָּתָה:

14 and said to him, "Do you know that King Baalis of Ammon has sent Ishmael son of Nethaniah to kill you?" But *Gedalya* son of *Achikam* would not believe them.

יד וַיֹּאמְרוּ אֵלָיו הֲיָדֹעַ תֵּדַע כִּי בַּעֲלִיס מֶלֶךְ בְּנֵי־עַמּוֹן שָׁלַח אֶת־יִשְׁמָעֵאל בֶּן־נְתַנְיָה לְהַכֹּתְךָ נָּפֶשׁ וְלֹא־הֶאֱמִין לָהֶם גְּדַלְיָהוּ בֶּן־אֲחִיקָם:

15 *Yochanan* son of Kareah also said secretly to *Gedalya* at *Mitzpa*, "Let me go and strike down Ishmael son of Nethaniah before anyone knows about it; otherwise he will kill you, and all the Judeans who have gathered about you will be dispersed, and the remnant of *Yehuda* will perish!"

טו וְיוֹחָנָן בֶּן־קָרֵחַ אָמַר אֶל־גְּדַלְיָהוּ בַסֵּתֶר בַּמִּצְפָּה לֵאמֹר אֵלְכָה נָּא וְאַכֶּה אֶת־יִשְׁמָעֵאל בֶּן־נְתַנְיָה וְאִישׁ לֹא יֵדָע לָמָּה יַכֶּכָּה נֶּפֶשׁ וְנָפֹצוּ כָּל־יְהוּדָה הַנִּקְבָּצִים אֵלֶיךָ וְאָבְדָה שְׁאֵרִית יְהוּדָה:

16 But *Gedalya* son of *Achikam* answered *Yochanan* son of Kareah, "Do not do such a thing: what you are saying about Ishmael is not true!"

טז וַיֹּאמֶר גְּדַלְיָהוּ בֶן־אֲחִיקָם אֶל־יוֹחָנָן בֶּן־קָרֵחַ אַל־תַּעַשׂ [תַּעֲשֵׂה] אֶת־הַדָּבָר הַזֶּה כִּי־שֶׁקֶר אַתָּה דֹבֵר אֶל־יִשְׁמָעֵאל:

41

1 In the seventh month, Ishmael son of Nethaniah son of Elishama, who was of royal descent and one of the king's commanders, came with ten men to *Gedalya* son of *Achikam* at *Mitzpa*; and they ate together there at *Mitzpa*.

מא א וַיְהִי בַּחֹדֶשׁ הַשְּׁבִיעִי בָּא יִשְׁמָעֵאל בֶּן־נְתַנְיָה בֶן־אֱלִישָׁמָע מִזֶּרַע הַמְּלוּכָה וְרַבֵּי הַמֶּלֶךְ וַעֲשָׂרָה אֲנָשִׁים אִתּוֹ אֶל־גְּדַלְיָהוּ בֶן־אֲחִיקָם הַמִּצְפָּתָה וַיֹּאכְלוּ שָׁם לֶחֶם יַחְדָּו בַּמִּצְפָּה:

2 Then Ishmael son of Nethaniah and the ten men who were with him arose and struck down *Gedalya* son of *Achikam* son of *Shafan* with the sword and killed him, because the king of Babylon had put him in charge of the land.

ב וַיָּקָם יִשְׁמָעֵאל בֶּן־נְתַנְיָה וַעֲשֶׂרֶת הָאֲנָשִׁים אֲשֶׁר־הָיוּ אִתּוֹ וַיַּכּוּ אֶת־גְּדַלְיָהוּ בֶן־אֲחִיקָם בֶּן־שָׁפָן בַּחֶרֶב וַיָּמֶת אֹתוֹ אֲשֶׁר־הִפְקִיד מֶלֶךְ־בָּבֶל בָּאָרֶץ:

va-YA-kom yish-ma-AYL ben n'-tan-YAH va-a-SE-ret ha-a-na-SHEEM a-sher ha-YU i-TO va-ya-KU et g'-dal-YA-hu ven a-khee-KAM ben sha-FAN ba-KHE-rev va-YA-met o-TO a-sher hif-KEED me-lekh ba-VEL ba-A-retz

3 Ishmael also killed all the Judeans who were with him – with *Gedalya* in *Mitzpa* – and the Chaldean soldiers who were stationed there.

ג וְאֵת כָּל־הַיְּהוּדִים אֲשֶׁר־הָיוּ אִתּוֹ אֶת־גְּדַלְיָהוּ בַּמִּצְפָּה וְאֶת־הַכַּשְׂדִּים אֲשֶׁר נִמְצְאוּ־שָׁם אֵת אַנְשֵׁי הַמִּלְחָמָה הִכָּה יִשְׁמָעֵאל:

Rabbi Abraham Isaac Kook (1865–1935)

41:2 And struck down *Gedalya* *Gedalya* son of *Achikam* is appointed by the Babylonians as governor of *Yehuda* after the destruction of *Yerushalayim*. A small band of Jewish fanatics, led by Ishmael the son of Nethaniah, take advantage of *Gedalya's* hospitality and assassinate him on *Rosh Hashana*, the Jewish new year. As a result, the few Jews remaining in Israel flee to Egypt to avoid the vengeance of the Babylonian army, ridding the Holy Land of a Jewish presence for the remainder of the Babylonian exile. The death of the last Jewish leader in Israel marked the end of the First Israelite Commonwealth. Since then, for over two thousand years, Jews have fasted in commemoration of *Gedalyah's* death on the day after *Rosh Hashana*, to remind them how hatred and zealousness cost them their sovereignty in the Land of Israel. Rabbi Abraham Isaac Kook taught that since *Yerushalayim* was destroyed on account of hatred and factionalism (*Yoma* 9b), it is through love and kindness that the Jews will return to the land and the *Beit Hamikdash* will be rebuilt.

Yirmiyahu/Jeremiah
Chapter 41

ירמיהו
פרק מא

4 The second day after *Gedalya* was killed, when no one yet knew about it,

ד וַיְהִי בַּיּוֹם הַשֵּׁנִי לְהָמִית אֶת־גְּדַלְיָהוּ וְאִישׁ לֹא יָדָע׃

5 eighty men came from *Shechem*, *Shilo*, and *Shomron*, their beards shaved, their garments torn, and their bodies gashed, carrying meal offerings and frankincense to present at the House of *Hashem*.

ה וַיָּבֹאוּ אֲנָשִׁים מִשְּׁכֶם מִשִּׁלוֹ וּמִשֹּׁמְרוֹן שְׁמֹנִים אִישׁ מְגֻלְּחֵי זָקָן וּקְרֻעֵי בְגָדִים וּמִתְגֹּדְדִים וּמִנְחָה וּלְבוֹנָה בְּיָדָם לְהָבִיא בֵּית יְהוָה׃

6 Ishmael son of Nethaniah went out from *Mitzpa* to meet them, weeping as he walked. As he met them, he said to them, "Come to *Gedalya* son of *Achikam.*"

ו וַיֵּצֵא יִשְׁמָעֵאל בֶּן־נְתַנְיָה לִקְרָאתָם מִן־הַמִּצְפָּה הֹלֵךְ הָלֹךְ וּבֹכֶה וַיְהִי כִּפְגֹשׁ אֹתָם וַיֹּאמֶר אֲלֵיהֶם בֹּאוּ אֶל־גְּדַלְיָהוּ בֶן־אֲחִיקָם׃

7 When they came inside the town, Ishmael son of Nethaniah and the men who were with him slaughtered them [and threw their bodies] into a cistern.

ז וַיְהִי כְּבוֹאָם אֶל־תּוֹךְ הָעִיר וַיִּשְׁחָטֵם יִשְׁמָעֵאל בֶּן־נְתַנְיָה אֶל־תּוֹךְ הַבּוֹר הוּא וְהָאֲנָשִׁים אֲשֶׁר־אִתּוֹ׃

8 But there were ten men among them who said to Ishmael, "Don't kill us! We have stores hidden in a field – wheat, barley, oil, and honey." So he stopped, and did not kill them along with their fellows. –

ח וַעֲשָׂרָה אֲנָשִׁים נִמְצְאוּ־בָם וַיֹּאמְרוּ אֶל־יִשְׁמָעֵאל אַל־תְּמִתֵנוּ כִּי־יֶשׁ־לָנוּ מַטְמֹנִים בַּשָּׂדֶה חִטִּים וּשְׂעֹרִים וְשֶׁמֶן וּדְבָשׁ וַיֶּחְדַּל וְלֹא הֱמִיתָם בְּתוֹךְ אֲחֵיהֶם׃

9 The cistern into which Ishmael threw all the corpses of the men he had killed in the affair of *Gedalya* was the one that King *Asa* had constructed on account of King *Basha* of *Yisrael*. That was the one which Ishmael son of Nethaniah filled with corpses. –

ט וְהַבּוֹר אֲשֶׁר הִשְׁלִיךְ שָׁם יִשְׁמָעֵאל אֵת כָּל־פִּגְרֵי הָאֲנָשִׁים אֲשֶׁר הִכָּה בְּיַד־גְּדַלְיָהוּ הוּא אֲשֶׁר עָשָׂה הַמֶּלֶךְ אָסָא מִפְּנֵי בַּעְשָׁא מֶלֶךְ־יִשְׂרָאֵל אֹתוֹ מִלֵּא יִשְׁמָעֵאל בֶּן־נְתַנְיָהוּ חֲלָלִים׃

10 Ishmael carried off all the rest of the people who were in *Mitzpa*, including the daughters of the king – all the people left in *Mitzpa*, over whom Nebuzaradan, the chief of the guards, had appointed *Gedalya* son of *Achikam*. Ishmael son of Nethaniah carried them off, and set out to cross over to the Amonites.

י וַיִּשְׁבְּ יִשְׁמָעֵאל אֶת־כָּל־שְׁאֵרִית הָעָם אֲשֶׁר בַּמִּצְפָּה אֶת־בְּנוֹת הַמֶּלֶךְ וְאֶת־כָּל־הָעָם הַנִּשְׁאָרִים בַּמִּצְפָּה אֲשֶׁר הִפְקִיד נְבוּזַרְאֲדָן רַב־טַבָּחִים אֶת־גְּדַלְיָהוּ בֶּן־אֲחִיקָם וַיִּשְׁבֵּם יִשְׁמָעֵאל בֶּן־נְתַנְיָה וַיֵּלֶךְ לַעֲבֹר אֶל־בְּנֵי עַמּוֹן׃

11 *Yochanan* son of Kareah, and all the army officers with him, heard of all the crimes committed by Ishmael son of Nethaniah.

יא וַיִּשְׁמַע יוֹחָנָן בֶּן־קָרֵחַ וְכָל־שָׂרֵי הַחֲיָלִים אֲשֶׁר אִתּוֹ אֵת כָּל־הָרָעָה אֲשֶׁר עָשָׂה יִשְׁמָעֵאל בֶּן־נְתַנְיָה׃

12 They took all their men and went to fight against Ishmael son of Nethaniah; and they encountered him by the great pool in *Givon*.

יב וַיִּקְחוּ אֶת־כָּל־הָאֲנָשִׁים וַיֵּלְכוּ לְהִלָּחֵם עִם־יִשְׁמָעֵאל בֶּן־נְתַנְיָה וַיִּמְצְאוּ אֹתוֹ אֶל־מַיִם רַבִּים אֲשֶׁר בְּגִבְעוֹן׃

13 When all the people held by Ishmael saw *Yochanan* son of Kareah and all the army officers with him, they were glad;

יג וַיְהִי כִּרְאוֹת כָּל־הָעָם אֲשֶׁר אֶת־יִשְׁמָעֵאל אֶת־יוֹחָנָן בֶּן־קָרֵחַ וְאֵת כָּל־שָׂרֵי הַחֲיָלִים אֲשֶׁר אִתּוֹ וַיִּשְׂמָחוּ׃

1174

Yirmiyahu/Jeremiah
Chapter 42

ירמיהו
פרק מב

14 all the people whom Ishmael had carried off from *Mitzpa* turned back and went over to *Yochanan* son of Kareah.

יד וַיָּסֹבּוּ כָּל־הָעָם אֲשֶׁר־שָׁבָה יִשְׁמָעֵאל מִן־הַמִּצְפָּה וַיָּשֻׁבוּ וַיֵּלְכוּ אֶל־יוֹחָנָן בֶּן־קָרֵחַ:

15 But Ishmael son of Nethaniah escaped from *Yochanan* with eight men, and went to the Amonites.

טו וְיִשְׁמָעֵאל בֶּן־נְתַנְיָה נִמְלַט בִּשְׁמֹנָה אֲנָשִׁים מִפְּנֵי יוֹחָנָן וַיֵּלֶךְ אֶל־בְּנֵי עַמּוֹן:

16 *Yochanan* son of Kareah and all the army officers with him took all the rest of the people whom he had rescued from Ishmael son of Nethaniah from *Mitzpa* after he had murdered *Gedalya* son of *Achikam* – the men, soldiers, women, children, and eunuchs whom [*Yochanan*] had brought back from *Givon*.

טז וַיִּקַּח יוֹחָנָן בֶּן־קָרֵחַ וְכָל־שָׂרֵי הַחֲיָלִים אֲשֶׁר־אִתּוֹ אֵת כָּל־שְׁאֵרִית הָעָם אֲשֶׁר הֵשִׁיב מֵאֵת יִשְׁמָעֵאל בֶּן־נְתַנְיָה מִן־הַמִּצְפָּה אַחַר הִכָּה אֶת־גְּדַלְיָה בֶּן־אֲחִיקָם גְּבָרִים אַנְשֵׁי הַמִּלְחָמָה וְנָשִׁים וְטַף וְסָרִסִים אֲשֶׁר הֵשִׁיב מִגִּבְעוֹן:

17 They set out, and they stopped at Geruth Chimham, near *Beit Lechem*, on their way to go to Egypt

יז וַיֵּלְכוּ וַיֵּשְׁבוּ בְּגֵרוּת כמוהם [כִּמְהָם] אֲשֶׁר־אֵצֶל בֵּית לָחֶם לָלֶכֶת לָבוֹא מִצְרָיִם:

18 because of the Chaldeans. For they were afraid of them, because Ishmael son of Nethaniah had killed *Gedalya* son of *Achikam*, whom the king of Babylon had put in charge of the land.

יח מִפְּנֵי הַכַּשְׂדִּים כִּי יָרְאוּ מִפְּנֵיהֶם כִּי־הִכָּה יִשְׁמָעֵאל בֶּן־נְתַנְיָה אֶת־גְּדַלְיָהוּ בֶּן־אֲחִיקָם אֲשֶׁר־הִפְקִיד מֶלֶךְ־בָּבֶל בָּאָרֶץ:

42

1 Then all the army officers, with *Yochanan* son of Kareah, Jezaniah son of Hoshaiah, and all the rest of the people, great and small, approached

א וַיִּגְּשׁוּ כָּל־שָׂרֵי הַחֲיָלִים וְיוֹחָנָן בֶּן־קָרֵחַ וִיזַנְיָה בֶּן־הוֹשַׁעְיָה וְכָל־הָעָם מִקָּטֹן וְעַד־גָּדוֹל:

2 the *Navi Yirmiyahu* and said, "Grant our plea, and pray for us to *Hashem* your God, for all this remnant! For we remain but a few out of many, as you can see.

ב וַיֹּאמְרוּ אֶל־יִרְמְיָהוּ הַנָּבִיא תִּפָּל־נָא תְחִנָּתֵנוּ לְפָנֶיךָ וְהִתְפַּלֵּל בַּעֲדֵנוּ אֶל־יְהֹוָה אֱלֹהֶיךָ בְּעַד כָּל־הַשְּׁאֵרִית הַזֹּאת כִּי־נִשְׁאַרְנוּ מְעַט מֵהַרְבֵּה כַּאֲשֶׁר עֵינֶיךָ רֹאוֹת אֹתָנוּ:

va-yo-m'-RU el yir-m'-YA-hu ha-na-VEE ti-pol NA t'-khi-na-TAY-nu l'-fa-NE-kha v'-hit-pa-LAYL ba-a-DAY-nu el a-do-NAI e-lo-HE-kha b'-AD kol ha-sh'-ay-REET ha-ZOT kee nish-AR-nu m'-AT may-har-BAY ka-a-SHER ay-NE-kha ro-OT o-TA-nu

3 Let *Hashem* your God tell us where we should go and what we should do."

ג וְיַגֶּד־לָנוּ יְהֹוָה אֱלֹהֶיךָ אֶת־הַדֶּרֶךְ אֲשֶׁר נֵלֶךְ־בָּהּ וְאֶת־הַדָּבָר אֲשֶׁר נַעֲשֶׂה:

42:2 For we remain but a few out of many The people, in panic over the upcoming invasion from Babylonia, turn to the prophet and ask him to pray for guidance. *Yirmiyahu* counsels them against going down to Egypt. However, in their final act of disobedience against God, they flee to Egypt, forcefully taking *Yirmiyahu* with them. Their statement that they were once many, but now have become few, represents an undoing of the divine promises. *Sefer Devarim* (10:22) describes how God took a few people, made them many, and brought them from Egypt to the Land of Israel. Now, they leave *Eretz Yisrael* headed for Egypt, few instead of many; a painful reminder of the damage caused by refusing to listen to the word of God.

Yirmiyahu/Jeremiah
Chapter 42

4 The *Navi Yirmiyahu* answered them, "Agreed: I will pray to *Hashem* your God as you request, and I will tell you whatever response *Hashem* gives for you. I will withhold nothing from you."

5 Thereupon they said to *Yirmiyahu*, "Let *Hashem* be a true and faithful witness against us! We swear that we will do exactly as *Hashem* your God instructs us through you –

6 Whether it is pleasant or unpleasant, we will obey *Hashem* our God to whom we send you, in order that it may go well with us when we obey *Hashem* our God."

7 After ten days, the word of *Hashem* came to *Yirmiyahu*.

8 He called *Yochanan* son of Kareah and all the army officers, and the rest of the people, great and small,

9 and said to them, "Thus said *Hashem*, the God of *Yisrael*, to whom you sent me to present your supplication before Him:

10 If you remain in this land, I will build you and not overthrow, I will plant you and not uproot; for I regret the punishment I have brought upon you.

11 Do not be afraid of the king of Babylon, whom you fear; do not be afraid of him – declares *Hashem* – for I am with you to save you and to rescue you from his hands.

12 I will dispose him to be merciful to you: he shall show you mercy and bring you back to your own land.

13 "But if you say, 'We will not stay in this land' – thus disobeying *Hashem* your God –

14 if you say, 'No! We will go to the land of Egypt, so that we may not see war or hear the sound of the *shofar*, and so that we may not hunger for bread; there we will stay,'

15 then hear the word of *Hashem*, O remnant of *Yehuda*! Thus said the Lord of Hosts, the God of *Yisrael*: If you turn your faces toward Egypt, and you go and sojourn there,

ירמיהו
פרק מב

ד וַיֹּאמֶר אֲלֵיהֶם יִרְמְיָהוּ הַנָּבִיא שָׁמַעְתִּי הִנְנִי מִתְפַּלֵּל אֶל־יְהֹוָה אֱלֹהֵיכֶם כְּדִבְרֵיכֶם וְהָיָה כָּל־הַדָּבָר אֲשֶׁר־יַעֲנֶה יְהֹוָה אֶתְכֶם אַגִּיד לָכֶם לֹא־אֶמְנַע מִכֶּם דָּבָר:

ה וְהֵמָּה אָמְרוּ אֶל־יִרְמְיָהוּ יְהִי יְהֹוָה בָּנוּ לְעֵד אֱמֶת וְנֶאֱמָן אִם־לֹא כְּכָל־הַדָּבָר אֲשֶׁר יִשְׁלָחֲךָ יְהֹוָה אֱלֹהֶיךָ אֵלֵינוּ כֵּן נַעֲשֶׂה:

ו אִם־טוֹב וְאִם־רָע בְּקוֹל יְהֹוָה אֱלֹהֵינוּ אֲשֶׁר אָנוּ [אֲנַחְנוּ] שֹׁלְחִים אֹתְךָ אֵלָיו נִשְׁמָע לְמַעַן אֲשֶׁר יִיטַב־לָנוּ כִּי נִשְׁמַע בְּקוֹל יְהֹוָה אֱלֹהֵינוּ:

ז וַיְהִי מִקֵּץ עֲשֶׂרֶת יָמִים וַיְהִי דְבַר־יְהֹוָה אֶל־יִרְמְיָהוּ:

ח וַיִּקְרָא אֶל־יוֹחָנָן בֶּן־קָרֵחַ וְאֶל כָּל־שָׂרֵי הַחֲיָלִים אֲשֶׁר אִתּוֹ וּלְכָל־הָעָם לְמִקָּטֹן וְעַד־גָּדוֹל:

ט וַיֹּאמֶר אֲלֵיהֶם כֹּה־אָמַר יְהֹוָה אֱלֹהֵי יִשְׂרָאֵל אֲשֶׁר שְׁלַחְתֶּם אֹתִי אֵלָיו לְהַפִּיל תְּחִנַּתְכֶם לְפָנָיו:

י אִם־שׁוֹב תֵּשְׁבוּ בָּאָרֶץ הַזֹּאת וּבָנִיתִי אֶתְכֶם וְלֹא אֶהֱרֹס וְנָטַעְתִּי אֶתְכֶם וְלֹא אֶתּוֹשׁ כִּי נִחַמְתִּי אֶל־הָרָעָה אֲשֶׁר עָשִׂיתִי לָכֶם:

יא אַל־תִּירְאוּ מִפְּנֵי מֶלֶךְ בָּבֶל אֲשֶׁר־אַתֶּם יְרֵאִים מִפָּנָיו אַל־תִּירְאוּ מִמֶּנּוּ נְאֻם־יְהֹוָה כִּי־אִתְּכֶם אָנִי לְהוֹשִׁיעַ אֶתְכֶם וּלְהַצִּיל אֶתְכֶם מִיָּדוֹ:

יב וְאֶתֵּן לָכֶם רַחֲמִים וְרִחַם אֶתְכֶם וְהֵשִׁיב אֶתְכֶם אֶל־אַדְמַתְכֶם:

יג וְאִם־אֹמְרִים אַתֶּם לֹא נֵשֵׁב בָּאָרֶץ הַזֹּאת לְבִלְתִּי שְׁמֹעַ בְּקוֹל יְהֹוָה אֱלֹהֵיכֶם:

יד לֵאמֹר לֹא כִּי אֶרֶץ מִצְרַיִם נָבוֹא אֲשֶׁר לֹא־נִרְאֶה מִלְחָמָה וְקוֹל שׁוֹפָר לֹא נִשְׁמָע וְלַלֶּחֶם לֹא־נִרְעָב וְשָׁם נֵשֵׁב:

טו וְעַתָּה לָכֵן שִׁמְעוּ דְבַר־יְהֹוָה שְׁאֵרִית יְהוּדָה כֹּה־אָמַר יְהֹוָה צְבָאוֹת אֱלֹהֵי יִשְׂרָאֵל אִם־אַתֶּם שׂוֹם תְּשִׂמוּן פְּנֵיכֶם לָבֹא מִצְרַיִם וּבָאתֶם לָגוּר שָׁם:

1176

Yirmiyahu/Jeremiah
Chapter 43

16 the sword that you fear shall overtake you there, in the land of Egypt, and the famine you worry over shall follow at your heels in Egypt too; and there you shall die.

17 All the men who turn their faces toward Egypt, in order to sojourn there, shall die by the sword, by famine, and by pestilence. They shall have no surviving remnant of the disaster that I will bring upon them.

18 For thus said the LORD of Hosts, the God of *Yisrael*: As My anger and wrath were poured out upon the inhabitants of *Yerushalayim*, so will My wrath be poured out on you if you go to Egypt. You shall become an execration of woe, a curse and a mockery; and you shall never again see this place.

19 *Hashem* has spoken against you, O remnant of *Yehuda*! Do not go to Egypt! Know well, then – for I warn you this day

20 that you were deceitful at heart when you sent me to *Hashem* your God, saying, 'Pray for us to *Hashem* our God; and whatever *Hashem* our God may say, just tell us and we will do it.'

21 I told you today, and you have not obeyed *Hashem* your God in respect to all that He sent me to tell you –

22 know well, then, that you shall die by the sword, by famine, and by pestilence in the place where you want to go and sojourn."

43 1 When *Yirmiyahu* had finished speaking all these words to all the people – all the words of *Hashem* their God, with which *Hashem* their God had sent him to them –

2 *Azarya* son of Hoshaiah and *Yochanan* son of Kareah and all the arrogant men said to *Yirmiyahu*, "You are lying! *Hashem* our God did not send you to say, 'Don't go to Egypt and sojourn there'!

3 It is *Baruch* son of *Nerya* who is inciting you against us, so that we will be delivered into the hands of the Chaldeans to be killed or to be exiled to Babylon!"

Yirmiyahu/Jeremiah
Chapter 43

4 So *Yochanan* son of Kareah and all the army officers and the rest of the people did not obey *Hashem*'s command to remain in the land of *Yehuda*.

5 Instead, *Yochanan* son of Kareah and all the army officers took the entire remnant of *Yehuda* – those who had returned from all the countries to which they had been scattered and had sojourned in the land of *Yehuda*,

6 men, women, and children; and the daughters of the king and all the people whom Nebuzaradan the chief of the guards had left with *Gedalya* son of *Achikam* son of *Shafan*, as well as the *Navi Yirmiyahu* and *Baruch* son of *Nerya* –

7 and they went to Egypt. They did not obey *Hashem*. They arrived at Tahpanhes,

8 and the word of *Hashem* came to *Yirmiyahu* in Tahpanhes:

9 Get yourself large stones, and embed them in mortar in the brick structure at the entrance to Pharaoh's palace in Tahpanhes, with some Judeans looking on.

10 And say to them: "Thus said the LORD of Hosts, the God of *Yisrael*: I am sending for My servant King Nebuchadrezzar of Babylon, and I will set his throne over these stones which I have embedded. He will spread out his pavilion over them.

v'-a-mar-TA a-lay-HEM koh a-MAR a-do-NAI tz'-va-OT e-lo-HAY yis-ra-AYL hi-n'-NEE sho-LAY-akh v'-la-kakh-TEE et n'-vu-khad-RE-tzar me-lekh ba-VEL av-DEE v'-sam-TEE khis-O mi-MA-al la-a-va-NEEM ha-AY-leh a-SHER ta-MAN-tee v'-na-TAH et shaf-ree-RO a-lay-HEM

11 He will come and attack the land of Egypt, delivering Those destined for the plague, to the plague, Those destined for captivity, to captivity, And those destined for the sword, to the sword.

43:10 And I will set his throne over these stones *Yirmiyahu* is commanded to embed giant stones into the mortar in front of Pharaoh's palace while men from *Yehuda* look on. This final symbolic act was performed with the hopes that the Jews who had fled to Egypt would regret their actions and return to Israel. The prophet declares that the gates of Egypt will not provide them protection, as the Babylonians will conquer Egypt as well. The only protection they can rely on is a return to *Hashem*'s will and the Land of Israel, or they too will be captured and destroyed. God's dominion, while concentrated in the Holy Land, extends everywhere; they cannot flee from His bidding.

Yirmiyahu/Jeremiah
Chapter 44

12 And I will set fire to the temples of the gods of Egypt; he will burn them down and carry them off. He shall wrap himself up in the land of Egypt, as a shepherd wraps himself up in his garment. And he shall depart from there in safety.

13 He shall smash the obelisks of the Temple of the Sun which is in the land of Egypt, and he shall burn down the temples of the gods of Egypt.

44

1 The word which came to *Yirmiyahu* for all the Judeans living in the land of Egypt, living in Migdol, Tahpanhes, and Noph, and in the land of Pathros:

2 Thus said the Lord of Hosts, the God of *Yisrael*: You have seen all the disaster that I brought on *Yerushalayim* and on all the towns of *Yehuda*. They are a ruin today, and no one inhabits them,

3 on account of the wicked things they did to vex Me, going to make offerings in worship of other gods which they had not known – neither they nor you nor your fathers.

4 Yet I persistently sent to you all My servants the *Neviim*, to say, "I beg you not to do this abominable thing which I hate."

5 But they would not listen or give ear, to turn back from their wickedness and not make offerings to other gods;

6 so My fierce anger was poured out, and it blazed against the towns of *Yehuda* and the streets of *Yerushalayim*. And they became a desolate ruin, as they still are today.

7 And now, thus said *Hashem*, the the Lord of Hosts, the God of *Yisrael*: Why are you doing such great harm to yourselves, so that every man and woman, child and infant of yours shall be cut off from the midst of *Yehuda*, and no remnant shall be left of you?

8 For you vex me by your deeds, making offering to other gods in the land of Egypt where you have come to sojourn, so that you shall be cut off and become a curse and a mockery among all the nations of earth.

ירמיהו
פרק מד

יב וְהִצַּתִּי אֵשׁ בְּבָתֵּי אֱלֹהֵי מִצְרַיִם וּשְׂרָפָם וְשָׁבָם וְעָטָה אֶת־אֶרֶץ מִצְרַיִם כַּאֲשֶׁר־יַעְטֶה הָרֹעֶה אֶת־בִּגְדוֹ וְיָצָא מִשָּׁם בְּשָׁלוֹם:

יג וְשִׁבַּר אֶת־מַצְּבוֹת בֵּית שֶׁמֶשׁ אֲשֶׁר בְּאֶרֶץ מִצְרָיִם וְאֶת־בָּתֵּי אֱלֹהֵי־מִצְרַיִם יִשְׂרֹף בָּאֵשׁ:

מד א הַדָּבָר אֲשֶׁר הָיָה אֶל־יִרְמְיָהוּ אֶל כָּל־הַיְּהוּדִים הַיֹּשְׁבִים בְּאֶרֶץ מִצְרָיִם הַיֹּשְׁבִים בְּמִגְדֹּל וּבְתַחְפַּנְחֵס וּבְנֹף וּבְאֶרֶץ פַּתְרוֹס לֵאמֹר:

ב כֹּה־אָמַר יְהֹוָה צְבָאוֹת אֱלֹהֵי יִשְׂרָאֵל אַתֶּם רְאִיתֶם אֵת כָּל־הָרָעָה אֲשֶׁר הֵבֵאתִי עַל־יְרוּשָׁלַ͏ִם וְעַל כָּל־עָרֵי יְהוּדָה וְהִנָּם חָרְבָּה הַיּוֹם הַזֶּה וְאֵין בָּהֶם יוֹשֵׁב:

ג מִפְּנֵי רָעָתָם אֲשֶׁר עָשׂוּ לְהַכְעִסֵנִי לָלֶכֶת לְקַטֵּר לַעֲבֹד לֵאלֹהִים אֲחֵרִים אֲשֶׁר לֹא יְדָעוּם הֵמָּה אַתֶּם וַאֲבֹתֵיכֶם:

ד וָאֶשְׁלַח אֲלֵיכֶם אֶת־כָּל־עֲבָדַי הַנְּבִיאִים הַשְׁכֵּים וְשָׁלֹחַ לֵאמֹר אַל־נָא תַעֲשׂוּ אֵת דְּבַר־הַתֹּעֵבָה הַזֹּאת אֲשֶׁר שָׂנֵאתִי:

ה וְלֹא שָׁמְעוּ וְלֹא־הִטּוּ אֶת־אָזְנָם לָשׁוּב מֵרָעָתָם לְבִלְתִּי קַטֵּר לֵאלֹהִים אֲחֵרִים:

ו וַתִּתַּךְ חֲמָתִי וְאַפִּי וַתִּבְעַר בְּעָרֵי יְהוּדָה וּבְחֻצוֹת יְרוּשָׁלָ͏ִם וַתִּהְיֶינָה לְחָרְבָּה לִשְׁמָמָה כַּיּוֹם הַזֶּה:

ז וְעַתָּה כֹּה־אָמַר יְהֹוָה אֱלֹהֵי צְבָאוֹת אֱלֹהֵי יִשְׂרָאֵל לָמָה אַתֶּם עֹשִׂים רָעָה גְדוֹלָה אֶל־נַפְשֹׁתֵכֶם לְהַכְרִית לָכֶם אִישׁ־וְאִשָּׁה עוֹלֵל וְיוֹנֵק מִתּוֹךְ יְהוּדָה לְבִלְתִּי הוֹתִיר לָכֶם שְׁאֵרִית:

ח לְהַכְעִסֵנִי בְּמַעֲשֵׂי יְדֵיכֶם לְקַטֵּר לֵאלֹהִים אֲחֵרִים בְּאֶרֶץ מִצְרַיִם אֲשֶׁר־אַתֶּם בָּאִים לָגוּר שָׁם לְמַעַן הַכְרִית לָכֶם וּלְמַעַן הֱיוֹתְכֶם לִקְלָלָה וּלְחֶרְפָּה בְּכֹל גּוֹיֵי הָאָרֶץ:

Yirmiyahu/Jeremiah
Chapter 44

9 Have you forgotten the wicked acts of your forefathers, of the kings of *Yehuda* and their wives, and your own wicked acts and those of your wives, which were committed in the land of *Yehuda* and in the streets of *Yerushalayim*?

10 No one has shown contrition to this day, and no one has shown reverence. You have not followed the Teaching and the laws that I set before you and before your fathers.

11 Assuredly, thus said the Lord of Hosts, the God of *Yisrael*: I am going to set My face against you for punishment, to cut off all of *Yehuda*.

12 I will take the remnant of *Yehuda* who turned their faces toward the land of Egypt, to go and sojourn there, and they shall be utterly consumed in the land of Egypt. They shall fall by the sword, they shall be consumed by famine; great and small alike shall die by the sword and by famine, and they shall become an execration and a desolation, a curse and a mockery.

13 I will punish those who live in the land of Egypt as I punished *Yerushalayim*, with the sword, with famine, and with pestilence.

14 Of the remnant of *Yehuda* who came to sojourn here in the land of Egypt, no survivor or fugitive shall be left to return to the land of *Yehuda*. Though they all long to return and dwell there, none shall return except [a few] survivors.

15 Thereupon they answered *Yirmiyahu* – all the men who knew that their wives made offerings to other gods; all the women present, a large gathering; and all the people who lived in Pathros in the land of Egypt:

16 "We will not listen to you in the matter about which you spoke to us in the name of *Hashem*.

17 On the contrary, we will do everything that we have vowed – to make offerings to the Queen of Heaven and to pour libations to her, as we used to do, we and our fathers, our kings and our officials, in the towns of *Yehuda* and the streets of *Yerushalayim*. For then we had plenty to eat, we were well-off, and suffered no misfortune.

Yirmiyahu/Jeremiah
Chapter 44

ירמיהו
פרק מד

18 But ever since we stopped making offerings to the Queen of Heaven and pouring libations to her, we have lacked everything, and we have been consumed by the sword and by famine.

יח וּמִן־אָז חָדַלְנוּ לְקַטֵּר לִמְלֶכֶת הַשָּׁמַיִם וְהַסֵּךְ־לָהּ נְסָכִים חָסַרְנוּ כֹל וּבַחֶרֶב וּבָרָעָב תָּמְנוּ׃

19 And when we make offerings to the Queen of Heaven and pour libations to her, is it without our husbands' approval that we have made cakes in her likeness and poured libations to her?"

יט וְכִי־אֲנַחְנוּ מְקַטְּרִים לִמְלֶכֶת הַשָּׁמַיִם וּלְהַסֵּךְ לָהּ נְסָכִים הֲמִבַּלְעֲדֵי אֲנָשֵׁינוּ עָשִׂינוּ לָהּ כַּוָּנִים לְהַעֲצִבָה וְהַסֵּךְ לָהּ נְסָכִים׃

20 *Yirmiyahu* replied to all the people, men and women — all the people who argued with him. He said,

כ וַיֹּאמֶר יִרְמְיָהוּ אֶל־כָּל־הָעָם עַל־הַגְּבָרִים וְעַל־הַנָּשִׁים וְעַל־כָּל־הָעָם הָעֹנִים אֹתוֹ דָּבָר לֵאמֹר׃

21 "Indeed, the offerings you presented in the towns of *Yehuda* and the streets of *Yerushalayim* — you, your fathers, your kings, your officials, and the people of the land — were remembered by *Hashem* and brought to mind!

כא הֲלוֹא אֶת־הַקִּטֵּר אֲשֶׁר קִטַּרְתֶּם בְּעָרֵי יְהוּדָה וּבְחֻצוֹת יְרוּשָׁלַםִ אַתֶּם וַאֲבוֹתֵיכֶם מַלְכֵיכֶם וְשָׂרֵיכֶם וְעַם הָאָרֶץ אֹתָם זָכַר יְהוָה וַתַּעֲלֶה עַל־לִבּוֹ׃

22 When *Hashem* could no longer bear your evil practices and the abominations you committed, your land became a desolate ruin and a curse, without inhabitant, as is still the case.

כב וְלֹא־יוּכַל יְהוָה עוֹד לָשֵׂאת מִפְּנֵי רֹעַ מַעַלְלֵיכֶם מִפְּנֵי הַתּוֹעֵבֹת אֲשֶׁר עֲשִׂיתֶם וַתְּהִי אַרְצְכֶם לְחָרְבָּה וּלְשַׁמָּה וְלִקְלָלָה מֵאֵין יוֹשֵׁב כְּהַיּוֹם הַזֶּה׃

v'-lo yu-KHAL a-do-NAI OD la-SAYT mi-p'-NAY RO-a ma-a-l'-lay-KHEM mi-p'-NAY ha-to-ay-VOT a-SHER a-see-TEM va-t'-HEE ar-z'-KHEM l'-khor-BAH ul-sha-MAH v'-lik-la-LAH may-AYN yo-SHAYV k'-ha-YOM ha-ZEH

23 Because you burned incense and sinned against *Hashem* and did not obey *Hashem*, and because you did not follow His Teaching, His laws, and His exhortations, therefore this disaster has befallen you, as is still the case."

כג מִפְּנֵי אֲשֶׁר קִטַּרְתֶּם וַאֲשֶׁר חֲטָאתֶם לַיהוָה וְלֹא שְׁמַעְתֶּם בְּקוֹל יְהוָה וּבְתֹרָתוֹ וּבְחֻקֹּתָיו וּבְעֵדְוֹתָיו לֹא הֲלַכְתֶּם עַל־כֵּן קָרָאת אֶתְכֶם הָרָעָה הַזֹּאת כַּיּוֹם הַזֶּה׃

24 *Yirmiyahu* further said to all the people and to all the women: "Hear the word of *Hashem*, all Judeans in the land of Egypt!

כד וַיֹּאמֶר יִרְמְיָהוּ אֶל־כָּל־הָעָם וְאֶל כָּל־הַנָּשִׁים שִׁמְעוּ דְּבַר־יְהוָה כָּל־יְהוּדָה אֲשֶׁר בְּאֶרֶץ מִצְרָיִם׃

44:22 Your land became a desolate ruin Even in Egypt, their country overrun by Babylon and their *Beit Hamikdash* destroyed, the remaining Jews turn to *Yirmiyahu* and say, "We will not listen to you in the matter about which you spoke to us in the name of *Hashem*" (verse 16). Despite the destruction and exile, they choose to maintain their wrongdoing and wayward belief in idolatry. *Yirmiyahu* responds that their land has been destroyed because of their sins. The connection between the Jewish people and *Eretz Yisrael* is not happenstance. Whether or not they are able to remain in the land is directly dependent on their behavior. Sinful behavior caused them to be kicked out, and their re-entry into the land is dependent upon prayer and repentance. As soon as the People of Israel are willing to change, God will bring them back with open arms. This is one of the most enduring lessons repeated throughout the *Tanakh*.

Yirmiyahu/Jeremiah
Chapter 45

25 Thus said the LORD of Hosts, the God of *Yisrael*: You and your wives have confirmed by deed what you spoke in words: 'We will fulfill the vows which we made, to burn incense to the Queen of Heaven and to pour libations to her.' So fulfill your vows; perform your vows!

26 "Yet hear the word of *Hashem*, all Judeans who dwell in the land of Egypt! Lo, I swear by My great name – said *Hashem* – that none of the men of *Yehuda* in all the land of Egypt shall ever again invoke My name, saying, 'As *Hashem* lives!'

27 I will be watchful over them to their hurt, not to their benefit; all the men of *Yehuda* in the land of Egypt shall be consumed by sword and by famine, until they cease to be.

28 Only the few who survive the sword shall return from the land of Egypt to the land of *Yehuda*. All the remnant of *Yehuda* who came to the land of Egypt to sojourn there shall learn whose word will be fulfilled – Mine or theirs!

29 "And this shall be the sign to you – declares *Hashem* – that I am going to deal with you in this place, so that you may know that My threats of punishment against you will be fulfilled:

30 Thus said *Hashem*: I will deliver Pharaoh Hophra, king of Egypt, into the hands of his enemies, those who seek his life, just as I delivered King *Tzidkiyahu* of *Yehuda* into the hands of King Nebuchadrezzar of Babylon, his enemy who sought his life."

45 1 The word which the *Navi Yirmiyahu* spoke to *Baruch* son of *Nerya*, when he was writing these words in a scroll at *Yirmiyahu*'s dictation, in the fourth year of King *Yehoyakim* son of *Yoshiyahu* of *Yehuda*:

2 Thus said *Hashem*, the God of *Yisrael*, concerning you, *Baruch*:

3 You say, "Woe is me! *Hashem* has added grief to my pain. I am worn out with groaning, and I have found no rest."

4 Thus shall you speak to him: "Thus said *Hashem*: I am going to overthrow what I have built, and uproot what I have planted – this applies to the whole land.

Yirmiyahu/Jeremiah
Chapter 46

ירמיהו
פרק מו

5 And do you expect great things for yourself? Don't expect them. For I am going to bring disaster upon all flesh – declares *Hashem* – but I will at least grant you your life in all the places where you may go."

ה וְאַתָּה תְּבַקֶּשׁ־לְךָ גְדֹלוֹת אַל־תְּבַקֵּשׁ כִּי הִנְנִי מֵבִיא רָעָה עַל־כָּל־בָּשָׂר נְאֻם־יְהֹוָה וְנָתַתִּי לְךָ אֶת־נַפְשְׁךָ לְשָׁלָל עַל כָּל־הַמְּקֹמוֹת אֲשֶׁר תֵּלֶךְ־שָׁם:

v'-a-TAH t'-va-kesh l'-KHA g'-do-LOT al t'-va-KESH KEE hi-n'-NEE may-VEE ra-AH al kol ba-SAR n'-um a-do-NAI v'-na-ta-TEE l'-KHA et naf-sh'-KHA l'-sha-LAL AL kol ha-m'-ko-MOT a-SHER tay-lekh SHAM

46 1 The word of *Hashem* to the *Navi Yirmiyahu* concerning the nations.

מו א אֲשֶׁר הָיָה דְבַר־יְהֹוָה אֶל־יִרְמְיָהוּ הַנָּבִיא עַל־הַגּוֹיִם:

2 Concerning Egypt, about the army of Pharaoh Neco, king of Egypt, which was at the river Euphrates near Carchemish, and which was defeated by King Nebuchadrezzar of Babylon, in the fourth year of King *Yehoyakim* son of *Yoshiyahu* of *Yehuda*.

ב לְמִצְרַיִם עַל־חֵיל פַּרְעֹה נְכוֹ מֶלֶךְ מִצְרַיִם אֲשֶׁר־הָיָה עַל־נְהַר־פְּרָת בְּכַרְכְּמִשׁ אֲשֶׁר הִכָּה נְבוּכַדְרֶאצַּר מֶלֶךְ בָּבֶל בִּשְׁנַת הָרְבִיעִית לִיהוֹיָקִים בֶּן־יֹאשִׁיָּהוּ מֶלֶךְ יְהוּדָה:

3 Get ready buckler and shield, And move forward to battle!

ג עִרְכוּ מָגֵן וְצִנָּה וּגְשׁוּ לַמִּלְחָמָה:

4 Harness the horses; Mount, you horsemen! Fall in line, helmets on! Burnish the lances, Don your armor!

ד אִסְרוּ הַסּוּסִים וַעֲלוּ הַפָּרָשִׁים וְהִתְיַצְּבוּ בְּכוֹבָעִים מִרְקוּ הָרְמָחִים לִבְשׁוּ הַסִּרְיֹנֹת:

5 Why do I see them dismayed, Yielding ground? Their fighters are crushed, They flee in haste And do not turn back – Terror all around! – declares *Hashem*.

ה מַדּוּעַ רָאִיתִי הֵמָּה חַתִּים נְסֹגִים אָחוֹר וְגִבּוֹרֵיהֶם יֻכַּתּוּ וּמָנוֹס נָסוּ וְלֹא הִפְנוּ מָגוֹר מִסָּבִיב נְאֻם־יְהֹוָה:

6 The swift cannot get away, The warrior cannot escape. In the north, by the river Euphrates, They stagger and fall.

ו אַל־יָנוּס הַקַּל וְאַל־יִמָּלֵט הַגִּבּוֹר צָפוֹנָה עַל־יַד נְהַר־פְּרָת כָּשְׁלוּ וְנָפָלוּ:

7 Who is this that rises like the Nile, Like streams whose waters surge?

ז מִי־זֶה כַּיְאֹר יַעֲלֶה כַּנְּהָרוֹת יִתְגָּעֲשׁוּ מֵימָיו:

8 It is Egypt that rises like the Nile, Like streams whose waters surge, That said, "I will rise, I will cover the earth, I will wipe out towns And those who dwell in them.

ח מִצְרַיִם כַּיְאֹר יַעֲלֶה וְכַנְּהָרוֹת יִתְגֹּעֲשׁוּ מָיִם וַיֹּאמֶר אַעֲלֶה אֲכַסֶּה־אֶרֶץ אֹבִידָה עִיר וְיֹשְׁבֵי בָהּ:

Rashi
(1040–1105)

45:5 And do you expect great things for yourself? In the midst of the calamity, *Yirmiyahu* rebukes his closest student, *Baruch* son of *Nerya*, for being concerned about his personal welfare at a time of national crisis. Some suggest that as his grandfather was *Maasayahu*, governor of *Yerushalayim* during *Yoshiyahu's* reign (II Chronicles 34:8), *Baruch* also hoped for high office, only to see his aspirations dissipate. *Rashi*, however, attributes a higher motivation to *Baruch*: He was hoping, like great students of prophets before him, such as *Yehoshua* and *Elisha*, to receive the gift of prophecy. However, *Yirmiyahu* reminds his student, at a time when the people are suffering, personal goals – even spiritual ones – must be set aside.

Yirmiyahu/Jeremiah
Chapter 46

9 Advance, O horses, Dash madly, O chariots! Let the warriors go forth, Cush and Put, that grasp the shield, And the Ludim who grasp and draw the bow!"

10 But that day shall be for the LORD of Hosts a day when He exacts retribution from His foes. The sword shall devour; it shall be sated and drunk with their blood. For the LORD of Hosts is preparing a sacrifice in the northland, by the river Euphrates.

11 Go up to *Gilad* and get balm, Fair Maiden Egypt. In vain do you seek many remedies, There is no healing for you.

12 Nations have heard your shame; The earth resounds with your screams. For warrior stumbles against warrior; The two fall down together.

13 The word which *Hashem* spoke to the *Navi Yirmiyahu* about the coming of King Nebuchadrezzar of Babylon to attack the land of Egypt:

14 Declare in Egypt, proclaim in Migdol, Proclaim in Noph and Tahpanhes! Say: Take your posts and stand ready, For the sword has devoured all around you!

15 Why are your stalwarts swept away? They did not stand firm, For *Hashem* thrust them down;

16 He made many stumble, They fell over one another. They said: "Up! let us return to our people, To the land of our birth, Because of the deadly sword."

17 There they called Pharaoh king of Egypt: "Braggart who let the hour go by."

18 As I live – declares the King, Whose name is LORD of Hosts – As surely as *Tavor* is among the mountains And *Carmel* is by the sea, So shall this come to pass.

19 Equip yourself for exile, Fair Egypt, you who dwell secure! For Noph shall become a waste, Desolate, without inhabitants.

20 Egypt is a handsome heifer – A gadfly from the north is coming, coming!

21 The mercenaries, too, in her midst Are like stall-fed calves; They too shall turn tail, Flee as one, and make no stand. Their day of disaster is upon them, The hour of their doom.

ירמיהו
פרק מו

ט עֲל֤וּ הַסּוּסִים֙ וְהִתְהֹלְל֣וּ הָרֶ֔כֶב וְיֵצְא֖וּ הַגִּבּוֹרִ֑ים כּ֤וּשׁ וּפוּט֙ תֹּפְשֵׂ֣י מָגֵ֔ן וְלוּדִ֕ים תֹּפְשֵׂ֖י דֹּ֥רְכֵי קָֽשֶׁת׃

י וְהַיּ֨וֹם הַה֜וּא לַֽאדֹנָ֧י יֱהוִ֣ה צְבָא֗וֹת י֤וֹם נְקָמָה֙ לְהִנָּקֵ֣ם מִצָּרָ֔יו וְאָכְלָ֥ה חֶ֙רֶב֙ וְשָׂ֣בְעָ֔ה וְרָוְתָ֖ה מִדָּמָ֑ם כִּ֣י זֶ֠בַח לַאדֹנָ֨י יֱהוִ֧ה צְבָא֛וֹת בְּאֶ֥רֶץ צָפ֖וֹן אֶל־נְהַר־פְּרָֽת׃

יא עֲלִ֤י גִלְעָד֙ וּקְחִ֣י צֳרִ֔י בְּתוּלַ֖ת בַּת־מִצְרָ֑יִם לַשָּׁוְא֙ הרביתי [הִרְבֵּ֣ית] רְפֻא֔וֹת תְּעָלָ֖ה אֵ֥ין לָֽךְ׃

יב שָׁמְע֤וּ גוֹיִם֙ קְלוֹנֵ֔ךְ וְצִוְחָתֵ֖ךְ מָלְאָ֣ה הָאָ֑רֶץ כִּֽי־גִבּ֤וֹר בְּגִבּוֹר֙ כָּשָׁ֔לוּ יַחְדָּ֖יו נָפְל֥וּ שְׁנֵיהֶֽם׃

יג הַדָּבָר֙ אֲשֶׁ֣ר דִּבֶּ֣ר יְהֹוָ֔ה אֶל־יִרְמְיָ֖הוּ הַנָּבִ֑יא לָב֗וֹא נְבֽוּכַדְרֶאצַּר֙ מֶ֣לֶךְ בָּבֶ֔ל לְהַכּ֖וֹת אֶת־אֶ֥רֶץ מִצְרָֽיִם׃

יד הַגִּ֤ידוּ בְמִצְרַ֙יִם֙ וְהַשְׁמִ֣יעוּ בְמִגְדּ֔וֹל וְהַשְׁמִ֥יעוּ בְנֹ֖ף וּבְתַחְפַּנְחֵ֑ס אִמְר֗וּ הִתְיַצֵּב֙ וְהָכֵ֣ן לָ֔ךְ כִּֽי־אָכְלָ֥ה חֶ֖רֶב סְבִיבֶֽיךָ׃

טו מַדּ֖וּעַ נִסְחַ֣ף אַבִּירֶ֑יךָ לֹ֣א עָמַ֔ד כִּ֥י יְהֹוָ֖ה הֲדָפֽוֹ׃

טז הִרְבָּ֖ה כּוֹשֵׁ֑ל גַּם־נָפַ֞ל אִ֣ישׁ אֶל־רֵעֵ֗הוּ וַיֹּֽאמְרוּ֙ ק֣וּמָה וְנָשֻׁ֣בָה אֶל־עַמֵּ֗נוּ וְאֶל־אֶ֙רֶץ֙ מֽוֹלַדְתֵּ֔נוּ מִפְּנֵ֖י חֶ֥רֶב הַיּוֹנָֽה׃

יז קָרְא֖וּ שָׁ֑ם פַּרְעֹ֤ה מֶֽלֶךְ־מִצְרַ֙יִם֙ שָׁא֔וֹן הֶעֱבִ֖יר הַמּוֹעֵֽד׃

יח חַי־אָ֙נִי֙ נְאֻם־הַמֶּ֔לֶךְ יְהֹוָ֥ה צְבָא֖וֹת שְׁמ֑וֹ כִּ֚י כְּתָב֣וֹר בֶּהָרִ֔ים וּכְכַרְמֶ֖ל בַּיָּ֥ם יָבֽוֹא׃

יט כְּלֵ֤י גוֹלָה֙ עֲשִׂ֣י לָ֔ךְ יוֹשֶׁ֖בֶת בַּת־מִצְרָ֑יִם כִּֽי־נֹף֙ לְשַׁמָּ֣ה תִֽהְיֶ֔ה וְנִצְּתָ֖ה מֵאֵ֥ין יוֹשֵֽׁב׃

כ עֶגְלָ֥ה יְפֵה־פִיָּ֖ה מִצְרָ֑יִם קֶ֥רֶץ מִצָּפ֖וֹן בָּ֥א בָֽא׃

כא גַּם־שְׂכִרֶ֤יהָ בְקִרְבָּהּ֙ כְּעֶגְלֵ֣י מַרְבֵּ֔ק כִּֽי־גַם־הֵ֧מָּה הִפְנ֛וּ נָ֥סוּ יַחְדָּ֖יו לֹ֣א עָמָ֑דוּ כִּ֣י י֥וֹם אֵידָ֛ם בָּ֥א עֲלֵיהֶ֖ם עֵ֥ת פְּקֻדָּתָֽם׃

1184

Yirmiyahu/Jeremiah
Chapter 46

22 She shall rustle away like a snake As they come marching in force; They shall come against her with axes, Like hewers of wood.

כב קוֹלָהּ כַּנָּחָשׁ יֵלֵךְ כִּי־בְחַיִל יֵלֵכוּ וּבְקַרְדֻּמּוֹת בָּאוּ לָהּ כְּחֹטְבֵי עֵצִים׃

23 They shall cut down her forest – declares *Hashem* – Though it cannot be measured; For they are more numerous than locusts, And cannot be counted.

כג כָּרְתוּ יַעְרָהּ נְאֻם־יְהֹוָה כִּי לֹא יֵחָקֵר כִּי רַבּוּ מֵאַרְבֶּה וְאֵין לָהֶם מִסְפָּר׃

24 Fair Egypt shall be shamed, Handed over to the people of the north.

כד הֹבִישָׁה בַּת־מִצְרָיִם נִתְּנָה בְּיַד עַם־צָפוֹן׃

25 The Lord of Hosts, the God of *Yisrael*, has said: I will inflict punishment on Ammon of No and on Pharaoh – on Egypt, her gods, and her kings – on Pharaoh and all who rely on him.

כה אָמַר יְהֹוָה צְבָאוֹת אֱלֹהֵי יִשְׂרָאֵל הִנְנִי פוֹקֵד אֶל־אָמוֹן מִנֹּא וְעַל־פַּרְעֹה וְעַל־מִצְרַיִם וְעַל־אֱלֹהֶיהָ וְעַל־מְלָכֶיהָ וְעַל־פַּרְעֹה וְעַל הַבֹּטְחִים בּוֹ׃

26 I will deliver them into the hands of those who seek to kill them, into the hands of King Nebuchadrezzar of Babylon and into the hands of his subjects. But afterward she shall be inhabited again as in former days, declares *Hashem*.

כו וּנְתַתִּים בְּיַד מְבַקְשֵׁי נַפְשָׁם וּבְיַד נְבוּכַדְרֶאצַּר מֶלֶךְ־בָּבֶל וּבְיַד־עֲבָדָיו וְאַחֲרֵי־כֵן תִּשְׁכֹּן כִּימֵי־קֶדֶם נְאֻם־יְהֹוָה׃

27 But you, Have no fear, My servant *Yaakov*, Be not dismayed, O *Yisrael*! I will deliver you from far away, Your folk from their land of captivity; And *Yaakov* again shall have calm And quiet, with none to trouble him.

כז וְאַתָּה אַל־תִּירָא עַבְדִּי יַעֲקֹב וְאַל־תֵּחַת יִשְׂרָאֵל כִּי הִנְנִי מוֹשִׁעֲךָ מֵרָחוֹק וְאֶת־זַרְעֲךָ מֵאֶרֶץ שִׁבְיָם וְשָׁב יַעֲקֹב וְשָׁקַט וְשַׁאֲנַן וְאֵין מַחֲרִיד׃

v'-a-TAH al tee-RA av-DEE ya-a-KOV v'-al tay-KHAT yis-ra-AYL KEE hin-n'-NEE mo-shi-a-KHA may-ra-KHOK m'-et zar-a-KHA may-E-retz shiv-YAM v'-SHAV ya-a-KOV v'-sha-KAT v'-sha-a-NAN v'-AYN ma-kha-REED

28 But you, have no fear, My servant *Yaakov* – declares *Hashem* – For I am with you. I will make an end of all the nations Among which I have banished you, But I will not make an end of you! I will not leave you unpunished, But I will chastise you in measure.

כח אַתָּה אַל־תִּירָא עַבְדִּי יַעֲקֹב נְאֻם־יְהֹוָה כִּי אִתְּךָ אָנִי כִּי אֶעֱשֶׂה כָלָה בְּכׇל־הַגּוֹיִם אֲשֶׁר הִדַּחְתִּיךָ שָּׁמָּה וְאֹתְךָ לֹא־אֶעֱשֶׂה כָלָה וְיִסַּרְתִּיךָ לַמִּשְׁפָּט וְנַקֵּה לֹא אֲנַקֶּךָּ׃

46:27 I will deliver you from far away *Yirmiyahu* once again prophesies against the nations of the world. He begins with Egypt, upon whom the Israelites relied for protection from Babylonia, instead of relying on God. After harsh words of destruction and doom directed at the Egyptians, he then addresses the Jewish people. Given the harsh fate that awaits those peoples who defy God, *Yirmiyahu* turns to console the Children of Israel. Though they have sinned against God and have been punished, God's love for them is eternal, and they will eventually return to their homeland.

Yirmiyahu/Jeremiah
Chapter 47

ירמיהו
פרק מז

47:1 The word of *Hashem* that came to the *Navi* Yirmiyahu concerning the Philistines, before Pharaoh conquered *Azza*.

א אֲשֶׁר הָיָה דְבַר־יְהֹוָה אֶל־יִרְמְיָהוּ הַנָּבִיא אֶל־פְּלִשְׁתִּים בְּטֶרֶם יַכֶּה פַרְעֹה אֶת־עַזָּה׃

a-SHER ha-YAH d'-var a-do-NAI el yir-m'-YA-hu ha-na-VEE el p'-lish-TEEM b'-TE-rem ya-KEH far-OH et a-ZAH

2 Thus said *Hashem*: See, waters are rising from the north, They shall become a raging torrent, They shall flood the land and its creatures, The towns and their inhabitants. Men shall cry out, All the inhabitants of the land shall howl,

ב כֹּה ׀ אָמַר יְהֹוָה הִנֵּה־מַיִם עֹלִים מִצָּפוֹן וְהָיוּ לְנַחַל שׁוֹטֵף וְיִשְׁטְפוּ אֶרֶץ וּמְלוֹאָהּ עִיר וְיֹשְׁבֵי בָהּ וְזָעֲקוּ הָאָדָם וְהֵילִל כֹּל יוֹשֵׁב הָאָרֶץ׃

3 At the clatter of the stamping hoofs of his stallions, At the noise of his chariots, The rumbling of their wheels, Fathers shall not look to their children Out of sheer helplessness

ג מִקּוֹל שַׁעֲטַת פַּרְסוֹת אַבִּירָיו מֵרַעַשׁ לְרִכְבּוֹ הֲמוֹן גַּלְגִּלָּיו לֹא־הִפְנוּ אָבוֹת אֶל־בָּנִים מֵרִפְיוֹן יָדָיִם׃

4 Because of the day that is coming For ravaging all the Philistines, For cutting off every last ally Of Tyre and Sidon. For *Hashem* will ravage the Philistines, The remnant from the island of Caphtor.

ד עַל־הַיּוֹם הַבָּא לִשְׁדוֹד אֶת־כׇּל־פְּלִשְׁתִּים לְהַכְרִית לְצֹר וּלְצִידוֹן כֹּל שָׂרִיד עֹזֵר כִּי־שֹׁדֵד יְהֹוָה אֶת־פְּלִשְׁתִּים שְׁאֵרִית אִי כַפְתּוֹר׃

5 Baldness has come upon *Azza*, Ashkelon is destroyed. O remnant of their valley, How long will you gash yourself?

ה בָּאָה קׇרְחָה אֶל־עַזָּה נִדְמְתָה אַשְׁקְלוֹן שְׁאֵרִית עִמְקָם עַד־מָתַי תִּתְגּוֹדָדִי׃

6 "O sword of *Hashem*, When will you be quiet at last? Withdraw into your sheath, Rest and be still!"

ו הוֹי חֶרֶב לַיהֹוָה עַד־אָנָה לֹא תִשְׁקֹטִי הֵאָסְפִי אַל־תַּעְרֵךְ הֵרָגְעִי וָדֹמִּי׃

7 How can it be quiet When *Hashem* has given it orders Against Ashkelon and the seacoast, Given it assignment there?

ז אֵיךְ תִּשְׁקֹטִי וַיהֹוָה צִוָּה־לָהּ אֶל־אַשְׁקְלוֹן וְאֶל־חוֹף הַיָּם שָׁם יְעָדָהּ׃

48:1 Concerning Moab. Thus said the Lord of Hosts, the God of *Yisrael*: Alas, that Nebo should be ravaged, Kiriathaim captured and shamed, The stronghold shamed and dismayed!

א לְמוֹאָב כֹּה־אָמַר יְהֹוָה צְבָאוֹת אֱלֹהֵי יִשְׂרָאֵל הוֹי אֶל־נְבוֹ כִּי שֻׁדָּדָה הֹבִישָׁה נִלְכְּדָה קִרְיָתָיִם הֹבִישָׁה הַמִּשְׂגָּב וָחָתָּה׃

2 Moab's glory is no more; In Heshbon they have planned evil against her: "Come, let us make an end of her as a nation!" You too, O Madmen, shall be silenced; The sword is following you.

ב אֵין עוֹד תְּהִלַּת מוֹאָב בְּחֶשְׁבּוֹן חָשְׁבוּ עָלֶיהָ רָעָה לְכוּ וְנַכְרִיתֶנָּה מִגּוֹי גַּם־מַדְמֵן תִּדֹּמִּי אַחֲרַיִךְ תֵּלֶךְ חָרֶב׃

47:1 Concerning the *Philistines* Yirmiyahu now prophesies about the destruction of the Philistines. The Philistines lived on the southwestern coast of Israel, and occupied the five cities of *Azza*, Ashkelon, Ashdod, Ekron, and Gath. In the Bible, they continuously appear as an enemy of the Israelites. While *Yirmiyahu* depicts their destruction, he does not provide a reason for the harsh decree against them. *Yechezkel* (25:15), however, provides a possible insight into why they deserve this punishment: "because the Philistines, in their ancient hatred, acted vengefully, and with utter scorn sought revenge and destruction."

Yirmiyahu/Jeremiah
Chapter 48

ירמיהו
פרק מח

3 Hark! an outcry from Horonaim, Destruction and utter ruin!

ג קוֹל צְעָקָה מֵחֹרוֹנָיִם שֹׁד וָשֶׁבֶר גָּדוֹל׃

4 Moab is broken; Her young ones cry aloud;

ד נִשְׁבְּרָה מוֹאָב הִשְׁמִיעוּ זְּעָקָה צְעוֹרֶיהָ [צְעִירֶיהָ]׃

5 They climb to Luhith Weeping continually; On the descent to Horonaim A distressing cry of anguish is heard:

ה כִּי מַעֲלֵה הַלֻּחוֹת [הַלּוּחִית] בִּבְכִי יַעֲלֶה־בֶּכִי כִּי בְּמוֹרַד חוֹרֹנַיִם צָרֵי צַעֲקַת־שֶׁבֶר שָׁמֵעוּ׃

6 Flee, save your lives! And be like Aroer in the desert.

ו נֻסוּ מַלְּטוּ נַפְשְׁכֶם וְתִהְיֶינָה כַּעֲרוֹעֵר בַּמִּדְבָּר׃

7 Surely, because of your trust In your wealth and in your treasures, You too shall be captured. And Chemosh shall go forth to exile, Together with his *Kohanim* and attendants.

ז כִּי יַעַן בִּטְחֵךְ בְּמַעֲשַׂיִךְ וּבְאוֹצְרוֹתָיִךְ גַּם־אַתְּ תִּלָּכֵדִי וְיָצָא כמיש [כְמוֹשׁ] בַּגּוֹלָה כֹּהֲנָיו וְשָׂרָיו יחד [יַחְדָּיו]׃

8 The ravager shall come to every town; No town shall escape. The valley shall be devastated And the tableland laid waste – because *Hashem* has spoken.

ח וְיָבֹא שֹׁדֵד אֶל־כָּל־עִיר וְעִיר לֹא תִמָּלֵט וְאָבַד הָעֵמֶק וְנִשְׁמַד הַמִּישֹׁר אֲשֶׁר אָמַר יְהֹוָה׃

9 Give wings to Moab, For she must go hence. Her towns shall become desolate, With no one living in them.

ט תְּנוּ־צִיץ לְמוֹאָב כִּי נָצֹא תֵּצֵא וְעָרֶיהָ לְשַׁמָּה תִהְיֶינָה מֵאֵין יוֹשֵׁב בָּהֵן׃

10 Cursed be he who is slack in doing *Hashem*'s work! Cursed be he who withholds his sword from blood!

י אָרוּר עֹשֶׂה מְלֶאכֶת יְהֹוָה רְמִיָּה וְאָרוּר מֹנֵעַ חַרְבּוֹ מִדָּם׃

11 Moab has been secure from his youth on – He is settled on his lees And has not been poured from vessel to vessel – He has never gone into exile. Therefore his fine flavor has remained And his bouquet is unspoiled.

יא שַׁאֲנַן מוֹאָב מִנְּעוּרָיו וְשֹׁקֵט הוּא אֶל־שְׁמָרָיו וְלֹא־הוּרַק מִכְּלִי אֶל־כֶּלִי וּבַגּוֹלָה לֹא הָלָךְ עַל־כֵּן עָמַד טַעְמוֹ בּוֹ וְרֵיחוֹ לֹא נָמָר׃

12 But days are coming – declares *Hashem* – when I will send men against him to tip him over; they shall empty his vessels and smash his jars.

יב לָכֵן הִנֵּה־יָמִים בָּאִים נְאֻם־יְהֹוָה וְשִׁלַּחְתִּי־לוֹ צֹעִים וְצֵעֻהוּ וְכֵלָיו יָרִיקוּ וְנִבְלֵיהֶם יְנַפֵּצוּ׃

13 And Moab shall be shamed because of Chemosh, as the House of *Yisrael* were shamed because of *Beit El*, on whom they relied.

יג וּבֹשׁ מוֹאָב מִכְּמוֹשׁ כַּאֲשֶׁר־בֹּשׁוּ בֵּית יִשְׂרָאֵל מִבֵּית אֵל מִבְטֶחָם׃

u-VOSH mo-AV mik-MOSH ka-a-sher BO-shu BAYT yis-ra-AYL mi-BAYT AYL miv-te-KHAM

48:13 As the House of *Yisrael* were shamed because of *Beit El* Yirmiyahu asserts that Moab will be as embarrassed about relying on their god, *Chemosh*, as the Jews were about relying on *Yerovam*'s golden calves. According to contemporary Israeli scholar Rabbi Amnon Bazak, *Yerovam*'s calves were intended to replace the two cherubs found on top of the ark in the *Beit Hamikdash*. He placed one in *Dan*, the northern border of his kingdom, and one in *Beit El*, at the southern border, to signify that the Divine Presence shall rest between the two calves, throughout his entire kingdom, just as it rests between the two cherubs on top of the

Yirmiyahu/Jeremiah
Chapter 48

14 How can you say: We are warriors, Valiant men for war?

15 Moab is ravaged, His towns have been entered, His choice young men Have gone down to the slaughter – declares the King whose name is Lord of Hosts.

16 The doom of Moab is coming close, His downfall is approaching swiftly.

17 Condole with him, all who live near him, All you who know him by name! Say: "Alas, the strong rod is broken, The lordly staff!"

18 Descend from glory And sit in thirst, O inhabitant of Fair Dibon; For the ravager of Moab has entered your town, He has destroyed your fortresses.

19 Stand by the road and look out, O inhabitant of Aroer. Ask of him who is fleeing And of her who is escaping: Say, "What has happened?"

20 Moab is shamed and dismayed; Howl and cry aloud! Tell at the Arnon That Moab is ravaged!

21 Judgment has come upon the tableland – upon Holon, Jahzah, and Mephaath;

22 upon Dibon, Nebo, and Beth-diblathaim;

23 upon Kiriathaim, Beth-gamul, and Beth-meon;

24 upon Kerioth and Bozrah – upon all the towns of the land of Moab, far and near.

25 The might of Moab has been cut down, His strength is broken, – declares *Hashem*.

26 Get him drunk For he vaunted himself against *Hashem*. Moab shall vomit till he is drained, And he too shall be a laughingstock.

27 Wasn't *Yisrael* a laughingstock to you? Was he ever caught among thieves, That you should shake your head Whenever you speak of him?

---

ark. *Yerovam* hoped that instead of viewing *Yerushalayim* and the *Beit Hamikdash* as the sole place of God's Presence, they would see the entire Land of Israel as the resting place for God's glory. The people, however, failed to internalize *Yerovam's* intended message and instead of worshipping *Hashem* throughout the land, they worshiped the calves themselves, angering God and eventually leading to their exile.

Yirmiyahu/Jeremiah
Chapter 48

28 Desert the cities And dwell in the crags, O inhabitants of Moab! Be like a dove that nests In the sides of a pit.

29 We have heard of Moab's pride – Most haughty is he – Of his arrogance and pride, His haughtiness and self-exaltation.

30 I know his insolence – declares *Hashem* – the wickedness that is in him, th wickedness he has committed.

31 Therefore I will howl for Moab, I will cry out for all Moab, I will moan for the men of Kir-heres.

32 With greater weeping than for Jazer I weep for you, O vine of Sibmah, Whose tendrils crossed the sea, Reached to the sea, to Jazer. A ravager has come down Upon your fig and grape harvests.

33 Rejoicing and gladness Are gone from the farm land, From the country of Moab; I have put an end to wine in the presses, No one treads [the grapes] with shouting – The shout is a shout no more.

34 There is an outcry from Heshbon to Elealeh, They raise their voices as far as Jahaz, From Zoar to Horonaim and Eglathshelishiah. The waters of Nimrim Shall also become desolation.

35 And I will make an end in Moab – declares *Hashem* – Of those who offer at a shrine And burn incense to their god.

36 Therefore, My heart moans for Moab like a flute; Like a flute my heart moans For the men of Kir-heres – Therefore, The gains they have made shall vanish –

37 For every head is bald And every beard is shorn; On all hands there are gashes, And on the loins sackcloth.

38 On all the roofs of Moab, And in its squares There is naught but lamentation; For I have broken Moab Like a vessel no one wants – declares *Hashem*.

39 How he is dismayed! Wail! How Moab has turned his back in shame! Moab shall be a laughingstock And a shock to all those near him.

40 For thus said *Hashem*: See, he soars like an eagle And spreads out his wings against Moab!

ירמיהו
פרק מח

כח עִזְבוּ עָרִים וְשִׁכְנוּ בַּסֶּלַע יֹשְׁבֵי מוֹאָב וִהְיוּ כְיוֹנָה תְּקַנֵּן בְּעֶבְרֵי פִי־פָחַת:

כט שָׁמַעְנוּ גְאוֹן־מוֹאָב גֵּאֶה מְאֹד גָּבְהוֹ וּגְאוֹנוֹ וְגַאֲוָתוֹ וְרֻם לִבּוֹ:

ל אֲנִי יָדַעְתִּי נְאֻם־יְהֹוָה עֶבְרָתוֹ וְלֹא־כֵן בַּדָּיו לֹא־כֵן עָשׂוּ:

לא עַל־כֵּן עַל־מוֹאָב אֲיֵלִיל וּלְמוֹאָב כֻּלֹּה אֶזְעָק אֶל־אַנְשֵׁי קִיר־חֶרֶשׂ יֶהְגֶּה:

לב מִבְּכִי יַעְזֵר אֶבְכֶּה־לָּךְ הַגֶּפֶן שִׂבְמָה נְטִישֹׁתַיִךְ עָבְרוּ יָם עַד יָם יַעְזֵר נָגָעוּ עַל־קֵיצֵךְ וְעַל־בְּצִירֵךְ שֹׁדֵד נָפָל:

לג וְנֶאֶסְפָה שִׂמְחָה וָגִיל מִכַּרְמֶל וּמֵאֶרֶץ מוֹאָב וְיַיִן מִיקָבִים הִשְׁבַּתִּי לֹא־יִדְרֹךְ הֵידָד הֵידָד לֹא הֵידָד:

לד מִזַּעֲקַת חֶשְׁבּוֹן עַד־אֶלְעָלֵה עַד־יַהַץ נָתְנוּ קוֹלָם מִצֹּעַר עַד־חֹרֹנַיִם עֶגְלַת שְׁלִשִׁיָּה כִּי גַּם־מֵי נִמְרִים לִמְשַׁמּוֹת יִהְיוּ:

לה וְהִשְׁבַּתִּי לְמוֹאָב נְאֻם־יְהֹוָה מַעֲלֶה בָמָה וּמַקְטִיר לֵאלֹהָיו:

לו עַל־כֵּן לִבִּי לְמוֹאָב כַּחֲלִלִים יֶהֱמֶה וְלִבִּי אֶל־אַנְשֵׁי קִיר־חֶרֶשׂ כַּחֲלִילִים יֶהֱמֶה עַל־כֵּן יִתְרַת עָשָׂה אָבָדוּ:

לז כִּי כָל־רֹאשׁ קָרְחָה וְכָל־זָקָן גְּרֻעָה עַל כָּל־יָדַיִם גְּדֻדֹת וְעַל־מָתְנַיִם שָׂק:

לח עַל כָּל־גַּגּוֹת מוֹאָב וּבִרְחֹבֹתֶיהָ כֻּלֹּה מִסְפֵּד כִּי־שָׁבַרְתִּי אֶת־מוֹאָב כִּכְלִי אֵין־חֵפֶץ בּוֹ נְאֻם־יְהֹוָה:

לט אֵיךְ חַתָּה הֵילִילוּ אֵיךְ הִפְנָה־עֹרֶף מוֹאָב בּוֹשׁ וְהָיָה מוֹאָב לִשְׂחֹק וְלִמְחִתָּה לְכָל־סְבִיבָיו:

מ כִּי־כֹה אָמַר יְהֹוָה הִנֵּה כַנֶּשֶׁר יִדְאֶה וּפָרַשׂ כְּנָפָיו אֶל־מוֹאָב:

Yirmiyahu/Jeremiah
Chapter 49

ירמיהו
פרק מט

41 Kerioth shall be captured And the strongholds shall be seized. In that day, the heart of Moab's warriors Shall be like the heart of a woman in travail.

מא נִלְכְּדָה הַקְּרִיּוֹת וְהַמְּצָדוֹת נִתְפָּשָׂה וְהָיָה לֵב גִּבּוֹרֵי מוֹאָב בַּיּוֹם הַהוּא כְּלֵב אִשָּׁה מְצֵרָה׃

42 And Moab shall be destroyed as a people, For he vaunted himself against *Hashem*.

מב וְנִשְׁמַד מוֹאָב מֵעָם כִּי עַל־יְהֹוָה הִגְדִּיל׃

43 Terror, and pit, and trap Upon you who dwell in Moab! – declares *Hashem*.

מג פַּחַד וָפַחַת וָפָח עָלֶיךָ יוֹשֵׁב מוֹאָב נְאֻם־יְהֹוָה׃

44 He who flees from the terror Shall fall into the pit; And he who climbs out of the pit Shall be caught in the trap. For I will bring upon Moab The year of their doom – declares *Hashem*.

מד הַנִּיס [הַנָּס] מִפְּנֵי הַפַּחַד יִפֹּל אֶל־הַפַּחַת וְהָעֹלֶה מִן־הַפַּחַת יִלָּכֵד בַּפָּח כִּי־אָבִיא אֵלֶיהָ אֶל־מוֹאָב שְׁנַת פְּקֻדָּתָם נְאֻם־יְהֹוָה׃

45 In the shelter of Heshbon Fugitives halt exhausted; For fire went forth from Heshbon, Flame from the midst of Sihon, Consuming the brow of Moab, The pate of the people of Shaon.

מה בְּצֵל חֶשְׁבּוֹן עָמְדוּ מִכֹּחַ נָסִים כִּי־אֵשׁ יָצָא מֵחֶשְׁבּוֹן וְלֶהָבָה מִבֵּין סִיחוֹן וַתֹּאכַל פְּאַת מוֹאָב וְקָדְקֹד בְּנֵי שָׁאוֹן׃

46 Woe to you, O Moab! The people of Chemosh are undone, For your sons are carried off into captivity, Your daughters into exile.

מו אוֹי־לְךָ מוֹאָב אָבַד עַם־כְּמוֹשׁ כִּי־לֻקְּחוּ בָנֶיךָ בַּשֶּׁבִי וּבְנֹתֶיךָ בַּשִּׁבְיָה׃

47 But I will restore the fortunes of Moab in the days to come – declares *Hashem*. Thus far is the judgment on Moab.

מז וְשַׁבְתִּי שְׁבוּת־מוֹאָב בְּאַחֲרִית הַיָּמִים נְאֻם־יְהֹוָה עַד־הֵנָּה מִשְׁפַּט מוֹאָב׃

49

1 Concerning the Amonites. Thus said *Hashem*: Has *Yisrael* no sons, Has he no heir? Then why has Milcom dispossessed *Gad*, And why have his people settled in *Gad*'s towns?

מט א לִבְנֵי עַמּוֹן כֹּה אָמַר יְהֹוָה הֲבָנִים אֵין לְיִשְׂרָאֵל אִם־יוֹרֵשׁ אֵין לוֹ מַדּוּעַ יָרַשׁ מַלְכָּם אֶת־גָּד וְעַמּוֹ בְּעָרָיו יָשָׁב׃

liv-NAY a-MON KOH a-MAR a-do-NAI ha-va-NEEM AYN l'-yis-ra-AYL im yo-RAYSH AYN LO ma-DU-a ya-RASH mal-KAM et GAD v'-a-MO b'-a-RAV ya-SHAV

2 Assuredly, days are coming – declares *Hashem* – When I will sound the alarm of war Against Rabbah of the Amonites; It shall become a desolate mound, And its villages shall be set on fire. And *Yisrael* shall dispossess Those who dispossessed him – said *Hashem*.

ב לָכֵן הִנֵּה יָמִים בָּאִים נְאֻם־יְהֹוָה וְהִשְׁמַעְתִּי אֶל־רַבַּת בְּנֵי־עַמּוֹן תְּרוּעַת מִלְחָמָה וְהָיְתָה לְתֵל שְׁמָמָה וּבְנֹתֶיהָ בָּאֵשׁ תִּצַּתְנָה וְיָרַשׁ יִשְׂרָאֵל אֶת־יֹרְשָׁיו אָמַר יְהֹוָה׃

49:1 Has *Yisrael* no sons After the deportation of the ten tribes of Israel to Assyria by Tiglat-pileser, Ammon occupies some of the lands that have been vacated. *Yirmiyahu* criticizes the Ammonites for taking Israeli land. The Ammonites assume that the tribes of Israel have disappeared, never to return. However, this reflects a misunderstanding of the eternal bond between the People of Israel and their inherited land. Even if the exiles themselves do not return, eventually their children will. Therefore, *Yirmiyahu* asks Ammon if Israel has no sons – do they not understand that the ancestral link between the People of Israel and the Land of Israel spans all generations?

Yirmiyahu/Jeremiah
Chapter 49

3 Howl, O Heshbon, for Ai is ravaged! Cry out, O daughters of Rabbah! Gird on sackcloth, lament, And run to and fro in the sheepfolds. For Milcom shall go into exile, Together with his *Kohanim* and attendants.

4 Why do you glory in strength, Your strength is drained, O rebellious daughter, You who relied on your treasures, [Who said:] Who dares attack me?

5 I am bringing terror upon you – declares the Lord of Hosts – From all those around you. Every one of you shall be driven in every direction, And none shall gather in the fugitives.

6 But afterward I will restore the fortunes of the Amonites – declares *Hashem*.

7 Concerning Edom. Thus said the Lord of Hosts: Is there no more wisdom in Teman? Has counsel vanished from the prudent? Has their wisdom gone stale?

8 Flee, turn away, sit down low, O inhabitants of Dedan, For I am bringing Esau's doom upon him, The time when I deal with him.

9 If vintagers were to come upon you, Would they leave no gleanings? Even thieves in the night Would destroy only for their needs!

10 But it is I who have bared Esau, Have exposed his place of concealment; He cannot hide. His offspring is ravaged, His kin and his neighbors – He is no more.

11 "Leave your orphans with me, I will rear them; Let your widows rely on me!"

12 For thus said *Hashem*: If they who rightly should not drink of the cup must drink it, are you the one to go unpunished? You shall not go unpunished: you will have to drink!

13 For by Myself I swear – declares *Hashem* – Bozrah shall become a desolation, a mockery, a ruin, and a curse; and all its towns shall be ruins for all time.

14 I have received tidings from *Hashem*, And an envoy is sent out among the nations: Assemble, and move against her, And rise up for war!

15 For I will make you least among nations, Most despised among men.

Yirmiyahu/Jeremiah
Chapter 49

16 Your horrible nature, Your arrogant heart has seduced you, You who dwell in clefts of the rock, Who occupy the height of the hill! Should you nest as high as the eagle, From there I will pull you down – declares *Hashem*.

17 And Edom shall be a cause of appallment; whoever passes by will be appalled and will hiss at all its wounds.

18 It shall be like the overthrow of Sodom and Gomorrah and their neighbors – said *Hashem*: no man shall live there, no human shall sojourn there.

19 It shall be as when a lion comes up out of the jungle of the *Yarden* against a secure pasture: in a moment I can harry him out of it and appoint over it anyone I choose. Then who is like Me? Who can summon Me? Who is the shepherd that can stand up against Me?

20 Hear, then, the plan which *Hashem* has devised against Edom, and what He has purposed against the inhabitants of Teman: Surely the shepherd boys Shall drag them away; Surely the pasture shall be Aghast because of them.

21 At the sound of their downfall The earth shall shake; The sound of screaming Shall be heard at the Sea of Reeds.

22 See, like an eagle he flies up, He soars and spreads his wings against Bozrah; And the heart of Edom's warriors in that day Shall be like the heart of a woman in travail.

23 Concerning Damascus. Hamath and Arpad are shamed, For they have heard bad news. They shake with anxiety, Like the sea which cannot rest.

24 Damascus has grown weak, She has turned around to flee; Trembling has seized her, Pain and anguish have taken hold of her, Like a woman in childbirth.

25 How has the glorious city not been deserted, The citadel of my joy!

26 Assuredly, her young men shall lie fallen in her squares. And all her warriors shall be stilled in that day – declares the LORD of Hosts.

27 I will set fire to the wall of Damascus, And it shall consume the fortresses of Ben-hadad.

Yirmiyahu/Jeremiah
Chapter 49

28 Concerning Kedar and the kingdoms of Hazor, which King Nebuchadrezzar of Babylon conquered. Thus said *Hashem*: Arise, march against Kedar, And ravage the Kedemites!

29 They will take away their tents and their flocks, Their tent cloths and all their gear; They shall carry off their camels, And shall proclaim against them: Terror all around!

30 Flee, wander far, Sit down low, O inhabitants of Hazor – says *Hashem*. For King Nebuchadrezzar of Babylon Has devised a plan against you And formed a purpose against you:

31 Rise up, attack a tranquil nation That dwells secure – says *Hashem* – That has no barred gates, That dwells alone.

32 Their camels shall become booty, And their abundant flocks a spoil; And I will scatter to every quarter Those who have their hair clipped; And from every direction I will bring Disaster upon them – says *Hashem*.

33 Hazor shall become a lair of jackals, A desolation for all time. No man shall live there, No human shall sojourn there.

34 The word of *Hashem* that came to the *Navi Yirmiyahu* concerning Elam, at the beginning of the reign of King *Tzidkiyahu* of *Yehuda*:

35 Thus said the Lord of Hosts: I am going to break the bow of Elam, the mainstay of their strength.

36 And I shall bring four winds against Elam from the four quarters of heaven, and scatter them to all those winds. There shall not be a nation to which the fugitives from Elam do not come.

37 And I will break Elam before their enemies, before those who seek their lives; and I will bring disaster upon them, My flaming wrath – declares *Hashem*. And I will dispatch the sword after them until I have consumed them.

38 And I will set My throne in Elam, And wipe out from there king and officials – says *Hashem*.

39 But in the days to come I will restore the fortunes of Elam – declares *Hashem*.

Yirmiyahu/Jeremiah
Chapter 50

ירמיהו
פרק נ

50 1 The word which *Hashem* spoke concerning Babylon, the land of the Chaldeans, through the *Navi Yirmiyahu*:

א הַדָּבָר אֲשֶׁר דִּבֶּר יְהֹוָה אֶל־בָּבֶל אֶל־אֶרֶץ כַּשְׂדִּים בְּיַד יִרְמְיָהוּ הַנָּבִיא:

2 Declare among the nations, and proclaim; Raise a standard, proclaim; Hide nothing! Say: Babylon is captured, Bel is shamed, Merodach is dismayed. Her idols are shamed, Her fetishes dismayed.

ב הַגִּידוּ בַגּוֹיִם וְהַשְׁמִיעוּ וּשְׂאוּ־נֵס הַשְׁמִיעוּ אַל־תְּכַחֵדוּ אִמְרוּ נִלְכְּדָה בָבֶל הֹבִישׁ בֵּל חַת מְרֹדָךְ הֹבִישׁוּ עֲצַבֶּיהָ חַתּוּ גִּלּוּלֶיהָ:

3 For a nation from the north has attacked her, It will make her land a desolation. No one shall dwell in it, Both man and beast shall wander away.

ג כִּי עָלָה עָלֶיהָ גּוֹי מִצָּפוֹן הוּא־יָשִׁית אֶת־אַרְצָהּ לְשַׁמָּה וְלֹא־יִהְיֶה יוֹשֵׁב בָּהּ מֵאָדָם וְעַד־בְּהֵמָה נָדוּ הָלָכוּ:

4 In those days and at that time – declares *Hashem* – the people of *Yisrael* together with the people of *Yehuda* shall come, and they shall weep as they go to seek *Hashem* their God.

ד בַּיָּמִים הָהֵמָּה וּבָעֵת הַהִיא נְאֻם־יְהֹוָה יָבֹאוּ בְנֵי־יִשְׂרָאֵל הֵמָּה וּבְנֵי־יְהוּדָה יַחְדָּו הָלוֹךְ וּבָכוֹ יֵלֵכוּ וְאֶת־יְהֹוָה אֱלֹהֵיהֶם יְבַקֵּשׁוּ:

5 They shall inquire for *Tzion*; in that direction their faces shall turn; they shall come and attach themselves to *Hashem* by a covenant for all time, which shall never be forgotten.

ה צִיּוֹן יִשְׁאָלוּ דֶּרֶךְ הֵנָּה פְנֵיהֶם בֹּאוּ וְנִלְווּ אֶל־יְהֹוָה בְּרִית עוֹלָם לֹא תִשָּׁכֵחַ:

tzi-YON yish-A-lu DE-rekh HAY-nah f'-nay-HEM BO-u v'-nil-VU el a-do-NAI b'-REET o-LAM LO ti-sha-KHAY-akh

6 My people were lost sheep: their shepherds led them astray, they drove them out to the mountains, they roamed from mount to hill, they forgot their own resting place.

ו צֹאן אֹבְדוֹת הָיָה [הָיוּ] עַמִּי רֹעֵיהֶם הִתְעוּם הָרִים שׁוֹבֵבִים [שׁוֹבְבוּם] מֵהַר אֶל־גִּבְעָה הָלָכוּ שָׁכְחוּ רִבְצָם:

7 All who encountered them devoured them; and their foes said, "We shall not be held guilty, because they have sinned against *Hashem*, the true Pasture, the Hope of their fathers – *Hashem*."

ז כָּל־מוֹצְאֵיהֶם אֲכָלוּם וְצָרֵיהֶם אָמְרוּ לֹא נֶאְשָׁם תַּחַת אֲשֶׁר חָטְאוּ לַיהֹוָה נְוֵה־צֶדֶק וּמִקְוֵה אֲבוֹתֵיהֶם יְהֹוָה:

8 Flee from Babylon, Leave the land of the Chaldeans, And be like he-goats that lead the flock!

ח נֻדוּ מִתּוֹךְ בָּבֶל וּמֵאֶרֶץ כַּשְׂדִּים יצאו [צֵאוּ] וִהְיוּ כְּעַתּוּדִים לִפְנֵי־צֹאן:

9 For see, I am rousing and leading An assemblage of great nations against Babylon From the lands of the north. They shall draw up their lines against her, There she shall be captured. Their arrows are like those of a skilled warrior Who does not turn back without hitting the mark.

ט כִּי הִנֵּה אָנֹכִי מֵעִיר וּמַעֲלֶה עַל־בָּבֶל קְהַל־גּוֹיִם גְּדֹלִים מֵאֶרֶץ צָפוֹן וְעָרְכוּ לָהּ מִשָּׁם תִּלָּכֵד חִצָּיו כְּגִבּוֹר מַשְׁכִּיל לֹא יָשׁוּב רֵיקָם:

50:5 A covenant for all time, which shall never be forgotten For most of *Yirmiyahu's* prophecies, the mighty nation of Babylonia serves as a messenger or agent, carrying out God's will. When the People of Israel wish to challenge Babylonia's rule over them, *Yirmiyahu* tells them that to do so is tantamount to challenging *Hashem* Himself. However, like the other nations before them, Babylonia will eventually be punished for its arrogance and sinful behavior. Like Israel, they shall face an enemy "from the north" (verse 3). When this occurs, Israel will once again be returned to its homeland. As *Yirmiyahu* says in verse 19, "And I will lead *Yisrael* back to his pasture." While nations come and go, the Jewish people remain connected to their beloved Land of Israel in "a covenant for all time, which shall never be forgotten."

Yirmiyahu/Jeremiah
Chapter 50

ירמיהו

פרק נ

10 Chaldea shall be despoiled, All her spoilers shall be sated – declares *Hashem*.

י וְהָיְתָה כַשְׂדִּים לְשָׁלָל כָּל־שֹׁלְלֶיהָ יִשְׂבָּעוּ נְאֻם־יְהֹוָה:

11 For you rejoiced, you exulted, You who plundered My possession; You stamped like a heifer treading grain, You neighed like steeds.

יא כִּי תִשְׂמְחִי [תִשְׂמְחוּ] כִּי תַעֲלְזִי [תַעֲלְזוּ] שֹׁסֵי נַחֲלָתִי כִּי תָפוּשִׁי [תָפוּשׁוּ] כְּעֶגְלָה דָשָׁה וְתִצְהֲלִי [וְתִצְהֲלוּ] כָּאֲבִּרִים:

12 So your mother will be utterly shamed, She who bore you will be disgraced. Behold the end of the nations – Wilderness, desert, and steppe!

יב בּוֹשָׁה אִמְּכֶם מְאֹד חָפְרָה יוֹלַדְתְּכֶם הִנֵּה אַחֲרִית גּוֹיִם מִדְבָּר צִיָּה וַעֲרָבָה:

13 Because of *Hashem*'s wrath she shall not be inhabited; She shall be utterly desolate. Whoever passes by Babylon will be appalled And will hiss at all her wounds.

יג מִקֶּצֶף יְהֹוָה לֹא תֵשֵׁב וְהָיְתָה שְׁמָמָה כֻלָּהּ כֹּל עֹבֵר עַל־בָּבֶל יִשֹּׁם וְיִשְׁרֹק עַל־כָּל־מַכּוֹתֶיהָ:

14 Range yourselves roundabout Babylon, All you who draw the bow; Shoot at her, don't spare arrows, For she has sinned against *Hashem*.

יד עִרְכוּ עַל־בָּבֶל סָבִיב כָּל־דֹּרְכֵי קֶשֶׁת יְדוּ אֵלֶיהָ אַל־תַּחְמְלוּ אֶל־חֵץ כִּי לַיהֹוָה חָטָאָה:

15 Raise a shout against her all about! She has surrendered; Her bastions have fallen, Her walls are thrown down – This is *Hashem*'s vengeance. Take vengeance on her, Do to her as she has done!

טו הָרִיעוּ עָלֶיהָ סָבִיב נָתְנָה יָדָהּ נָפְלוּ אָשְׁיוֹתֶיהָ [אָשְׁוִיּוֹתֶיהָ] נֶהֶרְסוּ חוֹמוֹתֶיהָ כִּי נִקְמַת יְהֹוָה הִיא הִנָּקְמוּ בָהּ כַּאֲשֶׁר עָשְׂתָה עֲשׂוּ־לָהּ:

16 Make an end in Babylon of sowers, And of wielders of the sickle at harvest time. Because of the deadly sword, Each man shall turn back to his people, They shall flee every one to his land.

טז כִּרְתוּ זוֹרֵעַ מִבָּבֶל וְתֹפֵשׂ מַגָּל בְּעֵת קָצִיר מִפְּנֵי חֶרֶב הַיּוֹנָה אִישׁ אֶל־עַמּוֹ יִפְנוּ וְאִישׁ לְאַרְצוֹ יָנֻסוּ:

17 *Yisrael* are scattered sheep, harried by lions. First the king of Assyria devoured them, and in the end King Nebuchadrezzar of Babylon crunched their bones.

יז שֶׂה פְזוּרָה יִשְׂרָאֵל אֲרָיוֹת הִדִּיחוּ הָרִאשׁוֹן אֲכָלוֹ מֶלֶךְ אַשּׁוּר וְזֶה הָאַחֲרוֹן עִצְּמוֹ נְבוּכַדְרֶאצַּר מֶלֶךְ בָּבֶל:

18 Assuredly, thus said the LORD of Hosts, the God of *Yisrael*: I will deal with the king of Babylon and his land as I dealt with the king of Assyria.

יח לָכֵן כֹּה־אָמַר יְהֹוָה צְבָאוֹת אֱלֹהֵי יִשְׂרָאֵל הִנְנִי פֹקֵד אֶל־מֶלֶךְ בָּבֶל וְאֶל־אַרְצוֹ כַּאֲשֶׁר פָּקַדְתִּי אֶל־מֶלֶךְ אַשּׁוּר:

19 And I will lead *Yisrael* back to his pasture, and he shall graze in *Carmel* and Bashan, and eat his fill in the hill country of *Efraim* and in *Gilad*.

יט וְשֹׁבַבְתִּי אֶת־יִשְׂרָאֵל אֶל־נָוֵהוּ וְרָעָה הַכַּרְמֶל וְהַבָּשָׁן וּבְהַר אֶפְרַיִם וְהַגִּלְעָד תִּשְׂבַּע נַפְשׁוֹ:

20 In those days and at that time – declares *Hashem* – The iniquity of *Yisrael* shall be sought, And there shall be none; The sins of *Yehuda*, And none shall be found; For I will pardon those I allow to survive.

כ בַּיָּמִים הָהֵם וּבָעֵת הַהִיא נְאֻם־יְהֹוָה יְבֻקַּשׁ אֶת־עֲוֹן יִשְׂרָאֵל וְאֵינֶנּוּ וְאֶת־חַטֹּאת יְהוּדָה וְלֹא תִמָּצֶאינָה כִּי אֶסְלַח לַאֲשֶׁר אַשְׁאִיר:

21 Advance against her – the land of Merathaim – And against the inhabitants of Pekod; Ruin and destroy after them to the last – says *Hashem* – Do just as I have commanded you.

כא עַל־הָאָרֶץ מְרָתַיִם עֲלֵה עָלֶיהָ וְאֶל־יוֹשְׁבֵי פְּקוֹד חֲרֹב וְהַחֲרֵם אַחֲרֵיהֶם נְאֻם־יְהֹוָה וַעֲשֵׂה כְּכֹל אֲשֶׁר צִוִּיתִיךָ:

22 Hark! War in the land And vast destruction!

כב קוֹל מִלְחָמָה בָּאָרֶץ וְשֶׁבֶר גָּדוֹל:

Yirmiyahu/Jeremiah
Chapter 50

23 How the hammer of the whole earth Has been hacked and shattered! How Babylon has become An appallment among the nations!

24 I set a snare for you, O Babylon And you were trapped unawares; You were found and caught, Because you challenged *Hashem*.

25 *Hashem* has opened His armory And brought out the weapons of His wrath; For that is the task Of my Lord God of Hosts In the land of the Chaldeans.

26 Come against her from every quarter; Break open her granaries, Pile her up like heaps of grain, And destroy her, let her have no remnant!

27 Destroy all her bulls, Let them go down to slaughter. Alas for them, their day is come, The hour of their doom!

28 Hark! fugitives are escaping From the land of Babylon, To tell in *Tzion* of the vengeance of *Hashem* our God, Vengeance for His Temple.

29 Summon archers against Babylon, All who draw the bow! Encamp against her roundabout, Let none of her people escape. Pay her back for her actions, Do to her just what she has done; For she has acted insolently against *Hashem*, The Holy One of *Yisrael*.

30 Assuredly, her young men shall fall in her squares, And all her warriors shall perish in that day — declares *Hashem*.

31 I am going to deal with you, O Insolence — declares the Lord of Hosts — For your day is come, the time when I doom you:

32 Insolence shall stumble and fall, With none to raise her up. I will set her cities on fire, And it shall consume everything around her.

33 Thus said the Lord of Hosts: The people of *Yisrael* are oppressed, And so too the people of *Yehuda*; All their captors held them, They refused to let them go.

34 Their Redeemer is mighty, His name is Lord of Hosts. He will champion their cause — So as to give rest to the earth, And unrest to the inhabitants of Babylon.

Yirmiyahu/Jeremiah
Chapter 50

35 A sword against the Chaldeans – declares *Hashem* – And against the inhabitants of Babylon, Against its officials and its wise men!

לה חֶרֶב עַל־כַּשְׂדִּים נְאֻם־יְהֹוָה וְאֶל־יֹשְׁבֵי בָבֶל וְאֶל־שָׂרֶיהָ וְאֶל־חֲכָמֶיהָ׃

36 A sword against the diviners, that they be made fools of! A sword against the warriors, that they be dismayed!

לו חֶרֶב אֶל־הַבַּדִּים וְנֹאָלוּ חֶרֶב אֶל־גִּבּוֹרֶיהָ וָחָתּוּ׃

37 A sword against its horses and chariots, And against all the motley crowd in its midst, That they become like women! A sword against its treasuries, that they be pillaged!

לז חֶרֶב אֶל־סוּסָיו וְאֶל־רִכְבּוֹ וְאֶל־כָּל־הָעֶרֶב אֲשֶׁר בְּתוֹכָהּ וְהָיוּ לְנָשִׁים חֶרֶב אֶל־אוֹצְרֹתֶיהָ וּבֻזָּזוּ׃

38 A drought against its waters, that they be dried up! For it is a land of idols; They are besotted by their dread images.

לח חֹרֶב אֶל־מֵימֶיהָ וְיָבֵשׁוּ כִּי אֶרֶץ פְּסִלִים הִיא וּבָאֵימִים יִתְהֹלָלוּ׃

39 Assuredly, Wildcats and hyenas shall dwell [there], And ostriches shall dwell there; It shall never be settled again, Nor inhabited throughout the ages.

לט לָכֵן יֵשְׁבוּ צִיִּים אֶת־אִיִּים וְיָשְׁבוּ בָהּ בְּנוֹת יַעֲנָה וְלֹא־תֵשֵׁב עוֹד לָנֶצַח וְלֹא תִשְׁכּוֹן עַד־דּוֹר וָדוֹר׃

40 It shall be as when *Hashem* overthrew Sodom and Gomorrah and their neighbors – declares *Hashem*; no man shall live there, no human shall sojourn there.

מ כְּמַהְפֵּכַת אֱלֹהִים אֶת־סְדֹם וְאֶת־עֲמֹרָה וְאֶת־שְׁכֵנֶיהָ נְאֻם־יְהֹוָה לֹא־יֵשֵׁב שָׁם אִישׁ וְלֹא־יָגוּר בָּהּ בֶּן־אָדָם׃

41 Lo, a people comes from the northland; A great nation and many kings are roused From the remotest parts of the earth.

מא הִנֵּה עַם בָּא מִצָּפוֹן וְגוֹי גָּדוֹל וּמְלָכִים רַבִּים יֵעֹרוּ מִיַּרְכְּתֵי־אָרֶץ׃

42 They grasp the bow and javelin, They are cruel, they show no mercy; The sound of them is like the roaring sea. They ride upon horses, Accoutered like a man for battle, Against you, O Fair Babylon!

מב קֶשֶׁת וְכִידֹן יַחֲזִיקוּ אַכְזָרִי הֵמָּה וְלֹא יְרַחֵמוּ קוֹלָם כַּיָּם יֶהֱמֶה וְעַל־סוּסִים יִרְכָּבוּ עָרוּךְ כְּאִישׁ לַמִּלְחָמָה עָלַיִךְ בַּת־בָּבֶל׃

43 The king of Babylon has heard the report of them And his hands are weakened; Anguish seizes him, Pangs like a woman in childbirth.

מג שָׁמַע מֶלֶךְ־בָּבֶל אֶת־שִׁמְעָם וְרָפוּ יָדָיו צָרָה הֶחֱזִיקַתְהוּ חִיל כַּיּוֹלֵדָה׃

44 It shall be as when a lion comes out of the jungle of the *Yarden* against a secure pasture: in a moment I can harry them out of it and appoint over it anyone I choose. Then who is like Me? Who can summon Me? Who is the shepherd that can stand up against Me?

מד הִנֵּה כְּאַרְיֵה יַעֲלֶה מִגְּאוֹן הַיַּרְדֵּן אֶל־נְוֵה אֵיתָן כִּי־אַרְגִּעָה אֲרוּצֵם [אֲרִיצֵם] מֵעָלֶיהָ וּמִי בָחוּר אֵלֶיהָ אֶפְקֹד כִּי מִי כָמוֹנִי וּמִי יוֹעִדֶנִּי וּמִי־זֶה רֹעֶה אֲשֶׁר יַעֲמֹד לְפָנָי׃

45 Hear, then, the plan that *Hashem* has devised against Babylon, and has purposed against the land of Chaldea: Surely the shepherd boys Shall drag them away; Surely the pasture shall be Aghast because of them.

מה לָכֵן שִׁמְעוּ עֲצַת־יְהֹוָה אֲשֶׁר יָעַץ אֶל־בָּבֶל וּמַחְשְׁבוֹתָיו אֲשֶׁר חָשַׁב אֶל־אֶרֶץ כַּשְׂדִּים אִם־לֹא יִסְחָבוּם צְעִירֵי הַצֹּאן אִם־לֹא יַשִּׁים עֲלֵיהֶם נָוֶה׃

46 At the sound of Babylon's capture The earth quakes, And an outcry is heard among the nations.

מו מִקּוֹל נִתְפְּשָׂה בָבֶל נִרְעֲשָׁה הָאָרֶץ וּזְעָקָה בַּגּוֹיִם נִשְׁמָע׃

Yirmiyahu / Jeremiah

Chapter 51

1 Thus said *Hashem*: See, I am rousing a destructive wind Against Babylon and the inhabitants of Leb-kamai.

2 I will send strangers against Babylon, and they shall winnow her. And they shall strip her land bare; They shall beset her on all sides On the day of disaster.

3 Let the archer draw his bow, And let him stand ready in his coat of mail! Show no pity to her young men, Wipe out all her host!

4 Let them fall slain in the land of Chaldea, Pierced through in her streets.

5 For *Yisrael* and *Yehuda* were not bereft Of their God the Lord of Hosts, But their land was filled with guilt Before the Holy One of *Yisrael*.

6 Flee from the midst of Babylon And save your lives, each of you! Do not perish for her iniquity; For this is a time of vengeance for *Hashem*, He will deal retribution to her.

7 Babylon was a golden cup in *Hashem*'s hand, It made the whole earth drunk; The nations drank of her wine – That is why the nations are mad.

8 Suddenly Babylon has fallen and is shattered; Howl over her! Get balm for her wounds: Perhaps she can be healed.

9 We tried to cure Babylon But she was incurable. Let us leave her and go, Each to his own land; For her punishment reaches to heaven, It is as high as the sky.

10 *Hashem* has proclaimed our vindication; Come, let us recount in *Tzion* The deeds of *Hashem* our God.

11 Polish the arrows, Fill the quivers! *Hashem* has roused the spirit of the kings of Media, For His plan against Babylon is to destroy her. This is the vengeance of *Hashem*, Vengeance for His Temple.

12 Raise a standard against the walls of Babylon! Set up a blockade; station watchmen; Prepare those in ambush. For *Hashem* has both planned and performed What He decreed against the inhabitants of Babylon.

13 O you who dwell by great waters, With vast storehouses, Your time is come, the hour of your end.

Yirmiyahu/Jeremiah
Chapter 51

14 The Lord of Hosts has sworn by Himself: I will fill you with men like a locust swarm, They will raise a shout against you.

נִשְׁבַּע יְהֹוָה צְבָאוֹת בְּנַפְשׁוֹ כִּי אִם־מִלֵּאתִיךְ אָדָם כַּיֶּלֶק וְעָנוּ עָלַיִךְ הֵידָד׃

15 He made the earth by His might, Established the world by His wisdom, And by His understanding stretched out the skies.

עֹשֵׂה אֶרֶץ בְּכֹחוֹ מֵכִין תֵּבֵל בְּחָכְמָתוֹ וּבִתְבוּנָתוֹ נָטָה שָׁמָיִם׃

16 When He makes His voice heard, There is a rumbling of waters in the skies; He makes vapors rise from the end of the earth, He makes lightning for the rain, And brings forth wind from His treasuries.

לְקוֹל תִּתּוֹ הֲמוֹן מַיִם בַּשָּׁמַיִם וַיַּעַל נְשִׂאִים מִקְצֵה־אָרֶץ בְּרָקִים לַמָּטָר עָשָׂה וַיֹּצֵא רוּחַ מֵאֹצְרֹתָיו׃

17 Every man is proved dull, without knowledge; Every goldsmith is put to shame because of the idol, For his molten image is a deceit – There is no breath in them.

נִבְעַר כָּל־אָדָם מִדַּעַת הֹבִישׁ כָּל־צֹרֵף מִפָּסֶל כִּי שֶׁקֶר נִסְכּוֹ וְלֹא־רוּחַ בָּם׃

18 They are delusion, a work of mockery; In their hour of doom, they shall perish.

הֶבֶל הֵמָּה מַעֲשֵׂה תַּעְתֻּעִים בְּעֵת פְּקֻדָּתָם יֹאבֵדוּ׃

19 Not like these in the Portion of *Yaakov*, For it is He who formed all things; And [*Yisrael* is] His very own tribe. Lord of Hosts is His name.

לֹא־כְאֵלֶּה חֵלֶק יַעֲקוֹב כִּי־יוֹצֵר הַכֹּל הוּא וְשֵׁבֶט נַחֲלָתוֹ יְהֹוָה צְבָאוֹת שְׁמוֹ׃

lo kh'-AY-leh KHAY-lek ya-a-KOV kee -yo-TZAYR ha-KOL HU v'-SHAY-vet na-kha-la-TO a-do-NAI tz'-va-OT sh'-MO

20 You are My war club, [My] weapons of battle; With you I clubbed nations, With you I destroyed kingdoms;

מַפֵּץ־אַתָּה לִי כְּלֵי מִלְחָמָה וְנִפַּצְתִּי בְךָ גּוֹיִם וְהִשְׁחַתִּי בְךָ מַמְלָכוֹת׃

21 With you I clubbed horse and rider, With you I clubbed chariot and driver,

וְנִפַּצְתִּי בְךָ סוּס וְרֹכְבוֹ וְנִפַּצְתִּי בְךָ רֶכֶב וְרֹכְבוֹ׃

22 With you I clubbed man and woman, With you I clubbed graybeard and boy, With you I clubbed youth and maiden;

וְנִפַּצְתִּי בְךָ אִישׁ וְאִשָּׁה וְנִפַּצְתִּי בְךָ זָקֵן וָנָעַר וְנִפַּצְתִּי בְךָ בָּחוּר וּבְתוּלָה׃

23 With you I clubbed shepherd and flock, With you I clubbed plowman and team, With you I clubbed governors and prefects.

וְנִפַּצְתִּי בְךָ רֹעֶה וְעֶדְרוֹ וְנִפַּצְתִּי בְךָ אִכָּר וְצִמְדּוֹ וְנִפַּצְתִּי בְךָ פַּחוֹת וּסְגָנִים׃

24 But I will requite Babylon and all the inhabitants of Chaldea For all the wicked things they did to *Tzion* before your eyes – declares *Hashem*.

וְשִׁלַּמְתִּי לְבָבֶל וּלְכֹל יוֹשְׁבֵי כַשְׂדִּים אֵת כָּל־רָעָתָם אֲשֶׁר־עָשׂוּ בְצִיּוֹן לְעֵינֵיכֶם נְאֻם יְהֹוָה׃

51:19 Not like these in the Portion of *Yaakov* For two long chapters, *Yirmiyahu* describes the utter destruction that will befall the Babylonians. However, it is the future of Israel that ultimately concerns God. The Babylonians put their trust in their idols (verse 17–18) and are let down in the end. Israel's fate is different because they trust in *Hashem*. Since *Hashem* created the world, it is His to distribute as He pleases. He chose to give the Land of Israel to the people of Israel, the "Portion of *Yaakov*," as an eternal inheritance that will remain theirs forever.

Yirmiyahu/Jeremiah
Chapter 51

25 See, I will deal with you, O mountain of the destroyer – declares *Hashem* – Destroyer of the whole earth! I will stretch out My hand against you And roll you down from the crags, And make you a burnt-out mountain.

26 They shall never take from you A cornerstone or foundation stone; You shall be a desolation for all time – declares *Hashem*.

27 Raise a standard on earth, Sound a *shofar* among the nations, Appoint nations against her, Assemble kingdoms against her – Ararat, Minni, and Ashkenaz – Designate a marshal against her, Bring up horses like swarming locusts!

28 Appoint nations for war against her – The kings of Media, Her governors and all her prefects, And all the lands they rule!

29 Then the earth quakes and writhes, For *Hashem*'s purpose is fulfilled against Babylon, To make the land of Babylon A waste without inhabitant.

30 The warriors of Babylon stop fighting, They sit in the strongholds, Their might is dried up, They become women. Her dwellings are set afire, Her bars are broken.

31 Runner dashes to meet runner, Messenger to meet messenger, To report to the king of Babylon That his city is captured, from end to end.

32 The fords are captured, And the swamp thickets are consumed in fire; And the fighting men are in panic.

33 For thus said the Lord of Hosts, the God of *Yisrael*: Fair Babylon is like a threshing floor Ready to be trodden; In a little while her harvesttime will come.

34 "Nebuchadrezzar king of Babylon Devoured me and discomfited me; He swallowed me like a dragon, He filled his belly with my dainties, And set me down like an empty dish; Then he rinsed me out.

35 Let the violence done me and my kindred Be upon Babylon," Says the inhabitant of *Tzion*; "And let my blood be upon the inhabitants of Chaldea," Says *Yerushalayim*.

36 Assuredly, thus said *Hashem*: I am going to uphold your cause And take vengeance for you; I will dry up her sea And make her fountain run dry.

Yirmiyahu/Jeremiah
Chapter 51

37 Babylon shall become rubble, A den for jackals, An object of horror and hissing, Without inhabitant.

38 Like lions, they roar together, They growl like lion cubs.

39 When they are heated, I will set out their drink And get them drunk, that they may become hilarious And then sleep an endless sleep, Never to awake – declares *Hashem*.

40 I will bring them down like lambs for slaughter, Like rams and he-goats.

41 How has Sheshach been captured, The praise of the whole earth been taken! How has Babylon become A horror to the nations!

42 The sea has risen over Babylon, She is covered by its roaring waves.

43 Her towns are a desolation, A land of desert and steppe, A land no man lives in And no human passes through.

44 And I will deal with Bel in Babylon, And make him disgorge what he has swallowed, And nations shall no more gaze on him with joy. Even the wall of Babylon shall fall.

45 Depart from there, O My people, Save your lives, each of you, From the furious anger of *Hashem*.

46 Do not be downhearted or afraid At the rumors heard in the land: A rumor will come one year, And another rumor the next year Of violence in the land, And of ruler against ruler.

47 Assuredly, days are coming, When I will deal with Babylon's images; Her whole land shall be shamed, And all her slain shall fall in her midst.

48 Heavens and earth and all that is in them Shall shout over Babylon; For the ravagers shall come upon her from the north – declares *Hashem*.

49 Yes, Babylon is to fall [For] the slain of *Yisrael*, As the slain of all the earth Have fallen through Babylon.

50 You fugitives from the sword, Go, don't delay! Remember *Hashem* from afar, And call *Yerushalayim* to mind.

Yirmiyahu/Jeremiah
Chapter 51

51 "We were shamed, we heard taunts; Humiliation covered our faces, When aliens entered The sacred areas of *Hashem*'s House."

52 Assuredly, days are coming – declares *Hashem* – When I will deal with her images, And throughout her land the dying shall groan.

53 Though Babylon should climb to the skies, Though she fortify her strongholds up to heaven, The ravagers would come against her from Me – declares *Hashem*.

54 Hark! an outcry from Babylon, Great destruction from the land of the Chaldeans.

55 For *Hashem* is ravaging Babylon; He will put an end to her great din, Whose roar is like waves of mighty waters, Whose tumultuous noise resounds.

56 For a ravager is coming upon Babylon, Her warriors shall be captured, their bows shall be snapped. For *Hashem* is a God of requital, He deals retribution.

57 I will make her officials and wise men drunk, Her governors and prefects and warriors; And they shall sleep an endless sleep, Never to awaken – declares the King whose name is Lord of Hosts.

58 Thus said the Lord of Hosts: Babylon's broad wall shall be knocked down, And her high gates set afire. Peoples shall labor for naught, And nations have wearied themselves for fire.

59 The instructions that the *Navi Yirmiyahu* gave to *Seraya* son of *Nerya* son of *Machseya*, when the latter went with King *Tzidkiyahu* of *Yehuda* to Babylonia, in the fourth year of [*Tzidkiyahu*'s] reign. *Seraya* was quartermaster.

60 *Yirmiyahu* wrote down in one scroll all the disaster that would come upon Babylon, all these things that are written concerning Babylon.

61 And *Yirmiyahu* said to *Seraya*, "When you get to Babylon, see that you read out all these words.

62 And say, '*Hashem*, You Yourself have declared concerning this place that it shall be cut off, without inhabitant, man or beast; that it shall be a desolation for all time.'

Yirmiyahu/Jeremiah
Chapter 52

ירמיהו
פרק נב

63 And when you finish reading this scroll, tie a stone to it and hurl it into the Euphrates.

סג וְהָיָה כְּכַלֹּתְךָ לִקְרֹא אֶת־הַסֵּפֶר הַזֶּה תִּקְשֹׁר עָלָיו אֶבֶן וְהִשְׁלַכְתּוֹ אֶל־תּוֹךְ פְּרָת:

64 And say, 'Thus shall Babylon sink and never rise again, because of the disaster that I will bring upon it. And [nations] shall have wearied themselves [for fire].'" Thus far the words of *Yirmiyahu*.

סד וְאָמַרְתָּ כָּכָה תִּשְׁקַע בָּבֶל וְלֹא־תָקוּם מִפְּנֵי הָרָעָה אֲשֶׁר אָנֹכִי מֵבִיא עָלֶיהָ וְיָעֵפוּ עַד־הֵנָּה דִּבְרֵי יִרְמְיָהוּ:

52 1 *Tzidkiyahu* was twenty-one years old when he became king, and he reigned in *Yerushalayim* for eleven years. His mother's name was Hamutal, daughter of *Yirmiyahu* of Libnah.

נב א בֶּן־עֶשְׂרִים וְאַחַת שָׁנָה צִדְקִיָּהוּ בְמָלְכוֹ וְאַחַת עֶשְׂרֵה שָׁנָה מָלַךְ בִּירוּשָׁלָם וְשֵׁם אִמּוֹ חֲמִיטַל [חֲמוּטַל] בַּת־יִרְמְיָהוּ מִלִּבְנָה:

2 He did what was displeasing to *Hashem*, just as *Yehoyakim* had done.

ב וַיַּעַשׂ הָרַע בְּעֵינֵי יְהֹוָה כְּכֹל אֲשֶׁר־עָשָׂה יְהוֹיָקִים:

3 Indeed, *Yerushalayim* and *Yehuda* were a cause of anger for *Hashem*, so that He cast them out of His presence. *Tzidkiyahu* rebelled against the king of Babylon.

ג כִּי עַל־אַף יְהֹוָה הָיְתָה בִּירוּשָׁלַם וִיהוּדָה עַד־הִשְׁלִיכוֹ אוֹתָם מֵעַל פָּנָיו וַיִּמְרֹד צִדְקִיָּהוּ בְּמֶלֶךְ בָּבֶל:

KEE al AF a-do-NAI ha-y'-TAH bee-ru-sha-LA-im vee-hu-DAH ad hish-li-KHO o-TAM may-AL pa-NAV va-yim-ROD tzid-ki-YA-hu b'-ME-lekh ba-VEL

4 And in the ninth year of his reign, on the tenth day of the tenth month, King Nebuchadrezzar moved against *Yerushalayim* with his whole army. They besieged it and built towers against it all around.

ד וַיְהִי בַשָּׁנָה הַתְּשִׁעִית לְמָלְכוֹ בַּחֹדֶשׁ הָעֲשִׂירִי בֶּעָשׂוֹר לַחֹדֶשׁ בָּא נְבוּכַדְרֶאצַּר מֶלֶךְ־בָּבֶל הוּא וְכָל־חֵילוֹ עַל־יְרוּשָׁלַם וַיַּחֲנוּ עָלֶיהָ וַיִּבְנוּ עָלֶיהָ דָּיֵק סָבִיב:

5 The city continued in a state of siege until the eleventh year of King *Tzidkiyahu*.

ה וַתָּבֹא הָעִיר בַּמָּצוֹר עַד עַשְׁתֵּי עֶשְׂרֵה שָׁנָה לַמֶּלֶךְ צִדְקִיָּהוּ:

6 By the ninth day of the fourth month, the famine had become acute in the city; there was no food left for the common people.

ו בַּחֹדֶשׁ הָרְבִיעִי בְּתִשְׁעָה לַחֹדֶשׁ וַיֶּחֱזַק הָרָעָב בָּעִיר וְלֹא־הָיָה לֶחֶם לְעַם הָאָרֶץ:

7 Then [the wall of] the city was breached. All the soldiers fled; they left the city by night through the gate between the double walls, which is near the king's garden – the Chaldeans were all around the city – and they set out for the Arabah.

ז וַתִּבָּקַע הָעִיר וְכָל־אַנְשֵׁי הַמִּלְחָמָה יִבְרְחוּ וַיֵּצְאוּ מֵהָעִיר לַיְלָה דֶּרֶךְ שַׁעַר בֵּין־הַחֹמֹתַיִם אֲשֶׁר עַל־גַּן הַמֶּלֶךְ וְכַשְׂדִּים עַל־הָעִיר סָבִיב וַיֵּלְכוּ דֶּרֶךְ הָעֲרָבָה:

52:3 Indeed, *Yerushalayim* and *Yehuda* were a cause of anger for *Hashem* *Yirmiyahu*'s final chapter repeats the description of the downfall of *Yehuda* and *Yerushalayim* at the hands of the Babylonians. One might be tempted to separate *Hashem* from history, and state that politics and theology do not mix. What *Yirmiyahu* teaches is that the two work hand-in-hand. On the surface, Babylonia is another superpower overrunning a minor, vassal state. However, *Yehuda* is vulnerable not because of its small army, but because it refuses to perform justice and righteousness, and worships idols in *Hashem*'s holy land. It is their sinful behavior and God's corresponding anger that leads to Israel's exile, just as God's everlasting love for His people and His land will eventually lead to their full return and restoration, and to the redemption of the entire world.

Yirmiyahu/Jeremiah
Chapter 52

ירמיהו
פרק נב

8 But the Chaldean troops pursued the king, and they overtook *Tzidkiyahu* in the steppes of *Yericho*, as his entire force left him and scattered.

ח וַיִּרְדְּפוּ חֵיל־כַּשְׂדִּים אַחֲרֵי הַמֶּלֶךְ וַיַּשִּׂגוּ אֶת־צִדְקִיָּהוּ בְּעַרְבֹת יְרֵחוֹ וְכָל־חֵילוֹ נָפֹצוּ מֵעָלָיו:

9 They captured the king and brought him before the king of Babylon at Riblah, in the region of Hamath; and he put him on trial.

ט וַיִּתְפְּשׂוּ אֶת־הַמֶּלֶךְ וַיַּעֲלוּ אֹתוֹ אֶל־מֶלֶךְ בָּבֶל רִבְלָתָה בְּאֶרֶץ חֲמָת וַיְדַבֵּר אִתּוֹ מִשְׁפָּטִים:

10 The king of Babylon had *Tzidkiyahu*'s sons slaughtered before his eyes; he also had all the officials of *Yehuda* slaughtered at Riblah.

י וַיִּשְׁחַט מֶלֶךְ־בָּבֶל אֶת־בְּנֵי צִדְקִיָּהוּ לְעֵינָיו וְגַם אֶת־כָּל־שָׂרֵי יְהוּדָה שָׁחַט בְּרִבְלָתָה:

11 Then the eyes of *Tzidkiyahu* were put out, and he was chained in bronze fetters. The king of Babylon brought him to Babylon and put him in prison, [where he remained] to the day of his death.

יא וְאֶת־עֵינֵי צִדְקִיָּהוּ עִוֵּר וַיַּאַסְרֵהוּ בַנְחֻשְׁתַּיִם וַיְבִאֵהוּ מֶלֶךְ־בָּבֶל בָּבֶלָה וַיִּתְּנֵהוּ בבית־[בֵית־] הַפְּקֻדֹּת עַד־יוֹם מוֹתוֹ:

12 On the tenth day of the fifth month – that was the nineteenth year of King Nebuchadrezzar, the king of Babylon – Nebuzaradan, the chief of the guards, came to represent the king of Babylon in *Yerushalayim*.

יב וּבַחֹדֶשׁ הַחֲמִישִׁי בֶּעָשׂוֹר לַחֹדֶשׁ הִיא שְׁנַת תְּשַׁע־עֶשְׂרֵה שָׁנָה לַמֶּלֶךְ נְבוּכַדְרֶאצַּר מֶלֶךְ־בָּבֶל בָּא נְבוּזַרְאֲדָן רַב־טַבָּחִים עָמַד לִפְנֵי מֶלֶךְ־בָּבֶל בִּירוּשָׁלָ͏ִם:

13 He burned the House of *Hashem*, the king's palace, and all the houses of *Yerushalayim*; he burned down the house of every notable person.

יג וַיִּשְׂרֹף אֶת־בֵּית־יְהֹוָה וְאֶת־בֵּית הַמֶּלֶךְ וְאֵת כָּל־בָּתֵּי יְרוּשָׁלַ͏ִם וְאֶת־כָּל־בֵּית הַגָּדוֹל שָׂרַף בָּאֵשׁ:

14 The entire Chaldean force that was with the chief of the guards tore down all the walls of *Yerushalayim* on every side.

יד וְאֶת־כָּל־חֹמוֹת יְרוּשָׁלַ͏ִם סָבִיב נָתְצוּ כָּל־חֵיל כַּשְׂדִּים אֲשֶׁר אֶת־רַב־טַבָּחִים:

15 The remnant of the people left in the city, the defectors who had gone over to the king of Babylon, and what remained of the craftsmen were taken into exile by Nebuzaradan, the chief of the guards. But some of the poorest elements of the population –

טו וּמִדַּלּוֹת הָעָם וְאֶת־יֶתֶר הָעָם הַנִּשְׁאָרִים בָּעִיר וְאֶת־הַנֹּפְלִים אֲשֶׁר נָפְלוּ אֶל־מֶלֶךְ בָּבֶל וְאֵת יֶתֶר הָאָמוֹן הֶגְלָה נְבוּזַרְאֲדָן רַב־טַבָּחִים:

16 some of the poorest in the land – were left by Nebuzaradan, the chief of the guards, to be vinedressers and field hands.

טז וּמִדַּלּוֹת הָאָרֶץ הִשְׁאִיר נְבוּזַרְאֲדָן רַב־טַבָּחִים לְכֹרְמִים וּלְיֹגְבִים:

17 The Chaldeans broke up the bronze columns of the House of *Hashem*, the stands, and the bronze tank that was in the House of *Hashem*; and they carried all the bronze away to Babylon.

יז וְאֶת־עַמּוּדֵי הַנְּחֹשֶׁת אֲשֶׁר לְבֵית־יְהֹוָה וְאֶת־הַמְּכֹנוֹת וְאֶת־יָם הַנְּחֹשֶׁת אֲשֶׁר בְּבֵית־יְהֹוָה שִׁבְּרוּ כַשְׂדִּים וַיִּשְׂאוּ אֶת־כָּל־נְחֻשְׁתָּם בָּבֶלָה:

18 They also took the pails, scrapers, snuffers, sprinkling bowls, ladles, and all the other bronze vessels used in the service.

יח וְאֶת־הַסִּרוֹת וְאֶת־הַיָּעִים וְאֶת־הַמְזַמְּרוֹת וְאֶת־הַמִּזְרָקֹת וְאֶת־הַכַּפּוֹת וְאֵת כָּל־כְּלֵי הַנְּחֹשֶׁת אֲשֶׁר־יְשָׁרְתוּ בָהֶם לָקָחוּ:

Yirmiyahu/Jeremiah
Chapter 52

19 The chief of the guards took whatever was of gold and whatever was of silver: basins, fire pans, sprinkling bowls, pails, *menorahs*, ladles, and jars.

20 The two columns, the one tank and the twelve bronze oxen which supported it, and the stands, which King *Shlomo* had provided for the House of *Hashem* – all these objects contained bronze beyond weighing.

21 As for the columns, each was eighteen *amot* high and twelve *amot* in circumference; it was hollow, and [the metal] was four fingers thick.

22 It had a bronze capital above it; the height of each capital was five *amot*, and there was a meshwork [decorated] with pomegranates about the capital, all made of bronze; and so for the second column, also with pomegranates.

23 There were ninety-six pomegranates facing outward; all the pomegranates around the meshwork amounted to one hundred.

24 The chief of the guards also took *Seraya* the chief *Kohen* and *Tzefanya*, the deputy *Kohen*, and the three guardians of the threshold.

25 And from the city he took a eunuch who was in command of the soldiers; seven royal privy councilors, who were present in the city; the scribe of the army commander, who was in charge of mustering the people of the land; and sixty of the common people who were inside the city.

26 Nebuzaradan, the chief of the guards, took them and brought them to the king of Babylon at Riblah.

27 The king of Babylon had them struck down and put to death at Riblah, in the region of Hamath. Thus *Yehuda* was exiled from its land.

28 This is the number of those whom Nebuchadrezzar exiled in the seventh year: 3,023 Judeans.

29 In the eighteenth year of Nebuchadrezzar, 832 persons [were exiled] from *Yerushalayim*.

Yirmiyahu/Jeremiah
Chapter 52

30 And in the twenty-third year of Nebuchadrezzar, Nebuzaradan, the chief of the guards, exiled 745 Judeans. The total amounted to 4,600 persons.

31 In the thirty-seventh year of the exile of King Yehoyachin of Yehuda, on the twenty-fifth day of the twelfth month, King Evil-merodach of Babylon, in the year he became king, took note of King Yehoyachin of Yehuda and released him from prison.

32 He spoke kindly to him, and gave him a throne above those of other kings who were with him in Babylon.

33 He removed his prison garments and [Yehoyachin] ate regularly in his presence the rest of his life.

34 A regular allotment of food was given him by order of the king of Babylon, an allotment for each day, to the day of his death – all the days of his life.

ירמיהו
פרק נב

ל בִּשְׁנַת שָׁלֹשׁ וְעֶשְׂרִים לִנְבוּכַדְרֶאצַּר הֶגְלָה נְבוּזַרְאֲדָן רַב־טַבָּחִים יְהוּדִים נֶפֶשׁ שְׁבַע מֵאוֹת אַרְבָּעִים וַחֲמִשָּׁה כָּל־נֶפֶשׁ אַרְבַּעַת אֲלָפִים וְשֵׁשׁ מֵאוֹת:

לא וַיְהִי בִשְׁלֹשִׁים וָשֶׁבַע שָׁנָה לְגָלוּת יְהוֹיָכִן מֶלֶךְ־יְהוּדָה בִּשְׁנֵים עָשָׂר חֹדֶשׁ בְּעֶשְׂרִים וַחֲמִשָּׁה לַחֹדֶשׁ נָשָׂא אֱוִיל מְרֹדַךְ מֶלֶךְ בָּבֶל בִּשְׁנַת מַלְכֻתוֹ אֶת־רֹאשׁ יְהוֹיָכִין מֶלֶךְ־יְהוּדָה וַיֹּצֵא אוֹתוֹ מִבֵּית הכליא [הַכְּלוּא]:

לב וַיְדַבֵּר אִתּוֹ טֹבוֹת וַיִּתֵּן אֶת־כִּסְאוֹ מִמַּעַל לְכִסֵּא מלכים [הַמְּלָכִים] אֲשֶׁר אִתּוֹ בְּבָבֶל:

לג וְשִׁנָּה אֵת בִּגְדֵי כִלְאוֹ וְאָכַל לֶחֶם לְפָנָיו תָּמִיד כָּל־יְמֵי חַיָּו:

לד וַאֲרֻחָתוֹ אֲרֻחַת תָּמִיד נִתְּנָה־לּוֹ מֵאֵת מֶלֶךְ־בָּבֶל דְּבַר־יוֹם בְּיוֹמוֹ עַד־יוֹם מוֹתוֹ כֹּל יְמֵי חַיָּיו:

Sefer Yechezkel
The Book of Ezekiel

Introduction and commentary by Rabbi Yaakov Beasley

Sefer Yechezkel (Ezekiel) contains the prophecies *Yechezkel* received between the years 593–571 BCE. Since he provides exact dates for a number of his prophecies throughout the book, we can easily pinpoint the moment in history when they are delivered. His messages are intended mainly for the Jews already living in Babylonia, who were exiled from *Yerushalayim* in 597 BCE, and watch from afar as their *Beit Hamikdash* and homeland in *Yehuda* are destroyed. In addition to his prophecies of rebuke, one of *Yechezkel*'s central roles involves offering strength to these people who have been torn from the Holy Land. His name thus befits his role as prophet, since *Yechezkel* (יחזקאל) means 'God strengthens'. Hashem chose *Yechezkel* to give strength to His people.

Yechezkel descends from a priestly family in *Yerushalayim*. After being exiled from *Yerushalayim*, he lives in Babylonia, in the city of Tel Abib. His messages of rebuke fall mostly on deaf ears, as the Jews in Babylonia refuse to believe that *Hashem* will destroy His holy city of *Yerushalayim* and His Temple. They also do not accept his words of reproach justifying the upcoming tragedy. After the traumatic destruction, however, the people have become ready to listen to *Yechezkel*, and the focus of his message changes. Instead of emphasizing the catastrophe and its causes, he begins to outline a plan for the Jewish people to survive the temporary loss of their land and to prevail in exile. His messages refer equally to the ritual and the ethical, and he delivers a message of hope that echoes to this day.

Sefer Yechezkel, which is organized chronologically, can be divided into three major sections, paralleling the historical events which unfold around the prophet. Chapters 1–24 speak of the judgment that will befall *Yerushalayim* and provide an explanation for why God has chosen to chastise His people so harshly: The punishments are meant to cleanse His people from their accumulated sins so they can return in purity to their land. In that vein, the actual destruction of *Yerushalayim* is compared to an offering on the altar.

The second section, chapters 25–32, outlines a series of judgments that will befall the nations of the world, either for actively helping Babylonia destroy *Yerushalayim*, or for reveling in the downfall of Israel. Included among these nations are Ammon, Moab, Edom, Philistia, Tyre, Sidon, and Egypt.

The third and final section, chapters 33–48, provides hope for restoration of the exiled remnant of Israel. *Yechezkel* promises that they can, and will, return as a sovereign nation to the Holy Land. This message of deliverance and restoration can be further subdivided into two parts: chapters 33–40 describe the return to the soil of the land, and the final eight chapters envision the rebuilt *Beit Hamikdash* in all its glory, and the Messianic Age. *Yechezkel*'s most famous revelation can be found in this section: The vision of the valley of the dry bones (chapter 37).

Sefer Yechezkel is full of unusual symbolic acts and allegories which are intended to help the prophet convey his messages. For example, *Yechezkel* is told to lie on his side for over a year, to shave his hair, and to refrain from mourning for his deceased wife. *Yechezkel*'s extravagant, other-worldly descriptions of the "heavenly chariot" and court became the focal point for study of many esoteric mystical traditions. These pursuits have been considered spiritually dangerous for untrained or unprepared students, and studying these chapters was traditionally discouraged, except under the guidance of a master. In fact, there were many who felt that it was not appropriate to include *Sefer Yechezkel* within the biblical canon. The rabbis, however, chose to include *Sefer Yechezkel*, as it was deemed an authentic prophetic work whose eternal messages are meaningful for all generations.

Map of the Ancient Near East

Yechezkel was a contemporary of *Yirmiyahu*. Both lived at the time of the destruction of the first *Beit Hamikdash* and prophesied about its ruin. But while *Yirmiyahu* experienced the destruction in *Eretz Yisrael*, *Yechezkel* prophesied from Babylonia where he had been exiled prior to the final destruction. His presence in the exile, in addition to his prophecies of comfort, brought solace to the rest of the exiles who were eventually brought from *Eretz Yisrael* to Babylonia and reminded them that *Hashem* had not forsaken His people despite the banishment from the land.

The following is a map of the Ancient Near East, including the areas of *Eretz Yisrael,* from where the Jews were taken, and Babylonia, where *Yechezkel* prophesied and the exiled nation was settled.

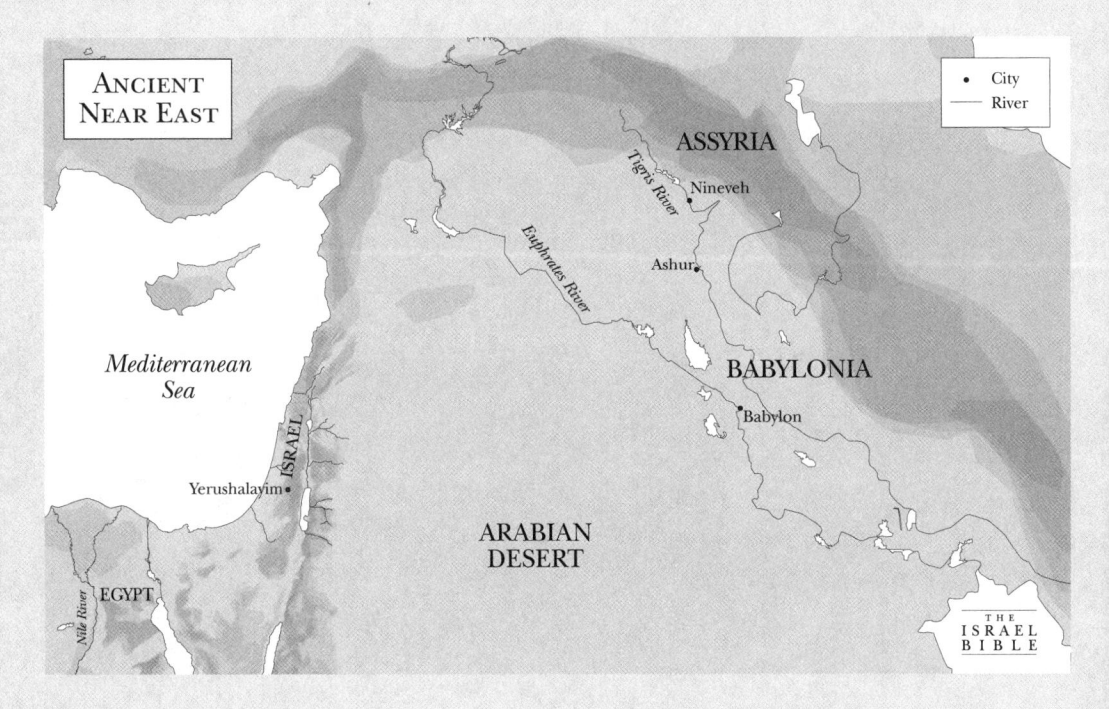

Yechezkel/Ezekiel
Chapter 1

יחזקאל
פרק א

1 ¹ In the thirtieth year, on the fifth day of the fourth month, when I was in the community of exiles by the Chebar Canal, the heavens opened and I saw visions of *Hashem*.

א וַיְהִי בִּשְׁלֹשִׁים שָׁנָה בָּרְבִיעִי בַּחֲמִשָּׁה לַחֹדֶשׁ וַאֲנִי בְתוֹךְ־הַגּוֹלָה עַל־נְהַר־כְּבָר נִפְתְּחוּ הַשָּׁמַיִם וָאֶרְאֶה מַרְאוֹת אֱלֹהִים:

² On the fifth day of the month – it was the fifth year of the exile of King *Yehoyachin* –

ב בַּחֲמִשָּׁה לַחֹדֶשׁ הִיא הַשָּׁנָה הַחֲמִישִׁית לְגָלוּת הַמֶּלֶךְ יוֹיָכִין:

³ the word of *Hashem* came to the *Kohen Yechezkel* son of *Buzi*, by the Chebar Canal, in the land of the Chaldeans. And the hand of *Hashem* came upon him there.

ג הָיֹה הָיָה דְבַר־יְהֹוָה אֶל־יְחֶזְקֵאל בֶּן־בּוּזִי הַכֹּהֵן בְּאֶרֶץ כַּשְׂדִּים עַל־נְהַר־כְּבָר וַתְּהִי עָלָיו שָׁם יַד־יְהֹוָה:

ha-YOH ha-YAH d'-var a-do-NAI el y'-khez-KAYL ben bu-ZEE ha-ko-HAYN b'-E-retz kas-DEEM al n'-har k'-VAR va-t'-HEE a-LAV SHAM yad a-do-NAI

⁴ I looked, and lo, a stormy wind came sweeping out of the north – a huge cloud and flashing fire, surrounded by a radiance; and in the center of it, in the center of the fire, a gleam as of amber.

ד וָאֵרֶא וְהִנֵּה רוּחַ סְעָרָה בָּאָה מִן־הַצָּפוֹן עָנָן גָּדוֹל וְאֵשׁ מִתְלַקַּחַת וְנֹגַהּ לוֹ סָבִיב וּמִתּוֹכָהּ כְּעֵין הַחַשְׁמַל מִתּוֹךְ הָאֵשׁ:

⁵ In the center of it were also the figures of four creatures. And this was their appearance They had the figures of human beings.

ה וּמִתּוֹכָהּ דְּמוּת אַרְבַּע חַיּוֹת וְזֶה מַרְאֵיהֶן דְּמוּת אָדָם לָהֵנָּה:

⁶ However, each had four faces, and each of them had four wings;

ו וְאַרְבָּעָה פָנִים לְאֶחָת וְאַרְבַּע כְּנָפַיִם לְאַחַת לָהֶם:

⁷ the legs of each were [fused into] a single rigid leg, and the feet of each were like a single calf's hoof; and their sparkle was like the luster of burnished bronze.

ז וְרַגְלֵיהֶם רֶגֶל יְשָׁרָה וְכַף רַגְלֵיהֶם כְּכַף רֶגֶל עֵגֶל וְנֹצְצִים כְּעֵין נְחֹשֶׁת קָלָל:

⁸ They had human hands below their wings. The four of them had their faces and their wings on their four sides.

ח וִידוֹ [וִידֵי] אָדָם מִתַּחַת כַּנְפֵיהֶם עַל אַרְבַּעַת רִבְעֵיהֶם וּפְנֵיהֶם וְכַנְפֵיהֶם לְאַרְבַּעְתָּם:

⁹ Each one's wings touched those of the other. They did not turn when they moved; each could move in the direction of any of its faces.

ט חֹבְרֹת אִשָּׁה אֶל־אֲחוֹתָהּ כַּנְפֵיהֶם לֹא־יִסַּבּוּ בְלֶכְתָּן אִישׁ אֶל־עֵבֶר פָּנָיו יֵלֵכוּ:

היה היה

1:3 The word of *Hashem* came to the *Kohen Yechezkel* *Yechezkel's* prophecy begins with the terrifying and esoteric vision of *Hashem's* holy chariot, symbolic of the Divine Presence leaving the *Beit Hamikdash* and following the Jewish people into exile. The people may be temporarily bereft of their land, but are never abandoned by God. According to Jewish tradition, a prophet cannot receive prophecy outside the Land of Israel, unless he has first received it inside of the land. Therefore, the early commentators such as *Rashi* and *Radak*, note that in Hebrew, the word for the past is doubled in the words *hayo haya* (הָיֹה הָיָה), translated here as "came to," since *Yechezkel's* current prophecy is a continuation of previous prophecies that visited him in *Yerushalayim*. Even when exiled, the people's connection to the holiness and spirituality of *Eretz Yisrael* is never severed or broken.

Yechezkel/Ezekiel
Chapter 1

יחזקאל
פרק א

10 Each of them had a human face [at the front]; each of the four had the face of a lion on the right; each of the four had the face of an ox on the left; and each of the four had the face of an eagle [at the back].

י וּדְמוּת פְּנֵיהֶם פְּנֵי אָדָם וּפְנֵי אַרְיֵה אֶל־הַיָּמִין לְאַרְבַּעְתָּם וּפְנֵי־שׁוֹר מֵהַשְּׂמֹאול לְאַרְבַּעְתָּן וּפְנֵי־נֶשֶׁר לְאַרְבַּעְתָּן:

11 Such were their faces. As for their wings, they were separated: above, each had two touching those of the others, while the other two covered its body.

יא וּפְנֵיהֶם וְכַנְפֵיהֶם פְּרֻדוֹת מִלְמָעְלָה לְאִישׁ שְׁתַּיִם חֹבְרוֹת אִישׁ וּשְׁתַּיִם מְכַסּוֹת אֵת גְּוִיֹּתֵיהֶנָה:

12 And each could move in the direction of any of its faces; they went wherever the spirit impelled them to go, without turning when they moved.

יב וְאִישׁ אֶל־עֵבֶר פָּנָיו יֵלֵכוּ אֶל אֲשֶׁר יִהְיֶה־שָּׁמָּה הָרוּחַ לָלֶכֶת יֵלֵכוּ לֹא יִסַּבּוּ בְּלֶכְתָּן:

13 Such then was the appearance of the creatures. With them was something that looked like burning coals of fire. This fire, suggestive of torches, kept moving about among the creatures; the fire had a radiance, and lightning issued from the fire.

יג וּדְמוּת הַחַיּוֹת מַרְאֵיהֶם כְּגַחֲלֵי־אֵשׁ בֹּעֲרוֹת כְּמַרְאֵה הַלַּפִּדִים הִיא מִתְהַלֶּכֶת בֵּין הַחַיּוֹת וְנֹגַהּ לָאֵשׁ וּמִן־הָאֵשׁ יוֹצֵא בָרָק:

14 Dashing to and fro [among] the creatures was something that looked like flares.

יד וְהַחַיּוֹת רָצוֹא וָשׁוֹב כְּמַרְאֵה הַבָּזָק:

15 As I gazed on the creatures, I saw one wheel on the ground next to each of the four-faced creatures.

טו וָאֵרֶא הַחַיּוֹת וְהִנֵּה אוֹפַן אֶחָד בָּאָרֶץ אֵצֶל הַחַיּוֹת לְאַרְבַּעַת פָּנָיו:

16 As for the appearance and structure of the wheels, they gleamed like beryl. All four had the same form; the appearance and structure of each was as of two wheels cutting through each other.

טז מַרְאֵה הָאוֹפַנִּים וּמַעֲשֵׂיהֶם כְּעֵין תַּרְשִׁישׁ וּדְמוּת אֶחָד לְאַרְבַּעְתָּן וּמַרְאֵיהֶם וּמַעֲשֵׂיהֶם כַּאֲשֶׁר יִהְיֶה הָאוֹפַן בְּתוֹךְ הָאוֹפָן:

17 And when they moved, each could move in the direction of any of its four quarters; they did not veer when they moved.

יז עַל־אַרְבַּעַת רִבְעֵיהֶן בְּלֶכְתָּם יֵלֵכוּ לֹא יִסַּבּוּ בְּלֶכְתָּן:

18 Their rims were tall and frightening, for the rims of all four were covered all over with eyes.

יח וְגַבֵּיהֶן וְגֹבַהּ לָהֶם וְיִרְאָה לָהֶם וְגַבֹּתָם מְלֵאֹת עֵינַיִם סָבִיב לְאַרְבַּעְתָּן:

19 And when the creatures moved forward, the wheels moved at their sides; and when the creatures were borne above the earth, the wheels were borne too.

יט וּבְלֶכֶת הַחַיּוֹת יֵלְכוּ הָאוֹפַנִּים אֶצְלָם וּבְהִנָּשֵׂא הַחַיּוֹת מֵעַל הָאָרֶץ יִנָּשְׂאוּ הָאוֹפַנִּים:

20 Wherever the spirit impelled them to go, they went – wherever the spirit impelled them – and the wheels were borne alongside them; for the spirit of the creatures was in the wheels.

כ עַל אֲשֶׁר יִהְיֶה־שָּׁם הָרוּחַ לָלֶכֶת יֵלֵכוּ שָׁמָּה הָרוּחַ לָלֶכֶת וְהָאוֹפַנִּים יִנָּשְׂאוּ לְעֻמָּתָם כִּי רוּחַ הַחַיָּה בָּאוֹפַנִּים:

21 When those moved, these moved; and when those stood still, these stood still; and when those were borne above the earth, the wheels were borne alongside them – for the spirit of the creatures was in the wheels.

כא בְּלֶכְתָּם יֵלֵכוּ וּבְעָמְדָם יַעֲמֹדוּ וּבְהִנָּשְׂאָם מֵעַל הָאָרֶץ יִנָּשְׂאוּ הָאוֹפַנִּים לְעֻמָּתָם כִּי רוּחַ הַחַיָּה בָּאוֹפַנִּים:

Yechezkel/Ezekiel
Chapter 2

22 Above the heads of the creatures was a form: an expanse, with an awe-inspiring gleam as of crystal, was spread out above their heads.

23 Under the expanse, each had one pair of wings extended toward those of the others; and each had another pair covering its body.

24 When they moved, I could hear the sound of their wings like the sound of mighty waters, like the sound of *Shaddai*, a tumult like the din of an army. When they stood still, they would let their wings droop.

25 From above the expanse over their heads came a sound. When they stood still, they would let their wings droop.

26 Above the expanse over their heads was the semblance of a throne, in appearance like sapphire; and on top, upon this semblance of a throne, there was the semblance of a human form.

27 From what appeared as his loins up, I saw a gleam as of amber – what looked like a fire encased in a frame; and from what appeared as his loins down, I saw what looked like fire. There was a radiance all about him.

28 Like the appearance of the bow which shines in the clouds on a day of rain, such was the appearance of the surrounding radiance. That was the appearance of the semblance of the Presence of *Hashem*. When I beheld it, I flung myself down on my face. And I heard the voice of someone speaking.

2

1 And He said to me, "O mortal, stand up on your feet that I may speak to you."

2 As He spoke to me, a spirit entered into me and set me upon my feet; and I heard what was being spoken to me.

3 He said to me, "O mortal, I am sending you to the people of *Yisrael*, that nation of rebels, who have rebelled against Me. – They as well as their fathers have defied Me to this very day;

va-YO-mer ay-LAI ben a-DAM sho-LAY-akh a-NEE o-t'-KHA el b'-NAY yis-ra-AYL el go-YIM ha-mo-r'-DEEM a-SHER ma-r'-du VEE HAY-mah va-a-vo-TAM PA-sh'-u VEE ad E-tzem ha-YOM ha-ZEH

בן אדם | **2:3** **'O mortal, I am sending you to the people of Yisrael** *Yechezkel* is addressed with the term *ben adam* (בן אדם) ninety-three times in his book. This expression literally means 'son of man,' and is translated

Yechezkel/Ezekiel
Chapter 3

4 for the sons are brazen of face and stubborn of heart. I send you to them, and you shall say to them: 'Thus said *Hashem*' –

5 whether they listen or not, for they are a rebellious breed – that they may know that there was a *Navi* among them.

6 "And you, mortal, do not fear them and do not fear their words, though thistles and thorns press against you, and you sit upon scorpions. Do not be afraid of their words and do not be dismayed by them, though they are a rebellious breed;

7 but speak My words to them, whether they listen or not, for they are rebellious.

8 "And you, mortal, heed what I say to you: Do not be rebellious like that rebellious breed. Open your mouth and eat what I am giving you."

9 As I looked, there was a hand stretched out to me, holding a written scroll.

10 He unrolled it before me, and it was inscribed on both the front and the back; on it were written lamentations, dirges, and woes.

3

1 He said to me, "Mortal, eat what is offered you; eat this scroll, and go speak to the House of *Yisrael*."

2 So I opened my mouth, and He gave me this scroll to eat,

3 as He said to me, "Mortal, feed your stomach and fill your belly with this scroll that I give you." I ate it, and it tasted as sweet as honey to me.

4 Then He said to me, "Mortal, go to the House of *Yisrael* and repeat My very words to them.

---

here as 'mortal'. This designation alludes to both his humility and mortality, but also to all of mankind's role at God's side in improving the world, as alluded to in *Tehillim* (80:18). As such, *Yechezkel's* messages are intended both for Israel and for the nations. While his message is specific to Israel, the truths it contains are meant for the betterment of all mankind.

Yechezkel/Ezekiel
Chapter 3

יחזקאל
פרק ג

5 For you are sent, not to a people of unintelligible speech and difficult language, but to the House of *Yisrael* –

ה כִּי לֹא אֶל־עַם עִמְקֵי שָׂפָה וְכִבְדֵי לָשׁוֹן אַתָּה שָׁלוּחַ אֶל־בֵּית יִשְׂרָאֵל:

6 not to the many peoples of unintelligible speech and difficult language, whose talk you cannot understand. If I sent you to them, they would listen to you.

ו לֹא ׀ אֶל־עַמִּים רַבִּים עִמְקֵי שָׂפָה וְכִבְדֵי לָשׁוֹן אֲשֶׁר לֹא־תִשְׁמַע דִּבְרֵיהֶם אִם־לֹא אֲלֵיהֶם שְׁלַחְתִּיךָ הֵמָּה יִשְׁמְעוּ אֵלֶיךָ:

7 But the House of *Yisrael* will refuse to listen to you, for they refuse to listen to Me; for the whole House of *Yisrael* are brazen of forehead and stubborn of heart.

ז וּבֵית יִשְׂרָאֵל לֹא יֹאבוּ לִשְׁמֹעַ אֵלֶיךָ כִּי־אֵינָם אֹבִים לִשְׁמֹעַ אֵלָי כִּי כָּל־בֵּית יִשְׂרָאֵל חִזְקֵי־מֵצַח וּקְשֵׁי־לֵב הֵמָּה:

8 But I will make your face as hard as theirs, and your forehead as brazen as theirs.

ח הִנֵּה נָתַתִּי אֶת־פָּנֶיךָ חֲזָקִים לְעֻמַּת פְּנֵיהֶם וְאֶת־מִצְחֲךָ חָזָק לְעֻמַּת מִצְחָם:

9 I will make your forehead like adamant, harder than flint. Do not fear them, and do not be dismayed by them, though they are a rebellious breed."

ט כְּשָׁמִיר חָזָק מִצֹּר נָתַתִּי מִצְחֶךָ לֹא־תִירָא אוֹתָם וְלֹא־תֵחַת מִפְּנֵיהֶם כִּי בֵּית־מְרִי הֵמָּה:

10 Then He said to me: "Mortal, listen with your ears and receive into your mind all the words that I speak to you.

י וַיֹּאמֶר אֵלָי בֶּן־אָדָם אֶת־כָּל־דְּבָרַי אֲשֶׁר אֲדַבֵּר אֵלֶיךָ קַח בִּלְבָבְךָ וּבְאָזְנֶיךָ שְׁמָע:

11 Go to your people, the exile community, and speak to them. Say to them: Thus says *Hashem* – whether they listen or not."

יא וְלֵךְ בֹּא אֶל־הַגּוֹלָה אֶל־בְּנֵי עַמֶּךָ וְדִבַּרְתָּ אֲלֵיהֶם וְאָמַרְתָּ אֲלֵיהֶם כֹּה אָמַר אֲדֹנָי יֱהֹוִה אִם־יִשְׁמְעוּ וְאִם־יֶחְדָּלוּ:

12 Then a spirit carried me away, and behind me I heard a great roaring sound: "Blessed is the Presence of *Hashem*, in His place,"

יב וַתִּשָּׂאֵנִי רוּחַ וָאֶשְׁמַע אַחֲרַי קוֹל רַעַשׁ גָּדוֹל בָּרוּךְ כְּבוֹד־יְהֹוָה מִמְּקוֹמוֹ:

13 with the sound of the wings of the creatures beating against one another, and the sound of the wheels beside them – a great roaring sound.

יג וְקוֹל ׀ כַּנְפֵי הַחַיּוֹת מַשִּׁיקוֹת אִשָּׁה אֶל־אֲחוֹתָהּ וְקוֹל הָאוֹפַנִּים לְעֻמָּתָם וְקוֹל רַעַשׁ גָּדוֹל:

14 A spirit seized me and carried me away. I went in bitterness, in the fury of my spirit, while the hand of *Hashem* was strong upon me.

יד וְרוּחַ נְשָׂאַתְנִי וַתִּקָּחֵנִי וָאֵלֵךְ מַר בַּחֲמַת רוּחִי וְיַד־יְהֹוָה עָלַי חָזָקָה:

15 And I came to the exile community that dwelt in Tel Abib by the Chebar Canal, and I remained where they dwelt. And for seven days I sat there stunned among them.

טו וָאָבוֹא אֶל־הַגּוֹלָה תֵּל אָבִיב הַיֹּשְׁבִים אֶל־נְהַר־כְּבָר ואשר [וָאֵשֵׁב] הֵמָּה יוֹשְׁבִים שָׁם וָאֵשֵׁב שָׁם שִׁבְעַת יָמִים מַשְׁמִים בְּתוֹכָם:

va-a-VO el ha-go-LAH TAYL a-VEEV ha-yo-sh'-VEEM el n'-har k'-VAR va-ay-SHAYV HAY-mah yo-sh'-VEEM SHAM va-ay-SHAYV SHAM shiv-AT ya-MEEM mash-MEEM b'-to-KHAM

3:15 And I came to the exile community that dwelt in Tel Abib *Yechezkel* goes to the Israelite captives at Tel Abib near the Chebar River. Before he delivers his message of doom, however, he simply sits with them for a week, empathizing with their suffering before sharing the divine message. The name Tel Abib has been linked to the Akkadian "mound of the flood," mentioned in ancient Babylonian sources, so called because it was

Tel Aviv

Yechezkel/Ezekiel
Chapter 3

יחזקאל
פרק ג

16 After those seven days, the word of Hashem came to me:

טז וַיְהִי מִקְצֵה שִׁבְעַת יָמִים וַיְהִי דְבַר־יְהֹוָה אֵלַי לֵאמֹר׃

17 "O mortal, I appoint you watchman for the House of Yisrael; and when you hear a word from My mouth, you must warn them for Me.

יז בֶּן־אָדָם צֹפֶה נְתַתִּיךָ לְבֵית יִשְׂרָאֵל וְשָׁמַעְתָּ מִפִּי דָּבָר וְהִזְהַרְתָּ אוֹתָם מִמֶּנִּי׃

18 If I say to a wicked man, 'You shall die,' and you do not warn him – you do not speak to warn the wicked man of his wicked course in order to save his life – he, the wicked man, shall die for his iniquity, but I will require a reckoning for his blood from you.

יח בְּאׇמְרִי לָרָשָׁע מוֹת תָּמוּת וְלֹא הִזְהַרְתּוֹ וְלֹא דִבַּרְתָּ לְהַזְהִיר רָשָׁע מִדַּרְכּוֹ הָרְשָׁעָה לְחַיֹּתוֹ הוּא רָשָׁע בַּעֲוֺנוֹ יָמוּת וְדָמוֹ מִיָּדְךָ אֲבַקֵּשׁ׃

19 But if you do warn the wicked man, and he does not turn back from his wickedness and his wicked course, he shall die for his iniquity, but you will have saved your own life.

יט וְאַתָּה כִּי־הִזְהַרְתָּ רָשָׁע וְלֹא־שָׁב מֵרִשְׁעוֹ וּמִדַּרְכּוֹ הָרְשָׁעָה הוּא בַּעֲוֺנוֹ יָמוּת וְאַתָּה אֶת־נַפְשְׁךָ הִצַּלְתָּ׃

20 Again, if a righteous man abandons his righteousness and does wrong, when I put a stumbling block before him, he shall die. He shall die for his sins; the righteous deeds that he did shall not be remembered; but because you did not warn him, I will require a reckoning for his blood from you.

כ וּבְשׁוּב צַדִּיק מִצִּדְקוֹ וְעָשָׂה עָוֶל וְנָתַתִּי מִכְשׁוֹל לְפָנָיו הוּא יָמוּת כִּי לֹא הִזְהַרְתּוֹ בְּחַטָּאתוֹ יָמוּת וְלֹא תִזָּכַרְןָ צִדְקֹתָו אֲשֶׁר עָשָׂה וְדָמוֹ מִיָּדְךָ אֲבַקֵּשׁ׃

21 If, however, you warn the righteous man not to sin, and he, the righteous, does not sin, he shall live because he took warning, and you will have saved your own life."

כא וְאַתָּה כִּי הִזְהַרְתּוֹ צַדִּיק לְבִלְתִּי חֲטֹא צַדִּיק וְהוּא לֹא־חָטָא חָיוֹ יִחְיֶה כִּי נִזְהָר וְאַתָּה אֶת־נַפְשְׁךָ הִצַּלְתָּ׃

22 Then the hand of Hashem came upon me there, and He said to me, "Arise, go out to the valley, and there I will speak with you."

כב וַתְּהִי עָלַי שָׁם יַד־יְהֹוָה וַיֹּאמֶר אֵלַי קוּם צֵא אֶל־הַבִּקְעָה וְשָׁם אֲדַבֵּר אוֹתָךְ׃

23 I arose and went out to the valley, and there stood the Presence of Hashem, like the Presence that I had seen at the Chebar Canal; and I flung myself down on my face.

כג וָאָקוּם וָאֵצֵא אֶל־הַבִּקְעָה וְהִנֵּה־שָׁם כְּבוֹד־יְהֹוָה עֹמֵד כַּכָּבוֹד אֲשֶׁר רָאִיתִי עַל־נְהַר־כְּבָר וָאֶפֹּל עַל־פָּנָי׃

---

flooded by the Euphrates River. The great irony is that the name of the city of the exiles has become the name of modern Israel's shining metropolis, Tel Aviv (תל אביב), which in modern Hebrew means 'the hill of spring.' The name for the city was borrowed from the title of Nahum Sokolow's Hebrew translation of Theodor Herzl's *Altneuland*, 'Old New Land.' It was chosen because the word *Tel*, a mound covering ruins of ancient settlements, conjures up images of that which is ancient, while the word *aviv*, spring, implies that which is fresh and new.

Yechezkel/Ezekiel Chapter 4

יחזקאל פרק ד

24 And a spirit entered into me and set me upon my feet. And He spoke to me, and said to me: "Go, shut yourself up in your house.

כד וַתָּבֹא־בִי רוּחַ וַתַּעֲמִדֵנִי עַל־רַגְלָי וַיְדַבֵּר אֹתִי וַיֹּאמֶר אֵלַי בֹּא הִסָּגֵר בְּתוֹךְ בֵּיתֶךָ:

25 As for you, O mortal, cords have been placed upon you, and you have been bound with them, and you shall not go out among them.

כה וְאַתָּה בֶן־אָדָם הִנֵּה נָתְנוּ עָלֶיךָ עֲבוֹתִים וַאֲסָרוּךָ בָּהֶם וְלֹא תֵצֵא בְּתוֹכָם:

26 And I will make your tongue cleave to your palate, and you shall be dumb; you shall not be a reprover to them, for they are a rebellious breed.

כו וּלְשׁוֹנְךָ אַדְבִּיק אֶל־חִכֶּךָ וְנֶאֱלַמְתָּ וְלֹא־תִהְיֶה לָהֶם לְאִישׁ מוֹכִיחַ כִּי בֵּית מְרִי הֵמָּה:

27 But when I speak with you, I will open your mouth, and you shall say to them, 'Thus says *Hashem*!' He who listens will listen, and he who does not will not – for they are a rebellious breed."

כז וּבְדַבְּרִי אוֹתְךָ אֶפְתַּח אֶת־פִּיךָ וְאָמַרְתָּ אֲלֵיהֶם כֹּה אָמַר אֲדֹנָי יֱהֹוִה הַשֹּׁמֵעַ יִשְׁמָע וְהֶחָדֵל יֶחְדָּל כִּי בֵּית מְרִי הֵמָּה:

4 1 "And you, O mortal, take a brick and put it in front of you, and incise on it a city, *Yerushalayim*.

א וְאַתָּה בֶן־אָדָם קַח־לְךָ לְבֵנָה וְנָתַתָּה אוֹתָהּ לְפָנֶיךָ וְחַקּוֹתָ עָלֶיהָ עִיר אֶת־יְרוּשָׁלָ͏ִם:

2 Set up a siege against it, and build towers against it, and cast a mound against it; pitch camps against it, and bring up battering rams roundabout it.

ב וְנָתַתָּה עָלֶיהָ מָצוֹר וּבָנִיתָ עָלֶיהָ דָּיֵק וְשָׁפַכְתָּ עָלֶיהָ סֹלְלָה וְנָתַתָּה עָלֶיהָ מַחֲנוֹת וְשִׂים־עָלֶיהָ כָּרִים סָבִיב:

3 Then take an iron plate and place it as an iron wall between yourself and the city, and set your face against it. Thus it shall be under siege, you shall besiege it. This shall be an omen for the House of *Yisrael*.

ג וְאַתָּה קַח־לְךָ מַחֲבַת בַּרְזֶל וְנָתַתָּה אוֹתָהּ קִיר בַּרְזֶל בֵּינְךָ וּבֵין הָעִיר וַהֲכִינֹתָה אֶת־פָּנֶיךָ אֵלֶיהָ וְהָיְתָה בַמָּצוֹר וְצַרְתָּ עָלֶיהָ אוֹת הִיא לְבֵית יִשְׂרָאֵל:

4 "Then lie on your left side, and let it bear the punishment of the House of *Yisrael*; for as many days as you lie on it you shall bear their punishment.

ד וְאַתָּה שְׁכַב עַל־צִדְּךָ הַשְּׂמָאלִי וְשַׂמְתָּ אֶת־עֲוֹן בֵּית־יִשְׂרָאֵל עָלָיו מִסְפַּר הַיָּמִים אֲשֶׁר תִּשְׁכַּב עָלָיו תִּשָּׂא אֶת־עֲוֹנָם:

5 For I impose upon you three hundred and ninety days, corresponding to the number of the years of their punishment; and so you shall bear the punishment for the House of *Yisrael*.

ה וַאֲנִי נָתַתִּי לְךָ אֶת־שְׁנֵי עֲוֹנָם לְמִסְפַּר יָמִים שְׁלֹשׁ־מֵאוֹת וְתִשְׁעִים יוֹם וְנָשָׂאתָ עֲוֹן בֵּית־יִשְׂרָאֵל:

6 When you have completed these, you shall lie another forty days on your right side, and bear the punishment of the House of *Yehuda*. I impose on you one day for each year.

ו וְכִלִּיתָ אֶת־אֵלֶּה וְשָׁכַבְתָּ עַל־צִדְּךָ הַיְמוֹנִי [הַיְמָנִי] שֵׁנִית וְנָשָׂאתָ אֶת־עֲוֹן בֵּית־יְהוּדָה אַרְבָּעִים יוֹם יוֹם לַשָּׁנָה יוֹם לַשָּׁנָה נְתַתִּיו לָךְ:

7 "Then, with bared arm, set your face toward besieged *Yerushalayim* and prophesy against it.

ז וְאֶל־מְצוֹר יְרוּשָׁלַ͏ִם תָּכִין פָּנֶיךָ וּזְרֹעֲךָ חֲשׂוּפָה וְנִבֵּאתָ עָלֶיהָ:

8 Now I put cords upon you, so that you cannot turn from side to side until you complete your days of siege.

ח וְהִנֵּה נָתַתִּי עָלֶיךָ עֲבוֹתִים וְלֹא־תֵהָפֵךְ מִצִּדְּךָ אֶל־צִדֶּךָ עַד־כַּלּוֹתְךָ יְמֵי מְצוּרֶךָ:

Yechezkel/Ezekiel
Chapter 4

יחזקאל
פרק ד

9 "Further, take wheat, barley, beans, lentils, millet, and emmer. Put them into one vessel and bake them into bread. Eat it as many days as you lie on your side: three hundred and ninety.

ט וְאַתָּה קַח־לְךָ חִטִּין וּשְׂעֹרִים וּפוֹל וַעֲדָשִׁים וְדֹחַן וְכֻסְּמִים וְנָתַתָּה אוֹתָם בִּכְלִי אֶחָד וְעָשִׂיתָ אוֹתָם לְךָ לְלָחֶם מִסְפַּר הַיָּמִים אֲשֶׁר־אַתָּה שׁוֹכֵב עַל־צִדְּךָ שְׁלֹשׁ־מֵאוֹת וְתִשְׁעִים יוֹם תֹּאכְלֶנּוּ:

v'-a-TAH kakh l'-KHA khi-TEEN us-o-REEM u-FOL va-a-da-SHEEM v'-DO-khan v'-khu-s'-MEEM v'-na-ta-TAH o-TAM bikh-LEE e-KHAD v'-a-SEE-ta o-TAM l'-KHA l'-LA-khem mis-PAR ha-ya-MEEM a-sher a-TAH sho-KHAYV al tzi-d'-KHA sh'-losh may-OT v'-tish-EEM YOM to-kh'-LE-nu

10 The food that you eat shall be by weight, twenty *shekalim* a day; this you shall eat in the space of a day.

י וּמַאֲכָלְךָ אֲשֶׁר תֹּאכְלֶנּוּ בְּמִשְׁקוֹל עֶשְׂרִים שֶׁקֶל לַיּוֹם מֵעֵת עַד־עֵת תֹּאכְלֶנּוּ:

11 And you shall drink water by measure; drink a sixth of a *hin* in the space of a day.

יא וּמַיִם בִּמְשׂוּרָה תִשְׁתֶּה שִׁשִּׁית הַהִין מֵעֵת עַד־עֵת תִּשְׁתֶּה:

12 "Eat it as a barley cake; you shall bake it on human excrement before their eyes.

יב וְעֻגַת שְׂעֹרִים תֹּאכְלֶנָּה וְהִיא בְּגֶלְלֵי צֵאַת הָאָדָם תְּעֻגֶנָה לְעֵינֵיהֶם:

13 So," said *Hashem*, "shall the people of *Yisrael* eat their bread, unclean, among the nations to which I will banish them."

יג וַיֹּאמֶר יְהֹוָה כָּכָה יֹאכְלוּ בְנֵי־יִשְׂרָאֵל אֶת־לַחְמָם טָמֵא בַּגּוֹיִם אֲשֶׁר אַדִּיחֵם שָׁם:

14 Then I said, "Ah, *Hashem*, my person was never defiled; nor have I eaten anything that died of itself or was torn by beasts from my youth until now, nor has foul flesh entered my mouth."

יד וָאֹמַר אֲהָהּ אֲדֹנָי יְהֹוִה הִנֵּה נַפְשִׁי לֹא מְטֻמָּאָה וּנְבֵלָה וּטְרֵפָה לֹא־אָכַלְתִּי מִנְּעוּרַי וְעַד־עַתָּה וְלֹא־בָא בְּפִי בְּשַׂר פִּגּוּל:

15 He answered me, "See, I allow you cow's dung instead of human excrement; prepare your bread on that."

טו וַיֹּאמֶר אֵלַי רְאֵה נָתַתִּי לְךָ אֶת־צפועי [צְפִיעֵי] הַבָּקָר תַּחַת גֶּלְלֵי הָאָדָם וְעָשִׂיתָ אֶת־לַחְמְךָ עֲלֵיהֶם:

16 And He said to me, "O mortal, I am going to break the staff of bread in *Yerushalayim*, and they shall eat bread by weight, in anxiety, and drink water by measure, in horror,

טז וַיֹּאמֶר אֵלַי בֶּן־אָדָם הִנְנִי שֹׁבֵר מַטֵּה־לֶחֶם בִּירוּשָׁלַםִ וְאָכְלוּ־לֶחֶם בְּמִשְׁקָל וּבִדְאָגָה וּמַיִם בִּמְשׂוּרָה וּבְשִׁמָּמוֹן יִשְׁתּוּ:

17 so that, lacking bread and water, they shall stare at each other, heartsick over their iniquity.

יז לְמַעַן יַחְסְרוּ לֶחֶם וָמָיִם וְנָשַׁמּוּ אִישׁ וְאָחִיו וְנָמַקּוּ בַּעֲוֺנָם:

4:9 And bake them into bread *Yechezkel* demonstrates to his listeners the dire straits the people from *Yerushalayim* are in during the final Babylonian siege against the city. According to the Talmud (*Eruvin* 81a), *Yechezkel* rations to himself inedible flour and inferior grains and limits his water in order to portray the austere conditions under which the people of *Yerushalayim* are suffering. As a final blow, these foods are prepared in an impure manner (verse 13), something repulsive to the sensitive prophet-priest. Indeed, bread and water were very scarce during the Babylonian siege of *Yerushalayim*, as the Bible indicates elsewhere: "The tongue of the suckling cleaves to its palate for thirst. Little children beg for bread; none gives them a morsel." (Lamentations 4:4).

Yechezkel/Ezekiel
Chapter 5

יחזקאל
פרק ה

5 ¹ And you, O mortal, take a sharp knife; use it as a barber's razor and pass it over your head and beard. Then take scales and divide the hair.

א וְאַתָּה בֶן־אָדָם קַח־לְךָ חֶרֶב חַדָּה תַּעַר הַגַּלָּבִים תִּקָּחֶנָּה לָּךְ וְהַעֲבַרְתָּ עַל־רֹאשְׁךָ וְעַל־זְקָנֶךָ וְלָקַחְתָּ לְךָ מֹאזְנֵי מִשְׁקָל וְחִלַּקְתָּם׃

² When the days of siege are completed, destroy a third part in fire in the city, take a third and strike it with the sword all around the city, and scatter a third to the wind and unsheathe a sword after them.

ב שְׁלִשִׁית בָּאוּר תַּבְעִיר בְּתוֹךְ הָעִיר כִּמְלֹאת יְמֵי הַמָּצוֹר וְלָקַחְתָּ אֶת־הַשְּׁלִשִׁית תַּכֶּה בַחֶרֶב סְבִיבוֹתֶיהָ וְהַשְּׁלִשִׁית תִּזְרֶה לָרוּחַ וְחֶרֶב אָרִיק אַחֲרֵיהֶם׃

³ "Take also a few [hairs] from there and tie them up in your skirts.

ג וְלָקַחְתָּ מִשָּׁם מְעַט בְּמִסְפָּר וְצַרְתָּ אוֹתָם בִּכְנָפֶיךָ׃

⁴ And take some more of them and cast them into the fire, and burn them in the fire. From this a fire shall go out upon the whole House of *Yisrael*."

ד וּמֵהֶם עוֹד תִּקָּח וְהִשְׁלַכְתָּ אוֹתָם אֶל־תּוֹךְ הָאֵשׁ וְשָׂרַפְתָּ אֹתָם בָּאֵשׁ מִמֶּנּוּ תֵצֵא־אֵשׁ אֶל־כָּל־בֵּית יִשְׂרָאֵל׃

⁵ Thus said *Hashem*: I set this *Yerushalayim* in the midst of nations, with countries round about her.

ה כֹּה אָמַר אֲדֹנָי יֱהֹוִה זֹאת יְרוּשָׁלַם בְּתוֹךְ הַגּוֹיִם שַׂמְתִּיהָ וּסְבִיבוֹתֶיהָ אֲרָצוֹת׃

KOH a-MAR a-do-NAI e-lo-HEEM ZOT y'-ru-sha-LA-im b'-TOKH ha-go-YIM sam-TEE-ha us-vee-vo-TE-ha a-ra-TZOT

⁶ But she rebelled against My rules and My laws, acting more wickedly than the nations and the countries round about her; she rejected My rules and disobeyed My laws.

ו וַתֶּמֶר אֶת־מִשְׁפָּטַי לְרִשְׁעָה מִן־הַגּוֹיִם וְאֶת־חֻקּוֹתַי מִן־הָאֲרָצוֹת אֲשֶׁר סְבִיבוֹתֶיהָ כִּי בְמִשְׁפָּטַי מָאָסוּ וְחֻקּוֹתַי לֹא־הָלְכוּ בָהֶם׃

⁷ Assuredly, thus said *Hashem*: Because you have outdone the nations that are round about you – you have not obeyed My laws or followed My rules, nor have you observed the rules of the nations round about you –

ז לָכֵן כֹּה־אָמַר אֲדֹנָי יֱהֹוִה יַעַן הֲמָנְכֶם מִן־הַגּוֹיִם אֲשֶׁר סְבִיבוֹתֵיכֶם בְּחֻקּוֹתַי לֹא הֲלַכְתֶּם וְאֶת־מִשְׁפָּטַי לֹא עֲשִׂיתֶם וּכְמִשְׁפְּטֵי הַגּוֹיִם אֲשֶׁר סְבִיבוֹתֵיכֶם לֹא עֲשִׂיתֶם׃

⁸ assuredly, thus said *Hashem*: I, in turn, am going to deal with you, and I will execute judgments in your midst in the sight of the nations.

ח לָכֵן כֹּה אָמַר אֲדֹנָי יֱהֹוִה הִנְנִי עָלַיִךְ גַּם־אָנִי וְעָשִׂיתִי בְתוֹכֵךְ מִשְׁפָּטִים לְעֵינֵי הַגּוֹיִם׃

⁹ On account of all your abominations, I will do among you what I have never done, and the like of which I will never do again.

ט וְעָשִׂיתִי בָךְ אֵת אֲשֶׁר לֹא־עָשִׂיתִי וְאֵת אֲשֶׁר־לֹא־אֶעֱשֶׂה כָמֹהוּ עוֹד יַעַן כָּל־תּוֹעֲבֹתָיִךְ׃

Rabbi Yitzchak Abarbanel (1437–1508)

5:5 I set this *Yerushalayim* in the midst of nations God tells *Yechezkel* that He has set *Yerushalayim* as the center of the world, the rest of the countries around it. In medieval times, *Yerushalayim* was literally thought of as the center of the world, and maps were drawn to reflect that understanding. *Yerushalayim* remains the religious and spiritual center of the world, as it says (Isaiah 2:3) "For instruction shall come forth from *Tzion*, the word of *Hashem* from *Yerushalayim*" Indeed, all the major monotheistic religions of the Western world consider *Yerushalayim* to be their holy city, and it contains their most sacred places. As Rabbi Yitzchak Abarbanel analogizes, "the heart is to the rest of the body as *Yerushalayim* is to the world."

Yechezkel/Ezekiel
Chapter 6

10 Assuredly, parents shall eat their children in your midst, and children shall eat their parents. I will execute judgments against you, and I will scatter all your survivors in every direction.

11 Assuredly, as I live – said *Hashem* – because you defiled My Sanctuary with all your detestable things and all your abominations, I in turn will shear [you] away and show no pity. I in turn will show no compassion:

12 One-third of you shall die of pestilence or perish in your midst by famine, one-third shall fall by the sword around you, and I will scatter one-third in every direction and will unsheathe the sword after them.

13 I will vent all My anger and satisfy My fury upon them; and when I vent all My fury upon them, they shall know that I *Hashem* have spoken in My passion.

14 I will make you a ruin and a mockery among the nations roundabout you, in the sight of every passerby.

15 And when I execute judgment upon you in anger and rage and furious chastisement, you shall be a mockery and a derision, a warning and a horror, to the nations roundabout you: I *Hashem* have spoken.

16 When I loose the deadly arrows of famine against those doomed to destruction, when I loose them against you to destroy you, I will heap more famine upon you and break your staff of bread.

17 I will let loose against you famine and wild beasts and they shall bereave you; pestilence and bloodshed shall sweep through you, and I will bring the sword upon you. I *Hashem* have spoken.

6

1 The word of *Hashem* came to me:

2 O mortal, turn your face toward the mountains of *Yisrael* and prophesy to them

ben a-DAM SEEM pa-NE-kha el ha-RAY yis-ra-AYL v'-hi-na-VAY a-lay-HEM

6:2 O mortal Throughout the book of *Yechezkel*, God consistently refers to *Yechezkel* as ben adam (בן אדם), meaning 'son of man' or 'mortal.' *Adam* (אדם) is the Hebrew word for 'man.' According to Rabbi Matityahu Glazerson, this word is reflective of the three partners who participate in the creation of a human being: the

Yechezkel/Ezekiel
Chapter 6

יחזקאל
פרק ו

3 and say: O mountains of *Yisrael*, hear the word of *Hashem*. Thus said *Hashem* to the mountains and the hills, to the streams and the valleys: See, I will bring a sword against you and destroy your shrines.

ג וְאָמַרְתָּ הָרֵי יִשְׂרָאֵל שִׁמְעוּ דְּבַר־אֲדֹנָי יֱהֹוִה כֹּה־אָמַר אֲדֹנָי יֱהֹוִה לֶהָרִים וְלַגְּבָעוֹת לָאֲפִיקִים וְלַגֵּאָיוֹת [וְלַגֵּאָיוֹת] הִנְנִי אֲנִי מֵבִיא עֲלֵיכֶם חֶרֶב וְאִבַּדְתִּי בָּמֽוֹתֵיכֶֽם׃

4 Your altars shall be wrecked and your incense stands smashed, and I will hurl down your slain in front of your fetishes.

ד וְנָשַׁמּוּ מִזְבְּחוֹתֵיכֶם וְנִשְׁבְּרוּ חַמָּנֵיכֶם וְהִפַּלְתִּי חַלְלֵיכֶם לִפְנֵי גִּלּוּלֵיכֶֽם׃

5 I will cast the corpses of the people of *Yisrael* in front of their fetishes, and scatter your bones around your altars

ה וְנָתַתִּי אֶת־פִּגְרֵי בְּנֵי יִשְׂרָאֵל לִפְנֵי גִּלּוּלֵיהֶם וְזֵרִיתִי אֶת־עַצְמֽוֹתֵיכֶם סְבִיבוֹת מִזְבְּחֽוֹתֵיכֶֽם׃

6 in all your settlements. The towns shall be laid waste and the shrines shall be devastated. Thus your altars shall be laid waste and bear their punishment; your fetishes shall be smashed and annihilated, your incense stands cut down, and your handiwork wiped out;

ו בְּכֹל מוֹשְׁבֽוֹתֵיכֶם הֶעָרִים תֶּחֱרַבְנָה וְהַבָּמוֹת תִּישָׁמְנָה לְמַעַן יֶחֶרְבוּ וְיֶאְשְׁמוּ מִזְבְּחֽוֹתֵיכֶם וְנִשְׁבְּרוּ וְנִשְׁבְּתוּ גִּלּוּלֵיכֶם וְנִגְדְּעוּ חַמָּנֵיכֶם וְנִמְחוּ מַעֲשֵׂיכֶֽם׃

7 and the slain shall fall in your midst. Then you shall know that I am *Hashem*.

ז וְנָפַל חָלָל בְּתוֹכְכֶם וִידַעְתֶּם כִּי־אֲנִי יְהֹוָֽה׃

8 Yet I will leave a remnant, in that some of you shall escape the sword among the nations and be scattered through the lands.

ח וְהוֹתַרְתִּי בִּהְיוֹת לָכֶם פְּלִיטֵי חֶרֶב בַּגּוֹיִם בְּהִזָּרוֹתֵיכֶם בָּאֲרָצֽוֹת׃

9 And those of you that escape will remember Me among the nations where they have been taken captive, how I was brokenhearted through their faithless hearts which turned away from Me, and through their eyes which lusted after their fetishes. And they shall loathe themselves for all the evil they committed and for all their abominable deeds.

ט וְזָכְרוּ פְלִיטֵיכֶם אוֹתִי בַּגּוֹיִם אֲשֶׁר נִשְׁבּוּ־שָׁם אֲשֶׁר נִשְׁבַּרְתִּי אֶת־לִבָּם הַזּוֹנֶה אֲשֶׁר־סָר מֵעָלַי וְאֵת עֵינֵיהֶם הַזֹּנוֹת אַחֲרֵי גִּלּוּלֵיהֶם וְנָקֹטּוּ בִּפְנֵיהֶם אֶל־הָרָעוֹת אֲשֶׁר עָשׂוּ לְכֹל תּוֹעֲבֹתֵיהֶֽם׃

10 Then they shall realize it was not without cause that I *Hashem* resolved to bring this evil upon them.

י וְיָדְעוּ כִּי־אֲנִי יְהֹוָה לֹא אֶל־חִנָּם דִּבַּרְתִּי לַעֲשׂוֹת לָהֶם הָרָעָה הַזֹּֽאת׃

11 Thus said *Hashem*: Strike your hands together and stamp your feet and cry: Aha! over all the vile abominations of the House of *Yisrael* who shall fall by the sword, by famine, and by pestilence.

יא כֹּֽה־אָמַר אֲדֹנָי יֱהֹוִה הַכֵּה בְכַפְּךָ וּרְקַע בְּרַגְלְךָ וֶאֱמָר־אָח אֶל כָּל־תּוֹעֲבוֹת רָעוֹת בֵּית יִשְׂרָאֵל אֲשֶׁר בַּחֶרֶב בָּרָעָב וּבַדֶּבֶר יִפֹּֽלוּ׃

12 He who is far away shall die of pestilence, and he who is near shall fall by the sword, and he who survives and is protected shall die of famine. Thus I will spend My fury upon them.

יב הָרָחוֹק בַּדֶּבֶר יָמוּת וְהַקָּרוֹב בַּחֶרֶב יִפּוֹל וְהַנִּשְׁאָר וְהַנָּצוּר בָּרָעָב יָמוּת וְכִלֵּיתִי חֲמָתִי בָּֽם׃

---

father, the mother and the Holy One, blessed is He. The letter *alef* (א), whose numerical value is one, represents, the Holy One who provides the spiritual component, the soul. The remaining two letters, *dalet* (ד) and *mem* (מ), spell *dam* (דם), meaning 'blood,' which symbolizes the physical aspect contributed by the father and mother.

1221

Yechezkel/Ezekiel

Chapter 6 (cont.)

13 And you shall know that I am *Hashem*, when your slain lie among the fetishes round about their altars, on every high hill, on all the mountaintops, under every green tree, and under every leafy oak – wherever they presented pleasing odors to all their fetishes.

14 I will stretch out My hand against them, and lay the land waste and desolate in all their settlements, from the wilderness as far as Diblah; then they shall know that I am *Hashem*.

Chapter 7

1 The word of *Hashem* came to me:

2 You, O mortal, [say:] Thus said *Hashem* to the land of *Yisrael*: Doom! Doom is coming upon the four corners of the land.

3 Now doom is upon you! I will let loose My anger against you and judge you according to your ways; I will requite you for all your abominations.

4 I will show you no pity and no compassion; but I will requite you for your ways and for the abominations in your midst. And you shall know that I am *Hashem*.

5 Thus said *Hashem*: A singular disaster; a disaster is coming.

6 Doom is coming! The hour of doom is coming! It stirs against you; there it comes!

7 The cycle has come around for you, O inhabitants of the land; the time has come; the day is near. There is panic on the mountains, not joy.

8 Very soon I will pour out My wrath upon you and spend My anger on you; I will judge you according to your ways, and I will requite you for all your abominations.

9 I will show you no pity and no compassion; but I will requite you for your ways, and for the abominations in your midst. And you shall know it was I *Hashem* who punished.

10 Here is the day! See, the cycle has come round; it has appeared. The rod has blossomed; arrogance has budded,

11 lawlessness has grown into a rod of wickedness. Nothing comes of them, nor of their abundance, nor of their wealth; nor is there preeminence among them.

Yechezkel/Ezekiel
Chapter 7

יחזקאל
פרק ז

12 The time has come, the day has arrived. Let not the buyer rejoice nor the seller mourn – for divine wrath shall overtake all her multitude.

יב בָּא הָעֵת הִגִּיעַ הַיּוֹם הַקּוֹנֶה אַל־יִשְׂמָח וְהַמּוֹכֵר אַל־יִתְאַבָּל כִּי חָרוֹן אֶל־כָּל־הֲמוֹנָהּ:

13 For the seller shall not return to what he sold so long as they remain among the living. For the vision concerns all her multitude, it shall not be revoked. And because of his guilt, no man shall hold fast to his life.

יג כִּי הַמּוֹכֵר אֶל־הַמִּמְכָּר לֹא יָשׁוּב וְעוֹד בַּחַיִּים חַיָּתָם כִּי־חָזוֹן אֶל־כָּל־הֲמוֹנָהּ לֹא יָשׁוּב וְאִישׁ בַּעֲוֹנוֹ חַיָּתוֹ לֹא יִתְחַזָּקוּ:

> KEE ha-mo-KHAYR el ha-mim-KAR LO ya-SHUV v'-OD ba-kha-YEEM kha-ya-TAM kee kha-ZON el kol ha-mo-NAH LO ya-SHUV v'-EESH ba-a-vo-NO kha-ya-TO lo yit-kha-ZA-ku

14 They have sounded the horn, and all is prepared; but no one goes to battle, for My wrath is directed against all her multitude.

יד תָּקְעוּ בַתָּקוֹעַ וְהָכִין הַכֹּל וְאֵין הֹלֵךְ לַמִּלְחָמָה כִּי חֲרוֹנִי אֶל־כָּל־הֲמוֹנָהּ:

15 The sword is outside and pestilence and famine are inside; he who is in the open shall die by the sword, he who is in the town shall be devoured by famine and pestilence.

טו הַחֶרֶב בַּחוּץ וְהַדֶּבֶר וְהָרָעָב מִבָּיִת אֲשֶׁר בַּשָּׂדֶה בַּחֶרֶב יָמוּת וַאֲשֶׁר בָּעִיר רָעָב וָדֶבֶר יֹאכְלֶנּוּ:

16 And if any survive, they shall take to the mountains; they shall be like doves of the valley, moaning together – every one for his iniquity.

טז וּפָלְטוּ פְּלִיטֵיהֶם וְהָיוּ אֶל־הֶהָרִים כְּיוֹנֵי הַגֵּאָיוֹת כֻּלָּם הֹמוֹת אִישׁ בַּעֲוֹנוֹ:

17 All hands shall grow weak, and all knees shall turn to water.

יז כָּל־הַיָּדַיִם תִּרְפֶּינָה וְכָל־בִּרְכַּיִם תֵּלַכְנָה מָּיִם:

18 They shall gird on sackcloth, and horror shall cover them; every face shall betray shame, and every head shall be made bald.

יח וְחָגְרוּ שַׂקִּים וְכִסְּתָה אוֹתָם פַּלָּצוּת וְאֶל כָּל־פָּנִים בּוּשָׁה וּבְכָל־רָאשֵׁיהֶם קָרְחָה:

19 They shall throw their silver into the streets, and their gold shall be treated as something unclean. Their silver and gold shall not avail to save them in the day of *Hashem*'s wrath – to satisfy their hunger or to fill their stomachs. Because they made them stumble into guilt –

יט כַּסְפָּם בַּחוּצוֹת יַשְׁלִיכוּ וּזְהָבָם לְנִדָּה יִהְיֶה כַּסְפָּם וּזְהָבָם לֹא־יוּכַל לְהַצִּילָם בְּיוֹם עֶבְרַת יְהֹוָה נַפְשָׁם לֹא יְשַׂבֵּעוּ וּמֵעֵיהֶם לֹא יְמַלֵּאוּ כִּי־מִכְשׁוֹל עֲוֹנָם הָיָה:

20 for out of their beautiful adornments, in which they took pride, they made their images and their detestable abominations – therefore I will make them an unclean thing to them.

כ וּצְבִי עֶדְיוֹ לְגָאוֹן שָׂמָהוּ וְצַלְמֵי תוֹעֲבֹתָם שִׁקּוּצֵיהֶם עָשׂוּ בוֹ עַל־כֵּן נְתַתִּיו לָהֶם לְנִדָּה:

7:13 For the seller shall not return to what he sold The Land of Israel is a sacred trust from *Hashem*, and in biblical times familial properties could be sold only in times of dire necessity. These sales were always considered temporary, and the family would make extreme efforts to redeem their property, their physical connection to the Holy Land (Leviticus 25). During the *yovel*, the Jubilee year, even lands which had not been redeemed would be returned to the original owners. In this bitter prophecy, *Yechezkel* warns that the upcoming exile will prevent both buyer and seller from enjoying the land, since they will be exiled from *Eretz Yisrael*.

Yechezkel/Ezekiel
Chapter 8

21 I will give them as spoil to strangers, and as plunder to the wicked of the earth; and they shall defile them.

22 I will turn My face from them, and My treasures shall be defiled; ruffians shall invade it and defile it.

23 Forge the chain, for the land is full of bloody crimes, and the city is full of lawlessness.

24 I will bring in the worst of the nations to take possession of their houses; so shall I turn to naught the pride of the powerful, and their sanctuaries shall be defiled.

25 Horror comes, and they shall seek safety, but there shall be none.

26 Calamity shall follow calamity, and rumor follow rumor. Then they shall seek vision from the *Navi* in vain; instruction shall perish from the *Kohen*, and counsel from the elders.

27 The king shall mourn, the prince shall clothe himself with desolation, and the hands of the people of the land shall tremble. I will treat them in accordance with their own ways and judge them according to their deserts. And they shall know that I am *Hashem*.

8

1 In the sixth year, on the fifth day of the sixth month, I was sitting at home, and the elders of *Yehuda* were sitting before me, and there the hand of *Hashem* fell upon me.

2 As I looked, there was a figure that had the appearance of fire: from what appeared as his loins down, [he was] fire; and from his loins up, his appearance was resplendent and had the color of amber.

3 He stretched out the form of a hand, and took me by the hair of my head. A spirit lifted me up between heaven and earth and brought me in visions of *Hashem* to *Yerushalayim*, to the entrance of the Penimith Gate that faces north; that was the site of the infuriating image that provokes fury.

4 And the Presence of the God of *Yisrael* appeared there, like the vision that I had seen in the valley.

5 And He said to me, "O mortal, turn your eyes northward." I turned my eyes northward, and there, north of the gate of the *Mizbayach*, was that infuriating image on the approach.

Yechezkel/Ezekiel
Chapter 8

יחזקאל
פרק ח

6 And He said to me, "Mortal, do you see what they are doing, the terrible abominations that the House of *Yisrael* is practicing here, to drive Me far from My Sanctuary? You shall yet see even greater abominations!"

ו וַיֹּאמֶר אֵלַי בֶּן־אָדָם הֲרֹאֶה אַתָּה מֵהֶם [מָה] [הֵם] עֹשִׂים תּוֹעֵבוֹת גְּדֹלוֹת אֲשֶׁר בֵּית־יִשְׂרָאֵל עֹשִׂים פֹּה לְרָחֳקָה מֵעַל מִקְדָּשִׁי וְעוֹד תָּשׁוּב תִּרְאֶה תּוֹעֵבוֹת גְּדֹלוֹת:

7 Then He brought me to the entrance of the court; and I looked, and there was a hole in the wall.

ז וַיָּבֵא אֹתִי אֶל־פֶּתַח הֶחָצֵר וָאֶרְאֶה וְהִנֵּה חֹר־אֶחָד בַּקִּיר:

8 He said to me, "Mortal, break through the wall"; so I broke through the wall and found an entrance.

ח וַיֹּאמֶר אֵלַי בֶּן־אָדָם חֲתָר־נָא בַקִּיר וָאֶחְתֹּר בַּקִּיר וְהִנֵּה פֶּתַח אֶחָד:

9 And He said to me, "Enter and see the vile abominations that they are practicing here."

ט וַיֹּאמֶר אֵלָי בֹּא וּרְאֵה אֶת־הַתּוֹעֵבוֹת הָרָעוֹת אֲשֶׁר הֵם עֹשִׂים פֹּה:

10 I entered and looked, and there all detestable forms of creeping things and beasts and all the fetishes of the House of *Yisrael* were depicted over the entire wall.

י וָאָבוֹא וָאֶרְאֶה וְהִנֵּה כָל־תַּבְנִית רֶמֶשׂ וּבְהֵמָה שֶׁקֶץ וְכָל־גִּלּוּלֵי בֵּית יִשְׂרָאֵל מְחֻקֶּה עַל־הַקִּיר סָבִיב סָבִיב:

11 Before them stood seventy men, elders of the House of *Yisrael*, with Jaazaniah son of *Shafan* standing in their midst. Everyone had a censer in his hand, and a thick cloud of incense smoke ascended.

יא וְשִׁבְעִים אִישׁ מִזִּקְנֵי בֵית־יִשְׂרָאֵל וְיַאֲזַנְיָהוּ בֶן־שָׁפָן עֹמֵד בְּתוֹכָם עֹמְדִים לִפְנֵיהֶם וְאִישׁ מִקְטַרְתּוֹ בְּיָדוֹ וַעֲתַר עֲנַן־הַקְּטֹרֶת עֹלֶה:

12 Again He spoke to me, "O mortal, have you seen what the elders of the House of *Yisrael* are doing in the darkness, everyone in his image-covered chamber? For they say, '*Hashem* does not see us; *Hashem* has abandoned the country.'"

יב וַיֹּאמֶר אֵלַי הֲרָאִיתָ בֶן־אָדָם אֲשֶׁר זִקְנֵי בֵית־יִשְׂרָאֵל עֹשִׂים בַּחֹשֶׁךְ אִישׁ בְּחַדְרֵי מַשְׂכִּיתוֹ כִּי אֹמְרִים אֵין יְהֹוָה רֹאֶה אֹתָנוּ עָזַב יְהֹוָה אֶת־הָאָרֶץ:

va-YO-mer ay-LAI ha-ra-EE-ta ven a-DAM a-SHER zik-NAY vayt yis-ra-AYL o-SEEM ba-KHO-shekh EESH b'-khad-RAY mas-kee-TO KEE o-m'-REEM AYN a-do-NAI ro-EH o-TA-nu a-ZAV a-do-NAI et ha-A-retz

13 And He said to me, "You shall see even more terrible abominations which they practice."

יג וַיֹּאמֶר אֵלָי עוֹד תָּשׁוּב תִּרְאֶה תּוֹעֵבוֹת גְּדֹלוֹת אֲשֶׁר־הֵמָּה עֹשִׂים:

14 Next He brought me to the entrance of the north gate of the House of *Hashem*; and there sat the women bewailing Tammuz.

יד וַיָּבֵא אֹתִי אֶל־פֶּתַח שַׁעַר בֵּית־יְהֹוָה אֲשֶׁר אֶל־הַצָּפוֹנָה וְהִנֵּה־שָׁם הַנָּשִׁים יֹשְׁבוֹת מְבַכּוֹת אֶת־הַתַּמּוּז:

15 He said to me, "Have you seen, O mortal? You shall see even more terrible abominations than these."

טו וַיֹּאמֶר אֵלַי הֲרָאִיתָ בֶן־אָדָם עוֹד תָּשׁוּב תִּרְאֶה תּוֹעֵבוֹת גְּדֹלוֹת מֵאֵלֶּה:

8:12 Have you seen what the elders of the House of *Yisrael* are doing To explain the upcoming destruction of *Yerushalayim*, *Yechezkel* is shown a scene of the city's elders secretly practicing idolatry within the confines of the Temple. Though they hide their abominations from the public, they do not hesitate to engage in this repugnant behavior. They see the upcoming downfall of *Yehuda* and *Yerushalayim*, but instead of concluding that repentance is needed, the corrupt elders choose to believe that God has rejected His people and "abandoned the country," which leads them to forsake *Hashem* and engage in idolatry.

Yechezkel/Ezekiel
Chapter 9

יחזקאל
פרק ט

16 Then He brought me into the inner court of the House of *Hashem*, and there, at the entrance to the Temple of *Hashem*, between the portico and the *Mizbayach*, were about twenty-five men, their backs to the Temple of *Hashem* and their faces to the east; they were bowing low to the sun in the east.

טז וַיָּבֵא אֹתִי אֶל־חֲצַר בֵּית־יְהֹוָה הַפְּנִימִית וְהִנֵּה־פֶתַח הֵיכַל יְהֹוָה בֵּין הָאוּלָם וּבֵין הַמִּזְבֵּחַ כְּעֶשְׂרִים וַחֲמִשָּׁה אִישׁ אֲחֹרֵיהֶם אֶל־הֵיכַל יְהֹוָה וּפְנֵיהֶם קֵדְמָה וְהֵמָּה מִשְׁתַּחֲוִיתֶם קֵדְמָה לַשָּׁמֶשׁ:

17 And He said to me, "Do you see, O mortal? Is it not enough for the House of *Yehuda* to practice the abominations that they have committed here, that they must fill the country with lawlessness and provoke Me still further and thrust the branch to their nostrils?

יז וַיֹּאמֶר אֵלַי הֲרָאִיתָ בֶן־אָדָם הֲנָקֵל לְבֵית יְהוּדָה מֵעֲשׂוֹת אֶת־הַתּוֹעֵבוֹת אֲשֶׁר עָשׂוּ־פֹה כִּי־מָלְאוּ אֶת־הָאָרֶץ חָמָס וַיָּשֻׁבוּ לְהַכְעִיסֵנִי וְהִנָּם שֹׁלְחִים אֶת־הַזְּמוֹרָה אֶל־אַפָּם:

18 I in turn will act with fury, I will show no pity or compassion; though they cry aloud to Me, I will not listen to them."

יח וְגַם־אֲנִי אֶעֱשֶׂה בְחֵמָה לֹא־תָחוֹס עֵינִי וְלֹא אֶחְמֹל וְקָרְאוּ בְאָזְנַי קוֹל גָּדוֹל וְלֹא אֶשְׁמַע אוֹתָם:

9 1 Then He called loudly in my hearing, saying, "Approach, you men in charge of the city, each bearing his weapons of destruction!"

ט א וַיִּקְרָא בְאָזְנַי קוֹל גָּדוֹל לֵאמֹר קָרְבוּ פְּקֻדּוֹת הָעִיר וְאִישׁ כְּלִי מַשְׁחֵתוֹ בְּיָדוֹ:

2 And six men entered by way of the upper gate that faces north, each with his club in his hand; and among them was another, clothed in linen, with a writing case at his waist. They came forward and stopped at the bronze *Mizbayach*.

ב וְהִנֵּה שִׁשָּׁה אֲנָשִׁים בָּאִים מִדֶּרֶךְ־שַׁעַר הָעֶלְיוֹן אֲשֶׁר מָפְנֶה צָפוֹנָה וְאִישׁ כְּלִי מַפָּצוֹ בְּיָדוֹ וְאִישׁ־אֶחָד בְּתוֹכָם לָבֻשׁ בַּדִּים וְקֶסֶת הַסֹּפֵר בְּמָתְנָיו וַיָּבֹאוּ וַיַּעַמְדוּ אֵצֶל מִזְבַּח הַנְּחֹשֶׁת:

3 Now the Presence of the God of *Yisrael* had moved from the cherub on which it had rested to the platform of the House. He called to the man clothed in linen with the writing case at his waist;

ג וּכְבוֹד אֱלֹהֵי יִשְׂרָאֵל נַעֲלָה מֵעַל הַכְּרוּב אֲשֶׁר הָיָה עָלָיו אֶל מִפְתַּן הַבָּיִת וַיִּקְרָא אֶל־הָאִישׁ הַלָּבֻשׁ הַבַּדִּים אֲשֶׁר קֶסֶת הַסֹּפֵר בְּמָתְנָיו:

4 and *Hashem* said to him, "Pass through the city, through *Yerushalayim*, and put a mark on the foreheads of the men who moan and groan because of all the abominations that are committed in it."

ד וַיֹּאמֶר יְהֹוָה אֵלָו [אֵלָיו] עֲבֹר בְּתוֹךְ הָעִיר בְּתוֹךְ יְרוּשָׁלָ͏ִם וְהִתְוִיתָ תָּו עַל־מִצְחוֹת הָאֲנָשִׁים הַנֶּאֱנָחִים וְהַנֶּאֱנָקִים עַל כָּל־הַתּוֹעֵבוֹת הַנַּעֲשׂוֹת בְּתוֹכָהּ:

va-YO-mer a-do-NAI ay-LAV a-VOR b'-TOKH ha-EER b'-TOKH y'-ru-sha-LA-im v'-hit-VEE-ta TAV al mitz-KHOT ha-a-na-SHEEM ha-ne-e-na-KHEEM v'-ha-ne-e-na-KEEM AL kol ha-TO-ay-VOT ha-na-a-SOT b'-to-KHAH

9:4 And put a mark on the foreheads of the men who moan and groan *Yechezkel* is shown a vision of the death of the guilty in *Yerushalayim*. Before the executions commence, he sees a messenger in white linen mark the foreheads of those who grieve and lament over the destruction, ensuring that a righteous remnant remains. 'To set a mark' in Hebrew is *vihitveeta tav* (התוית תו), based on which the sages explain that the mark that was made was the Hebrew letter *tav* (ת). Like the mark of Cain, which, according to *Rashi* was also a Hebrew letter, this mark is intended to save its bearers from harm.

תו

Yechezkel/Ezekiel
Chapter 10

יחזקאל
פרק י

5 To the others He said in my hearing, "Follow him through the city and strike; show no pity or compassion.

ה וּלְאֵ֙לֶּה֙ אָמַ֣ר בְּאָזְנַ֔י עִבְר֥וּ בָעִ֖יר אַחֲרָ֑יו וְהַכּ֕וּ עַל־[אַל־] תָּחֹ֥ס עֵינֵיכֶ֖ם [עֵינְכֶ֖ם] וְאַל־תַּחְמֹֽלוּ׃

6 Kill off graybeard, youth and maiden, women and children; but do not touch any person who bears the mark. Begin here at My Sanctuary." So they began with the elders who were in front of the House.

ו זָקֵ֡ן בָּח֣וּר וּבְתוּלָה֩ וְטַ֨ף וְנָשִׁ֜ים תַּהַרְג֣וּ לְמַשְׁחִ֗ית וְעַל־כׇּל־אִ֨ישׁ אֲשֶׁר־עָלָ֤יו הַתָּו֙ אַל־תִּגַּ֔שׁוּ וּמִמִּקְדָּשִׁ֖י תָּחֵ֑לּוּ וַיָּחֵ֙לּוּ֙ בָּאֲנָשִׁ֣ים הַזְּקֵנִ֔ים אֲשֶׁ֖ר לִפְנֵ֥י הַבָּֽיִת׃

7 And He said to them, "Defile the House and fill the courts with the slain. Then go forth." So they went forth and began to kill in the city.

ז וַיֹּ֣אמֶר אֲלֵיהֶ֗ם טַמְּא֤וּ אֶת־הַבַּ֙יִת֙ וּמַלְא֥וּ אֶת־הַחֲצֵר֖וֹת חֲלָלִ֑ים צֵ֥אוּ וְיָצְא֖וּ וְהִכּ֥וּ בָעִֽיר׃

8 When they were out killing, and I remained alone, I flung myself on my face and cried out, "Ah, *Hashem*! Are you going to annihilate all that is left of *Yisrael*, pouring out Your fury upon *Yerushalayim*?"

ח וַיְהִי֙ כְּהַכּוֹתָ֔ם וְנֵאשֲׁאַ֖ר אָ֑נִי וָאֶפְּלָ֨ה עַל־פָּנַ֜י וָאֶזְעַ֗ק וָאֹמַר֙ אֲהָהּ֙ אֲדֹנָ֣י יֱהֹוִ֔ה הֲמַשְׁחִ֣ית אַתָּ֔ה אֵ֖ת כׇּל־שְׁאֵרִ֣ית יִשְׂרָאֵ֑ל בְּשׇׁפְכְּךָ֥ אֶת־חֲמָתְךָ֖ עַל־יְרוּשָׁלָֽ͏ִם׃

9 He answered me, "The iniquity of the Houses of *Yehuda* and *Yisrael* is very very great, the land is full of crime and the city is full of corruption. For they say, '*Hashem* has forsaken the land, and *Hashem* does not see.'

ט וַיֹּ֣אמֶר אֵלַ֗י עֲוֺ֨ן בֵּית־יִשְׂרָאֵ֤ל וִיהוּדָה֙ גָּד֣וֹל בִּמְאֹ֣ד מְאֹ֔ד וַתִּמָּלֵ֤א הָאָ֙רֶץ֙ דָּמִ֔ים וְהָעִ֖יר מָֽלְאָ֣ה מֻטֶּ֑ה כִּ֣י אָמְר֗וּ עָזַ֤ב יְהֹוָה֙ אֶת־הָאָ֔רֶץ וְאֵ֥ין יְהֹוָ֖ה רֹאֶֽה׃

10 I, in turn, will show no pity or compassion; I will give them their deserts."

י וְגַ֨ם־אֲנִ֔י לֹא־תָח֥וֹס עֵינִ֖י וְלֹ֣א אֶחְמֹ֑ל דַּרְכָּ֖ם בְּרֹאשָׁ֥ם נָתָֽתִּי׃

11 And then the man clothed in linen with the writing case at his waist brought back word, saying, "I have done as You commanded me."

יא וְהִנֵּ֣ה הָאִ֣ישׁ ׀ לְבֻ֣שׁ הַבַּדִּ֗ים אֲשֶׁ֤ר הַקֶּ֙סֶת֙ בְּמׇתְנָ֔יו מֵשִׁ֥יב דָּבָ֖ר לֵאמֹ֑ר עָשִׂ֕יתִי כַּאֲשֶׁר [כְּכֹ֖ל] [אֲשֶׁ֥ר] צִוִּיתָֽנִי׃

10

1 I looked, and on the expanse over the heads of the cherubs, there was something like a sapphire stone; an appearance resembling a throne could be seen over them.

י א וָאֶרְאֶ֗ה וְהִנֵּ֤ה אֶל־הָרָקִ֙יעַ֙ אֲשֶׁר֙ עַל־רֹ֣אשׁ הַכְּרֻבִ֔ים כְּאֶ֣בֶן סַפִּ֔יר כְּמַרְאֵ֖ה דְּמ֣וּת כִּסֵּ֑א נִרְאָ֖ה עֲלֵיהֶֽם׃

va-er-EH v'-hi-NAY el ha-ra-KEE-a a-SHER al ROSH ha-k'-ru-VEEM k'-E-ven sa-PEER k'-mar-AY d'-MUT ki-SAY nir-AH a-lay-HEM

10:1 On the expanse over the heads of the cherubs Chapter 10 contains the second description of God's throne departing from *Yerushalayim*. The man in white linen, mentioned in chapter 9, takes coals from between the cherubim to set the city ablaze, and the glory of *Hashem* then moves away while fire purges the city. In the Bible, cherubim appear as dividers between *Hashem* and humanity. The first time they appear, they block the entrance to the Garden of Eden (Genesis 3:24). They are also found on the veil that separates the holy places in the *Mishkan* and the *Beit Hamikdash* from the Holy of Holies (Exodus 36:35, 1 Kings 6:23). Here, the cherubim appear again, as *Hashem* separates Himself from the sinful city.

Yechezkel/Ezekiel
Chapter 10

יחזקאל
פרק י

2 He spoke to the man clothed in linen and said, "Step inside the wheelwork, under the cherubs, and fill your hands with glowing coals from among the cherubs, and scatter them over the city." And he went in as I looked on.

ב וַיֹּאמֶר אֶל־הָאִישׁ לְבֻשׁ הַבַּדִּים וַיֹּאמֶר בֹּא אֶל־בֵּינוֹת לַגַּלְגַּל אֶל־תַּחַת לַכְּרוּב וּמַלֵּא חָפְנֶיךָ גַחֲלֵי־אֵשׁ מִבֵּינוֹת לַכְּרֻבִים וּזְרֹק עַל־הָעִיר וַיָּבֹא לְעֵינָי׃

3 Now the cherubs were standing on the south side of the House when the man entered, and the cloud filled the inner court.

ג וְהַכְּרֻבִים עֹמְדִים מִימִין לַבַּיִת בְּבֹאוֹ הָאִישׁ וְהֶעָנָן מָלֵא אֶת־הֶחָצֵר הַפְּנִימִית׃

4 But when the Presence of *Hashem* moved from the cherubs to the platform of the House, the House was filled with the cloud, and the court was filled with the radiance of the Presence of *Hashem*.

ד וַיָּרָם כְּבוֹד־יְהֹוָה מֵעַל הַכְּרוּב עַל מִפְתַּן הַבָּיִת וַיִּמָּלֵא הַבַּיִת אֶת־הֶעָנָן וְהֶחָצֵר מָלְאָה אֶת־נֹגַהּ כְּבוֹד יְהֹוָה׃

5 The sound of the cherubs' wings could be heard as far as the outer court, like the voice of *ElShaddai* when He speaks.

ה וְקוֹל כַּנְפֵי הַכְּרוּבִים נִשְׁמַע עַד־הֶחָצֵר הַחִיצֹנָה כְּקוֹל אֵל־שַׁדַּי בְּדַבְּרוֹ׃

6 When He commanded the man dressed in linen: "Take fire from among the cherubs within the wheelwork," he went in and stood beside a wheel.

ו וַיְהִי בְּצַוֺּתוֹ אֶת־הָאִישׁ לְבֻשׁ־הַבַּדִּים לֵאמֹר קַח אֵשׁ מִבֵּינוֹת לַגַּלְגַּל מִבֵּינוֹת לַכְּרוּבִים וַיָּבֹא וַיַּעֲמֹד אֵצֶל הָאוֹפָן׃

7 And a cherub stretched out his hand among the cherubs to the fire that was among the cherubs; he took some and put it into the hands of him who was clothed in linen, who took it and went out.

ז וַיִּשְׁלַח הַכְּרוּב אֶת־יָדוֹ מִבֵּינוֹת לַכְּרוּבִים אֶל־הָאֵשׁ אֲשֶׁר בֵּינוֹת הַכְּרֻבִים וַיִּשָּׂא וַיִּתֵּן אֶל־חָפְנֵי לְבֻשׁ הַבַּדִּים וַיִּקַּח וַיֵּצֵא׃

8 The cherubs appeared to have the form of a man's hand under their wings.

ח וַיֵּרָא לַכְּרֻבִים תַּבְנִית יַד־אָדָם תַּחַת כַּנְפֵיהֶם׃

9 I could see that there were four wheels beside the cherubs, one wheel beside each of the cherubs; as for the appearance of the wheels, they gleamed like the beryl stone.

ט וָאֶרְאֶה וְהִנֵּה אַרְבָּעָה אוֹפַנִּים אֵצֶל הַכְּרוּבִים אוֹפַן אֶחָד אֵצֶל הַכְּרוּב אֶחָד וְאוֹפַן אֶחָד אֵצֶל הַכְּרוּב אֶחָד וּמַרְאֵה הָאוֹפַנִּים כְּעֵין אֶבֶן תַּרְשִׁישׁ׃

10 In appearance, the four had the same form, as if there were two wheels cutting through each other.

י וּמַרְאֵיהֶם דְּמוּת אֶחָד לְאַרְבַּעְתָּם כַּאֲשֶׁר יִהְיֶה הָאוֹפַן בְּתוֹךְ הָאוֹפָן׃

11 And when they moved, each could move in the direction of any of its four quarters; they did not veer as they moved. The [cherubs] moved in the direction in which one of the heads faced, without turning as they moved.

יא בְּלֶכְתָּם אֶל־אַרְבַּעַת רִבְעֵיהֶם יֵלֵכוּ לֹא יִסַּבּוּ בְּלֶכְתָּם כִּי הַמָּקוֹם אֲשֶׁר־יִפְנֶה הָרֹאשׁ אַחֲרָיו יֵלֵכוּ לֹא יִסַּבּוּ בְּלֶכְתָּם׃

12 Their entire bodies – backs, hands, and wings – and the wheels, the wheels of the four of them, were covered all over with eyes.

יב וְכָל־בְּשָׂרָם וְגַבֵּהֶם וִידֵיהֶם וְכַנְפֵיהֶם וְהָאוֹפַנִּים מְלֵאִים עֵינַיִם סָבִיב לְאַרְבַּעְתָּם אוֹפַנֵּיהֶם׃

13 It was these wheels that I had heard called "the wheelwork."

יג לָאוֹפַנִּים לָהֶם קוֹרָא הַגַּלְגַּל בְּאָזְנָי׃

14 Each one had four faces: One was a cherub's face, the second a human face, the third a lion's face, and the fourth an eagle's face.

יד וְאַרְבָּעָה פָנִים לְאֶחָד פְּנֵי הָאֶחָד פְּנֵי הַכְּרוּב וּפְנֵי הַשֵּׁנִי פְּנֵי אָדָם וְהַשְּׁלִישִׁי פְּנֵי אַרְיֵה וְהָרְבִיעִי פְּנֵי־נָשֶׁר׃

Yechezkel/Ezekiel

Chapter 11

יחזקאל

פרק יא

15 The cherubs ascended; those were the creatures that I had seen by the Chebar Canal.

טו וַיֵּרֹמּוּ הַכְּרוּבִים הִיא הַחַיָּה אֲשֶׁר רָאִיתִי בִּנְהַר־כְּבָר׃

16 Whenever the cherubs went, the wheels went beside them; and when the cherubs lifted their wings to ascend from the earth, the wheels did not roll away from their side.

טז וּבְלֶכֶת הַכְּרוּבִים יֵלְכוּ הָאוֹפַנִּים אֶצְלָם וּבִשְׂאֵת הַכְּרוּבִים אֶת־כַּנְפֵיהֶם לָרוּם מֵעַל הָאָרֶץ לֹא־יִסַּבּוּ הָאוֹפַנִּים גַּם־הֵם מֵאֶצְלָם׃

17 When those stood still, these stood still; and when those ascended, these ascended with them, for the spirit of the creature was in them.

יז בְּעָמְדָם יַעֲמֹדוּ וּבְרוֹמָם יֵרוֹמּוּ אוֹתָם כִּי רוּחַ הַחַיָּה בָּהֶם׃

18 Then the Presence of *Hashem* left the platform of the House and stopped above the cherubs.

יח וַיֵּצֵא כְּבוֹד יְהֹוָה מֵעַל מִפְתַּן הַבָּיִת וַיַּעֲמֹד עַל־הַכְּרוּבִים׃

19 And I saw the cherubs lift their wings and rise from the earth, with the wheels beside them as they departed; and they stopped at the entrance of the eastern gate of the House of *Hashem*, with the Presence of the God of *Yisrael* above them.

יט וַיִּשְׂאוּ הַכְּרוּבִים אֶת־כַּנְפֵיהֶם וַיֵּרֹמּוּ מִן־הָאָרֶץ לְעֵינַי בְּצֵאתָם וְהָאוֹפַנִּים לְעֻמָּתָם וַיַּעֲמֹד פֶּתַח שַׁעַר בֵּית־יְהֹוָה הַקַּדְמוֹנִי וּכְבוֹד אֱלֹהֵי־יִשְׂרָאֵל עֲלֵיהֶם מִלְמָעְלָה׃

20 They were the same creatures that I had seen below the God of *Yisrael* at the Chebar Canal; so now I knew that they were cherubs.

כ הִיא הַחַיָּה אֲשֶׁר רָאִיתִי תַּחַת אֱלֹהֵי־יִשְׂרָאֵל בִּנְהַר־כְּבָר וָאֵדַע כִּי כְרוּבִים הֵמָּה׃

21 Each one had four faces and each had four wings, with the form of human hands under the wings.

כא אַרְבָּעָה אַרְבָּעָה פָנִים לְאֶחָד וְאַרְבַּע כְּנָפַיִם לְאֶחָד וּדְמוּת יְדֵי אָדָם תַּחַת כַּנְפֵיהֶם׃

22 As for the form of their faces, they were the very faces that I had seen by the Chebar Canal – their appearance and their features – and each could move in the direction of any of its faces.1

כב וּדְמוּת פְּנֵיהֶם הֵמָּה הַפָּנִים אֲשֶׁר רָאִיתִי עַל־נְהַר־כְּבָר מַרְאֵיהֶם וְאוֹתָם אִישׁ אֶל־עֵבֶר פָּנָיו יֵלֵכוּ׃

11 1 Then a spirit lifted me up and brought me to the east gate of the House of *Hashem*, which faces eastward; and there, at the entrance of the gate, were twenty-five men, among whom I saw Jaazaniah son of Azzur and Pelatiah son of Benaiah, leaders of the people.

יא א וַתִּשָּׂא אֹתִי רוּחַ וַתָּבֵא אֹתִי אֶל־שַׁעַר בֵּית־יְהֹוָה הַקַּדְמוֹנִי הַפּוֹנֶה קָדִימָה וְהִנֵּה בְּפֶתַח הַשַּׁעַר עֶשְׂרִים וַחֲמִשָּׁה אִישׁ וָאֶרְאֶה בְתוֹכָם אֶת־יַאֲזַנְיָה בֶן־עַזֻּר וְאֶת־פְּלַטְיָהוּ בֶן־בְּנָיָהוּ שָׂרֵי הָעָם׃

2 [*Hashem*] said to me, "O mortal, these are the men who plan iniquity and plot wickedness in this city,

ב וַיֹּאמֶר אֵלָי בֶּן־אָדָם אֵלֶּה הָאֲנָשִׁים הַחֹשְׁבִים אָוֶן וְהַיֹּעֲצִים עֲצַת־רָע בָּעִיר הַזֹּאת׃

3 who say: 'There is no need now to build houses; this [city] is the pot, and we are the meat.'

ג הָאֹמְרִים לֹא בְקָרוֹב בְּנוֹת בָּתִּים הִיא הַסִּיר וַאֲנַחְנוּ הַבָּשָׂר׃

4 I adjure you, prophesy against them; prophesy, O mortal!"

ד לָכֵן הִנָּבֵא עֲלֵיהֶם הִנָּבֵא בֶּן־אָדָם׃

5 Thereupon the spirit of *Hashem* fell upon me, and He said to me, "Speak: Thus said *Hashem*: Such are your thoughts, O House of *Yisrael*; I know what comes into your mind.

ה וַתִּפֹּל עָלַי רוּחַ יְהֹוָה וַיֹּאמֶר אֵלַי אֱמֹר כֹּה־אָמַר יְהֹוָה כֵּן אֲמַרְתֶּם בֵּית יִשְׂרָאֵל וּמַעֲלוֹת רוּחֲכֶם אֲנִי יְדַעְתִּיהָ׃

Yechezkel/Ezekiel

Chapter 11

6 Many have you slain in this city; you have filled its streets with corpses.

7 Assuredly, thus says *Hashem*: The corpses that you have piled up in it are the meat for which it is the pot; but you shall be taken out of it.

8 You feared the sword, and the sword I will bring upon you – declares *Hashem*.

9 I will take you out of it and deliver you into the hands of strangers, and I will execute judgments upon you.

10 You shall fall by the sword; I will punish you at the border of *Yisrael*. And you shall know that I am *Hashem*.

11 This [city] shall not be a pot for you, nor you the meat in it; I will punish you at the border of *Yisrael*.

12 Then you shall know that I am *Hashem*, whose laws you did not follow and whose rules you did not obey, acting instead according to the rules of the nations around you."

13 Now, as I prophesied, Pelatiah son of Benaiah dropped dead. I threw myself upon my face and cried out aloud, "Ah, *Hashem*! You are wiping out the remnant of *Yisrael*!"

14 Then the word of *Hashem* came to me:

15 "O mortal, [I will save] your brothers, your brothers, the men of your kindred, all of that very House of *Yisrael* to whom the inhabitants of *Yerushalayim* say, 'Keep far from *Hashem*; the land has been given as a heritage to us.'

16 Say then: Thus said *Hashem*: I have indeed removed them far among the nations and have scattered them among the countries, and I have become to them a diminished sanctity in the countries whither they have gone.

17 Yet say: Thus said *Hashem*: I will gather you from the peoples and assemble you out of the countries where you have been scattered, and I will give you the Land of *Yisrael*.

18 And they shall return there, and do away with all its detestable things and all its abominations.

יחזקאל

פרק יא

ו הִרְבֵּיתֶם חַלְלֵיכֶם בָּעִיר הַזֹּאת וּמִלֵּאתֶם חוּצֹתֶיהָ חָלָל:

ז לָכֵן כֹּה־אָמַר אֲדֹנָי יֱהֹוִה חַלְלֵיכֶם אֲשֶׁר שַׂמְתֶּם בְּתוֹכָהּ הֵמָּה הַבָּשָׂר וְהִיא הַסִּיר וְאֶתְכֶם הוֹצִיא מִתּוֹכָהּ:

ח חֶרֶב יְרֵאתֶם וְחֶרֶב אָבִיא עֲלֵיכֶם נְאֻם אֲדֹנָי יֱהֹוִה:

ט וְהוֹצֵאתִי אֶתְכֶם מִתּוֹכָהּ וְנָתַתִּי אֶתְכֶם בְּיַד־זָרִים וְעָשִׂיתִי בָכֶם שְׁפָטִים:

י בַּחֶרֶב תִּפֹּלוּ עַל־גְּבוּל יִשְׂרָאֵל אֶשְׁפּוֹט אֶתְכֶם וִידַעְתֶּם כִּי־אֲנִי יְהֹוָה:

יא הִיא לֹא־תִהְיֶה לָכֶם לְסִיר וְאַתֶּם תִּהְיוּ בְּתוֹכָהּ לְבָשָׂר אֶל־גְּבוּל יִשְׂרָאֵל אֶשְׁפֹּט אֶתְכֶם:

יב וִידַעְתֶּם כִּי־אֲנִי יְהֹוָה אֲשֶׁר בְּחֻקַּי לֹא הֲלַכְתֶּם וּמִשְׁפָּטַי לֹא עֲשִׂיתֶם וּכְמִשְׁפְּטֵי הַגּוֹיִם אֲשֶׁר סְבִיבוֹתֵיכֶם עֲשִׂיתֶם:

יג וַיְהִי כְּהִנָּבְאִי וּפְלַטְיָהוּ בֶן־בְּנָיָה מֵת וָאֶפֹּל עַל־פָּנַי וָאֶזְעַק קוֹל־גָּדוֹל וָאֹמַר אֲהָהּ אֲדֹנָי יֱהֹוִה כָּלָה אַתָּה עֹשֶׂה אֵת שְׁאֵרִית יִשְׂרָאֵל:

יד וַיְהִי דְבַר־יְהֹוָה אֵלַי לֵאמֹר:

טו בֶּן־אָדָם אַחֶיךָ אַחֶיךָ אַנְשֵׁי גְאֻלָּתֶךָ וְכָל־בֵּית יִשְׂרָאֵל כֻּלֹּה אֲשֶׁר אָמְרוּ לָהֶם יֹשְׁבֵי יְרוּשָׁלַיִם רַחֲקוּ מֵעַל יְהֹוָה לָנוּ הִיא נִתְּנָה הָאָרֶץ לְמוֹרָשָׁה:

טז לָכֵן אֱמֹר כֹּה־אָמַר אֲדֹנָי יֱהֹוִה כִּי הִרְחַקְתִּים בַּגּוֹיִם וְכִי הֲפִיצוֹתִים בָּאֲרָצוֹת וָאֱהִי לָהֶם לְמִקְדָּשׁ מְעַט בָּאֲרָצוֹת אֲשֶׁר־בָּאוּ שָׁם:

יז לָכֵן אֱמֹר כֹּה־אָמַר אֲדֹנָי יֱהֹוִה וְקִבַּצְתִּי אֶתְכֶם מִן־הָעַמִּים וְאָסַפְתִּי אֶתְכֶם מִן־הָאֲרָצוֹת אֲשֶׁר נְפֹצוֹתֶם בָּהֶם וְנָתַתִּי לָכֶם אֶת־אַדְמַת יִשְׂרָאֵל:

יח וּבָאוּ־שָׁמָּה וְהֵסִירוּ אֶת־כָּל־שִׁקּוּצֶיהָ וְאֶת־כָּל־תּוֹעֲבוֹתֶיהָ מִמֶּנָּה:

Yechezkel/Ezekiel
Chapter 12

יחזקאל
פרק יב

19 I will give them one heart and put a new spirit in them; I will remove the heart of stone from their bodies and give them a heart of flesh,

יט וְנָתַתִּי לָהֶם לֵב אֶחָד וְרוּחַ חֲדָשָׁה אֶתֵּן בְּקִרְבְּכֶם וַהֲסִרֹתִי לֵב הָאֶבֶן מִבְּשָׂרָם וְנָתַתִּי לָהֶם לֵב בָּשָׂר:

20 that they may follow My laws and faithfully observe My rules. Then they shall be My people and I will be their God.

כ לְמַעַן בְּחֻקֹּתַי יֵלֵכוּ וְאֶת־מִשְׁפָּטַי יִשְׁמְרוּ וְעָשׂוּ אֹתָם וְהָיוּ־לִי לְעָם וַאֲנִי אֶהְיֶה לָהֶם לֵאלֹהִים:

21 But as for them whose heart is set upon their detestable things and their abominations, I will repay them for their conduct – declares *Hashem*."

כא וְאֶל־לֵב שִׁקּוּצֵיהֶם וְתוֹעֲבוֹתֵיהֶם לִבָּם הֹלֵךְ דַּרְכָּם בְּרֹאשָׁם נָתַתִּי נְאֻם אֲדֹנָי יֱהוִֹה:

22 Then the cherubs, with the wheels beside them, lifted their wings, while the Presence of the God of *Yisrael* rested above them.

כב וַיִּשְׂאוּ הַכְּרוּבִים אֶת־כַּנְפֵיהֶם וְהָאוֹפַנִּים לְעֻמָּתָם וּכְבוֹד אֱלֹהֵי־יִשְׂרָאֵל עֲלֵיהֶם מִלְמָעְלָה:

23 The Presence of *Hashem* ascended from the midst of the city and stood on the hill east of the city.

כג וַיַּעַל כְּבוֹד יְהוָֹה מֵעַל תּוֹךְ הָעִיר וַיַּעֲמֹד עַל־הָהָר אֲשֶׁר מִקֶּדֶם לָעִיר:

24 A spirit carried me away and brought me in a vision by the spirit of *Hashem* to the exile community in Chaldea. Then the vision that I had seen left me,

כד וְרוּחַ נְשָׂאַתְנִי וַתְּבִיאֵנִי כַשְׂדִּימָה אֶל־הַגּוֹלָה בַּמַּרְאֶה בְּרוּחַ אֱלֹהִים וַיַּעַל מֵעָלַי הַמַּרְאֶה אֲשֶׁר רָאִיתִי:

25 and I told the exiles all the things that *Hashem* had shown me.

כה וָאֲדַבֵּר אֶל־הַגּוֹלָה אֵת כָּל־דִּבְרֵי יְהוָֹה אֲשֶׁר הֶרְאָנִי:

va-a-da-BAYR el ha-go-LAH AYT kol div-RAY a-do-NAI a-SHER her-A-nee

12

1 The word of *Hashem* came to me:

יב א וַיְהִי דְבַר־יְהוָֹה אֵלַי לֵאמֹר:

2 O mortal, you dwell among the rebellious breed. They have eyes to see but see not, ears to hear but hear not; for they are a rebellious breed.

ב בֶּן־אָדָם בְּתוֹךְ בֵּית־הַמֶּרִי אַתָּה יֹשֵׁב אֲשֶׁר עֵינַיִם לָהֶם לִרְאוֹת וְלֹא רָאוּ אָזְנַיִם לָהֶם לִשְׁמֹעַ וְלֹא שָׁמֵעוּ כִּי בֵּית מְרִי הֵם:

3 Therefore, mortal, get yourself gear for exile, and go into exile by day before their eyes. Go into exile from your home to another place before their very eyes; perhaps they will take note, even though they are a rebellious breed.

ג וְאַתָּה בֶן־אָדָם עֲשֵׂה לְךָ כְּלֵי גוֹלָה וּגְלֵה יוֹמָם לְעֵינֵיהֶם וְגָלִיתָ מִמְּקוֹמְךָ אֶל־מָקוֹם אַחֵר לְעֵינֵיהֶם אוּלַי יִרְאוּ כִּי בֵּית מְרִי הֵמָּה:

11:25 And I told the exiles In verses 16–17, *Hashem* promises that though He has exiled the Children of Israel and scattered them among the nations, in the future He will gather and redeem them: "I will gather you from the peoples and assemble you out of the countries where you have been scattered, and I will give you the Land of Israel." In this verse, *Yechezkel* shares *Hashem*'s promise with the Children of Israel already in captivity, giving them hope for the future. The Hebrew word for 'captivity' or 'exile', found in this verse, is *gola* (גולה), while the term for 'redemption' is *geula* (גאולה). Rabbi Benjamin Blech notes that the two words are spelled almost identically, with the only difference between them being the single letter *aleph* (א). The numerical value of the *aleph* is one, representing the one true God who must be incorporated into the mentality of the *gola* (exile) in order to bring about the *geula* (redemption).

גאולה

Rabbi Benjamin Blech (b. 1933)

Yechezkel/Ezekiel
Chapter 12

יחזקאל
פרק יב

4 Carry out your gear as gear for exile by day before their very eyes; and go out again in the evening before their eyes, as one who goes out into exile.

ד וְהוֹצֵאתָ כֵלֶיךָ כִּכְלֵי גוֹלָה יוֹמָם לְעֵינֵיהֶם וְאַתָּה תֵּצֵא בָעֶרֶב לְעֵינֵיהֶם כְּמוֹצָאֵי גּוֹלָה׃

5 Before their eyes, break through the wall and carry [the gear] out through it;

ה לְעֵינֵיהֶם חֲתָר־לְךָ בַקִּיר וְהוֹצֵאתָ בּוֹ׃

6 before their eyes, carry it on your shoulder. Take it out in the dark, and cover your face that you may not see the land; for I make you a portent to the House of Yisrael.

ו לְעֵינֵיהֶם עַל־כָּתֵף תִּשָּׂא בָּעֲלָטָה תוֹצִיא פָּנֶיךָ תְכַסֶּה וְלֹא תִרְאֶה אֶת־הָאָרֶץ כִּי־מוֹפֵת נְתַתִּיךָ לְבֵית יִשְׂרָאֵל׃

7 I did just as I was ordered: I took out my gear by day as gear for exile, and in the evening I broke through the wall with my own hands. In the darkness I carried [the gear] out on my shoulder, carrying it before their eyes.

ז וָאַעַשׂ כֵּן כַּאֲשֶׁר צֻוֵּיתִי כֵּלַי הוֹצֵאתִי כִּכְלֵי גוֹלָה יוֹמָם וּבָעֶרֶב חָתַרְתִּי־לִי בַקִּיר בְּיָד בָּעֲלָטָה הוֹצֵאתִי עַל־כָּתֵף נָשָׂאתִי לְעֵינֵיהֶם׃

8 In the morning, the word of Hashem came to me:

ח וַיְהִי דְבַר־יְהוָה אֵלַי בַּבֹּקֶר לֵאמֹר׃

9 O mortal, did not the House of Yisrael, that rebellious breed, ask you, "What are you doing?"

ט בֶּן־אָדָם הֲלֹא אָמְרוּ אֵלֶיךָ בֵּית יִשְׂרָאֵל בֵּית הַמֶּרִי מָה אַתָּה עֹשֶׂה׃

10 Say to them: "Thus said Hashem: This pronouncement concerns the prince in Yerushalayim and all the House of Yisrael who are in it."

י אֱמֹר אֲלֵיהֶם כֹּה אָמַר אֲדֹנָי יְהוִֹה הַנָּשִׂיא הַמַּשָּׂא הַזֶּה בִּירוּשָׁלַ͏ִם וְכָל־בֵּית יִשְׂרָאֵל אֲשֶׁר־הֵמָּה בְתוֹכָם׃

e-MOR a-lay-HEM KOH a-MAR a-do-NAI e-lo-HEEM ha-na-SEE ha-ma-SA ha-ZEH bee-ru-sha-LA-im v'-khol BAYT yis-ra-AYL a-sher HAY-mah v'-to-KHAM

11 Say: "I am a portent for you: As I have done, so shall it be done to them; they shall go into exile, into captivity.

יא אֱמֹר אֲנִי מוֹפֶתְכֶם כַּאֲשֶׁר עָשִׂיתִי כֵּן יֵעָשֶׂה לָהֶם בַּגּוֹלָה בַשְּׁבִי יֵלֵכוּ׃

12 And the prince among them shall carry his gear on his shoulder as he goes out in the dark. He shall break through the wall in order to carry [his gear] out through it; he shall cover his face, because he himself shall not see the land with his eyes."

יב וְהַנָּשִׂיא אֲשֶׁר־בְּתוֹכָם אֶל־כָּתֵף יִשָּׂא בָּעֲלָטָה וְיֵצֵא בַּקִּיר יַחְתְּרוּ לְהוֹצִיא בוֹ פָּנָיו יְכַסֶּה יַעַן אֲשֶׁר לֹא־יִרְאֶה לַעַיִן הוּא אֶת־הָאָרֶץ׃

13 I will spread My net over him, and he shall be caught in My snare. I will bring him to Babylon, the land of the Chaldeans, but he shall not see it; and there he shall die.

יג וּפָרַשְׂתִּי אֶת־רִשְׁתִּי עָלָיו וְנִתְפַּשׂ בִּמְצוּדָתִי וְהֵבֵאתִי אֹתוֹ בָבֶלָה אֶרֶץ כַּשְׂדִּים וְאוֹתָהּ לֹא־יִרְאֶה וְשָׁם יָמוּת׃

12:10 This pronouncement concerns the prince In this chapter, Yechezkel acts out the scene of a person carrying the barest provisions, digging a hole under a stone wall. According to the Malbim, these actions reflect the behavior of King Tzidkiyahu. Instead of listening to the prophet Yirmiyahu and submitting to Babylonia, the Babylonian-appointed king of Yehuda attempts to abandon his people by disguising himself and fleeing the siege. However, he is apprehended by the enemy and brought to Babylonia in chains. As hard as it was to surrender, it was the will of God. By refusing to listen and running away, Tzidkiyahu seals his fate. We must follow Hashem's will even when is not easy, because that path is ultimately best for us.

Malbim (1809–1879)

Yechezkel/Ezekiel
Chapter 12

14 And all those around him, his helpers and all his troops, I will scatter in every direction; and I will unsheathe the sword after them.

15 Then, when I have scattered them among the nations and dispersed them through the countries, they shall know that I am *Hashem*.

16 But I will spare a few of them from the sword, from famine, and from pestilence, that they may recount all their abominable deeds among the nations to which they come; and they shall know that I am *Hashem*!

17 The word of *Hashem* came to me:

18 O mortal, eat your bread in trembling and drink your water in fear and anxiety.

19 And say to the people of the land: Thus said *Hashem* concerning the inhabitants of *Yerushalayim* in the land of *Yisrael*: They shall eat their bread in anxiety and drink their water in desolation, because their land will be desolate of its multitudes on account of the lawlessness of all its inhabitants.

20 The inhabited towns shall be laid waste and the land shall become a desolation; then you shall know that I am *Hashem*.

21 The word of *Hashem* came to me:

22 O mortal, what is this proverb that you have in the land of *Yisrael*, that you say, "The days grow many and every vision comes to naught?"

23 Assuredly, say to them, Thus said *Hashem*: I will put an end to this proverb; it shall not be used in *Yisrael* any more. Speak rather to them: The days draw near, and the fulfillment of every vision.

24 For there shall no longer be any false vision or soothing divination in the House of *Yisrael*.

25 But whenever I *Hashem* speak what I speak, that word shall be fulfilled without any delay; in your days, O rebellious breed, I will fulfill every word I speak – declares *Hashem*.

26 The word of *Hashem* came to me:

27 See, O mortal, the House of *Yisrael* says, "The vision that he sees is far ahead, and he prophesies for the distant future."

Yechezkel/Ezekiel
Chapter 13

28 Assuredly, say to them: Thus said *Hashem*: There shall be no more delay; whenever I speak a word, that word shall be fulfilled – declares *Hashem*.

יחזקאל
פרק יג

כח לָכֵן אֱמֹר אֲלֵיהֶם כֹּה אָמַר אֲדֹנָי יֱהֹוִה לֹא־תִמָּשֵׁךְ עוֹד כָּל־דְּבָרָי אֲשֶׁר אֲדַבֵּר דָּבָר וְיֵעָשֶׂה נְאֻם אֲדֹנָי יֱהֹוִה׃

13 1 The word of *Hashem* came to me:

יג א וַיְהִי דְבַר־יְהֹוָה אֵלַי לֵאמֹר׃

2 O mortal, prophesy against the *Neviim* of *Yisrael* who prophesy; say to those who prophesy out of their own imagination: Hear the word of *Hashem*!

ב בֶּן־אָדָם הִנָּבֵא אֶל־נְבִיאֵי יִשְׂרָאֵל הַנִּבָּאִים וְאָמַרְתָּ לִנְבִיאֵי מִלִּבָּם שִׁמְעוּ דְּבַר־יְהֹוָה׃

3 Thus said *Hashem*: Woe to the degenerate *Neviim*, who follow their own fancy, without having had a vision!

ג כֹּה אָמַר אֲדֹנָי יֱהֹוִה הוֹי עַל־הַנְּבִיאִים הַנְּבָלִים אֲשֶׁר הֹלְכִים אַחַר רוּחָם וּלְבִלְתִּי רָאוּ׃

4 Your *Neviim*, O *Yisrael*, have been like jackals among ruins.

ד כְּשֻׁעָלִים בָּחֳרָבוֹת נְבִיאֶיךָ יִשְׂרָאֵל הָיוּ׃

k'-shu-a-LEEM ba-kha-ra-VOT n'-vee-E-kha yis-ra-AYL ha-YU

5 You did not enter the breaches and repair the walls for the House of *Yisrael*, that they might stand up in battle in the day of *Hashem*.

ה לֹא עֲלִיתֶם בַּפְּרָצוֹת וַתִּגְדְּרוּ גָדֵר עַל־בֵּית יִשְׂרָאֵל לַעֲמֹד בַּמִּלְחָמָה בְּיוֹם יְהֹוָה׃

6 They prophesied falsehood and lying divination; they said, "Declares *Hashem*," when *Hashem* did not send them, and then they waited for their word to be fulfilled.

ו חָזוּ שָׁוְא וְקֶסֶם כָּזָב הָאֹמְרִים נְאֻם־יְהֹוָה וַיהֹוָה לֹא שְׁלָחָם וְיִחֲלוּ לְקַיֵּם דָּבָר׃

7 It was false visions you prophesied and lying divination you uttered, saying, "Declares *Hashem*," when I had not spoken.

ז הֲלוֹא מַחֲזֵה־שָׁוְא חֲזִיתֶם וּמִקְסַם כָּזָב אֲמַרְתֶּם וְאֹמְרִים נְאֻם־יְהֹוָה וַאֲנִי לֹא דִבַּרְתִּי׃

8 Assuredly, thus said *Hashem*: Because you speak falsehood and prophesy lies, assuredly, I will deal with you – declares *Hashem*.

ח לָכֵן כֹּה אָמַר אֲדֹנָי יֱהֹוִה יַעַן דַּבֶּרְכֶם שָׁוְא וַחֲזִיתֶם כָּזָב לָכֵן הִנְנִי אֲלֵיכֶם נְאֻם אֲדֹנָי יֱהֹוִה׃

9 My hand will be against the *Neviim* who prophesy falsehood and utter lying divination. They shall not remain in the assembly of My people, they shall not be inscribed in the lists of the House of *Yisrael*, and they shall not come back to the land of *Yisrael*. Thus shall you know that I am *Hashem*.

ט וְהָיְתָה יָדִי אֶל־הַנְּבִיאִים הַחֹזִים שָׁוְא וְהַקֹּסְמִים כָּזָב בְּסוֹד עַמִּי לֹא־יִהְיוּ וּבִכְתָב בֵּית־יִשְׂרָאֵל לֹא יִכָּתֵבוּ וְאֶל־אַדְמַת יִשְׂרָאֵל לֹא יָבֹאוּ וִידַעְתֶּם כִּי אֲנִי אֲדֹנָי יֱהֹוִה׃

13:4 Your *Neviim*, O *Yisrael*, have been like jackals among ruins *Yechezkel* compares the false prophets who led Israel astray to jackals lurking among the ruins. While the image of animals prowling among ruins symbolizes destruction, the Talmud (*Makkot* 24b) also sees these animals as harbingers of redemption. It relates that the great Rabbi Akiva was walking with some other Sages near the remnants of the destroyed Temple. When he saw a jackal emerge from the site of the Holy of Holies, he laughed with joy, while the others who were with him wept. The Sages were shocked by his laughter, but Rabbi Akiva explained that just as *Hashem* faithfully fulfilled His prophecies of destruction, so too He will be faithful to fulfill the prophecies of redemption, restoration and renewal.

A golden Jackal in Revivim, Israel

Yechezkel/Ezekiel
Chapter 13

10 Inasmuch as they have misled My people, saying, "It is well," when nothing is well, daubing with plaster the flimsy wall which the people were building,

11 say to those daubers of plaster: It shall collapse; a driving rain shall descend – and you, O great hailstones, shall fall – and a hurricane wind shall rend it.

12 Then, when the wall collapses, you will be asked, "What became of the plaster you daubed on?"

13 Assuredly, thus said *Hashem*: In My fury I will let loose hurricane winds; in My anger a driving rain shall descend, and great hailstones in destructive fury.

14 I will throw down the wall that you daubed with plaster, and I will raze it to the ground so that its foundation is exposed; and when it falls, you shall perish in its midst; then you shall know that I am *Hashem*.

15 And when I have spent My fury upon the wall and upon those who daubed it with plaster, I will say to you: Gone is the wall and gone are its daubers,

16 the *Neviim* of *Yisrael* who prophesy about *Yerushalayim* and see a vision of well-being for her when there is no well-being – declares *Hashem*.

17 And you, O mortal, set your face against the women of your people, who prophesy out of their own imagination. Prophesy against them

18 and say: Thus said *Hashem*: Woe to those who sew pads on all arm-joints and make bonnets for the head of every person, in order to entrap! Can you hunt down lives among My people, while you preserve your own lives?

19 You have profaned My name among My people in return for handfuls of barley and morsels of bread; you have announced the death of persons who will not die and the survival of persons who will not live – lying to My people, who listen to your lies.

20 Assuredly, thus said *Hashem*: I am going to deal with your pads, by which you hunt down lives like birds, and I will tear them from your arms and free the persons whose lives you hunt down like birds.

יחזקאל
פרק יג

י יַעַן וּבְיַעַן הִטְעוּ אֶת־עַמִּי לֵאמֹר שָׁלוֹם וְאֵין שָׁלוֹם וְהוּא בֹּנֶה חַיִץ וְהִנָּם טָחִים אֹתוֹ תָּפֵל:

יא אֱמֹר אֶל־טָחֵי תָפֵל וְיִפֹּל הָיָה גֶּשֶׁם שׁוֹטֵף וְאַתֵּנָה אַבְנֵי אֶלְגָּבִישׁ תִּפֹּלְנָה וְרוּחַ סְעָרוֹת תְּבַקֵּעַ:

יב וְהִנֵּה נָפַל הַקִּיר הֲלוֹא יֵאָמֵר אֲלֵיכֶם אַיֵּה הַטִּיחַ אֲשֶׁר טַחְתֶּם:

יג לָכֵן כֹּה אָמַר אֲדֹנָי יֱהֹוִה וּבִקַּעְתִּי רוּחַ־סְעָרוֹת בַּחֲמָתִי וְגֶשֶׁם שֹׁטֵף בְּאַפִּי יִהְיֶה וְאַבְנֵי אֶלְגָּבִישׁ בְּחֵמָה לְכָלָה:

יד וְהָרַסְתִּי אֶת־הַקִּיר אֲשֶׁר־טַחְתֶּם תָּפֵל וְהִגַּעְתִּיהוּ אֶל־הָאָרֶץ וְנִגְלָה יְסֹדוֹ וְנָפְלָה וּכְלִיתֶם בְּתוֹכָהּ וִידַעְתֶּם כִּי־אֲנִי יְהֹוָה:

טו וְכִלֵּיתִי אֶת־חֲמָתִי בַּקִּיר וּבַטָּחִים אֹתוֹ תָּפֵל וְאֹמַר לָכֶם אֵין הַקִּיר וְאֵין הַטָּחִים אֹתוֹ:

טז נְבִיאֵי יִשְׂרָאֵל הַנִּבְּאִים אֶל־יְרוּשָׁלַםִ וְהַחֹזִים לָהּ חֲזוֹן שָׁלֹם וְאֵין שָׁלֹם נְאֻם אֲדֹנָי יֱהֹוִה:

יז וְאַתָּה בֶן־אָדָם שִׂים פָּנֶיךָ אֶל־בְּנוֹת עַמְּךָ הַמִּתְנַבְּאוֹת מִלִּבְּהֶן וְהִנָּבֵא עֲלֵיהֶן:

יח וְאָמַרְתָּ כֹּה־אָמַר אֲדֹנָי יֱהֹוִה הוֹי לִמְתַפְּרוֹת כְּסָתוֹת עַל כָּל־אַצִּילֵי יָדַי וְעֹשׂוֹת הַמִּסְפָּחוֹת עַל־רֹאשׁ כָּל־קוֹמָה לְצוֹדֵד נְפָשׁוֹת הַנְּפָשׁוֹת תְּצוֹדֵדְנָה לְעַמִּי וּנְפָשׁוֹת לָכֶנָה תְחַיֶּינָה:

יט וַתְּחַלֶּלְנָה אֹתִי אֶל־עַמִּי בְּשַׁעֲלֵי שְׂעֹרִים וּבִפְתוֹתֵי לֶחֶם לְהָמִית נְפָשׁוֹת אֲשֶׁר לֹא־תְמוּתֶנָה וּלְחַיּוֹת נְפָשׁוֹת אֲשֶׁר לֹא־תִחְיֶינָה בְּכַזֶּבְכֶם לְעַמִּי שֹׁמְעֵי כָזָב:

כ לָכֵן כֹּה־אָמַר אֲדֹנָי יֱהֹוִה הִנְנִי אֶל־כִּסְּתוֹתֵיכֶנָה אֲשֶׁר אַתֵּנָה מְצֹדְדוֹת שָׁם אֶת־הַנְּפָשׁוֹת לְפֹרְחוֹת וְקָרַעְתִּי אֹתָם מֵעַל זְרוֹעֹתֵיכֶם וְשִׁלַּחְתִּי אֶת־הַנְּפָשׁוֹת אֲשֶׁר אַתֶּם מְצֹדְדוֹת אֶת־נְפָשִׁים לְפֹרְחֹת:

1235

Yechezkel/Ezekiel
Chapter 14

21 I will tear off your bonnets and rescue My people from your hands, and they shall no longer be prey in your hands; then you shall know that I am *Hashem*.

22 Because you saddened the heart of the innocent with lies, when I would not inflict suffering on him, and encouraged the wicked not to repent of his evil ways and so gain life –

23 assuredly, you shall no longer prophesy lies or practice divination! I will save My people from your hands, and you shall know that I am *Hashem*.

14 1 Certain elders of *Yisrael* came to me and sat down before me.

2 And the word of *Hashem* came to me:

3 O mortal, these men have turned their thoughts upon their fetishes and set their minds upon the sin through which they stumbled: Shall I respond to their inquiry?

4 Now speak to them and tell them: Thus said *Hashem*: If anyone of the House of *Yisrael* turns his thoughts upon his fetishes and sets his mind upon the sin through which he stumbled, and yet comes to the *Navi*, I *Hashem* will respond to him as he comes with his multitude of fetishes.

5 Thus I will hold the House of *Yisrael* to account for their thoughts, because they have all been estranged from Me through their fetishes.

6 Now say to the House of *Yisrael*: Thus said *Hashem*: Repent, and turn back from your fetishes and turn your minds away from all your abominations.

7 For if any man of the House of *Yisrael*, or of the strangers who dwell in *Yisrael*, breaks away from Me and turns his thoughts upon his fetishes and sets his mind upon the sins through which he stumbled, and then goes to the *Navi* to inquire of Me through him, I *Hashem* will respond to him directly.

8 I will set My face against that man and make him a sign and a byword, and I will cut him off from the midst of My people. Then you shall know that I am *Hashem*.

יחזקאל
פרק יד

כא וְקָרַעְתִּי אֶת־מִסְפְּחֹתֵיכֶם וְהִצַּלְתִּי אֶת־עַמִּי מִיֶּדְכֶן וְלֹא־יִהְיוּ עוֹד בְּיֶדְכֶן לִמְצוּדָה וִידַעְתֶּן כִּי־אֲנִי יְהֹוָה:

כב יַעַן הַכְאוֹת לֵב־צַדִּיק שֶׁקֶר וַאֲנִי לֹא הִכְאַבְתִּיו וּלְחַזֵּק יְדֵי רָשָׁע לְבִלְתִּי־שׁוּב מִדַּרְכּוֹ הָרָע לְהַחֲיֹתוֹ:

כג לָכֵן שָׁוְא לֹא תֶחֱזֶינָה וְקֶסֶם לֹא־תִקְסַמְנָה עוֹד וְהִצַּלְתִּי אֶת־עַמִּי מִיֶּדְכֶן וִידַעְתֶּן כִּי־אֲנִי יְהֹוָה:

יד א וַיָּבוֹא אֵלַי אֲנָשִׁים מִזִּקְנֵי יִשְׂרָאֵל וַיֵּשְׁבוּ לְפָנָי:

ב וַיְהִי דְבַר־יְהֹוָה אֵלַי לֵאמֹר:

ג בֶּן־אָדָם הָאֲנָשִׁים הָאֵלֶּה הֶעֱלוּ גִלּוּלֵיהֶם עַל־לִבָּם וּמִכְשׁוֹל עֲוֹנָם נָתְנוּ נֹכַח פְּנֵיהֶם הַאִדָּרֹשׁ אִדָּרֵשׁ לָהֶם:

ד לָכֵן דַּבֵּר־אוֹתָם וְאָמַרְתָּ אֲלֵיהֶם כֹּה־אָמַר אֲדֹנָי יְהֹוָה אִישׁ אִישׁ מִבֵּית יִשְׂרָאֵל אֲשֶׁר יַעֲלֶה אֶת־גִּלּוּלָיו אֶל־לִבּוֹ וּמִכְשׁוֹל עֲוֹנוֹ יָשִׂים נֹכַח פָּנָיו וּבָא אֶל־הַנָּבִיא אֲנִי יְהֹוָה נַעֲנֵיתִי לוֹ בָהּ [בָא] בְּרֹב גִּלּוּלָיו:

ה לְמַעַן תְּפֹשׂ אֶת־בֵּית־יִשְׂרָאֵל בְּלִבָּם אֲשֶׁר נָזֹרוּ מֵעָלַי בְּגִלּוּלֵיהֶם כֻּלָּם:

ו לָכֵן אֱמֹר אֶל־בֵּית יִשְׂרָאֵל כֹּה אָמַר אֲדֹנָי יְהֹוִה שׁוּבוּ וְהָשִׁיבוּ מֵעַל גִּלּוּלֵיכֶם וּמֵעַל כָּל־תּוֹעֲבֹתֵיכֶם הָשִׁיבוּ פְנֵיכֶם:

ז כִּי אִישׁ אִישׁ מִבֵּית יִשְׂרָאֵל וּמֵהַגֵּר אֲשֶׁר־יָגוּר בְּיִשְׂרָאֵל וְיִנָּזֵר מֵאַחֲרַי וְיַעַל גִּלּוּלָיו אֶל־לִבּוֹ וּמִכְשׁוֹל עֲוֹנוֹ יָשִׂים נֹכַח פָּנָיו וּבָא אֶל־הַנָּבִיא לִדְרָשׁ־לוֹ בִי אֲנִי יְהֹוָה נַעֲנֶה־לּוֹ בִּי:

ח וְנָתַתִּי פָנַי בָּאִישׁ הַהוּא וַהֲשִׁמֹתִיהוּ לְאוֹת וְלִמְשָׁלִים וְהִכְרַתִּיו מִתּוֹךְ עַמִּי וִידַעְתֶּם כִּי־אֲנִי יְהֹוָה:

Yechezkel/Ezekiel
Chapter 14

יחזקאל
פרק יד

9 And if a *Navi* is seduced and does speak a word [to such a man], it was I *Hashem* who seduced that *Navi*; I will stretch out My hand against him and destroy him from among My people *Yisrael*.

ט וְהַנָּבִיא כִי־יְפֻתֶּה וְדִבֶּר דָּבָר אֲנִי יְהֹוָה פִּתֵּיתִי אֵת הַנָּבִיא הַהוּא וְנָטִיתִי אֶת־יָדִי עָלָיו וְהִשְׁמַדְתִּיו מִתּוֹךְ עַמִּי יִשְׂרָאֵל׃

10 Thus they shall bear their punishment: The punishment of the inquirer and the punishment of the *Navi* shall be the same,

י וְנָשְׂאוּ עֲוֺנָם כַּעֲוֺן הַדֹּרֵשׁ כַּעֲוֺן הַנָּבִיא יִהְיֶה׃

11 so that the House of *Yisrael* may never again stray from Me and defile itself with all its transgressions. Then they shall be My people and I will be their God – declares *Hashem*.

יא לְמַעַן לֹא־יִתְעוּ עוֹד בֵּית־יִשְׂרָאֵל מֵאַחֲרַי וְלֹא־יִטַּמְּאוּ עוֹד בְּכָל־פִּשְׁעֵיהֶם וְהָיוּ לִי לְעָם וַאֲנִי אֶהְיֶה לָהֶם לֵאלֹהִים נְאֻם אֲדֹנָי יְהוִה׃

12 The word of *Hashem* came to me:

יב וַיְהִי דְבַר־יְהֹוָה אֵלַי לֵאמֹר׃

13 O mortal, if a land were to sin against Me and commit a trespass, and I stretched out My hand against it and broke its staff of bread, and sent famine against it and cut off man and beast from it,

יג בֶּן־אָדָם אֶרֶץ כִּי תֶחֱטָא־לִי לִמְעָל־מַעַל וְנָטִיתִי יָדִי עָלֶיהָ וְשָׁבַרְתִּי לָהּ מַטֵּה־לָחֶם וְהִשְׁלַחְתִּי־בָהּ רָעָב וְהִכְרַתִּי מִמֶּנָּה אָדָם וּבְהֵמָה׃

14 even if these three men – *Noach*, *Daniel*, and *Iyov* – should be in it, they would by their righteousness save only themselves – declares *Hashem*.

יד וְהָיוּ שְׁלֹשֶׁת הָאֲנָשִׁים הָאֵלֶּה בְּתוֹכָהּ נֹחַ דָּנִאֵל [דָּנִיֵּאל] וְאִיּוֹב הֵמָּה בְצִדְקָתָם יְנַצְּלוּ נַפְשָׁם נְאֻם אֲדֹנָי יְהוִה׃

v'-ha-YU sh'-LO-shet ha-a-na-SHEEM ha-AY-leh b'-to-KHAH NO-akh da-ni-AYL v'-i-YOV HAY-mah v'-tzid-ka-TAM y'-na-tz'-LU naf-SHAM n'-UM a-do-NAI e-lo-HEEM

15 Or, if I were to send wild beasts to roam the land and they depopulated it, and it became a desolation with none passing through it because of the beasts,

טו לוּ־חַיָּה רָעָה אַעֲבִיר בָּאָרֶץ וְשִׁכְּלָתָּה וְהָיְתָה שְׁמָמָה מִבְּלִי עוֹבֵר מִפְּנֵי הַחַיָּה׃

16 as I live – declares *Hashem* – those three men in it would save neither sons nor daughters; they alone would be saved, but the land would become a desolation.

טז שְׁלֹשֶׁת הָאֲנָשִׁים הָאֵלֶּה בְּתוֹכָהּ חַי־אָנִי נְאֻם אֲדֹנָי יְהוִה אִם־בָּנִים וְאִם־בָּנוֹת יַצִּילוּ הֵמָּה לְבַדָּם יִנָּצֵלוּ וְהָאָרֶץ תִּהְיֶה שְׁמָמָה׃

17 Or, if I were to bring the sword upon that land and say, "Let a sword sweep through the land so that I may cut off from it man and beast,"

יז אוֹ חֶרֶב אָבִיא עַל־הָאָרֶץ הַהִיא וְאָמַרְתִּי חֶרֶב תַּעֲבֹר בָּאָרֶץ וְהִכְרַתִּי מִמֶּנָּה אָדָם וּבְהֵמָה׃

14:14 They would by their righteousness save only themselves Hearing of *Yerushalayim*'s imminent demise, one can imagine that *Yechezkel* would have entreated God go save the city, as *Avraham* had before Sodom was destroyed, by means of the following plea: Could the presence of righteous people in the city perhaps prevent its destruction? *Hashem* responds by listing three great people, *Noach*, *Daniel*, and *Iyov*, whose personal piety was beyond reproach. *Noach* was faced with the destruction of mankind, *Daniel* was faced with the destruction of the nation and *Iyov* was confronted by the destruction of his family. However, each one was able to save only themselves, but not the others around them. The presence of the righteous can only assist others who are willing to learn and be influenced by them.

Yechezkel/Ezekiel
Chapter 15

18 if those three men should be in it, as I live – declares *Hashem* – they would save neither sons nor daughters, but they alone would be saved.

19 Or, if I let loose a pestilence against that land, and poured out My fury upon it in blood, cutting off from it man and beast,

20 should *Noach*, *Daniel*, and *Iyov* be in it, as I live – declares *Hashem* – they would save neither son nor daughter; they would save themselves alone by their righteousness.

21 Assuredly, thus said *Hashem*: How much less [should any escape] now that I have let loose against *Yerushalayim* all four of My terrible punishments – the sword, famine, wild beasts, and pestilence – to cut off man and beast from it!

22 Yet there are survivors left of it, sons and daughters who are being brought out. They are coming out to you; and when you see their ways and their deeds, you will be consoled for the disaster that I brought on *Yerushalayim*, for all that I brought on it.

23 You will be consoled through them, when you see their ways and their deeds and realize that not without cause did I do all that I did in it – declares *Hashem*.

15

1 The word of *Hashem* came to me:

2 O mortal, how is the wood of the grapevine better than the wood of any branch to be found among the trees of the forest?

3 Can wood be taken from it for use in any work? Can one take a peg from it to hang any vessel on?

4 Now suppose it was thrown into the fire as fuel and the fire consumed its two ends and its middle was charred – is it good for any use?

5 Even when it was whole it could not be used for anything; how much less when fire has consumed it and it is charred! Can it still be used for anything?

6 Assuredly, thus said *Hashem*: Like the wood of the grapevine among the trees of the forest, which I have designated to be fuel for fire, so will I treat the inhabitants of *Yerushalayim*.

Yechezkel/Ezekiel
Chapter 16

יחזקאל
פרק טז

la-KHAYN KOH a-MAR a-do-NAI e-lo-HEEM ka-a-SHER aytz ha-GE-fen b'-AYTZ ha-YA-ar a-sher n'-ta-TEEV la-AYSH l'-okh-LAH KAYN na-TA-tee et yo-sh'-VAY y'-ru-sha-LA-im

7 I will set My face against them; they escaped from fire, but fire shall consume them. When I set my face against them, you shall know that I am *Hashem*.

ז וְנָתַתִּי אֶת־פָּנַי בָּהֶם מֵהָאֵשׁ יָצָאוּ וְהָאֵשׁ תֹּאכְלֵם וִידַעְתֶּם כִּי־אֲנִי יְהֹוָה בְּשׂוּמִי אֶת־פָּנַי בָּהֶם:

8 I will make the land a desolation, because they committed trespass – declares *Hashem*.

ח וְנָתַתִּי אֶת־הָאָרֶץ שְׁמָמָה יַעַן מָעֲלוּ מַעַל נְאֻם אֲדֹנָי יְהֹוִה:

16
1 The word of *Hashem* came to me:

א וַיְהִי דְבַר־יְהֹוָה אֵלַי לֵאמֹר:

2 O mortal, proclaim *Yerushalayim*'s abominations to her,

ב בֶּן־אָדָם הוֹדַע אֶת־יְרוּשָׁלַםִ אֶת־תּוֹעֲבֹתֶיהָ:

3 and say: Thus said *Hashem* to *Yerushalayim*: By origin and birth you are from the land of the Canaanites – your father was an Amorite and your mother a Hittite.

ג וְאָמַרְתָּ כֹּה־אָמַר אֲדֹנָי יְהֹוִה לִירוּשָׁלַםִ מְכֹרֹתַיִךְ וּמֹלְדֹתַיִךְ מֵאֶרֶץ הַכְּנַעֲנִי אָבִיךְ הָאֱמֹרִי וְאִמֵּךְ חִתִּית:

4 As for your birth, when you were born your navel cord was not cut, and you were not bathed in water to smooth you; you were not rubbed with salt, nor were you swaddled.

ד וּמוֹלְדוֹתַיִךְ בְּיוֹם הוּלֶּדֶת אֹתָךְ לֹא־כָרַּת שָׁרֵּךְ וּבְמַיִם לֹא־רֻחַצְתְּ לְמִשְׁעִי וְהָמְלֵחַ לֹא הֻמְלַחַתְּ וְהָחְתֵּל לֹא חֻתָּלְתְּ:

5 No one pitied you enough to do any one of these things for you out of compassion for you; on the day you were born, you were left lying, rejected, in the open field.

ה לֹא־חָסָה עָלַיִךְ עַיִן לַעֲשׂוֹת לָךְ אַחַת מֵאֵלֶּה לְחֻמְלָה עָלָיִךְ וַתֻּשְׁלְכִי אֶל־פְּנֵי הַשָּׂדֶה בְּגֹעַל נַפְשֵׁךְ בְּיוֹם הֻלֶּדֶת אֹתָךְ:

6 When I passed by you and saw you wallowing in your blood, I said to you: "Live in spite of your blood." Yea, I said to you: "Live in spite of your blood."

ו וָאֶעֱבֹר עָלַיִךְ וָאֶרְאֵךְ מִתְבּוֹסֶסֶת בְּדָמָיִךְ וָאֹמַר לָךְ בְּדָמַיִךְ חֲיִי וָאֹמַר לָךְ בְּדָמַיִךְ חֲיִי:

7 I let you grow like the plants of the field; and you continued to grow up until you attained to womanhood, until your breasts became firm and your hair sprouted. You were still naked and bare

ז רְבָבָה כְּצֶמַח הַשָּׂדֶה נְתַתִּיךְ וַתִּרְבִּי וַתִּגְדְּלִי וַתָּבֹאִי בַּעֲדִי עֲדָיִים שָׁדַיִם נָכֹנוּ וּשְׂעָרֵךְ צִמֵּחַ וְאַתְּ עֵרֹם וְעֶרְיָה:

8 when I passed by you [again] and saw that your time for love had arrived. So I spread My robe over you and covered your nakedness, and I entered into a covenant with you by oath – declares *Hashem*; thus you became Mine.

ח וָאֶעֱבֹר עָלַיִךְ וָאֶרְאֵךְ וְהִנֵּה עִתֵּךְ עֵת דֹּדִים וָאֶפְרֹשׂ כְּנָפִי עָלַיִךְ וָאֲכַסֶּה עֶרְוָתֵךְ וָאֶשָּׁבַע לָךְ וָאָבוֹא בִבְרִית אֹתָךְ נְאֻם אֲדֹנָי יְהֹוִה וַתִּהְיִי לִי:

15:6 Like the wood of the grapevine among the trees of the forest Grapes are one of the seven special agricultural products of *Eretz Yisrael*, and they can teach us a vital life lesson. Contemporary author Rabbi Natan Slifkin explains that grapes must be totally crushed, either underfoot or in a press, to produce valuable wine. He states, "The same is true of the righteous. The difficult question of how bad things can happen to good people is partially resolved through realizing that it is precisely through trials of suffering that latent potential is brought to fruition." In this prophecy, *Yechezkel* promises that the inhabitants of *Yerushalayim* will be destroyed just as a vine that no longer produces grapes is burned for fuel. The message of the grape, however, is that the suffering

A vineyard near Beit Shemesh

Yechezkel/Ezekiel
Chapter 16

9 I bathed you in water, and washed the blood off you, and anointed you with oil.

10 I clothed you with embroidered garments, and gave you sandals of dolphin leather to wear, and wound fine linen about your head, and dressed you in silks.

11 I decked you out in finery and put bracelets on your arms and a chain around your neck.

12 I put a ring in your nose, and earrings in your ears, and a splendid crown on your head.

13 You adorned yourself with gold and silver, and your apparel was of fine linen, silk, and embroidery. Your food was choice flour, honey, and oil. You grew more and more beautiful, and became fit for royalty.

14 Your beauty won you fame among the nations, for it was perfected through the splendor which I set upon you – declares *Hashem*.

15 But confident in your beauty and fame, you played the harlot: you lavished your favors on every passerby; they were his.

16 You even took some of your cloths and made yourself tapestried platforms and fornicated on them – not in the future; not in time to come.

17 You took your beautiful things, made of the gold and silver that I had given you, and you made yourself phallic images and fornicated with them.

18 You took your embroidered cloths to cover them; and you set My oil and My incense before them.

19 The food that I had given you – the choice flour, the oil, and the honey, which I had provided for you to eat – you set it before them for a pleasing odor. And so it went – declares *Hashem*.

20 You even took the sons and daughters that you bore to Me and sacrificed them to those [images] as food – as if your harlotries were not enough,

21 you slaughtered My children and presented them as offerings to them!

22 In all your abominations and harlotries, you did not remember the days of your youth, when you were naked and bare, and lay wallowing in your blood.

---

and hardships are not intended merely as punishments. Rather, *Hashem* hopes that the pain and anguish will eventually bring out the best in them, and inspire their return to Him.

Yechezkel/Ezekiel
Chapter 16

יְחֶזְקֵאל
פרק טז

23 After all your wickedness (woe, woe to you!) – declares *Hashem* –

כג וַיְהִי אַחֲרֵי כָּל־רָעָתֵךְ אוֹי אוֹי לָךְ נְאֻם אֲדֹנָי יֱהֹוִה:

24 you built yourself an eminence and made yourself a mound in every square.

כד וַתִּבְנִי־לָךְ גֶּב וַתַּעֲשִׂי־לָךְ רָמָה בְּכָל־רְחוֹב:

25 You built your mound at every crossroad; and you sullied your beauty and spread your legs to every passerby, and you multiplied your harlotries.

כה אֶל־כָּל־רֹאשׁ דֶּרֶךְ בָּנִית רָמָתֵךְ וַתְּתַעֲבִי אֶת־יָפְיֵךְ וַתְּפַשְּׂקִי אֶת־רַגְלַיִךְ לְכָל־עוֹבֵר וַתַּרְבִּי אֶת־תזנתך [תַּזְנוּתָיִךְ]:

26 You played the whore with your neighbors, the lustful Egyptians – you multiplied your harlotries to anger Me.

כו וַתִּזְנִי אֶל־בְּנֵי־מִצְרַיִם שְׁכֵנַיִךְ גִּדְלֵי בָשָׂר וַתַּרְבִּי אֶת־תַּזְנֻתֵךְ לְהַכְעִיסֵנִי:

27 Now, I will stretch out My arm against you and withhold your maintenance; and I will surrender you to the will of your enemies, the Philistine women, who are shocked by your lewd behavior.

כז וְהִנֵּה נָטִיתִי יָדִי עָלַיִךְ וָאֶגְרַע חֻקֵּךְ וָאֶתְּנֵךְ בְּנֶפֶשׁ שֹׂנְאוֹתַיִךְ בְּנוֹת פְּלִשְׁתִּים הַנִּכְלָמוֹת מִדַּרְכֵּךְ זִמָּה:

28 In your insatiable lust you also played the whore with the Assyrians; you played the whore with them, but were still unsated.

כח וַתִּזְנִי אֶל־בְּנֵי אַשּׁוּר מִבִּלְתִּי שָׂבְעָתֵךְ וַתִּזְנִים וְגַם לֹא שָׂבָעַתְּ:

29 You multiplied your harlotries with Chaldea, that land of traders; yet even with this you were not satisfied.

כט וַתַּרְבִּי אֶת־תַּזְנוּתֵךְ אֶל־אֶרֶץ כְּנַעַן כַּשְׂדִּימָה וְגַם־בְּזֹאת לֹא שָׂבָעַתְּ:

30 How sick was your heart – declares *Hashem* – when you did all those things, the acts of a self-willed whore,

ל מָה אֲמֻלָה לִבָּתֵךְ נְאֻם אֲדֹנָי יֱהֹוִה בַּעֲשׂוֹתֵךְ אֶת־כָּל־אֵלֶּה מַעֲשֵׂה אִשָּׁה־זוֹנָה שַׁלָּטֶת:

31 building your eminence at every crossroad and setting your mound in every square! Yet you were not like a prostitute, for you spurned fees;

לא בִּבְנוֹתַיִךְ גַּבֵּךְ בְּרֹאשׁ כָּל־דֶּרֶךְ וְרָמָתֵךְ עשיתי [עָשִׂית] בְּכָל־רְחוֹב וְלֹא־הָיִית [הָיִיתְ] כַּזּוֹנָה לְקַלֵּס אֶתְנָן:

32 [you were like] the adulterous wife who welcomes strangers instead of her husband.

לב הָאִשָּׁה הַמְּנָאָפֶת תַּחַת אִישָׁהּ תִּקַּח אֶת־זָרִים:

33 Gifts are made to all prostitutes, but you made gifts to all your lovers, and bribed them to come to you from every quarter for your harlotries.

לג לְכָל־זֹנוֹת יִתְּנוּ־נֵדֶה וְאַתְּ נָתַתְּ אֶת־נְדָנַיִךְ לְכָל־מְאַהֲבַיִךְ וַתִּשְׁחֳדִי אוֹתָם לָבוֹא אֵלַיִךְ מִסָּבִיב בְּתַזְנוּתָיִךְ:

34 You were the opposite of other women: you solicited instead of being solicited; you paid fees instead of being paid fees. Thus you were just the opposite!

לד וַיְהִי־בָךְ הֵפֶךְ מִן־הַנָּשִׁים בְּתַזְנוּתַיִךְ וְאַחֲרַיִךְ לֹא זוּנָּה וּבְתִתֵּךְ אֶתְנָן וְאֶתְנַן לֹא נִתַּן־לָךְ וַתְּהִי לְהֶפֶךְ:

35 Now, O harlot, hear the word of *Hashem*.

לה לָכֵן זוֹנָה שִׁמְעִי דְּבַר־יְהֹוָה:

36 Thus said *Hashem*: Because of your brazen effrontery, offering your nakedness to your lovers for harlotry – just like the blood of your children, which you gave to all your abominable fetishes: –

לו כֹּה־אָמַר אֲדֹנָי יֱהֹוִה יַעַן הִשָּׁפֵךְ נְחֻשְׁתֵּךְ וַתִּגָּלֶה עֶרְוָתֵךְ בְּתַזְנוּתַיִךְ עַל־מְאַהֲבָיִךְ וְעַל כָּל־גִּלּוּלֵי תוֹעֲבוֹתַיִךְ וְכִדְמֵי בָנַיִךְ אֲשֶׁר נָתַתְּ לָהֶם:

Yechezkel/Ezekiel
Chapter 16

37 I will assuredly assemble all the lovers to whom you gave your favors, along with everybody you accepted and everybody you rejected. I will assemble them against you from every quarter, and I will expose your nakedness to them, and they shall see all your nakedness.

38 I will inflict upon you the punishment of women who commit adultery and murder, and I will direct bloody and impassioned fury against you.

39 I will deliver you into their hands, and they shall tear down your eminence and level your mounds; and they shall strip you of your clothing and take away your dazzling jewels, leaving you naked and bare.

40 Then they shall assemble a mob against you to pelt you with stones and pierce you with their swords.

41 They shall put your houses to the flames and execute punishment upon you in the sight of many women; thus I will put a stop to your harlotry, and you shall pay no more fees.

42 When I have satisfied My fury upon you and My rage has departed from you, then I will be tranquil; I will be angry no more.

43 Because you did not remember the days of your youth, but infuriated Me with all those things, I will pay you back for your conduct – declares *Hashem*. Have you not committed depravity on top of all your other abominations?

44 Why, everyone who uses proverbs applies to you the proverb "Like mother, like daughter."

45 You are the daughter of your mother, who rejected her husband and children. And you are the sister of your sisters, who rejected their husbands and children; for you are daughters of a Hittite mother and an Amorite father.

46 Your elder sister was *Shomron*, who lived with her daughters to the north of you; your younger sister was Sodom, who lived with her daughters to the south of you.

47 Did you not walk in their ways and practice their abominations? Why, you were almost more corrupt than they in all your ways.

יחזקאל
פרק טז

לז לָכֵן הִנְנִי מְקַבֵּץ אֶת־כָּל־מְאַהֲבַיִךְ אֲשֶׁר עָרַבְתְּ עֲלֵיהֶם וְאֵת כָּל־אֲשֶׁר אָהַבְתְּ עַל כָּל־אֲשֶׁר שָׂנֵאת וְקִבַּצְתִּי אֹתָם עָלַיִךְ מִסָּבִיב וְגִלֵּיתִי עֶרְוָתֵךְ אֲלֵהֶם וְרָאוּ אֶת־כָּל־עֶרְוָתֵךְ:

לח וּשְׁפַטְתִּיךְ מִשְׁפְּטֵי נֹאֲפוֹת וְשֹׁפְכֹת דָּם וּנְתַתִּיךְ דַּם חֵמָה וְקִנְאָה:

לט וְנָתַתִּי אוֹתָךְ בְּיָדָם וְהָרְסוּ גַבֵּךְ וְנִתְּצוּ רָמֹתַיִךְ וְהִפְשִׁיטוּ אוֹתָךְ בְּגָדַיִךְ וְלָקְחוּ כְּלֵי תִפְאַרְתֵּךְ וְהִנִּיחוּךְ עֵירֹם וְעֶרְיָה:

מ וְהֶעֱלוּ עָלַיִךְ קָהָל וְרָגְמוּ אוֹתָךְ בָּאָבֶן וּבִתְּקוּךְ בְּחַרְבוֹתָם:

מא וְשָׂרְפוּ בָתַּיִךְ בָּאֵשׁ וְעָשׂוּ־בָךְ שְׁפָטִים לְעֵינֵי נָשִׁים רַבּוֹת וְהִשְׁבַּתִּיךְ מִזּוֹנָה וְגַם־אֶתְנַן לֹא תִתְּנִי־עוֹד:

מב וַהֲנִחֹתִי חֲמָתִי בָּךְ וְסָרָה קִנְאָתִי מִמֵּךְ וְשָׁקַטְתִּי וְלֹא אֶכְעַס עוֹד:

מג יַעַן אֲשֶׁר לֹא־זָכַרְתִּי [זָכַרְתְּ] אֶת־יְמֵי נְעוּרַיִךְ וַתִּרְגְּזִי־לִי בְּכָל־אֵלֶּה וְגַם־אֲנִי הֵא דַּרְכֵּךְ בְּרֹאשׁ נָתַתִּי נְאֻם אֲדֹנָי יְהוִה וְלֹא עָשִׂיתִי [עָשִׂית] אֶת־הַזִּמָּה עַל כָּל־תּוֹעֲבֹתָיִךְ:

מד הִנֵּה כָּל־הַמֹּשֵׁל עָלַיִךְ יִמְשֹׁל לֵאמֹר כְּאִמָּה בִּתָּהּ:

מה בַּת־אִמֵּךְ אַתְּ גֹּעֶלֶת אִישָׁהּ וּבָנֶיהָ וַאֲחוֹת אֲחוֹתֵךְ אַתְּ אֲשֶׁר גָּעֲלוּ אַנְשֵׁיהֶן וּבְנֵיהֶן אִמְּכֶן חִתִּית וַאֲבִיכֶן אֱמֹרִי:

מו וַאֲחוֹתֵךְ הַגְּדוֹלָה שֹׁמְרוֹן הִיא וּבְנוֹתֶיהָ הַיּוֹשֶׁבֶת עַל־שְׂמֹאולֵךְ וַאֲחוֹתֵךְ הַקְּטַנָּה מִמֵּךְ הַיּוֹשֶׁבֶת מִימִינֵךְ סְדֹם וּבְנוֹתֶיהָ:

מז וְלֹא בְדַרְכֵיהֶן הָלַכְתְּ וּבְתוֹעֲבוֹתֵיהֶן עָשִׂיתִי [עָשִׂית] כִּמְעַט קָט וַתַּשְׁחִתִי מֵהֵן בְּכָל־דְּרָכָיִךְ:

Yechezkel/Ezekiel
Chapter 16

48 As I live – declares *Hashem* – your sister Sodom and her daughters did not do what you and your daughters did.

49 Only this was the sin of your sister Sodom: arrogance! She and her daughters had plenty of bread and untroubled tranquillity; yet she did not support the poor and the needy.

50 In their haughtiness, they committed abomination before Me; and so I removed them, as you saw.

51 Nor did *Shomron* commit even half your sins. You committed more abominations than they, and by all the abominations that you committed you made your sisters look righteous.

52 Truly, you must bear the disgrace of serving as your sisters' advocate: Since you have sinned more abominably than they, they appear righteous in comparison. So be ashamed and bear your disgrace, because you have made your sisters look righteous.

53 I will restore their fortunes – the fortunes of Sodom and her daughters and the fortunes of *Shomron* and her daughters – and your fortunes along with theirs.

54 Thus you shall bear your disgrace and feel your disgrace for behaving in such a way that they could take comfort.

55 Then your sister Sodom and her daughters shall return to their former state, and *Shomron* and her daughters shall return to their former state, and you and your daughters shall return to your former state.

56 Was not your sister Sodom a byword in your mouth in the days of your pride,

57 before your own wickedness was exposed? So must you now bear the mockery of the daughters of Aram and all her neighbors, the daughters of Philistia who jeer at you on every side.

58 You yourself must bear your depravity and your abominations – declares *Hashem*.

59 Truly, thus said *Hashem*: I will deal with you as you have dealt, for you have spurned the pact and violated the covenant.

יחזקאל
פרק טז

מח חַי־אָ֗נִי נְאֻם֮ אֲדֹנָ֣י יֱהֹוִה֒ אִם־עָֽשְׂתָה֙ סְדֹ֣ם אֲחוֹתֵ֔ךְ הִ֖יא וּבְנוֹתֶ֑יהָ כַּאֲשֶׁ֣ר עָשִׂ֔ית אַ֖תְּ וּבְנוֹתָֽיִךְ׃

מט הִנֵּה־זֶ֣ה הָיָ֔ה עֲוֺ֖ן סְדֹ֣ם אֲחוֹתֵ֑ךְ גָּא֨וֹן שִׂבְעַת־לֶ֜חֶם וְשַׁלְוַ֣ת הַשְׁקֵ֗ט הָ֤יָה לָהּ֙ וְלִבְנוֹתֶ֔יהָ וְיַד־עָנִ֥י וְאֶבְי֖וֹן לֹ֥א הֶחֱזִֽיקָה׃

נ וַֽתִּגְבְּהֶ֔ינָה וַתַּעֲשֶׂ֥ינָה תוֹעֵבָ֖ה לְפָנָ֑י וָאָסִ֥יר אֶתְהֶ֖ן כַּאֲשֶׁ֥ר רָאִֽיתִי׃

נא וְשֹׁ֣מְר֔וֹן כַּחֲצִ֥י חַטֹּאתַ֖יִךְ לֹ֣א חָטָ֑אָה וַתַּרְבִּ֤י אֶת־תּוֹעֲבוֹתַ֙יִךְ֙ מֵהֵ֔נָּה וַתְּצַדְּקִי֙ אֶת־אֲחוֹתֵ֔ךְ [אֲחוֹתַ֔יִךְ] בְּכׇל־תּוֹעֲבוֹתַ֖יִךְ אֲשֶׁ֥ר עָשִׂ֖ית [עָשִֽׂית]׃

נב גַּם־אַ֣תְּ ׀ שְׂאִ֣י כְלִמָּתֵ֗ךְ אֲשֶׁ֤ר פִּלַּלְתְּ֙ לַאֲחוֹתֵ֔ךְ בְּחַטֹּאתַ֛יִךְ אֲשֶׁר־הִתְעַ֥בְתְּ מֵהֵ֖ן תִּצְדַּ֣קְנָה מִמֵּ֑ךְ וְגַם־אַ֥תְּ בּ֛וֹשִׁי וּשְׂאִ֥י כְלִמָּתֵ֖ךְ בְּצַדֶּקְתֵּ֥ךְ אַחְיוֹתֵֽךְ׃

נג וְשַׁבְתִּי֙ אֶת־שְׁבִ֣יתְהֶ֔ן אֶת־שְׁב֤וּת [שְׁבִ֤ית] סְדֹם֙ וּבְנוֹתֶ֔יהָ וְאֶת־שְׁב֥וּת [שְׁבִ֥ית] שֹׁמְר֖וֹן וּבְנוֹתֶ֑יהָ וּשְׁב֥וּת [וּשְׁבִ֥ית] שְׁבִיתַ֖יִךְ בְּתוֹכָֽהְנָה׃

נד לְמַ֙עַן֙ תִּשְׂאִ֣י כְלִמָּתֵ֔ךְ וְנִכְלַ֕מְתְּ מִכֹּ֖ל אֲשֶׁ֣ר עָשִׂ֑ית בְּנַחֲמֵ֖ךְ אֹתָֽן׃

נה וַאֲחוֹתַ֗יִךְ סְדֹ֤ם וּבְנוֹתֶ֙יהָ֙ תָּשֹׁ֣בְןָ לְקַדְמָתָ֔ן וְשֹֽׁמְרוֹן֙ וּבְנוֹתֶ֔יהָ תָּשֹׁ֖בְןָ לְקַדְמָתָ֑ן וְאַ֣תְּ וּבְנוֹתַ֔יִךְ תְּשֻׁבֶ֖ינָה לְקַדְמַתְכֶֽן׃

נו וְל֤וֹא הָֽיְתָה֙ סְדֹ֣ם אֲחוֹתֵ֔ךְ לִשְׁמוּעָ֖ה בְּפִ֑יךְ בְּי֖וֹם גְּאוֹנָֽיִךְ׃

נז בְּטֶ֩רֶם֩ תִּגָּלֶ֨ה רָעָתֵ֜ךְ כְּמ֣וֹ עֵ֗ת חֶרְפַּ֤ת בְּנוֹת־אֲרָם֙ וְכׇל־סְבִיבוֹתֶ֣יהָ בְּנ֣וֹת פְּלִשְׁתִּ֑ים הַשָּׁא֥טוֹת אוֹתָ֖ךְ מִסָּבִֽיב׃

נח אֶת־זִמָּתֵ֥ךְ וְאֶת־תּוֹעֲבוֹתַ֖יִךְ אַ֣תְּ נְשָׂאתִ֑ים נְאֻ֖ם יְהֹוָֽה׃

נט כִּ֣י כֹ֤ה אָמַר֙ אֲדֹנָ֣י יֱהֹוִ֔ה וְעָשִׂ֥יתִי [וְעָשִׂ֥יתִֽי] אוֹתָ֖ךְ כַּאֲשֶׁ֣ר עָשִׂ֑ית אֲשֶׁר־בָּזִ֥ית אָלָ֖ה לְהָפֵ֥ר בְּרִֽית׃

Yechezkel/Ezekiel

Chapter 17

60 Nevertheless, I will remember the covenant I made with you in the days of your youth, and I will establish it with you as an everlasting covenant.

v'-za-khar-TEE a-NEE et b'-ree-TEE o-TAKH bee-MAY n'-u-RA-yikh va-ha-kee-mo-TEE LAKH b'-REET o-LAM

61 You shall remember your ways and feel ashamed, when you receive your older sisters and your younger sisters, and I give them to you as daughters, though they are not of your covenant.

62 I will establish My covenant with you, and you shall know that I am *Hashem*.

63 Thus you shall remember and feel shame, and you shall be too abashed to open your mouth again, when I have forgiven you for all that you did – declares *Hashem*.

17

1 The word of *Hashem* came to me:

2 O mortal, propound a riddle and relate an allegory to the House of *Yisrael*.

3 Say: Thus said *Hashem*: The great eagle with the great wings and the long pinions, with the full plumage and the brilliant colors, came to the Lebanon range and seized the top of the cedar.

4 He plucked off its topmost bough and carried it off to the land of traders and set it in a city of merchants.

5 He then took some of the seed of the land and planted it in a fertile field; he planted and set it like a willow beside abundant waters.

6 It grew and became a spreading vine of low stature; it became a vine, produced branches, and sent out boughs. [He had intended] that its twigs should turn to him, and that its roots should stay under him.

16:60 I will establish it with you as an everlasting covenant This chapter is *Yechezkel's* longest. To explain the unfolding tragedy of destruction and exile, *Yechezkel* employs another metaphor, portraying Israel as a baby abandoned in the wilderness. Ignored by most, a kind passerby picks her up, protects her and cares for her. Upon her reaching the age of maturity, he marries her. Nevertheless, despite his dedication and affection, the young woman becomes unfaithful. Such has been the relationship between the People of Israel and *Hashem*. He saved them from slavery, cared for them and protected them in the desert, entered into a covenant with them at Mount Sinai and brought them to their own land. In return, though, they betrayed Him and abandoned Him, favoring other gods over their own. Unlike mortal man, however, God does not change His mind. He promises that He will renew His relationship with them in an "everlasting covenant" and return them to their land.

Yechezkel/Ezekiel

Chapter 17

7 But there was another great eagle with great wings and full plumage; and this vine now bent its roots in his direction and sent out its twigs toward him, that he might water it more than the bed where it was planted –

8 though it was planted in rich soil beside abundant water – so that it might grow branches and produce boughs and be a noble vine.

9 Say: Thus said *Hashem*: Will it thrive? Will he not tear out its roots and rip off its crown, so that its entire foliage withers? It shall wither, despite any strong arm or mighty army [that may come] to remove it from its roots.

10 And suppose it is transplanted, will it thrive? When the east wind strikes it, it shall wither – wither upon the bed where it is growing.

11 Then the word of *Hashem* came to me:

12 Say to the rebellious breed: Do you not know what these things mean? Say: The king of Babylon came to *Yerushalayim*, and carried away its king and its officers and brought them back with him to Babylon.

13 He took one of the seed royal and made a covenant with him and imposed an oath on him, and he carried away the nobles of the land –

14 so that it might be a humble kingdom and not exalt itself, but keep his covenant and so endure.

15 But [that prince] rebelled against him and sent his envoys to Egypt to get horses and a large army. Will he succeed? Will he who does such things escape? Shall he break a covenant and escape?

16 As I live – declares *Hashem* – in the very homeland of the king who made him king, whose oath he flouted and whose covenant he broke – right there, in Babylon, he shall die.

17 Pharaoh will not fight at his side with a great army and with numerous troops in the war, when mounds are thrown up and siege towers erected to destroy many lives.

18 He flouted a pact and broke a covenant; he gave his promise and did all these things – he shall not escape.

Yechezkel/Ezekiel
Chapter 18

19 Assuredly, thus said *Hashem*: As I live, I will pay him back for flouting My pact and breaking My covenant.

יט לָכֵ֞ן כֹּֽה־אָמַ֨ר אֲדֹנָ֤י יְהֹוִה֙ חַי־אָ֔נִי אִם־לֹ֗א אָלָתִי֙ אֲשֶׁ֣ר בָּזָ֔ה וּבְרִיתִ֖י אֲשֶׁ֣ר הֵפִ֑יר וּנְתַתִּ֖יו בְּרֹאשֽׁוֹ:

20 I will spread My net over him and he shall be caught in My snare; I will carry him to Babylon and enter with him into judgment there for the trespass which he committed against Me.

כ וּפָרַשְׂתִּ֤י עָלָיו֙ רִשְׁתִּ֔י וְנִתְפַּ֖שׂ בִּמְצֽוּדָתִ֑י וַהֲבִיאוֹתִ֣יהוּ בָבֶ֗לָה וְנִשְׁפַּטְתִּ֤י אִתּוֹ֙ שָׁ֔ם מַעֲל֖וֹ אֲשֶׁ֥ר מָעַל־בִּֽי:

21 And all the fugitives of all his battalions shall fall by the sword, and those who remain shall scatter in every direction; then you will know that I *Hashem* have spoken.

כא וְאֵ֨ת כָּל־מברחו [מִבְרָחָ֜יו] בְּכָל־אֲגַפָּ֗יו בַּחֶ֣רֶב יִפֹּ֔לוּ וְהַנִּשְׁאָרִ֖ים לְכָל־ר֣וּחַ יִפָּרֵ֑שׂוּ וִידַעְתֶּ֕ם כִּ֛י אֲנִ֥י יְהֹוָ֖ה דִּבַּֽרְתִּי:

22 Thus said *Hashem*: Then I in turn will take and set [in the ground a slip] from the lofty top of the cedar; I will pluck a tender twig from the tip of its crown, and I will plant it on a tall, towering mountain.

כב כֹּ֤ה אָמַר֙ אֲדֹנָ֣י יְהֹוִ֔ה וְלָקַ֣חְתִּי אָ֗נִי מִצַּמֶּ֧רֶת הָאֶ֛רֶז הָרָמָ֖ה וְנָתָ֑תִּי מֵרֹ֤אשׁ יֹֽנְקוֹתָיו֙ רַ֣ךְ אֶקְטֹ֔ף וְשָׁתַ֣לְתִּי אָ֔נִי עַ֥ל הַר־גָּבֹ֖הַּ וְתָלֽוּל:

23 I will plant it in *Yisrael*'s lofty highlands, and it shall bring forth boughs and produce branches and grow into a noble cedar. Every bird of every feather shall take shelter under it, shelter in the shade of its boughs.

כג בְּהַ֨ר מְר֤וֹם יִשְׂרָאֵל֙ אֶשְׁתֳּלֶ֔נּוּ וְנָשָׂ֥א עָנָ֖ף וְעָ֣שָׂה פֶ֑רִי וְהָיָ֖ה לְאֶ֣רֶז אַדִּ֑יר וְשָׁכְנ֣וּ תַחְתָּ֗יו כֹּ֚ל צִפּ֣וֹר כָּל־כָּנָ֔ף בְּצֵ֥ל דָּלִיּֽוֹתָ֖יו תִּשְׁכֹּֽנָּה:

b'-HAR m'-ROM yis-ra-AYL esh-to-LE-nu v'-na-SA a-NAF v'-A-sah FE-ree v'-ha-YAH l'-E-rez a-DEER v'-sha-kh'-NU takh-TAV KOL tzi-POR kol ka-NAF b'-TZAYL da-li-yo-TAV tish-KO-nah

24 Then shall all the trees of the field know that it is I *Hashem* who have abased the lofty tree and exalted the lowly tree, who have dried up the green tree and made the withered tree bud. I *Hashem* have spoken, and I will act.

כד וְֽיָדְע֞וּ כָּל־עֲצֵ֣י הַשָּׂדֶ֗ה כִּ֣י אֲנִ֤י יְהֹוָה֙ הִשְׁפַּ֣לְתִּי ׀ עֵ֣ץ גָּבֹ֗הַּ הִגְבַּ֙הְתִּי֙ עֵ֣ץ שָׁפָ֔ל הוֹבַ֙שְׁתִּי֙ עֵ֣ץ לָ֔ח וְהִפְרַ֖חְתִּי עֵ֣ץ יָבֵ֑שׁ אֲנִ֥י יְהֹוָ֖ה דִּבַּ֥רְתִּי וְעָשִֽׂיתִי:

18

1 The word of *Hashem* came to me:

א וַיְהִ֥י דְבַר־יְהֹוָ֖ה אֵלַ֥י לֵאמֹֽר:

2 What do you mean by quoting this proverb upon the soil of *Yisrael*, "Parents eat sour grapes and their children's teeth are blunted"?

ב מַה־לָּכֶ֗ם אַתֶּ֤ם מֹֽשְׁלִים֙ אֶת־הַמָּשָׁ֣ל הַזֶּ֔ה עַל־אַדְמַ֥ת יִשְׂרָאֵ֖ל לֵאמֹ֑ר אָבוֹת֙ יֹ֣אכְלוּ בֹ֔סֶר וְשִׁנֵּ֥י הַבָּנִ֖ים תִּקְהֶֽינָה:

ma la-KHEM a-TEM mo-sh'-LEEM et ha-ma-SHAL ha-ZEH al ad-MAT yis-ra-AYL lay-MOR a-VOT YO-kh'-lu VO-ser v'-shi-NAY ha-ba-NEEM tik-HE-nah

---

17:23 Every bird of every feather shall take shelter under it *Yechezkel* reverses the negative prophecies and includes a vision of hope. Referring to *Mashiach*, he describes a small cedar shoot which will be restored to the high mountain of *Yerushalayim*. This tree will grow, bear fruit, and provide protection for all those who seek it. *Yechezkel* is teaching that in the time of redemption, not only will Israel seek out *Hashem*, but all the nations of the world will travel to *Yerushalayim* to seek Israel's friendship and to acknowledge God's sovereignty.

18:2 What do you mean by quoting this proverb upon the soil of *Yisrael* The sinful nation complains that they are being punished for transgressions committed by their

Yechezkel/Ezekiel
Chapter 18

יחזקאל
פרק יח

3 As I live – declares *Hashem* – this proverb shall no longer be current among you in *Yisrael*.

ג חַי־אָ֣נִי נְאֻם֮ אֲדֹנָ֣י יֱהֹוִה֒ אִם־יִֽהְיֶ֣ה לָכֶ֗ם ע֛וֹד מְשֹׁ֥ל הַמָּשָׁ֖ל הַזֶּ֑ה בְּיִשְׂרָאֵֽל:

4 Consider, all lives are Mine; the life of the parent and the life of the child are both Mine. The person who sins, only he shall die.

ד הֵ֤ן כׇּל־הַנְּפָשׁוֹת֙ לִ֣י הֵ֔נָּה כְּנֶ֧פֶשׁ הָאָ֛ב וּכְנֶ֥פֶשׁ הַבֵּ֖ן לִי־הֵ֑נָּה הַנֶּ֥פֶשׁ הַחֹטֵ֖את הִ֥יא תָמֽוּת:

5 Thus, if a man is righteous and does what is just and right:

ה וְאִ֖ישׁ כִּי־יִֽהְיֶ֣ה צַדִּ֑יק וְעָשָׂ֛ה מִשְׁפָּ֖ט וּצְדָקָֽה:

6 If he has not eaten on the mountains or raised his eyes to the fetishes of the House of *Yisrael*; if he has not defiled another man's wife or approached a menstruous woman;

ו אֶל־הֶֽהָרִים֙ לֹ֣א אָכָ֔ל וְעֵינָיו֙ לֹ֣א נָשָׂ֔א אֶל־גִּלּוּלֵ֖י בֵּ֣ית יִשְׂרָאֵ֑ל וְאֶת־אֵ֤שֶׁת רֵעֵ֙הוּ֙ לֹ֣א טִמֵּ֔א וְאֶל־אִשָּׁ֥ה נִדָּ֖ה לֹ֥א יִקְרָֽב:

7 if he has not wronged anyone; if he has returned the debtor's pledge to him and has taken nothing by robbery; if he has given bread to the hungry and clothed the naked;

ז וְאִישׁ֙ לֹ֣א יוֹנֶ֔ה חֲבֹלָת֥וֹ חוֹב֙ יָשִׁ֔יב גְּזֵלָ֖ה לֹ֣א יִגְזֹ֑ל לַחְמוֹ֙ לְרָעֵ֣ב יִתֵּ֔ן וְעֵירֹ֖ם יְכַסֶּה־בָּֽגֶד:

8 if he has not lent at advance interest or exacted accrued interest; if he has abstained from wrongdoing and executed true justice between man and man;

ח בַּנֶּ֣שֶׁךְ לֹֽא־יִתֵּ֗ן וְתַרְבִּית֙ לֹ֣א יִקָּ֔ח מֵעָ֖וֶל יָשִׁ֣יב יָד֑וֹ מִשְׁפַּ֤ט אֱמֶת֙ יַעֲשֶׂ֔ה בֵּ֥ין אִ֖ישׁ לְאִֽישׁ:

9 if he has followed My laws and kept My rules and acted honestly – he is righteous. Such a man shall live – declares *Hashem*.

ט בְּחֻקּוֹתַ֧י יְהַלֵּ֛ךְ וּמִשְׁפָּטַ֥י שָׁמַ֖ר לַעֲשׂ֣וֹת אֱמֶ֑ת צַדִּ֥יק הוּא֙ חָיֹ֣ה יִֽחְיֶ֔ה נְאֻ֖ם אֲדֹנָ֥י יֱהֹוִֽה:

10 Suppose, now, that he has begotten a son who is a ruffian, a shedder of blood, who does any of these things,

י וְהוֹלִ֥יד בֵּן־פָּרִ֖יץ שֹׁפֵ֣ךְ דָּ֑ם וְעָ֣שָׂה אָ֔ח מֵאַחַ֖ד מֵאֵֽלֶּה:

11 whereas he himself did none of these things. That is, [the son] has eaten on the mountains, has defiled another man's wife,

יא וְה֕וּא אֶת־כׇּל־אֵ֖לֶּה לֹ֣א עָשָׂ֑ה כִּ֣י גַ֤ם אֶל־הֶהָרִים֙ אָכָ֔ל וְאֶת־אֵ֥שֶׁת רֵעֵ֖הוּ טִמֵּֽא:

12 has wronged the poor and the needy, has taken by robbery, has not returned a pledge, has raised his eyes to the fetishes, has committed abomination,

יב עָנִ֤י וְאֶבְיוֹן֙ הוֹנָ֔ה גְּזֵל֣וֹת גָּזָ֔ל חֲבֹ֖ל לֹ֣א יָשִׁ֑יב וְאֶל־הַגִּלּוּלִים֙ נָשָׂ֣א עֵינָ֔יו תּוֹעֵבָ֖ה עָשָֽׂה:

13 has lent at advance interest, or exacted accrued interest – shall he live? He shall not live! If he has committed any of these abominations, he shall die; he has forfeited his life.

יג בַּנֶּ֧שֶׁךְ נָתַ֛ן וְתַרְבִּ֥ית לָקַ֖ח וָחָ֑י לֹ֣א יִֽחְיֶ֗ה אֵ֣ת כׇּל־הַתּוֹעֵב֤וֹת הָאֵ֙לֶּה֙ עָשָׂ֔ה מ֣וֹת יוּמָ֔ת דָּמָ֖יו בּ֥וֹ יִֽהְיֶֽה:

---

ancestors. *Yechezkel* explains that this is inaccurate; they are being held accountable because they have continued their parents' evil deeds. The prophet specifically reprimands the people for uttering this complaint in the Land of Israel. The fallacy in the children's complaint that they are being punished for their father's sins motivates *Yechezkel* to speak, as the Holy Land cannot tolerate falsehood.

Yechezkel/Ezekiel
Chapter 18

יחזקאל
פרק יח

14 Now suppose that he, in turn, has begotten a son who has seen all the sins that his father committed, but has taken heed and has not imitated them:

יד וְהִנֵּה הוֹלִיד בֵּן וַיַּרְא אֶת־כָּל־חַטֹּאת אָבִיו אֲשֶׁר עָשָׂה וַיִּרְאֶה וְלֹא יַעֲשֶׂה כָּהֵן׃

15 He has not eaten on the mountains or raised his eyes to the fetishes of the House of Yisrael; he has not defiled another man's wife;

טו עַל־הֶהָרִים לֹא אָכָל וְעֵינָיו לֹא נָשָׂא אֶל־גִּלּוּלֵי בֵּית יִשְׂרָאֵל אֶת־אֵשֶׁת רֵעֵהוּ לֹא טִמֵּא׃

16 he has not wronged anyone; he has not seized a pledge or taken anything by robbery; he has given his bread to the hungry and clothed the naked;

טז וְאִישׁ לֹא הוֹנָה חֲבֹל לֹא חָבָל וּגְזֵלָה לֹא גָזָל לַחְמוֹ לְרָעֵב נָתָן וְעֵרוֹם כִּסָּה־בָגֶד׃

17 he has refrained from oppressing the poor; he has not exacted advance or accrued interest; he has obeyed My rules and followed My laws – he shall not die for the iniquity of his father, but shall live.

יז מֵעָנִי הֵשִׁיב יָדוֹ נֶשֶׁךְ וְתַרְבִּית לֹא לָקָח מִשְׁפָּטַי עָשָׂה בְּחֻקּוֹתַי הָלָךְ הוּא לֹא יָמוּת בַּעֲוֺן אָבִיו חָיֹה יִחְיֶה׃

18 To be sure, his father, because he practiced fraud, robbed his brother, and acted wickedly among his kin, did die for his iniquity;

יח אָבִיו כִּי־עָשַׁק עֹשֶׁק גָּזַל גֵּזֶל אָח וַאֲשֶׁר לֹא־טוֹב עָשָׂה בְּתוֹךְ עַמָּיו וְהִנֵּה־מֵת בַּעֲוֺנוֹ׃

19 and now you ask, "Why has not the son shared the burden of his father's guilt?" But the son has done what is right and just, and has carefully kept all My laws: he shall live!

יט וַאֲמַרְתֶּם מַדֻּעַ לֹא־נָשָׂא הַבֵּן בַּעֲוֺן הָאָב וְהַבֵּן מִשְׁפָּט וּצְדָקָה עָשָׂה אֵת כָּל־חֻקּוֹתַי שָׁמַר וַיַּעֲשֶׂה אֹתָם חָיֹה יִחְיֶה׃

20 The person who sins, he alone shall die. A child shall not share the burden of a parent's guilt, nor shall a parent share the burden of a child's guilt; the righteousness of the righteous shall be accounted to him alone, and the wickedness of the wicked shall be accounted to him alone.

כ הַנֶּפֶשׁ הַחֹטֵאת הִיא תָמוּת בֵּן לֹא־יִשָּׂא בַּעֲוֺן הָאָב וְאָב לֹא יִשָּׂא בַּעֲוֺן הַבֵּן צִדְקַת הַצַּדִּיק עָלָיו תִּהְיֶה וְרִשְׁעַת רשע [הָרָשָׁע] עָלָיו תִּהְיֶה׃

21 Moreover, if the wicked one repents of all the sins that he committed and keeps all My laws and does what is just and right, he shall live; he shall not die.

כא וְהָרָשָׁע כִּי יָשׁוּב מִכָּל־חַטֹּאתוֹ [חַטֹּאתָיו] אֲשֶׁר עָשָׂה וְשָׁמַר אֶת־כָּל־חֻקּוֹתַי וְעָשָׂה מִשְׁפָּט וּצְדָקָה חָיֹה יִחְיֶה לֹא יָמוּת׃

22 None of the transgressions he committed shall be remembered against him; because of the righteousness he has practiced, he shall live.

כב כָּל־פְּשָׁעָיו אֲשֶׁר עָשָׂה לֹא יִזָּכְרוּ לוֹ בְּצִדְקָתוֹ אֲשֶׁר־עָשָׂה יִחְיֶה׃

23 Is it my desire that a wicked person shall die? – says Hashem. It is rather that he shall turn back from his ways and live.

כג הֶחָפֹץ אֶחְפֹּץ מוֹת רָשָׁע נְאֻם אֲדֹנָי יֱהֹוִה הֲלוֹא בְּשׁוּבוֹ מִדְּרָכָיו וְחָיָה׃

24 So, too, if a righteous person turns away from his righteousness and does wrong, practicing the very abominations that the wicked person practiced, shall he live? None of the righteous deeds that he did shall be remembered; because of the treachery he has practiced and the sins he has committed – because of these, he shall die.

כד וּבְשׁוּב צַדִּיק מִצִּדְקָתוֹ וְעָשָׂה עָוֶל כְּכֹל הַתּוֹעֵבוֹת אֲשֶׁר־עָשָׂה הָרָשָׁע יַעֲשֶׂה וָחָי כָּל־צדקתו [צִדְקֹתָיו] אֲשֶׁר־עָשָׂה לֹא תִזָּכַרְנָה בְּמַעֲלוֹ אֲשֶׁר־מָעַל וּבְחַטָּאתוֹ אֲשֶׁר־חָטָא בָּם יָמוּת׃

1248

Yechezkel/Ezekiel
Chapter 19

25 Yet you say, "The way of *Hashem* is unfair." Listen, O House of *Yisrael*: Is My way unfair? It is your ways that are unfair!

26 When a righteous person turns away from his righteousness and does wrong, he shall die for it; he shall die for the wrong he has done.

27 And if a wicked person turns back from the wickedness that he practiced and does what is just and right, such a person shall save his life.

28 Because he took heed and turned back from all the transgressions that he committed, he shall live; he shall not die.

29 Yet the House of *Yisrael* say, "The way of *Hashem* is unfair." Are My ways unfair, O House of *Yisrael*? It is your ways that are unfair!

30 Be assured, O House of *Yisrael*, I will judge each one of you according to his ways – declares *Hashem*. Repent and turn back from your transgressions; let them not be a stumbling block of guilt for you.

31 Cast away all the transgressions by which you have offended, and get yourselves a new heart and a new spirit, that you may not die, O House of *Yisrael*.

32 For it is not My desire that anyone shall die – declares *Hashem*. Repent, therefore, and live!

19

1 And you are to intone a dirge over the princes of *Yisrael*,

2 and say: What a lioness was your mother Among the lions! Crouching among the great beasts, She reared her cubs.

3 She raised up one of her cubs, He became a great beast; He learned to hunt prey – He devoured men.

4 Nations heeded [the call] against him; He was caught in their snare. They dragged him off with hooks To the land of Egypt.

5 When she saw herself frustrated, Her hope defeated, She took another of her cubs And set him up as a great beast.

6 He stalked among the lions, He was a great beast; He learned to hunt prey – He devoured men.

Yechezkel/Ezekiel
Chapter 20

יחזקאל
פרק כ

7 He ravished their widows, Laid waste their cities; The land and all in it were appalled At the sound of his roaring.

ז וַיֵּדַע אַלְמְנוֹתָיו וְעָרֵיהֶם הֶחֱרִיב וַתֵּשַׁם אֶרֶץ וּמְלֹאָהּ מִקּוֹל שַׁאֲגָתוֹ׃

va-YAY-da al-m'-no-TAV v'-a-ray-HEM he-khe-REEV va-tay-SHAM E-retz um-lo-AH mi-KOL sha-a-ga-TO

8 Nations from the countries roundabout Arrayed themselves against him. They spread their net over him, He was caught in their snare.

ח וַיִּתְּנוּ עָלָיו גּוֹיִם סָבִיב מִמְּדִינוֹת וַיִּפְרְשׂוּ עָלָיו רִשְׁתָּם בְּשַׁחְתָּם נִתְפָּשׂ׃

9 With hooks he was put in a cage, They carried him off to the king of Babylon And confined him in a fortress, So that never again should his roar be heard On the hills of *Yisrael*.

ט וַיִּתְּנֻהוּ בַסּוּגַר בַּחַחִים וַיְבִאֻהוּ אֶל־מֶלֶךְ בָּבֶל יְבִאֻהוּ בַּמְּצֹדוֹת לְמַעַן לֹא־יִשָּׁמַע קוֹלוֹ עוֹד אֶל־הָרֵי יִשְׂרָאֵל׃

10 Your mother was like a vine in your blood, Planted beside streams, With luxuriant boughs and branches Thanks to abundant waters.

י אִמְּךָ כַגֶּפֶן בְּדָמְךָ עַל־מַיִם שְׁתוּלָה פֹּרִיָּה וַעֲנֵפָה הָיְתָה מִמַּיִם רַבִּים׃

11 And she had a mighty rod Fit for a ruler's scepter. It towered highest among the leafy trees, It was conspicuous by its height, By the abundance of its boughs.

יא וַיִּהְיוּ־לָהּ מַטּוֹת עֹז אֶל־שִׁבְטֵי מֹשְׁלִים וַתִּגְבַּהּ קוֹמָתוֹ עַל־בֵּין עֲבֹתִים וַיֵּרָא בְגָבְהוֹ בְּרֹב דָּלִיֹּתָיו׃

12 But plucked up in a fury, She was hurled to the ground. The east wind withered her branches, They broke apart and dried up; And her mighty rod was consumed by fire.

יב וַתֻּתַּשׁ בְּחֵמָה לָאָרֶץ הֻשְׁלָכָה וְרוּחַ הַקָּדִים הוֹבִישׁ פִּרְיָהּ הִתְפָּרְקוּ וְיָבֵשׁוּ מַטֵּה עֻזָּהּ אֵשׁ אֲכָלָתְהוּ׃

13 Now she is planted in the desert, In ground that is arid and parched.

יג וְעַתָּה שְׁתוּלָה בַמִּדְבָּר בְּאֶרֶץ צִיָּה וְצָמָא׃

14 Fire has issued from her twig-laden branch And has consumed her boughs, She is left without a mighty rod, A scepter to rule with. This is a dirge, and it has become a [familiar] dirge.

יד וַתֵּצֵא אֵשׁ מִמַּטֵּה בַדֶּיהָ פִּרְיָהּ אָכָלָה וְלֹא־הָיָה בָהּ מַטֵּה־עֹז שֵׁבֶט לִמְשׁוֹל קִינָה הִיא וַתְּהִי לְקִינָה׃

20

1 In the seventh year, on the tenth day of the fifth month, certain elders of *Yisrael* came to inquire of *Hashem*, and sat down before me.

כ א וַיְהִי בַּשָּׁנָה הַשְּׁבִיעִית בַּחֲמִשִׁי בֶּעָשׂוֹר לַחֹדֶשׁ בָּאוּ אֲנָשִׁים מִזִּקְנֵי יִשְׂרָאֵל לִדְרֹשׁ אֶת־יְהֹוָה וַיֵּשְׁבוּ לְפָנָי׃

2 And the word of *Hashem* came to me:

ב וַיְהִי דְבַר־יְהֹוָה אֵלַי לֵאמֹר׃

3 O mortal, speak to the elders of *Yisrael* and say to them: Thus said *Hashem*: Have you come to inquire of Me? As I live, I will not respond to your inquiry – declares *Hashem*.

ג בֶּן־אָדָם דַּבֵּר אֶת־זִקְנֵי יִשְׂרָאֵל וְאָמַרְתָּ אֲלֵהֶם כֹּה אָמַר אֲדֹנָי יְהֹוִה הֲלִדְרֹשׁ אֹתִי אַתֶּם בָּאִים חַי־אָנִי אִם־אִדָּרֵשׁ לָכֶם נְאֻם אֲדֹנָי יְהֹוִה׃

19:7 At the sound of his roaring *Yechezkel* laments the final kings of *Yehuda*, whose royal family sign was the lion, and blames King *Yehoyakim* for turning the land to waste. *Rashi* suggests that through the policy of excessive taxation he instituted in order to pay tribute to Egypt, *Yehoyakim* impoverished the cities, leading to their destruction. A leader has great responsibilities towards his people and the Kings of *Yehuda* are held accountable for impoverishing the nation.

Rashi
(1040–1105)

Yechezkel/Ezekiel
Chapter 20

יְחֶזְקֵאל
פרק כ

4 Arraign, arraign them, O mortal! Declare to them the abhorrent deeds of their fathers.

ד הֲתִשְׁפֹּט אֹתָם הֲתִשְׁפּוֹט בֶּן־אָדָם אֶת־תּוֹעֲבֹת אֲבוֹתָם הוֹדִיעֵם׃

5 Say to them: Thus said *Hashem*: On the day that I chose *Yisrael*, I gave My oath to the stock of the House of *Yaakov*; when I made Myself known to them in the land of Egypt, I gave my oath to them. When I said, "I *Hashem* am your God,"

ה וְאָמַרְתָּ אֲלֵיהֶם כֹּה־אָמַר אֲדֹנָי יְהֹוִה בְּיוֹם בָּחֳרִי בְיִשְׂרָאֵל וָאֶשָּׂא יָדִי לְזֶרַע בֵּית יַעֲקֹב וָאִוָּדַע לָהֶם בְּאֶרֶץ מִצְרָיִם וָאֶשָּׂא יָדִי לָהֶם לֵאמֹר אֲנִי יְהֹוָה אֱלֹהֵיכֶם׃

6 that same day I swore to them to take them out of the land of Egypt into a land flowing with milk and honey, a land which I had sought out for them, the fairest of all lands.

ו בַּיּוֹם הַהוּא נָשָׂאתִי יָדִי לָהֶם לְהוֹצִיאָם מֵאֶרֶץ מִצְרָיִם אֶל־אֶרֶץ אֲשֶׁר־תַּרְתִּי לָהֶם זָבַת חָלָב וּדְבַשׁ צְבִי הִיא לְכָל־הָאֲרָצוֹת׃

ba-YOM ha-HU na-SA-tee ya-DEE la-HEM l'-ho-tzee-AM may-E-retz mitz-RA-yim el E-retz a-sher TAR-tee la-HEM za-VAT kha-LAV ud-VASH tz'-VEE HEE l'-khol ha-a-ra-TZOT

7 I also said to them: Cast away, every one of you, the detestable things that you are drawn to, and do not defile yourselves with the fetishes of Egypt – I *Hashem* am your God.

ז וָאֹמַר אֲלֵהֶם אִישׁ שִׁקּוּצֵי עֵינָיו הַשְׁלִיכוּ וּבְגִלּוּלֵי מִצְרַיִם אַל־תִּטַּמָּאוּ אֲנִי יְהֹוָה אֱלֹהֵיכֶם׃

8 But they defied Me and refused to listen to Me. They did not cast away the detestable things they were drawn to, nor did they give up the fetishes of Egypt. Then I resolved to pour out My fury upon them, to vent all My anger upon them there, in the land of Egypt.

ח וַיַּמְרוּ־בִי וְלֹא אָבוּ לִשְׁמֹעַ אֵלַי אִישׁ אֶת־שִׁקּוּצֵי עֵינֵיהֶם לֹא הִשְׁלִיכוּ וְאֶת־גִּלּוּלֵי מִצְרַיִם לֹא עָזָבוּ וָאֹמַר לִשְׁפֹּךְ חֲמָתִי עֲלֵיהֶם לְכַלּוֹת אַפִּי בָּהֶם בְּתוֹךְ אֶרֶץ מִצְרָיִם׃

9 But I acted for the sake of My name, that it might not be profaned in the sight of the nations among whom they were. For it was before their eyes that I had made Myself known to *Yisrael* to bring them out of the land of Egypt.

ט וָאַעַשׂ לְמַעַן שְׁמִי לְבִלְתִּי הֵחֵל לְעֵינֵי הַגּוֹיִם אֲשֶׁר־הֵמָּה בְתוֹכָם אֲשֶׁר נוֹדַעְתִּי אֲלֵיהֶם לְעֵינֵיהֶם לְהוֹצִיאָם מֵאֶרֶץ מִצְרָיִם׃

10 I brought them out of the land of Egypt and I led them into the wilderness.

י וָאוֹצִיאֵם מֵאֶרֶץ מִצְרָיִם וָאֲבִאֵם אֶל־הַמִּדְבָּר׃

11 I gave them My laws and taught them My rules, by the pursuit of which a man shall live.

יא וָאֶתֵּן לָהֶם אֶת־חֻקּוֹתַי וְאֶת־מִשְׁפָּטַי הוֹדַעְתִּי אוֹתָם אֲשֶׁר יַעֲשֶׂה אוֹתָם הָאָדָם וָחַי בָּהֶם׃

20:6 The fairest of all lands *Eretz Yisrael* is described here as 'fair' or 'beautiful,' in Hebrew *tzvi* (צבי). The word *tzvi* also means 'gazelle,' which prompts the Talmud (*Ketubot* 112a) to compare the Land of Israel to the skin of a gazelle (see also Daniel 11:16 where the Land of Israel is referred to as *eretz ha-tzvi*, 'the beautiful land'). Just as its skin stretches to fit over the body of the gazelle but shrinks when removed, so do the physical borders of *Eretz Yisrael* stretch to fit its Jewish inhabitants, but shrink when they are exiled from the land. Perhaps a deeper message can be applied for Israel's inhabitants as well. Unlike other places in the world, the inhabitants of Israel must "stretch" themselves morally and spiritually to appreciate the holiness of the Land of the Gazelle, "the fairest of all lands."

A gazelle in the Negev dessert

Yechezkel/Ezekiel
Chapter 20

12 Moreover, I gave them My *Shabbatot* to serve as a sign between Me and them, that they might know that it is I *Hashem* who sanctify them.

13 But the House of *Yisrael* rebelled against Me in the wilderness; they did not follow My laws and they rejected My rules – by the pursuit of which a man shall live – and they grossly desecrated My *Shabbatot*. Then I thought to pour out My fury upon them in the wilderness and to make an end of them;

14 but I acted for the sake of My name, that it might not be profaned in the sight of the nations before whose eyes I had led them out.

15 However, I swore to them in the wilderness that I would not bring them into the land flowing with milk and honey, the fairest of all lands, which I had assigned [to them],

16 for they had rejected My rules, disobeyed My laws, and desecrated My *Shabbatot*; their hearts followed after their fetishes.

17 But I had pity on them and did not destroy them; I did not make an end of them in the wilderness.

18 I warned their children in the wilderness: Do not follow the practices of your fathers, do not keep their ways, and do not defile yourselves with their fetishes.

19 I *Hashem* am your God: Follow My laws and be careful to observe My rules.

20 And hallow My *Shabbatot*, that they may be a sign between Me and you, that you may know that I *Hashem* am your God.

21 But the children rebelled against Me: they did not follow My laws and did not faithfully observe My rules, by the pursuit of which man shall live; they profaned My *Shabbatot*. Then I resolved to pour out My fury upon them, to vent all My anger upon them, in the wilderness.

22 But I held back My hand and acted for the sake of My name, that it might not be profaned in the sight of the nations before whose eyes I had led them out.

23 However, I swore to them in the wilderness that I would scatter them among the nations and disperse them through the lands,

יחזקאל
פרק כ

יב וְגַם אֶת־שַׁבְּתוֹתַי נָתַתִּי לָהֶם לִהְיוֹת לְאוֹת בֵּינִי וּבֵינֵיהֶם לָדַעַת כִּי אֲנִי יְהֹוָה מְקַדְּשָׁם׃

יג וַיַּמְרוּ־בִי בֵית־יִשְׂרָאֵל בַּמִּדְבָּר בְּחֻקּוֹתַי לֹא־הָלָכוּ וְאֶת־מִשְׁפָּטַי מָאָסוּ אֲשֶׁר יַעֲשֶׂה אֹתָם הָאָדָם וָחַי בָּהֶם וְאֶת־שַׁבְּתֹתַי חִלְּלוּ מְאֹד וָאֹמַר לִשְׁפֹּךְ חֲמָתִי עֲלֵיהֶם בַּמִּדְבָּר לְכַלּוֹתָם׃

יד וָאֶעֱשֶׂה לְמַעַן שְׁמִי לְבִלְתִּי הֵחֵל לְעֵינֵי הַגּוֹיִם אֲשֶׁר הוֹצֵאתִים לְעֵינֵיהֶם׃

טו וְגַם־אֲנִי נָשָׂאתִי יָדִי לָהֶם בַּמִּדְבָּר לְבִלְתִּי הָבִיא אוֹתָם אֶל־הָאָרֶץ אֲשֶׁר־נָתַתִּי זָבַת חָלָב וּדְבַשׁ צְבִי הִיא לְכָל־הָאֲרָצוֹת׃

טז יַעַן בְּמִשְׁפָּטַי מָאָסוּ וְאֶת־חֻקּוֹתַי לֹא־הָלְכוּ בָהֶם וְאֶת־שַׁבְּתוֹתַי חִלֵּלוּ כִּי אַחֲרֵי גִלּוּלֵיהֶם לִבָּם הֹלֵךְ׃

יז וַתָּחָס עֵינִי עֲלֵיהֶם מִשַּׁחֲתָם וְלֹא־עָשִׂיתִי אוֹתָם כָּלָה בַּמִּדְבָּר׃

יח וָאֹמַר אֶל־בְּנֵיהֶם בַּמִּדְבָּר בְּחוּקֵּי אֲבוֹתֵיכֶם אַל־תֵּלֵכוּ וְאֶת־מִשְׁפְּטֵיהֶם אַל־תִּשְׁמֹרוּ וּבְגִלּוּלֵיהֶם אַל־תִּטַּמָּאוּ׃

יט אֲנִי יְהֹוָה אֱלֹהֵיכֶם בְּחֻקּוֹתַי לֵכוּ וְאֶת־מִשְׁפָּטַי שִׁמְרוּ וַעֲשׂוּ אוֹתָם׃

כ וְאֶת־שַׁבְּתוֹתַי קַדֵּשׁוּ וְהָיוּ לְאוֹת בֵּינִי וּבֵינֵיכֶם לָדַעַת כִּי אֲנִי יְהֹוָה אֱלֹהֵיכֶם׃

כא וַיַּמְרוּ־בִי הַבָּנִים בְּחֻקּוֹתַי לֹא־הָלָכוּ וְאֶת־מִשְׁפָּטַי לֹא־שָׁמְרוּ לַעֲשׂוֹת אוֹתָם אֲשֶׁר יַעֲשֶׂה אוֹתָם הָאָדָם וָחַי בָּהֶם אֶת־שַׁבְּתוֹתַי חִלֵּלוּ וָאֹמַר לִשְׁפֹּךְ חֲמָתִי עֲלֵיהֶם לְכַלּוֹת אַפִּי בָּם בַּמִּדְבָּר׃

כב וַהֲשִׁבֹתִי אֶת־יָדִי וָאַעַשׂ לְמַעַן שְׁמִי לְבִלְתִּי הֵחֵל לְעֵינֵי הַגּוֹיִם אֲשֶׁר הוֹצֵאתִי אוֹתָם לְעֵינֵיהֶם׃

כג גַּם־אֲנִי נָשָׂאתִי אֶת־יָדִי לָהֶם בַּמִּדְבָּר לְהָפִיץ אֹתָם בַּגּוֹיִם וּלְזָרוֹת אוֹתָם בָּאֲרָצוֹת׃

Yechezkel/Ezekiel

Chapter 20

24 because they did not obey My rules, but rejected My laws, profaned My *Shabbatot*, and looked with longing to the fetishes of their fathers.

25 Moreover, I gave them laws that were not good and rules by which they could not live:

26 When they set aside every first issue of the womb, I defiled them by their very gifts – that I might render them desolate, that they might know that I am *Hashem*.

27 Now, O mortal, speak to the House of *Yisrael* and say to them: Thus said *Hashem*: By this too your fathers affronted Me and committed trespass against Me:

28 When I brought them to the land that I had sworn to give them, and they saw any high hill or any leafy tree, they slaughtered their sacrifices there and presented their offensive offerings there; there they produced their pleasing odors and poured out their libations.

29 Then I said to them, "What is this shrine which you visit?" (Therefore such [a shrine] is called bamah to this day.)

30 Now say to the House of *Yisrael*: Thus said *Hashem*: If you defile yourselves as your fathers did and go astray after their detestable things,

31 and if to this very day you defile yourselves in the presentation of your gifts by making your children pass through the fire to all your fetishes, shall I respond to your inquiry, O House of *Yisrael*? As I live – declares *Hashem* – I will not respond to you.

32 And what you have in mind shall never come to pass – when you say, "We will be like the nations, like the families of the lands, worshiping wood and stone."

33 As I live – declares *Hashem* – I will reign over you with a strong hand, and with an outstretched arm, and with overflowing fury.

34 With a strong hand and an outstretched arm and overflowing fury I will bring you out from the peoples and gather you from the lands where you are scattered,

יחזקאל

פרק כ

כד יַעַן מִשְׁפָּטַי לֹא־עָשׂוּ וְחֻקּוֹתַי מָאָסוּ וְאֶת־שַׁבְּתוֹתַי חִלֵּלוּ וְאַחֲרֵי גִּלּוּלֵי אֲבוֹתָם הָיוּ עֵינֵיהֶם:

כה וְגַם־אֲנִי נָתַתִּי לָהֶם חֻקִּים לֹא טוֹבִים וּמִשְׁפָּטִים לֹא יִחְיוּ בָּהֶם:

כו וָאֲטַמֵּא אוֹתָם בְּמַתְּנוֹתָם בְּהַעֲבִיר כָּל־פֶּטֶר רָחַם לְמַעַן אֲשִׁמֵּם לְמַעַן אֲשֶׁר יֵדְעוּ אֲשֶׁר אֲנִי יְהֹוָה:

כז לָכֵן דַּבֵּר אֶל־בֵּית יִשְׂרָאֵל בֶּן־אָדָם וְאָמַרְתָּ אֲלֵיהֶם כֹּה אָמַר אֲדֹנָי יְהֹוִה עוֹד זֹאת גִּדְּפוּ אוֹתִי אֲבוֹתֵיכֶם בְּמַעֲלָם בִּי מָעַל:

כח וָאֲבִיאֵם אֶל־הָאָרֶץ אֲשֶׁר נָשָׂאתִי אֶת־יָדִי לָתֵת אוֹתָהּ לָהֶם וַיִּרְאוּ כָל־גִּבְעָה רָמָה וְכָל־עֵץ עָבֹת וַיִּזְבְּחוּ־שָׁם אֶת־זִבְחֵיהֶם וַיִּתְּנוּ־שָׁם כַּעַס קָרְבָּנָם וַיָּשִׂימוּ שָׁם רֵיחַ נִיחוֹחֵיהֶם וַיַּסִּיכוּ שָׁם אֶת־נִסְכֵּיהֶם:

כט וָאֹמַר אֲלֵהֶם מָה הַבָּמָה אֲשֶׁר־אַתֶּם הַבָּאִים שָׁם וַיִּקָּרֵא שְׁמָהּ בָּמָה עַד הַיּוֹם הַזֶּה:

ל לָכֵן אֱמֹר אֶל־בֵּית יִשְׂרָאֵל כֹּה אָמַר אֲדֹנָי יְהֹוִה הַבְּדֶרֶךְ אֲבוֹתֵיכֶם אַתֶּם נִטְמְאִים וְאַחֲרֵי שִׁקּוּצֵיהֶם אַתֶּם זֹנִים:

לא וּבִשְׂאֵת מַתְּנֹתֵיכֶם בְּהַעֲבִיר בְּנֵיכֶם בָּאֵשׁ אַתֶּם נִטְמְאִים לְכָל־גִּלּוּלֵיכֶם עַד־הַיּוֹם וַאֲנִי אִדָּרֵשׁ לָכֶם בֵּית יִשְׂרָאֵל חַי־אָנִי נְאֻם אֲדֹנָי יְהֹוִה אִם־אִדָּרֵשׁ לָכֶם:

לב וְהָעֹלָה עַל־רוּחֲכֶם הָיוֹ לֹא תִהְיֶה אֲשֶׁר אַתֶּם אֹמְרִים נִהְיֶה כַגּוֹיִם כְּמִשְׁפְּחוֹת הָאֲרָצוֹת לְשָׁרֵת עֵץ וָאָבֶן:

לג חַי־אָנִי נְאֻם אֲדֹנָי יְהֹוִה אִם־לֹא בְּיָד חֲזָקָה וּבִזְרוֹעַ נְטוּיָה וּבְחֵמָה שְׁפוּכָה אֶמְלוֹךְ עֲלֵיכֶם:

לד וְהוֹצֵאתִי אֶתְכֶם מִן־הָעַמִּים וְקִבַּצְתִּי אֶתְכֶם מִן־הָאֲרָצוֹת אֲשֶׁר נְפוֹצֹתֶם בָּם בְּיָד חֲזָקָה וּבִזְרוֹעַ נְטוּיָה וּבְחֵמָה שְׁפוּכָה:

Yechezkel/Ezekiel
Chapter 20

יחזקאל
פרק כ

35 and I will bring you into the wilderness of the peoples; and there I will enter into judgment with you face to face.

לה וְהֵבֵאתִי אֶתְכֶם אֶל־מִדְבַּר הָעַמִּים וְנִשְׁפַּטְתִּי אִתְּכֶם שָׁם פָּנִים אֶל־פָּנִים:

36 As I entered into judgment with your fathers in the wilderness of the land of Egypt, so will I enter into judgment with you – declares *Hashem*.

לו כַּאֲשֶׁר נִשְׁפַּטְתִּי אֶת־אֲבוֹתֵיכֶם בְּמִדְבַּר אֶרֶץ מִצְרָיִם כֵּן אִשָּׁפֵט אִתְּכֶם נְאֻם אֲדֹנָי יֱהֹוִה:

37 I will make you pass under the shepherd's staff, and I will bring you into the bond of the covenant.

לז וְהַעֲבַרְתִּי אֶתְכֶם תַּחַת הַשָּׁבֶט וְהֵבֵאתִי אֶתְכֶם בְּמָסֹרֶת הַבְּרִית:

38 I will remove from you those who rebel and transgress against Me; I will take them out of the countries where they sojourn, but they shall not enter the land of *Yisrael*. Then you shall know that I am *Hashem*.

לח וּבָרוֹתִי מִכֶּם הַמֹּרְדִים וְהַפּוֹשְׁעִים בִּי מֵאֶרֶץ מְגוּרֵיהֶם אוֹצִיא אוֹתָם וְאֶל־אַדְמַת יִשְׂרָאֵל לֹא יָבוֹא וִידַעְתֶּם כִּי־אֲנִי יְהֹוָה:

39 As for you, O House of *Yisrael*, thus said *Hashem*: Go, every one of you, and worship his fetishes and continue, if you will not obey Me; but do not profane My holy name any more with your idolatrous gifts.

לט וְאַתֶּם בֵּית־יִשְׂרָאֵל כֹּה־אָמַר אֲדֹנָי יֱהֹוִה אִישׁ גִּלּוּלָיו לְכוּ עֲבֹדוּ וְאַחַר אִם־אֵינְכֶם שֹׁמְעִים אֵלָי וְאֶת־שֵׁם קָדְשִׁי לֹא תְחַלְּלוּ־עוֹד בְּמַתְּנוֹתֵיכֶם וּבְגִלּוּלֵיכֶם:

40 For only on My holy mountain, on the lofty mount of *Yisrael* – declares *Hashem* – there, in the land, the entire House of *Yisrael*, all of it, must worship Me. There I will accept them, and there I will take note of your contributions and the choicest offerings of all your sacred things.

מ כִּי בְהַר־קָדְשִׁי בְּהַר מְרוֹם יִשְׂרָאֵל נְאֻם אֲדֹנָי יֱהֹוִה שָׁם יַעַבְדֻנִי כָּל־בֵּית יִשְׂרָאֵל כֻּלֹּה בָּאָרֶץ שָׁם אֶרְצֵם וְשָׁם אֶדְרוֹשׁ אֶת־תְּרוּמֹתֵיכֶם וְאֶת־רֵאשִׁית מַשְׂאוֹתֵיכֶם בְּכָל־קָדְשֵׁיכֶם:

41 When I bring you out from the peoples and gather you from the lands in which you are scattered, I will accept you as a pleasing odor; and I will be sanctified through you in the sight of the nations.

מא בְּרֵיחַ נִיחֹחַ אֶרְצֶה אֶתְכֶם בְּהוֹצִיאִי אֶתְכֶם מִן־הָעַמִּים וְקִבַּצְתִּי אֶתְכֶם מִן־הָאֲרָצוֹת אֲשֶׁר נְפֹצֹתֶם בָּם וְנִקְדַּשְׁתִּי בָכֶם לְעֵינֵי הַגּוֹיִם:

b'-RAY-akh nee-KHO-akh er-TZEH et-KHEM b'-ho-tzee-EE et-KHEM min ha-a-MEEM v'-ki-batz-TEE et-KHEM min ha-a-ra-TZOT a-SHER n'-fo-tzo-TEM BAM v'-nik-dash-TEE va-KHEM l'-ay-NAY ha-go-YIM

20:41 When I bring you out from the peoples and gather you Having already lived in exile, the prophet *Yechezkel* describes the future miraculous ingathering of the exiles, a miraculous event our generation has been privileged to witness. Yitzhak Ben-Zvi (1884–1963), historian, Zionist leader and the second President of Israel, reflected on the role of the State in this biblical promise: "The ingathering of the exiles is the most central and lofty ideal of this country. The redemptive reestablishment of Israel – this is a complete revolution in the annals of our days, in the chronicles of our entire nation. It serves as a counterweight, opposing our destruction and our extended exile." For 2,000 years, Jews pondered the *"When?"* of these events, and Yitzhak Ben Zvi's founding generation of Zionists dealt with the question of *"How?"* – how could they enable the process to succeed? Now, it is our generation's mission to ask the next question: *"Why?"* – Why is it that we have merited to witness, and be involved in, such wondrous episodes? The key to appreciating our present day opportunities, and the path to enhancing our future, lies in seeking these answers and working towards their fulfillment.

President Yitzchak Ben-Zvi (1884–1963)

Yechezkel/Ezekiel
Chapter 21

יחזקאל
פרק כא

42 Then, when I have brought you to the land of *Yisrael*, to the country that I swore to give to your fathers, you shall know that I am *Hashem*.

מב וִידַעְתֶּ֞ם כִּֽי־אֲנִ֣י יְהֹוָ֗ה בַּהֲבִיאִ֤י אֶתְכֶם֙ אֶל־אַדְמַ֣ת יִשְׂרָאֵ֔ל אֶל־הָאָ֕רֶץ אֲשֶׁ֤ר נָשָׂ֙אתִי֙ אֶת־יָדִ֔י לָתֵ֥ת אוֹתָ֖הּ לַאֲבֽוֹתֵיכֶֽם׃

43 There you will recall your ways and all the acts by which you defiled yourselves; and you will loathe yourselves for all the evils that you committed.

מג וּזְכַרְתֶּם־שָׁ֗ם אֶת־דַּרְכֵיכֶם֙ וְאֵת֙ כׇּל־עֲלִילֽוֹתֵיכֶ֔ם אֲשֶׁ֥ר נִטְמֵאתֶ֖ם בָּ֑ם וּנְקֹֽטֹתֶם֙ בִּפְנֵיכֶ֔ם בְּכׇל־רָעוֹתֵיכֶ֖ם אֲשֶׁ֥ר עֲשִׂיתֶֽם׃

44 Then, O House of *Yisrael*, you shall know that I am *Hashem*, when I deal with you for My name's sake – not in accordance with your evil ways and corrupt acts – declares *Hashem*.

מד וִידַעְתֶּ֞ם כִּֽי־אֲנִ֣י יְהֹוָ֗ה בַּעֲשׂוֹתִ֤י אִתְּכֶם֙ לְמַ֣עַן שְׁמִ֔י לֹא֩ כְדַרְכֵיכֶ֨ם הָרָעִ֜ים וְכַעֲלִילוֹתֵיכֶ֤ם הַנִּשְׁחָתוֹת֙ בֵּ֣ית יִשְׂרָאֵ֔ל נְאֻ֖ם אֲדֹנָ֥י יְהֹוִֽה׃

21
1 The word of *Hashem* came to me:

כא א וַיְהִ֥י דְבַר־יְהֹוָ֖ה אֵלַ֥י לֵאמֹֽר׃

2 O mortal, set your face toward Teman, and proclaim to Darom, and prophesy against the brushland of the *Negev*.

ben a-DAM SEEM pa-NE-kha DE-rekh tay-MA-nah v'-ha-TAYF el da-ROM v'-hi-na-VAY el YA-ar ha-sa-DEH NE-gev

ב בֶּן־אָדָ֗ם שִׂ֤ים פָּנֶ֙יךָ֙ דֶּ֣רֶךְ תֵּימָ֔נָה וְהַטֵּ֖ף אֶל־דָּר֑וֹם וְהִנָּבֵ֕א אֶל־יַ֥עַר הַשָּׂדֶ֖ה נֶֽגֶב׃

3 Say to the brushland of the *Negev*: Hear the word of *Hashem*. Thus said *Hashem*: I am going to kindle a fire in you, which shall devour every tree of yours, both green and withered. Its leaping flame shall not go out, and every face from south to north shall be scorched by it.

ג וְאָמַרְתָּ֙ לְיַ֣עַר הַנֶּ֔גֶב שְׁמַ֖ע דְּבַר־יְהֹוָ֑ה כֹּֽה־אָמַ֣ר אֲדֹנָ֣י יְהֹוִ֡ה הִנְנִי־מַצִּֽית־בְּךָ֣ אֵ֡שׁ וְאָכְלָ֣ה בְךָ֣ כׇל־עֵֽץ־לַח֩ וְכׇל־עֵ֨ץ יָבֵ֤שׁ לֹֽא־תִכְבֶּה֙ לַהֶ֣בֶת שַׁלְהֶ֔בֶת וְנִצְרְבוּ־בָ֥הּ כׇּל־פָּנִ֖ים מִנֶּ֥גֶב צָפֽוֹנָה׃

4 Then all flesh shall recognize that I *Hashem* have kindled it; it shall not go out.

ד וְרָאוּ֙ כׇּל־בָּשָׂ֔ר כִּ֛י אֲנִ֥י יְהֹוָ֖ה בִּעַרְתִּ֑יהָ לֹ֖א תִּכְבֶּֽה׃

5 And I said, "Ah, *Hashem*! They say of me: He is just a riddlemonger."

ה וָאֹמַ֕ר אֲהָ֖הּ אֲדֹנָ֣י יְהֹוִ֑ה הֵ֚מָּה אֹמְרִ֣ים לִ֔י הֲלֹ֛א מְמַשֵּׁ֥ל מְשָׁלִ֖ים הֽוּא׃

6 Then the word of *Hashem* came to me:

ו וַיְהִ֥י דְבַר־יְהֹוָ֖ה אֵלַ֥י לֵאמֹֽר׃

7 O mortal, set your face toward *Yerushalayim* and proclaim against her sanctuaries and prophesy against the land of *Yisrael*.

ז בֶּן־אָדָ֗ם שִׂ֤ים פָּנֶ֙יךָ֙ אֶל־יְר֣וּשָׁלַ֔͏ִם וְהַטֵּ֖ף אֶל־מִקְדָּשִׁ֑ים וְהִנָּבֵ֖א אֶל־אַדְמַ֥ת יִשְׂרָאֵֽל׃

Ein Avdat in the Negov

21:2 Prophesy against the brushland of the *Negev* Repeating his warning of *Yerushalayim*'s imminent destruction, *Yechezkel* uses the metaphor of a forest fire that will burn without control until all the trees of the forest, dry and healthy alike, are consumed. In Israel's arid climate, forest fires are extremely dangerous, spreading quickly and leaving behind tremendous destruction. Before giving him this prophecy, *Hashem* tells *Yechezkel* to look southward in the direction of Israel, and uses three Hebrew words for 'south,' *tayman* (תימן), *darom* (דרום) and *negev* (נגב). In the following verse, however, only the word *negev* is used. In addition to 'south,' *negev* also means 'dry,' and refers to the desert region of southern Israel. After the fire, all of Israel will be like the *negev* – a barren, lifeless desert.

נגב

Yechezkel/Ezekiel
Chapter 21

יחזקאל
פרק כא

ח וְאָמַרְתָּ לְאַדְמַת יִשְׂרָאֵל כֹּה אָמַר יְהֹוָה הִנְנִי אֵלַיִךְ וְהוֹצֵאתִי חַרְבִּי מִתַּעְרָהּ וְהִכְרַתִּי מִמֵּךְ צַדִּיק וְרָשָׁע:

8 Say to the land of *Yisrael*: Thus said *Hashem*: I am going to deal with you! I will draw My sword from its sheath, and I will wipe out from you both the righteous and the wicked.

ט יַעַן אֲשֶׁר־הִכְרַתִּי מִמֵּךְ צַדִּיק וְרָשָׁע לָכֵן תֵּצֵא חַרְבִּי מִתַּעְרָהּ אֶל־כָּל־בָּשָׂר מִנֶּגֶב צָפוֹן:

9 In order to wipe out from you both the righteous and the wicked, My sword shall assuredly be unsheathed against all flesh from south to north;

י וְיָדְעוּ כָּל־בָּשָׂר כִּי אֲנִי יְהֹוָה הוֹצֵאתִי חַרְבִּי מִתַּעְרָהּ לֹא תָשׁוּב עוֹד:

10 and all flesh shall know that I *Hashem* have drawn My sword from its sheath, not to be sheathed again.

יא וְאַתָּה בֶן־אָדָם הֵאָנַח בְּשִׁבְרוֹן מָתְנַיִם וּבִמְרִירוּת תֵּאָנַח לְעֵינֵיהֶם:

11 And you, O mortal, sigh; with tottering limbs and bitter grief, sigh before their eyes.

יב וְהָיָה כִּי־יֹאמְרוּ אֵלֶיךָ עַל־מָה אַתָּה נֶאֱנָח וְאָמַרְתָּ אֶל־שְׁמוּעָה כִי־בָאָה וְנָמֵס כָּל־לֵב וְרָפוּ כָל־יָדַיִם וְכִהֲתָה כָל־רוּחַ וְכָל־בִּרְכַּיִם תֵּלַכְנָה מַּיִם הִנֵּה בָאָה וְנִהְיָתָה נְאֻם אֲדֹנָי יְהֹוִה:

12 And when they ask you, "Why do you sigh?" answer, "Because of the tidings that have come." Every heart shall sink and all hands hang nerveless; every spirit shall grow faint and all knees turn to water because of the tidings that have come. It is approaching, it shall come to pass – declares *Hashem*.

יג וַיְהִי דְבַר־יְהֹוָה אֵלַי לֵאמֹר:

13 The word of *Hashem* came to me:

יד בֶּן־אָדָם הִנָּבֵא וְאָמַרְתָּ כֹּה אָמַר אֲדֹנָי אֱמֹר חֶרֶב חֶרֶב הוּחַדָּה וְגַם־מְרוּטָה:

14 O mortal, prophesy and say: Thus said *Hashem*: A sword! A sword has been whetted and polished.

טו לְמַעַן טְבֹחַ טֶבַח הוּחַדָּה לְמַעַן־הֱיֵה־לָהּ בָּרָק מֹרָטָה אוֹ נָשִׂישׂ שֵׁבֶט בְּנִי מֹאֶסֶת כָּל־עֵץ:

15 It has been whetted to wreak slaughter; [therefore] it has been ground to a brilliant polish. How can we rejoice? My son, it scorns the rod and every stick.

טז וַיִּתֵּן אֹתָהּ לְמָרְטָה לִתְפֹּשׂ בַּכָּף הִיא־הוּחַדָּה חֶרֶב וְהִיא מֹרָטָה לָתֵת אוֹתָהּ בְּיַד־הוֹרֵג:

16 It has been given to be polished and then grasped in the hand; for this has the sword been whetted, for this polished – to be put into the hand of a slayer.

יז זְעַק וְהֵילֵל בֶּן־אָדָם כִּי־הִיא הָיְתָה בְעַמִּי הִיא בְּכָל־נְשִׂיאֵי יִשְׂרָאֵל מְגוּרֵי אֶל־חֶרֶב הָיוּ אֶת־עַמִּי לָכֵן סְפֹק אֶל־יָרֵךְ:

17 Cry and wail, O mortal, for this shall befall My people, this shall befall all the chieftains of *Yisrael*: they shall be cast before the sword together with My people; oh, strike the thigh [in grief].

יח כִּי בֹחַן וּמָה אִם־גַּם־שֵׁבֶט מֹאֶסֶת לֹא יִהְיֶה נְאֻם אֲדֹנָי יְהֹוִה:

18 Consider: How shall it fail to happen, seeing that it even scorns the rod? – says *Hashem*.

יט וְאַתָּה בֶן־אָדָם הִנָּבֵא וְהַךְ כַּף אֶל־כָּף וְתִכָּפֵל חֶרֶב שְׁלִישִׁתָה חֶרֶב חֲלָלִים הִיא חֶרֶב חָלָל הַגָּדוֹל הַחֹדֶרֶת לָהֶם:

19 Further, O mortal, prophesy, striking hand against hand. Let the sword strike a second time and yet a third time; it is a sword for massacre, a sword for great carnage, that presses upon them.

כ לְמַעַן לָמוּג לֵב וְהַרְבֵּה הַמִּכְשֹׁלִים עַל כָּל־שַׁעֲרֵיהֶם נָתַתִּי אִבְחַת־חָרֶב אָח עֲשׂוּיָה לְבָרָק מְעֻטָּה לְטָבַח:

20 Thus hearts shall lose courage and many shall fall. At all their gates I have appointed slaughter by the sword. Ah! it is made to flash brilliantly, it is honed for slaughter.

Yechezkel/Ezekiel
Chapter 21

יחזקאל

פרק כא

21 Be united, go to the right, turn left; whither are you bound?

כא הִתְאַחֲדִי הֵימִנִי הָשִׂימִי הַשְׂמִילִי אָנָה פָּנַיִךְ מֻעָדוֹת:

22 I, too, will strike hand against hand and will satisfy My fury upon you; I *Hashem* have spoken.

כב וְגַם־אֲנִי אַכֶּה כַפִּי אֶל־כַּפִּי וַהֲנִחֹתִי חֲמָתִי אֲנִי יְהוָה דִּבַּרְתִּי:

23 The word of *Hashem* came to me:

כג וַיְהִי דְבַר־יְהוָה אֵלַי לֵאמֹר:

24 And you, O mortal, choose two roads on which the sword of the king of Babylon may advance, both issuing from the same country; and select a spot, select it where roads branch off to [two] cities.

כד וְאַתָּה בֶן־אָדָם שִׂים־לְךָ שְׁנַיִם דְּרָכִים לָבוֹא חֶרֶב מֶלֶךְ־בָּבֶל מֵאֶרֶץ אֶחָד יֵצְאוּ שְׁנֵיהֶם וְיָד בָּרֵא בְּרֹאשׁ דֶּרֶךְ־עִיר בָּרֵא:

25 Choose a way for the sword to advance on Rabbah of the Amonites or on fortified *Yerushalayim* in *Yehuda*.

כה דֶּרֶךְ תָּשִׂים לָבוֹא חֶרֶב אֵת רַבַּת בְּנֵי־עַמּוֹן וְאֶת־יְהוּדָה בִירוּשָׁלַםִ בְּצוּרָה:

26 For the king of Babylon has stood at the fork of the road, where two roads branch off, to perform divination: He has shaken arrows, consulted teraphim, and inspected the liver.

כו כִּי־עָמַד מֶלֶךְ־בָּבֶל אֶל־אֵם הַדֶּרֶךְ בְּרֹאשׁ שְׁנֵי הַדְּרָכִים לִקְסָם־קָסֶם קִלְקַל בַּחִצִּים שָׁאַל בַּתְּרָפִים רָאָה בַּכָּבֵד:

27 In his right hand came up the omen against *Yerushalayim* – to set battering rams, to proclaim murder, to raise battle shouts, to set battering rams against the gates, to cast up mounds, to erect towers.

כז בִּימִינוֹ הָיָה הַקֶּסֶם יְרוּשָׁלַםִ לָשׂוּם כָּרִים לִפְתֹּחַ פֶּה בְּרֶצַח לְהָרִים קוֹל בִּתְרוּעָה לָשׂוּם כָּרִים עַל־שְׁעָרִים לִשְׁפֹּךְ סֹלְלָה לִבְנוֹת דָּיֵק:

28 In their eyes, the oaths they had sworn to them were like empty divination; but this shall serve to recall their guilt, for which they shall be taken to task.

כח וְהָיָה לָהֶם כקסום־[כִּקְסָם־] שָׁוְא בְּעֵינֵיהֶם שְׁבֻעֵי שְׁבֻעוֹת לָהֶם וְהוּא־מַזְכִּיר עָוֺן לְהִתָּפֵשׂ:

29 Assuredly, thus said *Hashem*: For causing your guilt to be recalled, your transgressions to be uncovered, and your sins to be revealed – all your misdeeds – because you have brought yourselves to [My] mind, you shall be taken to task.

כט לָכֵן כֹּה־אָמַר אֲדֹנָי יְהוִה יַעַן הַזְכַּרְכֶם עֲוֺנְכֶם בְּהִגָּלוֹת פִּשְׁעֵיכֶם לְהֵרָאוֹת חַטֹּאותֵיכֶם בְּכֹל עֲלִילוֹתֵיכֶם יַעַן הִזָּכֶרְכֶם בַּכַּף תִּתָּפֵשׂוּ:

30 And to you, O dishonored wicked prince of *Yisrael*, whose day has come – the time set for your punishment –

ל וְאַתָּה חָלָל רָשָׁע נְשִׂיא יִשְׂרָאֵל אֲשֶׁר־בָּא יוֹמוֹ בְּעֵת עֲוֺן קֵץ:

31 thus said *Hashem*: Remove the turban and lift off the crown! This shall not remain as it is; exalt the low and abase the high.

לא כֹּה אָמַר אֲדֹנָי יְהוִה הָסִיר הַמִּצְנֶפֶת וְהָרִים הָעֲטָרָה זֹאת לֹא־זֹאת הַשָּׁפָלָה הַגְבֵּהַּ וְהַגָּבֹהַּ הַשְׁפִּיל:

32 Ruin, an utter ruin I will make it. It shall be no more until he comes to whom it rightfully belongs; and I will give it to him.

לב עַוָּה עַוָּה עַוָּה אֲשִׂימֶנָּה גַּם־זֹאת לֹא הָיָה עַד־בֹּא אֲשֶׁר־לוֹ הַמִּשְׁפָּט וּנְתַתִּיו:

33 Further, O mortal, prophesy and say: Thus said *Hashem* concerning the Amonites and their blasphemies: Proclaim: O sword! O sword unsheathed for slaughter, polished to the utmost, to a flashing brilliance!

לג וְאַתָּה בֶן־אָדָם הִנָּבֵא וְאָמַרְתָּ כֹּה אָמַר אֲדֹנָי יְהוִה אֶל־בְּנֵי עַמּוֹן וְאֶל־חֶרְפָּתָם וְאָמַרְתָּ חֶרֶב חֶרֶב פְּתוּחָה לְטֶבַח מְרוּטָה לְהָכִיל לְמַעַן בָּרָק:

Yechezkel/Ezekiel

Chapter 22

34 Because they have prophesied falsely about you and have divined deceitfully concerning you, you shall be wielded over the necks of the dishonored wicked ones, for their day has come, the time set for their punishment.

35 Return it to its sheath! In the place where you were created, in the land of your origin, I will judge you.

36 I will pour out My indignation upon you, I will blow upon you with the fire of My wrath; and I will deliver you into the hands of barbarians, craftsmen of destruction.

37 You shall be fuel for the fire, your blood shall sink into the earth, you shall not be remembered, for I *Hashem* have spoken.

22

1 The word of *Hashem* came to me:

2 Further, O mortal, arraign, arraign the city of bloodshed; declare to her all her abhorrent deeds!

3 Say: Thus said *Hashem*: O city in whose midst blood is shed, so that your hour is approaching; within which fetishes are made, so that you have become unclean!

4 You stand guilty of the blood you have shed, defiled by the fetishes you have made. You have brought on your day; you have reached your year. Therefore I will make you the mockery of the nations and the scorn of all the lands.

5 Both the near and the far shall scorn you, O besmirched of name, O laden with iniquity!

6 Every one of the princes of *Yisrael* in your midst used his strength for the shedding of blood.

7 Fathers and mothers have been humiliated within you; strangers have been cheated in your midst; orphans and widows have been wronged within you.

8 You have despised My holy things and profaned My *Shabbatot*.

9 Base men in your midst were intent on shedding blood; in you they have eaten upon the mountains; and they have practiced depravity in your midst.

יחזקאל

פרק כב

לד בַּחֲזוֹת לָךְ שָׁוְא בִּקְסָם־לָךְ כָּזָב לָתֵת אוֹתָךְ אֶל־צַוְּארֵי חַלְלֵי רְשָׁעִים אֲשֶׁר־בָּא יוֹמָם בְּעֵת עֲוֹן קֵץ:

לה הָשֵׁב אֶל־תַּעְרָהּ בִּמְקוֹם אֲשֶׁר־נִבְרֵאת בְּאֶרֶץ מְכֻרוֹתַיִךְ אֶשְׁפֹּט אֹתָךְ:

לו וְשָׁפַכְתִּי עָלַיִךְ זַעְמִי בְּאֵשׁ עֶבְרָתִי אָפִיחַ עָלָיִךְ וּנְתַתִּיךְ בְּיַד אֲנָשִׁים בֹּעֲרִים חָרָשֵׁי מַשְׁחִית:

לז לָאֵשׁ תִּהְיֶה לְאָכְלָה דָּמֵךְ יִהְיֶה בְּתוֹךְ הָאָרֶץ לֹא תִזָּכֵרִי כִּי אֲנִי יְהוָה דִּבַּרְתִּי:

כב א וַיְהִי דְבַר־יְהוָה אֵלַי לֵאמֹר:

ב וְאַתָּה בֶן־אָדָם הֲתִשְׁפֹּט הֲתִשְׁפֹּט אֶת־עִיר הַדָּמִים וְהוֹדַעְתָּהּ אֵת כָּל־תּוֹעֲבוֹתֶיהָ:

ג וְאָמַרְתָּ כֹּה אָמַר אֲדֹנָי יְהוִה עִיר שֹׁפֶכֶת דָּם בְּתוֹכָהּ לָבוֹא עִתָּהּ וְעָשְׂתָה גִלּוּלִים עָלֶיהָ לְטָמְאָה:

ד בְּדָמֵךְ אֲשֶׁר־שָׁפַכְתְּ אָשַׁמְתְּ וּבְגִלּוּלַיִךְ אֲשֶׁר־עָשִׂית טָמֵאת וַתַּקְרִיבִי יָמַיִךְ וַתָּבוֹא עַד־שְׁנוֹתָיִךְ עַל־כֵּן נְתַתִּיךְ חֶרְפָּה לַגּוֹיִם וְקַלָּסָה לְכָל־הָאֲרָצוֹת:

ה הַקְּרֹבוֹת וְהָרְחֹקוֹת מִמֵּךְ יִתְקַלְּסוּ־בָךְ טְמֵאַת הַשֵּׁם רַבַּת הַמְּהוּמָה:

ו הִנֵּה נְשִׂיאֵי יִשְׂרָאֵל אִישׁ לִזְרֹעוֹ הָיוּ בָךְ לְמַעַן שְׁפָךְ־דָּם:

ז אָב וָאֵם הֵקַלּוּ בָךְ לַגֵּר עָשׂוּ בַעֹשֶׁק בְּתוֹכֵךְ יָתוֹם וְאַלְמָנָה הוֹנוּ בָךְ:

ח קָדָשַׁי בָּזִית וְאֶת־שַׁבְּתֹתַי חִלָּלְתְּ:

ט אַנְשֵׁי רָכִיל הָיוּ בָךְ לְמַעַן שְׁפָךְ־דָּם וְאֶל־הֶהָרִים אָכְלוּ בָךְ זִמָּה עָשׂוּ בְתוֹכֵךְ:

1258

Yechezkel/Ezekiel
Chapter 22

10 In you they have uncovered their fathers' nakedness; in you they have ravished women during their impurity.

11 They have committed abhorrent acts with other men's wives; in their depravity they have defiled their own daughters-in-law; in you they have ravished their own sisters, daughters of their fathers.

12 They have taken bribes within you to shed blood. You have taken advance and accrued interest; you have defrauded your countrymen to your profit. You have forgotten Me – declares *Hashem*.

13 Lo, I will strike My hands over the ill-gotten gains that you have amassed, and over the bloodshed that has been committed in your midst.

14 Will your courage endure, will your hands remain firm in the days when I deal with you? I *Hashem* have spoken and I will act.

15 I will scatter you among the nations and disperse you through the lands; I will consume the uncleanness out of you.

16 You shall be dishonored in the sight of nations, and you shall know that I am *Hashem*.

17 The word of *Hashem* came to me:

18 O mortal, the House of *Yisrael* has become dross to Me; they are all copper, tin, iron, and lead. But in a crucible, the dross shall turn into silver.

19 Assuredly, thus said *Hashem*: Because you have all become dross, I will gather you into *Yerushalayim*.

20 As silver, copper, iron, lead, and tin are gathered into a crucible to blow the fire upon them, so as to melt them, so will I gather you in My fierce anger and cast you [into the fire] and melt you.

21 I will gather you and I will blow upon you the fire of My fury, and you shall be melted in it.

22 As silver is melted in a crucible, so shall you be melted in it. And you shall know that I *Hashem* have poured out My fury upon you.

23 The word of *Hashem* came to me:

Yechezkel/Ezekiel
Chapter 23

24 O mortal, say to her: You are an uncleansed land, not to be washed with rain on the day of indignation.

ben a-DAM e-mor LAH AT E-retz LO m'-to-ha-RAH HEE LO gush-MAH b'-YOM ZA-am

25 Her gang of *Neviim* are like roaring lions in her midst, rending prey. They devour human beings; they seize treasure and wealth; they have widowed many women in her midst.

26 Her *Kohanim* have violated My Teaching: they have profaned what is sacred to Me, they have not distinguished between the sacred and the profane, they have not taught the difference between the unclean and the clean, and they have closed their eyes to My *Shabbatot*. I am profaned in their midst.

27 Her officials are like wolves rending prey in her midst; they shed blood and destroy lives to win ill-gotten gain.

28 Her *Neviim*, too, daub the wall for them with plaster: They prophesy falsely and divine deceitfully for them; they say, "Thus said *Hashem*," when *Hashem* has not spoken.

29 And the people of the land have practiced fraud and committed robbery; they have wronged the poor and needy, have defrauded the stranger without redress.

30 And I sought a man among them to repair the wall or to stand in the breach before Me in behalf of this land, that I might not destroy it; but I found none.

31 I have therefore poured out My indignation upon them; I will consume them with the fire of My fury. I will repay them for their conduct – declares *Hashem*.

23

1 The word of *Hashem* came to me:

2 O mortal, once there were two women, daughters of one mother.

22:24 You are an uncleansed land In describing how the entire nation became corrupt, *Hashem* declares "You are an uncleansed land." This is reflective of the extreme spiritual sensitivity of Israel, a special characteristic of the land that appears throughout the Bible. Sinning inside the Holy Land affects not only the sinner, but the land itself becomes defiled as well (see Leviticus 18:24, Numbers 35:34). Thus, because of the sins of the nation, the land has become impure. Conversely, every act of goodness and kindness in Israel strengthens the land in addition to the people.

Yechezkel/Ezekiel
Chapter 23

יְחֶזְקֵאל
פרק כג

3 They played the whore in Egypt; they played the whore while still young. There their breasts were squeezed, and there their virgin nipples were handled.

ג וַתִּזְנֶינָה בְמִצְרַיִם בִּנְעוּרֵיהֶן זָנוּ שָׁמָּה מֹעֲכוּ שְׁדֵיהֶן וְשָׁם עִשּׂוּ דַּדֵּי בְּתוּלֵיהֶן:

4 Their names were: the elder one, *Ohola*; and her sister, *Oholiva*. They became Mine, and they bore sons and daughters. As for their names, *Ohola* is Shomron, and *Oholiva* is Yerushalayim.

ד וּשְׁמוֹתָן אָהֳלָה הַגְּדוֹלָה וְאָהֳלִיבָה אֲחוֹתָהּ וַתִּהְיֶינָה לִי וַתֵּלַדְנָה בָּנִים וּבָנוֹת וּשְׁמוֹתָן שֹׁמְרוֹן אָהֳלָה וִירוּשָׁלַיִם אָהֳלִיבָה:

ush-mo-TAN a-ho-LAH ha-g'-do-LAH v'-a-ho-lee-VAH a-kho-TAH va-tih-YE-nah LEE va-tay-LAD-nah ba-NEEM u-va-NOT ush-mo-TAN sho-m'-RON a-ho-LAH vee-ru-sha-LA-im a-ho-lee-VAH

5 *Ohola* whored while she was Mine, and she lusted after her lovers, after the Assyrians, warriors

ה וַתִּזֶן אָהֳלָה תַּחְתָּי וַתַּעְגַּב עַל־מְאַהֲבֶיהָ אֶל־אַשּׁוּר קְרוֹבִים:

6 clothed in blue, governors and prefects, horsemen mounted on steeds – all of them handsome young fellows.

ו לְבֻשֵׁי תְכֵלֶת פַּחוֹת וּסְגָנִים בַּחוּרֵי חֶמֶד כֻּלָּם פָּרָשִׁים רֹכְבֵי סוּסִים:

7 She bestowed her favors upon them – upon all the pick of the Assyrians – and defiled herself with all their fetishes after which she lusted.

ז וַתִּתֵּן תַּזְנוּתֶיהָ עֲלֵיהֶם מִבְחַר בְּנֵי־אַשּׁוּר כֻּלָּם וּבְכֹל אֲשֶׁר־עָגְבָה בְּכָל־גִּלּוּלֵיהֶם נִטְמָאָה:

8 She did not give up the whoring she had begun with the Egyptians; for they had lain with her in her youth, and they had handled her virgin nipples and had poured out their lust upon her.

ח וְאֶת־תַּזְנוּתֶיהָ מִמִּצְרַיִם לֹא עָזָבָה כִּי אוֹתָהּ שָׁכְבוּ בִנְעוּרֶיהָ וְהֵמָּה עִשּׂוּ דַּדֵּי בְתוּלֶיהָ וַיִּשְׁפְּכוּ תַזְנוּתָם עָלֶיהָ:

9 Therefore I delivered her into the hands of her lovers, into the hands of the Assyrians after whom she lusted.

ט לָכֵן נְתַתִּיהָ בְּיַד־מְאַהֲבֶיהָ בְּיַד בְּנֵי אַשּׁוּר אֲשֶׁר עָגְבָה עֲלֵיהֶם:

10 They exposed her nakedness; they seized her sons and daughters, and she herself was put to the sword. And because of the punishment inflicted upon her, she became a byword among women.

י הֵמָּה גִלּוּ עֶרְוָתָהּ בָּנֶיהָ וּבְנוֹתֶיהָ לָקָחוּ וְאוֹתָהּ בַּחֶרֶב הָרָגוּ וַתְּהִי־שֵׁם לַנָּשִׁים וּשְׁפוּטִים עָשׂוּ בָהּ:

11 Her sister *Oholiva* saw this; yet her lusting was more depraved than her sister's, and her whoring more debased.

יא וַתֵּרֶא אֲחוֹתָהּ אָהֳלִיבָה וַתַּשְׁחֵת עַגְבָתָהּ מִמֶּנָּה וְאֶת־תַּזְנוּתֶיהָ מִזְּנוּנֵי אֲחוֹתָהּ:

23:4 *Ohola* is *Shomron*, and *Oholiva* is *Yerushalayim* Yechezkel compares the two kingdoms of Israel to two unfaithful sisters named *Ohola* and *Oholiva*. The northern kingdom is represented by the older sister, as it was the first to officially institute idolatrous worship (I Kings 12) and to establish alliances with deceitful foreign powers instead of trusting in God (Hosea 8:9). The southern kingdom of *Yehuda* followed, also worshipping idols and making alliances with foreign nations against God's will. The covenantal relationship between *Hashem* and the Children of Israel is likened to a marriage. By worshipping other gods and relying on foreign powers, the Israelites are being unfaithful to *Hashem* and defiling His land.

Yechezkel/Ezekiel
Chapter 23

יחזקאל
פרק כג

12 She lusted after the Assyrians, governors and prefects, warriors gorgeously clad, horsemen mounted on steeds – all of them handsome young fellows.

יב אֶל־בְּנֵי אַשּׁוּר עָגָבָה פַּחוֹת וּסְגָנִים קְרֹבִים לְבֻשֵׁי מִכְלוֹל פָּרָשִׁים רֹכְבֵי סוּסִים בַּחוּרֵי חֶמֶד כֻּלָּם׃

13 And I saw how she had defiled herself. Both of them followed the same course,

יג וָאֵרֶא כִּי נִטְמָאָה דֶּרֶךְ אֶחָד לִשְׁתֵּיהֶן׃

14 but she carried her harlotries further. For she saw men sculptured upon the walls, figures of Chaldeans drawn in vermilion,

יד וַתּוֹסֶף אֶל־תַּזְנוּתֶיהָ וַתֵּרֶא אַנְשֵׁי מְחֻקֶּה עַל־הַקִּיר צַלְמֵי כשדיים [כַשְׂדִּים] חֲקֻקִים בַּשָּׁשַׁר׃

15 girded with belts round their waists, and with flowing turbans on their heads, all of them looking like officers – a picture of Babylonians whose native land was Chaldea.

טו חֲגוֹרֵי אֵזוֹר בְּמָתְנֵיהֶם סְרוּחֵי טְבוּלִים בְּרָאשֵׁיהֶם מַרְאֵה שָׁלִשִׁים כֻּלָּם דְּמוּת בְּנֵי־בָבֶל כַּשְׂדִּים אֶרֶץ מוֹלַדְתָּם׃

16 At the very sight of them she lusted after them, and she sent messengers for them to Chaldea.

טז ותעגב [וַתַּעְגְּבָה] עֲלֵיהֶם לְמַרְאֵה עֵינֶיהָ וַתִּשְׁלַח מַלְאָכִים אֲלֵיהֶם כַּשְׂדִּימָה׃

17 So the Babylonians came to her for lovemaking and defiled her with their whoring; and she defiled herself with them until she turned from them in disgust.

יז וַיָּבֹאוּ אֵלֶיהָ בְנֵי־בָבֶל לְמִשְׁכַּב דֹּדִים וַיְטַמְּאוּ אוֹתָהּ בְּתַזְנוּתָם וַתִּטְמָא־בָם וַתֵּקַע נַפְשָׁהּ מֵהֶם׃

18 She flaunted her harlotries and exposed her nakedness, and I turned from her in disgust, as I had turned disgusted from her sister.

יח וַתְּגַל תַּזְנוּתֶיהָ וַתְּגַל אֶת־עֶרְוָתָהּ וַתֵּקַע נַפְשִׁי מֵעָלֶיהָ כַּאֲשֶׁר נָקְעָה נַפְשִׁי מֵעַל אֲחוֹתָהּ׃

19 But she whored still more, remembering how in her youth she had played the whore in the land of Egypt;

יט וַתַּרְבֶּה אֶת־תַּזְנוּתֶיהָ לִזְכֹּר אֶת־יְמֵי נְעוּרֶיהָ אֲשֶׁר זָנְתָה בְּאֶרֶץ מִצְרָיִם׃

20 she lusted for concubinage with them, whose members were like those of asses and whose organs were like those of stallions.

כ וַתַּעְגְּבָה עַל פִּלַגְשֵׁיהֶם אֲשֶׁר בְּשַׂר־חֲמוֹרִים בְּשָׂרָם וְזִרְמַת סוּסִים זִרְמָתָם׃

21 Thus you reverted to the wantonness of your youth, remembering your youthful breasts, when the men of Egypt handled your nipples.

כא וַתִּפְקְדִי אֵת זִמַּת נְעוּרָיִךְ בַּעְשׂוֹת מִמִּצְרַיִם דַּדַּיִךְ לְמַעַן שְׁדֵי נְעוּרָיִךְ׃

22 Assuredly, *Oholiva*, thus said *Hashem*: I am going to rouse against you the lovers from whom you turned in disgust, and I will bring them upon you from all around –

כב לָכֵן אָהֳלִיבָה כֹּה־אָמַר אֲדֹנָי יֱהֹוִה הִנְנִי מֵעִיר אֶת־מְאַהֲבַיִךְ עָלַיִךְ אֵת אֲשֶׁר־נָקְעָה נַפְשֵׁךְ מֵהֶם וַהֲבֵאתִים עָלַיִךְ מִסָּבִיב׃

23 the Babylonians and all the Chaldeans, [the people of] Pekod, Shoa, and Koa, and all the Assyrians with them, all of them handsome young fellows, governors and prefects, officers and warriors, all of them riding on horseback.

כג בְּנֵי בָבֶל וְכָל־כַּשְׂדִּים פְּקוֹד וְשׁוֹעַ וְקוֹעַ כָּל־בְּנֵי אַשּׁוּר אוֹתָם בַּחוּרֵי חֶמֶד פַּחוֹת וּסְגָנִים כֻּלָּם שָׁלִשִׁים וּקְרוּאִים רֹכְבֵי סוּסִים כֻּלָּם׃

1262

Yechezkel/Ezekiel
Chapter 23

24 They shall attack you with fleets of wheeled chariots and a host of troops; they shall set themselves against you on all sides with bucklers, shields, and helmets. And I will entrust your punishment to them, and they shall inflict their punishments on you.

25 I will direct My passion against you, and they shall deal with you in fury: they shall cut off your nose and ears. The last of you shall fall by the sword; they shall take away your sons and daughters, and your remnant shall be devoured by fire.

26 They shall strip you of your clothing and take away your dazzling jewels.

27 I will put an end to your wantonness and to your whoring in the land of Egypt, and you shall not long for them or remember Egypt any more.

28 For thus said *Hashem*: I am going to deliver you into the hands of those you hate, into the hands of those from whom you turned in disgust.

29 They shall treat you with hate, and they shall take away all you have toiled for, and leave you naked and bare; your naked whoredom, wantonness, and harlotry will be exposed.

30 These things shall be done to you for your harlotries with the nations, for defiling yourself with their fetishes.

31 You walked in your sister's path; therefore I will put her cup into your hand.

32 Thus said *Hashem*: You shall drink of your sister's cup, So deep and wide; It shall cause derision and scorn, It holds so much.

33 You shall be filled with drunkenness and woe. The cup of desolation and horror, The cup of your sister *Shomron* –

34 You shall drink it and drain it, And gnaw its shards; And you shall tear your breasts. For I have spoken – declares *Hashem*.

35 Assuredly, thus said *Hashem*: Because you have forgotten Me and cast Me behind your back, you in turn must suffer for your wanton whoring.

36 Then *Hashem* said to me: O mortal, arraign *Ohola* and *Oholiva*, and charge them with their abominations.

Yechezkel/Ezekiel
Chapter 23

37 For they have committed adultery, and blood is on their hands; truly they have committed adultery with their fetishes, and have even offered to them as food the children they bore to Me.

38 At the same time they also did this to Me: they defiled My Sanctuary and profaned My *Shabbatot*.

39 On the very day that they slaughtered their children to their fetishes, they entered My Sanctuary to desecrate it. That is what they did in My House.

40 Moreover, they sent for men to come from afar, [men] to whom a messenger was sent; and they came. For them, [*Oholiva,*] you bathed, painted your eyes, and donned your finery;

41 and you sat on a grand couch with a set table in front of it – and it was My incense and My oil you laid upon it.

42 And the noise of a carefree multitude was there, of numerous men brought drunk from the desert; and they put bracelets on their arms and splendid crowns upon their heads.

43 Then I said, "To destruction with adultery! Look, they are still going on with those same fornications of hers."

44 And they would go to her as one goes to a prostitute; that is how they went to *Ohola* and *Oholiva,* wanton women.

45 But righteous men shall punish them with the punishments for adultery and for bloodshed, for they are adulteresses and have blood on their hands.

46 For thus said *Hashem*: Summon an assembly against them, and make them an object of horror and plunder.

47 Let the assembly pelt them with stones and cut them down with their swords; let them kill their sons and daughters, and burn down their homes.

48 I will put an end to wantonness in the land; and all the women shall take warning not to imitate your wantonness.

49 They shall punish you for your wantonness, and you shall suffer the penalty for your sinful idolatry. And you shall know that I am *Hashem*.

יחזקאל
פרק כג

לז כִּי נִאֵפוּ וְדָם בִּידֵיהֶן וְאֶת־גִּלּוּלֵיהֶן נִאֵפוּ וְגַם אֶת־בְּנֵיהֶן אֲשֶׁר יָלְדוּ־לִי הֶעֱבִירוּ לָהֶם לְאָכְלָה:

לח עוֹד זֹאת עָשׂוּ לִי טִמְּאוּ אֶת־מִקְדָּשִׁי בַּיּוֹם הַהוּא וְאֶת־שַׁבְּתוֹתַי חִלֵּלוּ:

לט וּבְשַׁחֲטָם אֶת־בְּנֵיהֶם לְגִלּוּלֵיהֶם וַיָּבֹאוּ אֶל־מִקְדָּשִׁי בַּיּוֹם הַהוּא לְחַלְּלוֹ וְהִנֵּה־כֹה עָשׂוּ בְּתוֹךְ בֵּיתִי:

מ וְאַף כִּי תִשְׁלַחְנָה לַאֲנָשִׁים בָּאִים מִמֶּרְחָק אֲשֶׁר מַלְאָךְ שָׁלוּחַ אֲלֵיהֶם וְהִנֵּה־בָאוּ לַאֲשֶׁר רָחַצְתְּ כָּחַלְתְּ עֵינַיִךְ וְעָדִית עֶדִי:

מא וְיָשַׁבְתְּ עַל־מִטָּה כְבוּדָּה וְשֻׁלְחָן עָרוּךְ לְפָנֶיהָ וּקְטָרְתִּי וְשַׁמְנִי שַׂמְתְּ עָלֶיהָ:

מב וְקוֹל הָמוֹן שָׁלֵו בָהּ וְאֶל־אֲנָשִׁים מֵרֹב אָדָם מוּבָאִים סוֹבָאִים [סָבָאִים] מִמִּדְבָּר וַיִּתְּנוּ צְמִידִים אֶל־יְדֵיהֶן וַעֲטֶרֶת תִּפְאֶרֶת עַל־רָאשֵׁיהֶן:

מג וָאֹמַר לַבָּלָה נִאוּפִים עת [עַתָּה] יזנה [יִזְנוּ] תַזְנוּתֶהָ וָהִיא:

מד וַיָּבוֹא אֵלֶיהָ כְּבוֹא אֶל־אִשָּׁה זוֹנָה כֵּן בָּאוּ אֶל־אׇהֳלָה וְאֶל־אׇהֳלִיבָה אִשֹּׁת הַזִּמָּה:

מה וַאֲנָשִׁים צַדִּיקִם הֵמָּה יִשְׁפְּטוּ אוֹתְהֶם מִשְׁפַּט נֹאֲפוֹת וּמִשְׁפַּט שֹׁפְכוֹת דָּם כִּי נֹאֲפֹת הֵנָּה וְדָם בִּידֵיהֶן:

מו כִּי כֹּה אָמַר אֲדֹנָי יֱהֹוִה הַעֲלֵה עֲלֵיהֶם קָהָל וְנָתֹן אֶתְהֶן לְזַעֲוָה וְלָבַז:

מז וְרָגְמוּ עֲלֵיהֶן אֶבֶן קָהָל וּבָרֵא אוֹתְהֶן בְּחַרְבוֹתָם בְּנֵיהֶם וּבְנוֹתֵיהֶם יַהֲרֹגוּ וּבָתֵּיהֶן בָּאֵשׁ יִשְׂרֹפוּ:

מח וְהִשְׁבַּתִּי זִמָּה מִן־הָאָרֶץ וְנִוַּסְּרוּ כׇּל־הַנָּשִׁים וְלֹא תַעֲשֶׂינָה כְּזִמַּתְכֶנָה:

מט וְנָתְנוּ זִמַּתְכֶנָה עֲלֵיכֶן וַחֲטָאֵי גִלּוּלֵיכֶן תִּשֶּׂאינָה וִידַעְתֶּם כִּי אֲנִי אֲדֹנָי יֱהֹוִה:

Yechezkel/Ezekiel

Chapter 24

יחזקאל

פרק כד

24 ¹ In the ninth year, on the tenth day of the tenth month, the word of *Hashem* came to me:

וַיְהִי דְבַר־יְהֹוָה אֵלַי בַּשָּׁנָה הַתְּשִׁיעִית בַּחֹדֶשׁ הָעֲשִׂירִי בֶּעָשׂוֹר לַחֹדֶשׁ לֵאמֹר׃ א

vai-HEE d'-var a-do-NAI ay-LAI ba-sha-NAH ha-t'-shee-EET ba-KHO-desh ha-a-see-REE be-a-SOR la-KHO-desh lay-MOR

2 O mortal, record this date, this exact day; for this very day the king of Babylon has laid siege to *Yerushalayim*.

בֶּן־אָדָם כתוב־[כְּתָב־] לְךָ אֶת־שֵׁם הַיּוֹם אֶת־עֶצֶם הַיּוֹם הַזֶּה סָמַךְ מֶלֶךְ־בָּבֶל אֶל־יְרוּשָׁלַ͏ִם בְּעֶצֶם הַיּוֹם הַזֶּה׃ ב

3 Further, speak in an allegory to the rebellious breed and say to them: Thus said *Hashem*: Put the caldron [on the fire], put it on, And then pour water into it.

וּמְשֹׁל אֶל־בֵּית־הַמֶּרִי מָשָׁל וְאָמַרְתָּ אֲלֵיהֶם כֹּה אָמַר אֲדֹנָי יְהֹוִה שְׁפֹת הַסִּיר שְׁפֹת וְגַם־יְצֹק בּוֹ מָיִם׃ ג

4 Collect in it the pieces [of meat]. Every choice piece, thigh and shoulder; Fill it with the best cuts –

אֱסֹף נְתָחֶיהָ אֵלֶיהָ כָּל־נֵתַח טוֹב יָרֵךְ וְכָתֵף מִבְחַר עֲצָמִים מַלֵּא׃ ד

5 Take the best of the flock. Also pile the cuts under it; Get it boiling briskly, And cook the cuts in it.

מִבְחַר הַצֹּאן לָקוֹחַ וְגַם דּוּר הָעֲצָמִים תַּחְתֶּיהָ רַתַּח רְתָחֶיהָ גַּם־בָּשְׁלוּ עֲצָמֶיהָ בְּתוֹכָהּ׃ ה

6 Assuredly, thus said *Hashem*: Woe to the city of blood – A caldron whose scum is in it, Whose scum has not been cleaned out! Empty it piece by piece; No lot has fallen upon it.

לָכֵן כֹּה־אָמַר אֲדֹנָי יְהֹוִה אוֹי עִיר הַדָּמִים סִיר אֲשֶׁר חֶלְאָתָהּ בָהּ וְחֶלְאָתָהּ לֹא יָצְאָה מִמֶּנָּה לִנְתָחֶיהָ לִנְתָחֶיהָ הוֹצִיאָהּ לֹא־נָפַל עָלֶיהָ גּוֹרָל׃ ו

7 For the blood she shed is still in her; She set it upon a bare rock; She did not pour it out on the ground To cover it with earth.

כִּי דָמָהּ בְּתוֹכָהּ הָיָה עַל־צְחִיחַ סֶלַע שָׂמָתְהוּ לֹא שְׁפָכַתְהוּ עַל־הָאָרֶץ לְכַסּוֹת עָלָיו עָפָר׃ ז

8 She set her blood upon the bare rock, So that it was not covered, So that it may stir up [My] fury To take vengeance.

לְהַעֲלוֹת חֵמָה לִנְקֹם נָקָם נָתַתִּי אֶת־דָּמָהּ עַל־צְחִיחַ סָלַע לְבִלְתִּי הִכָּסוֹת׃ ח

9 Assuredly, thus said *Hashem*: Woe to the city of blood! I in turn will make a great blaze.

לָכֵן כֹּה אָמַר אֲדֹנָי יְהֹוִה אוֹי עִיר הַדָּמִים גַּם־אֲנִי אַגְדִּיל הַמְּדוּרָה׃ ט

10 Pile on the logs, Kindle the fire, Cook the meat through And stew it completely, And let the bones be charred.

הַרְבֵּה הָעֵצִים הַדְלֵק הָאֵשׁ הָתֵם הַבָּשָׂר וְהַרְקַח הַמֶּרְקָחָה וְהָעֲצָמוֹת יֵחָרוּ׃ י

11 Let it stand empty on the coals, Until it becomes so hot That the copper glows. Then its uncleanness shall melt away in it, And its rust be consumed.

וְהַעֲמִידֶהָ עַל־גֶּחָלֶיהָ רֵקָה לְמַעַן תֵּחַם וְחָרָה נְחֻשְׁתָּהּ וְנִתְּכָה בְתוֹכָהּ טֻמְאָתָהּ תִּתֻּם חֶלְאָתָהּ׃ יא

24:1 On the tenth day of the tenth month In the final chapter describing *Yerushalayim's* downfall, the prophet mentions the date of the start of the Babylonian siege of *Yerushalayim*, describing it as the tenth day of the tenth month. This day, the tenth of the month of *Tevet*, is one of the four fast days mentioned in *Zecharya* (8:19) that were instituted after the destruction of the *Beit Hamikdash*, in commemoration of various stages of its destruction. Until today, Jews all over the world fast on the tenth of *Tevet*, to remember the Babylonian siege of *Yerushalayim*, to mourn over its destruction and to pray for it to be rebuilt.

Yechezkel/Ezekiel
Chapter 24

יחזקאל
פרק כד

12 It has frustrated all effort, Its thick scum will not leave it – Into the fire with its scum!

יב תְּאֻנִים הֶלְאָת וְלֹא־תֵצֵא מִמֶּנָּה רַבַּת חֶלְאָתָהּ בְּאֵשׁ חֶלְאָתָהּ׃

13 For your vile impurity – because I sought to cleanse you of your impurity, but you would not be cleansed – you shall never be clean again until I have satisfied My fury upon you.

יג בְּטֻמְאָתֵךְ זִמָּה יַעַן טִהַרְתִּיךְ וְלֹא טָהַרְתְּ מִטֻּמְאָתֵךְ לֹא תִטְהֲרִי־עוֹד עַד־הֲנִיחִי אֶת־חֲמָתִי בָּךְ׃

14 I *Hashem* have spoken: It shall come to pass and I will do it. I will not refrain or spare or relent. You shall be punished according to your ways and your deeds – declares *Hashem*.

יד אֲנִי יְהֹוָה דִּבַּרְתִּי בָּאָה וְעָשִׂיתִי לֹא־אֶפְרַע וְלֹא־אָחוּס וְלֹא אֶנָּחֵם כִּדְרָכַיִךְ וְכַעֲלִילוֹתַיִךְ שְׁפָטוּךְ נְאֻם אֲדֹנָי יְהֹוִה׃

15 The word of *Hashem* came to me:

טו וַיְהִי דְבַר־יְהֹוָה אֵלַי לֵאמֹר׃

16 O mortal, I am about to take away the delight of your eyes from you through pestilence; but you shall not lament or weep or let your tears flow.

טז בֶּן־אָדָם הִנְנִי לֹקֵחַ מִמְּךָ אֶת־מַחְמַד עֵינֶיךָ בְּמַגֵּפָה וְלֹא תִסְפֹּד וְלֹא תִבְכֶּה וְלוֹא תָבוֹא דִּמְעָתֶךָ׃

17 Moan softly; observe no mourning for the dead: Put on your turban and put your sandals on your feet; do not cover over your upper lip, and do not eat the bread of comforters."

יז הֵאָנֵק דֹּם מֵתִים אֵבֶל לֹא־תַעֲשֶׂה פְּאֵרְךָ חֲבוֹשׁ עָלֶיךָ וּנְעָלֶיךָ תָּשִׂים בְּרַגְלֶיךָ וְלֹא תַעְטֶה עַל־שָׂפָם וְלֶחֶם אֲנָשִׁים לֹא תֹאכֵל׃

18 In the evening my wife died, and in the morning I did as I had been commanded. And when I spoke to the people that morning,

יח וָאֲדַבֵּר אֶל־הָעָם בַּבֹּקֶר וַתָּמָת אִשְׁתִּי בָּעָרֶב וָאַעַשׂ בַּבֹּקֶר כַּאֲשֶׁר צֻוֵּיתִי׃

19 the people asked me, "Will you not tell us what these things portend for us, that you are acting so?"

יט וַיֹּאמְרוּ אֵלַי הָעָם הֲלֹא־תַגִּיד לָנוּ מָה־אֵלֶּה לָּנוּ כִּי אַתָּה עֹשֶׂה׃

20 I answered them, "The word of *Hashem* has come to me:

כ וָאֹמַר אֲלֵיהֶם דְּבַר־יְהֹוָה הָיָה אֵלַי לֵאמֹר׃

21 Tell the House of *Yisrael*: Thus said *Hashem*: 'I am going to desecrate My Sanctuary, your pride and glory, the delight of your eyes and the desire of your heart; and the sons and daughters you have left behind shall fall by the sword.

כא אֱמֹר לְבֵית יִשְׂרָאֵל כֹּה־אָמַר אֲדֹנָי יְהֹוִה הִנְנִי מְחַלֵּל אֶת־מִקְדָּשִׁי גְּאוֹן עֻזְּכֶם מַחְמַד עֵינֵיכֶם וּמַחְמַל נַפְשְׁכֶם וּבְנֵיכֶם וּבְנוֹתֵיכֶם אֲשֶׁר עֲזַבְתֶּם בַּחֶרֶב יִפֹּלוּ׃

24* And *Yechezkel* shall become a portent for you: you shall do just as he has done, when it happens; and you shall know that I am *Hashem*.'

22 Accordingly, you shall do as I have done: you shall not cover over your upper lips or eat the bread of comforters;

כב וַעֲשִׂיתֶם כַּאֲשֶׁר עָשִׂיתִי עַל־שָׂפָם לֹא תַעְטוּ וְלֶחֶם אֲנָשִׁים לֹא תֹאכֵלוּ׃

23 and your turbans shall remain on your heads, and your sandals upon your feet. You shall not lament or weep, but you shall be heartsick because of your iniquities and shall moan to one another."

כג וּפְאֵרֵכֶם עַל־רָאשֵׁיכֶם וְנַעֲלֵיכֶם בְּרַגְלֵיכֶם לֹא תִסְפְּדוּ וְלֹא תִבְכּוּ וּנְמַקֹּתֶם בַּעֲוֺנֹתֵיכֶם וּנְהַמְתֶּם אִישׁ אֶל־אָחִיו׃

And *Yechezkel* shall become a portent for you: you shall do just as he has done, when it happens; and you shall know that I am *Hashem*.'

כד וְהָיָה יְחֶזְקֵאל לָכֶם לְמוֹפֵת כְּכֹל אֲשֶׁר־עָשָׂה תַּעֲשׂוּ בְּבֹאָהּ וִידַעְתֶּם כִּי אֲנִי אֲדֹנָי יְהֹוִה׃

* Verse 24 moved up for clarity

1266

Yechezkel/Ezekiel
Chapter 25

יחזקאל
פרק כה

25 You, O mortal, take note: On the day that I take their stronghold from them, their pride and joy, the delight of their eyes and the longing of their hearts – their sons and daughters –

כה וְאַתָּה בֶן־אָדָם הֲלוֹא בְּיוֹם קַחְתִּי מֵהֶם אֶת־מָעוּזָּם מְשׂוֹשׂ תִּפְאַרְתָּם אֶת־מַחְמַד עֵינֵיהֶם וְאֶת־מַשָּׂא נַפְשָׁם בְּנֵיהֶם וּבְנוֹתֵיהֶם:

26 on that day a fugitive will come to you, to let you hear it with your own ears.

כו בַּיּוֹם הַהוּא יָבוֹא הַפָּלִיט אֵלֶיךָ לְהַשְׁמָעוּת אָזְנָיִם:

27 On that day your mouth shall be opened to the fugitive, and you shall speak and no longer be dumb. So you shall be a portent for them, and they shall know that I am *Hashem*.

כז בַּיּוֹם הַהוּא יִפָּתַח פִּיךָ אֶת־הַפָּלִיט וּתְדַבֵּר וְלֹא תֵאָלֵם עוֹד וְהָיִיתָ לָהֶם לְמוֹפֵת וְיָדְעוּ כִּי־אֲנִי יְהוָה:

25

1 The word of *Hashem* came to me:

כה א וַיְהִי דְבַר־יְהוָה אֵלַי לֵאמֹר:

2 O mortal, set your face toward the Amonites and prophesy against them.

ב בֶּן־אָדָם שִׂים פָּנֶיךָ אֶל־בְּנֵי עַמּוֹן וְהִנָּבֵא עֲלֵיהֶם:

3 Say to the Amonites: Hear the word of *Hashem*! Thus said *Hashem*: Because you cried "Aha!" over My Sanctuary when it was desecrated, and over the land of *Yisrael* when it was laid waste, and over the House of *Yehuda* when it went into exile –

ג וְאָמַרְתָּ לִבְנֵי עַמּוֹן שִׁמְעוּ דְּבַר־אֲדֹנָי יְהוִה כֹּה־אָמַר אֲדֹנָי יְהוִה יַעַן אָמְרֵךְ הֶאָח אֶל־מִקְדָּשִׁי כִי־נִחָל וְאֶל־אַדְמַת יִשְׂרָאֵל כִּי נָשַׁמָּה וְאֶל־בֵּית יְהוּדָה כִּי הָלְכוּ בַּגּוֹלָה:

4 assuredly, I will deliver you to the Kedemites as a possession. They shall set up their encampments among you and pitch their dwellings in your midst; they shall eat your produce and they shall drink your milk.

ד לָכֵן הִנְנִי נֹתְנָךְ לִבְנֵי־קֶדֶם לְמוֹרָשָׁה וְיִשְּׁבוּ טִירוֹתֵיהֶם בָּךְ וְנָתְנוּ בָךְ מִשְׁכְּנֵיהֶם הֵמָּה יֹאכְלוּ פִרְיֵךְ וְהֵמָּה יִשְׁתּוּ חֲלָבֵךְ:

5 I will make Rabbah a pasture for camels and Ammon a place for sheep to lie down. And you shall know that I am *Hashem*.

ה וְנָתַתִּי אֶת־רַבָּה לִנְוֵה גְמַלִּים וְאֶת־בְּנֵי עַמּוֹן לְמִרְבַּץ־צֹאן וִידַעְתֶּם כִּי־אֲנִי יְהוָה:

6 For thus said *Hashem*: Because you clapped your hands and stamped your feet and rejoiced over the land of *Yisrael* with such utter scorn –

ו כִּי כֹה אָמַר אֲדֹנָי יְהוִה יַעַן מַחְאֲךָ יָד וְרַקְעֲךָ בְּרָגֶל וַתִּשְׂמַח בְּכָל־שָׁאטְךָ בְּנֶפֶשׁ אֶל־אַדְמַת יִשְׂרָאֵל:

7 assuredly, I will stretch out My hand against you and give you as booty to the nations; I will cut you off from among the peoples and wipe you out from among the countries and destroy you. And you shall know that I am *Hashem*.

ז לָכֵן הִנְנִי נָטִיתִי אֶת־יָדִי עָלֶיךָ וּנְתַתִּיךָ לְבַז [לְבַג] לַגּוֹיִם וְהִכְרַתִּיךָ מִן־הָעַמִּים וְהַאֲבַדְתִּיךָ מִן־הָאֲרָצוֹת אַשְׁמִידְךָ וְיָדַעְתָּ כִּי־אֲנִי יְהוָה:

8 Thus said *Hashem*: Because Moab and Seir said, "See, the House of *Yehuda* is like all other nations" –

ח כֹּה אָמַר אֲדֹנָי יְהוִה יַעַן אָמֹר מוֹאָב וְשֵׂעִיר הִנֵּה כְּכָל־הַגּוֹיִם בֵּית יְהוּדָה:

9 assuredly, I will lay bare the flank of Moab, all its towns to the last one – Beth-jeshimoth, Baal-meon, and Kiriathaim, the glory of the country.

ט לָכֵן הִנְנִי פֹתֵחַ אֶת־כֶּתֶף מוֹאָב מֵהֶעָרִים מֵעָרָיו מִקָּצֵהוּ צְבִי אֶרֶץ בֵּית הַיְשִׁימֹת בַּעַל מְעוֹן וקריתמה [וְקִרְיָתָיְמָה]:

Yechezkel/Ezekiel
Chapter 26

10 I will deliver it, together with Ammon, to the Kedemites as their possession. Thus Ammon shall not be remembered among the nations,

לִבְנֵי־קֶדֶם עַל־בְּנֵי עַמּוֹן וּנְתַתִּיהָ לְמוֹרָשָׁה לְמַעַן לֹא־תִזָּכֵר בְּנֵי־עַמּוֹן בַּגּוֹיִם: י

11 and I will mete out punishments to Moab. And they shall know that I am *Hashem*.

וּבְמוֹאָב אֶעֱשֶׂה שְׁפָטִים וְיָדְעוּ כִּי־אֲנִי יְהֹוָה: יא

12 Thus said *Hashem*: Because Edom acted vengefully against the House of *Yehuda* and incurred guilt by wreaking revenge upon it –

כֹּה אָמַר אֲדֹנָי יֱהֹוִה יַעַן עֲשׂוֹת אֱדוֹם בִּנְקֹם נָקָם לְבֵית יְהוּדָה וַיֶּאְשְׁמוּ אָשׁוֹם וְנִקְּמוּ בָהֶם: יב

13 assuredly, thus said *Hashem*: I will stretch out My hand against Edom and cut off from it man and beast, and I will lay it in ruins; from Tema to Dedan they shall fall by the sword.

לָכֵן כֹּה אָמַר אֲדֹנָי יֱהֹוִה וְנָטִתִי יָדִי עַל־אֱדוֹם וְהִכְרַתִּי מִמֶּנָּה אָדָם וּבְהֵמָה וּנְתַתִּיהָ חָרְבָּה מִתֵּימָן וּדְדָנֶה בַּחֶרֶב יִפֹּלוּ: יג

14 I will wreak My vengeance on Edom through My people *Yisrael*, and they shall take action against Edom in accordance with My blazing anger; and they shall know My vengeance – declares *Hashem*.

וְנָתַתִּי אֶת־נִקְמָתִי בֶּאֱדוֹם בְּיַד עַמִּי יִשְׂרָאֵל וְעָשׂוּ בֶאֱדוֹם כְּאַפִּי וְכַחֲמָתִי וְיָדְעוּ אֶת־נִקְמָתִי נְאֻם אֲדֹנָי יֱהֹוִה: יד

15 Thus said *Hashem*: Because the Philistines, in their ancient hatred, acted vengefully, and with utter scorn sought revenge and destruction –

כֹּה אָמַר אֲדֹנָי יֱהֹוִה יַעַן עֲשׂוֹת פְּלִשְׁתִּים בִּנְקָמָה וַיִּנָּקְמוּ נָקָם בִּשְׁאָט בְּנֶפֶשׁ לְמַשְׁחִית אֵיבַת עוֹלָם: טו

16 assuredly, thus said *Hashem*: I will stretch out My hand against the Philistines and cut off the Cherethites and wipe out the last survivors of the seacoast.

לָכֵן כֹּה אָמַר אֲדֹנָי יֱהֹוִה הִנְנִי נוֹטֶה יָדִי עַל־פְּלִשְׁתִּים וְהִכְרַתִּי אֶת־כְּרֵתִים וְהַאֲבַדְתִּי אֶת־שְׁאֵרִית חוֹף הַיָּם: טז

17 I will wreak frightful vengeance upon them by furious punishment; and when I inflict My vengeance upon them, they shall know that I am *Hashem*.

וְעָשִׂיתִי בָם נְקָמוֹת גְּדֹלוֹת בְּתוֹכְחוֹת חֵמָה וְיָדְעוּ כִּי־אֲנִי יְהֹוָה בְּתִתִּי אֶת־נִקְמָתִי בָּם: יז

v'-a-SEE-tee VAM n'-ka-MOT g'-do-LOT b'-to-kh'-KHOT khay-MAH v'-ya-d'-U kee a-NEE a-do-NAI b'-ti-TEE et nik-ma-TEE BAM

26

1 In the eleventh year, on the first of the month, the word of *Hashem* came to me:

וַיְהִי בְּעַשְׁתֵּי־עֶשְׂרֵה שָׁנָה בְּאֶחָד לַחֹדֶשׁ הָיָה דְבַר־יְהֹוָה אֵלַי לֵאמֹר: א

25:17 They shall know that I am *Hashem* *Yechezkel* begins a series of prophecies against the nations who either assisted the Babylonian destruction of *Yehuda*, or who rejoiced upon *Yehuda's* downfall. *Yechezkel* describes how the Philistines "with utter scorn sought revenge" (verse 15). Therefore, God promises to execute a great vengeance on Philistia. The retribution will be so great that it will be clear that it came from Heaven. *Hashem* loves His people, Israel, even in times of punishment, and He personally involves Himself in their redemption and the downfall of their enemies.

Yechezkel/Ezekiel
Chapter 26

יחזקאל
פרק כו

2 O mortal, because Tyre gloated over *Yerushalayim*, "Aha! The gateway of the peoples is broken, it has become mine; I shall be filled, now that it is laid in ruins" –

בֶּן־אָדָם יַעַן אֲשֶׁר־אָמְרָה צֹר עַל־יְרוּשָׁלַ͏ִם הֶאָח נִשְׁבְּרָה דַּלְתוֹת הָעַמִּים נָסֵבָּה אֵלָי אִמָּלְאָה הָחֳרָבָה:

ben a-DAM YA-an a-sher A-m'-rah TZOR al y'-ru-sha-LA-im he-AKH nish-b'-RAH dal-TOT ha-a-MEEM na-SAY-bah ay-LAI i-ma-l'-AH ha-kho-ra-VAH

3 assuredly, thus said *Hashem*: I am going to deal with you, O Tyre! I will hurl many nations against you, As the sea hurls its waves.

לָכֵן כֹּה אָמַר אֲדֹנָי יֱהֹוִה הִנְנִי עָלַיִךְ צֹר וְהַעֲלֵיתִי עָלַיִךְ גּוֹיִם רַבִּים כְּהַעֲלוֹת הַיָּם לְגַלָּיו:

4 They shall destroy the walls of Tyre And demolish her towers; And I will scrape her soil off her And leave her a naked rock.

וְשִׁחֲתוּ חֹמוֹת צֹר וְהָרְסוּ מִגְדָּלֶיהָ וְסִחֵיתִי עֲפָרָהּ מִמֶּנָּה וְנָתַתִּי אוֹתָהּ לִצְחִיחַ סָלַע:

5 She shall be in the heart of the sea A place for drying nets; For I have spoken it – declares *Hashem*. She shall become spoil for the nations,

מִשְׁטַח חֲרָמִים תִּהְיֶה בְּתוֹךְ הַיָּם כִּי אֲנִי דִבַּרְתִּי נְאֻם אֲדֹנָי יֱהֹוִה וְהָיְתָה לְבַז לַגּוֹיִם:

6 And her daughter-towns in the country Shall be put to the sword. And they shall know that I am *Hashem*.

וּבְנוֹתֶיהָ אֲשֶׁר בַּשָּׂדֶה בַּחֶרֶב תֵּהָרַגְנָה וְיָדְעוּ כִּי־אֲנִי יְהֹוָה:

7 For thus said *Hashem*: I will bring from the north, against Tyre, King Nebuchadrezzar of Babylon, a king of kings, with horses, chariots, and horsemen – a great mass of troops.

כִּי כֹה אָמַר אֲדֹנָי יֱהֹוִה הִנְנִי מֵבִיא אֶל־צֹר נְבוּכַדְרֶאצַּר מֶלֶךְ־בָּבֶל מִצָּפוֹן מֶלֶךְ מְלָכִים בְּסוּס וּבְרֶכֶב וּבְפָרָשִׁים וְקָהָל וְעַם־רָב:

8 Your daughter-towns in the country He shall put to the sword; He shall erect towers against you, And cast up mounds against you, And raise [a wall of] bucklers against you.

בְּנוֹתַיִךְ בַּשָּׂדֶה בַּחֶרֶב יַהֲרֹג וְנָתַן עָלַיִךְ דָּיֵק וְשָׁפַךְ עָלַיִךְ סֹלְלָה וְהֵקִים עָלַיִךְ צִנָּה:

9 He shall turn the force of his battering rams Against your walls And smash your towers with his axes.

וּמְחִי קָבָלּוֹ יִתֵּן בְּחֹמוֹתָיִךְ וּמִגְדְּלֹתַיִךְ יִתֹּץ בְּחַרְבוֹתָיו:

10 From the cloud raised by his horses Dust shall cover you; From the clatter of horsemen And wheels and chariots, Your walls shall shake – When he enters your gates As men enter a breached city.

מִשִּׁפְעַת סוּסָיו יְכַסֵּךְ אֲבָקָם מִקּוֹל פָּרַשׁ וְגַלְגַּל וָרֶכֶב תִּרְעַשְׁנָה חוֹמוֹתַיִךְ בְּבֹאוֹ בִּשְׁעָרַיִךְ כִּמְבוֹאֵי עִיר מְבֻקָּעָה:

26:2 Because Tyre gloated over *Yerushalayim* Tyre, the capital city of the Phoenician empire, was besieged by Nebuchadnezzar and ultimately destroyed by Alexander the Great. Tyre was a great commercial center, with a rock fortress located offshore that was nearly impregnable. Its ability to withstand great armies made Tyre's inhabitants arrogant and insensitive. They rejoice at the misfortune of their neighbors, trying to profit from the sufferings of others. Since their attitude towards *Yerushalayim* is described as "I shall be filled, now that it is laid in ruins," Tyre is deserving of the divine punishments that will befall it.

Yechezkel/Ezekiel
Chapter 26

11 With the hoofs of his steeds He shall trample all your streets. He shall put your people to the sword, And your mighty pillars shall crash to the ground.

12 They shall plunder your wealth And loot your merchandise. They shall raze your walls And tear down your splendid houses, And they shall cast into the water Your stones and timber and soil.

13 I will put an end to the murmur of your songs, And the sound of your lyres shall be heard no more.

14 I will make you a naked rock, You shall be a place for drying nets; You shall never be rebuilt. For I have spoken – declares *Hashem*.

15 Thus said *Hashem* to Tyre: The coastlands shall quake at the sound of your downfall, when the wounded groan, when slaughter is rife within you.

16 All the rulers of the sea shall descend from their thrones; they shall remove their robes and strip off their embroidered garments. They shall clothe themselves with trembling, and shall sit on the ground; they shall tremble every moment, and they shall be aghast at you.

17 And they shall intone a dirge over you, and they shall say to you: How you have perished, you who were peopled from the seas, O renowned city! Mighty on the sea were she and her inhabitants, Who cast their terror on all its inhabitants.

18 Now shall the coastlands tremble On the day of your downfall, And the coastlands by the sea Be terrified at your end.

19 For thus said *Hashem*: When I make you a ruined city, like cities empty of inhabitants; when I bring the deep over you, and its mighty waters cover you,

20 then I will bring you down, with those who go down to the Pit, to the people of old. I will install you in the netherworld, with those that go down to the Pit, like the ruins of old, so that you shall not be inhabited and shall not radiate splendor in the land of the living.

21 I will make you a horror, and you shall cease to be; you shall be sought, but shall never be found again – declares *Hashem*.

יחזקאל
פרק כו

יא בְּפַרְסוֹת סוּסָיו יִרְמֹס אֶת־כָּל־חוּצוֹתָיִךְ עַמֵּךְ בַּחֶרֶב יַהֲרֹג וּמַצְּבוֹת עֻזֵּךְ לָאָרֶץ תֵּרֵד׃

יב וְשָׁלְלוּ חֵילֵךְ וּבָזְזוּ רְכֻלָּתֵךְ וְהָרְסוּ חוֹמוֹתַיִךְ וּבָתֵּי חֶמְדָּתֵךְ יִתֹּצוּ וַאֲבָנַיִךְ וְעֵצַיִךְ וַעֲפָרֵךְ בְּתוֹךְ מַיִם יָשִׂימוּ׃

יג וְהִשְׁבַּתִּי הֲמוֹן שִׁירָיִךְ וְקוֹל כִּנּוֹרַיִךְ לֹא יִשָּׁמַע עוֹד׃

יד וּנְתַתִּיךְ לִצְחִיחַ סֶלַע מִשְׁטַח חֲרָמִים תִּהְיֶה לֹא תִבָּנֶה עוֹד כִּי אֲנִי יְהוָה דִּבַּרְתִּי נְאֻם אֲדֹנָי יְהוִה׃

טו כֹּה אָמַר אֲדֹנָי יְהוִה לְצוֹר הֲלֹא מִקּוֹל מַפַּלְתֵּךְ בֶּאֱנֹק חָלָל בֵּהָרֵג הֶרֶג בְּתוֹכֵךְ יִרְעֲשׁוּ הָאִיִּים׃

טז וְיָרְדוּ מֵעַל כִּסְאוֹתָם כֹּל נְשִׂיאֵי הַיָּם וְהֵסִירוּ אֶת־מְעִילֵיהֶם וְאֶת־בִּגְדֵי רִקְמָתָם יִפְשֹׁטוּ חֲרָדוֹת יִלְבָּשׁוּ עַל־הָאָרֶץ יֵשֵׁבוּ וְחָרְדוּ לִרְגָעִים וְשָׁמְמוּ עָלָיִךְ׃

יז וְנָשְׂאוּ עָלַיִךְ קִינָה וְאָמְרוּ לָךְ אֵיךְ אָבַדְתְּ נוֹשֶׁבֶת מִיַּמִּים הָעִיר הַהֻלָּלָה אֲשֶׁר הָיְתָה חֲזָקָה בַיָּם הִיא וְיֹשְׁבֶיהָ אֲשֶׁר־נָתְנוּ חִתִּיתָם לְכָל־יוֹשְׁבֶיהָ׃

יח עַתָּה יֶחְרְדוּ הָאִיִּן יוֹם מַפַּלְתֵּךְ וְנִבְהֲלוּ הָאִיִּים אֲשֶׁר־בַּיָּם מִצֵּאתֵךְ׃

יט כִּי כֹה אָמַר אֲדֹנָי יְהוִה בְּתִתִּי אֹתָךְ עִיר נֶחֱרֶבֶת כֶּעָרִים אֲשֶׁר לֹא־נוֹשָׁבוּ בְּהַעֲלוֹת עָלַיִךְ אֶת־תְּהוֹם וְכִסּוּךְ הַמַּיִם הָרַבִּים׃

כ וְהוֹרַדְתִּיךְ אֶת־יוֹרְדֵי בוֹר אֶל־עַם עוֹלָם וְהוֹשַׁבְתִּיךְ בְּאֶרֶץ תַּחְתִּיּוֹת כָּחֳרָבוֹת מֵעוֹלָם אֶת־יוֹרְדֵי בוֹר לְמַעַן לֹא תֵשֵׁבִי וְנָתַתִּי צְבִי בְּאֶרֶץ חַיִּים׃

כא בַּלָּהוֹת אֶתְּנֵךְ וְאֵינֵךְ וּתְבֻקְשִׁי וְלֹא־תִמָּצְאִי עוֹד לְעוֹלָם נְאֻם אֲדֹנָי יְהוִה׃

Yechezkel/Ezekiel
Chapter 27

יְחֶזְקֵאל
פֶּרֶק כז

27 1 The word of *Hashem* came to me:

וַיְהִי דְבַר־יְהֹוָה אֵלַי לֵאמֹר׃

2 Now you, O mortal, intone a dirge over Tyre.

וְאַתָּה בֶן־אָדָם שָׂא עַל־צֹר קִינָה׃

3 Say to Tyre: O you who dwell at the gateway of the sea, Who trade with the peoples on many coastlands: Thus said *Hashem*: O Tyre, you boasted, I am perfect in beauty.

וְאָמַרְתָּ לְצוֹר הַיֹּשַׁבְתִּי [הַיֹּשֶׁבֶת] עַל־מְבוֹאֹת יָם רֹכֶלֶת הָעַמִּים אֶל־אִיִּים רַבִּים כֹּה אָמַר אֲדֹנָי יְהֹוִה צוֹר אַתְּ אָמַרְתְּ אֲנִי כְּלִילַת יֹפִי׃

v'-a-mar-TA l'-TZOR ha-yo-SHE-vet al m'-vo-OT YAM ro-KHE-let ha-a-MEEM el i-YEEM ra-BEEM KOH a-MAR a-do-NAI e-lo-HEEM TZOR AT a-MAR-t' a-NEE k'-LEE-lat YO-fee

4 Your frontiers were on the high seas, Your builders perfected your beauty.

בְּלֵב יַמִּים גְּבוּלָיִךְ בֹּנַיִךְ כָּלְלוּ יָפְיֵךְ׃

5 From cypress trees of Senir They fashioned your planks; They took a cedar from Lebanon To make a mast for you.

בְּרוֹשִׁים מִשְּׂנִיר בָּנוּ לָךְ אֵת כָּל־לֻחֹתָיִם אֶרֶז מִלְּבָנוֹן לָקָחוּ לַעֲשׂוֹת תֹּרֶן עָלָיִךְ׃

6 From oak trees of Bashan They made your oars; Of boxwood from the isles of Kittim, Inlaid with ivory, They made your decks.

אַלּוֹנִים מִבָּשָׁן עָשׂוּ מִשּׁוֹטָיִךְ קַרְשֵׁךְ עָשׂוּ־שֵׁן בַּת־אֲשֻׁרִים מֵאִיֵּי כתים [כִּתִּיִּים]׃

7 Embroidered linen from Egypt Was the cloth That served you for sails; Of blue and purple from the coasts of Elishah Were your awnings.

שֵׁשׁ־בְּרִקְמָה מִמִּצְרַיִם הָיָה מִפְרָשֵׂךְ לִהְיוֹת לָךְ לְנֵס תְּכֵלֶת וְאַרְגָּמָן מֵאִיֵּי אֱלִישָׁה הָיָה מְכַסֵּךְ׃

8 The inhabitants of Sidon and Arvad Were your rowers; Your skilled men, O Tyre, were within you, They were your pilots.

יֹשְׁבֵי צִידוֹן וְאַרְוַד הָיוּ שָׁטִים לָךְ חֲכָמַיִךְ צוֹר הָיוּ בָךְ הֵמָּה חֹבְלָיִךְ׃

9 Gebal's elders and craftsmen were within you, Making your repairs. All the ships of the sea, with their crews, Were in your harbor To traffic in your wares.

זִקְנֵי גְבַל וַחֲכָמֶיהָ הָיוּ בָךְ מַחֲזִיקֵי בִּדְקֵךְ כָּל־אֳנִיּוֹת הַיָּם וּמַלָּחֵיהֶם הָיוּ בָךְ לַעֲרֹב מַעֲרָבֵךְ׃

10 Men of Persia, Lud, and Put Were in your army, Your fighting men; They hung shields and helmets in your midst, They lent splendor to you.

פָּרַס וְלוּד וּפוּט הָיוּ בְחֵילֵךְ אַנְשֵׁי מִלְחַמְתֵּךְ מָגֵן וְכוֹבַע תִּלּוּ־בָךְ הֵמָּה נָתְנוּ הֲדָרֵךְ׃

11 Men of Arvad and Helech Manned your walls all around, And men of Gammad were stationed in your towers; They hung their quivers all about your walls; They perfected your beauty.

בְּנֵי אַרְוַד וְחֵילֵךְ עַל־חוֹמוֹתַיִךְ סָבִיב וְגַמָּדִים בְּמִגְדְּלוֹתַיִךְ הָיוּ שִׁלְטֵיהֶם תִּלּוּ עַל־חוֹמוֹתַיִךְ סָבִיב הֵמָּה כָּלְלוּ יָפְיֵךְ׃

27:3 I am perfect in beauty *Yechezkel* laments the downfall of Tyre, blaming her ruin on arrogance. He compares Tyre to a beautiful ship, made of the finest materials by expert craftsmen (verses 4–11). He then gives a detailed description of the commercial activity that enriched the port city (verses 12–25). However, the proud ship, reliant on its wealth for its success and safety, was too full and heavy, a dangerous state for a vessel in deep waters. It therefore sank at the first storm (verses 26–36). As an expression of her arrogance, Tyre says about herself "I am perfect in beauty," a biblical phrase that had been used by *Yirmiyahu* to describe *Yerushalayim* (Lamentations 2:15).

Yechezkel/Ezekiel

Chapter 27

12 Tarshish traded with you because of your wealth of all kinds of goods; they bartered silver, iron, tin, and lead for your wares.

13 Javan, Tubal, and Meshech – they were your merchants; they trafficked with you in human beings and copper utensils.

14 From Beth-togarmah they bartered horses, horsemen, and mules for your wares.

15 The people of Dedan were your merchants; many coastlands traded under your rule and rendered you tribute in ivory tusks and ebony.

16 Aram traded with you because of your wealth of merchandise, dealing with you in turquoise, purple stuff, embroidery, fine linen, coral, and agate.

17 *Yehuda* and the land of *Yisrael* were your merchants; they trafficked with you in wheat of Minnith and Pannag, honey, oil, and balm.

18 Because of your wealth of merchandise, because of your great wealth, Damascus traded with you in Helbon wine and white wool.

19 Vedan and Javan from Uzal traded for your wares; they trafficked with you in polished iron, cassia, and calamus.

20 Dedan was your merchant in saddlecloths for riding.

21 Arabia and all Kedar's chiefs were traders under your rule; they traded with you in lambs, rams, and goats.

22 The merchants of Sheba and Raamah were your merchants; they bartered for your wares all the finest spices, all kinds of precious stones, and gold.

23 Haran, Canneh, and Eden, the merchants of Sheba, Assyria, and Chilmad traded with you.

24 These were your merchants in choice fabrics, embroidered cloaks of blue, and many-colored carpets tied up with cords and preserved with cedar – among your wares.

25 The ships of Tarshish were in the service of your trade. So you were full and richly laden On the high seas.

26 Your oarsmen brought you out Into the mighty waters; The tempest wrecked you On the high seas.

Yechezkel/Ezekiel
Chapter 28

יחזקאל
פרק כח

27 Your wealth, your wares, your merchandise, Your sailors and your pilots, The men who made your repairs, Those who carried on your traffic, And all the fighting men within you – All the multitude within you – Shall go down into the depths of the sea On the day of your downfall.

כז הוֹנֵךְ וְעִזְבוֹנַיִךְ מַעֲרָבֵךְ מַלָּחַיִךְ וְחֹבְלָיִךְ מַחֲזִיקֵי בִדְקֵךְ וְעֹרְבֵי מַעֲרָבֵךְ וְכָל־אַנְשֵׁי מִלְחַמְתֵּךְ אֲשֶׁר־בָּךְ וּבְכָל־קְהָלֵךְ אֲשֶׁר בְּתוֹכֵךְ יִפְּלוּ בְּלֵב יַמִּים בְּיוֹם מַפַּלְתֵּךְ:

28 At the outcry of your pilots The billows shall heave;

כח לְקוֹל זַעֲקַת חֹבְלָיִךְ יִרְעֲשׁוּ מִגְרֹשׁוֹת:

29 And all the oarsmen and mariners, All the pilots of the sea, Shall come down from their ships And stand on the ground.

כט וְיָרְדוּ מֵאֳנִיּוֹתֵיהֶם כֹּל תֹּפְשֵׂי מָשׁוֹט מַלָּחִים כֹּל חֹבְלֵי הַיָּם אֶל־הָאָרֶץ יַעֲמֹדוּ:

30 They shall raise their voices over you And cry out bitterly; They shall cast dust on their heads And strew ashes on themselves.

ל וְהִשְׁמִיעוּ עָלַיִךְ בְּקוֹלָם וְיִזְעֲקוּ מָרָה וְיַעֲלוּ עָפָר עַל־רָאשֵׁיהֶם בָּאֵפֶר יִתְפַּלָּשׁוּ:

31 On your account, they shall make Bald patches on their heads, And shall gird themselves with sackcloth. They shall weep over you, brokenhearted, With bitter lamenting;

לא וְהִקְרִיחוּ אֵלַיִךְ קָרְחָה וְחָגְרוּ שַׂקִּים וּבָכוּ אֵלַיִךְ בְּמַר־נֶפֶשׁ מִסְפֵּד מָר:

32 They shall intone a dirge over you as they wail, And lament for you thus: Who was like Tyre when she was silenced In the midst of the sea?

לב וְנָשְׂאוּ אֵלַיִךְ בְּנִיהֶם קִינָה וְקוֹנְנוּ עָלָיִךְ מִי כְצוֹר כְּדֻמָה בְּתוֹךְ הַיָּם:

33 When your wares were unloaded from the seas, You satisfied many peoples; With your great wealth and merchandise You enriched the kings of the earth.

לג בְּצֵאת עִזְבוֹנַיִךְ מִיַּמִּים הִשְׂבַּעַתְּ עַמִּים רַבִּים בְּרֹב הוֹנַיִךְ וּמַעֲרָבַיִךְ הֶעֱשַׁרְתְּ מַלְכֵי־אָרֶץ:

34 But when you were wrecked on the seas, In the deep waters sank your merchandise And all the crew aboard you.

לד עֵת נִשְׁבֶּרֶת מִיַּמִּים בְּמַעֲמַקֵּי־מָיִם מַעֲרָבֵךְ וְכָל־קְהָלֵךְ בְּתוֹכֵךְ נָפָלוּ:

35 All the inhabitants of the coastlands Are appalled over you; Their kings are aghast, Their faces contorted.

לה כֹּל יֹשְׁבֵי הָאִיִּים שָׁמְמוּ עָלָיִךְ וּמַלְכֵיהֶם שָׂעֲרוּ שַׂעַר רָעֲמוּ פָּנִים:

36 The merchants among the peoples hissed at you; You have become a horror, And have ceased to be forever.

לו סֹחֲרִים בָּעַמִּים שָׁרְקוּ עָלָיִךְ בַּלָּהוֹת הָיִית וְאֵינֵךְ עַד־עוֹלָם:

28 1 The word of *Hashem* came to me:

כח א וַיְהִי דְבַר־יְהֹוָה אֵלַי לֵאמֹר:

2 O mortal, say to the prince of Tyre: Thus said *Hashem*: Because you have been so haughty and have said, "I am a god; I sit enthroned like a god in the heart of the seas," whereas you are not a god but a man, though you deemed your mind equal to a god's –

ב בֶּן־אָדָם אֱמֹר לִנְגִיד צֹר כֹּה־אָמַר אֲדֹנָי יֱהֹוִה יַעַן גָּבַהּ לִבְּךָ וַתֹּאמֶר אֵל אָנִי מוֹשַׁב אֱלֹהִים יָשַׁבְתִּי בְּלֵב יַמִּים וְאַתָּה אָדָם וְלֹא־אֵל וַתִּתֵּן לִבְּךָ כְּלֵב אֱלֹהִים:

3 Yes, you are wiser than *Daniel*; In no hidden matter can anyone Compare to you.

ג הִנֵּה חָכָם אַתָּה מדנאל [מִדָּנִיֵּאל] כָּל־סָתוּם לֹא עֲמָמוּךָ:

Yechezkel/Ezekiel
Chapter 28

4 By your shrewd understanding You have gained riches, And have amassed gold and silver In your treasuries.

5 By your great shrewdness in trade You have increased your wealth, And you have grown haughty Because of your wealth.

6 Assuredly, thus said *Hashem*: Because you have deemed your mind equal to a god's,

7 I swear I will bring against you Strangers, the most ruthless of nations. They shall unsheathe their swords Against your prized shrewdness, And they shall strike down your splendor.

8 They shall bring you down to the Pit; In the heart of the sea you shall die The death of the slain.

9 Will you still say, "I am a god" Before your slayers, When you are proved a man, not a god, At the hands of those who strike you down?

10 By the hands of strangers you shall die The death of the uncircumcised; For I have spoken – declares *Hashem*.

11 The word of *Hashem* came to me:

12 O mortal, intone a dirge over the king of Tyre and say to him: Thus said *Hashem*: You were the seal of perfection, Full of wisdom and flawless in beauty.

13 You were in Eden, the garden of *Hashem*; Every precious stone was your adornment: Carnelian, chrysolite, and amethyst; Beryl, lapis lazuli, and jasper; Sapphire, turquoise, and emerald; And gold beautifully wrought for you, Mined for you, prepared the day you were created.

14 I created you as a cherub With outstretched shielding wings; And you resided on *Hashem*'s holy mountain; You walked among stones of fire.

15 You were blameless in your ways, From the day you were created Until wrongdoing was found in you.

16 By your far-flung commerce You were filled with lawlessness And you sinned. So I have struck you down From the mountain of *Hashem*, And I have destroyed you, O shielding cherub, From among the stones of fire.

17 You grew haughty because of your beauty, You debased your wisdom for the sake of your splendor; I have cast you to the ground, I have made you an object for kings to stare at.

Yechezkel/Ezekiel
Chapter 28

יחזקאל
פרק כח

18 By the greatness of your guilt, Through the dishonesty of your trading, You desecrated your sanctuaries. So I made a fire issue from you, And it has devoured you; I have reduced you to ashes on the ground, In the sight of all who behold you.

יח מֵרֹב עֲוֺנֶיךָ בְּעֶוֶל רְכֻלָּתְךָ חִלַּלְתָּ מִקְדָּשֶׁיךָ וָאוֹצִא־אֵשׁ מִתּוֹכְךָ הִיא אֲכָלַתְךָ וָאֶתֶּנְךָ לְאֵפֶר עַל־הָאָרֶץ לְעֵינֵי כָּל־רֹאֶיךָ׃

19 All who knew you among the peoples Are appalled at your doom. You have become a horror And have ceased to be, forever.

יט כָּל־יוֹדְעֶיךָ בָּעַמִּים שָׁמְמוּ עָלֶיךָ בַּלָּהוֹת הָיִיתָ וְאֵינְךָ עַד־עוֹלָם׃

20 The word of *Hashem* came to me:

כ וַיְהִי דְבַר־יְהֹוָה אֵלַי לֵאמֹר׃

21 O mortal, set your face toward Sidon and prophesy against her.

כא בֶּן־אָדָם שִׂים פָּנֶיךָ אֶל־צִידוֹן וְהִנָּבֵא עָלֶיהָ׃

22 Say: Thus said *Hashem*: I am going to deal with you, O Sidon. I will gain glory in your midst; And they shall know that I am *Hashem*, When I wreak punishment upon her And show Myself holy through her.

כב וְאָמַרְתָּ כֹּה אָמַר אֲדֹנָי יְהֹוִה הִנְנִי עָלַיִךְ צִידוֹן וְנִכְבַּדְתִּי בְּתוֹכֵךְ וְיָדְעוּ כִּי־אֲנִי יְהֹוָה בַּעֲשׂוֹתִי בָהּ שְׁפָטִים וְנִקְדַּשְׁתִּי בָהּ׃

23 I will let pestilence loose against her And bloodshed into her streets. And the slain shall fall in her midst When the sword comes upon her from all sides. And they shall know that I am *Hashem*.

כג וְשִׁלַּחְתִּי־בָהּ דֶּבֶר וָדָם בְּחוּצוֹתֶיהָ וְנִפְלַל חָלָל בְּתוֹכָהּ בְּחֶרֶב עָלֶיהָ מִסָּבִיב וְיָדְעוּ כִּי־אֲנִי יְהֹוָה׃

24 Then shall the House of *Yisrael* no longer be afflicted with prickling briers and lacerating thorns from all the neighbors who despise them; and they shall know that I am *Hashem*.

כד וְלֹא־יִהְיֶה עוֹד לְבֵית יִשְׂרָאֵל סִלּוֹן מַמְאִיר וְקוֹץ מַכְאִב מִכֹּל סְבִיבֹתָם הַשָּׁאטִים אוֹתָם וְיָדְעוּ כִּי אֲנִי אֲדֹנָי יְהֹוִה׃

25 Thus said *Hashem*: When I have gathered the House of *Yisrael* from the peoples among which they have been dispersed, and have shown Myself holy through them in the sight of the nations, they shall settle on their own soil, which I gave to My servant *Yaakov*,

כה כֹּה־אָמַר אֲדֹנָי יְהֹוִה בְּקַבְּצִי אֶת־בֵּית יִשְׂרָאֵל מִן־הָעַמִּים אֲשֶׁר נָפֹצוּ בָם וְנִקְדַּשְׁתִּי בָם לְעֵינֵי הַגּוֹיִם וְיָשְׁבוּ עַל־אַדְמָתָם אֲשֶׁר נָתַתִּי לְעַבְדִּי לְיַעֲקֹב׃

koh a-MAR a-do-NAI e-lo-HEEM b'-ka-b'-TZEE et BAYT yis-ra-AYL min ha-a-MEEM a-SHER na-FO-tzu VAM v'-nik-DASH-tee VAM l'-ay-NAY ha-go-YIM v'-ya-sh'-VU al ad-ma-TAM a-SHER na-TA-tee l'-av-DEE l'-ya-a-KOV

28:25 When I have gathered the House of *Yisrael* This verse describes the future redemption of the Jewish people from all the nations amongst whom they are scattered. The "ingathering of the exiles" was the stated goal of the first Zionist Congress in 1897, and remains a central mission of the State of Israel. This objective is reflected in the Knesset's 1950 "Law of Return," which grants full automatic citizenship to any Jew who desires to settle in the Jewish State. Modern Israel was founded to serve as the homeland for the Jewish people scattered throughout the earth. Over the past several decades, millions of Jews from over one-hundred countries have returned home in dramatic fulfillment of this prophecy.

The original Law of Return

Yechezkel/Ezekiel

Chapter 29

26 and they shall dwell on it in security. They shall build houses and plant vineyards, and shall dwell on it in security, when I have meted out punishment to all those about them who despise them. And they shall know that I *Hashem* am their God.

כו וְיָשְׁבוּ עָלֶיהָ לָבֶטַח וּבָנוּ בָתִּים וְנָטְעוּ כְרָמִים וְיָשְׁבוּ לָבֶטַח בַּעֲשׂוֹתִי שְׁפָטִים בְּכֹל הַשָּׁאטִים אֹתָם מִסְּבִיבוֹתָם וְיָדְעוּ כִּי אֲנִי יְהוָה אֱלֹהֵיהֶם׃

29

1 In the tenth year, on the twelfth day of the tenth month, the word of *Hashem* came to me:

א בַּשָּׁנָה הָעֲשִׂירִית בָּעֲשִׂרִי בִּשְׁנֵים עָשָׂר לַחֹדֶשׁ הָיָה דְבַר־יְהוָה אֵלַי לֵאמֹר׃

2 O mortal, turn your face against Pharaoh king of Egypt, and prophesy against him and against all Egypt.

ב בֶּן־אָדָם שִׂים פָּנֶיךָ עַל־פַּרְעֹה מֶלֶךְ מִצְרָיִם וְהִנָּבֵא עָלָיו וְעַל־מִצְרַיִם כֻּלָּהּ׃

3 Speak these words: Thus said *Hashem*: I am going to deal with you, O Pharaoh king of Egypt, Mighty monster, sprawling in your channels, Who said, My Nile is my own I made it for myself.

ג דַּבֵּר וְאָמַרְתָּ כֹּה־אָמַר אֲדֹנָי יְהוִה הִנְנִי עָלֶיךָ פַּרְעֹה מֶלֶךְ־מִצְרַיִם הַתַּנִּים הַגָּדוֹל הָרֹבֵץ בְּתוֹךְ יְאֹרָיו אֲשֶׁר אָמַר לִי יְאֹרִי וַאֲנִי עֲשִׂיתִנִי׃

da-BAYR v'-a-mar-TA koh a-MAR a-do-NAI e-lo-HEEM hi-n'-NEE a-LE-kha par-OH me-lekh mitz-RA-yim ha-ta-NEEM ha-ga-DOL ha-ro-VAYTZ b'-TOKH y'-o-RAV a-SHER a-MAR LEE y'-o-REE va-a-NEE a-see-TI-nee

4 I will put hooks in your jaws, And make the fish of your channels Cling to your scales; I will haul you up from your channels, With all the fish of your channels Clinging to your scales.

ד וְנָתַתִּי חחיים [חַחִים] בִּלְחָיֶיךָ וְהִדְבַּקְתִּי דְגַת־יְאֹרֶיךָ בְּקַשְׂקְשֹׂתֶיךָ וְהַעֲלִיתִיךָ מִתּוֹךְ יְאֹרֶיךָ וְאֵת כָּל־דְּגַת יְאֹרֶיךָ בְּקַשְׂקְשֹׂתֶיךָ תִּדְבָּק׃

5 And I will fling you into the desert, With all the fish of your channels. You shall be left lying in the open, Ungathered and unburied: I have given you as food To the beasts of the earth And the birds of the sky.

ה וּנְטַשְׁתִּיךָ הַמִּדְבָּרָה אוֹתְךָ וְאֵת כָּל־דְּגַת יְאֹרֶיךָ עַל־פְּנֵי הַשָּׂדֶה תִּפּוֹל לֹא תֵאָסֵף וְלֹא תִקָּבֵץ לְחַיַּת הָאָרֶץ וּלְעוֹף הַשָּׁמַיִם נְתַתִּיךָ לְאָכְלָה׃

6 Then all the inhabitants of Egypt shall know That I am *Hashem*. Because you were a staff of reed To the House of *Yisrael*:

ו וְיָדְעוּ כָּל־יֹשְׁבֵי מִצְרַיִם כִּי אֲנִי יְהוָה יַעַן הֱיוֹתָם מִשְׁעֶנֶת קָנֶה לְבֵית יִשְׂרָאֵל׃

7 When they grasped you with the hand, you would splinter, And wound all their shoulders, And when they leaned on you, you would break, And make all their loins unsteady.

ז בְּתָפְשָׂם בְּךָ בכפך [בַכַּף] תֵּרוֹץ וּבָקַעְתָּ לָהֶם כָּל־כָּתֵף וּבְהִשָּׁעֲנָם עָלֶיךָ תִּשָּׁבֵר וְהַעֲמַדְתָּ לָהֶם כָּל־מָתְנָיִם׃

8 Assuredly, thus said *Hashem*: Lo, I will bring a sword against you, and will cut off man and beast from you,

ח לָכֵן כֹּה אָמַר אֲדֹנָי יְהוִה הִנְנִי מֵבִיא עָלַיִךְ חָרֶב וְהִכְרַתִּי מִמֵּךְ אָדָם וּבְהֵמָה׃

29:3 My Nile is my own The wicked Pharaoh boasts that he has no need for heavenly powers, as his nation does not depend on rainfall for its sustenance. Each year, the mighty Nile river would overflow, ensuring the irrigation and growth of Egyptian crops. In contrast, *Eretz Yisrael* does not have a water source that it can depend on; rather it "soaks up its water from the rains of heaven" (Deuteronomy 11:11). While at first glance it may appear that the Nile is entirely reliable, Pharaoh fails to recognize that he is missing the singular relationship with God which exists in the Land of Israel. As the *Torah* states, since *Eretz Yisrael* is dependent on rainfall, it is the land "which *Hashem* your God looks after, on which *Hashem* your God always keeps His eye" (ibid 12).

Yechezkel/Ezekiel
Chapter 29

9 so that the land of Egypt shall fall into desolation and ruin. And they shall know that I am *Hashem* – because he boasted, "The Nile is mine, and I made it."

10 Assuredly, I am going to deal with you and your channels, and I will reduce the land of Egypt to utter ruin and desolation, from Migdol to Syene, all the way to the border of Nubia.

11 No foot of man shall traverse it, and no foot of beast shall traverse it; and it shall remain uninhabited for forty years.

12 For forty years I will make the land of Egypt the most desolate of desolate lands, and its cities shall be the most desolate of ruined cities. And I will scatter the Egyptians among the nations and disperse them throughout the countries.

13 Further, thus said *Hashem*: After a period of forty years I will gather the Egyptians from the peoples among whom they were dispersed.

14 I will restore the fortunes of the Egyptians and bring them back to the land of their origin, the land of Pathros, and there they shall be a lowly kingdom.

15 It shall be the lowliest of all the kingdoms, and shall not lord it over the nations again. I will reduce the Egyptians, so that they shall have no dominion over the nations.

16 Never again shall they be the trust of the House of *Yisrael*, recalling its guilt in having turned to them. And they shall know that I am *Hashem*.

17 In the twenty-seventh year, on the first day of the first month, the word of *Hashem* came to me:

18 O mortal, King Nebuchadrezzar of Babylon has made his army expend vast labor on Tyre; every head is rubbed bald and every shoulder scraped. But he and his army have had no return for the labor he expended on Tyre.

19 Assuredly, thus said *Hashem*: I will give the land of Egypt to Nebuchadrezzar, king of Babylon. He shall carry off her wealth and take her spoil and seize her booty; and she shall be the recompense of his army.

יחזקאל
פרק כט

ט וְהָיְתָה אֶרֶץ־מִצְרַיִם לִשְׁמָמָה וְחָרְבָּה וְיָדְעוּ כִּי־אֲנִי יְהֹוָה יַעַן אָמַר יְאֹר לִי וַאֲנִי עָשִׂיתִי:

י לָכֵן הִנְנִי אֵלֶיךָ וְאֶל־יְאֹרֶיךָ וְנָתַתִּי אֶת־אֶרֶץ מִצְרַיִם לְחָרְבוֹת חֹרֶב שְׁמָמָה מִמִּגְדֹּל סְוֵנֵה וְעַד־גְּבוּל כּוּשׁ:

יא לֹא תַעֲבָר־בָּהּ רֶגֶל אָדָם וְרֶגֶל בְּהֵמָה לֹא תַעֲבָר־בָּהּ וְלֹא תֵשֵׁב אַרְבָּעִים שָׁנָה:

יב וְנָתַתִּי אֶת־אֶרֶץ מִצְרַיִם שְׁמָמָה בְּתוֹךְ אֲרָצוֹת נְשַׁמּוֹת וְעָרֶיהָ בְּתוֹךְ עָרִים מׇחֳרָבוֹת תִּהְיֶיןָ שְׁמָמָה אַרְבָּעִים שָׁנָה וַהֲפִצֹתִי אֶת־מִצְרַיִם בַּגּוֹיִם וְזֵרִיתִים בָּאֲרָצוֹת:

יג כִּי כֹּה אָמַר אֲדֹנָי יְהֹוִה מִקֵּץ אַרְבָּעִים שָׁנָה אֲקַבֵּץ אֶת־מִצְרַיִם מִן־הָעַמִּים אֲשֶׁר־נָפֹצוּ שָׁמָּה:

יד וְשַׁבְתִּי אֶת־שְׁבוּת מִצְרַיִם וַהֲשִׁבֹתִי אֹתָם אֶרֶץ פַּתְרוֹס עַל־אֶרֶץ מְכוּרָתָם וְהָיוּ שָׁם מַמְלָכָה שְׁפָלָה:

טו מִן־הַמַּמְלָכוֹת תִּהְיֶה שְׁפָלָה וְלֹא־תִתְנַשֵּׂא עוֹד עַל־הַגּוֹיִם וְהִמְעַטְתִּים לְבִלְתִּי רְדוֹת בַּגּוֹיִם:

טז וְלֹא יִהְיֶה־עוֹד לְבֵית יִשְׂרָאֵל לְמִבְטָח מַזְכִּיר עָוֺן בִּפְנוֹתָם אַחֲרֵיהֶם וְיָדְעוּ כִּי אֲנִי אֲדֹנָי יְהֹוִה:

יז וַיְהִי בְּעֶשְׂרִים וָשֶׁבַע שָׁנָה בָּרִאשׁוֹן בְּאֶחָד לַחֹדֶשׁ הָיָה דְבַר־יְהֹוָה אֵלַי לֵאמֹר:

יח בֶּן־אָדָם נְבוּכַדְרֶאצַּר מֶלֶךְ־בָּבֶל הֶעֱבִיד אֶת־חֵילוֹ עֲבֹדָה גְדֹלָה אֶל־צֹר כׇּל־רֹאשׁ מֻקְרָח וְכׇל־כָּתֵף מְרוּטָה וְשָׂכָר לֹא־הָיָה לּוֹ וּלְחֵילוֹ מִצֹּר עַל־הָעֲבֹדָה אֲשֶׁר־עָבַד עָלֶיהָ:

יט לָכֵן כֹּה אָמַר אֲדֹנָי יְהֹוִה הִנְנִי נֹתֵן לִנְבוּכַדְרֶאצַּר מֶלֶךְ־בָּבֶל אֶת־אֶרֶץ מִצְרָיִם וְנָשָׂא הֲמֹנָהּ וְשָׁלַל שְׁלָלָהּ וּבָזַז בִּזָּהּ וְהָיְתָה שָׂכָר לְחֵילוֹ:

Yechezkel/Ezekiel

Chapter 30

20 As the wage for which he labored, for what they did for Me, I give him the land of Egypt – declares *Hashem*.

21 On that day I will endow the House of *Yisrael* with strength, and you shall be vindicated among them. And they shall know that I am *Hashem*.

30

1 The word of *Hashem* came to me:

2 O mortal, prophesy and say: Thus said *Hashem*: Wail, alas for the day!

3 For a day is near; A day of *Hashem* is near. It will be a day of cloud, An hour of [invading] nations.

4 A sword shall pierce Egypt, And Nubia shall be seized with trembling, When men fall slain in Egypt And her wealth is seized And her foundations are overthrown.

5 Nubia, Put, and Lud, and all the mixed populations, and Cub, and the inhabitants of the allied countries shall fall by the sword with them.

6 Thus said *Hashem*: Those who support Egypt shall fall, And her proud strength shall sink; There they shall fall by the sword, From Migdol to Syene – declares *Hashem*.

7 They shall be the most desolate of desolate lands, and her cities shall be the most ruined of cities,

8 when I set fire to Egypt and all who help her are broken. Thus they shall know that I am *Hashem*.

9 On that day, messengers shall set out at My bidding to strike terror into confident Nubia. And they shall be seized with trembling on Egypt's day [of doom] – for it is at hand.

10 Thus said *Hashem*: I will put an end to the wealth of Egypt through King Nebuchadrezzar of Babylon.

11 He, together with his troops, the most ruthless of the nations, shall be brought to ravage the land. And they shall unsheathe the sword against Egypt and fill the land with the slain.

12 I will turn the channels into dry ground, and I will deliver the land into the hands of evil men. I will lay waste the land and everything in it by the hands of strangers. I *Hashem* have spoken.

יחזקאל
פרק ל

כ אֶת־פְּעֻלָּתוֹ אֲשֶׁר־עָבַד בָּהּ נָתַתִּי לוֹ אֶת־אֶרֶץ מִצְרָיִם אֲשֶׁר עָשׂוּ לִי נְאֻם אֲדֹנָי יֱהֹוִה׃

כא בַּיּוֹם הַהוּא אַצְמִיחַ קֶרֶן לְבֵית יִשְׂרָאֵל וּלְךָ אֶתֵּן פִּתְחוֹן־פֶּה בְּתוֹכָם וְיָדְעוּ כִּי־אֲנִי יְהֹוָה׃

ל א וַיְהִי דְבַר־יְהֹוָה אֵלַי לֵאמֹר׃

ב בֶּן־אָדָם הִנָּבֵא וְאָמַרְתָּ כֹּה אָמַר אֲדֹנָי יֱהֹוִה הֵילִילוּ הָהּ לַיּוֹם׃

ג כִּי־קָרוֹב יוֹם וְקָרוֹב יוֹם לַיהֹוָה יוֹם עָנָן עֵת גּוֹיִם יִהְיֶה׃

ד וּבָאָה חֶרֶב בְּמִצְרַיִם וְהָיְתָה חַלְחָלָה בְּכוּשׁ בִּנְפֹל חָלָל בְּמִצְרָיִם וְלָקְחוּ הֲמוֹנָהּ וְנֶהֶרְסוּ יְסוֹדֹתֶיהָ׃

ה כּוּשׁ וּפוּט וְלוּד וְכָל־הָעֶרֶב וְכוּב וּבְנֵי אֶרֶץ הַבְּרִית אִתָּם בַּחֶרֶב יִפֹּלוּ׃

ו כֹּה אָמַר יְהֹוָה וְנָפְלוּ סֹמְכֵי מִצְרַיִם וְיָרַד גְּאוֹן עֻזָּהּ מִמִּגְדֹּל סְוֵנֵה בַּחֶרֶב יִפְּלוּ־בָהּ נְאֻם אֲדֹנָי יֱהֹוִה׃

ז וְנָשַׁמּוּ בְּתוֹךְ אֲרָצוֹת נְשַׁמּוֹת וְעָרָיו בְּתוֹךְ־עָרִים נַחֲרָבוֹת תִּהְיֶינָה׃

ח וְיָדְעוּ כִּי־אֲנִי יְהֹוָה בְּתִתִּי־אֵשׁ בְּמִצְרַיִם וְנִשְׁבְּרוּ כָּל־עֹזְרֶיהָ׃

ט בַּיּוֹם הַהוּא יֵצְאוּ מַלְאָכִים מִלְּפָנַי בַּצִּים לְהַחֲרִיד אֶת־כּוּשׁ בֶּטַח וְהָיְתָה חַלְחָלָה בָהֶם בְּיוֹם מִצְרַיִם כִּי הִנֵּה בָּאָה׃

י כֹּה אָמַר אֲדֹנָי יְהֹוִה וְהִשְׁבַּתִּי אֶת־הֲמוֹן מִצְרַיִם בְּיַד נְבוּכַדְרֶאצַּר מֶלֶךְ־בָּבֶל׃

יא הוּא וְעַמּוֹ אִתּוֹ עָרִיצֵי גוֹיִם מוּבָאִים לְשַׁחֵת הָאָרֶץ וְהֵרִיקוּ חַרְבוֹתָם עַל־מִצְרַיִם וּמָלְאוּ אֶת־הָאָרֶץ חָלָל׃

יב וְנָתַתִּי יְאֹרִים חָרָבָה וּמָכַרְתִּי אֶת־הָאָרֶץ בְּיַד־רָעִים וַהֲשִׁמֹּתִי אֶרֶץ וּמְלֹאָהּ בְּיַד־זָרִים אֲנִי יְהֹוָה דִּבַּרְתִּי׃

Yechezkel/Ezekiel
Chapter 30

יחזקאל
פרק ל

13 Thus said *Hashem*: I will destroy the fetishes and make an end of the idols in Noph; and no longer shall there be a prince in the land of Egypt; and I will strike the land of Egypt with fear.

יג כֹּה־אָמַר אֲדֹנָי יְהֹוִה וְהַאֲבַדְתִּי גִלּוּלִים וְהִשְׁבַּתִּי אֱלִילִים מִנֹּף וְנָשִׂיא מֵאֶרֶץ־מִצְרַיִם לֹא יִהְיֶה־עוֹד וְנָתַתִּי יִרְאָה בְּאֶרֶץ מִצְרָיִם:

14 I will lay Pathros waste, I will set fire to Zoan, and I will execute judgment on No.

יד וַהֲשִׁמֹּתִי אֶת־פַּתְרוֹס וְנָתַתִּי אֵשׁ בְּצֹעַן וְעָשִׂיתִי שְׁפָטִים בְּנֹא:

15 I will pour out my anger upon Sin, the stronghold of Egypt, and I will destroy the wealth of No.

טו וְשָׁפַכְתִּי חֲמָתִי עַל־סִין מָעוֹז מִצְרָיִם וְהִכְרַתִּי אֶת־הֲמוֹן נֹא:

16 I will set fire to Egypt; Sin shall writhe in anguish and No shall be torn apart; and Noph [shall face] adversaries in broad daylight.

טז וְנָתַתִּי אֵשׁ בְּמִצְרַיִם חוּל תָּחִיל [תָּחוּל] סִין וְנֹא תִּהְיֶה לְהִבָּקֵעַ וְנֹף צָרֵי יוֹמָם:

17 The young men of Aven and Pi-beseth shall fall by the sword, and those [towns] shall go into captivity.

יז בַּחוּרֵי אָוֶן וּפִי־בֶסֶת בַּחֶרֶב יִפֹּלוּ וְהֵנָּה בַּשְּׁבִי תֵלַכְנָה:

18 In Tehaphnehes daylight shall be withheld, when I break there the power of Egypt, and there her proud strength comes to an end. [The city] itself shall be covered with cloud, and its daughter towns shall go into captivity.

יח וּבִתְחַפְנְחֵס חָשַׂךְ הַיּוֹם בְּשִׁבְרִי־שָׁם אֶת־מֹטוֹת מִצְרַיִם וְנִשְׁבַּת־בָּהּ גְּאוֹן עֻזָּהּ הִיא עָנָן יְכַסֶּנָּה וּבְנוֹתֶיהָ בַּשְּׁבִי תֵלַכְנָה:

19 Thus I will execute judgment on Egypt; And they shall know that I am *Hashem*.

יט וְעָשִׂיתִי שְׁפָטִים בְּמִצְרָיִם וְיָדְעוּ כִּי־אֲנִי יְהֹוָה:

20 In the eleventh year, on the seventh day of the first month, the word of *Hashem* came to me:

כ וַיְהִי בְּאַחַת עֶשְׂרֵה שָׁנָה בָּרִאשׁוֹן בְּשִׁבְעָה לַחֹדֶשׁ הָיָה דְבַר־יְהֹוָה אֵלַי לֵאמֹר:

21 O mortal, I have broken the arm of Pharaoh king of Egypt; it has not been bound up to be healed nor firmly bandaged to make it strong enough to grasp the sword.

כא בֶּן־אָדָם אֶת־זְרוֹעַ פַּרְעֹה מֶלֶךְ־מִצְרַיִם שָׁבָרְתִּי וְהִנֵּה לֹא־חֻבְּשָׁה לָתֵת רְפֻאוֹת לָשׂוּם חִתּוּל לְחָבְשָׁהּ לְחָזְקָהּ לִתְפֹּשׂ בֶּחָרֶב:

22 Assuredly, thus said *Hashem*: I am going to deal with Pharaoh king of Egypt. I will break his arms, both the sound one and the injured, and make the sword drop from his hand.

כב לָכֵן כֹּה־אָמַר אֲדֹנָי יְהֹוִה הִנְנִי אֶל־פַּרְעֹה מֶלֶךְ־מִצְרַיִם וְשָׁבַרְתִּי אֶת־זְרֹעֹתָיו אֶת־הַחֲזָקָה וְאֶת־הַנִּשְׁבָּרֶת וְהִפַּלְתִּי אֶת־הַחֶרֶב מִיָּדוֹ:

la-KHAYN koh a-MAR a-do-NAI e-lo-HEEM hi-n'-NEE el par-OH me-lekh mitz-RA-yim v'-sha-var-TEE et z'-ro-o-TAV et ha-kha-za-KAH v'-et ha-nish-BA-ret v'-hi-pal-TEE et ha-KHE-rev mi-ya-DO

30:22 And make the sword drop from his hand This prophecy was stated in the spring of 587 BCE, one year before the destruction of the first *Beit Hamikdash*. When Nebuchadnezzar first attacks *Yerushalayim* in 588 BCE, Pharaoh Hophra comes to assist *Tzidkiyahu*. However, Hophra's armies are soundly defeated, and he retreats, leaving *Yerushalayim* alone against the onslaught. *Yechezkel* portrays Egypt as having one broken arm, unable to hold a sword to defend itself (verse 21). He then states that Babylonia will finish the conquest, breaking Egypt's good arm as well. Indeed, after its defeat by Nebuchadnezzar, Egypt never regains its status as a superpower in the ancient world. As the prophets had predicted, relying on foreign powers for help instead of turning to God was of no benefit to *Yehuda*.

Yechezkel/Ezekiel
Chapter 31

יחזקאל
פרק לא

23 I will scatter the Egyptians among the nations and disperse them throughout the countries.

כג וַהֲפִצוֹתִי אֶת־מִצְרַיִם בַּגּוֹיִם וְזֵרִיתִם בָּאֲרָצוֹת׃

24 I will strengthen the arms of the king of Babylon and put My sword in his hand; and I will break the arms of Pharaoh, and he shall groan before him with the groans of one struck down.

כד וְחִזַּקְתִּי אֶת־זְרֹעוֹת מֶלֶךְ בָּבֶל וְנָתַתִּי אֶת־חַרְבִּי בְּיָדוֹ וְשָׁבַרְתִּי אֶת־זְרֹעוֹת פַּרְעֹה וְנָאַק נַאֲקוֹת חָלָל לְפָנָיו׃

25 I will make firm the arms of the king of Babylon, but the arms of Pharaoh shall fail. And they shall know that I am *Hashem*, when I put My sword into the hand of the king of Babylon, and he lifts it against the land of Egypt.

כה וְהַחֲזַקְתִּי אֶת־זְרֹעוֹת מֶלֶךְ בָּבֶל וּזְרֹעוֹת פַּרְעֹה תִּפֹּלְנָה וְיָדְעוּ כִּי־אֲנִי יְהֹוָה בְּתִתִּי חַרְבִּי בְּיַד־מֶלֶךְ בָּבֶל וְנָטָה אוֹתָהּ אֶל־אֶרֶץ מִצְרָיִם׃

26 I will scatter the Egyptians among the nations and disperse them throughout the countries. Thus they shall know that I am *Hashem*.

כו וַהֲפִצוֹתִי אֶת־מִצְרַיִם בַּגּוֹיִם וְזֵרִיתִי אוֹתָם בָּאֲרָצוֹת וְיָדְעוּ כִּי־אֲנִי יְהֹוָה׃

31

1 In the eleventh year, on the first day of the third month, the word of *Hashem* came to me:

לא א וַיְהִי בְּאַחַת עֶשְׂרֵה שָׁנָה בַּשְּׁלִישִׁי בְּאֶחָד לַחֹדֶשׁ הָיָה דְבַר־יְהֹוָה אֵלַי לֵאמֹר׃

2 O mortal, say to Pharaoh king of Egypt and his hordes: Who was comparable to you in greatness?

ב בֶּן־אָדָם אֱמֹר אֶל־פַּרְעֹה מֶלֶךְ־מִצְרַיִם וְאֶל־הֲמוֹנוֹ אֶל־מִי דָמִיתָ בְגָדְלֶךָ׃

3 Assyria was a cedar in Lebanon With beautiful branches and shady thickets, Of lofty stature, With its top among leafy trees.

ג הִנֵּה אַשּׁוּר אֶרֶז בַּלְּבָנוֹן יְפֵה עָנָף וְחֹרֶשׁ מֵצַל וּגְבַהּ קוֹמָה וּבֵין עֲבֹתִים הָיְתָה צַמַּרְתּוֹ׃

hi-NAY a-SHUR E-rez ba-l'-va-NON y'-FAY a-NAF v'-KHO-resh may-TZAL ug-VAH ko-MAH u-VAYN a-vo-TEEM ha-y'-TAH tza-mar-TO

4 Waters nourished it, The deep made it grow tall, Washing with its streams The place where it was planted, Making its channels well up To all the trees of the field.

ד מַיִם גִּדְּלוּהוּ תְּהוֹם רֹמְמָתְהוּ אֶת־נַהֲרֹתֶיהָ הֹלֵךְ סְבִיבוֹת מַטָּעָהּ וְאֶת־תְּעָלֹתֶיהָ שִׁלְחָה אֶל כָּל־עֲצֵי הַשָּׂדֶה׃

5 Therefore it exceeded in stature All the trees of the field; Its branches multiplied and its boughs grew long Because of the abundant water That welled up for it.

ה עַל־כֵּן גָּבְהָא קֹמָתוֹ מִכֹּל עֲצֵי הַשָּׂדֶה וַתִּרְבֶּינָה סַרְעַפֹּתָיו וַתֶּאֱרַכְנָה פֹארֹתָו [פֹארֹתָיו] מִמַּיִם רַבִּים בְּשַׁלְּחוֹ׃

6 In its branches nested All the birds of the sky; All the beasts of the field Bore their young under its boughs, And in its shadow lived All the great nations.

ו בִּסְעַפֹּתָיו קִנְנוּ כָּל־עוֹף הַשָּׁמַיִם וְתַחַת פֹּארֹתָיו יָלְדוּ כֹּל חַיַּת הַשָּׂדֶה וּבְצִלּוֹ יֵשְׁבוּ כֹּל גּוֹיִם רַבִּים׃

31:3 Assyria was a cedar in Lebanon For people who refused to believe that Egypt could be defeated after centuries of hegemony, *Yechezkel* points to Assyria. The mighty Assyrians had ruled for centuries, secure in their dominant position as a world power, like a solid and strong cedar tree. Yet they were ultimately chopped down and quickly fell. The cedar trees from Lebanon are remarkably thick and tall trees, reaching up to ninety feet in height and having a girth of over thirty feet. Because of its quality and resistance to decay and worms, cedar wood was a highly valued construction material. Indeed, King *Shlomo* imported cedars from Lebanon to use in the construction of his own palace, as well the *Beit Hamikdash*.

Yechezkel/Ezekiel

Chapter 31

יחזקאל
פרק לא

7 It was beautiful in its height, In the length of its branches, Because its stock stood By abundant waters.

ז וַיְּיִף בְּגָדְלוֹ בְּאֹרֶךְ דָּלִיּוֹתָיו כִּי־הָיָה שָׁרְשׁוֹ אֶל־מַיִם רַבִּים׃

8 Cedars in the garden of *Hashem* Could not compare with it; Cypresses could not match its boughs, And plane trees could not vie with its branches; No tree in the garden of *Hashem* Was its peer in beauty.

ח אֲרָזִים לֹא־עֲמָמֻהוּ בְּגַן־אֱלֹהִים בְּרוֹשִׁים לֹא דָמוּ אֶל־סְעַפֹּתָיו וְעַרְמֹנִים לֹא־הָיוּ כְּפֹארֹתָיו כָּל־עֵץ בְּגַן־אֱלֹהִים לֹא־דָמָה אֵלָיו בְּיָפְיוֹ׃

9 I made it beautiful In the profusion of its branches; And all the trees of Eden envied it In the garden of *Hashem*.

ט יָפֶה עֲשִׂיתִיו בְּרֹב דָּלִיּוֹתָיו וַיְקַנְאֻהוּ כָּל־עֲצֵי־עֵדֶן אֲשֶׁר בְּגַן הָאֱלֹהִים׃

10 Assuredly, thus said *Hashem*: Because it towered high in stature, and thrust its top up among the leafy trees, and it was arrogant in its height,

י לָכֵן כֹּה אָמַר אֲדֹנָי יֱהֹוִה יַעַן אֲשֶׁר גָּבַהְתָּ בְּקוֹמָה וַיִּתֵּן צַמַּרְתּוֹ אֶל־בֵּין עֲבוֹתִים וְרָם לְבָבוֹ בְּגָבְהוֹ׃

11 I delivered it into the hands of the mightiest of nations. They treated it as befitted its wickedness. I banished it.

יא וְאֶתְּנֵהוּ בְּיַד אֵיל גּוֹיִם עָשׂוֹ יַעֲשֶׂה לוֹ כְּרִשְׁעוֹ גֵּרַשְׁתִּהוּ׃

12 Strangers, the most ruthless of nations, cut it down and abandoned it; its branches fell on the mountains and in every valley; its boughs were splintered in every watercourse of the earth; and all the peoples of the earth departed from its shade and abandoned it.

יב וַיִּכְרְתֻהוּ זָרִים עָרִיצֵי גוֹיִם וַיִּטְּשֻׁהוּ אֶל־הֶהָרִים וּבְכָל־גֵּאָיוֹת נָפְלוּ דָלִיּוֹתָיו וַתִּשָּׁבַרְנָה פֹארֹתָיו בְּכֹל אֲפִיקֵי הָאָרֶץ וַיֵּרְדוּ מִצִּלּוֹ כָּל־עַמֵּי הָאָרֶץ וַיִּטְּשֻׁהוּ׃

13 Upon its fallen trunk all the birds of the sky nest, and all the beasts of the field lodge among its boughs –

יג עַל־מַפַּלְתּוֹ יִשְׁכְּנוּ כָּל־עוֹף הַשָּׁמָיִם וְאֶל־פֹּארֹתָיו הָיוּ כֹּל חַיַּת הַשָּׂדֶה׃

14 so that no trees by water should exalt themselves in stature or set their tops among the leafy trees, and that no well-watered tree may reach up to them in height. For they are all consigned to death, to the lowest part of the netherworld, together with human beings who descend into the Pit.

יד לְמַעַן אֲשֶׁר לֹא־יִגְבְּהוּ בְקוֹמָתָם כָּל־עֲצֵי־מַיִם וְלֹא־יִתְּנוּ אֶת־צַמַּרְתָּם אֶל־בֵּין עֲבֹתִים וְלֹא־יַעַמְדוּ אֲלֵיהֶם בְּגָבְהָם כָּל־שֹׁתֵי מָיִם כִּי־כֻלָּם נִתְּנוּ לַמָּוֶת אֶל־אֶרֶץ תַּחְתִּית בְּתוֹךְ בְּנֵי אָדָם אֶל־יוֹרְדֵי בוֹר׃

15 Thus said *Hashem*: On the day it went down to Sheol, I closed the deep over it and covered it; I held back its streams, and the great waters were checked. I made Lebanon mourn deeply for it, and all the trees of the field languished on its account.

טו כֹּה־אָמַר אֲדֹנָי יֱהֹוִה בְּיוֹם רִדְתּוֹ שְׁאוֹלָה הֶאֱבַלְתִּי כִּסֵּתִי עָלָיו אֶת־תְּהוֹם וָאֶמְנַע נַהֲרוֹתֶיהָ וַיִּכָּלְאוּ מַיִם רַבִּים וָאַקְדִּר עָלָיו לְבָנוֹן וְכָל־עֲצֵי הַשָּׂדֶה עָלָיו עֻלְפֶּה׃

16 I made nations quake at the crash of its fall, when I cast it down to Sheol with those who descend into the Pit; and all the trees of Eden, the choicest and best of Lebanon, all that were well watered, were consoled in the lowest part of the netherworld.

טז מִקּוֹל מַפַּלְתּוֹ הִרְעַשְׁתִּי גוֹיִם בְּהוֹרִדִי אֹתוֹ שְׁאוֹלָה אֶת־יוֹרְדֵי בוֹר וַיִּנָּחֲמוּ בְּאֶרֶץ תַּחְתִּית כָּל־עֲצֵי־עֵדֶן מִבְחַר וְטוֹב־לְבָנוֹן כָּל־שֹׁתֵי מָיִם׃

Yechezkel/Ezekiel
Chapter 32

יחזקאל
פרק לב

17 They also descended with it into Sheol, to those slain by the sword, together with its supporters, they who had lived under its shadow among the nations.

יז גַּם־הֵם אִתּוֹ יָרְדוּ שְׁאוֹלָה אֶל־חַלְלֵי־חָרֶב וּזְרֹעוֹ יָשְׁבוּ בְצִלּוֹ בְּתוֹךְ גּוֹיִם:

18 [Now you know] who is comparable to you in glory and greatness among the trees of Eden. And you too shall be brought down with the trees of Eden to the lowest part of the netherworld; you shall lie among the uncircumcised and those slain by the sword. Such shall be [the fate of] Pharaoh and all his hordes – declares *Hashem*.

יח אֶל־מִי דָמִיתָ כָּכָה בְּכָבוֹד וּבְגֹדֶל בַּעֲצֵי־עֵדֶן וְהוּרַדְתָּ אֶת־עֲצֵי־עֵדֶן אֶל־אֶרֶץ תַּחְתִּית בְּתוֹךְ עֲרֵלִים תִּשְׁכַּב אֶת־חַלְלֵי־חֶרֶב הוּא פַרְעֹה וְכָל־הֲמוֹנֹה נְאֻם אֲדֹנָי יֱהֹוִה:

32

1 In the twelfth year, on the first day of the twelfth month, the word of *Hashem* came to me:

לב א וַיְהִי בִּשְׁתֵּי עֶשְׂרֵה שָׁנָה בִּשְׁנֵי־עָשָׂר חֹדֶשׁ בְּאֶחָד לַחֹדֶשׁ הָיָה דְבַר־יְהֹוָה אֵלַי לֵאמֹר:

2 O mortal, intone a dirge over Pharaoh king of Egypt. Say to him: O great beast among the nations, you are doomed! You are like the dragon in the seas, Thrusting through their streams, Stirring up the water with your feet And muddying their streams!

ב בֶּן־אָדָם שָׂא קִינָה עַל־פַּרְעֹה מֶלֶךְ־מִצְרַיִם וְאָמַרְתָּ אֵלָיו כְּפִיר גּוֹיִם נִדְמֵיתָ וְאַתָּה כַּתַּנִּים בַּיַּמִּים וַתָּגַח בְּנַהֲרוֹתֶיךָ וַתִּדְלַח־מַיִם בְּרַגְלֶיךָ וַתִּרְפֹּס נַהֲרוֹתָם:

ben a-DAM SA kee-NAH al par-OH me-lekh mitz-RA-yim v'-a-mar-TA ay-LAV k'-FEER go-YIM nid-MAY-ta v'-a-TAH ka-ta-NEEM ba-ya-MEEM va-TA-gakh b'-na-ha-ro-TE-kha va-tid-lakh MA-yim b'-rag-LE-kha va-tir-POS na-ha-ro-TAM

3 Thus said *Hashem*: I will cast My net over you In an assembly of many peoples, And you shall be hauled up in My toils.

ג כֹּה אָמַר אֲדֹנָי יֱהֹוִה וּפָרַשְׂתִּי עָלֶיךָ אֶת־רִשְׁתִּי בִּקְהַל עַמִּים רַבִּים וְהֶעֱלוּךָ בְּחֶרְמִי:

4 And I will fling you to the ground, Hurl you upon the open field. I will cause all the birds of the sky To settle upon you. I will cause the beasts of all the earth To batten on you.

ד וּנְטַשְׁתִּיךָ בָאָרֶץ עַל־פְּנֵי הַשָּׂדֶה אֲטִילֶךָ וְהִשְׁכַּנְתִּי עָלֶיךָ כָּל־עוֹף הַשָּׁמַיִם וְהִשְׂבַּעְתִּי מִמְּךָ חַיַּת כָּל־הָאָרֶץ:

5 I will cast your carcass upon the hill And fill the valleys with your rotting flesh.

ה וְנָתַתִּי אֶת־בְּשָׂרְךָ עַל־הֶהָרִים וּמִלֵּאתִי הַגֵּאָיוֹת רָמוּתֶךָ:

6 I will drench the earth With your oozing blood upon the hills, And the watercourses shall be filled with your [gore].

ו וְהִשְׁקֵיתִי אֶרֶץ צָפָתְךָ מִדָּמְךָ אֶל־הֶהָרִים וַאֲפִקִים יִמָּלְאוּן מִמֶּךָּ:

32:2 You are like the dragon in the seas With the exile and destruction of Israel and *Yehuda* complete, *Yechezkel* turns his attention to the other nations. Though Egypt views itself as a fierce lion among the nations, able to roam freely and terrorize its neighbors, *Yechezkel* taunts them, saying that they are nothing more than a wretched beast in a swamp who will be thrashed like a crocodile away from the water. Though Israel has suffered at the hands of many enemies, they have no reason to fear. Ultimately, all the enemy nations will fall and Israel will return triumphantly to the Promised Land.

Crocodiles at Hamat Gader

Yechezkel/Ezekiel
Chapter 32

יחזקאל

פרק לב

7 When you are snuffed out, I will cover the sky And darken its stars; I will cover the sun with clouds And the moon shall not give its light.

ז וְכִסֵּיתִי בְכַבּוֹתְךָ שָׁמַיִם וְהִקְדַּרְתִּי אֶת־כֹּכְבֵיהֶם שֶׁמֶשׁ בֶּעָנָן אֲכַסֶּנּוּ וְיָרֵחַ לֹא־יָאִיר אוֹרוֹ׃

8 All the lights that shine in the sky I will darken above you; And I will bring darkness upon your land – declares *Hashem*.

ח כָּל־מְאוֹרֵי אוֹר בַּשָּׁמַיִם אַקְדִּירֵם עָלֶיךָ וְנָתַתִּי חֹשֶׁךְ עַל־אַרְצְךָ נְאֻם אֲדֹנָי יֱהֹוִה׃

9 I will vex the hearts of many peoples When I bring your shattered remnants among the nations, To countries which you never knew.

ט וְהִכְעַסְתִּי לֵב עַמִּים רַבִּים בַּהֲבִיאִי שִׁבְרְךָ בַּגּוֹיִם עַל־אֲרָצוֹת אֲשֶׁר לֹא־יְדַעְתָּם׃

10 I will strike many peoples with horror over your fate; And their kings shall be aghast over you, When I brandish My sword before them. They shall tremble continually, Each man for his own life, On the day of your downfall.

י וַהֲשִׁמּוֹתִי עָלֶיךָ עַמִּים רַבִּים וּמַלְכֵיהֶם יִשְׂעֲרוּ עָלֶיךָ שַׂעַר בְּעוֹפְפִי חַרְבִּי עַל־פְּנֵיהֶם וְחָרְדוּ לִרְגָעִים אִישׁ לְנַפְשׁוֹ בְּיוֹם מַפַּלְתֶּךָ׃

11 For thus said *Hashem*: The sword of the king of Babylon shall come upon you.

יא כִּי כֹּה אָמַר אֲדֹנָי יֱהֹוִה חֶרֶב מֶלֶךְ־בָּבֶל תְּבוֹאֶךָ׃

12 I will cause your multitude to fall By the swords of warriors, All the most ruthless among the nations. They shall ravage the splendor of Egypt, And all her masses shall be wiped out.

יב בְּחַרְבוֹת גִּבּוֹרִים אַפִּיל הֲמוֹנֶךָ עָרִיצֵי גוֹיִם כֻּלָּם וְשָׁדְדוּ אֶת־גְּאוֹן מִצְרַיִם וְנִשְׁמַד כָּל־הֲמוֹנָהּ׃

13 I will make all her cattle vanish from beside abundant waters; The feet of man shall not muddy them any more, Nor shall the hoofs of cattle muddy them.

יג וְהַאֲבַדְתִּי אֶת־כָּל־בְּהֶמְתָּהּ מֵעַל מַיִם רַבִּים וְלֹא תִדְלָחֵם רֶגֶל־אָדָם עוֹד וּפַרְסוֹת בְּהֵמָה לֹא תִדְלָחֵם׃

14 Then I will let their waters settle, And make their rivers flow like oil – declares *Hashem*:

יד אָז אַשְׁקִיעַ מֵימֵיהֶם וְנַהֲרוֹתָם כַּשֶּׁמֶן אוֹלִיךְ נְאֻם אֲדֹנָי יֱהֹוִה׃

15 When I lay the land of Egypt waste, When the land is emptied of [the life] that filled it, When I strike down all its inhabitants. And they shall know that I am *Hashem*.

טו בְּתִתִּי אֶת־אֶרֶץ מִצְרַיִם שְׁמָמָה וּנְשַׁמָּה אֶרֶץ מִמְּלֹאָהּ בְּהַכּוֹתִי אֶת־כָּל־יוֹשְׁבֵי בָהּ וְיָדְעוּ כִּי־אֲנִי יְהֹוָה׃

16 This is a dirge, and it shall be intoned; The women of the nations shall intone it, They shall intone it over Egypt and all her multitude – declares *Hashem*.

טז קִינָה הִיא וְקוֹנְנוּהָ בְּנוֹת הַגּוֹיִם תְּקוֹנֵנָּה אוֹתָהּ עַל־מִצְרַיִם וְעַל־כָּל־הֲמוֹנָהּ תְּקוֹנֵנָּה אוֹתָהּ נְאֻם אֲדֹנָי יֱהֹוִה׃

17 In the twelfth year, on the fifteenth day of the month, the word of *Hashem* came to me:

יז וַיְהִי בִּשְׁתֵּי עֶשְׂרֵה שָׁנָה בַּחֲמִשָּׁה עָשָׂר לַחֹדֶשׁ הָיָה דְבַר־יְהֹוָה אֵלַי לֵאמֹר׃

18 O mortal, wail [the dirge] – along with the women of the mighty nations – over the masses of Egypt, accompanying their descent to the lowest part of the netherworld, among those who have gone down into the Pit.

יח בֶּן־אָדָם נְהֵה עַל־הֲמוֹן מִצְרַיִם וְהוֹרִדֵהוּ אוֹתָהּ וּבְנוֹת גּוֹיִם אַדִּרִם אֶל־אֶרֶץ תַּחְתִּיּוֹת אֶת־יוֹרְדֵי בוֹר׃

19 Whom do you surpass in beauty? Down with you, and be laid to rest with the uncircumcised!

יט מִמִּי נָעָמְתָּ רְדָה וְהָשְׁכְּבָה אֶת־עֲרֵלִים׃

Yechezkel/Ezekiel
Chapter 32

יחזקאל
פרק לב

20 They shall lie amid those slain by the sword, [amid those slain by] the sword [Egypt] has been dragged and left with all her masses.

כ בְּתוֹךְ חַלְלֵי־חֶרֶב יִפֹּלוּ חֶרֶב נִתָּנָה מָשְׁכוּ אוֹתָהּ וְכָל־הֲמוֹנֶיהָ:

21 From the depths of Sheol the mightiest of warriors speak to him and his allies; the uncircumcised, the slain by the sword, have gone down and lie [there].

כא יְדַבְּרוּ־לוֹ אֵלֵי גִבּוֹרִים מִתּוֹךְ שְׁאוֹל אֶת־עֹזְרָיו יָרְדוּ שָׁכְבוּ הָעֲרֵלִים חַלְלֵי־חָרֶב:

22 Assyria is there with all her company, their graves round about, all of them slain, fallen by the sword.

כב שָׁם אַשּׁוּר וְכָל־קְהָלָהּ סְבִיבוֹתָיו קִבְרֹתָיו כֻּלָּם חֲלָלִים הַנֹּפְלִים בֶּחָרֶב:

23 Their graves set in the farthest recesses of the Pit, all her company are round about her tomb, all of them slain, fallen by the sword – they who struck terror in the land of the living.

כג אֲשֶׁר נִתְּנוּ קִבְרֹתֶיהָ בְּיַרְכְּתֵי־בוֹר וַיְהִי קְהָלָהּ סְבִיבוֹת קְבֻרָתָהּ כֻּלָּם חֲלָלִים נֹפְלִים בַּחֶרֶב אֲשֶׁר־נָתְנוּ חִתִּית בְּאֶרֶץ חַיִּים:

24 There too is Elam and all her masses round about her tomb, all of them slain, fallen by the sword – they who descended uncircumcised to the lowest part of the netherworld, who struck terror in the land of the living – now they bear their shame with those who have gone down to the Pit.

כד שָׁם עֵילָם וְכָל־הֲמוֹנָהּ סְבִיבוֹת קְבֻרָתָהּ כֻּלָּם חֲלָלִים הַנֹּפְלִים בַּחֶרֶב אֲשֶׁר־יָרְדוּ עֲרֵלִים אֶל־אֶרֶץ תַּחְתִּיּוֹת אֲשֶׁר נָתְנוּ חִתִּיתָם בְּאֶרֶץ חַיִּים וַיִּשְׂאוּ כְלִמָּתָם אֶת־יוֹרְדֵי בוֹר:

25 They made a bed for her among the slain, with all her masses; their graves are round about her. They are all uncircumcised, slain by the sword. Though their terror was once spread over the land of the living, they bear their shame with those who have gone into the Pit; they are placed among the slain.

כה בְּתוֹךְ חֲלָלִים נָתְנוּ מִשְׁכָּב לָהּ בְּכָל־הֲמוֹנָהּ סְבִיבוֹתָיו קִבְרֹתֶהָ כֻּלָּם עֲרֵלִים חַלְלֵי־חֶרֶב כִּי־נִתַּן חִתִּיתָם בְּאֶרֶץ חַיִּים וַיִּשְׂאוּ כְלִמָּתָם אֶת־יוֹרְדֵי בוֹר בְּתוֹךְ חֲלָלִים נִתָּן:

26 Meshech and Tubal and all their masses are there; their graves are round about. They are all uncircumcised, pierced through by the sword – they who once struck terror in the land of the living.

כו שָׁם מֶשֶׁךְ תֻּבַל וְכָל־הֲמוֹנָהּ סְבִיבוֹתָיו קִבְרוֹתֶיהָ כֻּלָּם עֲרֵלִים מְחֻלְלֵי חֶרֶב כִּי־נָתְנוּ חִתִּיתָם בְּאֶרֶץ חַיִּים:

27 And they do not lie with the fallen uncircumcised warriors, who went down to Sheol with their battle gear, who put their swords beneath their heads and their iniquities upon thei bones – for the terror of the warriors was upon the land of the living.

כז וְלֹא יִשְׁכְּבוּ אֶת־גִּבּוֹרִים נֹפְלִים מֵעֲרֵלִים אֲשֶׁר יָרְדוּ־שְׁאוֹל בִּכְלֵי־מִלְחַמְתָּם וַיִּתְּנוּ אֶת־חַרְבוֹתָם תַּחַת רָאשֵׁיהֶם וַתְּהִי עֲוֹנֹתָם עַל־עַצְמוֹתָם כִּי־חִתִּית גִּבּוֹרִים בְּאֶרֶץ חַיִּים:

28 And you too shall be shattered amid the uncircumcised, and lie among those slain by the sword.

כח וְאַתָּה בְּתוֹךְ עֲרֵלִים תִּשָּׁבַר וְתִשְׁכַּב אֶת־חַלְלֵי־חָרֶב:

29 Edom is there, her kings and all her chieftains, who, for all their might, are laid among those who are slain by the sword; they too lie with the uncircumcised and with those who have gone down to the Pit.

כט שָׁמָּה אֱדוֹם מְלָכֶיהָ וְכָל־נְשִׂיאֶיהָ אֲשֶׁר־נִתְּנוּ בִגְבוּרָתָם אֶת־חַלְלֵי־חָרֶב הֵמָּה אֶת־עֲרֵלִים יִשְׁכָּבוּ וְאֶת־יֹרְדֵי בוֹר:

Yechezkel/Ezekiel
Chapter 33

יחזקאל
פרק לג

30 All the princes of the north and all the Sidonians are there, who went down in disgrace with the slain, in spite of the terror that their might inspired; and they lie, uncircumcised, with those who are slain by the sword, and bear their shame with those who have gone down to the Pit.

שָׁמָּה נְסִיכֵי צָפוֹן כֻּלָּם וְכָל־צִדֹנִי אֲשֶׁר־יָרְדוּ אֶת־חֲלָלִים בְּחִתִּיתָם מִגְּבוּרָתָם בּוֹשִׁים וַיִּשְׁכְּבוּ עֲרֵלִים אֶת־חַלְלֵי־חֶרֶב וַיִּשְׂאוּ כְלִמָּתָם אֶת־יוֹרְדֵי בוֹר:

31 These Pharaoh shall see, and he shall be consoled for all his masses, those of Pharaoh's men slain by the sword and all his army – declares *Hashem*.

אוֹתָם יִרְאֶה פַרְעֹה וְנִחַם עַל־כָּל־הֲמוֹנֹה [הֲמוֹנוֹ] חַלְלֵי־חֶרֶב פַּרְעֹה וְכָל־חֵילוֹ נְאֻם אֲדֹנָי יֱהֹוִה:

32 I strike terror into the land of the living; Pharaoh and all his masses are laid among the uncircumcised, along with those who were slain by the sword – said *Hashem*.

כִּי־נָתַתִּי אֶת־חִתִּיתוֹ [חִתִּיתִי] בְּאֶרֶץ חַיִּים וְהֻשְׁכַּב בְּתוֹךְ עֲרֵלִים אֶת־חַלְלֵי־חֶרֶב פַּרְעֹה וְכָל־הֲמוֹנֹה נְאֻם אֲדֹנָי יֱהֹוִה:

33

1 The word of *Hashem* came to me:

וַיְהִי דְבַר־יְהֹוָה אֵלַי לֵאמֹר:

2 O mortal, speak to your fellow countrymen and say to them: When I bring the sword against a country, the citizens of that country take one of their number and appoint him their watchman.

בֶּן־אָדָם דַּבֵּר אֶל־בְּנֵי־עַמְּךָ וְאָמַרְתָּ אֲלֵיהֶם אֶרֶץ כִּי־אָבִיא עָלֶיהָ חָרֶב וְלָקְחוּ עַם־הָאָרֶץ אִישׁ אֶחָד מִקְצֵיהֶם וְנָתְנוּ אֹתוֹ לָהֶם לְצֹפֶה:

3 Suppose he sees the sword advancing against the country, and he blows the *shofar* and warns the people.

וְרָאָה אֶת־הַחֶרֶב בָּאָה עַל־הָאָרֶץ וְתָקַע בַּשּׁוֹפָר וְהִזְהִיר אֶת־הָעָם:

v'-ra-AH et ha-KHE-rev ba-AH al ha-A-retz v'-ta-KA ba-sho-FAR v'-hiz-HEER et ha-AM

4 If anybody hears the sound of the *shofar* but ignores the warning, and the sword comes and dispatches him, his blood shall be on his own head.

וְשָׁמַע הַשֹּׁמֵעַ אֶת־קוֹל הַשּׁוֹפָר וְלֹא נִזְהָר וַתָּבוֹא חֶרֶב וַתִּקָּחֵהוּ דָּמוֹ בְרֹאשׁוֹ יִהְיֶה:

5 Since he heard the sound of the *shofar* but ignored the warning, his bloodguilt shall be upon himself; had he taken the warning, he would have saved his life.

אֵת קוֹל הַשּׁוֹפָר שָׁמַע וְלֹא נִזְהָר דָּמוֹ בּוֹ יִהְיֶה וְהוּא נִזְהָר נַפְשׁוֹ מִלֵּט:

6 But if the watchman sees the sword advancing and does not blow the *shofar*, so that the people are not warned, and the sword comes and destroys one of them, that person was destroyed for his own sins; however, I will demand a reckoning for his blood from the watchman.

וְהַצֹּפֶה כִּי־יִרְאֶה אֶת־הַחֶרֶב בָּאָה וְלֹא־תָקַע בַּשּׁוֹפָר וְהָעָם לֹא־נִזְהָר וַתָּבוֹא חֶרֶב וַתִּקַּח מֵהֶם נָפֶשׁ הוּא בַּעֲוֹנוֹ נִלְקָח וְדָמוֹ מִיַּד־הַצֹּפֶה אֶדְרֹשׁ:

Man blowing the shofar at the Western Wall

33:3 He blows the horn At the beginning of this chapter, *Yechezkel* compares the job of a prophet to a city's watchman. Just as the guard alerts the townsfolk of impending danger, so is the prophet responsible for warning the people about the consequences of their actions. Ancient Israelite cities were built with towers connected to their walls where the watchmen would sit. In order to warn inhabitants of approaching enemies, the watchman would blow a 'horn', in Hebrew *shofar* (שופר). In Judaism, the shofar has both military significance (see also Joshua 6), and religious significance, as it is sounded on *Rosh Hashana*, the Jewish New Year. By using the image of a *shofar*, *Yechezkel* deftly combines the two themes of military and spiritual preparedness.

Yechezkel/Ezekiel
Chapter 33

7 Now, O mortal, I have appointed you a watchman for the House of *Yisrael*; and whenever you hear a message from My mouth, you must transmit My warning to them.

8 When I say to the wicked, "Wicked man, you shall die," but you have not spoken to warn the wicked man against his way, he, that wicked man, shall die for his sins, but I will demand a reckoning for his blood from you.

9 But if you have warned the wicked man to turn back from his way, and he has not turned from his way, he shall die for his own sins, but you will have saved your life.

10 Now, O mortal, say to the House of *Yisrael*: This is what you have been saying: "Our transgressions and our sins weigh heavily upon us; we are sick at heart about them. How can we survive?"

11 Say to them: As I live – declares *Hashem* – it is not My desire that the wicked shall die, but that the wicked turn from his [evil] ways and live. Turn back, turn back from your evil ways, that you may not die, O House of *Yisrael*!

12 Now, O mortal, say to your fellow countrymen: The righteousness of the righteous shall not save him when he transgresses, nor shall the wickedness of the wicked cause him to stumble when he turns back from his wickedness. The righteous shall not survive through his righteousness when he sins.

13 When I say of the righteous "He shall surely live," and, relying on his righteousness, he commits iniquity, none of his righteous deeds shall be remembered; but for the iniquity that he has committed he shall die.

14 So, too, when I say to the wicked, "You shall die," and he turns back from his sinfulness and does what is just and right –

15 if the wicked man restores a pledge, makes good what he has taken by robbery, follows the laws of life, and does not commit iniquity – he shall live, he shall not die.

16 None of the sins that he committed shall be remembered against him; since he does what is just and right, he shall live.

Yechezkel/Ezekiel
Chapter 33

יחזקאל
פרק לג

17 Your fellow countrymen say, "The way of *Hashem* is unfair." But it is their way that is unfair!

יז וְאָמְרוּ בְּנֵי עַמְּךָ לֹא יִתָּכֵן דֶּרֶךְ אֲדֹנָי וְהֵמָּה דַּרְכָּם לֹא־יִתָּכֵן:

18 When a righteous man turns away from his righteous deeds and commits iniquity, he shall die for it.

יח בְּשׁוּב־צַדִּיק מִצִּדְקָתוֹ וְעָשָׂה עָוֶל וּמֵת בָּהֶם:

19 And when a wicked man turns back from his wickedness and does what is just and right, it is he who shall live by virtue of these things.

יט וּבְשׁוּב רָשָׁע מֵרִשְׁעָתוֹ וְעָשָׂה מִשְׁפָּט וּצְדָקָה עֲלֵיהֶם הוּא יִחְיֶה:

20 And will you say, "The way of *Hashem* is unfair"? I will judge each one of you according to his ways, O House of *Yisrael*!

כ וַאֲמַרְתֶּם לֹא יִתָּכֵן דֶּרֶךְ אֲדֹנָי אִישׁ כִּדְרָכָיו אֶשְׁפּוֹט אֶתְכֶם בֵּית יִשְׂרָאֵל:

21 In the twelfth year of our exile, on the fifth day of the tenth month, a fugitive came to me from *Yerushalayim* and reported, "The city has fallen."

כא וַיְהִי בִּשְׁתֵּי עֶשְׂרֵה שָׁנָה בָּעֲשִׂרִי בַּחֲמִשָּׁה לַחֹדֶשׁ לְגָלוּתֵנוּ בָּא־אֵלַי הַפָּלִיט מִירוּשָׁלַ͏ִם לֵאמֹר הֻכְּתָה הָעִיר:

22 Now the hand of *Hashem* had come upon me the evening before the fugitive arrived, and He opened my mouth before he came to me in the morning; thus my mouth was opened and I was no longer speechless.

כב וְיַד־יְהֹוָה הָיְתָה אֵלַי בָּעֶרֶב לִפְנֵי בּוֹא הַפָּלִיט וַיִּפְתַּח אֶת־פִּי עַד־בּוֹא אֵלַי בַּבֹּקֶר וַיִּפָּתַח פִּי וְלֹא נֶאֱלַמְתִּי עוֹד:

23 The word of *Hashem* came to me:

כג וַיְהִי דְבַר־יְהֹוָה אֵלַי לֵאמֹר:

24 O mortal, those who live in these ruins in the land of *Yisrael* argue, "*Avraham* was but one man, yet he was granted possession of the land. We are many; surely, the land has been given as a possession to us."

כד בֶּן־אָדָם יֹשְׁבֵי הֶחֳרָבוֹת הָאֵלֶּה עַל־אַדְמַת יִשְׂרָאֵל אֹמְרִים לֵאמֹר אֶחָד הָיָה אַבְרָהָם וַיִּירַשׁ אֶת־הָאָרֶץ וַאֲנַחְנוּ רַבִּים לָנוּ נִתְּנָה הָאָרֶץ לְמוֹרָשָׁה:

25 Therefore say to them: Thus said *Hashem*: You eat with the blood, you raise your eyes to your fetishes, and you shed blood – yet you expect to possess the land!

כה לָכֵן אֱמֹר אֲלֵיהֶם כֹּה־אָמַר אֲדֹנָי יְהֹוִה עַל־הַדָּם תֹּאכֵלוּ וְעֵינֵכֶם תִּשְׂאוּ אֶל־גִּלּוּלֵיכֶם וְדָם תִּשְׁפֹּכוּ וְהָאָרֶץ תִּירָשׁוּ:

26 You have relied on your sword, you have committed abominations, you have all defiled other men's wives – yet you expect to possess the land!

כו עֲמַדְתֶּם עַל־חַרְבְּכֶם עֲשִׂיתֶן תּוֹעֵבָה וְאִישׁ אֶת־אֵשֶׁת רֵעֵהוּ טִמֵּאתֶם וְהָאָרֶץ תִּירָשׁוּ:

27 Thus shall you speak to them: Thus said *Hashem*: As I live, those who are in the ruins shall fall by the sword, and those who are in the open I have allotted as food to the beasts, and those who are in the strongholds and caves shall die by pestilence.

כז כֹּה־תֹאמַר אֲלֵהֶם כֹּה־אָמַר אֲדֹנָי יְהֹוִה חַי־אָנִי אִם־לֹא אֲשֶׁר בֶּחֳרָבוֹת בַּחֶרֶב יִפֹּלוּ וַאֲשֶׁר עַל־פְּנֵי הַשָּׂדֶה לַחַיָּה נְתַתִּיו לְאָכְלוֹ וַאֲשֶׁר בַּמְּצָדוֹת וּבַמְּעָרוֹת בַּדֶּבֶר יָמוּתוּ:

28 I will make the land a desolate waste, and her proud glory shall cease; and the mountains of *Yisrael* shall be desolate, with none passing through.

כח וְנָתַתִּי אֶת־הָאָרֶץ שְׁמָמָה וּמְשַׁמָּה וְנִשְׁבַּת גְּאוֹן עֻזָּהּ וְשָׁמְמוּ הָרֵי יִשְׂרָאֵל מֵאֵין עוֹבֵר:

Yechezkel/Ezekiel
Chapter 34

יחזקאל
פרק לד

29 And they shall know that I am *Hashem*, when I make the land a desolate waste on account of all the abominations which they have committed.

כט וְיָדְעוּ כִּי־אֲנִי יְהֹוָה בְּתִתִּי אֶת־הָאָרֶץ שְׁמָמָה וּמְשַׁמָּה עַל כׇּל־תּוֹעֲבֹתָם אֲשֶׁר עָשׂוּ׃

30 Note well, O mortal: your fellow countrymen who converse about you by the walls and in the doorways of their houses and say to each other and propose to one another, "Come and hear what word has issued from *Hashem*."

ל וְאַתָּה בֶן־אָדָם בְּנֵי עַמְּךָ הַנִּדְבָּרִים בְּךָ אֵצֶל הַקִּירוֹת וּבְפִתְחֵי הַבָּתִּים וְדִבֶּר־חַד אֶת־אַחַד אִישׁ אֶת־אָחִיו לֵאמֹר בֹּאוּ־נָא וְשִׁמְעוּ מָה הַדָּבָר הַיּוֹצֵא מֵאֵת יְהֹוָה׃

31 They will come to you in crowds and sit before you in throngs and will hear your words, but they will not obey them. For they produce nothing but lust with their mouths; and their hearts pursue nothing but gain.

לא וְיָבוֹאוּ אֵלֶיךָ כִּמְבוֹא־עָם וְיֵשְׁבוּ לְפָנֶיךָ עַמִּי וְשָׁמְעוּ אֶת־דְּבָרֶיךָ וְאוֹתָם לֹא יַעֲשׂוּ כִּי־עֲגָבִים בְּפִיהֶם הֵמָּה עֹשִׂים אַחֲרֵי בִצְעָם לִבָּם הֹלֵךְ׃

32 To them you are just a singer of bawdy songs, who has a sweet voice and plays skillfully; they hear your words, but will not obey them.

לב וְהִנְּךָ לָהֶם כְּשִׁיר עֲגָבִים יְפֵה קוֹל וּמֵטִב נַגֵּן וְשָׁמְעוּ אֶת־דְּבָרֶיךָ וְעֹשִׂים אֵינָם אוֹתָם׃

33 But when it comes – and come it will – they shall know that a *Navi* has been among them.

לג וּבְבֹאָהּ הִנֵּה בָאָה וְיָדְעוּ כִּי נָבִיא הָיָה בְתוֹכָם׃

34 1 The word of *Hashem* came to me:

לד א וַיְהִי דְבַר־יְהֹוָה אֵלַי לֵאמֹר׃

2 O mortal, prophesy against the shepherds of *Yisrael*. Prophesy, and say to them: To the shepherds: Thus said *Hashem*: Ah, you shepherds of *Yisrael*, who have been tending yourselves! Is it not the flock that the shepherds ought to tend?

ב בֶּן־אָדָם הִנָּבֵא עַל־רוֹעֵי יִשְׂרָאֵל הִנָּבֵא וְאָמַרְתָּ אֲלֵיהֶם לָרֹעִים כֹּה אָמַר אֲדֹנָי יֱהֹוִה הוֹי רֹעֵי־יִשְׂרָאֵל אֲשֶׁר הָיוּ רֹעִים אוֹתָם הֲלוֹא הַצֹּאן יִרְעוּ הָרֹעִים׃

3 You partake of the fat, you clothe yourselves with the wool, and you slaughter the fatlings; but you do not tend the flock

ג אֶת־הַחֵלֶב תֹּאכֵלוּ וְאֶת־הַצֶּמֶר תִּלְבָּשׁוּ הַבְּרִיאָה תִּזְבָּחוּ הַצֹּאן לֹא תִרְעוּ׃

4 You have not sustained the weak, healed the sick, or bandaged the injured; you have not brought back the strayed, or looked for the lost; but you have driven them with harsh rigor,

ד אֶת־הַנַּחְלוֹת לֹא חִזַּקְתֶּם וְאֶת־הַחוֹלָה לֹא־רִפֵּאתֶם וְלַנִּשְׁבֶּרֶת לֹא חֲבַשְׁתֶּם וְאֶת־הַנִּדַּחַת לֹא הֲשֵׁבֹתֶם וְאֶת־הָאֹבֶדֶת לֹא בִקַּשְׁתֶּם וּבְחׇזְקָה רְדִיתֶם אֹתָם וּבְפָרֶךְ׃

5 and they have been scattered for want of anyone to tend them; scattered, they have become prey for every wild beast.

ה וַתְּפוּצֶינָה מִבְּלִי רֹעֶה וַתִּהְיֶינָה לְאׇכְלָה לְכׇל־חַיַּת הַשָּׂדֶה וַתְּפוּצֶינָה׃

6 My sheep stray through all the mountains and over every lofty hill; My flock is scattered all over the face of the earth, with none to take thought of them and none to seek them.

ו יִשְׁגּוּ צֹאנִי בְּכׇל־הֶהָרִים וְעַל כׇּל־גִּבְעָה רָמָה וְעַל כׇּל־פְּנֵי הָאָרֶץ נָפֹצוּ צֹאנִי וְאֵין דּוֹרֵשׁ וְאֵין מְבַקֵּשׁ׃

7 Hear then, O shepherds, the word of *Hashem*!

ז לָכֵן רֹעִים שִׁמְעוּ אֶת־דְּבַר יְהֹוָה׃

1288

Yechezkel/Ezekiel
Chapter 34

יחזקאל פרק לד

8 As I live – declares *Hashem*: Because My flock has been a spoil – My flock has been a prey for all the wild beasts, for want of anyone to tend them since My shepherds have not taken thought of My flock, for the shepherds tended themselves instead of tending the flock –

ח חַי־אָנִי נְאֻם אֲדֹנָי יֱהֹוִה אִם־לֹא יַעַן הֱיוֹת־צֹאנִי ׀ לָבַז וַתִּהְיֶינָה צֹאנִי לְאׇכְלָה לְכׇל־חַיַּת הַשָּׂדֶה מֵאֵין רֹעֶה וְלֹא־דָרְשׁוּ רֹעַי אֶת־צֹאנִי וַיִּרְעוּ הָרֹעִים אוֹתָם וְאֶת־צֹאנִי לֹא רָעוּ׃

9 hear indeed, O shepherds, the word of *Hashem*:

ט לָכֵן הָרֹעִים שִׁמְעוּ דְּבַר־יְהֹוָה׃

10 Thus said *Hashem*: I am going to deal with the shepherds! I will demand a reckoning of them for My flock, and I will dismiss them from tending the flock. The shepherds shall not tend themselves any more; for I will rescue My flock from their mouths, and it shall not be their prey.

י כֹּה־אָמַר אֲדֹנָי יֱהֹוִה הִנְנִי אֶל־הָרֹעִים וְדָרַשְׁתִּי אֶת־צֹאנִי מִיָּדָם וְהִשְׁבַּתִּים מֵרְעוֹת צֹאן וְלֹא־יִרְעוּ עוֹד הָרֹעִים אוֹתָם וְהִצַּלְתִּי צֹאנִי מִפִּיהֶם וְלֹא־תִהְיֶיןָ לָהֶם לְאׇכְלָה׃

11 For thus said *Hashem*: Here am I! I am going to take thought for My flock and I will seek them out.

יא כִּי כֹּה אָמַר אֲדֹנָי יֱהֹוִה הִנְנִי־אָנִי וְדָרַשְׁתִּי אֶת־צֹאנִי וּבִקַּרְתִּים׃

12 As a shepherd seeks out his flock when some [animals] in his flock have gotten separated, so I will seek out My flock, I will rescue them from all the places to which they were scattered on a day of cloud and gloom.

יב כְּבַקָּרַת רֹעֶה עֶדְרוֹ בְּיוֹם־הֱיוֹתוֹ בְתוֹךְ־צֹאנוֹ נִפְרָשׁוֹת כֵּן אֲבַקֵּר אֶת־צֹאנִי וְהִצַּלְתִּי אֶתְהֶם מִכׇּל־הַמְּקוֹמֹת אֲשֶׁר נָפֹצוּ שָׁם בְּיוֹם עָנָן וַעֲרָפֶל׃

13 I will take them out from the peoples and gather them from the countries, and I will bring them to their own land, and will pasture them on the mountains of *Yisrael*, by the watercourses and in all the settled portions of the land.

יג וְהוֹצֵאתִים מִן־הָעַמִּים וְקִבַּצְתִּים מִן־הָאֲרָצוֹת וַהֲבִיאֹתִים אֶל־אַדְמָתָם וּרְעִיתִים אֶל־הָרֵי יִשְׂרָאֵל בָּאֲפִיקִים וּבְכֹל מוֹשְׁבֵי הָאָרֶץ׃

v'-ho-tzay-TEEM min ha-a-MEEM v'-ki-batz-TEEM min ha-a-ra-TZOT va-ha-vee-o-TEEM el ad-ma-TAM ur-ee-TEEM el ha-RAY yis-ra-AYL ba-a-fee-KEEM uv-KHOL mo-sh'-VAY ha-A-retz

14 I will feed them in good grazing land, and the lofty hills of *Yisrael* shall be their pasture. There, in the hills of *Yisrael*, they shall lie down in a good pasture and shall feed on rich grazing land.

יד בְּמִרְעֶה־טּוֹב אֶרְעֶה אֹתָם וּבְהָרֵי מְרוֹם־יִשְׂרָאֵל יִהְיֶה נְוֵהֶם שָׁם תִּרְבַּצְנָה בְּנָוֶה טּוֹב וּמִרְעֶה שָׁמֵן תִּרְעֶינָה אֶל־הָרֵי יִשְׂרָאֵל׃

15 I Myself will graze My flock, and I Myself will let them lie down – declares *Hashem*.

טו אֲנִי אֶרְעֶה צֹאנִי וַאֲנִי אַרְבִּיצֵם נְאֻם אֲדֹנָי יֱהֹוִה׃

34:13 I will take them out from the peoples and gather them The "ingathering of the exiles," known in Hebrew as *kibbutz galuyot* (קיבוץ גלויות), is promised in multiple places throughout the Bible. Although they are scattered throughout the four corners of the earth, *Yechezkel* declares that one day, God will gather the People of Israel and return them to their ancient soil, the Land of Israel. For centuries, Jews have been praying three times daily for the fulfillment of this prophecy in their central prayer, known as the *amidah*. With the establishment of the State of Israel and the many waves of immigration that have taken place in recent history, we are fortunate to witness the beginning of the fulfillment of this tremendous miracle.

North American immigrants

Yechezkel/Ezekiel

Chapter 34

יחזקאל
פרק לד

16 I will look for the lost, and I will bring back the strayed; I will bandage the injured, and I will sustain the weak; and the fat and healthy ones I will destroy. I will tend them rightly.

טז אֶת־הָאֹבֶדֶת אֲבַקֵּשׁ וְאֶת־הַנִּדַּחַת אָשִׁיב וְלַנִּשְׁבֶּרֶת אֶחֱבֹשׁ וְאֶת־הַחוֹלָה אֲחַזֵּק וְאֶת־הַשְּׁמֵנָה וְאֶת־הַחֲזָקָה אַשְׁמִיד אֶרְעֶנָּה בְמִשְׁפָּט:

17 And as for you, My flock, thus said *Hashem*: I am going to judge between one animal and another. To the rams and the bucks:

יז וְאַתֵּנָה צֹאנִי כֹּה אָמַר אֲדֹנָי יֱהֹוִה הִנְנִי שֹׁפֵט בֵּין־שֶׂה לָשֶׂה לָאֵילִים וְלָעַתּוּדִים:

18 Is it not enough for you to graze on choice grazing ground, but you must also trample with your feet what is left from your grazing? And is it not enough for you to drink clear water, but you must also muddy with your feet what is left?

יח הַמְעַט מִכֶּם הַמִּרְעֶה הַטּוֹב תִּרְעוּ וְיֶתֶר מִרְעֵיכֶם תִּרְמְסוּ בְּרַגְלֵיכֶם וּמִשְׁקַע־מַיִם תִּשְׁתּוּ וְאֵת הַנּוֹתָרִים בְּרַגְלֵיכֶם תִּרְפֹּשׂוּן:

19 And must My flock graze on what your feet have trampled and drink what your feet have muddied?

יט וְצֹאנִי מִרְמַס רַגְלֵיכֶם תִּרְעֶינָה וּמִרְפַּשׂ רַגְלֵיכֶם תִּשְׁתֶּינָה:

20 Assuredly, thus said *Hashem* to them: Here am I, I am going to decide between the stout animals and the lean.

כ לָכֵן כֹּה אָמַר אֲדֹנָי יֱהֹוִה אֲלֵיהֶם הִנְנִי־אָנִי וְשָׁפַטְתִּי בֵּין־שֶׂה בִרְיָה וּבֵין שֶׂה רָזָה:

21 Because you pushed with flank and shoulder against the feeble ones and butted them with your horns until you scattered them abroad,

כא יַעַן בְּצַד וּבְכָתֵף תֶּהְדֹּפוּ וּבְקַרְנֵיכֶם תְּנַגְּחוּ כָּל־הַנַּחְלוֹת עַד אֲשֶׁר הֲפִיצוֹתֶם אוֹתָנָה אֶל־הַחוּצָה:

22 I will rescue My flock and they shall no longer be a spoil. I will decide between one animal and another.

כב וְהוֹשַׁעְתִּי לְצֹאנִי וְלֹא־תִהְיֶינָה עוֹד לָבַז וְשָׁפַטְתִּי בֵּין שֶׂה לָשֶׂה:

23 Then I will appoint a single shepherd over them to tend them – My servant *David*. He shall tend them, he shall be a shepherd to them.

כג וַהֲקִמֹתִי עֲלֵיהֶם רֹעֶה אֶחָד וְרָעָה אֶתְהֶן אֵת עַבְדִּי דָוִיד הוּא יִרְעֶה אֹתָם וְהוּא־יִהְיֶה לָהֶן לְרֹעֶה:

24 I *Hashem* will be their God, and My servant *David* shall be a ruler among them – I *Hashem* have spoken.

כד וַאֲנִי יְהֹוָה אֶהְיֶה לָהֶם לֵאלֹהִים וְעַבְדִּי דָוִד נָשִׂיא בְתוֹכָם אֲנִי יְהֹוָה דִּבַּרְתִּי:

25 And I will grant them a covenant of friendship. I will banish vicious beasts from their land, and they shall live secure in the wasteland, they shall even sleep in the woodland.

כה וְכָרַתִּי לָהֶם בְּרִית שָׁלוֹם וְהִשְׁבַּתִּי חַיָּה־רָעָה מִן־הָאָרֶץ וְיָשְׁבוּ בַמִּדְבָּר לָבֶטַח וְיָשְׁנוּ בַּיְּעָרִים:

26 I will make these and the environs of My hill a blessing: I will send down the rain in its season, rains that bring blessing.

כו וְנָתַתִּי אוֹתָם וּסְבִיבוֹת גִּבְעָתִי בְּרָכָה וְהוֹרַדְתִּי הַגֶּשֶׁם בְּעִתּוֹ גִּשְׁמֵי בְרָכָה יִהְיוּ:

27 The trees of the field shall yield their fruit and the land shall yield its produce. [My people] shall continue secure on its own soil. They shall know that I am *Hashem* when I break the bars of their yoke and rescue them from those who enslave them.

כז וְנָתַן עֵץ הַשָּׂדֶה אֶת־פִּרְיוֹ וְהָאָרֶץ תִּתֵּן יְבוּלָהּ וְהָיוּ עַל־אַדְמָתָם לָבֶטַח וְיָדְעוּ כִּי־אֲנִי יְהֹוָה בְּשִׁבְרִי אֶת־מֹטוֹת עֻלָּם וְהִצַּלְתִּים מִיַּד הָעֹבְדִים בָּהֶם:

Yechezkel/Ezekiel
Chapter 35

יחזקאל
פרק לה

28 They shall no longer be a spoil for the nations, and the beasts of the earth shall not devour them; they shall dwell secure and untroubled.

וְלֹא־יִהְיוּ עוֹד בַּז לַגּוֹיִם וְחַיַּת הָאָרֶץ לֹא תֹאכְלֵם וְיָשְׁבוּ לָבֶטַח וְאֵין מַחֲרִיד:

29 I shall establish for them a planting of renown; they shall no more be carried off by famine, and they shall not have to bear again the taunts of the nations.

וַהֲקִמֹתִי לָהֶם מַטָּע לְשֵׁם וְלֹא־יִהְיוּ עוֹד אֲסֻפֵי רָעָב בָּאָרֶץ וְלֹא־יִשְׂאוּ עוֹד כְּלִמַּת הַגּוֹיִם:

30 They shall know that I *Hashem* their God am with them and they, the House of *Yisrael*, are My people – declares *Hashem*.

וְיָדְעוּ כִּי אֲנִי יְהוָה אֱלֹהֵיהֶם אִתָּם וְהֵמָּה עַמִּי בֵּית יִשְׂרָאֵל נְאֻם אֲדֹנָי יֱהוִה:

31 For you, My flock, flock that I tend, are men; and I am your God – declares *Hashem*.

וְאַתֵּן צֹאנִי צֹאן מַרְעִיתִי אָדָם אַתֶּם אֲנִי אֱלֹהֵיכֶם נְאֻם אֲדֹנָי יֱהוִה:

35

1 The word of *Hashem* came to me:

וַיְהִי דְבַר־יְהוָה אֵלַי לֵאמֹר:

2 O mortal, set your face against Mount Seir and prophesy against it.

בֶּן־אָדָם שִׂים פָּנֶיךָ עַל־הַר שֵׂעִיר וְהִנָּבֵא עָלָיו:

3 Say to it: Thus said *Hashem*: I am going to deal with you, Mount Seir: I will stretch out My hand against you and make you an utter waste.

וְאָמַרְתָּ לּוֹ כֹּה אָמַר אֲדֹנָי יֱהוִה הִנְנִי אֵלֶיךָ הַר־שֵׂעִיר וְנָטִיתִי יָדִי עָלֶיךָ וּנְתַתִּיךָ שְׁמָמָה וּמְשַׁמָּה:

4 I will turn your towns into ruins, and you shall be a desolation; then you shall know that I am *Hashem*.

עָרֶיךָ חָרְבָּה אָשִׂים וְאַתָּה שְׁמָמָה תִהְיֶה וְיָדַעְתָּ כִּי־אֲנִי יְהוָה:

5 Because you harbored an ancient hatred and handed the people of *Yisrael* over to the sword in their time of calamity, the time set for their punishment –

יַעַן הֱיוֹת לְךָ אֵיבַת עוֹלָם וַתַּגֵּר אֶת־בְּנֵי־יִשְׂרָאֵל עַל־יְדֵי־חָרֶב בְּעֵת אֵידָם בְּעֵת עֲוֹן קֵץ:

YA-an he-YOT l'-KHA ay-VAT o-LAM va-ta-GAYR et b'-nay yis-ra-AYL al y'-DAY KHA-rev b'-AYT ay-DAM b'-AYT a-VON KAYTZ

6 assuredly, as I live, declares *Hashem*, I will doom you with blood; blood shall pursue you; I swear that, for your bloodthirsty hatred, blood shall pursue you.

לָכֵן חַי־אָנִי נְאֻם אֲדֹנָי יֱהוִה כִּי־לְדָם אֶעֶשְׂךָ וְדָם יִרְדֲּפֶךָ אִם־לֹא דָם שָׂנֵאתָ וְדָם יִרְדֲּפֶךָ:

7 I will make Mount Seir an utter waste, and I will keep all passersby away from it.

וְנָתַתִּי אֶת־הַר שֵׂעִיר לְשִׁמְמָה וּשְׁמָמָה וְהִכְרַתִּי מִמֶּנּוּ עֹבֵר וָשָׁב:

8 I will cover its mountains with the slain; men slain by the sword shall lie on your hills, in your valleys, and in all your watercourses.

וּמִלֵּאתִי אֶת־הָרָיו חֲלָלָיו גִּבְעוֹתֶיךָ וְגֵאוֹתֶיךָ וְכָל־אֲפִיקֶיךָ חַלְלֵי־חֶרֶב יִפְּלוּ בָהֶם:

35:5 Because you harbored an ancient hatred Although chapter 32 ended *Yechezkel's* prophecies against the nations, he returns with one final chapter against the nation of Edom. The Edomites were descendants of Esau whose animosity towards his brother *Yaakov* was perpetuated throughout history. Esau inhabited the mountainous region on the east side of the Arava valley, around Mount Seir – a dry, barren, rocky landscape. *Yechezkel* explains that since the Edomites constantly assisted Israel's enemies, God was personally against them (verse 3), and would ensure that their country would remain desolate (verse 4).

Yechezkel/Ezekiel
Chapter 36

9 I will make you a desolation for all time; your towns shall never be inhabited. And you shall know that I am *Hashem*.

10 Because you thought "The two nations and the two lands shall be mine and we shall possess them" – although *Hashem* was there –

11 assuredly, as I live, declares *Hashem*, I will act with the same anger and passion that you acted with in your hatred of them. And I will make Myself known through them when I judge you.

12 You shall know that I *Hashem* have heard all the taunts you uttered against the hills of *Yisrael*: "They have been laid waste; they have been given to us as prey."

13 And you spoke arrogantly against Me and multiplied your words against Me: I have heard it.

14 Thus said *Hashem*: When the whole earth rejoices, I will make you a desolation.

15 As you rejoiced when the heritage of the House of *Yisrael* was laid waste, so will I treat you: the hill country of Seir and the whole of Edom, all of it, shall be laid waste. And they shall know that I am *Hashem*.

36

1 And you, O mortal, prophesy to the mountains of *Yisrael* and say: O mountains of *Yisrael*, hear the word of *Hashem*:

2 Thus said *Hashem*: Because the enemy gloated over you, "Aha! Those ancient heights have become our possession!"

3 therefore prophesy, and say: Thus said *Hashem*: Just because they eagerly lusted to see you become a possession of the other nations round about, so that you have become the butt of gossip in every language and of the jibes from every people –

4 truly, you mountains of *Yisrael*, hear the word of *Hashem*: Thus said *Hashem* to the mountains and the hills, to the watercourses and the valleys, and to the desolate wastes and deserted cities which have become a prey and a laughingstock to the other nations round about:

יחזקאל
פרק לו

ט שְׁמְמוֹת עוֹלָם אֶתְּנֵךְ וְעָרַיִךְ לֹא תִישַׁבְנָה [תָשֹׁבְנָה] וִידַעְתֶּם כִּי־אֲנִי יְהוָה:

י יַעַן אֲמָרֵךְ אֶת־שְׁנֵי הַגּוֹיִם וְאֶת־שְׁתֵּי הָאֲרָצוֹת לִי תִהְיֶינָה וִירַשְׁנוּהָ וַיהוָה שָׁם הָיָה:

יא לָכֵן חַי־אָנִי נְאֻם אֲדֹנָי יְהוִה וְעָשִׂיתִי כְּאַפְּךָ וּכְקִנְאָתְךָ אֲשֶׁר עָשִׂיתָה מִשִּׂנְאָתֶיךָ בָּם וְנוֹדַעְתִּי בָם כַּאֲשֶׁר אֶשְׁפְּטֶךָ:

יב וְיָדַעְתָּ כִּי־אֲנִי יְהוָה שָׁמַעְתִּי אֶת־כָּל־ נָאָצוֹתֶיךָ אֲשֶׁר אָמַרְתָּ עַל־הָרֵי יִשְׂרָאֵל לֵאמֹר שממה [שָׁמֵמוּ] לָנוּ נִתְּנוּ לְאָכְלָה:

יג וַתַּגְדִּילוּ עָלַי בְּפִיכֶם וְהַעְתַּרְתֶּם עָלַי דִּבְרֵיכֶם אֲנִי שָׁמָעְתִּי:

יד כֹּה אָמַר אֲדֹנָי יְהוִה כִּשְׂמֹחַ כָּל־הָאָרֶץ שְׁמָמָה אֶעֱשֶׂה־לָּךְ:

טו כְּשִׂמְחָתְךָ לְנַחֲלַת בֵּית־יִשְׂרָאֵל עַל אֲשֶׁר־שָׁמֵמָה כֵּן אֶעֱשֶׂה־לָּךְ שְׁמָמָה תִהְיֶה הַר־שֵׂעִיר וְכָל־אֱדוֹם כֻּלָּהּ וְיָדְעוּ כִּי־אֲנִי יְהוָה:

לו א וְאַתָּה בֶן־אָדָם הִנָּבֵא אֶל־הָרֵי יִשְׂרָאֵל וְאָמַרְתָּ הָרֵי יִשְׂרָאֵל שִׁמְעוּ דְּבַר־יְהוָה:

ב כֹּה אָמַר אֲדֹנָי יְהוִה יַעַן אָמַר הָאוֹיֵב עֲלֵיכֶם הֶאָח וּבָמוֹת עוֹלָם לְמוֹרָשָׁה הָיְתָה לָּנוּ:

ג לָכֵן הִנָּבֵא וְאָמַרְתָּ כֹּה אָמַר אֲדֹנָי יְהוִה יַעַן בְּיַעַן שַׁמּוֹת וְשָׁאֹף אֶתְכֶם מִסָּבִיב לִהְיוֹתְכֶם מוֹרָשָׁה לִשְׁאֵרִית הַגּוֹיִם וַתֵּעֲלוּ עַל־שְׂפַת לָשׁוֹן וְדִבַּת־עָם:

ד לָכֵן הָרֵי יִשְׂרָאֵל שִׁמְעוּ דְּבַר־אֲדֹנָי יְהוִה כֹּה־אָמַר אֲדֹנָי יְהוִה לֶהָרִים וְלַגְּבָעוֹת לָאֲפִיקִים וְלַגֵּאָיוֹת וְלֶחֳרָבוֹת הַשֹּׁמְמוֹת וְלֶעָרִים הַנֶּעֱזָבוֹת אֲשֶׁר הָיוּ לְבַז וּלְלַעַג לִשְׁאֵרִית הַגּוֹיִם אֲשֶׁר מִסָּבִיב:

Yechezkel/Ezekiel
Chapter 36

יחזקאל
פרק לו

5 Assuredly, thus said *Hashem*: I have indeed spoken in My blazing wrath against the other nations and against all of Edom which, with wholehearted glee and with contempt, have made My land a possession for themselves for pasture and for prey.

ה לָכֵן כֹּה־אָמַר אֲדֹנָי יֱהֹוִה אִם־לֹא בְּאֵשׁ קִנְאָתִי דִבַּרְתִּי עַל־שְׁאֵרִית הַגּוֹיִם וְעַל־אֱדוֹם כֻּלָּא אֲשֶׁר נָתְנוּ אֶת־אַרְצִי ׀ לָהֶם לְמוֹרָשָׁה בְּשִׂמְחַת כָּל־לֵבָב בִּשְׁאָט נֶפֶשׁ לְמַעַן מִגְרָשָׁהּ לָבַז׃

6 Yes, prophesy about the land of *Yisrael*, and say to the mountains and the hills, to the watercourses and to the valleys, Thus said *Hashem*: Behold, I declare in My blazing wrath: Because you have suffered the taunting of the nations,

ו לָכֵן הִנָּבֵא עַל־אַדְמַת יִשְׂרָאֵל וְאָמַרְתָּ לֶהָרִים וְלַגְּבָעוֹת לָאֲפִיקִים וְלַגֵּאָיוֹת כֹּה־אָמַר ׀ אֲדֹנָי יֱהֹוִה הִנְנִי בְקִנְאָתִי וּבַחֲמָתִי דִּבַּרְתִּי יַעַן כְּלִמַּת גּוֹיִם נְשָׂאתֶם׃

7 thus said *Hashem*: I hereby swear that the nations which surround you shall, in their turn, suffer disgrace.

ז לָכֵן כֹּה אָמַר אֲדֹנָי יֱהֹוִה אֲנִי נָשָׂאתִי אֶת־יָדִי אִם־לֹא הַגּוֹיִם אֲשֶׁר לָכֶם מִסָּבִיב הֵמָּה כְּלִמָּתָם יִשָּׂאוּ׃

8 But you, O mountains of *Yisrael*, shall yield your produce and bear your fruit for My people *Yisrael*, for their return is near.

ח וְאַתֶּם הָרֵי יִשְׂרָאֵל עַנְפְּכֶם תִּתֵּנוּ וּפֶרְיְכֶם תִּשְׂאוּ לְעַמִּי יִשְׂרָאֵל כִּי קֵרְבוּ לָבוֹא׃

v'-a-TEM ha-RAY yis-ra-AYL an-p'-KHEM ti-TAY-nu u-fer-y'-KHEM tis-U l'-a-MEE yis-ra-AYL kee kay-r'-VU la-VO

9 For I will care for you: I will turn to you, and you shall be tilled and sown.

ט כִּי הִנְנִי אֲלֵיכֶם וּפָנִיתִי אֲלֵיכֶם וְנֶעֱבַדְתֶּם וְנִזְרַעְתֶּם׃

10 I will settle a large population on you, the whole House of *Yisrael*; the towns shall be resettled, and the ruined sites rebuilt.

י וְהִרְבֵּיתִי עֲלֵיכֶם אָדָם כָּל־בֵּית יִשְׂרָאֵל כֻּלֹּה וְנֹשְׁבוּ הֶעָרִים וְהֶחֳרָבוֹת תִּבָּנֶינָה׃

11 I will multiply men and beasts upon you, and they shall increase and be fertile, and I will resettle you as you were formerly, and will make you more prosperous than you were at first. And you shall know that I am *Hashem*.

יא וְהִרְבֵּיתִי עֲלֵיכֶם אָדָם וּבְהֵמָה וְרָבוּ וּפָרוּ וְהוֹשַׁבְתִּי אֶתְכֶם כְּקַדְמוֹתֵיכֶם וְהֵטִבֹתִי מֵרִאשֹׁתֵיכֶם וִידַעְתֶּם כִּי־אֲנִי יְהֹוָה׃

12 I will lead men – My people *Yisrael* – to you, and they shall possess you. You shall be their heritage, and you shall not again cause them to be bereaved.

יב וְהוֹלַכְתִּי עֲלֵיכֶם אָדָם אֶת־עַמִּי יִשְׂרָאֵל וִירֵשׁוּךָ וְהָיִיתָ לָהֶם לְנַחֲלָה וְלֹא־תוֹסִף עוֹד לְשַׁכְּלָם׃

13 Thus said *Hashem*: Because they say to you, "You are [a land] that devours men, you have been a bereaver of your nations,"

יג כֹּה אָמַר אֲדֹנָי יֱהֹוִה יַעַן אֹמְרִים לָכֶם אֹכֶלֶת אָדָם אתי [אָתְּ] וּמְשַׁכֶּלֶת גּויִךְ [גּוֹיַיִךְ] הָיִית׃

Eshtaol Forest planted by the Jewish National Fund

36:8 But you, O mountains of *Yisrael*, shall yield your produce In this prophecy, *Hashem* promises that the land will again be inhabited by the house of Israel and that it will flourish, pledging that the mountains will grow trees and produce fruits for the sake of His returning nation. Since the Jewish people have returned to Israel, the land has indeed begun to flourish, and there are once again trees growing throughout the land. In fact, under the direction of the Jewish National Fund, over 250,000,000 trees have been planted in Israel since 1901. While the world struggles with deforestation, Israel is the only country that ended the twentieth century with more trees than it had at its start. According to Rabbi Abba of the Talmud (*Sanhedrin* 98a), the flourishing of the Land of Israel described in this verse is a clear sign that the complete and final redemption is near.

Yechezkel/Ezekiel
Chapter 36

יחזקאל
פרק לו

14 assuredly, you shall devour men no more, you shall never again bereave your nations – declares *Hashem*.

יד לָכֵן אָדָם לֹא־תֹאכְלִי עוֹד וְגוֹיַיִךְ [וְגוֹיַיִךְ] לֹא תְכַשְּׁלִי־[תְשַׁכְּלִי־] עוֹד נְאֻם אֲדֹנָי יֱהֹוִה:

15 No more will I allow the jibes of the nations to be heard against you, no longer shall you suffer the taunting of the peoples; and never again shall you cause your nations to stumble – declares *Hashem*.

טו וְלֹא־אַשְׁמִיעַ אֵלַיִךְ עוֹד כְּלִמַּת הַגּוֹיִם וְחֶרְפַּת עַמִּים לֹא תִשְׂאִי־עוֹד וְגוֹיַיִךְ [וְגוֹיַיִךְ] לֹא־תַכְשִׁלִי עוֹד נְאֻם אֲדֹנָי יֱהֹוִה:

16 The word of *Hashem* came to me:

טז וַיְהִי דְבַר־יְהֹוָה אֵלַי לֵאמֹר:

17 O mortal, when the House of *Yisrael* dwelt on their own soil, they defiled it with their ways and their deeds; their ways were in My sight like the uncleanness of a menstruous woman.

יז בֶּן־אָדָם בֵּית יִשְׂרָאֵל יֹשְׁבִים עַל־אַדְמָתָם וַיְטַמְּאוּ אוֹתָהּ בְּדַרְכָּם וּבַעֲלִילוֹתָם כְּטֻמְאַת הַנִּדָּה הָיְתָה דַרְכָּם לְפָנָי:

18 So I poured out My wrath on them for the blood which they shed upon their land, and for the fetishes with which they defiled it.

יח וָאֶשְׁפֹּךְ חֲמָתִי עֲלֵיהֶם עַל־הַדָּם אֲשֶׁר־שָׁפְכוּ עַל־הָאָרֶץ וּבְגִלּוּלֵיהֶם טִמְּאוּהָ:

19 I scattered them among the nations, and they were dispersed through the countries: I punished them in accordance with their ways and their deeds.

יט וָאָפִיץ אֹתָם בַּגּוֹיִם וַיִּזָּרוּ בָּאֲרָצוֹת כְּדַרְכָּם וְכַעֲלִילוֹתָם שְׁפַטְתִּים:

20 But when they came to those nations, they caused My holy name to be profaned, in that it was said of them, "These are the people of *Hashem*, yet they had to leave His land."

כ וַיָּבוֹא אֶל־הַגּוֹיִם אֲשֶׁר־בָּאוּ שָׁם וַיְחַלְּלוּ אֶת־שֵׁם קָדְשִׁי בֶּאֱמֹר לָהֶם עַם־יְהֹוָה אֵלֶּה וּמֵאַרְצוֹ יָצָאוּ:

va-ya-VO el ha-go-YIM a-sher BA-u SHAM vai-kha-l'-LU et SHAYM kod-SHEE be-e-MOR la-HEM am a-do-NAI AY-leh u-may-ar-TZO ya-TZA-u

21 Therefore I am concerned for My holy name, which the House of *Yisrael* have caused to be profaned among the nations to which they have come.

כא וָאֶחְמֹל עַל־שֵׁם קָדְשִׁי אֲשֶׁר חִלְּלוּהוּ בֵּית יִשְׂרָאֵל בַּגּוֹיִם אֲשֶׁר־בָּאוּ שָׁמָּה:

22 Say to the House of *Yisrael*: Thus said *Hashem*: Not for your sake will I act, O House of *Yisrael*, but for My holy name, which you have caused to be profaned among the nations to which you have come.

כב לָכֵן אֱמֹר לְבֵית־יִשְׂרָאֵל כֹּה אָמַר אֲדֹנָי יֱהֹוִה לֹא לְמַעַנְכֶם אֲנִי עֹשֶׂה בֵּית יִשְׂרָאֵל כִּי אִם־לְשֵׁם־קָדְשִׁי אֲשֶׁר חִלַּלְתֶּם בַּגּוֹיִם אֲשֶׁר־בָּאתֶם שָׁם:

36:20 They caused My holy name to be profaned *Yechezkel* writes that the exile of the People of Israel among the nations caused a 'desecration of God's name,' in Hebrew, *chilul Hashem* (חילול השם). *Rashi* explains that in response to the exile, the nations of the world would say "these are the Lord's people and they left His land; apparently, He did not have the power to save His people and His land." Hence, the exile of the people from *Eretz Yisrael* causes the name of the Lord to be profaned. It therefore follows that the redemption of this people and their return to their homeland results in a *kiddush Hashem* (קידוש השם), 'sanctification of God's name.' As *Yechezkel* writes (verses 23–24), "And I will sanctify My great name, which has been profaned among the nations…I will take you from among the nations and gather you from all the countries, and I will bring you back to your own land."

Yechezkel/Ezekiel
Chapter 36

יחזקאל
פרק לו

23 I will sanctify My great name which has been profaned among the nations – among whom you have caused it to be profaned. And the nations shall know that I am *Hashem* – declares *Hashem* – when I manifest My holiness before their eyes through you.

כג וְקִדַּשְׁתִּי אֶת־שְׁמִי הַגָּדוֹל הַמְחֻלָּל בַּגּוֹיִם אֲשֶׁר חִלַּלְתֶּם בְּתוֹכָם וְיָדְעוּ הַגּוֹיִם כִּי־אֲנִי יְהֹוָה נְאֻם אֲדֹנָי יֱהֹוִה בְּהִקָּדְשִׁי בָכֶם לְעֵינֵיהֶם:

v'-ki-dash-TEE et sh'-MEE ha-ga-DOL ham-khu-LAL ba-go-YIM a-SHER khi-lal-TEM b'-to-KHAM v'-ya-d'-U ha-go-YIM kee a-NEE a-do-NAI n'-UM a-do-NAI e-lo-HEEM b'-hi-ka-d'-SHEE va-KHEM l'-ay-nay-HEM

24 I will take you from among the nations and gather you from all the countries, and I will bring you back to your own land.

כד וְלָקַחְתִּי אֶתְכֶם מִן־הַגּוֹיִם וְקִבַּצְתִּי אֶתְכֶם מִכָּל־הָאֲרָצוֹת וְהֵבֵאתִי אֶתְכֶם אֶל־אַדְמַתְכֶם:

25 I will sprinkle clean water upon you, and you shall be clean: I will cleanse you from all your uncleanness and from all your fetishes.

כה וְזָרַקְתִּי עֲלֵיכֶם מַיִם טְהוֹרִים וּטְהַרְתֶּם מִכֹּל טֻמְאוֹתֵיכֶם וּמִכָּל־גִּלּוּלֵיכֶם אֲטַהֵר אֶתְכֶם:

26 And I will give you a new heart and put a new spirit into you: I will remove the heart of stone from your body and give you a heart of flesh;

כו וְנָתַתִּי לָכֶם לֵב חָדָשׁ וְרוּחַ חֲדָשָׁה אֶתֵּן בְּקִרְבְּכֶם וַהֲסִרֹתִי אֶת־לֵב הָאֶבֶן מִבְּשַׂרְכֶם וְנָתַתִּי לָכֶם לֵב בָּשָׂר:

27 and I will put My spirit into you. Thus I will cause you to follow My laws and faithfully to observe My rules.

כז וְאֶת־רוּחִי אֶתֵּן בְּקִרְבְּכֶם וְעָשִׂיתִי אֵת אֲשֶׁר־בְּחֻקַּי תֵּלֵכוּ וּמִשְׁפָּטַי תִּשְׁמְרוּ וַעֲשִׂיתֶם:

28 Then you shall dwell in the land which I gave to your fathers, and you shall be My people and I will be your God.

כח וִישַׁבְתֶּם בָּאָרֶץ אֲשֶׁר נָתַתִּי לַאֲבֹתֵיכֶם וִהְיִיתֶם לִי לְעָם וְאָנֹכִי אֶהְיֶה לָכֶם לֵאלֹהִים:

29 And when I have delivered you from all your uncleanness, I will summon the grain and make it abundant, and I will not bring famine upon you.

כט וְהוֹשַׁעְתִּי אֶתְכֶם מִכֹּל טֻמְאוֹתֵיכֶם וְקָרָאתִי אֶל־הַדָּגָן וְהִרְבֵּיתִי אֹתוֹ וְלֹא־אֶתֵּן עֲלֵיכֶם רָעָב:

30 I will make the fruit of your trees and the crops of your fields abundant, so that you shall never again be humiliated before the nations because of famine.

ל וְהִרְבֵּיתִי אֶת־פְּרִי הָעֵץ וּתְנוּבַת הַשָּׂדֶה לְמַעַן אֲשֶׁר לֹא תִקְחוּ עוֹד חֶרְפַּת רָעָב בַּגּוֹיִם:

31 Then you shall recall your evil ways and your base conduct, and you shall loathe yourselves for your iniquities and your abhorrent practices.

לא וּזְכַרְתֶּם אֶת־דַּרְכֵיכֶם הָרָעִים וּמַעַלְלֵיכֶם אֲשֶׁר לֹא־טוֹבִים וּנְקֹטֹתֶם בִּפְנֵיכֶם עַל עֲוֺנֹתֵיכֶם וְעַל תּוֹעֲבוֹתֵיכֶם:

32 Not for your sake will I act – declares *Hashem* – take good note! Be ashamed and humiliated because of your ways, O House of *Yisrael*!

לב לֹא לְמַעַנְכֶם אֲנִי־עֹשֶׂה נְאֻם אֲדֹנָי יֱהֹוִה יִוָּדַע לָכֶם בּוֹשׁוּ וְהִכָּלְמוּ מִדַּרְכֵיכֶם בֵּית יִשְׂרָאֵל:

33 Thus said *Hashem*: When I have cleansed you of all your iniquities, I will people your settlements, and the ruined places shall be rebuilt;

לג כֹּה אָמַר אֲדֹנָי יֱהֹוִה בְּיוֹם טַהֲרִי אֶתְכֶם מִכֹּל עֲוֺנוֹתֵיכֶם וְהוֹשַׁבְתִּי אֶת־הֶעָרִים וְנִבְנוּ הֶחֳרָבוֹת:

34 and the desolate land, after lying waste in the sight of every passerby, shall again be tilled.

לד וְהָאָרֶץ הַנְּשַׁמָּה תֵּעָבֵד תַּחַת אֲשֶׁר הָיְתָה שְׁמָמָה לְעֵינֵי כָּל־עוֹבֵר:

Yechezkel/Ezekiel
Chapter 37

יחזקאל
פרק לז

35 And men shall say, "That land, once desolate, has become like the garden of Eden and the cities, once ruined, desolate, and ravaged, are now populated and fortified."

לה וְאָמְרוּ הָאָרֶץ הַלֵּזוּ הַנְּשַׁמָּה הָיְתָה כְּגַן־עֵדֶן וְהֶעָרִים הֶחֳרֵבוֹת וְהַנְשַׁמּוֹת וְהַנֶּהֱרָסוֹת בְּצוּרוֹת יָשָׁבוּ׃

36 And the nations that are left around you shall know that I *Hashem* have rebuilt the ravaged places and replanted the desolate land. I *Hashem* have spoken and will act.

לו וְיָדְעוּ הַגּוֹיִם אֲשֶׁר יִשָּׁאֲרוּ סְבִיבוֹתֵיכֶם כִּי אֲנִי יְהֹוָה בָּנִיתִי הַנֶּהֱרָסוֹת נָטַעְתִּי הַנְּשַׁמָּה אֲנִי יְהֹוָה דִּבַּרְתִּי וְעָשִׂיתִי׃

37 Thus said *Hashem*: Moreover, in this I will respond to the House of *Yisrael* and act for their sake: I will multiply their people like sheep.

לז כֹּה אָמַר אֲדֹנָי יְהֹוִה עוֹד זֹאת אִדָּרֵשׁ לְבֵית־יִשְׂרָאֵל לַעֲשׂוֹת לָהֶם אַרְבֶּה אֹתָם כַּצֹּאן אָדָם׃

38 As *Yerushalayim* is filled with sacrificial sheep during her festivals, so shall the ruined cities be filled with flocks of people. And they shall know that I am *Hashem*. 1

לח כְּצֹאן קֳדָשִׁים כְּצֹאן יְרוּשָׁלַיִם בְּמוֹעֲדֶיהָ כֵּן תִּהְיֶינָה הֶעָרִים הֶחֳרֵבוֹת מְלֵאוֹת צֹאן אָדָם וְיָדְעוּ כִּי־אֲנִי יְהֹוָה׃

37

1 The hand of *Hashem* came upon me. He took me out by the spirit of *Hashem* and set me down in the valley. It was full of bones.

לז א הָיְתָה עָלַי יַד־יְהֹוָה וַיּוֹצִאֵנִי בְרוּחַ יְהֹוָה וַיְנִיחֵנִי בְּתוֹךְ הַבִּקְעָה וְהִיא מְלֵאָה עֲצָמוֹת׃

2 He led me all around them; there were very many of them spread over the valley, and they were very dry.

ב וְהֶעֱבִירַנִי עֲלֵיהֶם סָבִיב סָבִיב וְהִנֵּה רַבּוֹת מְאֹד עַל־פְּנֵי הַבִּקְעָה וְהִנֵּה יְבֵשׁוֹת מְאֹד׃

3 He said to me, "O mortal, can these bones live again?" I replied, "O *Hashem*, only You know."

ג וַיֹּאמֶר אֵלַי בֶּן־אָדָם הֲתִחְיֶינָה הָעֲצָמוֹת הָאֵלֶּה וָאֹמַר אֲדֹנָי יְהֹוִה אַתָּה יָדָעְתָּ׃

va-YO-mer ay-LAI ben a-DAM ha-tikh-YE-nah ha-a-tza-MOT ha-AY-leh va-o-MAR a-do-NAI e-lo-HEEM a-TAH ya-DA-ta

4 And He said to me, "Prophesy over these bones and say to them: O dry bones, hear the word of *Hashem*!

ד וַיֹּאמֶר אֵלַי הִנָּבֵא עַל־הָעֲצָמוֹת הָאֵלֶּה וְאָמַרְתָּ אֲלֵיהֶם הָעֲצָמוֹת הַיְבֵשׁוֹת שִׁמְעוּ דְּבַר־יְהֹוָה׃

5 Thus said *Hashem* to these bones: I will cause breath to enter you and you shall live again.

ה כֹּה אָמַר אֲדֹנָי יְהֹוִה לָעֲצָמוֹת הָאֵלֶּה הִנֵּה אֲנִי מֵבִיא בָכֶם רוּחַ וִחְיִיתֶם׃

37:3 'O mortal, can these bones live again?' This chapter contains *Yechezkel*'s well-known vision of the valley in which dry bones come to life. There could be no greater metaphor for the restoration of the Jewish people to their land. *Yisrael* and *Yehuda* have been destroyed, the people scattered to the four corners of the earth. Just as no one could imagine that dead bones could live again, the exiles cannot imagine that they will survive as a nation, let alone ever return to their homeland. Yet, when God asks *Yechezkel* "can these bones live?" he doesn't express doubt or hopelessness. He answers that anything can happen if it is God's will. And so the dry bones arise from the dead. In a similarly miraculous fashion, in the years immediately following the Holocaust, the People of Israel cameback to life in the Land of Israel. In fact, these verses are read on Israeli radio every year on Holocaust Remembrance Day.

Yechezkel/Ezekiel
Chapter 37

6 I will lay sinews upon you, and cover you with flesh, and form skin over you. And I will put breath into you, and you shall live again. And you shall know that I am *Hashem*!"

7 I prophesied as I had been commanded. And while I was prophesying, suddenly there was a sound of rattling, and the bones came together, bone to matching bone.

8 I looked, and there were sinews on them, and flesh had grown, and skin had formed over them; but there was no breath in them.

9 Then He said to me, "Prophesy to the breath, prophesy, O mortal! Say to the breath: Thus said *Hashem*: Come, O breath, from the four winds, and breathe into these slain, that they may live again."

10 I prophesied as He commanded me. The breath entered them, and they came to life and stood up on their feet, a vast multitude.

11 And He said to me, "O mortal, these bones are the whole House of *Yisrael*. They say, 'Our bones are dried up, our hope is gone; we are doomed.'

12 Prophesy, therefore, and say to them: Thus said *Hashem*: I am going to open your graves and lift you out of the graves, O My people, and bring you to the land of *Yisrael*.

13 You shall know, O My people, that I am *Hashem*, when I have opened your graves and lifted you out of your graves.

14 I will put My breath into you and you shall live again, and I will set you upon your own soil. Then you shall know that I *Hashem* have spoken and have acted" – declares *Hashem*.

15 The word of *Hashem* came to me:

16 And you, O mortal, take a stick and write on it, "Of *Yehuda* and the Israelites associated with him"; and take another stick and write on it, "Of *Yosef* – the stick of *Efraim* – and all the House of *Yisrael* associated with him."

17 Bring them close to each other, so that they become one stick, joined together in your hand.

Yechezkel/Ezekiel
Chapter 37

יחזקאל
פרק לז

18 And when any of your people ask you, "Won't you tell us what these actions of yours mean?"

יח וְכַאֲשֶׁר יֹאמְרוּ אֵלֶיךָ בְּנֵי עַמְּךָ לֵאמֹר הֲלוֹא־תַגִּיד לָנוּ מָה־אֵלֶּה לָּךְ׃

19 answer them, "Thus said *Hashem*: I am going to take the stick of *Yosef* – which is in the hand of *Efraim* – and of the tribes of *Yisrael* associated with him, and I will place the stick of *Yehuda* upon it and make them into one stick; they shall be joined in My hand."

יט דַּבֵּר אֲלֵהֶם כֹּה־אָמַר אֲדֹנָי יְהֹוִה הִנֵּה אֲנִי לֹקֵחַ אֶת־עֵץ יוֹסֵף אֲשֶׁר בְּיַד־אֶפְרַיִם וְשִׁבְטֵי יִשְׂרָאֵל חברו [חֲבֵרָיו] וְנָתַתִּי אוֹתָם עָלָיו אֶת־עֵץ יְהוּדָה וַעֲשִׂיתִם לְעֵץ אֶחָד וְהָיוּ אֶחָד בְּיָדִי׃

da-BAYR a-lay-HEM koh a-MAR a-do-NAI e-lo-HEEM hi-NAY a-NEE lo-KAY-akh et AYTZ yo-SAYF a-SHER b'-YAD ef-RA-yim v'-shiv-TAY yis-ra-AYL kha-vay-RAV v'-na-ta-TEE o-TAM a-LAV et AYTZ y'-hu-DAH va-a-see-TEEM l'-AYTZ e-KHAD v'-ha-YU e-KHAD b'-ya-DEE

20 You shall hold up before their eyes the sticks which you have inscribed,

כ וְהָיוּ הָעֵצִים אֲשֶׁר־תִּכְתֹּב עֲלֵיהֶם בְּיָדְךָ לְעֵינֵיהֶם׃

21 and you shall declare to them: Thus said *Hashem*: I am going to take *B'nei Yisrael* from among the nations they have gone to, and gather them from every quarter, and bring them to their own land.

כא וְדַבֵּר אֲלֵיהֶם כֹּה־אָמַר אֲדֹנָי יְהֹוִה הִנֵּה אֲנִי לֹקֵחַ אֶת־בְּנֵי יִשְׂרָאֵל מִבֵּין הַגּוֹיִם אֲשֶׁר הָלְכוּ־שָׁם וְקִבַּצְתִּי אֹתָם מִסָּבִיב וְהֵבֵאתִי אוֹתָם אֶל־אַדְמָתָם׃

22 I will make them a single nation in the land, on the hills of *Yisrael*, and one king shall be king of them all. Never again shall they be two nations, and never again shall they be divided into two kingdoms.

כב וְעָשִׂיתִי אֹתָם לְגוֹי אֶחָד בָּאָרֶץ בְּהָרֵי יִשְׂרָאֵל וּמֶלֶךְ אֶחָד יִהְיֶה לְכֻלָּם לְמֶלֶךְ וְלֹא יהיה־[יִהְיוּ־] עוֹד לִשְׁנֵי גוֹיִם וְלֹא יֵחָצוּ עוֹד לִשְׁתֵּי מַמְלָכוֹת עוֹד׃

23 Nor shall they ever again defile themselves by their fetishes and their abhorrent things, and by their other transgressions. I will save them in all their settlements where they sinned, and I will cleanse them. Then they shall be My people, and I will be their God.

כג וְלֹא יִטַּמְּאוּ עוֹד בְּגִלּוּלֵיהֶם וּבְשִׁקּוּצֵיהֶם וּבְכֹל פִּשְׁעֵיהֶם וְהוֹשַׁעְתִּי אֹתָם מִכֹּל מוֹשְׁבֹתֵיהֶם אֲשֶׁר חָטְאוּ בָהֶם וְטִהַרְתִּי אוֹתָם וְהָיוּ־לִי לְעָם וַאֲנִי אֶהְיֶה לָהֶם לֵאלֹהִים׃

24 My servant *David* shall be king over them; there shall be one shepherd for all of them. They shall follow My rules and faithfully obey My laws.

כד וְעַבְדִּי דָוִד מֶלֶךְ עֲלֵיהֶם וְרוֹעֶה אֶחָד יִהְיֶה לְכֻלָּם וּבְמִשְׁפָּטַי יֵלֵכוּ וְחֻקֹּתַי יִשְׁמְרוּ וְעָשׂוּ אוֹתָם׃

25 Thus they shall remain in the land which I gave to My servant *Yaakov* and in which your fathers dwelt; they and their children and their children's children shall dwell there forever, with My servant *David* as their prince for all time.

כה וְיָשְׁבוּ עַל־הָאָרֶץ אֲשֶׁר נָתַתִּי לְעַבְדִּי לְיַעֲקֹב אֲשֶׁר יָשְׁבוּ־בָהּ אֲבוֹתֵיכֶם וְיָשְׁבוּ עָלֶיהָ הֵמָּה וּבְנֵיהֶם וּבְנֵי בְנֵיהֶם עַד־עוֹלָם וְדָוִד עַבְדִּי נָשִׂיא לָהֶם לְעוֹלָם׃

37:19 They shall be joined in My hand *Yechezkel* again prophesies about the ingathering of the exiles. He stresses that this a promise for all of Israel; not only for the members of the kingdom of *Yehuda*, but also for the tribes from kingdom of *Yisrael* whose people have been considered lost since the Assyrian conquest of the northern kingdom. During the final redemption, all twelve tribes of Israel will return to the Promised Land, and they will re-unite to form one nation unified under one leader. Today, Jews are returning to *Eretz Yisrael* from all over the world, and are joining together to reestablish the Nation of Israel in the Land of Israel.

Members of the Bnei Menashe tribe arrive in Israel

Yechezkel/Ezekiel — Chapter 38

26 I will make a covenant of friendship with them – it shall be an everlasting covenant with them – I will establish them and multiply them, and I will place My Sanctuary among them forever.

27 My Presence shall rest over them; I will be their God and they shall be My people.

28 And when My Sanctuary abides among them forever, the nations shall know that I *Hashem* do sanctify *Yisrael*.

38

1 The word of *Hashem* came to me:

2 O mortal, turn your face toward Gog of the land of Magog, the chief prince of Meshech and Tubal. Prophesy against him

3 and say: Thus said *Hashem*: Lo, I am coming to deal with you, O Gog, chief prince of Meshech and Tubal!

4 I will turn you around and put hooks in your jaws, and lead you out with all your army, horses, and horsemen, all of them clothed in splendor, a vast assembly, all of them with bucklers and shields, wielding swords.

5 Among them shall be Persia, Nubia, and Put, everyone with shield and helmet;

6 Gomer and all its cohorts, Beth-togarmah [in] the remotest parts of the north and all its cohorts – the many peoples with you.

7 Be ready, prepare yourselves, you and all the battalions mustered about you, and hold yourself in reserve for them.

8 After a long time you shall be summoned; in the distant future you shall march against the land [of a people] restored from the sword, gathered from the midst of many peoples – against the mountains of *Yisrael*, which have long lain desolate – [a people] liberated from the nations, and now all dwelling secure.

9 You shall advance, coming like a storm; you shall be like a cloud covering the earth, you and all your cohorts, and the many peoples with you.

10 Thus said *Hashem*: On that day, a thought will occur to you, and you will conceive a wicked design.

Yechezkel/Ezekiel
Chapter 38

יחזקאל
פרק לח

11 You will say, "I will invade a land of open towns, I will fall upon a tranquil people living secure, all of them living in unwalled towns and lacking bars and gates,

יא וְאָמַרְתָּ אֶעֱלֶה עַל־אֶרֶץ פְּרָזוֹת אָבוֹא הַשֹּׁקְטִים יֹשְׁבֵי לָבֶטַח כֻּלָּם יֹשְׁבִים בְּאֵין חוֹמָה וּבְרִיחַ וּדְלָתַיִם אֵין לָהֶם׃

12 in order to take spoil and seize plunder" – to turn your hand against repopulated wastes, and against a people gathered from among nations, acquiring livestock and possessions, living at the center of the earth.

יב לִשְׁלֹל שָׁלָל וְלָבֹז בַּז לְהָשִׁיב יָדְךָ עַל־חֳרָבוֹת נוֹשָׁבֹת וְאֶל־עַם מְאֻסָּף מִגּוֹיִם עֹשֶׂה מִקְנֶה וְקִנְיָן יֹשְׁבֵי עַל־טַבּוּר הָאָרֶץ׃

13 Sheba and Dedan, and the merchants and all the magnates of Tarshish will say to you, "Have you come to take spoil? Is it to seize plunder that you assembled your hordes – to carry off silver and gold, to make off with livestock and goods, to gather an immense booty?"

יג שְׁבָא וּדְדָן וְסֹחֲרֵי תַרְשִׁישׁ וְכָל־כְּפִרֶיהָ יֹאמְרוּ לְךָ הֲלִשְׁלֹל שָׁלָל אַתָּה בָא הֲלָבֹז בַּז הִקְהַלְתָּ קְהָלֶךָ לָשֵׂאת כֶּסֶף וְזָהָב לָקַחַת מִקְנֶה וְקִנְיָן לִשְׁלֹל שָׁלָל גָּדוֹל׃

14 Therefore prophesy, O mortal, and say to Gog: Thus said *Hashem*: Surely, on that day, when My people *Yisrael* are living secure, you will take note,

יד לָכֵן הִנָּבֵא בֶן־אָדָם וְאָמַרְתָּ לְגוֹג כֹּה אָמַר אֲדֹנָי יְהוִה הֲלוֹא בַּיּוֹם הַהוּא בְּשֶׁבֶת עַמִּי יִשְׂרָאֵל לָבֶטַח תֵּדָע׃

la-KHAYN hi-na-VAY ven a-DAM v'-a-mar-TA l'-GOG KOH a-MAR a-do-NAI e-lo-HEEM ha-LO ba-YOM ha-HU b'-SHE-vet a-MEE yis-ra-AYL la-VE-takh tay-DA

15 and you will come from your home in the farthest north, you and many peoples with you – all of them mounted on horses, a vast horde, a mighty army –

טו וּבָאתָ מִמְּקוֹמְךָ מִיַּרְכְּתֵי צָפוֹן אַתָּה וְעַמִּים רַבִּים אִתָּךְ רֹכְבֵי סוּסִים כֻּלָּם קָהָל גָּדוֹל וְחַיִל רָב׃

16 and you will advance upon My people *Yisrael*, like a cloud covering the earth. This shall happen on that distant day: I will bring you to My land, that the nations may know Me when, before their eyes, I manifest My holiness through you, O Gog!

טז וְעָלִיתָ עַל־עַמִּי יִשְׂרָאֵל כֶּעָנָן לְכַסּוֹת הָאָרֶץ בְּאַחֲרִית הַיָּמִים תִּהְיֶה וַהֲבִאוֹתִיךָ עַל־אַרְצִי לְמַעַן דַּעַת הַגּוֹיִם אֹתִי בְּהִקָּדְשִׁי בְךָ לְעֵינֵיהֶם גּוֹג׃

17 Thus said *Hashem*: Why, you are the one I spoke of in ancient days through My servants, the *Neviim* of *Yisrael*, who prophesied for years in those days that I would bring you against them!

יז כֹּה־אָמַר אֲדֹנָי יְהוִה הַאַתָּה־הוּא אֲשֶׁר־דִּבַּרְתִּי בְּיָמִים קַדְמוֹנִים בְּיַד עֲבָדַי נְבִיאֵי יִשְׂרָאֵל הַנִּבְּאִים בַּיָּמִים הָהֵם שָׁנִים לְהָבִיא אֹתְךָ עֲלֵיהֶם׃

38:14 When My people *Yisrael* are living secure In *Yechezkel's* final apocalyptic vision, Gog and Magog make their evil preparations to invade Israel. They see the people dwelling in the land in security and prosperity, and feel that the time is ripe to attack. *Hashem* tells Gog and Magog that through their evil, they will be destroyed, and God's name will be sanctified throughout the world (verse 16). This verse gives us a hint into the mind of Israel's enemies. The sight of the People of Israel living in peace and quiet in *Eretz Yisrael* motivates them to attack. Although Israel poses no threat, her enemies are prepared to risk everything to see her destroyed. But as God makes clear, He will never allow that to happen.

Yechezkel/Ezekiel
Chapter 39

18 On that day, when Gog sets foot on the soil of *Yisrael* – declares *Hashem* – My raging anger shall flare up.

19 For I have decreed in My indignation and in My blazing wrath: On that day, a terrible earthquake shall befall the land of *Yisrael*.

20 The fish of the sea, the birds of the sky, the beasts of the field, all creeping things that move on the ground, and every human being on earth shall quake before Me. Mountains shall be overthrown, cliffs shall topple, and every wall shall crumble to the ground.

21 I will then summon the sword against him throughout My mountains – declares *Hashem* – and every man's sword shall be turned against his brother.

22 I will punish him with pestilence and with bloodshed; and I will pour torrential rain, hailstones, and sulfurous fire upon him and his hordes and the many peoples with him.

23 Thus will I manifest My greatness and My holiness, and make Myself known in the sight of many nations. And they shall know that I am *Hashem*.

39 1 And you, O mortal, prophesy against Gog and say: Thus said *Hashem*: I am going to deal with you, O Gog, chief prince of Meshech and Tubal!

2 I will turn you around and drive you on, and I will take you from the far north and lead you toward the mountains of *Yisrael*.

3 I will strike your bow from your left hand and I will loosen the arrows from your right hand.

4 You shall fall on the mountains of *Yisrael*, you and all your battalions and the peoples who are with you; and I will give you as food to carrion birds of every sort and to the beasts of the field,

5 as you lie in the open field. For I have spoken – declares *Hashem*.

6 And I will send a fire against Magog and against those who dwell secure in the coastlands. And they shall know that I am *Hashem*.

Yechezkel/Ezekiel
Chapter 39

7 I will make My holy name known among My people *Yisrael*, and never again will I let My holy name be profaned. And the nations shall know that I *Hashem* am holy in *Yisrael*.

8 Ah! it has come, it has happened – declares *Hashem*: this is that day that I decreed.

9 Then the inhabitants of the cities of *Yisrael* will go out and make fires and feed them with the weapons – shields and bucklers, bows and arrows, clubs and spears; they shall use them as fuel for seven years.

10 They will not gather firewood in the fields or cut any in the forests, but will use the weapons as fuel for their fires. They will despoil those who despoiled them and plunder those who plundered them – declares *Hashem*.

11 On that day I will assign to Gog a burial site there in *Yisrael* – the Valley of the Travelers, east of the Sea. It shall block the path of travelers, for there Gog and all his multitude will be buried. It shall be called the Valley of Gog's Multitude.

12 The House of *Yisrael* shall spend seven months burying them, in order to cleanse the land;

13 all the people of the land shall bury them. The day I manifest My glory shall bring renown to them – declares *Hashem*.

14 And they shall appoint men to serve permanently, to traverse the land and bury any invaders who remain above ground, in order to cleanse it. The search shall go on for a period of seven months.

15 As those who traverse the country make their rounds, any one of them who sees a human bone shall erect a marker beside it, until the buriers have interred them in the Valley of Gog's Multitude.

16 There shall also be a city named Multitude. And thus the land shall be cleansed.

17 And you, O mortal, say to every winged bird and to all the wild beasts: Thus said *Hashem*: Assemble, come and gather from all around for the sacrificial feast that I am preparing for you – a great sacrificial feast – upon the mountains of *Yisrael*, and eat flesh and drink blood.

יחזקאל
פרק לט

ז וְאֶת־שֵׁם קָדְשִׁי אוֹדִיעַ בְּתוֹךְ עַמִּי יִשְׂרָאֵל וְלֹא־אַחֵל אֶת־שֵׁם־קָדְשִׁי עוֹד וְיָדְעוּ הַגּוֹיִם כִּי־אֲנִי יְהֹוָה קָדוֹשׁ בְּיִשְׂרָאֵל׃

ח הִנֵּה בָאָה וְנִהְיָתָה נְאֻם אֲדֹנָי יֱהֹוִה הוּא הַיּוֹם אֲשֶׁר דִּבַּרְתִּי׃

ט וְיָצְאוּ יֹשְׁבֵי עָרֵי יִשְׂרָאֵל וּבִעֲרוּ וְהִשִּׂיקוּ בְּנֶשֶׁק וּמָגֵן וְצִנָּה בְּקֶשֶׁת וּבְחִצִּים וּבְמַקֵּל יָד וּבְרֹמַח וּבִעֲרוּ בָהֶם אֵשׁ שֶׁבַע שָׁנִים׃

י וְלֹא־יִשְׂאוּ עֵצִים מִן־הַשָּׂדֶה וְלֹא יַחְטְבוּ מִן־הַיְּעָרִים כִּי בַנֶּשֶׁק יְבַעֲרוּ־אֵשׁ וְשָׁלְלוּ אֶת־שֹׁלְלֵיהֶם וּבָזְזוּ אֶת־בֹּזְזֵיהֶם נְאֻם אֲדֹנָי יֱהֹוִה׃

יא וְהָיָה בַיּוֹם הַהוּא אֶתֵּן לְגוֹג מְקוֹם־שָׁם קֶבֶר בְּיִשְׂרָאֵל גֵּי הָעֹבְרִים קִדְמַת הַיָּם וְחֹסֶמֶת הִיא אֶת־הָעֹבְרִים וְקָבְרוּ שָׁם אֶת־גּוֹג וְאֶת־כָּל־הֲמוֹנֹה וְקָרְאוּ גֵּיא הֲמוֹן גּוֹג׃

יב וּקְבָרוּם בֵּית יִשְׂרָאֵל לְמַעַן טַהֵר אֶת־הָאָרֶץ שִׁבְעָה חֳדָשִׁים׃

יג וְקָבְרוּ כָּל־עַם הָאָרֶץ וְהָיָה לָהֶם לְשֵׁם יוֹם הִכָּבְדִי נְאֻם אֲדֹנָי יֱהֹוִה׃

יד וְאַנְשֵׁי תָמִיד יַבְדִּילוּ עֹבְרִים בָּאָרֶץ מְקַבְּרִים אֶת־הָעֹבְרִים אֶת־הַנּוֹתָרִים עַל־פְּנֵי הָאָרֶץ לְטַהֲרָהּ מִקְצֵה שִׁבְעָה־חֳדָשִׁים יַחְקֹרוּ׃

טו וְעָבְרוּ הָעֹבְרִים בָּאָרֶץ וְרָאָה עֶצֶם אָדָם וּבָנָה אֶצְלוֹ צִיּוּן עַד קָבְרוּ אֹתוֹ הַמְקַבְּרִים אֶל־גֵּיא הֲמוֹן גּוֹג׃

טז וְגַם שֶׁם־עִיר הֲמוֹנָה וְטִהֲרוּ הָאָרֶץ׃

יז וְאַתָּה בֶן־אָדָם כֹּה־אָמַר אֲדֹנָי יֱהֹוִה אֱמֹר לְצִפּוֹר כָּל־כָּנָף וּלְכֹל חַיַּת הַשָּׂדֶה הִקָּבְצוּ וָבֹאוּ הֵאָסְפוּ מִסָּבִיב עַל־זִבְחִי אֲשֶׁר אֲנִי זֹבֵחַ לָכֶם זֶבַח גָּדוֹל עַל הָרֵי יִשְׂרָאֵל וַאֲכַלְתֶּם בָּשָׂר וּשְׁתִיתֶם דָּם׃

Yechezkel/Ezekiel
Chapter 39

יחזקאל
פרק לט

18 You shall eat the flesh of warriors and drink the blood of the princes of the earth: rams, lambs, he-goats, and bulls – fatlings of Bashan all of them.

יח בְּשַׂר גִּבּוֹרִים תֹּאכֵלוּ וְדַם־נְשִׂיאֵי הָאָרֶץ תִּשְׁתּוּ אֵילִים כָּרִים וְעַתּוּדִים פָּרִים מְרִיאֵי בָשָׁן כֻּלָּם:

19 You shall eat fat to satiety and drink your fill of blood from the sacrificial feast that I have prepared for you.

יט וַאֲכַלְתֶּם־חֵלֶב לְשָׂבְעָה וּשְׁתִיתֶם דָּם לְשִׁכָּרוֹן מִזִּבְחִי אֲשֶׁר־זָבַחְתִּי לָכֶם:

20 And you shall sate yourselves at My table with horses, charioteers, warriors, and all fighting men – declares *Hashem*.

כ וּשְׂבַעְתֶּם עַל־שֻׁלְחָנִי סוּס וָרֶכֶב גִּבּוֹר וְכָל־אִישׁ מִלְחָמָה נְאֻם אֲדֹנָי יֱהֹוִה:

21 Thus will I manifest My glory among the nations, and all the nations shall see the judgment that I executed and the power that I wielded against them.

כא וְנָתַתִּי אֶת־כְּבוֹדִי בַּגּוֹיִם וְרָאוּ כָל־הַגּוֹיִם אֶת־מִשְׁפָּטִי אֲשֶׁר עָשִׂיתִי וְאֶת־יָדִי אֲשֶׁר־שַׂמְתִּי בָהֶם:

22 From that time on, the House of *Yisrael* shall know that I *Hashem* am their God.

כב וְיָדְעוּ בֵּית יִשְׂרָאֵל כִּי אֲנִי יֱהֹוָה אֱלֹהֵיהֶם מִן־הַיּוֹם הַהוּא וָהָלְאָה:

23 And the nations shall know that the House of *Yisrael* were exiled only for their iniquity, because they trespassed against Me, so that I hid My face from them and delivered them into the hands of their adversaries, and they all fell by the sword.

כג וְיָדְעוּ הַגּוֹיִם כִּי בַעֲוֺנָם גָּלוּ בֵית־יִשְׂרָאֵל עַל אֲשֶׁר מָעֲלוּ־בִי וָאַסְתִּר פָּנַי מֵהֶם וָאֶתְּנֵם בְּיַד צָרֵיהֶם וַיִּפְּלוּ בַחֶרֶב כֻּלָּם:

24 When I hid My face from them, I dealt with them according to their uncleanness and their transgressions.

כד כְּטֻמְאָתָם וּכְפִשְׁעֵיהֶם עָשִׂיתִי אֹתָם וָאַסְתִּר פָּנַי מֵהֶם:

25 Assuredly, thus said *Hashem*: I will now restore the fortunes of *Yaakov* and take the whole House of *Yisrael* back in love; and I will be zealous for My holy name.

כה לָכֵן כֹּה אָמַר אֲדֹנָי יֱהֹוִה עַתָּה אָשִׁיב אֶת־שְׁבִית [שְׁבוּת] יַעֲקֹב וְרִחַמְתִּי כָּל־בֵּית יִשְׂרָאֵל וְקִנֵּאתִי לְשֵׁם קָדְשִׁי:

la-KHAYN KOH a-MAR a-do-NAI e-lo-HEEM a-TAH a-SHEEV et sh'-VUT ya-a-KOV v'-ri-kham-TEE kol BAYT yis-ra-AYL v'-ki-nay-TEE l'-SHAYM kod-SHEE

26 They will bear their shame and all their trespasses that they committed against Me, when they dwell in their land secure and untroubled,

כו וְנָשׂוּ אֶת־כְּלִמָּתָם וְאֶת־כָּל־מַעֲלָם אֲשֶׁר מָעֲלוּ־בִי בְּשִׁבְתָּם עַל־אַדְמָתָם לָבֶטַח וְאֵין מַחֲרִיד:

27 when I have brought them back from among the peoples and gathered them out of the lands of their enemies and have manifested My holiness through them in the sight of many nations.

כז בְּשׁוֹבְבִי אוֹתָם מִן־הָעַמִּים וְקִבַּצְתִּי אֹתָם מֵאַרְצוֹת אֹיְבֵיהֶם וְנִקְדַּשְׁתִּי בָם לְעֵינֵי הַגּוֹיִם רַבִּים:

רחמים

39:25 Take the whole House of *Yisrael* back in love The root of the Hebrew word for 'compassion,' *rachamim* (רחמים), is from the same root as the word *rekhem* (רחם), which means 'womb.' The connection between these two ideas is that a mother has innate compassion for her children, the fruit of her womb, as it says in Isaiah (49:15), "Can a woman forget her baby, or disown the child of her womb?" *Yechezkel* teaches that when *Hashem* returns the captivity of *Yaakov*, He will shower them with mercy and compassion, comparable to the natural compassion a mother has for her child.

Yechezkel/Ezekiel
Chapter 40

יחזקאל
פרק מ

28 They shall know that I *Hashem* am their God when, having exiled them among the nations, I gather them back into their land and leave none of them behind.

כח וְיָדְעוּ כִּי אֲנִי יְהֹוָה אֱלֹהֵיהֶם בְּהַגְלוֹתִי אֹתָם אֶל־הַגּוֹיִם וְכִנַּסְתִּים עַל־אַדְמָתָם וְלֹא־אוֹתִיר עוֹד מֵהֶם שָׁם׃

29 I will never again hide My face from them, for I will pour out My spirit upon the House of *Yisrael* – declares *Hashem*.

כט וְלֹא־אַסְתִּיר עוֹד פָּנַי מֵהֶם אֲשֶׁר שָׁפַכְתִּי אֶת־רוּחִי עַל־בֵּית יִשְׂרָאֵל נְאֻם אֲדֹנָי יְהֹוִה׃

40 1 In the twenty-fifth year of our exile, the fourteenth year after the city had fallen, at the beginning of the year, the tenth day of the month – on that very day – the hand of *Hashem* came upon me, and He brought me there.

א בְּעֶשְׂרִים וְחָמֵשׁ שָׁנָה לְגָלוּתֵנוּ בְּרֹאשׁ הַשָּׁנָה בֶּעָשׂוֹר לַחֹדֶשׁ בְּאַרְבַּע עֶשְׂרֵה שָׁנָה אַחַר אֲשֶׁר הֻכְּתָה הָעִיר בְּעֶצֶם הַיּוֹם הַזֶּה הָיְתָה עָלַי יַד־יְהֹוָה וַיָּבֵא אֹתִי שָׁמָּה׃

2 He brought me, in visions of *Hashem*, to the Land of *Yisrael*, and He set me down on a very high mountain on which there seemed to be the outline of a city on the south.

ב בְּמַרְאוֹת אֱלֹהִים הֱבִיאַנִי אֶל־אֶרֶץ יִשְׂרָאֵל וַיְנִיחֵנִי אֶל־הַר גָּבֹהַּ מְאֹד וְעָלָיו כְּמִבְנֵה־עִיר מִנֶּגֶב׃

b'-mar-OT e-lo-HEEM he-vee-A-nee el E-retz yis-ra-AYL vai-nee-KHAY-nee el HAR ga-VO-ha m'-OD v'-a-LAV k'-miv-nay EER mi-NE-gev

3 He brought me over to it, and there, standing at the gate, was a man who shone like copper. In his hand were a cord of linen and a measuring rod.

ג וַיָּבֵיא אוֹתִי שָׁמָּה וְהִנֵּה־אִישׁ מַרְאֵהוּ כְּמַרְאֵה נְחֹשֶׁת וּפְתִיל־פִּשְׁתִּים בְּיָדוֹ וּקְנֵה הַמִּדָּה וְהוּא עֹמֵד בַּשָּׁעַר׃

4 The man spoke to me: "Mortal, look closely and listen attentively and note well everything I am going to show you – for you have been brought here in order to be shown – and report everything you see to the House of *Yisrael*."

ד וַיְדַבֵּר אֵלַי הָאִישׁ בֶּן־אָדָם רְאֵה בְעֵינֶיךָ וּבְאָזְנֶיךָ שְּׁמָע וְשִׂים לִבְּךָ לְכֹל אֲשֶׁר־אֲנִי מַרְאֶה אוֹתָךְ כִּי לְמַעַן הַרְאוֹתְכָה הֻבָאתָה הֵנָּה הַגֵּד אֶת־כָּל־אֲשֶׁר־אַתָּה רֹאֶה לְבֵית יִשְׂרָאֵל׃

5 Along the outside of the Temple [area] ran a wall on every side. The rod that the man held was six *amot* long, plus one *tefach* for each *amah*; and when he applied it to that structure, it measured one rod deep and one rod high.

ה וְהִנֵּה חוֹמָה מִחוּץ לַבַּיִת סָבִיב סָבִיב וּבְיַד הָאִישׁ קְנֵה הַמִּדָּה שֵׁשׁ־אַמּוֹת בָּאַמָּה וָטֹפַח וַיָּמָד אֶת־רֹחַב הַבִּנְיָן קָנֶה אֶחָד וְקוֹמָה קָנֶה אֶחָד׃

40:2 And He set me down on a very high mountain The final section of *Yechezkel*'s prophecy describes the building of the third *Beit Hamikdash*, its operation, and the re-division of the Land of Israel among the people. These chapters contain the prophet's hopes for his people, and represent the closing of a circle that began in chapter 1. Decades earlier, *Yechezkel* envisioned the Divine Presence leaving *Eretz Yisrael* and the Temple prior to its destruction. Now, perched on the high mountain, the Temple Mount in *Yerushalayim*, *Yechezkel* can foresee the return of the People of Israel to the Land of Israel, and God's Presence returning to His city. According to the sages, this vision comes to *Yechezkel* at the beginning of the *yovel*, the Jubilee year. *Radak* emphasizes how appropriate the timing of this vision is, since during the *yovel*, all people are freed and returned to their ancestral homes.

Yechezkel / Ezekiel

Chapter 40

6 He went up to the gate that faced eastward and mounted its steps. He measured the threshold of the gate; it was one rod deep – the one threshold was one rod deep.

7 Each recess was one rod wide and one rod deep, with [a partition of] 5 *amot* between recesses; and the threshold of the gate, at the inner vestibule of the gate, was one rod deep.

8 For when he measured it at the inner vestibule of the gate, it was one rod [deep].

9 Next he measured the vestibule of the gate, and it measured 8 *amot* and its supports 2 *amot*; the vestibule of the gate was at its inner end.

10 On either side of this eastern gate there were three recesses, all three of the same size; of identical sizes were also the supports on either side.

11 He measured the opening of the gate and found it 10 *amot* wide, while the gate itself measured 13 *amot* across.

12 At the fronts of the recesses on either side were barriers of one *amah*; the recesses on either side were 6 *amot* [deep].

13 Their openings faced each other directly across the gate passage, so that when he measured from rear of recess to rear of recess he obtained a width of 25 *amot*.

14 He made the vestibule – 60 *amot* – and the gate next to the support on every side of the court.

15 And [the distance] from the front of the outer gate to the front of the inner vestibule of the gate was 50 *amot*.

16 The recesses – and their supports – had windows with frames on the interior of the gate complex on both sides, and the interiors of the vestibules also had windows on both sides; and the supports were adorned with palms.

17 He took me into the outer court. There were chambers there, and there was a pavement laid out all around the court. There were 30 chambers on the pavement.

18 The pavements flanked the gates; the depth of the lower pavements paralleled that of the gates.

יחזקאל

פרק מ

א וַיָּבוֹא אֶל־שַׁעַר אֲשֶׁר פָּנָיו דֶּרֶךְ הַקָּדִימָה וַיַּעַל במעלותו [בְּמַעֲלוֹתָיו] וַיָּמָד אֶת־סַף הַשַּׁעַר קָנֶה אֶחָד רֹחַב וְאֵת סַף אֶחָד קָנֶה אֶחָד רֹחַב׃

ז וְהַתָּא קָנֶה אֶחָד אֹרֶךְ וְקָנֶה אֶחָד רֹחַב וּבֵין הַתָּאִים חָמֵשׁ אַמּוֹת וְסַף הַשַּׁעַר מֵאֵצֶל אוּלָם הַשַּׁעַר מֵהַבַּיִת קָנֶה אֶחָד׃

ח וַיָּמָד אֶת־אֻלָם הַשַּׁעַר מֵהַבַּיִת קָנֶה אֶחָד׃

ט וַיָּמָד אֶת־אֻלָם הַשַּׁעַר שְׁמֹנֶה אַמּוֹת ואילו [וְאֵילָיו] שְׁתַּיִם אַמּוֹת וְאֻלָם הַשַּׁעַר מֵהַבָּיִת׃

י וְתָאֵי הַשַּׁעַר דֶּרֶךְ הַקָּדִים שְׁלֹשָׁה מִפֹּה וּשְׁלֹשָׁה מִפֹּה מִדָּה אַחַת לִשְׁלָשְׁתָּם וּמִדָּה אַחַת לָאֵילִם מִפֹּה וּמִפּוֹ׃

יא וַיָּמָד אֶת־רֹחַב פֶּתַח־הַשַּׁעַר עֶשֶׂר אַמּוֹת אֹרֶךְ הַשַּׁעַר שְׁלוֹשׁ עֶשְׂרֵה אַמּוֹת׃

יב וּגְבוּל לִפְנֵי הַתָּאוֹת אַמָּה אֶחָת וְאַמָּה־אַחַת גְּבוּל מִפֹּה וְהַתָּא שֵׁשׁ־אַמּוֹת מִפּוֹ וְשֵׁשׁ אַמּוֹת מִפּוֹ׃

יג וַיָּמָד אֶת־הַשַּׁעַר מִגַּג הַתָּא לְגַגּוֹ רֹחַב עֶשְׂרִים וְחָמֵשׁ אַמּוֹת פֶּתַח נֶגֶד פָּתַח׃

יד וַיַּעַשׂ אֶת־אֵילִים שִׁשִּׁים אַמָּה וְאֶל־אֵיל הֶחָצֵר הַשַּׁעַר סָבִיב סָבִיב׃

טו וְעַל פְּנֵי הַשַּׁעַר היאתון [הָאִיתוֹן] עַל־לִפְנֵי אֻלָם הַשַּׁעַר הַפְּנִימִי חֲמִשִּׁים אַמָּה׃

טז וְחַלֹּנוֹת אֲטֻמוֹת אֶל־הַתָּאִים וְאֶל אֵלֵיהֵמָה לִפְנִימָה לַשַּׁעַר סָבִיב סָבִיב וְכֵן לָאֵלַמּוֹת וְחַלּוֹנוֹת סָבִיב סָבִיב לִפְנִימָה וְאֶל־אַיִל תִּמֹרִים׃

יז וַיְבִיאֵנִי אֶל־הֶחָצֵר הַחִיצוֹנָה וְהִנֵּה לְשָׁכוֹת וְרִצְפָה עָשׂוּי לֶחָצֵר סָבִיב סָבִיב שְׁלֹשִׁים לְשָׁכוֹת אֶל־הָרִצְפָה׃

יח וְהָרִצְפָה אֶל־כֶּתֶף הַשְּׁעָרִים לְעֻמַּת אֹרֶךְ הַשְּׁעָרִים הָרִצְפָה הַתַּחְתּוֹנָה׃

Yechezkel/Ezekiel
Chapter 40

יחזקאל
פרק מ

19 Then he measured the width of the lower court, from in front of the inner gate to in front of the outer gate – 100 *amot*. After the east [gate], the north [gate].

יט וַיָּמָד רֹחַב מִלִּפְנֵי הַשַּׁעַר הַתַּחְתּוֹנָה לִפְנֵי הֶחָצֵר הַפְּנִימִי מִחוּץ מֵאָה אַמָּה הַקָּדִים וְהַצָּפוֹן:

20 Next he measured the gate of the outer court that faced north: its length and its width,

כ וְהַשַּׁעַר אֲשֶׁר פָּנָיו דֶּרֶךְ הַצָּפוֹן לֶחָצֵר הַחִיצוֹנָה מָדַד אָרְכּוֹ וְרָחְבּוֹ:

21 its three recesses on either side and its supports, as also its vestibule. It measured, like the first gate, 50 *amot* in length and 25 *amot* in width.

כא וְתָאָו [וְתָאָיו] שְׁלוֹשָׁה מִפּוֹ וּשְׁלֹשָׁה מִפּוֹ וְאֵילוֹ [וְאֵילָיו] וְאֵלַמּוֹ [וְאֵלַמָּיו] הָיָה כְּמִדַּת הַשַּׁעַר הָרִאשׁוֹן חֲמִשִּׁים אַמָּה אָרְכּוֹ וְרֹחַב חָמֵשׁ וְעֶשְׂרִים בָּאַמָּה:

22 Its windows and [those of] its vestibule, as also its palm trees, corresponded to those of the gate that faced east. [From the outside] one had to climb 7 steps to reach it, and its vestibule was ahead of them.

כב וְחַלּוֹנוֹ [וְחַלּוֹנָיו] וְאֵלַמּוֹ [וְאֵלַמָּיו] וְתִמֹרוֹ [וְתִמֹרָיו] כְּמִדַּת הַשַּׁעַר אֲשֶׁר פָּנָיו דֶּרֶךְ הַקָּדִים וּבְמַעֲלוֹת שֶׁבַע יַעֲלוּ בוֹ וְאֵלַמּוֹ [וְאֵלַמָּיו] לִפְנֵיהֶם:

23 Like the east gate, the north gate faced a gate leading into the inner forecourt; and when he measured the distance from gate to gate, it was 100 *amot*.

כג וְשַׁעַר לֶחָצֵר הַפְּנִימִי נֶגֶד הַשַּׁעַר לַצָּפוֹן וְלַקָּדִים וַיָּמָד מִשַּׁעַר אֶל־שַׁעַר מֵאָה אַמָּה:

24 Then he took me to the south side. There was also a gate on the south side, and he got the same measurements as before for its supports and its vestibule.

כד וַיּוֹלִכֵנִי דֶּרֶךְ הַדָּרוֹם וְהִנֵּה־שַׁעַר דֶּרֶךְ הַדָּרוֹם וּמָדַד אֵילוֹ [אֵילָיו] וְאֵלַמּוֹ [וְאֵלַמָּיו] כַּמִּדּוֹת הָאֵלֶּה:

25 Both it and its vestibule had windows like the aforementioned ones. It was 50 *amot* long and 25 *amot* wide.

כה וְחַלּוֹנִים לוֹ וּלְאֵלַמּוֹ [וּלְאֵלַמָּיו] סָבִיב סָבִיב כְּהַחֲלֹּנוֹת הָאֵלֶּה חֲמִשִּׁים אַמָּה אֹרֶךְ וְרֹחַב חָמֵשׁ וְעֶשְׂרִים אַמָּה:

26 Its staircase consisted of 7 steps; its vestibule was ahead of them, and its supports were decorated on both sides with palm trees.

כו וּמַעֲלוֹת שִׁבְעָה עֹלוֹתוֹ [עֹלוֹתָיו] וְאֵלַמּוֹ [וְאֵלַמָּיו] לִפְנֵיהֶם וְתִמֹרִים לוֹ אֶחָד מִפּוֹ וְאֶחָד מִפּוֹ אֶל־אֵילוֹ [אֵילָיו]:

27 The inner court likewise had a gate facing south; and on the south side, too, he measured a distance of 100 *amot* from the [outer] gate to the [inner] gate.

כז וְשַׁעַר לֶחָצֵר הַפְּנִימִי דֶּרֶךְ הַדָּרוֹם וַיָּמָד מִשַּׁעַר אֶל־הַשַּׁעַר דֶּרֶךְ הַדָּרוֹם מֵאָה אַמּוֹת:

28 He now took me into the inner forecourt through its south gate. When he measured this south gate, it had the same measurements as the foregoing.

כח וַיְבִיאֵנִי אֶל־חָצֵר הַפְּנִימִי בְּשַׁעַר הַדָּרוֹם וַיָּמָד אֶת־הַשַּׁעַר הַדָּרוֹם כַּמִּדּוֹת הָאֵלֶּה:

29 Its recesses, its supports, and its vestibule had the same measurements. Both it and its vestibule had windows on both sides; it was 50 *amot* long and 25 *amot* wide –

כט וְתָאָו [וְתָאָיו] וְאֵילוֹ [וְאֵילָיו] וְאֵלַמּוֹ [וְאֵלַמָּיו] כַּמִּדּוֹת הָאֵלֶּה וְחַלּוֹנוֹת לוֹ וּלְאֵלַמּוֹ [וּלְאֵלַמָּיו] סָבִיב סָבִיב חֲמִשִּׁים אַמָּה אֹרֶךְ וְרֹחַב עֶשְׂרִים וְחָמֵשׁ אַמּוֹת:

30 vestibules on both sides, 25 *amot* long, 5 *amot* wide.

ל וְאֵלַמּוֹת סָבִיב סָבִיב אֹרֶךְ חָמֵשׁ וְעֶשְׂרִים אַמָּה וְרֹחַב חָמֵשׁ אַמּוֹת:

Yechezkel/Ezekiel
Chapter 40

31 Its vestibule, however, gave on the outer court. Its supports were adorned on either side with palms, and its staircase consisted of 8 steps.

32 Then he took me to the eastern side of the inner forecourt; and when he measured the gate there, he got the same measurements:

33 its recesses, supports, and vestibule had the above measurements. Both it and its vestibule had windows on both sides; it was 50 *amot* long and 25 *amot* wide,

34 and its vestibule gave on the outer court. Its supports were decorated on both sides with palm trees, and its staircase consisted of 8 steps.

35 Then he took me to the north gate, and found its measurements to be identical,

36 with the same recesses, supports, vestibule, windows on both sides, and a length of 50 *amot* and a width of 25 *amot*.

37 Its supports gave on the outer court; its supports were decorated on both sides with palm trees; and its staircase consisted of eight steps.

38 A chamber opened into the gate; there the burnt offering would be washed.

39 And inside the vestibule of the gate, there were two tables on each side, at which the burnt offering, the sin offering, and the guilt offering were to be slaughtered;

40 while outside – as one goes up toward the opening of the north gate – there were two tables on one side, and there were two tables on the other side of the gate's vestibule.

41 Thus there were four tables on either flank of the gate – eight tables in all – at which [the sacrifices] were to be slaughtered.

42 As for the four tables for the burnt offering – they were of hewn stone, one and a half *amot* long, one and a half *amot* wide, and one *amah* high – on them were laid out the instruments with which burnt offerings and sacrifices were slaughtered.

יחזקאל
פרק מ

לא וְאֵלַמָּו אֶל־חָצֵר הַחִצוֹנָה וְתִמֹרִים אֶל־אֵילָו [אֵילָיו] וּמַעֲלוֹת שְׁמוֹנֶה מַעֲלוֹ [מַעֲלָיו]:

לב וַיְבִיאֵנִי אֶל־הֶחָצֵר הַפְּנִימִי דֶּרֶךְ הַקָּדִים וַיָּמָד אֶת־הַשַּׁעַר כַּמִּדּוֹת הָאֵלֶּה:

לג וְתָאָו [וְתָאָיו] וְאֵלָו [וְאֵלָיו] וְאֵלַמָּו [וְאֵלַמָּיו] כַּמִּדּוֹת הָאֵלֶּה וְחַלּוֹנוֹת לוֹ וּלְאֵלַמָּו [וּלְאֵלַמָּיו] סָבִיב סָבִיב אֹרֶךְ חֲמִשִּׁים אַמָּה וְרֹחַב חָמֵשׁ וְעֶשְׂרִים אַמָּה:

לד וְאֵלַמָּו [וְאֵלַמָּיו] לֶחָצֵר הַחִיצוֹנָה וְתִמֹרִים אֶל־אֵלוֹ [אֵילָיו] מִפּוֹ וּמִפּוֹ וּשְׁמֹנֶה מַעֲלוֹת מַעֲלוֹ [מַעֲלָיו]:

לה וַיְבִיאֵנִי אֶל־שַׁעַר הַצָּפוֹן וּמָדַד כַּמִּדּוֹת הָאֵלֶּה:

לו תָּאָו [תָּאָיו] אֵלָו [אֵילָיו] וְאֵלַמָּו [וְאֵלַמָּיו] וְחַלּוֹנוֹת לוֹ סָבִיב סָבִיב אֹרֶךְ חֲמִשִּׁים אַמָּה וְרֹחַב חָמֵשׁ וְעֶשְׂרִים אַמָּה:

לז וְאֵילָו [וְאֵילָיו] לֶחָצֵר הַחִיצוֹנָה וְתִמֹרִים אֶל־אֵילָו [אֵילָיו] מִפּוֹ וּמִפּוֹ וּשְׁמֹנֶה מַעֲלוֹת מַעֲלוֹ [מַעֲלָיו]:

לח וְלִשְׁכָּה וּפִתְחָהּ בְּאֵילִים הַשְּׁעָרִים שָׁם יָדִיחוּ אֶת־הָעֹלָה:

לט וּבְאֻלָם הַשַּׁעַר שְׁנַיִם שֻׁלְחָנוֹת מִפּוֹ וּשְׁנַיִם שֻׁלְחָנוֹת מִפֹּה לִשְׁחוֹט אֲלֵיהֶם הָעוֹלָה וְהַחַטָּאת וְהָאָשָׁם:

מ וְאֶל־הַכָּתֵף מִחוּצָה לָעוֹלֶה לְפֶתַח הַשַּׁעַר הַצָּפוֹנָה שְׁנַיִם שֻׁלְחָנוֹת וְאֶל־הַכָּתֵף הָאַחֶרֶת אֲשֶׁר לְאֻלָם הַשַּׁעַר שְׁנַיִם שֻׁלְחָנוֹת:

מא אַרְבָּעָה שֻׁלְחָנוֹת מִפֹּה וְאַרְבָּעָה שֻׁלְחָנוֹת מִפֹּה לְכֶתֶף הַשָּׁעַר שְׁמוֹנָה שֻׁלְחָנוֹת אֲלֵיהֶם יִשְׁחָטוּ:

מב וְאַרְבָּעָה שֻׁלְחָנוֹת לָעוֹלָה אַבְנֵי גָזִית אֹרֶךְ אַמָּה אַחַת וָחֵצִי וְרֹחַב אַמָּה אַחַת וָחֵצִי וְגֹבַהּ אַמָּה אֶחָת וְיַנִּיחוּ אֶת־הַכֵּלִים אֲשֶׁר יִשְׁחֲטוּ אֶת־הָעוֹלָה בָּם וְהַזָּבַח:

1307

Yechezkel/Ezekiel
Chapter 41

יחזקאל
פרק מא

מג וְהַשְׁפַתַּיִם טֹפַח אֶחָד מוּכָנִים בַּבַּיִת סָבִיב ׀ סָבִיב וְאֶל־הַשֻּׁלְחָנוֹת בְּשַׂר הַקָּרְבָּן׃

43 Shelves, one *tefach* wide, were attached all around the inside; and the sacrificial flesh was [laid] on the tables.

מד וּמִחוּצָה לַשַּׁעַר הַפְּנִימִי לִשְׁכוֹת שָׁרִים בֶּחָצֵר הַפְּנִימִי אֲשֶׁר אֶל־כֶּתֶף שַׁעַר הַצָּפוֹן וּפְנֵיהֶם דֶּרֶךְ הַדָּרוֹם אֶחָד אֶל־כֶּתֶף שַׁעַר הַקָּדִים פְּנֵי דֶּרֶךְ הַצָּפֹן׃

44 There were chambers for singers in the inner forecourt: [one] beside the north gate facing south, and one beside the east gate facing north.

מה וַיְדַבֵּר אֵלָי זֹה הַלִּשְׁכָּה אֲשֶׁר פָּנֶיהָ דֶּרֶךְ הַדָּרוֹם לַכֹּהֲנִים שֹׁמְרֵי מִשְׁמֶרֶת הַבָּיִת׃

45 [The man] explained to me: "The chamber that faces south is for the *Kohanim* who perform the duties of the Temple;

מו וְהַלִּשְׁכָּה אֲשֶׁר פָּנֶיהָ דֶּרֶךְ הַצָּפוֹן לַכֹּהֲנִים שֹׁמְרֵי מִשְׁמֶרֶת הַמִּזְבֵּחַ הֵמָּה בְנֵי־צָדוֹק הַקְּרֵבִים מִבְּנֵי־לֵוִי אֶל־יְהֹוָה לְשָׁרְתוֹ׃

46 and the chamber that faces north is for the *Kohanim* who perform the duties of the *Mizbayach* – they are the descendants of *Tzadok*, who alone of the descendants of *Levi* may approach *Hashem* to minister to Him."

מז וַיָּמָד אֶת־הֶחָצֵר אֹרֶךְ ׀ מֵאָה אַמָּה וְרֹחַב מֵאָה אַמָּה מְרֻבָּעַת וְהַמִּזְבֵּחַ לִפְנֵי הַבָּיִת׃

47 He then measured the forecourt: 100 *amot* long and 100 *amot* broad – foursquare. In front of the Temple stood the *Mizbayach*.

מח וַיְבִאֵנִי אֶל־אֻלָם הַבַּיִת וַיָּמָד אֵל אֻלָם חָמֵשׁ אַמּוֹת מִפֹּה וְחָמֵשׁ אַמּוֹת מִפֹּה וְרֹחַב הַשַּׁעַר שָׁלֹשׁ אַמּוֹת מִפּוֹ וְשָׁלֹשׁ אַמּוֹת מִפּוֹ׃

48 He took me into the portico of the Temple and measured it. The jambs of the portico were 5 *amot* deep on either side. The width of the gate-opening was [14 *amot*, and the flanking wall of the gate was] 3 *amot* on either side.

מט אֹרֶךְ הָאֻלָם עֶשְׂרִים אַמָּה וְרֹחַב עַשְׁתֵּי עֶשְׂרֵה אַמָּה וּבַמַּעֲלוֹת אֲשֶׁר יַעֲלוּ אֵלָיו וְעַמֻּדִים אֶל־הָאֵילִים אֶחָד מִפֹּה וְאֶחָד מִפֹּה׃

49 The portico was 20 *amot* wide and 11 *amot* deep, and it was by steps that it was reached. There were columns by the jambs on either side.

41

א וַיְבִיאֵנִי אֶל־הַהֵיכָל וַיָּמָד אֶת־הָאֵילִים שֵׁשׁ־אַמּוֹת רֹחַב־מִפּוֹ וְשֵׁשׁ־אַמּוֹת רֹחַב־מִפּוֹ רֹחַב הָאֹהֶל׃

1 He then led me into the great hall. He measured the jambs, 6 *amot* on either side; such was the depth of each jamb.

ב וְרֹחַב הַפֶּתַח עֶשֶׂר אַמּוֹת וְכִתְפוֹת הַפֶּתַח חָמֵשׁ אַמּוֹת מִפּוֹ וְחָמֵשׁ אַמּוֹת מִפּוֹ וַיָּמָד אָרְכּוֹ אַרְבָּעִים אַמָּה וְרֹחַב עֶשְׂרִים אַמָּה׃

2 The entrance was 10 *amot* wide, and the flanking walls of the entrance were each 5 *amot* wide. Next he measured the depth [of the hall], 40 *amot*, and the width, 20 *amot*.

ג וּבָא לִפְנִימָה וַיָּמָד אֵיל־הַפֶּתַח שְׁתַּיִם אַמּוֹת וְהַפֶּתַח שֵׁשׁ אַמּוֹת וְרֹחַב הַפֶּתַח שֶׁבַע אַמּוֹת׃

3 And then he entered the inner room. He measured each jamb of the entrance, 2 *amot* [deep]; the entrance itself, 6 *amot* across; and the width of [the flanking wall on either side of] the entrance, 7 *amot*.

ד וַיָּמָד אֶת־אָרְכּוֹ עֶשְׂרִים אַמָּה וְרֹחַב עֶשְׂרִים אַמָּה אֶל־פְּנֵי הַהֵיכָל וַיֹּאמֶר אֵלַי זֶה קֹדֶשׁ הַקֳּדָשִׁים׃

4 Then he measured the depth, 20 *amot*; and the width at the inner end of the great hall was also 20 *amot*. And he said to me, "This is the Holy of Holies."

Yechezkel/Ezekiel
Chapter 41

5 Then he measured the wall of the Temple. [It was] 6 *amot* [thick] on every side of the Temple, and the side-chamber measured 4 *amot* [across].

6 The side chambers were arranged one above the other, in 33 sections. All around, there were projections in the Temple wall to serve the side chambers as supports, so that [their] supports should not be the Temple wall itself.

7 The winding passage of the side chambers widened from story to story; and since the structure was furnished all over with winding passages from story to story, the structure itself became wider from story to story. It was by this means that one ascended from the bottom story to the top one by way of the middle one.

8 I observed that the Temple was surrounded by a raised pavement – the foundations of the side chambers; its elevation was a rod's length, or 6 *amot*.

9 The outer wall of the side chamber was 5 *amot* thick, and that which served as a walk between the Temple's side chambers

10 and the chamber complexes was 20 *amot* wide all around the Temple.

11 Of entrances to the side chambers giving on the walk, there was one entrance on the north side and one entrance on the south side; and the space of the walk was 5 *amot* thick all around.

12 And the structure that fronted on the vacant space at the [Temple's] western end was 70 *amot* deep; the walls of the structure were 5 *amot* thick on every side; and it was 90 *amot* wide.

13 He measured the [total] depth of the Temple, 100 *amot*; and the depth of the vacant space and of the structure, with its walls, also came to 100 *amot*.

14 The front side of the Temple, like the vacant space on the east, was 100 *amot* wide.

15 He also measured the width of the structure facing the vacant space in the rear, inclusive of its ledges, 100 *amot*. Both the great hall inside and the portico next to the court –

יחזקאל
פרק מא

ה וַיָּמָד קִיר־הַבַּיִת שֵׁשׁ אַמּוֹת וְרֹחַב הַצֵּלָע אַרְבַּע אַמּוֹת סָבִיב ׀ סָבִיב לַבַּיִת סָבִיב׃

ו וְהַצְּלָעוֹת צֵלָע אֶל־צֵלָע שָׁלוֹשׁ וּשְׁלֹשִׁים פְּעָמִים וּבָאוֹת בַּקִּיר אֲשֶׁר־לַבַּיִת לַצְּלָעוֹת סָבִיב ׀ סָבִיב לִהְיוֹת אֲחוּזִים וְלֹא־יִהְיוּ אֲחוּזִים בְּקִיר הַבָּיִת׃

ז וְרָחֲבָה וְנָסְבָה לְמַעְלָה לְמַעְלָה לַצְּלָעוֹת כִּי מוּסַב־הַבַּיִת לְמַעְלָה לְמַעְלָה סָבִיב ׀ סָבִיב לַבַּיִת עַל־כֵּן רֹחַב־לַבַּיִת לְמָעְלָה וְכֵן הַתַּחְתּוֹנָה יַעֲלֶה עַל־הָעֶלְיוֹנָה לַתִּיכוֹנָה׃

ח וְרָאִיתִי לַבַּיִת גֹּבַהּ סָבִיב ׀ סָבִיב מֵיסְדוֹת [מוּסְדוֹת] הַצְּלָעוֹת מְלוֹ הַקָּנֶה שֵׁשׁ אַמּוֹת אַצִּילָה׃

ט רֹחַב הַקִּיר אֲשֶׁר־לַצֵּלָע אֶל־הַחוּץ חָמֵשׁ אַמּוֹת וַאֲשֶׁר מֻנָּח בֵּית צְלָעוֹת אֲשֶׁר לַבָּיִת׃

י וּבֵין הַלְּשָׁכוֹת רֹחַב עֶשְׂרִים אַמָּה סָבִיב לַבַּיִת סָבִיב ׀ סָבִיב׃

יא וּפֶתַח הַצֵּלָע לַמֻּנָּח פֶּתַח אֶחָד דֶּרֶךְ הַצָּפוֹן וּפֶתַח אֶחָד לַדָּרוֹם וְרֹחַב מְקוֹם הַמֻּנָּח חָמֵשׁ אַמּוֹת סָבִיב ׀ סָבִיב׃

יב וְהַבִּנְיָן אֲשֶׁר אֶל־פְּנֵי הַגִּזְרָה פְּאַת דֶּרֶךְ־הַיָּם רֹחַב שִׁבְעִים אַמָּה וְקִיר הַבִּנְיָן חָמֵשׁ־אַמּוֹת רֹחַב סָבִיב ׀ סָבִיב וְאָרְכּוֹ תִּשְׁעִים אַמָּה׃

יג וּמָדַד אֶת־הַבַּיִת אֹרֶךְ מֵאָה אַמָּה וְהַגִּזְרָה וְהַבִּנְיָה וְקִירוֹתֶיהָ אֹרֶךְ מֵאָה אַמָּה׃

יד וְרֹחַב פְּנֵי הַבַּיִת וְהַגִּזְרָה לַקָּדִים מֵאָה אַמָּה׃

טו וּמָדַד אֹרֶךְ־הַבִּנְיָן אֶל־פְּנֵי הַגִּזְרָה אֲשֶׁר עַל־אַחֲרֶיהָ וְאַתּוּקֵיהָא [וְאַתִּיקֶיהָא] מִפּוֹ וּמִפּוֹ מֵאָה אַמָּה וְהַהֵיכָל הַפְּנִימִי וְאֻלַמֵּי הֶחָצֵר׃

Yechezkel/Ezekiel
Chapter 41

יחזקאל
פרק מא

טז הַסִּפִּים וְהַחַלּוֹנִים הָאֲטֻמוֹת וְהָאַתִּיקִים סָבִיב לִשְׁלָשְׁתָּם נֶגֶד הַסַּף שְׂחִיף עֵץ סָבִיב ׀ סָבִיב וְהָאָרֶץ עַד־הַחַלֹּנוֹת וְהַחַלֹּנוֹת מְכֻסּוֹת:

16 the thresholds – and the windows with frames and the ledges at the threshold, all over the three parts of each, were completely overlaid with wood. There was wainscoting from the floor to the windows, including the window [frame]s

יז עַל־מֵעַל הַפֶּתַח וְעַד־הַבַּיִת הַפְּנִימִי וְלַחוּץ וְאֶל־כָּל־הַקִּיר סָבִיב ׀ סָבִיב בַּפְּנִימִי וּבַחִיצוֹן מִדּוֹת:

17 and extending above the openings, both in the inner Temple and outside. And all over the wall, both in the inner one and in the outer, ran a pattern.

יח וְעָשׂוּי כְּרוּבִים וְתִמֹרִים וְתִמֹרָה בֵּין־כְּרוּב לִכְרוּב וּשְׁנַיִם פָּנִים לַכְּרוּב:

18 It consisted of cherubs and palm trees, with a palm tree between every two cherubs. Each cherub had two faces:

v'-a-SUY k'-ru-VEEM v'-ti-mo-REEM v'-ti-mo-RAH bayn k'-RUV likh-RUV ush-NA-yim pa-NEEM la-k'-RUV

יט וּפְנֵי אָדָם אֶל־הַתִּמֹרָה מִפּוֹ וּפְנֵי־כְפִיר אֶל־הַתִּמֹרָה מִפּוֹ עָשׂוּי אֶל־כָּל־הַבַּיִת סָבִיב ׀ סָבִיב:

19 a human face turned toward the palm tree on one side and a lion's face turned toward the palm tree on the other side. This was repeated all over the Temple;

כ מֵהָאָרֶץ עַד־מֵעַל הַפֶּתַח הַכְּרוּבִים וְהַתִּמֹרִים עֲשׂוּיִם וְקִיר הַהֵיכָל:

20 the cherubs and the palm trees were carved on the wall from the floor to above the openings. As regards the great hall,

כא הַהֵיכָל מְזוּזַת רְבֻעָה וּפְנֵי הַקֹּדֶשׁ הַמַּרְאֶה כַּמַּרְאֶה:

21 the great hall had four doorposts; and before the Shrine was something resembling

כב הַמִּזְבֵּחַ עֵץ שָׁלוֹשׁ אַמּוֹת גָּבֹהַּ וְאָרְכּוֹ שְׁתַּיִם־אַמּוֹת וּמִקְצֹעוֹתָיו לוֹ וְאָרְכּוֹ וְקִירֹתָיו עֵץ וַיְדַבֵּר אֵלַי זֶה הַשֻּׁלְחָן אֲשֶׁר לִפְנֵי יְהוָה:

22 a wooden *Mizbayach* 3 *amot* high and 2 *amot* long and having inner corners; and its length and its walls were of wood. And he said to me, "This is the table that stands before *Hashem*."

כג וּשְׁתַּיִם דְּלָתוֹת לַהֵיכָל וְלַקֹּדֶשׁ:

23 The great hall had a double door, and the Shrine likewise had

כד וּשְׁתַּיִם דְּלָתוֹת לַדְּלָתוֹת שְׁתַּיִם מוּסַבּוֹת דְּלָתוֹת שְׁתַּיִם לְדֶלֶת אֶחָת וּשְׁתֵּי דְלָתוֹת לָאַחֶרֶת:

24 a double door, and each door had two swinging leaves: two for the one door and two such leaves for the other.

41:18 It consisted of cherubs and palm trees On the walls of the inner and outer chambers of the *Beit Hamikdash* in *Yechezkel's* vision are cherubs and palm trees. These two items also appear in *Shlomo's* Temple (II Kings 6:29–36). The significance of the cherubs as dividers between mankind and God has been discussed in chapter 10. The palm tree symbolizes both righteousness (Psalms 92:13) and longevity. In fact, in 2005, a date palm was successfully grown from a two-thousand-year-old seed found on Masada, becoming the oldest seed ever to be brought back to life. The tree, nicknamed "Methuselah" after the longest-living figure in the Bible (Genesis 5:27), is now over two meters tall and has sprouted flowers. Ancient Judean dates were known to have healing properties and Israeli researchers are hoping that Methuselah will also have medicinal qualities that will benefit future generations.

Methuselah date plam tree

Yechezkel/Ezekiel
Chapter 42

יחזקאל
פרק מב

25 Cherubs and palm trees were carved on these – on the doors of the hall – just as they were carved on the walls; and there was a lattice of wood outside in front of the portico.

כה וַעֲשׂוּיָה אֲלֵיהֶן אֶל־דַּלְתוֹת הַהֵיכָל כְּרוּבִים וְתִמֹרִים כַּאֲשֶׁר עֲשׂוּיִם לַקִּירוֹת וְעָב עֵץ אֶל־פְּנֵי הָאוּלָם מֵהַחוּץ׃

26 And there were windows with frames and palm trees on the flanking walls of the portico on either side [of the entrance] and [on] the Temple's side chambers and [on] the lattices.

כו וְחַלּוֹנִים אֲטֻמוֹת וְתִמֹרִים מִפּוֹ וּמִפּוֹ אֶל־כִּתְפוֹת הָאוּלָם וְצַלְעוֹת הַבַּיִת וְהָעֻבִּים׃

42 1 He took me out, by way of the northern gate, into the outer court, and he led me [westward] up to a complex of chambers that ran parallel to the northern ends of the vacant space and the structure.

מב א וַיּוֹצִאֵנִי אֶל־הֶחָצֵר הַחִיצוֹנָה הַדֶּרֶךְ דֶּרֶךְ הַצָּפוֹן וַיְבִאֵנִי אֶל־הַלִּשְׁכָּה אֲשֶׁר נֶגֶד הַגִּזְרָה וַאֲשֶׁר־נֶגֶד הַבִּנְיָן אֶל־הַצָּפוֹן׃

2 The width of its façade – its north side, the one from which it was entered – was 100 *amot*, and its depth was 50 *amot*.

ב אֶל־פְּנֵי־אֹרֶךְ אַמּוֹת הַמֵּאָה פֶּתַח הַצָּפוֹן וְהָרֹחַב חֲמִשִּׁים אַמּוֹת׃

3 At right angles to the 20 *amot* of the inner court and to the pavement of the outer court, the complex rose ledge by ledge in three tiers.

ג נֶגֶד הָעֶשְׂרִים אֲשֶׁר לֶחָצֵר הַפְּנִימִי וְנֶגֶד רִצְפָה אֲשֶׁר לֶחָצֵר הַחִיצוֹנָה אַתִּיק אֶל־פְּנֵי־אַתִּיק בַּשְּׁלִשִׁים׃

4 There was an areaway, 10 *amot* wide and a road of one *amah*, running along the inner-court side of the chamber complex, but its entrances were on its north side.

ד וְלִפְנֵי הַלְּשָׁכוֹת מַהֲלַךְ עֶשֶׂר אַמּוֹת רֹחַב אֶל־הַפְּנִימִית דֶּרֶךְ אַמָּה אֶחָת וּפִתְחֵיהֶם לַצָּפוֹן׃

5 Here its upper chambers were cut back, because ledges took away from them as construction proceeded backward from the bottom ones and then from the middle ones.

ה וְהַלְּשָׁכוֹת הָעֶלְיוֹנֹת קְצֻרוֹת כִּי־יוֹכְלוּ אַתִּיקִים מֵהֵנָּה מֵהַתַּחְתֹּנוֹת וּמֵהַתִּכֹנוֹת בִּנְיָן׃

6 For they were arranged in three tiers, and they had no columns like those of the chambers in the courts. That is why the rise proceeded by stages: from the ground, from the bottom ones, and from the middle ones.

ו כִּי מְשֻׁלָּשׁוֹת הֵנָּה וְאֵין לָהֶן עַמּוּדִים כְּעַמּוּדֵי הַחֲצֵרוֹת עַל־כֵּן נֶאֱצַל מֵהַתַּחְתּוֹנוֹת וּמֵהַתִּיכֹנוֹת מֵהָאָרֶץ׃

7 In the outer court, a wall 50 *amot* long ran parallel to the chamber complex up to the chambers in the outer court;

ז וְגָדֵר אֲשֶׁר־לַחוּץ לְעֻמַּת הַלְּשָׁכוֹת דֶּרֶךְ הֶחָצֵר הַחִצוֹנָה אֶל־פְּנֵי הַלְּשָׁכוֹת אָרְכּוֹ חֲמִשִּׁים אַמָּה׃

8 for the chambers in the outer court were themselves 50 *amot* deep, thus completing 100 *amot* alongside the edifice.

ח כִּי־אֹרֶךְ הַלְּשָׁכוֹת אֲשֶׁר לֶחָצֵר הַחִצוֹנָה חֲמִשִּׁים אַמָּה וְהִנֵּה עַל־פְּנֵי הַהֵיכָל מֵאָה אַמָּה׃

9 Thus, at the foot of that complex of chambers ran a passage – of a width set by the wall in the outer court – which one entered from the east in order to gain access to them from the outer court.*

ט וּמִתַּחְתָּה לְשָׁכוֹת [וּמִתַּחַת] [הַלְּשָׁכוֹת] הָאֵלֶּה הַמָּבוֹא [הַמֵּבִיא] מֵהַקָּדִים בְּבֹאוֹ לָהֵנָּה מֵהֶחָצֵר הַחִצֹנָה׃

10 There was another chamber complex to the east of the vacant space and the structure,

י בְּרֹחַב גֶּדֶר הֶחָצֵר דֶּרֶךְ הַקָּדִים אֶל־פְּנֵי הַגִּזְרָה וְאֶל־פְּנֵי הַבִּנְיָן לְשָׁכוֹת׃

---

* "of a width set by the wall in the outer court" moved up from verse 10 for clarity

Yechezkel/Ezekiel
Chapter 42

יחזקאל
פרק מב

11 likewise with a passage in front – just like the complex on the north side, with which this one agreed in width and depth and in the exact layout of its exits and entrances.

יא וְדֶרֶךְ לִפְנֵיהֶם כְּמַרְאֵה הַלְּשָׁכוֹת אֲשֶׁר דֶּרֶךְ הַצָּפוֹן כְּאָרְכָּן כֵּן רָחְבָּן וְכֹל מוֹצָאֵיהֶן וּכְמִשְׁפְּטֵיהֶן וּכְפִתְחֵיהֶן:

12 Accordingly, the entrances to the chamber complex on the south side were approached from the east by the entrance at the head of the corresponding passage along the matching wall.

יב וּכְפִתְחֵי הַלְּשָׁכוֹת אֲשֶׁר דֶּרֶךְ הַדָּרוֹם פֶּתַח בְּרֹאשׁ דָּרֶךְ דֶּרֶךְ בִּפְנֵי הַגְּדֶרֶת הֲגִינָה דֶּרֶךְ הַקָּדִים בְּבוֹאָן:

13 And he said to me, "The northern chambers and the southern chambers by the vacant space are the consecrated chambers in which the *Kohanim* who have access to *Hashem* shall eat the most holy offerings. There they shall deposit the most holy offerings – the meal offerings, the sin offerings, and the guilt offerings, for the place is consecrated.

יג וַיֹּאמֶר אֵלַי לִשְׁכוֹת הַצָּפוֹן לִשְׁכוֹת הַדָּרוֹם אֲשֶׁר אֶל־פְּנֵי הַגִּזְרָה הֵנָּה לִשְׁכוֹת הַקֹּדֶשׁ אֲשֶׁר יֹאכְלוּ־שָׁם הַכֹּהֲנִים אֲשֶׁר־קְרוֹבִים לַיהוָה קָדְשֵׁי הַקֳּדָשִׁים שָׁם יַנִּיחוּ קָדְשֵׁי הַקֳּדָשִׁים וְהַמִּנְחָה וְהַחַטָּאת וְהָאָשָׁם כִּי הַמָּקוֹם קָדֹשׁ:

14 When the *Kohanim* enter, they shall not proceed from the consecrated place to the outer court without first leaving here the vestments in which they minister; for the [vestments] are consecrated. Before proceeding to the area open to the people, they shall put on other garments."

יד בְּבֹאָם הַכֹּהֲנִים וְלֹא־יֵצְאוּ מֵהַקֹּדֶשׁ אֶל־הֶחָצֵר הַחִיצוֹנָה וְשָׁם יַנִּיחוּ בִגְדֵיהֶם אֲשֶׁר־יְשָׁרְתוּ בָהֶן כִּי־קֹדֶשׁ הֵנָּה יִלְבְּשׁוּ [וְלָבְשׁוּ] בְּגָדִים אֲחֵרִים וְקָרְבוּ אֶל־אֲשֶׁר לָעָם:

15 When he had finished the measurements of the inner Temple [area], he led me out by way of the gate which faces east, and he measured off the entire area.

טו וְכִלָּה אֶת־מִדּוֹת הַבַּיִת הַפְּנִימִי וְהוֹצִיאַנִי דֶּרֶךְ הַשַּׁעַר אֲשֶׁר פָּנָיו דֶּרֶךְ הַקָּדִים וּמְדָדוֹ סָבִיב סָבִיב:

16 He measured the east side with the measuring rod, 500 [*amot*] – in rods, by the measuring rod. He turned

טז מָדַד רוּחַ הַקָּדִים בִּקְנֵה הַמִּדָּה חֲמֵשׁ־אֵמוֹת [מֵאוֹת] קָנִים בִּקְנֵה הַמִּדָּה סָבִיב:

17 [and] measured the north side: 500 [*amot*] – in rods, by the measuring rod. He turned

יז מָדַד רוּחַ הַצָּפוֹן חֲמֵשׁ־מֵאוֹת קָנִים בִּקְנֵה הַמִּדָּה סָבִיב:

18 [and] measured the south side: 500 [*amot*] – in rods, by the measuring rod.

יח אֵת רוּחַ הַדָּרוֹם מָדַד חֲמֵשׁ־מֵאוֹת קָנִים בִּקְנֵה הַמִּדָּה:

19 Then he turned to the west side [and] measured it: 500 *amot* – in rods, by the measuring rod.

יט סָבַב אֶל־רוּחַ הַיָּם מָדַד חֲמֵשׁ־מֵאוֹת קָנִים בִּקְנֵה הַמִּדָּה:

20 Thus he measured it on the four sides; it had a wall completely surrounding it, 500 [*amot*] long on each side, to separate the consecrated from the unconsecrated.

כ לְאַרְבַּע רוּחוֹת מְדָדוֹ חוֹמָה לוֹ סָבִיב סָבִיב אֹרֶךְ חֲמֵשׁ מֵאוֹת וְרֹחַב חֲמֵשׁ מֵאוֹת לְהַבְדִּיל בֵּין הַקֹּדֶשׁ לְחֹל:

42:20 To separate the consecrated from the unconsecrated *Yechezkel*'s vision of the rebuilt *Beit Hamikdash* concludes with a description of its surrounding walls. These walls form a perfect square, five-hundred cubits on each side, and serve to distinguish between the holiness of *Har Habayit*, the Temple Mount,

1312

Yechezkel/Ezekiel
Chapter 43

יְחֶזְקֵאל
פֶּרֶק מג

l'-ar-BA ru-KHOT m'-da-DO KHO-mah LO sa-VEEV sa-VEEV O-rekh kha-MAYSH may-OT v'-RO-khav kha-MAYSH may-OT l'-hav-DEEL BAYN ha-KO-desh l'-KHOL

43 **1** Then he led me to a gate, the gate that faced east.

א וַיּוֹלִכֵנִי אֶל־הַשָּׁעַר שַׁעַר אֲשֶׁר פֹּנֶה דֶּרֶךְ הַקָּדִים:

2 And there, coming from the east with a roar like the roar of mighty waters, was the Presence of the God of *Yisrael*, and the earth was lit up by His Presence.

ב וְהִנֵּה כְּבוֹד אֱלֹהֵי יִשְׂרָאֵל בָּא מִדֶּרֶךְ הַקָּדִים וְקוֹלוֹ כְּקוֹל מַיִם רַבִּים וְהָאָרֶץ הֵאִירָה מִכְּבֹדוֹ:

3 The vision was like the vision I had seen when I came to destroy the city, the very same vision that I had seen by the Chebar Canal. Forthwith, I fell on my face.

ג וּכְמַרְאֵה הַמַּרְאֶה אֲשֶׁר רָאִיתִי כַּמַּרְאֶה אֲשֶׁר־רָאִיתִי בְּבֹאִי לְשַׁחֵת אֶת־הָעִיר וּמַרְאוֹת כַּמַּרְאֶה אֲשֶׁר רָאִיתִי אֶל־נְהַר־כְּבָר וָאֶפֹּל אֶל־פָּנָי:

4 The Presence of *Hashem* entered the Temple by the gate that faced eastward.

ד וּכְבוֹד יְהֹוָה בָּא אֶל־הַבָּיִת דֶּרֶךְ שַׁעַר אֲשֶׁר פָּנָיו דֶּרֶךְ הַקָּדִים:

5 A spirit carried me into the inner court, and lo, the Presence of *Hashem* filled the Temple;

ה וַתִּשָּׂאֵנִי רוּחַ וַתְּבִיאֵנִי אֶל־הֶחָצֵר הַפְּנִימִי וְהִנֵּה מָלֵא כְבוֹד־יְהֹוָה הַבָּיִת:

6 and I heard speech addressed to me from the Temple, though [the] man was standing beside me.

ו וָאֶשְׁמַע מִדַּבֵּר אֵלַי מֵהַבָּיִת וְאִישׁ הָיָה עֹמֵד אֶצְלִי:

7 It said to me: O mortal, this is the place of My throne and the place for the soles of My feet, where I will dwell in the midst of the people *Yisrael* forever. The House of *Yisrael* and their kings must not again defile My holy name by their apostasy and by the corpses of their kings at their death.

ז וַיֹּאמֶר אֵלַי בֶּן־אָדָם אֶת־מְקוֹם כִּסְאִי וְאֶת־מְקוֹם כַּפּוֹת רַגְלַי אֲשֶׁר אֶשְׁכָּן־שָׁם בְּתוֹךְ בְּנֵי־יִשְׂרָאֵל לְעוֹלָם וְלֹא יְטַמְּאוּ עוֹד בֵּית־יִשְׂרָאֵל שֵׁם קָדְשִׁי הֵמָּה וּמַלְכֵיהֶם בִּזְנוּתָם וּבְפִגְרֵי מַלְכֵיהֶם בָּמוֹתָם:

8 When they placed their threshold next to My threshold and their doorposts next to My doorposts with only a wall between Me and them, they would defile My holy name by the abominations that they committed, and I consumed them in My anger.

ח בְּתִתָּם סִפָּם אֶת־סִפִּי וּמְזוּזָתָם אֵצֶל מְזוּזָתִי וְהַקִּיר בֵּינִי וּבֵינֵיהֶם וְטִמְּאוּ אֶת־שֵׁם קָדְשִׁי בְּתוֹעֲבוֹתָם אֲשֶׁר עָשׂוּ וָאֲכַל אֹתָם בְּאַפִּי:

9 Therefore, let them put their apostasy and the corpses of their kings far from Me, and I will dwell among them forever.

ט עַתָּה יְרַחֲקוּ אֶת־זְנוּתָם וּפִגְרֵי מַלְכֵיהֶם מִמֶּנִּי וְשָׁכַנְתִּי בְתוֹכָם לְעוֹלָם:

10 [Now] you, O mortal, describe the Temple to the House of *Yisrael*, and let them measure its design. But let them be ashamed of their iniquities:

י אַתָּה בֶן־אָדָם הַגֵּד אֶת־בֵּית־יִשְׂרָאֵל אֶת־הַבַּיִת וְיִכָּלְמוּ מֵעֲוֺנוֹתֵיהֶם וּמָדְדוּ אֶת־תָּכְנִית:

and the rest of *Yerushalayim*, where sacrifices could not be offered. The *Mishna* (*Keilim* 1:6–9) teaches that the Land of Israel possesses ten ascending levels of holiness, starting from the outskirts of the country and culminating with the Holy of Holies, the resting place of God's Divine Presence.

Yechezkel/Ezekiel
Chapter 43

יחזקאל
פרק מג

11 When they are ashamed of all they have done, make known to them the plan of the Temple and its layout, its exits and entrances – its entire plan, and all the laws and instructions pertaining to its entire plan. Write it down before their eyes, that they may faithfully follow its entire plan and all its laws.

יא וְאִם־נִכְלְמוּ מִכֹּל אֲשֶׁר־עָשׂוּ צוּרַת הַבַּיִת וּתְכוּנָתוֹ וּמוֹצָאָיו וּמוֹבָאָיו וְכָל־צוּרֹתָו וְאֵת כָּל־חֻקֹּתָיו וְכָל־צוּרֹתָו [צוּרֹתָיו] וְכָל־תֹּורֹתָו [תּוֹרֹתָיו] הוֹדַע אוֹתָם וּכְתֹב לְעֵינֵיהֶם וְיִשְׁמְרוּ אֶת־כָּל־צוּרָתוֹ וְאֶת־כָּל־חֻקֹּתָיו וְעָשׂוּ אוֹתָם:

v'-im nikh-l'-MU mi-KOL a-sher a-SU tzu-RAT ha-BA-yit ut-khu-na-TO u-mo-tza-AV u-mo-va-AV v'-khol tzu-ro-TAV v'-AYT kol khu-ko-TAV v'-khol tzu-ro-TAV v'-khol to-ro-TAV ho-DA o-TAM ukh-TOV l'-ay-nay-HEM v'-yish-m'-RU et kol tzu-ra-TO v'-et kol khu-ko-TAV v'-a-SU o-TAM

12 Such are the instructions for the Temple on top of the mountain: the entire area of its enclosure shall be most holy. Thus far the instructions for the Temple.

יב זֹאת תּוֹרַת הַבָּיִת עַל־רֹאשׁ הָהָר כָּל־גְּבֻלוֹ סָבִיב סָבִיב קֹדֶשׁ קָדָשִׁים הִנֵּה־זֹאת תּוֹרַת הַבָּיִת:

13 And these are the dimensions of the *Mizbayach*, in *amot* where each is an *amah* and a *tefach*. The trench shall be an *amah* deep and an *amah* wide, with a rim one *zeret* high around its edge. And the height shall be as follows:

יג וְאֵלֶּה מִדּוֹת הַמִּזְבֵּחַ בָּאַמּוֹת אַמָּה אַמָּה וָטֹפַח וְחֵיק הָאַמָּה וְאַמָּה־רֹחַב וּגְבוּלָהּ אֶל־שְׂפָתָהּ סָבִיב זֶרֶת הָאֶחָד וְזֶה גַּב הַמִּזְבֵּחַ:

14 From the trench in the ground to the lower ledge, which shall be an *amah* wide: 2 *amot*; from the lower ledge to the upper ledge, which shall likewise be an *amah* wide: 4 *amot*;

יד וּמֵחֵיק הָאָרֶץ עַד־הָעֲזָרָה הַתַּחְתּוֹנָה שְׁתַּיִם אַמּוֹת וְרֹחַב אַמָּה אֶחָת וּמֵהֲעֲזָרָה הַקְּטַנָּה עַד־הָעֲזָרָה הַגְּדוֹלָה אַרְבַּע אַמּוֹת וְרֹחַב הָאַמָּה:

15 and the height of the *Mizbayach* hearth shall be 4 *amot*, with 4 horns projecting upward from the hearth: 4 *amot*.

טו וְהַהַרְאֵל אַרְבַּע אַמּוֹת וּמֵהָאֲרִיאֵל וּלְמַעְלָה הַקְּרָנוֹת אַרְבַּע:

16 Now the hearth shall be 12 *amot* long and 12 broad, square, with 4 equal sides.

טז וְהָאֲרִאֵיל [וְהָאֲרִיאֵל] שְׁתֵּים עֶשְׂרֵה אֹרֶךְ בִּשְׁתֵּים עֶשְׂרֵה רֹחַב רָבוּעַ אֶל אַרְבַּעַת רְבָעָיו:

17 Hence, the [upper] base shall be 14 *amot* broad, with 4 equal sides. The surrounding rim shall be half an *amah* [high], and the surrounding trench shall measure one *amah*. And the ramp shall face east.

יז וְהָעֲזָרָה אַרְבַּע עֶשְׂרֵה אֹרֶךְ בְּאַרְבַּע עֶשְׂרֵה רֹחַב אֶל אַרְבַּעַת רְבָעֶיהָ וְהַגְּבוּל סָבִיב אוֹתָהּ חֲצִי הָאַמָּה וְהַחֵיק־לָהּ אַמָּה סָבִיב וּמַעֲלֹתֵהוּ פְּנוֹת קָדִים:

43:11 Make known to them the plan of the Temple and its layout The Sages describe a conversation that took place between *Hashem* and *Yechezkel* after the prophet had been exiled to Babylonia. The Lord tells *Yechezkel* to teach the design of the third *Beit Hamikdash* to the Children of Israel. *Yechezkel* answers, "Let it wait until we return to the Land of Israel … we cannot build it here in Babylonia." *Hashem* turns to the prophet and responds, "No, teach it to the people now, because when the people study the design of your *Beit Hamikdash*, I will consider it as if they have already begun to build it." Today, scholars in Jerusalem are studying the design of the third Temple, and are already building vessels to use in it, including the solid gold *menorah* prominently displayed at the top of the stairs leading down to the *Kotel*.

Replica of the Temple menorah

Yechezkel/Ezekiel
Chapter 44

18 Then he said to me: O mortal, thus said *Hashem*: These are the directions for the *Mizbayach* on the day it is erected, so that burnt offerings may be offered up on it and blood dashed against it.

19 You shall give to the levitical *Kohanim* who are of the stock of *Tzadok*, and so eligible to minister to Me – declares *Hashem* – a young bull of the herd for a sin offering.

20 You shall take some of its blood and apply it to the four horns [of the *Mizbayach*], to the four corners of the base, and to the surrounding rim; thus you shall purge it and perform purification upon it.

21 Then you shall take the bull of sin offering and burn it in the designated area of the Temple, outside the Sanctuary.

22 On the following day, you shall offer a goat without blemish as a sin offering; and the *Mizbayach* shall be purged [with it] just as it was purged with the bull.

23 When you have completed the ritual of purging, you shall offer a bull of the herd without blemish and a ram of the flock without blemish.

24 Offer them to *Hashem*; let the *Kohanim* throw salt on them and offer them up as a burnt offering to *Hashem*.

25 Every day, for seven days, you shall present a goat of sin offering, as well as a bull of the herd and a ram of the flock; you shall present unblemished ones.

26 Seven days they shall purge the *Mizbayach* and cleanse it; thus shall it be consecrated.

27 And when these days are over, then from the eighth day onward the *Kohanim* shall offer your burnt offerings and your offerings of well-being on the *Mizbayach*; and I wil extend My favor to you – declares *Hashem*.

44 1 Then he led me back to the outer gate of the Sanctuary that faced eastward; it was shut.

2 And *Hashem* said to me: This gate is to be kept shut and is not to be opened! No one shall enter by it because *Hashem*, the God of *Yisrael*, has entered by it; therefore it shall remain shut.

יחזקאל
פרק מד

יח וַיֹּאמֶר אֵלַי בֶּן־אָדָם כֹּה אָמַר אֲדֹנָי יְהֹוִה אֵלֶּה חֻקּוֹת הַמִּזְבֵּחַ בְּיוֹם הֵעָשׂוֹתוֹ לְהַעֲלוֹת עָלָיו עוֹלָה וְלִזְרֹק עָלָיו דָּם:

יט וְנָתַתָּה אֶל־הַכֹּהֲנִים הַלְוִיִּם אֲשֶׁר הֵם מִזֶּרַע צָדוֹק הַקְּרֹבִים אֵלַי נְאֻם אֲדֹנָי יְהֹוִה לְשָׁרְתֵנִי פַּר בֶּן־בָּקָר לְחַטָּאת:

כ וְלָקַחְתָּ מִדָּמוֹ וְנָתַתָּה עַל־אַרְבַּע קַרְנֹתָיו וְאֶל־אַרְבַּע פִּנּוֹת הָעֲזָרָה וְאֶל־הַגְּבוּל סָבִיב וְחִטֵּאתָ אוֹתוֹ וְכִפַּרְתָּהוּ:

כא וְלָקַחְתָּ אֵת הַפָּר הַחַטָּאת וּשְׂרָפוֹ בְּמִפְקַד הַבַּיִת מִחוּץ לַמִּקְדָּשׁ:

כב וּבַיּוֹם הַשֵּׁנִי תַּקְרִיב שְׂעִיר־עִזִּים תָּמִים לְחַטָּאת וְחִטְּאוּ אֶת־הַמִּזְבֵּחַ כַּאֲשֶׁר חִטְּאוּ בַּפָּר:

כג בְּכַלּוֹתְךָ מֵחַטֵּא תַּקְרִיב פַּר בֶּן־בָּקָר תָּמִים וְאַיִל מִן־הַצֹּאן תָּמִים:

כד וְהִקְרַבְתָּם לִפְנֵי יְהֹוָה וְהִשְׁלִיכוּ הַכֹּהֲנִים עֲלֵיהֶם מֶלַח וְהֶעֱלוּ אוֹתָם עֹלָה לַיהֹוָה:

כה שִׁבְעַת יָמִים תַּעֲשֶׂה שְׂעִיר־חַטָּאת לַיּוֹם וּפַר בֶּן־בָּקָר וְאַיִל מִן־הַצֹּאן תְּמִימִים יַעֲשׂוּ:

כו שִׁבְעַת יָמִים יְכַפְּרוּ אֶת־הַמִּזְבֵּחַ וְטִהֲרוּ אֹתוֹ וּמִלְאוּ יָדוֹ [יָדָיו]:

כז וִיכַלּוּ אֶת־הַיָּמִים וְהָיָה בַיּוֹם הַשְּׁמִינִי וָהָלְאָה יַעֲשׂוּ הַכֹּהֲנִים עַל־הַמִּזְבֵּחַ אֶת־עוֹלוֹתֵיכֶם וְאֶת־שַׁלְמֵיכֶם וְרָצִאתִי אֶתְכֶם נְאֻם אֲדֹנָי יְהֹוִה:

מד א וַיָּשֶׁב אֹתִי דֶּרֶךְ שַׁעַר הַמִּקְדָּשׁ הַחִיצוֹן הַפֹּנֶה קָדִים וְהוּא סָגוּר:

ב וַיֹּאמֶר אֵלַי יְהֹוָה הַשַּׁעַר הַזֶּה סָגוּר יִהְיֶה לֹא יִפָּתֵחַ וְאִישׁ לֹא־יָבֹא בוֹ כִּי יְהֹוָה אֱלֹהֵי־יִשְׂרָאֵל בָּא בוֹ וְהָיָה סָגוּר:

Yechezkel/Ezekiel
Chapter 44

3 Only the prince may sit in it and eat bread before *Hashem*, since he is a prince; he shall enter by way of the vestibule of the gate, and shall depart by the same way.

4 Then he led me, by way of the north gate, to the front of the Temple. I looked, and lo! the Presence of *Hashem* filled the Temple of *Hashem*; and I fell upon my face.

5 Then *Hashem* said to me: O mortal, mark well, look closely and listen carefully to everything that I tell you regarding all the laws of the Temple of *Hashem* and all the instructions regarding it. Note well who may enter the Temple and all who must be excluded from the Sanctuary.

6 And say to the rebellious House of *Yisrael*: Thus said *Hashem*: Too long, O House of *Yisrael*, have you committed all your abominations,

7 admitting aliens, uncircumcised of spirit and uncircumcised of flesh, to be in My Sanctuary and profane My very Temple, when you offer up My food – the fat and the blood. You have broken My covenant with all your abominations.

8 You have not discharged the duties concerning My sacred offerings, but have appointed them to discharge the duties of My Sanctuary for you.

9 Thus said *Hashem*: Let no alien, uncircumcised in spirit and flesh, enter My Sanctuary – no alien whatsoever among the people of *Yisrael*.

10 But the *Leviim* who forsook Me when *Yisrael* went astray – straying from Me to follow their fetishes – shall suffer their punishment:

11 They shall be servitors in My Sanctuary, appointed over the Temple gates, and performing the chores of My Temple; they shall slaughter the burnt offerings and the sacrifices for the people. They shall attend on them and serve them.

12 Because they served the House of *Yisrael* in the presence of their fetishes and made them stumble into guilt, therefore – declares *Hashem* – I have sworn concerning them that they shall suffer their punishment:

יחזקאל
פרק מד

ג אֶת־הַנָּשִׂיא נָשִׂיא הוּא יֵשֶׁב־בּוֹ לֶאֱכָל־
לֶחֶם לִפְנֵי יְהֹוָה מִדֶּרֶךְ אֻלָם הַשַּׁעַר
יָבוֹא וּמִדַּרְכּוֹ יֵצֵא:

ד וַיְבִיאֵנִי דֶּרֶךְ־שַׁעַר הַצָּפוֹן אֶל־פְּנֵי הַבַּיִת
וָאֵרֶא וְהִנֵּה מָלֵא כְבוֹד־יְהֹוָה אֶת־בֵּית
יְהֹוָה וָאֶפֹּל אֶל־פָּנָי:

ה וַיֹּאמֶר אֵלַי יְהֹוָה בֶּן־אָדָם שִׂים לִבְּךָ
וּרְאֵה בְעֵינֶיךָ וּבְאָזְנֶיךָ שְּׁמָע אֵת כָּל־
אֲשֶׁר אֲנִי מְדַבֵּר אֹתָךְ לְכָל־חֻקּוֹת
בֵּית־יְהֹוָה וּלְכָל־תּוֹרֹתוֹ [תּוֹרֹתָיו]
וְשַׂמְתָּ לִבְּךָ לִמְבוֹא הַבַּיִת בְּכֹל מוֹצָאֵי
הַמִּקְדָּשׁ:

ו וְאָמַרְתָּ אֶל־מֶרִי אֶל־בֵּית יִשְׂרָאֵל
כֹּה אָמַר אֲדֹנָי יְהֹוִה רַב־לָכֶם מִכָּל־
תּוֹעֲבוֹתֵיכֶם בֵּית יִשְׂרָאֵל:

ז בַּהֲבִיאֲכֶם בְּנֵי־נֵכָר עַרְלֵי־לֵב וְעַרְלֵי
בָשָׂר לִהְיוֹת בְּמִקְדָּשִׁי לְחַלְּלוֹ אֶת־בֵּיתִי
בְּהַקְרִיבְכֶם אֶת־לַחְמִי חֵלֶב וָדָם וַיָּפֵרוּ
אֶת־בְּרִיתִי אֶל כָּל־תּוֹעֲבוֹתֵיכֶם:

ח וְלֹא שְׁמַרְתֶּם מִשְׁמֶרֶת קָדָשָׁי וַתְּשִׂימוּן
לְשֹׁמְרֵי מִשְׁמַרְתִּי בְּמִקְדָּשִׁי לָכֶם:

ט כֹּה־אָמַר אֲדֹנָי יְהֹוִה כָּל־בֶּן־נֵכָר עֶרֶל לֵב
וְעֶרֶל בָּשָׂר לֹא יָבוֹא אֶל־מִקְדָּשִׁי לְכָל־
בֶּן־נֵכָר אֲשֶׁר בְּתוֹךְ בְּנֵי יִשְׂרָאֵל:

י כִּי אִם־הַלְוִיִּם אֲשֶׁר רָחֲקוּ מֵעָלַי
בִּתְעוֹת יִשְׂרָאֵל אֲשֶׁר תָּעוּ מֵעָלַי אַחֲרֵי
גִּלּוּלֵיהֶם וְנָשְׂאוּ עֲוֹנָם:

יא וְהָיוּ בְמִקְדָּשִׁי מְשָׁרְתִים פְּקֻדּוֹת אֶל־
שַׁעֲרֵי הַבַּיִת וּמְשָׁרְתִים אֶת־הַבָּיִת הֵמָּה
יִשְׁחֲטוּ אֶת־הָעֹלָה וְאֶת־הַזֶּבַח לָעָם
וְהֵמָּה יַעַמְדוּ לִפְנֵיהֶם לְשָׁרְתָם:

יב יַעַן אֲשֶׁר יְשָׁרְתוּ אוֹתָם לִפְנֵי גִלּוּלֵיהֶם
וְהָיוּ לְבֵית־יִשְׂרָאֵל לְמִכְשׁוֹל עָוֹן עַל־כֵּן
נָשָׂאתִי יָדִי עֲלֵיהֶם נְאֻם אֲדֹנָי יְהֹוִה
וְנָשְׂאוּ עֲוֹנָם:

Yechezkel/Ezekiel
Chapter 44

יחזקאל
פרק מד

13 They shall not approach Me to serve Me as *Kohanim*, to come near any of My sacred offerings, the most holy things. They shall bear their shame for the abominations that they committed.

וְלֹא־יִגְּשׁוּ אֵלַי לְכַהֵן לִי וְלָגֶשֶׁת עַל־כָּל־קָדָשַׁי אֶל־קָדְשֵׁי הַקֳּדָשִׁים וְנָשְׂאוּ כְּלִמָּתָם וְתוֹעֲבוֹתָם אֲשֶׁר עָשׂוּ׃

14 I will make them watchmen of the Temple, to perform all its chores, everything that needs to be done in it.

וְנָתַתִּי אוֹתָם שֹׁמְרֵי מִשְׁמֶרֶת הַבָּיִת לְכֹל עֲבֹדָתוֹ וּלְכֹל אֲשֶׁר יֵעָשֶׂה בּוֹ׃

15 But the levitical *Kohanim* descended from *Tzadok*, who maintained the service of My Sanctuary when the people of *Yisrael* went astray from Me – they shall approach Me to minister to Me; they shall stand before Me to offer Me fat and blood – declares *Hashem*.

וְהַכֹּהֲנִים הַלְוִיִּם בְּנֵי צָדוֹק אֲשֶׁר שָׁמְרוּ אֶת־מִשְׁמֶרֶת מִקְדָּשִׁי בִּתְעוֹת בְּנֵי־יִשְׂרָאֵל מֵעָלַי הֵמָּה יִקְרְבוּ אֵלַי לְשָׁרְתֵנִי וְעָמְדוּ לְפָנַי לְהַקְרִיב לִי חֵלֶב וָדָם נְאֻם אֲדֹנָי יֱהוִה׃

v'-ha-ko-ha-NEEM hal-vi-YIM b'-NAY tza-DOK a-SHER sha-m'-RU et mish-ME-ret mik-da-SHEE bit-OT b'-nay yis-ra-AYL may-a-LAI HAY-mah yik-r'-VU ay-LAI l'-sha-r'-TAY-nee v'-a-m'-DU l'-fa-NAI l'-hak-REEV LEE KHAY-lev va-DAM n'-UM a-do-NAI e-lo-HEEM

16 They alone may enter My Sanctuary and they alone shall approach My table to minister to Me; and they shall keep My charge.

הֵמָּה יָבֹאוּ אֶל־מִקְדָּשִׁי וְהֵמָּה יִקְרְבוּ אֶל־שֻׁלְחָנִי לְשָׁרְתֵנִי וְשָׁמְרוּ אֶת־מִשְׁמַרְתִּי׃

17 And when they enter the gates of the inner court, they shall wear linen vestments: they shall have nothing woolen upon them when they minister inside the gates of the inner court.

וְהָיָה בְּבוֹאָם אֶל־שַׁעֲרֵי הֶחָצֵר הַפְּנִימִית בִּגְדֵי פִשְׁתִּים יִלְבָּשׁוּ וְלֹא־יַעֲלֶה עֲלֵיהֶם צֶמֶר בְּשָׁרְתָם בְּשַׁעֲרֵי הֶחָצֵר הַפְּנִימִית וָבָיְתָה׃

18 They shall have linen turbans on their heads and linen breeches on their loins; they shall not gird themselves with anything that causes sweat.

פַּאֲרֵי פִשְׁתִּים יִהְיוּ עַל־רֹאשָׁם וּמִכְנְסֵי פִשְׁתִּים יִהְיוּ עַל־מָתְנֵיהֶם לֹא יַחְגְּרוּ בַּיָּזַע׃

19 When they go out to the outer court – the outer court where the people are – they shall remove the vestments in which they minister and shall deposit them in the sacred chambers; they shall put on other garments, lest they make the people consecrated by [contact with] their vestments.

וּבְצֵאתָם אֶל־הֶחָצֵר הַחִיצוֹנָה אֶל־הֶחָצֵר הַחִיצוֹנָה אֶל־הָעָם יִפְשְׁטוּ אֶת־בִּגְדֵיהֶם אֲשֶׁר־הֵמָּה מְשָׁרְתִם בָּם וְהִנִּיחוּ אוֹתָם בְּלִשְׁכֹת הַקֹּדֶשׁ וְלָבְשׁוּ בְּגָדִים אֲחֵרִים וְלֹא־יְקַדְּשׁוּ אֶת־הָעָם בְּבִגְדֵיהֶם׃

20 They shall neither shave their heads nor let their hair go untrimmed; they shall keep their hair trimmed.

וְרֹאשָׁם לֹא יְגַלֵּחוּ וּפֶרַע לֹא יְשַׁלֵּחוּ כָּסוֹם יִכְסְמוּ אֶת־רָאשֵׁיהֶם׃

44:15 Descended from *Tzadok* For their loyalty to *Hashem*, *Yechezkel* nominates the members of the house of *Tzadok* to serve as teachers (verse 23) and judges (verse 24), and to serve in the *Beit Hamikdash*. Given their enhanced positions of power, it is not surprising that the house of *Tzadok* will face the burden of greater restrictions, as described in the rest of the chapter. Those who lead God's people in *Eretz Yisrael* must be prepared to make sacrifices others won't make, in order to maintain their character and purity.

Yechezkel/Ezekiel Chapter 45

21 No *Kohen* shall drink wine when he enters into the inner court.

כא וְיַיִן לֹא־יִשְׁתּוּ כָּל־כֹּהֵן בְּבוֹאָם אֶל־הֶחָצֵר הַפְּנִימִית׃

22 They shall not marry widows or divorced women; they may marry only virgins of the stock of the House of *Yisrael*, or widows who are widows of *Kohanim*.

כב וְאַלְמָנָה וּגְרוּשָׁה לֹא־יִקְחוּ לָהֶם לְנָשִׁים כִּי אִם־בְּתוּלֹת מִזֶּרַע בֵּית יִשְׂרָאֵל וְהָאַלְמָנָה אֲשֶׁר תִּהְיֶה אַלְמָנָה מִכֹּהֵן יִקָּחוּ׃

23 They shall declare to My people what is sacred and what is profane, and inform them what is clean and what is unclean.

כג וְאֶת־עַמִּי יוֹרוּ בֵּין קֹדֶשׁ לְחֹל וּבֵין־טָמֵא לְטָהוֹר יוֹדִעֻם׃

24 In lawsuits, too, it is they who shall act as judges; they shall decide them in accordance with My rules. They shall preserve My teachings and My laws regarding all My fixed occasions; and they shall maintain the sanctity of My *Shabbatot*.

כד וְעַל־רִיב הֵמָּה יַעַמְדוּ לשפט [לְמִשְׁפָּט] בְּמִשְׁפָּטַי ושפטהו [יִשְׁפְּטוּהוּ] וְאֶת־תּוֹרֹתַי וְאֶת־חֻקֹּתַי בְּכָל־מוֹעֲדַי יִשְׁמֹרוּ וְאֶת־שַׁבְּתוֹתַי יְקַדֵּשׁוּ׃

25 [A *Kohen*] shall not defile himself by entering [a house] where there is a dead person. He shall defile himself only for father or mother, son or daughter, brother or unmarried sister.

כה וְאֶל־מֵת אָדָם לֹא יָבוֹא לְטָמְאָה כִּי אִם־לְאָב וּלְאֵם וּלְבֵן וּלְבַת לְאָח וּלְאָחוֹת אֲשֶׁר־לֹא־הָיְתָה לְאִישׁ יִטַּמָּאוּ׃

26 After he has become clean, seven days shall be counted off for him;

כו וְאַחֲרֵי טָהֳרָתוֹ שִׁבְעַת יָמִים יִסְפְּרוּ־לוֹ׃

27 and on the day that he reenters the inner court of the Sanctuary to minister in the Sanctuary, he shall present his sin offering – declares *Hashem*.

כז וּבְיוֹם בֹּאוֹ אֶל־הַקֹּדֶשׁ אֶל־הֶחָצֵר הַפְּנִימִית לְשָׁרֵת בַּקֹּדֶשׁ יַקְרִיב חַטָּאתוֹ נְאֻם אֲדֹנָי יֱהֹוִה׃

28 This shall be their portion, for I am their portion; and no holding shall be given them in *Yisrael*, for I am their holding.

כח וְהָיְתָה לָהֶם לְנַחֲלָה אֲנִי נַחֲלָתָם וַאֲחֻזָּה לֹא־תִתְּנוּ לָהֶם בְּיִשְׂרָאֵל אֲנִי אֲחֻזָּתָם׃

29 The meal offerings, sin offerings, and guilt offerings shall be consumed by them. Everything proscribed in *Yisrael* shall be theirs.

כט הַמִּנְחָה וְהַחַטָּאת וְהָאָשָׁם הֵמָּה יֹאכְלוּם וְכָל־חֵרֶם בְּיִשְׂרָאֵל לָהֶם יִהְיֶה׃

30 All the choice first fruits of every kind, and all the gifts of every kind – of all your contributions – shall go to the *Kohanim*. You shall further give the first of the yield of your baking to the *Kohen*, that a blessing may rest upon your home.

ל וְרֵאשִׁית כָּל־בִּכּוּרֵי כֹל וְכָל־תְּרוּמַת כֹּל מִכֹּל תְּרוּמוֹתֵיכֶם לַכֹּהֲנִים יִהְיֶה וְרֵאשִׁית עֲרִסוֹתֵיכֶם תִּתְּנוּ לַכֹּהֵן לְהָנִיחַ בְּרָכָה אֶל־בֵּיתֶךָ׃

31 *Kohanim* shall not eat anything, whether bird or animal, that died or was torn by beasts.

לא כָּל־נְבֵלָה וּטְרֵפָה מִן־הָעוֹף וּמִן־הַבְּהֵמָה לֹא יֹאכְלוּ הַכֹּהֲנִים׃

45

1 When you allot the land as an inheritance, you shall set aside from the land, as a gift sacred to *Hashem*, an area 25,000 [*amot*] long and 10,000 wide: this shall be holy through its entire extent.

מה א וּבְהַפִּילְכֶם אֶת־הָאָרֶץ בְּנַחֲלָה תָּרִימוּ תְרוּמָה לַיהֹוָה קֹדֶשׁ מִן־הָאָרֶץ אֹרֶךְ חֲמִשָּׁה וְעֶשְׂרִים אֶלֶף אֹרֶךְ וְרֹחַב עֲשָׂרָה אָלֶף קֹדֶשׁ־הוּא בְכָל־גְּבוּלָהּ סָבִיב׃

Yechezkel/Ezekiel
Chapter 45

יְחֶזְקֵאל
פרק מה

2 Of this, a square measuring a full 500 by 500 shall be reserved for the Sanctuary, and 50 *amot* for an open space all around it.

ב יִהְיֶה מִזֶּה אֶל־הַקֹּדֶשׁ חֲמֵשׁ מֵאוֹת בַּחֲמֵשׁ מֵאוֹת מְרֻבָּע סָבִיב וַחֲמִשִּׁים אַמָּה מִגְרָשׁ לוֹ סָבִיב׃

3 Of the aforesaid area, you shall measure off, as most holy and destined to include the Sanctuary, [a space] 25,000 long by 10,000 wide;

ג וּמִן־הַמִּדָּה הַזֹּאת תָּמוֹד אֹרֶךְ חמש [חֲמִשָּׁה] וְעֶשְׂרִים אֶלֶף וְרֹחַב עֲשֶׂרֶת אֲלָפִים וּבוֹ־יִהְיֶה הַמִּקְדָּשׁ קֹדֶשׁ קָדָשִׁים׃

4 it is a sacred portion of the land; it shall provide space for houses for the *Kohanim*, the ministrants of the Sanctuary who are qualified to minister to *Hashem*, as well as holy ground for the Sanctuary.

ד קֹדֶשׁ מִן־הָאָרֶץ הוּא לַכֹּהֲנִים מְשָׁרְתֵי הַמִּקְדָּשׁ יִהְיֶה הַקְּרֵבִים לְשָׁרֵת אֶת־יְהוָה וְהָיָה לָהֶם מָקוֹם לְבָתִּים וּמִקְדָּשׁ לַמִּקְדָּשׁ׃

5 Another [space], 25,000 long by 10,000 wide, shall be the property of the *Leviim*, the servants of the Temple – twenty chambers.

ה וַחֲמִשָּׁה וְעֶשְׂרִים אֶלֶף אֹרֶךְ וַעֲשֶׂרֶת אֲלָפִים רֹחַב יהיה [וְהָיָה] לַלְוִיִּם מְשָׁרְתֵי הַבַּיִת לָהֶם לַאֲחֻזָּה עֶשְׂרִים לְשָׁכֹת׃

6 Alongside the sacred reserve, you shall set aside [a space] 25,000 long by 5,000 wide, as the property of the city; it shall belong to the whole House of *Yisrael*.

ו וַאֲחֻזַּת הָעִיר תִּתְּנוּ חֲמֵשֶׁת אֲלָפִים רֹחַב וְאֹרֶךְ חֲמִשָּׁה וְעֶשְׂרִים אֶלֶף לְעֻמַּת תְּרוּמַת הַקֹּדֶשׁ לְכָל־בֵּית יִשְׂרָאֵל יִהְיֶה׃

7 And to the prince shall belong, on both sides of the sacred reserve and the property of the city and alongside the sacred reserve and the property of the city, on the west extending westward and on the east extending eastward, a portion corresponding to one of the [tribal] portions that extend from the western border to the eastern border

ז וְלַנָּשִׂיא מִזֶּה וּמִזֶּה לִתְרוּמַת הַקֹּדֶשׁ וְלַאֲחֻזַּת הָעִיר אֶל־פְּנֵי תְרוּמַת־הַקֹּדֶשׁ וְאֶל־פְּנֵי אֲחֻזַּת הָעִיר מִפְּאַת־יָם יָמָּה וּמִפְּאַת־קֵדְמָה קָדִימָה וְאֹרֶךְ לְעֻמּוֹת אַחַד הַחֲלָקִים מִגְּבוּל יָם אֶל־גְּבוּל קָדִימָה׃

8 of the land. That shall be his property in *Yisrael*; and My princes shall no more defraud My people, but shall leave the rest of the land to the several tribes of the House of *Yisrael*.

ח לָאָרֶץ יִהְיֶה־לּוֹ לַאֲחֻזָּה בְּיִשְׂרָאֵל וְלֹא־יוֹנוּ עוֹד נְשִׂיאַי אֶת־עַמִּי וְהָאָרֶץ יִתְּנוּ לְבֵית־יִשְׂרָאֵל לְשִׁבְטֵיהֶם׃

9 Thus said *Hashem*: Enough, princes of *Yisrael*! Make an end of lawlessness and rapine, and do what is right and just! Put a stop to your evictions of My people – declares *Hashem*.

ט כֹּה־אָמַר אֲדֹנָי יְהוִה רַב־לָכֶם נְשִׂיאֵי יִשְׂרָאֵל חָמָס וָשֹׁד הָסִירוּ וּמִשְׁפָּט וּצְדָקָה עֲשׂוּ הָרִימוּ גְרֻשֹׁתֵיכֶם מֵעַל עַמִּי נְאֻם אֲדֹנָי יְהוִה׃

koh a-MAR a-do-NAI e-lo-HEEM rav la-KHEM n'-see-AY yis-ra-AYL kha-MAS va-SHOD ha-SEE-ru u-mish-PAT utz-da-KAH a-SU ha-REE-mu g'-ru-sho-tay-KHEM may-AL a-MEE n'-UM a-do-NAI e-lo-HEEM

45:9 Do what is right and just In the middle of discussing the division of the land between the priests, princes, and the people, *Yechezkel* suddenly stops to warn the leaders against false weights and measures.

The previous *Beit Hamikdash* fell because of dishonesty and injustice (see Amos 8). *Yechezkel* understands that the strongest foundation for rebuilding the *Beit Hamikdash*, and residing in *Eretz Yisrael*, is a sense of

Yechezkel/Ezekiel
Chapter 45

יחזקאל
פרק מה

10 Have honest balances, an honest *efah*, and an honest *bat*.

י מֹאזְנֵי־צֶדֶק וְאֵיפַת־צֶדֶק וּבַת־צֶדֶק יְהִי לָכֶם׃

11 The *efah* and the *bat* shall comprise the same volume, the *bat* a tenth of a *chomer* and the *efah* a tenth of a *chomer*; their capacity shall be gauged by the *chomer*.

יא הָאֵיפָה וְהַבַּת תֹּכֶן אֶחָד יִהְיֶה לָשֵׂאת מַעְשַׂר הַחֹמֶר הַבָּת וַעֲשִׂירִת הַחֹמֶר הָאֵיפָה אֶל־הַחֹמֶר יִהְיֶה מַתְכֻּנְתּוֹ׃

12 And the *shekel* shall weigh 20 *geira*. 20 *shekalim*, 25 *shekalim* [and] 10 plus 5 *shekalim* shall count with you as a *maneh*.

יב וְהַשֶּׁקֶל עֶשְׂרִים גֵּרָה עֶשְׂרִים שְׁקָלִים חֲמִשָּׁה וְעֶשְׂרִים שְׁקָלִים עֲשָׂרָה וַחֲמִשָּׁה שֶׁקֶל הַמָּנֶה יִהְיֶה לָכֶם׃

13 This is the contribution you shall make: One-sixth of an *efah* from every *chomer* of wheat and one-sixth of an *efah* from every *chomer* of barley,

יג זֹאת הַתְּרוּמָה אֲשֶׁר תָּרִימוּ שִׁשִּׁית הָאֵיפָה מֵחֹמֶר הַחִטִּים וְשִׁשִּׁיתֶם הָאֵיפָה מֵחֹמֶר הַשְּׂעֹרִים׃

14 while the due from the oil – the oil being measured by the *bat* – shall be one-tenth of a *bat* from every *kor*. – As 10 *batim* make a *chomer*, so 10 *batim* make a *chomer*. –

יד וְחֹק הַשֶּׁמֶן הַבַּת הַשֶּׁמֶן מַעְשַׂר הַבַּת מִן־הַכֹּר עֲשֶׂרֶת הַבַּתִּים חֹמֶר כִּי־עֲשֶׂרֶת הַבַּתִּים חֹמֶר׃

15 And [the due] from the flock shall be one animal from every 200. [All these shall be contributed] from *Yisrael*'s products for meal offerings, burnt offerings, and offerings of well-being, to make expiation for them – declares *Hashem*.

טו וְשֶׂה־אַחַת מִן־הַצֹּאן מִן־הַמָּאתַיִם מִמַּשְׁקֵה יִשְׂרָאֵל לְמִנְחָה וּלְעוֹלָה וְלִשְׁלָמִים לְכַפֵּר עֲלֵיהֶם נְאֻם אֲדֹנָי יְהוִה׃

16 In this contribution, the entire population must join with the prince in *Yisrael*.

טז כֹּל הָעָם הָאָרֶץ יִהְיוּ אֶל־הַתְּרוּמָה הַזֹּאת לַנָּשִׂיא בְּיִשְׂרָאֵל׃

17 But the burnt offerings, the meal offerings, and the libations on festivals, new moons, *Shabbatot* – all fixed occasions – of the House of *Yisrael* shall be the obligation of the prince; he shall provide the sin offerings, the meal offerings, the burnt offerings, and the offerings of well-being, to make expiation for the House of *Yisrael*.

יז וְעַל־הַנָּשִׂיא יִהְיֶה הָעוֹלוֹת וְהַמִּנְחָה וְהַנֶּסֶךְ בַּחַגִּים וּבֶחֳדָשִׁים וּבַשַּׁבָּתוֹת בְּכָל־מוֹעֲדֵי בֵּית יִשְׂרָאֵל הוּא־יַעֲשֶׂה אֶת־הַחַטָּאת וְאֶת־הַמִּנְחָה וְאֶת־הָעוֹלָה וְאֶת־הַשְּׁלָמִים לְכַפֵּר בְּעַד בֵּית־יִשְׂרָאֵל׃

18 Thus said *Hashem*: On the first day of the first month, you shall take a bull of the herd without blemish, and you shall cleanse the Sanctuary.

יח כֹּה־אָמַר אֲדֹנָי יְהוִה בָּרִאשׁוֹן בְּאֶחָד לַחֹדֶשׁ תִּקַּח פַּר־בֶּן־בָּקָר תָּמִים וְחִטֵּאתָ אֶת־הַמִּקְדָּשׁ׃

19 The *Kohen* shall take some of the blood of the sin offering and apply it to the doorposts of the Temple, to the four corners of the ledge of the *Mizbayach*, and to the doorposts of the gate of the inner court.

יט וְלָקַח הַכֹּהֵן מִדַּם הַחַטָּאת וְנָתַן אֶל־מְזוּזַת הַבַּיִת וְאֶל־אַרְבַּע פִּנּוֹת הָעֲזָרָה לַמִּזְבֵּחַ וְעַל־מְזוּזַת שַׁעַר הֶחָצֵר הַפְּנִימִית׃

---

justice. The same rules of honesty and integrity that apply in the marketplace (see Leviticus 19) apply in the *Beit Hamikdash*, and throughout the Land of Israel. *Yechezkel* therefore interrupts his division of the land to emphasize the importance of honest dealings in settling Israel. Just as dishonesty and injustice led to the destruction of the *Beit Hamikdash* and exile from the land, it is through honesty and justice that the people will merit resettling and dwelling in *Eretz Yisrael*.

Yechezkel/Ezekiel Chapter 46

יחזקאל
פרק מו

20 You shall do the same on the seventh day of the month to purge the Temple from uncleanness caused by unwitting or ignorant persons.

כ וְכֵן תַּעֲשֶׂה בְּשִׁבְעָה בַחֹדֶשׁ מֵאִישׁ שֹׁגֶה וּמִפֶּתִי וְכִפַּרְתֶּם אֶת־הַבָּיִת:

21 On the fourteenth day of the first month you shall have the *Pesach* sacrifice; and during a festival of seven days unleavened bread shall be eaten.

כא בָּרִאשׁוֹן בְּאַרְבָּעָה עָשָׂר יוֹם לַחֹדֶשׁ יִהְיֶה לָכֶם הַפָּסַח חָג שְׁבֻעוֹת יָמִים מַצּוֹת יֵאָכֵל:

22 On that day, the prince shall provide a bull of sin offering on behalf of himself and of the entire population;

כב וְעָשָׂה הַנָּשִׂיא בַּיּוֹם הַהוּא בַּעֲדוֹ וּבְעַד כָּל־עַם הָאָרֶץ פַּר חַטָּאת:

23 and during the seven days of the festival, he shall provide daily – for seven days – seven bulls and seven rams, without blemish, for a burnt offering to *Hashem*, and one goat daily for a sin offering.

כג וְשִׁבְעַת יְמֵי־הֶחָג יַעֲשֶׂה עוֹלָה לַיהוָה שִׁבְעַת פָּרִים וְשִׁבְעַת אֵילִים תְּמִימִם לַיּוֹם שִׁבְעַת הַיָּמִים וְחַטָּאת שְׂעִיר עִזִּים לַיּוֹם:

24 He shall provide a meal offering of an *efah* for each bull and an *efah* for each ram, with a *hin* of oil to every *efah*.

כד וּמִנְחָה אֵיפָה לַפָּר וְאֵיפָה לָאַיִל יַעֲשֶׂה וְשֶׁמֶן הִין לָאֵיפָה:

25 So, too, during the festival of the seventh month, for seven days from the fifteenth day on, he shall provide the same sin offerings, burnt offerings, meal offerings, and oil.

כה בַּשְּׁבִיעִי בַּחֲמִשָּׁה עָשָׂר יוֹם לַחֹדֶשׁ בֶּחָג יַעֲשֶׂה כָאֵלֶּה שִׁבְעַת הַיָּמִים כַּחַטָּאת כָּעֹלָה וְכַמִּנְחָה וְכַשָּׁמֶן:

46 1 Thus said *Hashem*: The gate of the inner court which faces east shall be closed on the six working days; it shall be opened on the *Shabbat* day and it shall be opened on the day of the new moon.

מו א כֹּה־אָמַר אֲדֹנָי יְהוִה שַׁעַר הֶחָצֵר הַפְּנִימִית הַפֹּנֶה קָדִים יִהְיֶה סָגוּר שֵׁשֶׁת יְמֵי הַמַּעֲשֶׂה וּבְיוֹם הַשַּׁבָּת יִפָּתֵחַ וּבְיוֹם הַחֹדֶשׁ יִפָּתֵחַ:

2 The prince shall enter by way of the vestibule outside the gate, and shall attend at the gatepost while the *Kohanim* sacrifice his burnt offering and his offering of well-being; he shall then bow low at the threshold of the gate and depart. The gate, however, shall not be closed until evening.

ב וּבָא הַנָּשִׂיא דֶּרֶךְ אוּלָם הַשַּׁעַר מִחוּץ וְעָמַד עַל־מְזוּזַת הַשַּׁעַר וְעָשׂוּ הַכֹּהֲנִים אֶת־עוֹלָתוֹ וְאֶת־שְׁלָמָיו וְהִשְׁתַּחֲוָה עַל־מִפְתַּן הַשַּׁעַר וְיָצָא וְהַשַּׁעַר לֹא־יִסָּגֵר עַד־הָעָרֶב:

3 The common people shall worship before *Hashem* on *Shabbatot* and new moons at the entrance of the same gate.

ג וְהִשְׁתַּחֲווּ עַם־הָאָרֶץ פֶּתַח הַשַּׁעַר הַהוּא בַּשַּׁבָּתוֹת וּבֶחֳדָשִׁים לִפְנֵי יְהוָה:

4 The burnt offering which the prince presents to *Hashem* on the *Shabbat* day shall consist of six lambs without blemish and one ram without blemish –

ד וְהָעֹלָה אֲשֶׁר־יַקְרִב הַנָּשִׂיא לַיהוָה בְּיוֹם הַשַּׁבָּת שִׁשָּׁה כְבָשִׂים תְּמִימִם וְאַיִל תָּמִים:

5 with a meal offering of an *efah* for the ram, a meal offering of as much as he wishes for the lambs, and a *hin* of oil with every *efah*.

ה וּמִנְחָה אֵיפָה לָאַיִל וְלַכְּבָשִׂים מִנְחָה מַתַּת יָדוֹ וְשֶׁמֶן הִין לָאֵיפָה:

6 And on the day of the new moon, it shall consist of a bull of the herd without blemish, and six lambs and a ram – they shall be without blemish.

ו וּבְיוֹם הַחֹדֶשׁ פַּר בֶּן־בָּקָר תְּמִימִם וְשֵׁשֶׁת כְּבָשִׂם וָאַיִל תְּמִימִם יִהְיוּ:

Yechezkel/Ezekiel
Chapter 46

7 And he shall provide a meal offering of an *efah* for the bull, an *efah* for the ram, and as much as he can afford for the lambs, with a *hin* of oil to every *efah*.

ז וְאֵיפָה לַפָּר וְאֵיפָה לָאַיִל יַעֲשֶׂה מִנְחָה וְלַכְּבָשִׂים כַּאֲשֶׁר תַּשִּׂיג יָדוֹ וְשֶׁמֶן הִין לָאֵיפָה׃

8 When the prince enters, he shall come in by way of the vestibule of the gate, and he shall go out the same way.

ח וּבְבוֹא הַנָּשִׂיא דֶּרֶךְ אוּלָם הַשַּׁעַר יָבוֹא וּבְדַרְכּוֹ יֵצֵא׃

9 But on the fixed occasions, when the common people come before *Hashem*, whoever enters by the north gate to bow low shall leave by the south gate; and whoever enters by the south gate shall leave by the north gate. They shall not go back through the gate by which they came in, but shall go out by the opposite one.

ט וּבְבוֹא עַם־הָאָרֶץ לִפְנֵי יְהֹוָה בַּמּוֹעֲדִים הַבָּא דֶּרֶךְ־שַׁעַר צָפוֹן לְהִשְׁתַּחֲוֺת יֵצֵא דֶּרֶךְ־שַׁעַר נֶגֶב וְהַבָּא דֶּרֶךְ־שַׁעַר נֶגֶב יֵצֵא דֶּרֶךְ־שַׁעַר צָפוֹנָה לֹא יָשׁוּב דֶּרֶךְ הַשַּׁעַר אֲשֶׁר־בָּא בוֹ כִּי נִכְחוֹ יצאו [יֵצֵא]׃

u-v'-VO am ha-A-retz lif-NAY a-do-NAI ba-mo-a-DEEM ha-BA DE-rekh SHA-ar tza-FON l'-hish-ta-kha-VOT yay-TZAY de-rekh SHA-ar NE-gev v'-ha-BA de-rekh SHA-ar NE-gev yay-TZAY de-rekh SHA-ar tza-FO-nah LO ya-SHUV DE-rekh ha-SHA-ar a-sher BA VO KEE nikh-KHO yay-TZAY

10 And as for the prince, he shall enter with them when they enter and leave when they leave.

י וְהַנָּשִׂיא בְּתוֹכָם בְּבוֹאָם יָבוֹא וּבְצֵאתָם יֵצֵאוּ׃

11 On festivals and fixed occasions, the meal offering shall be an *efah* for each bull, an *efah* for each ram, and as much as he wishes for the lambs, with a *hin* of oil for every *efah*.

יא וּבַחַגִּים וּבַמּוֹעֲדִים תִּהְיֶה הַמִּנְחָה אֵיפָה לַפָּר וְאֵיפָה לָאַיִל וְלַכְּבָשִׂים מַתַּת יָדוֹ וְשֶׁמֶן הִין לָאֵיפָה׃

12 The gate that faces east shall also be opened for the prince whenever he offers a freewill offering – be it burnt offering or offering of well-being – freely offered to *Hashem*, so that he may offer his burnt offering or his offering of well-being just as he does on the *Shabbat* day. Then he shall leave, and the gate shall be closed after he leaves.

יב וְכִי־יַעֲשֶׂה הַנָּשִׂיא נְדָבָה עוֹלָה אוֹ־שְׁלָמִים נְדָבָה לַיהֹוָה וּפָתַח לוֹ אֶת הַשַּׁעַר הַפֹּנֶה קָדִים וְעָשָׂה אֶת־עֹלָתוֹ וְאֶת־שְׁלָמָיו כַּאֲשֶׁר יַעֲשֶׂה בְּיוֹם הַשַּׁבָּת וְיָצָא וְסָגַר אֶת־הַשַּׁעַר אַחֲרֵי צֵאתוֹ׃

13 Each day you shall offer a lamb of the first year without blemish, as a daily burnt offering to *Hashem*; you shall offer one every morning.

יג וְכֶבֶשׂ בֶּן־שְׁנָתוֹ תָּמִים תַּעֲשֶׂה עוֹלָה לַיּוֹם לַיהֹוָה בַּבֹּקֶר בַּבֹּקֶר תַּעֲשֶׂה אֹתוֹ׃

46:9 They shall not go back through the gate by which they came in *Yechezkel* outlines a series of regulations regarding the orderly flow of worship in the third Temple. Though his instructions appear technical in nature, they contain important spiritual messages. The people are required to come to *Yerushalayim* three times a year during the pilgrimage festivals of *Pesach*, *Shavuot*, and *Sukkot*. All pilgrims were expected to leave the *Beit Hamikdash* courtyard from the gate on the opposite side from where they had entered. One suggestion to explain this procedure is that it incorporates a sense of variety, so that worshippers at the Holy Temple will feel enhanced excitement as they enter, and even as they exit, the complex.

1322

Yechezkel/Ezekiel
Chapter 46

יחזקאל
פרק מו

14 And every morning regularly you shall offer a meal offering with it: a sixth of an *efah*, with a third of a *hin* of oil to moisten the choice flour, as a meal offering to *Hashem* – a law for all time.

יד וּמִנְחָה תַעֲשֶׂה עָלָיו בַּבֹּקֶר בַּבֹּקֶר שִׁשִּׁית הָאֵיפָה וְשֶׁמֶן שְׁלִישִׁית הַהִין לָרֹס אֶת־הַסֹּלֶת מִנְחָה לַיהֹוָה חֻקּוֹת עוֹלָם תָּמִיד:

15 The lamb, the meal offering, and oil shall be presented every morning as a regular burnt offering.

טו וְעָשׂוּ [יַעֲשׂוּ] אֶת־הַכֶּבֶשׂ וְאֶת־הַמִּנְחָה וְאֶת־הַשֶּׁמֶן בַּבֹּקֶר בַּבֹּקֶר עוֹלַת תָּמִיד:

16 Thus said *Hashem*: If the prince makes a gift to any of his sons, it shall become the latter's inheritance; it shall pass on to his sons; it is their holding by inheritance.

טז כֹּה־אָמַר אֲדֹנָי יְהֹוִה כִּי־יִתֵּן הַנָּשִׂיא מַתָּנָה לְאִישׁ מִבָּנָיו נַחֲלָתוֹ הִיא לְבָנָיו תִּהְיֶה אֲחֻזָּתָם הִיא בְּנַחֲלָה:

17 But if he makes a gift from his inheritance to any of his subjects, it shall only belong to the latter until the year of release. Then it shall revert to the prince; his inheritance must by all means pass on to his sons.

יז וְכִי־יִתֵּן מַתָּנָה מִנַּחֲלָתוֹ לְאַחַד מֵעֲבָדָיו וְהָיְתָה לּוֹ עַד־שְׁנַת הַדְּרוֹר וְשָׁבַת לַנָּשִׂיא אַךְ נַחֲלָתוֹ בָּנָיו לָהֶם תִּהְיֶה:

18 But the prince shall not take property away from any of the people and rob them of their holdings. Only out of his own holdings shall he endow his sons, in order that My people may not be dispossessed of their holdings.

יח וְלֹא־יִקַּח הַנָּשִׂיא מִנַּחֲלַת הָעָם לְהוֹנֹתָם מֵאֲחֻזָּתָם מֵאֲחֻזָּתוֹ יַנְחִל אֶת־בָּנָיו לְמַעַן אֲשֶׁר לֹא־יָפֻצוּ עַמִּי אִישׁ מֵאֲחֻזָּתוֹ:

19 Then he led me into the passage at the side of the gate to the sacred chambers of the *Kohanim*, which face north, and there, at the rear of it, in the west, I saw a space.

יט וַיְבִיאֵנִי בַמָּבוֹא אֲשֶׁר עַל־כֶּתֶף הַשַּׁעַר אֶל־הַלִּשְׁכוֹת הַקֹּדֶשׁ אֶל־הַכֹּהֲנִים הַפֹּנוֹת צָפוֹנָה וְהִנֵּה־שָׁם מָקוֹם בירכתם [בַּיַּרְכָתַיִם] יָמָּה:

20 He said to me, "This is the place where the *Kohanim* shall boil the guilt offerings and the sin offerings, and where they shall bake the meal offerings, so as not to take them into the outer court and make the people consecrated."

כ וַיֹּאמֶר אֵלַי זֶה הַמָּקוֹם אֲשֶׁר יְבַשְּׁלוּ־שָׁם הַכֹּהֲנִים אֶת־הָאָשָׁם וְאֶת־הַחַטָּאת אֲשֶׁר יֹאפוּ אֶת־הַמִּנְחָה לְבִלְתִּי הוֹצִיא אֶל־הֶחָצֵר הַחִיצוֹנָה לְקַדֵּשׁ אֶת־הָעָם:

21 Then he led me into the outer court and led me past the four corners of the court; and in each corner of the court there was an enclosure.

כא וַיּוֹצִיאֵנִי אֶל־הֶחָצֵר הַחִיצֹנָה וַיַּעֲבִירֵנִי אֶל־אַרְבַּעַת מִקְצוֹעֵי הֶחָצֵר וְהִנֵּה חָצֵר בְּמִקְצֹעַ הֶחָצֵר חָצֵר בְּמִקְצֹעַ הֶחָצֵר:

22 These unroofed enclosures, [each] 40 [*amot*] long and 30 wide, were in the four corners of the court; the four corner enclosures had the same measurements.

כב בְּאַרְבַּעַת מִקְצֹעוֹת הֶחָצֵר חֲצֵרוֹת קְטֻרוֹת אַרְבָּעִים אֹרֶךְ וּשְׁלֹשִׁים רֹחַב מִדָּה אַחַת לְאַרְבַּעְתָּם מְהֻקְצָעוֹת:

23 [On the inside,] running round the four of them, there was a row of masonry, equipped with hearths under the rows all around.

כג וְטוּר סָבִיב בָּהֶם סָבִיב לְאַרְבַּעְתָּם וּמְבַשְּׁלוֹת עָשׂוּי מִתַּחַת הַטִּירוֹת סָבִיב:

24 He said to me, "These are the kitchens where the Temple servitors shall boil the sacrifices of the people."

כד וַיֹּאמֶר אֵלָי אֵלֶּה בֵּית הַמְבַשְּׁלִים אֲשֶׁר יְבַשְּׁלוּ־שָׁם מְשָׁרְתֵי הַבַּיִת אֶת־זֶבַח הָעָם:

Yechezkel/Ezekiel

Chapter 47

47 1 He led me back to the entrance of the Temple, and I found that water was issuing from below the platform of the Temple – eastward, since the Temple faced east – but the water was running out at the south of the *Mizbayach*, under the south wall of the Temple.

2 Then he led me out by way of the northern gate and led me around to the outside of the outer gate that faces in the direction of the east; and I found that water was gushing from [under] the south wall.

3 As the man went on eastward with a measuring line in his hand, he measured off a thousand *amot* and led me across the water; the water was ankle deep.

4 Then he measured off another thousand and led me across the water; the water was knee deep. He measured off a further thousand and led me across the water; the water was up to the waist.

5 When he measured yet another thousand, it was a stream I could not cross; for the water had swollen into a stream that could not be crossed except by swimming.

6 "Do you see, O mortal?" he said to me; and he led me back to the bank of the stream.

7 As I came back, I saw trees in great profusion on both banks of the stream.

8 "This water," he told me, "runs out to the eastern region, and flows into the Arabah; and when it comes into the sea, into the sea of foul waters, the water will become wholesome.

9 Every living creature that swarms will be able to live wherever this stream goes; the fish will be very abundant once these waters have reached there. It will be wholesome, and everything will live wherever this stream goes.

10 Fishermen shall stand beside it all the way from *Ein Gedi* to En-eglaim; it shall be a place for drying nets; and the fish will be of various kinds [and] most plentiful, like the fish of the Great Sea.

11 But its swamps and marshes shall not become wholesome; they will serve to [supply] salt.

יחזקאל
פרק מז

מז א וַיְשִׁבֵנִי אֶל־פֶּתַח הַבַּיִת וְהִנֵּה־מַיִם יֹצְאִים מִתַּחַת מִפְתַּן הַבַּיִת קָדִימָה כִּי־פְנֵי הַבַּיִת קָדִים וְהַמַּיִם יֹרְדִים מִתַּחַת מִכֶּתֶף הַבַּיִת הַיְמָנִית מִנֶּגֶב לַמִּזְבֵּחַ:

ב וַיּוֹצִאֵנִי דֶּרֶךְ־שַׁעַר צָפוֹנָה וַיְסִבֵּנִי דֶּרֶךְ חוּץ אֶל־שַׁעַר הַחוּץ דֶּרֶךְ הַפּוֹנֶה קָדִים וְהִנֵּה־מַיִם מְפַכִּים מִן־הַכָּתֵף הַיְמָנִית:

ג בְּצֵאת־הָאִישׁ קָדִים וְקָו בְּיָדוֹ וַיָּמָד אֶלֶף בָּאַמָּה וַיַּעֲבִרֵנִי בַמַּיִם מֵי אָפְסָיִם:

ד וַיָּמָד אֶלֶף וַיַּעֲבִרֵנִי בַמַּיִם מַיִם בִּרְכָּיִם וַיָּמָד אֶלֶף וַיַּעֲבִרֵנִי מֵי מָתְנָיִם:

ה וַיָּמָד אֶלֶף נַחַל אֲשֶׁר לֹא־אוּכַל לַעֲבֹר כִּי־גָאוּ הַמַּיִם מֵי שָׂחוּ נַחַל אֲשֶׁר לֹא־יֵעָבֵר:

ו וַיֹּאמֶר אֵלַי הֲרָאִיתָ בֶן־אָדָם וַיּוֹלִכֵנִי וַיְשִׁבֵנִי שְׂפַת הַנָּחַל:

ז בְּשׁוּבֵנִי וְהִנֵּה אֶל־שְׂפַת הַנַּחַל עֵץ רַב מְאֹד מִזֶּה וּמִזֶּה:

ח וַיֹּאמֶר אֵלַי הַמַּיִם הָאֵלֶּה יוֹצְאִים אֶל־הַגְּלִילָה הַקַּדְמוֹנָה וְיָרְדוּ עַל־הָעֲרָבָה וּבָאוּ הַיָּמָּה אֶל־הַיָּמָּה הַמּוּצָאִים וְנִרְפְּאוּ [וְנִרְפּוּ] הַמָּיִם:

ט וְהָיָה כָל־נֶפֶשׁ חַיָּה אֲשֶׁר־יִשְׁרֹץ אֶל כָּל־אֲשֶׁר יָבוֹא שָׁם נַחֲלַיִם יִחְיֶה וְהָיָה הַדָּגָה רַבָּה מְאֹד כִּי בָאוּ שָׁמָּה הַמַּיִם הָאֵלֶּה וְיֵרָפְאוּ וָחָי כֹּל אֲשֶׁר־יָבוֹא שָׁמָּה הַנָּחַל:

י וְהָיָה יַעַמְדוּ [עָמְדוּ] עָלָיו דַּוָּגִים מֵעֵין גֶּדִי וְעַד־עֵין עֶגְלַיִם מִשְׁטוֹחַ לַחֲרָמִים יִהְיוּ לְמִינָה תִּהְיֶה דְגָתָם כִּדְגַת הַיָּם הַגָּדוֹל רַבָּה מְאֹד:

יא בִּצֹּאתוֹ [בִּצֹּאתָיו] וּגְבָאָיו וְלֹא יֵרָפְאוּ לְמֶלַח נִתָּנוּ:

1324

Yechezkel/Ezekiel
Chapter 47

יחזקאל
פרק מז

12 All kinds of trees for food will grow up on both banks of the stream. Their leaves will not wither nor their fruit fail; they will yield new fruit every month, because the water for them flows from the Temple. Their fruit will serve for food and their leaves for healing."

יב וְעַל־הַנַּחַל יַעֲלֶה עַל־שְׂפָתוֹ מִזֶּה וּמִזֶּה כָּל־עֵץ־מַאֲכָל לֹא־יִבּוֹל עָלֵהוּ וְלֹא־יִתֹּם פִּרְיוֹ לָחֳדָשָׁיו יְבַכֵּר כִּי מֵימָיו מִן־הַמִּקְדָּשׁ הֵמָּה יוֹצְאִים וְהָיוּ [וְהָיָה] פִרְיוֹ לְמַאֲכָל וְעָלֵהוּ לִתְרוּפָה:

13 Thus said *Hashem*: These shall be the boundaries of the land that you shall allot to the twelve tribes of *Yisrael*. *Yosef* shall receive two portions,

יג כֹּה אָמַר אֲדֹנָי יְהוִה גֵּה גְבוּל אֲשֶׁר תִּתְנַחֲלוּ אֶת־הָאָרֶץ לִשְׁנֵי עָשָׂר שִׁבְטֵי יִשְׂרָאֵל יוֹסֵף חֲבָלִים:

14 and you shall share the rest equally. As I swore to give it to your fathers, so shall this land fall to you as your heritage.

יד וּנְחַלְתֶּם אוֹתָהּ אִישׁ כְּאָחִיו אֲשֶׁר נָשָׂאתִי אֶת־יָדִי לְתִתָּהּ לַאֲבֹתֵיכֶם וְנָפְלָה הָאָרֶץ הַזֹּאת לָכֶם בְּנַחֲלָה:

un-khal-TEM o-TAH EESH k'-a-KHEEV a-SHER na-SA-tee et ya-DEE l'-ti-TAH la-a-vo-tay-KHEM v'-NA-f'-LAH ha-A-retz ha-ZOT la-KHEM b'-na-kha-LAH

15 These are the boundaries of the land: As the northern limit: From the Great Sea by way of Hethlon, Lebo-hamath,* Zedad,

טו וְזֶה גְּבוּל הָאָרֶץ לִפְאַת צָפוֹנָה מִן־הַיָּם הַגָּדוֹל הַדֶּרֶךְ חֶתְלֹן לְבוֹא צְדָדָה:

16 Berathah, Sibraim – which lies between the border of Damascus and the border of Hamath – [down to] Hazer-hatticon, which is on the border of Hauran.

טז חֲמָת בֵּרוֹתָה סִבְרַיִם אֲשֶׁר בֵּין־גְּבוּל דַּמֶּשֶׂק וּבֵין גְּבוּל חֲמָת חָצֵר הַתִּיכוֹן אֲשֶׁר אֶל־גְּבוּל חַוְרָן:

17 Thus the boundary shall run from the Sea to Hazar-enon, to the north of the territory of Damascus, with the territory of Hamath to the north of it. That shall be the northern limit.

יז וְהָיָה גְבוּל מִן־הַיָּם חֲצַר עֵינוֹן גְּבוּל דַּמֶּשֶׂק וְצָפוֹן צָפוֹנָה וּגְבוּל חֲמָת וְאֵת פְּאַת צָפוֹן:

18 As the eastern limit: A line between Hauran and Damascus, and between *Gilad* and the land of *Yisrael*: with the *Yarden* as a boundary, you shall measure down to the Eastern Sea. That shall be the eastern limit.

יח וּפְאַת קָדִים מִבֵּין חַוְרָן וּמִבֵּין־דַּמֶּשֶׂק וּמִבֵּין הַגִּלְעָד וּמִבֵּין אֶרֶץ יִשְׂרָאֵל הַיַּרְדֵּן מִגְּבוּל עַל־הַיָּם הַקַּדְמוֹנִי תָּמֹדּוּ וְאֵת פְּאַת קָדִימָה:

19 The southern limit shall run: A line from Tamar to the waters of Meriboth-kadesh, along the Wadi [of Egypt and] the Great Sea. That is the southern limit.

יט וּפְאַת נֶגֶב תֵּימָנָה מִתָּמָר עַד־מֵי מְרִיבוֹת קָדֵשׁ נַחֲלָה אֶל־הַיָּם הַגָּדוֹל וְאֵת פְּאַת־תֵּימָנָה נֶגְבָּה:

20 And as the western limit: The Great Sea shall be the boundary up to a point opposite Lebo-hamath. That shall be the western limit.

כ וּפְאַת־יָם הַיָּם הַגָּדוֹל מִגְּבוּל עַד־נֹכַח לְבוֹא חֲמָת זֹאת פְּאַת־יָם:

---

* "hamath" brought up from verse 16 for clarity

נחלה
נחל

47:14 So shall this land fall to you as your heritage. In biblical Hebrew, the word for 'inheritance' is *nachalah* (נחלה). The root of this word, *nakhal* (נחל), also means 'a flowing stream,' as in *Devarim* (8:7), "a land with streams and springs and fountains." These two ideas are connected: Just like a stream of water flows downward, so too, the inheritance of a precious legacy passes from one generation to the next. Such is the connection between the Children of Israel and the Land of Israel. Their inheritance was given to *Avraham* to be passed down to *Yitzchak* and to all subsequent generations.

Yechezkel/Ezekiel
Chapter 48

יחזקאל
פרק מח

21 This land you shall divide for yourselves among the tribes of *Yisrael*.

כא וְחִלַּקְתֶּם אֶת־הָאָרֶץ הַזֹּאת לָכֶם לְשִׁבְטֵי יִשְׂרָאֵל׃

22 You shall allot it as a heritage for yourselves and for the strangers who reside among you, who have begotten children among you. You shall treat them as Israelite citizens; they shall receive allotments along with you among the tribes of *Yisrael*.

כב וְהָיָה תַּפִּלוּ אוֹתָהּ בְּנַחֲלָה לָכֶם וּלְהַגֵּרִים הַגָּרִים בְּתוֹכְכֶם אֲשֶׁר־הוֹלִדוּ בָנִים בְּתוֹכְכֶם וְהָיוּ לָכֶם כְּאֶזְרָח בִּבְנֵי יִשְׂרָאֵל אִתְּכֶם יִפְּלוּ בְנַחֲלָה בְּתוֹךְ שִׁבְטֵי יִשְׂרָאֵל׃

23 You shall give the stranger an allotment within the tribe where he resides – declares *Hashem*.

כג וְהָיָה בַשֵּׁבֶט אֲשֶׁר־גָּר הַגֵּר אִתּוֹ שָׁם תִּתְּנוּ נַחֲלָתוֹ נְאֻם אֲדֹנָי יֱהֹוִה׃

48

1 These are the names of the tribes: At the northern end, along the Hethlon road, [from] Lebo-hamath to Hazar-enan – which is the border of Damascus, with Hamath to the north – from the eastern border to the Sea: *Dan* – one [tribe].

א וְאֵלֶּה שְׁמוֹת הַשְּׁבָטִים מִקְצֵה צָפוֹנָה אֶל־יַד דֶּרֶךְ־חֶתְלֹן לְבוֹא־חֲמָת חֲצַר עֵינָן גְּבוּל דַּמֶּשֶׂק צָפוֹנָה אֶל־יַד חֲמָת וְהָיוּ־לוֹ פְאַת־קָדִים הַיָּם דָּן אֶחָד׃

v'-AY-leh sh'-MOT ha-sh'-va-TEEM mik-TZAY tza-FO-nah el YAD de-rekh khet-LON l'-vo kha-MAT kha-TZAR ay-NAN g'-VUL da-ME-sek tza-FO-nah el YAD kha-MAT v'-ha-yu LO f'-at ka-DEEM ha-YAM DAN e-KHAD

2 Adjoining the territory of *Dan*, from the eastern border to the western border: *Asher* – one.

ב וְעַל גְּבוּל דָּן מִפְּאַת קָדִים עַד־פְּאַת־יָמָּה אָשֵׁר אֶחָד׃

3 Adjoining the territory of *Asher*, from the eastern border to the western border: *Naftali* – one.

ג וְעַל גְּבוּל אָשֵׁר מִפְּאַת קָדִימָה וְעַד־פְּאַת־יָמָּה נַפְתָּלִי אֶחָד׃

4 Adjoining the territory of *Naftali*, from the eastern border to the western border: *Menashe* – one.

ד וְעַל גְּבוּל נַפְתָּלִי מִפְּאַת קָדְמָה עַד־פְּאַת־יָמָּה מְנַשֶּׁה אֶחָד׃

5 Adjoining the territory of *Menashe*, from the eastern border to the western border: *Efraim* – one.

ה וְעַל גְּבוּל מְנַשֶּׁה מִפְּאַת קָדְמָה עַד־פְּאַת־יָמָּה אֶפְרַיִם אֶחָד׃

6 Adjoining the territory of *Efraim*, from the eastern border to the western border: *Reuven* – one.

ו וְעַל גְּבוּל אֶפְרַיִם מִפְּאַת קָדִים וְעַד־פְּאַת־יָמָּה רְאוּבֵן אֶחָד׃

7 Adjoining the territory of *Reuven*, from the eastern border to the western border: *Yehuda* – one.

ז וְעַל גְּבוּל רְאוּבֵן מִפְּאַת קָדִים עַד־פְּאַת־יָמָּה יְהוּדָה אֶחָד׃

8 Adjoining the territory of *Yehuda*, from the eastern border to the western border, shall be the reserve that you set aside: 25,000 [*amot*] in breadth and in length equal to one of the portions from the eastern border to the western border; the Sanctuary shall be in the middle of it.

ח וְעַל גְּבוּל יְהוּדָה מִפְּאַת קָדִים עַד־פְּאַת־יָמָּה תִּהְיֶה הַתְּרוּמָה אֲשֶׁר־תָּרִימוּ חֲמִשָּׁה וְעֶשְׂרִים אֶלֶף רֹחַב וְאֹרֶךְ כְּאַחַד הַחֲלָקִים מִפְּאַת קָדִימָה עַד־פְּאַת־יָמָּה וְהָיָה הַמִּקְדָּשׁ בְּתוֹכוֹ׃

48:1 From the eastern border to the Sea The final chapter of *Yechezkel* begins with the inheritance of the land and apportionment among the twelve tribes. By returning to the tribal arrangement, *Yechezkel* promises a return to traditional family groupings. This final lesson of *Yechezkel* teaches that the viability of Israel's existence in their ancestral land is intimately connected to the strength of the families who dwell within it. When feelings of love permeate and strengthen the families of Israel in *Eretz Yisrael*, then the God of Israel blesses His people and dwells among them in eternal harmony.

Yechezkel/Ezekiel
Chapter 48

9 The reserve that you set aside for *Hashem* shall be 25,000 long and 10,000 wide.

10 It shall be apportioned to the following: The sacred reserve for the *Kohanim* shall measure 25,000 [*amot*] on the north, 10,000 on the west, 10,000 on the east, and 25,000 on the south, with *Hashem*'s Sanctuary in the middle of it.

11 This consecrated area shall be for the *Kohanim* of the line of *Tzadok*, who kept My charge and did not go astray, as the *Leviim* did when the people of *Yisrael* went astray.

12 It shall be a special reserve for them out of the [total] reserve from the land, most holy, adjoining the territory of the *Leviim*.

13 Alongside the territory of the *Kohanim*, the *Leviim* shall have [an area] 25,000 long by 10,000 wide; the total length shall be 25,000 and the breadth 10,000.

14 None of it – the choicest of the land – may be sold, exchanged, or transferred; it is sacred to *Hashem*.

15 The remaining 5,000 in breadth by 25,000 shall be for common use – serving the city for dwellings and pasture. The city itself shall be in the middle of it;

16 and these shall be its measurements: On the north side 4,500 *amot*, on the south side 4,500, on the east side 4,500, and on the west side 4,500.

17 The pasture shall extend 250 *amot* to the north of the city, 250 to the south, 250 to the east, and 250 to the west.

18 As for the remaining 10,000 to the east and 10,000 to the west, adjoining the long side of the sacred reserve, the produce of these areas adjoining the sacred reserve shall serve as food for the workers in the city;

19 the workers in the city from all the tribes of *Yisrael* shall cultivate it.

יחזקאל
פרק מח

ט הַתְּרוּמָה אֲשֶׁר תָּרִימוּ לַיהוָה אֹרֶךְ חֲמִשָּׁה וְעֶשְׂרִים אֶלֶף וְרֹחַב עֲשֶׂרֶת אֲלָפִים:

י וּלְאֵלֶּה תִּהְיֶה תְרוּמַת־הַקֹּדֶשׁ לַכֹּהֲנִים צָפוֹנָה חֲמִשָּׁה וְעֶשְׂרִים אֶלֶף וְיָמָּה רֹחַב עֲשֶׂרֶת אֲלָפִים וְקָדִימָה רֹחַב עֲשֶׂרֶת אֲלָפִים וְנֶגְבָּה אֹרֶךְ חֲמִשָּׁה וְעֶשְׂרִים אָלֶף וְהָיָה מִקְדַּשׁ־יְהוָה בְּתוֹכוֹ:

יא לַכֹּהֲנִים הַמְקֻדָּשׁ מִבְּנֵי צָדוֹק אֲשֶׁר שָׁמְרוּ מִשְׁמַרְתִּי אֲשֶׁר לֹא־תָעוּ בִּתְעוֹת בְּנֵי יִשְׂרָאֵל כַּאֲשֶׁר תָּעוּ הַלְוִיִּם:

יב וְהָיְתָה לָהֶם תְּרוּמִיָּה מִתְּרוּמַת הָאָרֶץ קֹדֶשׁ קָדָשִׁים אֶל־גְּבוּל הַלְוִיִּם:

יג וְהַלְוִיִּם לְעֻמַּת גְּבוּל הַכֹּהֲנִים חֲמִשָּׁה וְעֶשְׂרִים אֶלֶף אֹרֶךְ וְרֹחַב עֲשֶׂרֶת אֲלָפִים כָּל־אֹרֶךְ חֲמִשָּׁה וְעֶשְׂרִים אֶלֶף וְרֹחַב עֲשֶׂרֶת אֲלָפִים:

יד וְלֹא־יִמְכְּרוּ מִמֶּנּוּ וְלֹא יָמֵר וְלֹא יַעֲבוֹר [יַעֲבִיר] רֵאשִׁית הָאָרֶץ כִּי־קֹדֶשׁ לַיהוָה:

טו וַחֲמֵשֶׁת אֲלָפִים הַנּוֹתָר בָּרֹחַב עַל־פְּנֵי חֲמִשָּׁה וְעֶשְׂרִים אֶלֶף חֹל־הוּא לָעִיר לְמוֹשָׁב וּלְמִגְרָשׁ וְהָיְתָה הָעִיר בְּתוֹכֹה [בְּתוֹכוֹ]:

טז וְאֵלֶּה מִדּוֹתֶיהָ פְּאַת צָפוֹן חֲמֵשׁ מֵאוֹת וְאַרְבַּעַת אֲלָפִים וּפְאַת־נֶגֶב חֲמֵשׁ חֲמֵשׁ מֵאוֹת וְאַרְבַּעַת אֲלָפִים וּמִפְּאַת קָדִים חֲמֵשׁ מֵאוֹת וְאַרְבַּעַת אֲלָפִים וּפְאַת־יָמָּה חֲמֵשׁ מֵאוֹת וְאַרְבַּעַת אֲלָפִים:

יז וְהָיָה מִגְרָשׁ לָעִיר צָפוֹנָה חֲמִשִּׁים וּמָאתַיִם וְנֶגְבָּה חֲמִשִּׁים וּמָאתָיִם וְקָדִימָה חֲמִשִּׁים וּמָאתַיִם וְיָמָּה חֲמִשִּׁים וּמָאתָיִם:

יח וְהַנּוֹתָר בָּאֹרֶךְ לְעֻמַּת תְּרוּמַת הַקֹּדֶשׁ עֲשֶׂרֶת אֲלָפִים קָדִימָה וַעֲשֶׂרֶת אֲלָפִים יָמָּה וְהָיָה לְעֻמַּת תְּרוּמַת הַקֹּדֶשׁ וְהָיְתָה תְבוּאָתֹה [תְבוּאָתוֹ] לְלֶחֶם לְעֹבְדֵי הָעִיר:

יט וְהָעֹבֵד הָעִיר יַעַבְדוּהוּ מִכֹּל שִׁבְטֵי יִשְׂרָאֵל:

Yechezkel/Ezekiel
Chapter 48

יחזקאל
פרק מח

20 The entire reserve, 25,000 square, you shall set aside as the sacred reserve plus the city property.

כ כָּל־הַתְּרוּמָה חֲמִשָּׁה וְעֶשְׂרִים אֶלֶף בַּחֲמִשָּׁה וְעֶשְׂרִים אָלֶף רְבִיעִית תָּרִימוּ אֶת־תְּרוּמַת הַקֹּדֶשׁ אֶל־אֲחֻזַּת הָעִיר:

21 What remains on either side of the sacred reserve and the city property shall belong to the prince. The prince shall own [the land] from the border of the 25,000 of the reserve up to the eastern boundary, and from the border of the 25,000 on the west up to the western boundary, corresponding to the [tribal] portions. The sacred reserve, with the Temple Sanctuary in the middle of it

כא וְהַנּוֹתָר לַנָּשִׂיא מִזֶּה וּמִזֶּה לִתְרוּמַת־הַקֹּדֶשׁ וְלַאֲחֻזַּת הָעִיר אֶל־פְּנֵי חֲמִשָּׁה וְעֶשְׂרִים אֶלֶף תְּרוּמָה עַד־גְּבוּל קָדִימָה וְיָמָּה עַל־פְּנֵי חֲמִשָּׁה וְעֶשְׂרִים אֶלֶף עַל־גְּבוּל יָמָּה לְעֻמַּת חֲלָקִים לַנָּשִׂיא וְהָיְתָה תְּרוּמַת הַקֹּדֶשׁ וּמִקְדַּשׁ הַבַּיִת בתוכה [בְּתוֹכוֹ]:

22 and the property of the *Leviim* and the city property as well, shall be in the middle of the [area belonging] to the prince; [the rest of the land] between the territory of *Yehuda* and the territory of *Binyamin* shall belong to the prince.

כב וּמֵאֲחֻזַּת הַלְוִיִּם וּמֵאֲחֻזַּת הָעִיר בְּתוֹךְ אֲשֶׁר לַנָּשִׂיא יִהְיֶה בֵּין גְּבוּל יְהוּדָה וּבֵין גְּבוּל בִּנְיָמִן לַנָּשִׂיא יִהְיֶה:

23 As for the remaining tribes: From the eastern border to the western border: *Binyamin* – one.

כג וְיֶתֶר הַשְּׁבָטִים מִפְּאַת קָדִימָה עַד־פְּאַת־יָמָּה בִּנְיָמִן אֶחָד:

24 Adjoining the territory of *Binyamin*, from the eastern border to the western border: *Shimon* – one.

כד וְעַל גְּבוּל בִּנְיָמִן מִפְּאַת קָדִימָה עַד־פְּאַת־יָמָּה שִׁמְעוֹן אֶחָד:

25 Adjoining the territory of *Shimon*, from the eastern border to the western border: *Yissachar* – one.

כה וְעַל גְּבוּל שִׁמְעוֹן מִפְּאַת קָדִימָה עַד־פְּאַת־יָמָּה יִשָּׂשכָר אֶחָד:

26 Adjoining the territory of *Yissachar*, from the eastern border to the western border: *Zevulun* – one.

כו וְעַל גְּבוּל יִשָּׂשכָר מִפְּאַת קָדִימָה עַד־פְּאַת־יָמָּה זְבוּלֻן אֶחָד:

27 Adjoining the territory of *Zevulun*, from the eastern border to the western border: *Gad* – one.

כז וְעַל גְּבוּל זְבוּלֻן מִפְּאַת קָדִמָה עַד־פְּאַת־יָמָּה גָּד אֶחָד:

28 The other border of *Gad* shall be the southern boundary. This boundary shall run from *Tamar* to the waters of Meribath-kadesh, to the Wadi [of Egypt], and to the Great Sea.

כח וְעַל גְּבוּל גָּד אֶל־פְּאַת נֶגֶב תֵּימָנָה וְהָיָה גְבוּל מִתָּמָר מֵי מְרִיבַת קָדֵשׁ נַחֲלָה עַל־הַיָּם הַגָּדוֹל:

29 That is the land which you shall allot as a heritage to the tribes of *Yisrael*, and those are their portions – declares *Hashem*.

כט זֹאת הָאָרֶץ אֲשֶׁר־תַּפִּילוּ מִנַּחֲלָה לְשִׁבְטֵי יִשְׂרָאֵל וְאֵלֶּה מַחְלְקוֹתָם נְאֻם אֲדֹנָי יֱהֹוִה:

30 And these are the exits from the city: On its northern side, measuring 4,500 *amot*,

ל וְאֵלֶּה תּוֹצְאֹת הָעִיר מִפְּאַת צָפוֹן חֲמֵשׁ מֵאוֹת וְאַרְבַּעַת אֲלָפִים מִדָּה:

31 the gates of the city shall be – three gates on the north – named for the tribes of *Yisrael*: the *Reuven* Gate: one; the *Yehuda* Gate: one; the *Levi* Gate: one.

לא וְשַׁעֲרֵי הָעִיר עַל־שְׁמוֹת שִׁבְטֵי יִשְׂרָאֵל שְׁעָרִים שְׁלוֹשָׁה צָפוֹנָה שַׁעַר רְאוּבֵן אֶחָד שַׁעַר יְהוּדָה אֶחָד שַׁעַר לֵוִי אֶחָד:

Yechezkel/Ezekiel
Chapter 48

32 On the eastern side, [measuring] 4,500 *amot* – there shall be three gates: the *Yosef* Gate: one; the *Binyamin* Gate: one; and the *Dan* Gate: one.

33 On the southern side, measuring 4,500 *amot*, there shall be three gates: the *Shimon* Gate: one; the *Yissachar* Gate: one; and the *Zevulun* Gate: one.

34 And on the western side, [measuring] 4,500 *amot* – there shall be three gates: the *Gad* Gate: one; the *Asher* Gate: one; the *Naftali* Gate: one.

35 Its circumference [shall be] 18,000 [*amot*]; and the name of the city from that day on shall be "Hashem Is There."

יחזקאל
פרק מח

לב וְאֶל־פְּאַת קָדִימָה חֲמֵשׁ מֵאוֹת וְאַרְבַּעַת אֲלָפִים וּשְׁעָרִים שְׁלֹשָׁה וְשַׁעַר יוֹסֵף אֶחָד שַׁעַר בִּנְיָמִן אֶחָד שַׁעַר דָּן אֶחָד׃

לג וּפְאַת־נֶגְבָּה חֲמֵשׁ מֵאוֹת וְאַרְבַּעַת אֲלָפִים מִדָּה וּשְׁעָרִים שְׁלֹשָׁה שַׁעַר שִׁמְעוֹן אֶחָד שַׁעַר יִשָּׂשכָר אֶחָד שַׁעַר זְבוּלֻן אֶחָד׃

לד פְּאַת־יָמָּה חֲמֵשׁ מֵאוֹת וְאַרְבַּעַת אֲלָפִים שַׁעֲרֵיהֶם שְׁלֹשָׁה שַׁעַר גָּד אֶחָד שַׁעַר אָשֵׁר אֶחָד שַׁעַר נַפְתָּלִי אֶחָד׃

לה סָבִיב שְׁמֹנָה עָשָׂר אָלֶף וְשֵׁם־הָעִיר מִיּוֹם יְהוָֹה שָׁמָּה׃

Sefer Trei Asar
The Book of the Twelve Prophets

Introduction and commentary by Rabbi Yaakov Beasley

The last book of the Prophets contains the prophecies of twelve distinct prophets, and is known as *Trei Asar* (תרי עשר), meaning 'twelve' in Aramaic. In English, it is sometimes referred to as the "Twelve Minor Prophets," a moniker that describes only their relatively short messages, but not their importance.

From the Dead Sea Scrolls and the work of Ben Sirach, we know that these twelve prophetic texts were grouped together as one book already by the second century BCE. The era of the *Trei Asar* ranges from the middle of the eighth century BCE to the beginning of the fourth century BCE. *Hoshea, Yoel, Amos, Ovadya, Yona* and *Micha* prophesied during the eighth century BCE, when Assyria terrorized the entire Middle East including the kingdoms of *Yisrael* and *Yehuda*. *Nachum, Chavakuk* and *Tzefanya* lived in the seventh century BCE, when Assyria's even more vicious successor, Babylonia, threatened and eventually exiled the tiny kingdom of *Yehuda*. The final three prophets, *Chagai, Zecharya* and *Malachi* lived during the period of the return to *Tzion*, when the Jewish people returned to the Land of Israel after seventy years of Babylonian exile. These three prophets were active during a period spanning from the middle of the sixth century to the beginning of the fourth century BCE, and with the final prophecies of *Malachi* came the end of the age of prophecy.

Despite being separated from each other by over five hundred years, these prophets shared several messages which are relevant to this very day: Concern for the poor, an emphasis on justice and morality over uninspired ritual, the enduring bond between *Hashem* and His people, and the eternal relationship of the Jewish people to *Eretz Yisrael*.

Chart of the Twelve Prophets and When They Lived

Name	Time Period
Hoshea	A contemporary of the prophets *Yeshayahu*, *Amos* and *Micha*, *Hoshea* prophesied during the reigns of *Uzziyahu*, *Yotam*, *Achaz* and *Chizkiyahu* of the kingdom of *Yehuda*, and *Yerovam* son of *Yoash* of the kingdom of *Yisrael* (Hosea 1:1).
Yoel	*Rashi* quotes three different opinions from the Sages regarding when *Yoel* lived: (1) He was the son of *Shmuel* (see I Samuel 8:2), (2) He was a contemporary of *Elisha*, and (3) He prophesied during the reign of *Menashe*, king of *Yehuda*, along with *Nachum* and *Chavakuk*.
Amos	*Amos* was a contemporary of *Hoshea*, *Micha* and *Yeshayahu*. He prophesied to the kingdom of *Yisrael* during the reigns of *Uzziyahu* king of *Yehuda* and *Yerovam* son of *Yoash* king of *Yisrael* (Amos 1:1).
Ovadya	According to the Sages (*Sanhedrin* 39b), *Ovadya* was a convert from Edom who lived during the time of *Yehoshafat* king of *Yehuda* and *Achav* king of *Yisrael*. He was in charge of *Achav*'s household and hid 100 prophets from the wicked king and queen in order to save them from death (I Kings 18). They suggest that it is because he risked his own life to save the prophets that he merited prophecy. According to this opinion, he was a contemporary of the prophet *Eliyahu*.
Yona	*Yona* is mentioned in *Sefer Melachim* II 14:25 as a prophet who lived during the reign of *Yerovam* son of *Yoash* in the northern kingdom of Israel.
Micha	*Micha* was a contemporary of *Yeshayahu*, *Hoshea* and *Amos*. He prophesied to the kingdom of *Yehuda* during the reigns of *Yotam*, *Achaz* and *Chizkiyahu* (Micah 1:1).
Nachum	According to the Sages, *Nachum* prophesied during the reign of *Menashe* king of *Yehuda* and was a contemporary of *Yoel* and *Chavakuk*.
Chavakuk	According to the Sages, *Chavakuk* prophesied during the reign of *Menashe* king of *Yehuda* along with *Yoel* and *Nachum*.
Tzefanya	*Tzefanya* prophesied during the reign of *Yoshiyahu* son of *Amon*, king of *Yehuda* (Zephaniah 1:1). He was a contemporary of *Yirmiyahu* and *Chulda* the prophetess.
Chagai	*Chagai* lived during the time of Darius, king of Persia (Haggai 1:1). He was a contemporary of *Zecharya*, and together they prophesied to the people of *Yehuda* who had returned to the Land of Israel in order to rebuild the *Beit Hamikdash* following the proclamation of Cyrus king of Persia. During his time, and because of his encouragement, the second *Beit Hamikdash* was built (Ezra 6:14).
Zecharya	*Zecharya* lived during the time of Darius, king of Persia (*Zecharya* 1:1). He was a contemporary of *Chagai*, and together they prophesied to the people of *Yehuda* who had returned to the Land of Israel in order to rebuild the *Beit Hamikdash* following the proclamation of Cyrus king of Persia. During his time, and because of his encouragement, the second *Beit Hamikdash* was built (Ezra 6:14).
Malachi	*Malachi* was the last of the prophets and lived at the beginning of the Second Temple period. Following his death, the period of prophecy ceased.

Sefer Hoshea
The Book of Hosea

The first of the *Trei Asar*, the book of *Hoshea* (Hosea) son of *Be'eri*, is one of the longest of the twelve, comprising fourteen chapters. *Hoshea* prophesies to the last generation before the Assyrian destruction of the northern kingdom of *Yisrael* in 722 BCE. In his prophecies, *Hoshea* denounces the corruption of the rich and powerful, whose indifference to injustice is leading the people towards certain destruction. While still outwardly powerful, the country's foundations have been weakened and undermined during years of lawlessness and violence. Though his message is stark and dire, his belief in the people's ability to repent and return is even greater, and *Hoshea* tries to convince them of the possibility of salvation, even when all seems lost. In its barest form, God's relationship with the people is founded on love, the love of a parent for an infant that He taught to walk (11:3), and the love of a husband for His betrothed (2:16).

The first three chapters of the book are autobiographical; *Hoshea* is commanded by God to marry a woman described as a harlot, and to have children with her. Through this marriage and the naming of his children, *Hoshea* creates one of the most powerful metaphors for the relationship between *Hashem* and Israel. The following chapters, 4–13, describe a litany of sins that the people committed, and the punishments that will inevitably follow. The final chapter is one of the most sublime calls for repentance in the Bible, and is traditionally read in synagogues on the Sabbath which occurs during the Days of Repentance, between *Rosh Hashana* and *Yom Kippur*.

Hoshea/Hosea
Chapter 1

הושע
פרק א

1 ¹ The word of *Hashem* that came to *Hoshea* son of *Be'eri*, in the reigns of Kings *Uzziyahu*, *Yotam*, *Achaz*, and *Chizkiyahu* of *Yehuda*, and in the reign of King *Yerovam* son of *Yoash* of *Yisrael*.

א דְּבַר־יְהֹוָה אֲשֶׁר הָיָה אֶל־הוֹשֵׁעַ בֶּן־בְּאֵרִי בִּימֵי עֻזִּיָּה יוֹתָם אָחָז יְחִזְקִיָּה מַלְכֵי יְהוּדָה וּבִימֵי יָרָבְעָם בֶּן־יוֹאָשׁ מֶלֶךְ יִשְׂרָאֵל׃

² When *Hashem* first spoke to *Hoshea*, *Hashem* said to *Hoshea*, "Go, get yourself a wife of whoredom and children of whoredom; for the land will stray from following *Hashem*."

ב תְּחִלַּת דִּבֶּר־יְהֹוָה בְּהוֹשֵׁעַ וַיֹּאמֶר יְהֹוָה אֶל־הוֹשֵׁעַ לֵךְ קַח־לְךָ אֵשֶׁת זְנוּנִים וְיַלְדֵי זְנוּנִים כִּי־זָנֹה תִזְנֶה הָאָרֶץ מֵאַחֲרֵי יְהֹוָה׃

³ So he went and married Gomer daughter of Diblaim. She conceived and bore him a son,

ג וַיֵּלֶךְ וַיִּקַּח אֶת־גֹּמֶר בַּת־דִּבְלָיִם וַתַּהַר וַתֵּלֶד־לוֹ בֵּן׃

⁴ and *Hashem* instructed him, "Name him *Yizrael*; for, I will soon punish the House of *Yehu* for the bloody deeds at *Yizrael* and put an end to the monarchy of the House of *Yisrael*.

ד וַיֹּאמֶר יְהֹוָה אֵלָיו קְרָא שְׁמוֹ יִזְרְעֶאל כִּי־עוֹד מְעַט וּפָקַדְתִּי אֶת־דְּמֵי יִזְרְעֶאל עַל־בֵּית יֵהוּא וְהִשְׁבַּתִּי מַמְלְכוּת בֵּית יִשְׂרָאֵל׃

va-YO-mer a-do-NAI ay-LAV k'-RA sh'-MO yiz-r'-EL kee OD m'-AT u-FA-kad-TEE et d'-MAY yiz-r'-EL al BAYT yay-HU v'-HISH-ba-TEE mam-l'-KHUT BAYT yis-ra-AYL

⁵ In that day, I will break the bow of *Yisrael* in the Valley of *Yizrael*."

ה וְהָיָה בַּיּוֹם הַהוּא וְשָׁבַרְתִּי אֶת־קֶשֶׁת יִשְׂרָאֵל בְּעֵמֶק יִזְרְעֶאל׃

⁶ She conceived again and bore a daughter; and He said to him, "Name her Lo-ruhamah; for I will no longer accept the House of *Yisrael* or pardon them.

ו וַתַּהַר עוֹד וַתֵּלֶד בַּת וַיֹּאמֶר לוֹ קְרָא שְׁמָהּ לֹא רֻחָמָה כִּי לֹא אוֹסִיף עוֹד אֲרַחֵם אֶת־בֵּית יִשְׂרָאֵל כִּי־נָשֹׂא אֶשָּׂא לָהֶם׃

⁷ But I will accept the House of *Yehuda*. And I will give them victory through *Hashem* their God; I will not give them victory with bow and sword and battle, by horses and riders.)"

ז וְאֶת־בֵּית יְהוּדָה אֲרַחֵם וְהוֹשַׁעְתִּים בַּיהֹוָה אֱלֹהֵיהֶם וְלֹא אוֹשִׁיעֵם בְּקֶשֶׁת וּבְחֶרֶב וּבְמִלְחָמָה בְּסוּסִים וּבְפָרָשִׁים׃

⁸ After weaning Lo-ruhamah, she conceived and bore a son.

ח וַתִּגְמֹל אֶת־לֹא רֻחָמָה וַתַּהַר וַתֵּלֶד בֵּן׃

⁹ Then He said, "Name him Lo-ammi; for you are not My people, and I will not be your [*Hashem*]."

ט וַיֹּאמֶר קְרָא שְׁמוֹ לֹא עַמִּי כִּי אַתֶּם לֹא עַמִּי וְאָנֹכִי לֹא־אֶהְיֶה לָכֶם׃

1:4 I will soon punish the House of *Yehu* for the bloody deeds at *Yizrael* *Hoshea* describes how the nation's present troubles stem from the manner in which the ruling dynasty of the kingdom of Israel, the house of *Yehu*, had achieved power. The *Yizrael* valley runs through the northern hills of Israel, from Megiddo to *Beit Shean*, and was one of the major highways in antiquity. The ancient city of *Yizrael*, located on the western edge of the Gilboa mountain range, overlooked the valley and was a very important city for the northern kingdom of *Yisrael*. It was strategically located, affording great military advantage, and the nearby *Yizrael* spring provided ample water for the city as well as for travellers. It was there that the *coup d'état*, in which *Yehu* overthrew the idolatrous house of *Achav*, took place. Though originally supported by the prophet *Elisha*, the takeover became exceedingly violent and bloodthirsty, and *Hoshea* promises that *Yehu* will be punished accordingly. *Hoshea* reminds us that even when beginning with good intentions, power and authority can easily corrupt.

Tel Yizrael looking east toward Gilboa

Hoshea/Hosea
Chapter 2

הושע
פרק ב

2

1 The number of the people of *Yisrael* shall be like that of the sands of the sea, which cannot be measured or counted; and instead of being told, "You are Not-My-People," they shall be called Children-of-the-Living-*Hashem*.

א וְהָיָה מִסְפַּר בְּנֵי־יִשְׂרָאֵל כְּחוֹל הַיָּם אֲשֶׁר לֹא־יִמַּד וְלֹא יִסָּפֵר וְהָיָה בִּמְקוֹם אֲשֶׁר־יֵאָמֵר לָהֶם לֹא־עַמִּי אַתֶּם יֵאָמֵר לָהֶם בְּנֵי אֵל־חָי׃

2 The people of *Yehuda* and the people of *Yisrael* shall assemble together and appoint one head over them; and they shall rise from the ground – for marvelous shall be the day of *Yizrael*!

ב וְנִקְבְּצוּ בְּנֵי־יְהוּדָה וּבְנֵי־יִשְׂרָאֵל יַחְדָּו וְשָׂמוּ לָהֶם רֹאשׁ אֶחָד וְעָלוּ מִן־הָאָרֶץ כִּי גָדוֹל יוֹם יִזְרְעֶאל׃

3 Oh, call your brothers "My People," And your sisters "Lovingly Accepted!"

ג אִמְרוּ לַאֲחֵיכֶם עַמִּי וְלַאֲחוֹתֵיכֶם רֻחָמָה׃

4 Rebuke your mother, rebuke her – For she is not My wife And I am not her husband – And let her put away her harlotry from her face And her adultery from between her breasts.

ד רִיבוּ בְאִמְּכֶם רִיבוּ כִּי־הִיא לֹא אִשְׁתִּי וְאָנֹכִי לֹא אִישָׁהּ וְתָסֵר זְנוּנֶיהָ מִפָּנֶיהָ וְנַאֲפוּפֶיהָ מִבֵּין שָׁדֶיהָ׃

5 Else will I strip her naked And leave her as on the day she was born: And I will make her like a wilderness, Render her like desert land, And let her die of thirst.

ה פֶּן־אַפְשִׁיטֶנָּה עֲרֻמָּה וְהִצַּגְתִּיהָ כְּיוֹם הִוָּלְדָהּ וְשַׂמְתִּיהָ כַמִּדְבָּר וְשַׁתִּהָ כְּאֶרֶץ צִיָּה וַהֲמִתִּיהָ בַּצָּמָא׃

6 I will also disown her children; For they are now a harlot's brood,

ו וְאֶת־בָּנֶיהָ לֹא אֲרַחֵם כִּי־בְנֵי זְנוּנִים הֵמָּה׃

7 In that their mother has played the harlot, She that conceived them has acted shamelessly – Because she thought, "I will go after my lovers, Who supply my bread and my water, My wool and my linen, My oil and my drink."

ז כִּי זָנְתָה אִמָּם הֹבִישָׁה הוֹרָתָם כִּי אָמְרָה אֵלְכָה אַחֲרֵי מְאַהֲבַי נֹתְנֵי לַחְמִי וּמֵימַי צַמְרִי וּפִשְׁתִּי שַׁמְנִי וְשִׁקּוּיָי׃

8 Assuredly, I will hedge up her roads with thorns And raise walls against her, And she shall not find her paths.

ח לָכֵן הִנְנִי־שָׂךְ אֶת־דַּרְכֵּךְ בַּסִּירִים וְגָדַרְתִּי אֶת־גְּדֵרָהּ וּנְתִיבוֹתֶיהָ לֹא תִמְצָא׃

9 Pursue her lovers as she will, She shall not overtake them; And seek them as she may, She shall never find them. Then she will say, "I will go and return To my first husband, For then I fared better than now."

ט וְרִדְּפָה אֶת־מְאַהֲבֶיהָ וְלֹא־תַשִּׂיג אֹתָם וּבִקְשָׁתַם וְלֹא תִמְצָא וְאָמְרָה אֵלְכָה וְאָשׁוּבָה אֶל־אִישִׁי הָרִאשׁוֹן כִּי טוֹב לִי אָז מֵעָתָּה׃

10 And she did not consider this: It was I who bestowed on her The new grain and wine and oil; I who lavished silver on her And gold – which they used for Baal.

י וְהִיא לֹא יָדְעָה כִּי אָנֹכִי נָתַתִּי לָהּ הַדָּגָן וְהַתִּירוֹשׁ וְהַיִּצְהָר וְכֶסֶף הִרְבֵּיתִי לָהּ וְזָהָב עָשׂוּ לַבָּעַל׃

v'-HEE LO ya-d'-AH KEE a-no-KHEE na-TA-tee LAH ha-da-GAN v'-ha-tee-ROSH v'-ha-yitz-HAR v'-KHE-sef hir-BAY-tee LAH v'-za-HAV a-SU la-BA-al

2:10 And she did not consider this: It was I who bestowed on her the new grain One of the greatest sins of the wayward wife is that she attributes to her lovers the gifts that were actually given to her by her husband.

Hoshea/Hosea
Chapter 2

הוֹשֵׁעַ
פרק ב

11 Assuredly, I will take back My new grain in its time And My new wine in its season, And I will snatch away My wool and My linen That serve to cover her nakedness.

יא לָכֵן אָשׁוּב וְלָקַחְתִּי דְגָנִי בְּעִתּוֹ וְתִירוֹשִׁי בְּמוֹעֲדוֹ וְהִצַּלְתִּי צַמְרִי וּפִשְׁתִּי לְכַסּוֹת אֶת־עֶרְוָתָהּ:

12 Now will I uncover her shame In the very sight of her lovers, And none shall save her from Me.

יב וְעַתָּה אֲגַלֶּה אֶת־נַבְלֻתָהּ לְעֵינֵי מְאַהֲבֶיהָ וְאִישׁ לֹא־יַצִּילֶנָּה מִיָּדִי:

13 And I will end all her rejoicing: Her festivals, new moons, and *Shabbatot* – All her festive seasons.

יג וְהִשְׁבַּתִּי כָּל־מְשׂוֹשָׂהּ חַגָּהּ חָדְשָׁהּ וְשַׁבַּתָּהּ וְכֹל מוֹעֲדָהּ:

14 I will lay waste her vines and her fig trees, Which she thinks are a fee She received from her lovers; I will turn them into brushwood, And beasts of the field shall devour them.

יד וַהֲשִׁמֹּתִי גַּפְנָהּ וּתְאֵנָתָהּ אֲשֶׁר אָמְרָה אֶתְנָה הֵמָּה לִי אֲשֶׁר נָתְנוּ־לִי מְאַהֲבָי וְשַׂמְתִּים לְיַעַר וַאֲכָלָתַם חַיַּת הַשָּׂדֶה:

15 Thus will I punish her For the days of the Baalim, On which she brought them offerings; When, decked with earrings and jewels, She would go after her lovers, Forgetting Me – declares *Hashem*.

טו וּפָקַדְתִּי עָלֶיהָ אֶת־יְמֵי הַבְּעָלִים אֲשֶׁר תַּקְטִיר לָהֶם וַתַּעַד נִזְמָהּ וְחֶלְיָתָהּ וַתֵּלֶךְ אַחֲרֵי מְאַהֲבֶיהָ וְאֹתִי שָׁכְחָה נְאֻם־יְהוָה:

16 Assuredly, I will speak coaxingly to her And lead her through the wilderness And speak to her tenderly.

טז לָכֵן הִנֵּה אָנֹכִי מְפַתֶּיהָ וְהֹלַכְתִּיהָ הַמִּדְבָּר וְדִבַּרְתִּי עַל־לִבָּהּ:

17 I will give her her vineyards from there, And the Valley of Achor as a plowland of hope. There she shall respond as in the days of her youth, When she came up from the land of Egypt.

יז וְנָתַתִּי לָהּ אֶת־כְּרָמֶיהָ מִשָּׁם וְאֶת־עֵמֶק עָכוֹר לְפֶתַח תִּקְוָה וְעָנְתָה שָּׁמָּה כִּימֵי נְעוּרֶיהָ וּכְיוֹם עֲלוֹתָהּ מֵאֶרֶץ־מִצְרָיִם:

18 And in that day – declares *Hashem* – You will call [Me] Ishi, And no more will you call Me Baali.

יח וְהָיָה בַיּוֹם־הַהוּא נְאֻם־יְהוָה תִּקְרְאִי אִישִׁי וְלֹא־תִקְרְאִי־לִי עוֹד בַּעְלִי:

19 For I will remove the names of the Baalim from her mouth, And they shall nevermore be mentioned by name.

יט וַהֲסִרֹתִי אֶת־שְׁמוֹת הַבְּעָלִים מִפִּיהָ וְלֹא־יִזָּכְרוּ עוֹד בִּשְׁמָם:

20 In that day, I will make a covenant for them with the beasts of the field, the birds of the air, and the creeping things of the ground; I will also banish bow, sword, and war from the land. Thus I will let them lie down in safety.

כ וְכָרַתִּי לָהֶם בְּרִית בַּיּוֹם הַהוּא עִם־חַיַּת הַשָּׂדֶה וְעִם־עוֹף הַשָּׁמַיִם וְרֶמֶשׂ הָאֲדָמָה וְקֶשֶׁת וְחֶרֶב וּמִלְחָמָה אֶשְׁבּוֹר מִן־הָאָרֶץ וְהִשְׁכַּבְתִּים לָבֶטַח:

21 And I will espouse you forever: I will espouse you with righteousness and justice, And with goodness and mercy,

כא וְאֵרַשְׂתִּיךְ לִי לְעוֹלָם וְאֵרַשְׂתִּיךְ לִי בְּצֶדֶק וּבְמִשְׁפָּט וּבְחֶסֶד וּבְרַחֲמִים:

Symbolically, this means that Israel should have recognized that her prosperity comes not from the other nations, but from *Hashem*. The gifts mentioned in the verse include not only grains, wine and oil, the traditional crops of the Land of Israel, but also valuable metals which are not native to the land, and symbolize God's extra love for His people. One must learn to identify and appreciate everything *Hashem* does, especially those aspects of his life which reflect His showering of kindness beyond what is deserved.

Hoshea/Hosea
Chapter 3

הושע
פרק ג

22 And I will espouse you with faithfulness; Then you shall be devoted to *Hashem*.

כב וְאֵרַשְׂתִּיךְ לִי בֶּאֱמוּנָה וְיָדַעַתְּ אֶת־יְהֹוָה׃

23 In that day, I will respond – declares *Hashem* – I will respond to the sky, And it shall respond to the earth;

כג וְהָיָה ׀ בַּיּוֹם הַהוּא אֶעֱנֶה נְאֻם־יְהֹוָה אֶעֱנֶה אֶת־הַשָּׁמָיִם וְהֵם יַעֲנוּ אֶת־הָאָרֶץ׃

24 And the earth shall respond With new grain and wine and oil, And they shall respond to *Yizrael*.

כד וְהָאָרֶץ תַּעֲנֶה אֶת־הַדָּגָן וְאֶת־הַתִּירוֹשׁ וְאֶת־הַיִּצְהָר וְהֵם יַעֲנוּ אֶת־יִזְרְעֶאל׃

25 I will sow her in the land as My own; And take Lo-ruhamah back in favor; And I will say to Lo-ammi, "You are My people," And he will respond, "[You are] my God."

כה וּזְרַעְתִּיהָ לִּי בָּאָרֶץ וְרִחַמְתִּי אֶת־לֹא רֻחָמָה וְאָמַרְתִּי לְלֹא־עַמִּי עַמִּי־אַתָּה וְהוּא יֹאמַר אֱלֹהָי׃

3 1 *Hashem* said to me further, "Go, befriend a woman who, while befriended by a companion, consorts with others, just as *Hashem* befriends the Israelites, but they turn to other gods and love the cups of the grape."

ג א וַיֹּאמֶר יְהֹוָה אֵלַי עוֹד לֵךְ אֱהַב־אִשָּׁה אֲהֻבַת רֵעַ וּמְנָאָפֶת כְּאַהֲבַת יְהֹוָה אֶת־בְּנֵי יִשְׂרָאֵל וְהֵם פֹּנִים אֶל־אֱלֹהִים אֲחֵרִים וְאֹהֲבֵי אֲשִׁישֵׁי עֲנָבִים׃

2 Then I hired her for fifteen [*shekalim* of] silver, a *chomer* of barley, and a *letek* of barley;

ב וָאֶכְּרֶהָ לִּי בַּחֲמִשָּׁה עָשָׂר כָּסֶף וְחֹמֶר שְׂעֹרִים וְלֵתֶךְ שְׂעֹרִים׃

3 and I stipulated with her, "In return, you are to go a long time without either fornicating or marrying; even I [shall not cohabit] with you."

ג וָאֹמַר אֵלֶיהָ יָמִים רַבִּים תֵּשְׁבִי לִי לֹא תִזְנִי וְלֹא תִהְיִי לְאִישׁ וְגַם־אֲנִי אֵלָיִךְ׃

4 For the Israelites shall go a long time without king and without officials, without sacrifice and without cult pillars, and without ephod and teraphim.

ד כִּי ׀ יָמִים רַבִּים יֵשְׁבוּ בְּנֵי יִשְׂרָאֵל אֵין מֶלֶךְ וְאֵין שָׂר וְאֵין זֶבַח וְאֵין מַצֵּבָה וְאֵין אֵפוֹד וּתְרָפִים׃

5 Afterward, the Israelites will turn back and will seek *Hashem* their God and *David* their king – and they will thrill over *Hashem* and over His bounty in the days to come.

ה אַחַר יָשֻׁבוּ בְּנֵי יִשְׂרָאֵל וּבִקְשׁוּ אֶת־יְהֹוָה אֱלֹהֵיהֶם וְאֵת דָּוִד מַלְכָּם וּפָחֲדוּ אֶל־יְהֹוָה וְאֶל־טוּבוֹ בְּאַחֲרִית הַיָּמִים׃

a-KHAR ya-SHU-vu b'-NAY yis-ra-AYL u-vik-SHU et a-do-NAI e-lo-hay-HEM v'-AYT da-VEED mal-KAM u-fa-kha-DU el a-do-NAI v'-el tu-VO b'-a-kha-REET ha-ya-MEEM

3:5 In the days to come *Hoshea* promises that despite the period of punishment and separation, ultimately Israel will return and seek *Hashem*, their God and *David*, their king. He says this will take place *b'acharit ha'yamim* (באחרית הימים), translated here as 'in the days to come,' but often translated as 'the end of days.' However, as Prime Minister Menachem Begin pointed out in a speech to the delegates of the United Nations Disarmament Conference in 1982, "*Acharit hayamim* does not mean 'the last days' or 'the end of days.' On the contrary! The key word, *acharit*, is a synonym for a bright future. It means *hatikva*, 'hope,' as we find in Jeremiah (29:11): *latet lachem acharit v'tikva* (לתת לכם אחרית ותקוה) – 'to give to you a future and a hope,' or, 'to give you a hopeful future.' *Acharit* can also mean progeny, as we find in Ezekiel (23:25), and in progeny there is future. Hence, *b'acharit hayamim* really means the days of redemption, when mankind shall enjoy the full blessings of eternal peace for all generations to come." The Prime Minister taught the UN delegates that no matter how difficult the present may be, one must maintain our hope for a bright future and the days of redemption.

Prime Minister Menachem Begin (1913–1992)

Hoshea/Hosea
Chapter 4

הושע
פרק ד

4 1 Hear the word of *Hashem*, O people of *Yisrael*! For *Hashem* has a case Against the inhabitants of this land, Because there is no honesty and no goodness And no obedience to *Hashem* in the land.

א שִׁמְעוּ דְבַר־יְהֹוָה בְּנֵי יִשְׂרָאֵל כִּי רִיב לַיהֹוָה עִם־יוֹשְׁבֵי הָאָרֶץ כִּי אֵין־אֱמֶת וְאֵין־חֶסֶד וְאֵין־דַּעַת אֱלֹהִים בָּאָרֶץ:

shim-U d'-var a-do-NAI b'-NAY yis-ra-AYL KEE REEV la-do-NAI im yo-sh'-VAY ha-A-retz KEE ayn e-MET v'-ayn KHE-sed v'-ayn DA-at e-lo-HEEM ba-A-retz

2 [False] swearing, dishonesty, and murder, And theft and adultery are rife; Crime follows upon crime!

ב אָלֹה וְכַחֵשׁ וְרָצֹחַ וְגָנֹב וְנָאֹף פָּרָצוּ וְדָמִים בְּדָמִים נָגָעוּ:

3 For that, the earth is withered: Everything that dwells on it languishes – Beasts of the field and birds of the sky – Even the fish of the sea perish.

ג עַל־כֵּן תֶּאֱבַל הָאָרֶץ וְאֻמְלַל כָּל־יוֹשֵׁב בָּהּ בְּחַיַּת הַשָּׂדֶה וּבְעוֹף הַשָּׁמָיִם וְגַם־דְּגֵי הַיָּם יֵאָסֵפוּ:

4 "Let no man rebuke, let no man protest!" For this your people has a grievance against [you], O *Kohen*!

ד אַךְ אִישׁ אַל־יָרֵב וְאַל־יוֹכַח אִישׁ וְעַמְּךָ כִּמְרִיבֵי כֹהֵן:

5 So you shall stumble by day, And by night a *Navi* shall stumble as well, And I will destroy your kindred.

ה וְכָשַׁלְתָּ הַיּוֹם וְכָשַׁל גַּם־נָבִיא עִמְּךָ לָיְלָה וְדָמִיתִי אִמֶּךָ:

6 My people is destroyed because of [your] disobedience! Because you have rejected obedience, I reject you as My *Kohen*; Because you have spurned the teaching of your God, I, in turn, will spurn your children.

ו נִדְמוּ עַמִּי מִבְּלִי הַדָּעַת כִּי־אַתָּה הַדַּעַת מָאַסְתָּ וְאֶמְאָסְאךָ מִכַּהֵן לִי וַתִּשְׁכַּח תּוֹרַת אֱלֹהֶיךָ אֶשְׁכַּח בָּנֶיךָ גַּם־אָנִי:

7 The more they increased, the more they sinned against Me: I will change their dignity to dishonor.

ז כְּרֻבָּם כֵּן חָטְאוּ־לִי כְּבוֹדָם בְּקָלוֹן אָמִיר:

8 They feed on My people's sin offerings, And so they desire its iniquity.

ח חַטַּאת עַמִּי יֹאכֵלוּ וְאֶל־עֲוֺנָם יִשְׂאוּ נַפְשׁוֹ:

9 Therefore, the people shall fare like the *Kohanim*: I will punish it for its conduct, I will requite it for its deeds.

ט וְהָיָה כָעָם כַּכֹּהֵן וּפָקַדְתִּי עָלָיו דְּרָכָיו וּמַעֲלָלָיו אָשִׁיב לוֹ:

10 Truly, they shall eat, but not be sated; They shall swill, but not be satisfied, Because they have forsaken *Hashem* To practice

י וְאָכְלוּ וְלֹא יִשְׂבָּעוּ הִזְנוּ וְלֹא יִפְרֹצוּ כִּי־אֶת־יְהֹוָה עָזְבוּ לִשְׁמֹר:

דעת

4:1 No obedience to *Hashem* in the land Hoshea begins to outline *Hashem*'s case against His people by stating that there is no truth, no mercy, and no "*da'at Elokim*" in the land. *Da'at Elokim* is translated here as 'obedience to *Hashem*,' but literally means 'knowledge of *Hashem*.' From this negative statement, we can see *Hoshea*'s conception of the ideal person: One who is honest, kind, and "knows" God. To "know God" is reminiscent of the Bible's description of the ideal, intimate relationship between husband and wife, described as, "Now the man knew his wife *Chava*" (Genesis 4:1). The ideal relationship described by this term encompasses not only the physical dimension, but includes total comprehension or knowledge of the other. Through study of the Bible and the world which God created, we can come as close as possible to understand and to know *Hashem*.

Hoshea/Hosea
Chapter 5

הושע
פרק ה

11 lechery. Wine and new wine destroy The mind of

יא זְנוּת וְיַיִן וְתִירוֹשׁ יִקַּח־לֵב:

12 My people: It consults its stick, Its rod directs it! A lecherous impulse has made them go wrong, And they have strayed from submission to their God.

יב עַמִּי בְּעֵצוֹ יִשְׁאָל וּמַקְלוֹ יַגִּיד לוֹ כִּי רוּחַ זְנוּנִים הִתְעָה וַיִּזְנוּ מִתַּחַת אֱלֹהֵיהֶם:

13 They sacrifice on the mountaintops And offer on the hills, Under oaks, poplars, and terebinths Whose shade is so pleasant. That is why their daughters fornicate And their daughters-in-law commit adultery!

יג עַל־רָאשֵׁי הֶהָרִים יְזַבֵּחוּ וְעַל־הַגְּבָעוֹת יְקַטֵּרוּ תַּחַת אַלּוֹן וְלִבְנֶה וְאֵלָה כִּי טוֹב צִלָּהּ עַל־כֵּן תִּזְנֶינָה בְּנוֹתֵיכֶם וְכַלּוֹתֵיכֶם תְּנָאַפְנָה:

14 I will not punish their daughters for fornicating Nor their daughters-in-law for committing adultery; For they themselves turn aside with whores And sacrifice with prostitutes, And a people that is without sense must stumble.

יד לֹא־אֶפְקוֹד עַל־בְּנוֹתֵיכֶם כִּי תִזְנֶינָה וְעַל־כַּלּוֹתֵיכֶם כִּי תְנָאַפְנָה כִּי־הֵם עִם־הַזֹּנוֹת יְפָרֵדוּ וְעִם־הַקְּדֵשׁוֹת יְזַבֵּחוּ וְעָם לֹא־יָבִין יִלָּבֵט:

15 If you are a lecher, *Yisrael* – Let not *Yehuda* incur guilt – Do not come to *Gilgal*, Do not make pilgrimages to *Beit Aven*, And do not swear by *Hashem*!

טו אִם־זֹנֶה אַתָּה יִשְׂרָאֵל אַל־יֶאְשַׁם יְהוּדָה וְאַל־תָּבֹאוּ הַגִּלְגָּל וְאַל־תַּעֲלוּ בֵּית אָוֶן וְאַל־תִּשָּׁבְעוּ חַי־יְהֹוָה:

16 Ah, *Yisrael* has balked Like a stubborn cow; Therefore, *Hashem* will graze him On the range, like a sheep.

טז כִּי כְּפָרָה סֹרֵרָה סָרַר יִשְׂרָאֵל עַתָּה יִרְעֵם יְהֹוָה כְּכֶבֶשׂ בַּמֶּרְחָב:

17 *Efraim* is addicted to images – Let him be.

יז חֲבוּר עֲצַבִּים אֶפְרָיִם הַנַּח־לוֹ:

18 They drink to excess – Their liquor turns against them. They "love" beyond measure – Disgrace is the "gift"

יח סָר סָבְאָם הַזְנֵה הִזְנוּ אָהֲבוּ הֵבוּ קָלוֹן מָגִנֶּיהָ:

19 Which the wind is bringing; They shall garner shame from their sacrifices.

יט צָרַר רוּחַ אוֹתָהּ בִּכְנָפֶיהָ וְיֵבֹשׁוּ מִזִּבְחוֹתָם:

5 1 Hear this, O *Kohanim*, Attend, O House of *Yisrael*, And give ear, O royal house; For right conduct is your responsibility! But you have been a snare to *Mitzpa* And a net spread out over *Tavor*;

ה א שִׁמְעוּ־זֹאת הַכֹּהֲנִים וְהַקְשִׁיבוּ בֵּית יִשְׂרָאֵל וּבֵית הַמֶּלֶךְ הַאֲזִינוּ כִּי לָכֶם הַמִּשְׁפָּט כִּי־פַח הֱיִיתֶם לְמִצְפָּה וְרֶשֶׁת פְּרוּשָׂה עַל־תָּבוֹר:

shim-u ZOT ha-ko-ha-NEEM v'-hak-SHEE-vu BAYT yis-ra-AYL u-VAYT ha-ME-lekh ha-a-ZEE-nu KEE la-KHEM ha-mish-PAT kee FAKH he-yee-TEM l'-mitz-PAH v'-RE-shet p'-ru-SAH al ta-VOR

5:1 But you have been a snare to *Mitzpa* and a net spread out over *Tavor* *Hoshea* targets the leadership of Israel for failing the people, calling them "a snare to *Mitzpa* and a net spread out over *Tavor*." These two places carry strong echoes from Israel's history. *Mitzpa* is a site of Israelite worship of God in the times of the Judges (Judges 20:1). *Hashem* saves His people at *Mitzpa* during the time of *Shmuel* (I Samuel 7:10–11), and it is the place where the tribes gather to demand the appointment of Israel's first king, *Shaul* (I Samuel 8–12). The mountain of *Tavor* is where the tribes gather together to fight *Yavin*, king of Hazor and his general *Sisera* (Judges 4–5). The same places where *Hashem* brought salvation to His people in the past, are now used as sites of sin and rebellion against Him.

Mount Tavor

Hoshea/Hosea
Chapter 5

הושע
פרק ה

2 For when trappers dug deep pitfalls, I was the only reprover of them all.

ב וְשַׁחֲטָה שֵׂטִים הֶעְמִיקוּ וַאֲנִי מוּסָר לְכֻלָּם:

3 Yes, I have watched *Efraim*, *Yisrael* has not escaped my notice: Behold, you have fornicated, O *Efraim*; *Yisrael* has defiled himself!

ג אֲנִי יָדַעְתִּי אֶפְרַיִם וְיִשְׂרָאֵל לֹא־נִכְחַד מִמֶּנִּי כִּי עַתָּה הִזְנֵיתָ אֶפְרַיִם נִטְמָא יִשְׂרָאֵל:

4 Their habits do not let them Turn back to their God; Because of the lecherous impulse within them, They pay no heed to *Hashem*.

ד לֹא יִתְּנוּ מַעַלְלֵיהֶם לָשׁוּב אֶל־אֱלֹהֵיהֶם כִּי רוּחַ זְנוּנִים בְּקִרְבָּם וְאֶת־יְהֹוָה לֹא יָדָעוּ:

5 *Yisrael*'s pride shall be humbled before his very eyes, As *Yisrael* and *Efraim* fall because of their sin (And *Yehuda* falls with them).

ה וְעָנָה גְאוֹן־יִשְׂרָאֵל בְּפָנָיו וְיִשְׂרָאֵל וְאֶפְרַיִם יִכָּשְׁלוּ בַּעֲוֹנָם כָּשַׁל גַּם־יְהוּדָה עִמָּם:

6 Then they will go with their sheep and cattle To seek *Hashem*, but they will not find Him. He has cast them off:

ו בְּצֹאנָם וּבִבְקָרָם יֵלְכוּ לְבַקֵּשׁ אֶת־יְהֹוָה וְלֹא יִמְצָאוּ חָלַץ מֵהֶם:

7 [Because] they have broken faith with *Hashem*, Because they have begotten Alien children. Therefore, the new moon Shall devour their portion.

ז בַּיהֹוָה בָּגָדוּ כִּי־בָנִים זָרִים יָלָדוּ עַתָּה יֹאכְלֵם חֹדֶשׁ אֶת־חֶלְקֵיהֶם:

8 Sound a *shofar* in *Giva*, A trumpet in *Rama*; Give the alarm in *Beit Aven*; After you, *Binyamin*!

ח תִּקְעוּ שׁוֹפָר בַּגִּבְעָה חֲצֹצְרָה בָּרָמָה הָרִיעוּ בֵּית אָוֶן אַחֲרֶיךָ בִּנְיָמִין:

9 *Efraim* is stricken with horror On a day of chastisement. Against the tribes of *Yisrael* I proclaim certainties:

ט אֶפְרַיִם לְשַׁמָּה תִהְיֶה בְּיוֹם תּוֹכֵחָה בְּשִׁבְטֵי יִשְׂרָאֵל הוֹדַעְתִּי נֶאֱמָנָה:

10 The officers of *Yehuda* have acted Like shifters of field boundaries; On them I will pour out My wrath like water.

י הָיוּ שָׂרֵי יְהוּדָה כְּמַסִּיגֵי גְּבוּל עֲלֵיהֶם אֶשְׁפּוֹךְ כַּמַּיִם עֶבְרָתִי:

11 *Efraim* is defrauded Robbed of redress, Because he has witlessly Gone after futility.

יא עָשׁוּק אֶפְרַיִם רְצוּץ מִשְׁפָּט כִּי הוֹאִיל הָלַךְ אַחֲרֵי־צָו:

12 For it is I who am like rot to *Efraim*, Like decay to the House of *Yehuda*;

יב וַאֲנִי כָעָשׁ לְאֶפְרָיִם וְכָרָקָב לְבֵית יְהוּדָה:

13 Yet when *Efraim* became aware of his sickness, *Yehuda* of his sores, *Efraim* repaired to Assyria – He sent envoys to a patron king! He will never be able to cure you, Will not heal you of your sores.

יג וַיַּרְא אֶפְרַיִם אֶת־חָלְיוֹ וִיהוּדָה אֶת־מְזֹרוֹ וַיֵּלֶךְ אֶפְרַיִם אֶל־אַשּׁוּר וַיִּשְׁלַח אֶל־מֶלֶךְ יָרֵב וְהוּא לֹא יוּכַל לִרְפֹּא לָכֶם וְלֹא־יִגְהֶה מִכֶּם מָזוֹר:

14 No, I will be like a lion to *Efraim*, Like a great beast to the House of *Yehuda*; I, I will attack and stride away, Carrying the prey that no one can rescue;

יד כִּי אָנֹכִי כַשַּׁחַל לְאֶפְרַיִם וְכַכְּפִיר לְבֵית יְהוּדָה אֲנִי אֲנִי אֶטְרֹף וְאֵלֵךְ אֶשָּׂא וְאֵין מַצִּיל:

15 And I will return to My abode – Till they realize their guilt. In their distress, they will seek Me And beg for My favor.

טו אֵלֵךְ אָשׁוּבָה אֶל־מְקוֹמִי עַד אֲשֶׁר־יֶאְשְׁמוּ וּבִקְשׁוּ פָנָי בַּצַּר לָהֶם יְשַׁחֲרֻנְנִי:

Hoshea/Hosea
Chapter 6

הושע
פרק ו

6 1 "Come, let us turn back to *Hashem*: He attacked, and He can heal us; He wounded, and He can bind us up.

א לְכוּ וְנָשׁוּבָה אֶל־יְהֹוָה כִּי הוּא טָרָף וְיִרְפָּאֵנוּ יַךְ וְיַחְבְּשֵׁנוּ׃

2 In two days He will make us whole again; On the third day He will raise us up, And we shall be whole by His favor.

ב יְחַיֵּנוּ מִיֹּמָיִם בַּיּוֹם הַשְּׁלִישִׁי יְקִמֵנוּ וְנִחְיֶה לְפָנָיו׃

3 Let us pursue obedience to *Hashem*, And we shall become obedient. His appearance is as sure as daybreak, And He will come to us like rain, Like latter rain that refreshes the earth."

ג וְנֵדְעָה נִרְדְּפָה לָדַעַת אֶת־יְהֹוָה כְּשַׁחַר נָכוֹן מוֹצָאוֹ וְיָבוֹא כַגֶּשֶׁם לָנוּ כְּמַלְקוֹשׁ יוֹרֶה אָרֶץ׃

4 What can I do for you, *Efraim*, What can I do for you, *Yehuda*, When your goodness is like morning clouds, Like dew so early gone?

ד מָה אֶעֱשֶׂה־לְּךָ אֶפְרַיִם מָה אֶעֱשֶׂה־לְּךָ יְהוּדָה וְחַסְדְּכֶם כַּעֲנַן־בֹּקֶר וְכַטַּל מַשְׁכִּים הֹלֵךְ׃

5 That is why I have hewn down the *Neviim*, Have slain them with the words of My mouth: And the day that dawned [brought on] your punishment.

ה עַל־כֵּן חָצַבְתִּי בַּנְּבִיאִים הֲרַגְתִּים בְּאִמְרֵי־פִי וּמִשְׁפָּטֶיךָ אוֹר יֵצֵא׃

6 For I desire goodness, not sacrifice; Obedience to *Hashem*, rather than burnt offerings.

ו כִּי חֶסֶד חָפַצְתִּי וְלֹא־זָבַח וְדַעַת אֱלֹהִים מֵעֹלוֹת׃

KEE KHE-sed kha-FATZ-tee v'-lo ZA-vakh v'-DA-at e-lo-HEEM may-o-LOT

7 But they, to a man, have transgressed the Covenant. This is where they have been false to Me:

ז וְהֵמָּה כְּאָדָם עָבְרוּ בְרִית שָׁם בָּגְדוּ בִי׃

8 *Gilad* is a city of evildoers, Tracked up with blood.

ח גִּלְעָד קִרְיַת פֹּעֲלֵי אָוֶן עֲקֻבָּה מִדָּם׃

9 The gang of *Kohanim* is Like the ambuscade of bandits Who murder on the road to *Shechem*, For they have encouraged depravity.

ט וּכְחַכֵּי אִישׁ גְּדוּדִים חֶבֶר כֹּהֲנִים דֶּרֶךְ יְרַצְּחוּ־שֶׁכְמָה כִּי זִמָּה עָשׂוּ׃

10 In the House of *Yisrael* I have seen A horrible thing; *Efraim* has fornicated there, *Yisrael* has defiled himself.

י בְּבֵית יִשְׂרָאֵל רָאִיתִי שַׁעֲרִירִיָּה [שַׁעֲרוּרִיָּה] שָׁם זְנוּת לְאֶפְרַיִם נִטְמָא יִשְׂרָאֵל׃

11 Even *Yehuda* has reaped a harvest of you! When I would restore My people's fortunes,

יא גַּם־יְהוּדָה שָׁת קָצִיר לָךְ בְּשׁוּבִי שְׁבוּת עַמִּי׃

6:6 For I desire goodness, not sacrifice Chapter 6 explains *Hashem*'s reluctance to answer His people in their distress, despite their apparent repentance (6:1–3). God points to the fleeting and superficial nature of their request, stating, "your goodness is like morning clouds" (6:4). *Hoshea* then makes one of his most revolutionary declarations: Sacrificial acts alone, the basis of all ancient religions, have no value without an accompanying commitment to living a moral life. He says "For I desire goodness, not sacrifice, obedience to *Hashem* rather than burnt offerings." Although we no longer offer sacrifices, to this day there are those who get caught up in the superficial, ritual aspects of religion at the expense of ethical behavior. In this verse, *Hoshea* calls on us to act properly in our dealings with other people and to strengthen our awareness of, and commitment to, *Hashem*. Once these values are ingrained in us, then rituals become meaningful.

Hoshea/Hosea
Chapter 7

הושע
פרק ז

7 ¹ When I would heal *Yisrael*, The guilt of *Efraim* reveals itself And the wickedness of *Shomron*. For they have acted treacherously, With thieves breaking in And bands raiding outside.

א כְּרָפְאִי לְיִשְׂרָאֵל וְנִגְלָה עֲוֹן אֶפְרַיִם וְרָעוֹת שֹׁמְרוֹן כִּי פָעֲלוּ שָׁקֶר וְגַנָּב יָבוֹא פָּשַׁט גְּדוּד בַּחוּץ׃

² And they do not consider That I remembered all their wickedness. Why, their misdeeds have been all around them, They have been ever before Me.

ב וּבַל־יֹאמְרוּ לִלְבָבָם כָּל־רָעָתָם זָכָרְתִּי עַתָּה סְבָבוּם מַעַלְלֵיהֶם נֶגֶד פָּנַי הָיוּ׃

³ In malice they make a king merry, And officials in treachery.

ג בְּרָעָתָם יְשַׂמְּחוּ־מֶלֶךְ וּבְכַחֲשֵׁיהֶם שָׂרִים׃

⁴ They commit adultery, all of them, Like an oven fired by a baker, Who desists from stoking only From the kneading of the dough to its leavening.

ד כֻּלָּם מְנָאֲפִים כְּמוֹ תַנּוּר בֹּעֵרָה מֵאֹפֶה יִשְׁבּוֹת מֵעִיר מִלּוּשׁ בָּצֵק עַד־חֻמְצָתוֹ׃

⁵ The day they made our king sick [And] officials with the poison of wine, He gave his hand to traitors.

ה יוֹם מַלְכֵּנוּ הֶחֱלוּ שָׂרִים חֲמַת מִיָּיִן מָשַׁךְ יָדוֹ אֶת־לֹצְצִים׃

⁶ For they approach their ambush With their hearts like an oven: Through the night Their baker has slept; In the morning, it flares up Like a blazing fire.

ו כִּי־קֵרְבוּ כַתַּנּוּר לִבָּם בְּאָרְבָּם כָּל־הַלַּיְלָה יָשֵׁן אֹפֵהֶם בֹּקֶר הוּא בֹעֵר כְּאֵשׁ לֶהָבָה׃

⁷ They all get heated like an oven And devour their rulers – None of them calls to Me. All their kings have fallen [by their hand].

ז כֻּלָּם יֵחַמּוּ כַּתַּנּוּר וְאָכְלוּ אֶת־שֹׁפְטֵיהֶם כָּל־מַלְכֵיהֶם נָפָלוּ אֵין־קֹרֵא בָהֶם אֵלָי׃

ku-LAM yay-KHA-mu ka-ta-NUR v'-a-kh'-LU et sho-f'-tay-HEM kol mal-khay-HEM na-FA-lu ayn ko-RAY va-HEM ay-LAI

⁸ *Efraim* is among the peoples; He is rotting away. *Efraim* is like a cake – Incapable of turning.

ח אֶפְרַיִם בָּעַמִּים הוּא יִתְבּוֹלָל אֶפְרַיִם הָיָה עֻגָה בְּלִי הֲפוּכָה׃

⁹ Strangers have consumed his strength, But he has taken no notice; Also, mold is scattered over him, But he has taken no notice.

ט אָכְלוּ זָרִים כֹּחוֹ וְהוּא לֹא יָדָע גַּם־שֵׂיבָה זָרְקָה בּוֹ וְהוּא לֹא יָדָע׃

¹⁰ Though *Yisrael*'s pride has been humbled Before his very eyes, They have not turned back To their God *Hashem*; They have not sought Him In spite of everything.

י וְעָנָה גְאוֹן־יִשְׂרָאֵל בְּפָנָיו וְלֹא־שָׁבוּ אֶל־יְהוָה אֱלֹהֵיהֶם וְלֹא בִקְשֻׁהוּ בְּכָל־זֹאת׃

7:7 None of them calls to Me In its final years, the northern kingdom suffers from political instability, with four kings assassinated in less than fifteen years (746–732 BCE). Chapter 7 describes how the dishonest princes and nobles constantly conspire against their leaders, devouring their judges and killing their kings. Indeed, of the northern kingdom's seventeen rulers, only eight died naturally. *Hoshea* criticizes this, but adds poignantly that in the efforts to establish a lasting kingship, no one thought to call upon *Hashem*, the only King whose protection is guaranteed and everlasting.

Hoshea/Hosea
Chapter 8

11 Instead, *Efraim* has acted Like a silly dove with no mind: They have appealed to Egypt! They have gone to Assyria!

12 When they go, I will spread My net over them, I will bring them down Like birds of the sky; I will chastise them When I hear their bargaining.

13 Woe to them For straying from Me; Destruction to them For rebelling against Me! For I was their Redeemer; Yet they have plotted treason against Me.

14 But they did not cry out to Me sincerely As they lay wailing. They debauch over new grain and new wine, They are faithless to Me.

15 I braced, I strengthened their arms, And they plot evil against Me!

16 They come back; They have been of no use, Like a slack bow. Their officers shall fall by the sword, Because of the stammering of their tongues. Such shall be [the results of] their jabbering In the land of Egypt.

8 1 [Put] a *shofar* to your mouth – Like an eagle over the House of *Hashem*; Because they have transgressed My covenant And been faithless to My teaching.

2 *Yisrael* cries out to Me, "O my God, we are devoted to You."

3 *Yisrael* rejects what is good; An enemy shall pursue him.

4 They have made kings, But not with My sanction; They have made officers, But not of My choice. Of their silver and gold They have made themselves images, To their own undoing.

5 He rejects your calf, *Shomron*! I am furious with them! Will they never be capable of purity?

6 For it was *Yisrael*'s doing; It was only made by a joiner, It is not a god. No, the calf of *Shomron* shall be Reduced to splinters!

7 They sow wind, And they shall reap whirlwind – Standing stalks devoid of ears And yielding no flour. If they do yield any, Strangers shall devour it.

הושע
פרק ח

יא וַיְהִ֤י אֶפְרַ֙יִם֙ כְּיוֹנָ֣ה פוֹתָ֔ה אֵ֖ין לֵ֑ב מִצְרַ֥יִם קָרָ֖אוּ אַשּׁ֥וּר הָלָֽכוּ׃

יב כַּאֲשֶׁ֣ר יֵלֵ֗כוּ אֶפְר֤וֹשׂ עֲלֵיהֶם֙ רִשְׁתִּ֔י כְּע֥וֹף הַשָּׁמַ֖יִם אֽוֹרִידֵ֑ם אַיְסִרֵ֕ם כְּשֵׁ֖מַע לַעֲדָתָֽם׃

יג א֣וֹי לָהֶ֤ם כִּי־נָדְדוּ֙ מִמֶּ֔נִּי שֹׁ֥ד לָהֶ֖ם כִּי־פָ֣שְׁעוּ בִ֑י וְאָנֹכִ֣י אֶפְדֵּ֔ם וְהֵ֕מָּה דִּבְּר֥וּ עָלַ֖י כְּזָבִֽים׃

יד וְלֹא־זָעֲק֤וּ אֵלַי֙ בְּלִבָּ֔ם כִּ֥י יְיֵלִ֖ילוּ עַל־מִשְׁכְּבוֹתָ֑ם עַל־דָּגָ֧ן וְתִיר֛וֹשׁ יִתְגּוֹרָ֖רוּ יָס֥וּרוּ בִֽי׃

טו וַאֲנִ֣י יִסַּ֔רְתִּי חִזַּ֖קְתִּי זְרֽוֹעֹתָ֑ם וְאֵלַ֖י יְחַשְּׁבוּ־רָֽע׃

טז יָשׁ֣וּבוּ ׀ לֹ֣א עָ֗ל הָיוּ֙ כְּקֶ֣שֶׁת רְמִיָּ֔ה יִפְּל֥וּ בַחֶ֛רֶב שָׂרֵיהֶ֖ם מִזַּ֣עַם לְשׁוֹנָ֑ם ז֥וֹ לַעְגָּ֖ם בְּאֶ֥רֶץ מִצְרָֽיִם׃

ח א אֶל־חִכְּךָ֣ שֹׁפָ֔ר כַּנֶּ֖שֶׁר עַל־בֵּ֣ית יְהֹוָ֑ה יַ֚עַן עָבְר֣וּ בְרִיתִ֔י וְעַל־תּוֹרָתִ֖י פָּשָֽׁעוּ׃

ב לִ֖י יִזְעָ֑קוּ אֱלֹהַ֥י יְֽדַעֲנ֖וּךָ יִשְׂרָאֵֽל׃

ג זָנַ֥ח יִשְׂרָאֵ֖ל ט֑וֹב אוֹיֵ֖ב יִרְדְּפֽוֹ׃

ד הֵ֤ם הִמְלִ֙יכוּ֙ וְלֹ֣א מִמֶּ֔נִּי הֵשִׂ֖ירוּ וְלֹ֣א יָדָ֑עְתִּי כַּסְפָּ֣ם וּזְהָבָ֗ם עָשׂ֤וּ לָהֶם֙ עֲצַבִּ֔ים לְמַ֖עַן יִכָּרֵֽת׃

ה זָנַח֙ עֶגְלֵ֣ךְ שֹׁמְר֔וֹן חָרָ֥ה אַפִּ֖י בָּ֑ם עַד־מָתַ֕י לֹ֥א יוּכְל֖וּ נִקָּיֹֽן׃

ו כִּ֣י מִיִּשְׂרָאֵ֔ל וְה֖וּא חָרָ֣שׁ עָשָׂ֑הוּ וְלֹ֥א אֱלֹהִ֖ים ה֑וּא כִּֽי־שְׁבָבִ֣ים יִֽהְיֶ֔ה עֵ֖גֶל שֹׁמְרֽוֹן׃

ז כִּ֛י ר֥וּחַ יִזְרָ֖עוּ וְסוּפָ֣תָה יִקְצֹ֑רוּ קָמָ֣ה אֵֽין־ל֗וֹ צֶ֚מַח בְּלִ֣י יַעֲשֶׂה־קֶּ֔מַח אוּלַ֣י יַעֲשֶׂ֔ה זָרִ֖ים יִבְלָעֻֽהוּ׃

Hoshea/Hosea
Chapter 9

הושע
פרק ט

8 *Yisrael* is bewildered; They have now become among the nations Like an unwanted vessel,

ח נִבְלַע יִשְׂרָאֵל עַתָּה הָיוּ בַגּוֹיִם כִּכְלִי אֵין־חֵפֶץ בּוֹ:

niv-LA yis-ra-AYL a-TAH ha-YU va-go-YIM kikh-LEE ayn KHAY-fetz BO

9 [Like] a lonely wild ass. For they have gone up to Assyria, *Efraim* has courted friendship.

ט כִּי־הֵמָּה עָלוּ אַשּׁוּר פֶּרֶא בּוֹדֵד לוֹ אֶפְרַיִם הִתְנוּ אֲהָבִים:

10 And while they are courting among the nations, There I will hold them fast; And they shall begin to diminish in number From the burden of king [and] officers.

י גַּם כִּי־יִתְנוּ בַגּוֹיִם עַתָּה אֲקַבְּצֵם וַיָּחֵלּוּ מְּעָט מִמַּשָּׂא מֶלֶךְ שָׂרִים:

11 For *Efraim* has multiplied altars – for guilt; His altars have redounded to his guilt:

יא כִּי־הִרְבָּה אֶפְרַיִם מִזְבְּחֹת לַחֲטֹא הָיוּ־לוֹ מִזְבְּחוֹת לַחֲטֹא:

12 The many teachings I wrote for him Have been treated as something alien.

יב אֶכְתָּב־[אֶכְתָּב־] לוֹ רֻבּוֹ [רֻבֵּי] תּוֹרָתִי כְּמוֹ־זָר נֶחְשָׁבוּ:

13 When they present sacrifices to Me, It is but flesh for them to eat: *Hashem* has not accepted them. Behold, He remembers their iniquity, He will punish their sins: Back to Egypt with them!

יג זִבְחֵי הַבְהָבַי יִזְבְּחוּ בָשָׂר וַיֹּאכֵלוּ יְהֹוָה לֹא רָצָם עַתָּה יִזְכֹּר עֲוֹנָם וְיִפְקֹד חַטֹּאותָם הֵמָּה מִצְרַיִם יָשׁוּבוּ:

14 *Yisrael* has ignored his Maker And built temples (And *Yehuda* has fortified many cities). So I will set fire to his cities, And it shall consume their fortresses.

יד וַיִּשְׁכַּח יִשְׂרָאֵל אֶת־עֹשֵׂהוּ וַיִּבֶן הֵיכָלוֹת וִיהוּדָה הִרְבָּה עָרִים בְּצֻרוֹת וְשִׁלַּחְתִּי־אֵשׁ בְּעָרָיו וְאָכְלָה אַרְמְנֹתֶיהָ:

9

1 Rejoice not, O *Yisrael*, As other peoples exult; For you have strayed Away from your God: You have loved a harlot's fee By every threshing floor of new grain.

ט א אַל־תִּשְׂמַח יִשְׂרָאֵל אֶל־גִּיל כָּעַמִּים כִּי זָנִיתָ מֵעַל אֱלֹהֶיךָ אָהַבְתָּ אֶתְנָן עַל כָּל־גָּרְנוֹת דָּגָן:

2 Threshing floor and winepress Shall not join them, And the new wine shall betray her.

ב גֹּרֶן וָיֶקֶב לֹא יִרְעֵם וְתִירוֹשׁ יְכַחֶשׁ בָּהּ:

3 They shall not be able to remain In the land of *Hashem*. But *Efraim* shall return to Egypt And shall eat unclean food in Assyria.

ג לֹא יֵשְׁבוּ בְּאֶרֶץ יְהֹוָה וְשָׁב אֶפְרַיִם מִצְרַיִם וּבְאַשּׁוּר טָמֵא יֹאכֵלוּ:

4 It shall be for them like the food of mourners, All who partake of which are defiled. They will offer no libations of wine to *Hashem*, And no sacrifices of theirs will be pleasing to Him; But their food will be only for their hunger, It shall not come into the House of *Hashem*.

ד לֹא־יִסְּכוּ לַיהֹוָה יַיִן וְלֹא יֶעֶרְבוּ־לוֹ זִבְחֵיהֶם כְּלֶחֶם אוֹנִים לָהֶם כָּל־אֹכְלָיו יִטַּמָּאוּ כִּי־לַחְמָם לְנַפְשָׁם לֹא יָבוֹא בֵּית יְהֹוָה:

8:8 Like an unwanted vessel *Hoshea* likens Israel to an empty vessel; once its contents are gone, the container has no value and can be discarded. So too Israel, having paid protection money to Assyria and Egypt for years, is now bereft of gold and riches. Hence, Assyria no longer sees any benefit in keeping Israel alive. Furthermore, in verse 9, *Hoshea* compares the relationship between Israel and Assyria to a person searching for love through the hire of prostitutes. The tragedy of this relationship is that the Israelites turn to other nations, buying their false and fleeting love, while everlasting love is freely available from God. *Hashem* loves them unconditionally, yet they turn away from Him.

Hoshea/Hosea
Chapter 9

5 What will you do about feast days, About the festivals of *Hashem*?

ה מַה־תַּעֲשׂוּ לְיוֹם מוֹעֵד וּלְיוֹם חַג־יְהֹוָה׃

6 Behold, they have gone from destruction [With] the silver they treasure. Egypt shall hold them fast, Moph shall receive them in burial. Weeds are their heirs; Prickly shrubs occupy their [old] homes.

ו כִּי־הִנֵּה הָלְכוּ מִשֹּׁד מִצְרַיִם תְּקַבְּצֵם מֹף תְּקַבְּרֵם מַחְמַד לְכַסְפָּם קִמּוֹשׂ יִירָשֵׁם חוֹחַ בְּאׇהֳלֵיהֶם׃

7 The days of punishment have come For your heavy guilt; The days of requital have come – Let *Yisrael* know it! The *Navi* was distraught, The inspired man driven mad By constant harassment.

ז בָּאוּ יְמֵי הַפְּקֻדָּה בָּאוּ יְמֵי הַשִּׁלֻּם יֵדְעוּ יִשְׂרָאֵל אֱוִיל הַנָּבִיא מְשֻׁגָּע אִישׁ הָרוּחַ עַל רֹב עֲוֺנְךָ וְרַבָּה מַשְׂטֵמָה׃

8 *Efraim* watches for my God. As for the *Navi*, Fowlers' snares are on all his paths, Harassment in the House of his God.

ח צֹפֶה אֶפְרַיִם עִם־אֱלֹהָי נָבִיא פַּח יָקוֹשׁ עַל־כׇּל־דְּרָכָיו מַשְׂטֵמָה בְּבֵית אֱלֹהָיו׃

9 They have been as grievously corrupt As in the days of *Giva*; He will remember their iniquity, He will punish their sins.

ט הֶעְמִיקוּ־שִׁחֵתוּ כִּימֵי הַגִּבְעָה יִזְכּוֹר עֲוֺנָם יִפְקוֹד חַטֹּאותָם׃

10 I found *Yisrael* [as pleasing] As grapes in the wilderness; Your fathers seemed to Me Like the first fig to ripen on a fig tree. But when they came to Baal-peor, They turned aside to shamefulness; Then they became as detested As they had been loved.

י כַּעֲנָבִים בַּמִּדְבָּר מָצָאתִי יִשְׂרָאֵל כְּבִכּוּרָה בִתְאֵנָה בְּרֵאשִׁיתָהּ רָאִיתִי אֲבוֹתֵיכֶם הֵמָּה בָּאוּ בַעַל־פְּעוֹר וַיִּנָּזְרוּ לַבֹּשֶׁת וַיִּהְיוּ שִׁקּוּצִים כְּאׇהֳבָם׃

ka-a-na-VEEM ba-mid-BAR ma-TZA-tee yis-ra-AYL k'-vi-ku-RAH vit-ay-NAH b'-ray-shee-TAH ra-EE-tee a-vo-tay-KHEM HAY-mah BA-u va-al p'-OR va-yi-na-z'-RU la-BO-shet va-yih-YU shi-ku-TZEEM k'-a-ho-VAM

11 From birth, from the womb, from conception *Efraim*'s glory shall be Like birds that fly away.

יא אֶפְרַיִם כָּעוֹף יִתְעוֹפֵף כְּבוֹדָם מִלֵּדָה וּמִבֶּטֶן וּמֵהֵרָיוֹן׃

12 Even if they rear their infants, I will bereave them of men. Woe to them indeed When I turn away from them!

יב כִּי אִם־יְגַדְּלוּ אֶת־בְּנֵיהֶם וְשִׁכַּלְתִּים מֵאָדָם כִּי־גַם־אוֹי לָהֶם בְּשׂוּרִי מֵהֶם׃

13 It shall go with *Efraim* As I have seen it go with Tyre, Which was planted in a meadow; *Efraim* too must bring out His children to slayers.

יג אֶפְרַיִם כַּאֲשֶׁר־רָאִיתִי לְצוֹר שְׁתוּלָה בְנָוֶה וְאֶפְרַיִם לְהוֹצִיא אֶל־הֹרֵג בָּנָיו׃

14 Give them, *Hashem* – give them what? Give them a womb that miscarries, And shriveled breasts!

יד תֵּן־לָהֶם יְהֹוָה מַה־תִּתֵּן תֵּן־לָהֶם רֶחֶם מַשְׁכִּיל וְשָׁדַיִם צֹמְקִים׃

9:10 Then they became as detested as they had been loved *Hoshea*'s rebukes increasingly draw upon the history of Israel to emphasize their message. The prophet mentions the tragedy of *Giva* (verse 9), when the licentiousness of members of the tribe of *Binyamin* led to a deadly civil war (Judges 20), and their behavior in the desert at *Baal Pe'or* (Numbers 25), where the people succumbed to the charms of the Moabite and Midianite women and brought a plague upon themselves. Though they are God's first fruits, the tastiest on the vine, Israel forgot the clear warning of *Sefer Vayikra* 18, that sexual immorality and inappropriate behavior will inevitably lead to their expulsion from the Land of Israel.

Hoshea/Hosea
Chapter 10

הושע
פרק י

15 All their misfortune [began] at *Gilgal*, For there I disowned them. For their evil deeds I will drive them out of My House. I will accept them no more; All their officials are disloyal.

טו כׇּל־רָעָתָם בַּגִּלְגָּל כִּי־שָׁם שְׂנֵאתִים עַל רֹעַ מַעַלְלֵיהֶם מִבֵּיתִי אֲגָרְשֵׁם לֹא אוֹסֵף אַהֲבָתָם כׇּל־שָׂרֵיהֶם סֹרְרִים׃

16 *Efraim* is stricken, Their stock is withered; They can produce no fruit. Even if they do bear children, I will slay their cherished offspring.

טז הֻכָּה אֶפְרַיִם שׇׁרְשָׁם יָבֵשׁ פְּרִי בלי־[בַל־]יַעֲשׂוּן גַּם כִּי יֵלֵדוּן וְהֵמַתִּי מַחֲמַדֵּי בִטְנָם׃

17 My *Hashem* rejects them Because they have not obeyed Him, And they shall go wandering Among the nations.

יז יִמְאָסֵם אֱלֹהַי כִּי לֹא שָׁמְעוּ לוֹ וְיִהְיוּ נֹדְדִים בַּגּוֹיִם׃

10 1 *Yisrael* is a ravaged vine And its fruit is like it. When his fruit was plentiful, He made altars aplenty; When his land was bountiful, Cult pillars abounded.

א גֶּפֶן בּוֹקֵק יִשְׂרָאֵל פְּרִי יְשַׁוֶּה־לּוֹ כְּרֹב לְפִרְיוֹ הִרְבָּה לַמִּזְבְּחוֹת כְּטוֹב לְאַרְצוֹ הֵיטִיבוּ מַצֵּבוֹת׃

GE-fen bo-KAYK yis-ra-AYL p'-REE y'-sha-veh LO k'-ROV l'-fir-YO hir-BAH la-miz-b'-KHOT k'-TOV l'-ar-TZO hay-TEE-vu ma-tzay-VOT

2 Now that his boughs are broken up, He feels his guilt; He himself pulls apart his altars, Smashes his pillars.

ב חָלַק לִבָּם עַתָּה יֶאְשָׁמוּ הוּא יַעֲרֹף מִזְבְּחוֹתָם יְשֹׁדֵד מַצֵּבוֹתָם׃

3 Truly, now they say, "We have no king; For, since we do not fear *Hashem*, What can a king do to us?"

ג כִּי עַתָּה יֹאמְרוּ אֵין מֶלֶךְ לָנוּ כִּי לֹא יָרֵאנוּ אֶת־יְהֹוָה וְהַמֶּלֶךְ מַה־יַּעֲשֶׂה־לָּנוּ׃

4 So they conclude agreements and make covenants With false oaths, And justice degenerates into poison weeds, Breaking out on the furrows of the fields.

ד דִּבְּרוּ דְבָרִים אָלוֹת שָׁוְא כָּרֹת בְּרִית וּפָרַח כָּרֹאשׁ מִשְׁפָּט עַל תַּלְמֵי שָׂדָי׃

5 The inhabitants of *Shomron* fear For the calf of *Beit Aven*; Indeed, its people and priestlings, Whose joy it once was, Mourn over it for the glory That is departed from it.

ה לְעֶגְלוֹת בֵּית אָוֶן יָגוּרוּ שְׁכַן שֹׁמְרוֹן כִּי־אָבַל עָלָיו עַמּוֹ וּכְמָרָיו עָלָיו יָגִילוּ עַל־כְּבוֹדוֹ כִּי־גָלָה מִמֶּנּוּ׃

6 It too shall be brought to Assyria As tribute to a patron king; *Efraim* shall be chagrined, *Yisrael* shall be dismayed Because of his plans.

ו גַּם־אוֹתוֹ לְאַשּׁוּר יוּבָל מִנְחָה לְמֶלֶךְ יָרֵב בׇּשְׁנָה אֶפְרַיִם יִקָּח וְיֵבוֹשׁ יִשְׂרָאֵל מֵעֲצָתוֹ׃

7 *Shomron*'s monarchy is vanishing Like foam upon water,

ז נִדְמֶה שֹׁמְרוֹן מַלְכָּהּ כְּקֶצֶף עַל־פְּנֵי־מָיִם׃

Grapes on a vine in Shtula, Israel

10:1 Yisrael is a ravaged vine Throughout the Bible, Israel is compared to a grapevine (see, for example, Isaiah 5). *Hoshea* uses this metaphor to describe how as Israel prospered, they lavished even more money on their idolatries, shedding their relationship with God like an overburdened vine casts off its grapes. The Hebrew word for 'ravaged,' *bokek* (בוקק), is a play on words, and means both 'to empty' and 'to lay waste' (see Isaiah 24:1, Nahum 2:3), and also 'luxuriant.' Though originally prosperous, the people use their wealth inappropriately, which leads to exile of the people and to the land becoming empty and barren.

בוקק

Hoshea/Hosea
Chapter 11

הושע
פרק יא

8 Ruined shall be the shrines of [Beth-]aven, That sin of *Yisrael*. Thorns and thistles Shall grow on their altars. They shall call to the mountains, "Bury us!" To the hills, "Fall on us!"

ח וְנִשְׁמְדוּ בָּמוֹת אָוֶן חַטַּאת יִשְׂרָאֵל קוֹץ וְדַרְדַּר יַעֲלֶה עַל־מִזְבְּחוֹתָם וְאָמְרוּ לֶהָרִים כַּסּוּנוּ וְלַגְּבָעוֹת נִפְלוּ עָלֵינוּ:

9 You have sinned more, O *Yisrael*, Than in the days of *Giva*. There they stand [as] at *Giva*! Shall they not be overtaken By a war upon scoundrels

ט מִימֵי הַגִּבְעָה חָטָאתָ יִשְׂרָאֵל שָׁם עָמָדוּ לֹא־תַשִּׂיגֵם בַּגִּבְעָה מִלְחָמָה עַל־בְּנֵי עַלְוָה:

10 As peoples gather against them? When I chose [them], I broke them in, Harnessing them for two furrows.

י בְּאַוָּתִי וְאֶסֳּרֵם וְאֻסְּפוּ עֲלֵיהֶם עַמִּים בְּאָסְרָם לִשְׁתֵּי עֵינֹתָם [עוֹנֹתָם:]

11 *Efraim* became a trained heifer, But preferred to thresh; I placed a yoke Upon her sleek neck. I will make *Efraim* do advance plowing; *Yehuda* shall do [main] plowing! *Yaakov* shall do final plowing!

יא וְאֶפְרַיִם עֶגְלָה מְלֻמָּדָה אֹהַבְתִּי לָדוּשׁ וַאֲנִי עָבַרְתִּי עַל־טוּב צַוָּארָהּ אַרְכִּיב אֶפְרַיִם יַחֲרוֹשׁ יְהוּדָה יְשַׂדֶּד־לוֹ יַעֲקֹב:

12 "Sow righteousness for yourselves; Reap the fruits of goodness; Break for yourselves betimes fresh ground Of seeking *Hashem*, So that you may obtain a teacher of righteousness."

יב זִרְעוּ לָכֶם לִצְדָקָה קִצְרוּ לְפִי־חֶסֶד נִירוּ לָכֶם נִיר וְעֵת לִדְרוֹשׁ אֶת־יְהוָה עַד־יָבוֹא וְיֹרֶה צֶדֶק לָכֶם:

13 You have plowed wickedness, You have reaped iniquity – [And] you shall eat the fruits of treachery – Because you relied on your way, On your host of warriors.

יג חֲרַשְׁתֶּם־רֶשַׁע עַוְלָתָה קְצַרְתֶּם אֲכַלְתֶּם פְּרִי־כָחַשׁ כִּי־בָטַחְתָּ בְדַרְכְּךָ בְּרֹב גִּבּוֹרֶיךָ:

14 But the din of war shall arise in your own people, And all your fortresses shall be ravaged As Betharbel was ravaged by *Shalman* On a day of battle, When mothers and babes were dashed to death together.

יד וְקָאם שָׁאוֹן בְּעַמֶּךָ וְכָל־מִבְצָרֶיךָ יוּשַּׁד כְּשֹׁד שַׁלְמַן בֵּית אַרְבֵאל בְּיוֹם מִלְחָמָה אֵם עַל־בָּנִים רֻטָּשָׁה:

15 This is what *Beit El* has done to you For your horrible wickedness: At dawn shall *Yisrael*'s monarchy Utterly perish.

טו כָּכָה עָשָׂה לָכֶם בֵּית־אֵל מִפְּנֵי רָעַת רָעַתְכֶם בַּשַּׁחַר נִדְמֹה נִדְמָה מֶלֶךְ יִשְׂרָאֵל:

11 1 I fell in love with *Yisrael* When he was still a child; And I have called [him] My son Ever since Egypt.

יא א כִּי נַעַר יִשְׂרָאֵל וָאֹהֲבֵהוּ וּמִמִּצְרַיִם קָרָאתִי לִבְנִי:

2 Thus were they called, But they went their own way; They sacrifice to Baalim And offer to carved images.

ב קָרְאוּ לָהֶם כֵּן הָלְכוּ מִפְּנֵיהֶם לַבְּעָלִים יְזַבֵּחוּ וְלַפְּסִלִים יְקַטֵּרוּן:

3 I have pampered *Efraim*, Taking them in My arms; But they have ignored My healing care.

ג וְאָנֹכִי תִרְגַּלְתִּי לְאֶפְרַיִם קָחָם עַל־זְרוֹעֹתָיו וְלֹא יָדְעוּ כִּי רְפָאתִים:

4 I drew them with human ties, With cords of love; But I seemed to them as one Who imposed a yoke on their jaws, Though I was offering them food.

ד בְּחַבְלֵי אָדָם אֶמְשְׁכֵם בַּעֲבֹתוֹת אַהֲבָה וָאֶהְיֶה לָהֶם כִּמְרִימֵי עֹל עַל לְחֵיהֶם וְאַט אֵלָיו אוֹכִיל:

5 No! They return to the land of Egypt, And Assyria is their king. Because they refuse to repent,

ה לֹא יָשׁוּב אֶל־אֶרֶץ מִצְרַיִם וְאַשּׁוּר הוּא מַלְכּוֹ כִּי מֵאֲנוּ לָשׁוּב:

Hoshea/Hosea
Chapter 12

הושע
פרק יב

6 A sword shall descend upon their towns And consume their limbs And devour [them] because of their designs.

וְחָלָה חֶרֶב בְּעָרָיו וְכִלְּתָה בַדָּיו וְאָכֵלָה מִמֹּעֲצוֹתֵיהֶם:

7 For My people persists In its defection from Me; When it is summoned upward, It does not rise at all.

וְעַמִּי תְלוּאִים לִמְשׁוּבָתִי וְאֶל־עַל יִקְרָאֻהוּ יַחַד לֹא יְרוֹמֵם:

8 How can I give you up, O *Efraim*? How surrender you, O *Yisrael*? How can I make you like Admah, Render you like Zeboiim? I have had a change of heart, All My tenderness is stirred.

אֵיךְ אֶתֶּנְךָ אֶפְרַיִם אֲמַגֶּנְךָ יִשְׂרָאֵל אֵיךְ אֶתֶּנְךָ כְאַדְמָה אֲשִׂימְךָ כִּצְבֹאיִם נֶהְפַּךְ עָלַי לִבִּי יַחַד נִכְמְרוּ נִחוּמָי:

9 I will not act on My wrath, Will not turn to destroy *Efraim*. For I am *Hashem*, not man, The Holy One in your midst: I will not come in fury.

לֹא אֶעֱשֶׂה חֲרוֹן אַפִּי לֹא אָשׁוּב לְשַׁחֵת אֶפְרָיִם כִּי אֵל אָנֹכִי וְלֹא־אִישׁ בְּקִרְבְּךָ קָדוֹשׁ וְלֹא אָבוֹא בְּעִיר:

LO e-e-SEH kha-RON a-PEE LO a-SHUV l'-sha-KHAYT ef-RA-yim KEE AYL a-no-KHEE v'-lo EESH b'-kir-b'-KHA ka-DOSH v'-LO a-VO b'-EER

10 *Hashem* will roar like a lion, And they shall march behind Him; When He roars, His children shall come Fluttering out of the west.

אַחֲרֵי יְהוָה יֵלְכוּ כְּאַרְיֵה יִשְׁאָג כִּי־הוּא יִשְׁאַג וְיֶחֶרְדוּ בָנִים מִיָּם:

11 They shall flutter from Egypt like sparrows, From the land of Assyria like doves; And I will settle them in their homes – declares *Hashem*.

יֶחֶרְדוּ כְצִפּוֹר מִמִּצְרַיִם וּכְיוֹנָה מֵאֶרֶץ אַשּׁוּר וְהוֹשַׁבְתִּים עַל־בָּתֵּיהֶם נְאֻם־יְהוָה:

12 1 *Efraim* surrounds Me with deceit, The House of *Yisrael* with guile. (But *Yehuda* stands firm with *Hashem* And is faithful to the Holy One.)

סְבָבֻנִי בְכַחַשׁ אֶפְרַיִם וּבְמִרְמָה בֵּית יִשְׂרָאֵל וִיהוּדָה עֹד רָד עִם־אֵל וְעִם־קְדוֹשִׁים נֶאֱמָן:

2 *Efraim* tends the wind And pursues the gale; He is forever adding Illusion to calamity. Now they make a covenant with Assyria, Now oil is carried to Egypt.

אֶפְרַיִם רֹעֶה רוּחַ וְרֹדֵף קָדִים כָּל־הַיּוֹם כָּזָב וָשֹׁד יַרְבֶּה וּבְרִית עִם־אַשּׁוּר יִכְרֹתוּ וְשֶׁמֶן לְמִצְרַיִם יוּבָל:

3 *Hashem* once indicted *Yehuda*, And punished *Yaakov* for his conduct, Requited him for his deeds.

וְרִיב לַיהוָה עִם־יְהוּדָה וְלִפְקֹד עַל־יַעֲקֹב כִּדְרָכָיו כְּמַעֲלָלָיו יָשִׁיב לוֹ:

4 In the womb he tried to supplant his brother; Grown to manhood, he strove with a divine being,

בַּבֶּטֶן עָקַב אֶת־אָחִיו וּבְאוֹנוֹ שָׂרָה אֶת־אֱלֹהִים:

Rashi (1040–1105)

11:9 I will not act on My wrath *Hoshea* compares Israel to a son that *Hashem* lovingly carried in His arms, healed when sick, and taught to walk (verse 3). Therefore, as an expression of His love, *Hashem* states that He will not express the fullness of His anger at Israel's rebellion, for He is not like man. *Rashi* explains that unlike man, God never regrets any good that He performs or promises to carry out. Therefore, despite their rebellion, He will not go back on His promise of an eternal bond with the Children of Israel, nor His promise of redemption. Instead, He will call out to them with a roar like that of a lion, which will be heard in all the places of their exile. They will return to Him like a bird that returns to its nest, and He will ultimately "settle them in their homes" (verse 11) when He brings them back to the Land of Israel.

Hoshea/Hosea
Chapter 12

הושע
פרק יב

5 He strove with an angel and prevailed – The other had to weep and implore him. At *Beit El* [*Yaakov*] would meet him, There to commune with him.

ה וַיָּשַׂר אֶל־מַלְאָךְ וַיֻּכָל בָּכָה וַיִּתְחַנֶּן־לוֹ בֵּית־אֵל יִמְצָאֶנּוּ וְשָׁם יְדַבֵּר עִמָּנוּ:

6 Yet *Hashem*, the God of Hosts, Must be invoked as "*Hashem*."

ו וַיהֹוָה אֱלֹהֵי הַצְּבָאוֹת יְהֹוָה זִכְרוֹ:

7 You must return to your God! Practice goodness and justice, And constantly trust in your God.

ז וְאַתָּה בֵּאלֹהֶיךָ תָשׁוּב חֶסֶד וּמִשְׁפָּט שְׁמֹר וְקַוֵּה אֶל־אֱלֹהֶיךָ תָּמִיד:

8 A trader who uses false balances, Who loves to overreach,

ח כְּנַעַן בְּיָדוֹ מֹאזְנֵי מִרְמָה לַעֲשֹׁק אָהֵב:

9 *Efraim* thinks, "Ah, I have become rich; I have gotten power! All my gains do not amount To an offense which is real guilt."

ט וַיֹּאמֶר אֶפְרַיִם אַךְ עָשַׁרְתִּי מָצָאתִי אוֹן לִי כָּל־יְגִיעַי לֹא יִמְצְאוּ־לִי עָוֹן אֲשֶׁר־חֵטְא:

10 I *Hashem* have been your God Ever since the land of Egypt. I will let you dwell in your tents again As in the days of old,

י וְאָנֹכִי יְהֹוָה אֱלֹהֶיךָ מֵאֶרֶץ מִצְרָיִם עֹד אוֹשִׁיבְךָ בָאֳהָלִים כִּימֵי מוֹעֵד:

11 When I spoke to the *Neviim*; For I granted many visions, And spoke parables through the *Neviim*.

יא וְדִבַּרְתִּי עַל־הַנְּבִיאִים וְאָנֹכִי חָזוֹן הִרְבֵּיתִי וּבְיַד הַנְּבִיאִים אֲדַמֶּה:

12 As for *Gilad*, it is worthless; And to no purpose have they Been sacrificing oxen in *Gilgal*: The altars of these are also Like stone heaps upon a plowed field.

יב אִם־גִּלְעָד אָוֶן אַךְ־שָׁוְא הָיוּ בַּגִּלְגָּל שְׁוָרִים זִבֵּחוּ גַּם מִזְבְּחוֹתָם כְּגַלִּים עַל תַּלְמֵי שָׂדָי:

13 Then *Yaakov* had to flee to the land of *Aram*; There *Yisrael* served for a wife, For a wife he had to guard [sheep].

יג וַיִּבְרַח יַעֲקֹב שְׂדֵה אֲרָם וַיַּעֲבֹד יִשְׂרָאֵל בְּאִשָּׁה וּבְאִשָּׁה שָׁמָר:

14 But when *Hashem* Brought *Yisrael* up from Egypt, It was through a *Navi*; Through a *Navi* they were guarded.

יד וּבְנָבִיא הֶעֱלָה יְהֹוָה אֶת־יִשְׂרָאֵל מִמִּצְרָיִם וּבְנָבִיא נִשְׁמָר:

uv-na-VEE he-e-LAH a-do-NAI et yis-ra-AYL mi-mitz-RA-yim uv-na-VEE nish-MAR

15 *Efraim* gave bitter offense, And his Lord cast his crimes upon him And requited him for his mockery.

טו הִכְעִיס אֶפְרַיִם תַּמְרוּרִים וְדָמָיו עָלָיו יִטּוֹשׁ וְחֶרְפָּתוֹ יָשִׁיב לוֹ אֲדֹנָיו:

12:14 Through a *Navi* they were guarded In verses 13 and 14, *Hoshea* ties together two stories from Israel's history: *Yaakov*'s sojourn in Aram and Israel's slavery in Egypt. Both places served as refuge. Aram was *Yaakov*'s asylum from his brother's wrath, and Egypt provided sustenance for *Yaakov*'s family during the famine. However, in both of those places, the experiences turned sour. *Yaakov* was deceived by Laban into working for his wives under strenuous conditions, and ultimately had to flee back to Israel. The Egyptians also took advantage of their guests and enslaved the Israelites. *Hoshea* uses the Hebrew word *shamar* (שמר), meaning 'to keep' or 'to guard,' to connect the two episodes. At the end of verse 13, he writes that *Yaakov* guarded Laban's sheep from danger, while at the end of verse 14, he says that *Hashem* guarded Israel through His prophet and led them out of Egypt to safety.

שמר

Hoshea/Hosea
Chapter 13

הושע
פרק יג

13 ¹ When *Efraim* spoke piety, He was exalted in *Yisrael*; But he incurred guilt through Baal, And so he died.

א כְּדַבֵּר אֶפְרַיִם רְתֵת נָשָׂא הוּא בְּיִשְׂרָאֵל וַיֶּאְשַׁם בַּבַּעַל וַיָּמֹת:

² And now they go on sinning; They have made them molten images, Idols, by their skill, from their silver, Wholly the work of craftsmen. Yet for these they appoint men to sacrifice; They are wont to kiss calves!

ב וְעַתָּה יוֹסִפוּ לַחֲטֹא וַיַּעֲשׂוּ לָהֶם מַסֵּכָה מִכַּסְפָּם כִּתְבוּנָם עֲצַבִּים מַעֲשֵׂה חָרָשִׁים כֻּלֹּה לָהֶם הֵם אֹמְרִים זֹבְחֵי אָדָם עֲגָלִים יִשָּׁקוּן:

³ Assuredly, They shall be like morning clouds, Like dew so early gone; Like chaff whirled away from the threshing floor. And like smoke from a lattice.

ג לָכֵן יִהְיוּ כַּעֲנַן־בֹּקֶר וְכַטַּל מַשְׁכִּים הֹלֵךְ כְּמֹץ יְסֹעֵר מִגֹּרֶן וּכְעָשָׁן מֵאֲרֻבָּה:

⁴ Only I *Hashem* have been your God Ever since the land of Egypt; You have never known a [true] *Hashem* but Me, You have never had a helper other than Me.

ד וְאָנֹכִי יְהוָה אֱלֹהֶיךָ מֵאֶרֶץ מִצְרָיִם וֵאלֹהִים זוּלָתִי לֹא תֵדָע וּמוֹשִׁיעַ אַיִן בִּלְתִּי:

⁵ I looked after you in the desert, In a thirsty land.

ה אֲנִי יְדַעְתִּיךָ בַּמִּדְבָּר בְּאֶרֶץ תַּלְאֻבוֹת:

⁶ When they grazed, they were sated; When they were sated, they grew haughty; And so they forgot Me.

ו כְּמַרְעִיתָם וַיִּשְׂבָּעוּ שָׂבְעוּ וַיָּרָם לִבָּם עַל־כֵּן שְׁכֵחוּנִי:

⁷ So I am become like a lion to them, Like a leopard I lurk on the way;

ז וָאֱהִי לָהֶם כְּמוֹ־שָׁחַל כְּנָמֵר עַל־דֶּרֶךְ אָשׁוּר:

⁸ **Like a bear robbed of her young I attack them And rip open the casing of their hearts; I will devour them there like a lion, The beasts of the field shall mangle them.**

ef-g'-SHAYM k'-DOV sha-KUL v'-ek-RA s'-GOR li-BAM v'-o-kh'-LAYM SHAM k'-la-VEE kha-YAT ha-sa-DEH t'-va-k'-AYM

ח אֶפְגְּשֵׁם כְּדֹב שַׁכּוּל וְאֶקְרַע סְגוֹר לִבָּם וְאֹכְלֵם שָׁם כְּלָבִיא חַיַּת הַשָּׂדֶה תְּבַקְּעֵם:

⁹ You are undone, O *Yisrael*! You had no help but Me.

ט שִׁחֶתְךָ יִשְׂרָאֵל כִּי־בִי בְעֶזְרֶךָ:

¹⁰ Where now is your king? Let him save you! Where are the chieftains in all your towns Whom you demanded: "Give me a king and officers"?

י אֱהִי מַלְכְּךָ אֵפוֹא וְיוֹשִׁיעֲךָ בְּכָל־עָרֶיךָ וְשֹׁפְטֶיךָ אֲשֶׁר אָמַרְתָּ תְּנָה־לִּי מֶלֶךְ וְשָׂרִים:

¹¹ I give you kings in my ire, And take them away in My wrath.

יא אֶתֶּן־לְךָ מֶלֶךְ בְּאַפִּי וְאֶקַּח בְּעֶבְרָתִי:

¹² *Efraim*'s guilt is bound up, His sin is stored away.

יב צָרוּר עֲוֺן אֶפְרָיִם צְפוּנָה חַטָּאתוֹ:

13:8 Like a bear robbed of her young Hoshea portrays *Hashem* in His ferocious anger at the Children of Israel, as a female bear whose cubs have been stolen. *Radak* notes that the mother bear takes care of her young cubs much more than most other animals. Therefore, the sense of anger at the loss of her cubs is correspondingly much stronger. Similarly, God cared for Israel for so long that His sense of loss at their rejection of Him is enormous.

Syrian brown bears at the Jerusalem Zoo

Hoshea/Hosea
Chapter 14

הושע
פרק יד

13 Pangs of childbirth assail him, And the babe is not wise – For this is no time to survive At the birthstool of babes.

יג חֶבְלֵי יוֹלֵדָה יָבֹאוּ לוֹ הוּא־בֵן לֹא חָכָם כִּי־עֵת לֹא־יַעֲמֹד בְּמִשְׁבַּר בָּנִים׃

14 From Sheol itself I will save them, Redeem them from very Death. Where, O Death, are your plagues? Your pestilence where, O Sheol? Revenge shall be far from My thoughts.

יד מִיַּד שְׁאוֹל אֶפְדֵּם מִמָּוֶת אֶגְאָלֵם אֱהִי דְבָרֶיךָ מָוֶת אֱהִי קָטָבְךָ שְׁאוֹל נֹחַם יִסָּתֵר מֵעֵינָי׃

15 For though he flourish among reeds, A blast, a wind of *Hashem*, Shall come blowing up from the wilderness; His fountain shall be parched, His spring dried up. That [wind] shall plunder treasures, Every lovely object.

טו כִּי הוּא בֵּן אַחִים יַפְרִיא יָבוֹא קָדִים רוּחַ יְהֹוָה מִמִּדְבָּר עֹלֶה וְיֵבוֹשׁ מְקוֹרוֹ וְיֶחֱרַב מַעְיָנוֹ הוּא יִשְׁסֶה אוֹצַר כָּל־כְּלִי חֶמְדָּה׃

14

1 *Shomron* must bear her guilt, For she has defied her God. They shall fall by the sword, Their infants shall be dashed to death, And their women with child ripped open.

יד א תֶּאְשַׁם שֹׁמְרוֹן כִּי מָרְתָה בֵּאלֹהֶיהָ בַּחֶרֶב יִפֹּלוּ עֹלְלֵיהֶם יְרֻטָּשׁוּ וְהָרִיּוֹתָיו יְבֻקָּעוּ׃

2 Return, O *Yisrael*, to *Hashem* your God, For you have fallen because of your sin.

ב שׁוּבָה יִשְׂרָאֵל עַד יְהֹוָה אֱלֹהֶיךָ כִּי כָשַׁלְתָּ בַּעֲוֺנֶךָ׃

SHU-vah yis-ra-AYL AD a-do-NAI e-lo-HE-kha KEE kha-SHAL-ta ba-a-vo-NE-kha

3 Take words with you And return to *Hashem*. Say to Him: "Forgive all guilt And accept what is good; Instead of bulls we will pay [The offering of] our lips.

ג קְחוּ עִמָּכֶם דְּבָרִים וְשׁוּבוּ אֶל־יְהֹוָה אִמְרוּ אֵלָיו כָּל־תִּשָּׂא עָוֺן וְקַח־טוֹב וּנְשַׁלְּמָה פָרִים שְׂפָתֵינוּ׃

4 Assyria shall not save us, No more will we ride on steeds; Nor ever again will we call Our handiwork our god, Since in You alone orphans find pity!"

ד אַשּׁוּר ׀ לֹא יוֹשִׁיעֵנוּ עַל־סוּס לֹא נִרְכָּב וְלֹא־נֹאמַר עוֹד אֱלֹהֵינוּ לְמַעֲשֵׂה יָדֵינוּ אֲשֶׁר־בְּךָ יְרֻחַם יָתוֹם׃

5 I will heal their affliction, Generously will I take them back in love; For My anger has turned away from them.

ה אֶרְפָּא מְשׁוּבָתָם אֹהֲבֵם נְדָבָה כִּי שָׁב אַפִּי מִמֶּנּוּ׃

6 I will be to *Yisrael* like dew; He shall blossom like the lily, He shall strike root like a Lebanon tree.

ו אֶהְיֶה כַטַּל לְיִשְׂרָאֵל יִפְרַח כַּשּׁוֹשַׁנָּה וְיַךְ שָׁרָשָׁיו כַּלְּבָנוֹן׃

14:2 Return, O *Yisrael*, to *Hashem* your God *Hoshea* concludes his prophecy with a direct cry to Israel to repent and return to *Hashem*. This is a central theme of *Hoshea*'s prophecies; in this short book, the Hebrew word for 'return,' *shuv* (שוב), appears twenty-five times. *Hoshea* holds out hope that if the people wholeheartedly repent and return, the upcoming devastation can still be avoided. But for that to happen, two things must occur. First, the people must recognize that their sinfulness has led to their predicament, as he says "you have fallen because of your sin." More importantly, the commentators note that *Hoshea* uses the word *ad* (עד), which means 'to,' instead of *el* (אל) which means 'towards.' For repentance to work, it cannot be a fleeting fancy or a mere turning in God's direction. Rather, the people must embrace a sincere commitment to renew the relationship with God and return, not just towards, but all the way to *Hashem*.

שוב

Hoshea/Hosea

Chapter 14

7 His boughs shall spread out far, His beauty shall be like the olive tree's, His fragrance like that of Lebanon.

8 They who sit in his shade shall be revived: They shall bring to life new grain, They shall blossom like the vine; His scent shall be like the wine of Lebanon.

9 *Efraim* [shall say]: "What more have I to do with idols? When I respond and look to Him, I become like a verdant cypress." Your fruit is provided by Me.

10 He who is wise will consider these words, He who is prudent will take note of them. For the paths of *Hashem* are smooth; The righteous can walk on them, While sinners stumble on them.

הושע

פרק יד

ז יֵלְכוּ יֹנְקוֹתָיו וִיהִי כַזַּיִת הוֹדוֹ וְרֵיחַ לוֹ כַּלְּבָנוֹן:

ח יָשֻׁבוּ יֹשְׁבֵי בְצִלּוֹ יְחַיּוּ דָגָן וְיִפְרְחוּ כַגָּפֶן זִכְרוֹ כְּיֵין לְבָנוֹן:

ט אֶפְרַיִם מַה־לִּי עוֹד לָעֲצַבִּים אֲנִי עָנִיתִי וַאֲשׁוּרֶנּוּ אֲנִי כִּבְרוֹשׁ רַעֲנָן מִמֶּנִּי פֶּרְיְךָ נִמְצָא:

י מִי חָכָם וְיָבֵן אֵלֶּה נָבוֹן וְיֵדָעֵם כִּי־יְשָׁרִים דַּרְכֵי יְהֹוָה וְצַדִּקִים יֵלְכוּ בָם וּפֹשְׁעִים יִכָּשְׁלוּ בָם:

Sefer Yoel
The Book of Joel

The second book of the *Trei Asar*, *Sefer Yoel* (Joel), consists of four small chapters. Aside from his father's name, we know nothing of the prophet's personal life, and the absence of historical references in the book make pinpointing when he lived near impossible. However, *Yoel*'s message is clear: Through repentance, disaster can be averted and judgment can be transformed to mercy. Indeed, *Yoel* is one of the few prophets who successfully effects a transformation among the people.

The book has an easily identifiable structure. The first two chapters describe an impending invasion of locusts in *Yehuda*, a manifestation of God's judgment. This plague of locusts is metaphorically compared to an invading army from the north. However, when the people repent, rains fall and restore the land, and the invasion is repelled. In the third chapter, the outpouring of rain becomes a metaphor for an outpouring of God's spirit among the people, as the "day of *Hashem*," judgment day, approaches. In the final chapter, *Hashem* punishes the nations who hated Israel and threatened *Yerushalayim*. Ultimately, the land is restored and the People of Israel will dwell securely on it.

Yoel/Joel
Chapter 1

יוֹאֵל
פרק א

1 ¹ The word of *Hashem* that came to *Yoel* son of *Petuel*.

א דְּבַר־יְהֹוָה אֲשֶׁר הָיָה אֶל־יוֹאֵל בֶּן־פְּתוּאֵל:

² Listen to this, O elders, Give ear, all inhabitants of the land. Has the like of this happened in your days Or in the days of your fathers?

ב שִׁמְעוּ־זֹאת הַזְּקֵנִים וְהַאֲזִינוּ כֹּל יוֹשְׁבֵי הָאָרֶץ הֶהָיְתָה זֹּאת בִּימֵיכֶם וְאִם בִּימֵי אֲבֹתֵיכֶם:

³ Tell your children about it, And let your children tell theirs, And their children the next generation!

ג עָלֶיהָ לִבְנֵיכֶם סַפֵּרוּ וּבְנֵיכֶם לִבְנֵיהֶם וּבְנֵיהֶם לְדוֹר אַחֵר:

⁴ **What the cutter has left, the locust has devoured; What the locust has left, the grub has devoured; And what the grub has left, the hopper has devoured.**

ד יֶתֶר הַגָּזָם אָכַל הָאַרְבֶּה וְיֶתֶר הָאַרְבֶּה אָכַל הַיָּלֶק וְיֶתֶר הַיֶּלֶק אָכַל הֶחָסִיל:

YE-ter ha-ga-ZAM a-KHAL ha-ar-BEH v'-YE-ter ha-ar-BEH a-KHAL ha-YA-lek v'-YE-ter ha-YE-lek a-KHAL he-kha-SEEL

⁵ Wake up, you drunkards, and weep, Wail, all you swillers of wine – For the new wine that is denied you!

ה הָקִיצוּ שִׁכּוֹרִים וּבְכוּ וְהֵילִלוּ כָּל־שֹׁתֵי יָיִן עַל־עָסִיס כִּי נִכְרַת מִפִּיכֶם:

⁶ For a nation has invaded my land, Vast beyond counting, With teeth like the teeth of a lion, With the fangs of a lion's breed.

ו כִּי־גוֹי עָלָה עַל־אַרְצִי עָצוּם וְאֵין מִסְפָּר שִׁנָּיו שִׁנֵּי אַרְיֵה וּמְתַלְּעוֹת לָבִיא לוֹ:

⁷ They have laid my vines waste And splintered my fig trees: They have stripped off their bark and thrown [it] away; Their runners have turned white.

ז שָׂם גַּפְנִי לְשַׁמָּה וּתְאֵנָתִי לִקְצָפָה חָשֹׂף חֲשָׂפָהּ וְהִשְׁלִיךְ הִלְבִּינוּ שָׂרִיגֶיהָ:

⁸ Lament – like a maiden girt with sackcloth For the husband of her youth!

ח אֱלִי כִּבְתוּלָה חֲגֻרַת־שַׂק עַל־בַּעַל נְעוּרֶיהָ:

⁹ Offering and libation have ceased From the House of *Hashem*; The *Kohanim* must mourn Who minister to *Hashem*.

ט הָכְרַת מִנְחָה וָנֶסֶךְ מִבֵּית יְהֹוָה אָבְלוּ הַכֹּהֲנִים מְשָׁרְתֵי יְהֹוָה:

¹⁰ The country is ravaged, The ground must mourn; For the new grain is ravaged, The new wine is dried up, The new oil has failed.

י שֻׁדַּד שָׂדֶה אָבְלָה אֲדָמָה כִּי שֻׁדַּד דָּגָן הוֹבִישׁ תִּירוֹשׁ אֻמְלַל יִצְהָר:

Twelve Prophets

A swarm of locusts over the town of Naveh, Israel

1:4 What the cutter has left, the locust has devoured In Israel and the Middle East, swarms of locusts are not uncommon. The insects appear in the spring, sweeping across northern Africa into Egypt, and from there across the Sinai Peninsula into Israel. Today, we can predict their arrival and control the damage they cause, but in ancient times, they could wreak havoc and cause massive devastation, even destroying an entire year's crop. In this verse, *Yoel* describes a plague of four different species of locusts, each one more destructive than the one that preceded it. Some commentators understand this prophecy literally. Others see it as a metaphor for the different enemy nations that attack the people in their land. Indeed, the prophet Amos writes about a plague of locusts devouring the crops of the northern kingdom (Amos 7:1–3). Either way, *Yoel* calls upon the people to wake up from their drunken stupor (verse 5) to meet the threat, recognizing that it is a result of their sins.

1357

Yoel/Joel
Chapter 2

יואל
פרק ב

11 Farmers are dismayed And vine dressers wail Over wheat and barley; For the crops of the field are lost.

יא הֹבִישׁוּ אִכָּרִים הֵילִילוּ כֹּרְמִים עַל־חִטָּה וְעַל־שְׂעֹרָה כִּי אָבַד קְצִיר שָׂדֶה:

12 The vine has dried up, The fig tree withers, Pomegranate, palm, and apple – All the trees of the field are sear. And joy has dried up Among men.

יב הַגֶּפֶן הוֹבִישָׁה וְהַתְּאֵנָה אֻמְלָלָה רִמּוֹן גַּם־תָּמָר וְתַפּוּחַ כָּל־עֲצֵי הַשָּׂדֶה יָבֵשׁוּ כִּי־הֹבִישׁ שָׂשׂוֹן מִן־בְּנֵי אָדָם:

13 Gird yourselves and lament, O *Kohanim*, Wail, O ministers of the *Mizbayach*; Come, spend the night in sackcloth, O ministers of my God For offering and libation are withheld From the House of your God.

יג חִגְרוּ וְסִפְדוּ הַכֹּהֲנִים הֵילִילוּ מְשָׁרְתֵי מִזְבֵּחַ בֹּאוּ לִינוּ בַשַּׂקִּים מְשָׁרְתֵי אֱלֹהָי כִּי נִמְנַע מִבֵּית אֱלֹהֵיכֶם מִנְחָה וָנָסֶךְ:

14 Solemnize a fast, Proclaim an assembly; Gather the elders – all the inhabitants of the land – In the House of *Hashem* your God, And cry out to *Hashem*.

יד קַדְּשׁוּ־צוֹם קִרְאוּ עֲצָרָה אִסְפוּ זְקֵנִים כֹּל יֹשְׁבֵי הָאָרֶץ בֵּית יְהוָה אֱלֹהֵיכֶם וְזַעֲקוּ אֶל־יְהוָה:

15 Alas for the day! For the day of *Hashem* is near; It shall come like havoc from *Shaddai*.

טו אֲהָהּ לַיּוֹם כִּי קָרוֹב יוֹם יְהוָה וּכְשֹׁד מִשַּׁדַּי יָבוֹא:

16 For food is cut off Before our very eyes, And joy and gladness From the House of our God.

טז הֲלוֹא נֶגֶד עֵינֵינוּ אֹכֶל נִכְרָת מִבֵּית אֱלֹהֵינוּ שִׂמְחָה וָגִיל:

17 The seeds have shriveled Under their clods. The granaries are desolate, Barns are in ruins, For the new grain has failed.

יז עָבְשׁוּ פְרֻדוֹת תַּחַת מֶגְרְפֹתֵיהֶם נָשַׁמּוּ אֹצָרוֹת נֶהֶרְסוּ מַמְּגֻרוֹת כִּי הֹבִישׁ דָּגָן:

18 How the beasts groan! The herds of cattle are bewildered Because they have no pasture, And the flocks of sheep are dazed.

יח מַה־נֶּאֶנְחָה בְהֵמָה נָבֹכוּ עֶדְרֵי בָקָר כִּי אֵין מִרְעֶה לָהֶם גַּם־עֶדְרֵי הַצֹּאן נֶאְשָׁמוּ:

19 To You, *Hashem*, I call. For fire has consumed The pastures in the wilderness, And flame has devoured All the trees of the countryside.

יט אֵלֶיךָ יְהוָה אֶקְרָא כִּי אֵשׁ אָכְלָה נְאוֹת מִדְבָּר וְלֶהָבָה לִהֲטָה כָּל־עֲצֵי הַשָּׂדֶה:

20 The very beasts of the field Cry out to You; For the watercourses are dried up, And fire has consumed The pastures in the wilderness.

כ גַּם־בַּהֲמוֹת שָׂדֶה תַּעֲרוֹג אֵלֶיךָ כִּי יָבְשׁוּ אֲפִיקֵי מָיִם וְאֵשׁ אָכְלָה נְאוֹת הַמִּדְבָּר:

2

1 Blow a *shofar* in *Tzion*, Sound an alarm on My holy mount! Let all dwellers on earth tremble, For the day of *Hashem* has come! It is close –

ב א תִּקְעוּ שׁוֹפָר בְּצִיּוֹן וְהָרִיעוּ בְּהַר קָדְשִׁי יִרְגְּזוּ כֹּל יֹשְׁבֵי הָאָרֶץ כִּי־בָא יוֹם־יְהוָה כִּי קָרוֹב:

2 A day of darkness and gloom, A day of densest cloud Spread like soot over the hills. A vast, enormous horde – Nothing like it has ever happened, And it shall never happen again Through the years and ages.

ב יוֹם חֹשֶׁךְ וַאֲפֵלָה יוֹם עָנָן וַעֲרָפֶל כְּשַׁחַר פָּרֻשׂ עַל־הֶהָרִים עַם רַב וְעָצוּם כָּמֹהוּ לֹא נִהְיָה מִן־הָעוֹלָם וְאַחֲרָיו לֹא יוֹסֵף עַד־שְׁנֵי דּוֹר וָדוֹר:

3 Their vanguard is a consuming fire, Their rear guard a devouring flame. Before them the land was like the Garden of Eden, Behind them, a desolate waste: Nothing has escaped them.

ג לְפָנָיו אָכְלָה אֵשׁ וְאַחֲרָיו תְּלַהֵט לֶהָבָה כְּגַן־עֵדֶן הָאָרֶץ לְפָנָיו וְאַחֲרָיו מִדְבַּר שְׁמָמָה וְגַם־פְּלֵיטָה לֹא־הָיְתָה לּוֹ:

Yoel/Joel
Chapter 2

יואל
פרק ב

4 They have the appearance of horses, They gallop just like steeds.

ד כְּמַרְאֵה סוּסִים מַרְאֵהוּ וּכְפָרָשִׁים כֵּן יְרוּצוּן׃

5 With a clatter as of chariots They bound on the hilltops, With a noise like a blazing fire Consuming straw; Like an enormous horde Arrayed for battle.

ה כְּקוֹל מַרְכָּבוֹת עַל־רָאשֵׁי הֶהָרִים יְרַקֵּדוּן כְּקוֹל לַהַב אֵשׁ אֹכְלָה קָשׁ כְּעַם עָצוּם עֱרוּךְ מִלְחָמָה׃

6 Peoples tremble before them, All faces turn ashen.

ו מִפָּנָיו יָחִילוּ עַמִּים כָּל־פָּנִים קִבְּצוּ פָארוּר׃

7 They rush like warriors, They scale a wall like fighters. And each keeps to his own track. Their paths never cross;

ז כְּגִבּוֹרִים יְרֻצוּן כְּאַנְשֵׁי מִלְחָמָה יַעֲלוּ חוֹמָה וְאִישׁ בִּדְרָכָיו יֵלֵכוּן וְלֹא יְעַבְּטוּן אֹרְחוֹתָם׃

8 No one jostles another, Each keeps to his own course. And should they fall through a loophole, They do not get hurt.

ח וְאִישׁ אָחִיו לֹא יִדְחָקוּן גֶּבֶר בִּמְסִלָּתוֹ יֵלֵכוּן וּבְעַד הַשֶּׁלַח יִפֹּלוּ לֹא יִבְצָעוּ׃

9 They rush up the wall, They dash about in the city; They climb into the houses, They enter like thieves By way of the windows.

ט בָּעִיר יָשֹׁקּוּ בַּחוֹמָה יְרֻצוּן בַּבָּתִּים יַעֲלוּ בְּעַד הַחַלּוֹנִים יָבֹאוּ כַּגַּנָּב׃

10 Before them earth trembles, Heaven shakes, Sun and moon are darkened, And stars withdraw their brightness.

י לְפָנָיו רָגְזָה אֶרֶץ רָעֲשׁוּ שָׁמָיִם שֶׁמֶשׁ וְיָרֵחַ קָדָרוּ וְכוֹכָבִים אָסְפוּ נָגְהָם׃

11 And *Hashem* roars aloud At the head of His army; For vast indeed is His host, Numberless are those that do His bidding. For great is the day of *Hashem*, Most terrible – who can endure it?

יא וַיהוָה נָתַן קוֹלוֹ לִפְנֵי חֵילוֹ כִּי רַב מְאֹד מַחֲנֵהוּ כִּי עָצוּם עֹשֵׂה דְבָרוֹ כִּי־גָדוֹל יוֹם־יְהוָה וְנוֹרָא מְאֹד וּמִי יְכִילֶנּוּ׃

12 "Yet even now" – says *Hashem* – "Turn back to Me with all your hearts, And with fasting, weeping, and lamenting."

יב וְגַם־עַתָּה נְאֻם־יְהוָה שֻׁבוּ עָדַי בְּכָל־לְבַבְכֶם וּבְצוֹם וּבִבְכִי וּבְמִסְפֵּד׃

13 Rend your hearts Rather than your garments, And turn back to *Hashem* your God. For He is gracious and compassionate, Slow to anger, abounding in kindness, And renouncing punishment.

יג וְקִרְעוּ לְבַבְכֶם וְאַל־בִּגְדֵיכֶם וְשׁוּבוּ אֶל־יְהוָה אֱלֹהֵיכֶם כִּי־חַנּוּן וְרַחוּם הוּא אֶרֶךְ אַפַּיִם וְרַב־חֶסֶד וְנִחָם עַל־הָרָעָה׃

v'-kir-U l'-vav-KHEM v'-al big-day-KHEM v'-SHU-vu el a-do-NAI e-lo-hay-KHEM kee kha-NUN v'-ra-KHUM HU E-rekh a-PA-yim v'-rav KHE-sed v'-ni-KHAM al ha-ra-AH

2:13 Rend your hearts rather than your garments *Yoel* tells the Children of Israel that all is not lost; if they repent, the impending disaster can be averted. However, the repentance must not focus on external symbols and behavior, but rather must consist of a genuine change in thoughts and actions. Tearing one's clothing is a sign of mourning (see for example II Samuel 3:31), but *Yoel* cautions that these actions must reflect genuine feelings of remorse. He then references the divine attributes of mercy detailed in *Shemot* (34:6–7) in the context of the giving of the second set of tablets of the Law, which symbolizes the renewal of the covenant. By mentioning the divine attributes, *Yoel* reminds his people that God gives second chances, and also hints to them how they should behave in order to once again find favor in His eyes.

Yoel/Joel
Chapter 2

יואל
פרק ב

14 Who knows but He may turn and relent, And leave a blessing behind For meal offering and drink offering To *Hashem* your God?

מִי יוֹדֵעַ יָשׁוּב וְנִחָם וְהִשְׁאִיר אַחֲרָיו בְּרָכָה מִנְחָה וָנֶסֶךְ לַיהוָה אֱלֹהֵיכֶם:

15 Blow a *shofar* in *Tzion*, Solemnize a fast, Proclaim an assembly!

תִּקְעוּ שׁוֹפָר בְּצִיּוֹן קַדְּשׁוּ־צוֹם קִרְאוּ עֲצָרָה:

16 Gather the people, Bid the congregation purify themselves. Bring together the old, Gather the babes And the sucklings at the breast; Let the bridegroom come out of his chamber, The bride from her canopied couch.

אִסְפוּ־עָם קַדְּשׁוּ קָהָל קִבְצוּ זְקֵנִים אִסְפוּ עוֹלָלִים וְיֹנְקֵי שָׁדָיִם יֵצֵא חָתָן מֵחֶדְרוֹ וְכַלָּה מֵחֻפָּתָהּ:

17 Between the portico and the *Mizbayach*, Let the *Kohanim*, *Hashem*'s ministers, weep And say: "Oh, spare Your people, *Hashem*! Let not Your possession become a mockery, To be taunted by nations! Let not the peoples say, 'Where is their God?'"

בֵּין הָאוּלָם וְלַמִּזְבֵּחַ יִבְכּוּ הַכֹּהֲנִים מְשָׁרְתֵי יְהוָה וְיֹאמְרוּ חוּסָה יְהוָה עַל־עַמֶּךָ וְאַל־תִּתֵּן נַחֲלָתְךָ לְחֶרְפָּה לִמְשָׁל־בָּם גּוֹיִם לָמָּה יֹאמְרוּ בָעַמִּים אַיֵּה אֱלֹהֵיהֶם:

18 Then *Hashem* was roused On behalf of His land And had compassion Upon His people.

וַיְקַנֵּא יְהוָה לְאַרְצוֹ וַיַּחְמֹל עַל־עַמּוֹ:

19 In response to His people *Hashem* declared: "I will grant you the new grain, The new wine, and the new oil, And you shall have them in abundance. Nevermore will I let you be A mockery among the nations.

וַיַּעַן יְהוָה וַיֹּאמֶר לְעַמּוֹ הִנְנִי שֹׁלֵחַ לָכֶם אֶת־הַדָּגָן וְהַתִּירוֹשׁ וְהַיִּצְהָר וּשְׂבַעְתֶּם אֹתוֹ וְלֹא־אֶתֵּן אֶתְכֶם עוֹד חֶרְפָּה בַּגּוֹיִם:

20 I will drive the northerner far from you, I will thrust it into a parched and desolate land – Its van to the Eastern Sea And its rear to the Western Sea; And the stench of it shall go up, And the foul smell rise." For [*Hashem*] shall work great deeds.

וְאֶת־הַצְּפוֹנִי אַרְחִיק מֵעֲלֵיכֶם וְהִדַּחְתִּיו אֶל־אֶרֶץ צִיָּה וּשְׁמָמָה אֶת־פָּנָיו אֶל־הַיָּם הַקַּדְמֹנִי וְסֹפוֹ אֶל־הַיָּם הָאַחֲרוֹן וְעָלָה בָאְשׁוֹ וְתַעַל צַחֲנָתוֹ כִּי הִגְדִּיל לַעֲשׂוֹת:

21 Fear not, O soil, rejoice and be glad; For *Hashem* has wrought great deeds.

אַל־תִּירְאִי אֲדָמָה גִּילִי וּשְׂמָחִי כִּי־הִגְדִּיל יְהוָה לַעֲשׂוֹת:

22 Fear not, O beasts of the field, For the pastures in the wilderness Are clothed with grass. The trees have borne their fruit; Fig tree and vine Have yielded their strength.

אַל־תִּירְאוּ בַּהֲמוֹת שָׂדַי כִּי דָשְׁאוּ נְאוֹת מִדְבָּר כִּי־עֵץ נָשָׂא פִרְיוֹ תְּאֵנָה וָגֶפֶן נָתְנוּ חֵילָם:

23 O children of *Tzion*, be glad, Rejoice in *Hashem* your God. For He has given you the early rain in [His] kindness, Now He makes the rain fall [as] formerly – The early rain and the late –

וּבְנֵי צִיּוֹן גִּילוּ וְשִׂמְחוּ בַּיהוָה אֱלֹהֵיכֶם כִּי־נָתַן לָכֶם אֶת־הַמּוֹרֶה לִצְדָקָה וַיּוֹרֶד לָכֶם גֶּשֶׁם מוֹרֶה וּמַלְקוֹשׁ בָּרִאשׁוֹן:

24 And threshing floors shall be piled with grain, And vats shall overflow with new wine and oil.

וּמָלְאוּ הַגֳּרָנוֹת בָּר וְהֵשִׁיקוּ הַיְקָבִים תִּירוֹשׁ וְיִצְהָר:

25 "I will repay you for the years Consumed by swarms and hoppers, By grubs and locusts, The great army I let loose against you.

וְשִׁלַּמְתִּי לָכֶם אֶת־הַשָּׁנִים אֲשֶׁר אָכַל הָאַרְבֶּה הַיֶּלֶק וְהֶחָסִיל וְהַגָּזָם חֵילִי הַגָּדוֹל אֲשֶׁר שִׁלַּחְתִּי בָּכֶם:

Yoel/Joel

Chapter 3

יואל

פרק ג

26 And you shall eat your fill And praise the name of *Hashem* your God Who dealt so wondrously with you – My people shall be shamed no more.

כו וַאֲכַלְתֶּם אָכוֹל וְשָׂבוֹעַ וְהִלַּלְתֶּם אֶת־שֵׁם יְהֹוָה אֱלֹהֵיכֶם אֲשֶׁר־עָשָׂה עִמָּכֶם לְהַפְלִיא וְלֹא־יֵבֹשׁוּ עַמִּי לְעוֹלָם׃

27 And you shall know That I am in the midst of *Yisrael*: That I *Hashem* am your God And there is no other. And My people shall be shamed no more."

כז וִידַעְתֶּם כִּי בְקֶרֶב יִשְׂרָאֵל אָנִי וַאֲנִי יְהֹוָה אֱלֹהֵיכֶם וְאֵין עוֹד וְלֹא־יֵבֹשׁוּ עַמִּי לְעוֹלָם׃

3 1 After that, I will pour out My spirit on all flesh; Your sons and daughters shall prophesy; Your old men shall dream dreams, And your young men shall see visions.

ג א וְהָיָה אַחֲרֵי־כֵן אֶשְׁפּוֹךְ אֶת־רוּחִי עַל־כָּל־בָּשָׂר וְנִבְּאוּ בְּנֵיכֶם וּבְנוֹתֵיכֶם זִקְנֵיכֶם חֲלֹמוֹת יַחֲלֹמוּן בַּחוּרֵיכֶם חֶזְיֹנוֹת יִרְאוּ׃

v'-ha-YAH a-kha-ray KHAYN esh-POKH et ru-KHEE al kol ba-SAR v'-ni-b'-U b'-nay-KHEM uv-no-tay-KHEM zik-nay-KHEM kha-lo-MOT ya-kha-lo-MUN ba-KHU-ray-KHEM khez-yo-NOT yir-U

2 I will even pour out My spirit Upon male and female slaves in those days.

ב וְגַם עַל־הָעֲבָדִים וְעַל־הַשְּׁפָחוֹת בַּיָּמִים הָהֵמָּה אֶשְׁפּוֹךְ אֶת־רוּחִי׃

3 Before the great and terrible day of *Hashem* comes,* I will set portents in the sky and on earth: Blood and fire and pillars of smoke;

ג וְנָתַתִּי מוֹפְתִים בַּשָּׁמַיִם וּבָאָרֶץ דָּם וָאֵשׁ וְתִימְרוֹת עָשָׁן׃

4 The sun shall turn into darkness And the moon into blood.

ד הַשֶּׁמֶשׁ יֵהָפֵךְ לְחֹשֶׁךְ וְהַיָּרֵחַ לְדָם לִפְנֵי בּוֹא יוֹם יְהֹוָה הַגָּדוֹל וְהַנּוֹרָא׃

5 But everyone who invokes the name of *Hashem* shall escape; for there shall be a remnant on Mount *Tzion* and in *Yerushalayim*, as *Hashem* promised. Anyone who invokes *Hashem* will be among the survivors.

ה וְהָיָה כֹּל אֲשֶׁר־יִקְרָא בְּשֵׁם יְהֹוָה יִמָּלֵט כִּי בְּהַר־צִיּוֹן וּבִירוּשָׁלַםִ תִּהְיֶה פְלֵיטָה כַּאֲשֶׁר אָמַר יְהֹוָה וּבַשְּׂרִידִים אֲשֶׁר יְהֹוָה קֹרֵא׃

4 1 For lo! in those days 1 And in that time, When I restore the fortunes Of *Yehuda* and *Yerushalayim*,

ד א כִּי הִנֵּה בַּיָּמִים הָהֵמָּה וּבָעֵת הַהִיא אֲשֶׁר אשוב [אָשִׁיב] אֶת־שְׁבוּת יְהוּדָה וִירוּשָׁלָםִ׃

2 I will gather all the nations And bring them down to the Valley of *Yehoshafat*. There I will contend with them Over My very own people, *Yisrael*, Which they scattered among the nations. For they divided My land among themselves

ב וְקִבַּצְתִּי אֶת־כָּל־הַגּוֹיִם וְהוֹרַדְתִּים אֶל־עֵמֶק יְהוֹשָׁפָט וְנִשְׁפַּטְתִּי עִמָּם שָׁם עַל־עַמִּי וְנַחֲלָתִי יִשְׂרָאֵל אֲשֶׁר פִּזְּרוּ בַגּוֹיִם וְאֶת־אַרְצִי חִלֵּקוּ׃

---

* "Before the great and terrible day of *Hashem* comes" brought up from verse 4 for clarity

Rabbi Abraham Ibn Ezra (1089–1167)

3:1 I will pour out My spirit on all flesh *Yoel* describes how, in the end of days, there will be an outpouring of God's spirit and prophecy among all people, young and old, male and female. This is, in fact, *Moshe's* fervent wish when *Yehoshua* confronts him with the complaint that *Eldad* and *Medad* are prophesying in the camp. *Moshe* responds "would that all *Hashem's* people were prophets, that *Hashem* put His spirit upon them!" (Numbers 11:29). The medieval commentator *Ibn Ezra* narrows the meaning of *Yoel's* prophecy to those who reside in the Land of Israel. Only in the Holy Land can one reach the spiritual heights necessary to communicate with the Divine.

Yoel/Joel
Chapter 4

יואל
פרק ד

3 And cast lots over My people; And they bartered a boy for a whore, And sold a girl for wine, which they drank.

ג וְאֶל־עַמִּי יַדּוּ גוֹרָל וַיִּתְּנוּ הַיֶּלֶד בַּזּוֹנָה וְהַיַּלְדָּה מָכְרוּ בַיַּיִן וַיִּשְׁתּוּ:

4 What is this you are doing to Me, O Tyre, Sidon, and all the districts of Philistia? Are you requiting Me for something I have done, or are you doing something for My benefit? Quick as a flash, I will pay you back;

ד וְגַם מָה־אַתֶּם לִי צֹר וְצִידוֹן וְכֹל גְּלִילוֹת פְּלָשֶׁת הַגְּמוּל אַתֶּם מְשַׁלְּמִים עָלָי וְאִם־גֹּמְלִים אַתֶּם עָלַי קַל מְהֵרָה אָשִׁיב גְּמֻלְכֶם בְּרֹאשְׁכֶם:

5 for you have taken My gold and My silver, and have carried off My precious treasures to your palaces;

ה אֲשֶׁר־כַּסְפִּי וּזְהָבִי לְקַחְתֶּם וּמַחֲמַדַּי הַטֹּבִים הֲבֵאתֶם לְהֵיכְלֵיכֶם:

6 and you have sold the people of Yehuda and the people of Yerushalayim to the Ionians, so that you have removed them far away from their homeland.

ו וּבְנֵי יְהוּדָה וּבְנֵי יְרוּשָׁלַםִ מְכַרְתֶּם לִבְנֵי הַיְּוָנִים לְמַעַן הַרְחִיקָם מֵעַל גְּבוּלָם:

7 Behold, I will rouse them to leave the place you have sold them to, and I will pay you back:

ז הִנְנִי מְעִירָם מִן־הַמָּקוֹם אֲשֶׁר־מְכַרְתֶּם אֹתָם שָׁמָּה וַהֲשִׁבֹתִי גְמֻלְכֶם בְּרֹאשְׁכֶם:

8 I will deliver your sons and daughters into the hands of the people of Yehuda, and they will sell them into captivity to a distant nation – for Hashem has spoken.

ח וּמָכַרְתִּי אֶת־בְּנֵיכֶם וְאֶת־בְּנוֹתֵיכֶם בְּיַד בְּנֵי יְהוּדָה וּמְכָרוּם לִשְׁבָאיִם אֶל־גּוֹי רָחוֹק כִּי יְהֹוָה דִּבֵּר:

9 Proclaim this among the nations: Prepare for battle! Arouse the warriors, Let all the fighters come and draw near!

ט קִרְאוּ־זֹאת בַּגּוֹיִם קַדְּשׁוּ מִלְחָמָה הָעִירוּ הַגִּבּוֹרִים יִגְּשׁוּ יַעֲלוּ כֹּל אַנְשֵׁי הַמִּלְחָמָה:

10 Beat your plowshares into swords, And your pruning hooks into spears. Let even the weakling say, "I am strong."

י כֹּתּוּ אִתֵּיכֶם לַחֲרָבוֹת וּמַזְמְרֹתֵיכֶם לִרְמָחִים הַחַלָּשׁ יֹאמַר גִּבּוֹר אָנִי:

11 Rouse yourselves and come, All you nations; Come together From roundabout. There bring down Your warriors, Hashem!

יא עוּשׁוּ וָבֹאוּ כָל־הַגּוֹיִם מִסָּבִיב וְנִקְבָּצוּ שָׁמָּה הַנְחַת יְהֹוָה גִּבּוֹרֶיךָ:

12 Let the nations rouse themselves and march up To the Valley of Yehoshafat; For there I will sit in judgment Over all the nations roundabout.

יב יֵעוֹרוּ וְיַעֲלוּ הַגּוֹיִם אֶל־עֵמֶק יְהוֹשָׁפָט כִּי שָׁם אֵשֵׁב לִשְׁפֹּט אֶת־כָּל־הַגּוֹיִם מִסָּבִיב:

13 Swing the sickle, For the crop is ripe; Come and tread, For the winepress is full, The vats are overflowing! For great is their wickedness.

יג שִׁלְחוּ מַגָּל כִּי בָשַׁל קָצִיר בֹּאוּ רְדוּ כִּי־מָלְאָה גַּת הֵשִׁיקוּ הַיְקָבִים כִּי רַבָּה רָעָתָם:

14 Multitudes upon multitudes In the Valley of Decision! For the day of Hashem is at hand In the Valley of Decision.

יד הֲמוֹנִים הֲמוֹנִים בְּעֵמֶק הֶחָרוּץ כִּי קָרוֹב יוֹם יְהֹוָה בְּעֵמֶק הֶחָרוּץ:

15 Sun and moon are darkened, And stars withdraw their brightness.

טו שֶׁמֶשׁ וְיָרֵחַ קָדָרוּ וְכוֹכָבִים אָסְפוּ נָגְהָם:

16 And Hashem will roar from Tzion, And shout aloud from Yerushalayim, So that heaven and earth tremble. But Hashem will be a shelter to His people, A refuge to the children of Yisrael.

טז וַיהֹוָה מִצִּיּוֹן יִשְׁאָג וּמִירוּשָׁלַםִ יִתֵּן קוֹלוֹ וְרָעֲשׁוּ שָׁמַיִם וָאָרֶץ וַיהֹוָה מַחֲסֶה לְעַמּוֹ וּמָעוֹז לִבְנֵי יִשְׂרָאֵל:

Yoel/Joel
Chapter 4

יואל
פרק ד

17 And you shall know that I *Hashem* your God Dwell in *Tzion*, My holy mount. And *Yerushalayim* shall be holy; Nevermore shall strangers pass through it.

יז וִידַעְתֶּם כִּי אֲנִי יְהֹוָה אֱלֹהֵיכֶם שֹׁכֵן בְּצִיּוֹן הַר־קָדְשִׁי וְהָיְתָה יְרוּשָׁלַם קֹדֶשׁ וְזָרִים לֹא־יַעַבְרוּ־בָהּ עוֹד:

18 And in that day, The mountains shall drip with wine, The hills shall flow with milk, And all the watercourses of *Yehuda* shall flow with water; A spring shall issue from the House of *Hashem* And shall water the Wadi of the Acacias.

יח וְהָיָה בַיּוֹם הַהוּא יִטְּפוּ הֶהָרִים עָסִיס וְהַגְּבָעוֹת תֵּלַכְנָה חָלָב וְכָל־אֲפִיקֵי יְהוּדָה יֵלְכוּ מָיִם וּמַעְיָן מִבֵּית יְהֹוָה יֵצֵא וְהִשְׁקָה אֶת־נַחַל הַשִּׁטִּים:

19 Egypt shall be a desolation, And Edom a desolate waste, Because of the outrage to the people of *Yehuda*, In whose land they shed the blood of the innocent.

יט מִצְרַיִם לִשְׁמָמָה תִהְיֶה וֶאֱדוֹם לְמִדְבַּר שְׁמָמָה תִּהְיֶה מֵחֲמַס בְּנֵי יְהוּדָה אֲשֶׁר־שָׁפְכוּ דָם־נָקִיא בְּאַרְצָם:

20 But *Yehuda* shall be inhabited forever, And *Yerushalayim* throughout the ages.

כ וִיהוּדָה לְעוֹלָם תֵּשֵׁב וִירוּשָׁלַם לְדוֹר וָדוֹר:

vee-hu-DAH l'-o-LAM tay-SHAYV vee-ru-sha-LA-im l'-DOR va-DOR

21 Thus I will treat as innocent their blood Which I have not treated as innocent; And *Hashem* shall dwell in *Tzion*.

כא וְנִקֵּיתִי דָּמָם לֹא־נִקֵּיתִי וַיהֹוָה שֹׁכֵן בְּצִיּוֹן:

4:20 But *Yehuda* shall be inhabited forever *Yehuda* is *Yaakov*'s fourth son. When the land is divided amongst the tribes of Israel, *Yehuda* receives the vast territory south of *Yerushalayim*, extending from the Dead Sea in the east to the Mediterranean in the west. For centuries, this area has been known as the region of *Yehuda*, or Judea. Though many people seek to sever the bond between the Jewish people and Judea, the biblical heartland of the Jewish people, through His prophet *Yoel* God promises that *Yehuda* will exist forever.

Sefer Amos
The Book of Amos

The third book of *Trei Asar*, *Sefer Amos* (Amos), contains some of the strongest calls for social justice in the Bible, and indeed, in all of human history. Like his contemporaries *Yeshayahu*, *Hoshea* and *Micha*, *Amos* prophesied in the middle of the eighth century BCE, in the generation preceding the destruction of the northern kingdom of Israel at the hands of Assyria in 722 BCE. This was the period of *Yerovam* II, whose rule represented the last era of stability and prosperity the kingdom of Israel enjoyed before its descent into instability and eventual dissolution. The superscription to his book mentions that he prophesied "two years before the earthquake." Excavations at Hazor have uncovered evidence of a major earthquake that caused extensive damage to the region in the year 760 BCE.

Amos describes himself as both a shepherd (1:1) and as a "tender of sycamore figs" (7:14). Accordingly, his prophecies often draw their metaphors from nature. Though he himself is wealthy, he is especially sympathetic to the plight of the working-class farmers, who find themselves paying full tribute to the ruling functionaries in the capital and to the shrine at *Beit El*, even when suffering from drought, plague and famine. They were compelled to take out heavy loans to continue farming, and their clothes and their children are taken as pledges to secure their debts (2:6–8, 8:4–6).

The book contains three main sections. The first two chapters state that just as other nations courted disaster through their failure to behave morally, Israel will not escape a similar fate. The next four chapters wrestle with the people's claim that their prosperity is evidence of God's favor. The final three chapters describe in clear detail the prophet's visions of the disasters that await the people should they refuse to heed his warning and repent.

Amos/Amos
Chapter 1

עמוס
פרק א

1 ¹ The words of *Amos*, a sheepbreeder from *Tekoa*, who prophesied concerning *Yisrael* in the reigns of Kings *Uzziyahu* of *Yehuda* and *Yerovam* son of *Yoash* of *Yisrael*, two years before the earthquake.

א דִּבְרֵי עָמוֹס אֲשֶׁר־הָיָה בַנֹּקְדִים מִתְּקוֹעַ אֲשֶׁר חָזָה עַל־יִשְׂרָאֵל בִּימֵי עֻזִּיָּה מֶלֶךְ־יְהוּדָה וּבִימֵי יָרָבְעָם בֶּן־יוֹאָשׁ מֶלֶךְ יִשְׂרָאֵל שְׁנָתַיִם לִפְנֵי הָרָעַשׁ:

² He proclaimed: *Hashem* roars from *Tzion*, Shouts aloud from *Yerushalayim*; And the pastures of the shepherds shall languish, And the summit of *Carmel* shall wither.

ב וַיֹּאמַר יְהֹוָה מִצִּיּוֹן יִשְׁאָג וּמִירוּשָׁלַם יִתֵּן קוֹלוֹ וְאָבְלוּ נְאוֹת הָרֹעִים וְיָבֵשׁ רֹאשׁ הַכַּרְמֶל:

³ hus said *Hashem*: For three transgressions of Damascus, For four, I will not revoke it: Because they threshed *Gilad* With threshing boards of iron.

ג כֹּה אָמַר יְהֹוָה עַל־שְׁלֹשָׁה פִּשְׁעֵי דַמֶּשֶׂק וְעַל־אַרְבָּעָה לֹא אֲשִׁיבֶנּוּ עַל־דּוּשָׁם בַּחֲרֻצוֹת הַבַּרְזֶל אֶת־הַגִּלְעָד:

⁴ I will send down fire upon the palace of Hazael, And it shall devour the fortresses of Ben-hadad.

ד וְשִׁלַּחְתִּי אֵשׁ בְּבֵית חֲזָאֵל וְאָכְלָה אַרְמְנוֹת בֶּן־הֲדָד:

⁵ I will break the gate bars of Damascus, And wipe out the inhabitants from the Vale of Aven And the sceptered ruler of Beth-eden; And the people of Aram shall be exiled to Kir – said *Hashem*.

ה וְשָׁבַרְתִּי בְּרִיחַ דַּמֶּשֶׂק וְהִכְרַתִּי יוֹשֵׁב מִבִּקְעַת־אָוֶן וְתוֹמֵךְ שֵׁבֶט מִבֵּית עֶדֶן וְגָלוּ עַם־אֲרָם קִירָה אָמַר יְהֹוָה:

⁶ Thus said *Hashem*: For three transgressions of *Azza*, For four, I will not revoke it: Because they exiled an entire population, Which they delivered to Edom.

ו כֹּה אָמַר יְהֹוָה עַל־שְׁלֹשָׁה פִּשְׁעֵי עַזָּה וְעַל־אַרְבָּעָה לֹא אֲשִׁיבֶנּוּ עַל־הַגְלוֹתָם גָּלוּת שְׁלֵמָה לְהַסְגִּיר לֶאֱדוֹם:

⁷ I will send down fire upon the wall of *Azza*, And it shall devour its fortresses;

ז וְשִׁלַּחְתִּי אֵשׁ בְּחוֹמַת עַזָּה וְאָכְלָה אַרְמְנֹתֶיהָ:

⁸ And I will wipe out the inhabitants of *Ashdod* And the sceptered ruler of *Ashkelon*; And I will turn My hand against Ekron, And the Philistines shall perish to the last man – said *Hashem*.

ח וְהִכְרַתִּי יוֹשֵׁב מֵאַשְׁדּוֹד וְתוֹמֵךְ שֵׁבֶט מֵאַשְׁקְלוֹן וַהֲשִׁיבוֹתִי יָדִי עַל־עֶקְרוֹן וְאָבְדוּ שְׁאֵרִית פְּלִשְׁתִּים אָמַר אֲדֹנָי יְהֹוִה:

⁹ Thus said *Hashem*: For three transgressions of Tyre, For four, I will not revoke it: Because they handed over An entire population to Edom, Ignoring the covenant of brotherhood.

ט כֹּה אָמַר יְהֹוָה עַל־שְׁלֹשָׁה פִּשְׁעֵי־צֹר וְעַל־אַרְבָּעָה לֹא אֲשִׁיבֶנּוּ עַל־הַסְגִּירָם גָּלוּת שְׁלֵמָה לֶאֱדוֹם וְלֹא זָכְרוּ בְּרִית אַחִים:

¹⁰ I will send down fire upon the wall of Tyre, And it shall devour its fortresses.

י וְשִׁלַּחְתִּי אֵשׁ בְּחוֹמַת צֹר וְאָכְלָה אַרְמְנֹתֶיהָ:

¹¹ Thus said *Hashem*: For three transgressions of Edom, For four, I will not revoke it: Because he pursued his brother with the sword And repressed all pity, Because his anger raged unceasing And his fury stormed unchecked.

יא כֹּה אָמַר יְהֹוָה עַל־שְׁלֹשָׁה פִּשְׁעֵי אֱדוֹם וְעַל־אַרְבָּעָה לֹא אֲשִׁיבֶנּוּ עַל־רָדְפוֹ בַחֶרֶב אָחִיו וְשִׁחֵת רַחֲמָיו וַיִּטְרֹף לָעַד אַפּוֹ וְעֶבְרָתוֹ שְׁמָרָה נֶצַח:

KOH a-MAR a-do-NAI al sh'-lo-SHAH pish-AY e-DOM v'-al ar-ba-AH LO a-shee-VE-nu al rod-FO va-KHE-rev a-KHEEV v'-shi-KHAYT ra-kha-MAV va-yit-ROF la-AD a-PO v'-ev-ra-TO sh'-ma-RAH NE-tzakh

1:11 Because his anger raged unceasing *Amos* delivers a harsh prophecy against the southern nation of Edom. When the Land of Israel could no longer bear to have both *Yaakov* and Esau dwell there together,

Amos/Amos
Chapter 2

12 I will send down fire upon Teman, And it shall devour the fortresses of Bozrah.

13 Thus said *Hashem*: For three transgressions of the Amonites, For four, I will not revoke it: Because they ripped open the pregnant women of *Gilad* In order to enlarge their own territory.

14 I will set fire to the wall of Rabbah, And it shall devour its fortresses, Amid shouting on a day of battle, On a day of violent tempest.

15 Their king and his officers shall go Into exile together – said *Hashem*.

2:1 Thus said *Hashem*: For three transgressions of Moab, For four, I will not revoke it: Because he burned the bones Of the king of Edom to lime.

2 I will send down fire upon Moab, And it shall devour the fortresses of Kerioth. And Moab shall die in tumult, Amid shouting and the blare of *shofarot*;

3 I will wipe out the ruler from within her And slay all her officials along with him – said *Hashem*.

4 Thus said *Hashem*: For three transgressions of *Yehuda*, For four, I will not revoke it: Because they have spurned the Teaching of *Hashem* And have not observed His laws; They are beguiled by the delusions After which their fathers walked.

5 I will send down fire upon *Yehuda*, And it shall devour the fortresses of *Yerushalayim*.

עמוס

פרק ב

יב וְשִׁלַּחְתִּי אֵשׁ בְּתֵימָן וְאָכְלָה אַרְמְנוֹת בָּצְרָה:

יג כֹּה אָמַר יְהֹוָה עַל־שְׁלֹשָׁה פִּשְׁעֵי בְנֵי־עַמּוֹן וְעַל־אַרְבָּעָה לֹא אֲשִׁיבֶנּוּ עַל־בִּקְעָם הָרוֹת הַגִּלְעָד לְמַעַן הַרְחִיב אֶת־גְּבוּלָם:

יד וְהִצַּתִּי אֵשׁ בְּחוֹמַת רַבָּה וְאָכְלָה אַרְמְנוֹתֶיהָ בִּתְרוּעָה בְּיוֹם מִלְחָמָה בְּסַעַר בְּיוֹם סוּפָה:

טו וְהָלַךְ מַלְכָּם בַּגּוֹלָה הוּא וְשָׂרָיו יַחְדָּו אָמַר יְהֹוָה:

א כֹּה אָמַר יְהֹוָה עַל־שְׁלֹשָׁה פִּשְׁעֵי מוֹאָב וְעַל־אַרְבָּעָה לֹא אֲשִׁיבֶנּוּ עַל־שָׂרְפוֹ עַצְמוֹת מֶלֶךְ־אֱדוֹם לַשִּׂיד:

ב וְשִׁלַּחְתִּי־אֵשׁ בְּמוֹאָב וְאָכְלָה אַרְמְנוֹת הַקְּרִיּוֹת וּמֵת בְּשָׁאוֹן מוֹאָב בִּתְרוּעָה בְּקוֹל שׁוֹפָר:

ג וְהִכְרַתִּי שׁוֹפֵט מִקִּרְבָּהּ וְכָל־שָׂרֶיהָ אֶהֱרוֹג עִמּוֹ אָמַר יְהֹוָה:

ד כֹּה אָמַר יְהֹוָה עַל־שְׁלֹשָׁה פִּשְׁעֵי יְהוּדָה וְעַל־אַרְבָּעָה לֹא אֲשִׁיבֶנּוּ עַל־מָאֳסָם אֶת־תּוֹרַת יְהֹוָה וְחֻקָּיו לֹא שָׁמָרוּ וַיַּתְעוּם כִּזְבֵיהֶם אֲשֶׁר־הָלְכוּ אֲבוֹתָם אַחֲרֵיהֶם:

ה וְשִׁלַּחְתִּי אֵשׁ בִּיהוּדָה וְאָכְלָה אַרְמְנוֹת יְרוּשָׁלָ͏ִם:

Esau chose to leave for Mount Seir, which became the territory of Edom (Genesis 36:6–8). The Edomites are traditionally thought to be descendants of Esau, and are held accountable for maintaining the fires of enmity and hatred towards *Yaakov's* descendants. Their hatred for *Yaakov's* descendants was so great, and lasted so long, that during *Yehuda's* downfall at the hands of the Babylonians, the Edomites rejoiced and cheered, took spoils from the war and even helped the Babylonians capture Israelites who tried to escape (Obadiah 1:10–15). Their sin was even more heinous because Israel was proscribed from attacking them (Deuteronomy 2:4), and because they refused to abandon old hatreds. Once a prosperous area (I Samuel 14:47), the land of Edom is today a desolate desert, as promised in *Yechezkel* (35:9), "I will make you a desolation for all time; your towns shall never be inhabited, and you shall know that I am *Hashem*."

Amos / Amos
Chapter 2

עָמוֹס
פֶּרֶק ב

6 Thus said *Hashem*: For three transgressions of *Yisrael*, For four, I will not revoke it: Because they have sold for silver Those whose cause was just, And the needy for a pair of sandals.

א כֹּה אָמַר יְהֹוָה עַל־שְׁלֹשָׁה פִּשְׁעֵי יִשְׂרָאֵל וְעַל־אַרְבָּעָה לֹא אֲשִׁיבֶנּוּ עַל־מִכְרָם בַּכֶּסֶף צַדִּיק וְאֶבְיוֹן בַּעֲבוּר נַעֲלָיִם:

KOH a-MAR a-do-NAI al sh'-lo-SHAH pish-AY yis-ra-AYL v'-alar-ba-AH LO a-shee-VE-nu al mikh-RAM ba-KE-sef tza-DEEK v'-ev-YON ba-a-VUR na-a-LA-yim

7 [Ah,] you who trample the heads of the poor Into the dust of the ground, And make the humble walk a twisted course! Father and son go to the same girl, And thereby profane My holy name.

ז הַשֹּׁאֲפִים עַל־עֲפַר־אֶרֶץ בְּרֹאשׁ דַּלִּים וְדֶרֶךְ עֲנָוִים יַטּוּ וְאִישׁ וְאָבִיו יֵלְכוּ אֶל־הַנַּעֲרָה לְמַעַן חַלֵּל אֶת־שֵׁם קׇדְשִׁי:

8 They recline by every altar On garments taken in pledge, And drink in the House of their God Wine bought with fines they imposed.

ח וְעַל־בְּגָדִים חֲבֻלִים יַטּוּ אֵצֶל כׇּל־מִזְבֵּחַ וְיֵין עֲנוּשִׁים יִשְׁתּוּ בֵּית אֱלֹהֵיהֶם:

9 Yet I Destroyed the Amorite before them, Whose stature was like the cedar's And who was stout as the oak, Destroying his boughs above And his trunk below!

ט וְאָנֹכִי הִשְׁמַדְתִּי אֶת־הָאֱמֹרִי מִפְּנֵיהֶם אֲשֶׁר כְּגֹבַהּ אֲרָזִים גׇּבְהוֹ וְחָסֹן הוּא כָּאַלּוֹנִים וָאַשְׁמִיד פִּרְיוֹ מִמַּעַל וְשָׁרָשָׁיו מִתָּחַת:

10 And I Brought you up from the land of Egypt And led you through the wilderness forty years, To possess the land of the Amorite!

י וְאָנֹכִי הֶעֱלֵיתִי אֶתְכֶם מֵאֶרֶץ מִצְרָיִם וָאוֹלֵךְ אֶתְכֶם בַּמִּדְבָּר אַרְבָּעִים שָׁנָה לָרֶשֶׁת אֶת־אֶרֶץ הָאֱמֹרִי:

11 And I raised up *Neviim* from among your sons And nazirites from among your young men. Is that not so, O people of *Yisrael*? – says *Hashem*.

יא וָאָקִים מִבְּנֵיכֶם לִנְבִיאִים וּמִבַּחוּרֵיכֶם לִנְזִרִים הַאַף אֵין־זֹאת בְּנֵי יִשְׂרָאֵל נְאֻם־יְהֹוָה:

12 But you made the nazirites drink wine And ordered the *Neviim* not to prophesy.

יב וַתַּשְׁקוּ אֶת־הַנְּזִרִים יָיִן וְעַל־הַנְּבִיאִים צִוִּיתֶם לֵאמֹר לֹא תִּנָּבְאוּ:

13 Ah, I will slow your movements As a wagon is slowed When it is full of cut grain.

יג הִנֵּה אָנֹכִי מֵעִיק תַּחְתֵּיכֶם כַּאֲשֶׁר תָּעִיק הָעֲגָלָה הַמְלֵאָה לָהּ עָמִיר:

14 Flight shall fail the swift, The strong shall find no strength, And the warrior shall not save his life.

יד וְאָבַד מָנוֹס מִקָּל וְחָזָק לֹא־יְאַמֵּץ כֹּחוֹ וְגִבּוֹר לֹא־יְמַלֵּט נַפְשׁוֹ:

Twelve Prophets

Rashi (1040–1105)

2:6 Because they have sold for silver those whose cause was just *Amos* begins his denunciation of Israel's crimes with the statement that "they have sold for silver those whose cause was just, and the needy for a pair of sandals ". The earliest commentators took this as an allusion to the sale of *Yosef* by his brothers. *Rashi*, however, suggests an alternative explanation based on the Hebrew word for 'shoe', *na'al* (נעל), which also means 'to lock' or 'close in'. According to *Rashi*, the rich would "close in" the property of the poor by purchasing all the land surrounding a poor person's field, preventing him from accessing his lot. They would then compel the poor man to sell his property at heavily discounted prices, forcing him into poverty. In this way, not only did the rich take advantage of the less fortunate, but they forced them into selling their ancestral property. The crime of appropriating a person's ancestral property, his connection to the Land of Israel, is denounced in I Kings chapter 21 and Isaiah 5:8.

1369

Amos/Amos
Chapter 3

עמוס
פרק ג

15 The bowman shall not hold his ground, And the fleet-footed shall not escape, Nor the horseman save his life.

טו וְתֹפֵשׂ הַקֶּשֶׁת לֹא יַעֲמֹד וְקַל בְּרַגְלָיו לֹא יְמַלֵּט וְרֹכֵב הַסּוּס לֹא יְמַלֵּט נַפְשׁוֹ׃

16 Even the most stouthearted warrior Shall run away unarmed that day – declares *Hashem*.

טז וְאַמִּיץ לִבּוֹ בַּגִּבּוֹרִים עָרוֹם יָנוּס בַּיּוֹם־הַהוּא נְאֻם־יְהֹוָה׃

3

1 Hear this word, O people of *Yisrael*, That *Hashem* has spoken concerning you, Concerning the whole family that I brought up from the land of Egypt:

א שִׁמְעוּ אֶת־הַדָּבָר הַזֶּה אֲשֶׁר דִּבֶּר יְהֹוָה עֲלֵיכֶם בְּנֵי יִשְׂרָאֵל עַל כָּל־הַמִּשְׁפָּחָה אֲשֶׁר הֶעֱלֵיתִי מֵאֶרֶץ מִצְרַיִם לֵאמֹר׃

2 You alone have I singled out Of all the families of the earth – That is why I will call you to account For all your iniquities.

ב רַק אֶתְכֶם יָדַעְתִּי מִכֹּל מִשְׁפְּחוֹת הָאֲדָמָה עַל־כֵּן אֶפְקֹד עֲלֵיכֶם אֵת כָּל־עֲוֺנֹתֵיכֶם׃

3 Can two walk together Without having met?

ג הֲיֵלְכוּ שְׁנַיִם יַחְדָּו בִּלְתִּי אִם־נוֹעָדוּ׃

4 Does a lion roar in the forest When he has no prey? Does a great beast let out a cry from its den Without having made a capture?

ד הֲיִשְׁאַג אַרְיֵה בַּיַּעַר וְטֶרֶף אֵין לוֹ הֲיִתֵּן כְּפִיר קוֹלוֹ מִמְּעֹנָתוֹ בִּלְתִּי אִם־לָכָד׃

ha-yish-AG ar-YAY ba-YA-ar v'-TE-ref AYN LO ha-yi-TAYN k'-FEER ko-LO mi-m'-o-na-TO bil-TEE im la-KHAD

5 Does a bird drop on the ground – in a trap – With no snare there? Does a trap spring up from the ground Unless it has caught something?

ה הֲתִפֹּל צִפּוֹר עַל־פַּח הָאָרֶץ וּמוֹקֵשׁ אֵין לָהּ הֲיַעֲלֶה־פַּח מִן־הָאֲדָמָה וְלָכוֹד לֹא יִלְכּוֹד׃

6 When a *shofar* is sounded in a town, Do the people not take alarm? Can misfortune come to a town If *Hashem* has not caused it?

ו אִם־יִתָּקַע שׁוֹפָר בְּעִיר וְעָם לֹא יֶחֱרָדוּ אִם־תִּהְיֶה רָעָה בְּעִיר וַיהֹוָה לֹא עָשָׂה׃

7 Indeed, my God does nothing Without having revealed His purpose To His servants the *Neviim*.

ז כִּי לֹא יַעֲשֶׂה אֲדֹנָי יְהֹוִה דָּבָר כִּי אִם־גָּלָה סוֹדוֹ אֶל־עֲבָדָיו הַנְּבִיאִים׃

8 A lion has roared, Who can but fear? My *Hashem* has spoken, Who can but prophesy?

ח אַרְיֵה שָׁאָג מִי לֹא יִירָא אֲדֹנָי יְהֹוִה דִּבֶּר מִי לֹא יִנָּבֵא׃

9 Proclaim in the fortresses of *Ashdod* And in the fortresses of the land of Egypt! Say: Gather on the hill of *Shomron* And witness the great outrages within her And the oppression in her midst.

ט הַשְׁמִיעוּ עַל־אַרְמְנוֹת בְּאַשְׁדּוֹד וְעַל־אַרְמְנוֹת בְּאֶרֶץ מִצְרָיִם וְאִמְרוּ הֵאָסְפוּ עַל־הָרֵי שֹׁמְרוֹן וּרְאוּ מְהוּמֹת רַבּוֹת בְּתוֹכָהּ וַעֲשׁוּקִים בְּקִרְבָּהּ׃

10 They are incapable of doing right – declares *Hashem*; They store up lawlessness and rapine In their fortresses.

י וְלֹא־יָדְעוּ עֲשׂוֹת־נְכֹחָה נְאֻם־יְהֹוָה הָאוֹצְרִים חָמָס וָשֹׁד בְּאַרְמְנוֹתֵיהֶם׃

3:4 Does a lion roar in the forest when he has no prey? In ancient Israel, lions inhabited the forested areas of the country, and are therefore commonly used as metaphors in the Bible. A lion roars when he is about to attack his prey. An astute animal who hears a roar understands that the lion is about to attack, and rushes to escape. An unperceptive animal, on the other hand, will get caught and destroyed. The message to the Jewish people is to pay attention to the warning signs of impending destruction, and do what is necessary to prevent it. Those who choose to ignore these signs will suffer the consequences.

A lion at the Ramat Gan safari

Amos/Amos
Chapter 4

עמוס
פרק ד

11 Assuredly, Thus said my God: An enemy, all about the land! He shall strip you of your splendor, And your fortresses shall be plundered.

יא לָכֵן כֹּה אָמַר אֲדֹנָי יְהוִה צַר וּסְבִיב הָאָרֶץ וְהוֹרִד מִמֵּךְ עֻזֵּךְ וְנָבֹזּוּ אַרְמְנוֹתָיִךְ׃

12 Thus said *Hashem*: As a shepherd rescues from the lion's jaws Two shank bones or the tip of an ear, So shall the Israelites escape Who dwell in *Shomron* – With the leg of a bed or the head of a couch.

יב כֹּה אָמַר יְהוָה כַּאֲשֶׁר יַצִּיל הָרֹעֶה מִפִּי הָאֲרִי שְׁתֵּי כְרָעַיִם אוֹ בְדַל־אֹזֶן כֵּן יִנָּצְלוּ בְּנֵי יִשְׂרָאֵל הַיֹּשְׁבִים בְּשֹׁמְרוֹן בִּפְאַת מִטָּה וּבִדְמֶשֶׁק עָרֶשׂ׃

13 Hear [this], and warn the House of *Yaakov* – says my Lord *Hashem*, the God of Hosts –

יג שִׁמְעוּ וְהָעִידוּ בְּבֵית יַעֲקֹב נְאֻם־אֲדֹנָי יְהוִה אֱלֹהֵי הַצְּבָאוֹת׃

14 That when I punish *Yisrael* for its transgressions, I will wreak judgment on the altar of *Beit El*, And the horns of the altar shall be cut off And shall fall to the ground.

יד כִּי בְּיוֹם פָּקְדִי פִשְׁעֵי־יִשְׂרָאֵל עָלָיו וּפָקַדְתִּי עַל־מִזְבְּחוֹת בֵּית־אֵל וְנִגְדְּעוּ קַרְנוֹת הַמִּזְבֵּחַ וְנָפְלוּ לָאָרֶץ׃

15 I will wreck the winter palace Together with the summer palace; The ivory palaces shall be demolished, And the great houses shall be destroyed – declares *Hashem*.

טו וְהִכֵּיתִי בֵית־הַחֹרֶף עַל־בֵּית הַקָּיִץ וְאָבְדוּ בָּתֵּי הַשֵּׁן וְסָפוּ בָּתִּים רַבִּים נְאֻם־יְהוָה׃

4

1 Hear this word, you cows of Bashan On the hill of *Shomron* – Who defraud the poor, Who rob the needy; Who say to your husbands, "Bring, and let's carouse!"

א שִׁמְעוּ הַדָּבָר הַזֶּה פָּרוֹת הַבָּשָׁן אֲשֶׁר בְּהַר שֹׁמְרוֹן הָעֹשְׁקוֹת דַּלִּים הָרֹצְצוֹת אֶבְיוֹנִים הָאֹמְרֹת לַאֲדֹנֵיהֶם הָבִיאָה וְנִשְׁתֶּה׃

shim-U ha-da-VAR ha-ZEH pa-ROT ha-ba-SHAN a-SHER b'-HAR sho-m'-RON ha-o-sh'-KOT da-LEEM ha-ro-tz'-TZOT ev-yo-NEEM ha-o-m'-ROT la-a-do-nay-HEM ha-VEE-ah v'-nish-TEH

2 My *Hashem* swears by His holiness: Behold, days are coming upon you When you will be carried off in baskets, And, to the last one, in fish baskets,

ב נִשְׁבַּע אֲדֹנָי יְהוִה בְּקָדְשׁוֹ כִּי הִנֵּה יָמִים בָּאִים עֲלֵיכֶם וְנִשָּׂא אֶתְכֶם בְּצִנּוֹת וְאַחֲרִיתְכֶן בְּסִירוֹת דּוּגָה׃

3 And taken out [of the city] – Each one through a breach straight ahead – And flung on the refuse heap – declares *Hashem*.

ג וּפְרָצִים תֵּצֶאנָה אִשָּׁה נֶגְדָּהּ וְהִשְׁלַכְתֶּנָה הַהַרְמוֹנָה נְאֻם־יְהוָה׃

4 Come to *Beit El* and transgress; To *Gilgal*, and transgress even more: Present your sacrifices the next morning And your tithes on the third day;

ד בֹּאוּ בֵית־אֵל וּפִשְׁעוּ הַגִּלְגָּל הַרְבּוּ לִפְשֹׁעַ וְהָבִיאוּ לַבֹּקֶר זִבְחֵיכֶם לִשְׁלֹשֶׁת יָמִים מַעְשְׂרֹתֵיכֶם׃

5 And burn a thank offering of leavened bread; And proclaim freewill offerings loudly. For you love that sort of thing, O Israelites – declares my God.

ה וְקַטֵּר מֵחָמֵץ תּוֹדָה וְקִרְאוּ נְדָבוֹת הַשְׁמִיעוּ כִּי כֵן אֲהַבְתֶּם בְּנֵי יִשְׂרָאֵל נְאֻם אֲדֹנָי יְהוִה׃

4:1 You cows of Bashan Sparing no one in his denunciations, *Amos* speaks against the women of *Shomron*. Their selfish lifestyle and constant consumption forces their husbands to continually extort money from the poor to satisfy their extravagant tastes. He compares these women to the cattle of Bashan, who constantly consume grains and ask the masters for more to drink. The plains of Bashan are located east of the Sea of Galilee, on the banks of the Yarmuk river in Trans-Jordan. They were considered among the richest lands in biblical times (Deuteronomy 32:14, Ezekiel 39:18, Psalms 22:13).

Amos/Amos
Chapter 5

6 I, on My part, have given you Cleanness of teeth in all your towns, And lack of food in all your settlements. Yet you did not turn back to Me – declares *Hashem*.

7 I therefore withheld the rain from you Three months before harvesttime: I would make it rain on one town And not on another; One field would be rained upon While another on which it did not rain Would wither.

8 So two or three towns would wander To a single town to drink water, But their thirst would not be slaked. Yet you did not turn back to Me – declares *Hashem*.

9 I scourged you with blight and mildew; Repeatedly your gardens and vineyards, Your fig trees and olive trees Were devoured by locusts. Yet you did not turn back to Me – declares *Hashem*.

10 I sent against you pestilence In the manner of Egypt; I slew your young men with the sword, Together with your captured horses, And I made the stench of your armies Rise in your very nostrils. Yet you did not turn back to Me – declares *Hashem*.

11 I have wrought destruction among you As when *Hashem* destroyed Sodom and Gomorrah; You have become like a brand plucked from burning. Yet you have not turned back to Me – declares *Hashem*.

12 Assuredly, Because I am doing that to you, Even so will I act toward you, O *Yisrael* – Prepare to meet your God, O *Yisrael*!

13 Behold, He who formed the mountains, And created the wind, And has told man what His wish is, Who turns blackness into daybreak, And treads upon the high places of the earth – His name is *Hashem*, the God of Hosts.

5

1 Hear this word which I intone As a dirge over you, O House of *Yisrael*:

2 Fallen, not to rise again, Is Maiden *Yisrael*; Abandoned on her soil With none to lift her up.

3 For thus said my God About the House of *Yisrael*: The town that marches out a thousand strong Shall have a hundred left, And the one that marches out a hundred strong Shall have but ten left.

4 Thus said *Hashem* To the House of *Yisrael*: Seek Me, and you will live.

Amos/Amos
Chapter 5

עמוס
פרק ה

5 Do not seek *Beit El*, Nor go to *Gilgal*, Nor cross over to *Be'er Sheva*; For *Gilgal* shall go into exile, And *Beit El* shall become a delusion.

ה וְאַל־תִּדְרְשׁוּ בֵּית־אֵל וְהַגִּלְגָּל לֹא תָבֹאוּ וּבְאֵר שֶׁבַע לֹא תַעֲבֹרוּ כִּי הַגִּלְגָּל גָּלֹה יִגְלֶה וּבֵית־אֵל יִהְיֶה לְאָוֶן:

6 Seek *Hashem*, and you will live, Else He will rush like fire upon the House of *Yosef* And consume *Beit El* with none to quench it.

ו דִּרְשׁוּ אֶת־יְהֹוָה וִחְיוּ פֶּן־יִצְלַח כָּאֵשׁ בֵּית יוֹסֵף וְאָכְלָה וְאֵין־מְכַבֶּה לְבֵית־אֵל:

7 [Ah,] you who turn justice into wormwood And hurl righteousness to the ground! [Seek *Hashem*,]

ז הַהֹפְכִים לְלַעֲנָה מִשְׁפָּט וּצְדָקָה לָאָרֶץ הִנִּיחוּ:

8 Who made the Pleiades and Orion, Who turns deep darkness into dawn And darkens day into night, Who summons the waters of the sea And pours them out upon the earth – His name is *Hashem*!

ח עֹשֵׂה כִימָה וּכְסִיל וְהֹפֵךְ לַבֹּקֶר צַלְמָוֶת וְיוֹם לַיְלָה הֶחְשִׁיךְ הַקּוֹרֵא לְמֵי־הַיָּם וַיִּשְׁפְּכֵם עַל־פְּנֵי הָאָרֶץ יְהֹוָה שְׁמוֹ:

9 It is He who hurls destruction upon strongholds, So that ruin comes upon fortresses!

ט הַמַּבְלִיג שֹׁד עַל־עָז וְשֹׁד עַל־מִבְצָר יָבוֹא:

10 They hate the arbiter in the gate, And detest him whose plea is just.

י שָׂנְאוּ בַשַּׁעַר מוֹכִיחַ וְדֹבֵר תָּמִים יְתָעֵבוּ:

11 Assuredly, Because you impose a tax on the poor And exact from him a levy of grain, You have built houses of hewn stone, But you shall not live in them; You have planted delightful vineyards, But shall not drink their wine.

יא לָכֵן יַעַן בּוֹשַׁסְכֶם עַל־דָּל וּמַשְׂאַת־בַּר תִּקְחוּ מִמֶּנּוּ בָּתֵּי גָזִית בְּנִיתֶם וְלֹא־תֵשְׁבוּ בָם כַּרְמֵי־חֶמֶד נְטַעְתֶּם וְלֹא תִשְׁתּוּ אֶת־יֵינָם:

12 For I have noted how many are your crimes, And how countless your sins – You enemies of the righteous, You takers of bribes, You who subvert in the gate The cause of the needy!

יב כִּי יָדַעְתִּי רַבִּים פִּשְׁעֵיכֶם וַעֲצֻמִים חַטֹּאתֵיכֶם צֹרְרֵי צַדִּיק לֹקְחֵי כֹפֶר וְאֶבְיוֹנִים בַּשַּׁעַר הִטּוּ:

13 Assuredly, At such a time the prudent man keeps silent, For it is an evil time.

יג לָכֵן הַמַּשְׂכִּיל בָּעֵת הַהִיא יִדֹּם כִּי עֵת רָעָה הִיא:

14 Seek good and not evil, That you may live, And that *Hashem*, the God of Hosts, May truly be with you, As you think.

יד דִּרְשׁוּ־טוֹב וְאַל־רָע לְמַעַן תִּחְיוּ וִיהִי־כֵן יְהֹוָה אֱלֹהֵי־צְבָאוֹת אִתְּכֶם כַּאֲשֶׁר אֲמַרְתֶּם:

15 Hate evil and love good, And establish justice in the gate; Perhaps *Hashem*, the God of Hosts, Will be gracious to the remnant of *Yosef*.

טו שִׂנְאוּ־רָע וְאֶהֱבוּ טוֹב וְהַצִּיגוּ בַשַּׁעַר מִשְׁפָּט אוּלַי יֶחֱנַן יְהֹוָה אֱלֹהֵי־צְבָאוֹת שְׁאֵרִית יוֹסֵף:

16 Assuredly, Thus said *Hashem*, My Lord, the God of Hosts: In every square there shall be lamenting, In every street cries of "Ah, woe!" And the farm hand shall be Called to mourn, And those skilled in wailing To lament;

טז לָכֵן כֹּה־אָמַר יְהֹוָה אֱלֹהֵי צְבָאוֹת אֲדֹנָי בְּכָל־רְחֹבוֹת מִסְפֵּד וּבְכָל־חוּצוֹת יֹאמְרוּ הוֹ־הוֹ וְקָרְאוּ אִכָּר אֶל־אֵבֶל וּמִסְפֵּד אֶל־יוֹדְעֵי נֶהִי:

17 For there shall be lamenting In every vineyard, too, When I pass through your midst – said *Hashem*.

יז וּבְכָל־כְּרָמִים מִסְפֵּד כִּי־אֶעֱבֹר בְּקִרְבְּךָ אָמַר יְהֹוָה:

Amos / Amos
Chapter 5

18 Ah, you who wish For the day of *Hashem*! Why should you want The day of *Hashem*? It shall be darkness, not light! –

יח הוֹי הַמִּתְאַוִּים אֶת־יוֹם יְהֹוָה לָמָּה־זֶּה לָכֶם יוֹם יְהֹוָה הוּא־חֹשֶׁךְ וְלֹא־אוֹר:

19 As if a man should run from a lion And be attacked by a bear; Or if he got indoors, Should lean his hand on the wall And be bitten by a snake!

יט כַּאֲשֶׁר יָנוּס אִישׁ מִפְּנֵי הָאֲרִי וּפְגָעוֹ הַדֹּב וּבָא הַבַּיִת וְסָמַךְ יָדוֹ עַל־הַקִּיר וּנְשָׁכוֹ הַנָּחָשׁ:

20 Surely the day of *Hashem* shall be Not light, but darkness, Blackest night without a glimmer.

כ הֲלֹא־חֹשֶׁךְ יוֹם יְהֹוָה וְלֹא־אוֹר וְאָפֵל וְלֹא־נֹגַהּ לוֹ:

21 I loathe, I spurn your festivals, I am not appeased by your solemn assemblies.

כא שָׂנֵאתִי מָאַסְתִּי חַגֵּיכֶם וְלֹא אָרִיחַ בְּעַצְּרֹתֵיכֶם:

22 If you offer Me burnt offerings – or your meal offerings – I will not accept them; I will pay no heed To your gifts of fatlings.

כב כִּי אִם־תַּעֲלוּ־לִי עֹלוֹת וּמִנְחֹתֵיכֶם לֹא אֶרְצֶה וְשֶׁלֶם מְרִיאֵיכֶם לֹא אַבִּיט:

23 Spare Me the sound of your hymns, And let Me not hear the music of your lutes.

כג הָסֵר מֵעָלַי הֲמוֹן שִׁרֶיךָ וְזִמְרַת נְבָלֶיךָ לֹא אֶשְׁמָע:

24 But let justice well up like water, Righteousness like an unfailing stream.

כד וְיִגַּל כַּמַּיִם מִשְׁפָּט וּצְדָקָה כְּנַחַל אֵיתָן:

v'-yi-GAL ka-MA-yim mish-PAT utz-da-KAH k'-NA-khal ay-TAN

25 Did you offer sacrifice and oblation to Me Those forty years in the wilderness, O House of *Yisrael*?

כה הַזְּבָחִים וּמִנְחָה הִגַּשְׁתֶּם־לִי בַמִּדְבָּר אַרְבָּעִים שָׁנָה בֵּית יִשְׂרָאֵל:

26 And you shall carry off your "king" – Sikkuth and Kiyyun, The images you have made for yourselves Of your astral deity –

כו וּנְשָׂאתֶם אֵת סִכּוּת מַלְכְּכֶם וְאֵת כִּיּוּן צַלְמֵיכֶם כּוֹכַב אֱלֹהֵיכֶם אֲשֶׁר עֲשִׂיתֶם לָכֶם:

27 As I drive you into exile beyond Damascus – Said *Hashem*, whose name is God of Hosts.

כז וְהִגְלֵיתִי אֶתְכֶם מֵהָלְאָה לְדַמָּשֶׂק אָמַר יְהֹוָה אֱלֹהֵי־צְבָאוֹת שְׁמוֹ:

Chapter 6

6:1 Ah, you who are at ease in *Tzion* And confident on the hill of *Shomron*, You notables of the leading nation On whom the House of *Yisrael* pin their hopes:

א הוֹי הַשַּׁאֲנַנִּים בְּצִיּוֹן וְהַבֹּטְחִים בְּהַר שֹׁמְרוֹן נְקֻבֵי רֵאשִׁית הַגּוֹיִם וּבָאוּ לָהֶם בֵּית יִשְׂרָאֵל:

HOY ha-sha-a-na-NEEM b'-tzi-YON v'-ha-bo-t'-KHEEM b'-HAR sho-m'-RON n'-ku-VAY ray-SHEET ha-go-YIM u-VA-u la-HEM BAYT yis-ra-AYL

5:24 Righteousness like an unfailing stream Having rejected rote ritual worship that is not accompanied by moral behavior (verse 22), *Amos* makes a simple statement: He declares that *Hashem* desires justice and righteousness. Though the Land of Israel has only one rainy season, when the rainfall builds up and finally overflows, the creeks and brooks are filled from the swiftly flowing rivers and there are even flash floods. So too, the desire for justice and righteousness should build up in the people until it overflows "like an unfailing stream".

6:1 And confident on the hill of *Shomron* While the poor suffer under heavy taxation and injustice, the rich remain blissfully unaware of the conditions

Flash flood water in the Judean desert

Amos / Amos
Chapter 6

2 Cross over to Calneh and see, Go from there to Great Hamath, And go down to Gath of the Philistines: Are [you] better than those kingdoms, Or is their territory larger than yours?

3 Yet you ward off [the thought of] a day of woe And convene a session of lawlessness.

4 They lie on ivory beds, Lolling on their couches, Feasting on lambs from the flock And on calves from the stalls.

5 They hum snatches of song To the tune of the lute – They account themselves musicians like *David*.

6 They drink [straight] from the wine bowls And anoint themselves with the choicest oils – But they are not concerned about the ruin of *Yosef*.

7 Assuredly, right soon They shall head the column of exiles; They shall loll no more at festive meals.

8 My *Hashem* swears by Himself: I loathe the Pride of *Yaakov*, And I detest his fortresses. I will declare forfeit city and inhabitants alike – declares *Hashem*, the God of Hosts.

9 If ten people are left in one house, they shall die.

10 And if someone's kinsman – who is to burn incense for him – comes to carry the remains out of a house, and he calls to the one at the rear of the house, "Are there any alive besides you?" he will answer, "No, none." And he will say, "Hush!" – so that no one may utter the name of *Hashem*.

11 For *Hashem* will command, And the great house shall be smashed to bits, And the little house to splinters.

12 Can horses gallop on a rock? Can it be plowed with oxen? Yet you have turned justice into poison weed And the fruit of righteousness to wormwood.

עמוס
פרק ו

ב עִבְרוּ כַלְנֵה וּרְאוּ וּלְכוּ מִשָּׁם חֲמַת רַבָּה וּרְדוּ גַת־פְּלִשְׁתִּים הֲטוֹבִים מִן־הַמַּמְלָכוֹת הָאֵלֶּה אִם־רַב גְּבוּלָם מִגְּבֻלְכֶם׃

ג הַמְנַדִּים לְיוֹם רָע וַתַּגִּישׁוּן שֶׁבֶת חָמָס׃

ד הַשֹּׁכְבִים עַל־מִטּוֹת שֵׁן וּסְרֻחִים עַל־עַרְשֹׂתָם וְאֹכְלִים כָּרִים מִצֹּאן וַעֲגָלִים מִתּוֹךְ מַרְבֵּק׃

ה הַפֹּרְטִים עַל־פִּי הַנָּבֶל כְּדָוִיד חָשְׁבוּ לָהֶם כְּלֵי־שִׁיר׃

ו הַשֹּׁתִים בְּמִזְרְקֵי יַיִן וְרֵאשִׁית שְׁמָנִים יִמְשָׁחוּ וְלֹא נֶחְלוּ עַל־שֵׁבֶר יוֹסֵף׃

ז לָכֵן עַתָּה יִגְלוּ בְּרֹאשׁ גֹּלִים וְסָר מִרְזַח סְרוּחִים׃

ח נִשְׁבַּע אֲדֹנָי יְהוִה בְּנַפְשׁוֹ נְאֻם־יְהוָה אֱלֹהֵי צְבָאוֹת מְתָאֵב אָנֹכִי אֶת־גְּאוֹן יַעֲקֹב וְאַרְמְנֹתָיו שָׂנֵאתִי וְהִסְגַּרְתִּי עִיר וּמְלֹאָהּ׃

ט וְהָיָה אִם־יִוָּתְרוּ עֲשָׂרָה אֲנָשִׁים בְּבַיִת אֶחָד וָמֵתוּ׃

י וּנְשָׂאוֹ דּוֹדוֹ וּמְסָרְפוֹ לְהוֹצִיא עֲצָמִים מִן־הַבַּיִת וְאָמַר לַאֲשֶׁר בְּיַרְכְּתֵי הַבַּיִת הַעוֹד עִמָּךְ וְאָמַר אָפֶס וְאָמַר הָס כִּי לֹא לְהַזְכִּיר בְּשֵׁם יְהוָה׃

יא כִּי־הִנֵּה יְהוָה מְצַוֶּה וְהִכָּה הַבַּיִת הַגָּדוֹל רְסִיסִים וְהַבַּיִת הַקָּטֹן בְּקִעִים׃

יב הַיְרֻצוּן בַּסֶּלַע סוּסִים אִם־יַחֲרוֹשׁ בַּבְּקָרִים כִּי־הֲפַכְתֶּם לְרֹאשׁ מִשְׁפָּט וּפְרִי צְדָקָה לְלַעֲנָה׃

The hills of Shomron

outside their palaces and the impending doom that awaits them. *Shomron* was situated in the central hills of the country, surrounded by an array of mountains, which gave its inhabitants a feeling of security. *Amos* uses this geographical fact to mock the leadership's lack of awareness of the events transpiring on the other side of these mountains.

Amos/Amos
Chapter 7

עמוס
פרק ז

13 [Ah,] those who are so happy about Lo-dabar, Who exult, "By our might We have captured Karnaim"!

הַשְּׂמֵחִים לְלֹא דָבָר הָאֹמְרִים הֲלוֹא בְחָזְקֵנוּ לָקַחְנוּ לָנוּ קַרְנָיִם׃

14 But I, O House of *Yisrael*, Will raise up a nation against you – declares *Hashem*, the God of Hosts – Who will harass you from Lebo-Hamath To the Wadi Arabah. 1

כִּי הִנְנִי מֵקִים עֲלֵיכֶם בֵּית יִשְׂרָאֵל נְאֻם־יְהֹוָה אֱלֹהֵי הַצְּבָאוֹת גּוֹי וְלָחֲצוּ אֶתְכֶם מִלְּבוֹא חֲמָת עַד־נַחַל הָעֲרָבָה׃

7 1 This is what my God showed me: He was creating [a plague of] locusts at the time when the late-sown crops were beginning to sprout – the late-sown crops after the king's reaping.

ז א כֹּה הִרְאַנִי אֲדֹנָי יֱהֹוִה וְהִנֵּה יוֹצֵר גֹּבַי בִּתְחִלַּת עֲלוֹת הַלָּקֶשׁ וְהִנֵּה־לֶקֶשׁ אַחַר גִּזֵּי הַמֶּלֶךְ׃

2 When it had finished devouring the herbage in the land, I said, "O *Hashem*, pray forgive. How will *Yaakov* survive? He is so small."

ב וְהָיָה אִם־כִּלָּה לֶאֱכוֹל אֶת־עֵשֶׂב הָאָרֶץ וָאֹמַר אֲדֹנָי יֱהֹוִה סְלַח־נָא מִי יָקוּם יַעֲקֹב כִּי קָטֹן הוּא׃

3 *Hashem* relented concerning this. "It shall not come to pass," said *Hashem*.

ג נִחַם יְהֹוָה עַל־זֹאת לֹא תִהְיֶה אָמַר יְהֹוָה׃

4 This is what *Hashem* showed me: Lo, my God was summoning to contend by fire which consumed the Great Deep and was consuming the fields.

ד כֹּה הִרְאַנִי אֲדֹנָי יֱהֹוִה וְהִנֵּה קֹרֵא לָרִב בָּאֵשׁ אֲדֹנָי יֱהֹוִה וַתֹּאכַל אֶת־תְּהוֹם רַבָּה וְאָכְלָה אֶת־הַחֵלֶק׃

5 I said, "Oh, *Hashem*, refrain! How will *Yaakov* survive? He is so small."

ה וָאֹמַר אֲדֹנָי יֱהֹוִה חֲדַל־נָא מִי יָקוּם יַעֲקֹב כִּי קָטֹן הוּא׃

6 *Hashem* relented concerning this. "That shall not come to pass, either," said my God.

ו נִחַם יְהֹוָה עַל־זֹאת גַּם־הִיא לֹא תִהְיֶה אָמַר אֲדֹנָי יֱהֹוִה׃

7 This is what He showed me: He was standing on a wall checked with a plumb line and He was holding a plumb line.

ז כֹּה הִרְאַנִי וְהִנֵּה אֲדֹנָי נִצָּב עַל־חוֹמַת אֲנָךְ וּבְיָדוֹ אֲנָךְ׃

8 And *Hashem* asked me, "What do you see, *Amos*?" "A plumb line," I replied. And my Lord declared, "I am going to apply a plumb line to My people *Yisrael*; I will pardon them no more.

ח וַיֹּאמֶר יְהֹוָה אֵלַי מָה־אַתָּה רֹאֶה עָמוֹס וָאֹמַר אֲנָךְ וַיֹּאמֶר אֲדֹנָי הִנְנִי שָׂם אֲנָךְ בְּקֶרֶב עַמִּי יִשְׂרָאֵל לֹא־אוֹסִיף עוֹד עֲבוֹר לוֹ׃

va-YO-mer a-do-NAI ay-LAI mah a-TAH ro-EH a-MOS va-o-MAR a-NAKH va-YO-mer a-do-NAI hi-n'-NEE SAM a-NAKH b'-KE-rev a-MEE yis-ra-AYL lo o-SEEF OD a-VOR LO

7:8 I am going to apply a plumb line to My people *Yisrael* *Amos* is shown a vision of a plumb line, a construction tool used to measure the vertical straightness of a wall by means of a string with a piece of lead tied to it. This is important, because if the wall is leaning or uneven, it will be unstable and may eventually collapse under its own weight as it is being built, or afterwards. Here, the plumb line is a symbol of God's examination of the people's moral uprightness. Their pretensions of integrity are symbolized by a wall being built higher and higher. When He checks it, he finds the measurements lacking.

Amos/Amos
Chapter 8

9 The shrines of *Yitzchak* shall be laid waste, and the sanctuaries of *Yisrael* reduced to ruins; and I will turn upon the House of *Yerovam* with the sword."

10 *Amatzya*, the *Kohen* of *Beit El*, sent this message to King *Yerovam* of *Yisrael*: "*Amos* is conspiring against you within the House of *Yisrael*. The country cannot endure the things he is saying.

11 For *Amos* has said, '*Yerovam* shall die by the sword, and *Yisrael* shall be exiled from its soil.'"

12 *Amatzya* also said to *Amos*, "Seer, off with you to the land of *Yehuda*! Earn your living there, and do your prophesying there.

13 But don't ever prophesy again at *Beit El*; for it is a king's sanctuary and a royal palace."

14 *Amos* answered *Amatzya*: "I am not a *Navi*, and I am not a *Navi*'s disciple. I am a cattle breeder and a tender of sycamore figs.

15 But *Hashem* took me away from following the flock, and *Hashem* said to me, 'Go, prophesy to My people *Yisrael*.'

16 And so, hear the word of *Hashem*. You say I must not prophesy about the House of *Yisrael* or preach about the House of *Yitzchak*;

17 but this, I swear, is what *Hashem* said: Your wife shall play the harlot in the town, your sons and daughters shall fall by the sword, and your land shall be divided up with a measuring line. And you yourself shall die on unclean soil; for *Yisrael* shall be exiled from its soil."

8
1 This is what my God showed me: There was a basket of figs.

KOH hir-A-nee a-do-NAI e-lo-HEEM v'-hi-NAY k'-LUV KA-yitz

8:1 A basket of figs *Amos* is shown a vision of a basket of figs, in Hebrew a *k'luv ka-yitz* (כלוב קיץ), which literally means 'a basket of summer fruit.' The fruits were harvested during the transition from summer to the rainy season, and brought to the *Beit Hamikdash* during the *Sukkot* holiday in the seventh month of the year. *Hashem*'s explanation of the vision: "The hour of doom has come for My people *Yisrael*; I will not pardon them again" (verse 2), is a play on words. In Hebrew, 'summer' is pronounced *ka-yitz* (קיץ), while 'end,' or 'hour of doom' as it is translated here, is pronounced *kaytz* (קץ). The *Malbim* explains that the prophet is warning that just as the summer marks the end of the fruit harvest, so too the end of the kingdom of Israel is approaching.

Malbim (1809–1879)

Amos/Amos
Chapter 8

עמוס
פרק ח

2 He said, "What do you see, *Amos*?" "A basket of figs," I replied. And *Hashem* said to me: "The hour of doom has come for My people *Yisrael*; I will not pardon them again.

ב וַיֹּאמֶר מָה־אַתָּה רֹאֶה עָמוֹס וָאֹמַר כְּלוּב קָיִץ וַיֹּאמֶר יְהֹוָה אֵלַי בָּא הַקֵּץ אֶל־עַמִּי יִשְׂרָאֵל לֹא־אוֹסִיף עוֹד עֲבוֹר לוֹ:

3 And the singing women of the palace shall howl on that day – declares my God: So many corpses Left lying everywhere! Hush!"

ג וְהֵילִילוּ שִׁירוֹת הֵיכָל בַּיּוֹם הַהוּא נְאֻם אֲדֹנָי יְהֹוִה רַב הַפֶּגֶר בְּכָל־מָקוֹם הִשְׁלִיךְ הָס:

4 Listen to this, you who devour the needy, annihilating the poor of the land,

ד שִׁמְעוּ־זֹאת הַשֹּׁאֲפִים אֶבְיוֹן וְלַשְׁבִּית עֲנִוֵּי [עֲנִיֵּי] אָרֶץ:

5 saying, "If only the new moon were over, so that we could sell grain; the *Shabbat*, so that we could offer wheat for sale, using an *efah* that is too small, and a *shekel* that is too big, tilting a dishonest scale,

ה לֵאמֹר מָתַי יַעֲבֹר הַחֹדֶשׁ וְנַשְׁבִּירָה שֶּׁבֶר וְהַשַּׁבָּת וְנִפְתְּחָה־בָּר לְהַקְטִין אֵיפָה וּלְהַגְדִּיל שֶׁקֶל וּלְעַוֵּת מֹאזְנֵי מִרְמָה:

6 and selling grain refuse as grain! We will buy the poor for silver, the needy for a pair of sandals."

ו לִקְנוֹת בַּכֶּסֶף דַּלִּים וְאֶבְיוֹן בַּעֲבוּר נַעֲלָיִם וּמַפַּל בַּר נַשְׁבִּיר:

7 *Hashem* swears by the Pride of *Yaakov*: "I will never forget any of their doings."

ז נִשְׁבַּע יְהֹוָה בִּגְאוֹן יַעֲקֹב אִם־אֶשְׁכַּח לָנֶצַח כָּל־מַעֲשֵׂיהֶם:

8 Shall not the earth shake for this And all that dwell on it mourn? Shall it not all rise like the Nile And surge and subside like the Nile of Egypt?

ח הַעַל זֹאת לֹא־תִרְגַּז הָאָרֶץ וְאָבַל כָּל־יוֹשֵׁב בָּהּ וְעָלְתָה כָאֹר כֻּלָּהּ וְנִגְרְשָׁה וְנִשְׁקְעָה [וְנִשְׁקָעָה] כִּיאוֹר מִצְרָיִם:

9 And in that day – declares my God – I will make the sun set at noon, I will darken the earth on a sunny day.

ט וְהָיָה בַּיּוֹם הַהוּא נְאֻם אֲדֹנָי יְהֹוִה וְהֵבֵאתִי הַשֶּׁמֶשׁ בַּצָּהֳרָיִם וְהַחֲשַׁכְתִּי לָאָרֶץ בְּיוֹם אוֹר:

10 I will turn your festivals into mourning And all your songs into dirges; I will put sackcloth on all loins And tonsures on every head. I will make it mourn as for an only child, All of it as on a bitter day.

י וְהָפַכְתִּי חַגֵּיכֶם לְאֵבֶל וְכָל־שִׁירֵיכֶם לְקִינָה וְהַעֲלֵיתִי עַל־כָּל־מָתְנַיִם שָׂק וְעַל־כָּל־רֹאשׁ קָרְחָה וְשַׂמְתִּיהָ כְּאֵבֶל יָחִיד וְאַחֲרִיתָהּ כְּיוֹם מָר:

11 A time is coming – declares my God – when I will send a famine upon the land: not a hunger for bread or a thirst for water, but for hearing the words of *Hashem*.

יא הִנֵּה יָמִים בָּאִים נְאֻם אֲדֹנָי יְהֹוִה וְהִשְׁלַחְתִּי רָעָב בָּאָרֶץ לֹא־רָעָב לַלֶּחֶם וְלֹא־צָמָא לַמַּיִם כִּי אִם־לִשְׁמֹעַ אֵת דִּבְרֵי יְהֹוָה:

12 Men shall wander from sea to sea and from north to east to seek the word of *Hashem*, but they shall not find it.

יב וְנָעוּ מִיָּם עַד־יָם וּמִצָּפוֹן וְעַד־מִזְרָח יְשׁוֹטְטוּ לְבַקֵּשׁ אֶת־דְּבַר־יְהֹוָה וְלֹא יִמְצָאוּ:

13 In that day, the beautiful maidens and the young men shall faint with thirst –

יג בַּיּוֹם הַהוּא תִּתְעַלַּפְנָה הַבְּתוּלֹת הַיָּפוֹת וְהַבַּחוּרִים בַּצָּמָא:

14 Those who swear by the guilt of *Shomron*, Saying, "As your god lives, *Dan*," And "As the way to *Be'er Sheva* lives" – They shall fall to rise no more.

יד הַנִּשְׁבָּעִים בְּאַשְׁמַת שֹׁמְרוֹן וְאָמְרוּ חֵי אֱלֹהֶיךָ דָּן וְחֵי דֶּרֶךְ בְּאֵר־שָׁבַע וְנָפְלוּ וְלֹא־יָקוּמוּ עוֹד:

Amos / Amos
Chapter 9

עמוס
פרק ט

9 1 I saw *Hashem* standing by the *Mizbayach*, and He said: Strike the capitals so that the thresholds quake, and make an end of the first of them all. And I will slay the last of them with the sword; not one of them shall escape, and not one of them shall survive.

א רָאִיתִי אֶת־אֲדֹנָי נִצָּב עַל־הַמִּזְבֵּחַ וַיֹּאמֶר הַךְ הַכַּפְתּוֹר וְיִרְעֲשׁוּ הַסִּפִּים וּבְצַעַם בְּרֹאשׁ כֻּלָּם וְאַחֲרִיתָם בַּחֶרֶב אֶהֱרֹג לֹא־יָנוּס לָהֶם נָס וְלֹא־יִמָּלֵט לָהֶם פָּלִיט:

2 If they burrow down to Sheol, From there My hand shall take them; And if they ascend to heaven, From there I will bring them down.

ב אִם־יַחְתְּרוּ בִשְׁאוֹל מִשָּׁם יָדִי תִקָּחֵם וְאִם־יַעֲלוּ הַשָּׁמַיִם מִשָּׁם אוֹרִידֵם:

3 If they hide on the top of *Carmel*, There I will search them out and seize them; And if they conceal themselves from My sight At the bottom of the sea, There I will command The serpent to bite them.

ג וְאִם־יֵחָבְאוּ בְּרֹאשׁ הַכַּרְמֶל מִשָּׁם אֲחַפֵּשׂ וּלְקַחְתִּים וְאִם־יִסָּתְרוּ מִנֶּגֶד עֵינַי בְּקַרְקַע הַיָּם מִשָּׁם אֲצַוֶּה אֶת־הַנָּחָשׁ וּנְשָׁכָם:

4 And if they go into captivity Before their enemies, There I will command The sword to slay them. I will fix My eye on them for evil And not for good.

ד וְאִם־יֵלְכוּ בַשְּׁבִי לִפְנֵי אֹיְבֵיהֶם מִשָּׁם אֲצַוֶּה אֶת־הַחֶרֶב וַהֲרָגָתַם וְשַׂמְתִּי עֵינִי עֲלֵיהֶם לְרָעָה וְלֹא לְטוֹבָה:

5 It is my Lord the God of Hosts At whose touch the earth trembles And all who dwell on it mourn, And all of it swells like the Nile And subsides like the Nile of Egypt;

ה וַאדֹנָי יֱהֹוִה הַצְּבָאוֹת הַנּוֹגֵעַ בָּאָרֶץ וַתָּמוֹג וְאָבְלוּ כָּל־יוֹשְׁבֵי בָהּ וְעָלְתָה כַיְאֹר כֻּלָּהּ וְשָׁקְעָה כִּיאֹר מִצְרָיִם:

6 Who built His chambers in heaven And founded His vault on the earth, Who summons the waters of the sea And pours them over the land – His name is *Hashem*.

ו הַבּוֹנֶה בַשָּׁמַיִם מַעֲלוֹתוֹ [מַעֲלוֹתָיו] וַאֲגֻדָּתוֹ עַל־אֶרֶץ יְסָדָהּ הַקֹּרֵא לְמֵי־הַיָּם וַיִּשְׁפְּכֵם עַל־פְּנֵי הָאָרֶץ יְהֹוָה שְׁמוֹ:

7 To Me, O Israelites, you are Just like the Ethiopians – declares *Hashem*. True, I brought *Yisrael* up From the land of Egypt, But also the Philistines from Caphtor And the Arameans from Kir.

ז הֲלוֹא כִבְנֵי כֻשִׁיִּים אַתֶּם לִי בְּנֵי יִשְׂרָאֵל נְאֻם־יְהֹוָה הֲלוֹא אֶת־יִשְׂרָאֵל הֶעֱלֵיתִי מֵאֶרֶץ מִצְרַיִם וּפְלִשְׁתִּיִּים מִכַּפְתּוֹר וַאֲרָם מִקִּיר:

8 Behold, *Hashem* has His eye Upon the sinful kingdom: I will wipe it off The face of the earth! But, I will not wholly wipe out The House of *Yaakov* – declares *Hashem*.

ח הִנֵּה עֵינֵי אֲדֹנָי יֱהֹוִה בַּמַּמְלָכָה הַחַטָּאָה וְהִשְׁמַדְתִּי אֹתָהּ מֵעַל פְּנֵי הָאֲדָמָה אֶפֶס כִּי לֹא הַשְׁמֵיד אַשְׁמִיד אֶת־בֵּית יַעֲקֹב נְאֻם־יְהֹוָה:

9 For I will give the order And shake the House of *Yisrael* – Through all the nations – As one shakes [sand] in a sieve, And not a pebble falls to the ground.

ט כִּי־הִנֵּה אָנֹכִי מְצַוֶּה וַהֲנִעוֹתִי בְכָל־הַגּוֹיִם אֶת־בֵּית יִשְׂרָאֵל כַּאֲשֶׁר יִנּוֹעַ בַּכְּבָרָה וְלֹא־יִפּוֹל צְרוֹר אָרֶץ:

10 All the sinners of My people Shall perish by the sword, Who boast, "Never shall the evil Overtake us or come near us."

י בַּחֶרֶב יָמוּתוּ כֹּל חַטָּאֵי עַמִּי הָאֹמְרִים לֹא־תַגִּישׁ וְתַקְדִּים בַּעֲדֵינוּ הָרָעָה:

Amos/Amos
Chapter 9

עמוס
פרק ט

11 In that day, I will set up again the fallen booth of *David*: I will mend its breaches and set up its ruins anew. I will build it firm as in the days of old,

יא בַּיּוֹם הַהוּא אָקִים אֶת־סֻכַּת דָּוִיד הַנֹּפֶלֶת וְגָדַרְתִּי אֶת־פִּרְצֵיהֶן וַהֲרִסֹתָיו אָקִים וּבְנִיתִיהָ כִּימֵי עוֹלָם:

12 So that they shall possess the rest of Edom And all the nations once attached to My name – declares *Hashem* who will bring this to pass.

יב לְמַעַן יִירְשׁוּ אֶת־שְׁאֵרִית אֱדוֹם וְכָל־הַגּוֹיִם אֲשֶׁר־נִקְרָא שְׁמִי עֲלֵיהֶם נְאֻם־יְהֹוָה עֹשֶׂה זֹּאת:

13 A time is coming – declares *Hashem* – When the plowman shall meet the reaper, And the treader of grapes Him who holds the [bag of] seed; When the mountains shall drip wine And all the hills shall wave [with grain].

יג הִנֵּה יָמִים בָּאִים נְאֻם־יְהֹוָה וְנִגַּשׁ חוֹרֵשׁ בַּקֹּצֵר וְדֹרֵךְ עֲנָבִים בְּמֹשֵׁךְ הַזָּרַע וְהִטִּיפוּ הֶהָרִים עָסִיס וְכָל־הַגְּבָעוֹת תִּתְמוֹגַגְנָה:

14 I will restore My people *Yisrael*. They shall rebuild ruined cities and inhabit them; They shall plant vineyards and drink their wine; They shall till gardens and eat their fruits.

יד וְשַׁבְתִּי אֶת־שְׁבוּת עַמִּי יִשְׂרָאֵל וּבָנוּ עָרִים נְשַׁמּוֹת וְיָשָׁבוּ וְנָטְעוּ כְרָמִים וְשָׁתוּ אֶת־יֵינָם וְעָשׂוּ גַנּוֹת וְאָכְלוּ אֶת־פְּרִיהֶם:

15 And I will plant them upon their soil, Nevermore to be uprooted From the soil I have given them – said *Hashem* your God.

טו וּנְטַעְתִּים עַל־אַדְמָתָם וְלֹא יִנָּתְשׁוּ עוֹד מֵעַל אַדְמָתָם אֲשֶׁר נָתַתִּי לָהֶם אָמַר יְהֹוָה אֱלֹהֶיךָ:

un-ta-TEEM al ad-ma-TAM v'-LO yi-na-t'-SHU OD may-AL ad-ma-TAM a-SHER na-TA-tee la-HEM a-MAR a-do-NAI e-lo-HE-kha

---

9:15 Nevermore to be uprooted from the soil I have given them Despite the predictions of punishments that will befall the Children of Israel, *Amos* ends his prophecy with a message of hope. He proclaims that the day will come when the people will return to the Land of Israel, build houses, plant vineyards and trees, and enjoy their fruits. This is reminiscent of the idyllic times described by *Micha* (4:4) when every man shall sit "Under his grapevine or fig tree with no one to disturb him." *Amos* concludes by comparing the people to a sapling planted firmly in the ground. Their connection to the Land of Israel will never again be uprooted.

Sefer Ovadya
The Book of Obadiah

The fourth book of the *Trei Asar*, *Sefer Ovadya* (Obadiah), is the shortest book in the *Tanakh*. It contains one stark message consisting of invective against Edom. Throughout history, Edom remained Israel's implacable enemy, a hatred made even more unforgivable due to their close blood relationship: The Edomites were descendants of Esau, *Yaakov's* brother. The loathing for Edom became engraved in the Jewish mind, and in rabbinic thought, all of Israel's enemies are considered to be Edom's spiritual descendants.

It is impossible to identify who *Ovadya* was, or the time in which he lived. Some traditions connect him with the righteous treasurer of *Achav's* court, who hid the prophets from Jezebel's murderous wrath (I Kings 18:3–4). However, it is difficult to imagine a prophecy against Edom being uttered at that time, in the ninth century BCE, when Edom was a backward region consisting mostly of desert sands. Furthermore, the focus of the book is on *Yehuda* and *Yerushalayim*, and not on *Achav's* northern kingdom.

Therefore, others suggest that *Ovadya* prophesied after the destruction of the first Temple in 586 BCE, when Edom not only broke their alliance with *Yehuda* to betray them to the Babylonian conquerors (see Psalms 137:7 and Isaiah 34:5–17), but then moved across the Jordan Valley to the area west of the Dead Sea, invading and occupying territory that had previously been the inheritance of the exiled Judeans.

The single chapter of *Ovadya* contains several smaller sections, including the prophecy and call against Edom, the grounds for the upcoming punishment, and the punishment itself.

Ovadya/Obaddiah
Chapter 1

עוֹבַדְיָה
פרק א

1 ¹ The prophecy of *Ovadya*. We have received tidings from *Hashem*, And an envoy has been sent out among the nations: "Up! Let us rise up against her for battle." Thus said my God concerning Edom:

א חֲזוֹן עֹבַדְיָה כֹּה־אָמַר אֲדֹנָי יֱהֹוִה לֶאֱדוֹם שְׁמוּעָה שָׁמַעְנוּ מֵאֵת יְהוָה וְצִיר בַּגּוֹיִם שֻׁלָּח קוּמוּ וְנָקוּמָה עָלֶיהָ לַמִּלְחָמָה׃

² I will make you least among nations, You shall be most despised.

ב הִנֵּה קָטֹן נְתַתִּיךָ בַּגּוֹיִם בָּזוּי אַתָּה מְאֹד׃

³ Your arrogant heart has seduced you, You who dwell in clefts of the rock, In your lofty abode. You think in your heart, "Who can pull me down to earth?"

ג זְדוֹן לִבְּךָ הִשִּׁיאֶךָ שֹׁכְנִי בְחַגְוֵי־סֶלַע מְרוֹם שִׁבְתּוֹ אֹמֵר בְּלִבּוֹ מִי יוֹרִדֵנִי אָרֶץ׃

⁴ Should you nest as high as the eagle, Should your eyrie be lodged 'mong the stars, Even from there I will pull you down – declares *Hashem*.

ד אִם־תַּגְבִּיהַּ כַּנֶּשֶׁר וְאִם־בֵּין כּוֹכָבִים שִׂים קִנֶּךָ מִשָּׁם אוֹרִידְךָ נְאֻם־יְהוָה׃

⁵ If thieves were to come to you, Marauders by night, They would steal no more than they needed. If vintagers came to you, They would surely leave some gleanings. How utterly you are destroyed!

ה אִם־גַּנָּבִים בָּאוּ־לְךָ אִם־שׁוֹדְדֵי לַיְלָה אֵיךְ נִדְמֵיתָה הֲלוֹא יִגְנְבוּ דַּיָּם אִם־בֹּצְרִים בָּאוּ לָךְ הֲלוֹא יַשְׁאִירוּ עֹלֵלוֹת׃

⁶ How thoroughly rifled is Esau, How ransacked his hoards!

ו אֵיךְ נֶחְפְּשׂוּ עֵשָׂו נִבְעוּ מַצְפֻּנָיו׃

⁷ All your allies turned you back At the frontier; Your own confederates Have duped and overcome you; [Those who ate] your bread Have planted snares under you. He is bereft of understanding.

ז עַד־הַגְּבוּל שִׁלְּחוּךָ כֹּל אַנְשֵׁי בְרִיתֶךָ הִשִּׁיאוּךָ יָכְלוּ לְךָ אַנְשֵׁי שְׁלֹמֶךָ לַחְמְךָ יָשִׂימוּ מָזוֹר תַּחְתֶּיךָ אֵין תְּבוּנָה בּוֹ׃

⁸ In that day – declares *Hashem* – I will make the wise vanish from Edom, Understanding from Esau's mount.

ח הֲלוֹא בַּיּוֹם הַהוּא נְאֻם־יְהוָה וְהַאֲבַדְתִּי חֲכָמִים מֵאֱדוֹם וּתְבוּנָה מֵהַר עֵשָׂו׃

⁹ Your warriors shall lose heart, O Teman, And not a man on Esau's mount Shall survive the slaughter.

ט וְחַתּוּ גִבּוֹרֶיךָ תֵּימָן לְמַעַן יִכָּרֶת־אִישׁ מֵהַר עֵשָׂו מִקָּטֶל׃

v'-kha-TU gi-bo-RE-kha tay-MAN l'-MA-an yi-KA-ret eesh may-HAR ay-SAV mi-KA-tel

¹⁰ For the outrage to your brother *Yaakov*, Disgrace shall engulf you, And you shall perish forever

י מֵחֲמַס אָחִיךָ יַעֲקֹב תְּכַסְּךָ בוּשָׁה וְנִכְרַתָּ לְעוֹלָם׃

1:9 Not a man on Esau's mount shall survive the slaughter In the conclusion of *Ovadya*'s description of Edom's downfall, two mountains face off against each other: Mount *Tzion*, the symbol of justice and peace, and the Mountain of Esau or Mount Seir, which is the symbol of Esau's treachery and greed. When *Tzion* defeats Seir, God's rule over the world will be complete. The end of this prophecy is reminiscent of other verses in the Bible that foretell *Hashem*'s dominion over the world in future times, with *Tzion* the seat of His reign. For example, King David writes: "*Hashem* shall reign forever, your God, O *Tzion*, for all generations" (Psalms 146:10). *Zecharya* prophesies: "*Hashem* shall be King over all the earth" (Zecharya 14:9), and *Yeshayahu* and *Micha* envision a time when "Many peoples shall go and say: 'Come, Let us go up to the Mount of *Hashem*, to the House of the God of *Yaakov*, that He may instruct us in His ways, and that we may walk in His paths; for instruction shall come forth from *Tzion*, the word of *Hashem* from *Yerushalayim*" (Isaiah 2:3, Micah 4:2).

Ovadya/Obadiah
Chapter 1

11 On that day when you stood aloof, When aliens carried off his goods, When foreigners entered his gates And cast lots for *Yerushalayim*, You were as one of them.

12 How could you gaze with glee On your brother that day, On his day of calamity! How could you gloat Over the people of *Yehuda* On that day of ruin! How could you loudly jeer On a day of anguish!

13 How could you enter the gate of My people On its day of disaster, Gaze in glee with the others On its misfortune On its day of disaster, And lay hands on its wealth On its day of disaster!

14 How could you stand at the passes To cut down its fugitives! How could you betray those who fled On that day of anguish!

15 As you did, so shall it be done to you; Your conduct shall be requited. Yea, against all nations The day of *Hashem* is at hand.

16 That same cup that you drank on My Holy Mount Shall all nations drink evermore, Drink till their speech grows thick, And they become as though they had never been.

17 But on *Tzion*'s mount a remnant shall survive, And it shall be holy. The House of *Yaakov* shall dispossess Those who dispossessed them.

uv-HAR tzi-YON tih-YEH f'-lay-TAH v'-HA-yah KO-desh v'-ya-r'-SHU BAYT ya-a-KOV AYT mo-ra-shay-HEM

עובדיה
פרק א

יא בְּיוֹם עֲמָדְךָ מִנֶּגֶד בְּיוֹם שְׁבוֹת זָרִים חֵילוֹ וְנָכְרִים בָּאוּ שערו [שְׁעָרָיו] וְעַל־יְרוּשָׁלַם יַדּוּ גוֹרָל גַּם־אַתָּה כְּאַחַד מֵהֶם:

יב וְאַל־תֵּרֶא בְיוֹם־אָחִיךָ בְּיוֹם נָכְרוֹ וְאַל־תִּשְׂמַח לִבְנֵי־יְהוּדָה בְּיוֹם אָבְדָם וְאַל־תַּגְדֵּל פִּיךָ בְּיוֹם צָרָה:

יג אַל־תָּבוֹא בְשַׁעַר־עַמִּי בְּיוֹם אֵידָם אַל־תֵּרֶא גַם־אַתָּה בְּרָעָתוֹ בְּיוֹם אֵידוֹ וְאַל־תִּשְׁלַחְנָה בְחֵילוֹ בְּיוֹם אֵידוֹ:

יד וְאַל־תַּעֲמֹד עַל־הַפֶּרֶק לְהַכְרִית אֶת־פְּלִיטָיו וְאַל־תַּסְגֵּר שְׂרִידָיו בְּיוֹם צָרָה:

טו כִּי־קָרוֹב יוֹם־יְהוָה עַל־כָּל־הַגּוֹיִם כַּאֲשֶׁר עָשִׂיתָ יֵעָשֶׂה לָּךְ גְּמֻלְךָ יָשׁוּב בְּרֹאשֶׁךָ:

טז כִּי כַּאֲשֶׁר שְׁתִיתֶם עַל־הַר קָדְשִׁי יִשְׁתּוּ כָל־הַגּוֹיִם תָּמִיד וְשָׁתוּ וְלָעוּ וְהָיוּ כְּלוֹא הָיוּ:

יז וּבְהַר צִיּוֹן תִּהְיֶה פְלֵיטָה וְהָיָה קֹדֶשׁ וְיָרְשׁוּ בֵּית יַעֲקֹב אֵת מוֹרָשֵׁיהֶם:

1:17 But on *Tzion*'s mount a remnant shall survive. *Ovadya* uses the same Hebrew word, *playta* (פליטה), 'remnant,' that *Yaakov* originally used to describe his confrontation with his brother: "If Esau comes to the one camp and attacks it, the other camp may yet escape *(playta)*" (Genesis 32:9). When the same Hebrew word is used to describe unrelated events, this means that the *Tanakh* is alluding to a deep connection between them. *Ovadya* is invoking the great confrontation between *Yaakov* and Esau to describe the final encounter between the Jews and their enemies, and teaching us the ultimate secret to the survival of *Yaakov*'s descendants, the Jewish people. When the European Jewish community realized the grave danger Hitler posed, they found solace in the words of the *Tanakh* and recognized that "on *Tzion*'s mount a remnant shall survive." The saintly Rabbi Israel Meir Kagen (1839–1933), known as the *Chofetz Chaim*, told his students that the survival of the Jewish people would be through the Land of Israel. In fact, the great Ponevezh Yeshiva in *Bnei Brak*, one of the largest centers of *Torah* study in the world, has this verse etched on its front wall, reminding its students never to forget that *Tzion* is the only refuge from persecution and the wrath of Esau.

Front wall of the Ponovezh Yeshiva in Bnei Brak

Ovadya/Obadiah
Chapter 1

עוֹבַדְיָה
פרק א

18 The House of *Yaakov* shall be fire, And the House of *Yosef* flame, And the House of Esau shall be straw; They shall burn it and devour it, And no survivor shall be left of the House of Esau – for *Hashem* has spoken.

יח וְהָיָה בֵית־יַעֲקֹב אֵשׁ וּבֵית יוֹסֵף לֶהָבָה וּבֵית עֵשָׂו לְקַשׁ וְדָלְקוּ בָהֶם וַאֲכָלוּם וְלֹא־יִהְיֶה שָׂרִיד לְבֵית עֵשָׂו כִּי יְהֹוָה דִּבֵּר:

19 Thus they shall possess the *Negev* and Mount Esau as well, the Shephelah and Philistia. They shall possess the Ephraimite country and the district of *Shomron*, and *Binyamin* along with *Gilad*.

יט וְיָרְשׁוּ הַנֶּגֶב אֶת־הַר עֵשָׂו וְהַשְּׁפֵלָה אֶת־פְּלִשְׁתִּים וְיָרְשׁוּ אֶת־שְׂדֵה אֶפְרַיִם וְאֵת שְׂדֵה שֹׁמְרוֹן וּבִנְיָמִן אֶת־הַגִּלְעָד:

20 And that exiled force of Israelites [shall possess] what belongs to the Phoenicians as far as Zarephath, while the Jerusalemite exile community of Sepharad shall possess the towns of the *Negev*.

כ וְגָלֻת הַחֵל־הַזֶּה לִבְנֵי יִשְׂרָאֵל אֲשֶׁר־כְּנַעֲנִים עַד־צָרְפַת וְגָלֻת יְרוּשָׁלִַם אֲשֶׁר בִּסְפָרַד יִרְשׁוּ אֵת עָרֵי הַנֶּגֶב:

21 For liberators shall march up on Mount *Tzion* to wreak judgment on Mount Esau; and dominion shall be *Hashem*'s.

כא וְעָלוּ מוֹשִׁעִים בְּהַר צִיּוֹן לִשְׁפֹּט אֶת־הַר עֵשָׂו וְהָיְתָה לַיהֹוָה הַמְּלוּכָה:

v'-a-LU mo-shi-EEM b'-HAR tzi-YON lish-POT et HAR ay-SAV v'-ha-y'-TAH la-do-NAI ha-m'-lu-KHAH

1:21 For liberators shall march up on Mount Tzion Who are the liberators who will march upon Mount Zion and judge the enemies of the Jewish people? Rabbi David Stavsky (1929–2004) quotes several commentators including *Radak*, *Malbim* and *Mezudat David*, who agree that these saviors are the *Mashiach* and his ministers. He writes that especially in our own times, following the Holocaust and the establishment of the State of Israel, "We must analyze and understand every nuance of this verse, for I believe we are living in a time when *Ovadya's* prophecy is at last being realized... These seem to be the days of a Messianic era. If not, how else can we explain the awakening from a coma of millions of Soviet Jews, a resuscitation, a life after spiritual death, a return to a Judaism that they knew of, but could not practice. We feel in the depths of our souls, in the marrow of our bones, that we are living in Messianic times."

Rabbi David Stavsky (1930–2004)

Sefer Yona
The Book of Jonah

The fifth book of the *Trei Asar, Sefer Yona* (Jonah), is one of the most famous books of the Bible and one of the least understood. The excitement of the giant fish that swallows the runaway prophet, the suspense about whether or not the people of Nineveh will repent, and the question if God will carry out his threat to overturn the city, all tend to overshadow the resounding moral message contained in the book: *Hashem* is merciful, patient, and forgiving, even to the worst scoundrels and enemies that humanity knows, as long as they take steps towards justice, righteousness, and repentance.

Yona, son of *Amittai*, is mentioned in *Melachim* II (14:25) as a prophet who lived during the reign of *Yerovam* II in the northern kingdom of Israel. His reign at the beginning of the eighth century BCE was one of relative peace and quiet. However, the shadow of Assyrian domination and conquest, which had been long dormant, was beginning to raise its terrible head. Nineveh was the capital of Assyria, and one can only imagine the feelings of the prophet when asked to prophesy to save the city of Nineveh, Israel's most bitter enemy who would become the instrument of its annihilation. In *Yona's* mind, saving the city of Nineveh would make him complicit in the destruction of his people. Is this something he can do?

The book can be divided into two sections of two chapters each. Each section contains a request by God that *Yona* prophesy to the people of Nineveh, the Assyrian capital, and *Yona's* response. The first time, *Yona* refuses to deliver the message and attempts to flee, only to be stopped by *Hashem*. The second time *Hashem* calls him, *Yona* acquiesces, and tells the people of Nineveh that their end is near. They repent, and God chooses to forgive them. When the prophet complains, God demonstrates to him that His mercy extends to all the world's inhabitants and creatures.

Yona/Jonah
Chapter 1

יונה
פרק א

1 **1** The word of *Hashem* came to *Yona* son of *Amitai*:

א וַיְהִי דְּבַר־יְהֹוָה אֶל־יוֹנָה בֶן־אֲמִתַּי לֵאמֹר׃

2 Go at once to Nineveh, that great city, and proclaim judgment upon it; for their wickedness has come before Me.

ב קוּם לֵךְ אֶל־נִינְוֵה הָעִיר הַגְּדוֹלָה וּקְרָא עָלֶיהָ כִּי־עָלְתָה רָעָתָם לְפָנָי׃

3 *Yona*, however, started out to flee to Tarshish from *Hashem*'s service. He went down to *Yaffo* and found a ship going to Tarshish. He paid the fare and went aboard to sail with the others to Tarshish, away from the service of *Hashem*.

ג וַיָּקׇם יוֹנָה לִבְרֹחַ תַּרְשִׁישָׁה מִלִּפְנֵי יְהֹוָה וַיֵּרֶד יָפוֹ וַיִּמְצָא אֳנִיָּה ׀ בָּאָה תַרְשִׁישׁ וַיִּתֵּן שְׂכָרָהּ וַיֵּרֶד בָּהּ לָבוֹא עִמָּהֶם תַּרְשִׁישָׁה מִלִּפְנֵי יְהֹוָה׃

va-YA-kom yo-NAH liv-RO-akh tar-SHEE-shah mi-lif-NAY a-do-NAI va-YAY-red ya-FO va-yim-TZA o-ni-YAH ba-AH tar-SHEESH va-yi-TAYN s'-kha-RAH va-YAY-red BAH la-VO i-ma-HEM tar-SHEE-shah mi-lif-NAY a-do-NAI

4 But *Hashem* cast a mighty wind upon the sea, and such a great tempest came upon the sea that the ship was in danger of breaking up.

ד וַיהֹוָה הֵטִיל רוּחַ־גְּדוֹלָה אֶל־הַיָּם וַיְהִי סַעַר־גָּדוֹל בַּיָּם וְהָאֳנִיָּה חִשְּׁבָה לְהִשָּׁבֵר׃

5 In their fright, the sailors cried out, each to his own god; and they flung the ship's cargo overboard to make it lighter for them. *Yona*, meanwhile, had gone down into the hold of the vessel where he lay down and fell asleep.

ה וַיִּירְאוּ הַמַּלָּחִים וַיִּזְעֲקוּ אִישׁ אֶל־אֱלֹהָיו וַיָּטִלוּ אֶת־הַכֵּלִים אֲשֶׁר בָּאֳנִיָּה אֶל־הַיָּם לְהָקֵל מֵעֲלֵיהֶם וְיוֹנָה יָרַד אֶל־יַרְכְּתֵי הַסְּפִינָה וַיִּשְׁכַּב וַיֵּרָדַם׃

6 The captain went over to him and cried out, "How can you be sleeping so soundly! Up, call upon your god! Perhaps the god will be kind to us and we will not perish."

ו וַיִּקְרַב אֵלָיו רַב הַחֹבֵל וַיֹּאמֶר לוֹ מַה־לְּךָ נִרְדָּם קוּם קְרָא אֶל־אֱלֹהֶיךָ אוּלַי יִתְעַשֵּׁת הָאֱלֹהִים לָנוּ וְלֹא נֹאבֵד׃

7 The men said to one another, "Let us cast lots and find out on whose account this misfortune has come upon us." They cast lots and the lot fell on *Yona*.

ז וַיֹּאמְרוּ אִישׁ אֶל־רֵעֵהוּ לְכוּ וְנַפִּילָה גוֹרָלוֹת וְנֵדְעָה בְּשֶׁלְּמִי הָרָעָה הַזֹּאת לָנוּ וַיַּפִּלוּ גּוֹרָלוֹת וַיִּפֹּל הַגּוֹרָל עַל־יוֹנָה׃

8 They said to him, "Tell us, you who have brought this misfortune upon us, what is your business? Where have you come from? What is your country, and of what people are you?"

ח וַיֹּאמְרוּ אֵלָיו הַגִּידָה־נָּא לָנוּ בַּאֲשֶׁר לְמִי־הָרָעָה הַזֹּאת לָנוּ מַה־מְּלַאכְתְּךָ וּמֵאַיִן תָּבוֹא מָה אַרְצֶךָ וְאֵי־מִזֶּה עַם אָתָּה׃

9 "I am a Hebrew," he replied. "I worship *Hashem*, the God of Heaven, who made both sea and land."

ט וַיֹּאמֶר אֲלֵיהֶם עִבְרִי אָנֹכִי וְאֶת־יְהֹוָה אֱלֹהֵי הַשָּׁמַיִם אֲנִי יָרֵא אֲשֶׁר־עָשָׂה אֶת־הַיָּם וְאֶת־הַיַּבָּשָׁה׃

1:3 *Yona*, however, started out to flee to Tarshish from *Hashem*'s service How could *Yona* even entertain the possibility that he could flee from God? Doesn't *Hashem*'s providence and dominion extend over all the earth? Many commentators, such as *Rashi*, *Radak*, *Malbim*, and others explain that while *Yona* knew that *Hashem*'s rule extends everywhere, the highest level of spiritual consciousness, necessary for direct prophetic communication, is possible only in the Holy Land. By leaving *Eretz Yisrael*, *Yona* thought that he had managed to disqualify himself from receiving future prophecies, and that *Hashem* would have to turn to another prophet to deliver His message.

Yona/Jonah
Chapter 2

יונה
פרק ב

10 The men were greatly terrified, and they asked him, "What have you done?" And when the men learned that he was fleeing from the service of *Hashem* – for so he told them –

י וַיִּירְאוּ הָאֲנָשִׁים יִרְאָה גְדוֹלָה וַיֹּאמְרוּ אֵלָיו מַה־זֹּאת עָשִׂיתָ כִּי־יָדְעוּ הָאֲנָשִׁים כִּי־מִלִּפְנֵי יְהוָה הוּא בֹרֵחַ כִּי הִגִּיד לָהֶם׃

11 they said to him, "What must we do to you to make the sea calm around us?" For the sea was growing more and more stormy.

יא וַיֹּאמְרוּ אֵלָיו מַה־נַּעֲשֶׂה לָּךְ וְיִשְׁתֹּק הַיָּם מֵעָלֵינוּ כִּי הַיָּם הוֹלֵךְ וְסֹעֵר׃

12 He answered, "Heave me overboard, and the sea will calm down for you; for I know that this terrible storm came upon you on my account."

יב וַיֹּאמֶר אֲלֵיהֶם שָׂאוּנִי וַהֲטִילֻנִי אֶל־הַיָּם וְיִשְׁתֹּק הַיָּם מֵעֲלֵיכֶם כִּי יוֹדֵעַ אָנִי כִּי בְשֶׁלִּי הַסַּעַר הַגָּדוֹל הַזֶּה עֲלֵיכֶם׃

13 Nevertheless, the men rowed hard to regain the shore, but they could not, for the sea was growing more and more stormy about them.

יג וַיַּחְתְּרוּ הָאֲנָשִׁים לְהָשִׁיב אֶל־הַיַּבָּשָׁה וְלֹא יָכֹלוּ כִּי הַיָּם הוֹלֵךְ וְסֹעֵר עֲלֵיהֶם׃

14 Then they cried out to *Hashem*: "Oh, please, *Hashem*, do not let us perish on account of this man's life. Do not hold us guilty of killing an innocent person! For You, *Hashem*, by Your will, have brought this about."

יד וַיִּקְרְאוּ אֶל־יְהוָה וַיֹּאמְרוּ אָנָּה יְהוָה אַל־נָא נֹאבְדָה בְּנֶפֶשׁ הָאִישׁ הַזֶּה וְאַל־תִּתֵּן עָלֵינוּ דָּם נָקִיא כִּי־אַתָּה יְהוָה כַּאֲשֶׁר חָפַצְתָּ עָשִׂיתָ׃

15 And they heaved *Yona* overboard, and the sea stopped raging.

טו וַיִּשְׂאוּ אֶת־יוֹנָה וַיְטִלֻהוּ אֶל־הַיָּם וַיַּעֲמֹד הַיָּם מִזַּעְפּוֹ׃

16 The men feared *Hashem* greatly; they offered a sacrifice to *Hashem* and they made vows.

טז וַיִּירְאוּ הָאֲנָשִׁים יִרְאָה גְדוֹלָה אֶת־יְהוָה וַיִּזְבְּחוּ־זֶבַח לַיהוָה וַיִּדְּרוּ נְדָרִים׃

2
1 *Hashem* provided a huge fish to swallow *Yona*; and *Yona* remained in the fish's belly three days and three nights.

ב א וַיְמַן יְהוָה דָּג גָּדוֹל לִבְלֹעַ אֶת־יוֹנָה וַיְהִי יוֹנָה בִּמְעֵי הַדָּג שְׁלֹשָׁה יָמִים וּשְׁלֹשָׁה לֵילוֹת׃

2 *Yona* prayed to *Hashem* his God from the belly of the fish.

ב וַיִּתְפַּלֵּל יוֹנָה אֶל־יְהוָה אֱלֹהָיו מִמְּעֵי הַדָּגָה׃

3 He said: In my trouble I called to *Hashem*, And He answered me; From the belly of Sheol I cried out, And You heard my voice.

ג וַיֹּאמֶר קָרָאתִי מִצָּרָה לִי אֶל־יְהוָה וַיַּעֲנֵנִי מִבֶּטֶן שְׁאוֹל שִׁוַּעְתִּי שָׁמַעְתָּ קוֹלִי׃

4 You cast me into the depths, Into the heart of the sea, The floods engulfed me; All Your breakers and billows Swept over me.

ד וַתַּשְׁלִיכֵנִי מְצוּלָה בִּלְבַב יַמִּים וְנָהָר יְסֹבְבֵנִי כָּל־מִשְׁבָּרֶיךָ וְגַלֶּיךָ עָלַי עָבָרוּ׃

5 I thought I was driven away Out of Your sight: Would I ever gaze again Upon Your holy Temple?

ה וַאֲנִי אָמַרְתִּי נִגְרַשְׁתִּי מִנֶּגֶד עֵינֶיךָ אַךְ אוֹסִיף לְהַבִּיט אֶל־הֵיכַל קָדְשֶׁךָ׃

6 The waters closed in over me, The deep engulfed me. Weeds twined around my head.

ו אֲפָפוּנִי מַיִם עַד־נֶפֶשׁ תְּהוֹם יְסֹבְבֵנִי סוּף חָבוּשׁ לְרֹאשִׁי׃

7 I sank to the base of the mountains; The bars of the earth closed upon me forever. Yet You brought my life up from the pit, *Hashem* my God!

ז לְקִצְבֵי הָרִים יָרַדְתִּי הָאָרֶץ בְּרִחֶיהָ בַעֲדִי לְעוֹלָם וַתַּעַל מִשַּׁחַת חַיַּי יְהוָה אֱלֹהָי׃

Yona/Jonah
Chapter 3

יונה
פרק ג

8 When my life was ebbing away, I called *Hashem* to mind; And my prayer came before You, Into Your holy Temple.

בְּהִתְעַטֵּף עָלַי נַפְשִׁי אֶת־יְהֹוָה זָכָרְתִּי וַתָּבוֹא אֵלֶיךָ תְּפִלָּתִי אֶל־הֵיכַל קָדְשֶׁךָ׃

b'-hit-a-TAYF a-LAI naf-SHEE et a-do-NAI za-KHAR-tee va-ta-VO ay-LE-kha t'-fi-la-TEE el hay-KHAL kod-SHE-kha

9 They who cling to empty folly Forsake their own welfare,

מְשַׁמְּרִים הַבְלֵי־שָׁוְא חַסְדָּם יַעֲזֹבוּ׃

10 But I, with loud thanksgiving, Will sacrifice to You; What I have vowed I will perform. Deliverance is *Hashem*'s!

וַאֲנִי בְּקוֹל תּוֹדָה אֶזְבְּחָה־לָּךְ אֲשֶׁר נָדַרְתִּי אֲשַׁלֵּמָה יְשׁוּעָתָה לַיהֹוָה׃

11 *Hashem* commanded the fish, and it spewed *Yona* out upon dry land.

וַיֹּאמֶר יְהֹוָה לַדָּג וַיָּקֵא אֶת־יוֹנָה אֶל־הַיַּבָּשָׁה׃

3 1 The word of *Hashem* came to *Yona* a second time:

וַיְהִי דְבַר־יְהֹוָה אֶל־יוֹנָה שֵׁנִית לֵאמֹר׃

2 "Go at once to Nineveh, that great city, and proclaim to it what I tell you."

קוּם לֵךְ אֶל־נִינְוֵה הָעִיר הַגְּדוֹלָה וּקְרָא אֵלֶיהָ אֶת־הַקְּרִיאָה אֲשֶׁר אָנֹכִי דֹּבֵר אֵלֶיךָ׃

3 *Yona* went at once to Nineveh in accordance with *Hashem*'s command. Nineveh was an enormously large city a three days' walk across.

וַיָּקׇם יוֹנָה וַיֵּלֶךְ אֶל־נִינְוֵה כִּדְבַר יְהֹוָה וְנִינְוֵה הָיְתָה עִיר־גְּדוֹלָה לֵאלֹהִים מַהֲלַךְ שְׁלֹשֶׁת יָמִים׃

4 *Yona* started out and made his way into the city the distance of one day's walk, and proclaimed: "Forty days more, and Nineveh shall be overthrown!"

וַיָּחֶל יוֹנָה לָבוֹא בָעִיר מַהֲלַךְ יוֹם אֶחָד וַיִּקְרָא וַיֹּאמַר עוֹד אַרְבָּעִים יוֹם וְנִינְוֵה נֶהְפָּכֶת׃

5 The people of Nineveh believed *Hashem*. They proclaimed a fast, and great and small alike put on sackcloth.

וַיַּאֲמִינוּ אַנְשֵׁי נִינְוֵה בֵּאלֹהִים וַיִּקְרְאוּ־צוֹם וַיִּלְבְּשׁוּ שַׂקִּים מִגְּדוֹלָם וְעַד־קְטַנָּם׃

6 When the news reached the king of Nineveh, he rose from his throne, took off his robe, put on sackcloth, and sat in ashes.

וַיִּגַּע הַדָּבָר אֶל־מֶלֶךְ נִינְוֵה וַיָּקׇם מִכִּסְאוֹ וַיַּעֲבֵר אַדַּרְתּוֹ מֵעָלָיו וַיְכַס שַׂק וַיֵּשֶׁב עַל־הָאֵפֶר׃

7 And he had the word cried through Nineveh: "By decree of the king and his nobles: No man or beast – of flock or herd – shall taste anything! They shall not graze, and they shall not drink water!

וַיַּזְעֵק וַיֹּאמֶר בְּנִינְוֵה מִטַּעַם הַמֶּלֶךְ וּגְדֹלָיו לֵאמֹר הָאָדָם וְהַבְּהֵמָה הַבָּקָר וְהַצֹּאן אַל־יִטְעֲמוּ מְאוּמָה אַל־יִרְעוּ וּמַיִם אַל־יִשְׁתּוּ׃

2:8 And my prayer came before You, into Your holy Temple Such is the heart of a true prophet. Trapped inside the belly of the large fish, with no hope of escape, *Yona* does not despair. Instead, he pours out his prayer to God. Though he has run away from *Hashem* and His mission, *Yona* hopes that he will not only survive, but once again become worthy to stand before God in his Holy Temple in *Yerushalayim*, to bring offerings and to pray (verse 10). This prayer anticipates the lesson that *Hashem* later imparts to *Yona*. Though man may stumble in sin, he can always pick himself up and recover, as it is written, "Seven times the righteous man falls and gets up, while the wicked are tripped by one misfortune" (Proverbs 24:16). Even after our biggest failures, God lovingly awaits our return, if only we have the will to do so.

Yona/Jonah
Chapter 4

יוֹנָה
פֶּרֶק ד

8 They shall be covered with sackcloth – man and beast – and shall cry mightily to *Hashem*. Let everyone turn back from his evil ways and from the injustice of which he is guilty.

ח וְיִתְכַּסּוּ שַׂקִּים הָאָדָם וְהַבְּהֵמָה וְיִקְרְאוּ אֶל־אֱלֹהִים בְּחָזְקָה וְיָשֻׁבוּ אִישׁ מִדַּרְכּוֹ הָרָעָה וּמִן־הֶחָמָס אֲשֶׁר בְּכַפֵּיהֶם׃

9 Who knows but that *Hashem* may turn and relent? He may turn back from His wrath, so that we do not perish."

ט מִי־יוֹדֵעַ יָשׁוּב וְנִחַם הָאֱלֹהִים וְשָׁב מֵחֲרוֹן אַפּוֹ וְלֹא נֹאבֵד׃

10 *Hashem* saw what they did, how they were turning back from their evil ways. And *Hashem* renounced the punishment He had planned to bring upon them, and did not carry it out.

י וַיַּרְא הָאֱלֹהִים אֶת־מַעֲשֵׂיהֶם כִּי־שָׁבוּ מִדַּרְכָּם הָרָעָה וַיִּנָּחֶם הָאֱלֹהִים עַל־הָרָעָה אֲשֶׁר־דִּבֶּר לַעֲשׂוֹת־לָהֶם וְלֹא עָשָׂה׃

va-YAR ha-e-lo-HEEM et ma-a-say-HEM kee SHA-vu mi-dar-KAM ha-ra-AH va-yi-NA-khem ha-e-lo-HEEM al ha-ra-AH a-sher di-BER la-a-sot la-HEM v'-LO a-SAH

4

1 This displeased *Yona* greatly, and he was grieved.

א וַיֵּרַע אֶל־יוֹנָה רָעָה גְדוֹלָה וַיִּחַר לוֹ׃

2 He prayed to *Hashem*, saying, "*Hashem*! Isn't this just what I said when I was still in my own country? That is why I fled beforehand to Tarshish. For I know that You are a compassionate and gracious God, slow to anger, abounding in kindness, renouncing punishment.

ב וַיִּתְפַּלֵּל אֶל־יְהֹוָה וַיֹּאמַר אָנָּה יְהֹוָה הֲלוֹא־זֶה דְבָרִי עַד־הֱיוֹתִי עַל־אַדְמָתִי עַל־כֵּן קִדַּמְתִּי לִבְרֹחַ תַּרְשִׁישָׁה כִּי יָדַעְתִּי כִּי אַתָּה אֵל־חַנּוּן וְרַחוּם אֶרֶךְ אַפַּיִם וְרַב־חֶסֶד וְנִחָם עַל־הָרָעָה׃

3 Please, *Hashem*, take my life, for I would rather die than live."

ג וְעַתָּה יְהֹוָה קַח־נָא אֶת־נַפְשִׁי מִמֶּנִּי כִּי טוֹב מוֹתִי מֵחַיָּי׃

4 *Hashem* replied, "Are you that deeply grieved?"

ד וַיֹּאמֶר יְהֹוָה הַהֵיטֵב חָרָה לָךְ׃

5 Now *Yona* had left the city and found a place east of the city. He made a booth there and sat under it in the shade, until he should see what happened to the city.

ה וַיֵּצֵא יוֹנָה מִן־הָעִיר וַיֵּשֶׁב מִקֶּדֶם לָעִיר וַיַּעַשׂ לוֹ שָׁם סֻכָּה וַיֵּשֶׁב תַּחְתֶּיהָ בַּצֵּל עַד אֲשֶׁר יִרְאֶה מַה־יִּהְיֶה בָּעִיר׃

3:10 How they were turning back from their evil ways The people of Nineveh don sackcloth, fast, and sit in dust and ashes, in the hope that this will bring *Hashem* to forgive them. What *Yona* teaches us, however, is that it is not these external actions that bring about their forgiveness. Instead, what impresses *Hashem* is the fact that these actions reflected, and perhaps helped bring about, a fundamental change in their mentality. They abandon their evil ways and make a true commitment to behave righteously and justly in the future. Without such a genuine change of heart, the external signs remain empty gestures. The Sages of the Talmud (*Taanit* 16a) derive this lesson from the fact that the verse does not say "God saw their sackcloth and fasting," but rather, "*Hashem* saw what they did, how they were turning back from their evil ways".

Yona/Jonah
Chapter 4

יונה
פרק ד

6 *Hashem* provided a ricinus plant, which grew up over *Yona*, to provide shade for his head and save him from discomfort. *Yona* was very happy about the plant.

וַיְמַן יְהֹוָה־אֱלֹהִים קִיקָיוֹן וַיַּעַל מֵעַל לְיוֹנָה לִהְיוֹת צֵל עַל־רֹאשׁוֹ לְהַצִּיל לוֹ מֵרָעָתוֹ וַיִּשְׂמַח יוֹנָה עַל־הַקִּיקָיוֹן שִׂמְחָה גְדוֹלָה׃

vai-MAN a-do-nai e-lo-HEEM kee-ka-YON va-YA-al may-AL l'-yo-NAH lih-YOT TZAYL al ro-SHO l'-ha-TZEEL LO may-ra-a-TO va-yis-MAKH yo-NAH al ha-kee-ka-YON sim-KHAH g'-do-LAH

7 But the next day at dawn *Hashem* provided a worm, which attacked the plant so that it withered.

וַיְמַן הָאֱלֹהִים תּוֹלַעַת בַּעֲלוֹת הַשַּׁחַר לַמׇּחֳרָת וַתַּךְ אֶת־הַקִּיקָיוֹן וַיִּיבָשׁ׃

8 And when the sun rose, *Hashem* provided a sultry east wind; the sun beat down on *Yona*'s head, and he became faint. He begged for death, saying, "I would rather die than live."

וַיְהִי כִּזְרֹחַ הַשֶּׁמֶשׁ וַיְמַן אֱלֹהִים רוּחַ קָדִים חֲרִישִׁית וַתַּךְ הַשֶּׁמֶשׁ עַל־רֹאשׁ יוֹנָה וַיִּתְעַלָּף וַיִּשְׁאַל אֶת־נַפְשׁוֹ לָמוּת וַיֹּאמֶר טוֹב מוֹתִי מֵחַיָּי׃

9 Then *Hashem* said to *Yona*, "Are you so deeply grieved about the plant?" "Yes," he replied, "so deeply that I want to die."

וַיֹּאמֶר אֱלֹהִים אֶל־יוֹנָה הַהֵיטֵב חָרָה־לְךָ עַל־הַקִּיקָיוֹן וַיֹּאמֶר הֵיטֵב חָרָה־לִי עַד־מָוֶת׃

10 Then *Hashem* said: "You cared about the plant, which you did not work for and which you did not grow, which appeared overnight and perished overnight.

וַיֹּאמֶר יְהֹוָה אַתָּה חַסְתָּ עַל־הַקִּיקָיוֹן אֲשֶׁר לֹא־עָמַלְתָּ בּוֹ וְלֹא גִדַּלְתּוֹ שֶׁבִּן־לַיְלָה הָיָה וּבִן־לַיְלָה אָבָד׃

11 And should not I care about Nineveh, that great city, in which there are more than a hundred and twenty thousand persons who do not yet know their right hand from their left, and many beasts as well!"

וַאֲנִי לֹא אָחוּס עַל־נִינְוֵה הָעִיר הַגְּדוֹלָה אֲשֶׁר יֶשׁ־בָּהּ הַרְבֵּה מִשְׁתֵּים־עֶשְׂרֵה רִבּוֹ אָדָם אֲשֶׁר לֹא־יָדַע בֵּין־יְמִינוֹ לִשְׂמֹאלוֹ וּבְהֵמָה רַבָּה׃

4:6 Hashem provided a ricinus plant As *Yona* sulks over God's compassion to those he views as sinners, *Hashem* prepares for him a large plant, a *kikayon* (קיקיון), to provide *Yona* with shade. The identity of this plant has long fascinated commentators. According to some, it is the castor oil plant, which is common in Israel. This plant has large leaves and grows to a considerable height in a short amount of time, so that a sprout quickly attains the appearance of a small tree, much like *Yona*'s *kikayon* which appeared suddenly and provided him with ample shade. The scientific name of this plant is *Ricinus Communis*. In Egyptian, the plant is called kiki, which is similar to the Hebrew word used here: *Kikayon*.

Castor oil plant seedling in Israel

Sefer Micha
The Book of Micah

The sixth of the *Trei Asar*, *Sefer Micha* (Micah), records the prophecies of *Micha* the Morashite. A contemporary of *Yeshayahu* and *Hoshea*, he lived in the second half of the eighth century BCE, a time which saw the Assyrians become a superpower in the Middle East, defeating and subjecting the nations and countries that stood in its path of conquest. The northern kingdom of Israel, *Shomron*, is conquered and exiled by the Assyrian king Sargon II in 722 BCE, and just over twenty years later, in 701 BCE, his son Sennacherib embarks on his own campaign of conquest, capturing all of *Yehuda's* fortified cities and laying siege to *Yerushalayim*. Only through God's miraculous intervention described in *Sefer Melachim* II 19, bringing a plague that strikes the Assyrian army at night, killing hundreds of thousands and causing their retreat, is the country saved.

The brilliance of the Hebrew prophets is expressed in their understanding that these events were not accidental, but were directly linked to the level of righteousness and justice among the nation. *Yehuda*, unlike the idolatrous *Yisrael*, continued to worship *Hashem*. Like their northern brethren, however, unscrupulous officials in the cities profited from the labor of the hard-working farmers in the countryside. The prophet *Micha* was a strong opponent of these wealthy and powerful men, denouncing them at every opportunity. It is thus not surprising that scholars have referred to him as the "*Amos* of the southern kingdom". However, unlike *Amos*, *Micha* was somewhat successful in effecting a change among his people. When, a century later, *Yirmiyahu* is tried for sedition, the elders protested, reminding them: "*Micha* the Morashtite, who prophesied in the days of King *Chizkiyahu* of *Yehuda*, said to all the people of *Yehuda*: 'Thus said the LORD of Hosts: *Tzion* shall be plowed as a field, *Yerushalayim* shall become heaps of ruins, and the Temple Mount a shrine in the woods.' "Did King *Chizkiyahu* of *Yehuda*, and all *Yehuda*, put him to death? Did he not rather fear *Hashem* and implore *Hashem*, so that *Hashem* renounced the punishment He had decreed against them? We are about to do great injury to ourselves!" (Jeremiah 26:18–19).

The structure of the book is straightforward. It contains three sections beginning in chapters 1, 3, and 6. In each section, *Micha* outlines God's complaint before the people, clarifies what *Hashem* wants from them, and concludes with a message of hope and salvation.

Micha/Micah
Chapter 1

מיכה
פרק א

1 The word of *Hashem* that came to *Micha* the Morashtite, who prophesied concerning *Shomron* and *Yerushalayim* in the reigns of Kings *Yotam*, *Achaz*, and *Chizkiyahu* of *Yehuda*.

א דְּבַר־יְהֹוָה ׀ אֲשֶׁר הָיָה אֶל־מִיכָה הַמֹּרַשְׁתִּי בִּימֵי יוֹתָם אָחָז יְחִזְקִיָּה מַלְכֵי יְהוּדָה אֲשֶׁר־חָזָה עַל־שֹׁמְרוֹן וִירוּשָׁלָ͏ִם:

2 Listen, all you peoples, Give heed, O earth, and all it holds; And let my God be your accuser – My Lord from His holy abode.

ב שִׁמְעוּ עַמִּים כֻּלָּם הַקְשִׁיבִי אֶרֶץ וּמְלֹאָהּ וִיהִי אֲדֹנָי יְהֹוִה בָּכֶם לְעֵד אֲדֹנָי מֵהֵיכַל קָדְשׁוֹ:

3 For lo! *Hashem* Is coming forth from His dwelling-place, He will come down and stride Upon the heights of the earth.

ג כִּי־הִנֵּה יְהֹוָה יֹצֵא מִמְּקוֹמוֹ וְיָרַד וְדָרַךְ עַל־במותי [בָּמֳתֵי] אָרֶץ:

4 The mountains shall melt under Him And the valleys burst open – Like wax before fire, Like water cascading down a slope.

ד וְנָמַסּוּ הֶהָרִים תַּחְתָּיו וְהָעֲמָקִים יִתְבַּקָּעוּ כַּדּוֹנַג מִפְּנֵי הָאֵשׁ כְּמַיִם מֻגָּרִים בְּמוֹרָד:

5 All this is for the transgression of *Yaakov*, And for the sins of the House of *Yisrael*. What is the transgression of *Yaakov* But *Shomron*, And what the shrines of *Yehuda* But *Yerushalayim*?

ה בְּפֶשַׁע יַעֲקֹב כָּל־זֹאת וּבְחַטֹּאות בֵּית יִשְׂרָאֵל מִי־פֶשַׁע יַעֲקֹב הֲלוֹא שֹׁמְרוֹן וּמִי בָּמוֹת יְהוּדָה הֲלוֹא יְרוּשָׁלָ͏ִם:

6 So I will turn *Shomron* Into a ruin in open country, Into ground for planting vineyards; For I will tumble her stones into the valley And lay her foundations bare.

ו וְשַׂמְתִּי שֹׁמְרוֹן לְעִי הַשָּׂדֶה לְמַטָּעֵי כָרֶם וְהִגַּרְתִּי לַגַּי אֲבָנֶיהָ וִיסֹדֶיהָ אֲגַלֶּה:

7 All her sculptured images shall be smashed, And all her harlot's wealth be burned, And I will make a waste heap of all her idols, For they were amassed from fees for harlotry, And they shall become harlots' fees again.

ז וְכָל־פְּסִילֶיהָ יֻכַּתּוּ וְכָל־אֶתְנַנֶּיהָ יִשָּׂרְפוּ בָאֵשׁ וְכָל־עֲצַבֶּיהָ אָשִׂים שְׁמָמָה כִּי מֵאֶתְנַן זוֹנָה קִבָּצָה וְעַד־אֶתְנַן זוֹנָה יָשׁוּבוּ:

8 Because of this I will lament and wail; I will go stripped and naked! I will lament as sadly as the jackals, As mournfully as the ostriches.

ח עַל־זֹאת אֶסְפְּדָה וְאֵילִילָה אֵילְכָה שילל [שׁוֹלָל] וְעָרוֹם אֶעֱשֶׂה מִסְפֵּד כַּתַּנִּים וְאֵבֶל כִּבְנוֹת יַעֲנָה:

9 For her wound is incurable, It has reached *Yehuda*, It has spread to the gate of my people, To *Yerushalayim*.

ט כִּי אֲנוּשָׁה מַכּוֹתֶיהָ כִּי־בָאָה עַד־יְהוּדָה נָגַע עַד־שַׁעַר עַמִּי עַד־יְרוּשָׁלָ͏ִם:

10 Tell it not in Gath, Refrain from weeping; In Beth-leaphrah, Strew dust over your [head].

י בְּגַת אַל־תַּגִּידוּ בָּכוֹ אַל־תִּבְכּוּ בְּבֵית לְעַפְרָה עָפָר התפלשתי [הִתְפַּלָּשִׁי]:

11 Pass on, inhabitants of Shaphir! Did not the inhabitants of Zaanan Have to go forth naked in shame? There is lamentation in Beth-ezel – It will withdraw its support from you.

יא עִבְרִי לָכֶם יוֹשֶׁבֶת שָׁפִיר עֶרְיָה־בֹשֶׁת לֹא יָצְאָה יוֹשֶׁבֶת צַאֲנָן מִסְפַּד בֵּית הָאֵצֶל יִקַּח מִכֶּם עֶמְדָּתוֹ:

12 Though the inhabitants of Maroth Hoped for good, Yet disaster from *Hashem* descended Upon the gate of *Yerushalayim*.

יב כִּי־חָלָה לְטוֹב יוֹשֶׁבֶת מָרוֹת כִּי־יָרַד רָע מֵאֵת יְהֹוָה לְשַׁעַר יְרוּשָׁלָ͏ִם:

Micha/Micah
Chapter 2

מיכה
פרק ב

13 Hitch the steeds to the chariot, Inhabitant of *Lachish*! It is the beginning Of Fair *Tzion*'s guilt; *Yisrael*'s transgressions Can be traced to you!

יג רְתֹם הַמֶּרְכָּבָה לָרֶכֶשׁ יוֹשֶׁבֶת לָכִישׁ רֵאשִׁית חַטָּאת הִיא לְבַת־צִיּוֹן כִּי־בָךְ נִמְצְאוּ פִּשְׁעֵי יִשְׂרָאֵל:

r'-TOM ha-mer-ka-VAH la-RE-khesh yo-SHE-vet la-KHEESH ray-SHEET kha-TAT HEE l'-vat tzi-YON kee VAKH nim-tz'-U pish-AY yis-ra-AYL

14 Truly, you must give a farewell gift To Moresheth-gath. The houses of Achzib are To the kings of *Yisrael* Like a spring that fails.

יד לָכֵן תִּתְּנִי שִׁלּוּחִים עַל מוֹרֶשֶׁת גַּת בָּתֵּי אַכְזִיב לְאַכְזָב לְמַלְכֵי יִשְׂרָאֵל:

15 A dispossessor will I bring to you Who dwell in Mareshah; At *Adulam* the glory Of *Yisrael* shall set.

טו עֹד הַיֹּרֵשׁ אָבִי לָךְ יוֹשֶׁבֶת מָרֵשָׁה עַד־עֲדֻלָּם יָבוֹא כְּבוֹד יִשְׂרָאֵל:

16 Shear off your hair and make yourself bald For the children you once delighted in; Make yourself as bald as a vulture, For they have been banished from you.

טז קָרְחִי וָגֹזִּי עַל־בְּנֵי תַּעֲנוּגָיִךְ הַרְחִבִי קָרְחָתֵךְ כַּנֶּשֶׁר כִּי גָלוּ מִמֵּךְ:

2

1 Ah, those who plan iniquity And design evil on their beds; When morning dawns, they do it, For they have the power.

ב א הוֹי חֹשְׁבֵי־אָוֶן וּפֹעֲלֵי רָע עַל־מִשְׁכְּבוֹתָם בְּאוֹר הַבֹּקֶר יַעֲשׂוּהָ כִּי יֶשׁ־לְאֵל יָדָם:

2 They covet fields, and seize them; Houses, and take them away. They defraud men of their homes, And people of their land.

ב וְחָמְדוּ שָׂדוֹת וְגָזָלוּ וּבָתִּים וְנָשָׂאוּ וְעָשְׁקוּ גֶּבֶר וּבֵיתוֹ וְאִישׁ וְנַחֲלָתוֹ:

3 Assuredly, thus said *Hashem*: I am planning such a misfortune against this clan that you will not be able to free your necks from it. You will not be able to walk erect; it will be such a time of disaster.

ג לָכֵן כֹּה אָמַר יְהֹוָה הִנְנִי חֹשֵׁב עַל־הַמִּשְׁפָּחָה הַזֹּאת רָעָה אֲשֶׁר לֹא־תָמִישׁוּ מִשָּׁם צַוְּארֹתֵיכֶם וְלֹא תֵלְכוּ רוֹמָה כִּי עֵת רָעָה הִיא:

4 In that day, One shall recite a poem about you, And utter a bitter lament, And shall say: "My people's portion changes hands; How it slips away from me! Our field is allotted to a rebel. We are utterly ravaged."

ד בַּיּוֹם הַהוּא יִשָּׂא עֲלֵיכֶם מָשָׁל וְנָהָה נְהִי נִהְיָה אָמַר שָׁדוֹד נְשַׁדֻּנוּ חֵלֶק עַמִּי יָמִיר אֵיךְ יָמִישׁ לִי לְשׁוֹבֵב שָׂדֵינוּ יְחַלֵּק:

5 Truly, none of you Shall cast a lot cord In the assembly of *Hashem*!

ה לָכֵן לֹא־יִהְיֶה לְךָ מַשְׁלִיךְ חֶבֶל בְּגוֹרָל בִּקְהַל יְהֹוָה:

6 "Stop preaching!" they preach. "That's no way to preach; Shame shall not overtake [us]."

ו אַל־תַּטִּפוּ יַטִּיפוּן לֹא־יַטִּפוּ לָאֵלֶּה לֹא יִסַּג כְּלִמּוֹת:

1:13 Inhabitant of *Lachish* *Micha* tells the inhabitants of *Lachish* to prepare to flee the oncoming enemy, and states that this onslaught will be the beginning of *Yehuda*'s downfall. *Lachish*, located thirty miles southwest of *Yerushalayim*, was fortified by *Rechovam* (II Chronicles 11:5–12), and was the southern kingdom's second largest city. Its location was strategic, as it guarded the mountain pass from the southern coastal plain to *Yerushalayim* and the interior of the kingdom of *Yehuda*. *Lachish* was captured and demolished by Sennacherib, king of the Assyrians, during his campaign to capture *Yerushalayim* and conquer the entire kingdom during the reign of King *Chizkiyahu*. Today, excavations at *Lachish* have revealed the largest siege ramp discovered in the Middle East, as well as the largest Iron Age structure discovered in the Land of Israel. Predicting the destruction of this large and powerful city, *Micha* mocks the Israelites' trust in their horses and military prowess instead of *Hashem*'s protection.

Assyrian siege ramp at Tel Lachish

Micha/Micah
Chapter 3

מיכה
פרק ג

7 Is the House of *Yaakov* condemned? Is *Hashem*'s patience short? Is such His practice?" To be sure, My words are friendly To those who walk in rectitude;

הֶאָמוּר בֵּית־יַעֲקֹב הֲקָצַר רוּחַ יְהֹוָה אִם־אֵלֶּה מַעֲלָלָיו הֲלוֹא דְבָרַי יֵיטִיבוּ עִם הַיָּשָׁר הוֹלֵךְ׃

he-a-MUR bayt ya-a-KOV ha-ka-TZAR RU-akh a-do-NAI im AY-leh ma-a-la-LAV ha-LO d'-va-RAI yay-TEE-vu IM ha-ya-SHAR ho-LAYKH

8 But an enemy arises against My people. You strip the mantle with the cloak Off such as pass unsuspecting, Who are turned away from war.

וְאֶתְמוּל עַמִּי לְאוֹיֵב יְקוֹמֵם מִמּוּל שַׂלְמָה אֶדֶר תַּפְשִׁטוּן מֵעֹבְרִים בֶּטַח שׁוּבֵי מִלְחָמָה׃

9 You drive the women of My people away From their pleasant homes; You deprive their infants Of My glory forever.

נְשֵׁי עַמִּי תְּגָרְשׁוּן מִבֵּית תַּעֲנֻגֶיהָ מֵעַל עֹלָלֶיהָ תִּקְחוּ הֲדָרִי לְעוֹלָם׃

10 Up and depart! This is no resting place Because of [your] defilement. Terrible destruction shall befall.

קוּמוּ וּלְכוּ כִּי לֹא־זֹאת הַמְּנוּחָה בַּעֲבוּר טָמְאָה תְּחַבֵּל וְחֶבֶל נִמְרָץ׃

11 If a man were to go about uttering Windy, baseless falsehoods: "I'll preach to you in favor of wine and liquor" – He would be a preacher [acceptable] to that people.

לוּ־אִישׁ הֹלֵךְ רוּחַ וָשֶׁקֶר כִּזֵּב אַטִּף לְךָ לַיַּיִן וְלַשֵּׁכָר וְהָיָה מַטִּיף הָעָם הַזֶּה׃

12 I will assemble *Yaakov*, all of you; I will bring together the remnant of *Yisrael*; I will make them all like sheep of Bozrah, Like a flock inside its pen – They will be noisy with people.

אָסֹף אֶאֱסֹף יַעֲקֹב כֻּלָּךְ קַבֵּץ אֲקַבֵּץ שְׁאֵרִית יִשְׂרָאֵל יַחַד אֲשִׂימֶנּוּ כְּצֹאן בָּצְרָה כְּעֵדֶר בְּתוֹךְ הַדָּבְרוֹ תְּהִימֶנָה מֵאָדָם׃

13 One who makes a breach Goes before them; They enlarge it to a gate And leave by it. Their king marches before them, *Hashem* at their head.

עָלָה הַפֹּרֵץ לִפְנֵיהֶם פָּרְצוּ וַיַּעֲבֹרוּ שַׁעַר וַיֵּצְאוּ בוֹ וַיַּעֲבֹר מַלְכָּם לִפְנֵיהֶם וַיהֹוָה בְּרֹאשָׁם׃

3

1 I said: Listen, you rulers of *Yaakov*, You chiefs of the House of *Yisrael*! For you ought to know what is right,

וָאֹמַר שִׁמְעוּ־נָא רָאשֵׁי יַעֲקֹב וּקְצִינֵי בֵּית יִשְׂרָאֵל הֲלוֹא לָכֶם לָדַעַת אֶת־הַמִּשְׁפָּט׃

2 But you hate good and love evil.

שֹׂנְאֵי טוֹב וְאֹהֲבֵי רעה [רָע] גֹּזְלֵי עוֹרָם מֵעֲלֵיהֶם וּשְׁאֵרָם מֵעַל עַצְמוֹתָם׃

3 You have devoured My people's flesh; You have flayed the skin off them, And their flesh off their bones. And after tearing their skins off them, And their flesh off their bones,* And breaking their bones to bits, You have cut it up as into a pot, Like meat in a caldron.

וַאֲשֶׁר אָכְלוּ שְׁאֵר עַמִּי וְעוֹרָם מֵעֲלֵיהֶם הִפְשִׁיטוּ וְאֶת־עַצְמֹתֵיהֶם פִּצֵּחוּ וּפָרְשׂוּ כַּאֲשֶׁר בַּסִּיר וּכְבָשָׂר בְּתוֹךְ קַלָּחַת׃

---

* "And after tearing their skins off them, And their flesh off their bones" brought down from verse 2 for clarity

---

2:7 To be sure, My words are friendly to those who walk in rectitude *Micha* answers the false prophets who attempt to quiet his warnings. They claim that *Hashem*'s patience is forever, and that since Israel is God's people, they will never come to harm. *Micha* explains that for God's blessings to rest on the people, they must "walk in rectitude," and not on the crooked path. If they do not heed this warning, He will punish them and exile them from the Land of Israel, which cannot tolerate evil behavior. In verse 12, however, *Micha* promises that once the people have been punished, they will be returned to the Land of Israel from all the places of their exile, and placed under God's protection like a flock of sheep safe in its pen.

Micha/Micah
Chapter 3

מיכה
פרק ג

4 Someday they shall cry out to *Hashem*, But He will not answer them; At that time He will hide His face from them, In accordance with the wrongs they have done.

אָז יִזְעֲקוּ אֶל־יְהֹוָה וְלֹא יַעֲנֶה אוֹתָם וְיַסְתֵּר פָּנָיו מֵהֶם בָּעֵת הַהִיא כַּאֲשֶׁר הֵרֵעוּ מַעַלְלֵיהֶם׃

5 Thus said *Hashem* to the *Neviim* Who lead My people astray, Who cry "Peace!" When they have something to chew, But launch a war on him Who fails to fill their mouths:

כֹּה אָמַר יְהֹוָה עַל־הַנְּבִיאִים הַמַּתְעִים אֶת־עַמִּי הַנֹּשְׁכִים בְּשִׁנֵּיהֶם וְקָרְאוּ שָׁלוֹם וַאֲשֶׁר לֹא־יִתֵּן עַל־פִּיהֶם וְקִדְּשׁוּ עָלָיו מִלְחָמָה׃

6 Assuredly, It shall be night for you So that you cannot prophesy, And it shall be dark for you So that you cannot divine; The sun shall set on the *Neviim*, And the day shall be darkened for them.

לָכֵן לַיְלָה לָכֶם מֵחָזוֹן וְחָשְׁכָה לָכֶם מִקְּסֹם וּבָאָה הַשֶּׁמֶשׁ עַל־הַנְּבִיאִים וְקָדַר עֲלֵיהֶם הַיּוֹם׃

7 The seers shall be shamed And the diviners confounded; They shall cover their upper lips, Because no response comes from *Hashem*.

וּבֹשׁוּ הַחֹזִים וְחָפְרוּ הַקֹּסְמִים וְעָטוּ עַל־שָׂפָם כֻּלָּם כִּי אֵין מַעֲנֵה אֱלֹהִים׃

8 But I, I am filled with strength by the spirit of *Hashem*, And with judgment and courage, To declare to *Yaakov* his transgressions And to *Yisrael* his sin.

וְאוּלָם אָנֹכִי מָלֵאתִי כֹחַ אֶת־רוּחַ יְהֹוָה וּמִשְׁפָּט וּגְבוּרָה לְהַגִּיד לְיַעֲקֹב פִּשְׁעוֹ וּלְיִשְׂרָאֵל חַטָּאתוֹ׃

9 Hear this, you rulers of the House of *Yaakov*, You chiefs of the House of *Yisrael*, Who detest justice And make crooked all that is straight,

שִׁמְעוּ־נָא זֹאת רָאשֵׁי בֵּית יַעֲקֹב וּקְצִינֵי בֵּית יִשְׂרָאֵל הַמְתַעֲבִים מִשְׁפָּט וְאֵת כָּל־הַיְשָׁרָה יְעַקֵּשׁוּ׃

10 Who build *Tzion* with crime, *Yerushalayim* with iniquity!

בֹּנֶה צִיּוֹן בְּדָמִים וִירוּשָׁלַ͏ִם בְּעַוְלָה׃

bo-NEH tzi-YON b'-da-MEEM vee-ru-sha-LA-im b'-av-LAH

11 Her rulers judge for gifts, Her *Kohanim* give rulings for a fee, And her *Neviim* divine for pay; Yet they rely upon *Hashem*, saying, "*Hashem* is in our midst; No calamity shall overtake us."

רָאשֶׁיהָ בְּשֹׁחַד יִשְׁפֹּטוּ וְכֹהֲנֶיהָ בִּמְחִיר יוֹרוּ וּנְבִיאֶיהָ בְּכֶסֶף יִקְסֹמוּ וְעַל־יְהֹוָה יִשָּׁעֵנוּ לֵאמֹר הֲלוֹא יְהֹוָה בְּקִרְבֵּנוּ לֹא־תָבוֹא עָלֵינוּ רָעָה׃

12 Assuredly, because of you *Tzion* shall be plowed as a field, And *Yerushalayim* shall become heaps of ruins, And the *Har Habayit* A shrine in the woods.

לָכֵן בִּגְלַלְכֶם צִיּוֹן שָׂדֶה תֵחָרֵשׁ וִירוּשָׁלַ͏ִם עִיִּין תִּהְיֶה וְהַר הַבַּיִת לְבָמוֹת יָעַר׃

3:10 Who build *Tzion* with crime In the eighth century BCE, wealthy landowners and traders began to build lavishes mansions, summer and winter houses in the cities. They did this with wealth they had acquired through crime and dishonesty, by oppressing the poor and expropriating the properties of smaller landowners. *Micha* describes the sickness: "Who build *Tzion* with crime, *Yerushalayim* with iniquity!", and his contemporary *Yeshayahu* described the cure: "*Tzion* shall be saved in the judgment; Her repentant ones, in the retribution" (Isaiah. 1:27).

Micha/Micah
Chapter 4

מיכה
פרק ד

4 ¹ In the days to come, The Mount of *Hashem*'s House shall stand Firm above the mountains; And it shall tower above the hills. The peoples shall gaze on it with joy,

א וְהָיָה בְּאַחֲרִית הַיָּמִים יִהְיֶה הַר בֵּית־יְהֹוָה נָכוֹן בְּרֹאשׁ הֶהָרִים וְנִשָּׂא הוּא מִגְּבָעוֹת וְנָהֲרוּ עָלָיו עַמִּים׃

² And the many nations shall go and shall say: "Come, Let us go up to the Mount of *Hashem*, To the House of the God of *Yaakov*; That He may instruct us in His ways, And that we may walk in His paths." For instruction shall come forth from *Tzion*, The word of *Hashem* from *Yerushalayim*.

ב וְהָלְכוּ גּוֹיִם רַבִּים וְאָמְרוּ לְכוּ וְנַעֲלֶה אֶל־הַר־יְהֹוָה וְאֶל־בֵּית אֱלֹהֵי יַעֲקֹב וְיוֹרֵנוּ מִדְּרָכָיו וְנֵלְכָה בְּאֹרְחֹתָיו כִּי מִצִּיּוֹן תֵּצֵא תוֹרָה וּדְבַר־יְהֹוָה מִירוּשָׁלָ͏ִם׃

³ Thus He will judge among the many peoples, And arbitrate for the multitude of nations, However distant; And they shall beat their swords into plowshares And their spears into pruning hooks. Nation shall not take up Sword against nation; They shall never again know war;

ג וְשָׁפַט בֵּין עַמִּים רַבִּים וְהוֹכִיחַ לְגוֹיִם עֲצֻמִים עַד־רָחוֹק וְכִתְּתוּ חַרְבֹתֵיהֶם לְאִתִּים וַחֲנִיתֹתֵיהֶם לְמַזְמֵרוֹת לֹא־יִשְׂאוּ גּוֹי אֶל־גּוֹי חֶרֶב וְלֹא־יִלְמְדוּן עוֹד מִלְחָמָה׃

⁴ But every man shall sit Under his grapevine or fig tree With no one to disturb him. For it was God the LORD of Hosts who spoke.

ד וְיָשְׁבוּ אִישׁ תַּחַת גַּפְנוֹ וְתַחַת תְּאֵנָתוֹ וְאֵין מַחֲרִיד כִּי־פִי יְהֹוָה צְבָאוֹת דִּבֵּר׃

v'-ya-sh'-VU EESH TA-khat gaf-NO v'-TA-khat t'-ay-na-TO v'-AYN ma-kha-REED kee FEE a-do-NAI tz'-va-OT di-BAYR

⁵ Though all the peoples walk Each in the names of its gods, We will walk In the name of *Hashem* our God Forever and ever.

ה כִּי כָּל־הָעַמִּים יֵלְכוּ אִישׁ בְּשֵׁם אֱלֹהָיו וַאֲנַחְנוּ נֵלֵךְ בְּשֵׁם־יְהֹוָה אֱלֹהֵינוּ לְעוֹלָם וָעֶד׃

⁶ In that day – declares *Hashem* – I will assemble the lame [sheep] And will gather the outcast And those I have treated harshly;

ו בַּיּוֹם הַהוּא נְאֻם־יְהֹוָה אֹסְפָה הַצֹּלֵעָה וְהַנִּדָּחָה אֲקַבֵּצָה וַאֲשֶׁר הֲרֵעֹתִי׃

⁷ And I will turn the lame into a remnant And the expelled into a populous nation. And *Hashem* will reign over them on Mount *Tzion* Now and for evermore.

ז וְשַׂמְתִּי אֶת־הַצֹּלֵעָה לִשְׁאֵרִית וְהַנַּהֲלָאָה לְגוֹי עָצוּם וּמָלַךְ יְהֹוָה עֲלֵיהֶם בְּהַר צִיּוֹן מֵעַתָּה וְעַד־עוֹלָם׃

⁸ And you, O Migdal-eder, Outpost of Fair *Tzion*, It shall come to you: The former monarchy shall return – The kingship of Fair *Yerushalayim*.

ח וְאַתָּה מִגְדַּל־עֵדֶר עֹפֶל בַּת־צִיּוֹן עָדֶיךָ תֵּאתֶה וּבָאָה הַמֶּמְשָׁלָה הָרִאשֹׁנָה מַמְלֶכֶת לְבַת־יְרוּשָׁלָ͏ִם׃

4:4 But every man shall sit under his grapevine or fig tree Figs are one of the seven agricultural species that are special products of the Land of Israel (Deuteronomy 8:8). They are first mentioned in the Bible in the beginning of *Sefer Bereishit* (3:7), when *Adam* and *Chava* cover their nakedness with fig leaves. The Talmud compares the *Torah* itself to a fig tree. Just as one always finds figs on the tree since the fruits do not all ripen at the same time, similarly, one will always find new flavor in the *Torah* he is studying (*Eruvin* 54). During King *Shlomo*'s reign, all of Israel lived in safety, "everyone under his own vine and under his own fig tree" (I Kings 5:5), a phrase that indicates national prosperity and also demonstrates that, in biblical tradition, the fig tree serves as a symbol of peace and tranquility. In this verse, the prophet *Micha* promises the same peace and tranquility in the time of the redemption.

Fig tree in Jerusalem

Micha/Micah
Chapter 5

9 Now why do you utter such cries? Is there no king in you, Have your advisors perished, That you have been seized by writhing Like a woman in travail?

עַתָּה לָמָּה תָרִיעִי רֵעַ הֲמֶלֶךְ אֵין־בָּךְ אִם־יוֹעֲצֵךְ אָבָד כִּי־הֶחֱזִיקֵךְ חִיל כַּיּוֹלֵדָה׃

10 Writhe and scream, Fair *Tzion*, Like a woman in travail! For now you must leave the city And dwell in the country – And you will reach Babylon. There you shall be saved, There *Hashem* will redeem you From the hands of your foes.

חוּלִי וָגֹחִי בַּת־צִיּוֹן כַּיּוֹלֵדָה כִּי־עַתָּה תֵצְאִי מִקִּרְיָה וְשָׁכַנְתְּ בַּשָּׂדֶה וּבָאת עַד־בָּבֶל שָׁם תִּנָּצֵלִי שָׁם יִגְאָלֵךְ יְהֹוָה מִכַּף אֹיְבָיִךְ׃

11 Indeed, many nations Have assembled against you Who think, "Let our eye Obscenely gaze on *Tzion*."

וְעַתָּה נֶאֶסְפוּ עָלַיִךְ גּוֹיִם רַבִּים הָאֹמְרִים תֶּחֱנָף וְתַחַז בְּצִיּוֹן עֵינֵינוּ׃

12 But they do not know The design of *Hashem*, They do not divine His intent: He has gathered them Like cut grain to the threshing floor.

וְהֵמָּה לֹא יָדְעוּ מַחְשְׁבוֹת יְהֹוָה וְלֹא הֵבִינוּ עֲצָתוֹ כִּי קִבְּצָם כֶּעָמִיר גֹּרְנָה׃

v'-HAY-mah LO ya-d'-U makh-sh'-VOT a-do-NAI v'-LO hay-VEE-nu a-tza-TO KEE ki-b'-TZAM ke-a-MEER go-r'-NAH

13 Up and thresh, Fair *Tzion*! For I will give you horns of iron And provide you with hoofs of bronze, And you will crush the many peoples. You will devote their riches to *Hashem*, Their wealth to the Lord of all the earth.

קוּמִי וָדוֹשִׁי בַת־צִיּוֹן כִּי־קַרְנֵךְ אָשִׂים בַּרְזֶל וּפַרְסֹתַיִךְ אָשִׂים נְחוּשָׁה וַהֲדִקּוֹת עַמִּים רַבִּים וְהַחֲרַמְתִּי לַיהֹוָה בִּצְעָם וְחֵילָם לַאֲדוֹן כָּל־הָאָרֶץ׃

14 Now you gash yourself in grief. They have laid siege to us; They strike the ruler of *Yisrael* On the cheek with a staff.

עַתָּה תִּתְגֹּדְדִי בַת־גְּדוּד מָצוֹר שָׂם עָלֵינוּ בַּשֵּׁבֶט יַכּוּ עַל־הַלְּחִי אֵת שֹׁפֵט יִשְׂרָאֵל׃

5 1 And you, O *Beit Lechem* of *Efrat*, Least among the clans of *Yehuda*, From you one shall come forth To rule *Yisrael* for Me – One whose origin is from of old, From ancient times.

וְאַתָּה בֵּית־לֶחֶם אֶפְרָתָה צָעִיר לִהְיוֹת בְּאַלְפֵי יְהוּדָה מִמְּךָ לִי יֵצֵא לִהְיוֹת מוֹשֵׁל בְּיִשְׂרָאֵל וּמוֹצָאֹתָיו מִקֶּדֶם מִימֵי עוֹלָם׃

v'-a-TAH bayt LE-khem ef-RA-tah tza-EER lih-YOT b'-al-FAY y'-hu-DAH mi-m'-KHA LEE yay-TZAY lih-YOT mo-SHAYL b'-yis-ra-AYL u-mo-tza-o-TAV mi-KE-dem mee-MAY o-LAM

4:12 He has gathered them like cut grain to the threshing floor Though the Jewish people will eventually be taken into exile, *Micha* warns the nations of the world not to celebrate too quickly, for they do not understand *Hashem*'s ways. Those who dare attack the Holy Land and God's holy city are gathered "like cut grain to the threshing floor." God is the harvester, and those nations who "gathered" to celebrate Israel's downfall will ultimately be "gathered" together to be destroyed, their joy becoming the basis for their own destruction.

5:1 And you, O *Beit Lechem* of *Efrat* At the beginning of chapter 5, a young child appears who will lead the people to victory. He is born in *Beit Lechem* of *Efrat* in *Yehuda*. The city of *Beit Lechem*, which means 'House of Bread,' sits five miles south of *Yerushalayim*. In this verse, *Efrat* is either another name for *Beit Lechem* or refers to the larger district in which it is found. The present day city of *Efrat* was established in 1983, adjacent to the *Beit Lechem*, and is home to over 8,000 residents. *Micha* writes that *Beit Lechem* is in *Yehuda*, to distinguish it from another city called *Beit Lechem* in the north of the country in the territory of *Zevulun* (Joshua 19:15). The young one is described as "Least among the clans of *Yehuda*," but nevertheless, "he will deliver us from Assyria" (verse 5). *Micha*'s allusion to King *David*, the youngest of all his brothers who nevertheless

בית לחם

Micha/Micah
Chapter 5

מיכה
פרק ה

2 Truly, He will leave them [helpless] Until she who is to bear has borne; Then the rest of his countrymen Shall return to the children of *Yisrael*.

ב לָכֵן יִתְּנֵם עַד־עֵת יוֹלֵדָה יָלָדָה וְיֶתֶר אֶחָיו יְשׁוּבוּן עַל־בְּנֵי יִשְׂרָאֵל׃

3 He shall stand and shepherd By the might of *Hashem*, By the power of the name Of *Hashem* his God, And they shall dwell [secure]. For lo, he shall wax great To the ends of the earth;

ג וְעָמַד וְרָעָה בְּעֹז יְהוָה בִּגְאוֹן שֵׁם יְהוָה אֱלֹהָיו וְיָשָׁבוּ כִּי־עַתָּה יִגְדַּל עַד־אַפְסֵי־אָרֶץ׃

4 And that shall afford safety. Should Assyria invade our land And tread upon our fortresses, We will set up over it seven shepherds, Eight princes of men,

ד וְהָיָה זֶה שָׁלוֹם אַשּׁוּר כִּי־יָבוֹא בְאַרְצֵנוּ וְכִי יִדְרֹךְ בְּאַרְמְנוֹתֵינוּ וַהֲקֵמֹנוּ עָלָיו שִׁבְעָה רֹעִים וּשְׁמֹנָה נְסִיכֵי אָדָם׃

5 Who will shepherd Assyria's land with swords, The land of Nimrod in its gates. Thus he will deliver [us] From Assyria, should it invade our land, And should it trample our country.

ה וְרָעוּ אֶת־אֶרֶץ אַשּׁוּר בַּחֶרֶב וְאֶת־אֶרֶץ נִמְרֹד בִּפְתָחֶיהָ וְהִצִּיל מֵאַשּׁוּר כִּי־יָבוֹא בְאַרְצֵנוּ וְכִי יִדְרֹךְ בִּגְבוּלֵנוּ׃

6 The remnant of *Yaakov* shall be, In the midst of the many peoples, Like dew from *Hashem*, Like droplets on grass – Which do not look to any man Nor place their hope in mortals.

ו וְהָיָה שְׁאֵרִית יַעֲקֹב בְּקֶרֶב עַמִּים רַבִּים כְּטַל מֵאֵת יְהוָה כִּרְבִיבִים עֲלֵי־עֵשֶׂב אֲשֶׁר לֹא־יְקַוֶּה לְאִישׁ וְלֹא יְיַחֵל לִבְנֵי אָדָם׃

7 The remnant of *Yaakov* Shall be among the nations, In the midst of the many peoples, Like a lion among beasts of the wild, Like a fierce lion among flocks of sheep, Which tramples wherever it goes And rends, with none to deliver.

ז וְהָיָה שְׁאֵרִית יַעֲקֹב בַּגּוֹיִם בְּקֶרֶב עַמִּים רַבִּים כְּאַרְיֵה בְּבַהֲמוֹת יַעַר כִּכְפִיר בְּעֶדְרֵי־צֹאן אֲשֶׁר אִם עָבַר וְרָמַס וְטָרַף וְאֵין מַצִּיל׃

8 Your hand shall prevail over your foes, And all your enemies shall be cut down!

ח תָּרֹם יָדְךָ עַל־צָרֶיךָ וְכָל־אֹיְבֶיךָ יִכָּרֵתוּ׃

9 In that day – declares *Hashem* – I will destroy the horses in your midst And wreck your chariots.

ט וְהָיָה בַיּוֹם־הַהוּא נְאֻם־יְהוָה וְהִכְרַתִּי סוּסֶיךָ מִקִּרְבֶּךָ וְהַאֲבַדְתִּי מַרְכְּבֹתֶיךָ׃

10 I will destroy the cities of your land And demolish all your fortresses.

י וְהִכְרַתִּי עָרֵי אַרְצֶךָ וְהָרַסְתִּי כָּל־מִבְצָרֶיךָ׃

11 I will destroy the sorcery you practice, And you shall have no more soothsayers.

יא וְהִכְרַתִּי כְשָׁפִים מִיָּדֶךָ וּמְעוֹנְנִים לֹא יִהְיוּ־לָךְ׃

12 I will destroy your idols And the sacred pillars in your midst; And no more shall you bow down To the work of your hands.

יב וְהִכְרַתִּי פְסִילֶיךָ וּמַצֵּבוֹתֶיךָ מִקִּרְבֶּךָ וְלֹא־תִשְׁתַּחֲוֶה עוֹד לְמַעֲשֵׂה יָדֶיךָ׃

13 I will tear down the sacred posts in your midst And destroy your cities.

יג וְנָתַשְׁתִּי אֲשֵׁירֶיךָ מִקִּרְבֶּךָ וְהִשְׁמַדְתִּי עָרֶיךָ׃

14 In anger and wrath Will I wreak retribution On the nations that have not obeyed.

יד וְעָשִׂיתִי בְּאַף וּבְחֵמָה נָקָם אֶת־הַגּוֹיִם אֲשֶׁר לֹא שָׁמֵעוּ׃

---

brought salvation from Israel's enemies, is unmistakable. Indeed, this young lad will be a descendant of King

David, son of "*Yishai of Beit Lechem*" (I Samuel 16:1).

Micha/Micah
Chapter 6

6 ¹ Hear what *Hashem* is saying: Come, present [My] case before the mountains, And let the hills hear you pleading.

² Hear, you mountains, the case of *Hashem* – You firm foundations of the earth! For *Hashem* has a case against His people, He has a suit against *Yisrael*.

³ "My people! What wrong have I done you? What hardship have I caused you? Testify against Me.

⁴ In fact, I brought you up from the land of Egypt, I redeemed you from the house of bondage, And I sent before you *Moshe*, *Aharon*, and *Miriam*.

⁵ "My people, Remember what Balak king of Moab Plotted against you, And how Balaam son of Beor Responded to him. [Recall your passage] From Shittim to *Gilgal* – And you will recognize The gracious acts of *Hashem*."

⁶ With what shall I approach *Hashem*, Do homage to *Hashem* on high? Shall I approach Him with burnt offerings, With calves a year old?

⁷ Would *Hashem* be pleased with thousands of rams, With myriads of streams of oil? Shall I give my firstborn for my transgression, The fruit of my body for my sins?

⁸ "He has told you, O man, what is good, And what *Hashem* requires of you: Only to do justice And to love goodness, And to walk modestly with your God;

   hi-GEED l'-KHA a-DAM mah TOV u-mah a-do-NAI do-RAYSH mi-m'-KHA KEE im a-SOT mish-PAT v'-A-ha-vat KHE-sed v'-hatz-NAY-a LE-khet im e-lo-HE-kha

⁹ Then will your name achieve wisdom." Hark! *Hashem* Summons the city: Hear, O scepter; For who can direct her

---

6:8 Walk modestly with your God The people search for *Hashem*, earnestly but blindly, by increasing their offerings and bringing more sacrifices. *Micha* replies with the most sublime verse of his book, linking piety with ethics and righteousness with empathy. What God wants from man is that he act justly, love kindness, and walk humbly with *Hashem*. Based on this verse, the Sages extol the virtues of modesty in all areas of life, such as the importance of giving charity anonymously or dressing in clothing that conceals more than reveals. In ultra-Orthodox neighborhoods in Israel, this verse is often quoted on signs that welcome tourists but request that visitors abide by the sensitivities of the community by dressing modestly.

Micha/Micah

Chapter 7

מיכה

פרק ז

10 but you? Will I overlook, in the wicked man's house, The granaries of wickedness And the accursed short *efah*?

י עוֹד הַאִשׁ בֵּית רָשָׁע אֹצְרוֹת רֶשַׁע וְאֵיפַת רָזוֹן זְעוּמָה׃

11 Shall he be acquitted despite wicked balances And a bag of fraudulent weights? –

יא הַאֶזְכֶּה בְּמֹאזְנֵי רֶשַׁע וּבְכִיס אַבְנֵי מִרְמָה׃

12 Whose rich men are full of lawlessness, And whose inhabitants speak treachery, With tongues of deceit in their mouths.

יב אֲשֶׁר עֲשִׁירֶיהָ מָלְאוּ חָמָס וְיֹשְׁבֶיהָ דִּבְּרוּ־שָׁקֶר וּלְשׁוֹנָם רְמִיָּה בְּפִיהֶם׃

13 I, in turn, have beaten you sore, Have stunned [you] for your sins:

יג וְגַם־אֲנִי הֶחֱלֵיתִי הַכּוֹתֶךָ הַשְׁמֵם עַל־חַטֹּאתֶךָ׃

14 You have been eating without getting your fill, And there is a gnawing at your vitals; You have been conceiving without bearing young, And what you bore I would deliver to the sword.

יד אַתָּה תֹאכַל וְלֹא תִשְׂבָּע וְיֶשְׁחֲךָ בְּקִרְבֶּךָ וְתַסֵּג וְלֹא תַפְלִיט וַאֲשֶׁר תְּפַלֵּט לַחֶרֶב אֶתֵּן׃

15 You have been sowing, but have nothing to reap; You have trod olives, but have no oil for rubbing, And grapes but have no wine to drink.

טו אַתָּה תִזְרַע וְלֹא תִקְצוֹר אַתָּה תִדְרֹךְ־זַיִת וְלֹא־תָסוּךְ שֶׁמֶן וְתִירוֹשׁ וְלֹא תִשְׁתֶּה־יָּיִן׃

16 Yet you have kept the laws of *Omri*, And all the practices of the House of *Achav*, And have followed what they devised. Therefore I will make you an object of horror And her inhabitants an object of hissing; And you shall bear the mockery of peoples.

טז וְיִשְׁתַּמֵּר חֻקּוֹת עָמְרִי וְכֹל מַעֲשֵׂה בֵית־אַחְאָב וַתֵּלְכוּ בְּמֹעֲצוֹתָם לְמַעַן תִּתִּי אֹתְךָ לְשַׁמָּה וְיֹשְׁבֶיהָ לִשְׁרֵקָה וְחֶרְפַּת עַמִּי תִּשָּׂאוּ׃

7

1 Woe is me! I am become like leavings of a fig harvest, Like gleanings when the vintage is over, There is not a cluster to eat, Not a ripe fig I could desire.

ז א אַלְלַי לִי כִּי הָיִיתִי כְּאָסְפֵּי־קַיִץ כְּעֹלְלֹת בָּצִיר אֵין־אֶשְׁכּוֹל לֶאֱכוֹל בִּכּוּרָה אִוְּתָה נַפְשִׁי׃

2 The pious are vanished from the land, None upright are left among men; All lie in wait to commit crimes, One traps the other in his net.

ב אָבַד חָסִיד מִן־הָאָרֶץ וְיָשָׁר בָּאָדָם אָיִן כֻּלָּם לְדָמִים יֶאֱרֹבוּ אִישׁ אֶת־אָחִיהוּ יָצוּדוּ חֵרֶם׃

3 They are eager to do evil: The magistrate makes demands, And the judge [judges] for a fee; The rich man makes his crooked plea, And they grant it.

ג עַל־הָרַע כַּפַּיִם לְהֵיטִיב הַשַּׂר שֹׁאֵל וְהַשֹּׁפֵט בַּשִּׁלּוּם וְהַגָּדוֹל דֹּבֵר הַוַּת נַפְשׁוֹ הוּא וַיְעַבְּתוּהָ׃

4 The best of them is like a prickly shrub; The [most] upright, worse than a barrier of thorns. On the day you waited for, your doom has come – Now their confusion shall come to pass.

ד טוֹבָם כְּחֵדֶק יָשָׁר מִמְּסוּכָה יוֹם מְצַפֶּיךָ פְּקֻדָּתְךָ בָאָה עַתָּה תִהְיֶה מְבוּכָתָם׃

5 Trust no friend, Rely on no intimate; Be guarded in speech With her who lies in your bosom.

ה אַל־תַּאֲמִינוּ בְרֵעַ אַל־תִּבְטְחוּ בְּאַלּוּף מִשֹּׁכֶבֶת חֵיקֶךָ שְׁמֹר פִּתְחֵי־פִיךָ׃

6 For son spurns father, Daughter rises up against mother, Daughter-in-law against mother-in-law – A man's own household Are his enemies.

ו כִּי־בֵן מְנַבֵּל אָב בַּת קָמָה בְאִמָּהּ כַּלָּה בַּחֲמֹתָהּ אֹיְבֵי אִישׁ אַנְשֵׁי בֵיתוֹ׃

Micha/Micah
Chapter 7

מיכה
פרק ז

7 Yet I will look to *Hashem*, I will wait for the God who saves me, My *Hashem* will hear me.

ז וַאֲנִי בַּיהֹוָה אֲצַפֶּה אוֹחִילָה לֵאלֹהֵי יִשְׁעִי יִשְׁמָעֵנִי אֱלֹהָי:

8 Do not rejoice over me, O my enemy! Though I have fallen, I rise again; Though I sit in darkness, *Hashem* is my light.

ח אַל־תִּשְׂמְחִי אֹיַבְתִּי לִי כִּי נָפַלְתִּי קָמְתִּי כִּי־אֵשֵׁב בַּחֹשֶׁךְ יְהֹוָה אוֹר לִי:

9 I must bear the anger of *Hashem*, Since I have sinned against Him, Until He champions my cause And upholds my claim. He will let me out into the light; I will enjoy vindication by Him.

ט זַעַף יְהֹוָה אֶשָּׂא כִּי חָטָאתִי לוֹ עַד אֲשֶׁר יָרִיב רִיבִי וְעָשָׂה מִשְׁפָּטִי יוֹצִיאֵנִי לָאוֹר אֶרְאֶה בְּצִדְקָתוֹ:

10 When my enemy sees it, She shall be covered with shame, She who taunts me with "Where is He, *Hashem* your God?" My eyes shall behold her [downfall]; Lo, she shall be for trampling Like mud in the streets.

י וְתֵרֶא אֹיַבְתִּי וּתְכַסֶּהָ בוּשָׁה הָאֹמְרָה אֵלַי אַיּוֹ יְהֹוָה אֱלֹהָיִךְ עֵינַי תִּרְאֶינָּה בָּהּ עַתָּה תִּהְיֶה לְמִרְמָס כְּטִיט חוּצוֹת:

11 A day for mending your walls – That is a far-off day.

יא יוֹם לִבְנוֹת גְּדֵרָיִךְ יוֹם הַהוּא יִרְחַק־חֹק:

12 This is rather a day when to you [Tramplers] will come streaming From Assyria and the towns of Egypt – From [every land from] Egypt to the Euphrates, From sea to sea and from mountain to mountain –

יב יוֹם הוּא וְעָדֶיךָ יָבוֹא לְמִנִּי אַשּׁוּר וְעָרֵי מָצוֹר וּלְמִנִּי מָצוֹר וְעַד־נָהָר וְיָם מִיָּם וְהַר הָהָר:

13 And your land shall become a desolation – Because of those who dwell in it – As the fruit of their misdeeds.

יג וְהָיְתָה הָאָרֶץ לִשְׁמָמָה עַל־יֹשְׁבֶיהָ מִפְּרִי מַעַלְלֵיהֶם:

14 Oh, shepherd Your people with Your staff, Your very own flock. May they who dwell isolated In a woodland surrounded by farmland Graze Bashan and *Gilad* As in olden days.

יד רְעֵה עַמְּךָ בְשִׁבְטֶךָ צֹאן נַחֲלָתֶךָ שֹׁכְנִי לְבָדָד יַעַר בְּתוֹךְ כַּרְמֶל יִרְעוּ בָשָׁן וְגִלְעָד כִּימֵי עוֹלָם:

15 I will show him wondrous deeds As in the days when You sallied forth from the land of Egypt.

טו כִּימֵי צֵאתְךָ מֵאֶרֶץ מִצְרָיִם אַרְאֶנּוּ נִפְלָאוֹת:

16 Let nations behold and be ashamed Despite all their might; Let them put hand to mouth; Let their ears be deafened!

טז יִרְאוּ גוֹיִם וְיֵבֹשׁוּ מִכֹּל גְּבוּרָתָם יָשִׂימוּ יָד עַל־פֶּה אָזְנֵיהֶם תֶּחֱרַשְׁנָה:

17 Let them lick dust like snakes, Like crawling things on the ground! Let them come trembling out of their strongholds To *Hashem* our God; Let them fear and dread You!

יז יְלַחֲכוּ עָפָר כַּנָּחָשׁ כְּזֹחֲלֵי אֶרֶץ יִרְגְּזוּ מִמִּסְגְּרֹתֵיהֶם אֶל־יְהֹוָה אֱלֹהֵינוּ יִפְחָדוּ וְיִרְאוּ מִמֶּךָּ:

Micha/Micah
Chapter 7

מיכה
פרק ז

18 Who is a *Hashem* like You, Forgiving iniquity And remitting transgression; Who has not maintained His wrath forever Against the remnant of His own people, Because He loves graciousness!

יח מִי־אֵל כָּמוֹךָ נֹשֵׂא עָוֺן וְעֹבֵר עַל־פֶּשַׁע לִשְׁאֵרִית נַחֲלָתוֹ לֹא־הֶחֱזִיק לָעַד אַפּוֹ כִּי־חָפֵץ חֶסֶד הוּא:

mee AYL ka-MO-kha no-SAY a-VON v'-o-VAYR al PE-sha lish-ay-REET na-kha-la-TO lo he-khe-ZEEK la-AD a-PO kee kha-FAYTZ KHE-sed HU

19 He will take us back in love; He will cover up our iniquities, You will hurl all our sins Into the depths of the sea.

יט יָשׁוּב יְרַחֲמֵנוּ יִכְבֹּשׁ עֲוֺנֹתֵינוּ וְתַשְׁלִיךְ בִּמְצֻלוֹת יָם כָּל־חַטֹּאותָם:

20 You will keep faith with *Yaakov*, Loyalty to *Avraham*, As You promised on oath to our fathers In days gone by.

כ תִּתֵּן אֱמֶת לְיַעֲקֹב חֶסֶד לְאַבְרָהָם אֲשֶׁר־נִשְׁבַּעְתָּ לַאֲבֹתֵינוּ מִימֵי קֶדֶם:

7:18 Forgiving iniquity and remitting transgression
Micha concludes his prophecies by declaring his belief in God's loyalty to His people and His land. This verse echoes the thirteen attributes of mercy that God presented to *Moshe* after the sin of the golden calf (see Exodus 34:5–7). By recalling these attributes, the prophet also expresses his confidence in the people's ability to repent and return. He is certain that in the future, they will be deserving of forgiveness and restoration to their land. *Hashem* will trample the sins of Israel underfoot and cast them into the sea, just as He cast Pharaoh's chariots to the bottom of the sea so many years earlier.

Sefer Nachum
The Book of Nahum

The seventh of the *Trei Asar*, *Sefer Nachum* (Nahum), begins, "A pronouncement on Nineveh: The book of the prophecy of *Nachum* the Elkoshite." We know nothing about the person behind the prophecy, nor can we identify the location of Elkosh.

What this small book does, however, is concentrate upon the upcoming downfall of the Assyrian empire, which had brutally dominated the Middle East for over five centuries. The book provides a general outline of the period in which it was written; it mentions the Assyrian conquest of Thebes (No-Amon) in 663 BCE, and prophesies about the future ransacking of the Assyrian capital Nineveh, which fell in the combined assault of Babylonia and Media in 612 BCE. These references position *Nachum* in the middle of the seventh century BCE, a time when the emasculated kingdom of *Yehuda* barely enjoyed vassal status in the vast Assyrian empire.

The empty fields of the exiled kingdom of *Yisrael* to the north of *Yehuda* served as a grim reminder of what awaited them should they similarly choose disobedience. Indeed, King *Menashe*, who ruled *Yehuda* at the time, behaved no better, religiously or morally, than the Assyrian overlords he served; the Bible relates that he was guilty of idolatry, licentiousness and murder (see II Kings Chapter 20).

The message of *Nachum's* prophecy is empowered by its single-mindedness: Uncompromising abhorrence of Israel's perfidious foe. The first chapter describes God's judgment – those who trust in *Hashem* will find shelter while the rest of the world trembles. The second chapter provides glimpses and flashes of Nineveh's upcoming destruction. The final chapter explains the reason for Nineveh's sudden fall.

Nachum/Nahum
Chapter 1

נחום
פרק א

1 ¹ A pronouncement on Nineveh: The Book of the Prophecy of *Nachum* the Elkoshite.

א מַשָּׂא נִינְוֵה סֵפֶר חֲזוֹן נַחוּם הָאֶלְקֹשִׁי׃

² *Hashem* is a passionate, avenging *Hashem*; *Hashem* is vengeful and fierce in wrath. *Hashem* takes vengeance on His enemies, He rages against His foes.

ב אֵל קַנּוֹא וְנֹקֵם יְהֹוָה נֹקֵם יְהֹוָה וּבַעַל חֵמָה נֹקֵם יְהֹוָה לְצָרָיו וְנוֹטֵר הוּא לְאֹיְבָיו׃

³ *Hashem* is slow to anger and of great forbearance, But *Hashem* does not remit all punishment. He travels in whirlwind and storm, And clouds are the dust on His feet.

ג יְהֹוָה אֶרֶךְ אַפַּיִם וּגְדל־[וּגְדָל־] כֹּחַ וְנַקֵּה לֹא יְנַקֶּה יְהֹוָה בְּסוּפָה וּבִשְׂעָרָה דַּרְכּוֹ וְעָנָן אֲבַק רַגְלָיו׃

⁴ He rebukes the sea and dries it up, And He makes all rivers fail; Bashan and *Carmel* languish, And the blossoms of Lebanon wither.

ד גּוֹעֵר בַּיָּם וַיַּבְּשֵׁהוּ וְכָל־הַנְּהָרוֹת הֶחֱרִיב אֻמְלַל בָּשָׁן וְכַרְמֶל וּפֶרַח לְבָנוֹן אֻמְלָל׃

go-AYR ba-YAM va-ya-b'-SHAY-hu v'-khol ha-n'-ha-ROT he-khe-REEV um-LAL ba-SHAN v'-khar-MEL u-FE-rakh l'-va-NON um-LAL

⁵ The mountains quake because of Him, And the hills melt. The earth heaves before Him, The world and all that dwell therein.

ה הָרִים רָעֲשׁוּ מִמֶּנּוּ וְהַגְּבָעוֹת הִתְמֹגָגוּ וַתִּשָּׂא הָאָרֶץ מִפָּנָיו וְתֵבֵל וְכָל־יֹשְׁבֵי בָהּ׃

⁶ Who can stand before His wrath? Who can resist His fury? His anger pours out like fire, And rocks are shattered because of Him.

ו לִפְנֵי זַעְמוֹ מִי יַעֲמוֹד וּמִי יָקוּם בַּחֲרוֹן אַפּוֹ חֲמָתוֹ נִתְּכָה כָאֵשׁ וְהַצֻּרִים נִתְּצוּ מִמֶּנּוּ׃

⁷ *Hashem* is good to [those who hope in Him], A haven on a day of distress; He is mindful of those who seek refuge in Him.

ז טוֹב יְהֹוָה לְמָעוֹז בְּיוֹם צָרָה וְיֹדֵעַ חֹסֵי בוֹ׃

⁸ And with a sweeping flood He makes an end of her place, And chases His enemies into darkness.

ח וּבְשֶׁטֶף עֹבֵר כָּלָה יַעֲשֶׂה מְקוֹמָהּ וְאֹיְבָיו יְרַדֶּף־חֹשֶׁךְ׃

⁹ Why will you plot against *Hashem*? He wreaks utter destruction: No adversary opposes Him twice!

ט מַה־תְּחַשְּׁבוּן אֶל־יְהֹוָה כָּלָה הוּא עֹשֶׂה לֹא־תָקוּם פַּעֲמַיִם צָרָה׃

¹⁰ For like men besotted with drink, They are burned up like tangled thorns, Like straw that is thoroughly dried.

י כִּי עַד־סִירִים סְבֻכִים וּכְסָבְאָם סְבוּאִים אֻכְּלוּ כְּקַשׁ יָבֵשׁ מָלֵא׃

Cows grazing in the Golan Heights, part of biblical Bashan

1:4 Bashan and *Carmel* languish *Nachum* begins his prophecy by addressing Nineveh, the capital of Assyria. He depicts *Hashem*'s control over nature, and indicates that just as He rules over nature, He also rules over humanity and will punish Israel's enemies. In this verse, *Nachum* first describes how *Hashem* dries up the seas and the rivers, a reference to the miracles of the splitting of the Sea of Reeds (Exodus 15) and the crossing of the *Yarden* river (Joshua 3). He then says that Bashan, *Carmel*, and Lebanon, three of the most luxuriant areas of the Holy Land, thought to be immune to drought, will dry up before *Hashem*'s presence. Biblical Bashan was located on the east side of the Jordan river in modern day Syria and the Israeli Golan Heights. It was captured by the Israelites from Og, king of Bashan, who came out against them as they prepared to enter the Land of Israel (Numbers 21:33–35), and given as part of the inheritance of half the tribe of *Menashe* (Joshua 13:29–31). The land of Bashan is known in the Bible for its rich pastures (Jeremiah 50:19), oak forests (Isaiah 2:13) and majestic mountains (Psalms 68:16).

Nachum/Nahum
Chapter 2

נחום
פרק ב

11 The base plotter Who designed evil against *Hashem* Has left you.

יא מִמֵּךְ יָצָא חֹשֵׁב עַל־יְהֹוָה רָעָה יֹעֵץ בְּלִיָּעַל׃

12 Thus said *Hashem*: "Even as they were full and many, Even so are they over and gone; As surely as I afflicted you, I will afflict you no more."

יב כֹּה ׀ אָמַר יְהֹוָה אִם־שְׁלֵמִים וְכֵן רַבִּים וְכֵן נָגֹזּוּ וְעָבָר וְעִנִּתִךְ לֹא אֲעַנֵּךְ עוֹד׃

13 And now I will break off his yoke bar from you And burst your cords apart.

יג וְעַתָּה אֶשְׁבֹּר מֹטֵהוּ מֵעָלָיִךְ וּמוֹסְרֹתַיִךְ אֲנַתֵּק׃

14 *Hashem* has commanded concerning him: No posterity shall continue your name. I will do away with The carved and graven images In the temples of your gods; I will make your grave Accord with your worthlessness.

יד וְצִוָּה עָלֶיךָ יְהֹוָה לֹא־יִזָּרַע מִשִּׁמְךָ עוֹד מִבֵּית אֱלֹהֶיךָ אַכְרִית פֶּסֶל וּמַסֵּכָה אָשִׂים קִבְרֶךָ כִּי קַלּוֹתָ׃

2 1 Behold on the hills The footsteps of a herald Announcing good fortune! "Celebrate your festivals, O *Yehuda*, Fulfill your vows. Never again shall scoundrels invade you, They have totally vanished."

ב א הִנֵּה עַל־הֶהָרִים רַגְלֵי מְבַשֵּׂר מַשְׁמִיעַ שָׁלוֹם חָגִּי יְהוּדָה חַגַּיִךְ שַׁלְּמִי נְדָרָיִךְ כִּי לֹא יוֹסִיף עוֹד לעבור־[לַעֲבָר־] בָּךְ בְּלִיַּעַל כֻּלֹּה נִכְרָת׃

2 A shatterer has come up against you. Man the guard posts, Watch the road; Steady your loins, Brace all your strength!

ב עָלָה מֵפִיץ עַל־פָּנַיִךְ נָצוֹר מְצֻרָה צַפֵּה־דֶרֶךְ חַזֵּק מָתְנַיִם אַמֵּץ כֹּחַ מְאֹד׃

3 For *Hashem* has restored the Pride of *Yaakov* As well as the Pride of *Yisrael*, Though marauders have laid them waste And ravaged their branches.

ג כִּי שָׁב יְהֹוָה אֶת־גְּאוֹן יַעֲקֹב כִּגְאוֹן יִשְׂרָאֵל כִּי בְקָקוּם בֹּקְקִים וּזְמֹרֵיהֶם שִׁחֵתוּ׃

4 His warriors' shields are painted red, And the soldiers are clothed in crimson; The chariots are like flaming torches, On the day they are made ready. The [arrows of] cypress wood are poisoned,

ד מָגֵן גִּבֹּרֵיהוּ מְאָדָּם אַנְשֵׁי־חַיִל מְתֻלָּעִים בְּאֵשׁ־פְּלָדוֹת הָרֶכֶב בְּיוֹם הֲכִינוֹ וְהַבְּרֹשִׁים הָרְעָלוּ׃

5 The chariots dash about frenzied in the fields, They rush through the meadows. They appear like torches, They race like streaks of lightning.

ה בַּחוּצוֹת יִתְהוֹלְלוּ הָרֶכֶב יִשְׁתַּקְשְׁקוּן בָּרְחֹבוֹת מַרְאֵיהֶן כַּלַּפִּידִם כַּבְּרָקִים יְרוֹצֵצוּ׃

6 He commands his burly men; They stumble as they advance, They hasten up to her wall, Where wheeled shelters are set up.

ו יִזְכֹּר אַדִּירָיו יִכָּשְׁלוּ בהלכותם [בַּהֲלִיכָתָם] יְמַהֲרוּ חוֹמָתָהּ וְהֻכַן הַסֹּכֵךְ׃

7 The floodgates are opened, And the palace is deluged.

ז שַׁעֲרֵי הַנְּהָרוֹת נִפְתָּחוּ וְהַהֵיכָל נָמוֹג׃

sha-a-RAY ha-n'-ha-ROT nif-TA-khu v'-ha-hay-KHAL na-MOG

2:7 The floodgates are opened In this chapter, *Nachum* envisions something that almost no one else at that time could dream of: The defeat of evil, and the downfall of Assyria after five centuries of hegemony in the Middle East. During their reign, the Assyrians exiled the ten tribes of the northern kingdom of *Yisrael*, and ruled over *Yehuda* as well. Their downfall is therefore greatly anticipated by the Children of Israel. *Nachum* carefully

Nachum/Nahum
Chapter 3

נחום
פרק ג

8 And Huzzab is exiled and carried away, While her handmaidens escort [her] As with the voices of doves, Beating their breasts.

ח וְהֻצַּב גֻּלְּתָה הֹעֲלָתָה וְאַמְהֹתֶיהָ מְנַהֲגוֹת כְּקוֹל יוֹנִים מְתֹפְפֹת עַל־לִבְבֵהֶן׃

9 Nineveh has been like a [placid] pool of water From earliest times; Now they flee. "Stop! Stop!" – But none can turn them back.

ט וְנִינְוֵה כִבְרֵכַת־מַיִם מִימֵי הִיא וְהֵמָּה נָסִים עִמְדוּ עֲמֹדוּ וְאֵין מַפְנֶה׃

10 "Plunder silver! Plunder gold!" There is no limit to the treasure; It is a hoard of all precious objects.

י בֹּזּוּ כֶסֶף בֹּזּוּ זָהָב וְאֵין קֵצֶה לַתְּכוּנָה כָּבֹד מִכֹּל כְּלִי חֶמְדָּה׃

11 Desolation, devastation, and destruction! Spirits sink, Knees buckle, All loins tremble, All faces turn ashen.

יא בּוּקָה וּמְבוּקָה וּמְבֻלָּקָה וְלֵב נָמֵס וּפִק בִּרְכַּיִם וְחַלְחָלָה בְּכָל־מָתְנַיִם וּפְנֵי כֻלָּם קִבְּצוּ פָארוּר׃

12 What has become of that lions' den, That pasture of great beasts, Where lion and lion's breed walked, And lion's cub – with none to disturb them?

יב אַיֵּה מְעוֹן אֲרָיוֹת וּמִרְעֶה הוּא לַכְּפִרִים אֲשֶׁר הָלַךְ אַרְיֵה לָבִיא שָׁם גּוּר אַרְיֵה וְאֵין מַחֲרִיד׃

13 [Where is] the lion that tore victims for his cubs And strangled for his lionesses, And filled his lairs with prey And his dens with mangled flesh?

יג אַרְיֵה טֹרֵף בְּדֵי גֹרוֹתָיו וּמְחַנֵּק לְלִבְאֹתָיו וַיְמַלֵּא־טֶרֶף חֹרָיו וּמְעֹנֹתָיו טְרֵפָה׃

14 I am going to deal with you – declares the Lord of Hosts: I will burn down her chariots in smoke, And the sword shall devour your great beasts; I will stamp out your killings from the earth, And the sound of your messengers Shall be heard no more.

יד הִנְנִי אֵלַיִךְ נְאֻם יְהוָה צְבָאוֹת וְהִבְעַרְתִּי בֶעָשָׁן רִכְבָּהּ וּכְפִירַיִךְ תֹּאכַל חָרֶב וְהִכְרַתִּי מֵאֶרֶץ טַרְפֵּךְ וְלֹא־יִשָּׁמַע עוֹד קוֹל מַלְאָכֵכֵה׃

3 1 Ah, city of crime, Utterly treacherous, Full of violence, Where killing never stops!

ג א הוֹי עִיר דָּמִים כֻּלָּהּ כַּחַשׁ פֶּרֶק מְלֵאָה לֹא יָמִישׁ טָרֶף׃

2 Crack of whip And rattle of wheel, Galloping steed And bounding chariot!

ב קוֹל שׁוֹט וְקוֹל רַעַשׁ אוֹפָן וְסוּס דֹּהֵר וּמֶרְכָּבָה מְרַקֵּדָה׃

3 Charging horsemen, Flashing swords, And glittering spears! Hosts of slain And heaps of corpses, Dead bodies without number – They stumble over bodies.

ג פָּרָשׁ מַעֲלֶה וְלַהַב חֶרֶב וּבְרַק חֲנִית וְרֹב חָלָל וְכֹבֶד פָּגֶר וְאֵין קֵצֶה לַגְּוִיָּה יִכְשְׁלוּ [וְכָשְׁלוּ] בִּגְוִיָּתָם׃

4 Because of the countless harlotries of the harlot, The winsome mistress of sorcery, Who ensnared nations with her harlotries And peoples with her sorcery,

ד מֵרֹב זְנוּנֵי זוֹנָה טוֹבַת חֵן בַּעֲלַת כְּשָׁפִים הַמֹּכֶרֶת גּוֹיִם בִּזְנוּנֶיהָ וּמִשְׁפָּחוֹת בִּכְשָׁפֶיהָ׃

---

records every detail of the capital's collapse, from the colorful descriptions of the onrushing soldiers (verse 4), to the chariots rushing through the streets (verse 5). In this verse, Nachum describes the opening of the river gates and the collapse of the palace. Nineveh, the capital of Assyria, was located on the east bank of the Tigris River, and the river Huser ran through it. A series of moats and channels protected the city, but the Greek historian Diodorus Siculus writes that when the invaders opened the river gates, the rushing waters washed away several of the ramparts defending the city. Once the invading armies entered the outer wall of the city they fought to capture the palace, which they eventually burned.

Nachum/Nahum
Chapter 3

נחום
פרק ג

5 I am going to deal with you – declares the Lord of Hosts. I will lift up your skirts over your face And display your nakedness to the nations And your shame to kingdoms.

הִנְנִי אֵלַיִךְ נְאֻם יְהֹוָה צְבָאוֹת וְגִלֵּיתִי שׁוּלַיִךְ עַל־פָּנָיִךְ וְהַרְאֵיתִי גוֹיִם מַעְרֵךְ וּמַמְלָכוֹת קְלוֹנֵךְ:

hi-n'-NEE ay-LA-yikh n'-UM a-do-NAI tz'-va-OT v'-gi-lay-TEE shu-LA-yikh al pa-NA-yikh v'-har-ay-TEE go-YIM ma-RAYKH u-mam-la-KHOT k'-lo-NAYKH

6 I will throw loathsome things over you And disfigure you And make a spectacle of you.

וְהִשְׁלַכְתִּי עָלַיִךְ שִׁקֻּצִים וְנִבַּלְתִּיךְ וְשַׂמְתִּיךְ כְּרֹאִי:

7 All who see you will recoil from you And will say, "Nineveh has been ravaged!" Who will console her? Where shall I look for Anyone to comfort you?

וְהָיָה כָל־רֹאַיִךְ יִדּוֹד מִמֵּךְ וְאָמַר שָׁדְּדָה נִינְוֵה מִי יָנוּד לָהּ מֵאַיִן אֲבַקֵּשׁ מְנַחֲמִים לָךְ:

8 Were you any better than No-amon, Which sat by the Nile, Surrounded by water – Its rampart a river, Its wall consisting of sea?

הֲתֵיטְבִי מִנֹּא אָמוֹן הַיֹּשְׁבָה בַּיְאֹרִים מַיִם סָבִיב לָהּ אֲשֶׁר־חֵיל יָם מִיָּם חוֹמָתָהּ:

9 Populous Nubia And teeming Egypt, Put and the Libyans – They were her helpers.

כּוּשׁ עָצְמָה וּמִצְרַיִם וְאֵין קֵצֶה פּוּט וְלוּבִים הָיוּ בְּעֶזְרָתֵךְ:

10 Yet even she was exiled, She went into captivity. Her babes, too, were dashed in pieces At every street corner. Lots were cast for her honored men, And all her nobles were bound in chains.

גַּם־הִיא לַגֹּלָה הָלְכָה בַשֶּׁבִי גַּם עֹלָלֶיהָ יְרֻטְּשׁוּ בְּרֹאשׁ כָּל־חוּצוֹת וְעַל־נִכְבַּדֶּיהָ יַדּוּ גוֹרָל וְכָל־גְּדוֹלֶיהָ רֻתְּקוּ בַזִּקִּים:

11 You too shall be drunk And utterly overcome; You too shall seek A refuge from the enemy.

גַּם־אַתְּ תִּשְׁכְּרִי תְּהִי נַעֲלָמָה גַּם־אַתְּ תְּבַקְשִׁי מָעוֹז מֵאוֹיֵב:

12 All your forts are fig trees With ripe fruit; If shaken they will fall Into the mouths of devourers.

כָּל־מִבְצָרַיִךְ תְּאֵנִים עִם־בִּכּוּרִים אִם־יִנּוֹעוּ וְנָפְלוּ עַל־פִּי אוֹכֵל:

13 Truly, the troops within you are women; The gates of your land have opened themselves To your enemies; Fire has consumed your gate bars.

הִנֵּה עַמֵּךְ נָשִׁים בְּקִרְבֵּךְ לְאֹיְבַיִךְ פָּתוֹחַ נִפְתְּחוּ שַׁעֲרֵי אַרְצֵךְ אָכְלָה אֵשׁ בְּרִיחָיִךְ:

14 Draw water for the siege, Strengthen your forts; Tread the clay, Trample the mud, Grasp the brick mold!

מֵי מָצוֹר שַׁאֲבִי־לָךְ חַזְּקִי מִבְצָרָיִךְ בֹּאִי בַטִּיט וְרִמְסִי בַחֹמֶר הַחֲזִיקִי מַלְבֵּן:

15 There fire will devour you, The sword will put an end to you; It will devour you like the grub. Multiply like grubs, Multiply like locusts!

שָׁם תֹּאכְלֵךְ אֵשׁ תַּכְרִיתֵךְ חֶרֶב תֹּאכְלֵךְ כַּיָּלֶק הִתְכַּבֵּד כַּיֶּלֶק הִתְכַּבְּדִי כָּאַרְבֶּה:

3:5 I am going to deal with you – declares the Lord of Hosts In *Nachum's* final prophecy against Nineveh, *Hashem* addresses Assyria directly. The statement "I am going to deal with you" testifies that the nations set to fight against Assyria are only the agents of God, Who is ultimately controlling global events. The punishment of uncovering the nakedness of Assyria mirrors the punishment traditionally given to unfaithful spouses (Hosea 2:5). Assyria gained power by "seducing" smaller nations, enticing them into alliances and then breaking their word and enslaving them. Assyria acted unfaithfully, and will therefore receive the punishment of the unfaithful. Those who were humiliated by Assyria will now witness its downfall.

Nachum/Nahum
Chapter 3

נחום
פרק ג

טז הַרְבֵּית רֹכְלַיִךְ מִכּוֹכְבֵי הַשָּׁמָיִם יֶלֶק פָּשַׁט וַיָּעֹף:

16 You had more traders Than the sky has stars – The grubs cast their skins and fly away.

יז מִנְּזָרַיִךְ כָּאַרְבֶּה וְטַפְסְרַיִךְ כְּגוֹב גֹּבָי הַחוֹנִים בַּגְּדֵרוֹת בְּיוֹם קָרָה שֶׁמֶשׁ זָרְחָה וְנוֹדַד וְלֹא־נוֹדַע מְקוֹמוֹ אַיָּם:

17 Your guards were like locusts, Your marshals like piles of hoppers Which settle on the stone fences On a chilly day; When the sun comes out, they fly away, And where they are nobody knows.

יח נָמוּ רֹעֶיךָ מֶלֶךְ אַשּׁוּר יִשְׁכְּנוּ אַדִּירֶיךָ נָפֹשׁוּ עַמְּךָ עַל־הֶהָרִים וְאֵין מְקַבֵּץ:

18 Your shepherds are slumbering, O king of Assyria; Your sheepmasters are lying inert; Your people are scattered over the hills, And there is none to gather them.

יט אֵין־כֵּהָה לְשִׁבְרֶךָ נַחְלָה מַכָּתֶךָ כֹּל שֹׁמְעֵי שִׁמְעֲךָ תָּקְעוּ כַף עָלֶיךָ כִּי עַל־מִי לֹא־עָבְרָה רָעָתְךָ תָּמִיד:

19 There is no healing for your injury; Your wound is grievous. All who hear the news about you, Clap their hands over you. For who has not suffered From your constant malice?

Twelve Prophets

1415

Sefer Chavakuk
The Book of Habakkuk

The eighth of the *Trei Asar*, *Sefer Chavakuk* (Habakkuk), is unique among the prophetic works of the Bible. In most works, the prophets convey God's message to the people. *Chavakuk*, though, conveys the people's questions to *Hashem*. He saw that evil remained unpunished and unbowed, and challenged Heaven for a response. God does respond, and challenges *Chavakuk* to wait and see how the divine plan plays out through history. Until then, "the righteous man is rewarded with life for his fidelity" (2:4).

We know little about the prophet's personal life. His name, from the Hebrew word to 'embrace', appears only here. Most scholars place him near the end of Assyria's reign. That superpower, which brutally enslaved the Middle East for centuries, was about to collapse. Unlike his predecessor *Nachum*, who rejoiced in Assyria's upcoming downfall, *Chavakuk* saw that an even crueler and more vicious foe, Babylonia, would arise and take its place. Some suggest that he prophesied after the shocking and tragic death of *Yehuda's* most righteous king, *Yoshiyahu*, at the hands of the Egyptian invaders at Megiddo in 608 BCE.

Ancient traditions identify *Chavakuk* as the son of the Shunamite woman who *Elisha* revived in *Melachim* II 4, and also as one who was called by angels to feed *Daniel* in the lion's den. What this teaches is that his message was understood to span generations. Each era faces its own challenges to their beliefs, but we are called upon to trust in *Hashem* and His righteousness.

This short book contains three sections; a two-part dialogue with *Hashem*, a series of taunts towards Israel's former oppressors, and a final request of God to overthrow all evil and injustice in the world.

Chavakuk/Habakkuk
Chapter 1

חבקוק
פרק א

1 ¹ The pronouncement made by the *Navi Chavakuk*.

א הַמַּשָּׂא אֲשֶׁר חָזָה חֲבַקּוּק הַנָּבִיא:

² How long, *Hashem*, shall I cry out And You not listen, Shall I shout to You, "Violence!" And You not save?

ב עַד־אָנָה יְהֹוָה שִׁוַּעְתִּי וְלֹא תִשְׁמָע אֶזְעַק אֵלֶיךָ חָמָס וְלֹא תוֹשִׁיעַ:

³ Why do You make me see iniquity [Why] do You look upon wrong? – Raiding and violence are before me, Strife continues and contention goes on.

ג לָמָּה תַרְאֵנִי אָוֶן וְעָמָל תַּבִּיט וְשֹׁד וְחָמָס לְנֶגְדִּי וַיְהִי רִיב וּמָדוֹן יִשָּׂא:

⁴ That is why decision fails And justice never emerges; For the villain hedges in the just man – Therefore judgment emerges deformed.

ד עַל־כֵּן תָּפוּג תּוֹרָה וְלֹא־יֵצֵא לָנֶצַח מִשְׁפָּט כִּי רָשָׁע מַכְתִּיר אֶת־הַצַּדִּיק עַל־כֵּן יֵצֵא מִשְׁפָּט מְעֻקָּל:

al KAYN ta-FUG to-RAH v'-lo yay-TZAY la-NE-tzakh mish-PAT KEE ra-SHA makh-TEER et ha-tza-DEEK al KAYN yay-TZAY mish-PAT m'-u-KAL

⁵ "Look among the nations, Observe well and be utterly astounded; For a work is being wrought in your days Which you would not believe if it were told.

ה רְאוּ בַגּוֹיִם וְהַבִּיטוּ וְהִתַּמְּהוּ תְּמָהוּ כִּי־פֹעַל פֹּעֵל בִּימֵיכֶם לֹא תַאֲמִינוּ כִּי יְסֻפָּר:

⁶ For lo, I am raising up the Chaldeans, That fierce, impetuous nation, Who cross the earth's wide spaces To seize homes not their own.

ו כִּי־הִנְנִי מֵקִים אֶת־הַכַּשְׂדִּים הַגּוֹי הַמַּר וְהַנִּמְהָר הַהוֹלֵךְ לְמֶרְחֲבֵי־אֶרֶץ לָרֶשֶׁת מִשְׁכָּנוֹת לֹא־לוֹ:

⁷ They are terrible, dreadful; They make their own laws and rules.

ז אָיֹם וְנוֹרָא הוּא מִמֶּנּוּ מִשְׁפָּטוֹ וּשְׂאֵתוֹ יֵצֵא:

⁸ Their horses are swifter than leopards, Fleeter than wolves of the steppe. Their steeds gallop – their steeds Come flying from afar. Like vultures rushing toward food,

ח וְקַלּוּ מִנְּמֵרִים סוּסָיו וְחַדּוּ מִזְּאֵבֵי עֶרֶב וּפָשׁוּ פָּרָשָׁיו וּפָרָשָׁיו מֵרָחוֹק יָבֹאוּ יָעֻפוּ כְּנֶשֶׁר חָשׁ לֶאֱכוֹל:

⁹ They all come, bent on rapine. The thrust of their van is forward, And they amass captives like sand.

ט כֻּלֹּה לְחָמָס יָבוֹא מְגַמַּת פְּנֵיהֶם קָדִימָה וַיֶּאֱסֹף כַּחוֹל שֶׁבִי:

¹⁰ Kings they hold in derision, And princes are a joke to them; They laugh at every fortress, They pile up earth and capture it.

י וְהוּא בַּמְּלָכִים יִתְקַלָּס וְרֹזְנִים מִשְׂחָק לוֹ הוּא לְכָל־מִבְצָר יִשְׂחָק וַיִּצְבֹּר עָפָר וַיִּלְכְּדָהּ:

¹¹ Then they pass on like the wind, They transgress and incur guilt, For they ascribe their might to their god."

יא אָז חָלַף רוּחַ וַיַּעֲבֹר וְאָשֵׁם זוּ כֹחוֹ לֵאלֹהוֹ:

1:4 That is why decision fails and justice never emerges Having acknowledged the existence of evil, *Chavakuk* presents the key issue of the book: when the wicked prevail, not only do righteous people suffer, but the law, the *Torah* itself, is weakened. In the Bible, justice and righteousness are intertwined. Without one or the other, the law is used by evildoers to entrap the righteous for their own selfish gain. When people see that evil succeeds at the expense of the righteous, then God's teachings cannot influence others to be righteous and just.

Chavakuk/Habakkuk
Chapter 2

חבקוק
פרק ב

12 You, *Hashem*, are from everlasting; My holy *Hashem*, You never die. *Hashem*, You have made them a subject of contention; O Rock, You have made them a cause for complaint.

יב הֲלוֹא אַתָּה מִקֶּדֶם יְהֹוָה אֱלֹהַי קְדֹשִׁי לֹא נָמוּת יְהֹוָה לְמִשְׁפָּט שַׂמְתּוֹ וְצוּר לְהוֹכִיחַ יְסַדְתּוֹ׃

13 You whose eyes are too pure to look upon evil, Who cannot countenance wrongdoing, Why do You countenance treachery, And stand by idle While the one in the wrong devours The one in the right?

יג טְהוֹר עֵינַיִם מֵרְאוֹת רָע וְהַבִּיט אֶל־עָמָל לֹא תוּכָל לָמָּה תַבִּיט בּוֹגְדִים תַּחֲרִישׁ בְּבַלַּע רָשָׁע צַדִּיק מִמֶּנּוּ׃

14 You have made mankind like the fish of the sea, Like creeping things that have no ruler.

יד וַתַּעֲשֶׂה אָדָם כִּדְגֵי הַיָּם כְּרֶמֶשׂ לֹא־מֹשֵׁל בּוֹ׃

15 He has fished them all up with a line, Pulled them up in his trawl, And gathered them in his net. That is why he rejoices and is glad.

טו כֻּלֹּה בְּחַכָּה הֵעֲלָה יְגֹרֵהוּ בְחֶרְמוֹ וְיַאַסְפֵהוּ בְּמִכְמַרְתּוֹ עַל־כֵּן יִשְׂמַח וְיָגִיל׃

16 That is why he sacrifices to his trawl And makes offerings to his net; For through them his portion is rich And his nourishment fat.

טז עַל־כֵּן יְזַבֵּחַ לְחֶרְמוֹ וִיקַטֵּר לְמִכְמַרְתּוֹ כִּי בָהֵמָּה שָׁמֵן חֶלְקוֹ וּמַאֲכָלוֹ בְּרִאָה׃

17 Shall he then keep emptying his trawl, And slaying nations without pity?

יז הַעַל כֵּן יָרִיק חֶרְמוֹ וְתָמִיד לַהֲרֹג גּוֹיִם לֹא יַחְמוֹל׃

2

1 I will stand on my watch, Take up my station at the post, And wait to see what He will say to me, What He will reply to my complaint.

א עַל־מִשְׁמַרְתִּי אֶעֱמֹדָה וְאֶתְיַצְּבָה עַל־מָצוֹר וַאֲצַפֶּה לִרְאוֹת מַה־יְדַבֶּר־בִּי וּמָה אָשִׁיב עַל־תּוֹכַחְתִּי׃

2 *Hashem* answered me and said: Write the prophecy down, Inscribe it clearly on tablets, So that it can be read easily.

ב וַיַּעֲנֵנִי יְהֹוָה וַיֹּאמֶר כְּתוֹב חָזוֹן וּבָאֵר עַל־הַלֻּחוֹת לְמַעַן יָרוּץ קוֹרֵא בוֹ׃

3 For there is yet a prophecy for a set term, A truthful witness for a time that will come. Even if it tarries, wait for it still; For it will surely come, without delay:

ג כִּי עוֹד חָזוֹן לַמּוֹעֵד וְיָפֵחַ לַקֵּץ וְלֹא יְכַזֵּב אִם־יִתְמַהְמָהּ חַכֵּה־לוֹ כִּי־בֹא יָבֹא לֹא יְאַחֵר׃

4 Lo, his spirit within him is puffed up, not upright, But the righteous man is rewarded with life For his fidelity.

ד הִנֵּה עֻפְּלָה לֹא־יָשְׁרָה נַפְשׁוֹ בּוֹ וְצַדִּיק בֶּאֱמוּנָתוֹ יִחְיֶה׃

hi-NAY u-p'-LAH lo ya-sh'-RAH naf-SHO BO v'-tza-DEEK be-e-mu-na-TO yikh-YEH

2:4 But the righteous man is rewarded with life for his fidelity With these words, *Chavakuk* asserts that it is the faith of the righteous person that grants him life. Israel's acclaimed national poet, Chaim Nachman Bialik, a pioneer of Zionist Hebrew poetry wrote: "This particular people called Israel has, despite all the vicissitudes which for two thousand years have daily, yea hourly, attempted to expel it from its own milieu and uproot it from its spiritual climate – this people, I assert, has accepted upon its body and soul the burdens of eternal allegiance to the Kingdom of the Spirit." Bialik is alluding to this same idea. Even more than the People of Israel have adhered to their faith as they have lived, it is their adherence to their faith that has granted them life.

Chaim Nachman Bialik
(1873–1934)

Chavakuk/Habakkuk
Chapter 2

חבקוק
פרק ב

5 How much less then shall the defiant go unpunished, The treacherous, arrogant man Who has made his maw as wide as Sheol, Who is as insatiable as Death, Who has harvested all the nations And gathered in all the peoples!

ה וְאַף כִּי־הַיַּיִן בּוֹגֵד גֶּבֶר יָהִיר וְלֹא יִנְוֶה אֲשֶׁר הִרְחִיב כִּשְׁאוֹל נַפְשׁוֹ וְהוּא כַמָּוֶת וְלֹא יִשְׂבָּע וַיֶּאֱסֹף אֵלָיו כָּל־הַגּוֹיִם וַיִּקְבֹּץ אֵלָיו כָּל־הָעַמִּים׃

6 Surely all these shall pronounce a satire against him, A pointed epigram concerning him. They shall say: Ah, you who pile up what is not yours – How much longer? – And make ever heavier your load of indebtedness!

ו הֲלוֹא־אֵלֶּה כֻלָּם עָלָיו מָשָׁל יִשָּׂאוּ וּמְלִיצָה חִידוֹת לוֹ וְיֹאמַר הוֹי הַמַּרְבֶּה לֹּא־לוֹ עַד־מָתַי וּמַכְבִּיד עָלָיו עַבְטִיט׃

7 Right suddenly will your creditors arise, And those who remind you will awake, And you will be despoiled by them.

ז הֲלוֹא פֶתַע יָקוּמוּ נֹשְׁכֶיךָ וְיִקְצוּ מְזַעְזְעֶיךָ וְהָיִיתָ לִמְשִׁסּוֹת לָמוֹ׃

8 Because you plundered many nations, All surviving peoples shall plunder you – For crimes against men and wrongs against lands, Against cities and all their inhabitants.

ח כִּי אַתָּה שַׁלּוֹתָ גּוֹיִם רַבִּים יְשָׁלּוּךָ כָּל־יֶתֶר עַמִּים מִדְּמֵי אָדָם וַחֲמַס־אֶרֶץ קִרְיָה וְכָל־יֹשְׁבֵי בָהּ׃

9 Ah, you who have acquired gains To the detriment of your own house, Who have destroyed many peoples* In order to set your nest on high To escape disaster!

ט הוֹי בֹּצֵעַ בֶּצַע רָע לְבֵיתוֹ לָשׂוּם בַּמָּרוֹם קִנּוֹ לְהִנָּצֵל מִכַּף־רָע׃

10 You have plotted shame for your own house, And guilt for yourself;

י יָעַצְתָּ בֹּשֶׁת לְבֵיתֶךָ קְצוֹת־עַמִּים רַבִּים וְחוֹטֵא נַפְשֶׁךָ׃

11 For a stone shall cry out from the wall, And a rafter shall answer it from the woodwork.

יא כִּי־אֶבֶן מִקִּיר תִּזְעָק וְכָפִיס מֵעֵץ יַעֲנֶנָּה׃

12 Ah, you who have built a town with crime, And established a city with infamy,

יב הוֹי בֹּנֶה עִיר בְּדָמִים וְכוֹנֵן קִרְיָה בְּעַוְלָה׃

13 So that peoples have had to toil for the fire, And nations to weary themselves for naught! Behold, it is from the Lord of Hosts:

יג הֲלוֹא הִנֵּה מֵאֵת יְהֹוָה צְבָאוֹת וְיִיגְעוּ עַמִּים בְּדֵי־אֵשׁ וּלְאֻמִּים בְּדֵי־רִיק יִעָפוּ׃

14 For the earth shall be filled With awe for the glory of *Hashem* As water covers the sea.

יד כִּי תִּמָּלֵא הָאָרֶץ לָדַעַת אֶת־כְּבוֹד יְהֹוָה כַּמַּיִם יְכַסּוּ עַל־יָם׃

KEE ti-ma-LAY ha-A-retz la-DA-at et k'-VOD a-do-NAI ka-MA-yim y'-kha-SU al YAM

---

* "Who have destroyed many peoples" brought up from verse 10 for clarity

Yigal Allon (1918–1980)

2:14 For the earth shall be filled with awe for the glory of *Hashem* Here *Chavakuk* describes a great future for the entire world upon the return of the Jewish people to *Eretz Yisrael*. One of Israel's leading statesmen, Yigal Allon (1918–1980), eloquently defined Modern Zionism for world leaders in an address to the United Nations in 1975: "Zionism is the modern expression of the ancient Jewish heritage. Zionism is the national liberation movement of a people exiled from its historic homeland and dispersed among the nations of the world. Zionism is the redemption of an ancient nation from a tragic lot and the redemption of a land neglected for centuries. Zionism is the revival of an ancient language and culture, in which the vision of a

Chavakuk/Habakkuk

Chapter 3

15 Ah, you who make others drink to intoxication As you pour out your wrath, In order to gaze upon their nakedness!

16 You shall be sated with shame Rather than glory: Drink in your turn and stagger! The cup in the right hand of *Hashem* Shall come around to you, And disgrace to your glory.

17 For the lawlessness against Lebanon shall cover you, The destruction of beasts shall overwhelm you — For crimes against men and wrongs against lands, Against cities and all their inhabitants.

18 What has the carved image availed, That he who fashioned it has carved it For an image and a false oracle — That he who fashioned his product has trusted in it, Making dumb idols?

19 Ah, you who say, "Wake up" to wood, "Awaken," to inert stone! Can that give an oracle? Why, it is encased in gold and silver, But there is no breath inside it.

20 But *Hashem* in His holy Abode — Be silent before Him all the earth!

3

1 A prayer of the *Navi Chavakuk*. In the mode of Shigionoth.

2 O *Hashem*! I have learned of Your renown; I am awed, *Hashem*, by Your deeds. Renew them in these years, Oh, make them known in these years! Though angry, may You remember compassion.

3 *Hashem* is coming from Teman, The Holy One from Mount Paran. Selah. His majesty covers the skies, His splendor fills the earth:

4 It is a brilliant light Which gives off rays on every side — And therein His glory is enveloped.

v'-NO-gah ka-OR tih-YEH kar-NA-yim mi-ya-DO LO v'-SHAM khev-YON u-ZOH

---

universal peace has been a central theme. Zionism is the embodiment of a unique pioneering spirit, of the dignity of labor, and of enduring human values. Zionism is creating a society, however, imperfect it may still be, which tries to implement the highest ideal of democracy – political, social and cultural – for all the inhabitants of Israel, irrespective of religious belief, race or sex. Zionism is, in sum, the constant and unrelenting effort to realize the national and universal vision of the prophets of Israel."

3:4 It is a brilliant light The Hebrew word for 'light', *ohr* (אור), is very similar to the word for 'awaken', *ayr* (ער). According to Rabbi Michael Munk in his book *The Wisdom in the Hebrew Alphabet*, this teaches that light is the element that awakens creation to development. Just as physical light stimulates the growth of plants, spiritual and intellectual light prods man to achieve his potential.

אור
ער

Chavakuk/Habakkuk
Chapter 3

חבקוק
פרק ג

5 Pestilence marches before Him, And plague comes forth at His heels.

ה לְפָנָיו יֵלֶךְ דָּבֶר וְיֵצֵא רֶשֶׁף לְרַגְלָיו:

6 When He stands, He makes the earth shake; When He glances, He makes nations tremble. The age-old mountains are shattered, The primeval hills sink low. His are the ancient routes:

ו עָמַד וַיְמֹדֶד אֶרֶץ רָאָה וַיַּתֵּר גּוֹיִם וַיִּתְפֹּצְצוּ הַרְרֵי־עַד שַׁחוּ גִּבְעוֹת עוֹלָם הֲלִיכוֹת עוֹלָם לוֹ:

7 As a scene of havoc I behold The tents of Cushan; Shaken are the pavilions Of the land of Midian!

ז תַּחַת אָוֶן רָאִיתִי אָהֳלֵי כוּשָׁן יִרְגְּזוּן יְרִיעוֹת אֶרֶץ מִדְיָן:

8 Are You wroth, *Hashem*, with Neharim? Is Your anger against Neharim, Your rage against Yam – That You are driving Your steeds, Your victorious chariot?

ח הֲבִנְהָרִים חָרָה יְהֹוָה אִם בַּנְּהָרִים אַפֶּךָ אִם־בַּיָּם עֶבְרָתֶךָ כִּי תִרְכַּב עַל־סוּסֶיךָ מַרְכְּבֹתֶיךָ יְשׁוּעָה:

9 All bared and ready is Your bow. Sworn are the rods of the word. Selah. You make the earth burst into streams,

ט עֶרְיָה תֵעוֹר קַשְׁתֶּךָ שְׁבֻעוֹת מַטּוֹת אֹמֶר סֶלָה נְהָרוֹת תְּבַקַּע־אָרֶץ:

10 The mountains rock at the sight of You, A torrent of rain comes down; Loud roars the deep, The sky returns the echo.

י רָאוּךָ יָחִילוּ הָרִים זֶרֶם מַיִם עָבָר נָתַן תְּהוֹם קוֹלוֹ רוֹם יָדֵיהוּ נָשָׂא:

11 Sun [and] moon stand still on high As Your arrows fly in brightness, Your flashing spear in brilliance.

יא שֶׁמֶשׁ יָרֵחַ עָמַד זְבֻלָה לְאוֹר חִצֶּיךָ יְהַלֵּכוּ לְנֹגַהּ בְּרַק חֲנִיתֶךָ:

12 You tread the earth in rage, You trample nations in fury.

יב בְּזַעַם תִּצְעַד־אָרֶץ בְּאַף תָּדוּשׁ גּוֹיִם:

13 You have come forth to deliver Your people, To deliver Your anointed. You will smash the roof of the villain's house, Raze it from foundation to top. Selah.

יג יָצָאתָ לְיֵשַׁע עַמֶּךָ לְיֵשַׁע אֶת־מְשִׁיחֶךָ מָחַצְתָּ רֹּאשׁ מִבֵּית רָשָׁע עָרוֹת יְסוֹד עַד־צַוָּאר סֶלָה:

14 You will crack [his] skull with Your bludgeon; Blown away shall be his warriors, Whose delight is to crush me suddenly, To devour a poor man in an ambush.

יד נָקַבְתָּ בְמַטָּיו רֹאשׁ פְּרָזָו [פְּרָזָיו] יִסְעֲרוּ לַהֲפִיצֵנִי עֲלִיצֻתָם כְּמוֹ־לֶאֱכֹל עָנִי בַּמִּסְתָּר:

15 You will make Your steeds tread the sea, Stirring the mighty waters.

טו דָּרַכְתָּ בַיָּם סוּסֶיךָ חֹמֶר מַיִם רַבִּים:

16 I heard and my bowels quaked, My lips quivered at the sound; Rot entered into my bone, I trembled where I stood. Yet I wait calmly for the day of distress, For a people to come to attack us.

טז שָׁמַעְתִּי וַתִּרְגַּז בִּטְנִי לְקוֹל צָלֲלוּ שְׂפָתַי יָבוֹא רָקָב בַּעֲצָמַי וְתַחְתַּי אֶרְגָּז אֲשֶׁר אָנוּחַ לְיוֹם צָרָה לַעֲלוֹת לְעַם יְגוּדֶנּוּ:

17 Though the fig tree does not bud And no yield is on the vine, Though the olive crop has failed And the fields produce no grain, Though sheep have vanished from the fold And no cattle are in the pen,

יז כִּי־תְאֵנָה לֹא־תִפְרָח וְאֵין יְבוּל בַּגְּפָנִים כִּחֵשׁ מַעֲשֵׂה־זַיִת וּשְׁדֵמוֹת לֹא־עָשָׂה אֹכֶל גָּזַר מִמִּכְלָה צֹאן וְאֵין בָּקָר בָּרְפָתִים:

18 Yet will I rejoice in *Hashem*, Exult in the God who delivers me.

יח וַאֲנִי בַּיהֹוָה אֶעְלוֹזָה אָגִילָה בֵּאלֹהֵי יִשְׁעִי:

19 My *Hashem* is my strength: He makes my feet like the deer's And lets me stride upon the heights. For the leader; with instrumental music.

יט יְהֹוִה אֲדֹנָי חֵילִי וַיָּשֶׂם רַגְלַי כָּאַיָּלוֹת וְעַל בָּמוֹתַי יַדְרִכֵנִי לַמְנַצֵּחַ בִּנְגִינוֹתָי:

Sefer Tzefanya
The Book of Zephaniah

The ninth of the *Trei Asar*, *Sefer Tzefanya* (Zephaniah), describes the last of the twelve prophets to speak before *Yehuda's* final disintegration and dissolution by Babylonia at the end of the seventh century BCE. In the year 638 BCE, the young child *Yoshiyahu* ascended the throne of *Yehuda*. For over half a century under his grandfather *Menashe*, *Yehuda* was a subservient vassal to the Assyrian Empire, and lost most vestiges of its sovereignty, including its religious autonomy. Instead of the pure worship of God, *Menashe* brought Assyrian idols and cultic practices into *Yehuda*, and even into the *Beit Hamikdash* itself.

In the country, rich courtiers profited from the toil of the oppressed citizenry. However, by the time *Yoshiyahu* comes to power, Assyrian influence is on the wane. The young child king senses that the moment is right to remove all vestiges of foreign rule from the country, engaging in the most comprehensive religious and political reform that *Yehuda* has ever seen. Within two decades, the righteous *Yoshiyahu* will rule over a country as big as that of *David* and *Shlomo*. Among those guiding him was the prophet *Tzefanya*, about whom we know little.

Tzefanya speaks about how the people of God must live in righteousness, which involves respecting the needs of the poor and engaging in genuine worship. Otherwise, he warns, *Hashem* is preparing a day of judgment, a "Day of *Hashem*". It is up to the people to decide whether that judgment will befall them, or their enemies.

The book contains five sections in its three chapters. Chapter 1 warns about the approach of divine judgment on the world, including *Yehuda*. Chapter 2 repeats the warning for other countries, excluding *Yehuda*. Chapter 3 then begins with *Yehuda's* call to judgment, continues with *Hashem*'s punishment and concludes with the prophet urging *Tzion* and *Yisrael* to rejoice, for after the judgment, God's love and care for them will become evident to all.

Tzefanya/Zephaniah
Chapter 1

צפניה
פרק א

1 ¹ The word of *Hashem* that came to *Tzefanya* son of *Kushi* son of *Gedalya* son of Amariah son of *Chizkiyahu*, during the reign of King *Yoshiyahu* son of *Amon* of *Yehuda*.

א דְּבַר־יְהֹוָה אֲשֶׁר הָיָה אֶל־צְפַנְיָה בֶּן־כּוּשִׁי בֶן־גְּדַלְיָה בֶּן־אֲמַרְיָה בֶּן־חִזְקִיָּה בִּימֵי יֹאשִׁיָּהוּ בֶן־אָמוֹן מֶלֶךְ יְהוּדָה:

2 I will sweep everything away From the face of the earth – declares *Hashem*.

ב אָסֹף אָסֵף כֹּל מֵעַל פְּנֵי הָאֲדָמָה נְאֻם־יְהֹוָה:

3 I will sweep away man and beast; I will sweep away the birds of the sky And the fish of the sea. I will make the wicked stumble, And I will destroy mankind From the face of the earth – declares *Hashem*.

ג אָסֵף אָדָם וּבְהֵמָה אָסֵף עוֹף־הַשָּׁמַיִם וּדְגֵי הַיָּם וְהַמַּכְשֵׁלוֹת אֶת־הָרְשָׁעִים וְהִכְרַתִּי אֶת־הָאָדָם מֵעַל פְּנֵי הָאֲדָמָה נְאֻם־יְהֹוָה:

4 I will stretch out My arm against *Yehuda* And against all who dwell in *Yerushalayim*; And I will wipe out from this place Every vestige of Baal, And the name of the priestlings along with the *Kohanim*;

ד וְנָטִיתִי יָדִי עַל־יְהוּדָה וְעַל כָּל־יוֹשְׁבֵי יְרוּשָׁלָ͏ִם וְהִכְרַתִּי מִן־הַמָּקוֹם הַזֶּה אֶת־שְׁאָר הַבַּעַל אֶת־שֵׁם הַכְּמָרִים עִם־הַכֹּהֲנִים:

5 And those who bow down on the roofs To the host of heaven; And those who bow down and swear to *Hashem* But also swear by Malcam;

ה וְאֶת־הַמִּשְׁתַּחֲוִים עַל־הַגַּגּוֹת לִצְבָא הַשָּׁמָיִם וְאֶת־הַמִּשְׁתַּחֲוִים הַנִּשְׁבָּעִים לַיהֹוָה וְהַנִּשְׁבָּעִים בְּמַלְכָּם:

6 And those who have forsaken *Hashem*, And those who have not sought *Hashem* And have not turned to Him.

ו וְאֶת־הַנְּסוֹגִים מֵאַחֲרֵי יְהֹוָה וַאֲשֶׁר לֹא־בִקְשׁוּ אֶת־יְהֹוָה וְלֹא דְרָשֻׁהוּ:

7 Be silent before my God, For the day of *Hashem* is approaching; For *Hashem* has prepared a sacrificial feast, Has bidden His guests purify themselves.

ז הַס מִפְּנֵי אֲדֹנָי יְהֹוִה כִּי קָרוֹב יוֹם יְהֹוָה כִּי־הֵכִין יְהֹוָה זֶבַח הִקְדִּישׁ קְרֻאָיו:

8 And on the day of *Hashem*'s sacrifice I will punish the officials And the king's sons, And all who don a foreign vestment.

ח וְהָיָה בְּיוֹם זֶבַח יְהֹוָה וּפָקַדְתִּי עַל־הַשָּׂרִים וְעַל־בְּנֵי הַמֶּלֶךְ וְעַל כָּל־הַלֹּבְשִׁים מַלְבּוּשׁ נָכְרִי:

9 I will also punish on that day Everyone who steps over the threshold, Who fill their master's palace With lawlessness and fraud.

ט וּפָקַדְתִּי עַל כָּל־הַדּוֹלֵג עַל־הַמִּפְתָּן בַּיּוֹם הַהוּא הַמְמַלְאִים בֵּית אֲדֹנֵיהֶם חָמָס וּמִרְמָה:

10 In that day there shall be – declares *Hashem* – A loud outcry from the Fish Gate, And howling from the Mishneh, And a sound of great anguish from the hills.

י וְהָיָה בַיּוֹם הַהוּא נְאֻם־יְהֹוָה קוֹל צְעָקָה מִשַּׁעַר הַדָּגִים וִילָלָה מִן־הַמִּשְׁנֶה וְשֶׁבֶר גָּדוֹל מֵהַגְּבָעוֹת:

11 The dwellers of the Machtesh howl; For all the tradesmen have perished, All who weigh silver are wiped out.

יא הֵילִילוּ יֹשְׁבֵי הַמַּכְתֵּשׁ כִּי נִדְמָה כָּל־עַם כְּנַעַן נִכְרְתוּ כָּל־נְטִילֵי כָסֶף:

12 At that time, I will search *Yerushalayim* with lamps; And I will punish the men Who rest untroubled on their lees, Who say to themselves, "*Hashem* will do nothing, good or bad."

יב וְהָיָה בָּעֵת הַהִיא אֲחַפֵּשׂ אֶת־יְרוּשָׁלַ͏ִם בַּנֵּרוֹת וּפָקַדְתִּי עַל־הָאֲנָשִׁים הַקֹּפְאִים עַל־שִׁמְרֵיהֶם הָאֹמְרִים בִּלְבָבָם לֹא־יֵיטִיב יְהֹוָה וְלֹא יָרֵעַ:

Tzefanya/Zephaniah
Chapter 2

צפניה
פרק ב

13 Their wealth shall be plundered And their homes laid waste. They shall build houses and not dwell in them, Plant vineyards and not drink their wine.

וְהָיָה חֵילָם לִמְשִׁסָּה וּבָתֵּיהֶם לִשְׁמָמָה וּבָנוּ בָתִּים וְלֹא יֵשֵׁבוּ וְנָטְעוּ כְרָמִים וְלֹא יִשְׁתּוּ אֶת־יֵינָם׃

14 The great day of *Hashem* is approaching, Approaching most swiftly. Hark, the day of *Hashem*! It is bitter: There a warrior shrieks!

קָרוֹב יוֹם־יְהֹוָה הַגָּדוֹל קָרוֹב וּמַהֵר מְאֹד קוֹל יוֹם יְהֹוָה מַר צֹרֵחַ שָׁם גִּבּוֹר׃

15 That day shall be a day of wrath, A day of trouble and distress, A day of calamity and desolation, A day of darkness and deep gloom, A day of densest clouds,

יוֹם עֶבְרָה הַיּוֹם הַהוּא יוֹם צָרָה וּמְצוּקָה יוֹם שֹׁאָה וּמְשׁוֹאָה יוֹם חֹשֶׁךְ וַאֲפֵלָה יוֹם עָנָן וַעֲרָפֶל׃

YOM ev-RAH ha-YOM ha-HU YOM tza-RAH um-tzu-KAH YOM sho-AH um-sho-AH YOM KHO-shekh va-a-fay-LAH YOM a-NAN va-a-ra-FEL

16 A day of *shofar* blasts and alarms – Against the fortified towns And the lofty corner towers.

יוֹם שׁוֹפָר וּתְרוּעָה עַל הֶעָרִים הַבְּצֻרוֹת וְעַל הַפִּנּוֹת הַגְּבֹהוֹת׃

17 I will bring distress on the people, And they shall walk like blind men, Because they sinned against *Hashem*; Their blood shall be spilled like dust, And their fat like dung.

וַהֲצֵרֹתִי לָאָדָם וְהָלְכוּ כַּעִוְרִים כִּי לַיהֹוָה חָטָאוּ וְשֻׁפַּךְ דָּמָם כֶּעָפָר וּלְחֻמָם כַּגְּלָלִים׃

18 Moreover, their silver and gold Shall not avail to save them. On the day of *Hashem*'s wrath, In the fire of His passion, The whole land shall be consumed; For He will make a terrible end Of all who dwell in the land.

גַּם־כַּסְפָּם גַּם־זְהָבָם לֹא־יוּכַל לְהַצִּילָם בְּיוֹם עֶבְרַת יְהֹוָה וּבְאֵשׁ קִנְאָתוֹ תֵּאָכֵל כָּל־הָאָרֶץ כִּי־כָלָה אַךְ־נִבְהָלָה יַעֲשֶׂה אֵת כָּל־יֹשְׁבֵי הָאָרֶץ׃

2

1 Gather together, gather, O nation without shame,

הִתְקוֹשְׁשׁוּ וָקוֹשּׁוּ הַגּוֹי לֹא נִכְסָף׃

2 Before the day the decree is born – The day flies by like chaff – Before the fierce anger Of *Hashem* overtakes you, Before the day of anger Of *Hashem* overtakes you.

בְּטֶרֶם לֶדֶת חֹק כְּמֹץ עָבַר יוֹם בְּטֶרֶם לֹא־יָבוֹא עֲלֵיכֶם חֲרוֹן אַף־יְהֹוָה בְּטֶרֶם לֹא־יָבוֹא עֲלֵיכֶם יוֹם אַף־יְהֹוָה׃

3 Seek *Hashem*, All you humble of the land Who have fulfilled His law; Seek righteousness, Seek humility. Perhaps you will find shelter On the day of *Hashem*'s anger.

בַּקְּשׁוּ אֶת־יְהֹוָה כָּל־עַנְוֵי הָאָרֶץ אֲשֶׁר מִשְׁפָּטוֹ פָּעָלוּ בַּקְּשׁוּ־צֶדֶק בַּקְּשׁוּ עֲנָוָה אוּלַי תִּסָּתְרוּ בְּיוֹם אַף־יְהֹוָה׃

1:15 A day of calamity and desolation The Hebrew name of Israel's Holocaust Remembrance Day, *Yom Hashoah* (יום השואה), comes from this verse. When describing the devastating destruction of *Yerushalayim*, *Tzefanya* refers to that day as *yom shoah umishoah* (יום שואה ומשואה), 'A day of calamity and desolation.' *Yom Hashoah* was established by the Knesset in memory of the six million Jews murdered by the Nazis during World War II. It coincides with the anniversary of the Warsaw ghetto uprising, remembering not only the destruction of European Jewry, but also the heroic revolt which serves as a symbol of defiance against oppression. *Yom Hashoah* is commemorated in Israel with a siren that is sounded in the morning, bringing everyone, even highway traffic, to a standstill for a minute of silence in memory of those who perished in the Holocaust. Memorial ceremonies are held throughout the country, and entertainment establishments are closed in the evening, to focus on the solemnness of the day.

2:3 Seek *Hashem*, all you humble of the land The "humble of the land" are the few who rejected idolatry,

Standing for the Yom Hashoah siren in Jerusalem

Tzefanya/Zephaniah
Chapter 2

צפניה
פרק ב

ba-k'-SHU et a-do-NAI kol an-VAY ha-A-retz a-SHER mish-pa-TO pa-A-lu ba-k'-shu TZE-dek ba-k'-SHU a-na-VAH u-LAI ti-sa-t'-RU b'-YOM af a-do-NAI

4 Indeed, *Azza* shall be deserted And *Ashkelon* desolate; *Ashdod*'s people shall be expelled in broad daylight, And Ekron shall be uprooted.

כִּי עַזָּה עֲזוּבָה תִהְיֶה וְאַשְׁקְלוֹן לִשְׁמָמָה אַשְׁדּוֹד בַּצׇּהֳרַיִם יְגָרְשׁוּהָ וְעֶקְרוֹן תֵּעָקֵר:

5 Ah, nation of Cherethites Who inhabit the seacoast! There is a word of *Hashem* against you, O Canaan, land of the Philistines: I will lay you waste Without inhabitants.

הוֹי יֹשְׁבֵי חֶבֶל הַיָּם גּוֹי כְּרֵתִים דְּבַר־יְהֹוָה עֲלֵיכֶם כְּנַעַן אֶרֶץ פְּלִשְׁתִּים וְהַאֲבַדְתִּיךְ מֵאֵין יוֹשֵׁב:

6 The seacoast Cheroth shall become An abode for shepherds and folds for flocks,

וְהָיְתָה חֶבֶל הַיָּם נְוֺת כְּרֹת רֹעִים וְגִדְרוֹת צֹאן:

7 And shall be a portion for the remnant of the House of *Yehuda*; On these [pastures] they shall graze [their flocks], They shall lie down at eventide In the houses of *Ashkelon*. For *Hashem* their God will take note of them And restore their fortunes.

וְהָיָה חֶבֶל לִשְׁאֵרִית בֵּית יְהוּדָה עֲלֵיהֶם יִרְעוּן בְּבָתֵּי אַשְׁקְלוֹן בָּעֶרֶב יִרְבָּצוּן כִּי יִפְקְדֵם יְהֹוָה אֱלֹהֵיהֶם וְשָׁב שבותם [שְׁבִיתָם:]

8 I have heard the insults of Moab And the jeers of the Amonites, Who have insulted My people And gloated over their country.

שָׁמַעְתִּי חֶרְפַּת מוֹאָב וְגִדּוּפֵי בְּנֵי עַמּוֹן אֲשֶׁר חֵרְפוּ אֶת־עַמִּי וַיַּגְדִּילוּ עַל־גְּבוּלָם:

9 Assuredly, as I live – declares the Lord of Hosts, the God of *Yisrael* – Moab shall become like Sodom And the Amonites like Gomorrah: Clumps of weeds and patches of salt, And desolation evermore. The remnant of My people shall plunder them, The remainder o My nation shall possess them.

לָכֵן חַי־אָנִי נְאֻם יְהֹוָה צְבָאוֹת אֱלֹהֵי יִשְׂרָאֵל כִּי־מוֹאָב כִּסְדֹם תִּהְיֶה וּבְנֵי עַמּוֹן כַּעֲמֹרָה מִמְשַׁק חָרוּל וּמִכְרֵה־מֶלַח וּשְׁמָמָה עַד־עוֹלָם שְׁאֵרִית עַמִּי יְבָזּוּם וְיֶתֶר גּוֹי [גּוֹיִי] יִנְחָלוּם:

10 That is what they'll get for their haughtiness, For insulting and jeering At the people of the Lord of Hosts.

זֹאת לָהֶם תַּחַת גְּאוֹנָם כִּי חֵרְפוּ וַיַּגְדִּלוּ עַל־עַם יְהֹוָה צְבָאוֹת:

11 *Hashem* will show Himself terrible against them, Causing all the gods on earth to shrivel; And all the coastlands of the nations Shall bow down to Him – Every man in his own home.

נוֹרָא יְהֹוָה עֲלֵיהֶם כִּי רִזָּה אֵת כָּל־אֱלֹהֵי הָאָרֶץ וְיִשְׁתַּחֲווּ־לוֹ אִישׁ מִמְּקוֹמוֹ כֹּל אִיֵּי הַגּוֹיִם:

12 You Cushites too – They shall be slain by My sword.

גַּם־אַתֶּם כּוּשִׁים חַלְלֵי חַרְבִּי הֵמָּה:

---

quietly serving God in the Land of Israel despite the hardships. *Tzefanya* encourages them to continue their loyalty to *Hashem* despite the decree of destruction and exile soon to take effect. He uses the command "seek" three times: To seek the Lord, to seek righteousness, and to seek humility. The three go together. One cannot seek God without striving for righteousness, or without behaving with humility, since the way we treat others automatically affects how we treat God. If they continue to seek out *Hashem*, "Perhaps you will find shelter on the day of *Hashem*'s anger." *Tzefanya* teaches that the safest refuge from God's anger is with *Hashem* Himself.

Tzefanya/Zephaniah
Chapter 3

צְפַנְיָה

פֶּרֶק ג

13 And He will stretch out His arm against the north And destroy Assyria; He will make Nineveh a desolation, Arid as the desert.

וְיֵ֣ט יָד֗וֹ עַל־צָפ֛וֹן וִֽיאַבֵּ֖ד אֶת־אַשּׁ֑וּר וְיָשֵׂ֤ם אֶת־נִֽינְוֵה֙ לִשְׁמָמָ֔ה צִיָּ֖ה כַּמִּדְבָּֽר׃

14 In it flocks shall lie down, Every species of beast, While jackdaws and owls roost on its capitals, The great owl hoots in the window, And the raven [croaks] on the threshold. For he has stripped its cedarwork bare.

וְרָבְצ֨וּ בְתוֹכָ֤הּ עֲדָרִים֙ כׇּל־חַיְתוֹ־ג֔וֹי גַּם־קָאַת֙ גַּם־קִפֹּ֔ד בְּכַפְתֹּרֶ֖יהָ יָלִ֑ינוּ ק֠וֹל יְשׁוֹרֵ֨ר בַּחַלּ֜וֹן חֹ֤רֶב בַּסַּף֙ כִּ֣י אַרְזָ֥ה עֵרָֽה׃

15 Is this the gay city That dwelt secure, That thought in her heart, "I am, and there is none but me"? Alas, she is become a waste, A lair of wild beasts! Everyone who passes by her Hisses and gestures with his hand.

זֹ֠את הָעִ֤יר הָעַלִּיזָה֙ הַיּוֹשֶׁ֣בֶת לָבֶ֔טַח הָאֹֽמְרָה֙ בִּלְבָבָ֔הּ אֲנִ֖י וְאַפְסִ֣י ע֑וֹד אֵ֣יךְ ׀ הָיְתָ֣ה לְשַׁמָּ֗ה מַרְבֵּץ֙ לַֽחַיָּ֔ה כֹּ֚ל עוֹבֵ֣ר עָלֶ֔יהָ יִשְׁרֹ֖ק יָנִ֥יעַ יָדֽוֹ׃

3 1 Ah, sullied, polluted, Overbearing city!

ה֥וֹי מֹרְאָ֖ה וְנִגְאָלָ֑ה הָעִ֖יר הַיּוֹנָֽה׃

2 She has been disobedient, Has learned no lesson; She has not trusted in *Hashem*, Has not drawn near to her God.

לֹ֤א שָֽׁמְעָה֙ בְּק֔וֹל לֹ֥א לָקְחָ֖ה מוּסָ֑ר בַּֽיהֹוָה֙ לֹ֣א בָטָ֔חָה אֶל־אֱלֹהֶ֖יהָ לֹ֥א קָרֵֽבָה׃

3 The officials within her Are roaring lions; Her judges are wolves of the steppe, They leave no bone until morning.

שָׂרֶ֣יהָ בְקִרְבָּ֔הּ אֲרָי֖וֹת שֹׁאֲגִ֑ים שֹׁפְטֶ֙יהָ֙ זְאֵ֣בֵי עֶ֔רֶב לֹ֥א גָרְמ֖וּ לַבֹּֽקֶר׃

4 Her *Neviim* are reckless, Faithless fellows; Her *Kohanim* profane what is holy, They give perverse rulings.

נְבִיאֶ֙יהָ֙ פֹּחֲזִ֔ים אַנְשֵׁ֖י בֹּגְד֑וֹת כֹּהֲנֶ֙יהָ֙ חִלְּלוּ־קֹ֔דֶשׁ חָמְס֖וּ תּוֹרָֽה׃

5 But *Hashem* in her midst is righteous, He does no wrong; He issues judgment every morning, As unfailing as the light. The wrongdoer knows no shame!

יְהֹוָ֤ה צַדִּיק֙ בְּקִרְבָּ֔הּ לֹ֥א יַעֲשֶׂ֖ה עַוְלָ֑ה בַּבֹּ֨קֶר בַּבֹּ֜קֶר מִשְׁפָּט֨וֹ יִתֵּ֤ן לָאוֹר֙ לֹ֣א נֶעְדָּ֔ר וְלֹא־יוֹדֵ֥עַ עַוָּ֖ל בֹּֽשֶׁת׃

6 I wiped out nations: Their corner towers are desolate; I turned their thoroughfares into ruins, With none passing by; Their towns lie waste without people, Without inhabitants.

הִכְרַ֣תִּי גוֹיִ֗ם נָשַׁ֙מּוּ֙ פִּנּוֹתָ֔ם הֶחֱרַ֥בְתִּי חֽוּצוֹתָ֖ם מִבְּלִ֣י עוֹבֵ֑ר נִצְדּ֧וּ עָרֵיהֶ֛ם מִבְּלִי־אִ֖ישׁ מֵאֵ֥ין יוֹשֵֽׁב׃

7 And I thought that she would fear Me, Would learn a lesson, And that the punishment I brought on them Would not be lost on her. Instead, all the more eagerly They have practiced corruption in all their deeds.

אָמַ֜רְתִּי אַךְ־תִּֽירְאִ֤י אוֹתִי֙ תִּקְחִ֣י מוּסָ֔ר וְלֹֽא־יִכָּרֵ֣ת מְעוֹנָ֔הּ כֹּ֥ל אֲשֶׁר־פָּקַ֖דְתִּי עָלֶ֑יהָ אָכֵן֙ הִשְׁכִּ֣ימוּ הִשְׁחִ֔יתוּ כֹּ֖ל עֲלִילוֹתָֽם׃

8 But wait for Me – says *Hashem* – For the day when I arise as an accuser; When I decide to gather nations, To bring kingdoms together, To pour out My indignation on them, All My blazing anger. Indeed, by the fire of My passion All the earth shall be consumed.

לָכֵ֤ן חַכּוּ־לִי֙ נְאֻם־יְהֹוָ֔ה לְי֖וֹם קוּמִ֣י לְעַ֑ד כִּ֣י מִשְׁפָּטִי֩ לֶאֱסֹ֨ף גּוֹיִ֜ם לְקׇבְצִ֣י מַמְלָכ֗וֹת לִשְׁפֹּ֨ךְ עֲלֵיהֶ֤ם זַעְמִי֙ כֹּ֚ל חֲר֣וֹן אַפִּ֔י כִּ֚י בְּאֵ֣שׁ קִנְאָתִ֔י תֵּאָכֵ֖ל כׇּל־הָאָֽרֶץ׃

Tzefanya/Zephaniah
Chapter 3

צפניה
פרק ג

9 For then I will make the peoples pure of speech, So that they all invoke *Hashem* by name And serve Him with one accord.

כִּי־אָז אֶהְפֹּךְ אֶל־עַמִּים שָׂפָה בְרוּרָה לִקְרֹא כֻלָּם בְּשֵׁם יְהֹוָה לְעָבְדוֹ שְׁכֶם אֶחָד:

kee AZ eh-POKH el a-MEEM sa-FAH v'-ru-RAH lik-RO khu-LAM b-SHAYM a-do-NAI l'-ov-DO sh'-KHEM e-KHAD

10 From beyond the rivers of Cush, My suppliants Shall bring offerings to Me in Fair Puzai.

מֵעֵבֶר לְנַהֲרֵי־כוּשׁ עֲתָרַי בַּת־פּוּצַי יוֹבִלוּן מִנְחָתִי:

11 In that day, You will no longer be shamed for all the deeds By which you have defied Me. For then I will remove The proud and exultant within you, And you will be haughty no more On My sacred mount.

בַּיּוֹם הַהוּא לֹא תֵבוֹשִׁי מִכֹּל עֲלִילֹתַיִךְ אֲשֶׁר פָּשַׁעַתְּ בִּי כִּי־אָז אָסִיר מִקִּרְבֵּךְ עַלִּיזֵי גַּאֲוָתֵךְ וְלֹא־תוֹסִפִי לְגָבְהָה עוֹד בְּהַר קָדְשִׁי:

12 But I will leave within you A poor, humble folk, And they shall find refuge In the name of *Hashem*.

וְהִשְׁאַרְתִּי בְקִרְבֵּךְ עַם עָנִי וָדָל וְחָסוּ בְּשֵׁם יְהֹוָה:

13 The remnant of *Yisrael* Shall do no wrong And speak no falsehood; A deceitful tongue Shall not be in their mouths. Only such as these shall graze and lie down, With none to trouble them.

שְׁאֵרִית יִשְׂרָאֵל לֹא־יַעֲשׂוּ עַוְלָה וְלֹא־יְדַבְּרוּ כָזָב וְלֹא־יִמָּצֵא בְּפִיהֶם לְשׁוֹן תַּרְמִית כִּי־הֵמָּה יִרְעוּ וְרָבְצוּ וְאֵין מַחֲרִיד:

14 Shout for joy, Fair *Tzion*, Cry aloud, O *Yisrael*! Rejoice and be glad with all your heart, Fair *Yerushalayim*!

רָנִּי בַּת־צִיּוֹן הָרִיעוּ יִשְׂרָאֵל שִׂמְחִי וְעָלְזִי בְּכָל־לֵב בַּת יְרוּשָׁלָ͏ִם:

15 *Hashem* has annulled the judgment against you, He has swept away your foes. *Yisrael*'s Sovereign *Hashem* is within you; You need fear misfortune no more.

הֵסִיר יְהֹוָה מִשְׁפָּטַיִךְ פִּנָּה אֹיְבֵךְ מֶלֶךְ יִשְׂרָאֵל יְהֹוָה בְּקִרְבֵּךְ לֹא־תִירְאִי רָע עוֹד:

16 In that day, This shall be said to *Yerushalayim*: Have no fear, O *Tzion*; Let not your hands droop!

בַּיּוֹם הַהוּא יֵאָמֵר לִירוּשָׁלַ͏ִם אַל־תִּירָאִי צִיּוֹן אַל־יִרְפּוּ יָדָיִךְ:

17 Your God *Hashem* is in your midst, A warrior who brings triumph. He will rejoice over you and be glad, He will shout over you with jubilation. He will soothe with His love

יְהֹוָה אֱלֹהַיִךְ בְּקִרְבֵּךְ גִּבּוֹר יוֹשִׁיעַ יָשִׂישׂ עָלַיִךְ בְּשִׂמְחָה יַחֲרִישׁ בְּאַהֲבָתוֹ יָגִיל עָלַיִךְ בְּרִנָּה:

a-do-NAI e-lo-HA-yikh b'-kir-BAYKH gi-BOR yo-SHEE-a ya-SEES a-LA-yikh b'-sim-KHAH ya-kha-REESH b'-A-ha-va-TO ya-GIL a-LA-yikh b'-ri-NAH

שפה ברורה

3:9 Pure of speech The prophet describes how in the future, all the nations of the world will have 'pure speech,' *safa b'rurah* (שפה ברורה). Ibn Ezra, among other commentators, maintains that the pure speech that *Tzefanya* promises is the language of Hebrew, and that in future times the whole world will begin to learn Hebrew, the language of Creation. Biblical Hebrew is known as *lashon hakodesh* (לשון הקודש), 'the holy language.' The *Maharal* (Deuteronomy 1:23) writes that each language reflects the essence of the nation who speaks it. Since the Jewish people are a holy people, they speak the holy language, and since it is holy and pure, it contains no vulgar or shameful words. The *Ramban* (Exodus 30:13) adds that what makes this language holy is that "it is the language with which God speaks with His prophets and His nation." This verse is another incredible example of an obscure prophecy that has come to prominent fruition in our generation, as millions of people all over the world, both Jews and gentiles, are learning Hebrew in order to speak *lashon hakodesh*.

3:17 He will shout over you with jubilation. He will soothe with His love *Tzefanya* describes the result of *Hashem*'s judgement in triumphant terms.

Tzefanya/Zephaniah
Chapter 3

צפניה
פרק ג

18 Those long disconsolate. I will take away from you the woe Over which you endured mockery.

יח נוּגֵי מִמּוֹעֵד אָסַפְתִּי מִמֵּךְ הָיוּ מַשְׂאֵת עָלֶיהָ חֶרְפָּה׃

19 At that time I will make [an end] Of all who afflicted you. And I will rescue the lame [sheep] And gather the strayed; And I will exchange their disgrace For fame and renown in all the earth.

יט הִנְנִי עֹשֶׂה אֶת־כָּל־מְעַנַּיִךְ בָּעֵת הַהִיא וְהוֹשַׁעְתִּי אֶת־הַצֹּלֵעָה וְהַנִּדָּחָה אֲקַבֵּץ וְשַׂמְתִּים לִתְהִלָּה וּלְשֵׁם בְּכָל־הָאָרֶץ בָּשְׁתָּם׃

20 At that time I will gather you, And at [that] time I will bring you [home]; For I will make you renowned and famous Among all the peoples on earth, When I restore you fortunes Before their very eyes – said *Hashem*

כ בָּעֵת הַהִיא אָבִיא אֶתְכֶם וּבָעֵת קַבְּצִי אֶתְכֶם כִּי־אֶתֵּן אֶתְכֶם לְשֵׁם וְלִתְהִלָּה בְּכֹל עַמֵּי הָאָרֶץ בְּשׁוּבִי אֶת־שְׁבוּתֵיכֶם לְעֵינֵיכֶם אָמַר יְהֹוָה׃

Having removed evil from the world, He will allow the remnant of Israel to live safely in its land, knowing that God dwells among the People of Israel in the Land of Israel. *Hashem* himself will rejoice and sing when He sees His people dwelling in the land without fear of evil. The phrase *yacharish b'ahavato* (באהבתו יחריש), translated here as 'He will soothe with His love,' literally means that God 'will be silent in His love.' This wording intrigues many. *Rashi* suggest that the message behind these words is that in His love, *Hashem* will be silent even should Israel sin again. Sometimes, the greatest demonstration of love in a relationship is when one side can ignore the shortcomings of the other.

Sefer Chagai
The Book of Haggai

The tenth of the *Trei Asar*, *Sefer Chagai* (Haggai), is the first book written after the first wave of exiles return to *Eretz Yisrael* in 536 BCE.

After the Persian empire defeated the Babylonians, Cyrus the Great allowed the Jewish exiles to return home. Those Jews who returned to their ancestral land did so filled with idealism and hope, but soon the harsh reality of rebuilding their destroyed homes and repairing their scorched fields overtook them. The land was parched, the rains did not fall, and the returnees were barely capable of sustaining themselves. At the same time, the Persian empire was shaken by a series of revolts (522–520 BCE), and the people who had moved into the Land of Israel in their absence began making trouble for the returnees.

Into this picture stepped *Chagai*. He carried a brief, direct message. The people who lived in Israel were not sinners, but they were so concerned with their individual lives, needs and wants that they forgot the primary purpose of the return. The reason the People of Israel were to dwell in the Land of Israel was to proclaim the name of the God of Israel. Instead of concerning themselves with their personal needs, the people must dedicate their efforts to building a second Temple, where *Hashem*'s Presence can rest and from there, emanate all over the world.

If the People of Israel would recognize the cosmic significance of their actions and efforts, not only would they receive rains of blessing, but they would also affect change the world over. As described in *Sefer Ezra* (chapter 6), *Chagai*'s efforts were not in vain; through his encouragement and that offered by his contemporary prophet *Zecharya*, the people completed building the *Beit Hamikdash* and dedicated it in 516 BCE.

Chagai/Haggai
Chapter 1

חגי
פרק א

1 ¹ In the second year of King Darius, on the first day of the sixth month, this word of *Hashem* came through the *Navi Chagai* to *Zerubavel* son of *Shealtiel*, the governor of *Yehuda*, and to *Yehoshua* son of *Yehotzadak*, the *Kohen Gadol*:

א בִּשְׁנַת שְׁתַּיִם לְדָרְיָוֶשׁ הַמֶּלֶךְ בַּחֹדֶשׁ הַשִּׁשִּׁי בְּיוֹם אֶחָד לַחֹדֶשׁ הָיָה דְבַר־יְהֹוָה בְּיַד־חַגַּי הַנָּבִיא אֶל־זְרֻבָּבֶל בֶּן־שְׁאַלְתִּיאֵל פַּחַת יְהוּדָה וְאֶל־יְהוֹשֻׁעַ בֶּן־יְהוֹצָדָק הַכֹּהֵן הַגָּדוֹל לֵאמֹר׃

² Thus said the Lord of Hosts: These people say, "The time has not yet come for rebuilding the House of *Hashem*."

ב כֹּה אָמַר יְהֹוָה צְבָאוֹת לֵאמֹר הָעָם הַזֶּה אָמְרוּ לֹא עֶת־בֹּא עֵת־בֵּית יְהֹוָה לְהִבָּנוֹת׃

³ And the word of *Hashem* through the *Navi Chagai* continued:

ג וַיְהִי דְּבַר־יְהֹוָה בְּיַד־חַגַּי הַנָּבִיא לֵאמֹר׃

⁴ Is it a time for you to dwell in your paneled houses, while this House is lying in ruins?

ד הַעֵת לָכֶם אַתֶּם לָשֶׁבֶת בְּבָתֵּיכֶם סְפוּנִים וְהַבַּיִת הַזֶּה חָרֵב׃

ha-AYT la-KHEM a-TEM la-SHE-vet b'-va-tay-KHEM s'-fu-NEEM v'-ha-BA-yit ha-ZEH kha-RAYV

⁵ Now thus said the Lord of Hosts: Consider how you have been faring!

ה וְעַתָּה כֹּה אָמַר יְהֹוָה צְבָאוֹת שִׂימוּ לְבַבְכֶם עַל־דַּרְכֵיכֶם׃

⁶ You have sowed much and brought in little; you eat without being satisfied; you drink without getting your fill; you clothe yourselves, but no one gets warm; and he who earns anything earns it for a leaky purse.

ו זְרַעְתֶּם הַרְבֵּה וְהָבֵא מְעָט אָכוֹל וְאֵין־לְשָׂבְעָה שָׁתוֹ וְאֵין־לְשָׁכְרָה לָבוֹשׁ וְאֵין־לְחֹם לוֹ וְהַמִּשְׂתַּכֵּר מִשְׂתַּכֵּר אֶל־צְרוֹר נָקוּב׃

⁷ Thus said the Lord of Hosts: Consider how you have fared:

ז כֹּה אָמַר יְהֹוָה צְבָאוֹת שִׂימוּ לְבַבְכֶם עַל־דַּרְכֵיכֶם׃

⁸ Go up to the hills and get timber, and rebuild the House; then I will look on it with favor and I will be glorified – said *Hashem*.

ח עֲלוּ הָהָר וַהֲבֵאתֶם עֵץ וּבְנוּ הַבָּיִת וְאֶרְצֶה־בּוֹ וְאֶכָּבֵד [וְאֶכָּבְדָה] אָמַר יְהֹוָה׃

⁹ You have been expecting much and getting little; and when you brought it home, I would blow on it! Because of what? – says the Lord of Hosts. Because of My House which lies in ruins, while you all hurry to your own houses!

ט פָּנֹה אֶל־הַרְבֵּה וְהִנֵּה לִמְעָט וַהֲבֵאתֶם הַבַּיִת וְנָפַחְתִּי בוֹ יַעַן מֶה נְאֻם יְהֹוָה צְבָאוֹת יַעַן בֵּיתִי אֲשֶׁר־הוּא חָרֵב וְאַתֶּם רָצִים אִישׁ לְבֵיתוֹ׃

ספונים

1:4 Is it a time for you to dwell in your paneled houses Addressing the Jews who returned to the Land of Israel after seventy years of Babylonian exile, *Chagai's* mission is to motivate them to resume construction of the second Temple. He begins by challenging them to reflect on their priorities, and to consider what is more important: Their comfort, or God's? While they dwell in paneled houses, *Hashem's* house lies in ruins. The Hebrew term for 'paneled' is *sefunim* (ספונים). According to some, the panels were made out of cedar wood, imported from Lebanon. *Chagai* is accusing the people of not learning from King *David*, who said to the prophet *Natan*, "Here I am dwelling in a house of cedar, while the *Aron* of *Hashem* abides in a tent!" (II Samuel 7). *David* longed to overcome that disparity and build the first *Beit Hamikdash*, while the Israelites in *Chagai's* time are unconcerned. *Chagai* tries to break their complacency.

Chagai/Haggai
Chapter 2

10 That is why the skies above you have withheld [their] moisture and the earth has withheld its yield,

11 and I have summoned fierce heat upon the land – upon the hills, upon the new grain and wine and oil, upon all that the ground produces, upon man and beast, and upon all the fruits of labor.

12 *Zerubavel* son of *Shealtiel* and the *Kohen Gadol Yehoshua* son of *Yehotzadak* and all the rest of the people gave heed to the summons of *Hashem* their God and to the words of the *Navi Chagai*, when *Hashem* their God sent him; the people feared *Hashem*.

13 And *Chagai*, *Hashem*'s messenger, fulfilling *Hashem*'s mission, spoke to the people, "I am with you – declares *Hashem*."

14 Then *Hashem* roused the spirit of *Zerubavel* son of *Shealtiel*, the governor of *Yehuda*, and the spirit of the *Kohen Gadol Yehoshua* son of *Yehotzadak*, and the spirit of all the rest of the people: They came and set to work on the House of the Lord of Hosts, their God,

15 on the twenty-fourth day of the sixth month. In the second year of King Darius,

2

1 on the twenty-first day of the seventh month, the word of *Hashem* came through the *Navi Chagai*:

2 Speak to *Zerubavel* son of *Shealtiel*, the governor of *Yehuda*, and to the *Kohen Gadol Yehoshua* son of *Yehotzadak*, and to the rest of the people:

3 Who is there left among you who saw this House in its former splendor? How does it look to you now? It must seem like nothing to you.

4 But be strong, O *Zerubavel* – says *Hashem* – be strong, O *Kohen Gadol Yehoshua* son of *Yehotzadak*; be strong, all you people of the land – says *Hashem* – and act! For I am with you – says the Lord of Hosts.

5 So I promised you when you came out of Egypt, and My spirit is still in your midst. Fear not!

6 For thus said the Lord of Hosts: In just a little while longer I will shake the heavens and the earth, the sea and the dry land;

חגי

פרק ב

י עַל־כֵּן עֲלֵיכֶם כָּלְאוּ שָׁמַיִם מִטָּל וְהָאָרֶץ כָּלְאָה יְבוּלָהּ:

יא וָאֶקְרָא חֹרֶב עַל־הָאָרֶץ וְעַל־הֶהָרִים וְעַל־הַדָּגָן וְעַל־הַתִּירוֹשׁ וְעַל־הַיִּצְהָר וְעַל אֲשֶׁר תּוֹצִיא הָאֲדָמָה וְעַל־הָאָדָם וְעַל־הַבְּהֵמָה וְעַל כָּל־יְגִיעַ כַּפָּיִם:

יב וַיִּשְׁמַע זְרֻבָּבֶל ׀ בֶּן־שַׁלְתִּיאֵל וִיהוֹשֻׁעַ בֶּן־יְהוֹצָדָק הַכֹּהֵן הַגָּדוֹל וְכֹל ׀ שְׁאֵרִית הָעָם בְּקוֹל יְהוָה אֱלֹהֵיהֶם וְעַל־דִּבְרֵי חַגַּי הַנָּבִיא כַּאֲשֶׁר שְׁלָחוֹ יְהוָה אֱלֹהֵיהֶם וַיִּירְאוּ הָעָם מִפְּנֵי יְהוָה:

יג וַיֹּאמֶר חַגַּי מַלְאַךְ יְהוָה בְּמַלְאֲכוּת יְהוָה לָעָם לֵאמֹר אֲנִי אִתְּכֶם נְאֻם־יְהוָה:

יד וַיָּעַר יְהוָה אֶת־רוּחַ זְרֻבָּבֶל בֶּן־שַׁלְתִּיאֵל פַּחַת יְהוּדָה וְאֶת־רוּחַ יְהוֹשֻׁעַ בֶּן־יְהוֹצָדָק הַכֹּהֵן הַגָּדוֹל וְאֶת־רוּחַ כֹּל שְׁאֵרִית הָעָם וַיָּבֹאוּ וַיַּעֲשׂוּ מְלָאכָה בְּבֵית־יְהוָה צְבָאוֹת אֱלֹהֵיהֶם:

טו בְּיוֹם עֶשְׂרִים וְאַרְבָּעָה לַחֹדֶשׁ בַּשִּׁשִּׁי בִּשְׁנַת שְׁתַּיִם לְדָרְיָוֶשׁ הַמֶּלֶךְ:

ב א בַּשְּׁבִיעִי בְּעֶשְׂרִים וְאֶחָד לַחֹדֶשׁ הָיָה דְּבַר־יְהוָה בְּיַד־חַגַּי הַנָּבִיא לֵאמֹר:

ב אֱמָר־נָא אֶל־זְרֻבָּבֶל בֶּן־שַׁלְתִּיאֵל פַּחַת יְהוּדָה וְאֶל־יְהוֹשֻׁעַ בֶּן־יְהוֹצָדָק הַכֹּהֵן הַגָּדוֹל וְאֶל־שְׁאֵרִית הָעָם לֵאמֹר:

ג מִי בָכֶם הַנִּשְׁאָר אֲשֶׁר רָאָה אֶת־הַבַּיִת הַזֶּה בִּכְבוֹדוֹ הָרִאשׁוֹן וּמָה אַתֶּם רֹאִים אֹתוֹ עַתָּה הֲלוֹא כָמֹהוּ כְּאַיִן בְּעֵינֵיכֶם:

ד וְעַתָּה חֲזַק זְרֻבָּבֶל ׀ נְאֻם־יְהוָה וַחֲזַק יְהוֹשֻׁעַ בֶּן־יְהוֹצָדָק הַכֹּהֵן הַגָּדוֹל וַחֲזַק כָּל־עַם הָאָרֶץ נְאֻם־יְהוָה וַעֲשׂוּ כִּי־אֲנִי אִתְּכֶם נְאֻם יְהוָה צְבָאוֹת:

ה אֶת־הַדָּבָר אֲשֶׁר־כָּרַתִּי אִתְּכֶם בְּצֵאתְכֶם מִמִּצְרַיִם וְרוּחִי עֹמֶדֶת בְּתוֹכְכֶם אַל־תִּירָאוּ:

ו כִּי כֹה אָמַר יְהוָה צְבָאוֹת עוֹד אַחַת מְעַט הִיא וַאֲנִי מַרְעִישׁ אֶת־הַשָּׁמַיִם וְאֶת־הָאָרֶץ וְאֶת־הַיָּם וְאֶת־הֶחָרָבָה:

Chagai/Haggai
Chapter 2

חגי
פרק ב

7 I will shake all the nations. And the precious things of all the nations shall come [here], and I will fill this House with glory, said the Lord of Hosts.

וְהִרְעַשְׁתִּי אֶת־כָּל־הַגּוֹיִם וּבָאוּ חֶמְדַּת כָּל־הַגּוֹיִם וּמִלֵּאתִי אֶת־הַבַּיִת הַזֶּה כָּבוֹד אָמַר יְהֹוָה צְבָאוֹת׃

8 Silver is Mine and gold is Mine – says the Lord of Hosts.

לִי הַכֶּסֶף וְלִי הַזָּהָב נְאֻם יְהֹוָה צְבָאוֹת׃

9 The glory of this latter House shall be greater than that of the former one, said the Lord of Hosts; and in this place I will grant prosperity – declares the Lord of Hosts.

גָּדוֹל יִהְיֶה כְּבוֹד הַבַּיִת הַזֶּה הָאַחֲרוֹן מִן־הָרִאשׁוֹן אָמַר יְהֹוָה צְבָאוֹת וּבַמָּקוֹם הַזֶּה אֶתֵּן שָׁלוֹם נְאֻם יְהֹוָה צְבָאוֹת׃

ga-DOL yih-YEH k'-VOD ha-BA-yit ha-ZEH ha-a-kha-RON min HA-ri-SHON a-MAR a-do-NAI tz'-va-OT u-va-ma-KOM ha-ZEH e-TAYN sha-LOM n'-UM a-do-NAI tz'-va-OT

10 On the twenty-fourth day of the ninth [month], in the second year of Darius, the word of *Hashem* came to the *Navi Chagai*:

בְּעֶשְׂרִים וְאַרְבָּעָה לַתְּשִׁיעִי בִּשְׁנַת שְׁתַּיִם לְדָרְיָוֶשׁ הָיָה דְּבַר־יְהֹוָה אֶל־חַגַּי הַנָּבִיא לֵאמֹר׃

11 Thus said the Lord of Hosts: Seek a ruling from the *Kohanim*, as follows:

כֹּה אָמַר יְהֹוָה צְבָאוֹת שְׁאַל־נָא אֶת־הַכֹּהֲנִים תּוֹרָה לֵאמֹר׃

12 If a man is carrying sacrificial flesh in a fold of his garment, and with that fold touches bread, stew, wine, oil, or any other food, will the latter become holy? In reply, the *Kohanim* said, "No."

הֵן יִשָּׂא־אִישׁ בְּשַׂר־קֹדֶשׁ בִּכְנַף בִּגְדוֹ וְנָגַע בִּכְנָפוֹ אֶל־הַלֶּחֶם וְאֶל־הַנָּזִיד וְאֶל־הַיַּיִן וְאֶל־שֶׁמֶן וְאֶל־כָּל־מַאֲכָל הֲיִקְדָּשׁ וַיַּעֲנוּ הַכֹּהֲנִים וַיֹּאמְרוּ לֹא׃

13 *Chagai* went on, "If someone defiled by a corpse touches any of these, will it be defiled?" And the *Kohanim* responded, "Yes."

וַיֹּאמֶר חַגַּי אִם־יִגַּע טְמֵא־נֶפֶשׁ בְּכָל־אֵלֶּה הֲיִטְמָא וַיַּעֲנוּ הַכֹּהֲנִים וַיֹּאמְרוּ יִטְמָא׃

14 Thereupon *Chagai* said: That is how this people and that is how this nation looks to Me – declares *Hashem* – and so, too, the work of their hands: Whatever they offer there is defiled.

וַיַּעַן חַגַּי וַיֹּאמֶר כֵּן הָעָם־הַזֶּה וְכֵן־הַגּוֹי הַזֶּה לְפָנַי נְאֻם־יְהֹוָה וְכֵן כָּל־מַעֲשֵׂה יְדֵיהֶם וַאֲשֶׁר יַקְרִיבוּ שָׁם טָמֵא הוּא׃

15 And now take thought, from this day backward: As long as no stone had been laid on another in the House of *Hashem*,

וְעַתָּה שִׂימוּ־נָא לְבַבְכֶם מִן־הַיּוֹם הַזֶּה וָמָעְלָה מִטֶּרֶם שׂוּם־אֶבֶן אֶל־אֶבֶן בְּהֵיכַל יְהֹוָה׃

v'-a-TAH SEE-mu NA l'-vav-KHEM min ha-YOM ha-ZEH va-MA-lah mi-TE-rem sum E-ven el E-ven b'-hay-KHAL a-do-NAI

Jerusalem, city of peace

2:9 And in this place I will grant prosperity *Chagai* prophesies of a time when all the nations of the world will recognize *Hashem*, Whose glory rests on the *Beit Hamikdash* in *Yerushalayim* (ירושלים). *Chagai* promises that "in this place I will grant *shalom* (שלום)," translated here as 'prosperity' but generally meaning 'peace.' The word *makom* (מקום), 'place,' often refers to a sacred place that God chooses (see for example Deuteronomy 12:5, 1 Kings 8:29, 30), and specifically refers to *Yerushalayim* (see for example II Kings 22:16). This promise of peace in *Yerushalayim* corresponds with the tradition that *Yerushalayim* is the city of peace, and is reflected in the Hebrew name of the city. *Yerushalayim* is derived from two words, *yerush* – *shalom* (ירוש־שלום), 'an inheritance of peace.'

2:15 No stone had been laid on another in the House of *Hashem* In this verse, the prophet ad-

Chagai/Haggai
Chapter 2

16 if one came to a heap of twenty measures, it would yield only ten; and if one came to a wine vat to skim off fifty measures, the press would yield only twenty.

17 I struck you – all the works of your hands – with blight and mildew and hail, but you did not return to Me – declares *Hashem*.

18 Take note, from this day forward – from the twenty-fourth day of the ninth month, from the day when the foundation was laid for *Hashem*'s Temple – take note

19 while the seed is still in the granary, and the vine, fig tree, pomegranate, and olive tree have not yet borne fruit. For from this day on I will send blessings.

20 And the word of *Hashem* came to *Chagai* a second time on the twenty-fourth day of the month:

21 Speak to *Zerubavel* the governor of *Yehuda*: I am going to shake the heavens and the earth.

22 And I will overturn the thrones of kingdoms and destroy the might of the kingdoms of the nations. I will overturn chariots and their drivers. Horses and their riders shall fall, each by the sword of his fellow.

23 On that day – declares the LORD of Hosts – I will take you, O My servant *Zerubavel* son of *Shealtiel* – declares *Hashem* – and make you as a signet; for I have chosen you – declares the LORD of Hosts.

---

dresses the masons' job of laying bricks to build the *Beit Hamikdash*, but it is likely that he is also speaking metaphorically about laying the "bricks" that "construct" society. Yitzchak Navon (1921–2015), a leading Israeli diplomat and playwright and Israel's fifth president, wrote beautifully about contributing "bricks" to the building of the State of Israel: "The angel Gabriel, according to tradition, is responsible for the ferrying of souls in the Land of Israel. If Gabriel came to me and said, 'Look, I'm willing to take your soul now and give it back to you at any period of time in the history of the Nation of Israel, from the very beginning to this very day' – I would not think of any other time other than Moses and the Ten Commandments at Mount Sinai.... But other than that, there is no more important period in the history of Israel, more interesting, and also tragic, like the redemption after two thousand years in exile. To be born at such a historical point in time! I'm glad that is what happened, and I could say, in this colossal endeavor called the State of Israel, I too contributed a brick to this important wall."

President Yitzchak Navon (1921–2015)

Sefer Zecharya
The Book of Zechariah

The eleventh of the *Trei Asar*, *Sefer Zecharya* (Zechariah), is one of the most esoteric books of the Bible. It is the second of the three books written during the period of return to the Land of Israel after the Persians defeated the Babylonians in 538 BCE. Several of *Zecharya's* prophecies are dated to the second and fourth years of the reign of Darius (520 and 518 BCE), at the time when the construction of the second *Beit Hamikdash* had begun in earnest under the Persian-appointed governor Zerubbabel. As such, it is not surprising that many of the visions in the book describe the significance of the Temple and its reconstruction, and how it could potentially allow divine sovereignty to spread throughout the world.

We know more about *Zecharya* than we do most other prophets. Like *Yechezkel* and *Yirmiyahu*, he was a priest, and his grandfather, *Ido*, is mentioned among the *Kohanim* in *Ezra* chapter 5 and *Nechemya* chapter 12. His contemporaries include the prophet *Chagai*, who began prophesying two months before him, and the high priest *Yehoshua*. However, his message differs from that of *Chagai*, whose single-minded focus was the encouragement of the Jewish people to build the Temple, so that *Hashem*'s rule could spread over the world. To this message, *Zecharya* adds a religious and moral dimension. He encourages the people to repent, emphasizes that God's rule stands in contrast to military might – "Not by might, nor by power, but by My spirit" (4:6) – and stresses that ritual fast days have no value unless accompanied by spiritual improvement.

Zecharya/Zechariah
Chapter 1

זכריה
פרק א

1 **1** In the eighth month of the second year of Darius, this word of *Hashem* came to the *Navi Zecharya* son of *Berechya* son of *Ido*:

א בַּחֹדֶשׁ הַשְּׁמִינִי בִּשְׁנַת שְׁתַּיִם לְדָרְיָוֶשׁ הָיָה דְבַר־יְהֹוָה אֶל־זְכַרְיָה בֶּן־בֶּרֶכְיָה בֶּן־עִדּוֹ הַנָּבִיא לֵאמֹר:

2 *Hashem* was very angry with your fathers.

ב קָצַף יְהֹוָה עַל־אֲבוֹתֵיכֶם קָצֶף:

3 Say to them further: Thus said the Lord of Hosts: Turn back to me – says the Lord of Hosts – and I will turn back to you – said the Lord of Hosts.

ג וְאָמַרְתָּ אֲלֵהֶם כֹּה אָמַר יְהֹוָה צְבָאוֹת שׁוּבוּ אֵלַי נְאֻם יְהֹוָה צְבָאוֹת וְאָשׁוּב אֲלֵיכֶם אָמַר יְהֹוָה צְבָאוֹת:

4 Do not be like your fathers! For when the earlier *Neviim* called to them, "Thus said the Lord of Hosts: Come, turn back from your evil ways and your evil deeds, they did not obey or give heed to Me – declares *Hashem*.

ד אַל־תִּהְיוּ כַאֲבֹתֵיכֶם אֲשֶׁר קָרְאוּ־אֲלֵיהֶם הַנְּבִיאִים הָרִאשֹׁנִים לֵאמֹר כֹּה אָמַר יְהֹוָה צְבָאוֹת שׁוּבוּ נָא מִדַּרְכֵיכֶם הָרָעִים וּמַעֲלִילֵיכֶם [וּמַעַלְלֵיכֶם] הָרָעִים וְלֹא שָׁמְעוּ וְלֹא־הִקְשִׁיבוּ אֵלַי נְאֻם־יְהֹוָה:

5 Where are your fathers now? And did the *Neviim* live forever?

ה אֲבוֹתֵיכֶם אַיֵּה־הֵם וְהַנְּבִאִים הַלְעוֹלָם יִחְיוּ:

6 But the warnings and the decrees with which I charged My servants the *Neviim* overtook your fathers – did they not? – and in the end they had to admit, '*Hashem* has dealt with us according to our ways and our deeds, just as He purposed.'"

ו אַךְ דְּבָרַי וְחֻקַּי אֲשֶׁר צִוִּיתִי אֶת־עֲבָדַי הַנְּבִיאִים הֲלוֹא הִשִּׂיגוּ אֲבֹתֵיכֶם וַיָּשׁוּבוּ וַיֹּאמְרוּ כַּאֲשֶׁר זָמַם יְהֹוָה צְבָאוֹת לַעֲשׂוֹת לָנוּ כִּדְרָכֵינוּ וּכְמַעֲלָלֵינוּ כֵּן עָשָׂה אִתָּנוּ:

7 On the twenty-fourth day of the eleventh month of the second year of Darius – the month of *Shevat* – this word of *Hashem* came to the *Navi Zecharya* son of *Berechya* son of *Ido*:

ז בְּיוֹם עֶשְׂרִים וְאַרְבָּעָה לְעַשְׁתֵּי־עָשָׂר חֹדֶשׁ הוּא־חֹדֶשׁ שְׁבָט בִּשְׁנַת שְׁתַּיִם לְדָרְיָוֶשׁ הָיָה דְבַר־יְהֹוָה אֶל־זְכַרְיָה בֶּן־בֶּרֶכְיָהוּ בֶּן־עִדּוֹא הַנָּבִיא לֵאמֹר:

8 In the night, I had a vision. I saw a man, mounted on a bay horse, standing among the myrtles in the Deep, and behind him were bay, sorrel, and white horses.

ח רָאִיתִי הַלַּיְלָה וְהִנֵּה־אִישׁ רֹכֵב עַל־סוּס אָדֹם וְהוּא עֹמֵד בֵּין הַהֲדַסִּים אֲשֶׁר בַּמְּצֻלָה וְאַחֲרָיו סוּסִים אֲדֻמִּים שְׂרֻקִּים וּלְבָנִים:

9 I asked, "What are those, my lord?" And the angel who talked with me answered, "I will let you know what they are."

ט וָאֹמַר מָה־אֵלֶּה אֲדֹנִי וַיֹּאמֶר אֵלַי הַמַּלְאָךְ הַדֹּבֵר בִּי אֲנִי אַרְאֶךָּ מָה־הֵמָּה אֵלֶּה:

10 Then the man who was standing among the myrtles spoke up and said, "These were sent out by *Hashem* to roam the earth."

י וַיַּעַן הָאִישׁ הָעֹמֵד בֵּין־הַהֲדַסִּים וַיֹּאמַר אֵלֶּה אֲשֶׁר שָׁלַח יְהֹוָה לְהִתְהַלֵּךְ בָּאָרֶץ:

11 And in fact, they reported to the angel of *Hashem* who was standing among the myrtles, "We have roamed the earth, and have found all the earth dwelling in tranquility."

יא וַיַּעֲנוּ אֶת־מַלְאַךְ יְהֹוָה הָעֹמֵד בֵּין הַהֲדַסִּים וַיֹּאמְרוּ הִתְהַלַּכְנוּ בָאָרֶץ וְהִנֵּה כׇל־הָאָרֶץ יֹשֶׁבֶת וְשֹׁקָטֶת:

12 Thereupon the angel of *Hashem* exclaimed, "O Lord of Hosts! How long will You withhold pardon from *Yerushalayim* and the towns of *Yehuda*, which You placed under a curse seventy years ago?"

יב וַיַּעַן מַלְאַךְ־יְהֹוָה וַיֹּאמַר יְהֹוָה צְבָאוֹת עַד־מָתַי אַתָּה לֹא־תְרַחֵם אֶת־יְרוּשָׁלַ͏ִם וְאֵת עָרֵי יְהוּדָה אֲשֶׁר זָעַמְתָּה זֶה שִׁבְעִים שָׁנָה:

Zecharya/Zechariah
Chapter 2

זכריה
פרק ב

13 *Hashem* replied with kind, comforting words to the angel who talked with me.

יג וַיַּ֣עַן יְהֹוָ֗ה אֶת־הַמַּלְאָ֛ךְ הַדֹּבֵ֥ר בִּ֖י דְּבָרִ֣ים טוֹבִ֑ים דְּבָרִ֖ים נִחֻמִֽים׃

14 Then the angel who talked with me said to me: "Proclaim! Thus said the Lord of Hosts: I am very jealous for *Yerushalayim* – for *Tzion* –

יד וַיֹּ֣אמֶר אֵלַ֗י הַמַּלְאָ֛ךְ הַדֹּבֵ֥ר בִּ֖י קְרָ֣א לֵאמֹ֑ר כֹּ֤ה אָמַר֙ יְהֹוָ֣ה צְבָא֔וֹת קִנֵּ֧אתִי לִירוּשָׁלַ֛͏ִם וּלְצִיּ֖וֹן קִנְאָ֥ה גְדוֹלָֽה׃

15 and I am very angry with those nations that are at ease; for I was only angry a little, but they overdid the punishment.

טו וְקֶ֤צֶף גָּדוֹל֙ אֲנִ֣י קֹצֵ֔ף עַל־הַגּוֹיִ֖ם הַשַּׁאֲנַנִּ֑ים אֲשֶׁ֤ר אֲנִי֙ קָצַ֣פְתִּי מְּעָ֔ט וְהֵ֖מָּה עָזְר֥וּ לְרָעָֽה׃

16 Assuredly, thus said *Hashem*: I graciously return to *Yerushalayim*. My House shall be built in her – declares the Lord of Hosts – the measuring line is being applied to *Yerushalayim*.

טז לָכֵ֞ן כֹּֽה־אָמַ֣ר יְהֹוָ֗ה שַׁ֤בְתִּי לִירוּשָׁלַ֙͏ִם֙ בְּֽרַחֲמִ֔ים בֵּיתִי֙ יִבָּ֣נֶה בָּ֔הּ נְאֻ֖ם יְהֹוָ֣ה צְבָא֑וֹת וְקָ֥ו [וְקָ֖ו] יִנָּטֶ֥ה עַל־יְרוּשָׁלָֽ͏ִם׃

17 Proclaim further: Thus said the Lord of Hosts: My towns shall yet overflow with bounty. For *Hashem* will again comfort *Tzion*; He will choose *Yerushalayim* again."

יז ע֣וֹד ׀ קְרָ֣א לֵאמֹ֗ר כֹּ֤ה אָמַר֙ יְהֹוָ֣ה צְבָא֔וֹת ע֛וֹד תְּפוּצֶ֥נָה עָרַ֖י מִטּ֑וֹב וְנִחַ֨ם יְהֹוָ֥ה עוֹד֙ אֶת־צִיּ֔וֹן וּבָחַ֥ר ע֖וֹד בִּירוּשָׁלָֽ͏ִם׃

OD k'-RA lay-MOR KOH a-MAR a-do-NAI tz'-va-OT OD t'-fu-TZE-nah a-RAI mi-TOV v'-ni-KHAM a-do-NAI OD et tzi-YON u-va-KHAR OD bee-ru-sha-LA-im

2

1 I looked up, and I saw four horns.

ב א וָאֶשָּׂ֥א אֶת־עֵינַ֖י וָאֵ֑רֶא וְהִנֵּ֖ה אַרְבַּ֥ע קְרָנֽוֹת׃

2 I asked the angel who talked with me, "What are those?" "Those," he replied, "are the horns that tossed *Yehuda*, *Yisrael*, and *Yerushalayim*."

ב וָאֹמַ֗ר אֶל־הַמַּלְאָ֛ךְ הַדֹּבֵ֥ר בִּ֖י מָה־אֵ֑לֶּה וַיֹּ֣אמֶר אֵלַ֔י אֵ֚לֶּה הַקְּרָנ֔וֹת אֲשֶׁ֣ר זֵר֗וּ אֶת־יְהוּדָ֥ה אֶת־יִשְׂרָאֵ֖ל וִירוּשָׁלָֽ͏ִם׃

3 Then *Hashem* showed me four smiths.

ג וַיַּרְאֵ֣נִי יְהֹוָ֔ה אַרְבָּעָ֖ה חָרָשִֽׁים׃

4 "What are they coming to do?" I asked. He replied: "Those are the horns that tossed *Yehuda*, so that no man could raise his head; and these men have come to throw them into a panic, to hew down the horns of the nations that raise a horn against the land of *Yehuda*, to toss it."

ד וָאֹמַ֕ר מָ֛ה אֵ֥לֶּה בָאִ֖ים לַעֲשׂ֑וֹת וַיֹּ֣אמֶר לֵאמֹ֗ר אֵ֣לֶּה הַקְּרָנ֞וֹת אֲשֶׁר־זֵ֣רוּ אֶת־יְהוּדָ֗ה כְּפִי־אִישׁ֙ לֹא־נָשָׂ֣א רֹאשׁ֔וֹ וַיָּבֹ֤אוּ אֵ֙לֶּה֙ לְהַחֲרִ֣יד אֹתָ֔ם לְיַדּ֞וֹת אֶת־קַרְנ֣וֹת הַגּוֹיִ֗ם הַנֹּשְׂאִ֥ים קֶ֛רֶן אֶל־אֶ֥רֶץ יְהוּדָ֖ה לְזָרוֹתָֽהּ׃

5 I looked up, and I saw a man holding a measuring line.

ה וָאֶשָּׂ֥א עֵינַ֛י וָאֵ֖רֶא וְהִנֵּה־אִ֑ישׁ וּבְיָד֖וֹ חֶ֥בֶל מִדָּֽה׃

1:17 My towns shall yet overflow with bounty
The prophet *Zecharya* lives at a very exciting time in Jewish history, when the Persian King Darius allows his Jewish subjects to return to *Yerushalayim* and rebuild the *Beit Hamikdash*. While there are some who heed the call, many do not respond with the proper enthusiasm. *Zecharya* tries to encourage the Children of Israel to return by reiterating God's promises and blessings regarding the Land of Israel. In this verse, *Hashem* promises, "My towns shall yet overflow with bounty. For *Hashem* will again comfort *Tzion*, He will choose *Yerushalayim* again." According to many commentators, such as *Malbim* and *Metzudat David*, these prophecies apply not only to the time of *Zecharya*, but also to the days of the future redemption. Recent years have begun to see the fulfillment of these prophecies, as many cities in Israel flourish again, and God has chosen *Yerushalayim* by returning His children to the holy city.

Zecharya/Zechariah
Chapter 2

6 "Where are you going?" I asked. "To measure *Yerushalayim*," he replied, "to see how long and wide it is to be."

7 But the angel who talked with me came forward, and another angel came forward to meet him.

8 The former said to him, "Run to that young man and tell him: "*Yerushalayim* shall be peopled as a city without walls, so many shall be the men and cattle it contains.

9 And I Myself – declares *Hashem* – will be a wall of fire all around it, and I will be a glory inside it.

10 "Away, away! Flee from the land of the north – says *Hashem* – though I swept you [there] like the four winds of heaven – declares *Hashem*."

11 Away, escape, O *Tzion*, you who dwell in Fair Babylon!

12 For thus said the Lord of Hosts – He who sent me after glory – concerning the nations that have taken you as spoil: "Whoever touches you touches the pupil of his own eye.

13 For I will lift My hand against them, and they shall be spoil for those they enslaved." – Then you shall know that I was sent by the Lord of Hosts.

14 Shout for joy, Fair *Tzion*! For lo, I come; and I will dwell in your midst – declares *Hashem*.

15 In that day many nations will attach themselves to *Hashem* and become His people, and He will dwell in your midst. Then you will know that I was sent to you by the Lord of Hosts.

16 *Hashem* will take *Yehuda* to Himself as His portion in the Holy Land, and He will choose *Yerushalayim* once more.

> v'-na-KHAL a-do-NAI et y'-hu-DAH khel-KO AL ad-MAT ha-KO-desh u-va-KHAR OD bee-ru-sha-LA-im

---

ירושלים
יראה
שלם

2:16 And He will choose *Yerushalayim* once more There are many explanations of the meaning of *Yerushalayim* (ירושלים), the Hebrew name for Jerusalem. According to the Sages, the name *Yerushalayim* comes from the words *Yirah* (יראה) and *Shalem* (שלם). *Yirah* is the Hebrew word for 'awe', and *shalem* means 'complete'. Rabbi Shlomo Carlebach explained that the name *Yerushalayim*, therefore, means complete, self-effacing awe; completely submitting oneself to God. The holy city is special and beloved to man because God loves it so much. This is also how we relate to the entire Land of Israel. We love it because He loves it.

Zecharya/Zechariah
Chapter 3

זכריה
פרק ג

17 Be silent, all flesh, before *Hashem*! For He is roused from His holy habitation.

הַס כָּל־בָּשָׂר מִפְּנֵי יְהֹוָה כִּי נֵעוֹר מִמְּעוֹן קָדְשׁוֹ׃

3 ¹ He further showed me *Yehoshua*, the *Kohen Gadol*, standing before the angel of *Hashem*, and the Accuser standing at his right to accuse him.

וַיַּרְאֵנִי אֶת־יְהוֹשֻׁעַ הַכֹּהֵן הַגָּדוֹל עֹמֵד לִפְנֵי מַלְאַךְ יְהֹוָה וְהַשָּׂטָן עֹמֵד עַל־יְמִינוֹ לְשִׂטְנוֹ׃

² But [the angel of] *Hashem* said to the Accuser, "*Hashem* rebuke you, O Accuser; may *Hashem* who has chosen *Yerushalayim* rebuke you! For this is a brand plucked from the fire."

וַיֹּאמֶר יְהֹוָה אֶל־הַשָּׂטָן יִגְעַר יְהֹוָה בְּךָ הַשָּׂטָן וְיִגְעַר יְהֹוָה בְּךָ הַבֹּחֵר בִּירוּשָׁלָ͏ִם הֲלוֹא זֶה אוּד מֻצָּל מֵאֵשׁ׃

³ Now *Yehoshua* was clothed in filthy garments when he stood before the angel.

וִיהוֹשֻׁעַ הָיָה לָבֻשׁ בְּגָדִים צוֹאִים וְעֹמֵד לִפְנֵי הַמַּלְאָךְ׃

⁴ The latter spoke up and said to his attendants, "Take the filthy garments off him!" And he said to him, "See, I have removed your guilt from you, and you shall be clothed in [priestly] robes."

וַיַּעַן וַיֹּאמֶר אֶל־הָעֹמְדִים לְפָנָיו לֵאמֹר הָסִירוּ הַבְּגָדִים הַצֹּאִים מֵעָלָיו וַיֹּאמֶר אֵלָיו רְאֵה הֶעֱבַרְתִּי מֵעָלֶיךָ עֲוֹנֶךָ וְהַלְבֵּשׁ אֹתְךָ מַחֲלָצוֹת׃

⁵ Then he gave the order, "Let a pure diadem be placed on his head." And they placed the pure diadem on his head and clothed him in [priestly] garments, as the angel of *Hashem* stood by.

וָאֹמַר יָשִׂימוּ צָנִיף טָהוֹר עַל־רֹאשׁוֹ וַיָּשִׂימוּ הַצָּנִיף הַטָּהוֹר עַל־רֹאשׁוֹ וַיַּלְבִּשֻׁהוּ בְּגָדִים וּמַלְאַךְ יְהֹוָה עֹמֵד׃

⁶ And the angel of *Hashem* charged *Yehoshua* as follows:

וַיָּעַד מַלְאַךְ יְהֹוָה בִּיהוֹשֻׁעַ לֵאמֹר׃

⁷ "Thus said the Lord of Hosts: If you walk in My paths and keep My charge, you in turn will rule My House and guard My courts, and I will permit you to move about among these attendants.

כֹּה־אָמַר יְהֹוָה צְבָאוֹת אִם־בִּדְרָכַי תֵּלֵךְ וְאִם אֶת־מִשְׁמַרְתִּי תִשְׁמֹר וְגַם־אַתָּה תָּדִין אֶת־בֵּיתִי וְגַם תִּשְׁמֹר אֶת־חֲצֵרָי וְנָתַתִּי לְךָ מַהְלְכִים בֵּין הָעֹמְדִים הָאֵלֶּה׃

koh a-MAR a-do-NAI tz'-va-OT im bid-ra-KHAI tay-LAYKH v'-IM et mish-mar-TEE tish-MOR v'-gam a-TAH ta-DEEN et bay-TEE v'-GAM tish-MOR et kha-tzay-RAI v'-na-ta-TEE l'-KHA mah-l'-KHEEM BAYN ha-o-m'-DEEM ha-AY-leh

⁸ Hearken well, O High Priest *Yehoshua*, you and your fellow *Kohanim* sitting before you! For those men are a sign that I am going to bring My servant the Branch.

שְׁמַע־נָא יְהוֹשֻׁעַ הַכֹּהֵן הַגָּדוֹל אַתָּה וְרֵעֶיךָ הַיֹּשְׁבִים לְפָנֶיךָ כִּי־אַנְשֵׁי מוֹפֵת הֵמָּה כִּי־הִנְנִי מֵבִיא אֶת־עַבְדִּי צֶמַח׃

3:7 And I will permit you to move about among these attendants In this chapter, *Yehoshua* the *Kohen Gadol* ('High Priest') has his dirty clothes removed, symbolic of the removal of his sins. *Yehoshua* is told that if he walks in the ways of *Hashem* and follows His commandments, he will be allowed to "move about these attendants." These attendants refers to the angels in the vision, implying that *Yehoshua* will be granted the ability to engage in direct communion with *Hashem*, just as the angels do. Some, however, interpret this to mean that *Yehoshua* will be given the right to enter Israel's most sacred spot – the Holy of Holies in the *Beit Hamikdash* in *Yerushalayim*, where the *Kohen Gadol* would enter once a year on *Yom Kippur*, the Day of Atonement (Leviticus 16).

Zecharya/Zechariah
Chapter 4

9 For mark well this stone which I place before *Yehoshua*, a single stone with seven eyes. I will execute its engraving – declares the Lord of Hosts – and I will remove that country's guilt in a single day.

10 In that day – declares the Lord of Hosts – you will be inviting each other to the shade of vines and fig trees."

4 **1** The angel who talked with me came back and woke me as a man is wakened from sleep.

2 He said to me, "What do you see?" And I answered, "I see a *menorah* all of gold, with a bowl above it. The lamps on it are seven in number, and the lamps above it have seven pipes;

va-YO-mer ay-LAI MAH a-TAH ro-EH va-o-MAR ra-EE-tee v'-hi-NAY m'-no-RAT za-HAV ku-LAH v'-gu-LAH al ro-SHAH v'-shiv-AH nay-ro-TE-ha a-LE-ha shiv-AH v'-shiv-AH mu-tza-KOT la-nay-ROT a-SHER al ro-SHAH

3 and by it are two olive trees, one on the right of the bowl and one on its left."

4 I, in turn, asked the angel who talked with me, "What do those things mean, my lord?"

5 "Do you not know what those things mean?" asked the angel who talked with me; and I said, "No, my lord."

6 Then he explained to me as follows: "This is the word of *Hashem* to *Zerubavel*: Not by might, nor by power, but by My spirit – said the Lord of Hosts.

7 Whoever you are, O great mountain in the path of *Zerubavel*, turn into level ground! For he shall produce that excellent stone; it shall be greeted with shouts of 'Beautiful! Beautiful!'"

8 And the word of *Hashem* came to me:

Replica of the Temple menorah

4:2 A menorah all of gold The Sages refer to *Yerushalyim* as 'the light of the world,' *ohro shel olam* (אורו של עולם). The symbol of this holy spiritual light was the Temple lamp, the *menorah* (מנורה), which emanated light through the unusual windows of the Sanctuary. These windows were made narrower on the inside, bringing less sunlight into the Sanctuary, but maximizing the spiritual light that burst forth to the world. This is symbolic of Israel's mission to be a "light of nations" (Isaiah 42:6).

Zecharya/Zechariah
Chapter 5

9 "*Zerubavel*'s hands have founded this House and *Zerubavel*'s hands shall complete it. Then you shall know that it was the Lord of Hosts who sent me to you.

10 Does anyone scorn a day of small beginnings? When they see the stone of distinction in the hand of *Zerubavel*, they shall rejoice. "Those seven are the eyes of *Hashem*, ranging over the whole earth."

11 "And what," I asked him, "are those two olive trees, one on the right and one on the left of the *menorah*?"

va-A-an va-o-MAR ay-LAV mah sh'-NAY ha-zay-TEEM ha-AY-leh al y'-MEEN ha-m'-no-RAH v'-al s'-mo-LAH

12 And I further asked him, "What are the two tops of the olive trees that feed their gold through those two golden tubes?"

13 He asked me, "Don't you know what they are?" And I replied, "No, my lord."

14 Then he explained, "They are the two anointed dignitaries who attend the Lord of all the earth."

5 1 I looked up again, and I saw a flying scroll.

2 "What do you see?" he asked. And I replied, "A flying scroll, twenty *amot* long and ten *amot* wide."

3 "That," he explained to me, "is the curse which goes out over the whole land. For everyone who has stolen, as is forbidden on one side [of the scroll], has gone unpunished; and everyone who has sworn [falsely], as is forbidden on the other side of it, has gone unpunished.

4 [But] I have sent it forth – declares the Lord of Hosts – and [the curse] shall enter the house of the thief and the house of the one who swears falsely by My name, and it shall lodge inside their houses and shall consume them to the last timber and stone."

4:11 those two olive trees the *menorah* and olive branches depicted in *zecharya*'s vision were chosen as the centerpieces of the state of israel's emblem. according to its designers, the olive branches symbolize the state's peaceful intentions. the image of the *menorah*, copied from the arch of titus, attests to the link of the jewish people with their glorious past in their homeland, and israel's return to its former luster. there are perhaps no two better symbols to represent the jewish people. oil is extracted when pressure is applied. in a similar fashion, the jewish people are refined when faced with difficulty, as hardship allows one to become more sensitive to others and form a closer connection with *hashem*. it follows that olive oil is used to light the *menorah*, representing clarity and wisdom for the entire world.

Emblem of the State of Israel

Zecharya/Zechariah
Chapter 6

5 Then the angel who talked with me came forward and said, "Now look up and note this other object that is approaching."

ה וַיֵּצֵא הַמַּלְאָךְ הַדֹּבֵר בִּי וַיֹּאמֶר אֵלַי שָׂא נָא עֵינֶיךָ וּרְאֵה מָה הַיּוֹצֵאת הַזֹּאת׃

6 I asked, "What is it?" And he said, "This tub that is approaching – this," said he, "is their eye in all the land."

ו וָאֹמַר מַה־הִיא וַיֹּאמֶר זֹאת הָאֵיפָה הַיּוֹצֵאת וַיֹּאמֶר זֹאת עֵינָם בְּכָל־הָאָרֶץ׃

7 And behold, a disk of lead was lifted, revealing a woman seated inside the tub.

ז וְהִנֵּה כִּכַּר עֹפֶרֶת נִשֵּׂאת וְזֹאת אִשָּׁה אַחַת יוֹשֶׁבֶת בְּתוֹךְ הָאֵיפָה׃

8 "That," he said, "is Wickedness"; and, thrusting her down into the tub, he pressed the leaden weight into its mouth.

ח וַיֹּאמֶר זֹאת הָרִשְׁעָה וַיַּשְׁלֵךְ אֹתָהּ אֶל־תּוֹךְ הָאֵיפָה וַיַּשְׁלֵךְ אֶת־אֶבֶן הָעֹפֶרֶת אֶל־פִּיהָ׃

9 I looked up again and saw two women come soaring with the wind in their wings – they had wings like those of a stork – and carry off the tub between earth and sky.

ט וָאֶשָּׂא עֵינַי וָאֵרֶא וְהִנֵּה שְׁתַּיִם נָשִׁים יוֹצְאוֹת וְרוּחַ בְּכַנְפֵיהֶם וְלָהֵנָּה כְנָפַיִם כְּכַנְפֵי הַחֲסִידָה וַתִּשֶּׂאנָה אֶת־הָאֵיפָה בֵּין הָאָרֶץ וּבֵין הַשָּׁמָיִם׃

va-e-SA ay-NAI va-AY-re v'-hi-NAY sh'-TA-yim na-SHEEM yo-tz'-OT v'-RU-akh b'-khan-fay-HEM v'-la-HAY-nah kh'-na-FA-yim k'-khan-FAY ha-kha-see-DAH va-ti-SE-nah et HA-ay-FAH BAYN ha-A-retz u-VAYN ha-sha-MA-yim

10 "Where are they taking the tub?" I asked the angel who talked with me.

י וָאֹמַר אֶל־הַמַּלְאָךְ הַדֹּבֵר בִּי אָנָה הֵמָּה מוֹלִכוֹת אֶת־הָאֵיפָה׃

11 And he answered, "To build a shrine for it in the land of Shinar; [a stand] shall be erected for it, and it shall be set down there upon the stand."

יא וַיֹּאמֶר אֵלַי לִבְנוֹת־לָהּ בַיִת בְּאֶרֶץ שִׁנְעָר וְהוּכַן וְהֻנִּיחָה שָּׁם עַל־מְכֻנָתָהּ׃

6

1 I looked up again, and I saw: Four chariots were coming out from between the two mountains; the mountains were of copper.

א וָאָשֻׁב וָאֶשָּׂא עֵינַי וָאֶרְאֶה וְהִנֵּה אַרְבַּע מַרְכָּבוֹת יֹצְאוֹת מִבֵּין שְׁנֵי הֶהָרִים וְהֶהָרִים הָרֵי נְחֹשֶׁת׃

2 The horses of the first chariot were bay, the horses of the second chariot were black;

ב בַּמֶּרְכָּבָה הָרִאשֹׁנָה סוּסִים אֲדֻמִּים וּבַמֶּרְכָּבָה הַשֵּׁנִית סוּסִים שְׁחֹרִים׃

3 the horses of the third chariot were white, and the horses of the fourth chariot were spotted – dappled.

ג וּבַמֶּרְכָּבָה הַשְּׁלִשִׁית סוּסִים לְבָנִים וּבַמֶּרְכָּבָה הָרְבִעִית סוּסִים בְּרֻדִּים אֲמֻצִּים׃

4 And I spoke up and asked the angel who talked with me: "What are those, my lord?"

ד וָאַעַן וָאֹמַר אֶל־הַמַּלְאָךְ הַדֹּבֵר בִּי מָה־אֵלֶּה אֲדֹנִי׃

5 In reply, the angel said to me, "Those are the four winds of heaven coming out after presenting themselves to the Lord of all the earth.

ה וַיַּעַן הַמַּלְאָךְ וַיֹּאמֶר אֵלָי אֵלֶּה אַרְבַּע רֻחוֹת הַשָּׁמַיִם יוֹצְאוֹת מֵהִתְיַצֵּב עַל־אֲדוֹן כָּל־הָאָרֶץ׃

5:9 And saw two women come soaring with the wind Zecharya has a fantastic vision of a woman, who personifies evil, being thrust into a basket that is sealed with lead. She is then carried by two other women, portrayed as angels, who expel her from the *Beit Hamikdash* and carry her away to Babylonia. Some take this to symbolize the removal of the Babylonian cult, which worshipped the goddess Ishtar, from the Land of Israel. The Talmud (*Kiddushin* 49b) symbolically identifies these two women as pride and hypocrisy, who, together with evil, find themselves exiled from the Holy Land and sent to Babylonia.

Zecharya/Zechariah
Chapter 6

זכריה
פרק ו

6 The one with the black horses is going out to the region of the north; the white ones have gone out to what is to the west of them; the spotted ones have gone out to the region of the south;

ו אֲשֶׁר־בָּהּ הַסּוּסִים הַשְּׁחֹרִים יֹצְאִים אֶל־אֶרֶץ צָפוֹן וְהַלְּבָנִים יָצְאוּ אֶל־אַחֲרֵיהֶם וְהַבְּרֻדִּים יָצְאוּ אֶל־אֶרֶץ הַתֵּימָן:

7 and the dappled ones have gone out…" They were ready to start out and range the earth, and he gave them the order, "Start out and range the earth!" And they ranged the earth.

ז וְהָאֲמֻצִּים יָצְאוּ וַיְבַקְשׁוּ לָלֶכֶת לְהִתְהַלֵּךְ בָּאָרֶץ וַיֹּאמֶר לְכוּ הִתְהַלְּכוּ בָאָרֶץ וַתִּתְהַלַּכְנָה בָּאָרֶץ:

8 Then he alerted me, and said to me, "Take good note! Those that went out to the region of the north have done my pleasure in the region of the north."

ח וַיַּזְעֵק אֹתִי וַיְדַבֵּר אֵלַי לֵאמֹר רְאֵה הַיּוֹצְאִים אֶל־אֶרֶץ צָפוֹן הֵנִיחוּ אֶת־רוּחִי בְּאֶרֶץ צָפוֹן:

9 The word of *Hashem* came to me:

ט וַיְהִי דְבַר־יְהֹוָה אֵלַי לֵאמֹר:

10 Receive from the exiled community – from Heldai, Tobijah, and Jedaiah, who have come from Babylon – and you, in turn, proceed the same day to the house of *Yoshiyahu* son of *Tzefanya*.

י לָקוֹחַ מֵאֵת הַגּוֹלָה מֵחֶלְדַּי וּמֵאֵת טוֹבִיָּה וּמֵאֵת יְדַעְיָה וּבָאתָ אַתָּה בַּיּוֹם הַהוּא וּבָאתָ בֵּית יֹאשִׁיָּה בֶן־צְפַנְיָה אֲשֶׁר־בָּאוּ מִבָּבֶל:

11 Take silver and gold and make crowns. Place [one] on the head of High Priest *Yehoshua* son of *Yehotzadak*,

יא וְלָקַחְתָּ כֶסֶף־וְזָהָב וְעָשִׂיתָ עֲטָרוֹת וְשַׂמְתָּ בְּרֹאשׁ יְהוֹשֻׁעַ בֶּן־יְהוֹצָדָק הַכֹּהֵן הַגָּדוֹל:

12 and say to him, "Thus said the Lord of Hosts: Behold, a man called the Branch shall branch out from the place where he is, and he shall build the Temple of *Hashem*.

יב וְאָמַרְתָּ אֵלָיו לֵאמֹר כֹּה אָמַר יְהֹוָה צְבָאוֹת לֵאמֹר הִנֵּה־אִישׁ צֶמַח שְׁמוֹ וּמִתַּחְתָּיו יִצְמָח וּבָנָה אֶת־הֵיכַל יְהֹוָה:

13 He shall build the Temple of *Hashem* and shall assume majesty, and he shall sit on his throne and rule. And there shall also be a *Kohen* seated on his throne, and harmonious understanding shall prevail between them."

יג וְהוּא יִבְנֶה אֶת־הֵיכַל יְהֹוָה וְהוּא־יִשָּׂא הוֹד וְיָשַׁב וּמָשַׁל עַל־כִּסְאוֹ וְהָיָה כֹהֵן עַל־כִּסְאוֹ וַעֲצַת שָׁלוֹם תִּהְיֶה בֵּין שְׁנֵיהֶם:

14 The crowns shall remain in the Temple of *Hashem* as a memorial to Helem, Tobijah, Jedaiah, and Hen son of *Tzefanya*.

יד וְהָעֲטָרֹת תִּהְיֶה לְחֵלֶם וּלְטוֹבִיָּה וְלִידַעְיָה וּלְחֵן בֶּן־צְפַנְיָה לְזִכָּרוֹן בְּהֵיכַל יְהֹוָה:

15 Men from far away shall come and take part in the building of the Temple of *Hashem*, and you shall know that I have been sent to you by the Lord of Hosts – if only you will obey *Hashem* your God!

טו וּרְחוֹקִים יָבֹאוּ וּבָנוּ בְּהֵיכַל יְהֹוָה וִידַעְתֶּם כִּי־יְהֹוָה צְבָאוֹת שְׁלָחַנִי אֲלֵיכֶם וְהָיָה אִם־שָׁמוֹעַ תִּשְׁמְעוּן בְּקוֹל יְהֹוָה אֱלֹהֵיכֶם:

ur-kho-KEEM ya-VO-u u-va-NU b'-hay-KHAL a-do-NAI vee-da-TEM kee a-do-NAI tz'-va-OT sh'-la-KHA-nee a-lay-KHEM v'-ha-YAH im sha-MO-a tish-m'-UN b'-KOL a-do-NAI e-lo-hay-KHEM

6:15 Men from far away shall come and take part in the building of the Temple Verses 12–13 refer to the dual coronation of the king and the priest. Verse 13 ends with the words "and harmonious understanding shall prevail between them," implying that they will work together side by side; the spiritual and the physical

Zecharya/Zechariah
Chapter 7

זכריה
פרק ז

7 1 In the fourth year of King Darius, on the fourth day of the ninth month, *Kislev*, the word of *Hashem* came to *Zecharya* –

א וַיְהִי בִּשְׁנַת אַרְבַּע לְדָרְיָוֶשׁ הַמֶּלֶךְ הָיָה דְבַר־יְהֹוָה אֶל־זְכַרְיָה בְּאַרְבָּעָה לַחֹדֶשׁ הַתְּשִׁעִי בְּכִסְלֵו:

2 when *Beit El*-sharezer and Regem-melech and his men sent to entreat the favor of *Hashem*,

ב וַיִּשְׁלַח בֵּית־אֵל שַׂר־אֶצֶר וְרֶגֶם מֶלֶךְ וַאֲנָשָׁיו לְחַלּוֹת אֶת־פְּנֵי יְהֹוָה:

3 [and] to address this inquiry to the *Kohanim* of the House of *Hashem* and to the *Neviim*: "Shall I weep and practice abstinence in the fifth month, as I have been doing all these years?"

ג לֵאמֹר אֶל־הַכֹּהֲנִים אֲשֶׁר לְבֵית־יְהֹוָה צְבָאוֹת וְאֶל־הַנְּבִיאִים לֵאמֹר הַאֶבְכֶּה בַּחֹדֶשׁ הַחֲמִשִׁי הִנָּזֵר כַּאֲשֶׁר עָשִׂיתִי זֶה כַּמֶּה שָׁנִים:

4 Thereupon the word of the Lord of Hosts came to me:

ד וַיְהִי דְּבַר־יְהֹוָה צְבָאוֹת אֵלַי לֵאמֹר:

5 Say to all the people of the land and to the *Kohanim*: When you fasted and lamented in the fifth and seventh months all these seventy years, did you fast for my benefit?

e-MOR el kol AM ha-A-retz v'-el ha-ko-ha-NEEM lay-MOR kee tzam-TEM v'-sa-FOD ba-kha-mee-SHEE u-va-sh'-vee-EE v'-ZEH shiv-EEM sha-NAH ha-TZOM tzam-TU-nee A-nee

ה אֱמֹר אֶל־כָּל־עַם הָאָרֶץ וְאֶל־הַכֹּהֲנִים לֵאמֹר כִּי־צַמְתֶּם וְסָפוֹד בַּחֲמִישִׁי וּבַשְּׁבִיעִי וְזֶה שִׁבְעִים שָׁנָה הֲצוֹם צַמְתֻּנִי אָנִי:

6 And when you eat and drink, who but you does the eating, and who but you does the drinking?

ו וְכִי תֹאכְלוּ וְכִי תִשְׁתּוּ הֲלוֹא אַתֶּם הָאֹכְלִים וְאַתֶּם הַשֹּׁתִים:

7 Look, this is the message that *Hashem* proclaimed through the earlier *Neviim*, when *Yerushalayim* and the towns about her were peopled and tranquil, when the *Negev* and the Shephelah were peopled.

ז הֲלוֹא אֶת־הַדְּבָרִים אֲשֶׁר קָרָא יְהֹוָה בְּיַד הַנְּבִיאִים הָרִאשֹׁנִים בִּהְיוֹת יְרוּשָׁלַ͏ִם יֹשֶׁבֶת וּשְׁלֵוָה וְעָרֶיהָ סְבִיבֹתֶיהָ וְהַנֶּגֶב וְהַשְּׁפֵלָה יֹשֵׁב:

8 And the word of *Hashem* to *Zecharya* continued:

ח וַיְהִי דְּבַר־יְהֹוָה אֶל־זְכַרְיָה לֵאמֹר:

9 Thus said the Lord of Hosts: Execute true justice; deal loyally and compassionately with one another.

ט כֹּה אָמַר יְהֹוָה צְבָאוֹת לֵאמֹר מִשְׁפַּט אֱמֶת שְׁפֹטוּ וְחֶסֶד וְרַחֲמִים עֲשׂוּ אִישׁ אֶת־אָחִיו:

---

leaders complementing each other in the building of the *Beit Hamikdash* and the nation's service of God. If the Jewish people work together and remain obedient to *Hashem* and observant of His commandments, *Zecharya* promises that not only will support arrive from abroad, but more Jews from among the exiles of Babylonia and Assyria will return to the Holy Land. Eventually, the righteous of all the world (see 8:22) will flock to *Yerushalayim* in great numbers to learn the ways of *Hashem*.

Rabbi Yitzchak Abarbanel (1437–1508)

7:5 Did you fast for my benefit? In the fourth year of King Darius, a delegation is sent to the prophet in *Yerushalayim* by the Jews who remained behind in Babylonia. They come with the following question: since the Jewish people are back in the Land of Israel and the *Beit Hamikdash* is being rebuilt, is it appropriate to continue to fast and mourn over the destruction of the first Temple, as they have been doing annually for decades? The prophet's response is clear. In *Hashem*'s eyes, fasting and other external signs of mourning have no value if not accompanied by sincere repentance and ethical behavior (verses 9–10). The medieval commentator, Rabbi Yitzchak Abarbanel, notes that while the question originates from the Jews in Babylon, the answer is directed towards the inhabitants of *Eretz Yisrael*. They sacrificed to return to the land; it is their actions that carry the most spiritual significance for the world.

Zecharya/Zechariah
Chapter 8

10 Do not defraud the widow, the orphan, the stranger, and the poor; and do not plot evil against one another. –

11 But they refused to pay heed. They presented a balky back and turned a deaf ear.

12 They hardened their hearts like adamant against heeding the instruction and admonition that the LORD of Hosts sent to them by His spirit through the earlier *Neviim*; and a terrible wrath issued from the LORD of Hosts.

13 Even as He called and they would not listen, "So," said the LORD of Hosts, "let them call and I will not listen."

14 I dispersed them among all those nations which they had not known, and the land was left behind them desolate, without any who came and went. They caused a delightful land to be turned into a desolation.

8 1 The word of the LORD of Hosts came [to me]:

2 Thus said the LORD of Hosts: I am very jealous for *Tzion*, I am fiercely jealous for her.

3 Thus said *Hashem*: I have returned to *Tzion*, and I will dwell in *Yerushalayim*. *Yerushalayim* will be called the City of Faithfulness, and the mount of the LORD of Hosts the Holy Mount.

4 Thus said the LORD of Hosts: There shall yet be old men and women in the squares of *Yerushalayim*, each with staff in hand because of their great age.

5 And the squares of the city shall be crowded with boys and girls playing in the squares.

6 Thus said the LORD of Hosts: Though it will seem impossible to the remnant of this people in those days, shall it also be impossible to Me? – declares the LORD of Hosts.

7 Thus said the LORD of Hosts: I will rescue My people from the lands of the east and from the lands of the west,

8 and I will bring them home to dwell in *Yerushalayim*. They shall be My people, and I will be their God – in truth and sincerity.

Zecharya/Zechariah
Chapter 8

9 Thus said the Lord of Hosts: Take courage, you who now hear these words which the *Neviim* spoke when the foundations were laid for the rebuilding of the Temple, the House of the Lord of Hosts.

10 For before that time, the earnings of men were nil, and profits from beasts were nothing. It was not safe to go about one's business on account of enemies; and I set all men against one another.

11 But now I will not treat the remnant of this people as before – declares the Lord of Hosts –

12 but what it sows shall prosper: The vine shall produce its fruit, the ground shall produce its yield, and the skies shall provide their moisture. I will bestow all these things upon the remnant of this people.

13 And just as you were a curse among the nations, O House of *Yehuda* and House of *Yisrael*, so, when I vindicate you, you shall become a blessing. Have no fear; take courage!

14 For thus said the Lord of Hosts: Just as I planned to afflict you and did not relent when your fathers provoked Me to anger – said the Lord of Hosts –

15 so, at this time, I have turned and planned to do good to *Yerushalayim* and to the House of *Yehuda*. Have no fear!

16 These are the things you are to do: Speak the truth to one another, render true and perfect justice in your gates.

AY-leh ha-d'-va-REEM a-SHER ta-a-SU da-b'-RU e-MET EESH et ray-AY-hu e-MET u-mish-PAT sha-LOM shif-TU b'-sha-a-ray-KHEM

17 And do not contrive evil against one another, and do not love perjury, because all those are things that I hate – declares *Hashem*.

8:16 Render true and perfect justice in your gates
In order for *Yehuda* and *Yisrael* to become a blessing (verse 13), they have to perform *emet umishpat shalom* (אמת ומשפט שלום). While this phrase is translated here as "true and perfect justice," the words literally mean 'truth' and 'judgement of peace.' When two people each claim to represent truth, how does peace emerge? The Sages state that from here we learn the importance of compromise, as truth, justice, and peace are the three pillars upon which the world depends (*Ethics of the Fathers* 1:18). The commentator *Radak* suggests that when the judges in Israel mete out righteous justice, then even the losing parties in a quarrel will accept the judgment peacefully. This sense of justice and peace will cause the nations of the world to encourage each other to go to *Yerushalayim* for God's blessing (verses 20–22).

Zecharya/Zechariah
Chapter 9

זכריה
פרק ט

18 And the word of the Lord of Hosts came to me, saying,

יח וַיְהִי דְּבַר־יְהֹוָה צְבָאוֹת אֵלַי לֵאמֹר׃

19 Thus said the Lord of Hosts: The fast of the fourth month, the fast of the fifth month, the fast of the seventh month, and the fast of the tenth month shall become occasions for joy and gladness, happy festivals for the House of *Yehuda*; but you must love honesty and integrity.

יט כֹּה־אָמַר יְהֹוָה צְבָאוֹת צוֹם הָרְבִיעִי וְצוֹם הַחֲמִישִׁי וְצוֹם הַשְּׁבִיעִי וְצוֹם הָעֲשִׂירִי יִהְיֶה לְבֵית־יְהוּדָה לְשָׂשׂוֹן וּלְשִׂמְחָה וּלְמֹעֲדִים טוֹבִים וְהָאֱמֶת וְהַשָּׁלוֹם אֱהָבוּ׃

20 Thus said the Lord of Hosts: Peoples and the inhabitants of many cities shall yet come –

כ כֹּה אָמַר יְהֹוָה צְבָאוֹת עֹד אֲשֶׁר יָבֹאוּ עַמִּים וְיֹשְׁבֵי עָרִים רַבּוֹת׃

21 the inhabitants of one shall go to the other and say, "Let us go and entreat the favor of *Hashem*, let us seek the Lord of Hosts; I will go, too."

כא וְהָלְכוּ יֹשְׁבֵי אַחַת אֶל־אַחַת לֵאמֹר נֵלְכָה הָלוֹךְ לְחַלּוֹת אֶת־פְּנֵי יְהֹוָה וּלְבַקֵּשׁ אֶת־יְהֹוָה צְבָאוֹת אֵלְכָה גַּם־אָנִי׃

22 The many peoples and the multitude of nations shall come to seek the Lord of Hosts in *Yerushalayim* and to entreat the favor of *Hashem*.

כב וּבָאוּ עַמִּים רַבִּים וְגוֹיִם עֲצוּמִים לְבַקֵּשׁ אֶת־יְהֹוָה צְבָאוֹת בִּירוּשָׁלָ͏ִם וּלְחַלּוֹת אֶת־פְּנֵי יְהֹוָה׃

23 Thus said the Lord of Hosts: In those days, ten men from nations of every tongue will take hold – they will take hold of every *Yehudi* by a corner of his cloak and say, "Let us go with you, for we have heard that *Hashem* is with you."

כג כֹּה אָמַר יְהֹוָה צְבָאוֹת בַּיָּמִים הָהֵמָּה אֲשֶׁר יַחֲזִיקוּ עֲשָׂרָה אֲנָשִׁים מִכֹּל לְשֹׁנוֹת הַגּוֹיִם וְהֶחֱזִיקוּ בִּכְנַף אִישׁ יְהוּדִי לֵאמֹר נֵלְכָה עִמָּכֶם כִּי שָׁמַעְנוּ אֱלֹהִים עִמָּכֶם׃

9

1 A pronouncement: The word of *Hashem*. He will reside in the land of Hadrach and Damascus; For all men's eyes will turn to *Hashem* – Like all the tribes of *Yisrael* –

ט א מַשָּׂא דְבַר־יְהֹוָה בְּאֶרֶץ חַדְרָךְ וְדַמֶּשֶׂק מְנֻחָתוֹ כִּי לַיהֹוָה עֵין אָדָם וְכֹל שִׁבְטֵי יִשְׂרָאֵל׃

2 Including Hamath, which borders on it, And Tyre and Sidon, though they are very wise.

ב וְגַם־חֲמָת תִּגְבָּל־בָּהּ צֹר וְצִידוֹן כִּי חָכְמָה מְאֹד׃

3 Tyre has built herself a fortress; She has amassed silver like dust, And gold like the mud in the streets.

ג וַתִּבֶן צֹר מָצוֹר לָהּ וַתִּצְבָּר־כֶּסֶף כֶּעָפָר וְחָרוּץ כְּטִיט חוּצוֹת׃

4 But my Lord will impoverish her; He will defeat her forces at sea, And she herself shall be consumed by fire.

ד הִנֵּה אֲדֹנָי יוֹרִשֶׁנָּה וְהִכָּה בַיָּם חֵילָהּ וְהִיא בָּאֵשׁ תֵּאָכֵל׃

5 *Ashkelon* shall see it and be frightened, *Azza* shall tremble violently, And Ekron, at the collapse of her hopes. Kingship shall vanish from *Azza*, *Ashkelon* shall be without inhabitants,

ה תֵּרֶא אַשְׁקְלוֹן וְתִירָא וְעַזָּה וְתָחִיל מְאֹד וְעֶקְרוֹן כִּי־הֹבִישׁ מֶבָּטָהּ וְאָבַד מֶלֶךְ מֵעַזָּה וְאַשְׁקְלוֹן לֹא תֵשֵׁב׃

6 And a mongrel people shall settle in *Ashdod*. I will uproot the grandeur of Philistia.

ו וְיָשַׁב מַמְזֵר בְּאַשְׁדּוֹד וְהִכְרַתִּי גְּאוֹן פְּלִשְׁתִּים׃

7 But I will clean out the blood from its mouth, And the detestable things from between its teeth. Its survivors, too, shall belong to our God: They shall become like a clan in *Yehuda*, And Ekron shall be like the Jebusites.

ז וַהֲסִרֹתִי דָמָיו מִפִּיו וְשִׁקֻּצָיו מִבֵּין שִׁנָּיו וְנִשְׁאַר גַּם־הוּא לֵאלֹהֵינוּ וְהָיָה כְּאַלֻּף בִּיהוּדָה וְעֶקְרוֹן כִּיבוּסִי׃

Zecharya/Zechariah
Chapter 9

זכריה
פרק ט

8 And I will encamp in My House against armies, Against any that come and go, And no oppressor shall ever overrun them again; For I have now taken note with My own eyes.

ח וְחָנִיתִי לְבֵיתִי מִצָּבָה מֵעֹבֵר וּמִשָּׁב וְלֹא־יַעֲבֹר עֲלֵיהֶם עוֹד נֹגֵשׂ כִּי עַתָּה רָאִיתִי בְעֵינָי׃

9 Rejoice greatly, Fair *Tzion*; Raise a shout, Fair *Yerushalayim*! Lo, your king is coming to you. He is victorious, triumphant, Yet humble, riding on an ass, On a donkey foaled by a she-ass.

ט גִּילִי מְאֹד בַּת־צִיּוֹן הָרִיעִי בַּת יְרוּשָׁלַ͏ִם הִנֵּה מַלְכֵּךְ יָבוֹא לָךְ צַדִּיק וְנוֹשָׁע הוּא עָנִי וְרֹכֵב עַל־חֲמוֹר וְעַל־עַיִר בֶּן־אֲתֹנוֹת׃

gee-LEE m'-OD bat tzi-YON ha-REE-ee BAT y'-ru-sha-LA-im hi-NAY mal-KAYCH ya-VO LAKH tza-DIK v'-no-SHA HU a-NEE v'-ro-KHAYV al kha-MOR v'-al A-yir ben a-to-NOT

10 He shall banish chariots from *Efraim* And horses from *Yerushalayim*; The warrior's bow shall be banished. He shall call on the nations to surrender, And his rule shall extend from sea to sea And from ocean to land's end.

י וְהִכְרַתִּי־רֶכֶב מֵאֶפְרַיִם וְסוּס מִירוּשָׁלַ͏ִם וְנִכְרְתָה קֶשֶׁת מִלְחָמָה וְדִבֶּר שָׁלוֹם לַגּוֹיִם וּמָשְׁלוֹ מִיָּם עַד־יָם וּמִנָּהָר עַד־אַפְסֵי־אָרֶץ׃

11 You, for your part, have released Your prisoners from the dry pit, For the sake of the blood of your covenant,

יא גַּם־אַתְּ בְּדַם־בְּרִיתֵךְ שִׁלַּחְתִּי אֲסִירַיִךְ מִבּוֹר אֵין מַיִם בּוֹ׃

12 [Saying], "Return to Bizzaron, You prisoners of hope." In return [I] announce this day: I will repay you double.

יב שׁוּבוּ לְבִצָּרוֹן אֲסִירֵי הַתִּקְוָה גַּם־הַיּוֹם מַגִּיד מִשְׁנֶה אָשִׁיב לָךְ׃

13 For I have drawn *Yehuda* taut, And applied [My hand] to *Efraim* as to a bow, And I will arouse your sons, O *Tzion*, Against your sons, O Javan, And make you like a warrior's sword.

יג כִּי־דָרַכְתִּי לִי יְהוּדָה קֶשֶׁת מִלֵּאתִי אֶפְרַיִם וְעוֹרַרְתִּי בָנַיִךְ צִיּוֹן עַל־בָּנַיִךְ יָוָן וְשַׂמְתִּיךְ כְּחֶרֶב גִּבּוֹר׃

14 And *Hashem* will manifest Himself to them, And His arrows shall flash like lightning; My *Hashem* shall sound the *shofar* And advance in a stormy tempest.

יד וַיהֹוָה עֲלֵיהֶם יֵרָאֶה וְיָצָא כַבָּרָק חִצּוֹ וַאדֹנָי יְהֹוִה בַּשּׁוֹפָר יִתְקָע וְהָלַךְ בְּסַעֲרוֹת תֵּימָן׃

15 The Lord of Hosts will protect them: [His] slingstones shall devour and conquer; They shall drink, shall rage as with wine, And be filled [with it] like a dashing bowl, Like the corners of an *Mizbayach*.

טו יְהֹוָה צְבָאוֹת יָגֵן עֲלֵיהֶם וְאָכְלוּ וְכָבְשׁוּ אַבְנֵי־קֶלַע וְשָׁתוּ הָמוּ כְּמוֹ־יָיִן וּמָלְאוּ כַּמִּזְרָק כְּזָוִיּוֹת מִזְבֵּחַ׃

A donkey in Nachal Gerar

9:9 Yet humble, riding on an ass *Zecharya* describes the arrival in *Yerushalayim* of Israel's king *Mashiach*, to the cheers of the people after having defeated Israel's enemies. Though returning in miraculous victory, the Messiah will not enter the gates of Jerusalem on a glorious military steed. Instead, the *Mashiach* will ride on a humble donkey. Rabbi Menachem Mendel Schneerson, the Lubavitcher Rebbe, explains that a 'donkey' in Hebrew is *chamor* (חמור) which is similar to *chomer* (חומר) which means 'materialism.' This verse teaches that the *Mashiach*, who represents spirituality, will ride upon the donkey of materialism, for he will usher in a world where these two contrasting values will be fused together in the service of *Hashem*.

חמור
חומר

Zecharya/Zechariah
Chapter 10

16 *Hashem* their God shall prosper them On that day; [He shall pasture] His people like sheep. [They shall be] like crown jewels glittering on His soil.

17 How lovely, how beautiful they shall be, Producing young men like new grain, Young women like new wine!

10 1 Ask *Hashem* for rain In the season of late rain. It is *Hashem* who causes storms; And He will provide rainstorms for them, Grass in the fields for everyone.

sha-a-LU may-a-do-NAI ma-TAR b'-AYT mal-KOSH a-do-NAI o-SEH kha-zee-ZEEM um-tar GE-shem yi-TAYN la-HEM l'-EESH AY-sev ba-sa-DEH

2 For the teraphim spoke delusion, The augurs predicted falsely; And dreamers speak lies And console with illusions. That is why My people have strayed like a flock, They suffer for lack of a shepherd.

3 My anger is roused against the shepherds, And I will punish the he-goats. For the Lord of Hosts has taken thought In behalf of His flock, the House of *Yehuda*; He will make them like majestic chargers in battle.

4 From them shall come cornerstones, From them tent pegs, From them bows of combat, And every captain shall also arise from them.

5 And together they shall be like warriors in battle, Tramping in the dirt of the streets; They shall fight, for *Hashem* shall be with them, And they shall put horsemen to shame.

6 I will give victory to the House of *Yehuda*, And triumph to the House of *Yosef*. I will restore them, for I have pardoned them, And they shall be as though I had never disowned them; For I *Hashem* am their God, And I will answer their prayers.

Zechariah 10:1 Ask *Hashem* for rain in the season of late rain *Zecharya* begins this chapter by calling on the Children of Israel to pray for rain. Should they ask for rain, *Hashem* will gladly fulfill the request. It seems strange that the people are to pray for rain "in the season of late rain." Since it is the rainy season, the request seems unnecessary. However, in *Sefer Devarim* (11:10–11) the *Torah* describes how the Land of Israel is different than Egypt, in that it is dependant on rainfall for its sustenance: "For the land that you are about to enter and possess is not like the land of Egypt from which you have come. There the grain you sowed had to be watered by your own labors, like a vegetable garden; but the land you are about to cross into and possess, a land of hills and valleys, soaks up its water from the rains of heaven." However, because of the special nature of *Eretz Yisrael*, even in the winter the rains do not come naturally unless man turns to *Hashem* and prays for them. This reality strengthens the relationship between the God of Israel, the People of Israel and the Land of Israel.

Zecharya/Zechariah
Chapter 11

7 *Efraim* shall be like a warrior, And they shall exult as with wine; Their children shall see it and rejoice, They shall exult in *Hashem*.

8 I will whistle to them and gather them, For I will redeem them; They shall increase and continue increasing.

9 For though I sowed them among the nations, In the distant places they shall remember Me, They shall escape with their children and shall return.

10 I will bring them back from the land of Egypt And gather them from Assyria; And I will bring them to the lands of *Gilad* and Lebanon, And even they shall not suffice for them.

11 A hemmed-in force shall pass over the sea And shall stir up waves in the sea; And all the deeps of the Nile shall dry up. Down shall come the pride of Assyria, And the scepter of Egypt shall pass away.

12 But I will make them mighty through *Hashem*, And they shall march proudly in His name – declares *Hashem*.

11 1 Throw open your gates, O Lebanon, And let fire consume your cedars!

2 Howl, cypresses, for cedars have fallen! How the mighty are ravaged! Howl, you oaks of Bashan, For the stately forest is laid low!

3 Hark, the wailing of the shepherds, For their rich pastures are ravaged; Hark, the roaring of the great beasts, For the jungle of the *Yarden* is ravaged.

4 Thus said my God *Hashem*: Tend the sheep meant for slaughter,

5 whose buyers will slaughter them with impunity, whose seller will say, "Praised be *Hashem*! I'll get rich," and whose shepherd will not pity them.

6 For I will pity the inhabitants of the land no more – declares *Hashem* – but I will place every man at the mercy of every other man and at the mercy of his king; they shall break the country to bits, and I will not rescue it from their hands.

זכריה
פרק יא

ז וְהָיוּ כְגִבּוֹר אֶפְרַיִם וְשָׂמַח לִבָּם כְּמוֹ־יָיִן וּבְנֵיהֶם יִרְאוּ וְשָׂמֵחוּ יָגֵל לִבָּם בַּיהוָֹה:

ח אֶשְׁרְקָה לָהֶם וַאֲקַבְּצֵם כִּי פְדִיתִים וְרָבוּ כְּמוֹ רָבוּ:

ט וְאֶזְרָעֵם בָּעַמִּים וּבַמֶּרְחַקִּים יִזְכְּרוּנִי וְחָיוּ אֶת־בְּנֵיהֶם וָשָׁבוּ:

י וַהֲשִׁיבוֹתִים מֵאֶרֶץ מִצְרַיִם וּמֵאַשּׁוּר אֲקַבְּצֵם וְאֶל־אֶרֶץ גִּלְעָד וּלְבָנוֹן אֲבִיאֵם וְלֹא יִמָּצֵא לָהֶם:

יא וְעָבַר בַּיָּם צָרָה וְהִכָּה בַיָּם גַּלִּים וְהֹבִישׁוּ כֹּל מְצוּלוֹת יְאֹר וְהוּרַד גְּאוֹן אַשּׁוּר וְשֵׁבֶט מִצְרַיִם יָסוּר:

יב וְגִבַּרְתִּים בַּיהוָֹה וּבִשְׁמוֹ יִתְהַלָּכוּ נְאֻם יְהוָֹה:

יא א פְּתַח לְבָנוֹן דְּלָתֶיךָ וְתֹאכַל אֵשׁ בַּאֲרָזֶיךָ:

ב הֵילֵל בְּרוֹשׁ כִּי־נָפַל אֶרֶז אֲשֶׁר אַדִּרִים שֻׁדָּדוּ הֵילִילוּ אַלּוֹנֵי בָשָׁן כִּי יָרַד יַעַר הבצור [הַבָּצִיר]:

ג קוֹל יִלְלַת הָרֹעִים כִּי שֻׁדְּדָה אַדַּרְתָּם קוֹל שַׁאֲגַת כְּפִירִים כִּי שֻׁדַּד גְּאוֹן הַיַּרְדֵּן:

ד כֹּה אָמַר יְהוָֹה אֱלֹהָי רְעֵה אֶת־צֹאן הַהֲרֵגָה:

ה אֲשֶׁר קֹנֵיהֶן יַהֲרֹגֻן וְלֹא יֶאְשָׁמוּ וּמֹכְרֵיהֶן יֹאמַר בָּרוּךְ יְהוָֹה וַאעְשִׁר וְרֹעֵיהֶם לֹא יַחְמוֹל עֲלֵיהֶן:

ו כִּי לֹא אֶחְמוֹל עוֹד עַל־יֹשְׁבֵי הָאָרֶץ נְאֻם־יְהוָֹה וְהִנֵּה אָנֹכִי מַמְצִיא אֶת־הָאָדָם אִישׁ בְּיַד־רֵעֵהוּ וּבְיַד מַלְכּוֹ וְכִתְּתוּ אֶת־הָאָרֶץ וְלֹא אַצִּיל מִיָּדָם:

Zecharya/Zechariah
Chapter 11

זכריה
פרק יא

7 So I tended the sheep meant for slaughter, for those poor men of the sheep. I got two staffs, one of which I named Favor and the other Unity, and I proceeded to tend the sheep.

וָאֶרְעֶה אֶת־צֹאן הַהֲרֵגָה לָכֵן עֲנִיֵּי הַצֹּאן וָאֶקַּח־לִי שְׁנֵי מַקְלוֹת לְאַחַד קָרָאתִי נֹעַם וּלְאַחַד קָרָאתִי חֹבְלִים וָאֶרְעֶה אֶת־הַצֹּאן׃

va-er-EH et TZON ha-ha-ray-GAH la-KHAYN a-ni-YAY ha-TZON va-e-kakh LEE sh'-NAY mak-LOT l'-a-KHAD ka-RA-tee NO-am ul-a-KHAD ka-RA-tee kho-v'-LEEM va-er-EH et ha-TZON

8 But I lost the three shepherds in one month; then my patience with them was at an end, and they in turn were disgusted with me.

וָאַכְחִד אֶת־שְׁלֹשֶׁת הָרֹעִים בְּיֶרַח אֶחָד וַתִּקְצַר נַפְשִׁי בָּהֶם וְגַם־נַפְשָׁם בָּחֲלָה בִי׃

9 So I declared, "I am not going to tend you; let the one that is to die die and the one that is to get lost get lost; and let the rest devour each other's flesh!"

וָאֹמַר לֹא אֶרְעֶה אֶתְכֶם הַמֵּתָה תָמוּת וְהַנִּכְחֶדֶת תִּכָּחֵד וְהַנִּשְׁאָרוֹת תֹּאכַלְנָה אִשָּׁה אֶת־בְּשַׂר רְעוּתָהּ׃

10 Taking my staff Favor, I cleft it in two, so as to annul the covenant I had made with all the peoples;

וָאֶקַּח אֶת־מַקְלִי אֶת־נֹעַם וָאֶגְדַּע אֹתוֹ לְהָפֵיר אֶת־בְּרִיתִי אֲשֶׁר כָּרַתִּי אֶת־כָּל־הָעַמִּים׃

11 and when it was annulled that day, the same poor men of the sheep who watched me realized that it was a message from *Hashem*.

וַתֻּפַר בַּיּוֹם הַהוּא וַיֵּדְעוּ כֵן עֲנִיֵּי הַצֹּאן הַשֹּׁמְרִים אֹתִי כִּי דְבַר־יְהֹוָה הוּא׃

12 Then I said to them, "If you are satisfied, pay me my wages; if not, don't." So they weighed out my wages, thirty *shekalim* of silver —

וָאֹמַר אֲלֵיהֶם אִם־טוֹב בְּעֵינֵיכֶם הָבוּ שְׂכָרִי וְאִם־לֹא חֲדָלוּ וַיִּשְׁקְלוּ אֶת־שְׂכָרִי שְׁלֹשִׁים כָּסֶף׃

13 the noble sum that I was worth in their estimation. *Hashem* said to me, "Deposit it in the treasury." And I took the thirty *shekalim* and deposited it in the treasury in the House of *Hashem*.

וַיֹּאמֶר יְהֹוָה אֵלַי הַשְׁלִיכֵהוּ אֶל־הַיּוֹצֵר אֶדֶר הַיְקָר אֲשֶׁר יָקַרְתִּי מֵעֲלֵיהֶם וָאֶקְחָה שְׁלֹשִׁים הַכֶּסֶף וָאַשְׁלִיךְ אֹתוֹ בֵּית יְהֹוָה אֶל־הַיּוֹצֵר׃

14 Then I cleft in two my second staff, Unity, in order to annul the brotherhood between *Yehuda* and *Yisrael*.

וָאֶגְדַּע אֶת־מַקְלִי הַשֵּׁנִי אֵת הַחֹבְלִים לְהָפֵר אֶת־הָאַחֲוָה בֵּין יְהוּדָה וּבֵין יִשְׂרָאֵל׃

15 *Hashem* said to me further: Get yourself the gear of a foolish shepherd.

וַיֹּאמֶר יְהֹוָה אֵלָי עוֹד קַח־לְךָ כְּלִי רֹעֶה אֱוִלִי׃

16 For I am going to raise up in the land a shepherd who will neither miss the lost [sheep], nor seek the strayed, nor heal the injured, nor sustain the frail, but will feast on the flesh of the fat ones and tear off their hoofs.

כִּי הִנֵּה־אָנֹכִי מֵקִים רֹעֶה בָּאָרֶץ הַנִּכְחָדוֹת לֹא־יִפְקֹד הַנַּעַר לֹא־יְבַקֵּשׁ וְהַנִּשְׁבֶּרֶת לֹא יְרַפֵּא הַנִּצָּבָה לֹא יְכַלְכֵּל וּבְשַׂר הַבְּרִיאָה יֹאכַל וּפַרְסֵיהֶן יְפָרֵק׃

11:7 One of which I named Favor and the other Unity The prophet is asked to act as a shepherd to his people, since the previous shepherds had neglected them and were dismissed. In order to guide the flock, the shepherd must carry "two staffs." One staff is named *noam* (נעם), meaning 'favor,' and the second staff is named *chovlim* (חבלים). The word *chovlim* refers to something that ties two items together, and is a metaphor for unity. These staffs represent the characteristics of a good leader; dealing favorably and pleasantly with his people and keeping them united.

נעם
חבלים

Zecharya/Zechariah
Chapter 12

זכריה
פרק יב

17 Oh, the worthless shepherd Who abandons the flock! Let a sword descend upon his arm And upon his right eye! His arm shall shrivel up; His right eye shall go blind.

יז הוֹי רֹעִי הָאֱלִיל עֹזְבִי הַצֹּאן חֶרֶב עַל־זְרוֹעוֹ וְעַל־עֵין יְמִינוֹ זְרֹעוֹ יָבוֹשׁ תִּיבָשׁ וְעֵין יְמִינוֹ כָּהֹה תִכְהֶה׃

12 1 A pronouncement: The word of *Hashem* concerning *Yisrael*. The utterance of *Hashem*, Who stretched out the skies And made firm the earth, And created man's breath within him:

יב א מַשָּׂא דְבַר־יְהֹוָה עַל־יִשְׂרָאֵל נְאֻם־יְהֹוָה נֹטֶה שָׁמַיִם וְיֹסֵד אָרֶץ וְיֹצֵר רוּחַ־אָדָם בְּקִרְבּוֹ׃

2 Behold, I will make *Yerushalayim* a bowl of reeling for the peoples all around. *Yehuda* shall be caught up in the siege upon *Yerushalayim*,

ב הִנֵּה אָנֹכִי שָׂם אֶת־יְרוּשָׁלַ͏ִם סַף־רַעַל לְכָל־הָעַמִּים סָבִיב וְגַם עַל־יְהוּדָה יִהְיֶה בַמָּצוֹר עַל־יְרוּשָׁלָ͏ִם׃

3 when all the nations of the earth gather against her. In that day, I will make *Yerushalayim* a stone for all the peoples to lift; all who lift it shall injure themselves.

ג וְהָיָה בַיּוֹם־הַהוּא אָשִׂים אֶת־יְרוּשָׁלַ͏ִם אֶבֶן מַעֲמָסָה לְכָל־הָעַמִּים כָּל־עֹמְסֶיהָ שָׂרוֹט יִשָּׂרֵטוּ וְנֶאֶסְפוּ עָלֶיהָ כֹּל גּוֹיֵי הָאָרֶץ׃

v'-ha-YAH va-YOM ha-HU a-SEEM et y'-ru-sha-LA-im E-ven ma-a-ma-SAH l'-khol ha-a-MEEM kol o-m'-SE-ha sa-ROT yi-sa-RAY-tu v'-ne-es-FU a-LE-ha KOL go-YAY ha-A-retz

4 In that day – declares *Hashem* – I will strike every horse with panic and its rider with madness. But I will watch over the House of *Yehuda* while I strike every horse of the peoples with blindness.

ד בַּיּוֹם הַהוּא נְאֻם־יְהֹוָה אַכֶּה כָל־סוּס בַּתִּמָּהוֹן וְרֹכְבוֹ בַּשִּׁגָּעוֹן וְעַל־בֵּית יְהוּדָה אֶפְקַח אֶת־עֵינַי וְכֹל סוּס הָעַמִּים אַכֶּה בַּעִוָּרוֹן׃

5 And the clans of *Yehuda* will say to themselves, "The dwellers of *Yerushalayim* are a task set for us by their God, the Lord of Hosts."

ה וְאָמְרוּ אַלֻּפֵי יְהוּדָה בְּלִבָּם אַמְצָה לִי יֹשְׁבֵי יְרוּשָׁלַ͏ִם בַּיהֹוָה צְבָאוֹת אֱלֹהֵיהֶם׃

6 In that day, I will make the clans of *Yehuda* like a flaming brazier among sticks and like a flaming torch among sheaves. They shall devour all the besieging peoples right and left; and *Yerushalayim* shall continue on its site, in *Yerushalayim*.

ו בַּיּוֹם הַהוּא אָשִׂים אֶת־אַלֻּפֵי יְהוּדָה כְּכִיּוֹר אֵשׁ בְּעֵצִים וּכְלַפִּיד אֵשׁ בְּעָמִיר וְאָכְלוּ עַל־יָמִין וְעַל־שְׂמֹאול אֶת־כָּל־הָעַמִּים סָבִיב וְיָשְׁבָה יְרוּשָׁלַ͏ִם עוֹד תַּחְתֶּיהָ בִּירוּשָׁלָ͏ִם׃

7 *Hashem* will give victory to the tents of *Yehuda* first, so that the glory of the House of *David* and the glory of the inhabitants of *Yerushalayim* may not be too great for *Yehuda*.

ז וְהוֹשִׁיעַ יְהֹוָה אֶת־אָהֳלֵי יְהוּדָה בָּרִאשֹׁנָה לְמַעַן לֹא־תִגְדַּל תִּפְאֶרֶת בֵּית־דָּוִיד וְתִפְאֶרֶת יֹשֵׁב יְרוּשָׁלַ͏ִם עַל־יְהוּדָה׃

12:3 I will make *Yerushalayim* a stone for all the peoples to lift *Zecharya* prophesies about a future attack against *Yehuda* by the nations of the world. In that attack, the nations will besiege *Yerushalayim*, Israel's capital, only to be miraculously defeated by *Yehuda*. *Hashem* states that *Yerushalayim* will become "a stone for all the peoples to lift," and "all who lift it shall injure themselves." In ancient times, when heavy stones lay in a field, the farmers would have to remove them with great effort, often cutting themselves futilely, in order to plough. This verse means that the nations of the world that try to remove *Yehuda* and *Yerushalayim* will fail, injuring themselves while trying to destroy the holy city. Spiritually, *Yerushalayim* and *Yisrael* symbolize God and His word. Taking on *Yerushalayim* forces the nations to contend with *Hashem* and His goodness. Ultimately, they will be blocked from going off on their own path.

Zecharya/Zechariah
Chapter 13

זכריה
פרק יג

8 In that day, *Hashem* will shield the inhabitants of *Yerushalayim*; and the feeblest of them shall be in that day like *David*, and the House of *David* like a divine being – like an angel of *Hashem* – at their head.

ח בַּיּוֹם הַהוּא יָגֵן יְהֹוָה בְּעַד יוֹשֵׁב יְרוּשָׁלַ͏ִם וְהָיָה הַנִּכְשָׁל בָּהֶם בַּיּוֹם הַהוּא כְּדָוִיד וּבֵית דָּוִיד כֵּאלֹהִים כְּמַלְאַךְ יְהֹוָה לִפְנֵיהֶם׃

9 In that day I will all but annihilate all the nations that came up against *Yerushalayim*.

ט וְהָיָה בַּיּוֹם הַהוּא אֲבַקֵּשׁ לְהַשְׁמִיד אֶת־כָּל־הַגּוֹיִם הַבָּאִים עַל־יְרוּשָׁלָ͏ִם׃

10 But I will fill the House of *David* and the inhabitants of *Yerushalayim* with a spirit of pity and compassion; and they shall lament to Me about those who are slain, wailing over them as over a favorite son and showing bitter grief as over a first-born.

י וְשָׁפַכְתִּי עַל־בֵּית דָּוִיד וְעַל יוֹשֵׁב יְרוּשָׁלַ͏ִם רוּחַ חֵן וְתַחֲנוּנִים וְהִבִּיטוּ אֵלַי אֵת אֲשֶׁר־דָּקָרוּ וְסָפְדוּ עָלָיו כְּמִסְפֵּד עַל־הַיָּחִיד וְהָמֵר עָלָיו כְּהָמֵר עַל־הַבְּכוֹר׃

11 In that day, the wailing in *Yerushalayim* shall be as great as the wailing at Hadad-rimmon in the plain of Megiddon.

יא בַּיּוֹם הַהוּא יִגְדַּל הַמִּסְפֵּד בִּירוּשָׁלַ͏ִם כְּמִסְפַּד הֲדַדְ־רִמּוֹן בְּבִקְעַת מְגִדּוֹן׃

12 The land shall wail, each family by itself: The family of the House of *David* by themselves, and their womenfolk by themselves; the family of the House of *Natan* by themselves, and their womenfolk by themselves;

יב וְסָפְדָה הָאָרֶץ מִשְׁפָּחוֹת מִשְׁפָּחוֹת לְבָד מִשְׁפַּחַת בֵּית־דָּוִיד לְבָד וּנְשֵׁיהֶם לְבָד מִשְׁפַּחַת בֵּית־נָתָן לְבָד וּנְשֵׁיהֶם לְבָד׃

13 the family of the House of *Levi* by themselves, and their women-folk by themselves; the family of the Shim'ites by themselves, and their womenfolk by themselves;

יג מִשְׁפַּחַת בֵּית־לֵוִי לְבָד וּנְשֵׁיהֶם לְבָד מִשְׁפַּחַת הַשִּׁמְעִי לְבָד וּנְשֵׁיהֶם לְבָד׃

14 and all the other families, every family by itself, with their womenfolk by themselves.

יד כֹּל הַמִּשְׁפָּחוֹת הַנִּשְׁאָרוֹת מִשְׁפָּחֹת מִשְׁפָּחֹת לְבָד וּנְשֵׁיהֶם לְבָד׃

13

1 In that day a fountain shall be open to the House of *David* and the inhabitants of *Yerushalayim* for purging and cleansing.

יג א בַּיּוֹם הַהוּא יִהְיֶה מָקוֹר נִפְתָּח לְבֵית דָּוִיד וּלְיֹשְׁבֵי יְרוּשָׁלָ͏ִם לְחַטַּאת וּלְנִדָּה׃

ba-YOM ha-HU yih-YEH ma-KOR nif-TAKH l'-VAYT da-VEED ul-yo-sh'-VAY y'-ru-sha-LA-im l'-kha-TAT ul-ni-DAH

13:1 In that day a fountain shall be open This chapter describes the upcoming purification of *Yehuda* and *Yisrael*, as the impure spirit is removed from the land. The purification will take place in *Yerushalayim* through the waters of a fountain that will gush up from the earth and stream over the countryside, purifying the people and the land. Although it is not explicitly named as such, perhaps the source of this fountain is Jerusalem's *Gichon* spring where *Shlomo* was anointed (I Kings 1:38–39), and which provided drinking water as well as irrigation for the gardens in the nearby Kidron valley. The *Gichon* spring was also one of the rivers that flowed from the Garden of Eden mentioned in *Sefer Bereishit* (2:13).

The Kidron Valley

Zecharya/Zechariah
Chapter 14

2 In that day, too – declares the Lord of Hosts – I will erase the very names of the idols from the land; they shall not be uttered any more. And I will also make the "*Neviim*" and the unclean spirit vanish from the land.

3 If anyone "prophesies" thereafter, his own father and mother, who brought him into the world, will say to him, "You shall die, for you have lied in the name of *Hashem*"; and his own father and mother, who brought him into the world, will put him to death when he "prophesies."

4 In that day, every "*Navi*" will be ashamed of the "visions" [he had] when he "prophesied." In order to deceive, he will not wear a hairy mantle,

5 and he will declare, "I am not a '*Navi*'; I am a tiller of the soil; you see, I was plied with the red stuff from my youth on."

6 And if he is asked, "What are those sores on your back?" he will reply, "From being beaten in the homes of my friends."

7 O sword! Rouse yourself against My shepherd, The man in charge of My flock – says the Lord of Hosts. Strike down the shepherd And let the flock scatter; And I will also turn My hand Against all the shepherd boys.

8 Throughout the land – declares *Hashem* – Two-thirds shall perish, shall die, And one-third of it shall survive.

9 That third I will put into the fire, And I will smelt them as one smelts silver And test them as one tests gold. They will invoke Me by name, And I will respond to them. I will declare, "You are My people," And they will declare, "*Hashem* is our God!"

14 1 Lo, a day of *Hashem* is coming when your spoil shall be divided in your very midst!

2 For I will gather all the nations to *Yerushalayim* for war: The city shall be captured, the houses plundered, and the women violated; and a part of the city shall go into exile. But the rest of the population shall not be uprooted from the city.

3 Then *Hashem* will come forth and make war on those nations as He is wont to make war on a day of battle.

זכריה
פרק יד

ב וְהָיָה בַיּוֹם הַהוּא נְאֻם יְהֹוָה צְבָאוֹת אַכְרִית אֶת־שְׁמוֹת הָעֲצַבִּים מִן־הָאָרֶץ וְלֹא יִזָּכְרוּ עוֹד וְגַם אֶת־הַנְּבִיאִים וְאֶת־רוּחַ הַטֻּמְאָה אַעֲבִיר מִן־הָאָרֶץ:

ג וְהָיָה כִּי־יִנָּבֵא אִישׁ עוֹד וְאָמְרוּ אֵלָיו אָבִיו וְאִמּוֹ יֹלְדָיו לֹא תִחְיֶה כִּי שֶׁקֶר דִּבַּרְתָּ בְּשֵׁם יְהֹוָה וּדְקָרֻהוּ אָבִיהוּ וְאִמּוֹ יֹלְדָיו בְּהִנָּבְאוֹ:

ד וְהָיָה בַּיּוֹם הַהוּא יֵבֹשׁוּ הַנְּבִיאִים אִישׁ מֵחֶזְיֹנוֹ בְּהִנָּבְאֹתוֹ וְלֹא יִלְבְּשׁוּ אַדֶּרֶת שֵׂעָר לְמַעַן כַּחֵשׁ:

ה וְאָמַר לֹא נָבִיא אָנֹכִי אִישׁ־עֹבֵד אֲדָמָה אָנֹכִי כִּי אָדָם הִקְנַנִי מִנְּעוּרָי:

ו וְאָמַר אֵלָיו מָה הַמַּכּוֹת הָאֵלֶּה בֵּין יָדֶיךָ וְאָמַר אֲשֶׁר הֻכֵּיתִי בֵּית מְאַהֲבָי:

ז חֶרֶב עוּרִי עַל־רֹעִי וְעַל־גֶּבֶר עֲמִיתִי נְאֻם יְהֹוָה צְבָאוֹת הַךְ אֶת־הָרֹעֶה וּתְפוּצֶיןָ הַצֹּאן וַהֲשִׁבֹתִי יָדִי עַל־הַצֹּעֲרִים:

ח וְהָיָה בְכָל־הָאָרֶץ נְאֻם־יְהֹוָה פִּי־שְׁנַיִם בָּהּ יִכָּרֵתוּ יִגְוָעוּ וְהַשְּׁלִשִׁית יִוָּתֶר בָּהּ:

ט וְהֵבֵאתִי אֶת־הַשְּׁלִשִׁית בָּאֵשׁ וּצְרַפְתִּים כִּצְרֹף אֶת־הַכֶּסֶף וּבְחַנְתִּים כִּבְחֹן אֶת־הַזָּהָב הוּא יִקְרָא בִשְׁמִי וַאֲנִי אֶעֱנֶה אֹתוֹ אָמַרְתִּי עַמִּי הוּא וְהוּא יֹאמַר יְהֹוָה אֱלֹהָי:

יד א הִנֵּה יוֹם־בָּא לַיהֹוָה וְחֻלַּק שְׁלָלֵךְ בְּקִרְבֵּךְ:

ב וְאָסַפְתִּי אֶת־כָּל־הַגּוֹיִם אֶל־יְרוּשָׁלַם לַמִּלְחָמָה וְנִלְכְּדָה הָעִיר וְנָשַׁסּוּ הַבָּתִּים וְהַנָּשִׁים תשגלנה [תִּשָּׁכַבְנָה] וְיָצָא חֲצִי הָעִיר בַּגּוֹלָה וְיֶתֶר הָעָם לֹא יִכָּרֵת מִן־הָעִיר:

ג וְיָצָא יְהֹוָה וְנִלְחַם בַּגּוֹיִם הָהֵם כְּיוֹם הִלָּחֲמוֹ בְּיוֹם קְרָב:

Zecharya/Zechariah
Chapter 14

זכריה
פרק יד

4 On that day, He will set His feet on the Mount of Olives, near *Yerushalayim* on the east; and the Mount of Olives shall split across from east to west, and one part of the Mount shall shift to the north and the other to the south, a huge gorge.

ד וְעָמְדוּ רַגְלָיו בַּיּוֹם־הַהוּא עַל־הַר הַזֵּיתִים אֲשֶׁר עַל־פְּנֵי יְרוּשָׁלַ͏ִם מִקֶּדֶם וְנִבְקַע הַר הַזֵּיתִים מֵחֶצְיוֹ מִזְרָחָה וָיָמָּה גֵּיא גְּדוֹלָה מְאֹד וּמָשׁ חֲצִי הָהָר צָפוֹנָה וְחֶצְיוֹ־נֶגְבָּה׃

5 And the Valley in the Hills shall be stopped up, for the Valley of the Hills shall reach only to Azal; it shall be stopped up as it was stopped up as a result of the earthquake in the days of King *Uzziyahu* of *Yehuda*. – And *Hashem* my God, with all the holy beings, will come to you.

ה וְנַסְתֶּם גֵּיא־הָרַי כִּי־יַגִּיעַ גֵּי־הָרִים אֶל־אָצַל וְנַסְתֶּם כַּאֲשֶׁר נַסְתֶּם מִפְּנֵי הָרַעַשׁ בִּימֵי עֻזִּיָּה מֶלֶךְ־יְהוּדָה וּבָא יְהֹוָה אֱלֹהַי כׇּל־קְדֹשִׁים עִמָּךְ׃

6 In that day, there shall be neither sunlight nor cold moonlight,

ו וְהָיָה בַּיּוֹם הַהוּא לֹא־יִהְיֶה אוֹר יְקָרוֹת יקפאון [וְקִפָּאוֹן׃]

7 but there shall be a continuous day – only *Hashem* knows when – of neither day nor night, and there shall be light at eventide.

ז וְהָיָה יוֹם־אֶחָד הוּא יִוָּדַע לַיהֹוָה לֹא־יוֹם וְלֹא־לָיְלָה וְהָיָה לְעֵת־עֶרֶב יִהְיֶה־אוֹר׃

8 In that day, fresh water shall flow from *Yerushalayim*, part of it to the Eastern Sea and part to the Western Sea, throughout the summer and winter.

ח וְהָיָה בַּיּוֹם הַהוּא יֵצְאוּ מַיִם־חַיִּים מִירוּשָׁלַ͏ִם חֶצְיָם אֶל־הַיָּם הַקַּדְמוֹנִי וְחֶצְיָם אֶל־הַיָּם הָאַחֲרוֹן בַּקַּיִץ וּבָחֹרֶף יִהְיֶה׃

9 And *Hashem* shall be king over all the earth; in that day there shall be one *Hashem* with one name.

ט וְהָיָה יְהֹוָה לְמֶלֶךְ עַל־כׇּל־הָאָרֶץ בַּיּוֹם הַהוּא יִהְיֶה יְהֹוָה אֶחָד וּשְׁמוֹ אֶחָד׃

10 Then the whole country shall become like the Arabah, from Geba to Rimmon south of *Yerushalayim*. The latter, however, shall perch high up where it is, and shall be inhabited* from the Gate of *Binyamin* to the site of the Old Gate, down to the Corner Gate, and from the Tower of Hananel to the king's winepresses.

י יִסּוֹב כׇּל־הָאָרֶץ כָּעֲרָבָה מִגֶּבַע לְרִמּוֹן נֶגֶב יְרוּשָׁלָ͏ִם וְרָאֲמָה וְיָשְׁבָה תַחְתֶּיהָ לְמִשַּׁעַר בִּנְיָמִן עַד־מְקוֹם שַׁעַר הָרִאשׁוֹן עַד־שַׁעַר הַפִּנִּים וּמִגְדַּל חֲנַנְאֵל עַד יִקְבֵי הַמֶּלֶךְ׃

11 Never again shall destruction be decreed, and *Yerushalayim* shall dwell secure.

יא וְיָשְׁבוּ בָהּ וְחֵרֶם לֹא יִהְיֶה־עוֹד וְיָשְׁבָה יְרוּשָׁלַ͏ִם לָבֶטַח׃

12 As for those peoples that warred against *Yerushalayim*, *Hashem* will smite them with this plague: Their flesh shall rot away while they stand on their feet; their eyes shall rot away in their sockets; and their tongues shall rot away in their mouths.

יב וְזֹאת תִּהְיֶה הַמַּגֵּפָה אֲשֶׁר יִגֹּף יְהֹוָה אֶת־כׇּל־הָעַמִּים אֲשֶׁר צָבְאוּ עַל־יְרוּשָׁלָ͏ִם הָמֵק בְּשָׂרוֹ וְהוּא עֹמֵד עַל־רַגְלָיו וְעֵינָיו תִּמַּקְנָה בְחֹרֵיהֶן וּלְשׁוֹנוֹ תִּמַּק בְּפִיהֶם׃

13 In that day, a great panic from *Hashem* shall fall upon them, and everyone shall snatch at the hand of another, and everyone shall raise his hand against everyone else's hand.

יג וְהָיָה בַּיּוֹם הַהוּא תִּהְיֶה מְהוּמַת־יְהֹוָה רַבָּה בָּהֶם וְהֶחֱזִיקוּ אִישׁ יַד רֵעֵהוּ וְעָלְתָה יָדוֹ עַל־יַד רֵעֵהוּ׃

---

* "shall be inhabited" brought up from verse 11 for clarity

Zecharya/Zechariah
Chapter 14

זכריה
פרק יד

14 *Yehuda* shall join the fighting in *Yerushalayim*, and the wealth of all the nations roundabout – vast quantities of gold, silver, and clothing – shall be gathered in.

יד וְגַם־יְהוּדָה תִּלָּחֵם בִּירוּשָׁלָ͏ִם וְאֻסַּף חֵיל כָּל־הַגּוֹיִם סָבִיב זָהָב וָכֶסֶף וּבְגָדִים לָרֹב מְאֹד׃

15 The same plague shall strike the horses, the mules, the camels, and the asses; the plague shall affect all the animals in those camps.

טו וְכֵן תִּהְיֶה מַגֵּפַת הַסּוּס הַפֶּרֶד הַגָּמָל וְהַחֲמוֹר וְכָל־הַבְּהֵמָה אֲשֶׁר יִהְיֶה בַּמַּחֲנוֹת הָהֵמָּה כַּמַּגֵּפָה הַזֹּאת׃

16 All who survive of all those nations that came up against *Yerushalayim* shall make a pilgrimage year by year to bow low to the King LORD of Hosts and to observe the festival of *Sukkot*.

טז וְהָיָה כָּל־הַנּוֹתָר מִכָּל־הַגּוֹיִם הַבָּאִים עַל־יְרוּשָׁלָ͏ִם וְעָלוּ מִדֵּי שָׁנָה בְשָׁנָה לְהִשְׁתַּחֲוֺת לְמֶלֶךְ יְהֹוָה צְבָאוֹת וְלָחֹג אֶת־חַג הַסֻּכּוֹת׃

v'-ha-YAH kol ha-no-TAR mi-kol ha-go-YIM ha-ba-EEM al y'-ru-sha-LA-im v'-a-LU mi-DAY sha-NAH v'-sha-NAH l'-hish-ta-kha-VOT l'-ME-lekh a-do-NAI tz'-va-OT v'-la-KHOG et KHAG ha-su-KOT

17 Any of the earth's communities that does not make the pilgrimage to *Yerushalayim* to bow low to the King LORD of Hosts shall receive no rain.

יז וְהָיָה אֲשֶׁר לֹא־יַעֲלֶה מֵאֵת מִשְׁפְּחוֹת הָאָרֶץ אֶל־יְרוּשָׁלַ͏ִם לְהִשְׁתַּחֲוֺת לְמֶלֶךְ יְהֹוָה צְבָאוֹת וְלֹא עֲלֵיהֶם יִהְיֶה הַגָּשֶׁם׃

18 However, if the community of Egypt does not make this pilgrimage, it shall not be visited by the same affliction with which *Hashem* will strike the other nations that do not come up to observe the festival of *Sukkot*.

יח וְאִם־מִשְׁפַּחַת מִצְרַיִם לֹא־תַעֲלֶה וְלֹא בָאָה וְלֹא עֲלֵיהֶם תִּהְיֶה הַמַּגֵּפָה אֲשֶׁר יִגֹּף יְהֹוָה אֶת־הַגּוֹיִם אֲשֶׁר לֹא יַעֲלוּ לָחֹג אֶת־חַג הַסֻּכּוֹת׃

19 Such shall be the punishment of Egypt and of all other nations that do not come up to observe the festival of *Sukkot*.

יט זֹאת תִּהְיֶה חַטַּאת מִצְרָיִם וְחַטַּאת כָּל־הַגּוֹיִם אֲשֶׁר לֹא יַעֲלוּ לָחֹג אֶת־חַג הַסֻּכּוֹת׃

20 In that day, even the bells on the horses shall be inscribed "Holy to *Hashem*." The metal pots in the House of *Hashem* shall be like the basins before the *Mizbayach*;

כ בַּיּוֹם הַהוּא יִהְיֶה עַל־מְצִלּוֹת הַסּוּס קֹדֶשׁ לַיהֹוָה וְהָיָה הַסִּירוֹת בְּבֵית יְהֹוָה כַּמִּזְרָקִים לִפְנֵי הַמִּזְבֵּחַ׃

21 indeed, every metal pot in *Yerushalayim* and in *Yehuda* shall be holy to the LORD of Hosts. And all those who sacrifice shall come and take of these to boil [their sacrificial meat] in; in that day there shall be no more traders in the House of the LORD of Hosts.

כא וְהָיָה כָּל־סִיר בִּירוּשָׁלַ͏ִם וּבִיהוּדָה קֹדֶשׁ לַיהֹוָה צְבָאוֹת וּבָאוּ כָּל־הַזֹּבְחִים וְלָקְחוּ מֵהֶם וּבִשְּׁלוּ בָהֶם וְלֹא־יִהְיֶה כְנַעֲנִי עוֹד בְּבֵית־יְהֹוָה צְבָאוֹת בַּיּוֹם הַהוּא׃

14:16 All who survive of all those nations At the end of days, the righteous from amongst the nations will make a pilgrimage to *Yerushalayim* on *Sukkot*, the feast of Tabernacles. On this universal holiday, Israel prays for winter rain and offers sacrifices in the *Beit Hamikdash* on behalf of the seventy nations of the world. Today, one of the most beautiful events in *Yerushalayim* during *Sukkot* is the massive parade through the streets of the holy city where thousands of non-Jews, representatives of the nations of the world, fulfill these moving words of *Zecharya*.

Chinese delegation at the Jerusalem March

Sefer Malachi
The Book of Malachi

The last of the *Trei Asar*, *Sefer Malachi* (Malachi), not only concludes the twelve prophets in this book, but also represents the end of the era of prophecy in Israel. As such, this book must be understood as a transition. The people are adjusting to life in the resettled Land of Israel, and to a world without prophecy. The book's theme is outlined at the outset – God's love for His people Israel has never waned. The prophet is motivated to rebuke the Children of Israel so that they again become worthy of receiving His love.

It is difficult to pinpoint exactly when *Malachi* lived, or even if this was his personal name or a title of some sort, as it means "my messenger." The Talmud (*Megila* 15a) even suggests that he was *Ezra*. However, we do know that he prophesied sometime after the second *Beit Hamikdash* had been built in *Yerushalayim*. The enthusiasm that had accompanied the original pilgrims and returnees had dissipated, and the people's moral standards had slipped. Offerings were given at the Temple, but only perfunctorily, without emotion or passion. Gifts and tithes were only occasionally brought to *Yerushalayim*. There was a problem of intermarriage between Jewish men and local Canaanite women and other foreigners, similar to the problems faced by *Ezra* when he arrived in Israel in 458 BCE. The underlying malaise that gripped the people was that they did not consider themselves special or worthy of *Hashem*'s attention or affection. This sense permeated their lives, and the commandments were performed by rote, if at all.

Malachi/Malachi
Chapter 1

מלאכי
פרק א

1 ¹ A pronouncement: The word of *Hashem* to *Yisrael* through *Malachi*.

א מַשָּׂא דְבַר־יְהֹוָה אֶל־יִשְׂרָאֵל בְּיַד מַלְאָכִֽי׃

² I have shown you love, said *Hashem*. But you ask, "How have You shown us love?" After all – declares *Hashem* – Esau is *Yaakov*'s brother; yet I have accepted *Yaakov*

ב אָהַבְתִּי אֶתְכֶם אָמַר יְהֹוָה וַאֲמַרְתֶּם בַּמָּה אֲהַבְתָּנוּ הֲלוֹא־אָח עֵשָׂו לְיַעֲקֹב נְאֻם־יְהֹוָה וָאֹהַב אֶת־יַעֲקֹֽב׃

³ and have rejected Esau. I have made his hills a desolation, his territory a home for beasts of the desert.

ג וְאֶת־עֵשָׂו שָׂנֵאתִי וָאָשִׂים אֶת־הָרָיו שְׁמָמָה וְאֶת־נַחֲלָתוֹ לְתַנּוֹת מִדְבָּֽר׃

⁴ If Edom thinks, "Though crushed, we can build the ruins again," thus said the Lord of Hosts: They may build, but I will tear down. And so they shall be known as the region of wickedness, the people damned forever of *Hashem*.

ד כִּי־תֹאמַר אֱדוֹם רֻשַּׁשְׁנוּ וְנָשׁוּב וְנִבְנֶה חֳרָבוֹת כֹּה אָמַר יְהֹוָה צְבָאוֹת הֵמָּה יִבְנוּ וַאֲנִי אֶהֱרוֹס וְקָרְאוּ לָהֶם גְּבוּל רִשְׁעָה וְהָעָם אֲשֶׁר־זָעַם יְהֹוָה עַד־עוֹלָֽם׃

⁵ Your eyes shall behold it, and you shall declare, "Great is *Hashem* beyond the borders of *Yisrael*!"

ה וְעֵינֵיכֶם תִּרְאֶינָה וְאַתֶּם תֹּאמְרוּ יִגְדַּל יְהֹוָה מֵעַל לִגְבוּל יִשְׂרָאֵֽל׃

v'-ay-nay-KHEM tir-E-nah v'-a-TEM to-m'-RU yig-DAL a-do-NAI may-AL lig-VUL yis-ra-AYL

⁶ A son should honor his father, and a slave his master. Now if I am a father, where is the honor due Me? And if I am a master, where is the reverence due Me? – said the Lord of Hosts to you, O *Kohanim* who scorn My name. But you ask, "How have we scorned Your name?"

ו בֵּן יְכַבֵּד אָב וְעֶבֶד אֲדֹנָיו וְאִם־אָב אָנִי אַיֵּה כְבוֹדִי וְאִם־אֲדוֹנִים אָנִי אַיֵּה מוֹרָאִי אָמַר יְהֹוָה צְבָאוֹת לָכֶם הַכֹּהֲנִים בּוֹזֵי שְׁמִי וַאֲמַרְתֶּם בַּמֶּה בָזִינוּ אֶת־שְׁמֶֽךָ׃

⁷ You offer defiled food on My *Mizbayach*. But you ask, "How have we defiled You?" By saying, "The table of *Hashem* can be treated with scorn."

ז מַגִּישִׁים עַל־מִזְבְּחִי לֶחֶם מְגֹאָל וַאֲמַרְתֶּם בַּמֶּה גֵאַלְנוּךָ בֶּאֱמׇרְכֶם שֻׁלְחַן יְהֹוָה נִבְזֶה הֽוּא׃

⁸ When you present a blind animal for sacrifice – it doesn't matter! When you present a lame or sick one – it doesn't matter! Just offer it to your governor: Will he accept you? Will he show you favor? – said the Lord of Hosts.

ח וְכִי־תַגִּשׁוּן עִוֵּר לִזְבֹּחַ אֵין רָע וְכִי תַגִּישׁוּ פִּסֵּחַ וְחֹלֶה אֵין רָע הַקְרִיבֵהוּ נָא לְפֶחָתֶךָ הֲיִרְצְךָ אוֹ הֲיִשָּׂא פָנֶיךָ אָמַר יְהֹוָה צְבָאֽוֹת׃

⁹ And now implore the favor of *Hashem*! Will He be gracious to us? This is what you have done – will He accept any of you? the Lord of Hosts has said:

ט וְעַתָּה חַלּוּ־נָא פְנֵי־אֵל וִיחׇנֵּנוּ מִיֶּדְכֶם הָיְתָה זֹּאת הֲיִשָּׂא מִכֶּם פָּנִים אָמַר יְהֹוָה צְבָאֽוֹת׃

Rabbi Abraham Ibn Ezra (1089–1167)

1:5 Great is *Hashem* beyond the borders of *Yisrael* Unlike the people of Edom, whose evil behavior causes God to cast them away repeatedly and call their boundary "the region of wickedness" (verses 3–4), *Hashem*'s love for Israel is unending and unconditional (verse 2). When the Jewish people recognize this, it will be declared that "*Hashem* is great beyond the border of Israel." These words can be understood in two ways. The commentator *Ibn Ezra* suggests that it means even those outside of Israel will say "*Hashem* is great." More likely, it means that the People of Israel themselves will call out excitedly "Great is *Hashem*, beyond the borders of *Yisrael*."

Malachi/Malachi
Chapter 2

מלאכי
פרק ב

10 If only you would lock My doors, and not kindle fire on My *Mizbayach* to no purpose! I take no pleasure in you – said the Lord of Hosts – and I will accept no offering from you.

י מִי גַם־בָּכֶם וְיִסְגֹּר דְּלָתַיִם וְלֹא־תָאִירוּ מִזְבְּחִי חִנָּם אֵין־לִי חֵפֶץ בָּכֶם אָמַר יְהוָה צְבָאוֹת וּמִנְחָה לֹא־אֶרְצֶה מִיֶּדְכֶם׃

11 For from where the sun rises to where it sets, My name is honored among the nations, and everywhere incense and pure oblation are offered to My name; for My name is honored among the nations – said the Lord of Hosts.

יא כִּי מִמִּזְרַח־שֶׁמֶשׁ וְעַד־מְבוֹאוֹ גָּדוֹל שְׁמִי בַּגּוֹיִם וּבְכָל־מָקוֹם מֻקְטָר מֻגָּשׁ לִשְׁמִי וּמִנְחָה טְהוֹרָה כִּי־גָדוֹל שְׁמִי בַּגּוֹיִם אָמַר יְהוָה צְבָאוֹת׃

12 But you profane it when you say, "The table of *Hashem* is defiled and the meat, the food, can be treated with scorn."

יב וְאַתֶּם מְחַלְּלִים אוֹתוֹ בֶּאֱמָרְכֶם שֻׁלְחַן אֲדֹנָי מְגֹאָל הוּא וְנִיבוֹ נִבְזֶה אָכְלוֹ׃

13 You say, "Oh, what a bother!" And so you degrade it – said the Lord of Hosts – and you bring the stolen, the lame, and the sick; and you offer such as an oblation. Will I accept it from you? – said *Hashem*.

יג וַאֲמַרְתֶּם הִנֵּה מַתְּלָאָה וְהִפַּחְתֶּם אוֹתוֹ אָמַר יְהוָה צְבָאוֹת וַהֲבֵאתֶם גָּזוּל וְאֶת־הַפִּסֵּחַ וְאֶת־הַחוֹלֶה וַהֲבֵאתֶם אֶת־הַמִּנְחָה הַאֶרְצֶה אוֹתָהּ מִיֶּדְכֶם אָמַר יְהוָה׃

14 A curse on the cheat who has an [unblemished] male in his flock, but for his vow sacrifices a blemished animal to *Hashem*! For I am a great King – said the Lord of Hosts – and My name is revered among the nations.

יד וְאָרוּר נוֹכֵל וְיֵשׁ בְּעֶדְרוֹ זָכָר וְנֹדֵר וְזֹבֵחַ מָשְׁחָת לַאדֹנָי כִּי מֶלֶךְ גָּדוֹל אָנִי אָמַר יְהוָה צְבָאוֹת וּשְׁמִי נוֹרָא בַגּוֹיִם׃

2 1 And now, O *Kohanim*, this charge is for you:

ב א וְעַתָּה אֲלֵיכֶם הַמִּצְוָה הַזֹּאת הַכֹּהֲנִים׃

2 Unless you obey and unless you lay it to heart, and do honor to My name – said the Lord of Hosts – I will send a curse and turn your blessings into curses. (Indeed, I have turned them into curses, because you do not lay it to heart.)

ב אִם־לֹא תִשְׁמְעוּ וְאִם־לֹא תָשִׂימוּ עַל־לֵב לָתֵת כָּבוֹד לִשְׁמִי אָמַר יְהוָה צְבָאוֹת וְשִׁלַּחְתִּי בָכֶם אֶת־הַמְּאֵרָה וְאָרוֹתִי אֶת־בִּרְכוֹתֵיכֶם וְגַם אָרוֹתִיהָ כִּי אֵינְכֶם שָׂמִים עַל־לֵב׃

3 I will put your seed under a ban, and I will strew dung upon your faces, the dung of your festal sacrifices, and you shall be carried out to its [heap].

ג הִנְנִי גֹעֵר לָכֶם אֶת־הַזֶּרַע וְזֵרִיתִי פֶרֶשׁ עַל־פְּנֵיכֶם פֶּרֶשׁ חַגֵּיכֶם וְנָשָׂא אֶתְכֶם אֵלָיו׃

4 Know, then, that I have sent this charge to you that My covenant with *Levi* may endure – said the Lord of Hosts.

ד וִידַעְתֶּם כִּי שִׁלַּחְתִּי אֲלֵיכֶם אֵת הַמִּצְוָה הַזֹּאת לִהְיוֹת בְּרִיתִי אֶת־לֵוִי אָמַר יְהוָה צְבָאוֹת׃

5 I had with him a covenant of life and well-being, which I gave to him, and of reverence, which he showed Me. For he stood in awe of My name.

ה בְּרִיתִי הָיְתָה אִתּוֹ הַחַיִּים וְהַשָּׁלוֹם וָאֶתְּנֵם־לוֹ מוֹרָא וַיִּירָאֵנִי וּמִפְּנֵי שְׁמִי נִחַת הוּא׃

6 Proper rulings were in his mouth, And nothing perverse was on his lips; He served Me with complete loyalty And held the many back from iniquity.

ו תּוֹרַת אֱמֶת הָיְתָה בְּפִיהוּ וְעַוְלָה לֹא־נִמְצָא בִשְׂפָתָיו בְּשָׁלוֹם וּבְמִישׁוֹר הָלַךְ אִתִּי וְרַבִּים הֵשִׁיב מֵעָוֺן׃

Malachi/Malachi
Chapter 2

מלאכי
פרק ב

7 For the lips of a *Kohen* guard knowledge, And men seek rulings from his mouth; For he is a messenger of the Lord of Hosts.

כִּֽי־שִׂפְתֵ֤י כֹהֵן֙ יִשְׁמְרוּ־דַ֔עַת וְתוֹרָ֖ה יְבַקְשׁ֣וּ מִפִּ֑יהוּ כִּ֛י מַלְאַ֥ךְ יְהֹוָֽה־צְבָא֖וֹת הֽוּא׃

kee sif-TAY kho-HAYN yish-m'-ru DA-at v'-to-RAH y'-vak-SHU mi-PEE-hu KEE mal-AKH a-do-nai tz'-va-OT HU

8 But you have turned away from that course: You have made the many stumble through your rulings; you have corrupted the covenant of the *Leviim* – said the Lord of Hosts.

וְאַתֶּם֙ סַרְתֶּ֣ם מִן־הַדֶּ֔רֶךְ הִכְשַׁלְתֶּ֥ם רַבִּ֖ים בַּתּוֹרָ֑ה שִֽׁחַתֶּם֙ בְּרִ֣ית הַלֵּוִ֔י אָמַ֖ר יְהֹוָ֥ה צְבָאֽוֹת׃

9 And I, in turn, have made you despicable and vile in the eyes of all the people, because you disregard My ways and show partiality in your rulings.

וְגַם־אֲנִ֞י נָתַ֧תִּי אֶתְכֶ֛ם נִבְזִ֥ים וּשְׁפָלִ֖ים לְכׇל־הָעָ֑ם כְּפִ֗י אֲשֶׁ֤ר אֵֽינְכֶם֙ שֹׁמְרִ֣ים אֶת־דְּרָכַ֔י וְנֹשְׂאִ֥ים פָּנִ֖ים בַּתּוֹרָֽה׃

10 Have we not all one Father? Did not one *Hashem* create us? Why do we break faith with one another, profaning the covenant of our ancestors?

הֲל֨וֹא אָ֤ב אֶחָד֙ לְכֻלָּ֔נוּ הֲל֛וֹא אֵ֥ל אֶחָ֖ד בְּרָאָ֑נוּ מַדּ֗וּעַ נִבְגַּד֙ אִ֣ישׁ בְּאָחִ֔יו לְחַלֵּ֖ל בְּרִ֥ית אֲבֹתֵֽינוּ׃

11 *Yehuda* has broken faith; abhorrent things have been done in *Yisrael* and in *Yerushalayim*. For *Yehuda* has profaned what is holy to *Hashem* – what He desires – and espoused daughters of alien gods.

בָּגְדָ֣ה יְהוּדָ֔ה וְתוֹעֵבָ֛ה נֶעֶשְׂתָ֥ה בְיִשְׂרָאֵ֖ל וּבִירֽוּשָׁלָ֑͏ִם כִּ֣י ׀ חִלֵּ֣ל יְהוּדָ֗ה קֹ֤דֶשׁ יְהֹוָה֙ אֲשֶׁ֣ר אָהֵ֔ב וּבָעַ֖ל בַּת־אֵ֥ל נֵכָֽר׃

12 May *Hashem* leave to him who does this no descendants dwelling in the tents of *Yaakov* and presenting offerings to the Lord of Hosts.

יַכְרֵ֨ת יְהֹוָ֜ה לָאִ֨ישׁ אֲשֶׁ֣ר יַעֲשֶׂ֗נָּה עֵ֤ר וְעֹנֶה֙ מֵאׇהֳלֵ֣י יַעֲקֹ֔ב וּמַגִּ֥ישׁ מִנְחָ֖ה לַיהֹוָ֥ה צְבָאֽוֹת׃

13 And this you do as well: You cover the *Mizbayach* of *Hashem* with tears, weeping, and moaning, so that He refuses to regard the oblation any more and to accept what you offer.

וְזֹאת֙ שֵׁנִ֣ית תַּעֲשׂ֔וּ כַּסּ֤וֹת דִּמְעָה֙ אֶת־מִזְבַּ֣ח יְהֹוָ֔ה בְּכִ֖י וַֽאֲנָקָ֑ה מֵאֵ֣ין ע֗וֹד פְּנוֹת֙ אֶל־הַמִּנְחָ֔ה וְלָקַ֥חַת רָצ֖וֹן מִיֶּדְכֶֽם׃

14 But you ask, "Because of what?" Because *Hashem* is a witness between you and the wife of your youth with whom you have broken faith, though she is your partner and covenanted spouse.

וַאֲמַרְתֶּ֖ם עַל־מָ֑ה עַ֡ל כִּי־יְהֹוָה֩ הֵעִ֨יד בֵּינְךָ֜ וּבֵ֣ין ׀ אֵ֣שֶׁת נְעוּרֶ֗יךָ אֲשֶׁ֤ר אַתָּה֙ בָּגַ֣דְתָּה בָּ֔הּ וְהִ֥יא חֲבֶרְתְּךָ֖ וְאֵ֥שֶׁת בְּרִיתֶֽךָ׃

15 Did not the One make [all,] so that all remaining life-breath is His? And what does that One seek but godly folk? So be careful of your life-breath, and let no one break faith with the wife of his youth.

וְלֹא־אֶחָ֣ד עָשָׂ֗ה וּשְׁאָ֥ר ר֙וּחַ֙ ל֔וֹ וּמָה֙ הָֽאֶחָ֔ד מְבַקֵּ֖שׁ זֶ֣רַע אֱלֹהִ֑ים וְנִשְׁמַרְתֶּם֙ בְּרֽוּחֲכֶ֔ם וּבְאֵ֥שֶׁת נְעוּרֶ֖יךָ אַל־יִבְגֹּֽד׃

2:7 For the lips of a *Kohen* guard knowledge Malachi explains that the priests' responsibilities extend beyond service in the *Beit Hamikdash* to include teaching *Hashem*'s law to the people. Knowledge is not just conveyed; it is guarded and preserved so that the message is transmitted faithfully. That can be done only if the *Kohanim* themselves are men of integrity and truth. Just as water can be contaminated if kept in a rusty container, God's teaching must be protected and spread by men about whom it can be said "nothing perverse was on his lips; he served Me with complete loyalty" (verse 6).

Malachi/Malachi
Chapter 3

16 For I detest divorce – said *Hashem*, the God of *Yisrael* – and covering oneself with lawlessness as with a garment – said the Lord of Hosts. So be careful of your life-breath and do not act treacherously.

17 You have wearied *Hashem* with your talk. But you ask, "By what have we wearied [Him]?" By saying, "All who do evil are good in the sight of *Hashem*, and in them He delights," or else, "Where is the God of justice?"

3 1 Behold, I am sending My messenger to clear the way before Me, and the Lord whom you seek shall come to His Temple suddenly. As for the angel of the covenant that you desire, he is already coming.

2 But who can endure the day of his coming, and who can hold out when he appears? For he is like a smelter's fire and like fuller's lye.

3 He shall act like a smelter and purger of silver; and he shall purify the descendants of *Levi* and refine them like gold and silver, so that they shall present offerings in righteousness.

4 Then the offerings of *Yehuda* and *Yerushalayim* shall be pleasing to *Hashem* as in the days of yore and in the years of old.

5 But [first] I will step forward to contend against you, and I will act as a relentless accuser against those who have no fear of Me: Who practice sorcery, who commit adultery, who swear falsely, who cheat laborers of their hire, and who subvert [the cause of] the widow, orphan, and stranger, said the Lord of Hosts.

6 For I am *Hashem* – I have not changed; and you are the children of *Yaakov* – you have not ceased to be.

7 From the very days of your fathers you have turned away from My laws and have not observed them. Turn back to Me, and I will turn back to you – said the Lord of Hosts. But you ask, "How shall we turn back?"

8 Ought man to defraud *Hashem*? Yet you are defrauding Me. And you ask, "How have we been defrauding You?" In tithe and contribution.

9 You are suffering under a curse, yet you go on defrauding Me – the whole nation of you.

Malachi / Malachi
Chapter 3

10 Bring the full tithe into the storehouse, and let there be food in My House, and thus put Me to the test – said the Lord of Hosts. I will surely open the floodgates of the sky for you and pour down blessings on you;

11 and I will banish the locusts from you, so that they will not destroy the yield of your soil; and your vines in the field shall no longer miscarry – said the Lord of Hosts.

12 And all the nations shall account you happy, for you shall be the most desired of lands – said the Lord of Hosts.

13 You have spoken hard words against Me – said *Hashem*. But you ask, "What have we been saying among ourselves against You?"

14 You have said, "It is useless to serve *Hashem*. What have we gained by keeping His charge and walking in abject awe of the Lord of Hosts?

15 And so, we account the arrogant happy: they have indeed done evil and endured; they have indeed dared *Hashem* and escaped."

16 In this vein have those who revere *Hashem* been talking to one another. *Hashem* has heard and noted it, and a scroll of remembrance has been written at His behest concerning those who revere *Hashem* and esteem His name.

17 And on the day that I am preparing, said the Lord of Hosts, they shall be My treasured possession; I will be tender toward them as a man is tender toward a son who ministers to him.

18 And you shall come to see the difference between the righteous and the wicked, between him who has served *Hashem* and him who has not served Him.

19 For lo! That day is at hand, burning like an oven. All the arrogant and all the doers of evil shall be straw, and the day that is coming – said the Lord of Hosts – shall burn them to ashes and leave of them neither stock nor boughs.

20 But for you who revere My name a sun of victory shall rise to bring healing. You shall go forth and stamp like stall-fed calves,

מלאכי
פרק ג

י הָבִ֨יאוּ אֶת־כׇּל־הַֽמַּעֲשֵׂ֜ר אֶל־בֵּ֣ית הָאוֹצָ֗ר וִיהִ֥י טֶ֙רֶף֙ בְּבֵיתִ֔י וּבְחָנ֤וּנִי נָא֙ בָּזֹ֔את אָמַ֖ר יְהֹוָ֣ה צְבָא֑וֹת אִם־לֹ֧א אֶפְתַּ֣ח לָכֶ֗ם אֵ֚ת אֲרֻבּ֣וֹת הַשָּׁמַ֔יִם וַהֲרִיקֹתִ֥י לָכֶ֛ם בְּרָכָ֖ה עַד־בְּלִי־דָֽי׃

יא וְגָעַרְתִּ֤י לָכֶם֙ בָּֽאֹכֵ֔ל וְלֹֽא־יַשְׁחִ֥ת לָכֶ֖ם אֶת־פְּרִ֣י הָאֲדָמָ֑ה וְלֹא־תְשַׁכֵּ֨ל לָכֶ֤ם הַגֶּ֙פֶן֙ בַּשָּׂדֶ֔ה אָמַ֖ר יְהֹוָ֥ה צְבָאֽוֹת׃

יב וְאִשְּׁר֥וּ אֶתְכֶ֖ם כׇּל־הַגּוֹיִ֑ם כִּֽי־תִהְי֤וּ אַתֶּם֙ אֶ֣רֶץ חֵ֔פֶץ אָמַ֖ר יְהֹוָ֥ה צְבָאֽוֹת׃

יג חָזְק֥וּ עָלַ֛י דִּבְרֵיכֶ֖ם אָמַ֣ר יְהֹוָ֑ה וַאֲמַרְתֶּ֕ם מַה־נִּדְבַּ֖רְנוּ עָלֶֽיךָ׃

יד אֲמַרְתֶּ֕ם שָׁ֖וְא עֲבֹ֣ד אֱלֹהִ֑ים וּמַה־בֶּ֗צַע כִּ֤י שָׁמַ֙רְנוּ֙ מִשְׁמַרְתּ֔וֹ וְכִ֤י הָלַ֙כְנוּ֙ קְדֹ֣רַנִּ֔ית מִפְּנֵ֖י יְהֹוָ֥ה צְבָאֽוֹת׃

טו וְעַתָּ֕ה אֲנַ֖חְנוּ מְאַשְּׁרִ֣ים זֵדִ֑ים גַּם־נִבְנוּ֙ עֹשֵׂ֣י רִשְׁעָ֔ה גַּ֥ם בָּחֲנ֛וּ אֱלֹהִ֖ים וַיִּמָּלֵֽטוּ׃

טז אָ֧ז נִדְבְּר֛וּ יִרְאֵ֥י יְהֹוָ֖ה אִ֣ישׁ אֶת־רֵעֵ֑הוּ וַיַּקְשֵׁ֤ב יְהֹוָה֙ וַיִּשְׁמָ֔ע וַ֠יִּכָּתֵ֠ב סֵ֣פֶר זִכָּר֤וֹן לְפָנָיו֙ לְיִרְאֵ֣י יְהֹוָ֔ה וּלְחֹשְׁבֵ֖י שְׁמֽוֹ׃

יז וְהָ֣יוּ לִ֗י אָמַר֙ יְהֹוָ֣ה צְבָא֔וֹת לַיּ֕וֹם אֲשֶׁ֥ר אֲנִ֖י עֹשֶׂ֣ה סְגֻלָּ֑ה וְחָמַלְתִּ֣י עֲלֵיהֶ֔ם כַּֽאֲשֶׁר֙ יַחְמֹ֣ל אִ֔ישׁ עַל־בְּנ֖וֹ הָעֹבֵ֥ד אֹתֽוֹ׃

יח וְשַׁבְתֶּם֙ וּרְאִיתֶ֔ם בֵּ֥ין צַדִּ֖יק לְרָשָׁ֑ע בֵּ֚ין עֹבֵ֣ד אֱלֹהִ֔ים לַאֲשֶׁ֖ר לֹ֥א עֲבָדֽוֹ׃

יט כִּֽי־הִנֵּ֤ה הַיּוֹם֙ בָּ֔א בֹּעֵ֖ר כַּתַּנּ֑וּר וְהָי֨וּ כׇל־זֵדִ֜ים וְכׇל־עֹשֵׂ֤ה רִשְׁעָה֙ קַ֔שׁ וְלִהַ֨ט אֹתָ֜ם הַיּ֣וֹם הַבָּ֗א אָמַר֙ יְהֹוָ֣ה צְבָא֔וֹת אֲשֶׁ֛ר לֹא־יַעֲזֹ֥ב לָהֶ֖ם שֹׁ֥רֶשׁ וְעָנָֽף׃

כ וְזָרְחָ֨ה לָכֶ֜ם יִרְאֵ֤י שְׁמִי֙ שֶׁ֣מֶשׁ צְדָקָ֔ה וּמַרְפֵּ֖א בִּכְנָפֶ֑יהָ וִיצָאתֶ֥ם וּפִשְׁתֶּ֖ם כְּעֶגְלֵ֥י מַרְבֵּֽק׃

Malachi/Malachi

Chapter 3

מלאכי

פרק ג

21 and you shall trample the wicked to a pulp, for they shall be dust beneath your feet on the day that I am preparing – said the Lord of Hosts.

כא וְעַסּוֹתֶ֣ם רְשָׁעִ֔ים כִּֽי־יִהְי֣וּ אֵ֔פֶר תַּ֖חַת כַּפּ֣וֹת רַגְלֵיכֶ֑ם בַּיּוֹם֙ אֲשֶׁ֣ר אֲנִ֣י עֹשֶׂ֔ה אָמַ֖ר יְהֹוָ֥ה צְבָאֽוֹת׃

22 Be mindful of the Teaching of My servant *Moshe*, whom I charged at Horeb with laws and rules for all *Yisrael*.

כב זִכְר֕וּ תּוֹרַ֖ת מֹשֶׁ֣ה עַבְדִּ֑י אֲשֶׁר֩ צִוִּ֨יתִי אוֹת֤וֹ בְחֹרֵב֙ עַל־כָּל־יִשְׂרָאֵ֔ל חֻקִּ֖ים וּמִשְׁפָּטִֽים׃

23 Lo, I will send the *Navi Eliyahu* to you before the coming of the awesome, fearful day of *Hashem*.

כג הִנֵּ֤ה אָֽנֹכִי֙ שֹׁלֵ֣חַ לָכֶ֔ם אֵ֖ת אֵלִיָּ֣ה הַנָּבִ֑יא לִפְנֵ֗י בּ֚וֹא י֣וֹם יְהֹוָ֔ה הַגָּד֖וֹל וְהַנּוֹרָֽא׃

hi-NAY a-no-KHEE sho-LAY-akh la-KHEM AYT ay-li-YAH ha-na-VEE lif-NAY BO YOM a-do-NAI ha-ga-DOL v'-ha-no-RA

24 He shall reconcile parents with children and children with their parents, so that, when I come, I do not strike the whole land with utter destruction. Lo, I will send the *Navi Eliyahu* to you before the coming of the awesome, fearful day of *Hashem*.

כד וְהֵשִׁ֤יב לֵב־אָבוֹת֙ עַל־בָּנִ֔ים וְלֵ֥ב בָּנִ֖ים עַל־אֲבוֹתָ֑ם פֶּן־אָב֕וֹא וְהִכֵּיתִ֥י אֶת־הָאָ֖רֶץ חֵֽרֶם׃ [הנה אנכי שלח לכם את אליה הנביא לפני בוא יום יהוה הגדול והנורא]

Twelve Prophets

3:23 Lo, I will send the *Navi Eliyahu* *Malachi*'s last words mark the closing of the era of prophecy. He ends his final message by stating that the day of *Hashem* is coming, preceded by the arrival of *Eliyahu* the prophet. On that day, the prophet's role will not be to overthrow nations, but as verse 24 continues, to "reconcile parents with children and children with their parents." Only when our homes are filled with harmony and love, teaches *Malachi*, can we begin to dream of peace and understanding on a global scale.

1470

Sefer Tehillim
The Book of Psalms

Introduction and commentary by Rabbi Avi Baumol

Sefer Tehillim (Psalms) is first and foremost a shining example of biblical poetry. This genre conveys the word of God in a different medium than narrative; it focuses not on what one reads or hears but rather on what one feels and intuits. The Bible integrates poetry throughout its 24 books, reminding the reader of the infinite nature of *Hashem* and the multivalent dimensions of His word. The addition of poetry to the biblical landscape teaches the reader to gauge the cadence, rhythm, rhyme and meter in the divine expressions. If modern poets taught that form complements content, they predicated their sentiments on ancient biblical sources.

Moshe himself refers to the *Torah* as poetry: "Therefore, write down this poem, and teach it to the People of Israel" (Deuteronomy 31:19). Based on this declaration, it seems that the receiver of *Torah* must not only "learn" the divine words, but also "sing" the heavenly song.

Jewish tradition says that the entire *Torah* (Five Books of Moses) contains the actual word of God, while the *Nevi'im* (Prophets) consist of the prophets' own formulations as well as direct quotations from *Hashem* Himself. The *Ketuvim* (Writings) though, present us with a third dimension in Godly revelation: That of humans speaking with divine inspiration.

It is this third category into which *Sefer Tehillim* falls. Written, according to the Talmud (*Bava Batra* 14b), by King *David* and ten elders, each poem exposes the raw emotion of the Israelites attempting to feel God's presence, while at the same time contending with external and internal foes. The medium of poetry, with its wordplays and metaphors, acrostics and flowery language, offers a universal subjective aspect to the written word. Each generation finds inspiration, spirit and solace in *David*'s song. Each psalm, according to tradition, while authored by human beings, nevertheless possesses a divine spark, a spiritual note.

While the Talmud refers to additional 'elder' authors, general Jewish tradition views the *Sefer Tehillim* as the work of King *David*. He authored the overwhelming majority. He is described in the Bible as "one who fashioned psalms" (II Chronicles 29:25,30), he was "skilled at playing the lyre" (I Samuel 16:16), and through his poems we find an entire system of worshiping *Hashem* in the *Beit Hamikdash* as well as throughout Israel.

Where did *David* find the tools to craft this profound, yet eclectic, book of praise to God? The answer is that the poets' quiver was filled with his sights, senses and experiences. And specifically in *Eretz Yisrael*, where almost all of the Psalms were penned, the flora, fauna, rivers, mountains, cities, caves, kings and nations were his muse.

In *Sefer Tehillim*, God, the Nation of Israel and the Land of Israel are inextricably linked. When *David* speaks of the Judean desert, we know to which he refers; when *David* runs to the mountains, we can access that geographical context and be doubly enriched. Thus, every psalm is also somewhat of a history lesson, teaching of the Children of Israel and their deep relationship with the Land of Israel, the God of Israel, with their enemies and with each other.

The Israel Bible presents you the chapters of *Sefer Tehillim* and their connection to *Eretz Yisrael*, perhaps the most authentic context in which to view these precious words. Your task is to be attuned to the magic of Israel, God's chosen land, and to peruse each chapter in Hebrew or in English, with an eye to the poetry, history, spirit and divine spark. Then, as with every other book of the Bible, you are challenged to apply these eternal messages to your own life.

Map of Places in *Sefer Tehillim*

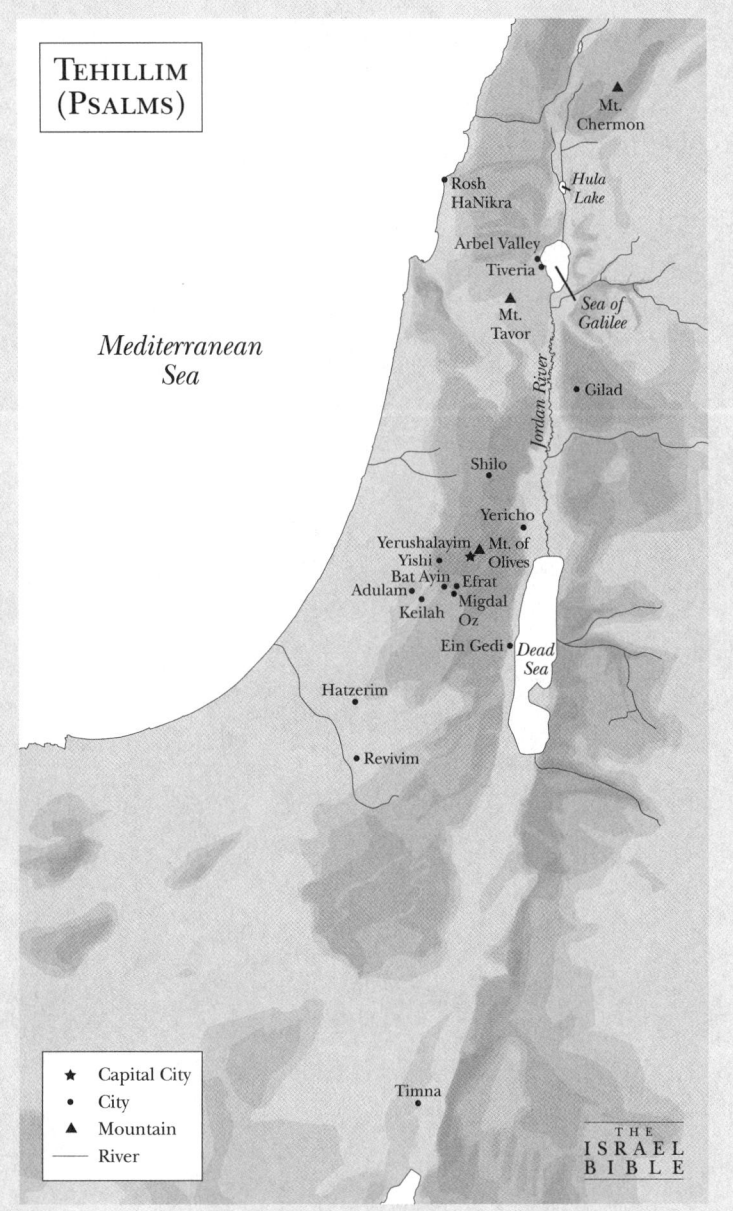

Tehillim (Psalms)

Place	Related Comment in *Sefer Tehillim*
Adulam	142:1
Arbel Valley	19:6
Bat Ayin	17:8
Chermon	42:7, 89:13, 121:1
Dead Sea	11:6, 18:8
Efrat	132:6
Ein Gedi	55:8, 57:1
Gilad	108:9
Mount of Olives	3:1
Hatzerim	10:8
Hula Lake Park	8:9
Jordan River	139:14
Keilah	31:22
Migdal Oz	61:4
Revivim	65:11
Rosh Hanikra	93:4, 98:8
Shilo	43:3, 78:60
Tavor	68:9, 89:13
Timna Park	12:7
Tiveria	47:5
Yericho	128:6
Yerushalayim	48:9, 87:2, 101:8, 122:6, 125:2, 135:21, 137:5, 137:6
Yishi	25:5

Tehillim/Psalms
Chapter 1

1 ¹ Happy is the man who has not followed the counsel of the wicked, or taken the path of sinners, or joined the company of the insolent;

אַשְׁרֵי־הָאִישׁ אֲשֶׁר לֹא הָלַךְ בַּעֲצַת רְשָׁעִים וּבְדֶרֶךְ חַטָּאִים לֹא עָמָד וּבְמוֹשַׁב לֵצִים לֹא יָשָׁב:

ash-ray ha-EESH a-SHER LO ha-LAKH ba-a-TZAT r'-sha-EEM uv-DE-rekh KHA-ta-eem LO a-MAD uv-mo-SHAV lay-TZEEM LO ya-SHAV

² rather, the teaching of *Hashem* is his delight, and he studies that teaching day and night.

כִּי אִם בְּתוֹרַת יְהֹוָה חֶפְצוֹ וּבְתוֹרָתוֹ יֶהְגֶּה יוֹמָם וָלָיְלָה:

³ He is like a tree planted beside streams of water, which yields its fruit in season, whose foliage never fades, and whatever it produces thrives.

וְהָיָה כְּעֵץ שָׁתוּל עַל־פַּלְגֵי מָיִם אֲשֶׁר פִּרְיוֹ יִתֵּן בְּעִתּוֹ וְעָלֵהוּ לֹא־יִבּוֹל וְכֹל אֲשֶׁר־יַעֲשֶׂה יַצְלִיחַ:

⁴ Not so the wicked; rather, they are like chaff that wind blows away.

לֹא־כֵן הָרְשָׁעִים כִּי אִם־כַּמֹּץ אֲשֶׁר־תִּדְּפֶנּוּ רוּחַ:

⁵ Therefore the wicked will not survive judgment, nor will sinners, in the assembly of the righteous.

עַל־כֵּן לֹא־יָקֻמוּ רְשָׁעִים בַּמִּשְׁפָּט וְחַטָּאִים בַּעֲדַת צַדִּיקִים:

⁶ For *Hashem* cherishes the way of the righteous, but the way of the wicked is doomed.

כִּי־יוֹדֵעַ יְהֹוָה דֶּרֶךְ צַדִּיקִים וְדֶרֶךְ רְשָׁעִים תֹּאבֵד:

2 ¹ Why do nations assemble, and peoples plot vain things;

לָמָּה רָגְשׁוּ גוֹיִם וּלְאֻמִּים יֶהְגּוּ־רִיק:

² kings of the earth take their stand, and regents intrigue together against *Hashem* and against His anointed?

יִתְיַצְּבוּ מַלְכֵי־אֶרֶץ וְרוֹזְנִים נוֹסְדוּ־יָחַד עַל־יְהֹוָה וְעַל־מְשִׁיחוֹ:

³ "Let us break the cords of their yoke, shake off their ropes from us!"

נְנַתְּקָה אֶת־מוֹסְרוֹתֵימוֹ וְנַשְׁלִיכָה מִמֶּנּוּ עֲבֹתֵימוֹ:

⁴ He who is enthroned in heaven laughs; *Hashem* mocks at them.

יוֹשֵׁב בַּשָּׁמַיִם יִשְׂחָק אֲדֹנָי יִלְעַג־לָמוֹ:

⁵ Then He speaks to them in anger, terrifying them in His rage,

אָז יְדַבֵּר אֵלֵימוֹ בְאַפּוֹ וּבַחֲרוֹנוֹ יְבַהֲלֵמוֹ:

⁶ "But I have installed My king on *Tzion*, My holy mountain!"

וַאֲנִי נָסַכְתִּי מַלְכִּי עַל־צִיּוֹן הַר־קָדְשִׁי:

va-a-NEE na-SAKH-tee mal-KEE al tzi-YON har kod-SHEE

1:1 Happy is the man who has not followed the counsel of the wicked King *David* begins *Sefer Tehillim*, a collection of songs of praise for the Lord, by focusing on man. His first action is to walk, in Hebrew *halakh* (הלך), and immediately upon setting out on his journey is forced to decide which path he should take: righteous or wicked, fruitful or barren. This 'walking' reminds us of God's first words to *Avraham* directing him to travel to the Land of Israel, *lech lecha* (לך לך), 'Go forth' (Genesis 12:1), and more significantly, *kum hithalekh ba'aretz* (קום התהלך בארץ), 'Arise, walk about the land' (Genesis 13:17). *David* may have been reminding us that while praising God transcends time and place, *Sefer Tehillim* was written in the Land of Israel, the ancient walking grounds of our forefathers.

2:6 My king on *Tzion* As opposed to Psalm 1 which heralds the man who walks in the ways of *Hashem*, Psalm 2 is directed to nations and kings, rebuking those derelict peoples who reject the Lord and seek to destroy Israel. The Sages suggest various possibilities to explain to which enemy the psalm refers: Nimrod,

Tehillim/Psalms
Chapter 3

תהלים
פרק ג

7 Let me tell of the decree: *Hashem* said to me, "You are My son, I have fathered you this day.

ז אֲסַפְּרָה אֶל חֹק יְהֹוָה אָמַר אֵלַי בְּנִי אַתָּה אֲנִי הַיּוֹם יְלִדְתִּיךָ:

8 Ask it of Me, and I will make the nations your domain; your estate, the limits of the earth.

ח שְׁאַל מִמֶּנִּי וְאֶתְּנָה גוֹיִם נַחֲלָתֶךָ וַאֲחֻזָּתְךָ אַפְסֵי־אָרֶץ:

9 You can smash them with an iron mace, shatter them like potter's ware."

ט תְּרֹעֵם בְּשֵׁבֶט בַּרְזֶל כִּכְלִי יוֹצֵר תְּנַפְּצֵם:

10 So now, O kings, be prudent; accept discipline, you rulers of the earth!

י וְעַתָּה מְלָכִים הַשְׂכִּילוּ הִוָּסְרוּ שֹׁפְטֵי אָרֶץ:

11 Serve *Hashem* in awe; tremble with fright,

יא עִבְדוּ אֶת־יְהֹוָה בְּיִרְאָה וְגִילוּ בִּרְעָדָה:

12 pay homage in good faith, lest He be angered, and your way be doomed in the mere flash of His anger. Happy are all who take refuge in Him.

יב נַשְּׁקוּ־בַר פֶּן־יֶאֱנַף וְתֹאבְדוּ דֶרֶךְ כִּי־יִבְעַר כִּמְעַט אַפּוֹ אַשְׁרֵי כָּל־חוֹסֵי בוֹ:

3 1 A psalm of *David* when he fled from his son *Avshalom*.

א מִזְמוֹר לְדָוִד בְּבָרְחוֹ מִפְּנֵי אַבְשָׁלוֹם בְּנוֹ:

miz-MOR l'-da-VID b'-vor-KHO mi-p'-NAY av-sha-LOM b'-NO

2 *Hashem*, my foes are so many! Many are those who attack me;

ב יְהֹוָה מָה־רַבּוּ צָרָי רַבִּים קָמִים עָלָי:

3 many say of me, "There is no deliverance for him through *Hashem*." *Selah*.

ג רַבִּים אֹמְרִים לְנַפְשִׁי אֵין יְשׁוּעָתָה לּוֹ בֵאלֹהִים סֶלָה:

4 But You, *Hashem*, are a shield about me, my glory, He who holds my head high.

ד וְאַתָּה יְהֹוָה מָגֵן בַּעֲדִי כְּבוֹדִי וּמֵרִים רֹאשִׁי:

5 I cry aloud to *Hashem*, and He answers me from His holy mountain. *Selah*.

ה קוֹלִי אֶל־יְהֹוָה אֶקְרָא וַיַּעֲנֵנִי מֵהַר קָדְשׁוֹ סֶלָה:

6 I lie down and sleep and wake again, for *Hashem* sustains me.

ו אֲנִי שָׁכַבְתִּי וָאִישָׁנָה הֱקִיצוֹתִי כִּי יְהֹוָה יִסְמְכֵנִי:

Pharaoh, or Gog and Magog. But regardless who the enemy is, he is ultimately doomed to destruction. *Hashem* has chosen a king from among the Children of Israel who will serve as His anointed one on *Tzion*, His holy mountain. Once the People of Israel conquer and settle the land, the anointed one, king of Israel, will assume the role of defender of his people and will protect Israel from harm.

3:1 When he fled from his son *Avshalom* *David* writes his psalms, expressing both his darkest fears and his greatest expressions of gratitude to God, during the tumultuous times in his life. As punishment for sinning with *Batsheva*, *David* is warned that *Hashem* will "make a calamity rise against you from within your own house" (II Samuel 12:11). A few years later, *David* finds himself driven out of his capital city by his son *Avshalom*. As he ascends the Mount of Olives crying and downtrodden (II Samuel 15:30), he turns to *Hashem* in pain and suffering and calls out with this psalm. The Mount of Olives is a mountain ridge adjacent to the Old City of *Yerushalayim*. After the destruction of the second *Beit Hamikdash*, a custom emerged to make a pilgrimage to the Mount of Olives on the ninth day of the Hebrew month of *Av*, the day which commemorates the destruction of the Temple, in order to gaze upon *Har HaBayit* and cry. In the modern State of Israel, while we still mourn the loss of the *Beit Hamikdash*, we are privileged to be able to rejoice over the return to Jerusalem and its surrounding mountains.

Mount of Olives

Tehillim/Psalms
Chapter 4

תהלים
פרק ד

7 I have no fear of the myriad forces arrayed against me on every side.

ז לֹא־אִירָא מֵרִבְבוֹת עָם אֲשֶׁר סָבִיב שָׁתוּ עָלָי׃

8 Rise, *Hashem*! Deliver me, O my God! For You slap all my enemies in the face; You break the teeth of the wicked.

ח קוּמָה יְהֹוָה הוֹשִׁיעֵנִי אֱלֹהַי כִּי־הִכִּיתָ אֶת־כָּל־אֹיְבַי לֶחִי שִׁנֵּי רְשָׁעִים שִׁבַּרְתָּ׃

9 Deliverance is *Hashem*'s; Your blessing be upon Your people! *Selah*.

ט לַיהֹוָה הַיְשׁוּעָה עַל־עַמְּךָ בִרְכָתֶךָ סֶּלָה׃

4 1 For the leader; with instrumental music. A psalm of *David*.

lam-na-TZAY-akh bin-gee-NOT miz-MOR l'-da-VID

ד א לַמְנַצֵּחַ בִּנְגִינוֹת מִזְמוֹר לְדָוִד׃

2 Answer me when I call, O *Hashem*, my vindicator! You freed me from distress; have mercy on me and hear my prayer.

ב בְּקָרְאִי עֲנֵנִי אֱלֹהֵי צִדְקִי בַּצָּר הִרְחַבְתָּ לִּי חָנֵּנִי וּשְׁמַע תְּפִלָּתִי׃

3 You men, how long will my glory be mocked, will you love illusions, have recourse to frauds? *Selah*.

ג בְּנֵי אִישׁ עַד־מֶה כְבוֹדִי לִכְלִמָּה תֶּאֱהָבוּן רִיק תְּבַקְשׁוּ כָזָב סֶלָה׃

4 Know that *Hashem* singles out the faithful for Himself; *Hashem* hears when I call to Him.

ד וּדְעוּ כִּי־הִפְלָה יְהֹוָה חָסִיד לוֹ יְהֹוָה יִשְׁמַע בְּקָרְאִי אֵלָיו׃

5 So tremble, and sin no more; ponder it on your bed, and sigh.

ה רִגְזוּ וְאַל־תֶּחֱטָאוּ אִמְרוּ בִלְבַבְכֶם עַל־מִשְׁכַּבְכֶם וְדֹמּוּ סֶלָה׃

6 Offer sacrifices in righteousness and trust in *Hashem*.

ו זִבְחוּ זִבְחֵי־צֶדֶק וּבִטְחוּ אֶל־יְהֹוָה׃

7 Many say, "O for good days!" Bestow Your favor on us, *Hashem*.

ז רַבִּים אֹמְרִים מִי־יַרְאֵנוּ טוֹב נְסָה־עָלֵינוּ אוֹר פָּנֶיךָ יְהֹוָה׃

8 You put joy into my heart when their grain and wine show increase.

ח נָתַתָּה שִׂמְחָה בְלִבִּי מֵעֵת דְּגָנָם וְתִירוֹשָׁם רָבּוּ׃

9 Safe and sound, I lie down and sleep, for You alone, *Hashem*, keep me secure.

ט בְּשָׁלוֹם יַחְדָּו אֶשְׁכְּבָה וְאִישָׁן כִּי־אַתָּה יְהֹוָה לְבָדָד לָבֶטַח תּוֹשִׁיבֵנִי׃

5 1 For the leader; on nechiloth. A psalm of *David*.

ה א לַמְנַצֵּחַ אֶל־הַנְּחִילוֹת מִזְמוֹר לְדָוִד׃

2 Give ear to my speech, *Hashem*; consider my utterance.

ב אֲמָרַי הַאֲזִינָה יְהֹוָה בִּינָה הֲגִיגִי׃

3 Heed the sound of my cry, my king and *Hashem*, for I pray to You.

ג הַקְשִׁיבָה לְקוֹל שַׁוְעִי מַלְכִּי וֵאלֹהָי כִּי־אֵלֶיךָ אֶתְפַּלָּל׃

למנצח

4:1 For the leader The title of this psalm is *lamnatzeakh* (למנצח), translated as "for the leader." The root of the word *menatzeakh* is נ-צ-ח, which means 'victory.' What does the Lord consider a victory? According to the Sages, a victory for God is achieved when the Nation of Israel is living on its land, engaged in self-actualization and maturation, and evolves from a miracle-reliant culture into a self-sustaining and law-abiding nation. Then, *Hashem* smiles down on them from heaven.

Tehillim/Psalms
Chapter 6

תהלים
פרק ו

4 Hear my voice, *Hashem*, at daybreak; at daybreak I plead before You, and wait.

ד יְהֹוָה בֹּקֶר תִּשְׁמַע קוֹלִי בֹּקֶר אֶעֱרָךְ־לְךָ וַאֲצַפֶּה׃

5 For You are not a *Hashem* who desires wickedness; evil cannot abide with You;

ה כִּי לֹא אֵל־חָפֵץ רֶשַׁע אָתָּה לֹא יְגֻרְךָ רָע׃

6 wanton men cannot endure in Your sight. You detest all evildoers;

ו לֹא־יִתְיַצְּבוּ הוֹלְלִים לְנֶגֶד עֵינֶיךָ שָׂנֵאתָ כָּל־פֹּעֲלֵי אָוֶן׃

7 You doom those who speak lies; murderous, deceitful men *Hashem* abhors.

ז תְּאַבֵּד דֹּבְרֵי כָזָב אִישׁ־דָּמִים וּמִרְמָה יְתָעֵב יְהֹוָה׃

8 But I, through Your abundant love, enter Your house; I bow down in awe at Your holy temple.

ח וַאֲנִי בְּרֹב חַסְדְּךָ אָבוֹא בֵיתֶךָ אֶשְׁתַּחֲוֶה אֶל־הֵיכַל־קָדְשְׁךָ בְּיִרְאָתֶךָ׃

9 *Hashem*, lead me along Your righteous [path] because of my watchful foes; make Your way straight before me.

ט יְהֹוָה נְחֵנִי בְצִדְקָתֶךָ לְמַעַן שׁוֹרְרָי הוֹשַׁר [הַיְשַׁר] לְפָנַי דַּרְכֶּךָ׃

10 For there is no sincerity on their lips; their heart is [filled with] malice; their throat is an open grave; their tongue slippery.

י כִּי אֵין בְּפִיהוּ נְכוֹנָה קִרְבָּם הַוּוֹת קֶבֶר־פָּתוּחַ גְּרוֹנָם לְשׁוֹנָם יַחֲלִיקוּן׃

11 Condemn them, O *Hashem*; let them fall by their own devices; cast them out for their many crimes, for they defy You.

יא הַאֲשִׁימֵם אֱלֹהִים יִפְּלוּ מִמֹּעֲצוֹתֵיהֶם בְּרֹב פִּשְׁעֵיהֶם הַדִּיחֵמוֹ כִּי־מָרוּ בָךְ׃

12 But let all who take refuge in You rejoice, ever jubilant as You shelter them; and let those who love Your name exult in You.

יב וְיִשְׂמְחוּ כָל־חוֹסֵי בָךְ לְעוֹלָם יְרַנֵּנוּ וְתָסֵךְ עָלֵימוֹ וְיַעְלְצוּ בְךָ אֹהֲבֵי שְׁמֶךָ׃

v'-yis-m'-KHU khol KHO-say VAKH l'-o-LAM y'-ra-NAY-nu v'-ta-SAYKH a-LAY-mo v'-ya-l'-TZU v'-KHA o-ha-VAY sh'-ME-kha

13 For You surely bless the righteous man, *Hashem*, encompassing him with favor like a shield.

יג כִּי־אַתָּה תְּבָרֵךְ צַדִּיק יְהֹוָה כַּצִּנָּה רָצוֹן תַּעְטְרֶנּוּ׃

6

1 For the leader; with instrumental music on the sheminith. A psalm of *David*.

א לַמְנַצֵּחַ בִּנְגִינוֹת עַל־הַשְּׁמִינִית מִזְמוֹר לְדָוִד׃

2 *Hashem*, do not punish me in anger, do not chastise me in fury.

ב יְהֹוָה אַל־בְּאַפְּךָ תוֹכִיחֵנִי וְאַל־בַּחֲמָתְךָ תְיַסְּרֵנִי׃

3 Have mercy on me, *Hashem*, for I languish; heal me, *Hashem*, for my bones shake with terror.

ג חָנֵּנִי יְהֹוָה כִּי אֻמְלַל אָנִי רְפָאֵנִי יְהֹוָה כִּי נִבְהֲלוּ עֲצָמָי׃

5:12 But let all who take refuge in You rejoice Despite all the dangerous threats surrounding the modern Jewish State, Israeli citizens consistently rate extremely high in global surveys measuring quality of life and happiness. While their sense of purpose in helping to reclaim the land of their forefathers certainly contributes to Israelis' high levels of satisfaction, the key to happiness in life is found in this verse: "all who take refuge in You rejoice." Israelis have no choice but to rely on the salvation of *Hashem*. By placing their trust in the Lord, they achieve true happiness and set an example for the rest of the world.

Tehillim/Psalms
Chapter 7

תהלים
פרק ז

4 My whole being is stricken with terror, while You, *Hashem* – O, how long!

וְנַפְשִׁי נִבְהֲלָה מְאֹד וְאַתְּ [וְאַתָּה] יְהֹוָה עַד־מָתָי:

v'-naf-SHEE niv-ha-LAH m'-OD v'-a-TAH a-do-NAI ad ma-TAI

5 *Hashem*, turn! Rescue me! Deliver me as befits Your faithfulness.

שׁוּבָה יְהֹוָה חַלְּצָה נַפְשִׁי הוֹשִׁיעֵנִי לְמַעַן חַסְדֶּךָ:

6 For there is no praise of You among the dead; in Sheol, who can acclaim You?

כִּי אֵין בַּמָּוֶת זִכְרֶךָ בִּשְׁאוֹל מִי יוֹדֶה־לָּךְ:

7 I am weary with groaning; every night I drench my bed, I melt my couch in tears.

יָגַעְתִּי בְּאַנְחָתִי אַשְׂחֶה בְכָל־לַיְלָה מִטָּתִי בְּדִמְעָתִי עַרְשִׂי אַמְסֶה:

8 My eyes are wasted by vexation, worn out because of all my foes.

עָשְׁשָׁה מִכַּעַס עֵינִי עָתְקָה בְּכָל־צוֹרְרָי:

9 Away from me, all you evildoers, for *Hashem* heeds the sound of my weeping.

סוּרוּ מִמֶּנִּי כָּל־פֹּעֲלֵי אָוֶן כִּי־שָׁמַע יְהֹוָה קוֹל בִּכְיִי:

10 *Hashem* heeds my plea, *Hashem* accepts my prayer.

שָׁמַע יְהֹוָה תְּחִנָּתִי יְהֹוָה תְּפִלָּתִי יִקָּח:

11 All my enemies will be frustrated and stricken with terror; they will turn back in an instant, frustrated.

יֵבֹשׁוּ וְיִבָּהֲלוּ מְאֹד כָּל־אֹיְבָי יָשֻׁבוּ יֵבֹשׁוּ רָגַע:

7

1 *Shiggaion* of *David*, which he sang to *Hashem*, concerning Cush, a Benjaminite.

שִׁגָּיוֹן לְדָוִד אֲשֶׁר־שָׁר לַיהֹוָה עַל־דִּבְרֵי־כוּשׁ בֶּן־יְמִינִי:

shi-ga-YON l'-da-VID a-sher SHAR la-do-NAI al div-ray KHUSH ben y'-mee-NEE

2 *Hashem*, my God, in You I seek refuge; deliver me from all my pursuers and save me,

יְהֹוָה אֱלֹהַי בְּךָ חָסִיתִי הוֹשִׁיעֵנִי מִכָּל־רֹדְפַי וְהַצִּילֵנִי:

3 lest, like a lion, they tear me apart, rending in pieces, and no one save me.

פֶּן־יִטְרֹף כְּאַרְיֵה נַפְשִׁי פֹּרֵק וְאֵין מַצִּיל:

4 *Hashem*, my God, if I have done such things, if my hands bear the guilt of wrongdoing,

יְהֹוָה אֱלֹהַי אִם־עָשִׂיתִי זֹאת אִם־יֶשׁ־עָוֶל בְּכַפָּי:

בהלה

6:4 My whole being is stricken with terror *David* mentions the idea of *behala* (בהלה) meaning 'terror' or 'fear', three times in this short, sad psalm. The first two times, he laments being in this melancholy state. The third time, he wishes it upon his enemies. The same term appears in the *Torah* as the first punishment for the Children of Israel when they begin to sin in the Land of Israel. In *Vayikra* (26:16), God begins His list of punishments for not listening to the Lord and abandoning His commandments by saying, "I will wreak misery upon you," using the same Hebrew word *behala*. Yet, despite the long list of punishments delineated in that section, it ends with a divine promise to remember the covenant made with the forefathers and *Eretz Yisrael*: "Then will I remember My covenant with *Yaakov*; also My covenant with *Yitzchak*, and also My covenant with *Avraham* I will remember; and I will remember the land" (Leviticus 26:42).

7:1 Concerning Cush, a Benjaminite Sometimes our enemies come from without, such as neighboring kingdoms or other nations. Other times, our enemies appear from within as our own brethren seek to harm us. The title of Psalm 7 refers to 'Cush a Benjamite.' According to some, this refers to *Shaul* king of Israel, *David*'s father in-law, who came from the tribe of *Binyamin*. *David* is no stranger to internal rivalry. He struggled with King *Shaul* who sought to destroy him, and was not able to live freely in the Land of Israel until *Shaul*'s death. This psalm reminds us of the extreme measures *David* took to protect himself from harm, while at the same time being careful not cause harm or disrespect to the appointed leader of Israel.

Tehillim/Psalms
Chapter 8

תהלים
פרק ח

5 if I have dealt evil to my ally – I who rescued my foe without reward –

ה אִם־גָּמַלְתִּי שׁוֹלְמִי רָע וָאֲחַלְּצָה צוֹרְרִי רֵיקָם:

6 then let the enemy pursue and overtake me; let him trample my life to the ground, and lay my body in the dust. *Selah*.

ו יִרַדֹּף אוֹיֵב נַפְשִׁי וְיַשֵּׂג וְיִרְמֹס לָאָרֶץ חַיָּי וּכְבוֹדִי לֶעָפָר יַשְׁכֵּן סֶלָה:

7 Rise, *Hashem*, in Your anger; assert Yourself against the fury of my foes; bestir Yourself on my behalf; You have ordained judgment.

ז קוּמָה יְהֹוָה בְּאַפֶּךָ הִנָּשֵׂא בְּעַבְרוֹת צוֹרְרָי וְעוּרָה אֵלַי מִשְׁפָּט צִוִּיתָ:

8 Let the assembly of peoples gather about You, with You enthroned above, on high.

ח וַעֲדַת לְאֻמִּים תְּסוֹבְבֶךָּ וְעָלֶיהָ לַמָּרוֹם שׁוּבָה:

9 *Hashem* judges the peoples; vindicate me, *Hashem*, for the righteousness and blamelessness that are mine.

ט יְהֹוָה יָדִין עַמִּים שָׁפְטֵנִי יְהֹוָה כְּצִדְקִי וּכְתֻמִּי עָלָי:

10 Let the evil of the wicked come to an end, but establish the righteous; he who probes the mind and conscience is *Hashem* the righteous.

י יִגְמָר־נָא רַע רְשָׁעִים וּתְכוֹנֵן צַדִּיק וּבֹחֵן לִבּוֹת וּכְלָיוֹת אֱלֹהִים צַדִּיק:

11 I look to *Hashem* to shield me; the deliverer of the upright.

יא מָגִנִּי עַל־אֱלֹהִים מוֹשִׁיעַ יִשְׁרֵי־לֵב:

12 *Hashem* vindicates the righteous; *Hashem* pronounces doom each day.

יב אֱלֹהִים שׁוֹפֵט צַדִּיק וְאֵל זֹעֵם בְּכָל־יוֹם:

13 If one does not turn back, but whets his sword, bends his bow and aims it,

יג אִם־לֹא יָשׁוּב חַרְבּוֹ יִלְטוֹשׁ קַשְׁתּוֹ דָרַךְ וַיְכוֹנְנֶהָ:

14 then against himself he readies deadly weapons, and makes his arrows sharp.

יד וְלוֹ הֵכִין כְּלֵי־מָוֶת חִצָּיו לְדֹלְקִים יִפְעָל:

15 See, he hatches evil, conceives mischief, and gives birth to fraud.

טו הִנֵּה יְחַבֶּל־אָוֶן וְהָרָה עָמָל וְיָלַד שָׁקֶר:

16 He has dug a pit and deepened it, and will fall into the trap he made.

טז בּוֹר כָּרָה וַיַּחְפְּרֵהוּ וַיִּפֹּל בְּשַׁחַת יִפְעָל:

17 His mischief will recoil upon his own head; his lawlessness will come down upon his skull.

יז יָשׁוּב עֲמָלוֹ בְרֹאשׁוֹ וְעַל קָדְקֳדוֹ חֲמָסוֹ יֵרֵד:

18 I will praise *Hashem* for His righteousness, and sing a hymn to the name of *Hashem* Most High.

יח אוֹדֶה יְהֹוָה כְּצִדְקוֹ וַאֲזַמְּרָה שֵׁם־יְהֹוָה עֶלְיוֹן:

8 1 For the leader; on the gittith. A psalm of *David*.

ח א לַמְנַצֵּחַ עַל־הַגִּתִּית מִזְמוֹר לְדָוִד:

2 *Hashem*, our Lord, How majestic is Your name throughout the earth, You who have covered the heavens with Your splendor!

ב יְהֹוָה אֲדֹנֵינוּ מָה־אַדִּיר שִׁמְךָ בְּכָל־הָאָרֶץ אֲשֶׁר תְּנָה הוֹדְךָ עַל־הַשָּׁמָיִם:

3 From the mouths of infants and sucklings You have founded strength on account of Your foes, to put an end to enemy and avenger.

ג מִפִּי עוֹלְלִים וְיֹנְקִים יִסַּדְתָּ עֹז לְמַעַן צוֹרְרֶיךָ לְהַשְׁבִּית אוֹיֵב וּמִתְנַקֵּם:

4 When I behold Your heavens, the work of Your fingers, the moon and stars that You set in place,

ד כִּי־אֶרְאֶה שָׁמֶיךָ מַעֲשֵׂי אֶצְבְּעֹתֶיךָ יָרֵחַ וְכוֹכָבִים אֲשֶׁר כּוֹנָנְתָּה:

1480

Tehillim/Psalms
Chapter 9

תהילים
פרק ט

5 what is man that You have been mindful of him, mortal man that You have taken note of him,

מָה־אֱנוֹשׁ כִּי־תִזְכְּרֶנּוּ וּבֶן־אָדָם כִּי תִפְקְדֶנּוּ:

6 that You have made him little less than divine, and adorned him with glory and majesty;

וַתְּחַסְּרֵהוּ מְּעַט מֵאֱלֹהִים וְכָבוֹד וְהָדָר תְּעַטְּרֵהוּ:

7 You have made him master over Your handiwork, laying the world at his feet,

תַּמְשִׁילֵהוּ בְּמַעֲשֵׂי יָדֶיךָ כֹּל שַׁתָּה תַחַת־רַגְלָיו:

8 sheep and oxen, all of them, and wild beasts, too;

צֹנֶה וַאֲלָפִים כֻּלָּם וְגַם בַּהֲמוֹת שָׂדָי:

9 the birds of the heavens, the fish of the sea, whatever travels the paths of the seas.

צִפּוֹר שָׁמַיִם וּדְגֵי הַיָּם עֹבֵר אָרְחוֹת יַמִּים:

tzi-POR sha-MA-yim ud-GAY ha-YAM o-VAYR or-KHOT ya-MEEM

10 *Hashem*, our Lord, how majestic is Your name throughout the earth!

יְהוָה אֲדֹנֵינוּ מָה־אַדִּיר שִׁמְךָ בְּכָל־הָאָרֶץ:

9 1 For the leader; *'almuth labben*. A psalm of *David*.

לַמְנַצֵּחַ עַלְמוּת לַבֵּן מִזְמוֹר לְדָוִד:

2 I will praise You, *Hashem*, with all my heart; I will tell all Your wonders.

אוֹדֶה יְהוָה בְּכָל־לִבִּי אֲסַפְּרָה כָּל־נִפְלְאוֹתֶיךָ:

3 I will rejoice and exult in You, singing a hymn to Your name, O Most High.

אֶשְׂמְחָה וְאֶעֶלְצָה בָךְ אֲזַמְּרָה שִׁמְךָ עֶלְיוֹן:

4 When my enemies retreat, they stumble to their doom at Your presence.

בְּשׁוּב־אוֹיְבַי אָחוֹר יִכָּשְׁלוּ וְיֹאבְדוּ מִפָּנֶיךָ:

5 For You uphold my right and claim, enthroned as righteous judge.

כִּי־עָשִׂיתָ מִשְׁפָּטִי וְדִינִי יָשַׁבְתָּ לְכִסֵּא שׁוֹפֵט צֶדֶק:

6 You blast the nations; You destroy the wicked; You blot out their name forever.

גָּעַרְתָּ גוֹיִם אִבַּדְתָּ רָשָׁע שְׁמָם מָחִיתָ לְעוֹלָם וָעֶד:

7 The enemy is no more – ruins everlasting; You have torn down their cities; their very names are lost.

הָאוֹיֵב תַּמּוּ חֳרָבוֹת לָנֶצַח וְעָרִים נָתַשְׁתָּ אָבַד זִכְרָם הֵמָּה:

8 But *Hashem* abides forever; He has set up His throne for judgment;

וַיהוָה לְעוֹלָם יֵשֵׁב כּוֹנֵן לַמִּשְׁפָּט כִּסְאוֹ:

Migrating birds in the Hula Valley

8:9 The birds of the heavens What birds did *David* see passing through the Land of Israel? Israeli ornithologists tell us that there were many. Israel lies along a main route of the bird migration connecting three adjacent continents: Africa, Asia and Europe. Indeed, the prophet *Yirmiyahu* speaks of the stork knowing her appointed times of migration (8:7), and *Iyov* (39:26) speaks of the hawk's migration when he says, "Is it by your wisdom that the hawk grows pinions, spreads his wings to the south?" Today, over 500 million birds from 390 different species pass through Israel's air space twice a year. The Hula Lake Park in the Upper Galilee is a popular destination for bird watching in modern Israel.

Tehillim/Psalms
Chapter 9

תהלים
פרק ט

9	it is He who judges the world with righteousness, rules the peoples with equity.	וְהוּא יִשְׁפֹּט־תֵּבֵל בְּצֶדֶק יָדִין לְאֻמִּים בְּמֵישָׁרִים:	ט

v'-HU yish-pot tay-VAYL b'-TZE-dek ya-DEEN l'-u-MEEM b'-may-sha-REEM

10	Hashem is a haven for the oppressed, a haven in times of trouble.	וִיהִי יְהֹוָה מִשְׂגָּב לַדָּךְ מִשְׂגָּב לְעִתּוֹת בַּצָּרָה:	י
11	Those who know Your name trust You, for You do not abandon those who turn to You, Hashem.	וְיִבְטְחוּ בְךָ יוֹדְעֵי שְׁמֶךָ כִּי לֹא־עָזַבְתָּ דֹרְשֶׁיךָ יְהֹוָה:	יא
12	Sing a hymn to Hashem, who reigns in Tzion; declare His deeds among the peoples.	זַמְּרוּ לַיהֹוָה יֹשֵׁב צִיּוֹן הַגִּידוּ בָעַמִּים עֲלִילוֹתָיו:	יב
13*	For He does not ignore the cry of the afflicted; He who requites bloodshed is mindful of them.	כִּי־דֹרֵשׁ דָּמִים אוֹתָם זָכָר לֹא־שָׁכַח צַעֲקַת עניים [עֲנָוִים:]	יג
14	Have mercy on me, Hashem; see my affliction at the hands of my foes, You who lift me from the gates of death,	חָנְנֵנִי יְהֹוָה רְאֵה עָנְיִי מִשֹּׂנְאָי מְרוֹמְמִי מִשַּׁעֲרֵי מָוֶת:	יד
15	so that in the gates of Fair Tzion I might tell all Your praise, I might exult in Your deliverance.	לְמַעַן אֲסַפְּרָה כָּל־תְּהִלָּתֶיךָ בְּשַׁעֲרֵי בַת־צִיּוֹן אָגִילָה בִּישׁוּעָתֶךָ:	טו
16	The nations sink in the pit they have made; their own foot is caught in the net they have hidden.	טָבְעוּ גוֹיִם בְּשַׁחַת עָשׂוּ בְּרֶשֶׁת־זוּ טָמָנוּ נִלְכְּדָה רַגְלָם:	טז
17	Hashem has made Himself known: He works judgment; the wicked man is snared by his own devices. Higgaion. Selah.	נוֹדַע יְהֹוָה מִשְׁפָּט עָשָׂה בְּפֹעַל כַּפָּיו נוֹקֵשׁ רָשָׁע הִגָּיוֹן סֶלָה:	יז
18	Let the wicked be in Sheol, all the nations who ignore Hashem!	יָשׁוּבוּ רְשָׁעִים לִשְׁאוֹלָה כָּל־גּוֹיִם שְׁכֵחֵי אֱלֹהִים:	יח
19	Not always shall the needy be ignored, nor the hope of the afflicted forever lost.	כִּי לֹא לָנֶצַח יִשָּׁכַח אֶבְיוֹן תִּקְוַת ענוים [עֲנִיִּים] תֹּאבַד לָעַד:	יט
20	Rise, Hashem! Let not men have power; let the nations be judged in Your presence.	קוּמָה יְהֹוָה אַל־יָעֹז אֱנוֹשׁ יִשָּׁפְטוּ גוֹיִם עַל־פָּנֶיךָ:	כ
21	Strike fear into them, Hashem; let the nations know they are only men. Selah.	שִׁיתָה יְהֹוָה מוֹרָה לָהֶם יֵדְעוּ גוֹיִם אֱנוֹשׁ הֵמָּה סֶּלָה:	כא

* order of clauses inverted for clarity

9:9 It is He who judges the world The Sages comment that Hashem judges the nations of the world according to their capabilities, but at the same time reminds them of the position of righteous gentiles in Israel's history. God asks the nations, "why have you not come close to me?" If they say I was too iniquitous, idolatrous or distant from You, He responds, "were you more iniquitous than Rahab the harlot who ultimately came close to Israel and produced prophets and righteous people? Were you more idolatrous than Jethro the priest who came close and produced prophets and righteous people? Were you more distant than Rut the Moabite who came close and produced kings of Israel?" The desire for the nations of the world to work together and establish positive relationships with the Nation of Israel was echoed in Israel's Declaration of Independence: "We extend our hand to all neighboring states and their peoples in an offer of peace and good neighborliness, and appeal to them to establish bonds of cooperation and mutual help with the sovereign Jewish people settled in its own land."

PM David Ben Gurion signing the Declaration of Independence

Tehillim/Psalms
Chapter 10

תהלים
פרק י

10 1 Why, *Hashem*, do You stand aloof, heedless in times of trouble?

א לָמָה יְהוָה תַּעֲמֹד בְּרָחוֹק תַּעְלִים לְעִתּוֹת בַּצָּרָה:

2 The wicked in his arrogance hounds the lowly – may they be caught in the schemes they devise!

ב בְּגַאֲוַת רָשָׁע יִדְלַק עָנִי יִתָּפְשׂוּ בִּמְזִמּוֹת זוּ חָשָׁבוּ:

3 The wicked crows about his unbridled lusts; the grasping man reviles and scorns *Hashem*.

ג כִּי־הִלֵּל רָשָׁע עַל־תַּאֲוַת נַפְשׁוֹ וּבֹצֵעַ בֵּרֵךְ נִאֵץ יְהוָה:

4 The wicked, arrogant as he is, in all his scheming [thinks], "He does not call to account; *Hashem* does not care."

ד רָשָׁע כְּגֹבַהּ אַפּוֹ בַּל־יִדְרֹשׁ אֵין אֱלֹהִים כָּל־מְזִמּוֹתָיו:

5 His ways prosper at all times; Your judgments are far beyond him; he snorts at all his foes.

ה יָחִילוּ דרכו [דְרָכָיו] בְּכָל־עֵת מָרוֹם מִשְׁפָּטֶיךָ מִנֶּגְדּוֹ כָּל־צוֹרְרָיו יָפִיחַ בָּהֶם:

6 He thinks, "I shall not be shaken, through all time never be in trouble."

ו אָמַר בְּלִבּוֹ בַּל־אֶמּוֹט לְדֹר וָדֹר אֲשֶׁר לֹא־בְרָע:

7 His mouth is full of oaths, deceit, and fraud; mischief and evil are under his tongue.

ז אָלָה פִּיהוּ מָלֵא וּמִרְמוֹת וָתֹךְ תַּחַת לְשׁוֹנוֹ עָמָל וָאָוֶן:

8 He lurks in outlying places; from a covert he slays the innocent; his eyes spy out the hapless.

ח יֵשֵׁב בְּמַאְרַב חֲצֵרִים בַּמִּסְתָּרִים יַהֲרֹג נָקִי עֵינָיו לְחֵלְכָה יִצְפֹּנוּ:

yay-SHAYV b'-ma-RAV kha-tzay-REEM ba-mis-ta-REEM ya-ha-ROG na-KEE ay-NAV l'-khay-l'-KHA yitz-PO-nu

9 He waits in a covert like a lion in his lair; waits to seize the lowly; he seizes the lowly as he pulls his net shut;

ט יֶאֱרֹב בַּמִּסְתָּר כְּאַרְיֵה בְסֻכֹּה יֶאֱרֹב לַחֲטוֹף עָנִי יַחְטֹף עָנִי בְּמָשְׁכוֹ בְרִשְׁתּוֹ:

10 he stoops, he crouches, and the hapless fall prey to his might.

י ודכה [יִדְכֶּה] יָשֹׁחַ וְנָפַל בַּעֲצוּמָיו חלכאים [חֵיל] [כָּאִים]:

11 He thinks, "*Hashem* is not mindful, He hides His face, He never looks."

יא אָמַר בְּלִבּוֹ שָׁכַח אֵל הִסְתִּיר פָּנָיו בַּל־רָאָה לָנֶצַח:

12 Rise, *Hashem*! Strike at him, O *Hashem*! Do not forget the lowly.

יב קוּמָה יְהוָה אֵל נְשָׂא יָדֶךָ אַל־תִּשְׁכַּח עניים [עֲנָוִים]:

13 Why should the wicked man scorn *Hashem*, thinking You do not call to account?

יג עַל־מֶה נִאֵץ רָשָׁע אֱלֹהִים אָמַר בְּלִבּוֹ לֹא תִּדְרֹשׁ:

Drip irrigation in Hatzerim, Israel

10:8 He lurks in outlying places This psalm depicts the enemies of Israel who use the land's hidden spaces, marav chatzayrim (מארב חצרים), to attack *Hashem*'s people. In 1946, before the establishment of the State of Israel, Jews courageously went out on the night after *Yom Kippur*, the 'Day of Atonement,' and created new settlements that became known as the "eleven points in the Negev," in order to establish a presence on the ground to prevent attacks by Arabs, and hegemony of Arabs over the Jews, in southern Israel. One of the places chosen for Jewish settlement was Hatzerim (חצרים), founded with just fifty inhabitants who struggled agriculturally due to the land's brackish soil. Ultimately, however, they changed their focus from agriculture to industrial development and quickly established one of the leading agricultural companies in Israel. Today, the Netafim corporation, which developed drip-irrigation technology and is based in Hatzerim, provides solutions for many water-scarce countries around the world.

Tehillim / Psalms
Chapter 11

תהלים
פרק יא

14 You do look! You take note of mischief and vexation! To requite is in Your power. To You the hapless can entrust himself; You have ever been the orphan's help.

יד רָאִתָה כִּי־אַתָּה עָמָל וָכַעַס תַּבִּיט לָתֵת בְּיָדֶךָ עָלֶיךָ יַעֲזֹב חֵלְכָה יָתוֹם אַתָּה הָיִיתָ עוֹזֵר:

15 O break the power of the wicked and evil man, so that when You look for his wickedness You will find it no more.

טו שְׁבֹר זְרוֹעַ רָשָׁע וָרָע תִּדְרוֹשׁ־רִשְׁעוֹ בַל־תִּמְצָא:

16 *Hashem* is king for ever and ever; the nations will perish from His land.

טז יְהוָה מֶלֶךְ עוֹלָם וָעֶד אָבְדוּ גוֹיִם מֵאַרְצוֹ:

17 You will listen to the entreaty of the lowly, *Hashem*, You will make their hearts firm; You will incline Your ear

יז תַּאֲוַת עֲנָוִים שָׁמַעְתָּ יְהוָה תָּכִין לִבָּם תַּקְשִׁיב אָזְנֶךָ:

18 to Champion the orphan and the downtrodden, that men who are of the earth tyrannize no more.

יח לִשְׁפֹּט יָתוֹם וָדָךְ בַּל־יוֹסִיף עוֹד לַעֲרֹץ אֱנוֹשׁ מִן־הָאָרֶץ:

11

1 For the leader. Of *David*. In *Hashem* I take refuge; how can you say to me, "Take to the hills like a bird!

יא א לַמְנַצֵּחַ לְדָוִד בַּיהוָה חָסִיתִי אֵיךְ תֹּאמְרוּ לְנַפְשִׁי נוּדוּ [נוּדִי] הַרְכֶם צִפּוֹר:

2 For see, the wicked bend the bow, they set their arrow on the string to shoot from the shadows at the upright.

ב כִּי הִנֵּה הָרְשָׁעִים יִדְרְכוּן קֶשֶׁת כּוֹנְנוּ חִצָּם עַל־יֶתֶר לִירוֹת בְּמוֹ־אֹפֶל לְיִשְׁרֵי־לֵב:

3 When the foundations are destroyed, what can the righteous man do?"

ג כִּי הַשָּׁתוֹת יֵהָרֵסוּן צַדִּיק מַה־פָּעָל:

4 *Hashem* is in His holy palace; *Hashem* – His throne is in heaven; His eyes behold, His gaze searches mankind.

ד יְהוָה בְּהֵיכַל קָדְשׁוֹ יְהוָה בַּשָּׁמַיִם כִּסְאוֹ עֵינָיו יֶחֱזוּ עַפְעַפָּיו יִבְחֲנוּ בְּנֵי אָדָם:

5 *Hashem* seeks out the righteous man, but loathes the wicked one who loves injustice.

ה יְהוָה צַדִּיק יִבְחָן וְרָשָׁע וְאֹהֵב חָמָס שָׂנְאָה נַפְשׁוֹ:

6 He will rain down upon the wicked blazing coals and sulfur; a scorching wind shall be their lot.

ו יַמְטֵר עַל־רְשָׁעִים פַּחִים אֵשׁ וְגָפְרִית וְרוּחַ זִלְעָפוֹת מְנָת כּוֹסָם:

yam-TAYR al r'-sha-EEM pa-KHEEM AYSH v'-gof-REET v'-RU-akh zil-a-FOT m'-NAT ko-SAM

11:6 Blazing coals and sulfur The words *aish v'gofreet* (אש וגפרית), 'blazing coals and sulfur,' remind us of when the Lord rained down burning sulfuric coals on Sodom and Gomorrah in order to destroy them, as described in *Sefer Bereishit* (19:24). There, the Torah uses the expression *gofreet va-aish* (גפרית ואש), 'sulfurous fire.' In the Bible, *Hashem* sends down from the heavens rain to sustain, manna to nourish, and burning fires to eradicate evil from the land. While in *Sefer Bereishit* sulfuric fire is associated with death and destruction, in the modern State of Israel it represents life, rejuvenation and prosperity. In 1911, Moshe Novomeysky, a European industrialist, visited the Dead Sea for the first time and understood its potential as a treasure trove for minerals, phosphates, sulfurs and potash. He created the Palestine Potash Company which would later turn into Dead Sea Works, one of Israel's most important export companies and one of the world's largest producers of potash products.

Dead Sea Works factory

Tehillim/Psalms
Chapter 12

7 For *Hashem* is righteous; He loves righteous deeds; the upright shall behold His face.

12 1 For the leader; on the sheminith. A psalm of *David*.

2 Help, *Hashem*! For the faithful are no more; the loyal have vanished from among men.

3 Men speak lies to one another; their speech is smooth; they talk with duplicity.

4 May *Hashem* cut off all flattering lips, every tongue that speaks arrogance.

5 They say, "By our tongues we shall prevail; with lips such as ours, who can be our master?"

6 "Because of the groans of the plundered poor and needy, I will now act," says *Hashem*. "I will give help," He affirms to him.

7 The words of *Hashem* are pure words, silver purged in an earthen crucible, refined sevenfold.

im-ROT a-do-NAI a-ma-ROT t'-ho-ROT KE-sef tza-RUF ba-a-LEEL la-A-retz m'-zu-KAK shiv-a-TA-yim

8 You, *Hashem*, will keep them, guarding each from this age evermore.

9 On every side the wicked roam when baseness is exalted among men.

13 1 For the leader. A psalm of *David*.

2 How long, *Hashem*; will You ignore me forever? How long will You hide Your face from me?

3 How long will I have cares on my mind, grief in my heart all day? How long will my enemy have the upper hand?

Copper mines in Timna Valley

12:7 Silver purged in an earthen crucible, refined sevenfold This psalm contrasts the language of the wicked, who speak duplicitously with a forked tongue, with the pure unadulterated words of God. To express the level of purity of *Hashem*'s words, the verse uses the metaphor of metal mined from the earth, which goes through seven stages of refinement in order to arrive at a level of purity worthy of a precious metal. It is not surprising that the psalmist would be aware of the process of metallurgy. Archaeology at Timna Park in southern Israel reveals evidence of copper mining going back thousands of years. In 1959, an archeo-metallurgical expedition under the leadership of Dr. Beno Othenberg began, and ultimately revealed over 10,000 copper mines in the southern Arava region of Israel. More contemporary discoveries date some of the mines to the eleventh to ninth centuries BCE, which coincides with the period of the Israelite kingdom.

Tehillim/Psalms
Chapter 14

תהילים
פרק יד

4 Look at me, answer me, *Hashem*, my God! Restore the luster to my eyes, lest I sleep the sleep of death;

ד הַבִּיטָה עֲנֵנִי יְהוָה אֱלֹהָי הָאִירָה עֵינַי פֶּן־אִישַׁן הַמָּוֶת׃

5 lest my enemy say, "I have overcome him," my foes exult when I totter.

ה פֶּן־יֹאמַר אֹיְבִי יְכָלְתִּיו צָרַי יָגִילוּ כִּי אֶמּוֹט׃

6 But I trust in Your faithfulness, my heart will exult in Your deliverance. I will sing to *Hashem*, for He has been good to me.

ו וַאֲנִי בְּחַסְדְּךָ בָטַחְתִּי יָגֵל לִבִּי בִּישׁוּעָתֶךָ אָשִׁירָה לַיהוָה כִּי גָמַל עָלָי׃

va-a-NEE b'-khas-d'-KHA va-takh-TEE ya-GAYL li-BEE bee-shu-a-TE-kha a-SHEE-ra la-do-NAI KEE ga-MAL a-LAI

14

1 For the leader. Of *David*. The benighted man thinks, "*Hashem* does not care." Man's deeds are corrupt and loathsome; no one does good.

א לַמְנַצֵּחַ לְדָוִד אָמַר נָבָל בְּלִבּוֹ אֵין אֱלֹהִים הִשְׁחִיתוּ הִתְעִיבוּ עֲלִילָה אֵין עֹשֵׂה־טוֹב׃

lam-na-TZAY-akh l'-da-VID a-MAR na-VAL b'-li-BO AYN e-lo-HEEM hish-KHEE-tu hit-EE-vu a-lee-LAH AYN o-SAY TOV

2 *Hashem* looks down from heaven on mankind to find a man of understanding, a man mindful of *Hashem*.

ב יְהוָה מִשָּׁמַיִם הִשְׁקִיף עַל־בְּנֵי־אָדָם לִרְאוֹת הֲיֵשׁ מַשְׂכִּיל דֹּרֵשׁ אֶת־אֱלֹהִים׃

3 All have turned bad, altogether foul; there is none who does good, not even one.

ג הַכֹּל סָר יַחְדָּו נֶאֱלָחוּ אֵין עֹשֵׂה־טוֹב אֵין גַּם־אֶחָד׃

4 Are they so witless, all those evildoers, who devour my people as they devour food, and do not invoke *Hashem*?

ד הֲלֹא יָדְעוּ כָּל־פֹּעֲלֵי אָוֶן אֹכְלֵי עַמִּי אָכְלוּ לֶחֶם יְהוָה לֹא קָרָאוּ׃

13:6 But I trust in Your faithfulness, my heart will exult in Your deliverance King *David*'s psalms can be applied to every situation in a person's life, capturing one's joy and grief, disappointments and hopes. Since King *David* himself experiences the travails of every person and expresses his feelings through the verses of his psalms, a person can always find words to respond to his own experiences within *Tehillim*'s heartfelt verses. King *David* serves as a model of strength of character and belief in *Hashem*, because no matter what he goes through, he never gives up hope. Even at his lowest points, feeling abandoned and discouraged (verse 2), he is still able to say "I trust in Your faithfulness." And no matter what emotions he feels, he is still able to announce "I will sing to *Hashem*, for He has been good to me." This has been the source of the Jews' strength over the millennia: No matter how much pain and suffering they endure, they maintain an unwavering belief in the Lord and His salvation, and hope for the time when their tears will transform to laughter and joy. In 1950, a group of Sephardic Jews from Iraq and Kurdistan created a joint settlement in the heart of the country which they called *Yagel*, the word in this verse that means 'will exult.'

14:1 The benighted man thinks The psalmist paints a dim picture of humanity with corruption in command and desire reigning. *Hashem* peers from the heavens and wonders if any people still contemplate and seek the Creator. The Hebrew word for 'benighted' used in this verse is *naval* (נבל), which means 'foolish' or 'senseless.' It is also the name of the infamous wicked man described in *Sefer Shmuel* I 25. *David* encounters *Naval*, who lives only to please his desires and spares nobody his evil plans. He is indeed a fool, corrupt, immoral and unjust, and is ultimately condemned by his own hubris. His wife *Avigail*, however, acts with kindness and love. *David* sees redemption in *Avigail* and eventually, after *Naval*'s death, makes her his wife. The psalm concludes with the hope of the ultimate redemption, as the salvation of Israel will come when the nation of God returns to the land. Then, *Yaakov* will rejoice, Israel will be happy (verse 7).

Entrance to Yagel, Israel

Tehillim/Psalms
Chapter 15

תהלים
פרק טו

5 There they will be seized with fright, for *Hashem* is present in the circle of the righteous.

ה שָׁם פָּחֲדוּ פָחַד כִּי־אֱלֹהִים בְּדוֹר צַדִּיק:

6 You may set at naught the counsel of the lowly, but *Hashem* is his refuge.

ו עֲצַת־עָנִי תָבִישׁוּ כִּי יְהֹוָה מַחְסֵהוּ:

7 O that the deliverance of *Yisrael* might come from *Tzion*! When *Hashem* restores the fortunes of His people, *Yaakov* will exult, *Yisrael* will rejoice.

ז מִי יִתֵּן מִצִּיּוֹן יְשׁוּעַת יִשְׂרָאֵל בְּשׁוּב יְהֹוָה שְׁבוּת עַמּוֹ יָגֵל יַעֲקֹב יִשְׂמַח יִשְׂרָאֵל:

15

1 A psalm of *David*. *Hashem*, who may sojourn in Your tent, who may dwell on Your holy mountain?

א מִזְמוֹר לְדָוִד יְהֹוָה מִי־יָגוּר בְּאׇהֳלֶךָ מִי־יִשְׁכֹּן בְּהַר קׇדְשֶׁךָ:

2 He who lives without blame, who does what is right, and in his heart acknowledges the truth;

ho-LAYKH ta-MEEM u-fo-AYL TZE-dek v'-do-VAYR e-MET bil-va-VO

ב הוֹלֵךְ תָּמִים וּפֹעֵל צֶדֶק וְדֹבֵר אֱמֶת בִּלְבָבוֹ:

3 whose tongue is not given to evil; who has never done harm to his fellow, or borne reproach for [his acts toward] his neighbor;

ג לֹא־רָגַל עַל־לְשֹׁנוֹ לֹא־עָשָׂה לְרֵעֵהוּ רָעָה וְחֶרְפָּה לֹא־נָשָׂא עַל־קְרֹבוֹ:

4 for whom a contemptible man is abhorrent, but who honors those who fear *Hashem*; who stands by his oath even to his hurt;

ד נִבְזֶה בְּעֵינָיו נִמְאָס וְאֶת־יִרְאֵי יְהֹוָה יְכַבֵּד נִשְׁבַּע לְהָרַע וְלֹא יָמִר:

5 who has never lent money at interest, or accepted a bribe against the innocent. The man who acts thus shall never be shaken.

ה כַּסְפּוֹ לֹא־נָתַן בְּנֶשֶׁךְ וְשֹׁחַד עַל־נָקִי לֹא לָקָח עֹשֵׂה־אֵלֶּה לֹא יִמּוֹט לְעוֹלָם:

16

1 A michtam of *David*. Protect me, O *Hashem*, for I seek refuge in You.

א מִכְתָּם לְדָוִד שָׁמְרֵנִי אֵל כִּי־חָסִיתִי בָךְ:

2 I say to *Hashem*, "You are my Lord, my benefactor; there is none above You."

ב אָמַרְתְּ לַיהֹוָה אֲדֹנָי אָתָּה טוֹבָתִי בַּל־עָלֶיךָ:

3 As to the holy and mighty ones that are in the land, my whole desire concerning them is that

ג לִקְדוֹשִׁים אֲשֶׁר־בָּאָרֶץ הֵמָּה וְאַדִּירֵי כׇּל־חֶפְצִי־בָם:

4 those who espouse another [god] may have many sorrows! I will have no part of their bloody libations; their names will not pass my lips.

ד יִרְבּוּ עַצְּבוֹתָם אַחֵר מָהָרוּ בַּל־אַסִּיךְ נִסְכֵּיהֶם מִדָּם וּבַל־אֶשָּׂא אֶת־שְׁמוֹתָם עַל־שְׂפָתָי:

5 *Hashem* is my allotted share and portion; You control my fate.

ה יְהֹוָה מְנָת־חֶלְקִי וְכוֹסִי אַתָּה תּוֹמִיךְ גּוֹרָלִי:

15:2 And in his heart acknowledges the truth
This verse teaches that one who does what is right and 'acknowledges the truth,' *do-vayr emet* (דבר אמת), will merit to dwell with the Lord. The words *doveir emet* literally mean 'speak the truth,' and according to *Radak*, imply that it is not enough to think or know the truth; one must also speak about it and spread it. Finding the truth in a world of falsehood is a constant challenge. Especially with regard to Israel today, an abundance of lies and misinformation is constantly being spread. It is therefore important to learn effective tools for speaking up on Israel's behalf and countering false and unfair claims commonly made against Israel. Spreading the truth about Israel will bring the world closer to peace and closer to *Hashem*.

Tehillim/Psalms
Chapter 17

תהלים
פרק יז

6 Delightful country has fallen to my lot; lovely indeed is my estate.

חֲבָלִים נָפְלוּ־לִי בַּנְּעִמִים אַף־נַחֲלָת שָׁפְרָה עָלָי: ו

kha-va-LEEM na-f'-lu LEE ba-n'-i-MEEM af na-kha-LAT sha-f'-RAH a-LAI

7 I bless *Hashem* who has guided me; my conscience admonishes me at night.

אֲבָרֵךְ אֶת־יְהֹוָה אֲשֶׁר יְעָצָנִי אַף־לֵילוֹת יִסְּרוּנִי כִלְיוֹתָי: ז

8 I am ever mindful of *Hashem*'s presence; He is at my right hand; I shall never be shaken.

שִׁוִּיתִי יְהֹוָה לְנֶגְדִּי תָמִיד כִּי מִימִינִי בַּל־אֶמּוֹט: ח

9 So my heart rejoices, my whole being exults, and my body rests secure.

לָכֵן שָׂמַח לִבִּי וַיָּגֶל כְּבוֹדִי אַף־בְּשָׂרִי יִשְׁכֹּן לָבֶטַח: ט

10 For You will not abandon me to Sheol, or let Your faithful one see the Pit.

כִּי לֹא־תַעֲזֹב נַפְשִׁי לִשְׁאוֹל לֹא־תִתֵּן חֲסִידְךָ לִרְאוֹת שָׁחַת: י

11 You will teach me the path of life. In Your presence is perfect joy; delights are ever in Your right hand.

תּוֹדִיעֵנִי אֹרַח חַיִּים שֹׂבַע שְׂמָחוֹת אֶת־פָּנֶיךָ נְעִמוֹת בִּימִינְךָ נֶצַח: יא

17

1 A prayer of *David*. Hear, *Hashem*, what is just; heed my cry, give ear to my prayer, uttered without guile.

תְּפִלָּה לְדָוִד שִׁמְעָה יְהֹוָה צֶדֶק הַקְשִׁיבָה רִנָּתִי הַאֲזִינָה תְפִלָּתִי בְּלֹא שִׂפְתֵי מִרְמָה: א

2 My vindication will come from You; Your eyes will behold what is right.

מִלְּפָנֶיךָ מִשְׁפָּטִי יֵצֵא עֵינֶיךָ תֶּחֱזֶינָה מֵישָׁרִים: ב

3 You have visited me at night, probed my mind, You have tested me and found nothing amiss; I determined that my mouth should not transgress.

בָּחַנְתָּ לִבִּי פָּקַדְתָּ לַּיְלָה צְרַפְתַּנִי בַל־תִּמְצָא זַמֹּתִי בַּל־יַעֲבָר־פִּי: ג

4 As for man's dealings, in accord with the command of Your lips, I have kept in view the fate of the lawless.

לִפְעֻלּוֹת אָדָם בִּדְבַר שְׂפָתֶיךָ אֲנִי שָׁמַרְתִּי אָרְחוֹת פָּרִיץ: ד

5 My feet have held to Your paths; my legs have not given way.

תָּמֹךְ אֲשֻׁרַי בְּמַעְגְּלוֹתֶיךָ בַּל־נָמוֹטּוּ פְעָמָי: ה

6 I call on You; You will answer me, *Hashem*; turn Your ear to me, hear what I say.

אֲנִי־קְרָאתִיךָ כִי־תַעֲנֵנִי אֵל הַט־אָזְנְךָ לִי שְׁמַע אִמְרָתִי: ו

16:6 Delightful country has fallen to my lot; lovely indeed is my estate The Land of Israel is divided into portions, one for each tribe. In *Bamidbar* (26:52–56), the Bible delineates the process by which each tribe was awarded its specific inheritance. On the one hand, the leaders of the nation are commanded to apportion the land with careful attention paid to ensure that each receives an appropriate inheritance: "With larger groups, increase the share; with smaller groups, reduce the share." In addition, some tribes were seafarers, while others were vintners; some were mountain people and others preferred the planes, and the land was divided accordingly. On the other hand, though, the *Torah* tells us that a special divine lottery would be held to determine the inheritance of each tribe: "Each portion shall be assigned by lot, whether for larger or smaller groups." This apparent contradiction contains a message to the tribes of Israel. On the one hand, conquering and colonizing the land is dependent on the effort and involvement of each individual. On the other hand, they must always be aware of the divine element in settling *Eretz Yisrael*.

Tehillim/Psalms
Chapter 18

תהלים
פרק יח

7 Display Your faithfulness in wondrous deeds, You who deliver with Your right hand those who seek refuge from assailants.

ז הַפְלֵה חֲסָדֶיךָ מוֹשִׁיעַ חוֹסִים מִמִּתְקוֹמְמִים בִּימִינֶךָ:

8 Guard me like the apple of Your eye; hide me in the shadow of Your wings

ח שָׁמְרֵנִי כְּאִישׁוֹן בַּת־עָיִן בְּצֵל כְּנָפֶיךָ תַּסְתִּירֵנִי:

shom-RAY-nee k'-ee-SHON bat A-yin b'-TZAYL k'-na-FE-kha tas-tee-RAY-nee

9 from the wicked who despoil me, my mortal enemies who encircle me.

ט מִפְּנֵי רְשָׁעִים זוּ שַׁדּוּנִי אֹיְבַי בְּנֶפֶשׁ יַקִּיפוּ עָלָי:

10 Their hearts are closed to pity; they mouth arrogance;

י חֶלְבָּמוֹ סָגְרוּ פִּימוֹ דִּבְּרוּ בְגֵאוּת:

11 now they hem in our feet on every side; they set their eyes roaming over the land.

יא אַשֻּׁרֵינוּ עַתָּה סבבוני [סְבָבוּנוּ] עֵינֵיהֶם יָשִׁיתוּ לִנְטוֹת בָּאָרֶץ:

12 He is like a lion eager for prey, a king of beasts lying in wait.

יב דִּמְיֹנוֹ כְּאַרְיֵה יִכְסוֹף לִטְרוֹף וְכִכְפִיר יֹשֵׁב בְּמִסְתָּרִים:

13 Rise, *Hashem*! Go forth to meet him. Bring him down; rescue me from the wicked with Your sword,

יג קוּמָה יְהוָה קַדְּמָה פָנָיו הַכְרִיעֵהוּ פַּלְּטָה נַפְשִׁי מֵרָשָׁע חַרְבֶּךָ:

14 from men, *Hashem*, with Your hand, from men whose share in life is fleeting. But as to Your treasured ones, fill their bellies. Their sons too shall be satisfied, and have something to leave over for their young.

יד מִמְתִים יָדְךָ יְהוָה מִמְתִים מֵחֶלֶד חֶלְקָם בַּחַיִּים וצפינך [וּצְפוּנְךָ] תְּמַלֵּא בִטְנָם יִשְׂבְּעוּ בָנִים וְהִנִּיחוּ יִתְרָם לְעוֹלְלֵיהֶם:

15 Then I, justified, will behold Your face; awake, I am filled with the vision of You.

טו אֲנִי בְּצֶדֶק אֶחֱזֶה פָנֶיךָ אֶשְׂבְּעָה בְהָקִיץ תְּמוּנָתֶךָ:

18

1 For the leader. Of *David*, the servant of *Hashem*, who addressed the words of this song to *Hashem* after *Hashem* had saved him from the hands of all his enemies and from the clutches of *Shaul*.

יח א לַמְנַצֵּחַ לְעֶבֶד יְהוָה לְדָוִד אֲשֶׁר דִּבֶּר לַיהוָה אֶת־דִּבְרֵי הַשִּׁירָה הַזֹּאת בְּיוֹם הִצִּיל־יְהוָה אוֹתוֹ מִכַּף כָּל־אֹיְבָיו וּמִיַּד שָׁאוּל:

2 He said: I adore you, *Hashem*, my strength,

ב וַיֹּאמַר אֶרְחָמְךָ יְהוָה חִזְקִי:

Ariel view of Bat Ayin

17:8 The apple of Your eye The term *eeshon bat ayin* (אישון בת־עין), 'the apple of the eye', refers to the pupil, and is used by the psalmist to reflect the divine protection he seeks: "Guard me like the apple of Your eye". The eye is the most sensitive part of the body, and therefore the most protected part of the face. There are eyelids and eyelashes to protect the eyes from foreign intrusion, eyebrows to protect from sweat, and the forehead and nose to protect them from impact. The psalmist asks that *Hashem* protect him fully like the eye that is surrounded on all sides. A more profound interpretation of this expression recognizes that the eye is also the window to the soul. By asking the Lord to protect his eyes, the psalmist is thus asking God to guard his soul. In 1989, a group of settlers created a new community in *Gush Etzion* under the guidance of Rabbi Yitzchak Ginsburg. The residents of the community, called *Bat Ayin*, are mostly Jews with Hassidic tendencies, who place great emphasis on spirituality and the soul and aim to recognize and spread the light of *Hashem* in this world. Today, close to 200 families live in *Bat Ayin*, representing Jews of all walks of life, from rabbis and teachers, to artists and musicians, builders, farmers, doctors and writers.

Tehillim/Psalms
Chapter 18

תהלים
פרק יח

3 *Hashem*, my crag, my fortress, my rescuer, my God, my rock in whom I seek refuge, my shield, my mighty Champion, my haven.

ג יְהֹוָה סַלְעִי וּמְצוּדָתִי וּמְפַלְטִי אֵלִי צוּרִי אֶחֱסֶה־בּוֹ מָגִנִּי וְקֶרֶן־יִשְׁעִי מִשְׂגַּבִּי׃

4 All praise! I called on *Hashem* and was delivered from my enemies.

ד מְהֻלָּל אֶקְרָא יְהֹוָה וּמִן־אֹיְבַי אִוָּשֵׁעַ׃

5 Ropes of Death encompassed me; torrents of Belial terrified me;

ה אֲפָפוּנִי חֶבְלֵי־מָוֶת וְנַחֲלֵי בְלִיַּעַל יְבַעֲתוּנִי׃

6 ropes of Sheol encircled me; snares of Death confronted me.

ו חֶבְלֵי שְׁאוֹל סְבָבוּנִי קִדְּמוּנִי מוֹקְשֵׁי מָוֶת׃

7 In my distress I called on *Hashem*, cried out to my God; in His temple He heard my voice; my cry to Him reached His ears.

ז בַּצַּר־לִי אֶקְרָא יְהֹוָה וְאֶל־אֱלֹהַי אֲשַׁוֵּעַ יִשְׁמַע מֵהֵיכָלוֹ קוֹלִי וְשַׁוְעָתִי לְפָנָיו תָּבוֹא בְאָזְנָיו׃

8 Then the earth rocked and quaked; the foundations of the mountains shook, rocked by His indignation;

ח וַתִּגְעַשׁ וַתִּרְעַשׁ הָאָרֶץ וּמוֹסְדֵי הָרִים יִרְגָּזוּ וַיִּתְגָּעֲשׁוּ כִּי־חָרָה לוֹ׃

va-tig-ASH va-tir-ASH ha-A-retz u-mo-s'-DAY ha-REEM yir-GA-zu va-yit-ga-a-SHU kee KHA-rah LO

9 smoke went up from His nostrils, from His mouth came devouring fire; live coals blazed forth from Him.

ט עָלָה עָשָׁן בְּאַפּוֹ וְאֵשׁ־מִפִּיו תֹּאכֵל גֶּחָלִים בָּעֲרוּ מִמֶּנּוּ׃

10 He bent the sky and came down, thick cloud beneath His feet.

י וַיֵּט שָׁמַיִם וַיֵּרַד וַעֲרָפֶל תַּחַת רַגְלָיו׃

11 He mounted a cherub and flew, gliding on the wings of the wind.

יא וַיִּרְכַּב עַל־כְּרוּב וַיָּעֹף וַיֵּדֶא עַל־כַּנְפֵי־רוּחַ׃

12 He made darkness His screen; dark thunderheads, dense clouds of the sky were His pavilion round about Him.

יב יָשֶׁת חֹשֶׁךְ סִתְרוֹ סְבִיבוֹתָיו סֻכָּתוֹ חֶשְׁכַת־מַיִם עָבֵי שְׁחָקִים׃

13 Out of the brilliance before Him, hail and fiery coals pierced His clouds.

יג מִנֹּגַהּ נֶגְדּוֹ עָבָיו עָבְרוּ בָּרָד וְגַחֲלֵי־אֵשׁ׃

14 Then *Hashem* thundered from heaven, the Most High gave forth His voice – hail and fiery coals.

יד וַיַּרְעֵם בַּשָּׁמַיִם יְהֹוָה וְעֶלְיוֹן יִתֵּן קֹלוֹ בָּרָד וְגַחֲלֵי־אֵשׁ׃

15 He let fly His shafts and scattered them; He discharged lightning and routed them.

טו וַיִּשְׁלַח חִצָּיו וַיְפִיצֵם וּבְרָקִים רָב וַיְהֻמֵּם׃

18:8 Then the earth rocked and quaked David sings a song of gratitude to *Hashem* after defeating his enemies. Sometimes God's support appears in the form of a "a soft murmuring sound" (I Kings 19:12); other times it "rocked and quaked" the very foundations of the world. In Israel over the centuries there have been many quakes which shook the earth. The Dead Sea, for example, is a result of a cataclysmic rift in the earth's crust, a result of the tectonic plates shifting under the surface. This shift produced mountain ranges and volcanoes in the Golan Heights, as well as deep fissures, one of which is filled with the deepest hypersaline lake in the world.

The Dead Sea

Tehillim/Psalms
Chapter 18

תהלים
פרק יח

16 The ocean bed was exposed; the foundations of the world were laid bare by You mighty roaring, *Hashem*, at the blast of the breath of Your nostrils.

טז וַיֵּרָאוּ אֲפִיקֵי מַיִם וַיִּגָּלוּ מוֹסְדוֹת תֵּבֵל מִגַּעֲרָתְךָ יְהֹוָה מִנִּשְׁמַת רוּחַ אַפֶּךָ׃

17 He reached down from on high, He took me; He drew me out of the mighty waters;

יז יִשְׁלַח מִמָּרוֹם יִקָּחֵנִי יַמְשֵׁנִי מִמַּיִם רַבִּים׃

18 He saved me from my fierce enemy, from foes too strong for me.

יח יַצִּילֵנִי מֵאֹיְבִי עָז וּמִשֹּׂנְאַי כִּי־אָמְצוּ מִמֶּנִּי׃

19 They confronted me on the day of my calamity, but *Hashem* was my support.

יט יְקַדְּמוּנִי בְיוֹם־אֵידִי וַיְהִי־יְהֹוָה לְמִשְׁעָן לִי׃

20 He brought me out to freedom; He rescued me because He was pleased with me.

כ וַיּוֹצִיאֵנִי לַמֶּרְחָב יְחַלְּצֵנִי כִּי חָפֵץ בִּי׃

21 *Hashem* rewarded me according to my merit; He requited the cleanness of my hands;

כא יִגְמְלֵנִי יְהֹוָה כְּצִדְקִי כְּבֹר יָדַי יָשִׁיב לִי׃

22 for I have kept to the ways of *Hashem*, and have not been guilty before my God;

כב כִּי־שָׁמַרְתִּי דַּרְכֵי יְהֹוָה וְלֹא־רָשַׁעְתִּי מֵאֱלֹהָי׃

23 for I am mindful of all His rules; I have not disregarded His laws.

כג כִּי כָל־מִשְׁפָּטָיו לְנֶגְדִּי וְחֻקֹּתָיו לֹא־אָסִיר מֶנִּי׃

24 I have been blameless toward Him, and have guarded myself against sinning;

כד וָאֱהִי תָמִים עִמּוֹ וָאֶשְׁתַּמֵּר מֵעֲוֺנִי׃

25 and *Hashem* has requited me according to my merit, the cleanness of my hands in His sight.

כה וַיָּשֶׁב־יְהֹוָה לִי כְצִדְקִי כְּבֹר יָדַי לְנֶגֶד עֵינָיו׃

26 With the loyal, You deal loyally; with the blameless man, blamelessly.

כו עִם־חָסִיד תִּתְחַסָּד עִם־גְּבַר תָּמִים תִּתַּמָּם׃

27 With the pure, You act purely, and with the perverse, You are wily.

כז עִם־נָבָר תִּתְבָּרָר וְעִם־עִקֵּשׁ תִּתְפַּתָּל׃

28 It is You who deliver lowly folk, but haughty eyes You humble.

כח כִּי־אַתָּה עַם־עָנִי תוֹשִׁיעַ וְעֵינַיִם רָמוֹת תַּשְׁפִּיל׃

29 It is You who light my lamp; *Hashem*, my God, lights up my darkness.

כט כִּי־אַתָּה תָּאִיר נֵרִי יְהֹוָה אֱלֹהַי יַגִּיהַּ חָשְׁכִּי׃

30 With You, I can rush a barrier; with my God I can scale a wall;

ל כִּי־בְךָ אָרֻץ גְּדוּד וּבֵאלֹהַי אֲדַלֶּג־שׁוּר׃

31 the way of *Hashem* is perfect; the word of *Hashem* is pure; He is a shield to all who seek refuge in Him.

לא הָאֵל תָּמִים דַּרְכּוֹ אִמְרַת־יְהֹוָה צְרוּפָה מָגֵן הוּא לְכֹל הַחֹסִים בּוֹ׃

32 Truly, who is a god except *Hashem*, who is a rock but our God? –

לב כִּי מִי אֱלוֹהַּ מִבַּלְעֲדֵי יְהֹוָה וּמִי צוּר זוּלָתִי אֱלֹהֵינוּ׃

33 the God who girded me with might, who made my way perfect;

לג הָאֵל הַמְאַזְּרֵנִי חָיִל וַיִּתֵּן תָּמִים דַּרְכִּי׃

34 who made my legs like a deer's, and let me stand firm on the heights;

לד מְשַׁוֶּה רַגְלַי כָּאַיָּלוֹת וְעַל בָּמֹתַי יַעֲמִידֵנִי׃

1491

Tehillim/Psalms
Chapter 19

#	English	Hebrew
35	who trained my hands for battle; my arms can bend a bow of bronze.	לה מְלַמֵּד יָדַי לַמִּלְחָמָה וְנִחֲתָה קֶשֶׁת־נְחוּשָׁה זְרוֹעֹתָי:
36	You have given me the shield of Your protection; Your right hand has sustained me, Your care has made me great.	לו וַתִּתֶּן־לִי מָגֵן יִשְׁעֶךָ וִימִינְךָ תִסְעָדֵנִי וְעַנְוַתְךָ תַרְבֵּנִי:
37	You have let me stride on freely; my feet have not slipped.	לז תַּרְחִיב צַעֲדִי תַחְתָּי וְלֹא מָעֲדוּ קַרְסֻלָּי:
38	I pursued my enemies and overtook them; I did not turn back till I destroyed them.	לח אֶרְדּוֹף אוֹיְבַי וְאַשִּׂיגֵם וְלֹא־אָשׁוּב עַד־כַּלּוֹתָם:
39	I struck them down, and they could rise no more; they lay fallen at my feet.	לט אֶמְחָצֵם וְלֹא־יֻכְלוּ קוּם יִפְּלוּ תַּחַת רַגְלָי:
40	You have girded me with strength for battle, brought my adversaries low before me,	מ וַתְּאַזְּרֵנִי חַיִל לַמִּלְחָמָה תַּכְרִיעַ קָמַי תַּחְתָּי:
41	made my enemies turn tail before me; I wiped out my foes.	מא וְאֹיְבַי נָתַתָּה לִּי עֹרֶף וּמְשַׂנְאַי אַצְמִיתֵם:
42	They cried out, but there was none to deliver; [cried] to *Hashem*, but He did not answer them.	מב יְשַׁוְּעוּ וְאֵין־מוֹשִׁיעַ עַל־יְהוָה וְלֹא עָנָם:
43	I ground them fine as windswept dust; I trod them flat as dirt of the streets.	מג וְאֶשְׁחָקֵם כְּעָפָר עַל־פְּנֵי־רוּחַ כְּטִיט חוּצוֹת אֲרִיקֵם:
44	You have rescued me from the strife of people; You have set me at the head of nations; peoples I knew not must serve me.	מד תְּפַלְּטֵנִי מֵרִיבֵי עָם תְּשִׂימֵנִי לְרֹאשׁ גּוֹיִם עַם לֹא־יָדַעְתִּי יַעַבְדוּנִי:
45	At the mere report of me they are submissive; foreign peoples cower before me;	מה לְשֵׁמַע אֹזֶן יִשָּׁמְעוּ לִי בְּנֵי־נֵכָר יְכַחֲשׁוּ־לִי:
46	foreign peoples lose courage, and come trembling out of their strongholds.	מו בְּנֵי־נֵכָר יִבֹּלוּ וְיַחְרְגוּ מִמִּסְגְּרוֹתֵיהֶם:
47	*Hashem* lives! Blessed is my rock! Exalted be *Hashem*, my deliverer,	מז חַי־יְהוָה וּבָרוּךְ צוּרִי וְיָרוּם אֱלֹהֵי יִשְׁעִי:
48	the God who has vindicated me and made peoples subject to me,	מח הָאֵל הַנּוֹתֵן נְקָמוֹת לִי וַיַּדְבֵּר עַמִּים תַּחְתָּי:
49	who rescued me from my enemies, who raised me clear of my adversaries, saved me from lawless men.	מט מְפַלְּטִי מֵאֹיְבָי אַף מִן־קָמַי תְּרוֹמְמֵנִי מֵאִישׁ חָמָס תַּצִּילֵנִי:
50	For this I sing Your praise among the nations, *Hashem*, and hymn Your name:	נ עַל־כֵּן אוֹדְךָ בַגּוֹיִם יְהוָה וּלְשִׁמְךָ אֲזַמֵּרָה:
51	He accords great victories to His king, keeps faith with His anointed, with *David* and his offspring forever.	נא מַגְדִּל [מִגְדּוֹל] יְשׁוּעוֹת מַלְכּוֹ וְעֹשֶׂה חֶסֶד לִמְשִׁיחוֹ לְדָוִד וּלְזַרְעוֹ עַד־עוֹלָם:

19 1 For the leader. A psalm of *David*.   **יט** א לַמְנַצֵּחַ מִזְמוֹר לְדָוִד:

2 The heavens declare the glory of *Hashem*, the sky proclaims His handiwork.   ב הַשָּׁמַיִם מְסַפְּרִים כְּבוֹד־אֵל וּמַעֲשֵׂה יָדָיו מַגִּיד הָרָקִיעַ:

Tehillim/Psalms
Chapter 19

תהלים
פרק יט

3 Day to day makes utterance, night to night speaks out.

ג יוֹם לְיוֹם יַבִּיעַ אֹמֶר וְלַיְלָה לְּלַיְלָה יְחַוֶּה־דָּעַת׃

4 There is no utterance, there are no words, whose sound goes unheard.

ד אֵין־אֹמֶר וְאֵין דְּבָרִים בְּלִי נִשְׁמָע קוֹלָם׃

5 Their voice carries throughout the earth, their words to the end of the world. He placed in them a tent for the sun,

ה בְּכָל־הָאָרֶץ יָצָא קַוָּם וּבִקְצֵה תֵבֵל מִלֵּיהֶם לַשֶּׁמֶשׁ שָׂם־אֹהֶל בָּהֶם׃

6 who is like a groom coming forth from the chamber, like a hero, eager to run his course.

ו וְהוּא כְּחָתָן יֹצֵא מֵחֻפָּתוֹ יָשִׂישׂ כְּגִבּוֹר לָרוּץ אֹרַח׃

v'-HU k'-kha-TAN yo-TZAY may-khu-pa-TO ya-SEES k'-gi-BOR la-RUTZ O-rakh

7 His rising-place is at one end of heaven, and his circuit reaches the other; nothing escapes his heat.

ז מִקְצֵה הַשָּׁמַיִם מוֹצָאוֹ וּתְקוּפָתוֹ עַל־קְצוֹתָם וְאֵין נִסְתָּר מֵחַמָּתוֹ׃

8 The teaching of *Hashem* is perfect, renewing life; the decrees of *Hashem* are enduring, making the simple wise;

ח תּוֹרַת יְהֹוָה תְּמִימָה מְשִׁיבַת נָפֶשׁ עֵדוּת יְהֹוָה נֶאֱמָנָה מַחְכִּימַת פֶּתִי׃

9 The precepts of *Hashem* are just, rejoicing the heart; the instruction of *Hashem* is lucid, making the eyes light up.

ט פִּקּוּדֵי יְהֹוָה יְשָׁרִים מְשַׂמְּחֵי־לֵב מִצְוַת יְהֹוָה בָּרָה מְאִירַת עֵינָיִם׃

10 The fear of *Hashem* is pure, abiding forever; the judgments of *Hashem* are true, righteous altogether,

י יִרְאַת יְהֹוָה טְהוֹרָה עוֹמֶדֶת לָעַד מִשְׁפְּטֵי־יְהֹוָה אֱמֶת צָדְקוּ יַחְדָּו׃

11 more desirable than gold, than much fine gold; sweeter than honey, than drippings of the comb.

יא הַנֶּחֱמָדִים מִזָּהָב וּמִפַּז רָב וּמְתוּקִים מִדְּבַשׁ וְנֹפֶת צוּפִים׃

12 Your servant pays them heed; in obeying them there is much reward.

יב גַּם־עַבְדְּךָ נִזְהָר בָּהֶם בְּשָׁמְרָם עֵקֶב רָב׃

13 Who can be aware of errors? Clear me of unperceived guilt,

יג שְׁגִיאוֹת מִי־יָבִין מִנִּסְתָּרוֹת נַקֵּנִי׃

14 and from willful sins keep Your servant; let them not dominate me; then shall I be blameless and clear of grave offense.

יד גַּם מִזֵּדִים חֲשֹׂךְ עַבְדֶּךָ אַל־יִמְשְׁלוּ־בִי אָז אֵיתָם וְנִקֵּיתִי מִפֶּשַׁע רָב׃

Arbel Valley

19:6 Who is like a groom coming forth from the chamber The psalm begins with a description of nature praising *Hashem*. The king of nature, the sun, is portrayed as a glorious symbol of God's magnificence on this earth, described as "a groom coming forth from the chamber." The rising of the sun is also seen as a metaphor for the redemption of the Jewish people. The Jerusalem Talmud (*Berachot* 1:1) relates a story of two righteous rabbinic scholars, Rabbi Hiyya and Rabbi Shimon, walking in the Arbel Valley in the Lower Galilee, in the early hours of the morning. As the first rays of dawn appeared, Rabbi Hiyya remarked to Rabbi Shimon that this is how the redemption of Israel will take place. At first it comes very slowly, but as it progresses, its light increases. This lesson is important to keep in mind when we look critically at current events or the imperfect political reality confronting Israel, both domestically and internationally. The redemption of Israel is coming. It develops slowly, but surely.

Tehillim/Psalms
Chapter 20

15 May the words of my mouth and the prayer of my heart be acceptable to You, *Hashem*, my rock and my redeemer.

תהלים
פרק כ

טו יִהְיוּ לְרָצוֹן אִמְרֵי־פִי וְהֶגְיוֹן לִבִּי לְפָנֶיךָ יְהֹוָה צוּרִי וְגֹאֲלִי:

20 1 For the leader. A psalm of *David*.

כ א לַמְנַצֵּחַ מִזְמוֹר לְדָוִד:

2 May *Hashem* answer you in time of trouble, the name of *Yaakov's Hashem* keep you safe.

ב יַעַנְךָ יְהֹוָה בְּיוֹם צָרָה יְשַׂגֶּבְךָ שֵׁם אֱלֹהֵי יַעֲקֹב:

3 May He send you help from the sanctuary, and sustain you from *Tzion*.

ג יִשְׁלַח־עֶזְרְךָ מִקֹּדֶשׁ וּמִצִּיּוֹן יִסְעָדֶךָּ:

4 May He receive the tokens of all your meal offerings, and approve your burn offerings. *Selah*.

ד יִזְכֹּר כָּל־מִנְחֹתֶךָ וְעוֹלָתְךָ יְדַשְּׁנֶה סֶלָה:

5 May He grant you your desire, and fulfill your every plan.

ה יִתֶּן־לְךָ כִלְבָבֶךָ וְכָל־עֲצָתְךָ יְמַלֵּא:

6 May we shout for joy in your victory, arrayed by standards in the name of our God. May *Hashem* fulfill your every wish.

ו נְרַנְּנָה בִּישׁוּעָתֶךָ וּבְשֵׁם־אֱלֹהֵינוּ נִדְגֹּל יְמַלֵּא יְהֹוָה כָּל־מִשְׁאֲלוֹתֶיךָ:

7 Now I know that *Hashem* will give victory to His anointed, will answer him from His heavenly sanctuary with the mighty victories of His right arm.

ז עַתָּה יָדַעְתִּי כִּי הוֹשִׁיעַ יְהֹוָה מְשִׁיחוֹ יַעֲנֵהוּ מִשְּׁמֵי קָדְשׁוֹ בִּגְבֻרוֹת יֵשַׁע יְמִינוֹ:

a-TAH ya-DA-tee KEE ho-SHEE-a a-do-NAI m'-shee-KHO ya-a-NAY-hu mi-sh'-MAY kod-SHO big-vu-ROT YAY-sha y'-mee-NO

8 They [call] on chariots, they [call] on horses, but we call on the name of *Hashem* our God.

ח אֵלֶּה בָרֶכֶב וְאֵלֶּה בַסּוּסִים וַאֲנַחְנוּ בְּשֵׁם־יְהֹוָה אֱלֹהֵינוּ נַזְכִּיר:

9 They collapse and lie fallen, but we rally and gather strength.

ט הֵמָּה כָּרְעוּ וְנָפָלוּ וַאֲנַחְנוּ קַּמְנוּ וַנִּתְעוֹדָד:

10 *Hashem*, grant victory! May the King answer us when we call.

י יְהֹוָה הוֹשִׁיעָה הַמֶּלֶךְ יַעֲנֵנוּ בְיוֹם־קָרְאֵנוּ:

21 1 For the leader. A psalm of *David*.

כא א לַמְנַצֵּחַ מִזְמוֹר לְדָוִד:

2 *Hashem*, the king rejoices in Your strength; how greatly he exults in Your victory!

ב יְהֹוָה בְּעָזְּךָ יִשְׂמַח־מֶלֶךְ וּבִישׁוּעָתְךָ מַה־יָּגִיל [יָגֶל] מְאֹד:

20:7 *Hashem* will give victory to His anointed The *Torah* predicts a time when the Children of Israel, settled in the Land of Israel, will seek a king (Deuteronomy 17:14). God acquiesces to the request on condition that His anointed will be different from the kings of the other nations, in that he will be chosen by God (verse 15). This prediction came true in the times of the prophet *Shmuel* (I Samuel 8), as *Shaul*, followed by *David* and *Shlomo*, were chosen by *Hashem* as the first Jewish kings. The selection and anointing of the monarch reflects the vital relationship that the Jewish king must have with the priest, who is also anointed, and the prophet, God's messenger who selects and anoints the king. Together, these three represent the political, ritual and spiritual leadership of Israel. In order to lead the nation on the right path, the three leaders must work together and recognize the importance of each one's role. When, as in the case of *David*, the nation reveres the king and he, in turn, recognizes that his power comes from the Holy One, then "*Hashem* will give victory to His anointed."

Tomb of King David in Jerusalem

Tehillim/Psalms
Chapter 22

תהלים
פרק כב

3 You have granted him the desire of his heart, have not denied the request of his lips. *Selah*.

ג תַּאֲוַת לִבּוֹ נָתַתָּה לּוֹ וַאֲרֶשֶׁת שְׂפָתָיו בַּל־מָנַעְתָּ סֶּלָה:

4 You have proffered him blessings of good things, have set upon his head a crown of fine gold.

ד כִּי־תְקַדְּמֶנּוּ בִּרְכוֹת טוֹב תָּשִׁית לְרֹאשׁוֹ עֲטֶרֶת פָּז:

kee t'-ka-d'-ME-nu bir-KHOT TOV ta-SHEET l'-ro-SHO a-TE-ret PAZ

5 He asked You for life; You granted it; a long life, everlasting.

ה חַיִּים שָׁאַל מִמְּךָ נָתַתָּה לּוֹ אֹרֶךְ יָמִים עוֹלָם וָעֶד:

6 Great is his glory through Your victory; You have endowed him with splendor and majesty.

ו גָּדוֹל כְּבוֹדוֹ בִּישׁוּעָתֶךָ הוֹד וְהָדָר תְּשַׁוֶּה עָלָיו:

7 You have made him blessed forever, gladdened him with the joy of Your presence.

ז כִּי־תְשִׁיתֵהוּ בְרָכוֹת לָעַד תְּחַדֵּהוּ בְשִׂמְחָה אֶת־פָּנֶיךָ:

8 For the king trusts in *Hashem*; Through the faithfulness of the Most High he will not be shaken.

ח כִּי־הַמֶּלֶךְ בֹּטֵחַ בַּיהוָה וּבְחֶסֶד עֶלְיוֹן בַּל־יִמּוֹט:

9 Your hand is equal to all Your enemies; Your right hand overpowers Your foes.

ט תִּמְצָא יָדְךָ לְכָל־אֹיְבֶיךָ יְמִינְךָ תִּמְצָא שֹׂנְאֶיךָ:

10 You set them ablaze like a furnace when You show Your presence. *Hashem* in anger destroys them; fire consumes them.

י תְּשִׁיתֵמוֹ כְּתַנּוּר אֵשׁ לְעֵת פָּנֶיךָ יְהוָה בְּאַפּוֹ יְבַלְּעֵם וְתֹאכְלֵם אֵשׁ:

11 You wipe their offspring from the earth, their issue from among men.

יא פִּרְיָמוֹ מֵאֶרֶץ תְּאַבֵּד וְזַרְעָם מִבְּנֵי אָדָם:

12 For they schemed against You; they laid plans, but could not succeed.

יב כִּי־נָטוּ עָלֶיךָ רָעָה חָשְׁבוּ מְזִמָּה בַּל־יוּכָלוּ:

13 For You make them turn back by Your bows aimed at their face.

יג כִּי תְּשִׁיתֵמוֹ שֶׁכֶם בְּמֵיתָרֶיךָ תְּכוֹנֵן עַל־פְּנֵיהֶם:

14 Be exalted, *Hashem*, through Your strength; we will sing and chant the praises of Your mighty deeds.

יד רוּמָה יְהוָה בְעֻזֶּךָ נָשִׁירָה וּנְזַמְּרָה גְּבוּרָתֶךָ:

22 1 For the leader; on ayyeleth ha-shachar. A psalm of *David*.

כב א לַמְנַצֵּחַ עַל־אַיֶּלֶת הַשַּׁחַר מִזְמוֹר לְדָוִד:

2 My *Hashem*, my God, why have You abandoned me; why so far from delivering me and from my anguished roaring?

ב אֵלִי אֵלִי לָמָה עֲזַבְתָּנִי רָחוֹק מִישׁוּעָתִי דִּבְרֵי שַׁאֲגָתִי:

21:4 Set upon his head a crown of fine gold This psalm praises the king of Israel and prays that he conquer Israel's enemies. *Hashem* places a gold crown on his head, as a symbol of His protection and providence. The first king of Israel, *Shaul*, came from the tribe of *Binyamin*. The prophet *Shmuel* anoints him in the hills of *Efraim* and the nation rallies behind him and crowns him king. In 1981, a few families established a new community in the land of the tribe of *Binyamin*. They called the village *Ateret*, the Hebrew word used in this verse for 'crown.' Over the years, the settlement has grown and now boasts hundreds of people, synthesizing working the land with a commitment to God and the nation.

Welcome sign, Ateret, Israel

1495

Tehillim/Psalms
Chapter 22

תהלים
פרק כב

3 My *Hashem*, I cry by day – You answer not; by night, and have no respite.

ג אֱלֹהַי אֶקְרָא יוֹמָם וְלֹא תַעֲנֶה וְלַיְלָה וְלֹא־דוּמִיָּה לִי:

4 But You are the Holy One, enthroned, the Praise of *Yisrael*.

ד וְאַתָּה קָדוֹשׁ יוֹשֵׁב תְּהִלּוֹת יִשְׂרָאֵל:

5 In You our fathers trusted; they trusted, and You rescued them.

ה בְּךָ בָּטְחוּ אֲבֹתֵינוּ בָּטְחוּ וַתְּפַלְּטֵמוֹ:

6 To You they cried out and they escaped; in You they trusted and were not disappointed.

ו אֵלֶיךָ זָעֲקוּ וְנִמְלָטוּ בְּךָ בָטְחוּ וְלֹא־בוֹשׁוּ:

7 But I am a worm, less than human; scorned by men, despised by people.

ז וְאָנֹכִי תוֹלַעַת וְלֹא־אִישׁ חֶרְפַּת אָדָם וּבְזוּי עָם:

v'-a-no-KHEE to-LA-at v'-lo EESH kher-PAT a-DAM uv-ZUY AM

8 All who see me mock me; they curl their lips, they shake their heads.

ח כָּל־רֹאַי יַלְעִגוּ לִי יַפְטִירוּ בְשָׂפָה יָנִיעוּ רֹאשׁ:

9 "Let him commit himself to *Hashem*; let Him rescue him, let Him save him, for He is pleased with him."

ט גֹּל אֶל־יְהוָה יְפַלְּטֵהוּ יַצִּילֵהוּ כִּי חָפֵץ בּוֹ:

10 You drew me from the womb, made me secure at my mother's breast.

י כִּי־אַתָּה גֹחִי מִבָּטֶן מַבְטִיחִי עַל־שְׁדֵי אִמִּי:

11 I became Your charge at birth; from my mother's womb You have been my God.

יא עָלֶיךָ הָשְׁלַכְתִּי מֵרָחֶם מִבֶּטֶן אִמִּי אֵלִי אָתָּה:

12 Do not be far from me, for trouble is near, and there is none to help.

יב אַל־תִּרְחַק מִמֶּנִּי כִּי־צָרָה קְרוֹבָה כִּי־אֵין עוֹזֵר:

13 Many bulls surround me, mighty ones of Bashan encircle me.

יג סְבָבוּנִי פָּרִים רַבִּים אַבִּירֵי בָשָׁן כִּתְּרוּנִי:

14 They open their mouths at me like tearing, roaring lions.

יד פָּצוּ עָלַי פִּיהֶם אַרְיֵה טֹרֵף וְשֹׁאֵג:

15 My life ebbs away: all my bones are disjointed; my heart is like wax, melting within me;

טו כַּמַּיִם נִשְׁפַּכְתִּי וְהִתְפָּרְדוּ כָּל־עַצְמוֹתָי הָיָה לִבִּי כַּדּוֹנָג נָמֵס בְּתוֹךְ מֵעָי:

16 my vigor dries up like a shard; my tongue cleaves to my palate; You commit me to the dust of death.

טז יָבֵשׁ כַּחֶרֶשׂ כֹּחִי וּלְשׁוֹנִי מֻדְבָּק מַלְקוֹחָי וְלַעֲפַר־מָוֶת תִּשְׁפְּתֵנִי:

22:7 But I am a worm, less than human The Talmud (*Chullin* 89a) states that *Hashem* grants greatness to the righteous but they humble themselves. *Avraham* calls himself "dust of the earth" (Genesis 18:27), *Moshe* and *Aharon* say "For who are we" (Exodus 16:7), *Shaul* calls himself a "simple son of the small tribe of *Binyamin*" (I Samuel 9:21), and *Gidon* says "But I am only a Benjaminite, from the smallest of the tribes of *Yisrael*, and my clan is the least of all the clans of the tribe of *Binyamin*!" (Judges 6:15). But when the Lord grants greatness to the wicked, they lash out against Him and Israel in arrogance. Pharaoh says "Who is *Hashem* that I should heed Him?" (Exodus 5:2), Goliath says "I herewith defy the ranks of *Yisrael*" (I Samuel 17:10), Sennacherib asks "Which among all the gods of [those] countries saved their countries from me, that *Hashem* should save *Yerushalayim* from me?" (II Kings 18:35), and Nebuchadnezzar says "and what god is there that can save you from my power?" (Daniel 3:15). *David* reminds us of the value of humility that leaders must display in their lives.

Tehillim/Psalms
Chapter 23

תהלים
פרק כג

17 Dogs surround me; a pack of evil ones closes in on me, like lions [they maul] my hands and feet.

יז כִּי סְבָבוּנִי כְּלָבִים עֲדַת מְרֵעִים הִקִּיפוּנִי כָּאֲרִי יָדַי וְרַגְלָי:

18 I take the count of all my bones while they look on and gloat.

יח אֲסַפֵּר כָּל־עַצְמוֹתָי הֵמָּה יַבִּיטוּ יִרְאוּ־בִי:

19 They divide my clothes among themselves, casting lots for my garments.

יט יְחַלְּקוּ בְגָדַי לָהֶם וְעַל־לְבוּשִׁי יַפִּילוּ גוֹרָל:

20 But You, *Hashem*, be not far off; my strength, hasten to my aid.

כ וְאַתָּה יְהֹוָה אַל־תִּרְחָק אֱיָלוּתִי לְעֶזְרָתִי חוּשָׁה:

21 Save my life from the sword, my precious life from the clutches of a dog.

כא הַצִּילָה מֵחֶרֶב נַפְשִׁי מִיַּד־כֶּלֶב יְחִידָתִי:

22 Deliver me from a lion's mouth; from the horns of wild oxen rescue me.

כב הוֹשִׁיעֵנִי מִפִּי אַרְיֵה וּמִקַּרְנֵי רֵמִים עֲנִיתָנִי:

23 Then will I proclaim Your fame to my brethren, praise You in the congregation.

כג אֲסַפְּרָה שִׁמְךָ לְאֶחָי בְּתוֹךְ קָהָל אֲהַלְלֶךָּ:

24 You who fear *Hashem*, praise Him! All you offspring of *Yaakov*, honor Him! Be in dread of Him, all you offspring of *Yisrael*!

כד יִרְאֵי יְהֹוָה הַלְלוּהוּ כָּל־זֶרַע יַעֲקֹב כַּבְּדוּהוּ וְגוּרוּ מִמֶּנּוּ כָּל־זֶרַע יִשְׂרָאֵל:

25 For He did not scorn, He did not spurn the plea of the lowly; He did not hide His face from him; when he cried out to Him, He listened.

כה כִּי לֹא־בָזָה וְלֹא שִׁקַּץ עֱנוּת עָנִי וְלֹא־הִסְתִּיר פָּנָיו מִמֶּנּוּ וּבְשַׁוְּעוֹ אֵלָיו שָׁמֵעַ:

26 Because of You I offer praise in the great congregation; I pay my vows in the presence of His worshipers.

כו מֵאִתְּךָ תְהִלָּתִי בְּקָהָל רָב נְדָרַי אֲשַׁלֵּם נֶגֶד יְרֵאָיו:

27 Let the lowly eat and be satisfied; let all who seek *Hashem* praise Him. Always be of good cheer!

כז יֹאכְלוּ עֲנָוִים וְיִשְׂבָּעוּ יְהַלְלוּ יְהֹוָה דֹּרְשָׁיו יְחִי לְבַבְכֶם לָעַד:

28 Let all the ends of the earth pay heed and turn to *Hashem*, and the peoples of all nations prostrate themselves before You;

כח יִזְכְּרוּ וְיָשֻׁבוּ אֶל־יְהֹוָה כָּל־אַפְסֵי־אָרֶץ וְיִשְׁתַּחֲווּ לְפָנֶיךָ כָּל־מִשְׁפְּחוֹת גּוֹיִם:

29 for kingship is *Hashem*'s and He rules the nations.

כט כִּי לַיהֹוָה הַמְּלוּכָה וּמֹשֵׁל בַּגּוֹיִם:

30 All those in full vigor shall eat and prostrate themselves; all those at death's door, whose spirits flag, shall bend the knee before Him.

ל אָכְלוּ וַיִּשְׁתַּחֲווּ כָּל־דִּשְׁנֵי־אֶרֶץ לְפָנָיו יִכְרְעוּ כָּל־יוֹרְדֵי עָפָר וְנַפְשׁוֹ לֹא חִיָּה:

31 Offspring shall serve Him; *Hashem*'s fame shall be proclaimed to the generation

לא זֶרַע יַעַבְדֶנּוּ יְסֻפַּר לַאדֹנָי לַדּוֹר:

32 to come; they shall tell of His beneficence to people yet to be born, for He has acted.

לב יָבֹאוּ וְיַגִּידוּ צִדְקָתוֹ לְעַם נוֹלָד כִּי עָשָׂה:

23 1 A psalm of *David*. *Hashem* is my shepherd; I lack nothing.

כג א מִזְמוֹר לְדָוִד יְהֹוָה רֹעִי לֹא אֶחְסָר:

2 He makes me lie down in green pastures; He leads me to water in places of repose;

ב בִּנְאוֹת דֶּשֶׁא יַרְבִּיצֵנִי עַל־מֵי מְנֻחוֹת יְנַהֲלֵנִי:

1497

Tehillim/Psalms
Chapter 24

תהלים
פרק כד

3 He renews my life; He guides me in right paths as befits His name.

ג נַפְשִׁי יְשׁוֹבֵב יַנְחֵנִי בְמַעְגְּלֵי־צֶדֶק לְמַעַן שְׁמוֹ:

4 Though I walk through a valley of deepest darkness, I fear no harm, for You are with me; Your rod and Your staff – they comfort me.

ד גַּם כִּי־אֵלֵךְ בְּגֵיא צַלְמָוֶת לֹא־אִירָא רָע כִּי־אַתָּה עִמָּדִי שִׁבְטְךָ וּמִשְׁעַנְתֶּךָ הֵמָּה יְנַחֲמֻנִי:

5 You spread a table for me in full view of my enemies; You anoint my head with oil; my drink is abundant.

ה תַּעֲרֹךְ לְפָנַי שֻׁלְחָן נֶגֶד צֹרְרָי דִּשַּׁנְתָּ בַשֶּׁמֶן רֹאשִׁי כּוֹסִי רְוָיָה:

6 Only goodness and steadfast love shall pursue me all the days of my life, and I shall dwell in the house of *Hashem* for many long years.

ו אַךְ טוֹב וָחֶסֶד יִרְדְּפוּנִי כָּל־יְמֵי חַיָּי וְשַׁבְתִּי בְּבֵית־יְהֹוָה לְאֹרֶךְ יָמִים:

AKH TOV va-KHE-sed yir-d'-FU-nee kol y'-MAY kha-YAI v'-shav-TEE b'-vayt a-do-NAI l-O-rekh ya-MEEM

24

1 Of *David*. A psalm. The earth is *Hashem*'s and all that it holds, the world and its inhabitants.

כד א לְדָוִד מִזְמוֹר לַיהֹוָה הָאָרֶץ וּמְלוֹאָהּ תֵּבֵל וְיֹשְׁבֵי בָהּ:

l'-da-VID miz-MOR la-do-NAI ha-A-retz um-lo-AH tay-VAYL v'-yo-sh'-VAY VAH

2 For He founded it upon the ocean, set it on the nether-streams.

ב כִּי־הוּא עַל־יַמִּים יְסָדָהּ וְעַל־נְהָרוֹת יְכוֹנְנֶהָ:

3 Who may ascend the mountain of *Hashem*? Who may stand in His holy place? –

ג מִי־יַעֲלֶה בְהַר־יְהֹוָה וּמִי־יָקוּם בִּמְקוֹם קָדְשׁוֹ:

4 He who has clean hands and a pure heart, who has not taken a false oath by My life or sworn deceitfully.

ד נְקִי כַפַּיִם וּבַר־לֵבָב אֲשֶׁר לֹא־נָשָׂא לַשָּׁוְא נַפְשִׁי וְלֹא נִשְׁבַּע לְמִרְמָה:

5 He shall carry away a blessing from *Hashem*, a just reward from *Hashem*, his deliverer.

ה יִשָּׂא בְרָכָה מֵאֵת יְהֹוָה וּצְדָקָה מֵאֱלֹהֵי יִשְׁעוֹ:

6 Such is the circle of those who turn to Him, *Yaakov*, who seek Your presence. *Selah*.

ו זֶה דּוֹר דֹּרְשָׁיו [דֹּרְשׁוֹ] מְבַקְשֵׁי פָנֶיךָ יַעֲקֹב סֶלָה:

23:6 And I shall dwell in the house of *Hashem* for many long years Psalm 23 has stood by the Jewish people as their support through the darkest days of persecution and exile. Over the centuries, no evil murderer or terrible tragedy has been able to crush the resilient spirit of the Jews, when they remember that "You are with me" (verse 4). King *David* certainly has a difficult life. While he never gives up hope, as he knows that *Hashem* is with him, he longs for times when he can live comfortably in the Holy Land while "goodness and steadfast love shall pursue me all the days of my life." The concluding phrase "I shall dwell in the house of *Hashem* for many long years" uses the Hebrew word *v'shavtee* (ושבתי), 'to dwell.' However, the word also means 'I will return.' Here, King *David* prays not only to dwell in God's palace, but that he will be found worthy of returning there frequently.

24:1 The earth is *Hashem*'s and all that it holds As King *David* says in this verse, "The earth is *Hashem*'s and all that it holds." Just as the creator of a piece of art is the owner of his masterpiece, God, as creator, is the owner of the entire world. Only a creator can see the full potential of his creation, have a vision for its destiny and decide with whom to share it. Such is *Hashem*'s relationship with the world. He built it with a vision and shared it with mankind. As is stated over and over in the *Tanakh*, He chose to give the Land of Israel to the Jewish people.

Tehillim/Psalms
Chapter 25

תהילים
פרק כה

7 O gates, lift up your heads! Up high, you everlasting doors, so the King of glory may come in!

ז שְׂאוּ שְׁעָרִים רָאשֵׁיכֶם וְהִנָּשְׂאוּ פִּתְחֵי עוֹלָם וְיָבוֹא מֶלֶךְ הַכָּבוֹד:

8 Who is the King of glory? – *Hashem*, mighty and valiant, *Hashem*, valiant in battle.

ח מִי זֶה מֶלֶךְ הַכָּבוֹד יְהֹוָה עִזּוּז וְגִבּוֹר יְהֹוָה גִּבּוֹר מִלְחָמָה:

9 O gates, lift up your heads! Lift them up, you everlasting doors, so the King of glory may come in!

ט שְׂאוּ שְׁעָרִים רָאשֵׁיכֶם וּשְׂאוּ פִּתְחֵי עוֹלָם וְיָבֹא מֶלֶךְ הַכָּבוֹד:

10 Who is the King of glory? – the Lord of hosts, He is the King of glory! *Selah*.

י מִי הוּא זֶה מֶלֶךְ הַכָּבוֹד יְהֹוָה צְבָאוֹת הוּא מֶלֶךְ הַכָּבוֹד סֶלָה:

25

1 Of *David*. *Hashem*, I set my hope on You;

א לְדָוִד אֵלֶיךָ יְהֹוָה נַפְשִׁי אֶשָּׂא:

2 my God, in You I trust; may I not be disappointed, may my enemies not exult over me.

ב אֱלֹהַי בְּךָ בָטַחְתִּי אַל־אֵבוֹשָׁה אַל־יַעַלְצוּ אֹיְבַי לִי:

3 O let none who look to You be disappointed; let the faithless be disappointed, empty-handed.

ג גַּם כָּל־קֹוֶיךָ לֹא יֵבֹשׁוּ יֵבֹשׁוּ הַבּוֹגְדִים רֵיקָם:

4 Let me know Your paths, *Hashem*; teach me Your ways;

ד דְּרָכֶיךָ יְהֹוָה הוֹדִיעֵנִי אֹרְחוֹתֶיךָ לַמְּדֵנִי:

5 guide me in Your true way and teach me, for You are *Hashem*, my deliverer; it is You I look to at all times.

ה הַדְרִיכֵנִי בַאֲמִתֶּךָ וְלַמְּדֵנִי כִּי־אַתָּה אֱלֹהֵי יִשְׁעִי אוֹתְךָ קִוִּיתִי כָּל־הַיּוֹם:

had-ree-KHAY-nee va-a-mi-TE-kha v'-la-m'-DAY-nee kee a-TAH e-lo-HAY yish-EE o-t'-KHA ki-VEE-ti kol ha-YOM

6 *Hashem*, be mindful of Your compassion and Your faithfulness; they are old as time.

ו זְכֹר־רַחֲמֶיךָ יְהֹוָה וַחֲסָדֶיךָ כִּי מֵעוֹלָם הֵמָּה:

7 Be not mindful of my youthful sins and transgressions; in keeping with Your faithfulness consider what is in my favor, as befits Your goodness, *Hashem*.

ז חַטֹּאות נְעוּרַי וּפְשָׁעַי אַל־תִּזְכֹּר כְּחַסְדְּךָ זְכָר־לִי־אַתָּה לְמַעַן טוּבְךָ יְהֹוָה:

8 Good and upright is *Hashem*; therefore He shows sinners the way.

ח טוֹב־וְיָשָׁר יְהֹוָה עַל־כֵּן יוֹרֶה חַטָּאִים בַּדָּרֶךְ:

9 He guides the lowly in the right path, and teaches the lowly His way.

ט יַדְרֵךְ עֲנָוִים בַּמִּשְׁפָּט וִילַמֵּד עֲנָוִים דַּרְכּוֹ:

10 All *Hashem*'s paths are steadfast love for those who keep the decrees of His covenant.

י כָּל־אָרְחוֹת יְהֹוָה חֶסֶד וֶאֱמֶת לְנֹצְרֵי בְרִיתוֹ וְעֵדֹתָיו:

25:5 For You are *Hashem*, my deliverer This psalm is an acrostic, describing and praising the one who fears *Hashem*. Together with a statement of faith, it contains a desire to know God's ways, a plea for compassion, a confession of sins, and a request for deliverance from enemies and salvation for all Israel. In 1950, when the State of Israel was newly established and new settlements were emerging, a group of Yemenite Jews came to the lowlands near *Beit Shemesh* and desired to set up an agricultural settlement. They named it *Yishi*, meaning 'God is my deliverer'. Today, the Yemenite community still works the land and recites the *Tehillim* daily, continuously hoping for the complete salvation.

Village of Yishi

Tehillim/Psalms
Chapter 26

תהלים
פרק כו

11 As befits Your name, *Hashem*, pardon my iniquity though it be great.

יא לְמַעַן־שִׁמְךָ יְהֹוָה וְסָלַחְתָּ לַעֲוֺנִי כִּי רַב־הוּא׃

12 Whoever fears *Hashem*, he shall be shown what path to choose.

יב מִי־זֶה הָאִישׁ יְרֵא יְהֹוָה יוֹרֶנּוּ בְּדֶרֶךְ יִבְחָר׃

13 He shall live a happy life, and his children shall inherit the land.

יג נַפְשׁוֹ בְּטוֹב תָּלִין וְזַרְעוֹ יִירַשׁ אָרֶץ׃

14 The counsel of *Hashem* is for those who fear Him; to them He makes known His covenant.

יד סוֹד יְהֹוָה לִירֵאָיו וּבְרִיתוֹ לְהוֹדִיעָם׃

15 My eyes are ever toward *Hashem*, for He will loose my feet from the net.

טו עֵינַי תָּמִיד אֶל־יְהֹוָה כִּי הוּא־יוֹצִיא מֵרֶשֶׁת רַגְלָי׃

16 Turn to me, have mercy on me, for I am alone and afflicted.

טז פְּנֵה־אֵלַי וְחָנֵּנִי כִּי־יָחִיד וְעָנִי אָנִי׃

17 My deep distress increases; deliver me from my straits.

יז צָרוֹת לְבָבִי הִרְחִיבוּ מִמְּצוּקוֹתַי הוֹצִיאֵנִי׃

18 Look at my affliction and suffering, and forgive all my sins.

יח רְאֵה עָנְיִי וַעֲמָלִי וְשָׂא לְכָל־חַטֹּאותָי׃

19 See how numerous my enemies are, and how unjustly they hate me!

יט רְאֵה־אוֹיְבַי כִּי־רָבּוּ וְשִׂנְאַת חָמָס שְׂנֵאוּנִי׃

20 Protect me and save me; let me not be disappointed, for I have sought refuge in You.

כ שָׁמְרָה נַפְשִׁי וְהַצִּילֵנִי אַל־אֵבוֹשׁ כִּי־חָסִיתִי בָךְ׃

21 May integrity and uprightness watch over me, for I look to You.

כא תֹּם־וָיֹשֶׁר יִצְּרוּנִי כִּי קִוִּיתִיךָ׃

22 O *Hashem*, redeem *Yisrael* from all its distress.

כב פְּדֵה אֱלֹהִים אֶת־יִשְׂרָאֵל מִכֹּל צָרוֹתָיו׃

26 1 Of *David*. Vindicate me, *Hashem*, for I have walked without blame; I have trusted in *Hashem*; I have not faltered.

כו א לְדָוִד שָׁפְטֵנִי יְהֹוָה כִּי־אֲנִי בְּתֻמִּי הָלַכְתִּי וּבַיהֹוָה בָּטַחְתִּי לֹא אֶמְעָד׃

l'-da-VID shof-TAY-nee a-do-NAI kee a-NEE b'-tu-MEE ha-LAKH-tee u-va-do-NAI ba-TAKH-tee LO em-AD

2 Probe me, *Hashem*, and try me, test my heart and mind;

ב בְּחָנֵנִי יְהֹוָה וְנַסֵּנִי צרופה [צָרְפָה] כִלְיוֹתַי וְלִבִּי׃

3 for my eyes are on Your steadfast love; I have set my course by it.

ג כִּי־חַסְדְּךָ לְנֶגֶד עֵינָי וְהִתְהַלַּכְתִּי בַּאֲמִתֶּךָ׃

26:1 Vindicate me Rarely do we find a psalm which unabashedly calls out to *Hashem* for judgment. King *David* teaches us to always be introspective, and to find ways to improve ourselves and to remain humble before God. However, sometimes, when the circumstances are dire and the enemy is at the door, *David* will turn to God and ask for judgment. *David* states that he walked with innocence, truth, and praise of *Hashem*. He did not surround himself with liars, thieves or wicked men. Rather, he encircled the altar of God, speaking His praise and seeking His final home. Ultimately, in a choir of the multitudes *David* sings out to *Hashem* for vindication, and awaits His comforting response.

1500

Tehillim/Psalms
Chapter 27

4 I do not consort with scoundrels, or mix with hypocrites;

5 I detest the company of evil men, and do not consort with the wicked;

6 I wash my hands in innocence, and walk around Your *Mizbayach*, *Hashem*,

7 raising my voice in thanksgiving, and telling all Your wonders.

8 *Hashem*, I love Your temple abode, the dwelling-place of Your glory.

9 Do not sweep me away with sinners, or [snuff out] my life with murderers,

10 who have schemes at their fingertips, and hands full of bribes.

11 But I walk without blame; redeem me, have mercy on me!

12 My feet are on level ground. In assemblies I will bless *Hashem*.

27

1 Of *David*. *Hashem* is my light and my help; whom should I fear? *Hashem* is the stronghold of my life, whom should I dread?

2 When evil men assail me to devour my flesh – it is they, my foes and my enemies, who stumble and fall.

3 Should an army besiege me, my heart would have no fear; should war beset me, still would I be confident.

4 One thing I ask of *Hashem*, only that do I seek: to live in the house of *Hashem* all the days of my life, to gaze upon the beauty of *Hashem*, to frequent His temple.

5 He will shelter me in His pavilion on an evil day, grant me the protection of His tent, raise me high upon a rock.

6 Now is my head high over my enemies roundabout; I sacrifice in His tent with shouts of joy, singing and chanting a hymn to *Hashem*.

7 Hear, *Hashem*, when I cry aloud; have mercy on me, answer me.

8 In Your behalf my heart says: "Seek My face!" *Hashem*, I seek Your face.

תהילים
פרק כז

ד לֹא־יָשַׁבְתִּי עִם־מְתֵי־שָׁוְא וְעִם נַעֲלָמִים לֹא אָבוֹא׃

ה שָׂנֵאתִי קְהַל מְרֵעִים וְעִם־רְשָׁעִים לֹא אֵשֵׁב׃

ו אֶרְחַץ בְּנִקָּיוֹן כַּפָּי וַאֲסֹבְבָה אֶת־מִזְבַּחֲךָ יְהֹוָה׃

ז לַשְׁמִעַ בְּקוֹל תּוֹדָה וּלְסַפֵּר כׇּל־נִפְלְאוֹתֶיךָ׃

ח יְהֹוָה אָהַבְתִּי מְעוֹן בֵּיתֶךָ וּמְקוֹם מִשְׁכַּן כְּבוֹדֶךָ׃

ט אַל־תֶּאֱסֹף עִם־חַטָּאִים נַפְשִׁי וְעִם־אַנְשֵׁי דָמִים חַיָּי׃

י אֲשֶׁר־בִּידֵיהֶם זִמָּה וִימִינָם מָלְאָה שֹּׁחַד׃

יא וַאֲנִי בְּתֻמִּי אֵלֵךְ פְּדֵנִי וְחָנֵּנִי׃

יב רַגְלִי עָמְדָה בְמִישׁוֹר בְּמַקְהֵלִים אֲבָרֵךְ יְהֹוָה׃

כז א לְדָוִד ׀ יְהֹוָה ׀ אוֹרִי וְיִשְׁעִי מִמִּי אִירָא יְהֹוָה מָעוֹז־חַיַּי מִמִּי אֶפְחָד׃

ב בִּקְרֹב עָלַי ׀ מְרֵעִים לֶאֱכֹל אֶת־בְּשָׂרִי צָרַי וְאֹיְבַי לִי הֵמָּה כָשְׁלוּ וְנָפָלוּ׃

ג אִם־תַּחֲנֶה עָלַי ׀ מַחֲנֶה לֹא־יִירָא לִבִּי אִם־תָּקוּם עָלַי מִלְחָמָה בְּזֹאת אֲנִי בוֹטֵחַ׃

ד אַחַת ׀ שָׁאַלְתִּי מֵאֵת־יְהֹוָה אוֹתָהּ אֲבַקֵּשׁ שִׁבְתִּי בְּבֵית־יְהֹוָה כׇּל־יְמֵי חַיַּי לַחֲזוֹת בְּנֹעַם־יְהֹוָה וּלְבַקֵּר בְּהֵיכָלוֹ׃

ה כִּי יִצְפְּנֵנִי ׀ בְּסֻכֹּה בְּיוֹם רָעָה יַסְתִּרֵנִי בְּסֵתֶר אׇהֳלוֹ בְּצוּר יְרוֹמְמֵנִי׃

ו וְעַתָּה יָרוּם רֹאשִׁי עַל אֹיְבַי סְבִיבוֹתַי וְאֶזְבְּחָה בְאׇהֳלוֹ זִבְחֵי תְרוּעָה אָשִׁירָה וַאֲזַמְּרָה לַיהֹוָה׃

ז שְׁמַע־יְהֹוָה קוֹלִי אֶקְרָא וְחָנֵּנִי וַעֲנֵנִי׃

ח לְךָ ׀ אָמַר לִבִּי בַּקְּשׁוּ פָנָי אֶת־פָּנֶיךָ יְהֹוָה אֲבַקֵּשׁ׃

Tehillim/Psalms
Chapter 28

תהילים
פרק כח

9 Do not hide Your face from me; do not thrust aside Your servant in anger; You have ever been my help. Do not forsake me, do not abandon me, O *Hashem*, my deliverer.

ט אַל־תַּסְתֵּ֬ר פָּנֶ֨יךָ ׀ מִמֶּנִּי֮ אַֽל־תַּט־בְּאַ֗ף עַ֫בְדֶּ֥ךָ עֶזְרָתִ֥י הָיִ֑יתָ אַֽל־תִּטְּשֵׁ֥נִי וְאַל־תַּֽ֝עַזְבֵ֗נִי אֱלֹהֵ֥י יִשְׁעִֽי:

10 Though my father and mother abandon me, *Hashem* will take me in.

י כִּי־אָבִ֣י וְאִמִּ֣י עֲזָב֑וּנִי וַֽיהֹוָ֣ה יַאַסְפֵֽנִי:

11 Show me Your way, *Hashem*, and lead me on a level path because of my watchful foes.

יא ה֤וֹרֵ֥נִי יְהֹוָ֗ה דַּ֫רְכֶּ֥ךָ וּ֭נְחֵנִי בְּאֹ֣רַח מִישׁ֑וֹר לְ֝מַ֗עַן שֽׁוֹרְרָֽי:

12 Do not subject me to the will of my foes, for false witnesses and unjust accusers have appeared against me.

יב אַֽל־תִּ֭תְּנֵנִי בְּנֶ֣פֶשׁ צָרָ֑י כִּ֥י קָֽמוּ־בִ֥י עֵֽדֵי־שֶׁ֝֗קֶר וִיפֵ֥חַ חָמָֽס:

13 Had I not the assurance that I would enjoy the goodness of *Hashem* in the land of the living…

יג לׅׄוּלֵׅׄ֗אׅׄ הֶ֭אֱמַנְתִּי לִרְא֥וֹת בְּֽטוּב־יְהֹוָ֗ה בְּאֶ֣רֶץ חַיִּֽים:

14 Look to *Hashem*; be strong and of good courage! O look to *Hashem*!

יד קַוֵּ֗ה אֶל־יְהֹ֫וָ֥ה חֲ֭זַק וְיַאֲמֵ֣ץ לִבֶּ֑ךָ וְ֝קַוֵּ֗ה אֶל־יְהֹוָֽה:

ka-VAY el a-do-NAI kha-ZAK v'-ya-a-MAYTZ li-BE-kha v'-ka-VAY el a-do-NAI

28 1 Of *David*. *Hashem*, I call to You; my rock, do not disregard me, for if You hold aloof from me, I shall be like those gone down into the Pit.

כח א לְדָוִ֨ד ׀ אֵ֘לֶ֤יךָ יְהֹוָ֨ה ׀ אֶקְרָ֗א צוּרִי֮ אַֽל־תֶּחֱרַ֢שׁ מִ֫מֶּ֥נִּי פֶּן־תֶּחֱשֶׁ֥ה מִמֶּ֑נִּי וְ֝נִמְשַׁ֗לְתִּי עִם־י֥וֹרְדֵי בֽוֹר:

l'-da-VID ay-LE-kha a-do-NAI ek-RA tzu-REE al te-khe-RASH mi-ME-nee pen te-khe-SHEH mi-ME-nee v'-nim-SHAL-tee im yo-r'-DAY VOR

27:14 Look to *Hashem* In this psalm, which Jews recite each day during the Hebrew month of *Elul*, immediately prior to the High Holidays and the Ten Days of Repentance, King *David* serves as a model of faith. Despite terrible enemies and feelings of abandonment, he never gives up hope in the Lord. Instead, he longs for a time when he will dwell permanently in the house of *Hashem* and behold his graciousness (verse 4), and instructs his readers to maintain similar hope and faith in God, and wait for His salvation (verse 14). The People of Israel have always taken this exhortation seriously, and though they waited a long time for Him, they never gave up their hope and trust in the Lord. Prime Minister Menachem Begin once said about the return of the Jews to Israel: "The miracle of Return was accompanied by the miracle of Revival. Within a generation there developed within the Jewish people the strength to take up arms, to rise against alien rule, to throw off the yoke of oppression. How long, how endless were the years of exile, of humiliation and destruction. And how short, in comparison, were the years of revival, reinvigoration and armed uprising. History has no parallels in its record!" They waited faithfully for Him, and in our generation, He has brought them home.

28:1 I shall be like those gone down into the Pit In this verse, King *David* declares that if *Hashem* remains silent to his request he will die. The metaphor he uses for death is descent into a pit. *Sefer Bereishit* (chapter 37) describes the descent of *Yosef* into a pit at the suggestion of *Reuven*. *Rashi* (Genesis 37:28) explains that though the pit was empty of water, it was filled with snakes and scorpions. By Jewish law, *Yosef* would be considered dead, due to the extreme danger of the situation. However, the verse says that by throwing him into the pit, *Reuven* actually saved *Yosef* from his brothers (Genesis 37:21), while the Sages criticize *Yehuda* for taking *Yosef* out of the pit and selling him into slavery. Rabbi Chaim of Volozhin explains that living in *Eretz Yisrael*, even surrounded by dangers such as snakes and scorpions, is better than living outside of Israel in relative security.

Prime Minister Menachem Begin (1913–1992)

Tehillim/Psalms
Chapter 29

תהלים
פרק כט

2 Listen to my plea for mercy when I cry out to You, when I lift my hands toward Your inner sanctuary.

ב שְׁמַע קוֹל תַּחֲנוּנַי בְּשַׁוְּעִי אֵלֶיךָ בְּנָשְׂאִי יָדַי אֶל־דְּבִיר קָדְשֶׁךָ:

3 Do not count me with the wicked and evildoers who profess goodwill toward their fellows while malice is in their heart.

ג אַל־תִּמְשְׁכֵנִי עִם־רְשָׁעִים וְעִם־פֹּעֲלֵי אָוֶן דֹּבְרֵי שָׁלוֹם עִם־רֵעֵיהֶם וְרָעָה בִּלְבָבָם:

4 Pay them according to their deeds, their malicious acts; according to their handiwork pay them, give them their deserts.

ד תֶּן־לָהֶם כְּפָעֳלָם וּכְרֹעַ מַעַלְלֵיהֶם כְּמַעֲשֵׂה יְדֵיהֶם תֵּן לָהֶם הָשֵׁב גְּמוּלָם לָהֶם:

5 For they do not consider Hashem's deeds, the work of His hands. May He tear them down, never to rebuild them!

ה כִּי לֹא יָבִינוּ אֶל־פְּעֻלֹּת יְהֹוָה וְאֶל־מַעֲשֵׂה יָדָיו יֶהֶרְסֵם וְלֹא יִבְנֵם:

6 Blessed is Hashem, for He listens to my plea for mercy.

ו בָּרוּךְ יְהֹוָה כִּי־שָׁמַע קוֹל תַּחֲנוּנָי:

7 Hashem is my strength and my shield; my heart trusts in Him. I was helped, and my heart exulted, so I will glorify Him with my song.

ז יְהֹוָה עֻזִּי וּמָגִנִּי בּוֹ בָטַח לִבִּי וְנֶעֱזָרְתִּי וַיַּעֲלֹז לִבִּי וּמִשִּׁירִי אֲהוֹדֶנּוּ:

8 Hashem is their strength; He is a stronghold for the deliverance of His anointed.

ח יְהֹוָה עֹז־לָמוֹ וּמָעוֹז יְשׁוּעוֹת מְשִׁיחוֹ הוּא:

9 Deliver and bless Your very own people; tend them and sustain them forever.

ט הוֹשִׁיעָה אֶת־עַמֶּךָ וּבָרֵךְ אֶת־נַחֲלָתֶךָ וּרְעֵם וְנַשְּׂאֵם עַד־הָעוֹלָם:

29 1 A psalm of David. Ascribe to Hashem, O divine beings, ascribe to Hashem glory and strength.

כט א מִזְמוֹר לְדָוִד הָבוּ לַיהֹוָה בְּנֵי אֵלִים הָבוּ לַיהֹוָה כָּבוֹד וָעֹז:

2 Ascribe to Hashem the glory of His name; bow down to Hashem, majestic in holiness.

ב הָבוּ לַיהֹוָה כְּבוֹד שְׁמוֹ הִשְׁתַּחֲווּ לַיהֹוָה בְּהַדְרַת־קֹדֶשׁ:

3 The voice of Hashem is over the waters; the God of glory thunders, Hashem, over the mighty waters.

ג קוֹל יְהֹוָה עַל־הַמָּיִם אֵל־הַכָּבוֹד הִרְעִים יְהֹוָה עַל־מַיִם רַבִּים:

KOL a-do-NAI al ha-MA-yim ayl ha-ka-VOD hir-EEM a-do-NAI al MA-yim ra-BEEM

4 The voice of Hashem is power; the voice of Hashem is majesty;

ד קוֹל־יְהֹוָה בַּכֹּחַ קוֹל יְהֹוָה בֶּהָדָר:

5 the voice of Hashem breaks cedars; Hashem shatters the cedars of Lebanon.

ה קוֹל יְהֹוָה שֹׁבֵר אֲרָזִים וַיְשַׁבֵּר יְהֹוָה אֶת־אַרְזֵי הַלְּבָנוֹן:

מים

29:3 The voice of Hashem is over the waters According to Rabbi Matityahu Glazerson, the word for 'water,' *mayim* (מים), provides an interesting example of the unique way in which the Hebrew word expresses the essence of the object it names. This word is spelled with two instances of the letter *mem* (מ), and one letter *yud* (י) in between them. Science tells us that a water molecule, represented by the notation H_2O, is made up of two atoms of hydrogen surrounding one atom of oxygen. In the Hebrew word, this exact structure is reflected; the letter 'מ' represents the hydrogen while the 'י' represents the oxygen.

Tehillim/Psalms
Chapter 30

תהלים
פרק ל

6 He makes Lebanon skip like a calf, Sirion, like a young wild ox.

ו וַיַּרְקִידֵם כְּמוֹ־עֵגֶל לְבָנוֹן וְשִׂרְיֹן כְּמוֹ בֶן־רְאֵמִים:

7 The voice of *Hashem* kindles flames of fire;

ז קוֹל־יְהֹוָה חֹצֵב לַהֲבוֹת אֵשׁ:

8 the voice of *Hashem* convulses the wilderness; *Hashem* convulses the wilderness of Kadesh;

ח קוֹל יְהֹוָה יָחִיל מִדְבָּר יָחִיל יְהֹוָה מִדְבַּר קָדֵשׁ:

9 the voice of *Hashem* causes hinds to calve, and strips forests bare; while in His temple all say "Glory!"

ט קוֹל יְהֹוָה יְחוֹלֵל אַיָּלוֹת וַיֶּחֱשֹׂף יְעָרוֹת וּבְהֵיכָלוֹ כֻּלּוֹ אֹמֵר כָּבוֹד:

10 *Hashem* sat enthroned at the Flood; *Hashem* sits enthroned, king forever.

י יְהֹוָה לַמַּבּוּל יָשָׁב וַיֵּשֶׁב יְהֹוָה מֶלֶךְ לְעוֹלָם:

11 May *Hashem* grant strength to His people; may *Hashem* bestow on His people wellbeing.

יא יְהֹוָה עֹז לְעַמּוֹ יִתֵּן יְהֹוָה יְבָרֵךְ אֶת־עַמּוֹ בַשָּׁלוֹם:

30

1 A psalm of *David*. A song for the dedication of the House.

א מִזְמוֹר שִׁיר־חֲנֻכַּת הַבַּיִת לְדָוִד:

miz-MOR sheer kha-nu-KAT ha-BA-yit l'-da-VID

2 I extol You, *Hashem*, for You have lifted me up, and not let my enemies rejoice over me.

ב אֲרוֹמִמְךָ יְהֹוָה כִּי דִלִּיתָנִי וְלֹא־שִׂמַּחְתָּ אֹיְבַי לִי:

3 *Hashem*, my God, I cried out to You, and You healed me.

ג יְהֹוָה אֱלֹהָי שִׁוַּעְתִּי אֵלֶיךָ וַתִּרְפָּאֵנִי:

4 *Hashem*, You brought me up from Sheol, preserved me from going down into the Pit.

ד יְהֹוָה הֶעֱלִיתָ מִן־שְׁאוֹל נַפְשִׁי חִיִּיתַנִי מִיּוֹרְדִי־[מִיָּרְדִי־] בוֹר:

5 O you faithful of *Hashem*, sing to Him, and praise His holy name.

ה זַמְּרוּ לַיהֹוָה חֲסִידָיו וְהוֹדוּ לְזֵכֶר קָדְשׁוֹ:

6 For He is angry but a moment, and when He is pleased there is life. One may lie down weeping at nightfall; but at dawn there are shouts of joy.

ו כִּי רֶגַע בְּאַפּוֹ חַיִּים בִּרְצוֹנוֹ בָּעֶרֶב יָלִין בֶּכִי וְלַבֹּקֶר רִנָּה:

7 When I was untroubled, I thought, "I shall never be shaken,"

ז וַאֲנִי אָמַרְתִּי בְשַׁלְוִי בַּל־אֶמּוֹט לְעוֹלָם:

8 for You, O *Hashem*, when You were pleased, made [me] firm as a mighty mountain. When You hid Your face, I was terrified.

ח יְהֹוָה בִּרְצוֹנְךָ הֶעֱמַדְתָּה לְהַרְרִי עֹז הִסְתַּרְתָּ פָנֶיךָ הָיִיתִי נִבְהָל:

9 I called to You, *Hashem*; to my Lord I made appeal,

ט אֵלֶיךָ יְהֹוָה אֶקְרָא וְאֶל־אֲדֹנָי אֶתְחַנָּן:

30:1 A song for the dedication of the House
Which house did *David* dedicate? Rabbi Avraham Ibn Ezra says that this psalm refers to the dedication of his own house, the "house of cedar" that he built for himself (II Samuel 7:2). While King *David* was instructed by God not to build the *Beit Hamikdash*, he nonetheless built a palace for himself right next to *Har HaBayit*. In 2005, archaeologist Dr. Eilat Mazar announced she had uncovered the remnants of King *David*'s palace. She maintains that the large structure she discovered was built during the tenth century BCE, as she found artifacts from that era, in addition to important bullae, clay seal impressions, with names of royal officials mentioned in the Bible.

Remains of King David's palace

Tehillim/Psalms

Chapter 31

10 "What is to be gained from my death, from my descent into the Pit? Can dust praise You? Can it declare Your faithfulness?

11 Hear, *Hashem*, and have mercy on me; *Hashem*, be my help!"

12 You turned my lament into dancing, you undid my sackcloth and girded me with joy,

13 that [my] whole being might sing hymns to You endlessly; *Hashem* my God, I will praise You forever.

31

1 For the leader. A psalm of *David*.

2 I seek refuge in You, *Hashem*; may I never be disappointed; as You are righteous, rescue me.

3 Incline Your ear to me; be quick to save me; be a rock, a stronghold for me, a citadel, for my deliverance.

4 For You are my rock and my fortress; You lead me and guide me as befits Your name.

5 You free me from the net laid for me, for You are my stronghold.

6 Into Your hand I entrust my spirit; You redeem me, *Hashem*, faithful *Hashem*.

7 I detest those who rely on empty folly, but I trust in *Hashem*.

8 Let me exult and rejoice in Your faithfulness when You notice my affliction, are mindful of my deep distress,

9 and do not hand me over to my enemy, but grant me relief.

10 Have mercy on me, *Hashem*, for I am in distress; my eyes are wasted by vexation, my substance and body too.

11 My life is spent in sorrow, my years in groaning; my strength fails because of my iniquity, my limbs waste away.

12 Because of all my foes I am the particular butt of my neighbors, a horror to my friends; those who see me on the street avoid me.

13 I am put out of mind like the dead; I am like an object given up for lost.

תהלים

פרק לא

י מַה־בֶּצַע בְּדָמִי בְּרִדְתִּי אֶל־שָׁחַת הֲיוֹדְךָ עָפָר הֲיַגִּיד אֲמִתֶּךָ:

יא שְׁמַע־יְהֹוָה וְחָנֵּנִי יְהֹוָה הֱיֵה־עֹזֵר לִי:

יב הָפַכְתָּ מִסְפְּדִי לְמָחוֹל לִי פִּתַּחְתָּ שַׂקִּי וַתְּאַזְּרֵנִי שִׂמְחָה:

יג לְמַעַן יְזַמֶּרְךָ כָבוֹד וְלֹא יִדֹּם יְהֹוָה אֱלֹהַי לְעוֹלָם אוֹדֶךָּ:

לא

א לַמְנַצֵּחַ מִזְמוֹר לְדָוִד:

ב בְּךָ יְהֹוָה חָסִיתִי אַל־אֵבוֹשָׁה לְעוֹלָם בְּצִדְקָתְךָ פַלְּטֵנִי:

ג הַטֵּה אֵלַי ׀ אָזְנְךָ מְהֵרָה הַצִּילֵנִי הֱיֵה לִי ׀ לְצוּר־מָעוֹז לְבֵית מְצוּדוֹת לְהוֹשִׁיעֵנִי:

ד כִּי־סַלְעִי וּמְצוּדָתִי אָתָּה וּלְמַעַן שִׁמְךָ תַּנְחֵנִי וּתְנַהֲלֵנִי:

ה תּוֹצִיאֵנִי מֵרֶשֶׁת זוּ טָמְנוּ לִי כִּי־אַתָּה מָעוּזִּי:

ו בְּיָדְךָ אַפְקִיד רוּחִי פָּדִיתָה אוֹתִי יְהֹוָה אֵל אֱמֶת:

ז שָׂנֵאתִי הַשֹּׁמְרִים הַבְלֵי־שָׁוְא וַאֲנִי אֶל־יְהֹוָה בָּטָחְתִּי:

ח אָגִילָה וְאֶשְׂמְחָה בְּחַסְדֶּךָ אֲשֶׁר רָאִיתָ אֶת־עָנְיִי יָדַעְתָּ בְּצָרוֹת נַפְשִׁי:

ט וְלֹא הִסְגַּרְתַּנִי בְּיַד־אוֹיֵב הֶעֱמַדְתָּ בַמֶּרְחָב רַגְלָי:

י חָנֵּנִי יְהֹוָה כִּי צַר־לִי עָשְׁשָׁה בְכַעַס עֵינִי נַפְשִׁי וּבִטְנִי:

יא כִּי כָלוּ בְיָגוֹן חַיַּי וּשְׁנוֹתַי בַּאֲנָחָה כָּשַׁל בַּעֲוֹנִי כֹחִי וַעֲצָמַי עָשֵׁשׁוּ:

יב מִכָּל־צֹרְרַי הָיִיתִי חֶרְפָּה וְלִשֲׁכֵנַי ׀ מְאֹד וּפַחַד לִמְיֻדָּעָי רֹאַי בַּחוּץ נָדְדוּ מִמֶּנִּי:

יג נִשְׁכַּחְתִּי כְּמֵת מִלֵּב הָיִיתִי כִּכְלִי אֹבֵד:

Tehillim/Psalms
Chapter 31

תהלים
פרק לא

14 I hear the whisperings of many, intrigue on every side, as they scheme together against me, plotting to take my life. / יד כִּי שָׁמַעְתִּי דִּבַּת רַבִּים מָגוֹר מִסָּבִיב בְּהִוָּסְדָם יַחַד עָלַי לָקַחַת נַפְשִׁי זָמָמוּ׃

15 But I trust in You, *Hashem*; I say, "You are my God!" / טו וַאֲנִי עָלֶיךָ בָטַחְתִּי יְהֹוָה אָמַרְתִּי אֱלֹהַי אָתָּה׃

16 My fate is in Your hand; save me from the hand of my enemies and pursuers. / טז בְּיָדְךָ עִתֹּתָי הַצִּילֵנִי מִיַּד־אוֹיְבַי וּמֵרֹדְפָי׃

17 Show favor to Your servant; as You are faithful, deliver me. / יז הָאִירָה פָנֶיךָ עַל־עַבְדֶּךָ הוֹשִׁיעֵנִי בְחַסְדֶּךָ׃

18 *Hashem*, let me not be disappointed when I call You; let the wicked be disappointed; let them be silenced in Sheol; / יח יְהֹוָה אַל־אֵבוֹשָׁה כִּי קְרָאתִיךָ יֵבֹשׁוּ רְשָׁעִים יִדְּמוּ לִשְׁאוֹל׃

19 let lying lips be stilled that speak haughtily against the righteous with arrogance and contempt. / יט תֵּאָלַמְנָה שִׂפְתֵי שָׁקֶר הַדֹּבְרוֹת עַל־צַדִּיק עָתָק בְּגַאֲוָה וָבוּז׃

20 How abundant is the good that You have in store for those who fear You, that You do in the full view of men for those who take refuge in You. / כ מָה רַב־טוּבְךָ אֲשֶׁר־צָפַנְתָּ לִּירֵאֶיךָ פָּעַלְתָּ לַחֹסִים בָּךְ נֶגֶד בְּנֵי אָדָם׃

21 You grant them the protection of Your presence against scheming men; You shelter them in Your pavilion from contentious tongues. / כא תַּסְתִּירֵם בְּסֵתֶר פָּנֶיךָ מֵרֻכְסֵי אִישׁ תִּצְפְּנֵם בְּסֻכָּה מֵרִיב לְשֹׁנוֹת׃

22 Blessed is *Hashem*, for He has been wondrously faithful to me, a veritable bastion. / כב בָּרוּךְ יְהֹוָה כִּי הִפְלִיא חַסְדּוֹ לִי בְּעִיר מָצוֹר׃

ba-RUKH a-do-NAI KEE hif-LEE khas-DO LEE b'-EER ma-TZOR

23 Alarmed, I had thought, "I am thrust out of Your sight"; yet You listened to my plea for mercy when I cried out to You. / כג וַאֲנִי אָמַרְתִּי בְחָפְזִי נִגְרַזְתִּי מִנֶּגֶד עֵינֶיךָ אָכֵן שָׁמַעְתָּ קוֹל תַּחֲנוּנַי בְּשַׁוְּעִי אֵלֶיךָ׃

24 So love *Hashem*, all you faithful; *Hashem* guards the loyal, and more than requites him who acts arrogantly. / כד אֶהֱבוּ אֶת־יְהֹוָה כָּל־חֲסִידָיו אֱמוּנִים נֹצֵר יְהֹוָה וּמְשַׁלֵּם עַל־יֶתֶר עֹשֵׂה גַאֲוָה׃

25 Be strong and of good courage, all you who wait for *Hashem*. / כה חִזְקוּ וְיַאֲמֵץ לְבַבְכֶם כָּל־הַמְיַחֲלִים לַיהֹוָה׃

31:22 For He has been wondrously faithful to me, a veritable bastion King *David* sings *Hashem*'s praise for being by his side during the most trying times, especially when King *Shaul* seeks to destroy him. *David* teaches us the recipe for protecting against enemies even from within: Keep God close by, and heed His words. In this verse, he praises the Lord for being faithful to him *b'eer matzor* (בעיר מצור). Though translated here a 'a veritable bastion,' these words can also mean 'a besieged city.' According to *Rashi*, this is a reference to the city of Keilah, described in *Shmuel* I (chapter 23). After saving that city from the Philistines, *David* learns that *Shaul* is on the chase. He wonders if the people of Keilah will turn him over to *Shaul*, and asks *Hashem* for guidance because Keilah is "a town with gates and bars" (I Samuel 23:7) and once *Shaul* arrives he will be trapped inside. God tells *David* that *Shaul* is indeed on the way, and that the people of Keilah will turn on him if he remains in the 'besieged city.' David gathers his men and leaves the city at once, causing *Shaul* to give up the chase. Once again, *David*, saved by *Hashem*'s counsel, sings a song of praise to his redeemer.

Rashi
(1040–1105)

Tehillim / Psalms
Chapter 32

32 ¹ Of *David*. A maskil. Happy is he whose transgression is forgiven, whose sin is covered over.

l'-da-VID mas-KEEL ash-RAY n'-suy PE-sha k'-SUY kha-ta-AH

² Happy the man whom *Hashem* does not hold guilty, and in whose spirit there is no deceit.

³ As long as I said nothing, my limbs wasted away from my anguished roaring all day long.

⁴ For night and day Your hand lay heavy on me; my vigor waned as in the summer drought. *Selah.*

⁵ Then I acknowledged my sin to You; I did not cover up my guilt; I resolved, "I will confess my transgressions to *Hashem*," and You forgave the guilt of my sin. *Selah.*

⁶ Therefore let every faithful man pray to You upon discovering [his sin], that the rushing mighty waters not overtake him.

⁷ You are my shelter; You preserve me from distress; You surround me with the joyous shouts of deliverance. *Selah.*

⁸ Let me enlighten you and show you which way to go; let me offer counsel; my eye is on you.

⁹ Be not like a senseless horse or mule whose movement must be curbed by bit and bridle; far be it from you!

¹⁰ Many are the torments of the wicked, but he who trusts in *Hashem* shall be surrounded with favor.

¹¹ Rejoice in *Hashem* and exult, O you righteous; shout for joy, all upright men!

33 ¹ Sing forth, O you righteous, to *Hashem*; it is fit that the upright acclaim Him.

אשרי

32:1 Happy The word *ashrei* (אשרי), 'happy,' which begins this psalm, reminds us of the first word of the opening chapter of the book of *Tehillim*, which speaks of the happy person who veers away from sin and chooses the godly path. Unlike Psalm 1, which refers to the person who avoids sin, this psalm expresses the power of repentance, referring to the individual who already sinned and suffers punishment. However, if he returns to God, he, too, is happy, since his sins are forgiven and he can again enjoy a close relationship with the Almighty. Two of the metaphors used to describe the process of sin and repentance relate to weather conditions in Israel. The "summer drought" (verse 4) and the "rushing mighty waters" (verse 6) refer to Israel's semi-arid and desert areas, and to the mountainous regions where waters rush through streams. Both environments play a role in the physical and spiritual cleansing of the individual in the Land of Israel.

Tehillim/Psalms
Chapter 33

תהלים
פרק לג

2 Praise *Hashem* with the lyre; with the ten-stringed harp sing to Him;

ב הוֹדוּ לַיהוָה בְּכִנּוֹר בְּנֵבֶל עָשׂוֹר זַמְּרוּ־לוֹ:

3 sing Him a new song; play sweetly with shouts of joy.

ג שִׁירוּ־לוֹ שִׁיר חָדָשׁ הֵיטִיבוּ נַגֵּן בִּתְרוּעָה:

SHEE-ru LO SHEER kha-DASH hay-TEE-vu na-GAYN bit-ru-AH

4 For the word of *Hashem* is right; His every deed is faithful.

ד כִּי־יָשָׁר דְּבַר־יְהוָה וְכָל־מַעֲשֵׂהוּ בֶּאֱמוּנָה:

5 He loves what is right and just; the earth is full of *Hashem*'s faithful care.

ה אֹהֵב צְדָקָה וּמִשְׁפָּט חֶסֶד יְהוָה מָלְאָה הָאָרֶץ:

6 By the word of *Hashem* the heavens were made, by the breath of His mouth, all their host.

ו בִּדְבַר יְהוָה שָׁמַיִם נַעֲשׂוּ וּבְרוּחַ פִּיו כָּל־צְבָאָם:

7 He heaps up the ocean waters like a mound, stores the deep in vaults.

ז כֹּנֵס כַּנֵּד מֵי הַיָּם נֹתֵן בְּאוֹצָרוֹת תְּהוֹמוֹת:

8 Let all the earth fear *Hashem*; let all the inhabitants of the world dread Him.

ח יִירְאוּ מֵיְהוָה כָּל־הָאָרֶץ מִמֶּנּוּ יָגוּרוּ כָּל־יֹשְׁבֵי תֵבֵל:

9 For He spoke, and it was; He commanded, and it endured.

ט כִּי הוּא אָמַר וַיֶּהִי הוּא־צִוָּה וַיַּעֲמֹד:

10 *Hashem* frustrates the plans of nations, brings to naught the designs of peoples.

י יְהוָה הֵפִיר עֲצַת־גּוֹיִם הֵנִיא מַחְשְׁבוֹת עַמִּים:

11 What *Hashem* plans endures forever, what He designs, for ages on end.

יא עֲצַת יְהוָה לְעוֹלָם תַּעֲמֹד מַחְשְׁבוֹת לִבּוֹ לְדֹר וָדֹר:

12 Happy the nation whose *Hashem* is *Hashem*, the people He has chosen to be His own.

יב אַשְׁרֵי הַגּוֹי אֲשֶׁר־יְהוָה אֱלֹהָיו הָעָם בָּחַר לְנַחֲלָה לוֹ:

13 *Hashem* looks down from heaven; He sees all mankind.

יג מִשָּׁמַיִם הִבִּיט יְהוָה רָאָה אֶת־כָּל־בְּנֵי הָאָדָם:

14 From His dwelling-place He gazes on all the inhabitants of the earth –

יד מִמְּכוֹן־שִׁבְתּוֹ הִשְׁגִּיחַ אֶל כָּל־יֹשְׁבֵי הָאָרֶץ:

15 He who fashions the hearts of them all, who discerns all their doings.

טו הַיֹּצֵר יַחַד לִבָּם הַמֵּבִין אֶל־כָּל־מַעֲשֵׂיהֶם:

16 Kings are not delivered by a large force; warriors are not saved by great strength;

טז אֵין־הַמֶּלֶךְ נוֹשָׁע בְּרָב־חָיִל גִּבּוֹר לֹא־יִנָּצֵל בְּרָב־כֹּחַ:

33:3 A new song Music has always played a significant role in the Bible. The earliest instruments are mentioned in *Sefer Bereishit* (4:21). *Moshe* and the Jewish people sing a great song of gratitude after the splitting of the sea, and Israel sings a similar song after being saved from peril in the desert (Numbers 21:17). *Kohanim* and *Leviim* use instruments on holidays and to signal important meetings for the camp. *Elisha* asks for a harpist in order to receive the divine word (II Kings 3:15). But above all, King *David* is the musician par excellence, who would play his instrument to soothe the soul of *Shaul* (I Samuel 16:23). Later, he composes music, writes psalms and even invents new instruments to be used in the *Beit Hamikdash* (I Chronicles 23:5).

Tehillim/Psalms
Chapter 34

17 horses are a false hope for deliverance; for all their great power they provide no escape.

יז שֶׁ֣קֶר הַ֭סּוּס לִתְשׁוּעָ֑ה וּבְרֹ֥ב חֵ֝יל֗וֹ לֹ֣א יְמַלֵּֽט׃

18 Truly the eye of *Hashem* is on those who fear Him, who wait for His faithful care

יח הִנֵּ֤ה עֵ֣ין יְ֭הוָה אֶל־יְרֵאָ֑יו לַֽמְיַחֲלִ֥ים לְחַסְדּֽוֹ׃

19 to save them from death, to sustain them in famine.

יט לְהַצִּ֣יל מִמָּ֣וֶת נַפְשָׁ֑ם וּ֝לְחַיּוֹתָ֗ם בָּרָעָֽב׃

20 We set our hope on *Hashem*, He is our help and shield;

כ נַ֭פְשֵׁנוּ חִכְּתָ֣ה לַיהוָ֑ה עֶזְרֵ֖נוּ וּמָגִנֵּ֣נוּ הֽוּא׃

21 in Him our hearts rejoice, for in His holy name we trust.

כא כִּי־ב֭וֹ יִשְׂמַ֣ח לִבֵּ֑נוּ כִּ֖י בְשֵׁ֥ם קָדְשׁ֣וֹ בָטָֽחְנוּ׃

22 May we enjoy, *Hashem*, Your faithful care, as we have put our hope in You.

כב יְהִֽי־חַסְדְּךָ֣ יְהוָ֣ה עָלֵ֑ינוּ כַּ֝אֲשֶׁ֗ר יִחַ֥לְנוּ לָֽךְ׃

34

1 Of *David*, when he feigned madness in the presence of Abimelech, who turned him out, and he left.

לד א לְדָוִ֗ד בְּשַׁנּוֹת֣וֹ אֶת־טַ֭עְמוֹ לִפְנֵ֣י אֲבִימֶ֑לֶךְ וַֽ֝יְגָרֲשֵׁ֗הוּ וַיֵּלַֽךְ׃

2 I bless *Hashem* at all times; praise of Him is ever in my mouth.

ב אֲבָרֲכָ֣ה אֶת־יְהוָ֣ה בְּכָל־עֵ֑ת תָּ֝מִ֗יד תְּֽהִלָּת֥וֹ בְּפִֽי׃

3 I glory in *Hashem*; let the lowly hear it and rejoice.

ג בַּ֭יהוָה תִּתְהַלֵּ֣ל נַפְשִׁ֑י יִשְׁמְע֖וּ עֲנָוִ֣ים וְיִשְׂמָֽחוּ׃

4 Exalt *Hashem* with me let us extol His name together.

ד גַּדְּל֣וּ לַיהוָ֣ה אִתִּ֑י וּנְרוֹמְמָ֖ה שְׁמ֣וֹ יַחְדָּֽו׃

5 I turned to *Hashem*, and He answered me; He saved me from all my terrors.

ה דָּרַ֣שְׁתִּי אֶת־יְהוָ֣ה וְעָנָ֑נִי וּמִכָּל־מְ֝גוּרוֹתַ֗י הִצִּילָֽנִי׃

6 Men look to Him and are radiant; let their faces not be downcast.

ו הִבִּ֣יטוּ אֵלָ֣יו וְנָהָ֑רוּ וּ֝פְנֵיהֶ֗ם אַל־יֶחְפָּֽרוּ׃

7 Here was a lowly man who called, and *Hashem* listened, and delivered him from all his troubles.

ז זֶ֤ה עָנִ֣י קָ֭רָא וַיהוָ֣ה שָׁמֵ֑עַ וּמִכָּל־צָ֝רוֹתָ֗יו הוֹשִׁיעֽוֹ׃

8 The angel of *Hashem* camps around those who fear Him and rescues them.

ח חֹנֶ֤ה מַלְאַךְ־יְהוָ֓ה סָ֘בִ֤יב לִֽירֵאָ֗יו וַֽיְחַלְּצֵֽם׃

9 Taste and see how good *Hashem* is; happy the man who takes refuge in Him!

ט טַעֲמ֣וּ וּ֭רְאוּ כִּי־ט֣וֹב יְהוָ֑ה אַֽשְׁרֵ֥י הַ֝גֶּ֗בֶר יֶחֱסֶה־בּֽוֹ׃

10 Fear *Hashem*, you His consecrated ones, for those who fear Him lack nothing.

י יְר֣אוּ אֶת־יְהוָ֣ה קְדֹשָׁ֑יו כִּי־אֵ֥ין מַ֝חְס֗וֹר לִירֵאָֽיו׃

11 Lions have been reduced to starvation, but those who turn to *Hashem* shall not lack any good.

יא כְּ֭פִירִים רָשׁ֣וּ וְרָעֵ֑בוּ וְדֹרְשֵׁ֥י יְ֝הוָ֗ה לֹא־יַחְסְר֥וּ כָל־טֽוֹב׃

12 Come, my sons, listen to me; I will teach you what it is to fear *Hashem*.

יב לְֽכוּ־בָ֭נִים שִׁמְעוּ־לִ֑י יִֽרְאַ֥ת יְ֝הוָ֗ה אֲלַמֶּדְכֶֽם׃

1509

Tehillim/Psalms
Chapter 35

תהילים
פרק לה

13 Who is the man who is eager for life, who desires years of good fortune?

מִי־הָאִישׁ הֶחָפֵץ חַיִּים אֹהֵב יָמִים לִרְאוֹת טוֹב:

mee ha-EESH he-kha-FAYTZ kha-YIM o-HAYV ya-MEEM lir-OT TOV

14 Guard your tongue from evil, your lips from deceitful speech.

נְצֹר לְשׁוֹנְךָ מֵרָע וּשְׂפָתֶיךָ מִדַּבֵּר מִרְמָה:

15 Shun evil and do good, seek amity and pursue it.

סוּר מֵרָע וַעֲשֵׂה־טוֹב בַּקֵּשׁ שָׁלוֹם וְרָדְפֵהוּ:

16 The eyes of *Hashem* are on the righteous, His ears attentive to their cry.

עֵינֵי יְהוָה אֶל־צַדִּיקִים וְאָזְנָיו אֶל־שַׁוְעָתָם:

17 The face of *Hashem* is set against evildoers, to erase their names from the earth.

פְּנֵי יְהוָה בְּעֹשֵׂי רָע לְהַכְרִית מֵאֶרֶץ זִכְרָם:

18 They cry out, and *Hashem* hears, and saves them from all their troubles.

צָעֲקוּ וַיהוָה שָׁמֵעַ וּמִכָּל־צָרוֹתָם הִצִּילָם:

19 *Hashem* is close to the brokenhearted; those crushed in spirit He delivers.

קָרוֹב יְהוָה לְנִשְׁבְּרֵי־לֵב וְאֶת־דַּכְּאֵי־רוּחַ יוֹשִׁיעַ:

20 Though the misfortunes of the righteous be many, *Hashem* will save him from them all,

רַבּוֹת רָעוֹת צַדִּיק וּמִכֻּלָּם יַצִּילֶנּוּ יְהוָה:

21 Keeping all his bones intact, not one of them being broken.

שֹׁמֵר כָּל־עַצְמוֹתָיו אַחַת מֵהֵנָּה לֹא נִשְׁבָּרָה:

22 One misfortune is the deathblow of the wicked; the foes of the righteous shall be ruined.

תְּמוֹתֵת רָשָׁע רָעָה וְשֹׂנְאֵי צַדִּיק יֶאְשָׁמוּ:

23 *Hashem* redeems the life of His servants; all who take refuge in Him shall not be ruined.

פּוֹדֶה יְהוָה נֶפֶשׁ עֲבָדָיו וְלֹא יֶאְשְׁמוּ כָּל־הַחֹסִים בּוֹ:

35

1 Of *David*. *Hashem*, strive with my adversaries, give battle to my foes,

לְדָוִד רִיבָה יְהוָה אֶת־יְרִיבַי לְחַם אֶת־לֹחֲמָי:

2 take up shield and buckler, and come to my defense;

הַחֲזֵק מָגֵן וְצִנָּה וְקוּמָה בְּעֶזְרָתִי:

3 ready the spear and javelin against my pursuers; tell me, "I am your deliverance."

וְהָרֵק חֲנִית וּסְגֹר לִקְרַאת רֹדְפָי אֱמֹר לְנַפְשִׁי יְשֻׁעָתֵךְ אָנִי:

34:13 Who is eager for life The *kibbutz* movement, which began in the 1920's, was primarily a secular enterprise. Jewish pioneers sought to create an ideal living environment guided by brotherhood and shared idealism. However, there was also a religious *kibbutz* movement. In 1944, a group of religious Jews founded a *kibbutz* on the principles of *Torah* and religious idealism. They named their *kibbutz* in honor of one of the most towering rabbinic personalities of the century, Rabbi Israel Meir HaKohen Kagan, otherwise known as the *Chafetz Chaim*, the name of his book about the laws of guarding one's speech. *Chafetz Chaim* means one "who is eager for life." The name stems from this chapter in *Tehillim* where a question is raised, *mee ha-eesh hechafeitz chaim* (מי האיש החפץ חיים), 'Who is the man who is eager for life?' The response is found the next verse: One who guards his tongue from evil and his lips from deceitful speech.

Members of Kibbutz Chafetz Chaim studying Torah, 1945

Tehillim/Psalms
Chapter 35

תהלים
פרק לה

4 Let those who seek my life be frustrated and put to shame; let those who plan to harm me fall back in disgrace.

ד יֵבֹשׁוּ וְיִכָּלְמוּ מְבַקְשֵׁי נַפְשִׁי יִסֹּגוּ אָחוֹר וְיַחְפְּרוּ חֹשְׁבֵי רָעָתִי:

5 Let them be as chaff in the wind, *Hashem*'s angel driving them on.

ה יִהְיוּ כְּמֹץ לִפְנֵי־רוּחַ וּמַלְאַךְ יְהֹוָה דּוֹחֶה:

6 Let their path be dark and slippery, with *Hashem*'s angel in pursuit.

ו יְהִי־דַרְכָּם חֹשֶׁךְ וַחֲלַקְלַקֹּת וּמַלְאַךְ יְהֹוָה רֹדְפָם:

7 For without cause they hid a net to trap me; without cause they dug a pit* for me.

ז כִּי־חִנָּם טָמְנוּ־לִי שַׁחַת רִשְׁתָּם חִנָּם חָפְרוּ לְנַפְשִׁי:

8 Let disaster overtake them unawares; let the net they hid catch them; let them fall into it when disaster [strikes].

ח תְּבוֹאֵהוּ שׁוֹאָה לֹא־יֵדָע וְרִשְׁתּוֹ אֲשֶׁר־טָמַן תִּלְכְּדוֹ בְּשׁוֹאָה יִפָּל־בָּהּ:

9 Then shall I exult in *Hashem*, rejoice in His deliverance.

ט וְנַפְשִׁי תָּגִיל בַּיהֹוָה תָּשִׂישׂ בִּישׁוּעָתוֹ:

10 All my bones shall say, "*Hashem*, who is like You? You save the poor from one stronger than he, the poor and needy from his despoiler."

י כָּל עַצְמוֹתַי תֹּאמַרְנָה יְהֹוָה מִי כָמוֹךָ מַצִּיל עָנִי מֵחָזָק מִמֶּנּוּ וְעָנִי וְאֶבְיוֹן מִגֹּזְלוֹ:

KOL atz-mo-TAI to-mar-NAH a-do-NAI MEE kha-MO-kha ma-TZEEL a-NEE may-kha-ZAK mi-ME-nu v'-a-NEE v'-ev-YON mi-go-z'-LO

11 Malicious witnesses appear who question me about things I do not know.

יא יְקוּמוּן עֵדֵי חָמָס אֲשֶׁר לֹא־יָדַעְתִּי יִשְׁאָלוּנִי:

12 They repay me evil for good, [seeking] my bereavement.

יב יְשַׁלְּמוּנִי רָעָה תַּחַת טוֹבָה שְׁכוֹל לְנַפְשִׁי:

13 Yet, when they were ill, my dress was sackcloth, I kept a fast – may what I prayed for happen to me!

יג וַאֲנִי בַּחֲלוֹתָם לְבוּשִׁי שָׂק עִנֵּיתִי בַצּוֹם נַפְשִׁי וּתְפִלָּתִי עַל־חֵיקִי תָשׁוּב:

14 I walked about as though it were my friend or my brother; I was bowed with gloom, like one mourning for his mother.

יד כְּרֵעַ־כְּאָח לִי הִתְהַלָּכְתִּי כַּאֲבֶל־אֵם קֹדֵר שַׁחוֹתִי:

15 But when I stumble, they gleefully gather; wretches gather against me, I know not why; they tear at me without end.

טו וּבְצַלְעִי שָׂמְחוּ וְנֶאֱסָפוּ עָלַי נֵכִים וְלֹא יָדַעְתִּי קָרְעוּ וְלֹא־דָמּוּ:

16 With impious, mocking grimace they gnash their teeth at me.

טז בְּחַנְפֵי לַעֲגֵי מָעוֹג חָרֹק עָלַי שִׁנֵּימוֹ:

---

* "pit" transferred from first clause for clarity

35:10 All my bones shall say, "*Hashem*, who is like You?" *David*, surrounded by enemies and troubles, seeks out *Hashem* and prays for greener pastures. He poetically yearns for a time when all of his bones will engage in praising God. The Sages wonder what situation would allow him to serve *Hashem* with all his bones. Some commandments are done with one's mind, others with the mouth and some with one's limbs, but what commandment encompasses the entire body? The answer is the command to settle the Land of Israel. King *David* was yearning to live in Israel, where one's entire body is completely immersed in the land, God's chosen land.

Tehillim/Psalms
Chapter 36

17 O *Hashem*, how long will You look on? Rescue me from their attacks, my precious life, from the lions,

18 that I may praise You in a great congregation, acclaim You in a mighty throng.

19 Let not my treacherous enemies rejoice over me, or those who hate me without reason wink their eyes.

20 For they do not offer amity, but devise fraudulent schemes against harmless folk.

21 They open wide their mouths at me, saying, "Aha, aha, we have seen it!"

22 You have seen it, *Hashem*; do not hold aloof! O *Hashem*, be not far from me!

23 Wake, rouse Yourself for my cause, for my claim, O my God and my Lord!

24 Take up my cause, *Hashem* my God, as You are beneficent, and let them not rejoice over me.

25 Let them not think, "Aha, just what we wished!" Let them not say, "We have destroyed him!"

26 May those who rejoice at my misfortune be frustrated and utterly disgraced; may those who vaunt themselves over me be clad in frustration and shame.

27 May those who desire my vindication sing forth joyously; may they always say, "Extolled be *Hashem* who desires the well-being of His servant,"

28 while my tongue shall recite Your beneficent acts, Your praises all day long.

36 1 For the leader. Of the servant of *Hashem*, of *David*.

2 I know what Transgression says to the wicked; he has no sense of the dread of *Hashem*,

3 because its speech is seductive to him till his iniquity be found out and he be hated.

4 His words are evil and deceitful; he will not consider doing good.

5 In bed he plots mischief; he is set on a path of no good, he does not reject evil.

6 *Hashem*, Your faithfulness reaches to heaven; Your steadfastness to the sky;

Tehillim / Psalms
Chapter 37

תהלים
פרק לז

7 Your beneficence is like the high mountains; Your justice like the great deep; man and beast You deliver, *Hashem*.

צִדְקָתְךָ כְּהַרְרֵי־אֵל מִשְׁפָּטֶךָ תְּהוֹם רַבָּה אָדָם־וּבְהֵמָה תוֹשִׁיעַ יְהֹוָה:

tzid-ka-t'-KHA k'-ha-r'-ray AYL mish-pa-TE-kha t'-HOM ra-BAH a-DAM uv-hay-MAH to-SHEE-a a-do-NAI

8 How precious is Your faithful care, O *Hashem*! Mankind shelters in the shadow of Your wings.

מַה־יָּקָר חַסְדְּךָ אֱלֹהִים וּבְנֵי אָדָם בְּצֵל כְּנָפֶיךָ יֶחֱסָיוּן:

9 They feast on the rich fare of Your house; You let them drink at Your refreshing stream.

יִרְוְיֻן מִדֶּשֶׁן בֵּיתֶךָ וְנַחַל עֲדָנֶיךָ תַשְׁקֵם:

10 With You is the fountain of life; by Your light do we see light.

כִּי־עִמְּךָ מְקוֹר חַיִּים בְּאוֹרְךָ נִרְאֶה־אוֹר:

11 Bestow Your faithful care on those devoted to You, and Your beneficence on upright men.

מְשֹׁךְ חַסְדְּךָ לְיֹדְעֶיךָ וְצִדְקָתְךָ לְיִשְׁרֵי־לֵב:

12 Let not the foot of the arrogant tread on me, or the hand of the wicked drive me away.

אַל־תְּבוֹאֵנִי רֶגֶל גַּאֲוָה וְיַד־רְשָׁעִים אַל־תְּנִדֵנִי:

13 There lie the evildoers, fallen, thrust down, unable to rise.

שָׁם נָפְלוּ פֹּעֲלֵי אָוֶן דֹּחוּ וְלֹא־יָכְלוּ קוּם:

37

1 Of *David*. Do not be vexed by evil men; do not be incensed by wrongdoers;

לְדָוִד אַל־תִּתְחַר בַּמְּרֵעִים אַל־תְּקַנֵּא בְּעֹשֵׂי עַוְלָה:

2 for they soon wither like grass, like verdure fade away.

כִּי כֶחָצִיר מְהֵרָה יִמָּלוּ וּכְיֶרֶק דֶּשֶׁא יִבּוֹלוּן:

3 Trust in *Hashem* and do good, abide in the land and remain loyal.

בְּטַח בַּיהֹוָה וַעֲשֵׂה־טוֹב שְׁכָן־אֶרֶץ וּרְעֵה אֱמוּנָה:

4 Seek the favor of *Hashem*, and He will grant you the desires of your heart.

וְהִתְעַנַּג עַל־יְהֹוָה וְיִתֶּן־לְךָ מִשְׁאֲלֹת לִבֶּךָ:

5 Leave all to *Hashem*; trust in Him; He will do it.

גּוֹל עַל־יְהֹוָה דַּרְכֶּךָ וּבְטַח עָלָיו וְהוּא יַעֲשֶׂה:

6 He will cause your vindication to shine forth like the light, the justice of your case, like the noonday sun.

וְהוֹצִיא כָאוֹר צִדְקֶךָ וּמִשְׁפָּטֶךָ כַּצָּהֳרָיִם:

7 Be patient and wait for *Hashem*, do not be vexed by the prospering man who carries out his schemes.

דּוֹם לַיהֹוָה וְהִתְחוֹלֵל לוֹ אַל־תִּתְחַר בְּמַצְלִיחַ דַּרְכּוֹ בְּאִישׁ עֹשֶׂה מְזִמּוֹת:

Rabbi Samson R. Hirsch (1808–1888)

36:7 Man and beast You deliver, *Hashem* Rabbi Samson Raphael Hirsch writes that God created a world in which man and animal alike can live and prosper. Had *Hashem* desired that only the animals would roam the world, there would have been no notion of *mishpatecha* (משפטיך), 'your justice,' nor *tzidkatcha* (צדקתך) 'your beneficence.' However, as the verse says, "Man and beast You deliver, *Hashem*." Man, with the capacity to veer from evil and to become educated, was set on the land to fulfill God's will. With man as part of the balance, it is necessary for *Hashem* to judge the world based on man's actions. Similarly, since since man has the ability to choose good, God's world can also be encompassed by *tzedaka*, 'beneficence' and 'righteousness.'

Tehillim/Psalms
Chapter 37

8 Give up anger, abandon fury, do not be vexed; it can only do harm.

9 For evil men will be cut off, but those who look to *Hashem* – they shall inherit the land.

10 A little longer and there will be no wicked man; you will look at where he was – he will be gone.

11 But the lowly shall inherit the land, and delight in abundant well-being.

12 The wicked man schemes against the righteous, and gnashes his teeth at him.

13 *Hashem* laughs at him, for He knows that his day will come.

14 The wicked draw their swords, bend their bows, to bring down the lowly and needy, to slaughter upright men.

15 Their swords shall pierce their own hearts, and their bows shall be broken.

16 Better the little that the righteous man has than the great abundance of the wicked.

17 For the arms of the wicked shall be broken, but *Hashem* is the support of the righteous.

18 *Hashem* is concerned for the needs of the blameless; their portion lasts forever;

19 they shall not come to grief in bad times; in famine, they shall eat their fill.

20 But the wicked shall perish, and the enemies of *Hashem* shall be consumed, like meadow grass consumed in smoke.

21 The wicked man borrows and does not repay; the righteous is generous and keeps giving.

22 Those blessed by Him shall inherit the land, but those cursed by Him shall be cut off.

23 The steps of a man are made firm by *Hashem*, when He delights in his way.

24 Though he stumbles, he does not fall down, for *Hashem* gives him support.

25 I have been young and am now old, but I have never seen a righteous man abandoned, or his children seeking bread.

Tehillim/Psalms
Chapter 37

תהלים
פרק לז

26 He is always generous, and lends, and his children are held blessed.

כו כָּל־הַיּוֹם חוֹנֵן וּמַלְוֶה וְזַרְעוֹ לִבְרָכָה:

27 Shun evil and do good, and you shall abide forever.

כז סוּר מֵרָע וַעֲשֵׂה־טוֹב וּשְׁכֹן לְעוֹלָם:

28 For *Hashem* loves what is right, He does not abandon His faithful ones. They are preserved forever, while the children of the wicked will be cut off.

כח כִּי יְהֹוָה אֹהֵב מִשְׁפָּט וְלֹא־יַעֲזֹב אֶת־חֲסִידָיו לְעוֹלָם נִשְׁמָרוּ וְזֶרַע רְשָׁעִים נִכְרָת:

29 The righteous shall inherit the land, and abide forever in it.

כט צַדִּיקִים יִירְשׁוּ־אָרֶץ וְיִשְׁכְּנוּ לָעַד עָלֶיהָ:

30 The mouth of the righteous utters wisdom, and his tongue speaks what is right.

ל פִּי־צַדִּיק יֶהְגֶּה חָכְמָה וּלְשׁוֹנוֹ תְּדַבֵּר מִשְׁפָּט:

31 The teaching of his God is in his heart; his feet do not slip.

לא תּוֹרַת אֱלֹהָיו בְּלִבּוֹ לֹא תִמְעַד אֲשֻׁרָיו:

32 The wicked watches for the righteous, seeking to put him to death;

לב צוֹפֶה רָשָׁע לַצַּדִּיק וּמְבַקֵּשׁ לַהֲמִיתוֹ:

33 *Hashem* will not abandon him to his power; He will not let him be condemned in judgment.

לג יְהֹוָה לֹא־יַעַזְבֶנּוּ בְיָדוֹ וְלֹא יַרְשִׁיעֶנּוּ בְּהִשָּׁפְטוֹ:

34 Look to *Hashem* and keep to His way, and He will raise you high that you may inherit the land; when the wicked are cut off, you shall see it.

ka-VAY el a-do-NAI ush-MOR dar-KO vee-ro-mim-KHA la-RE-shet A-retz b'-hi-ka-RAYT r'-sha-EEM tir-EH

לד קַוֵּה אֶל־יְהֹוָה וּשְׁמֹר דַּרְכּוֹ וִירוֹמִמְךָ לָרֶשֶׁת אָרֶץ בְּהִכָּרֵת רְשָׁעִים תִּרְאֶה:

35 I saw a wicked man, powerful, well-rooted like a robust native tree.

לה רָאִיתִי רָשָׁע עָרִיץ וּמִתְעָרֶה כְּאֶזְרָח רַעֲנָן:

36 Suddenly he vanished and was gone; I sought him, but he was not to be found.

לו וַיַּעֲבֹר וְהִנֵּה אֵינֶנּוּ וָאֲבַקְשֵׁהוּ וְלֹא נִמְצָא:

37 Mark the blameless, note the upright, for there is a future for the man of integrity.

לז שְׁמָר־תָּם וּרְאֵה יָשָׁר כִּי־אַחֲרִית לְאִישׁ שָׁלוֹם:

38 But transgressors shall be utterly destroyed, the future of the wicked shall be cut off.

לח וּפֹשְׁעִים נִשְׁמְדוּ יַחְדָּו אַחֲרִית רְשָׁעִים נִכְרָתָה:

39 The deliverance of the righteous comes from *Hashem*, their stronghold in time of trouble.

לט וּתְשׁוּעַת צַדִּיקִים מֵיְהֹוָה מָעוּזָּם בְּעֵת צָרָה:

37:34 He will raise you high that you may inherit the land Who is worthy to inherit the Land of Israel? The psalmist comforts the righteous one who sees only the arrogant succeeding in the world. He speaks of the fleeting existence of the wicked and notes that they will ultimately fall. However, those who have faith in *Hashem*, wait patiently for Him, who are humble, veer from evil and engage in acts of righteousness, will eventually inherit *Eretz Yisrael* and inhabit it.

Tehillim / Psalms
Chapter 38

תהלים
פרק לח

40 *Hashem* helps them and rescues them, rescues them from the wicked and delivers them, for they seek refuge in Him.

מ וַיַּעְזְרֵם יְהֹוָה וַיְפַלְּטֵם יְפַלְּטֵם מֵרְשָׁעִים וְיוֹשִׁיעֵם כִּי־חָסוּ בוֹ:

38 1 A psalm of *David*. Lehazkir.

לח א מִזְמוֹר לְדָוִד לְהַזְכִּיר:

2 *Hashem*, do not punish me in wrath; do not chastise me in fury.

ב יְהֹוָה אַל־בְּקֶצְפְּךָ תוֹכִיחֵנִי וּבַחֲמָתְךָ תְיַסְּרֵנִי:

3 For Your arrows have struck me; Your blows have fallen upon me.

ג כִּי־חִצֶּיךָ נִחֲתוּ בִי וַתִּנְחַת עָלַי יָדֶךָ:

4 There is no soundness in my flesh because of Your rage, no wholeness in my bones because of my sin.

ד אֵין־מְתֹם בִּבְשָׂרִי מִפְּנֵי זַעְמֶךָ אֵין־שָׁלוֹם בַּעֲצָמַי מִפְּנֵי חַטָּאתִי:

5 For my iniquities have overwhelmed me; they are like a heavy burden, more than I can bear.

ה כִּי עֲוֺנֹתַי עָבְרוּ רֹאשִׁי כְּמַשָּׂא כָבֵד יִכְבְּדוּ מִמֶּנִּי:

6 My wounds stink and fester because of my folly.

ו הִבְאִישׁוּ נָמַקּוּ חַבּוּרֹתָי מִפְּנֵי אִוַּלְתִּי:

7 I am all bent and bowed; I walk about in gloom all day long.

ז נַעֲוֵיתִי שַׁחֹתִי עַד־מְאֹד כָּל־הַיּוֹם קֹדֵר הִלָּכְתִּי:

8 For my sinews are full of fever; there is no soundness in my flesh.

ח כִּי־כְסָלַי מָלְאוּ נִקְלֶה וְאֵין מְתֹם בִּבְשָׂרִי:

9 I am all benumbed and crushed; I roar because of the turmoil in my mind.

ט נְפוּגוֹתִי וְנִדְכֵּיתִי עַד־מְאֹד שָׁאַגְתִּי מִנַּהֲמַת לִבִּי:

10 O *Hashem*, You are aware of all my entreaties; my groaning is not hidden from You.

י אֲדֹנָי נֶגְדְּךָ כָל־תַּאֲוָתִי וְאַנְחָתִי מִמְּךָ לֹא־נִסְתָּרָה:

11 My mind reels; my strength fails me; my eyes too have lost their luster.

יא לִבִּי סְחַרְחַר עֲזָבַנִי כֹחִי וְאוֹר־עֵינַי גַּם־הֵם אֵין אִתִּי:

12 My friends and companions stand back from my affliction; my kinsmen stand far off.

יב אֹהֲבַי וְרֵעַי מִנֶּגֶד נִגְעִי יַעֲמֹדוּ וּקְרוֹבַי מֵרָחֹק עָמָדוּ:

13 Those who seek my life lay traps; those who wish me harm speak malice; they utter deceit all the time.

יג וַיְנַקְשׁוּ מְבַקְשֵׁי נַפְשִׁי וְדֹרְשֵׁי רָעָתִי דִּבְּרוּ הַוּוֹת וּמִרְמוֹת כָּל־הַיּוֹם יֶהְגּוּ:

14 But I am like a deaf man, unhearing, like a dumb man who cannot speak up;

יד וַאֲנִי כְחֵרֵשׁ לֹא אֶשְׁמָע וּכְאִלֵּם לֹא יִפְתַּח־פִּיו:

va-a-NEE kh'-khay-RAYSH LO esh-MA ukh-ee-LAYM LO yif-takh PEEV

38:14 Like a dumb man who cannot speak up Psalm 38 is difficult to read, as it is almost entirely an expression of pain written by an individual who is suffering, physically and spiritually. While his bones have no peace and his sins are too much to bear, his friends stand afar, unable or unwilling to help, and his enemies seek to hurt him. His response is: I am deaf and mute. I pretend not to hear their taunts nor do I respond to their calls of malice and deceit. Instead, he calls out only to the Lord for salvation and deliverance. In the thirteenth century, Rabbi Menachem Meiri wrote that this psalm refers to the Jews in exile. He commented profoundly: "The psalm refers to our long exile in which our enemies are many and our nemeses ridicule us and

Tehillim/Psalms
Chapter 39

תהלים
פרק לט

15 I am like one who does not hear, who has no retort on his lips.

טו וָאֱהִי כְּאִישׁ אֲשֶׁר לֹא־שֹׁמֵעַ וְאֵין בְּפִיו תּוֹכָחוֹת׃

16 But I wait for You, *Hashem*; You will answer, O *Hashem*, my God.

טז כִּי־לְךָ יְהוָה הוֹחָלְתִּי אַתָּה תַעֲנֶה אֲדֹנָי אֱלֹהָי׃

17 For I fear they will rejoice over me; when my foot gives way they will vaunt themselves against me.

יז כִּי־אָמַרְתִּי פֶּן־יִשְׂמְחוּ־לִי בְּמוֹט רַגְלִי עָלַי הִגְדִּילוּ׃

18 For I am on the verge of collapse; my pain is always with me.

יח כִּי־אֲנִי לְצֶלַע נָכוֹן וּמַכְאוֹבִי נֶגְדִּי תָמִיד׃

19 I acknowledge my iniquity; I am fearful over my sin;

יט כִּי־עֲוֹנִי אַגִּיד אֶדְאַג מֵחַטָּאתִי׃

20 for my mortal enemies are numerous; my treacherous foes are many.

כ וְאֹיְבַי חַיִּים עָצֵמוּ וְרַבּוּ שֹׂנְאַי שָׁקֶר׃

21 Those who repay evil for good harass me for pursuing good.

כא וּמְשַׁלְּמֵי רָעָה תַּחַת טוֹבָה יִשְׂטְנוּנִי תַּחַת רדופי־[רָדְפִי־] טוֹב׃

22 Do not abandon me, *Hashem*; my God, be not far from me;

כב אַל־תַּעַזְבֵנִי יְהוָה אֱלֹהַי אַל־תִּרְחַק מִמֶּנִּי׃

23 hasten to my aid, O *Hashem*, my deliverance.

כג חוּשָׁה לְעֶזְרָתִי אֲדֹנָי תְּשׁוּעָתִי׃

39

1 For the leader; for *Yedutun*. A psalm of *David*.

לט א לַמְנַצֵּחַ לידיתון [לִידוּתוּן] מִזְמוֹר לְדָוִד׃

2 I resolved I would watch my step lest I offend by my speech; I would keep my mouth muzzled while the wicked man was in my presence.

ב אָמַרְתִּי אֶשְׁמְרָה דְרָכַי מֵחֲטוֹא בִלְשׁוֹנִי אֶשְׁמְרָה לְפִי מַחְסוֹם בְּעֹד רָשָׁע לְנֶגְדִּי׃

a-MAR-tee esh-m'-RAH d'-ra-KHAI may-kha-TO vil-sho-NEE esh-m'-RAH l'-FEE makh-SOM b'-OD ra-SHA l'-neg-DEE

3 I was dumb, silent; I was very still while my pain was intense.

ג נֶאֱלַמְתִּי דוּמִיָּה הֶחֱשֵׁיתִי מִטּוֹב וּכְאֵבִי נֶעְכָּר׃

4 My mind was in a rage, my thoughts were all aflame; I spoke out:

ד חַם־לִבִּי בְּקִרְבִּי בַּהֲגִיגִי תִבְעַר־אֵשׁ דִּבַּרְתִּי בִּלְשׁוֹנִי׃

---

sit in their serenity. We are hated and have no recourse but we pray that our salvation and redemption will come soon. *Amen.*" Eight centuries later, the redemption has begun and the Jewish people are no longer mute.

39:2 Lest I offend by my speech The Sages of the Talmud ask (*Yoma* 9b) why the second *Beit Hamikdash* was destroyed if there were plenty of people studying the *Torah*, following *Hashem*'s commandments and performing acts of kindness for others. They answer that it was because people spoke ill of each other due to baseless hatred. This teaches that such animosity and foul-mouthed behavior is worse than idolatry, sexual immorality and murder, which are the reasons given for the destruction of the first *Beit Hamikdash*. The Sages then ask, was there no slander or baseless hatred among the people in the first Temple period? They answer that, in fact, there was, but those who lived during the first *Beit Hamikdash* were open with their bitter feelings, thus their punishment was shorter. During the second *Beit Hamikdash*, the people hid their resentments, secretly slandering and speaking hate, and therefore their exile lasted much longer.

Tehillim/Psalms
Chapter 40

5 Tell me, *Hashem*, what my term is, what is the measure of my days; I would know how fleeting my life is.

ה הוֹדִיעֵנִי יְהֹוָה קִצִּי וּמִדַּת יָמַי מַה־הִיא אֵדְעָה מֶה־חָדֵל אָנִי׃

6 You have made my life just handbreadths long; its span is as nothing in Your sight; no man endures any longer than a breath. *Selah*.

ו הִנֵּה טְפָחוֹת נָתַתָּה יָמַי וְחֶלְדִּי כְאַיִן נֶגְדֶּךָ אַךְ כָּל־הֶבֶל כָּל־אָדָם נִצָּב סֶלָה׃

7 Man walks about as a mere shadow; mere futility is his hustle and bustle, amassing and not knowing who will gather in.

ז אַךְ־בְּצֶלֶם ׀ יִתְהַלֶּךְ־אִישׁ אַךְ־הֶבֶל יֶהֱמָיוּן יִצְבֹּר וְלֹא־יֵדַע מִי־אֹסְפָם׃

8 What, then, can I count on, O *Hashem*? In You my hope lies.

ח וְעַתָּה מַה־קִּוִּיתִי אֲדֹנָי תּוֹחַלְתִּי לְךָ הִיא׃

9 Deliver me from all my transgressions; make me not the butt of the benighted.

ט מִכָּל־פְּשָׁעַי הַצִּילֵנִי חֶרְפַּת נָבָל אַל־תְּשִׂימֵנִי׃

10 I am dumb, I do not speak up, for it is Your doing.

י נֶאֱלַמְתִּי לֹא אֶפְתַּח־פִּי כִּי אַתָּה עָשִׂיתָ׃

11 Take away Your plague from me; I perish from Your blows.

יא הָסֵר מֵעָלַי נִגְעֶךָ מִתִּגְרַת יָדְךָ אֲנִי כָלִיתִי׃

12 You chastise a man in punishment for his sin, consuming like a moth what he treasures. No man is more than a breath. *Selah*.

יב בְּתוֹכָחוֹת עַל־עָוֹן ׀ יִסַּרְתָּ אִישׁ וַתֶּמֶס כָּעָשׁ חֲמוּדוֹ אַךְ הֶבֶל כָּל־אָדָם סֶלָה׃

13 Hear my prayer, *Hashem*; give ear to my cry; do not disregard my tears; for like all my forebears I am an alien, resident with You.

יג שִׁמְעָה־תְפִלָּתִי ׀ יְהֹוָה וְשַׁוְעָתִי ׀ הַאֲזִינָה אֶל־דִּמְעָתִי אַל־תֶּחֱרַשׁ כִּי גֵר אָנֹכִי עִמָּךְ תּוֹשָׁב כְּכָל־אֲבוֹתָי׃

14 Look away from me, that I may recover, before I pass away and am gone.

יד הָשַׁע מִמֶּנִּי וְאַבְלִיגָה בְּטֶרֶם אֵלֵךְ וְאֵינֶנִּי׃

40

1 For the leader. A psalm of *David*.

א לַמְנַצֵּחַ לְדָוִד מִזְמוֹר׃

2 I put my hope in *Hashem*; He inclined toward me, and heeded my cry.

ב קַוֹּה קִוִּיתִי יְהֹוָה וַיֵּט אֵלַי וַיִּשְׁמַע שַׁוְעָתִי׃

ka-VOH ki-VEE-tee a-do-NAI va-YAYT ay-LAI va-yish-MA shav-a-TEE

3 He lifted me out of the miry pit, the slimy clay, and set my feet on a rock, steadied my legs.

ג וַיַּעֲלֵנִי ׀ מִבּוֹר שָׁאוֹן מִטִּיט הַיָּוֵן וַיָּקֶם עַל־סֶלַע רַגְלַי כּוֹנֵן אֲשֻׁרָי׃

40:2 I put my hope in *Hashem* In *Tehillim*, King *David* often calls out to *Hashem* in pain; expressing his suffering and calling for salvation. Here, *David* reminds us that God not only listens to his pleas, but also responds. Psalm 40 opens with a direct response to Psalm 27's last line: "Look to *Hashem*; be strong and of good courage! O look to *Hashem*!" *David* tells us that he indeed put his hope in *Hashem*, and *Hashem* listened, heard his cry and saved him. Perhaps in this verse *David* is acknowledging his salvation from *Shaul*, perhaps he is rejoicing in the return of the Ark to *Yerushalayim*, or perhaps he is just sharing the momentary bliss of his wives, his children or his nation. We believe that our prayers are always heard by God; sometimes the time is right for Him only to listen, and sometimes He responds with great salvation. Those times require us to sing great praise to Him.

Tehillim/Psalms
Chapter 40

תהלים
פרק מ

4 He put a new song into my mouth, a hymn to our God. May many see it and stand in awe, and trust in *Hashem*.

ד וַיִּתֵּן בְּפִי שִׁיר חָדָשׁ תְּהִלָּה לֵאלֹהֵינוּ יִרְאוּ רַבִּים וְיִירָאוּ וְיִבְטְחוּ בַּיהוָה:

5 Happy is the man who makes *Hashem* his trust, who turns not to the arrogant or to followers of falsehood.

ה אַשְׁרֵי הַגֶּבֶר אֲשֶׁר־שָׂם יְהוָֹה מִבְטַחוֹ וְלֹא־פָנָה אֶל־רְהָבִים וְשָׂטֵי כָזָב:

6 You, *Hashem* my God, have done many things; the wonders You have devised for us cannot be set out before You; I would rehearse the tale of them, but they are more than can be told.

ו רַבּוֹת עָשִׂיתָ אַתָּה יְהוָה אֱלֹהַי נִפְלְאֹתֶיךָ וּמַחְשְׁבֹתֶיךָ אֵלֵינוּ אֵין עֲרֹךְ אֵלֶיךָ אַגִּידָה וַאֲדַבֵּרָה עָצְמוּ מִסַּפֵּר:

7 You gave me to understand that You do not desire sacrifice and meal offering; You do not ask for burnt offering and sin offering.

ז זֶבַח וּמִנְחָה לֹא־חָפַצְתָּ אָזְנַיִם כָּרִיתָ לִּי עוֹלָה וַחֲטָאָה לֹא שָׁאָלְתָּ:

8 Then I said, "See, I will bring a scroll recounting what befell me."

ח אָז אָמַרְתִּי הִנֵּה־בָאתִי בִּמְגִלַּת־סֵפֶר כָּתוּב עָלָי:

9 To do what pleases You, my God, is my desire; Your teaching is in my inmost parts.

ט לַעֲשׂוֹת־רְצוֹנְךָ אֱלֹהַי חָפָצְתִּי וְתוֹרָתְךָ בְּתוֹךְ מֵעָי:

10 I proclaimed [Your] righteousness in a great congregation; see, I did not withhold my words; *Hashem*, You must know it.

י בִּשַּׂרְתִּי צֶדֶק בְּקָהָל רָב הִנֵּה שְׂפָתַי לֹא אֶכְלָא יְהוָה אַתָּה יָדָעְתָּ:

11 I did not keep Your beneficence to myself; I declared Your faithful deliverance; I did not fail to speak of Your steadfast love in a great congregation.

יא צִדְקָתְךָ לֹא־כִסִּיתִי בְּתוֹךְ לִבִּי אֱמוּנָתְךָ וּתְשׁוּעָתְךָ אָמָרְתִּי לֹא־כִחַדְתִּי חַסְדְּךָ וַאֲמִתְּךָ לְקָהָל רָב:

12 *Hashem*, You will not withhold from me Your compassion; Your steadfast love will protect me always.

יב אַתָּה יְהוָה לֹא־תִכְלָא רַחֲמֶיךָ מִמֶּנִּי חַסְדְּךָ וַאֲמִתְּךָ תָּמִיד יִצְּרוּנִי:

13 For misfortunes without number envelop me; my iniquities have caught up with me; I cannot see; they are more than the hairs of my head; I am at my wits' end.

יג כִּי אָפְפוּ־עָלַי רָעוֹת עַד־אֵין מִסְפָּר הִשִּׂיגוּנִי עֲוֹנֹתַי וְלֹא־יָכֹלְתִּי לִרְאוֹת עָצְמוּ מִשַּׂעֲרוֹת רֹאשִׁי וְלִבִּי עֲזָבָנִי:

14 O favor me, *Hashem*, and save me; *Hashem*, hasten to my aid.

יד רְצֵה יְהוָה לְהַצִּילֵנִי יְהוָה לְעֶזְרָתִי חוּשָׁה:

15 Let those who seek to destroy my life be frustrated and disgraced; let those who wish me harm fall back in shame.

טו יֵבֹשׁוּ וְיַחְפְּרוּ יַחַד מְבַקְשֵׁי נַפְשִׁי לִסְפּוֹתָהּ יִסֹּגוּ אָחוֹר וְיִכָּלְמוּ חֲפֵצֵי רָעָתִי:

16 Let those who say "Aha! Aha!" over me be desolate because of their frustration.

טז יָשֹׁמּוּ עַל־עֵקֶב בָּשְׁתָּם הָאֹמְרִים לִי הֶאָח הֶאָח:

17 But let all who seek You be glad and rejoice in You; let those who are eager for Your deliverance always say, "Extolled be *Hashem*!"

יז יָשִׂישׂוּ וְיִשְׂמְחוּ בְּךָ כָּל־מְבַקְשֶׁיךָ יֹאמְרוּ תָמִיד יִגְדַּל יְהוָה אֹהֲבֵי תְּשׁוּעָתֶךָ:

Tehillim/Psalms
Chapter 41

18 But I am poor and needy; may *Hashem* devise [deliverance] for me. You are my help and my rescuer; my God, do not delay.

41

1 For the leader. A psalm of *David*.

2 Happy is he who is thoughtful of the wretched; in bad times may *Hashem* keep him from harm.

3 May *Hashem* guard him and preserve him; and may he be thought happy in the land. Do not subject him to the will of his enemies.

4 *Hashem* will sustain him on his sickbed; You shall wholly transform his bed of suffering.

5 I said, "*Hashem*, have mercy on me, heal me, for I have sinned against You."

6 My enemies speak evilly of me, "When will he die and his name perish?"

7 If one comes to visit, he speaks falsely; his mind stores up evil thoughts; once outside, he speaks them.

8 All my enemies whisper together against me, imagining the worst for me.

9 "Something baneful has settled in him; he'll not rise from his bed again."

10 My ally in whom I trusted, even he who shares my bread, has been utterly false to me.

11 But You, *Hashem*, have mercy on me; let me rise again and repay them.

12 Then shall I know that You are pleased with me: when my enemy cannot shout in triumph over me.

13 You will support me because of my integrity, and let me abide in Your presence forever.

14 Blessed is *Hashem*, God of *Yisrael*, from eternity to eternity. *Amen* and *Amen*.

ba-RUKH a-do-NAI e-lo-HAY yis-ra-AYL may-ha-o-LAM v'-ad ha-o-LAM a-MAYN v'-a-MAYN

41:14 Blessed is Hashem Sefer Tehillim is traditionally subdivided into five books, parallel to the five books of the *Torah*. Psalm 41 concludes the first of these five books with a blessing. The word for blessing, *beracha* (ברכה), comes from the root ב-ר-כ which also produces words like 'crevice', 'tunnel', and 'knees'. All these reflect the notion of going from above to something below. In his book *Jewish Meditation*, Rabbi Aryeh

Tehillim/Psalms
Chapter 42

תהלים
פרק מב

42 1 For the leader. A maskil of the Korahites.

א לַמְנַצֵּחַ מַשְׂכִּיל לִבְנֵי־קֹרַח:

2 Like a hind crying for water, my soul cries for You, O *Hashem*;

ב כְּאַיָּל תַּעֲרֹג עַל־אֲפִיקֵי־מָיִם כֵּן נַפְשִׁי תַעֲרֹג אֵלֶיךָ אֱלֹהִים:

3 my soul thirsts for *Hashem*, the living *Hashem*; O when will I come to appear before *Hashem*!

ג צָמְאָה נַפְשִׁי לֵאלֹהִים לְאֵל חָי מָתַי אָבוֹא וְאֵרָאֶה פְּנֵי אֱלֹהִים:

4 My tears have been my food day and night; I am ever taunted with, "Where is your God?"

ד הָיְתָה־לִּי דִמְעָתִי לֶחֶם יוֹמָם וָלָיְלָה בֶּאֱמֹר אֵלַי כָּל־הַיּוֹם אַיֵּה אֱלֹהֶיךָ:

5 When I think of this, I pour out my soul: how I walked with the crowd, moved with them, the festive throng, to the House of *Hashem* with joyous shouts of praise.

ה אֵלֶּה אֶזְכְּרָה וְאֶשְׁפְּכָה עָלַי נַפְשִׁי כִּי אֶעֱבֹר בַּסָּךְ אֶדַּדֵּם עַד־בֵּית אֱלֹהִים בְּקוֹל־רִנָּה וְתוֹדָה הָמוֹן חוֹגֵג:

6 Why so downcast, my soul, why disquieted within me? Have hope in *Hashem*; I will yet praise Him for His saving presence.

ו מַה־תִּשְׁתּוֹחֲחִי נַפְשִׁי וַתֶּהֱמִי עָלָי הוֹחִילִי לֵאלֹהִים כִּי־עוֹד אוֹדֶנּוּ יְשׁוּעוֹת פָּנָיו:

7 O my God, my soul is downcast; therefore I think of You in this land of *Yarden* and *Chermon*, in Mount Mizar,

ז אֱלֹהַי עָלַי נַפְשִׁי תִשְׁתּוֹחָח עַל־כֵּן אֶזְכָּרְךָ מֵאֶרֶץ יַרְדֵּן וְחֶרְמוֹנִים מֵהַר מִצְעָר:

e-lo-HAI a-LAI naf-SHEE tish-to-KHAKH al KAYN ez-ko-r'-KHA may-E-retz yar-DAYN v'-kher-mo-NEEM may-HAR mitz-AR

8 where deep calls to deep in the roar of Your cataracts; all Your breakers and billows have swept over me.

ח תְּהוֹם־אֶל־תְּהוֹם קוֹרֵא לְקוֹל צִנּוֹרֶיךָ כָּל־מִשְׁבָּרֶיךָ וְגַלֶּיךָ עָלַי עָבָרוּ:

9 By day may *Hashem* vouchsafe His faithful care, so that at night a song to Him may be with me, a prayer to the God of my life.

ט יוֹמָם יְצַוֶּה יְהֹוָה חַסְדּוֹ וּבַלַּיְלָה שִׁירֹה [שִׁירוֹ] עִמִּי תְּפִלָּה לְאֵל חַיָּי:

10 I say to *Hashem*, my rock, "Why have You forgotten me, why must I walk in gloom, oppressed by my enemy?"

י אוֹמְרָה לְאֵל סַלְעִי לָמָה שְׁכַחְתָּנִי לָמָּה־קֹדֵר אֵלֵךְ בְּלַחַץ אוֹיֵב:

Kaplan explains that our mission is to bring *Hashem* down from above to become an integral part of our lives. In contrast, the word *tehilla* (תהילה), meaning 'praise,' implies God's transcendence. Yet, the two words together, *tehilla* and *beracha*, 'praise' and 'blessing,' are the essence of man's relationship with the Lord. We must strive to both praise *Hashem* as transcendent above place and time, and bless Him as being very immanent and closely involved in our lives.

42:7 And *Chermon*, in Mount Mizar A young man living in the northern region of Israel longs for *Yerushalayim*, his soul thirsting for closeness to God. Unable to reach the holy city, he finds his inspiration in Mount *Chermon*. Soaring over two thousand eight hundred meters above sea level, this mountain range is covered in snow for much of the year, and the runoff of melting snow is a major source of freshwater for the Jordan River which flows into the Sea of Galilee. The runoff from the top of the *Chermon* also enables a fertile plant life and rich vegetation below the snow line of the mountain, and the southern slopes of the mountains extend to the northern Golan Heights. Yet despite the richness in rain, vegetation and awe-inspiring vistas, the psalmist still seeks spiritual inspiration two hundred kilometers southward, from a small hill upon which stands the *Beit Hamikdash* and from where the word of *Hashem* emanates to the entire world: *Yerushalayim*.

Mount Chermon

Tehillim/Psalms
Chapter 43

תהלים
פרק מג

11 Crushing my bones, my foes revile me, taunting me always with, "Where is your God?"

יא בְּרֶ֤צַח ׀ בְּֽעַצְמוֹתַ֗י חֵרְפ֥וּנִי צוֹרְרָ֑י בְּאָמְרָ֥ם אֵלַ֥י כָּל־הַ֝יּ֗וֹם אַיֵּ֥ה אֱלֹהֶֽיךָ׃

12 Why so downcast, my soul, why disquieted within me? Have hope in *Hashem*; I will yet praise Him, my ever-present help, my God.

יב מַה־תִּשְׁתּ֬וֹחֲחִ֨י ׀ נַפְשִׁי֮ וּֽמַה־תֶּהֱמִ֢י עָ֫לָ֥י הוֹחִ֣ילִי לֵֽ֭אלֹהִים כִּי־ע֣וֹד אוֹדֶ֑נּוּ יְשׁוּעֹ֥ת פָּ֝נַ֗י וֵאלֹהָֽי׃

43

1 Vindicate me, O *Hashem*, Champion my cause against faithless people; rescue me from the treacherous, dishonest man.

מג א שָׁפְטֵ֤נִי אֱלֹהִ֨ים ׀ וְרִ֘יבָ֤ה רִיבִ֗י מִגּ֥וֹי לֹֽא־חָסִ֑יד מֵ֤אִישׁ־מִרְמָ֖ה וְעַוְלָ֣ה תְפַלְּטֵֽנִי׃

2 For You are my God, my stronghold; why have You rejected me? Why must I walk in gloom, oppressed by the enemy?

ב כִּֽי־אַתָּ֤ה ׀ אֱלֹהֵ֣י מָֽעוּזִּי֮ לָמָ֢ה זְנַ֫חְתָּ֥נִי לָֽמָּה־קֹדֵ֥ר אֶתְהַלֵּ֗ךְ בְּלַ֣חַץ אוֹיֵֽב׃

3 Send forth Your light and Your truth; they will lead me; they will bring me to Your holy mountain, to Your dwelling-place,

ג שְׁלַח־אוֹרְךָ֣ וַ֭אֲמִתְּךָ הֵ֣מָּה יַנְח֑וּנִי יְבִיא֥וּנִי אֶל־הַר־קָ֝דְשְׁךָ֗ וְאֶל־מִשְׁכְּנוֹתֶֽיךָ׃

sh'-lakh o-r'-KHA va-a-mi-t'-KHA HAY-mah yan-KHU-nee y'-vee-U-nee el har kod-sh'-KHA v'-el mish-k'-no-TE-kha

4 that I may come to the *Mizbayach* of *Hashem*, *Hashem*, my delight, my joy; that I may praise You with the lyre, O *Hashem*, my God.

ד וְאָב֤וֹאָה ׀ אֶל־מִזְבַּ֬ח אֱלֹהִ֗ים אֶל־אֵל֮ שִׂמְחַ֢ת גִּ֫ילִ֥י וְאוֹדְךָ֥ בְכִנּ֗וֹר אֱלֹהִ֥ים אֱלֹהָֽי׃

5 Why so downcast, my soul, why disquieted within me? Have hope in *Hashem*; I will yet praise Him, my ever-present help, my God.

ה מַה־תִּשְׁתּ֬וֹחֲחִ֨י ׀ נַפְשִׁי֮ וּֽמַה־תֶּהֱמִ֢י עָ֫לָ֥י הוֹחִ֣ילִי לֵֽ֭אלֹהִים כִּי־ע֣וֹד אוֹדֶ֑נּוּ יְשׁוּעֹ֥ת פָּ֝נַ֗י וֵֽאלֹהָֽי׃

44

1 For the leader. Of the Korahites. A maskil.

מד א לַמְנַצֵּ֬חַ לִבְנֵי־קֹ֬רַח מַשְׂכִּֽיל׃

2 We have heard, O *Hashem*, our fathers have told us the deeds You performed in their time, in days of old.

ב אֱלֹהִ֤ים ׀ בְּאָזְנֵ֬ינוּ שָׁמַ֗עְנוּ אֲבוֹתֵ֥ינוּ סִפְּרוּ־לָ֑נוּ פֹּ֥עַל פָּעַ֥לְתָּ בִֽ֝ימֵיהֶ֗ם בִּ֣ימֵי קֶֽדֶם׃

e-lo-HEEM b'-oz-NAY-nu sha-MA-nu a-vo-TAY-nu si-p'-ru LA-nu PO-al pa-AL-ta vee-may-HEM BEE-may KE-dem

---

משכן

43:3 Your dwelling-place The word for Tabernacle is *Mishkan* (משכן), from the Hebrew root ש-כ-נ, which means 'to dwell.' The *Mishkan* was erected in the desert as a temporary dwelling for *Hashem*, which was ultimately replaced by a permanent resting place, in the form of the *Beit Hamikdash* on Mount Moriah. But getting there took some time. The Sages trace the travels of the *Mishkan* in the Land of Israel: Fourteen years in *Gilgal*, 369 years in *Shilo*, and another 57 years in *Nov* and *Givon*. Altogether, it took 440 years from the entry of the Children of Israel into *Eretz Yisrael* until *Shlomo* built the *Beit Hamikdash*. In this psalm, the psalmist asks God for light and truth to help him return to the holy mountain, to the resting place of the Lord.

44:2 Our fathers have told us Walking through the Land of Israel is an educational experience. Every kilometer tells another story of ancient, medieval or modern history. The empires that have passed through this land are many: Canaanite, Israelite, Assyrian, Babylonian, Persian, Greek, Hasmonean, Roman, Byzantine, Muslim, Mamluk, Ottoman, British. Today, Israel is holy to many religions. Each one passes down their sacred stories from one generation to the next,

Tehillim/Psalms
Chapter 44

3 With Your hand You planted them, displacing nations; You brought misfortune on peoples, and drove them out.

4 It was not by their sword that they took the land, their arm did not give them victory, but Your right hand, Your arm, and Your goodwill, for You favored them.

5 You are my king, O *Hashem*; decree victories for *Yaakov*!

6 Through You we gore our foes; by Your name we trample our adversaries;

7 I do not trust in my bow; it is not my sword that gives me victory;

8 You give us victory over our foes; You thwart those who hate us.

9 In *Hashem* we glory at all times, and praise Your name unceasingly. *Selah*.

10 Yet You have rejected and disgraced us; You do not go with our armies.

11 You make us retreat before our foe; our enemies plunder us at will.

12 You let them devour us like sheep; You disperse us among the nations.

13 You sell Your people for no fortune, You set no high price on them.

14 You make us the butt of our neighbors the scorn and derision of those around us.

15 You make us a byword among the nations, a laughingstock among the peoples.

16 I am always aware of my disgrace; I am wholly covered with shame

17 at the sound of taunting revilers, in the presence of the vengeful foe.

18 All this has come upon us, yet we have not forgotten You, or been false to Your covenant.

תהילים
פרק מד

ג אַתָּה יָדְךָ גּוֹיִם הוֹרַשְׁתָּ וַתִּטָּעֵם תָּרַע לְאֻמִּים וַתְּשַׁלְּחֵם:

ד כִּי לֹא בְחַרְבָּם יָרְשׁוּ אָרֶץ וּזְרוֹעָם לֹא־הוֹשִׁיעָה לָּמוֹ כִּי־יְמִינְךָ וּזְרוֹעֲךָ וְאוֹר פָּנֶיךָ כִּי רְצִיתָם:

ה אַתָּה־הוּא מַלְכִּי אֱלֹהִים צַוֵּה יְשׁוּעוֹת יַעֲקֹב:

ו בְּךָ צָרֵינוּ נְנַגֵּחַ בְּשִׁמְךָ נָבוּס קָמֵינוּ:

ז כִּי לֹא בְקַשְׁתִּי אֶבְטָח וְחַרְבִּי לֹא תוֹשִׁיעֵנִי:

ח כִּי הוֹשַׁעְתָּנוּ מִצָּרֵינוּ וּמְשַׂנְאֵינוּ הֱבִישׁוֹתָ:

ט בֵּאלֹהִים הִלַּלְנוּ כָל־הַיּוֹם וְשִׁמְךָ לְעוֹלָם נוֹדֶה סֶלָה:

י אַף־זָנַחְתָּ וַתַּכְלִימֵנוּ וְלֹא־תֵצֵא בְּצִבְאוֹתֵינוּ:

יא תְּשִׁיבֵנוּ אָחוֹר מִנִּי־צָר וּמְשַׂנְאֵינוּ שָׁסוּ לָמוֹ:

יב תִּתְּנֵנוּ כְּצֹאן מַאֲכָל וּבַגּוֹיִם זֵרִיתָנוּ:

יג תִּמְכֹּר־עַמְּךָ בְלֹא־הוֹן וְלֹא־רִבִּיתָ בִּמְחִירֵיהֶם:

יד תְּשִׂימֵנוּ חֶרְפָּה לִשְׁכֵנֵינוּ לַעַג וָקֶלֶס לִסְבִיבוֹתֵינוּ:

טו תְּשִׂימֵנוּ מָשָׁל בַּגּוֹיִם מְנוֹד־רֹאשׁ בַּל־אֻמִּים:

טז כָּל־הַיּוֹם כְּלִמָּתִי נֶגְדִּי וּבֹשֶׁת פָּנַי כִּסָּתְנִי:

יז מִקּוֹל מְחָרֵף וּמְגַדֵּף מִפְּנֵי אוֹיֵב וּמִתְנַקֵּם:

יח כָּל־זֹאת בָּאַתְנוּ וְלֹא שְׁכַחֲנוּךָ וְלֹא־שִׁקַּרְנוּ בִּבְרִיתֶךָ:

reads their holy texts and experiences the magic of the Holy Land. In times of great joy we revel in the aura of the Holy Land and connect it to bygone years. In times of pain and distress, we suffer at our present and recall the tranquility of Israel's past.

1523

Tehillim/Psalms
Chapter 45

תהלים
פרק מה

19 Our hearts have not gone astray, nor have our feet swerved from Your path,

יט לֹא־נָסוֹג אָחוֹר לִבֵּנוּ וַתֵּט אֲשֻׁרֵינוּ מִנִּי אָרְחֶךָ:

20 though You cast us, crushed, to where the sea monster is, and covered us over with deepest darkness.

כ כִּי דִכִּיתָנוּ בִּמְקוֹם תַּנִּים וַתְּכַס עָלֵינוּ בְצַלְמָוֶת:

21 If we forgot the name of our God and spread forth our hands to a foreign god,

כא אִם־שָׁכַחְנוּ שֵׁם אֱלֹהֵינוּ וַנִּפְרֹשׂ כַּפֵּינוּ לְאֵל זָר:

22 *Hashem* would surely search it out, for He knows the secrets of the heart.

כב הֲלֹא אֱלֹהִים יַחֲקָר־זֹאת כִּי־הוּא יֹדֵעַ תַּעֲלֻמוֹת לֵב:

23 It is for Your sake that we are slain all day long, that we are regarded as sheep to be slaughtered.

כג כִּי־עָלֶיךָ הֹרַגְנוּ כָל־הַיּוֹם נֶחְשַׁבְנוּ כְּצֹאן טִבְחָה:

24 Rouse Yourself; why do You sleep, O *Hashem*? Awaken, do not reject us forever!

כד עוּרָה לָמָּה תִישַׁן אֲדֹנָי הָקִיצָה אַל־תִּזְנַח לָנֶצַח:

25 Why do You hide Your face, ignoring our affliction and distress?

כה לָמָּה־פָנֶיךָ תַסְתִּיר תִּשְׁכַּח עָנְיֵנוּ וְלַחֲצֵנוּ:

26 We lie prostrate in the dust; our body clings to the ground.

כו כִּי שָׁחָה לֶעָפָר נַפְשֵׁנוּ דָּבְקָה לָאָרֶץ בִּטְנֵנוּ:

27 Arise and help us, redeem us, as befits Your faithfulness.

כז קוּמָה עֶזְרָתָה לָּנוּ וּפְדֵנוּ לְמַעַן חַסְדֶּךָ:

45

1 For the leader; on shoshannim. Of the Korahites. A maskil. A love song.

מה א לַמְנַצֵּחַ עַל־שֹׁשַׁנִּים לִבְנֵי־קֹרַח מַשְׂכִּיל שִׁיר יְדִידֹת:

2 My heart is astir with gracious words; I speak my poem to a king; my tongue is the pen of an expert scribe.

ב רָחַשׁ לִבִּי דָּבָר טוֹב אֹמֵר אָנִי מַעֲשַׂי לְמֶלֶךְ לְשׁוֹנִי עֵט סוֹפֵר מָהִיר:

3 You are fairer than all men; your speech is endowed with grace; rightly has *Hashem* given you an eternal blessing.

ג יָפְיָפִיתָ מִבְּנֵי אָדָם הוּצַק חֵן בְּשִׂפְתוֹתֶיךָ עַל־כֵּן בֵּרַכְךָ אֱלֹהִים לְעוֹלָם:

4 Gird your sword upon your thigh, O hero, in your splendor and glory;

ד חֲגוֹר־חַרְבְּךָ עַל־יָרֵךְ גִּבּוֹר הוֹדְךָ וַהֲדָרֶךָ:

5 in your glory, win success; ride on in the cause of truth and meekness and right; and let your right hand lead you to awesome deeds.

ה וַהֲדָרְךָ צְלַח רְכַב עַל־דְּבַר־אֱמֶת וְעַנְוָה־צֶדֶק וְתוֹרְךָ נוֹרָאוֹת יְמִינֶךָ:

6 Your arrows, sharpened, [pierce] the breast of the king's enemies; peoples fall at your feet.*

ו חִצֶּיךָ שְׁנוּנִים עַמִּים תַּחְתֶּיךָ יִפְּלוּ בְּלֵב אוֹיְבֵי הַמֶּלֶךְ:

7 Your divine throne is everlasting; your royal scepter is a scepter of equity.

ז כִּסְאֲךָ אֱלֹהִים עוֹלָם וָעֶד שֵׁבֶט מִישֹׁר שֵׁבֶט מַלְכוּתֶךָ:

---

* order of clauses inverted for clarity

Tehillim/Psalms
Chapter 46

תהלים
פרק מו

8 You love righteousness and hate wickedness; rightly has *Hashem*, your God, chosen to anoint you with oil of gladness over all your peers.

אָהַבְתָּ צֶּדֶק וַתִּשְׂנָא רֶשַׁע עַל־כֵּן מְשָׁחֲךָ אֱלֹהִים אֱלֹהֶיךָ שֶׁמֶן שָׂשׂוֹן מֵחֲבֵרֶיךָ: ח

a-HAV-ta TZE-dek va-tis-NA RE-sha al KAYN m'-sha-kha-KHA e-lo-HEEM e-lo-HE-kha SHE-men sa-SON may-kha-vay-RE-kha

9 All your robes [are fragrant] with myrrh and aloes and cassia; from ivoried palaces lutes entertain you.

מֹר־וַאֲהָלוֹת קְצִיעוֹת כָּל־בִּגְדֹתֶיךָ מִן־הֵיכְלֵי שֵׁן מִנִּי שִׂמְּחוּךָ: ט

10 Royal princesses are your favorites; the consort stands at your right hand, decked in gold of Ophir.

בְּנוֹת מְלָכִים בְּיִקְּרוֹתֶיךָ נִצְּבָה שֵׁגַל לִימִינְךָ בְּכֶתֶם אוֹפִיר: י

11 Take heed, lass, and note, incline your ear: forget your people and your father's house,

שִׁמְעִי־בַת וּרְאִי וְהַטִּי אָזְנֵךְ וְשִׁכְחִי עַמֵּךְ וּבֵית אָבִיךְ: יא

12 and let the king be aroused by your beauty; since he is your lord, bow to him.

וְיִתְאָו הַמֶּלֶךְ יָפְיֵךְ כִּי־הוּא אֲדֹנַיִךְ וְהִשְׁתַּחֲוִי־לוֹ: יב

13 O Tyrian lass, the wealthiest people will court your favor with gifts,

וּבַת־צֹר בְּמִנְחָה פָּנַיִךְ יְחַלּוּ עֲשִׁירֵי עָם: יג

14 goods of all sorts. The royal princess, her dress embroidered with golden mountings,

כָּל־כְּבוּדָּה בַת־מֶלֶךְ פְּנִימָה מִמִּשְׁבְּצוֹת זָהָב לְבוּשָׁהּ: יד

15 is led inside to the king; maidens in her train, her companions, are presented to you.

לִרְקָמוֹת תּוּבַל לַמֶּלֶךְ בְּתוּלוֹת אַחֲרֶיהָ רֵעוֹתֶיהָ מוּבָאוֹת לָךְ: טו

16 They are led in with joy and gladness; they enter the palace of the king.

תּוּבַלְנָה בִּשְׂמָחֹת וָגִיל תְּבֹאֶינָה בְּהֵיכַל מֶלֶךְ: טז

17 Your sons will succeed your ancestors; you will appoint them princes throughout the land.

תַּחַת אֲבֹתֶיךָ יִהְיוּ בָנֶיךָ תְּשִׁיתֵמוֹ לְשָׂרִים בְּכָל־הָאָרֶץ: יז

18 I commemorate your fame for all generations, so peoples will praise you forever and ever.

אַזְכִּירָה שִׁמְךָ בְּכָל־דֹּר וָדֹר עַל־כֵּן עַמִּים יְהוֹדֻךָ לְעֹלָם וָעֶד: יח

46 1 For the leader. Of the Korahites; on alamoth. A song.

לַמְנַצֵּחַ לִבְנֵי־קֹרַח עַל־עֲלָמוֹת שִׁיר: א מו

2 *Hashem* is our refuge and stronghold, a help in trouble, very near.

אֱלֹהִים לָנוּ מַחֲסֶה וָעֹז עֶזְרָה בְצָרוֹת נִמְצָא מְאֹד: ב

e-lo-HEEM LA-nu ma-kha-SEH va-OZ ez-RAH v'-tza-ROT nim-TZA m'-OD

45:8 Oil of gladness Throughout Israel one will find ancient olive presses made by Canaanites, Israelites, Hellenists and others, and many from the Byzantine era. Olive oil is heralded in the Bible as one of the great agricultural products of the Land of Israel (Deuteronomy 8:8), and there is a special commandment to use oil made of olives, with additional ingredients such as myrrh and cinnamon (Exodus 30:22–25), to anoint kings, priests and the holy vessels of the *Mishkan* and *Beit Hamikdash*. The psalmist praises the king who is chosen by God and anointed with Israel-grown olive oil, bringing joy to all.

46:2 Our refuge and stronghold Since it lies on the fault line of the Syrian-African rift, many earthquakes have hit the Land of Israel over the course of its history. In fact, *Sefer Amos* (1:1) refers to a major earthquake that shook *Eretz Yisrael* in Biblical times. The psalmist, aware of this

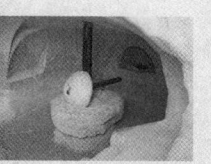

Ancient olive press Beit Guvrin, Israel

Tehillim/Psalms
Chapter 47

3 Therefore we are not afraid though the earth reels, though mountains topple into the sea –

ג עַל־כֵּן לֹא־נִירָא בְּהָמִיר אָרֶץ וּבְמוֹט הָרִים בְּלֵב יַמִּים:

4 its waters rage and foam; in its swell mountains quake. *Selah.*

ד יֶהֱמוּ יֶחְמְרוּ מֵימָיו יִרְעֲשׁוּ־הָרִים בְּגַאֲוָתוֹ סֶלָה:

5 There is a river whose streams gladden *Hashem*'s city, the holy dwelling-place of the Most High.

ה נָהָר פְּלָגָיו יְשַׂמְּחוּ עִיר־אֱלֹהִים קְדֹשׁ מִשְׁכְּנֵי עֶלְיוֹן:

6 *Hashem* is in its midst, it will not be toppled; by daybreak *Hashem* will come to its aid.

ו אֱלֹהִים בְּקִרְבָּהּ בַּל־תִּמּוֹט יַעְזְרֶהָ אֱלֹהִים לִפְנוֹת בֹּקֶר:

7 Nations rage, kingdoms topple; at the sound of His thunder the earth dissolves.

ז הָמוּ גוֹיִם מָטוּ מַמְלָכוֹת נָתַן בְּקוֹלוֹ תָּמוּג אָרֶץ:

8 The LORD of hosts is with us; the God of *Yaakov* is our haven. *Selah.*

ח יְהֹוָה צְבָאוֹת עִמָּנוּ מִשְׂגָּב־לָנוּ אֱלֹהֵי יַעֲקֹב סֶלָה:

9 Come and see what *Hashem* has done, how He has wrought desolation on the earth.

ט לְכוּ־חֲזוּ מִפְעֲלוֹת יְהֹוָה אֲשֶׁר־שָׂם שַׁמּוֹת בָּאָרֶץ:

10 He puts a stop to wars throughout the earth, breaking the bow, snapping the spear, consigning wagons to the flames.

י מַשְׁבִּית מִלְחָמוֹת עַד־קְצֵה הָאָרֶץ קֶשֶׁת יְשַׁבֵּר וְקִצֵּץ חֲנִית עֲגָלוֹת יִשְׂרֹף בָּאֵשׁ:

11 "Desist! Realize that I am *Hashem*! I dominate the nations; I dominate the earth."

יא הַרְפּוּ וּדְעוּ כִּי־אָנֹכִי אֱלֹהִים אָרוּם בַּגּוֹיִם אָרוּם בָּאָרֶץ:

12 The LORD of hosts is with us; the God of *Yaakov* is our haven. *Selah.*

יב יְהֹוָה צְבָאוֹת עִמָּנוּ מִשְׂגָּב־לָנוּ אֱלֹהֵי יַעֲקֹב סֶלָה:

47 1 For the leader. Of the Korahites. A psalm.

מז א לַמְנַצֵּחַ לִבְנֵי־קֹרַח מִזְמוֹר:

2 All you peoples, clap your hands, raise a joyous shout for *Hashem*.

ב כָּל־הָעַמִּים תִּקְעוּ־כָף הָרִיעוּ לֵאלֹהִים בְּקוֹל רִנָּה:

3 For *Hashem* Most High is awesome, great king over all the earth;

ג כִּי־יְהֹוָה עֶלְיוֹן נוֹרָא מֶלֶךְ גָּדוֹל עַל־כָּל־הָאָרֶץ:

4 He subjects peoples to us, sets nations at our feet.

ד יַדְבֵּר עַמִּים תַּחְתֵּינוּ וּלְאֻמִּים תַּחַת רַגְלֵינוּ:

---

phenomenon, will not fear when the earth overturns or when the mountains take over the seas and vice versa (verses 3–4), because "*Hashem* is our refuge and stronghold, a help in trouble, very near." Perhaps what he means by this is that not only does the Lord protect His people in times of trouble, but these 'natural' phenomenon, seen as disasters, are really *Hashem*'s mysterious way of offering protection to His people. One theory about this psalm is that it was written after the miraculous destruction of Sennacherib's army during their attack on *Yerushalayim* (II Kings 19:35), when the Lord caused a war to cease (verse 10) overnight. Indeed, the Lord protected the Children of Israel and helped them in their time of trouble.

Tehillim/Psalms
Chapter 48

5 He chose our heritage for us, the pride of *Yaakov* whom He loved. *Selah*.

yiv-khar LA-nu et na-kha-la-TAY-nu ET g'-ON ya-a-KOV a-sher a-HAYV SE-lah

6 *Hashem* ascends midst acclamation; *Hashem*, to the blasts of the *shofar*.

7 Sing, O sing to *Hashem*; sing, O sing to our king;

8 for *Hashem* is king over all the earth; sing a hymn.

9 *Hashem* reigns over the nations; *Hashem* is seated on His holy throne.

10 The great of the peoples are gathered together, the retinue of *Avraham*'s *Hashem*; for the guardians of the earth belong to *Hashem*; He is greatly exalted.

48

1 A song. A psalm of the Korahites.

2 *Hashem* is great and much acclaimed in the city of our God, His holy mountain –

3 fair-crested, joy of all the earth, Mount *Tzion*, summit of Zaphon, city of the great king.

4 Through its citadels, *Hashem* has made Himself known as a haven.

5 See, the kings joined forces; they advanced together.

6 At the mere sight of it they were stunned, they were terrified, they panicked;

7 they were seized there with a trembling, like a woman in the throes of labor,

8 as the Tarshish fleet was wrecked in an easterly gale.

47:5 Pride of *Yaakov* "The Pride of *Yaakov*" was the name of a famous academy of *Torah* learning in the Land of Israel. Also, called *Yeshivat Eretz Yisrael*, it lasted from the sixth until the twelfth century CE. It began in *Tiveria* (Tiberias), the center of Jewish intellectual life from the second to tenth centuries CE, under the tutelage of Rabbi Yehuda Nesiah, grandson of Rabbi Yehuda the Prince. *Tiveria* was the last headquarters of the High Court of Israel, called the *Sanhedrin*, which left *Yerushalyim* after it fell to the Romans in 70 CE. It saw the development of the Jerusalem Talmud, the diacritics for Hebrew writing, cantillation and many other Jewish intellectual activities. The academy went through many iterations and was housed in different locations but maintained a strong, central position in Jewish life and scholarship for close to six hundred years.

Tehillim/Psalms
Chapter 49

תהלים
פרק מט

9 The likes of what we heard we have now witnessed in the city of the Lord of hosts, in the city of our God – may *Hashem* preserve it forever! *Selah*.

ט כַּאֲשֶׁר שָׁמַעְנוּ כֵּן רָאִינוּ בְּעִיר־יְהֹוָה צְבָאוֹת בְּעִיר אֱלֹהֵינוּ אֱלֹהִים יְכוֹנְנֶהָ עַד־עוֹלָם סֶלָה:

ka-a-SHER sha-MA-nu KAYN ra-EE-nu b'-EER a-do-NAI tz'-va-OT b'-EER e-lo-HAY-nu e-lo-HEEM y'-kho-n'-NE-ha ad o-LAM SE-lah

10 In Your temple, *Hashem*, we meditate upon Your faithful care.

י דִּמִּינוּ אֱלֹהִים חַסְדֶּךָ בְּקֶרֶב הֵיכָלֶךָ:

11 The praise of You, *Hashem*, like Your name, reaches to the ends of the earth; Your right hand is filled with beneficence.

יא כְּשִׁמְךָ אֱלֹהִים כֵּן תְּהִלָּתְךָ עַל־קַצְוֵי־אֶרֶץ צֶדֶק מָלְאָה יְמִינֶךָ:

12 Let Mount *Tzion* rejoice! Let the towns of *Yehuda* exult, because of Your judgments.

יב יִשְׂמַח הַר־צִיּוֹן תָּגֵלְנָה בְּנוֹת יְהוּדָה לְמַעַן מִשְׁפָּטֶיךָ:

13 Walk around *Tzion*, circle it; count its towers,

יג סֹבּוּ צִיּוֹן וְהַקִּיפוּהָ סִפְרוּ מִגְדָּלֶיהָ:

14 take note of its ramparts; go through its citadels, that you may recount it to a future age.

יד שִׁיתוּ לִבְּכֶם לְחֵילָה פַּסְּגוּ אַרְמְנוֹתֶיהָ לְמַעַן תְּסַפְּרוּ לְדוֹר אַחֲרוֹן:

15 For *Hashem* – He is our God forever; He will lead us evermore.

טו כִּי זֶה אֱלֹהִים אֱלֹהֵינוּ עוֹלָם וָעֶד הוּא יְנַהֲגֵנוּ עַל־מוּת:

49

1 For the leader. Of the Korahites. A psalm.

א לַמְנַצֵּחַ לִבְנֵי־קֹרַח מִזְמוֹר:

מט

2 Hear this, all you peoples; give ear, all inhabitants of the world,

ב שִׁמְעוּ־זֹאת כָּל־הָעַמִּים הַאֲזִינוּ כָּל־יֹשְׁבֵי חָלֶד:

3 men of all estates, rich and poor alike.

ג גַּם־בְּנֵי אָדָם גַּם־בְּנֵי־אִישׁ יַחַד עָשִׁיר וְאֶבְיוֹן:

4 My mouth utters wisdom, my speech is full of insight.

ד פִּי יְדַבֵּר חָכְמוֹת וְהָגוּת לִבִּי תְבוּנוֹת:

5 I will turn my attention to a theme, set forth my lesson to the music of a lyre.

ה אַטֶּה לְמָשָׁל אָזְנִי אֶפְתַּח בְּכִנּוֹר חִידָתִי:

6 In time of trouble, why should I fear the encompassing evil of those who would supplant me –

ו לָמָּה אִירָא בִּימֵי רָע עֲוֺן עֲקֵבַי יְסוּבֵּנִי:

7 men who trust in their riches, who glory in their great wealth?

ז הַבֹּטְחִים עַל־חֵילָם וּבְרֹב עָשְׁרָם יִתְהַלָּלוּ:

8 Ah, it cannot redeem a man, or pay his ransom to *Hashem*;

ח אָח לֹא־פָדֹה יִפְדֶּה אִישׁ לֹא־יִתֵּן לֵאלֹהִים כָּפְרוֹ:

48:9 May *Hashem* preserve it forever In the times of the *Beit Hamikdash*, a special psalm was sung by the *Leviim* on each of the seven days of the week. In the absence of the *Beit Hamikdash*, Jews continue to say these daily *Tehillim* at the end of the morning prayers, in memory of the times when the Temple stood and in hopes of its redemption and restoration. Psalm 48 is recited on Mondays, and, as Rabbi Lord Jonathan Sacks writes, is "a hymn of praise to the beauty and endurance of *Yerushalayim*, the city that outlived all those who sought to conquer it." He adds in the name of Rabbi Joseph Hertz, "it is the Eternal City of the Eternal People."

Rabbi Lord Jonathan Sacks (1948–2020)

1528

Tehillim/Psalms
Chapter 50

9 the price of life is too high; and so one ceases to be, forever. וְיֵקַר פִּדְיוֹן נַפְשָׁם וְחָדַל לְעוֹלָם:

10 Shall he live eternally, and never see the grave? וִיחִי־עוֹד לָנֶצַח לֹא יִרְאֶה הַשָּׁחַת:

11 For one sees that the wise die, that the foolish and ignorant both perish, leaving their wealth to others. כִּי יִרְאֶה חֲכָמִים יָמוּתוּ יַחַד כְּסִיל וָבַעַר יֹאבֵדוּ וְעָזְבוּ לַאֲחֵרִים חֵילָם:

12 Their grave is their eternal home, the dwelling-place for all generations of those once famous on earth. קִרְבָּם בָּתֵּימוֹ לְעוֹלָם מִשְׁכְּנֹתָם לְדֹר וָדֹר קָרְאוּ בִשְׁמוֹתָם עֲלֵי אֲדָמוֹת:

13 Man does not abide in honor; he is like the beasts that perish. וְאָדָם בִּיקָר בַּל־יָלִין נִמְשַׁל כַּבְּהֵמוֹת נִדְמוּ:

14 Such is the fate of those who are self-confident, the end of those pleased with their own talk. *Selah*. זֶה דַרְכָּם כֵּסֶל לָמוֹ וְאַחֲרֵיהֶם בְּפִיהֶם יִרְצוּ סֶלָה:

15 Sheeplike they head for Sheol, with Death as their shepherd. The upright shall rule over them at daybreak, and their form shall waste away in Sheol till its nobility be gone. כַּצֹּאן לִשְׁאוֹל שַׁתּוּ מָוֶת יִרְעֵם וַיִּרְדּוּ בָם יְשָׁרִים לַבֹּקֶר וְצִירָם [וְצוּרָם] לְבַלּוֹת שְׁאוֹל מִזְּבֻל לוֹ:

16 But *Hashem* will redeem my life from the clutches of Sheol, for He will take me. *Selah*. אַךְ־אֱלֹהִים יִפְדֶּה נַפְשִׁי מִיַּד־שְׁאוֹל כִּי יִקָּחֵנִי סֶלָה:

17 Do not be afraid when a man becomes rich, when his household goods increase; אַל־תִּירָא כִּי־יַעֲשִׁר אִישׁ כִּי־יִרְבֶּה כְּבוֹד בֵּיתוֹ:

18 for when he dies he can take none of it along; his goods cannot follow him down. כִּי לֹא בְמוֹתוֹ יִקַּח הַכֹּל לֹא־יֵרֵד אַחֲרָיו כְּבוֹדוֹ:

KEE LO b'-mo-TO yi-KAKH ha-KOL lo yay-RAYD a-kha-RAV k'-vo-DO

19 Though he congratulates himself in his lifetime – "They must admit that you did well by yourself" – כִּי־נַפְשׁוֹ בְּחַיָּיו יְבָרֵךְ וְיוֹדֻךָ כִּי־תֵיטִיב לָךְ:

20 yet he must join the company of his ancestors, who will never see daylight again. תָּבוֹא עַד־דּוֹר אֲבוֹתָיו עַד־נֵצַח לֹא יִרְאוּ־אוֹר:

21 Man does not understand honor; he is like the beasts that perish. אָדָם בִּיקָר וְלֹא יָבִין נִמְשַׁל כַּבְּהֵמוֹת נִדְמוּ:

50

1 A psalm of *Asaf*. *Hashem*, *Hashem* spoke and summoned the world from east to west. מִזְמוֹר לְאָסָף אֵל אֱלֹהִים יְהוָה דִּבֶּר וַיִּקְרָא־אָרֶץ מִמִּזְרַח־שֶׁמֶשׁ עַד־מְבֹאוֹ:

2 From *Tzion*, perfect in beauty, *Hashem* appeared מִצִּיּוֹן מִכְלַל־יֹפִי אֱלֹהִים הוֹפִיעַ:

49:18 His goods cannot follow him down The Bible relates that after *Shlomo* becomes king of Israel, he has a dream. In his dream, *Hashem* appears and offers to grant him one wish. Instead of requesting wealth or long life, *Shlomo* humbly asks for wisdom so that he can properly judge the people. God is pleased with his decision, and rewards him not only with wisdom, but with wealth and honor as well. Upon waking the next morning, he comes to *Yerushalayim* and offers sacrifices, expressing his gratitude to the Lord (I Kings 3:5–14). In making his request, *Shlomo* demonstrates that he understands the message of this verse: Those things that most people chase, wealth and fortune, are the most fleeting.

Tehillim/Psalms
Chapter 50

תהלים
פרק נ

mi-tzi-YON mikh-lal YO-fee e-lo-HEEM ho-FEE-a

3 – let our God come and not fail to act! Devouring fire preceded Him; it stormed around Him fiercely.

ג יָבֹא אֱלֹהֵינוּ וְאַל־יֶחֱרַשׁ אֵשׁ־לְפָנָיו תֹּאכֵל וּסְבִיבָיו נִשְׂעֲרָה מְאֹד:

4 He summoned the heavens above, and the earth, for the trial of His people.

ד יִקְרָא אֶל־הַשָּׁמַיִם מֵעָל וְאֶל־הָאָרֶץ לָדִין עַמּוֹ:

5 "Bring in My devotees, who made a covenant with Me over sacrifice!"

ה אִסְפוּ־לִי חֲסִידָי כֹּרְתֵי בְרִיתִי עֲלֵי־זָבַח:

6 Then the heavens proclaimed His righteousness, for He is a *Hashem* who judges. *Selah*.

ו וַיַּגִּידוּ שָׁמַיִם צִדְקוֹ כִּי־אֱלֹהִים שֹׁפֵט הוּא סֶלָה:

7 "Pay heed, My people, and I will speak, O *Yisrael*, and I will arraign you. I am *Hashem*, your God.

ז שִׁמְעָה עַמִּי וַאֲדַבֵּרָה יִשְׂרָאֵל וְאָעִידָה בָּךְ אֱלֹהִים אֱלֹהֶיךָ אָנֹכִי:

8 I censure you not for your sacrifices, and your burnt offerings, made to Me daily;

ח לֹא עַל־זְבָחֶיךָ אוֹכִיחֶךָ וְעוֹלֹתֶיךָ לְנֶגְדִּי תָמִיד:

9 I claim no bull from your estate, no he-goats from your pens.

ט לֹא־אֶקַּח מִבֵּיתְךָ פָר מִמִּכְלְאֹתֶיךָ עַתּוּדִים:

10 For Mine is every animal of the forest, the beasts on a thousand mountains.

י כִּי־לִי כָל־חַיְתוֹ־יָעַר בְּהֵמוֹת בְּהַרְרֵי־אָלֶף:

11 I know every bird of the mountains, the creatures of the field are subject to Me.

יא יָדַעְתִּי כָּל־עוֹף הָרִים וְזִיז שָׂדַי עִמָּדִי:

12 Were I hungry, I would not tell you, for Mine is the world and all it holds.

יב אִם־אֶרְעַב לֹא־אֹמַר לָךְ כִּי־לִי תֵבֵל וּמְלֹאָהּ:

13 Do I eat the flesh of bulls, or drink the blood of he-goats?

יג הַאוֹכַל בְּשַׂר אַבִּירִים וְדַם עַתּוּדִים אֶשְׁתֶּה:

14 Sacrifice a thank offering to *Hashem*, and pay your vows to the Most High.

יד זְבַח לֵאלֹהִים תּוֹדָה וְשַׁלֵּם לְעֶלְיוֹן נְדָרֶיךָ:

15 Call upon Me in time of trouble; I will rescue you, and you shall honor Me."

טו וּקְרָאֵנִי בְּיוֹם צָרָה אֲחַלֶּצְךָ וּתְכַבְּדֵנִי:

16 And to the wicked, *Hashem* said: "Who are you to recite My laws, and mouth the terms of My covenant,

טז וְלָרָשָׁע אָמַר אֱלֹהִים מַה־לְּךָ לְסַפֵּר חֻקָּי וַתִּשָּׂא בְרִיתִי עֲלֵי־פִיךָ:

17 seeing that you spurn My discipline, and brush My words aside?

יז וְאַתָּה שָׂנֵאתָ מוּסָר וַתַּשְׁלֵךְ דְּבָרַי אַחֲרֶיךָ:

50:2 From *Tzion*, perfect in beauty The Sages of the Talmud wonder (*Yoma* 54b), from where did God fashion the entire world? "Rabbi Eliezer says: The world was created from its center… Rabbi *Yehoshua* said: The world was created from its sides… Rabbi Yitzchak the Smith said: The Holy One, blessed be He, cast a stone into the ocean, from which the world then was founded… But the Sages said: The world was created from Zion, as it is said: … 'Out of *Tzion*, the perfection of the beauty,' that means from *Tzion* was the beauty of the world perfected."

Tehillim/Psalms
Chapter 51

18 When you see a thief, you fall in with him, and throw in your lot with adulterers; אִם־רָאִיתָ גַּנָּב וַתִּרֶץ עִמּוֹ וְעִם מְנָאֲפִים חֶלְקֶךָ׃

19 you devote your mouth to evil, and yoke your tongue to deceit; פִּיךָ שָׁלַחְתָּ בְרָעָה וּלְשׁוֹנְךָ תַּצְמִיד מִרְמָה׃

20 you are busy maligning your brother, defaming the son of your mother. תֵּשֵׁב בְּאָחִיךָ תְדַבֵּר בְּבֶן־אִמְּךָ תִּתֶּן־דֹּפִי׃

21 If I failed to act when you did these things, you would fancy that I was like you; so I censure you and confront you with charges. אֵלֶּה עָשִׂיתָ וְהֶחֱרַשְׁתִּי דִּמִּיתָ הֱיוֹת־אֶהְיֶה כָמוֹךָ אוֹכִיחֲךָ וְאֶעֶרְכָה לְעֵינֶיךָ׃

22 Mark this, you who are unmindful of *Hashem*, lest I tear you apart and no one save you. בִּינוּ־נָא זֹאת שֹׁכְחֵי אֱלוֹהַּ פֶּן־אֶטְרֹף וְאֵין מַצִּיל׃

23 He who sacrifices a thank offering honors Me, and to him who improves his way I will show the salvation of *Hashem*." זֹבֵחַ תּוֹדָה יְכַבְּדָנְנִי וְשָׂם דֶּרֶךְ אַרְאֶנּוּ בְּיֵשַׁע אֱלֹהִים׃

51 1 For the leader. A psalm of *David*, לַמְנַצֵּחַ מִזְמוֹר לְדָוִד׃

2 when *Natan* the *Navi* came to him after he had come to *Batsheva*.

b'-VO ay-LAV na-TAN ha-na-VEE ka-a-sher BA el bat SHA-va

בְּבוֹא־אֵלָיו נָתָן הַנָּבִיא כַּאֲשֶׁר־בָּא אֶל־בַּת־שָׁבַע׃

3 Have mercy upon me, O *Hashem*, as befits Your faithfulness; in keeping with Your abundant compassion, blot out my transgressions. חָנֵּנִי אֱלֹהִים כְּחַסְדֶּךָ כְּרֹב רַחֲמֶיךָ מְחֵה פְשָׁעָי׃

4 Wash me thoroughly of my iniquity, and purify me of my sin; הרבה [הֶרֶב] כַּבְּסֵנִי מֵעֲוֹנִי וּמֵחַטָּאתִי טַהֲרֵנִי׃

5 for I recognize my transgressions, and am ever conscious of my sin. כִּי־פְשָׁעַי אֲנִי אֵדָע וְחַטָּאתִי נֶגְדִּי תָמִיד׃

6 Against You alone have I sinned, and done what is evil in Your sight; so You are just in Your sentence, and right in Your judgment. לְךָ לְבַדְּךָ חָטָאתִי וְהָרַע בְּעֵינֶיךָ עָשִׂיתִי לְמַעַן תִּצְדַּק בְּדָבְרֶךָ תִּזְכֶּה בְשָׁפְטֶךָ׃

7 Indeed I was born with iniquity; with sin my mother conceived me. הֵן־בְּעָווֹן חוֹלָלְתִּי וּבְחֵטְא יֶחֱמַתְנִי אִמִּי׃

51:2 Batsheva King *David* teaches us about man's vulnerability and his desires, as well as his ability to soar to the heavens and redeem his sins through repentance. While sin is hidden, repentance, in the eyes of *David*, must not be clandestine; it should be public. When *David* is confronted by the prophet *Natan* with rebuke (II Samuel 12), he responds with a single word: *Chatati* (חטאתי), 'I have sinned.' Psalm 51, however, is his public response. It begins with a glaring title with which *David* indicts himself right from the start: *Natan* the prophet came to me after I had gone in to *Batsheva* (verse 2). In verse 5, he declares that his sin is always with him while he begs the Lord to cleanse him of his iniquity. *David* is not satisfied with his own personal repentance but he declares that he will teach others the path towards repentance and atonement as well (verse 15). Though he erred, because of his commitment to return and to bring others closer to *Hashem*, we continue to herald King *David* as the greatest king of Israel.

Tehillim/Psalms
Chapter 52

תהלים
פרק נב

8 Indeed You desire truth about that which is hidden; teach me wisdom about secret things.

ח הֵן־אֱמֶת חָפַצְתָּ בַטֻּחוֹת וּבְסָתֻם חָכְמָה תוֹדִיעֵנִי׃

9 Purge me with hyssop till I am pure; wash me till I am whiter than snow.

ט תְּחַטְּאֵנִי בְאֵזוֹב וְאֶטְהָר תְּכַבְּסֵנִי וּמִשֶּׁלֶג אַלְבִּין׃

10 Let me hear tidings of joy and gladness; let the bones You have crushed exult.

י תַּשְׁמִיעֵנִי שָׂשׂוֹן וְשִׂמְחָה תָּגֵלְנָה עֲצָמוֹת דִּכִּיתָ׃

11 Hide Your face from my sins; blot out all my iniquities.

יא הַסְתֵּר פָּנֶיךָ מֵחֲטָאָי וְכָל־עֲוֺנֹתַי מְחֵה׃

12 Fashion a pure heart for me, O *Hashem*; create in me a steadfast spirit.

יב לֵב טָהוֹר בְּרָא־לִי אֱלֹהִים וְרוּחַ נָכוֹן חַדֵּשׁ בְּקִרְבִּי׃

13 Do not cast me out of Your presence, or take Your holy spirit away from me.

יג אַל־תַּשְׁלִיכֵנִי מִלְּפָנֶיךָ וְרוּחַ קָדְשְׁךָ אַל־תִּקַּח מִמֶּנִּי׃

14 Let me again rejoice in Your help; let a vigorous spirit sustain me.

יד הָשִׁיבָה לִּי שְׂשׂוֹן יִשְׁעֶךָ וְרוּחַ נְדִיבָה תִסְמְכֵנִי׃

15 I will teach transgressors Your ways, that sinners may return to You.

טו אֲלַמְּדָה פֹשְׁעִים דְּרָכֶיךָ וְחַטָּאִים אֵלֶיךָ יָשׁוּבוּ׃

16 Save me from bloodguilt, O *Hashem*, *Hashem*, my deliverer, that I may sing forth Your beneficence.

טז הַצִּילֵנִי מִדָּמִים אֱלֹהִים אֱלֹהֵי תְּשׁוּעָתִי תְּרַנֵּן לְשׁוֹנִי צִדְקָתֶךָ׃

17 O *Hashem*, open my lips, and let my mouth declare Your praise.

יז אֲדֹנָי שְׂפָתַי תִּפְתָּח וּפִי יַגִּיד תְּהִלָּתֶךָ׃

18 You do not want me to bring sacrifices; You do not desire burnt offerings;

יח כִּי לֹא־תַחְפֹּץ זֶבַח וְאֶתֵּנָה עוֹלָה לֹא תִרְצֶה׃

19 True sacrifice to *Hashem* is a contrite spirit; *Hashem*, You will not despise a contrite and crushed heart.

יט זִבְחֵי אֱלֹהִים רוּחַ נִשְׁבָּרָה לֵב־נִשְׁבָּר וְנִדְכֶּה אֱלֹהִים לֹא תִבְזֶה׃

20 May it please You to make *Tzion* prosper; rebuild the walls of *Yerushalayim*.

כ הֵיטִיבָה בִרְצוֹנְךָ אֶת־צִיּוֹן תִּבְנֶה חוֹמוֹת יְרוּשָׁלָ͏ִם׃

21 Then You will want sacrifices offered in righteousness, burnt and whole offerings; then bulls will be offered on Your *Mizbayach*.

כא אָז תַּחְפֹּץ זִבְחֵי־צֶדֶק עוֹלָה וְכָלִיל אָז יַעֲלוּ עַל־מִזְבַּחֲךָ פָרִים׃

52

1 For the leader. A *maskil* of *David*,

נב א לַמְנַצֵּחַ מַשְׂכִּיל לְדָוִד׃

2 when *Doeg Ha'adomi* came and informed *Shaul*, telling him, "*David* came to *Achimelech*'s house."

ב בְּבוֹא דּוֹאֵג הָאֲדֹמִי וַיַּגֵּד לְשָׁאוּל וַיֹּאמֶר לוֹ בָּא דָוִד אֶל־בֵּית אֲחִימֶלֶךְ׃

b'-VO do-AYG ha-a-do-MEE va-ya-GAYD l'-sha-UL va-YO-mer LO BA da-VID el BAYT a-khee-ME-lekh

52:2 *Doeg Ha'adomi* came and informed *Shaul* What is the definition of derogatory speech, known in Hebrew as *lashon hara* (לשון הרע)? It is often assumed that this refers to a person who makes up terrible things about someone else. That, however, is a different transgression, called 'slander.' The term *lashon hara* refers to a

Tehillim/Psalms Chapter 53

תהלים
פרק נג

3 Why do you boast of your evil, brave fellow? *Hashem*'s faithfulness never ceases.

ג מַה־תִּתְהַלֵּל בְּרָעָה הַגִּבּוֹר חֶסֶד אֵל כָּל־הַיּוֹם:

4 Your tongue devises mischief, like a sharpened razor that works treacherously.

ד הַוּוֹת תַּחְשֹׁב לְשׁוֹנֶךָ כְּתַעַר מְלֻטָּשׁ עֹשֵׂה רְמִיָּה:

5 You prefer evil to good, the lie, to speaking truthfully. *Selah*.

ה אָהַבְתָּ רָּע מִטּוֹב שֶׁקֶר מִדַּבֵּר צֶדֶק סֶלָה:

6 You love all pernicious words, treacherous speech.

ו אָהַבְתָּ כָל־דִּבְרֵי־בָלַע לְשׁוֹן מִרְמָה:

7 So *Hashem* will tear you down for good, will break you and pluck you from your tent, and root you out of the land of the living. *Selah*.

ז גַּם־אֵל יִתָּצְךָ לָנֶצַח יַחְתְּךָ וְיִסָּחֲךָ מֵאֹהֶל וְשֵׁרֶשְׁךָ מֵאֶרֶץ חַיִּים סֶלָה:

8 The righteous, seeing it, will be awestruck; they will jibe at him, saying,

ח וְיִרְאוּ צַדִּיקִים וְיִירָאוּ וְעָלָיו יִשְׂחָקוּ:

9 "Here was a fellow who did not make *Hashem* his refuge, but trusted in his great wealth, relied upon his mischief."

ט הִנֵּה הַגֶּבֶר לֹא יָשִׂים אֱלֹהִים מָעוּזּוֹ וַיִּבְטַח בְּרֹב עָשְׁרוֹ יָעֹז בְּהַוָּתוֹ:

10 But I am like a thriving olive tree in *Hashem*'s house; I trust in the faithfulness of *Hashem* forever and ever.

י וַאֲנִי כְּזַיִת רַעֲנָן בְּבֵית אֱלֹהִים בָּטַחְתִּי בְחֶסֶד־אֱלֹהִים עוֹלָם וָעֶד:

11 I praise You forever, for You have acted; I declare that Your name is good in the presence of Your faithful ones.

יא אוֹדְךָ לְעוֹלָם כִּי עָשִׂיתָ וַאֲקַוֶּה שִׁמְךָ כִי־טוֹב נֶגֶד חֲסִידֶיךָ:

53

1 For the leader; on mahalath. A maskil of *David*.

נג א לַמְנַצֵּחַ עַל־מָחֲלַת מַשְׂכִּיל לְדָוִד:

2 The benighted man thinks, "*Hashem* does not care." Man's wrongdoing is corrupt and loathsome; no one does good.

ב אָמַר נָבָל בְּלִבּוֹ אֵין אֱלֹהִים הִשְׁחִיתוּ וְהִתְעִיבוּ עָוֶל אֵין עֹשֵׂה־טוֹב:

3 *Hashem* looks down from heaven on mankind to find a man of understanding, a man mindful of *Hashem*.

ג אֱלֹהִים מִשָּׁמַיִם הִשְׁקִיף עַל־בְּנֵי אָדָם לִרְאוֹת הֲיֵשׁ מַשְׂכִּיל דֹּרֵשׁ אֶת־אֱלֹהִים:

4 Everyone is dross, altogether foul; there is none who does good, not even one.

ד כֻּלּוֹ סָג יַחְדָּו נֶאֱלָחוּ אֵין עֹשֵׂה־טוֹב אֵין גַּם־אֶחָד:

5 Are they so witless, those evildoers, who devour my people as they devour food, and do not invoke *Hashem*?

ה הֲלֹא יָדְעוּ פֹּעֲלֵי אָוֶן אֹכְלֵי עַמִּי אָכְלוּ לֶחֶם אֱלֹהִים לֹא קָרָאוּ:

---

situation where one person harms others, intentionally or unintentionally, through true statements. A case in point is the biblical story of Doeg the Edomite, chief herdsman of King *Shaul* (I Samuel 22). When asked by *Shaul* if he knew the whereabouts of *David*, he replied that *David* is in the city of *Nov*, together with the High Priest *Achimelech*. To *Shaul*, it sounded like *David* and *Achimelech* were conspiring to rebel, and thus *Shaul* gave a directive to destroy all the priests of the city of *Nov*. Doeg's misspoken words caused great sorrow, as it says in verse 4, "Your tongue devises mischief, like a sharpened razor that works treacherously." In this psalm, *David* addresses a great man who falls because he used the power of his tongue inappropriately.

Tehillim/Psalms
Chapter 54

תהלים
פרק נד

6 There they will be seized with fright – never was there such a fright – for *Hashem* has scattered the bones of your besiegers; you have put them to shame, for *Hashem* has rejected them.

שָׁם ׀ פָּחֲדוּ־פַחַד לֹא־הָיָה פָחַד כִּי־אֱלֹהִים פִּזַּר עַצְמוֹת חֹנָךְ הֱבִשֹׁתָה כִּי־אֱלֹהִים מְאָסָם:

7 O that the deliverance of *Yisrael* might come from *Tzion*! When *Hashem* restores the fortunes of His people, *Yaakov* will exult, *Yisrael* will rejoice.

מִי יִתֵּן מִצִּיּוֹן יְשֻׁעוֹת יִשְׂרָאֵל בְּשׁוּב אֱלֹהִים שְׁבוּת עַמּוֹ יָגֵל יַעֲקֹב יִשְׂמַח יִשְׂרָאֵל:

MEE yi-TAYN mi-tzi-YON y'-shu-OT yis-ra-AYL b'-SHUV e-lo-HEEM sh'-VUT
a-MO ya-GAYL ya-a-KOV yis-MAKH yis-ra-AYL

54 1 For the leader; with instrumental music. A *maskil* of *David*,

נד א לַמְנַצֵּחַ בִּנְגִינֹת מַשְׂכִּיל לְדָוִד:

2 when the Ziphites came and told *Shaul*, "Know, *David* is in hiding among us."

ב בְּבוֹא הַזִּיפִים וַיֹּאמְרוּ לְשָׁאוּל הֲלֹא דָוִד מִסְתַּתֵּר עִמָּנוּ:

b'-VO ha-zee-FEEM va-yo-m'-RU l'-sha-UL ha-LO da-VID mis-ta-TAYR i-MA-nu

3 O *Hashem*, deliver me by Your name; by Your power vindicate me.

ג אֱלֹהִים בְּשִׁמְךָ הוֹשִׁיעֵנִי וּבִגְבוּרָתְךָ תְדִינֵנִי:

4 O *Hashem*, hear my prayer; give ear to the words of my mouth.

ד אֱלֹהִים שְׁמַע תְּפִלָּתִי הַאֲזִינָה לְאִמְרֵי־פִי:

5 For strangers have risen against me, and ruthless men seek my life; they are unmindful of *Hashem*. Selah.

ה כִּי זָרִים קָמוּ עָלַי וְעָרִיצִים בִּקְשׁוּ נַפְשִׁי לֹא שָׂמוּ אֱלֹהִים לְנֶגְדָּם סֶלָה:

6 See, *Hashem* is my helper; *Hashem* is my support.

ו הִנֵּה אֱלֹהִים עֹזֵר לִי אֲדֹנָי בְּסֹמְכֵי נַפְשִׁי:

7 He will repay the evil of my watchful foes; by Your faithfulness, destroy them!

ז יָשׁוּב [יָשִׁיב] הָרַע לְשֹׁרְרָי בַּאֲמִתְּךָ הַצְמִיתֵם:

8 Then I will offer You a freewill sacrifice; I will praise Your name, *Hashem*, for it is good,

ח בִּנְדָבָה אֶזְבְּחָה־לָּךְ אוֹדֶה שִּׁמְךָ יְהֹוָה כִּי־טוֹב:

53:7 The fortunes of His people In the first years after Israel's independence, close to seven-hundred thousand Jews moved to the country, including many survivors of the Holocaust looking to build a new life in God's Promised Land. Under the leadership of future Prime Minister Levi Eshkol, the Jewish Agency built absorption settlements throughout the country to accommodate the staggering numbers. One was appropriately named *Sh'vut Am* (שבות עם), 'the return of the people,' taken from Psalm 53. Though translated here as "the fortunes of His people," the words *sh'vut amo* (שבות עמו) in this verse also mean 'the return of His people.' Over the course of a few years, over one-hundred thousand new immigrants lived in *Sh'vut Am*, and from there went on to build Israel's future. Indeed, when salvation came to Israel with the return of the captivity, Israel did rejoice.

54:2 The *Ziphites* *David* sings in times of sadness, danger and fright, and of course he also sings in times of salvation, joy and triumph. One such episode of salvation is described in *Shmuel* I 23. The people of Ziph, a city in the portion of *Yehuda*, report *David*'s location to *Shaul*. Unaware of this betrayal, *David* dwells among the Ziphites until *Shaul* is close by, ready to end *David*'s life. The story reaches its climax with *David* on one side of a mountain in the wilderness of Maon, and *Shaul* on the other about to pounce. Miraculously, just as he is ready to strike, a messenger appears to *Shaul*, informing him that the Philistines are attacking and that he is needed elsewhere in the kingdom. *David* is able to flee, and later acknowledges *Hashem*'s graciousness and salvation in this psalm.

Prime Minister Levi Eshkol (1895–1969)

Tehillim/Psalms
Chapter 55

תהילים
פרק נה

9 for it has saved me from my foes, and let me gaze triumphant upon my enemies.

ט כִּי מִכָּל־צָרָה הִצִּילָנִי וּבְאֹיְבַי רָאֲתָה עֵינִי:

55 1 For the leader; with instrumental music. A maskil of *David*.

נה א לַמְנַצֵּחַ בִּנְגִינֹת מַשְׂכִּיל לְדָוִד:

2 Give ear, O *Hashem*, to my prayer; do not ignore my plea;

ב הַאֲזִינָה אֱלֹהִים תְּפִלָּתִי וְאַל־תִּתְעַלַּם מִתְּחִנָּתִי:

3 pay heed to me and answer me. I am tossed about, complaining and moaning

ג הַקְשִׁיבָה לִּי וַעֲנֵנִי אָרִיד בְּשִׂיחִי וְאָהִימָה:

4 at the clamor of the enemy, because of the oppression of the wicked; for they bring evil upon me and furiously harass me.

ד מִקּוֹל אוֹיֵב מִפְּנֵי עָקַת רָשָׁע כִּי־יָמִיטוּ עָלַי אָוֶן וּבְאַף יִשְׂטְמוּנִי:

5 My heart is convulsed within me; terrors of death assail me.

ה לִבִּי יָחִיל בְּקִרְבִּי וְאֵימוֹת מָוֶת נָפְלוּ עָלָי:

6 Fear and trembling invade me; I am clothed with horror.

ו יִרְאָה וָרַעַד יָבֹא בִי וַתְּכַסֵּנִי פַּלָּצוּת:

7 I said, "O that I had the wings of a dove I would fly away and find rest;

ז וָאֹמַר מִי־יִתֶּן־לִּי אֵבֶר כַּיּוֹנָה אָעוּפָה וְאֶשְׁכֹּנָה:

8 surely, I would flee far off; I would lodge in the wilderness; *Selah*

ח הִנֵּה אַרְחִיק נְדֹד אָלִין בַּמִּדְבָּר סֶלָה:

hi-NAY ar-KHEEK n'-DOD a-LEEN ba-mid-BAR SE-lah

9 I would soon find me a refuge from the sweeping wind, from the tempest."

ט אָחִישָׁה מִפְלָט לִי מֵרוּחַ סֹעָה מִסָּעַר:

10 O *Hashem*, confound their speech, confuse it! For I see lawlessness and strife in the city;

י בַּלַּע אֲדֹנָי פַּלַּג לְשׁוֹנָם כִּי־רָאִיתִי חָמָס וְרִיב בָּעִיר:

11 day and night they make their rounds on its walls; evil and mischief are inside it.

יא יוֹמָם וָלַיְלָה יְסוֹבְבֻהָ עַל־חוֹמֹתֶיהָ וְאָוֶן וְעָמָל בְּקִרְבָּהּ:

12 Malice is within it; fraud and deceit never leave its square.

יב הַוּוֹת בְּקִרְבָּהּ וְלֹא־יָמִישׁ מֵרְחֹבָהּ תֹּךְ וּמִרְמָה:

13 It is not an enemy who reviles me – I could bear that; it is not my foe who vaunts himself against me – I could hide from him

יג כִּי לֹא־אוֹיֵב יְחָרְפֵנִי וְאֶשָּׂא לֹא־מְשַׂנְאִי עָלַי הִגְדִּיל וְאֶסָּתֵר מִמֶּנּוּ:

55:8 Lodge in the wilderness In times of great danger, *David* yearns to escape to the wilderness. At the end of *Shmuel* I chapter 23, having almost met his demise at the hands of *Shaul*, *David* flees to a fortresses in the hills above *Ein Gedi*, located in the Judean desert. The desert is a place of solitude and shelter. *Shaul* will have great difficulty finding *David* among the cliffs and caves of the Judean desert. Five hundred years later, *Yirmiyahu* yearns for a respite from rebuking the Nation of Israel in *Yerushalayim* and he also desires to escape to the desert (Jeremiah 9:1). Over a thousand years later, Simon Bar Kokhba flees to the same mountains, and from there he plans his rebellion against the Roman regime controlling the Land of Israel. In ancient times, the wilderness was a place in which to disappear. Today, as a result of *Hashem*'s blessings, it is filled with life.

Tehillim/Psalms
Chapter 56

14 but it is you, my equal, my companion, my friend; יד וְאַתָּה אֱנוֹשׁ כְּעֶרְכִּי אַלּוּפִי וּמְיֻדָּעִי׃

15 sweet was our fellowship; we walked together in *Hashem*'s house. טו אֲשֶׁר יַחְדָּו נַמְתִּיק סוֹד בְּבֵית אֱלֹהִים נְהַלֵּךְ בְּרָגֶשׁ׃

16 Let Him incite death against them; may they go down alive into Sheol! For where they dwell, there evil is. טז יַשִּׁימָוֶת [יַשִּׁי] [מָוֶת] עָלֵימוֹ יֵרְדוּ שְׁאוֹל חַיִּים כִּי־רָעוֹת בִּמְגוּרָם בְּקִרְבָּם׃

17 As for me, I call to *Hashem*; *Hashem* will deliver me. יז אֲנִי אֶל־אֱלֹהִים אֶקְרָא וַיהֹוָה יוֹשִׁיעֵנִי׃

18 Evening, morning, and noon, I complain and moan, and He hears my voice. יח עֶרֶב וָבֹקֶר וְצׇהֳרַיִם אָשִׂיחָה וְאֶהֱמֶה וַיִּשְׁמַע קוֹלִי׃

19 He redeems me unharmed from the battle against me; it is as though many are on my side. יט פָּדָה בְשָׁלוֹם נַפְשִׁי מִקְּרׇב־לִי כִּי־בְרַבִּים הָיוּ עִמָּדִי׃

20 *Hashem* who has reigned from the first, who will have no successor, hears and humbles those who have no fear of *Hashem*. Selah. כ יִשְׁמַע ׀ אֵל ׀ וְיַעֲנֵם וְיֹשֵׁב קֶדֶם סֶלָה אֲשֶׁר אֵין חֲלִיפוֹת לָמוֹ וְלֹא יָרְאוּ אֱלֹהִים׃

21 He harmed his ally, he broke his pact; כא שָׁלַח יָדָיו בִּשְׁלֹמָיו חִלֵּל בְּרִיתוֹ׃

22 his talk was smoother than butter, yet his mind was on war; his words were more soothing than oil, yet they were drawn swords. כב חָלְקוּ ׀ מַחְמָאֹת פִּיו וּקְרׇב־לִבּוֹ רַכּוּ דְבָרָיו מִשֶּׁמֶן וְהֵמָּה פְתִחוֹת׃

23 Cast your burden on *Hashem* and He will sustain you; He will never let the righteous man collapse. כג הַשְׁלֵךְ עַל־יְהֹוָה ׀ יְהָבְךָ וְהוּא יְכַלְכְּלֶךָ לֹא־יִתֵּן לְעוֹלָם מוֹט לַצַּדִּיק׃

24 For You, O *Hashem*, will bring them down to the nethermost Pit – those murderous, treacherous men; they shall not live out half their days; but I trust in You. כד וְאַתָּה אֱלֹהִים ׀ תּוֹרִדֵם ׀ לִבְאֵר שַׁחַת אַנְשֵׁי דָמִים וּמִרְמָה לֹא־יֶחֱצוּ יְמֵיהֶם וַאֲנִי אֶבְטַח־בָּךְ׃

56

1 For the leader; on yonath elem rechokim. Of David. A michtam; when the Philistines seized him in Gath. א לַמְנַצֵּחַ ׀ עַל־יוֹנַת אֵלֶם רְחֹקִים לְדָוִד מִכְתָּם בֶּאֱחֹז אֹתוֹ פְלִשְׁתִּים בְּגַת׃

lam-na-TZAY-akh al yo-NAT AY-lem r'-kho-KEEM l'-da-VID mikh-TAM be-e-KHOZ o-TO f'-lish-TEEM b'-GAT

2 Have mercy on me, O *Hashem*, for men persecute me; all day long my adversary oppresses me. ב חׇנֵּנִי אֱלֹהִים כִּי־שְׁאָפַנִי אֱנוֹשׁ כׇּל־הַיּוֹם לֹחֵם יִלְחָצֵנִי׃

56:1 When the Philistines seized him in Gath Constantly on the run in a very small Israelite kingdom, *David* does the irrational; he escapes to the Philistine city of Gath (I Samuel 21:11–16). The Philistines were the main enemy of the Israelites at the time, and *David* himself had slain Goliath, who was from the same city. How does *David* survive when the advisors of King Achish reveal that this is the same *David* who was responsible for the defeat of the Philistines? *David* feigns insanity. He dances uncontrollably, foams at the mouth and sputters unintelligible words. His behavior leads the king of Gath to make his famous statement "Do I lack madmen, that you have brought this fellow to rave for me? Should this fellow enter my house?" (I Samuel 21:16). He lets *David* free, and *David* responds to this near-death experience in the best way he knows: With a psalm of gratitude to *Hashem*.

1536

Tehillim/Psalms
Chapter 57

תהילים
פרק נז

3 My watchful foes persecute me all day long; many are my adversaries, O Exalted One.

ג שָׁאֲפוּ שׁוֹרְרַי כָּל־הַיּוֹם כִּי־רַבִּים לֹחֲמִים לִי מָרוֹם׃

4 When I am afraid, I trust in You,

ד יוֹם אִירָא אֲנִי אֵלֶיךָ אֶבְטָח׃

5 in *Hashem*, whose word I praise, in *Hashem* I trust; I am not afraid; what can mortals do to me?

ה בֵּאלֹהִים אֲהַלֵּל דְּבָרוֹ בֵּאלֹהִים בָּטַחְתִּי לֹא אִירָא מַה־יַּעֲשֶׂה בָשָׂר לִי׃

6 All day long they cause me grief in my affairs, they plan only evil against me.

ו כָּל־הַיּוֹם דְּבָרַי יְעַצֵּבוּ עָלַי כָּל־מַחְשְׁבֹתָם לָרָע׃

7 They plot, they lie in ambush; they watch my every move, hoping for my death.

ז יָגוּרוּ יִצְפֹּנוּ [יִצְפּוֹנוּ] הֵמָּה עֲקֵבַי יִשְׁמֹרוּ כַּאֲשֶׁר קִוּוּ נַפְשִׁי׃

8 Cast them out for their evil; subdue peoples in Your anger, O *Hashem*.

ח עַל־אָוֶן פַּלֶּט־לָמוֹ בְּאַף עַמִּים הוֹרֵד אֱלֹהִים׃

9 You keep count of my wanderings; put my tears into Your flask, into Your record.

ט נֹדִי סָפַרְתָּה אָתָּה שִׂימָה דִמְעָתִי בְנֹאדֶךָ הֲלֹא בְּסִפְרָתֶךָ׃

10 Then my enemies will retreat when I call on You; this I know, that *Hashem* is for me.

י אָז יָשׁוּבוּ אוֹיְבַי אָחוֹר בְּיוֹם אֶקְרָא זֶה־יָדַעְתִּי כִּי־אֱלֹהִים לִי׃

11 In *Hashem*, whose word I praise, in *Hashem*, whose word I praise,

יא בֵּאלֹהִים אֲהַלֵּל דָּבָר בַּיהוָה אֲהַלֵּל דָּבָר׃

12 in *Hashem* I trust; I am not afraid; what can man do to me?

יב בֵּאלֹהִים בָּטַחְתִּי לֹא אִירָא מַה־יַּעֲשֶׂה אָדָם לִי׃

13 I must pay my vows to You, O *Hashem*; I will render thank offerings to You.

יג עָלַי אֱלֹהִים נְדָרֶיךָ אֲשַׁלֵּם תּוֹדֹת לָךְ׃

14 For You have saved me from death, my foot from stumbling, that I may walk before *Hashem* in the light of life.

יד כִּי הִצַּלְתָּ נַפְשִׁי מִמָּוֶת הֲלֹא רַגְלַי מִדֶּחִי לְהִתְהַלֵּךְ לִפְנֵי אֱלֹהִים בְּאוֹר הַחַיִּים׃

57
1 For the leader; al tashcheth. Of *David*. A michtam; when he fled from *Shaul* into a cave.

נז א לַמְנַצֵּחַ אַל־תַּשְׁחֵת לְדָוִד מִכְתָּם בְּבָרְחוֹ מִפְּנֵי־שָׁאוּל בַּמְּעָרָה׃

lam-na-TZAY-akh al tash-KHAYT l'-da-VID mikh-T'AM b'-vor-KHO mi-p'-NAY sha-UL ba-m'-a-RAH

2 Have mercy on me, O *Hashem*, have mercy on me, for I seek refuge in You, I seek refuge in the shadow of Your wings, until danger passes.

ב חָנֵּנִי אֱלֹהִים חָנֵּנִי כִּי בְךָ חָסָיָה נַפְשִׁי וּבְצֵל־כְּנָפֶיךָ אֶחְסֶה עַד יַעֲבֹר הַוּוֹת׃

57:1 When he fled from *Shaul*, into a cave Even in the wilderness of *Ein Gedi*, *David* is chased down by *Shaul*, as someone informed the king of his location. *Shaul* takes three-thousand soldiers and plans to destroy *David* once and for all. The *Tanakh* records (I Samuel 24:3) that *Shaul* goes alone into a cave to relieve himself, unaware that *David* is hiding there. Though he has the opportunity, *David* does not kill *Shaul*. Rather, he cuts off a piece of *Shaul's* royal garment and then confronts *Shaul*, stating that he had the chance to kill him but did not. *Shaul* breaks down and weeps, hugging *David* and wishing him only well, until the next time he seeks to kill him again. *David* chooses to show restraint and respect for the king of Israel despite being continually chased by him. This psalm is another testimony of *Hashem's* salvation and *David's* acknowledgment of His constant protection.

Tehillim/Psalms
Chapter 58

3 I call to *Hashem* Most High, to *Hashem* who is good to me.

4 He will reach down from heaven and deliver me: *Hashem* will send down His steadfast love; my persecutor reviles. *Selah.*

5 As for me, I lie down among man-eating lions whose teeth are spears and arrows, whose tongue is a sharp sword.

6 Exalt Yourself over the heavens, O *Hashem*, let Your glory be over all the earth!

7 They prepared a net for my feet to ensnare me; they dug a pit for me, but they fell into it. *Selah.*

8 My heart is firm, O *Hashem*; my heart is firm; I will sing, I will chant a hymn.

9 Awake, O my soul! Awake, O harp and lyre! I will wake the dawn.

10 I will praise You among the peoples, O *Hashem*; I will sing a hymn to You among the nations;

11 for Your faithfulness is as high as heaven; Your steadfastness reaches to the sky.

12 Exalt Yourself over the heavens, O *Hashem*, let Your glory be over all the earth!

58 1 For the leader; al tashcheth. Of *David*. A michtam.

2 O mighty ones, do you really decree what is just? Do you judge mankind with equity?

3 In your minds you devise wrongdoing in the land; with your hands you deal out lawlessness.

4 The wicked are defiant from birth; the liars go astray from the womb.

5 Their venom is like that of a snake, a deaf viper that stops its ears

6 so as not to hear the voice of charmers or the expert mutterer of spells.

7 O *Hashem*, smash their teeth in their mouth; shatter the fangs of lions, *Hashem*;

8 let them melt, let them vanish like water; let Him aim His arrows that they be cut down;

9 like a snail that melts away as it moves; like a woman's stillbirth, may they never see the sun!

תהלים
פרק נח

ג אֶקְרָא לֵאלֹהִים עֶלְיוֹן לָאֵל גֹּמֵר עָלָי׃

ד יִשְׁלַח מִשָּׁמַיִם וְיוֹשִׁיעֵנִי חֵרֵף שֹׁאֲפִי סֶלָה יִשְׁלַח אֱלֹהִים חַסְדּוֹ וַאֲמִתּוֹ׃

ה נַפְשִׁי בְּתוֹךְ לְבָאִם אֶשְׁכְּבָה לֹהֲטִים בְּנֵי־אָדָם שִׁנֵּיהֶם חֲנִית וְחִצִּים וּלְשׁוֹנָם חֶרֶב חַדָּה׃

ו רוּמָה עַל־הַשָּׁמַיִם אֱלֹהִים עַל כָּל־הָאָרֶץ כְּבוֹדֶךָ׃

ז רֶשֶׁת הֵכִינוּ לִפְעָמַי כָּפַף נַפְשִׁי כָּרוּ לְפָנַי שִׁיחָה נָפְלוּ בְתוֹכָהּ סֶלָה׃

ח נָכוֹן לִבִּי אֱלֹהִים נָכוֹן לִבִּי אָשִׁירָה וַאֲזַמֵּרָה׃

ט עוּרָה כְבוֹדִי עוּרָה הַנֵּבֶל וְכִנּוֹר אָעִירָה שָּׁחַר׃

י אוֹדְךָ בָעַמִּים אֲדֹנָי אֲזַמֶּרְךָ בַּל־אֻמִּים׃

יא כִּי־גָדֹל עַד־שָׁמַיִם חַסְדֶּךָ וְעַד־שְׁחָקִים אֲמִתֶּךָ׃

יב רוּמָה עַל־שָׁמַיִם אֱלֹהִים עַל כָּל־הָאָרֶץ כְּבוֹדֶךָ׃

נח א לַמְנַצֵּחַ אַל־תַּשְׁחֵת לְדָוִד מִכְתָּם׃

ב הַאֻמְנָם אֵלֶם צֶדֶק תְּדַבֵּרוּן מֵישָׁרִים תִּשְׁפְּטוּ בְּנֵי אָדָם׃

ג אַף־בְּלֵב עוֹלֹת תִּפְעָלוּן בָּאָרֶץ חֲמַס יְדֵיכֶם תְּפַלֵּסוּן׃

ד זֹרוּ רְשָׁעִים מֵרָחֶם תָּעוּ מִבֶּטֶן דֹּבְרֵי כָזָב׃

ה חֲמַת־לָמוֹ כִּדְמוּת חֲמַת־נָחָשׁ כְּמוֹ־פֶתֶן חֵרֵשׁ יַאְטֵם אָזְנוֹ׃

ו אֲשֶׁר לֹא־יִשְׁמַע לְקוֹל מְלַחֲשִׁים חוֹבֵר חֲבָרִים מְחֻכָּם׃

ז אֱלֹהִים הֲרָס־שִׁנֵּימוֹ בְּפִימוֹ מַלְתְּעוֹת כְּפִירִים נְתֹץ יְהוָה׃

ח יִמָּאֲסוּ כְמוֹ־מַיִם יִתְהַלְּכוּ־לָמוֹ יִדְרֹךְ חִצָּו [חִצָּיו] כְּמוֹ יִתְמֹלָלוּ׃

ט כְּמוֹ שַׁבְּלוּל תֶּמֶס יַהֲלֹךְ נֵפֶל אֵשֶׁת בַּל־חָזוּ שָׁמֶשׁ׃

1538

Tehillim/Psalms
Chapter 59

תהלים
פרק נט

10 Before the thorns grow into a bramble, may He whirl them away alive in fury.

בְּטֶרֶם יָבִינוּ סִירֹתֵיכֶם אָטָד כְּמוֹ־חַי כְּמוֹ־חָרוֹן יִשְׂעָרֶנּוּ:

b'-TE-rem ya-VEE-nu see-ro-tay-KHEM a-TAD k'-mo KHAI k'-MO kha-RON yis-a-RE-nu

11 The righteous man will rejoice when he sees revenge; he will bathe his feet in the blood of the wicked.

יִשְׂמַח צַדִּיק כִּי־חָזָה נָקָם פְּעָמָיו יִרְחַץ בְּדַם הָרָשָׁע:

12 Men will say, "There is, then, a reward for the righteous; there is, indeed, divine justice on earth."

וְיֹאמַר אָדָם אַךְ־פְּרִי לַצַּדִּיק אַךְ יֵשׁ־אֱלֹהִים שֹׁפְטִים בָּאָרֶץ:

59 1 For the leader; *al tashcheth*. Of *David*. A *michtam*; when *Shaul* sent men to watch his house in order to put him to death.

לַמְנַצֵּחַ אַל־תַּשְׁחֵת לְדָוִד מִכְתָּם בִּשְׁלֹחַ שָׁאוּל וַיִּשְׁמְרוּ אֶת־הַבַּיִת לַהֲמִיתוֹ:

lam-na-TZAY-akh al tash-KHAYT l'-da-VID mikh-TAM bish-LO-akh sha-UL va-yish-m'-RU et ha-BA-yit la-ha-mee-TO

2 Save me from my enemies, O my God; secure me against my assailants.

הַצִּילֵנִי מֵאֹיְבַי אֱלֹהָי מִמִּתְקוֹמְמַי תְּשַׂגְּבֵנִי:

3 Save me from evildoers; deliver me from murderers.

הַצִּילֵנִי מִפֹּעֲלֵי אָוֶן וּמֵאַנְשֵׁי דָמִים הוֹשִׁיעֵנִי:

4 For see, they lie in wait for me; fierce men plot against me for no offense of mine, for no transgression, *Hashem*;

כִּי הִנֵּה אָרְבוּ לְנַפְשִׁי יָגוּרוּ עָלַי עַזִּים לֹא־פִשְׁעִי וְלֹא־חַטָּאתִי יְהֹוָה:

5 for no guilt of mine, do they rush to array themselves against me. Look, rouse Yourself on my behalf!

בְּלִי־עָוֹן יְרוּצוּן וְיִכּוֹנָנוּ עוּרָה לִקְרָאתִי וּרְאֵה:

6 You, O Lord God of hosts, God of *Yisrael*, bestir Yourself to bring all nations to account; have no mercy on any treacherous villain. *Selah*.

וְאַתָּה יְהֹוָה־אֱלֹהִים צְבָאוֹת אֱלֹהֵי יִשְׂרָאֵל הָקִיצָה לִפְקֹד כָּל־הַגּוֹיִם אַל־תָּחֹן כָּל־בֹּגְדֵי אָוֶן סֶלָה:

A boxthron shrub by Nitzana stream

58:10 Before the thorns grow into a bramble Throughout his psalms, *David* struggles with the reality that righteous people sometimes suffer while the wicked thrive. Psalm 58 is directed at the wicked, chastising them for their corruption and deceit. He warns that *Hashem* will bring retribution upon them for their sins, and he invokes several metaphors from nature to express his sentiment. The *atad* (אטד), 'boxthorn tree,' grows in the desert and is quite thorny. It seems to defy nature, as it is strong and durable despite growing in unfavorable conditions. The wicked might prick like the boxthorn and seem invincible, but *David* tells them that before they mature into a large, strong bramble, God will hurl them away and destroy them.

59:1 To watch his house in order to put him to death Although he is being chased by *Shaul* who openly states his desire to kill him, *David* is saved by individuals who love him and seek his welfare. Two such personalities appear in *Shmuel* I 19, and are, ironically, *Shaul*'s son *Yonatan* and his daughter *Michal*, *David*'s wife. When *Shaul* reveals his desire to kill *David* to his son, *Yonatan* recognizes the impending danger and warns *David* to hide. And when *Shaul* sends assassins to kill *David* in his home, *Michal* lowers her husband from the bedroom window by a rope and saves him from harm. *David* concludes his psalm with a declaration that he will continue to sing of God's greatness, since *Hashem* continues to save him and have mercy on him.

Tehillim/Psalms
Chapter 60

7 They come each evening growling like dogs, roaming the city.

ז יָשׁוּבוּ לָעֶרֶב יֶהֱמוּ כַכָּלֶב וִיסוֹבְבוּ עִיר:

8 They rave with their mouths, sharp words are on their lips; [they think,] "Who hears?"

ח הִנֵּה יַבִּיעוּן בְּפִיהֶם חֲרָבוֹת בְּשִׂפְתוֹתֵיהֶם כִּי־מִי שֹׁמֵעַ:

9 But You, *Hashem*, laugh at them; You mock all the nations.

ט וְאַתָּה יְהוָה תִּשְׂחַק־לָמוֹ תִּלְעַג לְכָל־גּוֹיִם:

10 O my strength, I wait for You; for *Hashem* is my haven.

י עֻזּוֹ אֵלֶיךָ אֶשְׁמֹרָה כִּי־אֱלֹהִים מִשְׂגַּבִּי:

11 My faithful God will come to aid me; *Hashem* will let me gloat over my watchful foes.

יא אֱלֹהֵי חסדו [חַסְדִּי] יְקַדְּמֵנִי אֱלֹהִים יַרְאֵנִי בְשֹׁרְרָי:

12 Do not kill them lest my people be unmindful; with Your power make wanderers of them; bring them low, O our shield, *Hashem*,

יב אַל־תַּהַרְגֵם פֶּן־יִשְׁכְּחוּ עַמִּי הֲנִיעֵמוֹ בְחֵילְךָ וְהוֹרִידֵמוֹ מָגִנֵּנוּ אֲדֹנָי:

13 because of their sinful mouths, the words on their lips. Let them be trapped by their pride, and by the imprecations and lies they utter.

יג חַטַּאת־פִּימוֹ דְּבַר־שְׂפָתֵימוֹ וְיִלָּכְדוּ בִגְאוֹנָם וּמֵאָלָה וּמִכַּחַשׁ יְסַפֵּרוּ:

14 In Your fury put an end to them; put an end to them that they be no more; that it may be known to the ends of the earth that *Hashem* does rule over Yaakov. Selah.

יד כַּלֵּה בְחֵמָה כַּלֵּה וְאֵינֵמוֹ וְיֵדְעוּ כִּי־אֱלֹהִים מֹשֵׁל בְּיַעֲקֹב לְאַפְסֵי הָאָרֶץ סֶלָה:

15 They come each evening growling like dogs, roaming the city.

טו וְיָשֻׁבוּ לָעֶרֶב יֶהֱמוּ כַכָּלֶב וִיסוֹבְבוּ עִיר:

16 They wander in search of food; and whine if they are not satisfied.

טז הֵמָּה ינועון [יְנִיעוּן] לֶאֱכֹל אִם־לֹא יִשְׂבְּעוּ וַיָּלִינוּ:

17 But I will sing of Your strength, extol each morning Your faithfulness; for You have been my haven, a refuge in time of trouble.

יז וַאֲנִי אָשִׁיר עֻזֶּךָ וַאֲרַנֵּן לַבֹּקֶר חַסְדֶּךָ כִּי־הָיִיתָ מִשְׂגָּב לִי וּמָנוֹס בְּיוֹם צַר־לִי:

18 O my strength, to You I sing hymns; for *Hashem* is my haven, my faithful *Hashem*.

יח עֻזִּי אֵלֶיךָ אֲזַמֵּרָה כִּי־אֱלֹהִים מִשְׂגַּבִּי אֱלֹהֵי חַסְדִּי:

60 1 For the leader; on shushan eduth. A michtam of *David* (to be taught),

א לַמְנַצֵּחַ עַל־שׁוּשַׁן עֵדוּת מִכְתָּם לְדָוִד לְלַמֵּד:

2 when he fought with Aram-Naharaim and Aram-Zobah, and *Yoav* returned and defeated Edom – [an army] of twelve thousand men – in the Valley of Salt.

ב בְּהַצּוֹתוֹ אֶת אֲרַם נַהֲרַיִם וְאֶת־אֲרַם צוֹבָה וַיָּשָׁב יוֹאָב וַיַּךְ אֶת־אֱדוֹם בְּגֵיא־מֶלַח שְׁנֵים עָשָׂר אָלֶף:

b'-ha-tzo-TO ET a-RAM na-ha-RA-yim v'-et a-RAM tzo-VAH va-YA-shov yo-AV va-YAKH et e-DOM b'-gay ME-lakh sh'-NAYM a-SAR A-lef

60:2 When he fought with Aram-Naharaim As king of Israel, *David* has to contend with neighboring countries, sometimes as allies but often as enemies. The Land of Israel is surrounded by other countries on three sides. To the south, Israel borders Egypt. In ancient times, the eastern lands were dominated by

Tehillim/Psalms

Chapter 61

3 O *Hashem*, You have rejected us, You have made a breach in us; You have been angry; restore us!

4 You have made the land quake; You have torn it open. Mend its fissures, for it is collapsing.

5 You have made Your people suffer hardship; You have given us wine that makes us reel.

6 Give those who fear You because of Your truth a banner for rallying. *Selah*.

7 That those whom You love might be rescued, deliver with Your right hand and answer me.

8 *Hashem* promised in His sanctuary that I would exultingly divide up *Shechem*, and measure the Valley of Sukkoth;

9 *Gilad* and *Menashe* would be mine, *Efraim* my chief stronghold, *Yehuda* my scepter;

10 Moab would be my washbasin; on Edom I would cast my shoe; acclaim me, O Philistia!

11 Would that I were brought to the bastion! Would that I were led to Edom!

12 But You have rejected us, O *Hashem*; *Hashem*, You do not march with our armies.

13 Grant us Your aid against the foe, for the help of man is worthless.

14 With *Hashem* we shall triumph; He will trample our foes.

61

1 For the leader; with instrumental music. Of *David*.

2 Hear my cry, O *Hashem*, heed my prayer.

3 From the end of the earth I call to You; when my heart is faint, You lead me to a rock that is high above me.

---

the kingdoms of Edom, Moab, Ammon, Bashan, and Aram. In the northeast was Aram Naharaim, the land from which *Avraham* began his journey towards the Promised Land. As recorded in the books of *Shmuel* and *Divrei Hayamim*, *David* conducts battles and expands his kingdom to include the eastern bank of the Jordan River, where the tribes of *Reuven*, *Gad* and *Menashe* had settled hundreds of years earlier. This verse makes reference to some of the battles *David* fights against his neighbors.

Tehillim/Psalms
Chapter 62

4 For You have been my refuge, a tower of strength against the enemy.

kee ha-YEE-ta makh-SEH LEE mig-dal OZ mi-p'-NAY o-YAYV

5 O that I might dwell in Your tent forever, take refuge under Your protecting wings. *Selah*.

6 O *Hashem*, You have heard my vows; grant the request of those who fear Your name.

7 Add days to the days of the king; may his years extend through generations;

8 may he dwell in *Hashem*'s presence forever; appoint steadfast love to guard him.

9 So I will sing hymns to Your name forever, as I fulfill my vows day after day.

62

1 For the leader; on *Yedutun*. A psalm of *David*.

lam-na-TZAY-akh al y'-du-TUN miz-MOR l'-da-VID

2 Truly my soul waits quietly for *Hashem*; my deliverance comes from Him.

3 Truly He is my rock and deliverance, my haven; I shall never be shaken.

4 How long will all of you attack a man, to crush him, as though he were a leaning wall, a tottering fence?

61:4 Tower of strength In the early period of Zionism, Jews sought to build up the Land of Israel, setting up agricultural settlements and hoping to live in peace with their neighbors in the Holy Land. In 1927, a group of Jews formed an association, purchased a plot of land south of *Beit Lechem*, settled there and called their new community *Migdal Eder*, the name of a biblical-era place in the same area which *Yaakov* passed on his journeys through the land. Unfortunately, during the Arab riots in 1929, the settlement was destroyed. Fifty years later, a new *kibbutz* (collective agricultural community) was established on the same site. It was given a similar name to its predecessor, which was taken from this verse in Psalm 61, in which *David* describes *Hashem* as his *migdal oz*, 'tower of strength,' against his enemies. Today, *Migdal Oz* has grown substantially. The main agricultural pursuits of this religious *kibbutz* include turkey coops, a dairy, fruit orchards and olive farming. In addition, it hosts a women's seminary for advanced *Torah* study.

62:1 *Yedutun* Who sang these *Tehillim*, and where? The name *Yedutun*, mentioned in the title of this psalm, might provide some insight. In *Sefer Divrei Hayamim* I 25, we find a listing of positions that *David* gives to the *Leviim* as part of their service in the house of the Lord. The three main Levite families mentioned are the house of *Asaf*, the house of *Hayman* and the house of *Yedutun*, "who prophesied to the accompaniment of lyres, harps, and cymbals... who, accompanied on the harp, prophesied, praising and extolling *Hashem*" (25:1,3). The house of God in Jerusalem, will become a permanent structure when his son, *Shlomo*, builds the *Beit Hamikdash* on Mount *Moriah*. There, the *Leviim* will fill the steps of the *Beit Hamikdash* with songs of praise, musical accompaniment and rejoicing.

1542

Tehillim/Psalms Chapter 63

תהילים פרק סג

5 They lay plans to topple him from his rank; they delight in falsehood; they bless with their mouths, while inwardly they curse. *Selah.*

6 Truly, wait quietly for *Hashem*, O my soul, for my hope comes from Him.

7 He is my rock and deliverance, my haven; I shall not be shaken.

8 I rely on *Hashem*, my deliverance and glory, my rock of strength; in *Hashem* is my refuge.

9 Trust in Him at all times, O people; pour out your hearts before Him; *Hashem* is our refuge. *Selah.*

10 Men are mere breath; mortals, illusion; placed on a scale all together, they weigh even less than a breath.

11 Do not trust in violence, or put false hopes in robbery; if force bears fruit pay it no mind.

12 One thing *Hashem* has spoken; two things have I heard: that might belongs to *Hashem*,

13 and faithfulness is Yours, O *Hashem*, to reward each man according to his deeds.

63

1 A psalm of *David*, when he was in the Wilderness of *Yehuda*.

miz-MOR l'-da-VID bih-yo-TO b'-mid-BAR y'-hu-DAH

2 *Hashem*, You are my God; I search for You, my soul thirsts for You, my body yearns for You, as a parched and thirsty land that has no water.

3 I shall behold You in the sanctuary, and see Your might and glory,

---

63:1 Wilderness of *Yehuda* Fleeing from *Shaul*, *David* goes south to the wilderness of *Yehuda*, where he quickly needs to contend with a scarcity of water. The Judean desert is unique due to its proximity to the Jerusalem mountains which receive ample rainfall; within a few kilometers, the amount of rain decreases dramatically as a result of a geological phenomenon called a "rain shadow desert." The clouds drifting westward across *Eretz Yisrael* from the Mediterranean Sea rise and cool, bringing rain over the Judean Hills and *Yerushalayim*. Then, as they continue east over the Judean desert, the clouds dissipate due to the extreme drop of almost a thousand meters within a short distance, condensing again and beginning to give significant rain only when they reach the mountains of Jordan. This psalm, therefore, begins with a focus on thirst. He experiences physical desire for water in "a parched and thirsty land," but more significantly, a spiritual yearning for *Hashem*'s presence, which he describes with the phrase, "my soul thirsts for You" (verse 2). *David* recognizes the threat of scarcity of water, but says it pales in comparison to the absence of God's presence.

Tehillim/Psalms
Chapter 64

תהלים
פרק סד

4 Truly Your faithfulness is better than life; my lips declare Your praise.

ד כִּי־טוֹב חַסְדְּךָ מֵחַיִּים שְׂפָתַי יְשַׁבְּחוּנְךָ׃

5 I bless You all my life; I lift up my hands, invoking Your name.

ה כֵּן אֲבָרֶכְךָ בְחַיָּי בְּשִׁמְךָ אֶשָּׂא כַפָּי׃

6 I am sated as with a rich feast, I sing praises with joyful lips

ו כְּמוֹ חֵלֶב וָדֶשֶׁן תִּשְׂבַּע נַפְשִׁי וְשִׂפְתֵי רְנָנוֹת יְהַלֶּל־פִּי׃

7 when I call You to mind upon my bed, when I think of You in the watches of the night;

ז אִם־זְכַרְתִּיךָ עַל־יְצוּעָי בְּאַשְׁמֻרוֹת אֶהְגֶּה־בָּךְ׃

8 for You are my help, and in the shadow of Your wings I shout for joy.

ח כִּי־הָיִיתָ עֶזְרָתָה לִּי וּבְצֵל כְּנָפֶיךָ אֲרַנֵּן׃

9 My soul is attached to You; Your right hand supports me.

ט דָּבְקָה נַפְשִׁי אַחֲרֶיךָ בִּי תָּמְכָה יְמִינֶךָ׃

10 May those who seek to destroy my life enter the depths of the earth.

י וְהֵמָּה לְשׁוֹאָה יְבַקְשׁוּ נַפְשִׁי יָבֹאוּ בְּתַחְתִּיּוֹת הָאָרֶץ׃

11 May they be gutted by the sword; may they be prey to jackals.

יא יַגִּירֻהוּ עַל־יְדֵי־חָרֶב מְנָת שֻׁעָלִים יִהְיוּ׃

12 But the king shall rejoice in *Hashem*; all who swear by Him shall exult, when the mouth of liars is stopped.

יב וְהַמֶּלֶךְ יִשְׂמַח בֵּאלֹהִים יִתְהַלֵּל כָּל־הַנִּשְׁבָּע בּוֹ כִּי יִסָּכֵר פִּי דוֹבְרֵי־שָׁקֶר׃

64 ¹ For the leader. A psalm of *David*.

סד א לַמְנַצֵּחַ מִזְמוֹר לְדָוִד׃

² Hear my voice, O *Hashem*, when I plead; guard my life from the enemy's terror.

ב שְׁמַע־אֱלֹהִים קוֹלִי בְשִׂיחִי מִפַּחַד אוֹיֵב תִּצֹּר חַיָּי׃

³ Hide me from a band of evil men, from a crowd of evildoers,

ג תַּסְתִּירֵנִי מִסּוֹד מְרֵעִים מֵרִגְשַׁת פֹּעֲלֵי אָוֶן׃

⁴ who whet their tongues like swords; they aim their arrows – cruel words –

ד אֲשֶׁר שָׁנְנוּ כַחֶרֶב לְשׁוֹנָם דָּרְכוּ חִצָּם דָּבָר מָר׃

a-SHER sha-n'-NU kha-KHE-rev l'-sho-NAM da-r'-KHU khi-TZAM da-VAR MAR

⁵ to shoot from hiding at the blameless man; they shoot him suddenly and without fear.

ה לִירֹת בַּמִּסְתָּרִים תָּם פִּתְאֹם יֹרֻהוּ וְלֹא יִירָאוּ׃

64:4 Cruel words King *David*'s enemies attack him in different ways; sometimes physically, sometimes verbally. From this psalm it appears that the verbal assaults affected him more than any other. When *David* is defamed and maligned, he lashes out using a metaphor of swords and arrows. *David* is no stranger to battle. The throngs of voices singing "*Shaul* hath slain his thousands, and *David* his tens of thousands" (I Samuel 21:12) attest to his prowess with the sword, the sling and the arrow. And yet, in his time of darkness when all his friends and confidants have disappeared, the arrow of his enemies is filled with poisoned words, slicing through his armor and penetrating his soul.

Tehillim/Psalms
Chapter 65

6 They arm themselves with an evil word; when they speak, it is to conceal traps; they think, "Who will see them?"

7 Let the wrongdoings they have concealed, each one inside him, his secret thoughts, be wholly exposed.

8 *Hashem* shall shoot them with arrows; they shall be struck down suddenly.

9 Their tongue shall be their downfall; all who see them shall recoil in horror;

10 all men shall stand in awe; they shall proclaim the work of *Hashem* and His deed which they perceived.

11 The righteous shall rejoice in *Hashem*, and take refuge in Him; all the upright shall exult.

65

1 For the leader. A psalm of *David*. A song.

2 Praise befits You in *Tzion*, O *Hashem*; vows are paid to You;

3 all mankind comes to You, You who hear prayer.

4 When all manner of sins overwhelm me, it is You who forgive our iniquities.

5 Happy is the man You choose and bring near to dwell in Your courts; may we be sated with the blessings of Your house, Your holy temple.

6 Answer us with victory through awesome deeds, O *Hashem*, our deliverer, in whom all the ends of the earth and the distant seas put their trust;

7 who by His power fixed the mountains firmly, who is girded with might,

8 who stills the raging seas, the raging waves, and tumultuous peoples.

9 Those who live at the ends of the earth are awed by Your signs; You make the lands of sunrise and sunset shout for joy.

10 You take care of the earth and irrigate it; You enrich it greatly, with the channel of *Hashem* full of water; You provide grain for men; for so do You prepare it.

תהילים
פרק סה

א יְחַזְּקוּ־לָמוֹ דָּבָר רָע יְסַפְּרוּ לִטְמוֹן מוֹקְשִׁים אָמְרוּ מִי יִרְאֶה־לָּמוֹ׃

ז יַחְפְּשׂוּ־עוֹלֹת תַּמְנוּ חֵפֶשׂ מְחֻפָּשׂ וְקֶרֶב אִישׁ וְלֵב עָמֹק׃

ח וַיֹּרֵם אֱלֹהִים חֵץ פִּתְאוֹם הָיוּ מַכּוֹתָם׃

ט וַיַּכְשִׁילוּהוּ עָלֵימוֹ לְשׁוֹנָם יִתְנֹדֲדוּ כָּל־רֹאֵה בָם׃

י וַיִּירְאוּ כָּל־אָדָם וַיַּגִּידוּ פֹּעַל אֱלֹהִים וּמַעֲשֵׂהוּ הִשְׂכִּילוּ׃

יא יִשְׂמַח צַדִּיק בַּיהוָה וְחָסָה בוֹ וְיִתְהַלְלוּ כָּל־יִשְׁרֵי־לֵב׃

סה א לַמְנַצֵּחַ מִזְמוֹר לְדָוִד שִׁיר׃

ב לְךָ דֻמִיָּה תְהִלָּה אֱלֹהִים בְּצִיּוֹן וּלְךָ יְשֻׁלַּם־נֶדֶר׃

ג שֹׁמֵעַ תְּפִלָּה עָדֶיךָ כָּל־בָּשָׂר יָבֹאוּ׃

ד דִּבְרֵי עֲוֺנֹת גָּבְרוּ מֶנִּי פְּשָׁעֵינוּ אַתָּה תְכַפְּרֵם׃

ה אַשְׁרֵי תִּבְחַר וּתְקָרֵב יִשְׁכֹּן חֲצֵרֶיךָ נִשְׂבְּעָה בְּטוּב בֵּיתֶךָ קְדֹשׁ הֵיכָלֶךָ׃

ו נוֹרָאוֹת בְּצֶדֶק תַּעֲנֵנוּ אֱלֹהֵי יִשְׁעֵנוּ מִבְטָח כָּל־קַצְוֵי־אֶרֶץ וְיָם רְחֹקִים׃

ז מֵכִין הָרִים בְּכֹחוֹ נֶאְזָר בִּגְבוּרָה׃

ח מַשְׁבִּיחַ שְׁאוֹן יַמִּים שְׁאוֹן גַּלֵּיהֶם וַהֲמוֹן לְאֻמִּים׃

ט וַיִּירְאוּ יֹשְׁבֵי קְצָווֹת מֵאוֹתֹתֶיךָ מוֹצָאֵי־בֹקֶר וָעֶרֶב תַּרְנִין׃

י פָּקַדְתָּ הָאָרֶץ וַתְּשֹׁקְקֶהָ רַבַּת תַּעְשְׁרֶנָּה פֶּלֶג אֱלֹהִים מָלֵא מָיִם תָּכִין דְּגָנָם כִּי־כֵן תְּכִינֶהָ׃

Tehillim/Psalms
Chapter 66

11 Saturating its furrows, leveling its ridges, You soften it with showers, You bless its growth.

t'-la-ME-ha ra-VAY na-KHAYT g'-du-DE-ha bir-vee-VEEM t'-mo-g'-GE-nah tzim-KHAH t'-va-RAYKH

12 You crown the year with Your bounty; fatness is distilled in Your paths;

13 the pasturelands distill it; the hills are girded with joy.

14 The meadows are clothed with flocks, the valleys mantled with grain; they raise a shout, they break into song.

66

1 For the leader. A song. A psalm. Raise a shout for *Hashem*, all the earth;

2 sing the glory of His name, make glorious His praise.

3 Say to *Hashem*, "How awesome are Your deeds, Your enemies cower before Your great strength;

4 all the earth bows to You, and sings hymns to You; all sing hymns to Your name." Selah.

5 Come and see the works of *Hashem*, who is held in awe by men for His acts.

6 He turned the sea into dry land; they crossed the river on foot; we therefore rejoice in Him.

ha-FAKH YAM l'-ya-ba-SHAH ba-na-HAR ya-av-RU v'-RA-gel SHAM nis-m'-khah BO

65:11 You soften it with showers This psalm offers blessings of gratitude to *Hashem* for abundant rains. It was sung in the *Beit Hamikdash* after especially rainy seasons, which were always viewed as a direct sign of God's beneficence. The word *revivim* (רביבים), 'showers,' refers to abundant rains, and was used by early Zionists as the name of a new settlement founded in the *Negev* desert in 1943. As the British were limiting immigration and new settlements on the land, the early Zionists built lookout points which would later become full-fledged settlements. These settlements were the beginning of habitation in the *Negev*, the desert region in southern Israel, and initiated the settling of the arid desert area of the Land of Israel. The name *Revivim* was chosen as a sign of their readiness to contend with the most formidable aspect of desert living: scarcity of water. They hearkened back to *Tehillim*, hoping for *Hashem's* bountiful rains to strengthen their presence in the land.

66:6 Turned the sea into dry land This psalm rejoices in *Hashem's* wondrous miracles performed for the People of Israel throughout the generations. Verse 6 marks two significant, parallel, wonders relating to water. "He turned the sea into dry land" reminds us of the splitting of the Sea of Reeds (Exodus 14). "They crossed the river on foot" reminds us of a similar phenomenon forty years later when the Children of Israel crossed the Jordan River. As recorded in *Sefer Yehoshua* 3, the waters of the *Yarden* stood and allowed the Israelites to traverse. The coupling of these two miracles here, and again in Psalm 114, reminds us that God had prepared a two-step mission for *Moshe*, only one of which he was able to fulfill by himself: He was supposed to lead Israel up from Egyptian bondage, and then bring them into the Land of Israel.

Ariel view of Kibbutz Revivim

Tehillim/Psalms
Chapter 67

תהילים
פרק סז

7 He rules forever in His might; His eyes scan the nations; let the rebellious not assert themselves. *Selah*.

ז מֹשֵׁל בִּגְבוּרָתוֹ עוֹלָם עֵינָיו בַּגּוֹיִם תִּצְפֶּינָה הַסּוֹרְרִים אַל־ירימו [יָרוּמוּ] לָמוֹ סֶלָה:

8 O peoples, bless our God, celebrate His praises;

ח בָּרְכוּ עַמִּים אֱלֹהֵינוּ וְהַשְׁמִיעוּ קוֹל תְּהִלָּתוֹ:

9 who has granted us life, and has not let our feet slip.

ט הַשָּׂם נַפְשֵׁנוּ בַּחַיִּים וְלֹא־נָתַן לַמּוֹט רַגְלֵנוּ:

10 You have tried us, O *Hashem*, refining us, as one refines silver.

י כִּי־בְחַנְתָּנוּ אֱלֹהִים צְרַפְתָּנוּ כִּצְרָף־כָּסֶף:

11 You have caught us in a net, caught us in trammels.

יא הֲבֵאתָנוּ בַמְּצוּדָה שַׂמְתָּ מוּעָקָה בְמָתְנֵינוּ:

12 You have let men ride over us; we have endured fire and water, and You have brought us through to prosperity.

יב הִרְכַּבְתָּ אֱנוֹשׁ לְרֹאשֵׁנוּ בָּאנוּ־בָאֵשׁ וּבַמַּיִם וַתּוֹצִיאֵנוּ לָרְוָיָה:

13 I enter Your house with burnt offerings, I pay my vows to You,

יג אָבוֹא בֵיתְךָ בְעוֹלוֹת אֲשַׁלֵּם לְךָ נְדָרָי:

14 [vows] that my lips pronounced, that my mouth uttered in my distress.

יד אֲשֶׁר־פָּצוּ שְׂפָתָי וְדִבֶּר־פִּי בַּצַּר־לִי:

15 I offer up fatlings to You, with the odor of burning rams; I sacrifice bulls and he-goats. *Selah*.

טו עֹלוֹת מֵחִים אַעֲלֶה־לָּךְ עִם־קְטֹרֶת אֵילִים אֶעֱשֶׂה בָקָר עִם־עַתּוּדִים סֶלָה:

16 Come and hear, all *Hashem*-fearing men, as I tell what He did for me.

טז לְכוּ־שִׁמְעוּ וַאֲסַפְּרָה כָּל־יִרְאֵי אֱלֹהִים אֲשֶׁר עָשָׂה לְנַפְשִׁי:

17 I called aloud to Him, glorification on my tongue.

יז אֵלָיו פִּי־קָרָאתִי וְרוֹמַם תַּחַת לְשׁוֹנִי:

18 Had I an evil thought in my mind, *Hashem* would not have listened.

יח אָוֶן אִם־רָאִיתִי בְלִבִּי לֹא יִשְׁמַע אֲדֹנָי:

19 But *Hashem* did listen; He paid heed to my prayer.

יט אָכֵן שָׁמַע אֱלֹהִים הִקְשִׁיב בְּקוֹל תְּפִלָּתִי:

20 Blessed is *Hashem* who has not turned away my prayer, or His faithful care from me.

כ בָּרוּךְ אֱלֹהִים אֲשֶׁר לֹא־הֵסִיר תְּפִלָּתִי וְחַסְדּוֹ מֵאִתִּי:

67

1 For the leader; with instrumental music. A psalm. A song.

סז א לַמְנַצֵּחַ בִּנְגִינֹת מִזְמוֹר שִׁיר:

2 May *Hashem* be gracious to us and bless us; may He show us favor, *selah*

ב אֱלֹהִים יְחָנֵּנוּ וִיבָרְכֵנוּ יָאֵר פָּנָיו אִתָּנוּ סֶלָה:

3 that Your way be known on earth, Your deliverance among all nations.

ג לָדַעַת בָּאָרֶץ דַּרְכֶּךָ בְּכָל־גּוֹיִם יְשׁוּעָתֶךָ:

4 Peoples will praise You, O *Hashem*; all peoples will praise You.

ד יוֹדוּךָ עַמִּים אֱלֹהִים יוֹדוּךָ עַמִּים כֻּלָּם:

5 Nations will exult and shout for joy, for You rule the peoples with equity, You guide the nations of the earth. *Selah*.

ה יִשְׂמְחוּ וִירַנְּנוּ לְאֻמִּים כִּי־תִשְׁפֹּט עַמִּים מִישׁוֹר וּלְאֻמִּים בָּאָרֶץ תַּנְחֵם סֶלָה:

Tehillim/Psalms
Chapter 68

תהלים
פרק סח

6 The peoples will praise You, O *Hashem*; all peoples will praise You.

ו יוֹד֣וּךָ עַמִּ֣ים ׀ אֱלֹהִ֑ים י֝וֹד֗וּךָ עַמִּ֥ים כֻּלָּֽם׃

7 May the earth yield its produce; may *Hashem*, our God, bless us.

ז אֶ֭רֶץ נָתְנָ֣ה יְבוּלָ֑הּ יְ֝בָרְכֵ֗נוּ אֱלֹהִ֥ים אֱלֹהֵֽינוּ׃

E-retz na-t'-NAH y'-vu-LAH y'-va-r'-KHAY-nu e-lo-HEEM e-lo-HAY-nu

8 May *Hashem* bless us, and be revered to the ends of the earth.

ח יְבָרְכֵ֥נוּ אֱלֹהִ֑ים וְיִ֥ירְא֥וּ אֹ֝ת֗וֹ כָּל־אַפְסֵי־אָֽרֶץ׃

68 1 For the leader. Of *David*. A psalm. A song.

סח א לַמְנַצֵּ֬חַ לְדָוִ֖ד מִזְמ֣וֹר שִֽׁיר׃

2 *Hashem* will arise, His enemies shall be scattered, His foes shall flee before Him.

ב יָק֣וּם אֱ֭לֹהִים יָפ֣וּצוּ אוֹיְבָ֑יו וְיָנ֥וּסוּ מְ֝שַׂנְאָ֗יו מִפָּנָֽיו׃

3 Disperse them as smoke is dispersed; as wax melts at fire, so the wicked shall perish before *Hashem*.

ג כְּהִנְדֹּ֥ף עָשָׁ֗ן תִּ֫נְדֹּ֥ף כְּהִמֵּ֣ס דּ֭וֹנַג מִפְּנֵי־אֵ֑שׁ יֹאבְד֥וּ רְ֝שָׁעִ֗ים מִפְּנֵ֥י אֱלֹהִֽים׃

4 But the righteous shall rejoice; they shall exult in the presence of *Hashem*; they shall be exceedingly joyful.

ד וְֽצַדִּיקִ֗ים יִשְׂמְח֣וּ יַ֭עַלְצוּ לִפְנֵ֥י אֱלֹהִ֗ים וְיָשִׂ֥ישׂוּ בְשִׂמְחָֽה׃

5 Sing to *Hashem*, chant hymns to His name; extol Him who rides the clouds; *Hashem* is His name. Exult in His presence –

ה שִׁ֤ירוּ ׀ לֵֽאלֹהִים֮ זַמְּר֪וּ שְׁ֫מ֥וֹ סֹ֡לּוּ לָרֹכֵ֣ב בָּ֭עֲרָבוֹת בְּיָ֥הּ שְׁמ֗וֹ וְעִלְז֥וּ לְפָנָֽיו׃

6 the father of orphans, the Champion of widows, *Hashem*, in His holy habitation.

ו אֲבִ֣י יְ֭תוֹמִים וְדַיַּ֣ן אַלְמָנ֑וֹת אֱ֝לֹהִ֗ים בִּמְע֥וֹן קָדְשֽׁוֹ׃

7 *Hashem* restores the lonely to their homes, sets free the imprisoned, safe and sound, while the rebellious must live in a parched land.

ז אֱלֹהִ֤ים ׀ מ֘וֹשִׁ֤יב יְחִידִ֨ים ׀ בַּ֗יְתָה מוֹצִ֣יא אֲ֭סִירִים בַּכּוֹשָׁר֑וֹת אַ֥ךְ ס֝וֹרְרִ֗ים שָׁכְנ֥וּ צְחִיחָֽה׃

8 O *Hashem*, when You went at the head of Your army, when You marched through the desert, *selah*

ח אֱֽלֹהִ֗ים בְּ֭צֵאתְךָ לִפְנֵ֣י עַמֶּ֑ךָ בְּצַעְדְּךָ֖ בִישִׁימ֣וֹן סֶֽלָה׃

9 the earth trembled, the sky rained because of *Hashem*, yon Sinai, because of *Hashem*, the God of *Yisrael*.

ט אֶ֤רֶץ רָעָ֨שָׁה ׀ אַף־שָׁמַ֣יִם נָטְפוּ֮ מִפְּנֵ֪י אֱלֹ֫הִ֥ים זֶ֥ה סִינַ֑י מִפְּנֵ֥י אֱ֝לֹהִ֗ים אֱלֹהֵ֥י יִשְׂרָאֵֽל׃

E-retz ra-a-SHAH af sha-MA-yim na-t'-FU mi-p'-NAY e-lo-HEEM ZEH see-NAI mi-p'-NAY e-lo-HEEM e-lo-HAY yis-ra-AYL

67:7 May the earth yield its produce The amount of produce that the Land of Israel gives is a direct response to the behavior of its inhabitants. *Hashem* makes this point very clear throughout the Bible, specifically in *Sefer Devarim* (11:13–15), in which He links the concept of reward and punishment with the successful produce of the land. If the children of7 God veer from His path and reject Him for idolatry, divine anger will arise and the land will not give its produce. This reaction is actually a blessing, since the inhabitants of *Eretz Yisrael* are thereby granted a barometer for their spiritual behavior. If there is famine and drought, they know that *Hashem* is angry, and they must inspect their actions. If there is plenty, God is happy with His nation and it is appropriate to sing praises to the Lord for His wonderful bounty.

68:9 The earth trembled, the sky rained because of *Hashem* The psalm opens with a paraphrase of *Sefer Bamidbar* (10:35), which explains that as the Aron traveled in the desert, *Moshe* called out, "Advance, *Hashem*!

Tehillim/Psalms
Chapter 68

10 You released a bountiful rain, O *Hashem*; when Your own land languished, You sustained it.

11 Your tribe dwells there; O *Hashem*, in Your goodness You provide for the needy.

12 *Hashem* gives a command; the women who bring the news are a great host:

13 "The kings and their armies are in headlong flight; housewives are sharing in the spoils;

14 even for those of you who lie among the sheepfolds there are wings of a dove sheathed in silver, its pinions in fine gold."

15 When *Shaddai* scattered the kings, it seemed like a snowstorm in Zalmon.

16 O majestic mountain, Mount Bashan; O jagged mountain, Mount Bashan;

17 why so hostile, O jagged mountains, toward the mountain *Hashem* desired as His dwelling? *Hashem* shall abide there forever.

18 *Hashem*'s chariots are myriads upon myriads, thousands upon thousands; *Hashem* is among them as in Sinai in holiness.

19 You went up to the heights, having taken captives, having received tribute of men, even of those who rebel against *Hashem*'s abiding there.

20 Blessed is *Hashem*. Day by day He supports us, *Hashem*, our deliverance. *Selah*.

21 *Hashem* is for us a God of deliverance; *Hashem* the Lord provides an escape from death.

22 *Hashem* will smash the heads of His enemies, the hairy crown of him who walks about in his guilt.

May Your enemies be scattered, And may Your foes flee before You!" The psalmist acknowledges that Israel goes into battle with God at the helm, smiting the enemy and miraculously scattering the cowardly foe. This is illustrated in a remarkable biblical story concerning the prophetess and judge *Devora*, and the battle fought by Israel against the Canaanites at Mount *Tavor* (Judges 4,5). *Devora* signals to the general *Barak* that *Hashem* is fighting with Israel and victory is at hand. The Canaanite army is defeated and Sisera the Canaanite general is ultimately killed by *Yael*, wife of *Chever* the Kenite in her tent. After the Israelite victory, *Devora* praises God with words that are strikingly similar to this verse: "*Hashem*, when You came forth from Seir, advanced from the country of Edom, the earth trembled; the heavens dripped, Yea, the clouds dripped water, the mountains quaked before *Hashem*, Him of Sinai, before *Hashem*, God of *Yisrael*" (Judges 5:4–3). The earth shakes at the realization that in Israel, God Himself fights together with His people.

Tehillim/Psalms
Chapter 69

23 *Hashem* said, "I will retrieve from Bashan, I will retrieve from the depths of the sea;

24 that your feet may wade through blood; that the tongue of your dogs may have its portion of your enemies."

25 Men see Your processions, O *Hashem*, the processions of my God, my king, into the sanctuary.

26 First come singers, then musicians, amidst maidens playing timbrels.

27 In assemblies bless *Hashem*, *Hashem*, O you who are from the fountain of *Yisrael*.

28 There is little *Binyamin* who rules them, the princes of *Yehuda* who command them, the princes of *Zevulun* and *Naftali*.

29 Your God has ordained strength for you, the strength, O *Hashem*, which You displayed for us

30 from Your temple above *Yerushalayim*. The kings bring You tribute.

31 Blast the beast of the marsh, the herd of bulls among the peoples, the calves, till they come cringing with pieces of silver. Scatter the peoples who delight in wars!

32 Tribute-bearers shall come from Egypt; Cush shall hasten its gifts to *Hashem*.

33 O kingdoms of the earth, sing to *Hashem*; chant hymns to *Hashem*, selah

34 to Him who rides the ancient highest heavens, who thunders forth with His mighty voice.

35 Ascribe might to *Hashem*, whose majesty is over *Yisrael*, whose might is in the skies.

36 You are awesome, O *Hashem*, in Your holy places; it is the God of *Yisrael* who gives might and power to the people. Blessed is *Hashem*.

69 1 For the leader. On shoshannim. Of *David*.

2 Deliver me, O *Hashem*, for the waters have reached my neck;

3 I am sinking into the slimy deep and find no foothold; I have come into the watery depths; the flood sweeps me away.

Tehillim/Psalms
Chapter 69

תהילים
פרק סט

4 I am weary with calling; my throat is dry; my eyes fail while I wait for *Hashem*.

ד יָגַעְתִּי בְקָרְאִי נִחַר גְּרוֹנִי כָּלוּ עֵינַי מְיַחֵל לֵאלֹהָי:

5 More numerous than the hairs of my head are those who hate me without reason; many are those who would destroy me, my treacherous enemies. Must I restore what I have not stolen?

ה רַבּוּ מִשַּׂעֲרוֹת רֹאשִׁי שֹׂנְאַי חִנָּם עָצְמוּ מַצְמִיתַי אֹיְבַי שֶׁקֶר אֲשֶׁר לֹא־גָזַלְתִּי אָז אָשִׁיב:

6 *Hashem*, You know my folly; my guilty deeds are not hidden from You.

ו אֱלֹהִים אַתָּה יָדַעְתָּ לְאִוַּלְתִּי וְאַשְׁמוֹתַי מִמְּךָ לֹא־נִכְחָדוּ:

7 Let those who look to You, O *Hashem*, God of hosts, not be disappointed on my account; let those who seek You, O God of *Yisrael*, not be shamed because of me.

ז אַל־יֵבֹשׁוּ בִי קֹוֶיךָ אֲדֹנָי יֱהֹוִה צְבָאוֹת אַל־יִכָּלְמוּ בִי מְבַקְשֶׁיךָ אֱלֹהֵי יִשְׂרָאֵל:

8 It is for Your sake that I have been reviled, that shame covers my face;

ח כִּי־עָלֶיךָ נָשָׂאתִי חֶרְפָּה כִּסְּתָה כְלִמָּה פָנָי:

9 I am a stranger to my brothers, an alien to my kin.

ט מוּזָר הָיִיתִי לְאֶחָי וְנָכְרִי לִבְנֵי אִמִּי:

10 My zeal for Your house has been my undoing; the reproaches of those who revile You have fallen upon me.

י כִּי־קִנְאַת בֵּיתְךָ אֲכָלָתְנִי וְחֶרְפּוֹת חוֹרְפֶיךָ נָפְלוּ עָלָי:

11 When I wept and fasted, I was reviled for it.

יא וָאֶבְכֶּה בַצּוֹם נַפְשִׁי וַתְּהִי לַחֲרָפוֹת לִי:

12 I made sackcloth my garment; I became a byword among them.

יב וָאֶתְּנָה לְבוּשִׁי שָׂק וָאֱהִי לָהֶם לְמָשָׁל:

13 Those who sit in the gate talk about me; I am the taunt of drunkards.

יג יָשִׂיחוּ בִי יֹשְׁבֵי שָׁעַר וּנְגִינוֹת שׁוֹתֵי שֵׁכָר:

14 As for me, may my prayer come to You, *Hashem*, at a favorable moment; O *Hashem*, in Your abundant faithfulness, answer me with Your sure deliverance.

יד וַאֲנִי תְפִלָּתִי־לְךָ יְהֹוָה עֵת רָצוֹן אֱלֹהִים בְּרָב־חַסְדֶּךָ עֲנֵנִי בֶּאֱמֶת יִשְׁעֶךָ:

15 Rescue me from the mire; let me not sink; let me be rescued from my enemies, and from the watery depths.

טו הַצִּילֵנִי מִטִּיט וְאַל־אֶטְבָּעָה אִנָּצְלָה מִשֹּׂנְאַי וּמִמַּעֲמַקֵּי־מָיִם:

16 Let the floodwaters not sweep me away; let the deep not swallow me; let the mouth of the Pit not close over me.

טז אַל־תִּשְׁטְפֵנִי שִׁבֹּלֶת מַיִם וְאַל־תִּבְלָעֵנִי מְצוּלָה וְאַל־תֶּאְטַר־עָלַי בְּאֵר פִּיהָ:

17 Answer me, *Hashem*, according to Your great steadfastness; in accordance with Your abundant mercy turn to me;

יז עֲנֵנִי יְהֹוָה כִּי־טוֹב חַסְדֶּךָ כְּרֹב רַחֲמֶיךָ פְּנֵה אֵלָי:

18 do not hide Your face from Your servant, for I am in distress; answer me quickly.

יח וְאַל־תַּסְתֵּר פָּנֶיךָ מֵעַבְדֶּךָ כִּי־צַר־לִי מַהֵר עֲנֵנִי:

19 Come near to me and redeem me; free me from my enemies.

יט קָרְבָה אֶל־נַפְשִׁי גְאָלָהּ לְמַעַן אֹיְבַי פְּדֵנִי:

20 You know my reproach, my shame, my disgrace; You are aware of all my foes.

כ אַתָּה יָדַעְתָּ חֶרְפָּתִי וּבָשְׁתִּי וּכְלִמָּתִי נֶגְדְּךָ כָּל־צוֹרְרָי:

Tehillim/Psalms
Chapter 69

תהלים
פרק סט

21 Reproach breaks my heart, I am in despair; I hope for consolation, but there is none, for comforters, but find none.

כא חֶרְפָּה ׀ שָׁבְרָה לִבִּי וָאָנוּשָׁה וָאֲקַוֶּה לָנוּד וָאַיִן וְלַמְנַחֲמִים וְלֹא מָצָאתִי:

22 They give me gall for food, vinegar to quench my thirst.

כב וַיִּתְּנוּ בְּבָרוּתִי רֹאשׁ וְלִצְמָאִי יַשְׁקוּנִי חֹמֶץ:

23 May their table be a trap for them, a snare for their allies.

כג יְהִי־שֻׁלְחָנָם לִפְנֵיהֶם לְפָח וְלִשְׁלוֹמִים לְמוֹקֵשׁ:

24 May their eyes grow dim so that they cannot see; may their loins collapse continually.

כד תֶּחְשַׁכְנָה עֵינֵיהֶם מֵרְאוֹת וּמָתְנֵיהֶם תָּמִיד הַמְעַד:

25 Pour out Your wrath on them; may Your blazing anger overtake them;

כה שְׁפָךְ־עֲלֵיהֶם זַעְמֶךָ וַחֲרוֹן אַפְּךָ יַשִּׂיגֵם:

26 may their encampments be desolate; may their tents stand empty.

כו תְּהִי־טִירָתָם נְשַׁמָּה בְּאָהֳלֵיהֶם אַל־יְהִי יֹשֵׁב:

27 For they persecute those You have struck; they talk about the pain of those You have felled.

כז כִּי־אַתָּה אֲשֶׁר־הִכִּיתָ רָדָפוּ וְאֶל־מַכְאוֹב חֲלָלֶיךָ יְסַפֵּרוּ:

28 Add that to their guilt; let them have no share of Your beneficence;

כח תְּנָה־עָוֹן עַל־עֲוֹנָם וְאַל־יָבֹאוּ בְּצִדְקָתֶךָ:

29 may they be erased from the book of life, and not be inscribed with the righteous.

כט יִמָּחוּ מִסֵּפֶר חַיִּים וְעִם צַדִּיקִים אַל־יִכָּתֵבוּ:

30 But I am lowly and in pain; Your help, O *Hashem*, keeps me safe.

ל וַאֲנִי עָנִי וְכוֹאֵב יְשׁוּעָתְךָ אֱלֹהִים תְּשַׂגְּבֵנִי:

31 I will extol *Hashem*'s name with song, and exalt Him with praise.

לא אֲהַלְלָה שֵׁם־אֱלֹהִים בְּשִׁיר וַאֲגַדְּלֶנּוּ בְתוֹדָה:

32 That will please *Hashem* more than oxen, than bulls with horns and hooves.

לב וְתִיטַב לַיהוָה מִשּׁוֹר פָּר מַקְרִן מַפְרִיס:

33 The lowly will see and rejoice; you who are mindful of *Hashem*, take heart!

לג רָאוּ עֲנָוִים יִשְׂמָחוּ דֹּרְשֵׁי אֱלֹהִים וִיחִי לְבַבְכֶם:

34 For *Hashem* listens to the needy, and does not spurn His captives.

לד כִּי־שֹׁמֵעַ אֶל־אֶבְיוֹנִים יְהוָה וְאֶת־אֲסִירָיו לֹא בָזָה:

35 Heaven and earth shall extol Him, the seas, and all that moves in them.

לה יְהַלְלוּהוּ שָׁמַיִם וָאָרֶץ יַמִּים וְכָל־רֹמֵשׂ בָּם:

36 For *Hashem* will deliver *Tzion* and rebuild the cities of *Yehuda*; they shall live there and inherit it;

KEE e-lo-HEEM yo-SHEE-a tzi-YON v'-yiv-NEH a-RAY y'-hu-DAH v'-YA-sh'vu SHAM vee-ray-SHU-ha

לו כִּי אֱלֹהִים ׀ יוֹשִׁיעַ צִיּוֹן וְיִבְנֶה עָרֵי יְהוּדָה וְיָשְׁבוּ שָׁם וִירֵשׁוּהָ:

69:36 They shall live there and inherit it Historically, the Israelites lived and prospered in the central mountain region of Israel, the area of Judea and Samaria. *Avraham* traveled from the north through the Samarian hills down to *Chevron*, his future eternal resting place. *Yitzchak* and *Yaakov*, as well as King *David*

Tehillim / Psalms
Chapter 70

37 the offspring of His servants shall possess it; those who cherish His name shall dwell there. | לְזֶרַע עֲבָדָיו יִנְחָלוּהָ וְאֹהֲבֵי שְׁמוֹ יִשְׁכְּנוּ־בָהּ׃

70 1 For the leader. Of *David*. Lehazkir. | א לַמְנַצֵּחַ לְדָוִד לְהַזְכִּיר׃

2 Hasten, O *Hashem*, to save me; *Hashem*, to aid me! | ב אֱלֹהִים לְהַצִּילֵנִי יְהוָה לְעֶזְרָתִי חוּשָׁה׃

3 Let those who seek my life be frustrated and disgraced; let those who wish me harm, fall back in shame. | ג יֵבֹשׁוּ וְיַחְפְּרוּ מְבַקְשֵׁי נַפְשִׁי יִסֹּגוּ אָחוֹר וְיִכָּלְמוּ חֲפֵצֵי רָעָתִי׃

yay-VO-shu v'-yakh-p'-RU m'-vak-SHAY naf-SHEE yi-SO-gu a-KHOR v'-yi-kal-MU kha-fay-TZAY ra-a-TEE

4 Let those who say, "Aha! Aha!" turn back because of their frustration. | ד יָשׁוּבוּ עַל־עֵקֶב בָּשְׁתָּם הָאֹמְרִים הֶאָח הֶאָח׃

5 But let all who seek You be glad and rejoice in You; let those who are eager for Your deliverance always say, "Extolled be *Hashem*!" | ה יָשִׂישׂוּ וְיִשְׂמְחוּ בְּךָ כָּל־מְבַקְשֶׁיךָ וְיֹאמְרוּ תָמִיד יִגְדַּל אֱלֹהִים אֹהֲבֵי יְשׁוּעָתֶךָ׃

6 But I am poor and needy; O *Hashem*, hasten to me! You are my help and my rescuer; *Hashem*, do not delay. | ו וַאֲנִי עָנִי וְאֶבְיוֹן אֱלֹהִים חוּשָׁה־לִּי עֶזְרִי וּמְפַלְטִי אַתָּה יְהוָה אַל־תְּאַחַר׃

71 1 I seek refuge in You, *Hashem*; may I never be disappointed. | א בְּךָ־יְהוָה חָסִיתִי אַל־אֵבוֹשָׁה לְעוֹלָם׃

2 As You are beneficent, save me and rescue me; incline Your ear to me and deliver me. | ב בְּצִדְקָתְךָ תַּצִּילֵנִי וּתְפַלְּטֵנִי הַטֵּה־אֵלַי אָזְנְךָ וְהוֹשִׁיעֵנִי׃

3 Be a sheltering rock for me to which I may always repair; decree my deliverance, for You are my rock and my fortress. | ג הֱיֵה לִי לְצוּר מָעוֹן לָבוֹא תָּמִיד צִוִּיתָ לְהוֹשִׁיעֵנִי כִּי־סַלְעִי וּמְצוּדָתִי אָתָּה׃

4 My *Hashem*, rescue me from the hand of the wicked, from the grasp of the unjust and the lawless. | ד אֱלֹהַי פַּלְּטֵנִי מִיַּד רָשָׁע מִכַּף מְעַוֵּל וְחוֹמֵץ׃

A Roman milestone on the Path of the Patriarchs

Rabbi Samson R. Hirsch (1808–1888)

and the Maccabees, hovered around the mountainous area, with its springs and grass for grazing. The psalmist reminds us of the close connection Israel has with the hills of Judea, and delivers a charge to settle the mountains and redeem them as their inheritance. An ancient road traverses the hilltops of Judea, connecting *Yerushalayim* with the southern *Chevron* hills. This road is called the Path of the Patriarchs, as it is most probably the route taken by *Avraham*, *Yitzchak* and *Yaakov* when traveling between *Beersheva*, *Chevron*, Mount *Moriah*, *Beit El*, and *Shechem*. Walking on it, one finds Roman milestones, an ancient ritual bath and archaeological remnants of years past. One also sees the beautiful, populated, modern cities of *Efrat*, *Neve Daniel*, *Elazar*, *Alon Shevut*, *K'far Etzion* and many other settlements in the area of Judea.

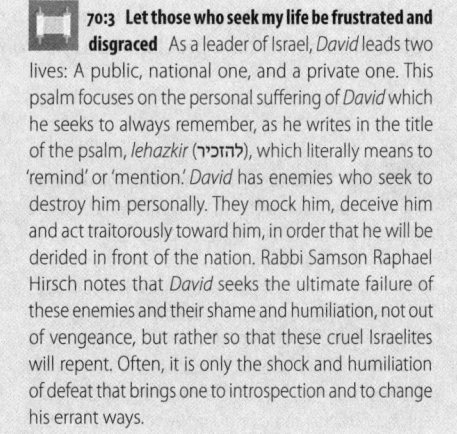

70:3 Let those who seek my life be frustrated and disgraced As a leader of Israel, *David* leads two lives: A public, national one, and a private one. This psalm focuses on the personal suffering of *David* which he seeks to always remember, as he writes in the title of the psalm, *lehazkir* (להזכיר), which literally means to 'remind' or 'mention.' *David* has enemies who seek to destroy him personally. They mock him, deceive him and act traitorously toward him, in order that he will be derided in front of the nation. Rabbi Samson Raphael Hirsch notes that *David* seeks the ultimate failure of these enemies and their shame and humiliation, not out of vengeance, but rather so that these cruel Israelites will repent. Often, it is only the shock and humiliation of defeat that brings one to introspection and to change his errant ways.

Tehillim/Psalms
Chapter 71

תהלים
פרק עא

5 For You are my hope, O *Hashem*, my trust from my youth.

ה כִּי־אַתָּה תִקְוָתִי אֲדֹנָי יֱהוִה מִבְטַחִי מִנְּעוּרָי:

6 While yet unborn, I depended on You; in the womb of my mother, You were my support; I sing Your praises always.

ו עָלֶיךָ נִסְמַכְתִּי מִבֶּטֶן מִמְּעֵי אִמִּי אַתָּה גוֹזִי בְּךָ תְהִלָּתִי תָמִיד:

a-LE-kha nis-MAKH-tee mi-BE-ten mi-m'-AY i-MEE a-TAH go-ZEE b'-KHA t'-hi-la-TEE ta-MEED

7 I have become an example for many, since You are my mighty refuge.

ז כְּמוֹפֵת הָיִיתִי לְרַבִּים וְאַתָּה מַחֲסִי־עֹז:

8 My mouth is full of praise to You, glorifying You all day long.

ח יִמָּלֵא פִי תְּהִלָּתֶךָ כָּל־הַיּוֹם תִּפְאַרְתֶּךָ:

9 Do not cast me off in old age; when my strength fails, do not forsake me!

ט אַל־תַּשְׁלִיכֵנִי לְעֵת זִקְנָה כִּכְלוֹת כֹּחִי אַל־תַּעַזְבֵנִי:

10 For my enemies talk against me; those who wait for me are of one mind,

י כִּי־אָמְרוּ אוֹיְבַי לִי וְשֹׁמְרֵי נַפְשִׁי נוֹעֲצוּ יַחְדָּו:

11 saying, "*Hashem* has forsaken him; chase him and catch him, for no one will save him!"

יא לֵאמֹר אֱלֹהִים עֲזָבוֹ רִדְפוּ וְתִפְשׂוּהוּ כִּי־אֵין מַצִּיל:

12 O *Hashem*, be not far from me; my God, hasten to my aid!

יב אֱלֹהִים אַל־תִּרְחַק מִמֶּנִּי אֱלֹהַי לְעֶזְרָתִי חִישָׁה [חוּשָׁה]:

13 Let my accusers perish in frustration; let those who seek my ruin be clothed in reproach and disgrace!

יג יֵבֹשׁוּ יִכְלוּ שֹׂטְנֵי נַפְשִׁי יַעֲטוּ חֶרְפָּה וּכְלִמָּה מְבַקְשֵׁי רָעָתִי:

14 As for me, I will hope always, and add to the many praises of You.

יד וַאֲנִי תָּמִיד אֲיַחֵל וְהוֹסַפְתִּי עַל־כָּל־תְּהִלָּתֶךָ:

15 My mouth tells of Your beneficence, of Your deliverance all day long, though I know not how to tell it.

טו פִּי יְסַפֵּר צִדְקָתֶךָ כָּל־הַיּוֹם תְּשׁוּעָתֶךָ כִּי לֹא יָדַעְתִּי סְפֹרוֹת:

16 I come with praise of Your mighty acts, O *Hashem*; I celebrate Your beneficence, Yours alone.

טז אָבוֹא בִּגְבֻרוֹת אֲדֹנָי יֱהוִה אַזְכִּיר צִדְקָתְךָ לְבַדֶּךָ:

17 You have let me experience it, *Hashem*, from my youth; until now I have proclaimed Your wondrous deeds,

יז אֱלֹהִים לִמַּדְתַּנִי מִנְּעוּרָי וְעַד־הֵנָּה אַגִּיד נִפְלְאוֹתֶיךָ:

א 71:6 In the womb of my mother, You were my support *David* praises the Lord, saying he relied on God from the earliest age. The Hebrew phrase *ata gozi* (אתה גוזי), translated here as 'You were my support,' is hard to explain. Rabbi Samson Raphael Hirsch raises the possibility that it comes from the root word ג-ז-ז, meaning 'to cut,' resulting in the image of *David* being cut from the womb at birth. Hirsch, however, rejects this idea and suggests that the root ג-ז-ז not only connotes cutting but also 'removing' and 'separating.' *David* is expressing the idea that from the time of his birth he was always different from everyone else, set aside by God for something grand and significant. Indeed, we find *David* separate from his brothers when his father *Yishai* doesn't even bring him in with the rest of his brothers to be considered as *Hashem*'s choice for king (I Samuel 16). However, in this moment of reflection, perhaps at the end of his life, *David* recalls the constant feelings of *Hashem*'s presence in his life and a mission of greatness.

גזז

Tehillim/Psalms
Chapter 72

18 and even in hoary old age do not forsake me, *Hashem*, until I proclaim Your strength to the next generation, Your mighty acts, to all who are to come,

19 Your beneficence, high as the heavens, O *Hashem*, You who have done great things; O *Hashem*, who is Your peer!

20 You who have made me undergo many troubles and misfortunes will revive me again, and raise me up from the depths of the earth.

21 You will grant me much greatness, You will turn and comfort me.

22 Then I will acclaim You to the music of the lyre for Your faithfulness, O my God; I will sing a hymn to You with a harp, O Holy One of *Yisrael*.

23 My lips shall be jubilant, as I sing a hymn to You, my whole being, which You have redeemed.

24 All day long my tongue shall recite Your beneficent acts, how those who sought my ruin were frustrated and disgraced.

72 1 Of *Shlomo*. O *Hashem*, endow the king with Your judgments, the king's son with Your righteousness;

2 that he may judge Your people rightly, Your lowly ones, justly.

3 Let the mountains produce well-being for the people, the hills, the reward of justice.

4 Let him Champion the lowly among the people, deliver the needy folk, and crush those who wrong them.

5 Let them fear You as long as the sun shines, while the moon lasts, generations on end.

6 Let him be like rain that falls on a mown field, like a downpour of rain on the ground,

7 that the righteous may flourish in his time, and well-being abound, till the moon is no more.

8 Let him rule from sea to sea, from the river to the ends of the earth.

9 Let desert-dwellers kneel before him, and his enemies lick the dust.

10 Let kings of Tarshish and the islands pay tribute, kings of Sheba and Seba offer gifts.

Tehillim/Psalms
Chapter 73

תהלים
פרק עג

11 Let all kings bow to him, and all nations serve him.

יא וְיִשְׁתַּחֲווּ־לוֹ כָל־מְלָכִים כָּל־גּוֹיִם יַעַבְדוּהוּ׃

12 For he saves the needy who cry out, the lowly who have no helper.

יב כִּי־יַצִּיל אֶבְיוֹן מְשַׁוֵּעַ וְעָנִי וְאֵין־עֹזֵר לוֹ׃

13 He cares about the poor and the needy; He brings the needy deliverance.

יג יָחֹס עַל־דַּל וְאֶבְיוֹן וְנַפְשׁוֹת אֶבְיוֹנִים יוֹשִׁיעַ׃

14 He redeems them from fraud and lawlessness; the shedding of their blood weighs heavily upon him.

יד מִתּוֹךְ וּמֵחָמָס יִגְאַל נַפְשָׁם וְיֵיקַר דָּמָם בְּעֵינָיו׃

15 So let him live, and receive gold of Sheba; let prayers for him be said always, blessings on him invoked at all times.

טו וִיחִי וְיִתֶּן־לוֹ מִזְּהַב שְׁבָא וְיִתְפַּלֵּל בַּעֲדוֹ תָמִיד כָּל־הַיּוֹם יְבָרֲכֶנְהוּ׃

16 Let abundant grain be in the land, to the tops of the mountains; let his crops thrive like the forest of Lebanon; and let men sprout up in towns like country grass.

טז יְהִי פִסַּת־בַּר בָּאָרֶץ בְּרֹאשׁ הָרִים יִרְעַשׁ כַּלְּבָנוֹן פִּרְיוֹ וְיָצִיצוּ מֵעִיר כְּעֵשֶׂב הָאָרֶץ׃

17 May his name be eternal; while the sun lasts, may his name endure; let men invoke his blessedness upon themselves; let all nations count him happy.

יז יְהִי שְׁמוֹ לְעוֹלָם לִפְנֵי־שֶׁמֶשׁ ינין [יִנּוֹן] שְׁמוֹ וְיִתְבָּרֲכוּ בוֹ כָּל־גּוֹיִם יְאַשְּׁרוּהוּ׃

18 Blessed is *Hashem*, God of *Yisrael*, who alone does wondrous things;

יח בָּרוּךְ יְהֹוָה אֱלֹהִים אֱלֹהֵי יִשְׂרָאֵל עֹשֵׂה נִפְלָאוֹת לְבַדּוֹ׃

19 Blessed is His glorious name forever; His glory fills the whole world. *Amen* and *Amen*.

יט וּבָרוּךְ שֵׁם כְּבוֹדוֹ לְעוֹלָם וְיִמָּלֵא כְבוֹדוֹ אֶת־כָּל הָאָרֶץ אָמֵן וְאָמֵן׃

u-va-RUKH SHAYM k'-vo-DO l'-o-LAM v'-yi-ma-LAY kh'-vo-DO et kol ha-A-retz a-MAYN v'-a-MAYN

20 End of the prayers of *David* son of *Yishai*.

כ כָּלּוּ תְפִלּוֹת דָּוִד בֶּן־יִשָׁי׃

73 1 A psalm of *Asaf*. *Hashem* is truly good to *Yisrael*, to those whose heart is pure.

עג א מִזְמוֹר לְאָסָף אַךְ טוֹב לְיִשְׂרָאֵל אֱלֹהִים לְבָרֵי לֵבָב׃

miz-MOR l'-a-SAF AKH TOV l'-yis-ra-AYL e-lo-HEEM l'-va-RAY lay-VAV

אמן

72:19 Amen, and Amen The word *Amen* is used in the Bible to connote agreement, faithfulness and certainty. It is often translated as "so be it." *Amen* is one of the most common examples of an English word that comes from biblical Hebrew. According to the movement of Edenics, which believes that English is a derivative of biblical Hebrew, the English word amenable, which means "willing to believe and submit," is also a direct offshoot of the word Hebrew word *Amen*. In Hebrew, *Amen* (אמן) shares a root with the word *emunah* (אמונה), which means 'faith' or 'trust'. The word *emunah* is used to describe eternal belief and great confidence in *Hashem*. The Talmud (*Shabbat* 119b) teaches that the three Hebrew letters of the word *Amen* (א-מ-נ) also stand for אל מלך נאמן (*el melech ne'eman*), which means 'God is a trustworthy king.' 20th-century American Rabbi David Stavsky pointed out in his book of sermons that every time we say the word *Amen*, we are not only affirming our agreement, but we are actually saying "I trust in you, God."

Rabbi David Stavsky (1929–2004)

73:1 A Psalm of Asaf *Asaf* is mentioned in *Sefer Divrei Hayamim* I (15:16–17) as one of the *Leviim* whom *David* appointed to sing in the *Beit Hamikdash*, and he is the author of the next ten psalms. In this psalm, he contrasts the suffering of the righteous in this world with

Tehillim/Psalms
Chapter 73

תהלים
פרק עג

2 As for me, my feet had almost strayed, my steps were nearly led off course,

ב וַאֲנִי כִּמְעַט נָטוּי [נָטָיוּ] רַגְלָי כְּאַיִן שֻׁפְּכָה [שֻׁפְּכוּ] אֲשֻׁרָי:

3 for I envied the wanton; I saw the wicked at ease.

ג כִּי־קִנֵּאתִי בַּהוֹלְלִים שְׁלוֹם רְשָׁעִים אֶרְאֶה:

4 Death has no pangs for them; their body is healthy.

ד כִּי אֵין חַרְצֻבּוֹת לְמוֹתָם וּבָרִיא אוּלָם:

5 They have no part in the travail of men; they are not afflicted like the rest of mankind.

ה בַּעֲמַל אֱנוֹשׁ אֵינֵמוֹ וְעִם־אָדָם לֹא יְנֻגָּעוּ:

6 So pride adorns their necks, lawlessness enwraps them as a mantle.

ו לָכֵן עֲנָקַתְמוֹ גַאֲוָה יַעֲטָף־שִׁית חָמָס לָמוֹ:

7 Fat shuts out their eyes; their fancies are extravagant.

ז יָצָא מֵחֵלֶב עֵינֵמוֹ עָבְרוּ מַשְׂכִּיּוֹת לֵבָב:

8 They scoff and plan evil; from their eminence they plan wrongdoing.

ח יָמִיקוּ וִידַבְּרוּ בְרָע עֹשֶׁק מִמָּרוֹם יְדַבֵּרוּ:

9 They set their mouths against heaven, and their tongues range over the earth.

ט שַׁתּוּ בַשָּׁמַיִם פִּיהֶם וּלְשׁוֹנָם תִּהֲלַךְ בָּאָרֶץ:

10 So they pound His people again and again, until they are drained of their very last tear.

י לָכֵן יָשִׁיב [יָשׁוּב] עַמּוֹ הֲלֹם וּמֵי מָלֵא יִמָּצוּ לָמוֹ:

11 Then they say, "How could *Hashem* know? Is there knowledge with the Most High?"

יא וְאָמְרוּ אֵיכָה יָדַע־אֵל וְיֵשׁ דֵּעָה בְעֶלְיוֹן:

12 Such are the wicked; ever tranquil, they amass wealth.

יב הִנֵּה־אֵלֶּה רְשָׁעִים וְשַׁלְוֵי עוֹלָם הִשְׂגּוּ־חָיִל:

13 It was for nothing that I kept my heart pure and washed my hands in innocence,

יג אַךְ־רִיק זִכִּיתִי לְבָבִי וָאֶרְחַץ בְּנִקָּיוֹן כַּפָּי:

14 seeing that I have been constantly afflicted, that each morning brings new punishments.

יד וָאֱהִי נָגוּעַ כָּל־הַיּוֹם וְתוֹכַחְתִּי לַבְּקָרִים:

15 Had I decided to say these things, I should have been false to the circle of Your disciples.

טו אִם־אָמַרְתִּי אֲסַפְּרָה כְמוֹ הִנֵּה דוֹר בָּנֶיךָ בָגָדְתִּי:

16 So I applied myself to understand this, but it seemed a hopeless task

טז וָאֲחַשְּׁבָה לָדַעַת זֹאת עָמָל הִיא [הוּא] בְעֵינָי:

17 till I entered *Hashem*'s sanctuary and reflected on their fate.

יז עַד־אָבוֹא אֶל־מִקְדְּשֵׁי־אֵל אָבִינָה לְאַחֲרִיתָם:

the success of the wicked, and notes that the wicked are "at ease" (verse 3) though he experiences difficult times. The way *Asaf* begins the psalm, however, is most significant. He speaks of *Hashem*'s greatness and his belief that God rewards His servants with good: "*Hashem* is truly good to *Yisrael*, to those whose heart is pure." The question of theodicy is as old as time. Though *Asaf* struggles with the fact that his enemies rejoice, relax and persevere while he has been "constantly afflicted" (verse 14), he nevertheless begins with an acknowledgment that ultimately, what the Lord does to His faithful servants is good, even if the benefit is not immediately obvious. In the meantime, *Asaf* concludes that although he suffers, just being close to the Lord is good, as he states "nearness to *Hashem* is good" (verse 28).

Tehillim/Psalms
Chapter 74

18 You surround them with flattery; You make them fall through blandishments.

אַךְ בַּחֲלָקוֹת תָּשִׁית לָמוֹ הִפַּלְתָּם לְמַשּׁוּאוֹת׃

19 How suddenly are they ruined, wholly swept away by terrors.

אֵיךְ הָיוּ לְשַׁמָּה כְרָגַע סָפוּ תַמּוּ מִן־בַּלָּהוֹת׃

20 When You are aroused You despise their image, as one does a dream after waking, O *Hashem*.

כַּחֲלוֹם מֵהָקִיץ אֲדֹנָי בָּעִיר צַלְמָם תִּבְזֶה׃

21 My mind was stripped of its reason, my feelings were numbed.

כִּי יִתְחַמֵּץ לְבָבִי וְכִלְיוֹתַי אֶשְׁתּוֹנָן׃

22 I was a dolt, without knowledge; I was brutish toward You.

וַאֲנִי־בַעַר וְלֹא אֵדָע בְּהֵמוֹת הָיִיתִי עִמָּךְ׃

23 Yet I was always with You, You held my right hand;

וַאֲנִי תָמִיד עִמָּךְ אָחַזְתָּ בְּיַד־יְמִינִי׃

24 You guided me by Your counsel and led me toward honor.

בַּעֲצָתְךָ תַנְחֵנִי וְאַחַר כָּבוֹד תִּקָּחֵנִי׃

25 Whom else have I in heaven? And having You, I want no one on earth.

מִי־לִי בַשָּׁמָיִם וְעִמְּךָ לֹא־חָפַצְתִּי בָאָרֶץ׃

26 My body and mind fail; but *Hashem* is the stay of my mind, my portion forever.

כָּלָה שְׁאֵרִי וּלְבָבִי צוּר־לְבָבִי וְחֶלְקִי אֱלֹהִים לְעוֹלָם׃

27 Those who keep far from You perish; You annihilate all who are untrue to You.

כִּי־הִנֵּה רְחֵקֶיךָ יֹאבֵדוּ הִצְמַתָּה כָּל־זוֹנֶה מִמֶּךָּ׃

28 As for me, nearness to *Hashem* is good; I have made *Hashem* my refuge, that I may recount all Your works.

וַאֲנִי קִרֲבַת אֱלֹהִים לִי־טוֹב שַׁתִּי בַּאדֹנָי יְהוִֹה מַחְסִי לְסַפֵּר כָּל־מַלְאֲכוֹתֶיךָ׃

74

1 A *maskil* of *Asaf*. Why, O *Hashem*, do You forever reject us, do You fume in anger at the flock that You tend?

מַשְׂכִּיל לְאָסָף לָמָה אֱלֹהִים זָנַחְתָּ לָנֶצַח יֶעְשַׁן אַפְּךָ בְּצֹאן מַרְעִיתֶךָ׃

mas-KEEL l'-a-SAF LA-mah e-lo-HEEM za-NAKH-ta la-NE-tzakh ye-SHAN a-p'-KHA b'-TZON mar-ee-TE-kha

2 Remember the community You made Yours long ago, Your very own tribe that You redeemed, Mount *Tzion*, where You dwell.

זְכֹר עֲדָתְךָ קָנִיתָ קֶּדֶם גָּאַלְתָּ שֵׁבֶט נַחֲלָתֶךָ הַר־צִיּוֹן זֶה שָׁכַנְתָּ בּוֹ׃

3 Bestir Yourself because of the perpetual tumult, all the outrages of the enemy in the sanctuary.

הָרִימָה פְעָמֶיךָ לְמַשֻּׁאוֹת נֶצַח כָּל־הֵרַע אוֹיֵב בַּקֹּדֶשׁ׃

74:1 Why, O *Hashem*, do You forever reject us
Amos Hakham, a modern Israeli Bible scholar and author of the contemporary *Daat Mikra* commentary on *Sefer Tehillim*, sees this chapter as an elegy over the destruction of the first *Beit Hamikdash*. The language is reminiscent of *Yirmiyahu's Megillat Eicha* (see Lamentations 5:20), and verse 2 calls on *Hashem* to remember "Mount *Tzion*, where you dwell." This implies that something disastrous happened there, possibly referring to the rampage of Nebuchadnezzar in 586 BCE. Furthermore, verses 3 and 7 refer to evil done in the sanctuary as well as the sanctuary being set on fire. The psalmist calls out to God in pain, "Why, O *Hashem*, do You forever reject us?" The picture of *Yerushalayim* in ruins was too much for the Israelites to behold, especially after having witnessed the splendor of King *Shlomo's Beit Hamikdash*.

Tehillim/Psalms
Chapter 74

4 Your foes roar inside Your meeting-place; they take their signs for true signs.

5 It is like men wielding axes against a gnarled tree;

6 with hatchet and pike they hacked away at its carved work.

7 They made Your sanctuary go up in flames; they brought low in dishonor the dwelling-place of Your presence.

8 They resolved, "Let us destroy them altogether!" They burned all *Hashem*'s *Mishkan*s in the land.

9 No signs appear for us; there is no longer any *Navi*; no one among us knows for how long.

10 Till when, O *Hashem*, will the foe blaspheme, will the enemy forever revile Your name?

11 Why do You hold back Your hand, Your right hand? Draw it out of Your bosom!

12 O *Hashem*, my King from of old, who brings deliverance throughout the land;

13 it was You who drove back the sea with Your might, who smashed the heads of the monsters in the waters;

14 it was You who crushed the heads of Leviathan, who left him as food for the denizens of the desert;

15 it was You who released springs and torrents, who made mighty rivers run dry;

16 the day is Yours, the night also; it was You who set in place the orb of the sun;

17 You fixed all the boundaries of the earth; summer and winter – You made them.

18 Be mindful of how the enemy blasphemes *Hashem*, how base people revile Your name.

19 Do not deliver Your dove to the wild beast; do not ignore forever the band of Your lowly ones.

20 Look to the covenant! For the dark places of the land are full of the haunts of lawlessness.

21 Let not the downtrodden turn away disappointed; let the poor and needy praise Your name.

תהלים
פרק עד

ד שָׁאֲגוּ צֹרְרֶיךָ בְּקֶרֶב מוֹעֲדֶךָ שָׂמוּ אוֹתֹתָם אֹתוֹת:

ה יִוָּדַע כְּמֵבִיא לְמָעְלָה בִּסְבָךְ־עֵץ קַרְדֻּמּוֹת:

ו ועת [וְעַתָּה] פִּתּוּחֶיהָ יָּחַד בְּכַשִּׁיל וְכֵילַפֹּת יַהֲלֹמוּן:

ז שִׁלְחוּ בָאֵשׁ מִקְדָּשֶׁךָ לָאָרֶץ חִלְּלוּ מִשְׁכַּן־שְׁמֶךָ:

ח אָמְרוּ בְלִבָּם נִינָם יָחַד שָׂרְפוּ כָל־מוֹעֲדֵי־אֵל בָּאָרֶץ:

ט אוֹתֹתֵינוּ לֹא רָאִינוּ אֵין־עוֹד נָבִיא וְלֹא־אִתָּנוּ יֹדֵעַ עַד־מָה:

י עַד־מָתַי אֱלֹהִים יְחָרֶף צָר יְנָאֵץ אוֹיֵב שִׁמְךָ לָנֶצַח:

יא לָמָּה תָשִׁיב יָדְךָ וִימִינֶךָ מִקֶּרֶב חוקך [חֵיקְךָ] כַלֵּה:

יב וֵאלֹהִים מַלְכִּי מִקֶּדֶם פֹּעֵל יְשׁוּעוֹת בְּקֶרֶב הָאָרֶץ:

יג אַתָּה פוֹרַרְתָּ בְעָזְּךָ יָם שִׁבַּרְתָּ רָאשֵׁי תַנִּינִים עַל־הַמָּיִם:

יד אַתָּה רִצַּצְתָּ רָאשֵׁי לִוְיָתָן תִּתְּנֶנּוּ מַאֲכָל לְעָם לְצִיִּים:

טו אַתָּה בָקַעְתָּ מַעְיָן וָנָחַל אַתָּה הוֹבַשְׁתָּ נַהֲרוֹת אֵיתָן:

טז לְךָ יוֹם אַף־לְךָ לָיְלָה אַתָּה הֲכִינוֹתָ מָאוֹר וָשָׁמֶשׁ:

יז אַתָּה הִצַּבְתָּ כָּל־גְּבוּלוֹת אָרֶץ קַיִץ וָחֹרֶף אַתָּה יְצַרְתָּם:

יח זְכָר־זֹאת אוֹיֵב חֵרֵף יְהֹוָה וְעַם נָבָל נִאֲצוּ שְׁמֶךָ:

יט אַל־תִּתֵּן לְחַיַּת נֶפֶשׁ תּוֹרֶךָ חַיַּת עֲנִיֶּיךָ אַל־תִּשְׁכַּח לָנֶצַח:

כ הַבֵּט לַבְּרִית כִּי מָלְאוּ מַחֲשַׁכֵּי־אֶרֶץ נְאוֹת חָמָס:

כא אַל־יָשֹׁב דַּךְ נִכְלָם עָנִי וְאֶבְיוֹן יְהַלְלוּ שְׁמֶךָ:

Tehillim/Psalms
Chapter 75

תהלים
פרק עה

22 Rise, O *Hashem*, Champion Your cause; be mindful that You are blasphemed by base men all day long.

כב קוּמָה אֱלֹהִים רִיבָה רִיבֶךָ זְכֹר חֶרְפָּתְךָ מִנִּי־נָבָל כָּל־הַיּוֹם:

23 Do not ignore the shouts of Your foes, the din of Your adversaries that ascends all the time.

כג אַל־תִּשְׁכַּח קוֹל צֹרְרֶיךָ שְׁאוֹן קָמֶיךָ עֹלֶה תָמִיד:

75 1 For the leader; *al tashcheth*. A psalm of *Asaf*, a song.

עה א לַמְנַצֵּחַ אַל־תַּשְׁחֵת מִזְמוֹר לְאָסָף שִׁיר:

2 We praise You, O *Hashem*; we praise You; Your presence is near; men tell of Your wondrous deeds.

ב הוֹדִינוּ לְּךָ אֱלֹהִים הוֹדִינוּ וְקָרוֹב שְׁמֶךָ סִפְּרוּ נִפְלְאוֹתֶיךָ:

3 "At the time I choose, I will give judgment equitably.

ג כִּי אֶקַּח מוֹעֵד אֲנִי מֵישָׁרִים אֶשְׁפֹּט:

4 Earth and all its inhabitants dissolve; it is I who keep its pillars firm. *Selah*.

ד נְמֹגִים אֶרֶץ וְכָל־יֹשְׁבֶיהָ אָנֹכִי תִכַּנְתִּי עַמּוּדֶיהָ סֶּלָה:

5 To wanton men I say, 'Do not be wanton!' to the wicked, 'Do not lift up your horns!'"

ה אָמַרְתִּי לַהוֹלְלִים אַל־תָּהֹלּוּ וְלָרְשָׁעִים אַל־תָּרִימוּ קָרֶן:

6 Do not lift your horns up high in vainglorious bluster.

ו אַל־תָּרִימוּ לַמָּרוֹם קַרְנְכֶם תְּדַבְּרוּ בְצַוָּאר עָתָק:

7 For what lifts a man comes not from the east or the west or the wilderness;

ז כִּי לֹא מִמּוֹצָא וּמִמַּעֲרָב וְלֹא מִמִּדְבַּר הָרִים:

KEE LO mi-mo-TZA u-mi-ma-a-RAV v'-LO mid-BAR ha-REEM

8 for *Hashem* it is who gives judgment; He brings down one man, He lifts up another.

ח כִּי־אֱלֹהִים שֹׁפֵט זֶה יַשְׁפִּיל וְזֶה יָרִים:

9 There is a cup in *Hashem*'s hand with foaming wine fully mixed; from this He pours; all the wicked of the earth drink, draining it to the very dregs.

ט כִּי כוֹס בְּיַד־יְהֹוָה וְיַיִן חָמַר מָלֵא מֶסֶךְ וַיַּגֵּר מִזֶּה אַךְ־שְׁמָרֶיהָ יִמְצוּ יִשְׁתּוּ כֹּל רִשְׁעֵי־אָרֶץ:

10 As for me, I will declare forever, I will sing a hymn to the God of *Yaakov*.

י וַאֲנִי אַגִּיד לְעֹלָם אֲזַמְּרָה לֵאלֹהֵי יַעֲקֹב:

11 "All the horns of the wicked I will cut; but the horns of the righteous shall be lifted up."

יא וְכָל־קַרְנֵי רְשָׁעִים אֲגַדֵּעַ תְּרוֹמַמְנָה קַרְנוֹת צַדִּיק:

א 75:7 For what lifts a man comes not from the east or the west The psalmist addresses the wealthy, telling them that they should not think their riches result from their own doing. Rather, *Hashem* alone "brings down one man, He lifts up another" (verse 8). In this context, the psalmist tells the affluent not to look to the east or west for the source of their prosperity, and ends with the words *v'lo mimidbar harim* (ולא ממדבר הרים). Commentators struggle to understand this expression. One explanation places a comma between *midbar*, 'wilderness,' and *harim*, 'mountains,' using them as geographical poles, similar to east and west. Based on this interpretation the verse means 'your wealth does not come from the east or west, nor does it come from the desert or the mountains.' A second interpretation understands the word *harim* as a verb meaning 'to lift up.' According to this explanation, the verse means 'not from east or west, nor from the desert will you be lifted up (i.e. become wealthy).' Regardless of the precise interpretation of the phrase, its message is to recognize that *Hashem* is the one who provides bounty and wealth.

1560

Tehillim/Psalms
Chapter 76

76 1 For the leader; with instrumental music. A psalm of *Asaf*, a song.

2 *Hashem* has made Himself known in *Yehuda*, His name is great in *Yisrael*;

no-DA bee-hu-DAH e-lo-HEEM b'-yis-ra-AYL ga-DOL sh'-MO

3 *Shalem* became His abode; *Tzion*, His den.

4 There He broke the fiery arrows of the bow, the shield and the sword of war. *Selah*.

5 You were resplendent, glorious, on the mountains of prey.

6 The stout-hearted were despoiled; they were in a stupor; the bravest of men could not lift a hand.

7 At Your blast, O God of *Yaakov*, horse and chariot lay stunned.

8 O You! You are awesome! Who can withstand You when You are enraged?

9 In heaven You pronounced sentence; the earth was numbed with fright

10 as *Hashem* rose to execute judgment, to deliver all the lowly of the earth. *Selah*.

11 The fiercest of men shall acknowledge You, when You gird on the last bit of fury.

12 Make vows and pay them to *Hashem* your God; all who are around Him shall bring tribute to the Awesome One.

13 He curbs the spirit of princes, inspires awe in the kings of the earth.

תהילים
פרק עו

עו א לַמְנַצֵּחַ בִּנְגִינֹת מִזְמוֹר לְאָסָף שִׁיר׃

ב נוֹדָע בִּיהוּדָה אֱלֹהִים בְּיִשְׂרָאֵל גָּדוֹל שְׁמוֹ׃

ג וַיְהִי בְשָׁלֵם סֻכּוֹ וּמְעוֹנָתוֹ בְצִיּוֹן׃

ד שָׁמָּה שִׁבַּר רִשְׁפֵי־קָשֶׁת מָגֵן וְחֶרֶב וּמִלְחָמָה סֶלָה׃

ה נָאוֹר אַתָּה אַדִּיר מֵהַרְרֵי־טָרֶף׃

ו אֶשְׁתּוֹלְלוּ אַבִּירֵי לֵב נָמוּ שְׁנָתָם וְלֹא־מָצְאוּ כָל־אַנְשֵׁי־חַיִל יְדֵיהֶם׃

ז מִגַּעֲרָתְךָ אֱלֹהֵי יַעֲקֹב נִרְדָּם וְרֶכֶב וָסוּס׃

ח אַתָּה נוֹרָא אַתָּה וּמִי־יַעֲמֹד לְפָנֶיךָ מֵאָז אַפֶּךָ׃

ט מִשָּׁמַיִם הִשְׁמַעְתָּ דִּין אֶרֶץ יָרְאָה וְשָׁקָטָה׃

י בְּקוּם־לַמִּשְׁפָּט אֱלֹהִים לְהוֹשִׁיעַ כָּל־עַנְוֵי־אֶרֶץ סֶלָה׃

יא כִּי־חֲמַת אָדָם תּוֹדֶךָּ שְׁאֵרִית חֵמֹת תַּחְגֹּר׃

יב נִדְרוּ וְשַׁלְּמוּ לַיהוָה אֱלֹהֵיכֶם כָּל־סְבִיבָיו יוֹבִילוּ שַׁי לַמּוֹרָא׃

יג יִבְצֹר רוּחַ נְגִידִים נוֹרָא לְמַלְכֵי־אָרֶץ׃

76:2 His name is great in *Yisrael* This psalm is a song of praise to *Hashem* for saving the Nation of Israel from its enemies. Though it is unclear to which specific battle this psalm refers, contemporary author Amos Hakham points to the Septuagint, which adds the words "regarding the Assyrian" into the title of the psalm. This certainly refers to the battle recorded in *Sefer Melachim* II (18–19), which took place in the eighth century BCE between Sennacherib, king of Assyria, and the kingdom of *Yehuda* under the leadership of King *Chizkiyahu*. Assyria had conquered Mesopotamia and the ten tribes of *Yisrael*, dispersing them throughout his empire. Their emissaries stood at the gates of *Yerushalayim* and warned *Chizkiyahu* of impending doom. The prophet *Yeshayahu* assured the king that God would bring salvation to *Yehuda* and protect them from harm. Miraculously, Sennacherib's army mysteriously died overnight and the Assyrians returned home without conquering *Yerushalayim*. This might explain the statement "*Hashem* has made Himself known in *Yehuda*," since as a result of this incident, all kingdoms heard that *Hashem* battles on behalf of *Yehuda* and *Yerushalayim*. God is known to be in *Yehuda*.

Tehillim/Psalms
Chapter 77

תהלים
פרק עז

77 1 For the leader; on *Yedutun*. Of *Asaf*. A psalm.

א לַמְנַצֵּחַ עַל־יְדִיתוּן [יְדוּתוּן] לְאָסָף מִזְמוֹר:

2 I cry aloud to *Hashem*; I cry to *Hashem* that He may give ear to me.

ב קוֹלִי אֶל־אֱלֹהִים וְאֶצְעָקָה קוֹלִי אֶל־אֱלֹהִים וְהַאֲזִין אֵלָי:

3 In my time of distress I turn to *Hashem*, with my hand [uplifted]; [my eyes] flow all night without respite; I will not be comforted.

ג בְּיוֹם צָרָתִי אֲדֹנָי דָּרָשְׁתִּי יָדִי לַיְלָה נִגְּרָה וְלֹא תָפוּג מֵאֲנָה הִנָּחֵם נַפְשִׁי:

4 I call *Hashem* to mind, I moan, I complain, my spirit fails. *Selah*.

ד אֶזְכְּרָה אֱלֹהִים וְאֶהֱמָיָה אָשִׂיחָה וְתִתְעַטֵּף רוּחִי סֶלָה:

5 You have held my eyelids open; I am overwrought, I cannot speak.

ה אָחַזְתָּ שְׁמֻרוֹת עֵינָי נִפְעַמְתִּי וְלֹא אֲדַבֵּר:

6 My thoughts turn to days of old, to years long past.

ו חִשַּׁבְתִּי יָמִים מִקֶּדֶם שְׁנוֹת עוֹלָמִים:

7 I recall at night their jibes at me; I commune with myself; my spirit inquires,

ז אֶזְכְּרָה נְגִינָתִי בַּלָּיְלָה עִם־לְבָבִי אָשִׂיחָה וַיְחַפֵּשׂ רוּחִי:

8 "Will *Hashem* reject forever and never again show favor?

ח הַלְעוֹלָמִים יִזְנַח אֲדֹנָי וְלֹא־יֹסִיף לִרְצוֹת עוֹד:

9 Has His faithfulness disappeared forever? Will His promise be unfulfilled for all time?

ט הֶאָפֵס לָנֶצַח חַסְדּוֹ גָּמַר אֹמֶר לְדֹר וָדֹר:

10 Has *Hashem* forgotten how to pity? Has He in anger stifled His compassion?" *Selah*.

י הֲשָׁכַח חַנּוֹת אֵל אִם־קָפַץ בְּאַף רַחֲמָיו סֶלָה:

11 And I said, "It is my fault that the right hand of the Most High has changed."

יא וָאֹמַר חַלּוֹתִי הִיא שְׁנוֹת יְמִין עֶלְיוֹן:

12 I recall the deeds of *Hashem*; yes, I recall Your wonders of old;

יב אַזְכִּיר [אֶזְכּוֹר] מַעַלְלֵי־יָהּ כִּי־אֶזְכְּרָה מִקֶּדֶם פִּלְאֶךָ:

13 I recount all Your works; I speak of Your acts.

יג וְהָגִיתִי בְכָל־פָּעֳלֶךָ וּבַעֲלִילוֹתֶיךָ אָשִׂיחָה:

14 O *Hashem*, Your ways are holiness; what god is as great as *Hashem*?

יד אֱלֹהִים בַּקֹּדֶשׁ דַּרְכֶּךָ מִי־אֵל גָּדוֹל כֵּאלֹהִים:

15 You are the God who works wonders; You have manifested Your strength among the peoples.

טו אַתָּה הָאֵל עֹשֵׂה פֶלֶא הוֹדַעְתָּ בָעַמִּים עֻזֶּךָ:

16 By Your arm You redeemed Your people, the children of *Yaakov* and *Yosef*. *Selah*.

טז גָּאַלְתָּ בִּזְרוֹעַ עַמֶּךָ בְּנֵי־יַעֲקֹב וְיוֹסֵף סֶלָה:

17 The waters saw You, O *Hashem*, the waters saw You and were convulsed; the very deep quaked as well.

יז רָאוּךָ מַּיִם אֱלֹהִים רָאוּךָ מַּיִם יָחִילוּ אַף יִרְגְּזוּ תְהֹמוֹת:

18 Clouds streamed water; the heavens rumbled; Your arrows flew about;

יח זֹרְמוּ מַיִם עָבוֹת קוֹל נָתְנוּ שְׁחָקִים אַף־חֲצָצֶיךָ יִתְהַלָּכוּ:

Tehillim/Psalms
Chapter 78

19 Your thunder rumbled like wheels; lightning lit up the world; the earth quaked and trembled.

KOL ra-am-KHA ba-gal-GAL hay-EE-ru v'-ra-KEEM tay-VAYL ra-g'-ZAH va-tir-ASH ha-A-retz

20 Your way was through the sea, Your path, through the mighty waters; Your tracks could not be seen.

21 You led Your people like a flock in the care of *Moshe* and *Aharon*.

78 1 A *maskil* of *Asaf*. Give ear, my people, to my teaching, turn your ear to what I say.

2 I will expound a theme, hold forth on the lessons of the past,

3 things we have heard and known, that our fathers have told us.

4 We will not withhold them from their children, telling the coming generation the praises of *Hashem* and His might, and the wonders He performed.

5 He established a decree in *Yaakov*, ordained a teaching in *Yisrael*, charging our fathers to make them known to their children,

6 that a future generation might know – children yet to be born – and in turn tell their children

7 that they might put their confidence in *Hashem*, and not forget *Hashem*'s great deeds, but observe His commandments,

8 and not be like their fathers, a wayward and defiant generation, a generation whose heart was inconstant, whose spirit was not true to *Hashem*.

77:19 Your thunder rumbled like wheels In our day-to-day lives, we rely on the predictable laws of nature, such as the rising and setting of the sun. In His great kindness, God wanted us to be able to regulate our lives, and therefore He gave us a system that we can depend on. But in spite of the apparently predictable laws of nature, in reality *Hashem* is orchestrating everything directly, behind the scenes. This can be demonstrated by His control over nature during the exodus from Egypt and the splitting of the sea. This is not only true about nature, but about everything that happens in this world. As much as we try to control our lives, our efforts are overshadowed by the divine will that invariably makes the final decision. There is no place where this truth is more apparent than in the Land of Israel. *Hashem* reminds us in *Sefer Devarim* (11:10), "For the land that you are about to enter and possess is not like the land of Egypt from which you have come. There the grain you sowed had to be watered by your own labors, like a vegetable garden." The fact that *Eretz Yisrael* is dependent upon the rainfall for its survival ensures that its citizens live with the constant reminder that they are dependent on God for their sustenance and livelihood.

Tehillim/Psalms
Chapter 78

תהלים
פרק עח

9 Like the Ephraimite bowmen who played false in the day of battle,

ט בְּנֵי־אֶפְרַיִם נוֹשְׁקֵי רוֹמֵי־קָשֶׁת הָפְכוּ בְּיוֹם קְרָב:

10 they did not keep *Hashem*'s covenant, they refused to follow His instruction;

י לֹא שָׁמְרוּ בְּרִית אֱלֹהִים וּבְתוֹרָתוֹ מֵאֲנוּ לָלֶכֶת:

11 they forgot His deeds and the wonders that He showed them.

יא וַיִּשְׁכְּחוּ עֲלִילוֹתָיו וְנִפְלְאוֹתָיו אֲשֶׁר הֶרְאָם:

12 He performed marvels in the sight of their fathers, in the land of Egypt, the plain of Zoan.

יב נֶגֶד אֲבוֹתָם עָשָׂה פֶלֶא בְּאֶרֶץ מִצְרַיִם שְׂדֵה־צֹעַן:

13 He split the sea and took them through it; He made the waters stand like a wall.

יג בָּקַע יָם וַיַּעֲבִירֵם וַיַּצֶּב־מַיִם כְּמוֹ־נֵד:

14 He led them with a cloud by day, and throughout the night by the light of fire.

יד וַיַּנְחֵם בֶּעָנָן יוֹמָם וְכָל־הַלַּיְלָה בְּאוֹר אֵשׁ:

15 He split rocks in the wilderness and gave them drink as if from the great deep.

טו יְבַקַּע צֻרִים בַּמִּדְבָּר וַיַּשְׁקְ כִּתְהֹמוֹת רַבָּה:

16 He brought forth streams from a rock and made them flow down like a river.

טז וַיּוֹצִא נוֹזְלִים מִסָּלַע וַיּוֹרֶד כַּנְּהָרוֹת מָיִם:

17 But they went on sinning against Him, defying the Most High in the parched land.

יז וַיּוֹסִיפוּ עוֹד לַחֲטֹא־לוֹ לַמְרוֹת עֶלְיוֹן בַּצִּיָּה:

18 To test *Hashem* was in their mind when they demanded food for themselves.

יח וַיְנַסּוּ־אֵל בִּלְבָבָם לִשְׁאָל־אֹכֶל לְנַפְשָׁם:

19 They spoke against *Hashem*, saying, "Can *Hashem* spread a feast in the wilderness?

יט וַיְדַבְּרוּ בֵּאלֹהִים אָמְרוּ הֲיוּכַל אֵל לַעֲרֹךְ שֻׁלְחָן בַּמִּדְבָּר:

20 True, He struck the rock and waters flowed, streams gushed forth; but can He provide bread? Can He supply His people with meat?"

כ הֵן הִכָּה־צוּר וַיָּזוּבוּ מַיִם וּנְחָלִים יִשְׁטֹפוּ הֲגַם־לֶחֶם יוּכַל תֵּת אִם־יָכִין שְׁאֵר לְעַמּוֹ:

21 *Hashem* heard and He raged; fire broke out against *Yaakov*, anger flared up at *Yisrael*,

כא לָכֵן שָׁמַע יְהוָה וַיִּתְעַבָּר וְאֵשׁ נִשְּׂקָה בְיַעֲקֹב וְגַם־אַף עָלָה בְיִשְׂרָאֵל:

22 because they did not put their trust in *Hashem*, did not rely on His deliverance.

כב כִּי לֹא הֶאֱמִינוּ בֵּאלֹהִים וְלֹא בָטְחוּ בִּישׁוּעָתוֹ:

23 So He commanded the skies above, He opened the doors of heaven

כג וַיְצַו שְׁחָקִים מִמָּעַל וְדַלְתֵי שָׁמַיִם פָּתָח:

24 and rained manna upon them for food, giving them heavenly grain.

כד וַיַּמְטֵר עֲלֵיהֶם מָן לֶאֱכֹל וּדְגַן־שָׁמַיִם נָתַן לָמוֹ:

25 Each man ate a hero's meal; He sent them provision in plenty.

כה לֶחֶם אַבִּירִים אָכַל אִישׁ צֵידָה שָׁלַח לָהֶם לָשֹׂבַע:

26 He set the east wind moving in heaven, and drove the south wind by His might.

כו יַסַּע קָדִים בַּשָּׁמָיִם וַיְנַהֵג בְּעֻזּוֹ תֵימָן:

27 He rained meat on them like dust, winged birds like the sands of the sea,

כז וַיַּמְטֵר עֲלֵיהֶם כֶּעָפָר שְׁאֵר וּכְחוֹל יַמִּים עוֹף כָּנָף:

Tehillim/Psalms
Chapter 78

28 making them come down inside His camp, around His dwelling-place.

29 They ate till they were sated; He gave them what they craved.

30 They had not yet wearied of what they craved, the food was still in their mouths

31 when *Hashem*'s anger flared up at them. He slew their sturdiest, struck down the youth of *Yisrael*.

32 Nonetheless, they went on sinning and had no faith in His wonders.

33 He made their days end in futility, their years in sudden death.

34 When He struck them, they turned to Him and sought *Hashem* once again.

35 They remembered that *Hashem* was their rock, *Hashem* Most High, their Redeemer.

36 Yet they deceived Him with their speech, lied to Him with their words;

37 their hearts were inconstant toward Him; they were untrue to His covenant.

38 But He, being merciful, forgave iniquity and would not destroy; He restrained His wrath time and again and did not give full vent to His fury;

39 for He remembered that they were but flesh, a passing breath that does not return.

40 How often did they defy Him in the wilderness, did they grieve Him in the wasteland!

41 Again and again they tested *Hashem*, vexed the Holy One of *Yisrael*.

42 They did not remember His strength, or the day He redeemed them from the foe;

43 how He displayed His signs in Egypt, His wonders in the plain of Zoan.

44 He turned their rivers into blood; He made their waters undrinkable.

45 He inflicted upon them swarms of insects to devour them, frogs to destroy them.

46 He gave their crops over to grubs, their produce to locusts.

תהלים
פרק עח

כח וַיַּפֵּל בְּקֶרֶב מַחֲנֵהוּ סָבִיב לְמִשְׁכְּנֹתָיו:

כט וַיֹּאכְלוּ וַיִּשְׂבְּעוּ מְאֹד וְתַאֲוָתָם יָבִא לָהֶם:

ל לֹא־זָרוּ מִתַּאֲוָתָם עוֹד אָכְלָם בְּפִיהֶם:

לא וְאַף אֱלֹהִים עָלָה בָהֶם וַיַּהֲרֹג בְּמִשְׁמַנֵּיהֶם וּבַחוּרֵי יִשְׂרָאֵל הִכְרִיעַ:

לב בְּכָל־זֹאת חָטְאוּ־עוֹד וְלֹא־הֶאֱמִינוּ בְּנִפְלְאוֹתָיו:

לג וַיְכַל־בַּהֶבֶל יְמֵיהֶם וּשְׁנוֹתָם בַּבֶּהָלָה:

לד אִם־הֲרָגָם וּדְרָשׁוּהוּ וְשָׁבוּ וְשִׁחֲרוּ־אֵל:

לה וַיִּזְכְּרוּ כִּי־אֱלֹהִים צוּרָם וְאֵל עֶלְיוֹן גֹּאֲלָם:

לו וַיְפַתּוּהוּ בְּפִיהֶם וּבִלְשׁוֹנָם יְכַזְּבוּ־לוֹ:

לז וְלִבָּם לֹא־נָכוֹן עִמּוֹ וְלֹא נֶאֶמְנוּ בִּבְרִיתוֹ:

לח וְהוּא רַחוּם יְכַפֵּר עָוֹן וְלֹא־יַשְׁחִית וְהִרְבָּה לְהָשִׁיב אַפּוֹ וְלֹא־יָעִיר כָּל־חֲמָתוֹ:

לט וַיִּזְכֹּר כִּי־בָשָׂר הֵמָּה רוּחַ הוֹלֵךְ וְלֹא יָשׁוּב:

מ כַּמָּה יַמְרוּהוּ בַמִּדְבָּר יַעֲצִיבוּהוּ בִּישִׁימוֹן:

מא וַיָּשׁוּבוּ וַיְנַסּוּ אֵל וּקְדוֹשׁ יִשְׂרָאֵל הִתְווּ:

מב לֹא־זָכְרוּ אֶת־יָדוֹ יוֹם אֲשֶׁר־פָּדָם מִנִּי־צָר:

מג אֲשֶׁר־שָׂם בְּמִצְרַיִם אֹתוֹתָיו וּמוֹפְתָיו בִּשְׂדֵה־צֹעַן:

מד וַיַּהֲפֹךְ לְדָם יְאֹרֵיהֶם וְנֹזְלֵיהֶם בַּל־יִשְׁתָּיוּן:

מה יְשַׁלַּח בָּהֶם עָרֹב וַיֹּאכְלֵם וּצְפַרְדֵּעַ וַתַּשְׁחִיתֵם:

מו וַיִּתֵּן לֶחָסִיל יְבוּלָם וִיגִיעָם לָאַרְבֶּה:

1565

Tehillim/Psalms
Chapter 78

47	He killed their vines with hail, their sycamores with frost.	מז יַהֲרֹג בַּבָּרָד גַּפְנָם וְשִׁקְמוֹתָם בַּחֲנָמַל:
48	He gave their beasts over to hail, their cattle to lightning bolts.	מח וַיַּסְגֵּר לַבָּרָד בְּעִירָם וּמִקְנֵיהֶם לָרְשָׁפִים:
49	He inflicted His burning anger upon them, wrath, indignation, trouble, a band of deadly messengers.	מט יְשַׁלַּח־בָּם חֲרוֹן אַפּוֹ עֶבְרָה וָזַעַם וְצָרָה מִשְׁלַחַת מַלְאֲכֵי רָעִים:
50	He cleared a path for His anger; He did not stop short of slaying them, but gave them over to pestilence.	נ יְפַלֵּס נָתִיב לְאַפּוֹ לֹא־חָשַׂךְ מִמָּוֶת נַפְשָׁם וְחַיָּתָם לַדֶּבֶר הִסְגִּיר:
51	He struck every first-born in Egypt, the first fruits of their vigor in the tents of Ham.	נא וַיַּךְ כָּל־בְּכוֹר בְּמִצְרָיִם רֵאשִׁית אוֹנִים בְּאָהֳלֵי־חָם:
52	He set His people moving like sheep, drove them like a flock in the wilderness.	נב וַיַּסַּע כַּצֹּאן עַמּוֹ וַיְנַהֲגֵם כַּעֵדֶר בַּמִּדְבָּר:
53	He led them in safety; they were unafraid; as for their enemies, the sea covered them.	נג וַיַּנְחֵם לָבֶטַח וְלֹא פָחָדוּ וְאֶת־אוֹיְבֵיהֶם כִּסָּה הַיָּם:
54	He brought them to His holy realm the mountain His right hand had acquired.	נד וַיְבִיאֵם אֶל־גְּבוּל קָדְשׁוֹ הַר־זֶה קָנְתָה יְמִינוֹ:
55	He expelled nations before them, settled the tribes of *Yisrael* in their tents, allotting them their portion by the line.*	נה וַיְגָרֶשׁ מִפְּנֵיהֶם גּוֹיִם וַיַּפִּילֵם בְּחֶבֶל נַחֲלָה וַיַּשְׁכֵּן בְּאָהֳלֵיהֶם שִׁבְטֵי יִשְׂרָאֵל:
56	Yet they defiantly tested *Hashem* Most High, and did not observe His decrees.	נו וַיְנַסּוּ וַיַּמְרוּ אֶת־אֱלֹהִים עֶלְיוֹן וְעֵדוֹתָיו לֹא שָׁמָרוּ:
57	They fell away, disloyal like their fathers; they played false like a treacherous bow.	נז וַיִּסֹּגוּ וַיִּבְגְּדוּ כַּאֲבוֹתָם נֶהְפְּכוּ כְּקֶשֶׁת רְמִיָּה:
58	They vexed Him with their high places; they incensed Him with their idols.	נח וַיַּכְעִיסוּהוּ בְּבָמוֹתָם וּבִפְסִילֵיהֶם יַקְנִיאוּהוּ:
59	*Hashem* heard it and was enraged; He utterly rejected *Yisrael*.	נט שָׁמַע אֱלֹהִים וַיִּתְעַבָּר וַיִּמְאַס מְאֹד בְּיִשְׂרָאֵל:
60	He forsook the *Mishkan* of *Shilo*, the tent He had set among men.	ס וַיִּטֹּשׁ מִשְׁכַּן שִׁלוֹ אֹהֶל שִׁכֵּן בָּאָדָם:

va-yi-TOSH mish-KAN shi-LO O-hel shi-KAYN ba-a-DAM

---

* order of clauses inverted for clarity

78:60 The *Mishkan* of *Shilo* Psalm 78 rebukes the Nation of Israel with a history lesson. The psalmist reminds his audience about the days of old, to exhort them to follow *Hashem*'s commandments. Much of the psalm is dedicated to the plight of the Israelites in exile during the period of servitude in Egypt and afterwards in the desert. The rebuke continues with the period after Israel entered the Promised Land. There, as well, they provoked *Hashem* by following their hearts that led them astray. In response, God removed His presence from the *Mishkan* in *Shilo*. Due to the corruption of the priests and the ignorance of the populace, the Tabernacle was destroyed (see Samuel I 4), the Ark of the Covenant was taken in battle by the Philistines and the high priest, *Eli*, and his two sons died.

Tehillim/Psalms
Chapter 79

תהלים
פרק עט

61 He let His might go into captivity, His glory into the hands of the foe.

סא וַיִּתֵּן לַשְּׁבִי עֻזּוֹ וְתִפְאַרְתּוֹ בְיַד־צָר:

62 He gave His people over to the sword; He was enraged at His very own.

סב וַיַּסְגֵּר לַחֶרֶב עַמּוֹ וּבְנַחֲלָתוֹ הִתְעַבָּר:

63 Fire consumed their young men, and their maidens remained unwed.

סג בַּחוּרָיו אָכְלָה־אֵשׁ וּבְתוּלֹתָיו לֹא הוּלָּלוּ:

64 Their *Kohanim* fell by the sword, and their widows could not weep.

סד כֹּהֲנָיו בַּחֶרֶב נָפָלוּ וְאַלְמְנֹתָיו לֹא תִבְכֶּינָה:

65 *Hashem* awoke as from sleep, like a warrior shaking off wine.

סה וַיִּקַץ כְּיָשֵׁן אֲדֹנָי כְּגִבּוֹר מִתְרוֹנֵן מִיָּיִן:

66 He beat back His foes, dealing them lasting disgrace.

סו וַיַּךְ־צָרָיו אָחוֹר חֶרְפַּת עוֹלָם נָתַן לָמוֹ:

67 He rejected the clan of *Yosef*; He did not choose the tribe of *Efraim*.

סז וַיִּמְאַס בְּאֹהֶל יוֹסֵף וּבְשֵׁבֶט אֶפְרַיִם לֹא בָחָר:

68 He did choose the tribe of *Yehuda*, Mount *Tzion*, which He loved.

סח וַיִּבְחַר אֶת־שֵׁבֶט יְהוּדָה אֶת־הַר צִיּוֹן אֲשֶׁר אָהֵב:

69 He built His Sanctuary like the heavens, like the earth that He established forever.

סט וַיִּבֶן כְּמוֹ־רָמִים מִקְדָּשׁוֹ כְּאֶרֶץ יְסָדָהּ לְעוֹלָם:

70 He chose *David*, His servant, and took him from the sheepfolds.

ע וַיִּבְחַר בְּדָוִד עַבְדּוֹ וַיִּקָּחֵהוּ מִמִּכְלְאֹת צֹאן:

71 He brought him from minding the nursing ewes to tend His people *Yaakov*, *Yisrael*, His very own.

עא מֵאַחַר עָלוֹת הֱבִיאוֹ לִרְעוֹת בְּיַעֲקֹב עַמּוֹ וּבְיִשְׂרָאֵל נַחֲלָתוֹ:

72 He tended them with blameless heart; with skillful hands he led them.

עב וַיִּרְעֵם כְּתֹם לְבָבוֹ וּבִתְבוּנוֹת כַּפָּיו יַנְחֵם:

79 1 A psalm of *Asaf*. O *Hashem*, heathens have entered Your domain, defiled Your holy temple, and turned *Yerushalayim* into ruins.

עט א מִזְמוֹר לְאָסָף אֱלֹהִים בָּאוּ גוֹיִם בְּנַחֲלָתֶךָ טִמְּאוּ אֶת־הֵיכַל קָדְשֶׁךָ שָׂמוּ אֶת־יְרוּשָׁלַםִ לְעִיִּים:

miz-MOR l'-a-SAF e-lo-HEEM BA-u go-YIM b'-na-kha-la-TE-kha ti-m'-U et hay-KHAL kod-SHE-kha SA-mu et y'-ru-sha-LA-im l'-i-YEEM

79:1 Defiled Your holy temple In some Jewish communities, this psalm is recited on the ninth of the Hebrew month of *Av*, which is the saddest day of the year as it commemorates the destruction of the *Beit Hamikdash*. As *Yirmiyahu* does in *Megillat Eicha*, the psalmist laments the day when Nebuchadnezzar, king of Babylonia, and his general Nebuzaradan entered the city of *Yerushalayim*. Nebuchadnezzar and Nebuzaradan defiled and burned the *Beit Hamikdash*, destroyed the city, slaughtered many of its inhabitants and exiled the rest of the nation. This grave day has been etched into the consciousness of every Jew throughout history. The conclusion of the psalm is a plea for God's vengeance so that the nations of the world will know the true justice of *Hashem*, and His name will remain glorified in the world.

Tehillim/Psalms
Chapter 80

2 They have left Your servants' corpses as food for the fowl of heaven, and the flesh of Your faithful for the wild beasts.

3 Their blood was shed like water around *Yerushalayim*, with none to bury them.

4 We have become the butt of our neighbors, the scorn and derision of those around us.

5 How long, *Hashem*, will You be angry forever, will Your indignation blaze like fire?

6 Pour out Your fury on the nations that do not know You, upon the kingdoms that do not invoke Your name,

7 for they have devoured *Yaakov* and desolated his home.

8 Do not hold our former iniquities against us; let Your compassion come swiftly toward us, for we have sunk very low.

9 Help us, O *Hashem*, our deliverer, for the sake of the glory of Your name. Save us and forgive our sin, for the sake of Your name.

10 Let the nations not say, "Where is their God?" Before our eyes let it be known among the nations that You avenge the spilled blood of Your servants.

11 Let the groans of the prisoners reach You; reprieve those condemned to death, as befits Your great strength.

12 Pay back our neighbors sevenfold for the abuse they have flung at You, O *Hashem*.

13 Then we, Your people, the flock You shepherd, shall glorify You forever; for all time we shall tell Your praises.

80 1 For the leader; on shoshannim, eduth. Of *Asaf*. A psalm.

2 Give ear, O shepherd of *Yisrael* who leads *Yosef* like a flock! Appear, You who are enthroned on the cherubim,

3 at the head of *Efraim*, *Binyamin*, and *Menashe*! Rouse Your might and come to our help!

4 Restore us, O *Hashem*; show Your favor that we may be delivered.

ב נָתְנוּ אֶת־נִבְלַת עֲבָדֶיךָ מַאֲכָל לְעוֹף הַשָּׁמָיִם בְּשַׂר חֲסִידֶיךָ לְחַיְתוֹ־אָרֶץ׃

ג שָׁפְכוּ דָמָם כַּמַּיִם סְבִיבוֹת יְרוּשָׁלָ͏ִם וְאֵין קוֹבֵר׃

ד הָיִינוּ חֶרְפָּה לִשְׁכֵנֵינוּ לַעַג וָקֶלֶס לִסְבִיבוֹתֵינוּ׃

ה עַד־מָה יְהוָה תֶּאֱנַף לָנֶצַח תִּבְעַר כְּמוֹ־אֵשׁ קִנְאָתֶךָ׃

ו שְׁפֹךְ חֲמָתְךָ אֶל־הַגּוֹיִם אֲשֶׁר לֹא־יְדָעוּךָ וְעַל מַמְלָכוֹת אֲשֶׁר בְּשִׁמְךָ לֹא קָרָאוּ׃

ז כִּי אָכַל אֶת־יַעֲקֹב וְאֶת־נָוֵהוּ הֵשַׁמּוּ׃

ח אַל־תִּזְכָּר־לָנוּ עֲוֺנֹת רִאשֹׁנִים מַהֵר יְקַדְּמוּנוּ רַחֲמֶיךָ כִּי דַלּוֹנוּ מְאֹד׃

ט עָזְרֵנוּ אֱלֹהֵי יִשְׁעֵנוּ עַל־דְּבַר כְּבוֹד־שְׁמֶךָ וְהַצִּילֵנוּ וְכַפֵּר עַל־חַטֹּאתֵינוּ לְמַעַן שְׁמֶךָ׃

י לָמָּה יֹאמְרוּ הַגּוֹיִם אַיֵּה אֱלֹהֵיהֶם יִוָּדַע בַּגֹּיִים [בַּגּוֹיִם] לְעֵינֵינוּ נִקְמַת דַּם־עֲבָדֶיךָ הַשָּׁפוּךְ׃

יא תָּבוֹא לְפָנֶיךָ אֶנְקַת אָסִיר כְּגֹדֶל זְרוֹעֲךָ הוֹתֵר בְּנֵי תְמוּתָה׃

יב וְהָשֵׁב לִשְׁכֵנֵינוּ שִׁבְעָתַיִם אֶל־חֵיקָם חֶרְפָּתָם אֲשֶׁר חֵרְפוּךָ אֲדֹנָי׃

יג וַאֲנַחְנוּ עַמְּךָ וְצֹאן מַרְעִיתֶךָ נוֹדֶה לְּךָ לְעוֹלָם לְדֹר וָדֹר נְסַפֵּר תְּהִלָּתֶךָ׃

פ א לַמְנַצֵּחַ אֶל־שֹׁשַׁנִּים עֵדוּת לְאָסָף מִזְמוֹר׃

ב רֹעֵה יִשְׂרָאֵל הַאֲזִינָה נֹהֵג כַּצֹּאן יוֹסֵף יֹשֵׁב הַכְּרוּבִים הוֹפִיעָה׃

ג לִפְנֵי אֶפְרַיִם וּבִנְיָמִן וּמְנַשֶּׁה עוֹרְרָה אֶת־גְּבוּרָתֶךָ וּלְכָה לִישֻׁעָתָה לָּנוּ׃

ד אֱלֹהִים הֲשִׁיבֵנוּ וְהָאֵר פָּנֶיךָ וְנִוָּשֵׁעָה׃

Tehillim / Psalms
Chapter 80

תהלים
פרק פ

5 O *Hashem*, God of hosts, how long will You be wrathful toward the prayers of Your people?

ה יְהֹוָה אֱלֹהִים צְבָאוֹת עַד־מָתַי עָשַׁנְתָּ בִּתְפִלַּת עַמֶּךָ:

6 You have fed them tears as their daily bread, made them drink great measures of tears.

ו הֶאֱכַלְתָּם לֶחֶם דִּמְעָה וַתַּשְׁקֵמוֹ בִּדְמָעוֹת שָׁלִישׁ:

7 You set us at strife with our neighbors; our enemies mock us at will.

ז תְּשִׂימֵנוּ מָדוֹן לִשְׁכֵנֵינוּ וְאֹיְבֵינוּ יִלְעֲגוּ־לָמוֹ:

8 O God of hosts, restore us; show Your favor that we may be delivered.

ח אֱלֹהִים צְבָאוֹת הֲשִׁיבֵנוּ וְהָאֵר פָּנֶיךָ וְנִוָּשֵׁעָה:

9 You plucked up a vine from Egypt; You expelled nations and planted it.

ט גֶּפֶן מִמִּצְרַיִם תַּסִּיעַ תְּגָרֵשׁ גּוֹיִם וַתִּטָּעֶהָ:

GE-fen mi-mitz-RA-yim ta-SEE-a t'-ga-RAYSH go-YIM va-ti-ta-E-ha

10 You cleared a place for it; it took deep root and filled the land.

י פִּנִּיתָ לְפָנֶיהָ וַתַּשְׁרֵשׁ שָׁרָשֶׁיהָ וַתְּמַלֵּא־אָרֶץ:

11 The mountains were covered by its shade, mighty cedars by its boughs.

יא כָּסוּ הָרִים צִלָּהּ וַעֲנָפֶיהָ אַרְזֵי־אֵל:

12 Its branches reached the sea, its shoots, the river.

יב תְּשַׁלַּח קְצִירֶהָ עַד־יָם וְאֶל־נָהָר יוֹנְקוֹתֶיהָ:

13 Why did You breach its wall so that every passerby plucks its fruit,

יג לָמָּה פָּרַצְתָּ גְדֵרֶיהָ וְאָרוּהָ כָּל־עֹבְרֵי דָרֶךְ:

14 wild boars gnaw at it, and creatures of the field feed on it?

יד יְכַרְסְמֶנָּה חֲזִיר מִיָּעַר וְזִיז שָׂדַי יִרְעֶנָּה:

15 O God of hosts, turn again, look down from heaven and see; take note of that vine,

טו אֱלֹהִים צְבָאוֹת שׁוּב־נָא הַבֵּט מִשָּׁמַיִם וּרְאֵה וּפְקֹד גֶּפֶן זֹאת:

16 the stock planted by Your right hand, the stem you have taken as Your own.

טז וְכַנָּה אֲשֶׁר־נָטְעָה יְמִינֶךָ וְעַל־בֵּן אִמַּצְתָּה לָּךְ:

17 For it is burned by fire and cut down, perishing before Your angry blast.

יז שְׂרֻפָה בָאֵשׁ כְּסוּחָה מִגַּעֲרַת פָּנֶיךָ יֹאבֵדוּ:

18 Grant Your help to the man at Your right hand, the one You have taken as Your own.

יח תְּהִי־יָדְךָ עַל־אִישׁ יְמִינֶךָ עַל־בֶּן־אָדָם אִמַּצְתָּ לָּךְ:

19 We will not turn away from You; preserve our life that we may invoke Your name.

יט וְלֹא־נָסוֹג מִמֶּךָּ תְּחַיֵּנוּ וּבְשִׁמְךָ נִקְרָא:

80:9 You plucked up a vine from Egypt In this psalm, *Asaf* employs a refrain asking *Hashem* to shine His infinite, glorious light upon His downtrodden people. He dreams of God's miraculous and overt return to the people. Just as *Hashem* took the vine, representing the entire Nation of Israel, out of Egypt and re-planted it in Canaan, so too should they receive His immediate deliverance in a complete and absolute fashion. The psalmist repeats the nation's desire for *Hashem* to shine His face upon them and bring them salvation. The next psalm, Psalm 81, records God's response to this plea.

Tehillim/Psalms
Chapter 81

20	O *Hashem*, God of hosts, restore us; show Your favor that we may be delivered.	יְהֹוָה אֱלֹהִים צְבָאוֹת הֲשִׁיבֵנוּ הָאֵר פָּנֶיךָ וְנִוָּשֵׁעָה:

81

1 For the leader; on the gittith. Of *Asaf*.

lam-na-TZAY-akh al ha-gi-TEET l'-a-SAF

לַמְנַצֵּחַ עַל־הַגִּתִּית לְאָסָף:

2 Sing joyously to *Hashem*, our strength; raise a shout for the God of *Yaakov*.
הַרְנִינוּ לֵאלֹהִים עוּזֵּנוּ הָרִיעוּ לֵאלֹהֵי יַעֲקֹב:

3 Take up the song, sound the timbrel, the melodious lyre and harp.
שְׂאוּ־זִמְרָה וּתְנוּ־תֹף כִּנּוֹר נָעִים עִם־נָבֶל:

4 Blow the *shofar* on the new moon, on the full moon for our feast day.
תִּקְעוּ בַחֹדֶשׁ שׁוֹפָר בַּכֶּסֶה לְיוֹם חַגֵּנוּ:

5 For it is a law for *Yisrael*, a ruling of the God of *Yaakov*;
כִּי חֹק לְיִשְׂרָאֵל הוּא מִשְׁפָּט לֵאלֹהֵי יַעֲקֹב:

6 He imposed it as a decree upon *Yosef* when he went forth from the land of Egypt; I heard a language that I knew not.
עֵדוּת בִּיהוֹסֵף שָׂמוֹ בְּצֵאתוֹ עַל־אֶרֶץ מִצְרָיִם שְׂפַת לֹא־יָדַעְתִּי אֶשְׁמָע:

7 I relieved his shoulder of the burden, his hands were freed from the basket.
הֲסִירוֹתִי מִסֵּבֶל שִׁכְמוֹ כַּפָּיו מִדּוּד תַּעֲבֹרְנָה:

8 In distress you called and I rescued you; I answered you from the secret place of thunder I tested you at the waters of Meribah. *Selah*.
בַּצָּרָה קָרָאתָ וָאֲחַלְּצֶךָּ אֶעֶנְךָ בְּסֵתֶר רַעַם אֶבְחָנְךָ עַל־מֵי מְרִיבָה סֶלָה:

9 Hear, My people, and I will admonish you; *Yisrael*, if you would but listen to Me!
שְׁמַע עַמִּי וְאָעִידָה בָּךְ יִשְׂרָאֵל אִם־תִּשְׁמַע־לִי:

10 You shall have no foreign god, you shall not bow to an alien god.
לֹא־יִהְיֶה בְךָ אֵל זָר וְלֹא תִשְׁתַּחֲוֶה לְאֵל נֵכָר:

11 I *Hashem* am your God who brought you out of the land of Egypt; open your mouth wide and I will fill it.
אָנֹכִי יְהֹוָה אֱלֹהֶיךָ הַמַּעַלְךָ מֵאֶרֶץ מִצְרָיִם הַרְחֶב־פִּיךָ וַאֲמַלְאֵהוּ:

12 But My people would not listen to Me, *Yisrael* would not obey Me.
וְלֹא־שָׁמַע עַמִּי לְקוֹלִי וְיִשְׂרָאֵל לֹא־אָבָה לִי:

13 So I let them go after their willful heart that they might follow their own devices.
וָאֲשַׁלְּחֵהוּ בִּשְׁרִירוּת לִבָּם יֵלְכוּ בְּמוֹעֲצוֹתֵיהֶם:

81:1 On the gittith According to some, the gittith, upon which this psalm is uttered, refers to a *gat* (גת), 'wine press.' This psalm, which presents *Hashem*'s response to the previous psalm, opts for a much slower, methodical process of salvation. As opposed to the metaphor of a vine being lifted up whole and then planted again in the land, the nation is not yet ready for, or deserving of, immediate salvation. Rather, like the procedure for producing wine from grapes, salvation will take time. The process requires several stages, and it requires a passage of time until the final product is ready. The message of this psalm is that redemption does not occur instantaneously. Just as winemaking requires a process involving various stages such as laborious harvesting, crushing, selecting, fermenting and ultimately waiting, before producing the finished product, so does redemption. But just as with fine wine, it is well worth the wait.

Ancient wine press in Shivta, Israel

Tehillim/Psalms
Chapter 82

14 If only My people would listen to Me, if *Yisrael* would follow My paths,

15 then would I subdue their enemies at once, strike their foes again and again.

16 Those who hate *Hashem* shall cower before Him; their doom shall be eternal.

17 He fed them the finest wheat; I sated you with honey from the rock.

82

1 A psalm of *Asaf*. *Hashem* stands in the divine assembly; among the divine beings He pronounces judgment.

2 How long will you judge perversely, showing favor to the wicked? *Selah*.

ad ma-TAI tish-p'-tu A-vel uf-NAY r'-sha-EEM tis-u SE-lah

3 Judge the wretched and the orphan, vindicate the lowly and the poor,

4 rescue the wretched and the needy; save them from the hand of the wicked.

5 They neither know nor understand, they go about in darkness; all the foundations of the earth totter.

6 I had taken you for divine beings, sons of the Most High, all of you;

7 but you shall die as men do, fall like any prince.

8 Arise, O *Hashem*, judge the earth, for all the nations are Your possession.

83

1 A song, a psalm of *Asaf*.

2 O *Hashem*, do not be silent; do not hold aloof; do not be quiet, O *Hashem*!

3 For Your enemies rage, Your foes assert themselves.

82:2 How long will you judge perversely A nation without a proper justice system will crumble. The prophet *Yeshayahu* criticizes the people, pointing out that while they love to offer sacrifices, they do not judge the orphan, widow and stranger with compassion. In a most biting simile, he compares the people to Sodom and Gomorrah (Isaiah 1:10–17). This psalm is directed at the corrupt judges who pander to the wealthy and influential. *Asaf* ridicules these judges, who take themselves to be of great importance, and reminds them that their demise will surely come. In the end, he calls out to *Hashem* to return to Israel and take His rightful place as the true Judge of the land.

Tehillim / Psalms
Chapter 83

תהלים
פרק פג

4 They plot craftily against Your people, take counsel against Your treasured ones.

ד עַל־עַמְּךָ יַעֲרִימוּ סוֹד וְיִתְיָעֲצוּ עַל־צְפוּנֶיךָ:

5 They say, "Let us wipe them out as a nation; *Yisrael*'s name will be mentioned no more."

ה אָמְרוּ לְכוּ וְנַכְחִידֵם מִגּוֹי וְלֹא־יִזָּכֵר שֵׁם־יִשְׂרָאֵל עוֹד:

6 Unanimous in their counsel they have made an alliance against You –

ו כִּי נוֹעֲצוּ לֵב יַחְדָּו עָלֶיךָ בְּרִית יִכְרֹתוּ:

7 the clans of Edom and the Ishmaelites, Moab and the Hagrites,

ז אָהֳלֵי אֱדוֹם וְיִשְׁמְעֵאלִים מוֹאָב וְהַגְרִים:

8 Gebal, Ammon, and Amalek, Philistia with the inhabitants of Tyre;

ח גְּבָל וְעַמּוֹן וַעֲמָלֵק פְּלֶשֶׁת עִם־יֹשְׁבֵי צוֹר:

9 Assyria too joins forces with them; they give support to the sons of Lot. *Selah*.

ט גַּם־אַשּׁוּר נִלְוָה עִמָּם הָיוּ זְרוֹעַ לִבְנֵי־לוֹט סֶלָה:

10 Deal with them as You did with Midian, with Sisera, with Jabin, at the brook Kishon –

י עֲשֵׂה־לָהֶם כְּמִדְיָן כְּסִיסְרָא כְיָבִין בְּנַחַל קִישׁוֹן:

11 who were destroyed at En-dor, who became dung for the field.

יא נִשְׁמְדוּ בְעֵין־דֹּאר הָיוּ דֹּמֶן לָאֲדָמָה:

12 Treat their great men like Oreb and Zeeb, all their princes like Zebah and Zalmunna,

יב שִׁיתֵמוֹ נְדִיבֵמוֹ כְּעֹרֵב וְכִזְאֵב וּכְזֶבַח וּכְצַלְמֻנָּע כָּל־נְסִיכֵמוֹ:

shee-TAY-mo n'-dee-VAY-mo k'-o-RAYV v'-khiz-AYV ukh-ZE-vakh ukh-tzal-mu-NA kol n'-see-KHAY-mo

13 who said, "Let us take the meadows of *Hashem* as our possession."

יג אֲשֶׁר אָמְרוּ נִירְשָׁה לָּנוּ אֵת נְאוֹת אֱלֹהִים:

14 O my God, make them like thistledown, like stubble driven by the wind.

יד אֱלֹהַי שִׁיתֵמוֹ כַגַּלְגַּל כְּקַשׁ לִפְנֵי־רוּחַ:

15 As a fire burns a forest, as flames scorch the hills,

טו כְּאֵשׁ תִּבְעַר־יָעַר וּכְלֶהָבָה תְּלַהֵט הָרִים:

16 pursue them with Your tempest, terrify them with Your storm.

טז כֵּן תִּרְדְּפֵם בְּסַעֲרֶךָ וּבְסוּפָתְךָ תְבַהֲלֵם:

17 Cover their faces with shame so that they seek Your name, *Hashem*.

יז מַלֵּא פְנֵיהֶם קָלוֹן וִיבַקְשׁוּ שִׁמְךָ יְהוָה:

18 May they be frustrated and terrified, disgraced and doomed forever.

יח יֵבֹשׁוּ וְיִבָּהֲלוּ עֲדֵי־עַד וְיַחְפְּרוּ וְיֹאבֵדוּ:

19 May they know that Your name, Yours alone, is *Hashem*, supreme over all the earth.

יט וְיֵדְעוּ כִּי־אַתָּה שִׁמְךָ יְהוָה לְבַדֶּךָ עֶלְיוֹן עַל־כָּל־הָאָרֶץ:

83:12 Treat their great men like Oreb and Zeeb The psalm lists eleven enemies of Israel who, throughout history, have sought to destroy the Nation of Israel. *Asaf* seeks *Hashem*'s vengeance, and asks that He come down in a grand display of omnipotence to smite all of Israel's enemies. He invokes the incidents recorded in *Sefer Shoftim*, when the Lord helped the judges destroy all the arrogant leaders of their adversaries. Oreb and Zeeb were two princes of Midian who were killed by *Gidon* during the defeat of the Midianites recorded in *Sefer Shoftim* (7:25), while Zebah and Zalmunna were two kings of Midian killed during this war as well (8:10–12).

Tehillim / Psalms
Chapter 84

84 1 For the leader; on the gittith. Of the Korahites. A psalm.

2 How lovely is Your dwelling-place, Lord of hosts.

3 I long, I yearn for the courts of *Hashem*; my body and soul shout for joy to the living *Hashem*.

4 Even the sparrow has found a home, and the swallow a nest for herself in which to set her young, near Your *Mizbayach*, O Lord of hosts, my king and my God.

5 Happy are those who dwell in Your house; they forever praise You. *Selah*.

6 Happy is the man who finds refuge in You, whose mind is on the [pilgrim] highways.

7 They pass through the Valley of Baca, regarding it as a place of springs, as if the early rain had covered it with blessing.

o-v'-RAY b'-AY-mek ha-ba-KHA ma-YAN y'-shee-TU-hu gam b'-ra-KHOT ya-TEH mo-REH

8 They go from rampart to rampart, appearing before *Hashem* in *Tzion*.

9 O *Hashem*, God of hosts, hear my prayer; give ear, O God of *Yaakov*. *Selah*.

10 O *Hashem*, behold our shield, look upon the face of Your anointed.

11 Better one day in Your courts than a thousand [anywhere else]; I would rather stand at the threshold of *Hashem*'s house than dwell in the tents of the wicked.

א לַמְנַצֵּחַ עַל־הַגִּתִּית לִבְנֵי־קֹרַח מִזְמוֹר׃
ב מַה־יְּדִידוֹת מִשְׁכְּנוֹתֶיךָ יְהֹוָה צְבָאוֹת׃
ג נִכְסְפָה וְגַם־כָּלְתָה נַפְשִׁי לְחַצְרוֹת יְהֹוָה לִבִּי וּבְשָׂרִי יְרַנְּנוּ אֶל אֵל־חָי׃
ד גַּם־צִפּוֹר מָצְאָה בַיִת וּדְרוֹר קֵן לָהּ אֲשֶׁר־שָׁתָה אֶפְרֹחֶיהָ אֶת־מִזְבְּחוֹתֶיךָ יְהֹוָה צְבָאוֹת מַלְכִּי וֵאלֹהָי׃
ה אַשְׁרֵי יוֹשְׁבֵי בֵיתֶךָ עוֹד יְהַלְלוּךָ סֶּלָה׃
ו אַשְׁרֵי אָדָם עוֹז־לוֹ בָךְ מְסִלּוֹת בִּלְבָבָם׃
ז עֹבְרֵי בְּעֵמֶק הַבָּכָא מַעְיָן יְשִׁיתוּהוּ גַּם־בְּרָכוֹת יַעְטֶה מוֹרֶה׃
ח יֵלְכוּ מֵחַיִל אֶל־חָיִל יֵרָאֶה אֶל־אֱלֹהִים בְּצִיּוֹן׃
ט יְהֹוָה אֱלֹהִים צְבָאוֹת שִׁמְעָה תְפִלָּתִי הַאֲזִינָה אֱלֹהֵי יַעֲקֹב סֶלָה׃
י מָגִנֵּנוּ רְאֵה אֱלֹהִים וְהַבֵּט פְּנֵי מְשִׁיחֶךָ׃
יא כִּי טוֹב־יוֹם בַּחֲצֵרֶיךָ מֵאָלֶף בָּחַרְתִּי הִסְתּוֹפֵף בְּבֵית אֱלֹהַי מִדּוּר בְּאָהֳלֵי־רֶשַׁע׃

84:7 They pass through the Valley of Baca The sons of *Korach* write a psalm depicting the longing for the *Beit Hamikdash* and the desire to make the great pilgrimage to *Yerushalayim* three times a year. From all corners of the land, pilgrims make their way to the Holy City for the three festivals, bearing gifts to present in the *Beit Hamikdash*. Some traverse long distances, while others walk a short way to get to Jerusalem and the *Beit Hamikdash*. The psalmist writes how the pilgrims would pass through the *Emek Habakha*, literally 'the valley of tears,' struggling to make their way home. In modern times, the name *Emek Habakha* has been applied to a strip of land in the Golan Heights that was the site of a major battle during the 1973 *Yom Kippur* War. Though vastly outnumbered, the Israeli soldiers of Battalion 77 held their positions against the Syrian army until the Syrians eventually withdrew. While they sacrificed many soldiers, the IDF prevented the Syrian army from breaking through and traveling south to destroy the heartLand of Israel.

Valley of Tears in the Golan Heights

Tehillim/Psalms
Chapter 85

תהלים
פרק פה

12	For *Hashem* is sun and shield; *Hashem* bestows grace and glory; He does not withhold His bounty from those who live without blame.	כִּי שֶׁמֶשׁ וּמָגֵן יְהֹוָה אֱלֹהִים חֵן וְכָבוֹד יִתֵּן יְהֹוָה לֹא יִמְנַע־טוֹב לַהֹלְכִים בְּתָמִים: יב
13	O Lord of hosts, happy is the man who trusts in You.	יְהֹוָה צְבָאוֹת אַשְׁרֵי אָדָם בֹּטֵחַ בָּךְ: יג

85

1. For the leader. Of the Korahites. A psalm.

   לַמְנַצֵּחַ לִבְנֵי־קֹרַח מִזְמוֹר: א

2. *Hashem*, You will favor Your land, restore *Yaakov's* fortune;

   רָצִיתָ יְהֹוָה אַרְצֶךָ שַׁבְתָּ שְׁבוּת [שְׁבִית] יַעֲקֹב: ב

   ra-TZEE-ta a-do-NAI ar-TZE-kha SHAV-ta sh'-VEET ya-a-KOV

3. You will forgive Your people's iniquity, pardon all their sins; *selah*

   נָשָׂאתָ עֲוֹן עַמֶּךָ כִּסִּיתָ כָל־חַטָּאתָם סֶלָה: ג

4. You will withdraw all Your anger, turn away from Your rage.

   אָסַפְתָּ כָל־עֶבְרָתֶךָ הֱשִׁיבוֹתָ מֵחֲרוֹן אַפֶּךָ: ד

5. Turn again, O *Hashem*, our helper, revoke Your displeasure with us.

   שׁוּבֵנוּ אֱלֹהֵי יִשְׁעֵנוּ וְהָפֵר כַּעַסְךָ עִמָּנוּ: ה

6. Will You be angry with us forever, prolong Your wrath for all generations?

   הַלְעוֹלָם תֶּאֱנַף־בָּנוּ תִּמְשֹׁךְ אַפְּךָ לְדֹר וָדֹר: ו

7. Surely You will revive us again, so that Your people may rejoice in You.

   הֲלֹא־אַתָּה תָּשׁוּב תְּחַיֵּנוּ וְעַמְּךָ יִשְׂמְחוּ־בָךְ: ז

8. Show us, *Hashem*, Your faithfulness; grant us Your deliverance.

   הַרְאֵנוּ יְהֹוָה חַסְדֶּךָ וְיֶשְׁעֲךָ תִּתֶּן־לָנוּ: ח

9. Let me hear what *Hashem*, *Hashem*, will speak; He will promise well-being to His people, His faithful ones; may they not turn to folly.

   אֶשְׁמְעָה מַה־יְדַבֵּר הָאֵל יְהֹוָה כִּי יְדַבֵּר שָׁלוֹם אֶל־עַמּוֹ וְאֶל־חֲסִידָיו וְאַל־יָשׁוּבוּ לְכִסְלָה: ט

10. His help is very near those who fear Him, to make His glory dwell in our land.

    אַךְ קָרוֹב לִירֵאָיו יִשְׁעוֹ לִשְׁכֹּן כָּבוֹד בְּאַרְצֵנוּ: י

11. Faithfulness and truth meet; justice and well-being kiss.

    חֶסֶד־וֶאֱמֶת נִפְגָּשׁוּ צֶדֶק וְשָׁלוֹם נָשָׁקוּ: יא

12. Truth springs up from the earth; justice looks down from heaven.

    אֱמֶת מֵאֶרֶץ תִּצְמָח וְצֶדֶק מִשָּׁמַיִם נִשְׁקָף: יב

13. *Hashem* also bestows His bounty; our land yields its produce.

    גַּם־יְהֹוָה יִתֵּן הַטּוֹב וְאַרְצֵנוּ תִּתֵּן יְבוּלָהּ: יג

85:2 Restore *Yaakov's* fortune After a period of exile, the Children of Israel return home. Contemporary commentator Amos Hakham sees this as a reference to the return of the Jews to the Land of Israel after seventy years of Babylonian exile. In 538 BCE, Cyrus the Great, king of the Persian empire, defeats the Babylonian empire and issues a declaration that the Jews may return to their homeland and rebuild the *Beit Hamikdash* (Ezra chapter 1). This is considered the beginning of the second Temple period. The psalmist acknowledges *Hashem's* desire for His nation to return to the Promised Land. Upon their return, the land will again bring forth its bountiful produce and flourish (verse 13).

Tehillim / Psalms
Chapter 86

14 Justice goes before Him as He sets out on His way.

יד צֶדֶק לְפָנָיו יְהַלֵּךְ וְיָשֵׂם לְדֶרֶךְ פְּעָמָיו:

86 1 A prayer of *David*. Incline Your ear, O *Hashem*, answer me, for I am poor and needy.

פו א תְּפִלָּה לְדָוִד הַטֵּה־יְהֹוָה אָזְנְךָ עֲנֵנִי כִּי־עָנִי וְאֶבְיוֹן אָנִי:

2 Preserve my life, for I am steadfast; O You, my God, deliver Your servant who trusts in You.

ב שָׁמְרָה נַפְשִׁי כִּי־חָסִיד אָנִי הוֹשַׁע עַבְדְּךָ אַתָּה אֱלֹהַי הַבּוֹטֵחַ אֵלֶיךָ:

3 Have mercy on me, O *Hashem*, for I call to You all day long;

ג חָנֵּנִי אֲדֹנָי כִּי אֵלֶיךָ אֶקְרָא כָּל־הַיּוֹם:

4 bring joy to Your servant's life, for on You, *Hashem*, I set my hope.

ד שַׂמֵּחַ נֶפֶשׁ עַבְדֶּךָ כִּי אֵלֶיךָ אֲדֹנָי נַפְשִׁי אֶשָּׂא:

5 For You, *Hashem*, are good and forgiving, abounding in steadfast love to all who call on You.

ה כִּי־אַתָּה אֲדֹנָי טוֹב וְסַלָּח וְרַב־חֶסֶד לְכָל־קֹרְאֶיךָ:

6 Give ear, *Hashem*, to my prayer; heed my plea for mercy.

ו הַאֲזִינָה יְהֹוָה תְּפִלָּתִי וְהַקְשִׁיבָה בְּקוֹל תַּחֲנוּנוֹתָי:

7 In my time of trouble I call You, for You will answer me.

ז בְּיוֹם צָרָתִי אֶקְרָאֶךָּ כִּי תַעֲנֵנִי:

8 There is none like You among the gods, O *Hashem*, and there are no deeds like Yours.

ח אֵין־כָּמוֹךָ בָאֱלֹהִים אֲדֹנָי וְאֵין כְּמַעֲשֶׂיךָ:

9 All the nations You have made will come to bow down before You, O *Hashem*, and they will pay honor to Your name.

ט כָּל־גּוֹיִם אֲשֶׁר עָשִׂיתָ יָבוֹאוּ וְיִשְׁתַּחֲווּ לְפָנֶיךָ אֲדֹנָי וִיכַבְּדוּ לִשְׁמֶךָ:

kol go-YIM a-SHER a-SEE-ta ya-VO-u v'-yish-ta-kha-VU l'-fa-NE-kha a-do-NAI vee-kha-b'-DU lish-ME-kha

10 For You are great and perform wonders; You alone are God.

י כִּי־גָדוֹל אַתָּה וְעֹשֵׂה נִפְלָאוֹת אַתָּה אֱלֹהִים לְבַדֶּךָ:

11 Teach me Your way, O *Hashem*; I will walk in Your truth; let my heart be undivided in reverence for Your name.

יא הוֹרֵנִי יְהֹוָה דַּרְכֶּךָ אֲהַלֵּךְ בַּאֲמִתֶּךָ יַחֵד לְבָבִי לְיִרְאָה שְׁמֶךָ:

12 I will praise You, O *Hashem*, my God, with all my heart and pay honor to Your name forever.

יב אוֹדְךָ אֲדֹנָי אֱלֹהַי בְּכָל־לְבָבִי וַאֲכַבְּדָה שִׁמְךָ לְעוֹלָם:

13 For Your steadfast love toward me is great; You have saved me from the depths of Sheol.

יג כִּי־חַסְדְּךָ גָּדוֹל עָלָי וְהִצַּלְתָּ נַפְשִׁי מִשְּׁאוֹל תַּחְתִּיָּה:

86:9 All the nations King *Shlomo* built the *Beit Hamikdash* in a very unique way, which allowed all the nations of the world to come and be inspired by the light of *Hashem*. In *Sefer Melachim* I 6:4, the windows of the *Beit Hamikdash* are described as both transparent and opaque at the same time. The Talmud (*Menachot* 86b) explains that as opposed to ordinary buildings whose windows are built to allow light to enter, the windows of the *Beit Hamikdash* were constructed to allow the light from inside to shine outwards. This symbolized the divine light that emanated from within the *Beit Hamikdash* and illuminated the entire world. Thus, when looking at the *Beit Hamikdash*, one experienced its reflective light, while inside the Temple it was opaque. This is a manifestation of *David's* desire, expressed here, that all the nations of the world will come to experience the light of God shining from the Temple.

Tehillim / Psalms
Chapter 87

תהלים
פרק פז

14 O *Hashem*, arrogant men have risen against me; a band of ruthless men seek my life; they are not mindful of You.

אֱלֹהִים זֵדִים קָמוּ־עָלַי וַעֲדַת עָרִיצִים בִּקְשׁוּ נַפְשִׁי וְלֹא שָׂמוּךָ לְנֶגְדָּם:

15 But You, O *Hashem*, are a God compassionate and merciful, slow to anger, abounding in steadfast love and faithfulness.

וְאַתָּה אֲדֹנָי אֵל־רַחוּם וְחַנּוּן אֶרֶךְ אַפַּיִם וְרַב־חֶסֶד וֶאֱמֶת:

16 Turn to me and have mercy on me; grant Your strength to Your servant and deliver the son of Your maidservant.

פְּנֵה אֵלַי וְחָנֵּנִי תְּנָה־עֻזְּךָ לְעַבְדֶּךָ וְהוֹשִׁיעָה לְבֶן־אֲמָתֶךָ:

17 Show me a sign of Your favor, that my enemies may see and be frustrated because You, *Hashem*, have given me aid and comfort.

עֲשֵׂה־עִמִּי אוֹת לְטוֹבָה וְיִרְאוּ שֹׂנְאַי וְיֵבֹשׁוּ כִּי־אַתָּה יְהוָה עֲזַרְתַּנִי וְנִחַמְתָּנִי:

87

1 Of the Korahites. A psalm. A song. His foundation is on the holy mountains.

לִבְנֵי־קֹרַח מִזְמוֹר שִׁיר יְסוּדָתוֹ בְּהַרְרֵי־קֹדֶשׁ:

2 *Hashem* loves the gates of *Tzion*, more than all the dwellings of *Yaakov*.

אֹהֵב יְהוָה שַׁעֲרֵי צִיּוֹן מִכֹּל מִשְׁכְּנוֹת יַעֲקֹב:

o-HAYV a-do-NAI sha-a-RAY tzi-YON mi-KOL mish-k'-NOT ya-a-KOV

3 Glorious things are spoken of you, O city of *Hashem*. Selah.

נִכְבָּדוֹת מְדֻבָּר בָּךְ עִיר הָאֱלֹהִים סֶלָה:

4 I mention Rahab and Babylon among those who acknowledge Me; Philistia, and Tyre, and Cush – each was born there.

אַזְכִּיר רַהַב וּבָבֶל לְיֹדְעָי הִנֵּה פְלֶשֶׁת וְצוֹר עִם־כּוּשׁ זֶה יֻלַּד־שָׁם:

5 Indeed, it shall be said of *Tzion*, "Every man was born there." He, the Most High, will preserve it.

וּלְצִיּוֹן יֵאָמַר אִישׁ וְאִישׁ יֻלַּד־בָּהּ וְהוּא יְכוֹנְנֶהָ עֶלְיוֹן:

ul-tzi-YON yay-a-MAR EESH v'-EESH yu-lad BAH v'-HU y'-kho-n'-NE-ha el-YON

87:2 The gates of *Tzion* This short psalm praises *Hashem*'s connection to *Tzion*. In order to express God's love for *Yerushalayim*, the psalmist writes: "*Hashem* loves the gates of *Tzion*, more than all the dwellings of *Yaakov*." The wall currently surrounding Jerusalem's Old City, built in 1538 by the Ottoman sultan Suleiman the Magnificent, has several gates around its perimeter, each of which is known by a different name. The gate at the southwestern corner of the wall is called "Zion Gate," or *Shaar Tzion* (שער ציון) in Hebrew, based on this verse. Thus, it has the oldest biblical name of any of the gates. However, the Arabic name for this gate is *David's* Gate, referring to the traditional location of *David's* tomb. The Zion Gate is also quite significant in modern Israeli history; it was through this gate that the Palmach Brigade of the Israeli army broke into the Old City during the 1948 War of Independence, releasing the Jewish quarter from its isolation. The Jordanians, however, re-conquered the Old City shortly afterwards, and Jews were forced to leave the walls of Jerusalem for the next nineteen years. Only after it was recaptured during the 1967 Six Day War were Jews again able to enter the Old City of *Yerushalayim*.

87:5 Indeed it shall be said of *Tzion*, "Every man was born there." What does this verse mean when it says that "every man" will be considered to have been born in *Tzion*? Rabbi Meisha, quoted in the Talmud (*Ketubot* 75a), explains that it is not only those who are physically born in the Land of Israel who are considered her children. Rather, those who yearn for the Land of Israel and long to see it are also considered *b'nei Tzion*, 'Children of Zion.' This idea is reflected in the words of the famous Israeli writer and Nobel Prize laureate S.Y. Agnon, who said in his Nobel Prize acceptance speech, "Through a historical catastrophe – the destruction of

Zion Gate

S.Y. Agnon (1888–1970)

1576

Tehillim / Psalms
Chapter 88

6 *Hashem* will inscribe in the register of peoples that each was born there. *Selah*.

7 Singers and dancers alike [will say]: "All my roots are in You."

88

1 A song. A psalm of the Korahites. For the leader; on mahalath leannoth. A maskil of *Hayman* the Ezrahite.

2 *Hashem*, God of my deliverance, when I cry out in the night before You,

3 let my prayer reach You; incline Your ear to my cry.

4 For I am sated with misfortune; I am at the brink of Sheol.

5 I am numbered with those who go down to the Pit; I am a helpless man

6 abandoned among the dead, like bodies lying in the grave of whom You are mindful no more, and who are cut off from Your care.

7 You have put me at the bottom of the Pit, in the darkest places, in the depths.

8 Your fury lies heavy upon me; You afflict me with all Your breakers. *Selah*.

9 You make my companions shun me; You make me abhorrent to them; I am shut in and do not go out.

10 My eyes pine away from affliction; I call to You, *Hashem*, each day; I stretch out my hands to You.

11 Do You work wonders for the dead? Do the shades rise to praise You? *Selah*.

12 Is Your faithful care recounted in the grave, Your constancy in the place of perdition?

13 Are Your wonders made known in the netherworld, Your beneficent deeds in the land of oblivion?

14 As for me, I cry out to You, *Hashem*; each morning my prayer greets You.

15 Why, *Hashem*, do You reject me, do You hide Your face from me?

16 From my youth I have been afflicted and near death; I suffer Your terrors wherever I turn.

17 Your fury overwhelms me; Your terrors destroy me.

תהלים
פרק פח

ו יְהֹוָה יִסְפֹּר בִּכְתוֹב עַמִּים זֶה יֻלַּד־שָׁם סֶלָה:

ז וְשָׁרִים כְּחֹלְלִים כָּל־מַעְיָנַי בָּךְ:

פח א שִׁיר מִזְמוֹר לִבְנֵי קֹרַח לַמְנַצֵּחַ עַל־מָחֲלַת לְעַנּוֹת מַשְׂכִּיל לְהֵימָן הָאֶזְרָחִי:

ב יְהֹוָה אֱלֹהֵי יְשׁוּעָתִי יוֹם־צָעַקְתִּי בַלַּיְלָה נֶגְדֶּךָ:

ג תָּבוֹא לְפָנֶיךָ תְּפִלָּתִי הַטֵּה־אָזְנְךָ לְרִנָּתִי:

ד כִּי־שָׂבְעָה בְרָעוֹת נַפְשִׁי וְחַיַּי לִשְׁאוֹל הִגִּיעוּ:

ה נֶחְשַׁבְתִּי עִם־יוֹרְדֵי בוֹר הָיִיתִי כְּגֶבֶר אֵין־אֱיָל:

ו בַּמֵּתִים חָפְשִׁי כְּמוֹ חֲלָלִים שֹׁכְבֵי קֶבֶר אֲשֶׁר לֹא זְכַרְתָּם עוֹד וְהֵמָּה מִיָּדְךָ נִגְזָרוּ:

ז שַׁתַּנִי בְּבוֹר תַּחְתִּיּוֹת בְּמַחֲשַׁכִּים בִּמְצֹלוֹת:

ח עָלַי סָמְכָה חֲמָתֶךָ וְכָל־מִשְׁבָּרֶיךָ עִנִּיתָ סֶּלָה:

ט הִרְחַקְתָּ מְיֻדָּעַי מִמֶּנִּי שַׁתַּנִי תוֹעֵבוֹת לָמוֹ כָּלֻא וְלֹא אֵצֵא:

י עֵינִי דָאֲבָה מִנִּי עֹנִי קְרָאתִיךָ יְהֹוָה בְּכָל־יוֹם שִׁטַּחְתִּי אֵלֶיךָ כַפָּי:

יא הֲלַמֵּתִים תַּעֲשֶׂה־פֶּלֶא אִם־רְפָאִים יָקוּמוּ יוֹדוּךָ סֶּלָה:

יב הַיְסֻפַּר בַּקֶּבֶר חַסְדֶּךָ אֱמוּנָתְךָ בָּאֲבַדּוֹן:

יג הֲיִוָּדַע בַּחֹשֶׁךְ פִּלְאֶךָ וְצִדְקָתְךָ בְּאֶרֶץ נְשִׁיָּה:

יד וַאֲנִי אֵלֶיךָ יְהֹוָה שִׁוַּעְתִּי וּבַבֹּקֶר תְּפִלָּתִי תְקַדְּמֶךָּ:

טו לָמָה יְהֹוָה תִּזְנַח נַפְשִׁי תַּסְתִּיר פָּנֶיךָ מִמֶּנִּי:

טז עָנִי אֲנִי וְגֹוֵעַ מִנֹּעַר נָשָׂאתִי אֵמֶיךָ אָפוּנָה:

יז עָלַי עָבְרוּ חֲרוֹנֶיךָ בִּעוּתֶיךָ צִמְּתוּתֻנִי:

Jerusalem by the emperor of Rome – I was born in one of the cities in the diaspora. But I always deemed myself a child of Jerusalem, one who is in reality a native of Jerusalem."

Tehillim/Psalms
Chapter 89

תהלים
פרק פט

18	They swirl about me like water all day long; they encircle me on every side.	סַבּוּנִי כַמַּיִם כָּל־הַיּוֹם הִקִּיפוּ עָלַי יָחַד:	יח
19	You have put friend and neighbor far from me and my companions out of my sight.	הִרְחַקְתָּ מִמֶּנִּי אֹהֵב וָרֵעַ מְיֻדָּעַי מַחְשָׁךְ:	יט

hir-KHAK-ta mi-ME-nee o-HAYV va-RAY-a m'-yu-da-AI makh-SHAKH

89

1	A maskil of Ethan the Ezrahite.	מַשְׂכִּיל לְאֵיתָן הָאֶזְרָחִי:	א
2	I will sing of *Hashem*'s steadfast love forever; to all generations I will proclaim Your faithfulness with my mouth.	חַסְדֵי יְהֹוָה עוֹלָם אָשִׁירָה לְדֹר וָדֹר אוֹדִיעַ אֱמוּנָתְךָ בְּפִי:	ב
3	I declare, "Your steadfast love is confirmed forever; there in the heavens You establish Your faithfulness."	כִּי־אָמַרְתִּי עוֹלָם חֶסֶד יִבָּנֶה שָׁמַיִם תָּכִן אֱמוּנָתְךָ בָהֶם:	ג
4	"I have made a covenant with My chosen one; I have sworn to My servant *David*:	כָּרַתִּי בְרִית לִבְחִירִי נִשְׁבַּעְתִּי לְדָוִד עַבְדִּי:	ד
5	I will establish your offspring forever, I will confirm your throne for all generations." *Selah*.	עַד־עוֹלָם אָכִין זַרְעֶךָ וּבָנִיתִי לְדֹר־וָדוֹר כִּסְאֲךָ סֶלָה:	ה
6	Your wonders, *Hashem*, are praised by the heavens, Your faithfulness, too, in the assembly of holy beings.	וְיוֹדוּ שָׁמַיִם פִּלְאֲךָ יְהֹוָה אַף־אֱמוּנָתְךָ בִּקְהַל קְדֹשִׁים:	ו
7	For who in the skies can equal *Hashem*, can compare with *Hashem* among the divine beings,	כִּי מִי בַשַּׁחַק יַעֲרֹךְ לַיהֹוָה יִדְמֶה לַיהֹוָה בִּבְנֵי אֵלִים:	ז
8	a *Hashem* greatly dreaded in the council of holy beings, held in awe by all around Him?	אֵל נַעֲרָץ בְּסוֹד־קְדֹשִׁים רַבָּה וְנוֹרָא עַל־כָּל־סְבִיבָיו:	ח
9	O *Hashem*, God of hosts, who is mighty like You, *Hashem*? Your faithfulness surrounds You;	יְהֹוָה אֱלֹהֵי צְבָאוֹת מִי־כָמוֹךָ חֲסִין יָהּ וֶאֱמוּנָתְךָ סְבִיבוֹתֶיךָ:	ט
10	You rule the swelling of the sea; when its waves surge, You still them.	אַתָּה מוֹשֵׁל בְּגֵאוּת הַיָּם בְּשׂוֹא גַלָּיו אַתָּה תְשַׁבְּחֵם:	י
11	You crushed Rahab; he was like a corpse; with Your powerful arm You scattered Your enemies.	אַתָּה דִכִּאתָ כֶחָלָל רָהַב בִּזְרוֹעַ עֻזְּךָ פִּזַּרְתָּ אוֹיְבֶיךָ:	יא
12	The heaven is Yours, the earth too; the world and all it holds – You established them.	לְךָ שָׁמַיִם אַף־לְךָ אָרֶץ תֵּבֵל וּמְלֹאָהּ אַתָּה יְסַדְתָּם:	יב

88:19 And my companions out of my sight This psalm is similar to a lamentation, as it ends on a very sad note. Though unusual, this type of psalm also belongs in the Psalter, which depicts a range of human experiences, and not only those with "happy endings." While scholars debate the identity of the authors of the psalm, since verse 1 attributes it to both the sons of *Korach* and *Hayman* the Ezrahite, the Sages suggest that the psalm was authored by the congregation of Israel as a whole. At times of total darkness and exile, the Jewish people struggle to find words to express faith in God's ultimate salvation. While the last words reflect this horrible state of bleak loneliness, we should note that the entire psalm was directed to *Hashem*, God of salvation (verse 2). God desires our expressions of suffering and our cries. This, too, is His praise.

Tehillim / Psalms
Chapter 89

13 North and south – You created them; *Tavor* and *Chermon* sing forth Your name.

tza-FON v'-ya-MEEN a-TAH v'-ra-TAM ta-VOR v'-kher-MON b'-shim-KHA y'-ra-NAY-nu

צָפוֹן וְיָמִין אַתָּה בְרָאתָם תָּבוֹר וְחֶרְמוֹן בְּשִׁמְךָ יְרַנֵּנוּ:

14 Yours is an arm endowed with might; Your hand is strong; Your right hand, exalted.

לְךָ זְרוֹעַ עִם־גְּבוּרָה תָּעֹז יָדְךָ תָּרוּם יְמִינֶךָ:

15 Righteousness and justice are the base of Your throne; steadfast love and faithfulness stand before You.

צֶדֶק וּמִשְׁפָּט מְכוֹן כִּסְאֶךָ חֶסֶד וֶאֱמֶת יְקַדְּמוּ פָנֶיךָ:

16 Happy is the people who know the joyful shout; *Hashem*, they walk in the light of Your presence.

אַשְׁרֵי הָעָם יוֹדְעֵי תְרוּעָה יְהוָה בְּאוֹר־פָּנֶיךָ יְהַלֵּכוּן:

17 They rejoice in Your name all day long; they are exalted through Your righteousness.

בְּשִׁמְךָ יְגִילוּן כָּל־הַיּוֹם וּבְצִדְקָתְךָ יָרוּמוּ:

18 For You are their strength in which they glory; our horn is exalted through Your favor.

כִּי־תִפְאֶרֶת עֻזָּמוֹ אָתָּה וּבִרְצֹנְךָ תָּרִים [תָּרוּם] קַרְנֵנוּ:

19 Truly our shield is of *Hashem*, our king, of the Holy One of *Yisrael*.

כִּי לַיהוָה מָגִנֵּנוּ וְלִקְדוֹשׁ יִשְׂרָאֵל מַלְכֵּנוּ:

20 Then You spoke to Your faithful ones in a vision and said, "I have conferred power upon a warrior; I have exalted one chosen out of the people.

אָז דִּבַּרְתָּ־בְחָזוֹן לַחֲסִידֶיךָ וַתֹּאמֶר שִׁוִּיתִי עֵזֶר עַל־גִּבּוֹר הֲרִימוֹתִי בָחוּר מֵעָם:

21 I have found *David*, My servant; anointed him with My sacred oil.

מָצָאתִי דָּוִד עַבְדִּי בְּשֶׁמֶן קָדְשִׁי מְשַׁחְתִּיו:

22 My hand shall be constantly with him and My arm shall strengthen him.

אֲשֶׁר יָדִי תִּכּוֹן עִמּוֹ אַף־זְרוֹעִי תְאַמְּצֶנּוּ:

23 No enemy shall oppress him, no vile man afflict him.

לֹא־יַשִּׁא אוֹיֵב בּוֹ וּבֶן־עַוְלָה לֹא יְעַנֶּנּוּ:

24 I will crush his adversaries before him; I will strike down those who hate him.

וְכַתּוֹתִי מִפָּנָיו צָרָיו וּמְשַׂנְאָיו אֶגּוֹף:

25 My faithfulness and steadfast love shall be with him; his horn shall be exalted through My name.

וֶאֱמוּנָתִי וְחַסְדִּי עִמּוֹ וּבִשְׁמִי תָּרוּם קַרְנוֹ:

26 I will set his hand upon the sea, his right hand upon the rivers.

וְשַׂמְתִּי בַיָּם יָדוֹ וּבַנְּהָרוֹת יְמִינוֹ:

89:13 *Tavor* and *Chermon* sing forth Your name The first segment of this psalm calls out to *Hashem* in praise of the wonderful acts of kindness and love He does for the world. While praising God and acknowledging that He is Creator and Master of the world, the psalmist turns to the great mountains *Tavor* and *Chermon*. Mount *Tavor* is where the great battle of *Barak* against the army of Sisera, king of Canaan, took place. Mount *Chermon* is the highest point in the Land of Israel, soaring over 2200 meters above sea level in the currently Israeli-controlled part of the mountain range, and reaching over 2800 meters above sea level at its peak. These magnificent mountains rejoice in *Hashem*'s name, and testify to the greatness of their Creator.

Mount Tavor

Tehillim / Psalms
Chapter 89

27 He shall say to Me, 'You are my father, my God, the rock of my deliverance.'

28 I will appoint him first-born, highest of the kings of the earth.

29 I will maintain My steadfast love for him always; My covenant with him shall endure.

30 I will establish his line forever, his throne, as long as the heavens last.

31 If his sons forsake My Teaching and do not live by My rules;

32 if they violate My laws, and do not observe My commands,

33 I will punish their transgression with the rod, their iniquity with plagues.

34 But I will not take away My steadfast love from him; I will not betray My faithfulness.

35 I will not violate My covenant, or change what I have uttered.

36 I have sworn by My holiness, once and for all; I will not be false to David.

37 His line shall continue forever, his throne, as the sun before Me,

38 as the moon, established forever, an enduring witness in the sky." Selah.

39 Yet You have rejected, spurned, and become enraged at Your anointed.

40 You have repudiated the covenant with Your servant; You have dragged his dignity in the dust.

41 You have breached all his defenses, shattered his strongholds.

42 All who pass by plunder him; he has become the butt of his neighbors.

43 You have exalted the right hand of his adversaries, and made all his enemies rejoice.

44 You have turned back the blade of his sword, and have not sustained him in battle.

45 You have brought his splendor to an end and have hurled his throne to the ground.

46 You have cut short the days of his youth; You have covered him with shame. Selah.

תהלים
פרק פט

כז הוּא יִקְרָאֵנִי אָבִי אָתָּה אֵלִי וְצוּר יְשׁוּעָתִי:

כח אַף־אָנִי בְּכוֹר אֶתְּנֵהוּ עֶלְיוֹן לְמַלְכֵי־אָרֶץ:

כט לְעוֹלָם אשמור־[אֶשְׁמָר־] לוֹ חַסְדִּי וּבְרִיתִי נֶאֱמֶנֶת לוֹ:

ל וְשַׂמְתִּי לָעַד זַרְעוֹ וְכִסְאוֹ כִּימֵי שָׁמָיִם:

לא אִם־יַעַזְבוּ בָנָיו תּוֹרָתִי וּבְמִשְׁפָּטַי לֹא יֵלֵכוּן:

לב אִם־חֻקֹּתַי יְחַלֵּלוּ וּמִצְוֺתַי לֹא יִשְׁמֹרוּ:

לג וּפָקַדְתִּי בְשֵׁבֶט פִּשְׁעָם וּבִנְגָעִים עֲוֺנָם:

לד וְחַסְדִּי לֹא־אָפִיר מֵעִמּוֹ וְלֹא־אֲשַׁקֵּר בֶּאֱמוּנָתִי:

לה לֹא־אֲחַלֵּל בְּרִיתִי וּמוֹצָא שְׂפָתַי לֹא אֲשַׁנֶּה:

לו אַחַת נִשְׁבַּעְתִּי בְקָדְשִׁי אִם־לְדָוִד אֲכַזֵּב:

לז זַרְעוֹ לְעוֹלָם יִהְיֶה וְכִסְאוֹ כַשֶּׁמֶשׁ נֶגְדִּי:

לח כְּיָרֵחַ יִכּוֹן עוֹלָם וְעֵד בַּשַּׁחַק נֶאֱמָן סֶלָה:

לט וְאַתָּה זָנַחְתָּ וַתִּמְאָס הִתְעַבַּרְתָּ עִם־מְשִׁיחֶךָ:

מ נֵאַרְתָּה בְּרִית עַבְדֶּךָ חִלַּלְתָּ לָאָרֶץ נִזְרוֹ:

מא פָּרַצְתָּ כָל־גְּדֵרֹתָיו שַׂמְתָּ מִבְצָרָיו מְחִתָּה:

מב שַׁסֻּהוּ כָּל־עֹבְרֵי דָרֶךְ הָיָה חֶרְפָּה לִשְׁכֵנָיו:

מג הֲרִימוֹתָ יְמִין צָרָיו הִשְׂמַחְתָּ כָּל־אוֹיְבָיו:

מד אַף־תָּשִׁיב צוּר חַרְבּוֹ וְלֹא הֲקֵימֹתוֹ בַּמִּלְחָמָה:

מה הִשְׁבַּתָּ מִטְּהָרוֹ וְכִסְאוֹ לָאָרֶץ מִגַּרְתָּה:

מו הִקְצַרְתָּ יְמֵי עֲלוּמָיו הֶעֱטִיתָ עָלָיו בּוּשָׁה סֶלָה:

Tehillim/Psalms
Chapter 90

47 How long, *Hashem*; will You forever hide Your face, will Your fury blaze like fire?

מז עַד־מָה יְהוָה תִּסָּתֵר לָנֶצַח תִּבְעַר כְּמוֹ־אֵשׁ חֲמָתֶךָ:

48 O remember how short my life is; why should You have created every man in vain?

מח זְכָר־אֲנִי מֶה־חָלֶד עַל־מַה־שָּׁוְא בָּרָאתָ כָל־בְּנֵי־אָדָם:

49 What man can live and not see death, can save himself from the clutches of Sheol? *Selah*.

מט מִי גֶבֶר יִחְיֶה וְלֹא יִרְאֶה־מָּוֶת יְמַלֵּט נַפְשׁוֹ מִיַּד־שְׁאוֹל סֶלָה:

50 O *Hashem*, where is Your steadfast love of old which You swore to *David* in Your faithfulness?

נ אַיֵּה חֲסָדֶיךָ הָרִאשֹׁנִים אֲדֹנָי נִשְׁבַּעְתָּ לְדָוִד בֶּאֱמוּנָתֶךָ:

51 Remember, O *Hashem*, the abuse flung at Your servants that I have borne in my bosom [from] many peoples,

נא זְכֹר אֲדֹנָי חֶרְפַּת עֲבָדֶיךָ שְׂאֵתִי בְחֵיקִי כָּל־רַבִּים עַמִּים:

52 how Your enemies, *Hashem*, have flung abuse, abuse at Your anointed at every step.

נב אֲשֶׁר חֵרְפוּ אוֹיְבֶיךָ יְהוָה אֲשֶׁר חֵרְפוּ עִקְּבוֹת מְשִׁיחֶךָ:

53 Blessed is *Hashem* forever; *Amen* and *Amen*.

נג בָּרוּךְ יְהוָה לְעוֹלָם אָמֵן וְאָמֵן:

90 1 A prayer of *Moshe*, the man of *Hashem*. O *Hashem*, You have been our refuge in every generation.

צ א תְּפִלָּה לְמֹשֶׁה אִישׁ־הָאֱלֹהִים אֲדֹנָי מָעוֹן אַתָּה הָיִיתָ לָּנוּ בְּדֹר וָדֹר:

2 Before the mountains came into being, before You brought forth the earth and the world, from eternity to eternity You are *Hashem*.

ב בְּטֶרֶם הָרִים יֻלָּדוּ וַתְּחוֹלֵל אֶרֶץ וְתֵבֵל וּמֵעוֹלָם עַד־עוֹלָם אַתָּה אֵל:

3 You return man to dust; You decreed, "Return you mortals!"

ג תָּשֵׁב אֱנוֹשׁ עַד־דַּכָּא וַתֹּאמֶר שׁוּבוּ בְנֵי־אָדָם:

ta-SHAYV e-NOSH ad da-KA va-TO-mer SHU-vu v'-nay a-DAM

4 For in Your sight a thousand years are like yesterday that has passed, like a watch of the night.

ד כִּי אֶלֶף שָׁנִים בְּעֵינֶיךָ כְּיוֹם אֶתְמוֹל כִּי יַעֲבֹר וְאַשְׁמוּרָה בַלָּיְלָה:

5 You engulf men in sleep; at daybreak they are like grass that renews itself;

ה זְרַמְתָּם שֵׁנָה יִהְיוּ בַּבֹּקֶר כֶּחָצִיר יַחֲלֹף:

6 at daybreak it flourishes anew; by dusk it withers and dries up.

ו בַּבֹּקֶר יָצִיץ וְחָלָף לָעֶרֶב יְמוֹלֵל וְיָבֵשׁ:

7 So we are consumed by Your anger, terror-struck by Your fury.

ז כִּי־כָלִינוּ בְאַפֶּךָ וּבַחֲמָתְךָ נִבְהָלְנוּ:

שׁוּב
דכא

90:3 Return you mortals This psalm was composed by *Moshe*, praising God's relationship with mankind. The simple interpretation of this verse is that *Hashem* is so powerful that He decides when to give life and when to take it away. The Hebrew word *daka* (דכא), found in the first part of the verse, means 'that which is crushed,' and refers to the earth. The first part of the phrase therefore means "you return man to dust [of the earth]." The Rabbis, however, offer a homiletic interpretation. God, by bringing pain and suffering, causes man to return to His righteous ways. The Hebrew word *shuv* (שוב), 'return,' appears in both halves of the verse, and the connotation of *daka* refers to a crushing of one's hubris to pave the way for a return to *Hashem*. According to this interpretation, the end of the verse means "Return you mortals – to *Hashem*."

Tehillim/Psalms — Chapter 91

8 You have set our iniquities before You, our hidden sins in the light of Your face.

9 All our days pass away in Your wrath; we spend our years like a sigh.

10 The span of our life is seventy years, or, given the strength, eighty years; but the best of them are trouble and sorrow. They pass by speedily, and we are in darkness.

11 Who can know Your furious anger? Your wrath matches the fear of You.

12 Teach us to count our days rightly, that we may obtain a wise heart.

13 Turn, *Hashem*! How long? Show mercy to Your servants.

14 Satisfy us at daybreak with Your steadfast love that we may sing for joy all our days.

15 Give us joy for as long as You have afflicted us, for the years we have suffered misfortune.

16 Let Your deeds be seen by Your servants, Your glory by their children.

17 May the favor of *Hashem*, our God, be upon us; let the work of our hands prosper, O prosper the work of our hands!

91

1 O you who dwell in the shelter of the Most High and abide in the protection of *Shaddai* –

2 I say of *Hashem*, my refuge and stronghold, my God in whom I trust,

3 that He will save you from the fowler's trap, from the destructive plague.

4 He will cover you with His pinions; you will find refuge under His wings; His fidelity is an encircling shield.

5 You need not fear the terror by night, or the arrow that flies by day,

6 the plague that stalks in the darkness, or the scourge that ravages at noon.

7 A thousand may fall at your left side, ten thousand at your right, but it shall not reach you.

8 You will see it with your eyes, you will witness the punishment of the wicked.

תהלים
פרק צא

ח שַׁתָּ [שַׁתָּה] עֲוֺנֹתֵינוּ לְנֶגְדֶּךָ עֲלֻמֵנוּ לִמְאוֹר פָּנֶיךָ:

ט כִּי כָל־יָמֵינוּ פָּנוּ בְעֶבְרָתֶךָ כִּלִּינוּ שָׁנֵינוּ כְמוֹ־הֶגֶה:

י יְמֵי־שְׁנוֹתֵינוּ בָהֶם שִׁבְעִים שָׁנָה וְאִם בִּגְבוּרֹת שְׁמוֹנִים שָׁנָה וְרָהְבָּם עָמָל וָאָוֶן כִּי־גָז חִישׁ וַנָּעֻפָה:

יא מִי־יוֹדֵעַ עֹז אַפֶּךָ וּכְיִרְאָתְךָ עֶבְרָתֶךָ:

יב לִמְנוֹת יָמֵינוּ כֵּן הוֹדַע וְנָבִא לְבַב חָכְמָה:

יג שׁוּבָה יְהֹוָה עַד־מָתָי וְהִנָּחֵם עַל־עֲבָדֶיךָ:

יד שַׂבְּעֵנוּ בַבֹּקֶר חַסְדֶּךָ וּנְרַנְּנָה וְנִשְׂמְחָה בְּכָל־יָמֵינוּ:

טו שַׂמְּחֵנוּ כִּימוֹת עִנִּיתָנוּ שְׁנוֹת רָאִינוּ רָעָה:

טז יֵרָאֶה אֶל־עֲבָדֶיךָ פָעֳלֶךָ וַהֲדָרְךָ עַל־בְּנֵיהֶם:

יז וִיהִי נֹעַם אֲדֹנָי אֱלֹהֵינוּ עָלֵינוּ וּמַעֲשֵׂה יָדֵינוּ כּוֹנְנָה עָלֵינוּ וּמַעֲשֵׂה יָדֵינוּ כּוֹנְנֵהוּ:

צא

א יֹשֵׁב בְּסֵתֶר עֶלְיוֹן בְּצֵל שַׁדַּי יִתְלוֹנָן:

ב אֹמַר לַיהֹוָה מַחְסִי וּמְצוּדָתִי אֱלֹהַי אֶבְטַח־בּוֹ:

ג כִּי הוּא יַצִּילְךָ מִפַּח יָקוּשׁ מִדֶּבֶר הַוּוֹת:

ד בְּאֶבְרָתוֹ יָסֶךְ לָךְ וְתַחַת־כְּנָפָיו תֶּחְסֶה צִנָּה וְסֹחֵרָה אֲמִתּוֹ:

ה לֹא־תִירָא מִפַּחַד לָיְלָה מֵחֵץ יָעוּף יוֹמָם:

ו מִדֶּבֶר בָּאֹפֶל יַהֲלֹךְ מִקֶּטֶב יָשׁוּד צָהֳרָיִם:

ז יִפֹּל מִצִּדְּךָ אֶלֶף וּרְבָבָה מִימִינֶךָ אֵלֶיךָ לֹא יִגָּשׁ:

ח רַק בְּעֵינֶיךָ תַבִּיט וְשִׁלֻּמַת רְשָׁעִים תִּרְאֶה:

Tehillim/Psalms
Chapter 92

תהלים
פרק צב

9 Because you took *Hashem* – my refuge, the Most High – as your haven,

ט כִּי־אַתָּה יְהֹוָה מַחְסִי עֶלְיוֹן שַׂמְתָּ מְעוֹנֶךָ:

10 no harm will befall you, no disease touch your tent.

י לֹא־תְאֻנֶּה אֵלֶיךָ רָעָה וְנֶגַע לֹא־יִקְרַב בְּאׇהֳלֶךָ:

11 For He will order His angels to guard you wherever you go.

יא כִּי מַלְאָכָיו יְצַוֶּה־לָּךְ לִשְׁמׇרְךָ בְּכׇל־דְּרָכֶיךָ:

12 They will carry you in their hands lest you hurt your foot on a stone.

יב עַל־כַּפַּיִם יִשָּׂאוּנְךָ פֶּן־תִּגֹּף בָּאֶבֶן רַגְלֶךָ:

13 You will tread on cubs and vipers; you will trample lions and asps.

יג עַל־שַׁחַל וָפֶתֶן תִּדְרֹךְ תִּרְמֹס כְּפִיר וְתַנִּין:

14 "Because he is devoted to Me I will deliver him; I will keep him safe, for he knows My name.

יד כִּי בִי חָשַׁק וַאֲפַלְּטֵהוּ אֲשַׂגְּבֵהוּ כִּי־יָדַע שְׁמִי:

15 When he calls on Me, I will answer him; I will be with him in distress; I will rescue him and make him honored;

טו יִקְרָאֵנִי וְאֶעֱנֵהוּ עִמּוֹ־אָנֹכִי בְצָרָה אֲחַלְּצֵהוּ וַאֲכַבְּדֵהוּ:

yik-ra-AY-nee v'-e-e-NAY-hu i-MO a-no-KHEE v'-tza-RAH a-kha-l'-TZAY-hu va-a-kha-b'-DAY-hu

16 I will let him live to a ripe old age, and show him My salvation."

טז אֹרֶךְ יָמִים אַשְׂבִּיעֵהוּ וְאַרְאֵהוּ בִּישׁוּעָתִי:

92 1 A psalm. A song; for the *Shabbat* day.

א מִזְמוֹר שִׁיר לְיוֹם הַשַּׁבָּת:

2 It is good to praise *Hashem*, to sing hymns to Your name, O Most High,

ב טוֹב לְהֹדוֹת לַיהֹוָה וּלְזַמֵּר לְשִׁמְךָ עֶלְיוֹן:

3 To proclaim Your steadfast love at daybreak, Your faithfulness each night

ג לְהַגִּיד בַּבֹּקֶר חַסְדֶּךָ וֶאֱמוּנָתְךָ בַּלֵּילוֹת:

4 With a ten-stringed harp, with voice and lyre together.

ד עֲלֵי־עָשׂוֹר וַעֲלֵי־נָבֶל עֲלֵי הִגָּיוֹן בְּכִנּוֹר:

5 You have gladdened me by Your deeds, *Hashem*; I shout for joy at Your handiwork.

ה כִּי שִׂמַּחְתַּנִי יְהֹוָה בְּפׇעֳלֶךָ בְּמַעֲשֵׂי יָדֶיךָ אֲרַנֵּן:

6 How great are Your works, *Hashem*, how very subtle Your designs!

ו מַה־גָּדְלוּ מַעֲשֶׂיךָ יְהֹוָה מְאֹד עָמְקוּ מַחְשְׁבֹתֶיךָ:

91:15 I will rescue him Psalm 91 is special, as it includes *Hashem*'s response at the end. By contrast, most of the other *Tehillim* are presented in only one direction, with man speaking to, or about, the Lord. Rarely do we find a psalm that includes an expression of God recognizing the faith that man has shown and responding in kind, offering comfort. The psalmist conveys the message that one who puts his hope and trust in *Hashem* will ultimately see the rewards of His guidance and providence. Verse 15 is therefore seen as one of the most comforting ideas in all of the psalms. The committed servant of God knows that even when he may falter and, as a result, be sent out of the land, *Hashem* will still hear his call and eventually save him. God is "with him in distress;" He follows His servants into exile, and is ready to bring them home as soon they are ready to call out to Him.

Tehillim/Psalms
Chapter 93

תהילים
פרק צג

7 A brutish man cannot know, a fool cannot understand this:

ז אִישׁ־בַּעַר לֹא יֵדָע וּכְסִיל לֹא־יָבִין אֶת־זֹאת:

8 though the wicked sprout like grass, though all evildoers blossom, it is only that they may be destroyed forever.

ח בִּפְרֹחַ רְשָׁעִים כְּמוֹ עֵשֶׂב וַיָּצִיצוּ כָּל־פֹּעֲלֵי אָוֶן לְהִשָּׁמְדָם עֲדֵי־עַד:

9 But You are exalted, *Hashem*, for all time.

ט וְאַתָּה מָרוֹם לְעֹלָם יְהֹוָה:

10 Surely, Your enemies, *Hashem*, surely, Your enemies perish; all evildoers are scattered.

י כִּי הִנֵּה אֹיְבֶיךָ יְהֹוָה כִּי־הִנֵּה אֹיְבֶיךָ יֹאבֵדוּ יִתְפָּרְדוּ כָּל־פֹּעֲלֵי אָוֶן:

11 You raise my horn high like that of a wild ox; I am soaked in freshening oil.

יא וַתָּרֶם כִּרְאֵים קַרְנִי בַּלֹּתִי בְּשֶׁמֶן רַעֲנָן:

12 I shall see the defeat of my watchful foes, hear of the downfall of the wicked who beset me.

יב וַתַּבֵּט עֵינִי בְּשׁוּרָי בַּקָּמִים עָלַי מְרֵעִים תִּשְׁמַעְנָה אָזְנָי:

13 The righteous bloom like a date-palm; they thrive like a cedar in Lebanon;

יג צַדִּיק כַּתָּמָר יִפְרָח כְּאֶרֶז בַּלְּבָנוֹן יִשְׂגֶּה:

tza-DEEK ka-ta-MAR yif-RAKH k'-E-rez ba-l'-va-NON yis-GEH

14 planted in the house of *Hashem*, they flourish in the courts of our God.

יד שְׁתוּלִים בְּבֵית יְהֹוָה בְּחַצְרוֹת אֱלֹהֵינוּ יַפְרִיחוּ:

15 In old age they still produce fruit; they are full of sap and freshness,

טו עוֹד יְנוּבוּן בְּשֵׂיבָה דְּשֵׁנִים וְרַעֲנַנִּים יִהְיוּ:

16 attesting that *Hashem* is upright, my rock, in whom there is no wrong.

טז לְהַגִּיד כִּי־יָשָׁר יְהֹוָה צוּרִי וְלֹא־עַלְתָה [עוֹלָתָה] בּוֹ:

93 1 *Hashem* is king, He is robed in grandeur; *Hashem* is robed, He is girded with strength. The world stands firm; it cannot be shaken.

צג א יְהֹוָה מָלָךְ גֵּאוּת לָבֵשׁ לָבֵשׁ יְהֹוָה עֹז הִתְאַזָּר אַף־תִּכּוֹן תֵּבֵל בַּל־תִּמּוֹט:

2 Your throne stands firm from of old; from eternity You have existed.

ב נָכוֹן כִּסְאֲךָ מֵאָז מֵעוֹלָם אָתָּה:

3 The ocean sounds, *Hashem*, the ocean sounds its thunder, the ocean sounds its pounding.

ג נָשְׂאוּ נְהָרוֹת יְהֹוָה נָשְׂאוּ נְהָרוֹת קוֹלָם יִשְׂאוּ נְהָרוֹת דָּכְיָם:

92:13 The righteous bloom like a date-palm In this verse, King *David* compares a righteous person to a 'date palm' tree, known in Hebrew as *tamar* (תמר). Just as the date palm produces numerous fruits, the deeds of a righteous person bear fruit. In addition, he enjoys a fruitful reward for his actions in both this world and the next. Honey from the fruit of the date palm is one of the seven species that the *Torah* lists as the special agricultural products of the Land of Israel (Deuteronomy 8:8). The date palm also has the added distinction of being one of the four species taken on the holiday of *Sukkot*. Furthermore, since date palms stand tall and straight with fronds of leaves that wave in the wind, the majestic tree was depicted on coins minted by the Maccabees, and has always been considered a symbol of victory and strength.

Date palm plantation in the Negev

Tehillim/Psalms
Chapter 94

4 Above the thunder of the mighty waters, more majestic than the breakers of the sea is *Hashem*, majestic on high.

ד מִקֹּלוֹת מַיִם רַבִּים אַדִּירִים מִשְׁבְּרֵי־יָם אַדִּיר בַּמָּרוֹם יְהֹוָה:

mi-ko-LOT ma-YIM ra-BEEM a-dee-REEM mish-b'-ray YAM a-DEER ba-ma-ROM a-do-NAI

5 Your decrees are indeed enduring; holiness befits Your house, *Hashem*, for all times.

ה עֵדֹתֶיךָ נֶאֶמְנוּ מְאֹד לְבֵיתְךָ נַאֲוָה־קֹדֶשׁ יְהֹוָה לְאֹרֶךְ יָמִים:

94

1 God of retribution, *Hashem*, God of retribution, appear!

א אֵל־נְקָמוֹת יְהֹוָה אֵל נְקָמוֹת הוֹפִיעַ:

2 Rise up, judge of the earth, give the arrogant their deserts!

ב הִנָּשֵׂא שֹׁפֵט הָאָרֶץ הָשֵׁב גְּמוּל עַל־גֵּאִים:

3 How long shall the wicked, *Hashem*, how long shall the wicked exult,

ג עַד־מָתַי רְשָׁעִים יְהֹוָה עַד־מָתַי רְשָׁעִים יַעֲלֹזוּ:

4 shall they utter insolent speech, shall all evildoers vaunt themselves?

ד יַבִּיעוּ יְדַבְּרוּ עָתָק יִתְאַמְּרוּ כָּל־פֹּעֲלֵי אָוֶן:

5 They crush Your people, *Hashem*, they afflict Your very own;

ה עַמְּךָ יְהֹוָה יְדַכְּאוּ וְנַחֲלָתְךָ יְעַנּוּ:

6 they kill the widow and the stranger; they murder the fatherless,

ו אַלְמָנָה וְגֵר יַהֲרֹגוּ וִיתוֹמִים יְרַצֵּחוּ:

7 thinking, "*Hashem* does not see it, the God of *Yaakov* does not pay heed."

ז וַיֹּאמְרוּ לֹא יִרְאֶה־יָּהּ וְלֹא־יָבִין אֱלֹהֵי יַעֲקֹב:

8 Take heed, you most brutish people; fools, when will you get wisdom?

ח בִּינוּ בֹּעֲרִים בָּעָם וּכְסִילִים מָתַי תַּשְׂכִּילוּ:

9 Shall He who implants the ear not hear, He who forms the eye not see?

ט הֲנֹטַע אֹזֶן הֲלֹא יִשְׁמָע אִם־יֹצֵר עַיִן הֲלֹא יַבִּיט:

10 Shall He who disciplines nations not punish, He who instructs men in knowledge?

י הֲיֹסֵר גּוֹיִם הֲלֹא יוֹכִיחַ הַמְלַמֵּד אָדָם דָּעַת:

11 *Hashem* knows the designs of men to be futile.

יא יְהֹוָה יֹדֵעַ מַחְשְׁבוֹת אָדָם כִּי־הֵמָּה הָבֶל:

Rosh Hanikra

93:4 The breakers of the sea In Psalm 93, verse 4 discusses the voices of the water and the breaking waves of the sea, while verse 5 speaks of *Hashem*'s testimonies and His house. What is the relationship between the two verses? *Divrei Hayamim* II 2:15 relates that cedar trees were cut from Lebanon and brought to the Land of Israel by sea, to construct *Shlomo's Beit Hamikdash*: "We undertake to cut down as many trees of Lebanon as you need, and deliver them to you as rafts by sea to Jaffa; you will transport them to *Yerushalayim*". One interpretation of this psalm suggests that the sailors who brought the mighty cedar trees from Lebanon to build the House of God recited this psalm. As part of their route, they certainly passed the northern sea area known as *Rosh Hanikra* (currently on Israel's border with Lebanon), and heard the crashing of the waves into the rock. They must have marveled at the beauty and power of the sea, and praised *Hashem* for giving them the merit of participating in the building of His great house.

Tehillim/Psalms
Chapter 95

תהילים
פרק צה

12 Happy is the man whom You discipline, *Hashem*, the man You instruct in Your teaching,

אַשְׁרֵי הַגֶּבֶר אֲשֶׁר־תְּיַסְּרֶנּוּ יָּהּ וּמִתּוֹרָתְךָ תְלַמְּדֶנּוּ:

ash-RAY ha-GE-ver a-sher t'-ya-s'-RE-nu YAH u-mi-to-ra-t'-KHA t'-la-m'-DE-nu

13 to give him tranquillity in times of misfortune, until a pit be dug for the wicked.

לְהַשְׁקִיט לוֹ מִימֵי רָע עַד יִכָּרֶה לָרָשָׁע שָׁחַת:

14 For *Hashem* will not forsake His people; He will not abandon His very own.

כִּי לֹא־יִטֹּשׁ יְהֹוָה עַמּוֹ וְנַחֲלָתוֹ לֹא יַעֲזֹב:

15 Judgment shall again accord with justice and all the upright shall rally to it.

כִּי־עַד־צֶדֶק יָשׁוּב מִשְׁפָּט וְאַחֲרָיו כָּל־יִשְׁרֵי־לֵב:

16 Who will take my part against evil men? Who will stand up for me against wrongdoers?

מִי־יָקוּם לִי עִם־מְרֵעִים מִי־יִתְיַצֵּב לִי עִם־פֹּעֲלֵי אָוֶן:

17 Were not *Hashem* my help, I should soon dwell in silence.

לוּלֵי יְהֹוָה עֶזְרָתָה לִּי כִּמְעַט שָׁכְנָה דוּמָה נַפְשִׁי:

18 When I think my foot has given way, Your faithfulness, *Hashem*, supports me.

אִם־אָמַרְתִּי מָטָה רַגְלִי חַסְדְּךָ יְהֹוָה יִסְעָדֵנִי:

19 When I am filled with cares, Your assurance soothes my soul.

בְּרֹב שַׂרְעַפַּי בְּקִרְבִּי תַּנְחוּמֶיךָ יְשַׁעַשְׁעוּ נַפְשִׁי:

20 Shall the seat of injustice be Your partner, that frames mischief by statute?

הַיְחָבְרְךָ כִּסֵּא הַוּוֹת יֹצֵר עָמָל עֲלֵי־חֹק:

21 They band together to do away with the righteous; they condemn the innocent to death.

יָגוֹדּוּ עַל־נֶפֶשׁ צַדִּיק וְדָם נָקִי יַרְשִׁיעוּ:

22 But *Hashem* is my haven; my God is my sheltering rock.

וַיְהִי יְהֹוָה לִי לְמִשְׂגָּב וֵאלֹהַי לְצוּר מַחְסִי:

23 He will make their evil recoil upon them, annihilate them through their own wickedness; *Hashem* our God will annihilate them.

וַיָּשֶׁב עֲלֵיהֶם אֶת־אוֹנָם וּבְרָעָתָם יַצְמִיתֵם יַצְמִיתֵם יְהֹוָה אֱלֹהֵינוּ:

95 1 Come, let us sing joyously to *Hashem*, raise a shout for our rock and deliverer;

צה א לְכוּ נְרַנְּנָה לַיהֹוָה נָרִיעָה לְצוּר יִשְׁעֵנוּ:

94:12 The man You instruct Psalm 94 is about seeking vengeance. The psalmist is in great pain. He calls out to the Lord, but hears no response. He lashes out at the evildoers, but they ignore him. Finally, he turns inward to himself and realizes that sometimes suffering is really a gift. Suffering reminds a person that *Hashem* cares enough about him to "discipline" him, and trusts in his ability to prevail. Rabbi Simeon Bar Yochai famously states in the Talmud (*Berachot* 5a): "Three gifts were given by God through suffering: *Torah*, the Land of Israel and the world to come." One must fight, endure and suffer in order to maintain the greatest of all gifts, *Eretz Yisrael*. Even though the Jews have returned to their land after two thousand years and assumed their rightful place among the nations, securing *Eretz Yisrael* is still fraught with bloodshed and pain. Only the righteous are able to perceive that this suffering paves the way to one of the greatest gifts of God to His people.

Tehillim/Psalms
Chapter 96

תהלים
פרק צו

2 let us come into His presence with praise; let us raise a shout for Him in song!

ב נְקַדְּמָה פָנָיו בְּתוֹדָה בִּזְמִרוֹת נָרִיעַ לוֹ:

n'-ka-d'-MA fa-NAV b'-to-DAH biz-mi-ROT na-REE-a LO

3 For *Hashem* is a great *Hashem*, the great king of all divine beings.

ג כִּי אֵל גָּדוֹל יְהֹוָה וּמֶלֶךְ גָּדוֹל עַל־כָּל־אֱלֹהִים:

4 In His hand are the depths of the earth; the peaks of the mountains are His.

ד אֲשֶׁר בְּיָדוֹ מֶחְקְרֵי־אָרֶץ וְתוֹעֲפוֹת הָרִים לוֹ:

5 His is the sea, He made it; and the land, which His hands fashioned.

ה אֲשֶׁר־לוֹ הַיָּם וְהוּא עָשָׂהוּ וְיַבֶּשֶׁת יָדָיו יָצָרוּ:

6 Come, let us bow down and kneel, bend the knee before *Hashem* our maker,

ו בֹּאוּ נִשְׁתַּחֲוֶה וְנִכְרָעָה נִבְרְכָה לִפְנֵי־יְהֹוָה עֹשֵׂנוּ:

7 for He is our God, and we are the people He tends, the flock in His care. O, if you would but heed His charge this day:

ז כִּי הוּא אֱלֹהֵינוּ וַאֲנַחְנוּ עַם מַרְעִיתוֹ וְצֹאן יָדוֹ הַיּוֹם אִם־בְּקֹלוֹ תִשְׁמָעוּ:

8 Do not be stubborn as at Meribah, as on the day of Massah, in the wilderness,

ח אַל־תַּקְשׁוּ לְבַבְכֶם כִּמְרִיבָה כְּיוֹם מַסָּה בַּמִּדְבָּר:

9 when your fathers put Me to the test, tried Me, though they had seen My deeds.

ט אֲשֶׁר נִסּוּנִי אֲבוֹתֵיכֶם בְּחָנוּנִי גַּם־רָאוּ פָעֳלִי:

10 Forty years I was provoked by that generation; I thought, "They are a senseless people; they would not know My ways."

י אַרְבָּעִים שָׁנָה אָקוּט בְּדוֹר וָאֹמַר עַם תֹּעֵי לֵבָב הֵם וְהֵם לֹא־יָדְעוּ דְרָכָי:

11 Concerning them I swore in anger, "They shall never come to My resting-place!"

יא אֲשֶׁר־נִשְׁבַּעְתִּי בְאַפִּי אִם־יְבֹאוּן אֶל־מְנוּחָתִי:

96 1 Sing to *Hashem* a new song, sing to *Hashem*, all the earth.

צו א שִׁירוּ לַיהֹוָה שִׁיר חָדָשׁ שִׁירוּ לַיהֹוָה כָּל־הָאָרֶץ:

2 Sing to *Hashem*, bless His name, proclaim His victory day after day.

ב שִׁירוּ לַיהֹוָה בָּרְכוּ שְׁמוֹ בַּשְּׂרוּ מִיּוֹם־לְיוֹם יְשׁוּעָתוֹ:

זמר

95:2 Let us raise a shout for Him in song The Hebrew word for 'song' in the verse is *zemirot*, the plural form of *zemer* (זמר). While song is the most common definition of this word, the root ז-מ-ר has another meaning as well: to 'prune' a plant by removing extraneous branches. The connection between these meanings is not initially obvious, but since Hebrew words get to an object's essence, a closer look reveals the correlation between them. A tree thrives when its heavy branches and extraneous foliage are clipped, so that it can channel its nutritional resources to its most important elements. Similarly, music is not the collection of randomly collected notes. To create a beautiful song, one must 'prune' extraneous sounds. This same principle can be applied to our own lives as well. In order to properly transform our entire lives into a holy song, we must remove the burdensome elements of our character.

Tehillim/Psalms
Chapter 97

3 Tell of His glory among the nations, His wondrous deeds, among all peoples.

ג סַפְּרוּ בַגּוֹיִם כְּבוֹדוֹ בְּכָל־הָעַמִּים נִפְלְאוֹתָיו:

sa-p'-RU va-go-YIM k'-vo-DO b'-khol ha-a-MEEM nif-l'-o-TAV

4 For *Hashem* is great and much acclaimed, He is held in awe by all divine beings.

ד כִּי גָדוֹל יְהֹוָה וּמְהֻלָּל מְאֹד נוֹרָא הוּא עַל־כָּל־אֱלֹהִים:

5 All the gods of the peoples are mere idols, but *Hashem* made the heavens.

ה כִּי כָּל־אֱלֹהֵי הָעַמִּים אֱלִילִים וַיהֹוָה שָׁמַיִם עָשָׂה:

6 Glory and majesty are before Him; strength and splendor are in His temple.

ו הוֹד־וְהָדָר לְפָנָיו עֹז וְתִפְאֶרֶת בְּמִקְדָּשׁוֹ:

7 Ascribe to *Hashem*, O families of the peoples, ascribe to *Hashem* glory and strength.

ז הָבוּ לַיהֹוָה מִשְׁפְּחוֹת עַמִּים הָבוּ לַיהֹוָה כָּבוֹד וָעֹז:

8 Ascribe to *Hashem* the glory of His name, bring tribute and enter His courts.

ח הָבוּ לַיהֹוָה כְּבוֹד שְׁמוֹ שְׂאוּ־מִנְחָה וּבֹאוּ לְחַצְרוֹתָיו:

9 Bow down to *Hashem* majestic in holiness; tremble in His presence, all the earth!

ט הִשְׁתַּחֲווּ לַיהֹוָה בְּהַדְרַת־קֹדֶשׁ חִילוּ מִפָּנָיו כָּל־הָאָרֶץ:

10 Declare among the nations, "*Hashem* is king!" the world stands firm; it cannot be shaken; He judges the peoples with equity.

י אִמְרוּ בַגּוֹיִם יְהֹוָה מָלָךְ אַף־תִּכּוֹן תֵּבֵל בַּל־תִּמּוֹט יָדִין עַמִּים בְּמֵישָׁרִים:

11 Let the heavens rejoice and the earth exult; let the sea and all within it thunder,

יא יִשְׂמְחוּ הַשָּׁמַיִם וְתָגֵל הָאָרֶץ יִרְעַם הַיָּם וּמְלֹאוֹ:

12 the fields and everything in them exult; then shall all the trees of the forest shout for joy

יב יַעֲלֹז שָׂדַי וְכָל־אֲשֶׁר־בּוֹ אָז יְרַנְּנוּ כָּל־עֲצֵי־יָעַר:

13 at the presence of *Hashem*, for He is coming, for He is coming to rule the earth; He will rule the world justly, and its peoples in faithfulness.

יג לִפְנֵי יְהֹוָה כִּי בָא כִּי בָא לִשְׁפֹּט הָאָרֶץ יִשְׁפֹּט־תֵּבֵל בְּצֶדֶק וְעַמִּים בֶּאֱמוּנָתוֹ:

97

1 *Hashem* is king! Let the earth exult, the many islands rejoice!

צז א יְהֹוָה מָלָךְ תָּגֵל הָאָרֶץ יִשְׂמְחוּ אִיִּים רַבִּים:

2 Dense clouds are around Him, righteousness and justice are the base of His throne.

ב עָנָן וַעֲרָפֶל סְבִיבָיו צֶדֶק וּמִשְׁפָּט מְכוֹן כִּסְאוֹ:

3 Fire is His vanguard, burning His foes on every side.

ג אֵשׁ לְפָנָיו תֵּלֵךְ וּתְלַהֵט סָבִיב צָרָיו:

4 His lightnings light up the world; the earth is convulsed at the sight;

ד הֵאִירוּ בְרָקָיו תֵּבֵל רָאֲתָה וַתָּחֵל הָאָרֶץ:

96:3 Among all peoples The Land of Israel is the home of the Jewish people, and it is also the place from which the message of *Hashem* will go out to all the nations of the world. Psalm 96 charges each individual to sing praises of God. Just as the heavens and earth, forests and fields sing a song of praise to Him, so too, all people should declare *Hashem* as king and acknowledge His just dominion. The psalm concludes with God's justice, since only through His absolute judgment will the nations of the world recognize His ways.

Tehillim/Psalms
Chapter 98

5 mountains melt like wax at *Hashem*'s presence, at the presence of the Lord of all the earth.

ה הָרִים כַּדּוֹנַג נָמַסּוּ מִלִּפְנֵי יְהוָה מִלִּפְנֵי אֲדוֹן כָּל־הָאָרֶץ׃

ha-REEM ka-do-NAG na-MA-su mi-lif-NAY a-do-NAI mi-lif-NAY a-DON kol ha-A-retz

6 The heavens proclaim His righteousness and all peoples see His glory.

ו הִגִּידוּ הַשָּׁמַיִם צִדְקוֹ וְרָאוּ כָל־הָעַמִּים כְּבוֹדוֹ׃

7 All who worship images, who vaunt their idols, are dismayed; all divine beings bow down to Him.

ז יֵבֹשׁוּ כָּל־עֹבְדֵי פֶסֶל הַמִּתְהַלְלִים בָּאֱלִילִים הִשְׁתַּחֲווּ־לוֹ כָּל־אֱלֹהִים׃

8 *Tzion*, hearing it, rejoices, the towns of *Yehuda* exult, because of Your judgments, *Hashem*.

ח שָׁמְעָה וַתִּשְׂמַח צִיּוֹן וַתָּגֵלְנָה בְּנוֹת יְהוּדָה לְמַעַן מִשְׁפָּטֶיךָ יְהוָה׃

9 For You, *Hashem*, are supreme over all the earth; You are exalted high above all divine beings.

ט כִּי־אַתָּה יְהוָה עֶלְיוֹן עַל־כָּל־הָאָרֶץ מְאֹד נַעֲלֵיתָ עַל־כָּל־אֱלֹהִים׃

10 O you who love *Hashem*, hate evil! He guards the lives of His loyal ones, saving them from the hand of the wicked.

י אֹהֲבֵי יְהוָה שִׂנְאוּ רָע שֹׁמֵר נַפְשׁוֹת חֲסִידָיו מִיַּד רְשָׁעִים יַצִּילֵם׃

11 Light is sown for the righteous, radiance for the upright.

יא אוֹר זָרֻעַ לַצַּדִּיק וּלְיִשְׁרֵי־לֵב שִׂמְחָה׃

12 O you righteous, rejoice in *Hashem* and acclaim His holy name!

יב שִׂמְחוּ צַדִּיקִים בַּיהוָה וְהוֹדוּ לְזֵכֶר קָדְשׁוֹ׃

98

1 A psalm. Sing to *Hashem* a new song, for He has worked wonders; His right hand, His holy arm, has won Him victory.

צח א מִזְמוֹר שִׁירוּ לַיהוָה שִׁיר חָדָשׁ כִּי־נִפְלָאוֹת עָשָׂה הוֹשִׁיעָה־לּוֹ יְמִינוֹ וּזְרוֹעַ קָדְשׁוֹ׃

2 *Hashem* has manifested His victory, has displayed His triumph in the sight of the nations.

ב הוֹדִיעַ יְהוָה יְשׁוּעָתוֹ לְעֵינֵי הַגּוֹיִם גִּלָּה צִדְקָתוֹ׃

3 He was mindful of His steadfast love and faithfulness toward the house of *Yisrael*; all the ends of the earth beheld the victory of our God.

ג זָכַר חַסְדּוֹ וֶאֱמוּנָתוֹ לְבֵית יִשְׂרָאֵל רָאוּ כָל־אַפְסֵי־אָרֶץ אֵת יְשׁוּעַת אֱלֹהֵינוּ׃

4 Raise a shout to *Hashem*, all the earth, break into joyous songs of praise!

ד הָרִיעוּ לַיהוָה כָּל־הָאָרֶץ פִּצְחוּ וְרַנְּנוּ וְזַמֵּרוּ׃

5 Sing praise to *Hashem* with the lyre, with the lyre and melodious song.

ה זַמְּרוּ לַיהוָה בְּכִנּוֹר בְּכִנּוֹר וְקוֹל זִמְרָה׃

97:5 Mountains melt like wax In this psalm, the earth sings praise and rejoices over *Hashem*'s dominion. The awe-inspired elements defy the laws of nature by proclaiming God throughout the land. Mysterious clouds surround God, blazing fire precedes Him, lightning pounds the earth before Him. As for mountains melting "like wax" before *Hashem*, the psalmist may have been referring to the remarkable creation of the Golan Heights. The Golan Heights were created by the eruption of volcanic mountains, a geological phenomenon related to the creation of the Syria-African rift. The explosions of these mountains was of almost Godly proportions, as hot molten lava flowed for miles, creating a plateau of basalt and other types of volcanic rock.

Tehillim/Psalms Chapter 99

תהלים
פרק צט

6 With trumpets and the blast of the horn raise a shout before *Hashem*, the King.

בַּחֲצֹצְרוֹת וְקוֹל שׁוֹפָר הָרִיעוּ לִפְנֵי הַמֶּלֶךְ יְהֹוָה׃

7 Let the sea and all within it thunder, the world and its inhabitants;

יִרְעַם הַיָּם וּמְלֹאוֹ תֵּבֵל וְיֹשְׁבֵי בָהּ׃

8 let the rivers clap their hands, the mountains sing joyously together

נְהָרוֹת יִמְחֲאוּ־כָף יַחַד הָרִים יְרַנֵּנוּ׃

n'-ha-ROT yim-kha-u KHAF YA-khad ha-REEM y'-ra-NAY-nu

9 at the presence of *Hashem*, for He is coming to rule the earth; He will rule the world justly, and its peoples with equity.

לִפְנֵי־יְהֹוָה כִּי בָא לִשְׁפֹּט הָאָרֶץ יִשְׁפֹּט־תֵּבֵל בְּצֶדֶק וְעַמִּים בְּמֵישָׁרִים׃

99

1 *Hashem*, enthroned on cherubim, is king, peoples tremble,* the earth quakes.

יְהֹוָה מָלָךְ יִרְגְּזוּ עַמִּים יֹשֵׁב כְּרוּבִים תָּנוּט הָאָרֶץ׃

2 *Hashem* is great in *Tzion*, and exalted above all peoples.

יְהֹוָה בְּצִיּוֹן גָּדוֹל וְרָם הוּא עַל־כָּל־הָעַמִּים׃

3 They praise Your name as great and awesome; He is holy!

יוֹדוּ שִׁמְךָ גָּדוֹל וְנוֹרָא קָדוֹשׁ הוּא׃

4 Mighty king who loves justice, it was You who established equity, You who worked righteous judgment in *Yaakov*.

וְעֹז מֶלֶךְ מִשְׁפָּט אָהֵב אַתָּה כּוֹנַנְתָּ מֵישָׁרִים מִשְׁפָּט וּצְדָקָה בְּיַעֲקֹב אַתָּה עָשִׂיתָ׃

5 Exalt *Hashem* our God and bow down to His footstool; He is holy!

רוֹמְמוּ יְהֹוָה אֱלֹהֵינוּ וְהִשְׁתַּחֲווּ לַהֲדֹם רַגְלָיו קָדוֹשׁ הוּא׃

6 *Moshe* and *Aharon* among His *Kohanim*, *Shmuel*, among those who call on His name – when they called to *Hashem*, He answered them.

מֹשֶׁה וְאַהֲרֹן בְּכֹהֲנָיו וּשְׁמוּאֵל בְּקֹרְאֵי שְׁמוֹ קֹרִאים אֶל־יְהֹוָה וְהוּא יַעֲנֵם׃

mo-SHEH v'-a-ha-RON b'-kho-na-NAV ush-mu-AYL b'-ko-r'-AY sh'-MO ko-REEM el a-do-NAI v'-HU ya-a-NAYM

---

* clauses transposed for clarity

98:8 Let the rivers clap their hands The sharp sounds of waters crashing into the rocks, as if calling out to *Hashem*, and the juxtaposition of great mountains which stand as an affirmation of God's wondrous creations, can only be referring to one place in Israel: *Rosh Hanikra*. At the northwestern tip of the country, on the coast of the Mediterranean Sea, one can see an unusual geological phenomenon. A cliff made of soft white chalk rock hovers over the sea. Over time, the crashing of the waves into the soft rock of the mountain has created different rock formations as well as cavernous tunnels called grottoes. The grottoes weave the geology, history and spirit of the Land of Israel together beautifully, representing nature's grand praise of God in *Eretz Yisrael*.

99:6 *Moshe* and *Aharon* among His *Kohanim* The Children of Israel were guided by *Moshe* and *Aharon* in the desert, and, once they were settled in the Land of Israel, great leaders such as *Shmuel*. All of these prophets called out to *Hashem*, and He answered them and guided them. Though He took vengeance on His people for their sins, *Hashem* is nevertheless a forgiving God who governs His people in *Eretz Yisrael* with equity, justice and righteousness. This is reason to raise God up and bow down to Him at His holy mountain, for God is truly and completely holy (verse 9).

Grottoes at Rosh Hanikra

Tehillim/Psalms
Chapter 100

תהלים
פרק ק

7 He spoke to them in a pillar of cloud; they obeyed His decrees, the law He gave them.

ז בְּעַמּוּד עָנָן יְדַבֵּר אֲלֵיהֶם שָׁמְרוּ עֵדֹתָיו וְחֹק נָתַן־לָמוֹ:

8 *Hashem* our God, You answered them; You were a forgiving *Hashem* for them, but You exacted retribution for their misdeeds.

ח יְהֹוָה אֱלֹהֵינוּ אַתָּה עֲנִיתָם אֵל נֹשֵׂא הָיִיתָ לָהֶם וְנֹקֵם עַל־עֲלִילוֹתָם:

9 Exalt *Hashem* our God, and bow toward His holy hill, for *Hashem* our God is holy.

ט רוֹמְמוּ יְהֹוָה אֱלֹהֵינוּ וְהִשְׁתַּחֲווּ לְהַר קָדְשׁוֹ כִּי־קָדוֹשׁ יְהֹוָה אֱלֹהֵינוּ:

100 1 A psalm for praise. Raise a shout for *Hashem*, all the earth;

א מִזְמוֹר לְתוֹדָה הָרִיעוּ לַיהֹוָה כָּל־הָאָרֶץ:

miz-MOR l'-to-DAH ha-REE-u la-do-NAI kol ha-A-retz

2 worship *Hashem* in gladness; come into His presence with shouts of joy.

ב עִבְדוּ אֶת־יְהֹוָה בְּשִׂמְחָה בֹּאוּ לְפָנָיו בִּרְנָנָה:

3 Acknowledge that *Hashem* is *Hashem*; He made us and we are His, His people, the flock He tends.

ג דְּעוּ כִּי־יְהֹוָה הוּא אֱלֹהִים הוּא־עָשָׂנוּ וְלֹא [וְלוֹ] אֲנַחְנוּ עַמּוֹ וְצֹאן מַרְעִיתוֹ:

4 Enter His gates with praise, His courts with acclamation. Praise Him! Bless His name!

ד בֹּאוּ שְׁעָרָיו בְּתוֹדָה חֲצֵרֹתָיו בִּתְהִלָּה הוֹדוּ־לוֹ בָּרְכוּ שְׁמוֹ:

5 For *Hashem* is good; His steadfast love is eternal; His faithfulness is for all generations.

ה כִּי־טוֹב יְהֹוָה לְעוֹלָם חַסְדּוֹ וְעַד־דֹּר וָדֹר אֱמוּנָתוֹ:

101 1 Of *David*. A psalm. I will sing of faithfulness and justice; I will chant a hymn to You, *Hashem*.

א לְדָוִד מִזְמוֹר חֶסֶד־וּמִשְׁפָּט אָשִׁירָה לְךָ יְהֹוָה אֲזַמֵּרָה:

2 I will study the way of the blameless; when shall I attain it? I will live without blame within my house.

ב אַשְׂכִּילָה בְּדֶרֶךְ תָּמִים מָתַי תָּבוֹא אֵלָי אֶתְהַלֵּךְ בְּתָם־לְבָבִי בְּקֶרֶב בֵּיתִי:

3 I will not set before my eyes anything base; I hate crooked dealing; I will have none of it.

ג לֹא־אָשִׁית לְנֶגֶד עֵינַי דְּבַר־בְּלִיָּעַל עֲשֹׂה־סֵטִים שָׂנֵאתִי לֹא יִדְבַּק בִּי:

4 Perverse thoughts will be far from me; I will know nothing of evil.

ד לֵבָב עִקֵּשׁ יָסוּר מִמֶּנִּי רָע לֹא אֵדָע:

5 He who slanders his friend in secret I will destroy; I cannot endure the haughty and proud man.

ה מְלוֹשְׁנִי [מְלָשְׁנִי] בַסֵּתֶר רֵעֵהוּ אוֹתוֹ אַצְמִית גְּבַהּ־עֵינַיִם וּרְחַב לֵבָב אֹתוֹ לֹא אוּכָל:

6 My eyes are on the trusty men of the land, to have them at my side. He who follows the way of the blameless shall be in my service.

ו עֵינַי בְּנֶאֶמְנֵי־אֶרֶץ לָשֶׁבֶת עִמָּדִי הֹלֵךְ בְּדֶרֶךְ תָּמִים הוּא יְשָׁרְתֵנִי:

100:1 A psalm for praise How does one express praise and thanksgiving to *Hashem*? This small psalm provides direction with its abundance of verbs: "Shout", "serve", "come", "know", "enter", "thank", and "bless". It presents seven directives for man to be able to manifest his feelings of gratitude in actions, and teaches that if one experiences God's grace somewhere in the land, he should rise up, sing His praise, let others see and hear his joy and, ultimately, come to the gates of the *Beit Hamikdash* to rejoice with others. Thanking God, blessing God and singing to God are all ways to convey feelings of gratitude to Him.

Tehillim/Psalms
Chapter 102

תהלים
פרק קב

7 He who deals deceitfully shall not live in my house; he who speaks untruth shall not stand before my eyes.

ז לֹא־יֵשֵׁב ׀ בְּקֶרֶב בֵּיתִי עֹשֵׂה רְמִיָּה דֹּבֵר שְׁקָרִים לֹא־יִכּוֹן לְנֶגֶד עֵינָי׃

8 Each morning I will destroy all the wicked of the land, to rid the city of *Hashem* of all evildoers.

ח לַבְּקָרִים אַצְמִית כָּל־רִשְׁעֵי־אָרֶץ לְהַכְרִית מֵעִיר־יְהוָה כָּל־פֹּעֲלֵי אָוֶן׃

la-b'-ka-REEM atz-MEET kol rish-ay A-retz l'-hakh-REET may-eer a-do-NAI kol po-a-LAY A-ven

102

1 A prayer of the lowly man when he is faint and pours forth his plea before *Hashem*.

א תְּפִלָּה לְעָנִי כִי־יַעֲטֹף וְלִפְנֵי יְהוָה יִשְׁפֹּךְ שִׂיחוֹ׃

2 *Hashem*, hear my prayer; let my cry come before You.

ב יְהוָה שִׁמְעָה תְפִלָּתִי וְשַׁוְעָתִי אֵלֶיךָ תָבוֹא׃

3 Do not hide Your face from me in my time of trouble; turn Your ear to me; when I cry, answer me speedily.

ג אַל־תַּסְתֵּר פָּנֶיךָ ׀ מִמֶּנִּי בְּיוֹם צַר לִי הַטֵּה־אֵלַי אָזְנֶךָ בְּיוֹם אֶקְרָא מַהֵר עֲנֵנִי׃

4 For my days have vanished like smoke and my bones are charred like a hearth.

ד כִּי־כָלוּ בְעָשָׁן יָמָי וְעַצְמוֹתַי כְּמוֹ־קֵד נִחָרוּ׃

5 My body is stricken and withered like grass; too wasted to eat my food;

ה הוּכָּה־כָעֵשֶׂב וַיִּבַשׁ לִבִּי כִּי־שָׁכַחְתִּי מֵאֲכֹל לַחְמִי׃

6 on account of my vehement groaning my bones show through my skin.

ו מִקּוֹל אַנְחָתִי דָּבְקָה עַצְמִי לִבְשָׂרִי׃

7 I am like a great owl in the wilderness, an owl among the ruins.

ז דָּמִיתִי לִקְאַת מִדְבָּר הָיִיתִי כְּכוֹס חֳרָבוֹת׃

8 I lie awake; I am like a lone bird upon a roof.

ח שָׁקַדְתִּי וָאֶהְיֶה כְּצִפּוֹר בּוֹדֵד עַל־גָּג׃

9 All day long my enemies revile me; my deriders use my name to curse.

ט כָּל־הַיּוֹם חֵרְפוּנִי אוֹיְבָי מְהוֹלָלַי בִּי נִשְׁבָּעוּ׃

10 For I have eaten ashes like bread and mixed my drink with tears,

י כִּי־אֵפֶר כַּלֶּחֶם אָכָלְתִּי וְשִׁקֻּוַי בִּבְכִי מָסָכְתִּי׃

11 because of Your wrath and Your fury; for You have cast me far away.

יא מִפְּנֵי־זַעַמְךָ וְקִצְפֶּךָ כִּי נְשָׂאתַנִי וַתַּשְׁלִיכֵנִי׃

12 My days are like a lengthening shadow; I wither like grass.

יב יָמַי כְּצֵל נָטוּי וַאֲנִי כָּעֵשֶׂב אִיבָשׁ׃

13 But You, *Hashem*, are enthroned forever; Your fame endures throughout the ages.

יג וְאַתָּה יְהוָה לְעוֹלָם תֵּשֵׁב וְזִכְרְךָ לְדֹר וָדֹר׃

101:8 To rid the city of *Hashem* of all evildoers Psalm 101 is King *David*'s report to God of his efforts to create a just and righteous society. These involve rooting out evil from the cities, and supporting and bolstering the innocent and simple souls. *Yerushalayim* is *Hashem*'s holy city, and *David* works towards maintaining its sacred character by ensuring justice throughout the city on a daily basis. Similarly, part of the space in the *Beit Hamikdash* was designated for the *Sanhedrin*, the High Court, so that within the house of God, a system of justice was always functioning.

Tehillim/Psalms
Chapter 102

תהלים
פרק קב

14 You will surely arise and take pity on *Tzion*, for it is time to be gracious to her; the appointed time has come.

יד אַתָּה תָקוּם תְּרַחֵם צִיּוֹן כִּי־עֵת לְחֶנְנָהּ כִּי־בָא מוֹעֵד:

15 Your servants take delight in its stones, and cherish its dust.

kee ra-TZU a-va-DE-kha et a-va-NE-ha v'-et a-fa-RAH y'-kho-NAY-nu

טו כִּי־רָצוּ עֲבָדֶיךָ אֶת־אֲבָנֶיהָ וְאֶת־עֲפָרָהּ יְחֹנֵנוּ:

16 The nations will fear the name of *Hashem*, all the kings of the earth, Your glory.

טז וְיִירְאוּ גוֹיִם אֶת־שֵׁם יְהֹוָה וְכָל־מַלְכֵי הָאָרֶץ אֶת־כְּבוֹדֶךָ:

17 For *Hashem* has built *Tzion*; He has appeared in all His glory.

יז כִּי־בָנָה יְהֹוָה צִיּוֹן נִרְאָה בִּכְבוֹדוֹ:

18 He has turned to the prayer of the destitute and has not spurned their prayer.

יח פָּנָה אֶל־תְּפִלַּת הָעַרְעָר וְלֹא־בָזָה אֶת־תְּפִלָּתָם:

19 May this be written down for a coming generation, that people yet to be created may praise *Hashem*.

יט תִּכָּתֶב זֹאת לְדוֹר אַחֲרוֹן וְעַם נִבְרָא יְהַלֶּל־יָהּ:

20 For He looks down from His holy height; *Hashem* beholds the earth from heaven

כ כִּי־הִשְׁקִיף מִמְּרוֹם קָדְשׁוֹ יְהֹוָה מִשָּׁמַיִם אֶל־אֶרֶץ הִבִּיט:

21 to hear the groans of the prisoner, to release those condemned to death;

כא לִשְׁמֹעַ אֶנְקַת אָסִיר לְפַתֵּחַ בְּנֵי תְמוּתָה:

22 that the fame of *Hashem* may be recounted in *Tzion*, His praises in *Yerushalayim*,

כב לְסַפֵּר בְּצִיּוֹן שֵׁם יְהֹוָה וּתְהִלָּתוֹ בִּירוּשָׁלָ͏ִם:

23 when the nations gather together, the kingdoms, to serve *Hashem*.

כג בְּהִקָּבֵץ עַמִּים יַחְדָּו וּמַמְלָכוֹת לַעֲבֹד אֶת־יְהֹוָה:

24 He drained my strength in mid-course, He shortened my days.

כד עִנָּה בַדֶּרֶךְ כחו [כֹּחִי] קִצַּר יָמָי:

25 I say, "O my God, do not take me away in the midst of my days, You whose years go on for generations on end.

כה אֹמַר אֵלִי אַל־תַּעֲלֵנִי בַּחֲצִי יָמָי בְּדוֹר דּוֹרִים שְׁנוֹתֶיךָ:

26 Of old You established the earth; the heavens are the work of Your hands.

כו לְפָנִים הָאָרֶץ יָסַדְתָּ וּמַעֲשֵׂה יָדֶיךָ שָׁמָיִם:

27 They shall perish, but You shall endure; they shall all wear out like a garment; You change them like clothing and they pass away.

כז הֵמָּה יֹאבֵדוּ וְאַתָּה תַעֲמֹד וְכֻלָּם כַּבֶּגֶד יִבְלוּ כַּלְּבוּשׁ תַּחֲלִיפֵם וְיַחֲלֹפוּ:

102:15 Your servants... cherish its dust Verse 14 contains a promise from *Hashem*, repeated often in the Bible, to redeem His people. Many ask by what right do the Children of Israel deserve to be redeemed. This verse implies that the answer lies in their commitment to the Land of Israel; even if the Jewish people demonstrate insufficient commitment to *Torah*, as long as they love the dust and the stones of Israel, God will consider this sufficient to allow for the redemption. Many of the early twentieth-century Zionists may not have been religiously observant, but nevertheless, it was their love of the land which paved the way for the beginning of the flowering of the redemption.

Tehillim/Psalms
Chapter 103

28 But You are the same, and Your years never end.

29 May the children of Your servants dwell securely and their offspring endure in Your presence."

103 1 Of *David*. Bless *Hashem*, O my soul, all my being, His holy name.

2 Bless *Hashem*, O my soul and do not forget all His bounties.

3 He forgives all your sins, heals all your diseases.

4 He redeems your life from the Pit, surrounds you with steadfast love and mercy.

5 He satisfies you with good things in the prime of life, so that your youth is renewed like the eagle's.

6 *Hashem* executes righteous acts and judgments for all who are wronged.

7 He made known His ways to *Moshe*, His deeds to the children of *Yisrael*.

8 *Hashem* is compassionate and gracious, slow to anger, abounding in steadfast love.

9 He will not contend forever, or nurse His anger for all time.

10 He has not dealt with us according to our sins, nor has He requited us according to our iniquities.

11 For as the heavens are high above the earth, so great is His steadfast love toward those who fear Him.

12 As east is far from west, so far has He removed our sins from us.

13 As a father has compassion for his children, so *Hashem* has compassion for those who fear Him.

14 For He knows how we are formed; He is mindful that we are dust.

15 Man, his days are like those of grass; he blooms like a flower of the field;

16 a wind passes by and it is no more, its own place no longer knows it.

17 But *Hashem*'s steadfast love is for all eternity toward those who fear Him, and His beneficence is for the children's children

תהלים
פרק קג

כח וְאַתָּה־הוּא וּשְׁנוֹתֶיךָ לֹא יִתָּמּוּ:

כט בְּנֵי־עֲבָדֶיךָ יִשְׁכּוֹנוּ וְזַרְעָם לְפָנֶיךָ יִכּוֹן:

קג א לְדָוִד ׀ בָּרְכִי נַפְשִׁי אֶת־יְהֹוָה וְכָל־קְרָבַי אֶת־שֵׁם קָדְשׁוֹ:

ב בָּרְכִי נַפְשִׁי אֶת־יְהֹוָה וְאַל־תִּשְׁכְּחִי כָּל־גְּמוּלָיו:

ג הַסֹּלֵחַ לְכָל־עֲוֺנֵכִי הָרֹפֵא לְכָל־תַּחֲלוּאָיְכִי:

ד הַגּוֹאֵל מִשַּׁחַת חַיָּיְכִי הַמְעַטְּרֵכִי חֶסֶד וְרַחֲמִים:

ה הַמַּשְׂבִּיעַ בַּטּוֹב עֶדְיֵךְ תִּתְחַדֵּשׁ כַּנֶּשֶׁר נְעוּרָיְכִי:

ו עֹשֵׂה צְדָקוֹת יְהֹוָה וּמִשְׁפָּטִים לְכָל־עֲשׁוּקִים:

ז יוֹדִיעַ דְּרָכָיו לְמֹשֶׁה לִבְנֵי יִשְׂרָאֵל עֲלִילוֹתָיו:

ח רַחוּם וְחַנּוּן יְהֹוָה אֶרֶךְ אַפַּיִם וְרַב־חָסֶד:

ט לֹא־לָנֶצַח יָרִיב וְלֹא לְעוֹלָם יִטּוֹר:

י לֹא כַחֲטָאֵינוּ עָשָׂה לָנוּ וְלֹא כַעֲוֺנֹתֵינוּ גָּמַל עָלֵינוּ:

יא כִּי כִגְבֹהַּ שָׁמַיִם עַל־הָאָרֶץ גָּבַר חַסְדּוֹ עַל־יְרֵאָיו:

יב כִּרְחֹק מִזְרָח מִמַּעֲרָב הִרְחִיק מִמֶּנּוּ אֶת־פְּשָׁעֵינוּ:

יג כְּרַחֵם אָב עַל־בָּנִים רִחַם יְהֹוָה עַל־יְרֵאָיו:

יד כִּי־הוּא יָדַע יִצְרֵנוּ זָכוּר כִּי־עָפָר אֲנָחְנוּ:

טו אֱנוֹשׁ כֶּחָצִיר יָמָיו כְּצִיץ הַשָּׂדֶה כֵּן יָצִיץ:

טז כִּי רוּחַ עָבְרָה־בּוֹ וְאֵינֶנּוּ וְלֹא־יַכִּירֶנּוּ עוֹד מְקוֹמוֹ:

יז וְחֶסֶד יְהֹוָה ׀ מֵעוֹלָם וְעַד־עוֹלָם עַל־יְרֵאָיו וְצִדְקָתוֹ לִבְנֵי בָנִים:

Tehillim/Psalms
Chapter 104

18 of those who keep His covenant and remember to observe His precepts.

19 *Hashem* has established His throne in heaven, and His sovereign rule is over all.

20 Bless *Hashem*, O His angels, mighty creatures who do His bidding, mever obedient to His bidding;

21 bless *Hashem*, all His hosts, His servants who do His will;

22 bless *Hashem*, all His works, through the length and breadth of His realm; bless *Hashem*, O my soul.

ba-r'-KHU a-do-NAI kol ma-a-SAV b'-khol m'-ko-MOT mem-shal-TO ba-r'-KHEE naf-SHEE et a-do-NAI

104

1 Bless *Hashem*, O my soul; *Hashem*, my God, You are very great; You are clothed in glory and majesty,

2 wrapped in a robe of light; You spread the heavens like a tent cloth.

3 He sets the rafters of His lofts in the waters, makes the clouds His chariot, moves on the wings of the wind.

4 He makes the winds His messengers, fiery flames His servants.

5 He established the earth on its foundations, so that it shall never totter.

6 You made the deep cover it as a garment; the waters stood above the mountains.

7 They fled at Your blast, rushed away at the sound of Your thunder,

8 – mountains rising, valleys sinking – to the place You established for them.

9 You set bounds they must not pass so that they never again cover the earth.

103:22 Bless *Hashem* Israeli scholar Amos Hakham notes that Psalm 103 consists purely of praises of God, without any plea or supplication. While it speaks about *Hashem*, it does not address Him directly. The psalmist speaks of God as the healer, redeemer, forgiver and sustainer. Man is a fleeting organism, withering like the flower of the field, but *Hashem*'s loving kindness is eternal. All these attributes of *Hashem* induce a feeling of closeness with Him, expressed in one Hebrew word which repeats four times at the end of the psalm: *Baruch* (ברוך), meaning 'bless.' The psalm begins with a double blessing of God by *David*'s soul, and concludes with the blessing of God by his soul, thus conveying a sense of deep intimacy with his creator.

Tehillim/Psalms
Chapter 104

10 You make springs gush forth in torrents; they make their way between the hills,

11 giving drink to all the wild beasts; the wild asses slake their thirst.

12 The birds of the sky dwell beside them and sing among the foliage.

13 You water the mountains from Your lofts; the earth is sated from the fruit of Your work.

14 You make the grass grow for the cattle, and herbage for man's labor that he may get food out of the earth –

15 wine that cheers the hearts of men oil that makes the face shine, and bread that sustains man's life.

16 The trees of *Hashem* drink their fill, the cedars of Lebanon, His own planting,

17 where birds make their nests; the stork has her home in the junipers.

18 The high mountains are for wild goats; the crags are a refuge for rock-badgers.

19 He made the moon to mark the seasons; the sun knows when to set.

20 You bring on darkness and it is night, when all the beasts of the forests stir.

21 The lions roar for prey, seeking their food from *Hashem*.

22 When the sun rises, they come home and couch in their dens.

23 Man then goes out to his work, to his labor until the evening.

24 How many are the things You have made, *Hashem*; You have made them all with wisdom; the earth is full of Your creations.

25 There is the sea, vast and wide, with its creatures beyond number, living things, small and great.

26 There go the ships, and Leviathan that You formed to sport with.

27 All of them look to You to give them their food when it is due.

28 Give it to them, they gather it up; open Your hand, they are well satisfied;

תהלים
פרק קד

י הַמְשַׁלֵּחַ מַעְיָנִים בַּנְּחָלִים בֵּין הָרִים יְהַלֵּכוּן:

יא יַשְׁקוּ כָּל־חַיְתוֹ שָׂדָי יִשְׁבְּרוּ פְרָאִים צְמָאָם:

יב עֲלֵיהֶם עוֹף־הַשָּׁמַיִם יִשְׁכּוֹן מִבֵּין עֳפָאיִם יִתְּנוּ־קוֹל:

יג מַשְׁקֶה הָרִים מֵעֲלִיּוֹתָיו מִפְּרִי מַעֲשֶׂיךָ תִּשְׂבַּע הָאָרֶץ:

יד מַצְמִיחַ חָצִיר לַבְּהֵמָה וְעֵשֶׂב לַעֲבֹדַת הָאָדָם לְהוֹצִיא לֶחֶם מִן־הָאָרֶץ:

טו וְיַיִן יְשַׂמַּח לְבַב־אֱנוֹשׁ לְהַצְהִיל פָּנִים מִשָּׁמֶן וְלֶחֶם לְבַב־אֱנוֹשׁ יִסְעָד:

טז יִשְׂבְּעוּ עֲצֵי יְהֹוָה אַרְזֵי לְבָנוֹן אֲשֶׁר נָטָע:

יז אֲשֶׁר־שָׁם צִפֳּרִים יְקַנֵּנוּ חֲסִידָה בְּרוֹשִׁים בֵּיתָהּ:

יח הָרִים הַגְּבֹהִים לַיְּעֵלִים סְלָעִים מַחְסֶה לַשְׁפַנִּים:

יט עָשָׂה יָרֵחַ לְמוֹעֲדִים שֶׁמֶשׁ יָדַע מְבוֹאוֹ:

כ תָּשֶׁת־חֹשֶׁךְ וִיהִי לָיְלָה בּוֹ־תִרְמֹשׂ כָּל־חַיְתוֹ־יָעַר:

כא הַכְּפִירִים שֹׁאֲגִים לַטָּרֶף וּלְבַקֵּשׁ מֵאֵל אָכְלָם:

כב תִּזְרַח הַשֶּׁמֶשׁ יֵאָסֵפוּן וְאֶל־מְעוֹנֹתָם יִרְבָּצוּן:

כג יֵצֵא אָדָם לְפָעֳלוֹ וְלַעֲבֹדָתוֹ עֲדֵי־עָרֶב:

כד מָה־רַבּוּ מַעֲשֶׂיךָ יְהֹוָה כֻּלָּם בְּחָכְמָה עָשִׂיתָ מָלְאָה הָאָרֶץ קִנְיָנֶךָ:

כה זֶה הַיָּם גָּדוֹל וּרְחַב יָדָיִם שָׁם־רֶמֶשׂ וְאֵין מִסְפָּר חַיּוֹת קְטַנּוֹת עִם־גְּדֹלוֹת:

כו שָׁם אֳנִיּוֹת יְהַלֵּכוּן לִוְיָתָן זֶה־יָצַרְתָּ לְשַׂחֶק־בּוֹ:

כז כֻּלָּם אֵלֶיךָ יְשַׂבֵּרוּן לָתֵת אָכְלָם בְּעִתּוֹ:

כח תִּתֵּן לָהֶם יִלְקֹטוּן תִּפְתַּח יָדְךָ יִשְׂבְּעוּן טוֹב:

1596

Tehillim/Psalms
Chapter 105

תהלים
פרק קה

29 hide Your face, they are terrified; take away their breath, they perish and turn again into dust;

כט תַּסְתִּיר פָּנֶיךָ יִבָּהֵלוּן תֹּסֵף רוּחָם יִגְוָעוּן וְאֶל־עֲפָרָם יְשׁוּבוּן׃

30 send back Your breath, they are created, and You renew the face of the earth.

ל תְּשַׁלַּח רוּחֲךָ יִבָּרֵאוּן וּתְחַדֵּשׁ פְּנֵי אֲדָמָה׃

31 May the glory of *Hashem* endure forever; may *Hashem* rejoice in His works!

לא יְהִי כְבוֹד יְהוָה לְעוֹלָם יִשְׂמַח יְהוָה בְּמַעֲשָׂיו׃

32 He looks at the earth and it trembles; He touches the mountains and they smoke.

לב הַמַּבִּיט לָאָרֶץ וַתִּרְעָד יִגַּע בֶּהָרִים וְיֶעֱשָׁנוּ׃

33 I will sing to *Hashem* as long as I live; all my life I will chant hymns to my God.

לג אָשִׁירָה לַיהוָה בְּחַיָּי אֲזַמְּרָה לֵאלֹהַי בְּעוֹדִי׃

34 May my prayer be pleasing to Him; I will rejoice in *Hashem*.

לד יֶעֱרַב עָלָיו שִׂיחִי אָנֹכִי אֶשְׂמַח בַּיהוָה׃

35 May sinners disappear from the earth, and the wicked be no more. Bless *Hashem*, O my soul. Hallelujah.

לה יִתַּמּוּ חַטָּאִים מִן־הָאָרֶץ וּרְשָׁעִים עוֹד אֵינָם בָּרֲכִי נַפְשִׁי אֶת־יְהוָה הַלְלוּ־יָהּ׃

yi-TA-mu kha-ta-EEM min ha-A-retz ur-sha-EEM OD ay-NAM ba-r'-KHEE naf-SHEE et a-do-NAI ha-l'-lu-YAH

105

1 Praise *Hashem*; call on His name; proclaim His deeds among the peoples.

א הוֹדוּ לַיהוָה קִרְאוּ בִשְׁמוֹ הוֹדִיעוּ בָעַמִּים עֲלִילוֹתָיו׃

2 Sing praises to Him; speak of all His wondrous acts.

ב שִׁירוּ־לוֹ זַמְּרוּ־לוֹ שִׂיחוּ בְּכָל־נִפְלְאוֹתָיו׃

3 Exult in His holy name; let all who seek *Hashem* rejoice.

ג הִתְהַלְלוּ בְּשֵׁם קָדְשׁוֹ יִשְׂמַח לֵב מְבַקְשֵׁי יְהוָה׃

4 Turn to *Hashem*, to His might; seek His presence constantly.

ד דִּרְשׁוּ יְהוָה וְעֻזּוֹ בַּקְּשׁוּ פָנָיו תָּמִיד׃

5 Remember the wonders He has done, His portents and the judgments He has pronounced,

ה זִכְרוּ נִפְלְאוֹתָיו אֲשֶׁר־עָשָׂה מֹפְתָיו וּמִשְׁפְּטֵי־פִיו׃

6 O offspring of *Avraham*, His servant, O descendants of *Yaakov*, His chosen ones.

ו זֶרַע אַבְרָהָם עַבְדּוֹ בְּנֵי יַעֲקֹב בְּחִירָיו׃

7 He is *Hashem* our God; His judgments are throughout the earth.

ז הוּא יְהוָה אֱלֹהֵינוּ בְּכָל־הָאָרֶץ מִשְׁפָּטָיו׃

8 He is ever mindful of His covenant, the promise He gave for a thousand generations,

ח זָכַר לְעוֹלָם בְּרִיתוֹ דָּבָר צִוָּה לְאֶלֶף דּוֹר׃

104:35 May sinners disappear from the earth The Talmud (*Berachot* 10a) records a story about a remarkable woman named Bruriah, who lived in the Land of Israel shortly after the second Temple period with her husband, the great sage Rabbi Meir. Rabbi Meir had been abused by vagrants, and he prayed for their destruction. Bruriah quoted this psalm, and noted that the verse should be understood as saying, "May sins disappear from the earth," instead of wishing for the actual destruction of the sinners themselves. Once their evil behavior ends, they will no longer be sinners, for they will return to *Hashem*. Rabbi Meir accepted his wife's advice and instead prayed for his enemies to repent. God accepted his prayers and they returned from their evil ways.

Tehillim/Psalms
Chapter 105

9	that He made with *Avraham*, swore to *Yitzchak*,	ט אֲשֶׁר כָּרַת אֶת־אַבְרָהָם וּשְׁבוּעָתוֹ לְיִשְׂחָק:
10	and confirmed in a decree for *Yaakov*, for *Yisrael*, as an eternal covenant,	י וַיַּעֲמִידֶהָ לְיַעֲקֹב לְחֹק לְיִשְׂרָאֵל בְּרִית עוֹלָם:
11	saying, "To you I will give the land of Canaan as your allotted heritage."	יא לֵאמֹר לְךָ אֶתֵּן אֶת־אֶרֶץ־כְּנָעַן חֶבֶל נַחֲלַתְכֶם:
12	They were then few in number, a mere handful, sojourning there,	יב בִּהְיוֹתָם מְתֵי מִסְפָּר כִּמְעַט וְגָרִים בָּהּ:
13	wandering from nation to nation, from one kingdom to another.	יג וַיִּתְהַלְּכוּ מִגּוֹי אֶל־גּוֹי מִמַּמְלָכָה אֶל־עַם אַחֵר:
14	He allowed no one to oppress them; He reproved kings on their account,	יד לֹא־הִנִּיחַ אָדָם לְעָשְׁקָם וַיּוֹכַח עֲלֵיהֶם מְלָכִים:
15	"Do not touch My anointed ones; do not harm My *neviim*."	טו אַל־תִּגְּעוּ בִמְשִׁיחָי וְלִנְבִיאַי אַל־תָּרֵעוּ:
16	He called down a famine on the land, destroyed every staff of bread.	טז וַיִּקְרָא רָעָב עַל־הָאָרֶץ כָּל־מַטֵּה־לֶחֶם שָׁבָר:
17	He sent ahead of them a man, *Yosef*, sold into slavery.	יז שָׁלַח לִפְנֵיהֶם אִישׁ לְעֶבֶד נִמְכַּר יוֹסֵף:
18	His feet were subjected to fetters; an iron collar was put on his neck.	יח עִנּוּ בַכֶּבֶל רגליו [רַגְלוֹ] בַּרְזֶל בָּאָה נַפְשׁוֹ:
19	Until his prediction came true the decree of *Hashem* purged him.	יט עַד־עֵת בֹּא־דְבָרוֹ אִמְרַת יְהֹוָה צְרָפָתְהוּ:
20	The king sent to have him freed; the ruler of nations released him.	כ שָׁלַח מֶלֶךְ וַיַּתִּירֵהוּ מֹשֵׁל עַמִּים וַיְפַתְּחֵהוּ:
21	He made him the lord of his household, empowered him over all his possessions,	כא שָׂמוֹ אָדוֹן לְבֵיתוֹ וּמֹשֵׁל בְּכָל־קִנְיָנוֹ:
22	to discipline his princes at will, to teach his elders wisdom.	כב לֶאְסֹר שָׂרָיו בְּנַפְשׁוֹ וּזְקֵנָיו יְחַכֵּם:
23	Then *Yisrael* came to Egypt; *Yaakov* sojourned in the land of Ham.	כג וַיָּבֹא יִשְׂרָאֵל מִצְרָיִם וְיַעֲקֹב גָּר בְּאֶרֶץ־חָם:
24	He made His people very fruitful, more numerous than their foes.	כד וַיֶּפֶר אֶת־עַמּוֹ מְאֹד וַיַּעֲצִמֵהוּ מִצָּרָיו:
25	He changed their heart to hate His people, to plot against His servants.	כה הָפַךְ לִבָּם לִשְׂנֹא עַמּוֹ לְהִתְנַכֵּל בַּעֲבָדָיו:
26	He sent His servant *Moshe*, and *Aharon*, whom He had chosen.	כו שָׁלַח מֹשֶׁה עַבְדּוֹ אַהֲרֹן אֲשֶׁר בָּחַר־בּוֹ:
27	They performed His signs among them, His wonders, against the land of Ham.	כז שָׂמוּ־בָם דִּבְרֵי אֹתוֹתָיו וּמֹפְתִים בְּאֶרֶץ חָם:
28	He sent darkness; it was very dark; did they not defy His word?	כח שָׁלַח חֹשֶׁךְ וַיַּחְשִׁךְ וְלֹא־מָרוּ אֶת־דברו [דְּבָרוֹ]:

Tehillim/Psalms
Chapter 105

29 He turned their waters into blood and killed their fish.

כט הָפַךְ אֶת־מֵימֵיהֶם לְדָם וַיָּמֶת אֶת־דְּגָתָם׃

30 Their land teemed with frogs, even the rooms of their king.

ל שָׁרַץ אַרְצָם צְפַרְדְּעִים בְּחַדְרֵי מַלְכֵיהֶם׃

31 Swarms of insects came at His command, lice, throughout their country.

לא אָמַר וַיָּבֹא עָרֹב כִּנִּים בְּכָל־גְּבוּלָם׃

32 He gave them hail for rain, and flaming fire in their land.

לב נָתַן גִּשְׁמֵיהֶם בָּרָד אֵשׁ לֶהָבוֹת בְּאַרְצָם׃

33 He struck their vines and fig trees, broke down the trees of their country.

לג וַיַּךְ גַּפְנָם וּתְאֵנָתָם וַיְשַׁבֵּר עֵץ גְּבוּלָם׃

34 Locusts came at His command, grasshoppers without number.

לד אָמַר וַיָּבֹא אַרְבֶּה וְיֶלֶק וְאֵין מִסְפָּר׃

35 They devoured every green thing in the land; they consumed the produce of the soil.

לה וַיֹּאכַל כָּל־עֵשֶׂב בְּאַרְצָם וַיֹּאכַל פְּרִי אַדְמָתָם׃

36 He struck down every first-born in the land, the first fruit of their vigor.

לו וַיַּךְ כָּל־בְּכוֹר בְּאַרְצָם רֵאשִׁית לְכָל־אוֹנָם׃

37 He led *Yisrael* out with silver and gold; none among their tribes faltered.

לז וַיּוֹצִיאֵם בְּכֶסֶף וְזָהָב וְאֵין בִּשְׁבָטָיו כּוֹשֵׁל׃

38 Egypt rejoiced when they left, for dread of *Yisrael* had fallen upon them.

לח שָׂמַח מִצְרַיִם בְּצֵאתָם כִּי־נָפַל פַּחְדָּם עֲלֵיהֶם׃

39 He spread a cloud for a cover, and fire to light up the night.

לט פָּרַשׂ עָנָן לְמָסָךְ וְאֵשׁ לְהָאִיר לָיְלָה׃

40 They asked and He brought them quail, and satisfied them with food from heaven.

מ שָׁאַל וַיָּבֵא שְׂלָו וְלֶחֶם שָׁמַיִם יַשְׂבִּיעֵם׃

41 He opened a rock so that water gushed forth; it flowed as a stream in the parched land.

מא פָּתַח צוּר וַיָּזוּבוּ מָיִם הָלְכוּ בַּצִּיּוֹת נָהָר׃

42 Mindful of His sacred promise to His servant *Avraham*,

מב כִּי־זָכַר אֶת־דְּבַר קָדְשׁוֹ אֶת־אַבְרָהָם עַבְדּוֹ׃

43 He led His people out in gladness, His chosen ones with joyous song.

מג וַיּוֹצִא עַמּוֹ בְשָׂשׂוֹן בְּרִנָּה אֶת־בְּחִירָיו׃

44 He gave them the lands of nations; they inherited the wealth of peoples,

מד וַיִּתֵּן לָהֶם אַרְצוֹת גּוֹיִם וַעֲמַל לְאֻמִּים יִירָשׁוּ׃

45 that they might keep His laws and observe His teachings. Hallelujah.

מה בַּעֲבוּר יִשְׁמְרוּ חֻקָּיו וְתוֹרֹתָיו יִנְצֹרוּ הַלְלוּ־יָהּ׃

ba-a-VUR yish-m'-RU khu-KAV v'-to-ro-TAV yin-TZO-ru ha-l'-lu-YAH

105:45 That they might keep His laws and observe His teachings Psalm 105 reviews the early history of the People of Israel, from the promise to give the Land of Israel to *Avraham* and his descendants through the exodus from Egypt. It is framed as a praise to *Hashem*, and the first twelve verses express gratitude to God for

Tehillim/Psalms
Chapter 106

106

1 Hallelujah. Praise *Hashem* for He is good; His steadfast love is eternal.

2 Who can tell the mighty acts of *Hashem*, proclaim all His praises?

3 Happy are those who act justly, who do right at all times.

4 Be mindful of me, *Hashem*, when You favor Your people; take note of me when You deliver them,

5 that I may enjoy the prosperity of Your chosen ones, share the joy of Your nation, glory in Your very own people.

lir-OT b'-to-VAT b'-khee-RE-kha lis-MO-akh b'-sim-KHAT go-YE-kha l'-hit-ha-LAYL im na-kha-la-TE-kha

6 We have sinned like our forefathers; we have gone astray, done evil.

7 Our forefathers in Egypt did not perceive Your wonders; they did not remember Your abundant love, but rebelled at the sea, at the Sea of Reeds.

8 Yet He saved them, as befits His name, to make known His might.

9 He sent His blast against the Sea of Reeds; it became dry; He led them through the deep as through a wilderness.

10 He delivered them from the foe, redeemed them from the enemy.

11 Water covered their adversaries; not one of them was left.

12 Then they believed His promise, and sang His praises.

---

all His wonders, His miracles, and bestowing the land to the children of *Avraham* as an inheritance. After a detailed account of the plagues and emergence from Egypt, the final verses remind us of the reason why *Eretz Yisrael* was given to the children of *Avraham*: So that the Nation of Israel will observe *Hashem*'s laws and protect His holy *Torah*.

106:5 Glory in Your very own people This chapter is an inverse of the previous one, continuing the history lesson with all the shame that the Children of Israel endured over time, due to their sins. The psalm begins with the desire to behold God's goodness and to enjoy the great inheritance promised to the children of *Avraham*, the Land of Israel. However, the people sin, indulge and become corrupt, causing great discredit to their heritage. Instead of *Hashem* rejoicing in the inheritance He bestowed on His people, this psalm records His wrath and disgust with the land whose inhabitants shirk His ways. Ultimately, though, God remembers His covenant and has compassion for all who return to Him. The psalm ends with a plea for salvation and praise of *Hashem* who continuously shows mercy to His people.

Tehillim/Psalms
Chapter 106

13 But they soon forgot His deeds; they would not wait to learn His plan.

יג מִהֲרוּ שָׁכְחוּ מַעֲשָׂיו לֹא־חִכּוּ לַעֲצָתוֹ:

14 They were seized with craving in the wilderness, and put *Hashem* to the test in the wasteland.

יד וַיִּתְאַוּוּ תַאֲוָה בַּמִּדְבָּר וַיְנַסּוּ־אֵל בִּישִׁימוֹן:

15 He gave them what they asked for, then made them waste away.

טו וַיִּתֵּן לָהֶם שֶׁאֱלָתָם וַיְשַׁלַּח רָזוֹן בְּנַפְשָׁם:

16 There was envy of *Moshe* in the camp, and of *Aharon*, the holy one of *Hashem*.

טז וַיְקַנְאוּ לְמֹשֶׁה בַּמַּחֲנֶה לְאַהֲרֹן קְדוֹשׁ יְהֹוָה:

17 The earth opened up and swallowed *Datan*, closed over the party of *Aviram*.

יז תִּפְתַּח־אֶרֶץ וַתִּבְלַע דָּתָן וַתְּכַס עַל־עֲדַת אֲבִירָם:

18 A fire blazed among their party, a flame that consumed the wicked.

יח וַתִּבְעַר־אֵשׁ בַּעֲדָתָם לֶהָבָה תְּלַהֵט רְשָׁעִים:

19 They made a calf at Horeb and bowed down to a molten image.

יט יַעֲשׂוּ־עֵגֶל בְּחֹרֵב וַיִּשְׁתַּחֲווּ לְמַסֵּכָה:

20 They exchanged their glory for the image of a bull that feeds on grass.

כ וַיָּמִירוּ אֶת־כְּבוֹדָם בְּתַבְנִית שׁוֹר אֹכֵל עֵשֶׂב:

21 They forgot *Hashem* who saved them, who performed great deeds in Egypt,

כא שָׁכְחוּ אֵל מוֹשִׁיעָם עֹשֶׂה גְדֹלוֹת בְּמִצְרָיִם:

22 wondrous deeds in the land of Ham, awesome deeds at the Sea of Reeds.

כב נִפְלָאוֹת בְּאֶרֶץ חָם נוֹרָאוֹת עַל־יַם־סוּף:

23 He would have destroyed them had not *Moshe* His chosen one confronted Him in the breach to avert His destructive wrath.

כג וַיֹּאמֶר לְהַשְׁמִידָם לוּלֵי מֹשֶׁה בְחִירוֹ עָמַד בַּפֶּרֶץ לְפָנָיו לְהָשִׁיב חֲמָתוֹ מֵהַשְׁחִית:

24 They rejected the desirable land, and put no faith in His promise.

כד וַיִּמְאֲסוּ בְּאֶרֶץ חֶמְדָּה לֹא־הֶאֱמִינוּ לִדְבָרוֹ:

25 They grumbled in their tents and disobeyed *Hashem*.

כה וַיֵּרָגְנוּ בְאָהֳלֵיהֶם לֹא שָׁמְעוּ בְּקוֹל יְהֹוָה:

26 So He raised His hand in oath to make them fall in the wilderness,

כו וַיִּשָּׂא יָדוֹ לָהֶם לְהַפִּיל אוֹתָם בַּמִּדְבָּר:

27 to disperse their offspring among the nations and scatter them through the lands.

כז וּלְהַפִּיל זַרְעָם בַּגּוֹיִם וּלְזָרוֹתָם בָּאֲרָצוֹת:

28 They attached themselves to Baal Peor, ate sacrifices offered to the dead.

כח וַיִּצָּמְדוּ לְבַעַל פְּעוֹר וַיֹּאכְלוּ זִבְחֵי מֵתִים:

29 They provoked anger by their deeds, and a plague broke out among them.

כט וַיַּכְעִיסוּ בְּמַעַלְלֵיהֶם וַתִּפְרָץ־בָּם מַגֵּפָה:

30 *Pinchas* stepped forth and intervened, and the plague ceased.

ל וַיַּעֲמֹד פִּינְחָס וַיְפַלֵּל וַתֵּעָצַר הַמַּגֵּפָה:

31 It was reckoned to his merit for all generations, to eternity.

לא וַתֵּחָשֶׁב לוֹ לִצְדָקָה לְדֹר וָדֹר עַד־עוֹלָם:

Tehillim/Psalms
Chapter 107

32 They provoked wrath at the waters of Meribah and *Moshe* suffered on their account, לב וַיַּקְצִיפוּ עַל־מֵי מְרִיבָה וַיֵּרַע לְמֹשֶׁה בַּעֲבוּרָם:

33 because they rebelled against Him and he spoke rashly. לג כִּי־הִמְרוּ אֶת־רוּחוֹ וַיְבַטֵּא בִּשְׂפָתָיו:

34 They did not destroy the nations as *Hashem* had commanded them, לד לֹא־הִשְׁמִידוּ אֶת־הָעַמִּים אֲשֶׁר אָמַר יְהוָה לָהֶם:

35 but mingled with the nations and learned their ways. לה וַיִּתְעָרְבוּ בַגּוֹיִם וַיִּלְמְדוּ מַעֲשֵׂיהֶם:

36 They worshiped their idols, which became a snare for them. לו וַיַּעַבְדוּ אֶת־עֲצַבֵּיהֶם וַיִּהְיוּ לָהֶם לְמוֹקֵשׁ:

37 Their own sons and daughters they sacrificed to demons. לז וַיִּזְבְּחוּ אֶת־בְּנֵיהֶם וְאֶת־בְּנוֹתֵיהֶם לַשֵּׁדִים:

38 They shed innocent blood, the blood of their sons and daughters, whom they sacrificed to the idols of Canaan; so the land was polluted with bloodguilt. לח וַיִּשְׁפְּכוּ דָם נָקִי דַּם־בְּנֵיהֶם וּבְנוֹתֵיהֶם אֲשֶׁר זִבְּחוּ לַעֲצַבֵּי כְנָעַן וַתֶּחֱנַף הָאָרֶץ בַּדָּמִים:

39 Thus they became defiled by their acts, debauched through their deeds. לט וַיִּטְמְאוּ בְמַעֲשֵׂיהֶם וַיִּזְנוּ בְּמַעַלְלֵיהֶם:

40 *Hashem* was angry with His people and He abhorred His inheritance. מ וַיִּחַר־אַף יְהוָה בְּעַמּוֹ וַיְתָעֵב אֶת־נַחֲלָתוֹ:

41 He handed them over to the nations; their foes ruled them. מא וַיִּתְּנֵם בְּיַד־גּוֹיִם וַיִּמְשְׁלוּ בָהֶם שֹׂנְאֵיהֶם:

42 Their enemies oppressed them and they were subject to their power. מב וַיִּלְחָצוּם אוֹיְבֵיהֶם וַיִּכָּנְעוּ תַּחַת יָדָם:

43 He saved them time and again, but they were deliberately rebellious, and so they were brought low by their iniquity. מג פְּעָמִים רַבּוֹת יַצִּילֵם וְהֵמָּה יַמְרוּ בַעֲצָתָם וַיָּמֹכּוּ בַּעֲוֺנָם:

44 When He saw that they were in distress, when He heard their cry, מד וַיַּרְא בַּצַּר לָהֶם בְּשָׁמְעוֹ אֶת־רִנָּתָם:

45 He was mindful of His covenant and in His great faithfulness relented. מה וַיִּזְכֹּר לָהֶם בְּרִיתוֹ וַיִּנָּחֶם כְּרֹב חֲסָדוֹ [חֲסָדָיו]:

46 He made all their captors kindly disposed toward them. מו וַיִּתֵּן אוֹתָם לְרַחֲמִים לִפְנֵי כָּל־שׁוֹבֵיהֶם:

47 Deliver us, *Hashem* our God, and gather us from among the nations, to acclaim Your holy name, to glory in Your praise. מז הוֹשִׁיעֵנוּ יְהוָה אֱלֹהֵינוּ וְקַבְּצֵנוּ מִן־הַגּוֹיִם לְהֹדוֹת לְשֵׁם קָדְשֶׁךָ לְהִשְׁתַּבֵּחַ בִּתְהִלָּתֶךָ:

48 Blessed is *Hashem*, God of *Yisrael*, From eternity to eternity. Let all the people say "*Amen*." Hallelujah. מח בָּרוּךְ־יְהוָה אֱלֹהֵי יִשְׂרָאֵל מִן־הָעוֹלָם וְעַד הָעוֹלָם וְאָמַר כָּל־הָעָם אָמֵן הַלְלוּ־יָהּ:

107

1 "Praise *Hashem*, for He is good; His steadfast love is eternal!" א הֹדוּ לַיהוָה כִּי־טוֹב כִּי לְעוֹלָם חַסְדּוֹ:

Tehillim/Psalms
Chapter 107

תהלים
פרק קז

2 Thus let the redeemed of *Hashem* say, those He redeemed from adversity,

ב יֹאמְרוּ גְּאוּלֵי יְהוָה אֲשֶׁר גְּאָלָם מִיַּד־צָר:

3 whom He gathered in from the lands, from east and west, from the north and from the sea.

ג וּמֵאֲרָצוֹת קִבְּצָם מִמִּזְרָח וּמִמַּעֲרָב מִצָּפוֹן וּמִיָּם:

4 Some lost their way in the wilderness, in the wasteland; they found no settled place.

ד תָּעוּ בַמִּדְבָּר בִּישִׁימוֹן דָּרֶךְ עִיר מוֹשָׁב לֹא מָצָאוּ:

5 Hungry and thirsty, their spirit failed.

ה רְעֵבִים גַּם־צְמֵאִים נַפְשָׁם בָּהֶם תִּתְעַטָּף:

6 In their adversity they cried to *Hashem*, and He rescued them from their troubles.

ו וַיִּצְעֲקוּ אֶל־יְהוָה בַּצַּר לָהֶם מִמְּצוּקוֹתֵיהֶם יַצִּילֵם:

7 He showed them a direct way to reach a settled place.

ז וַיַּדְרִיכֵם בְּדֶרֶךְ יְשָׁרָה לָלֶכֶת אֶל־עִיר מוֹשָׁב:

8 Let them praise *Hashem* for His steadfast love, His wondrous deeds for mankind;

yo-DU la-do-NAI khas-DO v'-nif-l'-o-TAV liv-NAY a-DAM

ח יוֹדוּ לַיהוָה חַסְדּוֹ וְנִפְלְאוֹתָיו לִבְנֵי אָדָם:

9 for He has satisfied the thirsty, filled the hungry with all good things.

ט כִּי־הִשְׂבִּיעַ נֶפֶשׁ שֹׁקֵקָה וְנֶפֶשׁ רְעֵבָה מִלֵּא־טוֹב:

10 Some lived in deepest darkness, bound in cruel irons,

י יֹשְׁבֵי חֹשֶׁךְ וְצַלְמָוֶת אֲסִירֵי עֳנִי וּבַרְזֶל:

11 because they defied the word of *Hashem*, spurned the counsel of the Most High.

יא כִּי־הִמְרוּ אִמְרֵי־אֵל וַעֲצַת עֶלְיוֹן נָאָצוּ:

12 He humbled their hearts through suffering; they stumbled with no one to help.

יב וַיַּכְנַע בֶּעָמָל לִבָּם כָּשְׁלוּ וְאֵין עֹזֵר:

13 In their adversity they cried to *Hashem*, and He rescued them from their troubles.

יג וַיִּזְעֲקוּ אֶל־יְהוָה בַּצַּר לָהֶם מִמְּצֻקוֹתֵיהֶם יוֹשִׁיעֵם:

14 He brought them out of deepest darkness, broke their bonds asunder.

יד יוֹצִיאֵם מֵחֹשֶׁךְ וְצַלְמָוֶת וּמוֹסְרוֹתֵיהֶם יְנַתֵּק:

15 Let them praise *Hashem* for His steadfast love, His wondrous deeds for mankind,

טו יוֹדוּ לַיהוָה חַסְדּוֹ וְנִפְלְאוֹתָיו לִבְנֵי אָדָם:

16 For He shattered gates of bronze, He broke their iron bars.

טז כִּי־שִׁבַּר דַּלְתוֹת נְחֹשֶׁת וּבְרִיחֵי בַרְזֶל גִּדֵּעַ:

107:8 Let them praise *Hashem* for His steadfast love In this beautiful psalm, King *David* describes the joy of seafarers who have been delivered from peril at sea. Upon arriving safely at port, they would publicly express their thanks to *Hashem*. Sharing the miracles in our lives with others, however big or small, leads more people to gain awareness of God's intervention in the world. Additionally, it opens our own eyes, enabling us to focus on the good and to see the many blessings we receive from the Lord each day. God's involvement in our lives is especially acute in the Land of Israel, "a land which *Hashem* your God looks after, on which *Hashem* your God always keeps His eye, from year's beginning to year's end" (Deuteronomy 11:12).

Tehillim/Psalms
Chapter 107

17 There were fools who suffered for their sinful way, and for their iniquities.

18 All food was loathsome to them; they reached the gates of death.

19 In their adversity they cried to *Hashem* and He saved them from their troubles.

20 He gave an order and healed them; He delivered them from the pits.

21 Let them praise *Hashem* for His steadfast love, His wondrous deeds for mankind.

22 Let them offer thanksgiving sacrifices, and tell His deeds in joyful song.

23 Others go down to the sea in ships, ply their trade in the mighty waters;

24 they have seen the works of *Hashem* and His wonders in the deep.

25 By His word He raised a storm wind that made the waves surge.

26 Mounting up to the heaven, plunging down to the depths, disgorging in their misery,

27 they reeled and staggered like a drunken man, all their skill to no avail.

28 In their adversity they cried to *Hashem*, and He saved them from their troubles.

29 He reduced the storm to a whisper; the waves were stilled.

30 They rejoiced when all was quiet, and He brought them to the port they desired.

31 Let them praise *Hashem* for His steadfast love, His wondrous deeds for mankind.

32 Let them exalt Him in the congregation of the people, acclaim Him in the assembly of the elders.

33 He turns the rivers into a wilderness, springs of water into thirsty land,

34 fruitful land into a salt marsh, because of the wickedness of its inhabitants.

35 He turns the wilderness into pools, parched land into springs of water.

36 There He settles the hungry; they build a place to settle in.

תהילים
פרק קז

יז אֱוִלִים מִדֶּרֶךְ פִּשְׁעָם וּמֵעֲוֺנֹתֵיהֶם יִתְעַנּוּ:

יח כָּל־אֹכֶל תְּתַעֵב נַפְשָׁם וַיַּגִּיעוּ עַד־שַׁעֲרֵי מָוֶת:

יט וַיִּזְעֲקוּ אֶל־יְהֹוָה בַּצַּר לָהֶם מִמְּצֻקוֹתֵיהֶם יוֹשִׁיעֵם:

כ יִשְׁלַח דְּבָרוֹ וְיִרְפָּאֵם וִימַלֵּט מִשְּׁחִיתוֹתָם:

כא יוֹדוּ לַיהֹוָה חַסְדּוֹ וְנִפְלְאוֹתָיו לִבְנֵי אָדָם:

כב וְיִזְבְּחוּ זִבְחֵי תוֹדָה וִיסַפְּרוּ מַעֲשָׂיו בְּרִנָּה:

כג יוֹרְדֵי הַיָּם בָּאֳנִיּוֹת עֹשֵׂי מְלָאכָה בְּמַיִם רַבִּים:

כד הֵמָּה רָאוּ מַעֲשֵׂי יְהֹוָה וְנִפְלְאוֹתָיו בִּמְצוּלָה:

כה וַיֹּאמֶר וַיַּעֲמֵד רוּחַ סְעָרָה וַתְּרוֹמֵם גַּלָּיו:

כו יַעֲלוּ שָׁמַיִם יֵרְדוּ תְהוֹמוֹת נַפְשָׁם בְּרָעָה תִתְמוֹגָג:

כז יָחוֹגּוּ וְיָנוּעוּ כַּשִּׁכּוֹר וְכָל־חָכְמָתָם תִּתְבַּלָּע:

כח וַיִּצְעֲקוּ אֶל־יְהֹוָה בַּצַּר לָהֶם וּמִמְּצוּקֹתֵיהֶם יוֹצִיאֵם:

כט יָקֵם סְעָרָה לִדְמָמָה וַיֶּחֱשׁוּ גַּלֵּיהֶם:

ל וַיִּשְׂמְחוּ כִי־יִשְׁתֹּקוּ וַיַּנְחֵם אֶל־מְחוֹז חֶפְצָם:

לא יוֹדוּ לַיהֹוָה חַסְדּוֹ וְנִפְלְאוֹתָיו לִבְנֵי אָדָם:

לב וִירֹמְמוּהוּ בִּקְהַל־עָם וּבְמוֹשַׁב זְקֵנִים יְהַלְלוּהוּ:

לג יָשֵׂם נְהָרוֹת לְמִדְבָּר וּמֹצָאֵי מַיִם לְצִמָּאוֹן:

לד אֶרֶץ פְּרִי לִמְלֵחָה מֵרָעַת יֹשְׁבֵי בָהּ:

לה יָשֵׂם מִדְבָּר לַאֲגַם־מַיִם וְאֶרֶץ צִיָּה לְמֹצָאֵי מָיִם:

לו וַיּוֹשֶׁב שָׁם רְעֵבִים וַיְכוֹנְנוּ עִיר מוֹשָׁב:

Tehillim/Psalms
Chapter 108

תהלים
פרק קח

37 They sow fields and plant vineyards that yield a fruitful harvest.

לז וַיִּזְרְעוּ שָׂדוֹת וַיִּטְּעוּ כְרָמִים וַיַּעֲשׂוּ פְּרִי תְבוּאָה׃

38 He blesses them and they increase greatly; and He does not let their cattle decrease,

לח וַיְבָרֲכֵם וַיִּרְבּוּ מְאֹד וּבְהֶמְתָּם לֹא יַמְעִיט׃

39 after they had been few and crushed by oppression, misery, and sorrow.

לט וַיִּמְעֲטוּ וַיָּשֹׁחוּ מֵעֹצֶר רָעָה וְיָגוֹן׃

40 He pours contempt on great men and makes them lose their way in trackless deserts;

מ שֹׁפֵךְ בּוּז עַל־נְדִיבִים וַיַּתְעֵם בְּתֹהוּ לֹא־דָרֶךְ׃

41 but the needy He secures from suffering, and increases their families like flocks.

מא וַיְשַׂגֵּב אֶבְיוֹן מֵעוֹנִי וַיָּשֶׂם כַּצֹּאן מִשְׁפָּחוֹת׃

42 The upright see it and rejoice; the mouth of all wrongdoers is stopped.

מב יִרְאוּ יְשָׁרִים וְיִשְׂמָחוּ וְכָל־עַוְלָה קָפְצָה פִּיהָ׃

43 The wise man will take note of these things; he will consider the steadfast love of *Hashem*.

מג מִי־חָכָם וְיִשְׁמָר־אֵלֶּה וְיִתְבּוֹנְנוּ חַסְדֵי יְהֹוָה׃

108

1 A song. A psalm of *David*.

קח א שִׁיר מִזְמוֹר לְדָוִד׃

2 My heart is firm, O *Hashem*; I will sing and chant a hymn with all my soul.

ב נָכוֹן לִבִּי אֱלֹהִים אָשִׁירָה וַאֲזַמְּרָה אַף־כְּבוֹדִי׃

3 Awake, O harp and lyre! I will wake the dawn.

ג עוּרָה הַנֵּבֶל וְכִנּוֹר אָעִירָה שָּׁחַר׃

4 I will praise You among the peoples, *Hashem*, sing a hymn to You among the nations;

ד אוֹדְךָ בָעַמִּים יְהֹוָה וַאֲזַמֶּרְךָ בַּל־אֻמִּים׃

5 for Your faithfulness is higher than the heavens; Your steadfastness reaches to the sky.

ה כִּי־גָדוֹל מֵעַל־שָׁמַיִם חַסְדֶּךָ וְעַד־שְׁחָקִים אֲמִתֶּךָ׃

6 Exalt Yourself over the heavens, O *Hashem*; let Your glory be over all the earth!

ו רוּמָה עַל־שָׁמַיִם אֱלֹהִים וְעַל כָּל־הָאָרֶץ כְּבוֹדֶךָ׃

7 That those whom You love may be rescued, deliver with Your right hand and answer me.

ז לְמַעַן יֵחָלְצוּן יְדִידֶיךָ הוֹשִׁיעָה יְמִינְךָ וַעֲנֵנִי׃

8 *Hashem* promised in His sanctuary that I would exultingly divide up *Shechem*, and measure the Valley of Sukkoth;

ח אֱלֹהִים דִּבֶּר בְּקָדְשׁוֹ אֶעְלֹזָה אֲחַלְּקָה שְׁכֶם וְעֵמֶק סֻכּוֹת אֲמַדֵּד׃

9 *Gilad* and *Menashe* would be mine, *Efraim* my chief stronghold, *Yehuda* my scepter;

ט לִי גִלְעָד לִי מְנַשֶּׁה וְאֶפְרַיִם מָעוֹז רֹאשִׁי יְהוּדָה מְחֹקְקִי׃

LEE gil-AD LEE m'-na-SHEH v'-ef-RA-yim ma-OZ ro-SHEE y'-hu-DAH m'-kho-k'-KEE

108:9 *Gilad* and *Menashe* would be mine In a moment of confidence, *David* rejoices at the great promise *Hashem* made to His people, to give them each a share in the Promised Land. He remarks "*Gilad* and *Menashe* would be mine," and speaks of controlling *Ephraim*, *Yehuda*, *Moab* and the land of the Philistines. He intends to fulfill the biblical command to conquer all the lands occupied by other kingdoms but bequeathed to Israel, or at one point conquered by Israel. *Gilad* is a mountainous strip of land on the eastern bank of the Jordan River which

Gilad mountains

1605

Tehillim/Psalms
Chapter 109

תהלים
פרק קט

10 Moab would be my washbasin; on Edom I would cast my shoe; I would raise a shout over Philistia.

י מוֹאָב ׀ סִיר רַחְצִי עַל־אֱדוֹם אַשְׁלִיךְ נַעֲלִי עָלַי פְּלֶשֶׁת אֶתְרוֹעָע׃

11 Would that I were brought to the bastion! Would that I were led to Edom!

יא מִי יֹבִלֵנִי עִיר מִבְצָר מִי נָחַנִי עַד־אֱדוֹם׃

12 But You have rejected us, O *Hashem*; *Hashem*, You do not march with our armies.

יב הֲלֹא־אֱלֹהִים זְנַחְתָּנוּ וְלֹא־תֵצֵא אֱלֹהִים בְּצִבְאוֹתֵינוּ׃

13 Grant us Your aid against the foe, for the help of man is worthless.

יג הָבָה־לָּנוּ עֶזְרָת מִצָּר וְשָׁוְא תְּשׁוּעַת אָדָם׃

14 With *Hashem* we shall triumph; He will trample our foes.

יד בֵּאלֹהִים נַעֲשֶׂה־חָיִל וְהוּא יָבוּס צָרֵינוּ׃

109

1 For the leader. Of *David*. A psalm. O God of my praise, do not keep aloof,

א לַמְנַצֵּחַ לְדָוִד מִזְמוֹר אֱלֹהֵי תְהִלָּתִי אַל־תֶּחֱרַשׁ׃

2 for the wicked and the deceitful open their mouth against me; they speak to me with lying tongue.

ב כִּי פִי רָשָׁע וּפִי־מִרְמָה עָלַי פָּתָחוּ דִּבְּרוּ אִתִּי לְשׁוֹן שָׁקֶר׃

3 They encircle me with words of hate; they attack me without cause.

ג וְדִבְרֵי שִׂנְאָה סְבָבוּנִי וַיִּלָּחֲמוּנִי חִנָּם׃

4 They answer my love with accusation but I am all prayer

ד תַּחַת־אַהֲבָתִי יִשְׂטְנוּנִי וַאֲנִי תְפִלָּה׃

TA-khat a-ha-va-TEE yis-t'-NU-nee va-a-NEE t'-fi-LAH

5 They repay me with evil for good, with hatred for my love.

ה וַיָּשִׂימוּ עָלַי רָעָה תַּחַת טוֹבָה וְשִׂנְאָה תַּחַת אַהֲבָתִי׃

6 Appoint a wicked man over him; may an accuser stand at his right side;

ו הַפְקֵד עָלָיו רָשָׁע וְשָׂטָן יַעֲמֹד עַל־יְמִינוֹ׃

7 may he be tried and convicted; may he be judged and found guilty.

ז בְּהִשָּׁפְטוֹ יֵצֵא רָשָׁע וּתְפִלָּתוֹ תִּהְיֶה לַחֲטָאָה׃

---

was conquered by Israel on their journey from Egypt to Canaan. After conquering the land of Sihon and Og, *Moshe* bequeathed it to the tribes of *Reuven* and *Gad* and to half the tribe of *Menashe*. *Yiftach* the judge came from this region, King *Shaul* defended the area from the kingdom of Ammon, and *Shlomo* also included this area in his kingdom. Once the Israelite kingdom split, however, this land was conquered by Aram.

109:4 I am all prayer According to Rabbi Samson Raphael Hirsch, this psalm is about evil people trying to eradicate *David's* very essence. Despite the love he has shown them and the good he has done for them, they pour curses and ridicule created from lies and hatred upon him. This psalm most likely refers to the events recorded in *Shmuel* II 16, when *David* flees his kingdom to escape his son *Avshalom* who wants to kill him. On his way out of the city, *Shim'i* the son of *Gera* from the house of *Shaul* spews vile curses at him, which the king accepts with resignation. This psalm, however, begins with *David* turning to *Hashem* with a plea not to stay silent. Only God's justice can eliminate the lies directed against *David*. Instead of hatred and vitriol, *David* says "I am all prayer." Only through God's intervention will his name be cleared.

Rabbi Samson R. Hirsch (1808–1888)

1606

Tehillim/Psalms
Chapter 109

8 May his days be few; may another take over his position.

9 May his children be orphans, his wife a widow.

10 May his children wander from their hovels, begging in search of [bread].

11 May his creditor seize all his possessions; may strangers plunder his wealth.

12 May no one show him mercy; may none pity his orphans;

13 may his posterity be cut off; may their names be blotted out in the next generation.

14 May *Hashem* be ever mindful of his father's iniquity, and may the sin of his mother not be blotted out.

15 May *Hashem* be aware of them always and cause their names to be cut off from the earth,

16 because he was not minded to act kindly, and hounded to death the poor and needy man, one crushed in spirit.

17 He loved to curse – may a curse come upon him! He would not bless – may blessing be far from him!

18 May he be clothed in a curse like a garment, may it enter his body like water, his bones like oil.

19 Let it be like the cloak he wraps around him, like the belt he always wears.

20 May *Hashem* thus repay my accusers, all those who speak evil against me.

21 Now You, O *Hashem*, my Lord, act on my behalf as befits Your name. Good and faithful as You are, save me.

22 For I am poor and needy, and my heart is pierced within me.

23 I fade away like a lengthening shadow; I am shaken off like locusts.

24 My knees give way from fasting; my flesh is lean, has lost its fat.

25 I am the object of their scorn; when they see me, they shake their head.

26 Help me, *Hashem*, my God; save me in accord with Your faithfulness,

Tehillim/Psalms
Chapter 110

תהלים
פרק קי

27 that men may know that it is Your hand, that You, *Hashem*, have done it.

וְיֵדְעוּ כִּי־יָדְךָ זֹּאת אַתָּה יְהֹוָה עֲשִׂיתָהּ׃

28 Let them curse, but You bless; let them rise up, but come to grief, while Your servant rejoices.

יְקַלְלוּ־הֵמָּה וְאַתָּה תְבָרֵךְ קָמוּ וַיֵּבֹשׁוּ וְעַבְדְּךָ יִשְׂמָח׃

29 My accusers shall be clothed in shame, wrapped in their disgrace as in a robe.

יִלְבְּשׁוּ שׂוֹטְנַי כְּלִמָּה וְיַעֲטוּ כַמְעִיל בָּשְׁתָּם׃

30 My mouth shall sing much praise to *Hashem*; I will acclaim Him in the midst of a throng,

אוֹדֶה יְהֹוָה מְאֹד בְּפִי וּבְתוֹךְ רַבִּים אֲהַלְלֶנּוּ׃

31 because He stands at the right hand of the needy, to save him from those who would condemn him.

כִּי־יַעֲמֹד לִימִין אֶבְיוֹן לְהוֹשִׁיעַ מִשֹּׁפְטֵי נַפְשׁוֹ׃

110 1 Of *David*. A psalm. *Hashem* said to my lord, "Sit at My right hand while I make your enemies your footstool."

קי א לְדָוִד מִזְמוֹר נְאֻם יְהֹוָה לַאדֹנִי שֵׁב לִימִינִי עַד־אָשִׁית אֹיְבֶיךָ הֲדֹם לְרַגְלֶיךָ׃

2 *Hashem* will stretch forth from *Tzion* your mighty scepter; hold sway over your enemies!

מַטֵּה־עֻזְּךָ יִשְׁלַח יְהֹוָה מִצִּיּוֹן רְדֵה בְּקֶרֶב אֹיְבֶיךָ׃

3 Your people come forward willingly on your day of battle. In majestic holiness, from the womb, from the dawn, yours was the dew of youth.

עַמְּךָ נְדָבֹת בְּיוֹם חֵילֶךָ בְּהַדְרֵי־קֹדֶשׁ מֵרֶחֶם מִשְׁחָר לְךָ טַל יַלְדֻתֶיךָ׃

4 *Hashem* has sworn and will not relent, "You are a *Kohen* forever, after the manner of Melchizedek."

נִשְׁבַּע יְהֹוָה וְלֹא יִנָּחֵם אַתָּה־כֹהֵן לְעוֹלָם עַל־דִּבְרָתִי מַלְכִּי־צֶדֶק׃

nish-BA a-do-NAI v'-LO yi-na-KHAYM a-TAH kho-HAYN l'-o-LAM al div-ra-TEE mal-kee TZE-dek

5 *Hashem* is at your right hand. He crushes kings in the day of His anger.

אֲדֹנָי עַל־יְמִינְךָ מָחַץ בְּיוֹם־אַפּוֹ מְלָכִים׃

6 He works judgment upon the nations, heaping up bodies, crushing heads far and wide.

יָדִין בַּגּוֹיִם מָלֵא גְוִיּוֹת מָחַץ רֹאשׁ עַל־אֶרֶץ רַבָּה׃

7 He drinks from the stream on his way; therefore he holds his head high.

מִנַּחַל בַּדֶּרֶךְ יִשְׁתֶּה עַל־כֵּן יָרִים רֹאשׁ׃

111 1 Hallelujah. I praise *Hashem* with all my heart in the assembled congregation of the upright.

קיא א הַלְלוּיָהּ אוֹדֶה יְהֹוָה בְּכָל־לֵבָב בְּסוֹד יְשָׁרִים וְעֵדָה׃

2 The works of *Hashem* are great, within reach of all who desire them.

גְּדֹלִים מַעֲשֵׂי יְהֹוָה דְּרוּשִׁים לְכָל־חֶפְצֵיהֶם׃

3 His deeds are splendid and glorious; His beneficence is everlasting;

הוֹד־וְהָדָר פָּעֳלוֹ וְצִדְקָתוֹ עֹמֶדֶת לָעַד׃

110:4 Melchizedek This psalm speaks of the coronation of a king, possibly *David*. It includes praises and blessings to the king of Israel who rules from *Tzion*, who will judge the nation, lead the army, and follow in the ways of *Hashem*. God sees the king as a kind of priest, as he serves the people and represents them to God, much like a priest does in the *Beit Hamikdash*. The first king-priest lived in the time of *Avraham*, though he was not from his family. The Bible praises Melchizedek, the great king of *Shalem*, which is the original name for *Yerushalayim*. Melchizedek recognizes *Avraham's* justice and blesses God in his presence (Genesis 14:18–20).

Tehillim/Psalms
Chapter 112

תהילים
פרק קיב

4 He has won renown for His wonders. *Hashem* is gracious and compassionate;

ד זֵכֶר עָשָׂה לְנִפְלְאֹתָיו חַנּוּן וְרַחוּם יְהֹוָה:

5 He gives food to those who fear Him; He is ever mindful of His covenant.

ה טֶרֶף נָתַן לִירֵאָיו יִזְכֹּר לְעוֹלָם בְּרִיתוֹ:

6 He revealed to His people His powerful works, in giving them the heritage of nations.

ו כֹּחַ מַעֲשָׂיו הִגִּיד לְעַמּוֹ לָתֵת לָהֶם נַחֲלַת גּוֹיִם:

KO-akh ma-a-SAV hi-GEED l'-a-MO la-TAYT la-HEM na-kha-LAT go-YIM

7 His handiwork is truth and justice; all His precepts are enduring,

ז מַעֲשֵׂי יָדָיו אֱמֶת וּמִשְׁפָּט נֶאֱמָנִים כָּל־פִּקּוּדָיו:

8 well-founded for all eternity, wrought of truth and equity.

ח סְמוּכִים לָעַד לְעוֹלָם עֲשׂוּיִם בֶּאֱמֶת וְיָשָׁר:

9 He sent redemption to His people; He ordained His covenant for all time; His name is holy and awesome.

ט פְּדוּת שָׁלַח לְעַמּוֹ צִוָּה לְעוֹלָם בְּרִיתוֹ קָדוֹשׁ וְנוֹרָא שְׁמוֹ:

10 The beginning of wisdom is the fear of *Hashem*; all who practice it gain sound understanding. Praise of Him is everlasting.

י רֵאשִׁית חָכְמָה יִרְאַת יְהֹוָה שֵׂכֶל טוֹב לְכָל־עֹשֵׂיהֶם תְּהִלָּתוֹ עֹמֶדֶת לָעַד:

112

1 Hallelujah. Happy is the man who fears *Hashem*, who is ardently devoted to His commandments.

קיב א הַלְלוּ יָהּ אַשְׁרֵי־אִישׁ יָרֵא אֶת־יְהֹוָה בְּמִצְוֹתָיו חָפֵץ מְאֹד:

ha-l'-lu-YAH ash-ray EESH ya-RAY et a-do-NAI b'-mitz-vo-TAV kha-FAYTZ m'-OD

2 His descendants will be mighty in the land, a blessed generation of upright men.

ב גִּבּוֹר בָּאָרֶץ יִהְיֶה זַרְעוֹ דּוֹר יְשָׁרִים יְבֹרָךְ:

3 Wealth and riches are in his house, and his beneficence lasts forever.

ג הוֹן־וָעֹשֶׁר בְּבֵיתוֹ וְצִדְקָתוֹ עֹמֶדֶת לָעַד:

4 A light shines for the upright in the darkness; he is gracious, compassionate, and beneficent.

ד זָרַח בַּחֹשֶׁךְ אוֹר לַיְשָׁרִים חַנּוּן וְרַחוּם וְצַדִּיק:

Rabbi Joseph B. Soloveitchik (1903–1993)

111:6 The heritage of nations This short psalm praises God in the form of an acrostic, each half verse beginning with a different letter of the Hebrew alphabet, in succession. The praises focus on *Hashem*'s justice, kindness, compassion and truth. The psalm also relates to the Lord's wondrous acts towards His nation. Verse 6 says that God declares His power to His nation by giving them *Eretz Yisrael*, but it does not explain what is so remarkable about this. The Sages explain: God said to the Children of Israel, "I could have created a new land for you; instead I chose to defeat your enemies and let you inherit their land, so that you will see My power." The Land of Israel is a gift from *Hashem*. It reminds the Jewish people of God's love for His people, His strength, and the fact that when they follow His ways, He causes their enemies to melt away from them.

112:1 Happy is the man who fears *Hashem* Psalm 111 is an acrostic praising *Hashem*, and Psalm 112 complements it with praises of man. Rabbi Joseph B. Soloveitchik once remarked that "Jewish law is theo-centric, but anthropo-oriented." He meant that while God is at the epicenter of the *Torah*, the Bible is really about human beings and how they interact with each other and with the Lord. Thus, while Psalm 111 dedicates itself to a complete praise of *Hashem*, Psalm 112 speaks of man and his capacity to live a life of praise and emulation of God. Man is happy and praiseworthy when all of his actions are focused on God, and oriented towards helping mankind.

Tehillim/Psalms
Chapter 113

תהלים
פרק קיג

5 All goes well with the man who lends generously, who conducts his affairs with equity.

ה טוֹב־אִישׁ חוֹנֵן וּמַלְוֶה יְכַלְכֵּל דְּבָרָיו בְּמִשְׁפָּט:

6 He shall never be shaken; the beneficent man will be remembered forever.

ו כִּי־לְעוֹלָם לֹא־יִמּוֹט לְזֵכֶר עוֹלָם יִהְיֶה צַדִּיק:

7 He is not afraid of evil tidings; his heart is firm, he trusts in *Hashem*.

ז מִשְּׁמוּעָה רָעָה לֹא יִירָא נָכוֹן לִבּוֹ בָּטֻחַ בַּיהֹוָה:

8 His heart is resolute, he is unafraid; in the end he will see the fall of his foes.

ח סָמוּךְ לִבּוֹ לֹא יִירָא עַד אֲשֶׁר־יִרְאֶה בְצָרָיו:

9 He gives freely to the poor; his beneficence lasts forever; his horn is exalted in honor.

ט פִּזַּר נָתַן לָאֶבְיוֹנִים צִדְקָתוֹ עֹמֶדֶת לָעַד קַרְנוֹ תָּרוּם בְּכָבוֹד:

10 The wicked man shall see it and be vexed; he shall gnash his teeth; his courage shall fail. The desire of the wicked shall come to nothing.

י רָשָׁע יִרְאֶה וְכָעָס שִׁנָּיו יַחֲרֹק וְנָמָס תַּאֲוַת רְשָׁעִים תֹּאבֵד:

113 1 Hallelujah. O servants of *Hashem*, give praise; praise the name of *Hashem*.

קיג א הַלְלוּ יָהּ הַלְלוּ עַבְדֵי יְהֹוָה הַלְלוּ אֶת־שֵׁם יְהֹוָה:

ha-l'-lu-YAH ha-l'-LU av-DAY a-do-NAI ha-l'-LU et SHAYM a-do-NAI

2 Let the name of *Hashem* be blessed now and forever.

ב יְהִי שֵׁם יְהֹוָה מְבֹרָךְ מֵעַתָּה וְעַד־עוֹלָם:

3 From east to west the name of *Hashem* is praised.

ג מִמִּזְרַח־שֶׁמֶשׁ עַד־מְבוֹאוֹ מְהֻלָּל שֵׁם יְהֹוָה:

4 *Hashem* is exalted above all nations; His glory is above the heavens.

ד רָם עַל־כָּל־גּוֹיִם יְהֹוָה עַל הַשָּׁמַיִם כְּבוֹדוֹ:

5 Who is like *Hashem* our God, who, enthroned on high,

ה מִי כַּיהֹוָה אֱלֹהֵינוּ הַמַּגְבִּיהִי לָשָׁבֶת:

6 sees what is below, in heaven and on earth?

ו הַמַּשְׁפִּילִי לִרְאוֹת בַּשָּׁמַיִם וּבָאָרֶץ:

7 He raises the poor from the dust, lifts up the needy from the refuse heap

ז מְקִימִי מֵעָפָר דָּל מֵאַשְׁפֹּת יָרִים אֶבְיוֹן:

8 to set them with the great, with the great men of His people.

ח לְהוֹשִׁיבִי עִם־נְדִיבִים עִם נְדִיבֵי עַמּוֹ:

9 He sets the childless woman among her household as a happy mother of children. Hallelujah.

ט מוֹשִׁיבִי עֲקֶרֶת הַבַּיִת אֵם־הַבָּנִים שְׂמֵחָה הַלְלוּ־יָהּ:

114 1 When *Yisrael* went forth from Egypt, the house of *Yaakov* from a people of strange speech,

קיד א בְּצֵאת יִשְׂרָאֵל מִמִּצְרָיִם בֵּית יַעֲקֹב מֵעַם לֹעֵז:

113:1 O servants of *Hashem*, give praise The first verse of this psalm calls on the servants of *Hashem* to bless the name of *Hashem*. This reflects a synthesis of the previous two psalms, one focusing on God, and the other on people who fear God. In this psalm, God is raised above all nations, and, at the same time, He raises up the humble and poor in status and in spirit. This is another expression of the vital partnership between *Hashem* and His people.

1610

Tehillim/Psalms
Chapter 115

2 *Yehuda* became His holy one, *Yisrael*, His dominion.

3 The sea saw them and fled, *Yarden* ran backward,

4 mountains skipped like rams, hills like sheep.

5 What alarmed you, O sea, that you fled, *Yarden*, that you ran backward,

6 mountains, that you skipped like rams, hills, like sheep?

7 Tremble, O earth, at the presence of *Hashem*, at the presence of the God of *Yaakov*,

8 who turned the rock into a pool of water, the flinty rock into a fountain.

ha-ho-f'-KHEE ha-TZUR a-gam MA-yim kha-la-MEESH l'-ma-y'-no MA-yim

115

1 Not to us, *Hashem*, not to us but to Your name bring glory for the sake of Your love and Your faithfulness.

2 Let the nations not say, "Where, now, is their God?"

3 when our God is in heaven and all that He wills He accomplishes.

4 Their idols are silver and gold, the work of men's hands.

5 They have mouths, but cannot speak, eyes, but cannot see;

6 they have ears, but cannot hear, noses, but cannot smell;

7 they have hands, but cannot touch, feet, but cannot walk; they can make no sound in their throats.

8 Those who fashion them, all who trust in them, shall become like them.

9 O *Yisrael*, trust in *Hashem*! He is their help and shield.

הצור
רוצה

114:8 Who turned the rock into a pool of water This verse describes the great strength of *Hashem*, Who can produce water from a rock. The Hebrew word for 'the rock,' *ha-tzur* (הצור), alludes to something that is unmoving or stubborn. Yet if read backwards, the word becomes *rotzeh* (רוצה) which means 'want' or 'willing.' Just as a rock can be turned into water, so too, obstinacy can be turned into willingness. And no matter how far a person is from God, he or she can always come closer. Additionally, *Tzur* is one of the Bible's names for the Almighty Himself. *Hashem*'s protection and kindness are as solid and unchanging as a rock.

Tehillim/Psalms
Chapter 116

10 O house of *Aharon*, trust in *Hashem*! He is their help and shield.

יא בֵּית אַהֲרֹן בִּטְחוּ בַיהֹוָה עֶזְרָם וּמָגִנָּם הוּא:

11 O you who fear *Hashem*, trust in *Hashem*! He is their help and shield.

יא יִרְאֵי יְהֹוָה בִּטְחוּ בַיהֹוָה עֶזְרָם וּמָגִנָּם הוּא:

12 *Hashem* is mindful of us. He will bless us; He will bless the house of *Yisrael*; He will bless the house of *Aharon*;

יב יְהֹוָה זְכָרָנוּ יְבָרֵךְ יְבָרֵךְ אֶת־בֵּית יִשְׂרָאֵל יְבָרֵךְ אֶת־בֵּית אַהֲרֹן:

13 He will bless those who fear *Hashem*, small and great alike.

יג יְבָרֵךְ יִרְאֵי יְהֹוָה הַקְּטַנִּים עִם־הַגְּדֹלִים:

14 May *Hashem* increase your numbers, yours and your children's also.

יד יֹסֵף יְהֹוָה עֲלֵיכֶם וְעַל־בְּנֵיכֶם:

15 May you be blessed by *Hashem*, Maker of heaven and earth.

טו בְּרוּכִים אַתֶּם לַיהֹוָה עֹשֵׂה שָׁמַיִם וָאָרֶץ:

16 The heavens belong to *Hashem*, but the earth He gave over to man.

טז הַשָּׁמַיִם שָׁמַיִם לַיהֹוָה וְהָאָרֶץ נָתַן לִבְנֵי־אָדָם:

ha-sha-MA-yim sha-MA-yim la-do-NAI v'-ha-A-retz na-TAN liv-NAY a-DAM

17 The dead cannot praise *Hashem*, nor any who go down into silence.

יז לֹא הַמֵּתִים יְהַלְלוּ־יָהּ וְלֹא כָּל־יֹרְדֵי דוּמָה:

18 But we will bless *Hashem* now and forever. Hallelujah.

יח וַאֲנַחְנוּ נְבָרֵךְ יָהּ מֵעַתָּה וְעַד־עוֹלָם הַלְלוּ־יָהּ:

116

1 I love *Hashem** for He hears my voice, my pleas;

א אָהַבְתִּי כִּי־יִשְׁמַע יְהֹוָה אֶת־קוֹלִי תַּחֲנוּנָי:

2 for He turns His ear to me whenever I call.

ב כִּי־הִטָּה אָזְנוֹ לִי וּבְיָמַי אֶקְרָא:

3 The bonds of death encompassed me; the torments of Sheol overtook me. I came upon trouble and sorrow

ג אֲפָפוּנִי חֶבְלֵי־מָוֶת וּמְצָרֵי שְׁאוֹל מְצָאוּנִי צָרָה וְיָגוֹן אֶמְצָא:

4 and I invoked the name of *Hashem*, "*Hashem*, save my life!"

ד וּבְשֵׁם־יְהֹוָה אֶקְרָא אָנָּה יְהֹוָה מַלְּטָה נַפְשִׁי:

5 *Hashem* is gracious and beneficent; our God is compassionate.

ה חַנּוּן יְהֹוָה וְצַדִּיק וֵאלֹהֵינוּ מְרַחֵם:

---

* "Hashem" transposed for clarity

115:16 But the earth He gave over to man
Though the heavens remain *Hashem*'s domain, He bestowed the earth to man, in order to spread His holy name. Rabbi Menachem Mendel of Kotzk, a nineteenth century Hasidic leader, explains beautifully: "The land was given to man to raise it up to the lofty level of the heavens." This is especially true in *Eretz Yisrael*. The Bible warns that there is a higher standard for one's behavior in the Land of Israel, as it says in *Sefer Vayikra* 18:26–28 "You must keep My laws and My rules, and you must not do any of those abhorrent things… So let not the land spew you out for defiling it, as it spewed out the nation that came before you."

Rabbi Menachem Mendel of Kotzk (1787–1859)

Tehillim/Psalms
Chapter 117

תהלים
פרק קיז

6 *Hashem* protects the simple; I was brought low and He saved me.

שֹׁמֵ֣ר פְּתָאיִ֣ם יְהֹוָ֑ה דַּ֝לּוֹתִ֗י וְלִ֣י יְהוֹשִֽׁיעַ׃

7 Be at rest, once again, O my soul, for *Hashem* has been good to you.

שׁוּבִ֣י נַ֭פְשִׁי לִמְנוּחָ֑יְכִי כִּֽי־יְ֝הֹוָ֗ה גָּמַ֥ל עָלָֽיְכִי׃

8 You have delivered me from death, my eyes from tears, my feet from stumbling.

כִּ֤י חִלַּ֥צְתָּ נַפְשִׁ֗י מִ֫מָּ֥וֶת אֶת־עֵינִ֥י מִן־דִּמְעָ֑ה אֶת־רַגְלִ֥י מִדֶּֽחִי׃

9 I shall walk before *Hashem* in the lands of the living.

אֶ֭תְהַלֵּךְ לִפְנֵ֣י יְהֹוָ֑ה בְּ֝אַרְצ֗וֹת הַֽחַיִּֽים׃

10 I trust [in *Hashem*]; out of great suffering I spoke

הֶ֭אֱמַנְתִּי כִּ֣י אֲדַבֵּ֑ר אֲ֝נִ֗י עָנִ֥יתִי מְאֹֽד׃

11 and said rashly, "All men are false."

אֲ֭נִי אָמַ֣רְתִּי בְחׇפְזִ֑י כׇּל־הָאָדָ֥ם כֹּזֵֽב׃

12 How can I repay *Hashem* for all His bounties to me?

מָה־אָשִׁ֥יב לַיהֹוָ֑ה כׇּֽל־תַּגְמוּל֥וֹהִי עָלָֽי׃

13 I raise the cup of deliverance and invoke the name of *Hashem*.

כּוֹס־יְשׁוּע֥וֹת אֶשָּׂ֑א וּבְשֵׁ֖ם יְהֹוָ֣ה אֶקְרָֽא׃

14 I will pay my vows to *Hashem* in the presence of all His people.

נְ֭דָרַי לַיהֹוָ֣ה אֲשַׁלֵּ֑ם נֶגְדָה־נָּ֝֗א לְכׇל־עַמּֽוֹ׃

n'-da-RAI la-do-NAI a-sha-LAYM neg-dah NA l'-khol a-MO

15 The death of His faithful ones is grievous in *Hashem*'s sight.

יָ֭קָר בְּעֵינֵ֣י יְהֹוָ֑ה הַ֝מָּ֗וְתָה לַחֲסִידָֽיו׃

16 *Hashem*, I am Your servant, Your servant, the son of Your maidservant; You have undone the cords that bound me.

אָנָּ֣ה יְהֹוָה֮ כִּֽי־אֲנִ֢י עַ֫בְדֶּ֥ךָ אֲֽנִי־עַ֭בְדְּךָ בֶּן־אֲמָתֶ֑ךָ פִּ֝תַּ֗חְתָּ לְמוֹסֵרָֽי׃

17 I will sacrifice a thank offering to You and invoke the name of *Hashem*.

לְֽךָ־אֶ֭זְבַּח זֶ֣בַח תּוֹדָ֑ה וּבְשֵׁ֖ם יְהֹוָ֣ה אֶקְרָֽא׃

18 I will pay my vows to *Hashem* in the presence of all His people,

נְ֭דָרַי לַיהֹוָ֣ה אֲשַׁלֵּ֑ם נֶגְדָה־נָּ֝֗א לְכׇל־עַמּֽוֹ׃

19 in the courts of the house of *Hashem*, in the midst of *Yerushalayim*. Hallelujah.

בְּחַצְר֤וֹת ׀ בֵּ֬ית יְהֹוָ֗ה בְּֽת֘וֹכֵ֤כִי יְֽרוּשָׁלָ֗͏ִם הַֽלְלוּ־יָֽהּ׃

117 1 Praise *Hashem*, all you nations; extol Him, all you peoples,

הַֽלְל֣וּ אֶת־יְ֭הֹוָה כׇּל־גּוֹיִ֑ם שַׁ֝בְּח֗וּהוּ כׇּל־הָאֻמִּֽים׃

2 for great is His steadfast love toward us; the faithfulness of *Hashem* endures forever. Hallelujah.

כִּ֥י גָ֘בַ֤ר עָלֵ֨ינוּ ׀ חַסְדּ֗וֹ וֶאֱמֶת־יְהֹוָ֥ה לְעוֹלָ֗ם הַֽלְלוּ־יָֽהּ׃

Model of the second Beit Hamikdash

116:14 I will pay my vows to *Hashem* God does not like liars. Time and again the Bible reminds us to heed our words, stay away from falsehood and to refrain from deception. Here, the psalmist is disgusted with liars, whom he finds everywhere (verse 11). In contrast, he intends to abide by his words and fulfill his obligations. He therefore comes to the courtyard of the *Beit Hamikdash* in *Yerushalayim* to fulfill his promises and oaths (verse 19). Only in this way can he truly bring praise to God and acknowledge all the good that He has done for him (verse 12).

Tehillim/Psalms
Chapter 118

תהלים
פרק קיח

KEE ga-VAR a-LAY-nu khas-DO ve-e-met a-do-NAI l'-o-LAM ha-l'-lu-YAH

118 1 Praise *Hashem*, for He is good, His steadfast love is eternal.

א הוֹדוּ לַיהוָה כִּי־טוֹב כִּי לְעוֹלָם חַסְדּוֹ:

2 Let *Yisrael* declare, "His steadfast love is eternal."

ב יֹאמַר־נָא יִשְׂרָאֵל כִּי לְעוֹלָם חַסְדּוֹ:

3 Let the house of *Aharon* declare, "His steadfast love is eternal."

ג יֹאמְרוּ־נָא בֵית־אַהֲרֹן כִּי לְעוֹלָם חַסְדּוֹ:

4 Let those who fear *Hashem* declare, "His steadfast love is eternal."

ד יֹאמְרוּ־נָא יִרְאֵי יְהוָה כִּי לְעוֹלָם חַסְדּוֹ:

5 In distress I called on *Hashem*; *Hashem* answered me and brought me relief.

ה מִן־הַמֵּצַר קָרָאתִי יָּהּ עָנָנִי בַמֶּרְחָב יָהּ:

min ha-may-TZAR ka-RA-tee YAH a-NA-nee va-mer-KHAV YAH

6 *Hashem* is on my side, I have no fear; what can man do to me?

ו יְהוָה לִי לֹא אִירָא מַה־יַּעֲשֶׂה לִי אָדָם:

7 With *Hashem* on my side as my helper, I will see the downfall of my foes.

ז יְהוָה לִי בְּעֹזְרָי וַאֲנִי אֶרְאֶה בְשֹׂנְאָי:

8 It is better to take refuge in *Hashem* than to trust in mortals;

ח טוֹב לַחֲסוֹת בַּיהוָה מִבְּטֹחַ בָּאָדָם:

9 it is better to take refuge in *Hashem* than to trust in the great.

ט טוֹב לַחֲסוֹת בַּיהוָה מִבְּטֹחַ בִּנְדִיבִים:

10 All nations have beset me; by the name of *Hashem* I will surely cut them down.

י כָּל־גּוֹיִם סְבָבוּנִי בְּשֵׁם יְהוָה כִּי אֲמִילַם:

11 They beset me, they surround me; by the name of *Hashem* I will surely cut them down.

יא סַבּוּנִי גַם־סְבָבוּנִי בְּשֵׁם יְהוָה כִּי אֲמִילַם:

12 They have beset me like bees; they shall be extinguished like burning thorns; by the name of *Hashem* I will surely cut them down.

יב סַבּוּנִי כִדְבוֹרִים דֹּעֲכוּ כְּאֵשׁ קוֹצִים בְּשֵׁם יְהוָה כִּי אֲמִילַם:

חסד ואמת

א **117:2 For great is His steadfast love toward us** In this short psalm we learn of the interaction of two seemingly contradictory attributes of *Hashem*: *Chesed* (חסד), 'mercy,' which is translated here as 'steadfast love,' and *emet* (אמת), 'truth.' Each of these seems to annul the other, as it is often the case that in truth, a person does not deserve mercy. Yet the psalmist clearly highlights both at the same time. On the one hand, the quality of mercy is more pronounced in this verse, since it is described as "great". On the other hand, the concluding words of the verse herald the truth of God, which endures forever. Perhaps the two ideas are not as contradictory as it first appears, as a life dedicated to kindness and mercy ultimately engenders a legacy of eternal truth.

א **118:5 In distress I called on *Hashem*** Psalm 118 is recited towards the end of the *Pesach seder*, and uses a word that is central to the themes of *Pesach*: 'Maytzar' (מצר), meaning 'straits' or 'distress'. This word is closely related to the Hebrew word for Egypt, *Mitzrayim* (מצרים). On an emotional level, Egypt symbolizes the agonizing straits that constrict us. Each of us occasionally finds ourselves trapped. Sometimes this happens due to physical causes like poverty or illness, and sometimes for psychological reasons, such as depression or anxiety. *Pesach* is the festival of freedom and faith, teaching that the Almighty saves all from each of life's narrow confines. As the psalmist notes, "In distress I called on *Hashem*; *Hashem* answered me and brought me relief."

מצר

Tehillim/Psalms
Chapter 119

13 You pressed me hard, I nearly fell; but *Hashem* helped me. יג דָּחֹה דְחִיתַנִי לִנְפֹּל וַיהוָה עֲזָרָנִי:

14 *Hashem* is my strength and might; He has become my deliverance. יד עָזִּי וְזִמְרָת יָהּ וַיְהִי־לִי לִישׁוּעָה:

15 The tents of the victorious resound with joyous shouts of deliverance, "The right hand of *Hashem* is triumphant! טו קוֹל רִנָּה וִישׁוּעָה בְּאָהֳלֵי צַדִּיקִים יְמִין יְהוָה עֹשָׂה חָיִל:

16 The right hand of *Hashem* is exalted! The right hand of *Hashem* is triumphant!" טז יְמִין יְהוָה רוֹמֵמָה יְמִין יְהוָה עֹשָׂה חָיִל:

17 I shall not die but live and proclaim the works of *Hashem*. יז לֹא אָמוּת כִּי־אֶחְיֶה וַאֲסַפֵּר מַעֲשֵׂי יָהּ:

18 *Hashem* punished me severely, but did not hand me over to death. יח יַסֹּר יִסְּרַנִּי יָּהּ וְלַמָּוֶת לֹא נְתָנָנִי:

19 Open the gates of victory for me that I may enter them and praise *Hashem*. יט פִּתְחוּ־לִי שַׁעֲרֵי־צֶדֶק אָבֹא־בָם אוֹדֶה יָהּ:

20 This is the gateway to *Hashem* – the victorious shall enter through it. כ זֶה־הַשַּׁעַר לַיהוָה צַדִּיקִים יָבֹאוּ בוֹ:

21 I praise You, for You have answered me, and have become my deliverance. כא אוֹדְךָ כִּי עֲנִיתָנִי וַתְּהִי־לִי לִישׁוּעָה:

22 The stone that the builders rejected has become the chief cornerstone. כב אֶבֶן מָאֲסוּ הַבּוֹנִים הָיְתָה לְרֹאשׁ פִּנָּה:

23 This is *Hashem*'s doing; it is marvelous in our sight. כג מֵאֵת יְהוָה הָיְתָה זֹּאת הִיא נִפְלָאת בְּעֵינֵינוּ:

24 This is the day that *Hashem* has made – let us exult and rejoice on it. כד זֶה־הַיּוֹם עָשָׂה יְהוָה נָגִילָה וְנִשְׂמְחָה בוֹ:

25 *Hashem*, deliver us! *Hashem*, let us prosper! כה אָנָּא יְהוָה הוֹשִׁיעָה נָּא אָנָּא יְהוָה הַצְלִיחָה נָּא:

26 May he who enters be blessed in the name of *Hashem*; we bless you from the House of *Hashem*. כו בָּרוּךְ הַבָּא בְּשֵׁם יְהוָה בֵּרַכְנוּכֶם מִבֵּית יְהוָה:

27 *Hashem* is *Hashem*; He has given us light; bind the festal offering to the horns of the *Mizbayach* with cords. כז אֵל יְהוָה וַיָּאֶר לָנוּ אִסְרוּ־חַג בַּעֲבֹתִים עַד־קַרְנוֹת הַמִּזְבֵּחַ:

28 You are my God and I will praise You; You are my God and I will extol You. כח אֵלִי אַתָּה וְאוֹדֶךָּ אֱלֹהַי אֲרוֹמְמֶךָּ:

29 Praise *Hashem* for He is good, His steadfast love is eternal. כט הוֹדוּ לַיהוָה כִּי־טוֹב כִּי לְעוֹלָם חַסְדּוֹ:

119 1 Happy are those whose way is blameless, who follow the teaching of *Hashem*. קיט א אַשְׁרֵי תְמִימֵי־דָרֶךְ הַהֹלְכִים בְּתוֹרַת יְהוָה:

ash-RAY t'-mee-may DA-rekh ha-ho-l'-KHEEM b'-to-RAT a-do-NAI

Tehillim/Psalms
Chapter 119

תהלים
פרק קיט

#	English	Hebrew
2	Happy are those who observe His decrees, who turn to Him wholeheartedly.	ב אַשְׁרֵי נֹצְרֵי עֵדֹתָיו בְּכָל־לֵב יִדְרְשׁוּהוּ:
3	They have done no wrong, but have followed His ways.	ג אַף לֹא־פָעֲלוּ עַוְלָה בִּדְרָכָיו הָלָכוּ:
4	You have commanded that Your precepts be kept diligently.	ד אַתָּה צִוִּיתָה פִקֻּדֶיךָ לִשְׁמֹר מְאֹד:
5	Would that my ways were firm in keeping Your laws;	ה אַחֲלַי יִכֹּנוּ דְרָכָי לִשְׁמֹר חֻקֶּיךָ:
6	then I would not be ashamed when I regard all Your commandments.	ו אָז לֹא־אֵבוֹשׁ בְּהַבִּיטִי אֶל־כָּל־מִצְוֹתֶיךָ:
7	I will praise You with a sincere heart as I learn Your just rules.	ז אוֹדְךָ בְּיֹשֶׁר לֵבָב בְּלָמְדִי מִשְׁפְּטֵי צִדְקֶךָ:
8	I will keep Your laws; do not utterly forsake me.	ח אֶת־חֻקֶּיךָ אֶשְׁמֹר אַל־תַּעַזְבֵנִי עַד־מְאֹד:
9	How can a young man keep his way pure? – by holding to Your word.	ט בַּמֶּה יְזַכֶּה־נַּעַר אֶת־אָרְחוֹ לִשְׁמֹר כִּדְבָרֶךָ:
10	I have turned to You with all my heart; do not let me stray from Your commandments.	י בְּכָל־לִבִּי דְרַשְׁתִּיךָ אַל־תַּשְׁגֵּנִי מִמִּצְוֹתֶיךָ:
11	In my heart I treasure Your promise; therefore I do not sin against You.	יא בְּלִבִּי צָפַנְתִּי אִמְרָתֶךָ לְמַעַן לֹא אֶחֱטָא־לָךְ:
12	Blessed are You, *Hashem*; train me in Your laws.	יב בָּרוּךְ אַתָּה יְהוָה לַמְּדֵנִי חֻקֶּיךָ:
13	With my lips I rehearse all the rules You proclaimed.	יג בִּשְׂפָתַי סִפַּרְתִּי כֹּל מִשְׁפְּטֵי־פִיךָ:
14	I rejoice over the way of Your decrees as over all riches.	יד בְּדֶרֶךְ עֵדְוֹתֶיךָ שַׂשְׂתִּי כְּעַל כָּל־הוֹן:
15	I study Your precepts; I regard Your ways;	טו בְּפִקֻּדֶיךָ אָשִׂיחָה וְאַבִּיטָה אֹרְחֹתֶיךָ:
16	I take delight in Your laws; I will not neglect Your word.	טז בְּחֻקֹּתֶיךָ אֶשְׁתַּעֲשָׁע לֹא אֶשְׁכַּח דְּבָרֶךָ:

119:1 Happy are those whose way is blameless. This psalm contains 176 verses of praise of *Hashem*, making it the longest chapter in the entire *Tanach*. It is an alphabetic acrostic in which each group of eight verses all begin with the same letter of the Hebrew alphabet, and almost every verse focuses on the beauty of God's *Torah*. Why is each letter repeated eight times? Kabbalistic teachings note that the natural order of the world corresponds to the number seven. For example, there are seven days in a week. The number eight, therefore, reflects that which is above nature, meaning the supernatural or the metaphysical. The eighth day after birth, therefore, is the day when a Jewish baby boy is circumcised, because it reflects the meta-historical connection between the Jew and *Hashem*. The *Torah* was given on the fiftieth day after the exodus, representing the day following a series of seven sevens. *Eretz Yisrael* also has a fifty-year cycle, with the *yovel*, the Jubilee year, occurring after forty-nine years, to remind us of the unique connection between *Hashem* and the Holy Land. The Nation of Israel, the Land of Israel, and the *Torah* of Israel are all associated with the number eight. Each contains a supernatural element, and are all reflected in this unique psalm.

Tehillim / Psalms
Chapter 119

תהילים
פרק קיט

#	English	Hebrew
17	Deal kindly with Your servant, that I may live to keep Your word.	יז גְּמֹל עַל־עַבְדְּךָ אֶחְיֶה וְאֶשְׁמְרָה דְבָרֶךָ:
18	Open my eyes, that I may perceive the wonders of Your teaching.	יח גַּל־עֵינַי וְאַבִּיטָה נִפְלָאוֹת מִתּוֹרָתֶךָ:
19	I am only a sojourner in the land; do not hide Your commandments from me.	יט גֵּר אָנֹכִי בָאָרֶץ אַל־תַּסְתֵּר מִמֶּנִּי מִצְוֹתֶיךָ:
20	My soul is consumed with longing for Your rules at all times.	כ גָּרְסָה נַפְשִׁי לְתַאֲבָה אֶל־מִשְׁפָּטֶיךָ בְכָל־עֵת:
21	You blast the accursed insolent ones who stray from Your commandments.	כא גָּעַרְתָּ זֵדִים אֲרוּרִים הַשֹּׁגִים מִמִּצְוֹתֶיךָ:
22	Take away from me taunt and abuse, because I observe Your decrees.	כב גַּל מֵעָלַי חֶרְפָּה וָבוּז כִּי עֵדֹתֶיךָ נָצָרְתִּי:
23	Though princes meet and speak against me, Your servant studies Your laws.	כג גַּם יָשְׁבוּ שָׂרִים בִּי נִדְבָּרוּ עַבְדְּךָ יָשִׂיחַ בְּחֻקֶּיךָ:
24	For Your decrees are my delight, my intimate companions.	כד גַּם־עֵדֹתֶיךָ שַׁעֲשֻׁעָי אַנְשֵׁי עֲצָתִי:
25	My soul clings to the dust; revive me in accordance with Your word.	כה דָּבְקָה לֶעָפָר נַפְשִׁי חַיֵּנִי כִּדְבָרֶךָ:
26	I have declared my way, and You have answered me; train me in Your laws.	כו דְּרָכַי סִפַּרְתִּי וַתַּעֲנֵנִי לַמְּדֵנִי חֻקֶּיךָ:
27	Make me understand the way of Your precepts, that I may study Your wondrous acts.	כז דֶּרֶךְ־פִּקּוּדֶיךָ הֲבִינֵנִי וְאָשִׂיחָה בְּנִפְלְאוֹתֶיךָ:
28	I am racked with grief; sustain me in accordance with Your word.	כח דָּלְפָה נַפְשִׁי מִתּוּגָה קַיְּמֵנִי כִּדְבָרֶךָ:
29	Remove all false ways from me; favor me with Your teaching.	כט דֶּרֶךְ־שֶׁקֶר הָסֵר מִמֶּנִּי וְתוֹרָתְךָ חָנֵּנִי:
30	I have chosen the way of faithfulness; I have set Your rules before me.	ל דֶּרֶךְ־אֱמוּנָה בָחָרְתִּי מִשְׁפָּטֶיךָ שִׁוִּיתִי:
31	I cling to Your decrees; *Hashem*, do not put me to shame.	לא דָּבַקְתִּי בְעֵדְוֹתֶיךָ יְהוָה אַל־תְּבִישֵׁנִי:
32	I eagerly pursue Your commandments, for You broaden my understanding.	לב דֶּרֶךְ־מִצְוֹתֶיךָ אָרוּץ כִּי תַרְחִיב לִבִּי:
33	Teach me, *Hashem*, the way of Your laws; I will observe them to the utmost.	לג הוֹרֵנִי יְהוָה דֶּרֶךְ חֻקֶּיךָ וְאֶצְּרֶנָּה עֵקֶב:
34	Give me understanding, that I may observe Your teaching and keep it wholeheartedly.	לד הֲבִינֵנִי וְאֶצְּרָה תוֹרָתֶךָ וְאֶשְׁמְרֶנָּה בְכָל־לֵב:
35	Lead me in the path of Your commandments, for that is my concern.	לה הַדְרִיכֵנִי בִּנְתִיב מִצְוֹתֶיךָ כִּי־בוֹ חָפָצְתִּי:
36	Turn my heart to Your decrees and not to love of gain.	לו הַט־לִבִּי אֶל־עֵדְוֹתֶיךָ וְאַל אֶל־בָּצַע:

Tehillim/Psalms
Chapter 119

תהלים
פרק קיט

#	English	Hebrew	
37	Avert my eyes from seeing falsehood; by Your ways preserve me.	הַעֲבֵר עֵינַי מֵרְאוֹת שָׁוְא בִּדְרָכֶךָ חַיֵּנִי׃	לז
38	Fulfill Your promise to Your servant, which is for those who worship You.	הָקֵם לְעַבְדְּךָ אִמְרָתֶךָ אֲשֶׁר לְיִרְאָתֶךָ׃	לח
39	Remove the taunt that I dread, for Your rules are good.	הַעֲבֵר חֶרְפָּתִי אֲשֶׁר יָגֹרְתִּי כִּי מִשְׁפָּטֶיךָ טוֹבִים׃	לט
40	See, I have longed for Your precepts; by Your righteousness preserve me.	הִנֵּה תָּאַבְתִּי לְפִקֻּדֶיךָ בְּצִדְקָתְךָ חַיֵּנִי׃	מ
41	May Your steadfast love reach me, *Hashem*, Your deliverance, as You have promised.	וִיבֹאֻנִי חֲסָדֶךָ יְהוָה תְּשׁוּעָתְךָ כְּאִמְרָתֶךָ׃	מא
42	I shall have an answer for those who taunt me, for I have put my trust in Your word.	וְאֶעֱנֶה חֹרְפִי דָבָר כִּי בָטַחְתִּי בִּדְבָרֶךָ׃	מב
43	Do not utterly take the truth away from my mouth, for I have put my hope in Your rules.	וְאַל־תַּצֵּל מִפִּי דְבַר־אֱמֶת עַד־מְאֹד כִּי לְמִשְׁפָּטֶךָ יִחָלְתִּי׃	מג
44	I will always obey Your teaching, forever and ever.	וְאֶשְׁמְרָה תוֹרָתְךָ תָמִיד לְעוֹלָם וָעֶד׃	מד
45	I will walk about at ease, for I have turned to Your precepts.	וְאֶתְהַלְּכָה בָרְחָבָה כִּי פִקֻּדֶיךָ דָרָשְׁתִּי׃	מה
46	I will speak of Your decrees, and not be ashamed in the presence of kings.	וַאֲדַבְּרָה בְעֵדֹתֶיךָ נֶגֶד מְלָכִים וְלֹא אֵבוֹשׁ׃	מו
47	I will delight in Your commandments, which I love.	וְאֶשְׁתַּעֲשַׁע בְּמִצְוֹתֶיךָ אֲשֶׁר אָהָבְתִּי׃	מז
48	I reach out for Your commandments, which I love; I study Your laws.	וְאֶשָּׂא־כַפַּי אֶל־מִצְוֹתֶיךָ אֲשֶׁר אָהָבְתִּי וְאָשִׂיחָה בְחֻקֶּיךָ׃	מח
49	Remember Your word to Your servant through which You have given me hope.	זְכֹר־דָּבָר לְעַבְדֶּךָ עַל אֲשֶׁר יִחַלְתָּנִי׃	מט
50	This is my comfort in my affliction, that Your promise has preserved me.	זֹאת נֶחָמָתִי בְעָנְיִי כִּי אִמְרָתְךָ חִיָּתְנִי׃	נ
51	Though the arrogant have cruelly mocked me, I have not swerved from Your teaching.	זֵדִים הֱלִיצֻנִי עַד־מְאֹד מִתּוֹרָתְךָ לֹא נָטִיתִי׃	נא
52	I remember Your rules of old, *Hashem*, and find comfort in them.	זָכַרְתִּי מִשְׁפָּטֶיךָ מֵעוֹלָם יְהוָה וָאֶתְנֶחָם׃	נב
53	I am seized with rage because of the wicked who forsake Your teaching.	זַלְעָפָה אֲחָזַתְנִי מֵרְשָׁעִים עֹזְבֵי תּוֹרָתֶךָ׃	נג
54	Your laws are a source of strength to me wherever I may dwell.	זְמִרוֹת הָיוּ־לִי חֻקֶּיךָ בְּבֵית מְגוּרָי׃	נד
55	I remember Your name at night, *Hashem*, and obey Your teaching.	זָכַרְתִּי בַלַּיְלָה שִׁמְךָ יְהוָה וָאֶשְׁמְרָה תּוֹרָתֶךָ׃	נה
56	This has been my lot, for I have observed Your precepts.	זֹאת הָיְתָה־לִּי כִּי פִקֻּדֶיךָ נָצָרְתִּי׃	נו
57	*Hashem* is my portion; I have resolved to keep Your words.	חֶלְקִי יְהוָה אָמַרְתִּי לִשְׁמֹר דְּבָרֶיךָ׃	נז

Tehillim / Psalms
Chapter 119

תהלים
פרק קיט

נח	58 I have implored You with all my heart; have mercy on me, in accordance with Your promise.	חִלִּיתִי פָנֶיךָ בְכָל־לֵב חָנֵּנִי כְּאִמְרָתֶךָ:
נט	59 I have considered my ways, and have turned back to Your decrees.	חִשַּׁבְתִּי דְרָכָי וָאָשִׁיבָה רַגְלַי אֶל־עֵדֹתֶיךָ:
ס	60 I have hurried and not delayed to keep Your commandments.	חַשְׁתִּי וְלֹא הִתְמַהְמָהְתִּי לִשְׁמֹר מִצְוֹתֶיךָ:
סא	61 Though the bonds of the wicked are coiled round me, I have not neglected Your teaching.	חֶבְלֵי רְשָׁעִים עִוְּדֻנִי תּוֹרָתְךָ לֹא שָׁכָחְתִּי:
סב	62 I arise at midnight to praise You for Your just rules.	חֲצוֹת־לַיְלָה אָקוּם לְהוֹדוֹת לָךְ עַל מִשְׁפְּטֵי צִדְקֶךָ:
סג	63 I am a companion to all who fear You, to those who keep Your precepts.	חָבֵר אָנִי לְכָל־אֲשֶׁר יְרֵאוּךָ וּלְשֹׁמְרֵי פִּקּוּדֶיךָ:
סד	64 Your steadfast love, *Hashem*, fills the earth; teach me Your laws.	חַסְדְּךָ יְהֹוָה מָלְאָה הָאָרֶץ חֻקֶּיךָ לַמְּדֵנִי:
סה	65 You have treated Your servant well, according to Your word, *Hashem*.	טוֹב עָשִׂיתָ עִם־עַבְדְּךָ יְהֹוָה כִּדְבָרֶךָ:
סו	66 Teach me good sense and knowledge, for I have put my trust in Your commandments.	טוּב טַעַם וָדַעַת לַמְּדֵנִי כִּי בְמִצְוֹתֶיךָ הֶאֱמָנְתִּי:
סז	67 Before I was humbled I went astray, but now I keep Your word.	טֶרֶם אֶעֱנֶה אֲנִי שֹׁגֵג וְעַתָּה אִמְרָתְךָ שָׁמָרְתִּי:
סח	68 You are good and beneficent; teach me Your laws.	טוֹב־אַתָּה וּמֵטִיב לַמְּדֵנִי חֻקֶּיךָ:
סט	69 Though the arrogant have accused me falsely, I observe Your precepts wholeheartedly.	טָפְלוּ עָלַי שֶׁקֶר זֵדִים אֲנִי בְּכָל־לֵב אֶצֹּר פִּקּוּדֶיךָ:
ע	70 Their minds are thick like fat; as for me, Your teaching is my delight.	טָפַשׁ כַּחֵלֶב לִבָּם אֲנִי תּוֹרָתְךָ שִׁעֲשָׁעְתִּי:
עא	71 It was good for me that I was humbled, so that I might learn Your laws.	טוֹב־לִי כִי־עֻנֵּיתִי לְמַעַן אֶלְמַד חֻקֶּיךָ:
עב	72 I prefer the teaching You proclaimed to thousands of gold and silver pieces.	טוֹב־לִי תוֹרַת־פִּיךָ מֵאַלְפֵי זָהָב וָכָסֶף:
עג	73 Your hands made me and fashioned me; give me understanding that I may learn Your commandments.	יָדֶיךָ עָשׂוּנִי וַיְכוֹנְנוּנִי הֲבִינֵנִי וְאֶלְמְדָה מִצְוֹתֶיךָ:
עד	74 Those who fear You will see me and rejoice, for I have put my hope in Your word.	יְרֵאֶיךָ יִרְאוּנִי וְיִשְׂמָחוּ כִּי לִדְבָרְךָ יִחָלְתִּי:
עה	75 I know, *Hashem*, that Your rulings are just; rightly have You humbled me.	יָדַעְתִּי יְהֹוָה כִּי־צֶדֶק מִשְׁפָּטֶיךָ וֶאֱמוּנָה עִנִּיתָנִי:
עו	76 May Your steadfast love comfort me in accordance with Your promise to Your servant.	יְהִי־נָא חַסְדְּךָ לְנַחֲמֵנִי כְּאִמְרָתְךָ לְעַבְדֶּךָ:
עז	77 May Your mercy reach me, that I might live, for Your teaching is my delight.	יְבֹאוּנִי רַחֲמֶיךָ וְאֶחְיֶה כִּי־תוֹרָתְךָ שַׁעֲשֻׁעָי:

Tehillim/Psalms
Chapter 119

78	Let the insolent be dismayed, for they have wronged me without cause; I will study Your precepts.	עח יֵבֹשׁוּ זֵדִים כִּי־שֶׁקֶר עִוְּתוּנִי אֲנִי אָשִׂיחַ בְּפִקּוּדֶיךָ:
79	May those who fear You, those who know Your decrees, turn again to me.	עט יָשׁוּבוּ לִי יְרֵאֶיךָ וידעו [וְיֹדְעֵי] עֵדֹתֶיךָ:
80	May I wholeheartedly follow Your laws so that I do not come to grief.	פ יְהִי־לִבִּי תָמִים בְּחֻקֶּיךָ לְמַעַן לֹא אֵבוֹשׁ:
81	I long for Your deliverance; I hope for Your word.	פא כָּלְתָה לִתְשׁוּעָתְךָ נַפְשִׁי לִדְבָרְךָ יִחָלְתִּי:
82	My eyes pine away for Your promise; I say, "When will You comfort me?"	פב כָּלוּ עֵינַי לְאִמְרָתֶךָ לֵאמֹר מָתַי תְּנַחֲמֵנִי:
83	Though I have become like a water-skin dried in smoke, I have not neglected Your laws.	פג כִּי־הָיִיתִי כְּנֹאד בְּקִיטוֹר חֻקֶּיךָ לֹא שָׁכָחְתִּי:
84	How long has Your servant to live? when will You bring my persecutors to judgment?	פד כַּמָּה יְמֵי־עַבְדֶּךָ מָתַי תַּעֲשֶׂה בְרֹדְפַי מִשְׁפָּט:
85	The insolent have dug pits for me, flouting Your teaching.	פה כָּרוּ־לִי זֵדִים שִׁיחוֹת אֲשֶׁר לֹא כְתוֹרָתֶךָ:
86	All Your commandments are enduring; I am persecuted without cause; help me!	פו כָּל־מִצְוֹתֶיךָ אֱמוּנָה שֶׁקֶר רְדָפוּנִי עָזְרֵנִי:
87	Though they almost wiped me off the earth, I did not abandon Your precepts.	פז כִּמְעַט כִּלּוּנִי בָאָרֶץ וַאֲנִי לֹא־עָזַבְתִּי פִקּוּדֶיךָ:
88	As befits Your steadfast love, preserve me, so that I may keep the decree You proclaimed.	פח כְּחַסְדְּךָ חַיֵּנִי וְאֶשְׁמְרָה עֵדוּת פִּיךָ:
89	*Hashem* exists forever; Your word stands firm in heaven.	פט לְעוֹלָם יְהוָה דְּבָרְךָ נִצָּב בַּשָּׁמָיִם:
90	Your faithfulness is for all generations; You have established the earth, and it stands.	צ לְדֹר וָדֹר אֱמוּנָתֶךָ כּוֹנַנְתָּ אֶרֶץ וַתַּעֲמֹד:
91	They stand this day to [carry out] Your rulings, for all are Your servants.	צא לְמִשְׁפָּטֶיךָ עָמְדוּ הַיּוֹם כִּי הַכֹּל עֲבָדֶיךָ:
92	Were not Your teaching my delight I would have perished in my affliction.	צב לוּלֵי תוֹרָתְךָ שַׁעֲשֻׁעָי אָז אָבַדְתִּי בְעָנְיִי:
93	I will never neglect Your precepts, for You have preserved my life through them.	צג לְעוֹלָם לֹא־אֶשְׁכַּח פִּקּוּדֶיךָ כִּי בָם חִיִּיתָנִי:
94	I am Yours; save me! For I have turned to Your precepts.	צד לְךָ־אֲנִי הוֹשִׁיעֵנִי כִּי פִקּוּדֶיךָ דָרָשְׁתִּי:
95	The wicked hope to destroy me, but I ponder Your decrees.	צה לִי קִוּוּ רְשָׁעִים לְאַבְּדֵנִי עֵדֹתֶיךָ אֶתְבּוֹנָן:
96	I have seen that all things have their limit, but Your commandment is broad beyond measure.	צו לְכָל־תִּכְלָה רָאִיתִי קֵץ רְחָבָה מִצְוָתְךָ מְאֹד:
97	O how I love Your teaching! It is my study all day long.	צז מָה־אָהַבְתִּי תוֹרָתֶךָ כָּל־הַיּוֹם הִיא שִׂיחָתִי:

Tehillim / Psalms
Chapter 119

98 Your commandments make me wiser than my enemies; they always stand by me. מֵאֹיְבַי תְּחַכְּמֵנִי מִצְוֺתֶךָ כִּי לְעוֹלָם הִיא־לִי׃

99 I have gained more insight than all my teachers, for Your decrees are my study. מִכָּל־מְלַמְּדַי הִשְׂכַּלְתִּי כִּי עֵדְוֺתֶיךָ שִׂיחָה לִי׃

100 I have gained more understanding than my elders, for I observe Your precepts. מִזְּקֵנִים אֶתְבּוֹנָן כִּי פִקּוּדֶיךָ נָצָרְתִּי׃

101 I have avoided every evil way so that I may keep Your word. מִכָּל־אֹרַח רָע כָּלִאתִי רַגְלָי לְמַעַן אֶשְׁמֹר דְּבָרֶךָ׃

102 I have not departed from Your rules, for You have instructed me. מִמִּשְׁפָּטֶיךָ לֹא־סָרְתִּי כִּי־אַתָּה הוֹרֵתָנִי׃

103 How pleasing is Your word to my palate, sweeter than honey. מַה־נִּמְלְצוּ לְחִכִּי אִמְרָתֶךָ מִדְּבַשׁ לְפִי׃

104 I ponder Your precepts; therefore I hate every false way. מִפִּקּוּדֶיךָ אֶתְבּוֹנָן עַל־כֵּן שָׂנֵאתִי כָּל־אֹרַח שָׁקֶר׃

105 Your word is a lamp to my feet, a light for my path. נֵר־לְרַגְלִי דְבָרֶךָ וְאוֹר לִנְתִיבָתִי׃

106 I have firmly sworn to keep Your just rules. נִשְׁבַּעְתִּי וָאֲקַיֵּמָה לִשְׁמֹר מִשְׁפְּטֵי צִדְקֶךָ׃

107 I am very much afflicted; *Hashem*, preserve me in accordance with Your word. נַעֲנֵיתִי עַד־מְאֹד יְהֹוָה חַיֵּנִי כִדְבָרֶךָ׃

108 Accept, *Hashem*, my freewill offerings; teach me Your rules. נִדְבוֹת פִּי רְצֵה־נָא יְהֹוָה וּמִשְׁפָּטֶיךָ לַמְּדֵנִי׃

109 Though my life is always in danger, I do not neglect Your teaching. נַפְשִׁי בְכַפִּי תָמִיד וְתוֹרָתְךָ לֹא שָׁכָחְתִּי׃

110 Though the wicked have set a trap for me, I have not strayed from Your precepts. נָתְנוּ רְשָׁעִים פַּח לִי וּמִפִּקּוּדֶיךָ לֹא תָעִיתִי׃

111 Your decrees are my eternal heritage; they are my heart's delight. נָחַלְתִּי עֵדְוֺתֶיךָ לְעוֹלָם כִּי־שְׂשׂוֹן לִבִּי הֵמָּה׃

112 I am resolved to follow Your laws to the utmost forever. נָטִיתִי לִבִּי לַעֲשׂוֹת חֻקֶּיךָ לְעוֹלָם עֵקֶב׃

113 I hate men of divided heart, but I love Your teaching. סֵעֲפִים שָׂנֵאתִי וְתוֹרָתְךָ אָהָבְתִּי׃

114 You are my protection and my shield; I hope for Your word. סִתְרִי וּמָגִנִּי אָתָּה לִדְבָרְךָ יִחָלְתִּי׃

115 Keep away from me, you evildoers, that I may observe the commandments of my God. סוּרוּ־מִמֶּנִּי מְרֵעִים וְאֶצְּרָה מִצְוֺת אֱלֹהָי׃

116 Support me as You promised, so that I may live; do not thwart my expectation. סָמְכֵנִי כְאִמְרָתְךָ וְאֶחְיֶה וְאַל־תְּבִישֵׁנִי מִשִּׂבְרִי׃

117 Sustain me that I may be saved, and I will always muse upon Your laws. סְעָדֵנִי וְאִוָּשֵׁעָה וְאֶשְׁעָה בְחֻקֶּיךָ תָמִיד׃

Tehillim/Psalms
Chapter 119

118	You reject all who stray from Your laws, for they are false and deceitful.	קיח סָלִיתָ כָּל־שׁוֹגִים מֵחֻקֶּיךָ כִּי־שֶׁקֶר תַּרְמִיתָם:
119	You do away with the wicked as if they were dross; rightly do I love Your decrees.	קיט סִגִים הִשְׁבַּתָּ כָל־רִשְׁעֵי־אָרֶץ לָכֵן אָהַבְתִּי עֵדֹתֶיךָ:
120	My flesh creeps from fear of You; I am in awe of Your rulings.	קכ סָמַר מִפַּחְדְּךָ בְשָׂרִי וּמִמִּשְׁפָּטֶיךָ יָרֵאתִי:
121	I have done what is just and right; do not abandon me to those who would wrong me.	קכא עָשִׂיתִי מִשְׁפָּט וָצֶדֶק בַּל־תַּנִּיחֵנִי לְעֹשְׁקָי:
122	Guarantee Your servant's well-being; do not let the arrogant wrong me.	קכב עֲרֹב עַבְדְּךָ לְטוֹב אַל־יַעַשְׁקֻנִי זֵדִים:
123	My eyes pine away for Your deliverance, for Your promise of victory.	קכג עֵינַי כָּלוּ לִישׁוּעָתֶךָ וּלְאִמְרַת צִדְקֶךָ:
124	Deal with Your servant as befits Your steadfast love; teach me Your laws.	קכד עֲשֵׂה עִם־עַבְדְּךָ כְחַסְדֶּךָ וְחֻקֶּיךָ לַמְּדֵנִי:
125	I am Your servant; give me understanding, that I might know Your decrees.	קכה עַבְדְּךָ־אָנִי הֲבִינֵנִי וְאֵדְעָה עֵדֹתֶיךָ:
126	It is a time to act for *Hashem*, for they have violated Your teaching.	קכו עֵת לַעֲשׂוֹת לַיהוָה הֵפֵרוּ תּוֹרָתֶךָ:
127	Rightly do I love Your commandments more than gold, even fine gold.	קכז עַל־כֵּן אָהַבְתִּי מִצְוֹתֶיךָ מִזָּהָב וּמִפָּז:
128	Truly by all [Your] precepts I walk straight; I hate every false way.	קכח עַל־כֵּן כָּל־פִּקּוּדֵי כֹל יִשָּׁרְתִּי כָּל־אֹרַח שֶׁקֶר שָׂנֵאתִי:
129	Your decrees are wondrous; rightly do I observe them.	קכט פְּלָאוֹת עֵדְוֹתֶיךָ עַל־כֵּן נְצָרָתַם נַפְשִׁי:
130	The words You inscribed give light, and grant understanding to the simple.	קל פֵּתַח דְּבָרֶיךָ יָאִיר מֵבִין פְּתָיִים:
131	I open my mouth wide, I pant, longing for Your commandments.	קלא פִּי־פָעַרְתִּי וָאֶשְׁאָפָה כִּי לְמִצְוֹתֶיךָ יָאָבְתִּי:
132	Turn to me and be gracious to me, as is Your rule with those who love Your name.	קלב פְּנֵה־אֵלַי וְחָנֵּנִי כְּמִשְׁפָּט לְאֹהֲבֵי שְׁמֶךָ:
133	Make my feet firm through Your promise; do not let iniquity dominate me.	קלג פְּעָמַי הָכֵן בְּאִמְרָתֶךָ וְאַל־תַּשְׁלֶט־בִּי כָל־אָוֶן:
134	Redeem me from being wronged by man, that I may keep Your precepts.	קלד פְּדֵנִי מֵעֹשֶׁק אָדָם וְאֶשְׁמְרָה פִּקּוּדֶיךָ:
135	Show favor to Your servant, and teach me Your laws.	קלה פָּנֶיךָ הָאֵר בְּעַבְדֶּךָ וְלַמְּדֵנִי אֶת־חֻקֶּיךָ:
136	My eyes shed streams of water because men do not obey Your teaching.	קלו פַּלְגֵי־מַיִם יָרְדוּ עֵינָי עַל לֹא־שָׁמְרוּ תוֹרָתֶךָ:
137	You are righteous, *Hashem*; Your rulings are just.	קלז צַדִּיק אַתָּה יְהוָה וְיָשָׁר מִשְׁפָּטֶיךָ:

Tehillim/Psalms
Chapter 119

138 You have ordained righteous decrees they are firmly enduring.
קלח צִוִּיתָ צֶדֶק עֵדֹתֶיךָ וֶאֱמוּנָה מְאֹד:

139 I am consumed with rage over my foes' neglect of Your words.
קלט צִמְּתַתְנִי קִנְאָתִי כִּי־שָׁכְחוּ דְבָרֶיךָ צָרָי:

140 Your word is exceedingly pure, and Your servant loves it.
קמ צְרוּפָה אִמְרָתְךָ מְאֹד וְעַבְדְּךָ אֲהֵבָהּ:

141 Though I am belittled and despised, I have not neglected Your precepts.
קמא צָעִיר אָנֹכִי וְנִבְזֶה פִּקֻּדֶיךָ לֹא שָׁכָחְתִּי:

142 Your righteousness is eternal; Your teaching is true.
קמב צִדְקָתְךָ צֶדֶק לְעוֹלָם וְתוֹרָתְךָ אֱמֶת:

143 Though anguish and distress come upon me, Your commandments are my delight.
קמג צַר־וּמָצוֹק מְצָאוּנִי מִצְוֹתֶיךָ שַׁעֲשֻׁעָי:

144 Your righteous decrees are eternal; give me understanding, that I might live.
קמד צֶדֶק עֵדְוֹתֶיךָ לְעוֹלָם הֲבִינֵנִי וְאֶחְיֶה:

145 I call with all my heart; answer me, *Hashem*, that I may observe Your laws.
קמה קָרָאתִי בְכָל־לֵב עֲנֵנִי יְהֹוָה חֻקֶּיךָ אֶצֹּרָה:

146 I call upon You; save me, that I may keep Your decrees.
קמו קְרָאתִיךָ הוֹשִׁיעֵנִי וְאֶשְׁמְרָה עֵדֹתֶיךָ:

147 I rise before dawn and cry for help; I hope for Your word.
קמז קִדַּמְתִּי בַנֶּשֶׁף וָאֲשַׁוֵּעָה לדבריך [לִדְבָרְךָ] יִחָלְתִּי:

148 My eyes greet each watch of the night, as I meditate on Your promise.
קמח קִדְּמוּ עֵינַי אַשְׁמֻרוֹת לָשִׂיחַ בְּאִמְרָתֶךָ:

149 Hear my voice as befits Your steadfast love; *Hashem*, preserve me, as is Your rule.
קמט קוֹלִי שִׁמְעָה כְחַסְדֶּךָ יְהֹוָה כְּמִשְׁפָּטֶךָ חַיֵּנִי:

150 Those who pursue intrigue draw near; they are far from Your teaching.
קנ קָרְבוּ רֹדְפֵי זִמָּה מִתּוֹרָתְךָ רָחָקוּ:

151 You, *Hashem*, are near, and all Your commandments are true.
קנא קָרוֹב אַתָּה יְהֹוָה וְכָל־מִצְוֹתֶיךָ אֱמֶת:

152 I know from Your decrees of old that You have established them forever.
קנב קֶדֶם יָדַעְתִּי מֵעֵדֹתֶיךָ כִּי לְעוֹלָם יְסַדְתָּם:

153 See my affliction and rescue me, for I have not neglected Your teaching.
קנג רְאֵה־עָנְיִי וְחַלְּצֵנִי כִּי־תוֹרָתְךָ לֹא שָׁכָחְתִּי:

154 Champion my cause and redeem me; preserve me according to Your promise.
קנד רִיבָה רִיבִי וּגְאָלֵנִי לְאִמְרָתְךָ חַיֵּנִי:

155 Deliverance is far from the wicked, for they have not turned to Your laws.
קנה רָחוֹק מֵרְשָׁעִים יְשׁוּעָה כִּי־חֻקֶּיךָ לֹא דָרָשׁוּ:

156 Your mercies are great, *Hashem*; as is Your rule, preserve me.
קנו רַחֲמֶיךָ רַבִּים יְהֹוָה כְּמִשְׁפָּטֶיךָ חַיֵּנִי:

157 Many are my persecutors and foes; I have not swerved from Your decrees.
קנז רַבִּים רֹדְפַי וְצָרָי מֵעֵדְוֹתֶיךָ לֹא נָטִיתִי:

Tehillim/Psalms
Chapter 119

158 I have seen traitors and loathed them, because they did not keep Your word in mind.

159 See that I have loved Your precepts; *Hashem*, preserve me, as befits Your steadfast love.

160 Truth is the essence of Your word; Your just rules are eternal.

161 Princes have persecuted me without reason; my heart thrills at Your word.

162 I rejoice over Your promise as one who obtains great spoil.

163 I hate and abhor falsehood; I love Your teaching.

164 I praise You seven times each day for Your just rules.

165 Those who love Your teaching enjoy wellbeing; they encounter no adversity.

166 I hope for Your deliverance, *Hashem*; I observe Your commandments.

167 I obey Your decrees and love them greatly.

168 I obey Your precepts and decrees; all my ways are before You.

169 May my plea reach You, *Hashem*; grant me understanding according to Your word.

170 May my petition come before You; save me in accordance with Your promise.

171 My lips shall pour forth praise, for You teach me Your laws.

172 My tongue shall declare Your promise, for all Your commandments are just.

173 Lend Your hand to help me, for I have chosen Your precepts.

174 I have longed for Your deliverance, *Hashem*; Your teaching is my delight.

175 Let me live, that I may praise You; may Your rules be my help;

176 I have strayed like a lost sheep; search for Your servant, for I have not neglected Your commandments.

Tehillim/Psalms
Chapter 120

תהלים
פרק קכ

120

1 A song of ascents. In my distress I called to *Hashem* and He answered me.

שִׁיר הַמַּעֲלוֹת אֶל־יְהֹוָה בַּצָּרָתָה לִּי קָרָאתִי וַיַּעֲנֵנִי׃ א

SHEER ha-ma-a-LOT el a-do-NAI ba-tza-RA-tah LEE ka-RA-tee va-ya-a-NAY-nee

2 *Hashem*, save me from treacherous lips, from a deceitful tongue!

יְהֹוָה הַצִּילָה נַפְשִׁי מִשְּׂפַת־שֶׁקֶר מִלָּשׁוֹן רְמִיָּה׃ ב

3 What can you profit, what can you gain, O deceitful tongue?

מַה־יִּתֵּן לְךָ וּמַה־יֹּסִיף לָךְ לָשׁוֹן רְמִיָּה׃ ג

4 A warrior's sharp arrows, with hot coals of broom-wood.

חִצֵּי גִבּוֹר שְׁנוּנִים עִם גַּחֲלֵי רְתָמִים׃ ד

5 Woe is me, that I live with Meshech, that I dwell among the clans of Kedar.

אוֹיָה־לִי כִּי־גַרְתִּי מֶשֶׁךְ שָׁכַנְתִּי עִם־אָהֳלֵי קֵדָר׃ ה

6 Too long have I dwelt with those who hate peace.

רַבַּת שָׁכְנָה־לָּהּ נַפְשִׁי עִם שׂוֹנֵא שָׁלוֹם׃ ו

7 I am all peace; but when I speak, they are for war.

אֲנִי־שָׁלוֹם וְכִי אֲדַבֵּר הֵמָּה לַמִּלְחָמָה׃ ז

121

1 A song for ascents. I turn my eyes to the mountains; from where will my help come?

שִׁיר לַמַּעֲלוֹת אֶשָּׂא עֵינַי אֶל־הֶהָרִים מֵאַיִן יָבֹא עֶזְרִי׃ א

SHEER la-ma-a-LOT e-SA ay-NAI el he-ha-REEM may-A-yin ya-VO ez-REE

2 My help comes from *Hashem*, maker of heaven and earth.

עֶזְרִי מֵעִם יְהֹוָה עֹשֵׂה שָׁמַיִם וָאָרֶץ׃ ב

3 He will not let your foot give way; your guardian will not slumber;

אַל־יִתֵּן לַמּוֹט רַגְלֶךָ אַל־יָנוּם שֹׁמְרֶךָ׃ ג

4 See, the guardian of *Yisrael* neither slumbers nor sleeps!

הִנֵּה לֹא־יָנוּם וְלֹא יִישָׁן שׁוֹמֵר יִשְׂרָאֵל׃ ד

מעלות

Mount Chermon

120:1 A song of ascents What is the meaning the Hebrew word *maalot* (מעלות), translated here as 'ascents,' which appears in the opening phrases of the next fifteen psalms? According to *Rashi*, it is a reference to the fifteen steps in the *Beit Hamikdash* upon which the *Leviim* stood while reciting these fifteen psalms. Rabbi Samson Raphael Hirsch explains the ascent in a spiritual way. He understands it to mean that from our low spiritual depths, we call, pray, and sing to *Hashem* to lift us up, or to give us the ability to ascend to the greatest heights. According to this interpretation, one can see a clear reflection of this in the beginning of Psalm 130: "Out of the depths I call You, *Hashem*." Other commentators suggest that these *Tehillim* were sung by those who returned to *Eretz Yisrael* from the Babylonian exile in the times of *Ezra*, upon their ascent to the Holy Land, as reflected in Psalm 126:1 "A Song of Ascents. when *Hashem* restores the fortunes of *Tzion*…" Travelling to the Land of Israel is always considered an ascent, as the verse in *Ezra* 7:9 says: "On the first day of the first month, the journey up from Babylon was started." Even today, moving to Israel is referred to as making *aliyah*, i.e. 'ascending' to live in the Land of Israel.

121:1 I turn my eyes to the mountains When he composed this psalm, the psalmist might have been standing at the foot of a large mountain, perhaps the *Chermon* mountain range, about to embark on a long journey. As he looks up to the mountains, he stands in awe of their beauty, their massiveness, their sheer greatness. It makes him feel meek, and he wonders: From where did they come? Who is behind them? Who will protect him on his journey through them? When looking at the diverse natural wonders found in Israel, such as the majestic *Chermon* mountain, the *Banyas* waterfalls or the great *Carmel* forest, how many times do we stop and acknowledge the Creator who sustains it all? When travelling throughout the beautiful Land of Israel, how often do we call out, "My help comes from *Hashem*, Maker of heaven and earth"?

Tehillim / Psalms
Chapter 122

5 *Hashem* is your guardian, *Hashem* is your protection at your right hand. יְהוָה שֹׁמְרֶךָ יְהוָה צִלְּךָ עַל־יַד יְמִינֶךָ׃

6 By day the sun will not strike you, nor the moon by night. יוֹמָם הַשֶּׁמֶשׁ לֹא־יַכֶּכָּה וְיָרֵחַ בַּלָּיְלָה׃

7 *Hashem* will guard you from all harm; He will guard your life. יְהוָה יִשְׁמָרְךָ מִכָּל־רָע יִשְׁמֹר אֶת־נַפְשֶׁךָ׃

8 *Hashem* will guard your going and coming now and forever. יְהוָה יִשְׁמָר־צֵאתְךָ וּבוֹאֶךָ מֵעַתָּה וְעַד־עוֹלָם׃

122 1 A song of ascents. Of *David*. I rejoiced when they said to me, "We are going to the House of *Hashem*." שִׁיר הַמַּעֲלוֹת לְדָוִד שָׂמַחְתִּי בְּאֹמְרִים לִי בֵּית יְהוָה נֵלֵךְ׃

2 Our feet stood inside your gates, O *Yerushalayim*, עֹמְדוֹת הָיוּ רַגְלֵינוּ בִּשְׁעָרַיִךְ יְרוּשָׁלָםִ׃

3 *Yerushalayim* built up, a city knit together, יְרוּשָׁלַםִ הַבְּנוּיָה כְּעִיר שֶׁחֻבְּרָה־לָּהּ יַחְדָּו׃

4 to which tribes would make pilgrimage, the tribes of *Hashem*, – as was enjoined upon *Yisrael* – to praise the name of *Hashem*. שֶׁשָּׁם עָלוּ שְׁבָטִים שִׁבְטֵי־יָהּ עֵדוּת לְיִשְׂרָאֵל לְהֹדוֹת לְשֵׁם יְהוָה׃

5 There the thrones of judgment stood, thrones of the house of *David*. כִּי שָׁמָּה יָשְׁבוּ כִסְאוֹת לְמִשְׁפָּט כִּסְאוֹת לְבֵית דָּוִיד׃

6 Pray for the well-being of *Yerushalayim*; "May those who love you be at peace. שַׁאֲלוּ שְׁלוֹם יְרוּשָׁלָםִ יִשְׁלָיוּ אֹהֲבָיִךְ׃

sha-a-LU sh'-LOM y'-ru-sha-LA-im yish-LA-yu o-ha-VA-yikh

7 May there be well-being within your ramparts, peace in your citadels." יְהִי־שָׁלוֹם בְּחֵילֵךְ שַׁלְוָה בְּאַרְמְנוֹתָיִךְ׃

8 For the sake of my kin and friends, I pray for your well-being; לְמַעַן אַחַי וְרֵעָי אֲדַבְּרָה־נָּא שָׁלוֹם בָּךְ׃

9 for the sake of the house of *Hashem* our God, I seek your good. לְמַעַן בֵּית־יְהוָה אֱלֹהֵינוּ אֲבַקְשָׁה טוֹב לָךְ׃

123 1 A song of ascents. To You, enthroned in heaven, I turn my eyes. שִׁיר הַמַּעֲלוֹת אֵלֶיךָ נָשָׂאתִי אֶת־עֵינַי הַיֹּשְׁבִי בַּשָּׁמָיִם׃

122:6 Pray for the well-being of *Yerushalayim*
This psalm starts with the words *sha'alu sh'lom Yerushalayim*, 'Pray for the well-being of Yerushalayim.' *Shalom* (שלום), translated here as 'well-being,' is the first Hebrew word many people learn. It actually has three meanings: 'hello,' 'goodbye' and 'peace.' It is the word with which friends greet one another, but *shalom* is more than a greeting; it is also a blessing. Peace is the most important gift we can ask from *Hashem*, on an individual level, as families, and between nations. It is therefore of utmost significance that the world's holiest city, *Yerushalayim* (ירושלים), has the word *shalom* at its core, because it is meant to be the source of all peace on earth. King *David* exhorts "Pray for the well-being of *Yerushalayim*," for when *Yerushalayim* is confronted with conflict, the whole world suffers. Conversely, though, when *Yerushalayim* is at peace, the entire world enjoys serenity.

שלום
ירושלים

Tehillim/Psalms

Chapter 124

תהלים
פרק קכד

2 As the eyes of slaves follow their master's hand, as the eyes of a slave-girl follow the hand of her mistress, so our eyes are toward *Hashem* our God, awaiting His favor.

ב הִנֵּה כְעֵינֵי עֲבָדִים אֶל־יַד אֲדוֹנֵיהֶם כְּעֵינֵי שִׁפְחָה אֶל־יַד גְּבִרְתָּהּ כֵּן עֵינֵינוּ אֶל־יְהֹוָה אֱלֹהֵינוּ עַד שֶׁיְּחָנֵּנוּ׃

3 Show us favor, *Hashem*, show us favor! We have had more than enough of contempt.

ג חָנֵּנוּ יְהֹוָה חָנֵּנוּ כִּי־רַב שָׂבַעְנוּ בוּז׃

kha-NAY-nu a-do-NAI kha-NAY-nu kee RAV sa-VA-nu VUZ

4 Long enough have we endured the scorn of the complacent, the contempt of th haughty.

ד רַבַּת שָׂבְעָה־לָּהּ נַפְשֵׁנוּ הַלַּעַג הַשַּׁאֲנַנִּים הַבּוּז לִגְאֵיוֹנִים׃

124 1 A song of ascents. Of *David*. Were it not for *Hashem*, who was on our side, let *Yisrael* now declare,

קכד א שִׁיר הַמַּעֲלוֹת לְדָוִד לוּלֵי יְהֹוָה שֶׁהָיָה לָנוּ יֹאמַר־נָא יִשְׂרָאֵל׃

2 were it not for *Hashem*, who was on our side when men assailed us,

ב לוּלֵי יְהֹוָה שֶׁהָיָה לָנוּ בְּקוּם עָלֵינוּ אָדָם׃

3 they would have swallowed us alive in their burning rage against us;

ג אֲזַי חַיִּים בְּלָעוּנוּ בַּחֲרוֹת אַפָּם בָּנוּ׃

4 the waters would have carried us off, the torrent would have swept over us;

ד אֲזַי הַמַּיִם שְׁטָפוּנוּ נַחְלָה עָבַר עַל־נַפְשֵׁנוּ׃

5 over us would have swept the seething waters.

ה אֲזַי עָבַר עַל־נַפְשֵׁנוּ הַמַּיִם הַזֵּידוֹנִים׃

6 Blessed is *Hashem*, who did not let us be ripped apart by their teeth.

ו בָּרוּךְ יְהֹוָה שֶׁלֹּא נְתָנָנוּ טֶרֶף לְשִׁנֵּיהֶם׃

7 We are like a bird escaped from the fowler's trap; the trap broke and we escaped.

ז נַפְשֵׁנוּ כְּצִפּוֹר נִמְלְטָה מִפַּח יוֹקְשִׁים הַפַּח נִשְׁבָּר וַאֲנַחְנוּ נִמְלָטְנוּ׃

naf-SHAY-nu k'-tzi-POR nim-l'-TAH mi-PAKH yo-k'-SHEEM ha-PAKH nish-BAR va-a-NAKH-nu nim-LAT-nu

Rabbi Joseph B. Soloveitchik (1903–1993)

The Jerusalem Prism

123:3 We have had more than enough of contempt Rabbi Yosef Albo, a fifteenth century Spanish Jewish scholar, understands this psalm as a call to *Hashem* for mercy from the long, and difficult exile. The psalmist speaks of the shame he undergoes living in the protracted exile. In one of his most famous writings about the Land of Israel, called "Six Knocks," Rabbi Joseph B. Soloveitchik, leader of American Modern Orthodoxy in the twentieth century, speaks of the miraculous nature of the re-birth of the Jewish people in our times, with the State of Israel as the modern Jewish homeland. Rabbi Soloveitchik notes that finally, after thousands of years of exile, Jewish blood is no longer cheap, as a Jew can always find "a secure refuge in the land of his ancestors." The shame of being defenseless and landless is too much for the psalmist to handle, so he cries out to God for salvation. In modern times, we have begun to experience that salvation.

124:7 We are like a bird escaped from the fowler's trap In Psalm 124, the psalmist thanks God for saving him from imminent destruction: "Were it not for *Hashem*, who was on our side when men assailed us" (verse 2). The metaphor of a bird escaping a trap is interesting in light of an archaeological discovery called the Jerusalem Prism, housed today in the Israel Museum. It contains the annals of the Assyrian king Sennacherib. In it, he makes reference to the conquest of northern Israel and the exile of its inhabitants, and describes his conquest of many of the cities in the southern kingdom of *Yehuda*. When depicting the siege of *Yerushalayim* in the time of *Chizkiyahu*, he says that he confined *Chizkiyahu* "as a caged bird," employing language similar to this verse. Ultimately, though, a miracle took place and the Assyrian army mysteriously died, allowing King *Chizkiyahu* and *Yerushalayim* to be freed from the Assyrian snare (II Kings 18–19).

Tehillim/Psalms
Chapter 125

תהלים
פרק קכה

8 Our help is the name of *Hashem*, maker of heaven and earth.

עֶזְרֵנוּ בְּשֵׁם יְהֹוָה עֹשֵׂה שָׁמַיִם וָאָרֶץ:

125

1 A song of ascents. Those who trust in *Hashem* are like Mount *Tzion* that cannot be moved, enduring forever.

שִׁיר הַמַּעֲלוֹת הַבֹּטְחִים בַּיהֹוָה כְּהַר־צִיּוֹן לֹא־יִמּוֹט לְעוֹלָם יֵשֵׁב:

2 *Yerushalayim*, hills enfold it, and *Hashem* enfolds His people now and forever.

y'-ru-sha-LA-im ha-REEM sa-VEEV LAH va-do-NAI sa-VEEV l'-a-MO may-a-TAH v'-ad o-LAM

יְרוּשָׁלַ͏ִם הָרִים סָבִיב לָהּ וַיהֹוָה סָבִיב לְעַמּוֹ מֵעַתָּה וְעַד־עוֹלָם:

3 The scepter of the wicked shall never rest upon the land allotted to the righteous, that the righteous not set their hand to wrongdoing.

כִּי לֹא יָנוּחַ שֵׁבֶט הָרֶשַׁע עַל גּוֹרַל הַצַּדִּיקִים לְמַעַן לֹא־יִשְׁלְחוּ הַצַּדִּיקִים בְּעַוְלָתָה יְדֵיהֶם:

4 Do good, *Hashem*, to the good, to the upright in heart.

הֵיטִיבָה יְהֹוָה לַטּוֹבִים וְלִישָׁרִים בְּלִבּוֹתָם:

5 But those who in their crookedness act corruptly, let *Hashem* make them go the way of evildoers. May it be well with *Yisrael*!

וְהַמַּטִּים עֲקַלְקַלּוֹתָם יוֹלִיכֵם יְהֹוָה אֶת־פֹּעֲלֵי הָאָוֶן שָׁלוֹם עַל־יִשְׂרָאֵל:

126

1 A song of ascents. When *Hashem* restores the fortunes of *Tzion* – we see it as in a dream –

SHEER ha-ma-a-LOT b'-SHUV a-do-NAI et shee-VAT tzi-YON ha-YEE-nu k'-kho-l'-MEEM

שִׁיר הַמַּעֲלוֹת בְּשׁוּב יְהֹוָה אֶת־שִׁיבַת צִיּוֹן הָיִינוּ כְּחֹלְמִים:

2 our mouths shall be filled with laughter, our tongues, with songs of joy. Then shall they say among the nations, "*Hashem* has done great things for them!"

אָז יִמָּלֵא שְׂחוֹק פִּינוּ וּלְשׁוֹנֵנוּ רִנָּה אָז יֹאמְרוּ בַגּוֹיִם הִגְדִּיל יְהֹוָה לַעֲשׂוֹת עִם־אֵלֶּה:

3 *Hashem* will do great things for us and we shall rejoice.

הִגְדִּיל יְהֹוָה לַעֲשׂוֹת עִמָּנוּ הָיִינוּ שְׂמֵחִים:

125:2 *Yerushalayim* The Hebrew name for Jerusalem, *Yerushalayim* (ירושלים), incorporates the word *shalom*, 'peace.' And the root of *shalom* (שלום) is *shalem* (שלם), meaning 'whole' or 'complete.' People fight with one another because they are not whole, and are not at peace with themselves. Once one is able to achieve wholeness, he can find inner peace, and will be much more likely to live peacefully with others. Throughout history and to this very day, many people come to *Yerushalayim*, the city of peace, to become whole within themselves and to find inner peace.

126:1 When *Hashem* restores the fortunes of *Tzion* Psalm 126 refers to *Tzion* (ציון), one of the Bible's names for *Yerushalayim*, which is also used in a more general sense for the entire Land of Israel. This name is closely related to the word for 'special' and 'distinctive,' *m'tzuyan* (מצוין). This teaches that God's holy city is more than a location. According to former British Chief Rabbi Jonathan Sacks, "*Tzion* is not just a place. It is a way of life. Jews are called to moral excellence, to be different…" God created a special place on earth which would be the ideal incubator for spiritual growth. The word *Tzion*, therefore, describes not only where we live, but how we must live. Psalm 126 is recited by Jews upon completing a festive meal, connecting it with the eternal longing for physical redemption and spiritual greatness in Zion. When *Hashem* finally returns His people to Israel, they will be "as in a dream," as the actual redemption and heightened spirituality will be even greater than imagined, beyond our wildest dreams.

ירושלים

ציון

Rabbi Lord Jonathan Sacks (1948–2020)

1628

Tehillim / Psalms — Chapter 127

תהלים
פרק קכז

4 Restore our fortunes, *Hashem*, like watercourses in the *Negev*.

שׁוּבָ֣ה יְ֭הוָה אֶת־שבותנו [שְׁבִיתֵ֑נוּ] כַּאֲפִיקִ֥ים בַּנֶּֽגֶב׃

5 They who sow in tears shall reap with songs of joy.

הַזֹּרְעִ֥ים בְּדִמְעָ֗ה בְּרִנָּ֥ה יִקְצֹֽרוּ׃

6 Though he goes along weeping, carrying the seed-bag, he shall come back with songs of joy, carrying his sheaves.

הָ֘ל֤וֹךְ יֵלֵ֨ךְ ׀ וּבָכֹה֮ נֹשֵׂ֪א מֶֽשֶׁךְ־הַ֫זָּ֥רַע בֹּֽא־יָבֹ֥א בְרִנָּ֑ה נֹ֝שֵׂ֗א אֲלֻמֹּתָֽיו׃

127 1 A song of ascents. Of *Shlomo*. Unless *Hashem* builds the house, its builders labor in vain on it; unless *Hashem* watches over the city, the watchman keeps vigil in vain.

שִׁ֥יר הַֽמַּעֲל֗וֹת לִשְׁלֹ֫מֹ֥ה אִם־יְהוָ֤ה ׀ לֹא־יִבְנֶ֬ה בַ֗יִת שָׁ֤וְא ׀ עָמְל֣וּ בוֹנָ֣יו בּ֑וֹ אִם־יְהוָ֥ה לֹֽא־יִשְׁמָר־עִ֝֗יר שָׁ֤וְא ׀ שָׁקַ֬ד שׁוֹמֵֽר׃

SHEER ha-ma-a-LOT lish-lo-MOH im a-do-NAI lo yiv-NEH VA-yit SHAV a-m'-LU vo-NAV BO im a-do-NAI lo yish-MOR EER SHAV sha-KAD sho-MAYR

2 In vain do you rise early and stay up late, you who toil for the bread you eat; He provides as much for His loved ones while they sleep.

שָׁ֤וְא לָכֶ֨ם ׀ מַשְׁכִּ֪ימֵי ק֡וּם מְאַֽחֲרֵי־שֶׁ֗בֶת אֹ֭כְלֵי לֶ֣חֶם הָעֲצָבִ֑ים כֵּ֤ן יִתֵּ֖ן לִֽידִיד֣וֹ שֵׁנָֽא׃

3 Sons are the provision of *Hashem*; the fruit of the womb, His reward.

הִנֵּ֤ה נַחֲלַ֣ת יְהוָ֣ה בָּנִ֑ים שָׂ֝כָ֗ר פְּרִ֣י הַבָּֽטֶן׃

4 Like arrows in the hand of a warrior are sons born to a man in his youth.

כְּחִצִּ֥ים בְּיַד־גִּבּ֑וֹר כֵּ֝֗ן בְּנֵ֣י הַנְּעוּרִֽים׃

5 Happy is the man who fills his quiver with them; they shall not be put to shame when they contend with the enemy in the gate.

אַשְׁרֵ֤י הַגֶּ֗בֶר אֲשֶׁ֤ר מִלֵּ֥א אֶת־אַשְׁפָּת֗וֹ מֵ֫הֶ֥ם לֹא־יֵבֹ֑שׁוּ כִּֽי־יְדַבְּר֖וּ אֶת־אוֹיְבִ֣ים בַּשָּֽׁעַר׃

128 1 A song of ascents. Happy are all who fear *Hashem*, who follow His ways.

שִׁ֭יר הַֽמַּעֲל֑וֹת אַ֝שְׁרֵ֗י כָּל־יְרֵ֥א יְהוָ֗ה הַ֝הֹלֵ֗ךְ בִּדְרָכָֽיו׃

2 You shall enjoy the fruit of your labors; you shall be happy and you shall prosper.

יְגִ֣יעַ כַּ֭פֶּיךָ כִּ֣י תֹאכֵ֑ל אַ֝שְׁרֶ֗יךָ וְט֣וֹב לָֽךְ׃

3 Your wife shall be like a fruitful vine within your house; your sons, like olive saplings around your table.

אֶשְׁתְּךָ֤ ׀ כְּגֶ֥פֶן פֹּרִיָּה֮ בְּיַרְכְּתֵ֪י בֵ֫יתֶ֥ךָ בָּ֭נֶיךָ כִּשְׁתִלֵ֣י זֵיתִ֑ים סָ֝בִ֗יב לְשֻׁלְחָנֶֽךָ׃

4 So shall the man who fears *Hashem* be blessed.

הִנֵּ֣ה כִי־כֵ֭ן יְבֹ֥רַךְ גָּ֗בֶר יְרֵ֣א יְהוָֽה׃

5 May *Hashem* bless you from *Tzion*; may you share the prosperity of *Yerushalayim* all the days of your life,

יְבָרֶכְךָ֥ יְהוָ֗ה מִצִּ֫יּ֥וֹן וּ֭רְאֵה בְּט֣וּב יְרוּשָׁלָ֑͏ִם כֹּ֝֗ל יְמֵ֣י חַיֶּֽיךָ׃

Rabbi Abraham Ibn Ezra (1089–1167)

127:1 Of Shlomo Rabbi Avraham Ibn Ezra writes that this psalm was composed after it was told that *Shlomo*, not *David*, would build the *Beit Hamikdash*. In *Divrei Hayamim* I 22:7–16, *David* explains to his son *Shlomo* the immense responsibility *Hashem* has transferred to him with the task of building the *Beit Hamikdash*. *David* himself had been told by God that he would not be given that opportunity, for he had waged too many wars and shed too much blood. His son, however, would be a man of peace who would reign during an era of peace. His name will be *Shlomo*, meaning peace and tranquility. Therefore he, and not *David*, will be the one to build the *Beit Hamikdash*. Instead of being disappointed, *David* rejoices at God's decision and blesses his son for the upcoming grand endeavor.

Tehillim/Psalms
Chapter 129

6 and live to see your children's children. May all be well with *Yisrael*! | וּרְאֵה־בָנִים לְבָנֶיךָ שָׁלוֹם עַל־יִשְׂרָאֵל:

ur-AY va-NEEM l'-va-NE-kha sha-LOM al yis-ra-AYL

129

1 A song of ascents. Since my youth they have often assailed me, let *Yisrael* now declare, | שִׁיר הַמַּעֲלוֹת רַבַּת צְרָרוּנִי מִנְּעוּרַי יֹאמַר־נָא יִשְׂרָאֵל:

2 since my youth they have often assailed me, but they have never overcome me. | רַבַּת צְרָרוּנִי מִנְּעוּרָי גַּם לֹא־יָכְלוּ לִי:

3 Plowmen plowed across my back; they made long furrows. | עַל־גַּבִּי חָרְשׁוּ חֹרְשִׁים הֶאֱרִיכוּ למענותם [לְמַעֲנִיתָם]:

4 *Hashem*, the righteous one, has snapped the cords of the wicked. | יְהוָה צַדִּיק קִצֵּץ עֲבוֹת רְשָׁעִים:

5 Let all who hate *Tzion* fall back in disgrace. | יֵבֹשׁוּ וְיִסֹּגוּ אָחוֹר כֹּל שֹׂנְאֵי צִיּוֹן:

yay-VO-shu v'-yi-SO-gu a-KHOR KOL so-n'-AY tzi-YON

6 Let them be like grass on roofs that fades before it can be pulled up, | יִהְיוּ כַּחֲצִיר גַּגּוֹת שֶׁקַּדְמַת שָׁלַף יָבֵשׁ:

7 that affords no handful for the reaper, no armful for the gatherer of sheaves, | שֶׁלֹּא מִלֵּא כַפּוֹ קוֹצֵר וְחִצְנוֹ מְעַמֵּר:

8 no exchange with passersby: "The blessing of *Hashem* be upon you." "We bless you by the name of *Hashem*." | וְלֹא אָמְרוּ הָעֹבְרִים בִּרְכַּת־יְהוָה אֲלֵיכֶם בֵּרַכְנוּ אֶתְכֶם בְּשֵׁם יְהוָה:

130

1 A song of ascents. Out of the depths I call You, *Hashem*. | שִׁיר הַמַּעֲלוֹת מִמַּעֲמַקִּים קְרָאתִיךָ יְהוָה:

2 O *Hashem*, listen to my cry; let Your ears be attentive to my plea for mercy. | אֲדֹנָי שִׁמְעָה בְקוֹלִי תִּהְיֶינָה אָזְנֶיךָ קַשֻּׁבוֹת לְקוֹל תַּחֲנוּנָי:

128:6 May all be well with *Yisrael* In 1936, archaeological excavations in the city of *Yericho* revealed the remains of an ancient synagogue. A huge mosaic was uncovered with pictures of a *menorah* (candelabrum), a *shofar* (ram's horn) a *lulav* (palm branch), and the concluding words of this psalm, *shalom al Yisrael* ('May all be well with *Yisrael*' or more literally, 'peace be upon *Yisrael*.') The synagogue was dated to around the seventh century CE, during the Byzantine period. In fact, hundreds of Byzantine-era synagogues have been discovered all over Israel, most of them facing *Yerushalayim* and containing various artifacts demonstrating that synagogues were thriving in ancient times throughout the land. Unfortunately, the "*Shalom Al Yisrael* Synagogue," as it has come to be known, which is now under the control of the Palestinian Authority, remains largely off-limits to Jewish worshippers.

129:5 All who hate *Tzion* According to some commentators, this psalm was composed by the Babylonian exiles during their return to *Tzion*. Those who returned were met with great opposition from the inhabitants of the land. The psalmist prays that the haters of *Tzion* will be shamed and fall away, while those who support the return to *Tzion* will find blessing and life. *Sefer Ezra* records that only some forty-thousand Jews initially returned to *Tzion* after King Cyrus granted permission for them to do so. Over time, though, and especially after the building of the second *Beit Hamikdash*, the Jews of Babylonia started to return in larger numbers. They were the recipients of the great rewards of the return to *Tzion* and to the *Beit Hamikdash*.

Mosaic at the Shalom al Yisrael synagogue in Yericho

Tehillim/Psalms
Chapter 131

תהילים
פרק קלא

3 If You keep account of sins, *Hashem*, Lord, who will survive?

אִם־עֲוֺנוֹת תִּשְׁמָר־יָהּ אֲדֹנָי מִי יַעֲמֹד׃

4 Yours is the power to forgive so that You may be held in awe.

כִּי־עִמְּךָ הַסְּלִיחָה לְמַעַן תִּוָּרֵא׃

5 I look to *Hashem*; I look to Him; I await His word.

קִוִּיתִי יְהֹוָה קִוְּתָה נַפְשִׁי וְלִדְבָרוֹ הוֹחָלְתִּי׃

6 I am more eager for *Hashem* than watchmen for the morning, watchmen for the morning.

נַפְשִׁי לַאדֹנָי מִשֹּׁמְרִים לַבֹּקֶר שֹׁמְרִים לַבֹּקֶר׃

naf-SHEE la-do-NAI mi-sho-m'-REEM la-BO-ker sho-m'-REEM la-BO-ker

7 O *Yisrael*, wait for *Hashem*; for with *Hashem* is steadfast love and great power to redeem.

יַחֵל יִשְׂרָאֵל אֶל־יְהֹוָה כִּי־עִם־יְהֹוָה הַחֶסֶד וְהַרְבֵּה עִמּוֹ פְדוּת׃

8 It is He who will redeem *Yisrael* from all their iniquities.

וְהוּא יִפְדֶּה אֶת־יִשְׂרָאֵל מִכֹּל עֲוֺנֹתָיו׃

131

1 A song of ascents. Of *David*. *Hashem*, my heart is not proud nor my look haughty; I do not aspire to great things or to what is beyond me;

שִׁיר הַמַּעֲלוֹת לְדָוִד יְהֹוָה לֹא־גָבַהּ לִבִּי וְלֹא־רָמוּ עֵינַי וְלֹא־הִלַּכְתִּי בִּגְדֹלוֹת וּבְנִפְלָאוֹת מִמֶּנִּי׃

SHEER ha-ma-a-LOT l'-da-VID a-do-NAI lo ga-VAH li-BEE v'-LO ra-MU ay-NAI v'-LO hi-LAKH-tee big-do-LOT uv-nif-la-OT mi-ME-nee

2 but I have taught myself to be contented like a weaned child with its mother; like a weaned child am I in my mind.

אִם־לֹא שִׁוִּיתִי וְדוֹמַמְתִּי נַפְשִׁי כְּגָמֻל עֲלֵי אִמּוֹ כַּגָּמֻל עָלַי נַפְשִׁי׃

3 O *Yisrael*, wait for *Hashem* now and forever.

יַחֵל יִשְׂרָאֵל אֶל־יְהֹוָה מֵעַתָּה וְעַד־עוֹלָם׃

132

1 A song of ascents. *Hashem*, remember in *David*'s favor his extreme self-denial,

שִׁיר הַמַּעֲלוֹת זְכוֹר־יְהֹוָה לְדָוִד אֵת כָּל־עֻנּוֹתוֹ׃

Members of the Hashomer security force

130:6 Watchmen for the morning This psalm is recited by Jews all over the world in times of distress, as the psalmist calls out to *Hashem* "out of the depths" (verse 1). In times of trouble, we wait for God and His salvation even more than one who watches for the morning. The word *hashomer* (השומר), 'the watchman,' was taken as the name of the first modern Jewish security force in the Land of Israel. From 1909 until 1920, during the period known as the time of the Second Aliyah, a group of Jewish settlers formed *Hashomer* to protect Jewish towns from enemy incursions. After the group disbanded, its members formed the *Haganah* defense organization, precursor of the Israel Defense Forces. The Jewish people have been defending themselves in the land for over one hundred years, but the psalm reminds us that *Hashem* is the ultimate protector of Israel.

131:1 My heart is not proud In the Bible, confession refers not only to admitting the evil deeds one has committed, but also to acknowledging the positive commandments one has internalized. *David* "confesses" that he has not been haughty, and has never thought of himself as too great. This might be referring to the incident recorded in *Shmuel* II 6:14, when "*David* whirled with all his might before *Hashem*" as the ark of God was brought to Jerusalem. His wife *Michal* castigates him for what she saw as behavior inappropriate for a king, but *David* responds by asking rhetorically: Shall he not dance and prostrate himself before God, Who chose him as leader of all of Israel? Throughout his life, *David* subjugated himself before God out of respect and awe. He was not too proud to express himself to the Lord in the way he thought most appropriate.

Tehillim/Psalms
Chapter 132

2 how he swore to *Hashem*, vowed to the Mighty One of *Yaakov*, — ב אֲשֶׁר נִשְׁבַּע לַיהֹוָה נָדַר לַאֲבִיר יַעֲקֹב׃

3 "I will not enter my house, nor will I mount my bed, — ג אִם־אָבֹא בְּאֹהֶל בֵּיתִי אִם־אֶעֱלֶה עַל־עֶרֶשׂ יְצוּעָי׃

4 I will not give sleep to my eyes, or slumber to my eyelids — ד אִם־אֶתֵּן שְׁנַת לְעֵינָי לְעַפְעַפַּי תְּנוּמָה׃

5 until I find a place for *Hashem*, an abode for the Mighty One of *Yaakov*." — ה עַד־אֶמְצָא מָקוֹם לַיהֹוָה מִשְׁכָּנוֹת לַאֲבִיר יַעֲקֹב׃

6 We heard it was in *Efrat*; we came upon it in the region of Jaar. — ו הִנֵּה־שְׁמַעֲנוּהָ בְאֶפְרָתָה מְצָאנוּהָ בִּשְׂדֵי־יָעַר׃

hi-nay sh'-ma-a-NU-ha v'-ef-RA-tah m'-tza-NU-ha bis-day YA-ar

7 Let us enter His abode, bow at His footstool. — ז נָבוֹאָה לְמִשְׁכְּנוֹתָיו נִשְׁתַּחֲוֶה לַהֲדֹם רַגְלָיו׃

8 Advance, *Hashem*, to Your resting-place, You and Your mighty *Aron*! — ח קוּמָה יְהֹוָה לִמְנוּחָתֶךָ אַתָּה וַאֲרוֹן עֻזֶּךָ׃

9 Your *Kohanim* are clothed in triumph; Your loyal ones sing for joy. — ט כֹּהֲנֶיךָ יִלְבְּשׁוּ־צֶדֶק וַחֲסִידֶיךָ יְרַנֵּנוּ׃

10 For the sake of Your servant *David* do not reject Your anointed one. — י בַּעֲבוּר דָּוִד עַבְדֶּךָ אַל־תָּשֵׁב פְּנֵי מְשִׁיחֶךָ׃

11 *Hashem* swore to *David* a firm oath that He will not renounce, "One of your own issue I will set upon your throne. — יא נִשְׁבַּע־יְהֹוָה לְדָוִד אֱמֶת לֹא־יָשׁוּב מִמֶּנָּה מִפְּרִי בִטְנְךָ אָשִׁית לְכִסֵּא־לָךְ׃

12 If your sons keep My covenant and My decrees that I teach them, then their sons also, to the end of time, shall sit upon your throne." — יב אִם־יִשְׁמְרוּ בָנֶיךָ בְּרִיתִי וְעֵדֹתִי זוֹ אֲלַמְּדֵם גַּם־בְּנֵיהֶם עֲדֵי־עַד יֵשְׁבוּ לְכִסֵּא־לָךְ׃

13 For *Hashem* has chosen *Tzion*; He has desired it for His seat. — יג כִּי־בָחַר יְהֹוָה בְּצִיּוֹן אִוָּהּ לְמוֹשָׁב לוֹ׃

14 "This is my resting-place for all time; here I will dwell, for I desire it. — יד זֹאת־מְנוּחָתִי עֲדֵי־עַד פֹּה־אֵשֵׁב כִּי אִוִּתִיהָ׃

15 I will amply bless its store of food, give its needy their fill of bread. — טו צֵידָהּ בָּרֵךְ אֲבָרֵךְ אֶבְיוֹנֶיהָ אַשְׂבִּיעַ לָחֶם׃

132:6 We heard it was in *Efrat* This is the longest of the 15 chapters of *Tehillim* known as the "Songs of Ascent". It is dedicated to King *David* and his desire for a resting place for *Hashem*'s presence. *David*'s vow to bring the Aron of God to *Yerushalayim* was heard in *Efrat*, *David*'s birthplace, and its inhabitants helped him bring the holy ark to *Yerushalayim*. Also called *Beit Lechem*, the city of *Efrat* is mentioned in the Bible as the birthplace of *Binyamin* and the burial place of *Rachel* (Genesis 35:19). In 1983, the Israeli religious Zionist settlement of *Efrat* was established by Moshe Moskowitz and Rabbi Shlomo Riskin, its chief rabbi, near modern day Bethlehem. Today, with close to ten thousand residents, thirty synagogues and many educational and religious institutions, *Efrat* is a thriving community built on the principles of *Torah* and dedication to the Nation of Israel.

Tehillim/Psalms
Chapter 133

תהלים
פרק קלג

16 I will clothe its *Kohanim* in victory, its loyal ones shall sing for joy.

טז וְכֹהֲנֶיהָ אַלְבִּישׁ יֶשַׁע וַחֲסִידֶיהָ רַנֵּן יְרַנֵּנוּ:

17 There I will make a horn sprout for *David*; I have prepared a lamp for My anointed one.

יז שָׁם אַצְמִיחַ קֶרֶן לְדָוִד עָרַכְתִּי נֵר לִמְשִׁיחִי:

18 I will clothe his enemies in disgrace, while on him his crown shall sparkle."

יח אוֹיְבָיו אַלְבִּישׁ בֹּשֶׁת וְעָלָיו יָצִיץ נִזְרוֹ:

133

1 A song of ascents. Of *David*. How good and how pleasant it is that brothers dwell together.

קלג א שִׁיר הַמַּעֲלוֹת לְדָוִד הִנֵּה מַה־טּוֹב וּמַה־נָּעִים שֶׁבֶת אַחִים גַּם־יָחַד:

2 It is like fine oil on the head running down onto the beard, the beard of *Aharon*, that comes down over the collar of his robe;

ב כַּשֶּׁמֶן הַטּוֹב עַל־הָרֹאשׁ יֹרֵד עַל־הַזָּקָן זְקַן־אַהֲרֹן שֶׁיֹּרֵד עַל־פִּי מִדּוֹתָיו:

3 like the dew of *Chermon* that falls upon the mountains of *Tzion*. There *Hashe* ordained blessing, everlasting life.

ג כְּטַל־חֶרְמוֹן שֶׁיֹּרֵד עַל־הַרְרֵי צִיּוֹן כִּי שָׁם צִוָּה יְהֹוָה אֶת־הַבְּרָכָה חַיִּים עַד־הָעוֹלָם:

k'-tal kher-MON she-yo-RAYD al ha-r'-RAY tzi-YON KEE SHAM tzi-VAH a-do-NAI et ha-b'-ra-KHAH kha-YEEM ad ha-o-LAM

134

1 A song of ascents. Now bless *Hashem*, all you servants of *Hashem* who stand nightly in the house of *Hashem*.

קלד א שִׁיר הַמַּעֲלוֹת הִנֵּה בָּרְכוּ אֶת־יְהֹוָה כָּל־עַבְדֵי יְהֹוָה הָעֹמְדִים בְּבֵית־יְהֹוָה בַּלֵּילוֹת:

SHEER ha-ma-a-LOT hi-NAY ba-r'-KHU et a-do-NAI kol av-DAY a-do-NAI ha-o-m'-DEEM b'-VAYT a-do-NAI ba-lay-LOT

2 Lift your hands toward the sanctuary and bless *Hashem*.

ב שְׂאוּ־יְדֵכֶם קֹדֶשׁ וּבָרְכוּ אֶת־יְהֹוָה:

3 May *Hashem*, maker of heaven and earth, bless you from *Tzion*.

ג יְבָרֶכְךָ יְהֹוָה מִצִּיּוֹן עֹשֵׂה שָׁמַיִם וָאָרֶץ:

135

1 Hallelujah. Praise the name of *Hashem*; give praise, you servants of *Hashem*

קלה א הַלְלוּ יָהּ הַלְלוּ אֶת־שֵׁם יְהֹוָה הַלְלוּ עַבְדֵי יְהֹוָה:

Morning dew near Beit Shemesh

133:3 Like the dew of *Chermon* *Tal* (טל), 'dew,' is a common biblical symbol of *Hashem*'s bountiful blessings. Rain is another sign of God's love for mankind. What is the difference between rain and dew? According to Jewish mysticism, rain is a sign of God showering his abundant blessings freely from above. Dew, which forms below from condensation of atmospheric water vapor, is related to the divine blessings which are a result of man's own efforts and achievements. This psalm teaches that *Hashem*'s blessing from above allows for the flowering of man's work below.

134:1 Now bless *Hashem* Rabbi Samson Raphael Hirsch notes how similar in size, and complementary in message, this psalm is to the previous one. Each of these short psalms contains only three verses and focuses on Israel's dwelling in the Land of Israel. However, Psalm 133 speaks of the interpersonal element, while Psalm 134 reminds us that the spiritual element must be present as well. Psalm 133 presents the social component of Zionism, which is how the land was built up in the modern era: "How good and how pleasant it is that brothers dwell together." And each of the verses of Psalm 134 speaks of blessing *Hashem*, to remind us that the spiritual component of returning to the land must complement the social one. When both aspects are present, says Hirsch, God will bring down the heavenly blessing from *Tzion*.

Tehillim / Psalms
Chapter 135

תהלים
פרק קלה

ב שֶׁעֹמְדִים בְּבֵית יְהֹוָה בְּחַצְרוֹת בֵּית אֱלֹהֵינוּ:

2 who stand in the house of *Hashem*, in the courts of the house of our God.

ג הַלְלוּ־יָהּ כִּי־טוֹב יְהֹוָה זַמְּרוּ לִשְׁמוֹ כִּי נָעִים:

3 Praise *Hashem*, for *Hashem* is good; sing hymns to His name, for it is pleasant.

ד כִּי־יַעֲקֹב בָּחַר לוֹ יָהּ יִשְׂרָאֵל לִסְגֻלָּתוֹ:

4 For *Hashem* has chosen *Yaakov* for Himself, *Yisrael*, as His treasured possession.

ה כִּי אֲנִי יָדַעְתִּי כִּי־גָדוֹל יְהֹוָה וַאֲדֹנֵינוּ מִכָּל־אֱלֹהִים:

5 For I know that *Hashem* is great, that our Lord is greater than all gods.

ו כֹּל אֲשֶׁר־חָפֵץ יְהֹוָה עָשָׂה בַּשָּׁמַיִם וּבָאָרֶץ בַּיַּמִּים וְכָל־תְּהוֹמוֹת:

6 Whatever *Hashem* desires He does in heaven and earth, in the seas and all the depths.

ז מַעֲלֶה נְשִׂאִים מִקְצֵה הָאָרֶץ בְּרָקִים לַמָּטָר עָשָׂה מוֹצֵא־רוּחַ מֵאוֹצְרוֹתָיו:

7 He makes clouds rise from the end of the earth; He makes lightning for the rain; He releases the wind from His vaults.

ח שֶׁהִכָּה בְּכוֹרֵי מִצְרָיִם מֵאָדָם עַד־בְּהֵמָה:

8 He struck down the first-born of Egypt, man and beast alike;

ט שָׁלַח אוֹתֹת וּמֹפְתִים בְּתוֹכֵכִי מִצְרָיִם בְּפַרְעֹה וּבְכָל־עֲבָדָיו:

9 He sent signs and portents against Egypt, against Pharaoh and all his servants;

י שֶׁהִכָּה גּוֹיִם רַבִּים וְהָרַג מְלָכִים עֲצוּמִים:

10 He struck down many nations and slew numerous kings –

יא לְסִיחוֹן מֶלֶךְ הָאֱמֹרִי וּלְעוֹג מֶלֶךְ הַבָּשָׁן וּלְכֹל מַמְלְכוֹת כְּנָעַן:

11 Sihon, king of the Amorites, Og, king of Bashan, and all the royalty of Canaan –

יב וְנָתַן אַרְצָם נַחֲלָה נַחֲלָה לְיִשְׂרָאֵל עַמּוֹ:

12 and gave their lands as a heritage, as a heritage to His people *Yisrael*.

יג יְהֹוָה שִׁמְךָ לְעוֹלָם יְהֹוָה זִכְרְךָ לְדֹר־וָדֹר:

13 *Hashem*, Your name endures forever, Your fame, *Hashem*, through all generations;

יד כִּי־יָדִין יְהֹוָה עַמּוֹ וְעַל־עֲבָדָיו יִתְנֶחָם:

14 for *Hashem* will Champion His people, and obtain satisfaction for His servants.

טו עֲצַבֵּי הַגּוֹיִם כֶּסֶף וְזָהָב מַעֲשֵׂה יְדֵי אָדָם:

15 The idols of the nations are silver and gold, the work of men's hands.

טז פֶּה־לָהֶם וְלֹא יְדַבֵּרוּ עֵינַיִם לָהֶם וְלֹא יִרְאוּ:

16 They have mouths, but cannot speak; they have eyes, but cannot see;

יז אָזְנַיִם לָהֶם וְלֹא יַאֲזִינוּ אַף אֵין־יֶשׁ־רוּחַ בְּפִיהֶם:

17 they have ears, but cannot hear, nor is there breath in their mouths.

יח כְּמוֹהֶם יִהְיוּ עֹשֵׂיהֶם כֹּל אֲשֶׁר־בֹּטֵחַ בָּהֶם:

18 Those who fashion them, all who trust in them, shall become like them.

יט בֵּית יִשְׂרָאֵל בָּרְכוּ אֶת־יְהֹוָה בֵּית אַהֲרֹן בָּרְכוּ אֶת־יְהֹוָה:

19 O house of *Yisrael*, bless *Hashem*; O house of *Aharon*, bless *Hashem*;

כ בֵּית הַלֵּוִי בָּרְכוּ אֶת־יְהֹוָה יִרְאֵי יְהֹוָה בָּרְכוּ אֶת־יְהֹוָה:

20 O house of *Levi*, bless *Hashem*; you who fear *Hashem*, bless *Hashem*.

1634

Tehillim/Psalms
Chapter 136

21 Blessed is *Hashem* from *Tzion*, He who dwells in *Yerushalayim*. Hallelujah.

בָּרוּךְ יְהֹוָה מִצִּיּוֹן שֹׁכֵן יְרוּשָׁלָ͏ִם הַלְלוּ־יָהּ׃

ba-RUKH a-do-NAI mi-tzi-YON sho-KHAYN y'-ru-sha-LA-im ha-l'-lu-YAH

136

1 Praise *Hashem*; for He is good, His steadfast love is eternal.

הוֹדוּ לַיהֹוָה כִּי־טוֹב כִּי לְעוֹלָם חַסְדּוֹ׃

2 Praise the God of gods, His steadfast love is eternal.

הוֹדוּ לֵאלֹהֵי הָאֱלֹהִים כִּי לְעוֹלָם חַסְדּוֹ׃

3 Praise the Lord of lords, His steadfast love is eternal;

הוֹדוּ לַאֲדֹנֵי הָאֲדֹנִים כִּי לְעוֹלָם חַסְדּוֹ׃

4 Who alone works great marvels, His steadfast love is eternal;

לְעֹשֵׂה נִפְלָאוֹת גְּדֹלוֹת לְבַדּוֹ כִּי לְעוֹלָם חַסְדּוֹ׃

5 Who made the heavens with wisdom, His steadfast love is eternal;

לְעֹשֵׂה הַשָּׁמַיִם בִּתְבוּנָה כִּי לְעוֹלָם חַסְדּוֹ׃

6 Who spread the earth over the water, His steadfast love is eternal;

לְרֹקַע הָאָרֶץ עַל־הַמָּיִם כִּי לְעוֹלָם חַסְדּוֹ׃

7 Who made the great lights, His steadfast love is eternal;

לְעֹשֵׂה אוֹרִים גְּדֹלִים כִּי לְעוֹלָם חַסְדּוֹ׃

8 the sun to dominate the day, His steadfast love is eternal;

אֶת־הַשֶּׁמֶשׁ לְמֶמְשֶׁלֶת בַּיּוֹם כִּי לְעוֹלָם חַסְדּוֹ׃

9 the moon and the stars to dominate the night, His steadfast love is eternal;

אֶת־הַיָּרֵחַ וְכוֹכָבִים לְמֶמְשְׁלוֹת בַּלָּיְלָה כִּי לְעוֹלָם חַסְדּוֹ׃

10 Who struck Egypt through their first-born, His steadfast love is eternal;

לְמַכֵּה מִצְרַיִם בִּבְכוֹרֵיהֶם כִּי לְעוֹלָם חַסְדּוֹ׃

11 and brought *Yisrael* out of their midst, His steadfast love is eternal;

וַיּוֹצֵא יִשְׂרָאֵל מִתּוֹכָם כִּי לְעוֹלָם חַסְדּוֹ׃

12 with a strong hand and outstretched arm, His steadfast love is eternal;

בְּיָד חֲזָקָה וּבִזְרוֹעַ נְטוּיָה כִּי לְעוֹלָם חַסְדּוֹ׃

13 Who split apart the Sea of Reeds, His steadfast love is eternal;

לְגֹזֵר יַם־סוּף לִגְזָרִים כִּי לְעוֹלָם חַסְדּוֹ׃

14 and made *Yisrael* pass through it, His steadfast love is eternal;

וְהֶעֱבִיר יִשְׂרָאֵל בְּתוֹכוֹ כִּי לְעוֹלָם חַסְדּוֹ׃

135:21 He who dwells in *Yerushalayim* Why did *Hashem* choose *Yerushalayim* as His resting place? The Sages find two revealing biblical passages that, when synthesized, teach us the value and message of *Yerushalayim*. In Genesis, *Avraham* was asked by God to sacrifice his son, in order to prove his allegiance to the Lord. This profound, inexplicable test took place on a mountain which *Avraham* called "*Adonai yir'eh*," meaning 'on the mount of *Hashem* there is vision,' or 'the mount where *Hashem* is seen' (Genesis 22:14). A few years earlier, *Avraham* showed the world his allegiance to his family, to justice and to righteousness when he fought against the four kings and retrieved his nephew Lot. After that battle, Melchizedek, the King of *Shalem* (another name for Jerusalem), went out to greet *Avraham* and bless *Hashem* (Genesis 14:18–20). When these two names, *Yir'eh* and *Shalem* are combined, the result is *Yerushalayim*. The name of the holy city thus expresses the harmonization of man's selfless actions towards *Hashem* and towards other people, both of which were manifest in *Yerushalayim*. It was thus chosen as Hashem's resting place.

Tehillim / Psalms
Chapter 137

תהלים
פרק קלו

15 Who hurled Pharaoh and his army into the Sea of Reeds, His steadfast love is eternal;   וְנִעֵר פַּרְעֹה וְחֵילוֹ בְיַם־סוּף כִּי לְעוֹלָם חַסְדּוֹ:

16 Who led His people through the wilderness, His steadfast love is eternal;   לְמוֹלִיךְ עַמּוֹ בַּמִּדְבָּר כִּי לְעוֹלָם חַסְדּוֹ:

17 Who struck down great kings, His steadfast love is eternal;   לְמַכֵּה מְלָכִים גְּדֹלִים כִּי לְעוֹלָם חַסְדּוֹ:

18 and slew mighty kings – His steadfast love is eternal;   וַיַּהֲרֹג מְלָכִים אַדִּירִים כִּי לְעוֹלָם חַסְדּוֹ:

19 Sihon, king of the Amorites, His steadfast love is eternal;   לְסִיחוֹן מֶלֶךְ הָאֱמֹרִי כִּי לְעוֹלָם חַסְדּוֹ:

20 Og, king of Bashan – His steadfast love is eternal;   וּלְעוֹג מֶלֶךְ הַבָּשָׁן כִּי לְעוֹלָם חַסְדּוֹ:

21 and gave their land as a heritage, His steadfast love is eternal;   וְנָתַן אַרְצָם לְנַחֲלָה כִּי לְעוֹלָם חַסְדּוֹ:

22 a heritage to His servant *Yisrael*, His steadfast love is eternal;   נַחֲלָה לְיִשְׂרָאֵל עַבְדּוֹ כִּי לְעוֹלָם חַסְדּוֹ:

23 Who took note of us in our degradation, His steadfast love is eternal;   שֶׁבְּשִׁפְלֵנוּ זָכַר לָנוּ כִּי לְעוֹלָם חַסְדּוֹ:
    she-b'-shif-LAY-nu ZA-khar LA-nu KEE l'-o-LAM khas-DO

24 and rescued us from our enemies, His steadfast love is eternal;   וַיִּפְרְקֵנוּ מִצָּרֵינוּ כִּי לְעוֹלָם חַסְדּוֹ:

25 Who gives food to all flesh, His steadfast love is eternal.   נֹתֵן לֶחֶם לְכָל־בָּשָׂר כִּי לְעוֹלָם חַסְדּוֹ:

26 Praise the God of heaven, His steadfast love is eternal.   הוֹדוּ לְאֵל הַשָּׁמָיִם כִּי לְעוֹלָם חַסְדּוֹ:

37

קלז

1 By the rivers of Babylon, there we sat, sat and wept, as we thought of *Tzion*.   עַל נַהֲרוֹת בָּבֶל שָׁם יָשַׁבְנוּ גַּם־בָּכִינוּ בְּזָכְרֵנוּ אֶת־צִיּוֹן:

2 There on the poplars we hung up our lyres,   עַל־עֲרָבִים בְּתוֹכָהּ תָּלִינוּ כִּנֹּרוֹתֵינוּ:

3 for our captors asked us there for songs, our tormentors, for amusement, "Sing us one of the songs of *Tzion*."   כִּי שָׁם שְׁאֵלוּנוּ שׁוֹבֵינוּ דִּבְרֵי־שִׁיר וְתוֹלָלֵינוּ שִׂמְחָה שִׁירוּ לָנוּ מִשִּׁיר צִיּוֹן:

136:23 Who took note of us in our degradation This psalm praises *Hashem* for the kindness and mercy He has shown to the People of Israel throughout history. Each line praises God for a specific act of grace, and ends with the refrain, "His steadfast love is eternal." The psalm begins with an account of different aspects of creation, continues with the exodus from Egypt and the travels in the desert, and concludes with the conquest of the lands of the eastern side of the Jordan river. Though it mentions that God gave the lands of Sihon and Og to the People of Israel as an inheritance, the psalm does not contain a line that explicitly praises Him for bequeathing the actual Promised Land to His people. Instead, it speaks of *Hashem*'s constant presence in their lives, remembering His people even in their "degradation" and delivering them from their enemies. According to some interpretations, this refers to *Hashem*'s dedication to the people even after they sin and are expelled from the land. It seems that the psalmist takes for granted that God has designated the Land of Israel for His nation. Thus, he sings praises for all the events which led to the acquisition of the land, and about what happened after its settlement, but does not need to mention the actual settling of the land itself.

Tehillim/Psalms
Chapter 138

תהלים
פרק קלח

4 How can we sing a song of *Hashem* on alien soil?

אֵיךְ נָשִׁיר אֶת־שִׁיר־יְהֹוָה עַל אַדְמַת נֵכָר: ד

5 If I forget you, O *Yerushalayim*, let my right hand wither;

אִם־אֶשְׁכָּחֵךְ יְרוּשָׁלָ͏ִם תִּשְׁכַּח יְמִינִי: ה

im esh-ka-KHAYKH y'-ru-sha-LA-im tish-KAKH y'-mee-NEE

6 let my tongue stick to my palate if I cease to think of you, if I do not keep *Yerushalayim* in memory even at my happiest hour.

תִּדְבַּק־לְשׁוֹנִי לְחִכִּי אִם־לֹא אֶזְכְּרֵכִי אִם־לֹא אַעֲלֶה אֶת־יְרוּשָׁלַ͏ִם עַל רֹאשׁ שִׂמְחָתִי: ו

tid-BAK l'-sho-NEE l'-khi-KEE im LO ez-k'-RAY-khee im LO a-a-LEH et y'-ru-sha-LA-im AL ROSH sim-kha-TEE

7 Remember, *Hashem*, against the Edomites the day of *Yerushalayim*'s fall; how they cried, "Strip her, strip her to her very foundations!"

זְכֹר יְהֹוָה לִבְנֵי אֱדוֹם אֵת יוֹם יְרוּשָׁלָ͏ִם הָאֹמְרִים עָרוּ עָרוּ עַד הַיְסוֹד בָּהּ: ז

8 Fair Babylon, you predator, a blessing on him who repays you in kind what you have inflicted on us;

בַּת־בָּבֶל הַשְּׁדוּדָה אַשְׁרֵי שֶׁיְשַׁלֶּם־לָךְ אֶת־גְּמוּלֵךְ שֶׁגָּמַלְתְּ לָנוּ: ח

9 a blessing on him who seizes your babies and dashes them against the rocks!

אַשְׁרֵי שֶׁיֹּאחֵז וְנִפֵּץ אֶת־עֹלָלַיִךְ אֶל־הַסָּלַע: ט

138

1 Of *David*. I praise You with all my heart, sing a hymn to You before the divine beings;

לְדָוִד אוֹדְךָ בְכָל־לִבִּי נֶגֶד אֱלֹהִים אֲזַמְּרֶךָּ: א

l'-da-VID o-d'-KHA v'-khol li-BEE NE-ged e-lo-HEEM a-za-m'-RE-ka

---

137:5 If I forget you, O *Yerushalayim* Psalm 137 was written by the rivers of Babylon, where the exiled Jews wailed and lamented the destruction of the *Beit Hamikdash*. They wondered how they would continue to endure on foreign soil. How could they continue to sing the songs of *Hashem*, which were supposed to be sung in the Temple, in the exile? Their answer was an oath to never forget *Yerushalayim*. This psalm makes an oblique reference to *Sefer Devarim* 8:19, "If you do forget *Hashem* your God and follow other gods to serve them or bow down to them, I warn you this day that you shall certainly perish." Israel's exile came when they forgot God in their land. In Babylon, they promised themselves never to repeat that mistake, and never to forget *Yerushalayim*. Today, this psalm is recited at Jewish weddings just before the groom breaks a glass, ensuring that Jerusalem is always at the forefront of our minds and reminding us that no joyous occasion is complete until *Yerushalayim* is restored to its former glory.

Rabbi Aryeh Levin (1885–1969)

137:6 if I do not keep *Yerushalayim* in memory even at my happiest hour. Rabbi Aryeh Levin (1885–1969) was considered one of the most righteous and pious Jews of the 20th century. He was known as the "*Tzadik* (saint) of *Yerushalayim*" for his devotion to the needy and downtrodden of the Holy City. His passion for seeing only the goodness of people and his zeal for Jerusalem were part of his very fiber. As is the Jewish custom, Rabbi Levin would place ashes on the forehead of a bridegroom under the wedding canopy in order to keep the destruction of *Yerushalayim* at the forefront of everyone's mind "even at my happiest hour". Fittingly, he had the privilege of personally experiencing the fulfillment of Rabbinic adage: "All who mourn Jerusalem, merit to witness its rebuilding (Taanit 30b)." After the liberation of Jerusalem in 1967, the "*Tzadik* of *Yerushalayim*" would visit the Western Wall weekly, until his death two years later.

138:1 Sing a hymn to You before the divine beings King *David* begins this psalm by declaring that he will sing praises to *Hashem* "before the divine beings." The commentators wonder to which divine beings, in Hebrew *elohim* (אלהים), the verse refers? Often, the term *Elohim* refers to God, but in this context many medieval commentators, such as *Rashi* and Rabbi Avraham Ibn Ezra, translate *elohim* as 'ministers' or

Tehillim/Psalms
Chapter 139

2 I bow toward Your holy temple and praise Your name for Your steadfast love and faithfulness, because You have exalted Your name, Your word, above all.

3 When I called, You answered me, You inspired me with courage.

4 All the kings of the earth shall praise You, *Hashem*, for they have heard the words You spoke.

5 They shall sing of the ways of *Hashem*, "Great is the majesty of *Hashem*!"

6 High though *Hashem* is, He sees the lowly; lofty, He perceives from afar.

7 Though I walk among enemies, You preserve me in the face of my foes; You extend Your hand; with Your right hand You deliver me.

8 *Hashem* will settle accounts for me. *Hashem*, Your steadfast love is eternal; do not forsake the work of Your hands.

139

1 For the leader. Of *David*. A psalm. *Hashem*, You have examined me and know me.

2 When I sit down or stand up You know it; You discern my thoughts from afar.

3 You observe my walking and reclining, and are familiar with all my ways.

4 There is not a word on my tongue but that You, *Hashem*, know it well.

5 You hedge me before and behind; You lay Your hand upon me.

6 It is beyond my knowledge; it is a mystery; I cannot fathom it.

7 Where can I escape from Your spirit? Where can I flee from Your presence?

8 If I ascend to heaven, You are there; if I descend to Sheol, You are there too.

9 If I take wing with the dawn to come to rest on the western horizon,

---

'judges'. According to this understanding, *David* is praising *Hashem* in the presence of the ministers. Other interpretations say that it refers to prophets. Rabbi Samson Raphael Hirsch, on the other hand, understands the word *elohim* as a reference to false gods. According to Hirsch, *David* is juxtaposing God's true, virtuous acts with the false, inauthentic gods of the surrounding nations.

Tehillim / Psalms
Chapter 139

תהלים
פרק קלט

10 even there Your hand will be guiding me, Your right hand will be holding me fast.

גַּם־שָׁם יָדְךָ תַנְחֵנִי וְתֹאחֲזֵנִי יְמִינֶךָ׃

11 If I say, "Surely darkness will conceal me, night will provide me with cover,"

וָאֹמַר אַךְ־חֹשֶׁךְ יְשׁוּפֵנִי וְלַיְלָה אוֹר בַּעֲדֵנִי׃

12 darkness is not dark for You; night is as light as day; darkness and light are the same.

גַּם־חֹשֶׁךְ לֹא־יַחְשִׁיךְ מִמֶּךָ וְלַיְלָה כַּיּוֹם יָאִיר כַּחֲשֵׁיכָה כָּאוֹרָה׃

13 It was You who created my conscience; You fashioned me in my mother's womb.

כִּי־אַתָּה קָנִיתָ כִלְיֹתָי תְּסֻכֵּנִי בְּבֶטֶן אִמִּי׃

14 **I praise You, for I am awesomely, wondrously made; Your work is wonderful; I know it very well.**

אוֹדְךָ עַל כִּי נוֹרָאוֹת נִפְלֵיתִי נִפְלָאִים מַעֲשֶׂיךָ וְנַפְשִׁי יֹדַעַת מְאֹד׃

o-d'-KHA AL KEE no-ra-OT nif-LAY-tee nif-la-EEM ma-a-SE-kha v'-naf-SHEE yo-DA-at m'-OD

15 My frame was not concealed from You when I was shaped in a hidden place, knit together in the recesses of the earth.

לֹא־נִכְחַד עָצְמִי מִמֶּךָּ אֲשֶׁר־עֻשֵּׂיתִי בַסֵּתֶר רֻקַּמְתִּי בְּתַחְתִּיּוֹת אָרֶץ׃

16 Your eyes saw my unformed limbs; they were all recorded in Your book; in due time they were formed, to the very last one of them.

גָּלְמִי רָאוּ עֵינֶיךָ וְעַל־סִפְרְךָ כֻּלָּם יִכָּתֵבוּ יָמִים יֻצָּרוּ וְלֹא [וְלוֹ] אֶחָד בָּהֶם׃

17 How weighty Your thoughts seem to me, O *Hashem*, how great their number!

וְלִי מַה־יָּקְרוּ רֵעֶיךָ אֵל מֶה עָצְמוּ רָאשֵׁיהֶם׃

18 I count them – they exceed the grains of sand; I end – but am still with You.

אֶסְפְּרֵם מֵחוֹל יִרְבּוּן הֱקִיצֹתִי וְעוֹדִי עִמָּךְ׃

19 O *Hashem*, if You would only slay the wicked – you murderers, away from me! –

אִם־תִּקְטֹל אֱלוֹהַּ רָשָׁע וְאַנְשֵׁי דָמִים סוּרוּ מֶנִּי׃

20 who invoke You for intrigue, Your enemies who swear by You falsely.

אֲשֶׁר יֹאמְרֻךָ לִמְזִמָּה נָשֻׂא לַשָּׁוְא עָרֶיךָ׃

21 *Hashem*, You know I hate those who hate You, and loathe Your adversaries.

הֲלוֹא־מְשַׂנְאֶיךָ יְהוָה אֶשְׂנָא וּבִתְקוֹמְמֶיךָ אֶתְקוֹטָט׃

22 I feel a perfect hatred toward them; I count them my enemies.

תַּכְלִית שִׂנְאָה שְׂנֵאתִים לְאוֹיְבִים הָיוּ לִי׃

Ancient ruins at Beit Shean

139:14 Your work is wonderful Many of the Sages and commentators see references in this psalm to the story of *Adam* and *Chava*. The early awareness of *Hashem*, the fashioning of men, the ascending and descending to find God, as well as the notion of the first darkness to befall him, are all reminiscent of this biblical story. Where might this story of the Garden of Eden have taken place? According to *Resh Lakish*, a Babylonian scholar in the Talmud (*Eiruvin* 19a), "If the Garden of Eden is in the Land of Israel, then *Beit Shean* is its gate." Ancient *Beit Shean* was located at the intersection of the Jezreel valley and the Jordan Valley. There, the Gilboa mountain waters emerge into lush springs at the foot of the mountains creating an oasis of water, vegetation, and warm climate which served as the impetus for the thriving ancient city of *Beit Shean*. Perhaps it is this place, reminiscent of the Garden of Eden, which inspired the psalmist to write about the advent of man and his nascent relationship with *Hashem*.

Tehillim/Psalms
Chapter 140

23 Examine me, O *Hashem*, and know my mind; probe me and know my thoughts.

24 See if I have vexatious ways, and guide me in ways everlasting.

140

1 For the leader. A psalm of *David*.

2 Rescue me, *Hashem*, from evil men; save me from the lawless,

kha-l'-TZAY-nee a-do-NAI may-a-DAM RA may-EESH kha-ma-SEEM tin-tz'-RAY-nee

3 whose minds are full of evil schemes, who plot war every day.

4 They sharpen their tongues like serpents; spiders' poison is on their lips. *Selah.*

5 *Hashem*, keep me out of the clutches of the wicked; save me from lawless men who scheme to make me fall.

6 Arrogant men laid traps with ropes for me; they spread out a net along the way; they set snares for me. *Selah.*

7 I said to *Hashem*: You are my God; give ear, *Hashem*, to my pleas for mercy.

8 O *Hashem*, my Lord, the strength of my deliverance, You protected my head on the day of battle.

9 *Hashem*, do not grant the desires of the wicked; do not let their plan succeed, else they be exalted. *Selah.*

10 May the heads of those who beset me be covered with the mischief of their lips.

140:2 Rescue me, *Hashem*, from evil men This psalm is about evil men and their wicked plans. There are many terms for evil, but here the psalmist chooses a specific word, *chamas* (חמס), referring to a specific type of wickedness described elsewhere in the Bible. When, in the incipient stages of civilization, the generation of *Noach* began to cheat, steal, deceive and act with total corruption, the Bible laments that God saw *chamas* in the land (Genesis 6:11). Later, in the days of *Yona*, the people of Nineveh are also described as engaging in *chamas* (Jonah 3:8). The specific crimes described as "*chamas*" are particularly insidious, as they undermine the very framework of society. Here, as *David* lashes out at the depraved ones who wish to destroy him, he speaks about men of *chamas* with evil in their hearts, who constantly stir up violence. They use traps and speak with forked tongues. *David* asks *Hashem* to save him and all the innocents from these devious minds, and curses the evil men to fall into their own vicious traps and be torn asunder. Ultimately, *David* concludes that the righteous ones will acknowledge God's great name and merit the presence of the Almighty.

חמס

Tehillim/Psalms Chapter 141

תהלים
פרק קמא

11 may coals of fire drop down upon them, and they be cast into pits, never to rise again.

יא יִמּוֹטוּ [יַמּוֹטוּ] עֲלֵיהֶם גֶּחָלִים בָּאֵשׁ יַפִּלֵם בְּמַהֲמֹרוֹת בַּל־יָקוּמוּ:

12 Let slanderers have no place in the land; let the evil of the lawless man drive him into corrals.

יב אִישׁ לָשׁוֹן בַּל־יִכּוֹן בָּאָרֶץ אִישׁ־חָמָס רָע יְצוּדֶנּוּ לְמַדְחֵפֹת:

13 I know that *Hashem* will Champion the cause of the poor, the right of the needy.

יג יָדַעְתָּ [יָדַעְתִּי] כִּי־יַעֲשֶׂה יְהֹוָה דִּין עָנִי מִשְׁפַּט אֶבְיֹנִים:

14 Righteous men shall surely praise Your name; the upright shall dwell in Your presence.

יד אַךְ צַדִּיקִים יוֹדוּ לִשְׁמֶךָ יֵשְׁבוּ יְשָׁרִים אֶת־פָּנֶיךָ:

141 1 A psalm of *David*. I call You, *Hashem*, hasten to me; give ear to my cry when I call You.

מא א מִזְמוֹר לְדָוִד יְהֹוָה קְרָאתִיךָ חוּשָׁה לִּי הַאֲזִינָה קוֹלִי בְּקָרְאִי־לָךְ:

2 Take my prayer as an offering of incense, my upraised hands as an evening sacrifice.

ב תִּכּוֹן תְּפִלָּתִי קְטֹרֶת לְפָנֶיךָ מַשְׂאַת כַּפַּי מִנְחַת־עָרֶב:

ti-KON t'-fi-la-TEE k'-TO-ret l'-fa-NE-kha mas-AT ka-PAI min-khat A-rev

3 *Hashem*, set a guard over my mouth, a watch at the door of my lips;

ג שִׁיתָה יְהֹוָה שָׁמְרָה לְפִי נִצְּרָה עַל־דַּל שְׂפָתָי:

4 let my mind not turn to an evil thing, to practice deeds of wickedness with men who are evildoers; let me not feast on their dainties.

ד אַל־תַּט־לִבִּי לְדָבָר רָע לְהִתְעוֹלֵל עֲלִלוֹת בְּרֶשַׁע אֶת־אִישִׁים פֹּעֲלֵי־אָוֶן וּבַל־אֶלְחַם בְּמַנְעַמֵּיהֶם:

5 Let the righteous man strike me in loyalty, let him reprove me; let my head not refuse such choice oil. My prayers are still against their evil deeds.

ה יֶהֶלְמֵנִי־צַדִּיק חֶסֶד וְיוֹכִיחֵנִי שֶׁמֶן רֹאשׁ אַל־יָנִי רֹאשִׁי כִּי־עוֹד וּתְפִלָּתִי בְּרָעוֹתֵיהֶם:

6 May their judges slip on the rock, but let my words be heard, for they are sweet.

ו נִשְׁמְטוּ בִידֵי־סֶלַע שֹׁפְטֵיהֶם וְשָׁמְעוּ אֲמָרַי כִּי נָעֵמוּ:

7 As when the earth is cleft and broken up our bones are scattered at the mouth of Sheol.

ז כְּמוֹ פֹלֵחַ וּבֹקֵעַ בָּאָרֶץ נִפְזְרוּ עֲצָמֵינוּ לְפִי שְׁאוֹל:

8 My eyes are fixed upon You, O *Hashem* my Lord; I seek refuge in You, do not put me in jeopardy.

ח כִּי אֵלֶיךָ יְהֹוִה אֲדֹנָי עֵינָי בְּכָה חָסִיתִי אַל־תְּעַר נַפְשִׁי:

9 Keep me from the trap laid for me, and from the snares of evildoers.

ט שָׁמְרֵנִי מִידֵי פַח יָקְשׁוּ לִי וּמֹקְשׁוֹת פֹּעֲלֵי אָוֶן:

10 Let the wicked fall into their nets while I alone come through.

י יִפְּלוּ בְמַכְמֹרָיו רְשָׁעִים יַחַד אָנֹכִי עַד־אֶעֱבוֹר:

141:2 An evening sacrifice Rabbi Samson Raphael Hirsch explains the importance of the *mincha*, the meal offering (see Leviticus chapter 2) that accompanied the evening sacrifice. The *mincha* was made of flour, oil and wine, three important products of *Eretz Yisrael*. Flour represents life, oil represents wealth and wine represents spiritual joy. The three fruits of the land used for this offering symbolize the ideal state of the People of Israel: Living, working and flourishing in the Land of Israel, while worshipping the God of Israel.

Tehillim / Psalms

Chapter 142

142 1 A maskil of *David*, while he was in the cave. A prayer.

מַשְׂכִּיל לְדָוִד בִּהְיוֹתוֹ בַמְּעָרָה תְפִלָּה:

mas-KEEL l'-da-VID bih-yo-TO va-m'-a-RAH t'-fi-LAH

2 I cry aloud to *Hashem*; I appeal to *Hashem* loudly for mercy.

קוֹלִי אֶל־יְהוָה אֶזְעָק קוֹלִי אֶל־יְהוָה אֶתְחַנָּן:

3 I pour out my complaint before Him; I lay my trouble before Him

אֶשְׁפֹּךְ לְפָנָיו שִׂיחִי צָרָתִי לְפָנָיו אַגִּיד:

4 when my spirit fails within me. You know my course; they have laid a trap in the path I walk.

בְּהִתְעַטֵּף עָלַי רוּחִי וְאַתָּה יָדַעְתָּ נְתִיבָתִי בְּאֹרַח־זוּ אֲהַלֵּךְ טָמְנוּ פַח לִי:

5 Look at my right and see – I have no friend; there is nowhere I can flee, no one cares about me.

הַבֵּיט יָמִין וּרְאֵה וְאֵין־לִי מַכִּיר אָבַד מָנוֹס מִמֶּנִּי אֵין דּוֹרֵשׁ לְנַפְשִׁי:

6 So I cry to You, *Hashem*; I say, "You are my refuge, all I have in the land of the living."

זָעַקְתִּי אֵלֶיךָ יְהוָה אָמַרְתִּי אַתָּה מַחְסִי חֶלְקִי בְּאֶרֶץ הַחַיִּים:

7 Listen to my cry, for I have been brought very low; save me from my pursuers, for they are too strong for me.

הַקְשִׁיבָה אֶל־רִנָּתִי כִּי־דַלּוֹתִי מְאֹד הַצִּילֵנִי מֵרֹדְפַי כִּי אָמְצוּ מִמֶּנִּי:

8 Free me from prison, that I may praise Your name. The righteous shall glory in me for Your gracious dealings with me.

הוֹצִיאָה מִמַּסְגֵּר נַפְשִׁי לְהוֹדוֹת אֶת־שְׁמֶךָ בִּי יַכְתִּרוּ צַדִּיקִים כִּי תִגְמֹל עָלָי:

143 1 A psalm of *David*. *Hashem*, hear my prayer; give ear to my plea, as You are faithful; answer me, as You are beneficent.

מִזְמוֹר לְדָוִד יְהוָה שְׁמַע תְּפִלָּתִי הַאֲזִינָה אֶל־תַּחֲנוּנַי בֶּאֱמֻנָתְךָ עֲנֵנִי בְּצִדְקָתֶךָ:

2 Do not enter into judgment with Your servant, for before You no creature is in the right.

וְאַל־תָּבוֹא בְמִשְׁפָּט אֶת־עַבְדֶּךָ כִּי לֹא־יִצְדַּק לְפָנֶיךָ כָל־חָי:

3 My foe hounded me; he crushed me to the ground; he made me dwell in darkness like those long dead.

כִּי רָדַף אוֹיֵב נַפְשִׁי דִּכָּא לָאָרֶץ חַיָּתִי הוֹשִׁיבַנִי בְמַחֲשַׁכִּים כְּמֵתֵי עוֹלָם:

4 My spirit failed within me; my mind was numbed with horror.

וַתִּתְעַטֵּף עָלַי רוּחִי בְּתוֹכִי יִשְׁתּוֹמֵם לִבִּי:

142:1 While he was in the cave As recorded in *Sefer Shmuel* I 22, *David* runs for his life, escaping to a cave in *Adulam*. There, instead of solitude and fear, he finds compatriots and begins to build an army. Perhaps this prayer spurs a new resolve within him, not to be depressed or paralyzed by fear. The Bible speaks of 400 men who gathered in front of *David*, each one bitter and depressed, each without will or direction (*ibid.*, verse 2). Prayer can serve as a great unifier. It can give desperate people hope, help them focus on new goals and instill with them lofty ideals. The prayer leader, *David*, is inspired by this group and begins his path towards self-determination, and ultimately towards the monarchy itself. From a dark, dank, cave emerges a spark, a spirit, a king of Israel.

Tehillim / Psalms
Chapter 144

תהלים
פרק קמד

5 Then I thought of the days of old; I rehearsed all Your deeds, recounted the work of Your hands.

זָכַרְתִּי יָמִים מִקֶּדֶם הָגִיתִי בְכָל־פָּעֳלֶךָ בְּמַעֲשֵׂה יָדֶיךָ אֲשׂוֹחֵחַ:

za-KHAR-tee ya-MEEM mi-KE-dem ha-GEE-tee v-khol pa-a-LE-kha b'-ma-a-SAY ya-DE-kha a-so-KHAY-akh

6 I stretched out my hands to You, longing for You like thirsty earth. *Selah.*

פֵּרַשְׂתִּי יָדַי אֵלֶיךָ נַפְשִׁי כְּאֶרֶץ־עֲיֵפָה לְךָ סֶלָה:

7 Answer me quickly, *Hashem*; my spirit can endure no more. Do not hide Your face from me, or I shall become like those who descend into the Pit.

מַהֵר עֲנֵנִי יְהֹוָה כָּלְתָה רוּחִי אַל־תַּסְתֵּר פָּנֶיךָ מִמֶּנִּי וְנִמְשַׁלְתִּי עִם־יֹרְדֵי בוֹר:

8 Let me learn of Your faithfulness by daybreak, for in You I trust; let me know the road I must take, for on You I have set my hope.

הַשְׁמִיעֵנִי בַבֹּקֶר חַסְדֶּךָ כִּי־בְךָ בָטָחְתִּי הוֹדִיעֵנִי דֶּרֶךְ־זוּ אֵלֵךְ כִּי־אֵלֶיךָ נָשָׂאתִי נַפְשִׁי:

9 Save me from my foes, *Hashem*; to You I look for cover.

הַצִּילֵנִי מֵאֹיְבַי יְהֹוָה אֵלֶיךָ כִסִּתִי:

10 Teach me to do Your will, for You are my God. Let Your gracious spirit lead me on level ground.

לַמְּדֵנִי לַעֲשׂוֹת רְצוֹנֶךָ כִּי־אַתָּה אֱלוֹהָי רוּחֲךָ טוֹבָה תַּנְחֵנִי בְּאֶרֶץ מִישׁוֹר:

11 For the sake of Your name, *Hashem*, preserve me; as You are beneficent, free me from distress.

לְמַעַן־שִׁמְךָ יְהֹוָה תְּחַיֵּנִי בְּצִדְקָתְךָ תּוֹצִיא מִצָּרָה נַפְשִׁי:

12 As You are faithful, put an end to my foes; destroy all my mortal enemies, for I am Your servant.

וּבְחַסְדְּךָ תַּצְמִית אֹיְבָי וְהַאֲבַדְתָּ כָּל־צֹרֲרֵי נַפְשִׁי כִּי אֲנִי עַבְדֶּךָ:

144

1 Of *David*. Blessed is *Hashem*, my rock, who trains my hands for battle, my fingers for warfare;

לְדָוִד בָּרוּךְ יְהֹוָה צוּרִי הַמְלַמֵּד יָדַי לַקְרָב אֶצְבְּעוֹתַי לַמִּלְחָמָה:

2 my faithful one, my fortress, my haven and my deliverer, my shield, in whom I take shelter, who makes peoples subject to me.

חַסְדִּי וּמְצוּדָתִי מִשְׂגַּבִּי וּמְפַלְטִי לִי מָגִנִּי וּבוֹ חָסִיתִי הָרוֹדֵד עַמִּי תַחְתָּי:

3 *Hashem*, what is man that You should care about him, mortal man, that You should think of him?

יְהֹוָה מָה־אָדָם וַתֵּדָעֵהוּ בֶּן־אֱנוֹשׁ וַתְּחַשְּׁבֵהוּ:

4 Man is like a breath; his days are like a passing shadow.

אָדָם לַהֶבֶל דָּמָה יָמָיו כְּצֵל עוֹבֵר:

Reading the declaration of independence

143:5 Then I thought of the days of old Once again, *David* is in a perilous state. Enemies from close and far depress him and make him feel lost and alone. In this psalm, he invokes a different technique to lift himself out of the morass: Memory. Isolating one's consciousness to the here and now can be lonesome and disheartening. Remembering that one is part of something greater than the present, however, can be uplifting. A number of biblical laws are related to past events and the idea of remembering, such as *Shabbat*, which is intended to remind us of both the creation of the world (Exodus 31:17) and the exodus from Egypt (Deuteronomy 5:15). In 1948, the framers of Israel's Declaration of Independence knew precisely how to begin their journey towards nationhood, by recalling the past. They began the declaration of the establishment of the State of Israel as follows: "The Land of Israel was the birthplace of the Jewish people. Here their spiritual, religious and political identity was shaped. Here they first attained to statehood, created cultural values of national and universal significance and gave to the world the eternal Book of Books."

Tehillim/Psalms
Chapter 145

תהלים
פרק קמה

5 *Hashem*, bend Your sky and come down; touch the mountains and they will smoke.

ה יְהוָה הַט־שָׁמֶיךָ וְתֵרֵד גַּע בֶּהָרִים וְיֶעֱשָׁנוּ:

6 Make lightning flash and scatter them; shoot Your arrows and rout them.

ו בְּרוֹק בָּרָק וּתְפִיצֵם שְׁלַח חִצֶּיךָ וּתְהֻמֵּם:

7 Reach Your hand down from on high; rescue me, save me from the mighty waters, from the hands of foreigners,

ז שְׁלַח יָדֶיךָ מִמָּרוֹם פְּצֵנִי וְהַצִּילֵנִי מִמַּיִם רַבִּים מִיַּד בְּנֵי נֵכָר:

8 whose mouths speak lies, and whose oaths are false.

ח אֲשֶׁר פִּיהֶם דִּבֶּר־שָׁוְא וִימִינָם יְמִין שָׁקֶר:

9 O *Hashem*, I will sing You a new song, sing a hymn to You with a ten-stringed harp,

ט אֱלֹהִים שִׁיר חָדָשׁ אָשִׁירָה לָּךְ בְּנֵבֶל עָשׂוֹר אֲזַמְּרָה־לָּךְ:

10 to You who give victory to kings, who rescue His servant *David* from the deadly sword.

י הַנּוֹתֵן תְּשׁוּעָה לַמְּלָכִים הַפּוֹצֶה אֶת־דָּוִד עַבְדּוֹ מֵחֶרֶב רָעָה:

11 Rescue me, save me from the hands of foreigners, whose mouths speak lies, and whose oaths are false.

יא פְּצֵנִי וְהַצִּילֵנִי מִיַּד בְּנֵי־נֵכָר אֲשֶׁר פִּיהֶם דִּבֶּר־שָׁוְא וִימִינָם יְמִין שָׁקֶר:

12 For our sons are like saplings, well-tended in their youth; our daughters are like cornerstones trimmed to give shape to a palace.

יב אֲשֶׁר בָּנֵינוּ כִּנְטִעִים מְגֻדָּלִים בִּנְעוּרֵיהֶם בְּנוֹתֵינוּ כְזָוִיֹּת מְחֻטָּבוֹת תַּבְנִית הֵיכָל:

13 Our storehouses are full, supplying produce of all kinds; our flocks number thousands, even myriads, in our fields;

יג מְזָוֵינוּ מְלֵאִים מְפִיקִים מִזַּן אֶל־זַן צֹאונֵנוּ מַאֲלִיפוֹת מְרֻבָּבוֹת בְּחוּצוֹתֵינוּ:

14 our cattle are well cared for There is no breaching and no sortie, and no wailing in our streets.

יד אַלּוּפֵינוּ מְסֻבָּלִים אֵין־פֶּרֶץ וְאֵין יוֹצֵאת וְאֵין צְוָחָה בִּרְחֹבֹתֵינוּ:

15 Happy the people who have it so; happy the people whose God is *Hashem*.

טו אַשְׁרֵי הָעָם שֶׁכָּכָה לּוֹ אַשְׁרֵי הָעָם שֶׁיהוָה אֱלֹהָיו:

ash-RAY ha-AM she-KA-khah LO ash-RAY ha-AM she-a-do-NAI e-lo-HAV

145 1 A song of praise. Of *David*. I will extol You, my God and king, and bless Your name forever and ever.

קמה א תְּהִלָּה לְדָוִד אֲרוֹמִמְךָ אֱלוֹהַי הַמֶּלֶךְ וַאֲבָרְכָה שִׁמְךָ לְעוֹלָם וָעֶד:

2 Every day will I bless You and praise Your name forever and ever.

ב בְּכָל־יוֹם אֲבָרְכֶךָּ וַאֲהַלְלָה שִׁמְךָ לְעוֹלָם וָעֶד:

144:15 Happy the people who have it so The last five psalms of *Sefer Tehillim* represent a special unit of praise to *Hashem*, which some see a microcosm of all the psalms. If that is true, then Psalm 144, which immediately precedes the final summary unit, serves as a conclusion of sorts. The ending of this psalm forms a valuable and oft-used poetic tool called "inclusio," referring to the use at the conclusion of a song, chapter or book of the very same words with which it started. Psalm 1 began with the Hebrew word *ashrei*, 'happy,' and this psalm concludes with a verse beginning with the same word, *ashrei*. The inaugural psalm praises the individual who veers from the wicked path and finds solace in God's word. This psalm praises the nation who, having internalized the messages taught by *David*, conquers its land, establishes a just society and radiates *Hashem*'s spirit to the world. How fortunate is the reader of psalms, who traverses from the praise of the individual to the praise of the entire Nation of Israel as he progresses through *Sefer Tehillim*.

Tehillim/Psalms
Chapter 145

תהילים
פרק קמה

3 Great is *Hashem* and much acclaimed; His greatness cannot be fathomed.

ג גָּדוֹל יְהֹוָה וּמְהֻלָּל מְאֹד וְלִגְדֻלָּתוֹ אֵין חֵקֶר:

4 One generation shall laud Your works to another and declare Your mighty acts.

ד דּוֹר לְדוֹר יְשַׁבַּח מַעֲשֶׂיךָ וּגְבוּרֹתֶיךָ יַגִּידוּ:

5 The glorious majesty of Your splendor and Your wondrous acts will I recite.

ה הֲדַר כְּבוֹד הוֹדֶךָ וְדִבְרֵי נִפְלְאֹתֶיךָ אָשִׂיחָה:

6 Men shall talk of the might of Your awesome deeds, and I will recount Your greatness.

ו וֶעֱזוּז נוֹרְאֹתֶיךָ יֹאמֵרוּ וּגְדוּלָּתְךָ [וּגְדֻלָּתְךָ] אֲסַפְּרֶנָּה:

7 They shall celebrate Your abundant goodness, and sing joyously of Your beneficence.

ז זֵכֶר רַב־טוּבְךָ יַבִּיעוּ וְצִדְקָתְךָ יְרַנֵּנוּ:

8 *Hashem* is gracious and compassionate, slow to anger and abounding in kindness.

ח חַנּוּן וְרַחוּם יְהֹוָה אֶרֶךְ אַפַּיִם וּגְדָל־חָסֶד:

9 *Hashem* is good to all, and His mercy is upon all His works.

ט טוֹב־יְהֹוָה לַכֹּל וְרַחֲמָיו עַל־כָּל־מַעֲשָׂיו:

10 All Your works shall praise You, *Hashem*, and Your faithful ones shall bless You.

י יוֹדוּךָ יְהֹוָה כָּל־מַעֲשֶׂיךָ וַחֲסִידֶיךָ יְבָרְכוּכָה:

11 They shall talk of the majesty of Your kingship, and speak of Your might,

יא כְּבוֹד מַלְכוּתְךָ יֹאמֵרוּ וּגְבוּרָתְךָ יְדַבֵּרוּ:

12 to make His mighty acts known among men and the majestic glory of His kingship.

יב לְהוֹדִיעַ לִבְנֵי הָאָדָם גְּבוּרֹתָיו וּכְבוֹד הֲדַר מַלְכוּתוֹ:

13 Your kingship is an eternal kingship; Your dominion is for all generations.

יג מַלְכוּתְךָ מַלְכוּת כָּל־עֹלָמִים וּמֶמְשַׁלְתְּךָ בְּכָל־דּוֹר וָדֹר:

14 *Hashem* supports all who stumble, and makes all who are bent stand straight.

יד סוֹמֵךְ יְהֹוָה לְכָל־הַנֹּפְלִים וְזוֹקֵף לְכָל־הַכְּפוּפִים:

so-MAYKH a-do-NAI l'-khol ha-no-f'-LEEM v'-zo-KAYF l'-khol ha-k'-fu-FEEM

15 The eyes of all look to You expectantly, and You give them their food when it is due.

טו עֵינֵי־כֹל אֵלֶיךָ יְשַׂבֵּרוּ וְאַתָּה נוֹתֵן־לָהֶם אֶת־אָכְלָם בְּעִתּוֹ:

16 You give it openhandedly, feeding every creature to its heart's content.

טז פּוֹתֵחַ אֶת־יָדֶךָ וּמַשְׂבִּיעַ לְכָל־חַי רָצוֹן:

17 *Hashem* is beneficent in all His ways and faithful in all His works.

יז צַדִּיק יְהֹוָה בְּכָל־דְּרָכָיו וְחָסִיד בְּכָל־מַעֲשָׂיו:

145:14 Hashem supports all who stumble According to the Talmud (*Berachot* 4b), this psalm, which is arranged in alphabetical order, is the choicest of all psalms, because it includes a sweeping praise of *Hashem*, from the first letter *aleph* to the final letter *tav*, It also serves as a reminder of the universal message that God is the sustainer of all. Indeed, the word 'all,' referring to all peoples, appears sixteen times in the psalm. Though it follows the Hebrew alphabet, the letter *nun* (נ) is missing from the psalm. The Sages explain that since the *nun* connotes *nefila* (נפילה), 'falling,' it was omitted. They quote *Sefer Amos* 5:2: "Fallen, not to rise again, is Maiden *Yisrael*." Because this *nefila* has a negative connotation, the letter *nun* was omitted from this psalm. However, the Talmud quotes a second, more positive interpretation of this verse: "She has fallen and will no longer [fall]. Rise, O Maiden Israel!"

Tehillim/Psalms
Chapter 146

18 *Hashem* is near to all who call Him, to all who call Him with sincerity.

19 He fulfills the wishes of those who fear Him; He hears their cry and delivers them.

20 *Hashem* watches over all who love Him, but all the wicked He will destroy.

21 My mouth shall utter the praise of *Hashem*, and all creatures shall bless His holy name forever and ever.

146 1 Hallelujah. Praise *Hashem*, O my soul!

ha-l'-lu-YAH ha-l'-LEE naf-SHEE et a-do-NAI

2 I will praise *Hashem* all my life, sing hymns to my God while I exist.

3 Put not your trust in the great, in mortal man who cannot save.

4 His breath departs; he returns to the dust; on that day his plans come to nothing.

5 Happy is he who has the God of *Yaakov* for his help, whose hope is in *Hashem* his God,

6 maker of heaven and earth, the sea and all that is in them; who keeps faith forever;

7 who secures justice for those who are wronged, gives food to the hungry. *Hashem* sets prisoners free;

8 *Hashem* restores sight to the blind; *Hashem* makes those who are bent stand straight; *Hashem* loves the righteous;

9 *Hashem* watches over the stranger; He gives courage to the orphan and widow, but makes the path of the wicked tortuous.

10 *Hashem* shall reign forever, your God, O *Tzion*, for all generations. Hallelujah.

146:1 Praise *Hashem*, O my soul Man lives on earth in two different spheres: As an individual with his own personal struggles, and as part of something bigger; a family, community and a nation, each with its own dynamic. Psalms 146 and 147 present the individual and the communal praise of *Hashem*. In this psalm, the individual is confronted by the prince who has more power and influence than he does. He must decide to either follow these hollow leaders, or to stand apart and put his faith in God alone. The psalm praises the individual who chooses to follow *Hashem* and recognizes that he will merit God's reward.

Tehillim/Psalms
Chapter 147

תהלים
פרק קמז

147 1 Hallelujah. It is good to chant hymns to our God; it is pleasant to sing glorious praise.

א הַלְלוּ יָהּ כִּי־טוֹב זַמְּרָה אֱלֹהֵינוּ כִּי־נָעִים נָאוָה תְהִלָּה:

2 *Hashem* rebuilds *Yerushalayim*; He gathers in the exiles of *Yisrael*.

ב בּוֹנֵה יְרוּשָׁלַםִ יְהֹוָה נִדְחֵי יִשְׂרָאֵל יְכַנֵּס:

3 He heals their broken hearts, and binds up their wounds.

ג הָרֹפֵא לִשְׁבוּרֵי לֵב וּמְחַבֵּשׁ לְעַצְּבוֹתָם:

4 He reckoned the number of the stars; to each He gave its name.

ד מוֹנֶה מִסְפָּר לַכּוֹכָבִים לְכֻלָּם שֵׁמוֹת יִקְרָא:

5 Great is our Lord and full of power; His wisdom is beyond reckoning.

ה גָּדוֹל אֲדוֹנֵינוּ וְרַב־כֹּחַ לִתְבוּנָתוֹ אֵין מִסְפָּר:

6 *Hashem* gives courage to the lowly, and brings the wicked down to the dust.

ו מְעוֹדֵד עֲנָוִים יְהֹוָה מַשְׁפִּיל רְשָׁעִים עֲדֵי־אָרֶץ:

7 Sing to *Hashem* a song of praise, chant a hymn with a lyre to our God,

ז עֱנוּ לַיהֹוָה בְּתוֹדָה זַמְּרוּ לֵאלֹהֵינוּ בְכִנּוֹר:

8 who covers the heavens with clouds, provides rain for the earth, makes mountains put forth grass;

ח הַמְכַסֶּה שָׁמַיִם בְּעָבִים הַמֵּכִין לָאָרֶץ מָטָר הַמַּצְמִיחַ הָרִים חָצִיר:

9 who gives the beasts their food, to the raven's brood what they cry for.

ט נוֹתֵן לִבְהֵמָה לַחְמָהּ לִבְנֵי עֹרֵב אֲשֶׁר יִקְרָאוּ:

10 He does not prize the strength of horses, nor value the fleetness of men;

י לֹא בִגְבוּרַת הַסּוּס יֶחְפָּץ לֹא־בְשׁוֹקֵי הָאִישׁ יִרְצֶה:

11 but *Hashem* values those who fear Him, those who depend on His faithful care.

יא רוֹצֶה יְהֹוָה אֶת־יְרֵאָיו אֶת־הַמְיַחֲלִים לְחַסְדּוֹ:

12 O *Yerushalayim*, glorify *Hashem*; praise your God, O *Tzion*!

יב שַׁבְּחִי יְרוּשָׁלַםִ אֶת־יְהֹוָה הַלְלִי אֱלֹהַיִךְ צִיּוֹן:

13 For He made the bars of your gates strong, and blessed your children within you.

יג כִּי־חִזַּק בְּרִיחֵי שְׁעָרָיִךְ בֵּרַךְ בָּנַיִךְ בְּקִרְבֵּךְ:

14 He endows your realm with well-being, and satisfies you with choice wheat.

יד הַשָּׂם־גְּבוּלֵךְ שָׁלוֹם חֵלֶב חִטִּים יַשְׂבִּיעֵךְ:

ha-SAM g'-vu-LAYKH sha-LOM KHAY-lev khi-TEEM yas-bee-AYKH

147:14 He endows your realm with well-being While the Bible makes frequent mention of military affairs and speaks often of soldiers, the important principle that emerges is found in this verse: *Ha-sam g'vulaych shalom* (השם גבולך שלום). Translated here as 'He endows your realm with well-being,' these words literally mean 'He who makes your borders peaceful.' We must always remember that ultimately, our own efforts do not matter. Rather, *Hashem* is behind all of our successes. Though the modern Israeli army is one of the strongest in the world, it continuously remembers the true source of its strength. At their swearing-in ceremony, which often takes place at the Western Wall, each IDF soldier is handed a *Tanakh* and a gun, as a reminder that ultimately the One above is the source of their physical strength and their military success.

A new IDF recruit holding a Tanakh and a gun

Tehillim/Psalms Chapter 148

15 He sends forth His word to the earth; His command runs swiftly.

16 He lays down snow like fleece, scatters frost like ashes.

17 He tosses down hail like crumbs – who can endure His icy cold?

18 He issues a command – it melts them; He breathes – the waters flow.

19 He issued His commands to *Yaakov*, His statutes and rules to *Yisrael*.

20 He did not do so for any other nation; of such rules they know nothing. Halleluyah.

148 1 Halleluyah. Praise *Hashem* from the heavens; praise Him on high.

2 Praise Him, all His angels, praise Him, all His hosts.

3 Praise Him, sun and moon, praise Him, all bright stars.

4 Praise Him, highest heavens, and you waters that are above the heavens.

5 Let them praise the name of *Hashem*, for it was He who commanded that they be created.

6 He made them endure forever, establishing an order that shall never change.

7 Praise *Hashem*, O you who are on earth, all sea monsters and ocean depths,

8 fire and hail, snow and smoke, storm wind that executes His command,

9 all mountains and hills, all fruit trees and cedars,

10 all wild and tamed beasts, creeping things and winged birds,

11 all kings and peoples of the earth, all princes of the earth and its judges,

12 youths and maidens alike, old and young together.

תהלים
פרק קמח

טו הַשֹּׁלֵחַ אִמְרָתוֹ אָרֶץ עַד־מְהֵרָה יָרוּץ דְּבָרוֹ׃

טז הַנֹּתֵן שֶׁלֶג כַּצָּמֶר כְּפוֹר כָּאֵפֶר יְפַזֵּר׃

יז מַשְׁלִיךְ קַרְחוֹ כְפִתִּים לִפְנֵי קָרָתוֹ מִי יַעֲמֹד׃

יח יִשְׁלַח דְּבָרוֹ וְיַמְסֵם יַשֵּׁב רוּחוֹ יִזְּלוּ־מָיִם׃

יט מַגִּיד דברו [דְּבָרָיו] לְיַעֲקֹב חֻקָּיו וּמִשְׁפָּטָיו לְיִשְׂרָאֵל׃

כ לֹא עָשָׂה כֵן לְכָל־גּוֹי וּמִשְׁפָּטִים בַּל־יְדָעוּם הַלְלוּ־יָהּ׃

קמח א הַלְלוּ יָהּ הַלְלוּ אֶת־יְהֹוָה מִן־הַשָּׁמַיִם הַלְלוּהוּ בַּמְּרוֹמִים׃

ב הַלְלוּהוּ כָל־מַלְאָכָיו הַלְלוּהוּ כָּל־צְבָאוֹ [צְבָאָיו]׃

ג הַלְלוּהוּ שֶׁמֶשׁ וְיָרֵחַ הַלְלוּהוּ כָּל־כּוֹכְבֵי אוֹר׃

ד הַלְלוּהוּ שְׁמֵי הַשָּׁמָיִם וְהַמַּיִם אֲשֶׁר מֵעַל הַשָּׁמָיִם׃

ה יְהַלְלוּ אֶת־שֵׁם יְהֹוָה כִּי הוּא צִוָּה וְנִבְרָאוּ׃

ו וַיַּעֲמִידֵם לָעַד לְעוֹלָם חָק־נָתַן וְלֹא יַעֲבוֹר׃

ז הַלְלוּ אֶת־יְהֹוָה מִן־הָאָרֶץ תַּנִּינִים וְכָל־תְּהֹמוֹת׃

ח אֵשׁ וּבָרָד שֶׁלֶג וְקִיטוֹר רוּחַ סְעָרָה עֹשָׂה דְבָרוֹ׃

ט הֶהָרִים וְכָל־גְּבָעוֹת עֵץ פְּרִי וְכָל־אֲרָזִים׃

י הַחַיָּה וְכָל־בְּהֵמָה רֶמֶשׂ וְצִפּוֹר כָּנָף׃

יא מַלְכֵי־אֶרֶץ וְכָל־לְאֻמִּים שָׂרִים וְכָל־שֹׁפְטֵי אָרֶץ׃

יב בַּחוּרִים וְגַם־בְּתוּלוֹת זְקֵנִים עִם־נְעָרִים׃

Tehillim/Psalms
Chapter 149

13 Let them praise the name of *Hashem*, for His name, His alone, is sublime; His splendor covers heaven and earth.

y'-ha-l'-LU et SHAYM a-do-NAI kee nis-GAV sh'-MO l'-va-DO ho-DO al E-retz v'-sha-MA-yim

יְהַלְלוּ אֶת־שֵׁם יְהֹוָה כִּי־נִשְׂגָּב שְׁמוֹ לְבַדּוֹ הוֹדוֹ עַל־אֶרֶץ וְשָׁמָיִם:

14 He has exalted the horn of His people for the glory of all His faithful ones, *Yisrael*, the people close to Him. Hallelujah.

וַיָּרֶם קֶרֶן לְעַמּוֹ תְּהִלָּה לְכָל־חֲסִידָיו לִבְנֵי יִשְׂרָאֵל עַם־קְרֹבוֹ הַלְלוּ־יָהּ:

149

1 Hallelujah. Sing to *Hashem* a new song, His praises in the congregation of the faithful.

הַלְלוּ יָהּ שִׁירוּ לַיהֹוָה שִׁיר חָדָשׁ תְּהִלָּתוֹ בִּקְהַל חֲסִידִים:

2 Let *Yisrael* rejoice in its maker; let the children of *Tzion* exult in their king.

יִשְׂמַח יִשְׂרָאֵל בְּעֹשָׂיו בְּנֵי־צִיּוֹן יָגִילוּ בְמַלְכָּם:

3 Let them praise His name in dance; with timbrel and lyre let them chant His praises.

יְהַלְלוּ שְׁמוֹ בְמָחוֹל בְּתֹף וְכִנּוֹר יְזַמְּרוּ־לוֹ:

4 For *Hashem* delights in His people; He adorns the lowly with victory.

כִּי־רוֹצֶה יְהֹוָה בְּעַמּוֹ יְפָאֵר עֲנָוִים בִּישׁוּעָה:

5 Let the faithful exult in glory; let them shout for joy upon their couches,

יַעְלְזוּ חֲסִידִים בְּכָבוֹד יְרַנְּנוּ עַל־מִשְׁכְּבוֹתָם:

6 with paeans to *Hashem* in their throats and two-edged swords in their hands,

רוֹמְמוֹת אֵל בִּגְרוֹנָם וְחֶרֶב פִּיפִיּוֹת בְּיָדָם:

ro-m'-MOT AYL big-ro-NAM v'-KHE-rev pee-fi-YOT b'-ya-DAM

7 to impose retribution upon the nations, punishment upon the peoples,

לַעֲשׂוֹת נְקָמָה בַּגּוֹיִם תּוֹכֵחֹת בַּל־אֻמִּים:

8 binding their kings with shackles, their nobles with chains of iron,

לֶאְסֹר מַלְכֵיהֶם בְּזִקִּים וְנִכְבְּדֵיהֶם בְּכַבְלֵי בַרְזֶל:

148:13 Let them praise the name of *Hashem* Psalm 148 can be divided into two parts. The first half speaks of *Hashem* being praised in the celestial spheres, while the second half speaks of human praises of God. Though both seemingly exalt Him the same way, as it says, "let them praise the name of *Hashem*" (verses 5 and 13), the praises are actually very different. The angels exalt God "for it was He who commanded that they be created." They are robotically programmed to sing *Hashem's* praises. Humans, on the other hand, worship Him because they see the beauty of creation, understand God's compassion and voluntarily choose to sing His praises. We are all recipients of God's love and His bounty. It is our duty to recognize what He gives us and to sing His praises.

149:6 And two-edged swords in their hands Israel wants to live in peace in the Promised Land, but sometimes they are threatened by nations attempting to destroy them and their country. Israel can respond with might or with spirit, and it must do both, because each response is insufficient on its own. Psalm 149 emphasizes the true synthesis of power and prayer. This verse reminds us of the judge, *Ehud* the son of Gera, who, after killing the king of Moab with a double edged sword, rallied the People of Israel to fight, shouting "Follow me closely, for *Hashem* has delivered your enemies, the Moabites, into your hands" (Judges 3:28). The men *Ehud* rallied sought to elevate God's name in the world, eradicate evil and bring justice to the land. This is the message of the penultimate chapter in the book of Psalms.

Tehillim/Psalms
Chapter 150

9 executing the doom decreed against them. This is the glory of all His faithful. Hallelujah.

150 1 Hallelujah. Praise *Hashem* in His sanctuary; praise Him in the sky, His stronghold.

2 Praise Him for His mighty acts; praise Him for His exceeding greatness.

3 Praise Him with blasts of the *shofar*; praise Him with harp and lyre.

ha-l'-LU-hu b'-TAY-ka sho-FAR ha-l'-LU-hu b'-NAY-vel v'-khi-NOR

4 Praise Him with timbrel and dance; praise Him with lute and pipe.

5 Praise Him with resounding cymbals; praise Him with loud-clashing cymbals.

6 Let all that breathes praise *Hashem*. Hallelujah.

תהלים
פרק קנ

ט לַעֲשׂוֹת בָּהֶם מִשְׁפָּט כָּתוּב הָדָר הוּא לְכׇל־חֲסִידָיו הַלְלוּ־יָהּ׃

קנ א הַלְלוּ יָהּ ׀ הַלְלוּ־אֵל בְּקׇדְשׁוֹ הַלְלוּהוּ בִּרְקִיעַ עֻזּוֹ׃

ב הַלְלוּהוּ בִגְבוּרֹתָיו הַלְלוּהוּ כְּרֹב גֻּדְלוֹ׃

ג הַלְלוּהוּ בְּתֵקַע שׁוֹפָר הַלְלוּהוּ בְּנֵבֶל וְכִנּוֹר׃

ד הַלְלוּהוּ בְתֹף וּמָחוֹל הַלְלוּהוּ בְּמִנִּים וְעוּגָב׃

ה הַלְלוּהוּ בְצִלְצְלֵי־שָׁמַע הַלְלוּהוּ בְּצִלְצְלֵי תְרוּעָה׃

ו כֹּל הַנְּשָׁמָה תְּהַלֵּל יָהּ הַלְלוּ־יָהּ׃

150:3 Praise Him with harp and lyre The final chapter of *Sefer Tehillim* invokes the image of an orchestra full of instruments to praise the Lord. King *David*, author of Psalms, had a deep love for music. The Talmud (*Sanhedrin* 16a) teaches that he kept his harp hung over his bed while he slept, and in the middle of the night, the wind blowing through his open window would make the strings stir. We can learn a valuable life lesson from this harp: The harder one plucks the harp's strings, the sweeter its sound. According to the Talmud (*Sanhedrin* 107a), before his sin with *Batsheva*, King *David* asked *Hashem* to be tested and challenged like the forefathers had been because he knew that, like a harp, after confronting life's challenges he would emerge a better person and closer to God. Though he initially failed the test, after he admitted his sin and repented, his relationship with *Hashem* was even stronger than it had been previously. *David* serves as a model for all of repentance and worship of God. By studying the precious passages of *Sefer Tehillim*, we too can overcome any of life's challenges and achieve unmatched intimacy with *Hashem*.

A statue of King David with his harp on Mount Zion

Sefer Mishlei
The Book of Proverbs

Introduction and commentary by Ahuva Balofsky

The name of this book of wisdom, *Mishlei*, is translated to English as 'Proverbs,' but that is perhaps too limited a designation. The Hebrew word *mashal*, from which the name *Mishlei* is derived, is more akin to an extended metaphor than a pithy saying.

Sefer Mishlei contains the collected wisdom of *Shlomo*, the wisest king to sit on the throne in *Yerushalayim*. In *Melachim* I 3:5–14, the Bible relates how this son of King *David* achieved such greatness. *Hashem* appeared to *Shlomo* in a dream and offered him whatever his heart desired. Young King *Shlomo* asked only for the wisdom to guide God's people in righteousness. So pleased was the Lord with *Shlomo's* request that He granted *Shlomo's* wish and, in addition, also gave him great wealth and success.

Sefer Mishlei refers to the fear of *Hashem* as "the beginning of wisdom" (1:7), noting that recognition of His hand in the world is the source of all understanding. It admonishes the wise to seek out similar companions and to avoid the fool and the temptress, promising reward for the hard-working and dedicated, and suffering for the lazy and the wicked.

On the surface, the lessons of *Sefer Mishlei* seem straightforward, but in his own introduction to the book, King *Shlomo* promises that great secrets lie behind his words. The metaphors in the text can be understood both literally and figuratively, and can be projected onto a number of different situations.

Throughout the text, wisdom is personified as a righteous woman, while temptation is represented by the harlot. King *Shlomo* tells the reader that *Hashem* founded creation itself on wisdom, making order out of the chaos. That wisdom has been understood to be God's *Torah*, and following its precepts will earn the faithful His reward.

Later chapters of *Sefer Mishlei* cite *Agur* son of *Yakeh* and King *Lemuel* as sources for the parables contained within. Jewish tradition considers both to be monikers for King *Shlomo*, as *Agur* means "compiler" and *Lemuel* means "for God".

The final chapter of the book, chapter 31, includes the beautiful passage entitled "A Woman of Valor." This poem, like everything else in *Sefer Mishlei*, can be understood literally, as a description of the ideal woman. However, in Jewish tradition it has been explained as a reference to the matriarch *Sara*, the *Torah* or even the *Shabbat*. In fact, it is customary in many Jewish homes to sing this poem on Friday night around the *Shabbat* table, while welcoming the Sabbath Queen. According to *Metzudat David*, *Shlomo* chose to end his book of wisdom with a praise of the woman of valor as a tribute to his mother, *Batsheva*, from whom who learned much of the wisdom contained within.

**List of Opinions Regarding
When *Shlomo* (Solomon) Authored his Biblical Books**

King *Shlomo* authored three of the books of *Tanakh*: *Mishlei*, *Shir Hashirim* and *Kohelet*. The first two are attributed to him explicitly (Proverbs 1:1, Song of Songs 1:1). The third is attributed to *Kohelet* son of *David* (Ecclesiastes 1:1) who the Sages tell us was *Shlomo*. There are several possible sequences offered by the Sages regarding the order in which he wrote these books (*Shir Hashirim Rabba* 1:10).

1. *Shlomo* wrote *Mishlei* before *Shir Hashirim* and *Kohelet*. This approach is based on the verse in *Sefer Melachim* I 5:12 which mentions *Shlomo*'s proverbs before his songs.
2. *Shlomo* wrote them all around the same time.
3. *Shlomo* wrote his books following the pattern of human experience. In his youth, when one is more likely to fall passionately in love and write emotional love songs, *Shlomo* authored *Shir Hashirim*. He wrote *Mishlei* as a mature adult when one is most likely to develop parables of wisdom. Finally, *Kohelet* was written in his old age when one is likely to be more serious and somber and to see the vanity in the world.

Mishlei/Proverbs
Chapter 1

משלי
פרק א

1 1 The proverbs of *Shlomo* son of *David*, king of *Yisrael*:

א מִשְׁלֵי שְׁלֹמֹה בֶן־דָּוִד מֶלֶךְ יִשְׂרָאֵל:

2 For learning wisdom and discipline; For understanding words of discernment;

ב לָדַעַת חָכְמָה וּמוּסָר לְהָבִין אִמְרֵי בִינָה:

3 For acquiring the discipline for success, Righteousness, justice, and equity;

ג לָקַחַת מוּסַר הַשְׂכֵּל צֶדֶק וּמִשְׁפָּט וּמֵישָׁרִים:

4 For endowing the simple with shrewdness, The young with knowledge and foresight.

ד לָתֵת לִפְתָאיִם עָרְמָה לְנַעַר דַּעַת וּמְזִמָּה:

5 The wise man, hearing them, will gain more wisdom; The discerning man will learn to be adroit;

ה יִשְׁמַע חָכָם וְיוֹסֶף לֶקַח וְנָבוֹן תַּחְבֻּלוֹת יִקְנֶה:

6 For understanding proverb and epigram, The words of the wise and their riddles.

ו לְהָבִין מָשָׁל וּמְלִיצָה דִּבְרֵי חֲכָמִים וְחִידֹתָם:

7 **The fear of *Hashem* is the beginning of knowledge; Fools despise wisdom and discipline.**

ז יִרְאַת יְהֹוָה רֵאשִׁית דָּעַת חָכְמָה וּמוּסָר אֱוִילִים בָּזוּ:

yir-AT a-do-NAI ray-SHEET DA-at khokh-MAH u-mu-SAR e-vee-LEEM BA-zu

8 My son, heed the discipline of your father, And do not forsake the instruction of your mother;

ח שְׁמַע בְּנִי מוּסַר אָבִיךָ וְאַל־תִּטֹּשׁ תּוֹרַת אִמֶּךָ:

9 For they are a graceful wreath upon your head, A necklace about your throat.

ט כִּי לִוְיַת חֵן הֵם לְרֹאשֶׁךָ וַעֲנָקִים לְגַרְגְּרֹתֶיךָ:

10 My son, if sinners entice you, do not yield;

י בְּנִי אִם־יְפַתּוּךָ חַטָּאִים אַל־תֹּבֵא:

11 If they say, "Come with us, Let us set an ambush to shed blood, Let us lie in wait for the innocent (Without cause!)

יא אִם־יֹאמְרוּ לְכָה אִתָּנוּ נֶאֶרְבָה לְדָם נִצְפְּנָה לְנָקִי חִנָּם:

12 Like Sheol, let us swallow them alive; Whole, like those who go down into the Pit.

יב נִבְלָעֵם כִּשְׁאוֹל חַיִּים וּתְמִימִים כְּיוֹרְדֵי בוֹר:

13 We shall obtain every precious treasure; We shall fill our homes with loot.

יג כָּל־הוֹן יָקָר נִמְצָא נְמַלֵּא בָתֵּינוּ שָׁלָל:

14 Throw in your lot with us; We shall all have a common purse."

יד גּוֹרָלְךָ תַּפִּיל בְּתוֹכֵנוּ כִּיס אֶחָד יִהְיֶה לְכֻלָּנוּ:

15 My son, do not set out with them; Keep your feet from their path.

טו בְּנִי אַל־תֵּלֵךְ בְּדֶרֶךְ אִתָּם מְנַע רַגְלְךָ מִנְּתִיבָתָם:

16 For their feet run to evil; They hurry to shed blood.

טז כִּי רַגְלֵיהֶם לָרַע יָרוּצוּ וִימַהֲרוּ לִשְׁפָּךְ־דָּם:

1:7 The fear of *Hashem* is the beginning of knowledge *Sefer Mishlei* contains the collected wisdom of *Shlomo*, the wisest king to sit on the throne in Israel. This verse sets the tone for the entire book of *Mishlei*. Once King *Solomon* has set out his purpose – to impart wisdom – in writing, he begins by identifying fear of *Hashem* as the root of that wisdom. Without awe of God, knowledge is empty and can be twisted for any number of negative purposes.

Mishlei/Proverbs

Chapter 1

משלי

פרק א

17	In the eyes of every winged creature The outspread net means nothing.	יז כִּי־חִנָּם מְזֹרָה הָרָשֶׁת בְּעֵינֵי כָל־בַּעַל כָּנָף׃
18	But they lie in ambush for their own blood; They lie in wait for their own lives.	יח וְהֵם לְדָמָם יֶאֱרֹבוּ יִצְפְּנוּ לְנַפְשֹׁתָם׃
19	Such is the fate of all who pursue unjust gain; It takes the life of its possessor.	יט כֵּן אָרְחוֹת כָּל־בֹּצֵעַ בָּצַע אֶת־נֶפֶשׁ בְּעָלָיו יִקָּח׃
20	Wisdom cries aloud in the streets, Raises her voice in the squares.	כ חָכְמוֹת בַּחוּץ תָּרֹנָּה בָּרְחֹבוֹת תִּתֵּן קוֹלָהּ׃
21	At the head of the busy streets she calls; At the entrance of the gates, in the city, she speaks out:	כא בְּרֹאשׁ הֹמִיּוֹת תִּקְרָא בְּפִתְחֵי שְׁעָרִים בָּעִיר אֲמָרֶיהָ תֹאמֵר׃
22	"How long will you simple ones love simplicity, You scoffers be eager to scoff, You dullards hate knowledge?	כב עַד־מָתַי פְּתָיִם תְּאֵהֲבוּ פֶתִי וְלֵצִים לָצוֹן חָמְדוּ לָהֶם וּכְסִילִים יִשְׂנְאוּ־דָעַת׃
23	You are indifferent to my rebuke; I will now speak my mind to you, And let you know my thoughts.	כג תָּשׁוּבוּ לְתוֹכַחְתִּי הִנֵּה אַבִּיעָה לָכֶם רוּחִי אוֹדִיעָה דְבָרַי אֶתְכֶם׃
24	Since you refused me when I called, And paid no heed when I extended my hand,	כד יַעַן קָרָאתִי וַתְּמָאֵנוּ נָטִיתִי יָדִי וְאֵין מַקְשִׁיב׃
25	You spurned all my advice, And would not hear my rebuke,	כה וַתִּפְרְעוּ כָל־עֲצָתִי וְתוֹכַחְתִּי לֹא אֲבִיתֶם׃
26	I will laugh at your calamity, And mock when terror comes upon you,	כו גַּם־אֲנִי בְּאֵידְכֶם אֶשְׂחָק אֶלְעַג בְּבֹא פַחְדְּכֶם׃
27	When terror comes like a disaster, And calamity arrives like a whirlwind, When trouble and distress come upon you.	כז בְּבֹא כשאוה [כְשׁוֹאָה] פַּחְדְּכֶם וְאֵידְכֶם כְּסוּפָה יֶאֱתֶה בְּבֹא עֲלֵיכֶם צָרָה וְצוּקָה׃
28	Then they shall call me but I will not answer; They shall seek me but not find me.	כח אָז יִקְרָאֻנְנִי וְלֹא אֶעֱנֶה יְשַׁחֲרֻנְנִי וְלֹא יִמְצָאֻנְנִי׃
29	Because they hated knowledge, And did not choose fear of *Hashem*;	כט תַּחַת כִּי־שָׂנְאוּ דָעַת וְיִרְאַת יְהוָה לֹא בָחָרוּ׃
30	They refused my advice, And disdained all my rebukes,	ל לֹא־אָבוּ לַעֲצָתִי נָאֲצוּ כָּל־תּוֹכַחְתִּי׃
31	They shall eat the fruit of their ways, And have their fill of their own counsels.	לא וְיֹאכְלוּ מִפְּרִי דַרְכָּם וּמִמֹּעֲצֹתֵיהֶם יִשְׂבָּעוּ׃
32	The tranquillity of the simple will kill them, And the complacency of dullards will destroy them.	לב כִּי מְשׁוּבַת פְּתָיִם תַּהַרְגֵם וְשַׁלְוַת כְּסִילִים תְּאַבְּדֵם׃
33	But he who listens to me will dwell in safety, Untroubled by the terror of misfortune."	לג וְשֹׁמֵעַ לִי יִשְׁכָּן־בֶּטַח וְשַׁאֲנַן מִפַּחַד רָעָה׃

Mishlei/Proverbs
Chapter 2

משלי
פרק ב

2

1 My son, if you accept my words And treasure up my commandments;

א בְּנִי אִם־תִּקַּח אֲמָרָי וּמִצְוֺתַי תִּצְפֹּן אִתָּךְ:

2 If you make your ear attentive to wisdom And your mind open to discernment;

ב לְהַקְשִׁיב לַחָכְמָה אָזְנֶךָ תַּטֶּה לִבְּךָ לַתְּבוּנָה:

3 If you call to understanding And cry aloud to discernment,

ג כִּי אִם לַבִּינָה תִקְרָא לַתְּבוּנָה תִּתֵּן קוֹלֶךָ:

4 If you seek it as you do silver And search for it as for treasures,

ד אִם־תְּבַקְשֶׁנָּה כַכָּסֶף וְכַמַּטְמוֹנִים תַּחְפְּשֶׂנָּה:

5 Then you will understand the fear of *Hashem* And attain knowledge of *Hashem*.

ה אָז תָּבִין יִרְאַת יְהוָה וְדַעַת אֱלֹהִים תִּמְצָא:

6 For *Hashem* grants wisdom; Knowledge and discernment are by His decree.

ו כִּי־יְהוָה יִתֵּן חָכְמָה מִפִּיו דַּעַת וּתְבוּנָה:

7 He reserves ability for the upright And is a shield for those who live blamelessly,

ז וְצָפַן [יִצְפֹּן] לַיְשָׁרִים תּוּשִׁיָּה מָגֵן לְהֹלְכֵי תֹם:

8 Guarding the paths of justice, Protecting the way of those loyal to Him.

ח לִנְצֹר אָרְחוֹת מִשְׁפָּט וְדֶרֶךְ חֲסִידָו [חֲסִידָיו] יִשְׁמֹר:

9 You will then understand what is right, just, And equitable – every good course.

ט אָז תָּבִין צֶדֶק וּמִשְׁפָּט וּמֵישָׁרִים כָּל־מַעְגַּל־טוֹב:

10 For wisdom will enter your mind And knowledge will delight you.

י כִּי־תָבוֹא חָכְמָה בְלִבֶּךָ וְדַעַת לְנַפְשְׁךָ יִנְעָם:

11 Foresight will protect you, And discernment will guard you.

יא מְזִמָּה תִּשְׁמֹר עָלֶיךָ תְּבוּנָה תִנְצְרֶכָּה:

12 It will save you from the way of evil men, From men who speak duplicity,

יב לְהַצִּילְךָ מִדֶּרֶךְ רָע מֵאִישׁ מְדַבֵּר תַּהְפֻּכוֹת:

13 Who leave the paths of rectitude To follow the ways of darkness,

יג הַעֹזְבִים אָרְחוֹת יֹשֶׁר לָלֶכֶת בְּדַרְכֵי־חֹשֶׁךְ:

14 Who rejoice in doing evil And exult in the duplicity of evil men,

יד הַשְּׂמֵחִים לַעֲשׂוֹת רָע יָגִילוּ בְּתַהְפֻּכוֹת רָע:

15 Men whose paths are crooked And who are devious in their course.

טו אֲשֶׁר אָרְחֹתֵיהֶם עִקְּשִׁים וּנְלוֹזִים בְּמַעְגְּלוֹתָם:

16 It will save you from the forbidden woman, From the alien woman whose talk is smooth,

טז לְהַצִּילְךָ מֵאִשָּׁה זָרָה מִנָּכְרִיָּה אֲמָרֶיהָ הֶחֱלִיקָה:

17 Who forsakes the companion of her youth And disregards the covenant of her God.

יז הַעֹזֶבֶת אַלּוּף נְעוּרֶיהָ וְאֶת־בְּרִית אֱלֹהֶיהָ שָׁכֵחָה:

18 Her house sinks down to Death, And her course leads to the shades.

יח כִּי שָׁחָה אֶל־מָוֶת בֵּיתָהּ וְאֶל־רְפָאִים מַעְגְּלֹתֶיהָ:

19 All who go to her cannot return And find again the paths of life.

יט כָּל־בָּאֶיהָ לֹא יְשׁוּבוּן וְלֹא־יַשִּׂיגוּ אָרְחוֹת חַיִּים:

Mishlei/Proverbs
Chapter 3

משלי
פרק ג

20 So follow the way of the good And keep to the paths of the just.

כ לְמַעַן תֵּלֵךְ בְּדֶרֶךְ טוֹבִים וְאָרְחוֹת צַדִּיקִים תִּשְׁמֹר:

21 For the upright will inhabit the earth, The blameless will remain in it.

כא כִּי־יְשָׁרִים יִשְׁכְּנוּ אָרֶץ וּתְמִימִים יִוָּתְרוּ בָהּ:

kee y'-sha-REEM yish-k'-nu A-retz ut-mee-MEEM yi-va-t'-RU VAH

22 While the wicked will vanish from the land And the treacherous will be rooted out of it.

כב וּרְשָׁעִים מֵאֶרֶץ יִכָּרֵתוּ וּבוֹגְדִים יִסְּחוּ מִמֶּנָּה:

3 1 My son, do not forget my teaching, But let your mind retain my commandments;

ג א בְּנִי תּוֹרָתִי אַל־תִּשְׁכָּח וּמִצְוֺתַי יִצֹּר לִבֶּךָ:

2 For they will bestow on you length of days, Years of life and well-being.

ב כִּי אֹרֶךְ יָמִים וּשְׁנוֹת חַיִּים וְשָׁלוֹם יוֹסִיפוּ לָךְ:

3 Let fidelity and steadfastness not leave you; Bind them about your throat, Write them on the tablet of your mind,

ג חֶסֶד וֶאֱמֶת אַל־יַעַזְבֻךָ קָשְׁרֵם עַל־גַּרְגְּרוֹתֶיךָ כָּתְבֵם עַל־לוּחַ לִבֶּךָ:

4 And you will find favor and approbation In the eyes of *Hashem* and man.

ד וּמְצָא־חֵן וְשֵׂכֶל־טוֹב בְּעֵינֵי אֱלֹהִים וְאָדָם:

5 Trust in *Hashem* with all your heart, And do not rely on your own understanding.

ה בְּטַח אֶל־יְהֹוָה בְּכָל־לִבֶּךָ וְאֶל־בִּינָתְךָ אַל־תִּשָּׁעֵן:

6 In all your ways acknowledge Him, And He will make your paths smooth.

ו בְּכָל־דְּרָכֶיךָ דָעֵהוּ וְהוּא יְיַשֵּׁר אֹרְחֹתֶיךָ:

7 Do not be wise in your own eyes; Fear *Hashem* and shun evil.

ז אַל־תְּהִי חָכָם בְּעֵינֶיךָ יְרָא אֶת־יְהֹוָה וְסוּר מֵרָע:

8 It will be a cure for your body, A tonic for your bones.

ח רִפְאוּת תְּהִי לְשָׁרֶּךָ וְשִׁקּוּי לְעַצְמוֹתֶיךָ:

9 Honor *Hashem* with your wealth, With the best of all your income,

ט כַּבֵּד אֶת־יְהֹוָה מֵהוֹנֶךָ וּמֵרֵאשִׁית כָּל־תְּבוּאָתֶךָ:

ka-BAYD et a-do-NAI may-ho-NE-kha u-may-ray-SHEET kol t'-vu-a-TE-kha

10 And your barns will be filled with grain, Your vats will burst with new wine.

י וְיִמָּלְאוּ אֲסָמֶיךָ שָׂבָע וְתִירוֹשׁ יְקָבֶיךָ יִפְרֹצוּ:

2:21 For the upright will inhabit the earth The word *eretz*, translated here as 'earth,' also means 'land.' According to Yehuda Keel, author of the *Da'at Mikra* commentary on *Sefer Mishlei*, this is a reference to the Land of Israel. In this verse, King *Shlomo* reminds us of *Hashem*'s promise to the Israelites in the desert, that if they walk in His ways, they will remain in the land which He has given them (see Deuteronomy 4:1). *Eretz Yisrael* is promised to those who remain steadfast in their commitment to God's words, not only in deed, but also in thought.

3:9 With the best of all your income Reisheet kol t'vuatecha (ראשית כל תבואתך), translated here as 'the best of all your income,' literally means 'the first of your grain.' Offering the first of our crops to God reminds us how much we owe Him. It is easy to forget how much *Hashem* has given us, as we get caught up in our own efforts towards success. God commands us to bring the first of our harvest each year to the *Beit Hamikdash* in *Yerushalayim* (see Deuteronomy 26:2), to remind us that He is behind everything that happens to us, and the constant source of our success.

The seven species from which the first fruit offering was brought

Mishlei/Proverbs
Chapter 3

11 Do not reject the discipline of *Hashem*, my son; Do not abhor His rebuke.

12 For whom *Hashem* loves, He rebukes, As a father the son whom he favors.

13 Happy is the man who finds wisdom, The man who attains understanding.

14 Her value in trade is better than silver, Her yield, greater than gold.

15 She is more precious than rubies; All of your goods cannot equal her.

16 In her right hand is length of days, In her left, riches and honor.

17 Her ways are pleasant ways, And all her paths, peaceful.

18 She is a tree of life to those who grasp her, And whoever holds on to her is happy.

19 *Hashem* founded the earth by wisdom; He established the heavens by understanding;

20 By His knowledge the depths burst apart, And the skies distilled dew.

21 My son, do not lose sight of them; Hold on to resourcefulness and foresight.

22 They will give life to your spirit And grace to your throat.

23 Then you will go your way safely And not injure your feet.

24 When you lie down you will be unafraid; You will lie down and your sleep will be sweet.

25 You will not fear sudden terror Or the disaster that comes upon the wicked,

26 For *Hashem* will be your trust; He will keep your feet from being caught.

27 Do not withhold good from one who deserves it When you have the power to do it [for him].

28 Do not say to your fellow, "Come back again; I'll give it to you tomorrow," when you have it with you.

29 Do not devise harm against your fellow Who lives trustfully with you.

משלי
פרק ג

יא מוּסַר יְהוָה בְּנִי אַל־תִּמְאָס וְאַל־תָּקֹץ בְּתוֹכַחְתּוֹ׃

יב כִּי אֶת אֲשֶׁר יֶאֱהַב יְהוָה יוֹכִיחַ וּכְאָב אֶת־בֵּן יִרְצֶה׃

יג אַשְׁרֵי אָדָם מָצָא חָכְמָה וְאָדָם יָפִיק תְּבוּנָה׃

יד כִּי טוֹב סַחְרָהּ מִסְּחַר־כָּסֶף וּמֵחָרוּץ תְּבוּאָתָהּ׃

טו יְקָרָה הִיא מִפְּנִיִּים [מִפְּנִינִים] וְכָל־חֲפָצֶיךָ לֹא יִשְׁווּ־בָהּ׃

טז אֹרֶךְ יָמִים בִּימִינָהּ בִּשְׂמֹאולָהּ עֹשֶׁר וְכָבוֹד׃

יז דְּרָכֶיהָ דַרְכֵי־נֹעַם וְכָל־נְתִיבוֹתֶיהָ שָׁלוֹם׃

יח עֵץ־חַיִּים הִיא לַמַּחֲזִיקִים בָּהּ וְתֹמְכֶיהָ מְאֻשָּׁר׃

יט יְהוָה בְּחָכְמָה יָסַד־אָרֶץ כּוֹנֵן שָׁמַיִם בִּתְבוּנָה׃

כ בְּדַעְתּוֹ תְּהוֹמוֹת נִבְקָעוּ וּשְׁחָקִים יִרְעֲפוּ־טָל׃

כא בְּנִי אַל־יָלֻזוּ מֵעֵינֶיךָ נְצֹר תֻּשִׁיָּה וּמְזִמָּה׃

כב וְיִהְיוּ חַיִּים לְנַפְשֶׁךָ וְחֵן לְגַרְגְּרֹתֶיךָ׃

כג אָז תֵּלֵךְ לָבֶטַח דַּרְכֶּךָ וְרַגְלְךָ לֹא תִגּוֹף׃

כד אִם־תִּשְׁכַּב לֹא־תִפְחָד וְשָׁכַבְתָּ וְעָרְבָה שְׁנָתֶךָ׃

כה אַל־תִּירָא מִפַּחַד פִּתְאֹם וּמִשֹּׁאַת רְשָׁעִים כִּי תָבֹא׃

כו כִּי־יְהוָה יִהְיֶה בְכִסְלֶךָ וְשָׁמַר רַגְלְךָ מִלָּכֶד׃

כז אַל־תִּמְנַע־טוֹב מִבְּעָלָיו בִּהְיוֹת לְאֵל יָדֶיךָ [יָדְךָ] לַעֲשׂוֹת׃

כח אַל־תֹּאמַר לְרֵעֶיךָ [לְרֵעֲךָ] לֵךְ וָשׁוּב וּמָחָר אֶתֵּן וְיֵשׁ אִתָּךְ׃

כט אַל־תַּחֲרֹשׁ עַל־רֵעֲךָ רָעָה וְהוּא־יוֹשֵׁב לָבֶטַח אִתָּךְ׃

Mishlei/Proverbs
Chapter 4

משלי
פרק ד

30	Do not quarrel with a man for no cause, When he has done you no harm.	אַל־תָּרוֹב [תָּרִיב] עִם־אָדָם חִנָּם אִם־לֹא גְמָלְךָ רָעָה:
31	Do not envy a lawless man, Or choose any of his ways;	אַל־תְּקַנֵּא בְּאִישׁ חָמָס וְאַל־תִּבְחַר בְּכׇל־דְּרָכָיו:
32	For the devious man is an abomination to *Hashem*, But He is intimate with the straightforward.	כִּי תוֹעֲבַת יְהֹוָה נָלוֹז וְאֶת־יְשָׁרִים סוֹדוֹ:
33	The curse of *Hashem* is on the house of the wicked, But He blesses the abode of the righteous.	מְאֵרַת יְהֹוָה בְּבֵית רָשָׁע וּנְוֵה צַדִּיקִים יְבָרֵךְ:
34	At scoffers He scoffs, But to the lowly He shows grace.	אִם־לַלֵּצִים הוּא־יָלִיץ וְלַעֲנִיִּים [וְלַעֲנָוִים] יִתֶּן־חֵן:
35	The wise shall obtain honor, But dullards get disgrace as their portion.	כָּבוֹד חֲכָמִים יִנְחָלוּ וּכְסִילִים מֵרִים קָלוֹן:

4

1	Sons, heed the discipline of a father; Listen and learn discernment,	שִׁמְעוּ בָנִים מוּסַר אָב וְהַקְשִׁיבוּ לָדַעַת בִּינָה:
2	For I give you good instruction; Do not forsake my teaching.	כִּי לֶקַח טוֹב נָתַתִּי לָכֶם תּוֹרָתִי אַל־תַּעֲזֹבוּ:
3	Once I was a son to my father, The tender darling of my mother.	כִּי־בֵן הָיִיתִי לְאָבִי רַךְ וְיָחִיד לִפְנֵי אִמִּי:

kee VAYN ha-YEE-tee l'-a-VEE RAKH v'-ya-KHEED lif-NAY i-MEE

4	He instructed me and said to me, "Let your mind hold on to my words; Keep my commandments and you will live.	וַיֹּרֵנִי וַיֹּאמֶר לִי יִתְמׇךְ־דְּבָרַי לִבֶּךָ שְׁמֹר מִצְוֺתַי וֶחְיֵה:
5	Acquire wisdom, acquire discernment; Do not forget and do not swerve from my words.	קְנֵה חׇכְמָה קְנֵה בִינָה אַל־תִּשְׁכַּח וְאַל־תֵּט מֵאִמְרֵי־פִי:
6	Do not forsake her and she will guard you; Love her and she will protect you.	אַל־תַּעַזְבֶהָ וְתִשְׁמְרֶךָּ אֱהָבֶהָ וְתִצְּרֶךָּ:
7	The beginning of wisdom is – acquire wisdom; With all your acquisitions, acquire discernment.	רֵאשִׁית חׇכְמָה קְנֵה חׇכְמָה וּבְכׇל־קִנְיָנְךָ קְנֵה בִינָה:
8	Hug her to you and she will exalt you; She will bring you honor if you embrace her.	סַלְסְלֶהָ וּתְרוֹמְמֶךָּ תְּכַבֵּדְךָ כִּי תְחַבְּקֶנָּה:
9	She will adorn your head with a graceful wreath; Crown you with a glorious diadem."	תִּתֵּן לְרֹאשְׁךָ לִוְיַת־חֵן עֲטֶרֶת תִּפְאֶרֶת תְּמַגְּנֶךָּ:
10	My son, heed and take in my words, And you will have many years of life.	שְׁמַע בְּנִי וְקַח אֲמָרָי וְיִרְבּוּ לְךָ שְׁנוֹת חַיִּים:

4:3 Once I was a son to my father Although this verse can be understood literally, it also contains a parable. The speaker represents the Nation of Israel, described in the Bible (Exodus 4:22) as *Hashem*'s firstborn son. It is to that chosen child that God imparts the wisdom of His *Torah*, just as a father imparts precious wisdom to his son (see verse 4). Like the child in this verse, the Nation of Israel received the *Torah* at a tender stage, shortly after being released from the bondage of Egypt.

Mishlei/Proverbs
Chapter 5

משלי
פרק ה

11 I instruct you in the way of wisdom; I guide you in straight courses.

יא בְּדֶרֶךְ חָכְמָה הֹרֵתִיךָ הִדְרַכְתִּיךָ בְּמַעְגְּלֵי־יֹשֶׁר:

12 You will walk without breaking stride; When you run, you will not stumble.

יב בְּלֶכְתְּךָ לֹא־יֵצַר צַעֲדֶךָ וְאִם־תָּרוּץ לֹא תִכָּשֵׁל:

13 Hold fast to discipline; do not let go; Keep it; it is your life.

יג הַחֲזֵק בַּמּוּסָר אַל־תֶּרֶף נִצְּרֶהָ כִּי־הִיא חַיֶּיךָ:

14 Do not enter on the path of the wicked; Do not walk on the way of evil men.

יד בְּאֹרַח רְשָׁעִים אַל־תָּבֹא וְאַל־תְּאַשֵּׁר בְּדֶרֶךְ רָעִים:

15 Avoid it; do not pass through it; Turn away from it; pass it by.

טו פְּרָעֵהוּ אַל־תַּעֲבָר־בּוֹ שְׂטֵה מֵעָלָיו וַעֲבוֹר:

16 For they cannot sleep unless they have done evil; Unless they make someone fall they are robbed of sleep.

טז כִּי לֹא יִשְׁנוּ אִם־לֹא יָרֵעוּ וְנִגְזְלָה שְׁנָתָם אִם־לֹא יכשולו [יַכְשִׁילוּ]:

17 They eat the bread of wickedness And drink the wine of lawlessness.

יז כִּי לָחֲמוּ לֶחֶם רֶשַׁע וְיֵין חֲמָסִים יִשְׁתּוּ:

18 The path of the righteous is like radiant sunlight, Ever brightening until noon.

יח וְאֹרַח צַדִּיקִים כְּאוֹר נֹגַהּ הוֹלֵךְ וָאוֹר עַד־נְכוֹן הַיּוֹם:

19 The way of the wicked is all darkness; They do not know what will make them stumble.

יט דֶּרֶךְ רְשָׁעִים כָּאֲפֵלָה לֹא יָדְעוּ בַּמֶּה יִכָּשֵׁלוּ:

20 My son, listen to my speech; Incline your ear to my words.

כ בְּנִי לִדְבָרַי הַקְשִׁיבָה לַאֲמָרַי הַט־אָזְנֶךָ:

21 Do not lose sight of them; Keep them in your mind.

כא אַל־יַלִּיזוּ מֵעֵינֶיךָ שָׁמְרֵם בְּתוֹךְ לְבָבֶךָ:

22 They are life to him who finds them, Healing for his whole body.

כב כִּי־חַיִּים הֵם לְמֹצְאֵיהֶם וּלְכָל־בְּשָׂרוֹ מַרְפֵּא:

23 More than all that you guard, guard your mind, For it is the source of life.

כג מִכָּל־מִשְׁמָר נְצֹר לִבֶּךָ כִּי־מִמֶּנּוּ תּוֹצְאוֹת חַיִּים:

24 Put crooked speech away from you; Keep devious talk far from you.

כד הָסֵר מִמְּךָ עִקְּשׁוּת פֶּה וּלְזוּת שְׂפָתַיִם הַרְחֵק מִמֶּךָּ:

25 Let your eyes look forward, Your gaze be straight ahead.

כה עֵינֶיךָ לְנֹכַח יַבִּיטוּ וְעַפְעַפֶּיךָ יַיְשִׁרוּ נֶגְדֶּךָ:

26 Survey the course you take, And all your ways will prosper.

כו פַּלֵּס מַעְגַּל רַגְלֶךָ וְכָל־דְּרָכֶיךָ יִכֹּנוּ:

27 Do not swerve to the right or the left; Keep your feet from evil.

כז אַל־תֵּט־יָמִין וּשְׂמֹאול הָסֵר רַגְלְךָ מֵרָע:

5

1 My son, listen to my wisdom; Incline your ear to my insight,

ה א בְּנִי לְחָכְמָתִי הַקְשִׁיבָה לִתְבוּנָתִי הַט־אָזְנֶךָ:

2 That you may have foresight, While your lips hold fast to knowledge.

ב לִשְׁמֹר מְזִמּוֹת וְדַעַת שְׂפָתֶיךָ יִנְצֹרוּ:

Mishlei/Proverbs
Chapter 5

משלי
פרק ה

3 For the lips of a forbidden woman drip honey; Her mouth is smoother than oil;

ג כִּי נֹפֶת תִּטֹּפְנָה שִׂפְתֵי זָרָה וְחָלָק מִשֶּׁמֶן חִכָּהּ׃

4 But in the end she is as bitter as wormwood, Sharp as a two-edged sword.

ד וְאַחֲרִיתָהּ מָרָה כַלַּעֲנָה חַדָּה כְּחֶרֶב פִּיּוֹת׃

5 Her feet go down to Death; Her steps take hold of Sheol.

ה רַגְלֶיהָ יֹרְדוֹת מָוֶת שְׁאוֹל צְעָדֶיהָ יִתְמֹכוּ׃

6 She does not chart a path of life; Her course meanders for lack of knowledge.

ו אֹרַח חַיִּים פֶּן־תְּפַלֵּס נָעוּ מַעְגְּלֹתֶיהָ לֹא תֵדָע׃

7 So now, sons, pay heed to me, And do not swerve from the words of my mouth.

ז וְעַתָּה בָנִים שִׁמְעוּ־לִי וְאַל־תָּסוּרוּ מֵאִמְרֵי־פִי׃

8 Keep yourself far away from her; Do not come near the doorway of her house

ח הַרְחֵק מֵעָלֶיהָ דַרְכֶּךָ וְאַל־תִּקְרַב אֶל־פֶּתַח בֵּיתָהּ׃

9 Lest you give up your vigor to others, Your years to a ruthless one;

ט פֶּן־תִּתֵּן לַאֲחֵרִים הוֹדֶךָ וּשְׁנֹתֶיךָ לְאַכְזָרִי׃

10 Lest strangers eat their fill of your strength, And your toil be for the house of another;

י פֶּן־יִשְׂבְּעוּ זָרִים כֹּחֶךָ וַעֲצָבֶיךָ בְּבֵית נָכְרִי׃

11 And in the end you roar, When your flesh and body are consumed,

יא וְנָהַמְתָּ בְאַחֲרִיתֶךָ בִּכְלוֹת בְּשָׂרְךָ וּשְׁאֵרֶךָ׃

12 And say, "O how I hated discipline, And heartily spurned rebuke.

יב וְאָמַרְתָּ אֵיךְ שָׂנֵאתִי מוּסָר וְתוֹכַחַת נָאַץ לִבִּי׃

13 I did not pay heed to my teachers, Or incline my ear to my instructors.

יג וְלֹא־שָׁמַעְתִּי בְּקוֹל מוֹרָי וְלִמְלַמְּדַי לֹא־הִטִּיתִי אָזְנִי׃

14 Soon I was in dire trouble Amidst the assembled congregation."

יד כִּמְעַט הָיִיתִי בְכָל־רָע בְּתוֹךְ קָהָל וְעֵדָה׃

15 Drink water from your own cistern, Running water from your own well.

טו שְׁתֵה־מַיִם מִבּוֹרֶךָ וְנֹזְלִים מִתּוֹךְ בְּאֵרֶךָ׃

16 Your springs will gush forth In streams in the public squares.

טז יָפוּצוּ מַעְיְנֹתֶיךָ חוּצָה בָּרְחֹבוֹת פַּלְגֵי־מָיִם׃

17 They will be yours alone, Others having no part with you.

יז יִהְיוּ־לְךָ לְבַדֶּךָ וְאֵין לְזָרִים אִתָּךְ׃

18 Let your fountain be blessed; Find joy in the wife of your youth –

y'-HEE m'-ko-r'-KHA va-RUKH us-MAKH may-AY-shet n'-u-RE-kha

יח יְהִי־מְקוֹרְךָ בָרוּךְ וּשְׂמַח מֵאֵשֶׁת נְעוּרֶךָ׃

5:18 Find joy in the wife of your youth King *Shlomo* compares the wife of one's youth to a fountain, a source of life-giving water, because she is a source of continued life through the children she bears. Water is a precious commodity in Israel, as rain falls in unpredictable and sometimes limited quantities, and only in its season. Being dependent on the Lord for rain ensures that His children must maintain a close connection with Him in the Land of Israel, and recognize the He is the true source of life and all of its blessings.

Mishlei/Proverbs

Chapter 6

19 A loving doe, a graceful mountain goat. Let her breasts satisfy you at all times; Be infatuated with love of her always.

20 Why be infatuated, my son, with a forbidden woman? Why clasp the bosom of an alien woman?

21 For a man's ways are before the eyes of *Hashem*; He surveys his entire course.

22 The wicked man will be trapped in his iniquities; He will be caught up in the ropes of his sin.

23 He will die for lack of discipline, Infatuated by his great folly.

6

1 My son, if you have stood surety for your fellow, Given your hand for another,

2 You have been trapped by the words of your mouth, Snared by the words of your mouth.

3 Do this, then, my son, to extricate yourself, For you have come into the power of your fellow: Go grovel – and badger your fellow;

4 Give your eyes no sleep, Your pupils no slumber.

5 Save yourself like a deer out of the hand [of a hunter], Like a bird out of the hand of a fowler.

6 Lazybones, go to the ant; Study its ways and learn.

7 Without leaders, officers, or rulers,

8 It lays up its stores during the summer, Gathers in its food at the harvest.

9 How long will you lie there, lazybones; When will you wake from your sleep?

10 A bit more sleep, a bit more slumber, A bit more hugging yourself in bed,

11 And poverty will come calling upon you, And want, like a man with a shield.

12 A scoundrel, an evil man Lives by crooked speech,

13 Winking his eyes, Shuffling his feet, Pointing his finger.

14 Duplicity is in his heart; He plots evil all the time; He incites quarrels.

משלי

פרק ו

יט אַיֶּלֶת אֲהָבִים וְיַעֲלַת־חֵן דַּדֶּיהָ יְרַוֻּךָ בְכָל־עֵת בְּאַהֲבָתָהּ תִּשְׁגֶּה תָמִיד:

כ וְלָמָּה תִשְׁגֶּה בְנִי בְזָרָה וּתְחַבֵּק חֵק נָכְרִיָּה:

כא כִּי נֹכַח עֵינֵי יְהֹוָה דַּרְכֵי־אִישׁ וְכָל־מַעְגְּלֹתָיו מְפַלֵּס:

כב עֲווֹנוֹתָיו יִלְכְּדֻנוֹ אֶת־הָרָשָׁע וּבְחַבְלֵי חַטָּאתוֹ יִתָּמֵךְ:

כג הוּא יָמוּת בְּאֵין מוּסָר וּבְרֹב אִוַּלְתּוֹ יִשְׁגֶּה:

ו א בְּנִי אִם־עָרַבְתָּ לְרֵעֶךָ תָּקַעְתָּ לַזָּר כַּפֶּיךָ:

ב נוֹקַשְׁתָּ בְאִמְרֵי־פִיךָ נִלְכַּדְתָּ בְּאִמְרֵי־פִיךָ:

ג עֲשֵׂה זֹאת אֵפוֹא בְּנִי וְהִנָּצֵל כִּי בָאתָ בְכַף־רֵעֶךָ לֵךְ הִתְרַפֵּס וּרְהַב רֵעֶיךָ:

ד אַל־תִּתֵּן שֵׁנָה לְעֵינֶיךָ וּתְנוּמָה לְעַפְעַפֶּיךָ:

ה הִנָּצֵל כִּצְבִי מִיָּד וּכְצִפּוֹר מִיַּד יָקוּשׁ:

ו לֵךְ־אֶל־נְמָלָה עָצֵל רְאֵה דְרָכֶיהָ וַחֲכָם:

ז אֲשֶׁר אֵין־לָהּ קָצִין שֹׁטֵר וּמֹשֵׁל:

ח תָּכִין בַּקַּיִץ לַחְמָהּ אָגְרָה בַקָּצִיר מַאֲכָלָהּ:

ט עַד־מָתַי עָצֵל תִּשְׁכָּב מָתַי תָּקוּם מִשְּׁנָתֶךָ:

י מְעַט שֵׁנוֹת מְעַט תְּנוּמוֹת מְעַט חִבֻּק יָדַיִם לִשְׁכָּב:

יא וּבָא־כִמְהַלֵּךְ רֵאשֶׁךָ וּמַחְסֹרְךָ כְּאִישׁ מָגֵן:

יב אָדָם בְּלִיַּעַל אִישׁ אָוֶן הוֹלֵךְ עִקְּשׁוּת פֶּה:

יג קֹרֵץ בְּעֵינָו מֹלֵל בְּרַגְלָו מֹרֶה בְּאֶצְבְּעֹתָיו:

יד תַּהְפֻּכוֹת בְּלִבּוֹ חֹרֵשׁ רָע בְּכָל־עֵת מדנים [מִדְיָנִים] יְשַׁלֵּחַ:

1661

Mishlei/Proverbs
Chapter 6

משלי
פרק ו

15 Therefore calamity will come upon him without warning; Suddenly he will be broken beyond repair.

טו עַל־כֵּן פִּתְאֹם יָבוֹא אֵידוֹ פֶּתַע יִשָּׁבֵר וְאֵין מַרְפֵּא:

16 Six things *Hashem* hates; Seven are an abomination to Him:

טז שֶׁשׁ־הֵנָּה שָׂנֵא יְהוָה וְשֶׁבַע תּוֹעֲבוֹת [תּוֹעֲבַת] נַפְשׁוֹ:

17 A haughty bearing, A lying tongue, Hands that shed innocent blood,

יז עֵינַיִם רָמוֹת לְשׁוֹן שָׁקֶר וְיָדַיִם שֹׁפְכוֹת דָּם־נָקִי:

18 A mind that hatches evil plots, Feet quick to run to evil,

יח לֵב חֹרֵשׁ מַחְשְׁבוֹת אָוֶן רַגְלַיִם מְמַהֲרוֹת לָרוּץ לָרָעָה:

19 A false witness testifying lies, And one who incites brothers to quarrel.

יט יָפִיחַ כְּזָבִים עֵד שָׁקֶר וּמְשַׁלֵּחַ מְדָנִים בֵּין אַחִים:

20 My son, keep your father's commandment; Do not forsake your mother's teaching.

כ נְצֹר בְּנִי מִצְוַת אָבִיךָ וְאַל־תִּטֹּשׁ תּוֹרַת אִמֶּךָ:

21 Tie them over your heart always; Bind them around your throat.

כא קָשְׁרֵם עַל־לִבְּךָ תָמִיד עָנְדֵם עַל־גַּרְגְּרֹתֶךָ:

22 When you walk it will lead you; When you lie down it will watch over you; And when you are awake it will talk with you.

כב בְּהִתְהַלֶּכְךָ תַּנְחֶה אֹתָךְ בְּשָׁכְבְּךָ תִּשְׁמֹר עָלֶיךָ וַהֲקִיצוֹתָ הִיא תְשִׂיחֶךָ:

23 For the commandment is a lamp, The teaching is a light, And the way to life is the rebuke that disciplines.

כג כִּי נֵר מִצְוָה וְתוֹרָה אוֹר וְדֶרֶךְ חַיִּים תּוֹכְחוֹת מוּסָר:

KEE NAYR mitz-VAH v'-TO-rah OR v'-DE-rekh kha-YEEM to-kh'-KHOT mu-SAR

24 It will keep you from an evil woman, From the smooth tongue of a forbidden woman.

כד לִשְׁמָרְךָ מֵאֵשֶׁת רָע מֵחֶלְקַת לָשׁוֹן נָכְרִיָּה:

25 Do not lust for her beauty Or let her captivate you with her eyes.

כה אַל־תַּחְמֹד יָפְיָהּ בִּלְבָבֶךָ וְאַל־תִּקָּחֲךָ בְּעַפְעַפֶּיהָ:

26 The last loaf of bread will go for a harlot; A married woman will snare a person of honor.

כו כִּי בְעַד־אִשָּׁה זוֹנָה עַד־כִּכַּר לָחֶם וְאֵשֶׁת אִישׁ נֶפֶשׁ יְקָרָה תָצוּד:

27 Can a man rake embers into his bosom Without burning his clothes?

כז הֲיַחְתֶּה אִישׁ אֵשׁ בְּחֵיקוֹ וּבְגָדָיו לֹא תִשָּׂרַפְנָה:

6:23 For the commandment is a lamp, the teaching is a light The Talmud (*Bava Batra* 4a) quotes this verse in a passage explaining why the wicked King Herod was motivated to renovate and beautify the second *Beit Hamikdash*. Herod had engaged in a murderous rampage against the leading rabbis of his generation, only to regret his evil actions after he came to know and respect the Sage *Bava ben Buta*. "What can I do to repent my evil ways?" King Herod begged *Bava*. Quoting this verse, *Bava* responded, "You who extinguished the light of the world by killing so many *Torah* scholars, can atone by bringing more light into the world." Herod listened to the rabbi and immediately embarked upon a massive architectural project, restoring the glory of the *Beit Hamikdash*, and causing the second Temple to surpass even the beauty of the first Temple built by King *Shlomo*. In this way, he strengthened the light emanating to the world.

Model of Herod's Temple, Jerusalem

1662

Mishlei/Proverbs
Chapter 7

משלי
פרק ז

28 Can a man walk on live coals Without scorching his feet?

כח אִם־יְהַלֵּךְ אִישׁ עַל־הַגֶּחָלִים וְרַגְלָיו לֹא תִכָּוֶינָה׃

29 It is the same with one who sleeps with his fellow's wife; None who touches her will go unpunished.

כט כֵּן הַבָּא אֶל־אֵשֶׁת רֵעֵהוּ לֹא יִנָּקֶה כָּל־הַנֹּגֵעַ בָּהּ׃

30 A thief is not held in contempt For stealing to appease his hunger;

ל לֹא־יָבוּזוּ לַגַּנָּב כִּי יִגְנוֹב לְמַלֵּא נַפְשׁוֹ כִּי יִרְעָב׃

31 Yet if caught he must pay sevenfold; He must give up all he owns.

לא וְנִמְצָא יְשַׁלֵּם שִׁבְעָתָיִם אֶת־כָּל־הוֹן בֵּיתוֹ יִתֵּן׃

32 He who commits adultery is devoid of sense; Only one who would destroy himself does such a thing.

לב נֹאֵף אִשָּׁה חֲסַר־לֵב מַשְׁחִית נַפְשׁוֹ הוּא יַעֲשֶׂנָּה׃

33 He will meet with disease and disgrace; His reproach will never be expunged.

לג נֶגַע־וְקָלוֹן יִמְצָא וְחֶרְפָּתוֹ לֹא תִמָּחֶה׃

34 The fury of the husband will be passionate; He will show no pity on his day of vengeance.

לד כִּי־קִנְאָה חֲמַת־גָּבֶר וְלֹא־יַחְמוֹל בְּיוֹם נָקָם׃

35 He will not have regard for any ransom; He will refuse your bribe, however great.

לה לֹא־יִשָּׂא פְּנֵי כָל־כֹּפֶר וְלֹא־יֹאבֶה כִּי תַרְבֶּה־שֹׁחַד׃

7 1 My son, heed my words; And store up my commandments with you.

ז א בְּנִי שְׁמֹר אֲמָרָי וּמִצְוֺתַי תִּצְפֹּן אִתָּךְ׃

2 Keep my commandments and live, My teaching, as the apple of your eye.

ב שְׁמֹר מִצְוֺתַי וֶחְיֵה וְתוֹרָתִי כְּאִישׁוֹן עֵינֶיךָ׃

3 Bind them on your fingers; Write them on the tablet of your mind.

ג קָשְׁרֵם עַל־אֶצְבְּעֹתֶיךָ כָּתְבֵם עַל־לוּחַ לִבֶּךָ׃

4 Say to Wisdom, "You are my sister," And call Understanding a kinswoman.

ד אֱמֹר לַחָכְמָה אֲחֹתִי אָתְּ וּמֹדָע לַבִּינָה תִקְרָא׃

5 She will guard you from a forbidden woman; From an alien woman whose talk is smooth.

ה לִשְׁמָרְךָ מֵאִשָּׁה זָרָה מִנָּכְרִיָּה אֲמָרֶיהָ הֶחֱלִיקָה׃

6 From the window of my house, Through my lattice, I looked out

ו כִּי בְּחַלּוֹן בֵּיתִי בְּעַד אֶשְׁנַבִּי נִשְׁקָפְתִּי׃

7 And saw among the simple, Noticed among the youths, A lad devoid of sense.

ז וָאֵרֶא בַפְּתָאיִם אָבִינָה בַבָּנִים נַעַר חֲסַר־לֵב׃

8 He was crossing the street near her corner, Walking toward her house

ח עֹבֵר בַּשּׁוּק אֵצֶל פִּנָּהּ וְדֶרֶךְ בֵּיתָהּ יִצְעָד׃

9 In the dusk of evening, In the dark hours of night.

ט בְּנֶשֶׁף־בְּעֶרֶב יוֹם בְּאִישׁוֹן לַיְלָה וַאֲפֵלָה׃

10 A woman comes toward him Dressed like a harlot, with set purpose.

י וְהִנֵּה אִשָּׁה לִקְרָאתוֹ שִׁית זוֹנָה וּנְצֻרַת לֵב׃

11 She is bustling and restive; She is never at home.

יא הֹמִיָּה הִיא וְסֹרָרֶת בְּבֵיתָהּ לֹא־יִשְׁכְּנוּ רַגְלֶיהָ׃

12 Now in the street, now in the square, She lurks at every corner.

יב פַּעַם בַּחוּץ פַּעַם בָּרְחֹבוֹת וְאֵצֶל כָּל־פִּנָּה תֶאֱרֹב׃

Mishlei/Proverbs
Chapter 7

משלי
פרק ז

13 She lays hold of him and kisses him; Brazenly she says to him,

יג וְהֶחֱזִיקָה בּוֹ וְנָשְׁקָה־לּוֹ הֵעֵזָה פָנֶיהָ וַתֹּאמַר לוֹ:

14 "I had to make a sacrifice of well-being; Today I fulfilled my vows.

יד זִבְחֵי שְׁלָמִים עָלָי הַיּוֹם שִׁלַּמְתִּי נְדָרָי:

ziv-KHAY sh'-la-MEEM a-LAI ha-YOM shi-LAM-tee n'-da-RAI

15 Therefore I have come out to you, Seeking you, and have found you.

טו עַל־כֵּן יָצָאתִי לִקְרָאתֶךָ לְשַׁחֵר פָּנֶיךָ וָאֶמְצָאֶךָּ:

16 I have decked my couch with covers Of dyed Egyptian linen;

טז מַרְבַדִּים רָבַדְתִּי עַרְשִׂי חֲטֻבוֹת אֵטוּן מִצְרָיִם:

17 I have sprinkled my bed With myrrh, aloes, and cinnamon.

יז נַפְתִּי מִשְׁכָּבִי מֹר אֲהָלִים וְקִנָּמוֹן:

18 Let us drink our fill of love till morning; Let us delight in amorous embrace.

יח לְכָה נִרְוֶה דֹדִים עַד־הַבֹּקֶר נִתְעַלְּסָה בָּאֳהָבִים:

19 For the man of the house is away; He is off on a distant journey.

יט כִּי אֵין הָאִישׁ בְּבֵיתוֹ הָלַךְ בְּדֶרֶךְ מֵרָחוֹק:

20 He took his bag of money with him And will return only at mid-month."

כ צְרוֹר־הַכֶּסֶף לָקַח בְּיָדוֹ לְיוֹם הַכֵּסֶא יָבֹא בֵיתוֹ:

21 She sways him with her eloquence, Turns him aside with her smooth talk.

כא הִטַּתּוּ בְּרֹב לִקְחָהּ בְּחֵלֶק שְׂפָתֶיהָ תַּדִּיחֶנּוּ:

22 Thoughtlessly he follows her, Like an ox going to the slaughter, Like a fool to the stocks for punishment –

כב הוֹלֵךְ אַחֲרֶיהָ פִּתְאֹם כְּשׁוֹר אֶל־טֶבַח יָבֹא וּכְעֶכֶס אֶל־מוּסַר אֱוִיל:

23 Until the arrow pierces his liver. He is like a bird rushing into a trap, Not knowing his life is at stake.

כג עַד יְפַלַּח חֵץ כְּבֵדוֹ כְּמַהֵר צִפּוֹר אֶל־פָּח וְלֹא־יָדַע כִּי־בְנַפְשׁוֹ הוּא:

24 Now, sons, listen to me; Pay attention to my words;

כד וְעַתָּה בָנִים שִׁמְעוּ־לִי וְהַקְשִׁיבוּ לְאִמְרֵי־פִי:

25 Let your mind not wander down her ways; Do not stray onto her paths.

כה אַל־יֵשְׂטְ אֶל־דְּרָכֶיהָ לִבֶּךָ אַל־תֵּתַע בִּנְתִיבוֹתֶיהָ:

26 For many are those she has struck dead, And numerous are her victims.

כו כִּי־רַבִּים חֲלָלִים הִפִּילָה וַעֲצֻמִים כָּל־הֲרֻגֶיהָ:

א 7:14 Sacrifice of well-being The sacrifice of well-being is often called the 'peace-offering' based on its Hebrew name, *korban sh'lamim* (קרבן שלמים), which is related to the Hebrew word *shalom* (שלום), 'peace.' According to Jewish tradition, it is called this because the *korban sh'lamim* symbolizes peace and unity, as it is the only offering that is shared by all relevant parties: *Hashem*, via the portions burned on the altar, and the priest and the owner of the sacrifice who each consume part of the meat. It is not a coincidence that this is also the only offering that is not restricted to the *Beit Hamikdash*, but may be eaten anywhere in the city of Jerusalem. The Hebrew name for Jerusalem, *Yerushalayim*, also has the word *shalom* at its root, and indeed, Jerusalem is known as *ir shel shalom*, the city of peace. *Yerushalayim* is meant to be the source for all peace on earth, and is therefore closely connected with the well-being offering.

Jerusalem

קרבן שלמים

Mishlei/Proverbs
Chapter 8

משלי
פרק ח

27 Her house is a highway to Sheol Leading down to Death's inner chambers.

כז דַּרְכֵי שְׁאוֹל בֵּיתָהּ יֹרְדוֹת אֶל־חַדְרֵי־מָוֶת׃

8 1 It is Wisdom calling, Understanding raising her voice.

ח א הֲלֹא־חָכְמָה תִקְרָא וּתְבוּנָה תִּתֵּן קוֹלָהּ׃

2 She takes her stand at the topmost heights, By the wayside, at the crossroads,

ב בְּרֹאשׁ־מְרוֹמִים עֲלֵי־דָרֶךְ בֵּית נְתִיבוֹת נִצָּבָה׃

3 Near the gates at the city entrance; At the entryways, she shouts,

ג לְיַד־שְׁעָרִים לְפִי־קָרֶת מְבוֹא פְתָחִים תָּרֹנָּה׃

4 "O men, I call to you; My cry is to all mankind.

ד אֲלֵיכֶם אִישִׁים אֶקְרָא וְקוֹלִי אֶל־בְּנֵי אָדָם׃

5 O simple ones, learn shrewdness; O dullards, instruct your minds.

ה הָבִינוּ פְתָאיִם עָרְמָה וּכְסִילִים הָבִינוּ לֵב׃

6 Listen, for I speak noble things; Uprightness comes from my lips;

ו שִׁמְעוּ כִּי־נְגִידִים אֲדַבֵּר וּמִפְתַּח שְׂפָתַי מֵישָׁרִים׃

7 My mouth utters truth; Wickedness is abhorrent to my lips.

ז כִּי־אֱמֶת יֶהְגֶּה חִכִּי וְתוֹעֲבַת שְׂפָתַי רֶשַׁע׃

8 All my words are just, None of them perverse or crooked;

ח בְּצֶדֶק כָּל־אִמְרֵי־פִי אֵין בָּהֶם נִפְתָּל וְעִקֵּשׁ׃

9 All are straightforward to the intelligent man, And right to those who have attained knowledge.

ט כֻּלָּם נְכֹחִים לַמֵּבִין וִישָׁרִים לְמֹצְאֵי דָעַת׃

10 Accept my discipline rather than silver, Knowledge rather than choice gold.

י קְחוּ־מוּסָרִי וְאַל־כָּסֶף וְדַעַת מֵחָרוּץ נִבְחָר׃

11 For wisdom is better than rubies; No goods can equal her.

יא כִּי־טוֹבָה חָכְמָה מִפְּנִינִים וְכָל־חֲפָצִים לֹא יִשְׁווּ־בָהּ׃

12 "I, Wisdom, live with Prudence; I attain knowledge and foresight.

יב אֲנִי־חָכְמָה שָׁכַנְתִּי עָרְמָה וְדַעַת מְזִמּוֹת אֶמְצָא׃

13 To fear *Hashem* is to hate evil; I hate pride, arrogance, the evil way, And duplicity in speech.

יג יִרְאַת יְהֹוָה שְׂנֹאת רָע גֵּאָה וְגָאוֹן וְדֶרֶךְ רָע וּפִי תַהְפֻּכוֹת שָׂנֵאתִי׃

14 Mine are counsel and resourcefulness; I am understanding; courage is mine.

יד לִי־עֵצָה וְתוּשִׁיָּה אֲנִי בִינָה לִי גְבוּרָה׃

15 Through me kings reign And rulers decree just laws;

טו בִּי מְלָכִים יִמְלֹכוּ וְרוֹזְנִים יְחֹקְקוּ צֶדֶק׃

16 Through me princes rule, Great men and all the righteous judges.

טז בִּי שָׂרִים יָשֹׂרוּ וּנְדִיבִים כָּל־שֹׁפְטֵי צֶדֶק׃

17 Those who love me I love, And those who seek me will find me.

יז אֲנִי אֹהֲבֶיהָ [אֹהֲבַי] אֵהָב וּמְשַׁחֲרַי יִמְצָאֻנְנִי׃

18 Riches and honor belong to me, Enduring wealth and success.

יח עֹשֶׁר־וְכָבוֹד אִתִּי הוֹן עָתֵק וּצְדָקָה׃

Mishlei/Proverbs

Chapter 8

משלי

פרק ח

19 My fruit is better than gold, fine gold, And my produce better than choice silver.

טוֹב פִּרְיִי מֵחָרוּץ וּמִפָּז וּתְבוּאָתִי מִכֶּסֶף נִבְחָר׃

20 I walk on the way of righteousness, On the paths of justice.

בְּאֹרַח־צְדָקָה אֲהַלֵּךְ בְּתוֹךְ נְתִיבוֹת מִשְׁפָּט׃

21 I endow those who love me with substance; I will fill their treasuries.

לְהַנְחִיל אֹהֲבַי יֵשׁ וְאֹצְרֹתֵיהֶם אֲמַלֵּא׃

22 "*Hashem* created me at the beginning of His course As the first of His works of old.

יְהֹוָה קָנָנִי רֵאשִׁית דַּרְכּוֹ קֶדֶם מִפְעָלָיו מֵאָז׃

a-do-NAI ka-NA-nee ray-SHEET dar-KO KE-dem mif-a-LAV may-AZ

23 In the distant past I was fashioned, At the beginning, at the origin of earth.

מֵעוֹלָם נִסַּכְתִּי מֵרֹאשׁ מִקַּדְמֵי־אָרֶץ׃

24 There was still no deep when I was brought forth, No springs rich in water;

בְּאֵין־תְּהֹמוֹת חוֹלָלְתִּי בְּאֵין מַעְיָנוֹת נִכְבַּדֵּי־מָיִם׃

25 Before [the foundation of] the mountains were sunk, Before the hills I was born.

בְּטֶרֶם הָרִים הָטְבָּעוּ לִפְנֵי גְבָעוֹת חוֹלָלְתִּי׃

26 He had not yet made earth and fields, Or the world's first clumps of clay.

עַד־לֹא עָשָׂה אֶרֶץ וְחוּצוֹת וְרֹאשׁ עַפְרוֹת תֵּבֵל׃

27 I was there when He set the heavens into place; When He fixed the horizon upon the deep;

בַּהֲכִינוֹ שָׁמַיִם שָׁם אָנִי בְּחֻקוֹ חוּג עַל־פְּנֵי תְהוֹם׃

28 When He made the heavens above firm, And the fountains of the deep gushed forth;

בְּאַמְּצוֹ שְׁחָקִים מִמָּעַל בַּעֲזוֹז עִינוֹת תְּהוֹם׃

29 When He assigned the sea its limits, So that its waters never transgress His command; When He fixed the foundations of the earth,

בְּשׂוּמוֹ לַיָּם חֻקּוֹ וּמַיִם לֹא יַעַבְרוּ־פִיו בְּחוּקוֹ מוֹסְדֵי אָרֶץ׃

30 I was with Him as a confidant, A source of delight every day, Rejoicing before Him at all times,

וָאֶהְיֶה אֶצְלוֹ אָמוֹן וָאֶהְיֶה שַׁעֲשֻׁעִים יוֹם יוֹם מְשַׂחֶקֶת לְפָנָיו בְּכָל־עֵת׃

31 Rejoicing in His inhabited world, Finding delight with mankind.

מְשַׂחֶקֶת בְּתֵבֵל אַרְצוֹ וְשַׁעֲשֻׁעַי אֶת־בְּנֵי אָדָם׃

32 Now, sons, listen to me; Happy are they who keep my ways.

וְעַתָּה בָנִים שִׁמְעוּ־לִי וְאַשְׁרֵי דְּרָכַי יִשְׁמֹרוּ׃

33 Heed discipline and become wise; Do not spurn it.

שִׁמְעוּ מוּסָר וַחֲכָמוּ וְאַל־תִּפְרָעוּ׃

34 Happy is the man who listens to me, Coming early to my gates each day, Waiting outside my doors.

אַשְׁרֵי אָדָם שֹׁמֵעַ לִי לִשְׁקֹד עַל־דַּלְתֹתַי יוֹם יוֹם לִשְׁמֹר מְזוּזֹת פְּתָחָי׃

8:22 The beginning of His course The wisdom of the *Torah* is described in this verse as the "beginning of His course." The Hebrew word for 'beginning,' *reishit* (ראשית), is also used to describe the Children of Israel, called *reisheet t'vuato*, 'the first-fruits of His [*Hashem's*] harvest' (Jeremiah 2:3), and it is also the first word of *Sefer Bereishit*, describing the creation of the world. The Sages connect the three uses of this word and teach that *Hashem* created the world for the sake of Israel and of the *Torah*. God created a world in which the Children of Israel are to follow the *Torah*, and thereby serve as a model for the rest of the nations.

ראשית

Mishlei/Proverbs
Chapter 9

משלי
פרק ט

35 For he who finds me finds life And obtains favor from *Hashem*.

לה כִּי מֹצְאִי מצאי [מָצָא] חַיִּים וַיָּפֶק רָצוֹן מֵיהוָֹה:

36 But he who misses me destroys himself; All who hate me love death."

לו וְחֹטְאִי חֹמֵס נַפְשׁוֹ כָּל־מְשַׂנְאַי אָהֲבוּ מָוֶת:

9 1 Wisdom has built her house, She has hewn her seven pillars.

ט א חָכְמוֹת בָּנְתָה בֵיתָהּ חָצְבָה עַמּוּדֶיהָ שִׁבְעָה:

khokh-MOT ba-n'-TAH vay-TAH kha-tz'-VAH a-mu-DE-ha shiv-AH

2 She has prepared the feast, Mixed the wine, And also set the table.

ב טָבְחָה טִבְחָהּ מָסְכָה יֵינָהּ אַף עָרְכָה שֻׁלְחָנָהּ:

3 She has sent out her maids to announce On the heights of the town,

ג שָׁלְחָה נַעֲרֹתֶיהָ תִקְרָא עַל־גַּפֵּי מְרֹמֵי קָרֶת:

4 "Let the simple enter here"; To those devoid of sense she says,

ד מִי־פֶתִי יָסֻר הֵנָּה חֲסַר־לֵב אָמְרָה לּוֹ:

5 "Come, eat my food And drink the wine that I have mixed;

ה לְכוּ לַחֲמוּ בְלַחֲמִי וּשְׁתוּ בְּיַיִן מָסָכְתִּי:

6 Give up simpleness and live, Walk in the way of understanding."

ו עִזְבוּ פְתָאיִם וִחְיוּ וְאִשְׁרוּ בְּדֶרֶךְ בִּינָה:

7 To correct a scoffer, Or rebuke a wicked man for his blemish, Is to call down abuse on oneself.*

ז יֹסֵר לֵץ לֹקֵחַ לוֹ קָלוֹן וּמוֹכִיחַ לְרָשָׁע מוּמוֹ:

8 Do not rebuke a scoffer, for he will hate you; Reprove a wise man, and he will love you.

ח אַל־תּוֹכַח לֵץ פֶּן־יִשְׂנָאֶךָּ הוֹכַח לְחָכָם וְיֶאֱהָבֶךָּ:

9 Instruct a wise man, and he will grow wiser; Teach a righteous man, and he will gain in learning.

ט תֵּן לְחָכָם וְיֶחְכַּם־עוֹד הוֹדַע לְצַדִּיק וְיוֹסֶף לֶקַח:

10 The beginning of wisdom is fear of *Hashem*, And knowledge of the Holy One is understanding.

י תְּחִלַּת חָכְמָה יִרְאַת יְהוָה וְדַעַת קְדֹשִׁים בִּינָה:

11 For through me your days will increase, And years be added to your life.

יא כִּי־בִי יִרְבּוּ יָמֶיךָ וְיוֹסִיפוּ לְּךָ שְׁנוֹת חַיִּים:

12 If you are wise, you are wise for yourself; If you are a scoffer, you bear it alone.

יב אִם־חָכַמְתָּ חָכַמְתָּ לָּךְ וְלַצְתָּ לְבַדְּךָ תִשָּׂא:

13 The stupid woman bustles about; She is simple and knows nothing.

יג אֵשֶׁת כְּסִילוּת הֹמִיָּה פְּתַיּוּת וּבַל־יָדְעָה מָּה:

14 She sits in the doorway of her house, Or on a chair at the heights of the town,

יד וְיָשְׁבָה לְפֶתַח בֵּיתָהּ עַל־כִּסֵּא מְרֹמֵי קָרֶת:

---

* clauses transposed for clarity

Rashi (1040–1105)

9:1 She has hewn her seven pillars The number seven is a recurring motif in the Bible, typically representing nature. It is used in the book of *Mishlei* as a way of expressing multitudes, so here it means wisdom has many pillars. According to the medieval commentator *Rashi*, in this context the number seven represents the seven days of creation. When *Hashem* created the world, the "house" referred to in the first half of this verse, He created it with wisdom.

1667

Mishlei/Proverbs
Chapter 10

משלי
פרק י

15 Calling to all the wayfarers Who go about their own affairs,

טו לִקְרֹא לְעֹבְרֵי־דָרֶךְ הַמְיַשְּׁרִים אֹרְחוֹתָם׃

16 "Let the simple enter here"; And to those devoid of sense she says,

טז מִי־פֶתִי יָסֻר הֵנָּה וַחֲסַר־לֵב וְאָמְרָה לּוֹ׃

17 "Stolen waters are sweet, And bread eaten furtively is tasty."

יז מַיִם־גְּנוּבִים יִמְתָּקוּ וְלֶחֶם סְתָרִים יִנְעָם׃

18 He does not know that the shades are there, That her guests are in the depths of Sheol.

יח וְלֹא־יָדַע כִּי־רְפָאִים שָׁם בְּעִמְקֵי שְׁאוֹל קְרֻאֶיהָ׃

10 1 The proverbs of *Shlomo*: A wise son brings joy to his father; A dull son is his mother's sorrow.

י א מִשְׁלֵי שְׁלֹמֹה בֵּן חָכָם יְשַׂמַּח־אָב וּבֵן כְּסִיל תּוּגַת אִמּוֹ׃

2 Ill-gotten wealth is of no avail, But righteousness saves from death.

ב לֹא־יוֹעִילוּ אוֹצְרוֹת רֶשַׁע וּצְדָקָה תַּצִּיל מִמָּוֶת׃

3 *Hashem* will not let the righteous go hungry, But He denies the wicked what they crave.

ג לֹא־יַרְעִיב יְהוָה נֶפֶשׁ צַדִּיק וְהַוַּת רְשָׁעִים יֶהְדֹּף׃

4 Negligent hands cause poverty, But diligent hands enrich.

ד רָאשׁ עֹשֶׂה כַף־רְמִיָּה וְיַד חָרוּצִים תַּעֲשִׁיר׃

5 He who lays in stores during the summer is a capable son, But he who sleeps during the harvest is an incompetent.

ה אֹגֵר בַּקַּיִץ בֵּן מַשְׂכִּיל נִרְדָּם בַּקָּצִיר בֵּן מֵבִישׁ׃

6 Blessings light upon the head of the righteous, But lawlessness covers the mouth of the wicked.

ו בְּרָכוֹת לְרֹאשׁ צַדִּיק וּפִי רְשָׁעִים יְכַסֶּה חָמָס׃

7 The name of the righteous is invoked in blessing, But the fame of the wicked rots.

ז זֵכֶר צַדִּיק לִבְרָכָה וְשֵׁם רְשָׁעִים יִרְקָב׃

8 He whose heart is wise accepts commands, But he whose speech is foolish comes to grief.

ח חֲכַם־לֵב יִקַּח מִצְוֹת וֶאֱוִיל שְׂפָתַיִם יִלָּבֵט׃

9 He who lives blamelessly lives safely, But he who walks a crooked path will be found out.

ט הוֹלֵךְ בַּתֹּם יֵלֶךְ בֶּטַח וּמְעַקֵּשׁ דְּרָכָיו יִוָּדֵעַ׃

10 He who winks his eye causes sorrow; He whose speech is foolish comes to grief.

י קֹרֵץ עַיִן יִתֵּן עַצָּבֶת וֶאֱוִיל שְׂפָתַיִם יִלָּבֵט׃

11 The mouth of the righteous is a fountain of life, But lawlessness covers the mouth of the wicked.

יא מְקוֹר חַיִּים פִּי צַדִּיק וּפִי רְשָׁעִים יְכַסֶּה חָמָס׃

12 Hatred stirs up strife, But love covers up all faults.

יב שִׂנְאָה תְּעוֹרֵר מְדָנִים וְעַל כָּל־פְּשָׁעִים תְּכַסֶּה אַהֲבָה׃

13 Wisdom is to be found on the lips of the intelligent, But a rod is ready for the back of the senseless.

יג בְּשִׂפְתֵי נָבוֹן תִּמָּצֵא חָכְמָה וְשֵׁבֶט לְגֵו חֲסַר־לֵב׃

14 The wise store up knowledge; The mouth of the fool is an imminent ruin.

יד חֲכָמִים יִצְפְּנוּ־דָעַת וּפִי־אֱוִיל מְחִתָּה קְרֹבָה׃

15 The wealth of a rich man is his fortress; The poverty of the poor is his ruin.

טו הוֹן עָשִׁיר קִרְיַת עֻזּוֹ מְחִתַּת דַּלִּים רֵישָׁם׃

1668

Mishlei/Proverbs

Chapter 10

משלי
פרק י

16 The labor of the righteous man makes for life; The produce of the wicked man makes for want.

טז פְּעֻלַּת צַדִּיק לְחַיִּים תְּבוּאַת רָשָׁע לְחַטָּאת:

17 He who follows discipline shows the way to life, But he who ignores reproof leads astray.

יז אֹרַח לְחַיִּים שׁוֹמֵר מוּסָר וְעוֹזֵב תּוֹכַחַת מַתְעֶה:

18 He who conceals hatred has lying lips, While he who speaks forth slander is a dullard.

יח מְכַסֶּה שִׂנְאָה שִׂפְתֵי־שָׁקֶר וּמוֹצִא דִבָּה הוּא כְסִיל:

19 Where there is much talking, there is no lack of transgressing, But he who curbs his tongue shows sense.

יט בְּרֹב דְּבָרִים לֹא יֶחְדַּל־פָּשַׁע וְחוֹשֵׂךְ שְׂפָתָיו מַשְׂכִּיל:

20 The tongue of a righteous man is choice silver, But the mind of the wicked is of little worth.

כ כֶּסֶף נִבְחָר לְשׁוֹן צַדִּיק לֵב רְשָׁעִים כִּמְעָט:

21 The lips of the righteous sustain many, But fools die for lack of sense.

כא שִׂפְתֵי צַדִּיק יִרְעוּ רַבִּים וֶאֱוִילִים בַּחֲסַר־לֵב יָמוּתוּ:

22 It is the blessing of *Hashem* that enriches, And no toil can increase it.

כב בִּרְכַּת יְהוָה הִיא תַעֲשִׁיר וְלֹא־יוֹסִף עֶצֶב עִמָּהּ:

bir-KAT a-do-NAI HEE ta-a-SHEER v'-LO yo-SIF E-tzev i-MAH

23 As mischief is sport for the dullard, So is wisdom for the man of understanding.

כג כִּשְׂחוֹק לִכְסִיל עֲשׂוֹת זִמָּה וְחָכְמָה לְאִישׁ תְּבוּנָה:

24 What the wicked man plots overtakes him; What the righteous desire is granted.

כד מְגוֹרַת רָשָׁע הִיא תְבוֹאֶנּוּ וְתַאֲוַת צַדִּיקִים יִתֵּן:

25 When the storm passes the wicked man is gone, But the righteous is an everlasting foundation.

כה כַּעֲבוֹר סוּפָה וְאֵין רָשָׁע וְצַדִּיק יְסוֹד עוֹלָם:

26 Like vinegar to the teeth, Like smoke to the eyes, Is a lazy man to those who send him on a mission.

כו כַּחֹמֶץ לַשִּׁנַּיִם וְכֶעָשָׁן לָעֵינָיִם כֵּן הֶעָצֵל לְשֹׁלְחָיו:

27 The fear of *Hashem* prolongs life, While the years of the wicked will be shortened.

כז יִרְאַת יְהוָה תּוֹסִיף יָמִים וּשְׁנוֹת רְשָׁעִים תִּקְצֹרְנָה:

28 The righteous can look forward to joy, But the hope of the wicked is doomed.

כח תּוֹחֶלֶת צַדִּיקִים שִׂמְחָה וְתִקְוַת רְשָׁעִים תֹּאבֵד:

29 The way of *Hashem* is a stronghold for the blameless, But a ruin for evildoers.

כט מָעוֹז לַתֹּם דֶּרֶךְ יְהוָה וּמְחִתָּה לְפֹעֲלֵי אָוֶן:

30 The righteous will never be shaken; The wicked will not inhabit the earth.

ל צַדִּיק לְעוֹלָם בַּל־יִמּוֹט וּרְשָׁעִים לֹא יִשְׁכְּנוּ־אָרֶץ:

Granot water desalination plant

10:22 It is the blessing of *Hashem* that enriches In *Sefer Devarim* (11:10–12), the *Torah* describes how the Promised Land is different from Egypt. In Egypt, one could water his crops from the Nile by using his foot to easily direct water to his fields, but in the Land of Israel, the eyes of *Hashem* are on the land. It is only through His blessings, as our verse says, that the land enriches and provides its fruits. Modern Israel has compensated for its lack of natural water resources and limited rainfall through great technological breakthroughs such as water recycling and desalination. Nevertheless, we must always remember that even with great technology and innovation, "it is the blessing of *Hashem* that enriches."

Mishlei/Proverbs
Chapter 11

משלי
פרק יא

31 The mouth of the righteous produces wisdom, But the treacherous tongue shall be cut off.

לא פִּֽי־צַדִּיק יָנוּב חָכְמָה וּלְשׁוֹן תַּהְפֻּכוֹת תִּכָּרֵֽת׃

32 The lips of the righteous know what is pleasing; The mouth of the wicked [knows] duplicity.

לב שִׂפְתֵי צַדִּיק יֵדְעוּן רָצוֹן וּפִי רְשָׁעִים תַּהְפֻּכֽוֹת׃

11

1 False scales are an abomination to *Hashem*; An honest weight pleases Him.

א מֹאזְנֵי מִרְמָה תּוֹעֲבַת יְהֹוָה וְאֶבֶן שְׁלֵמָה רְצוֹנֽוֹ׃

2 When arrogance appears, disgrace follows, But wisdom is with those who are unassuming.

ב בָּֽא־זָדוֹן וַיָּבֹא קָלוֹן וְאֶת־צְנוּעִים חָכְמָֽה׃

3 The integrity of the upright guides them; The deviousness of the treacherous leads them to ruin.

ג תֻּמַּת יְשָׁרִים תַּנְחֵם וְסֶלֶף בּוֹגְדִים ושדם [יְשָׁדֵּֽם]׃

4 Wealth is of no avail on the day of wrath, But righteousness saves from death.

ד לֹא־יוֹעִיל הוֹן בְּיוֹם עֶבְרָה וּצְדָקָה תַּצִּיל מִמָּֽוֶת׃

5 The righteousness of the blameless man smooths his way, But the wicked man is felled by his wickedness.

ה צִדְקַת תָּמִים תְּיַשֵּׁר דַּרְכּוֹ וּבְרִשְׁעָתוֹ יִפֹּל רָשָֽׁע׃

6 The righteousness of the upright saves them, But the treacherous are trapped by their malice.

ו צִדְקַת יְשָׁרִים תַּצִּילֵם וּבְהַוַּת בֹּגְדִים יִלָּכֵֽדוּ׃

7 At death the hopes of a wicked man are doomed, And the ambition of evil men comes to nothing.

ז בְּמוֹת אָדָם רָשָׁע תֹּאבַד תִּקְוָה וְתוֹחֶלֶת אוֹנִים אָבָֽדָה׃

8 The righteous man is rescued from trouble And the wicked man takes his place.

ח צַדִּיק מִצָּרָה נֶחֱלָץ וַיָּבֹא רָשָׁע תַּחְתָּֽיו׃

9 The impious man destroys his neighbor through speech, But through their knowledge the righteous are rescued.

ט בְּפֶה חָנֵף יַשְׁחִת רֵעֵהוּ וּבְדַעַת צַדִּיקִים יֵחָלֵֽצוּ׃

10 When the righteous prosper the city exults; When the wicked perish there are shouts of joy.

י בְּטוּב צַדִּיקִים תַּעֲלֹץ קִרְיָה וּבַאֲבֹד רְשָׁעִים רִנָּֽה׃

11 A city is built up by the blessing of the upright, But it is torn down by the speech of the wicked.

יא בְּבִרְכַּת יְשָׁרִים תָּרוּם קָרֶת וּבְפִי רְשָׁעִים תֵּהָרֵֽס׃

12 He who speaks contemptuously of his fellowman is devoid of sense; A prudent man keeps his peace.

יב בָּז־לְרֵעֵהוּ חֲסַר־לֵב וְאִישׁ תְּבוּנוֹת יַחֲרִֽישׁ׃

13 A base fellow gives away secrets, But a trustworthy soul keeps a confidence.

יג הוֹלֵךְ רָכִיל מְגַלֶּה־סּוֹד וְנֶאֱמַן־רוּחַ מְכַסֶּה דָבָֽר׃

14 For want of strategy an army falls, But victory comes with much planning.

יד בְּאֵין תַּחְבֻּלוֹת יִפָּל־עָם וּתְשׁוּעָה בְּרֹב יוֹעֵֽץ׃

15 Harm awaits him who stands surety for another; He who spurns pledging shall be secure.

טו רַע־יֵרוֹעַ כִּי־עָרַב זָר וְשֹׂנֵא תֹקְעִים בּוֹטֵֽחַ׃

16 A graceful woman obtains honor; Ruthless men obtain wealth.

טז אֵֽשֶׁת־חֵן תִּתְמֹךְ כָּבוֹד וְעָרִיצִים יִתְמְכוּ־עֹֽשֶׁר׃

1670

Mishlei/Proverbs

Chapter 11

משלי
פרק יא

17 A kindly man benefits himself; A cruel man makes trouble for himself.

גֹּמֵל נַפְשׁוֹ אִישׁ חָסֶד וְעֹכֵר שְׁאֵרוֹ אַכְזָרִי:

18 The wicked man earns illusory wages, But he who sows righteousness has a true reward.

רָשָׁע עֹשֶׂה פְעֻלַּת־שָׁקֶר וְזֹרֵעַ צְדָקָה שֶׂכֶר אֱמֶת:

19 Righteousness is a prop of life, But to pursue evil leads to death.

כֵּן־צְדָקָה לְחַיִּים וּמְרַדֵּף רָעָה לְמוֹתוֹ:

20 Men of crooked mind are an abomination to *Hashem*, But those whose way is blameless please Him.

תּוֹעֲבַת יְהֹוָה עִקְּשֵׁי־לֵב וּרְצוֹנוֹ תְּמִימֵי דָרֶךְ:

21 Assuredly, the evil man will not escape, But the offspring of the righteous will be safe.

יָד לְיָד לֹא־יִנָּקֶה רָּע וְזֶרַע צַדִּיקִים נִמְלָט:

22 Like a gold ring in the snout of a pig Is a beautiful woman bereft of sense.

נֶזֶם זָהָב בְּאַף חֲזִיר אִשָּׁה יָפָה וְסָרַת טָעַם:

23 What the righteous desire can only be good; What the wicked hope for [stirs] wrath.

תַּאֲוַת צַדִּיקִים אַךְ־טוֹב תִּקְוַת רְשָׁעִים עֶבְרָה:

24 One man gives generously and ends with more; Another stints on doing the right thing and incurs a loss.

יֵשׁ מְפַזֵּר וְנוֹסָף עוֹד וְחוֹשֵׂךְ מִיֹּשֶׁר אַךְ־לְמַחְסוֹר:

25 A generous person enjoys prosperity; He who satisfies others shall himself be sated.

נֶפֶשׁ־בְּרָכָה תְדֻשָּׁן וּמַרְוֶה גַּם־הוּא יוֹרֶא:

26 **He who withholds grain earns the curses of the people, But blessings are on the head of the one who dispenses it.**

mo-NAY-a BAR yi-k'-VU-hu l'-OM uv-ra-KHAH l'-ROSH mash-BEER

מֹנֵעַ בָּר יִקְּבֻהוּ לְאוֹם וּבְרָכָה לְרֹאשׁ מַשְׁבִּיר:

27 He who earnestly seeks what is good pursues what is pleasing; He who is bent on evil, upon him it shall come.

שֹׁחֵר טוֹב יְבַקֵּשׁ רָצוֹן וְדֹרֵשׁ רָעָה תְבוֹאֶנּוּ:

28 He who trusts in his wealth shall fall, But the righteous shall flourish like foliage.

בּוֹטֵחַ בְּעָשְׁרוֹ הוּא יִפֹּל וְכֶעָלֶה צַדִּיקִים יִפְרָחוּ:

29 He who makes trouble for his household shall inherit the wind; A fool is a slave to the wise-hearted.

עֹכֵר בֵּיתוֹ יִנְחַל־רוּחַ וְעֶבֶד אֱוִיל לַחֲכַם־לֵב:

11:26 He who withholds grain earns the curses of the people The Bible commands the Israelites to set aside a certain portion of their crops, grown in the Land of Israel, for the poor. The corners of their fields, the forgotten sheaves and the grains that fall during harvest are all to be left for the needy (Leviticus 19:9–10, Deuteronomy 24:19). In *Megillat Rut*, *Boaz* sustains his community in this manner and *Rut*, the poor widow, gathers in his field (chapter 2). This biblical imperative is still practiced in Israel today. Each season, farmers throughout Israel leave over millions of pounds of produce from their fields, which are collected by volunteers and distributed to poor people all over the country.

Mishlei/Proverbs
Chapter 12

משלי
פרק יב

30 The fruit of the righteous is a tree of life; A wise man captivates people.

לֹ פְּרִי־צַדִּיק עֵץ חַיִּים וְלֹקֵחַ נְפָשׁוֹת חָכָם׃

31 If the righteous on earth get their deserts, How much more the wicked man and the sinner.

לֹא הֵן צַדִּיק בָּאָרֶץ יְשֻׁלָּם אַף כִּי־רָשָׁע וְחוֹטֵא׃

12

1 He who loves discipline loves knowledge; He who spurns reproof is a brutish man.

יב א אֹהֵב מוּסָר אֹהֵב דָּעַת וְשֹׂנֵא תוֹכַחַת בָּעַר׃

2 A good man earns the favor of *Hashem*, A man of intrigues, His condemnation.

ב טוֹב יָפִיק רָצוֹן מֵיְהוָה וְאִישׁ מְזִמּוֹת יַרְשִׁיעַ׃

3 A man cannot be established in wickedness, But the root of the righteous will not be shaken loose.

ג לֹא־יִכּוֹן אָדָם בְּרֶשַׁע וְשֹׁרֶשׁ צַדִּיקִים בַּל־יִמּוֹט׃

4 A capable wife is a crown for her husband, But an incompetent one is like rot in his bones.

ד אֵשֶׁת־חַיִל עֲטֶרֶת בַּעְלָהּ וּכְרָקָב בְּעַצְמוֹתָיו מְבִישָׁה׃

5 The purposes of the righteous are justice, The schemes of the wicked are deceit.

ה מַחְשְׁבוֹת צַדִּיקִים מִשְׁפָּט תַּחְבֻּלוֹת רְשָׁעִים מִרְמָה׃

6 The words of the wicked are a deadly ambush, But the speech of the upright saves them.

ו דִּבְרֵי רְשָׁעִים אֱרָב־דָּם וּפִי יְשָׁרִים יַצִּילֵם׃

7 Overturn the wicked and they are gone, But the house of the righteous will endure.

ז הָפוֹךְ רְשָׁעִים וְאֵינָם וּבֵית צַדִּיקִים יַעֲמֹד׃

8 A man is commended according to his intelligence; A twisted mind is held up to contempt.

ח לְפִי־שִׂכְלוֹ יְהֻלַּל־אִישׁ וְנַעֲוֵה־לֵב יִהְיֶה לָבוּז׃

9 Better to be lightly esteemed and have a servant Than to put on airs and have no food.

ט טוֹב נִקְלֶה וְעֶבֶד לוֹ מִמִּתְכַּבֵּד וַחֲסַר־לָחֶם׃

10 A righteous man knows the needs of his beast, But the compassion of the wicked is cruelty.

י יוֹדֵעַ צַדִּיק נֶפֶשׁ בְּהֶמְתּוֹ וְרַחֲמֵי רְשָׁעִים אַכְזָרִי׃

11 He who tills his land shall have food in plenty, But he who pursues vanities is devoid of sense.

יא עֹבֵד אַדְמָתוֹ יִשְׂבַּע־לָחֶם וּמְרַדֵּף רֵיקִים חֲסַר־לֵב׃

o-VAYD ad-ma-TO yis-ba LA-chem um-ra-DAYF ray-KEEM cha-sar LAYV

12 The wicked covet the catch of evil men; The root of the righteous yields [fruit].

יב חָמַד רָשָׁע מְצוֹד רָעִים וְשֹׁרֶשׁ צַדִּיקִים יִתֵּן׃

13 Sinful speech is a trap for the evil man, But the righteous escapes from trouble.

יג בְּפֶשַׁע שְׂפָתַיִם מוֹקֵשׁ רָע וַיֵּצֵא מִצָּרָה צַדִּיק׃

14 A man gets his fill of good from the fruit of his speech; One is repaid in kind for one's deeds.

יד מִפְּרִי פִי־אִישׁ יִשְׂבַּע־טוֹב וּגְמוּל יְדֵי־אָדָם ישוב [יָשִׁיב] לוֹ׃

12:11 He who tills his land shall have food in plenty Israel was intended to be an agrarian society, therefore in this verse, farming is seen as a worthy pursuit. The Bible strengthens the people's connection to the Land of Israel through various agricultural celebrations, commemorations and obligations. Rabbi Abraham Isaac Kook points out that it is not these laws, unique to *Eretz Yisrael*, which make the land holy. Rather, it is the intrinsic holiness of the land that inspires these special agricultural commandments.

Rabbi Abraham Isaac Kook (1865–1935)

1672

Mishlei/Proverbs
Chapter 13

15 The way of a fool is right in his own eyes; But the wise man accepts advice.

16 A fool's vexation is known at once, But a clever man conceals his humiliation.

17 He who testifies faithfully tells the truth, But a false witness, deceit.

18 There is blunt talk like sword-thrusts, But the speech of the wise is healing.

19 Truthful speech abides forever, A lying tongue for but a moment.

20 Deceit is in the minds of those who plot evil; For those who plan good there is joy.

21 No harm befalls the righteous, But the wicked have their fill of misfortune.

22 Lying speech is an abomination to *Hashem*, But those who act faithfully please Him.

23 A clever man conceals what he knows, But the mind of a dullard cries out folly.

24 The hand of the diligent wields authority; The negligent are held in subjection.

25 If there is anxiety in a man's mind let him quash it, And turn it into joy with a good word.

26 A righteous man gives his friend direction, But the way of the wicked leads astray.

27 A negligent man never has game to roast; A diligent man has precious wealth.

28 The road of righteousness leads to life; By way of its path there is no death.

13 1 A wise son – it is through the discipline of his father; A scoffer – he never heard reproof.

2 A man enjoys good from the fruit of his speech; But out of the throat of the treacherous comes lawlessness.

3 He who guards his tongue preserves his life; He who opens wide his lips, it is his ruin.

4 A lazy man craves, but has nothing; The diligent shall feast on rich fare.

משלי
פרק יג

טו דֶּרֶךְ אֱוִיל יָשָׁר בְּעֵינָיו וְשֹׁמֵעַ לְעֵצָה חָכָם:

טז אֱוִיל בַּיּוֹם יִוָּדַע כַּעְסוֹ וְכֹסֶה קָלוֹן עָרוּם:

יז יָפִיחַ אֱמוּנָה יַגִּיד צֶדֶק וְעֵד שְׁקָרִים מִרְמָה:

יח יֵשׁ בּוֹטֶה כְּמַדְקְרוֹת חָרֶב וּלְשׁוֹן חֲכָמִים מַרְפֵּא:

יט שְׂפַת־אֱמֶת תִּכּוֹן לָעַד וְעַד־אַרְגִּיעָה לְשׁוֹן שָׁקֶר:

כ מִרְמָה בְּלֶב־חֹרְשֵׁי רָע וּלְיֹעֲצֵי שָׁלוֹם שִׂמְחָה:

כא לֹא־יְאֻנֶּה לַצַּדִּיק כָּל־אָוֶן וּרְשָׁעִים מָלְאוּ רָע:

כב תּוֹעֲבַת יְהֹוָה שִׂפְתֵי־שָׁקֶר וְעֹשֵׂי אֱמוּנָה רְצוֹנוֹ:

כג אָדָם עָרוּם כֹּסֶה דָּעַת וְלֵב כְּסִילִים יִקְרָא אִוֶּלֶת:

כד יַד־חָרוּצִים תִּמְשׁוֹל וּרְמִיָּה תִּהְיֶה לָמַס:

כה דְּאָגָה בְלֶב־אִישׁ יַשְׁחֶנָּה וְדָבָר טוֹב יְשַׂמְּחֶנָּה:

כו יָתֵר מֵרֵעֵהוּ צַדִּיק וְדֶרֶךְ רְשָׁעִים תַּתְעֵם:

כז לֹא־יַחֲרֹךְ רְמִיָּה צֵידוֹ וְהוֹן־אָדָם יָקָר חָרוּץ:

כח בְּאֹרַח־צְדָקָה חַיִּים וְדֶרֶךְ נְתִיבָה אַל־מָוֶת:

יג א בֵּן חָכָם מוּסַר אָב וְלֵץ לֹא־שָׁמַע גְּעָרָה:

ב מִפְּרִי פִי־אִישׁ יֹאכַל טוֹב וְנֶפֶשׁ בֹּגְדִים חָמָס:

ג נֹצֵר פִּיו שֹׁמֵר נַפְשׁוֹ פֹּשֵׂק שְׂפָתָיו מְחִתָּה־לוֹ:

ד מִתְאַוָּה וָאַיִן נַפְשׁוֹ עָצֵל וְנֶפֶשׁ חָרֻצִים תְּדֻשָּׁן:

Mishlei/Proverbs
Chapter 13

משלי
פרק יג

5 A righteous man hates lies; The wicked man is vile and disgraceful.

ה דְּבַר־שֶׁקֶר יִשְׂנָא צַדִּיק וְרָשָׁע יַבְאִישׁ וְיַחְפִּיר׃

6 Righteousness protects him whose way is blameless; Wickedness subverts the sinner.

ו צְדָקָה תִּצֹּר תָּם־דָּרֶךְ וְרִשְׁעָה תְּסַלֵּף חַטָּאת׃

7 One man pretends to be rich and has nothing; Another professes to be poor and has much wealth.

ז יֵשׁ מִתְעַשֵּׁר וְאֵין כֹּל מִתְרוֹשֵׁשׁ וְהוֹן רָב׃

8 Riches are ransom for a man's life, The poor never heard a reproof.

ח כֹּפֶר נֶפֶשׁ־אִישׁ עָשְׁרוֹ וְרָשׁ לֹא־שָׁמַע גְּעָרָה׃

9 The light of the righteous is radiant; The lamp of the wicked is extinguished.

ט אוֹר־צַדִּיקִים יִשְׂמָח וְנֵר רְשָׁעִים יִדְעָךְ׃

10 Arrogance yields nothing but strife; Wisdom belongs to those who seek advice.

י רַק־בְּזָדוֹן יִתֵּן מַצָּה וְאֶת־נוֹעָצִים חָכְמָה׃

11 Wealth may dwindle to less than nothing, But he who gathers little by little increases it.

יא הוֹן מֵהֶבֶל יִמְעָט וְקֹבֵץ עַל־יָד יַרְבֶּה׃

12 Hope deferred sickens the heart, But desire realized is a tree of life.

יב תּוֹחֶלֶת מְמֻשָּׁכָה מַחֲלָה־לֵב וְעֵץ חַיִּים תַּאֲוָה בָאָה׃

13 He who disdains a precept will be injured thereby; He who respects a command will be rewarded.

יג בָּז לְדָבָר יֵחָבֶל לוֹ וִירֵא מִצְוָה הוּא יְשֻׁלָּם׃

14 The instruction of a wise man is a fountain of life, Enabling one to avoid deadly snares.

יד תּוֹרַת חָכָם מְקוֹר חַיִּים לָסוּר מִמֹּקְשֵׁי מָוֶת׃

15 Good sense wins favor; The way of treacherous men is unchanging.

טו שֵׂכֶל־טוֹב יִתֶּן־חֵן וְדֶרֶךְ בֹּגְדִים אֵיתָן׃

16 Every clever man acts knowledgeably, But a dullard exposes his stupidity.

טז כָּל־עָרוּם יַעֲשֶׂה בְדָעַת וּכְסִיל יִפְרֹשׂ אִוֶּלֶת׃

17 Harm befalls a wicked messenger; A faithful courier brings healing.

יז מַלְאָךְ רָשָׁע יִפֹּל בְּרָע וְצִיר אֱמוּנִים מַרְפֵּא׃

18 Poverty and humiliation are for him who spurns discipline; But he who takes reproof to heart gets honor.

יח רֵישׁ וְקָלוֹן פּוֹרֵעַ מוּסָר וְשׁוֹמֵר תּוֹכַחַת יְכֻבָּד׃

19 Desire realized is sweet to the soul; To turn away from evil is abhorrent to the stupid.

יט תַּאֲוָה נִהְיָה תֶּעֱרַב לְנָפֶשׁ וְתוֹעֲבַת כְּסִילִים סוּר מֵרָע׃

20 He who keeps company with the wise becomes wise, But he who consorts with dullards comes to grief.

כ הָלוֹךְ [הוֹלֵךְ] אֶת־חֲכָמִים וחכם [יֶחְכָּם] וְרֹעֶה כְסִילִים יֵרוֹעַ׃

21 Misfortune pursues sinners, But the righteous are well rewarded.

כא חַטָּאִים תְּרַדֵּף רָעָה וְאֶת־צַדִּיקִים יְשַׁלֶּם־טוֹב׃

1674

Mishlei/Proverbs
Chapter 14

משלי
פרק יד

22 A good man has what to bequeath to his grandchildren, For the wealth of sinners is stored up for the righteous.

כב טוֹב יַנְחִיל בְּנֵי־בָנִים וְצָפוּן לַצַּדִּיק חֵיל חוֹטֵא:

TOV yan-KHEEL b'-nay va-NEEM v'-tza-FUN la-tza-DEEK KHAYL kho-TAY

23 The tillage of the poor yields much food; But substance is swept away for lack of moderation.

כג רָב־אֹכֶל נִיר רָאשִׁים וְיֵשׁ נִסְפֶּה בְּלֹא מִשְׁפָּט:

24 He who spares the rod hates his son, But he who loves him disciplines him early.

כד חוֹשֵׂךְ שִׁבְטוֹ שׂוֹנֵא בְנוֹ וְאֹהֲבוֹ שִׁחֲרוֹ מוּסָר:

25 The righteous man eats to his heart's content, But the belly of the wicked is empty.

כה צַדִּיק אֹכֵל לְשֹׂבַע נַפְשׁוֹ וּבֶטֶן רְשָׁעִים תֶּחְסָר:

14 1 The wisest of women builds her house, But folly tears it down with its own hands.

יד א חַכְמוֹת נָשִׁים בָּנְתָה בֵיתָהּ וְאִוֶּלֶת בְּיָדֶיהָ תֶהֶרְסֶנּוּ:

2 He who maintains his integrity fears *Hashem*; A man of devious ways scorns Him.

ב הוֹלֵךְ בְּיָשְׁרוֹ יְרֵא יְהֹוָה וּנְלוֹז דְּרָכָיו בּוֹזֵהוּ:

3 In the mouth of a fool is a rod of haughtiness, But the lips of the wise protect them.

ג בְּפִי־אֱוִיל חֹטֶר גַּאֲוָה וְשִׂפְתֵי חֲכָמִים תִּשְׁמוּרֵם:

4 If there are no oxen the crib is clean, But a rich harvest comes through the strength of the ox.

ד בְּאֵין אֲלָפִים אֵבוּס בָּר וְרָב־תְּבוּאוֹת בְּכֹחַ שׁוֹר:

5 An honest witness will not lie; A false witness testifies lies.

ה עֵד אֱמוּנִים לֹא יְכַזֵּב וְיָפִיחַ כְּזָבִים עֵד שָׁקֶר:

6 A scoffer seeks wisdom in vain, But knowledge comes easily to the intelligent man.

ו בִּקֶּשׁ־לֵץ חָכְמָה וָאָיִן וְדַעַת לְנָבוֹן נָקָל:

7 Keep your distance from a dullard, For you will not learn wise speech.

ז לֵךְ מִנֶּגֶד לְאִישׁ כְּסִיל וּבַל־יָדַעְתָּ שִׂפְתֵי־דָעַת:

8 It is the wisdom of a clever man to understand his course; But the stupidity of the dullard is delusion.

ח חָכְמַת עָרוּם הָבִין דַּרְכּוֹ וְאִוֶּלֶת כְּסִילִים מִרְמָה:

9 Reparations mediate between fools, Between the upright, good will.

ט אֱוִלִים יָלִיץ אָשָׁם וּבֵין יְשָׁרִים רָצוֹן:

10 The heart alone knows its bitterness, And no outsider can share in its joy.

י לֵב יוֹדֵעַ מָרַּת נַפְשׁוֹ וּבְשִׂמְחָתוֹ לֹא־יִתְעָרַב זָר:

11 The house of the wicked will be demolished, But the tent of the upright will flourish.

יא בֵּית רְשָׁעִים יִשָּׁמֵד וְאֹהֶל יְשָׁרִים יַפְרִיחַ:

13:22 A good man has what to bequeath to his grandchildren A righteous man leaves more than a physical inheritance for his children and grandchildren, as the merit of his good deeds is also bequeathed to them. By contrast, though, the sinner's wealth will ultimately pass to more worthy hands. The greatest inheritance left to the Jewish people is the Land of Israel, not to be squandered or given away, but passed to down to their children's children for eternity.

Mishlei/Proverbs

Chapter 14

משלי

פרק יד

12 A road may seem right to a man, But in the end it is a road to death.

יב יֵשׁ דֶּרֶךְ יָשָׁר לִפְנֵי־אִישׁ וְאַחֲרִיתָהּ דַּרְכֵי־מָוֶת:

13 The heart may ache even in laughter, And joy may end in grief.

יג גַּם־בִּשְׂחוֹק יִכְאַב־לֵב וְאַחֲרִיתָהּ שִׂמְחָה תוּגָה:

14 An unprincipled man reaps the fruits of his ways; A good man, of his deeds.

יד מִדְּרָכָיו יִשְׂבַּע סוּג לֵב וּמֵעָלָיו אִישׁ טוֹב:

15 A simple person believes anything; A clever man ponders his course.

טו פֶּתִי יַאֲמִין לְכָל־דָּבָר וְעָרוּם יָבִין לַאֲשֻׁרוֹ:

16 A wise man is diffident and shuns evil, But a dullard rushes in confidently.

טז חָכָם יָרֵא וְסָר מֵרָע וּכְסִיל מִתְעַבֵּר וּבוֹטֵחַ:

17 An impatient man commits folly; A man of intrigues will be hated.

יז קְצַר־אַפַּיִם יַעֲשֶׂה אִוֶּלֶת וְאִישׁ מְזִמּוֹת יִשָּׂנֵא:

18 Folly is the lot of the simple, But clever men glory in knowledge.

יח נָחֲלוּ פְתָאיִם אִוֶּלֶת וַעֲרוּמִים יַכְתִּרוּ דָעַת:

19 Evil men are brought low before the good, So are the wicked at the gates of the righteous.

יט שַׁחוּ רָעִים לִפְנֵי טוֹבִים וּרְשָׁעִים עַל־שַׁעֲרֵי צַדִּיק:

20 A pauper is despised even by his peers, But a rich man has many friends.

כ גַּם־לְרֵעֵהוּ יִשָּׂנֵא רָשׁ וְאֹהֲבֵי עָשִׁיר רַבִּים:

21 He who despises his fellow is wrong; He who shows pity for the lowly is happy.

כא בָּז־לְרֵעֵהוּ חוֹטֵא וּמְחוֹנֵן עניים [עֲנָוִים] אַשְׁרָיו:

22 Surely those who plan evil go astray, While those who plan good earn steadfast love.

כב הֲלוֹא־יִתְעוּ חֹרְשֵׁי רָע וְחֶסֶד וֶאֱמֶת חֹרְשֵׁי טוֹב:

23 From all toil there is some gain, But idle chatter is pure loss.

כג בְּכָל־עֶצֶב יִהְיֶה מוֹתָר וּדְבַר־שְׂפָתַיִם אַךְ־לְמַחְסוֹר:

24 The ornament of the wise is their wealth; The stupidity of dullards is stupidity.

כד עֲטֶרֶת חֲכָמִים עָשְׁרָם אִוֶּלֶת כְּסִילִים אִוֶּלֶת:

25 A truthful witness saves lives; He who testifies lies [spreads] deceit.

כה מַצִּיל נְפָשׁוֹת עֵד אֱמֶת וְיָפִחַ כְּזָבִים מִרְמָה:

26 Fear of *Hashem* is a stronghold, A refuge for a man's children.

כו בְּיִרְאַת יְהֹוָה מִבְטַח־עֹז וּלְבָנָיו יִהְיֶה מַחְסֶה:

27 Fear of *Hashem* is a fountain of life, Enabling one to avoid deadly snares.

כז יִרְאַת יְהֹוָה מְקוֹר חַיִּים לָסוּר מִמֹּקְשֵׁי מָוֶת:

28 A numerous people is the glory of a king; Without a nation a ruler is ruined.

כח בְּרָב־עָם הַדְרַת־מֶלֶךְ וּבְאֶפֶס לְאֹם מְחִתַּת רָזוֹן:

b'-rov AM had-rat ME-lekh uv-E-fes l'-OM m'-khi-TAT ra-ZON

14:28 A numerous people is the glory of a king This verse is frequently understood in reference to *Hashem* Himself. His glory is increased when the multitudes of His people follow His ways, bringing Him

Mishlei/Proverbs
Chapter 15

משלי
פרק טו

29 Patience results in much understanding; Impatience gets folly as its portion.

כט אֶ֣רֶךְ אַ֭פַּיִם רַב־תְּבוּנָ֑ה וּקְצַר־ר֝֗וּחַ מֵרִ֥ים אִוֶּֽלֶת׃

30 A calm disposition gives bodily health; Passion is rot to the bones.

ל חַיֵּ֣י בְ֭שָׂרִים לֵ֣ב מַרְפֵּ֑א וּרְקַ֖ב עֲצָמ֣וֹת קִנְאָֽה׃

31 He who withholds what is due to the poor affronts his Maker; He who shows pity for the needy honors Him.

לא עֹשֵֽׁק־דָּ֭ל חֵרֵ֣ף עֹשֵׂ֑הוּ וּ֝מְכַבְּד֗וֹ חֹנֵ֥ן אֶבְיֽוֹן׃

32 The wicked man is felled by his own evil; The righteous man finds security in his death.

לב בְּ֭רָעָתוֹ יִדָּחֶ֣ה רָשָׁ֑ע וְחֹסֶ֖ה בְמוֹת֣וֹ צַדִּֽיק׃

33 Wisdom rests quietly in the mind of a prudent man, But among dullards it makes itself known.

לג בְּלֵ֣ב נָ֭בוֹן תָּנ֣וּחַ חָכְמָ֑ה וּבְקֶ֥רֶב כְּ֝סִילִ֗ים תִּוָּדֵֽעַ׃

34 Righteousness exalts a nation; Sin is a reproach to any people.

לד צְדָקָ֥ה תְרוֹמֵֽם־גּ֑וֹי וְחֶ֖סֶד לְאֻמִּ֣ים חַטָּֽאת׃

35 The king favors a capable servant; He rages at an incompetent one.

לה רְצוֹן־מֶ֭לֶךְ לְעֶ֣בֶד מַשְׂכִּ֑יל וְ֝עֶבְרָת֗וֹ תִּהְיֶ֥ה מֵבִֽישׁ׃

15 1 A gentle response allays wrath; A harsh word provokes anger.

טו א מַֽעֲנֶה־רַּ֭ךְ יָשִׁ֣יב חֵמָ֑ה וּדְבַר־עֶ֝֗צֶב יַעֲלֶה־אָֽף׃

2 The tongue of the wise produces much knowledge, But the mouth of dullards pours out folly.

ב לְשׁ֣וֹן חֲ֭כָמִים תֵּיטִ֣יב דָּ֑עַת וּפִ֥י כְ֝סִילִ֗ים יַבִּ֥יעַ אִוֶּֽלֶת׃

3 The eyes of *Hashem* are everywhere, Observing the bad and the good.

ג בְּֽכָל־מָ֭קוֹם עֵינֵ֣י יְהֹוָ֑ה צֹ֝פ֗וֹת רָעִ֥ים וְטוֹבִֽים׃

4 A healing tongue is a tree of life, But a devious one makes for a broken spirit.

ד מַרְפֵּ֣א לָ֭שׁוֹן עֵ֣ץ חַיִּ֑ים וְסֶ֥לֶף בָּ֝֗הּ שֶׁ֣בֶר בְּרֽוּחַ׃

5 A fool spurns the discipline of his father, But one who heeds reproof becomes clever.

ה אֱוִ֗יל יִ֭נְאַץ מוּסַ֣ר אָבִ֑יו וְשֹׁמֵ֖ר תּוֹכַ֣חַת יַעְרִֽם׃

6 In the house of the righteous there is much treasure, But in the harvest of the wicked there is trouble.

ו בֵּ֣ית צַ֭דִּיק חֹ֣סֶן רָ֑ב וּבִתְבוּאַ֖ת רָשָׁ֣ע נֶעְכָּֽרֶת׃

7 The lips of the wise disseminate knowledge; Not so the minds of dullards.

ז שִׂפְתֵ֣י חֲ֭כָמִים יְזָ֣רוּ דָ֑עַת וְלֵ֖ב כְּסִילִ֣ים לֹא־כֵֽן׃

8 The sacrifice of the wicked is an abomination to *Hashem*, But the prayer of the upright pleases Him.

ח זֶ֣בַח רְ֭שָׁעִים תּוֹעֲבַ֣ת יְהֹוָ֑ה וּתְפִלַּ֖ת יְשָׁרִ֣ים רְצוֹנֽוֹ׃

a good name in the eyes of the world. Based on this verse, Jewish tradition teaches that if a person has a choice of houses of worship in which he could pray, it is preferable to worship God in the larger congregation, for "A numerous people is the glory of a king." The ultimate expression of God's glory, however, can be learned from its inverse: The greatest disgrace to *Hashem*'s glory is when the Children of Israel are isolated, scattered and exiled from the land. The greatest glory to the King of Kings, therefore, is the return of the People of Israel to the Land of Israel in large numbers. How fortunate is our generation that has seen millions of Jews from the four corners of the world return *en masse* to live in Israel, thereby bringing glory to the King of Kings.

Mishlei/Proverbs
Chapter 15

משלי
פרק טו

9 The way of the wicked is an abomination to *Hashem*, But He loves him who pursues righteousness.

ט תּוֹעֲבַת יְהוָה דֶּרֶךְ רָשָׁע וּמְרַדֵּף צְדָקָה יֶאֱהָב:

10 Discipline seems bad to him who forsakes the way; He who spurns reproof will die.

י מוּסָר רָע לְעֹזֵב אֹרַח שׂוֹנֵא תוֹכַחַת יָמוּת:

11 Sheol and Abaddon lie exposed to *Hashem*, How much more the minds of men!

יא שְׁאוֹל וַאֲבַדּוֹן נֶגֶד יְהוָה אַף כִּי־לִבּוֹת בְּנֵי־אָדָם:

12 The scoffer dislikes being reproved; He will not resort to the wise.

יב לֹא יֶאֱהַב־לֵץ הוֹכֵחַ לוֹ אֶל־חֲכָמִים לֹא יֵלֵךְ:

13 A joyful heart makes a cheerful face; A sad heart makes a despondent mood.

יג לֵב שָׂמֵחַ יֵיטִב פָּנִים וּבְעַצְּבַת־לֵב רוּחַ נְכֵאָה:

14 The mind of a prudent man seeks knowledge; The mouth of the dullard pursues folly.

יד לֵב נָבוֹן יְבַקֶּשׁ־דָּעַת וּפִי [וּפְנֵי] כְסִילִים יִרְעֶה אִוֶּלֶת:

15 All the days of a poor man are wretched, But contentment is a feast without end.

טו כָּל־יְמֵי עָנִי רָעִים וְטוֹב־לֵב מִשְׁתֶּה תָמִיד:

16 **Better a little with fear of *Hashem* Than great wealth with confusion.**

טז טוֹב־מְעַט בְּיִרְאַת יְהוָה מֵאוֹצָר רָב וּמְהוּמָה בוֹ:

tov m'-AT b'-yir-AT a-do-NAI may-o-TZAR RAV um-HU-mah VO

17 Better a meal of vegetables where there is love Than a fattened ox where there is hate.

יז טוֹב אֲרֻחַת יָרָק וְאַהֲבָה־שָׁם מִשּׁוֹר אָבוּס וְשִׂנְאָה־בוֹ:

18 A hot-tempered man provokes a quarrel; A patient man calms strife.

יח אִישׁ חֵמָה יְגָרֶה מָדוֹן וְאֶרֶךְ אַפַּיִם יַשְׁקִיט רִיב:

19 The way of a lazy man is like a hedge of thorns, But the path of the upright is paved.

יט דֶּרֶךְ עָצֵל כִּמְשֻׂכַת חָדֶק וְאֹרַח יְשָׁרִים סְלֻלָה:

20 A wise son makes his father happy; A fool of a man humiliates his mother.

כ בֵּן חָכָם יְשַׂמַּח־אָב וּכְסִיל אָדָם בּוֹזֶה אִמּוֹ:

21 Folly is joy to one devoid of sense; A prudent man walks a straight path.

כא אִוֶּלֶת שִׂמְחָה לַחֲסַר־לֵב וְאִישׁ תְּבוּנָה יְיַשֶּׁר־לָכֶת:

22 Plans are foiled for want of counsel, But they succeed through many advisers.

כב הָפֵר מַחֲשָׁבוֹת בְּאֵין סוֹד וּבְרֹב יוֹעֲצִים תָּקוּם:

23 A ready response is a joy to a man, And how good is a word rightly timed!

כג שִׂמְחָה לָאִישׁ בְּמַעֲנֵה־פִיו וְדָבָר בְּעִתּוֹ מַה־טּוֹב:

15:16 Better a little with fear of *Hashem* *Shlomo* presents the reader an understanding of true value. It is better to have only a little, accompanied by faith in *Hashem*, than to have much wealth, but suffer from inner turmoil and doubt. This eternal truth is especially evident in today's celebrity culture, where so many people who seem to have it all suffer publicly from depression and family instability. In contrast to the constant and empty pursuit of fame and fortune, King *Shlomo* teaches "better a little with fear of *Hashem*."

Mishlei/Proverbs
Chapter 16

משלי
פרק טז

24 For an intelligent man the path of life leads upward, In order to avoid Sheol below.

אֹרַח חַיִּים לְמַעְלָה לְמַשְׂכִּיל לְמַעַן סוּר מִשְּׁאוֹל מָטָּה: כד

25 *Hashem* will tear down the house of the proud, But He will establish the homestead of the widow.

בֵּית גֵּאִים יִסַּח יְהֹוָה וְיַצֵּב גְּבוּל אַלְמָנָה: כה

26 Evil thoughts are an abomination to *Hashem*, But pleasant words are pure.

תּוֹעֲבַת יְהֹוָה מַחְשְׁבוֹת רָע וּטְהֹרִים אִמְרֵי־נֹעַם: כו

27 He who pursues ill-gotten gain makes trouble for his household; He who spurns gifts will live long.

עֹכֵר בֵּיתוֹ בּוֹצֵעַ בָּצַע וְשׂוֹנֵא מַתָּנֹת יִחְיֶה: כז

28 The heart of the righteous man rehearses his answer, But the mouth of the wicked blurts out evil things.

לֵב צַדִּיק יֶהְגֶּה לַעֲנוֹת וּפִי רְשָׁעִים יַבִּיעַ רָעוֹת: כח

29 *Hashem* is far from the wicked, But He hears the prayer of the righteous.

רָחוֹק יְהֹוָה מֵרְשָׁעִים וּתְפִלַּת צַדִּיקִים יִשְׁמָע: כט

30 What brightens the eye gladdens the heart; Good news puts fat on the bones.

מְאוֹר־עֵינַיִם יְשַׂמַּח־לֵב שְׁמוּעָה טוֹבָה תְּדַשֶּׁן־עָצֶם: ל

31 He whose ear heeds the discipline of life Lodges among the wise.

אֹזֶן שֹׁמַעַת תּוֹכַחַת חַיִּים בְּקֶרֶב חֲכָמִים תָּלִין: לא

32 He who spurns discipline hates himself; He who heeds reproof gains understanding.

פּוֹרֵעַ מוּסָר מוֹאֵס נַפְשׁוֹ וְשׁוֹמֵעַ תּוֹכַחַת קוֹנֶה לֵּב: לב

33 The fear of *Hashem* is the discipline of wisdom; Humility precedes honor.

יִרְאַת יְהֹוָה מוּסַר חָכְמָה וְלִפְנֵי כָבוֹד עֲנָוָה: לג

16

1 A man may arrange his thoughts, But what he says depends on *Hashem*.

לְאָדָם מַעַרְכֵי־לֵב וּמֵיְהֹוָה מַעֲנֵה לָשׁוֹן: א

טז

2 All the ways of a man seem right to him, But *Hashem* probes motives.

כָּל־דַּרְכֵי־אִישׁ זַךְ בְּעֵינָיו וְתֹכֵן רוּחוֹת יְהֹוָה: ב

3 Entrust your affairs to *Hashem*, And your plans will succeed.

גֹּל אֶל־יְהֹוָה מַעֲשֶׂיךָ וְיִכֹּנוּ מַחְשְׁבֹתֶיךָ: ג

4 *Hashem* made everything for a purpose, Even the wicked for an evil day.

כֹּל פָּעַל יְהֹוָה לַמַּעֲנֵהוּ וְגַם־רָשָׁע לְיוֹם רָעָה: ד

KOL pa-AL a-do-NAI l'-ma-a-NAY-hu v'-gam ra-SHA l'-YOM ra-AH

5 Every haughty person is an abomination to *Hashem*; Assuredly, he will not go unpunished.

תּוֹעֲבַת יְהֹוָה כָּל־גְּבַהּ־לֵב יָד לְיָד לֹא יִנָּקֶה: ה

16:4 ***Hashem* made everything for a purpose** Since we know that *Hashem* is good, sometimes we assume that bad things happen despite Him. This verse reminds us that everything, even that which we perceive as evil, was created by God for a purpose. Though the reason is not always clear, we must look for the good that comes from every situation. The slavery in Egypt, for example, led to the formation of the Nation of Israel, the giving of the Torah on Mount Sinai, and ultimately the acquisition of the Land of Israel. With this verse in mind, we can rest assured that Israel's many enemies and the threats facing the Jewish state today are also part of *Hashem*'s divine plan and will lead to the greatest good: The redemption of Israel and the world.

Mishlei/Proverbs
Chapter 16

משלי
פרק טז

6 Iniquity is expiated by loyalty and faithfulness, And evil is avoided through fear of *Hashem*.

ו בְּחֶסֶד וֶאֱמֶת יְכֻפַּר עָוֹן וּבְיִרְאַת יְהֹוָה סוּר מֵרָע׃

7 When *Hashem* is pleased with a man's conduct, He may turn even his enemies into allies.

ז בִּרְצוֹת יְהֹוָה דַּרְכֵי־אִישׁ גַּם־אוֹיְבָיו יַשְׁלִם אִתּוֹ׃

8 Better a little with righteousness Than a large income with injustice.

ח טוֹב־מְעַט בִּצְדָקָה מֵרֹב תְּבוּאוֹת בְּלֹא מִשְׁפָּט׃

9 A man may plot out his course, But it is *Hashem* who directs his steps.

ט לֵב אָדָם יְחַשֵּׁב דַּרְכּוֹ וַיהֹוָה יָכִין צַעֲדוֹ׃

10 There is magic on the lips of the king; He cannot err in judgment.

י קֶסֶם ׀ עַל־שִׂפְתֵי־מֶלֶךְ בְּמִשְׁפָּט לֹא יִמְעַל־פִּיו׃

11 Honest scales and balances are *Hashem*'s; All the weights in the bag are His work.

יא פֶּלֶס ׀ וּמֹאזְנֵי מִשְׁפָּט לַיהֹוָה מַעֲשֵׂהוּ כׇּל־אַבְנֵי־כִיס׃

12 Wicked deeds are an abomination to kings, For the throne is established by righteousness.

יב תּוֹעֲבַת מְלָכִים עֲשׂוֹת רֶשַׁע כִּי בִצְדָקָה יִכּוֹן כִּסֵּא׃

13 Truthful speech wins the favor of kings; They love those who speak honestly.

יג רְצוֹן מְלָכִים שִׂפְתֵי־צֶדֶק וְדֹבֵר יְשָׁרִים יֶאֱהָב׃

14 The king's wrath is a messenger of death, But a wise man can appease it.

יד חֲמַת־מֶלֶךְ מַלְאֲכֵי־מָוֶת וְאִישׁ חָכָם יְכַפְּרֶנָּה׃

15 The king's smile means life; His favor is like a rain cloud in spring.

טו בְּאוֹר־פְּנֵי־מֶלֶךְ חַיִּים וּרְצוֹנוֹ כְּעָב מַלְקוֹשׁ׃

16 How much better to acquire wisdom than gold; To acquire understanding is preferable to silver.

טז קְנֹה־חׇכְמָה מַה־טּוֹב מֵחָרוּץ וּקְנוֹת בִּינָה נִבְחָר מִכָּסֶף׃

17 The highway of the upright avoids evil; He who would preserve his life watches his way.

יז מְסִלַּת יְשָׁרִים סוּר מֵרָע שֹׁמֵר נַפְשׁוֹ נֹצֵר דַּרְכּוֹ׃

18 Pride goes before ruin, Arrogance, before failure.

יח לִפְנֵי־שֶׁבֶר גָּאוֹן וְלִפְנֵי כִשָּׁלוֹן גֹּבַהּ רוּחַ׃

19 Better to be humble and among the lowly Than to share spoils with the proud.

יט טוֹב שְׁפַל־רוּחַ אֶת־עֲנִיִּים [עֲנָוִים] מֵחַלֵּק שָׁלָל אֶת־גֵּאִים׃

20 He who is adept in a matter will attain success; Happy is he who trusts in *Hashem*.

כ מַשְׂכִּיל עַל־דָּבָר יִמְצָא־טוֹב וּבוֹטֵחַ בַּיהֹוָה אַשְׁרָיו׃

21 The wise-hearted is called discerning; One whose speech is pleasing gains wisdom.

כא לַחֲכַם־לֵב יִקָּרֵא נָבוֹן וּמֶתֶק שְׂפָתַיִם יֹסִיף לֶקַח׃

22 Good sense is a fountain of life to those who have it, And folly is the punishment of fools.

כב מְקוֹר חַיִּים שֵׂכֶל בְּעָלָיו וּמוּסַר אֱוִלִים אִוֶּלֶת׃

23 The mind of the wise man makes his speech effective And increases the wisdom on his lips.

כג לֵב חָכָם יַשְׂכִּיל פִּיהוּ וְעַל־שְׂפָתָיו יֹסִיף לֶקַח׃

24 Pleasant words are like a honeycomb, Sweet to the palate and a cure for the body.

כד צוּף־דְּבַשׁ אִמְרֵי־נֹעַם מָתוֹק לַנֶּפֶשׁ וּמַרְפֵּא לָעָצֶם׃

25 A road may seem right to a man, But in the end it is a road to death.

כה יֵשׁ דֶּרֶךְ יָשָׁר לִפְנֵי־אִישׁ וְאַחֲרִיתָהּ דַּרְכֵי־מָוֶת׃

Mishlei/Proverbs
Chapter 17

26 The appetite of a laborer labors for him, Because his hunger forces him on.

כו נֶ֣פֶשׁ עָ֭מֵל עָ֣מְלָה לּ֑וֹ כִּֽי־אָכַ֖ף עָלָ֣יו פִּֽיהוּ׃

27 A scoundrel plots evil; What is on his lips is like a scorching fire.

כז אִ֣ישׁ בְּ֭לִיַּעַל כֹּ֣רֶה רָעָ֑ה וְעַל־שְׂ֝פָתָ֗יו [שְׂפָת֗וֹ] כְּאֵ֣שׁ צָרָֽבֶת׃

28 A shifty man stirs up strife, And a querulous one alienates his friend.

כח אִ֣ישׁ תַּ֭הְפֻּכוֹת יְשַׁלַּ֣ח מָד֑וֹן וְ֝נִרְגָּ֗ן מַפְרִ֥יד אַלּֽוּף׃

29 A lawless man misleads his friend, Making him take the wrong way.

כט אִ֣ישׁ חָ֭מָס יְפַתֶּ֣ה רֵעֵ֑הוּ וְ֝הוֹלִיכ֗וֹ בְּדֶ֣רֶךְ לֹא־טֽוֹב׃

30 He closes his eyes while meditating deception; He purses his lips while deciding upon evil.

ל עֹצֶ֣ה עֵ֭ינָיו לַחְשֹׁ֣ב תַּהְפֻּכ֑וֹת קֹרֵ֥ץ שְׂ֝פָתָ֗יו כִּלָּ֥ה רָעָֽה׃

31 Gray hair is a crown of glory; It is attained by the way of righteousness.

לא עֲטֶ֣רֶת תִּפְאֶ֣רֶת שֵׂיבָ֑ה בְּדֶ֥רֶךְ צְ֝דָקָ֗ה תִּמָּצֵֽא׃

32 Better to be forbearing than mighty, To have self-control than to conquer a city.

לב ט֤וֹב אֶ֣רֶךְ אַ֭פַּיִם מִגִּבּ֑וֹר וּמֹשֵׁ֥ל בְּ֝רוּח֗וֹ מִלֹּכֵ֥ד עִֽיר׃

33 Lots are cast into the lap; The decision depends on *Hashem*.

לג בַּ֭חֵיק יוּטַ֣ל אֶת־הַגּוֹרָ֑ל וּ֝מֵיְהֹוָ֗ה כׇּל־מִשְׁפָּטֽוֹ׃

17

1 Better a dry crust with peace Than a house full of feasting with strife.

יז א ט֤וֹב פַּ֣ת חֲ֭רֵבָה וְשַׁלְוָה־בָ֑הּ מִ֝בַּ֗יִת מָלֵ֥א זִבְחֵי־רִֽיב׃

2 A capable servant will dominate an incompetent son And share the inheritance with the brothers.

ב עֶֽבֶד־מַ֭שְׂכִּיל יִ֭מְשֹׁל בְּבֵ֣ן מֵבִ֑ישׁ וּבְת֥וֹךְ אַ֝חִ֗ים יַחֲלֹ֥ק נַחֲלָֽה׃

3 For silver – the crucible; For gold – the furnace, And *Hashem* tests the mind.

ג מַצְרֵ֣ף לַ֭כֶּסֶף וְכ֣וּר לַזָּהָ֑ב וּבֹחֵ֖ן לִבּ֣וֹת יְהֹוָֽה׃

4 An evildoer listens to mischievous talk; A liar gives ear to malicious words.

ד מֵ֭רַע מַקְשִׁ֣יב עַל־שְׂפַת־אָ֑וֶן שֶׁ֥קֶר מֵ֝זִ֗ין עַל־לְשׁ֥וֹן הַוֺּֽת׃

5 He who mocks the poor affronts his Maker; He who rejoices over another's misfortune will not go unpunished.

ה לֹעֵ֣ג לָ֭רָשׁ חֵרֵ֣ף עֹשֵׂ֑הוּ שָׂמֵ֥חַ לְ֝אֵ֗יד לֹ֣א יִנָּקֶֽה׃

6 Grandchildren are the crown of their elders, And the glory of children is their parents.

ו עֲטֶ֣רֶת זְ֭קֵנִים בְּנֵ֣י בָנִ֑ים וְתִפְאֶ֖רֶת בָּנִ֣ים אֲבוֹתָֽם׃

a-TE-ret z'-kay-NEEM b'-NAY va-NEEM v'-tif-E-ret ba-NEEM a-vo-TAM

17:6 Grandchildren are the crown of their elders This verse extols the blessing of grandchildren, much like the passage in *Sefer Tehillim* (128:6). In *Sefer Tehillim*, however, the blessing of grandchildren is couched between references to the well-being of *Yerushalayim* and *Eretz Yisrael*: "May you share the prosperity of *Yerushalayim* all the days of your life, and live to see your children's children. May all be well with *Yisrael* (literally, 'may peace be upon *Yisrael*')" (Psalms 128:5- 6). What is the connection between children's children and the welfare of *Eretz Yisrael* and *Yerushalayim*? It has been suggested that verse 5 should be understood as a command rather than a promise: See the good of Jerusalem. We must emphasize and talk about what is special and precious about the Land of Israel, instead of complaining and focusing on the negative. If that is how we relate to land, and that is what we convey and pass down to our children and grandchildren, then there is a hope for a future in which peace will be upon Israel.

Mishlei/Proverbs

Chapter 17

משלי

פרק יז

7 Lofty words are not fitting for a villain; Much less lying words for a great man.

ז לֹא־נָאוָה לְנָבָל שְׂפַת־יֶתֶר אַף כִּי־לְנָדִיב שְׂפַת־שָׁקֶר׃

8 A bribe seems like a charm to him who uses it; He succeeds at every turn.

ח אֶבֶן־חֵן הַשֹּׁחַד בְּעֵינֵי בְעָלָיו אֶל־כָּל־אֲשֶׁר יִפְנֶה יַשְׂכִּיל׃

9 He who seeks love overlooks faults, But he who harps on a matter alienates his friend.

ט מְכַסֶּה־פֶּשַׁע מְבַקֵּשׁ אַהֲבָה וְשֹׁנֶה בְדָבָר מַפְרִיד אַלּוּף׃

10 A rebuke works on an intelligent man More than one hundred blows on a fool.

י תֵּחַת גְּעָרָה בְמֵבִין מֵהַכּוֹת כְּסִיל מֵאָה׃

11 An evil man seeks only to rebel; A ruthless messenger will be sent against him.

יא אַךְ־מְרִי יְבַקֶּשׁ־רָע וּמַלְאָךְ אַכְזָרִי יְשֻׁלַּח־בּוֹ׃

12 Sooner meet a bereaved she-bear Than a fool with his nonsense.

יב פָּגוֹשׁ דֹּב שַׁכּוּל בְּאִישׁ וְאַל־כְּסִיל בְּאִוַּלְתּוֹ׃

13 Evil will never depart from the house Of him who repays good with evil.

יג מֵשִׁיב רָעָה תַּחַת טוֹבָה לֹא־תמיש [תָמוּשׁ] רָעָה מִבֵּיתוֹ׃

14 To start a quarrel is to open a sluice; Before a dispute flares up, drop it.

יד פּוֹטֵר מַיִם רֵאשִׁית מָדוֹן וְלִפְנֵי הִתְגַּלַּע הָרִיב נְטוֹשׁ׃

15 To acquit the guilty and convict the innocent – Both are an abomination to *Hashem*.

טו מַצְדִּיק רָשָׁע וּמַרְשִׁיעַ צַדִּיק תּוֹעֲבַת יְהוָה גַּם־שְׁנֵיהֶם׃

16 What good is money in the hand of a fool To purchase wisdom, when he has no mind?

טז לָמָּה־זֶּה מְחִיר בְּיַד־כְּסִיל לִקְנוֹת חָכְמָה וְלֶב־אָיִן׃

17 A friend is devoted at all times; A brother is born to share adversity.

יז בְּכָל־עֵת אֹהֵב הָרֵעַ וְאָח לְצָרָה יִוָּלֵד׃

18 Devoid of sense is he who gives his hand To stand surety for his fellow.

יח אָדָם חֲסַר־לֵב תּוֹקֵעַ כָּף עֹרֵב עֲרֻבָּה לִפְנֵי רֵעֵהוּ׃

19 He who loves transgression loves strife; He who builds a high threshold invites broken bones.

יט אֹהֵב פֶּשַׁע אֹהֵב מַצָּה מַגְבִּיהַּ פִּתְחוֹ מְבַקֶּשׁ־שָׁבֶר׃

20 Man of crooked mind comes to no good, And he who speaks duplicity falls into trouble.

כ עִקֶּשׁ־לֵב לֹא יִמְצָא־טוֹב וְנֶהְפָּךְ בִּלְשׁוֹנוֹ יִפּוֹל בְּרָעָה׃

21 One begets a dullard to one's own grief; The father of a villain has no joy.

כא יֹלֵד כְּסִיל לְתוּגָה לוֹ וְלֹא־יִשְׂמַח אֲבִי נָבָל׃

22 A joyful heart makes for good health; Despondency dries up the bones.

כב לֵב שָׂמֵחַ יֵיטִב גֵּהָה וְרוּחַ נְכֵאָה תְּיַבֶּשׁ־גָּרֶם׃

23 The wicked man draws a bribe out of his bosom To pervert the course of justice.

כג שֹׁחַד מֵחֵיק רָשָׁע יִקָּח לְהַטּוֹת אָרְחוֹת מִשְׁפָּט׃

24 Wisdom lies before the intelligent man; The eyes of the dullard range to the ends of the earth.

כד אֶת־פְּנֵי מֵבִין חָכְמָה וְעֵינֵי כְסִיל בִּקְצֵה־אָרֶץ׃

25 A stupid son is vexation for his father And a heartache for the woman who bore him.

כה כַּעַס לְאָבִיו בֵּן כְּסִיל וּמֶמֶר לְיוֹלַדְתּוֹ׃

Mishlei/Proverbs

Chapter 18

משלי	
פרק יח	

26 To punish the innocent is surely not right, Or to flog the great for their uprightness.

כו גַּם עֲנוֹשׁ לַצַּדִּיק לֹא־טוֹב לְהַכּוֹת נְדִיבִים עַל־יֹשֶׁר׃

27 A knowledgeable man is sparing with his words; A man of understanding is reticent.

כז חוֹשֵׂךְ אֲמָרָיו יוֹדֵעַ דָּעַת וקר־ [וִיקַר־] רוּחַ אִישׁ תְּבוּנָה׃

28 Even a fool, if he keeps silent, is deemed wise; Intelligent, if he seals his lips.

כח גַּם אֱוִיל מַחֲרִישׁ חָכָם יֵחָשֵׁב אֹטֵם שְׂפָתָיו נָבוֹן׃

18 1 He who isolates himself pursues his desires; He disdains all competence.

יח א לְתַאֲוָה יְבַקֵּשׁ נִפְרָד בְּכָל־תּוּשִׁיָּה יִתְגַּלָּע׃

2 The fool does not desire understanding, But only to air his thoughts.

ב לֹא־יַחְפֹּץ כְּסִיל בִּתְבוּנָה כִּי אִם־בְּהִתְגַּלּוֹת לִבּוֹ׃

3 Comes the wicked man comes derision, And with the rogue, contempt.

ג בְּבוֹא־רָשָׁע בָּא גַם־בּוּז וְעִם־קָלוֹן חֶרְפָּה׃

4 The words a man speaks are deep waters, A flowing stream, a fountain of wisdom.

ד מַיִם עֲמֻקִּים דִּבְרֵי פִי־אִישׁ נַחַל נֹבֵעַ מְקוֹר חָכְמָה׃

5 It is not right to be partial to the guilty And subvert the innocent in judgment.

ה שְׂאֵת פְּנֵי־רָשָׁע לֹא־טוֹב לְהַטּוֹת צַדִּיק בַּמִּשְׁפָּט׃

6 The words of a fool lead to strife; His speech invites blows.

ו שִׂפְתֵי כְסִיל יָבֹאוּ בְרִיב וּפִיו לְמַהֲלֻמוֹת יִקְרָא׃

7 The fool's speech is his ruin; His words are a trap for him.

ז פִּי־כְסִיל מְחִתָּה־לוֹ וּשְׂפָתָיו מוֹקֵשׁ נַפְשׁוֹ׃

8 The words of a querulous man are bruising; They penetrate one's inmost parts.

ח דִּבְרֵי נִרְגָּן כְּמִתְלַהֲמִים וְהֵם יָרְדוּ חַדְרֵי־בָטֶן׃

9 One who is slack in his work Is a brother to a vandal.

ט גַּם מִתְרַפֶּה בִמְלַאכְתּוֹ אָח הוּא לְבַעַל מַשְׁחִית׃

10 The name of *Hashem* is a tower of strength To which the righteous man runs and is safe.

י מִגְדַּל־עֹז שֵׁם יְהוָה בּוֹ־יָרוּץ צַדִּיק וְנִשְׂגָּב׃

11 The wealth of a rich man is his fortress; In his fancy it is a protective wall.

יא הוֹן עָשִׁיר קִרְיַת עֻזּוֹ וּכְחוֹמָה נִשְׂגָּבָה בְּמַשְׂכִּיתוֹ׃

12 Before ruin a man's heart is proud; Humility goes before honor.

יב לִפְנֵי־שֶׁבֶר יִגְבַּהּ לֶב־אִישׁ וְלִפְנֵי כָבוֹד עֲנָוָה׃

13 To answer a man before hearing him out Is foolish and disgraceful.

יג מֵשִׁיב דָּבָר בְּטֶרֶם יִשְׁמָע אִוֶּלֶת הִיא־לוֹ וּכְלִמָּה׃

14 A man's spirit can sustain him through illness; But low spirits – who can bear them?

יד רוּחַ־אִישׁ יְכַלְכֵּל מַחֲלֵהוּ וְרוּחַ נְכֵאָה מִי יִשָּׂאֶנָּה׃

15 The mind of an intelligent man acquires knowledge; The ears of the wise seek out knowledge.

טו לֵב נָבוֹן יִקְנֶה־דָּעַת וְאֹזֶן חֲכָמִים תְּבַקֶּשׁ־דָּעַת׃

16 A man's gift eases his way And gives him access to the great.

טז מַתָּן אָדָם יַרְחִיב לוֹ וְלִפְנֵי גְדֹלִים יַנְחֶנּוּ׃

Mishlei/Proverbs
Chapter 19

משלי
פרק יט

17 The first to plead his case seems right Till the other party examines him.

צַדִּיק הָרִאשׁוֹן בְּרִיבוֹ יבא־[וּבָא־] רֵעֵהוּ וַחֲקָרוֹ׃

18 The lot puts an end to strife And separates those locked in dispute.

מִדְיָנִים יַשְׁבִּית הַגּוֹרָל וּבֵין עֲצוּמִים יַפְרִיד׃

19 A brother offended is more formidable than a stronghold; Such strife is like the bars of a fortress.

אָח נִפְשָׁע מִקִּרְיַת־עֹז ומדונים [וּמִדְיָנִים] כִּבְרִיחַ אַרְמוֹן׃

20 A man's belly is filled by the fruit of his mouth; He will be filled by the produce of his lips.

מִפְּרִי פִי־אִישׁ תִּשְׂבַּע בִּטְנוֹ תְּבוּאַת שְׂפָתָיו יִשְׂבָּע׃

21 Death and life are in the power of the tongue; Those who love it will eat its fruit.

מָוֶת וְחַיִּים בְּיַד־לָשׁוֹן וְאֹהֲבֶיהָ יֹאכַל פִּרְיָהּ׃

22 **He who finds a wife has found happiness And has won the favor of *Hashem*.**

מָצָא אִשָּׁה מָצָא טוֹב וַיָּפֶק רָצוֹן מֵיְהוָה׃

ma-TZA i-SHAH MA-tza TOV va-YA-fek ra-TZON may-a-do-NAI

23 The poor man speaks beseechingly; The rich man's answer is harsh.

תַּחֲנוּנִים יְדַבֶּר־רָשׁ וְעָשִׁיר יַעֲנֶה עַזּוֹת׃

24 There are companions to keep one company, And there is a friend more devoted than a brother.

אִישׁ רֵעִים לְהִתְרֹעֵעַ וְיֵשׁ אֹהֵב דָּבֵק מֵאָח׃

19

1 Better a poor man who lives blamelessly Than one who speaks perversely and is a dullard.

טוֹב־רָשׁ הוֹלֵךְ בְּתֻמּוֹ מֵעִקֵּשׁ שְׂפָתָיו וְהוּא כְסִיל׃

2 A person without knowledge is surely not good; He who moves hurriedly blunders.

גַּם בְּלֹא־דַעַת נֶפֶשׁ לֹא־טוֹב וְאָץ בְּרַגְלַיִם חוֹטֵא׃

3 A man's folly subverts his way, And his heart rages against *Hashem*.

אִוֶּלֶת אָדָם תְּסַלֵּף דַּרְכּוֹ וְעַל־יְהוָה יִזְעַף לִבּוֹ׃

4 Wealth makes many friends, But a poor man loses his last friend.

הוֹן יֹסִיף רֵעִים רַבִּים וְדָל מֵרֵעֵהוּ יִפָּרֵד׃

5 A false witness will not go unpunished; He who testifies lies will not escape.

עֵד שְׁקָרִים לֹא יִנָּקֶה וְיָפִיחַ כְּזָבִים לֹא יִמָּלֵט׃

6 Many court the favor of a great man, And all are the friends of a dispenser of gifts.

רַבִּים יְחַלּוּ פְנֵי־נָדִיב וְכָל־הָרֵעַ לְאִישׁ מַתָּן׃

7 All the brothers of a poor man despise him; How much more is he shunned by his friends! He who pursues words – they are of no avail.

כָּל אֲחֵי־רָשׁ שְׂנֵאֻהוּ אַף כִּי מְרֵעֵהוּ רָחֲקוּ מִמֶּנּוּ מְרַדֵּף אֲמָרִים לא־[לוֹ־] הֵמָּה׃

א **18:22 He who finds a wife has found happiness**
This verse is a parallel to the verse in which *Hashem* says, "It is not good for man to be alone; I will make a fitting helper for him" (Genesis 2:18). God wants man to find a wife who will serve as his partner in life. When he does, *Hashem* will bless that union, as it fulfils His will. The Hebrew word for 'man' is *eesh* (איש), and the word for 'woman' is *eeshah* (אשה). The two words share two out of three Hebrew letters, א and ש. The other two letters, י and ה, spell one of the names of God. The Sages (*Sotah* 17a) teach that when man and woman unite in marriage and work together, the presence of the Lord resides with them.

איש
אישה

1684

Mishlei/Proverbs
Chapter 19

משלי
פרק יט

8 He who acquires wisdom is his own best friend; He preserves understanding and attains happiness.

ח קֹנֶה־לֵּב אֹהֵב נַפְשׁוֹ שֹׁמֵר תְּבוּנָה לִמְצֹא־טוֹב:

9 A false witness will not go unpunished; He who testifies falsely is doomed.

ט עֵד שְׁקָרִים לֹא יִנָּקֶה וְיָפִיחַ כְּזָבִים יֹאבֵד:

10 Luxury is not fitting for a dullard, Much less that a servant rule over princes.

י לֹא־נָאוֶה לִכְסִיל תַּעֲנוּג אַף כִּי־לְעֶבֶד מְשֹׁל בְּשָׂרִים:

11 A man shows intelligence by his forebearance; It is his glory when he overlooks an offense.

יא שֵׂכֶל אָדָם הֶאֱרִיךְ אַפּוֹ וְתִפְאַרְתּוֹ עֲבֹר עַל־פָּשַׁע:

12 The rage of a king is like the roar of a lion; His favor is like dew upon the grass.

יב נַהַם כַּכְּפִיר זַעַף מֶלֶךְ וּכְטַל עַל־עֵשֶׂב רְצוֹנוֹ:

NA-ham ka-k'-FEER ZA-af ME-lekh ukh-TAL al AY-sev r'-tzo-NO

13 A stupid son is a calamity to his father; The nagging of a wife is like the endless dripping of water.

יג הַוֹּת לְאָבִיו בֵּן כְּסִיל וְדֶלֶף טֹרֵד מִדְיְנֵי אִשָּׁה:

14 Property and riches are bequeathed by fathers, But an efficient wife comes from *Hashem*.

יד בַּיִת וָהוֹן נַחֲלַת אָבוֹת וּמֵיהֹוָה אִשָּׁה מַשְׂכָּלֶת:

15 Laziness induces sleep, And a negligent person will go hungry.

טו עַצְלָה תַּפִּיל תַּרְדֵּמָה וְנֶפֶשׁ רְמִיָּה תִרְעָב:

16 He who has regard for his life pays regard to commandments; He who is heedless of his ways will die.

טז שֹׁמֵר מִצְוָה שֹׁמֵר נַפְשׁוֹ בּוֹזֵה דְרָכָיו יוּמָת [יָמוּת]:

17 He who is generous to the poor makes a loan to *Hashem*; He will repay him his due.

יז מַלְוֵה יְהֹוָה חוֹנֵן דָּל וּגְמֻלוֹ יְשַׁלֶּם־לוֹ:

18 Discipline your son while there is still hope, And do not set your heart on his destruction.

יח יַסֵּר בִּנְךָ כִּי־יֵשׁ תִּקְוָה וְאֶל־הֲמִיתוֹ אַל־תִּשָּׂא נַפְשֶׁךָ:

19 A hot-tempered man incurs punishment; If you try to save him you will only make it worse.

יט גְּרָל־[גְּדָל־] חֵמָה נֹשֵׂא עֹנֶשׁ כִּי אִם־תַּצִּיל וְעוֹד תּוֹסִף:

20 Listen to advice and accept discipline In order that you may be wise in the end.

כ שְׁמַע עֵצָה וְקַבֵּל מוּסָר לְמַעַן תֶּחְכַּם בְּאַחֲרִיתֶךָ:

21 Many designs are in a man's mind, But it is *Hashem*'s plan that is accomplished.

כא רַבּוֹת מַחֲשָׁבוֹת בְּלֶב־אִישׁ וַעֲצַת יְהֹוָה הִיא תָקוּם:

22 Greed is a reproach to a man; Better be poor than a liar.

כב תַּאֲוַת אָדָם חַסְדּוֹ וְטוֹב־רָשׁ מֵאִישׁ כָּזָב:

Morning dew near Beit Shemesh

19:12 His favor is like dew upon the grass Often, when the Bible mentions a king, it is a metaphor for *Hashem* Himself. Here, God's anger is likened to a lion's roar. A roar is frightening, but serves as a warning to its prey that the lion is present, and clever prey can escape. So too, *Hashem*'s anger is intended to warn us to correct our ways before it is too late. His blessing, however, is like dew which nurtures the grass. Unlike rain, which is a blessing but can also be destructive, dew serves only to help the grass grow. Similarly, the Lord's favor serves only to nurture, not to harm us.

Mishlei/Proverbs
Chapter 20

משלי
פרק כ

23 He who fears *Hashem* earns life; He shall abide in contentment, Free from misfortune.

כג יִרְאַת יְהֹוָה לְחַיִּים וְשָׂבֵעַ יָלִין בַּל־יִפָּקֶד רָע:

24 The lazy man buries his hand in the bowl; He will not even bring it to his mouth.

כד טָמַן עָצֵל יָדוֹ בַּצַּלָּחַת גַּם־אֶל־פִּיהוּ לֹא יְשִׁיבֶנָּה:

25 Beat the scoffer and the simple will become clever; Reprove an intelligent man and he gains knowledge.

כה לֵץ תַּכֶּה וּפֶתִי יַעְרִם וְהוֹכִיחַ לְנָבוֹן יָבִין דָּעַת:

26 A son who causes shame and disgrace Plunders his father, puts his mother to flight.

כו מְשַׁדֶּד־אָב יַבְרִיחַ אֵם בֵּן מֵבִישׁ וּמַחְפִּיר:

27 My son, cease to stray from words of knowledge And receive discipline.

כז חֲדַל־בְּנִי לִשְׁמֹעַ מוּסָר לִשְׁגוֹת מֵאִמְרֵי־דָעַת:

28 A malicious witness scoffs at justice, And the speech of the wicked conceals mischief.

כח עֵד בְּלִיַּעַל יָלִיץ מִשְׁפָּט וּפִי רְשָׁעִים יְבַלַּע־אָוֶן:

29 Punishments are in store for scoffers And blows for the backs of dullards.

כט נָכוֹנוּ לַלֵּצִים שְׁפָטִים וּמַהֲלֻמוֹת לְגֵו כְּסִילִים:

20 1 Wine is a scoffer, strong drink a roisterer; He who is muddled by them will not grow wise.

כ א לֵץ הַיַּיִן הֹמֶה שֵׁכָר וְכָל־שֹׁגֶה בּוֹ לֹא יֶחְכָּם:

2 The terror of a king is like the roar of a lion; He who provokes his anger risks his life.

ב נַהַם כַּכְּפִיר אֵימַת מֶלֶךְ מִתְעַבְּרוֹ חוֹטֵא נַפְשׁוֹ:

3 It is honorable for a man to desist from strife, But every fool becomes embroiled.

ג כָּבוֹד לָאִישׁ שֶׁבֶת מֵרִיב וְכָל־אֱוִיל יִתְגַּלָּע:

4 In winter the lazy man does not plow; At harvesttime he seeks, and finds nothing.

ד מֵחֹרֶף עָצֵל לֹא־יַחֲרֹשׁ ישאל [וְשָׁאַל] בַּקָּצִיר וָאָיִן:

5 The designs in a man's mind are deep waters But a man of understanding can draw them out.

ה מַיִם עֲמֻקִּים עֵצָה בְלֶב־אִישׁ וְאִישׁ תְּבוּנָה יִדְלֶנָּה:

6 He calls many a man his loyal friend, But who can find a faithful man?

ו רָב־אָדָם יִקְרָא אִישׁ חַסְדּוֹ וְאִישׁ אֱמוּנִים מִי יִמְצָא:

7 The righteous man lives blamelessly; Happy are his children who come after him.

ז מִתְהַלֵּךְ בְּתֻמּוֹ צַדִּיק אַשְׁרֵי בָנָיו אַחֲרָיו:

8 The king seated on the throne of judgment Can winnow out all evil by his glance.

ח מֶלֶךְ יוֹשֵׁב עַל־כִּסֵּא־דִין מְזָרֶה בְעֵינָיו כָּל־רָע:

9 Who can say, "I have cleansed my heart, I am purged of my sin"?

ט מִי־יֹאמַר זִכִּיתִי לִבִּי טָהַרְתִּי מֵחַטָּאתִי:

10 False weights and false measures, Both are an abomination to *Hashem*.

י אֶבֶן וָאֶבֶן אֵיפָה וְאֵיפָה תּוֹעֲבַת יְהֹוָה גַּם־שְׁנֵיהֶם:

11 A child may be dissembling in his behavior Even though his actions are blameless and proper.

יא גַּם בְּמַעֲלָלָיו יִתְנַכֶּר־נָעַר אִם־זַךְ וְאִם־יָשָׁר פָּעֳלוֹ:

12 The ear that hears, the eye that sees – *Hashem* made them both.

יב אֹזֶן שֹׁמַעַת וְעַיִן רֹאָה יְהֹוָה עָשָׂה גַם־שְׁנֵיהֶם:

Mishlei/Proverbs
Chapter 20

משלי
פרק כ

13 Do not love sleep lest you be impoverished; Keep your eyes open and you will have plenty of food.

יג אַל־תֶּאֱהַב שֵׁנָה פֶּן־תִּוָּרֵשׁ פְּקַח עֵינֶיךָ שְׂבַע־לָחֶם:

14 "Bad, bad," says the buyer, But having moved off, he congratulates himself.

יד רַע רַע יֹאמַר הַקּוֹנֶה וְאֹזֵל לוֹ אָז יִתְהַלָּל:

15 Gold is plentiful, jewels abundant, But wise speech is a precious object.

טו יֵשׁ זָהָב וְרָב־פְּנִינִים וּכְלִי יְקָר שִׂפְתֵי־דָעַת:

16 Seize his garment, for he stood surety for another; Take it as a pledge, [for he stood surety] for an unfamiliar woman.

טז לְקַח־בִּגְדוֹ כִּי־עָרַב זָר וּבְעַד נָכְרִים [נָכְרִיָּה] חַבְלֵהוּ:

17 Bread gained by fraud may be tasty to a man, But later his mouth will be filled with gravel.

יז עָרֵב לָאִישׁ לֶחֶם שָׁקֶר וְאַחַר יִמָּלֵא־פִיהוּ חָצָץ:

18 Plans laid in council will succeed; Wage war with stratagems.

יח מַחֲשָׁבוֹת בְּעֵצָה תִכּוֹן וּבְתַחְבֻּלוֹת עֲשֵׂה מִלְחָמָה:

19 He who gives away secrets is a base fellow; Do not take up with a garrulous man.

יט גּוֹלֶה־סּוֹד הוֹלֵךְ רָכִיל וּלְפֹתֶה שְׂפָתָיו לֹא תִתְעָרָב:

20 One who reviles his father or mother, Light will fail him when darkness comes.

כ מְקַלֵּל אָבִיו וְאִמּוֹ יִדְעַךְ נֵרוֹ באישון [בֶּאֱשׁוּן] חֹשֶׁךְ:

21 An estate acquired in haste at the outset Will not be blessed in the end.

כא נַחֲלָה מבחלת [מְבֹהֶלֶת] בָּרִאשׁוֹנָה וְאַחֲרִיתָהּ לֹא תְבֹרָךְ:

22 *Do not say, "I will requite evil"; Put your hope in* Hashem *and He will deliver you.*

כב אַל־תֹּאמַר אֲשַׁלְּמָה־רָע קַוֵּה לַיהוָה וְיֹשַׁע לָךְ:

al to-MAR a-sha-l'-mah RA ka-VAY la-do-NAI v'-YO-sha LAKH

23 False weights are an abomination to Hashem; Dishonest scales are not right.

כג תּוֹעֲבַת יְהוָה אֶבֶן וָאָבֶן וּמֹאזְנֵי מִרְמָה לֹא־טוֹב:

24 A man's steps are decided by Hashem; What does a man know about his own way?

כד מֵיְהוָה מִצְעֲדֵי־גָבֶר וְאָדָם מַה־יָּבִין דַּרְכּוֹ:

25 It is a snare for a man to pledge a sacred gift rashly And to give thought to his vows only after they have been made.

כה מוֹקֵשׁ אָדָם יָלַע קֹדֶשׁ וְאַחַר נְדָרִים לְבַקֵּר:

26 A wise king winnows out the wicked, And turns the wheel upon them.

כו מְזָרֶה רְשָׁעִים מֶלֶךְ חָכָם וַיָּשֶׁב עֲלֵיהֶם אוֹפָן:

27 The lifebreath of man is the lamp of Hashem Revealing all his inmost parts.

כז נֵר יְהוָה נִשְׁמַת אָדָם חֹפֵשׂ כָּל־חַדְרֵי־בָטֶן:

20:22 Put your hope in *Hashem* **and He will deliver you** Sometimes we see wrongdoing in this world, and it bothers us. This verse teaches that it is not up to man to avenge evil, rather, this is *Hashem*'s duty. However, the fourteenth-century sage Rabbi Levi ben Gershon, better known as *Ralbag*, points out that we should not wish for God's vengeance against our enemies, but only for salvation from their harm. Similarly, the Talmud (*Berachot* 10a) comments, regarding the verse in *Sefer Tehillim* (104:35), that we should not pray for our enemies' demise, but for them to repent of their evil ways.

Mishlei/Proverbs
Chapter 21

28 Faithfulness and loyalty protect the king; He maintains his throne by faithfulness.

29 The glory of youths is their strength; The majesty of old men is their gray hair.

30 Bruises and wounds are repayment for evil, Striking at one's inmost parts.

21 1 Like channeled water is the mind of the king in *Hashem*'s hand; He directs it to whatever He wishes.

2 All the ways of a man seem right to him, But *Hashem* probes the mind.

3 To do what is right and just Is more desired by *Hashem* than sacrifice.

4 Haughty looks, a proud heart — The tillage of the wicked is sinful.

5 The plans of the diligent make only for gain; All rash haste makes only for loss.

6 Treasures acquired by a lying tongue Are like driven vapor, heading for extinction.

7 The violence of the wicked sweeps them away, For they refuse to act justly.

8 The way of a man may be tortuous and strange, Though his actions are blameless and proper.

9 Dwelling in the corner of a roof is better Than a contentious wife in a spacious house.

10 The desire of the wicked is set upon evil; His fellowman finds no favor in his eyes.

11 When a scoffer is punished, the simple man is edified; When a wise man is taught, he gains insight.

12 The Righteous One observes the house of the wicked man; He subverts the wicked to their ruin.

13 Who stops his ears at the cry of the wretched, He too will call and not be answered.

14 A gift in secret subdues anger, A present in private, fierce rage.

15 Justice done is a joy to the righteous, To evildoers, ruination.

16 A man who strays from the path of prudence Will rest in the company of ghosts.

משלי
פרק כא

כח חֶסֶד וֶאֱמֶת יִצְּרוּ־מֶלֶךְ וְסָעַד בַּחֶסֶד כִּסְאוֹ׃

כט תִּפְאֶרֶת בַּחוּרִים כֹּחָם וַהֲדַר זְקֵנִים שֵׂיבָה׃

ל חַבֻּרוֹת פֶּצַע תַּמְרִיק [תַּמְרוּק] בְּרָע וּמַכּוֹת חַדְרֵי־בָטֶן׃

כא א פַּלְגֵי־מַיִם לֶב־מֶלֶךְ בְּיַד־יְהֹוָה עַל־כָּל־אֲשֶׁר יַחְפֹּץ יַטֶּנּוּ׃

ב כָּל־דֶּרֶךְ־אִישׁ יָשָׁר בְּעֵינָיו וְתֹכֵן לִבּוֹת יְהֹוָה׃

ג עֲשֹׂה צְדָקָה וּמִשְׁפָּט נִבְחָר לַיהֹוָה מִזָּבַח׃

ד רוּם־עֵינַיִם וּרְחַב־לֵב נֵר רְשָׁעִים חַטָּאת׃

ה מַחְשְׁבוֹת חָרוּץ אַךְ־לְמוֹתָר וְכָל־אָץ אַךְ־לְמַחְסוֹר׃

ו פֹּעַל אוֹצָרוֹת בִּלְשׁוֹן שָׁקֶר הֶבֶל נִדָּף מְבַקְשֵׁי־מָוֶת׃

ז שֹׁד־רְשָׁעִים יְגוֹרֵם כִּי מֵאֲנוּ לַעֲשׂוֹת מִשְׁפָּט׃

ח הֲפַכְפַּךְ דֶּרֶךְ אִישׁ וָזָר וְזַךְ יָשָׁר פָּעֳלוֹ׃

ט טוֹב לָשֶׁבֶת עַל־פִּנַּת־גָּג מֵאֵשֶׁת מִדְיָנִים וּבֵית חָבֶר׃

י נֶפֶשׁ רָשָׁע אִוְּתָה־רָע לֹא־יֻחַן בְּעֵינָיו רֵעֵהוּ׃

יא בַּעְנָשׁ־לֵץ יֶחְכַּם־פֶּתִי וּבְהַשְׂכִּיל לְחָכָם יִקַּח־דָּעַת׃

יב מַשְׂכִּיל צַדִּיק לְבֵית רָשָׁע מְסַלֵּף רְשָׁעִים לָרָע׃

יג אֹטֵם אָזְנוֹ מִזַּעֲקַת־דָּל גַּם־הוּא יִקְרָא וְלֹא יֵעָנֶה׃

יד מַתָּן בַּסֵּתֶר יִכְפֶּה־אָף וְשֹׁחַד בַּחֵק חֵמָה עַזָּה׃

טו שִׂמְחָה לַצַּדִּיק עֲשׂוֹת מִשְׁפָּט וּמְחִתָּה לְפֹעֲלֵי אָוֶן׃

טז אָדָם תּוֹעֶה מִדֶּרֶךְ הַשְׂכֵּל בִּקְהַל רְפָאִים יָנוּחַ׃

Mishlei/Proverbs
Chapter 22

משלי
פרק כב

17 He who loves pleasure comes to want; He who loves wine and oil does not grow rich.

יז אִישׁ מַחְסוֹר אֹהֵב שִׂמְחָה אֹהֵב יַיִן־וָשֶׁמֶן לֹא יַעֲשִׁיר:

18 The wicked are the ransom of the righteous; The traitor comes in place of the upright.

יח כֹּפֶר לַצַּדִּיק רָשָׁע וְתַחַת יְשָׁרִים בּוֹגֵד:

19 It is better to live in the desert Than with a contentious, vexatious wife.

יט טוֹב שֶׁבֶת בְּאֶרֶץ־מִדְבָּר מֵאֵשֶׁת מדונים [מִדְיָנִים] וָכָעַס:

20 Precious treasure and oil are in the house of the wise man, And a fool of a man will run through them.

כ אוֹצָר נֶחְמָד וָשֶׁמֶן בִּנְוֵה חָכָם וּכְסִיל אָדָם יְבַלְּעֶנּוּ:

21 He who strives to do good and kind deeds Attains life, success, and honor.

כא רֹדֵף צְדָקָה וָחָסֶד יִמְצָא חַיִּים צְדָקָה וְכָבוֹד:

22 One wise man prevailed over a city of warriors And brought down its mighty stronghold.

כב עִיר גִּבֹּרִים עָלָה חָכָם וַיֹּרֶד עֹז מִבְטֶחָה:

23 He who guards his mouth and tongue Guards himself from trouble.

כג שֹׁמֵר פִּיו וּלְשׁוֹנוֹ שֹׁמֵר מִצָּרוֹת נַפְשׁוֹ:

24 The proud, insolent man, scoffer is his name, Acts in a frenzy of insolence.

כד זֵד יָהִיר לֵץ שְׁמוֹ עוֹשֶׂה בְּעֶבְרַת זָדוֹן:

25 The craving of a lazy man kills him, For his hands refuse to work.

כה תַּאֲוַת עָצֵל תְּמִיתֶנּוּ כִּי־מֵאֲנוּ יָדָיו לַעֲשׂוֹת:

26 All day long he is seized with craving While the righteous man gives without stint.

כו כָּל־הַיּוֹם הִתְאַוָּה תַאֲוָה וְצַדִּיק יִתֵּן וְלֹא יַחְשֹׂךְ:

27 The sacrifice of the wicked man is an abomination, The more so as he offers it in depravity.

כז זֶבַח רְשָׁעִים תּוֹעֵבָה אַף כִּי־בְזִמָּה יְבִיאֶנּוּ:

28 A false witness is doomed, But one who really heard will testify with success.

כח עֵד־כְּזָבִים יֹאבֵד וְאִישׁ שׁוֹמֵעַ לָנֶצַח יְדַבֵּר:

29 The wicked man is brazen-faced; The upright man discerns his course.

כט הֵעֵז אִישׁ רָשָׁע בְּפָנָיו וְיָשָׁר הוּא יכין [יָבִין] דרכיו [דַּרְכּוֹ]:

30 No wisdom, no prudence, and no counsel Can prevail against *Hashem*.

ל אֵין חָכְמָה וְאֵין תְּבוּנָה וְאֵין עֵצָה לְנֶגֶד יְהוָה:

31 The horse is readied for the day of battle, But victory comes from *Hashem*.

לא סוּס מוּכָן לְיוֹם מִלְחָמָה וְלַיהוָה הַתְּשׁוּעָה:

SUS mu-KHAN l'-YOM mil-kha-MAH v'-la-do-NAI ha-t'-shu-AH

22

1 Repute is preferable to great wealth Grace is better than silver and gold.

כב א נִבְחָר שֵׁם מֵעֹשֶׁר רָב מִכֶּסֶף וּמִזָּהָב חֵן טוֹב:

21:31 But victory comes from *Hashem* Throughout the Bible, horses are mentioned as animals of war. Here, King *Shlomo* is emphasizing an important lesson that is no less true today than it was when he said it centuries ago: Man prepares as much as possible, but ultimately, all victory and success comes only from *Hashem*.

Mishlei/Proverbs
Chapter 22

משלי
פרק כב

2 Rich man and poor man meet; *Hashem* made them both.

ב עָשִׁיר וָרָשׁ נִפְגָּשׁוּ עֹשֵׂה כֻלָּם יְהֹוָה:

3 The shrewd man saw trouble and took cover; The simple kept going and paid the penalty.

ג עָרוּם רָאָה רָעָה ויסתר [וְנִסְתָּר] וּפְתָיִים עָבְרוּ וְנֶעֱנָשׁוּ:

4 The effect of humility is fear of *Hashem*, Wealth, honor, and life.

ד עֵקֶב עֲנָוָה יִרְאַת יְהֹוָה עֹשֶׁר וְכָבוֹד וְחַיִּים:

5 Thorns and snares are in the path of the crooked; He who values his life will keep far from them.

ה צִנִּים פַּחִים בְּדֶרֶךְ עִקֵּשׁ שׁוֹמֵר נַפְשׁוֹ יִרְחַק מֵהֶם:

6 Train a lad in the way he ought to go; He will not swerve from it even in old age.

ו חֲנֹךְ לַנַּעַר עַל־פִּי דַרְכּוֹ גַּם כִּי־יַזְקִין לֹא־יָסוּר מִמֶּנָּה:

7 The rich rule the poor, And the borrower is a slave to the lender.

ז עָשִׁיר בְּרָשִׁים יִמְשׁוֹל וְעֶבֶד לֹוֶה לְאִישׁ מַלְוֶה:

8 He who sows injustice shall reap misfortune; His rod of wrath shall fail.

ח זוֹרֵעַ עַוְלָה יקצור־[יִקְצׇר־] אָוֶן וְשֵׁבֶט עֶבְרָתוֹ יִכְלֶה:

9 The generous man is blessed, For he gives of his bread to the poor.

ט טוֹב־עַיִן הוּא יְבֹרָךְ כִּי־נָתַן מִלַּחְמוֹ לַדָּל:

10 Expel the scoffer and contention departs, Quarrel and contumely cease.

י גָּרֵשׁ לֵץ וְיֵצֵא מָדוֹן וְיִשְׁבֹּת דִּין וְקָלוֹן:

11 A pure-hearted friend, His speech is gracious; He has the king for his companion.

יא אֹהֵב טהור־[טְהׇר־] לֵב חֵן שְׂפָתָיו רֵעֵהוּ מֶלֶךְ:

12 The eyes of *Hashem* watch the wise man; He subverts the words of the treacherous.

יב עֵינֵי יְהֹוָה נָצְרוּ דָעַת וַיְסַלֵּף דִּבְרֵי בֹגֵד:

13 The lazy man says, "There's a lion in the street; I shall be killed if I step outside."

יג אָמַר עָצֵל אֲרִי בַחוּץ בְּתוֹךְ רְחֹבוֹת אֵרָצֵחַ:

14 The mouth of a forbidden woman is a deep pit; He who is doomed by *Hashem* falls into it.

יד שׁוּחָה עֲמֻקָּה פִּי זָרוֹת זְעוּם יְהֹוָה יפול־[יִפׇּל־] שָׁם:

15 If folly settles in the heart of a lad, The rod of discipline will remove it.

טו אִוֶּלֶת קְשׁוּרָה בְלֶב־נָעַר שֵׁבֶט מוּסָר יַרְחִיקֶנָּה מִמֶּנּוּ:

16 To profit by withholding what is due to the poor Is like making gifts to the rich – pure loss.

טז עֹשֵׁק דָּל לְהַרְבּוֹת לוֹ נֹתֵן לְעָשִׁיר אַךְ־לְמַחְסוֹר:

17 Incline your ear and listen to the words of the sages; Pay attention to my wisdom.

יז הַט אׇזְנְךָ וּשְׁמַע דִּבְרֵי חֲכָמִים וְלִבְּךָ תָּשִׁית לְדַעְתִּי:

18 It is good that you store them inside you, And that all of them be constantly on your lips,

יח כִּי־נָעִים כִּי־תִשְׁמְרֵם בְּבִטְנֶךָ יִכֹּנוּ יַחְדָּו עַל־שְׂפָתֶיךָ:

19 That you may put your trust in *Hashem*. I let you know today – yes, you –

יט לִהְיוֹת בַּיהֹוָה מִבְטַחֶךָ הוֹדַעְתִּיךָ הַיּוֹם אַף־אָתָּה:

20 Indeed, I wrote down for you a threefold lore, Wise counsel,

כ הֲלֹא כָתַבְתִּי לְךָ שלשום [שָׁלִישִׁים] בְּמוֹעֵצֹת וָדָעַת:

21 To let you know truly reliable words, That you may give a faithful reply to him who sent you.

כא לְהוֹדִיעֲךָ קֹשְׁטְ אִמְרֵי אֱמֶת לְהָשִׁיב אֲמָרִים אֱמֶת לְשֹׁלְחֶיךָ:

1690

Mishlei/Proverbs
Chapter 23

משלי
פרק כג

22 Do not rob the wretched because he is wretched; Do not crush the poor man in the gate;

כב אַל־תִּגְזָל־דָּל כִּי דַל־הוּא וְאַל־תְּדַכֵּא עָנִי בַשָּׁעַר׃

23 For *Hashem* will take up their cause And despoil those who despoil them of life.

כג כִּי־יְהֹוָה יָרִיב רִיבָם וְקָבַע אֶת־קֹבְעֵיהֶם נָפֶשׁ׃

24 Do not associate with an irascible man, Or go about with one who is hot-tempered,

כד אַל־תִּתְרַע אֶת־בַּעַל אָף וְאֶת־אִישׁ חֵמוֹת לֹא תָבוֹא׃

25 Lest you learn his ways And find yourself ensnared.

כה פֶּן־תֶּאֱלַף ארחתו [אֹרְחֹתָיו] וְלָקַחְתָּ מוֹקֵשׁ לְנַפְשֶׁךָ׃

26 Do not be one of those who give their hand, Who stand surety for debts,

כו אַל־תְּהִי בְתֹקְעֵי־כָף בַּעֹרְבִים מַשָּׁאוֹת׃

27 Lest your bed be taken from under you When you have no money to pay.

כז אִם־אֵין־לְךָ לְשַׁלֵּם לָמָּה יִקַּח מִשְׁכָּבְךָ מִתַּחְתֶּיךָ׃

28 Do not remove the ancient boundary stone That your ancestors set up.

כח אַל־תַּסֵּג גְּבוּל עוֹלָם אֲשֶׁר עָשׂוּ אֲבוֹתֶיךָ׃

al ta-SAYG g'-VUL o-LAM a-SHER a-SU a-vo-TE-kha

29 See a man skilled at his work – He shall attend upon kings; He shall not attend upon obscure men.

כט חָזִיתָ אִישׁ מָהִיר בִּמְלַאכְתּוֹ לִפְנֵי־מְלָכִים יִתְיַצָּב בַּל־יִתְיַצֵּב לִפְנֵי חֲשֻׁכִּים׃

23

1 When you sit down to dine with a ruler, Consider well who is before you.

כג א כִּי־תֵשֵׁב לִלְחוֹם אֶת־מוֹשֵׁל בִּין תָּבִין אֶת־אֲשֶׁר לְפָנֶיךָ׃

2 Thrust a knife into your gullet If you have a large appetite.

ב וְשַׂמְתָּ שַׂכִּין בְּלֹעֶךָ אִם־בַּעַל נֶפֶשׁ אָתָּה׃

3 Do not crave for his dainties, For they are counterfeit food.

ג אַל־תִּתְאָו לְמַטְעַמּוֹתָיו וְהוּא לֶחֶם כְּזָבִים׃

4 Do not toil to gain wealth; Have the sense to desist.

ד אַל־תִּיגַע לְהַעֲשִׁיר מִבִּינָתְךָ חֲדָל׃

5 You see it, then it is gone; It grows wings and flies away, Like an eagle, heavenward.

ה התעוף [הֲתָעִיף] עֵינֶיךָ בּוֹ וְאֵינֶנּוּ כִּי עָשֹׂה יַעֲשֶׂה־לּוֹ כְנָפַיִם כְּנֶשֶׁר ועיף [וְעוּף] הַשָּׁמָיִם׃

ha-ta-EEF ay-NE-kha BO v'-ay-NE-nu KEE a-SOH ya-a-seh LO kh'-na-FA-yim k'-NE-sher ya-UF ha-sha-MA-yim

An eagle in flight in the Golan Heights

22:28 Do not remove the ancient boundary stone This verse reinforces the significance of a heritage in the Promised Land. When the Israelites arrived there after leaving Egypt, *Hashem* instructed *Moshe* to divide the land by drawing lots. Each tribe was given a region, and each family was assigned a portion of their tribe's land to be passed down through the generations (Numbers 26:52–56). Israel's family bonds to the land are so great, that when *Tzelofchad* died without sons, his daughters demanded the right to inherit their father's portion (Numbers 27). They were granted the inheritance on condition that they marry within their tribe, so the land not be absorbed into another tribe's portion (Numbers 36:6–7).

23:5 Like an eagle, heavenward The eagle flies higher than other birds. According to the medieval commentator *Rashi*, this is the reason why *Hashem* uses the metaphor of an eagle when describing the Exodus from Egypt: "I bore you on eagles' wings and brought you to Me" (Exodus 19:4). As opposed to other birds who carry their young between their legs

Mishlei/Proverbs

Chapter 23

משלי

פרק כג

6	Do not eat of a stingy man's food; Do not crave for his dainties;	אַל־תִּלְחַם אֶת־לֶחֶם רַע עָיִן וְאַל־תתאו [תִּתְאָיו] לְמַטְעַמֹּתָיו: ו
7	He is like one keeping accounts; "Eat and drink," he says to you, But he does not really mean it.	כִּי כְּמוֹ־שָׁעַר בְּנַפְשׁוֹ כֶּן־הוּא אֱכֹל וּשְׁתֵה יֹאמַר לָךְ וְלִבּוֹ בַּל־עִמָּךְ: ז
8	The morsel you eat you will vomit; You will waste your courteous words.	פִּתְּךָ־אָכַלְתָּ תְקִיאֶנָּה וְשִׁחַתָּ דְּבָרֶיךָ הַנְּעִימִים: ח
9	Do not speak to a dullard, For he will disdain your sensible words.	בְּאָזְנֵי כְסִיל אַל־תְּדַבֵּר כִּי־יָבוּז לְשֵׂכֶל מִלֶּיךָ: ט
10	Do not remove ancient boundary stones; Do not encroach upon the field of orphans,	אַל־תַּסֵּג גְּבוּל עוֹלָם וּבִשְׂדֵי יְתוֹמִים אַל־תָּבֹא: י
11	For they have a mighty Kinsman, And He will surely take up their cause with you.	כִּי־גֹאֲלָם חָזָק הוּא־יָרִיב אֶת־רִיבָם אִתָּךְ: יא
12	Apply your mind to discipline And your ears to wise sayings.	הָבִיאָה לַמּוּסָר לִבֶּךָ וְאָזְנֶךָ לְאִמְרֵי־דָעַת: יב
13	Do not withhold discipline from a child; If you beat him with a rod he will not die.	אַל־תִּמְנַע מִנַּעַר מוּסָר כִּי־תַכֶּנּוּ בַשֵּׁבֶט לֹא יָמוּת: יג
14	Beat him with a rod And you will save him from the grave.	אַתָּה בַּשֵּׁבֶט תַּכֶּנּוּ וְנַפְשׁוֹ מִשְּׁאוֹל תַּצִּיל: יד
15	My son, if your mind gets wisdom, My mind, too, will be gladdened.	בְּנִי אִם־חָכַם לִבֶּךָ יִשְׂמַח לִבִּי גַם־אָנִי: טו
16	I shall rejoice with all my heart When your lips speak right things.	וְתַעְלֹזְנָה כִלְיוֹתָי בְּדַבֵּר שְׂפָתֶיךָ מֵישָׁרִים: טז
17	Do not envy sinners in your heart, But only *Hashem*-fearing men, at all times,	אַל־יְקַנֵּא לִבְּךָ בַּחַטָּאִים כִּי אִם־בְּיִרְאַת־יְהוָה כָּל־הַיּוֹם: יז
18	For then you will have a future, And your hope will never fail.	כִּי אִם־יֵשׁ אַחֲרִית וְתִקְוָתְךָ לֹא תִכָּרֵת: יח
19	Listen, my son, and get wisdom; Lead your mind in a [proper] path.	שְׁמַע־אַתָּה בְנִי וַחֲכָם וְאַשֵּׁר בַּדֶּרֶךְ לִבֶּךָ: יט
20	Do not be of those who guzzle wine, Or glut themselves on meat;	אַל־תְּהִי בְסֹבְאֵי־יָיִן בְּזֹלֲלֵי בָשָׂר לָמוֹ: כ
21	For guzzlers and gluttons will be impoverished, And drowsing will clothe you in tatters.	כִּי־סֹבֵא וְזוֹלֵל יִוָּרֵשׁ וּקְרָעִים תַּלְבִּישׁ נוּמָה: כא

---

to protect them from predators flying above them, an eagle carries its young on its back (see Deuteronomy 32:11). Since the eagle flies higher than other birds, it fears no other flying predators. Its only concern comes from people who might shoot at its young from below, so it uses its own body to protect its children from the arrows. Similarly, the Lord placed His angel between the Israelites and the Egyptians (Exodus 14:19–20) in order to protect His children by absorbing the Egyptian arrows and stones.

Mishlei / Proverbs
Chapter 24

22 Listen to your father who begot you; Do not disdain your mother when she is old.

23 Buy truth and never sell it, And wisdom, discipline, and understanding.

24 The father of a righteous man will exult; He who begets a wise son will rejoice in him.

25 Your father and mother will rejoice; She who bore you will exult.

26 Give your mind to me, my son; Let your eyes watch my ways.

27 A harlot is a deep pit; A forbidden woman is a narrow well.

28 She too lies in wait as if for prey, And destroys the unfaithful among men.

29 Who cries, "Woe!" who, "Alas!"; Who has quarrels, who complaints; Who has wounds without cause; Who has bleary eyes?

30 Those whom wine keeps till the small hours, Those who gather to drain the cups.

31 Do not ogle that red wine As it lends its color to the cup, As it flows on smoothly;

32 In the end, it bites like a snake; It spits like a basilisk.

33 Your eyes will see strange sights; Your heart will speak distorted things.

34 You will be like one lying in bed on high seas, Like one lying on top of the rigging.

35 "They struck me, but I felt no hurt; They beat me, but I was unaware; As often as I wake, I go after it again."

24
1 Do not envy evil men Do not desire to be with them;

2 For their hearts talk violence, And their lips speak mischief.

3 A house is built by wisdom, And is established by understanding;

4 By knowledge are its rooms filled With all precious and beautiful things.

משלי
פרק כד

כב שְׁמַע לְאָבִיךָ זֶה יְלָדֶךָ וְאַל־תָּבוּז כִּי־זָקְנָה אִמֶּךָ:

כג אֱמֶת קְנֵה וְאַל־תִּמְכֹּר חָכְמָה וּמוּסָר וּבִינָה:

כד גּוֹל [גִּיל] יָגוּל [יָגִיל] אֲבִי צַדִּיק יוֹלֵד [וְיוֹלֵד] חָכָם וישמח־ [וְיִשְׂמַח־] בּוֹ:

כה יִשְׂמַח־אָבִיךָ וְאִמֶּךָ וְתָגֵל יוֹלַדְתֶּךָ:

כו תְּנָה־בְנִי לִבְּךָ לִי וְעֵינֶיךָ דְּרָכַי תרצנה [תִּצֹּרְנָה]:

כז כִּי־שׁוּחָה עֲמֻקָּה זוֹנָה וּבְאֵר צָרָה נָכְרִיָּה:

כח אַף־הִיא כְּחֶתֶף תֶּאֱרֹב וּבוֹגְדִים בְּאָדָם תּוֹסִף:

כט לְמִי אוֹי לְמִי אֲבוֹי לְמִי מדונים [מִדְיָנִים] לְמִי שִׂיחַ לְמִי פְּצָעִים חִנָּם לְמִי חַכְלִלוּת עֵינָיִם:

ל לַמְאַחֲרִים עַל־הַיָּיִן לַבָּאִים לַחְקֹר מִמְסָךְ:

לא אַל־תֵּרֶא יַיִן כִּי יִתְאַדָּם כִּי־יִתֵּן בכיס [בַּכּוֹס] עֵינוֹ יִתְהַלֵּךְ בְּמֵישָׁרִים:

לב אַחֲרִיתוֹ כְּנָחָשׁ יִשָּׁךְ וּכְצִפְעֹנִי יַפְרִשׁ:

לג עֵינֶיךָ יִרְאוּ זָרוֹת וְלִבְּךָ יְדַבֵּר תַּהְפֻּכוֹת:

לד וְהָיִיתָ כְּשֹׁכֵב בְּלֶב־יָם וּכְשֹׁכֵב בְּרֹאשׁ חִבֵּל:

לה הִכּוּנִי בַל־חָלִיתִי הֲלָמוּנִי בַּל־יָדָעְתִּי מָתַי אָקִיץ אוֹסִיף אֲבַקְשֶׁנּוּ עוֹד:

כד א אַל־תְּקַנֵּא בְּאַנְשֵׁי רָעָה וְאַל־תתאו [תִּתְאָו] לִהְיוֹת אִתָּם:

ב כִּי־שֹׁד יֶהְגֶּה לִבָּם וְעָמָל שִׂפְתֵיהֶם תְּדַבֵּרְנָה:

ג בְּחָכְמָה יִבָּנֶה בָּיִת וּבִתְבוּנָה יִתְכּוֹנָן:

ד וּבְדַעַת חֲדָרִים יִמָּלְאוּ כָּל־הוֹן יָקָר וְנָעִים:

Mishlei/Proverbs
Chapter 24

משלי
פרק כד

5 A wise man is strength; A knowledgeable man exerts power;

ה גֶּבֶר־חָכָם בַּעוֹז וְאִישׁ־דַּעַת מְאַמֶּץ־כֹּחַ:

6 For by stratagems you wage war, And victory comes with much planning.

ו כִּי בְתַחְבֻּלוֹת תַּעֲשֶׂה־לְּךָ מִלְחָמָה וּתְשׁוּעָה בְּרֹב יוֹעֵץ:

7 Wisdom is too lofty for a fool; He does not open his mouth in the gate.

ז רָאמוֹת לֶאֱוִיל חָכְמוֹת בַּשַּׁעַר לֹא יִפְתַּח־פִּיהוּ:

8 He who lays plans to do harm Is called by men a schemer.

ח מְחַשֵּׁב לְהָרֵעַ לוֹ בַּעַל־מְזִמּוֹת יִקְרָאוּ:

9 The schemes of folly are sin, And a scoffer is an abomination to men.

ט זִמַּת אִוֶּלֶת חַטָּאת וְתוֹעֲבַת לְאָדָם לֵץ:

10 If you showed yourself slack in time of trouble, Wanting in power,

י הִתְרַפִּיתָ בְּיוֹם צָרָה צַר כֹּחֶכָה:

11 If you refrained from rescuing those taken off to death, Those condemned to slaughter –

יא הַצֵּל לְקֻחִים לַמָּוֶת וּמָטִים לַהֶרֶג אִם־תַּחְשׂוֹךְ:

12 If you say, "We knew nothing of it," Surely He who fathoms hearts will discern [the truth], He who watches over your life will know it, And He will pay each man as he deserves.

יב כִּי־תֹאמַר הֵן לֹא־יָדַעְנוּ זֶה הֲלֹא־תֹכֵן לִבּוֹת הוּא־יָבִין וְנֹצֵר נַפְשְׁךָ הוּא יֵדָע וְהֵשִׁיב לְאָדָם כְּפָעֳלוֹ:

13 My son, eat honey, for it is good; Let its sweet drops be on your palate.

יג אֱכָל־בְּנִי דְבַשׁ כִּי־טוֹב וְנֹפֶת מָתוֹק עַל־חִכֶּךָ:

14 Know: such is wisdom for your soul; If you attain it, there is a future; Your hope will not be cut off.

יד כֵּן דְּעֶה חָכְמָה לְנַפְשֶׁךָ אִם־מָצָאתָ וְיֵשׁ אַחֲרִית וְתִקְוָתְךָ לֹא תִכָּרֵת:

15 Wicked man! Do not lurk by the home of the righteous man; Do no violence to his dwelling.

טו אַל־תֶּאֱרֹב רָשָׁע לִנְוֵה צַדִּיק אַל־תְּשַׁדֵּד רִבְצוֹ:

16 Seven times the righteous man falls and gets up, While the wicked are tripped by one misfortune.

טז כִּי שֶׁבַע יִפּוֹל צַדִּיק וָקָם וּרְשָׁעִים יִכָּשְׁלוּ בְרָעָה:

17 If your enemy falls, do not exult; If he trips, let your heart not rejoice,

יז בִּנְפֹל אויביך [אוֹיִבְךָ] אַל־תִּשְׂמָח וּבִכָּשְׁלוֹ אַל־יָגֵל לִבֶּךָ:

bin-FOL o-yiv-KHA al tis-MAKH u-vi-ka-sh'-LO al ya-GAYL li-BE-kha

18 Lest *Hashem* see it and be displeased, And avert His wrath from him.

יח פֶּן־יִרְאֶה יְהוָה וְרַע בְּעֵינָיו וְהֵשִׁיב מֵעָלָיו אַפּוֹ:

19 Do not be vexed by evildoers; Do not be incensed by the wicked;

יט אַל־תִּתְחַר בַּמְּרֵעִים אַל־תְּקַנֵּא בָּרְשָׁעִים:

24:17 If your enemy falls, do not exult Sadly, it is not uncommon for Israel's enemies to celebrate news of terror attacks by handing out candy in the streets. Here, the Bible emphasizes universal feelings of sympathy and compassion for all, and warns against rejoicing at the downfall of our enemies. For this reason, when the Jewish people celebrate the Exodus at the *Pesach seder* each year, they remove some of the wine in their cups, to sympathize with the Egyptian suffering that happened in the process. In this way, even thousands of years later, the Jewish People symbolically diminish their joy because of the pain experienced by their Egyptian enemies.

Mishlei/Proverbs
Chapter 25

משלי
פרק כה

20 For there is no future for the evil man; The lamp of the wicked goes out.

כ כִּי ׀ לֹא־תִהְיֶ֣ה אַחֲרִ֣ית לָרָ֑ע נֵ֖ר רְשָׁעִ֣ים יִדְעָֽךְ׃

21 Fear *Hashem*, my son, and the king, And do not mix with dissenters,

כא יְרָֽא־אֶת־יְהֹוָ֣ה בְּנִ֣י וָמֶ֑לֶךְ עִם־שׁ֝וֹנִ֗ים אַל־תִּתְעָרָֽב׃

22 For disaster comes from them suddenly; The doom both decree who can foreknow?

כב כִּי־פִ֭תְאֹם יָק֣וּם אֵידָ֑ם וּפִ֥יד שְׁ֝נֵיהֶ֗ם מִ֣י יוֹדֵֽעַ׃

23 These also are by the sages: It is not right to be partial in judgment.

כג גַּם־אֵ֥לֶּה לַחֲכָמִ֑ים הַֽכֵּר־פָּנִ֖ים בְּמִשְׁפָּ֣ט בַּל־טֽוֹב׃

24 He who says to the guilty, "You are innocent," Shall be cursed by peoples, Damned by nations;

כד אֹ֤מֵ֨ר ׀ לְרָשָׁע֮ צַדִּ֪יק אָ֥תָּה יִקְּבֻ֥הוּ עַמִּ֑ים יִזְעָמ֥וּהוּ לְאֻמִּֽים׃

25 But it shall go well with them who decide justly; Blessings of good things will light upon them.

כה וְלַמּוֹכִיחִ֥ים יִנְעָ֑ם וַ֝עֲלֵיהֶ֗ם תָּב֥וֹא בִרְכַּת־טֽוֹב׃

26 Giving a straightforward reply Is like giving a kiss.

כו שְׂפָתַ֥יִם יִשָּׁ֑ק מֵ֝שִׁ֗יב דְּבָרִ֥ים נְכֹחִֽים׃

27 Put your external affairs in order, Get ready what you have in the field, Then build yourself a home.

כז הָ֘כֵ֤ן בַּח֨וּץ ׀ מְלַאכְתֶּ֗ךָ וְעַתְּדָ֥הּ בַּשָּׂדֶ֣ה לָ֑ךְ אַ֝חַ֗ר וּבָנִ֥יתָ בֵיתֶֽךָ׃

28 Do not be a witness against your fellow without good cause; Would you mislead with your speech?

כח אַל־תְּהִ֣י עֵד־חִנָּ֣ם בְּרֵעֶ֑ךָ וַ֝הֲפִתִּ֗יתָ בִּשְׂפָתֶֽיךָ׃

29 Do not say, "I will do to him what he did to me; I will pay the man what he deserves."

כט אַל־תֹּאמַ֗ר כַּאֲשֶׁ֣ר עָֽשָׂה־לִ֭י כֵּ֣ן אֶֽעֱשֶׂה־לּ֑וֹ אָשִׁ֖יב לָאִ֣ישׁ כְּפׇעֳלֽוֹ׃

30 I passed by the field of a lazy man, By the vineyard of a man lacking sense.

ל עַל־שְׂדֵ֣ה אִישׁ־עָצֵ֣ל עָבַ֑רְתִּי וְעַל־כֶּ֝֗רֶם אָדָ֥ם חֲסַר־לֵֽב׃

31 It was all overgrown with thorns; Its surface was covered with chickweed, And its stone fence lay in ruins.

לא וְהִנֵּ֨ה עָ֘לָ֤ה כֻלּ֨וֹ ׀ קִמְּשֹׂנִ֗ים כָּסּ֣וּ פָנָ֣יו חֲרֻלִּ֑ים וְגֶ֖דֶר אֲבָנָ֣יו נֶהֱרָֽסָה׃

32 I observed and took it to heart; I saw it and learned a lesson.

לב וָֽאֶחֱזֶ֣ה אָ֭נֹכִי אָשִׁ֣ית לִבִּ֑י רָ֝אִ֗יתִי לָקַ֥חְתִּי מוּסָֽר׃

33 A bit more sleep, a bit more slumber, A bit more hugging yourself in bed,

לג מְעַ֣ט שֵׁ֭נוֹת מְעַ֣ט תְּנוּמ֑וֹת מְעַ֓ט ׀ חִבֻּ֖ק יָדַ֣יִם לִשְׁכָּֽב׃

34 And poverty will come calling upon you, And want, like a man with a shield.

לד וּבָֽא־מִתְהַלֵּ֥ךְ רֵישֶׁ֑ךָ וּ֝מַחְסֹרֶ֗יךָ כְּאִ֣ישׁ מָגֵֽן׃

25

1 These too are proverbs of *Shlomo*, which the men of King *Chizkiyahu* of *Yehuda* copied:

כה א גַּם־אֵ֭לֶּה מִשְׁלֵ֣י שְׁלֹמֹ֑ה אֲשֶׁ֥ר הֶ֝עְתִּ֗יקוּ אַנְשֵׁ֤י ׀ חִזְקִיָּ֬ה מֶלֶךְ־יְהוּדָֽה׃

2 **It is the glory of *Hashem* to conceal a matter, And the glory of a king to plumb a matter.**

ב כְּבֹ֣ד אֱ֭לֹהִים הַסְתֵּ֣ר דָּבָ֑ר וּכְבֹ֥ד מְ֝לָכִ֗ים חֲקֹ֣ר דָּבָֽר׃

k'-VOD e-lo-HEEM has-TAYR da-VAR ukh-VOD m'-la-KHEEM kha-KOR da-VAR

25:2 It is the glory of *Hashem* to conceal a matter The glory of earthly kings is made greater through scrutiny and investigation, both on their own part and when conducted by others. When the kings search out the

1695

Mishlei/Proverbs

Chapter 25

משלי

פרק כה

3 Like the heavens in their height, like the earth in its depth, Is the mind of kings – unfathomable.

ג שָׁמַיִם לָרוּם וָאָרֶץ לָעֹמֶק וְלֵב מְלָכִים אֵין חֵקֶר׃

4 The dross having been separated from the silver, A vessel emerged for the smith.

ד הָגוֹ סִיגִים מִכָּסֶף וַיֵּצֵא לַצֹּרֵף כֶּלִי׃

5 Remove the wicked from the king's presence, And his throne will be established in justice.

ה הָגוֹ רָשָׁע לִפְנֵי־מֶלֶךְ וְיִכּוֹן בַּצֶּדֶק כִּסְאוֹ׃

6 Do not exalt yourself in the king's presence; Do not stand in the place of nobles.

ו אַל־תִּתְהַדַּר לִפְנֵי־מֶלֶךְ וּבִמְקוֹם גְּדֹלִים אַל־תַּעֲמֹד׃

7 For it is better to be told, "Step up here," Than to be degraded in the presence of the great. Do not let what your eyes have seen

ז כִּי טוֹב אֲמָר־לְךָ עֲלֵה הֵנָּה מֵהַשְׁפִּילְךָ לִפְנֵי נָדִיב אֲשֶׁר רָאוּ עֵינֶיךָ׃

8 Be vented rashly in a quarrel; Think of what it will effect in the end, When your fellow puts you to shame.

ח אַל־תֵּצֵא לָרִב מַהֵר פֶּן מַה־תַּעֲשֶׂה בְּאַחֲרִיתָהּ בְּהַכְלִים אֹתְךָ רֵעֶךָ׃

9 Defend your right against your fellow, But do not give away the secrets of another,

ט רִיבְךָ רִיב אֶת־רֵעֶךָ וְסוֹד אַחֵר אַל־תְּגָל׃

10 Lest he who hears it reproach you, And your bad repute never end.

י פֶּן־יְחַסֶּדְךָ שֹׁמֵעַ וְדִבָּתְךָ לֹא תָשׁוּב׃

11 Like golden apples in silver showpieces Is a phrase well turned.

יא תַּפּוּחֵי זָהָב בְּמַשְׂכִּיּוֹת כָּסֶף דָּבָר דָּבֻר עַל־אָפְנָיו׃

12 Like a ring of gold, a golden ornament, Is a wise man's reproof in a receptive ear.

יב נֶזֶם זָהָב וַחֲלִי־כָתֶם מוֹכִיחַ חָכָם עַל־אֹזֶן שֹׁמָעַת׃

13 Like the coldness of snow at harvesttime Is a trusty messenger to those who send him; He lifts his master's spirits.

יג כְּצִנַּת־שֶׁלֶג בְּיוֹם קָצִיר צִיר נֶאֱמָן לְשֹׁלְחָיו וְנֶפֶשׁ אֲדֹנָיו יָשִׁיב׃

14 Like clouds, wind – but no rain – Is one who boasts of gifts not given.

יד נְשִׂיאִים וְרוּחַ וְגֶשֶׁם אָיִן אִישׁ מִתְהַלֵּל בְּמַתַּת־שָׁקֶר׃

15 Through forbearance a ruler may be won over; A gentle tongue can break bones.

טו בְּאֹרֶךְ אַפַּיִם יְפֻתֶּה קָצִין וְלָשׁוֹן רַכָּה תִּשְׁבָּר־גָּרֶם׃

16 If you find honey, eat only what you need, Lest, surfeiting yourself, you throw it up.

טז דְּבַשׁ מָצָאתָ אֱכֹל דַּיֶּךָּ פֶּן־תִּשְׂבָּעֶנּוּ וַהֲקֵאתוֹ׃

17 Visit your neighbor sparingly, Lest he have his surfeit of you and loathe you.

יז הֹקַר רַגְלְךָ מִבֵּית רֵעֶךָ פֶּן־יִשְׂבָּעֲךָ וּשְׂנֵאֶךָ׃

truth in order to do justice, they bring honor to themselves, and when others look into their actions, they respect such leaders for their righteousness. *Hashem's* glory, on the other hand, is made greater by conceal- ment. His miracles and actions are beyond human understanding, and though they are recorded in the Bible, many are shrouded in mystery.

18 Like a club, a sword, a sharpened arrow, Is a man who testifies falsely against his fellow.

יח מֵפִיץ וְחֶרֶב וְחֵץ שָׁנוּן אִישׁ עֹנֶה בְרֵעֵהוּ עֵד שָׁקֶר׃

19 Like a loose tooth and an unsteady leg, Is a treacherous support in time of trouble.

יט שֵׁן רֹעָה וְרֶגֶל מוּעָדֶת מִבְטָח בּוֹגֵד בְּיוֹם צָרָה׃

20 Disrobing on a chilly day, Like vinegar on natron, Is one who sings songs to a sorrowful soul.

כ מַעֲדֶה בֶּגֶד בְּיוֹם קָרָה חֹמֶץ עַל־נָתֶר וְשָׁר בַּשִּׁרִים עַל לֶב־רָע׃

21 If your enemy is hungry, give him bread to eat; If he is thirsty, give him water to drink.

כא אִם־רָעֵב שֹׂנַאֲךָ הַאֲכִלֵהוּ לָחֶם וְאִם־צָמֵא הַשְׁקֵהוּ מָיִם׃

22 You will be heaping live coals on his head, And *Hashem* will reward you.

כב כִּי גֶחָלִים אַתָּה חֹתֶה עַל־רֹאשׁוֹ וַיהוָה יְשַׁלֶּם־לָךְ׃

23 A north wind produces rain, And whispered words, a glowering face.

כג רוּחַ צָפוֹן תְּחוֹלֵל גָּשֶׁם וּפָנִים נִזְעָמִים לְשׁוֹן סָתֶר׃

24 Dwelling in the corner of a roof is better Than a contentious woman in a spacious house.

כד טוֹב שֶׁבֶת עַל־פִּנַּת־גָּג מֵאֵשֶׁת מדונים [מִדְיָנִים] וּבֵית חָבֶר׃

25 Like cold water to a parched throat Is good news from a distant land.

כה מַיִם קָרִים עַל־נֶפֶשׁ עֲיֵפָה וּשְׁמוּעָה טוֹבָה מֵאֶרֶץ מֶרְחָק׃

26 Like a muddied spring, a ruined fountain, Is a righteous man fallen before a wicked one.

כו מַעְיָן נִרְפָּשׂ וּמָקוֹר מָשְׁחָת צַדִּיק מָט לִפְנֵי־רָשָׁע׃

27 It is not good to eat much honey, Nor is it honorable to search for honor.

כז אָכֹל דְּבַשׁ הַרְבּוֹת לֹא־טוֹב וְחֵקֶר כְּבֹדָם כָּבוֹד׃

28 Like an open city without walls Is a man whose temper is uncurbed.

כח עִיר פְּרוּצָה אֵין חוֹמָה אִישׁ אֲשֶׁר אֵין מַעְצָר לְרוּחוֹ׃

26 1 Like snow in summer and rain at harvest-time, So honor is not fitting for a dullard.

כו א כַּשֶּׁלֶג בַּקַּיִץ וְכַמָּטָר בַּקָּצִיר כֵּן לֹא־נָאוֶה לִכְסִיל כָּבוֹד׃

2 As a sparrow must flit and a swallow fly, So a gratuitous curse must backfire.

ב כַּצִּפּוֹר לָנוּד כַּדְּרוֹר לָעוּף כֵּן קִלְלַת חִנָּם לא [לוֹ] תָבֹא׃

3 A whip for a horse and a bridle for a donkey, And a rod for the back of dullards.

ג שׁוֹט לַסּוּס מֶתֶג לַחֲמוֹר וְשֵׁבֶט לְגֵו כְּסִילִים׃

4 Do not answer a dullard in accord with his folly, Else you will become like him.

ד אַל־תַּעַן כְּסִיל כְּאִוַּלְתּוֹ פֶּן־תִּשְׁוֶה־לּוֹ גַם־אָתָּה׃

5 Answer a dullard in accord with his folly, Else he will think himself wise.

ה עֲנֵה כְסִיל כְּאִוַּלְתּוֹ פֶּן־יִהְיֶה חָכָם בְּעֵינָיו׃

6 He who sends a message by a dullard Will wear out legs and must put up with lawlessness.

ו מְקַצֶּה רַגְלַיִם חָמָס שֹׁתֶה שֹׁלֵחַ דְּבָרִים בְּיַד־כְּסִיל׃

7 As legs hang limp on a cripple, So is a proverb in the mouth of dullards.

ז דַּלְיוּ שֹׁקַיִם מִפִּסֵּחַ וּמָשָׁל בְּפִי כְּסִילִים׃

8 Like a pebble in a sling, So is paying honor to a dullard.

ח כִּצְרוֹר אֶבֶן בְּמַרְגֵּמָה כֵּן־נוֹתֵן לִכְסִיל כָּבוֹד׃

Mishlei/Proverbs
Chapter 26

משלי
פרק כו

9 As a thorn comes to the hand of a drunkard, So a proverb to the mouth of a dullard.

ט חוֹחַ עָלָה בְיַד־שִׁכּוֹר וּמָשָׁל בְּפִי כְסִילִים׃

10 A master can produce anything, But he who hires a dullard is as one who hires transients.

י רַב מְחוֹלֵל־כֹּל וְשֹׂכֵר כְּסִיל וְשֹׂכֵר עֹבְרִים׃

11 As a dog returns to his vomit, So a dullard repeats his folly.

יא כְּכֶלֶב שָׁב עַל־קֵאוֹ כְּסִיל שׁוֹנֶה בְאִוַּלְתּוֹ׃

12 If you see a man who thinks himself wise, There is more hope for a dullard than for him.

יב רָאִיתָ אִישׁ חָכָם בְּעֵינָיו תִּקְוָה לִכְסִיל מִמֶּנּוּ׃

13 A lazy man says, "There's a cub on the road, a lion in the squares."

יג אָמַר עָצֵל שַׁחַל בַּדָּרֶךְ אֲרִי בֵּין הָרְחֹבוֹת׃

14 The door turns on its hinge, And the lazy man on his bed.

יד הַדֶּלֶת תִּסּוֹב עַל־צִירָהּ וְעָצֵל עַל־מִטָּתוֹ׃

15 The lazy man buries his hand in the bowl; He will not even bring it to his mouth.

טו טָמַן עָצֵל יָדוֹ בַּצַּלָּחַת נִלְאָה לַהֲשִׁיבָהּ אֶל־פִּיו׃

16 The lazy man thinks himself wiser Than seven men who give good advice.

טז חָכָם עָצֵל בְּעֵינָיו מִשִּׁבְעָה מְשִׁיבֵי טָעַם׃

17 A passerby who gets embroiled in someone else's quarrel Is like one who seizes a dog by its ears.

יז מַחֲזִיק בְּאָזְנֵי־כָלֶב עֹבֵר מִתְעַבֵּר עַל־רִיב לֹּא־לוֹ׃

18 Like a madman scattering deadly firebrands, arrows,

יח כְּמִתְלַהְלֵהַּ הַיֹּרֶה זִקִּים חִצִּים וָמָוֶת׃

19 Is one who cheats his fellow and says, "I was only joking."

יט כֵּן־אִישׁ רִמָּה אֶת־רֵעֵהוּ וְאָמַר הֲלֹא־מְשַׂחֵק אָנִי׃

20 For lack of wood a fire goes out, And without a querulous man contention is stilled.

כ בְּאֶפֶס עֵצִים תִּכְבֶּה־אֵשׁ וּבְאֵין נִרְגָּן יִשְׁתֹּק מָדוֹן׃

b'-E-fes ay-TZEEM tikh-beh AYSH uv-AYN nir-GAN yish-TOK ma-DON

21 Charcoal for embers and wood for a fire And a contentious man for kindling strife.

כא פֶּחָם לְגֶחָלִים וְעֵצִים לְאֵשׁ וְאִישׁ מדונים [מִדְיָנִים] לְחַרְחַר־רִיב׃

22 The words of a querulous man are bruising; They penetrate one's inmost parts.

כב דִּבְרֵי נִרְגָּן כְּמִתְלַהֲמִים וְהֵם יָרְדוּ חַדְרֵי־בָטֶן׃

26:20 And without a querulous man contention is stilled Rumors and slander add fuel to the fire of human contention. Just as a fire will burn itself out when it runs out of wood, so too, a disagreement will end naturally if the parties involved are not continually provoked by gossip. The *Torah* warns against speaking ill about others. The verse in *Sefer Vayikra* (19:16), "Do not deal basely with your countrymen," is usually translated as "thou shalt not go up and down as a talebearer among thy people." Speech is so powerful and potentially dangerous that, according to the Sages (*Erchin* 15a), the tongue had to be hidden behind two protective barriers, the lips and the teeth, in order to protect it from being used for slander. Indeed, it was the slander of the spies, who spoke evil about the Land of Israel, which delayed entry into the Holy Land and caused the Nation of Israel to wander in the desert for forty years.

Mishlei/Proverbs
Chapter 27

משלי
פרק כז

23 Base silver laid over earthenware Are ardent lips with an evil mind.

כֶּסֶף סִיגִים מְצֻפֶּה עַל־חָרֶשׂ שְׂפָתַיִם דֹּלְקִים וְלֶב־רָע:

24 An enemy dissembles with his speech, Inwardly he harbors deceit.

בשפתו [בִּשְׂפָתָיו] יִנָּכֵר שׂוֹנֵא וּבְקִרְבּוֹ יָשִׁית מִרְמָה:

25 Though he be fair-spoken do not trust him, For seven abominations are in his mind.

כִּי־יְחַנֵּן קוֹלוֹ אַל־תַּאֲמֶן־בּוֹ כִּי שֶׁבַע תּוֹעֵבוֹת בְּלִבּוֹ:

26 His hatred may be concealed by dissimulation, But his evil will be exposed to public view.

תִּכַּסֶּה שִׂנְאָה בְּמַשָּׁאוֹן תִּגָּלֶה רָעָתוֹ בְקָהָל:

27 He who digs a pit will fall in it, And whoever rolls a stone, it will roll back on him.

כֹּרֶה־שַּׁחַת בָּהּ יִפֹּל וְגֹלֵל אֶבֶן אֵלָיו תָּשׁוּב:

28 A lying tongue hates those crushed by it; Smooth speech throws one down.

לְשׁוֹן־שֶׁקֶר יִשְׂנָא דַכָּיו וּפֶה חָלָק יַעֲשֶׂה מִדְחֶה:

27

1 Do not boast of tomorrow For you do not know what the day will bring.

אַל־תִּתְהַלֵּל בְּיוֹם מָחָר כִּי לֹא־תֵדַע מַה־יֵּלֶד יוֹם:

2 Let the mouth of another praise you, not yours, The lips of a stranger, not your own.

יְהַלֶּלְךָ זָר וְלֹא־פִיךָ נָכְרִי וְאַל־שְׂפָתֶיךָ:

3 A stone has weight, sand is heavy, But a fool's vexation outweighs them both.

כֹּבֶד־אֶבֶן וְנֵטֶל הַחוֹל וְכַעַס אֱוִיל כָּבֵד מִשְּׁנֵיהֶם:

4 There is the cruelty of fury, the overflowing of anger, But who can withstand jealousy?

אַכְזְרִיּוּת חֵמָה וְשֶׁטֶף אָף וּמִי יַעֲמֹד לִפְנֵי קִנְאָה:

5 Open reproof is better than concealed love.

טוֹבָה תּוֹכַחַת מְגֻלָּה מֵאַהֲבָה מְסֻתָּרֶת:

6 Wounds by a loved one are long lasting; The kisses of an enemy are profuse.

נֶאֱמָנִים פִּצְעֵי אוֹהֵב וְנַעְתָּרוֹת נְשִׁיקוֹת שׂוֹנֵא:

ne-e-ma-NEEM pitz-AY o-HAYV v'-na-ta-ROT n'-shee-KOT so-NAY

7 A sated person disdains honey, But to a hungry man anything bitter seems sweet.

נֶפֶשׁ שְׂבֵעָה תָּבוּס נֹפֶת וְנֶפֶשׁ רְעֵבָה כָּל־מַר מָתוֹק:

8 Like a sparrow wandering from its nest Is a man who wanders from his home.

כְּצִפּוֹר נוֹדֶדֶת מִן־קִנָּהּ כֵּן־אִישׁ נוֹדֵד מִמְּקוֹמוֹ:

9 Oil and incense gladden the heart, And the sweetness of a friend is better than one's own counsel.

שֶׁמֶן וּקְטֹרֶת יְשַׂמַּח־לֵב וּמֶתֶק רֵעֵהוּ מֵעֲצַת־נָפֶשׁ:

27:6 The kisses of an enemy are profuse With a trusted friend, even actions that seem hurtful ultimately turn out to be beneficial. A well-timed reprimand from someone who loves you can guide you to a better course of action. An enemy, however, should not be trusted. Even if he appears to offer love and support, he will ultimately lead you astray. This idea is reflected in the words of the prophets who rebuke the Israelites for putting their trust in other nations, such as Assyria and Egypt, instead of *Hashem*. Ultimately, they were let down by their enemies who determined they had nothing more to gain from helping the Jewish people (see Hosea 8:8–9).

Mishlei/Proverbs
Chapter 27

משלי
פרק כז

10 Do not desert your friend and your father's friend; Do not enter your brother's house in your time of misfortune; A close neighbor is better than a distant brother.

י רֵעֲךָ וְרֵעֶה [וְרֵעַ] אָבִיךָ אַל־תַּעֲזֹב וּבֵית אָחִיךָ אַל־תָּבוֹא בְּיוֹם אֵידֶךָ טוֹב שָׁכֵן קָרוֹב מֵאָח רָחוֹק׃

11 Get wisdom, my son, and gladden my heart, That I may have what to answer those who taunt me.

יא חֲכַם בְּנִי וְשַׂמַּח לִבִּי וְאָשִׁיבָה חֹרְפִי דָבָר׃

12 The shrewd man saw trouble and took cover; The simple kept going and paid the penalty.

יב עָרוּם רָאָה רָעָה נִסְתָּר פְּתָאיִם עָבְרוּ נֶעֱנָשׁוּ׃

13 Seize his garment, for he stood surety for another; Take it as a pledge, [for he stood surety] for an unfamiliar woman.

יג קַח־בִּגְדוֹ כִּי־עָרַב זָר וּבְעַד נָכְרִיָּה חַבְלֵהוּ׃

14 He who greets his fellow loudly early in the morning Shall have it reckoned to him as a curse.

יד מְבָרֵךְ רֵעֵהוּ בְּקוֹל גָּדוֹל בַּבֹּקֶר הַשְׁכֵּים קְלָלָה תֵּחָשֶׁב לוֹ׃

15 An endless dripping on a rainy day And a contentious wife are alike;

טו דֶּלֶף טוֹרֵד בְּיוֹם סַגְרִיר וְאֵשֶׁת מְדוֹנִים [מִדְיָנִים] נִשְׁתָּוָה׃

16 As soon repress her as repress the wind, Or declare one's right hand to be oil.

טז צֹפְנֶיהָ צָפַן־רוּחַ וְשֶׁמֶן יְמִינוֹ יִקְרָא׃

17 As iron sharpens iron So a man sharpens the wit of his friend.

יז בַּרְזֶל בְּבַרְזֶל יָחַד וְאִישׁ יַחַד פְּנֵי־רֵעֵהוּ׃

18 He who tends a fig tree will enjoy its fruit, And he who cares for his master will be honored.

יח נֹצֵר תְּאֵנָה יֹאכַל פִּרְיָהּ וְשֹׁמֵר אֲדֹנָיו יְכֻבָּד׃

19 As face answers to face in water, So does one man's heart to another.

יט כַּמַּיִם הַפָּנִים לַפָּנִים כֵּן לֵב־הָאָדָם לָאָדָם׃

20 Sheol and Abaddon cannot be satisfied, Nor can the eyes of man be satisfied.

כ שְׁאוֹל וַאֲבַדֹּה [וַאֲבַדּוֹ] לֹא תִשְׂבַּעְנָה וְעֵינֵי הָאָדָם לֹא תִשְׂבַּעְנָה׃

21 For silver – the crucible, for gold – the furnace, And a man is tested by his praise.

כא מַצְרֵף לַכֶּסֶף וְכוּר לַזָּהָב וְאִישׁ לְפִי מַהֲלָלוֹ׃

22 Even if you pound the fool in a mortar With a pestle along with grain, His folly will not leave him.

כב אִם תִּכְתּוֹשׁ־אֶת־הָאֱוִיל בַּמַּכְתֵּשׁ בְּתוֹךְ הָרִיפוֹת בַּעֱלִי לֹא־תָסוּר מֵעָלָיו אִוַּלְתּוֹ׃

23 Mind well the looks of your flock; Pay attention to your herds;

כג יָדֹעַ תֵּדַע פְּנֵי צֹאנֶךָ שִׁית לִבְּךָ לַעֲדָרִים׃

24 For property does not last forever, Or a crown for all generations.

כד כִּי לֹא לְעוֹלָם חֹסֶן וְאִם־נֵזֶר לְדוֹר דּוֹר [וָדוֹר]׃

25 Grass vanishes, new grass appears, And the herbage of the hills is gathered in.

כה גָּלָה חָצִיר וְנִרְאָה־דֶשֶׁא וְנֶאֶסְפוּ עִשְּׂבוֹת הָרִים׃

26 The lambs will provide you with clothing, The he-goats, the price of a field.

כו כְּבָשִׂים לִלְבוּשֶׁךָ וּמְחִיר שָׂדֶה עַתּוּדִים׃

27 The goats' milk will suffice for your food, The food of your household, And the maintenance of your maids.

כז וְדֵי חֲלֵב עִזִּים לְלַחְמְךָ לְלֶחֶם בֵּיתֶךָ וְחַיִּים לְנַעֲרוֹתֶיךָ׃

Mishlei/Proverbs
Chapter 28

משלי
פרק כח

28 1 The wicked flee though no one gives chase, But the righteous are as confident as a lion.

א נָסוּ וְאֵין־רֹדֵף רָשָׁע וְצַדִּיקִים כִּכְפִיר יִבְטָח׃

2 When there is rebellion in the land, many are its rulers; But with a man who has understanding and knowledge, stability will last.

ב בְּפֶשַׁע אֶרֶץ רַבִּים שָׂרֶיהָ וּבְאָדָם מֵבִין יֹדֵעַ כֵּן יַאֲרִיךְ׃

3 A poor man who withholds what is due to the wretched Is like a destructive rain that leaves no food.

ג גֶּבֶר רָשׁ וְעֹשֵׁק דַּלִּים מָטָר סֹחֵף וְאֵין לָחֶם׃

4 Those who forsake instruction praise the wicked, But those who heed instruction fight them.

ד עֹזְבֵי תוֹרָה יְהַלְלוּ רָשָׁע וְשֹׁמְרֵי תוֹרָה יִתְגָּרוּ בָם׃

5 Evil men cannot discern judgment, But those who seek *Hashem* discern all things.

ה אַנְשֵׁי־רָע לֹא־יָבִינוּ מִשְׁפָּט וּמְבַקְשֵׁי יְהוָה יָבִינוּ כֹל׃

6 Better is a poor man who lives blamelessly Than a rich man whose ways are crooked.

ו טוֹב־רָשׁ הוֹלֵךְ בְּתֻמּוֹ מֵעִקֵּשׁ דְּרָכַיִם וְהוּא עָשִׁיר׃

7 An intelligent son heeds instruction, But he who keeps company with gluttons disgraces his father.

ז נוֹצֵר תּוֹרָה בֵּן מֵבִין וְרֹעֶה זוֹלְלִים יַכְלִים אָבִיו׃

8 He who increases his wealth by loans at discount or interest Amasses it for one who is generous to the poor.

ח מַרְבֶּה הוֹנוֹ בְּנֶשֶׁךְ וּבְתַרְבִּית [וְתַרְבִּית] לְחוֹנֵן דַּלִּים יִקְבְּצֶנּוּ׃

mar-BEH ho-NO b'-NE-shekh v'-tar-BEET l'-kho-NAYN da-LEEM yik-b'-TZE-nu

9 He who turns a deaf ear to instruction – His prayer is an abomination.

ט מֵסִיר אָזְנוֹ מִשְּׁמֹעַ תּוֹרָה גַּם־תְּפִלָּתוֹ תּוֹעֵבָה׃

10 He who misleads the upright into an evil course Will fall into his own pit, But the blameless will prosper.

י מַשְׁגֶּה יְשָׁרִים בְּדֶרֶךְ רָע בִּשְׁחוּתוֹ הוּא־יִפּוֹל וּתְמִימִים יִנְחֲלוּ־טוֹב׃

11 A rich man is clever in his own eyes, But a perceptive poor man can see through him.

יא חָכָם בְּעֵינָיו אִישׁ עָשִׁיר וְדַל מֵבִין יַחְקְרֶנּוּ׃

12 When the righteous exult there is great glory, But when the wicked rise up men make themselves scarce.

יב בַּעֲלֹץ צַדִּיקִים רַבָּה תִפְאָרֶת וּבְקוּם רְשָׁעִים יְחֻפַּשׂ אָדָם׃

13 He who covers up his faults will not succeed; He who confesses and gives them up will find mercy.

יג מְכַסֶּה פְשָׁעָיו לֹא יַצְלִיחַ וּמוֹדֶה וְעֹזֵב יְרֻחָם׃

14 Happy is the man who is anxious always, But he who hardens his heart falls into misfortune.

יד אַשְׁרֵי אָדָם מְפַחֵד תָּמִיד וּמַקְשֶׁה לִבּוֹ יִפּוֹל בְּרָעָה׃

28:8 Amasses it for one who is generous to the poor Despite sayings to the contrary, sometimes it seems that the wicked do prosper. After all, if crime didn't pay, nobody would bother to try. This concerned even the greatest of biblical personalities, such as *Yirmiyahu*, who asks, "Wherefore does the way of the wicked prosper?" (Jeremiah 12:1). However, King *Shlomo* reassures us, one who becomes rich through dishonest means merely accumulates the wealth for the benefit of the righteous, as *Hashem* will ensure it arrives in their possession in the end.

Mishlei/Proverbs

Chapter 29

משלי

פרק כט

15 A roaring lion and a prowling bear Is a wicked man ruling a helpless people.

טו אֲרִי־נֹהֵם וְדֹב שׁוֹקֵק מֹשֵׁל רָשָׁע עַל עַם־דָּל׃

16 A prince who lacks understanding is very oppressive; He who spurns ill-gotten gains will live long.

טז נָגִיד חֲסַר תְּבוּנוֹת וְרַב מַעֲשַׁקּוֹת שֹׂנְאֵי [שֹׂנֵא] בֶצַע יַאֲרִיךְ יָמִים׃

17 A man oppressed by bloodguilt will flee to a pit; Let none give him support.

יז אָדָם עָשֻׁק בְּדַם־נָפֶשׁ עַד־בּוֹר יָנוּס אַל־יִתְמְכוּ־בוֹ׃

18 He who lives blamelessly will be delivered, But he who is crooked in his ways will fall all at once.

יח הוֹלֵךְ תָּמִים יִוָּשֵׁעַ וְנֶעְקַשׁ דְּרָכַיִם יִפּוֹל בְּאֶחָת׃

19 He who tills his land will have food in plenty, But he who pursues vanities will have poverty in plenty.

יט עֹבֵד אַדְמָתוֹ יִשְׂבַּע־לָחֶם וּמְרַדֵּף רֵקִים יִשְׂבַּע־רִישׁ׃

20 A dependable man will receive many blessings, But one in a hurry to get rich will not go unpunished.

כ אִישׁ אֱמוּנוֹת רַב־בְּרָכוֹת וְאָץ לְהַעֲשִׁיר לֹא יִנָּקֶה׃

21 To be partial is not right; A man may do wrong for a piece of bread.

כא הַכֵּר־פָּנִים לֹא־טוֹב וְעַל־פַּת־לֶחֶם יִפְשַׁע־גָּבֶר׃

22 A miserly man runs after wealth; He does not realize that loss will overtake it.

כב נִבְהָל לַהוֹן אִישׁ רַע עָיִן וְלֹא־יֵדַע כִּי־חֶסֶר יְבֹאֶנּוּ׃

23 He who reproves a man will in the end Find more favor than he who flatters him.

כג מוֹכִיחַ אָדָם אַחֲרַי חֵן יִמְצָא מִמַּחֲלִיק לָשׁוֹן׃

24 He who robs his father and mother and says, "It is no offense," Is a companion to vandals.

כד גּוֹזֵל אָבִיו וְאִמּוֹ וְאֹמֵר אֵין־פָּשַׁע חָבֵר הוּא לְאִישׁ מַשְׁחִית׃

25 A greedy man provokes quarrels, But he who trusts *Hashem* shall enjoy prosperity.

כה רְחַב־נֶפֶשׁ יְגָרֶה מָדוֹן וּבוֹטֵחַ עַל־יְהֹוָה יְדֻשָּׁן׃

26 He who trusts his own instinct is a dullard, But he who lives by wisdom shall escape.

כו בּוֹטֵחַ בְּלִבּוֹ הוּא כְסִיל וְהוֹלֵךְ בְּחָכְמָה הוּא יִמָּלֵט׃

27 He who gives to the poor will not be in want, But he who shuts his eyes will be roundly cursed.

כז נוֹתֵן לָרָשׁ אֵין מַחְסוֹר וּמַעְלִים עֵינָיו רַב־מְאֵרוֹת׃

28 When the wicked rise up, men go into hiding, But when they perish the righteous increase.

כח בְּקוּם רְשָׁעִים יִסָּתֵר אָדָם וּבַאֲבָדָם יִרְבּוּ צַדִּיקִים׃

29

1 One oft reproved may become stiffnecked, But he will be suddenly broken beyond repair.

כט א אִישׁ תּוֹכָחוֹת מַקְשֶׁה־עֹרֶף פֶּתַע יִשָּׁבֵר וְאֵין מַרְפֵּא׃

2 When the righteous become great the people rejoice, But when the wicked dominate the people groan.

ב בִּרְבוֹת צַדִּיקִים יִשְׂמַח הָעָם וּבִמְשֹׁל רָשָׁע יֵאָנַח עָם׃

3 A man who loves wisdom brings joy to his father, But he who keeps company with harlots will lose his wealth.

ג אִישׁ־אֹהֵב חָכְמָה יְשַׂמַּח אָבִיו וְרֹעֶה זוֹנוֹת יְאַבֶּד־הוֹן׃

4 By justice a king sustains the land, But a fraudulent man tears it down.

ד מֶלֶךְ בְּמִשְׁפָּט יַעֲמִיד אָרֶץ וְאִישׁ תְּרוּמוֹת יֶהֶרְסֶנָּה׃

Mishlei/Proverbs

Chapter 29

משלי

פרק כט

5 A man who flatters his fellow Spreads a net for his feet.

ה גֶּבֶר מַחֲלִיק עַל־רֵעֵהוּ רֶשֶׁת פּוֹרֵשׂ עַל־פְּעָמָיו:

6 An evil man's offenses are a trap for himself, But the righteous sing out joyously.

ו בְּפֶשַׁע אִישׁ רָע מוֹקֵשׁ וְצַדִּיק יָרוּן וְשָׂמֵחַ:

7 A righteous man is concerned with the cause of the wretched; A wicked man cannot understand such concern.

ז יֹדֵעַ צַדִּיק דִּין דַּלִּים רָשָׁע לֹא־יָבִין דָּעַת:

8 Scoffers inflame a city, But the wise allay anger.

ח אַנְשֵׁי לָצוֹן יָפִיחוּ קִרְיָה וַחֲכָמִים יָשִׁיבוּ אָף:

9 When a wise man enters into litigation with a fool There is ranting and ridicule, but no satisfaction.

ט אִישׁ־חָכָם נִשְׁפָּט אֶת־אִישׁ אֱוִיל וְרָגַז וְשָׂחַק וְאֵין נָחַת:

10 Bloodthirsty men detest the blameless, But the upright seek them out.

י אַנְשֵׁי דָמִים יִשְׂנְאוּ־תָם וִישָׁרִים יְבַקְשׁוּ נַפְשׁוֹ:

11 A dullard vents all his rage, But a wise man calms it down.

יא כָּל־רוּחוֹ יוֹצִיא כְסִיל וְחָכָם בְּאָחוֹר יְשַׁבְּחֶנָּה:

12 A ruler who listens to lies, All his ministers will be wicked.

יב מֹשֵׁל מַקְשִׁיב עַל־דְּבַר־שָׁקֶר כָּל־מְשָׁרְתָיו רְשָׁעִים:

13 A poor man and a fraudulent man meet; *Hashem* gives luster to the eyes of both.

יג רָשׁ וְאִישׁ תְּכָכִים נִפְגָּשׁוּ מֵאִיר־עֵינֵי שְׁנֵיהֶם יְהֹוָה:

14 A king who judges the wretched honestly, His throne will be established forever.

יד מֶלֶךְ שׁוֹפֵט בֶּאֱמֶת דַּלִּים כִּסְאוֹ לָעַד יִכּוֹן:

15 Rod and reproof produce wisdom, But a lad out of control is a disgrace to his mother.

טו שֵׁבֶט וְתוֹכַחַת יִתֵּן חָכְמָה וְנַעַר מְשֻׁלָּח מֵבִישׁ אִמּוֹ:

16 When the wicked increase, offenses increase, But the righteous will see their downfall.

טז בִּרְבוֹת רְשָׁעִים יִרְבֶּה־פָּשַׁע וְצַדִּיקִים בְּמַפַּלְתָּם יִרְאוּ:

17 Discipline your son and he will give you peace; He will gratify you with dainties.

יז יַסֵּר בִּנְךָ וִינִיחֶךָ וְיִתֵּן מַעֲדַנִּים לְנַפְשֶׁךָ:

18 For lack of vision a people lose restraint, But happy is he who heeds instruction.

יח בְּאֵין חָזוֹן יִפָּרַע עָם וְשֹׁמֵר תּוֹרָה אַשְׁרֵהוּ:

19 A slave cannot be disciplined by words; Though he may comprehend, he does not respond.

יט בִּדְבָרִים לֹא־יִוָּסֶר עָבֶד כִּי־יָבִין וְאֵין מַעֲנֶה:

20 If you see a man hasty in speech, There is more hope for a fool than for him.

כ חָזִיתָ אִישׁ אָץ בִּדְבָרָיו תִּקְוָה לִכְסִיל מִמֶּנּוּ:

21 A slave pampered from youth Will come to a bad end.

כא מְפַנֵּק מִנֹּעַר עַבְדּוֹ וְאַחֲרִיתוֹ יִהְיֶה מָנוֹן:

22 An angry man provokes a quarrel; A hot-tempered man commits many offenses.

כב אִישׁ־אַף יְגָרֶה מָדוֹן וּבַעַל חֵמָה רַב־פָּשַׁע:

Mishlei/Proverbs
Chapter 30

משלי
פרק ל

23 A man's pride will humiliate him, But a humble man will obtain honor.

גַּאֲוַת אָדָם תַּשְׁפִּילֶנּוּ וּשְׁפַל־רוּחַ יִתְמֹךְ כָּבוֹד׃

ga-a-VAT a-DAM tash-pee-LE-nu ush-fal RU-akh yit-MOKH ka-VOD

24 He who shares with a thief is his own enemy; He hears the imprecation and does not tell.

חוֹלֵק עִם־גַּנָּב שׂוֹנֵא נַפְשׁוֹ אָלָה יִשְׁמַע וְלֹא יַגִּיד׃

25 A man's fears become a trap for him, But he who trusts in *Hashem* shall be safeguarded.

חֶרְדַּת אָדָם יִתֵּן מוֹקֵשׁ וּבוֹטֵחַ בַּיהֹוָה יְשֻׂגָּב׃

26 Many seek audience with a ruler, But it is from *Hashem* that a man gets justice.

רַבִּים מְבַקְשִׁים פְּנֵי־מוֹשֵׁל וּמֵיְהֹוָה מִשְׁפַּט־אִישׁ׃

27 The unjust man is an abomination to the righteous, And he whose way is straight is an abomination to the wicked.

תּוֹעֲבַת צַדִּיקִים אִישׁ עָוֶל וְתוֹעֲבַת רָשָׁע יְשַׁר־דָּרֶךְ׃

30

1 The words of *Agur* son of *Yakeh*, [man of] *Massa*; The speech of the man to *Itiel*, to *Itiel* and *Ukal*:

דִּבְרֵי אָגוּר בִּן־יָקֶה הַמַּשָּׂא נְאֻם הַגֶּבֶר לְאִיתִיאֵל לְאִיתִיאֵל וְאֻכָל׃

2 I am brutish, less than a man; I lack common sense.

כִּי בַעַר אָנֹכִי מֵאִישׁ וְלֹא־בִינַת אָדָם לִי׃

3 I have not learned wisdom, Nor do I possess knowledge of the Holy One.

וְלֹא־לָמַדְתִּי חָכְמָה וְדַעַת קְדֹשִׁים אֵדָע׃

4 Who has ascended heaven and come down? Who has gathered up the wind in the hollow of his hand? Who has wrapped the waters in his garment? Who has established all the extremities of the earth? What is his name or his son's name, if you know it?

מִי עָלָה־שָׁמַיִם וַיֵּרַד מִי אָסַף־רוּחַ בְּחָפְנָיו מִי צָרַר־מַיִם בַּשִּׂמְלָה מִי הֵקִים כָּל־אַפְסֵי־אָרֶץ מַה־שְּׁמוֹ וּמַה־שֶּׁם־בְּנוֹ כִּי תֵדָע׃

5 Every word of *Hashem* is pure, A shield to those who take refuge in Him.

כָּל־אִמְרַת אֱלוֹהַּ צְרוּפָה מָגֵן הוּא לַחֹסִים בּוֹ׃

6 Do not add to His words, Lest He indict you and you be proved a liar.

אַל־תּוֹסְףְּ עַל־דְּבָרָיו פֶּן־יוֹכִיחַ בְּךָ וְנִכְזָבְתָּ׃

7 Two things I ask of you; do not deny them to me before I die:

שְׁתַּיִם שָׁאַלְתִּי מֵאִתָּךְ אַל־תִּמְנַע מִמֶּנִּי בְּטֶרֶם אָמוּת׃

8 Keep lies and false words far from me; Give me neither poverty nor riches, But provide me with my daily bread,

שָׁוְא וּדְבַר־כָּזָב הַרְחֵק מִמֶּנִּי רֵאשׁ וָעֹשֶׁר אַל־תִּתֶּן־לִי הַטְרִיפֵנִי לֶחֶם חֻקִּי׃

SHAV ud-var ka-ZAV har-KHAYK mi-ME-nee RAYSH va-O-sher al TI-ten LEE hat-ree-FAY-nee LE-khem khu-KEE

29:23 But a humble man will obtain honor Honor is a funny thing. One who seeks it out is unlikely to earn it from others, but one who rejects it is likely to earn his fellows' respect. As the Sages of the Talmud teach (*Eiruvin* 13b), "One who chases after honor, honor eludes him; but one who runs away from honor, honor clings to him."

30:8 Give me neither poverty nor riches We often think how grateful we would be to have wealth or abundance. This verse points out that often, riches do not lead people to gratitude, but rather to smugness and self-satisfaction. If we have too much of a good thing, we may come to believe we have earned it, and forget *Hashem*'s hand in our lives. In fact, the Bible warns that

1704

Mishlei/Proverbs
Chapter 30

משלי
פרק ל

9 Lest, being sated, I renounce, saying, "Who is *Hashem*?" Or, being impoverished, I take to theft And profane the name of my God.

ט פֶּן אֶשְׂבַּע וְכִחַשְׁתִּי וְאָמַרְתִּי מִי יְהֹוָה וּפֶן־אִוָּרֵשׁ וְגָנַבְתִּי וְתָפַשְׂתִּי שֵׁם אֱלֹהָי:

10 Do not inform on a slave to his master, Lest he curse you and you incur guilt.

י אַל־תַּלְשֵׁן עֶבֶד אֶל־אדנו [אֲדֹנָיו] פֶּן־יְקַלֶּלְךָ וְאָשָׁמְתָּ:

11 There is a breed of men that brings a curse on its fathers And brings no blessing to its mothers,

יא דּוֹר אָבִיו יְקַלֵּל וְאֶת־אִמּוֹ לֹא יְבָרֵךְ:

12 A breed that thinks itself pure, Though it is not washed of its filth;

יב דּוֹר טָהוֹר בְּעֵינָיו וּמִצֹּאָתוֹ לֹא רֻחָץ:

13 A breed so haughty of bearing, so supercilious;

יג דּוֹר מָה־רָמוּ עֵינָיו וְעַפְעַפָּיו יִנָּשֵׂאוּ:

14 A breed whose teeth are swords, Whose jaws are knives, Ready to devour the poor of the land, The needy among men.

יד דּוֹר חֲרָבוֹת שִׁנָּיו וּמַאֲכָלוֹת מְתַלְּעֹתָיו לֶאֱכֹל עֲנִיִּים מֵאֶרֶץ וְאֶבְיוֹנִים מֵאָדָם:

15 The leech has two daughters, "Give!" and "Give!" Three things are insatiable; Four never say, "Enough!":

טו לַעֲלוּקָה שְׁתֵּי בָנוֹת הַב הַב שָׁלוֹשׁ הֵנָּה לֹא תִשְׂבַּעְנָה אַרְבַּע לֹא־אָמְרוּ הוֹן:

16 Sheol, a barren womb, Earth that cannot get enough water, And fire which never says, "Enough!"

טז שְׁאוֹל וְעֹצֶר רָחַם אֶרֶץ לֹא־שָׂבְעָה מַּיִם וְאֵשׁ לֹא־אָמְרָה הוֹן:

17 The eye that mocks a father And disdains the homage due a mother – The ravens of the brook will gouge it out, Young eagles will devour it.

יז עַיִן תִּלְעַג לְאָב וְתָבוּז לִיקֲּהַת־אֵם יִקְּרוּהָ עֹרְבֵי־נַחַל וְיֹאכְלוּהָ בְנֵי־נָשֶׁר:

18 Three things are beyond me; Four I cannot fathom:

יח שְׁלֹשָׁה הֵמָּה נִפְלְאוּ מִמֶּנִּי וארבע [וְאַרְבָּעָה] לֹא יְדַעְתִּים:

19 How an eagle makes its way over the sky; How a snake makes its way over a rock; How a ship makes its way through the high seas; How a man has his way with a maiden.

יט דֶּרֶךְ הַנֶּשֶׁר בַּשָּׁמַיִם דֶּרֶךְ נָחָשׁ עֲלֵי צוּר דֶּרֶךְ־אֳנִיָּה בְלֶב־יָם וְדֶרֶךְ גֶּבֶר בְּעַלְמָה:

20 Such is the way of an adulteress: She eats, wipes her mouth, And says, "I have done no wrong."

כ כֵּן דֶּרֶךְ אִשָּׁה מְנָאָפֶת אָכְלָה וּמָחֲתָה פִיהָ וְאָמְרָה לֹא־פָעַלְתִּי אָוֶן:

21 The earth shudders at three things, At four which it cannot bear:

כא תַּחַת שָׁלוֹשׁ רָגְזָה אֶרֶץ וְתַחַת אַרְבַּע לֹא־תוּכַל שְׂאֵת:

22 A slave who becomes king; A scoundrel sated with food;

כב תַּחַת־עֶבֶד כִּי יִמְלוֹךְ וְנָבָל כִּי יִשְׂבַּע־לָחֶם:

---

forgetting the Lord and attributing one's wealth to his own power and might is one of the dangers of the blessing of bounty in the Land of Israel (Deuteronomy 8:7–18). Conversely, if we lack something in our lives, we may come to curse God, forgetting He has our best interests at heart. Hence, we should hope to always have just enough for our needs – not to feel the strain of lack, but also not the pride of luxury.

Mishlei/Proverbs

Chapter 31

23	A loathsome woman who gets married; A slave-girl who supplants her mistress.
24	Four are among the tiniest on earth, Yet they are the wisest of the wise:
25	Ants are a folk without power, Yet they prepare food for themselves in summer;
26	The badger is a folk without strength, Yet it makes its home in the rock;
27	The locusts have no king, Yet they all march forth in formation;
28	You can catch the lizard in your hand, Yet it is found in royal palaces.
29	There are three that are stately of stride, Four that carry themselves well:
30	The lion is mightiest among the beasts, And recoils before none;
31	The greyhound, the he-goat, The king whom none dares resist.
32	If you have been scandalously arrogant, If you have been a schemer, Then clap your hand to your mouth.
33	As milk under pressure produces butter, And a nose under pressure produces blood, So patience under pressure produces strife.

משלי

פרק לא

כג תַּחַת שְׂנוּאָה כִּי תִבָּעֵל וְשִׁפְחָה כִּי־תִירַשׁ גְּבִרְתָּהּ:

כד אַרְבָּעָה הֵם קְטַנֵּי־אָרֶץ וְהֵמָּה חֲכָמִים מְחֻכָּמִים:

כה הַנְּמָלִים עַם לֹא־עָז וַיָּכִינוּ בַקַּיִץ לַחְמָם:

כו שְׁפַנִּים עַם לֹא־עָצוּם וַיָּשִׂימוּ בַסֶּלַע בֵּיתָם:

כז מֶלֶךְ אֵין לָאַרְבֶּה וַיֵּצֵא חֹצֵץ כֻּלּוֹ:

כח שְׂמָמִית בְּיָדַיִם תְּתַפֵּשׂ וְהִיא בְּהֵיכְלֵי מֶלֶךְ:

כט שְׁלֹשָׁה הֵמָּה מֵיטִיבֵי צָעַד וְאַרְבָּעָה מֵיטִבֵי לָכֶת:

ל לַיִשׁ גִּבּוֹר בַּבְּהֵמָה וְלֹא־יָשׁוּב מִפְּנֵי־כֹל:

לא זַרְזִיר מָתְנַיִם אוֹ־תָיִשׁ וּמֶלֶךְ אַלְקוּם עִמּוֹ:

לב אִם־נָבַלְתָּ בְהִתְנַשֵּׂא וְאִם־זַמּוֹתָ יָד לְפֶה:

לג כִּי מִיץ חָלָב יוֹצִיא חֶמְאָה וּמִיץ־אַף יוֹצִיא דָם וּמִיץ אַפַּיִם יוֹצִיא רִיב:

31 1	The words of *Lemuel*, king of Massa, with which his mother admonished him:
2	No, my son! No, O son of my womb! No, O son of my vows!
3	Do not give your strength to women, Your vigor, to those who destroy kings.
4	Wine is not for kings, O *Lemuel*; Not for kings to drink, Nor any strong drink for princes,
5	Lest they drink and forget what has been ordained, And infringe on the rights of the poor.
6	Give strong drink to the hapless And wine to the embittered.
7	Let them drink and forget their poverty, And put their troubles out of mind.
8	Speak up for the dumb, For the rights of all the unfortunate.

לא

א דִּבְרֵי לְמוּאֵל מֶלֶךְ מַשָּׂא אֲשֶׁר־יִסְּרַתּוּ אִמּוֹ:

ב מַה־בְּרִי וּמַה־בַּר־בִּטְנִי וּמֶה בַּר־נְדָרָי:

ג אַל־תִּתֵּן לַנָּשִׁים חֵילֶךָ וּדְרָכֶיךָ לַמְחוֹת מְלָכִין:

ד אַל לַמְלָכִים לְמוֹאֵל אַל לַמְלָכִים שְׁתוֹ־יָיִן וּלְרוֹזְנִים אוֹ [אֵי] שֵׁכָר:

ה פֶּן־יִשְׁתֶּה וְיִשְׁכַּח מְחֻקָּק וִישַׁנֶּה דִּין כָּל־בְּנֵי־עֹנִי:

ו תְּנוּ־שֵׁכָר לְאוֹבֵד וְיַיִן לְמָרֵי נָפֶשׁ:

ז יִשְׁתֶּה וְיִשְׁכַּח רִישׁוֹ וַעֲמָלוֹ לֹא יִזְכָּר־עוֹד:

ח פְּתַח־פִּיךָ לְאִלֵּם אֶל־דִּין כָּל־בְּנֵי חֲלוֹף:

Mishlei/Proverbs

Chapter 31

משלי

פרק לא

9 Speak up, judge righteously, Champion the poor and the needy.

ט פְּתַח־פִּיךָ שְׁפָט־צֶדֶק וְדִין עָנִי וְאֶבְיוֹן׃

10 What a rare find is a capable wife! Her worth is far beyond that of rubies.

י אֵשֶׁת־חַיִל מִי יִמְצָא וְרָחֹק מִפְּנִינִים מִכְרָהּ׃

AY-shet KHA-yil MEE yim-TZA v'-ra-KHOK mi-p'-nee-NEEM mikh-RAH

11 Her husband puts his confidence in her, And lacks no good thing.

יא בָּטַח בָּהּ לֵב בַּעְלָהּ וְשָׁלָל לֹא יֶחְסָר׃

12 She is good to him, never bad, All the days of her life.

יב גְּמָלַתְהוּ טוֹב וְלֹא־רָע כֹּל יְמֵי חַיֶּיהָ׃

13 She looks for wool and flax, And sets her hand to them with a will.

יג דָּרְשָׁה צֶמֶר וּפִשְׁתִּים וַתַּעַשׂ בְּחֵפֶץ כַּפֶּיהָ׃

14 She is like a merchant fleet, Bringing her food from afar.

יד הָיְתָה כָּאֳנִיּוֹת סוֹחֵר מִמֶּרְחָק תָּבִיא לַחְמָהּ׃

15 She rises while it is still night, And supplies provisions for her household, The daily fare of her maids.

טו וַתָּקָם ׀ בְּעוֹד לַיְלָה וַתִּתֵּן טֶרֶף לְבֵיתָהּ וְחֹק לְנַעֲרֹתֶיהָ׃

16 She sets her mind on an estate and acquires it; She plants a vineyard by her own labors.

טז זָמְמָה שָׂדֶה וַתִּקָּחֵהוּ מִפְּרִי כַפֶּיהָ נטע [נָטְעָה] כָּרֶם׃

17 She girds herself with strength, And performs her tasks with vigor.

יז חָגְרָה בְעוֹז מָתְנֶיהָ וַתְּאַמֵּץ זְרוֹעֹתֶיהָ׃

18 She sees that her business thrives; Her lamp never goes out at night.

יח טָעֲמָה כִּי־טוֹב סַחְרָהּ לֹא־יִכְבֶּה בליל [בַלַּיְלָה] נֵרָהּ׃

19 She sets her hand to the distaff; Her fingers work the spindle.

יט יָדֶיהָ שִׁלְּחָה בַכִּישׁוֹר וְכַפֶּיהָ תָּמְכוּ פָלֶךְ׃

20 She gives generously to the poor; Her hands are stretched out to the needy.

כ כַּפָּהּ פָּרְשָׂה לֶעָנִי וְיָדֶיהָ שִׁלְּחָה לָאֶבְיוֹן׃

21 She is not worried for her household because of snow, For her whole household is dressed in crimson.

כא לֹא־תִירָא לְבֵיתָהּ מִשָּׁלֶג כִּי כָל־בֵּיתָהּ לָבֻשׁ שָׁנִים׃

22 She makes covers for herself; Her clothing is linen and purple.

כב מַרְבַדִּים עָשְׂתָה־לָּהּ שֵׁשׁ וְאַרְגָּמָן לְבוּשָׁהּ׃

31:10 A capable wife This chapter contains an extended poem in praise of the *eishet chayil*, translated here as 'capable wife,' but generally referred to as the 'woman of valor' (verses 10–31). She provides for her family in all ways, both materially and spiritually, and her endeavors and accomplishments are praised by the members of her household and by others. This poem is sung by Jews around the world on Friday nights, as they begin the first *Shabbat* meal. It is often understood as a praise for the Jewish woman who works hard to care for her family and for others, and to prepare for the *Shabbat* each week. On a more mystical plane, it has been said in the name of the sixteenth century Kabbalist Rabbi Yitzchak Luria, who is known by the acronym *Arizal*, that "the Land of Israel is the earthly manifestation of the woman of valor." When the Children of Israel follow *Hashem* faithfully in this unique land, they are provided for, both materially and spiritually. And, the beauty and charm of *Eretz Yisrael* are recognized and praised by all, Jews and non-Jews alike.

Mishlei/Proverbs
Chapter 31

משלי
פרק לא

23 Her husband is prominent in the gates, As he sits among the elders of the land.

כג נוֹדָע בַּשְּׁעָרִים בַּעְלָהּ בְּשִׁבְתּוֹ עִם־זִקְנֵי־אָרֶץ׃

24 She makes cloth and sells it, And offers a girdle to the merchant.

כד סָדִין עָשְׂתָה וַתִּמְכֹּר וַחֲגוֹר נָתְנָה לַכְּנַעֲנִי׃

25 She is clothed with strength and splendor; She looks to the future cheerfully.

כה עֹז־וְהָדָר לְבוּשָׁהּ וַתִּשְׂחַק לְיוֹם אַחֲרוֹן׃

26 Her mouth is full of wisdom, Her tongue with kindly teaching.

כו פִּיהָ פָּתְחָה בְחָכְמָה וְתוֹרַת־חֶסֶד עַל־לְשׁוֹנָהּ׃

27 She oversees the activities of her household And never eats the bread of idleness.

כז צוֹפִיָּה הֲלִיכוֹת בֵּיתָהּ וְלֶחֶם עַצְלוּת לֹא תֹאכֵל׃

28 Her children declare her happy; Her husband praises her,

כח קָמוּ בָנֶיהָ וַיְאַשְּׁרוּהָ בַּעְלָהּ וַיְהַלְלָהּ׃

29 "Many women have done well, But you surpass them all."

כט רַבּוֹת בָּנוֹת עָשׂוּ חָיִל וְאַתְּ עָלִית עַל־כֻּלָּנָה׃

30 Grace is deceptive, Beauty is illusory; It is for her fear of *Hashem* That a woman is to be praised.

ל שֶׁקֶר הַחֵן וְהֶבֶל הַיֹּפִי אִשָּׁה יִרְאַת־יְהוָה הִיא תִתְהַלָּל׃

31 Extol her for the fruit of her hand, And let her works praise her in the gates.

לא תְּנוּ־לָהּ מִפְּרִי יָדֶיהָ וִיהַלְלוּהָ בַשְּׁעָרִים מַעֲשֶׂיהָ׃

Sefer Iyov
The Book of Job

Introduction and commentary by Alexander Jacob Tsykin

Sefer Iyov (Job) is a complex work. It poses the difficult and well-known question of theodicy: Why do bad things happen to good people? *Sefer Iyov* begins with a narrative about an extremely righteous person named *Iyov*, who is to be tormented by *Hashem*. But why is he to be afflicted? What is the reason for his suffering? The answer to these questions remain uncertain.

Chapter one describes a wager God made with the Adversary, known in Hebrew as *Satan* (שטן), a spiritual being who is given the divinely-assigned task of trying to cause people to stumble spiritually. *Hashem* insists that *Iyov* would remain true and loyal even if horribly tormented and knowing that he deserves no punishment. What follows is a description of how all of *Iyov*'s children die, and all of his property is lost. *Iyov* accepts this devastating news with equanimity. The *Satan* then afflicts *Iyov* with a horrible disease, but stops short of taking his life as instructed by *Hashem* (1:12). At this point *Iyov* can no longer cope. He begins to question God's justice, though he never questions God's existence, or even His power.

Iyov's friends come to reassure him, but their way of attempting to comfort him is by insisting that *Hashem*'s justice is absolute, and that he must therefore deserve his terrible suffering. Throughout this surprising remonstration, *Iyov* gets more upset, and continuously protests his innocence of the suggested wrongdoings. Eventually, *Hashem* appears and reprimands *Iyov* for doubting Him, and the friends for sinning against Him, and then *Iyov*'s formerly-happy life is restored.

Throughout the course of the book, *Iyov* is meant to learn humility, and to understand that it is not his place to evaluate or question God. By accepting his suffering, *Iyov* becomes a better person. As the commentary in *The Israel Bible* demonstrates, sometimes it is those who *Hashem* loves most that He causes to suffer, because by doing so, He makes them stronger.

Whether or not we can pinpoint a reason for *Iyov*'s suffering, one thing is clear at the end of the book. We must always remember that there is a divine ruler who controls the world with ultimate wisdom and a perfect sense of justice. Though we may not be able to understand His reasons for running the world as He does, we must put our trust in Him alone, and believe that everything He does is for the best.

There is a debate among the Sages of the Talmud (*Bava Batra* 15a) regarding the period during which *Iyov* lived. A number of opinions are recorded, differing from one another by many generations. There is even one opinion that says he did not live at all, and the story of his suffering is a parable, meant to serve as a model for dealing with suffering and understanding why it occurs. It has also been suggested that the focus of the book is not general, universal human suffering, but the specific suffering of the Jewish people.

Indeed, *Iyov*'s homeland, the land of *Utz*, is understood by many as another name for the Land of Israel. The Jewish people have suffered considerably over the ages. Throughout history, they have lost everything, from their families to their possessions, their homes and even their homeland. They have been afflicted physically, emotionally and spiritually, but like *Iyov*, have been promised that the light of the Jewish nation will never be extinguished. Also like *Iyov*, they have at times remained strong and at times have questioned, but through it all they clung to their belief in the Creator.

Though we might never be able to fully answer the question of why the Children of Israel had to suffer throughout history as much as they did, *Sefer Iyov* reminds us that we must always trust in *Hashem*. We believe that Israel's suffering is ultimately for the good, and we must have the confidence that ultimately, the Nation of Israel will be fully restored to its former glory, safe and secure in *Eretz Yisrael*.

List of Opinions Regarding When *Iyov* (Job) lived

Sefer Iyov does not give much identifying information about its main character. The Talmud (*Bava Batra* 15a–b) offers a number of different suggestions as to when *Iyov* lived, based on various verses in the book:

Opinion attributed to:	Suggestion
Rabbi *Levi* son of *Lachma*	*Iyov* lived in the time of *Moshe*
Rava	*Iyov* lived during the time of the 12 spies
Anonymous opinion	*Iyov* never existed, the story is a parable
Rabbi *Yochanan* and Rabbi *Elazar*	*Iyov* returned with the Jewish exiles from Babylon
Rabbi *Eliezer*	*Iyov* lived at the time of the Judges
Rabbi *Yehoshua* son of *Korcha*	*Iyov* lived at the time of Ahasuerus
Rabbi *Natan*	*Iyov* lived in the days of the kingdom of Sheba
The Sages	*Iyov* lived in the days of the Babylonians under the leadership of Nebuchadnezzar
Some say	*Iyov* lived in the days of *Yaakov* and married *Yaakov*'s daughter *Dina*

Iyov/Job
Chapter 1

איוב
פרק א

1 There was a man in the land of *Utz* named *Iyov*. That man was blameless and upright; he feared *Hashem* and shunned evil.

א אִישׁ הָיָה בְאֶרֶץ־עוּץ אִיּוֹב שְׁמוֹ וְהָיָה הָאִישׁ הַהוּא תָּם וְיָשָׁר וִירֵא אֱלֹהִים וְסָר מֵרָע:

EESH ha-YAH v'-E-retz UTZ i-YOV sh'-MO v'-ha-YAH ha-EESH ha-HU TAM v'-ya-SHAR vee-RAY e-lo-HEEM v'-SAR may-RA

2 Seven sons and three daughters were born to him;

ב וַיִּוָּלְדוּ לוֹ שִׁבְעָה בָנִים וְשָׁלוֹשׁ בָּנוֹת:

3 his possessions were seven thousand sheep, three thousand camels, five hundred yoke of oxen and five hundred she-asses, and a very large household. That man was wealthier than anyone in the East.

ג וַיְהִי מִקְנֵהוּ שִׁבְעַת אַלְפֵי־צֹאן וּשְׁלֹשֶׁת אַלְפֵי גְמַלִּים וַחֲמֵשׁ מֵאוֹת צֶמֶד־בָּקָר וַחֲמֵשׁ מֵאוֹת אֲתוֹנוֹת וַעֲבֻדָּה רַבָּה מְאֹד וַיְהִי הָאִישׁ הַהוּא גָּדוֹל מִכָּל־בְּנֵי־קֶדֶם:

4 It was the custom of his sons to hold feasts, each on his set day in his own home. They would invite their three sisters to eat and drink with them.

ד וְהָלְכוּ בָנָיו וְעָשׂוּ מִשְׁתֶּה בֵּית אִישׁ יוֹמוֹ וְשָׁלְחוּ וְקָרְאוּ לִשְׁלֹשֶׁת אַחְיֹתֵיהֶם [אַחְיוֹתֵיהֶם] לֶאֱכֹל וְלִשְׁתּוֹת עִמָּהֶם:

5 When a round of feast days was over, *Iyov* would send word to them to sanctify themselves, and, rising early in the morning, he would make burnt offerings, one for each of them; for *Iyov* thought, "Perhaps my children have sinned and blasphemed *Hashem* in their thoughts." This is what *Iyov* always used to do.

ה וַיְהִי כִּי הִקִּיפוּ יְמֵי הַמִּשְׁתֶּה וַיִּשְׁלַח אִיּוֹב וַיְקַדְּשֵׁם וְהִשְׁכִּים בַּבֹּקֶר וְהֶעֱלָה עֹלוֹת מִסְפַּר כֻּלָּם כִּי אָמַר אִיּוֹב אוּלַי חָטְאוּ בָנַי וּבֵרְכוּ אֱלֹהִים בִּלְבָבָם כָּכָה יַעֲשֶׂה אִיּוֹב כָּל־הַיָּמִים:

6 One day the divine beings presented themselves before *Hashem*, and the Adversary came along with them.

ו וַיְהִי הַיּוֹם וַיָּבֹאוּ בְּנֵי הָאֱלֹהִים לְהִתְיַצֵּב עַל־יְהֹוָה וַיָּבוֹא גַם־הַשָּׂטָן בְּתוֹכָם:

7 *Hashem* said to the Adversary, "Where have you been?" The Adversary answered *Hashem*, "I have been roaming all over the earth."

ז וַיֹּאמֶר יְהֹוָה אֶל־הַשָּׂטָן מֵאַיִן תָּבֹא וַיַּעַן הַשָּׂטָן אֶת־יְהֹוָה וַיֹּאמַר מִשּׁוּט בָּאָרֶץ וּמֵהִתְהַלֵּךְ בָּהּ:

8 *Hashem* said to the Adversary, "Have you noticed My servant *Iyov*? There is no one like him on earth, a blameless and upright man who fears *Hashem* and shuns evil!"

ח וַיֹּאמֶר יְהֹוָה אֶל־הַשָּׂטָן הֲשַׂמְתָּ לִבְּךָ עַל־עַבְדִּי אִיּוֹב כִּי אֵין כָּמֹהוּ בָּאָרֶץ אִישׁ תָּם וְיָשָׁר יְרֵא אֱלֹהִים וְסָר מֵרָע:

9 The Adversary answered *Hashem*, "Does *Iyov* not have good reason to fear *Hashem*?

ט וַיַּעַן הַשָּׂטָן אֶת־יְהֹוָה וַיֹּאמַר הַחִנָּם יָרֵא אִיּוֹב אֱלֹהִים:

Rashi (1040–1105)

1:1 There was a man in the land of *Utz* The word Uz, in Hebrew *utz* (עוץ), is derived from the Hebrew word *etz* (עץ), meaning 'tree.' The Sages of the Talmud (*Bava Batra* 15a) teach that phrase "land of *Utz*" refers to *Eretz Yisrael*, called *Utz* in honor of *Iyov*, who protected the people of his generation with his steadfast righteousness. Just as a tree provides shade and protection from the sun, *Iyov's* merit protected the inhabitants of the land. Similarly, before *Moshe* sent spies into *Eretz Yisrael*, he asked them to check whether or not there were any trees in the land (Numbers 13:20). The medieval commentator *Rashi* explains that *Moshe* was really asking, "Does the Land of Israel have a worthy man living in it, who will protect the inhabitants with his merit?"

עוץ

Iyov/Job
Chapter 1

10 Why, it is You who have fenced him round, him and his household and all that he has. You have blessed his efforts so that his possessions spread out in the land.

11 But lay Your hand upon all that he has and he will surely blaspheme You to Your face."

12 *Hashem* replied to the Adversary, "See, all that he has is in your power; only do not lay a hand on him." The Adversary departed from the presence of *Hashem*.

13 One day, as his sons and daughters were eating and drinking wine in the house of their eldest brother,

14 a messenger came to *Iyov* and said, "The oxen were plowing and the she-asses were grazing alongside them

15 when Sabeans attacked them and carried them off, and put the boys to the sword; I alone have escaped to tell you."

16 This one was still speaking when another came and said, "*Hashem*'s fire fell from heaven, took hold of the sheep and the boys, and burned them up; I alone have escaped to tell you."

17 This one was still speaking when another came and said, "A Chaldean formation of three columns made a raid on the camels and carried them off and put the boys to the sword; I alone have escaped to tell you."

18 This one was still speaking when another came and said, "Your sons and daughters were eating and drinking wine in the house of their eldest brother

19 when suddenly a mighty wind came from the wilderness. It struck the four corners of the house so that it collapsed upon the young people and they died; I alone have escaped to tell you."

20 Then *Iyov* arose, tore his robe, cut off his hair, and threw himself on the ground and worshiped.

21 He said, "Naked came I out of my mother's womb, and naked shall I return there; *Hashem* has given, and *Hashem* has taken away; blessed be the name of *Hashem*."

22 For all that, *Iyov* did not sin nor did he cast reproach on *Hashem*.

איוב
פרק א

י הֲלֹא־אַתָּ [אַתָּה] שַׂכְתָּ בַעֲדוֹ וּבְעַד־בֵּיתוֹ וּבְעַד כָּל־אֲשֶׁר־לוֹ מִסָּבִיב מַעֲשֵׂה יָדָיו בֵּרַכְתָּ וּמִקְנֵהוּ פָּרַץ בָּאָרֶץ:

יא וְאוּלָם שְׁלַח־נָא יָדְךָ וְגַע בְּכָל־אֲשֶׁר־לוֹ אִם־לֹא עַל־פָּנֶיךָ יְבָרְכֶךָּ:

יב וַיֹּאמֶר יְהֹוָה אֶל־הַשָּׂטָן הִנֵּה כָל־אֲשֶׁר־לוֹ בְּיָדֶךָ רַק אֵלָיו אַל־תִּשְׁלַח יָדֶךָ וַיֵּצֵא הַשָּׂטָן מֵעִם פְּנֵי יְהֹוָה:

יג וַיְהִי הַיּוֹם וּבָנָיו וּבְנֹתָיו אֹכְלִים וְשֹׁתִים יַיִן בְּבֵית אֲחִיהֶם הַבְּכוֹר:

יד וּמַלְאָךְ בָּא אֶל־אִיּוֹב וַיֹּאמַר הַבָּקָר הָיוּ חֹרְשׁוֹת וְהָאֲתֹנוֹת רֹעוֹת עַל־יְדֵיהֶם:

טו וַתִּפֹּל שְׁבָא וַתִּקָּחֵם וְאֶת־הַנְּעָרִים הִכּוּ לְפִי־חָרֶב וָאִמָּלְטָה רַק־אֲנִי לְבַדִּי לְהַגִּיד לָךְ:

טז עוֹד זֶה מְדַבֵּר וְזֶה בָּא וַיֹּאמַר אֵשׁ אֱלֹהִים נָפְלָה מִן־הַשָּׁמַיִם וַתִּבְעַר בַּצֹּאן וּבַנְּעָרִים וַתֹּאכְלֵם וָאִמָּלְטָה רַק־אֲנִי לְבַדִּי לְהַגִּיד לָךְ:

יז עוֹד זֶה מְדַבֵּר וְזֶה בָּא וַיֹּאמַר כַּשְׂדִּים שָׂמוּ שְׁלֹשָׁה רָאשִׁים וַיִּפְשְׁטוּ עַל־הַגְּמַלִּים וַיִּקָּחוּם וְאֶת־הַנְּעָרִים הִכּוּ לְפִי־חָרֶב וָאִמָּלְטָה רַק־אֲנִי לְבַדִּי לְהַגִּיד לָךְ:

יח עַד זֶה מְדַבֵּר וְזֶה בָּא וַיֹּאמַר בָּנֶיךָ וּבְנוֹתֶיךָ אֹכְלִים וְשֹׁתִים יַיִן בְּבֵית אֲחִיהֶם הַבְּכוֹר:

יט וְהִנֵּה רוּחַ גְּדוֹלָה בָּאָה מֵעֵבֶר הַמִּדְבָּר וַיִּגַּע בְּאַרְבַּע פִּנּוֹת הַבַּיִת וַיִּפֹּל עַל־הַנְּעָרִים וַיָּמוּתוּ וָאִמָּלְטָה רַק־אֲנִי לְבַדִּי לְהַגִּיד לָךְ:

כ וַיָּקָם אִיּוֹב וַיִּקְרַע אֶת־מְעִלוֹ וַיָּגָז אֶת־רֹאשׁוֹ וַיִּפֹּל אַרְצָה וַיִּשְׁתָּחוּ:

כא וַיֹּאמֶר עָרֹם יָצָתִי [יָצָאתִי] מִבֶּטֶן אִמִּי וְעָרֹם אָשׁוּב שָׁמָּה יְהֹוָה נָתַן וַיהֹוָה לָקָח יְהִי שֵׁם יְהֹוָה מְבֹרָךְ:

כב בְּכָל־זֹאת לֹא־חָטָא אִיּוֹב וְלֹא־נָתַן תִּפְלָה לֵאלֹהִים:

Iyov/Job
Chapter 2

1 One day the divine beings presented themselves before *Hashem*. The Adversary came along with them to present himself before *Hashem*.

2 *Hashem* said to the Adversary, "Where have you been?" The Adversary answered *Hashem*, "I have been roaming all over the earth."

3 *Hashem* said to the Adversary, "Have you noticed My servant *Iyov*? There is no one like him on earth, a blameless and upright man who fears *Hashem* and shuns evil. He still keeps his integrity; so you have incited Me against him to destroy him for no good reason."

4 The Adversary answered *Hashem*, "Skin for skin – all that a man has he will give up for his life.

5 But lay a hand on his bones and his flesh, and he will surely blaspheme You to Your face."

6 So *Hashem* said to the Adversary, "See, he is in your power; only spare his life."

7 The Adversary departed from the presence of *Hashem* and inflicted a severe inflammation on *Iyov* from the sole of his foot to the crown of his head.

va-yay-TZAY ha-sa-TAN may-AYT p'-NAY a-do-NAI va-YAKH et i-YOV bish-KHEEN RA mi-KAF rag-LO v'-AD kod-ko-DO

8 He took a potsherd to scratch himself as he sat in ashes.

9 His wife said to him, "You still keep your integrity! Blaspheme *Hashem* and die!"

2:7 And inflicted a severe inflammation on *Iyov* This is *Iyov's* final test before he reacts to all of his suffering. After losing his wealth and his children, he is now stricken with a painful condition all over his body. What was the cause of the righteous *Iyov's* suffering? The Sages (*Sotah* 11a) teach that *Iyov* was one of three advisors whom Pharaoh consulted to determine the most effective method to exterminate the People of Israel during their subjugation in Egypt. Though he opposed the persecution, *Iyov* chose to remain silent rather than voice his opposition to the powerful king's plan. The Sages suggest that *Iyov's* suffering was a punishment for remaining silent in the face of the oppression of the Israelites. Because *Iyov* remained silent against the suffering of others, he was afflicted to the point where he cried out due to his own anguish. Today, the People of Israel are still faced with many threats and experience many tragedies. We must learn from *Iyov's* mistake to never remain silent, even if we don't feel personally threatened or afflicted. Rather, we must feel the pain of others as our own.

Iyov/Job
Chapter 3

איוב
פרק ג

10 But he said to her, "You talk as any shameless woman might talk! Should we accept only good from *Hashem* and not accept evil?" For all that, *Iyov* said nothing sinful.

וַיֹּאמֶר אֵלֶיהָ כְּדַבֵּר אַחַת הַנְּבָלוֹת תְּדַבֵּרִי גַּם אֶת־הַטּוֹב נְקַבֵּל מֵאֵת הָאֱלֹהִים וְאֶת־הָרָע לֹא נְקַבֵּל בְּכָל־זֹאת לֹא־חָטָא אִיּוֹב בִּשְׂפָתָיו׃

11 When *Iyov*'s three friends heard about all these calamities that had befallen him, each came from his home – Eliphaz the Temanite, Bildad the Shuhite, and Zophar the Naamathite. They met together to go and console and comfort him.

וַיִּשְׁמְעוּ שְׁלֹשֶׁת רֵעֵי אִיּוֹב אֵת כָּל־הָרָעָה הַזֹּאת הַבָּאָה עָלָיו וַיָּבֹאוּ אִישׁ מִמְּקֹמוֹ אֱלִיפַז הַתֵּימָנִי וּבִלְדַּד הַשּׁוּחִי וְצוֹפַר הַנַּעֲמָתִי וַיִּוָּעֲדוּ יַחְדָּו לָבוֹא לָנוּד־לוֹ וּלְנַחֲמוֹ׃

12 When they saw him from a distance, they could not recognize him, and they broke into loud weeping; each one tore his robe and threw dust into the air onto his head.

וַיִּשְׂאוּ אֶת־עֵינֵיהֶם מֵרָחוֹק וְלֹא הִכִּירֻהוּ וַיִּשְׂאוּ קוֹלָם וַיִּבְכּוּ וַיִּקְרְעוּ אִישׁ מְעִלוֹ וַיִּזְרְקוּ עָפָר עַל־רָאשֵׁיהֶם הַשָּׁמָיְמָה׃

13 They sat with him on the ground seven days and seven nights. None spoke a word to him for they saw how very great was his suffering.

וַיֵּשְׁבוּ אִתּוֹ לָאָרֶץ שִׁבְעַת יָמִים וְשִׁבְעַת לֵילוֹת וְאֵין־דֹּבֵר אֵלָיו דָּבָר כִּי רָאוּ כִּי־גָדַל הַכְּאֵב מְאֹד׃

3

1 Afterward, *Iyov* began to speak and cursed the day of his birth.

אַחֲרֵי־כֵן פָּתַח אִיּוֹב אֶת־פִּיהוּ וַיְקַלֵּל אֶת־יוֹמוֹ׃

a-kha-ray KHAYN pa-TAKH i-YOV et PEE-hu vai-ka-LAYL et yo-MO

2 *Iyov* spoke up and said:

וַיַּעַן אִיּוֹב וַיֹּאמַר׃

3 Perish the day on which I was born, And the night it was announced, "A male has been conceived!"

יֹאבַד יוֹם אִוָּלֶד בּוֹ וְהַלַּיְלָה אָמַר הֹרָה גָבֶר׃

4 May that day be darkness; May *Hashem* above have no concern for it; May light not shine on it;

הַיּוֹם הַהוּא יְהִי חֹשֶׁךְ אַל־יִדְרְשֵׁהוּ אֱלוֹהַּ מִמָּעַל וְאַל־תּוֹפַע עָלָיו נְהָרָה׃

5 May darkness and deep gloom reclaim it; May a pall lie over it; May what blackens the day terrify it.

יִגְאָלֻהוּ חֹשֶׁךְ וְצַלְמָוֶת תִּשְׁכָּן־עָלָיו עֲנָנָה יְבַעֲתֻהוּ כִּמְרִירֵי יוֹם׃

6 May obscurity carry off that night; May it not be counted among the days of the year; May it not appear in any of its months;

הַלַּיְלָה הַהוּא יִקָּחֵהוּ אֹפֶל אַל־יִחַדְּ בִּימֵי שָׁנָה בְּמִסְפַּר יְרָחִים אַל־יָבֹא׃

7 May that night be desolate; May no sound of joy be heard in it;

הִנֵּה הַלַּיְלָה הַהוּא יְהִי גַלְמוּד אַל־תָּבֹא רְנָנָה בוֹ׃

8 May those who cast spells upon the day damn it, Those prepared to disable Leviathan;

יִקְּבֻהוּ אֹרְרֵי־יוֹם הָעֲתִידִים עֹרֵר לִוְיָתָן׃

3:1 Cursed the day of his birth The righteous *Iyov*'s initial reaction to the suffering that befell him was not to blaspheme God, but rather, to curse his own birth. Why be born, he calls out painfully, if one's labor on this earth is pointless? With his reaction, *Iyov* gives us a model for coping with trials and tribulations. While we may express our personal pain, we should not vent our frustration on our Creator.

Iyov/Job
Chapter 3

9 May its twilight stars remain dark; May it hope for light and have none; May it not see the glimmerings of the dawn –

10 Because it did not block my mother's womb, And hide trouble from my eyes.

11 Why did I not die at birth, Expire as I came forth from the womb?

12 Why were there knees to receive me, Or breasts for me to suck?

13 For now would I be lying in repose, asleep and at rest,

14 With the world's kings and counselors who rebuild ruins for themselves,

15 Or with nobles who possess gold and who fill their houses with silver.

16 Or why was I not like a buried stillbirth, Like babies who never saw the light?

17 There the wicked cease from troubling; There rest those whose strength is spent.

18 Prisoners are wholly at ease; They do not hear the taskmaster's voice.

19 Small and great alike are there, And the slave is free of his master.

20 Why does He give light to the sufferer And life to the bitter in spirit;

21 To those who wait for death but it does not come, Who search for it more than for treasure,

22 Who rejoice to exultation, And are glad to reach the grave;

23 To the man who has lost his way, Whom *Hashem* has hedged about?

24 My groaning serves as my bread; My roaring pours forth as water.

25 For what I feared has overtaken me; What I dreaded has come upon me.

26 I had no repose, no quiet, no rest, And trouble came.

איוב
פרק ג

ט יַחְשְׁכוּ כּוֹכְבֵי נִשְׁפּוֹ יְקַו־לְאוֹר וָאַיִן וְאַל־יִרְאֶה בְּעַפְעַפֵּי־שָׁחַר:

י כִּי לֹא סָגַר דַּלְתֵי בִטְנִי וַיַּסְתֵּר עָמָל מֵעֵינָי:

יא לָמָּה לֹּא מֵרֶחֶם אָמוּת מִבֶּטֶן יָצָאתִי וְאֶגְוָע:

יב מַדּוּעַ קִדְּמוּנִי בִרְכָּיִם וּמַה־שָּׁדַיִם כִּי אִינָק:

יג כִּי־עַתָּה שָׁכַבְתִּי וְאֶשְׁקוֹט יָשַׁנְתִּי אָז יָנוּחַ לִי:

יד עִם־מְלָכִים וְיֹעֲצֵי אָרֶץ הַבֹּנִים חֳרָבוֹת לָמוֹ:

טו אוֹ עִם־שָׂרִים זָהָב לָהֶם הַמְמַלְאִים בָּתֵּיהֶם כָּסֶף:

טז אוֹ כְנֵפֶל טָמוּן לֹא אֶהְיֶה כְּעֹלְלִים לֹא־רָאוּ אוֹר:

יז שָׁם רְשָׁעִים חָדְלוּ רֹגֶז וְשָׁם יָנוּחוּ יְגִיעֵי כֹחַ:

יח יַחַד אֲסִירִים שַׁאֲנָנוּ לֹא שָׁמְעוּ קוֹל נֹגֵשׂ:

יט קָטֹן וְגָדוֹל שָׁם הוּא וְעֶבֶד חָפְשִׁי מֵאֲדֹנָיו:

כ לָמָּה יִתֵּן לְעָמֵל אוֹר וְחַיִּים לְמָרֵי נָפֶשׁ:

כא הַמְחַכִּים לַמָּוֶת וְאֵינֶנּוּ וַיַּחְפְּרֻהוּ מִמַּטְמוֹנִים:

כב הַשְּׂמֵחִים אֱלֵי־גִיל יָשִׂישׂוּ כִּי יִמְצְאוּ־קָבֶר:

כג לְגֶבֶר אֲשֶׁר־דַּרְכּוֹ נִסְתָּרָה וַיָּסֶךְ אֱלוֹהַּ בַּעֲדוֹ:

כד כִּי־לִפְנֵי לַחְמִי אַנְחָתִי תָבֹא וַיִּתְּכוּ כַמַּיִם שַׁאֲגֹתָי:

כה כִּי פַחַד פָּחַדְתִּי וַיֶּאֱתָיֵנִי וַאֲשֶׁר יָגֹרְתִּי יָבֹא לִי:

כו לֹא שָׁלַוְתִּי וְלֹא שָׁקַטְתִּי וְלֹא־נָחְתִּי וַיָּבֹא רֹגֶז:

Iyov/Job
Chapter 4

איוב
פרק ד

4

1 Then Eliphaz the Temanite said in reply:

וַיַּעַן אֱלִיפַז הַתֵּימָנִי וַיֹּאמַר: א

va-YA-an e-lee-FAZ ha-tay-ma-NEE va-yo-MAR

2 If one ventures a word with you, will it be too much? But who can hold back his words?

הֲנִסָּה דָבָר אֵלֶיךָ תִּלְאֶה וַעְצֹר בְּמִלִּין מִי יוּכָל: ב

3 See, you have encouraged many; You have strengthened failing hands.

הִנֵּה יִסַּרְתָּ רַבִּים וְיָדַיִם רָפוֹת תְּחַזֵּק: ג

4 Your words have kept him who stumbled from falling; You have braced knees that gave way.

כּוֹשֵׁל יְקִימוּן מִלֶּיךָ וּבִרְכַּיִם כֹּרְעוֹת תְּאַמֵּץ: ד

5 But now that it overtakes you, it is too much; It reaches you, and you are unnerved.

כִּי עַתָּה תָּבוֹא אֵלֶיךָ וַתֵּלֶא תִּגַּע עָדֶיךָ וַתִּבָּהֵל: ה

6 Is not your piety your confidence, Your integrity your hope?

הֲלֹא יִרְאָתְךָ כִּסְלָתֶךָ תִּקְוָתְךָ וְתֹם דְּרָכֶיךָ: ו

7 Think now, what innocent man ever perished? Where have the upright been destroyed?

זְכָר־נָא מִי הוּא נָקִי אָבָד וְאֵיפֹה יְשָׁרִים נִכְחָדוּ: ז

8 As I have seen, those who plow evil And sow mischief reap them.

כַּאֲשֶׁר רָאִיתִי חֹרְשֵׁי אָוֶן וְזֹרְעֵי עָמָל יִקְצְרֻהוּ: ח

9 They perish by a blast from *Hashem*, Are gone at the breath of His nostrils.

מִנִּשְׁמַת אֱלוֹהַּ יֹאבֵדוּ וּמֵרוּחַ אַפּוֹ יִכְלוּ: ט

10 The lion may roar, the cub may howl, But the teeth of the king of beasts are broken.

שַׁאֲגַת אַרְיֵה וְקוֹל שָׁחַל וְשִׁנֵּי כְפִירִים נִתָּעוּ: י

11 The lion perishes for lack of prey, And its whelps are scattered.

לַיִשׁ אֹבֵד מִבְּלִי־טָרֶף וּבְנֵי לָבִיא יִתְפָּרָדוּ: יא

12 A word came to me in stealth; My ear caught a whisper of it.

וְאֵלַי דָּבָר יְגֻנָּב וַתִּקַּח אָזְנִי שֵׁמֶץ מֶנְהוּ: יב

13 In thought-filled visions of the night, When deep sleep falls on men,

בִּשְׂעִפִּים מֵחֶזְיֹנוֹת לָיְלָה בִּנְפֹל תַּרְדֵּמָה עַל־אֲנָשִׁים: יג

14 Fear and trembling came upon me, Causing all my bones to quake with fright.

פַּחַד קְרָאַנִי וּרְעָדָה וְרֹב עַצְמוֹתַי הִפְחִיד: יד

15 A wind passed by me, Making the hair of my flesh bristle.

וְרוּחַ עַל־פָּנַי יַחֲלֹף תְּסַמֵּר שַׂעֲרַת בְּשָׂרִי: טו

4:1 Then Eliphaz the Temanite said in reply Eliphaz the Temanite is the first of *Iyov*'s friends to respond to his suffering. He asserts that *Hashem* would not punish those who are free of sin, as *Iyov* seems to believe; since all people sin, *Iyov* must not be an exception. He urges *Iyov* to confess his secret sins in order to alleviate his suffering. Though he means well, Eliphaz's view of divine justice is criticized by God Himself at the end of the book (42:7). Eliphaz is called a Temanite, presumably because he is from the city called Teman, which belonged to the descendants of Esau, the Edomites, and is mentioned in *Sefer Ovadya* (1:9). Eliphaz was also the name of Esau's firstborn son (Genesis 36:4). Many therefore assume that Eliphaz is an Edomite, and in *Sefer Iyov* represents Edomite wisdom, which was well-known in biblical times (see Jeremiah 49:7).

Iyov/Job
Chapter 5

איוב
פרק ה

16 It halted; its appearance was strange to me; A form loomed before my eyes; I heard a murmur, a voice,

יַעֲמֹד וְלֹא־אַכִּיר מַרְאֵהוּ תְּמוּנָה לְנֶגֶד עֵינָי דְּמָמָה וָקוֹל אֶשְׁמָע: טז

17 "Can mortals be acquitted by *Hashem*? Can man be cleared by his Maker?

הַאֱנוֹשׁ מֵאֱלוֹהַּ יִצְדָּק אִם מֵעֹשֵׂהוּ יִטְהַר־גָּבֶר: יז

18 If He cannot trust His own servants, And casts reproach on His angels,

הֵן בַּעֲבָדָיו לֹא יַאֲמִין וּבְמַלְאָכָיו יָשִׂים תָּהֳלָה: יח

19 How much less those who dwell in houses of clay, Whose origin is dust, Who are crushed like the moth,

אַף שֹׁכְנֵי בָתֵּי־חֹמֶר אֲשֶׁר־בֶּעָפָר יְסוֹדָם יְדַכְּאוּם לִפְנֵי־עָשׁ: יט

20 Shattered between daybreak and evening, Perishing forever, unnoticed.

מִבֹּקֶר לָעֶרֶב יֻכַּתּוּ מִבְּלִי מֵשִׂים לָנֶצַח יֹאבֵדוּ: כ

21 Their cord is pulled up And they die, and not with wisdom."

הֲלֹא־נִסַּע יִתְרָם בָּם יָמוּתוּ וְלֹא בְחָכְמָה: כא

5

1 Call now! Will anyone answer you? To whom among the holy beings will you turn?

קְרָא־נָא הֲיֵשׁ עוֹנֶךָּ וְאֶל־מִי מִקְּדֹשִׁים תִּפְנֶה: א ה

2 Vexation kills the fool; Passion slays the simpleton.

כִּי־לֶאֱוִיל יַהֲרָג־כָּעַשׂ וּפֹתֶה תָּמִית קִנְאָה: ב

3 I myself saw a fool who had struck roots; Impulsively, I cursed his home:

אֲנִי־רָאִיתִי אֱוִיל מַשְׁרִישׁ וָאֶקּוֹב נָוֵהוּ פִתְאֹם: ג

4 May his children be far from success; May they be oppressed in the gate with none to deliver them;

יִרְחֲקוּ בָנָיו מִיֶּשַׁע וְיִדַּכְּאוּ בַשַּׁעַר וְאֵין מַצִּיל: ד

5 May the hungry devour his harvest, Carrying it off in baskets; May the thirsty swallow their wealth.

אֲשֶׁר קְצִירוֹ רָעֵב יֹאכֵל וְאֶל־מִצִּנִּים יִקָּחֵהוּ וְשָׁאַף צַמִּים חֵילָם: ה

6 Evil does not grow out of the soil, Nor does mischief spring from the ground;

כִּי לֹא־יֵצֵא מֵעָפָר אָוֶן וּמֵאֲדָמָה לֹא־יִצְמַח עָמָל: ו

KEE lo yay-TZAY may-a-FAR A-ven u-may-a-da-MAH lo yitz-MAKH a-MAL

7 For man is born to [do] mischief, Just as sparks fly upward.

כִּי־אָדָם לְעָמָל יוּלָּד וּבְנֵי־רֶשֶׁף יַגְבִּיהוּ עוּף: ז

8 But I would resort to *Hashem*; I would lay my case before *Hashem*,

אוּלָם אֲנִי אֶדְרֹשׁ אֶל־אֵל וְאֶל־אֱלֹהִים אָשִׂים דִּבְרָתִי: ח

9 Who performs great deeds which cannot be fathomed, Wondrous things without number;

עֹשֶׂה גְדֹלוֹת וְאֵין חֵקֶר נִפְלָאוֹת עַד־אֵין מִסְפָּר: ט

אדם
אדמה

5:6 Nor does mischief spring from the ground Eliphaz says that suffering does not spring forth out of the ground, but rather comes as a result of a person's sins. Since no one is free of sin, every person is born to tribulations (verse 7). Even *Iyov*'s location in the Land of Israel cannot free him from the taint of sin.

Eliphaz reminds *Iyov* that suffering is part of the human condition, intrinsic in being an *adam* (אדם), 'a person,' and not something which comes on its own out of the *adama* (אדמה), 'earth.' Only those who disconnect from their humanity, therefore, can escape affliction.

1719

Iyov/Job

Chapter 6

איוב

פרק ו

10 Who gives rain to the earth, And sends water over the fields;

י הַנֹּתֵן מָטָר עַל־פְּנֵי־אָרֶץ וְשֹׁלֵחַ מַיִם עַל־פְּנֵי חוּצוֹת׃

11 Who raises the lowly up high, So that the dejected are secure in victory;

יא לָשׂוּם שְׁפָלִים לְמָרוֹם וְקֹדְרִים שָׂגְבוּ יֶשַׁע׃

12 Who thwarts the designs of the crafty, So that their hands cannot gain success;

יב מֵפֵר מַחְשְׁבוֹת עֲרוּמִים וְלֹא־תַעֲשֶׂינָה יְדֵיהֶם תּוּשִׁיָּה׃

13 Who traps the clever in their own wiles; The plans of the crafty go awry.

יג לֹכֵד חֲכָמִים בְּעָרְמָם וַעֲצַת נִפְתָּלִים נִמְהָרָה׃

14 By day they encounter darkness, At noon they grope as in the night.

יד יוֹמָם יְפַגְּשׁוּ־חֹשֶׁךְ וְכַלַּיְלָה יְמַשְׁשׁוּ בַצָּהֳרָיִם׃

15 But He saves the needy from the sword of their mouth, From the clutches of the strong.

טו וַיֹּשַׁע מֵחֶרֶב מִפִּיהֶם וּמִיַּד חָזָק אֶבְיוֹן׃

16 So there is hope for the wretched; The mouth of wrongdoing is stopped.

טז וַתְּהִי לַדַּל תִּקְוָה וְעֹלָתָה קָפְצָה פִּיהָ׃

17 See how happy is the man whom *Hashem* reproves; Do not reject the discipline of the Almighty.

יז הִנֵּה אַשְׁרֵי אֱנוֹשׁ יוֹכִחֶנּוּ אֱלוֹהַּ וּמוּסַר שַׁדַּי אַל־תִּמְאָס׃

18 He injures, but He binds up; He wounds, but His hands heal.

יח כִּי הוּא יַכְאִיב וְיֶחְבָּשׁ יִמְחַץ וְיָדוֹ [וְיָדָיו] תִּרְפֶּינָה׃

19 He will deliver you from six troubles; In seven no harm will reach you:

יט בְּשֵׁשׁ צָרוֹת יַצִּילֶךָּ וּבְשֶׁבַע לֹא־יִגַּע בְּךָ רָע׃

20 In famine He will redeem you from death, In war, from the sword.

כ בְּרָעָב פָּדְךָ מִמָּוֶת וּבְמִלְחָמָה מִידֵי חָרֶב׃

21 You will be sheltered from the scourging tongue; You will have no fear when violence comes.

כא בְּשׁוֹט לָשׁוֹן תֵּחָבֵא וְלֹא־תִירָא מִשֹּׁד כִּי יָבוֹא׃

22 You will laugh at violence and starvation, And have no fear of wild beasts.

כב לְשֹׁד וּלְכָפָן תִּשְׂחָק וּמֵחַיַּת הָאָרֶץ אַל־תִּירָא׃

23 For you will have a pact with the rocks in the field, And the beasts of the field will be your allies.

כג כִּי עִם־אַבְנֵי הַשָּׂדֶה בְרִיתֶךָ וְחַיַּת הַשָּׂדֶה הָשְׁלְמָה־לָךְ׃

24 You will know that all is well in your tent; When you visit your wife you will never fail.

כד וְיָדַעְתָּ כִּי־שָׁלוֹם אָהֳלֶךָ וּפָקַדְתָּ נָוְךָ וְלֹא תֶחֱטָא׃

25 You will see that your offspring are many, Your descendants like the grass of the earth.

כה וְיָדַעְתָּ כִּי־רַב זַרְעֶךָ וְצֶאֱצָאֶיךָ כְּעֵשֶׂב הָאָרֶץ׃

26 You will come to the grave in ripe old age, As shocks of grain are taken away in their season.

כו תָּבוֹא בְכֶלַח אֱלֵי־קָבֶר כַּעֲלוֹת גָּדִישׁ בְּעִתּוֹ׃

27 See, we have inquired into this and it is so; Hear it and accept it.

כז הִנֵּה־זֹאת חֲקַרְנוּהָ כֶּן־הִיא שְׁמָעֶנָּה וְאַתָּה דַע־לָךְ׃

6

1 Then *Iyov* said in reply:

א וַיַּעַן אִיּוֹב וַיֹּאמַר׃

2 If my anguish were weighed, My full calamity laid on the scales,

ב לוּ שָׁקוֹל יִשָּׁקֵל כַּעְשִׂי וְהַיָּתִי [וְהַוָּתִי] בְּמֹאזְנַיִם יִשְׂאוּ־יָחַד׃

Iyov/Job
Chapter 6

איוב
פרק ו

3 It would be heavier than the sand of the sea; That is why I spoke recklessly.

ג כִּי־עַתָּה מֵחוֹל יַמִּים יִכְבָּד עַל־כֵּן דְּבָרַי לָעוּ׃

4 For the arrows of the Almighty are in me; My spirit absorbs their poison; *Hashem*'s terrors are arrayed against me.

ד כִּי חִצֵּי שַׁדַּי עִמָּדִי אֲשֶׁר חֲמָתָם שֹׁתָה רוּחִי בִּעוּתֵי אֱלוֹהַּ יַעַרְכוּנִי׃

5 Does a wild ass bray when he has grass? Does a bull bellow over his fodder?

ה הֲיִנְהַק־פֶּרֶא עֲלֵי־דֶשֶׁא אִם יִגְעֶה־שּׁוֹר עַל־בְּלִילוֹ׃

6 Can what is tasteless be eaten without salt? Does mallow juice have any flavor?

ו הֲיֵאָכֵל תָּפֵל מִבְּלִי־מֶלַח אִם־יֶשׁ־טַעַם בְּרִיר חַלָּמוּת׃

7 I refuse to touch them; They are like food when I am sick.

ז מֵאֲנָה לִנְגּוֹעַ נַפְשִׁי הֵמָּה כִּדְוֵי לַחְמִי׃

8 Would that my request were granted, That *Hashem* gave me what I wished for;

ח מִי־יִתֵּן תָּבוֹא שֶׁאֱלָתִי וְתִקְוָתִי יִתֵּן אֱלוֹהַּ׃

9 Would that *Hashem* consented to crush me, Loosed His hand and cut me off.

ט וְיֹאֵל אֱלוֹהַּ וִידַכְּאֵנִי יַתֵּר יָדוֹ וִיבַצְּעֵנִי׃

10 Then this would be my consolation, As I writhed in unsparing pains: That I did not suppress my words against the Holy One.

י וּתְהִי עוֹד נֶחָמָתִי וַאֲסַלְּדָה בְחִילָה לֹא יַחְמוֹל כִּי־לֹא כִחַדְתִּי אִמְרֵי קָדוֹשׁ׃

11 What strength have I, that I should endure? How long have I to live, that I should be patient?

יא מַה־כֹּחִי כִי־אֲיַחֵל וּמַה־קִּצִּי כִּי־אַאֲרִיךְ נַפְשִׁי׃

12 Is my strength the strength of rock? Is my flesh bronze?

יב אִם־כֹּחַ אֲבָנִים כֹּחִי אִם־בְּשָׂרִי נָחוּשׁ׃

13 Truly, I cannot help myself; I have been deprived of resourcefulness.

יג הַאִם אֵין עֶזְרָתִי בִי וְתֻשִׁיָּה נִדְּחָה מִמֶּנִּי׃

14 A friend owes loyalty to one who fails, Though he forsakes the fear of the Almighty;

יד לַמָּס מֵרֵעֵהוּ חָסֶד וְיִרְאַת שַׁדַּי יַעֲזוֹב׃

15 My comrades are fickle, like a wadi, Like a bed on which streams once ran.

טו אַחַי בָּגְדוּ כְמוֹ־נָחַל כַּאֲפִיק נְחָלִים יַעֲבֹרוּ׃

16 They are dark with ice; Snow obscures them;

טז הַקֹּדְרִים מִנִּי־קָרַח עָלֵימוֹ יִתְעַלֶּם־שָׁלֶג׃

17 But when they thaw, they vanish; In the heat, they disappear where they are.

יז בְּעֵת יְזֹרְבוּ נִצְמָתוּ בְּחֻמּוֹ נִדְעֲכוּ מִמְּקוֹמָם׃

18 Their course twists and turns; They run into the desert and perish.

יח יִלָּפְתוּ אָרְחוֹת דַּרְכָּם יַעֲלוּ בַתֹּהוּ וְיֹאבֵדוּ׃

19 Caravans from Tema look to them; Processions from Sheba count on them.

יט הִבִּיטוּ אָרְחוֹת תֵּמָא הֲלִיכֹת שְׁבָא קִוּוּ־לָמוֹ׃

20 They are disappointed in their hopes; When they reach the place, they stand aghast.

כ בֹּשׁוּ כִּי־בָטָח בָּאוּ עָדֶיהָ וַיֶּחְפָּרוּ׃

21 So you are as nothing: At the sight of misfortune, you take fright.

כא כִּי־עַתָּה הֱיִיתֶם לֹא [לוֹ] תִּרְאוּ חֲתַת וַתִּירָאוּ׃

Iyov/Job

Chapter 7

22	Did I say to you, "I need your gift; Pay a bribe for me out of your wealth;	כב הֲכִי־אָמַרְתִּי הָבוּ לִי וּמִכֹּחֲכֶם שִׁחֲדוּ בַעֲדִי:
23	Deliver me from the clutches of my enemy; Redeem me from violent men"?	כג וּמַלְּטוּנִי מִיַּד־צָר וּמִיַּד עָרִיצִים תִּפְדּוּנִי:
24	Teach me; I shall be silent; Tell me where I am wrong.	כד הוֹרוּנִי וַאֲנִי אַחֲרִישׁ וּמַה־שָּׁגִיתִי הָבִינוּ לִי:
25	How trenchant honest words are; But what sort of reproof comes from you?	כה מַה־נִּמְרְצוּ אִמְרֵי־יֹשֶׁר וּמַה־יּוֹכִיחַ הוֹכֵחַ מִכֶּם:
26	Do you devise words of reproof, But count a hopeless man's words as wind?	כו הַלְהוֹכַח מִלִּים תַּחְשֹׁבוּ וּלְרוּחַ אִמְרֵי נֹאָשׁ:
27	You would even cast lots over an orphan, Or barter away your friend.	כז אַף־עַל־יָתוֹם תַּפִּילוּ וְתִכְרוּ עַל־רֵיעֲכֶם:

af al ya-TOM ta-PEE-lu v'-tikh-RU al ray-a-KHEM

28	Now be so good as to face me; I will not lie to your face.	כח וְעַתָּה הוֹאִילוּ פְנוּ־בִי וְעַל־פְּנֵיכֶם אִם־אֲכַזֵּב:
29	Relent! Let there not be injustice; Relent! I am still in the right.	כט שֻׁבוּ־נָא אַל־תְּהִי עַוְלָה ושבי [וְשֻׁבוּ] עוֹד צִדְקִי־בָהּ:
30	Is injustice on my tongue? Can my palate not discern evil?	ל הֲיֵשׁ־בִּלְשׁוֹנִי עַוְלָה אִם־חִכִּי לֹא־יָבִין הַוּוֹת:

7

1	Truly man has a term of service on earth; His days are like those of a hireling –	א הֲלֹא־צָבָא לֶאֱנוֹשׁ על־[עֲלֵי־] אָרֶץ וְכִימֵי שָׂכִיר יָמָיו:
2	Like a slave who longs for [evening's] shadows, Like a hireling who waits for his wage.	ב כְּעֶבֶד יִשְׁאַף־צֵל וּכְשָׂכִיר יְקַוֶּה פָעֳלוֹ:
3	So have I been allotted months of futility; Nights of misery have been apportioned to me.	ג כֵּן הָנְחַלְתִּי לִי יַרְחֵי־שָׁוְא וְלֵילוֹת עָמָל מִנּוּ־לִי:
4	When I lie down, I think, "When shall I rise?" Night drags on, And I am sated with tossings till morning twilight.	ד אִם־שָׁכַבְתִּי וְאָמַרְתִּי מָתַי אָקוּם וּמִדַּד־עָרֶב וְשָׂבַעְתִּי נְדֻדִים עֲדֵי־נָשֶׁף:
5	My flesh is covered with maggots and clods of earth; My skin is broken and festering.	ה לָבַשׁ בְּשָׂרִי רִמָּה וגיש [וְגוּשׁ] עָפָר עוֹרִי רָגַע וַיִּמָּאֵס:
6	My days fly faster than a weaver's shuttle, And come to their end without hope.	ו יָמַי קַלּוּ מִנִּי־אָרֶג וַיִּכְלוּ בְּאֶפֶס תִּקְוָה:

6:27 You would even cast lots over an orphan In *Sefer Yeshayahu*, the impending destruction of the Land of Israel and exile of its people is attributed to the corruption of the residents of *Yerushalayim*. Yeshayahu illustrates this corruption with examples, such as failing to pursue justice for orphans (Isaiah 1:23). Similarly, *Iyov* warns his fellows that while they might view themselves as righteous, it is for their kindness to the needy, such as himself, that they will be rewarded, and for its lack that they will be punished.

Iyov/Job

Chapter 7

7 Consider that my life is but wind; I shall never see happiness again.	זְכֹר כִּי־רוּחַ חַיָּי לֹא־תָשׁוּב עֵינִי לִרְאוֹת טוֹב:
8 The eye that gazes on me will not see me; Your eye will seek me, but I shall be gone.	לֹא־תְשׁוּרֵנִי עֵין רֹאִי עֵינֶיךָ בִּי וְאֵינֶנִּי:
9 As a cloud fades away, So whoever goes down to Sheol does not come up;	כָּלָה עָנָן וַיֵּלַךְ כֵּן יוֹרֵד שְׁאוֹל לֹא יַעֲלֶה:
10 He returns no more to his home; His place does not know him.	לֹא־יָשׁוּב עוֹד לְבֵיתוֹ וְלֹא־יַכִּירֶנּוּ עוֹד מְקֹמוֹ:
11 On my part, I will not speak with restraint; I will give voice to the anguish of my spirit; I will complain in the bitterness of my soul.	גַּם־אֲנִי לֹא אֶחֱשָׂךְ פִּי אֲדַבְּרָה בְּצַר רוּחִי אָשִׂיחָה בְּמַר נַפְשִׁי:
12 Am I the sea or the Dragon, That You have set a watch over me?	הֲיָם־אָנִי אִם־תַּנִּין כִּי־תָשִׂים עָלַי מִשְׁמָר:
13 When I think, "My bed will comfort me, My couch will share my sorrow,"	כִּי־אָמַרְתִּי תְּנַחֲמֵנִי עַרְשִׂי יִשָּׂא בְשִׂיחִי מִשְׁכָּבִי:
14 You frighten me with dreams, And terrify me with visions,	וְחִתַּתַּנִי בַחֲלֹמוֹת וּמֵחֶזְיֹנוֹת תְּבַעֲתַנִּי:
15 Till I prefer strangulation, Death, to my wasted frame.	וַתִּבְחַר מַחֲנָק נַפְשִׁי מָוֶת מֵעַצְמוֹתָי:
16 I am sick of it. I shall not live forever; Let me be, for my days are a breath.	מָאַסְתִּי לֹא־לְעֹלָם אֶחְיֶה חֲדַל מִמֶּנִּי כִּי־הֶבֶל יָמָי:
17 **What is man, that You make much of him, That You fix Your attention upon him?**	מָה־אֱנוֹשׁ כִּי תְגַדְּלֶנּוּ וְכִי־תָשִׁית אֵלָיו לִבֶּךָ:
mah e-NOSH KEE t'-ga-d'-LE-nu v'-KHEE ta-SHEET ay-LAV li-BE-kha	
18 You inspect him every morning, Examine him every minute.	וַתִּפְקְדֶנּוּ לִבְקָרִים לִרְגָעִים תִּבְחָנֶנּוּ:
19 Will You not look away from me for a while, Let me be, till I swallow my spittle?	כַּמָּה לֹא־תִשְׁעֶה מִמֶּנִּי לֹא־תַרְפֵּנִי עַד־בִּלְעִי רֻקִּי:
20 If I have sinned, what have I done to You, Watcher of men? Why make of me Your target, And a burden to myself?	חָטָאתִי מָה אֶפְעַל לָךְ נֹצֵר הָאָדָם לָמָה שַׂמְתַּנִי לְמִפְגָּע לָךְ וָאֶהְיֶה עָלַי לְמַשָּׂא:

7:17 What is man, that You make much of him In his despair, *Iyov* doubts the very worth of humanity. He declares that because man is insignificant, he is unworthy of *Hashem*'s attention and should be free from punishment and suffering. These words parallel the famous words of the psalmist: "What is man, that You have been mindful of him, mortal man that You have taken note of him?" However, the psalmist's conclusion is very different from *Iyov*'s: "That You have made him little less than divine, and adorned him with glory and majesty" (Psalms 8:5–6). While *Iyov* bemoans the esteem given by God to man, the psalmist praises *Hashem* for granting man the capacity for greatness, though in reality he is undeserving.

Iyov/Job Chapter 8

21 Why do You not pardon my transgression And forgive my iniquity? For soon I shall lie down in the dust; When You seek me, I shall be gone.

8 1 Bildad the Shuhite said in reply:

2 How long will you speak such things? Your utterances are a mighty wind!

3 Will *Hashem* pervert the right? Will the Almighty pervert justice?

4 If your sons sinned against Him, He dispatched them for their transgression.

5 But if you seek *Hashem* And supplicate the Almighty,

6 If you are blameless and upright, He will protect you, And grant well-being to your righteous home.

7 Though your beginning be small, In the end you will grow very great.

8 Ask the generation past, Study what their fathers have searched out –

9 For we are of yesterday and know nothing; Our days on earth are a shadow –

10 Surely they will teach you and tell you, Speaking out of their understanding.

11 Can papyrus thrive without marsh? Can rushes grow without water?

12 While still tender, not yet plucked, They would wither before any other grass.

13 Such is the fate of all who forget *Hashem*; The hope of the impious man comes to naught –

14 Whose confidence is a thread of gossamer, Whose trust is a spider's web.

15 He leans on his house – it will not stand; He seizes hold of it, but it will not hold.

16 He stays fresh even in the sun; His shoots spring up in his garden;

17 His roots are twined around a heap, They take hold of a house of stones.

18 When he is uprooted from his place, It denies him, [saying,] "I never saw you."

איוב פרק ח

כא וּמֶה לֹא־תִשָּׂא פִשְׁעִי וְתַעֲבִיר אֶת־עֲוֺנִי כִּי־עַתָּה לֶעָפָר אֶשְׁכָּב וְשִׁחֲרְתַּנִי וְאֵינֶנִּי׃

ח א וַיַּעַן בִּלְדַּד הַשּׁוּחִי וַיֹּאמַר׃

ב עַד־אָן תְּמַלֶּל־אֵלֶּה וְרוּחַ כַּבִּיר אִמְרֵי־פִיךָ׃

ג הַאֵל יְעַוֵּת מִשְׁפָּט וְאִם־שַׁדַּי יְעַוֵּת־צֶדֶק׃

ד אִם־בָּנֶיךָ חָטְאוּ־לוֹ וַיְשַׁלְּחֵם בְּיַד־פִּשְׁעָם׃

ה אִם־אַתָּה תְּשַׁחֵר אֶל־אֵל וְאֶל־שַׁדַּי תִּתְחַנָּן׃

ו אִם־זַךְ וְיָשָׁר אָתָּה כִּי־עַתָּה יָעִיר עָלֶיךָ וְשִׁלַּם נְוַת צִדְקֶךָ׃

ז וְהָיָה רֵאשִׁיתְךָ מִצְעָר וְאַחֲרִיתְךָ יִשְׂגֶּה מְאֹד׃

ח כִּי־שְׁאַל־נָא לְדֹר רִישׁוֹן וְכוֹנֵן לְחֵקֶר אֲבוֹתָם׃

ט כִּי־תְמוֹל אֲנַחְנוּ וְלֹא נֵדָע כִּי צֵל יָמֵינוּ עֲלֵי־אָרֶץ׃

י הֲלֹא־הֵם יוֹרוּךָ יֹאמְרוּ לָךְ וּמִלִּבָּם יוֹצִאוּ מִלִּים׃

יא הֲיִגְאֶה־גֹּמֶא בְּלֹא בִצָּה יִשְׂגֶּה־אָחוּ בְלִי־מָיִם׃

יב עֹדֶנּוּ בְאִבּוֹ לֹא יִקָּטֵף וְלִפְנֵי כָל־חָצִיר יִיבָשׁ׃

יג כֵּן אָרְחוֹת כָּל־שֹׁכְחֵי אֵל וְתִקְוַת חָנֵף תֹּאבֵד׃

יד אֲשֶׁר־יָקוֹט כִּסְלוֹ וּבֵית עַכָּבִישׁ מִבְטַחוֹ׃

טו יִשָּׁעֵן עַל־בֵּיתוֹ וְלֹא יַעֲמֹד יַחֲזִיק בּוֹ וְלֹא יָקוּם׃

טז רָטֹב הוּא לִפְנֵי־שָׁמֶשׁ וְעַל גַּנָּתוֹ יֹנַקְתּוֹ תֵצֵא׃

יז עַל־גַּל שָׁרָשָׁיו יְסֻבָּכוּ בֵּית אֲבָנִים יֶחֱזֶה׃

יח אִם־יְבַלְּעֶנּוּ מִמְּקוֹמוֹ וְכִחֶשׁ בּוֹ לֹא רְאִיתִיךָ׃

Iyov/Job
Chapter 9

	Hebrew	
19	Such is his happy lot; And from the earth others will grow.	הֵן־הוּא מְשׂוֹשׂ דַּרְכּוֹ וּמֵעָפָר אַחֵר יִצְמָחוּ: יט
20	Surely *Hashem* does not despise the blameless; He gives no support to evildoers.	הֶן־אֵל לֹא יִמְאַס־תָּם וְלֹא־יַחֲזִיק בְּיַד־מְרֵעִים: כ
21	He will yet fill your mouth with laughter, And your lips with shouts of joy.	עַד־יְמַלֵּה שְׂחוֹק פִּיךָ וּשְׂפָתֶיךָ תְרוּעָה: כא

ad y'-ma-LAY s'-KHOK PEE-kha us-fa-TE-kha t'-ru-AH

| 22 | Your enemies will be clothed in disgrace; The tent of the wicked will vanish. | שֹׂנְאֶיךָ יִלְבְּשׁוּ־בֹשֶׁת וְאֹהֶל רְשָׁעִים אֵינֶנּוּ: כב |

9

1	*Iyov* said in reply:	וַיַּעַן אִיּוֹב וַיֹּאמַר: א
2	Indeed I know that it is so: Man cannot win a suit against *Hashem*.	אָמְנָם יָדַעְתִּי כִי־כֵן וּמַה־יִּצְדַּק אֱנוֹשׁ עִם־אֵל: ב
3	If he insisted on a trial with Him, He would not answer one charge in a thousand.	אִם־יַחְפֹּץ לָרִיב עִמּוֹ לֹא־יַעֲנֶנּוּ אַחַת מִנִּי־אָלֶף: ג
4	Wise of heart and mighty in power – Who ever challenged Him and came out whole? –	חֲכַם לֵבָב וְאַמִּיץ כֹּחַ מִי־הִקְשָׁה אֵלָיו וַיִּשְׁלָם: ד

kha-KHAM lay-VAV v'-a-MEETZ KO-akh mee hik-SHAH ay-LAV va-yish-LAM

5	Him who moves mountains without their knowing it, Who overturns them in His anger;	הַמַּעְתִּיק הָרִים וְלֹא יָדָעוּ אֲשֶׁר הֲפָכָם בְּאַפּוֹ: ה
6	Who shakes the earth from its place, Till its pillars quake;	הַמַּרְגִּיז אֶרֶץ מִמְּקוֹמָהּ וְעַמּוּדֶיהָ יִתְפַּלָּצוּן: ו
7	Who commands the sun not to shine; Who seals up the stars;	הָאֹמֵר לַחֶרֶס וְלֹא יִזְרָח וּבְעַד כּוֹכָבִים יַחְתֹּם: ז

8:21 He will yet fill your mouth with laughter *Bildad* attempts to comfort *Iyov* by telling him that if he is as righteous as he claims to be, his suffering will not last long. When the suffering ends, he will feel so happy that his mouth will be filled with laughter. These words are reminiscent of the description, found in *Sefer Tehillim* (126:2), of the return of the exiled Jews to the Land of Israel: "Our mouths shall be filled with laughter." It is often said that what causes someone to laugh is an unexpected ending. While he is in the midst of his suffering, it is almost impossible for *Iyov* to imagine relief from his misery. Similarly, the Jewish people in exile could not always envision an actual redemption. When it comes, therefore, it not only causes feelings of happiness and joy, but laughter as well.

9:4 Wise of heart and mighty in power The words in this verse, translated as "wise of heart," are understood by the Sages to mean "wise about hearts," or "wise about innermost thoughts." This means that *Hashem* knows what is in people's hearts, and judges them accordingly. While man has the capacity to judge his fellow only by what is obvious to the human eye, *Hashem* knows what is really in a person's heart. *Iyov's* friends understand this in a negative sense; while *Iyov* seems righteous externally, he must have committed sins in secret. However, the opposite is also true. Someone might seem evil on the outside, but might have good intentions in his heart. It is man's challenge to behave as God does, and instead of making assumptions solely on the basis of external appearances, to understand that there is more in a person's heart that might not be apparent from the outside. We are therefore called upon to judge others favorably by always giving them the benefit of the doubt.

Iyov/Job
Chapter 9

8 Who by Himself spread out the heavens, And trod on the back of the sea;

9 Who made the Bear and Orion, Pleiades, and the chambers of the south wind;

10 Who performs great deeds which cannot be fathomed, And wondrous things without number.

11 He passes me by – I do not see Him; He goes by me, but I do not perceive Him.

12 He snatches away – who can stop Him? Who can say to Him, "What are You doing?"

13 *Hashem* does not restrain His anger; Under Him Rahab's helpers sink down.

14 How then can I answer Him, Or choose my arguments against Him?

15 Though I were in the right, I could not speak out, But I would plead for mercy with my judge.

16 If I summoned Him and He responded, I do not believe He would lend me His ear.

17 For He crushes me for a hair; He wounds me much for no cause.

18 He does not let me catch my breath, But sates me with bitterness.

19 If a trial of strength – He is the strong one; If a trial in court – who will summon Him for me?

20 Though I were innocent, My mouth would condemn me; Though I were blameless, He would prove me crooked.

21 I am blameless – I am distraught; I am sick of life.

22 It is all one; therefore I say, "He destroys the blameless and the guilty."

23 When suddenly a scourge brings death, He mocks as the innocent fail.

24 The earth is handed over to the wicked one; He covers the eyes of its judges. If it is not He, then who?

25 My days fly swifter than a runner; They flee without seeing happiness;

26 They pass like reed-boats, Like an eagle swooping onto its prey.

איוב
פרק ט

ח נֹטֶה שָׁמַיִם לְבַדּוֹ וְדוֹרֵךְ עַל־בָּמֳתֵי יָם׃

ט עֹשֶׂה־עָשׁ כְּסִיל וְכִימָה וְחַדְרֵי תֵמָן׃

י עֹשֶׂה גְדֹלוֹת עַד־אֵין חֵקֶר וְנִפְלָאוֹת עַד־אֵין מִסְפָּר׃

יא הֵן יַעֲבֹר עָלַי וְלֹא אֶרְאֶה וְיַחֲלֹף וְלֹא־אָבִין לוֹ׃

יב הֵן יַחְתֹּף מִי יְשִׁיבֶנּוּ מִי־יֹאמַר אֵלָיו מַה־תַּעֲשֶׂה׃

יג אֱלוֹהַּ לֹא־יָשִׁיב אַפּוֹ תחתו [תַּחְתָּיו] שָׁחֲחוּ עֹזְרֵי רָהַב׃

יד אַף כִּי־אָנֹכִי אֶעֱנֶנּוּ אֶבְחֲרָה דְבָרַי עִמּוֹ׃

טו אֲשֶׁר אִם־צָדַקְתִּי לֹא אֶעֱנֶה לִמְשֹׁפְטִי אֶתְחַנָּן׃

טז אִם־קָרָאתִי וַיַּעֲנֵנִי לֹא־אַאֲמִין כִּי־יַאֲזִין קוֹלִי׃

יז אֲשֶׁר־בִּשְׂעָרָה יְשׁוּפֵנִי וְהִרְבָּה פְצָעַי חִנָּם׃

יח לֹא־יִתְּנֵנִי הָשֵׁב רוּחִי כִּי יַשְׂבִּעַנִי מַמְּרֹרִים׃

יט אִם־לְכֹחַ אַמִּיץ הִנֵּה וְאִם־לְמִשְׁפָּט מִי יוֹעִידֵנִי׃

כ אִם־אֶצְדָּק פִּי יַרְשִׁיעֵנִי תָּם־אָנִי וַיַּעְקְשֵׁנִי׃

כא תָּם־אָנִי לֹא־אֵדַע נַפְשִׁי אֶמְאַס חַיָּי׃

כב אַחַת הִיא עַל־כֵּן אָמַרְתִּי תָּם וְרָשָׁע הוּא מְכַלֶּה׃

כג אִם־שׁוֹט יָמִית פִּתְאֹם לְמַסַּת נְקִיִּם יִלְעָג׃

כד אֶרֶץ נִתְּנָה בְיַד־רָשָׁע פְּנֵי־שֹׁפְטֶיהָ יְכַסֶּה אִם־לֹא אֵפוֹא מִי־הוּא׃

כה וְיָמַי קַלּוּ מִנִּי־רָץ בָּרְחוּ לֹא־רָאוּ טוֹבָה׃

כו חָלְפוּ עִם־אֳנִיּוֹת אֵבֶה כְּנֶשֶׁר יָטוּשׂ עֲלֵי־אֹכֶל׃

Iyov/Job
Chapter 10

27 If I say, "I will forget my complaint; Abandon my sorrow and be diverted,"

28 I remain in dread of all my suffering; I know that You will not acquit me.

29 It will be I who am in the wrong; Why then should I waste effort?

30 If I washed with soap, Cleansed my hands with lye,

31 You would dip me in muck Till my clothes would abhor me.

32 He is not a man, like me, that I can answer Him, That we can go to law together.

33 No arbiter is between us To lay his hand on us both.

34 If He would only take His rod away from me And not let His terror frighten me,

35 Then I would speak out without fear of Him; For I know myself not to be so.

10 1 I am disgusted with life; I will give rein to my complaint, Speak in the bitterness of my soul.

2 I say to *Hashem*, "Do not condemn me; Let me know what You charge me with.

3 Does it benefit You to defraud, To despise the toil of Your hands, While smiling on the counsel of the wicked?

4 Do You have the eyes of flesh? Is Your vision that of mere men?

5 Are Your days the days of a mortal, Are Your years the years of a man,

6 That You seek my iniquity And search out my sin?

7 You know that I am not guilty, And that there is none to deliver from Your hand.

8 "Your hands shaped and fashioned me, Then destroyed every part of me.

9 Consider that You fashioned me like clay; Will You then turn me back into dust?

10 You poured me out like milk, Congealed me like cheese;

איוב
פרק י

כז אִם־אָמְרִי אֶשְׁכְּחָה שִׂיחִי אֶעֶזְבָה פָנַי וְאַבְלִיגָה׃

כח יָגֹרְתִּי כָל־עַצְּבֹתָי יָדַעְתִּי כִּי־לֹא תְנַקֵּנִי׃

כט אָנֹכִי אֶרְשָׁע לָמָּה־זֶּה הֶבֶל אִיגָע׃

ל אִם־הִתְרָחַצְתִּי במו־[בְמֵי־] שָׁלֶג וַהֲזִכּוֹתִי בְּבֹר כַּפָּי׃

לא אָז בַּשַּׁחַת תִּטְבְּלֵנִי וְתִעֲבוּנִי שַׂלְמוֹתָי׃

לב כִּי־לֹא־אִישׁ כָּמֹנִי אֶעֱנֶנּוּ נָבוֹא יַחְדָּו בַּמִּשְׁפָּט׃

לג לֹא יֵשׁ־בֵּינֵינוּ מוֹכִיחַ יָשֵׁת יָדוֹ עַל־שְׁנֵינוּ׃

לד יָסֵר מֵעָלַי שִׁבְטוֹ וְאֵמָתוֹ אַל־תְּבַעֲתַנִּי׃

לה אֲדַבְּרָה וְלֹא אִירָאֶנּוּ כִּי לֹא־כֵן אָנֹכִי עִמָּדִי׃

א נָקְטָה נַפְשִׁי בְּחַיָּי אֶעֶזְבָה עָלַי שִׂיחִי אֲדַבְּרָה בְּמַר נַפְשִׁי׃

ב אֹמַר אֶל־אֱלוֹהַּ אַל־תַּרְשִׁיעֵנִי הוֹדִיעֵנִי עַל מַה־תְּרִיבֵנִי׃

ג הֲטוֹב לְךָ כִּי־תַעֲשֹׁק כִּי־תִמְאַס יְגִיעַ כַּפֶּיךָ וְעַל־עֲצַת רְשָׁעִים הוֹפָעְתָּ׃

ד הַעֵינֵי בָשָׂר לָךְ אִם־כִּרְאוֹת אֱנוֹשׁ תִּרְאֶה׃

ה הֲכִימֵי אֱנוֹשׁ יָמֶיךָ אִם־שְׁנוֹתֶיךָ כִּימֵי גָבֶר׃

ו כִּי־תְבַקֵּשׁ לַעֲוֹנִי וּלְחַטָּאתִי תִדְרוֹשׁ׃

ז עַל־דַּעְתְּךָ כִּי־לֹא אֶרְשָׁע וְאֵין מִיָּדְךָ מַצִּיל׃

ח יָדֶיךָ עִצְּבוּנִי וַיַּעֲשׂוּנִי יַחַד סָבִיב וַתְּבַלְּעֵנִי׃

ט זְכָר־נָא כִּי־כַחֹמֶר עֲשִׂיתָנִי וְאֶל־עָפָר תְּשִׁיבֵנִי׃

י הֲלֹא כֶחָלָב תַּתִּיכֵנִי וְכַגְּבִנָּה תַּקְפִּיאֵנִי׃

Iyov/Job
Chapter 11

איוב
פרק יא

11 You clothed me with skin and flesh And wove me of bones and sinews;

יא עוֹר וּבָשָׂר תַּלְבִּישֵׁנִי וּבַעֲצָמוֹת וְגִידִים תְּסֹכְכֵנִי׃

12 You bestowed on me life and care; Your providence watched over my spirit.

יב חַיִּים וָחֶסֶד עָשִׂיתָ עִמָּדִי וּפְקֻדָּתְךָ שָׁמְרָה רוּחִי׃

13 Yet these things You hid in Your heart; I know that You had this in mind:

יג וְאֵלֶּה צָפַנְתָּ בִלְבָבֶךָ יָדַעְתִּי כִּי־זֹאת עִמָּךְ׃

14 To watch me when I sinned And not clear me of my iniquity;

יד אִם־חָטָאתִי וּשְׁמַרְתָּנִי וּמֵעֲוֺנִי לֹא תְנַקֵּנִי׃

15 Should I be guilty – the worse for me! And even when innocent, I cannot lift my head; So sated am I with shame, And drenched in my misery.

טו אִם־רָשַׁעְתִּי אַלְלַי לִי וְצָדַקְתִּי לֹא־אֶשָּׂא רֹאשִׁי שְׂבַע קָלוֹן וּרְאֵה עָנְיִי׃

16 It is something to be proud of to hunt me like a lion, To show Yourself wondrous through me time and again!

טז וְיִגְאֶה כַּשַּׁחַל תְּצוּדֵנִי וְתָשֹׁב תִּתְפַּלָּא־בִי׃

17 You keep sending fresh witnesses against me, Letting Your vexation with me grow. I serve my term and am my own replacement.

יז תְּחַדֵּשׁ עֵדֶיךָ נֶגְדִּי וְתֶרֶב כַּעַשְׂךָ עִמָּדִי חֲלִיפוֹת וְצָבָא עִמִּי׃

18 "Why did You let me come out of the womb? Better had I expired before any eye saw me,

יח וְלָמָּה מֵרֶחֶם הֹצֵאתָנִי אֶגְוַע וְעַיִן לֹא־תִרְאֵנִי׃

v'-LA-mah may-RE-khem ho-tzay-TA-nee eg-VA v'-A-yin lo tir-AY-nee

19 Had I been as though I never was, Had I been carried from the womb to the grave.

יט כַּאֲשֶׁר לֹא־הָיִיתִי אֶהְיֶה מִבֶּטֶן לַקֶּבֶר אוּבָל׃

20 My days are few, so desist! Leave me alone, let me be diverted a while

כ הֲלֹא־מְעַט יָמַי יֶחְדָּל [וַחֲדָל] יָשִׁית [וְשִׁית] מִמֶּנִּי וְאַבְלִיגָה מְּעָט׃

21 Before I depart – never to return – For the land of deepest gloom;

כא בְּטֶרֶם אֵלֵךְ וְלֹא אָשׁוּב אֶל־אֶרֶץ חֹשֶׁךְ וְצַלְמָוֶת׃

22 A land whose light is darkness, All gloom and disarray, Whose light is like darkness."

כב אֶרֶץ עֵיפָתָה כְּמוֹ אֹפֶל צַלְמָוֶת וְלֹא סְדָרִים וַתֹּפַע כְּמוֹ־אֹפֶל׃

11 1 Then Zophar the Naamathite said in reply:

יא א וַיַּעַן צֹפַר הַנַּעֲמָתִי וַיֹּאמַר׃

2 Is a multitude of words unanswerable? Must a loquacious person be right?

ב הֲרֹב דְּבָרִים לֹא יֵעָנֶה וְאִם־אִישׁ שְׂפָתַיִם יִצְדָּק׃

3 Your prattle may silence men; You may mock without being rebuked,

ג בַּדֶּיךָ מְתִים יַחֲרִישׁוּ וַתִּלְעַג וְאֵין מַכְלִם׃

10:18 Why did You let me come out of the womb? The Hebrew word for 'womb,' *rekhem* (רחם), shares a root with the word for 'compassion,' which is *rakhamim* (רחמים). While at first glance the connection between these two words may be unclear, upon further thought it becomes obvious. A mother has a natural love and compassion for her offspring, the fruit of her womb. *Iyov* wishes he had never been taken out of the womb, because he feels bereft not only of *Hashem*'s justice, but also of His compassion and mercy.

רחם
רחמים

Iyov/Job
Chapter 11

איוב
פרק יא

4 And say, "My doctrine is pure, And I have been innocent in Your sight."

ד וַתֹּאמֶר זַךְ לִקְחִי וּבַר הָיִיתִי בְעֵינֶיךָ׃

5 But would that *Hashem* might speak, And talk to you Himself.

ה וְאוּלָם מִי־יִתֵּן אֱלוֹהַּ דַּבֵּר וְיִפְתַּח שְׂפָתָיו עִמָּךְ׃

6 He would tell you the secrets of wisdom, For there are many sides to sagacity; And know that *Hashem* has overlooked for you some of your iniquity.

ו וְיַגֶּד־לְךָ תַּעֲלֻמוֹת חָכְמָה כִּי־כִפְלַיִם לְתוּשִׁיָּה וְדַע כִּי־יַשֶּׁה לְךָ אֱלוֹהַּ מֵעֲוֺנֶךָ׃

7 Would you discover the mystery of *Hashem*? Would you discover the limit of the Almighty?

ז הַחֵקֶר אֱלוֹהַּ תִּמְצָא אִם עַד־תַּכְלִית שַׁדַּי תִּמְצָא׃

ha-KHAY-ker e-LO-ha tim-TZA IM ad takh-LEET sha-DAI tim-TZA

8 Higher than heaven – what can you do? Deeper than Sheol – what can you know?

ח גָּבְהֵי שָׁמַיִם מַה־תִּפְעָל עֲמֻקָּה מִשְּׁאוֹל מַה־תֵּדָע׃

9 Its measure is longer than the earth And broader than the sea.

ט אֲרֻכָּה מֵאֶרֶץ מִדָּהּ וּרְחָבָה מִנִּי־יָם׃

10 Should He pass by, or confine, Or call an assembly, who can stop Him?

י אִם־יַחֲלֹף וְיַסְגִּיר וְיַקְהִיל וּמִי יְשִׁיבֶנּוּ׃

11 For He knows deceitful men; When He sees iniquity, does He not discern it?

יא כִּי־הוּא יָדַע מְתֵי־שָׁוְא וַיַּרְא־אָוֶן וְלֹא יִתְבּוֹנָן׃

12 A hollow man will get understanding, When a wild ass is born a man.

יב וְאִישׁ נָבוּב יִלָּבֵב וְעַיִר פֶּרֶא אָדָם יִוָּלֵד׃

13 But if you direct your mind, And spread forth your hands toward Him –

יג אִם־אַתָּה הֲכִינוֹתָ לִבֶּךָ וּפָרַשְׂתָּ אֵלָיו כַּפֶּךָ׃

14 If there is iniquity with you, remove it, And do not let injustice reside in your tent –

יד אִם־אָוֶן בְּיָדְךָ הַרְחִיקֵהוּ וְאַל־תַּשְׁכֵּן בְּאֹהָלֶיךָ עַוְלָה׃

15 Then, free of blemish, you will hold your head high, And, when in straits, be unafraid.

טו כִּי־אָז תִּשָּׂא פָנֶיךָ מִמּוּם וְהָיִיתָ מֻצָק וְלֹא תִירָא׃

16 You will then put your misery out of mind, Consider it as water that has flowed past.

טז כִּי־אַתָּה עָמָל תִּשְׁכָּח כְּמַיִם עָבְרוּ תִזְכֹּר׃

11:7 Would you discover the mystery of *Hashem*? Zophar questions *Iyov*'s insistence that he is innocent, suggesting that *Iyov* is perhaps not as pure as he thinks he is, since man cannot comprehend *Hashem*'s mind nor his desires of us. Even *Moshe*, the greatest prophet of all time, was denied his request to fully comprehend the ways of *Hashem*. After the sin of the golden calf, *Moshe* prays for the people and seeks closeness to God. Sensing that this was a time of mercy, he pleads with *Hashem* to let him understand His ways, and requests of Him: "Let me behold Your presence" (Exodus 33:18). God's response, however, is, "You cannot see My face, for man may not see Me and live" (ibid. verse 20). The Sages understand this request to see God's face as a metaphor for *Moshe*'s plea to understand *Hashem*. In fact, the Sages of the Talmud (*Berachot* 7a) suggest that *Moshe* was specifically seeking the answer to the question of theodicy, wondering why bad things happen to good people and vice versa. This is indeed the question that bothers *Iyov* throughout his book, and continues to trouble us for eternity. However, as *Moshe* is told, we cannot comprehend the ways of God and might never understand the answer to this question as long as we are living.

Iyov/Job
Chapter 12

17 Life will be brighter than noon; You will shine, you will be like the morning.

וּֽמִ֭צָּהֳרַיִם יָק֣וּם חָ֑לֶד תָּ֝עֻ֗פָה כַּבֹּ֥קֶר תִּהְיֶֽה׃

18 You will be secure, for there is hope, And, entrenched, you will rest secure;

וּֽ֭בָטַחְתָּ כִּי־יֵ֣שׁ תִּקְוָ֑ה וְ֝חָפַרְתָּ֗ לָבֶ֥טַח תִּשְׁכָּֽב׃

u-va-takh-TA kee YAYSH tik-VAH v'-kha-far-TA la-VE-takh tish-KAV

19 You will lie down undisturbed; The great will court your favor.

וְֽ֭רָבַצְתָּ וְאֵ֣ין מַחֲרִ֑יד וְחִלּ֖וּ פָנֶ֣יךָ רַבִּֽים׃

20 But the eyes of the wicked pine away; Escape is cut off from them; They have only their last breath to look forward to.

וְעֵינֵ֥י רְשָׁעִ֗ים תִּ֫כְלֶ֥ינָה וּ֭מָנוֹס אָבַ֣ד מִנְהֶ֑ם וְ֝תִקְוָתָ֗ם מַֽפַּח־נָֽפֶשׁ׃

12

1 Then *Iyov* said in reply:

וַיַּ֥עַן אִיּ֗וֹב וַיֹּאמַֽר׃

2 Indeed, you are the [voice of] the people, And wisdom will die with you.

אָ֭מְנָם כִּ֣י אַתֶּם־עָ֑ם וְ֝עִמָּכֶ֗ם תָּמ֥וּת חָכְמָֽה׃

3 But I, like you, have a mind, And am not less than you. Who does not know such things?

גַּם־לִ֤י לֵבָ֨ב ׀ כְּֽמוֹכֶ֗ם לֹא־נֹפֵ֣ל אָנֹכִ֣י מִכֶּ֑ם וְאֶת־מִי־אֵ֥ין כְּמוֹ־אֵֽלֶּה׃

4 I have become a laughingstock to my friend – "One who calls to *Hashem* and is answered, Blamelessly innocent" – a laughingstock.

שְׂחֹ֤ק לְרֵעֵ֨הוּ ׀ אֶהְיֶ֗ה קֹרֵ֣א לֶ֭אֱלוֹהַּ וַֽיַּעֲנֵ֑הוּ שְׂ֝ח֗וֹק צַדִּ֥יק תָּמִֽים׃

5 In the thought of the complacent there is contempt for calamity; It is ready for those whose foot slips.

לַפִּ֣יד בּ֭וּז לְעַשְׁתּ֣וּת שַׁאֲנָ֑ן נָ֝כ֗וֹן לְמ֣וֹעֲדֵי רָֽגֶל׃

6 Robbers live untroubled in their tents, And those who provoke *Hashem* are secure, Those whom *Hashem's* hands have produced.

יִשְׁלָ֤יוּ אֹהָלִ֨ים ׀ לְשֹׁ֥דְדִ֗ים וּֽ֭בַטֻּחוֹת לְמַרְגִּ֣יזֵי אֵ֑ל לַאֲשֶׁ֤ר הֵבִ֖יא אֱל֣וֹהַּ בְּיָדֽוֹ׃

yish-LA-yu o-ha-LEEM l'-sho-d'-DEEM u-va-tu-KHOT l'-mar-GEE-zay AYL la-a-SHER hay-VEE e-LO-ha b'-ya-DO

11:18 You will be secure, for there is hope In Jewish culture, hope is considered one of the most potent tools at humanity's disposal for fulfilling its mission of perfecting the world. Asher Ginsberg, better known by his pen-name, *Achad Ha'am* (literally, "One of the People"), was the 19th–20th century founder of the movement known as "Cultural Zionism." He envisioned the upcoming state as a Jewish spiritual center; not merely a State of Jews, but a Jewish State. On this topic, he writes: "The national self of a nation is the link between its past and future. Memories on the one hand, and hope on the other. Our prophets, and later our sages, implanted in the Jew hope in the future, and to the Jew this was not a fantastic hope, but a reality. And this was the best spiritual food to sustain our life. Without this hope, the Torah alone could not have preserved us." With these beautiful words, *Achad Ha'am* illustrates how hope and *Torah* are inherently, and eternally, intertwined.

12:6 Robbers live untroubled in their tents *Iyov* protests his friends' assertion that *Hashem* does not punish those who do not deserve to be punish. He boldly states what most people know inherently: The righteous do indeed suffer, and evil people are rewarded. Furthermore, says *Iyov*, even the animals are aware of this reality (verse 7). The desire to understand God as just has blinded *Iyov's* friends to the truth which is obvious to everyone else. However, as King *Shlomo* reassures us in *Mishlei* (28:8), the wicked who prosper in this world, those who get rich by inappropriate means, are merely accumulating wealth for the benefit of the righteous, as *Hashem* will ultimately ensure that it arrives in their possession.

Achad Ha'am
(1856–1927)

Iyov/Job
Chapter 12

7 But ask the beasts, and they will teach you; The birds of the sky, they will tell you,

8 Or speak to the earth, it will teach you; The fish of the sea, they will inform you.

9 Who among all these does not know That the hand of *Hashem* has done this?

10 In His hand is every living soul And the breath of all mankind.

11 Truly, the ear tests arguments As the palate tastes foods.

12 Is wisdom in the aged And understanding in the long-lived?

13 With Him are wisdom and courage; His are counsel and understanding.

14 Whatever He tears down cannot be rebuilt; Whomever He imprisons cannot be set free.

15 When He holds back the waters, they dry up; When He lets them loose, they tear up the land.

16 With Him are strength and resourcefulness; Erring and causing to err are from Him.

17 He makes counselors go about naked And causes judges to go mad.

18 He undoes the belts of kings, And fastens loincloths on them.

19 He makes *Kohanim* go about naked, And leads temple-servants astray.

20 He deprives trusty men of speech, And takes away the reason of elders.

21 He pours disgrace upon great men, And loosens the belt of the mighty.

22 He draws mysteries out of the darkness, And brings obscurities to light.

m'-ga-LEH a-mu-KOT mi-nee KHO-shekh va-yo-TZAY la-OR tzal-MA-vet

איוב
פרק יב

ז וְאוּלָם שְׁאַל־נָא בְהֵמוֹת וְתֹרֶךָּ וְעוֹף הַשָּׁמַיִם וְיַגֶּד־לָךְ:

ח אוֹ שִׂיחַ לָאָרֶץ וְתֹרֶךָּ וִיסַפְּרוּ לְךָ דְּגֵי הַיָּם:

ט מִי לֹא־יָדַע בְּכָל־אֵלֶּה כִּי יַד־יְהֹוָה עָשְׂתָה זֹּאת:

י אֲשֶׁר בְּיָדוֹ נֶפֶשׁ כָּל־חָי וְרוּחַ כָּל־בְּשַׂר־אִישׁ:

יא הֲלֹא־אֹזֶן מִלִּין תִּבְחָן וְחֵךְ אֹכֶל יִטְעַם־לוֹ:

יב בִּישִׁישִׁים חָכְמָה וְאֹרֶךְ יָמִים תְּבוּנָה:

יג עִמּוֹ חָכְמָה וּגְבוּרָה לוֹ עֵצָה וּתְבוּנָה:

יד הֵן יַהֲרֹס וְלֹא יִבָּנֶה יִסְגֹּר עַל־אִישׁ וְלֹא יִפָּתֵחַ:

טו הֵן יַעְצֹר בַּמַּיִם וְיִבָשׁוּ וִישַׁלְּחֵם וְיַהַפְכוּ אָרֶץ:

טז עִמּוֹ עֹז וְתוּשִׁיָּה לוֹ שֹׁגֵג וּמַשְׁגֶּה:

יז מוֹלִיךְ יוֹעֲצִים שׁוֹלָל וְשֹׁפְטִים יְהוֹלֵל:

יח מוּסַר מְלָכִים פִּתֵּחַ וַיֶּאְסֹר אֵזוֹר בְּמָתְנֵיהֶם:

יט מוֹלִיךְ כֹּהֲנִים שׁוֹלָל וְאֵתָנִים יְסַלֵּף:

כ מֵסִיר שָׂפָה לְנֶאֱמָנִים וְטַעַם זְקֵנִים יִקָּח:

כא שׁוֹפֵךְ בּוּז עַל־נְדִיבִים וּמְזִיחַ אֲפִיקִים רִפָּה:

כב מְגַלֶּה עֲמֻקוֹת מִנִּי־חֹשֶׁךְ וַיֹּצֵא לָאוֹר צַלְמָוֶת:

גלות

12:22 He draws mysteries out of the darkness The Hebrew words for "He draws mysteries" are *m'galeh amukot* (מגלה עמוקות). The word *m'galeh* comes from the root *legalot* (לגלות), which means to reveal or discover. The same Hebrew letters are also found in the word *galut* (גלות), meaning exile or expulsion. This similarity is no mere play on words. Rather, according to Rabbi David Stavsky, a profound lesson emerges from the connection between these two words. "Nothing is more difficult for a human being than to be exiled from his native land, yet nothing can be more rewarding than discovering a way out of exile."

Iyov/Job
Chapter 13

איוב
פרק יג

23 He exalts nations, then destroys them; He expands nations, then leads them away.

כג מַשְׂגִּיא לַגּוֹיִם וַיְאַבְּדֵם שֹׁטֵחַ לַגּוֹיִם וַיַּנְחֵם׃

24 He deranges the leaders of the people, And makes them wander in a trackless waste.

כד מֵסִיר לֵב רָאשֵׁי עַם־הָאָרֶץ וַיַּתְעֵם בְּתֹהוּ לֹא־דָרֶךְ׃

25 They grope without light in the darkness; He makes them wander as if drunk.

כה יְמַשְׁשׁוּ־חֹשֶׁךְ וְלֹא־אוֹר וַיַּתְעֵם כַּשִּׁכּוֹר׃

13 1 My eye has seen all this; My ear has heard and understood it.

יג א הֶן־כֹּל רָאֲתָה עֵינִי שָׁמְעָה אָזְנִי וַתָּבֶן לָהּ׃

2 What you know, I know also; I am not less than you.

ב כְּדַעְתְּכֶם יָדַעְתִּי גַם־אָנִי לֹא־נֹפֵל אָנֹכִי מִכֶּם׃

3 Indeed, I would speak to the Almighty; I insist on arguing with *Hashem*.

ג אוּלָם אֲנִי אֶל־שַׁדַּי אֲדַבֵּר וְהוֹכֵחַ אֶל־אֵל אֶחְפָּץ׃

4 But you invent lies; All of you are quacks.

ד וְאוּלָם אַתֶּם טֹפְלֵי־שָׁקֶר רֹפְאֵי אֱלִל כֻּלְּכֶם׃

5 If you would only keep quiet It would be considered wisdom on your part.

ה מִי־יִתֵּן הַחֲרֵשׁ תַּחֲרִישׁוּן וּתְהִי לָכֶם לְחָכְמָה׃

6 Hear now my arguments, Listen to my pleading.

ו שִׁמְעוּ־נָא תוֹכַחְתִּי וְרִבוֹת שְׂפָתַי הַקְשִׁיבוּ׃

7 Will you speak unjustly on *Hashem*'s behalf? Will you speak deceitfully for Him?

ז הַלְאֵל תְּדַבְּרוּ עַוְלָה וְלוֹ תְּדַבְּרוּ רְמִיָּה׃

8 Will you be partial toward Him? Will you plead *Hashem*'s cause?

ח הֲפָנָיו תִּשָּׂאוּן אִם־לָאֵל תְּרִיבוּן׃

9 Will it go well when He examines you? Will you fool Him as one fools men?

ט הֲטוֹב כִּי־יַחְקֹר אֶתְכֶם אִם־כְּהָתֵל בֶּאֱנוֹשׁ תְּהָתֵלּוּ בוֹ׃

10 He will surely reprove you If in your heart you are partial toward Him.

י הוֹכֵחַ יוֹכִיחַ אֶתְכֶם אִם־בַּסֵּתֶר פָּנִים תִּשָּׂאוּן׃

11 His threat will terrify you, And His fear will seize you.

יא הֲלֹא שְׂאֵתוֹ תְּבַעֵת אֶתְכֶם וּפַחְדּוֹ יִפֹּל עֲלֵיכֶם׃

12 Your briefs are empty platitudes; Your responses are unsubstantial.

יב זִכְרֹנֵיכֶם מִשְׁלֵי־אֵפֶר לְגַבֵּי־חֹמֶר גַּבֵּיכֶם׃

13 Keep quiet; I will have my say, Come what may upon me.

יג הַחֲרִישׁוּ מִמֶּנִּי וַאֲדַבְּרָה־אָנִי וְיַעֲבֹר עָלַי מָה׃

14 How long! I will take my flesh in my teeth; I will take my life in my hands.

יד עַל־מָה אֶשָּׂא בְשָׂרִי בְשִׁנָּי וְנַפְשִׁי אָשִׂים בְּכַפִּי׃

15 He may well slay me; I may have no hope; Yet I will argue my case before Him.

טו הֵן יִקְטְלֵנִי לֹא [לוֹ] אֲיַחֵל אַךְ־דְּרָכַי אֶל־פָּנָיו אוֹכִיחַ׃

In the connection between the Hebrew words for exile and discovery, we see the great aspiration of the Jewish people to end their exile through the discovery of, and return to, their native homeland.

Iyov/Job
Chapter 14

איוב
פרק יד

16 In this too is my salvation: That no impious man can come into His presence.

טז גַּם־הוּא־לִי לִישׁוּעָה כִּי־לֹא לְפָנָיו חָנֵף יָבוֹא:

gam hu LEE lee-shu-AH kee LO l'-fa-NAV kha-NAYF ya-VO

17 Listen closely to my words; Give ear to my discourse.

יז שִׁמְעוּ שָׁמוֹעַ מִלָּתִי וְאַחֲוָתִי בְּאָזְנֵיכֶם:

18 See now, I have prepared a case; I know that I will win it.

יח הִנֵּה־נָא עָרַכְתִּי מִשְׁפָּט יָדַעְתִּי כִּי־אֲנִי אֶצְדָּק:

19 For who is it that would challenge me? I should then keep silent and expire.

יט מִי־הוּא יָרִיב עִמָּדִי כִּי־עַתָּה אַחֲרִישׁ וְאֶגְוָע:

20 But two things do not do to me, So that I need not hide from You:

כ אַךְ־שְׁתַּיִם אַל־תַּעַשׂ עִמָּדִי אָז מִפָּנֶיךָ לֹא אֶסָּתֵר:

21 Remove Your hand from me, And let not Your terror frighten me.

כא כַּפְּךָ מֵעָלַי הַרְחַק וְאֵמָתְךָ אַל־תְּבַעֲתַנִּי:

22 Then summon me and I will respond, Or I will speak and You reply to me.

כב וּקְרָא וְאָנֹכִי אֶעֱנֶה אוֹ־אֲדַבֵּר וַהֲשִׁיבֵנִי:

23 How many are my iniquities and sins? Advise me of my transgression and sin.

כג כַּמָּה לִי עֲוֺנוֹת וְחַטָּאוֹת פִּשְׁעִי וְחַטָּאתִי הֹדִיעֵנִי:

24 Why do You hide Your face, And treat me like an enemy?

כד לָמָּה־פָנֶיךָ תַסְתִּיר וְתַחְשְׁבֵנִי לְאוֹיֵב לָךְ:

25 Will You harass a driven leaf, Will You pursue dried-up straw,

כה הֶעָלֶה נִדָּף תַּעֲרוֹץ וְאֶת־קַשׁ יָבֵשׁ תִּרְדֹּף:

26 That You decree for me bitter things And make me answer for the iniquities of my youth,

כו כִּי־תִכְתֹּב עָלַי מְרֹרוֹת וְתוֹרִישֵׁנִי עֲוֺנוֹת נְעוּרָי:

27 That You put my feet in the stocks And watch all my ways, Hemming in my footsteps?

כז וְתָשֵׂם בַּסַּד רַגְלַי וְתִשְׁמוֹר כָּל־אָרְחוֹתָי עַל־שָׁרְשֵׁי רַגְלַי תִּתְחַקֶּה:

28 Man wastes away like a rotten thing, Like a garment eaten by moths.

כח וְהוּא כְּרָקָב יִבְלֶה כְּבֶגֶד אֲכָלוֹ עָשׁ:

14

1 Man born of woman is short-lived and sated with trouble.

יד א אָדָם יְלוּד אִשָּׁה קְצַר יָמִים וּשְׂבַע־רֹגֶז:

2 He blossoms like a flower and withers; He vanishes like a shadow and does not endure.

ב כְּצִיץ יָצָא וַיִּמָּל וַיִּבְרַח כַּצֵּל וְלֹא יַעֲמוֹד:

Rabbi Joseph B. Soloveitchik (1903–1993)

13:16 That no impious man can come into His presence *Iyov* rebukes those who come to comfort him by telling them that although he challenges *Hashem's* justice and they do not, he is still more righteous than they are. He, at least, approaches God honestly, not hypocritically. Rabbi Joseph B. Soloveitchik explains that it was the prophet *Yirmiyahu* who set the precedent for challenging *Hashem* in difficult times. In *Megillat Eicha*, instead of merely accepting what has happened, *Yirmiyahu* demands of God an explanation for the ruin of *Yerushalayim* and the devastation of the Land of Israel. While it is permissible to question *Hashem*, this must be coupled with the firm belief that although we might not understand His ways, they are ultimately for the good.

Iyov/Job	איוב
Chapter 14	פרק יד

3 Do You fix Your gaze on such a one? Will You go to law with me?   אַף־עַל־זֶה פָּקַחְתָּ עֵינֶךָ וְאֹתִי תָבִיא בְמִשְׁפָּט עִמָּךְ:

4 Who can produce a clean thing out of an unclean one? No one!   מִי־יִתֵּן טָהוֹר מִטָּמֵא לֹא אֶחָד:

5 His days are determined; You know the number of his months; You have set him limits that he cannot pass.   אִם חֲרוּצִים יָמָיו מִסְפַּר־חֳדָשָׁיו אִתָּךְ חֻקָּו [חֻקָּיו] עָשִׂיתָ וְלֹא יַעֲבוֹר:

6 Turn away from him, that he may be at ease Until, like a hireling, he finishes out his day.   שְׁעֵה מֵעָלָיו וְיֶחְדָּל עַד־יִרְצֶה כְּשָׂכִיר יוֹמוֹ:

7 There is hope for a tree; If it is cut down it will renew itself; Its shoots will not cease.   כִּי יֵשׁ לָעֵץ תִּקְוָה אִם־יִכָּרֵת וְעוֹד יַחֲלִיף וְיֹנַקְתּוֹ לֹא תֶחְדָּל:

KEE YAYSH la-AYTZ tik-VAH im yi-ka-RAYT v'-OD ya-kha-LEEF v'-yo-nak-TO LO tekh-DAL

8 If its roots are old in the earth, And its stump dies in the ground,   אִם־יַזְקִין בָּאָרֶץ שָׁרְשׁוֹ וּבֶעָפָר יָמוּת גִּזְעוֹ:

9 At the scent of water it will bud And produce branches like a sapling.   מֵרֵיחַ מַיִם יַפְרִחַ וְעָשָׂה קָצִיר כְּמוֹ־נָטַע:

10 But mortals languish and die; Man expires; where is he?   וְגֶבֶר יָמוּת וַיֶּחֱלָשׁ וַיִּגְוַע אָדָם וְאַיּוֹ:

11 The waters of the sea fail, And the river dries up and is parched.   אָזְלוּ־מַיִם מִנִּי־יָם וְנָהָר יֶחֱרַב וְיָבֵשׁ:

12 So man lies down never to rise; He will awake only when the heavens are no more, Only then be aroused from his sleep.   וְאִישׁ שָׁכַב וְלֹא־יָקוּם עַד־בִּלְתִּי שָׁמַיִם לֹא יָקִיצוּ וְלֹא־יֵעֹרוּ מִשְּׁנָתָם:

13 O that You would hide me in Sheol, Conceal me until Your anger passes, Set me a fixed time to attend to me.   מִי יִתֵּן בִּשְׁאוֹל תַּצְפִּנֵנִי תַּסְתִּירֵנִי עַד־שׁוּב אַפֶּךָ תָּשִׁית לִי חֹק וְתִזְכְּרֵנִי:

14 If a man dies, can he live again? All the time of my service I wait Until my replacement comes.   אִם־יָמוּת גֶּבֶר הֲיִחְיֶה כָּל־יְמֵי צְבָאִי אֲיַחֵל עַד־בּוֹא חֲלִיפָתִי:

15 You would call and I would answer You; You would set Your heart on Your handiwork.   תִּקְרָא וְאָנֹכִי אֶעֱנֶךָּ לְמַעֲשֵׂה יָדֶיךָ תִכְסֹף:

16 Then You would not count my steps, Or keep watch over my sin.   כִּי־עַתָּה צְעָדַי תִּסְפּוֹר לֹא־תִשְׁמוֹר עַל־חַטָּאתִי:

14:7 There is hope for a tree *Iyov* contrasts the passing of man to the death of a tree. Once a man has departed from this world, he cannot be brought back to life. A tree, on the other hand, though seemingly lifeless, can be revived. Similarly, *Yeshayahu* writes (6:13) that though a tree appears dead after it sheds its leaves, the trunk remains, and from there, the tree will flower again in the spring. *Yeshayahu* compares the Children of Israel to a tree. Though at times it appears that they have been annihilated and will cease to exist, a holy remnant always remains, from which they will grow anew and flourish.

Iyov/Job
Chapter 15

אִיּוֹב
פרק טו

17 My transgression would be sealed up in a pouch; You would coat over my iniquity.

חָתֻם בִּצְרוֹר פִּשְׁעִי וַתִּטְפֹּל עַל־עֲוֺנִי׃

18 Mountains collapse and crumble; Rocks are dislodged from their place.

וְאוּלָם הַר־נוֹפֵל יִבּוֹל וְצוּר יֶעְתַּק מִמְּקֹמוֹ׃

19 Water wears away stone; Torrents wash away earth; So you destroy man's hope,

אֲבָנִים שָׁחֲקוּ מַיִם תִּשְׁטֹף־סְפִיחֶיהָ עֲפַר־אָרֶץ וְתִקְוַת אֱנוֹשׁ הֶאֱבַדְתָּ׃

20 You overpower him forever and he perishes; You alter his visage and dispatch him.

תִּתְקְפֵהוּ לָנֶצַח וַיַּהֲלֹךְ מְשַׁנֶּה פָנָיו וַתְּשַׁלְּחֵהוּ׃

21 His sons attain honor and he does not know it; They are humbled and he is not aware of it.

יִכְבְּדוּ בָנָיו וְלֹא יֵדָע וְיִצְעֲרוּ וְלֹא־יָבִין לָמוֹ׃

22 He feels only the pain of his flesh, And his spirit mourns in him.

אַךְ־בְּשָׂרוֹ עָלָיו יִכְאָב וְנַפְשׁוֹ עָלָיו תֶּאֱבָל׃

15

1 Eliphaz the Temanite said in reply:

וַיַּעַן אֱלִיפַז הַתֵּימָנִי וַיֹּאמַר׃

2 Does a wise man answer with windy opinions, And fill his belly with the east wind?

הֶחָכָם יַעֲנֶה דַעַת־רוּחַ וִימַלֵּא קָדִים בִּטְנוֹ׃

3 Should he argue with useless talk, With words that are of no worth?

הוֹכֵחַ בְּדָבָר לֹא יִסְכּוֹן וּמִלִּים לֹא־יוֹעִיל בָּם׃

4 You subvert piety And restrain prayer to *Hashem*.

אַף־אַתָּה תָּפֵר יִרְאָה וְתִגְרַע שִׂיחָה לִפְנֵי־אֵל׃

af a-TAH ta-FAYR yir-AH v'-tig-RA see-KHAH lif-nay AYL

5 Your sinfulness dictates your speech, So you choose crafty language.

כִּי יְאַלֵּף עֲוֺנְךָ פִיךָ וְתִבְחַר לְשׁוֹן עֲרוּמִים׃

6 Your own mouth condemns you — not I; Your lips testify against you.

יַרְשִׁיעֲךָ פִיךָ וְלֹא־אָנִי וּשְׂפָתֶיךָ יַעֲנוּ־בָךְ׃

7 Were you the first man born? Were you created before the hills?

הֲרִאישׁוֹן אָדָם תִּוָּלֵד וְלִפְנֵי גְבָעוֹת חוֹלָלְתָּ׃

8 Have you listened in on the council of *Hashem*? Have you sole possession of wisdom?

הַבְסוֹד אֱלוֹהַּ תִּשְׁמָע וְתִגְרַע אֵלֶיךָ חָכְמָה׃

9 What do you know that we do not know, Or understand that we do not?

מַה־יָּדַעְתָּ וְלֹא נֵדָע תָּבִין וְלֹא־עִמָּנוּ הוּא׃

10 Among us are gray-haired old men, Older by far than your father.

גַּם־שָׂב גַּם־יָשִׁישׁ בָּנוּ כַּבִּיר מֵאָבִיךָ יָמִים׃

יראה

15:4 You subvert piety *Yirah* (יראה), translated here as 'piety,' literally means 'fear' or 'awe.' Eliphaz tells *Iyov* that he has dispensed with fear of *Hashem*, and, in so doing, has also abandoned wisdom, as implied in verse 2. The link between these two concepts can be seen in *Sefer Mishlei* (1:7): "The fear of *Hashem* is the beginning of knowledge." Without awe of God, knowledge is empty and can be twisted for any number of negative purposes. However, knowledge rooted in fear of *Hashem* leads to scrupulous attention to His word, for which one is rewarded in both this world and the world to come.

Iyov/Job
Chapter 15

11 Are *Hashem*'s consolations not enough for you, And His gentle words to you?

יא הַמְעַט מִמְּךָ תַּנְחֻמוֹת אֵל וְדָבָר לָאַט עִמָּךְ:

12 How your heart has carried you away, How your eyes have failed you,

יב מַה־יִּקָּחֲךָ לִבֶּךָ וּמַה־יִּרְזְמוּן עֵינֶיךָ:

13 That you could vent your anger on *Hashem*, And let such words out of your mouth!

יג כִּי־תָשִׁיב אֶל־אֵל רוּחֶךָ וְהֹצֵאתָ מִפִּיךָ מִלִּין:

14 What is man that he can be cleared of guilt, One born of woman, that he be in the right?

יד מָה־אֱנוֹשׁ כִּי־יִזְכֶּה וְכִי־יִצְדַּק יְלוּד אִשָּׁה:

15 He puts no trust in His holy ones; The heavens are not guiltless in His sight;

טו הֵן בִּקְדֹשׁוֹ [בִּקְדֹשָׁיו] לֹא יַאֲמִין וְשָׁמַיִם לֹא־זַכּוּ בְעֵינָיו:

16 What then of one loathsome and foul, Man, who drinks wrongdoing like water!

טז אַף כִּי־נִתְעָב וְנֶאֱלָח אִישׁ־שֹׁתֶה כַמַּיִם עַוְלָה:

17 I will hold forth; listen to me; What I have seen, I will declare –

יז אֲחַוְךָ שְׁמַע־לִי וְזֶה־חָזִיתִי וַאֲסַפֵּרָה:

18 That which wise men have transmitted from their fathers, And have not withheld,

יח אֲשֶׁר־חֲכָמִים יַגִּידוּ וְלֹא כִחֲדוּ מֵאֲבוֹתָם:

19 To whom alone the land was given, No stranger passing among them:

יט לָהֶם לְבַדָּם נִתְּנָה הָאָרֶץ וְלֹא־עָבַר זָר בְּתוֹכָם:

20 The wicked man writhes in torment all his days; Few years are reserved for the ruthless.

כ כָּל־יְמֵי רָשָׁע הוּא מִתְחוֹלֵל וּמִסְפַּר שָׁנִים נִצְפְּנוּ לֶעָרִיץ:

21 Frightening sounds fill his ears; When he is at ease a robber falls upon him.

כא קוֹל־פְּחָדִים בְּאָזְנָיו בַּשָּׁלוֹם שׁוֹדֵד יְבוֹאֶנּוּ:

22 He is never sure he will come back from the dark; A sword stares him in the face.

כב לֹא־יַאֲמִין שׁוּב מִנִּי־חֹשֶׁךְ וְצָפוּ [וְצָפוּי] הוּא אֱלֵי־חָרֶב:

23 He wanders about for bread – where is it? He knows that the day of darkness has been readied for him.

כג נֹדֵד הוּא לַלֶּחֶם אַיֵּה יָדַע כִּי־נָכוֹן בְּיָדוֹ יוֹם־חֹשֶׁךְ:

24 Troubles terrify him, anxiety overpowers him, Like a king expecting a siege.

כד יְבַעֲתֻהוּ צַר וּמְצוּקָה תִּתְקְפֵהוּ כְּמֶלֶךְ עָתִיד לַכִּידוֹר:

25 For he has raised his arm against *Hashem* And played the hero against the Almighty.

כה כִּי־נָטָה אֶל־אֵל יָדוֹ וְאֶל־שַׁדַּי יִתְגַּבָּר:

26 He runs at Him defiantly With his thickly bossed shield.

כו יָרוּץ אֵלָיו בְּצַוָּאר בַּעֲבִי גַּבֵּי מָגִנָּיו:

27 His face is covered with fat And his loins with blubber.

כז כִּי־כִסָּה פָנָיו בְּחֶלְבּוֹ וַיַּעַשׂ פִּימָה עֲלֵי־כָסֶל:

28 He dwells in cities doomed to ruin, In houses that shall not be lived in, That are destined to become heaps of rubble.

כח וַיִּשְׁכּוֹן עָרִים נִכְחָדוֹת בָּתִּים לֹא־יֵשְׁבוּ לָמוֹ אֲשֶׁר הִתְעַתְּדוּ לְגַלִּים:

29 He will not be rich; His wealth will not endure; His produce shall not bend to the earth.

כט לֹא־יֶעְשַׁר וְלֹא־יָקוּם חֵילוֹ וְלֹא־יִטֶּה לָאָרֶץ מִנְלָם:

Iyov/Job
Chapter 16

30 He will never get away from the darkness; Flames will sear his shoots; He will pass away by the breath of His mouth.

31 He will not be trusted; He will be misled by falsehood, And falsehood will be his recompense.

32 He will wither before his time, His boughs never having flourished.

33 He will drop his unripe grapes like a vine; He will shed his blossoms like an olive tree.

34 For the company of the impious is desolate; Fire consumes the tents of the briber;

35 For they have conceived mischief, given birth to evil, And their womb has produced deceit.

16

1 *Iyov* said in reply:

2 I have often heard such things; You are all mischievous comforters.

3 Have windy words no limit? What afflicts you that you speak on?

4 I would also talk like you If you were in my place; I would barrage you with words, I would wag my head over you.

5 I would encourage you with words, My moving lips would bring relief.

6 If I speak, my pain will not be relieved, And if I do not – what have I lost?

7 Now He has truly worn me out; You have destroyed my whole community.

8 You have shriveled me; My gauntness serves as a witness, And testifies against me.

9 In His anger He tears and persecutes me; He gnashes His teeth at me; My foe stabs me with his eyes.

10 They open wide their mouths at me; Reviling me, they strike my cheeks; They inflame themselves against me.

11 *Hashem* hands me over to an evil man, Thrusts me into the clutches of the wicked.

12 I had been untroubled, and He broke me in pieces; He took me by the scruff and shattered me; He set me up as His target;

Iyov/Job
Chapter 17

איוב
פרק יז

13 His bowmen surrounded me; He pierced my kidneys; He showed no mercy; He spilled my bile onto the ground.

יג יָסֹבּוּ עָלַי ׀ רַבָּיו יְפַלַּח כִּלְיוֹתַי וְלֹא יַחְמֹל יִשְׁפֹּךְ לָאָרֶץ מְרֵרָתִי׃

14 He breached me, breach after breach; He rushed at me like a warrior.

יד יִפְרְצֵנִי פֶרֶץ עַל־פְּנֵי־פָרֶץ יָרֻץ עָלַי כְּגִבּוֹר׃

15 I sewed sackcloth over my skin; I buried my glory in the dust.

טו שַׂק תָּפַרְתִּי עֲלֵי גִלְדִּי וְעֹלַלְתִּי בֶעָפָר קַרְנִי׃

16 My face is red with weeping; Darkness covers my eyes

טז פָּנַי חֳמַרְמְרָה [חֳמַרְמְרוּ] מִנִּי־בֶכִי וְעַל עַפְעַפַּי צַלְמָוֶת׃

17 For no injustice on my part And for the purity of my prayer!

יז עַל לֹא־חָמָס בְּכַפָּי וּתְפִלָּתִי זַכָּה׃

18 Earth, do not cover my blood; Let there be no resting place for my outcry!

יח אֶרֶץ אַל־תְּכַסִּי דָמִי וְאַל־יְהִי מָקוֹם לְזַעֲקָתִי׃

E-retz al t'-kha-SEE da-MEE v'-AL y'-HEE ma-KOM l'-za-a-ka-TEE

19 Surely now my witness is in heaven; He who can testify for me is on high.

יט גַּם־עַתָּה הִנֵּה־בַשָּׁמַיִם עֵדִי וְשָׂהֲדִי בַּמְּרוֹמִים׃

20 O my advocates, my fellows, Before *Hashem* my eyes shed tears;

כ מְלִיצַי רֵעָי אֶל־אֱלוֹהַּ דָּלְפָה עֵינִי׃

21 Let Him arbitrate between a man and *Hashem* As between a man and his fellow.

כא וְיוֹכַח לְגֶבֶר עִם־אֱלוֹהַּ וּבֶן־אָדָם לְרֵעֵהוּ׃

22 For a few more years will pass, And I shall go the way of no return.

כב כִּי־שְׁנוֹת מִסְפָּר יֶאֱתָיוּ וְאֹרַח לֹא־אָשׁוּב אֶהֱלֹךְ׃

17

1 My spirit is crushed, my days run out; The graveyard waits for me.

יז א רוּחִי חֻבָּלָה יָמַי נִזְעָכוּ קְבָרִים לִי׃

2 Surely mocking men keep me company, And with their provocations I close my eyes.

ב אִם־לֹא הֲתֻלִים עִמָּדִי וּבְהַמְּרוֹתָם תָּלַן עֵינִי׃

3 Come now, stand surety for me! Who will give his hand on my behalf?

ג שִׂימָה־נָּא עָרְבֵנִי עִמָּךְ מִי הוּא לְיָדִי יִתָּקֵעַ׃

4 You have hidden understanding from their minds; Therefore You must not exalt [them].

ד כִּי־לִבָּם צָפַנְתָּ מִשָּׂכֶל עַל־כֵּן לֹא תְרֹמֵם׃

16:18 Earth, do not cover my blood By asking the earth not to cover up his blood, *Iyov* invokes the murder of Abel by Cain in response to which the ground "opened its mouth to receive… [Abel's] blood" (Genesis 4:11). The commentators wonder what argument led to the first murder in history, in which a person killed his own brother. According to Rabbi Yehuda Halevi, they were fighting over the Land of Israel. In his words, "They desired to know which of them would be *Adam*'s successor, and heir to his essence and intrinsic perfection, to inherit the land, and to stand in connection with the divine influence, while the other would be a nonentity." From the beginning of time, *Eretz Yisrael* has been the object of desire and the source of conflict among those who wish to inherit it. However, *Hashem* states explicitly in the Bible that He gave it to *Avraham* to pass on to the Children of Israel as their eternal inheritance (see, e.g., Genesis 13:15).

Rabbi Judah Halevi (1075–1141)

Iyov/Job

Chapter 18

איוב

פרק יח

#	English	Hebrew
5	He informs on his friends for a share [of their property], And his children's eyes pine away.	ה לְחֵלֶק יַגִּיד רֵעִים וְעֵינֵי בָנָיו תִּכְלֶנָה:
6	He made me a byword among people; I have become like Tophet of old.	ו וְהִצִּגַנִי לִמְשֹׁל עַמִּים וְתֹפֶת לְפָנִים אֶהְיֶה:
7	My eyes fail from vexation; All shapes seem to me like shadows.	ז וַתֵּכַהּ מִכַּעַשׂ עֵינִי וִיצֻרַי כַּצֵּל כֻּלָּם:
8	The upright are amazed at this; The pure are aroused against the impious.	ח יָשֹׁמּוּ יְשָׁרִים עַל־זֹאת וְנָקִי עַל־חָנֵף יִתְעֹרָר:
9	The righteous man holds to his way; He whose hands are clean grows stronger.	ט וְיֹאחֵז צַדִּיק דַּרְכּוֹ וּטְהָר־יָדַיִם יֹסִיף אֹמֶץ:
10	But all of you, come back now; I shall not find a wise man among you.	י וְאוּלָם כֻּלָּם תָּשֻׁבוּ וּבֹאוּ נָא וְלֹא־אֶמְצָא בָכֶם חָכָם:
11	My days are done, my tendons severed, The strings of my heart. ya-MAI a-v'-RU zi-mo-TAI ni-t'-KU mo-ra-SHAY l'-va-VEE	יא יָמַי עָבְרוּ זִמֹּתַי נִתְּקוּ מוֹרָשֵׁי לְבָבִי:
12	They say that night is day, That light is here – in the face of darkness.	יב לַיְלָה לְיוֹם יָשִׂימוּ אוֹר קָרוֹב מִפְּנֵי־חֹשֶׁךְ:
13	If I must look forward to Sheol as my home, And make my bed in the dark place,	יג אִם־אֲקַוֶּה שְׁאוֹל בֵּיתִי בַּחֹשֶׁךְ רִפַּדְתִּי יְצוּעִי:
14	Say to the Pit, "You are my father," To the maggots, "Mother," "Sister" –	יד לַשַּׁחַת קָרָאתִי אָבִי אָתָּה אִמִּי וַאֲחֹתִי לָרִמָּה:
15	Where, then, is my hope? Who can see hope for me?	טו וְאַיֵּה אֵפוֹ תִקְוָתִי וְתִקְוָתִי מִי יְשׁוּרֶנָּה:
16	Will it descend to Sheol? Shall we go down together to the dust?	טז בַּדֵּי שְׁאֹל תֵּרַדְנָה אִם־יַחַד עַל־עָפָר נָחַת:

18

#	English	Hebrew
1	Then Bildad the Shuhite said in reply:	א וַיַּעַן בִּלְדַּד הַשֻּׁחִי וַיֹּאמַר:
2	How long? Put an end to talk! Consider, and then we shall speak.	ב עַד־אָנָה תְּשִׂימוּן קִנְצֵי לְמִלִּין תָּבִינוּ וְאַחַר נְדַבֵּר:

Rabbi Abraham Isaac Kook (1865–1935)

17:11 My tendons severed *Iyov* begins to feel distanced from God, and to believe that he can no longer communicate meaningfully with Him. *Iyov* can no longer beg *Hashem* to give him succor and end his suffering, and therefore feels he is close to death. Similarly, the Sages (*Berachot* 32b) state that from the time of the destruction of the *Beit Hamikdash*, an iron wall separates mankind from their Father in Heaven. Rabbi Abraham Isaac Kook explains the symbolism of this image: Iron is symbolic of death and destruction, as it is a material used to make instruments of war and execution. Conversely, the goal of the *Beit Hamikdash* was to prolong life and to promote peace in the world. With the destruction of the Temple, its influence in the world was replaced by the influence of iron. Rabbi Kook concludes that only when justice and integrity will be restored will the iron wall come down, and then the *Beit Hamikdash* will resume its place as the center of prayer and inspiration for the entire world.

Iyov/Job
Chapter 18

אִיּוֹב
פֶּרֶק יח

#	English	Hebrew
3	Why are we thought of as brutes, Regarded by you as stupid?	ג מַדּוּעַ נֶחְשַׁבְנוּ כַבְּהֵמָה נִטְמִינוּ בְּעֵינֵיכֶם:
4	You who tear yourself to pieces in anger – Will earth's order be disrupted for your sake? Will rocks be dislodged from their place?	ד טֹרֵף נַפְשׁוֹ בְּאַפּוֹ הַלְמַעַנְךָ תֵּעָזַב אָרֶץ וְיֶעְתַּק־צוּר מִמְּקֹמוֹ:
5	Indeed, the light of the wicked fails; The flame of his fire does not shine.	ה גַּם אוֹר רְשָׁעִים יִדְעָךְ וְלֹא־יִגַּהּ שְׁבִיב אִשּׁוֹ:
6	The light in his tent darkens; His lamp fails him.	ו אוֹר חָשַׁךְ בְּאָהֳלוֹ וְנֵרוֹ עָלָיו יִדְעָךְ:
7	His iniquitous strides are hobbled; His schemes overthrow him.	ז יֵצְרוּ צַעֲדֵי אוֹנוֹ וְתַשְׁלִיכֵהוּ עֲצָתוֹ:
8	He is led by his feet into the net; He walks onto the toils.	ח כִּי־שֻׁלַּח בְּרֶשֶׁת בְּרַגְלָיו וְעַל־שְׂבָכָה יִתְהַלָּךְ:
9	The trap seizes his heel; The noose tightens on him.	ט יֹאחֵז בְּעָקֵב פָּח יַחֲזֵק עָלָיו צַמִּים:
10	The rope for him lies hidden on the ground; His snare, on the path.	י טָמוּן בָּאָרֶץ חַבְלוֹ וּמַלְכֻּדְתּוֹ עֲלֵי נָתִיב:
11	Terrors assault him on all sides And send his feet flying.	יא סָבִיב בִּעֲתֻהוּ בַלָּהוֹת וֶהֱפִיצֻהוּ לְרַגְלָיו:
12	His progeny hunger; Disaster awaits his wife.	יב יְהִי־רָעֵב אֹנוֹ וְאֵיד נָכוֹן לְצַלְעוֹ:
13	The tendons under his skin are consumed; Death's first-born consumes his tendons.	יג יֹאכַל בַּדֵּי עוֹרוֹ יֹאכַל בַּדָּיו בְּכוֹר מָוֶת:
14	He is torn from the safety of his tent; Terror marches him to the king.	יד יִנָּתֵק מֵאָהֳלוֹ מִבְטַחוֹ וְתַצְעִדֵהוּ לְמֶלֶךְ בַּלָּהוֹת:
15	It lodges in his desolate tent; Sulfur is strewn upon his home.	טו תִּשְׁכּוֹן בְּאָהֳלוֹ מִבְּלִי־לוֹ יְזֹרֶה עַל־נָוֵהוּ גָפְרִית:
16	His roots below dry up, And above, his branches wither.	טז מִתַּחַת שָׁרָשָׁיו יִבָשׁוּ וּמִמַּעַל יִמַּל קְצִירוֹ:
17	All mention of him vanishes from the earth; He has no name abroad.	יז זִכְרוֹ־אָבַד מִנִּי־אָרֶץ וְלֹא־שֵׁם לוֹ עַל־פְּנֵי־חוּץ:
18	He is thrust from light to darkness, Driven from the world.	יח יֶהְדְּפֻהוּ מֵאוֹר אֶל־חֹשֶׁךְ וּמִתֵּבֵל יְנִדֻּהוּ:
19	He has no seed or breed among his people, No survivor where he once lived.	יט לֹא נִין לוֹ וְלֹא־נֶכֶד בְּעַמּוֹ וְאֵין שָׂרִיד בִּמְגוּרָיו:
20	Generations to come will be appalled at his fate, As the previous ones are seized with horror.	כ עַל־יוֹמוֹ נָשַׁמּוּ אַחֲרֹנִים וְקַדְמֹנִים אָחֲזוּ שָׂעַר:

al YO-mo na-SHA-mu a-kha-ro-NEEM v'-kad-mo-NEEM A-kha-zu SA-ar

18:20 Generations to come will be appalled at his fate In this chapter, *Bildad* describes the pain and misery that he believes *Iyov* must endure because he has sinned. He assumes that since *Iyov* is suffering, he must be evil, and will therefore meet the fate of an evildoer, especially since he refuses to acknowledge his sins and repent.

Iyov/Job

Chapter 19

איוב
פרק יט

21 "These were the haunts of the wicked; Here was the place of him who knew not *Hashem*."

כא אַךְ־אֵלֶּה מִשְׁכְּנוֹת עַוָּל וְזֶה מְקוֹם לֹא־יָדַע־אֵל׃

19

1 *Iyov* said in reply:

א וַיַּעַן אִיּוֹב וַיֹּאמַר׃

2 How long will you grieve my spirit, And crush me with words?

ב עַד־אָנָה תּוֹגְיוּן נַפְשִׁי וּתְדַכְּאוּנַנִי בְמִלִּים׃

3 Time and again you humiliate me, And are not ashamed to abuse me.

ג זֶה עֶשֶׂר פְּעָמִים תַּכְלִימוּנִי לֹא־תֵבֹשׁוּ תַּהְכְּרוּ־לִי׃

4 If indeed I have erred, My error remains with me.

ד וְאַף־אָמְנָם שָׁגִיתִי אִתִּי תָּלִין מְשׁוּגָתִי׃

5 Though you are overbearing toward me, Reproaching me with my disgrace,

ה אִם־אָמְנָם עָלַי תַּגְדִּילוּ וְתוֹכִיחוּ עָלַי חֶרְפָּתִי׃

6 Yet know that *Hashem* has wronged me; He has thrown up siege works around me.

ו דְּעוּ־אֵפוֹ כִּי־אֱלוֹהַּ עִוְּתָנִי וּמְצוּדוֹ עָלַי הִקִּיף׃

7 I cry, "Violence!" but am not answered; I shout, but can get no justice.

ז הֵן אֶצְעַק חָמָס וְלֹא אֵעָנֶה אֲשַׁוַּע וְאֵין מִשְׁפָּט׃

HAYN etz-AK kha-MAS v'-LO ay-a-NEH a-sha-VA v'-AYN mish-PAT

8 He has barred my way; I cannot pass; He has laid darkness upon my path.

ח אָרְחִי גָדַר וְלֹא אֶעֱבוֹר וְעַל נְתִיבוֹתַי חֹשֶׁךְ יָשִׂים׃

9 He has stripped me of my glory, Removed the crown from my head.

ט כְּבוֹדִי מֵעָלַי הִפְשִׁיט וַיָּסַר עֲטֶרֶת רֹאשִׁי׃

10 He tears down every part of me; I perish; He uproots my hope like a tree.

י יִתְּצֵנִי סָבִיב וָאֵלַךְ וַיַּסַּע כָּעֵץ תִּקְוָתִי׃

11 He kindles His anger against me; He regards me as one of His foes.

יא וַיִּחַר עָלַי אַפּוֹ וַיַּחְשְׁבֵנִי לוֹ כְצָרָיו׃

12 His troops advance together; They build their road toward me And encamp around my tent.

יב יַחַד יָבֹאוּ גְדוּדָיו וַיָּסֹלּוּ עָלַי דַּרְכָּם וַיַּחֲנוּ סָבִיב לְאׇהֳלִי׃

Rabbi Samson R. Hirsch (1808–1888)

Bildad declares that the devastation will be so overwhelming that "Generations to come will be appalled at his fate." The idea of future generations being astonished implies complete ruin and devastation. Similarly, in response to the sins of the People of Israel, the *Torah* writes: "The children who succeed you, and foreigners who come from distant lands" will all be surprised by the complete ruin of the Land of Israel after its destruction (Deuteronomy 29:21). This, too, was caused by a lack of diligence in performing God's commands, and its reversal requires complete adherence to the word of *Hashem*.

חמס

19:7 I cry, "Violence!" The word *chamas* (חמס), 'violence,' appears a number of times in the Bible. It is used as a general term for violence, and in particular is also used as a term for robbery. The Bible tells us that it was *chamas* that almost led to the destruction of the city of Nineveh in the time of *Yona* (Jonah 3:8), and that *Hashem* brought the flood in the time of *Noach* because of *chamas* (Genesis 6:11). In fact, it was the *chamas* of the generation of the flood that sealed their fate, even though they were also guilty of sexual immorality and idolatry. Rabbi Samson Raphael Hirsch explains that this is because *chamas* refers to petty injustice and underhanded dealings which are not punishable in court. This is even worse than overt sin and immorality, as it corrodes the entire social framework of society.

Iyov/Job
Chapter 20

13	He alienated my kin from me; My acquaintances disown me.	אַחַי מֵעָלַי הִרְחִיק וְיֹדְעַי אַךְ־זָרוּ מִמֶּנִּי: יג
14	My relatives are gone; My friends have forgotten me.	חָדְלוּ קְרוֹבָי וּמְיֻדָּעַי שְׁכֵחוּנִי: יד
15	My dependents and maidservants regard me as a stranger; I am an outsider to them.	גָּרֵי בֵיתִי וְאַמְהֹתַי לְזָר תַּחְשְׁבֻנִי נָכְרִי הָיִיתִי בְעֵינֵיהֶם: טו
16	I summon my servant but he does not respond; I must myself entreat him.	לְעַבְדִּי קָרָאתִי וְלֹא יַעֲנֶה בְּמוֹ־פִי אֶתְחַנֶּן־לוֹ: טז
17	My odor is repulsive to my wife; I am loathsome to my children.	רוּחִי זָרָה לְאִשְׁתִּי וְחַנֹּתִי לִבְנֵי בִטְנִי: יז
18	Even youngsters disdain me; When I rise, they speak against me.	גַּם־עֲוִילִים מָאֲסוּ בִי אָקוּמָה וַיְדַבְּרוּ־בִי: יח
19	All my bosom friends detest me; Those I love have turned against me.	תִּעֲבוּנִי כָּל־מְתֵי סוֹדִי וְזֶה־אָהַבְתִּי נֶהְפְּכוּ־בִי: יט
20	My bones stick to my skin and flesh; I escape with the skin of my teeth.	בְּעוֹרִי וּבִבְשָׂרִי דָּבְקָה עַצְמִי וָאֶתְמַלְּטָה בְּעוֹר שִׁנָּי: כ
21	Pity me, pity me! You are my friends; For the hand of *Hashem* has struck me!	חָנֻּנִי חָנֻּנִי אַתֶּם רֵעָי כִּי יַד־אֱלוֹהַּ נָגְעָה בִּי: כא
22	Why do you pursue me like *Hashem*, Maligning me insatiably?	לָמָּה תִּרְדְּפֻנִי כְמוֹ־אֵל וּמִבְּשָׂרִי לֹא תִשְׂבָּעוּ: כב
23	O that my words were written down; Would they were inscribed in a record,	מִי־יִתֵּן אֵפוֹ וְיִכָּתְבוּן מִלָּי מִי־יִתֵּן בַּסֵּפֶר וְיֻחָקוּ: כג
24	Incised on a rock forever With iron stylus and lead!	בְּעֵט־בַּרְזֶל וְעֹפָרֶת לָעַד בַּצּוּר יֵחָצְבוּן: כד
25	But I know that my Vindicator lives; In the end He will testify on earth –	וַאֲנִי יָדַעְתִּי גֹּאֲלִי חָי וְאַחֲרוֹן עַל־עָפָר יָקוּם: כה
26	This, after my skin will have been peeled off. But I would behold *Hashem* while still in my flesh,	וְאַחַר עוֹרִי נִקְּפוּ־זֹאת וּמִבְּשָׂרִי אֶחֱזֶה אֱלוֹהַּ: כו
27	I myself, not another, would behold Him; Would see with my own eyes: My heart pines within me.	אֲשֶׁר אֲנִי אֶחֱזֶה־לִּי וְעֵינַי רָאוּ וְלֹא־זָר כָּלוּ כִלְיֹתַי בְּחֵקִי: כז
28	You say, "How do we persecute him? The root of the matter is in him."	כִּי תֹאמְרוּ מַה־נִּרְדָּף־לוֹ וְשֹׁרֶשׁ דָּבָר נִמְצָא־בִי: כח
29	Be in fear of the sword, For [your] fury is iniquity worthy of the sword; Know there is a judgment!	גּוּרוּ לָכֶם מִפְּנֵי־חֶרֶב כִּי־חֵמָה עֲוֹנוֹת חָרֶב לְמַעַן תֵּדְעוּן שַׁדִּין [שַׁדּוּן]: כט

20

1	Zophar the Naamathite said in reply:	וַיַּעַן צֹפַר הַנַּעֲמָתִי וַיֹּאמַר: א
2	In truth, my thoughts urge me to answer (It is because of my feelings	לָכֵן שְׂעִפַּי יְשִׁיבוּנִי וּבַעֲבוּר חוּשִׁי בִי: ב
3	When I hear reproof that insults me); A spirit out of my understanding makes me reply:	מוּסַר כְּלִמָּתִי אֶשְׁמָע וְרוּחַ מִבִּינָתִי יַעֲנֵנִי: ג

1742

Iyov/Job
Chapter 20

4 Do you not know this, that from time immemorial, Since man was set on earth,

ד הֲזֹאת יָדַעְתָּ מִנִּי־עַד מִנִּי שִׂים אָדָם עֲלֵי־אָרֶץ׃

5 The joy of the wicked has been brief, The happiness of the impious, fleeting?

ה כִּי רִנְנַת רְשָׁעִים מִקָּרוֹב וְשִׂמְחַת חָנֵף עֲדֵי־רָגַע׃

6 Though he grows as high as the sky, His head reaching the clouds,

ו אִם־יַעֲלֶה לַשָּׁמַיִם שִׂיאוֹ וְרֹאשׁוֹ לָעָב יַגִּיעַ׃

7 He perishes forever, like his dung; Those who saw him will say, "Where is he?"

ז כְּגֶלְלוֹ לָנֶצַח יֹאבֵד רֹאָיו יֹאמְרוּ אַיּוֹ׃

8 He flies away like a dream and cannot be found; He is banished like a night vision.

ח כַּחֲלוֹם יָעוּף וְלֹא יִמְצָאוּהוּ וְיֻדַּד כְּחֶזְיוֹן לָיְלָה׃

9 Eyes that glimpsed him do so no more; They cannot see him in his place any longer.

ט עַיִן שְׁזָפַתּוּ וְלֹא תוֹסִיף וְלֹא־עוֹד תְּשׁוּרֶנּוּ מְקוֹמוֹ׃

10 His sons ingratiate themselves with the poor; His own hands must give back his wealth.

י בָּנָיו יְרַצּוּ דַלִּים וְיָדָיו תָּשֵׁבְנָה אוֹנוֹ׃

11 His bones, still full of vigor, Lie down in the dust with him.

יא עַצְמוֹתָיו מָלְאוּ עלומו [עֲלוּמָיו] וְעִמּוֹ עַל־עָפָר תִּשְׁכָּב׃

12 Though evil is sweet to his taste, And he conceals it under his tongue;

יב אִם־תַּמְתִּיק בְּפִיו רָעָה יַכְחִידֶנָּה תַּחַת לְשׁוֹנוֹ׃

13 Though he saves it, does not let it go, Holds it inside his mouth,

יג יַחְמֹל עָלֶיהָ וְלֹא יַעַזְבֶנָּה וְיִמְנָעֶנָּה בְּתוֹךְ חִכּוֹ׃

14 His food in his bowels turns Into asps' venom within him.

יד לַחְמוֹ בְּמֵעָיו נֶהְפָּךְ מְרוֹרַת פְּתָנִים בְּקִרְבּוֹ׃

15 The riches he swallows he vomits; *Hashem* empties it out of his stomach.

טו חַיִל בָּלַע וַיְקִאֶנּוּ מִבִּטְנוֹ יוֹרִשֶׁנּוּ אֵל׃

16 He sucks the poison of asps; The tongue of the viper kills him.

טז רֹאשׁ־פְּתָנִים יִינָק תַּהַרְגֵהוּ לְשׁוֹן אֶפְעֶה׃

17 Let him not enjoy the streams, The rivers of honey, the brooks of cream.

יז אַל־יֵרֶא בִפְלַגּוֹת נַהֲרֵי נַחֲלֵי דְּבַשׁ וְחֶמְאָה׃

18 He will give back the goods unswallowed; The value of the riches, undigested.

יח מֵשִׁיב יָגָע וְלֹא יִבְלָע כְּחֵיל תְּמוּרָתוֹ וְלֹא יַעֲלֹס׃

19 Because he crushed and tortured the poor, He will not build up the house he took by force.

יט כִּי־רִצַּץ עָזַב דַּלִּים בַּיִת גָּזַל וְלֹא יִבְנֵהוּ׃

20 He will not see his children tranquil; He will not preserve one of his dear ones.

כ כִּי לֹא־יָדַע שָׁלֵו בְּבִטְנוֹ בַּחֲמוּדוֹ לֹא יְמַלֵּט׃

21 With no survivor to enjoy it, His fortune will not prosper.

כא אֵין־שָׂרִיד לְאָכְלוֹ עַל־כֵּן לֹא־יָחִיל טוּבוֹ׃

22 When he has all he wants, trouble will come; Misfortunes of all kinds will batter him.

כב בִּמְלֹאות שִׂפְקוֹ יֵצֶר לוֹ כָּל־יַד עָמֵל תְּבוֹאֶנּוּ׃

1743

Iyov/Job
Chapter 21

איוב
פרק כא

23 Let that fill his belly; Let Him loose His burning anger at him, And rain down His weapons upon him.

כג יְהִי לְמַלֵּא בִטְנוֹ יְשַׁלַּח־בּוֹ חֲרוֹן אַפּוֹ וְיַמְטֵר עָלֵימוֹ בִּלְחוּמוֹ׃

24 Fleeing from iron arrows, He is shot through from a bow of bronze.

כד יִבְרַח מִנֵּשֶׁק בַּרְזֶל תַּחְלְפֵהוּ קֶשֶׁת נְחוּשָׁה׃

25 Brandished and run through his body, The blade, through his gall, Strikes terror into him.

כה שָׁלַף וַיֵּצֵא מִגֵּוָה וּבָרָק מִמְּרֹרָתוֹ יַהֲלֹךְ עָלָיו אֵמִים׃

26 Utter darkness waits for his treasured ones; A fire fanned by no man will consume him; Who survives in his tent will be crushed.

כו כָּל־חֹשֶׁךְ טָמוּן לִצְפּוּנָיו תְּאָכְלֵהוּ אֵשׁ לֹא־נֻפָּח יֵרַע שָׂרִיד בְּאָהֳלוֹ׃

kol KHO-shekh ta-MUN litz-pu-NAV t'-a-kh'-LAY-hu AYSH lo nu-PAKH yay-RA sa-REED b'-a-ho-LO

27 Heaven will expose his iniquity; Earth will rise up against him.

כז יְגַלּוּ שָׁמַיִם עֲוֺנוֹ וְאֶרֶץ מִתְקוֹמָמָה לוֹ׃

28 His household will be cast forth by a flood, Spilled out on the day of His wrath.

כח יִגֶל יְבוּל בֵּיתוֹ נִגָּרוֹת בְּיוֹם אַפּוֹ׃

29 This is the wicked man's portion from *Hashem*, The lot *Hashem* has ordained for him.

כט זֶה חֵלֶק־אָדָם רָשָׁע מֵאֱלֹהִים וְנַחֲלַת אִמְרוֹ מֵאֵל׃

21

1 *Iyov* said in reply:

כא א וַיַּעַן אִיּוֹב וַיֹּאמַר׃

2 Listen well to what I say, And let that be your consolation.

ב שִׁמְעוּ שָׁמוֹעַ מִלָּתִי וּתְהִי־זֹאת תַּנְחוּמֹתֵיכֶם׃

3 Bear with me while I speak, And after I have spoken, you may mock.

ג שָׂאוּנִי וְאָנֹכִי אֲדַבֵּר וְאַחַר דַּבְּרִי תַלְעִיג׃

4 Is my complaint directed toward a man? Why should I not lose my patience?

ד הֶאָנֹכִי לְאָדָם שִׂיחִי וְאִם־מַדּוּעַ לֹא־תִקְצַר רוּחִי׃

5 Look at me and be appalled, And clap your hand to your mouth.

ה פְּנוּ־אֵלַי וְהָשַׁמּוּ וְשִׂימוּ יָד עַל־פֶּה׃

6 When I think of it I am terrified; My body is seized with shuddering.

ו וְאִם־זָכַרְתִּי וְנִבְהָלְתִּי וְאָחַז בְּשָׂרִי פַּלָּצוּת׃

20:26 Who survives in his tent will be crushed Zophar asserts that anyone associated with an evil person will be punished as a result of that association. Why is it so important to avoid associating with evildoers? Associating with a sinner can cause a desecration of God's name, since righteous people are thought to be less virtuous due to these inappropriate associations. Furthermore, a righteous person must avoid being influenced by evildoers, lest they lead him to sin. This idea is applied by *Rashi* (Numbers 3:29) to explain why the tribe of *Reuven* joined the rebellion of *Korach*, who was from the *Kehat* family of the tribe of *Levi*. "Since the tribe of *Reuven* was settled in the south when they camped, thus being neighbors of *Kehat* and his children who were also camped in the south, they joined with *Korach* in his rebellion. Woe to the wicked, and woe to his neighbor!"

Rashi
(1040–1105)

Iyov/Job
Chapter 21

איוב
פרק כא

#	English	Hebrew
7	Why do the wicked live on, Prosper and grow wealthy? *ma-DU-a r'-sha-EEM yikh-YU a-t'-KU gam ga-v'-RU KHA-yil*	ז מַדּוּעַ רְשָׁעִים יִחְיוּ עָתְקוּ גַּם־גָּבְרוּ חָיִל:
8	Their children are with them always, And they see their children's children.	ח זַרְעָם נָכוֹן לִפְנֵיהֶם עִמָּם וְצֶאֱצָאֵיהֶם לְעֵינֵיהֶם:
9	Their homes are secure, without fear; They do not feel the rod of *Hashem*.	ט בָּתֵּיהֶם שָׁלוֹם מִפָּחַד וְלֹא שֵׁבֶט אֱלוֹהַּ עֲלֵיהֶם:
10	Their bull breeds and does not fail; Their cow calves and never miscarries;	י שׁוֹרוֹ עִבַּר וְלֹא יַגְעִל תְּפַלֵּט פָּרָתוֹ וְלֹא תְשַׁכֵּל:
11	They let their infants run loose like sheep, And their children skip about.	יא יְשַׁלְּחוּ כַצֹּאן עֲוִילֵיהֶם וְיַלְדֵיהֶם יְרַקֵּדוּן:
12	They sing to the music of timbrel and lute, And revel to the tune of the pipe;	יב יִשְׂאוּ כְּתֹף וְכִנּוֹר וְיִשְׂמְחוּ לְקוֹל עוּגָב:
13	They spend their days in happiness, And go down to Sheol in peace.	יג יבלו [יְכַלּוּ] בַטּוֹב יְמֵיהֶם וּבְרֶגַע שְׁאוֹל יֵחָתּוּ:
14	They say to *Hashem*, "Leave us alone, We do not want to learn Your ways;	יד וַיֹּאמְרוּ לָאֵל סוּר מִמֶּנּוּ וְדַעַת דְּרָכֶיךָ לֹא חָפָצְנוּ:
15	What is *Shaddai* that we should serve Him? What will we gain by praying to Him?"	טו מַה־שַּׁדַּי כִּי־נַעַבְדֶנּוּ וּמַה־נּוֹעִיל כִּי נִפְגַּע־בּוֹ:
16	Their happiness is not their own doing. (The thoughts of the wicked are beyond me!)	טז הֵן לֹא בְיָדָם טוּבָם עֲצַת רְשָׁעִים רָחֲקָה מֶנִּי:
17	How seldom does the lamp of the wicked fail, Does the calamity they deserve befall them, Does He apportion [their] lot in anger!	יז כַּמָּה נֵר־רְשָׁעִים יִדְעָךְ וְיָבֹא עָלֵימוֹ אֵידָם חֲבָלִים יְחַלֵּק בְּאַפּוֹ:
18	Let them become like straw in the wind, Like chaff carried off by a storm.	יח יִהְיוּ כְּתֶבֶן לִפְנֵי־רוּחַ וּכְמֹץ גְּנָבַתּוּ סוּפָה:
19	[You say,] "*Hashem* is reserving his punishment for his sons"; Let it be paid back to him that he may feel it,	יט אֱלוֹהַּ יִצְפֹּן־לְבָנָיו אוֹנוֹ יְשַׁלֵּם אֵלָיו וְיֵדָע:
20	Let his eyes see his ruin, And let him drink the wrath of *Shaddai*!	כ יִרְאוּ עינו [עֵינָיו] כִּידוֹ וּמֵחֲמַת שַׁדַּי יִשְׁתֶּה:
21	For what does he care about the fate of his family, When his number of months runs out?	כא כִּי מַה־חֶפְצוֹ בְּבֵיתוֹ אַחֲרָיו וּמִסְפַּר חֳדָשָׁיו חֻצָּצוּ:

21:7 Why do the wicked live on This question that *Iyov* asks is the crux of the entire book: Why do the righteous suffer while the wicked go unpunished? Though *Iyov* is troubled by this because of his personal experiences, he does not abandon his faith in God. If he did, the question would lose its meaning, for the seeming randomness of good and bad fortunes presents a difficulty only if one supposes that the world is ruled by a benevolent God. *Iyov* teaches that while it is acceptable to ask the questions, they must come from a place of faith in *Hashem* and His integrity, rather than denial and doubt.

Iyov/Job
Chapter 22

איוב
פרק כב

22 Can *Hashem* be instructed in knowledge, He who judges from such heights?

כב הַלְאֵל יְלַמֶּד־דָּעַת וְהוּא רָמִים יִשְׁפּוֹט׃

23 One man dies in robust health, All tranquil and untroubled;

כג זֶה יָמוּת בְּעֶצֶם תֻּמּוֹ כֻּלּוֹ שַׁלְאֲנַן וְשָׁלֵיו׃

24 His pails are full of milk; The marrow of his bones is juicy.

כד עֲטִינָיו מָלְאוּ חָלָב וּמֹחַ עַצְמוֹתָיו יְשֻׁקֶּה׃

25 Another dies embittered, Never having tasted happiness.

כה וְזֶה יָמוּת בְּנֶפֶשׁ מָרָה וְלֹא־אָכַל בַּטּוֹבָה׃

26 They both lie in the dust And are covered with worms.

כו יַחַד עַל־עָפָר יִשְׁכָּבוּ וְרִמָּה תְּכַסֶּה עֲלֵיהֶם׃

27 Oh, I know your thoughts, And the tactics you will devise against me.

כז הֵן יָדַעְתִּי מַחְשְׁבוֹתֵיכֶם וּמְזִמּוֹת עָלַי תַּחְמֹסוּ׃

28 You will say, "Where is the house of the great man – And where the tent in which the wicked dwelled?"

כח כִּי תֹאמְרוּ אַיֵּה בֵית־נָדִיב וְאַיֵּה אֹהֶל מִשְׁכְּנוֹת רְשָׁעִים׃

29 You must have consulted the wayfarers; You cannot deny their evidence.

כט הֲלֹא שְׁאֶלְתֶּם עוֹבְרֵי דָרֶךְ וְאֹתֹתָם לֹא תְנַכֵּרוּ׃

30 For the evil man is spared on the day of calamity, On the day when wrath is led forth.

ל כִּי לְיוֹם אֵיד יֵחָשֶׂךְ רָע לְיוֹם עֲבָרוֹת יוּבָלוּ׃

31 Who will upbraid him to his face? Who will requite him for what he has done?

לא מִי־יַגִּיד עַל־פָּנָיו דַּרְכּוֹ וְהוּא־עָשָׂה מִי יְשַׁלֶּם־לוֹ׃

32 He is brought to the grave, While a watch is kept at his tomb.

לב וְהוּא לִקְבָרוֹת יוּבָל וְעַל־גָּדִישׁ יִשְׁקוֹד׃

33 The clods of the wadi are sweet to him, Everyone follows behind him, Innumerable are those who precede him.

לג מָתְקוּ־לוֹ רִגְבֵי נָחַל וְאַחֲרָיו כָּל־אָדָם יִמְשׁוֹךְ וּלְפָנָיו אֵין מִסְפָּר׃

34 Why then do you offer me empty consolation? Of your replies only the perfidy remains.

לד וְאֵיךְ תְּנַחֲמוּנִי הָבֶל וּתְשׁוּבֹתֵיכֶם נִשְׁאַר־מָעַל׃

22 1 Eliphaz the Temanite said in reply:

כב א וַיַּעַן אֱלִיפַז הַתֵּימָנִי וַיֹּאמַר׃

2 Can a man be of use to *Hashem*, A wise man benefit Him?

ב הַלְאֵל יִסְכָּן־גָּבֶר כִּי־יִסְכֹּן עָלֵימוֹ מַשְׂכִּיל׃

3 Does *Shaddai* gain if you are righteous? Does He profit if your conduct is blameless?

ג הַחֵפֶץ לְשַׁדַּי כִּי תִצְדָּק וְאִם־בֶּצַע כִּי־תַתֵּם דְּרָכֶיךָ׃

22:3 Does *Shaddai* gain if you are righteous? Eliphaz states that *Hashem* does not desire piety, but rather good deeds. This is reminiscent of the first chapter of *Sefer Yeshayahu*. In *Sefer Yeshayahu*, God is angry at the inhabitants of *Yerushalayim* because they are engaged in unacceptable behavior towards their fellow men, such as murder, even as they continue to worship *Hashem* through prayer and sacrifice (Isaiah 1:11,15). *Yeshayahu* declares: "Alas, she has become a harlot, the faithful city that was filled with justice, where righteousness

Iyov/Job
Chapter 22

איוב
פרק כב

ha-KHAY-fetz l'-sha-DAI KEE titz-DAK v'-im BE-tza kee ta-TAYM d'-ra-KHE-kha

4	Is it because of your piety that He arraigns you, And enters into judgment with you?	הֲמִיִּרְאָתְךָ יֹכִיחֶךָ יָבוֹא עִמְּךָ בַּמִּשְׁפָּט: ד
5	You know that your wickedness is great, And that your iniquities have no limit.	הֲלֹא רָעָתְךָ רַבָּה וְאֵין־קֵץ לַעֲוֺנֹתֶיךָ: ה
6	You exact pledges from your fellows without reason, And leave them naked, stripped of their clothes;	כִּי־תַחְבֹּל אַחֶיךָ חִנָּם וּבִגְדֵי עֲרוּמִּים תַּפְשִׁיט: ו
7	You do not give the thirsty water to drink; You deny bread to the hungry.	לֹא־מַיִם עָיֵף תַּשְׁקֶה וּמֵרָעֵב תִּמְנַע־לָחֶם: ז
8	The land belongs to the strong; The privileged occupy it.	וְאִישׁ זְרוֹעַ לוֹ הָאָרֶץ וּנְשׂוּא פָנִים יֵשֶׁב בָּהּ: ח
9	You have sent away widows empty-handed; The strength of the fatherless is broken.	אַלְמָנוֹת שִׁלַּחְתָּ רֵיקָם וּזְרֹעוֹת יְתֹמִים יְדֻכָּא: ט
10	Therefore snares are all around you, And sudden terrors frighten you,	עַל־כֵּן סְבִיבוֹתֶיךָ פַחִים וִיבַהֶלְךָ פַּחַד פִּתְאֹם: י
11	Or darkness, so you cannot see; A flood of waters covers you.	אוֹ־חֹשֶׁךְ לֹא־תִרְאֶה וְשִׁפְעַת־מַיִם תְּכַסֶּךָּ: יא
12	*Hashem* is in the heavenly heights; See the highest stars, how lofty!	הֲלֹא־אֱלוֹהַּ גֹּבַהּ שָׁמָיִם וּרְאֵה רֹאשׁ כּוֹכָבִים כִּי־רָמּוּ: יב
13	You say, "What can *Hashem* know? Can He govern through the dense cloud?	וְאָמַרְתָּ מַה־יָּדַע אֵל הַבְעַד עֲרָפֶל יִשְׁפּוֹט: יג
14	The clouds screen Him so He cannot see As He moves about the circuit of heaven."	עָבִים סֵתֶר־לוֹ וְלֹא יִרְאֶה וְחוּג שָׁמַיִם יִתְהַלָּךְ: יד
15	Have you observed the immemorial path That evil men have trodden;	הַאֹרַח עוֹלָם תִּשְׁמֹר אֲשֶׁר דָּרְכוּ מְתֵי־אָוֶן: טו
16	How they were shriveled up before their time And their foundation poured out like a river?	אֲשֶׁר־קֻמְּטוּ וְלֹא־עֵת נָהָר יוּצַק יְסוֹדָם: טז
17	They said to *Hashem*, "Leave us alone; What can *Shaddai* do about it?"	הָאֹמְרִים לָאֵל סוּר מִמֶּנּוּ וּמַה־יִּפְעַל שַׁדַּי לָמוֹ: יז
18	But it was He who filled their houses with good things. (The thoughts of the wicked are beyond me!)	וְהוּא מִלֵּא בָתֵּיהֶם טוֹב וַעֲצַת רְשָׁעִים רָחֲקָה מֶנִּי: יח

dwelt. But now [it is filled with] murderers" (1:21). While a righteous person might believe that his observance of the formal commandments is what brings *Hashem* close to him, what *Hashem* desires most is kindness to other human beings. The chapter in *Yeshayahu* continues: "I will restore your magistrates as of old, and your counselors as of yore… *Tzion* shall be saved in the judgment; Her repentant ones, in the retribution." (1:26–27). It is through kindness, righteousness and justice towards others that the redemption of *Tzion* will come.

1747

Iyov/Job

Chapter 23

איוב

פרק כג

19 The righteous, seeing it, rejoiced; The innocent laughed with scorn.	יט יִרְא֣וּ צַדִּיקִ֣ים וְיִשְׂמָ֑חוּ וְ֝נָקִ֗י יִלְעַג־לָֽמוֹ׃
20 Surely their substance was destroyed, And their remnant consumed by fire.	כ אִם־לֹ֣א נִכְחַ֣ד קִימָ֑נוּ וְ֝יִתְרָ֗ם אָ֣כְלָה אֵֽשׁ׃
21 Be close to Him and wholehearted; Good things will come to you thereby.	כא הַסְכֶּן־נָ֣א עִמּ֑וֹ וּשְׁלָ֑ם בָּ֝הֶ֗ם תְּֽבוֹאַתְךָ֥ טוֹבָֽה׃
22 Accept instruction from His mouth; Lay up His words in your heart.	כב קַח־נָ֣א מִפִּ֣יו תּוֹרָ֑ה וְשִׂ֥ים אֲ֝מָרָ֗יו בִּלְבָבֶֽךָ׃
23 If you return to *Shaddai* you will be restored, If you banish iniquity from your tent;	כג אִם־תָּשׁ֣וּב עַד־שַׁ֭דַּי תִּבָּנֶ֑ה תַּרְחִ֥יק עַ֝וְלָ֗ה מֵאׇהֳלֶֽךָ׃
24 If you regard treasure as dirt, Ophir-gold as stones of the wadi,	כד וְשִׁית־עַל־עָפָ֣ר בָּ֑צֶר וּבְצ֖וּר נְחָלִ֣ים אוֹפִֽיר׃
25 And *Shaddai* be your treasure And precious silver for you,	כה וְהָיָ֣ה שַׁדַּ֣י בְּצָרֶ֑יךָ וְכֶ֖סֶף תּוֹעָפ֣וֹת לָֽךְ׃
26 When you seek the favor of *Shaddai*, And lift up your face to *Hashem*,	כו כִּי־אָ֭ז עַל־שַׁדַּ֣י תִּתְעַנָּ֑ג וְתִשָּׂ֖א אֶל־אֱל֣וֹהַּ פָּנֶֽיךָ׃
27 You will pray to Him, and He will listen to you, And you will pay your vows.	כז תַּעְתִּ֣יר אֵ֭לָיו וְיִשְׁמָעֶ֑ךָּ וּנְדָרֶ֥יךָ תְשַׁלֵּֽם׃
28 You will decree and it will be fulfilled, And light will shine upon your affairs.	כח וְֽתִגְזַר־א֭וֹמֶר וְיָ֣קׇם לָ֑ךְ וְעַל־דְּ֝רָכֶ֗יךָ נָ֣גַֽהּ אֽוֹר׃
29 When others sink low, you will say it is pride; For He saves the humble.	כט כִּֽי־הִ֭שְׁפִּילוּ וַתֹּ֣אמֶר גֵּוָ֑ה וְשַׁ֖ח עֵינַ֣יִם יוֹשִֽׁעַ׃
30 He will deliver the guilty; He will be delivered through the cleanness of your hands.	ל יְֽמַלֵּ֥ט אִי־נָקִ֑י וְ֝נִמְלַ֗ט בְּבֹ֣ר כַּפֶּֽיךָ׃
23 1 *Iyov* said in reply:	**כג** א וַיַּ֥עַן אִיּ֗וֹב וַיֹּאמַֽר׃
2 Today again my complaint is bitter; My strength is spent on account of my groaning.	ב גַּם־הַ֭יּוֹם מְרִ֣י שִׂחִ֑י יָ֝דִ֗י כָּבְדָ֥ה עַל־אַנְחָתִֽי׃
3 Would that I knew how to reach Him, How to get to His dwelling-place.	ג מִֽי־יִתֵּ֣ן יָ֭דַעְתִּי וְאֶמְצָאֵ֑הוּ אָ֝ב֗וֹא עַד־תְּכוּנָתֽוֹ׃
4 I would set out my case before Him And fill my mouth with arguments.	ד אֶעֶרְכָ֣ה לְפָנָ֣יו מִשְׁפָּ֑ט וּ֝פִ֗י אֲמַלֵּ֥א תוֹכָחֽוֹת׃
5 I would learn what answers He had for me And know how He would reply to me.	ה אֵ֭דְעָה מִלִּ֣ים יַעֲנֵ֑נִי וְ֝אָבִ֗ינָה מַה־יֹּ֥אמַר לִֽי׃
6 Would He contend with me overbearingly? Surely He would not accuse me!	ו הַבְּרׇב־כֹּ֭חַ יָרִ֣יב עִמָּדִ֑י לֹ֥א אַךְ־ה֝֗וּא יָשִׂ֥ם בִּֽי׃
7 There the upright would be cleared by Him, And I would escape forever from my judge.	ז שָׁ֗ם יָ֭שָׁר נוֹכָ֣ח עִמּ֑וֹ וַאֲפַלְּטָ֥ה לָ֝נֶ֗צַח מִשֹּׁפְטִֽי׃

Iyov/Job
Chapter 24

איוב
פרק כד

8 But if I go East – He is not there; West – I still do not perceive Him; הֵן קֶדֶם אֶהֱלֹךְ וְאֵינֶנּוּ וְאָחוֹר וְלֹא־אָבִין לֽוֹ׃

HAYN KE-dem e-he-LOKH v'-ay-NE-nu v'-a-KHOR v'-LO a-VEEN LO

9 North – since He is concealed, I do not behold Him; South – He is hidden, and I cannot see Him. שְׂמֹאול בַּעֲשֹׂתוֹ וְלֹא־אָחַז יַעְטֹף יָמִין וְלֹא אֶרְאֶֽה׃

10 But He knows the way I take; Would He assay me, I should emerge pure as gold. כִּֽי־יָדַע דֶּרֶךְ עִמָּדִי בְּחָנַנִי כַּזָּהָב אֵצֵֽא׃

11 I have followed in His tracks, Kept His way without swerving, בַּאֲשֻׁרוֹ אָחֲזָה רַגְלִי דַּרְכּוֹ שָׁמַרְתִּי וְלֹא־אָֽט׃

12 I have not deviated from what His lips commanded; I have treasured His words more than my daily bread. מִצְוַת שְׂפָתָיו וְלֹא אָמִישׁ מֵחֻקִּי צָפַנְתִּי אִמְרֵי־פִֽיו׃

13 He is one; who can dissuade Him? Whatever He desires, He does. וְהוּא בְאֶחָד וּמִי יְשִׁיבֶנּוּ וְנַפְשׁוֹ אִוְּתָה וַיָּֽעַשׂ׃

14 For He will bring my term to an end, But He has many more such at His disposal. כִּי יַשְׁלִים חֻקִּי וְכָהֵנָּה רַבּוֹת עִמּֽוֹ׃

15 Therefore I am terrified at His presence; When I consider, I dread Him. עַל־כֵּן מִפָּנָיו אֶבָּהֵל אֶתְבּוֹנֵן וְאֶפְחַד מִמֶּֽנּוּ׃

16 *Hashem* has made me fainthearted; *Shaddai* has terrified me. וְאֵל הֵרַךְ לִבִּי וְשַׁדַּי הִבְהִילָֽנִי׃

17 Yet I am not cut off by the darkness; He has concealed the thick gloom from me. כִּֽי־לֹא נִצְמַתִּי מִפְּנֵי־חֹשֶׁךְ וּמִפָּנַי כִּסָּה־אֹֽפֶל׃

24 1 Why are times for judgment not reserved by *Shaddai*? Even those close to Him cannot foresee His actions. מַדּוּעַ מִשַּׁדַּי לֹא־נִצְפְּנוּ עִתִּים וְיֹדְעָו [וְיֹדְעָיו] לֹא־חָזוּ יָמָֽיו׃

ma-DU-a mi-sha-DAI lo nitz-p'-NU i-TEEM v'-yo-d'-AV lo KHA-zu ya-MAV

2 People remove boundary-stones; They carry off flocks and pasture them; גְּבֻלוֹת יַשִּׂיגוּ עֵדֶר גָּזְלוּ וַיִּרְעֽוּ׃

23:8 But if I go East – He is not there Throughout the book, *Iyov*'s bitterness at God's apparent abandonment of him has been very noticeable. Until now it seemed that *Iyov* was upset because he knew that he did not deserve the punishment he received. Now, however, he expresses concern over his distance from *Hashem*. For a God-fearing person, distance from *Hashem* is unbearable. Similarly, when *Yeshayahu* proclaims to the inhabitants of *Yerushalayim*: "Though you pray at length, I will not listen." (1:15), this was meant to motivate them towards repentance. As a truly righteous man, *Iyov* could bear a test from the Almighty, but he cannot bear the lack of response to his prayers.

24:1 Even those close to Him cannot foresee His actions A careful reading shows that *Iyov* is not complaining about his punishment, but about the fact that he cannot see the end of his suffering. Similarly, in *Sefer Tehillim* (44:24), the People of Israel complain to God about their long exile from the Land of Israel: "Rouse Yourself; why do You sleep, O *Hashem*? Awaken, do not reject us forever." They cannot bear the seemingly endless exile from their homeland. It is always much easier to suffer if the end is in sight.

Iyov/Job
Chapter 24

3 They lead away the donkeys of the fatherless, And seize the widow's bull as a pledge;

4 They chase the needy off the roads; All the poor of the land are forced into hiding.

5 Like the wild asses of the wilderness, They go about their tasks, seeking food; The wilderness provides each with food for his lads;

6 They harvest fodder in the field, And glean the late grapes in the vineyards of the wicked.

7 They pass the night naked for lack of clothing, They have no covering against the cold;

8 They are drenched by the mountain rains, And huddle against the rock for lack of shelter.

9 They snatch the fatherless infant from the breast, And seize the child of the poor as a pledge.

10 They go about naked for lack of clothing, And, hungry, carry sheaves;

11 Between rows [of olive trees] they make oil, And, thirsty, they tread the winepresses.

12 Men groan in the city; The souls of the dying cry out; Yet *Hashem* does not regard it as a reproach.

13 They are rebels against the light; They are strangers to its ways, And do not stay in its path.

14 The murderer arises in the evening To kill the poor and needy, And at night he acts the thief.

15 The eyes of the adulterer watch for twilight, Thinking, "No one will glimpse me then." He masks his face.

16 In the dark they break into houses; By day they shut themselves in; They do not know the light.

17 For all of them morning is darkness; It is then that they discern the terror of darkness.

18 May they be flotsam on the face of the water; May their portion in the land be cursed; May none turn aside by way of their vineyards.

19 May drought and heat snatch away their snow waters, And Sheol, those who have sinned.

20 May the womb forget him; May he be sweet to the worms; May he be no longer remembered; May wrongdoers be broken like a tree.

איוב
פרק כד

ג חֲמוֹר יְתוֹמִים יִנְהָגוּ יַחְבְּלוּ שׁוֹר אַלְמָנָה׃

ד יַטּוּ אֶבְיוֹנִים מִדָּרֶךְ יַחַד חֻבְּאוּ עֲנִיֵּי־אָרֶץ׃

ה הֵן פְּרָאִים בַּמִּדְבָּר יָצְאוּ בְּפׇעֳלָם מְשַׁחֲרֵי לַטָּרֶף עֲרָבָה לוֹ לֶחֶם לַנְּעָרִים׃

ו בַּשָּׂדֶה בְּלִילוֹ יקצירו [יִקְצוֹרוּ] וְכֶרֶם רָשָׁע יְלַקֵּשׁוּ׃

ז עָרוֹם יָלִינוּ מִבְּלִי לְבוּשׁ וְאֵין כְּסוּת בַּקָּרָה׃

ח מִזֶּרֶם הָרִים יִרְטָבוּ וּמִבְּלִי מַחְסֶה חִבְּקוּ־צוּר׃

ט יִגְזְלוּ מִשֹּׁד יָתוֹם וְעַל־עָנִי יַחְבֹּלוּ׃

י עָרוֹם הִלְּכוּ בְּלִי לְבוּשׁ וּרְעֵבִים נָשְׂאוּ עֹמֶר׃

יא בֵּין־שׁוּרֹתָם יַצְהִירוּ יְקָבִים דָּרְכוּ וַיִּצְמָאוּ׃

יב מֵעִיר מְתִים יִנְאָקוּ וְנֶפֶשׁ־חֲלָלִים תְּשַׁוֵּעַ וֶאֱלוֹהַּ לֹא־יָשִׂים תִּפְלָה׃

יג הֵמָּה הָיוּ בְּמֹרְדֵי־אוֹר לֹא־הִכִּירוּ דְרָכָיו וְלֹא יָשְׁבוּ בִּנְתִיבֹתָיו׃

יד לָאוֹר יָקוּם רוֹצֵחַ יִקְטָל־עָנִי וְאֶבְיוֹן וּבַלַּיְלָה יְהִי כַגַּנָּב׃

טו וְעֵין נֹאֵף שָׁמְרָה נֶשֶׁף לֵאמֹר לֹא־תְשׁוּרֵנִי עָיִן וְסֵתֶר פָּנִים יָשִׂים׃

טז חָתַר בַּחֹשֶׁךְ בָּתִּים יוֹמָם חִתְּמוּ־לָמוֹ לֹא־יָדְעוּ אוֹר׃

יז כִּי יַחְדָּו בֹּקֶר לָמוֹ צַלְמָוֶת כִּי־יַכִּיר בַּלְהוֹת צַלְמָוֶת׃

יח קַל־הוּא עַל־פְּנֵי־מַיִם תְּקֻלַּל חֶלְקָתָם בָּאָרֶץ לֹא־יִפְנֶה דֶּרֶךְ כְּרָמִים׃

יט צִיָּה גַם־חֹם יִגְזְלוּ מֵימֵי־שֶׁלֶג שְׁאוֹל חָטָאוּ׃

כ יִשְׁכָּחֵהוּ רֶחֶם מְתָקוֹ רִמָּה עוֹד לֹא־יִזָּכֵר וַתִּשָּׁבֵר כָּעֵץ עַוְלָה׃

Iyov/Job
Chapter 25

21 May he consort with a barren woman who bears no child, Leave his widow deprived of good.

22 Though he has the strength to seize bulls, May he live with no assurance of survival.

23 Yet [*Hashem*] gives him the security on which he relies, And keeps watch over his affairs.

24 Exalted for a while, let them be gone; Be brought low, and shrivel like mallows, And wither like the heads of grain.

25 Surely no one can confute me, Or prove that I am wrong.

25

1 Bildad the Shuhite said in reply:

2 Dominion and dread are His; He imposes peace in His heights.

ham-SHAYL va-FA-khad i-MO o-SEH sha-LOM bim-ro-MAV

3 Can His troops be numbered? On whom does His light not shine?

4 How can man be in the right before *Hashem*? How can one born of woman be cleared of guilt?

5 Even the moon is not bright, And the stars are not pure in His sight.

6 How much less man, a worm, The son-of-man, a maggot.

26

1 Then *Iyov* said in reply:

2 You would help without having the strength; You would deliver with arms that have no power.

meh a-ZAR-ta l'-lo KHO-akh ho-SHA-ta z'-RO-a lo OZ

שמים

25:2 He imposes peace in His heights The words *oseh shalom bimromav* (עשה שלום במרומיו), 'He imposes peace in His heights,' form the first part of a well-known Jewish prayer: "He who imposes peace in His heights, may He make peace upon us and upon all Israel. Now respond: *Amen*." The medieval commentator *Rashi* explains that the word for 'heaven,' *shamayim* (שמים), is derived from the words *aish* (אש), 'fire,' and *mayim* (מים), 'water,' as the two came together in harmony to make up the heavens (Genesis 1:8). This prayer representing hope for peace in this world is recited at the end of the *Amidah*, the central prayer of the Jewish liturgy. At times it seems that just as fire and water cannot coexist, mankind will never be able to live together harmoniously. Nevertheless, we beseech *Hashem* to make peace on earth just He has made peace between fire and water in the heavens.

26:2 You would deliver with arms that have no power *Iyov* acknowledges that while *Bildad*'s intentions are good, in reality his words are of no assistance, since they do not provide any comfort. Though *Bildad* and *Iyov*'s other friends are trying to help, *Iyov* finds their statements very hurtful. It is often difficult to

Iyov/Job
Chapter 27

אִיּוֹב
פרק כו

3 Without having the wisdom, you offer advice And freely give your counsel. ג מַה־יָּעַצְתָּ לְלֹא חָכְמָה וְתוּשִׁיָּה לָרֹב הוֹדָעְתָּ׃

4 To whom have you addressed words? Whose breath issued from you? ד אֶת־מִי הִגַּדְתָּ מִלִּין וְנִשְׁמַת־מִי יָצְאָה מִמֶּךָּ׃

5 The shades tremble Beneath the waters and their denizens. ה הָרְפָאִים יְחוֹלָלוּ מִתַּחַת מַיִם וְשֹׁכְנֵיהֶם׃

6 Sheol is naked before Him; Abaddon has no cover. ו עָרוֹם שְׁאוֹל נֶגְדּוֹ וְאֵין כְּסוּת לָאֲבַדּוֹן׃

7 He it is who stretched out Zaphon over chaos, Who suspended earth over emptiness. ז נֹטֶה צָפוֹן עַל־תֹּהוּ תֹּלֶה אֶרֶץ עַל־בְּלִי־מָה׃

8 He wrapped up the waters in His clouds; Yet no cloud burst under their weight. ח צֹרֵר־מַיִם בְּעָבָיו וְלֹא־נִבְקַע עָנָן תַּחְתָּם׃

9 He shuts off the view of His throne, Spreading His cloud over it. ט מְאַחֵז פְּנֵי־כִסֵּה פַּרְשֵׁז עָלָיו עֲנָנוֹ׃

10 He drew a boundary on the surface of the waters, At the extreme where light and darkness meet. י חֹק־חָג עַל־פְּנֵי־מָיִם עַד־תַּכְלִית אוֹר עִם־חֹשֶׁךְ׃

11 The pillars of heaven tremble, Astounded at His blast. יא עַמּוּדֵי שָׁמַיִם יְרוֹפָפוּ וְיִתְמְהוּ מִגַּעֲרָתוֹ׃

12 By His power He stilled the sea; By His skill He struck down Rahab. יב בְּכֹחוֹ רָגַע הַיָּם ובתבנתו [וּבִתְבוּנָתוֹ] מָחַץ רָהַב׃

13 By His wind the heavens were calmed; His hand pierced the Elusive Serpent. יג בְּרוּחוֹ שָׁמַיִם שִׁפְרָה חֹלְלָה יָדוֹ נָחָשׁ בָּרִיחַ׃

14 These are but glimpses of His rule, The mere whisper that we perceive of Him; Who can absorb the thunder of His mighty deeds? יד הֶן־אֵלֶּה קְצוֹת דרכו [דְּרָכָיו] וּמַה־שֵּׁמֶץ דָּבָר נִשְׁמַע־בּוֹ וְרַעַם גְּבוּרֹתָו [גְּבוּרוֹתָיו] מִי יִתְבּוֹנָן׃

27

1 Iyov again took up his theme and said: א וַיֹּסֶף אִיּוֹב שְׂאֵת מְשָׁלוֹ וַיֹּאמַר׃

2 By Hashem who has deprived me of justice! By Shaddai who has embittered my life! ב חַי־אֵל הֵסִיר מִשְׁפָּטִי וְשַׁדַּי הֵמַר נַפְשִׁי׃

3 As long as there is life in me, And Hashem's breath is in my nostrils, ג כִּי־כָל־עוֹד נִשְׁמָתִי בִי וְרוּחַ אֱלוֹהַּ בְּאַפִּי׃

4 My lips will speak no wrong, Nor my tongue utter deceit. ד אִם־תְּדַבֵּרְנָה שְׂפָתַי עַוְלָה וּלְשׁוֹנִי אִם־יֶהְגֶּה רְמִיָּה׃

---

find the right words to comfort a grieving friend. In Jewish practice, a traditional formula is said when trying to comfort a mourner: "May the Omnipresent comfort you among the mourners of *Tzion* and *Yerushalayim*." Since *Hashem* is the only One who can truly understand the suffering of the individual, and the only One who can really bring comfort, we call upon Him to comfort the mourner. The Hebrew word for 'Omnipresent' is *hamakom* (המקום), which literally means 'the place.' We pray that *Hashem* comforts the mourner, and that the mourner recognize God's presence even in the difficult place in which he currently finds himself.

המקום

Iyov/Job
Chapter 27

אִיוֹב
פרק כז

5 Far be it from me to say you are right; Until I die I will maintain my integrity.
ה חָלִילָה לִּי אִם־אַצְדִּיק אֶתְכֶם עַד־אֶגְוָע לֹא־אָסִיר תֻּמָּתִי מִמֶּנִּי:

6 I persist in my righteousness and will not yield; I shall be free of reproach as long as I live.
ו בְּצִדְקָתִי הֶחֱזַקְתִּי וְלֹא אַרְפֶּהָ לֹא־יֶחֱרַף לְבָבִי מִיָּמָי:

7 May my enemy be as the wicked; My assailant, as the wrongdoer.
ז יְהִי כְרָשָׁע אֹיְבִי וּמִתְקוֹמְמִי כְעַוָּל:

8 For what hope has the impious man when he is cut down, When *Hashem* takes away his life?
ח כִּי מַה־תִּקְוַת חָנֵף כִּי יִבְצָע כִּי יֵשֶׁל אֱלוֹהַּ נַפְשׁוֹ:

9 Will *Hashem* hear his cry When trouble comes upon him,
ט הַצַעֲקָתוֹ יִשְׁמַע אֵל כִּי־תָבוֹא עָלָיו צָרָה:

ha-tza-a-ka-TO yish-MA AYL kee ta-VO a-LAV tza-RAH

10 When he seeks the favor of *Shaddai*, Calls upon *Hashem* at all times?
י אִם־עַל־שַׁדַּי יִתְעַנָּג יִקְרָא אֱלוֹהַּ בְּכָל־עֵת:

11 I will teach you what is in *Hashem*'s power, And what is with *Shaddai* I will not conceal.
יא אוֹרֶה אֶתְכֶם בְּיַד־אֵל אֲשֶׁר עִם־שַׁדַּי לֹא אֲכַחֵד:

12 All of you have seen it, So why talk nonsense?
יב הֵן־אַתֶּם כֻּלְּכֶם חֲזִיתֶם וְלָמָּה־זֶּה הֶבֶל תֶּהְבָּלוּ:

13 This is the evil man's portion from *Hashem*, The lot that the ruthless receive from *Shaddai*:
יג זֶה חֵלֶק־אָדָם רָשָׁע עִם־אֵל וְנַחֲלַת עָרִיצִים מִשַּׁדַּי יִקָּחוּ:

14 Should he have many sons – they are marked for the sword; His descendants will never have their fill of bread;
יד אִם־יִרְבּוּ בָנָיו לְמוֹ־חָרֶב וְצֶאֱצָאָיו לֹא יִשְׂבְּעוּ־לָחֶם:

15 Those who survive him will be buried in a plague, And their widows will not weep;
טו שְׂרִידָיו בַּמָּוֶת יִקָּבֵרוּ וְאַלְמְנֹתָיו לֹא תִבְכֶּינָה:

16 Should he pile up silver like dust, Lay up clothing like dirt –
טז אִם־יִצְבֹּר כֶּעָפָר כָּסֶף וְכַחֹמֶר יָכִין מַלְבּוּשׁ:

17 He may lay it up, but the righteous will wear it, And the innocent will share the silver.
יז יָכִין וְצַדִּיק יִלְבָּשׁ וְכֶסֶף נָקִי יַחֲלֹק:

18 The house he built is like a bird's nest, Like the booth a watchman makes.
יח בָּנָה כָעָשׁ בֵּיתוֹ וּכְסֻכָּה עָשָׂה נֹצֵר:

19 He lies down, a rich man, with [his wealth] intact; When he opens his eyes it is gone.
יט עָשִׁיר יִשְׁכַּב וְלֹא יֵאָסֵף עֵינָיו פָּקַח וְאֵינֶנּוּ:

27:9 Will *Hashem* hear his cry In this chapter, *Iyov* indicates that his colleagues who came to comfort him have instead brought about the opposite effect. Contemporary Bible scholar Amos Hakham explains that *Iyov* is so hurt by his friends that he calls them his enemies. He declares that even *Hashem* will ignore their cries when they call out for help, since in trying to defend God, they have misrepresented Him and also offended their fellow. One must be careful with the words he chooses to comfort those who are grieving, for it is easy to cause pain and distress while intending to console. Sometimes remaining silent, as the friends did for the first seven days they sat with *Iyov*, is really the best response.

Iyov/Job
Chapter 28

20 Terror overtakes him like a flood; A storm wind makes off with him by night.

21 The east wind carries him far away, and he is gone; It sweeps him from his place.

22 Then it hurls itself at him without mercy; He tries to escape from its force.

23 It claps its hands at him, And whistles at him from its place.

28

1 There is a mine for silver, And a place where gold is refined.

2 Iron is taken out of the earth, And copper smelted from rock.

3 He sets bounds for darkness; To every limit man probes, To rocks in deepest darkness.

4 They open up a shaft far from where men live, [In places] forgotten by wayfarers, Destitute of men, far removed.

5 Earth, out of which food grows, Is changed below as if into fire.

6 Its rocks are a source of sapphires; It contains gold dust too.

7 No bird of prey knows the path to it; The falcon's eye has not gazed upon it.

8 The proud beasts have not reached it; The lion has not crossed it.

9 Man sets his hand against the flinty rock And overturns mountains by the roots.

10 He carves out channels through rock; His eyes behold every precious thing.

11 He dams up the sources of the streams So that hidden things may be brought to light.

12 But where can wisdom be found; Where is the source of understanding?

13 No man can set a value on it; It cannot be found in the land of the living.

14 The deep says, "It is not in me"; The sea says, "I do not have it."

15 It cannot be bartered for gold; Silver cannot be paid out as its price.

איוב
פרק כח

כ תַּשִּׂיגֵהוּ כַמַּיִם בַּלָּהוֹת לַיְלָה גְּנָבַתּוּ סוּפָה:

כא יִשָּׂאֵהוּ קָדִים וְיֵלַךְ וִישָׂעֲרֵהוּ מִמְּקֹמוֹ:

כב וְיַשְׁלֵךְ עָלָיו וְלֹא יַחְמֹל מִיָּדוֹ בָּרוֹחַ יִבְרָח:

כג יִשְׂפֹּק עָלֵימוֹ כַפֵּימוֹ וְיִשְׁרֹק עָלָיו מִמְּקֹמוֹ:

כח א כִּי יֵשׁ לַכֶּסֶף מוֹצָא וּמָקוֹם לַזָּהָב יָזֹקּוּ:

ב בַּרְזֶל מֵעָפָר יֻקָּח וְאֶבֶן יָצוּק נְחוּשָׁה:

ג קֵץ שָׂם לַחֹשֶׁךְ וּלְכָל־תַּכְלִית הוּא חוֹקֵר אֶבֶן אֹפֶל וְצַלְמָוֶת:

ד פָּרַץ נַחַל מֵעִם־גָּר הַנִּשְׁכָּחִים מִנִּי־רָגֶל דַּלּוּ מֵאֱנוֹשׁ נָעוּ:

ה אֶרֶץ מִמֶּנָּה יֵצֵא־לָחֶם וְתַחְתֶּיהָ נֶהְפַּךְ כְּמוֹ־אֵשׁ:

ו מְקוֹם־סַפִּיר אֲבָנֶיהָ וְעַפְרֹת זָהָב לוֹ:

ז נָתִיב לֹא־יְדָעוֹ עָיִט וְלֹא שְׁזָפַתּוּ עֵין אַיָּה:

ח לֹא־הִדְרִיכֻהוּ בְנֵי־שָׁחַץ לֹא־עָדָה עָלָיו שָׁחַל:

ט בַּחַלָּמִישׁ שָׁלַח יָדוֹ הָפַךְ מִשֹּׁרֶשׁ הָרִים:

י בַּצּוּרוֹת יְאֹרִים בִּקֵּעַ וְכָל־יְקָר רָאֲתָה עֵינוֹ:

יא מִבְּכִי נְהָרוֹת חִבֵּשׁ וְתַעֲלֻמָהּ יֹצִא אוֹר:

יב וְהַחָכְמָה מֵאַיִן תִּמָּצֵא וְאֵי זֶה מְקוֹם בִּינָה:

יג לֹא־יָדַע אֱנוֹשׁ עֶרְכָּהּ וְלֹא תִמָּצֵא בְּאֶרֶץ הַחַיִּים:

יד תְּהוֹם אָמַר לֹא בִי־הִיא וְיָם אָמַר אֵין עִמָּדִי:

טו לֹא־יֻתַּן סְגוֹר תַּחְתֶּיהָ וְלֹא יִשָּׁקֵל כֶּסֶף מְחִירָהּ:

Iyov/Job
Chapter 28

16 The finest gold of Ophir cannot be weighed against it, Nor precious onyx, nor sapphire.

טז לֹא־תְסֻלֶּה בְּכֶתֶם אוֹפִיר בְּשֹׁהַם יָקָר וְסַפִּיר׃

17 Gold or glass cannot match its value, Nor vessels of fine gold be exchanged for it.

יז לֹא־יַעַרְכֶנָּה זָהָב וּזְכוֹכִית וּתְמוּרָתָהּ כְּלִי־פָז׃

18 Coral and crystal cannot be mentioned with it; A pouch of wisdom is better than rubies.

יח רָאמוֹת וְגָבִישׁ לֹא יִזָּכֵר וּמֶשֶׁךְ חָכְמָה מִפְּנִינִים׃

ra-MOT v'-ga-VEESH LO yi-za-KHAYR u-ME-shekh khokh-MAH mi-p'-nee-NEEM

19 Topaz from Nubia cannot match its value; Pure gold cannot be weighed against it.

יט לֹא־יַעַרְכֶנָּה פִּטְדַת־כּוּשׁ בְּכֶתֶם טָהוֹר לֹא תְסֻלֶּה׃

20 But whence does wisdom come? Where is the source of understanding?

כ וְהַחָכְמָה מֵאַיִן תָּבוֹא וְאֵי זֶה מְקוֹם בִּינָה׃

21 It is hidden from the eyes of all living Concealed from the fowl of heaven.

כא וְנֶעֶלְמָה מֵעֵינֵי כָל־חָי וּמֵעוֹף הַשָּׁמַיִם נִסְתָּרָה׃

22 Abaddon and Death say, "We have only a report of it."

כב אֲבַדּוֹן וָמָוֶת אָמְרוּ בְּאָזְנֵינוּ שָׁמַעְנוּ שִׁמְעָהּ׃

23 *Hashem* understands the way to it; He knows its source;

כג אֱלֹהִים הֵבִין דַּרְכָּהּ וְהוּא יָדַע אֶת־מְקוֹמָהּ׃

24 For He sees to the ends of the earth, Observes all that is beneath the heavens.

כד כִּי־הוּא לִקְצוֹת־הָאָרֶץ יַבִּיט תַּחַת כָּל־הַשָּׁמַיִם יִרְאֶה׃

25 When He fixed the weight of the winds, Set the measure of the waters;

כה לַעֲשׂוֹת לָרוּחַ מִשְׁקָל וּמַיִם תִּכֵּן בְּמִדָּה׃

26 When He made a rule for the rain And a course for the thunderstorms,

כו בַּעֲשׂתוֹ לַמָּטָר חֹק וְדֶרֶךְ לַחֲזִיז קֹלוֹת׃

27 Then He saw it and gauged it; He measured it and probed it.

כז אָז רָאָהּ וַיְסַפְּרָהּ הֱכִינָהּ וְגַם־חֲקָרָהּ׃

28 He said to man, "See! Fear of *Hashem* is wisdom; To shun evil is understanding."

כח וַיֹּאמֶר לָאָדָם הֵן יִרְאַת אֲדֹנָי הִיא חָכְמָה וְסוּר מֵרָע בִּינָה׃

Rubies

28:18 A pouch of wisdom is better than rubies In several places, the Bible uses the ruby as an example of something precious. *Sefer Mishlei* (31:10) describes the worth of the "woman of valor" as "far beyond that of rubies," and in this verse the value of wisdom is described as "better than rubies." Rabbi Menachem Mendel Schneerson, the twentieth century leader of the Chabad-Lubavitch Hasidic movement, once told former Haifa mayor Arie Gurel: "In Haifa, there is a sea. One shouldn't become intimidated by something that is deep. This is the uniqueness of Haifa: It has a sea and there is a valley and in the valley are precious stones and gems. The Holy One, Blessed Be He, did a wondrous thing; He concealed them in the depths of the earth, and in any case, in the depth of the river." Based on that conversation, a company called Shefa Yamim was started for the purpose of searching for precious stones near Haifa. Over the years, Shefa Yamim has discovered diamonds and other precious stones hidden in the Land of Israel, among them rubies.

Iyov/Job
Chapter 29

29 ¹ *Iyov* again took up his theme and said:

² O that I were as in months gone by, In the days when *Hashem* watched over me,

³ When His lamp shone over my head, When I walked in the dark by its light,

⁴ When I was in my prime, When *Hashem*'s company graced my tent,

⁵ When *Shaddai* was still with me, When my lads surrounded me,

⁶ When my feet were bathed in cream, And rocks poured out streams of oil for me.

⁷ When I passed through the city gates To take my seat in the square,

⁸ Young men saw me and hid, Elders rose and stood;

⁹ Nobles held back their words; They clapped their hands to their mouths.

¹⁰ The voices of princes were hushed; Their tongues stuck to their palates.

¹¹ The ear that heard me acclaimed me; The eye that saw, commended me.

¹² For I saved the poor man who cried out, The orphan who had none to help him.

¹³ I received the blessing of the lost; I gladdened the heart of the widow.

¹⁴ I clothed myself in righteousness and it robed me; Justice was my cloak and turban.

¹⁵ I was eyes to the blind And feet to the lame.

¹⁶ I was a father to the needy, And I looked into the case of the stranger.

¹⁷ I broke the jaws of the wrongdoer, And I wrested prey from his teeth.

¹⁸ I thought I would end my days with my family, And be as long-lived as the phoenix,

¹⁹ My roots reaching water, And dew lying on my branches;

²⁰ My vigor refreshed, My bow ever new in my hand.

²¹ Men would listen to me expectantly, And wait for my counsel.

איוב
פרק כט

כט א וַיֹּסֶף אִיּוֹב שְׂאֵת מְשָׁלוֹ וַיֹּאמַר׃

ב מִי־יִתְּנֵנִי כְיַרְחֵי־קֶדֶם כִּימֵי אֱלוֹהַּ יִשְׁמְרֵנִי׃

ג בְּהִלּוֹ נֵרוֹ עֲלֵי רֹאשִׁי לְאוֹרוֹ אֵלֶךְ חֹשֶׁךְ׃

ד כַּאֲשֶׁר הָיִיתִי בִּימֵי חָרְפִּי בְּסוֹד אֱלוֹהַּ עֲלֵי אׇהֳלִי׃

ה בְּעוֹד שַׁדַּי עִמָּדִי סְבִיבוֹתַי נְעָרָי׃

ו בִּרְחֹץ הֲלִיכַי בְּחֵמָה וְצוּר יָצוּק עִמָּדִי פַּלְגֵי־שָׁמֶן׃

ז בְּצֵאתִי שַׁעַר עֲלֵי־קָרֶת בָּרְחוֹב אָכִין מוֹשָׁבִי׃

ח רָאוּנִי נְעָרִים וְנֶחְבָּאוּ וִישִׁישִׁים קָמוּ עָמָדוּ׃

ט שָׂרִים עָצְרוּ בְמִלִּים וְכַף יָשִׂימוּ לְפִיהֶם׃

י קוֹל־נְגִידִים נֶחְבָּאוּ וּלְשׁוֹנָם לְחִכָּם דָּבֵקָה׃

יא כִּי אֹזֶן שָׁמְעָה וַתְּאַשְּׁרֵנִי וְעַיִן רָאֲתָה וַתְּעִידֵנִי׃

יב כִּי־אֲמַלֵּט עָנִי מְשַׁוֵּעַ וְיָתוֹם וְלֹא־עֹזֵר לוֹ׃

יג בִּרְכַּת אֹבֵד עָלַי תָּבֹא וְלֵב אַלְמָנָה אַרְנִן׃

יד צֶדֶק לָבַשְׁתִּי וַיִּלְבָּשֵׁנִי כִּמְעִיל וְצָנִיף מִשְׁפָּטִי׃

טו עֵינַיִם הָיִיתִי לַעִוֵּר וְרַגְלַיִם לַפִּסֵּחַ אָנִי׃

טז אָב אָנֹכִי לָאֶבְיוֹנִים וְרִב לֹא־יָדַעְתִּי אֶחְקְרֵהוּ׃

יז וָאֲשַׁבְּרָה מְתַלְּעוֹת עַוָּל וּמִשִּׁנָּיו אַשְׁלִיךְ טָרֶף׃

יח וָאֹמַר עִם־קִנִּי אֶגְוָע וְכַחוֹל אַרְבֶּה יָמִים׃

יט שׇׁרְשִׁי פָתוּחַ אֱלֵי־מָיִם וְטַל יָלִין בִּקְצִירִי׃

כ כְּבוֹדִי חָדָשׁ עִמָּדִי וְקַשְׁתִּי בְּיָדִי תַחֲלִיף׃

כא לִי־שָׁמְעוּ וְיִחֵלּוּ וְיִדְּמוּ לְמוֹ עֲצָתִי׃

Iyov/Job

Chapter 30

איוב
פרק ל

22 After I spoke they had nothing to say; My words were as drops [of dew] upon them.

כב אַחֲרֵי דְבָרִי לֹא יִשְׁנוּ וְעָלֵימוֹ תִּטֹּף מִלָּתִי׃

23 They waited for me as for rain, For the late rain, their mouths open wide.

כג וְיִחֲלוּ כַמָּטָר לִי וּפִיהֶם פָּעֲרוּ לְמַלְקוֹשׁ׃

24 When I smiled at them, they would not believe it; They never expected a sign of my favor.

כד אֶשְׂחַק אֲלֵהֶם לֹא יַאֲמִינוּ וְאוֹר פָּנַי לֹא יַפִּילוּן׃

25 I decided their course and presided over them; I lived like a king among his troops, Like one who consoles mourners.

כה אֶבֲחַר דַּרְכָּם וְאֵשֵׁב רֹאשׁ וְאֶשְׁכּוֹן כְּמֶלֶךְ בַּגְּדוּד כַּאֲשֶׁר אֲבֵלִים יְנַחֵם׃

ev-KHAR dar-KAM v'-ay-SHAYV ROSH v'-esh-KON k'-ME-lekh ba-g'-DUD ka-a-SHER a-vay-LEEM y'-na-KHAYM

30

1 But now those younger than I deride me, [Men] whose fathers I would have disdained to put among my sheep dogs.

א וְעַתָּה שָׂחֲקוּ עָלַי צְעִירִים מִמֶּנִּי לְיָמִים אֲשֶׁר־מָאַסְתִּי אֲבוֹתָם לָשִׁית עִם־כַּלְבֵי צֹאנִי׃

2 Of what use to me is the strength of their hands? All their vigor is gone.

ב גַּם־כֹּחַ יְדֵיהֶם לָמָּה לִּי עָלֵימוֹ אָבַד כָּלַח׃

3 Wasted from want and starvation, They flee to a parched land, To the gloom of desolate wasteland.

ג בְּחֶסֶר וּבְכָפָן גַּלְמוּד הַעֹרְקִים צִיָּה אֶמֶשׁ שׁוֹאָה וּמְשֹׁאָה׃

4 They pluck saltwort and wormwood; The roots of broom are their food.

ד הַקֹּטְפִים מַלּוּחַ עֲלֵי־שִׂיחַ וְשֹׁרֶשׁ רְתָמִים לַחְמָם׃

5 Driven out from society, They are cried at like a thief.

ה מִן־גֵּו יְגֹרָשׁוּ יָרִיעוּ עָלֵימוֹ כַּגַּנָּב׃

6 They live in the gullies of wadis, In holes in the ground, and in rocks,

ו בַּעֲרוּץ נְחָלִים לִשְׁכֹּן חֹרֵי עָפָר וְכֵפִים׃

7 Braying among the bushes, Huddling among the nettles,

ז בֵּין־שִׂיחִים יִנְהָקוּ תַּחַת חָרוּל יְסֻפָּחוּ׃

8 Scoundrels, nobodies, Stricken from the earth.

ח בְּנֵי־נָבָל גַּם־בְּנֵי בְלִי־שֵׁם נִכְּאוּ מִן־הָאָרֶץ׃

9 Now I am the butt of their gibes; I have become a byword to them.

ט וְעַתָּה נְגִינָתָם הָיִיתִי וָאֱהִי לָהֶם לְמִלָּה׃

10 They abhor me; they keep their distance from me; They do not withhold spittle from my face.

י תִּעֲבוּנִי רָחֲקוּ מֶנִּי וּמִפָּנַי לֹא־חָשְׂכוּ רֹק׃

29:25 I lived like a king among his troops *Iyov* notes that he was able to comfort the mourners and to deal fairly with the poor and widows because he was respected among them. It is relatively easy to be merciful and kind from a high position. Perhaps part of *Iyov*'s test is to learn that his kindness should not be contingent on his feelings of superiority. Compassion and sensitivity to others is built into the nature of the Land of Israel, where the Sabbatical year (*Sh'mitta*) is observed every seven years, to remember and provide for the needy and less fortunate (see Leviticus 25, 6–7).

Iyov/Job
Chapter 30

אִיּוֹב
פרק ל

#	English	Hebrew
11	Because *Hashem* has disarmed and humbled me, They have thrown off restraint in my presence.	יא כִּי־יִתְרוֹ [יִתְרִי] פִּתַּח וַיְעַנֵּנִי וְרֶסֶן מִפָּנַי שִׁלֵּחוּ:
12	Mere striplings assail me at my right hand: They put me to flight; They build their roads for my ruin.	יב עַל־יָמִין פִּרְחַח יָקוּמוּ רַגְלַי שִׁלֵּחוּ וַיָּסֹלּוּ עָלַי אָרְחוֹת אֵידָם:
13	They tear up my path; They promote my fall, Although it does them no good.	יג נָתְסוּ נְתִיבָתִי לְהַוָּתִי יֹעִילוּ לֹא עֹזֵר לָמוֹ:
14	They come as through a wide breach; They roll in like raging billows.	יד כְּפֶרֶץ רָחָב יֶאֱתָיוּ תַּחַת שֹׁאָה הִתְגַּלְגָּלוּ:
15	Terror tumbles upon me; It sweeps away my honor like the wind; My dignity vanishes like a cloud.	טו הָהְפַּךְ עָלַי בַּלָּהוֹת תִּרְדֹּף כָּרוּחַ נְדִבָתִי וּכְעָב עָבְרָה יְשֻׁעָתִי:
16	So now my life runs out; Days of misery have taken hold of me.	טז וְעַתָּה עָלַי תִּשְׁתַּפֵּךְ נַפְשִׁי יֹאחֲזוּנִי יְמֵי־עֹנִי:
17	By night my bones feel gnawed; My sinews never rest.	יז לַיְלָה עֲצָמַי נִקַּר מֵעָלָי וְעֹרְקַי לֹא יִשְׁכָּבוּן:
18	With great effort I change clothing; The neck of my tunic fits my waist.	יח בְּרָב־כֹּחַ יִתְחַפֵּשׂ לְבוּשִׁי כְּפִי כֻתָּנְתִּי יַאַזְרֵנִי:
19	**He regarded me as clay, I have become like dust and ashes.** *ho-RA-nee la-KHO-mer va-et-ma-SHAYL ke-a-FAR va-AY-fer*	יט הֹרָנִי לַחֹמֶר וָאֶתְמַשֵּׁל כֶּעָפָר וָאֵפֶר:
20	I cry out to You, but You do not answer me; I wait, but You do [not] consider me.	כ אֲשַׁוַּע אֵלֶיךָ וְלֹא תַעֲנֵנִי עָמַדְתִּי וַתִּתְבֹּנֶן בִּי:
21	You have become cruel to me; With Your powerful hand You harass me.	כא תֵּהָפֵךְ לְאַכְזָר לִי בְּעֹצֶם יָדְךָ תִשְׂטְמֵנִי:
22	You lift me up and mount me on the wind; You make my courage melt.	כב תִּשָּׂאֵנִי אֶל־רוּחַ תַּרְכִּיבֵנִי וּתְמֹגְגֵנִי תֻּשִׁוָּה [תּוּשִׁיָּה]:
23	I know You will bring me to death, The house assigned for all the living.	כג כִּי־יָדַעְתִּי מָוֶת תְּשִׁיבֵנִי וּבֵית מוֹעֵד לְכָל־חָי:
24	Surely He would not strike at a ruin If, in calamity, one cried out to Him.	כד אַךְ לֹא־בְעִי יִשְׁלַח־יָד אִם־בְּפִידוֹ לָהֶן שׁוּעַ:

30:19 I have become like dust and ashes *Iyov* expresses his modesty with the same words used by *Avraham* when he beseeched *Hashem* to save the cities of Sodom and Gomorrah: "I am but dust and ashes" (Genesis 18:27). Because of *Avraham's* genuine sense of modesty, he is granted the Land of Israel as an eternal inheritance for his descendants. When they follow in the path of their father *Avraham* and carry themselves with humility, the Children of Israel in turn merit living peacefully in the land. However, when they are filled with pride, they stray from *Hashem*, follow other gods and are then punished with exile from the land. *Yeshayahu* declares that during the time of the ultimate redemption, arrogance and pride will be eradicated from among the Children of Israel: "Man's haughty look shall be brought low, And the pride of mortals shall be humbled. None but *Hashem* shall be exalted in that day" (Isaiah 2:11).

Iyov/Job
Chapter 31

איוב
פרק לא

25 Did I not weep for the unfortunate? Did I not grieve for the needy?

כה אִם־לֹא בָכִיתִי לִקְשֵׁה־יוֹם עָגְמָה נַפְשִׁי לָאֶבְיוֹן׃

26 I looked forward to good fortune, but evil came; I hoped for light, but darkness came.

כו כִּי טוֹב קִוִּיתִי וַיָּבֹא רָע וַאֲיַחֲלָה לְאוֹר וַיָּבֹא אֹפֶל׃

27 My bowels are in turmoil without respite; Days of misery confront me.

כז מֵעַי רֻתְּחוּ וְלֹא־דָמּוּ קִדְּמֻנִי יְמֵי־עֹנִי׃

28 I walk about in sunless gloom; I rise in the assembly and cry out.

כח קֹדֵר הִלַּכְתִּי בְּלֹא חַמָּה קַמְתִּי בַקָּהָל אֲשַׁוֵּעַ׃

29 I have become a brother to jackals, A companion to ostriches.

כט אָח הָיִיתִי לְתַנִּים וְרֵעַ לִבְנוֹת יַעֲנָה׃

30 My skin, blackened, is peeling off me; My bones are charred by the heat.

ל עוֹרִי שָׁחַר מֵעָלָי וְעַצְמִי־חָרָה מִנִּי־חֹרֶב׃

31 So my lyre is given over to mourning, My pipe, to accompany weepers.

לא וַיְהִי לְאֵבֶל כִּנֹּרִי וְעֻגָבִי לְקוֹל בֹּכִים׃

31

1 I have covenanted with my eyes Not to gaze on a maiden.

לא א בְּרִית כָּרַתִּי לְעֵינָי וּמָה אֶתְבּוֹנֵן עַל־בְּתוּלָה׃

2 What fate is decreed by *Hashem* above? What lot, by *Shaddai* in the heights?

ב וּמֶה חֵלֶק אֱלוֹהַּ מִמָּעַל וְנַחֲלַת שַׁדַּי מִמְּרֹמִים׃

3 Calamity is surely for the iniquitous; Misfortune, for the worker of mischief.

ג הֲלֹא־אֵיד לְעַוָּל וְנֵכֶר לְפֹעֲלֵי אָוֶן׃

4 Surely He observes my ways, Takes account of my every step.

ד הֲלֹא־הוּא יִרְאֶה דְרָכָי וְכָל־צְעָדַי יִסְפּוֹר׃

5 Have I walked with worthless men, Or my feet hurried to deceit?

ה אִם־הָלַכְתִּי עִם־שָׁוְא וַתַּחַשׁ עַל־מִרְמָה רַגְלִי׃

6 Let Him weigh me on the scale of righteousness; Let *Hashem* ascertain my integrity.

ו יִשְׁקְלֵנִי בְמֹאזְנֵי־צֶדֶק וְיֵדַע אֱלוֹהַּ תֻּמָּתִי׃

7 If my feet have strayed from their course, My heart followed after my eyes, And a stain sullied my hands,

ז אִם תִּטֶּה אַשֻּׁרִי מִנִּי הַדָּרֶךְ וְאַחַר עֵינַי הָלַךְ לִבִּי וּבְכַפַּי דָּבַק מאוּם׃

8 May I sow, but another reap, May the growth of my field be uprooted!

ח אֶזְרְעָה וְאַחֵר יֹאכֵל וְצֶאֱצָאַי יְשֹׁרָשׁוּ׃

9 If my heart was ravished by the wife of my neighbor, And I lay in wait at his door,

ט אִם־נִפְתָּה לִבִּי עַל־אִשָּׁה וְעַל־פֶּתַח רֵעִי אָרָבְתִּי׃

10 May my wife grind for another, May others kneel over her!

י תִּטְחַן לְאַחֵר אִשְׁתִּי וְעָלֶיהָ יִכְרְעוּן אֲחֵרִין׃

11 For that would have been debauchery, A criminal offense,

יא כִּי־הוּא [הִיא] זִמָּה והיא [וְהוּא] עָוֹן פְּלִילִים׃

12 A fire burning down to Abaddon, Consuming the roots of all my increase.

יב כִּי אֵשׁ הִיא עַד־אֲבַדּוֹן תֹּאכֵל וּבְכָל־תְּבוּאָתִי תְשָׁרֵשׁ׃

Iyov/Job
Chapter 31

איוב
פרק לא

13 Did I ever brush aside the case of my servants, man or maid, When they made a complaint against me?

יג אִם־אֶמְאַס מִשְׁפַּט עַבְדִּי וַאֲמָתִי בְּרִבָם עִמָּדִי׃

14 What then should I do when *Hashem* arises; When He calls me to account, what should I answer Him?

יד וּמָה אֶעֱשֶׂה כִּי־יָקוּם אֵל וְכִי־יִפְקֹד מָה אֲשִׁיבֶנּוּ׃

15 Did not He who made me in my mother's belly make him? Did not One form us both in the womb?

טו הֲלֹא־בַבֶּטֶן עֹשֵׂנִי עָשָׂהוּ וַיְכוּנֶנּוּ בָּרֶחֶם אֶחָד׃

16 Did I deny the poor their needs, Or let a widow pine away,

טז אִם־אֶמְנַע מֵחֵפֶץ דַּלִּים וְעֵינֵי אַלְמָנָה אֲכַלֶּה׃

17 By eating my food alone, The fatherless not eating of it also?

יז וְאֹכַל פִּתִּי לְבַדִּי וְלֹא־אָכַל יָתוֹם מִמֶּנָּה׃

18 Why, from my youth he grew up with me as though I were his father; Since I left my mother's womb I was her guide.

יח כִּי מִנְּעוּרַי גְּדֵלַנִי כְאָב וּמִבֶּטֶן אִמִּי אַנְחֶנָּה׃

19 I never saw an unclad wretch, A needy man without clothing,

יט אִם־אֶרְאֶה אוֹבֵד מִבְּלִי לְבוּשׁ וְאֵין כְּסוּת לָאֶבְיוֹן׃

20 Whose loins did not bless me As he warmed himself with the shearings of my sheep.

כ אִם־לֹא בֵרֲכוּנִי חֲלָצָו [חֲלָצָיו] וּמִגֵּז כְּבָשַׂי יִתְחַמָּם׃

21 If I raised my hand against the fatherless, Looking to my supporters in the gate,

כא אִם־הֲנִיפוֹתִי עַל־יָתוֹם יָדִי כִּי־אֶרְאֶה בַשַּׁעַר עֶזְרָתִי׃

22 May my arm drop off my shoulder; My forearm break off at the elbow.

כב כְּתֵפִי מִשִּׁכְמָה תִפּוֹל וְאֶזְרֹעִי מִקָּנָה תִשָּׁבֵר׃

23 For I am in dread of *Hashem*-sent calamity; I cannot bear His threat.

כג כִּי פַחַד אֵלַי אֵיד אֵל וּמִשְּׂאֵתוֹ לֹא אוּכָל׃

24 Did I put my reliance on gold, Or regard fine gold as my bulwark?

כד אִם־שַׂמְתִּי זָהָב כִּסְלִי וְלַכֶּתֶם אָמַרְתִּי מִבְטַחִי׃

25 Did I rejoice in my great wealth, In having attained plenty?

כה אִם־אֶשְׂמַח כִּי־רַב חֵילִי וְכִי־כַבִּיר מָצְאָה יָדִי׃

26 If ever I saw the light shining, The moon on its course in full glory,

כו אִם־אֶרְאֶה אוֹר כִּי יָהֵל וְיָרֵחַ יָקָר הֹלֵךְ׃

27 And I secretly succumbed, And my hand touched my mouth in a kiss,

כז וַיִּפְתְּ בַּסֵּתֶר לִבִּי וַתִּשַּׁק יָדִי לְפִי׃

28 That, too, would have been a criminal offense, For I would have denied *Hashem* above.

כח גַּם־הוּא עָוֹן פְּלִילִי כִּי־כִחַשְׁתִּי לָאֵל מִמָּעַל׃

29 Did I rejoice over my enemy's misfortune? Did I thrill because evil befell him?

כט אִם־אֶשְׂמַח בְּפִיד מְשַׂנְאִי וְהִתְעֹרַרְתִּי כִּי־מְצָאוֹ רָע׃

30 I never let my mouth sin By wishing his death in a curse.

ל וְלֹא־נָתַתִּי לַחֲטֹא חִכִּי לִשְׁאֹל בְּאָלָה נַפְשׁוֹ׃

31 (Indeed, the men of my clan said, "We would consume his flesh insatiably!")

לא אִם־לֹא אָמְרוּ מְתֵי אָהֳלִי מִי־יִתֵּן מִבְּשָׂרוֹ לֹא נִשְׂבָּע׃

1760

Iyov/Job
Chapter 32

32 No sojourner spent the night in the open; I opened my doors to the road.

33 Did I hide my transgressions like *Adam*, Bury my wrongdoing in my bosom,

34 That I should [now] fear the great multitude, And am shattered by the contempt of families, So that I keep silent and do not step outdoors?

35 O that I had someone to give me a hearing; O that *Shaddai* would reply to my writ, Or my accuser draw up a true bill!

36 I would carry it on my shoulder; Tie it around me for a wreath.

37 I would give him an account of my steps, Offer it as to a commander.

38 If my land cries out against me, Its furrows weep together;

39 If I have eaten its produce without payment, And made its [rightful] owners despair,

40 May nettles grow there instead of wheat; Instead of barley, stinkweed! The words of *Iyov* are at an end.

TA-khat khi-TAH yay-TZAY KHO-akh v'-TA-khat s'-o-RAH vo-SHAH TA-mu div-RAY i-YOV

32 1 These three men ceased replying to *Iyov*, for he considered himself right.

2 Then Elihu son of Barachel the Buzite, of the family of *Ram*, was angry – angry at *Iyov* because he thought himself right against *Hashem*.

3 He was angry as well at his three friends, because they found no reply, but merely condemned *Iyov*.

31:40 The words of *Iyov* are at an end These words depict *Iyov*'s exhaustion. After his long peroration lamenting his many misfortunes and speculating as to their possible causes, *Iyov* suddenly gives up. He no longer has the strength to fight or the energy to protest. *Iyov* spends a lot of time and emotional energy trying to make sense of his suffering. Due to his intense suffering, it was difficult for *Iyov* to recognize, as King *Shlomo* did, the truth that "For whom *Hashem* loves, He rebukes" (Proverbs 3:12). Often, suffering is brought upon a person as a mark of God's love, while He abandons those for whom He has no regard to the whims of chance. King *David* also realizes that sometimes suffering is really a gift, when he says "Happy is the man whom You discipline, *Hashem*," (Psalms 94:12). This idea is reflected in a well-known statement by Rabbi Simeon Bar Yochai (*Berachot* 5a): "Three gifts were given by God through suffering; *Torah*, the Land of Israel, and the world to come." The righteous are able to perceive that suffering paves the way to bearing the greatest gifts of God to His people.

Iyov/Job
Chapter 32

איוב
פרק לב

4 Elihu waited out *Iyov*'s speech, for they were all older than he.

ד וֶאֱלִיהוּ חִכָּה אֶת־אִיּוֹב בִּדְבָרִים כִּי זְקֵנִים־הֵמָּה מִמֶּנּוּ לְיָמִים׃

5 But when Elihu saw that the three men had nothing to reply, he was angry.

ה וַיַּרְא אֱלִיהוּא כִּי אֵין מַעֲנֶה בְּפִי שְׁלֹשֶׁת הָאֲנָשִׁים וַיִּחַר אַפּוֹ׃

6 Then Elihu son of Barachel the Buzite said in reply: I have but few years, while you are old; Therefore I was too awestruck and fearful To hold forth among you.

ו וַיַּעַן אֱלִיהוּא בֶן־בַּרַכְאֵל הַבּוּזִי וַיֹּאמַר צָעִיר אֲנִי לְיָמִים וְאַתֶּם יְשִׁישִׁים עַל־כֵּן זָחַלְתִּי וָאִירָא מֵחַוֺּת דֵּעִי אֶתְכֶם׃

va-YA-an e-lee-HU ven ba-rakh-AYL ha-bu-ZEE va-yo-MAR tza-EER a-NEE l'-ya-MEEM v'-a-TEM y'-shee-SHEEM al KAYN za-KHAL-tee va-ee-RA may-kha-VOT day-EE et-KHEM

7 I thought, "Let age speak; Let advanced years declare wise things."

ז אָמַרְתִּי יָמִים יְדַבֵּרוּ וְרֹב שָׁנִים יֹדִיעוּ חָכְמָה׃

8 But truly it is the spirit in men, The breath of *Shaddai*, that gives them understanding.

ח אָכֵן רוּחַ־הִיא בֶאֱנוֹשׁ וְנִשְׁמַת שַׁדַּי תְּבִינֵם׃

9 It is not the aged who are wise, The elders, who understand how to judge.

ט לֹא־רַבִּים יֶחְכָּמוּ וּזְקֵנִים יָבִינוּ מִשְׁפָּט׃

10 Therefore I say, "Listen to me; I too would hold forth."

י לָכֵן אָמַרְתִּי שִׁמְעָה־לִּי אֲחַוֶּה דֵּעִי אַף־אָנִי׃

11 Here I have waited out your speeches, I have given ear to your insights, While you probed the issues;

יא הֵן הוֹחַלְתִּי לְדִבְרֵיכֶם אָזִין עַד־תְּבוּנֹתֵיכֶם עַד־תַּחְקְרוּן מִלִּין׃

12 But as I attended to you, I saw that none of you could argue with *Iyov*, Or offer replies to his statements.

יב וְעָדֵיכֶם אֶתְבּוֹנָן וְהִנֵּה אֵין לְאִיּוֹב מוֹכִיחַ עוֹנֶה אֲמָרָיו מִכֶּם׃

13 I fear you will say, "We have found the wise course; *Hashem* will defeat him, not man."

יג פֶּן־תֹּאמְרוּ מָצָאנוּ חָכְמָה אֵל יִדְּפֶנּוּ לֹא־אִישׁ׃

14 He did not set out his case against me, Nor shall I use your reasons to reply to him.

יד וְלֹא־עָרַךְ אֵלַי מִלִּין וּבְאִמְרֵיכֶם לֹא אֲשִׁיבֶנּוּ׃

15 They have been broken and can no longer reply; Words fail them.

טו חַתּוּ לֹא־עָנוּ עוֹד הֶעְתִּיקוּ מֵהֶם מִלִּים׃

16 I have waited till they stopped speaking, Till they ended and no longer replied.

טז וְהוֹחַלְתִּי כִּי־לֹא יְדַבֵּרוּ כִּי עָמְדוּ לֹא־עָנוּ עוֹד׃

32:6 I have but few years, while you are old By allowing *Iyov*'s other friends to speak first and expressing his own opinion only afterwards, Elihu seems to be giving great respect to his elders. However, we quickly learn that his deference is just a show. Not only does he disagree with the others, but he even scolds them. This lack of concern for appropriate behavior is also clear in his condemnatory and unsympathetic stance towards *Iyov*. However, *Malachi* states that before the ultimate redemption occurs: "He shall reconcile parents with children and children with their parents, so that, when I come, I do not strike the whole land with utter destruction." (3:24). According to the Bible, the way to bring hope and happiness to the world, and to build up the Land of Israel, is by the young honoring their elders, in accordance with the fifth commandment.

Iyov/Job
Chapter 33

17 Now I also would have my say; I too would like to hold forth,

18 For I am full of words; The wind in my belly presses me.

19 My belly is like wine not yet opened, Like jugs of new wine ready to burst.

20 Let me speak, then, and get relief; Let me open my lips and reply.

21 I would not show regard for any man, Or temper my speech for anyone's sake;

22 For I do not know how to temper my speech – My Maker would soon carry me oV!

33 1 But now, *Iyov*, listen to my words, Give ear to all that I say.

2 Now I open my lips; My tongue forms words in my mouth.

3 My words bespeak the uprightness of my heart; My lips utter insight honestly.

4 The spirit of *Hashem* formed me; The breath of *Shaddai* sustains me.

5 If you can, answer me; Argue against me, take your stand.

6 You and I are the same before *Hashem*; I too was nipped from clay.

7 ou are not overwhelmed by fear of me; My pressure does not weigh heavily on you.

8 Indeed, you have stated in my hearing, I heard the words spoken,

9 "I am guiltless, free from transgression; I am innocent, without iniquity.

10 But He finds reasons to oppose me, Considers me His enemy.

11 He puts my feet in stocks, Watches all my ways."

12 In this you are not right; I will answer you: *Hashem* is greater than any man.

13 Why do you complain against Him That He does not reply to any of man's charges?

14 For *Hashem* speaks time and again – Though man does not perceive it –

איוב
פרק לג

יז אַעֲנֶה אַף־אֲנִי חֶלְקִי אֲחַוֶּה דֵעִי אַף־אָנִי׃

יח כִּי מָלֵתִי מִלִּים הֱצִיקַתְנִי רוּחַ בִּטְנִי׃

יט הִנֵּה־בִטְנִי כְּיַיִן לֹא־יִפָּתֵחַ כְּאֹבוֹת חֲדָשִׁים יִבָּקֵעַ׃

כ אֲדַבְּרָה וְיִרְוַח־לִי אֶפְתַּח שְׂפָתַי וְאֶעֱנֶה׃

כא אַל־נָא אֶשָּׂא פְנֵי־אִישׁ וְאֶל־אָדָם לֹא אֲכַנֶּה׃

כב כִּי לֹא יָדַעְתִּי אֲכַנֶּה כִּמְעַט יִשָּׂאֵנִי עֹשֵׂנִי׃

לג א וְאוּלָם שְׁמַע־נָא אִיּוֹב מִלָּי וְכָל־דְּבָרַי הַאֲזִינָה׃

ב הִנֵּה־נָא פָּתַחְתִּי פִי דִּבְּרָה לְשׁוֹנִי בְחִכִּי׃

ג יֹשֶׁר־לִבִּי אֲמָרָי וְדַעַת שְׂפָתַי בָּרוּר מִלֵּלוּ׃

ד רוּחַ־אֵל עָשָׂתְנִי וְנִשְׁמַת שַׁדַּי תְּחַיֵּנִי׃

ה אִם־תּוּכַל הֲשִׁיבֵנִי עֶרְכָה לְפָנַי הִתְיַצָּבָה׃

ו הֵן־אֲנִי כְפִיךָ לָאֵל מֵחֹמֶר קֹרַצְתִּי גַם־אָנִי׃

ז הִנֵּה אֵמָתִי לֹא תְבַעֲתֶךָּ וְאַכְפִּי עָלֶיךָ לֹא־יִכְבָּד׃

ח אַךְ אָמַרְתָּ בְאָזְנָי וְקוֹל מִלִּין אֶשְׁמָע׃

ט זַךְ אֲנִי בְּלִי פָשַׁע חַף אָנֹכִי וְלֹא עָוֺן לִי׃

י הֵן תְּנוּאוֹת עָלַי יִמְצָא יַחְשְׁבֵנִי לְאוֹיֵב לוֹ׃

יא יָשֵׂם בַּסַּד רַגְלָי יִשְׁמֹר כָּל־אָרְחֹתָי׃

יב הֶן־זֹאת לֹא־צָדַקְתָּ אֶעֱנֶךָּ כִּי־יִרְבֶּה אֱלוֹהַּ מֵאֱנוֹשׁ׃

יג מַדּוּעַ אֵלָיו רִיבוֹתָ כִּי כָל־דְּבָרָיו לֹא־יַעֲנֶה׃

יד כִּי־בְאַחַת יְדַבֶּר־אֵל וּבִשְׁתַּיִם לֹא יְשׁוּרֶנָּה׃

Iyov/Job
Chapter 33

איוב
פרק לג

15 In a dream, a night vision, When deep sleep falls on men, While they slumber on their beds.

טו בַּחֲלוֹם חֶזְיוֹן לַיְלָה בִּנְפֹל תַּרְדֵּמָה עַל־אֲנָשִׁים בִּתְנוּמוֹת עֲלֵי מִשְׁכָּב:

16 Then He opens men's understanding, And by disciplining them leaves His signature

טז אָז יִגְלֶה אֹזֶן אֲנָשִׁים וּבְמֹסָרָם יַחְתֹּם:

17 To turn man away from an action, To suppress pride in man.

יז לְהָסִיר אָדָם מַעֲשֶׂה וְגֵוָה מִגֶּבֶר יְכַסֶּה:

18 He spares him from the Pit, His person, from perishing by the sword.

יח יַחְשֹׂךְ נַפְשׁוֹ מִנִּי־שָׁחַת וְחַיָּתוֹ מֵעֲבֹר בַּשָּׁלַח:

19 He is reproved by pains on his bed, And the trembling in his bones is constant.

יט וְהוּכַח בְּמַכְאוֹב עַל־מִשְׁכָּבוֹ וְרִיב [וְרוֹב] עֲצָמָיו אֵתָן:

20 He detests food; Fine food [is repulsive] to him.

כ וְזִהֲמַתּוּ חַיָּתוֹ לָחֶם וְנַפְשׁוֹ מַאֲכַל תַּאֲוָה:

21 His flesh wastes away till it cannot be seen, And his bones are rubbed away till they are invisible.

כא יִכֶל בְּשָׂרוֹ מֵרֹאִי וְשֻׁפִּי [וְשֻׁפּוּ] עַצְמוֹתָיו לֹא רֻאּוּ:

22 He comes close to the Pit, His life [verges] on death.

כב וַתִּקְרַב לַשַּׁחַת נַפְשׁוֹ וְחַיָּתוֹ לַמְמִתִים:

23 If he has a representative, One advocate against a thousand To declare the man's uprightness,

כג אִם־יֵשׁ עָלָיו מַלְאָךְ מֵלִיץ אֶחָד מִנִּי־אָלֶף לְהַגִּיד לְאָדָם יָשְׁרוֹ:

24 Then He has mercy on him and decrees, "Redeem him from descending to the Pit, For I have obtained his ransom;

כד וַיְחֻנֶּנּוּ וַיֹּאמֶר פְּדָעֵהוּ מֵרֶדֶת שָׁחַת מָצָאתִי כֹפֶר:

25 Let his flesh be healthier than in his youth; Let him return to his younger days."

כה רֻטֲפַשׁ בְּשָׂרוֹ מִנֹּעַר יָשׁוּב לִימֵי עֲלוּמָיו:

26 He prays to *Hashem* and is accepted by Him; He enters His presence with shouts of joy, For He requites a man for his righteousness.

כו יֶעְתַּר אֶל־אֱלוֹהַּ וַיִּרְצֵהוּ וַיַּרְא פָּנָיו בִּתְרוּעָה וַיָּשֶׁב לֶאֱנוֹשׁ צִדְקָתוֹ:

27 He declares to men, "I have sinned; I have perverted what was right; But I was not paid back for it."

כז יָשֹׁר עַל־אֲנָשִׁים וַיֹּאמֶר חָטָאתִי וְיָשָׁר הֶעֱוֵיתִי וְלֹא־שָׁוָה לִי:

ya-SHOR al a-na-SHEEM va-YO-mer kha-TA-tee v'-ya-SHAR he-e-VAY-tee v'-lo SHA-vah LEE

33:27 I have sinned In order for a person to be forgiven and his soul to be redeemed (verse 28), he must repent his sins and return from his evil ways. This is true for individuals, and applies equally on a national level. The Bible tells us that after the Children of Israel have sinned and are scattered among the nations of the world, it is through repentance that they will merit redemption and return to their land: "You will return to *Hashem* your God, and you and your children will heed His command… then *Hashem* your God will restore your fortunes and take you back in love… And *Hashem* your God will bring you to the land that your fathers possessed, and you shall possess it" (Deuteronomy 30:2–5). It is through repentance that they will return to the Land of Israel and rebuild the *Beit Hamikdash* in *Yerushalayim*, the spiritual center of the world. Only then will we be able to truly bask in God's glory.

Iyov/Job
Chapter 34

איוב
פרק לד

28 He redeemed him from passing into the Pit; He will enjoy the light.

כח פָּדָה נַפְשִׁי [נַפְשׁוֹ] מֵעֲבֹר בַּשָּׁחַת וְחַיָּתִי [וְחַיָּתוֹ] בָּאוֹר תִּרְאֶה:

29 Truly, *Hashem* does all these things Two or three times to a man,

כט הֶן־כָּל־אֵלֶּה יִפְעַל־אֵל פַּעֲמַיִם שָׁלוֹשׁ עִם־גָּבֶר:

30 To bring him back from the Pit, That he may bask in the light of life.

ל לְהָשִׁיב נַפְשׁוֹ מִנִּי־שָׁחַת לֵאוֹר בְּאוֹר הַחַיִּים:

31 Pay heed, *Iyov*, and hear me; Be still, and I will speak;

לא הַקְשֵׁב אִיּוֹב שְׁמַע־לִי הַחֲרֵשׁ וְאָנֹכִי אֲדַבֵּר:

32 If you have what to say, answer me; Speak, for I am eager to vindicate you.

לב אִם־יֵשׁ־מִלִּין הֲשִׁיבֵנִי דַּבֵּר כִּי־חָפַצְתִּי צַדְּקֶךָּ:

33 But if not, you listen to me; Be still, and I will teach you wisdom.

לג אִם־אַיִן אַתָּה שְׁמַע־לִי הַחֲרֵשׁ וַאֲאַלֶּפְךָ חָכְמָה:

34 1 Elihu said in reply:

לד א וַיַּעַן אֱלִיהוּא וַיֹּאמַר:

2 Listen, O wise men, to my words; You who have knowledge, give ear to me.

ב שִׁמְעוּ חֲכָמִים מִלָּי וְיֹדְעִים הַאֲזִינוּ לִי:

shim-U kha-kha-MEEM mi-LAI v'-yo-d'-EEM ha-a-ZEE-nu LEE

3 For the ear tests arguments As the palate tastes food.

ג כִּי־אֹזֶן מִלִּין תִּבְחָן וְחֵךְ יִטְעַם לֶאֱכֹל:

4 Let us decide for ourselves what is just; Let us know among ourselves what is good.

ד מִשְׁפָּט נִבְחֲרָה־לָּנוּ נֵדְעָה בֵינֵינוּ מַה־טּוֹב:

5 For *Iyov* has said, "I am right; *Hashem* has deprived me of justice.

ה כִּי־אָמַר אִיּוֹב צָדַקְתִּי וְאֵל הֵסִיר מִשְׁפָּטִי:

6 I declare the judgment against me false; My arrow-wound is deadly, though I am free from transgression."

ו עַל־מִשְׁפָּטִי אֲכַזֵּב אָנוּשׁ חִצִּי בְלִי־פָשַׁע:

7 What man is like *Iyov*, Who drinks mockery like water;

ז מִי־גֶבֶר כְּאִיּוֹב יִשְׁתֶּה־לַּעַג כַּמָּיִם:

8 Who makes common cause with evildoers, And goes with wicked men?

ח וְאָרַח לְחֶבְרָה עִם־פֹּעֲלֵי אָוֶן וְלָלֶכֶת עִם־אַנְשֵׁי־רֶשַׁע:

9 For he says, "Man gains nothing When he is in *Hashem*'s favor."

ט כִּי־אָמַר לֹא יִסְכָּן־גָּבֶר בִּרְצֹתוֹ עִם־אֱלֹהִים:

34:2 Listen, O wise men, to my words Elihu calls on the wise men and those who have knowledge to 'listen' or 'hear', and also to 'give ear'. This pair of synonyms appear together in a number of places in the Bible, most prominently in *Sefer Devarim* 32:1. That verse introduces a song in which *Hashem* calls on heaven and earth to be the eternal witnesses to the covenant He has made with the Jewish people. If Israel follows His commandments, they will live peacefully in the land. If, however, they over-indulge, become morally corrupt and abandon the Lord, they will be sent into exile. The prophet *Yeshayahu* also calls on heaven and earth with these same words (Isaiah 1:2).

Iyov/Job
Chapter 34

10 Therefore, men of understanding, listen to me; Wickedness be far from *Hashem*, Wrongdoing, from *Shaddai*!

11 For He pays a man according to his actions, And provides for him according to his conduct;

12 For *Hashem* surely does not act wickedly; *Shaddai* does not pervert justice.

13 Who placed the earth in His charge? Who ordered the entire world?

14 If He but intends it, He can call back His spirit and breath;

15 All flesh would at once expire, And mankind return to dust.

16 If you would understand, listen to this; Give ear to what I say.

17 Would one who hates justice govern? Would you condemn the Just Mighty One?

18 Would you call a king a scoundrel, Great men, wicked?

19 He is not partial to princes; The noble are not preferred to the wretched; For all of them are the work of His hands.

20 Some die suddenly in the middle of the night; People are in turmoil and pass on; Even great men are removed – not by human hands.

21 For His eyes are upon a man's ways; He observes his every step.

22 Neither darkness nor gloom offers A hiding-place for evildoers.

23 He has no set time for man To appear before *Hashem* in judgment.

24 He shatters mighty men without number And sets others in their place.

25 Truly, He knows their deeds; Night is over, and they are crushed.

26 He strikes them down with the wicked Where people can see,

27 Because they have been disloyal to Him And have not understood any of His ways;

איוב
פרק לד

י לָכֵן אַנְשֵׁי לֵבָב שִׁמְעוּ לִי חָלִלָה לָאֵל מֵרֶשַׁע וְשַׁדַּי מֵעָוֶל׃

יא כִּי פֹעַל אָדָם יְשַׁלֶּם־לוֹ וּכְאֹרַח אִישׁ יַמְצִאֶנּוּ׃

יב אַף־אָמְנָם אֵל לֹא־יַרְשִׁיעַ וְשַׁדַּי לֹא־יְעַוֵּת מִשְׁפָּט׃

יג מִי־פָקַד עָלָיו אָרְצָה וּמִי שָׂם תֵּבֵל כֻּלָּהּ׃

יד אִם־יָשִׂים אֵלָיו לִבּוֹ רוּחוֹ וְנִשְׁמָתוֹ אֵלָיו יֶאֱסֹף׃

טו יִגְוַע כָּל־בָּשָׂר יָחַד וְאָדָם עַל־עָפָר יָשׁוּב׃

טז וְאִם־בִּינָה שִׁמְעָה־זֹּאת הַאֲזִינָה לְקוֹל מִלָּי׃

יז הַאַף שׂוֹנֵא מִשְׁפָּט יַחֲבוֹשׁ וְאִם־צַדִּיק כַּבִּיר תַּרְשִׁיעַ׃

יח הַאֲמֹר לְמֶלֶךְ בְּלִיָּעַל רָשָׁע אֶל־נְדִיבִים׃

יט אֲשֶׁר לֹא־נָשָׂא פְּנֵי שָׂרִים וְלֹא נִכַּר־שׁוֹעַ לִפְנֵי־דָל כִּי־מַעֲשֵׂה יָדָיו כֻּלָּם׃

כ רֶגַע יָמֻתוּ וַחֲצוֹת לָיְלָה יְגֹעֲשׁוּ עָם וְיַעֲבֹרוּ וְיָסִירוּ אַבִּיר לֹא בְיָד׃

כא כִּי־עֵינָיו עַל־דַּרְכֵי־אִישׁ וְכָל־צְעָדָיו יִרְאֶה׃

כב אֵין־חֹשֶׁךְ וְאֵין צַלְמָוֶת לְהִסָּתֶר שָׁם פֹּעֲלֵי אָוֶן׃

כג כִּי לֹא עַל־אִישׁ יָשִׂים עוֹד לַהֲלֹךְ אֶל־אֵל בַּמִּשְׁפָּט׃

כד יָרֹעַ כַּבִּירִים לֹא־חֵקֶר וַיַּעֲמֵד אֲחֵרִים תַּחְתָּם׃

כה לָכֵן יַכִּיר מַעְבָּדֵיהֶם וְהָפַךְ לַיְלָה וְיִדַּכָּאוּ׃

כו תַּחַת־רְשָׁעִים סְפָקָם בִּמְקוֹם רֹאִים׃

כז אֲשֶׁר עַל־כֵּן סָרוּ מֵאַחֲרָיו וְכָל־דְּרָכָיו לֹא הִשְׂכִּילוּ׃

Iyov/Job
Chapter 35

28 Thus He lets the cry of the poor come before Him; He listens to the cry of the needy.

29 When He is silent, who will condemn? If He hides His face, who will see Him, Be it nation or man?

30 The impious man rule no more, Nor do those who ensnare the people.

31 Has he said to *Hashem*, "I will bear [my punishment] and offend no more.

32 What I cannot see You teach me. If I have done iniquity, I shall not do so again"?

33 Should He requite as you see fit? But you have despised [Him]! You must decide, not I; Speak what you know.

34 Men of understanding say to me, Wise men who hear me,

35 "*Iyov* does not speak with knowledge; His words lack understanding."

36 Would that *Iyov* were tried to the limit For answers which befit sinful men.

37 He adds to his sin; He increases his transgression among us; He multiplies his statements against *Hashem*.

35

1 Elihu said in reply:

2 Do you think it just To say, "I am right against *Hashem*"?

3 If you ask how it benefits you, "What have I gained from not sinning?"

4 I shall give you a reply, You, along with your friends.

5 Behold the heavens and see; Look at the skies high above you.

6 If you sin, what do you do to Him? If your transgressions are many, How do you affect Him?

7 If you are righteous, What do you give Him; What does He receive from your hand?

8 Your wickedness affects men like yourself; Your righteousness, mortals.

9 Because of contention the oppressed cry out; They shout because of the power of the great.

Iyov/Job
Chapter 36

10 But none says, "Where is my God, my Maker, Who gives strength in the night;

v'-LO a-MAR a-YAY e-LO-ah o-SAI no-TAYN z'-mee-ROT ba-LAI-lah

וְלֹא־אָמַר אַיֵּה אֱלוֹהַּ עֹשָׂי נֹתֵן זְמִרוֹת בַּלָּיְלָה:

11 Who gives us more knowledge than the beasts of the earth, Makes us wiser than the birds of the sky?"

מַלְּפֵנוּ מִבַּהֲמוֹת אָרֶץ וּמֵעוֹף הַשָּׁמַיִם יְחַכְּמֵנוּ:

12 Then they cry out, but He does not respond Because of the arrogance of evil men.

שָׁם יִצְעֲקוּ וְלֹא יַעֲנֶה מִפְּנֵי גְאוֹן רָעִים:

13 Surely it is false that *Hashem* does not listen, That *Shaddai* does not take note of it.

אַךְ־שָׁוְא לֹא־יִשְׁמַע אֵל וְשַׁדַּי לֹא יְשׁוּרֶנָּה:

14 Though you say, "You do not take note of it," The case is before Him; So wait for Him.

אַף כִּי־תֹאמַר לֹא תְשׁוּרֶנּוּ דִּין לְפָנָיו וּתְחוֹלֵל לוֹ:

15 But since now it does not seem so, He vents his anger; He does not realize that it may be long drawn out.

וְעַתָּה כִּי־אַיִן פָּקַד אַפּוֹ וְלֹא־יָדַע בַּפַּשׁ מְאֹד:

16 Hence *Iyov* mouths empty words, And piles up words without knowledge.

וְאִיּוֹב הֶבֶל יִפְצֶה־פִּיהוּ בִּבְלִי־דַעַת מִלִּין יַכְבִּר:

36

1 Then Elihu spoke once more.

וַיֹּסֶף אֱלִיהוּא וַיֹּאמַר:

2 Wait a little and let me hold forth; There is still more to say for *Hashem*.

כַּתַּר־לִי זְעֵיר וַאֲחַוֶּךָּ כִּי עוֹד לֶאֱלוֹהַּ מִלִּים:

3 I will make my opinions widely known; I will justify my Maker.

אֶשָּׂא דֵעִי לְמֵרָחוֹק וּלְפֹעֲלִי אֶתֵּן־צֶדֶק:

4 In truth, my words are not false; A man of sound opinions is before you.

כִּי־אָמְנָם לֹא־שֶׁקֶר מִלָּי תְּמִים דֵּעוֹת עִמָּךְ:

5 See, *Hashem* is mighty; He is not contemptuous; He is mighty in strength and mind.

הֶן־אֵל כַּבִּיר וְלֹא יִמְאָס כַּבִּיר כֹּחַ לֵב:

6 He does not let the wicked live; He grants justice to the lowly.

לֹא־יְחַיֶּה רָשָׁע וּמִשְׁפַּט עֲנִיִּים יִתֵּן:

7 He does not withdraw His eyes from the righteous; With kings on thrones He seats them forever, and they are exalted.

לֹא־יִגְרַע מִצַּדִּיק עֵינָיו וְאֶת־מְלָכִים לַכִּסֵּא וַיֹּשִׁיבֵם לָנֶצַח וַיִּגְבָּהוּ:

א 35:10 Who gives strength in the night The Hebrew word for 'strength' in this verse is *zemirot* (זמירות). This word generally means 'songs', but its root (ז-מ-ר) also has another meaning: To prune a tree and remove its extraneous branches. The connection between these words is not initially obvious, but as the "mother of all languages," Hebrew words often get to the very essence of the object they are describing. A tree thrives when its heavy branches and extraneous foliage are clipped, so that it can most effectively apply its nutritional resources. Though it may seem that cutting a tree weakens it, this process actually strengthens it. Similarly, music is not merely a collection of randomly collected notes. To be left with a beautiful song, one must "prune" extraneous sounds. This same principle can be applied to our lives; in order to properly strengthen ourselves and transform our entire existence into holy song, we must remove the burdensome elements of our character.

זמר

Iyov/Job
Chapter 36

איוב
פרק לו

8 If they are bound in shackles And caught in trammels of affliction,	ח וְאִם־אֲסוּרִים בַּזִּקִּים יִלָּכְדוּן בְּחַבְלֵי־עֹֽנִי:
9 He declares to them what they have done, And that their transgressions are excessive;	ט וַיַּגֵּד לָהֶם פָּעֳלָם וּפִשְׁעֵיהֶם כִּי יִתְגַּבָּֽרוּ:
10 He opens their understanding by discipline, And orders them back from mischief.	י וַיִּגֶל אָזְנָם לַמּוּסָר וַיֹּאמֶר כִּי־יְשֻׁבוּן מֵאָֽוֶן:
11 If they will serve obediently, They shall spend their days in happiness, Their years in delight.	יא אִֽם־יִשְׁמְעוּ וְיַעֲבֹדוּ יְכַלּוּ יְמֵיהֶם בַּטּוֹב וּשְׁנֵיהֶם בַּנְּעִימִֽים:
12 But if they are not obedient, They shall perish by the sword, Die for lack of understanding.	יב וְאִם־לֹא יִשְׁמְעוּ בְּשֶׁלַח יַעֲבֹרוּ וְיִגְוְעוּ כִּבְלִי־דָֽעַת:
13 But the impious in heart become enraged; They do not cry for help when He afflicts them.	יג וְֽחַנְפֵי־לֵב יָשִׂימוּ אָף לֹא יְשַׁוְּעוּ כִּי אֲסָרָֽם:
14 They die in their youth; [Expire] among the depraved.	יד תָּמֹת בַּנֹּעַר נַפְשָׁם וְחַיָּתָם בַּקְּדֵשִֽׁים:
15 He rescues the lowly from their affliction, And opens their understanding through distress.	טו יְחַלֵּץ עָנִי בְעָנְיוֹ וְיִגֶל בַּלַּחַץ אָזְנָֽם:
16 Indeed, He draws you away from the brink of distress To a broad place where there is no constraint; Your table is laid out with rich food.	טז וְאַף הֲסִיתְךָ מִפִּי־צָר רַחַב לֹא־מוּצָק תַּחְתֶּיהָ וְנַחַת שֻׁלְחָנְךָ מָלֵא דָֽשֶׁן:
17 You are obsessed with the case of the wicked man, But the justice of the case will be upheld.	יז וְדִין־רָשָׁע מָלֵאתָ דִּין וּמִשְׁפָּט יִתְמֹֽכוּ:
18 Let anger at his affluence not mislead you; Let much bribery not turn you aside.	יח כִּי־חֵמָה פֶּן־יְסִיתְךָ בְסָפֶק וְרָב־כֹּפֶר אַל־יַטֶּֽךָּ:
19 Will your limitless wealth avail you, All your powerful efforts?	יט הֲיַעֲרֹךְ שׁוּעֲךָ לֹא בְצָר וְכֹל מַאֲמַצֵּי־כֹֽחַ:
20 Do not long for the night When peoples vanish where they are.	כ אַל־תִּשְׁאַף הַלָּיְלָה לַעֲלוֹת עַמִּים תַּחְתָּֽם:
21 Beware! Do not turn to mischief; Because of that you have been tried by affliction.	כא הִשָּׁמֶר אַל־תֵּפֶן אֶל־אָוֶן כִּי־עַל־זֶה בָּחַרְתָּ מֵעֹֽנִי:
22 See, *Hashem* is beyond reach in His power; Who governs like Him?	כב הֶן־אֵל יַשְׂגִּיב בְּכֹחוֹ מִי כָמֹהוּ מוֹרֶֽה:
23 Who ever reproached Him for His conduct? Who ever said, "You have done wrong"?	כג מִֽי־פָקַד עָלָיו דַּרְכּוֹ וּמִֽי־אָמַר פָּעַלְתָּ עַוְלָֽה:
24 Remember, then, to magnify His work, Of which men have sung,	כד זְכֹר כִּי־תַשְׂגִּיא פָעֳלוֹ אֲשֶׁר שֹׁרְרוּ אֲנָשִֽׁים:
25 Which all men have beheld, Men have seen, from a distance.	כה כָּל־אָדָם חָזוּ־בוֹ אֱנוֹשׁ יַבִּיט מֵרָחֽוֹק:
26 See, *Hashem* is greater than we can know; The number of His years cannot be counted.	כו הֶן־אֵל שַׂגִּיא וְלֹא נֵדָע מִסְפַּר שָׁנָיו וְלֹא־חֵֽקֶר:

Iyov/Job
Chapter 37

איוב
פרק לז

#	English	Hebrew
27	He forms the droplets of water, Which cluster into rain, from His mist.	כִּי יְגָרַע נִטְפֵי־מָיִם יָזֹקּוּ מָטָר לְאֵדוֹ: כז
28	The skies rain; They pour down on all mankind.	אֲשֶׁר־יִזְּלוּ שְׁחָקִים יִרְעֲפוּ עֲלֵי אָדָם רָב: כח
29	Can one, indeed, contemplate the expanse of clouds, The thunderings from His pavilion?	אַף אִם־יָבִין מִפְרְשֵׂי־עָב תְּשֻׁאוֹת סֻכָּתוֹ: כט
30	See, He spreads His lightning over it; It fills the bed of the sea.	הֵן־פָּרַשׂ עָלָיו אוֹרוֹ וְשָׁרְשֵׁי הַיָּם כִּסָּה: ל
31	By these things He controls peoples; He gives food in abundance.	כִּי־בָם יָדִין עַמִּים יִתֶּן־אֹכֶל לְמַכְבִּיר: לא

kee VAM ya-DEEN a-MEEM yi-TEN O-khel l'-makh-BEER

| 32 | Lightning fills His hands; He orders it to hit the mark. | עַל־כַּפַּיִם כִּסָּה־אוֹר וַיְצַו עָלֶיהָ בְמַפְגִּיעַ: לב |
| 33 | Its noise tells of Him. The kindling of anger against iniquity. | יַגִּיד עָלָיו רֵעוֹ מִקְנֶה אַף עַל־עוֹלֶה: לג |

37

1	Because of this, too, my heart quakes, And leaps from its place.	אַף־לְזֹאת יֶחֱרַד לִבִּי וְיִתַּר מִמְּקוֹמוֹ: א לז
2	Just listen to the noise of His rumbling, To the sound that comes out of His mouth.	שִׁמְעוּ שָׁמוֹעַ בְּרֹגֶז קֹלוֹ וְהֶגֶה מִפִּיו יֵצֵא: ב
3	He lets it loose beneath the entire heavens – His lightning, to the ends of the earth.	תַּחַת־כָּל־הַשָּׁמַיִם יִשְׁרֵהוּ וְאוֹרוֹ עַל־כַּנְפוֹת הָאָרֶץ: ג
4	After it, He lets out a roar; He thunders in His majestic voice. No one can find a trace of it by the time His voice is heard.	אַחֲרָיו יִשְׁאַג־קוֹל יַרְעֵם בְּקוֹל גְּאוֹנוֹ וְלֹא יְעַקְּבֵם כִּי־יִשָּׁמַע קוֹלוֹ: ד

a-kha-RAV yish-AG KOL yar-AYM b'-KOL g'-o-NO v'-LO y'-ak-VAYM kee yi-sha-MA ko-LO

| 5 | *Hashem* thunders marvelously with His voice; He works wonders that we cannot understand. | יַרְעֵם אֵל בְּקוֹלוֹ נִפְלָאוֹת עֹשֶׂה גְדֹלוֹת וְלֹא נֵדָע: ה |

36:31 He gives food in abundance *Hashem* uses His control over nature to punish people and to reward them. If He judges mankind favorably, then He will provide "food in abundance." This is especially true in the Land of Israel, as expressed in *Sefer Devarim* (11:13–17). God says that if the Children of Israel perform good deeds and follow His commands, He will reward them with rain at the proper times, which will produce bountiful crops. Conversely, drought and famine are the punishments for national sin. It is important to recognize that while rain and drought are seemingly natural phenomena, they are actually *Hashem*'s vehicle for reward and punishment, and for communicating with His children.

37:4 After it, He lets out a roar In this verse, the majestic voice of God roars, proclaiming His justice and goodness to all creatures. The Divine voice is often described in the Bible as a roar, frequently as an expression of His anger. In ancient Israel, lions were commonly found in the forested areas of the country. The lion is therefore often used as a metaphor in the Bible. Though the lion's roar is frightening, it serves as a warning to its prey that the lion is present, and clever prey can escape. So too, God communicates with His children to warn them to correct their ways before it is too late.

Iyov/Job
Chapter 37

6 He commands the snow, "Fall to the ground!" And the downpour of rain, His mighty downpour of rain,

7 Is as a sign on every man's hand, That all men may know His doings.

8 Then the beast enters its lair, And remains in its den.

9 The storm wind comes from its chamber, And the cold from the constellations.

10 By the breath of *Hashem* ice is formed, And the expanse of water becomes solid.

11 He also loads the clouds with moisture And scatters His lightning-clouds.

12 He keeps turning events by His stratagems, That they might accomplish all that He commands them Throughout the inhabited earth,

13 Causing each of them to happen to His land, Whether as a scourge or as a blessing.

14 Give ear to this, *Iyov*; Stop to consider the marvels of *Hashem*.

15 Do you know what charge *Hashem* lays upon them When His lightning-clouds shine?

16 Do you know the marvels worked upon the expanse of clouds By Him whose understanding is perfect,

17 Why your clothes become hot When the land is becalmed by the south wind?

18 Can you help him stretch out the heavens, Firm as a mirror of cast metal?

19 Inform us, then, what we may say to Him; We cannot argue because [we are in] darkness.

20 Is anything conveyed to Him when I speak? Can a man say anything when he is confused?

21 Now, then, one cannot see the sun, Though it be bright in the heavens, Until the wind comes and clears them [of clouds].

22 By the north wind the golden rays emerge; The splendor about *Hashem* is awesome.

23 Shaddai — we cannot attain to Him; He is great in power and justice And abundant in righteousness; He does not torment.

איוב
פרק לז

ו כִּי לַשֶּׁלַג ׀ יֹאמַר הֱוֵא אָרֶץ וְגֶשֶׁם מָטָר וְגֶשֶׁם מִטְרוֹת עֻזּוֹ:

ז בְּיַד־כָּל־אָדָם יַחְתּוֹם לָדַעַת כָּל־אַנְשֵׁי מַעֲשֵׂהוּ:

ח וַתָּבֹא חַיָּה בְמוֹ־אָרֶב וּבִמְעוֹנֹתֶיהָ תִשְׁכֹּן:

ט מִן־הַחֶדֶר תָּבוֹא סוּפָה וּמִמְּזָרִים קָרָה:

י מִנִּשְׁמַת־אֵל יִתֶּן־קָרַח וְרֹחַב מַיִם בְּמוּצָק:

יא אַף־בְּרִי יַטְרִיחַ עָב יָפִיץ עֲנַן אוֹרוֹ:

יב וְהוּא מְסִבּוֹת ׀ מִתְהַפֵּךְ בתחבולתו [בְּתַחְבּוּלֹתָיו] לְפָעֳלָם כֹּל אֲשֶׁר יְצַוֵּם ׀ עַל־פְּנֵי תֵבֵל אָרְצָה:

יג אִם־לְשֵׁבֶט אִם־לְאַרְצוֹ אִם־לְחֶסֶד יַמְצִאֵהוּ:

יד הַאֲזִינָה זֹּאת אִיּוֹב עֲמֹד וְהִתְבּוֹנֵן ׀ נִפְלְאוֹת אֵל:

טו הֲתֵדַע בְּשׂוּם־אֱלוֹהַּ עֲלֵיהֶם וְהוֹפִיעַ אוֹר עֲנָנוֹ:

טז הֲתֵדַע עַל־מִפְלְשֵׂי־עָב מִפְלְאוֹת תְּמִים דֵּעִים:

יז אֲשֶׁר־בְּגָדֶיךָ חַמִּים בְּהַשְׁקִט אֶרֶץ מִדָּרוֹם:

יח תַּרְקִיעַ עִמּוֹ לִשְׁחָקִים חֲזָקִים כִּרְאִי מוּצָק:

יט הוֹדִיעֵנוּ מַה־נֹּאמַר לוֹ לֹא־נַעֲרֹךְ מִפְּנֵי־חֹשֶׁךְ:

כ הַיְסֻפַּר־לוֹ כִּי אֲדַבֵּר אִם־אָמַר אִישׁ כִּי יְבֻלָּע:

כא וְעַתָּה ׀ לֹא רָאוּ אוֹר בָּהִיר הוּא בַּשְּׁחָקִים וְרוּחַ עָבְרָה וַתְּטַהֲרֵם:

כב מִצָּפוֹן זָהָב יֶאֱתֶה עַל־אֱלוֹהַּ נוֹרָא הוֹד:

כג שַׁדַּי לֹא־מְצָאנֻהוּ שַׂגִּיא־כֹחַ וּמִשְׁפָּט וְרֹב־צְדָקָה לֹא יְעַנֶּה:

Iyov/Job
Chapter 38

איוב
פרק לח

24 Therefore, men are in awe of Him Whom none of the wise can perceive.

כד לָכֵן יְרֵאוּהוּ אֲנָשִׁים לֹא־יִרְאֶה כָּל־חַכְמֵי־לֵב׃

38 1 Then *Hashem* replied to *Iyov* out of the tempest and said:

לח א וַיַּעַן־יְהֹוָה אֶת־אִיּוֹב מִן [מִן] [הַסְּעָרָה] וַיֹּאמַר׃

2 Who is this who darkens counsel, Speaking without knowledge?

ב מִי זֶה מַחְשִׁיךְ עֵצָה בְמִלִּין בְּלִי־דָעַת׃

3 Gird your loins like a man; I will ask and you will inform Me.

ג אֱזָר־נָא כְגֶבֶר חֲלָצֶיךָ וְאֶשְׁאָלְךָ וְהוֹדִיעֵנִי׃

4 Where were you when I laid the earth's foundations? Speak if you have understanding.

ד אֵיפֹה הָיִיתָ בְּיָסְדִי־אָרֶץ הַגֵּד אִם־יָדַעְתָּ בִינָה׃

ay-FOH ha-YEE-ta b'-yos-DEE A-retz ha-GAYD im ya-DA-ta vee-NAH

5 Do you know who fixed its dimensions Or who measured it with a line?

ה מִי־שָׂם מְמַדֶּיהָ כִּי תֵדָע אוֹ מִי־נָטָה עָלֶיהָ קָּו׃

6 Onto what were its bases sunk? Who set its cornerstone

ו עַל־מָה אֲדָנֶיהָ הָטְבָּעוּ אוֹ מִי־יָרָה אֶבֶן פִּנָּתָהּ׃

7 When the morning stars sang together And all the divine beings shouted for joy?

ז בְּרָן־יַחַד כּוֹכְבֵי בֹקֶר וַיָּרִיעוּ כָּל־בְּנֵי אֱלֹהִים׃

8 Who closed the sea behind doors When it gushed forth out of the womb,

ח וַיָּסֶךְ בִּדְלָתַיִם יָם בְּגִיחוֹ מֵרֶחֶם יֵצֵא׃

9 When I clothed it in clouds, Swaddled it in dense clouds,

ט בְּשׂוּמִי עָנָן לְבֻשׁוֹ וַעֲרָפֶל חֲתֻלָּתוֹ׃

10 When I made breakers My limit for it, And set up its bar and doors,

י וָאֶשְׁבֹּר עָלָיו חֻקִּי וָאָשִׂים בְּרִיחַ וּדְלָתָיִם׃

11 And said, "You may come so far and no farther; Here your surging waves will stop"?

יא וָאֹמַר עַד־פֹּה תָבוֹא וְלֹא תֹסִיף וּפֹא־יָשִׁית בִּגְאוֹן גַּלֶּיךָ׃

12 Have you ever commanded the day to break, Assigned the dawn its place,

יב הְמִיָּמֶיךָ צִוִּיתָ בֹּקֶר יִדַּעְתָּה שַׁחַר [יְדַעְתָּה] [הַשַּׁחַר] מְקֹמוֹ׃

13 So that it seizes the corners of the earth And shakes the wicked out of it?

יג לֶאֱחֹז בְּכַנְפוֹת הָאָרֶץ וְיִנָּעֲרוּ רְשָׁעִים מִמֶּנָּה׃

38:4 Where were you when I laid the earth's foundations? In this chapter, *Hashem* finally responds to *Iyov's* questioning of His justice. He says that since *Iyov* was not around when God created the world, he cannot possibly understand the way in which He runs the world. Rabbi Judah Halevi, in his book *The Kuzari*, suggests that precisely because man was not around to witness the creation of the world, *Hashem* introduces Himself in the first of the ten commandments as the God who took the Children of Israel out of Egypt, rather than the God who created the world (Exodus 20:2). The people could not relate to God as creator, since they did not explicitly know him as such. However, the Exodus, which was experienced by the entire Nation of Israel, proved God's existence to them beyond a shadow of a doubt. Furthermore, *Ramban* explains that *Hashem's* manipulation of nature during the Exodus proves that He is indeed the Creator of the natural order of the world, and that He continues to be involved in the running of the world and the lives of His people.

Rabbi Judah Halevi (1075–1141)

Iyov/Job
Chapter 38

14	It changes like clay under the seal Till [its hues] are fixed like those of a garment.	יד תִּתְהַפֵּךְ כְּחֹמֶר חוֹתָם וְיִתְיַצְּבוּ כְּמוֹ לְבוּשׁ:
15	Their light is withheld from the wicked, And the upraised arm is broken.	טו וְיִמָּנַע מֵרְשָׁעִים אוֹרָם וּזְרוֹעַ רָמָה תִּשָּׁבֵר:
16	Have you penetrated to the sources of the sea, Or walked in the recesses of the deep?	טז הֲבָאתָ עַד־נִבְכֵי־יָם וּבְחֵקֶר תְּהוֹם הִתְהַלָּכְתָּ:
17	Have the gates of death been disclosed to you? Have you seen the gates of deep darkness?	יז הֲנִגְלוּ לְךָ שַׁעֲרֵי־מָוֶת וְשַׁעֲרֵי צַלְמָוֶת תִּרְאֶה:
18	Have you surveyed the expanses of the earth? If you know of these – tell Me.	יח הִתְבֹּנַנְתָּ עַד־רַחֲבֵי־אָרֶץ הַגֵּד אִם־יָדַעְתָּ כֻלָּהּ:
19	Which path leads to where light dwells, And where is the place of darkness,	יט אֵי־זֶה הַדֶּרֶךְ יִשְׁכָּן־אוֹר וְחֹשֶׁךְ אֵי־זֶה מְקֹמוֹ:
20	That you may take it to its domain And know the way to its home?	כ כִּי תִקָּחֶנּוּ אֶל־גְּבוּלוֹ וְכִי־תָבִין נְתִיבוֹת בֵּיתוֹ:
21	Surely you know, for you were born then, And the number of your years is many!	כא יָדַעְתָּ כִּי־אָז תִּוָּלֵד וּמִסְפַּר יָמֶיךָ רַבִּים:
22	Have you penetrated the vaults of snow, Seen the vaults of hail,	כב הֲבָאתָ אֶל־אֹצְרוֹת שָׁלֶג וְאֹצְרוֹת בָּרָד תִּרְאֶה:
23	Which I have put aside for a time of adversity, For a day of war and battle?	כג אֲשֶׁר־חָשַׂכְתִּי לְעֶת־צָר לְיוֹם קְרָב וּמִלְחָמָה:
24	By what path is the west wind dispersed, The east wind scattered over the earth?	כד אֵי־זֶה הַדֶּרֶךְ יֵחָלֶק אוֹר יָפֵץ קָדִים עֲלֵי־אָרֶץ:
25	Who cut a channel for the torrents And a path for the thunderstorms,	כה מִי־פִלַּג לַשֶּׁטֶף תְּעָלָה וְדֶרֶךְ לַחֲזִיז קֹלוֹת:
26	To rain down on uninhabited land, On the wilderness where no man is,	כו לְהַמְטִיר עַל־אֶרֶץ לֹא־אִישׁ מִדְבָּר לֹא־אָדָם בּוֹ:
27	To saturate the desolate wasteland, And make the crop of grass sprout forth?	כז לְהַשְׂבִּיעַ שֹׁאָה וּמְשֹׁאָה וּלְהַצְמִיחַ מֹצָא דֶשֶׁא:
28	Does the rain have a father? Who begot the dewdrops?	כח הֲיֵשׁ־לַמָּטָר אָב אוֹ מִי־הוֹלִיד אֶגְלֵי־טָל:
29	From whose belly came forth the ice? Who gave birth to the frost of heaven?	כט מִבֶּטֶן מִי יָצָא הַקָּרַח וּכְפֹר שָׁמַיִם מִי יְלָדוֹ:
30	Water congeals like stone, And the surface of the deep compacts.	ל כָּאֶבֶן מַיִם יִתְחַבָּאוּ וּפְנֵי תְהוֹם יִתְלַכָּדוּ:
31	Can you tie cords to Pleiades Or undo the reins of Orion?	לא הַתְקַשֵּׁר מַעֲדַנּוֹת כִּימָה אוֹ־מֹשְׁכוֹת כְּסִיל תְּפַתֵּחַ:
32	Can you lead out Mazzaroth in its season, Conduct the Bear with her sons?	לב הֲתֹצִיא מַזָּרוֹת בְּעִתּוֹ וְעַיִשׁ עַל־בָּנֶיהָ תַנְחֵם:

Iyov/Job		איוב
Chapter 39		פרק לט

33 Do you know the laws of heaven Or impose its authority on earth? לג הֲיָדַעְתָּ חֻקּוֹת שָׁמָיִם אִם־תָּשִׂים מִשְׁטָרוֹ בָאָרֶץ׃

34 Can you send up an order to the clouds For an abundance of water to cover you? לד הֲתָרִים לָעָב קוֹלֶךָ וְשִׁפְעַת־מַיִם תְּכַסֶּךָּ׃

35 Can you dispatch the lightning on a mission And have it answer you, "I am ready"? לה הַתְשַׁלַּח בְּרָקִים וְיֵלֵכוּ וְיֹאמְרוּ לְךָ הִנֵּנוּ׃

36 Who put wisdom in the hidden parts? Who gave understanding to the mind? לו מִי־שָׁת בַּטֻּחוֹת חָכְמָה אוֹ מִי־נָתַן לַשֶּׂכְוִי בִינָה׃

37 Who is wise enough to give an account of the heavens? Who can tilt the bottles of the sky, לז מִי־יְסַפֵּר שְׁחָקִים בְּחָכְמָה וְנִבְלֵי שָׁמַיִם מִי יַשְׁכִּיב׃

38 Whereupon the earth melts into a mass, And its clods stick together. לח בְּצֶקֶת עָפָר לַמּוּצָק וּרְגָבִים יְדֻבָּקוּ׃

39 Can you hunt prey for the lion, And satisfy the appetite of the king of beasts? לט הֲתָצוּד לְלָבִיא טָרֶף וְחַיַּת כְּפִירִים תְּמַלֵּא׃

40 They crouch in their dens, Lie in ambush in their lairs. מ כִּי־יָשֹׁחוּ בַמְּעוֹנוֹת יֵשְׁבוּ בַסֻּכָּה לְמוֹ־אָרֶב׃

41 Who provides food for the raven When his young cry out to *Hashem* And wander about without food? מא מִי יָכִין לָעֹרֵב צֵידוֹ כִּי־יְלָדָו [יְלָדָיו] אֶל־אֵל יְשַׁוֵּעוּ יִתְעוּ לִבְלִי־אֹכֶל׃

39 1 Do you know the season when the mountain goats give birth? Can you mark the time when the hinds calve? **לט** א הֲיָדַעְתָּ עֵת לֶדֶת יַעֲלֵי־סָלַע חֹלֵל אַיָּלוֹת תִּשְׁמֹר׃

2 Can you count the months they must complete? Do you know the season they give birth, ב תִּסְפֹּר יְרָחִים תְּמַלֶּאנָה וְיָדַעְתָּ עֵת לִדְתָּנָה׃

3 When they couch to bring forth their offspring, To deliver their young? ג תִּכְרַעְנָה יַלְדֵיהֶן תְּפַלַּחְנָה חֶבְלֵיהֶם תְּשַׁלַּחְנָה׃

4 Their young are healthy; they grow up in the open; They leave and return no more. ד יַחְלְמוּ בְנֵיהֶם יִרְבּוּ בַבָּר יָצְאוּ וְלֹא־שָׁבוּ לָמוֹ׃

5 Who sets the wild ass free? Who loosens the bonds of the onager, ה מִי־שִׁלַּח פֶּרֶא חָפְשִׁי וּמֹסְרוֹת עָרוֹד מִי פִתֵּחַ׃

6 Whose home I have made the wilderness, The salt land his dwelling-place? ו אֲשֶׁר־שַׂמְתִּי עֲרָבָה בֵיתוֹ וּמִשְׁכְּנוֹתָיו מְלֵחָה׃

7 He scoffs at the tumult of the city, Does not hear the shouts of the driver. ז יִשְׂחַק לַהֲמוֹן קִרְיָה תְּשֻׁאוֹת נוֹגֵשׂ לֹא יִשְׁמָע׃

8 He roams the hills for his pasture; He searches for any green thing. ח יְתוּר הָרִים מִרְעֵהוּ וְאַחַר כָּל־יָרוֹק יִדְרוֹשׁ׃

9 Would the wild ox agree to serve you? Would he spend the night at your crib? ט הֲיֹאבֶה רֵּים עָבְדֶךָ אִם־יָלִין עַל־אֲבוּסֶךָ׃

10 Can you hold the wild ox by ropes to the furrow? Would he plow up the valleys behind you? י הֲתִקְשָׁר־רֵים בְּתֶלֶם עֲבֹתוֹ אִם־יְשַׂדֵּד עֲמָקִים אַחֲרֶיךָ׃

1774

Iyov/Job
Chapter 39

איוב
פרק לט

11 Would you rely on his great strength And leave your toil to him?

הֲתִבְטַח־בּוֹ כִּי־רַב כֹּחוֹ וְתַעֲזֹב אֵלָיו יְגִיעֶךָ׃

12 Would you trust him to bring in the seed And gather it in from your threshing floor?

הֲתַאֲמִין בּוֹ כִּי־יָשׁוּב [יָשִׁיב] זַרְעֶךָ וְגָרְנְךָ יֶאֱסֹף׃

13 **The wing of the ostrich beats joyously; Are her pinions and plumage like the stork's?**

כְּנַף־רְנָנִים נֶעֱלָסָה אִם־אֶבְרָה חֲסִידָה וְנֹצָה׃

k'-naf r'-na-NEEM ne-e-LA-sah im ev-RAH kha-see-DAH v'-no-TZAH

14 She leaves her eggs on the ground, Letting them warm in the dirt,

כִּי־תַעֲזֹב לָאָרֶץ בֵּצֶיהָ וְעַל־עָפָר תְּחַמֵּם׃

15 Forgetting they may be crushed underfoot, Or trampled by a wild beast.

וַתִּשְׁכַּח כִּי־רֶגֶל תְּזוּרֶהָ וְחַיַּת הַשָּׂדֶה תְּדוּשֶׁהָ׃

16 Her young are cruelly abandoned as if they were not hers; Her labor is in vain for lack of concern.

הִקְשִׁיחַ בָּנֶיהָ לְּלֹא־לָהּ לְרִיק יְגִיעָהּ בְּלִי־פָחַד׃

17 For *Hashem* deprived her of wisdom, Gave her no share of understanding,

כִּי־הִשָּׁהּ אֱלוֹהַּ חָכְמָה וְלֹא־חָלַק לָהּ בַּבִּינָה׃

18 Else she would soar on high, Scoffing at the horse and its rider.

כָּעֵת בַּמָּרוֹם תַּמְרִיא תִּשְׂחַק לַסּוּס וּלְרֹכְבוֹ׃

19 Do you give the horse his strength? Do you clothe his neck with a mane?

הֲתִתֵּן לַסּוּס גְּבוּרָה הֲתַלְבִּישׁ צַוָּארוֹ רַעְמָה׃

20 Do you make him quiver like locusts, His majestic snorting [spreading] terror?

הְתַרְעִישֶׁנּוּ כָּאַרְבֶּה הוֹד נַחְרוֹ אֵימָה׃

21 He paws with force, he runs with vigor, Charging into battle.

יַחְפְּרוּ בָעֵמֶק וְיָשִׂישׂ בְּכֹחַ יֵצֵא לִקְרַאת־נָשֶׁק׃

22 He scoffs at fear; he cannot be frightened; He does not recoil from the sword.

יִשְׂחַק לְפַחַד וְלֹא יֵחָת וְלֹא־יָשׁוּב מִפְּנֵי־חָרֶב׃

23 A quiverful of arrows whizzes by him, And the flashing spear and the javelin.

עָלָיו תִּרְנֶה אַשְׁפָּה לַהַב חֲנִית וְכִידוֹן׃

24 Trembling with excitement, he swallows the land; He does not turn aside at the blast of the trumpet.

בְּרַעַשׁ וְרֹגֶז יְגַמֶּא־אָרֶץ וְלֹא־יַאֲמִין כִּי־קוֹל שׁוֹפָר׃

25 As the trumpet sounds, he says, "Aha!" From afar he smells the battle, The roaring and shouting of the officers.

בְּדֵי שֹׁפָר יֹאמַר הֶאָח וּמֵרָחוֹק יָרִיחַ מִלְחָמָה רַעַם שָׂרִים וּתְרוּעָה׃

39:13 The wing of the ostrich beats joyously The Land of Israel used to be home to wild ostriches, until they became extinct in the region as a result of hunting. In fact, in 2006, four ancient ostrich eggs, thought to be at least 5,000 years old, were found in the Sharon region, just north of *Tel Aviv*. Because they were common in ancient Israel, ostriches are mentioned in a number of places in the Bible. Verses 13–18 make mention of the cruelty of the ostrich, which leaves its eggs to be trampled and is callous to its young (see also Lamentations 4:3). The ostrich is also listed among the non-kosher birds that are forbidden to be eaten (Leviticus 11:16 and Deuteronomy 14:15).

An ostrich in Southern Israel

Iyov/Job
Chapter 40

26 Is it by your wisdom that the hawk grows pinions, Spreads his wings to the south?

27 Does the eagle soar at your command, Building his nest high,

28 Dwelling in the rock, Lodging upon the fastness of a jutting rock?

29 From there he spies out his food; From afar his eyes see it.

30 His young gulp blood; Where the slain are, there is he.

40 1 *Hashem* said in reply to *Iyov*.

2 Shall one who should be disciplined complain against *Shaddai*? He who arraigns *Hashem* must respond.

3 *Iyov* said in reply to *Hashem*:

4 See, I am of small worth; what can I answer You? I clap my hand to my mouth.

5 I have spoken once, and will not reply; Twice, and will do so no more.

6 Then *Hashem* replied to *Iyov* out of the tempest and said:

7 Gird your loins like a man; I will ask, and you will inform Me.

8 Would you impugn My justice? Would you condemn Me that you may be right?

ha-AF ta-FAYR mish-pa-TEE tar-shee-AY-nee l'-MA-an titz-DAK

9 Have you an arm like *Hashem's*? Can you thunder with a voice like His?

איוב
פרק מ

כו הַמִבִּינָתְךָ יַאֲבֶר־נֵץ יִפְרֹשׂ כנפו [כְּנָפָיו] לְתֵימָן:

כז אִם־עַל־פִּיךָ יַגְבִּיהַּ נָשֶׁר וְכִי יָרִים קִנּוֹ:

כח סֶלַע יִשְׁכֹּן וְיִתְלֹנָן עַל־שֶׁן־סֶלַע וּמְצוּדָה:

כט מִשָּׁם חָפַר־אֹכֶל לְמֵרָחוֹק עֵינָיו יַבִּיטוּ:

ל ואפרחו [וְאֶפְרֹחָיו] יְעַלְעוּ־דָם וּבַאֲשֶׁר חֲלָלִים שָׁם הוּא:

מ א וַיַּעַן יְהֹוָה אֶת־אִיּוֹב וַיֹּאמַר:

ב הֲרֹב עִם־שַׁדַּי יִסּוֹר מוֹכִיחַ אֱלוֹהַּ יַעֲנֶנָּה:

ג וַיַּעַן אִיּוֹב אֶת־יְהֹוָה וַיֹּאמַר:

ד הֵן קַלֹּתִי מָה אֲשִׁיבֶךָּ יָדִי שַׂמְתִּי לְמוֹ־פִי:

ה אַחַת דִּבַּרְתִּי וְלֹא אֶעֱנֶה וּשְׁתַּיִם וְלֹא אוֹסִיף:

ו וַיַּעַן־יְהֹוָה אֶת־אִיּוֹב מנ סערה [מִן][סְעָרָה] וַיֹּאמַר:

ז אֱזָר־נָא כְגֶבֶר חֲלָצֶיךָ אֶשְׁאָלְךָ וְהוֹדִיעֵנִי:

ח הַאַף תָּפֵר מִשְׁפָּטִי תַּרְשִׁיעֵנִי לְמַעַן תִּצְדָּק:

ט וְאִם־זְרוֹעַ כָּאֵל לָךְ וּבְקוֹל כָּמֹהוּ תַרְעֵם:

40:8 Would you condemn Me that you may be right? The Sages of the Talmud (*Bava Batra* 15a) try to determine the time period in which *Iyov* lived. Although some opinions have him living during the period of the Exodus from Egypt (see commentary to 2:7), another suggests that he was among the Babylonian exiles who returned to the Land of Israel after the destruction of the first *Beit Hamikdash*. The identification of *Iyov* with the generation that experienced the destruction of the Temple and exile from *Eretz Yisrael* is fitting. Throughout the book, *Iyov* struggles with the reality that he is suffering, though seemingly righteous. He challenges God's justice, trying to make sense of the age-old question about why bad things happen to good people. Likewise, the Jews at the time of the exile also struggled to understand why they deserved to suffer as they did (see Ezekiel 18). Though the Jews sinned and *Iyov* did not, his personal suffering is seen as emblematic of the suffering of the Nation of Israel.

Iyov/Job
Chapter 40

10	Deck yourself now with grandeur and eminence; Clothe yourself in glory and majesty.
11	Scatter wide your raging anger; See every proud man and bring him low.
12	See every proud man and humble him, And bring them down where they stand.
13	Bury them all in the earth; Hide their faces in obscurity.
14	Then even I would praise you For the triumph your right hand won you.
15	Take now behemoth, whom I made as I did you; He eats grass, like the cattle.
16	His strength is in his loins, His might in the muscles of his belly.
17	He makes his tail stand up like a cedar; The sinews of his thighs are knit together.
18	His bones are like tubes of bronze, His limbs like iron rods.
19	He is the first of *Hashem*'s works; Only his Maker can draw the sword against him.
20	The mountains yield him produce, Where all the beasts of the field play.
21	He lies down beneath the lotuses, In the cover of the swamp reeds.
22	The lotuses embower him with shade; The willows of the brook surround him.
23	He can restrain the river from its rushing; He is confident the stream will gush at his command.
24	Can he be taken by his eyes? Can his nose be pierced by hooks?
25	Can you draw out Leviathan by a fishhook? Can you press down his tongue by a rope?
26	Can you put a ring through his nose, Or pierce his jaw with a barb?
27	Will he plead with you at length? Will he speak soft words to you?
28	Will he make an agreement with you To be taken as your lifelong slave?
29	Will you play with him like a bird, And tie him down for your girls?

איוב
פרק מ

י עֲדֵה נָא גָאוֹן וָגֹבַהּ וְהוֹד וְהָדָר תִּלְבָּשׁ:

יא הָפֵץ עֶבְרוֹת אַפֶּךָ וּרְאֵה כָל־גֵּאֶה וְהַשְׁפִּילֵהוּ:

יב רְאֵה כָל־גֵּאֶה הַכְנִיעֵהוּ וַהֲדֹךְ רְשָׁעִים תַּחְתָּם:

יג טָמְנֵם בֶּעָפָר יָחַד פְּנֵיהֶם חֲבֹשׁ בַּטָּמוּן:

יד וְגַם־אֲנִי אוֹדֶךָּ כִּי־תוֹשִׁעַ לְךָ יְמִינֶךָ:

טו הִנֵּה־נָא בְהֵמוֹת אֲשֶׁר־עָשִׂיתִי עִמָּךְ חָצִיר כַּבָּקָר יֹאכֵל:

טז הִנֵּה־נָא כֹחוֹ בְמָתְנָיו וְאֹנוֹ בִּשְׁרִירֵי בִטְנוֹ:

יז יַחְפֹּץ זְנָבוֹ כְמוֹ־אָרֶז גִּידֵי פחדו [פַחֲדָיו] יְשֹׂרָגוּ:

יח עֲצָמָיו אֲפִיקֵי נְחוּשָׁה גְּרָמָיו כִּמְטִיל בַּרְזֶל:

יט הוּא רֵאשִׁית דַּרְכֵי־אֵל הָעֹשׂוֹ יַגֵּשׁ חַרְבּוֹ:

כ כִּי־בוּל הָרִים יִשְׂאוּ־לוֹ וְכָל־חַיַּת הַשָּׂדֶה יְשַׂחֲקוּ־שָׁם:

כא תַּחַת־צֶאֱלִים יִשְׁכָּב בְּסֵתֶר קָנֶה וּבִצָּה:

כב יְסֻכֻּהוּ צֶאֱלִים צִלֲלוֹ יְסֻבּוּהוּ עַרְבֵי־נָחַל:

כג הֵן יַעֲשֹׁק נָהָר לֹא יַחְפּוֹז יִבְטַח כִּי־יָגִיחַ יַרְדֵּן אֶל־פִּיהוּ:

כד בְּעֵינָיו יִקָּחֶנּוּ בְּמוֹקְשִׁים יִנְקָב־אָף:

כה תִּמְשֹׁךְ לִוְיָתָן בְּחַכָּה וּבְחֶבֶל תַּשְׁקִיעַ לְשֹׁנוֹ:

כו הֲתָשִׂים אַגְמוֹן בְּאַפּוֹ וּבְחוֹחַ תִּקּוֹב לֶחֱיוֹ:

כז הֲיַרְבֶּה אֵלֶיךָ תַּחֲנוּנִים אִם־יְדַבֵּר אֵלֶיךָ רַכּוֹת:

כח הֲיִכְרֹת בְּרִית עִמָּךְ תִּקָּחֶנּוּ לְעֶבֶד עוֹלָם:

כט הַתְשַׂחֶק־בּוֹ כַּצִּפּוֹר וְתִקְשְׁרֶנּוּ לְנַעֲרוֹתֶיךָ:

Iyov/Job
Chapter 41

30 Shall traders traffic in him? Will he be divided up among merchants?

31 Can you fill his skin with darts Or his head with fish-spears?

32 Lay a hand on him, And you will never think of battle again.

41

1 See, any hope [of capturing] him must be disappointed; One is prostrated by the very sight of him.

2 There is no one so fierce as to rouse him; Who then can stand up to Me?

3 Whoever confronts Me I will requite, For everything under the heavens is Mine.

4 I will not be silent concerning him Or the praise of his martial exploits.

5 Who can uncover his outer garment? Who can penetrate the folds of his jowls?

6 Who can pry open the doors of his face? His bared teeth strike terror.

7 His protective scales are his pride, Locked with a binding seal.

8 One scale touches the other; Not even a breath can enter between them.

9 Each clings to each; They are interlocked so they cannot be parted.

10 His sneezings flash lightning, And his eyes are like the glimmerings of dawn.

11 Firebrands stream from his mouth; Fiery sparks escape.

mi-PEEV la-pee-DEEM ya-ha-LO-khu kee-DO-day AYSH yit-ma-LA-tu

12 Out of his nostrils comes smoke As from a steaming, boiling cauldron.

איוב
פרק מא

ל יִכְרוּ עָלָיו חַבָּרִים יֶחֱצוּהוּ בֵּין כְּנַעֲנִים׃

לא הַתְמַלֵּא בְשֻׂכּוֹת עוֹרוֹ וּבְצִלְצַל דָּגִים רֹאשׁוֹ׃

לב שִׂים־עָלָיו כַּפֶּךָ זְכֹר מִלְחָמָה אַל־תּוֹסַף׃

מא א הֵן־תֹּחַלְתּוֹ נִכְזָבָה הֲגַם אֶל־מַרְאָיו יֻטָל׃

ב לֹא־אַכְזָר כִּי יְעוּרֶנּוּ וּמִי הוּא לְפָנַי יִתְיַצָּב׃

ג מִי הִקְדִּימַנִי וַאֲשַׁלֵּם תַּחַת כָּל־הַשָּׁמַיִם לִי־הוּא׃

ד לֹא־[לוֹ־] אַחֲרִישׁ בַּדָּיו וּדְבַר־גְּבוּרוֹת וְחִין עֶרְכּוֹ׃

ה מִי־גִלָּה פְּנֵי לְבוּשׁוֹ בְּכֶפֶל רִסְנוֹ מִי יָבוֹא׃

ו דַּלְתֵי פָנָיו מִי פִתֵּחַ סְבִיבוֹת שִׁנָּיו אֵימָה׃

ז גַּאֲוָה אֲפִיקֵי מָגִנִּים סָגוּר חוֹתָם צָר׃

ח אֶחָד בְּאֶחָד יִגַּשׁוּ וְרוּחַ לֹא־יָבוֹא בֵינֵיהֶם׃

ט אִישׁ־בְּאָחִיהוּ יְדֻבָּקוּ יִתְלַכְּדוּ וְלֹא יִתְפָּרָדוּ׃

י עֲטִישֹׁתָיו תָּהֶל אוֹר וְעֵינָיו כְּעַפְעַפֵּי־שָׁחַר׃

יא מִפִּיו לַפִּידִים יַהֲלֹכוּ כִּידוֹדֵי אֵשׁ יִתְמַלָּטוּ׃

יב מִנְּחִירָיו יֵצֵא עָשָׁן כְּדוּד נָפוּחַ וְאַגְמֹן׃

41:11 Firebrands stream from his mouth This verse recalls the description of the revelation at Mount Sinai, in which *Hashem* revealed Himself with fire: "All the people witnessed the thunder and lightning" (Exodus 20:15). *Iyov* is echoing a theme repeated in this book, by indicating that God's glory is defined not just by the fact that He created the world and continues to rule it absolutely, but also on account of the giving of the *Torah*. The Jewish people worship God not just because He created the world, but because He intervened directly on their behalf by giving them the Law and because He is constantly involved in the day-to-day wellbeing of His people.

Iyov/Job — Chapter 42

13 His breath ignites coals; Flames blaze from his mouth.

יג נַפְשׁוֹ גֶּחָלִים תְּלַהֵט וְלַהַב מִפִּיו יֵצֵא׃

14 Strength resides in his neck; Power leaps before him.

יד בְּצַוָּארוֹ יָלִין עֹז וּלְפָנָיו תָּדוּץ דְּאָבָה׃

15 The layers of his flesh stick together; He is as though cast hard; he does not totter.

טו מַפְּלֵי בְשָׂרוֹ דָבֵקוּ יָצוּק עָלָיו בַּל־יִמּוֹט׃

16 His heart is cast hard as a stone, Hard as the nether millstone.

טז לִבּוֹ יָצוּק כְּמוֹ־אָבֶן וְיָצוּק כְּפֶלַח תַּחְתִּית׃

17 Divine beings are in dread as he rears up; As he crashes down, they cringe.

יז מִשֵּׂתוֹ יָגוּרוּ אֵלִים מִשְּׁבָרִים יִתְחַטָּאוּ׃

18 No sword that overtakes him can prevail, Nor spear, nor missile, nor lance.

יח מַשִּׂיגֵהוּ חֶרֶב בְּלִי תָקוּם חֲנִית מַסָּע וְשִׁרְיָה׃

19 He regards iron as straw, Bronze, as rotted wood.

יט יַחְשֹׁב לְתֶבֶן בַּרְזֶל לְעֵץ רִקָּבוֹן נְחוּשָׁה׃

20 No arrow can put him to flight; Slingstones turn into stubble for him.

כ לֹא־יַבְרִיחֶנּוּ בֶן־קָשֶׁת לְקַשׁ נֶהְפְּכוּ־לוֹ אַבְנֵי־קָלַע׃

21 Clubs are regarded as stubble; He scoffs at the quivering javelin.

כא כְּקַשׁ נֶחְשְׁבוּ תוֹתָח וְיִשְׂחַק לְרַעַשׁ כִּידוֹן׃

22 His underpart is jagged shards; It spreads a threshing-sledge on the mud.

כב תַּחְתָּיו חַדּוּדֵי חָרֶשׂ יִרְפַּד חָרוּץ עֲלֵי־טִיט׃

23 He makes the depths seethe like a cauldron; He makes the sea [boil] like an ointment-pot.

כג יַרְתִּיחַ כַּסִּיר מְצוּלָה יָם יָשִׂים כַּמֶּרְקָחָה׃

24 His wake is a luminous path; He makes the deep seem white-haired.

כד אַחֲרָיו יָאִיר נָתִיב יַחְשֹׁב תְּהוֹם לְשֵׂיבָה׃

25 There is no one on land who can dominate him, Made as he is without fear.

כה אֵין־עַל־עָפָר מָשְׁלוֹ הֶעָשׂוּ לִבְלִי־חָת׃

26 He sees all that is haughty; He is king over all proud beasts.

כו אֶת־כָּל־גָּבֹהַּ יִרְאֶה הוּא מֶלֶךְ עַל־כָּל־בְּנֵי־שָׁחַץ׃

42

1 *Iyov* said in reply to *Hashem*:

מב א וַיַּעַן אִיּוֹב אֶת־יְהֹוָה וַיֹּאמַר׃

2 I know that You can do everything, That nothing you propose is impossible for You.

ב יָדַעְת [יָדַעְתִּי] כִּי־כֹל תּוּכָל וְלֹא־יִבָּצֵר מִמְּךָ מְזִמָּה׃

3 Who is this who obscures counsel without knowledge? Indeed, I spoke without understanding Of things beyond me, which I did not know.

ג מִי זֶה מַעְלִים עֵצָה בְּלִי דָעַת לָכֵן הִגַּדְתִּי וְלֹא אָבִין נִפְלָאוֹת מִמֶּנִּי וְלֹא אֵדָע׃

4 Hear now, and I will speak; I will ask, and You will inform me.

ד שְׁמַע־נָא וְאָנֹכִי אֲדַבֵּר אֶשְׁאָלְךָ וְהוֹדִיעֵנִי׃

5 I had heard You with my ears, But now I see You with my eyes;

ה לְשֵׁמַע־אֹזֶן שְׁמַעְתִּיךָ וְעַתָּה עֵינִי רָאָתְךָ׃

6 Therefore, I recant and relent, Being but dust and ashes.

ו עַל־כֵּן אֶמְאַס וְנִחַמְתִּי עַל־עָפָר וָאֵפֶר׃

Iyov/Job
Chapter 42

7 After *Hashem* had spoken these words to *Iyov*, *Hashem* said to Eliphaz the Temanite, "I am incensed at you and your two friends, for you have not spoken the truth about Me as did My servant *Iyov*.

8 Now take seven bulls and seven rams and go to My servant *Iyov* and sacrifice a burnt offering for yourselves. And let *Iyov*, My servant, pray for you; for to him I will show favor and not treat you vilely, since you have not spoken the truth about Me as did My servant *Iyov*."

v'-a-TAH k'-KHU la-KHEM shiv-AH fa-REEM v'-shiv-AH ay-LEEM ul-KHU el av-DEE i-YOV v'-ha-a-lee-TEM o-LAH ba-ad-KHEM v'-i-YOV av-DEE yit-pa-LAYL a-lay-KHEM KEE im pa-NAV e-SA l'-vil-TEE a-SOT i-ma-KHEM n'-va-LAH KEE LO di-bar-TEM ay-LAI n'-kho-NAH k'-av-DEE i-YOV

9 Eliphaz the Temanite and Bildad the Shuhite and Zophar the Naamathite went and did as *Hashem* had told them, and *Hashem* showed favor to *Iyov*.

10 *Hashem* restored *Iyov*'s fortunes when he prayed on behalf of his friends, and *Hashem* gave *Iyov* twice what he had before.

11 All his brothers and sisters and all his former friends came to him and had a meal with him in his house. They consoled and comforted him for all the misfortune that *Hashem* had brought upon him. Each gave him one *kesita* and each one gold ring.

12 Thus *Hashem* blessed the latter years of *Iyov*'s life more than the former. He had fourteen thousand sheep, six thousand camels, one thousand yoke of oxen, and one thousand she-asses.

13 He also had seven sons and three daughters.

14 The first he named Jemimah, the second Keziah, and the third Keren-happuch.

42:8 And let *Iyov*, My servant, pray for you By praying for his friends who have sinned *Iyov* ultimately demonstrates compassion, thereby walking in the footsteps of *Avraham*. In *Sefer Bereishit* (chapter 20), *Avraham*'s wife *Sara* is taken by Abimelech, king of the Philistines, who thought she was *Avraham*'s sister. After Abimelech is punished and *Sara* is returned, *Avraham* prays for the Philistine king's return to good health and the amelioration of the punishment *Hashem* had inflicted upon him. The inclination to be kind and forgiving is one of the reasons *Avraham* merited the Land of Israel as a permanent inheritance for himself and his descendants. By emulating these traits of kindness and compassion *Iyov* proves his righteousness, even in the face of his pain and suffering.

Iyov/Job
Chapter 42

15 Nowhere in the land were women as beautiful as *Iyov*'s daughters to be found. Their father gave them estates together with their brothers.

16 Afterward, *Iyov* lived one hundred and forty years to see four generations of sons and grandsons.

17 So *Iyov* died old and contented.

איוב
פרק מב

טו וְלֹא נִמְצָא נָשִׁים יָפוֹת כִּבְנוֹת אִיּוֹב בְּכָל־הָאָרֶץ וַיִּתֵּן לָהֶם אֲבִיהֶם נַחֲלָה בְּתוֹךְ אֲחֵיהֶם׃

טז וַיְחִי אִיּוֹב אַחֲרֵי־זֹאת מֵאָה וְאַרְבָּעִים שָׁנָה ויראה [וַיִּרְאֶה] אֶת־בָּנָיו וְאֶת־בְּנֵי בָנָיו אַרְבָּעָה דֹּרוֹת׃

יז וַיָּמָת אִיּוֹב זָקֵן וּשְׂבַע יָמִים׃

Megillat Shir Hashirim
The Scroll of Song of Songs

Introduction and commentary by Batya Markowitz

At first glance, *Megillat Shir Hashirim* (Song of Songs) is a poignant love song between the *dod*, 'lover,' and his *re'aya*, 'beloved,' relating a lengthy dialogue between the couple. However, if it was only a simple love song, it would not be part of *Tanakh*. The canonization of the book indicates that it contains a much deeper meaning; it expresses a dialogue between *Hashem* and His people that spans history.

The *Mishna* records a debate among the Sages regarding whether or not *Megillat Shir Hashirim* should be included in the corpus of *Tanakh*. Rabbi Akiva declares that is it not only worthy of being part of the canon; it is actually holier than any of the other books in the Bible. In his words, "All the writings are holy, but *Shir Hashirim* is the holy of holies." What makes *Megillat Shir Hashirim* so special is precisely the fact that it speaks of the relationship and love between the Children of Israel and the Creator.

According to the interpretation of the classic commentaries, *Megillat Shir Hashirim* alludes to the Exodus, the time the Israelites spent traveling in the desert, the first and second Temple periods and the wandering of the Jews throughout the exile. The high points of history are remembered longingly, both by God and by His people in exile, distanced from their homeland and their connection with *Hashem*. Traditionally, *Megillat Shir Hashirim* is read publicly during the holiday of *Pesach*, since that is the time when God's love for the People of Israel was made manifest with outright miracles, and when the relationship between *Hashem* and His people began.

In chronicling the history of the relationship between God and the Children of Israel, *Megillat Shir Hashirim* is replete with imagery taken from the breathtaking landscape of *Eretz Yisrael*. The metaphors are based on its natural phenomena, its plants and wildlife. References are made to the gazelle and the deer, the horse, doves, ravens, pigeons, foxes, lions and leopards. Specific places are mentioned, such as *Ein Gedi*, the mountains of *Gilad*, *Snir* and *Chermon*, as well as other hills, deserts, streams and vineyards – all of which are integral parts of Israel's landscape. Furthermore, there are twenty-three types of plants mentioned in *Shir Hashirim*, including various spices, roses, nuts, apples and the classic "milk and honey" for which the land is well-known. Additionally, most of the seven species unique to Israel are mentioned in *Shir Hashirim*. Our commentary highlights the similarities between some of these fruits and the People of Israel.

While *Shir Hashirim* is mainly the dialogue between the lover (*Hashem*), and His beloved people, at times the book turns to "the daughters of *Yerushalayim*," which is understood as a reference to the other nations of the world. These nations are called "daughters of *Yerushalayim*" because eventually, all of mankind will come to recognize Jerusalem as the center of the world.

The book ends with a plea from the female: "Hurry, my beloved, swift as a gazelle or a young stag, to the hills of spices!" Though by the conclusion of *Megillat Shir Hashirim* the lovers have not yet managed to fulfill their desire to reunite, they continue to yearn for the fulfillment of this dream. Understood on a deeper level, this expresses the cry of the Jewish people asking that *Hashem* speedily redeem them from their lengthy exile, and bring them back to *Eretz Yisrael* and *Yerushalayim*.

Map of Places in *Shir Hashirim*

1. **Carmel** (Song of Songs 7:6) is a coastal mountain range in northern Israel that stretches from the Mediterranean Sea southeast. Mount Carmel is famous for being the mountain on which *Eliyahu* the prophet confronted the prophets of Baal (I Kings 18).
2. **Chermon** (Song of Songs 4:8) is a mountain range at the southern end of the Anti-Lebanon mountain range, whose southern slope extends into the northern Golan Heights. This slope is the highest point in the Land of Israel, soaring 2,300 meters above sea level.
3. **Damascus** (Song of Songs 7:5), a city at the foot of the *Chermon* mountain range.
4. **Ein Gedi** (Song of Songs 1:14), an oasis in the desert, is located on the western shores of the Dead Sea.
5. **Heshbon** (Song of Songs 7:5) was a city in the territory of *Reuven*. It was situated next to a river and had very nice pools of water.
6. **Yerushalayim** (Song of Songs 6:4) is the modern-day capital of the State of Israel and the ancestral capital of the Jewish people. In addition to this reference to the city of Jerusalem, Song of Songs also makes mention of the "daughters of Jerusalem" in a number of places (1:5, 2:7, 3:5, 3:10, 5:8, 5:16, 8:4).
7. **Lebanon** (Song of Songs 7:5), a reference to the mountains of Lebanon which could be seen above the houses and towers of Damascus. The Mount Lebanon range extends along the entire country parallel to the Mediterranean coast.
8. **Mount Gilad** (Song of Songs 4:1) is located on the east side of the Jordan River, and was known in biblical times as an excellent spot for grazing.
9. **Tirzah** (Song of Songs 6:4) was the capital of the northern kingdom of Israel during the reigns of *Basha, Elah, Zimri* and *Omri*.

Shir HaShirim (Song of Songs)

- City
▲ Mountain
— River

Damascus

▲ Mt. Chermon

Sea of Galilee

Mediterranean Sea

▲ Mt. Carmel

▲ Mt. Gilad

Tirtza

Jordan River

Yerushalayim

Heshbon

Ein Gedi • *Dead Sea*

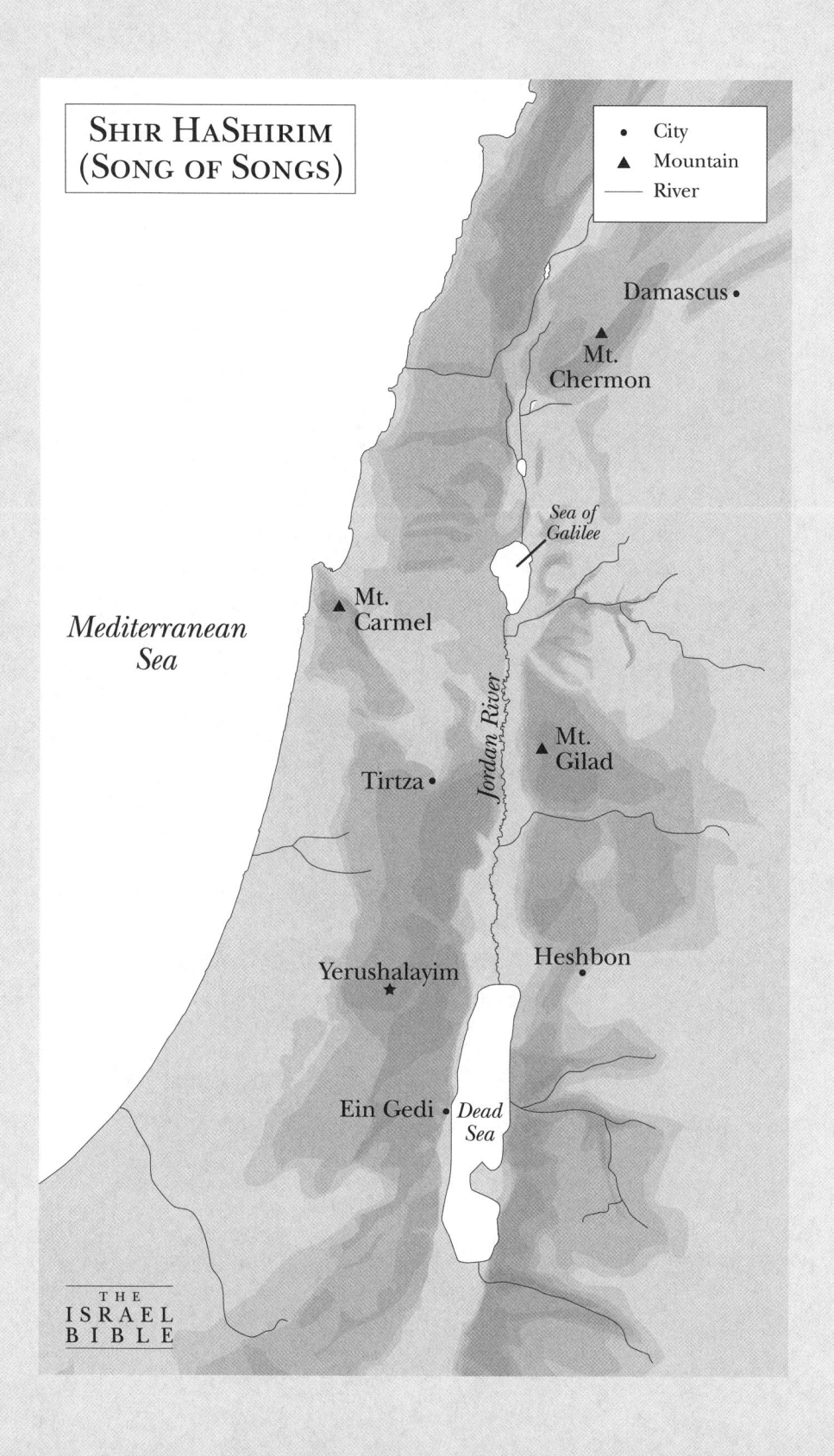

THE ISRAEL BIBLE

Shir Hashirim / Song of Songs
Chapter 1

שִׁיר הַשִּׁירִים
פרק א

1 ¹ The Song of Songs, by *Shlomo*.

א שִׁיר הַשִּׁירִים אֲשֶׁר לִשְׁלֹמֹה׃

² Oh, give me of the kisses of your mouth, For your love is more delightful than wine.

ב יִשָּׁקֵנִי מִנְּשִׁיקוֹת פִּיהוּ כִּי־טוֹבִים דֹּדֶיךָ מִיָּיִן׃

³ Your ointments yield a sweet fragrance, Your name is like finest oil – Therefore do maidens love you.

ג לְרֵיחַ שְׁמָנֶיךָ טוֹבִים שֶׁמֶן תּוּרַק שְׁמֶךָ עַל־כֵּן עֲלָמוֹת אֲהֵבוּךָ׃

⁴ Draw me after you, let us run! The king has brought me to his chambers. Let us delight and rejoice in your love, Savoring it more than wine – Like new wine they love you!

ד מָשְׁכֵנִי אַחֲרֶיךָ נָּרוּצָה הֱבִיאַנִי הַמֶּלֶךְ חֲדָרָיו נָגִילָה וְנִשְׂמְחָה בָּךְ נַזְכִּירָה דֹדֶיךָ מִיַּיִן מֵישָׁרִים אֲהֵבוּךָ׃

⁵ I am dark, but comely, O daughters of *Yerushalayim* – Like the tents of Kedar, Like the pavilions of *Shlomo*.

ה שְׁחוֹרָה אֲנִי וְנָאוָה בְּנוֹת יְרוּשָׁלָ͏ִם כְּאָהֳלֵי קֵדָר כִּירִיעוֹת שְׁלֹמֹה׃

⁶ Don't stare at me because I am swarthy, Because the sun has gazed upon me. My mother's sons quarreled with me, They made me guard the vineyards; My own vineyard I did not guard.

ו אַל־תִּרְאוּנִי שֶׁאֲנִי שְׁחַרְחֹרֶת שֶׁשְּׁזָפַתְנִי הַשָּׁמֶשׁ בְּנֵי אִמִּי נִחֲרוּ־בִי שָׂמֻנִי נֹטֵרָה אֶת־הַכְּרָמִים כַּרְמִי שֶׁלִּי לֹא נָטָרְתִּי׃

⁷ Tell me, you whom I love so well; Where do you pasture your sheep? Where do you rest them at noon? Let me not be as one who strays Beside the flocks of your fellows.

ז הַגִּידָה לִּי שֶׁאָהֲבָה נַפְשִׁי אֵיכָה תִרְעֶה אֵיכָה תַּרְבִּיץ בַּצָּהֳרָיִם שַׁלָּמָה אֶהְיֶה כְּעֹטְיָה עַל עֶדְרֵי חֲבֵרֶיךָ׃

⁸ If you do not know, O fairest of women, Go follow the tracks of the sheep, And graze your kids By the tents of the shepherds.

ח אִם־לֹא תֵדְעִי לָךְ הַיָּפָה בַּנָּשִׁים צְאִי־לָךְ בְּעִקְבֵי הַצֹּאן וּרְעִי אֶת־גְּדִיֹּתַיִךְ עַל מִשְׁכְּנוֹת הָרֹעִים׃

⁹ I have likened you, my darling, To a mare in Pharaoh's chariots:

ט לְסֻסָתִי בְּרִכְבֵי פַרְעֹה דִּמִּיתִיךְ רַעְיָתִי׃

¹⁰ Your cheeks are comely with plaited wreaths, Your neck with strings of jewels.

י נָאווּ לְחָיַיִךְ בַּתֹּרִים צַוָּארֵךְ בַּחֲרוּזִים׃

¹¹ We will add wreaths of gold To your spangles of silver.

יא תּוֹרֵי זָהָב נַעֲשֶׂה־לָּךְ עִם נְקֻדּוֹת הַכָּסֶף׃

¹² While the king was on his couch, My nard gave forth its fragrance.

יב עַד־שֶׁהַמֶּלֶךְ בִּמְסִבּוֹ נִרְדִּי נָתַן רֵיחוֹ׃

¹³ My beloved to me is a bag of myrrh Lodged between my breasts.

יג צְרוֹר הַמֹּר דּוֹדִי לִי בֵּין שָׁדַי יָלִין׃

¹⁴ My beloved to me is a spray of henna blooms From the vineyards of *Ein Gedi*.

יד אֶשְׁכֹּל הַכֹּפֶר דּוֹדִי לִי בְּכַרְמֵי עֵין גֶּדִי׃

esh-KOL ha-KO-fer do-DEE lee b'-khar-MAY ayn GE-dee

1:14 A spray of henna blooms from the vineyards of *Ein Gedi* *Ein Gedi* is located on the western shores of the Dead Sea. It is a lush oasis to this day, providing an abundance of water in a hot climate, surrounded in all directions by arid desert regions. According to the *Vilna Gaon*, this verse hints to the days of *Yehoshua*, when the Children of Israel entered *Eretz Yisrael*. Located near the Jordan river, *Ein Gedi* is near the

Ein Gedi waterfalls

Shir Hashirim / Song of Songs
Chapter 2

שיר השירים
פרק ב

15 Ah, you are fair, my darling, Ah, you are fair, With your dove-like eyes!

טו הִנָּךְ יָפָה רַעְיָתִי הִנָּךְ יָפָה עֵינַיִךְ יוֹנִים:

16 And you, my beloved, are handsome, Beautiful indeed! Our couch is in a bower;

טז הִנְּךָ יָפֶה דוֹדִי אַף נָעִים אַף־עַרְשֵׂנוּ רַעֲנָנָה:

17 Cedars are the beams of our house, Cypresses the rafters.

יז קֹרוֹת בָּתֵּינוּ אֲרָזִים רחיטנו [רַהִיטֵנוּ] בְּרוֹתִים:

2 1 I am a rose of *Sharon*, A lily of the valleys.

ב א אֲנִי חֲבַצֶּלֶת הַשָּׁרוֹן שׁוֹשַׁנַּת הָעֲמָקִים:

2 Like a lily among thorns, So is my darling among the maidens.

ב כְּשׁוֹשַׁנָּה בֵּין הַחוֹחִים כֵּן רַעְיָתִי בֵּין הַבָּנוֹת:

3 Like an apple tree among trees of the forest, So is my beloved among the youths. I delight to sit in his shade, And his fruit is sweet to my mouth.

ג כְּתַפּוּחַ בַּעֲצֵי הַיַּעַר כֵּן דּוֹדִי בֵּין הַבָּנִים בְּצִלּוֹ חִמַּדְתִּי וְיָשַׁבְתִּי וּפִרְיוֹ מָתוֹק לְחִכִּי:

4 He brought me to the banquet room And his banner of love was over me.

ד הֱבִיאַנִי אֶל־בֵּית הַיָּיִן וְדִגְלוֹ עָלַי אַהֲבָה:

5 "Sustain me with raisin cakes, Refresh me with apples, For I am faint with love."

ה סַמְּכוּנִי בָּאֲשִׁישׁוֹת רַפְּדוּנִי בַּתַּפּוּחִים כִּי־חוֹלַת אַהֲבָה אָנִי:

6 His left hand was under my head, His right arm embraced me.

ו שְׂמֹאלוֹ תַּחַת לְרֹאשִׁי וִימִינוֹ תְּחַבְּקֵנִי:

7 I adjure you, O maidens of *Yerushalayim*, By gazelles or by hinds of the field: Do not wake or rouse Love until it please!

ז הִשְׁבַּעְתִּי אֶתְכֶם בְּנוֹת יְרוּשָׁלַםִ בִּצְבָאוֹת אוֹ בְּאַיְלוֹת הַשָּׂדֶה אִם־תָּעִירוּ וְאִם־תְּעוֹרְרוּ אֶת־הָאַהֲבָה עַד שֶׁתֶּחְפָּץ:

8 Hark! My beloved! There he comes, Leaping over mountains, Bounding over hills.

ח קוֹל דּוֹדִי הִנֵּה־זֶה בָּא מְדַלֵּג עַל־הֶהָרִים מְקַפֵּץ עַל־הַגְּבָעוֹת:

9 My beloved is like a gazelle Or like a young stag. There he stands behind our wall, Gazing through the window, Peering through the lattice.

ט דּוֹמֶה דוֹדִי לִצְבִי אוֹ לְעֹפֶר הָאַיָּלִים הִנֵּה־זֶה עוֹמֵד אַחַר כָּתְלֵנוּ מַשְׁגִּיחַ מִן־הַחֲלֹּנוֹת מֵצִיץ מִן־הַחֲרַכִּים:

10 My beloved spoke thus to me, "Arise, my darling; My fair one, come away!

י עָנָה דוֹדִי וְאָמַר לִי קוּמִי לָךְ רַעְיָתִי יָפָתִי וּלְכִי־לָךְ:

11 For now the winter is past, The rains are over and gone.

יא כִּי־הִנֵּה הַסְּתָו [הַסְּתָיו] עָבָר הַגֶּשֶׁם חָלַף הָלַךְ לוֹ:

12 The blossoms have appeared in the land, The time of pruning has come; The song of the turtledove Is heard in our land.

יב הַנִּצָּנִים נִרְאוּ בָאָרֶץ עֵת הַזָּמִיר הִגִּיעַ וְקוֹל הַתּוֹר נִשְׁמַע בְּאַרְצֵנוּ:

---

border that the Israelites crossed upon entering the land. Just as the henna tree was a permanent fixture of this region, *Hashem*'s presence became a permanent fixture on earth when the People of Israel entered the Land of Israel as a nation for the first time.

Shir Hashirim / Song of Songs
Chapter 3

13 The green figs form on the fig tree, The vines in blossom give off fragrance. Arise, my darling; My fair one, come away!

יג הַתְּאֵנָה חָנְטָה פַגֶּיהָ וְהַגְּפָנִים סְמָדַר נָתְנוּ רֵיחַ קוּמִי לְכִי [לָךְ] רַעְיָתִי יָפָתִי וּלְכִי־לָךְ:

ha-t'-ay-NAH kha-n'-TAH fa-GE-ha v'-ha-g'-fa-NEEM s'-ma-DAR na-t'-NU RAY-akh KU-mee LAKH ra-ya-TEE ya-fa-TEE ul-khee LAKH

14 "O my dove, in the cranny of the rocks, Hidden by the cliff, Let me see your face, Let me hear your voice; For your voice is sweet And your face is comely."

יד יוֹנָתִי בְּחַגְוֵי הַסֶּלַע בְּסֵתֶר הַמַּדְרֵגָה הַרְאִינִי אֶת־מַרְאַיִךְ הַשְׁמִיעִנִי אֶת־קוֹלֵךְ כִּי־קוֹלֵךְ עָרֵב וּמַרְאֵיךְ נָאוֶה:

15 Catch us the foxes, The little foxes That ruin the vineyards – For our vineyard is in blossom.

טו אֶחֱזוּ־לָנוּ שׁוּעָלִים שׁוּעָלִים קְטַנִּים מְחַבְּלִים כְּרָמִים וּכְרָמֵינוּ סְמָדַר:

16 My beloved is mine And I am his Who browses among the lilies.

טז דּוֹדִי לִי וַאֲנִי לוֹ הָרֹעֶה בַּשּׁוֹשַׁנִּים:

17 When the day blows gently And the shadows flee, Set out, my beloved, Swift as a gazelle Or a young stag, For the hills of spices!

יז עַד שֶׁיָּפוּחַ הַיּוֹם וְנָסוּ הַצְּלָלִים סֹב דְּמֵה־לְךָ דוֹדִי לִצְבִי אוֹ לְעֹפֶר הָאַיָּלִים עַל־הָרֵי בָתֶר:

3

1 Upon my couch at night I sought the one I love – I sought, but found him not.

א עַל־מִשְׁכָּבִי בַּלֵּילוֹת בִּקַּשְׁתִּי אֵת שֶׁאָהֲבָה נַפְשִׁי בִּקַּשְׁתִּיו וְלֹא מְצָאתִיו:

2 "I must rise and roam the town, Through the streets and through the squares; I must seek the one I love." I sought but found him not.

ב אָקוּמָה נָּא וַאֲסוֹבְבָה בָעִיר בַּשְּׁוָקִים וּבָרְחֹבוֹת אֲבַקְשָׁה אֵת שֶׁאָהֲבָה נַפְשִׁי בִּקַּשְׁתִּיו וְלֹא מְצָאתִיו:

3 I met the watchmen Who patrol the town. "Have you seen the one I love?"

ג מְצָאוּנִי הַשֹּׁמְרִים הַסֹּבְבִים בָּעִיר אֵת שֶׁאָהֲבָה נַפְשִׁי רְאִיתֶם:

4 Scarcely had I passed them When I found the one I love. I held him fast, I would not let him go Till I brought him to my mother's house, To the chamber of her who conceived me

ד כִּמְעַט שֶׁעָבַרְתִּי מֵהֶם עַד שֶׁמָּצָאתִי אֵת שֶׁאָהֲבָה נַפְשִׁי אֲחַזְתִּיו וְלֹא אַרְפֶּנּוּ עַד־שֶׁהֲבֵיאתִיו אֶל־בֵּית אִמִּי וְאֶל־חֶדֶר הוֹרָתִי:

5 I adjure you, O maidens of *Yerushalayim*, By gazelles or by hinds of the field: Do not wake or rouse Love until it please!

ה הִשְׁבַּעְתִּי אֶתְכֶם בְּנוֹת יְרוּשָׁלַ͏ִם בִּצְבָאוֹת אוֹ בְּאַיְלוֹת הַשָּׂדֶה אִם־תָּעִירוּ וְאִם־תְּעוֹרְרוּ אֶת־הָאַהֲבָה עַד שֶׁתֶּחְפָּץ:

6 Who is she that comes up from the desert Like columns of smoke, In clouds of myrrh and frankincense, Of all the powders of the merchant?

ו מִי זֹאת עֹלָה מִן־הַמִּדְבָּר כְּתִימֲרוֹת עָשָׁן מְקֻטֶּרֶת מוֹר וּלְבוֹנָה מִכֹּל אַבְקַת רוֹכֵל:

2:13 The vines in blossom give off fragrance Grapes, like each of the other seven special agricultural species for which the Land of Israel is praised (Deuteronomy 8:8), are a symbol of the People of Israel. The Sages teach that the vine is the weakest and lowliest of trees, lacking even a trunk. To produce wine, which is served at royal banquets, grapes are crushed underfoot. Similarly, the Jewish people are a small, modest nation. Often, they are crushed and trampled by others, but ultimately they will be raised to royalty. Additionally, the largest grapes hang at the bottom of the cluster, similar to the greatest leaders such as *Moshe* who carried himself with great humility (Numbers 12:3).

A grape vine in Kfar Tabor, Israel

Shir Hashirim / Song of Songs
Chapter 4

שִׁיר הַשִּׁירִים
פֶּרֶק ד

7 There is *Shlomo*'s couch, Encircled by sixty warriors Of the warriors of *Yisrael*,

ז הִנֵּה מִטָּתוֹ שֶׁלִּשְׁלֹמֹה שִׁשִּׁים גִּבֹּרִים סָבִיב לָהּ מִגִּבֹּרֵי יִשְׂרָאֵל:

8 All of them trained in warfare, Skilled in battle, Each with sword on thigh Because of terror by night.

ח כֻּלָּם אֲחֻזֵי חֶרֶב מְלֻמְּדֵי מִלְחָמָה אִישׁ חַרְבּוֹ עַל־יְרֵכוֹ מִפַּחַד בַּלֵּילוֹת:

9 King *Shlomo* made him a palanquin Of wood from Lebanon.

ט אַפִּרְיוֹן עָשָׂה לוֹ הַמֶּלֶךְ שְׁלֹמֹה מֵעֲצֵי הַלְּבָנוֹן:

10 He made its posts of silver, Its back of gold, Its seat of purple wool. Within, it was decked with love By the maidens of *Yerushalayim*.

י עַמּוּדָיו עָשָׂה כֶסֶף רְפִידָתוֹ זָהָב מֶרְכָּבוֹ אַרְגָּמָן תּוֹכוֹ רָצוּף אַהֲבָה מִבְּנוֹת יְרוּשָׁלָ͏ִם:

a-mu-DAV a-SAH KHE-sef r'-fee-da-TO za-HAV mer-ka-VO ar-ga-MAN to-KHO ra-TZUF a-ha-VAH mi-b'-NOT y'-ru-sha-LA-im

11 O maidens of *Tzion*, go forth And gaze upon King *Shlomo* Wearing the crown that his mother Gave him on his wedding day, On his day of bliss.

יא צְאֶינָה וּרְאֶינָה בְּנוֹת צִיּוֹן בַּמֶּלֶךְ שְׁלֹמֹה בָּעֲטָרָה שֶׁעִטְּרָה־לּוֹ אִמּוֹ בְּיוֹם חֲתֻנָּתוֹ וּבְיוֹם שִׂמְחַת לִבּוֹ:

4 1 Ah, you are fair, my darling, Ah, you are fair. Your eyes are like doves Behind your veil. Your hair is like a flock of goats Streaming down Mount *Gilad*.

ד א הִנָּךְ יָפָה רַעְיָתִי הִנָּךְ יָפָה עֵינַיִךְ יוֹנִים מִבַּעַד לְצַמָּתֵךְ שַׂעְרֵךְ כְּעֵדֶר הָעִזִּים שֶׁגָּלְשׁוּ מֵהַר גִּלְעָד:

2 Your teeth are like a flock of ewes Climbing up from the washing pool; All of them bear twins, And not one loses her young.

ב שִׁנַּיִךְ כְּעֵדֶר הַקְּצוּבוֹת שֶׁעָלוּ מִן־הָרַחְצָה שֶׁכֻּלָּם מַתְאִימוֹת וְשַׁכֻּלָה אֵין בָּהֶם:

3 Your lips are like a crimson thread, Your mouth is lovely. Your brow behind your veil [Gleams] like a pomegranate split open.

ג כְּחוּט הַשָּׁנִי שִׂפְתוֹתַיִךְ וּמִדְבָּרֵיךְ נָאוֶה כְּפֶלַח הָרִמּוֹן רַקָּתֵךְ מִבַּעַד לְצַמָּתֵךְ:

4 Your neck is like the Tower of *David*, Built to hold weapons, Hung with a thousand shields – All the quivers of warriors.

ד כְּמִגְדַּל דָּוִיד צַוָּארֵךְ בָּנוּי לְתַלְפִּיּוֹת אֶלֶף הַמָּגֵן תָּלוּי עָלָיו כֹּל שִׁלְטֵי הַגִּבֹּרִים:

5 Your breasts are like two fawns, Twins of a gazelle, Browsing among the lilies.

ה שְׁנֵי שָׁדַיִךְ כִּשְׁנֵי עֳפָרִים תְּאוֹמֵי צְבִיָּה הָרוֹעִים בַּשּׁוֹשַׁנִּים:

6 When the day blows gently And the shadows flee, I will betake me to the mount of myrrh, To the hill of frankincense.

ו עַד שֶׁיָּפוּחַ הַיּוֹם וְנָסוּ הַצְּלָלִים אֵלֶךְ לִי אֶל־הַר הַמּוֹר וְאֶל־גִּבְעַת הַלְּבוֹנָה:

7 Every part of you is fair, my darling, There is no blemish in you

ז כֻּלָּךְ יָפָה רַעְיָתִי וּמוּם אֵין בָּךְ:

3:10 By the maidens of *Yerushalayim* In a number of places throughout *Shir Hashirim* in addition to this verse, the "maidens" or "daughters" of *Yerushalayim* represent the nations of the world (see 1:5, 2:7, 3:5, 5:8, 8:4). The medieval commentator *Rashi* explains that this is because in the future, *Yerushalayim* will be the metropolis of all countries, and all people will accept its centrality. Though the nations of the world will one day accept *Yerushalayim* as their political and religious capital, the Jewish people have always seen it as their eternal capital, providing inspiration and the means for fulfilling their spiritual needs even when they were in exile.

Jerusalem

Shir Hashirim / Song of Songs
Chapter 5

שיר השירים
פרק ה

ח אִתִּי מִלְּבָנוֹן כַּלָּה אִתִּי מִלְּבָנוֹן תָּבוֹאִי תָּשׁוּרִי מֵרֹאשׁ אֲמָנָה מֵרֹאשׁ שְׂנִיר וְחֶרְמוֹן מִמְּעֹנוֹת אֲרָיוֹת מֵהַרְרֵי נְמֵרִים:

8 From Lebanon come with me; From Lebanon, my bride, with me! Trip down from Amana's peak, From the peak of Senir and *Chermon*, From the dens of lions, From the hills of leopards.

ט לִבַּבְתִּנִי אֲחֹתִי כַלָּה לִבַּבְתִּינִי באחד [בְּאַחַת] מֵעֵינַיִךְ בְּאַחַד עֲנָק מִצַּוְּרֹנָיִךְ:

9 You have captured my heart, My own, my bride, You have captured my heart With one [glance] of your eyes, With one coil of your necklace.

י מַה־יָּפוּ דֹדַיִךְ אֲחֹתִי כַלָּה מַה־טֹּבוּ דֹדַיִךְ מִיַּיִן וְרֵיחַ שְׁמָנַיִךְ מִכָּל־בְּשָׂמִים:

10 How sweet is your love, My own, my bride! How much more delightful your love than wine, Your ointments more fragrant Than any spice!

יא נֹפֶת תִּטֹּפְנָה שִׂפְתוֹתַיִךְ כַּלָּה דְּבַשׁ וְחָלָב תַּחַת לְשׁוֹנֵךְ וְרֵיחַ שַׂלְמֹתַיִךְ כְּרֵיחַ לְבָנוֹן:

11 Sweetness drops From your lips, O bride; Honey and milk Are under your tongue And the scent of your robes Is like the scent of Lebanon.

יב גַּן נָעוּל אֲחֹתִי כַלָּה גַּל נָעוּל מַעְיָן חָתוּם:

12 A garden locked Is my own, my bride, A fountain locked, A sealed-up spring.

יג שְׁלָחַיִךְ פַּרְדֵּס רִמּוֹנִים עִם פְּרִי מְגָדִים כְּפָרִים עִם־נְרָדִים:

13 Your limbs are an orchard of pomegranates And of all luscious fruits, Of henna and of nard –

sh'-la-KHA-yikh par-DAYS ri-mo-NEEM IM p'-REE m'-ga-DEEM k'-fa-REEM im n'-ra-DEEM

יד נֵרְדְּ וְכַרְכֹּם קָנֶה וְקִנָּמוֹן עִם כָּל־עֲצֵי לְבוֹנָה מֹר וַאֲהָלוֹת עִם כָּל־רָאשֵׁי בְשָׂמִים:

14 Nard and saffron, Fragrant reed and cinnamon, With all aromatic woods, Myrrh and aloes – All the choice perfumes.

טו מַעְיַן גַּנִּים בְּאֵר מַיִם חַיִּים וְנֹזְלִים מִן־לְבָנוֹן:

15 You are] a garden spring, A well of fresh water, A rill of Lebanon.

טז עוּרִי צָפוֹן וּבוֹאִי תֵימָן הָפִיחִי גַנִּי יִזְּלוּ בְשָׂמָיו יָבֹא דוֹדִי לְגַנּוֹ וְיֹאכַל פְּרִי מְגָדָיו:

16 Awake, O north wind, Come, O south wind! Blow upon my garden, That its perfume may spread. Let my beloved come to his garden And enjoy its luscious fruits!

א בָּאתִי לְגַנִּי אֲחֹתִי כַלָּה אָרִיתִי מוֹרִי עִם־בְּשָׂמִי אָכַלְתִּי יַעְרִי עִם־דִּבְשִׁי שָׁתִיתִי יֵינִי עִם־חֲלָבִי אִכְלוּ רֵעִים שְׁתוּ וְשִׁכְרוּ דּוֹדִים:

5:1 I have come to my garden, My own, my bride; I have plucked my myrrh and spice, Eaten my honey and honeycomb, Drunk my wine and my milk. Eat, lovers, and drink: Drink deep of love!

4:13 An orchard of pomegranates The pomegranate is one of the seven special agricultural species of the Land of Israel (Deuteronomy 8:8). It has always been a symbol of beauty. Its unique shape is a favorite design element, appearing on the priestly garments and on the pillars at the entrance to the *Beit Hamikdash* in *Yerushalayim*, as well as in many forms of artwork to this day. At its crown, the pomegranate has a six-pointed star, which makes it the only place the *Magen David*, 'star of David,' appears in nature. According to Jewish teachings, the numerous seeds in the pomegranate represent the 613 biblical commandments of the *Torah*. On the Jewish New Year, *Rosh Hashana*, Jews say a special prayer over the beautiful fruit, "May our good deeds be as numerous as the seeds of a pomegranate."

Pomegranates in Beit Dagan

5:1 I have come to my garden According to *Metzudat David*, this verse is a metaphor for *Hashem* entering the *Beit Hamikdash* that the people

Shir Hashirim / Song of Songs
Chapter 5

שיר השירים
פרק ה

BA-tee l'-ga-NEE a-kho-TEE kha-LAH a-REE-tee mo-REE im b'-sa-MEE a-KHAL-tee ya-REE im div-SHEE sha-TEE-tee yay-NEE im kha-la-VEE ikh-LU ray-EEM sh'-TU v'-shikh-RU do-DEEM

2 I was asleep, But my heart was wakeful. Hark, my beloved knocks! "Let me in, my own, My darling, my faultless dove! For my head is drenched with dew, My locks with the damp of night."

ב אֲנִי יְשֵׁנָה וְלִבִּי עֵר קוֹל דּוֹדִי דוֹפֵק פִּתְחִי־לִי אֲחֹתִי רַעְיָתִי יוֹנָתִי תַמָּתִי שֶׁרֹאשִׁי נִמְלָא־טָל קְוֻצּוֹתַי רְסִיסֵי לָיְלָה:

a-NEE y'-shay-NAH v'-li-BEE ayr KOL do-DEE do-FAYK pit-khee LEE a-kho-TEE ra-ya-TEE yo-na-TEE ta-ma-TEE she-ro-SHEE nim-la TAL k'-vu-tzo-TAI r'-see-SAY LAI-lah

3 I had taken off my robe – Was I to don it again? I had bathed my feet – Was I to soil them again?

ג פָּשַׁטְתִּי אֶת־כֻּתָּנְתִּי אֵיכָכָה אֶלְבָּשֶׁנָּה רָחַצְתִּי אֶת־רַגְלַי אֵיכָכָה אֲטַנְּפֵם:

4 My beloved took his hand off the latch, And my heart was stirred for him.

ד דּוֹדִי שָׁלַח יָדוֹ מִן־הַחֹר וּמֵעַי הָמוּ עָלָיו:

5 I rose to let in my beloved; My hands dripped myrrh – My fingers, flowing myrrh – Upon the handles of the bolt.

ה קַמְתִּי אֲנִי לִפְתֹּחַ לְדוֹדִי וְיָדַי נָטְפוּ־מוֹר וְאֶצְבְּעֹתַי מוֹר עֹבֵר עַל כַּפּוֹת הַמַּנְעוּל:

6 I opened the door for my beloved, But my beloved had turned and gone. I was faint because of what he said. I sought, but found him not; I called, but he did not answer.

ו פָּתַחְתִּי אֲנִי לְדוֹדִי וְדוֹדִי חָמַק עָבָר נַפְשִׁי יָצְאָה בְדַבְּרוֹ בִּקַּשְׁתִּיהוּ וְלֹא מְצָאתִיהוּ קְרָאתִיו וְלֹא עָנָנִי:

7 I met the watchmen Who patrol the town; They struck me, they bruised me. The guards of the walls Stripped me of my mantle.

ז מְצָאֻנִי הַשֹּׁמְרִים הַסֹּבְבִים בָּעִיר הִכּוּנִי פְצָעוּנִי נָשְׂאוּ אֶת־רְדִידִי מֵעָלַי שֹׁמְרֵי הַחֹמוֹת:

8 I adjure you, O maidens of *Yerushalayim*! If you meet my beloved, tell him this: That I am faint with love.

ח הִשְׁבַּעְתִּי אֶתְכֶם בְּנוֹת יְרוּשָׁלָם אִם־תִּמְצְאוּ אֶת־דּוֹדִי מַה־תַּגִּידוּ לוֹ שֶׁחוֹלַת אַהֲבָה אָנִי:

9 How is your beloved better than another, O fairest of women? How is your beloved better than another That you adjure us so?

ט מַה־דּוֹדֵךְ מִדּוֹד הַיָּפָה בַּנָּשִׁים מַה־דּוֹדֵךְ מִדּוֹד שֶׁכָּכָה הִשְׁבַּעְתָּנוּ:

---

built for Him, and accepting the sacrifices they offer to Him. The garden is a reference to the Temple and the gathering of myrrh and spice to the acceptance of the incense offering that is brought in His honor. God metaphorically "eats" and "drinks" the offerings and libations, by means of a fire that descends from heaven to consume them. Finally, He calls upon his "friends," the loyal priests, to partake in their share of the offerings. The use of a garden as the image to represent the *Beit Hamikdash* paints a picture of beauty and harmony which befits the meeting place of God and mankind on earth.

5:2 Hark, my beloved knocks! The words: "My beloved knocks," in Hebrew *kol dodi dofek* (קוֹל דּוֹדִי דוֹפֵק), form the title and theme of Rabbi Joseph B. Soloveitchik's classic essay on religious Zionism. In this essay, Rabbi Soloveitchik highlights the miraculous events surrounding the establishment of the State of Israel and posits that God "knocked" six times to get our attention. He points to military successes, political opportunities, the theological awakening of the Christian world and other developments as contemporary signs that *Hashem* is beckoning the Jewish people to return to the Land of Israel. Rabbi Soloveitchik cautions that we must respond quickly to these knocks, unlike the beloved who hesitates in this chapter, and later regrets her lost opportunity.

Rabbi Joseph B. Soloveitchik (1903–1993)

Shir Hashirim / Song of Songs
Chapter 6

10 My beloved is clear-skinned and ruddy, Preeminent among ten thousand.

דּוֹדִי צַח וְאָדוֹם דָּגוּל מֵרְבָבָה:

11 His head is finest gold, His locks are curled And black as a raven.

רֹאשׁוֹ כֶּתֶם פָּז קְוֻצּוֹתָיו תַּלְתַּלִּים שְׁחֹרוֹת כָּעוֹרֵב:

12 His eyes are like doves By watercourses, Bathed in milk, Set by a brimming pool.

עֵינָיו כְּיוֹנִים עַל־אֲפִיקֵי מָיִם רֹחֲצוֹת בֶּחָלָב יֹשְׁבוֹת עַל־מִלֵּאת:

13 His cheeks are like beds of spices, Banks of perfume His lips are like lilies; They drip flowing myrrh.

לְחָיָו כַּעֲרוּגַת הַבֹּשֶׂם מִגְדְּלוֹת מֶרְקָחִים שִׂפְתוֹתָיו שׁוֹשַׁנִּים נֹטְפוֹת מוֹר עֹבֵר:

14 His hands are rods of gold, Studded with beryl; His belly a tablet of ivory, Adorned with sapphires.

יָדָיו גְּלִילֵי זָהָב מְמֻלָּאִים בַּתַּרְשִׁישׁ מֵעָיו עֶשֶׁת שֵׁן מְעֻלֶּפֶת סַפִּירִים:

15 His legs are like marble pillars Set in sockets of fine gold. He is majestic as Lebanon, Stately as the cedars.

שׁוֹקָיו עַמּוּדֵי שֵׁשׁ מְיֻסָּדִים עַל־אַדְנֵי־פָז מַרְאֵהוּ כַּלְּבָנוֹן בָּחוּר כָּאֲרָזִים:

16 His mouth is delicious And all of him is delightful. Such is my beloved, Such is my darling, O maidens of *Yerushalayim*!

חִכּוֹ מַמְתַקִּים וְכֻלּוֹ מַחֲמַדִּים זֶה דוֹדִי וְזֶה רֵעִי בְּנוֹת יְרוּשָׁלִָם:

6

1 "Whither has your beloved gone, O fairest of women? Whither has your beloved turned? Let us seek him with you."

אָנָה הָלַךְ דּוֹדֵךְ הַיָּפָה בַּנָּשִׁים אָנָה פָּנָה דוֹדֵךְ וּנְבַקְשֶׁנּוּ עִמָּךְ:

2 My beloved has gone down to his garden, To the beds of spices, To browse in the gardens And to pick lilies.

דּוֹדִי יָרַד לְגַנּוֹ לַעֲרוּגוֹת הַבֹּשֶׂם לִרְעוֹת בַּגַּנִּים וְלִלְקֹט שׁוֹשַׁנִּים:

3 I am my beloved's And my beloved is mine; He browses among the lilies.

אֲנִי לְדוֹדִי וְדוֹדִי לִי הָרֹעֶה בַּשּׁוֹשַׁנִּים:

4 You are beautiful, my darling, as *Tirtza*, Comely as *Yerushalayim*, Awesome as bannered hosts.

יָפָה אַתְּ רַעְיָתִי כְּתִרְצָה נָאוָה כִּירוּשָׁלִָם אֲיֻמָּה כַּנִּדְגָּלוֹת:

ya-FAH AT ra-ya-TEE k'-tir-TZAH na-VAH kee-ru-sha-LA-im a-yu-MAH ka-nid-ga-LOT

5 Turn your eyes away from me, For they overwhelm me! Your hair is like a flock of goats Streaming down from *Gilad*.

הָסֵבִּי עֵינַיִךְ מִנֶּגְדִּי שֶׁהֵם הִרְהִיבֻנִי שַׂעְרֵךְ כְּעֵדֶר הָעִזִּים שֶׁגָּלְשׁוּ מִן־הַגִּלְעָד:

6 Your teeth are like a flock of ewes Climbing up from the washing pool; All of them bear twins, And not one loses her young.

שִׁנַּיִךְ כְּעֵדֶר הָרְחֵלִים שֶׁעָלוּ מִן־הָרַחְצָה שֶׁכֻּלָּם מַתְאִימוֹת וְשַׁכֻּלָה אֵין בָּהֶם:

תרצה
ירושלים

6:4 You are beautiful, my darling, as *Tirtza*, comely as *Yerushalayim* *Tirtza* was an important city of the northern kingdom of *Yisrael*, which served as its capital during the reigns of the kings *Baasha*, *Elah*, *Zimri* and *Omri* (see I Kings 14:17). *Yerushalayim*, of course, was the capital of the kingdom of *Yehuda*. On a simple level, the lover says that his beloved is as beautiful as these capitals; that she is like a queen befitting the royal cities. On a deeper level, Rabbi Amos Hakham notes that the name *Tirza* (תרצה) is related to the word *ratza* (רצה), 'desire,' and the name *Yerushalayim* (ירושלים) is derived from the word *shalem* (שלם), meaning 'complete.' Hence, this verse also alludes to the fact that *Hashem* finds His people both 'desirable' and 'complete.'

Shir Hashirim / Song of Songs
Chapter 7

שיר השירים
פרק ז

7 Your brow behind your veil [Gleams] like a pomegranate split open.

ז כְּפֶלַח הָרִמּוֹן רַקָּתֵךְ מִבַּעַד לְצַמָּתֵךְ:

8 There are sixty queens, And eighty concubines, And damsels without number.

ח שִׁשִּׁים הֵמָּה מְלָכוֹת וּשְׁמֹנִים פִּילַגְשִׁים וַעֲלָמוֹת אֵין מִסְפָּר:

9 Only one is my dove, My perfect one, The only one of her mother, The delight of her who bore her. Maidens see and acclaim her; Queens and concubines, and praise her.

ט אַחַת הִיא יוֹנָתִי תַמָּתִי אַחַת הִיא לְאִמָּהּ בָּרָה הִיא לְיוֹלַדְתָּהּ רָאוּהָ בָנוֹת וַיְאַשְּׁרוּהָ מְלָכוֹת וּפִילַגְשִׁים וַיְהַלְלוּהָ:

10 Who is she that shines through like the dawn, Beautiful as the moon, Radiant as the sun Awesome as bannered hosts?

י מִי־זֹאת הַנִּשְׁקָפָה כְּמוֹ־שָׁחַר יָפָה כַלְּבָנָה בָּרָה כַּחַמָּה אֲיֻמָּה כַּנִּדְגָּלוֹת:

11 I went down to the nut grove To see the budding of the vale; To see if the vines had blossomed, If the pomegranates were in bloom.

יא אֶל־גִּנַּת אֱגוֹז יָרַדְתִּי לִרְאוֹת בְּאִבֵּי הַנָּחַל לִרְאוֹת הֲפָרְחָה הַגֶּפֶן הֵנֵצוּ הָרִמֹּנִים:

12 Before I knew it, My desire set me Mid the chariots of Ammi-nadib.

יב לֹא יָדַעְתִּי נַפְשִׁי שָׂמַתְנִי מַרְכְּבוֹת עַמִּי־נָדִיב:

7

1 Turn back, turn back, O maid of Shulem! Turn back, turn back, That we may gaze upon you. "Why will you gaze at the Shulammite In the Mahanaim dance?"

א שׁוּבִי שׁוּבִי הַשּׁוּלַמִּית שׁוּבִי שׁוּבִי וְנֶחֱזֶה־בָּךְ מַה־תֶּחֱזוּ בַּשּׁוּלַמִּית כִּמְחֹלַת הַמַּחֲנָיִם:

2 How lovely are your feet in sandals, O daughter of nobles! Your rounded thighs are like jewels, The work of a master's hand.

ב מַה־יָּפוּ פְעָמַיִךְ בַּנְּעָלִים בַּת־נָדִיב חַמּוּקֵי יְרֵכַיִךְ כְּמוֹ חֲלָאִים מַעֲשֵׂה יְדֵי אָמָּן:

3 Your navel is like a round goblet – Let mixed wine not be lacking! – Your belly like a heap of wheat Hedged about with lilies.

ג שָׁרְרֵךְ אַגַּן הַסַּהַר אַל־יֶחְסַר הַמָּזֶג בִּטְנֵךְ עֲרֵמַת חִטִּים סוּגָה בַּשּׁוֹשַׁנִּים:

4 Your breasts are like two fawns, Twins of a gazelle.

ד שְׁנֵי שָׁדַיִךְ כִּשְׁנֵי עֳפָרִים תָּאֳמֵי צְבִיָּה:

5 Your neck is like a tower of ivory, Your eyes like pools in Heshbon By the gate of Bath-rabbim, Your nose like the Lebanon tower That faces toward Damascus.

ה צַוָּארֵךְ כְּמִגְדַּל הַשֵּׁן עֵינַיִךְ בְּרֵכוֹת בְּחֶשְׁבּוֹן עַל־שַׁעַר בַּת־רַבִּים אַפֵּךְ כְּמִגְדַּל הַלְּבָנוֹן צוֹפֶה פְּנֵי דַמָּשֶׂק:

6 The head upon you is like crimson wool, The locks of your head are like purple – A king is held captive in the tresses.

ו רֹאשֵׁךְ עָלַיִךְ כַּכַּרְמֶל וְדַלַּת רֹאשֵׁךְ כָּאַרְגָּמָן מֶלֶךְ אָסוּר בָּרְהָטִים:

7 How fair you are, how beautiful! O Love, with all its rapture!

ז מַה־יָּפִית וּמַה־נָּעַמְתְּ אַהֲבָה בַּתַּעֲנוּגִים:

8 Your stately form is like the palm, Your breasts are like clusters.

ח זֹאת קוֹמָתֵךְ דָּמְתָה לְתָמָר וְשָׁדַיִךְ לְאַשְׁכֹּלוֹת:

ZOT ko-ma-TAYKH da-m'-TAH l'-ta-MAR v'-sha-DA-yikh l'-ash-ko-LOT

7:8 Your stately form is like the palm The date is one of the seven special species of *Eretz Yisrael* (Deuteronomy 8:8). Like each of the other species, the date, which grows from a palm tree, is also a symbol of the People of Israel. The Sages teach that the palm tree is unique, in that every part of the tree can be used

1794

Shir Hashirim / Song of Songs
Chapter 8

שיר השירים
פרק ח

9 I say: Let me climb the palm, Let me take hold of its branches; Let your breasts be like clusters of grapes, Your breath like the fragrance of apples,

ט אָמַרְתִּי אֶעֱלֶה בְתָמָר אֹחֲזָה בְּסַנְסִנָּיו וְיִהְיוּ־נָא שָׁדַיִךְ כְּאֶשְׁכְּלוֹת הַגֶּפֶן וְרֵיחַ אַפֵּךְ כַּתַּפּוּחִים:

10 And your mouth like choicest wine. "Let it flow to my beloved as new wine Gliding over the lips of sleepers."

י וְחִכֵּךְ כְּיֵין הַטּוֹב הוֹלֵךְ לְדוֹדִי לְמֵישָׁרִים דּוֹבֵב שִׂפְתֵי יְשֵׁנִים:

11 I am my beloved's, And his desire is for me.

יא אֲנִי לְדוֹדִי וְעָלַי תְּשׁוּקָתוֹ:

12 Come, my beloved, Let us go into the open; Let us lodge among the henna shrubs.

יב לְכָה דוֹדִי נֵצֵא הַשָּׂדֶה נָלִינָה בַּכְּפָרִים:

13 Let us go early to the vineyards; Let us see if the vine has flowered, If its blossoms have opened, If the pomegranates are in bloom. There I will give my love to you.

יג נַשְׁכִּימָה לַכְּרָמִים נִרְאֶה אִם פָּרְחָה הַגֶּפֶן פִּתַּח הַסְּמָדַר הֵנֵצוּ הָרִמּוֹנִים שָׁם אֶתֵּן אֶת־דֹּדַי לָךְ:

14 The mandrakes yield their fragrance, At our doors are all choice fruits; Both freshly picked and long-stored Have I kept, my beloved, for you.

יד הַדּוּדָאִים נָתְנוּ־רֵיחַ וְעַל־פְּתָחֵינוּ כָּל־מְגָדִים חֲדָשִׁים גַּם־יְשָׁנִים דּוֹדִי צָפַנְתִּי לָךְ:

8 1 If only it could be as with a brother, As if you had nursed at my mother's breast: Then I could kiss you When I met you in the street, And no one would despise me.

ח א מִי יִתֶּנְךָ כְּאָח לִי יוֹנֵק שְׁדֵי אִמִּי אֶמְצָאֲךָ בַחוּץ אֶשָּׁקְךָ גַּם לֹא־יָבֻזוּ לִי:

2 I would lead you, I would bring you To the house of my mother, Of her who taught me – I would let you drink of the spiced wine, Of my pomegranate juice.

ב אֶנְהָגֲךָ אֲבִיאֲךָ אֶל־בֵּית אִמִּי תְּלַמְּדֵנִי אַשְׁקְךָ מִיַּיִן הָרֶקַח מֵעֲסִיס רִמֹּנִי:

3 His left hand was under my head, His right hand caressed me.

ג שְׂמֹאלוֹ תַּחַת רֹאשִׁי וִימִינוֹ תְּחַבְּקֵנִי:

4 I adjure you, O maidens of *Yerushalayim*: Do not wake or rouse Love until it please!

ד הִשְׁבַּעְתִּי אֶתְכֶם בְּנוֹת יְרוּשָׁלָםִ מַה־תָּעִירוּ וּמַה־תְּעֹרְרוּ אֶת־הָאַהֲבָה עַד שֶׁתֶּחְפָּץ:

5 Who is she that comes up from the desert, Leaning upon her beloved? Under the apple tree I roused you; It was there your mother conceived you, There she who bore you conceived you.

ה מִי זֹאת עֹלָה מִן־הַמִּדְבָּר מִתְרַפֶּקֶת עַל־דּוֹדָהּ תַּחַת הַתַּפּוּחַ עוֹרַרְתִּיךָ שָׁמָּה חִבְּלַתְךָ אִמֶּךָ שָׁמָּה חִבְּלָה יְלָדַתְךָ:

6 Let me be a seal upon your heart, Like the seal upon your hand. For love is fierce as death, Passion is mighty as Sheol; Its darts are darts of fire, A blazing flame.

ו שִׂימֵנִי כַחוֹתָם עַל־לִבֶּךָ כַּחוֹתָם עַל־זְרוֹעֶךָ כִּי־עַזָּה כַמָּוֶת אַהֲבָה קָשָׁה כִשְׁאוֹל קִנְאָה רְשָׁפֶיהָ רִשְׁפֵּי אֵשׁ שַׁלְהֶבֶתְיָה:

Date palm in Northern Israel

for various purposes including food, shelter and fuel. Similarly, each member of the Jewish people has a unique mission involving various areas of endeavor, such as *Torah* study, charity and other good deeds. However, the date only has one pit, illustrating that while each individual has a separate mission, the nation has but one heart united by the common goal of fulfilling *Hashem*'s will in this world.

Shir Hashirim/Song of Songs
Chapter 8

שיר השירים
פרק ח

7 Vast floods cannot quench love, Nor rivers drown it. If a man offered all his wealth for love, He would be laughed to scorn.

ז מַיִם רַבִּים לֹא יוּכְלוּ לְכַבּוֹת אֶת־הָאַהֲבָה וּנְהָרוֹת לֹא יִשְׁטְפוּהָ אִם־יִתֵּן אִישׁ אֶת־כָּל־הוֹן בֵּיתוֹ בָּאַהֲבָה בּוֹז יָבוּזוּ לוֹ׃

8 "We have a little sister, Whose breasts are not yet formed. What shall we do for our sister When she is spoken for?

ח אָחוֹת לָנוּ קְטַנָּה וְשָׁדַיִם אֵין לָהּ מַה־נַּעֲשֶׂה לַאֲחֹתֵנוּ בַּיּוֹם שֶׁיְּדֻבַּר־בָּהּ׃

9 If she be a wall, We will build upon it a silver battlement; If she be a door, We will panel it in cedar."

ט אִם־חוֹמָה הִיא נִבְנֶה עָלֶיהָ טִירַת כָּסֶף וְאִם־דֶּלֶת הִיא נָצוּר עָלֶיהָ לוּחַ אָרֶז׃

10 I am a wall, My breasts are like towers. So I became in his eyes As one who finds favor.

י אֲנִי חוֹמָה וְשָׁדַי כַּמִּגְדָּלוֹת אָז הָיִיתִי בְעֵינָיו כְּמוֹצְאֵת שָׁלוֹם׃

11 *Shlomo* had a vineyard In Baal-hamon. He had to post guards in the vineyard: A man would give for its fruit A thousand pieces of silver.

יא כֶּרֶם הָיָה לִשְׁלֹמֹה בְּבַעַל הָמוֹן נָתַן אֶת־הַכֶּרֶם לַנֹּטְרִים אִישׁ יָבִא בְּפִרְיוֹ אֶלֶף כָּסֶף׃

12 I have my very own vineyard: You may have the thousand, O *Shlomo*, And the guards of the fruit two hundred!

יב כַּרְמִי שֶׁלִּי לְפָנָי הָאֶלֶף לְךָ שְׁלֹמֹה וּמָאתַיִם לְנֹטְרִים אֶת־פִּרְיוֹ׃

13 O you who linger in the garden, A lover is listening; Let me hear your voice.

יג הַיּוֹשֶׁבֶת בַּגַּנִּים חֲבֵרִים מַקְשִׁיבִים לְקוֹלֵךְ הַשְׁמִיעִנִי׃

14 "Hurry, my beloved, Swift as a gazelle or a young stag, To the hills of spices!"

יד בְּרַח דּוֹדִי וּדְמֵה־לְךָ לִצְבִי אוֹ לְעֹפֶר הָאַיָּלִים עַל הָרֵי בְשָׂמִים׃

b'-RAKH do-DEE ud-MAY l'-KHA litz-VEE O l'-O-fer ha-a-ya-LEEM AL ha-RAY v'-sa-MEEM

8:14 To the hills of spices Almost all commentators agree that the "hills of spices" mentioned in this verse are a reference to the Temple Mount in *Yerushalayim*. The spices refer to the incense offering that was offered in the *Beit Hamikdash*, which produced a sweet smell. The Talmud (*Yoma* 39b) relates that the scent of the incense was so strong that the women in *Yerushalayim* did not need to use perfume. In this verse, the people turn to *Hashem*, their beloved, and ask that he hurry like a gazelle "to the hills of spices." They wish to be redeemed quickly from their bitter exile. They beg for God to return them to the Land of Israel, and for His presence to also return to the Holy Land and to the *Beit Hamikdash* in *Yerushalayim*.

Megillat Rut
The Scroll of Ruth

Introduction and commentary by Rabbi Tuly Weisz

To most Jews, *Megillat Rut* (Ruth) immediately conjures up thoughts and memories of the holiday of *Shavuot*, when it is read publicly in synagogue.

Shavuot is one of the three central pilgrimage festivals and, according to Jewish tradition, is the day when the Children of Israel experienced revelation and received the *Torah* from *Hashem* at Mount Sinai. At first glance, it seems puzzling that, of all the books in the holy Bible, we specifically read *Megillat Rut* on the day that commemorates the giving of the *Torah*.

The giving of the *Torah* was the single most important moment in the history of civilization – not only for Jews, but for all of mankind. Long ago, the Sages wondered why, if the *Torah* is so holy, it wasn't given in the Holy Land? Why was the *Torah* given in a barren desert instead?

The ancient rabbis explained that since Israel is the Jewish homeland, had the *Torah* been given in there it would have belonged exclusively to the Jewish people. Instead, therefore, *Hashem* chose to transmit His moral code on a barren mountain in the ownerless wilderness, to emphasize that His Word is for everyone equally, because His instructions are the key to universal redemption.

In *Megillat Rut* we read about the Moabite princess *Rut* who forges her own path to Mount Sinai through her relationship with her mother-in-law *Naomi*. *Rut* is associated with the holiday of *Shavuot* because, with great self-sacrifice, she finds her way to the ultimate truth of the *Torah*. As she movingly declares to *Naomi*, "your people shall be my people, and your God my God" (Ruth 1:16).

This redemptive experience leads *Rut* to become the matriarch of King *David*'s royal lineage, and the ultimate ancestress of the *Mashiach*, who will bring the whole world to recognize *Hashem* and the *Torah* He gave on Mount Sinai on the holiday of *Shavuot*.

Map of Places in *Megillat Rut*

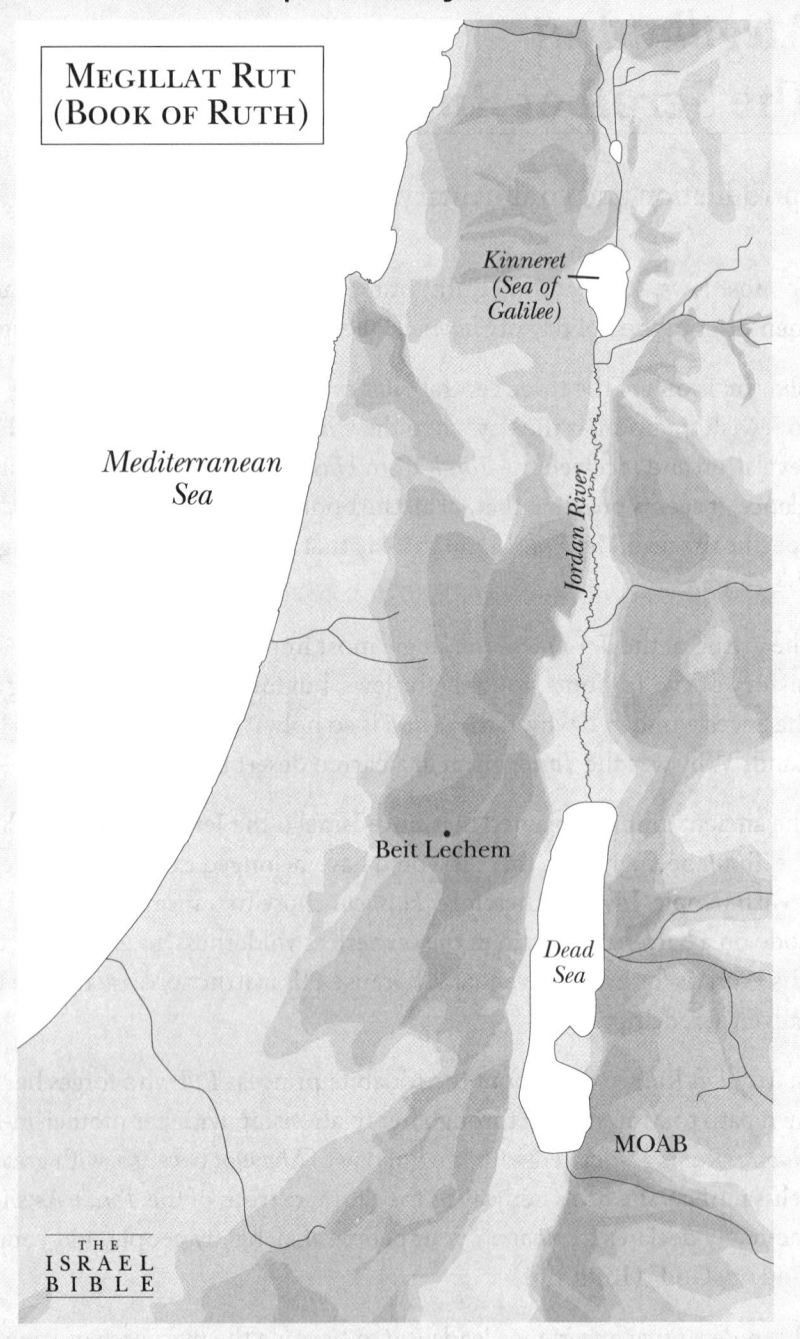

MEGILLAT RUT
(BOOK OF RUTH)

Kinneret (Sea of Galilee)

Mediterranean Sea

Jordan River

Beit Lechem

Dead Sea

MOAB

THE ISRAEL BIBLE

1. **Beit Lechem** – Part of the area of the tribe of *Yehuda*, it is the place where most of the events in the Book of Ruth transpire.
2. **Moab** – *Elimelech* escapes famine in Israel by bringing his family to Moab on the east side of the Jordan River (Ruth 1:1). In Moab, his children marry Moabite women, most notably *Rut*, who becomes the mother of Jewish royalty. *Elimelech* and his sons die in Moab.

Rut/Ruth

Chapter 1

רות
פרק א

1 ¹ In the days when the chieftains ruled, there was a famine in the land; and a man of *Beit Lechem* in *Yehuda*, with his wife and two sons, went to reside in the country of Moab.

א וַיְהִ֗י בִּימֵי֙ שְׁפֹ֣ט הַשֹּׁפְטִ֔ים וַיְהִ֥י רָעָ֖ב בָּאָ֑רֶץ וַיֵּ֨לֶךְ אִ֜ישׁ מִבֵּ֧ית לֶ֣חֶם יְהוּדָ֗ה לָגוּר֙ בִּשְׂדֵ֣י מוֹאָ֔ב ה֥וּא וְאִשְׁתּ֖וֹ וּשְׁנֵ֥י בָנָֽיו׃

² The man's name was *Elimelech*, his wife's name was *Naomi*, and his two sons were named *Machlon* and *Kilyon* – Ephrathites of *Beit Lechem* in *Yehuda*. They came to the country of Moab and remained there.

ב וְשֵׁ֣ם הָאִ֣ישׁ אֱ‍ֽלִימֶ֡לֶךְ וְשֵׁם֩ אִשְׁתּ֨וֹ נָעֳמִ֜י וְשֵׁ֥ם שְׁנֵֽי־בָנָ֣יו ׀ מַחְל֤וֹן וְכִלְיוֹן֙ אֶפְרָתִ֔ים מִבֵּ֥ית לֶ֖חֶם יְהוּדָ֑ה וַיָּבֹ֥אוּ שְׂדֵי־מוֹאָ֖ב וַיִּֽהְיוּ־שָֽׁם׃

³ *Elimelech*, *Naomi*'s husband, died; and she was left with her two sons.

ג וַיָּ֥מָת אֱלִימֶ֖לֶךְ אִ֣ישׁ נָעֳמִ֑י וַתִּשָּׁאֵ֥ר הִ֖יא וּשְׁנֵ֥י בָנֶֽיהָ׃

⁴ They married Moabite women, one named Orpah and the other *Rut*, and they lived there about ten years.

ד וַיִּשְׂא֣וּ לָהֶ֗ם נָשִׁים֙ מֹֽאֲבִיּ֔וֹת שֵׁ֤ם הָֽאַחַת֙ עָרְפָּ֔ה וְשֵׁ֥ם הַשֵּׁנִ֖ית ר֑וּת וַיֵּ֥שְׁבוּ שָׁ֖ם כְּעֶ֥שֶׂר שָׁנִֽים׃

⁵ Then those two – *Machlon* and *Kilyon* – also died; so the woman was left without her two sons and without her husband.

ה וַיָּמ֥וּתוּ גַם־שְׁנֵיהֶ֖ם מַחְל֣וֹן וְכִלְי֑וֹן וַתִּשָּׁאֵר֙ הָֽאִשָּׁ֔ה מִשְּׁנֵ֥י יְלָדֶ֖יהָ וּמֵאִישָֽׁהּ׃

va-ya-MU-tu gam sh'-nay-HEM makh-LON v'-khil-YON va-ti-sha-AYR ha-i-SHAH mi-sh'-NAY y'-la-DE-ha u-may-ee-SHAH

⁶ She started out with her daughters-in-law to return from the country of Moab; for in the country of Moab she had heard that *Hashem* had taken note of His people and given them food.

ו וַתָּ֤קָם הִיא֙ וְכַלֹּתֶ֔יהָ וַתָּ֖שָׁב מִשְּׂדֵ֣י מוֹאָ֑ב כִּ֤י שָֽׁמְעָה֙ בִּשְׂדֵ֣ה מוֹאָ֔ב כִּֽי־פָקַ֤ד יְהֹוָה֙ אֶת־עַמּ֔וֹ לָתֵ֥ת לָהֶ֖ם לָֽחֶם׃

⁷ Accompanied by her two daughters-in-law, she left the place where she had been living; and they set out on the road back to the land of *Yehuda*.

ז וַתֵּצֵ֗א מִן־הַמָּקוֹם֙ אֲשֶׁ֣ר הָיְתָה־שָּׁ֔מָּה וּשְׁתֵּ֥י כַלֹּתֶ֖יהָ עִמָּ֑הּ וַתֵּלַ֣כְנָה בַדֶּ֔רֶךְ לָשׁ֖וּב אֶל־אֶ֥רֶץ יְהוּדָֽה׃

⁸ But *Naomi* said to her two daughters-in-law, "Turn back, each of you to her mother's house. May *Hashem* deal kindly with you, as you have dealt with the dead and with me!

ח וַתֹּ֤אמֶר נׇעֳמִי֙ לִשְׁתֵּ֣י כַלֹּתֶ֔יהָ לֵ֣כְנָה שֹּׁ֔בְנָה אִשָּׁ֖ה לְבֵ֣ית אִמָּ֑הּ יעשה [יַ֣עַשׂ] יְהֹוָ֤ה עִמָּכֶם֙ חֶ֔סֶד כַּאֲשֶׁ֧ר עֲשִׂיתֶ֛ם עִם־הַמֵּתִ֖ים וְעִמָּדִֽי׃

⁹ May *Hashem* grant that each of you find security in the house of a husband!" And she kissed them farewell. They broke into weeping

ט יִתֵּ֤ן יְהֹוָה֙ לָכֶ֔ם וּמְצֶ֣אןָ מְנוּחָ֔ה אִשָּׁ֖ה בֵּ֣ית אִישָׁ֑הּ וַתִּשַּׁ֣ק לָהֶ֔ן וַתִּשֶּׂ֥אנָה קוֹלָ֖ן וַתִּבְכֶּֽינָה׃

¹⁰ and said to her, "No, we will return with you to your people."

י וַתֹּאמַ֖רְנָה־לָּ֑הּ כִּי־אִתָּ֥ךְ נָשׁ֖וּב לְעַמֵּֽךְ׃

Rashi (1040–1105)

1:5 So the woman was left without her two sons and without her husband The Sages teach that *Machlon*, *Kilyon* and their father *Elimelech* were all leaders of their generation, yet the text is silent regarding the reason for their untimely deaths. According to *Rashi*, their punishment was the result of the grave sin of abandoning the Land of Israel during a famine. Their actions greatly demoralized the struggling nation. This first lesson of *Megillat Rut* contains a valuable message for us today. We must not to turn our backs on the Promised Land, especially in her time of need.

Rut/Ruth
Chapter 1

רות
פרק א

11 But *Naomi* replied, "Turn back, my daughters! Why should you go with me? Have I any more sons in my body who might be husbands for you?

יא וַתֹּאמֶר נָעֳמִי שֹׁבְנָה בְנֹתַי לָמָּה תֵלַכְנָה עִמִּי הַעוֹד־לִי בָנִים בְּמֵעַי וְהָיוּ לָכֶם לַאֲנָשִׁים׃

12 Turn back, my daughters, for I am too old to be married. Even if I thought there was hope for me, even if I were married tonight and I also bore sons,

יב שֹׁבְנָה בְנֹתַי לֵכְןָ כִּי זָקַנְתִּי מִהְיוֹת לְאִישׁ כִּי אָמַרְתִּי יֶשׁ־לִי תִקְוָה גַּם הָיִיתִי הַלַּיְלָה לְאִישׁ וְגַם יָלַדְתִּי בָנִים׃

13 should you wait for them to grow up? Should you on their account debar yourselves from marriage? Oh no, my daughters! My lot is far more bitter than yours, for the hand of *Hashem* has struck out against me."

יג הֲלָהֵן תְּשַׂבֵּרְנָה עַד אֲשֶׁר יִגְדָּלוּ הֲלָהֵן תֵּעָגֵנָה לְבִלְתִּי הֱיוֹת לְאִישׁ אַל בְּנֹתַי כִּי־מַר־לִי מְאֹד מִכֶּם כִּי־יָצְאָה בִי יַד־יְהוָה׃

14 They broke into weeping again, and Orpah kissed her mother-in-law farewell. But *Rut* clung to her.

יד וַתִּשֶּׂנָה קוֹלָן וַתִּבְכֶּינָה עוֹד וַתִּשַּׁק עָרְפָּה לַחֲמוֹתָהּ וְרוּת דָּבְקָה בָּהּ׃

15 So she said, "See, your sister-in-law has returned to her people and her gods. Go follow your sister-in-law."

טו וַתֹּאמֶר הִנֵּה שָׁבָה יְבִמְתֵּךְ אֶל־עַמָּהּ וְאֶל־אֱלֹהֶיהָ שׁוּבִי אַחֲרֵי יְבִמְתֵּךְ׃

16 But *Rut* replied, "Do not urge me to leave you, to turn back and not follow you. For wherever you go, I will go; wherever you lodge, I will lodge; your people shall be my people, and your God my God.

טז וַתֹּאמֶר רוּת אַל־תִּפְגְּעִי־בִי לְעָזְבֵךְ לָשׁוּב מֵאַחֲרָיִךְ כִּי אֶל־אֲשֶׁר תֵּלְכִי אֵלֵךְ וּבַאֲשֶׁר תָּלִינִי אָלִין עַמֵּךְ עַמִּי וֵאלֹהַיִךְ אֱלֹהָי׃

va-TO-mer Ruth al tif-g'-ee VEE l'-oz-VAYKH la-SHUV may-a-kha-RA-yikh KEE el a-SHER tay-l'-KHEE ay-LAYKH u-va-a-SHER ta-LEE-nee a-LEEN a-MAYKH a-MEE vay-lo-HA-yikh e-lo-HAI

17 Where you die, I will die, and there I will be buried. Thus and more may *Hashem* do to me if anything but death parts me from you."

יז בַּאֲשֶׁר תָּמוּתִי אָמוּת וְשָׁם אֶקָּבֵר כֹּה יַעֲשֶׂה יְהוָה לִי וְכֹה יֹסִיף כִּי הַמָּוֶת יַפְרִיד בֵּינִי וּבֵינֵךְ׃

18 When [*Naomi*] saw how determined she was to go with her, she ceased to argue with her;

יח וַתֵּרֶא כִּי־מִתְאַמֶּצֶת הִיא לָלֶכֶת אִתָּהּ וַתֶּחְדַּל לְדַבֵּר אֵלֶיהָ׃

19 and the two went on until they reached *Beit Lechem*. When they arrived in *Beit Lechem*, the whole city buzzed with excitement over them. The women said, "Can this be *Naomi*?"

יט וַתֵּלַכְנָה שְׁתֵּיהֶם עַד־בֹּאָנָה בֵּית לָחֶם וַיְהִי כְּבֹאָנָה בֵּית לֶחֶם וַתֵּהֹם כָּל־הָעִיר עֲלֵיהֶן וַתֹּאמַרְנָה הֲזֹאת נָעֳמִי׃

20 "Do not call me *Naomi*," she replied. "Call me Mara, for *Shaddai* has made my lot very bitter.

כ וַתֹּאמֶר אֲלֵיהֶן אַל־תִּקְרֶאנָה לִי נָעֳמִי קְרֶאןָ לִי מָרָא כִּי־הֵמַר שַׁדַּי לִי מְאֹד׃

1:16 Your people shall be my people, and your God my God After *Naomi* begs her daughters-in-law not to follow her back to *Eretz Yisrael* and gives them compelling reasons to leave her, Orpah does what most people would do. She takes the easy way out, returns to her father's house and goes off to live a life of anonymity. *Rut*, on the other hand, answers the call in one of the most beautiful statements of faith and allegiance in the entire Bible. Her words and actions set her on the path of royalty, and have inspired the faithful for hundreds of years. *Rut* demonstrates for all time what it means to cast one's lot with the People of Israel, the Land of Israel and the God of Israel. For *Rut's* sacrifice, she was rewarded by becoming the matriarch of the Davidic dynasty, and the ancestress of the *Mashiach*.

Rut/Ruth
Chapter 2

רות
פרק ב

21 I went away full, and *Hashem* has brought me back empty. How can you call me *Naomi*, when *Hashem* has dealt harshly with me, when *Shaddai* has brought misfortune upon me!"

כא אֲנִי מְלֵאָה הָלַכְתִּי וְרֵיקָם הֱשִׁיבַנִי יְהֹוָה לָמָּה תִקְרֶאנָה לִי נָעֳמִי וַיהֹוָה עָנָה בִי וְשַׁדַּי הֵרַע לִי:

22 Thus *Naomi* returned from the country of Moab; she returned with her daughter-in-law *Rut* the Moabite. They arrived in *Beit Lechem* at the beginning of the barley harvest.

כב וַתָּשָׁב נָעֳמִי וְרוּת הַמּוֹאֲבִיָּה כַלָּתָהּ עִמָּהּ הַשָּׁבָה מִשְּׂדֵי מוֹאָב וְהֵמָּה בָּאוּ בֵּית לֶחֶם בִּתְחִלַּת קְצִיר שְׂעֹרִים:

2 1 Now *Naomi* had a kinsman on her husband's side, a man of substance, of the family of *Elimelech*, whose name was *Boaz*.

ב א וּלְנָעֳמִי מידע [מוֹדָע] לְאִישָׁהּ אִישׁ גִּבּוֹר חַיִל מִמִּשְׁפַּחַת אֱלִימֶלֶךְ וּשְׁמוֹ בֹּעַז:

2 *Rut* the Moabite said to *Naomi*, "I would like to go to the fields and glean among the ears of grain, behind someone who may show me kindness." "Yes, daughter, go," she replied;

ב וַתֹּאמֶר רוּת הַמּוֹאֲבִיָּה אֶל־נָעֳמִי אֵלְכָה־נָּא הַשָּׂדֶה וַאֲלַקֳטָה בַשִּׁבֳּלִים אַחַר אֲשֶׁר אֶמְצָא־חֵן בְּעֵינָיו וַתֹּאמֶר לָהּ לְכִי בִתִּי:

3 and off she went. She came and gleaned in a field, behind the reapers; and, as luck would have it, it was the piece of land belonging to *Boaz*, who was of *Elimelech*'s family.

ג וַתֵּלֶךְ וַתָּבוֹא וַתְּלַקֵּט בַּשָּׂדֶה אַחֲרֵי הַקֹּצְרִים וַיִּקֶר מִקְרֶהָ חֶלְקַת הַשָּׂדֶה לְבֹעַז אֲשֶׁר מִמִּשְׁפַּחַת אֱלִימֶלֶךְ:

4 Presently *Boaz* arrived from *Beit Lechem*. He greeted the reapers, "*Hashem* be with you!" And they responded, "*Hashem* bless you!"

ד וְהִנֵּה־בֹעַז בָּא מִבֵּית לֶחֶם וַיֹּאמֶר לַקּוֹצְרִים יְהֹוָה עִמָּכֶם וַיֹּאמְרוּ לוֹ יְבָרֶכְךָ יְהֹוָה:

v'-hi-nay VO-az BA mi-BAYT LE-khem va-YO-mer la-ko-tz'-REEM a-do-NAI i-ma-KHEM va-YO-m'-ru LO y'-va-re-kh'-KHA a-do-NAI

5 *Boaz* said to the servant who was in charge of the reapers, "Whose girl is that?"

ה וַיֹּאמֶר בֹּעַז לְנַעֲרוֹ הַנִּצָּב עַל־הַקּוֹצְרִים לְמִי הַנַּעֲרָה הַזֹּאת:

6 The servant in charge of the reapers replied, "She is a Moabite girl who came back with *Naomi* from the country of Moab.

ו וַיַּעַן הַנַּעַר הַנִּצָּב עַל־הַקּוֹצְרִים וַיֹּאמַר נַעֲרָה מוֹאֲבִיָּה הִיא הַשָּׁבָה עִם־נָעֳמִי מִשְּׂדֵה מוֹאָב:

7 She said, 'Please let me glean and gather among the sheaves behind the reapers.' She has been on her feet ever since she came this morning. She has rested but little in the hut."

ז וַתֹּאמֶר אֲלַקֳטָה־נָּא וְאָסַפְתִּי בָעֳמָרִים אַחֲרֵי הַקּוֹצְרִים וַתָּבוֹא וַתַּעֲמוֹד מֵאָז הַבֹּקֶר וְעַד־עַתָּה זֶה שִׁבְתָּהּ הַבַּיִת מְעָט:

2:4 Presently Boaz arrived from Beit Lechem In Hebrew, Bethlehem is *Beit Lechem* (בית לחם), which means 'House of Bread.' In ancient times, *Beit Lechem* was full of fields of wheat and grains for harvesting, which is why it is significant that so much of the story of *Rut* takes place during the harvest season, specifically in *Beit Lechem*. In 2012, archeological evidence of the biblical town of *Beit Lechem* was discovered. A clay seal was uncovered in the City of David in Jerusalem with the inscription "from *Beit Lechem* to the king," presumably sealing a package containing a tax payment in the seventh or eighth century BCE.

Rut/Ruth
Chapter 2

רות
פרק ב

8 *Boaz* said to *Rut*, "Listen to me, daughter. Don't go to glean in another field. Don't go elsewhere, but stay here close to my girls.

ח וַיֹּאמֶר בֹּעַז אֶל־רוּת הֲלוֹא שָׁמַעַתְּ בִּתִּי אַל־תֵּלְכִי לִלְקֹט בְּשָׂדֶה אַחֵר וְגַם לֹא תַעֲבוּרִי מִזֶּה וְכֹה תִדְבָּקִין עִם־נַעֲרֹתָי׃

9 Keep your eyes on the field they are reaping, and follow them. I have ordered the men not to molest you. And when you are thirsty, go to the jars and drink some of [the water] that the men have drawn."

ט עֵינַיִךְ בַּשָּׂדֶה אֲשֶׁר־יִקְצֹרוּן וְהָלַכְתְּ אַחֲרֵיהֶן הֲלוֹא צִוִּיתִי אֶת־הַנְּעָרִים לְבִלְתִּי נָגְעֵךְ וְצָמִת וְהָלַכְתְּ אֶל־הַכֵּלִים וְשָׁתִית מֵאֲשֶׁר יִשְׁאֲבוּן הַנְּעָרִים׃

10 She prostrated herself with her face to the ground, and said to him, "Why are you so kind as to single me out, when I am a foreigner?"

י וַתִּפֹּל עַל־פָּנֶיהָ וַתִּשְׁתַּחוּ אָרְצָה וַתֹּאמֶר אֵלָיו מַדּוּעַ מָצָאתִי חֵן בְּעֵינֶיךָ לְהַכִּירֵנִי וְאָנֹכִי נָכְרִיָּה׃

11 *Boaz* said in reply, "I have been told of all that you did for your mother-in-law after the death of your husband, how you left your father and mother and the land of your birth and came to a people you had not known before.

יא וַיַּעַן בֹּעַז וַיֹּאמֶר לָהּ הֻגֵּד הֻגַּד לִי כֹּל אֲשֶׁר־עָשִׂית אֶת־חֲמוֹתֵךְ אַחֲרֵי מוֹת אִישֵׁךְ וַתַּעַזְבִי אָבִיךְ וְאִמֵּךְ וְאֶרֶץ מוֹלַדְתֵּךְ וַתֵּלְכִי אֶל־עַם אֲשֶׁר לֹא־יָדַעַתְּ תְּמוֹל שִׁלְשׁוֹם׃

12 May *Hashem* reward your deeds. May you have a full recompense from *Hashem*, the God of *Yisrael*, under whose wings you have sought refuge!"

יב יְשַׁלֵּם יְהוָה פָּעֳלֵךְ וּתְהִי מַשְׂכֻּרְתֵּךְ שְׁלֵמָה מֵעִם יְהוָה אֱלֹהֵי יִשְׂרָאֵל אֲשֶׁר־בָּאת לַחֲסוֹת תַּחַת־כְּנָפָיו׃

13 She answered, "You are most kind, my lord, to comfort me and to speak gently to your maidservant – though I am not so much as one of your maidservants."

יג וַתֹּאמֶר אֶמְצָא־חֵן בְּעֵינֶיךָ אֲדֹנִי כִּי נִחַמְתָּנִי וְכִי דִבַּרְתָּ עַל־לֵב שִׁפְחָתֶךָ וְאָנֹכִי לֹא אֶהְיֶה כְּאַחַת שִׁפְחֹתֶיךָ׃

14 At mealtime, *Boaz* said to her, "Come over here and partake of the meal, and dip your morsel in the vinegar." So she sat down beside the reapers. He handed her roasted grain, and she ate her fill and had some left over.

יד וַיֹּאמֶר לָהּ בֹעַז לְעֵת הָאֹכֶל גֹּשִׁי הֲלֹם וְאָכַלְתְּ מִן־הַלֶּחֶם וְטָבַלְתְּ פִּתֵּךְ בַּחֹמֶץ וַתֵּשֶׁב מִצַּד הַקֹּצְרִים וַיִּצְבָּט־לָהּ קָלִי וַתֹּאכַל וַתִּשְׂבַּע וַתֹּתַר׃

15 When she got up again to glean, *Boaz* gave orders to his workers, "You are not only to let her glean among the sheaves, without interference,

טו וַתָּקָם לְלַקֵּט וַיְצַו בֹּעַז אֶת־נְעָרָיו לֵאמֹר גַּם בֵּין הָעֳמָרִים תְּלַקֵּט וְלֹא תַכְלִימוּהָ׃

16 but you must also pull some [stalks] out of the heaps and leave them for her to glean, and not scold her."

טז וְגַם שֹׁל־תָּשֹׁלּוּ לָהּ מִן־הַצְּבָתִים וַעֲזַבְתֶּם וְלִקְּטָה וְלֹא תִגְעֲרוּ־בָהּ׃

17 She gleaned in the field until evening. Then she beat out what she had gleaned – it was about an *'efah* of barley –

יז וַתְּלַקֵּט בַּשָּׂדֶה עַד־הָעָרֶב וַתַּחְבֹּט אֵת אֲשֶׁר־לִקֵּטָה וַיְהִי כְּאֵיפָה שְׂעֹרִים׃

va-t'-la-KAYT ba-sa-DEH ad ha-A-rev va-takh-BOT AYT a-sher li-KAY-tah vai-HEE k'-ay-FAH s'-o-REEM

שעורה

2:17 It was about an *efah* of barley Barley, the second of the special agricultural products of the Land of Israel (Deuteronomy 8:8), looks similar to wheat but is a smaller grain, and is surrounded by long, hair-like strands. This explains its Hebrew name *se'orah* (שעורה), which comes from the word *sei'ar* (שיער), meaning 'hair.' Additionally, barley requires less water and ripens earlier than wheat. In the Bible, the barley harvest signifies the

Barley in the Western Negev

Rut/Ruth
Chapter 3

רות
פרק ג

18 and carried it back with her to the town. When her mother-in-law saw what she had gleaned, and when she also took out and gave her what she had left over after eating her fill,	וַתִּשָּׂא וַתָּבוֹא הָעִיר וַתֵּרֶא חֲמוֹתָהּ אֵת אֲשֶׁר־לִקֵּטָה וַתּוֹצֵא וַתִּתֶּן־לָהּ אֵת אֲשֶׁר־הוֹתִרָה מִשָּׂבְעָהּ: יח
19 her mother-in-law asked her, "Where did you glean today? Where did you work? Blessed be he who took such generous notice of you!" So she told her mother-in-law whom she had worked with, saying, "The name of the man with whom I worked today is *Boaz*."	וַתֹּאמֶר לָהּ חֲמוֹתָהּ אֵיפֹה לִקַּטְתְּ הַיּוֹם וְאָנָה עָשִׂית יְהִי מַכִּירֵךְ בָּרוּךְ וַתַּגֵּד לַחֲמוֹתָהּ אֵת אֲשֶׁר־עָשְׂתָה עִמּוֹ וַתֹּאמֶר שֵׁם הָאִישׁ אֲשֶׁר עָשִׂיתִי עִמּוֹ הַיּוֹם בֹּעַז: יט
20 *Naomi* said to her daughter-in-law, "Blessed be he of *Hashem*, who has not failed in His kindness to the living or to the dead! For," *Naomi* explained to her daughter-in-law, "the man is related to us; he is one of our redeeming kinsmen."	וַתֹּאמֶר נָעֳמִי לְכַלָּתָהּ בָּרוּךְ הוּא לַיהֹוָה אֲשֶׁר לֹא־עָזַב חַסְדּוֹ אֶת־הַחַיִּים וְאֶת־הַמֵּתִים וַתֹּאמֶר לָהּ נָעֳמִי קָרוֹב לָנוּ הָאִישׁ מִגֹּאֲלֵנוּ הוּא: כ
21 *Rut* the Moabite said, "He even told me, 'Stay close by my workers until all my harvest is finished.'"	וַתֹּאמֶר רוּת הַמּוֹאֲבִיָּה גַּם כִּי־אָמַר אֵלַי עִם־הַנְּעָרִים אֲשֶׁר־לִי תִּדְבָּקִין עַד אִם־כִּלּוּ אֵת כָּל־הַקָּצִיר אֲשֶׁר־לִי: כא
22 And *Naomi* answered her daughter-in-law *Rut*, "It is best, daughter, that you go out with his girls, and not be annoyed in some other field."	וַתֹּאמֶר נָעֳמִי אֶל־רוּת כַּלָּתָהּ טוֹב בִּתִּי כִּי תֵצְאִי עִם־נַעֲרוֹתָיו וְלֹא יִפְגְּעוּ־בָךְ בְּשָׂדֶה אַחֵר: כב
23 So she stayed close to the maidservants of *Boaz*, and gleaned until the barley harvest and the wheat harvest were finished. Then she stayed at home with her mother-in-law.	וַתִּדְבַּק בְּנַעֲרוֹת בֹּעַז לְלַקֵּט עַד־כְּלוֹת קְצִיר־הַשְּׂעֹרִים וּקְצִיר הַחִטִּים וַתֵּשֶׁב אֶת־חֲמוֹתָהּ: כג

va-tid-BAK b'-na-a-ROT BO-az l'-la-KAYT ad k'-LOT k'-tzeer ha-s'-o-REEM uk-TZEER ha-khi-TEEM va-TAY-shev et kha-mo-TAH

3 1 *Naomi*, her mother-in-law, said to her, "Daughter, I must seek a home for you, where you may be happy.	וַתֹּאמֶר לָהּ נָעֳמִי חֲמוֹתָהּ בִּתִּי הֲלֹא אֲבַקֶּשׁ־לָךְ מָנוֹחַ אֲשֶׁר יִיטַב־לָךְ: א
2 Now there is our kinsman *Boaz*, whose girls you were close to. He will be winnowing barley on the threshing floor tonight.	וְעַתָּה הֲלֹא בֹעַז מֹדַעְתָּנוּ אֲשֶׁר הָיִית אֶת־נַעֲרוֹתָיו הִנֵּה־הוּא זֹרֶה אֶת־גֹּרֶן הַשְּׂעֹרִים הַלָּיְלָה: ב

---

beginning of spring, and barley would be brought to the *Beit Hamikdash* in *Yerushalayim* as part of the offerings of the holiday of *Pesach*. The barley offering in the Temple was a joyous ceremony that teaches us the importance of dedicating a portion of our crops to our Creator before we eat from them ourselves.

2:23 Until the barley harvest and the wheat harvest were finished One reason that *Megillat Rut* is read on the holiday of *Shavuot*, also known as the Feast of Weeks or Pentecost, is that the story took place during the barley and wheat harvest. *Shavuot* is referred to as the "Feast of the Harvest" (Exodus 23:16). It is the festival which began the season for Jewish farmers to make a pilgrimage to *Yerushalayim* to offer their first fruit and grain in the *Beit Hamikdash*, and when an offering of two loaves of bread was brought from the newly harvested wheat crop.

Rut/Ruth
Chapter 3

רות
פרק ג

3 So bathe, anoint yourself, dress up, and go down to the threshing floor. But do not disclose yourself to the man until he has finished eating and drinking.

ג וְרָחַצְתְּ וָסַכְתְּ וְשַׂמְתְּ שִׂמְלֹתַיִךְ [שִׂמְלֹתַיִךְ] עָלַיִךְ וירדתי [וְיָרַדְתְּ] הַגֹּרֶן אַל־תִּוָּדְעִי לָאִישׁ עַד כַּלֹּתוֹ לֶאֱכֹל וְלִשְׁתּוֹת:

4 When he lies down, note the place where he lies down, and go over and uncover his feet and lie down. He will tell you what you are to do."

ד וִיהִי בְשָׁכְבוֹ וְיָדַעַתְּ אֶת־הַמָּקוֹם אֲשֶׁר יִשְׁכַּב־שָׁם וּבָאת וְגִלִּית מַרְגְּלֹתָיו ושכבתי [וְשָׁכָבְתְּ] וְהוּא יַגִּיד לָךְ אֵת אֲשֶׁר תַּעֲשִׂין:

5 She replied, "I will do everything you tell me."

ה וַתֹּאמֶר אֵלֶיהָ כֹּל אֲשֶׁר־תֹּאמְרִי [אֵלַי] אֶעֱשֶׂה:

6 She went down to the threshing floor and did just as her mother-in-law had instructed her.

ו וַתֵּרֶד הַגֹּרֶן וַתַּעַשׂ כְּכֹל אֲשֶׁר־צִוַּתָּה חֲמוֹתָהּ:

7 Boaz ate and drank, and in a cheerful mood went to lie down beside the grainpile. Then she went over stealthily and uncovered his feet and lay down.

ז וַיֹּאכַל בֹּעַז וַיֵּשְׁתְּ וַיִּיטַב לִבּוֹ וַיָּבֹא לִשְׁכַּב בִּקְצֵה הָעֲרֵמָה וַתָּבֹא בַלָּט וַתְּגַל מַרְגְּלֹתָיו וַתִּשְׁכָּב:

8 In the middle of the night, the man gave a start and pulled back – there was a woman lying at his feet!

ח וַיְהִי בַּחֲצִי הַלַּיְלָה וַיֶּחֱרַד הָאִישׁ וַיִּלָּפֵת וְהִנֵּה אִשָּׁה שֹׁכֶבֶת מַרְגְּלֹתָיו:

9 "Who are you?" he asked. And she replied, "I am your handmaid Rut. Spread your robe over your handmaid, for you are a redeeming kinsman."

ט וַיֹּאמֶר מִי־אָתְּ וַתֹּאמֶר אָנֹכִי רוּת אֲמָתֶךָ וּפָרַשְׂתָּ כְנָפֶךָ עַל־אֲמָתְךָ כִּי גֹאֵל אָתָּה:

va-YO-mer mee AT va-TO-mer a-no-KHEE RUT a-ma-TE-kha u-fa-ras-TA kh'-na-FE-kha al a-ma-t'-KHA KEE go-AYL A-tah

10 He exclaimed, "Be blessed of Hashem, daughter! Your latest deed of loyalty is greater than the first, in that you have not turned to younger men, whether poor or rich.

י וַיֹּאמֶר בְּרוּכָה אַתְּ לַיהוָה בִּתִּי הֵיטַבְתְּ חַסְדֵּךְ הָאַחֲרוֹן מִן־הָרִאשׁוֹן לְבִלְתִּי־לֶכֶת אַחֲרֵי הַבַּחוּרִים אִם־דַּל וְאִם־עָשִׁיר:

11 And now, daughter, have no fear. I will do in your behalf whatever you ask, for all the elders of my town know what a fine woman you are.

יא וְעַתָּה בִּתִּי אַל־תִּירְאִי כֹּל אֲשֶׁר־תֹּאמְרִי אֶעֱשֶׂה־לָּךְ כִּי יוֹדֵעַ כָּל־שַׁעַר עַמִּי כִּי אֵשֶׁת חַיִל אָתְּ:

12 But while it is true I am a redeeming kinsman, there is another redeemer closer than I.

יב וְעַתָּה כִּי אָמְנָם כִּי אִם גֹּאֵל אָנֹכִי וְגַם יֵשׁ גֹּאֵל קָרוֹב מִמֶּנִּי:

3:9 For you are a redeeming kinsman The concept of the "redeeming kinsman," *goel* (גואל) in Hebrew, had great significance in biblical times. In *Megillat Rut*, the word *goel* is used to refer to a relative in the context of a levirate marriage, which occurs when a man dies without children. In such a case, his brother is supposed to marry his widow and perpetuate the name of the deceased. In the *Tanakh*, the term *goel* is also used in another context. *Vayikra* (25:25) says "his nearest redeemer shall come," referring to someone so deeply in debt that he is forced to sell his property until his closest relative comes to bail him out. Once again, a person's redeemer is his closest relative. *Hashem* has many names in the Bible, one of which is Redeemer, as in the "Redeemer of *Yisrael*" (Isaiah 49:7). By referring to God as our Redeemer, we are stating that He is even closer to us than any of our nearest relations.

גאל

Rut/Ruth
Chapter 4

13 Stay for the night. Then in the morning, if he will act as a redeemer, good! let him redeem. But if he does not want to act as redeemer for you, I will do so myself, as *Hashem* lives! Lie down until morning."

14 So she lay at his feet until dawn. She rose before one person could distinguish another, for he thought, "Let it not be known that the woman came to the threshing floor."

15 And he said, "Hold out the shawl you are wearing." She held it while he measured out six measures of barley, and he put it on her back. When she got back to the town,

16 she came to her mother-in-law, who asked, "How is it with you, daughter?" She told her all that the man had done for her;

17 and she added, "He gave me these six measures of barley, saying to me, 'Do not go back to your mother-in-law empty-handed.'"

18 And *Naomi* said, "Stay here, daughter, till you learn how the matter turns out. For the man will not rest, but will settle the matter today."

4 1 Meanwhile, *Boaz* had gone to the gate and sat down there. And now the redeemer whom *Boaz* had mentioned passed by. He called, "Come over and sit down here, So-and-so!" And he came over and sat down.

2 Then [*Boaz*] took ten elders of the town and said, "Be seated here"; and they sat down.

3 He said to the redeemer, "*Naomi*, now returned from the country of Moab, must sell the piece of land which belonged to our kinsman *Elimelech*.

4 I thought I should disclose the matter to you and say: Acquire it in the presence of those seated here and in the presence of the elders of my people. If you are willing to redeem it, redeem! But if you will not redeem, tell me, that I may know. For there is no one to redeem but you, and I come after you." "I am willing to redeem it," he replied.

5 *Boaz* continued, "When you acquire the property from *Naomi* and from *Rut* the Moabite, you must also acquire the wife of the deceased, so as to perpetuate the name of the deceased upon his estate."

רות

פרק ד

יג לִינִי הַלַּיְלָה וְהָיָה בַבֹּקֶר אִם־יִגְאָלֵךְ טוֹב יִגְאָל וְאִם־לֹא יַחְפֹּץ לְגָאֳלֵךְ וּגְאַלְתִּיךְ אָנֹכִי חַי־יְהֹוָה שִׁכְבִי עַד־הַבֹּקֶר׃

יד וַתִּשְׁכַּב מַרְגְּלוֹתָו [מַרְגְּלוֹתָיו] עַד־הַבֹּקֶר וַתָּקָם בְּטֶרוֹם [בְּטֶרֶם] יַכִּיר אִישׁ אֶת־רֵעֵהוּ וַיֹּאמֶר אַל־יִוָּדַע כִּי־בָאָה הָאִשָּׁה הַגֹּרֶן׃

טו וַיֹּאמֶר הָבִי הַמִּטְפַּחַת אֲשֶׁר־עָלַיִךְ וְאֶחֳזִי־בָהּ וַתֹּאחֶז בָּהּ וַיָּמָד שֵׁשׁ־שְׂעֹרִים וַיָּשֶׁת עָלֶיהָ וַיָּבֹא הָעִיר׃

טז וַתָּבוֹא אֶל־חֲמוֹתָהּ וַתֹּאמֶר מִי־אַתְּ בִּתִּי וַתַּגֶּד־לָהּ אֵת כָּל־אֲשֶׁר עָשָׂה־לָהּ הָאִישׁ׃

יז וַתֹּאמֶר שֵׁשׁ־הַשְּׂעֹרִים הָאֵלֶּה נָתַן לִי כִּי אָמַר [אֵלַי] אַל־תָּבוֹאִי רֵיקָם אֶל־חֲמוֹתֵךְ׃

יח וַתֹּאמֶר שְׁבִי בִתִּי עַד אֲשֶׁר תֵּדְעִין אֵיךְ יִפֹּל דָּבָר כִּי לֹא יִשְׁקֹט הָאִישׁ כִּי־אִם־כִּלָּה הַדָּבָר הַיּוֹם׃

ד א וּבֹעַז עָלָה הַשַּׁעַר וַיֵּשֶׁב שָׁם וְהִנֵּה הַגֹּאֵל עֹבֵר אֲשֶׁר דִּבֶּר־בֹּעַז וַיֹּאמֶר סוּרָה שְׁבָה־פֹּה פְּלֹנִי אַלְמֹנִי וַיָּסַר וַיֵּשֵׁב׃

ב וַיִּקַּח עֲשָׂרָה אֲנָשִׁים מִזִּקְנֵי הָעִיר וַיֹּאמֶר שְׁבוּ־פֹה וַיֵּשֵׁבוּ׃

ג וַיֹּאמֶר לַגֹּאֵל חֶלְקַת הַשָּׂדֶה אֲשֶׁר לְאָחִינוּ לֶאֱלִימֶלֶךְ מָכְרָה נָעֳמִי הַשָּׁבָה מִשְּׂדֵה מוֹאָב׃

ד וַאֲנִי אָמַרְתִּי אֶגְלֶה אָזְנְךָ לֵאמֹר קְנֵה נֶגֶד הַיֹּשְׁבִים וְנֶגֶד זִקְנֵי עַמִּי אִם־תִּגְאַל גְּאָל וְאִם־לֹא יִגְאַל הַגִּידָה לִּי וְאֵדְעָה [וְאֵדְעָה] כִּי אֵין זוּלָתְךָ לִגְאוֹל וְאָנֹכִי אַחֲרֶיךָ וַיֹּאמֶר אָנֹכִי אֶגְאָל׃

ה וַיֹּאמֶר בֹּעַז בְּיוֹם־קְנוֹתְךָ הַשָּׂדֶה מִיַּד נָעֳמִי וּמֵאֵת רוּת הַמּוֹאֲבִיָּה אֵשֶׁת־הַמֵּת קָנִיתִי [קָנִיתָה] לְהָקִים שֵׁם־הַמֵּת עַל־נַחֲלָתוֹ׃

Rut/Ruth

Chapter 4

6 The redeemer replied, "Then I cannot redeem it for myself, lest I impair my own estate. You take over my right of redemption, for I am unable to exercise it."

7 Now this was formerly done in *Yisrael* in cases of redemption or exchange: to validate any transaction, one man would take off his sandal and hand it to the other. Such was the practice in *Yisrael*.

8 So when the redeemer said to *Boaz*, "Acquire for yourself," he drew off his sandal.

9 And *Boaz* said to the elders and to the rest of the people, "You are witnesses today that I am acquiring from *Naomi* all that belonged to *Elimelech* and all that belonged to *Kilyon* and *Machlon*.

10 I am also acquiring *Rut* the Moabite, the wife of *Machlon*, as my wife, so as to perpetuate the name of the deceased upon his estate, that the name of the deceased may not disappear from among his kinsmen and from the gate of his home town. You are witnesses today."

11 All the people at the gate and the elders answered, "We are. May *Hashem* make the woman who is coming into your house like *Rachel* and *Leah*, both of whom built up the House of *Yisrael*! Prosper in *Efrat* and perpetuate your name in *Beit Lechem*!

12 And may your house be like the house of *Peretz* whom *Tamar* bore to *Yehuda* – through the offspring which *Hashem* will give you by this young woman."

13 So *Boaz* married *Rut*; she became his wife, and he cohabited with her. *Hashem* let her conceive, and she bore a son.

14 And the women said to *Naomi*, "Blessed be *Hashem*, who has not withheld a redeemer from you today! May his name be perpetuated in *Yisrael*!

15 He will renew your life and sustain your old age; for he is born of your daughter-in-law, who loves you and is better to you than seven sons."

16 *Naomi* took the child and held it to her bosom. She became its foster mother,

רות

פרק ד

ו וַיֹּאמֶר הַגֹּאֵל לֹא אוּכַל לִגְאָל־[לִגְאָל־] לִי פֶּן־אַשְׁחִית אֶת־נַחֲלָתִי גְּאַל־לְךָ אַתָּה אֶת־גְּאֻלָּתִי כִּי לֹא־אוּכַל לִגְאֹל׃

ז וְזֹאת לְפָנִים בְּיִשְׂרָאֵל עַל־הַגְּאוּלָּה וְעַל־הַתְּמוּרָה לְקַיֵּם כָּל־דָּבָר שָׁלַף אִישׁ נַעֲלוֹ וְנָתַן לְרֵעֵהוּ וְזֹאת הַתְּעוּדָה בְּיִשְׂרָאֵל׃

ח וַיֹּאמֶר הַגֹּאֵל לְבֹעַז קְנֵה־לָךְ וַיִּשְׁלֹף נַעֲלוֹ׃

ט וַיֹּאמֶר בֹּעַז לַזְּקֵנִים וְכָל־הָעָם עֵדִים אַתֶּם הַיּוֹם כִּי קָנִיתִי אֶת־כָּל־אֲשֶׁר לֶאֱלִימֶלֶךְ וְאֵת כָּל־אֲשֶׁר לְכִלְיוֹן וּמַחְלוֹן מִיַּד נָעֳמִי׃

י וְגַם אֶת־רוּת הַמֹּאֲבִיָּה אֵשֶׁת מַחְלוֹן קָנִיתִי לִי לְאִשָּׁה לְהָקִים שֵׁם־הַמֵּת עַל־נַחֲלָתוֹ וְלֹא־יִכָּרֵת שֵׁם־הַמֵּת מֵעִם אֶחָיו וּמִשַּׁעַר מְקוֹמוֹ עֵדִים אַתֶּם הַיּוֹם׃

יא וַיֹּאמְרוּ כָּל־הָעָם אֲשֶׁר־בַּשַּׁעַר וְהַזְּקֵנִים עֵדִים יִתֵּן יְהוָה אֶת־הָאִשָּׁה הַבָּאָה אֶל־בֵּיתֶךָ כְּרָחֵל וּכְלֵאָה אֲשֶׁר בָּנוּ שְׁתֵּיהֶם אֶת־בֵּית יִשְׂרָאֵל וַעֲשֵׂה־חַיִל בְּאֶפְרָתָה וּקְרָא־שֵׁם בְּבֵית לָחֶם׃

יב וִיהִי בֵיתְךָ כְּבֵית פֶּרֶץ אֲשֶׁר־יָלְדָה תָמָר לִיהוּדָה מִן־הַזֶּרַע אֲשֶׁר יִתֵּן יְהוָה לְךָ מִן־הַנַּעֲרָה הַזֹּאת׃

יג וַיִּקַּח בֹּעַז אֶת־רוּת וַתְּהִי־לוֹ לְאִשָּׁה וַיָּבֹא אֵלֶיהָ וַיִּתֵּן יְהוָה לָהּ הֵרָיוֹן וַתֵּלֶד בֵּן׃

יד וַתֹּאמַרְנָה הַנָּשִׁים אֶל־נָעֳמִי בָּרוּךְ יְהוָה אֲשֶׁר לֹא הִשְׁבִּית לָךְ גֹּאֵל הַיּוֹם וְיִקָּרֵא שְׁמוֹ בְּיִשְׂרָאֵל׃

טו וְהָיָה לָךְ לְמֵשִׁיב נֶפֶשׁ וּלְכַלְכֵּל אֶת־שֵׂיבָתֵךְ כִּי כַלָּתֵךְ אֲשֶׁר־אֲהֵבַתֶךְ יְלָדַתּוּ אֲשֶׁר־הִיא טוֹבָה לָךְ מִשִּׁבְעָה בָּנִים׃

טז וַתִּקַּח נָעֳמִי אֶת־הַיֶּלֶד וַתְּשִׁתֵהוּ בְחֵיקָהּ וַתְּהִי־לוֹ לְאֹמֶנֶת׃

Rut/Ruth
Chapter 4

רות
פרק ד

17 and the women neighbors gave him a name, saying, "A son is born to *Naomi*!" They named him *Oved*; he was the father of *Yishai*, father of *David*.

וַתִּקְרֶאנָה לוֹ הַשְּׁכֵנוֹת שֵׁם לֵאמֹר יֻלַּד־בֵּן לְנָעֳמִי וַתִּקְרֶאנָה שְׁמוֹ עוֹבֵד הוּא אֲבִי־יִשַׁי אֲבִי דָוִד:

18 This is the line of *Peretz*: *Peretz* begot *Chetzron*,

וְאֵלֶּה תּוֹלְדוֹת פָּרֶץ פֶּרֶץ הוֹלִיד אֶת־חֶצְרוֹן:

19 *Chetzron* begot *Ram*, *Ram* begot *Aminadav*,

וְחֶצְרוֹן הוֹלִיד אֶת־רָם וְרָם הוֹלִיד אֶת־עַמִּינָדָב:

20 *Aminadav* begot *Nachshon*, *Nachshon* begot *Salma*,

וְעַמִּינָדָב הוֹלִיד אֶת־נַחְשׁוֹן וְנַחְשׁוֹן הוֹלִיד אֶת־שַׂלְמָה:

21 *Salma* begot *Boaz*, *Boaz* begot *Oved*,

וְשַׂלְמוֹן הוֹלִיד אֶת־בֹּעַז וּבֹעַז הוֹלִיד אֶת־עוֹבֵד:

22 *Oved* begot *Yishai*, and *Yishai* begot *David*.

וְעֹבֵד הוֹלִיד אֶת־יִשַׁי וְיִשַׁי הוֹלִיד אֶת־דָּוִד:

v'-o-VAYD ho-LEED et yi-SHAI v'-yi-SHAI ho-LEED et da-VID

4:22 And *Yishai* begot *David* *Megillat Rut* ends by emphasizing *Rut*'s great reward for her selfless dedication to her mother-in-law and her late husband. She gives birth to a child who becomes the grandfather of King *David*, making *Rut* the ancestress of the Davidic dynasty as well as its future descendant, the *Mashiach*. Most other nations would have chosen a king with a perfect pedigree and impeccable lineage, yet King *David* descends from a Moabite convert. The lesson of King *David*'s humble origins is a powerful one. *Rut* teaches us that salvation and redemption can come from unlikely sources. No matter what our background is, we all have the ability to play a great role in history and make a difference in the world if we align ourselves with the God of Israel, the People of Israel and the Land of Israel.

Megillat Eicha
The Scroll of Lamentations

Introduction and commentary by Rabbi Noam Shapiro

In *Megillat Eicha* (Lamentations) the prophet *Yirmiyahu* records his impressions of the destruction of *Yerushalayim* and the first *Beit Hamikdash*, and the exile of the Jews from the Land of Israel. It is a very emotional book in which the prophet expresses feelings of intense loneliness, a sense of utter abandonment, desolation, desecration of that which was sacred, pain and suffering. There are times when *Yirmiyahu* even seems to challenge *Hashem* for allowing this to happen, yet the book also contains elements of prayer, faith and hope.

How did it happen? What led to the great destruction of the Holy Land and the exile of the Jews? Throughout the Bible, the Jews are told that *Eretz Yisrael* is their eternal inheritance, but that living in the land is dependent upon following God and His *Torah*. The prophets warn again and again that continuing to sin, abandoning *Hashem*, and treating others inappropriately will lead to destruction and exile. Ultimately, that is what happened. However, *Yirmiyahu* also reminds us that *Hashem* did not abandon His people and His land, even though He destroyed the place where they connect to Him most. Their new challenge is to find *Hashem* and rebuild their connection with Him, even in exile.

Amidst the mourning, sorrow and misery of *Megillat Eicha*, there are elements of faith and optimism. In the middle of chapter 3, the prophet declares "The kindness of *Hashem* has not ended, His mercies are not spent" (3:22). He continues a little further in the chapter: "For *Hashem* does not reject forever, but first afflicts, then pardons in His abundant kindness. For He does not willfully bring grief or affliction to man" (3:31–33). *Yirmiyahu* reminds us that destruction and exile from the Land of Israel is not an indication of a divorce between *Hashem* and His nation. Rather, the exile is meant to serve a rehabilitative function. It is meant to trigger introspection, evaluation of our behavior and relationship with *Hashem*, and to lead us to recommit ourselves to God and to each other. Indeed, *Yirmiyahu* himself composes a letter to the exiles in which he gives them the guidelines for surviving in exile, and promises redemption if they call out to *Hashem* (Jeremiah 28).

Similarly, the Talmud (*Makkot* 24b) relates that a number of leading Sages were visiting *Yerushalayim* following the destruction of the *Beit Hamikdash*, and they came upon the ruins of the Temple Mount. Seeing a jackal scamper across the holiest site in the world, three of the four rabbis started to cry. The great Rabbi Akiva, on the other hand, began to laugh joyously. Shocked, the others asked him to explain his behavior. Rabbi Akiva replied that if the prophecies of destruction have so clearly been fulfilled, we can be certain that the promises of redemption will also be fulfilled. *Megillat Eicha*, therefore, calls on us to "search and examine our ways, and turn back to *Hashem*" (3:40). It ends with a call to the Lord to fulfill those prophecies of redemption and "renew our days as of old" (5:21).

The Talmud (*Taanit* 30b) teaches that those who participate in mourning for the destruction of *Yerushalayim* will merit to participate in rejoicing over its rebuilding. Throughout the cycle of life, Jews express sorrow for the fact that the *Beit Hamikdash* is no longer with us, and that as a result, God's presence is more distant. For this reason, a glass is broken at Jewish weddings, to remember *Yerushalayim* even at the happiest of occasions. And once a year, on the ninth of the Hebrew month of *Av*, the mourning for *Yerushalayim* is particularly vivid. For more than twenty-four hours it is forbidden to eat or drink; Jews sit on the floor as an expression of mourning, and recall the events surrounding the destruction by reciting *Megillat Eicha* and other prayers of lament, as if the tragedy had just happened. In this way, it is possible to come to grips with what has been lost. *Megillat Eicha* is the text that best expresses our broken hearts as we call out again and again, *Eicha* (הכיא), 'alas,' or 'how [did this happen].'

For almost two thousand years, Jews have mourned over the destruction of *Yerushalayim* and the *Beit Hamikdash*. In modern times, we have begun to experience the rebirth of the Land of Israel and the Holy City. May we merit to quickly see *Hashem*'s comfort and the fulfillment of the rest of the redemption, through the coming of the *Mashiach* and the building of the third *Beit Hamikdash*.

Chart of Israel's Exiles, Persecutions and Wars

Megillat Eicha laments the destruction of *Yerushalayim* and the *Beit Hamikdash*, as well as the exile of the Jews from the Land of Israel at the hands of Nebuchadnezzar king of Babylon. This first exile of the Jews happened in stages, and is just one example of the many exiles, expulsions and persecutions of the Jewish people throughout history. The following is a partial list of persecutions and exiles of the Jewish people in the Land of Israel, as well as modern Israel's wars.

Event	Description	Perpetrator	Date	King of Israel/ Prime Minister	Relevant Verses
First stage of the exile of *Yisrael*	The Israelite populations of the Galilee, Gilad and the eastern side of the Jordan River are taken into exile.	Tiglath-Pileser king of Assyria	734 BCE	*Pekach*	II Kings 15:29, I Chronicles 5:26
Complete exile of the ten tribes of *Yisrael*	The remaining members of the ten tribes of *Yisrael* are exiled and scattered. Other populations are brought into the land to replace them.	Sennacherib king of Assyria	722 BCE	*Hoshea son of Eila*	II Kings 17:6, II Kings 18:9–12
First stage of the exile of *Yehuda*	The youths of the royal family are taken to Babylon	Nebuchadnezzar king of Babylon	604 BCE	*Yehoyakim*	Daniel 1:1–6
Second stage of the exile of *Yehuda* – Exile of the artisans and craftsmen	The king, the royal family, royal officials, warriors, artisans, and other distinguished people from *Yerushalayim* and *Yehuda* are exiled to Babylon	Nebuchadnezzar king of Babylon	597 BCE	*Yehoyachin*	II Kings 24:8–17
Third stage of the exile of *Yehuda*/ Destruction of *Yerushalayim* and the *Beit Hamikdash*	The *Beit Hamikdash* is destroyed and all the remaining inhabitants of *Yehuda* and *Yerushalayim*, aside from the poorest people, are exiled to Babylon	Nebuchadnezzar king of Babylon	586 BCE	*Tzidkiyahu*	II Kings 25:8–21, II Chronicles 36:15–20
Religious persecution by the Syrian-Greeks	The Jews in Israel are forbidden from *Torah* study and Jewish practice and the *Beit Hamikdash* is defiled. Those who continue to practice Judaism are killed.	Antiochus Epiphanes, king of the Seleucids (Syrian-Greek empire)	168–165 BCE		
Destruction of *Yerushalayim* and the Second *Beit Hamikdash*	The city of *Yerushalayim* is captured and the *Beit Hamikdash* is destroyed. Nearly one million Jews are killed in *Yerushalayim* alone and 100,000 taken captive	Titus of Rome	70 CE		
Bar Kochba Revolt	As a result of Bar Kochba's rebellion against the Romans, hundreds of thousands of Jews are slaughtered. Jews are banned from entering the city of *Yerushalayim* from the end of the Bar Kochba Revolt until the capture of *Yerushalayim* by the Muslims in 638 CE. Israel is renamed Syria Palaestina.	Hadrian, emperor of Rome	135 CE		

Event	Description	Perpetrator	Date	King of Israel/ Prime Minister	Relevant Verses
Chevron attacks	At the beginning of the Ottoman rule, the Sultan's deputy armies attack the Jews of *Chevron*. They are beaten, raped and murdered, and their homes and businesses are looted and pillaged. Jews do not return to *Chevron* for another 15 years.	Murad Bey, deputy of the Sultan from Jerusalem	1517 CE		
Tzfat Arab Pogrom	A 33 day pogrom against the Jews of *Tzfat* as part of the general rebellion against governor Muhammed Ali. Jews are raped and murdered, and their homes, synagogues and businesses are destroyed and looted.	Mobs of peasants	1834 CE		
Arab riots	At the encouragement of Haj Amin el-Husseini, Arabs begin rioting and carrying out murderous attacks against Jews throughout the Land of Israel, especially in the North, in *Yerushalayim* and in *Yaffo* and its environs.	Arab rioters encouraged by Haj Amin el-Husseini	1920– 1921		
Jihad against the Jews – *Chevron* Massacre and *Tzfat* Massacre	Accusing the Jews of trying to take over Muslim holy sites, especially the Temple Mount, Haj Amin el-Husseini calls for jihad against the Jews. Incitement spreads throughout the Land of Israel, especially in *Yerushalayim* and *Chevron*. The Jews of *Yerushalayim* suffer numerous attacks, and the Jewish community of *Chevron* is destroyed. One week later, the same thing happens to the Jews of *Tzfat*.	Arab rioters encouraged by Haj Amin el-Husseini	1929		
War of Independence	The Israeli War of Independence takes place along the entire border of the country. Israel fights against Lebanon and Syria in the north, Iraq and Jordan in the east, Egypt, assisted by Sudan, in the south, and Palestinians and Arab volunteers inside the country. Israel emerges victorious, defeating the invading Arab forces and capturing 5,000 square kilometers more than what was initially allocated by the United Nations. However, the Jews lose access to the eastern part of *Yerushalayim*, including the Western Wall and the Temple Mount, until 1967.	Egypt Transjordan Iraq Syria Lebanon	1947– 1949	David Ben-Gurion	
Sinai War	The Sinai War, or Sinai Campaign, is fought to end terrorist infiltrations and attacks in Israel, and to break the Egyptian blockade of *Eilat*. Israel's attack on Egypt is successful and Israel takes control of the Gaza Strip and the Sinai Peninsula before being pressured to give the Sinai Peninsula back to the Egyptians.	Egypt	1956	David Ben-Gurion	

Event	Description	Perpetrator	Date	King of Israel/ Prime Minister	Relevant Verses
Six-Day War	The Six-Day War begins in response to Egypt's mobilization of forces in the Sinai Peninsula, expelling of the UN forces and signing an agreement with Jordan. Israel launches a surprise attack which demolishes the Egyptian air force while it is still on the ground. In just six days, the IDF overruns the entire Sinai peninsula, takes the West Bank of the Jordan River, captures a great part of the Golan Heights, and regains control of the Old City of *Yerushalayim* and its Western Wall.	Egypt Syria Jordan Iraq Lebanon	1967	Levi Eshkol	
War of Attrition	The War of Attrition refers to the continuous, static fighting along the ceasefire borders of the Six-Day War, focused around the Bar Lev line on the Suez Canal. The fighting is initiated by Egypt in the hopes of regaining control of the Sinai Peninsula, lost to Israel in the Six-Day War. The war ends with a ceasefire in August 1970.	Egypt	1968–1970	Golda Meir	
Yom Kippur War	The Yom Kippur War begins with an attack by a coalition of Arab forces, led by Egypt and Syria, in both the Sinai Peninsula and the Golan Heights. The attack is carried out on *Yom Kippur*, the holiest day on the Jewish calendar, and takes Israel by surprise. While Egypt and Syria make significant initial gains, the IDF pushes them back. Within a few days, the Israeli army has crossed the Suez Canal into Egypt and are within artillery range of the airfields outside the Syrian capital of Damascus. The war ends by a ceasefire on October 25th.	Egypt Syria Jordan Iraq	1973	Golda Meir	
First Lebanon War	The First Lebanon War is Israel's response to continuous attacks on northern Israel carried out by Palestinian terror organizations in Lebanon. The war begins after an assassination attempt against Israel's ambassador to the United Kingdom, Shlomo Argov. As a result of the war, the Palestinian Liberation Organization (PLO) is expelled from Lebanon and an Israeli Security Zone is created in Southern Lebanon.	PLO	1982	Menachem Begin	
Second Lebanon War	The Second Lebanon War begins in response to the abduction of two Israeli soldiers by the Hezbollah terror organization. It lasts just over a month and results in the pacification of Southern Lebanon and a weakening of the Hezbollah terror group.	Hezbollah	2006	Ehud Olmert	

Event	Description	Perpetrator	Date	King of Israel/ Prime Minister	Relevant Verses
Operation Protective Edge	Operation Protective Edge begins in response to increased rocket fire by the Hamas terror organization from the Gaza Strip into Israel, following the abduction and murder of three Israeli teens. The operation begins with Israeli airstrikes into Gaza which are followed by a ground invasion aimed at destroying Hamas terror tunnels leading into Israel. As a result of the war, the Hamas terror organization is weakened and many of their tunnels are destroyed.	Hamas	2014	Benjamin Netanyahu	

Eicha/Lamentations
Chapter 1

איכה
פרק א

1 1 Alas! Lonely sits the city Once great with people! She that was great among nations Is become like a widow; The princess among states Is become a thrall.

א אֵיכָה יָשְׁבָה בָדָד הָעִיר רַבָּתִי עָם הָיְתָה כְּאַלְמָנָה רַבָּתִי בַגּוֹיִם שָׂרָתִי בַּמְּדִינוֹת הָיְתָה לָמַס׃

2 Bitterly she weeps in the night, Her cheek wet with tears. There is none to comfort her Of all her friends. All her allies have betrayed her; They have become her foes.

ב בָּכוֹ תִבְכֶּה בַּלַּיְלָה וְדִמְעָתָהּ עַל לֶחֱיָהּ אֵין־לָהּ מְנַחֵם מִכָּל־אֹהֲבֶיהָ כָּל־רֵעֶיהָ בָּגְדוּ בָהּ הָיוּ לָהּ לְאֹיְבִים׃

ba-KHO tiv-KEH ba-LAI-lah v'-dim-a-TAH AL le-khe-YAH ayn LAH m'-na-KHAYM mi-kol o-ha-VE-ha kol ray-E-ha BA-g'-du VAH ha-YU LAH l'-o-y'-VEEM

3 *Yehuda* has gone into exile Because of misery and harsh oppression; When she settled among the nations, She found no rest; All her pursuers overtook her In the narrow places.

ג גָּלְתָה יְהוּדָה מֵעֹנִי וּמֵרֹב עֲבֹדָה הִיא יָשְׁבָה בַגּוֹיִם לֹא מָצְאָה מָנוֹחַ כָּל־רֹדְפֶיהָ הִשִּׂיגוּהָ בֵּין הַמְּצָרִים׃

4 *Tzion*'s roads are in mourning, Empty of festival pilgrims; All her gates are deserted. Her *Kohanim* sigh, Her maidens are unhappy – She is utterly disconsolate!

ד דַּרְכֵי צִיּוֹן אֲבֵלוֹת מִבְּלִי בָּאֵי מוֹעֵד כָּל־שְׁעָרֶיהָ שׁוֹמֵמִין כֹּהֲנֶיהָ נֶאֱנָחִים בְּתוּלֹתֶיהָ נּוּגוֹת וְהִיא מַר־לָהּ׃

5 Her enemies are now the masters, Her foes are at ease, Because *Hashem* has afflicted her For her many transgressions; Her infants have gone into captivity Before the enemy.

ה הָיוּ צָרֶיהָ לְרֹאשׁ אֹיְבֶיהָ שָׁלוּ כִּי־יְהֹוָה הוֹגָהּ עַל רֹב־פְּשָׁעֶיהָ עוֹלָלֶיהָ הָלְכוּ שְׁבִי לִפְנֵי־צָר׃

6 Gone from Fair *Tzion* are all That were her glory; Her leaders were like stags That found no pasture; They could only walk feebly Before the pursuer.

ו וַיֵּצֵא מִן־[בַּת־]צִיּוֹן כָּל־הֲדָרָהּ הָיוּ שָׂרֶיהָ כְּאַיָּלִים לֹא־מָצְאוּ מִרְעֶה וַיֵּלְכוּ בְלֹא־כֹחַ לִפְנֵי רוֹדֵף׃

7 All the precious things she had In the days of old *Yerushalayim* recalled In her days of woe and sorrow, When her people fell by enemy hands With none to help her; When enemies looked on and gloated Over her downfall.

ז זָכְרָה יְרוּשָׁלַ͏ִם יְמֵי עָנְיָהּ וּמְרוּדֶיהָ כֹּל מַחֲמֻדֶיהָ אֲשֶׁר הָיוּ מִימֵי קֶדֶם בִּנְפֹל עַמָּהּ בְּיַד־צָר וְאֵין עוֹזֵר לָהּ רָאוּהָ צָרִים שָׂחֲקוּ עַל מִשְׁבַּתֶּהָ׃

1:2 All her allies have betrayed her; They have become her foes Jewish history has demonstrated time and time again just how drastically friends can indeed turn into enemies. Ever since the biblical account of Pharaoh inviting *Yosef*'s family down to Egypt, which eventually led to the bitter enslavement of the Israelites, we have seen one host country after another turn against her Jewish subjects. In the last century, for example, Jews were active contributors in all realms of European society: Politicians, academics, doctors, lawyers, artists, and more. It was thus all the more devastating when, in 1935, with Adolf Hitler's power steadily growing, the Nuremberg Laws were passed. These laws called for clear genetic definitions regarding who is a Jew, and all those defined as Jews were denied the right to German citizenship, demonstrating how dramatically a friend can turn into an enemy! In contrast, Israel's Law of Return was modified in 1970 to include anyone who would have been defined as a Jew under the Nuremberg Laws. According to the current law, anyone born a Jew, a child of a Jew or grandchild of a Jew, and their spouses, all have the right to attain citizenship in the State of Israel if they so desire.

The Law of Return

Eicha/Lamentations
Chapter 1

איכה
פרק א

8 *Yerushalayim* has greatly sinned, Therefore she is become a mockery. All who admired her despise her, For they have seen her disgraced; And she can only sigh And shrink back.

ח חֵטְא חָטְאָה יְרוּשָׁלַ͏ִם עַל־כֵּן לְנִידָה הָיָתָה כָּל־מְכַבְּדֶיהָ הִזִּילוּהָ כִּי־רָאוּ עֶרְוָתָהּ גַּם־הִיא נֶאֶנְחָה וַתָּשָׁב אָחוֹר:

9 Her uncleanness clings to her skirts. She gave no thought to her future; She has sunk appallingly, With none to comfort her. – See, *Hashem*, my misery; How the enemy jeers!

ט טֻמְאָתָהּ בְּשׁוּלֶיהָ לֹא זָכְרָה אַחֲרִיתָהּ וַתֵּרֶד פְּלָאִים אֵין מְנַחֵם לָהּ רְאֵה יְהֹוָה אֶת־עָנְיִי כִּי הִגְדִּיל אוֹיֵב:

10 The foe has laid hands On everything dear to her. She has seen her Sanctuary Invaded by nations Which You have denied admission Into Your community.

י יָדוֹ פָּרַשׂ צָר עַל כָּל־מַחֲמַדֶּיהָ כִּי־רָאֲתָה גוֹיִם בָּאוּ מִקְדָּשָׁהּ אֲשֶׁר צִוִּיתָה לֹא־יָבֹאוּ בַקָּהָל לָךְ:

11 All her inhabitants sigh, As they search for bread; They have bartered their treasures for food, To keep themselves alive. – See, *Hashem*, and behold, How abject I have become!

יא כָּל־עַמָּהּ נֶאֱנָחִים מְבַקְשִׁים לֶחֶם נָתְנוּ מַחֲמוֹדֵיהֶם [מַחֲמַדֵּיהֶם] בְּאֹכֶל לְהָשִׁיב נָפֶשׁ רְאֵה יְהֹוָה וְהַבִּיטָה כִּי הָיִיתִי זוֹלֵלָה:

12 May it never befall you, All who pass along the road – Look about and see: Is there any agony like mine, Which was dealt out to me When *Hashem* afflicted me On His day of wrath?

יב לוֹא אֲלֵיכֶם כָּל־עֹבְרֵי דֶרֶךְ הַבִּיטוּ וּרְאוּ אִם־יֵשׁ מַכְאוֹב כְּמַכְאֹבִי אֲשֶׁר עוֹלַל לִי אֲשֶׁר הוֹגָה יְהֹוָה בְּיוֹם חֲרוֹן אַפּוֹ:

13 From above He sent a fire Down into my bones. He spread a net for my feet, He hurled me backward; He has left me forlorn, In constant misery.

יג מִמָּרוֹם שָׁלַח־אֵשׁ בְּעַצְמֹתַי וַיִּרְדֶּנָּה פָּרַשׂ רֶשֶׁת לְרַגְלַי הֱשִׁיבַנִי אָחוֹר נְתָנַנִי שֹׁמֵמָה כָּל־הַיּוֹם דָּוָה:

14 The yoke of my offenses is bound fast, Lashed tight by His hand; Imposed upon my neck, It saps my strength; *Hashem* has delivered me into the hands Of those I cannot withstand.

יד נִשְׂקַד עֹל פְּשָׁעַי בְּיָדוֹ יִשְׂתָּרְגוּ עָלוּ עַל־צַוָּארִי הִכְשִׁיל כֹּחִי נְתָנַנִי אֲדֹנָי בִּידֵי לֹא־אוּכַל קוּם:

15 *Hashem* in my midst has rejected All my heroes; He has proclaimed a set time against me To crush my young men. As in a press *Hashem* has trodden Fair Maiden *Yehuda*.

טו סִלָּה כָל־אַבִּירַי אֲדֹנָי בְּקִרְבִּי קָרָא עָלַי מוֹעֵד לִשְׁבֹּר בַּחוּרָי גַּת דָּרַךְ אֲדֹנָי לִבְתוּלַת בַּת־יְהוּדָה:

16 For these things do I weep, My eyes flow with tears: Far from me is any comforter Who might revive my spirit; My children are forlorn, For the foe has prevailed.

טז עַל־אֵלֶּה אֲנִי בוֹכִיָּה עֵינִי עֵינִי יֹרְדָה מַּיִם כִּי־רָחַק מִמֶּנִּי מְנַחֵם מֵשִׁיב נַפְשִׁי הָיוּ בָנַי שׁוֹמֵמִים כִּי גָבַר אוֹיֵב:

al ay-LEH a-NEE vo-khi-YAH ay-NEE ay-NEE YO-r'-dah MA-yim kee ra-KHAK mi-ME-nee m'-na-KHAYM may-SHEEV naf-SHEE ha-YU va-NAI sho-may-MEEM KEE ga-VAR o-YAYV

1:16 For these things do I weep, my eyes flow with tears The Sages explain that *Hashem* intentionally selected the ninth of the month of *Av* as the day on which both the first and second Temples would be destroyed. According to Jewish tradition, the reason for this is that it was on the ninth of *Av* that the twelve spies returned from their mission to scout out the land of Israel. As reported in *Sefer Bamidbar* (13–14), following the spies' pessimistic and libelous report, the people fearfully cried out to God: "How will we ever conquer

Eicha/Lamentations
Chapter 1

איכה
פרק א

17 *Tzion* spreads out her hands, She has no one to comfort her; *Hashem* has summoned against *Yaakov* His enemies all about him; *Yerushalayim* has become among them A thing unclean.

יז פֵּרְשָׂה צִיּוֹן בְּיָדֶיהָ אֵין מְנַחֵם לָהּ צִוָּה יְהוָה לְיַעֲקֹב סְבִיבָיו צָרָיו הָיְתָה יְרוּשָׁלַ͏ִם לְנִדָּה בֵּינֵיהֶם׃

18 *Hashem* is in the right, For I have disobeyed Him. Hear, all you peoples, And behold my agony: My maidens and my youths Have gone into captivity!

יח צַדִּיק הוּא יְהוָה כִּי פִיהוּ מָרִיתִי שִׁמְעוּ־נָא כָל־עמים [הָעַמִּים] וּרְאוּ מַכְאֹבִי בְּתוּלֹתַי וּבַחוּרַי הָלְכוּ בַשֶּׁבִי׃

19 I cried out to my friends, But they played me false. My *Kohanim* and my elders Have perished in the city As they searched for food To keep themselves alive.

יט קָרָאתִי לַמְאַהֲבַי הֵמָּה רִמּוּנִי כֹּהֲנַי וּזְקֵנַי בָּעִיר גָּוָעוּ כִּי־בִקְשׁוּ אֹכֶל לָמוֹ וְיָשִׁיבוּ אֶת־נַפְשָׁם׃

20 See, *Hashem*, the distress I am in! My heart is in anguish, I know how wrong I was To disobey. Outside the sword deals death; Indoors, the plague.

כ רְאֵה יְהוָה כִּי־צַר־לִי מֵעַי חֳמַרְמָרוּ נֶהְפַּךְ לִבִּי בְּקִרְבִּי כִּי מָרוֹ מָרִיתִי מִחוּץ שִׁכְּלָה־חֶרֶב בַּבַּיִת כַּמָּוֶת׃

21 When they heard how I was sighing, There was none to comfort me; All my foes heard of my plight and exulted. For it is Your doing: You have brought on the day that You threatened. Oh, let them become like me!

כא שָׁמְעוּ כִּי נֶאֱנָחָה אָנִי אֵין מְנַחֵם לִי כָּל־אֹיְבַי שָׁמְעוּ רָעָתִי שָׂשׂוּ כִּי אַתָּה עָשִׂיתָ הֵבֵאתָ יוֹם־קָרָאתָ וְיִהְיוּ כָמוֹנִי׃

sha-m'-U KEE ne-e-na-KHAH A-nee AYN m'-na-KHAYM LEE kol o-y'-VAI sha-m'-U ra-a-TEE SA-su KEE a-TAH a-SEE-ta hay-VAY-ta yom ka-RA-ta v'-yih-YU kha-MO-nee

---

the land? Why did you take us out of Egypt to die at the hands of the Canaanites?" The Sages (*Taanit* 29a) record God's reprimand of the people for their lack of faith: "You cried on the ninth of *Av* for no reason, and so this day will become a day of crying for all generations." The events surrounding the destruction of the *Beit Hamikdash* are linked back to the biblical account of the twelve spies, to illustrate that all of Jewish history is inexorably interwoven; it all represents the unfolding of *Hashem*'s master plan. Furthermore, we must never forget that one of the keys to the rebuilding of the *Beit Hamikdash* and the commencement of the Messianic Era is our unquestioning trust in God and appreciation for *Eretz Yisrael*. This is the very trait that the spies and nation failed to exhibit when they rejected His land, and it is one which we must constantly seek to achieve.

Rabbi Joseph B. Soloveitchik (1903–1993)

1:21 When they heard how I was sighing, there was none to comfort me The prophet *Yirmiyahu* captures the sense of utter loneliness that prevailed after the destruction of *Yerushalayim* and the exile of the people. He describes their feeling that there was no one to stand by their side or to provide any sort of comfort in their time of need. Over many centuries of exile, Jews repeatedly experienced this same sense of abandonment. For example, over two and a half millennia following the destruction of *Yerushalayim* in *Yirmiyahu*'s time, as Hitler's persecution mounted in the late 1930's, many Jews desired to flee from Europe. Unfortunately, though, not a single country was willing to absorb Jewish refugees. In July of 1938, delegates from over thirty countries met in Évian-les-Bains, France, to discuss the refugee crisis. Despite many sympathetic speeches for the tragic plight of the Jews, no country was willing to significantly change their immigration quota to admit additional Jewish refugees. As this verse bemoans, the entire world had closed their doors to the Jewish people, abandoning them in their time of need. With the establishment of the State of Israel, however, the Jewish people now have a home. Never again will they be left alone with no one to protect and comfort them. As Rabbi Joseph B. Soloveitchik writes in his essay *Kol Dodi Dofek*, 'The Voice of my Beloved Knocks,' "A Jew who flees from a hostile country now knows that he can find a secure refuge in the land of his ancestors… Jews who have been uprooted from their homes can find lodging in the Holy Land."

Eicha/Lamentations
Chapter 2

איכה
פרק ב

22 Let all their wrongdoing come before You, And deal with them As You have dealt with me For all my transgressions. For my sighs are many, And my heart is sick.

כב תָּבֹא כָל־רָעָתָם לְפָנֶיךָ וְעוֹלֵל לָמוֹ כַּאֲשֶׁר עוֹלַלְתָּ לִי עַל כָּל־פְּשָׁעָי כִּי־רַבּוֹת אַנְחֹתַי וְלִבִּי דַוָּי׃

2

1 Alas! *Hashem* in His wrath Has shamed Fair *Tzion*, Has cast down from heaven to earth The majesty of *Yisrael*. He did not remember His Footstool On His day of wrath.

א אֵיכָה יָעִיב בְּאַפּוֹ אֲדֹנָי אֶת־בַּת־צִיּוֹן הִשְׁלִיךְ מִשָּׁמַיִם אֶרֶץ תִּפְאֶרֶת יִשְׂרָאֵל וְלֹא־זָכַר הֲדֹם־רַגְלָיו בְּיוֹם אַפּוֹ׃

ay-KHAH ya-EEV b'-a-PO a-do-NAI et bat tzi-YON hish-LEEKH mi-sha-MA-yim E-retz tif-E-ret yis-ra-AYL v'-LO za-KHAR ha-DOM rag-LAV b'-YOM a-PO

2 *Hashem* has laid waste without pity All the habitations of *Yaakov*; He has razed in His anger Fair *Yehuda*'s strongholds. He has brought low in dishonor The kingdom and its leaders.

ב בִּלַּע אֲדֹנָי לֹא [וְלֹא] חָמַל אֵת כָּל־נְאוֹת יַעֲקֹב הָרַס בְּעֶבְרָתוֹ מִבְצְרֵי בַת־יְהוּדָה הִגִּיעַ לָאָרֶץ חִלֵּל מַמְלָכָה וְשָׂרֶיהָ׃

3 In blazing anger He has cut down All the might of *Yisrael*; He has withdrawn His right hand In the presence of the foe; He has ravaged *Yaakov* like flaming fire, Consuming on all sides.

ג גָּדַע בָּחֳרִי אַף כֹּל קֶרֶן יִשְׂרָאֵל הֵשִׁיב אָחוֹר יְמִינוֹ מִפְּנֵי אוֹיֵב וַיִּבְעַר בְּיַעֲקֹב כְּאֵשׁ לֶהָבָה אָכְלָה סָבִיב׃

4 He bent His bow like an enemy, Poised His right hand like a foe; He slew all who delighted the eye. He poured out His wrath like fire In the Tent of Fair *Tzion*.

ד דָּרַךְ קַשְׁתּוֹ כְּאוֹיֵב נִצָּב יְמִינוֹ כְּצָר וַיַּהֲרֹג כֹּל מַחֲמַדֵּי־עָיִן בְּאֹהֶל בַּת־צִיּוֹן שָׁפַךְ כָּאֵשׁ חֲמָתוֹ׃

5 *Hashem* has acted like a foe, He has laid waste *Yisrael*, Laid waste all her citadels, Destroyed her strongholds. He has increased within Fair *Yehuda* Mourning and moaning.

ה הָיָה אֲדֹנָי כְּאוֹיֵב בִּלַּע יִשְׂרָאֵל בִּלַּע כָּל־אַרְמְנוֹתֶיהָ שִׁחֵת מִבְצָרָיו וַיֶּרֶב בְּבַת־יְהוּדָה תַּאֲנִיָּה וַאֲנִיָּה׃

6 He has stripped His Booth like a garden, He has destroyed His *Mishkan*; *Hashem* has ended in *Tzion* Festival and *Shabbat*; In His raging anger He has spurned King and *Kohen*.

ו וַיַּחְמֹס כַּגַּן שֻׂכּוֹ שִׁחֵת מוֹעֲדוֹ שִׁכַּח יְהוָה בְּצִיּוֹן מוֹעֵד וְשַׁבָּת וַיִּנְאַץ בְּזַעַם־אַפּוֹ מֶלֶךְ וְכֹהֵן׃

va-yakh-MOS ka-GAN su-KO shi-KHAYT mo-a-DO shi-KACH a-do-NAI b'-tzi-YON mo-AYD v'-sha-BAT va-yin-ATZ b'-ZA-am a-PO ME-lekh v'-kho-HAYN

2:1 He did not remember His Footstool on His day of wrath To explain the metaphor of the "footstool" referred to in this verse, many commentaries point to other places in the Bible where the *Beit Hamikdash* is referred to as God's footstool (see, e.g., Psalms 132:7). This image expresses the notion that while *Hashem*'s essence is incomprehensible to man, as He resides, as it were, in another realm, His presence can be felt in the *Beit Hamikdash*. There, we catch a glimpse of God's metaphorical "feet." Even in the absence of the *Beit Hamikdash*, the Bible tells us that God's presence can be felt most closely in the Land of Israel, "a land which *Hashem* your God looks after, on which *Hashem* your God always keeps His eyes, from year's beginning to year's end." (Deuteronomy 11:12).

2:6 *Hashem* has ended in *Tzion* festival and *Shabbat* The destruction of the *Beit Hamikdash* led to a drastic reduction of holiness in the world. This verse emphasizes the tragedy inherent in the elimination of the observance of *Shabbat* in the *Beit Hamikdash* due to the destruction. The famous Jewish author Achad

Achad Ha'am
(1856–1927)

Eicha/Lamentations
Chapter 2

איכה
פרק ב

7 *Hashem* has rejected His *Mizbayach*, Disdained His Sanctuary. He has handed over to the foe The walls of its citadels; They raised a shout in the House of *Hashem* As on a festival day.

ז זָנַח אֲדֹנָי מִזְבְּחוֹ נִאֵר מִקְדָּשׁוֹ הִסְגִּיר בְּיַד־אוֹיֵב חוֹמֹת אַרְמְנוֹתֶיהָ קוֹל נָתְנוּ בְּבֵית־יְהֹוָה כְּיוֹם מוֹעֵד:

8 *Hashem* resolved to destroy The wall of Fair *Tzion*; He measured with a line, refrained not From bringing destruction. He has made wall and rampart to mourn, Together they languish.

ח חָשַׁב יְהֹוָה לְהַשְׁחִית חוֹמַת בַּת־צִיּוֹן נָטָה קָו לֹא־הֵשִׁיב יָדוֹ מִבַּלֵּעַ וַיַּאֲבֶל־חֵל וְחוֹמָה יַחְדָּו אֻמְלָלוּ:

9 Her gates have sunk into the ground, He has smashed her bars to bits; Her king and her leaders are in exile, Instruction is no more; Her *neviim*, too, receive No vision from *Hashem*.

ט טָבְעוּ בָאָרֶץ שְׁעָרֶיהָ אִבַּד וְשִׁבַּר בְּרִיחֶיהָ מַלְכָּהּ וְשָׂרֶיהָ בַגּוֹיִם אֵין תּוֹרָה גַּם־נְבִיאֶיהָ לֹא־מָצְאוּ חָזוֹן מֵיְהֹוָה:

10 Silent sit on the ground The elders of Fair *Tzion*; They have strewn dust on their heads And girded themselves with sackcloth; The maidens of *Yerushalayim* have bowed Their heads to the ground.

י יֵשְׁבוּ לָאָרֶץ יִדְּמוּ זִקְנֵי בַת־צִיּוֹן הֶעֱלוּ עָפָר עַל־רֹאשָׁם חָגְרוּ שַׂקִּים הוֹרִידוּ לָאָרֶץ רֹאשָׁן בְּתוּלֹת יְרוּשָׁלָ͏ִם:

11 My eyes are spent with tears, My heart is in tumult, My being melts away Over the ruin of my poor people, As babes and sucklings languish In the squares of the city.

יא כָּלוּ בַדְּמָעוֹת עֵינַי חֳמַרְמְרוּ מֵעַי נִשְׁפַּךְ לָאָרֶץ כְּבֵדִי עַל־שֶׁבֶר בַּת־עַמִּי בֵּעָטֵף עוֹלֵל וְיוֹנֵק בִּרְחֹבוֹת קִרְיָה:

12 They keep asking their mothers, "Where is bread and wine?" As they languish like battle-wounded In the squares of the town, As their life runs out In their mothers' bosoms.

יב לְאִמֹּתָם יֹאמְרוּ אַיֵּה דָּגָן וָיָיִן בְּהִתְעַטְּפָם כֶּחָלָל בִּרְחֹבוֹת עִיר בְּהִשְׁתַּפֵּךְ נַפְשָׁם אֶל־חֵיק אִמֹּתָם:

13 What can I take as witness or liken To you, O Fair *Yerushalayim*? What can I match with you to console you, O Fair Maiden *Tzion*? For your ruin is vast as the sea: Who can heal you?

יג מָה־אֲעִידֵךְ מָה אֲדַמֶּה־לָּךְ הַבַּת יְרוּשָׁלַ͏ִם מָה אַשְׁוֶה־לָּךְ וַאֲנַחֲמֵךְ בְּתוּלַת בַּת־צִיּוֹן כִּי־גָדוֹל כַּיָּם שִׁבְרֵךְ מִי יִרְפָּא־לָךְ:

14 Your seers prophesied to you Delusion and folly. They did not expose your iniquity So as to restore your fortunes, But prophesied to you oracles Of delusion and deception.

יד נְבִיאַיִךְ חָזוּ לָךְ שָׁוְא וְתָפֵל וְלֹא־גִלּוּ עַל־עֲוֺנֵךְ לְהָשִׁיב שביתך [שְׁבוּתֵךְ] וַיֶּחֱזוּ לָךְ מַשְׂאוֹת שָׁוְא וּמַדּוּחִים:

Ha'am once remarked: "More than the Jews have kept the Sabbath, the Sabbath has kept the Jews." Indeed, in many ways, the tranquility and spiritual rejuvenation which *Shabbat* offers have proven invaluable to the Jew's ability to persevere in the face of so much oppression. Many of the Jewish people's worst enemies were aware of the power of the *Shabbat*, and thus sought to eradicate it from Jewish life. For example, Antiochus Epiphanes, the villain of the Hanukkah story, prohibited *Shabbat* observance, as did many subsequent oppressors. Despite the myriad attempts to erase the Sabbath from Jewish consciousness, it has remained a central and defining feature of Jewish life until this very day.

Eicha/Lamentations

Chapter 2

איכה

פרק ב

15 All who pass your way Clap their hands at you; They hiss and wag their head At Fair *Yerushalayim*: "Is this the city that was called Perfect in Beauty, Joy of All the Earth?"

סָפְקוּ עָלַיִךְ כַּפַּיִם כׇּל־עֹבְרֵי דֶרֶךְ שָׁרְקוּ וַיָּנִעוּ רֹאשָׁם עַל־בַּת יְרוּשָׁלָ͏ִם הֲזֹאת הָעִיר שֶׁיֹּאמְרוּ כְּלִילַת יֹפִי מָשׂוֹשׂ לְכׇל־הָאָרֶץ׃

sa-f'-KU a-LA-yikh ka-PA-yim kol O-v'-ray DE-rekh sha-r'-KU va-ya-NI-u ro-SHAM al BAT y'-ru-sha-LA-im ha-ZOT ha-EER she-yo-m'-RU k'-lee-LAT YO-fee ma-SOS l-khol ha-A-retz

16 All your enemies Jeer at you; They hiss and gnash their teeth, And cry: "We've ruined her! Ah, this is the day we hoped for; We have lived to see it!"

פָּצוּ עָלַיִךְ פִּיהֶם כׇּל־אוֹיְבַיִךְ שָׁרְקוּ וַיַּחַרְקוּ־שֵׁן אָמְרוּ בִּלָּעְנוּ אַךְ זֶה הַיּוֹם שֶׁקִּוִּינֻהוּ מָצָאנוּ רָאִינוּ׃

17 *Hashem* has done what He purposed, Has carried out the decree That He ordained long ago; He has torn down without pity. He has let the foe rejoice over you, Has exalted the might of your enemies.

עָשָׂה יְהֹוָה אֲשֶׁר זָמָם בִּצַּע אֶמְרָתוֹ אֲשֶׁר צִוָּה מִימֵי־קֶדֶם הָרַס וְלֹא חָמָל וַיְשַׂמַּח עָלַיִךְ אוֹיֵב הֵרִים קֶרֶן צָרָיִךְ׃

18 Their heart cried out to *Hashem*. O wall of Fair *Tzion*, Shed tears like a torrent Day and night! Give yourself no respite, Your eyes no rest.

צָעַק לִבָּם אֶל־אֲדֹנָי חוֹמַת בַּת־צִיּוֹן הוֹרִידִי כַנַּחַל דִּמְעָה יוֹמָם וָלַיְלָה אַל־תִּתְּנִי פוּגַת לָךְ אַל־תִּדֹּם בַּת־עֵינֵךְ׃

19 Arise, cry out in the night At the beginning of the watches, Pour out your heart like water In the presence of *Hashem*! Lift up your hands to Him For the life of your infants, Who faint for hunger At every street corner.

קוּמִי רֹנִּי בַלַּיְלָה [בַלַּיְלָה] לְרֹאשׁ אַשְׁמֻרוֹת שִׁפְכִי כַמַּיִם לִבֵּךְ נֹכַח פְּנֵי אֲדֹנָי שְׂאִי אֵלָיו כַּפַּיִךְ עַל־נֶפֶשׁ עוֹלָלַיִךְ הָעֲטוּפִים בְּרָעָב בְּרֹאשׁ כׇּל־חוּצוֹת׃

20 See, *Hashem*, and behold, To whom You have done this! Alas, women eat their own fruit, Their newborn babes! Alas, *Kohen* and *Navi* are slain In the Sanctuary of *Hashem*!

רְאֵה יְהֹוָה וְהַבִּיטָה לְמִי עוֹלַלְתָּ כֹּה אִם־תֹּאכַלְנָה נָשִׁים פִּרְיָם עֹלְלֵי טִפֻּחִים אִם־יֵהָרֵג בְּמִקְדַּשׁ אֲדֹנָי כֹּהֵן וְנָבִיא׃

21 Prostrate in the streets lie Both young and old. My maidens and youths Are fallen by the sword; You slew them on Your day of wrath, You slaughtered without pity.

שָׁכְבוּ לָאָרֶץ חוּצוֹת נַעַר וְזָקֵן בְּתוּלֹתַי וּבַחוּרַי נָפְלוּ בֶחָרֶב הָרַגְתָּ בְּיוֹם אַפֶּךָ טָבַחְתָּ לֹא חָמָלְתָּ׃

2:15 Is this the city that was called Perfect in Beauty, Joy of All the Earth? This verse demonstrates the grandeur that once was Jerusalem. However, it is peculiar that in the hands of Babylon and of numerous subsequent conquerors, the city of *Yerushalayim* and the entire Land of Israel lay almost completely in ruins. In his notes on *Sefer Vayikra* (26:32), the *Ramban* explains that *Eretz Yisrael* has a supernatural quality to it. While under foreign occupation, the land is little more than a barren desert. However, when it is under the sovereignty of the People of Israel, the land comes to life, flourishes, and yields great produce. Indeed, for nearly two millennia, as the land switched hands numerous times between various foreign occupiers, including Romans, Arabs, Turks and others, the land lay desolate. Amazingly, the modern rebirth of the Jewish homeland has brought with it an astounding development of the land, to the point where once again the Jewish people can claim a flourishing country. In agriculture, technology, and culture, contemporary Israel ranks among the most advanced countries of the world. Indeed, Jerusalem itself has returned to a point where visitors once again remark that the city is "Perfect in Beauty, Joy of All the Earth."

Ramban (1194–1270)

Eicha/Lamentations
Chapter 3

22 You summoned, as on a festival, My neighbors from roundabout. On the day of the wrath of *Hashem*, None survived or escaped; Those whom I bore and reared My foe has consumed.

כג תִּקְרָא כְיוֹם מוֹעֵד מְגוּרַי מִסָּבִיב וְלֹא הָיָה בְּיוֹם אַף־יְהֹוָה פָּלִיט וְשָׂרִיד אֲשֶׁר־טִפַּחְתִּי וְרִבִּיתִי אֹיְבִי כִלָּם׃

3 1 I am the man who has known affliction Under the rod of His wrath;

ג א אֲנִי הַגֶּבֶר רָאָה עֳנִי בְּשֵׁבֶט עֶבְרָתוֹ׃

2 Me He drove on and on In unrelieved darkness;

ב אוֹתִי נָהַג וַיֹּלַךְ חֹשֶׁךְ וְלֹא־אוֹר׃

3 On none but me He brings down His hand Again and again, without cease.

ג אַךְ בִּי יָשֻׁב יַהֲפֹךְ יָדוֹ כָּל־הַיּוֹם׃

4 He has worn away my flesh and skin; He has shattered my bones.

ד בִּלָּה בְשָׂרִי וְעוֹרִי שִׁבַּר עַצְמוֹתָי׃

5 All around me He has built Misery and hardship;

ה בָּנָה עָלַי וַיַּקַּף רֹאשׁ וּתְלָאָה׃

6 He has made me dwell in darkness, Like those long dead.

ו בְּמַחֲשַׁכִּים הוֹשִׁיבַנִי כְּמֵתֵי עוֹלָם׃

7 He has walled me in and I cannot break out; He has weighed me down with chains.

ז גָּדַר בַּעֲדִי וְלֹא אֵצֵא הִכְבִּיד נְחָשְׁתִּי׃

8 And when I cry and plead, He shuts out my prayer;

ח גַּם כִּי אֶזְעַק וַאֲשַׁוֵּעַ שָׂתַם תְּפִלָּתִי׃

GAM KEE ez-AK va-a-sha-VAY-a sa-TAM t'-fi-la-TEE

9 He has walled in my ways with hewn blocks, He has made my paths a maze.

ט גָּדַר דְּרָכַי בְּגָזִית נְתִיבֹתַי עִוָּה׃

10 He is a lurking bear to me, A lion in hiding;

י דֹּב אֹרֵב הוּא לִי אֲרִיה [אֲרִי] בְּמִסְתָּרִים׃

11 He has forced me off my way and mangled me, He has left me numb.

יא דְּרָכַי סוֹרֵר וַיְפַשְּׁחֵנִי שָׂמַנִי שֹׁמֵם׃

12 He has bent His bow and made me The target of His arrows:

יב דָּרַךְ קַשְׁתּוֹ וַיַּצִּיבֵנִי כַּמַּטָּרָא לַחֵץ׃

13 He has shot into my vitals The shafts of His quiver.

יג הֵבִיא בְּכִלְיוֹתָי בְּנֵי אַשְׁפָּתוֹ׃

14 I have become a laughingstock to all people, The butt of their gibes all day long.

יד הָיִיתִי שְּׂחֹק לְכָל־עַמִּי נְגִינָתָם כָּל־הַיּוֹם׃

15 He has filled me with bitterness, Sated me with wormwood.

טו הִשְׂבִּיעַנִי בַמְּרוֹרִים הִרְוַנִי לַעֲנָה׃

3:8 And when I cry and plead, He shuts out my prayer While God always hears our prayers, He doesn't always grant our requests. Even in difficult times, *Hashem* does not always respond to our prayers in the affirmative, but instead "He shuts out my prayer." It is noteworthy that in the central Jewish prayer, known as the *Amida* and recited three times a day, *Hashem* is referred to as, "He who listens to our prayers" and not, "He who answers our prayers." God's will is inscrutable. Like any parent, at times He says "no." But especially at those times, He is always there to listen with love and to hear our cries.

Eicha/Lamentations
Chapter 3

איכה
פרק ג

16 He has broken my teeth on gravel, Has ground me into the dust.

טז וַיַּגְרֵס בֶּחָצָץ שִׁנָּי הִכְפִּישַׁנִי בָּאֵפֶר׃

17 My life was bereft of peace, I forgot what happiness was.

יז וַתִּזְנַח מִשָּׁלוֹם נַפְשִׁי נָשִׁיתִי טוֹבָה׃

18 I thought my strength and hope Had perished before *Hashem*.

יח וָאֹמַר אָבַד נִצְחִי וְתוֹחַלְתִּי מֵיְהוָה׃

19 To recall my distress and my misery Was wormwood and poison;

יט זְכָר־עָנְיִי וּמְרוּדִי לַעֲנָה וָרֹאשׁ׃

20 Whenever I thought of them, I was bowed low.

כ זָכוֹר תִּזְכּוֹר וְתָשִׁיחַ [וְתָשׁוֹחַ] עָלַי נַפְשִׁי׃

21 But this do I call to mind, Therefore I have hope:

כא זֹאת אָשִׁיב אֶל־לִבִּי עַל־כֵּן אוֹחִיל׃

22 The kindness of *Hashem* has not ended, His mercies are not spent.

כב חַסְדֵי יְהוָה כִּי לֹא־תָמְנוּ כִּי לֹא־כָלוּ רַחֲמָיו׃

23 They are renewed every morning – Ample is Your grace!

כג חֲדָשִׁים לַבְּקָרִים רַבָּה אֱמוּנָתֶךָ׃

24 "*Hashem* is my portion," I say with full heart; Therefore will I hope in Him.

כד חֶלְקִי יְהוָה אָמְרָה נַפְשִׁי עַל־כֵּן אוֹחִיל לוֹ׃

25 *Hashem* is good to those who trust in Him, To the one who seeks Him;

כה טוֹב יְהוָה לְקוָֹו לְנֶפֶשׁ תִּדְרְשֶׁנּוּ׃

26 It is good to wait patiently Till rescue comes from *Hashem*.

כו טוֹב וְיָחִיל וְדוּמָם לִתְשׁוּעַת יְהוָה׃

27 It is good for a man, when young, To bear a yoke;

כז טוֹב לַגֶּבֶר כִּי־יִשָּׂא עֹל בִּנְעוּרָיו׃

28 Let him sit alone and be patient, When He has laid it upon him.

כח יֵשֵׁב בָּדָד וְיִדֹּם כִּי נָטַל עָלָיו׃

29 Let him put his mouth to the dust – There may yet be hope.

כט יִתֵּן בֶּעָפָר פִּיהוּ אוּלַי יֵשׁ תִּקְוָה׃

30 Let him offer his cheek to the smiter; Let him be surfeited with mockery.

ל יִתֵּן לְמַכֵּהוּ לֶחִי יִשְׂבַּע בְּחֶרְפָּה׃

31 For *Hashem* does not Reject forever,

לא כִּי לֹא יִזְנַח לְעוֹלָם אֲדֹנָי׃

KEE LO yiz-NAKH l'-o-LAM a-do-NAI

3:31 For the Lord does not reject forever Throughout the many episodes of persecution, Jews have remembered the critical message of this verse: The suffering of the Jewish people will not be eternal. Already in the days of *Moshe*, *Hashem* assured His people that though they may face His wrath and anger, though He may send nations to oppress them, they will always remain His chosen nation. Their suffering will eventually come to an end, and *Hashem* will redeem His people, as it says: "Yet, even then, when they are in the land of their enemies, I will not reject them or spurn them so as to destroy them, annulling My covenant with them: for I *Hashem* am their God" (Leviticus 26:44). To the contrary, "I will remember My covenant with *Yaakov*; I will remember also My covenant with *Yitzchak*, and also My covenant with *Avraham* I will remember; and I will remember the land" (Leviticus 26:42). Indeed, after years of persecution and suffering, the Jewish people are thriving and the Land of Israel is flourishing, thus demonstrating the eternal truth of this verse.

Eicha / Lamentations
Chapter 3

איכה
פרק ג

#	English	Hebrew
32	But first afflicts, then pardons In His abundant kindness.	לב כִּי אִם־הוֹגָה וְרִחַם כְּרֹב חֲסָדוֹ [חֲסָדָיו]:
33	For He does not willfully bring grief Or affliction to man,	לג כִּי לֹא עִנָּה מִלִּבּוֹ וַיַּגֶּה בְּנֵי־אִישׁ:
34	Crushing under His feet All the prisoners of the earth.	לד לְדַכֵּא תַּחַת רַגְלָיו כֹּל אֲסִירֵי אָרֶץ:
35	To deny a man his rights In the presence of the Most High,	לה לְהַטּוֹת מִשְׁפַּט־גָּבֶר נֶגֶד פְּנֵי עֶלְיוֹן:
36	To wrong a man in his cause — This *Hashem* does not choose.	לו לְעַוֵּת אָדָם בְּרִיבוֹ אֲדֹנָי לֹא רָאָה:
37	Whose decree was ever fulfilled, Unless *Hashem* willed it?	לז מִי זֶה אָמַר וַתֶּהִי אֲדֹנָי לֹא צִוָּה:
38	Is it not at the word of the Most High, That weal and woe befall?	לח מִפִּי עֶלְיוֹן לֹא תֵצֵא הָרָעוֹת וְהַטּוֹב:
39	Of what shall a living man complain? Each one of his own sins!	לט מַה־יִּתְאוֹנֵן אָדָם חָי גֶּבֶר עַל־חֲטָאוֹ [חֲטָאָיו]:
40	Let us search and examine our ways, And turn back to *Hashem*;	מ נַחְפְּשָׂה דְרָכֵינוּ וְנַחְקֹרָה וְנָשׁוּבָה עַד־יְהֹוָה:
41	Let us lift up our hearts with our hands To *Hashem* in heaven:	מא נִשָּׂא לְבָבֵנוּ אֶל־כַּפָּיִם אֶל־אֵל בַּשָּׁמָיִם:
42	We have transgressed and rebelled, And You have not forgiven.	מב נַחְנוּ פָשַׁעְנוּ וּמָרִינוּ אַתָּה לֹא סָלָחְתָּ:
43	You have clothed Yourself in anger and pursued us, You have slain without pity.	מג סַכֹּתָה בָאַף וַתִּרְדְּפֵנוּ הָרַגְתָּ לֹא חָמָלְתָּ:
44	You have screened Yourself off with a cloud, That no prayer may pass through.	מד סַכּוֹתָה בֶעָנָן לָךְ מֵעֲבוֹר תְּפִלָּה:
45	You have made us filth and refuse In the midst of the peoples.	מה סְחִי וּמָאוֹס תְּשִׂימֵנוּ בְּקֶרֶב הָעַמִּים:
46	All our enemies loudly Rail against us. *pa-TZU a-LAY-nu pee-HEM kol o-y'-VAY-nu*	מו פָּצוּ עָלֵינוּ פִּיהֶם כָּל־אֹיְבֵינוּ:

Abba Eban (1915–2002)

3:46 All our enemies loudly rail against us Many times, the enemies of the Jewish people eagerly awaited the day when the Jews would finally meet their demise. But these plans and expectations have always been divinely foiled. This verse reflects the hatred that Israel's enemies, both historical and contemporary, have always felt towards her. In the spring of 1967, for example, Israel's fate seemed truly doomed. Nearly all of her neighbors sought to wipe her off the map, including Egypt, Jordan, Syria, Iraq, and Saudi Arabia. Here is how Abba Eban, serving at that time as Israel's Foreign Minister, described the mood in the days leading up to the Six Day War: "There was no doubt that the howling mobs in Cairo, Damascus and Baghdad were seeing savage visions of murder and booty. Israel, for its part, had learned from Jewish history that no outrage against its men, women and children was inconceivable. Many things in Jewish history are too terrible to be believed, but nothing in that history is too terrible to have happened. Memories of the European slaughter were taking form and substance in countless Israeli hearts. They flowed into our room like turgid air and sat heavy on all our minds. As has always been the case, God had different plans, and the young State of Israel mightily and miraculously defeated its enemies."

Eicha/Lamentations
Chapter 3

#	English	Hebrew
47	Panic and pitfall are our lot, Death and destruction.	מז פַּחַד וָפַחַת הָיָה לָנוּ הַשֵּׁאת וְהַשָּׁבֶר:
48	My eyes shed streams of water Over the ruin of my poor people.	מח פַּלְגֵי־מַיִם תֵּרַד עֵינִי עַל־שֶׁבֶר בַּת־עַמִּי:
49	My eyes shall flow without cease, Without respite,	מט עֵינִי נִגְּרָה וְלֹא תִדְמֶה מֵאֵין הֲפֻגוֹת:
50	Until *Hashem* looks down And beholds from heaven.	נ עַד־יַשְׁקִיף וְיֵרֶא יְהֹוָה מִשָּׁמָיִם:
51	My eyes have brought me grief Over all the maidens of my city.	נא עֵינִי עוֹלְלָה לְנַפְשִׁי מִכֹּל בְּנוֹת עִירִי:
52	My foes have snared me like a bird, Without any cause.	נב צוֹד צָדוּנִי כַּצִּפּוֹר אֹיְבַי חִנָּם:
53	They have ended my life in a pit And cast stones at me.	נג צָמְתוּ בַבּוֹר חַיָּי וַיַּדּוּ־אֶבֶן בִּי:
54	Waters flowed over my head; I said: I am lost!	נד צָפוּ־מַיִם עַל־רֹאשִׁי אָמַרְתִּי נִגְזָרְתִּי:
55	I have called on Your name, *Hashem*, From the depths of the Pit.	נה קָרָאתִי שִׁמְךָ יְהֹוָה מִבּוֹר תַּחְתִּיּוֹת:
56	Hear my plea; Do not shut Your ear To my groan, to my cry!	נו קוֹלִי שָׁמָעְתָּ אַל־תַּעְלֵם אָזְנְךָ לְרַוְחָתִי לְשַׁוְעָתִי:
57	You have ever drawn nigh when I called You; You have said, "Do not fear!"	נז קָרַבְתָּ בְּיוֹם אֶקְרָאֶךָּ אָמַרְתָּ אַל־תִּירָא:
58	You championed my cause, O *Hashem*, You have redeemed my life. *RAV-ta a-do-NAI ree-VAY naf-SHEE ga-AL-ta kha-YAI*	נח רַבְתָּ אֲדֹנָי רִיבֵי נַפְשִׁי גָּאַלְתָּ חַיָּי:
59	You have seen, *Hashem*, the wrong done me; Oh, vindicate my right!	נט רָאִיתָה יְהֹוָה עַוָּתָתִי שָׁפְטָה מִשְׁפָּטִי:
60	You have seen all their malice, All their designs against me;	ס רָאִיתָה כָּל־נִקְמָתָם כָּל־מַחְשְׁבֹתָם לִי:
61	You have heard, *Hashem*, their taunts, All their designs against me,	סא שָׁמַעְתָּ חֶרְפָּתָם יְהֹוָה כָּל־מַחְשְׁבֹתָם עָלָי:
62	The mouthings and pratings of my adversaries Against me all day long.	סב שִׂפְתֵי קָמַי וְהֶגְיוֹנָם עָלַי כָּל־הַיּוֹם:

3:58 You have redeemed my life Indeed, God is the ultimate redeemer. Time and again, *Hashem* lifts the Jewish people up from the brink of destruction and depths of despair and helps them to stand upright once again. A shining example of this is the founding of the State of Israel. Merely three years following the end of the darkest period in Jewish history, when a third of world Jewry was brutally murdered and the future of the Jewish people seemed most bleak, God restored His nation to a position of dignity and strength. The significance of the founding of the State of Israel in 1948 was not just the return of the Jewish people to their homeland; it was the reestablishment of Jewish sovereignty, and the affirmation that *Hashem* did not break His word. He was, and remains, the redeemer of His people.

Eicha/Lamentations
Chapter 4

63 See how, at their ease or at work, I am the butt of their gibes.

64 Give them, *Hashem*, their deserts According to their deeds.

65 Give them anguish of heart; Your curse be upon them!

66 Oh, pursue them in wrath and destroy them From under the heavens of *Hashem*!

4 1 Alas! The gold is dulled, Debased the finest gold! The sacred gems are spilled At every street corner.

2 The precious children of *Tzion*; Once valued as gold – Alas, they are accounted as earthen pots, Work of a potter's hands!

3 Even jackals offer the breast And suckle their young; But my poor people has turned cruel, Like ostriches of the desert.

4 The tongue of the suckling cleaves To its palate for thirst. Little children beg for bread; None gives them a morsel.

5 Those who feasted on dainties Lie famished in the streets; Those who were reared in purple Have embraced refuse heaps.

6 The guilt of my poor people Exceeded the iniquity of Sodom, Which was overthrown in a moment, Without a hand striking it.

7 Her elect were purer than snow, Whiter than milk; Their limbs were ruddier than coral, Their bodies were like sapphire.

8 Now their faces are blacker than soot, They are not recognized in the streets; Their skin has shriveled on their bones, It has become dry as wood.

9 Better off were the slain of the sword Than those slain by famine, Who pined away, [as though] wounded, For lack of the fruits of the field.

10 With their own hands, tenderhearted women Have cooked their children; Such became their fare, In the disaster of my poor people.

11 *Hashem* vented all His fury, Poured out His blazing wrath; He kindled a fire in *Tzion* Which consumed its foundations.

איכה
פרק ד

סג שִׁבְתָּם וְקִימָתָם הַבִּיטָה אֲנִי מַנְגִּינָתָם:

סד תָּשִׁיב לָהֶם גְּמוּל יְהֹוָה כְּמַעֲשֵׂה יְדֵיהֶם:

סה תִּתֵּן לָהֶם מְגִנַּת־לֵב תַּאֲלָתְךָ לָהֶם:

סו תִּרְדֹּף בְּאַף וְתַשְׁמִידֵם מִתַּחַת שְׁמֵי יְהֹוָה:

א אֵיכָה יוּעַם זָהָב יִשְׁנֶא הַכֶּתֶם הַטּוֹב תִּשְׁתַּפֵּכְנָה אַבְנֵי־קֹדֶשׁ בְּרֹאשׁ כָּל־חוּצוֹת:

ב בְּנֵי צִיּוֹן הַיְקָרִים הַמְסֻלָּאִים בַּפָּז אֵיכָה נֶחְשְׁבוּ לְנִבְלֵי־חֶרֶשׂ מַעֲשֵׂה יְדֵי יוֹצֵר:

ג גַּם־תַּנִּין [תַּנִּים] חָלְצוּ שַׁד הֵינִיקוּ גּוּרֵיהֶן בַּת־עַמִּי לְאַכְזָר כִּי עֵנִים [כַּיְעֵנִים] בַּמִּדְבָּר:

ד דָּבַק לְשׁוֹן יוֹנֵק אֶל־חִכּוֹ בַּצָּמָא עוֹלָלִים שָׁאֲלוּ לֶחֶם פֹּרֵשׂ אֵין לָהֶם:

ה הָאֹכְלִים לְמַעֲדַנִּים נָשַׁמּוּ בַּחוּצוֹת הָאֱמֻנִים עֲלֵי תוֹלָע חִבְּקוּ אַשְׁפַּתּוֹת:

ו וַיִּגְדַּל עֲוֹן בַּת־עַמִּי מֵחַטַּאת סְדֹם הַהֲפוּכָה כְמוֹ־רָגַע וְלֹא־חָלוּ בָהּ יָדָיִם:

ז זַכּוּ נְזִירֶיהָ מִשֶּׁלֶג צַחוּ מֵחָלָב אָדְמוּ עֶצֶם מִפְּנִינִים סַפִּיר גִּזְרָתָם:

ח חָשַׁךְ מִשְּׁחוֹר תָּאֳרָם לֹא נִכְּרוּ בַּחוּצוֹת צָפַד עוֹרָם עַל־עַצְמָם יָבֵשׁ הָיָה כָעֵץ:

ט טוֹבִים הָיוּ חַלְלֵי־חֶרֶב מֵחַלְלֵי רָעָב שֶׁהֵם יָזוּבוּ מְדֻקָּרִים מִתְּנוּבֹת שָׂדָי:

י יְדֵי נָשִׁים רַחֲמָנִיּוֹת בִּשְּׁלוּ יַלְדֵיהֶן הָיוּ לְבָרוֹת לָמוֹ בְּשֶׁבֶר בַּת־עַמִּי:

יא כִּלָּה יְהֹוָה אֶת־חֲמָתוֹ שָׁפַךְ חֲרוֹן אַפּוֹ וַיַּצֶּת־אֵשׁ בְּצִיּוֹן וַתֹּאכַל יְסוֹדֹתֶיהָ:

Eicha/Lamentations
Chapter 4

איכה
פרק ד

12 The kings of the earth did not believe, Nor any of the inhabitants of the world, That foe or adversary could enter The gates of *Yerushalayim*.

לֹא הֶאֱמִינוּ מַלְכֵי־אֶרֶץ וְכֹל [כֹּל] יֹשְׁבֵי תֵבֵל כִּי יָבֹא צַר וְאוֹיֵב בְּשַׁעֲרֵי יְרוּשָׁלָ͏ִם:

13 It was for the sins of her *Neviim*, The iniquities of her *Kohanim*, Who had shed in her midst the blood of the just.

מֵחַטֹּאת נְבִיאֶיהָ עֲוֺנוֹת כֹּהֲנֶיהָ הַשֹּׁפְכִים בְּקִרְבָּהּ דַּם צַדִּיקִים:

14 They wandered blindly through the streets, Defiled with blood, So that no one was able To touch their garments.

נָעוּ עִוְרִים בַּחוּצוֹת נְגֹאֲלוּ בַּדָּם בְּלֹא יוּכְלוּ יִגְּעוּ בִּלְבֻשֵׁיהֶם:

15 "Away! Unclean!" people shouted at them, "Away! Away! Touch not!" So they wandered and wandered again; For the nations had resolved: "They shall stay here no longer."

סוּרוּ טָמֵא קָרְאוּ לָמוֹ סוּרוּ סוּרוּ אַל־תִּגָּעוּ כִּי נָצוּ גַּם־נָעוּ אָמְרוּ בַּגּוֹיִם לֹא יוֹסִפוּ לָגוּר:

SU-ru ta-MAY KA-r'-u LA-mo SU-ru SU-ru al ti-GA-u KEE na-TZU gam na-U a-m'-RU ba-go-YIM LO yo-SI-fu la-GUR

16 *Hashem*'s countenance has turned away from them, He will look on them no more. They showed no regard for *Kohanim*, No favor to elders.

פְּנֵי יְהֹוָה חִלְּקָם לֹא יוֹסִיף לְהַבִּיטָם פְּנֵי כֹהֲנִים לֹא נָשָׂאוּ זְקֵנִים [וּזְקֵנִים] לֹא חָנָנוּ:

17 Even now our eyes pine away In vain for deliverance. As we waited, still we wait For a nation that cannot help.

עוֹדֵינָה [עוֹדֵינוּ] תִּכְלֶינָה עֵינֵינוּ אֶל־עֶזְרָתֵנוּ הָבֶל בְּצִפִּיָּתֵנוּ צִפִּינוּ אֶל־גּוֹי לֹא יוֹשִׁעַ:

18 Our steps were checked, We could not walk in our squares. Our doom is near, our days are done – Alas, our doom has come!

צָדוּ צְעָדֵינוּ מִלֶּכֶת בִּרְחֹבֹתֵינוּ קָרַב קִצֵּינוּ מָלְאוּ יָמֵינוּ כִּי־בָא קִצֵּינוּ:

19 Our pursuers were swifter Than the eagles in the sky; They chased us in the mountains, Lay in wait for us in the wilderness.

קַלִּים הָיוּ רֹדְפֵינוּ מִנִּשְׁרֵי שָׁמָיִם עַל־הֶהָרִים דְּלָקֻנוּ בַּמִּדְבָּר אָרְבוּ לָנוּ:

ka-LEEM ha-YU ro-d'-FAY-nu mi-nish-RAY sha-MA-yim al he-ha-REEM d-la-KU-nu ba-mid-BAR a-r'-VU LA-nu

4:15 For the nations had resolved: "They shall stay here no longer." The insulting jeers described in this verse were repeated not too long ago. Following the liberation of the Nazi concentration camps, Jews were not only denied entry into many foreign countries, but even the borders of their homeland were closed. After the conclusion of World War II, Palestine (as the Land of Israel was then called) was under British sovereignty and the British government put a strict quota on the number of Jewish refugees allowed to enter. Furthermore, many of those who defied the quota and managed to cross the border into the Promised Land without British permission were rounded up and placed in detention camps, such as the one in the northern coastal city of Atlit. However, the will of *Hashem* could not be thwarted. After the founding of the State of Israel in 1948, the declaration "They shall stay here no longer" quickly became obsolete. With the Knesset's passing of the Law of Return, every Jew in the world became entitled to move to Israel and obtain citizenship in the new country. Since then, millions of Jews have moved from all corners of the globe to the Holy Land. For the first time in almost two thousand years, almost half of the Jews in the world now live in Israel and indeed, "they stay here" once again.

Atlit detention camp museum

4:19 They chased us in the mountains This verse conveys a sense that the enemy lurks on all terrains and in all locations, and is impossible to escape. Unfortunately, even after arriving on the shores of *Eretz*

Eicha/Lamentations
Chapter 5

20 The breath of our life, *Hashem*'s anointed, Was captured in their traps – He in whose shade we had thought To live among the nations.

21 Rejoice and exult, Fair Edom, Who dwell in the land of Uz! To you, too, the cup shall pass, You shall get drunk and expose your nakedness.

22 Your iniquity, Fair *Tzion*, is expiated; He will exile you no longer. Your iniquity, Fair Edom, He will note; He will uncover your sins.

5

1 Remember, *Hashem*, what has befallen us; Behold, and see our disgrace!

2 Our heritage has passed to aliens, Our homes to strangers.

na-kha-la-TAY-nu ne-hef-KHAH l'-za-REEM ba-TAY-nu l'-nokh-REEM

3 We have become orphans, fatherless; Our mothers are like widows.

4 We must pay to drink our own water, Obtain our own kindling at a price.

5 We are hotly pursued; Exhausted, we are given no rest.

6 We hold out a hand to Egypt; To Assyria, for our fill of bread.

7 Our fathers sinned and are no more; And we must bear their guilt.

8 Slaves are ruling over us, With none to rescue us from them.

איכה
פרק ה

כ רוּחַ אַפֵּינוּ מְשִׁיחַ יְהֹוָה נִלְכַּד בִּשְׁחִיתוֹתָם אֲשֶׁר אָמַרְנוּ בְּצִלּוֹ נִחְיֶה בַגּוֹיִם:

כא שִׂישִׂי וְשִׂמְחִי בַּת־אֱדוֹם יוֹשַׁבְתִּי [יוֹשֶׁבֶת] בְּאֶרֶץ עוּץ גַּם־עָלַיִךְ תַּעֲבָר־כּוֹס תִּשְׁכְּרִי וְתִתְעָרִי:

כב תַּם־עֲוֺנֵךְ בַּת־צִיּוֹן לֹא יוֹסִיף לְהַגְלוֹתֵךְ פָּקַד עֲוֺנֵךְ בַּת־אֱדוֹם גִּלָּה עַל־חַטֹּאתָיִךְ:

א זְכֹר יְהֹוָה מֶה־הָיָה לָנוּ הַבִּיט [הַבִּיטָה] וּרְאֵה אֶת־חֶרְפָּתֵנוּ:

ב נַחֲלָתֵנוּ נֶהֶפְכָה לְזָרִים בָּתֵּינוּ לְנָכְרִים:

ג יְתוֹמִים הָיִינוּ אִין [וְאֵין] אָב אִמֹּתֵינוּ כְּאַלְמָנוֹת:

ד מֵימֵינוּ בְּכֶסֶף שָׁתִינוּ עֵצֵינוּ בִּמְחִיר יָבֹאוּ:

ה עַל צַוָּארֵנוּ נִרְדָּפְנוּ יָגַעְנוּ לֹא [וְלֹא] הוּנַח לָנוּ:

ו מִצְרַיִם נָתַנּוּ יָד אַשּׁוּר לִשְׂבֹּעַ לָחֶם:

ז אֲבֹתֵינוּ חָטְאוּ אֵינָם [וְאֵינָם] אֲנַחְנוּ [וַאֲנַחְנוּ] עֲוֺנֹתֵיהֶם סָבָלְנוּ:

ח עֲבָדִים מָשְׁלוּ בָנוּ פֹּרֵק אֵין מִיָּדָם:

Battle hill of the 35 fallen soldiers in Gush Etzion

Yisrael following the Holocaust, Jewish refugees from Europe encountered a situation similar to that described in this verse. Having survived the Nazis, these Jews were met by a new enemy: The local Arab population, which fought violently to keep them away from their ancient homeland. This enemy also waged war on a number of fronts, including the mountains and the wilderness, as described in this verse. In January of 1948, a terrible tragedy took place in the Judean hills. A group of thirty-five soldiers was dispatched to bring provisions and food to the beleaguered communities of *Gush Etzion*, the Etzion bloc. They set out on foot at night to avoid detection, but the sun rose before they managed to reach their destination. Still in the vicinity of hostile villages, they were detected by some Arab women who had gone down to the valley to gather branches. Arab mobs were quickly deployed and after a lengthy battle, all thirty-five of the soldiers were killed in a bloody massacre. "They chased us in the mountains, lay in wait for us in the wilderness."

5:2 Our heritage has passed to aliens In the past century, we have merited to witness a reversal of this prophetic statement with our own eyes. Whereas *Yirmiyahu* bemoans the fact that Jewish land has been seized by foreigners, today, Jews have returned to their ancient homeland and reclaimed lands that have belonged to them from the time that they were promised by *Hashem* to *Avraham* and his descendants for eternity.

Eicha/Lamentations
Chapter 5

איכה
פרק ה

9 We get our bread at the peril of our lives, Because of the sword of the wilderness.

ט בְּנַפְשֵׁנוּ נָבִיא לַחְמֵנוּ מִפְּנֵי חֶרֶב הַמִּדְבָּר:

10 Our skin glows like an oven, With the fever of famine.

י עוֹרֵנוּ כְּתַנּוּר נִכְמָרוּ מִפְּנֵי זַלְעֲפוֹת רָעָב:

11 They have ravished women in *Tzion*, Maidens in the towns of *Yehuda*.

יא נָשִׁים בְּצִיּוֹן עִנּוּ בְּתֻלֹת בְּעָרֵי יְהוּדָה:

12 Princes have been hanged by them; No respect has been shown to elders.

יב שָׂרִים בְּיָדָם נִתְלוּ פְּנֵי זְקֵנִים לֹא נֶהְדָּרוּ:

13 Young men must carry millstones, And youths stagger under loads of wood.

יג בַּחוּרִים טְחוֹן נָשָׂאוּ וּנְעָרִים בָּעֵץ כָּשָׁלוּ:

14 The old men are gone from the gate, The young men from their music.

יד זְקֵנִים מִשַּׁעַר שָׁבָתוּ בַּחוּרִים מִנְּגִינָתָם:

15 Gone is the joy of our hearts; Our dancing is turned into mourning.

טו שָׁבַת מְשׂוֹשׂ לִבֵּנוּ נֶהְפַּךְ לְאֵבֶל מְחֹלֵנוּ:

16 The crown has fallen from our head; Woe to us that we have sinned!

טז נָפְלָה עֲטֶרֶת רֹאשֵׁנוּ אוֹי־נָא לָנוּ כִּי חָטָאנוּ:

17 Because of this our hearts are sick, Because of these our eyes are dimmed:

יז עַל־זֶה הָיָה דָוֶה לִבֵּנוּ עַל־אֵלֶּה חָשְׁכוּ עֵינֵינוּ:

18 Because of Mount *Tzion*, which lies desolate; Jackals prowl over it.

AL har tzi-YON she-sha-MAYM shu-a-LEEM hi-l'-khu VO

יח עַל הַר־צִיּוֹן שֶׁשָּׁמֵם שׁוּעָלִים הִלְּכוּ־בוֹ:

19 But You, *Hashem*, are enthroned forever, Your throne endures through the ages.

יט אַתָּה יְהֹוָה לְעוֹלָם תֵּשֵׁב כִּסְאֲךָ לְדֹר וָדוֹר:

20 Why have You forgotten us utterly, Forsaken us for all time?

כ לָמָּה לָנֶצַח תִּשְׁכָּחֵנוּ תַּעַזְבֵנוּ לְאֹרֶךְ יָמִים:

5:18 Because of Mount *Tzion*, which lies desolate; jackals prowl over it Though the image of jackals running freely on *Har HaBayit* certainly reflects the devastation and desolation of *Yerushalayim*, some find hope even in the depths of darkness. The Talmud (*Makkot* 24b) relates that a number of leading Sages were visiting *Yerushalayim* following the destruction of the Temple, and they came upon the ruins of the Temple Mount. Upon seeing a jackal scamper across the holiest site in the world, three of the four rabbis began to cry. The great Rabbi Akiva, on the other hand, began to laugh joyously. Shocked, they asked him to explain his behavior. Rabbi Akiva explained that if the prophecies of destruction had indeed been fulfilled, we can be certain that the promises of redemption will also be fulfilled. The Jews have always maintained immutable optimism and unwavering faith that the Almighty will preserve His covenant with them, and in modern times He has begun to fulfill His promises of redemption.

Eicha/Lamentations
Chapter 5

איכה
פרק ה

21 Take us back, *Hashem*, to Yourself, And let us come back; Renew our days as of old!

הֲשִׁיבֵ֨נוּ יְהֹוָ֤ה ׀ אֵלֶ֨יךָ֙ ונשוב [וְנָשׁ֔וּבָה] חַדֵּ֥שׁ יָמֵ֖ינוּ כְּקֶֽדֶם׃

ha-shee-VAY-nu a-do-NAI ay-LE-kha v'-na-SHU-vah kha-DAYSH ya-MAY-nu k'-KE-dem

22 For truly, You have rejected us, Bitterly raged against us. Take us back, *Hashem*, to Yourself, And let us come back; Renew our days as of old!

כִּ֚י אִם־מָאֹ֣ס מְאַסְתָּ֔נוּ קָצַ֥פְתָּ עָלֵ֖ינוּ עַד־מְאֹֽד׃ [הֲשִׁיבֵ֨נוּ יְהֹוָ֤ה אֵלֶ֨יךָ֙ וְנָשׁ֔וּבָה חַדֵּ֥שׁ יָמֵ֖ינוּ כְּקֶֽדֶם]

5:21 Take us back, *Hashem* This verse is one of the most significant verses in the entire book. Traditionally, when *Megillat Eicha* is read in synagogues on the ninth of *Av*, this verse is repeated at the conclusion of the reading, to highlight its significance and to end on a positive note. The verse emphasizes that *Hashem* will one day return the Jewish people to the Land of Israel, and renew the intimate relationship with Him centered around a rebuilt Temple in *Yerushalayim*. Moreover, it reminds us that a relationship with our Maker is a two-way street; we return to God, and God returns to us. Our generation has been blessed with the beginning of the fulfillment of this promise. The Jewish people have started their return to the land of their fathers, and the realization of the dream of redemption has begun. We sincerely pray for the fulfillment of the final redemption, a complete return to *Hashem* and the coming of the *Mashiach*.

Megillat Kohelet
The Scroll of Ecclesiastes

Introduction and commentary by Batya Markowitz

Megillat Kohelet (Ecclesiastes) gets its Hebrew name from its author King *Shlomo*, who calls himself *"Kohelet."* The name is related to the word *hak-hel* (הקהל), 'gathering', since *Shlomo* often shared his wisdom in public gatherings. *Megillat Kohelet* is a book of observations on life, made by the wisest man to ever live. According to the Sages, it was written towards the end of *Shlomo*'s life, after he had gathered much wisdom and life experience. Fitting for a book of insight, this book was written in *Yerushalayim*, a city known for its wisdom.

Throughout *Megillat Kohelet*, King *Shlomo* comments on the futility of life in this world. He warns not to be drawn to excessive celebration, and instructs that it is better to pursue knowledge than pleasure. He observes that *Hashem* created a perfect world in which "A season is set for everything" (3:1). Solomon ponders the age-old question of why righteous people suffer while the wicked prosper. He illustrates how meaningless the pursuit of wealth and luxuries is, and points out the things that really matter in life, such as a good reputation, charity and good deeds. He decries bad personality traits such as jealousy, stinginess, and anger.

At first glance, certain verses in *Megillat Kohelet* seem inherently contradictory or antithetical to Judaism, and for this reason the Sages considered not including it in the Bible. Ultimately, though, they arrived at the conclusion that *Kohelet* should be included, since its overall message is that life is infused with meaning when following the word of God and His *Torah*. *Megillat Kohelet* begins by saying that the physical world on its own is meaningless, and ends by stating: "The sum of the matter, when all is said and done: Revere *Hashem* and observe His commandments! For this applies to all mankind" (12:13).

Megillat Kohelet was originally read at the biblical *hak-hel* ceremony described in *Sefer Devarim* 31. Once every seven years, at the conclusion of the Sabbatical year, the king would address the people who had made the pilgrimage to *Yerushalayim* for the holiday of *Sukkot*. Traditionally, the king would read portions of the *Torah* at this ceremony. King *Shlomo* added the words of caution that are included in his book, *Megillat Kohelet*, and later kings read from this scroll as well.

To this day, *Megillat Kohelet* is read on *Sukkot* each year. In the Land of Israel, the holiday of *Sukkot* falls right before the rainy season. Crops that have been harvested and dried in the fields throughout the summer are stored before the first rains come. This time of year provides a great sense of accomplishment for the farmer who has toiled all year to finally reap the fruits of his labor. To avoid getting caught up in the self-satisfaction and the materialism, *Megillat Kohelet* is read specifically at this time, to warn a person that the goal of life is not material success, but rather the means to achieve the higher purpose of closeness with the Almighty.

Map of Ancient *Yerushalayim*

Kohelet (1:1) states that the book contains the words of *Kohelet* son of *David* who lived in *Yerushalayim*. The Sages identify *Kohelet* as *Shlomo*, who ruled in *Yerushalayim* following the death of his father *David*. The following is a map of *Yerushalayim* as it looked in the time of King *Shlomo*. For comparison, the map also contains the city limits at the end of the monarchy as well as the present day walls of the Old City of *Yerushalayim*.

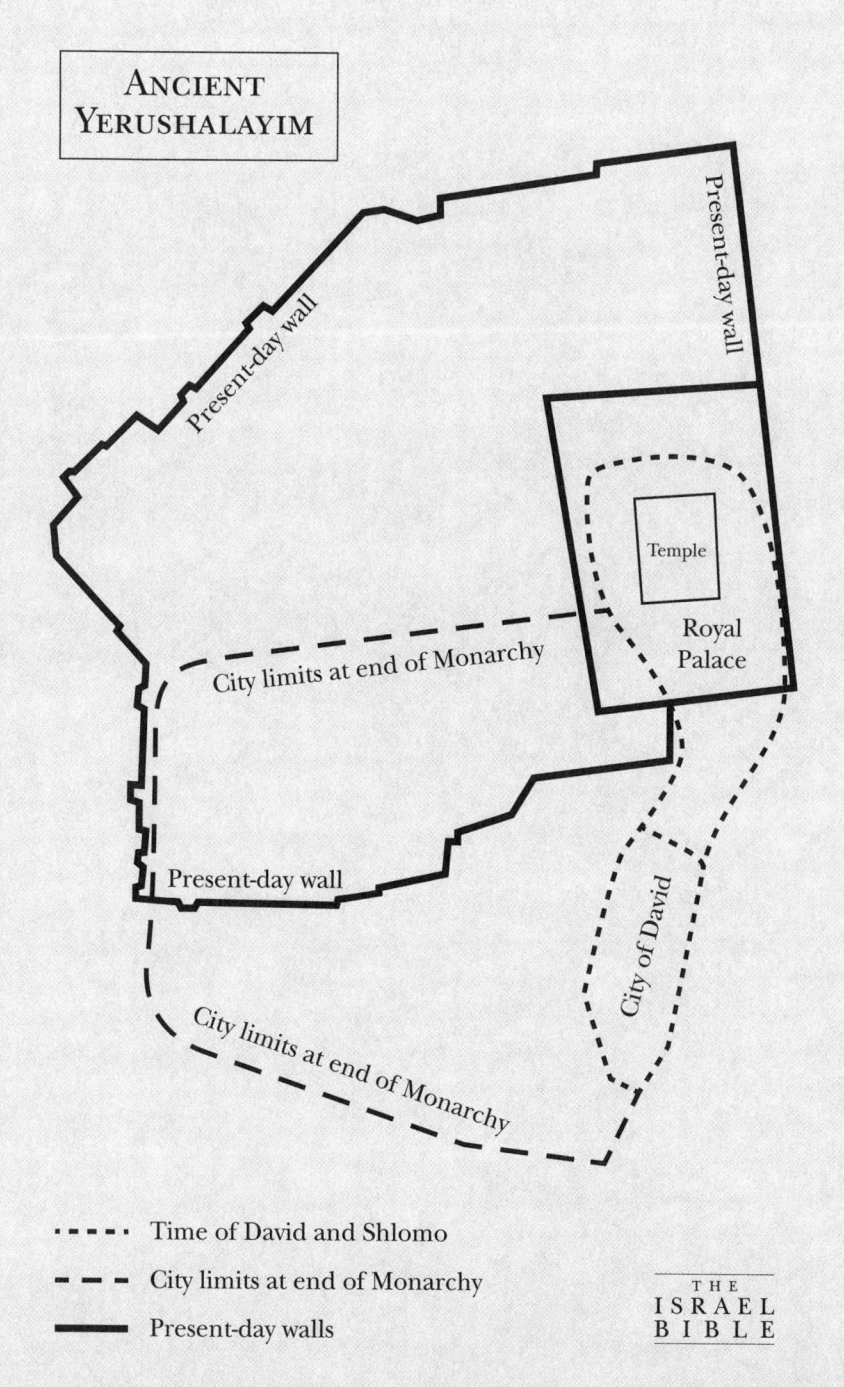

Ancient Yerushalayim

- ····· Time of David and Shlomo
- ---- City limits at end of Monarchy
- —— Present-day walls

THE ISRAEL BIBLE

Kohelet/Ecclesiastes
Chapter 1

קהלת
פרק א

1 ¹ The words of *Kohelet* son of *David*, king in *Yerushalayim*.

דִּבְרֵי קֹהֶלֶת בֶּן־דָּוִד מֶלֶךְ בִּירוּשָׁלָֽםִ׃

div-RAY ko-HE-let ben da-VID ME-lekh bee-ru-sha-LA-im

² Utter futility! – said *Kohelet* – Utter futility! All is futile!

הֲבֵל הֲבָלִים אָמַר קֹהֶלֶת הֲבֵל הֲבָלִים הַכֹּל הָֽבֶל׃

³ What real value is there for a man In all the gains he makes beneath the sun?

מַה־יִּתְרוֹן לָאָדָם בְּכָל־עֲמָלוֹ שֶׁיַּעֲמֹל תַּחַת הַשָּֽׁמֶשׁ׃

⁴ One generation goes, another comes, But the earth remains the same forever.

דּוֹר הֹלֵךְ וְדוֹר בָּא וְהָאָרֶץ לְעוֹלָם עֹמָֽדֶת׃

⁵ The sun rises, and the sun sets – And glides back to where it rises.

וְזָרַח הַשֶּׁמֶשׁ וּבָא הַשָּׁמֶשׁ וְאֶל־מְקוֹמוֹ שׁוֹאֵף זוֹרֵחַ הוּא שָֽׁם׃

⁶ Southward blowing, Turning northward, Ever turning blows the wind; On its rounds the wind returns.

הוֹלֵךְ אֶל־דָּרוֹם וְסוֹבֵב אֶל־צָפוֹן סוֹבֵב ׀ סֹבֵב הוֹלֵךְ הָרוּחַ וְעַל־סְבִיבֹתָיו שָׁב הָרֽוּחַ׃

⁷ All streams flow into the sea, Yet the sea is never full; To the place [from] which they flow The streams flow back again.

כָּל־הַנְּחָלִים הֹלְכִים אֶל־הַיָּם וְהַיָּם אֵינֶנּוּ מָלֵא אֶל־מְקוֹם שֶׁהַנְּחָלִים הֹלְכִים שָׁם הֵם שָׁבִים לָלָֽכֶת׃

⁸ All such things are wearisome: No man can ever state them; The eye never has enough of seeing, Nor the ear enough of hearing.

כָּל־הַדְּבָרִים יְגֵעִים לֹא־יוּכַל אִישׁ לְדַבֵּר לֹא־תִשְׂבַּע עַיִן לִרְאוֹת וְלֹא־תִמָּלֵא אֹזֶן מִשְּׁמֹֽעַ׃

⁹ Only that shall happen Which has happened, Only that occur Which has occurred; There is nothing new Beneath the sun!

מַה־שֶּֽׁהָיָה הוּא שֶׁיִּהְיֶה וּמַה־שֶּׁנַּֽעֲשָׂה הוּא שֶׁיֵּעָשֶׂה וְאֵין כָּל־חָדָשׁ תַּחַת הַשָּֽׁמֶשׁ׃

¹⁰ Sometimes there is a phenomenon of which they say, "Look, this one is new!" – it occurred long since, in ages that went by before us.

יֵשׁ דָּבָר שֶׁיֹּאמַר רְאֵה־זֶה חָדָשׁ הוּא כְּבָר הָיָה לְעֹלָמִים אֲשֶׁר הָיָה מִלְּפָנֵֽנוּ׃

¹¹ The earlier ones are not remembered; so too those that will occur later will no more be remembered than those that will occur at the very end.

אֵין זִכְרוֹן לָרִאשֹׁנִים וְגַם לָאַחֲרֹנִים שֶׁיִּהְיוּ לֹא־יִהְיֶה לָהֶם זִכָּרוֹן עִם שֶׁיִּהְיוּ לָאַחֲרֹנָֽה׃

¹² I, *Kohelet*, was king in *Yerushalayim* over *Yisrael*.

אֲנִי קֹהֶלֶת הָיִיתִי מֶלֶךְ עַל־יִשְׂרָאֵל בִּירוּשָׁלָֽםִ׃

1:1 King in *Yerushalayim* *Kohelet*, the Hebrew name of this book, is a title given to King *Shlomo*. Although he was king of all of Israel, the wisest of all men is called the "king in *Yerushalayim*" since *Yerushalayim* is known as a city of wisdom and a place that lends itself to deeper understanding. Furthermore, many sages resided in *Yerushalayim*, the political and spiritual capital of the united Kingdom of Israel. King *Shlomo* wants to add validity to his work by emphasizing that the observations recorded here were analyzed and approved by the wise residents of Jerusalem.

Kohelet/Ecclesiastes
Chapter 2

קהלת
פרק ב

13 I set my mind to study and to probe with wisdom all that happens under the sun. – An unhappy business, that, which *Hashem* gave men to be concerned with!

יג וְנָתַתִּי אֶת־לִבִּי לִדְרוֹשׁ וְלָתוּר בַּחָכְמָה עַל כָּל־אֲשֶׁר נַעֲשָׂה תַּחַת הַשָּׁמָיִם הוּא עִנְיַן רָע נָתַן אֱלֹהִים לִבְנֵי הָאָדָם לַעֲנוֹת בּוֹ׃

14 I observed all the happenings beneath the sun, and I found that all is futile and pursuit of wind:

יד רָאִיתִי אֶת־כָּל־הַמַּעֲשִׂים שֶׁנַּעֲשׂוּ תַּחַת הַשָּׁמֶשׁ וְהִנֵּה הַכֹּל הֶבֶל וּרְעוּת רוּחַ׃

15 A twisted thing that cannot be made straight, A lack that cannot be made good.

טו מְעֻוָּת לֹא־יוּכַל לִתְקֹן וְחֶסְרוֹן לֹא־יוּכַל לְהִמָּנוֹת׃

16 I said to myself: "Here I have grown richer and wiser than any that ruled before me over *Yerushalayim*, and my mind has zealously absorbed wisdom and learning."

טז דִּבַּרְתִּי אֲנִי עִם־לִבִּי לֵאמֹר אֲנִי הִנֵּה הִגְדַּלְתִּי וְהוֹסַפְתִּי חָכְמָה עַל כָּל־אֲשֶׁר־הָיָה לְפָנַי עַל־יְרוּשָׁלִָם וְלִבִּי רָאָה הַרְבֵּה חָכְמָה וָדָעַת׃

17 And so I set my mind to appraise wisdom and to appraise madness and folly. And I learned – that this too was pursuit of wind:

יז וָאֶתְּנָה לִבִּי לָדַעַת חָכְמָה וְדַעַת הוֹלֵלוֹת וְשִׂכְלוּת יָדַעְתִּי שֶׁגַּם־זֶה הוּא רַעְיוֹן רוּחַ׃

18 For as wisdom grows, vexation grows; To increase learning is to increase heartache.

יח כִּי בְּרֹב חָכְמָה רָב־כָּעַס וְיוֹסִיף דַּעַת יוֹסִיף מַכְאוֹב׃

2

1 I said to myself, "Come, I will treat you to merriment. Taste mirth!" That too, I found, was futile.

ב א אָמַרְתִּי אֲנִי בְּלִבִּי לְכָה־נָּא אֲנַסְּכָה בְשִׂמְחָה וּרְאֵה בְטוֹב וְהִנֵּה גַם־הוּא הָבֶל׃

2 Of revelry I said, "It's mad!" Of merriment, "What good is that?"

ב לִשְׂחוֹק אָמַרְתִּי מְהוֹלָל וּלְשִׂמְחָה מַה־זֹּה עֹשָׂה׃

3 I ventured to tempt my flesh with wine, and to grasp folly, while letting my mind direct with wisdom, to the end that I might learn which of the two was better for men to practice in their few days of life under heaven.

ג תַּרְתִּי בְלִבִּי לִמְשׁוֹךְ בַּיַּיִן אֶת־בְּשָׂרִי וְלִבִּי נֹהֵג בַּחָכְמָה וְלֶאֱחֹז בְּסִכְלוּת עַד אֲשֶׁר־אֶרְאֶה אֵי־זֶה טוֹב לִבְנֵי הָאָדָם אֲשֶׁר יַעֲשׂוּ תַּחַת הַשָּׁמַיִם מִסְפַּר יְמֵי חַיֵּיהֶם׃

4 I multiplied my possessions. I built myself houses and I planted vineyards.

ד הִגְדַּלְתִּי מַעֲשָׂי בָּנִיתִי לִי בָּתִּים נָטַעְתִּי לִי כְּרָמִים׃

5 I laid out gardens and groves, in which I planted every kind of fruit tree.

ה עָשִׂיתִי לִי גַּנּוֹת וּפַרְדֵּסִים וְנָטַעְתִּי בָהֶם עֵץ כָּל־פֶּרִי׃

a-SEE-tee LEE ga-NOT u-far-day-SEEM v'-na-TA-tee va-HEM AYTZ kol PE-ree

---

2:5 I planted every kind of fruit tree How is it possible that King *Shlomo* planted all kinds of fruit trees in his garden, if different trees require different climates in order to grow? The Sages of the *Midrash* say that in his wisdom, King *Shlomo* understood that *Yerushalayim* is the heart of the world, and the foundation from which the rest of the earth was created. Since it contains spiritual channels that lead to all other places, *Shlomo* was able to plant every kind of fruit tree in *Yerushalayim*. According to tradition, he knew which part of *Yerushalayim* gives its strength to Africa and which location is connected to India, and was able to plant the trees of these climates in those areas.

Kohelet/Ecclesiastes
Chapter 2

6 I constructed pools of water, enough to irrigate a forest shooting up with trees.

7 I bought male and female slaves, and I acquired stewards. I also acquired more cattle, both herds and flocks, than all who were before me in *Yerushalayim*.

8 I further amassed silver and gold and treasures of kings and provinces; and I got myself male and female singers, as well as the luxuries of commoners – coffers and coffers of them.

9 Thus, I gained more wealth than anyone before me in *Yerushalayim*. In addition, my wisdom remained with me:

10 I withheld from my eyes nothing they asked for, and denied myself no enjoyment; rather, I got enjoyment out of all my wealth. And that was all I got out of my wealth.

11 Then my thoughts turned to all the fortune my hands had built up, to the wealth I had acquired and won – and oh, it was all futile and pursuit of wind; there was no real value under the sun!

12 For what will the man be like who will succeed the one who is ruling over what was built up long ago? My thoughts also turned to appraising wisdom and madness and folly.*

13 I found that Wisdom is superior to folly As light is superior to darkness;

14 A wise man has his eyes in his head, Whereas a fool walks in darkness. But I also realized that the same fate awaits them both.

15 So I reflected: "The fate of the fool is also destined for me; to what advantage, then, have I been wise?" And I came to the conclusion that that too was futile,

16 because the wise man, just like the fool, is not remembered forever; for, as the succeeding days roll by, both are forgotten. Alas, the wise man dies, just like the fool!

17 And so I loathed life. For I was distressed by all that goes on under the sun, because everything is futile and pursuit of wind.

---

* order of the two sentences reversed for clarity

קהלת
פרק ב

ו עָשִׂיתִי לִי בְּרֵכוֹת מָיִם לְהַשְׁקוֹת מֵהֶם יַעַר צוֹמֵחַ עֵצִים:

ז קָנִיתִי עֲבָדִים וּשְׁפָחוֹת וּבְנֵי־בַיִת הָיָה לִי גַּם מִקְנֶה בָקָר וָצֹאן הַרְבֵּה הָיָה לִי מִכֹּל שֶׁהָיוּ לְפָנַי בִּירוּשָׁלָ͏ִם:

ח כָּנַסְתִּי לִי גַּם־כֶּסֶף וְזָהָב וּסְגֻלַּת מְלָכִים וְהַמְּדִינוֹת עָשִׂיתִי לִי שָׁרִים וְשָׁרוֹת וְתַעֲנוּגֹת בְּנֵי הָאָדָם שִׁדָּה וְשִׁדּוֹת:

ט וְגָדַלְתִּי וְהוֹסַפְתִּי מִכֹּל שֶׁהָיָה לְפָנַי בִּירוּשָׁלָ͏ִם אַף חָכְמָתִי עָמְדָה לִּי:

י וְכֹל אֲשֶׁר שָׁאֲלוּ עֵינַי לֹא אָצַלְתִּי מֵהֶם לֹא־מָנַעְתִּי אֶת־לִבִּי מִכָּל־שִׂמְחָה כִּי־לִבִּי שָׂמֵחַ מִכָּל־עֲמָלִי וְזֶה־הָיָה חֶלְקִי מִכָּל־עֲמָלִי:

יא וּפָנִיתִי אֲנִי בְּכָל־מַעֲשַׂי שֶׁעָשׂוּ יָדַי וּבֶעָמָל שֶׁעָמַלְתִּי לַעֲשׂוֹת וְהִנֵּה הַכֹּל הֶבֶל וּרְעוּת רוּחַ וְאֵין יִתְרוֹן תַּחַת הַשָּׁמֶשׁ:

יב וּפָנִיתִי אֲנִי לִרְאוֹת חָכְמָה וְהוֹלֵלוֹת וְסִכְלוּת כִּי מֶה הָאָדָם שֶׁיָּבוֹא אַחֲרֵי הַמֶּלֶךְ אֵת אֲשֶׁר־כְּבָר עָשׂוּהוּ:

יג וְרָאִיתִי אָנִי שֶׁיֵּשׁ יִתְרוֹן לַחָכְמָה מִן־הַסִּכְלוּת כִּיתְרוֹן הָאוֹר מִן־הַחֹשֶׁךְ:

יד הֶחָכָם עֵינָיו בְּרֹאשׁוֹ וְהַכְּסִיל בַּחֹשֶׁךְ הוֹלֵךְ וְיָדַעְתִּי גַם־אָנִי שֶׁמִּקְרֶה אֶחָד יִקְרֶה אֶת־כֻּלָּם:

טו וְאָמַרְתִּי אֲנִי בְּלִבִּי כְּמִקְרֵה הַכְּסִיל גַּם־אֲנִי יִקְרֵנִי וְלָמָּה חָכַמְתִּי אֲנִי אָז יוֹתֵר וְדִבַּרְתִּי בְלִבִּי שֶׁגַּם־זֶה הָבֶל:

טז כִּי אֵין זִכְרוֹן לֶחָכָם עִם־הַכְּסִיל לְעוֹלָם בְּשֶׁכְּבָר הַיָּמִים הַבָּאִים הַכֹּל נִשְׁכָּח וְאֵיךְ יָמוּת הֶחָכָם עִם־הַכְּסִיל:

יז וְשָׂנֵאתִי אֶת־הַחַיִּים כִּי רַע עָלַי הַמַּעֲשֶׂה שֶׁנַּעֲשָׂה תַּחַת הַשָּׁמֶשׁ כִּי־הַכֹּל הֶבֶל וּרְעוּת רוּחַ:

Kohelet/Ecclesiastes
Chapter 3

קהלת
פרק ג

18 So, too, I loathed all the wealth that I was gaining under the sun. For I shall leave it to the man who will succeed me –

יח וְשָׂנֵאתִי אֲנִי אֶת־כָּל־עֲמָלִי שֶׁאֲנִי עָמֵל תַּחַת הַשָּׁמֶשׁ שֶׁאַנִּיחֶנּוּ לָאָדָם שֶׁיִּהְיֶה אַחֲרָי:

19 and who knows whether he will be wise or foolish? – and he will control all the wealth that I gained by toil and wisdom under the sun. That too is futile.

יט וּמִי יוֹדֵעַ הֶחָכָם יִהְיֶה אוֹ סָכָל וְיִשְׁלַט בְּכָל־עֲמָלִי שֶׁעָמַלְתִּי וְשֶׁחָכַמְתִּי תַּחַת הַשָּׁמֶשׁ גַּם־זֶה הָבֶל:

20 And so I came to view with despair all the gains I had made under the sun.

כ וְסַבּוֹתִי אֲנִי לְיַאֵשׁ אֶת־לִבִּי עַל כָּל־הֶעָמָל שֶׁעָמַלְתִּי תַּחַת הַשָּׁמֶשׁ:

21 For sometimes a person whose fortune was made with wisdom, knowledge, and skill must hand it on to be the portion of somebody who did not toil for it. That too is futile, and a grave evil.

כא כִּי־יֵשׁ אָדָם שֶׁעֲמָלוֹ בְּחָכְמָה וּבְדַעַת וּבְכִשְׁרוֹן וּלְאָדָם שֶׁלֹּא עָמַל־בּוֹ יִתְּנֶנּוּ חֶלְקוֹ גַּם־זֶה הֶבֶל וְרָעָה רַבָּה:

22 For what does a man get for all the toiling and worrying he does under the sun?

כב כִּי מֶה־הֹוֶה לָאָדָם בְּכָל־עֲמָלוֹ וּבְרַעְיוֹן לִבּוֹ שֶׁהוּא עָמֵל תַּחַת הַשָּׁמֶשׁ:

23 All his days his thoughts are grief and heartache, and even at night his mind has no respite. That too is futile!

כג כִּי כָל־יָמָיו מַכְאֹבִים וָכַעַס עִנְיָנוֹ גַּם־בַּלַּיְלָה לֹא־שָׁכַב לִבּוֹ גַּם־זֶה הֶבֶל הוּא:

24 There is nothing worthwhile for a man but to eat and drink and afford himself enjoyment with his means. And even that, I noted, comes from *Hashem*.

כד אֵין־טוֹב בָּאָדָם שֶׁיֹּאכַל וְשָׁתָה וְהֶרְאָה אֶת־נַפְשׁוֹ טוֹב בַּעֲמָלוֹ גַּם־זֹה רָאִיתִי אָנִי כִּי מִיַּד הָאֱלֹהִים הִיא:

25 For who eats and who enjoys but myself?

כה כִּי מִי יֹאכַל וּמִי יָחוּשׁ חוּץ מִמֶּנִּי:

26 To the man, namely, who pleases Him He has given the wisdom and shrewdness to enjoy himself; and to him who displeases, He has given the urge to gather and amass – only for handing on to one who is pleasing to *Hashem*. That too is futile and pursuit of wind.

כו כִּי לְאָדָם שֶׁטּוֹב לְפָנָיו נָתַן חָכְמָה וְדַעַת וְשִׂמְחָה וְלַחוֹטֶא נָתַן עִנְיָן לֶאֱסוֹף וְלִכְנוֹס לָתֵת לְטוֹב לִפְנֵי הָאֱלֹהִים גַּם־זֶה הֶבֶל וּרְעוּת רוּחַ:

3 1 A season is set for everything, a time for every experience under heaven:

ג א לַכֹּל זְמָן וְעֵת לְכָל־חֵפֶץ תַּחַת הַשָּׁמָיִם:

2 A time for being born and a time for dying, A time for planting and a time for uprooting the planted;

ב עֵת לָלֶדֶת וְעֵת לָמוּת עֵת לָטַעַת וְעֵת לַעֲקוֹר נָטוּעַ:

3 A time for slaying and a time for healing, A time for tearing down and a time for building up;

ג עֵת לַהֲרוֹג וְעֵת לִרְפּוֹא עֵת לִפְרוֹץ וְעֵת לִבְנוֹת:

4 A time for weeping and a time for laughing, A time for wailing and a time for dancing;

ד עֵת לִבְכּוֹת וְעֵת לִשְׂחוֹק עֵת סְפוֹד וְעֵת רְקוֹד:

Kohelet/Ecclesiastes
Chapter 3

קהלת
פרק ג

5 A time for throwing stones and a time for gathering stones, A time for embracing and a time for shunning embraces;

ה עֵת לְהַשְׁלִיךְ אֲבָנִים וְעֵת כְּנוֹס אֲבָנִים עֵת לַחֲבוֹק וְעֵת לִרְחֹק מֵחַבֵּק:

AYT l'-hash-LEEKH a-va-NEEM v'-AYT k'-NOS a-va-NEEM AYT la-kha-VOK v'-AYT lir-KHOK may-kha-BAYK

6 A time for seeking and a time for losing, A time for keeping and a time for discarding;

ו עֵת לְבַקֵּשׁ וְעֵת לְאַבֵּד עֵת לִשְׁמוֹר וְעֵת לְהַשְׁלִיךְ:

7 A time for ripping and a time for sewing, A time for silence and a time for speaking;

ז עֵת לִקְרוֹעַ וְעֵת לִתְפּוֹר עֵת לַחֲשׁוֹת וְעֵת לְדַבֵּר:

8 A time for loving and a time for hating; A time for war and a time for peace.

ח עֵת לֶאֱהֹב וְעֵת לִשְׂנֹא עֵת מִלְחָמָה וְעֵת שָׁלוֹם:

9 What value, then, can the man of affairs get from what he earns?

ט מַה־יִּתְרוֹן הָעוֹשֶׂה בַּאֲשֶׁר הוּא עָמֵל:

10 I have observed the business that *Hashem* gave man to be concerned with:

י רָאִיתִי אֶת־הָעִנְיָן אֲשֶׁר נָתַן אֱלֹהִים לִבְנֵי הָאָדָם לַעֲנוֹת בּוֹ:

11 He brings everything to pass precisely at its time; He also puts eternity in their mind, but without man ever guessing, from first to last, all the things that *Hashem* brings to pass.

יא אֶת־הַכֹּל עָשָׂה יָפֶה בְעִתּוֹ גַּם אֶת־הָעֹלָם נָתַן בְּלִבָּם מִבְּלִי אֲשֶׁר לֹא־יִמְצָא הָאָדָם אֶת־הַמַּעֲשֶׂה אֲשֶׁר־עָשָׂה הָאֱלֹהִים מֵרֹאשׁ וְעַד־סוֹף:

12 Thus I realized that the only worthwhile thing there is for them is to enjoy themselves and do what is good in their lifetime;

יב יָדַעְתִּי כִּי אֵין טוֹב בָּם כִּי אִם־לִשְׂמוֹחַ וְלַעֲשׂוֹת טוֹב בְּחַיָּיו:

13 also, that whenever a man does eat and drink and get enjoyment out of all his wealth, it is a gift of *Hashem*.

יג וְגַם כָּל־הָאָדָם שֶׁיֹּאכַל וְשָׁתָה וְרָאָה טוֹב בְּכָל־עֲמָלוֹ מַתַּת אֱלֹהִים הִיא:

14 I realized, too, that whatever *Hashem* has brought to pass will recur evermore: Nothing can be added to it And nothing taken from it – and *Hashem* has brought to pass that men revere Him.

יד יָדַעְתִּי כִּי כָּל־אֲשֶׁר יַעֲשֶׂה הָאֱלֹהִים הוּא יִהְיֶה לְעוֹלָם עָלָיו אֵין לְהוֹסִיף וּמִמֶּנּוּ אֵין לִגְרֹעַ וְהָאֱלֹהִים עָשָׂה שֶׁיִּרְאוּ מִלְּפָנָיו:

15 What is occurring occurred long since, And what is to occur occurred long since: and *Hashem* seeks the pursued.

טו מַה־שֶּׁהָיָה כְּבָר הוּא וַאֲשֶׁר לִהְיוֹת כְּבָר הָיָה וְהָאֱלֹהִים יְבַקֵּשׁ אֶת־נִרְדָּף:

16 And, indeed, I have observed under the sun: Alongside justice there is wickedness, Alongside righteousness there is wickedness.

טז וְעוֹד רָאִיתִי תַּחַת הַשָּׁמֶשׁ מְקוֹם הַמִּשְׁפָּט שָׁמָּה הָרֶשַׁע וּמְקוֹם הַצֶּדֶק שָׁמָּה הָרָשַׁע:

3:5 A time for throwing stones According to the Sages, the phrase, "a time for throwing stones" is a reference to the destruction of *Yerushalayim*, when its grand walls were reduced to a heap of rocks. The phrase, "and a time to gather stones" refers to the second stage of exile, when King *Yechonya*, and those exiled with him, carried the stones and earth of *Yerushalayim* to Babylonia, in order to build synagogues and study halls from the precious and sacred earth of the Holy Land. Additionally, just as God allowed *Yerushalayim* to be destroyed and reduced to stones, He also allowed the stones to be gathered for *Yerushalayim* to be built once again.

Kohelet/Ecclesiastes
Chapter 4

קהלת
פרק ד

17 I mused: "Hashem will doom both righteous and wicked, for there is a time for every experience and for every happening."

יז אָמַרְתִּי אֲנִי בְּלִבִּי אֶת־הַצַּדִּיק וְאֶת־הָרָשָׁע יִשְׁפֹּט הָאֱלֹהִים כִּי־עֵת לְכָל־חֵפֶץ וְעַל כָּל־הַמַּעֲשֶׂה שָׁם:

18 So I decided, as regards men, to dissociate them [from] the divine beings and to face the fact that they are beasts.

יח אָמַרְתִּי אֲנִי בְּלִבִּי עַל־דִּבְרַת בְּנֵי הָאָדָם לְבָרָם הָאֱלֹהִים וְלִרְאוֹת שְׁהֶם־בְּהֵמָה הֵמָּה לָהֶם:

19 For in respect of the fate of man and the fate of beast, they have one and the same fate: as the one dies so dies the other, and both have the same lifebreath; man has no superiority over beast, since both amount to nothing.

יט כִּי מִקְרֶה בְנֵי־הָאָדָם וּמִקְרֶה הַבְּהֵמָה וּמִקְרֶה אֶחָד לָהֶם כְּמוֹת זֶה כֵּן מוֹת זֶה וְרוּחַ אֶחָד לַכֹּל וּמוֹתַר הָאָדָם מִן־הַבְּהֵמָה אָיִן כִּי הַכֹּל הָבֶל:

20 Both go to the same place; both came from dust and both return to dust.

כ הַכֹּל הוֹלֵךְ אֶל־מָקוֹם אֶחָד הַכֹּל הָיָה מִן־הֶעָפָר וְהַכֹּל שָׁב אֶל־הֶעָפָר:

21 Who knows if a man's lifebreath does rise upward and if a beast's breath does sink down into the earth?

כא מִי יוֹדֵעַ רוּחַ בְּנֵי הָאָדָם הָעֹלָה הִיא לְמָעְלָה וְרוּחַ הַבְּהֵמָה הַיֹּרֶדֶת הִיא לְמַטָּה לָאָרֶץ:

22 I saw that there is nothing better for man than to enjoy his possessions, since that is his portion. For who can enable him to see what will happen afterward?

כב וְרָאִיתִי כִּי אֵין טוֹב מֵאֲשֶׁר יִשְׂמַח הָאָדָם בְּמַעֲשָׂיו כִּי־הוּא חֶלְקוֹ כִּי מִי יְבִיאֶנּוּ לִרְאוֹת בְּמֶה שֶׁיִּהְיֶה אַחֲרָיו:

4

1 I further observed all the oppression that goes on under the sun: the tears of the oppressed, with none to comfort them; and the power of their oppressors – with none to comfort them.

א וְשַׁבְתִּי אֲנִי וָאֶרְאֶה אֶת־כָּל־הָעֲשֻׁקִים אֲשֶׁר נַעֲשִׂים תַּחַת הַשָּׁמֶשׁ וְהִנֵּה דִּמְעַת הָעֲשֻׁקִים וְאֵין לָהֶם מְנַחֵם וּמִיַּד עֹשְׁקֵיהֶם כֹּחַ וְאֵין לָהֶם מְנַחֵם:

v'-shav-TEE a-NEE va-er-EH et kol HA-a-shu-KEEM a-SHER na-a-SEEM TA-khat ha-SHA-mesh v'-hi-NAY dim-AT ha-a-shu-KEEM v'-AYN la-HEM m'-na-KHAYM u-mi-YAD o-sh'-kay-HEM KO-akh v'-AYN la-HEM m'-na-KHAYM

2 Then I accounted those who died long since more fortunate than those who are still living;

ב וְשַׁבֵּחַ אֲנִי אֶת־הַמֵּתִים שֶׁכְּבָר מֵתוּ מִן־הַחַיִּים אֲשֶׁר הֵמָּה חַיִּים עֲדֶנָה:

3 and happier than either are those who have not yet come into being and have never witnessed the miseries that go on under the sun.

ג וְטוֹב מִשְּׁנֵיהֶם אֵת אֲשֶׁר־עֲדֶן לֹא הָיָה אֲשֶׁר לֹא־רָאָה אֶת־הַמַּעֲשֶׂה הָרָע אֲשֶׁר נַעֲשָׂה תַּחַת הַשָּׁמֶשׁ:

4 I have also noted that all labor and skillful enterprise come from men's envy of each other – another futility and pursuit of wind!

ד וְרָאִיתִי אֲנִי אֶת־כָּל־עָמָל וְאֵת כָּל־כִּשְׁרוֹן הַמַּעֲשֶׂה כִּי הִיא קִנְאַת־אִישׁ מֵרֵעֵהוּ גַּם־זֶה הֶבֶל וּרְעוּת רוּחַ:

4:1 With none to comfort them When the verse mentions "all the oppression that goes on," it refers to the suffering of the Jewish people in exile. *Kohelet* observes, however, that not only do the people suffer in exile, but that they lack the leadership to comfort them. *Sforno* notes that the phrase "with none to comfort them" is repeated twice in this verse, hinting that they were lacking the leadership to teach them the two keys for redemption: repentance and prayer. First, the People of Israel need a leader who will guide them towards repentance, for sincere repentance leads to redemption. Second, they need a leader who will show them how to pray effectively so that their prayers will be answered, and they will be returned to the Land of Israel.

Kohelet/Ecclesiastes
Chapter 5

קהלת
פרק ה

5 [True,] The fool folds his hands together And has to eat his own flesh.

ה הַכְּסִיל חֹבֵק אֶת־יָדָיו וְאֹכֵל אֶת־בְּשָׂרוֹ:

6 [But no less truly,] Better is a handful of gratification Than two fistfuls of labor which is pursuit of wind.

ו טוֹב מְלֹא כַף נָחַת מִמְּלֹא חָפְנַיִם עָמָל וּרְעוּת רוּחַ:

7 And I have noted this further futility under the sun:

ז וְשַׁבְתִּי אֲנִי וָאֶרְאֶה הֶבֶל תַּחַת הַשָּׁמֶשׁ:

8 the case of the man who is alone, with no companion, who has neither son nor brother; yet he amasses wealth without limit, and his eye is never sated with riches. For whom, now, is he amassing it while denying himself enjoyment? That too is a futility and an unhappy business.

ח יֵשׁ אֶחָד וְאֵין שֵׁנִי גַּם בֵּן וָאָח אֵין־לוֹ וְאֵין קֵץ לְכָל־עֲמָלוֹ גַּם־עֵינָיו [עֵינוֹ] לֹא־תִשְׂבַּע עֹשֶׁר וּלְמִי אֲנִי עָמֵל וּמְחַסֵּר אֶת־נַפְשִׁי מִטּוֹבָה גַּם־זֶה הֶבֶל וְעִנְיַן רָע הוּא:

9 Two are better off than one, in that they have greater benefit from their earnings.

ט טוֹבִים הַשְּׁנַיִם מִן־הָאֶחָד אֲשֶׁר יֵשׁ־לָהֶם שָׂכָר טוֹב בַּעֲמָלָם:

10 For should they fall, one can raise the other; but woe betide him who is alone and falls with no companion to raise him!

י כִּי אִם־יִפֹּלוּ הָאֶחָד יָקִים אֶת־חֲבֵרוֹ וְאִילוֹ הָאֶחָד שֶׁיִּפּוֹל וְאֵין שֵׁנִי לַהֲקִימוֹ:

11 Further, when two lie together they are warm; but how can he who is alone get warm?

יא גַּם אִם־יִשְׁכְּבוּ שְׁנַיִם וְחַם לָהֶם וּלְאֶחָד אֵיךְ יֵחָם:

12 Also, if one attacks, two can stand up to him. A threefold cord is not readily broken!

יב וְאִם־יִתְקְפוֹ הָאֶחָד הַשְּׁנַיִם יַעַמְדוּ נֶגְדּוֹ וְהַחוּט הַמְשֻׁלָּשׁ לֹא בִמְהֵרָה יִנָּתֵק:

13 Better a poor but wise youth than an old but foolish king who no longer has the sense to heed warnings.

יג טוֹב יֶלֶד מִסְכֵּן וְחָכָם מִמֶּלֶךְ זָקֵן וּכְסִיל אֲשֶׁר לֹא־יָדַע לְהִזָּהֵר עוֹד:

14 For the former can emerge from a dungeon to become king; while the latter, even if born to kingship, can become a pauper.

יד כִּי־מִבֵּית הָסוּרִים יָצָא לִמְלֹךְ כִּי גַּם בְּמַלְכוּתוֹ נוֹלַד רָשׁ:

15 [However,] I reflected about all the living who walk under the sun with that youthful successor who steps into his place.

טו רָאִיתִי אֶת־כָּל־הַחַיִּים הַמְהַלְּכִים תַּחַת הַשָּׁמֶשׁ עִם הַיֶּלֶד הַשֵּׁנִי אֲשֶׁר יַעֲמֹד תַּחְתָּיו:

16 Unnumbered are the multitudes of all those who preceded them; and later generations will not acclaim him either. For that too is futile and pursuit of wind.

טז אֵין־קֵץ לְכָל־הָעָם לְכֹל אֲשֶׁר־הָיָה לִפְנֵיהֶם גַּם הָאַחֲרוֹנִים לֹא יִשְׂמְחוּ־בוֹ כִּי־גַם־זֶה הֶבֶל וְרַעְיוֹן רוּחַ:

17 Be not overeager to go to the House of *Hashem*: more acceptable is obedience than the offering of fools, for they know nothing [but] to do wrong.

יז שְׁמֹר רַגְלֶיךָ [רַגְלְךָ] כַּאֲשֶׁר תֵּלֵךְ אֶל־בֵּית הָאֱלֹהִים וְקָרוֹב לִשְׁמֹעַ מִתֵּת הַכְּסִילִים זָבַח כִּי־אֵינָם יוֹדְעִים לַעֲשׂוֹת רָע:

5 1 Keep your mouth from being rash, and let not your throat be quick to bring forth speech before *Hashem*. For *Hashem* is in heaven and you are on earth; that is why your words should be few.

ה א אַל־תְּבַהֵל עַל־פִּיךָ וְלִבְּךָ אַל־יְמַהֵר לְהוֹצִיא דָבָר לִפְנֵי הָאֱלֹהִים כִּי הָאֱלֹהִים בַּשָּׁמַיִם וְאַתָּה עַל־הָאָרֶץ עַל־כֵּן יִהְיוּ דְבָרֶיךָ מְעַטִּים:

Kohelet/Ecclesiastes
Chapter 5

קהלת
פרק ה

2 Just as dreams come with much brooding, so does foolish utterance come with much speech.

ב כִּי בָּא הַחֲלוֹם בְּרֹב עִנְיָן וְקוֹל כְּסִיל בְּרֹב דְּבָרִים:

3 When you make a vow to *Hashem*, do not delay to fulfill it. For He has no pleasure in fools; what you vow, fulfill.

ג כַּאֲשֶׁר תִּדֹּר נֶדֶר לֵאלֹהִים אַל־תְּאַחֵר לְשַׁלְּמוֹ כִּי אֵין חֵפֶץ בַּכְּסִילִים אֵת אֲשֶׁר־תִּדֹּר שַׁלֵּם:

4 It is better not to vow at all than to vow and not fulfill.

ד טוֹב אֲשֶׁר לֹא־תִדֹּר מִשֶּׁתִּדּוֹר וְלֹא תְשַׁלֵּם:

5 Don't let your mouth bring you into disfavor, and don't plead before the messenger that it was an error, but fear *Hashem*;* else *Hashem* may be angered by your talk and destroy your possessions.

ה אַל־תִּתֵּן אֶת־פִּיךָ לַחֲטִיא אֶת־בְּשָׂרֶךָ וְאַל־תֹּאמַר לִפְנֵי הַמַּלְאָךְ כִּי שְׁגָגָה הִיא לָמָּה יִקְצֹף הָאֱלֹהִים עַל־קוֹלֶךָ וְחִבֵּל אֶת־מַעֲשֵׂה יָדֶיךָ:

6 For much dreaming leads to futility and to superfluous talk.

ו כִּי בְרֹב חֲלֹמוֹת וַהֲבָלִים וּדְבָרִים הַרְבֵּה כִּי אֶת־הָאֱלֹהִים יְרָא:

7 If you see in a province oppression of the poor and suppression of right and justice, don't wonder at the fact; for one high official is protected by a higher one, and both of them by still higher ones.

ז אִם־עֹשֶׁק רָשׁ וְגֵזֶל מִשְׁפָּט וָצֶדֶק תִּרְאֶה בַמְּדִינָה אַל־תִּתְמַהּ עַל־הַחֵפֶץ כִּי גָבֹהַּ מֵעַל גָּבֹהַּ שֹׁמֵר וּגְבֹהִים עֲלֵיהֶם:

8 Thus the greatest advantage in all the land is his: he controls a field that is cultivated.

ח וְיִתְרוֹן אֶרֶץ בַּכֹּל הִיא [הוּא] מֶלֶךְ לְשָׂדֶה נֶעֱבָד:

9 A lover of money never has his fill of money, nor a lover of wealth his fill of income. That too is futile.

ט אֹהֵב כֶּסֶף לֹא־יִשְׂבַּע כֶּסֶף וּמִי־אֹהֵב בֶּהָמוֹן לֹא תְבוּאָה גַּם־זֶה הָבֶל:

o-HAYV KE-sef lo yis-BA KE-sef u-MEE o-HAYV be-ha-MON LO t'-vu-AH gam ZEH HA-vel

10 As his substance increases, so do those who consume it; what, then, does the success of its owner amount to but feasting his eyes?

י בִּרְבוֹת הַטּוֹבָה רַבּוּ אוֹכְלֶיהָ וּמַה־כִּשְׁרוֹן לִבְעָלֶיהָ כִּי אִם־רְאִית [רְאוּת] עֵינָיו:

11 A worker's sleep is sweet, whether he has much or little to eat; but the rich man's abundance doesn't let him sleep.

יא מְתוּקָה שְׁנַת הָעֹבֵד אִם־מְעַט וְאִם־הַרְבֵּה יֹאכֵל וְהַשָּׂבָע לֶעָשִׁיר אֵינֶנּוּ מַנִּיחַ לוֹ לִישׁוֹן:

12 Here is a grave evil I have observed under the sun: riches hoarded by their owner to his misfortune,

יב יֵשׁ רָעָה חוֹלָה רָאִיתִי תַּחַת הַשָּׁמֶשׁ עֹשֶׁר שָׁמוּר לִבְעָלָיו לְרָעָתוֹ:

13 in that those riches are lost in some unlucky venture; and if he begets a son, he has nothing in hand.

יג וְאָבַד הָעֹשֶׁר הַהוּא בְּעִנְיָן רָע וְהוֹלִיד בֵּן וְאֵין בְּיָדוֹ מְאוּמָה:

---

* "but fear Hashem" moved up from verse 6 for clarity

5:9 That too is futile The word *hevel* (הבל), 'futile,' appears many times throughout *Megillat Kohelet* as a description of the pursuit of various physical pleasures. Although the word is translated as 'futile,' it literally means 'vapor.' Vapor has the power to distort what a person sees. For example, the hot air rising from desert sands creates the mirage of an oasis. In this verse, Kohelet observes that amassing wealth is "*hevel.*" More than just futile, the pursuit of wealth is similar to vapor, since it has the power to distort a person's reality and values. *Kohelet* warns not to pursue wealth, because one who does so will never be satisfied.

הבל

Ecclesiastes

1842

Kohelet/Ecclesiastes
Chapter 6

קהלת
פרק ו

14 Another grave evil is this: He must depart just as he came.* As he came out of his mother's womb, so must he depart at last, naked as he came. He can take nothing of his wealth to carry with him.

כַּאֲשֶׁר יָצָא מִבֶּטֶן אִמּוֹ עָרוֹם יָשׁוּב לָלֶכֶת כְּשֶׁבָּא וּמְאוּמָה לֹא־יִשָּׂא בַעֲמָלוֹ שֶׁיֹּלֵךְ בְּיָדוֹ:

15 So what is the good of his toiling for the wind?

וְגַם־זֹה רָעָה חוֹלָה כָּל־עֻמַּת שֶׁבָּא כֵּן יֵלֵךְ וּמַה־יִּתְרוֹן לוֹ שֶׁיַּעֲמֹל לָרוּחַ:

16 Besides, all his days he eats in darkness, with much vexation and grief and anger.

גַּם כָּל־יָמָיו בַּחֹשֶׁךְ יֹאכֵל וְכָעַס הַרְבֵּה וְחָלְיוֹ וָקָצֶף:

17 Only this, I have found, is a real good: that one should eat and drink and get pleasure with all the gains he makes under the sun, during the numbered days of life that *Hashem* has given him; for that is his portion.

הִנֵּה אֲשֶׁר־רָאִיתִי אָנִי טוֹב אֲשֶׁר־יָפֶה לֶאֱכוֹל־וְלִשְׁתּוֹת וְלִרְאוֹת טוֹבָה בְּכָל־עֲמָלוֹ שֶׁיַּעֲמֹל תַּחַת־הַשֶּׁמֶשׁ מִסְפַּר יְמֵי־חַיָּו [חַיָּיו] אֲשֶׁר־נָתַן־לוֹ הָאֱלֹהִים כִּי־הוּא חֶלְקוֹ:

18 Also, whenever a man is given riches and property by *Hashem*, and is also permitted by Him to enjoy them and to take his portion and get pleasure for his gains – that is a gift of *Hashem*.

גַּם כָּל־הָאָדָם אֲשֶׁר נָתַן־לוֹ הָאֱלֹהִים עֹשֶׁר וּנְכָסִים וְהִשְׁלִיטוֹ לֶאֱכֹל מִמֶּנּוּ וְלָשֵׂאת אֶת־חֶלְקוֹ וְלִשְׂמֹחַ בַּעֲמָלוֹ זֹה מַתַּת אֱלֹהִים הִיא:

19 For [such a man] will not brood much over the days of his life, because *Hashem* keeps him busy enjoying himself.

כִּי לֹא הַרְבֵּה יִזְכֹּר אֶת־יְמֵי חַיָּיו כִּי הָאֱלֹהִים מַעֲנֶה בְּשִׂמְחַת לִבּוֹ:

6

1 There is an evil I have observed under the sun, and a grave one it is for man:

יֵשׁ רָעָה אֲשֶׁר רָאִיתִי תַּחַת הַשָּׁמֶשׁ וְרַבָּה הִיא עַל־הָאָדָם:

2 that *Hashem* sometimes grants a man riches, property, and wealth, so that he does not want for anything his appetite may crave, but *Hashem* does not permit him to enjoy it; instead, a stranger will enjoy it. That is futility and a grievous ill.

אִישׁ אֲשֶׁר יִתֶּן־לוֹ הָאֱלֹהִים עֹשֶׁר וּנְכָסִים וְכָבוֹד וְאֵינֶנּוּ חָסֵר לְנַפְשׁוֹ מִכֹּל אֲשֶׁר־יִתְאַוֶּה וְלֹא־יַשְׁלִיטֶנּוּ הָאֱלֹהִים לֶאֱכֹל מִמֶּנּוּ כִּי אִישׁ נָכְרִי יֹאכְלֶנּוּ זֶה הֶבֶל וָחֳלִי רָע הוּא:

EESH a-SHER yi-ten LO ha-e-lo-HEEM O-sher un-kha-SEEM v'-kha-VOD v'-ay-NE-nu kha-SAYR l'-naf-SHO mi-KOL a-sher yit-a-VEH v'-LO yash-lee-TE-nu ha-e-lo-HEEM le-e-KHOL mi-ME-nu KEE EESH nokh-REE yo-kh'-LE-nu ZEH HE-vel va-kho-LEE RA HU

3 Even if a man should beget a hundred children and live many years – no matter how many the days of his years may come to, if his gullet is not sated through his wealth, I say: The stillbirth, though it was not even accorded a burial, is more fortunate than he.

אִם־יוֹלִיד אִישׁ מֵאָה וְשָׁנִים רַבּוֹת יִחְיֶה וְרַב שֶׁיִּהְיוּ יְמֵי־שָׁנָיו וְנַפְשׁוֹ לֹא־תִשְׂבַּע מִן־הַטּוֹבָה וְגַם־קְבוּרָה לֹא־הָיְתָה לּוֹ אָמַרְתִּי טוֹב מִמֶּנּוּ הַנָּפֶל:

---

* "Another grave evil is this: He must depart just as he came" moved up from verse 15 for clarity

---

אושר
עושר

6:2 *Hashem* **sometimes grants a man riches** The Hebrew word for 'riches' is *osher*, spelled with the letter *ayin* (עושר). The Hebrew word for 'happiness' is also *osher*, but spelled with the letter *alef* (אושר). While the two words are homophones, they are not synonymous. Some people mistakenly believe that wealth leads to happiness. The Sages ("Ethics of the Fathers" 4:1), however, teach the exact opposite. "Who is wealthy? One who is happy with his lot." Only when a person is happy and satisfied with the material possessions that he has, no matter their value, can he be considered truly wealthy.

1843

Kohelet/Ecclesiastes
Chapter 7

4 Though it comes into futility and departs into darkness, and its very name is covered with darkness,

5 though it has never seen or experienced the sun, it is better off than he –

6 yes, even if the other lived a thousand years twice over but never had his fill of enjoyment! For are not both of them bound for the same place?

7 All of man's earning is for the sake of his mouth, yet his gullet is not sated.

8 What advantage then has the wise man over the fool, what advantage has the pauper who knows how to get on in life?

9 Is the feasting of the eyes more important than the pursuit of desire? That, too, is futility and pursuit of wind.

10 Whatever happens, it was designated long ago and it was known that it would happen; as for man, he cannot contend with what is stronger than he.

11 Often, much talk means much futility. How does it benefit a man?

12 Who can possibly know what is best for a man to do in life – the few days of his fleeting life? For who can tell him what the future holds for him under the sun?

7 1 A good name is better than fragrant oil, and the day of death than the day of birth.

2 It is better to go to a house of mourning than to a house of feasting; for that is the end of every man, and a living one should take it to heart.

3 Vexation is better than revelry; for though the face be sad, the heart may be glad.

4 Wise men are drawn to a house of mourning, and fools to a house of merrymaking.

5 It is better to listen to a wise man's reproof than to listen to the praise of fools.

6 For the levity of the fool is like the crackling of nettles under a kettle. But that too is illusory;

7 for cheating may rob the wise man of reason and destroy the prudence of the cautious.

Kohelet/Ecclesiastes
Chapter 7

קהלת
פרק ז

8 The end of a matter is better than the beginning of it. Better a patient spirit than a haughty spirit.

ח טוֹב אַחֲרִית דָּבָר מֵרֵאשִׁיתוֹ טוֹב אֶרֶךְ־רוּחַ מִגְּבַהּ־רוּחַ:

9 Don't let your spirit be quickly vexed, for vexation abides in the breasts of fools.

ט אַל־תְּבַהֵל בְּרוּחֲךָ לִכְעוֹס כִּי כַעַס בְּחֵיק כְּסִילִים יָנוּחַ:

10 Don't say, "How has it happened that former times were better than these?" For it is not wise of you to ask that question.

י אַל־תֹּאמַר מֶה הָיָה שֶׁהַיָּמִים הָרִאשֹׁנִים הָיוּ טוֹבִים מֵאֵלֶּה כִּי לֹא מֵחָכְמָה שָׁאַלְתָּ עַל־זֶה:

11 **Wisdom is as good as a patrimony, and even better, for those who behold the sun.**

יא טוֹבָה חָכְמָה עִם־נַחֲלָה וְיֹתֵר לְרֹאֵי הַשָּׁמֶשׁ:

to-VAH khokh-MAH im na-kha-LAH v'-yo-TAYR l'-ro-AY ha-SHA-mesh

12 For to be in the shelter of wisdom is to be also in the shelter of money, and the advantage of intelligence is that wisdom preserves the life of him who possesses it.

יב כִּי בְּצֵל הַחָכְמָה בְּצֵל הַכָּסֶף וְיִתְרוֹן דַּעַת הַחָכְמָה תְּחַיֶּה בְעָלֶיהָ:

13 Consider *Hashem*'s doing! Who can straighten what He has twisted?

יג רְאֵה אֶת־מַעֲשֵׂה הָאֱלֹהִים כִּי מִי יוּכַל לְתַקֵּן אֵת אֲשֶׁר עִוְּתוֹ:

14 So in a time of good fortune enjoy the good fortune; and in a time of misfortune, reflect: The one no less than the other was *Hashem*'s doing; consequently, man may find no fault with Him.

יד בְּיוֹם טוֹבָה הֱיֵה בְטוֹב וּבְיוֹם רָעָה רְאֵה גַּם אֶת־זֶה לְעֻמַּת־זֶה עָשָׂה הָאֱלֹהִים עַל־דִּבְרַת שֶׁלֹּא יִמְצָא הָאָדָם אַחֲרָיו מְאוּמָה:

15 In my own brief span of life, I have seen both these things: sometimes a good man perishes in spite of his goodness, and sometimes a wicked one endures in spite of his wickedness.

טו אֶת־הַכֹּל רָאִיתִי בִּימֵי הֶבְלִי יֵשׁ צַדִּיק אֹבֵד בְּצִדְקוֹ וְיֵשׁ רָשָׁע מַאֲרִיךְ בְּרָעָתוֹ:

16 So don't overdo goodness and don't act the wise man to excess, or you may be dumbfounded.

טז אַל־תְּהִי צַדִּיק הַרְבֵּה וְאַל־תִּתְחַכַּם יוֹתֵר לָמָּה תִּשּׁוֹמֵם:

17 Don't overdo wickedness and don't be a fool, or you may die before your time.

יז אַל־תִּרְשַׁע הַרְבֵּה וְאַל־תְּהִי סָכָל לָמָּה תָמוּת בְּלֹא עִתֶּךָ:

18 It is best that you grasp the one without letting go of the other, for one who fears *Hashem* will do his duty by both.

יח טוֹב אֲשֶׁר תֶּאֱחֹז בָּזֶה וְגַם־מִזֶּה אַל־תַּנַּח אֶת־יָדֶךָ כִּי־יְרֵא אֱלֹהִים יֵצֵא אֶת־כֻּלָּם:

Students studying Talmud in Tiveria

7:11 Wisdom is as good as a patrimony The Sages teach that the wisdom in this verse is the knowledge of the *Torah*, and the patrimony refers to the Land of Israel, which is the eternal inheritance of the Jewish people. *Tova chochma im nachala* (טובה חכמה עם נחלה), translated here as 'Wisdom is as good as a patrimony,' literally means "Wisdom is good with an inheritance." This means that the wisdom of the *Torah* is enhanced by the "inheritance" that is *Eretz Yisrael*. The Sages further teach that "there is no *Torah* like the *Torah* of the Land of Israel," since the very air of Israel makes a person wise. Israel is the Jews'"natural habitat," and it is therefore the place in which they can flourish and reach their spiritual potential. Mizrachi, the religious-Zionist movement founded in nineteenth century Vilna, reflected this sentiment in their motto: "The Land of Israel for the People of Israel, according to the *Torah* of Israel." Among other things, Mizrachi's mission, from its inception until today, has been working towards the economic and spiritual development of *Eretz Yisrael*.

1845

Kohelet/Ecclesiastes
Chapter 8

קהלת
פרק ח

19 Wisdom is more of a stronghold to a wise man than ten magnates that a city may contain.

יט הַחָכְמָה תָּעֹז לֶחָכָם מֵעֲשָׂרָה שַׁלִּיטִים אֲשֶׁר הָיוּ בָּעִיר:

20 For there is not one good man on earth who does what is best and doesn't err.

כ כִּי אָדָם אֵין צַדִּיק בָּאָרֶץ אֲשֶׁר יַעֲשֶׂה־טּוֹב וְלֹא יֶחֱטָא:

21 Finally, don't pay attention to everything that is said, so that you may not hear your slave reviling you;

כא גַּם לְכָל־הַדְּבָרִים אֲשֶׁר יְדַבֵּרוּ אַל־תִּתֵּן לִבֶּךָ אֲשֶׁר לֹא־תִשְׁמַע אֶת־עַבְדְּךָ מְקַלְלֶךָ:

22 for well you remember the many times that you yourself have reviled others.

כב כִּי גַּם־פְּעָמִים רַבּוֹת יָדַע לִבֶּךָ אֲשֶׁר גַּם־אַתְּ [אַתָּה] קִלַּלְתָּ אֲחֵרִים:

23 All this I tested with wisdom. I thought I could fathom it, but it eludes me.

כג כָּל־זֹה נִסִּיתִי בַחָכְמָה אָמַרְתִּי אֶחְכָּמָה וְהִיא רְחוֹקָה מִמֶּנִּי:

24 [The secret of] what happens is elusive and deep, deep down; who can discover it?

כד רָחוֹק מַה־שֶּׁהָיָה וְעָמֹק עָמֹק מִי יִמְצָאֶנּוּ:

25 I put my mind to studying, exploring, and seeking wisdom and the reason of things, and to studying wickedness, stupidity, madness, and folly.

כה סַבּוֹתִי אֲנִי וְלִבִּי לָדַעַת וְלָתוּר וּבַקֵּשׁ חָכְמָה וְחֶשְׁבּוֹן וְלָדַעַת רֶשַׁע כֶּסֶל וְהַסִּכְלוּת הוֹלֵלוֹת:

26 Now, I find woman more bitter than death; she is all traps, her hands are fetters and her heart is snares. He who is pleasing to *Hashem* escapes her, and he who is displeasing is caught by her.

כו וּמוֹצֵא אֲנִי מַר מִמָּוֶת אֶת־הָאִשָּׁה אֲשֶׁר־הִיא מְצוֹדִים וַחֲרָמִים לִבָּהּ אֲסוּרִים יָדֶיהָ טוֹב לִפְנֵי הָאֱלֹהִים יִמָּלֵט מִמֶּנָּה וְחוֹטֵא יִלָּכֶד בָּהּ:

27 See, this is what I found, said *Kohelet*, item by item in my search for the reason of things.

כז רְאֵה זֶה מָצָאתִי אָמְרָה קֹהֶלֶת אַחַת לְאַחַת לִמְצֹא חֶשְׁבּוֹן:

28 As for what I sought further but did not find, I found only one human being in a thousand, and the one I found among so many was never a woman.

כח אֲשֶׁר עוֹד־בִּקְשָׁה נַפְשִׁי וְלֹא מָצָאתִי אָדָם אֶחָד מֵאֶלֶף מָצָאתִי וְאִשָּׁה בְכָל־אֵלֶּה לֹא מָצָאתִי:

29 But, see, this I did find: *Hashem* made men plain, but they have engaged in too much reasoning.

כט לְבַד רְאֵה־זֶה מָצָאתִי אֲשֶׁר עָשָׂה הָאֱלֹהִים אֶת־הָאָדָם יָשָׁר וְהֵמָּה בִקְשׁוּ חִשְּׁבֹנוֹת רַבִּים:

8 1 Who is like the wise man, and who knows the meaning of the adage: "A man's wisdom lights up his face, So that his deep discontent is dissembled"?

ח א מִי כְּהֶחָכָם וּמִי יוֹדֵעַ פֵּשֶׁר דָּבָר חָכְמַת אָדָם תָּאִיר פָּנָיו וְעֹז פָּנָיו יְשֻׁנֶּא:

2 I do! "Obey the king's orders – and don't rush into uttering an oath by *Hashem*."

ב אֲנִי פִּי־מֶלֶךְ שְׁמוֹר וְעַל דִּבְרַת שְׁבוּעַת אֱלֹהִים:

3 Leave his presence; do not tarry in a dangerous situation, for he can do anything he pleases;

ג אַל־תִּבָּהֵל מִפָּנָיו תֵּלֵךְ אַל־תַּעֲמֹד בְּדָבָר רָע כִּי כָּל־אֲשֶׁר יַחְפֹּץ יַעֲשֶׂה:

4 inasmuch as a king's command is authoritative, and none can say to him, "What are you doing?"

ד בַּאֲשֶׁר דְּבַר־מֶלֶךְ שִׁלְטוֹן וּמִי יֹאמַר־לוֹ מַה־תַּעֲשֶׂה:

5 One who obeys orders will not suffer from the dangerous situation. A wise man, however, will bear in mind that there is a time of doom.

ה שׁוֹמֵר מִצְוָה לֹא יֵדַע דָּבָר רָע וְעֵת וּמִשְׁפָּט יֵדַע לֵב חָכָם:

Kohelet/Ecclesiastes
Chapter 8

קהלת
פרק ח

6 For there is a time for every experience, including the doom; for a man's calamity overwhelms him.

כִּי לְכָל־חֵפֶץ יֵשׁ עֵת וּמִשְׁפָּט כִּי־רָעַת הָאָדָם רַבָּה עָלָיו:

KEE l'-khol KHAY-fetz YAYSH AYT u-mish-PAT kee ra-AT ha-a-DAM ra-BAH a-LAV

7 Indeed, he does not know what is to happen; even when it is on the point of happening, who can tell him?

כִּי־אֵינֶנּוּ יֹדֵעַ מַה־שֶּׁיִּהְיֶה כִּי כַּאֲשֶׁר יִהְיֶה מִי יַגִּיד לוֹ:

8 No man has authority over the lifebreath – to hold back the lifebreath; there is no authority over the day of death. There is no mustering out from that war; wickedness is powerless to save its owner.

אֵין אָדָם שַׁלִּיט בָּרוּחַ לִכְלוֹא אֶת־הָרוּחַ וְאֵין שִׁלְטוֹן בְּיוֹם הַמָּוֶת וְאֵין מִשְׁלַחַת בַּמִּלְחָמָה וְלֹא־יְמַלֵּט רֶשַׁע אֶת־בְּעָלָיו:

9 All these things I observed; I noted all that went on under the sun, while men still had authority over men to treat them unjustly.

אֶת־כָּל־זֶה רָאִיתִי וְנָתוֹן אֶת־לִבִּי לְכָל־מַעֲשֶׂה אֲשֶׁר נַעֲשָׂה תַּחַת הַשָּׁמֶשׁ עֵת אֲשֶׁר שָׁלַט הָאָדָם בְּאָדָם לְרַע לוֹ:

10 And then I saw scoundrels coming from the Holy Site and being brought to burial, while such as had acted righteously were forgotten in the city. And here is another frustration:

וּבְכֵן רָאִיתִי רְשָׁעִים קְבֻרִים וָבָאוּ וּמִמְּקוֹם קָדוֹשׁ יְהַלֵּכוּ וְיִשְׁתַּכְּחוּ בָעִיר אֲשֶׁר כֵּן־עָשׂוּ גַּם־זֶה הָבֶל:

11 the fact that the sentence imposed for evil deeds is not executed swiftly, which is why men are emboldened to do evil –

אֲשֶׁר אֵין־נַעֲשָׂה פִתְגָם מַעֲשֵׂה הָרָעָה מְהֵרָה עַל־כֵּן מָלֵא לֵב בְּנֵי־הָאָדָם בָּהֶם לַעֲשׂוֹת רָע:

12 the fact that a sinner may do evil a hundred times and his [punishment] still be delayed. For although I am aware that "It will be well with those who revere *Hashem* since they revere Him,

אֲשֶׁר חֹטֶא עֹשֶׂה רָע מְאַת וּמַאֲרִיךְ לוֹ כִּי גַּם־יוֹדֵעַ אָנִי אֲשֶׁר יִהְיֶה־טּוֹב לְיִרְאֵי הָאֱלֹהִים אֲשֶׁר יִירְאוּ מִלְּפָנָיו:

13 and it will not be well with the scoundrel, and he will not live long, because he does not revere *Hashem*" –

וְטוֹב לֹא־יִהְיֶה לָרָשָׁע וְלֹא־יַאֲרִיךְ יָמִים כַּצֵּל אֲשֶׁר אֵינֶנּוּ יָרֵא מִלִּפְנֵי אֱלֹהִים:

14 here is a frustration that occurs in the world: sometimes an upright man is requited according to the conduct of the scoundrel; and sometimes the scoundrel is requited according to the conduct of the upright. I say all that is frustration.

יֶשׁ־הֶבֶל אֲשֶׁר נַעֲשָׂה עַל־הָאָרֶץ אֲשֶׁר יֵשׁ צַדִּיקִים אֲשֶׁר מַגִּיעַ אֲלֵהֶם כְּמַעֲשֵׂה הָרְשָׁעִים וְיֵשׁ רְשָׁעִים שֶׁמַּגִּיעַ אֲלֵהֶם כְּמַעֲשֵׂה הַצַּדִּיקִים אָמַרְתִּי שֶׁגַּם־זֶה הָבֶל:

8:6 For there is a time for every experience The word *chaifetz* (חפץ), translated here as 'experience,' also means 'desire.' *Sforno* explains that this verse means that God desires that various biblical commandments be observed at specific times of the year. Each season contains unique powers. The month of *Elul*, for example, which precedes the High Holidays, is conducive to repentance. *Adar*, the month in which the joyous holiday of *Purim* is celebrated, is a month of happiness, while *Av*, the month in which the two Temples in *Yerushalayim* were destroyed, is a month of mourning. Each year, a person can tap into the different powers corresponding to the different times of year. The Sages tell us that the exodus from Egypt took place in the month of *Nisan*, the month in which the holiday of *Pesach* is celebrated, and that the ultimate redemption will take place then as well. Therefore, a prayer for redemption is included in the *Pesach* seder, which ends with the words "next year in *Yerushalayim*."

Kohelet/Ecclesiastes
Chapter 9

15 I therefore praised enjoyment. For the only good a man can have under the sun is to eat and drink and enjoy himself. That much can accompany him, in exchange for his wealth, through the days of life that *Hashem* has granted him under the sun.

16 For I have set my mind to learn wisdom and to observe the business that goes on in the world – even to the extent of going without sleep day and night –

17 and I have observed all that *Hashem* brings to pass. Indeed, man cannot guess the events that occur under the sun. For man tries strenuously, but fails to guess them; and even if a sage should think to discover them he would not be able to guess them.

9 1 For all this I noted, and I ascertained all this: that the actions of even the righteous and the wise are determined by *Hashem*. Even love! Even hate! Man knows none of these in advance –

2 none! For the same fate is in store for all: for the righteous, and for the wicked; for the good and pure, and for the impure; for him who sacrifices, and for him who does not; for him who is pleasing, and for him who is displeasing; and for him who swears, and for him who shuns oaths.

3 That is the sad thing about all that goes on under the sun: that the same fate is in store for all. (Not only that, but men's hearts are full of sadness, and their minds of madness, while they live; and then – to the dead!)

4 For he who is reckoned among the living has something to look forward to – even a live dog is better than a dead lion –

5 since the living know they will die. But the dead know nothing; they have no more recompense, for even the memory of them has died.

6 Their loves, their hates, their jealousies have long since perished; and they have no more share till the end of time in all that goes on under the sun.

7 Go, eat your bread in gladness, and drink your wine in joy; for your action was long ago approved by *Hashem*.

קהלת
פרק ט

טו וְשִׁבַּחְתִּי אֲנִי אֶת־הַשִּׂמְחָה אֲשֶׁר אֵין־טוֹב לָאָדָם תַּחַת הַשֶּׁמֶשׁ כִּי אִם־לֶאֱכוֹל וְלִשְׁתּוֹת וְלִשְׂמוֹחַ וְהוּא יִלְוֶנּוּ בַעֲמָלוֹ יְמֵי חַיָּיו אֲשֶׁר־נָתַן־לוֹ הָאֱלֹהִים תַּחַת הַשָּׁמֶשׁ:

טז כַּאֲשֶׁר נָתַתִּי אֶת־לִבִּי לָדַעַת חָכְמָה וְלִרְאוֹת אֶת־הָעִנְיָן אֲשֶׁר נַעֲשָׂה עַל־הָאָרֶץ כִּי גַם בַּיּוֹם וּבַלַּיְלָה שֵׁנָה בְּעֵינָיו אֵינֶנּוּ רֹאֶה:

יז וְרָאִיתִי אֶת־כָּל־מַעֲשֵׂה הָאֱלֹהִים כִּי לֹא יוּכַל הָאָדָם לִמְצוֹא אֶת־הַמַּעֲשֶׂה אֲשֶׁר נַעֲשָׂה תַחַת־הַשֶּׁמֶשׁ בְּשֶׁל אֲשֶׁר יַעֲמֹל הָאָדָם לְבַקֵּשׁ וְלֹא יִמְצָא וְגַם אִם־יֹאמַר הֶחָכָם לָדַעַת לֹא יוּכַל לִמְצֹא:

ט א כִּי אֶת־כָּל־זֶה נָתַתִּי אֶל־לִבִּי וְלָבוּר אֶת־כָּל־זֶה אֲשֶׁר הַצַּדִּיקִים וְהַחֲכָמִים וַעֲבָדֵיהֶם בְּיַד הָאֱלֹהִים גַּם־אַהֲבָה גַם־שִׂנְאָה אֵין יוֹדֵעַ הָאָדָם הַכֹּל לִפְנֵיהֶם:

ב הַכֹּל כַּאֲשֶׁר לַכֹּל מִקְרֶה אֶחָד לַצַּדִּיק וְלָרָשָׁע לַטּוֹב וְלַטָּהוֹר וְלַטָּמֵא וְלַזֹּבֵחַ וְלַאֲשֶׁר אֵינֶנּוּ זֹבֵחַ כַּטּוֹב כַּחֹטֶא הַנִּשְׁבָּע כַּאֲשֶׁר שְׁבוּעָה יָרֵא:

ג זֶה רָע בְּכֹל אֲשֶׁר־נַעֲשָׂה תַּחַת הַשֶּׁמֶשׁ כִּי־מִקְרֶה אֶחָד לַכֹּל וְגַם לֵב בְּנֵי־הָאָדָם מָלֵא־רָע וְהוֹלֵלוֹת בִּלְבָבָם בְּחַיֵּיהֶם וְאַחֲרָיו אֶל־הַמֵּתִים:

ד כִּי־מִי אֲשֶׁר יְבֻחַר [יְחֻבַּר] אֶל כָּל־הַחַיִּים יֵשׁ בִּטָּחוֹן כִּי־לְכֶלֶב חַי הוּא טוֹב מִן־הָאַרְיֵה הַמֵּת:

ה כִּי הַחַיִּים יוֹדְעִים שֶׁיָּמֻתוּ וְהַמֵּתִים אֵינָם יוֹדְעִים מְאוּמָה וְאֵין־עוֹד לָהֶם שָׂכָר כִּי נִשְׁכַּח זִכְרָם:

ו גַּם אַהֲבָתָם גַּם־שִׂנְאָתָם גַּם־קִנְאָתָם כְּבָר אָבָדָה וְחֵלֶק אֵין־לָהֶם עוֹד לְעוֹלָם בְּכֹל אֲשֶׁר־נַעֲשָׂה תַּחַת הַשָּׁמֶשׁ:

ז לֵךְ אֱכֹל בְּשִׂמְחָה לַחְמֶךָ וּשְׁתֵה בְלֶב־טוֹב יֵינֶךָ כִּי כְבָר רָצָה הָאֱלֹהִים אֶת־מַעֲשֶׂיךָ:

Kohelet/Ecclesiastes
Chapter 9

קהלת
פרק ט

ח בְּכָל־עֵת יִהְיוּ בְגָדֶיךָ לְבָנִים וְשֶׁמֶן עַל־רֹאשְׁךָ אַל־יֶחְסָר׃

8 Let your clothes always be freshly washed, and your head never lack ointment.

b'-khol AYT yih-YU v'-ga-DE-kha l'-va-NEEM v'-SHE-men al ro-sh'-KHA al yekh-SAR

ט רְאֵה חַיִּים עִם־אִשָּׁה אֲשֶׁר־אָהַבְתָּ כָּל־יְמֵי חַיֵּי הֶבְלֶךָ אֲשֶׁר נָתַן־לְךָ תַּחַת הַשֶּׁמֶשׁ כֹּל יְמֵי הֶבְלֶךָ כִּי הוּא חֶלְקְךָ בַּחַיִּים וּבַעֲמָלְךָ אֲשֶׁר־אַתָּה עָמֵל תַּחַת הַשָּׁמֶשׁ׃

9 Enjoy happiness with a woman you love all the fleeting days of life that have been granted to you under the sun – all your fleeting days. For that alone is what you can get out of life and out of the means you acquire under the sun.

י כֹּל אֲשֶׁר תִּמְצָא יָדְךָ לַעֲשׂוֹת בְּכֹחֲךָ עֲשֵׂה כִּי אֵין מַעֲשֶׂה וְחֶשְׁבּוֹן וְדַעַת וְחָכְמָה בִּשְׁאוֹל אֲשֶׁר אַתָּה הֹלֵךְ שָׁמָּה׃

10 Whatever it is in your power to do, do with all your might. For there is no action, no reasoning, no learning, no wisdom in Sheol, where you are going.

יא שַׁבְתִּי וְרָאֹה תַחַת־הַשֶּׁמֶשׁ כִּי לֹא לַקַּלִּים הַמֵּרוֹץ וְלֹא לַגִּבּוֹרִים הַמִּלְחָמָה וְגַם לֹא לַחֲכָמִים לֶחֶם וְגַם לֹא לַנְּבֹנִים עֹשֶׁר וְגַם לֹא לַיֹּדְעִים חֵן כִּי־עֵת וָפֶגַע יִקְרֶה אֶת־כֻּלָּם׃

11 I have further observed under the sun that The race is not won by the swift, Nor the battle by the valiant; Nor is bread won by the wise, Nor wealth by the intelligent, Nor favor by the learned. For the time of mischance comes to all.

יב כִּי גַּם לֹא־יֵדַע הָאָדָם אֶת־עִתּוֹ כַּדָּגִים שֶׁנֶּאֱחָזִים בִּמְצוֹדָה רָעָה וְכַצִּפֳּרִים הָאֲחֻזוֹת בַּפָּח כָּהֵם יוּקָשִׁים בְּנֵי הָאָדָם לְעֵת רָעָה כְּשֶׁתִּפּוֹל עֲלֵיהֶם פִּתְאֹם׃

12 And a man cannot even know his time. As fishes are enmeshed in a fatal net, and as birds are trapped in a snare, so men are caught at the time of calamity, when it comes upon them without warning.

יג גַּם־זֹה רָאִיתִי חָכְמָה תַּחַת הַשָּׁמֶשׁ וּגְדוֹלָה הִיא אֵלָי׃

13 This thing too I observed under the sun about wisdom, and it affected me profoundly.

יד עִיר קְטַנָּה וַאֲנָשִׁים בָּהּ מְעָט וּבָא־אֵלֶיהָ מֶלֶךְ גָּדוֹל וְסָבַב אֹתָהּ וּבָנָה עָלֶיהָ מְצוֹדִים גְּדֹלִים׃

14 There was a little city, with few men in it; and to it came a great king, who invested it and built mighty siege works against it.

טו וּמָצָא בָהּ אִישׁ מִסְכֵּן חָכָם וּמִלַּט־הוּא אֶת־הָעִיר בְּחָכְמָתוֹ וְאָדָם לֹא זָכַר אֶת־הָאִישׁ הַמִּסְכֵּן הַהוּא׃

15 Present in the city was a poor wise man who might have saved it with his wisdom, but nobody thought of that poor man.

טז וְאָמַרְתִּי אָנִי טוֹבָה חָכְמָה מִגְּבוּרָה וְחָכְמַת הַמִּסְכֵּן בְּזוּיָה וּדְבָרָיו אֵינָם נִשְׁמָעִים׃

16 So I observed: Wisdom is better than valor; but A poor man's wisdom is scorned, And his words are not heeded.

9:8 Let your clothes always be freshly washed The word *l'vanim* (לבנים), translated here as 'freshly washed,' literally means 'white.' Some explain that this verse refers to the High Priest's service in the Temple on *Yom Kippur*, the Day of Atonement. When he entered the Holy of Holies on that holiest day of the year, the *Kohen Gadol* wore special clothing that were entirely white, instead of his regular colorful attire. The goal of his service was to bring atonement to the entire Jewish people. The High Priest conducted the service wearing white, which is synonymous with purity, as *Yeshayahu* states regarding the purification of sin: "Be your sins like crimson, they can turn snow-white" (Isaiah 1:18). This verse instructs every person that their garments should always be white and freshly washed, meaning that one should strive to be in a constant state of purity and innocence.

Kohelet/Ecclesiastes
Chapter 10

17 Words spoken softly by wise men are heeded sooner than those shouted by a lord in folly.

18 Wisdom is more valuable than weapons of war, but a single error destroys much of value.

10 1 Dead flies turn the perfumer's ointment fetid and putrid; so a little folly outweighs massive wisdom.

2 A wise man's mind tends toward the right hand, a fool's toward the left.

3 A fool's mind is also wanting when he travels, and he lets everybody know he is a fool.

4 If the wrath of a lord flares up against you, don't give up your post; for when wrath abates, grave offenses are pardoned.

5 Here is an evil I have seen under the sun as great as an error committed by a ruler:

6 Folly was placed on lofty heights, while rich men sat in low estate.

7 I have seen slaves on horseback, and nobles walking on the ground like slaves.

8 He who digs a pit will fall into it; he who breaches a stone fence will be bitten by a snake.

9 He who quarries stones will be hurt by them; he who splits wood will be harmed by it.

10 If the ax has become dull and he has not whetted the edge, he must exert more strength. Thus the advantage of a skill [depends on the exercise of] prudence.

11 If the snake bites because no spell was uttered, no advantage is gained by the trained charmer.

12 A wise man's talk brings him favor, but a fool's lips are his undoing.

13 His talk begins as silliness and ends as disastrous madness.

14 Yet the fool talks and talks! A man cannot know what will happen; who can tell him what the future holds?

15 A fool's exertions tire him out, for he doesn't know how to get to a town.

קהלת
פרק י

יז דִּבְרֵי חֲכָמִים בְּנַחַת נִשְׁמָעִים מִזַּעֲקַת מוֹשֵׁל בַּכְּסִילִים:

יח טוֹבָה חָכְמָה מִכְּלֵי קְרָב וְחוֹטֶא אֶחָד יְאַבֵּד טוֹבָה הַרְבֵּה:

י א זְבוּבֵי מָוֶת יַבְאִישׁ יַבִּיעַ שֶׁמֶן רוֹקֵחַ יָקָר מֵחָכְמָה מִכָּבוֹד סִכְלוּת מְעָט:

ב לֵב חָכָם לִימִינוֹ וְלֵב כְּסִיל לִשְׂמֹאלוֹ:

ג וְגַם־בַּדֶּרֶךְ כשהסכל [כְּשֶׁסָּכָל] הֹלֵךְ לִבּוֹ חָסֵר וְאָמַר לַכֹּל סָכָל הוּא:

ד אִם־רוּחַ הַמּוֹשֵׁל תַּעֲלֶה עָלֶיךָ מְקוֹמְךָ אַל־תַּנַּח כִּי מַרְפֵּא יַנִּיחַ חֲטָאִים גְּדוֹלִים:

ה יֵשׁ רָעָה רָאִיתִי תַּחַת הַשָּׁמֶשׁ כִּשְׁגָגָה שֶׁיֹּצָא מִלִּפְנֵי הַשַּׁלִּיט:

ו נִתַּן הַסֶּכֶל בַּמְּרוֹמִים רַבִּים וַעֲשִׁירִים בַּשֵּׁפֶל יֵשֵׁבוּ:

ז רָאִיתִי עֲבָדִים עַל־סוּסִים וְשָׂרִים הֹלְכִים כַּעֲבָדִים עַל־הָאָרֶץ:

ח חֹפֵר גּוּמָּץ בּוֹ יִפּוֹל וּפֹרֵץ גָּדֵר יִשְּׁכֶנּוּ נָחָשׁ:

ט מַסִּיעַ אֲבָנִים יֵעָצֵב בָּהֶם בּוֹקֵעַ עֵצִים יִסָּכֶן בָּם:

י אִם־קֵהָה הַבַּרְזֶל וְהוּא לֹא־פָנִים קִלְקַל וַחֲיָלִים יְגַבֵּר וְיִתְרוֹן הכשיר [הַכְשֵׁר] חָכְמָה:

יא אִם־יִשֹּׁךְ הַנָּחָשׁ בְּלוֹא־לָחַשׁ וְאֵין יִתְרוֹן לְבַעַל הַלָּשׁוֹן:

יב דִּבְרֵי פִי־חָכָם חֵן וְשִׂפְתוֹת כְּסִיל תְּבַלְּעֶנּוּ:

יג תְּחִלַּת דִּבְרֵי־פִיהוּ סִכְלוּת וְאַחֲרִית פִּיהוּ הוֹלֵלוּת רָעָה:

יד וְהַסָּכָל יַרְבֶּה דְבָרִים לֹא־יֵדַע הָאָדָם מַה־שֶּׁיִּהְיֶה וַאֲשֶׁר יִהְיֶה מֵאַחֲרָיו מִי יַגִּיד לוֹ:

טו עֲמַל הַכְּסִילִים תְּיַגְּעֶנּוּ אֲשֶׁר לֹא־יָדַע לָלֶכֶת אֶל־עִיר:

1850

Kohelet/Ecclesiastes
Chapter 11

קהלת
פרק יא

16 Alas for you, O land whose king is a lackey and whose ministers dine in the morning!

טז אִי־לָךְ אֶרֶץ שֶׁמַּלְכֵּךְ נָעַר וְשָׂרַיִךְ בַּבֹּקֶר יֹאכֵלוּ׃

17 Happy are you, O land whose king is a master and whose ministers dine at the proper time – with restraint, not with guzzling!

יז אַשְׁרֵיךְ אֶרֶץ שֶׁמַּלְכֵּךְ בֶּן־חוֹרִים וְשָׂרַיִךְ בָּעֵת יֹאכֵלוּ בִּגְבוּרָה וְלֹא בַשְּׁתִי׃

18 Through slothfulness the ceiling sags, Through lazy hands the house caves in.

יח בַּעֲצַלְתַּיִם יִמַּךְ הַמְּקָרֶה וּבְשִׁפְלוּת יָדַיִם יִדְלֹף הַבָּיִת׃

19 They make a banquet for revelry; wine makes life merry, and money answers every need.

יט לִשְׂחוֹק עֹשִׂים לֶחֶם וְיַיִן יְשַׂמַּח חַיִּים וְהַכֶּסֶף יַעֲנֶה אֶת־הַכֹּל׃

lis-KHOK o-SEEM LE-khem v'-YA-yin y'-sa-MAKH kha-YEEM v'-ha-KE-sef ya-a-NEH et ha-KOL

20 Don't revile a king even among your intimates. Don't revile a rich man even in your bedchamber; For a bird of the air may carry the utterance, And a winged creature may report the word.

כ גַּם בְּמַדָּעֲךָ מֶלֶךְ אַל־תְּקַלֵּל וּבְחַדְרֵי מִשְׁכָּבְךָ אַל־תְּקַלֵּל עָשִׁיר כִּי עוֹף הַשָּׁמַיִם יוֹלִיךְ אֶת־הַקּוֹל וּבַעַל הַכְּנָפַיִם [כְּנָפַיִם] יַגֵּיד דָּבָר׃

11

1 Send your bread forth upon the waters; for after many days you will find it.

יא א שַׁלַּח לַחְמְךָ עַל־פְּנֵי הַמָּיִם כִּי־בְרֹב הַיָּמִים תִּמְצָאֶנּוּ׃

2 Distribute portions to seven or even to eight, for you cannot know what misfortune may occur on earth.

ב תֶּן־חֵלֶק לְשִׁבְעָה וְגַם לִשְׁמוֹנָה כִּי לֹא תֵדַע מַה־יִּהְיֶה רָעָה עַל־הָאָרֶץ׃

3 If the clouds are filled, they will pour down rain on the earth; and if a tree falls to the south or to the north, the tree will stay where it falls.

ג אִם־יִמָּלְאוּ הֶעָבִים גֶּשֶׁם עַל־הָאָרֶץ יָרִיקוּ וְאִם־יִפּוֹל עֵץ בַּדָּרוֹם וְאִם בַּצָּפוֹן מְקוֹם שֶׁיִּפּוֹל הָעֵץ שָׁם יְהוּא׃

4 If one watches the wind, he will never sow; and if one observes the clouds, he will never reap.

ד שֹׁמֵר רוּחַ לֹא יִזְרָע וְרֹאֶה בֶעָבִים לֹא יִקְצוֹר׃

5 Just as you do not know how the lifebreath passes into the limbs within the womb of the pregnant woman, so you cannot foresee the actions of *Hashem*, who causes all things to happen.

ה כַּאֲשֶׁר אֵינְךָ יוֹדֵעַ מַה־דֶּרֶךְ הָרוּחַ כַּעֲצָמִים בְּבֶטֶן הַמְּלֵאָה כָּכָה לֹא תֵדַע אֶת־מַעֲשֵׂה הָאֱלֹהִים אֲשֶׁר יַעֲשֶׂה אֶת־הַכֹּל׃

6 Sow your seed in the morning, and don't hold back your hand in the evening, since you don't know which is going to succeed, the one or the other, or if both are equally good.

ו בַּבֹּקֶר זְרַע אֶת־זַרְעֶךָ וְלָעֶרֶב אַל־תַּנַּח יָדֶךָ כִּי אֵינְךָ יוֹדֵעַ אֵי זֶה יִכְשָׁר הֲזֶה אוֹ־זֶה וְאִם־שְׁנֵיהֶם כְּאֶחָד טוֹבִים׃

כסף **10:19 Money answers every need** Following the previous verse which opposes laziness, this verse encourages man to be industrious and to earn money. *Metzudat David* comments that unlike other pleasures, money is helpful in all situations. Whether a person is sick or healthy, happy or depressed, everybody benefits from financial stability. The Hebrew word for 'money' is *kesef* (כסף), related to the verb *kasaf* (כ-ס-ף) which means to 'yearn.' Money is something for which all people yearn, and that is what gives it its value. However, as King *Shlomo* warns in other verses (see 5:9), the pursuit of wealth for its own sake is futile; it must only be used in the service of *Hashem*.

Kohelet/Ecclesiastes
Chapter 12

7 How sweet is the light, what a delight for the eyes to behold the sun!

8 Even if a man lives many years, let him enjoy himself in all of them, remembering how many the days of darkness are going to be. The only future is nothingness!

9 O youth, enjoy yourself while you are young! Let your heart lead you to enjoyment in the days of your youth. Follow the desires of your heart and the glances of your eyes – but know well that *Hashem* will call you to account for all such things –

s'-MAKH ba-KHUR b'-yal-du-TE-kha vee-tee-v'-KHA li-b'-KHA bee-MAY v'-khu-ro-TE-kha v'-ha-LAYKH b'-dar-KHAY li-b'-KHA uv-mar-AY ay-NE-kha v'-DA KEE al kol AY-leh y'-vee-a-KHA ha-e-lo-HEEM ba-mish-PAT

10 and banish care from your mind, and pluck sorrow out of your flesh! For youth and black hair are fleeting.

12 1 So appreciate your vigor in the days of your youth, before those days of sorrow come and those years arrive of which you will say, "I have no pleasure in them";

2 before sun and light and moon and stars grow dark, and the clouds come back again after the rain:

3 When the guards of the house become shaky, And the men of valor are bent, And the maids that grind, grown few, are idle, And the ladies that peer through the windows grow dim,

4 And the doors to the street are shut – With the noise of the hand mill growing fainter, And the song of the bird growing feebler, And all the strains of music dying down;

א **11:9 O youth, enjoy yourself while you are young!** The Hebrew word for 'youth' is *bachur* (בחור), related to the word *bachar* (בחר) which means to 'chose.' The years of one's youth, from adolescence to early adulthood, are specifically a time of life-impacting choices. The young adult observes the world critically, and makes decisions that can impact the rest of his or her life regarding where to live, who to marry and what to do professionally. The young person mentioned here is encouraged to "follow the desires of your heart and the glances of your eyes," but is cautioned not to be led astray by desires, and is reminded that there will be accountability for these choices.

בחור
בחר

Kohelet/Ecclesiastes
Chapter 12

קהלת
פרק יב

5 When one is afraid of heights And there is terror on the road. – For the almond tree may blossom, The grasshopper be burdened, And the caper bush may bud again; But man sets out for his eternal abode, With mourners all around in the street. –

ה גַּם מִגָּבֹהַּ יִרָאוּ וְחַתְחַתִּים בַּדֶּרֶךְ וְיָנֵאץ הַשָּׁקֵד וְיִסְתַּבֵּל הֶחָגָב וְתָפֵר הָאֲבִיּוֹנָה כִּי־הֹלֵךְ הָאָדָם אֶל־בֵּית עוֹלָמוֹ וְסָבְבוּ בַשּׁוּק הַסֹּפְדִים:

6 Before the silver cord snaps And the golden bowl crashes, The jar is shattered at the spring, And the jug is smashed at the cistern.

ו עַד אֲשֶׁר לֹא־יֵרָחֵק [יֵרָתֵק] חֶבֶל הַכֶּסֶף וְתָרֻץ גֻּלַּת הַזָּהָב וְתִשָּׁבֶר כַּד עַל־הַמַּבּוּעַ וְנָרֹץ הַגַּלְגַּל אֶל־הַבּוֹר:

7 And the dust returns to the ground As it was, And the lifebreath returns to *Hashem* Who bestowed it.

ז וְיָשֹׁב הֶעָפָר עַל־הָאָרֶץ כְּשֶׁהָיָה וְהָרוּחַ תָּשׁוּב אֶל־הָאֱלֹהִים אֲשֶׁר נְתָנָהּ:

8 Utter futility – said *Kohelet* – All is futile!

ח הֲבֵל הֲבָלִים אָמַר הַקּוֹהֶלֶת הַכֹּל הָבֶל:

9 A further word: Because *Kohelet* was a sage, he continued to instruct the people. He listened to and tested the soundness of many maxims.

ט וְיֹתֵר שֶׁהָיָה קֹהֶלֶת חָכָם עוֹד לִמַּד־דַּעַת אֶת־הָעָם וְאִזֵּן וְחִקֵּר תִּקֵּן מְשָׁלִים הַרְבֵּה:

v'-yo-TAYR she-ha-YAH ko-HE-let kha-KHAM OD li-mad DA-at et ha-AM v'-i-ZAYN v'-khi-KAYR ti-KAYN m'-sha-LEEM har-BAY

10 *Kohelet* sought to discover useful sayings and recorded genuinely truthful sayings.

י בִּקֵּשׁ קֹהֶלֶת לִמְצֹא דִּבְרֵי־חֵפֶץ וְכָתוּב יֹשֶׁר דִּבְרֵי אֱמֶת:

11 The sayings of the wise are like goads, like nails fixed in prodding sticks. They were given by one Shepherd.

יא דִּבְרֵי חֲכָמִים כַּדָּרְבֹנוֹת וּכְמַשְׂמְרוֹת נְטוּעִים בַּעֲלֵי אֲסֻפּוֹת נִתְּנוּ מֵרֹעֶה אֶחָד:

12 A further word: Against them, my son, be warned! The making of many books is without limit And much study is a wearying of the flesh.

יב וְיֹתֵר מֵהֵמָּה בְּנִי הִזָּהֵר עֲשׂוֹת סְפָרִים הַרְבֵּה אֵין קֵץ וְלַהַג הַרְבֵּה יְגִעַת בָּשָׂר:

13 The sum of the matter, when all is said and done: Revere *Hashem* and observe His commandments! For this applies to all mankind:

יג סוֹף דָּבָר הַכֹּל נִשְׁמָע אֶת־הָאֱלֹהִים יְרָא וְאֶת־מִצְוֹתָיו שְׁמוֹר כִּי־זֶה כָּל־הָאָדָם:

14 that *Hashem* will call every creature to account for everything unknown, be it good or bad. The sum of the matter, when all is said and done: Revere *Hashem* and observe His commandments! For this applies to all mankind.

יד כִּי אֶת־כָּל־מַעֲשֶׂה הָאֱלֹהִים יָבִא בְמִשְׁפָּט עַל כָּל־נֶעְלָם אִם־טוֹב וְאִם־רָע: [סוף דבר הכל נשמע את־האלהים ירא ואת־מצותיו שמור כי־זה כל־האדם]

איזן
אוזן
אזנים

12:9 He listened The Hebrew word *izayn* (איזן), translated here as 'listened,' is related to the words *ozen* (אוזן), 'ear,' and *moznayim* (מאזנים), 'scale.' Commentators note that King *Shlomo*'s greatness was not that he heard and internalized much wisdom, but that he was also able to present it clearly, so that others could hear and understand it as well. Additionally, King *Shlomo* calculated and weighed the ideas presented to him in order to arrive at the ultimate truth. The deeper connection between the Hebrew words *ozen* and *moznayim* reflect the biological fact that the ear not only receives sound, but also aids a person's balance and equilibrium.

Megillat Esther
The Scroll of Esther

Introduction and commentary by Batya Markowitz

Esther comes from the Hebrew word *hester* (הסתר), which means 'hidden.' *Megilla* (מגילה), 'scroll,' is related to the word *ligalot* (לגלות), which means 'to reveal.' The challenge of reading *Megillat Esther* (Esther) is to reveal the hidden messages veiled within the exciting plot. At first glance, the story seems to be one of royal intrigue, power, wealth and politics. Superficially, the events of the *Megilla* seem to be the result of the whims of an intoxicated king. The name of God does not appear even once in the entire story, making *Megillat Esther* the only book of the *Tanakh* that does not mention His holy name. The reader's job, therefore, is to uncover *Hashem*'s hidden hand guiding what appears to be a string of coincidences.

Megillat Esther contains an account of events that took place when the Jewish people were living in Persia. Following the destruction of the first *Beit Hamikdash* at the hands of the Babylonians, the Jews were exiled to Babylon. Not long afterwards, the Babylonians were defeated by Cyrus, king of Persia, and the Jewish residents of Babylon found themselves under Persian rule. The story of *Esther* takes place against this backdrop of Persian exile.

Cyrus the Great was the first Persian king to control Babylon. In the first year of his reign he made a famous decree, granting permission for the Jews to return to *Yerushalayim* and rebuild their Temple (Ezra 1:1–3). Unfortunately, not many heeded the call. Though construction of the *Beit Hamikdash* begins soon after this first, small, wave of exiles return, it is quickly halted. It is not until the second year of King Darius's reign that construction of the Temple resumes, and it is finally completed in Darius's sixth year. Jewish tradition places King Ahasuerus between Cyrus and Darius. The Sages even suggest that Darius was the son of Ahasuerus and *Esther*. In their opinion, the story of *Esther* takes place after the Cyrus declaration, but before the reconstruction of the *Beit Hamikdash*. According to this opinion, the Jews of the story are the very ones who disregard the decree of Cyrus, and choose to remain in exile rather than returning to *Eretz Yisrael* to participate in the reconstruction of the Temple and *Yerushalayim*.

According to the Sages (*Megilla* 11a), Ahasuerus halted the reconstruction of the *Beit Hamikdash*, and he threw a feast when he believed that the Jews have been forsaken and would never return to *Yerushalayim*. He deliberately offered *Esther* only "half the kingdom," (Esther 5:3) refusing to restart the construction of the *Beit Hamikdash*. Meanwhile, *Mordechai*, a former citizen of *Yerushalayim* living in Shushan, the capital of the Persian empire, was teaching about the *Beit Hamikdash* and putting aside money for its construction. At the same time, however, the Jews of the Persian Empire have weakened their connection to *Eretz Yisrael*. They could have immigrated to Israel years before during Cyrus' rule, but instead opted to remain in exile. The opening of *Megillat Esther* even finds them at Ahasuerus's feast where the Temple vessels were on display. It has been suggested that the events of the story, and the evil decree of Haman, were Divine retribution for forsaking the Land of Israel and the *Beit Hamikdash*.

The miracle of the story of *Esther* carries an important message to the people of that time, and for all ages. Living in exile, the Jews felt physically distanced from their land, and spiritually distanced from their God. They no longer deserved the open miracles they had experienced in the past in their homeland. Nevertheless, the story of *Esther* teaches that *Hashem* has not, and will not, abandon His people. Although He is hidden in exile, He is very much present, pulling the strings from behind the scenes. The God who created the world and who split the sea is the same God who deposed Vashti, chose *Esther* and hanged Haman.

In a subtle way, *Megillat Esther* reminds exiled Jews throughout the ages of some very fundamental ideas. First, they must never forsake *Yerushalayim*, but must remember her no matter where they find themselves. Second, even outside of Israel, where *Hashem*'s presence is less obvious, they must discover and reveal the hidden God, and must see Him in all aspects of day-to-day life, not just in open miracles. And finally, they must always remember that *Hashem* will never forsake His promise to return the Children of Israel to the Land of Israel.

List of the *Neviim* (Prophets) and *Neviot* (Prophetesses)

Esther was not only a heroine of the Jewish people, but, according to the Sages, she was also a prophetess. The Talmud *(Megillah* 14a) states that there were 48 prophets and 7 prophetesses. The following is a list of prophets and prophetesses based on *Rashi*'s enumeration, as well as the main places in *Tanakh* that they are mentioned:

The 48 *Neviim*	Biblical Reference
Avraham	Genesis 11:26–25:11
Yitzchak	Genesis 21:1–28:9
Yaakov	Genesis 25:19–50:13
Moshe	Exodus 2-Deuteronomy 34
Aharon	Exodus 4:14-Numbers 20:29
Yehoshua son of *Nun*	The Book of Joshua
Pinchas son of *Elazar*	Numbers 25:1–15
Elkana	I Samuel 1
Eli	I Samuel 1–4:18
Shmuel son of *Elkana*	I Samuel 1–25:1
Gad	I Samuel 22:5, II Samuel 24:11,19
Natan	II Samuel 7, 12, II Kings 1
David son of *Yishai*	I Samuel 15-II Kings 2:13
Achiya the *Shilonite*	I Kings 11:29–39, 14:1–16
Shlomo son of *David*	I Kings 2–11
Ido	II Chronicles 12:15, 13:22
Shemaya	I Kings 12:22–24, II Chronicles 12:5–15
Eliyahu	I Kings 17:1-II Kings 2:12
Michaihu	I Kings 22
Ovadya	The Book of Obadiah
Chanani	II Chronicles 16:7–10
Yehu son of *Chanani*	I Kings 16:1–7
Azarya son of *Oded*	II Chronicles 15:1–8
Yachaziel son of *Zecharya*	II Chronicles 20:14–17
Eliezer son of *Dodavahu*	II Chronicles 20:37
Elisha son of *Shafat*	II Kings 2–9, 13:14–21
Yona son of *Amitai*	The Book of Jonah
Hoshea son of *B'eri*	The Book of Hosea

The 48 Neviim	Biblical Reference
Amos	The Book of Amos
Amotz	Father of *Yeshayahu** – Isaiah 1:1
Oded	II Chronicles 28:9–11
Yeshayahu son of *Amotz*	The Book of Isaiah
Micha of *Moreshet*	The Book of Micah
Yoel son of *Petuel*	The Book of Joel
Nachum	The Book of Nahum
Uriah son of *Shemaya*	Jeremiah 26:20–23
Chavakuk	The Book of Habakkuk
Tzefanya son of *Kushi*	The Book of Zephaniah
Yirmiyahu son of *Chilkiyahu*	The Book of Jeremiah
Yechezkel son of *Buzi*	The Book of Ezekiel
Neriya	Father of *Baruch* and *Seraya** – Jeremiah 32:12,16 36:4,8,14,32 43:3,6 45:1 51:59
Baruch son of *Neriya*	Jeremiah 32, 36, 43:2–7, 45
Seraya son of *Neriya*	Jeremiah 51:59–64
Machaseya	Father of *Neriya** – Jeremiah 32:12, 51:59
Chagai	The Book of Haggai
Zecharya	The Book of Zechariah
Malachi	The Book of Malachi
Mordechai	The Book of Esther

The 7 Neviot	
Sara	Genesis 11:29 – 23:20
Miriam	Exodus 2:1–9, 15:20–21 Numbers 12:1–15, 20:1
Devora	Judges 4–5
Chana	I Samuel 1:1–2:21
Avigail	I Samuel 25
Chulda	II Kings 22:14–20
Esther	The Book of Esther

* According to the Sages, if a prophet is identified with his father's name the father was also a prophet

Esther/Esther
Chapter 1

אסתר
פרק א

1

1 It happened in the days of Ahasuerus – that Ahasuerus who reigned over a hundred and twenty-seven provinces from India to Ethiopia.

א וַיְהִי בִּימֵי אֲחַשְׁוֵרוֹשׁ הוּא אֲחַשְׁוֵרוֹשׁ הַמֹּלֵךְ מֵהֹדּוּ וְעַד־כּוּשׁ שֶׁבַע וְעֶשְׂרִים וּמֵאָה מְדִינָה:

2 In those days, when King Ahasuerus occupied the royal throne in the fortress Shushan,

ב בַּיָּמִים הָהֵם כְּשֶׁבֶת הַמֶּלֶךְ אֲחַשְׁוֵרוֹשׁ עַל כִּסֵּא מַלְכוּתוֹ אֲשֶׁר בְּשׁוּשַׁן הַבִּירָה:

3 in the third year of his reign, he gave a banquet for all the officials and courtiers – the administration of Persia and Media, the nobles and the governors of the provinces in his service.

ג בִּשְׁנַת שָׁלוֹשׁ לְמָלְכוֹ עָשָׂה מִשְׁתֶּה לְכָל־שָׂרָיו וַעֲבָדָיו חֵיל פָּרַס וּמָדַי הַפַּרְתְּמִים וְשָׂרֵי הַמְּדִינוֹת לְפָנָיו:

bish-NAT sha-LOSH l'-mol-KHO a-SAH mish-TEH l'-khol sa-RAV va-a-va-DAV KHAYL pa-RAS u-ma-DAI ha-par-t'-MEEM v'-sa-RAY ha-m'-dee-NOT l'-fa-NAV

4 For no fewer than a hundred and eighty days he displayed the vast riches of his kingdom and the splendid glory of his majesty.

ד בְּהַרְאֹתוֹ אֶת־עֹשֶׁר כְּבוֹד מַלְכוּתוֹ וְאֶת־יְקָר תִּפְאֶרֶת גְּדוּלָּתוֹ יָמִים רַבִּים שְׁמוֹנִים וּמְאַת יוֹם:

5 At the end of this period, the king gave a banquet for seven days in the court of the king's palace garden for all the people who lived in the fortress Shushan, high and low alike.

ה וּבִמְלוֹאת הַיָּמִים הָאֵלֶּה עָשָׂה הַמֶּלֶךְ לְכָל־הָעָם הַנִּמְצְאִים בְּשׁוּשַׁן הַבִּירָה לְמִגָּדוֹל וְעַד־קָטָן מִשְׁתֶּה שִׁבְעַת יָמִים בַּחֲצַר גִּנַּת בִּיתַן הַמֶּלֶךְ:

6 [There were hangings of] white cotton and blue wool, caught up by cords of fine linen and purple wool to silver rods and alabaster columns; and there were couches of gold and silver on a pavement of marble, alabaster, mother-of-pearl, and mosaics.

ו חוּר כַּרְפַּס וּתְכֵלֶת אָחוּז בְּחַבְלֵי־בוּץ וְאַרְגָּמָן עַל־גְּלִילֵי כֶסֶף וְעַמּוּדֵי שֵׁשׁ מִטּוֹת זָהָב וָכֶסֶף עַל רִצְפַת בַּהַט־וָשֵׁשׁ וְדַר וְסֹחָרֶת:

7 Royal wine was served in abundance, as befits a king, in golden beakers, beakers of varied design.

ז וְהַשְׁקוֹת בִּכְלֵי זָהָב וְכֵלִים מִכֵּלִים שׁוֹנִים וְיֵין מַלְכוּת רָב כְּיַד הַמֶּלֶךְ:

8 And the rule for the drinking was, "No restrictions!" For the king had given orders to every palace steward to comply with each man's wishes.

ח וְהַשְּׁתִיָּה כַדָּת אֵין אֹנֵס כִּי־כֵן יִסַּד הַמֶּלֶךְ עַל כָּל־רַב בֵּיתוֹ לַעֲשׂוֹת כִּרְצוֹן אִישׁ־וָאִישׁ:

9 In addition, Queen Vashti gave a banquet for women, in the royal palace of King Ahasuerus.

ט גַּם וַשְׁתִּי הַמַּלְכָּה עָשְׂתָה מִשְׁתֵּה נָשִׁים בֵּית הַמַּלְכוּת אֲשֶׁר לַמֶּלֶךְ אֲחַשְׁוֵרוֹשׁ:

1:3 He gave a banquet What reason was there to celebrate in Ahasuerus's third year? The prophet *Yirmiyahu*, who lived at the end of the first Temple period, prophesied that the Children of Israel would be in exile for seventy years (Jeremiah 29:10). According to the Sages (*Megilla* 11b), Ahasuerus erroneously calculated that these seventy years had elapsed and that *Hashem* had forsaken the Jewish people and the Land of Israel. Not only did he host a celebratory banquet, but the Sages add that he donned the vestments of the high priest and used captured vessels from the *Beit Hamikdash* to emphasize this point. Punishment was exacted on Queen Vashti, wife of Ahasuerus and the granddaughter of Nebuchadnezzar, the wicked ruler who had destroyed the Temple. The Sages teach that Vashti convinced her husband not to allow the rebuilding of the *Beit Hamikdash* in *Yerushalayim* during his reign. Therefore, Vashti is punished.

Esther/Esther
Chapter 1

אסתר / פרק א

10	On the seventh day, when the king was merry with wine, he ordered Mehuman, Bizzetha, Harbona, Bigtha, Abagtha, Zethar, and Carcas, the seven eunuchs in attendance on King Ahasuerus,
11	to bring Queen Vashti before the king wearing a royal diadem, to display her beauty to the peoples and the officials; for she was a beautiful woman.
12	But Queen Vashti refused to come at the king's command conveyed by the eunuchs. The king was greatly incensed, and his fury burned within him.
13	Then the king consulted the sages learned in procedure. (For it was the royal practice [to turn] to all who were versed in law and precedent.
14	His closest advisers were Carshena, Shethar, Admatha, Tarshish, Meres, Marsena, and Memucan, the seven ministers of Persia and Media who had access to the royal presence and occupied the first place in the kingdom.)
15	"What," [he asked,] "shall be done, according to law, to Queen Vashti for failing to obey the command of King Ahasuerus conveyed by the eunuchs?"
16	Thereupon Memucan declared in the presence of the king and the ministers: "Queen Vashti has committed an offense not only against Your Majesty but also against all the officials and against all the peoples in all the provinces of King Ahasuerus.
17	For the queen's behavior will make all wives despise their husbands, as they reflect that King Ahasuerus himself ordered Queen Vashti to be brought before him, but she would not come.
18	This very day the ladies of Persia and Media, who have heard of the queen's behavior, will cite it to all Your Majesty's officials, and there will be no end of scorn and provocation!
19	"If it please Your Majesty, let a royal edict be issued by you, and let it be written into the laws of Persia and Media, so that it cannot be abrogated, that Vashti shall never enter the presence of King Ahasuerus. And let Your Majesty bestow her royal state upon another who is more worthy than she.

י בַּיּוֹם הַשְּׁבִיעִ֕י כְּט֥וֹב לֵב־הַמֶּ֖לֶךְ בַּיָּ֑יִן אָמַ֡ר לִ֠מְהוּמָ֠ן בִּזְּתָ֨א חַרְבוֹנָ֜א בִּגְתָ֤א וַאֲבַגְתָא֙ זֵתַ֣ר וְכַרְכַּ֔ס שִׁבְעַת֙ הַסָּ֣רִיסִ֔ים הַמְשָׁ֣רְתִ֔ים אֶת־פְּנֵ֖י הַמֶּ֥לֶךְ אֲחַשְׁוֵרֽוֹשׁ׃

יא לְ֠הָבִיא אֶת־וַשְׁתִּ֧י הַמַּלְכָּ֛ה לִפְנֵ֥י הַמֶּ֖לֶךְ בְּכֶ֣תֶר מַלְכ֑וּת לְהַרְא֨וֹת הָֽעַמִּ֤ים וְהַשָּׂרִים֙ אֶת־יָפְיָ֔הּ כִּֽי־טוֹבַ֥ת מַרְאֶ֖ה הִֽיא׃

יב וַתְּמָאֵ֞ן הַמַּלְכָּ֣ה וַשְׁתִּ֗י לָבוֹא֙ בִּדְבַ֣ר הַמֶּ֔לֶךְ אֲשֶׁ֖ר בְּיַ֣ד הַסָּרִיסִ֑ים וַיִּקְצֹ֤ף הַמֶּ֙לֶךְ֙ מְאֹ֔ד וַחֲמָת֖וֹ בָּעֲרָ֥ה בֽוֹ׃

יג וַיֹּ֣אמֶר הַמֶּ֔לֶךְ לַחֲכָמִ֖ים יֹדְעֵ֣י הָֽעִתִּ֑ים כִּי־כֵן֙ דְּבַ֣ר הַמֶּ֔לֶךְ לִפְנֵ֕י כׇּל־יֹדְעֵ֖י דָּ֥ת וָדִֽין׃

יד וְהַקָּרֹ֣ב אֵלָ֗יו כַּרְשְׁנָ֤א שֵׁתָר֙ אַדְמָ֣תָא תַרְשִׁ֔ישׁ מֶ֥רֶס מַרְסְנָ֖א מְמוּכָ֑ן שִׁבְעַ֞ת שָׂרֵ֣י ׀ פָּרַ֣ס וּמָדַ֗י רֹאֵי֙ פְּנֵ֣י הַמֶּ֔לֶךְ הַיֹּשְׁבִ֥ים רִאשֹׁנָ֖ה בַּמַּלְכֽוּת׃

טו כְּדָת֙ מַֽה־לַּעֲשׂ֔וֹת בַּמַּלְכָּ֖ה וַשְׁתִּ֑י עַ֣ל ׀ אֲשֶׁ֣ר לֹֽא־עָשְׂתָ֗ה אֶֽת־מַאֲמַר֙ הַמֶּ֣לֶךְ אֲחַשְׁוֵר֔וֹשׁ בְּיַ֖ד הַסָּרִיסִֽים׃

טז וַיֹּ֣אמֶר מומכן [מְמוּכָ֗ן] לִפְנֵ֤י הַמֶּ֙לֶךְ֙ וְהַשָּׂרִ֔ים לֹ֤א עַל־הַמֶּ֙לֶךְ֙ לְבַדּ֔וֹ עָוְתָ֖ה וַשְׁתִּ֣י הַמַּלְכָּ֑ה כִּ֤י עַל־כׇּל־הַשָּׂרִים֙ וְעַל־כׇּל־הָ֣עַמִּ֔ים אֲשֶׁ֕ר בְּכׇל־מְדִינ֖וֹת הַמֶּ֥לֶךְ אֲחַשְׁוֵרֽוֹשׁ׃

יז כִּֽי־יֵצֵ֤א דְבַר־הַמַּלְכָּה֙ עַל־כׇּל־הַנָּשִׁ֔ים לְהַבְז֥וֹת בַּעְלֵיהֶ֖ן בְּעֵינֵיהֶ֑ן בְּאׇמְרָ֗ם הַמֶּ֣לֶךְ אֲחַשְׁוֵר֡וֹשׁ אָמַ֞ר לְהָבִ֨יא אֶת־וַשְׁתִּ֧י הַמַּלְכָּ֛ה לְפָנָ֖יו וְלֹא־בָֽאָה׃

יח וְֽהַיּ֨וֹם הַזֶּ֜ה תֹּאמַ֣רְנָה ׀ שָׂר֣וֹת פָּֽרַס־וּמָדַ֗י אֲשֶׁ֤ר שָֽׁמְעוּ֙ אֶת־דְּבַ֣ר הַמַּלְכָּ֔ה לְכֹ֖ל שָׂרֵ֣י הַמֶּ֑לֶךְ וּכְדַ֖י בִּזָּי֥וֹן וָקָֽצֶף׃

יט אִם־עַל־הַמֶּ֣לֶךְ ט֗וֹב יֵצֵ֤א דְבַר־מַלְכוּת֙ מִלְּפָנָ֔יו וְיִכָּתֵ֛ב בְּדָתֵ֥י פָֽרַס־וּמָדַ֖י וְלֹ֣א יַעֲב֑וֹר אֲשֶׁ֨ר לֹֽא־תָב֜וֹא וַשְׁתִּ֗י לִפְנֵי֙ הַמֶּ֣לֶךְ אֲחַשְׁוֵר֔וֹשׁ וּמַלְכוּתָהּ֙ יִתֵּ֣ן הַמֶּ֔לֶךְ לִרְעוּתָ֖הּ הַטּוֹבָ֥ה מִמֶּֽנָּה׃

Esther/Esther
Chapter 2

אסתר
פרק ב

20 Then will the judgment executed by Your Majesty resound throughout your realm, vast though it is; and all wives will treat their husbands with respect, high and low alike."

וְנִשְׁמַע פִּתְגָם הַמֶּלֶךְ אֲשֶׁר־יַעֲשֶׂה בְּכָל־מַלְכוּתוֹ כִּי רַבָּה הִיא וְכָל־הַנָּשִׁים יִתְּנוּ יְקָר לְבַעְלֵיהֶן לְמִגָּדוֹל וְעַד־קָטָן׃

21 The proposal was approved by the king and the ministers, and the king did as Memucan proposed.

וַיִּיטַב הַדָּבָר בְּעֵינֵי הַמֶּלֶךְ וְהַשָּׂרִים וַיַּעַשׂ הַמֶּלֶךְ כִּדְבַר מְמוּכָן׃

22 Dispatches were sent to all the provinces of the king, to every province in its own script and to every nation in its own language, that every man should wield authority in his home and speak the language of his own people.

וַיִּשְׁלַח סְפָרִים אֶל־כָּל־מְדִינוֹת הַמֶּלֶךְ אֶל־מְדִינָה וּמְדִינָה כִּכְתָבָהּ וְאֶל־עַם וָעָם כִּלְשׁוֹנוֹ לִהְיוֹת כָּל־אִישׁ שֹׂרֵר בְּבֵיתוֹ וּמְדַבֵּר כִּלְשׁוֹן עַמּוֹ׃

2 1 Some time afterward, when the anger of King Ahasuerus subsided, he thought of Vashti and what she had done and what had been decreed against her.

אַחַר הַדְּבָרִים הָאֵלֶּה כְּשֹׁךְ חֲמַת הַמֶּלֶךְ אֲחַשְׁוֵרוֹשׁ זָכַר אֶת־וַשְׁתִּי וְאֵת אֲשֶׁר־עָשָׂתָה וְאֵת אֲשֶׁר־נִגְזַר עָלֶיהָ׃

2 The king's servants who attended him said, "Let beautiful young virgins be sought out for Your Majesty.

וַיֹּאמְרוּ נַעֲרֵי־הַמֶּלֶךְ מְשָׁרְתָיו יְבַקְשׁוּ לַמֶּלֶךְ נְעָרוֹת בְּתוּלוֹת טוֹבוֹת מַרְאֶה׃

3 Let Your Majesty appoint officers in every province of your realm to assemble all the beautiful young virgins at the fortress Shushan, in the harem under the supervision of Hege, the king's eunuch, guardian of the women. Let them be provided with their cosmetics.

וְיַפְקֵד הַמֶּלֶךְ פְּקִידִים בְּכָל־מְדִינוֹת מַלְכוּתוֹ וְיִקְבְּצוּ אֶת־כָּל־נַעֲרָה־בְתוּלָה טוֹבַת מַרְאֶה אֶל־שׁוּשַׁן הַבִּירָה אֶל־בֵּית הַנָּשִׁים אֶל־יַד הֵגֶא סְרִיס הַמֶּלֶךְ שֹׁמֵר הַנָּשִׁים וְנָתוֹן תַּמְרוּקֵיהֶן׃

4 And let the maiden who pleases Your Majesty be queen instead of Vashti." The proposal pleased the king, and he acted upon it.

וְהַנַּעֲרָה אֲשֶׁר תִּיטַב בְּעֵינֵי הַמֶּלֶךְ תִּמְלֹךְ תַּחַת וַשְׁתִּי וַיִּיטַב הַדָּבָר בְּעֵינֵי הַמֶּלֶךְ וַיַּעַשׂ כֵּן׃

5 In the fortress Shushan lived a *Yehudi* by the name of *Mordechai*, son of *Yair* son of *Shim'i* son of *Keesh*, a Benjaminite.

אִישׁ יְהוּדִי הָיָה בְּשׁוּשַׁן הַבִּירָה וּשְׁמוֹ מָרְדֳּכַי בֶּן יָאִיר בֶּן־שִׁמְעִי בֶּן־קִישׁ אִישׁ יְמִינִי׃

6 [*Keesh*] had been exiled from *Yerushalayim* in the group that was carried into exile along with King *Yechonya* of *Yehuda*, which had been driven into exile by King Nebuchadnezzar of Babylon. –

אֲשֶׁר הָגְלָה מִירוּשָׁלַיִם עִם־הַגֹּלָה אֲשֶׁר הָגְלְתָה עִם יְכָנְיָה מֶלֶךְ־יְהוּדָה אֲשֶׁר הֶגְלָה נְבוּכַדְנֶאצַּר מֶלֶךְ בָּבֶל׃

a-SHER hog-LAH mee-ru-sha-LA-im im ha-go-LAH a-SHER hog-l'-TAH IM y'-khon-YAH ME-lekh y'-hu-DAH a-SHER heg-LAH n'-vu-khad-ne-TZAR ME-lekh ba-VEL

Rabbi Elijah Kremer, the Vilna Gaon (1720–1797)

2:6 Had been exiled from *Yerushalayim* When chanted aloud in the synagogue on *Purim*, this verse is read in the same solemn tune as *Megillat Eicha*, since it mentions the exile of the Jewish people. The *Vilna Gaon* points out that the verb 'carried away' (ה-ג-ל) is mentioned three times in this verse, alluding to the fact that *Mordechai* was actually carried away from Israel three times. At the end of the first Temple period, the Jews were exiled from the Land of Israel in three stages, and *Mordechai* participated in all three of these. In love with the land, *Mordechai* returned after being forced to leave, was exiled again, and stubbornly returned once more until he was carried away a third time with the remaining Jews following the destruction of the first *Beit Hamikdash*.

Esther/Esther
Chapter 2

אסתר
פרק ב

7 He was foster father to *Hadassa* – that is, *Esther* – his uncle's daughter, for she had neither father nor mother. The maiden was shapely and beautiful; and when her father and mother died, *Mordechai* adopted her as his own daughter.

ז וַיְהִי אֹמֵן אֶת־הֲדַסָּה הִיא אֶסְתֵּר בַּת־דֹּדוֹ כִּי אֵין לָהּ אָב וָאֵם וְהַנַּעֲרָה יְפַת־תֹּאַר וְטוֹבַת מַרְאֶה וּבְמוֹת אָבִיהָ וְאִמָּהּ לְקָחָהּ מָרְדֳּכַי לוֹ לְבַת:

8 When the king's order and edict was proclaimed, and when many girls were assembled in the fortress Shushan under the supervision of Hegai, *Esther* too was taken into the king's palace under the supervision of Hegai, guardian of the women.

ח וַיְהִי בְּהִשָּׁמַע דְּבַר־הַמֶּלֶךְ וְדָתוֹ וּבְהִקָּבֵץ נְעָרוֹת רַבּוֹת אֶל־שׁוּשַׁן הַבִּירָה אֶל־יַד הֵגָי וַתִּלָּקַח אֶסְתֵּר אֶל־בֵּית הַמֶּלֶךְ אֶל־יַד הֵגַי שֹׁמֵר הַנָּשִׁים:

9 The girl pleased him and won his favor, and he hastened to furnish her with her cosmetics and her rations, as well as with the seven maids who were her due from the king's palace; and he treated her and her maids with special kindness in the harem.

ט וַתִּיטַב הַנַּעֲרָה בְעֵינָיו וַתִּשָּׂא חֶסֶד לְפָנָיו וַיְבַהֵל אֶת־תַּמְרוּקֶיהָ וְאֶת־מָנוֹתֶהָ לָתֵת לָהּ וְאֵת שֶׁבַע הַנְּעָרוֹת הָרְאֻיוֹת לָתֶת־לָהּ מִבֵּית הַמֶּלֶךְ וַיְשַׁנֶּהָ וְאֶת־נַעֲרוֹתֶיהָ לְטוֹב בֵּית הַנָּשִׁים:

10 *Esther* did not reveal her people or her kindred, for *Mordechai* had told her not to reveal it.

י לֹא־הִגִּידָה אֶסְתֵּר אֶת־עַמָּהּ וְאֶת־מוֹלַדְתָּהּ כִּי מָרְדֳּכַי צִוָּה עָלֶיהָ אֲשֶׁר לֹא־תַגִּיד:

11 Every single day *Mordechai* would walk about in front of the court of the harem, to learn how *Esther* was faring and what was happening to her.

יא וּבְכָל־יוֹם וָיוֹם מָרְדֳּכַי מִתְהַלֵּךְ לִפְנֵי חֲצַר בֵּית־הַנָּשִׁים לָדַעַת אֶת־שְׁלוֹם אֶסְתֵּר וּמַה־יֵּעָשֶׂה בָּהּ:

12 When each girl's turn came to go to King Ahasuerus at the end of the twelve months' treatment prescribed for women (for that was the period spent on beautifying them: six months with oil of myrrh and six months with perfumes and women's cosmetics,

יב וּבְהַגִּיעַ תֹּר נַעֲרָה וְנַעֲרָה לָבוֹא אֶל־הַמֶּלֶךְ אֲחַשְׁוֵרוֹשׁ מִקֵּץ הֱיוֹת לָהּ כְּדָת הַנָּשִׁים שְׁנֵים עָשָׂר חֹדֶשׁ כִּי כֵּן יִמְלְאוּ יְמֵי מְרוּקֵיהֶן שִׁשָּׁה חֳדָשִׁים בְּשֶׁמֶן הַמֹּר וְשִׁשָּׁה חֳדָשִׁים בַּבְּשָׂמִים וּבְתַמְרוּקֵי הַנָּשִׁים:

13 and it was after that that the girl would go to the king), whatever she asked for would be given her to take with her from the harem to the king's palace.

יג וּבָזֶה הַנַּעֲרָה בָּאָה אֶל־הַמֶּלֶךְ אֵת כָּל־אֲשֶׁר תֹּאמַר יִנָּתֵן לָהּ לָבוֹא עִמָּהּ מִבֵּית הַנָּשִׁים עַד־בֵּית הַמֶּלֶךְ:

14 She would go in the evening and leave in the morning for a second harem in charge of Shaashgaz, the king's eunuch, guardian of the concubines. She would not go again to the king unless the king wanted her, when she would be summoned by name.

יד בָּעֶרֶב הִיא בָאָה וּבַבֹּקֶר הִיא שָׁבָה אֶל־בֵּית הַנָּשִׁים שֵׁנִי אֶל־יַד שַׁעֲשְׁגַז סְרִיס הַמֶּלֶךְ שֹׁמֵר הַפִּילַגְשִׁים לֹא־תָבוֹא עוֹד אֶל־הַמֶּלֶךְ כִּי אִם־חָפֵץ בָּהּ הַמֶּלֶךְ וְנִקְרְאָה בְשֵׁם:

15 When the turn came for *Esther* daughter of *Avichayil* – the uncle of *Mordechai*, who had adopted her as his own daughter – to go to the king, she did not ask for anything but what Hegai, the king's eunuch, guardian of the women, advised. Yet *Esther* won the admiration of all who saw her.

טו וּבְהַגִּיעַ תֹּר־אֶסְתֵּר בַּת־אֲבִיחַיִל דֹּד מָרְדֳּכַי אֲשֶׁר לָקַח־לוֹ לְבַת לָבוֹא אֶל־הַמֶּלֶךְ לֹא בִקְשָׁה דָּבָר כִּי אִם אֶת־אֲשֶׁר יֹאמַר הֵגַי סְרִיס־הַמֶּלֶךְ שֹׁמֵר הַנָּשִׁים וַתְּהִי אֶסְתֵּר נֹשֵׂאת חֵן בְּעֵינֵי כָּל־רֹאֶיהָ:

Esther/Esther

Chapter 3

16 *Esther* was taken to King Ahasuerus, in his royal palace, in the tenth month, which is the month of *Tevet*, in the seventh year of his reign.

17 The king loved *Esther* more than all the other women, and she won his grace and favor more than all the virgins. So he set a royal diadem on her head and made her queen instead of Vashti.

18 The king gave a great banquet for all his officials and courtiers, "the banquet of *Esther*." He proclaimed a remission of taxes for the provinces and distributed gifts as befits a king.

19 When the virgins were assembled a second time, *Mordechai* sat in the palace gate.

20 But *Esther* still did not reveal her kindred or her people, as *Mordechai* had instructed her; for *Esther* obeyed *Mordechai*'s bidding, as she had done when she was under his tutelage.

21 At that time, when *Mordechai* was sitting in the palace gate, Bigthan and Teresh, two of the king's eunuchs who guarded the threshold, became angry, and plotted to do away with King Ahasuerus.

22 *Mordechai* learned of it and told it to Queen *Esther*, and *Esther* reported it to the king in *Mordechai*'s name.

23 The matter was investigated and found to be so, and the two were impaled on stakes. This was recorded in the book of annals at the instance of the king.

3 1 Some time afterward, King Ahasuerus promoted Haman son of Hammedatha the Agagite; he advanced him and seated him higher than any of his fellow officials.

2 All the king's courtiers in the palace gate knelt and bowed low to Haman, for such was the king's order concerning him; but *Mordechai* would not kneel or bow low.

3 Then the king's courtiers who were in the palace gate said to *Mordechai*, "Why do you disobey the king's order?"

4 When they spoke to him day after day and he would not listen to them, they told Haman, in order to see whether *Mordechai*'s resolve would prevail; for he had explained to them that he was a *Yehudi*.

אסתר

פרק ג

טז וַתִּלָּקַ֨ח אֶסְתֵּ֜ר אֶל־הַמֶּ֤לֶךְ אֲחַשְׁוֵר֙וֹשׁ אֶל־בֵּ֣ית מַלְכוּת֔וֹ בַּחֹ֥דֶשׁ הָעֲשִׂירִ֖י הוּא־חֹ֣דֶשׁ טֵבֵ֑ת בִּשְׁנַת־שֶׁ֖בַע לְמַלְכוּתֽוֹ׃

יז וַיֶּאֱהַ֨ב הַמֶּ֤לֶךְ אֶת־אֶסְתֵּר֙ מִכָּל־הַנָּשִׁ֔ים וַתִּשָּׂא־חֵ֥ן וָחֶ֛סֶד לְפָנָ֖יו מִכָּל־הַבְּתוּלֹ֑ת וַיָּ֤שֶׂם כֶּֽתֶר־מַלְכוּת֙ בְּרֹאשָׁ֔הּ וַיַּמְלִיכֶ֖הָ תַּ֥חַת וַשְׁתִּֽי׃

יח וַיַּ֨עַשׂ הַמֶּ֜לֶךְ מִשְׁתֶּ֣ה גָד֗וֹל לְכָל־שָׂרָיו֙ וַעֲבָדָ֔יו אֵ֖ת מִשְׁתֵּ֣ה אֶסְתֵּ֑ר וַהֲנָחָ֤ה לַמְּדִינוֹת֙ עָשָׂ֔ה וַיִּתֵּ֥ן מַשְׂאֵ֖ת כְּיַ֥ד הַמֶּֽלֶךְ׃

יט וּבְהִקָּבֵ֥ץ בְּתוּל֖וֹת שֵׁנִ֑ית וּמָרְדֳּכַ֖י יֹשֵׁ֥ב בְּשַֽׁעַר־הַמֶּֽלֶךְ׃

כ אֵ֣ין אֶסְתֵּ֗ר מַגֶּ֤דֶת מֽוֹלַדְתָּהּ֙ וְאֶת־עַמָּ֔הּ כַּאֲשֶׁ֛ר צִוָּ֥ה עָלֶ֖יהָ מָרְדֳּכָ֑י וְאֶת־מַאֲמַ֤ר מָרְדֳּכַי֙ אֶסְתֵּ֣ר עֹשָׂ֔ה כַּאֲשֶׁ֛ר הָיְתָ֥ה בְאָמְנָ֖ה אִתּֽוֹ׃

כא בַּיָּמִ֣ים הָהֵ֔ם וּמָרְדֳּכַ֖י יֹשֵׁ֣ב בְּשַֽׁעַר־הַמֶּ֑לֶךְ קָצַף֩ בִּגְתָ֨ן וָתֶ֜רֶשׁ שְׁנֵֽי־סָרִיסֵ֤י הַמֶּ֙לֶךְ֙ מִשֹּׁמְרֵ֣י הַסַּ֔ף וַיְבַקְשׁוּ֙ לִשְׁלֹ֣חַ יָ֔ד בַּמֶּ֖לֶךְ אֲחַשְׁוֵרֽוֹשׁ׃

כב וַיִּוָּדַ֤ע הַדָּבָר֙ לְמָרְדֳּכַ֔י וַיַּגֵּ֖ד לְאֶסְתֵּ֣ר הַמַּלְכָּ֑ה וַתֹּ֧אמֶר אֶסְתֵּ֛ר לַמֶּ֖לֶךְ בְּשֵׁ֥ם מָרְדֳּכָֽי׃

כג וַיְבֻקַּ֤שׁ הַדָּבָר֙ וַיִּמָּצֵ֔א וַיִּתָּל֥וּ שְׁנֵיהֶ֖ם עַל־עֵ֑ץ וַיִּכָּתֵ֗ב בְּסֵ֛פֶר דִּבְרֵ֥י הַיָּמִ֖ים לִפְנֵ֥י הַמֶּֽלֶךְ׃

ג א אַחַ֣ר ׀ הַדְּבָרִ֣ים הָאֵ֗לֶּה גִּדַּל֩ הַמֶּ֨לֶךְ אֲחַשְׁוֵר֜וֹשׁ אֶת־הָמָ֧ן בֶּֽן־הַמְּדָ֛תָא הָאֲגָגִ֖י וַֽיְנַשְּׂאֵ֑הוּ וַיָּ֙שֶׂם֙ אֶת־כִּסְא֔וֹ מֵעַ֕ל כָּל־הַשָּׂרִ֖ים אֲשֶׁ֥ר אִתּֽוֹ׃

ב וְכָל־עַבְדֵ֨י הַמֶּ֜לֶךְ אֲשֶׁר־בְּשַׁ֣עַר הַמֶּ֗לֶךְ כֹּרְעִ֤ים וּמִֽשְׁתַּחֲוִים֙ לְהָמָ֔ן כִּי־כֵ֖ן צִוָּה־ל֣וֹ הַמֶּ֑לֶךְ וּמָ֨רְדֳּכַ֔י לֹ֥א יִכְרַ֖ע וְלֹ֥א יִֽשְׁתַּחֲוֶֽה׃

ג וַיֹּ֨אמְר֜וּ עַבְדֵ֥י הַמֶּ֛לֶךְ אֲשֶׁר־בְּשַׁ֥עַר הַמֶּ֖לֶךְ לְמָרְדֳּכָ֑י מַדּ֙וּעַ֙ אַתָּ֣ה עוֹבֵ֔ר אֵ֖ת מִצְוַ֥ת הַמֶּֽלֶךְ׃

ד וַיְהִ֗י באמרם [כְּאָמְרָ֤ם] אֵלָיו֙ י֣וֹם וָי֔וֹם וְלֹ֥א שָׁמַ֖ע אֲלֵיהֶ֑ם וַיַּגִּ֣ידוּ לְהָמָ֗ן לִרְאוֹת֙ הֲיַֽעַמְדוּ֙ דִּבְרֵ֣י מָרְדֳּכַ֔י כִּֽי־הִגִּ֥יד לָהֶ֖ם אֲשֶׁר־ה֥וּא יְהוּדִֽי׃

Esther/Esther
Chapter 3

אסתר
פרק ג

5 When Haman saw that *Mordechai* would not kneel or bow low to him, Haman was filled with rage.

ה וַיַּרְא הָמָן כִּי־אֵין מָרְדֳּכַי כֹּרֵעַ וּמִשְׁתַּחֲוֶה לוֹ וַיִּמָּלֵא הָמָן חֵמָה׃

6 But he disdained to lay hands on *Mordechai* alone; having been told who *Mordechai*'s people were, Haman plotted to do away with all the *Yehudim*, *Mordechai*'s people, throughout the kingdom of Ahasuerus.

ו וַיִּבֶז בְּעֵינָיו לִשְׁלֹחַ יָד בְּמָרְדֳּכַי לְבַדּוֹ כִּי־הִגִּידוּ לוֹ אֶת־עַם מָרְדֳּכָי וַיְבַקֵּשׁ הָמָן לְהַשְׁמִיד אֶת־כָּל־הַיְּהוּדִים אֲשֶׁר בְּכָל־מַלְכוּת אֲחַשְׁוֵרוֹשׁ עַם מָרְדֳּכָי׃

7 In the first month, that is, the month of *Nisan*, in the twelfth year of King Ahasuerus, pur – which means "the lot" – was cast before Haman concerning every day and every month, [until it fell on] the twelfth month, that is, the month of *Adar*.

ז בַּחֹדֶשׁ הָרִאשׁוֹן הוּא־חֹדֶשׁ נִיסָן בִּשְׁנַת שְׁתֵּים עֶשְׂרֵה לַמֶּלֶךְ אֲחַשְׁוֵרוֹשׁ הִפִּיל פּוּר הוּא הַגּוֹרָל לִפְנֵי הָמָן מִיּוֹם לְיוֹם וּמֵחֹדֶשׁ לְחֹדֶשׁ שְׁנֵים־עָשָׂר הוּא־חֹדֶשׁ אֲדָר׃

8 Haman then said to King Ahasuerus, "There is a certain people, scattered and dispersed among the other peoples in all the provinces of your realm, whose laws are different from those of any other people and who do not obey the king's laws; and it is not in Your Majesty's interest to tolerate them.

ח וַיֹּאמֶר הָמָן לַמֶּלֶךְ אֲחַשְׁוֵרוֹשׁ יֶשְׁנוֹ עַם־אֶחָד מְפֻזָּר וּמְפֹרָד בֵּין הָעַמִּים בְּכֹל מְדִינוֹת מַלְכוּתֶךָ וְדָתֵיהֶם שֹׁנוֹת מִכָּל־עָם וְאֶת־דָּתֵי הַמֶּלֶךְ אֵינָם עֹשִׂים וְלַמֶּלֶךְ אֵין־שֹׁוֶה לְהַנִּיחָם׃

9 If it please Your Majesty, let an edict be drawn for their destruction, and I will pay ten thousand *kikarot* of silver to the stewards for deposit in the royal treasury."

ט אִם־עַל־הַמֶּלֶךְ טוֹב יִכָּתֵב לְאַבְּדָם וַעֲשֶׂרֶת אֲלָפִים כִּכַּר־כֶּסֶף אֶשְׁקוֹל עַל־יְדֵי עֹשֵׂי הַמְּלָאכָה לְהָבִיא אֶל־גִּנְזֵי הַמֶּלֶךְ׃

10 Thereupon the king removed his signet ring from his hand and gave it to Haman son of Hammedatha the Agagite, the foe of the *Yehudim*.

י וַיָּסַר הַמֶּלֶךְ אֶת־טַבַּעְתּוֹ מֵעַל יָדוֹ וַיִּתְּנָהּ לְהָמָן בֶּן־הַמְּדָתָא הָאֲגָגִי צֹרֵר הַיְּהוּדִים׃

11 And the king said, "The money and the people are yours to do with as you see fit."

יא וַיֹּאמֶר הַמֶּלֶךְ לְהָמָן הַכֶּסֶף נָתוּן לָךְ וְהָעָם לַעֲשׂוֹת בּוֹ כַּטּוֹב בְּעֵינֶיךָ׃

12 On the thirteenth day of the first month, the king's scribes were summoned and a decree was issued, as Haman directed, to the king's satraps, to the governors of every province, and to the officials of every people, to every province in its own script and to every people in its own language. The orders were issued in the name of King Ahasuerus and sealed with the king's signet.

יב וַיִּקָּרְאוּ סֹפְרֵי הַמֶּלֶךְ בַּחֹדֶשׁ הָרִאשׁוֹן בִּשְׁלוֹשָׁה עָשָׂר יוֹם בּוֹ וַיִּכָּתֵב כְּכָל־אֲשֶׁר־צִוָּה הָמָן אֶל אֲחַשְׁדַּרְפְּנֵי־הַמֶּלֶךְ וְאֶל־הַפַּחוֹת אֲשֶׁר עַל־מְדִינָה וּמְדִינָה וְאֶל־שָׂרֵי עַם וָעָם מְדִינָה וּמְדִינָה כִּכְתָבָהּ וְעַם וָעָם כִּלְשׁוֹנוֹ בְּשֵׁם הַמֶּלֶךְ אֲחַשְׁוֵרֹשׁ נִכְתָּב וְנֶחְתָּם בְּטַבַּעַת הַמֶּלֶךְ׃

13 Accordingly, written instructions were dispatched by couriers to all the king's provinces to destroy, massacre, and exterminate all the *Yehudim*, young

יג וְנִשְׁלוֹחַ סְפָרִים בְּיַד הָרָצִים אֶל־כָּל־מְדִינוֹת הַמֶּלֶךְ לְהַשְׁמִיד לַהֲרֹג וּלְאַבֵּד אֶת־כָּל־הַיְּהוּדִים מִנַּעַר וְעַד־זָקֵן טַף

3:13 To destroy, massacre, and exterminate all the *Yehudim* Usually, the Torah gives us the reason why an individual, or the nation as a whole, are punished. *Megillat Esther*, however, does not explicitly state what the people did to deserve the threat of annihilation. When viewed in historical context, it becomes clear that the Jews of Shushan were guilty for not having returned to *Eretz Yisrael* even though they had the

Esther/Esther
Chapter 4

and old, children and women, on a single day, on the thirteenth day of the twelfth month – that is, the month of *Adar* – and to plunder their possessions.	וְנָשִׁים בְּיוֹם אֶחָד בִּשְׁלוֹשָׁה עָשָׂר לְחֹדֶשׁ שְׁנֵים־עָשָׂר הוּא־חֹדֶשׁ אֲדָר וּשְׁלָלָם לָבוֹז:

v'-nish-LO-akh s'-fa-REEM b'-YAD ha-ra-TZEEM el kol m'-dee-NOT ha-ME-lekh l'-hash-MEED la-ha-ROG ul-a-BAYD et kol ha-y'-hu-DEEM mi-NA-ar v'-AD za-KAYN taf v'-na-SHEEM b'-YOM e-KHAD bish-lo-SHAH a-SAR l'-KHO-desh sh'-NAYM a-SAR hu KHO-desh a-DAR ush-la-LAM la-VOZ

14 The text of the document was to the effect that a law should be proclaimed in every single province; it was to be publicly displayed to all the peoples, so that they might be ready for that day.

פַּתְשֶׁגֶן הַכְּתָב לְהִנָּתֵן דָּת בְּכָל־מְדִינָה וּמְדִינָה גָּלוּי לְכָל־הָעַמִּים לִהְיוֹת עֲתִדִים לַיּוֹם הַזֶּה:

15 The couriers went out posthaste on the royal mission, and the decree was proclaimed in the fortress Shushan. The king and Haman sat down to feast, but the city of Shushan was dumfounded.

הָרָצִים יָצְאוּ דְחוּפִים בִּדְבַר הַמֶּלֶךְ וְהַדָּת נִתְּנָה בְּשׁוּשַׁן הַבִּירָה וְהַמֶּלֶךְ וְהָמָן יָשְׁבוּ לִשְׁתּוֹת וְהָעִיר שׁוּשָׁן נָבוֹכָה:

4 1 When *Mordechai* learned all that had happened, *Mordechai* tore his clothes and put on sackcloth and ashes. He went through the city, crying out loudly and bitterly,

וּמָרְדֳּכַי יָדַע אֶת־כָּל־אֲשֶׁר נַעֲשָׂה וַיִּקְרַע מָרְדֳּכַי אֶת־בְּגָדָיו וַיִּלְבַּשׁ שַׂק וָאֵפֶר וַיֵּצֵא בְּתוֹךְ הָעִיר וַיִּזְעַק זְעָקָה גְדֹלָה וּמָרָה:

2 until he came in front of the palace gate; for one could not enter the palace gate wearing sackcloth. –

וַיָּבוֹא עַד לִפְנֵי שַׁעַר־הַמֶּלֶךְ כִּי אֵין לָבוֹא אֶל־שַׁעַר הַמֶּלֶךְ בִּלְבוּשׁ שָׂק:

3 Also, in every province that the king's command and decree reached, there was great mourning among the *Yehudim*, with fasting, weeping, and wailing, and everybody lay in sackcloth and ashes. –

וּבְכָל־מְדִינָה וּמְדִינָה מְקוֹם אֲשֶׁר דְּבַר־הַמֶּלֶךְ וְדָתוֹ מַגִּיעַ אֵבֶל גָּדוֹל לַיְּהוּדִים וְצוֹם וּבְכִי וּמִסְפֵּד שַׂק וָאֵפֶר יֻצַּע לָרַבִּים:

4 When *Esther*'s maidens and eunuchs came and informed her, the queen was greatly agitated. She sent clothing for *Mordechai* to wear, so that he might take off his sackcloth; but he refused.

וַתָּבוֹאנָה נַעֲרוֹת אֶסְתֵּר וְסָרִיסֶיהָ וַיַּגִּידוּ לָהּ וַתִּתְחַלְחַל הַמַּלְכָּה מְאֹד וַתִּשְׁלַח בְּגָדִים לְהַלְבִּישׁ אֶת־מָרְדֳּכַי וּלְהָסִיר שַׂקּוֹ מֵעָלָיו וְלֹא קִבֵּל:

5 Thereupon *Esther* summoned Hathach, one of the eunuchs whom the king had appointed to serve her, and sent him to *Mordechai* to learn the why and wherefore of it all.

וַתִּקְרָא אֶסְתֵּר לַהֲתָךְ מִסָּרִיסֵי הַמֶּלֶךְ אֲשֶׁר הֶעֱמִיד לְפָנֶיהָ וַתְּצַוֵּהוּ עַל־מָרְדֳּכָי לָדַעַת מַה־זֶּה וְעַל־מַה־זֶּה:

6 Hathach went out to *Mordechai* in the city square in front of the palace gate;

וַיֵּצֵא הֲתָךְ אֶל־מָרְדֳּכָי אֶל־רְחוֹב הָעִיר אֲשֶׁר לִפְנֵי שַׁעַר־הַמֶּלֶךְ:

opportunity to do so. After the Persian king Cyrus conquered the Babylonians, he allowed the Children of Israel to return to the Land of Israel and begin reconstruction of the *Beit Hamikdash*. However, a mere 42,360 returned to *Yerushalayim* (Ezra 2:64) while close to a million remained in Babylonia. The generation was therefore punished for their lack of enthusiasm towards returning to Israel. This teaches us the importance of making every effort to embrace the land and to physically return to it whenever possible.

Esther/Esther

Chapter 4

אסתר

פרק ד

7 and *Mordechai* told him all that had happened to him, and all about the money that Haman had offered to pay into the royal treasury for the destruction of the *Yehudim*.

ז וַיַּגֶּד־לוֹ מָרְדֳּכַי אֵת כָּל־אֲשֶׁר קָרָהוּ וְאֵת פָּרָשַׁת הַכֶּסֶף אֲשֶׁר אָמַר הָמָן לִשְׁקוֹל עַל־גִּנְזֵי הַמֶּלֶךְ בַּיְּהוּדִיִּים [בַּיְּהוּדִים] לְאַבְּדָם׃

8 He also gave him the written text of the law that had been proclaimed in Shushan for their destruction. [He bade him] show it to *Esther* and inform her, and charge her to go to the king and to appeal to him and to plead with him for her people.

ח וְאֶת־פַּתְשֶׁגֶן כְּתָב־הַדָּת אֲשֶׁר־נִתַּן בְּשׁוּשָׁן לְהַשְׁמִידָם נָתַן לוֹ לְהַרְאוֹת אֶת־אֶסְתֵּר וּלְהַגִּיד לָהּ וּלְצַוּוֹת עָלֶיהָ לָבוֹא אֶל־הַמֶּלֶךְ לְהִתְחַנֶּן־לוֹ וּלְבַקֵּשׁ מִלְּפָנָיו עַל־עַמָּהּ׃

9 When Hathach came and delivered *Mordechai's* message to *Esther*,

ט וַיָּבוֹא הֲתָךְ וַיַּגֵּד לְאֶסְתֵּר אֵת דִּבְרֵי מָרְדֳּכָי׃

10 *Esther* told Hathach to take back to *Mordechai* the following reply:

י וַתֹּאמֶר אֶסְתֵּר לַהֲתָךְ וַתְּצַוֵּהוּ אֶל־מָרְדֳּכָי׃

11 "All the king's courtiers and the people of the king's provinces know that if any person, man or woman, enters the king's presence in the inner court without having been summoned, there is but one law for him – that he be put to death. Only if the king extends the golden scepter to him may he live. Now I have not been summoned to visit the king for the last thirty days."

יא כָּל־עַבְדֵי הַמֶּלֶךְ וְעַם־מְדִינוֹת הַמֶּלֶךְ יוֹדְעִים אֲשֶׁר כָּל־אִישׁ וְאִשָּׁה אֲשֶׁר יָבוֹא־אֶל־הַמֶּלֶךְ אֶל־הֶחָצֵר הַפְּנִימִית אֲשֶׁר לֹא־יִקָּרֵא אַחַת דָּתוֹ לְהָמִית לְבַד מֵאֲשֶׁר יוֹשִׁיט־לוֹ הַמֶּלֶךְ אֶת־שַׁרְבִיט הַזָּהָב וְחָיָה וַאֲנִי לֹא נִקְרֵאתִי לָבוֹא אֶל־הַמֶּלֶךְ זֶה שְׁלוֹשִׁים יוֹם׃

12 When *Mordechai* was told what *Esther* had said,

יב וַיַּגִּידוּ לְמָרְדֳּכָי אֵת דִּבְרֵי אֶסְתֵּר׃

13 *Mordechai* had this message delivered to *Esther*: "Do not imagine that you, of all the *Yehudim*, will escape with your life by being in the king's palace.

יג וַיֹּאמֶר מָרְדֳּכַי לְהָשִׁיב אֶל־אֶסְתֵּר אַל־תְּדַמִּי בְנַפְשֵׁךְ לְהִמָּלֵט בֵּית־הַמֶּלֶךְ מִכָּל־הַיְּהוּדִים׃

14 On the contrary, if you keep silent in this crisis, relief and deliverance will come to the *Yehudim* from another quarter, while you and your father's house will perish. And who knows, perhaps you have attained to royal position for just such a crisis."

יד כִּי אִם־הַחֲרֵשׁ תַּחֲרִישִׁי בָּעֵת הַזֹּאת רֶוַח וְהַצָּלָה יַעֲמוֹד לַיְּהוּדִים מִמָּקוֹם אַחֵר וְאַתְּ וּבֵית־אָבִיךְ תֹּאבֵדוּ וּמִי יוֹדֵעַ אִם־לְעֵת כָּזֹאת הִגַּעַתְּ לַמַּלְכוּת׃

KEE im ha-kha-RAYSH ta-kha-ree-SHEE ba-AYT ha-ZOT RE-vakh v'-ha-tza-LAH ya-a-MOD la-y'-hu-DEEM mi-ma-KOM a-KHAYR v'-AT u-VAYT a-VEEKH to-VAY-du u-MEE yo-DAY-a im l'-AYT ka-ZOT hi-GA-at la-mal-KHUT

15 Then *Esther* sent back this answer to *Mordechai*:

טו וַתֹּאמֶר אֶסְתֵּר לְהָשִׁיב אֶל־מָרְדֳּכָי׃

4:14 Relief and deliverance will come to the *Yehudim* *Mordechai's* inspiring words move *Esther* to courageously step up and defend her people. *Mordechai* does not say, "If you are silent now, then we are all doomed," because he knows that the God of Israel will never forsake His people. Instead, *Mordechai* empowers *Esther* to take a leading role in the redemption, and not to sit quietly on the sidelines as it unfolds. In every generation there are those who threaten the existence of the Nation of Israel. Ultimately, *Hashem* will defend His people and His land, but is up to each individual to decide if he or she will stand up, as Queen *Esther* did, on behalf of Israel.

Esther/Esther
Chapter 5

אסתר
פרק ה

16 "Go, assemble all the *Yehudim* who live in Shushan, and fast in my behalf; do not eat or drink for three days, night or day. I and my maidens will observe the same fast. Then I shall go to the king, though it is contrary to the law; and if I am to perish, I shall perish!"

טז לֵךְ כְּנוֹס אֶת־כָּל־הַיְּהוּדִים הַנִּמְצְאִים בְּשׁוּשָׁן וְצוּמוּ עָלַי וְאַל־תֹּאכְלוּ וְאַל־תִּשְׁתּוּ שְׁלֹשֶׁת יָמִים לַיְלָה וָיוֹם גַּם־אֲנִי וְנַעֲרֹתַי אָצוּם כֵּן וּבְכֵן אָבוֹא אֶל־הַמֶּלֶךְ אֲשֶׁר לֹא־כַדָּת וְכַאֲשֶׁר אָבַדְתִּי אָבָדְתִּי:

17 So *Mordechai* went about [the city] and did just as *Esther* had commanded him.

יז וַיַּעֲבֹר מָרְדֳּכָי וַיַּעַשׂ כְּכֹל אֲשֶׁר־צִוְּתָה עָלָיו אֶסְתֵּר:

5 1 On the third day, *Esther* put on royal apparel and stood in the inner court of the king's palace, facing the king's palace, while the king was sitting on his royal throne in the throne room facing the entrance of the palace.

ה א וַיְהִי בַּיּוֹם הַשְּׁלִישִׁי וַתִּלְבַּשׁ אֶסְתֵּר מַלְכוּת וַתַּעֲמֹד בַּחֲצַר בֵּית־הַמֶּלֶךְ הַפְּנִימִית נֹכַח בֵּית הַמֶּלֶךְ וְהַמֶּלֶךְ יוֹשֵׁב עַל־כִּסֵּא מַלְכוּתוֹ בְּבֵית הַמַּלְכוּת נֹכַח פֶּתַח הַבָּיִת:

2 As soon as the king saw Queen *Esther* standing in the court, she won his favor. The king extended to *Esther* the golden scepter which he had in his hand, and *Esther* approached and touched the tip of the scepter.

ב וַיְהִי כִרְאוֹת הַמֶּלֶךְ אֶת־אֶסְתֵּר הַמַּלְכָּה עֹמֶדֶת בֶּחָצֵר נָשְׂאָה חֵן בְּעֵינָיו וַיּוֹשֶׁט הַמֶּלֶךְ לְאֶסְתֵּר אֶת־שַׁרְבִיט הַזָּהָב אֲשֶׁר בְּיָדוֹ וַתִּקְרַב אֶסְתֵּר וַתִּגַּע בְּרֹאשׁ הַשַּׁרְבִיט:

3 "What troubles you, Queen *Esther*?" the king asked her. "And what is your request? Even to half the kingdom, it shall be granted you."

ג וַיֹּאמֶר לָהּ הַמֶּלֶךְ מַה־לָּךְ אֶסְתֵּר הַמַּלְכָּה וּמַה־בַּקָּשָׁתֵךְ עַד־חֲצִי הַמַּלְכוּת וְיִנָּתֵן לָךְ:

va-YO-mer LAH ha-ME-lekh mah LAKH es-TAYR ha-mal-KAH u-mah ba-ka-sha-TAYKH ad kha-TZEE ha-mal-KHUT v'-yi-na-TAYN LAKH

4 "If it please Your Majesty," *Esther* replied, "let Your Majesty and Haman come today to the feast that I have prepared for him."

ד וַתֹּאמֶר אֶסְתֵּר אִם־עַל־הַמֶּלֶךְ טוֹב יָבוֹא הַמֶּלֶךְ וְהָמָן הַיּוֹם אֶל־הַמִּשְׁתֶּה אֲשֶׁר־עָשִׂיתִי לוֹ:

5 The king commanded, "Tell Haman to hurry and do *Esther*'s bidding." So the king and Haman came to the feast that *Esther* had prepared.

ה וַיֹּאמֶר הַמֶּלֶךְ מַהֲרוּ אֶת־הָמָן לַעֲשׂוֹת אֶת־דְּבַר אֶסְתֵּר וַיָּבֹא הַמֶּלֶךְ וְהָמָן אֶל־הַמִּשְׁתֶּה אֲשֶׁר־עָשְׂתָה אֶסְתֵּר:

6 At the wine feast, the king asked *Esther*, "What is your wish? It shall be granted you. And what is your request? Even to half the kingdom, it shall be fulfilled."

ו וַיֹּאמֶר הַמֶּלֶךְ לְאֶסְתֵּר בְּמִשְׁתֵּה הַיַּיִן מַה־שְּׁאֵלָתֵךְ וְיִנָּתֵן לָךְ וּמַה־בַּקָּשָׁתֵךְ עַד־חֲצִי הַמַּלְכוּת וְתֵעָשׂ:

7 "My wish," replied *Esther*, "my request –

ז וַתַּעַן אֶסְתֵּר וַתֹּאמַר שְׁאֵלָתִי וּבַקָּשָׁתִי:

Rashi (1040–1105)

5:3 Even to half the kingdom When Ahasuerus offered *Esther* up to half of the kingdom, this was not merely an exaggerated show of generosity, but it referred to a specific geographic location. *Rashi* notes that the halfway mark of Ahasuerus' empire was the site of the *Beit Hamikdash*. Ahasuerus tells *Esther* that he is willing to do anything to make her happy, short of allowing the rebuilding of the Temple. Although Cyrus, his predecessor, had allowed the Children of Israel to return to Israel and begin reconstruction of the *Beit Hamikdash*, Ahasuerus was adamantly against it. Ironically, according to Jewish tradition it was his son Darius, born to him by *Esther*, who allowed the construction of the *Beit Hamikdash* to be completed.

Esther/Esther
Chapter 6

8 if Your Majesty will do me the favor, if it please Your Majesty to grant my wish and accede to my request – let Your Majesty and Haman come to the feast which I will prepare for them; and tomorrow I will do Your Majesty's bidding."

9 That day Haman went out happy and lighthearted. But when Haman saw *Mordechai* in the palace gate, and *Mordechai* did not rise or even stir on his account, Haman was filled with rage at him.

10 Nevertheless, Haman controlled himself and went home. He sent for his friends and his wife Zeresh,

11 and Haman told them about his great wealth and his many sons, and all about how the king had promoted him and advanced him above the officials and the king's courtiers.

12 "What is more," said Haman, "Queen *Esther* gave a feast, and besides the king she did not have anyone but me. And tomorrow too I am invited by her along with the king.

13 Yet all this means nothing to me every time I see that *Yehudi Mordechai* sitting in the palace gate."

14 Then his wife Zeresh and all his friends said to him, "Let a stake be put up, fifty *amot* high, and in the morning ask the king to have *Mordechai* impaled on it. Then you can go gaily with the king to the feast." The proposal pleased Haman, and he had the stake put up.

6 1 That night, sleep deserted the king, and he ordered the book of records, the annals, to be brought; and it was read to the king.

ba-LAI-lah ha-HU na-d'-DAH sh'-NAT ha-ME-lekh va-YO-mer l'-ha-VEE et SAY-fer ha-zikh-ro-NOT div-RAY ha-ya-MEEM va-yih-YU nik-ra-EEM lif-NAY ha-ME-lekh

---

6:1 That night Upon careful reading of *Megillat Esther*, it becomes clear that "that night" was the second night of *Pesach*. Since Haman's letters had been sent out on the thirteenth day of *Nisan*, and *Esther* called for three days of fasting, the first banquet took place on the sixteenth of *Nssan*. The Talmud (*Megila* 16a) relates that when Haman looked for *Mordechai* in order to lead him around the city, he found the Jewish Sage teaching the laws of the *Omer* offering, which was offered in the Temple on the second day of Passover. When granted permission to rebuild the *Beit Hamikdash* by Cyrus, the Jews did not heed the call, and only a small minority returned to *Yerushalayim*. Hoping to rectify this sin which potentially brought about Haman's

Esther / אסתר
Chapter 6 / פרק ו

2 There it was found written that *Mordechai* had denounced Bigthana and Teresh, two of the king's eunuchs who guarded the threshold, who had plotted to do away with King Ahasuerus.

ב וַיִּמָּצֵא כָתוּב אֲשֶׁר הִגִּיד מָרְדֳּכַי עַל־בִּגְתָנָא וָתֶרֶשׁ שְׁנֵי סָרִיסֵי הַמֶּלֶךְ מִשֹּׁמְרֵי הַסַּף אֲשֶׁר בִּקְשׁוּ לִשְׁלֹחַ יָד בַּמֶּלֶךְ אֲחַשְׁוֵרוֹשׁ:

3 "What honor or advancement has been conferred on *Mordechai* for this?" the king inquired. "Nothing at all has been done for him," replied the king's servants who were in attendance on him.

ג וַיֹּאמֶר הַמֶּלֶךְ מַה־נַּעֲשָׂה יְקָר וּגְדוּלָּה לְמָרְדֳּכַי עַל־זֶה וַיֹּאמְרוּ נַעֲרֵי הַמֶּלֶךְ מְשָׁרְתָיו לֹא־נַעֲשָׂה עִמּוֹ דָּבָר:

4 "Who is in the court?" the king asked. For Haman had just entered the outer court of the royal palace, to speak to the king about having *Mordechai* impaled on the stake he had prepared for him.

ד וַיֹּאמֶר הַמֶּלֶךְ מִי בֶחָצֵר וְהָמָן בָּא לַחֲצַר בֵּית־הַמֶּלֶךְ הַחִיצוֹנָה לֵאמֹר לַמֶּלֶךְ לִתְלוֹת אֶת־מָרְדֳּכַי עַל־הָעֵץ אֲשֶׁר־הֵכִין לוֹ:

5 "It is Haman standing in the court," the king's servants answered him. "Let him enter," said the king.

ה וַיֹּאמְרוּ נַעֲרֵי הַמֶּלֶךְ אֵלָיו הִנֵּה הָמָן עֹמֵד בֶּחָצֵר וַיֹּאמֶר הַמֶּלֶךְ יָבוֹא:

6 Haman entered, and the king asked him, "What should be done for a man whom the king desires to honor?" Haman said to himself, "Whom would the king desire to honor more than me?"

ו וַיָּבוֹא הָמָן וַיֹּאמֶר לוֹ הַמֶּלֶךְ מַה־לַעֲשׂוֹת בָּאִישׁ אֲשֶׁר הַמֶּלֶךְ חָפֵץ בִּיקָרוֹ וַיֹּאמֶר הָמָן בְּלִבּוֹ לְמִי יַחְפֹּץ הַמֶּלֶךְ לַעֲשׂוֹת יְקָר יוֹתֵר מִמֶּנִּי:

7 So Haman said to the king, "For the man whom the king desires to honor,

ז וַיֹּאמֶר הָמָן אֶל־הַמֶּלֶךְ אִישׁ אֲשֶׁר הַמֶּלֶךְ חָפֵץ בִּיקָרוֹ:

8 let royal garb which the king has worn be brought, and a horse on which the king has ridden and on whose head a royal diadem has been set;

ח יָבִיאוּ לְבוּשׁ מַלְכוּת אֲשֶׁר לָבַשׁ־בּוֹ הַמֶּלֶךְ וְסוּס אֲשֶׁר רָכַב עָלָיו הַמֶּלֶךְ וַאֲשֶׁר נִתַּן כֶּתֶר מַלְכוּת בְּרֹאשׁוֹ:

9 and let the attire and the horse be put in the charge of one of the king's noble courtiers. And let the man whom the king desires to honor be attired and paraded on the horse through the city square, while they proclaim before him: This is what is done for the man whom the king desires to honor!"

ט וְנָתוֹן הַלְּבוּשׁ וְהַסּוּס עַל־יַד־אִישׁ מִשָּׂרֵי הַמֶּלֶךְ הַפַּרְתְּמִים וְהִלְבִּישׁוּ אֶת־הָאִישׁ אֲשֶׁר הַמֶּלֶךְ חָפֵץ בִּיקָרוֹ וְהִרְכִּיבֻהוּ עַל־הַסּוּס בִּרְחוֹב הָעִיר וְקָרְאוּ לְפָנָיו כָּכָה יֵעָשֶׂה לָאִישׁ אֲשֶׁר הַמֶּלֶךְ חָפֵץ בִּיקָרוֹ:

10 "Quick, then!" said the king to Haman. "Get the garb and the horse, as you have said, and do this to *Mordechai* the *Yehudi*, who sits in the king's gate. Omit nothing of all you have proposed."

י וַיֹּאמֶר הַמֶּלֶךְ לְהָמָן מַהֵר קַח אֶת־הַלְּבוּשׁ וְאֶת־הַסּוּס כַּאֲשֶׁר דִּבַּרְתָּ וַעֲשֵׂה־כֵן לְמָרְדֳּכַי הַיְּהוּדִי הַיּוֹשֵׁב בְּשַׁעַר הַמֶּלֶךְ אַל־תַּפֵּל דָּבָר מִכֹּל אֲשֶׁר דִּבַּרְתָּ:

11 So Haman took the garb and the horse and arrayed *Mordechai* and paraded him through the city square; and he proclaimed before him: This is what is done for the man whom the king desires to honor!

יא וַיִּקַּח הָמָן אֶת־הַלְּבוּשׁ וְאֶת־הַסּוּס וַיַּלְבֵּשׁ אֶת־מָרְדֳּכָי וַיַּרְכִּיבֵהוּ בִּרְחוֹב הָעִיר וַיִּקְרָא לְפָנָיו כָּכָה יֵעָשֶׂה לָאִישׁ אֲשֶׁר הַמֶּלֶךְ חָפֵץ בִּיקָרוֹ:

---

decree of annihilation, *Mordechai* was teaching about the Temple and its laws. Though in exile, the Jews have remained connected to *Yerushalayim* and the Holy Temple through the study of *Torah*.

Esther/Esther
Chapter 7

אסתר
פרק ז

12 Then *Mordechai* returned to the king's gate, while Haman hurried home, his head covered in mourning.

יב וַיָּשָׁב מָרְדֳּכַי אֶל־שַׁעַר הַמֶּלֶךְ וְהָמָן נִדְחַף אֶל־בֵּיתוֹ אָבֵל וַחֲפוּי רֹאשׁ:

13 There Haman told his wife Zeresh and all his friends everything that had befallen him. His advisers and his wife Zeresh said to him, "If *Mordechai*, before whom you have begun to fall, is of Yehudiish stock, you will not overcome him; you will fall before him to your ruin."

יג וַיְסַפֵּר הָמָן לְזֶרֶשׁ אִשְׁתּוֹ וּלְכָל־אֹהֲבָיו אֵת כָּל־אֲשֶׁר קָרָהוּ וַיֹּאמְרוּ לוֹ חֲכָמָיו וְזֶרֶשׁ אִשְׁתּוֹ אִם מִזֶּרַע הַיְּהוּדִים מָרְדֳּכַי אֲשֶׁר הַחִלּוֹתָ לִנְפֹּל לְפָנָיו לֹא־תוּכַל לוֹ כִּי־נָפוֹל תִּפּוֹל לְפָנָיו:

14 While they were still speaking with him, the king's eunuchs arrived and hurriedly brought Haman to the banquet which *Esther* had prepared.

יד עוֹדָם מְדַבְּרִים עִמּוֹ וְסָרִיסֵי הַמֶּלֶךְ הִגִּיעוּ וַיַּבְהִלוּ לְהָבִיא אֶת־הָמָן אֶל־הַמִּשְׁתֶּה אֲשֶׁר־עָשְׂתָה אֶסְתֵּר:

7 1 So the king and Haman came to feast with Queen *Esther*.

ז א וַיָּבֹא הַמֶּלֶךְ וְהָמָן לִשְׁתּוֹת עִם־אֶסְתֵּר הַמַּלְכָּה:

va-ya-VO ha-ME-lekh v'-ha-MAN lish-TOT im es-TAYR ha-mal-KAH

2 On the second day, the king again asked *Esther* at the wine feast, "What is your wish, Queen *Esther*? It shall be granted you. And what is your request? Even to half the kingdom, it shall be fulfilled."

ב וַיֹּאמֶר הַמֶּלֶךְ לְאֶסְתֵּר גַּם בַּיּוֹם הַשֵּׁנִי בְּמִשְׁתֵּה הַיַּיִן מַה־שְּׁאֵלָתֵךְ אֶסְתֵּר הַמַּלְכָּה וְתִנָּתֵן לָךְ וּמַה־בַּקָּשָׁתֵךְ עַד־חֲצִי הַמַּלְכוּת וְתֵעָשׂ:

3 Queen *Esther* replied: "If Your Majesty will do me the favor, and if it pleases Your Majesty, let my life be granted me as my wish, and my people as my request.

ג וַתַּעַן אֶסְתֵּר הַמַּלְכָּה וַתֹּאמַר אִם־מָצָאתִי חֵן בְּעֵינֶיךָ הַמֶּלֶךְ וְאִם־עַל־הַמֶּלֶךְ טוֹב תִּנָּתֶן־לִי נַפְשִׁי בִּשְׁאֵלָתִי וְעַמִּי בְּבַקָּשָׁתִי:

4 For we have been sold, my people and I, to be destroyed, massacred, and exterminated. Had we only been sold as bondmen and bondwomen, I would have kept silent; for the adversary is not worthy of the king's trouble."

ד כִּי נִמְכַּרְנוּ אֲנִי וְעַמִּי לְהַשְׁמִיד לַהֲרוֹג וּלְאַבֵּד וְאִלּוּ לַעֲבָדִים וְלִשְׁפָחוֹת נִמְכַּרְנוּ הֶחֱרַשְׁתִּי כִּי אֵין הַצָּר שֹׁוֶה בְּנֵזֶק הַמֶּלֶךְ:

5 Thereupon King Ahasuerus demanded of Queen *Esther*, "Who is he and where is he who dared to do this?"

ה וַיֹּאמֶר הַמֶּלֶךְ אֲחַשְׁוֵרוֹשׁ וַיֹּאמֶר לְאֶסְתֵּר הַמַּלְכָּה מִי הוּא זֶה וְאֵי־זֶה הוּא אֲשֶׁר־מְלָאוֹ לִבּוֹ לַעֲשׂוֹת כֵּן:

6 "The adversary and enemy," replied *Esther*, "is this evil Haman!" And Haman cringed in terror before the king and the queen.

ו וַתֹּאמֶר אֶסְתֵּר אִישׁ צַר וְאוֹיֵב הָמָן הָרָע הַזֶּה וְהָמָן נִבְעַת מִלִּפְנֵי הַמֶּלֶךְ וְהַמַּלְכָּה:

7:1 So the king and Haman came to feast Why does *Esther* deem it necessary to invite Haman to her banquet with Ahasuerus? As long as the Jewish people knew that they had *Esther* in the palace, they were counting on her to reverse Haman's evil decree. Yet *Esther* wanted the people themselves to fully repent. Inviting Haman made it appear that she was abandoning her people and aligning with the wicked Haman. At that point, the terrified nation called out to *Hashem* with a new intensity that merited salvation. Throughout the ages, true redemption arrives when we realize that we have no one to rely on aside from God above.

Esther/Esther
Chapter 8

7 The king, in his fury, left the wine feast for the palace garden, while Haman remained to plead with Queen *Esther* for his life; for he saw that the king had resolved to destroy him.

8 When the king returned from the palace garden to the banquet room, Haman was lying prostrate on the couch on which *Esther* reclined. "Does he mean," cried the king, "to ravish the queen in my own palace?" No sooner did these words leave the king's lips than Haman's face was covered.

9 Then Harbonahh, one of the eunuchs in attendance on the king, said, "What is more, a stake is standing at Haman's house, fifty *amot* high, which Haman made for *Mordechai* – the man whose words saved the king." "Impale him on it!" the king ordered.

10 So they impaled Haman on the stake which he had put up for *Mordechai*, and the king's fury abated.

8 1 That very day King Ahasuerus gave the property of Haman, the enemy of the *Yehudim*, to Queen *Esther*. *Mordechai* presented himself to the king, for *Esther* had revealed how he was related to her.

2 The king slipped off his ring, which he had taken back from Haman, and gave it to *Mordechai*; and *Esther* put *Mordechai* in charge of Haman's property.

3 *Esther* spoke to the king again, falling at his feet and weeping, and beseeching him to avert the evil plotted by Haman the Agagite against the *Yehudim*.

4 The king extended the golden scepter to *Esther*, and *Esther* arose and stood before the king.

5 "If it please Your Majesty," she said, "and if I have won your favor and the proposal seems right to Your Majesty, and if I am pleasing to you – let dispatches be written countermanding those which were written by Haman son of Hammedatha the Agagite, embodying his plot to annihilate the *Yehudim* throughout the king's provinces.

6 For how can I bear to see the disaster which will befall my people! And how can I bear to see the destruction of my kindred!"

אסתר
פרק ח

ז וְהַמֶּלֶךְ קָם בַּחֲמָתוֹ מִמִּשְׁתֵּה הַיַּיִן אֶל־גִּנַּת הַבִּיתָן וְהָמָן עָמַד לְבַקֵּשׁ עַל־נַפְשׁוֹ מֵאֶסְתֵּר הַמַּלְכָּה כִּי רָאָה כִּי־כָלְתָה אֵלָיו הָרָעָה מֵאֵת הַמֶּלֶךְ:

ח וְהַמֶּלֶךְ שָׁב מִגִּנַּת הַבִּיתָן אֶל־בֵּית מִשְׁתֵּה הַיַּיִן וְהָמָן נֹפֵל עַל־הַמִּטָּה אֲשֶׁר אֶסְתֵּר עָלֶיהָ וַיֹּאמֶר הַמֶּלֶךְ הֲגַם לִכְבּוֹשׁ אֶת־הַמַּלְכָּה עִמִּי בַּבָּיִת הַדָּבָר יָצָא מִפִּי הַמֶּלֶךְ וּפְנֵי הָמָן חָפוּ:

ט וַיֹּאמֶר חַרְבוֹנָה אֶחָד מִן־הַסָּרִיסִים לִפְנֵי הַמֶּלֶךְ גַּם הִנֵּה־הָעֵץ אֲשֶׁר־עָשָׂה הָמָן לְמָרְדֳּכַי אֲשֶׁר דִּבֶּר־טוֹב עַל־הַמֶּלֶךְ עֹמֵד בְּבֵית הָמָן גָּבֹהַּ חֲמִשִּׁים אַמָּה וַיֹּאמֶר הַמֶּלֶךְ תְּלֻהוּ עָלָיו:

י וַיִּתְלוּ אֶת־הָמָן עַל־הָעֵץ אֲשֶׁר־הֵכִין לְמָרְדֳּכָי וַחֲמַת הַמֶּלֶךְ שָׁכָכָה:

ח א בַּיּוֹם הַהוּא נָתַן הַמֶּלֶךְ אֲחַשְׁוֵרוֹשׁ לְאֶסְתֵּר הַמַּלְכָּה אֶת־בֵּית הָמָן צֹרֵר היהודיים [הַיְּהוּדִים] וּמָרְדֳּכַי בָּא לִפְנֵי הַמֶּלֶךְ כִּי־הִגִּידָה אֶסְתֵּר מַה הוּא־לָהּ:

ב וַיָּסַר הַמֶּלֶךְ אֶת־טַבַּעְתּוֹ אֲשֶׁר הֶעֱבִיר מֵהָמָן וַיִּתְּנָהּ לְמָרְדֳּכָי וַתָּשֶׂם אֶסְתֵּר אֶת־מָרְדֳּכַי עַל־בֵּית הָמָן:

ג וַתּוֹסֶף אֶסְתֵּר וַתְּדַבֵּר לִפְנֵי הַמֶּלֶךְ וַתִּפֹּל לִפְנֵי רַגְלָיו וַתֵּבְךְּ וַתִּתְחַנֶּן־לוֹ לְהַעֲבִיר אֶת־רָעַת הָמָן הָאֲגָגִי וְאֵת מַחֲשַׁבְתּוֹ אֲשֶׁר חָשַׁב עַל־הַיְּהוּדִים:

ד וַיּוֹשֶׁט הַמֶּלֶךְ לְאֶסְתֵּר אֵת שַׁרְבִט הַזָּהָב וַתָּקָם אֶסְתֵּר וַתַּעֲמֹד לִפְנֵי הַמֶּלֶךְ:

ה וַתֹּאמֶר אִם־עַל־הַמֶּלֶךְ טוֹב וְאִם־מָצָאתִי חֵן לְפָנָיו וְכָשֵׁר הַדָּבָר לִפְנֵי הַמֶּלֶךְ וְטוֹבָה אֲנִי בְּעֵינָיו יִכָּתֵב לְהָשִׁיב אֶת־הַסְּפָרִים מַחֲשֶׁבֶת הָמָן בֶּן־הַמְּדָתָא הָאֲגָגִי אֲשֶׁר כָּתַב לְאַבֵּד אֶת־הַיְּהוּדִים אֲשֶׁר בְּכָל־מְדִינוֹת הַמֶּלֶךְ:

ו כִּי אֵיכָכָה אוּכַל וְרָאִיתִי בָּרָעָה אֲשֶׁר־יִמְצָא אֶת־עַמִּי וְאֵיכָכָה אוּכַל וְרָאִיתִי בְּאָבְדַן מוֹלַדְתִּי:

Esther/Esther
Chapter 8

אסתר
פרק ח

7 Then King Ahasuerus said to Queen *Esther* and Mordechai the *Yehudi*, "I have given Haman's property to *Esther*, and he has been impaled on the stake for scheming against the *Yehudim*.

ז וַיֹּאמֶר הַמֶּלֶךְ אֲחַשְׁוֵרֹשׁ לְאֶסְתֵּר הַמַּלְכָּה וּלְמׇרְדֳּכַי הַיְּהוּדִי הִנֵּה בֵית־הָמָן נָתַתִּי לְאֶסְתֵּר וְאֹתוֹ תָּלוּ עַל־הָעֵץ עַל אֲשֶׁר־שָׁלַח יָדוֹ בַּיְּהוּדִים [בַּיְּהוּדִים]:

8 And you may further write with regard to the *Yehudim* as you see fit. [Write it] in the king's name and seal it with the king's signet, for an edict that has been written in the king's name and sealed with the king's signet may not be revoked."

ח וְאַתֶּם כִּתְבוּ עַל־הַיְּהוּדִים כַּטּוֹב בְּעֵינֵיכֶם בְּשֵׁם הַמֶּלֶךְ וְחִתְמוּ בְּטַבַּעַת הַמֶּלֶךְ כִּי־כְתָב אֲשֶׁר־נִכְתָּב בְּשֵׁם־הַמֶּלֶךְ וְנַחְתּוֹם בְּטַבַּעַת הַמֶּלֶךְ אֵין לְהָשִׁיב:

9 So the king's scribes were summoned at that time, on the twenty-third day of the third month, that is, the month of *Sivan*; and letters were written, at *Mordechai*'s dictation, to the *Yehudim* and to the satraps, the governors and the officials of the one hundred and twenty-seven provinces from India to Ethiopia: to every province in its own script and to every people in its own language, and to the *Yehudim* in their own script and language.

ט וַיִּקָּרְאוּ סֹפְרֵי־הַמֶּלֶךְ בָּעֵת־הַהִיא בַּחֹדֶשׁ הַשְּׁלִישִׁי הוּא־חֹדֶשׁ סִיוָן בִּשְׁלוֹשָׁה וְעֶשְׂרִים בּוֹ וַיִּכָּתֵב כְּכׇל־אֲשֶׁר־צִוָּה מׇרְדֳּכַי אֶל־הַיְּהוּדִים וְאֶל הָאֲחַשְׁדַּרְפְּנִים־וְהַפַּחוֹת וְשָׂרֵי הַמְּדִינוֹת אֲשֶׁר מֵהֹדּוּ וְעַד־כּוּשׁ שֶׁבַע וְעֶשְׂרִים וּמֵאָה מְדִינָה מְדִינָה וּמְדִינָה כִּכְתָבָהּ וְעַם וָעָם כִּלְשֹׁנוֹ וְאֶל־הַיְּהוּדִים כִּכְתָבָם וְכִלְשׁוֹנָם:

va-yi-ka-r'-U so-f'-RAY ha-ME-lekh ba-ayt ha-HEE ba-KHO-desh ha-sh'-lee-SHEE hu KHO-desh see-VAN bish-lo-SHAH v'-es-REEM BO va-yi-ka-TAYV k'-khol a-sher tzi-VAH mor-d'-KHAI el ha-y'-hu-DEEM v'-EL ha-a-khash-dar-p'-NEEM v'-ha-pa-KHOT v'-sa-RAY ha-m'-dee-NOT a-SHER may-HO-du v'-ad KUSH SHE-va v'-es-REEM u-may-AH m'-dee-NAH m'-dee-NAH um-dee-NAH kikh-ta-VAH v'-AM va-AM kil-sho-NO v'-EL ha-y'-hu-DEEM kikh-ta-VAM v'-khil-sho-NAM

10 He had them written in the name of King Ahasuerus and sealed with the king's signet. Letters were dispatched by mounted couriers, riding steeds used in the king's service, bred of the royal stud,

י וַיִּכְתֹּב בְּשֵׁם הַמֶּלֶךְ אֲחַשְׁוֵרֹשׁ וַיַּחְתֹּם בְּטַבַּעַת הַמֶּלֶךְ וַיִּשְׁלַח סְפָרִים בְּיַד הָרָצִים בַּסּוּסִים רֹכְבֵי הָרֶכֶשׁ הָאֲחַשְׁתְּרָנִים בְּנֵי הָרַמָּכִים:

11 to this effect: The king has permitted the *Yehudim* of every city to assemble and fight for their lives; if any people or province attacks them, they may destroy, massacre, and exterminate its armed force together with women and children, and plunder their possessions –

יא אֲשֶׁר נָתַן הַמֶּלֶךְ לַיְּהוּדִים אֲשֶׁר בְּכׇל־עִיר־וָעִיר לְהִקָּהֵל וְלַעֲמֹד עַל־נַפְשָׁם לְהַשְׁמִיד וְלַהֲרֹג וּלְאַבֵּד אֶת־כׇּל־חֵיל עַם וּמְדִינָה הַצָּרִים אֹתָם טַף וְנָשִׁים וּשְׁלָלָם לָבוֹז:

8:9 Of the third month, that is, the month of Sivan This verse refers to the third month of the Jewish calendar, called *Sivan*. Throughout *Megillat Esther*, the Hebrew months are referred to by both number and name. *Ramban* (Exodus 12:2) teaches that originally the months were referred to by numbers, with the first month being the month of the redemption from Egypt, in order to commemorate the Exodus. During the Babylonian exile, however, the Jews adopted the Persian names for the months, which are used to this day. Just as the original numbering of the months included a reference to the Exodus from Egypt, the Persian names recall the return of the Jewish people from the Babylonian exile and the land of the Persians. In this way, all references to the Jewish calendar contain a subtle allusion to the first redemption from exile and the re-entry into the Land of Israel.

Ramban
(1194–1270)

Esther/Esther
Chapter 9

אסתר
פרק ט

12 on a single day in all the provinces of King Ahasuerus, namely, on the thirteenth day of the twelfth month, that is, the month of *Adar*.

יב בְּיוֹם אֶחָד בְּכָל־מְדִינוֹת הַמֶּלֶךְ אֲחַשְׁוֵרוֹשׁ בִּשְׁלוֹשָׁה עָשָׂר לְחֹדֶשׁ שְׁנֵים־עָשָׂר הוּא־חֹדֶשׁ אֲדָר:

13 The text of the document was to be issued as a law in every single province: it was to be publicly displayed to all the peoples, so that the *Yehudim* should be ready for that day to avenge themselves on their enemies.

יג פַּתְשֶׁגֶן הַכְּתָב לְהִנָּתֵן דָּת בְּכָל־מְדִינָה וּמְדִינָה גָּלוּי לְכָל־הָעַמִּים וְלִהְיוֹת היהודיים [הַיְּהוּדִים] עתודים [עֲתִידִים] לַיּוֹם הַזֶּה לְהִנָּקֵם מֵאֹיְבֵיהֶם:

14 The couriers, mounted on royal steeds, went out in urgent haste at the king's command; and the decree was proclaimed in the fortress Shushan.

יד הָרָצִים רֹכְבֵי הָרֶכֶשׁ הָאֲחַשְׁתְּרָנִים יָצְאוּ מְבֹהָלִים וּדְחוּפִים בִּדְבַר הַמֶּלֶךְ וְהַדָּת נִתְּנָה בְּשׁוּשַׁן הַבִּירָה:

15 *Mordechai* left the king's presence in royal robes of blue and white, with a magnificent crown of gold and a mantle of fine linen and purple wool. And the city of Shushan rang with joyous cries.

טו וּמָרְדֳּכַי יָצָא מִלִּפְנֵי הַמֶּלֶךְ בִּלְבוּשׁ מַלְכוּת תְּכֵלֶת וָחוּר וַעֲטֶרֶת זָהָב גְּדוֹלָה וְתַכְרִיךְ בּוּץ וְאַרְגָּמָן וְהָעִיר שׁוּשָׁן צָהֲלָה וְשָׂמֵחָה:

16 The *Yehudim* enjoyed light and gladness, happiness and honor.

טז לַיְּהוּדִים הָיְתָה אוֹרָה וְשִׂמְחָה וְשָׂשֹׂן וִיקָר:

17 And in every province and in every city, when the king's command and decree arrived, there was gladness and joy among the *Yehudim*, a feast and a holiday. And many of the people of the land professed to be *Yehudim*, for the fear of the *Yehudim* had fallen upon them.

יז וּבְכָל־מְדִינָה וּמְדִינָה וּבְכָל־עִיר וָעִיר מְקוֹם אֲשֶׁר דְּבַר־הַמֶּלֶךְ וְדָתוֹ מַגִּיעַ שִׂמְחָה וְשָׂשׂוֹן לַיְּהוּדִים מִשְׁתֶּה וְיוֹם טוֹב וְרַבִּים מֵעַמֵּי הָאָרֶץ מִתְיַהֲדִים כִּי־נָפַל פַּחַד־הַיְּהוּדִים עֲלֵיהֶם:

9 1 And so, on the thirteenth day of the twelfth month – that is, the month of *Adar* – when the king's command and decree were to be executed, the very day on which the enemies of the *Yehudim* had expected to get them in their power, the opposite happened, and the *Yehudim* got their enemies in their power.

ט א וּבִשְׁנֵים עָשָׂר חֹדֶשׁ הוּא־חֹדֶשׁ אֲדָר בִּשְׁלוֹשָׁה עָשָׂר יוֹם בּוֹ אֲשֶׁר הִגִּיעַ דְּבַר־הַמֶּלֶךְ וְדָתוֹ לְהֵעָשׂוֹת בַּיּוֹם אֲשֶׁר שִׂבְּרוּ אֹיְבֵי הַיְּהוּדִים לִשְׁלוֹט בָּהֶם וְנַהֲפוֹךְ הוּא אֲשֶׁר יִשְׁלְטוּ הַיְּהוּדִים הֵמָּה בְּשֹׂנְאֵיהֶם:

2 Throughout the provinces of King Ahasuerus, the *Yehudim* mustered in their cities to attack those who sought their hurt; and no one could withstand them, for the fear of them had fallen upon all the peoples.

ב נִקְהֲלוּ הַיְּהוּדִים בְּעָרֵיהֶם בְּכָל־מְדִינוֹת הַמֶּלֶךְ אֲחַשְׁוֵרוֹשׁ לִשְׁלֹחַ יָד בִּמְבַקְשֵׁי רָעָתָם וְאִישׁ לֹא־עָמַד לִפְנֵיהֶם כִּי־נָפַל פַּחְדָּם עַל־כָּל־הָעַמִּים:

3 Indeed, all the officials of the provinces – the satraps, the governors, and the king's stewards – showed deference to the *Yehudim*, because the fear of *Mordechai* had fallen upon them.

ג וְכָל־שָׂרֵי הַמְּדִינוֹת וְהָאֲחַשְׁדַּרְפְּנִים וְהַפַּחוֹת וְעֹשֵׂי הַמְּלָאכָה אֲשֶׁר לַמֶּלֶךְ מְנַשְּׂאִים אֶת־הַיְּהוּדִים כִּי־נָפַל פַּחַד־מָרְדֳּכַי עֲלֵיהֶם:

4 For *Mordechai* was now powerful in the royal palace, and his fame was spreading through all the provinces; the man *Mordechai* was growing ever more powerful.

ד כִּי־גָדוֹל מָרְדֳּכַי בְּבֵית הַמֶּלֶךְ וְשָׁמְעוֹ הוֹלֵךְ בְּכָל־הַמְּדִינוֹת כִּי־הָאִישׁ מָרְדֳּכַי הוֹלֵךְ וְגָדוֹל:

Esther/Esther
Chapter 9

5 So the *Yehudim* struck at their enemies with the sword, slaying and destroying; they wreaked their will upon their enemies.

6 In the fortress Shushan the *Yehudim* killed a total of five hundred men.

7 They also killed* Parshandatha, Dalphon, Aspatha,

8 Poratha, Adalia, Aridatha,

9 Parmashta, Arisai, Aridai, and Vaizatha,

10 the ten sons of Haman son of Hammedatha, the foe of the *Yehudim*. But they did not lay hands on the spoil.

11 When the number of those slain in the fortress Shushan was reported on that same day to the king,

12 the king said to Queen *Esther*, "In the fortress Shushan alone the *Yehudim* have killed a total of five hundred men, as well as the ten sons of Haman. What then must they have done in the provinces of the realm! What is your wish now? It shall be granted you. And what else is your request? It shall be fulfilled."

13 "If it please Your Majesty," *Esther* replied, "let the *Yehudim* in Shushan be permitted to act tomorrow also as they did today; and let Haman's ten sons be impaled on the stake."

14 The king ordered that this should be done, and the decree was proclaimed in Shushan. Haman's ten sons were impaled:

15 and the *Yehudim* in Shushan mustered again on the fourteenth day of *Adar* and slew three hundred men in Shushan. But they did not lay hands on the spoil.

16 The rest of the *Yehudim*, those in the king's provinces, likewise mustered and fought for their lives. They disposed of their enemies, killing seventy-five thousand of their foes; but they did not lay hands on the spoil.

---

* "They also killed" moved up from verse 10 for greater clarity

אסתר
פרק ט

ה וַיַּכּוּ הַיְּהוּדִים בְּכָל־אֹיְבֵיהֶם מַכַּת־חֶרֶב וְהֶרֶג וְאַבְדָן וַיַּעֲשׂוּ בְשֹׂנְאֵיהֶם כִּרְצוֹנָם:

ו וּבְשׁוּשַׁן הַבִּירָה הָרְגוּ הַיְּהוּדִים וְאַבֵּד חֲמֵשׁ מֵאוֹת אִישׁ:

ז וְאֵת פַּרְשַׁנְדָּתָא וְאֵת דַּלְפוֹן וְאֵת אַסְפָּתָא:

ח וְאֵת פּוֹרָתָא וְאֵת אֲדַלְיָא וְאֵת אֲרִידָתָא:

ט וְאֵת פַּרְמַשְׁתָּא וְאֵת אֲרִיסַי וְאֵת אֲרִדַי וְאֵת וַיְזָתָא:

י עֲשֶׂרֶת בְּנֵי הָמָן בֶּן־הַמְּדָתָא צֹרֵר הַיְּהוּדִים הָרָגוּ וּבַבִּזָּה לֹא שָׁלְחוּ אֶת־יָדָם:

יא בַּיּוֹם הַהוּא בָּא מִסְפַּר הַהֲרוּגִים בְּשׁוּשַׁן הַבִּירָה לִפְנֵי הַמֶּלֶךְ:

יב וַיֹּאמֶר הַמֶּלֶךְ לְאֶסְתֵּר הַמַּלְכָּה בְּשׁוּשַׁן הַבִּירָה הָרְגוּ הַיְּהוּדִים וְאַבֵּד חֲמֵשׁ מֵאוֹת אִישׁ וְאֵת עֲשֶׂרֶת בְּנֵי־הָמָן בִּשְׁאָר מְדִינוֹת הַמֶּלֶךְ מֶה עָשׂוּ וּמַה־שְּׁאֵלָתֵךְ וְיִנָּתֵן לָךְ וּמַה־בַּקָּשָׁתֵךְ עוֹד וְתֵעָשׂ:

יג וַתֹּאמֶר אֶסְתֵּר אִם־עַל־הַמֶּלֶךְ טוֹב יִנָּתֵן גַּם־מָחָר לַיְּהוּדִים אֲשֶׁר בְּשׁוּשָׁן לַעֲשׂוֹת כְּדָת הַיּוֹם וְאֵת עֲשֶׂרֶת בְּנֵי־הָמָן יִתְלוּ עַל־הָעֵץ:

יד וַיֹּאמֶר הַמֶּלֶךְ לְהֵעָשׂוֹת כֵּן וַתִּנָּתֵן דָּת בְּשׁוּשָׁן וְאֵת עֲשֶׂרֶת בְּנֵי־הָמָן תָּלוּ:

טו וַיִּקָּהֲלוּ הַיְּהוּדִיִּים [הַיְּהוּדִים] אֲשֶׁר־בְּשׁוּשָׁן גַּם בְּיוֹם אַרְבָּעָה עָשָׂר לְחֹדֶשׁ אֲדָר וַיַּהַרְגוּ בְשׁוּשָׁן שְׁלֹשׁ מֵאוֹת אִישׁ וּבַבִּזָּה לֹא שָׁלְחוּ אֶת־יָדָם:

טז וּשְׁאָר הַיְּהוּדִים אֲשֶׁר בִּמְדִינוֹת הַמֶּלֶךְ נִקְהֲלוּ וְעָמֹד עַל־נַפְשָׁם וְנוֹחַ מֵאֹיְבֵיהֶם וְהָרֹג בְּשֹׂנְאֵיהֶם חֲמִשָּׁה וְשִׁבְעִים אָלֶף וּבַבִּזָּה לֹא שָׁלְחוּ אֶת־יָדָם:

Esther/Esther
Chapter 9

אסתר
פרק ט

17 That was on the thirteenth day of the month of *Adar*; and they rested on the fourteenth day and made it a day of feasting and merrymaking.

יז בְּיוֹם־שְׁלֹשָׁה עָשָׂר לְחֹדֶשׁ אֲדָר וְנוֹחַ בְּאַרְבָּעָה עָשָׂר בּוֹ וְעָשֹׂה אֹתוֹ יוֹם מִשְׁתֶּה וְשִׂמְחָה׃

18 But the *Yehudim* in Shushan mustered on both the thirteenth and fourteenth days, and so rested on the fifteenth, and made it a day of feasting and merrymaking.)

יח וְהַיְּהוּדִיים [וְהַיְּהוּדִים] אֲשֶׁר־בְּשׁוּשָׁן נִקְהֲלוּ בִּשְׁלֹשָׁה עָשָׂר בּוֹ וּבְאַרְבָּעָה עָשָׂר בּוֹ וְנוֹחַ בַּחֲמִשָּׁה עָשָׂר בּוֹ וְעָשֹׂה אֹתוֹ יוֹם מִשְׁתֶּה וְשִׂמְחָה׃

19 That is why village *Yehudim*, who live in unwalled towns, observe the fourteenth day of the month of *Adar* and make it a day of merrymaking and feasting, and as a holiday and an occasion for sending gifts to one another.

יט עַל־כֵּן הַיְּהוּדִים הַפְּרוֹזִים [הַפְּרָזִים] הַיֹּשְׁבִים בְּעָרֵי הַפְּרָזוֹת עֹשִׂים אֵת יוֹם אַרְבָּעָה עָשָׂר לְחֹדֶשׁ אֲדָר שִׂמְחָה וּמִשְׁתֶּה וְיוֹם טוֹב וּמִשְׁלוֹחַ מָנוֹת אִישׁ לְרֵעֵהוּ׃

20 *Mordechai* recorded these events. And he sent dispatches to all the *Yehudim* throughout the provinces of King Ahasuerus, near and far,

כ וַיִּכְתֹּב מָרְדֳּכַי אֶת־הַדְּבָרִים הָאֵלֶּה וַיִּשְׁלַח סְפָרִים אֶל־כָּל־הַיְּהוּדִים אֲשֶׁר בְּכָל־מְדִינוֹת הַמֶּלֶךְ אֲחַשְׁוֵרוֹשׁ הַקְּרוֹבִים וְהָרְחוֹקִים׃

21 charging them to observe the fourteenth and fifteenth days of *Adar*, every year –

כא לְקַיֵּם עֲלֵיהֶם לִהְיוֹת עֹשִׂים אֵת יוֹם אַרְבָּעָה עָשָׂר לְחֹדֶשׁ אֲדָר וְאֵת יוֹם־חֲמִשָּׁה עָשָׂר בּוֹ בְּכָל־שָׁנָה וְשָׁנָה׃

l'-ka-YAYM a-lay-HEM lih-YOT o-SEEM AYT YOM ar-ba-AH a-SAR l'-KHO-desh a-DAR v'-AYT yom kha-mi-SHAH a-SAR BO b'-khol sha-NAH v'-sha-NAH

22 the same days on which the *Yehudim* enjoyed relief from their foes and the same month which had been transformed for them from one of grief and mourning to one of festive joy. They were to observe them as days of feasting and merrymaking, and as an occasion for sending gifts to one another and presents to the poor.

כב כַּיָּמִים אֲשֶׁר־נָחוּ בָהֶם הַיְּהוּדִים מֵאוֹיְבֵיהֶם וְהַחֹדֶשׁ אֲשֶׁר נֶהְפַּךְ לָהֶם מִיָּגוֹן לְשִׂמְחָה וּמֵאֵבֶל לְיוֹם טוֹב לַעֲשׂוֹת אוֹתָם יְמֵי מִשְׁתֶּה וְשִׂמְחָה וּמִשְׁלוֹחַ מָנוֹת אִישׁ לְרֵעֵהוּ וּמַתָּנוֹת לָאֶבְיוֹנִים׃

23 The *Yehudim* accordingly assumed as an obligation that which they had begun to practice and which *Mordechai* prescribed for them.

כג וְקִבֵּל הַיְּהוּדִים אֵת אֲשֶׁר־הֵחֵלּוּ לַעֲשׂוֹת וְאֵת אֲשֶׁר־כָּתַב מָרְדֳּכַי אֲלֵיהֶם׃

24 For Haman son of Hammedatha the Agagite, the foe of all the *Yehudim*, had plotted to destroy the *Yehudim*, and had cast pur – that is, the lot – with intent to crush and exterminate them.

כד כִּי הָמָן בֶּן־הַמְּדָתָא הָאֲגָגִי צֹרֵר כָּל־הַיְּהוּדִים חָשַׁב עַל־הַיְּהוּדִים לְאַבְּדָם וְהִפִּיל פּוּר הוּא הַגּוֹרָל לְהֻמָּם וּלְאַבְּדָם׃

Celebrating Purim in Jerusalem

9:21 To observe the fourteenth and fifteenth days of *Adar* *Purim* is the only Jewish holiday that is observed on two different days, depending on one's location. The residents of cities that were walled at the time that the Jewish people entered the Land of Israel with *Yehoshua* celebrate on the fifteenth of *Adar*, while the rest of the world celebrates on the fourteenth. Practically, the only city that celebrates Purim on the fifteenth of *Adar* is *Yerushalayim*. In establishing the holiday of *Purim*, *Esther* wanted to guarantee that the lesson of *Purim* would not be forgotten. In her time, the Children of Israel had forsaken *Yerushalayim* when they feasted at a party celebrating its destruction. Celebrating in *Yerushalayim* on a different day highlights its special status and its eternal connection to the People of Israel.

Esther/Esther
Chapter 10

25 But when [*Esther*] came before the king, he commanded: "With the promulgation of this decree, let the evil plot, which he devised against the *Yehudim*, recoil on his own head!" So they impaled him and his sons on the stake.

26 For that reason these days were named *Purim*, after pur. In view, then, of all the instructions in the said letter and of what they had experienced in that matter and what had befallen them,

27 the *Yehudim* undertook and irrevocably obligated themselves and their descendants, and all who might join them, to observe these two days in the manner prescribed and at the proper time each year.

28 Consequently, these days are recalled and observed in every generation: by every family, every province, and every city. And these days of *Purim* shall never cease among the *Yehudim*, and the memory of them shall never perish among their descendants.

29 Then Queen *Esther* daughter of *Avichayil* wrote a second letter of *Purim* for the purpose of confirming with full authority the aforementioned one of *Mordechai* the *Yehudi*.

30 Dispatches were sent to all the *Yehudim* in the hundred and twenty-seven provinces of the realm of Ahasuerus with an ordinance of "equity and honesty:"

31 These days of *Purim* shall be observed at their proper time, as *Mordechai* the *Yehudi* – and now Queen *Esther* – has obligated them to do, and just as they have assumed for themselves and their descendants the obligation of the fasts with their lamentations.

32 And *Esther*'s ordinance validating these observances of *Purim* was recorded in a scroll.

10

1 King Ahasuerus imposed tribute on the mainland and the islands.

2 All his mighty and powerful acts, and a full account of the greatness to which the king advanced *Mordechai*, are recorded in the Annals of the Kings of Media and Persia.

אסתר
פרק י

כה וּבְבֹאָהּ לִפְנֵי הַמֶּלֶךְ אָמַר עִם־הַסֵּפֶר יָשׁוּב מַחֲשַׁבְתּוֹ הָרָעָה אֲשֶׁר־חָשַׁב עַל־הַיְּהוּדִים עַל־רֹאשׁוֹ וְתָלוּ אֹתוֹ וְאֶת־בָּנָיו עַל־הָעֵץ:

כו עַל־כֵּן קָרְאוּ לַיָּמִים הָאֵלֶּה פוּרִים עַל־שֵׁם הַפּוּר עַל־כֵּן עַל־כָּל־דִּבְרֵי הָאִגֶּרֶת הַזֹּאת וּמָה־רָאוּ עַל־כָּכָה וּמָה הִגִּיעַ אֲלֵיהֶם:

כז קִיְּמוּ וקבל [וְקִבְּלוּ] הַיְּהוּדִים עֲלֵיהֶם וְעַל־זַרְעָם וְעַל כָּל־הַנִּלְוִים עֲלֵיהֶם וְלֹא יַעֲבוֹר לִהְיוֹת עֹשִׂים אֵת שְׁנֵי הַיָּמִים הָאֵלֶּה כִּכְתָבָם וְכִזְמַנָּם בְּכָל־שָׁנָה וְשָׁנָה:

כח וְהַיָּמִים הָאֵלֶּה נִזְכָּרִים וְנַעֲשִׂים בְּכָל־דּוֹר וָדוֹר מִשְׁפָּחָה וּמִשְׁפָּחָה מְדִינָה וּמְדִינָה וְעִיר וָעִיר וִימֵי הַפּוּרִים הָאֵלֶּה לֹא יַעַבְרוּ מִתּוֹךְ הַיְּהוּדִים וְזִכְרָם לֹא־יָסוּף מִזַּרְעָם:

כט וַתִּכְתֹּב אֶסְתֵּר הַמַּלְכָּה בַת־אֲבִיחַיִל וּמָרְדֳּכַי הַיְּהוּדִי אֶת־כָּל־תֹּקֶף לְקַיֵּם אֵת אִגֶּרֶת הַפּוּרִים הַזֹּאת הַשֵּׁנִית:

ל וַיִּשְׁלַח סְפָרִים אֶל־כָּל־הַיְּהוּדִים אֶל־שֶׁבַע וְעֶשְׂרִים וּמֵאָה מְדִינָה מַלְכוּת אֲחַשְׁוֵרוֹשׁ דִּבְרֵי שָׁלוֹם וֶאֱמֶת:

לא לְקַיֵּם אֶת־יְמֵי הַפֻּרִים הָאֵלֶּה בִּזְמַנֵּיהֶם כַּאֲשֶׁר קִיַּם עֲלֵיהֶם מָרְדֳּכַי הַיְּהוּדִי וְאֶסְתֵּר הַמַּלְכָּה וְכַאֲשֶׁר קִיְּמוּ עַל־נַפְשָׁם וְעַל־זַרְעָם דִּבְרֵי הַצּוֹמוֹת וְזַעֲקָתָם:

לב וּמַאֲמַר אֶסְתֵּר קִיַּם דִּבְרֵי הַפֻּרִים הָאֵלֶּה וְנִכְתָּב בַּסֵּפֶר:

י א וַיָּשֶׂם הַמֶּלֶךְ אחשרש [אֲחַשְׁוֵרוֹשׁ] מַס עַל־הָאָרֶץ וְאִיֵּי הַיָּם:

ב וְכָל־מַעֲשֵׂה תָקְפּוֹ וּגְבוּרָתוֹ וּפָרָשַׁת גְּדֻלַּת מָרְדֳּכַי אֲשֶׁר גִּדְּלוֹ הַמֶּלֶךְ הֲלוֹא־הֵם כְּתוּבִים עַל־סֵפֶר דִּבְרֵי הַיָּמִים לְמַלְכֵי מָדַי וּפָרָס:

Esther/Esther
Chapter 10

אסתר
פרק י

3 For *Mordechai* the *Yehudi* ranked next to King Ahasuerus and was highly regarded by the *Yehudim* and popular with the multitude of his brethren; he sought the good of his people and interceded for the welfare of all his kindred.

ג כִּי מָרְדֳּכַי הַיְּהוּדִי מִשְׁנֶה לַמֶּלֶךְ אֲחַשְׁוֵרוֹשׁ וְגָדוֹל לַיְּהוּדִים וְרָצוּי לְרֹב אֶחָיו דֹּרֵשׁ טוֹב לְעַמּוֹ וְדֹבֵר שָׁלוֹם לְכָל־זַרְעוֹ׃

KEE mor-d'-KHAI ha-y'-hu-DEE mish-NEH la-ME-lekh a-khash-vay-ROSH v'-ga-DOL la-y'-hu-DEEM v'-ra-TZUY l'-ROV e-KHAV do-RAYSH TOV l'-a-MO v'-do-VAYR sha-LOM l'-khol zar-O

10:3 For *Mordechai* the *Yehudi* ranked next to King Ahasuerus According to one opinion among the Sages, this verse describes two stages of *Mordechai's* life following the *Purim* miracle. He was "next to King Ahasuerus" until Darius, son of *Esther* and Ahasuerus, allowed the rebuilding of the *Beit Hamikdash*. At that point, he stepped down from his governmental position and became "highly regarded by the *Yehudim*," returning to the Land of Israel and assuming responsibility for the offerings in the *Beit Hamikdash* (see *Mishna Shekalim* 5:1). *Mordechai* did not let honor and fame stand in the way of his principles. Dismissing the glory, he jumped at the first opportunity to serve his people in *Eretz Yisrael*.

Sefer Daniel
The Book of Daniel

Introduction and commentary by Batya Markowitz

Sefer Daniel (Daniel) is the story of the People of Israel in exile, longing to return to the Land of Israel. Much of the book is even written in Aramaic, the language that was spoken in Babylonia during the seventy years of exile following the destruction of the first *Beit Hamikdash*.

The book opens with the exile of *Daniel* and his contemporaries from the Holy Land to Babylonia. There, he and his contemporaries are chosen to serve in Nebuchadnezzar's court. When *Daniel* succeeds at interpreting the king's dream, he is promoted to a high position. *Daniel* serves in the royal court throughout the reign of Nebuchadnezzar, until the downfall of Babylonia in the days of Belshazzar, Nebuchadnezzar's grandson, and retains a position of power even when Darius of Media ascends the throne.

Daniel is an extremely righteous and talented leader. When Darius's officials try to incriminate him, "they could find neither fault nor corruption, inasmuch as he was trustworthy, and no negligence or corruption was to be found in him" (Daniel 6:5). Throughout the second half of the book, *Daniel* mourns the destruction of the Temple and all the exiles that the Jews are to experience, and grieves over all the suffering they bring with them.

Sefer Daniel tells of the dangers, both physical and spiritual, encountered in the exile in foreign lands. Throughout the book, various attempts are made to sever the Jews' connection with their God and their land. *Chananya*, *Mishael* and *Azarya* are thrown into a furnace when they refuse to worship Nebuchadnezzar's idol. *Daniel* is thrown into a lions' den when he continues to pray to *Hashem* in violation of the king's decree. These righteous leaders are saved miraculously each time, showing the Jews that God has not abandoned them. This reassures the Jewish people that they are still connected to *Hashem* despite the exile, and that they will one day return to *Eretz Yisrael* as He promised.

The book is full of visions regarding the first exile, Nebuchadnezzar's reign, and all subsequent exiles until the arrival of the *Mashiach*. The Jews in exile are encouraged when they see that Nebuchadnezzar receives divine retribution for having destroyed *Yerushalayim* and the *Beit Hamikdash*. They see that the words of the prophets are indeed fulfilled when Babylonia's rule is terminated suddenly after seventy years, just as *Yirmiyahu* had predicted before they left the Land of Israel (Jeremiah 29:10). In the middle of a feast celebrating the fact that *Hashem* has forsaken the Jews in this foreign land, Belshazzar sees the "writing on the wall," showing that God has indeed calculated the seventy years, and that Babylon will be overrun by the Persian and Median empires.

The second half of the book is made up of the prophetic visions that *Daniel* received during this period. The visions are graphic and often ominous, foretelling the future exiles and suffering that the Jewish people will endure. At the same time, they are vague and obscure, allowing for various interpretations.

The medieval scholar Rabbi Yehuda Halevi writes in his philosophical work *The Kuzari*, that as a general rule, prophecy can only be received in *Eretz Yisrael*. *Daniel*, however, was able to receive prophetic visions in Babylonia because they were about, and for the sake of, *Eretz Yisrael*. They foretold the return of the Children of Israel to their homeland in the time of the second *Beit Hamikdash*, as well as their ultimate return at the end of days. These prophecies encouraged *Daniel* and the Jews of his generation, and they continue to serve as an encouragement that the God of Israel is a keeper of promises.

Throughout history, the People of Israel have been persecuted in foreign lands. *Sefer Daniel* is a study of Jewish survival in exile and the ultimate redemption.

Chart of the 70 Years of Babylonian Exile

It is well known that the Babylonian exile lasted 70 years. In fact, there were two sets of 70 years associated with the Babylonian exile and the destruction of the *Beit Hamikdash*. The following chart presents the two sets of 70 years and the relevant biblical verses relating to each. It is followed by a more detailed explanation.

70 Years	Beginning	End	Verse
Babylonian rule	605 BCE – Nebuchadnezzar defeats the Assyrians and Egyptians at the battle of Carchemish and then takes control of *Yehuda*.	538 BCE – The Babylonians fall to the Persians	Jeremiah 25:11 – And those nations shall serve the king of Babylon seventy years Ezra 1:1 – In the first year of King Cyrus of Persia, when the word of *Hashem* spoken by *Yirmiyahu* was fulfilled
Destruction of *Yerushalayim*	586 BCE – Destruction of *Yerushalayim* and the *Beit Hamikdash*	516 BCE – Construction of the second *Beit Hamikdash* is completed.	Jeremiah 29:10 – I will take note of you, and I will fulfill to you My promise of favor – to bring you back to this place Daniel 9:2 – the term of *Yerushalayim*'s desolation – seventy years

Sefer Daniel takes place during the Babylonian exile, which *Yirmiyahu* had predicted would last seventy years:

"This whole land shall be a desolate ruin. And those nations shall serve the king of Babylon seventy years. When the seventy years are over, I will punish the king of Babylon and that nation and the land of the Chaldeans for their sins – declares *Hashem* – and I will make it a desolation for all time" (Jeremiah 25:11–12).

"For thus said *Hashem*: When Babylon's seventy years are over, I will take note of you, and I will fulfill to you My promise of favor – to bring you back to this place" (Jeremiah 29:10).

Chapter 9 of *Sefer Daniel* starts with *Daniel*'s attempt to calculate the seventy years of Babylonian exile prophesied by the prophet *Yirmiyahu*:

"I, Daniel, consulted the books concerning the number of years that, according to the word of *Hashem* that had come to *Yirmiyahu* the prophet, were to be the term of *Yerushalayim*'s desolation – seventy years" (Daniel 9:2).

Many commentators, for example *Malbim*, explain that there were actually two different sets of seventy years. The first refers to seventy years of Babylonian reign. This began in the year 605 BCE, the fourth year of King *Yehoyakim*, when Nebuchadnezzar defeated the Assyrians and Egyptians in the battle at Carchemish and the Babylonians became the ruling world power, seizing control of *Yehuda* (see Jeremiah 25:1). It ended with the fall of the Babylonians to the Persians in 538 BCE. This understanding of the seventy years, as referring to seventy years of Babylonian rule, is reflected in the words of *Sefer Yirmiyahu* (25:11): "And those nations shall serve the king of Babylon seventy years." This also explains the first verse in *Sefer Ezra* which says "In the first year of King Cyrus of Persia, when the word of *Hashem* spoken by *Yirmiyahu* was fulfilled…" The defeat of the Babylonians by Cyrus of Persia marked the end of the seventy years of *Yirmiyahu*'s prophecy. Indeed, there were just about seventy years between the time that Nebuchadnezzar took control of *Yehuda* (605 BCE) until the Babylonia fell to the Persians (538 BCE). There are a number of ways of explaining the missing 3 years which are beyond the scope of this paragraph, but the simplest explanation is that the Bible often speaks in round numbers.

The second set of seventy years refers to the destruction of *Yerushalayim* and the *Beit Hamikdash*. This, according to the *Malbim*, is what *Daniel* was referring to when he said: "the term of *Yerushalayim*'s desolation – seventy years." He says that this understanding of 70 years is reflected in the words of *Yirmiyahu* (29:10): "I will take note of you, and I will fulfill to you My promise of favor – to bring you back to this place." The amount of time that passed from the destruction of *Yerushalayim* and the first *Beit Hamikdash* in 586 BCE, until the completion of the reconstruction of the second *Beit Hamikdash* in the sixth year of King Darius, 516 BCE, was indeed seventy years.

Daniel/Daniel

Chapter 1

דניאל
פרק א

1 1 In the third year of the reign of King *Yehoyakim* of *Yehuda*, King Nebuchadnezzar of Babylon came to *Yerushalayim* and laid siege to it.

א בִּשְׁנַת שָׁלוֹשׁ לְמַלְכוּת יְהוֹיָקִים מֶלֶךְ־יְהוּדָה בָּא נְבוּכַדְנֶאצַּר מֶלֶךְ־בָּבֶל יְרוּשָׁלַ͏ִם וַיָּצַר עָלֶיהָ׃

2 *Hashem* delivered King *Yehoyakim* of *Yehuda* into his power, together with some of the vessels of the House of *Hashem*, and he brought them to the land of Shinar to the house of his god; he deposited the vessels in the treasury of his god.

ב וַיִּתֵּן אֲדֹנָי בְּיָדוֹ אֶת־יְהוֹיָקִים מֶלֶךְ־יְהוּדָה וּמִקְצָת כְּלֵי בֵית־הָאֱלֹהִים וַיְבִיאֵם אֶרֶץ־שִׁנְעָר בֵּית אֱלֹהָיו וְאֶת־הַכֵּלִים הֵבִיא בֵּית אוֹצַר אֱלֹהָיו׃

> va-yi-TAYN a-do-NAI b'-ya-DO et y'-ho-ya-KEEM ME-lekh y'-hu-DAH u-mik-TZAT k'-LAY vayt ha-e-lo-HEEM vai-vee-AYM E-retz shin-AR BAYT e-lo-HAV v'-et ha-kay-LEEM hay-VEE BAYT o-TZAR e-lo-HAV

3 Then the king ordered Ashpenaz, his chief officer, to bring some Israelites of royal descent and of the nobility –

ג וַיֹּאמֶר הַמֶּלֶךְ לְאַשְׁפְּנַז רַב סָרִיסָיו לְהָבִיא מִבְּנֵי יִשְׂרָאֵל וּמִזֶּרַע הַמְּלוּכָה וּמִן־הַפַּרְתְּמִים׃

4 youths without blemish, handsome, proficient in all wisdom, knowledgeable and intelligent, and capable of serving in the royal palace – and teach them the writings and the language of the Chaldeans.

ד יְלָדִים אֲשֶׁר אֵין־בָּהֶם כָּל־מאום [מוּם] וְטוֹבֵי מַרְאֶה וּמַשְׂכִּילִים בְּכָל־חָכְמָה וְיֹדְעֵי דַעַת וּמְבִינֵי מַדָּע וַאֲשֶׁר כֹּחַ בָּהֶם לַעֲמֹד בְּהֵיכַל הַמֶּלֶךְ וּלֲלַמְּדָם סֵפֶר וּלְשׁוֹן כַּשְׂדִּים׃

5 The king allotted daily rations to them from the king's food and from the wine he drank. They were to be educated for three years, at the end of which they were to enter the king's service.

ה וַיְמַן לָהֶם הַמֶּלֶךְ דְּבַר־יוֹם בְּיוֹמוֹ מִפַּת־בַּג הַמֶּלֶךְ וּמִיֵּין מִשְׁתָּיו וּלְגַדְּלָם שָׁנִים שָׁלוֹשׁ וּמִקְצָתָם יַעַמְדוּ לִפְנֵי הַמֶּלֶךְ׃

6 Among them were the Judahites *Daniel*, *Chananya*, *Mishael* and *Azarya*.

ו וַיְהִי בָהֶם מִבְּנֵי יְהוּדָה דָּנִיֵּאל חֲנַנְיָה מִישָׁאֵל וַעֲזַרְיָה׃

7 The chief officer gave them new names; he named *Daniel* Belteshazzar, *Chananya* Shadrach, *Mishael* Meshach, and *Azarya* Abed-nego.

ז וַיָּשֶׂם לָהֶם שַׂר הַסָּרִיסִים שֵׁמוֹת וַיָּשֶׂם לְדָנִיֵּאל בֵּלְטְשַׁאצַּר וְלַחֲנַנְיָה שַׁדְרַךְ וּלְמִישָׁאֵל מֵישַׁךְ וְלַעֲזַרְיָה עֲבֵד נְגוֹ׃

8 *Daniel* resolved not to defile himself with the king's food or the wine he drank, so he sought permission of the chief officer not to defile himself,

ח וַיָּשֶׂם דָּנִיֵּאל עַל־לִבּוֹ אֲשֶׁר לֹא־יִתְגָּאַל בְּפַת־בַּג הַמֶּלֶךְ וּבְיֵין מִשְׁתָּיו וַיְבַקֵּשׁ מִשַּׂר הַסָּרִיסִים אֲשֶׁר לֹא יִתְגָּאָל׃

1:2 Hashem delivered King Yehoyakim of Yehuda into his power The exile from the Land of Israel to Babylonia happened in three stages. In the first stage, Nebuchadnezzar, king of Babylonia, deported King *Yehoyakim*, some young Judeans, and vessels from the *Beit Hamikdash*. *Hashem* hoped that the People of Israel would be shaken after this calamitous event, and that they would repent and avert further punishment. Unfortunately, the people ignored this message and were eventually exiled in two additional stages. The young Jews who arrived first in Babylonia were ultimately able to encourage their brothers who came in the subsequent rounds of exile. When the later stages of exile arrived, they found *Daniel*, *Chananya*, *Mishael*, and *Azarya*, in positions of power in the palace. This gave them the strength to survive, avoid assimilation, and not to despair of their eventual return to *Eretz Yisrael*.

Daniel/Daniel
Chapter 1

9 and *Hashem* disposed the chief officer to be kind and compassionate toward *Daniel*.

10 The chief officer said to *Daniel*, "I fear that my lord the king, who allotted food and drink to you, will notice that you look out of sorts, unlike the other youths of your age – and you will put my life in jeopardy with the king."

11 *Daniel* replied to the guard whom the chief officer had put in charge of *Daniel*, *Chananya*, *Mishael* and *Azarya*,

12 "Please test your servants for ten days, giving us legumes to eat and water to drink.

13 Then compare our appearance with that of the youths who eat of the king's food, and do with your servants as you see fit."

14 He agreed to this plan of theirs, and tested them for ten days.

15 When the ten days were over, they looked better and healthier than all the youths who were eating of the king's food.

16 So the guard kept on removing their food, and the wine they were supposed to drink, and gave them legumes.

17 *Hashem* made all four of these young men intelligent and proficient in all writings and wisdom, and *Daniel* had understanding of visions and dreams of all kinds.

18 When the time the king had set for their presentation had come, the chief officer presented them to Nebuchadnezzar.

19 The king spoke with them, and of them all none was equal to *Daniel*, *Chananya*, *Mishael* and *Azarya*; so these entered the king's service.

20 Whenever the king put a question to them requiring wisdom and understanding, he found them to be ten times better than all the magicians and exorcists throughout his realm.

21 *Daniel* was there until the first year of King Cyrus.

Daniel/Daniel
Chapter 2

דניאל
פרק ב

2 1 In the second year of the reign of Nebuchadnezzar, Nebuchadnezzar had a dream; his spirit was agitated, yet he was overcome by sleep.

א וּבִשְׁנַת שְׁתַּיִם לְמַלְכוּת נְבֻכַדְנֶצַּר חָלַם נְבֻכַדְנֶצַּר חֲלֹמוֹת וַתִּתְפָּעֶם רוּחוֹ וּשְׁנָתוֹ נִהְיְתָה עָלָיו:

2 The king ordered the magicians, exorcists, sorcerers, and Chaldeans to be summoned in order to tell the king what he had dreamed. They came and stood before the king,

ב וַיֹּאמֶר הַמֶּלֶךְ לִקְרֹא לַחַרְטֻמִּים וְלָאַשָּׁפִים וְלַמְכַשְּׁפִים וְלַכַּשְׂדִּים לְהַגִּיד לַמֶּלֶךְ חֲלֹמֹתָיו וַיָּבֹאוּ וַיַּעַמְדוּ לִפְנֵי הַמֶּלֶךְ:

3 and the king said to them, "I have had a dream and I am full of anxiety to know what I have dreamed."

ג וַיֹּאמֶר לָהֶם הַמֶּלֶךְ חֲלוֹם חָלָמְתִּי וַתִּפָּעֶם רוּחִי לָדַעַת אֶת־הַחֲלוֹם:

4 The Chaldeans spoke to the king in Aramaic, "O king, live forever! Relate the dream to your servants, and we will tell its meaning."

ד וַיְדַבְּרוּ הַכַּשְׂדִּים לַמֶּלֶךְ אֲרָמִית מַלְכָּא לְעָלְמִין חֱיִי אֱמַר חֶלְמָא לעבדיך [לְעַבְדָּךְ] וּפִשְׁרָא נְחַוֵּא:

5 The king said in reply to the Chaldeans, "I hereby decree: If you will not make the dream and its meaning known to me, you shall be torn limb from limb and your houses confiscated.

ה עָנֵה מַלְכָּא וְאָמַר לכשדיא [לְכַשְׂדָּאֵי] מִלְּתָא מִנִּי אַזְדָּא הֵן לָא תְהוֹדְעוּנַּנִי חֶלְמָא וּפִשְׁרֵהּ הַדָּמִין תִּתְעַבְדוּן וּבָתֵּיכוֹן נְוָלִי יִתְּשָׂמוּן:

6 But if you tell the dream and its meaning, you shall receive from me gifts, presents, and great honor; therefore, tell me the dream and its meaning."

ו וְהֵן חֶלְמָא וּפִשְׁרֵהּ תְּהַחֲוֹן מַתְּנָן וּנְבִזְבָּה וִיקָר שַׂגִּיא תְּקַבְּלוּן מִן־קֳדָמָי לָהֵן חֶלְמָא וּפִשְׁרֵהּ הַחֲוֹנִי:

7 Once again they answered, "Let the king relate the dream to his servants, and we will tell its meaning."

ז עֲנוֹ תִנְיָנוּת וְאָמְרִין מַלְכָּא חֶלְמָא יֵאמַר לְעַבְדוֹהִי וּפִשְׁרָה נְהַחֲוֵה:

8 The king said in reply, "It is clear to me that you are playing for time, since you see that I have decreed

ח עָנֵה מַלְכָּא וְאָמַר מִן־יַצִּיב יָדַע אֲנָה דִּי עִדָּנָא אַנְתּוּן זָבְנִין כָּל־קֳבֵל דִּי חֲזֵיתוֹן דִּי אַזְדָּא מִנִּי מִלְּתָא:

9 that if you do not make the dream known to me, there is but one verdict for you. You have conspired to tell me something false and fraudulent until circumstances change; so relate the dream to me, and I will then know that you can tell its meaning."

ט דִּי הֵן־חֶלְמָא לָא תְהוֹדְעֻנַּנִי חֲדָה־הִיא דָתְכוֹן וּמִלָּה כִדְבָה וּשְׁחִיתָה הִזְמִנְתּוּן [הִזְדְּמִנְתּוּן] לְמֵאמַר קָדָמַי עַד דִּי עִדָּנָא יִשְׁתַּנֵּא לָהֵן חֶלְמָא אֱמַרוּ לִי וְאִנְדַּע דִּי פִשְׁרֵהּ תְּהַחֲוֻנַּנִי:

10 The Chaldeans said in reply to the king, "There is no one on earth who can satisfy the king's demand, for great king or ruler – none has ever asked such a thing of any magician, exorcist, or Chaldean.

י עֲנוֹ כשדיא [כַשְׂדָּאֵי] קֳדָם־מַלְכָּא וְאָמְרִין לָא־אִיתַי אֱנָשׁ עַל־יַבֶּשְׁתָּא דִּי מִלַּת מַלְכָּא יוּכַל לְהַחֲוָיָה כָּל־קֳבֵל דִּי כָּל־מֶלֶךְ רַב וְשַׁלִּיט מִלָּה כִדְנָה לָא שְׁאֵל לְכָל־חַרְטֹם וְאָשַׁף וְכַשְׂדָּי:

11 The thing asked by the king is difficult; there is no one who can tell it to the king except the gods whose abode is not among mortals."

יא וּמִלְּתָא דִי־מַלְכָּה שָׁאֵל יַקִּירָה וְאָחֳרָן לָא אִיתַי דִּי יְחַוִּנַּהּ קֳדָם מַלְכָּא לָהֵן אֱלָהִין דִּי מְדָרְהוֹן עִם־בִּשְׂרָא לָא אִיתוֹהִי:

12 Whereupon the king flew into a violent rage, and gave an order to do away with all the wise men of Babylon.

יב כָּל־קֳבֵל דְּנָה מַלְכָּא בְּנַס וּקְצַף שַׂגִּיא וַאֲמַר לְהוֹבָדָה לְכֹל חַכִּימֵי בָבֶל:

Daniel/Daniel
Chapter 2

דניאל
פרק ב

13 The decree condemning the wise men to death was issued. *Daniel* and his companions were about to be put to death

יג וְדָתָא נֶפְקַת וְחַכִּימַיָּא מִתְקַטְּלִין וּבְעוֹ דָּנִיֵּאל וְחַבְרוֹהִי לְהִתְקְטָלָה:

14 when *Daniel* remonstrated with Arioch, the captain of the royal guard who had set out to put the wise men of Babylon to death.

יד בֵּאדַיִן דָּנִיֵּאל הֲתִיב עֵטָא וּטְעֵם לְאַרְיוֹךְ רַב־טַבָּחַיָּא דִּי מַלְכָּא דִּי נְפַק לְקַטָּלָה לְחַכִּימֵי בָּבֶל:

15 He spoke up and said to Arioch, the royal officer, "Why is the decree of the king so urgent?" Thereupon Arioch informed *Daniel* of the matter.

טו עָנֵה וְאָמַר לְאַרְיוֹךְ שַׁלִּיטָא דִּי־מַלְכָּא עַל־מָה דָתָא מְהַחְצְפָה מִן־קֳדָם מַלְכָּא אֱדַיִן מִלְּתָא הוֹדַע אַרְיוֹךְ לְדָנִיֵּאל:

16 So *Daniel* went to ask the king for time, that he might tell the meaning to the king.

טז וְדָנִיֵּאל עַל וּבְעָה מִן־מַלְכָּא דִּי זְמָן יִנְתֵּן־לֵהּ וּפִשְׁרָא לְהַחֲוָיָה לְמַלְכָּא:

17 Then *Daniel* went to his house and informed his companions, *Chananya*, *Mishael*, and *Azarya*, of the matter,

יז אֱדַיִן דָּנִיֵּאל לְבַיְתֵהּ אֲזַל וְלַחֲנַנְיָה מִישָׁאֵל וַעֲזַרְיָה חַבְרוֹהִי מִלְּתָא הוֹדַע:

18 that they might implore the God of Heaven for help regarding this mystery, so that *Daniel* and his colleagues would not be put to death together with the other wise men of Babylon.

יח וְרַחֲמִין לְמִבְעֵא מִן־קֳדָם אֱלָהּ שְׁמַיָּא עַל־רָזָה דְּנָה דִּי לָא יְהֹבְדוּן דָּנִיֵּאל וְחַבְרוֹהִי עִם־שְׁאָר חַכִּימֵי בָבֶל:

19 The mystery was revealed to *Daniel* in a night vision; then *Daniel* blessed the God of Heaven.

יט אֱדַיִן לְדָנִיֵּאל בְּחֶזְוָא דִי־לֵילְיָא רָזָה גֲלִי אֱדַיִן דָּנִיֵּאל בָּרִךְ לֶאֱלָהּ שְׁמַיָּא:

20 *Daniel* spoke up and said: "Let the name of *Hashem* be blessed forever and ever, For wisdom and power are His.

כ עָנֵה דָנִיֵּאל וְאָמַר לֶהֱוֵא שְׁמֵהּ דִּי־אֱלָהָא מְבָרַךְ מִן־עָלְמָא וְעַד־עָלְמָא דִּי חָכְמְתָא וּגְבוּרְתָא דִּי לֵהּ־הִיא:

21 He changes times and seasons, Removes kings and installs kings; He gives the wise their wisdom And knowledge to those who know.

כא וְהוּא מְהַשְׁנֵא עִדָּנַיָּא וְזִמְנַיָּא מְהַעְדֵּה מַלְכִין וּמְהָקֵים מַלְכִין יָהֵב חָכְמְתָא לְחַכִּימִין וּמַנְדְּעָא לְיָדְעֵי בִינָה:

22 He reveals deep and hidden things, Knows what is in the darkness, And light dwells with Him.

כב הוּא גָּלֵא עַמִּיקָתָא וּמְסַתְּרָתָא יָדַע מָה בַחֲשׁוֹכָא וּנְהִירָא [וּנְהוֹרָא] עִמֵּהּ שְׁרֵא:

23 I acknowledge and praise You, O God of my fathers, You who have given me wisdom and power, For now You have let me know what we asked of You; You have let us know what concerns the king."

כג לָךְ אֱלָהּ אֲבָהָתִי מְהוֹדֵא וּמְשַׁבַּח אֲנָה דִּי חָכְמְתָא וּגְבוּרְתָא יְהַבְתְּ לִי וּכְעַן הוֹדַעְתַּנִי דִּי־בְעֵינָא מִנָּךְ דִּי־מִלַּת מַלְכָּא הוֹדַעְתֶּנָא:

24 Thereupon *Daniel* went to Arioch, whom the king had appointed to do away with the wise men of Babylon; he came and said to him as follows, "Do not do away with the wise men of Babylon; bring me to the king and I will tell the king the meaning!"

כד כָּל־קֳבֵל דְּנָה דָּנִיֵּאל עַל עַל־אַרְיוֹךְ דִּי מַנִּי מַלְכָּא לְהוֹבָדָה לְחַכִּימֵי בָבֶל אֲזַל וְכֵן אֲמַר־לֵהּ לְחַכִּימֵי בָבֶל אַל־תְּהוֹבֵד הַעֵלְנִי קֳדָם מַלְכָּא וּפִשְׁרָא לְמַלְכָּא אֲחַוֵּא:

25 So Arioch rushed *Daniel* into the king's presence and said to him, "I have found among the exiles of *Yehuda* a man who can make the meaning known to the king!"

כה אֱדַיִן אַרְיוֹךְ בְּהִתְבְּהָלָה הַנְעֵל לְדָנִיֵּאל קֳדָם מַלְכָּא וְכֵן אֲמַר־לֵהּ דִּי־הַשְׁכַּחַת גְּבַר מִן־בְּנֵי גָלוּתָא דִּי יְהוּד דִּי פִשְׁרָא לְמַלְכָּא יְהוֹדַע:

Daniel/Daniel
Chapter 2

דניאל
פרק ב

26 The king said in reply to *Daniel* (who was called Belteshazzar), "Can you really make known to me the dream that I saw and its meaning?"

כו עָנֵה מַלְכָּא וְאָמַר לְדָנִיֵּאל דִּי שְׁמֵהּ בֵּלְטְשַׁאצַּר הַאִיתָיךְ [הַאִיתָךְ] כָּהֵל לְהוֹדָעֻתַנִי חֶלְמָא דִי־חֲזֵית וּפִשְׁרֵהּ:

27 *Daniel* answered the king and said, "The mystery about which the king has inquired – wise men, exorcists, magicians, and diviners cannot tell to the king.

כז עָנֵה דָנִיֵּאל קֳדָם מַלְכָּא וְאָמַר רָזָה דִּי־מַלְכָּא שָׁאֵל לָא חַכִּימִין אָשְׁפִין חַרְטֻמִּין גָּזְרִין יָכְלִין לְהַחֲוָיָה לְמַלְכָּא:

28 But there is a *Hashem* in heaven who reveals mysteries, and He has made known to King Nebuchadnezzar what is to be at the end of days. This is your dream and the vision that entered your mind in bed:

כח בְּרַם אִיתַי אֱלָהּ בִּשְׁמַיָּא גָּלֵא רָזִין וְהוֹדַע לְמַלְכָּא נְבוּכַדְנֶצַּר מָה דִּי לֶהֱוֵא בְּאַחֲרִית יוֹמַיָּא חֶלְמָךְ וְחֶזְוֵי רֵאשָׁךְ עַל־מִשְׁכְּבָךְ דְּנָה הוּא:

29 O king, the thoughts that came to your mind in your bed are about future events; He who reveals mysteries has let you know what is to happen.

כט אַנְתְּה מַלְכָּא רַעְיוֹנָךְ עַל־מִשְׁכְּבָךְ סְלִקוּ מָה דִּי לֶהֱוֵא אַחֲרֵי דְנָה וְגָלֵא רָזַיָּא הוֹדְעָךְ מָה־דִי לֶהֱוֵא:

30 Not because my wisdom is greater than that of other creatures has this mystery been revealed to me, but in order that the meaning should be made known to the king, and that you may know the thoughts of your mind.

ל וַאֲנָה לָא בְחָכְמָה דִּי־אִיתַי בִּי מִן־כָּל־חַיַּיָּא רָזָא דְנָה גֱּלִי לִי לָהֵן עַל־דִּבְרַת דִּי פִשְׁרָא לְמַלְכָּא יְהוֹדְעוּן וְרַעְיוֹנֵי לִבְבָךְ תִּנְדַּע:

31 "O king, as you looked on, there appeared a great statue. This statue, which was huge and its brightness surpassing, stood before you, and its appearance was awesome.

לא אַנְתְּה מַלְכָּא חָזֵה הֲוַיְתָ וַאֲלוּ צְלֵם חַד שַׂגִּיא צַלְמָא דִּכֵּן רַב וְזִיוֵהּ יַתִּיר קָאֵם לְקָבְלָךְ וְרֵוֵהּ דְּחִיל:

32 The head of that statue was of fine gold; its breast and arms were of silver; its belly and thighs, of bronze;

לב הוּא צַלְמָא רֵאשֵׁהּ דִּי־דְהַב טָב חֲדוֹהִי וּדְרָעוֹהִי דִּי כְסַף מְעוֹהִי וְיַרְכָתֵהּ דִּי נְחָשׁ:

33 its legs were of iron, and its feet part iron and part clay.

לג שָׁקוֹהִי דִּי פַרְזֶל רַגְלוֹהִי מִנְּהוֹן [מִנְּהֵין] דִּי פַרְזֶל וּמִנְּהוֹן [וּמִנְּהֵין] דִּי חֲסַף:

34 As you looked on, a stone was hewn out, not by hands, and struck the statue on its feet of iron and clay and crushed them.

לד חָזֵה הֲוַיְתָ עַד דִּי הִתְגְּזֶרֶת אֶבֶן דִּי־לָא בִידַיִן וּמְחָת לְצַלְמָא עַל־רַגְלוֹהִי דִּי פַרְזְלָא וְחַסְפָּא וְהַדֵּקֶת הִמּוֹן:

35 All at once, the iron, clay, bronze, silver, and gold were crushed, and became like chaff of the threshing floors of summer; a wind carried them off until no trace of them was left. But the stone that struck the statue became a great mountain and filled the whole earth.

לה בֵּאדַיִן דָּקוּ כַחֲדָה פַּרְזְלָא חַסְפָּא נְחָשָׁא כַּסְפָּא וְדַהֲבָא וַהֲווֹ כְּעוּר מִן־אִדְּרֵי־קַיִט וּנְשָׂא הִמּוֹן רוּחָא וְכָל־אֲתַר לָא־הִשְׁתְּכַח לְהוֹן וְאַבְנָא דִּי־מְחָת לְצַלְמָא הֲוָת לְטוּר רַב וּמְלָת כָּל־אַרְעָא:

36 "Such was the dream, and we will now tell the king its meaning.

לו דְּנָה חֶלְמָא וּפִשְׁרֵהּ נֵאמַר קֳדָם־מַלְכָּא:

37 You, O king – king of kings, to whom the God of Heaven has given kingdom, power, might, and glory;

לז אַנְתְּה מַלְכָּא מֶלֶךְ מַלְכַיָּא דִּי אֱלָהּ שְׁמַיָּא מַלְכוּתָא חִסְנָא וְתָקְפָּא וִיקָרָא יְהַב־לָךְ:

Daniel/Daniel
Chapter 2

דניאל
פרק ב

38 into whose hands He has given men, wild beasts, and the fowl of heaven, wherever they may dwell; and to whom He has given dominion over them all – you are the head of gold.

לח וּבְכָל־דִּי דָארִין [דָיְרִין] בְּנֵי־אֲנָשָׁא חֵיוַת בָּרָא וְעוֹף־שְׁמַיָּא יְהַב בִּידָךְ וְהַשְׁלְטָךְ בְּכָלְּהוֹן אַנְתְּה־הוּא רֵאשָׁה דִּי דַהֲבָא:

39 But another kingdom will arise after you, inferior to yours; then yet a third kingdom, of bronze, which will rule over the whole earth.

לט וּבָתְרָךְ תְּקוּם מַלְכוּ אָחֳרִי אֲרַעא מִנָּךְ וּמַלְכוּ תְלִיתָיא [תְלִיתָאָה] אָחֳרִי דִּי נְחָשָׁא דִּי תִשְׁלַט בְּכָל־אַרְעָא:

40 But the fourth kingdom will be as strong as iron; just as iron crushes and shatters everything – and like iron that smashes – so will it crush and smash all these.

מ וּמַלְכוּ רְבִיעָיה [רְבִיעָאָה] תֶּהֱוֵא תַּקִּיפָה כְּפַרְזְלָא כָּל־קֳבֵל דִּי פַרְזְלָא מְהַדֵּק וְחָשֵׁל כֹּלָּא וּכְפַרְזְלָא דִּי־מְרַעַע כָּל־אִלֵּין תַּדִּק וְתֵרֹעַ:

41 You saw the feet and the toes, part potter's clay and part iron; that means it will be a divided kingdom; it will have only some of the stability of iron, inasmuch as you saw iron mixed with common clay.

מא וְדִי־חֲזַיְתָה רַגְלַיָּא וְאֶצְבְּעָתָא מִנְּהוֹן [מִנְּהֵן] חֲסַף דִּי־פֶחָר וּמִנְּהוֹן [וּמִנְּהֵין] פַּרְזֶל מַלְכוּ פְלִיגָה תֶּהֱוֵה וּמִן־נִצְבְּתָא דִּי פַרְזְלָא לֶהֱוֵא־בַהּ כָּל־קֳבֵל דִּי חֲזַיְתָה פַּרְזְלָא מְעָרַב בַּחֲסַף טִינָא:

42 And the toes were part iron and part clay; that [means] the kingdom will be in part strong and in part brittle.

מב וְאֶצְבְּעָת רַגְלַיָּא מִנְּהוֹן [מִנְּהֵין] פַּרְזֶל וּמִנְּהוֹן [וּמִנְּהֵין] חֲסַף מִן־קְצָת מַלְכוּתָא תֶּהֱוֵה תַקִּיפָה וּמִנַּהּ תֶּהֱוֵה תְבִירָה:

43 You saw iron mixed with common clay; that means: they shall intermingle with the offspring of men, but shall not hold together, just as iron does not mix with clay.

מג דִּי [וְדִי] חֲזַיְתָ פַּרְזְלָא מְעָרַב בַּחֲסַף טִינָא מִתְעָרְבִין לֶהֱוֹן בִּזְרַע אֲנָשָׁא וְלָא־לֶהֱוֹן דָּבְקִין דְּנָה עִם־דְּנָה הֵא־כְדִי פַרְזְלָא לָא מִתְעָרַב עִם־חַסְפָּא:

44 And in the time of those kings, the God of Heaven will establish a kingdom that shall never be destroyed, a kingdom that shall not be transferred to another people. It will crush and wipe out all these kingdoms, but shall itself last forever –

מד וּבְיוֹמֵיהוֹן דִּי מַלְכַיָּא אִנּוּן יְקִים אֱלָהּ שְׁמַיָּא מַלְכוּ דִּי לְעָלְמִין לָא תִתְחַבַּל וּמַלְכוּתָה לְעַם אָחֳרָן לָא תִשְׁתְּבִק תַּדִּק וְתָסֵיף כָּל־אִלֵּין מַלְכְוָתָא וְהִיא תְּקוּם לְעָלְמַיָּא:

45 just as you saw how a stone was hewn from the mountain, not by hands, and crushed the iron, bronze, clay, silver, and gold. The great *Hashem* has made known to the king what will happen in the future. The dream is sure and its interpretation reliable."

מה כָּל־קֳבֵל דִּי־חֲזַיְתָ דִּי מִטּוּרָא אִתְגְּזֶרֶת אֶבֶן דִּי־לָא בִידַיִן וְהַדֶּקֶת פַּרְזְלָא נְחָשָׁא חַסְפָּא כַּסְפָּא וְדַהֲבָא אֱלָהּ רַב הוֹדַע לְמַלְכָּא מָה דִּי לֶהֱוֵא אַחֲרֵי דְנָה וְיַצִּיב חֶלְמָא וּמְהֵימַן פִּשְׁרֵהּ:

kol ko-VAYL dee kha-ZAI-ta DEE mi-tu-RA it-g'-ZE-ret E-ven dee LA vee-DA-yin v'-ha-DE-ket par-z'-LA n'-kha-SHA khas-PA kas-PA v'-da-ha-VA e-LAH RAV ho-DA l'-mal-KA MAH DEE le-he-VAY a-kha-RAY d'-NAH v'-ya-TZEEV khel-MA um-hay-MAN pish-RAY

2:45 A stone was hewn from the mountain, not by hands Nebuchadnezzar dreams of a statue whose body is comprised of various metals. This dream is a preview of world history. The metals correspond to

Daniel/Daniel
Chapter 3

46 Then King Nebuchadnezzar prostrated himself and paid homage to *Daniel* and ordered that a meal offering and pleasing offerings be made to him.

47 The king said in reply to *Daniel*, "Truly your God must be the God of gods and Lord of kings and the revealer of mysteries to have enabled you to reveal this mystery."

48 The king then elevated *Daniel* and gave him very many gifts, and made him governor of the whole province of Babylon and chief prefect of all the wise men of Babylon.

49 At *Daniel*'s request, the king appointed Shadrach, Meshach, and Abednego to administer the province of Babylon; while *Daniel* himself was at the king's court.

3 1 King Nebuchadnezzar made a statue of gold sixty *amot* high and six *amot* broad. He set it up in the plain of Dura in the province of Babylon.

2 King Nebuchadnezzar then sent word to gather the satraps, prefects, governors, counselors, treasurers, judges, officers, and all the provincial officials to attend the dedication of the statue that King Nebuchadnezzar had set up.

3 So the satraps, prefects, governors, counselors, treasurers, judges, officers, and all the provincial officials assembled for the dedication of the statue that King Nebuchadnezzar had set up, and stood before the statue that Nebuchadnezzar had set up.

4 The herald proclaimed in a loud voice, "You are commanded, O peoples and nations of every language,

---

דניאל
פרק ג

מו בֵּאדַיִן מַלְכָּא נְבוּכַדְנֶצַּר נְפַל עַל־אַנְפּוֹהִי וּלְדָנִיֵּאל סְגִד וּמִנְחָה וְנִיחֹחִין אֲמַר לְנַסָּכָה לֵהּ:

מז עָנֵה מַלְכָּא לְדָנִיֵּאל וְאָמַר מִן־קְשֹׁט דִּי אֱלָהֲכוֹן הוּא אֱלָהּ אֱלָהִין וּמָרֵא מַלְכִין וְגָלֵה רָזִין דִּי יְכֵלְתָּ לְמִגְלֵא רָזָה דְנָה:

מח אֱדַיִן מַלְכָּא לְדָנִיֵּאל רַבִּי וּמַתְּנָן רַבְרְבָן שַׂגִּיאָן יְהַב־לֵהּ וְהַשְׁלְטֵהּ עַל כָּל־מְדִינַת בָּבֶל וְרַב־סִגְנִין עַל כָּל־חַכִּימֵי בָבֶל:

מט וְדָנִיֵּאל בְּעָא מִן־מַלְכָּא וּמַנִּי עַל עֲבִידְתָּא דִּי מְדִינַת בָּבֶל לְשַׁדְרַךְ מֵישַׁךְ וַעֲבֵד נְגוֹ וְדָנִיֵּאל בִּתְרַע מַלְכָּא:

ג א נְבוּכַדְנֶצַּר מַלְכָּא עֲבַד צְלֵם דִּי־דְהַב רוּמֵהּ אַמִּין שִׁתִּין פְּתָיֵהּ אַמִּין שֵׁת אֲקִימֵהּ בְּבִקְעַת דּוּרָא בִּמְדִינַת בָּבֶל:

ב וּנְבוּכַדְנֶצַּר מַלְכָּא שְׁלַח לְמִכְנַשׁ לַאֲחַשְׁדַּרְפְּנַיָּא סִגְנַיָּא וּפַחֲוָתָא אֲדַרְגָּזְרַיָּא גְדָבְרַיָּא דְּתָבְרַיָּא תִּפְתָּיֵא וְכֹל שִׁלְטֹנֵי מְדִינָתָא לְמֵתֵא לַחֲנֻכַּת צַלְמָא דִּי הֲקֵים נְבוּכַדְנֶצַּר מַלְכָּא:

ג בֵּאדַיִן מִתְכַּנְּשִׁין אֲחַשְׁדַּרְפְּנַיָּא סִגְנַיָּא וּפַחֲוָתָא אֲדַרְגָּזְרַיָּא גְדָבְרַיָּא דְּתָבְרַיָּא תִּפְתָּיֵא וְכֹל שִׁלְטֹנֵי מְדִינָתָא לַחֲנֻכַּת צַלְמָא דִּי הֲקֵים נְבוּכַדְנֶצַּר מַלְכָּא וְקָאֲמִין [וְקָיְמִין] לָקֳבֵל צַלְמָא דִּי הֲקֵים נְבוּכַדְנֶצַּר:

ד וְכָרוֹזָא קָרֵא בְחָיִל לְכוֹן אָמְרִין עַמְמַיָּא אֻמַּיָּא וְלִשָּׁנַיָּא:

Rabbi Yitzchak Abarbanel (1437–1508)

the four main world powers: The head, made of gold, corresponds to Babylonia, the first kingdom to rule the entire known world and defeat the nation of Israel. The chest and arms, fashioned from silver, is symbolic of the Persian-Median empire which defeats the Babylonians. The bronze stomach and thighs represent the Greeks, and the iron legs symbolize the Romans. The clay toes allude to the fact that at the end of the final exile, the Arabs will gain power. As the vision continues, a rock cut from the mountain hits the toes, which symbolizes Israel and the rule of *Mashiach*. According to Rabbi Yitzchak Abarbanel, the rock is cut from the mountain without human intervention, teaching that the final redemption will come about directly from *Hashem*.

Daniel/Daniel
Chapter 3

5 when you hear the sound of the horn, pipe, zither, lyre, psaltery, bagpipe, and all other types of instruments, to fall down and worship the statue of gold that King Nebuchadnezzar has set up.

6 Whoever will not fall down and worship shall at once be thrown into a burning fiery furnace."

7 And so, as soon as all the peoples heard the sound of the horn, pipe, zither, lyre, psaltery, and all other types of instruments, all peoples and nations of every language fell down and worshiped the statue of gold that King Nebuchadnezzar had set up.

8 Seizing the occasion, certain Chaldeans came forward to slander the *Yehudim*.

9 They spoke up and said to King Nebuchadnezzar, "O king, live forever!

10 You, O king, gave an order that everyone who hears the horn, pipe, zither, lyre, psaltery, bagpipe, and all types of instruments must fall down and worship the golden statue,

11 and whoever does not fall down and worship shall be thrown into a burning fiery furnace.

12 There are certain *Yehudim* whom you appointed to administer the province of Babylon, Shadrach, Meshach, and Abed-nego; those men pay no heed to you, O king; they do not serve your god or worship the statue of gold that you have set up."

13 Then Nebuchadnezzar, in raging fury, ordered Shadrach, Meshach, and Abed-nego to be brought; so those men were brought before the king.

14 Nebuchadnezzar spoke to them and said, "Is it true, Shadrach, Meshach, and Abed-nego, that you do not serve my god or worship the statue of gold that I have set up?

15 Now if you are ready to fall down and worship the statue that I have made when you hear the sound of the horn, pipe, zither, lyre, psaltery, and bagpipe, and all other types of instruments, [well and good]; but if you will not worship, you shall at once

דניאל
פרק ג

ה בְּעִדָּנָא דִּי־תִשְׁמְעוּן קָל קַרְנָא מַשְׁרוֹקִיתָא קִיתָרוֹס [קַתְרוֹס] סַבְּכָא פְּסַנְתֵּרִין סוּמְפֹּנְיָה וְכֹל זְנֵי זְמָרָא תִּפְּלוּן וְתִסְגְּדוּן לְצֶלֶם דַּהֲבָא דִּי הֲקֵים נְבוּכַדְנֶצַּר מַלְכָּא:

ו וּמַן־דִּי־לָא יִפֵּל וְיִסְגֻּד בַּהּ־שַׁעֲתָא יִתְרְמֵא לְגוֹא־אַתּוּן נוּרָא יָקִדְתָּא:

ז כָּל־קֳבֵל דְּנָה בֵּהּ־זִמְנָא כְּדִי שָׁמְעִין כָּל־עַמְמַיָּא קָל קַרְנָא מַשְׁרוֹקִיתָא קִיתָרֹס [קַתְרוֹס] שַׂבְּכָא פְּסַנְטֵרִין וְכֹל זְנֵי זְמָרָא נָפְלִין כָּל־עַמְמַיָּא אֻמַּיָּא וְלִשָּׁנַיָּא סָגְדִין לְצֶלֶם דַּהֲבָא דִּי הֲקֵים נְבוּכַדְנֶצַּר מַלְכָּא:

ח כָּל־קֳבֵל דְּנָה בֵּהּ־זִמְנָא קְרִבוּ גֻּבְרִין כַּשְׂדָּאִין וַאֲכַלוּ קַרְצֵיהוֹן דִּי יְהוּדָיֵא:

ט עֲנוֹ וְאָמְרִין לִנְבוּכַדְנֶצַּר מַלְכָּא מַלְכָּא לְעָלְמִין חֱיִי:

י אנתה [אַנְתְּ] מַלְכָּא שָׂמְתָּ טְעֵם דִּי כָל־אֱנָשׁ דִּי־יִשְׁמַע קָל קַרְנָא מַשְׁרֹקִיתָא קִיתָרֹס [קַתְרוֹס] שַׂבְּכָא פְּסַנְתֵּרִין וסיפניה [וְסוּמְפֹּנְיָה] וְכֹל זְנֵי זְמָרָא יִפֵּל וְיִסְגֻּד לְצֶלֶם דַּהֲבָא:

יא וּמַן־דִּי־לָא יִפֵּל וְיִסְגֻּד יִתְרְמֵא לְגוֹא־אַתּוּן נוּרָא יָקִדְתָּא:

יב אִיתַי גֻּבְרִין יְהוּדָאיִן דִּי־מַנִּיתָ יָתְהוֹן עַל־עֲבִידַת מְדִינַת בָּבֶל שַׁדְרַךְ מֵישַׁךְ וַעֲבֵד נְגוֹ גֻּבְרַיָּא אִלֵּךְ לָא־שָׂמוּ עליך [עֲלָךְ] מַלְכָּא טְעֵם לֵאלָהָיִךְ [לֵאלָהָךְ] לָא פָלְחִין וּלְצֶלֶם דַּהֲבָא דִּי הֲקֵימְתָּ לָא סָגְדִין:

יג בֵּאדַיִן נְבוּכַדְנֶצַּר בִּרְגַז וַחֲמָה אֲמַר לְהַיְתָיָה לְשַׁדְרַךְ מֵישַׁךְ וַעֲבֵד נְגוֹ בֵּאדַיִן גֻּבְרַיָּא אִלֵּךְ הֵיתָיוּ קֳדָם מַלְכָּא:

יד עָנֵה נְבֻכַדְנֶצַּר וְאָמַר לְהוֹן הַצְדָּא שַׁדְרַךְ מֵישַׁךְ וַעֲבֵד נְגוֹ לֵאלָהַי לָא אִיתֵיכוֹן פָּלְחִין וּלְצֶלֶם דַּהֲבָא דִּי הֲקֵימֶת לָא סָגְדִין:

טו כְּעַן הֵן אִיתֵיכוֹן עֲתִידִין דִּי בְעִדָּנָא דִּי־תִשְׁמְעוּן קָל קַרְנָא מַשְׁרוֹקִיתָא קִיתָרֹס [קַתְרוֹס] שַׂבְּכָא פְּסַנְתֵּרִין וְסוּמְפֹּנְיָה וְכֹל זְנֵי זְמָרָא תִּפְּלוּן וְתִסְגְּדוּן לְצַלְמָא דִי־עַבְדֵת וְהֵן לָא תִסְגְּדוּן בַּהּ־שַׁעֲתָה

Daniel / דניאל
Chapter 3 / פרק ג

be thrown into a burning fiery furnace, and what god is there that can save you from my power?"

16 Shadrach, Meshach, and Abed-nego said in reply to the king, "O Nebuchadnezzar, we have no need to answer you in this matter,

17 for if so it must be, our God whom we serve is able to save us from the burning fiery furnace, and He will save us from your power, O king.

18 But even if He does not, be it known to you, O king, that we will not serve your god or worship the statue of gold that you have set up."

19 Nebuchadnezzar was so filled with rage at Shadrach, Meshach, and Abed-nego that his visage was distorted, and he gave an order to heat up the furnace to seven times its usual heat.

20 He commanded some of the strongest men of his army to bind Shadrach, Meshach, and Abed-nego, and to throw them into the burning fiery furnace.

21 So these men, in their shirts, trousers, hats, and other garments, were bound and thrown into the burning fiery furnace.

22 Because the king's order was urgent, and the furnace was heated to excess, a tongue of flame killed the men who carried up Shadrach, Meshach, and Abed-nego.

23 But those three men, Shadrach, Meshach, and Abed-nego, dropped, bound, into the burning fiery furnace.

24 Then King Nebuchadnezzar was astonished and, rising in haste, addressed his companions, saying, "Did we not throw three men, bound, into the fire?" They spoke in reply, "Surely, O king."

25 He answered, "But I see four men walking about unbound and unharmed in the fire and the fourth looks like a divine being."

תִּתְרְמוֹן לְגוֹא־אַתּוּן נוּרָא יָקִדְתָּא וּמַן־הוּא אֱלָהּ דֵּי יְשֵׁיזְבִנְכוֹן מִן־יְדָי:

טז עֲנוֹ שַׁדְרַךְ מֵישַׁךְ וַעֲבֵד נְגוֹ וְאָמְרִין לְמַלְכָּא נְבוּכַדְנֶצַּר לָא־חַשְׁחִין אֲנַחְנָה עַל־דְּנָה פִּתְגָם לַהֲתָבוּתָךְ:

יז הֵן אִיתַי אֱלָהַנָא דִּי־אֲנַחְנָא פָלְחִין יָכִל לְשֵׁיזָבוּתַנָא מִן־אַתּוּן נוּרָא יָקִדְתָּא וּמִן־יְדָךְ מַלְכָּא יְשֵׁיזִב:

יח וְהֵן לָא יְדִיעַ לֶהֱוֵא־לָךְ מַלְכָּא דִּי לֵאלָהָיךְ [לֵאלָהָךְ] לָא־אִיתַינָא [אִיתַנָא] פָלְחִין וּלְצֶלֶם דַּהֲבָא דִּי הֲקֵימְתָּ לָא נִסְגֻּד:

יט בֵּאדַיִן נְבוּכַדְנֶצַּר הִתְמְלִי חֱמָא וּצְלֵם אַנְפּוֹהִי אשתנו [אֶשְׁתַּנִּי] עַל־שַׁדְרַךְ מֵישַׁךְ וַעֲבֵד נְגוֹ עָנֵה וְאָמַר לְמֵזֵא לְאַתּוּנָא חַד־שִׁבְעָה עַל דִּי חֲזֵה לְמֵזְיֵהּ:

כ וּלְגֻבְרִין גִּבָּרֵי־חַיִל דִּי בְחַיְלֵהּ אֲמַר לְכַפָּתָה לְשַׁדְרַךְ מֵישַׁךְ וַעֲבֵד נְגוֹ לְמִרְמֵא לְאַתּוּן נוּרָא יָקִדְתָּא:

כא בֵּאדַיִן גֻּבְרַיָּא אִלֵּךְ כְּפִתוּ בְּסַרְבָּלֵיהוֹן פטישיהון [פַּטְּשֵׁיהוֹן] וְכַרְבְּלָתְהוֹן וּלְבֻשֵׁיהוֹן וּרְמִיו לְגוֹא־אַתּוּן נוּרָא יָקִדְתָּא:

כב כָּל־קֳבֵל דְּנָה מִן־דִּי מִלַּת מַלְכָּא מַחְצְפָה וְאַתּוּנָא אֵזֵה יַתִּירָא גֻּבְרַיָּא אִלֵּךְ דִּי הַסִּקוּ לְשַׁדְרַךְ מֵישַׁךְ וַעֲבֵד נְגוֹ קַטִּל הִמּוֹן שְׁבִיבָא דִּי נוּרָא:

כג וְגֻבְרַיָּא אִלֵּךְ תְּלָתֵּהוֹן שַׁדְרַךְ מֵישַׁךְ וַעֲבֵד נְגוֹ נְפַלוּ לְגוֹא־אַתּוּן־נוּרָא יָקִדְתָּא מְכַפְּתִין:

כד אֱדַיִן נְבוּכַדְנֶצַּר מַלְכָּא תְּוַהּ וְקָם בְּהִתְבְּהָלָה עָנֵה וְאָמַר לְהַדָּבְרוֹהִי הֲלָא גֻבְרִין תְּלָתָא רְמֵינָא לְגוֹא־נוּרָא מְכַפְּתִין עָנַיִן וְאָמְרִין לְמַלְכָּא יַצִּיבָא מַלְכָּא:

כה עָנֵה וְאָמַר הָא־אֲנָה חָזֵה גֻּבְרִין אַרְבְּעָה שְׁרַיִן מַהְלְכִין בְּגוֹא־נוּרָא וַחֲבָל לָא־אִיתַי בְּהוֹן וְרֵוֵהּ דִּי רביעיא [רְבִיעָאָה] דָּמֵה לְבַר־אֱלָהִין:

Daniel/Daniel
Chapter 3

דניאל
פרק ג

26 Nebuchadnezzar then approached the hatch of the burning fiery furnace and called, "Shadrach, Meshach, Abed-nego, servants of the Most High *Hashem*, come out!" So Shadrach, Meshach, and Abed-nego came out of the fire.

כו בֵּאדַיִן קְרֵב נְבוּכַדְנֶצַּר לִתְרַע אַתּוּן נוּרָא יָקִדְתָּא עָנֵה וְאָמַר שַׁדְרַךְ מֵישַׁךְ וַעֲבֵד־נְגוֹ עַבְדוֹהִי דִּי־אֱלָהָא עליא [עִלָּאָה] פֻּקוּ וֶאֱתוֹ בֵּאדַיִן נָפְקִין שַׁדְרַךְ מֵישַׁךְ וַעֲבֵד נְגוֹ מִן־גּוֹא נוּרָא:

27 The satraps, the prefects, the governors, and the royal companions gathered around to look at those men, on whose bodies the fire had had no effect, the hair of whose heads had not been singed, whose shirts looked no different, to whom not even the odor of fire clung.

כז וּמִתְכַּנְּשִׁין אֲחַשְׁדַּרְפְּנַיָּא סִגְנַיָּא וּפַחֲוָתָא וְהַדָּבְרֵי מַלְכָּא חָזַיִן לְגֻבְרַיָּא אִלֵּךְ דִּי לָא־שְׁלֵט נוּרָא בְּגֶשְׁמְהוֹן וּשְׂעַר רֵאשְׁהוֹן לָא הִתְחָרַךְ וְסָרְבָּלֵיהוֹן לָא שְׁנוֹ וְרֵיחַ נוּר לָא עֲדָת בְּהוֹן:

28 Nebuchadnezzar spoke up and said, "Blessed be the God of Shadrach, Meshach, and Abed-nego, who sent His angel to save His servants who, trusting in Him, flouted the king's decree at the risk of their lives rather than serve or worship any god but their own *Hashem*.

כח עָנֵה נְבוּכַדְנֶצַּר וְאָמַר בְּרִיךְ אֱלָהֲהוֹן דִּי־שַׁדְרַךְ מֵישַׁךְ וַעֲבֵד נְגוֹ דִּי־שְׁלַח מַלְאֲכֵהּ וְשֵׁיזִב לְעַבְדוֹהִי דִּי הִתְרְחִצוּ עֲלוֹהִי וּמִלַּת מַלְכָּא שַׁנִּיו וִיהַבוּ גשמיהון [גֶשְׁמְהוֹן] דִּי לָא־יִפְלְחוּן וְלָא־יִסְגְּדוּן לְכָל־אֱלָהּ לָהֵן לֵאלָהֲהוֹן:

29 I hereby give an order that [anyone of] any people or nation of whatever language who blasphemes the God of Shadrach, Meshach, and Abed-nego shall be torn limb from limb, and his house confiscated, for there is no other God who is able to save in this way."

כט וּמִנִּי שִׂים טְעֵם דִּי כָל־עַם אֻמָּה וְלִשָּׁן דִּי־יֵאמַר שלה [שָׁלוּ] עַל אֱלָהֲהוֹן דִּי־שַׁדְרַךְ מֵישַׁךְ וַעֲבֵד נְגוֹא הַדָּמִין יִתְעֲבֵד וּבַיְתֵהּ נְוָלִי יִשְׁתַּוֵּה כָּל־קֳבֵל דִּי לָא אִיתַי אֱלָהּ אָחֳרָן דִּי־יִכֻּל לְהַצָּלָה כִּדְנָה:

30 Thereupon the king promoted Shadrach, Meshach, and Abed-nego in the province of Babylon.

ל בֵּאדַיִן מַלְכָּא הַצְלַח לְשַׁדְרַךְ מֵישַׁךְ וַעֲבֵד נְגוֹ בִּמְדִינַת בָּבֶל:

bay-DA-yin mal-KA hatz-LAKH l'-shad-RAKH may-SHAKH va-a-VAYD n'-GO bim-dee-NAT ba-VEL

31 "King Nebuchadnezzar to all people and nations of every language that inhabit the whole earth: May your well-being abound!

לא נְבוּכַדְנֶצַּר מַלְכָּא לְכָל־עַמְמַיָּא אֻמַּיָּא וְלִשָּׁנַיָּא דִּי־דארין [דָיְרִין] בְּכָל־אַרְעָא שְׁלָמְכוֹן יִשְׂגֵּא:

3:30 The king promoted Shadrach, Meshach, and Abed-nego These are the Babylonian names of *Chananya*, *Mishael*, and *Azarya*, given to them by the Babylonian chief of officers after they arrived from Israel (1:7). This reference is the last time that *Chananya*, *Mishael*, and *Azarya* are mentioned in *Sefer Daniel*. One opinion in the Talmud (*Sanhedrin* 83a) suggests that this is because they returned to the Land of Israel. They were motivated practically by their fear of Nebuchadnezzar and what he may do to them next. In addition, they had been elevated spiritually by the miraculous deliverance from the fiery furnace and could no longer tolerate the impurities of Babylonia. Once in Israel, *Chananya*, *Mishael*, and *Azarya* learned *Torah* from *Yehoshua* the high priest, married and raised families. This incident contains a message for Jews throughout the ages: When the environment gets hostile in foreign countries, *Eretz Yisrael* provides a safe haven for the Jews. This is true today more than ever, when Jews living outside of Israel still suffer from anti-Semitism. As Prime Minister Golda Meir said about the State of Israel, "Above all, this country is our own. Nobody has to get up in the morning and worry what his neighbors think of him. Being a Jew is no problem here."

Prime Minister Golda Meir (1898–1978)

Daniel/Daniel
Chapter 4

32 The signs and wonders that the Most High *Hashem* has worked for me I am pleased to relate.

33 How great are His signs; how mighty His wonders! His kingdom is an everlasting kingdom, and His dominion endures throughout the generations."

4 1 I, Nebuchadnezzar, was living serenely in my house, flourishing in my palace.

2 I had a dream that frightened me, and my thoughts in bed and the vision of my mind alarmed me.

3 I gave an order to bring all the wise men of Babylon before me to let me know the meaning of the dream.

4 The magicians, exorcists, Chaldeans, and diviners came, and I related the dream to them, but they could not make its meaning known to me.

5 Finally, *Daniel*, called Belteshazzar after the name of my god, in whom the spirit of the holy gods was, came to me, and I related the dream to him, [saying],

6 "Belteshazzar, chief magician, in whom I know the spirit of the holy gods to be, and whom no mystery baffles, tell me the meaning of my dream vision that I have seen.

7 In the visions of my mind in bed I saw a tree of great height in the midst of the earth;

8 The tree grew and became mighty; Its top reached heaven, And it was visible to the ends of the earth.

9 Its foliage was beautiful And its fruit abundant; There was food for all in it. Beneath it the beasts of the field found shade, And the birds of the sky dwelt on its branches; All creatures fed on it.

10 In the vision of my mind in bed, I looked and saw a holy Watcher coming down from heaven.

11 He called loudly and said: 'Hew down the tree, lop off its branches, Strip off its foliage, scatter its fruit. Let the beasts of the field flee from beneath it And the birds from its branches,

12 But leave the stump with its roots in the ground. In fetters of iron and bronze Let him be drenched with the dew of heaven, And share earth's verdure with the beasts.

Daniel/Daniel
Chapter 4

13 Let his mind be altered from that of a man, And let him be given the mind of a beast, And let seven seasons pass over him.

14 This sentence is decreed by the Watchers; This verdict is commanded by the Holy Ones So that all creatures may know That the Most High is sovereign over the realm of man, And He gives it to whom He wishes And He may set over it even the lowest of men.'

15 "I, King Nebuchadnezzar, had this dream; now you, Belteshazzar, tell me its meaning, since all the wise men of my kingdom are not able to make its meaning known to me, but you are able, for the spirit of the holy gods is in you."

16 Then *Daniel*, called Belteshazzar, was perplexed for a while, and alarmed by his thoughts. The king addressed him, "Let the dream and its meaning not alarm you." Belteshazzar replied, "My lord, would that the dream were for your enemy and its meaning for your foe!

17 The tree that you saw grow and become mighty, whose top reached heaven, which was visible throughout the earth,

18 whose foliage was beautiful, whose fruit was so abundant that there was food for all in it, beneath which the beasts of the field dwelt, and in whose branches the birds of the sky lodged –

19 it is you, O king, you who have grown and become mighty, whose greatness has grown to reach heaven, and whose dominion is to the end of the earth.

20 The holy Watcher whom the king saw descend from heaven and say, Hew down the tree and destroy it, But leave the stump with its roots in the ground. In fetters of iron and bronze In the grass of the field, Let him be drenched with the dew of heaven, And share the lot of the beasts of the field Until seven seasons pass over him –

21 this is its meaning, O king; it is the decree of the Most High which has overtaken my lord the king.

דניאל
פרק ד

יג לִבְבֵהּ מִן־אנושא [אֲנָשָׁא] יְשַׁנּוֹן וּלְבַב חֵיוָה יִתְיְהִב לֵהּ וְשִׁבְעָה עִדָּנִין יַחְלְפוּן עֲלוֹהִי:

יד בִּגְזֵרַת עִירִין פִּתְגָמָא וּמֵאמַר קַדִּישִׁין שְׁאֵלְתָא עַד־דִּבְרַת דִּי יִנְדְּעוּן חַיַּיָּא דִּי־שַׁלִּיט עליא [עִלָּאָה] בְּמַלְכוּת אנושא [אֲנָשָׁא] וּלְמַן־דִּי יִצְבֵּא יִתְּנִנַּהּ וּשְׁפַל אֲנָשִׁים יְקִים עליה [עֲלַהּ]:

טו דְּנָה חֶלְמָא חֲזֵית אֲנָה מַלְכָּא נְבוּכַדְנֶצַּר ואנתה [וְאַנְתְּ] בֵּלְטְשַׁאצַּר פִּשְׁרֵא אֱמַר כָּל־קֳבֵל דִּי כָּל־חַכִּימֵי מַלְכוּתִי לָא־יָכְלִין פִּשְׁרָא לְהוֹדָעֻתַנִי ואנתה [וְאַנְתְּ] כָּהֵל דִּי רוּחַ־אֱלָהִין קַדִּישִׁין בָּךְ:

טז אֱדַיִן דָּנִיֵּאל דִּי־שְׁמֵהּ בֵּלְטְשַׁאצַּר אֶשְׁתּוֹמַם כְּשָׁעָה חֲדָה וְרַעְיֹנֹהִי יְבַהֲלֻנֵּהּ עָנֵה מַלְכָּא וְאָמַר בֵּלְטְשַׁאצַּר חֶלְמָא וּפִשְׁרֵא אַל־יְבַהֲלָךְ עָנֵה בֵלְטְשַׁאצַּר וְאָמַר מראי [מָרִי] חֶלְמָא לשנאיך [לְשָׂנְאָךְ] וּפִשְׁרֵהּ לעריך [לְעָרָךְ]:

יז אִילָנָא דִּי חֲזַיְתָ דִּי רְבָה וּתְקִף וְרוּמֵהּ יִמְטֵא לִשְׁמַיָּא וַחֲזוֹתֵהּ לְכָל־אַרְעָא:

יח וְעָפְיֵהּ שַׁפִּיר וְאִנְבֵּהּ שַׂגִּיא וּמָזוֹן לְכֹלָּא־בֵהּ תְּחֹתוֹהִי תְּדוּר חֵיוַת בָּרָא וּבְעַנְפוֹהִי יִשְׁכְּנָן צִפֲּרֵי שְׁמַיָּא:

יט אנתה־[אַנְתְּ־] הוּא מַלְכָּא דִּי רְבַית וּתְקֵפְתְּ וּרְבוּתָךְ רְבָת וּמְטָת לִשְׁמַיָּא וְשָׁלְטָנָךְ לְסוֹף אַרְעָא:

כ וְדִי חֲזָה מַלְכָּא עִיר וְקַדִּישׁ נָחִת מִן־שְׁמַיָּא וְאָמַר גֹּדּוּ אִילָנָא וְחַבְּלוּהִי בְּרַם עִקַּר שָׁרְשׁוֹהִי בְּאַרְעָא שְׁבֻקוּ וּבֶאֱסוּר דִּי־פַרְזֶל וּנְחָשׁ בְּדִתְאָא דִּי בָרָא וּבְטַל שְׁמַיָּא יִצְטַבַּע וְעִם־חֵיוַת בָּרָא חֲלָקֵהּ עַד דִּי־שִׁבְעָה עִדָּנִין יַחְלְפוּן עֲלוֹהִי:

כא דְּנָה פִשְׁרָא מַלְכָּא וּגְזֵרַת עליא [עִלָּאָה] הִיא דִּי מְטָת עַל־מראי [מָרִי] מַלְכָּא:

1894

Daniel/Daniel
Chapter 4
דניאל
פרק ד

22 You will be driven away from men and have your habitation with the beasts of the field. You will be fed grass like cattle, and be drenched with the dew of heaven; seven seasons will pass over you until you come to know that the Most High is sovereign over the realm of man, and He gives it to whom He wishes.

כב וְלָךְ טָרְדִין מִן־אֲנָשָׁא וְעִם־חֵיוַת בָּרָא לֶהֱוֵה מְדֹרָךְ וְעִשְׂבָּא כְתוֹרִין לָךְ יְטַעֲמוּן וּמִטַּל שְׁמַיָּא לָךְ מְצַבְּעִין וְשִׁבְעָה עִדָּנִין יַחְלְפוּן עֲלָיִךְ עַד דִּי־תִנְדַּע דִּי־שַׁלִּיט עִלָּיָא בְּמַלְכוּת אֲנָשָׁא וּלְמַן־דִּי יִצְבֵּא יִתְּנִנַּהּ:

23 And the meaning of the command to leave the stump of the tree with its roots is that the kingdom will remain yours from the time you come to know that Heaven is sovereign.

כג וְדִי אֲמַרוּ לְמִשְׁבַּק עִקַּר שָׁרְשׁוֹהִי דִּי אִילָנָא מַלְכוּתָךְ לָךְ קַיָּמָה מִן־דִּי תִנְדַּע דִּי שַׁלִּטִן שְׁמַיָּא:

24 Therefore, O king, may my advice be acceptable to you: Redeem your sins by beneficence and your iniquities by generosity to the poor; then your serenity may be extended."

כד לָהֵן מַלְכָּא מִלְכִּי יִשְׁפַּר עֲלָיִךְ [עֲלָךְ] וַחֲטָיָיךְ [וַחֲטָאָךְ] בְּצִדְקָה פְרֻק וַעֲוָיָתָךְ בְּמִחַן עֲנָיִן הֵן תֶּהֱוֵא אַרְכָה לִשְׁלֵוְתָךְ:

25 All this befell King Nebuchadnezzar.

כה כֹּלָּא מְּטָא עַל־נְבוּכַדְנֶצַּר מַלְכָּא:

26 Twelve months later, as he was walking on the roof of the royal palace at Babylon,

כו לִקְצָת יַרְחִין תְּרֵי־עֲשַׂר עַל־הֵיכַל מַלְכוּתָא דִּי בָבֶל מְהַלֵּךְ הֲוָה:

27 the king exclaimed, "There is great Babylon, which I have built by my vast power to be a royal residence for the glory of my majesty!"

כז עָנֵה מַלְכָּא וְאָמַר הֲלָא דָא־הִיא בָּבֶל רַבְּתָא דִּי־אֲנָה בֱנַיְתַהּ לְבֵית מַלְכוּ בִּתְקָף חִסְנִי וְלִיקָר הַדְרִי:

28 The words were still on the king's lips, when a voice fell from heaven, "It has been decreed for you, O King Nebuchadnezzar: The kingdom has passed out of your hands.

כח עוֹד מִלְּתָא בְּפֻם מַלְכָּא קָל מִן־שְׁמַיָּא נְפַל לָךְ אָמְרִין נְבוּכַדְנֶצַּר מַלְכָּא מַלְכוּתָה עֲדָת מִנָּךְ:

29 You are being driven away from men, and your habitation is to be with the beasts of the field. You are to be fed grass like cattle, and seven seasons will pass over you until you come to know that the Most High is sovereign over the realm of man and He gives it to whom He wishes."

כט וּמִן־אֲנָשָׁא לָךְ טָרְדִין וְעִם־חֵיוַת בָּרָא מְדֹרָךְ עִשְׂבָּא כְתוֹרִין לָךְ יְטַעֲמוּן וְשִׁבְעָה עִדָּנִין יַחְלְפוּן עֲלָיִךְ [עֲלָךְ] עַד דִּי־תִנְדַּע דִּי־שַׁלִּיט עִלָּיָא בְּמַלְכוּת אֲנָשָׁא וּלְמַן־דִּי יִצְבֵּא יִתְּנִנַּהּ:

u-min a-na-SHA LAKH ta-r'-DEEN v'-eem khay-VAT ba-RA m'-do-RAKH is-BA kh'-to-REEN LAKH y'-ta-a-MUN v'-shiv-AH i-da-NEEN yakh-l'-FUN a-LAKH AD dee tin-DA dee sha-LEET i-la-YA b'-mal-KHUT a-na-SHA ul-man DEE yitz-BAY yit-ni-NAH

4:29 And seven seasons will pass over you In this verse, Nebuchadnezzar is told that he will live with animals and act like a beast for a period of seven seasons. One explanation for this, suggested by the Sages, is that this is a punishment for the way he destroyed *Yerushalayim* and the *Beit Hamikdash*. Although *Hashem* had foretold that the destruction would take place, Nebuchadnezzar did much more than execute God's will. While he was meant to exile the People of Israel, he also killed many of them and treated them inhumanely. Furthermore, in addition to burning the *Beit Hamikdash*, he also destroyed the earth of *Eretz Yisrael* so that nothing could grow there for seven years. In retribution for his animalistic cruelty to the people and the land, Nebuchadnezzar actually became an animal for seven seasons. His punishment is a lesson about the sensitivity one must show to the People of Israel and the Land of Israel.

Daniel/Daniel
Chapter 5

דניאל
פרק ה

30 There and then the sentence was carried out upon Nebuchadnezzar. He was driven away from men, he ate grass like cattle, and his body was drenched with the dew of heaven until his hair grew like eagle's [feathers] and his nails like [the talons of] birds.

ל בַּהּ־שַׁעֲתָא מִלְּתָא סָפַת עַל־נְבוּכַדְנֶצַּר וּמִן־אֲנָשָׁא טְרִיד וְעִשְׂבָּא כְתוֹרִין יֵאכֻל וּמִטַּל שְׁמַיָּא גִּשְׁמֵהּ יִצְטַבַּע עַד דִּי שַׂעְרֵהּ כְּנִשְׁרִין רְבָה וְטִפְרוֹהִי כְצִפְּרִין:

31 "When the time had passed, I, Nebuchadnezzar, lifted my eyes to heaven, and my reason was restored to me. I blessed the Most High, and praised and glorified the Ever-Living One, Whose dominion is an everlasting dominion And whose kingdom endures throughout the generations.

לא וְלִקְצָת יוֹמַיָּה אֲנָה נְבוּכַדְנֶצַּר עַיְנַי לִשְׁמַיָּא נִטְלֵת וּמַנְדְּעִי עֲלַי יְתוּב וּלְעִלָּאָה [וּלְעִלָּאָה] בָּרְכֵת וּלְחַי עָלְמָא שַׁבְּחֵת וְהַדְּרֵת דִּי שָׁלְטָנֵהּ שָׁלְטָן עָלַם וּמַלְכוּתֵהּ עִם־דָּר וְדָר:

32 All the inhabitants of the earth are of no account. He does as He wishes with the host of heaven, And with the inhabitants of the earth. There is none to stay His hand Or say to Him, 'What have You done?'

לב וְכָל־דָּאֲרֵי [דָּיְרֵי] אַרְעָא כְּלָה חֲשִׁיבִין וּכְמִצְבְּיֵהּ עָבֵד בְּחֵיל שְׁמַיָּא וְדָארֵי [וְדָיְרֵי] אַרְעָא וְלָא אִיתַי דִּי־יְמַחֵא בִידֵהּ וְיֵאמַר לֵהּ מָה עֲבַדְתְּ:

33 There and then my reason was restored to me, and my majesty and splendor were restored to me for the glory of my kingdom. My companions and nobles sought me out, and I was reestablished over my kingdom, and added greatness was given me.

לג בֵּהּ־זִמְנָא מַנְדְּעִי יְתוּב עֲלַי וְלִיקַר מַלְכוּתִי הַדְרִי וְזִוִי יְתוּב עֲלַי וְלִי הַדָּבְרַי וְרַבְרְבָנַי יְבַעוֹן וְעַל־מַלְכוּתִי הָתְקְנַת וּרְבוּ יַתִּירָה הוּסְפַת לִי:

34 So now I, Nebuchadnezzar, praise, exalt, and glorify the King of Heaven, all of whose works are just and whose ways are right, and who is able to humble those who behave arrogantly."

לד כְּעַן אֲנָה נְבוּכַדְנֶצַּר מְשַׁבַּח וּמְרוֹמֵם וּמְהַדַּר לְמֶלֶךְ שְׁמַיָּא דִּי כָל־מַעֲבָדוֹהִי קְשֹׁט וְאֹרְחָתֵהּ דִּין וְדִי מַהְלְכִין בְּגֵוָה יָכִל לְהַשְׁפָּלָה:

5 1 King Belshazzar gave a great banquet for his thousand nobles, and in the presence of the thousand he drank wine.

ה א בֵּלְשַׁאצַּר מַלְכָּא עֲבַד לְחֶם רַב לְרַבְרְבָנוֹהִי אֲלַף וְלָקֳבֵל אַלְפָּא חַמְרָא שָׁתֵה:

bayl-sha-TZAR mal-KA a-vad l'-KHEM RAV l'-rav-r'-va-NO-hee a-LAF v'-la-ko-VAYL al-PA kham-RA sha-TAY

5:1 King Belshazzar gave a great banquet Years before, *Yirmiyahu* issued his famous prophecy that Babylonia would rule over the Jews for seventy years (Jeremiah 29:10). *Malbim* comments that according to Belshazzar's calculations, these seventy years have now elapsed and he is still in power. He therefore throws a feast to mark this milestone, and uses the holy vessels from the *Beit Hamikdash* in *Yerushalayim* to further illustrate this point (verse 2). *Hashem* responds with the famous writing that appears on the wall during the feast, and by morning, Belshazzar is dead. Rabbi Yitzchak Abrabanel adds that this incident plants much hope in the hearts of the People of Israel, who realize that God can turn events around in an instant. He coordinates everything and is precise in His calculations. The Jews of *Daniel*'s time witness that those who mistreat them will ultimately pay for their actions.

Malbim
(1809–1879)

Daniel/Daniel
Chapter 5

דניאל
פרק ה

2 Under the influence of the wine, Belshazzar ordered the gold and silver vessels that his father Nebuchadnezzar had taken out of the temple at *Yerushalayim* to be brought so that the king and his nobles, his consorts, and his concubines could drink from them.

ב בֵּלְשַׁאצַּר אֲמַר בִּטְעֵם חַמְרָא לְהַיְתָיָה לְמָאנֵי דַּהֲבָא וְכַסְפָּא דִּי הַנְפֵּק נְבוּכַדְנֶצַּר אֲבוּהִי מִן־הֵיכְלָא דִּי בִירוּשְׁלֶם וְיִשְׁתּוֹן בְּהוֹן מַלְכָּא וְרַבְרְבָנוֹהִי שֵׁגְלָתֵהּ וּלְחֵנָתֵהּ:

3 The golden vessels that had been taken out of the sanctuary of the House of *Hashem* in *Yerushalayim* were then brought, and the king, his nobles, his consorts, and his concubines drank from them.

ג בֵּאדַיִן הַיְתִיו מָאנֵי דַהֲבָא דִּי הַנְפִּקוּ מִן־הֵיכְלָא דִּי־בֵית אֱלָהָא דִּי בִירוּשְׁלֶם וְאִשְׁתִּיו בְּהוֹן מַלְכָּא וְרַבְרְבָנוֹהִי שֵׁגְלָתֵהּ וּלְחֵנָתֵהּ:

4 They drank wine and praised the gods of gold and silver, bronze, iron, wood, and stone.

ד אִשְׁתִּיו חַמְרָא וְשַׁבַּחוּ לֵאלָהֵי דַּהֲבָא וְכַסְפָּא נְחָשָׁא פַרְזְלָא אָעָא וְאַבְנָא:

5 Just then, the fingers of a human hand appeared and wrote on the plaster of the wall of the king's palace opposite the lampstand, so that the king could see the hand as it wrote.

ה בַּהּ־שַׁעֲתָה נְפַקוּ [נְפַקָה] אֶצְבְּעָן דִּי יַד־אֱנָשׁ וְכָתְבָן לָקֳבֵל נֶבְרַשְׁתָּא עַל־גִּירָא דִּי־כְתַל הֵיכְלָא דִּי מַלְכָּא וּמַלְכָּא חָזֵה פַּס יְדָה דִּי כָתְבָה:

6 The king's face darkened, and his thoughts alarmed him; the joints of his loins were loosened and his knees knocked together.

ו אֱדַיִן מַלְכָּא זִיוֹהִי שְׁנוֹהִי וְרַעְיֹנֹהִי יְבַהֲלוּנֵּהּ וְקִטְרֵי חַרְצֵהּ מִשְׁתָּרַיִן וְאַרְכֻבָּתֵהּ דָּא לְדָא נָקְשָׁן:

7 The king called loudly for the exorcists, Chaldeans, and diviners to be brought. The king addressed the wise men of Babylon, "Whoever can read this writing and tell me its meaning shall be clothed in purple and wear a golden chain on his neck, and shall rule as one of three in the kingdom."

ז קָרֵא מַלְכָּא בְּחַיִל לְהֶעָלָה לְאָשְׁפַיָּא כַשְׂדָּיֵא [כַּשְׂדָּאֵי] וְגָזְרַיָּא עָנֵה מַלְכָּא וְאָמַר לְחַכִּימֵי בָבֶל דִּי כָל־אֱנָשׁ דִּי־יִקְרֵה כְּתָבָה דְנָה וּפִשְׁרֵהּ יְחַוִּנַּנִי אַרְגְּוָנָא יִלְבַּשׁ וְהַמּוֹנְכָא [וְהַמְנִיכָא] דִי־דַהֲבָא עַל־צַוְּארֵהּ וְתַלְתִּי בְמַלְכוּתָא יִשְׁלַט:

8 Then all the king's wise men came, but they could not read the writing or make known its meaning to the king.

ח אֱדַיִן עללין [עָלִּין] כֹּל חַכִּימֵי מַלְכָּא וְלָא־כָהֲלִין כְּתָבָא לְמִקְרֵא וּפִשְׁרָא [וּפִשְׁרֵהּ] לְהוֹדָעָה לְמַלְכָּא:

9 King Belshazzar grew exceedingly alarmed and his face darkened, and his nobles were dismayed.

ט אֱדַיִן מַלְכָּא בֵלְשַׁאצַּר שַׂגִּיא מִתְבָּהַל וְזִיוֹהִי שָׁנַיִן עֲלוֹהִי וְרַבְרְבָנוֹהִי מִשְׁתַּבְּשִׁין:

10 Because of the state of the king and his nobles, the queen came to the banquet hall. The queen spoke up and said, "O king, live forever! Let your thoughts not alarm you or your face darken.

י מַלְכְּתָא לָקֳבֵל מִלֵּי מַלְכָּא וְרַבְרְבָנוֹהִי לְבֵית מִשְׁתְּיָא עללת [עַלַּת] עֲנָת מַלְכְּתָא וַאֲמֶרֶת מַלְכָּא לְעָלְמִין חֱיִי אַל־יְבַהֲלוּךְ רַעְיוֹנָךְ וְזִיוָיךְ אַל־יִשְׁתַּנּוֹ:

11 There is a man in your kingdom who has the spirit of the holy gods in him; in your father's time, illumination, understanding, and wisdom like that of the gods were to be found in him, and your father, King Nebuchadnezzar, appointed him chief of the magicians, exorcists, Chaldeans, and diviners.

יא אִיתַי גְּבַר בְּמַלְכוּתָךְ דִּי רוּחַ אֱלָהִין קַדִּישִׁין בֵּהּ וּבְיוֹמֵי אֲבוּךְ נַהִירוּ וְשָׂכְלְתָנוּ וְחָכְמָה כְּחָכְמַת־אֱלָהִין הִשְׁתְּכַחַת בֵּהּ וּמַלְכָּא נְבֻכַדְנֶצַּר אֲבוּךְ רַב חַרְטֻמִּין אָשְׁפִין כַּשְׂדָּאִין גָּזְרִין הֲקִימֵהּ אֲבוּךְ מַלְכָּא:

Daniel/Daniel
Chapter 5

דניאל
פרק ה

יב כָּל־קֳבֵל דִּי רוּחַ יַתִּירָה וּמַנְדַּע וְשָׂכְלְתָנוּ מְפַשַּׁר חֶלְמִין וַאֲחַוָיַת אֲחִידָן וּמְשָׁרֵא קִטְרִין הִשְׁתְּכַחַת בֵּהּ בְּדָנִיֵּאל דִּי־מַלְכָּא שָׂם־שְׁמֵהּ בֵּלְטְשַׁאצַּר כְּעַן דָּנִיֵּאל יִתְקְרֵי וּפִשְׁרָה יְהַחֲוֵה:

12 Seeing that there is to be found in *Daniel* (whom the king called Belteshazzar) extraordinary spirit, knowledge, and understanding to interpret dreams, to explain riddles and solve problems, let *Daniel* now be called to tell the meaning [of the writing]."

יג בֵּאדַיִן דָּנִיֵּאל הֻעַל קֳדָם מַלְכָּא עָנֵה מַלְכָּא וְאָמַר לְדָנִיֵּאל אנתה־[אַנְתְּ־] הוּא דָנִיֵּאל דִּי־מִן־בְּנֵי גָלוּתָא דִּי יְהוּד דִּי הַיְתִי מַלְכָּא אַבִי מִן־יְהוּד:

13 *Daniel* was then brought before the king. The king addressed *Daniel*, "You are *Daniel*, one of the exiles of *Yehuda* whom my father, the king, brought from *Yehuda*.

יד וְשִׁמְעֵת עליך [עֲלָךְ] דִּי רוּחַ אֱלָהִין בָּךְ וְנַהִירוּ וְשָׂכְלְתָנוּ וְחָכְמָה יַתִּירָה הִשְׁתְּכַחַת בָּךְ:

14 I have heard about you that you have the spirit of the gods in you, and that illumination, knowledge, and extraordinary wisdom are to be found in you.

טו וּכְעַן הֻעַלּוּ קָדָמַי חַכִּימַיָּא אָשְׁפַיָּא דִּי־כְתָבָה דְנָה יִקְרוֹן וּפִשְׁרֵהּ לְהוֹדָעֻתַנִי וְלָא־כָהֲלִין פְּשַׁר־מִלְּתָא לְהַחֲוָיָה:

15 Now the wise men and exorcists have been brought before me to read this writing and to make known its meaning to me. But they could not tell what it meant.

טז וַאֲנָה שִׁמְעֵת עליך [עֲלָךְ] דִּי־תוכל [תִיכּוּל] פִּשְׁרִין לְמִפְשַׁר וְקִטְרִין לְמִשְׁרֵא כְּעַן הֵן תוכל [תִּכוּל] כְּתָבָא לְמִקְרֵא וּפִשְׁרֵהּ לְהוֹדָעֻתַנִי אַרְגְּוָנָא תִלְבַּשׁ והמונכא [וְהַמְנִיכָא] דִי־דַהֲבָא עַל־צַוְּארָךְ וְתַלְתָּא בְמַלְכוּתָא תִּשְׁלַט:

16 I have heard about you, that you can give interpretations and solve problems. Now if you can read the writing and make known its meaning to me, you shall be clothed in purple and wear a golden chain on your neck and rule as one of three in the kingdom."

יז בֵּאדַיִן עָנֵה דָנִיֵּאל וְאָמַר קֳדָם מַלְכָּא מַתְּנָתָךְ לָךְ לֶהֶוְיָן וּנְבָזְבְּיָתָךְ לְאָחֳרָן הַב בְּרַם כְּתָבָא אֶקְרֵא לְמַלְכָּא וּפִשְׁרָא אֲהוֹדְעִנֵּהּ:

17 Then *Daniel* said in reply to the king, "You may keep your gifts for yourself, and give your presents to others. But I will read the writing for the king, and make its meaning known to him.

יח אנתה [אַנְתְּ] מַלְכָּא אֱלָהָא עליא [עִלָּאָה] מַלְכוּתָא וּרְבוּתָא וִיקָרָא וְהַדְרָה יְהַב לִנְבֻכַדְנֶצַּר אֲבוּךְ:

18 O king, the Most High *Hashem* bestowed kingship, grandeur, glory, and majesty upon your father Nebuchadnezzar.

יט וּמִן־רְבוּתָא דִּי יְהַב־לֵהּ כֹּל עַמְמַיָּא אֻמַּיָּא וְלִשָּׁנַיָּא הֲווֹ זאעין [זָיְעִין] וְדָחֲלִין מִן־קֳדָמוֹהִי דִּי־הֲוָה צָבֵא הֲוָא קָטֵל וְדִי־הֲוָה צָבֵא הֲוָה מַחֵא וְדִי־הֲוָה צָבֵא הֲוָה מָרִים וְדִי־הֲוָה צָבֵא הֲוָה מַשְׁפִּיל:

19 And because of the grandeur that He bestowed upon him, all the peoples and nations of every language trembled in fear of him. He put to death whom he wished, and whom he wished he let live; he raised high whom he wished and whom he wished he brought low.

כ וּכְדִי רִם לִבְבֵהּ וְרוּחֵהּ תִּקְפַת לַהֲזָדָה הָנְחַת מִן־כָּרְסֵא מַלְכוּתֵהּ וִיקָרָה הֶעְדִּיו מִנֵּהּ:

20 But when he grew haughty and willfully presumptuous, he was deposed from his royal throne and his glory was removed from him.

כא וּמִן־בְּנֵי אֲנָשָׁא טְרִיד וְלִבְבֵהּ עִם־חֵיוְתָא שוי [שַׁוִּיו] וְעִם־עֲרָדַיָּא מְדוֹרֵהּ עִשְׂבָּא כְתוֹרִין יְטַעֲמוּנֵּהּ וּמִטַּל שְׁמַיָּא גִּשְׁמֵהּ יִצְטַבַּע עַד דִּי־יְדַע דִּי־שַׁלִּיט אֱלָהָא עליא [עִלָּאָה] בְּמַלְכוּת אֲנָשָׁא וּלְמַן־דִּי יִצְבֵּה יְהָקֵים עליה [עֲלַהּ]:

21 He was driven away from men, and his mind made like that of a beast, and his habitation was with wild asses. He was fed grass like cattle, and his body was drenched with the dew of heaven until he came to know that the Most High *Hashem* is sovereign over the realm of man, and sets over it whom He wishes.

Daniel/Daniel

Chapter 6

22 But you, Belshazzar his son, did not humble yourself although you knew all this.

23 You exalted yourself against the Lord of Heaven, and had the vessels of His temple brought to you. You and your nobles, your consorts, and your concubines drank wine from them and praised the gods of silver and gold, bronze and iron, wood and stone, which do not see, hear, or understand; but the God who controls your lifebreath and every move you make – Him you did not glorify!

24 He therefore made the hand appear, and caused the writing to be inscribed.

25 This is the writing that is inscribed: mene mene tekel upharsin.

26 And this is its meaning: mene – *Hashem* has numbered [the days of] your kingdom and brought it to an end;

27 tekel – you have been weighed in the balance and found wanting;

28 peres – your kingdom has been divided and given to the Medes and the Persians."

29 Then, at Belshazzar's command, they clothed *Daniel* in purple, placed a golden chain on his neck, and proclaimed that he should rule as one of three in the kingdom.

30 That very night, Belshazzar, the Chaldean king, was killed,

6 1 and Darius the Mede received the kingdom, being about sixty-two years old.

2 It pleased Darius to appoint over the kingdom one hundred and twenty satraps to be in charge of the whole kingdom;

3 over them were three ministers, one of them *Daniel*, to whom these satraps reported, in order that the king not be troubled.

4 This man *Daniel* surpassed the other ministers and satraps by virtue of his extraordinary spirit, and the king considered setting him over the whole kingdom.

Daniel/דניאל
Chapter 6

פרק ו

5 The ministers and satraps looked for some fault in *Daniel*'s conduct in matters of state, but they could find neither fault nor corruption, inasmuch as he was trustworthy, and no negligence or corruption was to be found in him.

ה אֱדַיִן סָרְכַיָּא וַאֲחַשְׁדַּרְפְּנַיָּא הֲווֹ בָעַיִן עִלָּה לְהַשְׁכָּחָה לְדָנִיֵּאל מִצַּד מַלְכוּתָא וְכׇל־עִלָּה וּשְׁחִיתָה לָא־יָכְלִין לְהַשְׁכָּחָה כׇּל־קֳבֵל דִּי־מְהֵימַן הוּא וְכׇל־שָׁלוּ וּשְׁחִיתָה לָא הִשְׁתְּכַחַת עֲלוֹהִי׃

6 Those men then said, "We are not going to find any fault with this *Daniel*, unless we find something against him in connection with the laws of his God."

ו אֱדַיִן גֻּבְרַיָּא אִלֵּךְ אָמְרִין דִּי לָא נְהַשְׁכַּח לְדָנִיֵּאל דְּנָה כׇּל־עִלָּא לָהֵן הַשְׁכַּחְנָה עֲלוֹהִי בְּדָת אֱלָהֵהּ׃

7 Then these ministers and satraps came thronging in to the king and said to him, "O King Darius, live forever!

ז אֱדַיִן סָרְכַיָּא וַאֲחַשְׁדַּרְפְּנַיָּא אִלֵּן הַרְגִּשׁוּ עַל־מַלְכָּא וְכֵן אָמְרִין לֵהּ דָּרְיָוֶשׁ מַלְכָּא לְעָלְמִין חֱיִי׃

8 All the ministers of the kingdom, the prefects, satraps, companions, and governors are in agreement that a royal ban should be issued under sanction of an oath that whoever shall address a petition to any god or man, besides you, O king, during the next thirty days shall be thrown into a lions' den.

ח אִתְיָעַטוּ כֹּל סָרְכֵי מַלְכוּתָא סִגְנַיָּא וַאֲחַשְׁדַּרְפְּנַיָּא הַדָּבְרַיָּא וּפַחֲוָתָא לְקַיָּמָה קְיָם מַלְכָּא וּלְתַקָּפָה אֱסָר דִּי כׇל־דִּי־יִבְעֵה בָעוּ מִן־כׇּל־אֱלָהּ וֶאֱנָשׁ עַד־יוֹמִין תְּלָתִין לָהֵן מִנָּךְ מַלְכָּא יִתְרְמֵא לְגֹב אַרְיָוָתָא׃

9 So issue the ban, O king, and put it in writing so that it be unalterable as a law of the Medes and Persians that may not be abrogated."

ט כְּעַן מַלְכָּא תְּקִים אֱסָרָא וְתִרְשֻׁם כְּתָבָא דִּי לָא לְהַשְׁנָיָה כְּדָת־מָדַי וּפָרַס דִּי־לָא תֶעְדֵּא׃

10 Thereupon King Darius put the ban in writing.

י כׇּל־קֳבֵל דְּנָה מַלְכָּא דָּרְיָוֶשׁ רְשַׁם כְּתָבָא וֶאֱסָרָא׃

11 When *Daniel* learned that it had been put in writing, he went to his house, in whose upper chamber he had had windows made facing *Yerushalayim*, and three times a day he knelt down, prayed, and made confession to his God, as he had always done.

יא וְדָנִיֵּאל כְּדִי יְדַע דִּי־רְשִׁים כְּתָבָא עַל לְבַיְתֵהּ וְכַוִּין פְּתִיחָן לֵהּ בְּעִלִּיתֵהּ נֶגֶד יְרוּשְׁלֶם וְזִמְנִין תְּלָתָה בְיוֹמָא הוּא בָּרֵךְ עַל־בִּרְכוֹהִי וּמְצַלֵּא וּמוֹדֵא קֳדָם אֱלָהֵהּ כׇּל־קֳבֵל דִּי־הֲוָא עָבֵד מִן־קַדְמַת דְּנָה׃

v'-da-ni-YAYL k'-DEE y'-DA dee r'-SHEEM k'-ta-VA AL l'-vai-TAY v'-kha-VEEN p'-tee-KHAN LAY b'-i-lee-TAY NE-ged y'-ru-sh'-LEM v'-zim-NEEN t'-la-TA v'-yo-MA HU ba-RAYKH al bir-KHO-hee um-tza-LAY u-mo-DAY ko-DAM e-la-HAY kol ko-VAYL dee ha-VA a-VAYD min kad-MAT d'-NAH

6:11 He had windows made facing *Yerushalayim* Even though *Hashem*'s Temple had been destroyed for fifty years, *Daniel* continues to turn in its direction when praying. Indeed, Jews throughout the ages have maintained the tradition of praying facing *Yerushalayim*, showing their eternal connection with their holy city. This is a fulfillment of King *Shlomo*'s wish when dedicating the *Beit Hamikdash* (I Kings 8:48–49): "They turn back to You with all their heart and soul, in the land of the enemies… and they pray to You in the direction of their land which You gave to their fathers, of the city which You have chosen, and of the House which I have built to Your name – oh, give heed in Your heavenly abode to their prayer and supplication…" The deep bond between the Jewish people and the city of Jerusalem can be found throughout *Tanakh*.

Praying at the Western Wall in Jerusalem

Daniel/Daniel
Chapter 6

12 Then those men came thronging in and found *Daniel* petitioning his God in supplication.

13 They then approached the king and reminded him of the royal ban: "Did you not put in writing a ban that whoever addresses a petition to any god or man besides you, O king, during the next thirty days, shall be thrown into a lions' den?" The king said in reply, "The order stands firm, as a law of the Medes and Persians that may not be abrogated."

14 Thereupon they said to the king, "*Daniel*, one of the exiles of *Yehuda*, pays no heed to you, O king, or to the ban that you put in writing; three times a day he offers his petitions [to his God]."

15 Upon hearing that, the king was very disturbed, and he set his heart upon saving *Daniel*, and until the sun set made every effort to rescue him.

16 Then those men came thronging in to the king and said to the king, "Know, O king, that it is a law of the Medes and Persians that any ban that the king issues under sanction of oath is unalterable."

17 By the king's order, *Daniel* was then brought and thrown into the lions' den. The king spoke to *Daniel* and said, "Your God, whom you serve so regularly, will deliver you."

18 A rock was brought and placed over the mouth of the den; the king sealed it with his signet and with the signet of his nobles, so that nothing might be altered concerning *Daniel*.

19 The king then went to his palace and spent the night fasting; no diversions were brought to him, and his sleep fled from him.

20 Then, at the first light of dawn, the king arose and rushed to the lions' den.

21 As he approached the den, he cried to *Daniel* in a mournful voice; the king said to *Daniel*, "*Daniel*, servant of the living *Hashem*, was the God whom you served so regularly able to deliver you from the lions?"

22 *Daniel* then talked with the king, "O king, live forever!

Daniel/Daniel
Chapter 7

דניאל
פרק ז

23 My *Hashem* sent His angel, who shut the mouths of the lions so that they did not injure me, inasmuch as I was found innocent by Him, nor have I, O king, done you any injury."

כג אֱלָהִי שְׁלַח מַלְאֲכֵהּ וּסֲגַר פֻּם אַרְיָוָתָא וְלָא חַבְּלוּנִי כָּל־קֳבֵל דִּי קָדָמוֹהִי זָכוּ הִשְׁתְּכַחַת לִי וְאַף קָדָמָיךְ [קָדָמָךְ] מַלְכָּא חֲבוּלָה לָא עַבְדֵת:

24 The king was very glad, and ordered *Daniel* to be brought up out of the den. *Daniel* was brought up out of the den, and no injury was found on him, for he had trusted in his God.

כד בֵּאדַיִן מַלְכָּא שַׂגִּיא טְאֵב עֲלוֹהִי וּלְדָנִיֵּאל אֲמַר לְהַנְסָקָה מִן־גֻּבָּא וְהֻסַּק דָּנִיֵּאל מִן־גֻּבָּא וְכָל־חֲבָל לָא־הִשְׁתְּכַח בֵּהּ דִּי הֵימִן בֵּאלָהֵהּ:

25 Then, by order of the king, those men who had slandered *Daniel* were brought and, together with their children and wives, were thrown into the lions' den. They had hardly reached the bottom of the den when the lions overpowered them and crushed all their bones.

כה וַאֲמַר מַלְכָּא וְהַיְתִיו גֻּבְרַיָּא אִלֵּךְ דִּי־אֲכַלוּ קַרְצוֹהִי דִּי דָנִיֵּאל וּלְגֹב אַרְיָוָתָא רְמוֹ אִנּוּן בְּנֵיהוֹן וּנְשֵׁיהוֹן וְלָא־מְטוֹ לְאַרְעִית גֻּבָּא עַד דִּי־שְׁלִטוּ בְהוֹן אַרְיָוָתָא וְכָל־גַּרְמֵיהוֹן הַדִּקוּ:

26 Then King Darius wrote to all peoples and nations of every language that inhabit the earth, "May your well-being abound!

כו בֵּאדַיִן דָּרְיָוֶשׁ מַלְכָּא כְּתַב לְכָל־עַמְמַיָּא אֻמַּיָּא וְלִשָּׁנַיָּא דִּי־דָאֲרִין [דָּיְרִין] בְּכָל־אַרְעָא שְׁלָמְכוֹן יִשְׂגֵּא:

27 I have hereby given an order that throughout my royal domain men must tremble in fear before the God of *Daniel*, for He is the living *Hashem* who endures forever; His kingdom is indestructible, and His dominion is to the end of time;

כז מִן־קֳדָמַי שִׂים טְעֵם דִּי בְּכָל־שָׁלְטָן מַלְכוּתִי לֶהֱוֹן זָאֲעִין [זָיְעִין] וְדָחֲלִין מִן־קֳדָם אֱלָהֵהּ דִּי־דָנִיֵּאל דִּי־הוּא אֱלָהָא חַיָּא וְקַיָּם לְעָלְמִין וּמַלְכוּתֵהּ דִּי־לָא תִתְחַבַּל וְשָׁלְטָנֵהּ עַד־סוֹפָא:

28 He delivers and saves, and performs signs and wonders in heaven and on earth, for He delivered *Daniel* from the power of the lions."

כח מְשֵׁיזִב וּמַצִּל וְעָבֵד אָתִין וְתִמְהִין בִּשְׁמַיָּא וּבְאַרְעָא דִּי שֵׁיזִב לְדָנִיֵּאל מִן־יַד אַרְיָוָתָא:

29 Thus *Daniel* prospered during the reign of Darius and during the reign of Cyrus the Persian.

כט וְדָנִיֵּאל דְּנָה הַצְלַח בְּמַלְכוּת דָּרְיָוֶשׁ וּבְמַלְכוּת כּוֹרֶשׁ פַּרְסָיָא [פָּרְסָאָה]:

7
1 In the first year of King Belshazzar of Babylon, *Daniel* saw a dream and a vision of his mind in bed; afterward he wrote down the dream. Beginning the account,

א בִּשְׁנַת חֲדָה לְבֵלְאשַׁצַּר מֶלֶךְ בָּבֶל דָּנִיֵּאל חֵלֶם חֲזָה וְחֶזְוֵי רֵאשֵׁהּ עַל־מִשְׁכְּבֵהּ בֵּאדַיִן חֶלְמָא כְתַב רֵאשׁ מִלִּין אֲמַר:

bish-NAT kha-DAH l'-vayl-sha-TZAR ME-lekh ba-VEL da-ni-YAYL KHAY-lem kha-ZAH v'-khez-VAY ray-SHAY al mish-k'-VAY bay-DA-yin khel-MA kh'-TAV RAYSH mi-LEEN a-MAR

7:1 *Daniel* saw a dream Lest anyone think that history is coincidental, *Hashem* shows *Daniel* a preview of all that will transpire until the end of days. According to Rabbi Yitzchak Abrabanel, *Daniel's* visions are meant to comfort the Jewish people throughout their long and bitter exile. *Hashem* is like a doctor who explains a difficult treatment to his patient, but promises that all the painful symptoms guarantee a full recovery at the end. When we see that the predicted suffering has occurred, we can be assured that redemption, with all the promise it holds, will come true as well. For 2000 years history has been witness to much Jewish suffering. Finally, with the establishment of the State of Israel in 1948, the process of recovery has begun.

Daniel/Daniel
Chapter 7

דניאל
פרק ז

2 *Daniel* related the following: "In my vision at night, I saw the four winds of heaven stirring up the great sea.

ב עָנֵה דָנִיֵּאל וְאָמַר חָזֵה הֲוֵית בְּחֶזְוִי עִם־לֵילְיָא וַאֲרוּ אַרְבַּע רוּחֵי שְׁמַיָּא מְגִיחָן לְיַמָּא רַבָּא:

3 Four mighty beasts different from each other emerged from the sea.

ג וְאַרְבַּע חֵיוָן רַבְרְבָן סָלְקָן מִן־יַמָּא שָׁנְיָן דָּא מִן־דָּא:

4 The first was like a lion but had eagles' wings. As I looked on, its wings were plucked off, and it was lifted off the ground and set on its feet like a man and given the mind of a man.

ד קַדְמָיְתָא כְאַרְיֵה וְגַפִּין דִּי־נְשַׁר לַהּ חָזֵה הֲוֵית עַד דִּי־מְּרִיטוּ גַפַּיהּ וּנְטִילַת מִן־אַרְעָא וְעַל־רַגְלַיִן כֶּאֱנָשׁ הֳקִימַת וּלְבַב אֱנָשׁ יְהִיב לַהּ:

5 Then I saw a second, different beast, which was like a bear but raised on one side, and with three fangs in its mouth among its teeth; it was told, 'Arise, eat much meat!'

ה וַאֲרוּ חֵיוָה אָחֳרִי תִנְיָנָה דָּמְיָה לְדֹב וְלִשְׂטַר־חַד הֳקִמַת וּתְלָת עִלְעִין בְּפֻמַּהּ בֵּין שִׁנַּהּ [שִׁנַּיהּ] וְכֵן אָמְרִין לַהּ קוּמִי אֲכֻלִי בְּשַׂר שַׂגִּיא:

6 After that, as I looked on, there was another one, like a leopard, and it had on its back four wings like those of a bird; the beast had four heads, and dominion was given to it.

ו בָּאתַר דְּנָה חָזֵה הֲוֵית וַאֲרוּ אָחֳרִי כִּנְמַר וְלַהּ גַּפִּין אַרְבַּע דִּי־עוֹף עַל־גַּבַּיהּ [גַּבַּהּ] וְאַרְבְּעָה רֵאשִׁין לְחֵיוְתָא וְשָׁלְטָן יְהִיב לַהּ:

7 After that, as I looked on in the night vision, there was a fourth beast – fearsome, dreadful, and very powerful, with great iron teeth – that devoured and crushed, and stamped the remains with its feet. It was different from all the other beasts which had gone before it; and it had ten horns.

ז בָּאתַר דְּנָה חָזֵה הֲוֵית בְּחֶזְוֵי לֵילְיָא וַאֲרוּ חֵיוָה רְבִיעָיָה [רְבִיעָאָה] דְּחִילָה וְאֵימְתָנִי וְתַקִּיפָא יַתִּירָא וְשִׁנַּיִן דִּי־פַרְזֶל לַהּ רַבְרְבָן אָכְלָה וּמַדֱּקָה וּשְׁאָרָא בְּרַגְלַיהּ [בְּרַגְלַהּ] רָפְסָה וְהִיא מְשַׁנְּיָה מִן־כָּל־חֵיוָתָא דִּי קָדָמַיהּ וְקַרְנַיִן עֲשַׂר לַהּ:

8 While I was gazing upon these horns, a new little horn sprouted up among them; three of the older horns were uprooted to make room for it. There were eyes in this horn like those of a man, and a mouth that spoke arrogantly.

ח מִשְׂתַּכַּל הֲוֵית בְּקַרְנַיָּא וַאֲלוּ קֶרֶן אָחֳרִי זְעֵירָה סִלְקָת בֵּינֵיהוֹן [בֵּינֵיהֵן] וּתְלָת מִן־קַרְנַיָּא קַדְמָיָתָא אֶתְעֲקַרוּ [אֶתְעֲקַרָה] מִן־קֳדָמַיהּ [קֳדָמַהּ] וַאֲלוּ עַיְנִין כְּעַיְנֵי אֲנָשָׁא בְּקַרְנָא־דָא וּפֻם מְמַלִּל רַבְרְבָן:

9 As I looked on, Thrones were set in place, And the Ancient of Days took His seat. His garment was like white snow, And the hair of His head was like lamb's wool. His throne was tongues of flame; Its wheels were blazing fire.

ט חָזֵה הֲוֵית עַד דִּי כָרְסָוָן רְמִיו וְעַתִּיק יוֹמִין יְתִב לְבוּשֵׁהּ כִּתְלַג חִוָּר וּשְׂעַר רֵאשֵׁהּ כַּעֲמַר נְקֵא כָּרְסְיֵהּ שְׁבִיבִין דִּי־נוּר גַּלְגִּלּוֹהִי נוּר דָּלִק:

10 A river of fire streamed forth before Him; Thousands upon thousands served Him; Myriads upon myriads attended Him; The court sat and the books were opened.

י נְהַר דִּי־נוּר נָגֵד וְנָפֵק מִן־קֳדָמוֹהִי אֶלֶף אַלְפִים [אַלְפִין] יְשַׁמְּשׁוּנֵּהּ וְרִבּוֹ רִבְבָן [רִבְבָן] קָדָמוֹהִי יְקוּמוּן דִּינָא יְתִב וְסִפְרִין פְּתִיחוּ:

11 I looked on. Then, because of the arrogant words that the horn spoke, the beast was killed as I looked on; its body was destroyed and it was consigned to the flames.

יא חָזֵה הֲוֵית בֵּאדַיִן מִן־קָל מִלַּיָּא רַבְרְבָתָא דִּי קַרְנָא מְמַלֱּלָה חָזֵה הֲוֵית עַד דִּי קְטִילַת חֵיוְתָא וְהוּבַד גִּשְׁמַהּ וִיהִיבַת לִיקֵדַת אֶשָּׁא:

1903

Daniel/Daniel	דניאל
Chapter 7	פרק ז

12 The dominion of the other beasts was taken away, but an extension of life was given to them for a time and season.

יב וּשְׁאָר חֵיוָתָא הֶעְדִּיו שָׁלְטָנְהוֹן וְאַרְכָה בְחַיִּין יְהִיבַת לְהוֹן עַד־זְמַן וְעִדָּן:

13 As I looked on, in the night vision, One like a human being Came with the clouds of heaven; He reached the Ancient of Days And was presented to Him.

יג חָזֵה הֲוֵית בְּחֶזְוֵי לֵילְיָא וַאֲרוּ עִם־עֲנָנֵי שְׁמַיָּא כְּבַר אֱנָשׁ אָתֵה הֲוָה וְעַד־עַתִּיק יוֹמַיָּא מְטָה וּקְדָמוֹהִי הַקְרְבוּהִי:

14 Dominion, glory, and kingship were given to him; All peoples and nations of every language must serve him. His dominion is an everlasting dominion that shall not pass away, And his kingship, one that shall not be destroyed.

יד וְלֵהּ יְהִיב שָׁלְטָן וִיקָר וּמַלְכוּ וְכֹל עַמְמַיָּא אֻמַּיָּא וְלִשָּׁנַיָּא לֵהּ יִפְלְחוּן שָׁלְטָנֵהּ שָׁלְטָן עָלַם דִּי־לָא יֶעְדֵּה וּמַלְכוּתֵהּ דִּי־לָא תִתְחַבַּל:

15 As for me, *Daniel*, my spirit was disturbed within me and the vision of my mind alarmed me.

טו אֶתְכְּרִיַּת רוּחִי אֲנָה דָנִיֵּאל בְּגוֹא נִדְנֶה וְחֶזְוֵי רֵאשִׁי יְבַהֲלֻנַּנִי:

16 I approached one of the attendants and asked him the true meaning of all this. He gave me this interpretation of the matter:

טז קִרְבֵת עַל־חַד מִן־קָאֲמַיָּא וְיַצִּיבָא אֶבְעֵא־מִנֵּהּ עַל־כָּל־דְּנָה וַאֲמַר־לִי וּפְשַׁר מִלַּיָּא יְהוֹדְעִנַּנִי:

17 'These great beasts, four in number [mean] four kingdoms will arise out of the earth;

יז אִלֵּין חֵיוָתָא רַבְרְבָתָא דִּי אִנִּין אַרְבַּע אַרְבְּעָה מַלְכִין יְקוּמוּן מִן־אַרְעָא:

18 then holy ones of the Most High will receive the kingdom, and will possess the kingdom forever – forever and ever.'

יח וִיקַבְּלוּן מַלְכוּתָא קַדִּישֵׁי עֶלְיוֹנִין וְיַחְסְנוּן מַלְכוּתָא עַד־עָלְמָא וְעַד עָלַם עָלְמַיָּא:

19 Then I wanted to ascertain the true meaning of the fourth beast, which was different from them all, very fearsome, with teeth of iron, claws of bronze, that devoured and crushed, and stamped the remains;

יט אֱדַיִן צְבִית לְיַצָּבָא עַל־חֵיוְתָא רְבִיעָיְתָא דִּי־הֲוָת שָׁנְיָה מִן־כָּלְּהֵין [כָּלְּהֵן] דְּחִילָה יַתִּירָה שניה [שִׁנַּהּ] דִּי־פַרְזֶל וְטִפְרַיהּ דִּי־נְחָשׁ אָכְלָה מַדֲּקָה וּשְׁאָרָא בְּרַגְלַיהּ רָפְסָה:

20 and of the ten horns on its head; and of the new one that sprouted, to make room for which three fell – the horn that had eyes, and a mouth that spoke arrogantly, and which was more conspicuous than its fellows.

כ וְעַל־קַרְנַיָּא עֲשַׂר דִּי בְרֵאשַׁהּ וְאָחֳרִי דִּי סִלְקַת וּנְפַלוּ [וּנְפַלָה] מִן־קֳדָמַיהּ [קֳדָמַהּ] תְּלָת וְקַרְנָא דִכֵּן וְעַיְנִין לַהּ וְפֻם מְמַלִּל רַבְרְבָן וְחֶזְוַהּ רַב מִן־חַבְרָתַהּ:

21 (I looked on as that horn made war with the holy ones and overcame them,

כא חָזֵה הֲוֵית וְקַרְנָא דִכֵּן עָבְדָה קְרָב עִם־קַדִּישִׁין וְיָכְלָה לְהוֹן:

22 until the Ancient of Days came and judgment was rendered in favor of the holy ones of the Most High, for the time had come, and the holy ones took possession of the kingdom.)

כב עַד דִּי־אֲתָה עַתִּיק יוֹמַיָּא וְדִינָא יְהִב לְקַדִּישֵׁי עֶלְיוֹנִין וְזִמְנָא מְטָה וּמַלְכוּתָא הֶחֱסִנוּ קַדִּישִׁין:

23 This is what he said: 'The fourth beast [means] – there will be a fourth kingdom upon the earth which will be different from all the kingdoms; it will devour the whole earth, tread it down, and crush it.

כג כֵּן אֲמַר חֵיוְתָא רְבִיעָיְתָא מַלְכוּ רביעיא [רְבִיעָאָה] תֶּהֱוֵא בְאַרְעָא דִּי תִשְׁנֵא מִן־כָּל־מַלְכְוָתָא וְתֵאכֻל כָּל־אַרְעָא וּתְדוּשִׁנַּהּ וְתַדְּקִנַּהּ:

Daniel/Daniel
Chapter 8

דניאל
פרק ח

24 And the ten horns [mean] – from that kingdom, ten kings will arise, and after them another will arise. He will be different from the former ones, and will bring low three kings.

כד וְקַרְנַיָּא עֲשַׂר מִנַּהּ מַלְכוּתָהּ עַשְׂרָה מַלְכִין יְקֻמוּן וְאָחֳרָן יְקוּם אַחֲרֵיהוֹן וְהוּא יִשְׁנֵא מִן־קַדְמָיֵא וּתְלָתָה מַלְכִין יְהַשְׁפִּל:

25 He will speak words against the Most High, and will harass the holy ones of the Most High. He will think of changing times and laws, and they will be delivered into his power for a time, times, and half a time.

כה וּמִלִּין לְצַד עליא [עִלָּאָה] יְמַלִּל וּלְקַדִּישֵׁי עֶלְיוֹנִין יְבַלֵּא וְיִסְבַּר לְהַשְׁנָיָה זִמְנִין וְדָת וְיִתְיַהֲבוּן בִּידֵהּ עַד־עִדָּן וְעִדָּנִין וּפְלַג עִדָּן:

26 Then the court will sit and his dominion will be taken away, to be destroyed and abolished for all time.

כו וְדִינָא יִתִּב וְשָׁלְטָנֵהּ יְהַעְדּוֹן לְהַשְׁמָדָה וּלְהוֹבָדָה עַד־סוֹפָא:

27 The kingship and dominion and grandeur belonging to all the kingdoms under Heaven will be given to the people of the holy ones of the Most High. Their kingdom shall be an everlasting kingdom, and all dominions shall serve and obey them.'"

כז וּמַלְכוּתָה וְשָׁלְטָנָא וּרְבוּתָא דִּי מַלְכְוָת תְּחוֹת כָּל־שְׁמַיָּא יְהִיבַת לְעַם קַדִּישֵׁי עֶלְיוֹנִין מַלְכוּתֵהּ מַלְכוּת עָלַם וְכֹל שָׁלְטָנַיָּא לֵהּ יִפְלְחוּן וְיִשְׁתַּמְּעוּן:

28 Here the account ends. I, *Daniel*, was very alarmed by my thoughts, and my face darkened; and I could not put the matter out of my mind.

כח עַד־כָּה סוֹפָא דִי־מִלְּתָא אֲנָה דָנִיֵּאל שַׂגִּיא רַעְיוֹנַי יְבַהֲלֻנַּנִי וְזִיוַי יִשְׁתַּנּוֹן עֲלַי וּמִלְּתָא בְּלִבִּי נִטְרֵת:

8 1 In the third year of the reign of King Belshazzar, a vision appeared to me, to me, *Daniel*, after the one that had appeared to me earlier.

ח א בִּשְׁנַת שָׁלוֹשׁ לְמַלְכוּת בֵּלְאשַׁצַּר הַמֶּלֶךְ חָזוֹן נִרְאָה אֵלַי אֲנִי דָנִיֵּאל אַחֲרֵי הַנִּרְאָה אֵלַי בַּתְּחִלָּה:

2 I saw in the vision – at the time I saw it I was in the fortress of Shushan, in the province of Elam – I saw in the vision that I was beside the Ulai River.

ב וָאֶרְאֶה בֶּחָזוֹן וַיְהִי בִּרְאֹתִי וַאֲנִי בְּשׁוּשַׁן הַבִּירָה אֲשֶׁר בְּעֵילָם הַמְּדִינָה וָאֶרְאֶה בֶּחָזוֹן וַאֲנִי הָיִיתִי עַל־אוּבַל אוּלָי:

3 I looked and saw a ram standing between me and the river; he had two horns; the horns were high, with one higher than the other, and the higher sprouting last.

ג וָאֶשָּׂא עֵינַי וָאֶרְאֶה וְהִנֵּה אַיִל אֶחָד עֹמֵד לִפְנֵי הָאֻבָל וְלוֹ קְרָנָיִם וְהַקְּרָנַיִם גְּבֹהוֹת וְהָאַחַת גְּבֹהָה מִן־הַשֵּׁנִית וְהַגְּבֹהָה עֹלָה בָּאַחֲרֹנָה:

4 I saw the ram butting westward, northward, and southward. No beast could withstand him, and there was none to deliver from his power. He did as he pleased and grew great.

ד רָאִיתִי אֶת־הָאַיִל מְנַגֵּחַ יָמָּה וְצָפוֹנָה וָנֶגְבָּה וְכָל־חַיּוֹת לֹא־יַעַמְדוּ לְפָנָיו וְאֵין מַצִּיל מִיָּדוֹ וְעָשָׂה כִרְצֹנוֹ וְהִגְדִּיל:

5 As I looked on, a he-goat came from the west, passing over the entire earth without touching the ground. The goat had a conspicuous horn on its forehead.

ה וַאֲנִי הָיִיתִי מֵבִין וְהִנֵּה צְפִיר־הָעִזִּים בָּא מִן־הַמַּעֲרָב עַל־פְּנֵי כָל־הָאָרֶץ וְאֵין נוֹגֵעַ בָּאָרֶץ וְהַצָּפִיר קֶרֶן חָזוּת בֵּין עֵינָיו:

6 He came up to the two-horned ram that I had seen standing between me and the river and charged at him with furious force.

ו וַיָּבֹא עַד־הָאַיִל בַּעַל הַקְּרָנַיִם אֲשֶׁר רָאִיתִי עֹמֵד לִפְנֵי הָאֻבָל וַיָּרָץ אֵלָיו בַּחֲמַת כֹּחוֹ:

Daniel/Daniel
Chapter 8

דניאל
פרק ח

7 I saw him reach the ram and rage at him; he struck the ram and broke its two horns, and the ram was powerless to withstand him. He threw him to the ground and trampled him, and there was none to deliver the ram from his power.

ז וּרְאִיתִיו מַגִּיעַ אֵצֶל הָאַיִל וַיִּתְמַרְמַר אֵלָיו וַיַּךְ אֶת־הָאַיִל וַיְשַׁבֵּר אֶת־שְׁתֵּי קְרָנָיו וְלֹא־הָיָה כֹחַ בָּאַיִל לַעֲמֹד לְפָנָיו וַיַּשְׁלִיכֵהוּ אַרְצָה וַיִּרְמְסֵהוּ וְלֹא־הָיָה מַצִּיל לָאַיִל מִיָּדוֹ:

8 Then the he-goat grew very great, but at the peak of his power his big horn was broken. In its place, four conspicuous horns sprouted toward the four winds of heaven.

ח וּצְפִיר הָעִזִּים הִגְדִּיל עַד־מְאֹד וּכְעָצְמוֹ נִשְׁבְּרָה הַקֶּרֶן הַגְּדוֹלָה וַתַּעֲלֶנָה חָזוּת אַרְבַּע תַּחְתֶּיהָ לְאַרְבַּע רוּחוֹת הַשָּׁמָיִם:

9 From one of them emerged a small horn, which extended itself greatly toward the south, toward the east, and toward the beautiful land.

ט וּמִן־הָאַחַת מֵהֶם יָצָא קֶרֶן־אַחַת מִצְּעִירָה וַתִּגְדַּל־יֶתֶר אֶל־הַנֶּגֶב וְאֶל־הַמִּזְרָח וְאֶל־הַצֶּבִי:

10 It grew as high as the host of heaven and it hurled some stars of the [heavenly] host to the ground and trampled them.

י וַתִּגְדַּל עַד־צְבָא הַשָּׁמָיִם וַתַּפֵּל אַרְצָה מִן־הַצָּבָא וּמִן־הַכּוֹכָבִים וַתִּרְמְסֵם:

11 It vaunted itself against the very chief of the host; on its account the regular offering was suspended, and His holy place was abandoned.

יא וְעַד שַׂר־הַצָּבָא הִגְדִּיל וּמִמֶּנּוּ הרים [הוּרַם] הַתָּמִיד וְהֻשְׁלַךְ מְכוֹן מִקְדָּשׁוֹ:

12 An army was arrayed iniquitously against the regular offering; it hurled truth to the ground and prospered in what it did.

יב וְצָבָא תִּנָּתֵן עַל־הַתָּמִיד בְּפָשַׁע וְתַשְׁלֵךְ אֱמֶת אַרְצָה וְעָשְׂתָה וְהִצְלִיחָה:

13 Then I heard a holy being speaking, and another holy being said to whoever it was who was speaking, "How long will [what was seen in] the vision last – the regular offering be forsaken because of transgression; the sanctuary be surrendered and the [heavenly] host be trampled?"

יג וָאֶשְׁמְעָה אֶחָד־קָדוֹשׁ מְדַבֵּר וַיֹּאמֶר אֶחָד קָדוֹשׁ לַפַּלְמוֹנִי הַמְדַבֵּר עַד־מָתַי הֶחָזוֹן הַתָּמִיד וְהַפֶּשַׁע שֹׁמֵם תֵּת וְקֹדֶשׁ וְצָבָא מִרְמָס:

14 He answered me, "For twenty-three hundred evenings and mornings; then the sanctuary shall be cleansed."

יד וַיֹּאמֶר אֵלַי עַד עֶרֶב בֹּקֶר אַלְפַּיִם וּשְׁלֹשׁ מֵאוֹת וְנִצְדַּק קֹדֶשׁ:

15 While I, *Daniel*, was seeing the vision, and trying to understand it, there appeared before me one who looked like a man.

טו וַיְהִי בִּרְאֹתִי אֲנִי דָנִיֵּאל אֶת־הֶחָזוֹן וָאֲבַקְשָׁה בִינָה וְהִנֵּה עֹמֵד לְנֶגְדִּי כְּמַרְאֵה־גָבֶר:

16 I heard a human voice from the middle of Ulai calling out, "Gabriel, make that man understand the vision."

טז וָאֶשְׁמַע קוֹל־אָדָם בֵּין אוּלָי וַיִּקְרָא וַיֹּאמַר גַּבְרִיאֵל הָבֵן לְהַלָּז אֶת־הַמַּרְאֶה:

17 He came near to where I was standing, and as he came I was terrified, and fell prostrate. He said to me, "Understand, O man, that the vision refers to the time of the end."

יז וַיָּבֹא אֵצֶל עָמְדִי וּבְבֹאוֹ נִבְעַתִּי וָאֶפְּלָה עַל־פָּנָי וַיֹּאמֶר אֵלַי הָבֵן בֶּן־אָדָם כִּי לְעֶת־קֵץ הֶחָזוֹן:

18 When he spoke with me, I was overcome by a deep sleep as I lay prostrate on the ground. Then he touched me and made me stand up,

יח וּבְדַבְּרוֹ עִמִּי נִרְדַּמְתִּי עַל־פָּנַי אָרְצָה וַיִּגַּע־בִּי וַיַּעֲמִידֵנִי עַל־עָמְדִי:

Daniel/Daniel
Chapter 8

דניאל
פרק ח

19 and said, "I am going to inform you of what will happen when wrath is at an end, for [it refers] to the time appointed for the end.

יט וַיֹּאמֶר הִנְנִי מוֹדִיעֲךָ אֵת אֲשֶׁר־יִהְיֶה בְּאַחֲרִית הַזָּעַם כִּי לְמוֹעֵד קֵץ׃

20 "The two-horned ram that you saw [signifies] the kings of Media and Persia;

כ הָאַיִל אֲשֶׁר־רָאִיתָ בַּעַל הַקְּרָנָיִם מַלְכֵי מָדַי וּפָרָס׃

21 and the buck, the he-goat – the king of Greece; and the large horn on his forehead, that is the first king.

כא וְהַצָּפִיר הַשָּׂעִיר מֶלֶךְ יָוָן וְהַקֶּרֶן הַגְּדוֹלָה אֲשֶׁר בֵּין־עֵינָיו הוּא הַמֶּלֶךְ הָרִאשׁוֹן׃

v'-ha-tza-FEER ha-sa-EER ME-lekh ya-VAN v'-ha-KE-ren ha-g'-do-LAH a-SHER BAYN ay-NAV hu ha-ME-lekh ha-ri-SHON

22 One was broken and four came in its stead – that [means]: four kingdoms will arise out of a nation, but without its power.

כב וְהַנִּשְׁבֶּרֶת וַתַּעֲמֹדְנָה אַרְבַּע תַּחְתֶּיהָ אַרְבַּע מַלְכֻיוֹת מִגּוֹי יַעֲמֹדְנָה וְלֹא בְכֹחוֹ׃

23 When their kingdoms are at an end, when the measure of transgression has been filled, then a king will arise, impudent and versed in intrigue.

כג וּבְאַחֲרִית מַלְכוּתָם כְּהָתֵם הַפֹּשְׁעִים יַעֲמֹד מֶלֶךְ עַז־פָּנִים וּמֵבִין חִידוֹת׃

24 He will have great strength, but not through his own strength. He will be extraordinarily destructive; he will prosper in what he does, and destroy the mighty and the people of holy ones.

כד וְעָצַם כֹּחוֹ וְלֹא בְכֹחוֹ וְנִפְלָאוֹת יַשְׁחִית וְהִצְלִיחַ וְעָשָׂה וְהִשְׁחִית עֲצוּמִים וְעַם־קְדֹשִׁים׃

25 By his cunning, he will use deceit successfully. He will make great plans, will destroy many, taking them unawares, and will rise up against the chief of chiefs, but will be broken, not by [human] hands.

כה וְעַל־שִׂכְלוֹ וְהִצְלִיחַ מִרְמָה בְּיָדוֹ וּבִלְבָבוֹ יַגְדִּיל וּבְשַׁלְוָה יַשְׁחִית רַבִּים וְעַל־שַׂר־שָׂרִים יַעֲמֹד וּבְאֶפֶס יָד יִשָּׁבֵר׃

26 What was said in the vision about evenings and mornings is true. Now you keep the vision a secret, for it pertains to far-off days."

כו וּמַרְאֵה הָעֶרֶב וְהַבֹּקֶר אֲשֶׁר נֶאֱמַר אֱמֶת הוּא וְאַתָּה סְתֹם הֶחָזוֹן כִּי לְיָמִים רַבִּים׃

27 So I, *Daniel*, was stricken, and languished many days. Then I arose and attended to the king's business, but I was dismayed by the vision and no one could explain it.

כז וַאֲנִי דָנִיֵּאל נִהְיֵיתִי וְנֶחֱלֵיתִי יָמִים וָאָקוּם וָאֶעֱשֶׂה אֶת־מְלֶאכֶת הַמֶּלֶךְ וָאֶשְׁתּוֹמֵם עַל־הַמַּרְאֶה וְאֵין מֵבִין׃

8:21 And the buck, the he-goat – the king of Greece In *Daniel*'s first vision, the second and third kingdoms are represented by vicious beasts – a bear and a leopard. In this vision, they are represented by more tame animals – the ram and the he-goat. Rabbi Yitzchak Abrabanel explains that the first vision depicts the empires' objective strength, while the second vision portrays how these kingdoms treated the Jewish people and the Land of Israel. The Persian-Median empire, as well as the Greeks, were extremely powerful nations who conquered the entire known world at the time. Despite their might, these nations dealt relatively kindly with the Children of Israel. During Persian-Median rule, Cyrus encouraged the Jews to return to Israel. Darius allowed the completion of the Temple's construction and Xerxes provided material to help this cause. Alexander the Great, the first ruler of Greece, retreated peacefully from *Yerushalayim*. Only later, under the rule of Antiochus, did the Jews really begin to suffer.

Daniel/Daniel
Chapter 9

דניאל
פרק ט

9 1 In the first year of Darius son of Ahasuerus, of Median descent, who was made king over the kingdom of the Chaldeans –

2 in the first year of his reign, I, *Daniel*, consulted the books concerning the number of years that, according to the word of *Hashem* that had come to *Yirmiyahu* the *Navi*, were to be the term of *Yerushalayim*'s desolation – seventy years.

3 I turned my face to *Hashem*, devoting myself to prayer and supplication, in fasting, in sackcloth and ashes.

4 I prayed to *Hashem* my God, making confession thus: "O *Hashem*, great and awesome God, who stays faithful to His covenant with those who love Him and keep His commandments!

5 We have sinned; we have gone astray; we have acted wickedly; we have been rebellious and have deviated from Your commandments and Your rules,

6 and have not obeyed Your servants the *neviim* who spoke in Your name to our kings, our officers, our fathers, and all the people of the land.

7 With You, O *Hashem*, is the right, and the shame is on us to this very day, on the men of *Yehuda* and the inhabitants of *Yerushalayim*, all *Yisrael*, near and far, in all the lands where You have banished them, for the trespass they committed against You.

8 The shame, *Hashem*, is on us, on our kings, our officers, and our fathers, because we have sinned against You.

9 To *Hashem* our God belong mercy and forgiveness, for we rebelled against Him,

10 and did not obey *Hashem* our God by following His teachings that He set before us through His servants the *neviim*.

11 All *Yisrael* has violated Your teaching and gone astray, disobeying You; so the curse and the oath written in the Teaching of *Moshe*, the servant of *Hashem*, have been poured down upon us, for we have sinned against Him.

א בִּשְׁנַת אַחַת לְדָרְיָוֶשׁ בֶּן־אֲחַשְׁוֵרוֹשׁ מִזֶּרַע מָדָי אֲשֶׁר הָמְלַךְ עַל מַלְכוּת כַּשְׂדִּים:

ב בִּשְׁנַת אַחַת לְמָלְכוֹ אֲנִי דָּנִיֵּאל בִּינֹתִי בַּסְּפָרִים מִסְפַּר הַשָּׁנִים אֲשֶׁר הָיָה דְבַר־יְהֹוָה אֶל־יִרְמִיָה הַנָּבִיא לְמַלֹּאות לְחָרְבוֹת יְרוּשָׁלַםִ שִׁבְעִים שָׁנָה:

ג וָאֶתְּנָה אֶת־פָּנַי אֶל־אֲדֹנָי הָאֱלֹהִים לְבַקֵּשׁ תְּפִלָּה וְתַחֲנוּנִים בְּצוֹם וְשַׂק וָאֵפֶר:

ד וָאֶתְפַּלְלָה לַיהֹוָה אֱלֹהַי וָאֶתְוַדֶּה וָאֹמְרָה אָנָּא אֲדֹנָי הָאֵל הַגָּדוֹל וְהַנּוֹרָא שֹׁמֵר הַבְּרִית וְהַחֶסֶד לְאֹהֲבָיו וּלְשֹׁמְרֵי מִצְוֹתָיו:

ה חָטָאנוּ וְעָוִינוּ והרשענו [הִרְשַׁעְנוּ] וּמָרָדְנוּ וְסוֹר מִמִּצְוֹתֶךָ וּמִמִּשְׁפָּטֶיךָ:

ו וְלֹא שָׁמַעְנוּ אֶל־עֲבָדֶיךָ הַנְּבִיאִים אֲשֶׁר דִּבְּרוּ בְּשִׁמְךָ אֶל־מְלָכֵינוּ שָׂרֵינוּ וַאֲבֹתֵינוּ וְאֶל כָּל־עַם הָאָרֶץ:

ז לְךָ אֲדֹנָי הַצְּדָקָה וְלָנוּ בֹּשֶׁת הַפָּנִים כַּיּוֹם הַזֶּה לְאִישׁ יְהוּדָה וּלְיוֹשְׁבֵי יְרוּשָׁלַםִ וּלְכָל־יִשְׂרָאֵל הַקְּרֹבִים וְהָרְחֹקִים בְּכָל־הָאֲרָצוֹת אֲשֶׁר הִדַּחְתָּם שָׁם בְּמַעֲלָם אֲשֶׁר מָעֲלוּ־בָךְ:

ח יְהֹוָה לָנוּ בֹּשֶׁת הַפָּנִים לִמְלָכֵינוּ לְשָׂרֵינוּ וְלַאֲבֹתֵינוּ אֲשֶׁר חָטָאנוּ לָךְ:

ט לַאדֹנָי אֱלֹהֵינוּ הָרַחֲמִים וְהַסְּלִחוֹת כִּי מָרַדְנוּ בּוֹ:

י וְלֹא שָׁמַעְנוּ בְּקוֹל יְהֹוָה אֱלֹהֵינוּ לָלֶכֶת בְּתוֹרֹתָיו אֲשֶׁר נָתַן לְפָנֵינוּ בְּיַד עֲבָדָיו הַנְּבִיאִים:

יא וְכָל־יִשְׂרָאֵל עָבְרוּ אֶת־תּוֹרָתֶךָ וְסוֹר לְבִלְתִּי שְׁמוֹעַ בְּקֹלֶךָ וַתִּתַּךְ עָלֵינוּ הָאָלָה וְהַשְּׁבֻעָה אֲשֶׁר כְּתוּבָה בְּתוֹרַת מֹשֶׁה עֶבֶד־הָאֱלֹהִים כִּי חָטָאנוּ לוֹ:

Daniel/Daniel
Chapter 9

דניאל
פרק ט

12 He carried out the threat that He made against us, and against our rulers who ruled us, to bring upon us great misfortune; under the whole heaven there has never been done the like of what was done to *Yerushalayim*.

יב וַיָּקֶם אֶת־דבריו [דְּבָרוֹ ׀] אֲשֶׁר־דִּבֶּר עָלֵינוּ וְעַל שֹׁפְטֵינוּ אֲשֶׁר שְׁפָטוּנוּ לְהָבִיא עָלֵינוּ רָעָה גְדֹלָה אֲשֶׁר לֹא־נֶעֶשְׂתָה תַּחַת כָּל־הַשָּׁמַיִם כַּאֲשֶׁר נֶעֶשְׂתָה בִּירוּשָׁלָ͏ִם:

13 All that calamity, just as is written in the Teaching of *Moshe*, came upon us, yet we did not supplicate *Hashem* our God, did not repent of our iniquity or become wise through Your truth.

יג כַּאֲשֶׁר כָּתוּב בְּתוֹרַת מֹשֶׁה אֵת כָּל־הָרָעָה הַזֹּאת בָּאָה עָלֵינוּ וְלֹא־חִלִּינוּ אֶת־פְּנֵי ׀ יְהוָה אֱלֹהֵינוּ לָשׁוּב מֵעֲוֺנֵנוּ וּלְהַשְׂכִּיל בַּאֲמִתֶּךָ:

14 Hence *Hashem* was intent upon bringing calamity upon us, for *Hashem* our God is in the right in all that He has done, but we have not obeyed Him.

יד וַיִּשְׁקֹד יְהוָה עַל־הָרָעָה וַיְבִיאֶהָ עָלֵינוּ כִּי־צַדִּיק יְהוָה אֱלֹהֵינוּ עַל־כָּל־מַעֲשָׂיו אֲשֶׁר עָשָׂה וְלֹא שָׁמַעְנוּ בְּקֹלוֹ:

15 "Now, *Hashem* our God – You who brought Your people out of the land of Egypt with a mighty hand, winning fame for Yourself to this very day – we have sinned, we have acted wickedly.

טו וְעַתָּה ׀ אֲדֹנָי אֱלֹהֵינוּ אֲשֶׁר הוֹצֵאתָ אֶת־עַמְּךָ מֵאֶרֶץ מִצְרַיִם בְּיָד חֲזָקָה וַתַּעַשׂ־לְךָ שֵׁם כַּיּוֹם הַזֶּה חָטָאנוּ רָשָׁעְנוּ:

16 O *Hashem*, as befits Your abundant benevolence, let Your wrathful fury turn back from Your city *Yerushalayim*, Your holy mountain; for because of our sins and the iniquities of our fathers, *Yerushalayim* and Your people have become a mockery among all who are around us.

טז אֲדֹנָי כְּכָל־צִדְקֹתֶךָ יָשָׁב־נָא אַפְּךָ וַחֲמָתְךָ מֵעִירְךָ יְרוּשָׁלַ͏ִם הַר־קָדְשֶׁךָ כִּי בַחֲטָאֵינוּ וּבַעֲוֺנוֹת אֲבֹתֵינוּ יְרוּשָׁלַ͏ִם וְעַמְּךָ לְחֶרְפָּה לְכָל־סְבִיבֹתֵינוּ:

a-do-NAI k'-khol tzid-ko-TE-kha ya-shov NA a-p'-KHA va-kha-ma-t'-KHA may-ee-r'-KHA y'-ru-sha-LA-im har kod-SHE-kha KEE va-kha-ta-AY-nu u-va-a-vo-NOT a-vo-TAY-nu y'-ru-sha-LA-im v'-a-m'-KHA l'-kher-PAH l-khol s'-vee-vo-TAY-nu

17 "O our God, hear now the prayer of Your servant and his plea, and show Your favor to Your desolate sanctuary, for *Hashem*'s sake.

יז וְעַתָּה ׀ שְׁמַע אֱלֹהֵינוּ אֶל־תְּפִלַּת עַבְדְּךָ וְאֶל־תַּחֲנוּנָיו וְהָאֵר פָּנֶיךָ עַל־מִקְדָּשְׁךָ הַשָּׁמֵם לְמַעַן אֲדֹנָי:

Teddy Kollek
(1911–2007)

9:16 *Yerushalayim* and Your people have become a mockery In his prayer, *Daniel* lists three compelling reasons for *Hashem* to accept his prayer and redeem the people from Babylonia: For the sake of *Yerushalayim*, of the *Beit Hamikdash* and of the Jewish people. Rabbi Yitzchak Abrabanel elaborates on these points. Regarding *Yerushalayim*, *Daniel* points out that it is an embarrassment to God when His beautiful city lies in ruins. He further questions how *Hashem* can ignore the Temple Mount where His presence was manifest most clearly on earth. Lastly, it is a desecration of God's name when His chosen people are despised. *Daniel* groups *Yerushalayim* and the Jewish people together, "*Yerushalayim* and Your people have become a mockery among all who are around us," since the Jews and *Yerushalayim* are one. Without their holy city, how can they succeed in exile, and how can *Yerushalayim* flourish without her children? *Daniel*'s sentiments were echoed by Teddy Kollek, who served as mayor of *Yerushalayim* from 1967–1993: "For three thousand years, Jerusalem has been the center of Jewish hope and longing. No other city has played such a dominant role in the history, culture, religion and consciousness of a people as has Jerusalem in the life of Jewry and Judaism. Throughout centuries of exile, Jerusalem remained alive in the hearts of Jews everywhere as the focal point of Jewish history, the symbol of ancient glory, spiritual fulfillment and modern renewal. This heart and soul of the Jewish people engenders the thought that if you want one simple word to symbolize all of Jewish history, that word would be 'Jerusalem.'"

Daniel/Daniel
Chapter 9

דניאל
פרק ט

18 Incline Your ear, O my God, and hear; open Your eyes and see our desolation and the city to which Your name is attached. Not because of any merit of ours do we lay our plea before You but because of Your abundant mercies.

יח הַטֵּה אֱלֹהַי אָזְנְךָ וּשְׁמָע פקחה [פְּקַח] עֵינֶיךָ וּרְאֵה שֹׁמְמֹתֵינוּ וְהָעִיר אֲשֶׁר־נִקְרָא שִׁמְךָ עָלֶיהָ כִּי לֹא עַל־צִדְקֹתֵינוּ אֲנַחְנוּ מַפִּילִים תַּחֲנוּנֵינוּ לְפָנֶיךָ כִּי עַל־רַחֲמֶיךָ הָרַבִּים:

19 O *Hashem*, hear! O *Hashem*, forgive! O *Hashem*, listen, and act without delay for Your own sake, O my God; for Your name is attached to Your city and Your people!"

יט אֲדֹנָי שְׁמָעָה אֲדֹנָי סְלָחָה אֲדֹנָי הַקֲשִׁיבָה וַעֲשֵׂה אַל־תְּאַחַר לְמַעֲנְךָ אֱלֹהַי כִּי־שִׁמְךָ נִקְרָא עַל־עִירְךָ וְעַל־עַמֶּךָ:

20 While I was speaking, praying, and confessing my sin and the sin of my people *Yisrael*, and laying my supplication before *Hashem* my God on behalf of the holy mountain of my God –

כ וְעוֹד אֲנִי מְדַבֵּר וּמִתְפַּלֵּל וּמִתְוַדֶּה חַטָּאתִי וְחַטַּאת עַמִּי יִשְׂרָאֵל וּמַפִּיל תְּחִנָּתִי לִפְנֵי יְהֹוָה אֱלֹהַי עַל הַר־קֹדֶשׁ אֱלֹהָי:

21 while I was uttering my prayer, the man Gabriel, whom I had previously seen in the vision, was sent forth in flight and reached me about the time of the evening offering.

כא וְעוֹד אֲנִי מְדַבֵּר בַּתְּפִלָּה וְהָאִישׁ גַּבְרִיאֵל אֲשֶׁר רָאִיתִי בֶחָזוֹן בַּתְּחִלָּה מֻעָף בִּיעָף נֹגֵעַ אֵלַי כְּעֵת מִנְחַת־עָרֶב:

22 He made me understand by speaking to me and saying, "*Daniel*, I have just come forth to give you understanding.

כב וַיָּבֶן וַיְדַבֵּר עִמִּי וַיֹּאמַר דָּנִיֵּאל עַתָּה יָצָאתִי לְהַשְׂכִּילְךָ בִינָה:

23 A word went forth as you began your plea, and I have come to tell it, for you are precious; so mark the word and understand the vision.

כג בִּתְחִלַּת תַּחֲנוּנֶיךָ יָצָא דָבָר וַאֲנִי בָּאתִי לְהַגִּיד כִּי חֲמוּדוֹת אָתָּה וּבִין בַּדָּבָר וְהָבֵן בַּמַּרְאֶה:

24 "Seventy weeks have been decreed for your people and your holy city until the measure of transgression is filled and that of sin complete, until iniquity is expiated, and eternal righteousness ushered in; and prophetic vision ratified, and the Holy of Holies anointed.

כד שָׁבֻעִים שִׁבְעִים נֶחְתַּךְ עַל־עַמְּךָ וְעַל־עִיר קָדְשֶׁךָ לְכַלֵּא הַפֶּשַׁע ולחתם [וּלְהָתֵם] חטאות [חַטָּאת] וּלְכַפֵּר עָוֹן וּלְהָבִיא צֶדֶק עֹלָמִים וְלַחְתֹּם חָזוֹן וְנָבִיא וְלִמְשֹׁחַ קֹדֶשׁ קָדָשִׁים:

25 You must know and understand: From the issuance of the word to restore and rebuild *Yerushalayim* until the [time of the] anointed leader is seven weeks; and for sixty-two weeks it will be rebuilt, square and moat, but in a time of distress.

כה וְתֵדַע וְתַשְׂכֵּל מִן־מֹצָא דָבָר לְהָשִׁיב וְלִבְנוֹת יְרוּשָׁלַםִ עַד־מָשִׁיחַ נָגִיד שָׁבֻעִים שִׁבְעָה וְשָׁבֻעִים שִׁשִּׁים וּשְׁנַיִם תָּשׁוּב וְנִבְנְתָה רְחוֹב וְחָרוּץ וּבְצוֹק הָעִתִּים:

26 And after those sixty-two weeks, the anointed one will disappear and vanish. The army of a leader who is to come will destroy the city and the sanctuary, but its end will come through a flood. Desolation is decreed until the end of war.

כו וְאַחֲרֵי הַשָּׁבֻעִים שִׁשִּׁים וּשְׁנַיִם יִכָּרֵת מָשִׁיחַ וְאֵין לוֹ וְהָעִיר וְהַקֹּדֶשׁ יַשְׁחִית עַם נָגִיד הַבָּא וְקִצּוֹ בַשֶּׁטֶף וְעַד קֵץ מִלְחָמָה נֶחֱרֶצֶת שֹׁמֵמוֹת:

27 During one week he will make a firm covenant with many. For half a week he will put a stop to the sacrifice and the meal offering. At the corner [of the *Mizbayach*] will be an appalling abomination until the decreed destruction will be poured down upon the appalling thing."

כז וְהִגְבִּיר בְּרִית לָרַבִּים שָׁבוּעַ אֶחָד וַחֲצִי הַשָּׁבוּעַ יַשְׁבִּית זֶבַח וּמִנְחָה וְעַל כְּנַף שִׁקּוּצִים מְשֹׁמֵם וְעַד־כָּלָה וְנֶחֱרָצָה תִּתַּךְ עַל־שֹׁמֵם:

Daniel/Daniel
Chapter 10

דניאל
פרק י

10 ¹ In the third year of King Cyrus of Persia, an oracle was revealed to *Daniel*, who was called Belteshazzar. That oracle was true, but it was a great task to understand the prophecy; understanding came to him through the vision.

א בִּשְׁנַת שָׁלוֹשׁ לְכוֹרֶשׁ מֶלֶךְ פָּרַס דָּבָר נִגְלָה לְדָנִיֵּאל אֲשֶׁר־נִקְרָא שְׁמוֹ בֵּלְטְשַׁאצַּר וֶאֱמֶת הַדָּבָר וְצָבָא גָדוֹל וּבִין אֶת־הַדָּבָר וּבִינָה לוֹ בַּמַּרְאֶה:

² At that time, I, *Daniel*, kept three full weeks of mourning.

ב בַּיָּמִים הָהֵם אֲנִי דָנִיֵּאל הָיִיתִי מִתְאַבֵּל שְׁלֹשָׁה שָׁבֻעִים יָמִים:

ba-ya-MEEM ha-HAYM a-NEE da-ni-YAYL ha-YEE-tee mit-a-BAYL sh'-lo-SHAH sha-vu-EEM ya-MEEM

³ I ate no tasty food, nor did any meat or wine enter my mouth. I did not anoint myself until the three weeks were over.

ג לֶחֶם חֲמֻדוֹת לֹא אָכַלְתִּי וּבָשָׂר וָיַיִן לֹא־בָא אֶל־פִּי וְסוֹךְ לֹא־סָכְתִּי עַד־מְלֹאת שְׁלֹשֶׁת שָׁבֻעִים יָמִים:

⁴ It was on the twenty-fourth day of the first month, when I was on the bank of the great river – the Tigris –

ד וּבְיוֹם עֶשְׂרִים וְאַרְבָּעָה לַחֹדֶשׁ הָרִאשׁוֹן וַאֲנִי הָיִיתִי עַל יַד הַנָּהָר הַגָּדוֹל הוּא חִדָּקֶל:

⁵ that I looked and saw a man dressed in linen, his loins girt in fine gold.

ה וָאֶשָּׂא אֶת־עֵינַי וָאֵרֶא וְהִנֵּה אִישׁ־אֶחָד לָבוּשׁ בַּדִּים וּמָתְנָיו חֲגֻרִים בְּכֶתֶם אוּפָז:

⁶ His body was like beryl, his face had the appearance of lightning, his eyes were like flaming torches, his arms and legs had the color of burnished bronze, and the sound of his speech was like the noise of a multitude.

ו וּגְוִיָּתוֹ כְתַרְשִׁישׁ וּפָנָיו כְּמַרְאֵה בָרָק וְעֵינָיו כְּלַפִּידֵי אֵשׁ וּזְרֹעֹתָיו וּמַרְגְּלֹתָיו כְּעֵין נְחֹשֶׁת קָלָל וְקוֹל דְּבָרָיו כְּקוֹל הָמוֹן:

⁷ I, *Daniel*, alone saw the vision; the men who were with me did not see the vision, yet they were seized with a great terror and fled into hiding.

ז וְרָאִיתִי אֲנִי דָנִיֵּאל לְבַדִּי אֶת־הַמַּרְאָה וְהָאֲנָשִׁים אֲשֶׁר הָיוּ עִמִּי לֹא רָאוּ אֶת־הַמַּרְאָה אֲבָל חֲרָדָה גְדֹלָה נָפְלָה עֲלֵיהֶם וַיִּבְרְחוּ בְּהֵחָבֵא:

⁸ So I was left alone to see this great vision. I was drained of strength, my vigor was destroyed, and I could not summon up strength.

ח וַאֲנִי נִשְׁאַרְתִּי לְבַדִּי וָאֶרְאֶה אֶת־הַמַּרְאָה הַגְּדֹלָה הַזֹּאת וְלֹא נִשְׁאַר־בִּי כֹּחַ וְהוֹדִי נֶהְפַּךְ עָלַי לְמַשְׁחִית וְלֹא עָצַרְתִּי כֹּחַ:

Mourning the destruction of the Beit Hamikdash on the ninth of Av

10:2 I, Daniel, kept three full weeks of mourning
According to *Metzudat David*, Daniel mourns for three weeks over the cessation of the construction of the *Beit Hamikdash* during the reign of Cyrus (Ezra 4:24). Similarly, to this day Jews mourn the destruction of *Yerushalayim* and the *Beit Hamikdash* for three weeks each year. The mourning period starts with the seventeenth of the month of *Tammuz*, the day the walls of *Yerushalayim* were breached by the Romans in 70 CE, and culminates on the ninth of the next month, *Av*, when both the first and second Temples were set ablaze. Like *Daniel*, for part of this time Jews do not eat meat or drink wine, remembering the animal offerings and wine libations offered in the *Beit Hamikdash* that can no longer be brought. Mourning *Yerushalayim* strengthens the connection between the People of Israel and their holy city. It is said that Napoleon once passed a synagogue on the ninth of *Av* and inquired why the congregants were crying. When he was told that they were mourning their ancient Temple in Jerusalem, he is said to have responded: "Any people that can mourn an event that occurred thousands of years ago will one day return to their land."

Daniel/Daniel
Chapter 10

9 I heard him speaking; and when I heard him speaking, overcome by a deep sleep, I lay prostrate on the ground.

10 Then a hand touched me, and shook me onto my hands and knees.

11 He said to me, "O *Daniel*, precious man, mark what I say to you and stand up, for I have been sent to you." After he said this to me, I stood up, trembling.

12 He then said to me, "Have no fear, *Daniel*, for from the first day that you set your mind to get understanding, practicing abstinence before your God, your prayer was heard, and I have come because of your prayer.

13 However, the prince of the Persian kingdom opposed me for twenty-one days; now *Michael*, a prince of the first rank, has come to my aid, after I was detained there with the kings of Persia.

14 So I have come to make you understand what is to befall your people in the days to come, for there is yet a vision for those days."

15 While he was saying these things to me, I looked down and kept silent.

16 Then one who looked like a man touched my lips, and I opened my mouth and spoke, saying to him who stood before me, "My lord, because of the vision, I have been seized with pangs and cannot summon strength.

17 How can this servant of my lord speak with my lord, seeing that my strength has failed and no spirit is left in me?"

18 He who looked like a man touched me again, and strengthened me.

19 He said, "Have no fear, precious man, all will be well with you; be strong, be strong!" As he spoke with me, I was strengthened, and said, "Speak on, my lord, for you have strengthened me!"

20 Then he said, "Do you know why I have come to you? Now I must go back to fight the prince of Persia. When I go off, the prince of Greece will come in.

דניאל
פרק י

ט וָאֶשְׁמַע אֶת־קוֹל דְּבָרָיו וּכְשָׁמְעִי אֶת־קוֹל דְּבָרָיו וַאֲנִי הָיִיתִי נִרְדָּם עַל־פָּנַי וּפָנַי אָרְצָה:

י וְהִנֵּה־יָד נָגְעָה בִּי וַתְּנִיעֵנִי עַל־בִּרְכַּי וְכַפּוֹת יָדָי:

יא וַיֹּאמֶר אֵלַי דָּנִיֵּאל אִישׁ־חֲמֻדוֹת הָבֵן בַּדְּבָרִים אֲשֶׁר אָנֹכִי דֹבֵר אֵלֶיךָ וַעֲמֹד עַל־עָמְדֶךָ כִּי עַתָּה שֻׁלַּחְתִּי אֵלֶיךָ וּבְדַבְּרוֹ עִמִּי אֶת־הַדָּבָר הַזֶּה עָמַדְתִּי מַרְעִיד:

יב וַיֹּאמֶר אֵלַי אַל־תִּירָא דָנִיֵּאל כִּי מִן־הַיּוֹם הָרִאשׁוֹן אֲשֶׁר נָתַתָּ אֶת־לִבְּךָ לְהָבִין וּלְהִתְעַנּוֹת לִפְנֵי אֱלֹהֶיךָ נִשְׁמְעוּ דְבָרֶיךָ וַאֲנִי־בָאתִי בִּדְבָרֶיךָ:

יג וְשַׂר מַלְכוּת פָּרַס עֹמֵד לְנֶגְדִּי עֶשְׂרִים וְאֶחָד יוֹם וְהִנֵּה מִיכָאֵל אַחַד הַשָּׂרִים הָרִאשֹׁנִים בָּא לְעָזְרֵנִי וַאֲנִי נוֹתַרְתִּי שָׁם אֵצֶל מַלְכֵי פָרָס:

יד וּבָאתִי לַהֲבִינְךָ אֵת אֲשֶׁר־יִקְרָה לְעַמְּךָ בְּאַחֲרִית הַיָּמִים כִּי־עוֹד חָזוֹן לַיָּמִים:

טו וּבְדַבְּרוֹ עִמִּי כַּדְּבָרִים הָאֵלֶּה נָתַתִּי פָנַי אַרְצָה וְנֶאֱלָמְתִּי:

טז וְהִנֵּה כִּדְמוּת בְּנֵי אָדָם נֹגֵעַ עַל־שְׂפָתָי וָאֶפְתַּח־פִּי וָאֲדַבְּרָה וָאֹמְרָה אֶל־הָעֹמֵד לְנֶגְדִּי אֲדֹנִי בַּמַּרְאָה נֶהֶפְכוּ צִירַי עָלַי וְלֹא עָצַרְתִּי כֹחַ:

יז וְהֵיךְ יוּכַל עֶבֶד אֲדֹנִי זֶה לְדַבֵּר עִם־אֲדֹנִי זֶה וַאֲנִי מֵעַתָּה לֹא־יַעֲמָד־בִּי כֹחַ וּנְשָׁמָה לֹא נִשְׁאֲרָה־בִּי:

יח וַיֹּסֶף וַיִּגַּע־בִּי כְּמַרְאֵה אָדָם וַיְחַזְּקֵנִי:

יט וַיֹּאמֶר אַל־תִּירָא אִישׁ־חֲמֻדוֹת שָׁלוֹם לָךְ חֲזַק וַחֲזָק וּכְדַבְּרוֹ עִמִּי הִתְחַזַּקְתִּי וָאֹמְרָה יְדַבֵּר אֲדֹנִי כִּי חִזַּקְתָּנִי:

כ וַיֹּאמֶר הֲיָדַעְתָּ לָמָּה־בָּאתִי אֵלֶיךָ וְעַתָּה אָשׁוּב לְהִלָּחֵם עִם־שַׂר פָּרָס וַאֲנִי יוֹצֵא וְהִנֵּה שַׂר־יָוָן בָּא:

Daniel/Daniel
Chapter 11

דניאל
פרק יא

21 No one is helping me against them except your prince, *Michael*. However, I will tell you what is recorded in the book of truth.*

כא אֲבָל אַגִּיד לְךָ אֶת־הָרָשׁוּם בִּכְתָב אֱמֶת וְאֵין אֶחָד מִתְחַזֵּק עִמִּי עַל־אֵלֶּה כִּי אִם־מִיכָאֵל שַׂרְכֶם:

11

1 "In the first year of Darius the Mede, I took my stand to strengthen and fortify him.

יא א וַאֲנִי בִּשְׁנַת אַחַת לְדָרְיָוֶשׁ הַמָּדִי עָמְדִי לְמַחֲזִיק וּלְמָעוֹז לוֹ:

2 And now I will tell you the truth: Persia will have three more kings, and the fourth will be wealthier than them all; by the power he obtains through his wealth, he will stir everyone up against the kingdom of Greece.

ב וְעַתָּה אֱמֶת אַגִּיד לָךְ הִנֵּה־עוֹד שְׁלֹשָׁה מְלָכִים עֹמְדִים לְפָרַס וְהָרְבִיעִי יַעֲשִׁיר עֹשֶׁר־גָּדוֹל מִכֹּל וּכְחֶזְקָתוֹ בְעָשְׁרוֹ יָעִיר הַכֹּל אֵת מַלְכוּת יָוָן:

3 Then a warrior king will appear who will have an extensive dominion and do as he pleases.

ג וְעָמַד מֶלֶךְ גִּבּוֹר וּמָשַׁל מִמְשָׁל רַב וְעָשָׂה כִּרְצוֹנוֹ:

4 But after his appearance, his kingdom will be broken up and scattered to the four winds of heaven, but not for any of his posterity, nor with dominion like that which he had; for his kingdom will be uprooted and belong to others beside these.

ד וּכְעָמְדוֹ תִּשָּׁבֵר מַלְכוּתוֹ וְתֵחָץ לְאַרְבַּע רוּחוֹת הַשָּׁמָיִם וְלֹא לְאַחֲרִיתוֹ וְלֹא כְמָשְׁלוֹ אֲשֶׁר מָשָׁל כִּי תִנָּתֵשׁ מַלְכוּתוֹ וְלַאֲחֵרִים מִלְּבַד־אֵלֶּה:

5 "The king of the south will grow powerful; however, one of his officers will overpower him and rule, having an extensive dominion.

ה וְיֶחֱזַק מֶלֶךְ־הַנֶּגֶב וּמִן־שָׂרָיו וְיֶחֱזַק עָלָיו וּמָשָׁל מִמְשָׁל רַב מֶמְשַׁלְתּוֹ:

6 After some years, an alliance will be made, and the daughter of the king of the south will come to the king of the north to effect the agreement, but she will not maintain her strength, nor will his strength endure. She will be surrendered together with those who escorted her and the one who begot her and helped her during those times.

ו וּלְקֵץ שָׁנִים יִתְחַבָּרוּ וּבַת מֶלֶךְ־הַנֶּגֶב תָּבוֹא אֶל־מֶלֶךְ הַצָּפוֹן לַעֲשׂוֹת מֵישָׁרִים וְלֹא־תַעְצֹר כּוֹחַ הַזְּרוֹעַ וְלֹא יַעֲמֹד וּזְרֹעוֹ וְתִנָּתֵן הִיא וּמְבִיאֶיהָ וְהַיֹּלְדָהּ וּמַחֲזִקָהּ בָּעִתִּים:

7 A shoot from her stock will appear in his place, will come against the army and enter the fortress of the king of the north; he will fight and overpower them.

ז וְעָמַד מִנֵּצֶר שָׁרָשֶׁיהָ כַּנּוֹ וְיָבֹא אֶל־הַחַיִל וְיָבֹא בְּמָעוֹז מֶלֶךְ הַצָּפוֹן וְעָשָׂה בָהֶם וְהֶחֱזִיק:

8 He will also take their gods with their molten images and their precious vessels of silver and gold back to Egypt as booty. For some years he will leave the king of the north alone,

ח וְגַם אֱלֹהֵיהֶם עִם־נְסִכֵיהֶם עִם־כְּלֵי חֶמְדָּתָם כֶּסֶף וְזָהָב בַּשְּׁבִי יָבִא מִצְרָיִם וְהוּא שָׁנִים יַעֲמֹד מִמֶּלֶךְ הַצָּפוֹן:

9 who will [later] invade the realm of the king of the south, but will go back to his land.

ט וּבָא בְּמַלְכוּת מֶלֶךְ הַנֶּגֶב וְשָׁב אֶל־אַדְמָתוֹ:

10 "His sons will wage war, collecting a multitude of great armies; he will advance and sweep through as a flood, and will again wage war as far as his stronghold.

י וּבָנָו [וּבְנָיו] יִתְגָּרוּ וְאָסְפוּ הֲמוֹן חֲיָלִים רַבִּים וּבָא בוֹא וְשָׁטַף וְעָבָר וְיָשֹׁב וְיִתְגָּרוּ [וְיִתְגָּרֶה] עַד־מָעֻזֹּה [מָעֻזּוֹ]:

---

* order of clauses inverted for clarity

1913

Daniel/Daniel

Chapter 11

דניאל
פרק יא

11 Then the king of the south, in a rage, will go out to do battle with him, with the king of the north. He will muster a great multitude, but the multitude will be delivered into his [foe's] power.

יא וְיִתְמַרְמַר מֶלֶךְ הַנֶּגֶב וְיָצָא וְנִלְחַם עִמּוֹ עִם־מֶלֶךְ הַצָּפוֹן וְהֶעֱמִיד הָמוֹן רָב וְנִתַּן הֶהָמוֹן בְּיָדוֹ:

12 But when the multitude is carried off, he will grow arrogant; he will cause myriads to perish, but will not prevail.

יב וְנִשָּׂא הֶהָמוֹן ירום [וְרָם] לְבָבוֹ וְהִפִּיל רִבֹּאוֹת וְלֹא יָעוֹז:

13 Then the king of the north will again muster a multitude even greater than the first. After a time, a matter of years, he will advance with a great army and much baggage.

יג וְשָׁב מֶלֶךְ הַצָּפוֹן וְהֶעֱמִיד הָמוֹן רַב מִן־הָרִאשׁוֹן וּלְקֵץ הָעִתִּים שָׁנִים יָבוֹא בוֹא בְּחַיִל גָּדוֹל וּבִרְכוּשׁ רָב:

14 In those times, many will resist the king of the south, and the lawless sons of your people will assert themselves to confirm the vision, but they will fail.

יד וּבָעִתִּים הָהֵם רַבִּים יַעַמְדוּ עַל־מֶלֶךְ הַנֶּגֶב וּבְנֵי פָּרִיצֵי עַמְּךָ יִנַּשְּׂאוּ לְהַעֲמִיד חָזוֹן וְנִכְשָׁלוּ:

15 The king of the north will advance and throw up siege ramps and capture a fortress city, and the forces of the south will not hold out; even the elite of his army will be powerless to resist.

טו וְיָבֹא מֶלֶךְ הַצָּפוֹן וְיִשְׁפֹּךְ סוֹלֲלָה וְלָכַד עִיר מִבְצָרוֹת וּזְרֹעוֹת הַנֶּגֶב לֹא יַעֲמֹדוּ וְעַם מִבְחָרָיו וְאֵין כֹּחַ לַעֲמֹד:

16 His opponent will do as he pleases, for none will hold out against him; he will install himself in the beautiful land with destruction within his reach.

טז וְיַעַשׂ הַבָּא אֵלָיו כִּרְצוֹנוֹ וְאֵין עוֹמֵד לְפָנָיו וְיַעֲמֹד בְּאֶרֶץ־הַצְּבִי וְכָלָה בְיָדוֹ:

17 He will set his mind upon invading the strongholds throughout his [foe's] kingdom, but in order to destroy it he will effect an agreement with him and give him a daughter in marriage; he will not succeed at it and it will not come about.

יז וְיָשֵׂם פָּנָיו לָבוֹא בְּתֹקֶף כָּל־מַלְכוּתוֹ וִישָׁרִים עִמּוֹ וְעָשָׂה וּבַת הַנָּשִׁים יִתֶּן־לוֹ לְהַשְׁחִיתָהּ וְלֹא תַעֲמֹד וְלֹא־לוֹ תִהְיֶה:

18 He will turn to the coastlands and capture many; but a consul will put an end to his insults, nay pay him back for his insults.

יח וישב [וְיָשֵׂם] פָּנָיו לְאִיִּים וְלָכַד רַבִּים וְהִשְׁבִּית קָצִין חֶרְפָּתוֹ לוֹ בִּלְתִּי חֶרְפָּתוֹ יָשִׁיב לוֹ:

19 He will head back to the strongholds of his own land, but will stumble, and fall, and vanish.

יט וְיָשֵׁב פָּנָיו לְמָעוּזֵּי אַרְצוֹ וְנִכְשַׁל וְנָפַל וְלֹא יִמָּצֵא:

20 His place will be taken by one who will dispatch an officer to exact tribute for royal glory, but he will be broken in a few days, not by wrath or by war.

כ וְעָמַד עַל־כַּנּוֹ מַעֲבִיר נוֹגֵשׂ הֶדֶר מַלְכוּת וּבְיָמִים אֲחָדִים יִשָּׁבֵר וְלֹא בְאַפַּיִם וְלֹא בְמִלְחָמָה:

21 His place will be taken by a contemptible man, on whom royal majesty was not conferred; he will come in unawares and seize the kingdom through trickery.

כא וְעָמַד עַל־כַּנּוֹ נִבְזֶה וְלֹא־נָתְנוּ עָלָיו הוֹד מַלְכוּת וּבָא בְשַׁלְוָה וְהֶחֱזִיק מַלְכוּת בַּחֲלַקְלַקּוֹת:

22 The forces of the flood will be overwhelmed by him and will be broken, and so too the covenant leader.

כב וּזְרֹעוֹת הַשֶּׁטֶף יִשָּׁטְפוּ מִלְּפָנָיו וְיִשָּׁבֵרוּ וְגַם נְגִיד בְּרִית:

Daniel/Daniel

Chapter 11

דניאל

פרק יא

23 And, from the time an alliance is made with him, he will practice deceit; and he will rise to power with a small band.

כג וּמִן־הִתְחַבְּר֥וּת אֵלָ֖יו יַעֲשֶׂ֣ה מִרְמָ֑ה וְעָלָ֥ה וְעָצַ֖ם בִּמְעַט־גּֽוֹי׃

24 He will invade the richest of provinces unawares, and will do what his father and forefathers never did, lavishing on them spoil, booty, and wealth; he will have designs upon strongholds, but only for a time.

כד בְּשַׁלְוָ֞ה וּבְמִשְׁמַנֵּ֣י מְדִינָה֮ יָבוֹא֒ וְעָשָׂ֗ה אֲשֶׁ֨ר לֹא־עָשׂ֤וּ אֲבֹתָיו֙ וַאֲב֣וֹת אֲבֹתָ֔יו בִּזָּ֧ה וְשָׁלָ֛ל וּרְכ֖וּשׁ לָהֶ֣ם יִבְז֑וֹר וְעַ֧ל מִבְצָרִ֛ים יְחַשֵּׁ֥ב מַחְשְׁבֹתָ֖יו וְעַד־עֵֽת׃

25 "He will muster his strength and courage against the king of the south with a great army. The king of the south will wage war with a very great and powerful army but will not stand fast, for they will devise plans against him.

כה וְיָעֵר֩ כֹּח֨וֹ וּלְבָב֜וֹ עַל־מֶ֣לֶךְ הַנֶּגֶב֮ בְּחַ֣יִל גָּדוֹל֒ וּמֶ֣לֶךְ הַנֶּ֗גֶב יִתְגָּרֶה֙ לַמִּלְחָמָ֔ה בְּחַֽיִל־גָּד֥וֹל וְעָצ֖וּם עַד־מְאֹ֑ד וְלֹ֣א יַעֲמֹ֔ד כִּֽי־יַחְשְׁב֥וּ עָלָ֖יו מַחֲשָׁבֽוֹת׃

26 Those who eat of his food will ruin him. His army will be overwhelmed, and many will fall slain.

כו וְאֹכְלֵ֧י פַת־בָּג֛וֹ יִשְׁבְּר֖וּהוּ וְחֵיל֣וֹ יִשְׁט֑וֹף וְנָפְל֖וּ חֲלָלִ֥ים רַבִּֽים׃

27 The minds of both kings will be bent on evil; while sitting at the table together, they will lie to each other, but to no avail, for there is yet an appointed term.

כז וּשְׁנֵיהֶ֧ם הַמְּלָכִ֛ים לְבָבָ֖ם לְמֵרָ֑ע וְעַל־שֻׁלְחָ֤ן אֶחָד֙ כָּזָ֣ב יְדַבֵּ֔רוּ וְלֹ֣א תִצְלָ֔ח כִּי־ע֥וֹד קֵ֖ץ לַמּוֹעֵֽד׃

28 He will return to his land with great wealth, his mind set against the holy covenant. Having done his pleasure, he will return to his land.

כח וְיָשֹׁ֤ב אַרְצוֹ֙ בִּרְכ֣וּשׁ גָּד֔וֹל וּלְבָב֖וֹ עַל־בְּרִ֣ית קֹ֑דֶשׁ וְעָשָׂ֖ה וְשָׁ֥ב לְאַרְצֽוֹ׃

29 At the appointed time, he will again invade the south, but the second time will not be like the first.

כט לַמּוֹעֵ֥ד יָשׁ֖וּב וּבָ֣א בַנֶּ֑גֶב וְלֹֽא־תִהְיֶ֥ה כָרִאשֹׁנָ֖ה וְכָאַחֲרֹנָֽה׃

30 Ships from Kittim will come against him. He will be checked, and will turn back, raging against the holy covenant. Having done his pleasure, he will then attend to those who forsake the holy covenant.

ל וּבָ֣אוּ ב֗וֹ צִיִּים֙ כִּתִּ֔ים וְנִכְאָ֖ה וְשָׁ֑ב וְזָעַ֤ם עַל־בְּרִֽית־קוֹדֶשׁ֙ וְעָשָׂ֔ה וְשָׁ֣ב וְיָבֵ֔ן עַל־עֹזְבֵ֖י בְּרִ֥ית קֹֽדֶשׁ׃

31 Forces will be levied by him; they will desecrate the temple, the fortress; they will abolish the regular offering and set up the appalling abomination.

לא וּזְרֹעִ֖ים מִמֶּ֣נּוּ יַעֲמֹ֑דוּ וְחִלְּל֞וּ הַמִּקְדָּ֤שׁ הַמָּעוֹז֙ וְהֵסִ֣ירוּ הַתָּמִ֔יד וְנָתְנ֖וּ הַשִּׁקּ֥וּץ מְשֹׁמֵֽם׃

32 He will flatter with smooth words those who act wickedly toward the covenant, but the people devoted to their God will stand firm.

לב וּמַרְשִׁיעֵ֣י בְרִ֔ית יַחֲנִ֖יף בַּחֲלַקּ֑וֹת וְעַ֛ם יֹדְעֵ֥י אֱלֹהָ֖יו יַחֲזִ֥קוּ וְעָשֽׂוּ׃

33 The knowledgeable among the people will make the many understand; and for a while they shall fall by sword and flame, suffer captivity and spoliation.

לג וּמַשְׂכִּ֣ילֵי עָ֔ם יָבִ֖ינוּ לָרַבִּ֑ים וְנִכְשְׁל֞וּ בְּחֶ֧רֶב וּבְלֶהָבָ֛ה בִּשְׁבִ֥י וּבְבִזָּ֖ה יָמִֽים׃

34 In defeat, they will receive a little help, and many will join them insincerely.

לד וּבְהִכָּ֣שְׁלָ֔ם יֵעָזְר֖וּ עֵ֣זֶר מְעָ֑ט וְנִלְו֧וּ עֲלֵיהֶ֛ם רַבִּ֖ים בַּחֲלַקְלַקּֽוֹת׃

35 Some of the knowledgeable will fall, that they may be refined and purged and whitened until the time of the end, for an interval still remains until the appointed time.

לה וּמִן־הַמַּשְׂכִּילִ֣ים יִכָּֽשְׁל֗וּ לִצְר֥וֹף בָּהֶ֛ם וּלְבָרֵ֥ר וְלַלְבֵּ֖ן עַד־עֵ֣ת קֵ֑ץ כִּי־ע֖וֹד לַמּוֹעֵֽד׃

Daniel/Daniel
Chapter 11

דניאל
פרק יא

36 "The king will do as he pleases; he will exalt and magnify himself above every god, and he will speak awful things against the God of gods. He will prosper until wrath is spent, and what has been decreed is accomplished.

לו וְעָשָׂה כִרְצוֹנוֹ הַמֶּלֶךְ וְיִתְרוֹמֵם וְיִתְגַּדֵּל עַל־כָּל־אֵל וְעַל אֵל אֵלִים יְדַבֵּר נִפְלָאוֹת וְהִצְלִיחַ עַד־כָּלָה זַעַם כִּי נֶחֱרָצָה נֶעֱשָׂתָה׃

37 He will not have regard for the god of his ancestors or for the one dear to women; he will not have regard for any god, but will magnify himself above all.

לז וְעַל־אֱלֹהֵי אֲבֹתָיו לֹא יָבִין וְעַל־חֶמְדַּת נָשִׁים וְעַל־כָּל־אֱלוֹהַּ לֹא יָבִין כִּי עַל־כֹּל יִתְגַּדָּל׃

38 He will honor the god of fortresses on his stand; he will honor with gold and silver, with precious stones and costly things, a god that his ancestors never knew.

לח וְלֶאֱלֹהַּ מָעֻזִּים עַל־כַּנּוֹ יְכַבֵּד וְלֶאֱלוֹהַּ אֲשֶׁר לֹא־יְדָעֻהוּ אֲבֹתָיו יְכַבֵּד בְּזָהָב וּבְכֶסֶף וּבְאֶבֶן יְקָרָה וּבַחֲמֻדוֹת׃

39 He will deal with fortified strongholds with the help of an alien god. He will heap honor on those who acknowledge him, and will make them master over many; he will distribute land for a price.

לט וְעָשָׂה לְמִבְצְרֵי מָעֻזִּים עִם־אֱלוֹהַּ נֵכָר אֲשֶׁר הִכִּיר [יַכִּיר] יַרְבֶּה כָבוֹד וְהִמְשִׁילָם בָּרַבִּים וַאֲדָמָה יְחַלֵּק בִּמְחִיר׃

40 At the time of the end, the king of the south will lock horns with him, but the king of the north will attack him with chariots and riders and many ships. He will invade lands, sweeping through them like a flood;

מ וּבְעֵת קֵץ יִתְנַגַּח עִמּוֹ מֶלֶךְ הַנֶּגֶב וְיִשְׂתָּעֵר עָלָיו מֶלֶךְ הַצָּפוֹן בְּרֶכֶב וּבְפָרָשִׁים וּבָאֳנִיּוֹת רַבּוֹת וּבָא בַאֲרָצוֹת וְשָׁטַף וְעָבָר׃

41 he will invade the beautiful land, too, and many will fall, but these will escape his clutches: Edom, Moab, and the chief part of the Ammonites.

מא וּבָא בְּאֶרֶץ הַצְּבִי וְרַבּוֹת יִכָּשֵׁלוּ וְאֵלֶּה יִמָּלְטוּ מִיָּדוֹ אֱדוֹם וּמוֹאָב וְרֵאשִׁית בְּנֵי עַמּוֹן׃

u-VA b'-E-retz ha-tz'-VEE v'-ra-BOT yi-ka-SHAY-lu v'-AY-leh yi-ma-l'-TU mi-ya-DO e-DOM u-mo-AV v'-ray-SHEET b'-NAY a-MON

42 He will lay his hands on lands; not even the land of Egypt will escape.

מב וְיִשְׁלַח יָדוֹ בַּאֲרָצוֹת וְאֶרֶץ מִצְרַיִם לֹא תִהְיֶה לִפְלֵיטָה׃

43 He will gain control over treasures of gold and silver and over all the precious things of Egypt, and the Libyans and Cushites will follow at his heel.

מג וּמָשַׁל בְּמִכְמַנֵּי הַזָּהָב וְהַכֶּסֶף וּבְכֹל חֲמֻדוֹת מִצְרָיִם וְלֻבִים וְכֻשִׁים בְּמִצְעָדָיו׃

11:41 He will invade the beautiful land Many explanations are given for the term *eretz hatzvi* (ארץ הצבי), used in this verse as a description of the Land of Israel. Our translation reads 'beautiful land,' while other commentators say that it means 'desired land.' The Talmud (*Ketubot* 112a), following the literal translation 'land of the gazelle,' draws various parallels between the gazelle and *Eretz Yisrael*. For example, just as the gazelle is swift, Israel's fruits ripen quickly. Furthermore, just as the hide of the gazelle has the capacity to contain its body but shrinks when separated from it, so too the Land of Israel can expand to include its rightful inhabitants, but shrinks when the Jews are exiled from it. Perhaps a deeper message can be applied to Israel's inhabitants as well. In his book *Eretz Hatzvi*, Rabbi Zvi Teichman suggests that just as the land stretches to include its inhabitants, the inhabitants must also "stretch themselves" to appreciate the holiness and unique qualities of the "land of the gazelle."

ארץ הצבי

Daniel/Daniel
Chapter 12

דניאל
פרק יב

44 But reports from east and north will alarm him, and he will march forth in a great fury to destroy and annihilate many.

מד וּשְׁמֻעוֹת יְבַהֲלֻהוּ מִמִּזְרָח וּמִצָּפוֹן וְיָצָא בְּחֵמָא גְדֹלָה לְהַשְׁמִיד וּלְהַחֲרִים רַבִּים:

45 He will pitch his royal pavilion between the sea and the beautiful holy mountain, and he will meet his doom with no one to help him.

מה וְיִטַּע אָהֳלֵי אַפַּדְנוֹ בֵּין יַמִּים לְהַר־צְבִי־קֹדֶשׁ וּבָא עַד־קִצּוֹ וְאֵין עוֹזֵר לוֹ:

12

1 "At that time, the great prince, *Michael*, who stands beside the sons of your people, will appear. It will be a time of trouble, the like of which has never been since the nation came into being. At that time, your people will be rescued, all who are found inscribed in the book.

יב א וּבָעֵת הַהִיא יַעֲמֹד מִיכָאֵל הַשַּׂר הַגָּדוֹל הָעֹמֵד עַל־בְּנֵי עַמֶּךָ וְהָיְתָה עֵת צָרָה אֲשֶׁר לֹא־נִהְיְתָה מִהְיוֹת גּוֹי עַד הָעֵת הַהִיא וּבָעֵת הַהִיא יִמָּלֵט עַמְּךָ כָּל־הַנִּמְצָא כָּתוּב בַּסֵּפֶר:

2 Many of those that sleep in the dust of the earth will awake, some to eternal life, others to reproaches, to everlasting abhorrence.

ב וְרַבִּים מִיְּשֵׁנֵי אַדְמַת־עָפָר יָקִיצוּ אֵלֶּה לְחַיֵּי עוֹלָם וְאֵלֶּה לַחֲרָפוֹת לְדִרְאוֹן עוֹלָם:

3 And the knowledgeable will be radiant like the bright expanse of sky, and those who lead the many to righteousness will be like the stars forever and ever.

ג וְהַמַּשְׂכִּלִים יַזְהִרוּ כְּזֹהַר הָרָקִיעַ וּמַצְדִּיקֵי הָרַבִּים כַּכּוֹכָבִים לְעוֹלָם וָעֶד:

4 "But you, *Daniel*, keep the words secret, and seal the book until the time of the end. Many will range far and wide and knowledge will increase."

ד וְאַתָּה דָנִיֵּאל סְתֹם הַדְּבָרִים וַחֲתֹם הַסֵּפֶר עַד־עֵת קֵץ יְשֹׁטְטוּ רַבִּים וְתִרְבֶּה הַדָּעַת:

5 Then I, *Daniel*, looked and saw two others standing, one on one bank of the river, the other on the other bank of the river.

ה וְרָאִיתִי אֲנִי דָנִיֵּאל וְהִנֵּה שְׁנַיִם אֲחֵרִים עֹמְדִים אֶחָד הֵנָּה לִשְׂפַת הַיְאֹר וְאֶחָד הֵנָּה לִשְׂפַת הַיְאֹר:

6 One said to the man clothed in linen, who was above the water of the river, "How long until the end of these awful things?"

ו וַיֹּאמֶר לָאִישׁ לְבוּשׁ הַבַּדִּים אֲשֶׁר מִמַּעַל לְמֵימֵי הַיְאֹר עַד־מָתַי קֵץ הַפְּלָאוֹת:

7 Then I heard the man dressed in linen, who was above the water of the river, swear by the Ever-Living One as he lifted his right hand and his left hand to heaven: "For a time, times, and half a time; and when the breaking of the power of the holy people comes to an end, then shall all these things be fulfilled."

ז וָאֶשְׁמַע אֶת־הָאִישׁ לְבוּשׁ הַבַּדִּים אֲשֶׁר מִמַּעַל לְמֵימֵי הַיְאֹר וַיָּרֶם יְמִינוֹ וּשְׂמֹאלוֹ אֶל־הַשָּׁמַיִם וַיִּשָּׁבַע בְּחֵי הָעוֹלָם כִּי לְמוֹעֵד מוֹעֲדִים וָחֵצִי וּכְכַלּוֹת נַפֵּץ יַד־עַם־קֹדֶשׁ תִּכְלֶינָה כָל־אֵלֶּה:

8 I heard and did not understand, so I said, "My lord, what will be the outcome of these things?"

ח וַאֲנִי שָׁמַעְתִּי וְלֹא אָבִין וָאֹמְרָה אֲדֹנִי מָה אַחֲרִית אֵלֶּה:

9 He said, "Go, *Daniel*, for these words are secret and sealed to the time of the end.

ט וַיֹּאמֶר לֵךְ דָּנִיֵּאל כִּי־סְתֻמִים וַחֲתֻמִים הַדְּבָרִים עַד־עֵת קֵץ:

va-YO-mer LAYKH da-ni-YAYL kee s'-tu-MEEM va-kha-tu-MEEM ha-d'-va-REEM ad AYT KAYTZ

12:9 For these words are secret and sealed to the time of the end Generations of commentators have offered interpretations of the various visions in *Sefer Daniel*. Many different opinions have been suggested with regard to the specific events foretold in these prophesies. These distinct opinions do not contradict each other, however,

Daniel/Daniel
Chapter 12

דניאל
פרק יב

10 Many will be purified and purged and refined; the wicked will act wickedly and none of the wicked will understand; but the knowledgeable will understand.

י יִתְבָּרֲרוּ וְיִתְלַבְּנוּ וְיִצָּרְפוּ רַבִּים וְהִרְשִׁיעוּ רְשָׁעִים וְלֹא יָבִינוּ כָּל־רְשָׁעִים וְהַמַּשְׂכִּלִים יָבִינוּ:

11 From the time the regular offering is abolished, and an appalling abomination is set up – it will be a thousand two hundred and ninety days.

יא וּמֵעֵת הוּסַר הַתָּמִיד וְלָתֵת שִׁקּוּץ שֹׁמֵם יָמִים אֶלֶף מָאתַיִם וְתִשְׁעִים:

12 Happy the one who waits and reaches one thousand three hundred and thirty-five days.)

יב אַשְׁרֵי הַמְחַכֶּה וְיַגִּיעַ לְיָמִים אֶלֶף שְׁלֹשׁ מֵאוֹת שְׁלֹשִׁים וַחֲמִשָּׁה:

13 But you, go on to the end; you shall rest, and arise to your destiny at the end of the days."

יג וְאַתָּה לֵךְ לַקֵּץ וְתָנוּחַ וְתַעֲמֹד לְגֹרָלְךָ לְקֵץ הַיָּמִין:

because *Daniel*'s visions are deliberately vague, and hence, they can be fulfilled in numerous ways. Only in retrospect will it be possible to match up the visions with their actualization. The way in which they will ultimately be fulfilled in practice will be determined based on the Jewish people's actions, and their eagerness to return to the Land of Israel. Many possible dates for redemption have passed, but since the People of Israel were not ready, the final redemption has not yet come. At any point, however, they can improve their ways, fully embrace *Eretz Yisrael*, and return to their homeland, thus bringing about the redemption promised long ago in *Sefer Daniel*.

Sefer Ezra v'Nechemya
The Book of Ezra and Nehemiah

Introduction and commentary by Josh Even-Chen

Sefer Ezra v'Nechemya (Ezra and Nehemiah) is the penultimate book of the Hebrew Bible. Though comprised of two smaller books, *Sefer Ezra* and *Sefer Nechemya* were joined, as they concisely discuss the same general era, the final period included in the *Tanakh*. While some of the recorded events occur in faraway Persia, the focus of the book is the realization of the yearning of the Jewish exiles to return to *Eretz Yisrael*.

Many people associate the term "Zionism" only with the movement that began in the late nineteenth century, with the Jewish émigrés who returned to the Land of Israel in what became known as the "First *Aliya*." In truth, however, the first returnees to Zion were those who returned from the Babylonian exile in the time of *Ezra* and *Nechemya* some 2500 years ago, in what is referred to as *Shivat Tzion* (the return to Zion). Scholars have pointed out that the two events share similar characteristics. In both cases, the majority of exiles did not opt to return, and most of those who did come were young, driven by idealism and without strong ties to their host countries. Indeed, history, especially Jewish history, tends to repeat itself.

Seventy years before the reign of the Persian king Cyrus, Nebuchadnezzar and the Babylonians took control of the Land of Israel, exiling the inhabitants of *Yehuda* and destroying *Yerushalayim* and the *Beit Hamikdash*. One might have expected the Judean people to disappear in the Babylonian exile, as had happen to their brothers from the northern kingdom following the earlier exile at the hands of Assyria, but incredibly, as the prophet *Yirmiyahu* had predicted, they persisted. To assure their survival, they adopted a three-step approach: remember the past, live in the present, and hope for the future. And within that projected future, *Eretz Yisrael* was always central.

Sefer Ezra v'Nechemya begins with Cyrus's proclamation allowing the Jews to return to Israel and rebuild the *Beit Hamikdash*. While some Jews did heed the call, many chose to remain in Persia, where, over the years of Babylonian rule, they had become comfortable and had built a life for themselves. The returnees are met with resistance and hardship, and the construction of the Temple is halted until the second year of the reign of King Darius. In response to the encouragement of the prophets *Chagai* and *Zecharya*, construction of the *Beit Hamikdash* resumes and is finally completed in Darius's sixth year.

A short time later, in the seventh year of King Artaxerxes, *Ezra*, "a scribe expert in the Teaching of *Moshe*" (Ezra 7:6), brings a second wave of returnees to the Land of Israel, with *Nechemya* following thirteen years later. *Ezra* and *Nechemya* were both reformers, but while *Ezra* implemented spiritual reforms, *Nechemya* focused on pragmatic matters involving the country's material infrastructure. *Ezra's* attention turns to combating assimilation, promoting Jewish education and reestablishing a proper system of justice. *Nechemya* concentrates on physically reestablishing Jewish communities and reconstructing the fortifications of *Yerushalayim*. Both aspects were essential for the survival of the nation. Like *Nechemya*, the early twentieth-century Zionists were mostly responsible for building the country physically. However, as modern-day Israel's first Chief Rabbi, Abraham Isaac Kook, commented, even the most mundane tasks like plowing a field or building a home, if performed in Israel, constitute a fulfillment of the word of God.

All twenty-four books of the Hebrew Bible relate to *Eretz Yisrael*, but this is the only one that is dedicated to the rejuvenation of the land and its people, and the *Torah* laws. Our generation has merited seeing these words come to life before our eyes. It is therefore our privilege and obligation to study this book, in order to learn and benefit from the successes and failures, core messages, and divinely inspired wisdom that relates to the Jewish people's *first* attempt at resettling the Land of Israel, in the days of *Ezra* and *Nechemya*.

Chart of Important Milestones in the Settlement of the Land of Israel

Sefer Ezra v'Nechemya discusses the return of the Jews to the Land of Israel following 70 years of Babylonian exile. The return happened in stages and, to a certain degree, was incomplete. Over the years, small retorations of the Jewish people have taken place, each bringing us a little closer to the ultimate redemption. The following is a partial list of milestones in the settlement of the Jewish people in the Land of Israel:

Event	Description	Year	Relevant verses
Exodus from Egypt and entry into the Land of Israel	Under the leadership of *Moshe*, *Hashem* redeemed the Children of Israel from Egyptian slavery. After spending 40 years in the desert they reached their final destination – the Land of Israel.	Exodus – 2448 (Hebrew date) Entry into the land – 2488 (Hebrew date)	Exodus 6:6–8
Return to *Tzion*	Following Cyrus' proclamation allowing the Jews to return to Israel and rebuild the *Beit Hamikdash*, *Zerubavel*, along with *Yehoshua* the High Priest, led the first group of 42,360 returnees to the Land of Israel from the Babylonian exile. They re-settled the land and rebuilt the *Beit Hamikdash*. A number of years later, *Ezra* followed with a second wave of about 5,000 returnees. He worked hard to bring about religious reform among the Jews in Israel. Finally, *Nechemya* travelled to the Land of Israel to rebuild Jerusalem and repair its walls.	Zerubavel – 538 BCE Ezra – 458 BCE Nechemya – 445 BCE	Ezra 1–2, 7 Nehemiah 2, 13:6–7
Jewish independence – Hasmonean dynasty	The priestly Hasmonean family led a revolt against the Syrian-Greek rulers who had forbade the practice of Judaism and defiled the *Beit Hamikdash*. They won the battle for *Yerushalayim*, purified the *Beit Hamikdash*, and continued to fight their Seleucid oppressors. Eventually, the Hasmoneans were victorious, and, with the collapse of the Seleucid kingdom, Jewish independence was restored in the Land of Israel until its capture by the Romans in 63 BCE.	165 BCE – *Beit Hamikdash* is restored 142 BCE – Jews granted autonomy	
Aliyot	*Aliyah*, return to Israel, was always a national aspiration of the Jewish people but was not fulfilled on a large-scale until the rise of Zionism. From 1882 until the establishment of the State of Israel in 1948, over 550,000 Jews immigrated to the Land of Israel through several waves of *aliyah*.	1882–1948	
Declaration of the State of Israel	The State of Israel was officially declared by David Ben-Gurion on May, 14th 1948 (the 5th of *Iyar* 5708), and the Jews again have a national homeland in the Land of Israel. Many refer to this as the beginning of the final redemption.	1948	
Rescue Operations	Since the establishment of the State of Israel, there have been a number of rescue operations carried out by the Israel, bringing Jews all over the world to freedom in the Jewish State. Some of these operations include: Operation Magic Carpet, which brought approximately 50,000 Yemenite Jews to Israel, Operation Ezra and Nehemiah, which airlifted more than 120,000 Iraqi Jews to Israel, and Operation Moses, which brought approximately 8,000 Ethiopian Jews to the Jewish state.	Operation Magic Carpet – 1949–1950, Operation Ezra and Nehemiah – 1950–1951, Operation Moses – 1984	
Re-unification of *Yerushalayim*	The Six-Day war resulted in Israel's acquisition of the Sinai Peninsula and the Gaza Strip (both eventually given back), the West Bank, the Golan Heights, and East Jerusalem. For the first time since 1948, Jerusalem was reunited and Jews were able to pray at the Western Wall, the remaining outer wall of the Second *Beit Hamikdash*.	1967	
Jewish Immigration	Since 1948, more than 3 million Jews from all over the world have made *aliyah* to the Land of Israel. This is seen by many as a partial fulfillment of the prophecies of the ingathering of the exiles.	1948–present	

Ezra/Ezra

Chapter 1

עזרא

פרק א

1. **1** In the first year of King Cyrus of Persia, when the word of *Hashem* spoken by *Yirmiyahu* was fulfilled, *Hashem* roused the spirit of King Cyrus of Persia to issue a proclamation throughout his realm by word of mouth and in writing as follows:

א וּבִשְׁנַת אַחַת לְכוֹרֶשׁ מֶלֶךְ פָּרַס לִכְלוֹת דְּבַר־יְהֹוָה מִפִּי יִרְמְיָה הֵעִיר יְהֹוָה אֶת־רוּחַ כֹּרֶשׁ מֶלֶךְ־פָּרַס וַיַּעֲבֶר־קוֹל בְּכָל־מַלְכוּתוֹ וְגַם־בְּמִכְתָּב לֵאמֹר:

2. "Thus said King Cyrus of Persia: God of Heaven has given me all the kingdoms of the earth and has charged me with building Him a house in *Yerushalayim*, which is in *Yehuda*.

ב כֹּה אָמַר כֹּרֶשׁ מֶלֶךְ פָּרַס כֹּל מַמְלְכוֹת הָאָרֶץ נָתַן לִי יְהֹוָה אֱלֹהֵי הַשָּׁמָיִם וְהוּא־פָקַד עָלַי לִבְנוֹת־לוֹ בַיִת בִּירוּשָׁלַם אֲשֶׁר בִּיהוּדָה:

3. Anyone of you of all His people – may his God be with him, and let him go up to *Yerushalayim* that is in *Yehuda* and build the House of God of *Yisrael*, the God that is in *Yerushalayim*;

ג מִי־בָכֶם מִכָּל־עַמּוֹ יְהִי אֱלֹהָיו עִמּוֹ וְיַעַל לִירוּשָׁלַם אֲשֶׁר בִּיהוּדָה וְיִבֶן אֶת־בֵּית יְהֹוָה אֱלֹהֵי יִשְׂרָאֵל הוּא הָאֱלֹהִים אֲשֶׁר בִּירוּשָׁלָם:

4. and all who stay behind, wherever he may be living, let the people of his place assist him with silver, gold, goods, and livestock, besides the freewill offering to the House of *Hashem* that is in *Yerushalayim*."

ד וְכָל־הַנִּשְׁאָר מִכָּל־הַמְּקֹמוֹת אֲשֶׁר הוּא גָר־שָׁם יְנַשְּׂאוּהוּ אַנְשֵׁי מְקֹמוֹ בְּכֶסֶף וּבְזָהָב וּבִרְכוּשׁ וּבִבְהֵמָה עִם־הַנְּדָבָה לְבֵית הָאֱלֹהִים אֲשֶׁר בִּירוּשָׁלָם:

5. So the chiefs of the clans of *Yehuda* and *Binyamin*, and the *Kohanim* and *Leviim*, all whose spirit had been roused by *Hashem*, got ready to go up to build the House of *Hashem* that is in *Yerushalayim*.

ה וַיָּקוּמוּ רָאשֵׁי הָאָבוֹת לִיהוּדָה וּבִנְיָמִן וְהַכֹּהֲנִים וְהַלְוִיִּם לְכֹל הֵעִיר הָאֱלֹהִים אֶת־רוּחוֹ לַעֲלוֹת לִבְנוֹת אֶת־בֵּית יְהֹוָה אֲשֶׁר בִּירוּשָׁלָם:

6. All their neighbors supported them with silver vessels, with gold, with goods, with livestock, and with precious objects, besides what had been given as a freewill offering.

ו וְכָל־סְבִיבֹתֵיהֶם חִזְּקוּ בִידֵיהֶם בִּכְלֵי־כֶסֶף בַּזָּהָב בָּרְכוּשׁ וּבַבְּהֵמָה וּבַמִּגְדָּנוֹת לְבַד עַל־כָּל־הִתְנַדֵּב:

7. King Cyrus of Persia released the vessels of *Hashem*'s house which Nebuchadnezzar had taken away from *Yerushalayim* and had put in the house of his god.

ז וְהַמֶּלֶךְ כּוֹרֶשׁ הוֹצִיא אֶת־כְּלֵי בֵית־יְהֹוָה אֲשֶׁר הוֹצִיא נְבוּכַדְנֶצַּר מִירוּשָׁלַם וַיִּתְּנֵם בְּבֵית אֱלֹהָיו:

8. These King Cyrus of Persia released through the office of Mithredath the treasurer, who gave an inventory of them to *Sheshbatzar* the prince of *Yehuda*.

ח וַיּוֹצִיאֵם כּוֹרֶשׁ מֶלֶךְ פָּרַס עַל־יַד מִתְרְדָת הַגִּזְבָּר וַיִּסְפְּרֵם לְשֵׁשְׁבַּצַּר הַנָּשִׂיא לִיהוּדָה:

9. This is the inventory: 30 gold basins, 1,000 silver basins, 29 knives,

ט וְאֵלֶּה מִסְפָּרָם אֲגַרְטְלֵי זָהָב שְׁלֹשִׁים אֲגַרְטְלֵי־כֶסֶף אָלֶף מַחֲלָפִים תִּשְׁעָה וְעֶשְׂרִים:

10. 30 gold bowls, 410 silver double bowls, 1,000 other vessels;

י כְּפוֹרֵי זָהָב שְׁלֹשִׁים כְּפוֹרֵי כֶסֶף מִשְׁנִים אַרְבַּע מֵאוֹת וַעֲשָׂרָה כֵּלִים אֲחֵרִים אָלֶף:

Ezra/Ezra

Chapter 2

עזרא
פרק ב

11 in all, 5,400 gold and silver vessels. *Sheshbatzar* brought all these back when the exiles came back from Babylon to *Yerushalayim*.

יא כָּל־כֵּלִים לַזָּהָב וְלַכֶּסֶף חֲמֵשֶׁת אֲלָפִים וְאַרְבַּע מֵאוֹת הַכֹּל הֶעֱלָה שֵׁשְׁבַּצַּר עִם הֵעָלוֹת הַגּוֹלָה מִבָּבֶל לִירוּשָׁלָם׃

kol kay-LEEM la-za-HAV v'-la-KE-sef kha-MAY-shet a-la-FEEM v'-ar-BA may-OT ha-KOL he-e-LAH shaysh-ba-TZAR IM hay-a-LOT ha-go-LAH mi-ba-VEL lee-ru-sha-LA-im

2

1 These are the people of the province who came up from among the captive exiles whom King Nebuchadnezzar of Babylon had carried into exile to Babylon, who returned to *Yerushalayim* and *Yehuda*, each to his own city,

ב א וְאֵלֶּה בְּנֵי הַמְּדִינָה הָעֹלִים מִשְּׁבִי הַגּוֹלָה אֲשֶׁר הֶגְלָה נְבוּכַדְנֶצּוֹר [נְבוּכַדְנֶצַּר] מֶלֶךְ־בָּבֶל לְבָבֶל וַיָּשׁוּבוּ לִירוּשָׁלַם וִיהוּדָה אִישׁ לְעִירוֹ׃

2 who came with *Zerubavel*, *Yeshua*, *Nechemya*, *Seraya*, *Reelaiah*, *Mordechai*, *Bilshan*, *Mispar*, *Bigvai*, *Rehum*, *Baanah*: The list of the men of the people of *Yisrael*:

ב אֲשֶׁר־בָּאוּ עִם־זְרֻבָּבֶל יֵשׁוּעַ נְחֶמְיָה שְׂרָיָה רְעֵלָיָה מָרְדֳּכַי בִּלְשָׁן מִסְפָּר בִּגְוַי רְחוּם בַּעֲנָה מִסְפַּר אַנְשֵׁי עַם יִשְׂרָאֵל׃

3 the sons of Parosh – 2,172;

ג בְּנֵי פַרְעֹשׁ אַלְפַּיִם מֵאָה שִׁבְעִים וּשְׁנָיִם׃

4 the sons of Shephatiah – 372;

ד בְּנֵי שְׁפַטְיָה שְׁלֹשׁ מֵאוֹת שִׁבְעִים וּשְׁנָיִם׃

5 the sons of Arah – 775;

ה בְּנֵי אָרַח שְׁבַע מֵאוֹת חֲמִשָּׁה וְשִׁבְעִים׃

6 the sons of Pahath-moab: the sons of *Yeshua* and *Yoav* – 2,812;

ו בְּנֵי־פַחַת מוֹאָב לִבְנֵי יֵשׁוּעַ יוֹאָב אַלְפַּיִם שְׁמֹנֶה מֵאוֹת וּשְׁנֵים עָשָׂר׃

7 the sons of Elam – 1,254;

ז בְּנֵי עֵילָם אֶלֶף מָאתַיִם חֲמִשִּׁים וְאַרְבָּעָה׃

8 the sons of Zattu – 945;

ח בְּנֵי זַתּוּא תְּשַׁע מֵאוֹת וְאַרְבָּעִים וַחֲמִשָּׁה׃

9 the sons of Zaccai – 760;

ט בְּנֵי זַכָּי שְׁבַע מֵאוֹת וְשִׁשִּׁים׃

10 the sons of Bani – 642;

י בְּנֵי בָנִי שֵׁשׁ מֵאוֹת אַרְבָּעִים וּשְׁנָיִם׃

11 the sons of Bebai – 623;

יא בְּנֵי בֵבָי שֵׁשׁ מֵאוֹת עֶשְׂרִים וּשְׁלֹשָׁה׃

12 the sons of Azgad – 1,222;

יב בְּנֵי עַזְגָּד אֶלֶף מָאתַיִם עֶשְׂרִים וּשְׁנָיִם׃

13 the sons of Adonikam – 666;

יג בְּנֵי אֲדֹנִיקָם שֵׁשׁ מֵאוֹת שִׁשִּׁים וְשִׁשָּׁה׃

1:11 When the exiles came back from *Bavel* to *Yerushalayim*. The beloved Rabbi Shlomo Carlebach would quip, "Did you know that Jerusalem is the highest city in the world?" Many were skeptical, but he was correct – in the spiritual, if not topographical, sense. The Bible states that "*Avram* went *down* to Egypt" from Canaan (Genesis 12:10), and when the people returned to the Land of Israel from the Babylonian exile, although translated here as "the exiles *came back*," the more exacting translation is "the exiles *ascended*." Ever since the magnetic north has dictated the directional illustration of maps, people have said things like, "I'm going *down* south," or "I'm heading *up* north." However, this verse teaches that no matter where a person is in the world, his "spiritual compass" should always indicate that *Yerushalayim* is "up."

Rabbi Shlomo Carlebach (1925–1994)

Ezra/Ezra
Chapter 2

14	the sons of Bigvai – 2,056;	יד בְּנֵי בִגְוָי אַלְפַּיִם חֲמִשִּׁים וְשִׁשָּׁה:
15	the sons of Adin – 454;	טו בְּנֵי עָדִין אַרְבַּע מֵאוֹת חֲמִשִּׁים וְאַרְבָּעָה:
16	the sons of Ater: *Chizkiyahu* – 98;	טז בְּנֵי־אָטֵר לִיחִזְקִיָּה תִּשְׁעִים וּשְׁמֹנָה:
17	the sons of Bezai – 323;	יז בְּנֵי בֵצָי שְׁלֹשׁ מֵאוֹת עֶשְׂרִים וּשְׁלֹשָׁה:
18	the sons of Jorah – 112;	יח בְּנֵי יוֹרָה מֵאָה וּשְׁנֵים עָשָׂר:
19	the sons of Hashum – 223;	יט בְּנֵי חָשֻׁם מָאתַיִם עֶשְׂרִים וּשְׁלֹשָׁה:
20	the sons of Gibbar – 95;	כ בְּנֵי גִבָּר תִּשְׁעִים וַחֲמִשָּׁה:
21	the sons of *Beit Lechem* – 123;	כא בְּנֵי בֵית־לָחֶם מֵאָה עֶשְׂרִים וּשְׁלֹשָׁה:
22	the sons of Netophah – 56;	כב אַנְשֵׁי נְטֹפָה חֲמִשִּׁים וְשִׁשָּׁה:
23	the sons of *Anatot* – 128;	כג אַנְשֵׁי עֲנָתוֹת מֵאָה עֶשְׂרִים וּשְׁמֹנָה:
24	the sons of Azmaveth – 42;	כד בְּנֵי עַזְמָוֶת אַרְבָּעִים וּשְׁנָיִם:
25	the sons of Kiriath-arim: Chephirah and Beeroth – 743;	כה בְּנֵי קִרְיַת עָרִים כְּפִירָה וּבְאֵרוֹת שְׁבַע מֵאוֹת וְאַרְבָּעִים וּשְׁלֹשָׁה:
26	the sons of *Rama* and Geba – 621;	כו בְּנֵי הָרָמָה וָגָבַע שֵׁשׁ מֵאוֹת עֶשְׂרִים וְאֶחָד:
27	the men of Michmas – 122;	כז אַנְשֵׁי מִכְמָס מֵאָה עֶשְׂרִים וּשְׁנָיִם:
28	the men of *Beit El* and Ai – 223;	כח אַנְשֵׁי בֵית־אֵל וְהָעָי מָאתַיִם עֶשְׂרִים וּשְׁלֹשָׁה:
29	the men of Nebo – 52;	כט בְּנֵי נְבוֹ חֲמִשִּׁים וּשְׁנָיִם:
30	the sons of Magbish – 156;	ל בְּנֵי מַגְבִּישׁ מֵאָה חֲמִשִּׁים וְשִׁשָּׁה:
31	the sons of the other Elam – 1,254;	לא בְּנֵי עֵילָם אַחֵר אֶלֶף מָאתַיִם חֲמִשִּׁים וְאַרְבָּעָה:
32	the sons of Harim – 320;	לב בְּנֵי חָרִם שְׁלֹשׁ מֵאוֹת וְעֶשְׂרִים:
33	the sons of Lod, Hadid, and Ono – 725;	לג בְּנֵי־לֹד חָדִיד וְאוֹנוֹ שְׁבַע מֵאוֹת עֶשְׂרִים וַחֲמִשָּׁה:
34	the sons of *Yericho* – 345;	לד בְּנֵי יְרֵחוֹ שְׁלֹשׁ מֵאוֹת אַרְבָּעִים וַחֲמִשָּׁה:
35	the sons of Senaah – 3,630.	לה בְּנֵי סְנָאָה שְׁלֹשֶׁת אֲלָפִים וְשֵׁשׁ מֵאוֹת וּשְׁלֹשִׁים:
36	The *Kohanim*: the sons of Jedaiah: the house of *Yeshua* – 973;	לו הַכֹּהֲנִים בְּנֵי יְדַעְיָה לְבֵית יֵשׁוּעַ תְּשַׁע מֵאוֹת שִׁבְעִים וּשְׁלֹשָׁה:
37	the sons of Immer – 1,052;	לז בְּנֵי אִמֵּר אֶלֶף חֲמִשִּׁים וּשְׁנָיִם:
38	the sons of Pashhur – 1,247;	לח בְּנֵי פַשְׁחוּר אֶלֶף מָאתַיִם אַרְבָּעִים וְשִׁבְעָה:

Ezra/Ezra

Chapter 2

עזרא
פרק ב

39 the sons of Harim – 1,017.

מ הַלְוִיִּם בְּנֵי־יֵשׁוּעַ וְקַדְמִיאֵל לִבְנֵי הוֹדַוְיָה שִׁבְעִים וְאַרְבָּעָה:

לט בְּנֵי חָרִם אֶלֶף וְשִׁבְעָה עָשָׂר:

40 The *Leviim*: the sons of *Yeshua* and *Kadmiel*: the sons of Hodaviah – 74.

41 The singers: the sons of *Asaf* – 128.

מא הַמְשֹׁרְרִים בְּנֵי אָסָף מֵאָה עֶשְׂרִים וּשְׁמֹנָה:

42 The gatekeepers: the sons of *Shalum*, the sons of Ater, the sons of Talmon, the sons of Akkub, the sons of Hatita, the sons of Shobai, all told – 139.

מב בְּנֵי הַשֹּׁעֲרִים בְּנֵי־שַׁלּוּם בְּנֵי־אָטֵר בְּנֵי־טַלְמוֹן בְּנֵי־עַקּוּב בְּנֵי חֲטִיטָא בְּנֵי שֹׁבָי הַכֹּל מֵאָה שְׁלֹשִׁים וְתִשְׁעָה:

43 The temple servants: the sons of Ziha, the sons of Hasupha, the sons of Tabbaoth,

מג הַנְּתִינִים בְּנֵי־צִיחָא בְנֵי־חֲשׂוּפָא בְּנֵי טַבָּעוֹת:

44 the sons of Keros, the sons of Siaha, the sons of Padon,

מד בְּנֵי־קֵרֹס בְּנֵי־סִיעֲהָא בְּנֵי פָדוֹן:

45 the sons of Lebanah, the sons of Hagabah, the sons of Akkub,

מה בְּנֵי־לְבָנָה בְנֵי־חֲגָבָה בְּנֵי עַקּוּב:

46 the sons of Hagab, the sons of Salmai, the sons of Hanan,

מו בְּנֵי־חָגָב בְּנֵי־שַׁמְלַי [שַׂלְמַי] בְּנֵי חָנָן:

47 the sons of Giddel, the sons of Gahar, the sons of Reaiah,

מז בְּנֵי־גִדֵּל בְּנֵי־גַחַר בְּנֵי רְאָיָה:

48 the sons of Rezin, the sons of Nekoda, the sons of Gazzam,

מח בְּנֵי־רְצִין בְּנֵי־נְקוֹדָא בְּנֵי גַזָּם:

49 the sons of Uzza, the sons of Paseah, the sons of Besai,

מט בְּנֵי־עֻזָּא בְנֵי־פָסֵחַ בְּנֵי בֵסָי:

50 the sons of Asnah, the sons of Meunim, the sons of Nephusim,

נ בְּנֵי־אַסְנָה בְנֵי־מְעוּנִים [מְעִינִים] בְּנֵי נְפִיסִים [נְפוּסִים]:

51 the sons of Bakbuk, the sons of Hakupha, the sons of Harhur,

נא בְּנֵי־בַקְבּוּק בְּנֵי־חֲקוּפָא בְּנֵי חַרְחוּר:

52 the sons of Bazluth, the sons of Mehida, the sons of Harsha,

נב בְּנֵי־בַצְלוּת בְּנֵי־מְחִידָא בְּנֵי חַרְשָׁא:

53 the sons of Barkos, the sons of Sisera, the sons of Temah,

נג בְּנֵי־בַרְקוֹס בְּנֵי־סִיסְרָא בְּנֵי־תָמַח:

54 the sons of Neziah, the sons of Hatipha.

נד בְּנֵי נְצִיחַ בְּנֵי חֲטִיפָא:

55 The sons of *Shlomo*'s servants: the sons of Sotai, the sons of Hassophereth, the sons of Peruda,

נה בְּנֵי עַבְדֵי שְׁלֹמֹה בְּנֵי־סֹטַי בְּנֵי־הַסֹּפֶרֶת בְּנֵי פְרוּדָא:

56 the sons of Jaalah, the sons of Darkon, the sons of Giddel,

נו בְּנֵי־יַעֲלָה בְנֵי־דַרְקוֹן בְּנֵי גִדֵּל:

57 the sons of Shephatiah, the sons of Hattil, the sons of Pochereth-hazzebaim, the sons of Ami.

נז בְּנֵי שְׁפַטְיָה בְנֵי־חַטִּיל בְּנֵי פֹכֶרֶת הַצְּבָיִים בְּנֵי אָמִי:

58 The total of temple servants and the sons of *Shlomo*'s servants – 392.

נח כָּל־הַנְּתִינִים וּבְנֵי עַבְדֵי שְׁלֹמֹה שְׁלֹשׁ מֵאוֹת תִּשְׁעִים וּשְׁנָיִם:

Ezra / Chapter 2

⁵⁹ The following were those who came up from Tel-melah, Tel-harsha, Cherub, Addan, and Immer – they were unable to tell whether their father's house and descent were Israelite:

נט וְאֵלֶּה הָעֹלִים מִתֵּל מֶלַח תֵּל חַרְשָׁא כְּרוּב אַדָּן אִמֵּר וְלֹא יָכְלוּ לְהַגִּיד בֵּית־אֲבוֹתָם וְזַרְעָם אִם מִיִּשְׂרָאֵל הֵם:

⁶⁰ the sons of Delaiah, the sons of Tobiah, the sons of Nekoda – 652.

ס בְּנֵי־דְלָיָה בְנֵי־טוֹבִיָּה בְּנֵי נְקוֹדָא שֵׁשׁ מֵאוֹת חֲמִשִּׁים וּשְׁנָיִם:

⁶¹ Of the sons of the *Kohanim*, the sons of Habaiah, the sons of Hakkoz, the sons of *Barzilai* who had married a daughter of *Barzilai* and had taken his name –

סא וּמִבְּנֵי הַכֹּהֲנִים בְּנֵי חֲבַיָּה בְּנֵי הַקּוֹץ בְּנֵי בַרְזִלַּי אֲשֶׁר לָקַח מִבְּנוֹת בַּרְזִלַּי הַגִּלְעָדִי אִשָּׁה וַיִּקָּרֵא עַל־שְׁמָם:

⁶² these searched for their genealogical records, but they could not be found, so they were disqualified for the priesthood.

סב אֵלֶּה בִּקְשׁוּ כְתָבָם הַמִּתְיַחְשִׂים וְלֹא נִמְצָאוּ וַיְגֹאֲלוּ מִן־הַכְּהֻנָּה:

⁶³ The Tirshatha ordered them not to eat of the most holy things until a *Kohen* with Urim and Thummim should appear.

סג וַיֹּאמֶר הַתִּרְשָׁתָא לָהֶם אֲשֶׁר לֹא־יֹאכְלוּ מִקֹּדֶשׁ הַקֳּדָשִׁים עַד עֲמֹד כֹּהֵן לְאוּרִים וּלְתֻמִּים:

⁶⁴ The sum of the entire community was 42,360,

סד כָּל־הַקָּהָל כְּאֶחָד אַרְבַּע רִבּוֹא אַלְפַּיִם שְׁלֹשׁ־מֵאוֹת שִׁשִּׁים:

⁶⁵ not counting their male and female servants, those being 7,337; they also had 200 male and female singers.

סה מִלְּבַד עַבְדֵיהֶם וְאַמְהֹתֵיהֶם אֵלֶּה שִׁבְעַת אֲלָפִים שְׁלֹשׁ מֵאוֹת שְׁלֹשִׁים וְשִׁבְעָה וְלָהֶם מְשֹׁרְרִים וּמְשֹׁרְרוֹת מָאתָיִם:

⁶⁶ Their horses – 736; their mules – 245;

סו סוּסֵיהֶם שְׁבַע מֵאוֹת שְׁלֹשִׁים וְשִׁשָּׁה פִּרְדֵיהֶם מָאתַיִם אַרְבָּעִים וַחֲמִשָּׁה:

⁶⁷ their camels – 435; their asses – 6,720.

סז גְּמַלֵּיהֶם אַרְבַּע מֵאוֹת שְׁלֹשִׁים וַחֲמִשָּׁה חֲמֹרִים שֵׁשֶׁת אֲלָפִים שְׁבַע מֵאוֹת וְעֶשְׂרִים:

⁶⁸ Some of the chiefs of the clans, on arriving at the House of *Hashem* in *Yerushalayim*, gave a freewill offering to erect the House of *Hashem* on its site.

סח וּמֵרָאשֵׁי הָאָבוֹת בְּבוֹאָם לְבֵית יְהוָה אֲשֶׁר בִּירוּשָׁלָיִם הִתְנַדְּבוּ לְבֵית הָאֱלֹהִים לְהַעֲמִידוֹ עַל־מְכוֹנוֹ:

⁶⁹ In accord with their means, they donated to the treasury of the work: gold – 6,100 drachmas, silver – 5,000 *manim*, and priestly robes – 100.

סט כְּכֹחָם נָתְנוּ לְאוֹצַר הַמְּלָאכָה זָהָב דַּרְכְּמוֹנִים שֵׁשׁ־רִבֹּאות וָאֶלֶף וְכֶסֶף מָנִים חֲמֵשֶׁת אֲלָפִים וְכָתְנֹת כֹּהֲנִים מֵאָה:

⁷⁰ The *Kohanim*, the *Leviim* and some of the people, and the singers, gatekeepers, and the temple servants took up residence in their towns and all *Yisrael* in their towns.

ע וַיֵּשְׁבוּ הַכֹּהֲנִים וְהַלְוִיִּם וּמִן־הָעָם וְהַמְשֹׁרְרִים וְהַשּׁוֹעֲרִים וְהַנְּתִינִים בְּעָרֵיהֶם וְכָל־יִשְׂרָאֵל בְּעָרֵיהֶם:

va-yay-sh'-VU ha-ko-ha-NEEM v'-hal-vi-YIM u-min ha-AM v'-ham-sho-r'-REEM v'-ha-sho-a-REEM v'-ha-n'-tee-NEEM b'-a-ray-HEM v'-khol yis-ra-AYL b'-a-ray-HEM

2:70 And all *Yisrael* in their towns In this chapter we learn of the many Jewish families who return to their ancestral lands and villages, establishing new communities on the deserted and ruined old sites of the Land of Israel. As one travels across the landscape of the contemporary State of Israel, it is amazing to see

Ezra/Ezra
Chapter 3

עזרא
פרק ג

3 ¹ When the seventh month arrived – the Israelites being settled in their towns – the entire people assembled as one man in *Yerushalayim*.

א וַיִּגַּע הַחֹדֶשׁ הַשְּׁבִיעִי וּבְנֵי יִשְׂרָאֵל בֶּעָרִים וַיֵּאָסְפוּ הָעָם כְּאִישׁ אֶחָד אֶל־יְרוּשָׁלָ͏ִם׃

va-yi-GA ha-KHO-desh ha-sh'-vee-EE uv-NAY yis-ra-AYL be-a-REEM va-yay-a-s'-FU ha-AM k'-EESH e-KHAD el y'-ru-sha-LA-im

² Then *Yeshua* son of *Yotzadak* and his brother *Kohanim*, and *Zerubavel* son of *Shealtiel* and his brothers set to and built the *Mizbayach* of the God of *Yisrael* to offer burnt offerings upon it as is written in the Teaching of *Moshe*, the man of *Hashem*.

ב וַיָּקָם יֵשׁוּעַ בֶּן־יוֹצָדָק וְאֶחָיו הַכֹּהֲנִים וּזְרֻבָּבֶל בֶּן־שְׁאַלְתִּיאֵל וְאֶחָיו וַיִּבְנוּ אֶת־מִזְבַּח אֱלֹהֵי יִשְׂרָאֵל לְהַעֲלוֹת עָלָיו עֹלוֹת כַּכָּתוּב בְּתוֹרַת מֹשֶׁה אִישׁ־הָאֱלֹהִים׃

³ They set up the *Mizbayach* on its site because they were in fear of the peoples of the land, and they offered burnt offerings on it to *Hashem*, burnt offerings each morning and evening.

ג וַיָּכִינוּ הַמִּזְבֵּחַ עַל־מְכוֹנֹתָיו כִּי בְּאֵימָה עֲלֵיהֶם מֵעַמֵּי הָאֲרָצוֹת וַיַּעַל [וַיַּעֲלוּ] עָלָיו עֹלוֹת לַיהוָה עֹלוֹת לַבֹּקֶר וְלָעָרֶב׃

⁴ Then they celebrated the festival of *Sukkot* as is written, with its daily burnt offerings in the proper quantities, on each day as is prescribed for it,

ד וַיַּעֲשׂוּ אֶת־חַג הַסֻּכּוֹת כַּכָּתוּב וְעֹלַת יוֹם בְּיוֹם בְּמִסְפָּר כְּמִשְׁפַּט דְּבַר־יוֹם בְּיוֹמוֹ׃

⁵ followed by the regular burnt offering and the offerings for the new moons and for all the sacred fixed times of *Hashem*, and whatever freewill offerings were made to *Hashem*.

ה וְאַחֲרֵיכֵן עֹלַת תָּמִיד וְלֶחֳדָשִׁים וּלְכָל־מוֹעֲדֵי יְהוָה הַמְקֻדָּשִׁים וּלְכֹל מִתְנַדֵּב נְדָבָה לַיהוָה׃

⁶ From the first day of the seventh month they began to make burnt offerings to *Hashem*, though the foundation of the Temple of *Hashem* had not been laid.

ו מִיּוֹם אֶחָד לַחֹדֶשׁ הַשְּׁבִיעִי הֵחֵלּוּ לְהַעֲלוֹת עֹלוֹת לַיהוָה וְהֵיכַל יְהוָה לֹא יֻסָּד׃

---

this very process reoccurring. The communities of *Beersheva*, *Kibbutz Dan*, *Givon* and dozens of others were all constructed on the very same locations as their original, biblical namesakes. It is indeed wondrous to witness the fulfillment of the prophecy "… children shall return to *their* country" (Jeremiah 31:16), and to see "all *Yisrael* in their towns."

3:1 The entire people assembled as one man in *Yerushalayim* This particular wording recalls the Revelation at Mount Sinai, in reference to which it says: "They [plural] encamped in the wilderness; and there Israel [singular] encamped before the mount." (Exodus 19:2). The great medieval commentator, *Rashi*, points out that the transition from the plural to the singular form of the verb indicates that at Sinai, the Israelites were "as one person, with one heart." Just as the magnitude of the Sinai experience had the power to unite the multitudes of people from twelve independent tribes into one nation, such is the power of *Yerushalayim*. The Talmudic sage Rabbi Yehoshua ben Levi homiletically explains the verse "*Yerushalayim* built up, a city knit together," (Psalms 122:3), to mean that Jerusalem is a city "that makes all of Israel friends" (*Yerushalmi Chagiga* 3:6). As it did in the time of the return from Babylonia, today as well *Yerushalayim* has the power to bring Israel together as one, and to serve as a source of unity for all humanity.

Modern Beer Sheva

Ezra/Ezra Chapter 4

עזרא פרק ד

7 They paid the hewers and craftsmen with money, and the Sidonians and Tyrians with food, drink, and oil to bring cedarwood from Lebanon by sea to *Yaffo*, in accord with the authorization granted them by King Cyrus of Persia.

ז וַיִּתְּנוּ־כֶסֶף לַחֹצְבִים וְלֶחָרָשִׁים וּמַאֲכָל וּמִשְׁתֶּה וָשֶׁמֶן לַצִּדֹנִים וְלַצֹּרִים לְהָבִיא עֲצֵי אֲרָזִים מִן־הַלְּבָנוֹן אֶל־יָם יָפוֹא כְּרִשְׁיוֹן כּוֹרֶשׁ מֶלֶךְ־פָּרַס עֲלֵיהֶם׃

8 In the second year after their arrival at the House of *Hashem*, at *Yerushalayim*, in the second month, *Zerubavel* son of *Shealtiel* and *Yeshua* son of *Yotzadak*, and the rest of their brother *Kohanim* and *Leviim*, and all who had come from the captivity to *Yerushalayim*, as their first step appointed *Leviim* from the age of twenty and upward to supervise the work of the House of *Hashem*.

ח וּבַשָּׁנָה הַשֵּׁנִית לְבוֹאָם אֶל־בֵּית הָאֱלֹהִים לִירוּשָׁלַם בַּחֹדֶשׁ הַשֵּׁנִי הֵחֵלּוּ זְרֻבָּבֶל בֶּן־שְׁאַלְתִּיאֵל וְיֵשׁוּעַ בֶּן־יוֹצָדָק וּשְׁאָר אֲחֵיהֶם הַכֹּהֲנִים וְהַלְוִיִּם וְכָל־הַבָּאִים מֵהַשְּׁבִי יְרוּשָׁלַם וַיַּעֲמִידוּ אֶת־הַלְוִיִּם מִבֶּן עֶשְׂרִים שָׁנָה וָמַעְלָה לְנַצֵּחַ עַל־מְלֶאכֶת בֵּית־יְהוָה׃

9 *Yeshua*, his sons and brothers, *Kadmiel* and his sons, the sons of *Yehuda*, together were appointed in charge of those who did the work in the House of *Hashem*; also the sons of Henadad, their sons and brother *Leviim*.

ט וַיַּעֲמֹד יֵשׁוּעַ בָּנָיו וְאֶחָיו קַדְמִיאֵל וּבָנָיו בְּנֵי־יְהוּדָה כְּאֶחָד לְנַצֵּחַ עַל־עֹשֵׂה הַמְּלָאכָה בְּבֵית הָאֱלֹהִים בְּנֵי חֵנָדָד בְּנֵיהֶם וַאֲחֵיהֶם הַלְוִיִּם׃

10 When the builders had laid the foundation of the Temple of *Hashem*, *Kohanim* in their vestments with trumpets, and *Leviim* sons of *Asaf* with cymbals were stationed to give praise to *Hashem*, as King *David* of *Yisrael* had ordained.

י וְיִסְּדוּ הַבֹּנִים אֶת־הֵיכַל יְהוָה וַיַּעֲמִידוּ הַכֹּהֲנִים מְלֻבָּשִׁים בַּחֲצֹצְרוֹת וְהַלְוִיִּם בְּנֵי־אָסָף בַּמְצִלְתַּיִם לְהַלֵּל אֶת־יְהוָה עַל־יְדֵי דָּוִיד מֶלֶךְ־יִשְׂרָאֵל׃

11 They sang songs extolling and praising *Hashem*, "For He is good, His steadfast love for *Yisrael* is eternal." All the people raised a great shout extolling *Hashem* because the foundation of the House of *Hashem* had been laid.

יא וַיַּעֲנוּ בְּהַלֵּל וּבְהוֹדֹת לַיהוָה כִּי טוֹב כִּי־לְעוֹלָם חַסְדּוֹ עַל־יִשְׂרָאֵל וְכָל־הָעָם הֵרִיעוּ תְרוּעָה גְדוֹלָה בְהַלֵּל לַיהוָה עַל הוּסַד בֵּית־יְהוָה׃

12 Many of the *Kohanim* and *Leviim* and the chiefs of the clans, the old men who had seen the first house, wept loudly at the sight of the founding of this house. Many others shouted joyously at the top of their voices.

יב וְרַבִּים מֵהַכֹּהֲנִים וְהַלְוִיִּם וְרָאשֵׁי הָאָבוֹת הַזְּקֵנִים אֲשֶׁר רָאוּ אֶת־הַבַּיִת הָרִאשׁוֹן בְּיָסְדוֹ זֶה הַבַּיִת בְּעֵינֵיהֶם בֹּכִים בְּקוֹל גָּדוֹל וְרַבִּים בִּתְרוּעָה בְשִׂמְחָה לְהָרִים קוֹל׃

13 The people could not distinguish the shouts of joy from the people's weeping, for the people raised a great shout, the sound of which could be heard from afar.

יג וְאֵין הָעָם מַכִּירִים קוֹל תְּרוּעַת הַשִּׂמְחָה לְקוֹל בְּכִי הָעָם כִּי הָעָם מְרִיעִים תְּרוּעָה גְדוֹלָה וְהַקּוֹל נִשְׁמַע עַד־לְמֵרָחוֹק׃

4

1 When the adversaries of *Yehuda* and *Binyamin* heard that the returned exiles were building a temple to God of *Yisrael*,

א וַיִּשְׁמְעוּ צָרֵי יְהוּדָה וּבִנְיָמִן כִּי־בְנֵי הַגּוֹלָה בּוֹנִים הֵיכָל לַיהוָה אֱלֹהֵי יִשְׂרָאֵל׃

2 they approached *Zerubavel* and the chiefs of the clans and said to them, "Let us build with you, since we too worship your God, having offered sacrifices to Him since the time of King Esarhaddon of Assyria, who brought us here."

ב וַיִּגְּשׁוּ אֶל־זְרֻבָּבֶל וְאֶל־רָאשֵׁי הָאָבוֹת וַיֹּאמְרוּ לָהֶם נִבְנֶה עִמָּכֶם כִּי כָכֶם נִדְרוֹשׁ לֵאלֹהֵיכֶם וְלֹא [וְלוֹ] אֲנַחְנוּ זֹבְחִים מִימֵי אֵסַר חַדֹּן מֶלֶךְ אַשּׁוּר הַמַּעֲלֶה אֹתָנוּ פֹּה׃

Ezra/Ezra

Chapter 4

עזרא
פרק ד

3 *Zerubavel*, *Yeshua*, and the rest of the chiefs of the clans of *Yisrael* answered them, "It is not for you and us to build a House to our God, but we alone will build it to God of *Yisrael*, in accord with the charge that the king, King Cyrus of Persia, laid upon us."

ג וַיֹּאמֶר לָהֶם זְרֻבָּבֶל וְיֵשׁוּעַ וּשְׁאָר רָאשֵׁי הָאָבוֹת לְיִשְׂרָאֵל לֹא־לָכֶם וָלָנוּ לִבְנוֹת בַּיִת לֵאלֹהֵינוּ כִּי אֲנַחְנוּ יַחַד נִבְנֶה לַיהוָה אֱלֹהֵי יִשְׂרָאֵל כַּאֲשֶׁר צִוָּנוּ הַמֶּלֶךְ כּוֹרֶשׁ מֶלֶךְ־פָּרָס:

4 Thereupon the people of the land undermined the resolve of the people of *Yehuda*, and made them afraid to build.

ד וַיְהִי עַם־הָאָרֶץ מְרַפִּים יְדֵי עַם־יְהוּדָה וּמְבַלַהִים [וּמְבַהֲלִים] אוֹתָם לִבְנוֹת:

5 They bribed ministers in order to thwart their plans all the years of King Cyrus of Persia and until the reign of King Darius of Persia.

ה וְסֹכְרִים עֲלֵיהֶם יוֹעֲצִים לְהָפֵר עֲצָתָם כָּל־יְמֵי כּוֹרֶשׁ מֶלֶךְ פָּרַס וְעַד־מַלְכוּת דָּרְיָוֶשׁ מֶלֶךְ־פָּרָס:

6 And in the reign of Ahasuerus, at the start of his reign, they drew up an accusation against the inhabitants of *Yehuda* and *Yerushalayim*.

ו וּבְמַלְכוּת אֲחַשְׁוֵרוֹשׁ בִּתְחִלַּת מַלְכוּתוֹ כָּתְבוּ שִׂטְנָה עַל־יֹשְׁבֵי יְהוּדָה וִירוּשָׁלָ͏ִם:

7 And in the time of Artaxerxes, Bishlam, Mithredath, Tabeel, and the rest of their colleagues wrote to King Artaxerxes of Persia, a letter written in Aramaic and translated. Aramaic:

ז וּבִימֵי אַרְתַּחְשַׁשְׂתָּא כָּתַב בִּשְׁלָם מִתְרְדָת טָבְאֵל וּשְׁאָר כְּנוֹתוֹ [כְּנָוֺתָיו] עַל־אַרְתַּחְשַׁשְׂתְּא [אַרְתַּחְשַׁשְׂתְּ] מֶלֶךְ פָּרָס וּכְתָב הַנִּשְׁתְּוָן כָּתוּב אֲרָמִית וּמְתֻרְגָּם אֲרָמִית:

8 Rehum the commissioner and Shimshai the scribe wrote a letter concerning *Yerushalayim* to King Artaxerxes as follows:

ח רְחוּם בְּעֵל־טְעֵם וְשִׁמְשַׁי סָפְרָא כְּתַבוּ אִגְּרָה חֲדָה עַל־יְרוּשְׁלֶם לְאַרְתַּחְשַׁשְׂתְּא מַלְכָּא כְּנֵמָא:

9 (Then Rehum the commissioner and Shimshai the scribe, and the rest of their colleagues, the judges, officials, officers, and overseers, the men of Erech, and of Babylon, and of Susa – that is the Elamites –

ט אֱדַיִן רְחוּם בְּעֵל־טְעֵם וְשִׁמְשַׁי סָפְרָא וּשְׁאָר כְּנָוָתְהוֹן דִּינָיֵא וַאֲפַרְסַתְכָיֵא טַרְפְּלָיֵא אֲפָרְסָיֵא אַרְכְּוָי [אַרְכְּוָיֵא] בָּבְלָיֵא שׁוּשַׁנְכָיֵא דֶּהָוֵא [דֶּהָיֵא] עֵלְמָיֵא:

10 and other peoples whom the great and glorious Osnappar deported and settled in the city of *Shomron* and the rest of the province Beyond the River [wrote] – and now

י וּשְׁאָר אֻמַּיָּא דִּי הַגְלִי אָסְנַפַּר רַבָּא וְיַקִּירָא וְהוֹתֵב הִמּוֹ בְּקִרְיָה דִּי שָׁמְרָיִן וּשְׁאָר עֲבַר־נַהֲרָה וּכְעֶנֶת:

11 this is the text of the letter which they sent to him:) – "To King Artaxerxes [from] your servants, men of the province Beyond the River. And now

יא דְּנָה פַּרְשֶׁגֶן אִגַּרְתָּא דִּי שְׁלַחוּ עֲלוֹהִי עַל־אַרְתַּחְשַׁשְׂתְּא מַלְכָּא עַבְדָּךְ אֱנָשׁ עֲבַר־נַהֲרָה וּכְעֶנֶת:

12 be it known to the king that the *Yehudim* who came up from you to us have reached *Yerushalayim* and are rebuilding that rebellious and wicked city; they are completing the walls and repairing the foundation.

יב יְדִיעַ לֶהֱוֵא לְמַלְכָּא דִּי יְהוּדָיֵא דִּי סְלִקוּ מִן־לְוָתָךְ עֲלֶינָא אֲתוֹ לִירוּשְׁלֶם קִרְיְתָא מָרָדְתָּא וּבִאישְׁתָּא [וּבִישְׁתָּא] בָּנַיִן וְשׁוּרַיָּא [וְשׁוּרַיָּא] אשכללו [שַׁכְלִלוּ] וְאֻשַּׁיָּא יַחִיטוּ:

4:12 The *Yehudim* The chosen people have many biblical titles: Hebrews, children of *Yaakov*, and Israelites, to name a few. What is the origin of the branding 'Jew', in Hebrew *Yehudi* (יהודי)? The term is first

יהודים

Ezra/Ezra
Chapter 4

עזרא
פרק ד

y'-DEE-a le-he-VAY l'-mal-KA DEE y'-hu-da-YAY DEE s'-LI-ku min l'-va-TAKH a-LE-na a-TO lee-ru-sh'-LEM kir-y'-TA ma-ra-d'-TA u-veesh-TA ba-NA-yin v'-shu-ra-YA shakh-LEE-lu v'-u-sha-YA ya-KHEE-tu

13 Now be it known to the king that if this city is rebuilt and the walls completed, they will not pay tribute, poll-tax, or land-tax, and in the end it will harm the kingdom.

יג כְּעַן יְדִיעַ לֶהֱוֵא לְמַלְכָּא דִּי הֵן קִרְיְתָא דָךְ תִּתְבְּנֵא וְשׁוּרַיָּה יִשְׁתַּכְלְלוּן מִנְדָּה־בְלוֹ וַהֲלָךְ לָא יִנְתְּנוּן וְאַפְּתֹם מַלְכִים תְּהַנְזִק׃

14 Now since we eat the salt of the palace, and it is not right that we should see the king dishonored, we have written to advise the king [of this]

יד כְּעַן כָּל־קֳבֵל דִּי־מְלַח הֵיכְלָא מְלַחְנָא וְעַרְוַת מַלְכָּא לָא אֲרִיךְ לַנָא לְמֶחֱזֵא עַל־דְּנָה שְׁלַחְנָא וְהוֹדַעְנָא לְמַלְכָּא׃

15 so that you may search the records of your fathers and find in the records and know that this city is a rebellious city, harmful to kings and states. Sedition has been rife in it from early times; on that account this city was destroyed.

טו דִּי יְבַקַּר בִּסְפַר־דָּכְרָנַיָּא דִּי אֲבָהָתָךְ וּתְהַשְׁכַּח בִּסְפַר דָּכְרָנַיָּא וְתִנְדַּע דִּי קִרְיְתָא דָךְ קִרְיָא מָרָדָא וּמְהַנְזְקַת מַלְכִין וּמְדִנָן וְאֶשְׁתַּדּוּר עָבְדִין בְּגַוַּהּ מִן־יוֹמָת עָלְמָא עַל־דְּנָה קִרְיְתָא דָךְ הָחָרְבַת׃

16 We advise the king that if this city is rebuilt and its walls are completed, you will no longer have any portion in the province Beyond the River."

טז מְהוֹדְעִין אֲנַחְנָה לְמַלְכָּא דִּי הֵן קִרְיְתָא דָךְ תִּתְבְּנֵא וְשׁוּרַיָּה יִשְׁתַּכְלְלוּן לָקֳבֵל דְּנָה חֲלָק בַּעֲבַר נַהֲרָא לָא אִיתַי לָךְ׃

17 The king sent back the following message: "To Rehum the commissioner and Shimshai the scribe, and the rest of their colleagues, who dwell in *Shomron* and in the rest of the province of Beyond the River, greetings.

יז פִּתְגָמָא שְׁלַח מַלְכָּא עַל־רְחוּם בְּעֵל־טְעֵם וְשִׁמְשַׁי סָפְרָא וּשְׁאָר כְּנָוָתְהוֹן דִּי יָתְבִין בְּשָׁמְרָיִן וּשְׁאָר עֲבַר־נַהֲרָה שְׁלָם וּכְעֶת׃

18 Now the letter that you wrote me has been read to me in translation.

יח נִשְׁתְּוָנָא דִּי שְׁלַחְתּוּן עֲלֶינָא מְפָרַשׁ קֱרִי קָדָמָי׃

19 At my order a search has been made, and it has been found that this city has from earliest times risen against kings, and that rebellion and sedition have been rife in it.

יט וּמִנִּי שִׂים טְעֵם וּבַקַּרוּ וְהַשְׁכַּחוּ דִּי קִרְיְתָא דָךְ מִן־יוֹמָת עָלְמָא עַל־מַלְכִין מִתְנַשְּׂאָה וּמְרַד וְאֶשְׁתַּדּוּר מִתְעֲבֶד־בַּהּ׃

20 Powerful kings have ruled over *Yerushalayim* and exercised authority over the whole province of Beyond the River, and tribute, poll-tax, and land-tax were paid to them.

כ וּמַלְכִין תַּקִּיפִין הֲווֹ עַל־יְרוּשְׁלֶם וְשַׁלִּיטִין בְּכֹל עֲבַר נַהֲרָה וּמִדָּה בְלוֹ וַהֲלָךְ מִתְיְהֵב לְהוֹן׃

---

employed as a specific ethnic title during the Babylonian exile, as can be seen in this verse and also in the books of *Daniel* and *Esther*. Historically, this name indicated an association with the tribe of *Yehuda* (יהודה), from which most of the Babylonian exiles descended. However, the name ultimately derives from the Hebrew root which means to 'praise' or 'give thanks', as it says

"She [*Leah*] conceived again and bore a son, and declared, 'This time I will praise *Hashem*.' Therefore she named him *Yehudah*" (Genesis 29:35). The name thus highlights the inherent Jewish value of gratitude to God. The fact that this collective name was given in exile shows that sometimes one has to travel far away to discover who he really is.

Ezra/Ezra
Chapter 5

עזרא
פרק ה

21 Now issue an order to stop these men; this city is not to be rebuilt until I so order.

כא כְּעַן שִׂימוּ טְּעֵם לְבַטָּלָא גֻּבְרַיָּא אִלֵּךְ וְקִרְיְתָא דָךְ לָא תִתְבְּנֵא עַד־מִנִּי טַעְמָא יִתְּשָׂם:

22 Take care not to be lax in this matter or there will be much damage and harm to the kingdom."

כב וּזְהִירִין הֱווֹ שָׁלוּ לְמֶעְבַּד עַל־דְּנָה לְמָה יִשְׂגֵּא חֲבָלָא לְהַנְזָקַת מַלְכִין:

23 When the text of the letter of King Artaxerxes was read before Rehum and Shimshai the scribe and their colleagues, they hurried to *Yerushalayim*, to the *Yehudim*, and stopped them by main force.

כג אֱדַיִן מִן־דִּי פַּרְשֶׁגֶן נִשְׁתְּוָנָא דִּי ארתחששתא [אַרְתַּחְשַׁשְׂתְּ] מַלְכָּא קֱרִי קֳדָם־רְחוּם וְשִׁמְשַׁי סָפְרָא וּכְנָוָתְהוֹן אֲזַלוּ בִבְהִילוּ לִירוּשְׁלֶם עַל־יְהוּדָיֵא וּבַטִּלוּ הִמּוֹ בְּאֶדְרָע וְחָיִל:

24 At that time, work on the House of *Hashem* in *Yerushalayim* stopped and remained in abeyance until the second year of the reign of King Darius of Persia.

כד בֵּאדַיִן בְּטֵלַת עֲבִידַת בֵּית־אֱלָהָא דִּי בִּירוּשְׁלֶם וַהֲוָת בָּטְלָא עַד שְׁנַת תַּרְתֵּין לְמַלְכוּת דָּרְיָוֶשׁ מֶלֶךְ־פָּרָס:

5 1 Then the *Neviim*, *Chagai* the *Navi* and *Zecharya* son of *Ido*, prophesied to the *Yehudim* in *Yehuda* and *Yerushalayim*, inspired by the God of *Yisrael*.

ה א וְהִתְנַבִּי חַגַּי נביאה [נְבִיָּא] וּזְכַרְיָה בַר־עִדּוֹא נְבִיאַיָּא [נְבִיַּיָּא] עַל־יְהוּדָיֵא דִּי בִיהוּד וּבִירוּשְׁלֶם בְּשֻׁם אֱלָהּ יִשְׂרָאֵל עֲלֵיהוֹן:

2 Thereupon *Zerubavel* son of *Shealtiel* and *Yeshua* son of *Yotzadak* began rebuilding the House of *Hashem* in *Yerushalayim*, with the full support of the *Neviim* of *Hashem*.

ב בֵּאדַיִן קָמוּ זְרֻבָּבֶל בַּר־שְׁאַלְתִּיאֵל וְיֵשׁוּעַ בַּר־יוֹצָדָק וְשָׁרִיו לְמִבְנֵא בֵּית אֱלָהָא דִּי בִירוּשְׁלֶם וְעִמְּהוֹן נְבִיאַיָּא [נְבִיַּיָּא] דִי־אֱלָהָא מְסָעֲדִין לְהוֹן:

bay-DA-yin KA-mu z'-ru-ba-VEL bar sh'-al-tee-AYL v'-yay-SHU-a bar yo-tza-DAK v'-sha-REEV l'-miv-NAY BAYT e-la-HA DEE vee-ru-sh'-LEM v'-i-m'-HON n'-vi-ya-YA dee e-la-HA m'-sa-a-DEEN l'-HON

3 At once Tattenai, governor of the province of Beyond the River, Shethar-bozenai, and their colleagues descended upon them and said this to them, "Who issued orders to you to rebuild this house and complete its furnishing?"

ג בֵּהּ־זִמְנָא אֲתָא עֲלֵיהוֹן תַּתְּנַי פַּחַת עֲבַר־נַהֲרָה וּשְׁתַר בּוֹזְנַי וּכְנָוָתְהוֹן וְכֵן אָמְרִין לְהֹם מַן־שָׂם לְכֹם טְעֵם בַּיְתָא דְנָה לִבְּנֵא וְאֻשַּׁרְנָא דְנָה לְשַׁכְלָלָה:

4 Then we said to them, "What are the names of the men who are engaged in the building?"

ד אֱדַיִן כְּנֵמָא אֲמַרְנָא לְהֹם מַן־אִנּוּן שְׁמָהָת גֻּבְרַיָּא דִּי־דְנָה בִנְיָנָא בָּנַיִן:

5:2 With the full support of the *Neviim* of *Hashem*
Starting with chapter 4, verse 8, the language of *Sefer Ezra* switches from Hebrew to Aramaic. However, the *Neviim* of the time, *Chagai*, *Zecharya* and *Malachi*, address the nation exclusively in Hebrew. The Jewish people have been exiled to every corner of the world and, in the process, have learned many different languages. This is as true in the modern Diaspora as it was during the Babylonian and Persian eras. And yet, with the minor exceptions of the Aramaic sections of *Daniel* and *Ezra*, the *Tanakh* was written entirely in Hebrew. Although the Jews spoke other languages, Hebrew remained their essential language. Even if they did not speak it for everyday matter, it continued to be the language used for prayer and study, connecting to Hashem. The fact that Hebrew is again the vibrant and dynamic language of communication in contemporary Israel should not be underestimated. The revival of Hebrew as a spoken language in the 19th century, due largely to the efforts of Eliezer Ben-Yehuda, is as miraculous as the survival of the Hebrew people themselves. As Shimon Peres, former president of Israel, pointed out, "None in the Middle East speak their original language, except for Israel."

Eliezer Ben-Yehuda (1858–1922)

Ezra/Ezra
Chapter 5

עזרא
פרק ה

5 But *Hashem* watched over the elders of the *Yehudim* and they were not stopped while a report went to Darius and a letter was sent back in reply to it.

ה וְעֵין אֱלָהֲהֹם הֲוָת עַל־שָׂבֵי יְהוּדָיֵא וְלָא־בַטִּלוּ הִמּוֹ עַד־טַעְמָא לְדָרְיָוֶשׁ יְהָךְ וֶאֱדַיִן יְתִיבוּן נִשְׁתְּוָנָא עַל־דְּנָה׃

6 This is the text of the letter that Tattenai, governor of the province of Beyond the River, and Shethar-bozenai and his colleagues, the officials of Beyond the River, sent to King Darius.

ו פַּרְשֶׁגֶן אִגַּרְתָּא דִּי־שְׁלַח תַּתְּנַי פַּחַת עֲבַר־נַהֲרָה וּשְׁתַר בּוֹזְנַי וּכְנָוָתֵהּ אֲפַרְסְכָיֵא דִּי בַּעֲבַר נַהֲרָה עַל־דָּרְיָוֶשׁ מַלְכָּא׃

7 They sent a message to him and this is what was written in it: "To King Darius, greetings, and so forth.

ז פִּתְגָמָא שְׁלַחוּ עֲלוֹהִי וְכִדְנָה כְּתִיב בְּגַוֵּהּ לְדָרְיָוֶשׁ מַלְכָּא שְׁלָמָא כֹלָּא׃

8 Be it known to the king, that we went to the province of *Yehuda*, to the house of the great *Hashem*. It is being rebuilt of hewn stone, and wood is being laid in the walls. The work is being done with dispatch and is going well.

ח יְדִיעַ לֶהֱוֵא לְמַלְכָּא דִּי־אֲזַלְנָא לִיהוּד מְדִינְתָּא לְבֵית אֱלָהָא רַבָּא וְהוּא מִתְבְּנֵא אֶבֶן גְּלָל וְאָע מִתְּשָׂם בְּכֻתְלַיָּא וַעֲבִידְתָּא דָךְ אָסְפַּרְנָא מִתְעַבְדָא וּמַצְלַח בְּיֶדְהֹם׃

9 Thereupon we directed this question to these elders, 'Who issued orders to you to rebuild this house and to complete its furnishings?'

ט אֱדַיִן שְׁאֵלְנָא לְשָׂבַיָּא אִלֵּךְ כְּנֵמָא אֲמַרְנָא לְהֹם מַן־שָׂם לְכֹם טְעֵם בַּיְתָא דְנָה לְמִבְנְיָה וְאֻשַּׁרְנָא דְנָה לְשַׁכְלָלָה׃

10 We also asked their names so that we could write down the names of their leaders for your information.

י וְאַף שְׁמָהָתְהֹם שְׁאֵלְנָא לְהֹם לְהוֹדָעוּתָךְ דִּי נִכְתֻּב שֻׁם־גֻּבְרַיָּא דִּי בְרָאשֵׁיהֹם׃

11 This is what they answered us: 'We are the servants of the God of heaven and earth; we are rebuilding the house that was originally built many years ago; a great king of *Yisrael* built it and completed it.

יא וּכְנֵמָא פִתְגָמָא הֲתִיבוּנָא לְמֵמַר אֲנַחְנָא הִמּוֹ עַבְדוֹהִי דִי־אֱלָהּ שְׁמַיָּא וְאַרְעָא וּבָנַיִן בַּיְתָא דִּי־הֲוָא בְנֵה מִקַּדְמַת דְּנָה שְׁנִין שַׂגִּיאָן וּמֶלֶךְ לְיִשְׂרָאֵל רַב בְּנָהִי וְשַׁכְלְלֵהּ׃

12 But because our fathers angered the God of Heaven, He handed them over to Nebuchadnezzar the Chaldean, king of Babylon, who demolished this house and exiled the people to Babylon.

יב לָהֵן מִן־דִּי הַרְגִּזוּ אֲבָהֳתַנָא לֶאֱלָהּ שְׁמַיָּא יְהַב הִמּוֹ בְּיַד נְבוּכַדְנֶצַּר מֶלֶךְ־בָּבֶל כַּסְדָּיָא [כַּסְדָּאָה] וּבַיְתָה דְנָה סַתְרֵהּ וְעַמָּה הַגְלִי לְבָבֶל׃

13 But in the first year of King Cyrus of Babylon, King Cyrus issued an order to rebuild this House of *Hashem*.

יג בְּרַם בִּשְׁנַת חֲדָה לְכוֹרֶשׁ מַלְכָּא דִּי בָבֶל כּוֹרֶשׁ מַלְכָּא שָׂם טְעֵם בֵּית־אֱלָהָא דְנָה לִבְּנֵא׃

14 Also the silver and gold vessels of the House of *Hashem* that Nebuchadnezzar had taken away from the temple in *Yerushalayim* and brought to the temple in Babylon – King Cyrus released them from the temple in Babylon to be given to the one called *Sheshbatzar* whom he had appointed governor.

יד וְאַף מָאנַיָּא דִי־בֵית־אֱלָהָא דִּי דַהֲבָה וְכַסְפָּא דִּי נְבוּכַדְנֶצַּר הַנְפֵּק מִן־הֵיכְלָא דִּי בִירוּשְׁלֶם וְהֵיבֵל הִמּוֹ לְהֵיכְלָא דִּי בָבֶל הַנְפֵּק הִמּוֹ כּוֹרֶשׁ מַלְכָּא מִן־הֵיכְלָא דִּי בָבֶל וִיהִיבוּ לְשֵׁשְׁבַּצַּר שְׁמֵהּ דִּי פֶחָה שָׂמֵהּ׃

15 He said to him, "Take these vessels, go, deposit them in the temple in *Yerushalayim*, and let the House of *Hashem* be rebuilt on its original site."

טו וַאֲמַר־לֵהּ אֵלֶּה [אֵל] מָאנַיָּא שֵׂא אֵזֶל־אֲחֵת הִמּוֹ בְּהֵיכְלָא דִּי בִירוּשְׁלֶם וּבֵית אֱלָהָא יִתְבְּנֵא עַל־אַתְרֵהּ׃

Ezra/Ezra
Chapter 6

16 That same *Sheshbatzar* then came and laid the foundations for the House of *Hashem* in *Yerushalayim*; and ever since then it has been under construction, but is not yet finished.'

17 And now, if it please the king, let the royal archives there in Babylon be searched to see whether indeed an order had been issued by King Cyrus to rebuild this House of *Hashem* in *Yerushalayim*. May the king convey to us his pleasure in this matter."

6 1 Thereupon, at the order of King Darius, they searched the archives where the treasures were stored in Babylon.

2 But it was in the citadel of Ecbatana, in the province of Media, that a scroll was found in which the following was written: "Memorandum:

3 In the first year of King Cyrus, King Cyrus issued an order concerning the House of *Hashem* in *Yerushalayim*: 'Let the house be rebuilt, a place for offering sacrifices, with a base built up high. Let it be sixty *amot* high and sixty *amot* wide,

4 with a course of unused timber for each three courses of hewn stone. The expenses shall be paid by the palace.

5 And the gold and silver vessels of the House of *Hashem* which Nebuchadnezzar had taken away from the temple in *Yerushalayim* and transported to Babylon shall be returned, and let each go back to the temple in *Yerushalayim* where it belongs; you shall deposit it in the House of *Hashem*.'

6 "Now you, Tattenai, governor of the province of Beyond the River, Shethar-bozenai and colleagues, the officials of the province of Beyond the River, stay away from that place.

7 Allow the work of this House of *Hashem* to go on; let the governor of the *Yehudim* and the elders of the *Yehudim* rebuild this House of *Hashem* on its site.

8 And I hereby issue an order concerning what you must do to help these elders of the *Yehudim* rebuild this House of *Hashem*: the expenses are to be paid to these men with dispatch out of the resources of the king, derived from the taxes of the province of Beyond the River, so that the work not be stopped.

עזרא
פרק ו

טו אֱדַ֤יִן שֵׁשְׁבַּצַּר֙ דֵּ֔ךְ אֲתָ֗א יְהַ֤ב אֻשַּׁיָּא֙ דִּי־בֵ֤ית אֱלָהָא֙ דִּ֣י בִירוּשְׁלֶ֔ם וּמִן־אֱדַ֧יִן וְעַד־כְּעַ֛ן מִתְבְּנֵ֖א וְלָ֥א שְׁלִֽם׃

טז וּכְעַ֞ן הֵ֧ן עַל־מַלְכָּ֣א טָ֗ב יִתְבַּקַּ֞ר בְּבֵ֤ית גִּנְזַיָּא֙ דִּי־מַלְכָּ֣א תַמָּ֔ה דִּ֣י בְּבָבֶ֑ל הֵ֣ן אִיתַ֗י דִּי־מִן־כּ֤וֹרֶשׁ מַלְכָּא֙ שִׂ֣ים טְעֵ֔ם לְמִבְנֵ֛א בֵּית־אֱלָהָ֥א דֵ֖ךְ בִּירוּשְׁלֶ֑ם וּרְע֥וּת מַלְכָּ֛א עַל־דְּנָ֖ה יִשְׁלַ֥ח עֲלֶֽינָא׃

א בֵּאדַ֛יִן דָּרְיָ֥וֶשׁ מַלְכָּ֖א שָׂ֣ם טְעֵ֑ם וּבַקַּ֣רוּ ׀ בְּבֵ֣ית סִפְרַיָּ֗א דִּ֧י גִנְזַיָּ֛א מְהַחֲתִ֥ין תַּמָּ֖ה בְּבָבֶֽל׃

ב וְהִשְׁתְּכַ֣ח בְּאַחְמְתָ֗א בְּבִֽירְתָ֛א דִּ֛י בְּמָדַ֥י מְדִינְתָּ֖ה מְגִלָּ֣ה חֲדָ֑ה וְכֵן־כְּתִ֥יב בְּגַוַּ֖הּ דִּכְרוֹנָֽה׃

ג בִּשְׁנַ֨ת חֲדָ֜ה לְכ֣וֹרֶשׁ מַלְכָּ֗א כּ֣וֹרֶשׁ מַלְכָּא֮ שָׂ֣ם טְעֵם֒ בֵּית־אֱלָהָ֤א בִירֽוּשְׁלֶם֙ בַּיְתָ֣א יִתְבְּנֵ֔א אֲתַר֙ דִּֽי־דָבְחִ֣ין דִּבְחִ֔ין וְאֻשּׁ֖וֹהִי מְסוֹבְלִ֑ין רוּמֵהּ֙ אַמִּ֣ין שִׁתִּ֔ין פְּתָיֵ֖הּ אַמִּ֥ין שִׁתִּֽין׃

ד נִדְבָּכִ֞ין דִּי־אֶ֤בֶן גְּלָל֙ תְּלָתָ֔א וְנִדְבָּ֖ךְ דִּי־אָ֣ע חֲדַ֑ת וְנִ֨פְקְתָ֔א מִן־בֵּ֥ית מַלְכָּ֖א תִּתְיְהִֽב׃

ה וְ֠אַף מָאנֵ֣י בֵית־אֱלָהָא֮ דִּ֣י דַהֲבָ֣ה וְכַסְפָּא֒ דִּ֣י נְבוּכַדְנֶצַּ֗ר הַנְפֵּ֛ק מִן־הֵיכְלָ֥א דִי־בִירוּשְׁלֶ֖ם וְהֵיבֵ֣ל לְבָבֶ֑ל יַהֲתִיב֗וּן וִיהָ֤ךְ לְהֵיכְלָא֙ דִי־בִירוּשְׁלֶ֣ם לְאַתְרֵ֔הּ וְתַחֵ֖ת בְּבֵ֥ית אֱלָהָֽא׃

ו כְּעַ֡ן תַּ֠תְּנַי פַּחַ֨ת עֲבַֽר־נַהֲרָ֜ה שְׁתַ֤ר בּוֹזְנַי֙ וּכְנָוָ֣תְה֔וֹן אֲפַרְסְכָיֵ֔א דִּ֖י בַּעֲבַ֣ר נַהֲרָ֑ה רַחִיקִ֥ין הֲו֖וֹ מִן־תַּמָּֽה׃

ז שְׁבֻ֕קוּ לַעֲבִידַ֖ת בֵּית־אֱלָהָ֣א דֵ֑ךְ פַּחַ֤ת יְהוּדָיֵא֙ וּלְשָׂבֵ֣י יְהוּדָיֵ֔א בֵּית־אֱלָהָ֥א דֵ֖ךְ יִבְנ֥וֹן עַל־אַתְרֵֽהּ׃

ח וּמִנִּי֮ שִׂ֣ים טְעֵם֒ לְמָ֣א דִֽי־תַעַבְד֗וּן עִם־שָׂבֵ֤י יְהוּדָיֵא֙ אִלֵּ֔ךְ לְמִבְנֵ֖א בֵּית־אֱלָהָ֣א דֵ֑ךְ וּמִנִּכְסֵ֣י מַלְכָּ֗א דִּ֚י מִדַּת֙ עֲבַ֣ר נַהֲרָ֔ה אָסְפַּ֗רְנָא נִפְקְתָ֛א תֶּהֱוֵ֧א מִתְיַהֲבָ֛א לְגֻבְרַיָּ֥א אִלֵּ֖ךְ דִּי־לָ֥א לְבַטָּלָֽא׃

Ezra/Ezra
Chapter 6

עזרא
פרק ו

9 They are to be given daily, without fail, whatever they need of young bulls, rams, or lambs as burnt offerings for the God of Heaven, and wheat, salt, wine, and oil, at the order of the *Kohanim* in *Yerushalayim*,

ט וּמָה חַשְׁחָן וּבְנֵי תוֹרִין וְדִכְרִין וְאִמְּרִין לַעֲלָוָן לֶאֱלָהּ שְׁמַיָּא חִנְטִין מְלַח חֲמַר וּמְשַׁח כְּמֵאמַר כָּהֲנַיָּא דִי־בִירוּשְׁלֶם לֶהֱוֵא מִתְיְהֵב לְהֹם יוֹם בְּיוֹם דִּי־לָא שָׁלוּ:

10 so that they may offer pleasing sacrifices to the God of Heaven and pray for the life of the king and his sons.

י דִּי־לֶהֱוֹן מְהַקְרְבִין נִיחוֹחִין לֶאֱלָהּ שְׁמַיָּא וּמְצַלַּיִן לְחַיֵּי מַלְכָּא וּבְנוֹהִי:

11 I also issue an order that whoever alters this decree shall have a beam removed from his house, and he shall be impaled on it and his house confiscated.

יא וּמִנִּי שִׂים טְעֵם דִּי כָל־אֱנָשׁ דִּי יְהַשְׁנֵא פִּתְגָמָא דְנָה יִתְנְסַח אָע מִן־בַּיְתֵהּ וּזְקִיף יִתְמְחֵא עֲלֹהִי וּבַיְתֵהּ נְוָלוּ יִתְעֲבֵד עַל־דְּנָה:

12 And may the God who established His name there cause the downfall of any king or nation that undertakes to alter or damage that House of *Hashem* in *Yerushalayim*. I, Darius, have issued the decree; let it be carried out with dispatch."

יב וֵאלָהָא דִּי שַׁכִּן שְׁמֵהּ תַּמָּה יְמַגַּר כָּל־מֶלֶךְ וְעַם דִּי יִשְׁלַח יְדֵהּ לְהַשְׁנָיָה לְחַבָּלָה בֵּית־אֱלָהָא דֵךְ דִּי בִירוּשְׁלֶם אֲנָה דָרְיָוֶשׁ שָׂמֶת טְעֵם אָסְפַּרְנָא יִתְעֲבִד:

13 Then Tattenai, governor of the province of Beyond the River, Shethar-bozenai, and their colleagues carried out with dispatch what King Darius had written.

יג אֱדַיִן תַּתְּנַי פַּחַת עֲבַר־נַהֲרָה שְׁתַר בּוֹזְנַי וּכְנָוָתְהוֹן לָקֳבֵל דִּי־שְׁלַח דָּרְיָוֶשׁ מַלְכָּא כְּנֵמָא אָסְפַּרְנָא עֲבַדוּ:

14 So the elders of the *Yehudim* progressed in the building, urged on by the prophesying of *Chagai* the *Navi* and *Zecharya* son of *Ido*, and they brought the building to completion under the aegis of the God of *Yisrael* and by the order of Cyrus and Darius and King Artaxerxes of Persia.

יד וְשָׂבֵי יְהוּדָיֵא בָּנַיִן וּמַצְלְחִין בִּנְבוּאַת חַגַּי נְבִיאָה [נְבִיָּא] וּזְכַרְיָה בַּר־עִדּוֹא וּבְנוֹ וְשַׁכְלִלוּ מִן־טַעַם אֱלָהּ יִשְׂרָאֵל וּמִטְּעֵם כּוֹרֶשׁ וְדָרְיָוֶשׁ וְאַרְתַּחְשַׁשְׂתְּא מֶלֶךְ פָּרָס:

v'-sha-VAY y'-hu-da-YAY ba-NA-yin u-matz-l'-KHEEN bin-vu-AT kha-GAI n'-vi-YAH uz-khar-YAH bar i-DO uv-NO v'-shakh-LI-lu min TA-am e-LAH yis-ra-AYL u-mi-t'-AYM KO-resh v'-dar-YA-vesh v'-ar-takh-SHAS-t' ME-lekh pa-RAS

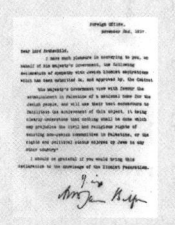

6:14 By the order of Cyrus and Darius and King Artaxerxes The autonomy of the Jewish people has often been subject to the blessings or restraints of foreigners. Cyrus's edict to allow the People of Israel to return to the Land of Israel and rebuild the *Beit Hamikdash* was a ray of hope in a bleak time. Persian approval of Jewish authority constituted a remarkable turning of the tide for the exiled Jews. Though construction of the Temple was temporarily halted, it was eventually completed in the sixth year of the reign of Darius, with his permission. The British Government's 1917 Balfour Declaration possessed similar promise when it declared: "His Majesty's government view with favour the establishment in Palestine of a national home for the Jewish people, and will use their best endeavours to facilitate the achievement of this object." In fact, Harry Truman said of his May 1948 recognition of the State of Israel as president of the United States: "I am Cyrus." In all these cases, it was non-Jews serving as God's agents who facilitated the return of the Jewish people to *Eretz Yisrael*.

The Balfour Declaration

Ezra/Ezra
Chapter 7

עזרא
פרק ז

15 The house was finished on the third of the month of *Adar* in the sixth year of the reign of King Darius.

טו וְשֵׁיצִיא בַּיְתָה דְנָה עַד יוֹם תְּלָתָה לִירַח אֲדָר דִּי־הִיא שְׁנַת־שֵׁת לְמַלְכוּת דָּרְיָוֶשׁ מַלְכָּא׃

16 The Israelites, the *Kohanim*, and the *Leviim*, and all the other exiles celebrated the dedication of the House of *Hashem* with joy.

טז וַעֲבַדוּ בְנֵי־יִשְׂרָאֵל כָּהֲנַיָּא וְלֵוָיֵא וּשְׁאָר בְּנֵי־גָלוּתָא חֲנֻכַּת בֵּית־אֱלָהָא דְנָה בְּחֶדְוָה׃

17 And they sacrificed for the dedication of this House of *Hashem* one hundred bulls, two hundred rams, four hundred lambs, and twelve goats as a purification offering for all of *Yisrael*, according to the number of the tribes of *Yisrael*.

יז וְהַקְרִבוּ לַחֲנֻכַּת בֵּית־אֱלָהָא דְנָה תּוֹרִין מְאָה דִּכְרִין מָאתַיִן אִמְּרִין אַרְבַּע מְאָה וּצְפִירֵי עִזִּין לחטיא [לְחַטָּאָה] עַל־כָּל־יִשְׂרָאֵל תְּרֵי־עֲשַׂר לְמִנְיָן שִׁבְטֵי יִשְׂרָאֵל׃

18 They appointed the *Kohanim* in their courses and the *Leviim* in their divisions for the service of *Hashem* in *Yerushalayim*, according to the prescription in the Book of *Moshe*.

יח וַהֲקִימוּ כָהֲנַיָּא בִּפְלֻגָּתְהוֹן וְלֵוָיֵא בְּמַחְלְקָתְהוֹן עַל־עֲבִידַת אֱלָהָא דִּי בִירוּשְׁלֶם כִּכְתָב סְפַר מֹשֶׁה׃

19 The returned exiles celebrated the *Pesach* on the fourteenth day of the first month,

יט וַיַּעֲשׂוּ בְנֵי־הַגּוֹלָה אֶת־הַפָּסַח בְּאַרְבָּעָה עָשָׂר לַחֹדֶשׁ הָרִאשׁוֹן׃

20 for the *Kohanim* and *Leviim* had purified themselves to a man; they were all pure. They slaughtered the *Pesach* offering for all the returned exiles, and for their brother *Kohanim* and for themselves.

כ כִּי הִטַּהֲרוּ הַכֹּהֲנִים וְהַלְוִיִּם כְּאֶחָד כֻּלָּם טְהוֹרִים וַיִּשְׁחֲטוּ הַפֶּסַח לְכָל־בְּנֵי הַגּוֹלָה וְלַאֲחֵיהֶם הַכֹּהֲנִים וְלָהֶם׃

21 The children of *Yisrael* who had returned from the exile, together with all who joined them in separating themselves from the uncleanliness of the nations of the lands to worship God of *Yisrael*, ate of it.

כא וַיֹּאכְלוּ בְנֵי־יִשְׂרָאֵל הַשָּׁבִים מֵהַגּוֹלָה וְכֹל הַנִּבְדָּל מִטֻּמְאַת גּוֹיֵ־הָאָרֶץ אֲלֵהֶם לִדְרֹשׁ לַיהוָה אֱלֹהֵי יִשְׂרָאֵל׃

22 They joyfully celebrated the festival of *Pesach* for seven days, for *Hashem* had given them cause for joy by inclining the heart of the Assyrian king toward them so as to give them support in the work of the House of *Hashem*, the God of *Yisrael*.

כב וַיַּעֲשׂוּ חַג־מַצּוֹת שִׁבְעַת יָמִים בְּשִׂמְחָה כִּי שִׂמְּחָם יְהוָה וְהֵסֵב לֵב מֶלֶךְ־אַשּׁוּר עֲלֵיהֶם לְחַזֵּק יְדֵיהֶם בִּמְלֶאכֶת בֵּית־הָאֱלֹהִים אֱלֹהֵי יִשְׂרָאֵל׃

7

1 After these events, during the reign of King Artaxerxes of Persia, *Ezra* son of *Seraya* son of *Azarya* son of *Chilkiya*

א וְאַחַר הַדְּבָרִים הָאֵלֶּה בְּמַלְכוּת אַרְתַּחְשַׁסְתְּא מֶלֶךְ־פָּרָס עֶזְרָא בֶּן־שְׂרָיָה בֶּן־עֲזַרְיָה בֶּן־חִלְקִיָּה׃

2 son of *Shalum* son of *Tzadok* son of *Achituv*

ב בֶּן־שַׁלּוּם בֶּן־צָדוֹק בֶּן־אֲחִיטוּב׃

3 son of Amariah son of *Azarya* son of Meraioth

ג בֶּן־אֲמַרְיָה בֶן־עֲזַרְיָה בֶּן־מְרָיוֹת׃

4 son of Zerahiah son of Uzzi son of Bukki

ד בֶּן־זְרַחְיָה בֶן־עֻזִּי בֶּן־בֻּקִּי׃

5 son of Abishua son of *Pinchas* son of *Elazar* son of *Aharon* the chief *Kohen* –

ה בֶּן־אֲבִישׁוּעַ בֶּן־פִּינְחָס בֶּן־אֶלְעָזָר בֶּן־אַהֲרֹן הַכֹּהֵן הָרֹאשׁ׃

Ezra/Ezra
Chapter 7

עזרא
פרק ז

6 that *Ezra* came up from Babylon, a scribe expert in the Teaching of *Moshe* which God of *Yisrael* had given, whose request the king had granted in its entirety, thanks to the benevolence of *Hashem* toward him.

הוּא עֶזְרָא עָלָה מִבָּבֶל וְהוּא־סֹפֵר מָהִיר בְּתוֹרַת מֹשֶׁה אֲשֶׁר־נָתַן יְהֹוָה אֱלֹהֵי יִשְׂרָאֵל וַיִּתֶּן־לוֹ הַמֶּלֶךְ כְּיַד־יְהֹוָה אֱלֹהָיו עָלָיו כֹּל בַּקָּשָׁתוֹ׃

HU ez-RA a-LAH mi-ba-VEL v'-hu so-FAYR ma-HEER b'-to-RAT mo-SHEH a-sher na-TAN a-do-NAI e-lo-HAY yis-ra-AYL va-yi-ten LO ha-ME-lekh k'-yad a-do-NAI e-lo-HAV a-LAV KOL ba-ka-sha-TO

7 Some of the Israelites, the *Kohanim* and *Leviim*, the singers, the gatekeepers, and the temple servants set out for *Yerushalayim* in the seventh year of King Artaxerxes,

וַיַּעֲלוּ מִבְּנֵי־יִשְׂרָאֵל וּמִן־הַכֹּהֲנִים וְהַלְוִיִּם וְהַמְשֹׁרְרִים וְהַשֹּׁעֲרִים וְהַנְּתִינִים אֶל־יְרוּשָׁלָם בִּשְׁנַת־שֶׁבַע לְאַרְתַּחְשַׁסְתְּא הַמֶּלֶךְ׃

8 arriving in *Yerushalayim* in the fifth month in the seventh year of the king.)

וַיָּבֹא יְרוּשָׁלַם בַּחֹדֶשׁ הַחֲמִישִׁי הִיא שְׁנַת הַשְּׁבִיעִית לַמֶּלֶךְ׃

9 On the first day of the first month the journey up from Babylon was started, and on the first day of the fifth month he arrived in *Yerushalayim*, thanks to the benevolent care of his God for him.

כִּי בְּאֶחָד לַחֹדֶשׁ הָרִאשׁוֹן הוּא יְסֻד הַמַּעֲלָה מִבָּבֶל וּבְאֶחָד לַחֹדֶשׁ הַחֲמִישִׁי בָּא אֶל־יְרוּשָׁלַם כְּיַד־אֱלֹהָיו הַטּוֹבָה עָלָיו׃

KEE b'-e-KHAD la-KHO-desh ha-ri-SHON HU y'-SUD ha-ma-a-LAH mi-ba-VEL uv-e-KHAD la-KHO-desh ha-kha-mee-SHEE BA el y'-ru-sha-LA-im k'-yad e-lo-HAV ha-to-VAH a-LAV

Ezra 7:6 A scribe expert in the Teaching of *Moshe*
Ezra was known as a *sofer* (סופר), a 'scribe' who reintroduced the *Torah* to public life in Jerusalem following the Babylonian exile. According to the Talmud (*Bava Kama* 82a), he instituted public reading of the *Torah* on *Shabbat* in order to make it more dear to the People of Israel. In modern times, another "scribe" made a great contribution to Israel's love for the *Torah*. Eliyahu Koren (1907–2001) was a master typographer who emigrated from Germany to Israel in 1933. He opened Koren Publishers Jerusalem in 1961, and the following year published the "Koren *Tanakh*," the first Bible edited, designed, produced and bound by Jews in nearly 500 years. David Ben Gurion responded to the publication of the *Tanakh*, "Israel is redeemed from shame." Koren, along with his team of experts, considered the precision of every letter, the placement of every word on every page and designed a new font to ensure maximum clarity and to signify the renewal of ancient Hebrew in modern times. The Koren *Tanakh*'s textual accuracy, innovative design and superior quality won it worldwide acclaim. After its publication, it became the Bible that IDF soldiers received, along with a gun, upon their induction into the Israel Defense Forces, and it is the Bible upon which Knesset members are sworn into office. As then Speaker of the Knesset Mr. Kadish Luz declared, "From this day forth, all of Israel's presidents shall take their oaths of office upon this Bible. We have been governed by a Provisional State Council, a Provisional Government and even now sit in the temporary Knesset building. To date, Israeli presidents have been sworn in using a temporary edition of the Bible. This occasion symbolizes our overcoming of foreign heritage and return to our origins".

Yesud Hamaala

7:9 The journey up from Babylon was started
The late nineteenth and twentieth centuries witnessed a series of massive waves of Jewish immigration to Israel, known as *aliyot*, literally, 'ascents.' Each *aliyah* had a specific demographic character. The nature of the returning Babylonian Jews was similar to the immigrants who came during the years 1882–1904 on what is known as the "First *Aliyah*". In both cases, the groups were mostly comprised of poor religious families. But to call these modern Zionists immigrants "first" is not entirely correct. Not only have there been waves of immigration to Israel throughout the centuries, but their forefathers returning from Babylon preceded them by two-thousand five-hundred years. In 1883, the first modern Jewish community in the northern Hula Valley

Ezra/Ezra
Chapter 7

עזרא
פרק ז

10 For *Ezra* had dedicated himself to study the Teaching of *Hashem* so as to observe it, and to teach laws and rules to *Yisrael*.

י כִּי עֶזְרָא הֵכִין לְבָבוֹ לִדְרוֹשׁ אֶת־תּוֹרַת יְהֹוָה וְלַעֲשֹׂת וּלְלַמֵּד בְּיִשְׂרָאֵל חֹק וּמִשְׁפָּט:

11 The following is the text of the letter which King Artaxerxes gave *Ezra* the *Kohen*-scribe, a scholar in matters concerning the commandments of *Hashem* and His laws to *Yisrael*:

יא וְזֶה פַּרְשֶׁגֶן הַנִּשְׁתְּוָן אֲשֶׁר נָתַן הַמֶּלֶךְ אַרְתַּחְשַׁסְתְּא לְעֶזְרָא הַכֹּהֵן הַסֹּפֵר סֹפֵר דִּבְרֵי מִצְוֹת־יְהֹוָה וְחֻקָּיו עַל־יִשְׂרָאֵל:

12 "Artaxerxes king of kings, to *Ezra* the *Kohen*, scholar in the law of the God of heaven, and so forth. And now,

יב אַרְתַּחְשַׁסְתְּא מֶלֶךְ מַלְכַיָּא לְעֶזְרָא כָהֲנָא סָפַר דָּתָא דִּי־אֱלָהּ שְׁמַיָּא גְּמִיר וּכְעֶנֶת:

13 I hereby issue an order that anyone in my kingdom who is of the people of *Yisrael* and its *Kohanim* and *Leviim* who feels impelled to go to *Yerushalayim* may go with you.

יג מִנִּי שִׂים טְעֵם דִּי כָל־מִתְנַדַּב בְּמַלְכוּתִי מִן־עַמָּה יִשְׂרָאֵל וְכָהֲנוֹהִי וְלֵוָיֵא לִמְהָךְ לִירוּשְׁלֶם עִמָּךְ יְהָךְ:

14 For you are commissioned by the king and his seven advisers to regulate *Yehuda* and *Yerushalayim* according to the law of your God, which is in your care,

יד כָּל־קֳבֵל דִּי מִן־קֳדָם מַלְכָּא וְשִׁבְעַת יָעֲטֹהִי שְׁלִיחַ לְבַקָּרָא עַל־יְהוּד וְלִירוּשְׁלֶם בְּדָת אֱלָהָךְ דִּי בִידָךְ:

15 and to bring the freewill offering of silver and gold, which the king and his advisers made to the God of *Yisrael*, whose dwelling is in *Yerushalayim*,

טו וּלְהֵיבָלָה כְּסַף וּדְהַב דִּי־מַלְכָּא וְיָעֲטוֹהִי הִתְנַדַּבוּ לֶאֱלָהּ יִשְׂרָאֵל דִּי בִירוּשְׁלֶם מִשְׁכְּנֵהּ:

16 and whatever silver and gold that you find throughout the province of Babylon, together with the freewill offerings that the people and the *Kohanim* will give for the House of their God, which is in *Yerushalayim*.

טז וְכֹל כְּסַף וּדְהַב דִּי תְהַשְׁכַּח בְּכֹל מְדִינַת בָּבֶל עִם הִתְנַדָּבוּת עַמָּא וְכָהֲנַיָּא מִתְנַדְּבִין לְבֵית אֱלָהֲהֹם דִּי בִירוּשְׁלֶם:

17 You shall, therefore, with dispatch acquire with this money bulls, rams, and lambs, with their meal offerings and libations, and offer them on the *Mizbayach* of the House of your God in *Yerushalayim*.

יז כָּל־קֳבֵל דְּנָה אָסְפַּרְנָא תִקְנֵא בְּכַסְפָּא דְנָה תּוֹרִין דִּכְרִין אִמְּרִין וּמִנְחָתְהוֹן וְנִסְכֵּיהוֹן וּתְקָרֵב הִמּוֹ עַל־מַדְבְּחָה דִּי בֵּית אֱלָהֲכֹם דִּי בִירוּשְׁלֶם:

18 And whatever you wish to do with the leftover silver and gold, you and your kinsmen may do, in accord with the will of your God.

יח וּמָה דִי עֲלָיִךְ [עֲלָךְ] וְעַל־אֶחָיִךְ [אֶחָךְ] יֵיטַב בִּשְׁאָר כַּסְפָּא וְדַהֲבָה לְמֶעְבַּד כִּרְעוּת אֱלָהֲכֹם תַּעַבְדוּן:

19 The vessels for the service of the House of your God that are given to you, deliver to *Hashem* in *Yerushalayim*,

יט וּמָאנַיָּא דִּי־מִתְיַהֲבִין לָךְ לְפָלְחָן בֵּית אֱלָהָךְ הַשְׁלֵם קֳדָם אֱלָהּ יְרוּשְׁלֶם:

---

was established by members of the "First aliyah." Inspired by this verse in *Ezra* describing the return of the Babylonian Jews, its founders named it *Yesud Ha'Ma'ala*, translated here as 'the journey up was started.'

Ezra/Ezra
Chapter 8

20 and any other needs of the House of your God that it falls to you to supply, do so from the royal treasury.

21 I, King Artaxerxes, for my part, hereby issue an order to all the treasurers in the province of Beyond the River that whatever request *Ezra* the *Kohen*, scholar in the law of the God of Heaven, makes of you is to be fulfilled with dispatch

22 up to the sum of one hundred *kikarot* of silver, one hundred *kor* of wheat, one hundred *batim* of wine, one hundred *batim* of oil, and salt without limit.

23 Whatever is by order of the God of Heaven must be carried out diligently for the House of the God of Heaven, else wrath will come upon the king and his sons.

24 We further advise you that it is not permissible to impose tribute, poll tax, or land tax on any *Kohen*, *Levi*, singer, gatekeeper, temple servant, or other servant of this House of *Hashem*.

25 And you, *Ezra*, by the divine wisdom you possess, appoint magistrates and judges to judge all the people in the province of Beyond the River who know the laws of your God, and to teach those who do not know them.

26 Let anyone who does not obey the law of your God and the law of the king be punished with dispatch, whether by death, corporal punishment, confiscation of possessions, or imprisonment."

27 Blessed is God of our fathers, who put it into the mind of the king to glorify the House of *Hashem* in *Yerushalayim*,

28 and who inclined the king and his counselors and the king's military officers to be favorably disposed toward me. For my part, thanks to the care of *Hashem* for me, I summoned up courage and assembled leading men in *Yisrael* to go with me.

8 1 These are the chiefs of the clans and the register of the genealogy of those who came up with me from Babylon in the reign of King Artaxerxes:

2 Of the sons of *Pinchas*, *Gershom*; of the sons of *Itamar*, *Daniel*; of the sons of *David*, Hattush.

עזרא
פרק ח

כ וּשְׁאָר חַשְׁחוּת בֵּית אֱלָהָךְ דִּי יִפֶּל־לָךְ לְמִנְתַּן תִּנְתֵּן מִן־בֵּית גִּנְזֵי מַלְכָּא:

כא וּמִנִּי אֲנָה אַרְתַּחְשַׁסְתְּא מַלְכָּא שִׂים טְעֵם לְכֹל גִּזַּבְרַיָּא דִּי בַּעֲבַר נַהֲרָה דִּי כָל־דִּי יִשְׁאֲלֶנְכוֹן עֶזְרָא כָהֲנָא סָפַר דָּתָא דִּי־אֱלָהּ שְׁמַיָּא אָסְפַּרְנָא יִתְעֲבִד:

כב עַד־כְּסַף כַּכְּרִין מְאָה וְעַד־חִנְטִין כֹּרִין מְאָה וְעַד־חֲמַר בַּתִּין מְאָה וְעַד־בַּתִּין מְשַׁח מְאָה וּמְלַח דִּי־לָא כְתָב:

כג כָּל־דִּי מִן־טַעַם אֱלָהּ שְׁמַיָּא יִתְעֲבֵד אַדְרַזְדָּא לְבֵית אֱלָהּ שְׁמַיָּא דִּי־לְמָה לֶהֱוֵא קְצַף עַל־מַלְכוּת מַלְכָּא וּבְנוֹהִי:

כד וּלְכֹם מְהוֹדְעִין דִּי כָל־כָּהֲנַיָּא וְלֵוָיֵא זַמָּרַיָּא תָרָעַיָּא נְתִינַיָּא וּפָלְחֵי בֵּית אֱלָהָא דְנָה מִנְדָּה בְלוֹ וַהֲלָךְ לָא שַׁלִּיט לְמִרְמֵא עֲלֵיהֹם:

כה וְאַנְתְּ עֶזְרָא כְּחָכְמַת אֱלָהָךְ דִּי־בִידָךְ מֶנִּי שָׁפְטִין וְדַיָּנִין דִּי־לֶהֱוֹן דָּאנִין [דָּאיְנִין] לְכָל־עַמָּה דִּי בַּעֲבַר נַהֲרָה לְכָל־יָדְעֵי דָּתֵי אֱלָהָךְ וְדִי לָא יָדַע תְּהוֹדְעוּן:

כו וְכָל־דִּי־לָא לֶהֱוֵא עָבֵד דָּתָא דִּי־אֱלָהָךְ וְדָתָא דִּי מַלְכָּא אָסְפַּרְנָא דִּינָה לֶהֱוֵא מִתְעֲבֵד מִנֵּהּ הֵן לְמוֹת הֵן לשרשו [לִשְׁרֹשִׁי] הֵן־לַעֲנָשׁ נִכְסִין וְלֶאֱסוּרִין:

כז בָּרוּךְ יְהֹוָה אֱלֹהֵי אֲבוֹתֵינוּ אֲשֶׁר נָתַן כָּזֹאת בְּלֵב הַמֶּלֶךְ לְפָאֵר אֶת־בֵּית יְהֹוָה אֲשֶׁר בִּירוּשָׁלָ͏ִם:

כח וְעָלַי הִטָּה־חֶסֶד לִפְנֵי הַמֶּלֶךְ וְיוֹעֲצָיו וּלְכָל־שָׂרֵי הַמֶּלֶךְ הַגִּבֹּרִים וַאֲנִי הִתְחַזַּקְתִּי כְּיַד־יְהֹוָה אֱלֹהַי עָלַי וָאֶקְבְּצָה מִיִּשְׂרָאֵל רָאשִׁים לַעֲלוֹת עִמִּי:

ח א וְאֵלֶּה רָאשֵׁי אֲבֹתֵיהֶם וְהִתְיַחְשָׂם הָעֹלִים עִמִּי בְּמַלְכוּת אַרְתַּחְשַׁסְתְּא הַמֶּלֶךְ מִבָּבֶל:

ב מִבְּנֵי פִינְחָס גֵּרְשֹׁם מִבְּנֵי אִיתָמָר דָּנִיֵּאל מִבְּנֵי דָוִיד חַטּוּשׁ:

Ezra/Ezra

Chapter 8

עזרא

פרק ח

3 Of the sons of *Shechanya*: of the sons of Parosh, *Zecharya*; through him the genealogy of 150 males was registered.

ג מִבְּנֵי שְׁכַנְיָה מִבְּנֵי פַרְעֹשׁ זְכַרְיָה וְעִמּוֹ הִתְיַחֵשׂ לִזְכָרִים מֵאָה וַחֲמִשִּׁים:

4 Eliehoenai son of Zerahiah, of the sons of Pahathmoab, and with him 200 males.

ד מִבְּנֵי פַחַת מוֹאָב אֶלְיְהוֹעֵינַי בֶּן־זְרַחְיָה וְעִמּוֹ מָאתַיִם הַזְּכָרִים:

5 Of the sons of *Shechanya* son of *Yachaziel*; and with him 300 males.

ה מִבְּנֵי שְׁכַנְיָה בֶּן־יַחֲזִיאֵל וְעִמּוֹ שְׁלֹשׁ מֵאוֹת הַזְּכָרִים:

6 And of the sons of Adin, Ebed son of *Yonatan*; and with him 50 males.

ו וּמִבְּנֵי עָדִין עֶבֶד בֶּן־יוֹנָתָן וְעִמּוֹ חֲמִשִּׁים הַזְּכָרִים:

7 And of the sons of Elam, Jeshaiah son of *Atalya*; and with him 70 males.

ז וּמִבְּנֵי עֵילָם יְשַׁעְיָה בֶּן־עֲתַלְיָה וְעִמּוֹ שִׁבְעִים הַזְּכָרִים:

8 And of the sons of Shephatiah, Zebadiah son of *Michael*; and with him 80 males.

ח וּמִבְּנֵי שְׁפַטְיָה זְבַדְיָה בֶּן־מִיכָאֵל וְעִמּוֹ שְׁמֹנִים הַזְּכָרִים:

9 Of the sons of *Yoav*, *Ovadya* son of *Yechiel*; and with him 218 males.

ט מִבְּנֵי יוֹאָב עֹבַדְיָה בֶּן־יְחִיאֵל וְעִמּוֹ מָאתַיִם וּשְׁמֹנָה עָשָׂר הַזְּכָרִים:

10 And of the sons of Shelomith, the son of Josiphiah; and with him 160 males.

י וּמִבְּנֵי שְׁלוֹמִית בֶּן־יוֹסִפְיָה וְעִמּוֹ מֵאָה וְשִׁשִּׁים הַזְּכָרִים:

11 And of the sons of Bebai, *Zecharya* son of Bebai; and with him 28 males.

יא וּמִבְּנֵי בֵבַי זְכַרְיָה בֶּן־בֵּבָי וְעִמּוֹ עֶשְׂרִים וּשְׁמֹנָה הַזְּכָרִים:

12 And of the sons of Azgad, *Yochanan* son of Hakkatan; and with him 110 males.

יב וּמִבְּנֵי עַזְגָּד יוֹחָנָן בֶּן־הַקָּטָן וְעִמּוֹ מֵאָה וַעֲשָׂרָה הַזְּכָרִים:

13 And of the sons of Adonikam, who were the last; and these are their names: Eliphelet, Jeiel, and *Shemaya*; and with them 60 males.

יג וּמִבְּנֵי אֲדֹנִיקָם אַחֲרֹנִים וְאֵלֶּה שְׁמוֹתָם אֱלִיפֶלֶט יְעִיאֵל וּשְׁמַעְיָה וְעִמָּהֶם שִׁשִּׁים הַזְּכָרִים:

14 And of the sons of Bigvai, Uthai and Zaccur; and with them 70 males.

יד וּמִבְּנֵי בִגְוַי עוּתַי וזבוד [וְזַכּוּר] וְעִמּוֹ שִׁבְעִים הַזְּכָרִים:

15 These I assembled by the river that enters Ahava, and we encamped there for three days. I reviewed the people and the *Kohanim*, but I did not find any *Leviim* there.

טו וָאֶקְבְּצֵם אֶל־הַנָּהָר הַבָּא אֶל־אַהֲוָא וַנַּחֲנֶה שָׁם יָמִים שְׁלֹשָׁה וָאָבִינָה בָעָם וּבַכֹּהֲנִים וּמִבְּנֵי לֵוִי לֹא־מָצָאתִי שָׁם:

16 I sent for *Eliezer*, Ariel, *Shemaya*, Elnathan, Jarib, Elnathan, *Natan*, *Zecharya*, and Meshullam, the leading men, and also for Joiarib and Elnathan, the instructors,

טז וָאֶשְׁלְחָה לֶאֱלִיעֶזֶר לַאֲרִיאֵל לִשְׁמַעְיָה וּלְאֶלְנָתָן וּלְיָרִיב וּלְאֶלְנָתָן וּלְנָתָן וְלִזְכַרְיָה וְלִמְשֻׁלָּם רָאשִׁים וּלְיוֹיָרִיב וּלְאֶלְנָתָן מְבִינִים:

17 and I gave them an order for *Ido*, the leader at the place [called] Casiphia. I gave them a message to convey to *Ido* [and] his brother, temple-servants at the place [called] Casiphia, that they should bring us attendants for the House of our God.

יז ואוצאה [וָאֲצַוֶּה] אוֹתָם עַל־אִדּוֹ הָרֹאשׁ בְּכָסִפְיָא הַמָּקוֹם וָאָשִׂימָה בְּפִיהֶם דְּבָרִים לְדַבֵּר אֶל־אִדּוֹ אָחִיו הנתונים [הַנְּתִינִים] בְּכָסִפְיָא הַמָּקוֹם לְהָבִיא־לָנוּ מְשָׁרְתִים לְבֵית אֱלֹהֵינוּ:

Ezra/Ezra
Chapter 8

עזרא
פרק ח

18 Thanks to the benevolent care of our God for us, they brought us a capable man of the family of Mahli son of *Levi* son of *Yisrael*, and Sherebiah and his sons and brothers, 18 in all,

יח וַיָּבִיאּוּ לָנוּ כְּיַד־אֱלֹהֵינוּ הַטּוֹבָה עָלֵינוּ אִישׁ שֶׂכֶל מִבְּנֵי מַחְלִי בֶּן־לֵוִי בֶּן־יִשְׂרָאֵל וְשֵׁרֵבְיָה וּבָנָיו וְאֶחָיו שְׁמֹנָה עָשָׂר׃

19 and Hashabiah, and with him Jeshaiah of the family of *Merari*, his brothers and their sons, 20 in all;

יט וְאֶת־חֲשַׁבְיָה וְאִתּוֹ יְשַׁעְיָה מִבְּנֵי מְרָרִי אֶחָיו וּבְנֵיהֶם עֶשְׂרִים׃

20 and of the temple servants whom *David* and the officers had appointed for the service of the *Leviim* – 220 temple servants, all of them listed by name.

כ וּמִן־הַנְּתִינִים שֶׁנָּתַן דָּוִיד וְהַשָּׂרִים לַעֲבֹדַת הַלְוִיִּם נְתִינִים מָאתַיִם וְעֶשְׂרִים כֻּלָּם נִקְּבוּ בְשֵׁמוֹת׃

21 I proclaimed a fast there by the Ahava River to afflict ourselves before our God to beseech Him for a smooth journey for us and for our children and for all our possessions;

כא וָאֶקְרָא שָׁם צוֹם עַל־הַנָּהָר אַהֲוָא לְהִתְעַנּוֹת לִפְנֵי אֱלֹהֵינוּ לְבַקֵּשׁ מִמֶּנּוּ דֶּרֶךְ יְשָׁרָה לָנוּ וּלְטַפֵּנוּ וּלְכָל־רְכוּשֵׁנוּ׃

22 for I was ashamed to ask the king for soldiers and horsemen to protect us against any enemy on the way, since we had told the king, "The benevolent care of our God is for all who seek Him, while His fierce anger is against all who forsake Him."

כב כִּי בֹשְׁתִּי לִשְׁאוֹל מִן־הַמֶּלֶךְ חַיִל וּפָרָשִׁים לְעָזְרֵנוּ מֵאוֹיֵב בַּדָּרֶךְ כִּי־אָמַרְנוּ לַמֶּלֶךְ לֵאמֹר יַד־אֱלֹהֵינוּ עַל־כָּל־מְבַקְשָׁיו לְטוֹבָה וְעֻזּוֹ וְאַפּוֹ עַל כָּל־עֹזְבָיו׃

23 So we fasted and besought our God for this, and He responded to our plea.

כג וַנָּצוּמָה וַנְּבַקְשָׁה מֵאֱלֹהֵינוּ עַל־זֹאת וַיֵּעָתֵר לָנוּ׃

24 Then I selected twelve of the chiefs of the *Kohanim*, namely Sherebiah and Hashabiah with ten of their brothers,

כד וָאַבְדִּילָה מִשָּׂרֵי הַכֹּהֲנִים שְׁנֵים עָשָׂר לְשֵׁרֵבְיָה חֲשַׁבְיָה וְעִמָּהֶם מֵאֲחֵיהֶם עֲשָׂרָה׃

25 and I weighed out to them the silver, the gold, and the vessels, the contribution to the House of our God which the king, his counselors and officers, and all *Yisrael* who were present had made.

כה ואשקולה [וָאֶשְׁקֳלָה] לָהֶם אֶת־הַכֶּסֶף וְאֶת־הַזָּהָב וְאֶת־הַכֵּלִים תְּרוּמַת בֵּית־אֱלֹהֵינוּ הַהֵרִימוּ הַמֶּלֶךְ וְיֹעֲצָיו וְשָׂרָיו וְכָל־יִשְׂרָאֵל הַנִּמְצָאִים׃

26 I entrusted to their safekeeping the weight of six hundred and fifty talents of silver, one hundred silver vessels of one talent each, one hundred talents of gold;

כו וָאֶשְׁקֳלָה עַל־יָדָם כֶּסֶף כִּכָּרִים שֵׁשׁ־מֵאוֹת וַחֲמִשִּׁים וּכְלֵי־כֶסֶף מֵאָה לְכִכָּרִים זָהָב מֵאָה כִכָּר׃

27 also, twenty gold bowls worth one thousand darics and two vessels of good, shining bronze, as precious as gold.

כז וּכְפֹרֵי זָהָב עֶשְׂרִים לַאֲדַרְכֹנִים אָלֶף וּכְלֵי נְחֹשֶׁת מֻצְהָב טוֹבָה שְׁנַיִם חֲמוּדֹת כַּזָּהָב׃

28 I said to them, "You are consecrated to *Hashem*, and the vessels are consecrated, and the silver and gold are a freewill offering to God of your fathers.

כח וָאֹמְרָה אֲלֵהֶם אַתֶּם קֹדֶשׁ לַיהוָה וְהַכֵּלִים קֹדֶשׁ וְהַכֶּסֶף וְהַזָּהָב נְדָבָה לַיהוָה אֱלֹהֵי אֲבֹתֵיכֶם׃

29 Guard them diligently until such time as you weigh them out in the presence of the officers of the *Kohanim* and the *Leviim* and the officers of the clans of *Yisrael* in *Yerushalayim* in the chambers of the House of *Hashem*."

כט שִׁקְדוּ וְשִׁמְרוּ עַד־תִּשְׁקְלוּ לִפְנֵי שָׂרֵי הַכֹּהֲנִים וְהַלְוִיִּם וְשָׂרֵי־הָאָבוֹת לְיִשְׂרָאֵל בִּירוּשָׁלָ͏ִם הַלִּשְׁכוֹת בֵּית יְהוָה׃

Ezra/Ezra
Chapter 9

עזרא
פרק ט

30 So the *Kohanim* and the *Leviim* received the cargo of silver and gold and vessels by weight, to bring them to *Yerushalayim* to the House of our God.

ל וְקִבְּלוּ הַכֹּהֲנִים וְהַלְוִיִּם מִשְׁקַל הַכֶּסֶף וְהַזָּהָב וְהַכֵּלִים לְהָבִיא לִירוּשָׁלַם לְבֵית אֱלֹהֵינוּ׃

31 We set out for *Yerushalayim* from the Ahava River on the twelfth of the first month. We enjoyed the care of our God, who saved us from enemy ambush on the journey.

לא וַנִּסְעָה מִנְּהַר אַהֲוָא בִּשְׁנֵים עָשָׂר לַחֹדֶשׁ הָרִאשׁוֹן לָלֶכֶת יְרוּשָׁלָם וְיַד־אֱלֹהֵינוּ הָיְתָה עָלֵינוּ וַיַּצִּילֵנוּ מִכַּף אוֹיֵב וְאוֹרֵב עַל־הַדָּרֶךְ׃

va-nis-AH mi-n'-HAR a-ha-VA bish-NAYM a-SAR la-KHO-desh ha-ri-SHON la-LE-khet y'-ru-sha-LA-im v'-YAD e-lo-HAY-nu ha-y'-TAH a-LAY-nu va-ya-tzee-LAY-nu mi-KAF o-YAYV v'-o-RAYV al ha-DA-rekh

32 We arrived in *Yerushalayim* and stayed there three days.

לב וַנָּבוֹא יְרוּשָׁלָם וַנֵּשֶׁב שָׁם יָמִים שְׁלֹשָׁה׃

33 On the fourth day the silver, gold, and vessels were weighed out in the House of our God into the keeping of Meremoth son of *Uriya* the *Kohen*, with whom was *Elazar* son of *Pinchas*. *Yozavad* son of *Yeshua*, and Noadiah son of Binnui, the *Leviim*, were with them.

לג וּבַיּוֹם הָרְבִיעִי נִשְׁקַל הַכֶּסֶף וְהַזָּהָב וְהַכֵּלִים בְּבֵית אֱלֹהֵינוּ עַל יַד־מְרֵמוֹת בֶּן־אוּרִיָּה הַכֹּהֵן וְעִמּוֹ אֶלְעָזָר בֶּן־פִּינְחָס וְעִמָּהֶם יוֹזָבָד בֶּן־יֵשׁוּעַ וְנוֹעַדְיָה בֶן־בִּנּוּי הַלְוִיִּם׃

34 Everything accorded as to number and weight, the entire cargo being recorded at that time.

לד בְּמִסְפָּר בְּמִשְׁקָל לַכֹּל וַיִּכָּתֵב כָּל־הַמִּשְׁקָל בָּעֵת הַהִיא׃

35 The returning exiles who arrived from captivity made burnt offerings to the God of *Yisrael*: twelve bulls for all *Yisrael*, ninety-six rams, seventy-seven lambs and twelve he-goats as a purification offering, all this a burnt offering to *Hashem*.

לה הַבָּאִים מֵהַשְּׁבִי בְנֵי־הַגּוֹלָה הִקְרִיבוּ עֹלוֹת לֵאלֹהֵי יִשְׂרָאֵל פָּרִים שְׁנֵים־עָשָׂר עַל־כָּל־יִשְׂרָאֵל אֵילִים תִּשְׁעִים וְשִׁשָּׁה כְּבָשִׂים שִׁבְעִים וְשִׁבְעָה צְפִירֵי חַטָּאת שְׁנֵים עָשָׂר הַכֹּל עוֹלָה לַיהוָה׃

36 They handed the royal orders to the king's satraps and the governors of the province of Beyond the River who gave support to the people and the House of *Hashem*.

לו וַיִּתְּנוּ אֶת־דָּתֵי הַמֶּלֶךְ לַאֲחַשְׁדַּרְפְּנֵי הַמֶּלֶךְ וּפַחֲווֹת עֵבֶר הַנָּהָר וְנִשְּׂאוּ אֶת־הָעָם וְאֶת־בֵּית־הָאֱלֹהִים׃

9

1 When this was over, the officers approached me, saying, "The people of *Yisrael* and the *Kohanim* and *Leviim* have not separated themselves from the peoples of the land whose abhorrent practices are like those of the Canaanites, the Hittites, the Perizzites, the Jebusites, the Ammonites, the Moabites, the Egyptians, and the Amorites.

ט א וּכְכַלּוֹת אֵלֶּה נִגְּשׁוּ אֵלַי הַשָּׂרִים לֵאמֹר לֹא־נִבְדְּלוּ הָעָם יִשְׂרָאֵל וְהַכֹּהֲנִים וְהַלְוִיִּם מֵעַמֵּי הָאֲרָצוֹת כְּתוֹעֲבֹתֵיהֶם לַכְּנַעֲנִי הַחִתִּי הַפְּרִזִּי הַיְבוּסִי הָעַמֹּנִי הַמֹּאָבִי הַמִּצְרִי וְהָאֱמֹרִי׃

8:31 We set out for *Yerushalayim* For the People of Israel, the past and present fuse together to create the most extraordinary future. Through *Ezra's* actions, it is clear that a carefully choreographed event was planned and designed to reflect the earlier exodus from Egypt. Just as the Jews left Egypt in the first month, the Hebrew month of *Nisan*, and crossed the Sea of Reeds, *Ezra's* exodus departed from a river in the first month. Certainly, the symbolism of recreating such a formative occurrence wasn't lost on the members of the entourage, giving them great courage and hope. In modern times, almost the entire Iraqi-Babylonian Jewish community immigrated to Israel in the early 1950s, essentially ending a continual presence there which had lasted for over 2800. This modern-day miracle was aptly named 'Operation Ezra and Nechemya'.

Iraqi immigrants arriving in Israel, 1950

1942

Ezra/Ezra
Chapter 9

עזרא
פרק ט

2 They have taken their daughters as wives for themselves and for their sons, so that the holy seed has become intermingled with the peoples of the land; and it is the officers and prefects who have taken the lead in this trespass."

ב כִּֽי־נָשְׂא֣וּ מִבְּנֹתֵיהֶ֗ם לָהֶם֙ וְלִבְנֵיהֶ֔ם וְהִתְעָֽרְבוּ֙ זֶ֣רַע הַקֹּ֔דֶשׁ בְּעַמֵּ֖י הָאֲרָצ֑וֹת וְיַ֧ד הַשָּׂרִ֣ים וְהַסְּגָנִ֗ים הָ֥יְתָ֛ה בַּמַּ֥עַל הַזֶּ֖ה רִאשׁוֹנָֽה׃

3 When I heard this, I rent my garment and robe, I tore hair out of my head and beard, and I sat desolate.

ג וּכְשָׁמְעִי֙ אֶת־הַדָּבָ֣ר הַזֶּ֔ה קָרַ֥עְתִּי אֶת־בִּגְדִ֖י וּמְעִילִ֑י וָאֶמְרְטָ֞ה מִשְּׂעַ֤ר רֹאשִׁי֙ וּזְקָנִ֔י וָאֵשְׁבָ֖ה מְשׁוֹמֵֽם׃

4 Around me gathered all who were concerned over the words of the God of *Yisrael* because of the returning exiles' trespass, while I sat desolate until the evening offering.

ד וְאֵלַ֣י יֵאָסְפ֗וּ כֹּ֚ל חָרֵד֙ בְּדִבְרֵ֣י אֱלֹהֵֽי־יִשְׂרָאֵ֔ל עַ֖ל מַ֣עַל הַגּוֹלָ֑ה וַאֲנִי֙ יֹשֵׁ֣ב מְשׁוֹמֵ֔ם עַ֖ד לְמִנְחַ֥ת הָעָֽרֶב׃

5 At the time of the evening offering I ended my self-affliction; still in my torn garment and robe, I got down on my knees and spread out my hands to *Hashem* my God,

ה וּבְמִנְחַ֣ת הָעֶ֗רֶב קַ֚מְתִּי מִתַּֽעֲנִיתִ֔י וּבְקָרְעִ֥י בִגְדִ֖י וּמְעִילִ֑י וָֽאֶכְרְעָה֙ עַל־בִּרְכַּ֔י וָאֶפְרְשָׂ֥ה כַפַּ֖י אֶל־יְהֹוָ֥ה אֱלֹהָֽי׃

6 and said, "O my God, I am too ashamed and mortified to lift my face to You, O my God, for our iniquities are overwhelming and our guilt has grown high as heaven.

ו וָאֹֽמְרָ֗ה אֱלֹהַי֙ בֹּ֣שְׁתִּי וְנִכְלַ֔מְתִּי לְהָרִ֧ים אֱלֹהַ֛י פָּנַ֖י אֵלֶ֑יךָ כִּ֣י עֲוֺנֹתֵ֤ינוּ רָבוּ֙ לְמַ֣עְלָה רֹּ֔אשׁ וְאַשְׁמָתֵ֥נוּ גָֽדְלָ֖ה עַ֥ד לַשָּׁמָֽיִם׃

7 From the time of our fathers to this very day we have been deep in guilt. Because of our iniquities, we, our kings, and our *Kohanim* have been handed over to foreign kings, to the sword, to captivity, to pillage, and to humiliation, as is now the case.

ז מִימֵ֣י אֲבֹתֵ֗ינוּ אֲנַ֙חְנוּ֙ בְּאַשְׁמָ֣ה גְדֹלָ֔ה עַ֖ד הַיּ֣וֹם הַזֶּ֑ה וּבַעֲוֺנֹתֵ֡ינוּ נִתַּ֣נּוּ אֲנַ֣חְנוּ מְלָכֵ֣ינוּ כֹהֲנֵ֡ינוּ בְּיַ֣ד ׀ מַלְכֵ֣י הָאֲרָצ֡וֹת בַּחֶ֜רֶב בַּשְּׁבִ֧י וּבַבִּזָּ֛ה וּבְבֹ֥שֶׁת פָּנִ֖ים כְּהַיּ֥וֹם הַזֶּֽה׃

8 "But now, for a short while, there has been a reprieve from *Hashem* our God, who has granted us a surviving remnant and given us a stake in His holy place; our God has restored the luster to our eyes and furnished us with a little sustenance in our bondage.

ח וְעַתָּ֡ה כִּמְעַט־רֶ֩גַע֩ הָיְתָ֨ה תְחִנָּ֜ה מֵאֵ֣ת ׀ יְהֹוָ֣ה אֱלֹהֵ֗ינוּ לְהַשְׁאִ֥יר לָ֙נוּ֙ פְּלֵיטָ֔ה וְלָתֶת־לָ֥נוּ יָתֵ֖ד בִּמְק֣וֹם קָדְשׁ֑וֹ לְהָאִ֤יר עֵינֵ֙ינוּ֙ אֱלֹהֵ֔ינוּ וּלְתִתֵּ֛נוּ מִֽחְיָ֥ה מְעַ֖ט בְּעַבְדֻתֵֽנוּ׃

v'-a-TAH kim-at RE-ga ha-y'-TAH t'-khi-NAH may-AYT a-do-NAI e-lo-HAY-nu l'-hash-EER LA-nu p'-lay-TAH v'-la-tet LA-nu ya-TAYD bim-KOM kod-SHO l'-ha-EER ay-NAY-nu e-lo-HAY-nu ul-ti-TAY-nu mikh-YAH m'-AT b'-av-du-TAY-nu

---

Rabbi Judah Halevi (1075–1141)

9:8 A Surviving Remnant In his admonition of the people who have returned to the Land of Israel only to abandon *Hashem* and intermarry with local women, Ezra praises God for providing them a reprieve from the years of exile and persecution. He thanks *Hashem* for causing the king of Persia to look favorably upon His people, and for the remnant of the nation that survived. However, even though Cyrus had granted permission to those who survived the destruction and exile, the "surviving remnant," to return home and reconstruct the *Beit Hamikdash*, a mere 42,360 people heeded the initial call to return and rebuild (Ezra 2:64). In just a short time, the Jews had become accustomed to living in exile, and had embraced its lifestyle. As Rabbi Yehuda Halevi writes in his work *The Kuzari*: "In reality, however, only a small portion returned.

Ezra/Ezra
Chapter 10

9 For bondsmen we are, though even in our bondage *Hashem* has not forsaken us, but has disposed the king of Persia favorably toward us, to furnish us with sustenance and to raise again the House of our God, repairing its ruins and giving us a hold in *Yehuda* and *Yerushalayim*.

10 "Now, what can we say in the face of this, O our God, for we have forsaken Your commandments,

11 which You gave us through Your servants the *Neviim* when You said, 'The land that you are about to possess is a land unclean through the uncleanness of the peoples of the land, through their abhorrent practices with which they, in their impurity, have filled it from one end to the other.

12 Now then, do not give your daughters in marriage to their sons or let their daughters marry your sons; do nothing for their well-being or advantage, then you will be strong and enjoy the bounty of the land and bequeath it to your children forever.'

13 After all that has happened to us because of our evil deeds and our deep guilt – though You, our God, have been forbearing, [punishing us] less than our iniquity [deserves] in that You have granted us such a remnant as this –

14 shall we once again violate Your commandments by intermarrying with these peoples who follow such abhorrent practices? Will You not rage against us till we are destroyed without remnant or survivor?

15 *Hashem*, God of *Yisrael*, You are benevolent, for we have survived as a remnant, as is now the case. We stand before You in all our guilt, for we cannot face You on this account."

10 1 While *Ezra* was praying and making confession, weeping and prostrating himself before the House of *Hashem*, a very great crowd of Israelites gathered about him, men, women, and children; the people were weeping bitterly.

עזרא
פרק י

ט כִּי־עֲבָדִים אֲנַחְנוּ וּבְעַבְדֻתֵנוּ לֹא עֲזָבָנוּ אֱלֹהֵינוּ וַיַּט־עָלֵינוּ חֶסֶד לִפְנֵי מַלְכֵי פָרַס לָתֶת־לָנוּ מִחְיָה לְרוֹמֵם אֶת־בֵּית אֱלֹהֵינוּ וּלְהַעֲמִיד אֶת־חָרְבֹתָיו וְלָתֶת־לָנוּ גָדֵר בִּיהוּדָה וּבִירוּשָׁלָיִם:

י וְעַתָּה מַה־נֹּאמַר אֱלֹהֵינוּ אַחֲרֵי־זֹאת כִּי עָזַבְנוּ מִצְוֹתֶיךָ:

יא אֲשֶׁר צִוִּיתָ בְּיַד עֲבָדֶיךָ הַנְּבִיאִים לֵאמֹר הָאָרֶץ אֲשֶׁר אַתֶּם בָּאִים לְרִשְׁתָּהּ אֶרֶץ נִדָּה הִיא בְּנִדַּת עַמֵּי הָאֲרָצוֹת בְּתוֹעֲבֹתֵיהֶם אֲשֶׁר מִלְאוּהָ מִפֶּה אֶל־פֶּה בְּטֻמְאָתָם:

יב וְעַתָּה בְּנוֹתֵיכֶם אַל־תִּתְּנוּ לִבְנֵיהֶם וּבְנֹתֵיהֶם אַל־תִּשְׂאוּ לִבְנֵיכֶם וְלֹא־תִדְרְשׁוּ שְׁלֹמָם וְטוֹבָתָם עַד־עוֹלָם לְמַעַן תֶּחֶזְקוּ וַאֲכַלְתֶּם אֶת־טוּב הָאָרֶץ וְהוֹרַשְׁתֶּם לִבְנֵיכֶם עַד־עוֹלָם:

יג וְאַחֲרֵי כָּל־הַבָּא עָלֵינוּ בְּמַעֲשֵׂינוּ הָרָעִים וּבְאַשְׁמָתֵנוּ הַגְּדֹלָה כִּי אַתָּה אֱלֹהֵינוּ חָשַׂכְתָּ לְמַטָּה מֵעֲוֺנֵנוּ וְנָתַתָּה לָּנוּ פְּלֵיטָה כָּזֹאת:

יד הֲנָשׁוּב לְהָפֵר מִצְוֺתֶיךָ וּלְהִתְחַתֵּן בְּעַמֵּי הַתֹּעֵבוֹת הָאֵלֶּה הֲלוֹא תֶאֱנַף־בָּנוּ עַד־כַּלֵּה לְאֵין שְׁאֵרִית וּפְלֵיטָה:

טו יְהוָה אֱלֹהֵי יִשְׂרָאֵל צַדִּיק אַתָּה כִּי־נִשְׁאַרְנוּ פְלֵיטָה כְּהַיּוֹם הַזֶּה הִנְנוּ לְפָנֶיךָ בְּאַשְׁמָתֵינוּ כִּי אֵין לַעֲמוֹד לְפָנֶיךָ עַל־זֹאת:

י א וּכְהִתְפַּלֵּל עֶזְרָא וּכְהִתְוַדֹּתוֹ בֹּכֶה וּמִתְנַפֵּל לִפְנֵי בֵּית הָאֱלֹהִים נִקְבְּצוּ אֵלָיו מִיִּשְׂרָאֵל קָהָל רַב־מְאֹד אֲנָשִׁים וְנָשִׁים וִילָדִים כִּי־בָכוּ הָעָם הַרְבֵּה־בֶכֶה:

The majority remained in *Bavel*, willfully accepting the exile, as they did not wish to leave their homes and businesses…" This is no less true in our own day and age. Jews have become very comfortable living in the Diaspora, yet they must take heed of *Ezra*'s stirring words to recognize the kindness *Hashem* has done for His people and return with their families to *Eretz Yisrael*.

Ezra/Ezra
Chapter 10

עזרא
פרק י

2 Then *Shechanya* son of *Yechiel* of the family of Elam spoke up and said to *Ezra*, "We have trespassed against our God by bringing into our homes foreign women from the peoples of the land; but there is still hope for *Yisrael* despite this.

ב וַיַּעַן שְׁכַנְיָה בֶן־יְחִיאֵל מִבְּנֵי עוֹלָם [עֵילָם] וַיֹּאמֶר לְעֶזְרָא אֲנַחְנוּ מָעַלְנוּ בֵאלֹהֵינוּ וַנֹּשֶׁב נָשִׁים נָכְרִיּוֹת מֵעַמֵּי הָאָרֶץ וְעַתָּה יֵשׁ־מִקְוֶה לְיִשְׂרָאֵל עַל־זֹאת:

3 Now then, let us make a covenant with our God to expel all these women and those who have been born to them, in accordance with the bidding of *Hashem* and of all who are concerned over the commandment of our God, and let the Teaching be obeyed.

ג וְעַתָּה נִכְרָת־בְּרִית לֵאלֹהֵינוּ לְהוֹצִיא כָל־נָשִׁים וְהַנּוֹלָד מֵהֶם בַּעֲצַת אֲדֹנָי וְהַחֲרֵדִים בְּמִצְוַת אֱלֹהֵינוּ וְכַתּוֹרָה יֵעָשֶׂה:

4 Take action, for the responsibility is yours and we are with you. Act with resolve!"

ד קוּם כִּי־עָלֶיךָ הַדָּבָר וַאֲנַחְנוּ עִמָּךְ חֲזַק וַעֲשֵׂה:

5 So *Ezra* at once put the officers of the *Kohanim* and the *Leviim* and all *Yisrael* under oath to act accordingly, and they took the oath.

ה וַיָּקָם עֶזְרָא וַיַּשְׁבַּע אֶת־שָׂרֵי הַכֹּהֲנִים הַלְוִיִּם וְכָל־יִשְׂרָאֵל לַעֲשׂוֹת כַּדָּבָר הַזֶּה וַיִּשָּׁבֵעוּ:

6 Then *Ezra* rose from his place in front of the House of *Hashem* and went into the Hamber of *Yehochanan* son of *Elyashiv*; there, he ate no bread and drank no water, for he was in mourning over the trespass of those who had returned from exile.

ו וַיָּקָם עֶזְרָא מִלִּפְנֵי בֵּית הָאֱלֹהִים וַיֵּלֶךְ אֶל־לִשְׁכַּת יְהוֹחָנָן בֶּן־אֶלְיָשִׁיב וַיֵּלֶךְ שָׁם לֶחֶם לֹא־אָכַל וּמַיִם לֹא־שָׁתָה כִּי מִתְאַבֵּל עַל־מַעַל הַגּוֹלָה:

7 Then a proclamation was issued in *Yehuda* and *Yerushalayim* that all who had returned from the exile should assemble in *Yerushalayim*,

ז וַיַּעֲבִירוּ קוֹל בִּיהוּדָה וִירוּשָׁלִַם לְכֹל בְּנֵי הַגּוֹלָה לְהִקָּבֵץ יְרוּשָׁלִָם:

8 and that anyone who did not come in three days would, by decision of the officers and elders, have his property confiscated and himself excluded from the congregation of the returning exiles.

ח וְכֹל אֲשֶׁר לֹא־יָבוֹא לִשְׁלֹשֶׁת הַיָּמִים כַּעֲצַת הַשָּׂרִים וְהַזְּקֵנִים יָחֳרַם כָּל־רְכוּשׁוֹ וְהוּא יִבָּדֵל מִקְּהַל הַגּוֹלָה:

9 All the men of *Yehuda* and *Binyamin* assembled in *Yerushalayim* in three days; it was the ninth month, the twentieth of the month. All the people sat in the square of the House of *Hashem*, trembling on account of the event and because of the rains.

ט וַיִּקָּבְצוּ כָל־אַנְשֵׁי־יְהוּדָה וּבִנְיָמִן יְרוּשָׁלִַם לִשְׁלֹשֶׁת הַיָּמִים הוּא חֹדֶשׁ הַתְּשִׁיעִי בְּעֶשְׂרִים בַּחֹדֶשׁ וַיֵּשְׁבוּ כָל־הָעָם בִּרְחוֹב בֵּית הָאֱלֹהִים מַרְעִידִים עַל־הַדָּבָר וּמֵהַגְּשָׁמִים:

va-yi-ka-v'-TZU khol an-SHAY y'-hu-DAH u-vin-ya-MIN y'-ru-sha-LA-im lish-LO-shet ha-ya-MEEM HU KHO-desh ha-t'-shee-EE b'-es-REEM ba-KHO-desh va-yay-sh'-VU khol ha-AM bir-KHOV BAYT ha-e-lo-HEEM mar-ee-DEEM al ha-da-VAR u-may-ha-g'-sha-MEEM

10:9 All the men of *Yehuda* and *Binyamin* assembled in *Yerushalayim* This verse only mentions the tribes of *Yehuda* and *Binyamin*, the two tribes that made up the ancient kingdom of *Yehuda* that had been exiled to Babylon. The other ten tribes who had formed the kingdom of *Yisrael* had been exiled earlier by the Assyrians, forced to assimilate and became lost to the Nation of Israel. Although today, almost all Jews are descendants of the ancient tribe of *Yehuda*, the modern Jewish state was called "Israel" and not "Judah." The su-

Ezra/Ezra
Chapter 10

עזרא
פרק י

10 Then *Ezra* the *Kohen* got up and said to them, "You have trespassed by bringing home foreign women, thus aggravating the guilt of *Yisrael*.

י וַיָּקָם עֶזְרָא הַכֹּהֵן וַיֹּאמֶר אֲלֵהֶם אַתֶּם מְעַלְתֶּם וַתֹּשִׁיבוּ נָשִׁים נָכְרִיּוֹת לְהוֹסִיף עַל־אַשְׁמַת יִשְׂרָאֵל׃

11 So now, make confession to *Hashem*, God of your fathers, and do His will, and separate yourselves from the peoples of the land and from the foreign women."

יא וְעַתָּה תְּנוּ תוֹדָה לַיהֹוָה אֱלֹהֵי־אֲבֹתֵיכֶם וַעֲשׂוּ רְצוֹנוֹ וְהִבָּדְלוּ מֵעַמֵּי הָאָרֶץ וּמִן־הַנָּשִׁים הַנָּכְרִיּוֹת׃

12 The entire congregation responded in a loud voice, "We must surely do just as you say.

יב וַיַּעֲנוּ כָל־הַקָּהָל וַיֹּאמְרוּ קוֹל גָּדוֹל כֵּן כדבריך [כִּדְבָרְךָ] עָלֵינוּ לַעֲשׂוֹת׃

13 However, many people are involved, and it is the rainy season; it is not possible to remain out in the open, nor is this the work of a day or two, because we have transgressed extensively in this matter.

יג אֲבָל הָעָם רָב וְהָעֵת גְּשָׁמִים וְאֵין כֹּחַ לַעֲמוֹד בַּחוּץ וְהַמְּלָאכָה לֹא־לְיוֹם אֶחָד וְלֹא לִשְׁנַיִם כִּי־הִרְבִּינוּ לִפְשֹׁעַ בַּדָּבָר הַזֶּה׃

14 Let our officers remain on behalf of the entire congregation, and all our townspeople who have brought home foreign women shall appear before them at scheduled times, together with the elders and judges of each town, in order to avert the burning anger of our God from us on this account."

יד יַעֲמְדוּ־נָא שָׂרֵינוּ לְכָל־הַקָּהָל וְכֹל אֲשֶׁר בֶּעָרֵינוּ הַהֹשִׁיב נָשִׁים נָכְרִיּוֹת יָבֹא לְעִתִּים מְזֻמָּנִים וְעִמָּהֶם זִקְנֵי־עִיר וָעִיר וְשֹׁפְטֶיהָ עַד לְהָשִׁיב חֲרוֹן אַף־אֱלֹהֵינוּ מִמֶּנּוּ עַד לַדָּבָר הַזֶּה׃

15 Only *Yonatan* son of *Asael* and Jahzeiah son of Tikvah remained for this purpose, assisted by Meshullam and Shabbethai, the *Leviim*.

טו אַךְ יוֹנָתָן בֶּן־עֲשָׂהאֵל וְיַחְזְיָה בֶן־תִּקְוָה עָמְדוּ עַל־זֹאת וּמְשֻׁלָּם וְשַׁבְּתַי הַלֵּוִי עֲזָרֻם׃

16 The returning exiles did so. *Ezra* the *Kohen* and the men who were the chiefs of the ancestral clans – all listed by name – sequestered themselves on the first day of the tenth month to study the matter.

טז וַיַּעֲשׂוּ־כֵן בְּנֵי הַגּוֹלָה וַיִּבָּדְלוּ עֶזְרָא הַכֹּהֵן אֲנָשִׁים רָאשֵׁי הָאָבוֹת לְבֵית אֲבֹתָם וְכֻלָּם בְּשֵׁמוֹת וַיֵּשְׁבוּ בְּיוֹם אֶחָד לַחֹדֶשׁ הָעֲשִׂירִי לְדַרְיוֹשׁ הַדָּבָר׃

17 By the first day of the first month they were done with all the men who had brought home foreign women.

יז וַיְכַלּוּ בַכֹּל אֲנָשִׁים הַהֹשִׁיבוּ נָשִׁים נָכְרִיּוֹת עַד יוֹם אֶחָד לַחֹדֶשׁ הָרִאשׁוֹן׃

18 Among the priestly families who were found to have brought foreign women were *Yeshua* son of *Yotzadak* and his brothers Maaseiah, *Eliezer*, Jarib, and *Gedalia*.

יח וַיִּמָּצֵא מִבְּנֵי הַכֹּהֲנִים אֲשֶׁר הֹשִׁיבוּ נָשִׁים נָכְרִיּוֹת מִבְּנֵי יֵשׁוּעַ בֶּן־יוֹצָדָק וְאֶחָיו מַעֲשֵׂיָה וֶאֱלִיעֶזֶר וְיָרִיב וּגְדַלְיָה׃

---

pratribal name "Israel" provides the most comprehensive framework for the realization of *Yechezkel's* vision: "Thus said *Hashem*: I am going to take the stick of *Yosef* – which is in the hand of *Efraim* and of the tribes of *Yisrael* associated with him – and I will place the stick of *Yehudah* upon it and make them into one stick; they shall be joined in My hand.... I will make them a single nation in the land, on the hills of *Yisrael*, and one king shall be king of them all. Never again shall they be two nations, and never again shall they be divided into two kingdoms" (Ezekiel 37:19, 22). The State's founders wished to be as inclusive as possible, allowing room for the vast cultural and ethnic diversity of the incoming exiles and thus fulfilling a role in the prophetic return of the lost ten tribes, along with the tribes of *Yehuda* and *Binyamin*, to the Land of Israel.

Ezra/Ezra
Chapter 10

19	They gave their word to expel their wives and, acknowledging their guilt, offered a ram from the flock to expiate it.	וַיִּתְּנוּ יָדָם לְהוֹצִיא נְשֵׁיהֶם וַאֲשֵׁמִים אֵיל־צֹאן עַל־אַשְׁמָתָם: יט
20	Of the sons of Immer: *Chanani* and Zebadiah;	וּמִבְּנֵי אִמֵּר חֲנָנִי וּזְבַדְיָה: כ
21	of the sons of Harim: Maaseiah, *Eliyahu, Shemaya, Yechiel,* and *Uzziyahu*;	וּמִבְּנֵי חָרִם מַעֲשֵׂיָה וְאֵלִיָּה וּשְׁמַעְיָה וִיחִיאֵל וְעֻזִּיָּה: כא
22	of the sons of Pashhur: Elioenai, Maaseiah, Ishmael, Nethanel, *Yozavad,* and Elasah;	וּמִבְּנֵי פַשְׁחוּר אֶלְיוֹעֵינַי מַעֲשֵׂיָה יִשְׁמָעֵאל נְתַנְאֵל יוֹזָבָד וְאֶלְעָשָׂה: כב
23	of the *Leviim: Yozavad, Shim'i,* Kelaiah who is Kelita, Pethahiah, *Yehuda,* and *Eliezer.*	וּמִן־הַלְוִיִּם יוֹזָבָד וְשִׁמְעִי וְקֵלָיָה הוּא קְלִיטָא פְּתַחְיָה יְהוּדָה וֶאֱלִיעֶזֶר: כג
24	Of the singers: *Elyashiv.* Of the gatekeepers: *Shalum,* Telem, and *Uri.*	וּמִן־הַמְשֹׁרְרִים אֶלְיָשִׁיב וּמִן־הַשֹּׁעֲרִים שַׁלֻּם וָטֶלֶם וְאוּרִי: כד
25	Of the Israelites: of the sons of Parosh: Ramiah, Izziah, Malchijah, Mijamin, *Elazar,* Malchijah, and Benaiah;	וּמִיִּשְׂרָאֵל מִבְּנֵי פַרְעֹשׁ רַמְיָה וְיִזִּיָּה וּמַלְכִּיָּה וּמִיָּמִן וְאֶלְעָזָר וּמַלְכִּיָּה וּבְנָיָה: כה
26	of the sons of Elam: Mattaniah, *Zecharya, Yechiel,* Abdi, Jeremoth, and *Eliyahu*;	וּמִבְּנֵי עֵילָם מַתַּנְיָה זְכַרְיָה וִיחִיאֵל וְעַבְדִּי וִירֵמוֹת וְאֵלִיָּה: כו
27	of the sons of Zattu: Elioenai, *Elyashiv,* Mattaniah, Jeremoth, Zabad, and Aziza;	וּמִבְּנֵי זַתּוּא אֶלְיוֹעֵנַי אֶלְיָשִׁיב מַתַּנְיָה וִירֵמוֹת וְזָבָד וַעֲזִיזָא: כז
28	of the sons of Bebai: *Yehochanan,* Chananya, Zabbai, and Athlai;	וּמִבְּנֵי בֵּבָי יְהוֹחָנָן חֲנַנְיָה זַבַּי עַתְלָי: כח
29	of the sons of Bani: Meshullam, Malluch, Adaiah, Yashuv, Sheal, and Ramoth;	וּמִבְּנֵי בָנִי מְשֻׁלָּם מַלּוּךְ וַעֲדָיָה יָשׁוּב וּשְׁאָל ירמות [וְרָמוֹת]: כט
30	of the sons of Pahathmoab: Adna, Chelal, Benaiah, Maaseiah, Mattaniah, *Betzalel,* Binnui, and *Menashe*;	וּמִבְּנֵי פַּחַת מוֹאָב עַדְנָא וּכְלָל בְּנָיָה מַעֲשֵׂיָה מַתַּנְיָה בְצַלְאֵל וּבִנּוּי וּמְנַשֶּׁה: ל
31	of the sons of Harim: *Eliezer,* Isshijah, Malchijah, Shemaya, and Shimeon;	וּבְנֵי חָרִם אֱלִיעֶזֶר יִשִּׁיָּה מַלְכִּיָּה שְׁמַעְיָה שִׁמְעוֹן: לא
32	also *Binyamin,* Malluch, and Shemariah;	בִּנְיָמִן מַלּוּךְ שְׁמַרְיָה: לב
33	of the sons of Hashum: Mattenai, Mattattah, Zabad, Eliphelet, Jeremai, *Menashe,* and *Shim'i*;	מִבְּנֵי חָשֻׁם מַתְּנַי מַתַּתָּה זָבָד אֱלִיפֶלֶט יְרֵמַי מְנַשֶּׁה שִׁמְעִי: לג
34	of the sons of Bani: Maadai, *Amram,* and Uel;	מִבְּנֵי בָנִי מַעֲדַי עַמְרָם וְאוּאֵל: לד
35	also Benaiah, Bedeiah, Cheluhu,	בְּנָיָה בֵדְיָה כלהי [כְּלוּהוּ]: לה
36	Vaniah, Meremoth, *Elyashiv*	וַנְיָה מְרֵמוֹת אֶלְיָשִׁיב: לו
37	Mattaniah, Mattenai, Jaasai,	מַתַּנְיָה מַתְּנַי ויעשו [וְיַעֲשָׂי]: לז
38	Bani, Binnui, *Shim'i,*	וּבָנִי וּבִנּוּי שִׁמְעִי: לח
39	Shelemiah, *Natan,* Adaiah,	וְשֶׁלֶמְיָה וְנָתָן וַעֲדָיָה: לט
40	Machnadebai, Shashai, Sharai,	מַכְנַדְבַי שָׁשַׁי שָׁרָי: מ

Ezra/Ezra
Chapter 10

עזרא
פרק י

41 Azarel, Shelemiah, Shemariah,

מא עֲזַרְאֵל וְשֶׁלֶמְיָהוּ שְׁמַרְיָה׃

42 *Shalum*, Amariah, and *Yosef*;

מב שַׁלּוּם אֲמַרְיָה יוֹסֵף׃

43 of the sons of Nebo: Jeiel, Mattithiah, Zabad, Zebina, Jaddai, *Yoel*, and Benaiah.

מג מִבְּנֵי נְבוֹ יְעִיאֵל מַתִּתְיָה זָבָד זְבִינָא ידו [יַדַּי] וְיוֹאֵל בְּנָיָה׃

44 All these had married foreign women, among whom were some women who had borne children.

מד כָּל־אֵלֶּה נשאי [נָשְׂאוּ] נָשִׁים נָכְרִיּוֹת וְיֵשׁ מֵהֶם נָשִׁים וַיָּשִׂימוּ בָּנִים׃

Nechemya/Nehemiah
Chapter 1

נחמיה
פרק א

1 1 The narrative of *Nechemya* son of *Chachalya*: In the month of *Kislev* of the twentieth year, when I was in the fortress of Shushan,

א דִּבְרֵי נְחֶמְיָה בֶּן־חֲכַלְיָה וַיְהִי בְחֹדֶשׁ־כסלו [כִּסְלֵיו] שְׁנַת עֶשְׂרִים וַאֲנִי הָיִיתִי בְּשׁוּשַׁן הַבִּירָה:

2 *Chanani*, one of my brothers, together with some men of *Yehuda*, arrived, and I asked them about the *Yehudim*, the remnant who had survived the captivity, and about *Yerushalayim*.

ב וַיָּבֹא חֲנָנִי אֶחָד מֵאַחַי הוּא וַאֲנָשִׁים מִיהוּדָה וָאֶשְׁאָלֵם עַל־הַיְּהוּדִים הַפְּלֵיטָה אֲשֶׁר־נִשְׁאֲרוּ מִן־הַשֶּׁבִי וְעַל־יְרוּשָׁלָם:

3 They replied, "The survivors who have survived the captivity there in the province are in dire trouble and disgrace; *Yerushalayim*'s wall is full of breaches, and its gates have been destroyed by fire."

ג וַיֹּאמְרוּ לִי הַנִּשְׁאָרִים אֲשֶׁר־נִשְׁאֲרוּ מִן־הַשְּׁבִי שָׁם בַּמְּדִינָה בְּרָעָה גְדֹלָה וּבְחֶרְפָּה וְחוֹמַת יְרוּשָׁלַםִ מְפֹרָצֶת וּשְׁעָרֶיהָ נִצְּתוּ בָאֵשׁ:

4 When I heard that, I sat and wept, and was in mourning for days, fasting and praying to the God of Heaven.

ד וַיְהִי כְּשָׁמְעִי אֶת־הַדְּבָרִים הָאֵלֶּה יָשַׁבְתִּי וָאֶבְכֶּה וָאֶתְאַבְּלָה יָמִים וָאֱהִי צָם וּמִתְפַּלֵּל לִפְנֵי אֱלֹהֵי הַשָּׁמָיִם:

5 I said, "*Hashem*, God of Heaven, great and awesome *Hashem*, who stays faithful to His covenant with those who love Him and keep His commandments!

ה וָאֹמַר אָנָּא יְהֹוָה אֱלֹהֵי הַשָּׁמַיִם הָאֵל הַגָּדוֹל וְהַנּוֹרָא שֹׁמֵר הַבְּרִית וָחֶסֶד לְאֹהֲבָיו וּלְשֹׁמְרֵי מִצְוֺתָיו:

6 Let Your ear be attentive and Your eyes open to receive the prayer of Your servant that I am praying to You now, day and night, on behalf of the Israelites, Your servants, confessing the sins that we Israelites have committed against You, sins that I and my father's house have committed.

ו תְּהִי נָא אָזְנְךָ־קַשֶּׁבֶת וְעֵינֶיךָ פְתוּחוֹת לִשְׁמֹעַ אֶל־תְּפִלַּת עַבְדְּךָ אֲשֶׁר אָנֹכִי מִתְפַּלֵּל לְפָנֶיךָ הַיּוֹם יוֹמָם וָלַיְלָה עַל־בְּנֵי יִשְׂרָאֵל עֲבָדֶיךָ וּמִתְוַדֶּה עַל־חַטֹּאות בְּנֵי־יִשְׂרָאֵל אֲשֶׁר חָטָאנוּ לָךְ וַאֲנִי וּבֵית־אָבִי חָטָאנוּ:

7 We have offended You by not keeping the commandments, the laws, and the rules that You gave to Your servant *Moshe*.

ז חֲבֹל חָבַלְנוּ לָךְ וְלֹא־שָׁמַרְנוּ אֶת־הַמִּצְוֺת וְאֶת־הַחֻקִּים וְאֶת־הַמִּשְׁפָּטִים אֲשֶׁר צִוִּיתָ אֶת־מֹשֶׁה עַבְדֶּךָ:

8 Be mindful of the promise You gave to Your servant *Moshe*: 'If you are unfaithful, I will scatter you among the peoples;

ח זְכָר־נָא אֶת־הַדָּבָר אֲשֶׁר צִוִּיתָ אֶת־מֹשֶׁה עַבְדְּךָ לֵאמֹר אַתֶּם תִּמְעָלוּ אֲנִי אָפִיץ אֶתְכֶם בָּעַמִּים:

9 but if you turn back to Me, faithfully keep My commandments, even if your dispersed are at the ends of the earth, I will gather them from there and bring them to the place where I have chosen to establish My name.'

ט וְשַׁבְתֶּם אֵלַי וּשְׁמַרְתֶּם מִצְוֺתַי וַעֲשִׂיתֶם אֹתָם אִם־יִהְיֶה נִדַּחֲכֶם בִּקְצֵה הַשָּׁמַיִם מִשָּׁם אֲקַבְּצֵם והבואתים [וַהֲבִיאוֹתִים] אֶל־הַמָּקוֹם אֲשֶׁר בָּחַרְתִּי לְשַׁכֵּן אֶת־שְׁמִי שָׁם:

v'-shav-TEM ay-LAI ush-mar-TEM mitz-vo-TAI va-a-see-TEM o-TAM im yih-YEH ni-da-kha-KHEM bik-TZAY ha-sha-MA-yim mi-SHAM a-ka-b'-TZAYM va-ha-vee-o-TEEM el ha-ma-KOM a-SHER ba-KHAR-tee l'-sha-KAYN et sh'-MEE SHAM

המקום

1:9 And bring them to the place where I have chosen to establish My name One thing that sets Judaism apart from other religions is the concept of a "chosen place." Many biblical commandments are relevant only in the Holy Land, and according to some Jewish philosophers, even other biblical laws have a qualitative superiority when performed in the land. Additionally, as seen in this verse, *Eretz Yisrael* is meant

Nechemya/Nehemiah
Chapter 2

10 For they are Your servants and Your people whom You redeemed by Your great power and Your mighty hand.

11 O *Hashem*! Let Your ear be attentive to the prayer of Your servant, and to the prayer of Your servants who desire to hold Your name in awe. Grant Your servant success today, and dispose that man to be compassionate toward him!" I was the king's cupbearer at the time.

2 1 In the month of *Nisan*, in the twentieth year of King Artaxerxes, wine was set before him; I took the wine and gave it to the king – I had never been out of sorts in his presence.

2 The king said to me, "How is it that you look bad, though you are not ill? It must be bad thoughts." I was very frightened,

3 but I answered the king, "May the king live forever! How should I not look bad when the city of the graveyard of my ancestors lies in ruins, and its gates have been consumed by fire?"

4 The king said to me, "What is your request?" With a prayer to the God of Heaven,

5 I answered the king, "If it please the king, and if your servant has found favor with you, send me to *Yehuda*, to the city of my ancestors' graves, to rebuild it."

6 With the consort seated at his side, the king said to me, "How long will you be gone and when will you return?" So it was agreeable to the king to send me, and I gave him a date.

7 Then I said to the king, "If it please the king, let me have letters to the governors of the province of Beyond the River, directing them to grant me passage until I reach *Yehuda*;

8 likewise, a letter to *Asaf*, the keeper of the King's Park, directing him to give me timber for roofing the gatehouses of the temple fortress and the city walls and for the house I shall occupy." The king gave me these, thanks to my God's benevolent care for me.

נחמיה
פרק ב

י וְהֵם עֲבָדֶיךָ וְעַמֶּךָ אֲשֶׁר פָּדִיתָ בְּכֹחֲךָ הַגָּדוֹל וּבְיָדְךָ הַחֲזָקָה:

יא אָנָּא אֲדֹנָי תְּהִי נָא אָזְנְךָ־קַשֶּׁבֶת אֶל־תְּפִלַּת עַבְדְּךָ וְאֶל־תְּפִלַּת עֲבָדֶיךָ הַחֲפֵצִים לְיִרְאָה אֶת־שְׁמֶךָ וְהַצְלִיחָה־נָּא לְעַבְדְּךָ הַיּוֹם וּתְנֵהוּ לְרַחֲמִים לִפְנֵי הָאִישׁ הַזֶּה וַאֲנִי הָיִיתִי מַשְׁקֶה לַמֶּלֶךְ:

ב א וַיְהִי בְּחֹדֶשׁ נִיסָן שְׁנַת עֶשְׂרִים לְאַרְתַּחְשַׁסְתְּא הַמֶּלֶךְ יַיִן לְפָנָיו וָאֶשָּׂא אֶת־הַיַּיִן וָאֶתְּנָה לַמֶּלֶךְ וְלֹא־הָיִיתִי רַע לְפָנָיו:

ב וַיֹּאמֶר לִי הַמֶּלֶךְ מַדּוּעַ פָּנֶיךָ רָעִים וְאַתָּה אֵינְךָ חוֹלֶה אֵין זֶה כִּי־אִם רֹעַ לֵב וָאִירָא הַרְבֵּה מְאֹד:

ג וָאֹמַר לַמֶּלֶךְ הַמֶּלֶךְ לְעוֹלָם יִחְיֶה מַדּוּעַ לֹא־יֵרְעוּ פָנַי אֲשֶׁר הָעִיר בֵּית־קִבְרוֹת אֲבֹתַי חֲרֵבָה וּשְׁעָרֶיהָ אֻכְּלוּ בָאֵשׁ:

ד וַיֹּאמֶר לִי הַמֶּלֶךְ עַל־מַה־זֶּה אַתָּה מְבַקֵּשׁ וָאֶתְפַּלֵּל אֶל־אֱלֹהֵי הַשָּׁמָיִם:

ה וָאֹמַר לַמֶּלֶךְ אִם־עַל־הַמֶּלֶךְ טוֹב וְאִם־יִיטַב עַבְדְּךָ לְפָנֶיךָ אֲשֶׁר תִּשְׁלָחֵנִי אֶל־יְהוּדָה אֶל־עִיר קִבְרוֹת אֲבֹתַי וְאֶבְנֶנָּה:

ו וַיֹּאמֶר לִי הַמֶּלֶךְ וְהַשֵּׁגַל יוֹשֶׁבֶת אֶצְלוֹ עַד־מָתַי יִהְיֶה מַהֲלָכְךָ וּמָתַי תָּשׁוּב וַיִּיטַב לִפְנֵי־הַמֶּלֶךְ וַיִּשְׁלָחֵנִי וָאֶתְּנָה לוֹ זְמָן:

ז וָאוֹמַר לַמֶּלֶךְ אִם־עַל־הַמֶּלֶךְ טוֹב אִגְּרוֹת יִתְּנוּ־לִי עַל־פַּחֲווֹת עֵבֶר הַנָּהָר אֲשֶׁר יַעֲבִירוּנִי עַד אֲשֶׁר־אָבוֹא אֶל־יְהוּדָה:

ח וְאִגֶּרֶת אֶל־אָסָף שֹׁמֵר הַפַּרְדֵּס אֲשֶׁר לַמֶּלֶךְ אֲשֶׁר יִתֶּן־לִי עֵצִים לְקָרוֹת אֶת־שַׁעֲרֵי הַבִּירָה אֲשֶׁר־לַבַּיִת וּלְחוֹמַת הָעִיר וְלַבַּיִת אֲשֶׁר־אָבוֹא אֵלָיו וַיִּתֶּן־לִי הַמֶּלֶךְ כְּיַד־אֱלֹהַי הַטּוֹבָה עָלָי:

---

to play a central role in the national redemption process, as it is the destination for the ingathering of the exiles. In the *Tanakh*, "the place," or *hamakom* (המקום) in Hebrew, refers both to the Land of Israel and the site of the *Beit Hamikdash*. Perhaps unsurprisingly, the Sages teach that this word is also one of God's seventy names.

1950

Nechemya/Nehemiah
Chapter 2

נחמיה
פרק ב

9 When I came to the governors of the province of Beyond the River I gave them the king's letters. The king also sent army officers and cavalry with me.

ט וָאָבוֹא אֶל־פַּחֲווֹת עֵבֶר הַנָּהָר וָאֶתְּנָה לָהֶם אֵת אִגְּרוֹת הַמֶּלֶךְ וַיִּשְׁלַח עִמִּי הַמֶּלֶךְ שָׂרֵי חַיִל וּפָרָשִׁים:

10 When Sanballat the Horonite and Tobiah the Ammonite servant heard, it displeased them greatly that someone had come, intent on improving the condition of the Israelites.

י וַיִּשְׁמַע סַנְבַלַּט הַחֹרֹנִי וְטוֹבִיָּה הָעֶבֶד הָעַמּוֹנִי וַיֵּרַע לָהֶם רָעָה גְדֹלָה אֲשֶׁר־בָּא אָדָם לְבַקֵּשׁ טוֹבָה לִבְנֵי יִשְׂרָאֵל:

11 I arrived in *Yerushalayim*. After I was there three days

יא וָאָבוֹא אֶל־יְרוּשָׁלָםִ וָאֱהִי־שָׁם יָמִים שְׁלֹשָׁה:

12 I got up at night, I and a few men with me, and telling no one what my God had put into my mind to do for *Yerushalayim*, and taking no other beast than the one on which I was riding,

יב וָאָקוּם לַיְלָה אֲנִי וַאֲנָשִׁים מְעַט עִמִּי וְלֹא־הִגַּדְתִּי לְאָדָם מָה אֱלֹהַי נֹתֵן אֶל־לִבִּי לַעֲשׂוֹת לִירוּשָׁלָםִ וּבְהֵמָה אֵין עִמִּי כִּי אִם־הַבְּהֵמָה אֲשֶׁר אֲנִי רֹכֵב בָּהּ:

13 I went out by the Valley Gate, at night, toward the Jackals' Spring and the Dung Gate; and I surveyed the walls of *Yerushalayim* that were breached, and its gates, consumed by fire.

יג וָאֵצְאָה בְשַׁעַר־הַגַּיְא לַיְלָה וְאֶל־פְּנֵי עֵין הַתַּנִּין וְאֶל־שַׁעַר הָאַשְׁפֹּת וָאֱהִי שֹׂבֵר בְּחוֹמֹת יְרוּשָׁלַםִ אֲשֶׁר־הֵמפרוּצִים [הֵם פְּרוּצִים] וּשְׁעָרֶיהָ אֻכְּלוּ בָאֵשׁ:

14 I proceeded to the Fountain Gate and to the King's Pool, where there was no room for the beast under me to continue.

יד וָאֶעֱבֹר אֶל־שַׁעַר הָעַיִן וְאֶל־בְּרֵכַת הַמֶּלֶךְ וְאֵין־מָקוֹם לַבְּהֵמָה לַעֲבֹר תַּחְתָּי:

15 So I went up the wadi by night, surveying the wall, and, entering again by the Valley Gate, I returned.

טו וָאֱהִי עֹלֶה בַנַּחַל לַיְלָה וָאֱהִי שֹׂבֵר בַּחוֹמָה וָאָשׁוּב וָאָבוֹא בְּשַׁעַר הַגַּיְא וָאָשׁוּב:

16 The prefects knew nothing of where I had gone or what I had done, since I had not yet divulged it to the *Yehudim* – the *Kohanim*, the nobles, the prefects, or the rest of the officials.

טז וְהַסְּגָנִים לֹא יָדְעוּ אָנָה הָלַכְתִּי וּמָה אֲנִי עֹשֶׂה וְלַיְּהוּדִים וְלַכֹּהֲנִים וְלַחֹרִים וְלַסְּגָנִים וּלְיֶתֶר עֹשֵׂה הַמְּלָאכָה עַד־כֵּן לֹא הִגַּדְתִּי:

17 Then I said to them, "You see the bad state we are in – *Yerushalayim* lying in ruins and its gates destroyed by fire. Come, let us rebuild the wall of *Yerushalayim* and suffer no more disgrace."

יז וָאוֹמַר אֲלֵהֶם אַתֶּם רֹאִים הָרָעָה אֲשֶׁר אֲנַחְנוּ בָהּ אֲשֶׁר יְרוּשָׁלַםִ חֲרֵבָה וּשְׁעָרֶיהָ נִצְּתוּ בָאֵשׁ לְכוּ וְנִבְנֶה אֶת־חוֹמַת יְרוּשָׁלַםִ וְלֹא־נִהְיֶה עוֹד חֶרְפָּה:

va-o-MAR a-lay-HEM a-TEM ro-EEM ha-ra-AH a-SHER a-NAKH-nu VAH a-SHER y'-ru-sha-LA-im kha-ray-VAH ush-a-RE-ha ni-tz'-TU va-AYSH l'-KHU v'-niv-NEH et KHO-mat y'-ru-sha-LA-im v'-lo nih-YEH OD kher-PAH

2:17 Come, let us rebuild the wall of *Yerushalayim* One of the Jewish prayers recited on the ninth day of the Hebrew month of *Av*, the day of the destruction of the *Beit Hamikdash*, states: "You destroyed Jerusalem by fire, so too will You rebuild it with fire." Near the Western Wall, archeologists uncovered a complex destroyed in the Roman fires of 70 CE, and spear-pierced skeletal remains found there gave silent testimony to the tragedy. Destruction by fire is comprehensible, but the idea of construction by fire is more difficult to understand. Perhaps it indicates the degree of passion necessary to engage in such a task. If this is the case, indeed we have merited living in a time where the latter fire is burning brighter, and many are answering *Nechemya*'s call: "Come, let us rebuild!"

Nechemya/Nehemiah
Chapter 3

נחמיה
פרק ג

18 I told them of my God's benevolent care for me, also of the things that the king had said to me, and they said, "Let us start building!" They were encouraged by [His] benevolence.

יח וָאַגִּיד לָהֶם אֶת־יַד אֱלֹהַי אֲשֶׁר־הִיא טוֹבָה עָלַי וְאַף־דִּבְרֵי הַמֶּלֶךְ אֲשֶׁר אָמַר־לִי וַיֹּאמְרוּ נָקוּם וּבָנִינוּ וַיְחַזְּקוּ יְדֵיהֶם לַטּוֹבָה׃

19 When Sanballat the Horonite and Tobiah the Ammonite servant and *Geshem* the Arab heard, they mocked us and held us in contempt and said, "What is this that you are doing? Are you rebelling against the king?"

יט וַיִּשְׁמַע סַנְבַלַּט הַחֹרֹנִי וְטֹבִיָּה הָעֶבֶד הָעַמּוֹנִי וְגֶשֶׁם הָעַרְבִי וַיַּלְעִגוּ לָנוּ וַיִּבְזוּ עָלֵינוּ וַיֹּאמְרוּ מָה־הַדָּבָר הַזֶּה אֲשֶׁר אַתֶּם עֹשִׂים הַעַל הַמֶּלֶךְ אַתֶּם מֹרְדִים׃

20 I said to them in reply, "The God of Heaven will grant us success, and we, His servants, will start building. But you have no share or claim or stake in *Yerushalayim*!"

כ וָאָשִׁיב אוֹתָם דָּבָר וָאוֹמַר לָהֶם אֱלֹהֵי הַשָּׁמַיִם הוּא יַצְלִיחַ לָנוּ וַאֲנַחְנוּ עֲבָדָיו נָקוּם וּבָנִינוּ וְלָכֶם אֵין־חֵלֶק וּצְדָקָה וְזִכָּרוֹן בִּירוּשָׁלָםִ׃

3 1 Then *Elyashiv* the *Kohen Gadol* and his fellow *Kohanim* set to and rebuilt the Sheep Gate; they consecrated it and set up its doors, consecrating it as far as the Hundred's Tower, as far as the Tower of Hananel.

ג א וַיָּקָם אֶלְיָשִׁיב הַכֹּהֵן הַגָּדוֹל וְאֶחָיו הַכֹּהֲנִים וַיִּבְנוּ אֶת־שַׁעַר הַצֹּאן הֵמָּה קִדְּשׁוּהוּ וַיַּעֲמִידוּ דַּלְתֹתָיו וְעַד־מִגְדַּל הַמֵּאָה קִדְּשׁוּהוּ עַד מִגְדַּל חֲנַנְאֵל׃

2 Next to him, the men of *Yericho* built. Next to them, Zaccur son of Imri.

ב וְעַל־יָדוֹ בָנוּ אַנְשֵׁי יְרֵחוֹ וְעַל־יָדוֹ בָנָה זַכּוּר בֶּן־אִמְרִי׃

3 The sons of Hassenaah rebuilt the Fish Gate; they roofed it and set up its doors, locks, and bars.

ג וְאֵת שַׁעַר הַדָּגִים בָּנוּ בְּנֵי הַסְּנָאָה הֵמָּה קֵרוּהוּ וַיַּעֲמִידוּ דַּלְתֹתָיו מַנְעוּלָיו וּבְרִיחָיו׃

4 Next to them, Meremoth son of *Uriya* son of Hakkoz repaired; and next to him, Meshullam son of *Berechya* son of Meshezabel. Next to him, *Tzadok* son of Baana repaired.

ד וְעַל־יָדָם הֶחֱזִיק מְרֵמוֹת בֶּן־אוּרִיָּה בֶּן־הַקּוֹץ וְעַל־יָדָם הֶחֱזִיק מְשֻׁלָּם בֶּן־בֶּרֶכְיָה בֶּן־מְשֵׁיזַבְאֵל וְעַל־יָדָם הֶחֱזִיק צָדוֹק בֶּן־בַּעֲנָא׃

5 Next to him, the Tekoites repaired, though their nobles would not take upon their shoulders the work of their lord.

ה וְעַל־יָדָם הֶחֱזִיקוּ הַתְּקוֹעִים וְאַדִּירֵיהֶם לֹא־הֵבִיאוּ צַוָּרָם בַּעֲבֹדַת אֲדֹנֵיהֶם׃

6 Joiada son of Paseah and Meshullam son of Besodeiah repaired the Jeshanah Gate; they roofed it and set up its doors, locks, and bars.

ו וְאֵת שַׁעַר הַיְשָׁנָה הֶחֱזִיקוּ יוֹיָדָע בֶּן־פָּסֵחַ וּמְשֻׁלָּם בֶּן־בְּסוֹדְיָה הֵמָּה קֵרוּהוּ וַיַּעֲמִידוּ דַּלְתֹתָיו וּמַנְעֻלָיו וּבְרִיחָיו׃

7 Next to them, Melatiah the Givonite and Jadon the Meronothite repaired, [with] the men of *Givon* and *Mitzpa*, under the jurisdiction of the governor of the province of Beyond the River.

ז וְעַל־יָדָם הֶחֱזִיק מְלַטְיָה הַגִּבְעֹנִי וְיָדוֹן הַמֵּרֹנֹתִי אַנְשֵׁי גִבְעוֹן וְהַמִּצְפָּה לְכִסֵּא פַּחַת עֵבֶר הַנָּהָר׃

8 Next to them, Uzziel son of Harhaiah, [of the] smiths, repaired. Next to him, *Chananya*, of the perfumers. They restored *Yerushalayim* as far as the Broad Wall.

ח עַל־יָדוֹ הֶחֱזִיק עֻזִּיאֵל בֶּן־חַרְהֲיָה צוֹרְפִים וְעַל־יָדוֹ הֶחֱזִיק חֲנַנְיָה בֶּן־הָרַקָּחִים וַיַּעַזְבוּ יְרוּשָׁלַםִ עַד הַחוֹמָה הָרְחָבָה׃

1952

Nechemya/Nehemiah
Chapter 3

נחמיה
פרק ג

9 Next to them, Rephaiah son of *Chur*, chief of half the district of *Yerushalayim*, repaired.

ט וְעַל־יָדָם הֶחֱזִיק רְפָיָה בֶן־חוּר שַׂר חֲצִי פֶּלֶךְ יְרוּשָׁלָֽם׃

10 Next to him, Jedaiah son of Harumaph repaired in front of his house. Next to him, Hattush son of Hashabneiah repaired.

י וְעַל־יָדָם הֶחֱזִיק יְדָיָה בֶן־חֲרוּמַף וְנֶגֶד בֵּיתוֹ וְעַל־יָדוֹ הֶחֱזִיק חַטּוּשׁ בֶּן־חֲשַׁבְנְיָֽה׃

11 Malchijah son of Harim and Hasshub son of Pahath-moab repaired a second stretch, including the Tower of Ovens.

יא מִדָּה שֵׁנִית הֶחֱזִיק מַלְכִּיָּה בֶן־חָרִם וְחַשּׁוּב בֶּן־פַּחַת מוֹאָב וְאֵת מִגְדַּל הַתַּנּוּרִֽים׃

12 Next to them, *Shalum* son of Hallohesh, chief of half the district of *Yerushalayim*, repaired – he and his daughters.

יב וְעַל־יָדוֹ הֶחֱזִיק שַׁלּוּם בֶּן־הַלּוֹחֵשׁ שַׂר חֲצִי פֶּלֶךְ יְרוּשָׁלָ͏ִם הוּא וּבְנוֹתָֽיו׃

13 Hanun and the inhabitants of *Zanoach* repaired the Valley Gate; they rebuilt it and set up its doors, locks, and bars. And [they also repaired] a thousand *amot* of wall to the Dung Gate.

יג אֵת שַׁעַר הַגַּיְא הֶחֱזִיק חָנוּן וְיֹשְׁבֵי זָנוֹחַ הֵמָּה בָנוּהוּ וַֽיַּעֲמִידוּ דַּלְתֹתָיו מַנְעֻלָיו וּבְרִיחָיו וְאֶלֶף אַמָּה בַּחוֹמָה עַד שַׁעַר הָשְׁפֽוֹת׃

14 Malchijah son of Rechab, chief of the district of Beth-haccerem, repaired the Dung Gate; he rebuilt it and set up its doors, locks, and bars.

יד וְאֵת שַׁעַר הָאַשְׁפּוֹת הֶחֱזִיק מַלְכִּיָּה בֶן־רֵכָב שַׂר פֶּלֶךְ בֵּית־הַכָּרֶם הוּא יִבְנֶנּוּ וְיַעֲמִיד דַּלְתֹתָיו מַנְעֻלָיו וּבְרִיחָֽיו׃

15 Shallun son of Col-hozeh, chief of the district of *Mitzpa*, repaired the Fountain Gate; he rebuilt it and covered it, and set up its doors, locks, and bars, as well as the wall of the irrigation pool of the King's Garden as far as the steps going down from the City of *David*.

טו וְאֵת שַׁעַר הָעַיִן הֶחֱזִיק שַׁלּוּן בֶּן־כָּל־חֹזֶה שַׂר פֶּלֶךְ הַמִּצְפָּה הוּא יִבְנֶנּוּ וִיטַֽלְלֶנּוּ וְיַעֲמִידוּ [וְיַעֲמִיד] דַּלְתֹתָיו מַנְעֻלָיו וּבְרִיחָיו וְאֵת חוֹמַת בְּרֵכַת הַשֶּׁלַח לְגַן־הַמֶּלֶךְ וְעַד־הַֽמַּעֲלוֹת הַיּוֹרְדוֹת מֵעִיר דָּוִֽיד׃

v'-AYT SHA-ar ha-A-yin he-khe-ZEEK sha-LUN ben kol kho-ZEH SAR PE-lekh ha-mitz-PAH HU yiv-NE-nu vee-ta-l'-LE-nu v'-ya-a-MEED dal-to-TAV man-u-LAV uv-ree-KHAV v'-AYT kho-MAT b'-ray-KHAT ha-SHE-lakh l'-gan ha-ME-lekh v'-ad ha-ma-a-LOT ha-yo-r'-DOT may-EER da-VEED

16 After him, *Nechemya* son of Azbuk, chief of half the district of Beth-zur, repaired, from in front of the graves of *David* as far as the artificial pool, and as far as the House of the Warriors.

טז אַחֲרָיו הֶחֱזִיק נְחֶמְיָה בֶן־עַזְבּוּק שַׂר חֲצִי פֶּלֶךְ בֵּית־צוּר עַד־נֶגֶד קִבְרֵי דָוִיד וְעַד־הַבְּרֵכָה הָעֲשׂוּיָה וְעַד בֵּית הַגִּבֹּרִֽים׃

3:15 As far as the steps going down from the City of David The most extraordinary site where one can see the merging of biblical text with archeology is Jerusalem's City of David National Park. Although identified in the mid-nineteenth century, many answers to biblical riddles still lay locked beneath its soil. In 2005, Israeli archeologist Eilat Mazar discover a large stone structure that she believes to be the foundations of King David's palace, illuminating the verse "*David* captured the stronghold of *Tzion*; it is now the City of *David*" (II Samuel 5:7). As one stands in this spot and gazes at the mountains in all directions, King David's words come to life: "*Yerushalayim*, hills enfold it, and *Hashem* enfolds His people now and forever" (Psalms 125:2).

Excavations at City of David National Park in Jerusalem

Nechemya/Nehemiah
Chapter 3

17 After him, the *Leviim* repaired: Rehum son of Bani. Next to him, Hashabiah, chief of half the district of Keilah, repaired for his district.

18 After him, their brothers repaired: Bavvai son of Henadad, chief of half the district of Keilah.

19 Next to him, Ezer son of *Yeshua*, the chief of *Mitzpa*, repaired a second stretch, from in front of the ascent to the armory [at] the angle [of the wall].

20 After him, *Baruch* son of Zaccai zealously repaired a second stretch, from the angle to the entrance to the house of *Elyashiv*, the *Kohen Gadol*.

21 After him, Meremoth son of *Uriya* son of Hakkoz repaired a second stretch, from the entrance to *Elyashiv*'s house to the end of *Elyashiv*'s house.

22 After him, the *Kohanim*, inhabitants of the plain, repaired.

23 After them, *Binyamin* and Hasshub repaired in front of their houses. After them, *Azarya* son of Maaseiah son of Ananiah repaired beside his house.

24 After him, Binnui son of Henadad repaired a second stretch, from the house of *Azarya* to the angle, to the corner.

25 Palal son of Uzai – from in front of the angle and the tower that juts out of the house of the king, the upper [tower] of the prison compound. After him, Pedaiah son of Parosh.

26 The temple servants were living on the Ophel, as far as a point in front of the Water Gate in the east, and the jutting tower.)

27 After him, the Tekoites repaired a second stretch, from in front of the great jutting tower to the wall of the Ophel.

28 Above the Horse Gate, the *Kohanim* repaired, each in front of his house.

29 After them, *Tzadok* son of Immer repaired in front of his house. After him, *Shemaya* son of Shechaniah, keeper of the East Gate, repaired.

נחמיה
פרק ג

יז אַחֲרָיו הֶחֱזִיקוּ הַלְוִיִּם רְחוּם בֶּן־בָּנִי עַל־יָדוֹ הֶחֱזִיק חֲשַׁבְיָה שַׂר־חֲצִי־פֶלֶךְ קְעִילָה לְפִלְכּוֹ׃

יח אַחֲרָיו הֶחֱזִיקוּ אֲחֵיהֶם בַּוַּי בֶּן־חֵנָדָד שַׂר חֲצִי פֶּלֶךְ קְעִילָה׃

יט וַיְחַזֵּק עַל־יָדוֹ עֵזֶר בֶּן־יֵשׁוּעַ שַׂר הַמִּצְפָּה מִדָּה שֵׁנִית מִנֶּגֶד עֲלֹת הַנֶּשֶׁק הַמִּקְצֹעַ׃

כ אַחֲרָיו הֶחֱרָה הֶחֱזִיק בָּרוּךְ בֶּן־זֹבַי [זַכַּי] מִדָּה שֵׁנִית מִן־הַמִּקְצוֹעַ עַד־פֶּתַח בֵּית אֶלְיָשִׁיב הַכֹּהֵן הַגָּדוֹל׃

כא אַחֲרָיו הֶחֱזִיק מְרֵמוֹת בֶּן־אוּרִיָּה בֶּן־הַקּוֹץ מִדָּה שֵׁנִית מִפֶּתַח בֵּית אֶלְיָשִׁיב וְעַד־תַּכְלִית בֵּית אֶלְיָשִׁיב׃

כב וְאַחֲרָיו הֶחֱזִיקוּ הַכֹּהֲנִים אַנְשֵׁי הַכִּכָּר׃

כג אַחֲרָיו הֶחֱזִיק בִּנְיָמִן וְחַשּׁוּב נֶגֶד בֵּיתָם אַחֲרָיו הֶחֱזִיק עֲזַרְיָה בֶן־מַעֲשֵׂיָה בֶּן־עֲנָנְיָה אֵצֶל בֵּיתוֹ׃

כד אַחֲרָיו הֶחֱזִיק בִּנּוּי בֶּן־חֵנָדָד מִדָּה שֵׁנִית מִבֵּית עֲזַרְיָה עַד־הַמִּקְצוֹעַ וְעַד־הַפִּנָּה׃

כה פָּלָל בֶּן־אוּזַי מִנֶּגֶד הַמִּקְצוֹעַ וְהַמִּגְדָּל הַיּוֹצֵא מִבֵּית הַמֶּלֶךְ הָעֶלְיוֹן אֲשֶׁר לַחֲצַר הַמַּטָּרָה אַחֲרָיו פְּדָיָה בֶן־פַּרְעֹשׁ׃

כו וְהַנְּתִינִים הָיוּ יֹשְׁבִים בָּעֹפֶל עַד נֶגֶד שַׁעַר הַמַּיִם לַמִּזְרָח וְהַמִּגְדָּל הַיּוֹצֵא׃

כז אַחֲרָיו הֶחֱזִיקוּ הַתְּקֹעִים מִדָּה שֵׁנִית מִנֶּגֶד הַמִּגְדָּל הַגָּדוֹל הַיּוֹצֵא וְעַד חוֹמַת הָעֹפֶל׃

כח מֵעַל שַׁעַר הַסּוּסִים הֶחֱזִיקוּ הַכֹּהֲנִים אִישׁ לְנֶגֶד בֵּיתוֹ׃

כט אַחֲרָיו הֶחֱזִיק צָדוֹק בֶּן־אִמֵּר נֶגֶד בֵּיתוֹ וְאַחֲרָיו הֶחֱזִיק שְׁמַעְיָה בֶן־שְׁכַנְיָה שֹׁמֵר שַׁעַר הַמִּזְרָח׃

1954

Nechemya/Nehemiah
Chapter 4

30 After him, *Chananya* son of Shelemiah and Hanun, the sixth son of Zalaph, repaired a second stretch. After them, Meshullam son of *Berechya* repaired in front of his chamber.

31 After him, Malchijah of the smiths repaired as far as the house of the temple servants and the merchants, [from] in front of the Muster Gate to the corner loft.

32 And between the corner loft to the Sheep Gate the smiths and the merchants repaired.

33 When Sanballat heard that we were rebuilding the wall, it angered him, and he was extremely vexed. He mocked the *Yehudim*,

34 saying in the presence of his brothers and the Shomronn force, "What are the miserable *Yehudim* doing? Will they restore, offer sacrifice, and finish one day? Can they revive those stones out of the dust heaps, burned as they are?"

35 Tobiah the Ammonite, alongside him, said, "That stone wall they are building – if a fox climbed it he would breach it!"

36 Hear, our God, how we have become a mockery, and return their taunts upon their heads! Let them be taken as spoil to a land of captivity!

37 Do not cover up their iniquity or let their sin be blotted out before You, for they hurled provocations at the builders.

38 We rebuilt the wall till it was continuous all around to half its height; for the people's heart was in the work.

4

1 When Sanballat and Tobiah, and the Arabs, the Ammonites, and the Ashdodites heard that healing had come to the walls of *Yerushalayim*, that the breached parts had begun to be filled, it angered them very much,

2 and they all conspired together to come and fight against *Yerushalayim* and to throw it into confusion.

3 Because of them we prayed to our God, and set up a watch over them day and night.

4 *Yehuda* was saying, "The strength of the basket-carrier has failed, And there is so much rubble; We are not able ourselves To rebuild the wall."

נחמיה
פרק ד

ל אַחֲרָיו [אַחֲרָיו] הֶחֱזִיק חֲנַנְיָה בֶן־שֶׁלֶמְיָה וְחָנוּן בֶּן־צָלָף הַשִּׁשִּׁי מִדָּה שֵׁנִי אַחֲרָיו הֶחֱזִיק מְשֻׁלָּם בֶּן־בֶּרֶכְיָה נֶגֶד נִשְׁכָּתוֹ׃

לא אַחֲרָיו [אַחֲרָיו] הֶחֱזִיק מַלְכִּיָּה בֶן־הַצֹּרְפִי עַד־בֵּית הַנְּתִינִים וְהָרֹכְלִים נֶגֶד שַׁעַר הַמִּפְקָד וְעַד עֲלִיַּת הַפִּנָּה׃

לב וּבֵין עֲלִיַּת הַפִּנָּה לְשַׁעַר הַצֹּאן הֶחֱזִיקוּ הַצֹּרְפִים וְהָרֹכְלִים׃

לג וַיְהִי כַּאֲשֶׁר שָׁמַע סַנְבַלַּט כִּי־אֲנַחְנוּ בוֹנִים אֶת־הַחוֹמָה וַיִּחַר לוֹ וַיִּכְעַס הַרְבֵּה וַיַּלְעֵג עַל־הַיְּהוּדִים׃

לד וַיֹּאמֶר לִפְנֵי אֶחָיו וְחֵיל שֹׁמְרוֹן וַיֹּאמֶר מָה הַיְּהוּדִים הָאֲמֵלָלִים עֹשִׂים הֲיַעַזְבוּ לָהֶם הֲיִזְבָּחוּ הַיְכַלּוּ בַיּוֹם הַיְחַיּוּ אֶת־הָאֲבָנִים מֵעֲרֵמוֹת הֶעָפָר וְהֵמָּה שְׂרוּפוֹת׃

לה וְטוֹבִיָּה הָעַמֹּנִי אֶצְלוֹ וַיֹּאמֶר גַּם אֲשֶׁר־הֵם בּוֹנִים אִם־יַעֲלֶה שׁוּעָל וּפָרַץ חוֹמַת אַבְנֵיהֶם׃

לו שְׁמַע אֱלֹהֵינוּ כִּי־הָיִינוּ בוּזָה וְהָשֵׁב חֶרְפָּתָם אֶל־רֹאשָׁם וּתְנֵם לְבִזָּה בְּאֶרֶץ שִׁבְיָה׃

לז וְאַל־תְּכַס עַל־עֲוֺנָם וְחַטָּאתָם מִלְּפָנֶיךָ אַל־תִּמָּחֶה כִּי הִכְעִיסוּ לְנֶגֶד הַבּוֹנִים׃

לח וַנִּבְנֶה אֶת־הַחוֹמָה וַתִּקָּשֵׁר כָּל־הַחוֹמָה עַד־חֶצְיָהּ וַיְהִי לֵב לָעָם לַעֲשׂוֹת׃

ד א וַיְהִי כַאֲשֶׁר שָׁמַע סַנְבַלַּט וְטוֹבִיָּה וְהָעַרְבִים וְהָעַמֹּנִים וְהָאַשְׁדּוֹדִים כִּי־עָלְתָה אֲרוּכָה לְחֹמוֹת יְרוּשָׁלִַם כִּי־הֵחֵלּוּ הַפְּרֻצִים לְהִסָּתֵם וַיִּחַר לָהֶם מְאֹד׃

ב וַיִּקְשְׁרוּ כֻלָּם יַחְדָּו לָבוֹא לְהִלָּחֵם בִּירוּשָׁלִָם וְלַעֲשׂוֹת לוֹ תּוֹעָה׃

ג וַנִּתְפַּלֵּל אֶל־אֱלֹהֵינוּ וַנַּעֲמִיד מִשְׁמָר עֲלֵיהֶם יוֹמָם וָלַיְלָה מִפְּנֵיהֶם׃

ד וַיֹּאמֶר יְהוּדָה כָּשַׁל כֹּחַ הַסַּבָּל וְהֶעָפָר הַרְבֵּה וַאֲנַחְנוּ לֹא נוּכַל לִבְנוֹת בַּחוֹמָה׃

Nechemya/Nehemiah
Chapter 4

נחמיה
פרק ד

5 And our foes were saying, "Before they know or see it, we shall be in among them and kill them, and put a stop to the work."

ה וַיֹּאמְרוּ צָרֵינוּ לֹא יֵדְעוּ וְלֹא יִרְאוּ עַד אֲשֶׁר־נָבוֹא אֶל־תּוֹכָם וַהֲרַגְנוּם וְהִשְׁבַּתְנוּ אֶת־הַמְּלָאכָה:

6 When the *Yehudim* living near them would arrive, they would tell us time and again "…from all the places where…you shall come back to us…"

ו וַיְהִי כַּאֲשֶׁר־בָּאוּ הַיְּהוּדִים הַיֹּשְׁבִים אֶצְלָם וַיֹּאמְרוּ לָנוּ עֶשֶׂר פְּעָמִים מִכָּל־הַמְּקֹמוֹת אֲשֶׁר־תָּשׁוּבוּ עָלֵינוּ:

7 I stationed, on the lower levels of the place, behind the walls, on the bare rock – I stationed the people by families with their swords, their lances, and their bows.

ז וָאַעֲמִיד מִתַּחְתִּיּוֹת לַמָּקוֹם מֵאַחֲרֵי לַחוֹמָה בַּצְּחִחִיִּים [בַּצְּחִיחִים] וָאַעֲמִיד אֶת־הָעָם לְמִשְׁפָּחוֹת עִם־חַרְבֹתֵיהֶם רָמְחֵיהֶם וְקַשְּׁתֹתֵיהֶם:

8 Then I decided to exhort the nobles, the prefects, and the rest of the people, "Do not be afraid of them! Think of the great and awesome *Hashem*, and fight for your brothers, your sons and daughters, your wives and homes!"

ח וָאֵרֶא וָאָקוּם וָאֹמַר אֶל־הַחֹרִים וְאֶל־הַסְּגָנִים וְאֶל־יֶתֶר הָעָם אַל־תִּירְאוּ מִפְּנֵיהֶם אֶת־אֲדֹנָי הַגָּדוֹל וְהַנּוֹרָא זְכֹרוּ וְהִלָּחֲמוּ עַל־אֲחֵיכֶם בְּנֵיכֶם וּבְנֹתֵיכֶם נְשֵׁיכֶם וּבָתֵּיכֶם:

9 When our enemies learned that it had become known to us, since *Hashem* had thus frustrated their plan, we could all return to the wall, each to his work.

ט וַיְהִי כַּאֲשֶׁר־שָׁמְעוּ אוֹיְבֵינוּ כִּי־נוֹדַע לָנוּ וַיָּפֶר הָאֱלֹהִים אֶת־עֲצָתָם ונשוב [וַנָּשָׁב] כֻּלָּנוּ אֶל־הַחוֹמָה אִישׁ אֶל־מְלַאכְתּוֹ:

10 From that day on, half my servants did work and half held lances and shields, bows and armor. And the officers stood behind the whole house of *Yehuda*

י וַיְהִי מִן־הַיּוֹם הַהוּא חֲצִי נְעָרַי עֹשִׂים בַּמְּלָאכָה וְחֶצְיָם מַחֲזִיקִים וְהָרְמָחִים הַמָּגִנִּים וְהַקְּשָׁתוֹת וְהַשִּׁרְיֹנִים וְהַשָּׂרִים אַחֲרֵי כָּל־בֵּית יְהוּדָה:

11 who were rebuilding the wall. The basket-carriers were burdened, doing work with one hand while the other held a weapon.

יא הַבּוֹנִים בַּחוֹמָה וְהַנֹּשְׂאִים בַּסֶּבֶל עֹמְשִׂים בְּאַחַת יָדוֹ עֹשֶׂה בַמְּלָאכָה וְאַחַת מַחֲזֶקֶת הַשָּׁלַח:

ha-bo-NEEM ba-kho-MAH v'-ha-no-s'-EEM ba-SE-vel o-m'-SEEM b'-a-KHAT ya-DO o-SEH va-m'-la-KHAH v'-a-KHAT ma-kha-ZE-ket ha-SHA-lakh

12 As for the builders, each had his sword girded at his side as he was building. The trumpeter stood beside me.

יב וְהַבּוֹנִים אִישׁ חַרְבּוֹ אֲסוּרִים עַל־מָתְנָיו וּבוֹנִים וְהַתּוֹקֵעַ בַּשּׁוֹפָר אֶצְלִי:

4:11 Doing work with one hand while the other held a weapon Throughout the *Tanakh*, God does wonders and miracles to save the Jewish people. Although perhaps one would think that a nation under *Hashem*'s direct protection should not need arms to defend itself, it is His will that people conduct themselves in a natural manner. Only when necessary will *Hashem* intervene with open miracles. This verse describes how in *Nechemya*'s time, those rebuilding the walls of *Yerushalayim* would work with one hand while holding weapons of self-defense in the other. Though they rely on their own strength for protection, they remember that the Lord is the source of their might and their success. As described earlier in verse 3, first they "prayed to our God," and then they "set up a watch" against their enemies. Today, the soldiers of the Israel Defense Forces are the ones protecting the Nation of Israel. At IDF swearing-in ceremonies, each soldier is given a *Tanakh* to hold in one hand, and a gun in the other. In this way, Israeli soldiers are the spiritual descendants of *Nechemya*'s work force who are reminded that it is not their strength alone that protects the nation, but *Hashem* above.

A new IDF recruit holding a Tanakh and a gun

Nechemya/Nehemiah
Chapter 5

נחמיה
פרק ה

13 I said to the nobles, the prefects, and the rest of the people, "There is much work and it is spread out; we are scattered over the wall, far from one another.

יג וָאֹמַר אֶל־הַחֹרִים וְאֶל־הַסְּגָנִים וְאֶל־יֶתֶר הָעָם הַמְּלָאכָה הַרְבֵּה וּרְחָבָה וַאֲנַחְנוּ נִפְרָדִים עַל־הַחוֹמָה רְחוֹקִים אִישׁ מֵאָחִיו:

14 When you hear a trumpet call, gather yourselves to me at that place; our God will fight for us!"

יד בִּמְקוֹם אֲשֶׁר תִּשְׁמְעוּ אֶת־קוֹל הַשּׁוֹפָר שָׁמָּה תִּקָּבְצוּ אֵלֵינוּ אֱלֹהֵינוּ יִלָּחֶם לָנוּ:

15 And so we worked on, while half were holding lances, from the break of day until the stars appeared.

טו וַאֲנַחְנוּ עֹשִׂים בַּמְּלָאכָה וְחֶצְיָם מַחֲזִיקִים בָּרְמָחִים מֵעֲלוֹת הַשַּׁחַר עַד צֵאת הַכּוֹכָבִים:

16 I further said to the people at that time, "Let every man with his servant lodge in *Yerushalayim*, that we may use the night to stand guard and the day to work."

טז גַּם בָּעֵת הַהִיא אָמַרְתִּי לָעָם אִישׁ וְנַעֲרוֹ יָלִינוּ בְּתוֹךְ יְרוּשָׁלָ͏ִם וְהָיוּ־לָנוּ הַלַּיְלָה מִשְׁמָר וְהַיּוֹם מְלָאכָה:

17 Nor did I, my brothers, my servants, or the guards following me ever take off our clothes, [or] each his weapon, even at the water.

יז וְאֵין אֲנִי וְאַחַי וּנְעָרַי וְאַנְשֵׁי הַמִּשְׁמָר אֲשֶׁר אַחֲרַי אֵין־אֲנַחְנוּ פֹשְׁטִים בְּגָדֵינוּ אִישׁ שִׁלְחוֹ הַמָּיִם:

5 1 There was a great outcry by the common folk and their wives against their brother *Yehudim*.

ה א וַתְּהִי צַעֲקַת הָעָם וּנְשֵׁיהֶם גְּדוֹלָה אֶל־אֲחֵיהֶם הַיְּהוּדִים:

2 Some said, "Our sons and daughters are numerous; we must get grain to eat in order that we may live!"

ב וְיֵשׁ אֲשֶׁר אֹמְרִים בָּנֵינוּ וּבְנֹתֵינוּ אֲנַחְנוּ רַבִּים וְנִקְחָה דָגָן וְנֹאכְלָה וְנִחְיֶה:

3 Others said, "We must pawn our fields, our vineyards, and our homes to get grain to stave off hunger."

ג וְיֵשׁ אֲשֶׁר אֹמְרִים שְׂדֹתֵינוּ וּכְרָמֵינוּ וּבָתֵּינוּ אֲנַחְנוּ עֹרְבִים וְנִקְחָה דָגָן בָּרָעָב:

4 Yet others said, "We have borrowed money against our fields and vineyards to pay the king's tax.

ד וְיֵשׁ אֲשֶׁר אֹמְרִים לָוִינוּ כֶסֶף לְמִדַּת הַמֶּלֶךְ שְׂדֹתֵינוּ וּכְרָמֵינוּ:

5 Now we are as good as our brothers, and our children as good as theirs; yet here we are subjecting our sons and daughters to slavery – some of our daughters are already subjected – and we are powerless, while our fields and vineyards belong to others."

ה וְעַתָּה כִּבְשַׂר אַחֵינוּ בְּשָׂרֵנוּ כִּבְנֵיהֶם בָּנֵינוּ וְהִנֵּה אֲנַחְנוּ כֹבְשִׁים אֶת־בָּנֵינוּ וְאֶת־בְּנֹתֵינוּ לַעֲבָדִים וְיֵשׁ מִבְּנֹתֵינוּ נִכְבָּשׁוֹת וְאֵין לְאֵל יָדֵנוּ וּשְׂדֹתֵינוּ וּכְרָמֵינוּ לַאֲחֵרִים:

6 It angered me very much to hear their outcry and these complaints.

ו וַיִּחַר לִי מְאֹד כַּאֲשֶׁר שָׁמַעְתִּי אֶת־זַעֲקָתָם וְאֵת הַדְּבָרִים הָאֵלֶּה:

7 After pondering the matter carefully, I censured the nobles and the prefects, saying, "Are you pressing claims on loans made to your brothers?" Then I raised a large crowd against them

ז וַיִּמָּלֵךְ לִבִּי עָלַי וָאָרִיבָה אֶת־הַחֹרִים וְאֶת־הַסְּגָנִים וָאֹמְרָה לָהֶם מַשָּׁא אִישׁ־בְּאָחִיו אַתֶּם נֹשְׁאִים [נֹשִׁים] וָאֶתֵּן עֲלֵיהֶם קְהִלָּה גְדוֹלָה:

8 and said to them, "We have done our best to buy back our Yehudiish brothers who were sold to the nations; will you now sell your brothers so that they must be sold [back] to us?" They kept silent, for they found nothing to answer.

ח וָאֹמְרָה לָהֶם אֲנַחְנוּ קָנִינוּ אֶת־אַחֵינוּ הַיְּהוּדִים הַנִּמְכָּרִים לַגּוֹיִם כְּדֵי בָנוּ וְגַם־אַתֶּם תִּמְכְּרוּ אֶת־אֲחֵיכֶם וְנִמְכְּרוּ־לָנוּ וַיַּחֲרִישׁוּ וְלֹא מָצְאוּ דָבָר:

Nechemya/Nehemiah
Chapter 5

9 So I continued, "What you are doing is not right. You ought to act in a *Hashem*-fearing way so as not to give our enemies, the nations, room to reproach us.

10 I, my brothers, and my servants also have claims of money and grain against them; let us now abandon those claims!

11 Give back at once their fields, their vineyards, their olive trees, and their homes, and [abandon] the claims for the hundred pieces of silver, the grain, the wine, and the oil that you have been pressing against them!"

12 They replied, "We shall give them back, and not demand anything of them; we shall do just as you say." Summoning the *Kohanim*, I put them under oath to keep this promise.

13 I also shook out the bosom of my garment and said, "So may *Hashem* shake free of his household and property any man who fails to keep this promise; may he be thus shaken out and stripped." All the assembled answered, "*Amen*," and praised *Hashem*. The people kept this promise.

14 Furthermore, from the day I was commissioned to be governor in the land of *Yehuda* – from the twentieth year of King Artaxerxes until his thirty-second year, twelve years in all – neither I nor my brothers ever ate of the governor's food allowance.

15 The former governors who preceded me laid heavy burdens on the people, and took from them for bread and wine more than forty *shekalim* of silver. Their servants also tyrannized over the people. But I, out of the fear of *Hashem*, did not do so.

v'-ha-pa-KHOT ha-ri-sho-NEEM a-sher l'-fa-NAI hikh-BEE-du al ha-AM va-yik-KHU may-HEM b'-LE-khem va-YA-yin a-KHAR KE-sef sh'-ka-LEEM ar-ba-EEM GAM na-a-ray-HEM sha-l'-TU al ha-AM va-a-NEE lo a-SEE-tee KHAYN mi-p'-NAY yir-AT e-lo-HEEM

5:15 And took from them for bread and wine More than any other food, bread and wine were the staples of ancient society. Bread provides basic nourishment, and wine, while in our lives considered a luxury, was an important source of calories, sugar and iron. Jews recite special benedictions over both bread and wine, and they are both utilized in spiritual rituals: Grains and wine were offered as Temple sacrifices, and today they are both used to mark the sanctity of the Shabbat and Jewish festivals, thus strengthening the connection between physical and spiritual sustenance. In addition, wheat and grapes are two of the seven special agricultural products associated with the Land of Israel (Deuteronomy 8:8). Today, after two thousand years of desolation, Israel boasts a booming agricultural industry and over 200 wineries that produce award-winning kosher wines.

Golan Heights Winery in Katzrin

Nechemya/Nehemiah
Chapter 6

16 I also supported the work on this wall; we did not buy any land, and all my servants were gathered there at the work.

טז וְגַם בִּמְלֶאכֶת הַחוֹמָה הַזֹּאת הֶחֱזַקְתִּי וְשָׂדֶה לֹא קָנִינוּ וְכָל־נְעָרַי קְבוּצִים שָׁם עַל־הַמְּלָאכָה׃

17 Although there were at my table, between *Yehudim* and prefects, one hundred and fifty men in all, beside those who came to us from surrounding nations;

יז וְהַיְּהוּדִים וְהַסְּגָנִים מֵאָה וַחֲמִשִּׁים אִישׁ וְהַבָּאִים אֵלֵינוּ מִן־הַגּוֹיִם אֲשֶׁר־סְבִיבֹתֵינוּ עַל־שֻׁלְחָנִי׃

18 and although what was prepared for each day came to one ox, six select sheep, and fowl, all prepared for me, and at ten-day intervals all sorts of wine in abundance – yet I did not resort to the governor's food allowance, for the [king's] service lay heavily on the people.

יח וַאֲשֶׁר הָיָה נַעֲשֶׂה לְיוֹם אֶחָד שׁוֹר אֶחָד צֹאן שֵׁשׁ־בְּרֻרוֹת וְצִפֳּרִים נַעֲשׂוּ־לִי וּבֵין עֲשֶׂרֶת יָמִים בְּכָל־יַיִן לְהַרְבֵּה וְעִם־זֶה לֶחֶם הַפֶּחָה לֹא בִקַּשְׁתִּי כִּי־כָבְדָה הָעֲבֹדָה עַל־הָעָם הַזֶּה׃

19 O my God, remember to my credit all that I have done for this people!

יט זָכְרָה־לִּי אֱלֹהַי לְטוֹבָה כֹּל אֲשֶׁר־עָשִׂיתִי עַל־הָעָם הַזֶּה׃

6 1 When word reached Sanballat, Tobiah, *Geshem* the Arab, and the rest of our enemies that I had rebuilt the wall and not a breach remained in it – though at that time I had not yet set up doors in the gateways –

ו א וַיְהִי כַאֲשֶׁר נִשְׁמַע לְסַנְבַלַּט וְטוֹבִיָּה וּלְגֶשֶׁם הָעַרְבִי וּלְיֶתֶר אֹיְבֵינוּ כִּי בָנִיתִי אֶת־הַחוֹמָה וְלֹא־נוֹתַר בָּהּ פָּרֶץ גַּם עַד־הָעֵת הַהִיא דְּלָתוֹת לֹא־הֶעֱמַדְתִּי בַּשְּׁעָרִים׃

vai-HEE kha-a-SHER nish-MA l'-san-va-LAT v'-to-vi-YAH ul-GE-shem ha-ar-VEE ul-YE-ter o-y'-VAY-nu KEE va-NEE-tee et ha-kho-MAH v'-lo NO-tar BAH PA-retz GAM ad ha-AYT ha-HEE d'-la-TOT lo he-e-MAD-tee va-sh'-a-REEM

2 Sanballat and *Geshem* sent a message to me, saying, "Come, let us get together in Kephirim in the Ono valley"; they planned to do me harm.

ב וַיִּשְׁלַח סַנְבַלַּט וְגֶשֶׁם אֵלַי לֵאמֹר לְכָה וְנִוָּעֲדָה יַחְדָּו בַּכְּפִירִים בְּבִקְעַת אוֹנוֹ וְהֵמָּה חֹשְׁבִים לַעֲשׂוֹת לִי רָעָה׃

3 I sent them messengers, saying, "I am engaged in a great work and cannot come down, for the work will stop if I leave it in order to come down to you."

ג וָאֶשְׁלְחָה עֲלֵיהֶם מַלְאָכִים לֵאמֹר מְלָאכָה גְדוֹלָה אֲנִי עֹשֶׂה וְלֹא אוּכַל לָרֶדֶת לָמָּה תִשְׁבַּת הַמְּלָאכָה כַּאֲשֶׁר אַרְפֶּהָ וְיָרַדְתִּי אֲלֵיכֶם׃

4 They sent me the same message four times, and I gave them the same answer.

ד וַיִּשְׁלְחוּ אֵלַי כַּדָּבָר הַזֶּה אַרְבַּע פְּעָמִים וָאָשִׁיב אוֹתָם כַּדָּבָר הַזֶּה׃

6:1 I had rebuilt the wall and not a breach remained in it Built, destroyed and rebuilt – this has repeatedly been the fate of *Yerushalayim*'s walls. Today's iconic Old City walls were renovated in 1538–42 by the Ottoman sultan Suleiman the Magnificent, whose dedicatory inscription adorns the Jaffa Gate. A more modest Hebrew inscription indicates another repair in 1970, quoting *Nechemya*, "Healing had come to the walls of *Yerushalayim*" (Nehemiah 4:1). Jerusalem's walls are significant in ways beyond what meets the eye; on a simple level, of course, they provide protection for the city. But on a more mystical plane, these walls provide a separation between what is inside and that which is outside. Though *Yerushalayim* and its inhabitants are supposed to influence the rest of the world with holiness and spirituality, the walls remind us that it is also important to separate and focus inward. Everyone has an obligation to make an impact and a contribution to the rest of the world, but one must remember not to neglect themselves and their own needs in the process.

Jerusalem's Old City walls

Nechemya/Nehemiah
Chapter 6

5 Sanballat sent me the same message a fifth time by his servant, who had an open letter with him.

6 Its text was: "Word has reached the nations, and *Geshem* too says that you and the *Yehudim* are planning to rebel – for which reason you are building the wall – and that you are to be their king. Such is the word.

7 You have also set up *Neviim* in *Yerushalayim* to proclaim about you, 'There is a king in *Yehuda*!' Word of these things will surely reach the king; so come, let us confer together."

8 I sent back a message to him, saying, "None of these things you mention has occurred; they are figments of your imagination" –

9 for they all wished to intimidate us, thinking, "They will desist from the work, and it will not get done." Now strengthen my hands!

10 Then I visited *Shemaya* son of Delaiah son of Mehetabel when he was housebound, and he said, "Let us meet in the House of *Hashem*, inside the sanctuary, And let us shut the doors of the sanctuary, for they are coming to kill you, By night they are coming to kill you."

11 I replied, "Will a man like me take flight? Besides, who such as I can go into the sanctuary and live? I will not go in."

12 Then I realized that it was not *Hashem* who sent him, but that he uttered that prophecy about me – Tobiah and Sanballat having hired him –

13 because he was a hireling, that I might be intimidated and act thus and commit a sin, and so provide them a scandal with which to reproach me.

14 "O my God, remember against Tobiah and Sanballat these deeds of theirs, and against Noadiah the prophetess, and against the other prophets that they wished to intimidate me!"

15 The wall was finished on the twenty-fifth of Elul, after fifty-two days.

16 When all our enemies heard it, all the nations round about us were intimidated, and fell very low in their own estimation; they realized that this work had been accomplished by the help of our God.

נחמיה
פרק ו

ה וַיִּשְׁלַח אֵלַי סַנְבַלַּט כַּדָּבָר הַזֶּה פַּעַם חֲמִישִׁית אֶת־נַעֲרוֹ וְאִגֶּרֶת פְּתוּחָה בְּיָדוֹ:

ו כָּתוּב בָּהּ בַּגּוֹיִם נִשְׁמָע וְגַשְׁמוּ אֹמֵר אַתָּה וְהַיְּהוּדִים חֹשְׁבִים לִמְרוֹד עַל־כֵּן אַתָּה בוֹנֶה הַחוֹמָה וְאַתָּה הֹוֶה לָהֶם לְמֶלֶךְ כַּדְּבָרִים הָאֵלֶּה:

ז וְגַם־נְבִיאִים הֶעֱמַדְתָּ לִקְרֹא עָלֶיךָ בִירוּשָׁלַם לֵאמֹר מֶלֶךְ בִּיהוּדָה וְעַתָּה יִשָּׁמַע לַמֶּלֶךְ כַּדְּבָרִים הָאֵלֶּה וְעַתָּה לְכָה וְנִוָּעֲצָה יַחְדָּו:

ח וָאֶשְׁלְחָה אֵלָיו לֵאמֹר לֹא נִהְיָה כַּדְּבָרִים הָאֵלֶּה אֲשֶׁר אַתָּה אוֹמֵר כִּי מִלִּבְּךָ אַתָּה בוֹדְאָם:

ט כִּי כֻלָּם מְיָרְאִים אוֹתָנוּ לֵאמֹר יִרְפּוּ יְדֵיהֶם מִן־הַמְּלָאכָה וְלֹא תֵעָשֶׂה וְעַתָּה חַזֵּק אֶת־יָדָי:

י וַאֲנִי־בָאתִי בֵּית שְׁמַעְיָה בֶן־דְּלָיָה בֶּן־מְהֵיטַבְאֵל וְהוּא עָצוּר וַיֹּאמֶר נִוָּעֵד אֶל־בֵּית הָאֱלֹהִים אֶל־תּוֹךְ הַהֵיכָל וְנִסְגְּרָה דַּלְתוֹת הַהֵיכָל כִּי בָּאִים לְהָרְגֶךָ וְלַיְלָה בָּאִים לְהָרְגֶךָ:

יא וָאֹמְרָה הַאִישׁ כָּמוֹנִי יִבְרָח וּמִי כָמוֹנִי אֲשֶׁר־יָבוֹא אֶל־הַהֵיכָל וָחָי לֹא אָבוֹא:

יב וָאַכִּירָה וְהִנֵּה לֹא־אֱלֹהִים שְׁלָחוֹ כִּי הַנְּבוּאָה דִּבֶּר עָלַי וְטוֹבִיָּה וְסַנְבַלַּט שְׂכָרוֹ:

יג לְמַעַן שָׂכוּר הוּא לְמַעַן־אִירָא וְאֶעֱשֶׂה־כֵּן וְחָטָאתִי וְהָיָה לָהֶם לְשֵׁם רָע לְמַעַן יְחָרְפוּנִי:

יד זָכְרָה אֱלֹהַי לְטוֹבִיָּה וּלְסַנְבַלַּט כְּמַעֲשָׂיו אֵלֶּה וְגַם לְנוֹעַדְיָה הַנְּבִיאָה וּלְיֶתֶר הַנְּבִיאִים אֲשֶׁר הָיוּ מְיָרְאִים אוֹתִי:

טו וַתִּשְׁלַם הַחוֹמָה בְּעֶשְׂרִים וַחֲמִשָּׁה לֶאֱלוּל לַחֲמִשִּׁים וּשְׁנַיִם יוֹם:

טז וַיְהִי כַּאֲשֶׁר שָׁמְעוּ כָּל־אוֹיְבֵינוּ וַיִּרְאוּ כָּל־הַגּוֹיִם אֲשֶׁר סְבִיבֹתֵינוּ וַיִּפְּלוּ מְאֹד בְּעֵינֵיהֶם וַיֵּדְעוּ כִּי מֵאֵת אֱלֹהֵינוּ נֶעֶשְׂתָה הַמְּלָאכָה הַזֹּאת:

Nechemya/Nehemiah
Chapter 7

נחמיה
פרק ז

17 Also in those days, the nobles of *Yehuda* kept up a brisk correspondence with Tobiah, and Tobiah with them.

יז גַּם ׀ בַּיָּמִים הָהֵם מַרְבִּים חֹרֵי יְהוּדָה אִגְּרֹתֵיהֶם הוֹלְכוֹת עַל־טוֹבִיָּה וַאֲשֶׁר לְטוֹבִיָּה בָּאוֹת אֲלֵיהֶם:

18 Many in *Yehuda* were his confederates, for he was a son-in-law of *Shechanya* son of Arah, and his son *Yehochanan* had married the daughter of Meshullam son of *Berechya*.

יח כִּי־רַבִּים בִּיהוּדָה בַּעֲלֵי שְׁבוּעָה לוֹ כִּי־חָתָן הוּא לִשְׁכַנְיָה בֶן־אָרַח וִיהוֹחָנָן בְּנוֹ לָקַח אֶת־בַּת־מְשֻׁלָּם בֶּן בֶּרֶכְיָה:

19 They would also speak well of him to me, and would divulge my affairs to him. Tobiah sent letters to intimidate me.

יט גַּם טוֹבֹתָיו הָיוּ אֹמְרִים לְפָנַי וּדְבָרַי הָיוּ מוֹצִיאִים לוֹ אִגְּרוֹת שָׁלַח טוֹבִיָּה לְיָרְאֵנִי:

7 1 When the wall was rebuilt and I had set up the doors, tasks were assigned to the gatekeepers, the singers, and the *Leviim*.

א וַיְהִי כַּאֲשֶׁר נִבְנְתָה הַחוֹמָה וָאַעֲמִיד הַדְּלָתוֹת וַיִּפָּקְדוּ הַשּׁוֹעֲרִים וְהַמְשֹׁרְרִים וְהַלְוִיִּם:

2 I put *Chanani* my brother and *Chananya*, the captain of the fortress, in charge of *Yerushalayim*, for he was a more trustworthy and *Hashem*-fearing man than most.

ב וָאֲצַוֶּה אֶת־חֲנָנִי אָחִי וְאֶת־חֲנַנְיָה שַׂר הַבִּירָה עַל־יְרוּשָׁלָ͏ִם כִּי־הוּא כְּאִישׁ אֱמֶת וְיָרֵא אֶת־הָאֱלֹהִים מֵרַבִּים:

3 I said to them, "The gates of *Yerushalayim* are not to be opened until the heat of the day, and before you leave your posts let the doors be closed and barred. And assign the inhabitants of *Yerushalayim* to watches, each man to his watch, and each in front of his own house."

ג וָאֹמַר [וָאֹמַר] לָהֶם לֹא יִפָּתְחוּ שַׁעֲרֵי יְרוּשָׁלַ͏ִם עַד־חֹם הַשֶּׁמֶשׁ וְעַד הֵם עֹמְדִים יָגִיפוּ הַדְּלָתוֹת וֶאֱחֹזוּ וְהַעֲמֵיד מִשְׁמְרוֹת יֹשְׁבֵי יְרוּשָׁלָ͏ִם אִישׁ בְּמִשְׁמָרוֹ וְאִישׁ נֶגֶד בֵּיתוֹ:

4 The city was broad and large, the people in it were few, and houses were not yet built.

ד וְהָעִיר רַחֲבַת יָדַיִם וּגְדוֹלָה וְהָעָם מְעַט בְּתוֹכָהּ וְאֵין בָּתִּים בְּנוּיִם:

v'-ha-EER ra-kha-VAT ya-DA-yim ug-do-LAH v'-ha-AM m'-AT b'-to-KHAH v'-AYN ba-TEEM b'-nu-YIM

5 My *Hashem* put it into my mind to assemble the nobles, the prefects, and the people, in order to register them by families. I found the genealogical register of those who were the first to come up, and there I found written:

ה וַיִּתֵּן אֱלֹהַי אֶל־לִבִּי וָאֶקְבְּצָה אֶת־הַחֹרִים וְאֶת־הַסְּגָנִים וְאֶת־הָעָם לְהִתְיַחֵשׂ וָאֶמְצָא סֵפֶר הַיַּחַשׂ הָעוֹלִים בָּרִאשׁוֹנָה וָאֶמְצָא כָּתוּב בּוֹ:

7:4 The city was broad and large, the people in it were few There must be a proper proportion between a city's size and its population. *Nechemya* is concerned that since too few people were living in *Yerushalayim*, it would be difficult to defend, even though it was surrounded by a wall. He therefore looks for more people to inhabit the city. Conversely, if the borders of a city encompass too small an area, it will become overcrowded. This was the case in the 1850s when, in a miraculous reversal of *Nechemya*'s time, *Yerushalayim* became so full of inhabitants that it was necessary to expand and build new neighborhoods outside the Old City walls, beginning with the neighborhood of *Mishkenot Sha'ananim* in 1860. As a land, however, the Land of Israel will always have room to contain her children. Also named *Eretz Hatzvi*, 'The Land of the Gazelle,' the Talmud (*Ketubot* 112a) states that just as a gazelle's hide stretches according to need, so too the Land of Israel will stretch to sustain any number of its people. Furthermore, King Solomon writes "my beloved is like a gazelle" (Song of Songs 2:9), inferring that just as a gazelle finds its way home from the ends of the world, so too will the dispersed Jews return. And when they do, *Eretz Yisrael* will contain them all.

Nechemya/Nehemiah
Chapter 7

נְחֶמְיָה
פרק ז

6 These are the people of the province who came up from among the captive exiles that Nebuchadnezzar, king of Babylon, had deported, and who returned to *Yerushalayim* and to *Yehuda*, each to his own city,

א אֵלֶּה ׀ בְּנֵי הַמְּדִינָה הָעֹלִים מִשְּׁבִי הַגּוֹלָה אֲשֶׁר הֶגְלָה נְבוּכַדְנֶצַּר מֶלֶךְ בָּבֶל וַיָּשׁוּבוּ לִירוּשָׁלַם וְלִיהוּדָה אִישׁ לְעִירוֹ׃

7 who came with *Zerubavel, Yeshua, Nechemya, Azarya*, Raamiah, Nahamani, *Mordechai*, Bilshan, Mispereth, Bigvai, Nehum, Baanah. The number of the men of the people of *Yisrael*:

ז הַבָּאִים עִם־זְרֻבָּבֶל יֵשׁוּעַ נְחֶמְיָה עֲזַרְיָה רַעַמְיָה נַחֲמָנִי מָרְדֳּכַי בִּלְשָׁן מִסְפֶּרֶת בִּגְוַי נְחוּם בַּעֲנָה מִסְפַּר אַנְשֵׁי עַם יִשְׂרָאֵל׃

8 the sons of Parosh – 2,172;

ח בְּנֵי פַרְעֹשׁ אַלְפַּיִם מֵאָה וְשִׁבְעִים וּשְׁנָיִם׃

9 the sons of Shephatiah – 372;

ט בְּנֵי שְׁפַטְיָה שְׁלֹשׁ מֵאוֹת שִׁבְעִים וּשְׁנָיִם׃

10 the sons of Arah – 652;

י בְּנֵי אָרַח שֵׁשׁ מֵאוֹת חֲמִשִּׁים וּשְׁנָיִם׃

11 the sons of Pahath-moab: the sons of *Yeshua* and *Yoav* – 2,818;

יא בְּנֵי־פַחַת מוֹאָב לִבְנֵי יֵשׁוּעַ וְיוֹאָב אַלְפַּיִם וּשְׁמֹנֶה מֵאוֹת שְׁמֹנָה עָשָׂר׃

12 the sons of Elam – 1,254;

יב בְּנֵי עֵילָם אֶלֶף מָאתַיִם חֲמִשִּׁים וְאַרְבָּעָה׃

13 the sons of Zattu – 845;

יג בְּנֵי זַתּוּא שְׁמֹנֶה מֵאוֹת אַרְבָּעִים וַחֲמִשָּׁה׃

14 the sons of Zaccai – 760;

יד בְּנֵי זַכָּי שְׁבַע מֵאוֹת וְשִׁשִּׁים׃

15 the sons of Binnui – 648;

טו בְּנֵי בִנּוּי שֵׁשׁ מֵאוֹת אַרְבָּעִים וּשְׁמֹנָה׃

16 the sons of Bebai – 628;

טז בְּנֵי בֵבָי שֵׁשׁ מֵאוֹת עֶשְׂרִים וּשְׁמֹנָה׃

17 the sons of Azgad – 2,322;

יז בְּנֵי עַזְגָּד אַלְפַּיִם שְׁלֹשׁ מֵאוֹת עֶשְׂרִים וּשְׁנָיִם׃

18 the sons of Adonikam – 667;

יח בְּנֵי אֲדֹנִיקָם שֵׁשׁ מֵאוֹת שִׁשִּׁים וְשִׁבְעָה׃

19 the sons of Bigvai – 2,067;

יט בְּנֵי בִגְוָי אַלְפַּיִם שִׁשִּׁים וְשִׁבְעָה׃

20 the sons of Adin – 655;

כ בְּנֵי עָדִין שֵׁשׁ מֵאוֹת חֲמִשִּׁים וַחֲמִשָּׁה׃

21 the sons of Ater: *Chizkiyahu* – 98;

כא בְּנֵי־אָטֵר לְחִזְקִיָּה תִּשְׁעִים וּשְׁמֹנָה׃

22 the sons of Hashum – 328;

כב בְּנֵי חָשֻׁם שְׁלֹשׁ מֵאוֹת עֶשְׂרִים וּשְׁמֹנָה׃

23 the sons of Bezai – 324;

כג בְּנֵי בֵצָי שְׁלֹשׁ מֵאוֹת עֶשְׂרִים וְאַרְבָּעָה׃

24 the sons of Hariph – 112;

כד בְּנֵי חָרִיף מֵאָה שְׁנֵים עָשָׂר׃

25 the sons of *Givon* – 95;

כה בְּנֵי גִבְעוֹן תִּשְׁעִים וַחֲמִשָּׁה׃

26 the men of *Beit Lechem* and Netophah – 188;

כו אַנְשֵׁי בֵית־לֶחֶם וּנְטֹפָה מֵאָה שְׁמֹנִים וּשְׁמֹנָה׃

27 the men of *Anatot* – 128;

כז אַנְשֵׁי עֲנָתוֹת מֵאָה עֶשְׂרִים וּשְׁמֹנָה׃

Nechemya/Nehemiah
Chapter 7

28 the men of Beth-azmaveth – 42;

29 the men of *Kiryat Ye'arim*, Chephirah, and Beeroth – 743;

30 the men of *Rama* and Geba – 621;

31 the men of Michmas – 122;

32 the men of *Beit El* and Ai – 123;

33 the men of the other Nebo – 52;

34 the sons of the other Elam – 1,254;

35 the sons of Harim – 320;

36 the sons of *Yericho* – 345;

37 the sons of Lod, Hadid, and Ono – 721;

38 the sons of Senaah – 3,930.

39 The *Kohanim*: the sons of Jedaiah: the house of Yeshua – 973;

40 the sons of Immer – 1,052;

41 the sons of Pashhur – 1,247;

42 the sons of Harim – 1,017.

43 The *Leviim*: the sons of *Yeshua*: *Kadmiel*, the sons of Hodeiah – 74.

44 The singers: the sons of *Asaf* – 148.

45 The gatekeepers: the sons of *Shalum*, the sons of Ater, the sons of Talmon, the sons of Akkub, the sons of Hatita, the sons of Shobai – 138.

46 The temple servants: the sons of Ziha, the sons of Hasupha, the sons of Tabbaoth,

47 the sons of Keros, the sons of Siah, the sons of Padon,

48 the sons of Lebanah, the sons of Hagabah, the sons of Shalmai,

Nechemya/Nehemiah
Chapter 7

נחמיה
פרק ז

49 the sons of Hanan, the sons of Giddel, the sons of Gahar,

מט בְּנֵי־חָנָן בְּנֵי־גִדֵּל בְּנֵי־גָחַר:

50 the sons of Reaiah, the sons of Rezin, the sons of Nekoda,

נ בְּנֵי־רְאָיָה בְנֵי־רְצִין בְּנֵי נְקוֹדָא:

51 the sons of Gazzam, the sons of Uzza, the sons of Paseah,

נא בְּנֵי־גַזָּם בְּנֵי־עֻזָּא בְּנֵי פָסֵחַ:

52 the sons of Besai, the sons of Meunim, the sons of Nephishesim,

נב בְּנֵי־בֵסַי בְנֵי־מְעוּנִים בְּנֵי נפושסים [נְפִישְׁסִים:]

53 the sons of Bakbuk, the sons of Hakupha, the sons of Harhur,

נג בְּנֵי־בַקְבּוּק בְּנֵי־חֲקוּפָא בְּנֵי חַרְחוּר:

54 the sons of Bazlith, the sons of Mehida, the sons of Harsha,

נד בְּנֵי־בַצְלִית בְּנֵי־מְחִידָא בְּנֵי חַרְשָׁא:

55 the sons of Barkos, the sons of Sisera, the sons of Temah,

נה בְּנֵי־בַרְקוֹס בְּנֵי־סִיסְרָא בְּנֵי־תָמַח:

56 the sons of Neziah, the sons of Hatipha.

נו בְּנֵי נְצִיחַ בְּנֵי חֲטִיפָא:

57 The sons of *Shlomo*'s servants: the sons of Sotai, the sons of Sophereth, the sons of Perida,

נז בְּנֵי עַבְדֵי שְׁלֹמֹה בְּנֵי־סוֹטַי בְּנֵי־סוֹפֶרֶת בְּנֵי פְרִידָא:

58 the sons of Jala, the sons of Darkon, the sons of Giddel,

נח בְּנֵי־יַעְלָא בְנֵי־דַרְקוֹן בְּנֵי גִדֵּל:

59 the sons of Shephatiah, the sons of Hattil, the sons of Pochereth-hazzebaim, the sons of Ammon.

נט בְּנֵי שְׁפַטְיָה בְנֵי־חַטִּיל בְּנֵי פֹּכֶרֶת הַצְּבָיִים בְּנֵי אָמוֹן:

60 The total of temple servants and the sons of *Shlomo*'s servants – 392.

ס כָּל־הַנְּתִינִים וּבְנֵי עַבְדֵי שְׁלֹמֹה שְׁלֹשׁ מֵאוֹת תִּשְׁעִים וּשְׁנָיִם:

61 The following were those who came up from Tel-melah, Tel-harsha, Cherub, Addon, and Immer – they were unable to tell whether their father's house and descent were Israelite:

סא וְאֵלֶּה הָעוֹלִים מִתֵּל מֶלַח תֵּל חַרְשָׁא כְּרוּב אַדּוֹן וְאִמֵּר וְלֹא יָכְלוּ לְהַגִּיד בֵּית־אֲבוֹתָם וְזַרְעָם אִם מִיִּשְׂרָאֵל הֵם:

62 the sons of Delaiah, the sons of Tobiah, the sons of Nekoda – 642.

סב בְּנֵי־דְלָיָה בְנֵי־טוֹבִיָּה בְּנֵי נְקוֹדָא שֵׁשׁ מֵאוֹת וְאַרְבָּעִים וּשְׁנָיִם:

63 Of the *Kohanim*: the sons of Habaiah, the sons of Hakkoz, the sons of *Barzilai* who had married a daughter of *Barzilai* the Giladite and had taken his name –

סג וּמִן־הַכֹּהֲנִים בְּנֵי חֲבַיָּה בְּנֵי הַקּוֹץ בְּנֵי בַרְזִלַּי אֲשֶׁר לָקַח מִבְּנוֹת בַּרְזִלַּי הַגִּלְעָדִי אִשָּׁה וַיִּקָּרֵא עַל־שְׁמָם:

64 these searched for their genealogical records, but they could not be found, so they were disqualified for the priesthood.

סד אֵלֶּה בִּקְשׁוּ כְתָבָם הַמִּתְיַחְשִׂים וְלֹא נִמְצָא וַיְגֹאֲלוּ מִן־הַכְּהֻנָּה:

65 The Tirshatha ordered them not to eat of the most holy things until a *Kohen* with Urim and Thummim should appear.

סה וַיֹּאמֶר הַתִּרְשָׁתָא לָהֶם אֲשֶׁר לֹא־יֹאכְלוּ מִקֹּדֶשׁ הַקֳּדָשִׁים עַד עֲמֹד הַכֹּהֵן לְאוּרִים וְתוּמִּים:

66 The sum of the entire community was 42,360,

סו כָּל־הַקָּהָל כְּאֶחָד אַרְבַּע רִבּוֹא אֲלָפִים שְׁלֹשׁ־מֵאוֹת וְשִׁשִּׁים:

Nechemya/Nehemiah
Chapter 8

67 not counting their male and female servants, these being 7,337; they also had 245 male and female singers.

68 [Their horses – 736, their mules – 245,] camels – 435, asses – 6,720.

69 Some of the heads of the clans made donations for the work. The Tirshatha donated to the treasury: gold – 1,000 drachmas, basins – 50, priestly robes – 530.

70 Some of the heads of the clans donated to the work treasury: gold – 20,000 drachmas, and silver – 2,200 *manim*.

71 The rest of the people donated: gold – 20,000 drachmas, silver – 2,000, and priestly robes – 67.

72 The *Kohanim*, the *Leviim*, the gatekeepers, the singers, some of the people, the temple servants, and all *Yisrael* took up residence in their towns. When the seventh month arrived – the Israelites being [settled] in their towns –

8 1 the entire people assembled as one man in the square before the Water Gate, and they asked *Ezra* the scribe to bring the scroll of the Teaching of *Moshe* with which *Hashem* had charged *Yisrael*.

2 On the first day of the seventh month, *Ezra* the *Kohen* brought the Teaching before the congregation, men and women and all who could listen with understanding.

3 He read from it, facing the square before the Water Gate, from the first light until midday, to the men and the women and those who could understand; the ears of all the people were given to the scroll of the Teaching.

4 *Ezra* the scribe stood upon a wooden tower made for the purpose, and beside him stood Mattithiah, Shema, Anaiah, *Uriya*, *Chilkiyahu*, and Maaseiah at his right, and at his left Pedaiah, *Mishael*, Malchijah, Hashum, Hashbaddanah, *Zecharya*, Meshullam.

נחמיה
פרק ח

סז מִלְּבַד עַבְדֵיהֶם וְאַמְהֹתֵיהֶם אֵלֶּה שִׁבְעַת אֲלָפִים שְׁלֹשׁ מֵאוֹת שְׁלֹשִׁים וְשִׁבְעָה וְלָהֶם מְשֹׁרְרִים וּמְשֹׁרְרוֹת מָאתַיִם וְאַרְבָּעִים וַחֲמִשָּׁה:

סח גְּמַלִּים אַרְבַּע מֵאוֹת שְׁלֹשִׁים וַחֲמִשָּׁה חֲמֹרִים שֵׁשֶׁת אֲלָפִים שְׁבַע מֵאוֹת וְעֶשְׂרִים:

סט וּמִקְצָת רָאשֵׁי הָאָבוֹת נָתְנוּ לַמְּלָאכָה הַתִּרְשָׁתָא נָתַן לָאוֹצָר זָהָב דַּרְכְּמֹנִים אֶלֶף מִזְרָקוֹת חֲמִשִּׁים כָּתְנוֹת כֹּהֲנִים שְׁלֹשִׁים וַחֲמֵשׁ מֵאוֹת:

ע וּמֵרָאשֵׁי הָאָבוֹת נָתְנוּ לְאוֹצַר הַמְּלָאכָה זָהָב דַּרְכְּמוֹנִים שְׁתֵּי רִבּוֹת וְכֶסֶף מָנִים אַלְפַּיִם וּמָאתָיִם:

עא וַאֲשֶׁר נָתְנוּ שְׁאֵרִית הָעָם זָהָב דַּרְכְּמוֹנִים שְׁתֵּי רִבּוֹא וְכֶסֶף מָנִים אַלְפָּיִם וְכָתְנֹת כֹּהֲנִים שִׁשִּׁים וְשִׁבְעָה:

עב וַיֵּשְׁבוּ הַכֹּהֲנִים וְהַלְוִיִּם וְהַשּׁוֹעֲרִים וְהַמְשֹׁרְרִים וּמִן הָעָם וְהַנְּתִינִים וְכָל יִשְׂרָאֵל בְּעָרֵיהֶם וַיִּגַּע הַחֹדֶשׁ הַשְּׁבִיעִי וּבְנֵי יִשְׂרָאֵל בְּעָרֵיהֶם:

ח א וַיֵּאָסְפוּ כָל הָעָם כְּאִישׁ אֶחָד אֶל הָרְחוֹב אֲשֶׁר לִפְנֵי שַׁעַר הַמָּיִם וַיֹּאמְרוּ לְעֶזְרָא הַסֹּפֵר לְהָבִיא אֶת סֵפֶר תּוֹרַת מֹשֶׁה אֲשֶׁר צִוָּה יְהוָה אֶת יִשְׂרָאֵל:

ב וַיָּבִיא עֶזְרָא הַכֹּהֵן אֶת הַתּוֹרָה לִפְנֵי הַקָּהָל מֵאִישׁ וְעַד אִשָּׁה וְכֹל מֵבִין לִשְׁמֹעַ בְּיוֹם אֶחָד לַחֹדֶשׁ הַשְּׁבִיעִי:

ג וַיִּקְרָא בוֹ לִפְנֵי הָרְחוֹב אֲשֶׁר לִפְנֵי שַׁעַר הַמַּיִם מִן הָאוֹר עַד מַחֲצִית הַיּוֹם נֶגֶד הָאֲנָשִׁים וְהַנָּשִׁים וְהַמְּבִינִים וְאָזְנֵי כָל הָעָם אֶל סֵפֶר הַתּוֹרָה:

ד וַיַּעֲמֹד עֶזְרָא הַסֹּפֵר עַל מִגְדַּל עֵץ אֲשֶׁר עָשׂוּ לַדָּבָר וַיַּעֲמֹד אֶצְלוֹ מַתִּתְיָה וְשֶׁמַע וַעֲנָיָה וְאוּרִיָּה וְחִלְקִיָּה וּמַעֲשֵׂיָה עַל יְמִינוֹ וּמִשְּׂמֹאלוֹ פְּדָיָה וּמִישָׁאֵל וּמַלְכִּיָּה וְחָשֻׁם וְחַשְׁבַּדָּנָה זְכַרְיָה מְשֻׁלָּם:

Nechemya/Nehemiah
Chapter 8

5 *Ezra* opened the scroll in the sight of all the people, for he was above all the people; as he opened it, all the people stood up.

6 *Ezra* blessed *Hashem*, the great *Hashem*, and all the people answered, "*Amen, Amen*," with hands upraised. Then they bowed their heads and prostrated themselves before *Hashem* with their faces to the ground.

7 *Yeshua*, Bani, Sherebiah, Jamin, Akkub, Shabbethai, Hodiah, Maaseiah, Kelita, *Azarya, Yozavad*, Hanan, Pelaiah, and the *Leviim* explained the Teaching to the people, while the people stood in their places.

8 They read from the scroll of the Teaching of *Hashem*, translating it and giving the sense; so they understood the reading.

9 *Nechemya* the Tirshatha, *Ezra* the *Kohen* and scribe, and the *Leviim* who were explaining to the people said to all the people, "This day is holy to *Hashem* your God: you must not mourn or weep," for all the people were weeping as they listened to the words of the Teaching.

10 He further said to them, "Go, eat choice foods and drink sweet drinks and send portions to whoever has nothing prepared, for the day is holy to our Lord. Do not be sad, for your rejoicing in *Hashem* is the source of your strength."

11 The *Leviim* were quieting the people, saying, "Hush, for the day is holy; do not be sad."

12 Then all the people went to eat and drink and send portions and make great merriment, for they understood the things they were told.

13 On the second day, the heads of the clans of all the people and the *Kohanim* and *Leviim* gathered to *Ezra* the scribe to study the words of the Teaching.

14 They found written in the Teaching that *Hashem* had commanded *Moshe* that the Israelites must dwell in booths during the festival of the seventh month,

Nechemya/Nehemiah
Chapter 9

נחמיה
פרק ט

15 and that they must announce and proclaim throughout all their towns and *Yerushalayim* as follows, "Go out to the mountains and bring leafy branches of olive trees, pine trees, myrtles, palms and [other] leafy trees to make booths, as it is written."

טו וַאֲשֶׁ֣ר יַשְׁמִ֗יעוּ וְיַעֲבִ֨ירוּ ק֥וֹל בְּכׇל־עָרֵיהֶ֘ם וּבִירוּשָׁלַ֣͏ִם לֵאמֹ֒ר צְא֣וּ הָהָ֗ר וְהָבִ֙יאוּ֙ עֲלֵי־זַ֙יִת֙ וַעֲלֵי־עֵ֣ץ שֶׁ֔מֶן וַעֲלֵ֤י הֲדַס֙ וַעֲלֵ֣י תְמָרִ֔ים וַעֲלֵ֖י עֵ֣ץ עָבֹ֑ת לַעֲשֹׂ֥ת סֻכֹּ֖ת כַּכָּתֽוּב׃

va-a-SHER yash-MEE-u v'-ya-a-VEE-ru KOL b'-khol a-ray-HEM u-vee-ru-sha-LA-im lay-MOR tz'-U ha-HAR v'-ha-VEE-u a-lay ZA-yit va-a-lay AYTZ SHE-men va-a-LAY ha-DAS va-a-LAY t'-ma-REEM va-a-LAY AYTZ a-VOT la-a-SOT su-KOT ka-ka-TUV

16 So the people went out and brought them, and made themselves booths on their roofs, in their courtyards, in the courtyards of the House of *Hashem*, in the square of the Water Gate and in the square of the *Efraim* Gate.

טז וַיֵּצְא֣וּ הָעָם֮ וַיָּבִ֒יאוּ֒ וַיַּעֲשׂ֩וּ לָהֶ֨ם סֻכּ֜וֹת אִ֤ישׁ עַל־גַּגּוֹ֙ וּבְחַצְרֹ֣תֵיהֶ֔ם וּבְחַצְר֖וֹת בֵּ֣ית הָאֱלֹהִ֑ים וּבִרְחוֹב֙ שַׁ֣עַר הַמַּ֔יִם וּבִרְח֖וֹב שַׁ֥עַר אֶפְרָֽיִם׃

17 The whole community that returned from the captivity made booths and dwelt in the booths – the Israelites had not done so from the days of *Yehoshua* son of *Nun* to that day – and there was very great rejoicing.

יז וַֽיַּעֲשׂ֣וּ כׇֽל־הַ֠קָּהָ֠ל הַשָּׁבִ֨ים מִן־הַשְּׁבִ֥י ׀ סֻכּוֹת֮ וַיֵּשְׁב֣וּ בַסֻּכּוֹת֒ כִּ֣י לֹֽא־עָשׂ֡וּ מִימֵי֩ יֵשׁ֨וּעַ בִּן־נ֥וּן כֵּן֙ בְּנֵ֣י יִשְׂרָאֵ֔ל עַ֖ד הַיּ֣וֹם הַה֑וּא וַתְּהִ֥י שִׂמְחָ֖ה גְּדוֹלָ֥ה מְאֹֽד׃

18 He read from the scroll of the Teaching of *Hashem* each day, from the first to the last day. They celebrated the festival seven days, and there was a solemn gathering on the eighth, as prescribed.

יח וַ֠יִּקְרָ֠א בְּסֵ֨פֶר תּוֹרַ֤ת הָאֱלֹהִים֙ י֣וֹם ׀ בְּי֔וֹם מִן־הַיּוֹם֙ הָרִ֣אשׁוֹן עַ֖ד הַיּ֣וֹם הָאַחֲר֑וֹן וַיַּעֲשׂוּ־חָג֙ שִׁבְעַ֣ת יָמִ֔ים וּבַיּ֧וֹם הַשְּׁמִינִ֛י עֲצֶ֖רֶת כַּמִּשְׁפָּֽט׃

9

1 On the twenty-fourth day of this month, the Israelites assembled, fasting, in sackcloth, and with earth upon them.

א וּבְיוֹם֩ עֶשְׂרִ֨ים וְאַרְבָּעָ֜ה לַחֹ֣דֶשׁ הַזֶּ֗ה נֶאֶסְפ֤וּ בְנֵֽי־יִשְׂרָאֵל֙ בְּצ֣וֹם וּבְשַׂקִּ֔ים וַאֲדָמָ֖ה עֲלֵיהֶֽם׃

2 Those of the stock of *Yisrael* separated themselves from all foreigners, and stood and confessed their sins and the iniquities of their fathers.

ב וַיִּבָּֽדְלוּ֙ זֶ֣רַע יִשְׂרָאֵ֔ל מִכֹּ֖ל בְּנֵ֣י נֵכָ֑ר וַיַּעַמְד֗וּ וַיִּתְוַדּוּ֙ עַל־חַטֹּ֣אתֵיהֶ֔ם וַעֲוֺנ֖וֹת אֲבֹתֵיהֶֽם׃

Olive branches in the Galilee

8:15 Go out to the mountains and bring leafy branches of olive trees Any species of tree may be used to construct the *sukkah*, the booth used to observe the holiday of *Sukkot*. For this particular *Sukkot*, though, the people specifically looked for olive branches. Besides being one of the seven special agricultural species of the Land of Israel (Deuteronomy 8:8), the olive also plays a significant role in the story of *Noach's* flood. After the rain stopped falling, *Noach* sent out a dove to see if the flood waters had receded. When the dove returned with a freshly plucked olive leaf, "*Noach* knew that the waters had decreased on the earth" (Genesis 8:11). Additionally, the *menorah* 'lamp' in the *Beit Hamikdash* is kindled daily exclusively with olive oil, and this oil is also used ceremoniously to anoint a new king. The common theme of these events is renewal. After the flood, the world was given a new start. Each time the *menorah* is lit, it is kindled anew, without any reliance on previous lightings, and the coronation of a new monarch also begins a new era for the kingdom. This symbolism was certainly not lost on the people in *Nechemya's* time, who were renewing their traditions in the God-given land of their forefathers.

Nechemya/Nehemiah
Chapter 9

נחמיה
פרק ט

3 Standing in their places, they read from the scroll of the Teaching of *Hashem* their God for one-fourth of the day, and for another fourth they confessed and prostrated themselves before *Hashem* their God.

ג וַיָּקוּמוּ עַל־עָמְדָם וַיִּקְרְאוּ בְּסֵפֶר תּוֹרַת יְהֹוָה אֱלֹהֵיהֶם רְבִעִית הַיּוֹם וּרְבִעִית מִתְוַדִּים וּמִשְׁתַּחֲוִים לַיהֹוָה אֱלֹהֵיהֶם׃

4 On the raised platform of the *Leviim* stood *Yeshua* and Bani, *Kadmiel*, Shebaniah, Bunni, Sherebiah, Bani, and Chenani, and cried in a loud voice to *Hashem* their God.

ד וַיָּקָם עַל־מַעֲלֵה הַלְוִיִּם יֵשׁוּעַ וּבָנִי קַדְמִיאֵל שְׁבַנְיָה בֻּנִּי שֵׁרֵבְיָה בָּנִי כְנָנִי וַיִּזְעֲקוּ בְּקוֹל גָּדוֹל אֶל־יְהֹוָה אֱלֹהֵיהֶם׃

5 The *Leviim Yeshua, Kadmiel*, Bani, Hashabniah, Sherebiah, Hodiah, and Pethahiah said, "Rise, bless *Hashem* your God who is from eternity to eternity: 'May Your glorious name be blessed, exalted though it is above every blessing and praise!'

ה וַיֹּאמְרוּ הַלְוִיִּם יֵשׁוּעַ וְקַדְמִיאֵל בָּנִי חֲשַׁבְנְיָה שֵׁרֵבְיָה הוֹדִיָּה שְׁבַנְיָה פְתַחְיָה קוּמוּ בָּרֲכוּ אֶת־יְהֹוָה אֱלֹהֵיכֶם מִן־הָעוֹלָם עַד־הָעוֹלָם וִיבָרֲכוּ שֵׁם כְּבוֹדֶךָ וּמְרוֹמַם עַל־כָּל־בְּרָכָה וּתְהִלָּה׃

6 "You alone are *Hashem*. You made the heavens, the highest heavens, and all their host, the earth and everything upon it, the seas and everything in them. You keep them all alive, and the host of heaven prostrate themselves before You.

ו אַתָּה־הוּא יְהֹוָה לְבַדֶּךָ אֵת [אַתָּה] עָשִׂיתָ אֶת־הַשָּׁמַיִם שְׁמֵי הַשָּׁמַיִם וְכָל־צְבָאָם הָאָרֶץ וְכָל־אֲשֶׁר עָלֶיהָ הַיַּמִּים וְכָל־אֲשֶׁר בָּהֶם וְאַתָּה מְחַיֶּה אֶת־כֻּלָּם וּצְבָא הַשָּׁמַיִם לְךָ מִשְׁתַּחֲוִים׃

7 You are *Hashem*, who chose *Avram*, who brought him out of Ur of the Chaldeans and changed his name to *Avraham*.

ז אַתָּה־הוּא יְהֹוָה הָאֱלֹהִים אֲשֶׁר בָּחַרְתָּ בְּאַבְרָם וְהוֹצֵאתוֹ מֵאוּר כַּשְׂדִּים וְשַׂמְתָּ שְּׁמוֹ אַבְרָהָם׃

8 Finding his heart true to You, You made a covenant with him to give the land of the Canaanite, the Hittite, the Amorite, the Perizzite, the Jebusite, and the Girgashite – to give it to his descendants. And You kept Your word, for You are righteous.

ח וּמָצָאתָ אֶת־לְבָבוֹ נֶאֱמָן לְפָנֶיךָ וְכָרוֹת עִמּוֹ הַבְּרִית לָתֵת אֶת־אֶרֶץ הַכְּנַעֲנִי הַחִתִּי הָאֱמֹרִי וְהַפְּרִזִּי וְהַיְבוּסִי וְהַגִּרְגָּשִׁי לָתֵת לְזַרְעוֹ וַתָּקֶם אֶת־דְּבָרֶיךָ כִּי צַדִּיק אָתָּה׃

9 You took note of our fathers' affliction in Egypt, and heard their cry at the Sea of Reeds.

ט וַתֵּרֶא אֶת־עֳנִי אֲבֹתֵינוּ בְּמִצְרָיִם וְאֶת־זַעֲקָתָם שָׁמַעְתָּ עַל־יַם־סוּף׃

10 You performed signs and wonders against Pharaoh, all his servants, and all the people of his land, for You knew that they acted presumptuously toward them. You made a name for Yourself that endures to this day.

י וַתִּתֵּן אֹתֹת וּמֹפְתִים בְּפַרְעֹה וּבְכָל־עֲבָדָיו וּבְכָל־עַם אַרְצוֹ כִּי יָדַעְתָּ כִּי הֵזִידוּ עֲלֵיהֶם וַתַּעַשׂ־לְךָ שֵׁם כְּהַיּוֹם הַזֶּה׃

11 You split the sea before them; they passed through the sea on dry land, but You threw their pursuers into the depths, like a stone into the raging waters.

יא וְהַיָּם בָּקַעְתָּ לִפְנֵיהֶם וַיַּעַבְרוּ בְתוֹךְ־הַיָּם בַּיַּבָּשָׁה וְאֶת־רֹדְפֵיהֶם הִשְׁלַכְתָּ בִמְצוֹלֹת כְּמוֹ־אֶבֶן בְּמַיִם עַזִּים׃

12 "You led them by day with a pillar of cloud, and by night with a pillar of fire, to give them light in the way they were to go.

יב וּבְעַמּוּד עָנָן הִנְחִיתָם יוֹמָם וּבְעַמּוּד אֵשׁ לַיְלָה לְהָאִיר לָהֶם אֶת־הַדֶּרֶךְ אֲשֶׁר יֵלְכוּ־בָהּ׃

13 You came down on *Har Sinai* and spoke to them from heaven; You gave them right rules and true teachings, good laws and commandments.

יג וְעַל הַר־סִינַי יָרַדְתָּ וְדַבֵּר עִמָּהֶם מִשָּׁמָיִם וַתִּתֵּן לָהֶם מִשְׁפָּטִים יְשָׁרִים וְתוֹרוֹת אֱמֶת חֻקִּים וּמִצְוֺת טוֹבִים׃

1968

Nechemya/Nehemiah
Chapter 9

נחמיה
פרק ט

14 You made known to them Your holy *Shabbat*, and You ordained for them laws, commandments and Teaching, through *Moshe* Your servant.

יד וְאֶת־שַׁבַּת קָדְשְׁךָ הוֹדַעְתָּ לָהֶם וּמִצְווֹת וְחֻקִּים וְתוֹרָה צִוִּיתָ לָהֶם בְּיַד מֹשֶׁה עַבְדֶּךָ׃

15 You gave them bread from heaven when they were hungry, and produced water from a rock when they were thirsty. You told them to go and possess the land that You swore to give them.

טו וְלֶחֶם מִשָּׁמַיִם נָתַתָּה לָהֶם לִרְעָבָם וּמַיִם מִסֶּלַע הוֹצֵאתָ לָהֶם לִצְמָאָם וַתֹּאמֶר לָהֶם לָבוֹא לָרֶשֶׁת אֶת־הָאָרֶץ אֲשֶׁר־נָשָׂאתָ אֶת־יָדְךָ לָתֵת לָהֶם׃

16 But they – our fathers – acted presumptuously; they stiffened their necks and did not obey Your commandments.

טז וְהֵם וַאֲבֹתֵינוּ הֵזִידוּ וַיַּקְשׁוּ אֶת־עָרְפָּם וְלֹא שָׁמְעוּ אֶל־מִצְוֺתֶיךָ׃

17 Refusing to obey, unmindful of Your wonders that You did for them, they stiffened their necks, and in their defiance resolved to return to their slavery. But You, being a forgiving *Hashem*, gracious and compassionate, long-suffering and abounding in faithfulness, did not abandon them.

יז וַיְמָאֲנוּ לִשְׁמֹעַ וְלֹא־זָכְרוּ נִפְלְאֹתֶיךָ אֲשֶׁר עָשִׂיתָ עִמָּהֶם וַיַּקְשׁוּ אֶת־עָרְפָּם וַיִּתְּנוּ־רֹאשׁ לָשׁוּב לְעַבְדֻתָם בְּמִרְיָם וְאַתָּה אֱלוֹהַּ סְלִיחוֹת חַנּוּן וְרַחוּם אֶרֶךְ־אַפַּיִם וְרַב־וָחֶסֶד [חֶסֶד] וְלֹא עֲזַבְתָּם׃

18 Even though they made themselves a molten calf and said, 'This is your God who brought you out of Egypt,' thus committing great impieties,

יח אַף כִּי־עָשׂוּ לָהֶם עֵגֶל מַסֵּכָה וַיֹּאמְרוּ זֶה אֱלֹהֶיךָ אֲשֶׁר הֶעֶלְךָ מִמִּצְרָיִם וַיַּעֲשׂוּ נֶאָצוֹת גְּדֹלוֹת׃

19 You, in Your abundant compassion, did not abandon them in the wilderness. The pillar of cloud did not depart from them to lead them on the way by day, nor the pillar of fire by night to give them light in the way they were to go.

יט וְאַתָּה בְּרַחֲמֶיךָ הָרַבִּים לֹא עֲזַבְתָּם בַּמִּדְבָּר אֶת־עַמּוּד הֶעָנָן לֹא־סָר מֵעֲלֵיהֶם בְּיוֹמָם לְהַנְחֹתָם בְּהַדֶּרֶךְ וְאֶת־עַמּוּד הָאֵשׁ בְּלַיְלָה לְהָאִיר לָהֶם וְאֶת־הַדֶּרֶךְ אֲשֶׁר יֵלְכוּ־בָהּ׃

20 You endowed them with Your good spirit to instruct them. You did not withhold Your manna from their mouth; You gave them water when they were thirsty.

כ וְרוּחֲךָ הַטּוֹבָה נָתַתָּ לְהַשְׂכִּילָם וּמַנְךָ לֹא־מָנַעְתָּ מִפִּיהֶם וּמַיִם נָתַתָּה לָהֶם לִצְמָאָם׃

21 Forty years You sustained them in the wilderness so that they lacked nothing; their clothes did not wear out, and their feet did not swell.

כא וְאַרְבָּעִים שָׁנָה כִּלְכַּלְתָּם בַּמִּדְבָּר לֹא חָסֵרוּ שַׂלְמֹתֵיהֶם לֹא בָלוּ וְרַגְלֵיהֶם לֹא בָצֵקוּ׃

22 "You gave them kingdoms and peoples, and allotted them territory. They took possession of the land of Sihon, the land of the king of Heshbon, and the land of Og, king of Bashan.

כב וַתִּתֵּן לָהֶם מַמְלָכוֹת וַעֲמָמִים וַתַּחְלְקֵם לְפֵאָה וַיִּירְשׁוּ אֶת־אֶרֶץ סִיחוֹן וְאֶת־אֶרֶץ מֶלֶךְ חֶשְׁבּוֹן וְאֶת־אֶרֶץ עוֹג מֶלֶךְ־הַבָּשָׁן׃

23 You made their children as numerous as the stars of heaven, and brought them to the land which You told their fathers to go and possess.

כג וּבְנֵיהֶם הִרְבִּיתָ כְּכֹכְבֵי הַשָּׁמָיִם וַתְּבִיאֵם אֶל־הָאָרֶץ אֲשֶׁר־אָמַרְתָּ לַאֲבֹתֵיהֶם לָבוֹא לָרָשֶׁת׃

24 The sons came and took possession of the land: You subdued the Canaanite inhabitants of the land before them; You delivered them into their power, both their kings and the peoples of the land, to do with them as they pleased.

כד וַיָּבֹאוּ הַבָּנִים וַיִּירְשׁוּ אֶת־הָאָרֶץ וַתַּכְנַע לִפְנֵיהֶם אֶת־יֹשְׁבֵי הָאָרֶץ הַכְּנַעֲנִים וַתִּתְּנֵם בְּיָדָם וְאֶת־מַלְכֵיהֶם וְאֶת־עַמְמֵי הָאָרֶץ לַעֲשׂוֹת בָּהֶם כִּרְצוֹנָם׃

Nechemya/Nehemiah — Chapter 9 / נחמיה פרק ט

25 They captured fortified cities and rich lands; they took possession of houses filled with every good thing, of hewn cisterns, vineyards, olive trees, and fruit trees in abundance. They ate, they were filled, they grew fat; they luxuriated in Your great bounty.

כה וַיִּלְכְּדוּ עָרִים בְּצֻרוֹת וַאֲדָמָה שְׁמֵנָה וַיִּירְשׁוּ בָּתִּים מְלֵאִים־כָּל־טוּב בֹּרוֹת חֲצוּבִים כְּרָמִים וְזֵיתִים וְעֵץ מַאֲכָל לָרֹב וַיֹּאכְלוּ וַיִּשְׂבְּעוּ וַיַּשְׁמִינוּ וַיִּתְעַדְּנוּ בְּטוּבְךָ הַגָּדוֹל:

26 Then, defying You, they rebelled; they cast Your Teaching behind their back. They killed Your *Neviim* who admonished them to turn them back to You; they committed great impieties.

כו וַיַּמְרוּ וַיִּמְרְדוּ בָּךְ וַיַּשְׁלִכוּ אֶת־תּוֹרָתְךָ אַחֲרֵי גַוָּם וְאֶת־נְבִיאֶיךָ הָרָגוּ אֲשֶׁר־הֵעִידוּ בָם לַהֲשִׁיבָם אֵלֶיךָ וַיַּעֲשׂוּ נֶאָצוֹת גְּדוֹלֹת:

27 "You delivered them into the power of their adversaries who oppressed them. In their time of trouble they cried to You; You in heaven heard them, and in Your abundant compassion gave them saviors who saved them from the power of their adversaries.

כז וַתִּתְּנֵם בְּיַד צָרֵיהֶם וַיָּצֵרוּ לָהֶם וּבְעֵת צָרָתָם יִצְעֲקוּ אֵלֶיךָ וְאַתָּה מִשָּׁמַיִם תִּשְׁמָע וּכְרַחֲמֶיךָ הָרַבִּים תִּתֵּן לָהֶם מוֹשִׁיעִים וְיוֹשִׁיעוּם מִיַּד צָרֵיהֶם:

28 But when they had relief, they again did what was evil in Your sight, so You abandoned them to the power of their enemies, who subjugated them. Again they cried to You, and You in heaven heard and rescued them in Your compassion, time after time.

כח וּכְנוֹחַ לָהֶם יָשׁוּבוּ לַעֲשׂוֹת רַע לְפָנֶיךָ וַתַּעַזְבֵם בְּיַד אֹיְבֵיהֶם וַיִּרְדּוּ בָהֶם וַיָּשׁוּבוּ וַיִּזְעָקוּךָ וְאַתָּה מִשָּׁמַיִם תִּשְׁמַע וְתַצִּילֵם כְּרַחֲמֶיךָ רַבּוֹת עִתִּים:

29 You admonished them in order to turn them back to Your Teaching, but they acted presumptuously and disobeyed Your commandments, and sinned against Your rules, by following which a man shall live. They turned a defiant shoulder, stiffened their neck, and would not obey.

כט וַתָּעַד בָּהֶם לַהֲשִׁיבָם אֶל־תּוֹרָתֶךָ וְהֵמָּה הֵזִידוּ וְלֹא־שָׁמְעוּ לְמִצְוֹתֶיךָ וּבְמִשְׁפָּטֶיךָ חָטְאוּ־בָם אֲשֶׁר־יַעֲשֶׂה אָדָם וְחָיָה בָהֶם וַיִּתְּנוּ כָתֵף סוֹרֶרֶת וְעָרְפָּם הִקְשׁוּ וְלֹא שָׁמֵעוּ:

30 You bore with them for many years, admonished them by Your spirit through Your *Neviim*, but they would not give ear, so You delivered them into the power of the peoples of the lands.

ל וַתִּמְשֹׁךְ עֲלֵיהֶם שָׁנִים רַבּוֹת וַתָּעַד בָּם בְּרוּחֲךָ בְּיַד־נְבִיאֶיךָ וְלֹא הֶאֱזִינוּ וַתִּתְּנֵם בְּיַד עַמֵּי הָאֲרָצֹת:

31 Still, in Your great compassion You did not make an end of them or abandon them, for You are a gracious and compassionate *Hashem*.

לא וּבְרַחֲמֶיךָ הָרַבִּים לֹא־עֲשִׂיתָם כָּלָה וְלֹא עֲזַבְתָּם כִּי אֵל־חַנּוּן וְרַחוּם אָתָּה:

32 "And now, our God, great, mighty, and awesome *Hashem*, who stays faithful to His covenant, do not treat lightly all the suffering that has overtaken us – our kings, our officers, our *Kohanim*, our *Neviim*, our fathers, and all Your people – from the time of the Assyrian kings to this day.

לב וְעַתָּה אֱלֹהֵינוּ הָאֵל הַגָּדוֹל הַגִּבּוֹר וְהַנּוֹרָא שׁוֹמֵר הַבְּרִית וְהַחֶסֶד אַל־יִמְעַט לְפָנֶיךָ אֵת כָּל־הַתְּלָאָה אֲשֶׁר־מְצָאַתְנוּ לִמְלָכֵינוּ לְשָׂרֵינוּ וּלְכֹהֲנֵינוּ וְלִנְבִיאֵנוּ וְלַאֲבֹתֵינוּ וּלְכָל־עַמֶּךָ מִימֵי מַלְכֵי אַשּׁוּר עַד הַיּוֹם הַזֶּה:

33 Surely You are in the right with respect to all that has come upon us, for You have acted faithfully, and we have been wicked.

לג וְאַתָּה צַדִּיק עַל כָּל־הַבָּא עָלֵינוּ כִּי־אֱמֶת עָשִׂיתָ וַאֲנַחְנוּ הִרְשָׁעְנוּ:

Nechemya/Nehemiah
Chapter 10

34 Our kings, officers, *Kohanim*, and fathers did not follow Your Teaching, and did not listen to Your commandments or to the warnings that You gave them.

35 When they had their own kings and enjoyed the good that You lavished upon them, and the broad and rich land that You put at their disposal, they would not serve You, and did not turn from their wicked deeds.

36 Today we are slaves, and the land that You gave our fathers to enjoy its fruit and bounty – here we are slaves on it!

> hi-NAY a-NAKH-nu ha-YOM a-va-DEEM v'-ha-A-retz a-sher na-TA-tah la-a-vo-TAY-nu le-e-KHOL et pir-YAH v'et tu-VAH hi-NAY a-NAKH-nu a-va-DEEM a-LE-ha

37 On account of our sins it yields its abundant crops to kings whom You have set over us. They rule over our bodies and our beasts as they please, and we are in great distress.

10 **1** "In view of all this, we make this pledge and put it in writing; and on the sealed copy [are subscribed] our officials, our *Leviim*, and our *Kohanim*.

2 "On the sealed copy [are subscribed]: *Nechemya* the Tirshatha son of *Chachalya* and *Tzidkiyahu*,

3 *Seraya*, *Azarya*, *Yirmiyahu*,

4 *Pashhur*, *Amariah*, *Malchijah*,

5 *Hattush*, *Shebaniah*, *Malluch*,

6 *Harim*, *Meremoth*, *Ovadya*,

7 *Daniel*, *Ginnethon*, *Baruch*,

8 *Meshullam*, *Aviya*, *Mijamin*,

9 *Maaziah*, *Bilgai*, *Shemaya*; these are the *Kohanim*.

9:36 Here we are slaves on it This chapter speaks of *Hashem*'s original promise to *Avraham* to grant the Land of Israel to his descendants as an inheritance (verse 8). It then continues with an overview of history, including the exodus from Egypt, the years in the desert, the acquisition of *Eretz Yisrael* and the many trials and tribulations that were the plight of the Israelites for many centuries. One might assume that *Hashem* gave the land to the People of Israel so that they could rest in it at ease, and yet this verse states that in fact "we are slaves on it." The Land of Israel is not just a homeland or national territory. It is a tool, a vehicle through which the people can fulfill their ultimate purpose: To serve God and serve as a light unto the nations (Isaiah 42:6) – a mission requiring much hard work.

Nechemya/Nehemiah
Chapter 10

10 "And the *Leviim*: *Yeshua* son of Azaniah, Binnui of the sons of Henadad, and *Kadmiel*.

11 And their brothers: Shebaniah, Hodiah, Kelita, Pelaiah, Hanan,

12 Mica, Rehob, Hashabiah,

13 Zaccur, Sherebiah, Shebaniah,

14 Hodiah, Bani, and Beninu.

15 "The heads of the people: Parosh, Pahath-moab, Elam, Zattu, Bani,

16 Bunni, Azgad, Bebai,

17 *Adoniyahu*, Bigvai, Adin,

18 Ater, *Chizkiyahu*, Azzur,

19 Hodiah, Hashum, Bezai,

20 Hariph, *Anatot*, Nebai,

21 Magpiash, Meshullam, Hezir,

22 Meshezabel, *Tzadok*, Jaddua,

23 Pelatiah, Hanan, Anaiah,

24 *Hoshea*, *Chananya*, Hasshub,

25 Hallohesh, Pilha, Shobek,

26 Rehum, Hashabnah, Maaseiah,

27 and Ahiah, Hanan, Anan,

28 Malluch, Harim, Baanah.

29 "And the rest of the people, the *Kohanim*, the *Leviim*, the gatekeepers, the singers, the temple servants, and all who separated themselves from the peoples of the lands to [follow] the Teaching of *Hashem*, their wives, sons and daughters, all who know enough to understand,

30 join with their noble brothers, and take an oath with sanctions to follow the Teaching of *Hashem*, given through *Moshe* the servant of *Hashem*, and to observe carefully all the commandments of *Hashem* our Lord, His rules and laws.

31 "Namely: We will not give our daughters in marriage to the peoples of the land, or take their daughters for our sons.

נחמיה
פרק י

י וְהַלְוִיִּם יֵשׁוּעַ בֶּן־אֲזַנְיָה בִּנּוּי מִבְּנֵי חֵנָדָד קַדְמִיאֵל׃

יא וַאֲחֵיהֶם שְׁבַנְיָה הוֹדִיָּה קְלִיטָא פְּלָאיָה חָנָן׃

יב מִיכָא רְחוֹב חֲשַׁבְיָה׃

יג זַכּוּר שֵׁרֵבְיָה שְׁבַנְיָה׃

יד הוֹדִיָּה בָנִי בְּנִינוּ׃

טו רָאשֵׁי הָעָם פַּרְעֹשׁ פַּחַת מוֹאָב עֵילָם זַתּוּא בָּנִי׃

טז בֻּנִּי עַזְגָּד בֵּבָי׃

יז אֲדֹנִיָּה בִגְוַי עָדִין׃

יח אָטֵר חִזְקִיָּה עַזּוּר׃

יט הוֹדִיָּה חָשֻׁם בֵּצָי׃

כ חָרִיף עֲנָתוֹת נוֹבִי [נֵיבָי׃]

כא מַגְפִּיעָשׁ מְשֻׁלָּם חֵזִיר׃

כב מְשֵׁיזַבְאֵל צָדוֹק יַדּוּעַ׃

כג פְּלַטְיָה חָנָן עֲנָיָה׃

כד הוֹשֵׁעַ חֲנַנְיָה חַשּׁוּב׃

כה הַלּוֹחֵשׁ פִּלְחָא שׁוֹבֵק׃

כו רְחוּם חֲשַׁבְנָה מַעֲשֵׂיָה׃

כז וַאֲחִיָּה חָנָן עָנָן׃

כח מַלּוּךְ חָרִם בַּעֲנָה׃

כט וּשְׁאָר הָעָם הַכֹּהֲנִים הַלְוִיִּם הַשּׁוֹעֲרִים הַמְשֹׁרְרִים הַנְּתִינִים וְכָל־הַנִּבְדָּל מֵעַמֵּי הָאֲרָצוֹת אֶל־תּוֹרַת הָאֱלֹהִים נְשֵׁיהֶם בְּנֵיהֶם וּבְנֹתֵיהֶם כֹּל יוֹדֵעַ מֵבִין׃

ל מַחֲזִיקִים עַל־אֲחֵיהֶם אַדִּירֵיהֶם וּבָאִים בְּאָלָה וּבִשְׁבוּעָה לָלֶכֶת בְּתוֹרַת הָאֱלֹהִים אֲשֶׁר נִתְּנָה בְּיַד מֹשֶׁה עֶבֶד־הָאֱלֹהִים וְלִשְׁמוֹר וְלַעֲשׂוֹת אֶת־כָּל־מִצְוֺת יְהֹוָה אֲדֹנֵינוּ וּמִשְׁפָּטָיו וְחֻקָּיו׃

לא וַאֲשֶׁר לֹא־נִתֵּן בְּנֹתֵינוּ לְעַמֵּי הָאָרֶץ וְאֶת־בְּנֹתֵיהֶם לֹא נִקַּח לְבָנֵינוּ׃

Nechemya/Nehemiah
Chapter 10

נחמיה
פרק י

32 "The peoples of the land who bring their wares and all sorts of foodstuff for sale on the *Shabbat* day – we will not buy from them on the *Shabbat* or a holy day. "We will forgo [the produce of] the seventh year, and every outstanding debt.

לב וְעַמֵּי הָאָרֶץ הַמְבִיאִים אֶת־הַמַּקָּחוֹת וְכָל־שֶׁבֶר בְּיוֹם הַשַּׁבָּת לִמְכּוֹר לֹא־נִקַּח מֵהֶם בַּשַּׁבָּת וּבְיוֹם קֹדֶשׁ וְנִטֹּשׁ אֶת־הַשָּׁנָה הַשְּׁבִיעִית וּמַשָּׁא כָל־יָד:

33 "We have laid upon ourselves obligations: To charge ourselves one-third of a *shekel* yearly for the service of the House of our God –

לג וְהֶעֱמַדְנוּ עָלֵינוּ מִצְוֹת לָתֵת עָלֵינוּ שְׁלִשִׁית הַשֶּׁקֶל בַּשָּׁנָה לַעֲבֹדַת בֵּית אֱלֹהֵינוּ:

34 for the rows of bread, for the regular meal offering and for the regular burnt offering, [for those of the] *Shabbatot*, new moons, festivals, for consecrations, for sin offerings to atone for *Yisrael*, and for all the work in the House of our God.

לד לְלֶחֶם הַמַּעֲרֶכֶת וּמִנְחַת הַתָּמִיד וּלְעוֹלַת הַתָּמִיד הַשַּׁבָּתוֹת הֶחֳדָשִׁים לַמּוֹעֲדִים וְלַקֳּדָשִׁים וְלַחַטָּאוֹת לְכַפֵּר עַל־יִשְׂרָאֵל וְכֹל מְלֶאכֶת בֵּית־אֱלֹהֵינוּ:

l'-LE-khem ha-ma-a-RE-khet u-min-KHAT ha-ta-MEED ul-o-LAT ha-ta-MEED ha-sha-ba-TOT he-kho-da-SHEEM la-mo-a-DEEM v'-la-ko-da-SHEEM v'-la-kha-TOT l'-kha-PAYR al yis-ra-AYL v'-KHOL m'-LE-khet bayt e-lo-HAY-nu

35 "We have cast lots [among] the *Kohanim*, the *Leviim*, and the people, to bring the wood offering to the House of our God by clans annually at set times in order to provide fuel for the *Mizbayach* of *Hashem* our God, as is written in the Teaching.

לה וְהַגּוֹרָלוֹת הִפַּלְנוּ עַל־קֻרְבַּן הָעֵצִים הַכֹּהֲנִים הַלְוִיִּם וְהָעָם לְהָבִיא לְבֵית אֱלֹהֵינוּ לְבֵית־אֲבֹתֵינוּ לְעִתִּים מְזֻמָּנִים שָׁנָה בְשָׁנָה לְבַעֵר עַל־מִזְבַּח יְהֹוָה אֱלֹהֵינוּ כַּכָּתוּב בַּתּוֹרָה:

36 "And [we undertake] to bring to the House of *Hashem* annually the first fruits of our soil, and of every fruit of every tree;

לו וּלְהָבִיא אֶת־בִּכּוּרֵי אַדְמָתֵנוּ וּבִכּוּרֵי כָּל־פְּרִי כָל־עֵץ שָׁנָה בְשָׁנָה לְבֵית יְהֹוָה:

37 also, the first-born of our sons and our beasts, as is written in the Teaching; and to bring the firstlings of our cattle and flocks to the House of our God for the *Kohanim* who minister in the House of our God.

לז וְאֶת־בְּכֹרוֹת בָּנֵינוּ וּבְהֶמְתֵּינוּ כַּכָּתוּב בַּתּוֹרָה וְאֶת־בְּכוֹרֵי בְקָרֵינוּ וְצֹאנֵינוּ לְהָבִיא לְבֵית אֱלֹהֵינוּ לַכֹּהֲנִים הַמְשָׁרְתִים בְּבֵית אֱלֹהֵינוּ:

38 "We will bring to the storerooms of the House of our God the first part of our dough, and our gifts [of grain], and of the fruit of every tree, wine and oil for the *Kohanim*, and the tithes of our land for the *Leviim* – the *Leviim* who collect the tithe in all our towns subject to royal service.

לח וְאֶת־רֵאשִׁית עֲרִיסֹתֵינוּ וּתְרוּמֹתֵינוּ וּפְרִי כָל־עֵץ תִּירוֹשׁ וְיִצְהָר נָבִיא לַכֹּהֲנִים אֶל־לִשְׁכוֹת בֵּית־אֱלֹהֵינוּ וּמַעְשַׂר אַדְמָתֵנוּ לַלְוִיִּם וְהֵם הַלְוִיִּם הַמְעַשְּׂרִים בְּכֹל עָרֵי עֲבֹדָתֵנוּ:

קרבן
קרוב

10:34 For the regular meal offering The last ten verses of this chapter focus on the pledge to revive the many sacrificial obligations. The word for 'sacrifice' or 'offering,' *korban* (קרבן), indicates its true purpose. *Korban* comes from the word *karov* (קרוב) which means 'close.' The *korban* facilitates a close relationship between man and God. Although the *korbanot* can only be brought in *Yerushalayim*, the core idea behind them is timeless and universal, intended for all humanity. In the absence of the *Beit Hamikdash* and its sacrifices, we use prayer as a means of coming close to our Father in Heaven. As the verse is *Hoshea* says "Instead of bulls we will pay [the offering of] our lips" (Hosea 14:3).

Nechemya/Nehemiah
Chapter 11

39 An Aaronite *Kohen* must be with the *Leviim* when they collect the tithe, and the *Leviim* must bring up a tithe of the tithe to the House of our God, to the storerooms of the treasury.

40 For it is to the storerooms that the Israelites and the *Leviim* must bring the gifts of grain, wine, and oil. The equipment of the sanctuary and of the ministering *Kohanim* and the gatekeepers and the singers is also there. "We will not neglect the House of our God."

11

1 The officers of the people settled in *Yerushalayim*; the rest of the people cast lots for one out of ten to come and settle in the holy city of *Yerushalayim*, and the other nine-tenths to stay in the towns.

va-yay-sh'-VU sa-RAY ha-AM bee-ru-sha-LA-im ush-AR ha-AM hi-PEE-lu go-ra-LOT l'-ha-VEE e-KHAD min ha-a-sa-RAH la-SHE-vet bee-ru-sha-LA-im EER ha-KO-desh v'-TAY-sha ha-ya-DOT be-a-REEM

2 The people gave their blessing to all the men who willingly settled in *Yerushalayim*.

3 These are the heads of the province who lived in *Yerushalayim* – in the countryside of *Yehuda*, the people lived in their towns, each on his own property, Israelites, *Kohanim*, *Leviim*, temple servants, and the sons of *Shlomo*'s servants,

4 while in *Yerushalayim* some of the Judahites and some of the Benjaminites lived: Of the Judahites: Athaiah son of *Uzziyahu* son of *Zecharya* son of Amariah son of Shephatiah son of *Mehalalel*, of the clan of Periz,

5 and Maaseiah son of *Baruch* son of Col-hozeh son of Hazaiah son of Adaiah son of Joiarib son of *Zecharya* son of the Shilohite.

11:1 In the holy city of *Yerushalayim* In addition to *Yerushalayim*, Jews recognize three other holy cities, *Tzfat* (Safed), *Teveria* (Tiberias), and *Chevron* (Hebron). The idea of four holy cities originated after the Ottoman conquest of Israel, and corresponds to the four centers of Jewish life at the time. Each city is holy for a different reason, and each corresponds to one of the four elements from which the ancients believed the world was created. *Chevron* is the burial site of the Patriarchs and Matriarchs, symbolic of earth. *Teveria*, where the Jerusalem Talmud was compiled, resides by the shores of the *Kinneret* and corresponds to water. *Tzfat*, located high up on the mountains, is the renowned center of mystical Judaism, the *Kabbalah*, and is therefore associated with air. And *Yerushalayim*, the site of the Temples which contained the altars and the *menorah* lamp, is associated with fire. In this way, the four holy cities of Israel contain all the elements for everything in heaven and earth.

Nechemya/Nehemiah
Chapter 11

נחמיה
פרק יא

6 All the clan of Periz who were living in *Yerushalayim* – 468 valorous men.

א כָּל־בְּנֵי־פֶרֶץ הַיֹּשְׁבִים בִּירוּשָׁלָ͏ִם אַרְבַּע מֵאוֹת שִׁשִּׁים וּשְׁמֹנָה אַנְשֵׁי־חָיִל:

7 These are the Binyaminites: Sallu son of Meshullam son of Joed son of Pedaiah son of Kolaiah son of Maaseiah son of *Itiel* son of Jesaiah.

ז וְאֵלֶּה בְּנֵי בִנְיָמִן סַלֻּא בֶּן־מְשֻׁלָּם בֶּן־יוֹעֵד בֶּן־פְּדָיָה בֶּן־קוֹלָיָה בֶּן־מַעֲשֵׂיָה בֶּן־אִיתִיאֵל בֶּן־יְשַׁעְיָה:

8 After him, Gabbai and Sallai – 928.

ח וְאַחֲרָיו גַּבַּי סַלָּי תְּשַׁע מֵאוֹת עֶשְׂרִים וּשְׁמֹנָה:

9 *Yoel* son of Zichri was the official in charge of them, and *Yehuda* son of Hassenuah was the second-in-command of the city.

ט וְיוֹאֵל בֶּן־זִכְרִי פָּקִיד עֲלֵיהֶם וִיהוּדָה בֶן־הַסְּנוּאָה עַל־הָעִיר מִשְׁנֶה:

10 Of the *Kohanim*: Jedaiah son of Joiarib, Jachin,

י מִן־הַכֹּהֲנִים יְדַעְיָה בֶן־יוֹיָרִיב יָכִין:

11 *Seraya* son of *Chilkiyahu* son of Meshullam son of *Tzadok* son of Meraioth son of *Achituv*, chief officer of the House of *Hashem*,

יא שְׂרָיָה בֶן־חִלְקִיָּה בֶּן־מְשֻׁלָּם בֶּן־צָדוֹק בֶּן־מְרָיוֹת בֶּן־אֲחִיטוּב נְגִד בֵּית הָאֱלֹהִים:

12 and their brothers, who did the work of the House – 822; and Adaiah son of Jeroham son of Pelaliah son of Amzi son of *Zecharya* son of Pashhur son of Malchijah,

יב וַאֲחֵיהֶם עֹשֵׂי הַמְּלָאכָה לַבַּיִת שְׁמֹנֶה מֵאוֹת עֶשְׂרִים וּשְׁנָיִם וַעֲדָיָה בֶּן־יְרֹחָם בֶּן־פְּלַלְיָה בֶּן־אַמְצִי בֶן־זְכַרְיָה בֶּן־פַּשְׁחוּר בֶּן־מַלְכִּיָּה:

13 and his brothers, heads of clans – 242; and Amashsai son of Azarel son of Ahzai son of Meshillemoth son of Immer,

יג וְאֶחָיו רָאשִׁים לְאָבוֹת מָאתַיִם אַרְבָּעִים וּשְׁנָיִם וַעֲמַשְׁסַי בֶּן־עֲזַרְאֵל בֶּן־אַחְזַי בֶּן־מְשִׁלֵּמוֹת בֶּן־אִמֵּר:

14 and their brothers, valorous warriors – 128. Zabdiel son of Haggedolim was the official in charge of them.

יד וַאֲחֵיהֶם גִּבּוֹרֵי חַיִל מֵאָה עֶשְׂרִים וּשְׁמֹנָה וּפָקִיד עֲלֵיהֶם זַבְדִּיאֵל בֶּן־הַגְּדוֹלִים:

15 Of the *Leviim*: *Shemaya* son of Hasshub son of Azrikam son of Hashabiah son of Bunni,

טו וּמִן־הַלְוִיִּם שְׁמַעְיָה בֶן־חַשּׁוּב בֶּן־עַזְרִיקָם בֶּן־חֲשַׁבְיָה בֶּן־בּוּנִּי:

16 and Shabbethai and *Yozavad* of the heads of the *Leviim* were in charge of the external work of the House of *Hashem*.

טז וְשַׁבְּתַי וְיוֹזָבָד עַל־הַמְּלָאכָה הַחִיצֹנָה לְבֵית הָאֱלֹהִים מֵרָאשֵׁי הַלְוִיִּם:

17 Mattaniah son of *Micha* son of Zabdi son of *Asaf* was the head; at prayer, he would lead off with praise; and Bakbukiah, one of his brothers, was his second-in-command; and Abda son of Shammua son of Galal son of *Yedutun*.

יז וּמַתַּנְיָה בֶן־מִיכָה בֶּן־זַבְדִּי בֶן־אָסָף רֹאשׁ הַתְּחִלָּה יְהוֹדֶה לַתְּפִלָּה וּבַקְבֻּקְיָה מִשְׁנֶה מֵאֶחָיו וְעַבְדָּא בֶּן־שַׁמּוּעַ בֶּן־גָּלָל בֶּן־יְדִיתוּן [יְדוּתוּן]:

18 All the *Leviim* in the holy city – 284.

יח כָּל־הַלְוִיִּם בְּעִיר הַקֹּדֶשׁ מָאתַיִם שְׁמֹנִים וְאַרְבָּעָה:

19 And the gatekeepers: Akkub, Talmon, and their brothers, who stood watch at the gates – 172.

יט וְהַשּׁוֹעֲרִים עַקּוּב טַלְמוֹן וַאֲחֵיהֶם הַשֹּׁמְרִים בַּשְּׁעָרִים מֵאָה שִׁבְעִים וּשְׁנָיִם:

20 And the rest of the Israelites, the *Kohanim*, and the *Leviim* in all the towns of *Yehuda* [lived] each on his estate.

כ וּשְׁאָר יִשְׂרָאֵל הַכֹּהֲנִים הַלְוִיִּם בְּכָל־עָרֵי יְהוּדָה אִישׁ בְּנַחֲלָתוֹ:

Nechemya/Nehemiah
Chapter 12

נחמיה
פרק יב

21 The temple servants lived on the Ophel; Ziha and Gishpa were in charge of the temple servants.

כא וְהַנְּתִינִים יֹשְׁבִים בָּעֹפֶל וְצִיחָא וְגִשְׁפָּא עַל־הַנְּתִינִים׃

22 The overseer of the *Leviim* in *Yerushalayim* was Uzzi son of Bani son of Hashabiah son of Mattaniah son of *Micha*, of the Asaphite singers, over the work of the House of *Hashem*.

כב וּפְקִיד הַלְוִיִּם בִּירוּשָׁלִַם עֻזִּי בֶן־בָּנִי בֶּן־חֲשַׁבְיָה בֶּן־מַתַּנְיָה בֶּן־מִיכָא מִבְּנֵי אָסָף הַמְשֹׁרְרִים לְנֶגֶד מְלֶאכֶת בֵּית־הָאֱלֹהִים׃

23 There was a royal order concerning them, a stipulation concerning the daily duties of the singers.

כג כִּי־מִצְוַת הַמֶּלֶךְ עֲלֵיהֶם וַאֲמָנָה עַל־הַמְשֹׁרְרִים דְּבַר־יוֹם בְּיוֹמוֹ׃

24 Petahiah son of Meshezabel, of the sons of *Zerach* son of *Yehuda*, advised the king concerning all the affairs of the people.

כד וּפְתַחְיָה בֶּן־מְשֵׁיזַבְאֵל מִבְּנֵי־זֶרַח בֶּן־יְהוּדָה לְיַד הַמֶּלֶךְ לְכָל־דָּבָר לָעָם׃

25 As concerns the villages with their fields: Some of the Judahites lived in *Kiryat Arba* and its outlying hamlets, in Dibon and its outlying hamlets, and in Jekabzeel and its villages;

כה וְאֶל־הַחֲצֵרִים בִּשְׂדֹתָם מִבְּנֵי יְהוּדָה יָשְׁבוּ בְּקִרְיַת הָאַרְבַּע וּבְנֹתֶיהָ וּבְדִיבֹן וּבְנֹתֶיהָ וּבִיקַבְצְאֵל וַחֲצֵרֶיהָ׃

26 in *Yeshua*, in Moladah, and in Beth-pelet;

כו וּבְיֵשׁוּעַ וּבְמוֹלָדָה וּבְבֵית פָּלֶט׃

27 in Hazar-shual, in *Be'er Sheva* and its outlying hamlets;

כז וּבַחֲצַר שׁוּעָל וּבִבְאֵר שֶׁבַע וּבְנֹתֶיהָ׃

28 and in *Tziklag* and in Meconah and its outlying hamlets,

כח וּבְצִקְלַג וּבִמְכֹנָה וּבִבְנֹתֶיהָ׃

29 in En-rimmon, in *Tzora* and in *Yarmut*;

כט וּבְעֵין רִמּוֹן וּבְצָרְעָה וּבְיַרְמוּת׃

30 *Zanoach, Adulam*, and their villages; *Lachish* and its fields; *Azeika* and its outlying hamlets. They settled from *Be'er Sheva* to the Valley of Hinnom.

ל זָנֹחַ עֲדֻלָּם וְחַצְרֵיהֶם לָכִישׁ וּשְׂדֹתֶיהָ עֲזֵקָה וּבְנֹתֶיהָ וַיַּחֲנוּ מִבְּאֵר־שֶׁבַע עַד־גֵּיא־הִנֹּם׃

31 The Benjaminites: from Geba, Michmash, Aija, and *Beit El* and its outlying hamlets;

לא וּבְנֵי בִנְיָמִן מִגָּבַע מִכְמָשׂ וְעַיָּה וּבֵית־אֵל וּבְנֹתֶיהָ׃

32 *Anatot, Nov*, Ananiah,

לב עֲנָתוֹת נֹב עֲנָנְיָה׃

33 Hazor, *Rama*, Gittaim,

לג חָצוֹר רָמָה גִּתָּיִם׃

34 Hadid, Zeboim, Neballat,

לד חָדִיד צְבֹעִים נְבַלָּט׃

35 Lod, Ono, Ge-harashim.

לה לֹד וְאוֹנוֹ גֵּי הַחֲרָשִׁים׃

36 Some of the Judahite divisions of *Leviim* were [shifted] to *Binyamin*.

לו וּמִן־הַלְוִיִּם מַחְלְקוֹת יְהוּדָה לְבִנְיָמִין׃

12

1 These are the *Kohanim* and the *Leviim* who came up with *Zerubavel* son of *Shealtiel* and *Yeshua*: *Seraya, Yirmiyahu, Ezra*,

יב א וְאֵלֶּה הַכֹּהֲנִים וְהַלְוִיִּם אֲשֶׁר עָלוּ עִם־זְרֻבָּבֶל בֶּן־שְׁאַלְתִּיאֵל וְיֵשׁוּעַ שְׂרָיָה יִרְמְיָה עֶזְרָא׃

2 Amariah, Malluch, Hattush,

ב אֲמַרְיָה מַלּוּךְ חַטּוּשׁ׃

3 *Shechanya*, Rehum, Meramoth,

ג שְׁכַנְיָה רְחֻם מְרֵמֹת׃

4 *Ido*, Ginnethoi, *Aviya*,

ד עִדּוֹא גִנְּתוֹי אֲבִיָּה׃

Nechemya/Nehemiah
Chapter 12

נחמיה
פרק יב

5 Mijamin, Maadiah, Bilgah,

ה מִיָּמִין מַעַדְיָה בִּלְגָּה:

6 *Shemaya*, Joiarib, Jedaiah,

ו שְׁמַעְיָה וְיוֹיָרִיב יְדַעְיָה:

7 Sallu, Amok, *Chilkiyahu*, Jedaiah. These were the heads of the *Kohanim* and their brothers in the time of *Yeshua*.

ז סַלּוּ עָמוֹק חִלְקִיָּה יְדַעְיָה אֵלֶּה רָאשֵׁי הַכֹּהֲנִים וַאֲחֵיהֶם בִּימֵי יֵשׁוּעַ:

8 The *Leviim*: *Yeshua*, Binnui, *Kadmiel*, Sherebiah, *Yehuda*, and Mattaniah, in charge of thanksgiving songs, he and his brothers;

ח וְהַלְוִיִּם יֵשׁוּעַ בִּנּוּי קַדְמִיאֵל שֵׁרֵבְיָה יְהוּדָה מַתַּנְיָה עַל־הֻיְּדוֹת הוּא וְאֶחָיו:

9 and Bakbukiah and Unni [and] their brothers served opposite them by shifts.

ט וּבַקְבֻּקְיָה וְעֻנּוֹ [וְעֻנִּי] אֲחֵיהֶם לְנֶגְדָּם לְמִשְׁמָרוֹת:

10 *Yeshua* begot Joiakim; Joiakim begot *Elyashiv*; *Elyashiv* begot Joiada.

י וְיֵשׁוּעַ הוֹלִיד אֶת־יוֹיָקִים וְיוֹיָקִים הוֹלִיד אֶת־אֶלְיָשִׁיב וְאֶלְיָשִׁיב אֶת־יוֹיָדָע:

11 Joiada begot *Yonatan*; *Yonatan* begot Jaddua.

יא וְיוֹיָדָע הוֹלִיד אֶת־יוֹנָתָן וְיוֹנָתָן הוֹלִיד אֶת־יַדּוּעַ:

12 In the time of Joiakim, the heads of the priestly clans were: Meriaiah – of the *Seraya* clan; *Chananya* – of the *Yirmiyahu* clan;

יב וּבִימֵי יוֹיָקִים הָיוּ כֹהֲנִים רָאשֵׁי הָאָבוֹת לִשְׂרָיָה מְרָיָה לְיִרְמְיָה חֲנַנְיָה:

13 Meshullam – of the *Ezra* clan; Yehochanan – of the Amariah clan;

יג לְעֶזְרָא מְשֻׁלָּם לַאֲמַרְיָה יְהוֹחָנָן:

14 *Yonatan* – of the Melicu clan; *Yosef* – of the Shebaniah clan;

יד לִמְלוּכִי [לִמְלִיכוּ] יוֹנָתָן לִשְׁבַנְיָה יוֹסֵף:

15 Adna – of the Harim clan; Helkai – of the Meraioth clan;

טו לְחָרִם עַדְנָא לִמְרָיוֹת חֶלְקָי:

16 *Zecharya* – of the *Ido* clan; Meshullam – of the Ginnethon clan;

טז לַעֲדָיָא [לְעִדּוֹא] זְכַרְיָה לְגִנְּתוֹן מְשֻׁלָּם:

17 Zichri – of the *Aviya* clan … of the Miniamin clan; Piltai – of the Moadiah clan;

יז לַאֲבִיָּה זִכְרִי לְמִנְיָמִין לְמוֹעַדְיָה פִּלְטָי:

18 Shammua – of the Bilgah clan; Jehonathan – of the *Shemaya* clan;

יח לְבִלְגָּה שַׁמּוּעַ לִשְׁמַעְיָה יְהוֹנָתָן:

19 Mattenai – of the Joiarib clan; Uzzi – of the Jedaiah clan;

יט וּלְיוֹיָרִיב מַתְּנַי לִידַעְיָה עֻזִּי:

20 Kallai – of the Sallai clan; Ever – of the Amok clan;

כ לְסַלַּי קַלָּי לְעָמוֹק עֵבֶר:

21 Hashabiah – of the *Chilkiyahu* clan; Nethanel – of the Jedaiah clan.

כא לְחִלְקִיָּה חֲשַׁבְיָה לִידַעְיָה נְתַנְאֵל:

22 The *Leviim* and the *Kohanim* were listed by heads of clans in the days of *Elyashiv*, Joiada, *Yochanan*, and Jaddua, down to the reign of Darius the Persian.

כב הַלְוִיִּם בִּימֵי אֶלְיָשִׁיב יוֹיָדָע וְיוֹחָנָן וְיַדּוּעַ כְּתוּבִים רָאשֵׁי אָבוֹת וְהַכֹּהֲנִים עַל־מַלְכוּת דָּרְיָוֶשׁ הַפָּרְסִי:

23 But the Levite heads of clans are listed in the book of the chronicles to the time of *Yochanan* son of *Elyashiv*.

כג בְּנֵי לֵוִי רָאשֵׁי הָאָבוֹת כְּתוּבִים עַל־סֵפֶר דִּבְרֵי הַיָּמִים וְעַד־יְמֵי יוֹחָנָן בֶּן־אֶלְיָשִׁיב:

Nechemya/Nehemiah
Chapter 12

נחמיה
פרק יב

24 The heads of the *Leviim*: Hashabiah, Sherebiah, Yeshua son of *Kadmiel*, and their brothers served opposite them, singing praise and thanksgiving hymns by the ordinance of *David* the man of *Hashem* – served opposite them in shifts;

כד וְרָאשֵׁי הַלְוִיִּם חֲשַׁבְיָה שֵׁרֵבְיָה וְיֵשׁוּעַ בֶּן־קַדְמִיאֵל וַאֲחֵיהֶם לְנֶגְדָּם לְהַלֵּל לְהוֹדוֹת בְּמִצְוַת דָּוִיד אִישׁ־הָאֱלֹהִים מִשְׁמָר לְעֻמַּת מִשְׁמָר׃

25 Mattaniah, Bakbukiah, *Ovadya*, Meshullam, Talmon, and Akkub, guarding as gatekeepers by shifts at the vestibules of the gates.

כה מַתַּנְיָה וּבַקְבֻּקְיָה עֹבַדְיָה מְשֻׁלָּם טַלְמוֹן עַקּוּב שֹׁמְרִים שׁוֹעֲרִים מִשְׁמָר בַּאֲסֻפֵּי הַשְּׁעָרִים׃

26 These were in the time of Joiakim son of *Yeshua* son of *Yotzadak*, and in the time of *Nechemya* the governor, and of *Ezra* the *Kohen*, the scribe.

כו אֵלֶּה בִּימֵי יוֹיָקִים בֶּן־יֵשׁוּעַ בֶּן־יוֹצָדָק וּבִימֵי נְחֶמְיָה הַפֶּחָה וְעֶזְרָא הַכֹּהֵן הַסּוֹפֵר׃

27 At the dedication of the wall of *Yerushalayim*, the *Leviim*, wherever they lived, were sought out and brought to *Yerushalayim* to celebrate a joyful dedication with thanksgiving and with song, accompanied by cymbals, harps, and lyres.

כז וּבַחֲנֻכַּת חוֹמַת יְרוּשָׁלַ͏ִם בִּקְשׁוּ אֶת־הַלְוִיִּם מִכָּל־מְקוֹמֹתָם לַהֲבִיאָם לִירוּשָׁלָ͏ִם לַעֲשֹׂת חֲנֻכָּה וְשִׂמְחָה וּבְתוֹדוֹת וּבְשִׁיר מְצִלְתַּיִם נְבָלִים וּבְכִנֹּרוֹת׃

28 The companies of singers assembled from the [*Yarden*] plain, the environs of *Yerushalayim*, and from the Netophathite villages;

כח וַיֵּאָסְפוּ בְּנֵי הַמְשֹׁרְרִים וּמִן־הַכִּכָּר סְבִיבוֹת יְרוּשָׁלַ͏ִם וּמִן־חַצְרֵי נְטֹפָתִי׃

29 from Beth-hagilgal, from the countryside of Geba and Azmaveth, for the singers built themselves villages in the environs of *Yerushalayim*.

כט וּמִבֵּית הַגִּלְגָּל וּמִשְּׂדוֹת גֶּבַע וְעַזְמָוֶת כִּי חֲצֵרִים בָּנוּ לָהֶם הַמְשֹׁרֲרִים סְבִיבוֹת יְרוּשָׁלָ͏ִם׃

30 The *Kohanim* and *Leviim* purified themselves; then they purified the people, and the gates, and the wall.

ל וַיִּטַּהֲרוּ הַכֹּהֲנִים וְהַלְוִיִּם וַיְטַהֲרוּ אֶת־הָעָם וְאֶת־הַשְּׁעָרִים וְאֶת־הַחוֹמָה׃

31 I had the officers of *Yehuda* go up onto the wall, and I appointed two large thanksgiving [choirs] and processions. [One marched] south on the wall, to the Dung Gate;

לא וָאַעֲלֶה אֶת־שָׂרֵי יְהוּדָה מֵעַל לַחוֹמָה וָאַעֲמִידָה שְׁתֵּי תוֹדֹת גְּדוֹלֹת וְתַהֲלֻכֹת לַיָּמִין מֵעַל לַחוֹמָה לְשַׁעַר הָאַשְׁפֹּת׃

32 behind them were Hoshaiah and half the officers of *Yehuda*,

לב וַיֵּלֶךְ אַחֲרֵיהֶם הוֹשַׁעְיָה וַחֲצִי שָׂרֵי יְהוּדָה׃

33 and *Azarya*, Ezra, Meshullam,

לג וַעֲזַרְיָה עֶזְרָא וּמְשֻׁלָּם׃

34 *Yehuda*, *Binyamin*, *Shemaya*, and *Yirmiyahu*,

לד יְהוּדָה וּבִנְיָמִן וּשְׁמַעְיָה וְיִרְמְיָה׃

35 and some of the young *Kohanim*, with trumpets; *Zecharya* son of *Yonatan* son of *Shemaya* son of Mattaniah son of *Michaihu* son of Zaccur son of *Asaf*,

לה וּמִבְּנֵי הַכֹּהֲנִים בַּחֲצֹצְרוֹת זְכַרְיָה בֶן־יוֹנָתָן בֶּן־שְׁמַעְיָה בֶּן־מַתַּנְיָה בֶּן־מִיכָיָה בֶּן־זַכּוּר בֶּן־אָסָף׃

36 and his brothers *Shemaya*, and Azarel, Milalai, Gilalai, Maai, Nethanel, *Yehuda*, and *Chanani*, with the musical instruments of *David*, the man of *Hashem*; and *Ezra* the scribe went ahead of them.

לו וְאֶחָיו שְׁמַעְיָה וַעֲזַרְאֵל מִלֲלַי גִּלֲלַי מָעַי נְתַנְאֵל וִיהוּדָה חֲנָנִי בִּכְלֵי־שִׁיר דָּוִיד אִישׁ הָאֱלֹהִים וְעֶזְרָא הַסּוֹפֵר לִפְנֵיהֶם׃

Nechemya/Nehemiah
Chapter 12

37 From there to the Fountain Gate, where they ascended the steps of the City of *David* directly before them, by the ascent on the wall, above the house of *David*, [and onward] to the Water Gate on the east.

לז וְעַל שַׁעַר הָעַיִן וְנֶגְדָּם עָלוּ עַל־מַעֲלוֹת עִיר דָּוִיד בַּמַּעֲלֶה לַחוֹמָה מֵעַל לְבֵית דָּוִיד וְעַד שַׁעַר הַמַּיִם מִזְרָח׃

38 The other thanksgiving [choir] marched on the wall in the opposite direction, with me and half the people behind it, above the Tower of Ovens to the Broad Wall;

לח וְהַתּוֹדָה הַשֵּׁנִית הַהוֹלֶכֶת לְמוֹאל וַאֲנִי אַחֲרֶיהָ וַחֲצִי הָעָם מֵעַל לְהַחוֹמָה מֵעַל לְמִגְדַּל הַתַּנּוּרִים וְעַד הַחוֹמָה הָרְחָבָה׃

v'-ha-to-DAH ha-shay-NEET ha-ho-LE-khet l'-MOL va-a-NEE a-kha-RE-ha va-kha-TZEE ha-AM may-AL l'-ha-kho-MAH may-AL l'-mig-DAL ha-ta-nu-REEM v'-AD ha-kho-MAH ha-r'-kha-VAH

39 and above the Gate of *Efraim*, the Jeshanah Gate, the Fish Gate, the Tower of Hananel, the Tower of the Hundred, to the Sheep Gate; and they halted at the Gate of the Prison Compound.

לט וּמֵעַל לְשַׁעַר־אֶפְרַיִם וְעַל־שַׁעַר הַיְשָׁנָה וְעַל־שַׁעַר הַדָּגִים וּמִגְדַּל חֲנַנְאֵל וּמִגְדַּל הַמֵּאָה וְעַד שַׁעַר הַצֹּאן וְעָמְדוּ בְּשַׁעַר הַמַּטָּרָה׃

40 Both thanksgiving choirs halted at the House of *Hashem*, and I and half the prefects with me,

מ וַתַּעֲמֹדְנָה שְׁתֵּי הַתּוֹדֹת בְּבֵית הָאֱלֹהִים וַאֲנִי וַחֲצִי הַסְּגָנִים עִמִּי׃

41 and the *Kohanim* Eliakim, Maaseiah, Miniamin, Michaihu, Elioenai, *Zecharya*, *Chananya*, with trumpets,

מא וְהַכֹּהֲנִים אֶלְיָקִים מַעֲשֵׂיָה מִנְיָמִין מִיכָיָה אֶלְיוֹעֵינַי זְכַרְיָה חֲנַנְיָה בַּחֲצֹצְרוֹת׃

42 and Maaseiah and *Shemaya*, *Elazar*, Uzzi, Yehochanan, Malchijah, Elam, and Ezer. Then the singers sounded forth, with Jezrahiah in charge.

מב וּמַעֲשֵׂיָה וּשְׁמַעְיָה וְאֶלְעָזָר וְעֻזִּי וִיהוֹחָנָן וּמַלְכִּיָּה וְעֵילָם וָעָזֶר וַיַּשְׁמִיעוּ הַמְשֹׁרְרִים וְיִזְרַחְיָה הַפָּקִיד׃

43 On that day, they offered great sacrifices and rejoiced, for *Hashem* made them rejoice greatly; the women and children also rejoiced, and the rejoicing in *Yerushalayim* could be heard from afar.

מג וַיִּזְבְּחוּ בַיּוֹם־הַהוּא זְבָחִים גְּדוֹלִים וַיִּשְׂמָחוּ כִּי הָאֱלֹהִים שִׂמְּחָם שִׂמְחָה גְדוֹלָה וְגַם הַנָּשִׁים וְהַיְלָדִים שָׂמֵחוּ וַתִּשָּׁמַע שִׂמְחַת יְרוּשָׁלַ͏ִם מֵרָחוֹק׃

44 At that time men were appointed over the chambers that served as treasuries for the gifts, the first fruits, and the tithes, into which the portions prescribed by the Teaching for the *Kohanim* and *Leviim* were gathered from the fields of the towns; for the people of *Yehuda* were grateful to the *Kohanim* and *Leviim* who were in attendance,

מד וַיִּפָּקְדוּ בַיּוֹם הַהוּא אֲנָשִׁים עַל־הַנְּשָׁכוֹת לָאוֹצָרוֹת לַתְּרוּמוֹת לָרֵאשִׁית וְלַמַּעַשְׂרוֹת לִכְנוֹס בָּהֶם לִשְׂדֵי הֶעָרִים מְנָאוֹת הַתּוֹרָה לַכֹּהֲנִים וְלַלְוִיִּם כִּי שִׂמְחַת יְהוּדָה עַל־הַכֹּהֲנִים וְעַל־הַלְוִיִּם הָעֹמְדִים׃

12:38 The broad wall In recording the procession of the wall's dedication ceremony, *Nechemya* mentions the "broad wall." During the 1948 War of Independence, the entire Jewish quarter of Jerusalem's Old City was utterly destroyed. After the 1967 liberation, the quarter's returning residents wished to rebuild their homes, and in the process, many archeological excavations were carried out. One of the many incredible finds was Dr. Nahman Avigad's discovery of the seven-meter-wide "broad wall," mentioned in this verse as well as earlier in *Sefer Nehemiah* (3:8). It is thought to have been built during the reign of King *Chizkiyahu* in the late eighth century BCE, as a defensive structure against the expected invasion by King Sennacherib of Assyria. Today, modern apartments surround the ancient wall, enabling a harmonious existence between Jerusalem's rich past and blessed present.

The broad wall in Jerusalem

Nechemya/Nehemiah
Chapter 13

נחמיה
פרק יג

45 who kept the charge of their God and the charge of purity, as well as to the singers and gatekeepers [serving] in accord with the ordinance of *David* and *Shlomo* his son –

מה וַיִּשְׁמְרוּ מִשְׁמֶרֶת אֱלֹהֵיהֶם וּמִשְׁמֶרֶת הַטָּהֳרָה וְהַמְשֹׁרְרִים וְהַשֹּׁעֲרִים כְּמִצְוַת דָּוִיד שְׁלֹמֹה בְנוֹ:

46 for the chiefs of the singers and songs of praise and thanksgiving to *Hashem* already existed in the time of *David* and *Asaf*.

מו כִּי־בִימֵי דָוִיד וְאָסָף מִקֶּדֶם ראש [רָאשֵׁי] הַמְשֹׁרְרִים וְשִׁיר־תְּהִלָּה וְהֹדוֹת לֵאלֹהִים:

47 And in the time of *Zerubavel*, and in the time of *Nechemya*, all *Yisrael* contributed the daily portions of the singers and the gatekeepers, and made sacred contributions for the *Leviim*, and the *Leviim* made sacred contributions for the Aaronites.

מז וְכָל־יִשְׂרָאֵל בִּימֵי זְרֻבָּבֶל וּבִימֵי נְחֶמְיָה נֹתְנִים מְנָיוֹת הַמְשֹׁרְרִים וְהַשֹּׁעֲרִים דְּבַר־יוֹם בְּיוֹמוֹ וּמַקְדִּשִׁים לַלְוִיִּם וְהַלְוִיִּם מַקְדִּשִׁים לִבְנֵי אַהֲרֹן:

13 1 At that time they read to the people from the Book of *Moshe*, and it was found written that no Ammonite or Moabite might ever enter the congregation of *Hashem*,

יג א בַּיּוֹם הַהוּא נִקְרָא בְּסֵפֶר מֹשֶׁה בְּאָזְנֵי הָעָם וְנִמְצָא כָּתוּב בּוֹ אֲשֶׁר לֹא־יָבוֹא עַמֹּנִי וּמֹאָבִי בִּקְהַל הָאֱלֹהִים עַד־עוֹלָם:

2 since they did not meet *Yisrael* with bread and water, and hired Balaam against them to curse them; but our God turned the curse into a blessing.

ב כִּי לֹא קִדְּמוּ אֶת־בְּנֵי יִשְׂרָאֵל בַּלֶּחֶם וּבַמָּיִם וַיִּשְׂכֹּר עָלָיו אֶת־בִּלְעָם לְקַלְלוֹ וַיַּהֲפֹךְ אֱלֹהֵינוּ הַקְּלָלָה לִבְרָכָה:

3 When they heard the Teaching, they separated all the alien admixture from *Yisrael*.

ג וַיְהִי כְּשָׁמְעָם אֶת־הַתּוֹרָה וַיַּבְדִּילוּ כָל־עֵרֶב מִיִּשְׂרָאֵל:

4 Earlier, the *Kohen Elyashiv*, a relative of Tobiah, who had been appointed over the rooms in the House of our God,

ד וְלִפְנֵי מִזֶּה אֶלְיָשִׁיב הַכֹּהֵן נָתוּן בְּלִשְׁכַּת בֵּית־אֱלֹהֵינוּ קָרוֹב לְטוֹבִיָּה:

5 had assigned to him a large room where they used to store the meal offering, the frankincense, the equipment, the tithes of grain, wine, and oil, the dues of the *Leviim*, singers and gatekeepers, and the gifts for the *Kohanim*.

ה וַיַּעַשׂ לוֹ לִשְׁכָּה גְדוֹלָה וְשָׁם הָיוּ לְפָנִים נֹתְנִים אֶת־הַמִּנְחָה הַלְּבוֹנָה וְהַכֵּלִים וּמַעְשַׂר הַדָּגָן הַתִּירוֹשׁ וְהַיִּצְהָר מִצְוַת הַלְוִיִּם וְהַמְשֹׁרְרִים וְהַשֹּׁעֲרִים וּתְרוּמַת הַכֹּהֲנִים:

6 During all this time, I was not in *Yerushalayim*, for in the thirty-second year of King Artaxerxes of Babylon, I went to the king, and only after a while did I ask leave of the king [to return].

ו וּבְכָל־זֶה לֹא הָיִיתִי בִּירוּשָׁלָם כִּי בִּשְׁנַת שְׁלֹשִׁים וּשְׁתַּיִם לְאַרְתַּחְשַׁסְתְּא מֶלֶךְ־בָּבֶל בָּאתִי אֶל־הַמֶּלֶךְ וּלְקֵץ יָמִים נִשְׁאַלְתִּי מִן־הַמֶּלֶךְ:

7 When I arrived in *Yerushalayim*, I learned of the outrage perpetrated by *Elyashiv* on behalf of Tobiah in assigning him a room in the courts of the House of *Hashem*.

ז וָאָבוֹא לִירוּשָׁלָ͏ִם וָאָבִינָה בָרָעָה אֲשֶׁר עָשָׂה אֶלְיָשִׁיב לְטוֹבִיָּה לַעֲשׂוֹת לוֹ נִשְׁכָּה בְּחַצְרֵי בֵּית הָאֱלֹהִים:

8 I was greatly displeased, and had all the household gear of Tobiah thrown out of the room;

ח וַיֵּרַע לִי מְאֹד וָאַשְׁלִיכָה אֶת־כָּל־כְּלֵי בֵית־טוֹבִיָּה הַחוּץ מִן־הַלִּשְׁכָּה:

1980

Nechemya/Nehemiah
Chapter 13

9 I gave orders to purify the rooms, and had the equipment of the House of *Hashem* and the meal offering and the frankincense put back.

10 I then discovered that the portions of the *Leviim* had not been contributed, and that the *Leviim* and the singers who performed the [temple] service had made off, each to his fields.

11 I censured the prefects, saying, "How is it that the House of *Hashem* has been neglected?" Then I recalled [the *Leviim*] and installed them again in their posts;

12 and all *Yehuda* brought the tithes of grain, wine, and oil into the treasuries.

13 I put the treasuries in the charge of the *Kohen* Shelemiah, the scribe *Tzadok*, and Pedaiah of the *Leviim*; and assisting them was Hanan son of Zaccur son of Mattaniah – for they were regarded as trustworthy persons, and it was their duty to distribute the portions to their brothers.

14 O my God, remember me favorably for this, and do not blot out the devotion I showed toward the House of my God and its attendants.

15 At that time I saw men in *Yehuda* treading winepresses on the *Shabbat*, and others bringing heaps of grain and loading them onto asses, also wine, grapes, figs, and all sorts of goods, and bringing them into *Yerushalayim* on the *Shabbat*. I admonished them there and then for selling provisions.

16 Tyrians who lived there brought fish and all sorts of wares and sold them on the *Shabbat* to the Judahites in *Yerushalayim*.

17 I censured the nobles of *Yehuda*, saying to them, "What evil thing is this that you are doing, profaning the *Shabbat* day!

18 This is just what your ancestors did, and for it *Hashem* brought all this misfortune on this city; and now you give cause for further wrath against *Yisrael* by profaning the *Shabbat*!"

נחמיה
פרק יג

ט וָאֹמְרָה וַיְטַהֲרוּ הַלְּשָׁכוֹת וָאָשִׁיבָה שָּׁם כְּלֵי בֵּית הָאֱלֹהִים אֶת־הַמִּנְחָה וְהַלְּבוֹנָה:

י וָאֵדְעָה כִּי־מְנָיוֹת הַלְוִיִּם לֹא נִתָּנָה וַיִּבְרְחוּ אִישׁ־לְשָׂדֵהוּ הַלְוִיִּם וְהַמְשֹׁרְרִים עֹשֵׂי הַמְּלָאכָה:

יא וָאָרִיבָה אֶת־הַסְּגָנִים וָאֹמְרָה מַדּוּעַ נֶעֱזַב בֵּית־הָאֱלֹהִים וָאֶקְבְּצֵם וָאַעֲמִדֵם עַל־עָמְדָם:

יב וְכָל־יְהוּדָה הֵבִיאוּ מַעְשַׂר הַדָּגָן וְהַתִּירוֹשׁ וְהַיִּצְהָר לָאוֹצָרוֹת:

יג וָאוֹצְרָה עַל־אוֹצָרוֹת שֶׁלֶמְיָה הַכֹּהֵן וְצָדוֹק הַסּוֹפֵר וּפְדָיָה מִן־הַלְוִיִּם וְעַל־יָדָם חָנָן בֶּן־זַכּוּר בֶּן־מַתַּנְיָה כִּי נֶאֱמָנִים נֶחְשָׁבוּ וַעֲלֵיהֶם לַחֲלֹק לַאֲחֵיהֶם:

יד זָכְרָה־לִּי אֱלֹהַי עַל־זֹאת וְאַל־תֶּמַח חֲסָדַי אֲשֶׁר עָשִׂיתִי בְּבֵית אֱלֹהַי וּבְמִשְׁמָרָיו:

טו בַּיָּמִים הָהֵמָּה רָאִיתִי בִיהוּדָה דֹּרְכִים־גִּתּוֹת בַּשַּׁבָּת וּמְבִיאִים הָעֲרֵמוֹת וְעֹמְסִים עַל־הַחֲמֹרִים וְאַף־יַיִן עֲנָבִים וּתְאֵנִים וְכָל־מַשָּׂא וּמְבִיאִים יְרוּשָׁלַ͏ִם בְּיוֹם הַשַּׁבָּת וָאָעִיד בְּיוֹם מִכְרָם צָיִד:

טז וְהַצֹּרִים יָשְׁבוּ בָהּ מְבִיאִים דָּאג וְכָל־מֶכֶר וּמֹכְרִים בַּשַּׁבָּת לִבְנֵי יְהוּדָה וּבִירוּשָׁלָ͏ִם:

יז וָאָרִיבָה אֵת חֹרֵי יְהוּדָה וָאֹמְרָה לָהֶם מָה־הַדָּבָר הָרָע הַזֶּה אֲשֶׁר אַתֶּם עֹשִׂים וּמְחַלְּלִים אֶת־יוֹם הַשַּׁבָּת:

יח הֲלוֹא כֹה עָשׂוּ אֲבֹתֵיכֶם וַיָּבֵא אֱלֹהֵינוּ עָלֵינוּ אֵת כָּל־הָרָעָה הַזֹּאת וְעַל הָעִיר הַזֹּאת וְאַתֶּם מוֹסִיפִים חָרוֹן עַל־יִשְׂרָאֵל לְחַלֵּל אֶת־הַשַּׁבָּת:

Nechemya/Nehemiah
Chapter 13

נחמיה
פרק יג

19 When shadows filled the gateways of *Yerushalayim* at the approach of the *Shabbat*, I gave orders that the doors be closed, and ordered them not to be opened until after the *Shabbat*. I stationed some of my servants at the gates, so that no goods should enter on the *Shabbat*.

יט וַיְהִי כַּאֲשֶׁר צָלֲלוּ שַׁעֲרֵי יְרוּשָׁלַםִ לִפְנֵי הַשַּׁבָּת וָאֹמְרָה וַיִּסָּגְרוּ הַדְּלָתוֹת וָאֹמְרָה אֲשֶׁר לֹא יִפְתָּחוּם עַד אַחַר הַשַּׁבָּת וּמִנְּעָרַי הֶעֱמַדְתִּי עַל־הַשְּׁעָרִים לֹא־יָבוֹא מַשָּׂא בְּיוֹם הַשַּׁבָּת:

vai-HEE ka-a-SHER tza-l'-LU sha-a-RAY y'-ru-sha-LA-im lif-NAY ha-sha-BAT va-o-m'-RAH va-yi-sa-g'-RU ha-d'-la-TOT va-o-m'-RAH a-SHER LO yif-ta-KHUM AD a-KHAR ha-sha-BAT u-mi-n'-a-RAI he-e-MAD-tee al ha-sh'-a-REEM lo ya-VO ma-SA b'-YOM ha-sha-BAT

20 Once or twice the merchants and the vendors of all sorts of wares spent the night outside *Yerushalayim*,

כ וַיָּלִינוּ הָרֹכְלִים וּמֹכְרֵי כָל־מִמְכָּר מִחוּץ לִירוּשָׁלָםִ פַּעַם וּשְׁתָּיִם:

21 but I warned them, saying, "What do you mean by spending the night alongside the wall? If you do so again, I will lay hands upon you!" From then on they did not come on the *Shabbat*.

כא וָאָעִידָה בָהֶם וָאֹמְרָה אֲלֵיהֶם מַדּוּעַ אַתֶּם לֵנִים נֶגֶד הַחוֹמָה אִם־תִּשְׁנוּ יָד אֶשְׁלַח בָּכֶם מִן־הָעֵת הַהִיא לֹא־בָאוּ בַּשַּׁבָּת:

22 I gave orders to the *Leviim* to purify themselves and come and guard the gates, to preserve the sanctity of the *Shabbat*. This too, O my God, remember to my credit, and spare me in accord with your abundant faithfulness.

כב וָאֹמְרָה לַלְוִיִּם אֲשֶׁר יִהְיוּ מִטַּהֲרִים וּבָאִים שֹׁמְרִים הַשְּׁעָרִים לְקַדֵּשׁ אֶת־יוֹם הַשַּׁבָּת גַּם־זֹאת זָכְרָה־לִּי אֱלֹהַי וְחוּסָה עָלַי כְּרֹב חַסְדֶּךָ:

23 Also at that time, I saw that *Yehudim* had married Ashdodite, Ammonite, and Moabite women;

כג גַּם בַּיָּמִים הָהֵם רָאִיתִי אֶת־הַיְּהוּדִים הֹשִׁיבוּ נָשִׁים אשדודיות [אַשְׁדֳּדִיּוֹת] עמוניות [עַמֳּנִיּוֹת] מוֹאֲבִיּוֹת:

13:19 I gave orders that the doors be closed Jerusalem's Old City constituted the entire city of *Yerushalayim* until the 1860s. There had always been a protective wall surrounding it, with gates allowing passage in and out. In *Nechemya's* time, the wall was reconstructed and the gates, with their strong doors, were closed to bar passage from evildoers. When the Crusaders ruled over *Yerushalayim*, the walls surrounding the city had only four gates, but when Suleiman the Magnificent of the Ottoman Turkish Empire renovated the walls of *Yerushalayim* from 1538–42, he ensured that there were six functional gates. In 1887, the New Gate was added and the Tanners' Gate was discovered, and opened during excavations in the 1990s. Like *Nechemya's* gates, until 1887 the current Old City gates were closed each day before sunset and opened again at sunrise. Today, however, seven of the gates remain open all the time and have no doors. Only the Gate of Mercy on the eastern side of the Temple Mount wall remains sealed and, according to tradition, will be reopened in the days of the *Mashiach*. According to *Yechezkel*, in the future there will be twelve gates leading to the city of *Yerushalayim*, one for each of the twelve tribes of Israel (Ezekiel 48:31–34). No matter how many gates there are, "*Hashem* loves the gates of *Tzion*, more than all the dwellings of *Yaakov*" (Psalms 87:2), for they lead to his most precious city, *Yerushalayim*.

Gate of Mercy

Nechemya/Nehemiah
Chapter 13

נחמיה
פרק יג

24 a good number of their children spoke the language of *Ashdod* and the language of those various peoples, and did not know how to speak Judean.

וּבְנֵיהֶם חֲצִי מְדַבֵּר אַשְׁדּוֹדִית וְאֵינָם מַכִּירִים לְדַבֵּר יְהוּדִית וְכִלְשׁוֹן עַם וָעָם: כד

uv-nay-HEM kha-TZEE m'-da-BAYR ash-do-DEET v'-ay-NAM ma-kee-REEM l'-da-BAYR y'-hu-DEET v'-khil-SHON am va-AM

25 I censured them, cursed them, flogged them, tore out their hair, and adjured them by *Hashem*, saying, "You shall not give your daughters in marriage to their sons, or take any of their daughters for your sons or yourselves.

וָאָרִיב עִמָּם וָאֲקַלְלֵם וָאַכֶּה מֵהֶם אֲנָשִׁים וָאֶמְרְטֵם וָאַשְׁבִּיעֵם בֵּאלֹהִים אִם־תִּתְּנוּ בְנֹתֵיכֶם לִבְנֵיהֶם וְאִם־תִּשְׂאוּ מִבְּנֹתֵיהֶם לִבְנֵיכֶם וְלָכֶם: כה

26 It was just in such things that King *Shlomo* of *Yisrael* sinned! Among the many nations there was not a king like him, and so well loved was he by his God that *Hashem* made him king of all *Yisrael*, yet foreign wives caused even him to sin.

הֲלוֹא עַל־אֵלֶּה חָטָא־שְׁלֹמֹה מֶלֶךְ יִשְׂרָאֵל וּבַגּוֹיִם הָרַבִּים לֹא־הָיָה מֶלֶךְ כָּמֹהוּ וְאָהוּב לֵאלֹהָיו הָיָה וַיִּתְּנֵהוּ אֱלֹהִים מֶלֶךְ עַל־כָּל־יִשְׂרָאֵל גַּם־אוֹתוֹ הֶחֱטִיאוּ הַנָּשִׁים הַנָּכְרִיּוֹת: כו

27 How, then, can we acquiesce in your doing this great wrong, breaking faith with our God by marrying foreign women?"

וְלָכֶם הֲנִשְׁמַע לַעֲשֹׂת אֵת כָּל־הָרָעָה הַגְּדוֹלָה הַזֹּאת לִמְעֹל בֵּאלֹהֵינוּ לְהֹשִׁיב נָשִׁים נָכְרִיּוֹת: כז

28 One of the sons of Joiada son of the *Kohen Gadol Elyashiv* was a son-in-law of Sanballat the Horonite; I drove him away from me.

וּמִבְּנֵי יוֹיָדָע בֶּן־אֶלְיָשִׁיב הַכֹּהֵן הַגָּדוֹל חָתָן לְסַנְבַלַּט הַחֹרֹנִי וָאַבְרִיחֵהוּ מֵעָלָי: כח

29 Remember to their discredit, O my God, how they polluted the priesthood, the covenant of the *Kohanim* and *Leviim*.

זָכְרָה לָהֶם אֱלֹהָי עַל גָּאֳלֵי הַכְּהֻנָּה וּבְרִית הַכְּהֻנָּה וְהַלְוִיִּם: כט

30 I purged them of every foreign element, and arranged for the *Kohanim* and the *Leviim* to work each at his task by shifts,

וְטִהַרְתִּים מִכָּל־נֵכָר וָאַעֲמִידָה מִשְׁמָרוֹת לַכֹּהֲנִים וְלַלְוִיִּם אִישׁ בִּמְלַאכְתּוֹ: ל

31 and for the wood offering [to be brought] at fixed times and for the first fruits. O my God, remember it to my credit!

וּלְקֻרְבַּן הָעֵצִים בְּעִתִּים מְזֻמָּנוֹת וְלַבִּכּוּרִים זָכְרָה־לִּי אֱלֹהַי לְטוֹבָה: לא

Eliezer Ben-Yehuda (1858–1922)

13:24 did not know how to speak Judean *Nechemya* bemoans the fact that in seventy years of exile the Jews of his generation forgot how to speak Hebrew. The situation was even worse in the modern era after 2,500 years of exile, when Hebrew was nearly extinct, reserved exclusively as the Jewish holy language for prayer and study. This all changed with the advent of the Zionist revival, thanks in large part to the efforts of one man, Eliezer Ben-Yehuda (1858–1922), who decided that "in order to have our own land and political life it is also necessary that we have a language to hold us together." Many scoffed at Ben-Yehuda's vision, but today Hebrew has been revived from the dustbin of history and is the official language of the State of Israel. Millions of Israeli Jews today converse in Hebrew, conduct their daily affairs in Hebrew, and can read the *Tanakh* in their original mother tongue as well. In the words of his biographer, "Before Ben-Yehuda people *could* speak Hebrew; after him, they *did*."

Sefer Divrei Hayamim
The Book of Chronicles

Introduction and commentary by Alexander Jacob Tsykin

Sefer Divrei Hayamim (Chronicles) is the final book of *Tanakh*, the Hebrew Bible. Like the books of *Shmuel* and *Melachim*, *Divrei Hayamim* is divided into two sections which together form a single book. It is traditionally attributed to *Ezra* the scribe. The first nine chapters of the book contain a series of genealogies, tracing the lineage of the Jews who returned from Babylon to *Eretz Yisrael*, starting from the time of creation. The second part of the book is mainly a review of events previously detailed in the books of *Shmuel* and *Melachim*, starting with the death of *Shaul* and focusing primarily on the kingdom of *Yehuda*. The book ends with a brief epilogue mentioning the proclamation of Cyrus allowing the Jews to return to *Eretz Yisrael* and rebuild the *Beit Hamikdash*, as described in the books of *Ezra* and *Nechemya*.

What is the connection between the genealogies and the rest of the book, and what is the purpose of the book which is, to a large extent, a repetition of other books of *Tanach*?

Perhaps part of the reason *Ezra* chose to include the genealogies in *Sefer Divrei Hayamim* is to demonstrate the legitimacy of Jewish settlement in *Eretz Yisrael* during the return from Babylonian exile. By enumerating the genealogies of so many people involved in the resettlement of the land and the re-construction of the *Beit Hamikdash* in *Yerushalayim*, *Ezra* sought to emphasize that the people who had come to Israel were not interlopers trying to seize the Holy Land and its trade routes. Rather, they were natives who had returned to their homeland as a matter of right. Additionally, these lists legitimized the status of the *Kohanim* and *Leviim* of that time, as these roles are hereditary, by showing that they were descendants of the original *Kohanim* and *Leviim* of the first Temple period.

Even though the return to the Land of Israel took place only several decades after the final exiles had left the land with the destruction of the first Temple, their claim to the land had already come under question. As described in *Sefer Ezra* chapter 4, the new inhabitants of the land were angry that the Jews were returning to reclaim some of their territory and rebuild the *Beit Hamikdash*, and they repeatedly tried to prevent that from occurring. As such, we can see why *Ezra* felt the need to prove the legitimacy of their claim to the land. This might also be the reason that *Sefer Divrei Hayamim* ends with the permission granted by Cyrus, king of Persia, for the Jews to return to Israel. This provided additional confirmation to the new residents of the land, and to the returning Jews, that *Eretz Yisrael* is indeed the property of the Jewish people.

Since the purpose of the book is to justify the Jewish claim to Israel, *Ezra* felt it necessary to repeat much of the history of the kingdom of *Yehuda*. In doing so, he sometimes repeated verbatim what it says in *Shmuel* and *Melachim,* and other times wrote about the events differently than the other books of *Tanakh,* in a way that reflects the purpose and messages of *Sefer Divrei Hayamim*. This historical account further strengthens the Jews' claim to the land. Additionally, the first leader of the return from exile, *Zerubavel*, descended from the Davidic dynasty (see I Chronicles 3:19). This fact further bolsters the legitimacy of the Jewish resettlement and sovereignty, as *Sefer Divrei Hayamim* continuously stresses that the Davidic line has an eternal claim to kingship in the Land of Israel. Finally, the accounts of the repeated sins of the Davidic monarchs, their repentance and *Hashem*'s forgiveness, shows that God did not give up on the Jewish people when he exiled them from *Eretz Yisrael*. Rather, He intended for the Jewish claim over the land to be everlasting.

Today, as in the time of *Ezra*, there are those who seek to delegitimize the Jewish people's claim to *Eretz Yisrael*. Like the "adversaries of *Yehuda* and *Binyamin*" in *Sefer Ezra* (Ezra 4:1), they contend that the Jews are no longer the rightful inhabitants of the land, that others have an equal or superior claim and that the Jews should be prevented from building and expanding Israel. The message of *Sefer Divrei Hayamim*, justifying the eternal Jewish claim to the Land of Israel, is therefore as relevant today as it was at the time it was written. Concluding *Tanakh* with *Sefer Divrei Hayamim*, which strongly supports the Jewish people's connection to their ancient homeland, confirms the centrality of the Land of Israel, which appears prominently in so many chapters of the Hebrew Bible, in the history and destiny of the Jewish people.

List of the Generations from *Adam* to King *David*

According to Rabbi Yitzchak Abrabanel, *Sefer Divrei Hayamim* was written to promote the stature of King *David* and the Davidic dynasty. It is from this lineage that *Mashiach* will come. *Divrei Hayamim* begins with a list of genealogies, starting with *Adam*, and then focuses on King *David* and the kingdom of *Yehuda*, whose kings were all descendants of *David*. The following is a list of generations from *Adam* through *David*.

Name	Years of life	Biblical Verse
Adam	930	Genesis 5:3–5
Shet	912	Genesis 5:6–8
Enosh	905	Genesis 5:9–11
Keinan	910	Genesis 5:12–14
Mahalalel	895	Genesis 5:15–17
Yered	962	Genesis 5:18–20
Enosh	365	Genesis 5:21–24
Metushelach	969	Genesis 5:25–27
Lemech	777	Genesis 5:28–31
Noach	950	Genesis 9:28–29
Shem	600	Genesis 11:10–11
Arpachshad	438	Genesis 11:12–13
Sheila	433	Genesis 11:14–15
Ever	464	Genesis 11:16–17
Peleg	239	Genesis 11:18–19
Re'u	239	Genesis 11:20–21
Serug	230	Genesis 11:22–23
Nachor	148	Genesis 11:24–25
Terach	205	Genesis 11:26–32
Avraham	175	Genesis 11:26, 25:7–10
Yitzchak	180	Genesis 25:19–20 Genesis 35:28–29
Yaakov	147	Genesis 47:28
Yehuda	119*	Genesis 29:35
Peretz	Unknown	Genesis 38
Chetzron	Unknown	Ruth 4:18

* Number based on the calculation of the Sages

Name	Years of life	Biblical Verse
Ram	Unknown	Ruth 4:19
Aminadav	Unknown	Ruth 4:19
Nachshon	Unknown	Ruth 4:20
Salma	Unknown	Ruth 4:20
Boaz	80*	Ruth 4:21
Oved	Unknown	Ruth 4:21
Yishai	Unknown	Ruth 4:22
David	70	Ruth 4:22

* Number based on the calculation of the Sages

Divrei Hayamim I / I Chronicles
Chapter 1

דברי הימים א
פרק א

1 ¹ *Adam, Shet, Enosh*;

א אָדָם שֵׁת אֱנוֹשׁ:

² *Keinan, Mehalalel, Yered*;

ב קֵינָן מַהֲלַלְאֵל יָרֶד:

³ *Chanoch, Metushelach, Lemech*;

ג חֲנוֹךְ מְתוּשֶׁלַח לָמֶךְ:

⁴ *Noach, Shem*, Ham, and Japheth.

ד נֹחַ שֵׁם חָם וָיָפֶת:

⁵ The sons of Japheth: Gomer, Magog, Media, Javan, Tubal, Meshech, and Tiras.

ה בְּנֵי יֶפֶת גֹּמֶר וּמָגוֹג וּמָדַי וְיָוָן וְתֻבָל וּמֶשֶׁךְ וְתִירָס:

⁶ The sons of Gomer: Ashkenaz, Diphath, and Togarmah.

ו וּבְנֵי גֹּמֶר אַשְׁכֲּנַז וְדִיפַת וְתוֹגַרְמָה:

⁷ The sons of Javan: Elishah, Tarshish, Kittim, and Rodanim.

ז וּבְנֵי יָוָן אֱלִישָׁה וְתַרְשִׁישָׁה כִּתִּים וְרוֹדָנִים:

⁸ The sons of Ham: Cush, Mizraim, Put, and Canaan.

ח בְּנֵי חָם כּוּשׁ וּמִצְרַיִם פּוּט וּכְנָעַן:

⁹ The sons of Cush: Seba, Havilah, Sabta, Raama, and Sabteca. The sons of Raama: Sheba and Dedan.

ט וּבְנֵי כוּשׁ סְבָא וַחֲוִילָה וְסַבְתָּא וְרַעְמָא וְסַבְתְּכָא וּבְנֵי רַעְמָא שְׁבָא וּדְדָן:

¹⁰ Cush begot Nimrod; he was the first mighty one on earth.

י וְכוּשׁ יָלַד אֶת־נִמְרוֹד הוּא הֵחֵל לִהְיוֹת גִּבּוֹר בָּאָרֶץ:

¹¹ Mizraim begot the Ludim, the Anamim, the Lehabim, the Naphtuhim,

יא וּמִצְרַיִם יָלַד אֶת־לודיים [לוּדִים] וְאֶת־עֲנָמִים וְאֶת־לְהָבִים וְאֶת־נַפְתֻּחִים:

¹² the Pathrusim, the Casluhim (whence the Philistines came forth), and the Caphtorim.

יב וְאֶת־פַּתְרֻסִים וְאֶת־כַּסְלֻחִים אֲשֶׁר יָצְאוּ מִשָּׁם פְּלִשְׁתִּים וְאֶת־כַּפְתֹּרִים:

¹³ Canaan begot Sidon his first-born, and Heth,

יג וּכְנַעַן יָלַד אֶת־צִידוֹן בְּכֹרוֹ וְאֶת־חֵת:

¹⁴ and the Jebusites, the Amorites, the Girgashites,

יד וְאֶת־הַיְבוּסִי וְאֶת־הָאֱמֹרִי וְאֵת הַגִּרְגָּשִׁי:

¹⁵ the Hivites, the Arkites, the Sinites,

טו וְאֶת־הַחִוִּי וְאֶת־הַעַרְקִי וְאֶת־הַסִּינִי:

¹⁶ the Arvadites, the Zemarites, and the Hamathites.

טז וְאֶת־הָאַרְוָדִי וְאֶת־הַצְּמָרִי וְאֶת־הַחֲמָתִי:

¹⁷ The sons of *Shem*: Elam, Assyria, *Arpachshad*, Lud, Aram, Uz, Hul, Gether, and Meshech.

יז בְּנֵי שֵׁם עֵילָם וְאַשּׁוּר וְאַרְפַּכְשַׁד וְלוּד וַאֲרָם וְעוּץ וְחוּל וְגֶתֶר וָמֶשֶׁךְ:

¹⁸ *Arpachshad* begot *Shelach*; and *Shelach* begot *Ever*.

יח וְאַרְפַּכְשַׁד יָלַד אֶת־שָׁלַח וְשֶׁלַח יָלַד אֶת־עֵבֶר:

¹⁹ Two sons were born to *Ever*: the name of the one was Peleg (for in his days the earth was divided), and the name of his brother Joktan.

יט וּלְעֵבֶר יֻלַּד שְׁנֵי בָנִים שֵׁם הָאֶחָד פֶּלֶג כִּי בְיָמָיו נִפְלְגָה הָאָרֶץ וְשֵׁם אָחִיו יָקְטָן:

²⁰ Joktan begot Almodad, Sheleph, Hazarmaveth, Jerah,

כ וְיָקְטָן יָלַד אֶת־אַלְמוֹדָד וְאֶת־שָׁלֶף וְאֶת־חֲצַרְמָוֶת וְאֶת־יָרַח:

²¹ Hadoram, Uzal, Diklah,

כא וְאֶת־הֲדוֹרָם וְאֶת־אוּזָל וְאֶת־דִּקְלָה:

²² Ebal, Abimael, Sheba,

כב וְאֶת־עֵיבָל וְאֶת־אֲבִימָאֵל וְאֶת־שְׁבָא:

²³ Ophir, Havilah, and Jobab; all these were the sons of Joktan.

כג וְאֶת־אוֹפִיר וְאֶת־חֲוִילָה וְאֶת־יוֹבָב כָּל־אֵלֶּה בְּנֵי יָקְטָן:

Divrei Hayamim I / I Chronicles
Chapter 1

24 Shem, Arpachshad, Shelach;

25 Ever, Peleg, Re'u;

26 Serug, Nachor, Terach;

27 Avram, that is, Avraham.

28 The sons of *Avraham*: *Yitzchak* and Ishmael.

29 This is their line: The first-born of Ishmael, Nebaioth; and Kedar, Abdeel, Mibsam,

30 Mishma, Dumah, Massa, Hadad, Tema,

31 Jetur, Naphish, and Kedmah. These are the sons of Ishmael.

32 The sons of Keturah, *Avraham*'s concubine: she bore Zimran, Jokshan, Medan, Midian, Ishbak, and Shuah. The sons of Jokshan: Sheba and Dedan.

33 The sons of Midian: Ephah, Epher, Enoch, Abida, and Eldaah. All these were the descendants of Keturah.

34 *Avraham* begot *Yitzchak*. The sons of *Yitzchak*: Esau and *Yisrael*.

35 The sons of Esau: Eliphaz, Reuel, Jeush, Jalam, and Korah.

36 The sons of Eliphaz: Teman, Omar, Zephi, Gatam, Kenaz, Timna, and Amalek.

37 The sons of Reuel: Nahath, Zerah, Shammah, and Mizzah.

38 The sons of Seir: Lotan, Shobal, Zibeon, Anah, Dishon, Ezer, and Dishan.

39 The sons of Lotan: Hori and Homam; and Lotan's sister was Timna.

40 The sons of Shobal: Alian, Manahath, Ebal, Shephi, and Onam. The sons of Zibeon: Aiah and Anah.

41 The sons of Anah: Dishon. The sons of Dishon: Hamran, Eshban, Ithran, and Cheran.

42 The sons of Ezer: Bilhan, Zaavan, and Jaakan. The sons of Dishan: Uz and Aran.

דברי הימים א
פרק א

כד שֵׁם אַרְפַּכְשַׁד שָׁלַח:

כה עֵבֶר פֶּלֶג רְעוּ:

כו שְׂרוּג נָחוֹר תָּרַח:

כז אַבְרָם הוּא אַבְרָהָם:

כח בְּנֵי אַבְרָהָם יִצְחָק וְיִשְׁמָעֵאל:

כט אֵלֶּה תֹּלְדוֹתָם בְּכוֹר יִשְׁמָעֵאל נְבָיוֹת וְקֵדָר וְאַדְבְּאֵל וּמִבְשָׂם:

ל מִשְׁמָע וְדוּמָה מַשָּׂא חֲדַד וְתֵימָא:

לא יְטוּר נָפִישׁ וָקֵדְמָה אֵלֶּה הֵם בְּנֵי יִשְׁמָעֵאל:

לב וּבְנֵי קְטוּרָה פִּילֶגֶשׁ אַבְרָהָם יָלְדָה אֶת־זִמְרָן וְיָקְשָׁן וּמְדָן וּמִדְיָן וְיִשְׁבָּק וְשׁוּחַ וּבְנֵי יָקְשָׁן שְׁבָא וּדְדָן:

לג וּבְנֵי מִדְיָן עֵיפָה וָעֵפֶר וַחֲנוֹךְ וַאֲבִידָע וְאֶלְדָּעָה כָּל־אֵלֶּה בְּנֵי קְטוּרָה:

לד וַיּוֹלֶד אַבְרָהָם אֶת־יִצְחָק בְּנֵי יִצְחָק עֵשָׂו וְיִשְׂרָאֵל:

לה בְּנֵי עֵשָׂו אֱלִיפַז רְעוּאֵל וִיעוּשׁ וְיַעְלָם וְקֹרַח:

לו בְּנֵי אֱלִיפָז תֵּימָן וְאוֹמָר צְפִי וְגַעְתָּם קְנַז וְתִמְנָע וַעֲמָלֵק:

לז בְּנֵי רְעוּאֵל נַחַת זֶרַח שַׁמָּה וּמִזָּה:

לח וּבְנֵי שֵׂעִיר לוֹטָן וְשׁוֹבָל וְצִבְעוֹן וַעֲנָה וְדִישֹׁן וְאֵצֶר וְדִישָׁן:

לט וּבְנֵי לוֹטָן חֹרִי וְהוֹמָם וַאֲחוֹת לוֹטָן תִּמְנָע:

מ בְּנֵי שׁוֹבָל עַלְיָן וּמָנַחַת וְעֵיבָל שְׁפִי וְאוֹנָם וּבְנֵי צִבְעוֹן אַיָּה וַעֲנָה:

מא בְּנֵי עֲנָה דִּישׁוֹן וּבְנֵי דִישׁוֹן חַמְרָן וְאֶשְׁבָּן וְיִתְרָן וּכְרָן:

מב בְּנֵי־אֵצֶר בִּלְהָן וְזַעֲוָן יַעֲקָן בְּנֵי דִישׁוֹן עוּץ וַאֲרָן:

Divrei Hayamim I / I Chronicles
Chapter 1

דברי הימים א
פרק א

43 These are the kings who reigned in the land of Edom before any king reigned over the Israelites: Bela son of Beor, and the name of his city was Dinhabah.

מג וְאֵלֶּה הַמְּלָכִים אֲשֶׁר מָלְכוּ בְּאֶרֶץ אֱדוֹם לִפְנֵי מְלָךְ־מֶלֶךְ לִבְנֵי יִשְׂרָאֵל בֶּלַע בֶּן־בְּעוֹר וְשֵׁם עִירוֹ דִּנְהָבָה:

v'-AY-leh ha-m'-la-KHEEM a-SHER ma-l'-KHU b'-E-retz e-DOM lif-NAY m'-lokh ME-lekh liv-NAY yis-ra-AYL BE-la ben b'-OR v'-SHAYM ee-RO din-HA-vah

44 When Bela died, Jobab son of Zerah from Bozrah succeeded him as king.

מד וַיָּמָת בָּלַע וַיִּמְלֹךְ תַּחְתָּיו יוֹבָב בֶּן־זֶרַח מִבָּצְרָה:

45 When Jobab died, Husham of the land of the Temanites succeeded him as king.

מה וַיָּמָת יוֹבָב וַיִּמְלֹךְ תַּחְתָּיו חוּשָׁם מֵאֶרֶץ הַתֵּימָנִי:

46 When Husham died, Hadad son of Bedad, who defeated the Midianites in the country of Moab, succeeded him as king, and the name of his city was Avith.

מו וַיָּמָת חוּשָׁם וַיִּמְלֹךְ תַּחְתָּיו הֲדַד בֶּן־בְּדַד הַמַּכֶּה אֶת־מִדְיָן בִּשְׂדֵה מוֹאָב וְשֵׁם עִירוֹ עֲיוֹת [עֲוִית:]

47 When Hadad died, Samlah of Masrekah succeeded him as king.

מז וַיָּמָת הֲדָד וַיִּמְלֹךְ תַּחְתָּיו שַׂמְלָה מִמַּשְׂרֵקָה:

48 When Samlah died, Saul of Rehoboth-on-the-River succeeded him as king.

מח וַיָּמָת שַׂמְלָה וַיִּמְלֹךְ תַּחְתָּיו שָׁאוּל מֵרְחֹבוֹת הַנָּהָר:

49 When Saul died, Baal-hanan son of Achbor succeeded him as king.

מט וַיָּמָת שָׁאוּל וַיִּמְלֹךְ תַּחְתָּיו בַּעַל חָנָן בֶּן־עַכְבּוֹר:

50 When Baal-hanan died, Hadad succeeded him as king; and the name of his city was Pai, and his wife's name Mehetabel daughter of Matred daughter of Me-zahab.

נ וַיָּמָת בַּעַל חָנָן וַיִּמְלֹךְ תַּחְתָּיו הֲדַד וְשֵׁם עִירוֹ פָּעִי וְשֵׁם אִשְׁתּוֹ מְהֵיטַבְאֵל בַּת־מַטְרֵד בַּת מֵי זָהָב:

51 And Hadad died. The clans of Edom were the clans of Timna, Alvah, Jetheth,

נא וַיָּמָת הֲדָד וַיִּהְיוּ אַלּוּפֵי אֱדוֹם אַלּוּף תִּמְנָע אַלּוּף עליה [עַלְוָה] אַלּוּף יְתֵת:

52 Oholibamah, Elah, Pinon,

נב אַלּוּף אָהֳלִיבָמָה אַלּוּף אֵלָה אַלּוּף פִּינֹן:

53 Kenaz, Teman, Mibzar,

נג אַלּוּף קְנַז אַלּוּף תֵּימָן אַלּוּף מִבְצָר:

54 Magdiel, and Iram; these are the clans of Edom.

נד אַלּוּף מַגְדִּיאֵל אַלּוּף עִירָם אֵלֶּה אַלּוּפֵי אֱדוֹם:

1:43 These are the kings who reigned in the land of Edom *Sefer Divrei Hayamim* begins with a record of the generations from *Adam* through the descendants of *Yaakov*. This verse introduces the leaders of the children of Esau, also known as Edom. By listing the heads of the family of Esau, the text confirms that *Hashem* fulfilled his promise to *Rivka* that she and *Yitzchak* would be the parents of two great nations (Genesis 25:23). Since God promised that both their sons would be become great nations, we are shown that *Hashem* kept his assurances and blessed Esau, regardless of Esau's choice to reject God and His covenant. The lesson is obvious. If God even keeps His promise with Esau, who rejected the path of his father *Yitzchak*, how much more so will *Hashem* keep His promise to *Yaakov*, who maintained the covenant.

Divrei Hayamim I / I Chronicles
Chapter 2

דברי הימים א
פרק ב

2 １ These are the sons of *Yisrael*: *Reuven*, *Shimon*, *Levi*, *Yehuda*, *Yissachar*, *Zevulun*,

א אֵלֶּה בְּנֵי יִשְׂרָאֵל רְאוּבֵן שִׁמְעוֹן לֵוִי וִיהוּדָה יִשָּׂשכָר וּזְבֻלוּן׃

2 *Dan*, *Yosef*, *Binyamin*, *Naftali*, *Gad*, and *Asher*.

ב דָּן יוֹסֵף וּבִנְיָמִן נַפְתָּלִי גָּד וְאָשֵׁר׃

3 The sons of *Yehuda*: *Er*, *Onan*, and *Sheila*; these three, Bath-shua the Canaanite woman bore to him. But *Er*, *Yehuda*'s first-born, was displeasing to *Hashem*, and He took his life.

ג בְּנֵי יְהוּדָה עֵר וְאוֹנָן וְשֵׁלָה שְׁלוֹשָׁה נוֹלַד לוֹ מִבַּת־שׁוּעַ הַכְּנַעֲנִית וַיְהִי עֵר בְּכוֹר יְהוּדָה רַע בְּעֵינֵי יְהֹוָה וַיְמִיתֵהוּ׃

4 His daughter-in-law *Tamar* also bore him *Peretz* and *Zerach*. *Yehuda*'s sons were five in all.

ד וְתָמָר כַּלָּתוֹ יָלְדָה לּוֹ אֶת־פֶּרֶץ וְאֶת־זָרַח כָּל־בְּנֵי יְהוּדָה חֲמִשָּׁה׃

v'-ta-MAR ka-la-TO ya-l'-DAH LO et PE-retz v'-et ZA-rakh kol b'-NAY y'-hu-DAH kha-mi-SHAH

5 The sons of *Peretz*: *Chetzron* and Hamul.

ה בְּנֵי־פֶרֶץ חֶצְרוֹן וְחָמוּל׃

6 The sons of *Zerach*: *Zimri*, Ethan, *Hayman*, Calcol, and Dara, five in all.

ו וּבְנֵי זֶרַח זִמְרִי וְאֵיתָן וְהֵימָן וְכַלְכֹּל וָדָרַע כֻּלָּם חֲמִשָּׁה׃

7 The sons of Carmi: Achar, the troubler of *Yisrael*, who committed a trespass against the proscribed thing;

ז וּבְנֵי כַּרְמִי עָכָר עוֹכֵר יִשְׂרָאֵל אֲשֶׁר מָעַל בַּחֵרֶם׃

8 and Ethan's son was *Azarya*.

ח וּבְנֵי אֵיתָן עֲזַרְיָה׃

9 The sons of *Chetzron* that were born to him: Jerahmeel, *Ram*, and Chelubai.

ט וּבְנֵי חֶצְרוֹן אֲשֶׁר נוֹלַד־לוֹ אֶת־יְרַחְמְאֵל וְאֶת־רָם וְאֶת־כְּלוּבָי׃

10 *Ram* begot *Aminadav*, and *Aminadav* begot *Nachshon*, prince of the sons of *Yehuda*.

י וְרָם הוֹלִיד אֶת־עַמִּינָדָב וְעַמִּינָדָב הוֹלִיד אֶת־נַחְשׁוֹן נְשִׂיא בְּנֵי יְהוּדָה׃

11 *Nachshon* was the father of *Salma*, *Salma* of *Boaz*,

יא וְנַחְשׁוֹן הוֹלִיד אֶת־שַׂלְמָא וְשַׂלְמָא הוֹלִיד אֶת־בֹּעַז׃

12 *Boaz* of *Oved*, *Oved* of *Yishai*.

יב וּבֹעַז הוֹלִיד אֶת־עוֹבֵד וְעוֹבֵד הוֹלִיד אֶת־יִשָׁי׃

13 *Yishai* begot *Eliav* his first-born, *Avinadav* the second, Shimea the third,

יג וְאִישַׁי הוֹלִיד אֶת־בְּכֹרוֹ אֶת־אֱלִיאָב וַאֲבִינָדָב הַשֵּׁנִי וְשִׁמְעָא הַשְּׁלִישִׁי׃

14 Nethanel the fourth, Raddai the fifth,

יד נְתַנְאֵל הָרְבִיעִי רַדַּי הַחֲמִישִׁי׃

2:4 His daughter-in-law *Tamar* also bore him *Peretz* and *Zerach* *Rashi* wonders why *Ezra* mentions the seemingly shameful incident of *Yehuda* and *Tamar*. Perhaps the answer is that rather than bringing shame upon *Yehuda*, this incident actually reveals his true greatness. Everyone, even the great heroes of the Bible, makes mistakes. However, it is to *Yehuda's* credit that he recognizes, admits and takes responsibility for his error rather than trying to cover it up, and also refrains from repeating his mistake (Genesis 38:26). This quality of humility is necessary in the forefather of the Davidic dynasty and, ultimately, the *Mashiach*. Many other nations would have chosen a king with an unblemished background and impeccable lineage, yet king *David* was a product of a troubling relationship. A powerful lesson can be learned from king *David's* humble origins: No matter what one's background is, all people have the ability to overcome their shortcomings and make a difference in the world.

Rashi
(1040–1105)

Divrei Hayamim I/I Chronicles
Chapter 2

15 Ozem the sixth, *David* the seventh;

16 their sisters were *Tzeruya* and *Avigail*. The sons of *Tzeruya*: *Avishai*, *Yoav*, and *Asael*, three.

17 *Avigail* bore Amasa, and the father of Amasa was Jether the Ishmaelite.

18 *Kalev* son of *Chetzron* had children by his wife Azubah, and by Jerioth; these were her sons: Jesher, Shobab, and Ardon.

19 When Azubah died, *Kalev* married *Efrat*, who bore him *Chur*.

20 *Chur* begot *Uri*, and *Uri* begot *Betzalel*.

21 Afterward *Chetzron* had relations with the daughter of Machir father of *Gilad* – he had married her when he was sixty years old – and she bore him Segub;

22 and Segub begot *Yair*; he had twenty-three cities in the land of *Gilad*.

23 But Geshur and Aram took from them Havvoth-jair, Kenath and its dependencies, sixty towns. All these were the sons of Machir, the father of *Gilad*.

24 After the death of *Chetzron*, in Caleb-ephrathah, *Aviya*, wife of *Chetzron*, bore Ashhur, the father of Tekoa.

25 The sons of Jerahmeel the first-born of *Chetzron*: *Ram* his first-born, Bunah, Oren, Ozem, and *Achiya*.

26 Jerahmeel had another wife, whose name was Atarah; she was the mother of Onam.

27 The sons of *Ram* the first-born of Jerahmeel: Maaz, Jamin, and Eker.

28 The sons of Onam: Shammai and Jada. The sons of Shammai: *Nadav* and Abishur.

29 The name of Abishur's wife was *Avichayil*, and she bore him Ahban and Molid.

30 The sons of *Nadav*: Seled and Appaim; Seled died childless.

31 The sons of Appaim: Ishi. The sons of Ishi: Sheshan. The sons of Sheshan: Ahlai.

Divrei Hayamim I/I Chronicles		דברי הימים א
Chapter 2		פרק ב

32 The sons of Jada, Shammai's brother: Jether and *Yonatan*; Jether died childless.

לב וּבְנֵי יָדָע אֲחִי שַׁמַּי יֶתֶר וְיוֹנָתָן וַיָּמָת יֶתֶר לֹא בָנִים׃

33 The sons of *Yonatan*: Peleth and Zaza. These were the descendants of Jerahmeel.

לג וּבְנֵי יוֹנָתָן פֶּלֶת וְזָזָא אֵלֶּה הָיוּ בְּנֵי יְרַחְמְאֵל׃

34 Sheshan had no sons, only daughters; Sheshan had an Egyptian slave, whose name was Jarha.

לד וְלֹא־הָיָה לְשֵׁשָׁן בָּנִים כִּי אִם־בָּנוֹת וּלְשֵׁשָׁן עֶבֶד מִצְרִי וּשְׁמוֹ יַרְחָע׃

35 So Sheshan gave his daughter in marriage to Jarha his slave; and she bore him Attai.

לה וַיִּתֵּן שֵׁשָׁן אֶת־בִּתּוֹ לְיַרְחָע עַבְדּוֹ לְאִשָּׁה וַתֵּלֶד לוֹ אֶת־עַתָּי׃

36 Attai begot *Natan*, and *Natan* begot Zabad.

לו וְעַתַּי הֹלִיד אֶת־נָתָן וְנָתָן הוֹלִיד אֶת־זָבָד׃

37 Zabad begot Ephlal, and Ephlal begot Oved.

לז וְזָבָד הוֹלִיד אֶת־אֶפְלָל וְאֶפְלָל הוֹלִיד אֶת־עוֹבֵד׃

38 Oved begot *Yehu*, and *Yehu* begot *Azarya*.

לח וְעוֹבֵד הוֹלִיד אֶת־יֵהוּא וְיֵהוּא הֹלִיד אֶת־עֲזַרְיָה׃

39 *Azarya* begot Helez, and Helez begot Eleasah.

לט וַעֲזַרְיָה הֹלִיד אֶת־חָלֶץ וְחֶלֶץ הֹלִיד אֶת־אֶלְעָשָׂה׃

40 Eleasah begot Sisamai, and Sisamai begot *Shalum*.

מ וְאֶלְעָשָׂה הֹלִיד אֶת־סִסְמָי וְסִסְמַי הֹלִיד אֶת־שַׁלּוּם׃

41 *Shalum* begot Jekamiah, and Jekamiah begot Elishama.

מא וְשַׁלּוּם הוֹלִיד אֶת־יְקַמְיָה וִיקַמְיָה הֹלִיד אֶת־אֱלִישָׁמָע׃

42 The sons of *Kalev* brother of Jerahmeel: Meshah his first-born, who was the father of Ziph. The sons of Mareshah father of *Chevron*.

מב וּבְנֵי כָלֵב אֲחִי יְרַחְמְאֵל מֵישָׁע בְּכֹרוֹ הוּא אֲבִי־זִיף וּבְנֵי מָרֵשָׁה אֲבִי חֶבְרוֹן׃

43 The sons of *Chevron*: *Korach*, Tappuah, Rekem, and Shema.

מג וּבְנֵי חֶבְרוֹן קֹרַח וְתַפֻּחַ וְרֶקֶם וָשָׁמַע׃

44 Shema begot Raham the father of Jorkeam, and Rekem begot Shammai.

מד וְשֶׁמַע הוֹלִיד אֶת־רַחַם אֲבִי יָרְקֳעָם וְרֶקֶם הוֹלִיד אֶת־שַׁמָּי׃

45 The son of Shammai: Maon, and Maon begot Bethzur.

מה וּבֶן־שַׁמַּי מָעוֹן וּמָעוֹן אֲבִי בֵית־צוּר׃

46 Ephah, *Kalev's* concubine, bore Haran, Moza, and Gazez; Haran begot Gazez.

מו וְעֵיפָה פִּילֶגֶשׁ כָּלֵב יָלְדָה אֶת־חָרָן וְאֶת־מוֹצָא וְאֶת־גָּזֵז וְחָרָן הֹלִיד אֶת־גָּזֵז׃

47 The sons of Jahdai: Regem, *Yotam*, Geshan, Pelet, Ephah, and Shaaph.

מז וּבְנֵי יָהְדָּי רֶגֶם וְיוֹתָם וְגֵישָׁן וָפֶלֶט וְעֵיפָה וָשָׁעַף׃

48 Maacah, *Kalev's* concubine, bore Sheber and Tirhanah.

מח פִּלֶגֶשׁ כָּלֵב מַעֲכָה יָלַד שֶׁבֶר וְאֶת־תִּרְחֲנָה׃

49 She also bore Shaaph father of Madmannah, Sheva father of Machbenah and father of Gibea; the daughter of *Kalev* was Achsah.

מט וַתֵּלֶד שַׁעַף אֲבִי מַדְמַנָּה אֶת־שְׁוָא אֲבִי מַכְבֵּנָה וַאֲבִי גִבְעָא וּבַת־כָּלֵב עַכְסָה׃

Divrei Hayamim I / I Chronicles
Chapter 3

דברי הימים א
פרק ג

50 These were the descendants of *Kalev*. The sons of *Chur* the first-born of *Efrat*: Shobal father of *Kiryat Ye'arim*,

נ אֵלֶּה הָיוּ בְּנֵי כָלֵב בֶּן־חוּר בְּכוֹר אֶפְרָתָה שׁוֹבָל אֲבִי קִרְיַת יְעָרִים:

51 Salma father of *Beit Lechem*, Hareph father of Beth-gader.

נא שַׂלְמָא אֲבִי בֵית־לָחֶם חָרֵף אֲבִי בֵית־גָּדֵר:

52 Shobal father of *Kiryat Ye'arim* had sons: Haroeh, half of the Menuhoth.

נב וַיִּהְיוּ בָנִים לְשׁוֹבָל אֲבִי קִרְיַת יְעָרִים הָרֹאֶה חֲצִי הַמְּנֻחוֹת:

53 And the families of *Kiryat Ye'arim*: the Ithrites, the Puthites, the Shumathites, and the Mishraites; from these came the Zorathites and the Eshtaolites.

נג וּמִשְׁפְּחוֹת קִרְיַת יְעָרִים הַיִּתְרִי וְהַפּוּתִי וְהַשֻּׁמָתִי וְהַמִּשְׁרָעִי מֵאֵלֶּה יָצְאוּ הַצָּרְעָתִי וְהָאֶשְׁתָּאֻלִי:

54 The sons of Salma: *Beit Lechem*, the Netophathites, Atroth-beth-joab, and half of the Manahathites, the Zorites.

נד בְּנֵי שַׂלְמָא בֵּית לֶחֶם וּנְטוֹפָתִי עַטְרוֹת בֵּית יוֹאָב וַחֲצִי הַמָּנַחְתִּי הַצָּרְעִי:

55 The families of the scribes that dwelt at Jabez: the Tirathites, the Shimeathites, the Sucathites; these are the Kenites who came from Hammath, father of the house of Rechab.

נה וּמִשְׁפְּחוֹת סֹפְרִים ישבו [יֹשְׁבֵי] יַעְבֵּץ תִּרְעָתִים שִׁמְעָתִים שׂוּכָתִים הֵמָּה הַקִּינִים הַבָּאִים מֵחַמַּת אֲבִי בֵית־רֵכָב:

3
1 These are the sons of *David* who were born to him in *Chevron*: the first-born *Amnon*, by Ahinoam the Yizraelite; the second *Daniel*, by *Avigail* the Carmelite;

א וְאֵלֶּה הָיוּ בְּנֵי דָוִיד אֲשֶׁר נוֹלַד־לוֹ בְּחֶבְרוֹן הַבְּכוֹר אַמְנֹן לַאֲחִינֹעַם הַיִּזְרְעֵאלִית שֵׁנִי דָּנִיֵּאל לַאֲבִיגַיִל הַכַּרְמְלִית:

2 the third *Avshalom*, son of Maacah daughter of King Talmai of Geshur; the fourth *Adoniyahu*, son of Haggith;

ב הַשְּׁלִשִׁי לְאַבְשָׁלוֹם בֶּן־מַעֲכָה בַּת־תַּלְמַי מֶלֶךְ גְּשׁוּר הָרְבִיעִי אֲדֹנִיָּה בֶן־חַגִּית:

3 the fifth Shephatiah, by Abital; the sixth Ithream, by his wife Eglah;

ג הַחֲמִישִׁי שְׁפַטְיָה לַאֲבִיטָל הַשִּׁשִּׁי יִתְרְעָם לְעֶגְלָה אִשְׁתּוֹ:

4 six were born to him in *Chevron*. He reigned there seven years and six months, and in *Yerushalayim* he reigned thirty-three years.

ד שִׁשָּׁה נוֹלַד־לוֹ בְחֶבְרוֹן וַיִּמְלָךְ־שָׁם שֶׁבַע שָׁנִים וְשִׁשָּׁה חֳדָשִׁים וּשְׁלֹשִׁים וְשָׁלוֹשׁ שָׁנָה מָלַךְ בִּירוּשָׁלָ͏ִם:

shi-SHAH no-lad LO v'-khev-RON va-YIM-lokh SHAM SHE-va sha-NEEM v'-shi-SHAH kho-da-SHEEM ush-lo-SHEEM v'-sha-LOSH sha-NAH ma-LAKH bee-ru-sha-LA-im

Chaim Weizmann (1874–1952)

3:4 And in *Yerushalayim* he reigned thirty-three years The text delineates exactly how many years of *David*'s reign were spent ruling in *Chevron*, and how many in *Yerushalayim*, because ruling in *Yerushalayim*, Hashem's chosen city, is qualitatively different than ruling anywhere else, even another city in *Eretz Yisrael*. *Yerushalayim* is the center of the world and the holiest place on earth. In December 1948, the first president of Israel, Chaim Weizmann, passionately declared: "Jerusalem holds a unique place in the heart of every Jew. Jerusalem is to us the quintessence of the Palestine idea. Its restoration symbolizes the redemption of Israel…To us Jerusalem has both a spiritual and a temporal significance. It is the City of God, the seat of our ancient sanctuary. But it is also the capital of David and Solomon, the City of the Great King, the metropolis of our ancient commonwealth…It is the center of our ancient national glory. It was our lodestar in all our

Divrei Hayamim I / I Chronicles
Chapter 3

דברי הימים א
פרק ג

5 These were born to him in *Yerushalayim*: Shimea, Shobab, *Natan*, and *Shlomo*, four by Bathshua daughter of Ammiel;

ה וְאֵלֶּה נוּלְּדוּ־לוֹ בִירוּשָׁלָיִם שִׁמְעָא וְשׁוֹבָב וְנָתָן וּשְׁלֹמֹה אַרְבָּעָה לְבַת־שׁוּעַ בַּת־עַמִּיאֵל:

6 then Ibhar, Elishama, Eliphelet,

ו וְיִבְחָר וֶאֱלִישָׁמָע וֶאֱלִיפָלֶט:

7 Nogah, Nepheg, Japhia,

ז וְנֹגַהּ וְנֶפֶג וְיָפִיעַ:

8 Elishama, Eliada, and Eliphelet – nine.

ח וֶאֱלִישָׁמָע וְאֶלְיָדָע וֶאֱלִיפֶלֶט תִּשְׁעָה:

9 All were *David's* sons, besides the sons of the concubines; and *Tamar* was their sister.

ט כֹּל בְּנֵי דָוִיד מִלְּבַד בְּנֵי־פִילַגְשִׁים וְתָמָר אֲחוֹתָם:

10 The son of *Shlomo*: *Rechovam*; his son *Aviya*, his son *Asa*, his son *Yehoshafat*,

י וּבֶן־שְׁלֹמֹה רְחַבְעָם אֲבִיָּה בְנוֹ אָסָא בְנוֹ יְהוֹשָׁפָט בְּנוֹ:

11 his son *Yoram*, his son *Achazyahu*, his son *Yoash*,

יא יוֹרָם בְּנוֹ אֲחַזְיָהוּ בְנוֹ יוֹאָשׁ בְּנוֹ:

12 his son *Amatzya*, his son *Azarya*, his son *Yotam*,

יב אֲמַצְיָהוּ בְנוֹ עֲזַרְיָה בְנוֹ יוֹתָם בְּנוֹ:

13 his son *Achaz*, his son *Chizkiyahu*, his son *Menashe*,

יג אָחָז בְּנוֹ חִזְקִיָּהוּ בְנוֹ מְנַשֶּׁה בְנוֹ:

14 his son *Amon*, and his son *Yoshiyahu*.

יד אָמוֹן בְּנוֹ יֹאשִׁיָּהוּ בְנוֹ:

15 The sons of *Yoshiyahu*: *Yochanan* the first-born, the second *Yehoyakim*, the third *Tzidkiyahu*, the fourth *Shalum*.

טו וּבְנֵי יֹאשִׁיָּהוּ הַבְּכוֹר יוֹחָנָן הַשֵּׁנִי יְהוֹיָקִים הַשְּׁלִשִׁי צִדְקִיָּהוּ הָרְבִיעִי שַׁלּוּם:

16 The descendants of *Yehoyakim*: his son *Yechonya*, his son *Tzidkiyahu*;

טז וּבְנֵי יְהוֹיָקִים יְכָנְיָה בְנוֹ צִדְקִיָּה בְנוֹ:

17 and the sons of *Yechonya*, the captive: *Shealtiel* his son,

יז וּבְנֵי יְכָנְיָה אַסִּר שְׁאַלְתִּיאֵל בְּנוֹ:

18 MalHiram, Pedaiah, Shenazzar, Jekamiah, Hoshama, and Nedabiah;

יח וּמַלְכִּירָם וּפְדָיָה וְשֶׁנְאַצַּר יְקַמְיָה הוֹשָׁמָע וּנְדַבְיָה:

19 the sons of Pedaiah: *Zerubavel* and *Shim'i*; the sons of *Zerubavel*: Meshullam and *Chananya*, and Shelomith was their sister;

יט וּבְנֵי פְדָיָה זְרֻבָּבֶל וְשִׁמְעִי וּבֶן־זְרֻבָּבֶל מְשֻׁלָּם וַחֲנַנְיָה וּשְׁלֹמִית אֲחוֹתָם:

20 Hashubah, Ohel, *Berechya*, Hasadiah, and Jushabhesed – five.

כ וַחֲשֻׁבָה וָאֹהֶל וּבֶרֶכְיָה וַחֲסַדְיָה יוּשַׁב חֶסֶד חָמֵשׁ:

21 And the sons of *Chananya*: Pelatiah and Jeshaiah; the sons of [Jeshaiah]: Rephaiah; the sons of [Rephaiah]: Arnan; the sons of [Arnan]: *Ovadya*; the sons of [*Ovadya*]: Shechanya.

כא וּבֶן־חֲנַנְיָה פְּלַטְיָה וִישַׁעְיָה בְּנֵי רְפָיָה בְּנֵי אַרְנָן בְּנֵי עֹבַדְיָה בְּנֵי שְׁכַנְיָה:

wanderings. It embodies all that is noblest in our hopes for the future. Jerusalem is the eternal mother of the Jewish people, precious and beloved even in its desolation. When David made Jerusalem the capital of Judea, on that day there began the Jewish Commonwealth… It seems inconceivable that the establishment of a Jewish State in Palestine should be accompanied by the detachment from it of its spiritual center and historical capital."

Divrei Hayamim I/I Chronicles
Chapter 4

דברי הימים א
פרק ד

22 And the sons of *Shechanya*: *Shemaya*; and the sons of *Shemaya*: Hattush, and Igal, and Bariah, and Neariah, and *Shafat* – six.

כב וּבְנֵי שְׁכַנְיָה שְׁמַעְיָה וּבְנֵי שְׁמַעְיָה חַטּוּשׁ וְיִגְאָל וּבָרִיחַ וּנְעַרְיָה וְשָׁפָט שִׁשָּׁה׃

23 And the sons of Neariah: Elioenai, and Hizkiah, and Azrikam – three.

כג וּבֶן־נְעַרְיָה אֶלְיוֹעֵינַי וְחִזְקִיָּה וְעַזְרִיקָם שְׁלֹשָׁה׃

24 And the sons of Elioenai: Hodaviah, and *Elyashiv*, and Pelaiah, and Akkub, and *Yochanan*, and Delaiah, and Anani – seven.

כד וּבְנֵי אֶלְיוֹעֵינַי הדיוהו [הוֹדַוְיָהוּ] וְאֶלְיָשִׁיב וּפְלָיָה וְעַקּוּב וְיוֹחָנָן וּדְלָיָה וַעֲנָנִי שִׁבְעָה׃

4 1 The sons of *Yehuda*: *Peretz*, *Chetzron*, Carmi, *Chur*, and Shobal.

ד א בְּנֵי יְהוּדָה פֶּרֶץ חֶצְרוֹן וְכַרְמִי וְחוּר וְשׁוֹבָל׃

2 Reaiah son of Shobal begot Jahath, and Jahath begot Ahumai and Lahad. These were the families of the Zorathites.

ב וּרְאָיָה בֶן־שׁוֹבָל הוֹלִיד אֶת־יַחַת וְיַחַת הֹלִיד אֶת־אֲחוּמַי וְאֶת־לָהַד אֵלֶּה מִשְׁפְּחוֹת הַצָּרְעָתִי׃

3 These were [the sons of] the father of Etam: *Yizrael*, Ishma, and Idbash; and the name of their sister was Hazlelponi,

ג וְאֵלֶּה אֲבִי עֵיטָם יִזְרְעֶאל וְיִשְׁמָא וְיִדְבָּשׁ וְשֵׁם אֲחוֹתָם הַצְלֶלְפּוֹנִי׃

4 and Penuel was the father of Gedor, and Ezer the father of Hushah. These were the sons of *Chur*, the first-born of *Efrat*, the father of *Beit Lechem*.

ד וּפְנוּאֵל אֲבִי גְדֹר וְעֵזֶר אֲבִי חוּשָׁה אֵלֶּה בְנֵי־חוּר בְּכוֹר אֶפְרָתָה אֲבִי בֵּית לָחֶם׃

5 Ashhur the father of Tekoa had two wives, Helah and Naarah;

ה וּלְאַשְׁחוּר אֲבִי תְקוֹעַ הָיוּ שְׁתֵּי נָשִׁים חֶלְאָה וְנַעֲרָה׃

6 Naarah bore him Ahuzam, Hepher, Temeni, and Ahashtari. These were the sons of Naarah.

ו וַתֵּלֶד לוֹ נַעֲרָה אֶת־אֲחֻזָּם וְאֶת־חֵפֶר וְאֶת־תֵּימְנִי וְאֶת־הָאֲחַשְׁתָּרִי אֵלֶּה בְּנֵי נַעֲרָה׃

7 The sons of Helah: Zereth, Zohar, and Ethnan.

ז וּבְנֵי חֶלְאָה צֶרֶת יצחר [וְצֹחַר] וְאֶתְנָן׃

8 Koz was the father of Anub, Zobebah, and the families of Aharhel son of Harum.

ח וְקוֹץ הוֹלִיד אֶת־עָנוּב וְאֶת־הַצֹּבֵבָה וּמִשְׁפְּחוֹת אֲחַרְחֵל בֶּן־הָרוּם׃

9 Jabez was more esteemed than his brothers; and his mother named him Jabez, "Because," she said, "I bore him in pain."

ט וַיְהִי יַעְבֵּץ נִכְבָּד מֵאֶחָיו וְאִמּוֹ קָרְאָה שְׁמוֹ יַעְבֵּץ לֵאמֹר כִּי יָלַדְתִּי בְּעֹצֶב׃

10 Jabez invoked the God of *Yisrael*, saying, "Oh, bless me, enlarge my territory, stand by me, and make me not suffer pain from misfortune!" And *Hashem* granted what he asked.

י וַיִּקְרָא יַעְבֵּץ לֵאלֹהֵי יִשְׂרָאֵל לֵאמֹר אִם־בָּרֵךְ תְּבָרֲכֵנִי וְהִרְבִּיתָ אֶת־גְּבוּלִי וְהָיְתָה יָדְךָ עִמִּי וְעָשִׂיתָ מֵּרָעָה לְבִלְתִּי עָצְבִּי וַיָּבֵא אֱלֹהִים אֵת אֲשֶׁר־שָׁאָל׃

11 Chelub the brother of Shuhah begot Mehir, who was the father of Eshton.

יא וּכְלוּב אֲחִי־שׁוּחָה הוֹלִיד אֶת־מְחִיר הוּא אֲבִי אֶשְׁתּוֹן׃

12 Eshton begot Bethrapha, Paseah, and Tehinnah father of Ir-nahash. These were the men of Recah.

יב וְאֶשְׁתּוֹן הוֹלִיד אֶת־בֵּית רָפָא וְאֶת־פָּסֵחַ וְאֶת־תְּחִנָּה אֲבִי עִיר נָחָשׁ אֵלֶּה אַנְשֵׁי רֵכָה׃

13 The sons of Kenaz: *Otniel* and *Seraya*; and the sons of *Otniel*:

יג וּבְנֵי קְנַז עָתְנִיאֵל וּשְׂרָיָה וּבְנֵי עָתְנִיאֵל חֲתַת׃

Divrei Hayamim I / I Chronicles
Chapter 4

14 Hathath and Meonothai. He begot Ophrah. *Seraya* begot *Yoav* father of Ge-harashim, so-called because they were craftsmen.

15 The sons of *Kalev* son of Jephunneh: Iru, Elah, and Naam; and the sons of Elah: Kenaz.

16 The sons of Jehallelel: Ziph, Ziphah, Tiria, and Asarel.

17 The sons of Ezrah: Jether, Mered, Epher, and Jalon. She conceived and bore *Miriam*, Shammai, and Ishbah father of Eshtemoa.

18 And his Judahite wife bore Jered father of Gedor, *Chever* father of Soco, and Jekuthiel father of *Zanoach*. These were the sons of Bithiah daughter of Pharaoh, whom Mered married.

19 The sons of the wife of Hodiah sister of Naham were the fathers of Keilah the Garmite and Eshtemoa the Maacathite.

20 The sons of *Shimon*: *Amnon*, Rinnah, Ben-hanan, and Tilon. The sons of Ishi: Zoheth and Ben-zoheth.

21 The sons of *Sheila* son of *Yehuda*: Er father of Lecah, Laadah father of Mareshah, and the families of the linen factory at Beth-ashbea;

22 and Jokim, and the men of Cozeba and *Yoash*, and Saraph, who married into Moab and Yashuvi Lehem (the records are ancient).

23 These were the potters who dwelt at Netaim and Gedera; they dwelt there in the king's service.

24 The sons of *Shimon*: Nemuel, Jamin, Jarib, *Zerach*, *Shaul*;

25 his son *Shalum*, his son Mibsam, his son Mishma.

26 The sons of Mishma: his son Hammuel, his son Zaccur, his son *Shim'i*.

27 *Shim'i* had sixteen sons and six daughters; but his brothers had not many children; in all, their families were not as prolific as the Judahites.

28 They dwelt in *Be'er Sheva*, Moladah, Hazar-shual,

29 Bilhah, Ezem, Tolad,

30 Bethuel, Hormah, *Tziklag*,

דברי הימים א
פרק ד

יד וּמְעוֹנֹתַי הוֹלִיד אֶת־עָפְרָה וּשְׂרָיָה הוֹלִיד אֶת־יוֹאָב אֲבִי גֵּיא חֲרָשִׁים כִּי חֲרָשִׁים הָיוּ:

טו וּבְנֵי כָלֵב בֶּן־יְפֻנֶּה עִירוּ אֵלָה וָנָעַם וּבְנֵי אֵלָה וּקְנַז:

טז וּבְנֵי יְהַלֶּלְאֵל זִיף וְזִיפָה תִּירְיָא וַאֲשַׂרְאֵל:

יז וּבֶן עֶזְרָה יֶתֶר וּמֶרֶד וְעֵפֶר וְיָלוֹן וַתַּהַר אֶת־מִרְיָם וְאֶת־שַׁמַּי וְאֶת־יִשְׁבָּח אֲבִי אֶשְׁתְּמֹעַ:

יח וְאִשְׁתּוֹ הַיְהֻדִיָּה יָלְדָה אֶת־יֶרֶד אֲבִי גְדוֹר וְאֶת־חֶבֶר אֲבִי שׂוֹכוֹ וְאֶת־יְקוּתִיאֵל אֲבִי זָנוֹחַ וְאֵלֶּה בְּנֵי בִּתְיָה בַת־פַּרְעֹה אֲשֶׁר לָקַח מָרֶד:

יט וּבְנֵי אֵשֶׁת הוֹדִיָּה אֲחוֹת נַחַם אֲבִי קְעִילָה הַגַּרְמִי וְאֶשְׁתְּמֹעַ הַמַּעֲכָתִי:

כ וּבְנֵי שִׁימוֹן אַמְנוֹן וְרִנָּה בֶּן־חָנָן וְתוֹלוֹן [וְתִילוֹן] וּבְנֵי יִשְׁעִי זוֹחֵת וּבֶן־זוֹחֵת:

כא בְּנֵי שֵׁלָה בֶן־יְהוּדָה עֵר אֲבִי לֵכָה וְלַעְדָּה אֲבִי מָרֵשָׁה וּמִשְׁפְּחוֹת בֵּית־עֲבֹדַת הַבֻּץ לְבֵית אַשְׁבֵּעַ:

כב וְיוֹקִים וְאַנְשֵׁי כֹזֵבָא וְיוֹאָשׁ וְשָׂרָף אֲשֶׁר־בָּעֲלוּ לְמוֹאָב וְיָשֻׁבִי לָחֶם וְהַדְּבָרִים עַתִּיקִים:

כג הֵמָּה הַיּוֹצְרִים וְיֹשְׁבֵי נְטָעִים וּגְדֵרָה עִם־הַמֶּלֶךְ בִּמְלַאכְתּוֹ יָשְׁבוּ שָׁם:

כד בְּנֵי שִׁמְעוֹן נְמוּאֵל וְיָמִין יָרִיב זֶרַח שָׁאוּל:

כה שַׁלֻּם בְּנוֹ מִבְשָׂם בְּנוֹ מִשְׁמָע בְּנוֹ:

כו וּבְנֵי מִשְׁמָע חַמּוּאֵל בְּנוֹ זַכּוּר בְּנוֹ שִׁמְעִי בְנוֹ:

כז וּלְשִׁמְעִי בָּנִים שִׁשָּׁה עָשָׂר וּבָנוֹת שֵׁשׁ וּלְאֶחָיו אֵין בָּנִים רַבִּים וְכֹל מִשְׁפַּחְתָּם לֹא הִרְבּוּ עַד־בְּנֵי יְהוּדָה:

כח וַיֵּשְׁבוּ בִּבְאֵר־שֶׁבַע וּמוֹלָדָה וַחֲצַר שׁוּעָל:

כט וּבְבִלְהָה וּבְעֶצֶם וּבְתוֹלָד:

ל וּבִבְתוּאֵל וּבְחָרְמָה וּבְצִיקְלָג:

Divrei Hayamim I / I Chronicles
Chapter 4

דברי הימים א
פרק ד

31 Beth-marcaboth, Hazar-susim, Beth-biri, and *Shaarayim*. These were their towns until *David* became king,

לא וּבְבֵית מַרְכָּבוֹת וּבַחֲצַר סוּסִים וּבְבֵית בִּרְאִי וּבְשַׁעֲרָיִם אֵלֶּה עָרֵיהֶם עַד־מְלֹךְ דָּוִיד:

32 together with their villages, Etam, Ain, Rimmon, Tochen, and Ashan – five towns,

לב וְחַצְרֵיהֶם עֵיטָם וָעַיִן רִמּוֹן וְתֹכֶן וְעָשָׁן עָרִים חָמֵשׁ:

33 along with all their villages that were around these towns as far as Baal; such were their settlements. Registered in their genealogy were:

לג וְכָל־חַצְרֵיהֶם אֲשֶׁר סְבִיבוֹת הֶעָרִים הָאֵלֶּה עַד־בָּעַל זֹאת מוֹשְׁבֹתָם וְהִתְיַחְשָׂם לָהֶם:

34 Meshobab, Jamlech, Joshah son of *Amatzya*,

לד וּמְשׁוֹבָב וְיַמְלֵךְ וְיוֹשָׁה בֶּן־אֲמַצְיָה:

35 *Yoel*, *Yehu* son of Joshibiah son of *Seraya* son of Asiel.

לה וְיוֹאֵל וְיֵהוּא בֶּן־יוֹשִׁבְיָה בֶּן־שְׂרָיָה בֶּן־עֲשִׂיאֵל:

36 Elioenai, Jaakobah, Jeshohaiah, Asaiah, Adiel, Jesimiel, Benaiah,

לו וְאֶלְיוֹעֵינַי וְיַעֲקֹבָה וִישׁוֹחָיָה וַעֲשָׂיָה וַעֲדִיאֵל וִישִׂימִאֵל וּבְנָיָה:

37 Ziza son of Shiphi son of Allon son of Jedaiah son of Shimri son of *Shemaya* –

לז וְזִיזָא בֶן־שִׁפְעִי בֶן־אַלּוֹן בֶּן־יְדָיָה בֶן־שִׁמְרִי בֶּן־שְׁמַעְיָה:

38 these mentioned by name were chiefs in their families, and their clans increased greatly.

לח אֵלֶּה הַבָּאִים בְּשֵׁמוֹת נְשִׂיאִים בְּמִשְׁפְּחוֹתָם וּבֵית אֲבוֹתֵיהֶם פָּרְצוּ לָרוֹב:

39 They went to the approaches to Gedor, to the eastern side of the valley, in search of pasture for their flocks.

לט וַיֵּלְכוּ לִמְבוֹא גְדֹר עַד לְמִזְרַח הַגָּיְא לְבַקֵּשׁ מִרְעֶה לְצֹאנָם:

40 They found rich, good pasture, and the land was ample, quiet, and peaceful. The former inhabitants were of Ham;

va-yim-tz'-U mir-EH sha-MAYN va-TOV v'-ha-A-retz ra-kha-VAT ya-DA-yim v'-sho-KE-tet ush-lay-VAH KEE min KHAM ha-yo-sh'-VEEM sham l'-fa-NEEM

מ וַיִּמְצְאוּ מִרְעֶה שָׁמֵן וָטוֹב וְהָאָרֶץ רַחֲבַת יָדַיִם וְשֹׁקֶטֶת וּשְׁלֵוָה כִּי מִן־חָם הַיֹּשְׁבִים שָׁם לְפָנִים:

41 those recorded by name came in the days of King *Chizkiyahu* of *Yehuda*, and attacked their encampments and the Meunim who were found there, and wiped them out forever, and settled in their place, because there was pasture there for their flocks.

מא וַיָּבֹאוּ אֵלֶּה הַכְּתוּבִים בְּשֵׁמוֹת בִּימֵי יְחִזְקִיָּהוּ מֶלֶךְ־יְהוּדָה וַיַּכּוּ אֶת־אָהֳלֵיהֶם וְאֶת־הַמְעִינִים [הַמְּעוּנִים] אֲשֶׁר נִמְצְאוּ־שָׁמָּה וַיַּחֲרִימֻם עַד־הַיּוֹם הַזֶּה וַיֵּשְׁבוּ תַּחְתֵּיהֶם כִּי־מִרְעֶה לְצֹאנָם שָׁם:

שלוה
שלום

4:40 The land was ample, quiet, and peaceful The Hebrew word for 'peaceful' in this verse is *shalva* (שלוה), rather than the more common word *'shalom'* (שלום). What is the difference between *shalom* and *shalva*? The 19th-century commentator *Malbim* explains that *shalom* refers an external peace, meaning that one is free from threats or harm. *Shalva*, on the other hand, refers to internal harmony. Accordingly, this verse teaches that the inhabitants of the cities of *Shimon* experienced not only a quiet security from outside threats, but also enjoyed peaceful coexistence with their brethren and neighbors. In his prayer for the peace of Jerusalem (Psalm 122:6) the Psalmist includes both terms: "Pray for the well-being (*shalom*) of *Yerushalayim*; may those who love you be at peace (*shalva*)."

Divrei Hayamim I / I Chronicles
Chapter 5

דברי הימים א
פרק ה

42 And some of them, five hundred of the Simeonites, went to Mount Seir, with Pelatiah, Neariah, Rephaiah, and Uzziel, sons of Ishi, at their head,

מב וּמֵהֶם מִן־בְּנֵי שִׁמְעוֹן הָלְכוּ לְהַר שֵׂעִיר אֲנָשִׁים חֲמֵשׁ מֵאוֹת וּפְלַטְיָה וּנְעַרְיָה וּרְפָיָה וְעֻזִּיאֵל בְּנֵי יִשְׁעִי בְּרֹאשָׁם:

43 and they destroyed the last surviving Amalekites, and they live there to this day.

מג וַיַּכּוּ אֶת־שְׁאֵרִית הַפְּלֵטָה לַעֲמָלֵק וַיֵּשְׁבוּ שָׁם עַד הַיּוֹם הַזֶּה:

5

1 The sons of *Reuven* the first-born of *Yisrael*. (He was the first-born; but when he defiled his father's bed, his birthright was given to the sons of *Yosef* son of *Yisrael*, so he is not reckoned as first-born in the genealogy;

א וּבְנֵי רְאוּבֵן בְּכוֹר־יִשְׂרָאֵל כִּי הוּא הַבְּכוֹר וּבְחַלְּלוֹ יְצוּעֵי אָבִיו נִתְּנָה בְּכֹרָתוֹ לִבְנֵי יוֹסֵף בֶּן־יִשְׂרָאֵל וְלֹא לְהִתְיַחֵשׂ לַבְּכֹרָה:

2 though *Yehuda* became more powerful than his brothers and a leader came from him, yet the birthright belonged to *Yosef*.)

ב כִּי יְהוּדָה גָּבַר בְּאֶחָיו וּלְנָגִיד מִמֶּנּוּ וְהַבְּכֹרָה לְיוֹסֵף:

3 The sons of *Reuven*, the first-born of *Yisrael*: Enoch, Pallu, *Chetzron*, and Carmi.

ג בְּנֵי רְאוּבֵן בְּכוֹר יִשְׂרָאֵל חֲנוֹךְ וּפַלּוּא חֶצְרוֹן וְכַרְמִי:

4 The sons of *Yoel*: his son *Shemaya*, his son Gog, his son *Shim'i*,

ד בְּנֵי יוֹאֵל שְׁמַעְיָה בְנוֹ גּוֹג בְּנוֹ שִׁמְעִי בְנוֹ:

5 his son *Micha*, his son Reaiah, his son Baal,

ה מִיכָה בְנוֹ רְאָיָה בְנוֹ בַּעַל בְּנוֹ:

6 his son Beerah – whom King Tillegath-pilneser of Assyria exiled – was chieftain of the Rebenites.

ו בְּאֵרָה בְנוֹ אֲשֶׁר הֶגְלָה תִּלְּגַת פִּלְנְאֶסֶר מֶלֶךְ אַשֻּׁר הוּא נָשִׂיא לָראוּבֵנִי:

7 And his kinsmen, by their families, according to their lines in the genealogy: the head, Jeiel, and *Zecharya*,

ז וְאֶחָיו לְמִשְׁפְּחֹתָיו בְּהִתְיַחֵשׂ לְתֹלְדוֹתָם הָרֹאשׁ יְעִיאֵל וּזְכַרְיָהוּ:

8 and Bela son of Azaz son of Shema son of *Yoel*; he dwelt in Aroer as far as Nebo and Baal-meon.

ח וּבֶלַע בֶּן־עָזָז בֶּן־שֶׁמַע בֶּן־יוֹאֵל הוּא יוֹשֵׁב בַּעֲרֹעֵר וְעַד־נְבוֹ וּבַעַל מְעוֹן:

9 He also dwelt to the east as far as the fringe of the wilderness this side of the Euphrates, because their cattle had increased in the land of *Gilad*.

ט וְלַמִּזְרָח יָשַׁב עַד־לְבוֹא מִדְבָּרָה לְמִן־הַנָּהָר פְּרָת כִּי מִקְנֵיהֶם רָבוּ בְּאֶרֶץ גִּלְעָד:

10 And in the days of *Shaul* they made war on the Hagrites, who fell by their hand; and they occupied their tents throughout all the region east of *Gilad*.

י וּבִימֵי שָׁאוּל עָשׂוּ מִלְחָמָה עִם־הַהַגְרִאִים וַיִּפְּלוּ בְּיָדָם וַיֵּשְׁבוּ בְּאָהֳלֵיהֶם עַל־כָּל־פְּנֵי מִזְרָח לַגִּלְעָד:

11 The sons of *Gad* dwelt facing them in the land of Bashan as far as Salcah:

יא וּבְנֵי־גָד לְנֶגְדָּם יָשְׁבוּ בְּאֶרֶץ הַבָּשָׁן עַד־סַלְכָה:

12 *Yoel* the chief, Shapham the second, Janai, and *Shafat* in Bashan.

יב יוֹאֵל הָרֹאשׁ וְשָׁפָם הַמִּשְׁנֶה וְיַעְנַי וְשָׁפָט בַּבָּשָׁן:

13 And by clans: *Michael*, Meshullam, Sheba, Jorai, Jacan, Zia, and *Ever* – seven.

יג וַאֲחֵיהֶם לְבֵית אֲבוֹתֵיהֶם מִיכָאֵל וּמְשֻׁלָּם וְשֶׁבַע וְיוֹרַי וְיַעְכָּן וְזִיעַ וָעֵבֶר שִׁבְעָה:

14 These were the sons of *Avichayil* son of Huri son of Jaroah son of *Gilad* son of *Michael* son of Jeshishai son of Jahdo son of Buz;

יד אֵלֶּה בְּנֵי אֲבִיחַיִל בֶּן־חוּרִי בֶּן־יָרוֹחַ בֶּן־גִּלְעָד בֶּן־מִיכָאֵל בֶּן־יְשִׁישַׁי בֶּן־יַחְדּוֹ בֶּן־בּוּז:

Divrei Hayamim I / I Chronicles
Chapter 5

דברי הימים א
פרק ה

15 Ahi son of Abdiel son of Guni was chief of their clan,

טו אֲחִי בֶּן־עַבְדִּיאֵל בֶּן־גּוּנִי רֹאשׁ לְבֵית אֲבוֹתָם:

16 and they dwelt in *Gilad*, in Bashan, and in its dependencies, and in all the pasturelands of Sharon, to their limits.

טז וַיֵּשְׁבוּ בַּגִּלְעָד בַּבָּשָׁן וּבִבְנֹתֶיהָ וּבְכָל־מִגְרְשֵׁי שָׁרוֹן עַל־תּוֹצְאוֹתָם:

17 All of them were registered by genealogies in the days of King *Yotam* of *Yehuda*, and in the days of King *Yerovam* of *Yisrael*.

יז כֻּלָּם הִתְיַחְשׂוּ בִּימֵי יוֹתָם מֶלֶךְ־יְהוּדָה וּבִימֵי יָרָבְעָם מֶלֶךְ־יִשְׂרָאֵל:

18 The Reubenites, the Gadites, and the half-tribe of *Menashe* had warriors who carried shield and sword, drew the bow, and were experienced at war – 44,760, ready for service.

יח בְּנֵי־רְאוּבֵן וְגָדִי וַחֲצִי שֵׁבֶט־מְנַשֶּׁה מִן־בְּנֵי־חַיִל אֲנָשִׁים נֹשְׂאֵי מָגֵן וְחֶרֶב וְדֹרְכֵי קֶשֶׁת וּלְמוּדֵי מִלְחָמָה אַרְבָּעִים וְאַרְבָּעָה אֶלֶף וּשְׁבַע־מֵאוֹת וְשִׁשִּׁים יֹצְאֵי צָבָא:

19 They made war on the Hagrites – Jetur, Naphish, and Nodab.

יט וַיַּעֲשׂוּ מִלְחָמָה עִם־הַהַגְרִיאִים וִיטוּר וְנָפִישׁ וְנוֹדָב:

20 They prevailed against them; the Hagrites and all who were with them were delivered into their hands, for they cried to *Hashem* in the battle, and He responded to their entreaty because they trusted in Him.

va-yay-a-z'-RU a-lay-HEM va-yi-na-t'-NU v'-ya-DAM ha-hag-ree-EEM v'-KHOL she-i-ma-HEM KEE lay-lo-HEEM za-a-KU ba-mil-kha-MAH v'-na-TOR la-HEM kee VA-t'-khu VO

כ וַיֵּעָזְרוּ עֲלֵיהֶם וַיִּנָּתְנוּ בְיָדָם הַהַגְרִיאִים וְכֹל שֶׁעִמָּהֶם כִּי לֵאלֹהִים זָעֲקוּ בַּמִּלְחָמָה וְנַעְתּוֹר לָהֶם כִּי־בָטְחוּ בוֹ:

21 They carried off their livestock: 50,000 of their camels, 250,000 sheep, 2,000 asses, and 100,000 people.

כא וַיִּשְׁבּוּ מִקְנֵיהֶם גְּמַלֵּיהֶם חֲמִשִּׁים אֶלֶף וְצֹאן מָאתַיִם וַחֲמִשִּׁים אֶלֶף וַחֲמוֹרִים אַלְפָּיִם וְנֶפֶשׁ אָדָם מֵאָה אָלֶף:

22 For many fell slain, because it was *Hashem*'s battle. And they dwelt in their place until the exile.

כב כִּי־חֲלָלִים רַבִּים נָפָלוּ כִּי מֵהָאֱלֹהִים הַמִּלְחָמָה וַיֵּשְׁבוּ תַחְתֵּיהֶם עַד־הַגֹּלָה:

23 The members of the half-tribe of *Menashe* dwelt in the land; they were very numerous from Bashan to Baal-hermon, Senir, and Mount *Chermon*.

כג וּבְנֵי חֲצִי שֵׁבֶט מְנַשֶּׁה יָשְׁבוּ בָּאָרֶץ מִבָּשָׁן עַד־בַּעַל חֶרְמוֹן וּשְׂנִיר וְהַר־חֶרְמוֹן הֵמָּה רָבוּ:

24 These were the chiefs of their clans: Epher, Ishi, Eliel, Azriel, *Yirmiyahu*, Hodaviah, and Jahdiel, men of substance, famous men, chiefs of their clans.

כד וְאֵלֶּה רָאשֵׁי בֵית־אֲבוֹתָם וְעֵפֶר וְיִשְׁעִי וֶאֱלִיאֵל וְעַזְרִיאֵל וְיִרְמְיָה וְהוֹדַוְיָה וְיַחְדִּיאֵל אֲנָשִׁים גִּבּוֹרֵי חַיִל אַנְשֵׁי שֵׁמוֹת רָאשִׁים לְבֵית אֲבוֹתָם:

5:20 For they cried to *Hashem* in the battle In the previous verses, we are told that the combined forces of the tribes of *Reuven*, *Gad* and *Menashe* numbered an impressive 44,760 troops of exceptional quality. And yet, we are told that the reason they were victorious in battle is because they trusted in *Hashem* and believed that He would help them and save them. As we have seen numerous times throughout *Tanakh*, success in the Land of Israel is not tied to physical capability and effort alone, though these are very important, but also to faith and trust in God.

Divrei Hayamim I / I Chronicles
Chapter 5

דברי הימים א
פרק ה

25 But they trespassed against the God of their fathers by going astray after the gods of the peoples of the land, whom *Hashem* had destroyed before them.

כה וַיִּמְעֲלוּ בֵּאלֹהֵי אֲבוֹתֵיהֶם וַיִּזְנוּ אַחֲרֵי אֱלֹהֵי עַמֵּי־הָאָרֶץ אֲשֶׁר־הִשְׁמִיד אֱלֹהִים מִפְּנֵיהֶם:

26 So the God of *Yisrael* roused the spirit of King Pul of Assyria – the spirit of King Tillegath-pilneser of Assyria – and he carried them away, namely, the Reubenites, the Gadites, and the half-tribe of *Menashe*, and brought them to Halah, Habor, Hara, and the river Gozan, to this day.

כו וַיָּעַר אֱלֹהֵי יִשְׂרָאֵל אֶת־רוּחַ פּוּל מֶלֶךְ־אַשּׁוּר וְאֶת־רוּחַ תִּלְּגַת פִּלְנֶסֶר מֶלֶךְ אַשּׁוּר וַיַּגְלֵם לָראוּבֵנִי וְלַגָּדִי וְלַחֲצִי שֵׁבֶט מְנַשֶּׁה וַיְבִיאֵם לַחְלַח וְחָבוֹר וְהָרָא וּנְהַר גּוֹזָן עַד הַיּוֹם הַזֶּה:

27 The sons of *Levi*: *Gershon*, *Kehat*, and *Merari*.

כז בְּנֵי לֵוִי גֵּרְשׁוֹן קְהָת וּמְרָרִי:

28 The sons of *Kehat*: *Amram*, *Izhar*, *Chevron*, and Uzziel.

כח וּבְנֵי קְהָת עַמְרָם יִצְהָר וְחֶבְרוֹן וְעֻזִּיאֵל:

29 The children of *Amram*: *Aharon*, *Moshe*, and *Miriam*. The sons of *Aharon*: *Nadav*, *Avihu*, *Elazar*, and *Itamar*.

כט וּבְנֵי עַמְרָם אַהֲרֹן וּמֹשֶׁה וּמִרְיָם וּבְנֵי אַהֲרֹן נָדָב וַאֲבִיהוּא אֶלְעָזָר וְאִיתָמָר:

30 *Elazar* begot *Pinchas*, *Pinchas* begot Abishua,

ל אֶלְעָזָר הוֹלִיד אֶת־פִּינְחָס פִּינְחָס הֹלִיד אֶת־אֲבִישׁוּעַ:

31 Abishua begot Bukki, Bukki begot Uzzi,

לא וַאֲבִישׁוּעַ הוֹלִיד אֶת־בֻּקִּי וּבֻקִּי הוֹלִיד אֶת־עֻזִּי:

32 Uzzi begot Zerahiah, Zerahiah begot Meraioth,

לב וְעֻזִּי הוֹלִיד אֶת־זְרַחְיָה וּזְרַחְיָה הוֹלִיד אֶת־מְרָיוֹת:

33 Meraioth begot Amariah, Amariah begot *Achituv*,

לג מְרָיוֹת הוֹלִיד אֶת־אֲמַרְיָה וַאֲמַרְיָה הוֹלִיד אֶת־אֲחִיטוּב:

34 *Achituv* begot *Tzadok*, *Tzadok* begot Ahimaaz,

לד וַאֲחִיטוּב הוֹלִיד אֶת־צָדוֹק וְצָדוֹק הוֹלִיד אֶת־אֲחִימָעַץ:

35 Ahimaaz begot *Azarya*, *Azarya* begot *Yochanan*,

לה וַאֲחִימַעַץ הוֹלִיד אֶת־עֲזַרְיָה וַעֲזַרְיָה הוֹלִיד אֶת־יוֹחָנָן:

36 and *Yochanan* begot *Azarya* (it was he who served as *Kohen* in the House that *Shlomo* built in *Yerushalayim*).

לו וְיוֹחָנָן הוֹלִיד אֶת־עֲזַרְיָה הוּא אֲשֶׁר כִּהֵן בַּבַּיִת אֲשֶׁר־בָּנָה שְׁלֹמֹה בִּירוּשָׁלָם:

37 *Azarya* begot Amariah, Amariah begot *Achituv*,

לז וַיּוֹלֶד עֲזַרְיָה אֶת־אֲמַרְיָה וַאֲמַרְיָה הוֹלִיד אֶת־אֲחִיטוּב:

38 *Achituv* begot *Tzadok*, *Tzadok* begot *Shalum*,

לח וַאֲחִיטוּב הוֹלִיד אֶת־צָדוֹק וְצָדוֹק הוֹלִיד אֶת־שַׁלּוּם:

39 *Shalum* begot *Chilkiyahu*, *Chilkiyahu* begot *Azarya*,

לט וְשַׁלּוּם הוֹלִיד אֶת־חִלְקִיָּה וְחִלְקִיָּה הוֹלִיד אֶת־עֲזַרְיָה:

40 *Azarya* begot *Seraya*, *Seraya* begot *Yehotzadak*;

מ וַעֲזַרְיָה הוֹלִיד אֶת־שְׂרָיָה וּשְׂרָיָה הוֹלִיד אֶת־יְהוֹצָדָק:

41 and *Yehotzadak* went into exile when *Hashem* exiled *Yehuda* and *Yerushalayim* by the hand of Nebuchadnezzar.

מא וִיהוֹצָדָק הָלַךְ בְּהַגְלוֹת יְהוָה אֶת־יְהוּדָה וִירוּשָׁלָם בְּיַד נְבֻכַדְנֶאצַּר:

Divrei Hayamim I / I Chronicles
Chapter 6

6

1 The sons of *Levi*: *Gershom*, *Kehat*, and *Merari*.

בְּנֵי לֵוִי גֵּרְשֹׁם קְהָת וּמְרָרִי׃

2 And these are the names of the sons of *Gershom*: Libni and *Shim'i*.

וְאֵלֶּה שְׁמוֹת בְּנֵי־גֵרְשׁוֹם לִבְנִי וְשִׁמְעִי׃

3 The sons of *Kehat*: *Amram*, Izhar, *Chevron*, and Uzziel.

וּבְנֵי קְהָת עַמְרָם וְיִצְהָר וְחֶבְרוֹן וְעֻזִּיאֵל׃

4 The sons of *Merari*: Mahli and Mushi. These were the families of the *Leviim* according to their clans.

בְּנֵי מְרָרִי מַחְלִי וּמֻשִׁי וְאֵלֶּה מִשְׁפְּחוֹת הַלֵּוִי לַאֲבוֹתֵיהֶם׃

5 Of *Gershom*: his son Libni, his son Jahath, his son Zimmah,

לְגֵרְשׁוֹם לִבְנִי בְנוֹ יַחַת בְּנוֹ זִמָּה בְנוֹ׃

6 his son Joah, his son *Ido*, his son *Zerach*, his son Jeatherai.

יוֹאָח בְּנוֹ עִדּוֹ בְנוֹ זֶרַח בְּנוֹ יְאָתְרַי בְּנוֹ׃

7 The sons of *Kehat*: his son *Aminadav*, his son *Korach*, his son Assir,

בְּנֵי קְהָת עַמִּינָדָב בְּנוֹ קֹרַח בְּנוֹ אַסִּיר בְּנוֹ׃

8 his son *Elkana*, his son Ebiasaph, his son Assir,

אֶלְקָנָה בְנוֹ וְאֶבְיָסָף בְּנוֹ וְאַסִּיר בְּנוֹ׃

9 his son Tahath, his son Uriel, his son *Uzziyahu*, and his son *Shaul*.

תַּחַת בְּנוֹ אוּרִיאֵל בְּנוֹ עֻזִּיָּה בְנוֹ וְשָׁאוּל בְּנוֹ׃

10 The sons of *Elkana*: Amasai and Ahimoth,

וּבְנֵי אֶלְקָנָה עֲמָשַׂי וַאֲחִימוֹת׃

11 his son *Elkana*, his son Zophai, his son Nahath,

אֶלְקָנָה בנו [בְּנוֹ] אֶלְקָנָה צוֹפַי בְּנוֹ וְנַחַת בְּנוֹ׃

12 his son *Eliav*, his son Jeroham, his son *Elkana*.

אֱלִיאָב בְּנוֹ יְרֹחָם בְּנוֹ אֶלְקָנָה בְנוֹ׃

13 The sons of *Shmuel*: his first-born Vashni, and *Aviya*.

וּבְנֵי שְׁמוּאֵל הַבְּכֹר וַשְׁנִי וַאֲבִיָּה׃

14 The sons of *Merari*: Mahli, his son Libni, his son *Shim'i*, his son Uzzah,

בְּנֵי מְרָרִי מַחְלִי לִבְנִי בְנוֹ שִׁמְעִי בְנוֹ עֻזָּה בְנוֹ׃

15 his son Shimea, his son Haggiah, and his son Asaiah.

שִׁמְעָא בְנוֹ חַגִּיָּה בְנוֹ עֲשָׂיָה בְנוֹ׃

16 These were appointed by *David* to be in charge of song in the House of *Hashem*, from the time the *Aron* came to rest.

וְאֵלֶּה אֲשֶׁר הֶעֱמִיד דָּוִיד עַל־יְדֵי־שִׁיר בֵּית יְהוָה מִמְּנוֹחַ הָאָרוֹן׃

v'-AY-leh a-SHER he-e-MEED da-VEED al y'-day SHEER BAYT a-do-NAI mi-m'-NO-akh ha-a-RON

6:16 From the time the *Aron* came to rest King *David* gives the *Leviim* their roles as singers after he brought the *Aron HaBrit* to rest in its eternal home, the holy city of *Yerushalayim*. Just as one does not assign chores in a temporary residence, it was not meaningful to set permanent tasks surrounding the Ark of the Covenant until it had been brought to its proper place. Only in *Yerushalayim*, the resting place of *Hashem*'s presence in the world and the source of His continuous revelation, could the *Aron* be deemed to have reached its permanent home.

Divrei Hayamim I / I Chronicles
Chapter 6

17 They served at the *Mishkan* of the Tent of Meeting with song until *Shlomo* built the House of *Hashem* in *Yerushalayim*; and they carried out their duties as prescribed for them.

18 Those were the appointed men; and their sons were: the Kohathites: *Hayman* the singer, son of *Yoel* son of *Shmuel*

19 son of *Elkana* son of Jeroham son of Eliel son of Toah

20 son of Zuph son of *Elkana* son of Mahath son of Amasai

21 son of *Elkana* son of *Yoel* son of *Azarya* son of *Tzefanya*

22 son of Tahath son of Assir son of Ebiasaph son of *Korach*

23 son of Izhar son of *Kehat* son of *Levi* son of *Yisrael*;

24 and his kinsman *Asaf*, who stood on his right, namely, *Asaf* son of *Berechya* son of Shimea

25 son of *Michael* son of Baaseiah son of Malchijah

26 son of Ethni son of *Zerach* son of Adaiah

27 son of Ethan son of Zimmah son of *Shim'i*

28 son of Jahath son of *Gershom* son of *Levi*.

29 On the left were their kinsmen: the sons of *Merari*: Ethan son of Kishi son of Abdi son of Malluch

30 son of Hashabiah son of *Amatzya* son of *Chilkiyahu*

31 son of Amzi son of Bani son of Shemer

32 son of Mahli son of Mushi son of *Merari* son of *Levi*;

33 and their kinsmen the *Leviim* were appointed for all the service of the *Mishkan* of the House of *Hashem*.

34 But *Aharon* and his sons made offerings upon the *Mizbayach* of burnt offering and upon the *Mizbayach* of incense, performing all the tasks of the most holy place, to make atonement for *Yisrael*, according to all that *Moshe* the servant of *Hashem* had commanded.

35 These are the sons of *Aharon*: his son *Elazar*, his son *Pinchas*, his son Abishua,

36 his son Bukki, his son Uzzi, his son Zerahiah,

יז וַיִּהְיוּ מְשָׁרְתִים לִפְנֵי מִשְׁכַּן אֹהֶל־מוֹעֵד בַּשִּׁיר עַד־בְּנוֹת שְׁלֹמֹה אֶת־בֵּית יְהֹוָה בִּירוּשָׁלָ͏ִם וַיַּעַמְדוּ כְמִשְׁפָּטָם עַל־עֲבוֹדָתָם:

יח וְאֵלֶּה הָעֹמְדִים וּבְנֵיהֶם מִבְּנֵי הַקְּהָתִי הֵימָן הַמְשׁוֹרֵר בֶּן־יוֹאֵל בֶּן־שְׁמוּאֵל:

יט בֶּן־אֶלְקָנָה בֶּן־יְרֹחָם בֶּן־אֱלִיאֵל בֶּן־תּוֹחַ:

כ בֶּן־צִיף [צוּף] בֶּן־אֶלְקָנָה בֶּן־מַחַת בֶּן־עֲמָשָׂי:

כא בֶּן־אֶלְקָנָה בֶּן־יוֹאֵל בֶּן־עֲזַרְיָה בֶּן־צְפַנְיָה:

כב בֶּן־תַּחַת בֶּן־אַסִּיר בֶּן־אֶבְיָסָף בֶּן־קֹרַח:

כג בֶּן־יִצְהָר בֶּן־קְהָת בֶּן־לֵוִי בֶּן־יִשְׂרָאֵל:

כד וְאָחִיו אָסָף הָעֹמֵד עַל־יְמִינוֹ אָסָף בֶּן־בֶּרֶכְיָהוּ בֶּן־שִׁמְעָא:

כה בֶּן־מִיכָאֵל בֶּן־בַּעֲשֵׂיָה בֶּן־מַלְכִּיָּה:

כו בֶּן־אֶתְנִי בֶן־זֶרַח בֶּן־עֲדָיָה:

כז בֶּן־אֵיתָן בֶּן־זִמָּה בֶּן־שִׁמְעִי:

כח בֶּן־יַחַת בֶּן־גֵּרְשֹׁם בֶּן־לֵוִי:

כט וּבְנֵי מְרָרִי אֲחֵיהֶם עַל־הַשְּׂמֹאול אֵיתָן בֶּן־קִישִׁי בֶּן־עַבְדִּי בֶּן־מַלּוּךְ:

ל בֶּן־חֲשַׁבְיָה בֶן־אֲמַצְיָה בֶּן־חִלְקִיָּה:

לא בֶּן־אַמְצִי בֶן־בָּנִי בֶּן־שָׁמֶר:

לב בֶּן־מַחְלִי בֶּן־מוּשִׁי בֶּן־מְרָרִי בֶּן־לֵוִי:

לג וַאֲחֵיהֶם הַלְוִיִּם נְתוּנִים לְכָל־עֲבוֹדַת מִשְׁכַּן בֵּית הָאֱלֹהִים:

לד וְאַהֲרֹן וּבָנָיו מַקְטִירִים עַל־מִזְבַּח הָעוֹלָה וְעַל־מִזְבַּח הַקְּטֹרֶת לְכֹל מְלֶאכֶת קֹדֶשׁ הַקֳּדָשִׁים וּלְכַפֵּר עַל־יִשְׂרָאֵל כְּכֹל אֲשֶׁר צִוָּה מֹשֶׁה עֶבֶד הָאֱלֹהִים:

לה וְאֵלֶּה בְּנֵי אַהֲרֹן אֶלְעָזָר בְּנוֹ פִינְחָס בְּנוֹ אֲבִישׁוּעַ בְּנוֹ:

לו בֻּקִּי בְנוֹ עֻזִּי בְנוֹ זְרַחְיָה בְנוֹ:

Divrei Hayamim I / I Chronicles

Chapter 6

דברי הימים א

פרק ו

37 his son Meraioth, his son Amariah, his son *Achituv*,

לז מְרָיוֹת בְּנוֹ אֲמַרְיָה בְנוֹ אֲחִיטוּב בְּנוֹ:

38 his son *Tzadok*, his son Ahimaaz.

לח צָדוֹק בְּנוֹ אֲחִימַעַץ בְּנוֹ:

39 These are their dwelling-places according to their settlements within their borders: to the sons of *Aharon* of the families of Kohathites, for theirs was the [first] lot;

לט וְאֵלֶּה מוֹשְׁבוֹתָם לְטִירוֹתָם בִּגְבוּלָם לִבְנֵי אַהֲרֹן לְמִשְׁפַּחַת הַקְּהָתִי כִּי לָהֶם הָיָה הַגּוֹרָל:

40 they gave them *Chevron* in the land of *Yehuda* and its surrounding pasturelands,

מ וַיִּתְּנוּ לָהֶם אֶת־חֶבְרוֹן בְּאֶרֶץ יְהוּדָה וְאֶת־מִגְרָשֶׁיהָ סְבִיבֹתֶיהָ:

41 but the fields of the city and its villages they gave to *Kalev* son of Jephunneh.

מא וְאֶת־שְׂדֵה הָעִיר וְאֶת־חֲצֵרֶיהָ נָתְנוּ לְכָלֵב בֶּן־יְפֻנֶּה:

42 To the sons of *Aharon* they gave the cities of refuge: *Chevron* and Libnah with its pasturelands, Jattir and Eshtemoa with its pasturelands,

מב וְלִבְנֵי אַהֲרֹן נָתְנוּ אֶת־עָרֵי הַמִּקְלָט אֶת־חֶבְרוֹן וְאֶת־לִבְנָה וְאֶת־מִגְרָשֶׁיהָ וְאֶת־יַתִּר וְאֶת־אֶשְׁתְּמֹעַ וְאֶת־מִגְרָשֶׁיהָ:

43 Hilen with its pasturelands, Debir with its pasturelands,

מג וְאֶת־חִילֵז וְאֶת־מִגְרָשֶׁיהָ אֶת־דְּבִיר וְאֶת־מִגְרָשֶׁיהָ:

44 Ashan with its pasturelands, and *Beit Shemesh* with its pasturelands.

מד וְאֶת־עָשָׁן וְאֶת־מִגְרָשֶׁיהָ וְאֶת־בֵּית שֶׁמֶשׁ וְאֶת־מִגְרָשֶׁיהָ:

45 From the tribe of *Binyamin*, Geba with its pasturelands, Alemeth with its pasturelands, and *Anatot* with its pasturelands. All their cities throughout their families were thirteen.

מה וּמִמַּטֵּה בִנְיָמִן אֶת־גֶּבַע וְאֶת־מִגְרָשֶׁיהָ וְאֶת־עָלֶמֶת וְאֶת־מִגְרָשֶׁיהָ וְאֶת־עֲנָתוֹת וְאֶת־מִגְרָשֶׁיהָ כָּל־עָרֵיהֶם שְׁלֹשׁ־עֶשְׂרֵה עִיר בְּמִשְׁפְּחוֹתֵיהֶם:

46 To the remaining Kohathites were given by lot out of the family of the tribe, out of the half-tribe, the half of *Menashe*, ten cities.

מו וְלִבְנֵי קְהָת הַנּוֹתָרִים מִמִּשְׁפַּחַת הַמַּטֶּה מִמַּחֲצִית מַטֵּה חֲצִי מְנַשֶּׁה בַּגּוֹרָל עָרִים עָשֶׂר:

47 To the Gershomites according to their families were allotted thirteen cities out of the tribes of *Yissachar, Asher, Naftali,* and *Menashe* in Bashan.

מז וְלִבְנֵי גֵרְשׁוֹם לְמִשְׁפְּחוֹתָם מִמַּטֵּה יִשָּׂשכָר וּמִמַּטֵּה אָשֵׁר וּמִמַּטֵּה נַפְתָּלִי וּמִמַּטֵּה מְנַשֶּׁה בַּבָּשָׁן עָרִים שְׁלֹשׁ עֶשְׂרֵה:

48 To the Merarites according to their families were allotted twelve cities out of the tribes of *Reuven, Gad,* and *Zevulun.*

מח לִבְנֵי מְרָרִי לְמִשְׁפְּחוֹתָם מִמַּטֵּה רְאוּבֵן וּמִמַּטֵּה־גָד וּמִמַּטֵּה זְבֻלוּן בַּגּוֹרָל עָרִים שְׁתֵּים עֶשְׂרֵה:

49 So the people of *Yisrael* gave the *Leviim* the cities with their pasturelands.

מט וַיִּתְּנוּ בְנֵי־יִשְׂרָאֵל לַלְוִיִּם אֶת־הֶעָרִים וְאֶת־מִגְרְשֵׁיהֶם:

50 They gave them by lot out of the tribe of the Judahites these cities that are mentioned by name, and out of the tribe of the Simeon, and out of the tribe of the Benjaminites.

נ וַיִּתְּנוּ בַגּוֹרָל מִמַּטֵּה בְנֵי־יְהוּדָה וּמִמַּטֵּה בְנֵי־שִׁמְעוֹן וּמִמַּטֵּה בְּנֵי בִנְיָמִן אֵת הֶעָרִים הָאֵלֶּה אֲשֶׁר־יִקְרְאוּ אֶתְהֶם בְּשֵׁמוֹת:

51 And some of the families of the sons of *Kehat* had cities of their territory out of the tribe of *Efraim*.

נא וּמִמִּשְׁפְּחוֹת בְּנֵי קְהָת וַיְהִי עָרֵי גְבוּלָם מִמַּטֵּה אֶפְרָיִם:

Divrei Hayamim I / I Chronicles

Chapter 7

52 They gave them the cities of refuge: *Shechem* with its pasturelands in the hill country of *Efraim*, Gezer with its pasturelands,

53 Jokmeam with its pasturelands, Beth-horon with its pasturelands,

54 Aijalon with its pasturelands, Gath-rimmon with its pasturelands;

55 and out of the half-tribe of *Menashe*: Aner with its pasturelands, and Bileam with its pasturelands, for the rest of the families of the Kohathites.

56 To the Gershomites; out of the half-tribe of *Menashe*: Golan in Bashan with its pasturelands and Ashtaroth with its pasturelands;

57 and out of the tribe of *Yissachar*: Kedesh with its pasturelands, Dobrath with its pasturelands,

58 Ramoth with its pasturelands, and Anem with its pasturelands;

59 out of the tribe of *Asher*: Mashal with its pasturelands, *Avdon* with its pasturelands,

60 Hukok with its pasturelands, and Rehob with its pasturelands;

61 and out of the tribe of *Naftali*: Kedesh in Galilee with its pasturelands; Hammon with its pasturelands, and Kiriathaim with its pasturelands.

62 To the rest of the Merarites, out of the tribe of *Zevulun*: Rimmono with its pasturelands, *Tavor* with its pasturelands;

63 and beyond the *Yarden* at *Yericho*, on the east side of the *Yarden*, out of the tribe of *Reuven*: Bezer in the wilderness with its pasturelands, Jahaz with its pasturelands,

64 Kedemoth with its pasturelands, and Mephaath with its pasture lands;

65 and out of the tribe of *Gad*: Ramoth in *Gilad* with its pasturelands, Mahanaim with its pasturelands,

66 Heshbon with its pasturelands, and Jazer with its pasturelands.

7 1 The sons of *Yissachar*: *Tola*, Puah, Yashuv, and Shimron – four.

Divrei HaYamim I/I Chronicles
Chapter 7

דברי הימים א
פרק ז

2 The sons of *Tola*: Uzzi, Rephaiah, Jeriel, Jahmai, Ibsam, Shemuel, chiefs of their clans, men of substance according to their lines; their number in the days of *David* was 22,600.

ב וּבְנֵי תוֹלָע עֻזִּי וּרְפָיָה וִירִיאֵל וְיַחְמַי וְיִבְשָׂם וּשְׁמוּאֵל רָאשִׁים לְבֵית־אֲבוֹתָם לְתוֹלָע גִּבּוֹרֵי חַיִל לְתֹלְדוֹתָם מִסְפָּרָם בִּימֵי דָוִיד עֶשְׂרִים־וּשְׁנַיִם אֶלֶף וְשֵׁשׁ מֵאוֹת:

3 The sons of Uzzi: Izrahiah. And the sons of Izrahiah: *Michael*, *Ovadya*, *Yoel*, and Isshiah – five. All of them were chiefs.

ג וּבְנֵי עֻזִּי יִזְרַחְיָה וּבְנֵי יִזְרַחְיָה מִיכָאֵל וְעֹבַדְיָה וְיוֹאֵל יִשִּׁיָּה חֲמִשָּׁה רָאשִׁים כֻּלָּם:

4 And together with them, by their lines, according to their clans, were units of the fighting force, 36,000, for they had many wives and sons.

ד וַעֲלֵיהֶם לְתֹלְדוֹתָם לְבֵית אֲבוֹתָם גְּדוּדֵי צְבָא מִלְחָמָה שְׁלֹשִׁים וְשִׁשָּׁה אָלֶף כִּי־הִרְבּוּ נָשִׁים וּבָנִים:

5 Their kinsmen belonging to all the families of *Yissachar* were in all 87,000 men of substance; they were all registered by genealogy.

ה וַאֲחֵיהֶם לְכֹל מִשְׁפְּחוֹת יִשָּׂשכָר גִּבּוֹרֵי חֲיָלִים שְׁמוֹנִים וְשִׁבְעָה אֶלֶף הִתְיַחְשָׂם לַכֹּל:

6 [The sons of] *Binyamin*: Bela, Becher, and Jediael – three.

ו בִּנְיָמִן בֶּלַע וָבֶכֶר וִידִיעֲאֵל שְׁלֹשָׁה:

7 The sons of Bela: Ezbon, Uzzi, Uzziel, Jerimoth, and Iri – five, chiefs of clans, men of substance, registered by genealogy – 22,034.

ז וּבְנֵי בֶלַע אֶצְבּוֹן וְעֻזִּי וְעֻזִּיאֵל וִירִימוֹת וְעִירִי חֲמִשָּׁה רָאשֵׁי בֵּית אָבוֹת גִּבּוֹרֵי חֲיָלִים וְהִתְיַחְשָׂם עֶשְׂרִים וּשְׁנַיִם אֶלֶף וּשְׁלֹשִׁים וְאַרְבָּעָה:

8 The sons of Becher: Zemirah, *Yoash*, *Eliezer*, Elioenai, *Omri*, Jeremoth, *Aviya*, *Anatot*, and Alemeth. All these were the sons of Becher;

ח וּבְנֵי בֶכֶר זְמִירָה וְיוֹעָשׁ וֶאֱלִיעֶזֶר וְאֶלְיוֹעֵינַי וְעָמְרִי וִירֵמוֹת וַאֲבִיָּה וַעֲנָתוֹת וָעָלָמֶת כָּל־אֵלֶּה בְּנֵי־בָכֶר:

9 and they were registered by genealogy according to their lines, as chiefs of their clans, men of substance – 20,200.

ט וְהִתְיַחְשָׂם לְתֹלְדוֹתָם רָאשֵׁי בֵּית אֲבוֹתָם גִּבּוֹרֵי חָיִל עֶשְׂרִים אֶלֶף וּמָאתָיִם:

10 The sons of Jediael: Bilhan. And the sons of Bilhan: Jeush, *Binyamin*, *Ehud*, Chenaanah, Zethan, Tarshish, and Ahishahar.

י וּבְנֵי יְדִיעֲאֵל בִּלְהָן וּבְנֵי בִלְהָן יעיש [יְעוּשׁ] וּבִנְיָמִן וְאֵהוּד וּכְנַעֲנָה וְזֵיתָן וְתַרְשִׁישׁ וַאֲחִישָׁחַר:

11 All these were the sons of Jediael, chiefs of the clans, men of substance – 17,200, who made up the fighting force.

יא כָּל־אֵלֶּה בְּנֵי יְדִיעֲאֵל לְרָאשֵׁי הָאָבוֹת גִּבּוֹרֵי חֲיָלִים שִׁבְעָה־עָשָׂר אֶלֶף וּמָאתַיִם יֹצְאֵי צָבָא לַמִּלְחָמָה:

12 And Shuppim and Huppim were the sons of Ir; Hushim the sons of Aher.

יב וְשֻׁפִּם וְחֻפִּם בְּנֵי עִיר חֻשִׁם בְּנֵי אַחֵר:

13 The sons of *Naftali*: Jahziel, Guni, Jezer, and *Shalum*, the descendants of *Bilha*.

יג בְּנֵי נַפְתָּלִי יַחֲצִיאֵל וְגוּנִי וְיֵצֶר וְשַׁלּוּם בְּנֵי בִלְהָה:

14 The sons of *Menashe*: Asriel, whom his Aramean concubine bore; she bore Machir the father of *Gilad*.

יד בְּנֵי מְנַשֶּׁה אַשְׂרִיאֵל אֲשֶׁר יָלָדָה פִּילַגְשׁוֹ הָאֲרַמִּיָּה יָלְדָה אֶת־מָכִיר אֲבִי גִלְעָד:

Divrei Hayamim I / I Chronicles
Chapter 7

15 And Machir took wives for Huppim and for Shuppim. The name of his sister was Maacah. And the name of the second was *Tzelofchad*; and *Tzelofchad* had daughters.

16 And Maacah the wife of Machir bore a son, and she named him Peresh; and the name of his brother was Sheresh; and his sons were Ulam and Rekem.

17 The sons of Ulam: Bedan. These were the sons of *Gilad* son of Machir son of *Menashe*.

18 And his sister Hammolecheth bore Ishhod, Abiezer, and *Machla*.

19 The sons of Shemida were Ahian, *Shechem*, Likhi, and Aniam.

20 The sons of *Efraim*: Shuthelah, his son Bered, his son Tahath, his son Eleadah, his son Tahath,

21 his son Zabad, his son Shuthelah, also Ezer and Elead. The men of Gath, born in the land, killed them because they had gone down to take their cattle.

22 And *Efraim* their father mourned many days, and his brothers came to comfort him.

23 He cohabited with his wife, who conceived and bore a son; and she named him Beriah, because it occurred when there was misfortune in his house.

24 His daughter was Sheerah, who built both Lower and Upper Beth-horon, and Uzzen-sheerah.

25 His son Rephah, his son Resheph, his son Telah, his son Tahan,

26 his son Ladan, his son Ammihud, his son Elishama,

27 his son Non, his son *Yehoshua*.

28 Their possessions and settlements were *Beit El* and its dependencies, and on the east Naaran, and on the west Gezer and its dependencies, *Shechem* and its dependencies, and Aiah and its dependencies;

29 also along the borders of the Manassites, *Beit-Shean* and its dependencies, Taanach and its dependencies, Megiddo and its dependencies, Dor and its dependencies. In these dwelt the sons of *Yosef* son of *Yisrael*.

30 The sons of *Asher*: Imnah, Ishvah, Ishvi, Beriah, and their sister Serah.

דברי הימים א
פרק ז

טו וּמָכִיר לָקַח אִשָּׁה לְחֻפִּים וּלְשֻׁפִּים וְשֵׁם אֲחֹתוֹ מַעֲכָה וְשֵׁם הַשֵּׁנִי צְלָפְחָד וַתִּהְיֶנָה לִצְלָפְחָד בָּנוֹת:

טז וַתֵּלֶד מַעֲכָה אֵשֶׁת־מָכִיר בֵּן וַתִּקְרָא שְׁמוֹ פֶּרֶשׁ וְשֵׁם אָחִיו שָׁרֶשׁ וּבָנָיו אוּלָם וָרָקֶם:

יז וּבְנֵי אוּלָם בְּדָן אֵלֶּה בְּנֵי גִלְעָד בֶּן־מָכִיר בֶּן־מְנַשֶּׁה:

יח וַאֲחֹתוֹ הַמֹּלֶכֶת יָלְדָה אֶת־אִישְׁהוֹד וְאֶת־אֲבִיעֶזֶר וְאֶת־מַחְלָה:

יט וַיִּהְיוּ בְּנֵי שְׁמִידָע אַחְיָן וָשֶׁכֶם וְלִקְחִי וַאֲנִיעָם:

כ וּבְנֵי אֶפְרַיִם שׁוּתָלַח וּבֶרֶד בְּנוֹ וְתַחַת בְּנוֹ וְאֶלְעָדָה בְנוֹ וְתַחַת בְּנוֹ:

כא וְזָבָד בְּנוֹ וְשׁוּתֶלַח בְּנוֹ וְעֵזֶר וְאֶלְעָד וַהֲרָגוּם אַנְשֵׁי־גַת הַנּוֹלָדִים בָּאָרֶץ כִּי יָרְדוּ לָקַחַת אֶת־מִקְנֵיהֶם:

כב וַיִּתְאַבֵּל אֶפְרַיִם אֲבִיהֶם יָמִים רַבִּים וַיָּבֹאוּ אֶחָיו לְנַחֲמוֹ:

כג וַיָּבֹא אֶל־אִשְׁתּוֹ וַתַּהַר וַתֵּלֶד בֵּן וַיִּקְרָא אֶת־שְׁמוֹ בְּרִיעָה כִּי בְרָעָה הָיְתָה בְּבֵיתוֹ:

כד וּבִתּוֹ שֶׁאֱרָה וַתִּבֶן אֶת־בֵּית־חוֹרוֹן הַתַּחְתּוֹן וְאֶת־הָעֶלְיוֹן וְאֵת אֻזֵּן שֶׁאֱרָה:

כה וְרֶפַח בְּנוֹ וְרֶשֶׁף וְתֶלַח בְּנוֹ וְתַחַן בְּנוֹ:

כו לַעְדָּן בְּנוֹ עַמִּיהוּד בְּנוֹ אֱלִישָׁמָע בְּנוֹ:

כז נוֹן בְּנוֹ יְהוֹשֻׁעַ בְּנוֹ:

כח וַאֲחֻזָּתָם וּמֹשְׁבוֹתָם בֵּית־אֵל וּבְנֹתֶיהָ וְלַמִּזְרָח נַעֲרָן וְלַמַּעֲרָב גֶּזֶר וּבְנֹתֶיהָ וּשְׁכֶם וּבְנֹתֶיהָ עַד־עַיָּה וּבְנֹתֶיהָ:

כט וְעַל־יְדֵי בְנֵי־מְנַשֶּׁה בֵּית־שְׁאָן וּבְנֹתֶיהָ תַּעְנַךְ וּבְנֹתֶיהָ מְגִדּוֹ וּבְנוֹתֶיהָ דּוֹר וּבְנוֹתֶיהָ בְּאֵלֶּה יָשְׁבוּ בְּנֵי יוֹסֵף בֶּן־יִשְׂרָאֵל:

ל בְּנֵי אָשֵׁר יִמְנָה וְיִשְׁוָה וְיִשְׁוִי וּבְרִיעָה וְשֶׂרַח אֲחוֹתָם:

Divrei Hayamim I/I Chronicles
Chapter 8

דברי הימים א
פרק ח

31 The sons of Beriah: *Chever* and Malchiel, who was the father of Birzaith.

לא וּבְנֵי בְרִיעָה חֶבֶר וּמַלְכִּיאֵל הוּא אֲבִי בִרְזָוִת [בִרְזָיִת]:

uv-NAY v'-ree-AH KHE-ver u-mal-kee-AYL HU a-VEE vir-ZA-yit

32 *Chever* begot Japhlet, Shomer, Hotham, and their sister, Shua.

לב וְחֶבֶר הוֹלִיד אֶת־יַפְלֵט וְאֶת־שׁוֹמֵר וְאֶת־חוֹתָם וְאֵת שׁוּעָא אֲחוֹתָם:

33 The sons of Japhlet: Pasach, Bimhal, and Ashvath. These were the sons of Japhlet.

לג וּבְנֵי יַפְלֵט פָּסַךְ וּבִמְהָל וְעַשְׁוָת אֵלֶּה בְּנֵי יַפְלֵט:

34 The sons of Shemer: Ahi, Rohgah, Hubbah, and Aram.

לד וּבְנֵי שָׁמֶר אֲחִי וְרוֹהֲגָה [וְרָהְגָּה] יַחְבָּה [וְחֻבָּה] וַאֲרָם:

35 The sons of Helem his brother: Zophah, Imna, Shelesh, and Amal.

לה וּבֶן־הֵלֶם אָחִיו צוֹפַח וְיִמְנָע וְשֵׁלֶשׁ וְעָמָל:

36 The sons of Zophah: Suah, Harnepher, Shual, Beri, Imrah,

לו בְּנֵי צוֹפַח סוּחַ וְחַרְנֶפֶר וְשׁוּעָל וּבֵרִי וְיִמְרָה:

37 Bezer, Hod, Shamma, Shilshah, Ithran, and Beera.

לז בֶּצֶר וָהוֹד וְשַׁמָּא וְשִׁלְשָׁה וְיִתְרָן וּבְאֵרָא:

38 The sons of Jether: Jephunneh, Pispa, and Ara.

לח וּבְנֵי יֶתֶר יְפֻנֶּה וּפִסְפָּה וַאֲרָא:

39 The sons of Ulla: Arah, Hanniel, and Rizia.

לט וּבְנֵי עֻלָּא אָרַח וְחַנִּיאֵל וְרִצְיָא:

40 All of these men of *Asher*, chiefs of the clans, select men, men of substance, heads of the chieftains. And they were registered by genealogy according to fighting force; the number of the men was 26,000 men.

מ כָּל־אֵלֶּה בְנֵי־אָשֵׁר רָאשֵׁי בֵית־הָאָבוֹת בְּרוּרִים גִּבּוֹרֵי חֲיָלִים רָאשֵׁי הַנְּשִׂיאִים וְהִתְיַחְשָׂם בַּצָּבָא בַּמִּלְחָמָה מִסְפָּרָם אֲנָשִׁים עֶשְׂרִים וְשִׁשָּׁה אָלֶף:

8 1 *Binyamin* begot Bela his first-born, Ashbel the second, Aharah the third,

ח א וּבִנְיָמִן הוֹלִיד אֶת־בֶּלַע בְּכֹרוֹ אַשְׁבֵּל הַשֵּׁנִי וְאַחְרַח הַשְּׁלִישִׁי:

2 Nohah the fourth, and Rapha the fifth.

ב נוֹחָה הָרְבִיעִי וְרָפָא הַחֲמִישִׁי:

3 And Bela had sons: Addar, Gera, *Avihud*,

ג וַיִּהְיוּ בָנִים לְבָלַע אַדָּר וְגֵרָא וַאֲבִיהוּד:

4 Abishua, Naaman, Ahoah,

ד וַאֲבִישׁוּעַ וְנַעֲמָן וַאֲחוֹחַ:

5 Gera, Shephuphan, and Huram.

ה וְגֵרָא וּשְׁפוּפָן וְחוּרָם:

Olives from the Upper Galilee, part of the land of the tribe of Asher

7:31 Birzaith In the list of the children of *Asher*, the name Birzaith (ברזית), which literally means 'of the oil,' appears. The Sages debate the significance of this name. Some say it means that this man's daughters were so beautiful that they married the High Priests, or the kings, who were anointed with the sacred oil made by *Moshe*. Other interpretations suggest that this is not the name of a person, rather the name of a place found in the tribe of *Asher*. Either way, the connection between the tribe of *Asher* and the sacred oil is celebrated in this verse. Indeed, *Asher* is blessed by both *Yaakov* and *Moshe* with an abundance of oil in his territory (see Genesis 49:20 and Deuteronomy 33:24). The Sages state (*Menachot* 85b) that olive oil would flow like a fountain in the lands of *Asher*, and its quality was so superior that people in search of high quality oil were sent to the tribe of *Asher*. Furthermore, they state that *Asher*'s land was so fertile that in times of shortage, such as during the Sabbatical year when it is prohibited to work the land, *Asher* would provide olive oil for the entire Nation of Israel.

Divrei Hayamim I / I Chronicles
Chapter 8

#	English	Hebrew
6	These were the sons of *Ehud* – they were chiefs of clans of the inhabitants of Geba, and they were exiled to Manahath:	וְאֵלֶּה בְּנֵי אֵחוּד אֵלֶּה הֵם רָאשֵׁי אָבוֹת לְיוֹשְׁבֵי גֶבַע וַיַּגְלוּם אֶל־מָנָחַת:
7	Naaman, *Achiya*, and Gera – he exiled them and begot Uzza and Ahihud.	וְנַעֲמָן וַאֲחִיָּה וְגֵרָא הוּא הֶגְלָם וְהוֹלִיד אֶת־עֻזָּא וְאֶת־אֲחִיחֻד:
8	And Shaharaim had sons in the country of Moab after he had sent away Hushim and Baara his wives.	וְשַׁחֲרַיִם הוֹלִיד בִּשְׂדֵה מוֹאָב מִן־שִׁלְחוֹ אֹתָם חוּשִׁים וְאֶת־בַּעֲרָא נָשָׁיו:
9	He had sons by Hodesh his wife: Jobab, Zibia, Mesha, Malcam,	וַיּוֹלֶד מִן־חֹדֶשׁ אִשְׁתּוֹ אֶת־יוֹבָב וְאֶת־צִבְיָא וְאֶת־מֵישָׁא וְאֶת־מַלְכָּם:
10	Jeuz, Sachiah, and Mirmah. These were his sons, chiefs of clans.	וְאֶת־יְעוּץ וְאֶת־שָׂכְיָה וְאֶת־מִרְמָה אֵלֶּה בָנָיו רָאשֵׁי אָבוֹת:
11	He also begot by Hushim: Abitub and Elpaal.	וּמֵחֻשִׁים הוֹלִיד אֶת־אֲבִיטוּב וְאֶת־אֶלְפָּעַל:
12	The sons of Elpaal: *Ever*, Misham, and Shemed, who built Ono and Lod with its dependencies,	וּבְנֵי אֶלְפַּעַל עֵבֶר וּמִשְׁעָם וָשָׁמֶד הוּא בָּנָה אֶת־אוֹנוֹ וְאֶת־לֹד וּבְנֹתֶיהָ:
13	and Beriah and Shema – they were chiefs of clans of the inhabitants of Aijalon, who put to flight the inhabitants of Gath;	וּבְרִעָה וָשֶׁמַע הֵמָּה רָאשֵׁי הָאָבוֹת לְיוֹשְׁבֵי אַיָּלוֹן הֵמָּה הִבְרִיחוּ אֶת־יוֹשְׁבֵי גַת:
14	and Ahio, Shashak, and Jeremoth.	וְאַחְיוֹ שָׁשָׁק וִירֵמוֹת:
15	Zebadiah, Arad, Eder,	וּזְבַדְיָה וַעֲרָד וָעָדֶר:
16	*Michael*, Ishpah, and Joha were sons of Beriah.	וּמִיכָאֵל וְיִשְׁפָּה וְיוֹחָא בְּנֵי בְרִיעָה:
17	Zebadiah, Meshullam, Hizki, *Chever*,	וּזְבַדְיָה וּמְשֻׁלָּם וְחִזְקִי וָחָבֶר:
18	Ishmerai, Izliah, and Jobab were the sons of Elpaal.	וְיִשְׁמְרַי וְיִזְלִיאָה וְיוֹבָב בְּנֵי אֶלְפָּעַל:
19	Jakim, Zichri, Zabdi,	וְיָקִים וְזִכְרִי וְזַבְדִּי:
20	Elienai, Zillethai, Eliel,	וֶאֱלִיעֵנַי וְצִלְּתַי וֶאֱלִיאֵל:
21	Adaiah, Beraiah, and Shimrath were the sons of *Shim'i*.	וַעֲדָיָה וּבְרָאיָה וְשִׁמְרָת בְּנֵי שִׁמְעִי:
22	Ishpan, *Ever*, Eliel,	וְיִשְׁפָּן וָעֵבֶר וֶאֱלִיאֵל:
23	*Avdon*, Zichri, Hanan,	וְעַבְדּוֹן וְזִכְרִי וְחָנָן:
24	*Chananya*, Elam, Anthothiah,	וַחֲנַנְיָה וְעֵילָם וְעַנְתֹתִיָּה:
25	Iphdeiah, and Penuel were the sons of Shashak.	וְיִפְדְיָה וּפְנִיאֵל [וּפְנוּאֵל] בְּנֵי שָׁשָׁק:
26	Shamsherai, Shehariah, *Atalya*,	וְשַׁמְשְׁרַי וּשְׁחַרְיָה וַעֲתַלְיָה:
27	Jaareshiah, *Eliyahu*, and Zichri were the sons of Jeroham.	וְיַעֲרֶשְׁיָה וְאֵלִיָּה וְזִכְרִי בְּנֵי יְרֹחָם:

Divrei Hayamim I / I Chronicles
Chapter 8

28	These were the chiefs of the clans, according to their lines. These chiefs dwelt in *Yerushalayim*.	אֵלֶּה רָאשֵׁי אָבוֹת לְתֹלְדוֹתָם רָאשִׁים אֵלֶּה יָשְׁבוּ בִירוּשָׁלָ͏ִם׃ כח

AY-leh ra-SHAY a-VOT l'-to-l'-do-TAM ra-SHEEM AY-leh ya-sh'-VU vee-ru-sha-LA-im

29 The father of *Givon* dwelt in *Givon*, and the name of his wife was Maacah.

וּבְגִבְעוֹן יָשְׁבוּ אֲבִי גִבְעוֹן וְשֵׁם אִשְׁתּוֹ מַעֲכָה׃ כט

30 His first-born son: *Avdon*; then Zur, *Keesh*, Baal, *Nadav*,

וּבְנוֹ הַבְּכוֹר עַבְדּוֹן וְצוּר וְקִישׁ וּבַעַל וְנָדָב׃ ל

31 Gedor, Ahio, Zecher.

וּגְדוֹר וְאַחְיוֹ וָזָכֶר׃ לא

32 Mikloth begot Shimeah. And they dwelt in *Yerushalayim* opposite their kinsmen, with their kinsmen.

וּמִקְלוֹת הוֹלִיד אֶת־שִׁמְאָה וְאַף־הֵמָּה נֶגֶד אֲחֵיהֶם יָשְׁבוּ בִירוּשָׁלַ͏ִם עִם־אֲחֵיהֶם׃ לב

33 Ner begot *Keesh*, *Keesh* begot *Shaul*, *Shaul* begot *Yehonatan*, Malchi-shua, *Avinadav*, and Eshbaal;

וְנֵר הוֹלִיד אֶת־קִישׁ וְקִישׁ הוֹלִיד אֶת־שָׁאוּל וְשָׁאוּל הוֹלִיד אֶת־יְהוֹנָתָן וְאֶת־מַלְכִּי־שׁוּעַ וְאֶת־אֲבִינָדָב וְאֶת־אֶשְׁבָּעַל׃ לג

34 and the son of *Yehonatan* was Merib-baal; and Merib-baal begot *Micha*.

וּבֶן־יְהוֹנָתָן מְרִיב בָּעַל וּמְרִיב בַּעַל הוֹלִיד אֶת־מִיכָה׃ לד

35 The sons of *Micha*: Pithon, Melech, Taarea, and Achaz.

וּבְנֵי מִיכָה פִּיתוֹן וָמֶלֶךְ וְתַאְרֵעַ וְאָחָז׃ לה

36 *Achaz* begot Jehoaddah; and Jehoaddah begot Alemeth, Azmaveth, and *Zimri*; *Zimri* begot Moza.

וְאָחָז הוֹלִיד אֶת־יְהוֹעַדָּה וִיהוֹעַדָּה הוֹלִיד אֶת־עָלֶמֶת וְאֶת־עַזְמָוֶת וְאֶת־זִמְרִי וְזִמְרִי הוֹלִיד אֶת־מוֹצָא׃ לו

37 Moza begot Binea; his son Raphah; his son Eleasah, his son Azel.

וּמוֹצָא הוֹלִיד אֶת־בִּנְעָא רָפָה בְנוֹ אֶלְעָשָׂה בְנוֹ אָצֵל בְּנוֹ׃ לז

38 Azel had six sons, and these are their names: Azrikam, Bocheru, Ishmael, Sheariah, *Ovadya*, and Hanan. All these were the sons of Azel.

וּלְאָצֵל שִׁשָּׁה בָנִים וְאֵלֶּה שְׁמוֹתָם עַזְרִיקָם בֹּכְרוּ וְיִשְׁמָעֵאל וּשְׁעַרְיָה וְעֹבַדְיָה וְחָנָן כָּל־אֵלֶּה בְּנֵי אָצַל׃ לח

39 The sons of Eshek his brother: Ulam his first-born, Jeush the second, and Eliphelet the third.

וּבְנֵי עֵשֶׁק אָחִיו אוּלָם בְּכֹרוֹ יְעוּשׁ הַשֵּׁנִי וֶאֱלִיפֶלֶט הַשְּׁלִשִׁי׃ לט

40 The descendants of Ulam – men of substance, who drew the bow, had many children and grandchildren – one hundred and fifty; all these were Benjaminites.

וַיִּהְיוּ בְנֵי־אוּלָם אֲנָשִׁים גִּבֹּרֵי־חַיִל דֹּרְכֵי קֶשֶׁת וּמַרְבִּים בָּנִים וּבְנֵי בָנִים מֵאָה וַחֲמִשִּׁים כָּל־אֵלֶּה מִבְּנֵי בִנְיָמִן׃ מ

8:28 These chiefs dwelt in *Yerushalayim* These members of the tribe of *Binyamin* chose to live in *Yerushalayim*. As *Radak* states, this is not surprising since the territory of *Binyamin* includes part of *Yerushalayim*. However, it becomes more difficult to understand when we look at the archaeological record, which shows that the only part of *Yerushalayim* included in the tribe of *Binyamin* was the area of *Har HaBayit*. The rest of the city, including the houses, extended southwards into the territory of *Yehuda*. Nevertheless, these Benjaminites chose to live outside their tribal lands since *Yerushalayim* was so beloved to them.

Divrei Hayamim I / I Chronicles
Chapter 9

דברי הימים א
פרק ט

9 **1** All *Yisrael* was registered by genealogies; and these are in the book of the kings of *Yisrael*. And *Yehuda* was taken into exile in Babylon because of their trespass.

א וְכָל־יִשְׂרָאֵל הִתְיַחְשׂוּ וְהִנָּם כְּתוּבִים עַל־סֵפֶר מַלְכֵי יִשְׂרָאֵל וִיהוּדָה הָגְלוּ לְבָבֶל בְּמַעֲלָם:

2 The first to settle in their towns, on their property, were Israelites, *Kohanim*, *Leviim*, and temple servants,

ב וְהַיּוֹשְׁבִים הָרִאשֹׁנִים אֲשֶׁר בַּאֲחֻזָּתָם בְּעָרֵיהֶם יִשְׂרָאֵל הַכֹּהֲנִים הַלְוִיִּם וְהַנְּתִינִים:

3 while some of the Judahites and some of the Benjaminites and some of the Ephraimites and Manassehites settled in *Yerushalayim*;

ג וּבִירוּשָׁלַםִ יָשְׁבוּ מִן־בְּנֵי יְהוּדָה וּמִן־בְּנֵי בִנְיָמִן וּמִן־בְּנֵי אֶפְרַיִם וּמְנַשֶּׁה:

u-vee-ru-sha-LA-im ya-sh'-VU min b'-NAY y'-hu-DAH u-min b'-NAY vin-ya-MIN u-min b'-NAY ef-RA-yim um-na-SHEH

4 Uthai son of Ammihud son of *Omri* son of Imri son of Bani, from the sons of *Peretz* son of *Yehuda*;

ד עוּתַי בֶּן־עַמִּיהוּד בֶּן־עָמְרִי בֶּן־אִמְרִי בֶן־בנימין [בָּנִי] [מִן־] בְּנֵי־פֶרֶץ בֶּן־יְהוּדָה:

5 and of the Shilonites: Asaiah the first-born and his sons.

ה וּמִן־הַשִּׁילוֹנִי עֲשָׂיָה הַבְּכוֹר וּבָנָיו:

6 Of the sons of *Zerach*: Jeuel and their kinsmen – 690.

ו וּמִן־בְּנֵי־זֶרַח יְעוּאֵל וַאֲחֵיהֶם שֵׁשׁ־מֵאוֹת וְתִשְׁעִים:

7 Of the Benjaminites: Sallu son of Meshullam son of Hodaviah son of Hassenuah,

ז וּמִן־בְּנֵי בִּנְיָמִן סַלּוּא בֶּן־מְשֻׁלָּם בֶּן־הוֹדַוְיָה בֶּן־הַסְּנֻאָה:

8 Ibneiah son of Jeroham, Elah son of Uzzi son of Michri, and Meshullam son of Shephatiah son of Reuel son of Ibneiah;

ח וְיִבְנְיָה בֶּן־יְרֹחָם וְאֵלָה בֶן־עֻזִּי בֶּן־מִכְרִי וּמְשֻׁלָּם בֶּן־שְׁפַטְיָה בֶּן־רְעוּאֵל בֶּן־יִבְנִיָּה:

9 and their kinsmen, according to their lines – 956. All these were chiefs of their ancestral clans.

ט וַאֲחֵיהֶם לְתֹלְדוֹתָם תְּשַׁע מֵאוֹת וַחֲמִשִּׁים וְשִׁשָּׁה כָּל־אֵלֶּה אֲנָשִׁים רָאשֵׁי אָבוֹת לְבֵית אֲבֹתֵיהֶם:

10 Of the *Kohanim*: Jedaiah, Jehoiarib, Jachin,

י וּמִן־הַכֹּהֲנִים יְדַעְיָה וִיהוֹיָרִיב וְיָכִין:

11 and *Azarya* son of *Chilkiyahu* son of Meshullam son of *Tzadok* son of Meraioth son of *Achituv*, chief officer of the House of *Hashem*;

יא וַעֲזַרְיָה בֶן־חִלְקִיָּה בֶּן־מְשֻׁלָּם בֶּן־צָדוֹק בֶּן־מְרָיוֹת בֶּן־אֲחִיטוּב נְגִיד בֵּית הָאֱלֹהִים:

9:3 Manassehites settled in *Yerushalayim* In *Sefer Nechemya* (chapter 11) we are told that the exiles who had returned from Babylonia drew lots to see which individuals would settle in *Yerushalayim*. Even though *Yerushalayim* did not belong to the territories of *Ephraim* and *Menashe*, it was important to have more people inhabiting the Holy City so that it would be secure and defensible. By bringing additional people to *Yerushalayim*, they also sought to fulfill the prophecy: "There shall yet be old men and women in the squares of *Yerushalayim*, each with staff in hand because of their great age. And the squares of the city shall be crowded with boys and girls playing in the squares" (Zechariah 8:4–5). Perhaps the fact that these members of the tribe of *Menashe* inhabited the city together with people from other tribes reflects the opinion in the Talmud (*Yoma* 12a) that the city of *Yerushalayim* was not divided among the tribes. Rather, everyone has a claim to the holiest city on earth.

Divrei Hayamim I / I Chronicles
Chapter 9

דברי הימים א
פרק ט

12 and Adaiah son of Jeroham son of Pashhur son of Malchijah, and Maasai son of Adiel son of Jahzerah son of Meshullam son of Meshillemith son of Immer,

יב וַעֲדָיָה בֶּן־יְרֹחָם בֶּן־פַּשְׁחוּר בֶּן־מַלְכִּיָּה וּמַעְשַׂי בֶּן־עֲדִיאֵל בֶּן־יַחְזֵרָה בֶּן־מְשֻׁלָּם בֶּן־מְשִׁלֵּמִית בֶּן־אִמֵּר:

13 together with their kinsmen, chiefs of their clans – 1,760, men of substance for the work of the service of the House of *Hashem*.

יג וַאֲחֵיהֶם רָאשִׁים לְבֵית אֲבוֹתָם אֶלֶף וּשְׁבַע מֵאוֹת וְשִׁשִּׁים גִּבּוֹרֵי חֵיל מְלֶאכֶת עֲבוֹדַת בֵּית הָאֱלֹהִים:

14 Of the *Leviim*: Shemaya son of Hasshub son of Azrikam son of Hashabiah, of the sons of *Merari*;

יד וּמִן־הַלְוִיִּם שְׁמַעְיָה בֶן־חַשּׁוּב בֶּן־עַזְרִיקָם בֶּן־חֲשַׁבְיָה מִן־בְּנֵי מְרָרִי:

15 and Bakbakkar, Heresh, Galal, and Mattaniah son of Mica son of Zichri son of *Asaf*;

טו וּבַקְבַּקַּר חֶרֶשׁ וְגָלָל וּמַתַּנְיָה בֶּן־מִיכָא בֶּן־זִכְרִי בֶּן־אָסָף:

16 and *Ovadya* son of *Shemaya* son of Galal son of *Yedutun*, and *Berechya* son of *Asa* son of *Elkana*, who dwelt in the villages of the Netophathites.

טז וְעֹבַדְיָה בֶּן־שְׁמַעְיָה בֶּן־גָּלָל בֶּן־יְדוּתוּן וּבֶרֶכְיָה בֶן־אָסָא בֶּן־אֶלְקָנָה הַיּוֹשֵׁב בְּחַצְרֵי נְטוֹפָתִי:

17 The gatekeepers were: *Shalum*, Akkub, Talmon, Ahiman; and their kinsman *Shalum* was the chief

יז וְהַשֹּׁעֲרִים שַׁלּוּם וְעַקּוּב וְטַלְמֹן וַאֲחִימָן וַאֲחִיהֶם שַׁלּוּם הָרֹאשׁ:

18 hitherto in the King's Gate on the east. They were the keepers belonging to the Levite camp.

יח וְעַד־הֵנָּה בְּשַׁעַר הַמֶּלֶךְ מִזְרָחָה הֵמָּה הַשֹּׁעֲרִים לְמַחֲנוֹת בְּנֵי לֵוִי:

19 *Shalum* son of Kore son of Ebiasaph son of *Korach*, and his kinsmen of his clan, the Korahites, were in charge of the work of the service, guards of the threshold of the Tent; their fathers had been guards of the entrance to the camp of *Hashem*.

יט וְשַׁלּוּם בֶּן־קוֹרֵא בֶּן־אֶבְיָסָף בֶּן־קֹרַח וְאֶחָיו לְבֵית־אָבִיו הַקָּרְחִים עַל מְלֶאכֶת הָעֲבוֹדָה שֹׁמְרֵי הַסִּפִּים לָאֹהֶל וַאֲבֹתֵיהֶם עַל־מַחֲנֵה יְהֹוָה שֹׁמְרֵי הַמָּבוֹא:

20 And *Pinchas* son of *Elazar* was the chief officer over them in time past; *Hashem* was with him.

כ וּפִינְחָס בֶּן־אֶלְעָזָר נָגִיד הָיָה עֲלֵיהֶם לְפָנִים יְהֹוָה עִמּוֹ:

21 *Zecharya* the son of Meshelemiah was gatekeeper at the entrance of the Tent of Meeting.

כא זְכַרְיָה בֶּן מְשֶׁלֶמְיָה שֹׁעֵר פֶּתַח לְאֹהֶל מוֹעֵד:

22 All these, who were selected as gatekeepers at the thresholds, were 212. They were selected by genealogies in their villages. *David* and *Shmuel* the seer established them in their office of trust.

כב כֻּלָּם הַבְּרוּרִים לְשֹׁעֲרִים בַּסִּפִּים מָאתַיִם וּשְׁנֵים עָשָׂר הֵמָּה בְחַצְרֵיהֶם הִתְיַחְשָׂם הֵמָּה יִסַּד דָּוִיד וּשְׁמוּאֵל הָרֹאֶה בֶּאֱמוּנָתָם:

23 They and their descendants were in charge of the gates of the House of *Hashem*, that is, the House of the Tent, as guards.

כג וְהֵם וּבְנֵיהֶם עַל־הַשְּׁעָרִים לְבֵית־יְהֹוָה לְבֵית־הָאֹהֶל לְמִשְׁמָרוֹת:

24 The gatekeepers were on the four sides, east, west, north, and south;

כד לְאַרְבַּע רוּחוֹת יִהְיוּ הַשֹּׁעֲרִים מִזְרָח יָמָּה צָפוֹנָה וָנֶגְבָּה:

25 and their kinsmen in their villages were obliged to join them every seven days, according to a fixed schedule.

כה וַאֲחֵיהֶם בְּחַצְרֵיהֶם לָבוֹא לְשִׁבְעַת הַיָּמִים מֵעֵת אֶל־עֵת עִם־אֵלֶּה:

26 The four chief gatekeepers, who were *Leviim*, were entrusted to be over the chambers and the treasuries of the House of *Hashem*.

כו כִּי בֶאֱמוּנָה הֵמָּה אַרְבַּעַת גִּבֹּרֵי הַשֹּׁעֲרִים הֵם הַלְוִיִּם וְהָיוּ עַל־הַלְּשָׁכוֹת וְעַל הָאֹצְרוֹת בֵּית הָאֱלֹהִים:

Divrei Hayamim I / I Chronicles
Chapter 9

27 They spent the night near the House of *Hashem*; for they had to do guard duty, and they were in charge of opening it every morning.

28 Some of them had charge of the service vessels, for they were counted when they were brought back and taken out.

29 Some of them were in charge of the vessels and all the holy vessels, and of the flour, wine, oil, incense, and spices.

30 Some of the *Kohanim* blended the compound of spices.

31 Mattithiah, one of the *Leviim*, the first-born of *Shalum* the Korahite, was entrusted with making the flat cakes.

32 Also some of their Kohathite kinsmen had charge of the rows of bread, to prepare them for each *Shabbat*.

33 Now these are the singers, the chiefs of Levitical clans who remained in the chambers free of other service, for they were on duty day and night.

34 These were chiefs of Levitical clans, according to their lines; these chiefs lived in *Yerushalayim*.

35 The father of *Givon*, Jeiel, lived in *Givon*, and the name of his wife was Maacah.

36 His first-born son, *Avdon*; then Zur, *Keesh*, Baal, Ner, *Nadav*,

37 Gedor, Ahio, *Zecharya*, and Mikloth;

38 Mikloth begot Shimeam; and they lived in *Yerushalayim* opposite their kinsmen, with their kinsmen.

39 Ner begot *Keesh*, Keesh begot *Shaul*, Shaul begot *Yehonatan*, Malchi-shua, *Avinadav*, and Eshbaal;

40 and the son of *Yehonatan* was Merib-baal; and Merib-baal begot *Micha*.

41 The sons of *Micha*: Pithon, Melech, Taharea;

42 *Achaz* begot Jarah, and Jarah begot Alemeth, Azmaveth, and *Zimri*; Zimri begot Moza.

Divrei Hayamim I / I Chronicles
Chapter 10

43 Moza begot Binea; his son was Rephaiah, his son Eleasah, his son Azel.

44 Azel had six sons and these were their names: Azrikam, Bocheru, Ishmael, Sheariah, *Ovadya*, and Hanan. These were the sons of Azel.

10

1 The Philistines attacked *Yisrael*, and the men of *Yisrael* fled before the Philistines and [many] fell on Mount Gilboa.

2 The Philistines pursued *Shaul* and his sons, and the Philistines struck down *Yonatan*, *Avinadav*, and Malchishua, sons of *Shaul*.

3 The battle raged around *Shaul*, and the archers hit him, and he was wounded by the archers.

4 *Shaul* said to his arms-bearer, "Draw your sword and run me through, so that these uncircumcised may not come and make sport of me." But his arms-bearer, out of great awe, refused; whereupon *Shaul* grasped the sword and fell upon it.

5 When the arms-bearer saw that *Shaul* was dead, he too fell on his sword and died.

6 Thus *Shaul* and his three sons and his entire house died together.

7 And when all the men of *Yisrael* who were in the valley saw that they had fled and that *Shaul* and his sons were dead, they abandoned their towns and fled; the Philistines then came and occupied them.

8 The next day the Philistines came to strip the slain, and they found *Shaul* and his sons lying on Mount Gilboa.

9 They stripped him, and carried off his head and his armor, and sent them throughout the land of the Philistines to spread the news to their idols and among the people.

10 They placed his armor in the temple of their god, and they impaled his head in the temple of Dagan.

11 When all Jabesh-gilead heard everything that the Philistines had done to *Shaul*,

12 all their stalwart men set out, removed the bodies of *Shaul* and his sons, and brought them to Jabesh. They buried the bones under the oak tree in Jabesh, and they fasted for seven days.

Divrei Hayamim I / I Chronicles
Chapter 11

דברי הימים א
פרק יא

13 *Shaul* died for the trespass that he had committed against *Hashem* in not having fulfilled the command of *Hashem*; moreover, he had consulted a ghost to seek advice,

יג וַיָּמָת שָׁאוּל בְּמַעֲלוֹ אֲשֶׁר מָעַל בַּיהוָה עַל־דְּבַר יְהוָה אֲשֶׁר לֹא־שָׁמָר וְגַם־לִשְׁאוֹל בָּאוֹב לִדְרוֹשׁ:

14 and did not seek advice of *Hashem*; so He had him slain and the kingdom transferred to *David* son of *Yishai*.

יד וְלֹא־דָרַשׁ בַּיהוָה וַיְמִיתֵהוּ וַיַּסֵּב אֶת־הַמְּלוּכָה לְדָוִיד בֶּן־יִשָׁי:

v'-LO da-RASH ba-do-NAI vai-mee-TAY-hu va-ya-SAYV et ha-m'-lu-KHAH l'-da-VEED ben yi-SHAI

11 1 All *Yisrael* gathered to *David* at *Chevron* and said, "We are your own flesh and blood.

יא א וַיִּקָּבְצוּ כָל־יִשְׂרָאֵל אֶל־דָּוִיד חֶבְרוֹנָה לֵאמֹר הִנֵּה עַצְמְךָ וּבְשָׂרְךָ אֲנָחְנוּ:

2 Long before now, even when *Shaul* was king, you were the leader of *Yisrael*; and *Hashem* your God said to you: You shall shepherd My people *Yisrael*; you shall be ruler of My people *Yisrael*."

ב גַּם־תְּמוֹל גַּם־שִׁלְשׁוֹם גַּם בִּהְיוֹת שָׁאוּל מֶלֶךְ אַתָּה הַמּוֹצִיא וְהַמֵּבִיא אֶת־יִשְׂרָאֵל וַיֹּאמֶר יְהוָה אֱלֹהֶיךָ לְךָ אַתָּה תִרְעֶה אֶת־עַמִּי אֶת־יִשְׂרָאֵל וְאַתָּה תִּהְיֶה נָגִיד עַל עַמִּי יִשְׂרָאֵל:

3 All the elders of *Yisrael* came to the king at *Chevron*, and *David* made a pact with them in *Chevron* before *Hashem*. And they anointed *David* king over *Yisrael*, according to the word of *Hashem* through *Shmuel*.

ג וַיָּבֹאוּ כָּל־זִקְנֵי יִשְׂרָאֵל אֶל־הַמֶּלֶךְ חֶבְרוֹנָה וַיִּכְרֹת לָהֶם דָּוִיד בְּרִית בְּחֶבְרוֹן לִפְנֵי יְהוָה וַיִּמְשְׁחוּ אֶת־דָּוִיד לְמֶלֶךְ עַל־יִשְׂרָאֵל כִּדְבַר יְהוָה בְּיַד־שְׁמוּאֵל:

4 *David* and all *Yisrael* set out for *Yerushalayim*, that is Jebus, where the Jebusite inhabitants of the land lived.

ד וַיֵּלֶךְ דָּוִיד וְכָל־יִשְׂרָאֵל יְרוּשָׁלַ͏ִם הִיא יְבוּס וְשָׁם הַיְבוּסִי יֹשְׁבֵי הָאָרֶץ:

va-YAY-lekh da-VEED v'-khol yis-ra-AYL y'-ru-sha-LA-yim hee y'-VUS v'-SHAM hai-vu-SEE yo-sh'-VAY ha-A-retz

5 *David* was told by the inhabitants of Jebus, "You will never get in here!" But *David* captured the stronghold of *Tzion*; it is now the City of *David*.

ה וַיֹּאמְרוּ יֹשְׁבֵי יְבוּס לְדָוִיד לֹא תָבוֹא הֵנָּה וַיִּלְכֹּד דָּוִיד אֶת־מְצֻדַת צִיּוֹן הִיא עִיר דָּוִיד:

10:14 The kingdom transferred to *David* son of *Yishai* *Shaul* was given a double punishment for the sins he had committed, which included consulting *Shmuel*'s spirit in contravention of *Torah* law (I Samuel 28): He died, and his kingdom was transferred to *David*. Consulting a spirit is a crime labeled as an abomination (Deuteronomy 18:9–12). Only someone with an outstanding record of righteousness is truly fit to lead the People of Israel in the Land of Israel.

11:4 *David* and all *Yisrael* set out for *Yerushalayim* This first action that the text informs us *David* took after becoming king was to capture *Yerushalayim* and establish it as his capital. However, this actually occurred several years into *David*'s reign, as he ruled in *Chevron* for seven years before moving to *Yerushalayim* (I Kings 2:11). Nonetheless, *Divrei Hayamim* does not record any of his accomplishments during those years. Conquering the Holy City from the idolatrous Jebusites and establishing his capital there was the most meaningful event of *David*'s reign until that point. By doing so, he began the process that would lead to the construction of the *Beit Hamikdash* and service of God in "the site that *Hashem* your God will choose amidst all your tribes as His habitation, to establish His name there" (Deuteronomy 12:5).

Divrei Hayamim I / I Chronicles
Chapter 11

דברי הימים א
פרק יא

6 *David* said, "Whoever attacks the Jebusites first will be the chief officer"; *Yoav* son of *Tzeruya* attacked first, and became the chief.

ו וַיֹּ֣אמֶר דָּוִ֗יד כָּל־מַכֵּ֤ה יְבוּסִי֙ בָּרִ֣אשׁוֹנָ֔ה יִהְיֶ֥ה לְרֹ֖אשׁ וּלְשָׂ֑ר וַיַּ֧עַל בָּרִאשׁוֹנָ֛ה יוֹאָ֥ב בֶּן־צְרוּיָ֖ה וַיְהִ֥י לְרֹֽאשׁ׃

7 *David* occupied the stronghold; therefore it was renamed the City of *David*.

ז וַיֵּ֥שֶׁב דָּוִ֖יד בַּמְצָ֑ד עַל־כֵּ֥ן קָרְאוּ־ל֖וֹ עִ֥יר דָּוִֽיד׃

8 *David* also fortified the surrounding area, from the Millo roundabout, and *Yoav* rebuilt the rest of the city.

ח וַיִּ֨בֶן הָעִ֜יר מִסָּבִ֗יב מִן־הַמִּלּ֖וֹא וְעַד־הַסָּבִ֑יב וְיוֹאָ֥ב יְחַיֶּ֖ה אֶת־שְׁאָ֥ר הָעִֽיר׃

9 *David* kept growing stronger, for the Lord of Hosts was with him.

ט וַיֵּ֥לֶךְ דָּוִ֖יד הָל֣וֹךְ וְגָד֑וֹל וַיהֹוָ֥ה צְבָא֖וֹת עִמּֽוֹ׃

10 And these were *David's* chief warriors who strongly supported him in his kingdom, together with all *Yisrael*, to make him king, according to the word of *Hashem* concerning *Yisrael*.

י וְאֵ֛לֶּה רָאשֵׁ֥י הַגִּבֹּרִ֖ים אֲשֶׁ֣ר לְדָוִ֑יד הַמִּתְחַזְּקִ֨ים עִמּ֤וֹ בְמַלְכוּתוֹ֙ עִם־כָּל־יִשְׂרָאֵ֔ל לְהַמְלִיכ֖וֹ כִּדְבַ֥ר יְהֹוָ֖ה עַל־יִשְׂרָאֵֽל׃

11 This is the list of *David's* warriors: Jashobeam son of Hachmoni, the chief officer; he wielded his spear against three hundred and slew them all on one occasion.

יא וְאֵ֛לֶּה מִסְפַּ֥ר הַגִּבֹּרִ֖ים אֲשֶׁ֣ר לְדָוִ֑יד יָשָׁבְעָ֣ם בֶּן־חַכְמוֹנִי֮ רֹ֣אשׁ הַשָּׁלִישִׁים֒ [הַשָּׁלִישִׁים] הֽוּא־עוֹרֵ֧ר אֶת־חֲנִית֛וֹ עַל־שְׁלֹשׁ־מֵא֥וֹת חָלָ֖ל בְּפַ֥עַם אֶחָֽת׃

12 Next to him was *Elazar* son of Dodo, the Ahohite; he was one of the three warriors.

יב וְאַחֲרָ֛יו אֶלְעָזָ֥ר בֶּן־דּוֹד֖וֹ הָאֲחוֹחִ֑י ה֖וּא בִּשְׁלוֹשָׁ֥ה הַגִּבֹּרִֽים׃

13 He was with *David* at Pas Dammim when the Philistines gathered there for battle. There was a plot of ground full of barley there; the troops had fled from the Philistines,

יג הֽוּא־הָיָ֥ה עִם־דָּוִ֖יד בַּפַּ֣ס דַּמִּ֑ים וְהַפְּלִשְׁתִּ֣ים נֶאֶסְפוּ־שָׁ֣ם לַמִּלְחָמָ֗ה וַתְּהִ֞י חֶלְקַ֤ת הַשָּׂדֶה֙ מְלֵאָ֣ה שְׂעוֹרִ֔ים וְהָעָ֥ם נָ֖סוּ מִפְּנֵ֥י פְלִשְׁתִּֽים׃

14 but they took their stand in the middle of the plot and defended it, and they routed the Philistines. Thus *Hashem* wrought a great victory.

יד וַיִּתְיַצְּב֤וּ בְתוֹךְ־הַחֶלְקָה֙ וַיַּצִּיל֔וּהָ וַיַּכּ֖וּ אֶת־פְּלִשְׁתִּ֑ים וַיּ֧וֹשַׁע יְהֹוָ֛ה תְּשׁוּעָ֥ה גְדוֹלָֽה׃

15 Three of the thirty chiefs went down to the rock to *David*, at the cave of *Adulam*, while a force of Philistines was encamped in the Valley of Rephaim.

טו וַיֵּרְד֡וּ שְׁלוֹשָׁה֩ מִן־הַשְּׁלוֹשִׁ֨ים רֹ֤אשׁ עַל־הַצֻּר֙ אֶל־דָּוִ֔יד אֶל־מְעָרַ֖ת עֲדֻלָּ֑ם וּמַחֲנֵ֣ה פְלִשְׁתִּ֔ים חֹנָ֖ה בְּעֵ֥מֶק רְפָאִֽים׃

16 *David* was then in the stronghold, and a Philistine garrison was then at *Beit Lechem*.

טז וְדָוִ֖יד אָ֣ז בַּמְּצוּדָ֑ה וּנְצִ֣יב פְּלִשְׁתִּ֔ים אָ֖ז בְּבֵ֥ית לָֽחֶם׃

17 *David* felt a craving and said, "If only I could get a drink of water from the cistern which is by the gate of *Beit Lechem*!"

יז ויתאו [וַיִּתְאָ֥יו] דָּוִ֖יד וַיֹּאמַ֑ר מִ֣י יַשְׁקֵ֗נִי מַ֚יִם מִבּ֣וֹר בֵּֽית־לֶ֔חֶם אֲשֶׁ֖ר בַּשָּֽׁעַר׃

18 So the three got through the Philistine camp, and drew water from the cistern which is by the gate of *Beit Lechem*, and they carried it back to *David*. But *David* would not drink it, and he poured it out as a libation to *Hashem*.

יח וַיִּבְקְע֨וּ הַשְּׁלֹשָׁ֜ה בְּמַחֲנֵ֣ה פְלִשְׁתִּ֗ים וַיִּֽשְׁאֲבוּ־מַ֙יִם֙ מִבּ֤וֹר בֵּֽית־לֶ֙חֶם֙ אֲשֶׁ֣ר בַּשַּׁ֔עַר וַיִּשְׂא֖וּ וַיָּבִ֣אוּ אֶל־דָּוִ֑יד וְלֹֽא־אָבָ֤ה דָוִיד֙ לִשְׁתּוֹתָ֔ם וַיְנַסֵּ֥ךְ אֹתָ֖ם לַיהֹוָֽה׃

Divrei Hayamim I/I Chronicles
Chapter 11

19	For he said, "*Hashem* forbid that I should do this! Can I drink the blood of these men who risked their lives?" – for they had brought it at the risk of their lives, and he would not drink it. Such were the exploits of the three warriors.
20	Abshai, the brother of *Yoav*, was head of another three. He once wielded his spear against three hundred and slew them. He won a name among the three;
21	among the three he was more highly regarded than the other two, and so he became their commander. However, he did not attain to the other three.
22	Benaiah son of *Yehoyada* from Kabzeel was a brave soldier who performed great deeds. He killed the two [sons] of Ariel of Moab. Once, on a snowy day, he went down into a pit and killed a lion.
23	He also killed an Egyptian, a giant of a man five *amot* tall. The Egyptian had a spear in his hand, like a weaver's beam, yet [Benaiah] went down against him with a club, wrenched the spear out of the Egyptian's hand, and killed him with his own spear.
24	Such were the exploits of Benaiah son of *Yehoyada*; and he won a name among the three warriors.
25	He was highly regarded among the thirty, but he did not attain to the three. *David* put him in charge of his bodyguard.
26	The valiant warriors: *Asael* brother of *Yoav*, *Elchanan* son of Dodo from *Beit Lechem*,
27	Shammoth the Harorite, Helez the Pelonite,
28	Ira son of Ikkesh from *Tekoa*, Abiezer of *Anatot*,
29	Sibbecai the Hushathite, Ilai the Ahohite,
30	Mahrai the Netophathite, Heled son of Baanah the Netophathite,
31	Ittai son of Ribai from *Giva* of the Benjaminites, Benaiah of Pirathon,
32	Hurai of Nahale-gaash, Abiel the Arbathite,
33	Azmaveth the Bahrumite, Eliahba of Shaalbon,
34	the sons of *Hashem* the Gizonite, *Yonatan* son of Shageh the Hararite,

דברי הימים א
פרק יא

יט וַיֹּאמֶר חָלִילָה לִּי מֵאֱלֹהַי מֵעֲשׂוֹת זֹאת הֲדַם הָאֲנָשִׁים הָאֵלֶּה אֶשְׁתֶּה בְנַפְשׁוֹתָם כִּי בְנַפְשׁוֹתָם הֱבִיאוּם וְלֹא אָבָה לִשְׁתּוֹתָם אֵלֶּה עָשׂוּ שְׁלֹשֶׁת הַגִּבֹּרִים׃

כ וְאַבְשַׁי אֲחִי־יוֹאָב הוּא הָיָה רֹאשׁ הַשְּׁלוֹשָׁה וְהוּא עוֹרֵר אֶת־חֲנִיתוֹ עַל־שְׁלֹשׁ מֵאוֹת חָלָל וְלֹא־[וְלוֹ־] שֵׁם בַּשְּׁלוֹשָׁה׃

כא מִן־הַשְּׁלוֹשָׁה בַשְּׁנַיִם נִכְבָּד וַיְהִי לָהֶם לְשָׂר וְעַד־הַשְּׁלוֹשָׁה לֹא־בָא׃

כב בְּנָיָה בֶן־יְהוֹיָדָע בֶּן־אִישׁ־חַיִל רַב־פְּעָלִים מִן־קַבְצְאֵל הוּא הִכָּה אֵת שְׁנֵי אֲרִיאֵל מוֹאָב וְהוּא יָרַד וְהִכָּה אֶת־הָאֲרִי בְּתוֹךְ הַבּוֹר בְּיוֹם הַשָּׁלֶג׃

כג וְהוּא־הִכָּה אֶת־הָאִישׁ הַמִּצְרִי אִישׁ מִדָּה חָמֵשׁ בָּאַמָּה וּבְיַד הַמִּצְרִי חֲנִית כִּמְנוֹר אֹרְגִים וַיֵּרֶד אֵלָיו בַּשָּׁבֶט וַיִּגְזֹל אֶת־הַחֲנִית מִיַּד הַמִּצְרִי וַיַּהַרְגֵהוּ בַּחֲנִיתוֹ׃

כד אֵלֶּה עָשָׂה בְּנָיָהוּ בֶּן־יְהוֹיָדָע וְלוֹ־שֵׁם בִּשְׁלוֹשָׁה הַגִּבֹּרִים׃

כה מִן־הַשְּׁלוֹשִׁים הִנּוֹ נִכְבָּד הוּא וְאֶל־הַשְּׁלוֹשָׁה לֹא־בָא וַיְשִׂימֵהוּ דָוִיד עַל־מִשְׁמַעְתּוֹ׃

כו וְגִבּוֹרֵי הַחֲיָלִים עֲשָׂה־אֵל אֲחִי יוֹאָב אֶלְחָנָן בֶּן־דּוֹדוֹ מִבֵּית לָחֶם׃

כז שַׁמּוֹת הַהֲרוֹרִי חֶלֶץ הַפְּלוֹנִי׃

כח עִירָא בֶן־עִקֵּשׁ הַתְּקוֹעִי אֲבִיעֶזֶר הָעַנְּתוֹתִי׃

כט סִבְּכַי הַחֻשָׁתִי עִילַי הָאֲחוֹחִי׃

ל מַהְרַי הַנְּטֹפָתִי חֵלֶד בֶּן־בַּעֲנָה הַנְּטוֹפָתִי׃

לא אִיתַי בֶּן־רִיבַי מִגִּבְעַת בְּנֵי בִנְיָמִן בְּנָיָה הַפִּרְעָתֹנִי׃

לב חוּרַי מִנַּחֲלֵי גָעַשׁ אֲבִיאֵל הָעַרְבָתִי׃

לג עַזְמָוֶת הַבַּחֲרוּמִי אֶלְיַחְבָּא הַשַּׁעַלְבֹנִי׃

לד בְּנֵי הָשֵׁם הַגִּזוֹנִי יוֹנָתָן בֶּן־שָׁגֵה הַהֲרָרִי׃

Divrei Hayamim I/I Chronicles
Chapter 12

35 Ahiam son of Sacar the Hararite, Eliphal son of Ur,   לה אֲחִיאָם בֶּן־שָׂכָר הַהֲרָרִי אֱלִיפַל בֶּן־אוּר:

36 Hepher the Mecherathite, *Achiya* the Pelonite,   לו חֵפֶר הַמְּכֵרָתִי אֲחִיָּה הַפְּלֹנִי:

37 Hezro the Carmelite, Naarai son of Ezbai,   לז חֶצְרוֹ הַכַּרְמְלִי נַעֲרַי בֶּן־אֶזְבָּי:

38 *Yoel* brother of *Natan*, Mibhar son of Hagri,   לח יוֹאֵל אֲחִי נָתָן מִבְחָר בֶּן־הַגְרִי:

39 Zelek the Ammonite, Naharai the Berothite – the arms-bearer of *Yoav* son of *Tzeruya* –   לט צֶלֶק הָעַמּוֹנִי נַחְרַי הַבֵּרֹתִי נֹשֵׂא כְּלֵי יוֹאָב בֶּן־צְרוּיָה:

40 Ira the Ithrite, Gareb the Ithrite,   מ עִירָא הַיִּתְרִי גָּרֵב הַיִּתְרִי:

41 *Uriya* the Hittite, Zabad son of Ahlai.   מא אוּרִיָּה הַחִתִּי זָבָד בֶּן־אַחְלָי:

42 Adina son of Shiza the Reubenite, a chief of the Reubenites, and thirty with him;   מב עֲדִינָא בֶן־שִׁיזָא הָראוּבֵנִי רֹאשׁ לָראוּבֵנִי וְעָלָיו שְׁלוֹשִׁים:

43 Hanan son of Maacah, and Joshaphat the Mithnite;   מג חָנָן בֶּן־מַעֲכָה וְיוֹשָׁפָט הַמִּתְנִי:

44 *Uzziyahu* the Ashterathite, Shama and Jeiel sons of Hotham the Aroerite;   מד עֻזִּיָּא הָעַשְׁתְּרָתִי שָׁמָע וִיעוּאֵל [וִיעִיאֵל] בְּנֵי חוֹתָם הָעֲרֹעֵרִי:

45 Jedaiael son of Shimri, and Joha his brother, the Tizite;   מה יְדִיעֲאֵל בֶּן־שִׁמְרִי וְיֹחָא אָחִיו הַתִּיצִי:

46 Eliel the Mahavite, and Jeribai and Joshaviah sons of Elnaam, and Ithmah the Moabite;   מו אֱלִיאֵל הַמַּחֲוִים וִירִיבַי וְיוֹשַׁוְיָה בְּנֵי אֶלְנָעַם וְיִתְמָה הַמּוֹאָבִי:

47 Eliel, Oved, and Jaassiel the Mezobaite.   מז אֱלִיאֵל וְעוֹבֵד וְיַעֲשִׂיאֵל הַמְּצֹבָיָה:

12 1 The following joined *David* at *Tziklag* while he was still in hiding from *Shaul* son of *Keesh*; these were the warriors who gave support in battle;   יב א וְאֵלֶּה הַבָּאִים אֶל־דָּוִיד לְצִיקְלַג עוֹד עָצוּר מִפְּנֵי שָׁאוּל בֶּן־קִישׁ וְהֵמָּה בַּגִּבּוֹרִים עֹזְרֵי הַמִּלְחָמָה:

2 they were armed with the bow and could use both right hand and left hand to sling stones or shoot arrows with the bow; they were kinsmen of *Shaul* from *Binyamin*.   ב נֹשְׁקֵי קֶשֶׁת מַיְמִינִים וּמַשְׂמִאלִים בָּאֲבָנִים וּבַחִצִּים בַּקָּשֶׁת מֵאֲחֵי שָׁאוּל מִבִּנְיָמִן:

3 At the head were Ahiezer and *Yoash*, sons of Shemaah of *Giva*; and Jeziel and Pelet, sons of Azmaveth; and Beracah and *Yehu* of *Anatot*;   ג הָרֹאשׁ אֲחִיעֶזֶר וְיוֹאָשׁ בְּנֵי הַשְּׁמָעָה הַגִּבְעָתִי וִיזוּאֵל [וִיזִיאֵל] וָפֶלֶט בְּנֵי עַזְמָוֶת וּבְרָכָה וְיֵהוּא הָעֲנְּתֹתִי:

4 Ishmaiah of *Givon*, a warrior among the thirty, leading the thirty;   ד וְיִשְׁמַעְיָה הַגִּבְעוֹנִי גִּבּוֹר בַּשְּׁלֹשִׁים וְעַל־הַשְּׁלֹשִׁים:

5 *Yirmiyahu*, *Yachaziel*, *Yochanan*, and *Yozavad* of Gedera;   ה וְיִרְמְיָה וְיַחֲזִיאֵל וְיוֹחָנָן וְיוֹזָבָד הַגְּדֵרָתִי:

6 Eluzai, Jerimoth, Bealiah, Shemariah, and Shephatiah the Hariphite;   ו אֶלְעוּזַי וִירִימוֹת וּבְעַלְיָה וּשְׁמַרְיָהוּ וּשְׁפַטְיָהוּ הַחֲרִיפִי [הַחֲרוּפִי]:

7 *Elkana*, Isshiah, Azarel, Joezer, and Jashobeam the Korahites;   ז אֶלְקָנָה וְיִשִּׁיָּהוּ וַעֲזַרְאֵל וְיוֹעֶזֶר וְיָשָׁבְעָם הַקָּרְחִים:

8 Yoelah and Zebadiah, sons of Jeroham of Gedor.   ח וְיוֹעֵאלָה וּזְבַדְיָה בְּנֵי יְרֹחָם מִן־הַגְּדוֹר:

Divrei Hayamim I / I Chronicles
Chapter 12

דברי הימים א
פרק יב

9 Of the Gadites, there withdrew to follow *David* to the wilderness stronghold valiant men, fighters fit for battle, armed with shield and spear; they had the appearance of lions, and were as swift as gazelles upon the mountains:

ט וּמִן־הַגָּדִי נִבְדְּלוּ אֶל־דָּוִיד לַמְצַד מִדְבָּרָה גִּבֹּרֵי הַחַיִל אַנְשֵׁי צָבָא לַמִּלְחָמָה עֹרְכֵי צִנָּה וָרֹמַח וּפְנֵי אַרְיֵה פְּנֵיהֶם וְכִצְבָאיִם עַל־הֶהָרִים לְמַהֵר:

10 *Ezer* the chief, *Ovadya* the second, *Eliav* the third,

י עֵזֶר הָרֹאשׁ עֹבַדְיָה הַשֵּׁנִי אֱלִיאָב הַשְּׁלִשִׁי:

11 *Mashmannah* the fourth, *Yirmiyahu* the fifth,

יא מִשְׁמַנָּה הָרְבִיעִי יִרְמְיָה הַחֲמִשִׁי:

12 *Attai* the sixth, *Eliel* the seventh,

יב עַתַּי הַשִּׁשִּׁי אֱלִיאֵל הַשְּׁבִעִי:

13 *Yochanan* the eighth, *Elzabad* the ninth,

יג יוֹחָנָן הַשְּׁמִינִי אֶלְזָבָד הַתְּשִׁיעִי:

14 *Yirmiyahu* the tenth, *Machbannai* the eleventh.

יד יִרְמְיָהוּ הָעֲשִׂירִי מַכְבַּנַּי עַשְׁתֵּי עָשָׂר:

15 Those were the Gadites, heads of the army. The least was equal to a hundred, the greatest to a thousand.

טו אֵלֶּה מִבְּנֵי־גָד רָאשֵׁי הַצָּבָא אֶחָד לְמֵאָה הַקָּטֹן וְהַגָּדוֹל לְאָלֶף:

16 These were the ones who crossed the *Yarden* in the first month, when it was at its crest, and they put to flight all the lowlanders to the east and west.

טז אֵלֶּה הֵם אֲשֶׁר עָבְרוּ אֶת־הַיַּרְדֵּן בַּחֹדֶשׁ הָרִאשׁוֹן וְהוּא מְמַלֵּא עַל־כָּל־גְּדִיתָיו [גְּדוֹתָיו] וַיַּבְרִיחוּ אֶת־כָּל־הָעֲמָקִים לַמִּזְרָח וְלַמַּעֲרָב:

AY-leh HAYM a-SHER a-v'-RU et ha-yar-DAYN ba-KHO-desh ha-ri-SHON v'-HU m'-ma-LAY al kol g'-do-TAV va-yav-REE-khu et kol HA-a-ma-KEEM la-miz-RAKH v'-la-ma-a-RAV

17 Some of the Benjaminites and Judahites came to the stronghold to *David*,

יז וַיָּבֹאוּ מִן־בְּנֵי בִנְיָמִן וִיהוּדָה עַד־לַמְצָד לְדָוִיד:

18 and *David* went out to meet them, saying to them, "If you come on a peaceful errand, to support me, then I will make common cause with you, but if to betray me to my foes, for no injustice on my part, then let the God of our fathers take notice and give judgment."

יח וַיֵּצֵא דָוִיד לִפְנֵיהֶם וַיַּעַן וַיֹּאמֶר לָהֶם אִם־לְשָׁלוֹם בָּאתֶם אֵלַי לְעָזְרֵנִי יִהְיֶה־לִּי עֲלֵיכֶם לֵבָב לְיָחַד וְאִם־לְרַמּוֹתַנִי לְצָרַי בְּלֹא חָמָס בְּכַפַּי יֵרֶא אֱלֹהֵי אֲבוֹתֵינוּ וְיוֹכַח:

19 Then the spirit seized *Amasai*, chief of the captains "We are yours, *David* On your side, son of *Yishai*

יט וְרוּחַ לָבְשָׁה אֶת־עֲמָשַׂי רֹאשׁ השלושים [הַשָּׁלִישִׁים] לְךָ דָוִיד וְעִמְּךָ

12:16 They put to flight all the lowlanders to the east and west The simple meaning of this verse is that the warriors who crossed the Jordan river routed all enemies from the nearby valleys. However, *Rashi* offers an alternative interpretation of this phrase. He suggests that the soldiers used their shields to push the water away, so that they could cross on dry land. This is reminiscent of two similar crossings recorded in the *Tanakh*: *Moshe* split the Sea of Reeds, rendering the area dry for the children of Israel to pass through (Exodus 14:21), and the waters of the Jordan river were also stopped so that the Children of Israel could cross on dry land into the Land of Israel under the leadership of *Yehoshua* (Joshua 3:16). By stating that *David*'s warriors did something similar, *Rashi* is telling us that *David* was the next link in a chain of great leaders which stretched back to *Moshe* and *Yehoshua*.

Rashi
(1040–1105)

Divrei Hayamim I / I Chronicles
Chapter 12

At peace, at peace with you And at peace with him who supports you For your God supports you. So *David* accepted them, and placed them at the head of his band.

20 Some Manassites went over to *David*'s side when he came with the Philistines to make war against *Shaul*, but they were of no help to them, because the lords of the Philistines in council dismissed him, saying, "He will go over to the side of his lord, *Shaul*, and it will cost us our heads";

21 when he went to *Tziklag*, these Manassites went over to his side – Adnah, *Yozavad*, Jediael, *Michael*, *Yozavad*, Elihu, and Zillethai, chiefs of the clans of *Menashe*.

22 It was they who gave support to *David* against the band, for all were valiant men; and they were officers of the force.

23 Day in day out, people came to *David* to give him support, until there was an army as vast as the army of *Hashem*.

24 These are the numbers of the [men of the] armed bands who joined *David* at *Chevron* to transfer *Shaul*'s kingdom to him, in accordance with the word of *Hashem*:

25 Judahites, equipped with shield and spear – 6,800 armed men;

26 Simeonites, valiant men, fighting troops – 7,100;

27 of the *Leviim* – 4,600;

28 *Yehoyada*, chief officer of the Aaronides; with him, 3,700;

29 *Tzadok*, a young valiant man, with his clan – 22 officers;

30 of the Benjaminites, kinsmen of *Shaul*, 3,000 in their great numbers, hitherto protecting the interests of the house of *Shaul*;

31 of the Ephraimites, 20,800 valiant men, famous in their clans;

דברי הימים א
פרק יב

בֶּן־יִשַׁי שָׁלוֹם שָׁלוֹם לְךָ וְשָׁלוֹם לְעֹזְרֶךָ כִּי עֲזָרְךָ אֱלֹהֶיךָ וַיְקַבְּלֵם דָּוִיד וַיִּתְּנֵם בְּרָאשֵׁי הַגְּדוּד:

כ וּמִמְּנַשֶּׁה נָפְלוּ עַל־דָּוִיד בְּבֹאוֹ עִם־פְּלִשְׁתִּים עַל־שָׁאוּל לַמִּלְחָמָה וְלֹא עֲזָרֻם כִּי בְעֵצָה שִׁלְּחֻהוּ סַרְנֵי פְלִשְׁתִּים לֵאמֹר בְּרָאשֵׁינוּ יִפּוֹל אֶל־אֲדֹנָיו שָׁאוּל:

כא בְּלֶכְתּוֹ אֶל־צִיקְלַג נָפְלוּ עָלָיו מִמְּנַשֶּׁה עַדְנַח וְיוֹזָבָד וִידִיעֲאֵל וּמִיכָאֵל וְיוֹזָבָד וֶאֱלִיהוּא וְצִלְּתָי רָאשֵׁי הָאֲלָפִים אֲשֶׁר לִמְנַשֶּׁה:

כב וְהֵמָּה עָזְרוּ עִם־דָּוִיד עַל־הַגְּדוּד כִּי־גִבּוֹרֵי חַיִל כֻּלָּם וַיִּהְיוּ שָׂרִים בַּצָּבָא:

כג כִּי לְעֶת־יוֹם בְּיוֹם יָבֹאוּ עַל־דָּוִיד לְעָזְרוֹ עַד־לְמַחֲנֶה גָדוֹל כְּמַחֲנֵה אֱלֹהִים:

כד וְאֵלֶּה מִסְפְּרֵי רָאשֵׁי הֶחָלוּץ לַצָּבָא בָּאוּ עַל־דָּוִיד חֶבְרוֹנָה לְהָסֵב מַלְכוּת שָׁאוּל אֵלָיו כְּפִי יְהֹוָה:

כה בְּנֵי יְהוּדָה נֹשְׂאֵי צִנָּה וָרֹמַח שֵׁשֶׁת אֲלָפִים וּשְׁמוֹנֶה מֵאוֹת חֲלוּצֵי צָבָא:

כו מִן־בְּנֵי שִׁמְעוֹן גִּבּוֹרֵי חַיִל לַצָּבָא שִׁבְעַת אֲלָפִים וּמֵאָה:

כז מִן־בְּנֵי הַלֵּוִי אַרְבַּעַת אֲלָפִים וְשֵׁשׁ מֵאוֹת:

כח וִיהוֹיָדָע הַנָּגִיד לְאַהֲרֹן וְעִמּוֹ שְׁלֹשֶׁת אֲלָפִים וּשְׁבַע מֵאוֹת:

כט וְצָדוֹק נַעַר גִּבּוֹר חָיִל וּבֵית־אָבִיו שָׂרִים עֶשְׂרִים וּשְׁנָיִם:

ל וּמִן־בְּנֵי בִנְיָמִן אֲחֵי שָׁאוּל שְׁלֹשֶׁת אֲלָפִים וְעַד־הֵנָּה מַרְבִּיתָם שֹׁמְרִים מִשְׁמֶרֶת בֵּית שָׁאוּל:

לא וּמִן־בְּנֵי אֶפְרַיִם עֶשְׂרִים אֶלֶף וּשְׁמוֹנֶה מֵאוֹת גִּבּוֹרֵי חַיִל אַנְשֵׁי שֵׁמוֹת לְבֵית אֲבוֹתָם:

Divrei Hayamim I/I Chronicles
Chapter 13

32 of the half-tribe of *Menashe*, 18,000, who were designated by name to come and make *David* king;	לב וּמֵחֲצִי מַטֵּה מְנַשֶּׁה שְׁמוֹנָה עָשָׂר אָלֶף אֲשֶׁר נִקְּבוּ בְּשֵׁמוֹת לָבוֹא לְהַמְלִיךְ אֶת־דָּוִיד:
33 of the Issacharites, men who knew how to interpret the signs of the times, to determine how *Yisrael* should act; their chiefs were 200, and all their kinsmen followed them;	לג וּמִבְּנֵי יִשָּׂשכָר יוֹדְעֵי בִינָה לַעִתִּים לָדַעַת מַה־יַּעֲשֶׂה יִשְׂרָאֵל רָאשֵׁיהֶם מָאתַיִם וְכָל־אֲחֵיהֶם עַל־פִּיהֶם:
34 of *Zevulun*, those ready for service, able to man a battle line with all kinds of weapons, 50,000, giving support wholeheartedly;	לד מִזְּבֻלוּן יוֹצְאֵי צָבָא עֹרְכֵי מִלְחָמָה בְּכָל־כְּלֵי מִלְחָמָה חֲמִשִּׁים אָלֶף וְלַעֲדֹר בְּלֹא־לֵב וָלֵב:
35 of *Naftali*, 1,000 chieftains with their shields and lances – 37,000;	לה וּמִנַּפְתָּלִי שָׂרִים אָלֶף וְעִמָּהֶם בְּצִנָּה וַחֲנִית שְׁלֹשִׁים וְשִׁבְעָה אָלֶף:
36 of the Danites, able to man the battle line – 28,600;	לו וּמִן־הַדָּנִי עֹרְכֵי מִלְחָמָה עֶשְׂרִים־וּשְׁמוֹנָה אֶלֶף וְשֵׁשׁ מֵאוֹת:
37 of *Asher*, those ready for service to man the battle line – 40,000;	לז וּמֵאָשֵׁר יוֹצְאֵי צָבָא לַעֲרֹךְ מִלְחָמָה אַרְבָּעִים אָלֶף:
38 from beyond the *Yarden*, of the Reubenites, the Gadites, and the half-tribe of *Menashe*, together with all kinds of military weapons – 120,000.	לח וּמֵעֵבֶר לַיַּרְדֵּן מִן־הָראוּבֵנִי וְהַגָּדִי וַחֲצִי שֵׁבֶט מְנַשֶּׁה בְּכֹל כְּלֵי צְבָא מִלְחָמָה מֵאָה וְעֶשְׂרִים אָלֶף:
39 All these, fighting men, manning the battle line with whole heart, came to *Chevron* to make *David* king over all *Yisrael*. Likewise, all the rest of *Yisrael* was of one mind to make *David* king.	לט כָּל־אֵלֶּה אַנְשֵׁי מִלְחָמָה עֹדְרֵי מַעֲרָכָה בְּלֵבָב שָׁלֵם בָּאוּ חֶבְרוֹנָה לְהַמְלִיךְ אֶת־דָּוִיד עַל־כָּל־יִשְׂרָאֵל וְגַם כָּל־שֵׁרִית יִשְׂרָאֵל לֵב אֶחָד לְהַמְלִיךְ אֶת־דָּוִיד:
40 They were there with *David* three days, eating and drinking, for their kinsmen had provided for them.	מ וַיִּהְיוּ־שָׁם עִם־דָּוִיד יָמִים שְׁלוֹשָׁה אֹכְלִים וְשׁוֹתִים כִּי־הֵכִינוּ לָהֶם אֲחֵיהֶם:
41 And also, their relatives as far away as *Yissachar*, *Zevulun*, and *Naftali* brought food by ass, camel, mule, and ox – provisions of flour, cakes of figs, raisin cakes, wine, oil, cattle, and sheep in abundance, for there was joy in *Yisrael*.	מא וְגַם הַקְּרוֹבִים־אֲלֵיהֶם עַד־יִשָּׂשכָר וּזְבֻלוּן וְנַפְתָּלִי מְבִיאִים לֶחֶם בַּחֲמוֹרִים וּבַגְּמַלִּים וּבַפְּרָדִים וּבַבָּקָר מַאֲכָל קֶמַח דְּבֵלִים וְצִמּוּקִים וְיַיִן־וְשֶׁמֶן וּבָקָר וְצֹאן לָרֹב כִּי שִׂמְחָה בְּיִשְׂרָאֵל:
13 1 Then *David* consulted with the officers of the thousands and the hundreds, with every chief officer.	יג א וַיִּוָּעַץ דָּוִיד עִם־שָׂרֵי הָאֲלָפִים וְהַמֵּאוֹת לְכָל־נָגִיד:
2 *David* said to the entire assembly of *Yisrael*, "If you approve, and if *Hashem* our God concurs, let us send far and wide to our remaining kinsmen throughout the territories of *Yisrael*, including the *Kohanim* and *Leviim* in the towns where they have pasturelands, that they should gather together to us	ב וַיֹּאמֶר דָּוִיד לְכֹל קְהַל יִשְׂרָאֵל אִם־עֲלֵיכֶם טוֹב וּמִן־יְהוָה אֱלֹהֵינוּ נִפְרְצָה נִשְׁלְחָה עַל־אַחֵינוּ הַנִּשְׁאָרִים בְּכָל אַרְצוֹת יִשְׂרָאֵל וְעִמָּהֶם הַכֹּהֲנִים וְהַלְוִיִּם בְּעָרֵי מִגְרְשֵׁיהֶם וְיִקָּבְצוּ אֵלֵינוּ:

Divrei Hayamim I / I Chronicles
Chapter 13

va-YO-mer da-VEED l'-KHOL k'-HAL yis-ra-AYL im a-lay-KHEM TOV u-min a-do-NAI e-lo-HAY-nu nif-r'-TZAH nish-l'-KHAH al a-KHAY-nu ha-nish-a-REEM b'-KHOL ar-TZOT yis-ra-AYL v'-i-ma-HEM ha-ko-ha-NEEM v'-hal-vi-YIM b'-a-RAY mig-r'-shay-HEM v'-yi-ka-v'-TZU ay-LAY-nu

3 in order to transfer the *Aron* of our God to us, for throughout the days of *Shaul* we paid no regard to it."

ג וְנָסֵבָּה אֶת־אֲרוֹן אֱלֹהֵינוּ אֵלֵינוּ כִּי־לֹא דְרַשְׁנֻהוּ בִּימֵי שָׁאוּל׃

4 The entire assembly agreed to do so, for the proposal pleased all the people.

ד וַיֹּאמְרוּ כָל־הַקָּהָל לַעֲשׂוֹת כֵּן כִּי־יָשַׁר הַדָּבָר בְּעֵינֵי כָל־הָעָם׃

5 *David* then assembled all *Yisrael* from Shihor of Egypt to Lebo-hamath, in order to bring the *Aron* of *Hashem* from *Kiryat Ye'arim*.

ה וַיַּקְהֵל דָּוִיד אֶת־כָּל־יִשְׂרָאֵל מִן־שִׁיחוֹר מִצְרַיִם וְעַד־לְבוֹא חֲמָת לְהָבִיא אֶת־אֲרוֹן הָאֱלֹהִים מִקִּרְיַת יְעָרִים׃

6 *David* and all *Yisrael* went up to Baalah, *Kiryat Ye'arim* of *Yehuda*, to bring up from there the *Aron* of *Hashem*, *Hashem*, Enthroned on the *Keruvim*, to which the Name was attached.

ו וַיַּעַל דָּוִיד וְכָל־יִשְׂרָאֵל בַּעֲלָתָה אֶל־קִרְיַת יְעָרִים אֲשֶׁר לִיהוּדָה לְהַעֲלוֹת מִשָּׁם אֵת אֲרוֹן הָאֱלֹהִים יְהֹוָה יוֹשֵׁב הַכְּרוּבִים אֲשֶׁר־נִקְרָא שֵׁם׃

7 They transported the *Aron* of *Hashem* on a new cart from the house of *Avinadav*; Uzza and Ahio guided the cart,

ז וַיַּרְכִּיבוּ אֶת־אֲרוֹן הָאֱלֹהִים עַל־עֲגָלָה חֲדָשָׁה מִבֵּית אֲבִינָדָב וְעֻזָּא וְאַחְיוֹ נֹהֲגִים בָּעֲגָלָה׃

8 and *David* and all *Yisrael* danced before *Hashem* with all their might – with songs, lyres, harps, timbrels, cymbals, and trumpets.

ח וְדָוִיד וְכָל־יִשְׂרָאֵל מְשַׂחֲקִים לִפְנֵי הָאֱלֹהִים בְּכָל־עֹז וּבְשִׁירִים וּבְכִנֹּרוֹת וּבִנְבָלִים וּבְתֻפִּים וּבִמְצִלְתַּיִם וּבַחֲצֹצְרוֹת׃

9 But when they came to the threshing floor of Chidon, Uzza put out his hand to hold the *Aron* of *Hashem* because the oxen had stumbled.

ט וַיָּבֹאוּ עַד־גֹּרֶן כִּידֹן וַיִּשְׁלַח עֻזָּא אֶת־יָדוֹ לֶאֱחֹז אֶת־הָאָרוֹן כִּי שָׁמְטוּ הַבָּקָר׃

10 *Hashem* was incensed at Uzza, and struck him down, because he laid a hand on the *Aron*; and so he died there before *Hashem*.

י וַיִּחַר־אַף יְהֹוָה בְּעֻזָּא וַיַּכֵּהוּ עַל אֲשֶׁר־שָׁלַח יָדוֹ עַל־הָאָרוֹן וַיָּמָת שָׁם לִפְנֵי אֱלֹהִים׃

11 *David* was distressed because *Hashem* had burst out against Uzza; and that place was named Perez-uzzah, as it is still called.

יא וַיִּחַר לְדָוִיד כִּי־פָרַץ יְהֹוָה פֶּרֶץ בְּעֻזָּא וַיִּקְרָא לַמָּקוֹם הַהוּא פֶּרֶץ עֻזָּא עַד הַיּוֹם הַזֶּה׃

13:2 That they should gather together to us King *David* assembled the People of Israel before bringing the *Aron HaBrit* to its resting place in *Yerushalayim*. The Ark is the symbol of the covenant between the Children of Israel and God, as it says, "And deposit in the *Aron* [the tablets of] the Pact which I will give you" (Exodus 25:16). The verses in Exodus continue to elaborate about the function of the *Aron*: "There I will meet with you, and I will impart to you – from above the cover, from between the two cherubim that are on top of the *Aron HaBrit*" (Exodus 25:22). Since the Lord continues to communicate with the people from above the *Aron* after the revelation at Sinai, this means that the Ark is the means through which He expresses His continued commitment to the covenant and His closeness with the people. *David* therefore felt that the entire nation should take part in the ceremony marking the transference of the Ark to *Yerushalayim*.

Divrei Hayamim I / I Chronicles
Chapter 14

דברי הימים א
פרק יד

12 *David* was afraid of *Hashem* that day; he said, "How can I bring the *Aron* of *Hashem* here?"

יב וַיִּרָא דָוִיד אֶת־הָאֱלֹהִים בַּיּוֹם הַהוּא לֵאמֹר הֵיךְ אָבִיא אֵלַי אֵת אֲרוֹן הָאֱלֹהִים:

13 So *David* did not remove the *Aron* to his place in the City of *David*; instead, he diverted it to the house of *Oved Edom* the Gittite.

יג וְלֹא־הֵסִיר דָּוִיד אֶת־הָאָרוֹן אֵלָיו אֶל־עִיר דָּוִיד וַיַּטֵּהוּ אֶל־בֵּית עֹבֵד־אֱדֹם הַגִּתִּי:

14 The *Aron* of *Hashem* remained in the house of *Oved Edom*, in its own abode, three months, and *Hashem* blessed the house of *Oved Edom* and all he had.

יד וַיֵּשֶׁב אֲרוֹן הָאֱלֹהִים עִם־בֵּית עֹבֵד אֱדֹם בְּבֵיתוֹ שְׁלֹשָׁה חֳדָשִׁים וַיְבָרֶךְ יְהוָה אֶת־בֵּית עֹבֵד־אֱדֹם וְאֶת־כָּל־אֲשֶׁר־לוֹ:

14

1 King Hiram of Tyre sent envoys to *David* with cedar logs, stonemasons, and carpenters to build a palace for him.

א וַיִּשְׁלַח חִירָם [חוּרָם] מֶלֶךְ־צֹר מַלְאָכִים אֶל־דָּוִיד וַעֲצֵי אֲרָזִים וְחָרָשֵׁי קִיר וְחָרָשֵׁי עֵצִים לִבְנוֹת לוֹ בָּיִת:

2 Thus *David* knew that *Hashem* had established him as king over *Yisrael*, and that his kingship was highly exalted for the sake of His people *Yisrael*.

ב וַיֵּדַע דָּוִיד כִּי־הֱכִינוֹ יְהוָה לְמֶלֶךְ עַל־יִשְׂרָאֵל כִּי־נִשֵּׂאת לְמַעְלָה מַלְכוּתוֹ בַּעֲבוּר עַמּוֹ יִשְׂרָאֵל:

3 *David* took more wives in *Yerushalayim*, and *David* begot more sons and daughters.

ג וַיִּקַּח דָּוִיד עוֹד נָשִׁים בִּירוּשָׁלָםִ וַיּוֹלֶד דָּוִיד עוֹד בָּנִים וּבָנוֹת:

4 These are the names of the children born to him in *Yerushalayim*: Shammua, Shobab, *Natan*, and *Shlomo*;

ד וְאֵלֶּה שְׁמוֹת הַיְלוּדִים אֲשֶׁר הָיוּ־לוֹ בִּירוּשָׁלָםִ שַׁמּוּעַ וְשׁוֹבָב נָתָן וּשְׁלֹמֹה:

5 Ibhar, Elishua, and Elpelet;

ה וְיִבְחָר וֶאֱלִישׁוּעַ וְאֶלְפָּלֶט:

6 Nogah, Nepheg, and Japhia;

ו וְנֹגַהּ וְנֶפֶג וְיָפִיעַ:

7 Elishama, Beeliada, and Eliphelet.

ז וֶאֱלִישָׁמָע וּבְעֶלְיָדָע וֶאֱלִיפָלֶט:

8 When the Philistines heard that *David* had been anointed king over all *Yisrael*, all the Philistines went up in search of *David*; but *David* heard of it, and he went out to them.

ח וַיִּשְׁמְעוּ פְלִשְׁתִּים כִּי־נִמְשַׁח דָּוִיד לְמֶלֶךְ עַל־כָּל־יִשְׂרָאֵל וַיַּעֲלוּ כָל־פְּלִשְׁתִּים לְבַקֵּשׁ אֶת־דָּוִיד וַיִּשְׁמַע דָּוִיד וַיֵּצֵא לִפְנֵיהֶם:

9 The Philistines came and raided the Valley of Rephaim.

ט וּפְלִשְׁתִּים בָּאוּ וַיִּפְשְׁטוּ בְּעֵמֶק רְפָאִים:

10 *David* inquired of *Hashem*, "Shall I go up against the Philistines? Will You deliver them into my hands?" And *Hashem* answered him, "Go up, and I will deliver them into your hands."

י וַיִּשְׁאַל דָּוִיד בֵּאלֹהִים לֵאמֹר הַאֶעֱלֶה עַל־פְּלִשְׁתִּיִּים [פְּלִשְׁתִּים] וּנְתַתָּם בְּיָדִי וַיֹּאמֶר לוֹ יְהוָה עֲלֵה וּנְתַתִּים בְּיָדֶךָ:

va-yish-AL da-VEED bay-lo-HEEM lay-MOR ha-e-e-LEH al p'-lish-TEEM un-ta-TAM b'-ya-DEE va-YO-mer LO a-do-NAI a-LAY un-ta-TEEM b'-ya-DE-kha

---

14:10 Shall I go up against the Philistines *David* understood that success is dependent upon God's consent and aid. Therefore, although he is a superior warrior and general, he asks the Almighty if he should proceed before attacking the Philistines. By doing so, *David* teaches a crucial lesson about the importance of acting within the bounds of divine consent, especially in God's chosen land.

Divrei Hayamim I / I Chronicles

Chapter 15

11 Thereupon *David* ascended Baal-perazim, and *David* defeated them there. *David* said, "*Hashem* burst out against my enemies by my hands as waters burst out." That is why that place was named Baal-perazim.

12 They abandoned their gods there, and *David* ordered these to be burned.

13 Once again the Philistines raided the valley.

14 *David* inquired of *Hashem* once more, and *Hashem* answered, "Do not go up after them, but circle around them and confront them at the baca trees.

15 And when you hear the sound of marching in the tops of the baca trees, then go out to battle, for *Hashem* will be going in front of you to attack the Philistine forces."

16 *David* did as *Hashem* had commanded him; and they routed the Philistines from *Givon* all the way to Gezer.

17 *David* became famous throughout the lands, and *Hashem* put the fear of him in all the nations.

15

1 He had houses made for himself in the City of *David*, and he prepared a place for the *Aron* of *Hashem*, and pitched a tent for it.

2 Then *David* gave orders that none but the *Leviim* were to carry the *Aron* of *Hashem*, for *Hashem* had chosen them to carry the *Aron* of *Hashem* and to minister to Him forever.

3 *David* assembled all *Yisrael* in *Yerushalayim* to bring up the *Aron* of *Hashem* to its place, which he had prepared for it.

va-yak-HAYL da-VEED et kol yis-ra-AYL el y'-ru-sha-LA-im l'-ha-a-LOT et a-RON a-do-NAI el m'-ko-MO a-sher hay-KHEEN LO

4 Then *David* gathered together the Aaronides and the *Leviim*:

15:3 *David* assembled all *Yisrael* in *Yerushalayim* *David* summoned the entire Nation of Israel to bring the *Aron HaBrit* to its place in the heart of *Yerushalayim*. Such a public demonstration was necessary because this was a truly momentous event: King *David* was bringing the spiritual center, or focal point, of the people to the spiritual center of the land. This highlights the never-ending bond between the People of Israel and the Land of Israel, which is cemented by their covenant with the God of Israel.

Divrei Hayamim I / I Chronicles
Chapter 15

דברי הימים א
פרק טו

5 the sons of *Kehat*: Uriel the officer and his kinsmen – 120;

ה לִבְנֵי קְהָת אוּרִיאֵל הַשָּׂר וְאֶחָיו מֵאָה וְעֶשְׂרִים:

6 the sons of *Merari*: Asaiah the officer and his kinsmen – 220;

ו לִבְנֵי מְרָרִי עֲשָׂיָה הַשָּׂר וְאֶחָיו מָאתַיִם וְעֶשְׂרִים:

7 the sons of *Gershom*: Yoel the officer and his kinsmen – 130;

ז לִבְנֵי גֵרְשׁוֹם יוֹאֵל הַשָּׂר וְאֶחָיו מֵאָה וּשְׁלֹשִׁים:

8 the sons of Elizaphan: *Shemaya* the officer and his kinsmen – 200;

ח לִבְנֵי אֱלִיצָפָן שְׁמַעְיָה הַשָּׂר וְאֶחָיו מָאתָיִם:

9 the sons of *Chevron*: Eliel the officer and his kinsmen – 80;

ט לִבְנֵי חֶבְרוֹן אֱלִיאֵל הַשָּׂר וְאֶחָיו שְׁמוֹנִים:

10 the sons of *Uzziel*: *Aminadav* the officer and his kinsmen – 112.

י לִבְנֵי עֻזִּיאֵל עַמִּינָדָב הַשָּׂר וְאֶחָיו מֵאָה וּשְׁנֵים עָשָׂר:

11 *David* sent for *Tzadok* and *Evyatar* the *Kohanim*, and for the *Leviim*: Uriel, Asaiah, Yoel, Shemaya, Eliel, and *Aminadav*.

יא וַיִּקְרָא דָוִיד לְצָדוֹק וּלְאֶבְיָתָר הַכֹּהֲנִים וְלַלְוִיִּם לְאוּרִיאֵל עֲשָׂיָה וְיוֹאֵל שְׁמַעְיָה וֶאֱלִיאֵל וְעַמִּינָדָב:

12 He said to them, "You are the heads of the clans of the *Leviim*; sanctify yourselves, you and your kinsmen, and bring up the *Aron* of *Hashem* God of *Yisrael* to [the place] I have prepared for it.

יב וַיֹּאמֶר לָהֶם אַתֶּם רָאשֵׁי הָאָבוֹת לַלְוִיִּם הִתְקַדְּשׁוּ אַתֶּם וַאֲחֵיכֶם וְהַעֲלִיתֶם אֵת אֲרוֹן יְהוָה אֱלֹהֵי יִשְׂרָאֵל אֶל־הֲכִינוֹתִי לוֹ:

13 Because you were not there the first time, *Hashem* our God burst out against us, for we did not show due regard for Him."

יג כִּי לְמַבָּרִאשׁוֹנָה לֹא אַתֶּם פָּרַץ יְהוָה אֱלֹהֵינוּ בָּנוּ כִּי־לֹא דְרַשְׁנֻהוּ כַּמִּשְׁפָּט:

14 The *Kohanim* and *Leviim* sanctified themselves in order to bring up the *Aron* of *Hashem* God of *Yisrael*.

יד וַיִּתְקַדְּשׁוּ הַכֹּהֲנִים וְהַלְוִיִּם לְהַעֲלוֹת אֶת־אֲרוֹן יְהוָה אֱלֹהֵי יִשְׂרָאֵל:

15 The *Leviim* carried the *Aron* of *Hashem* by means of poles on their shoulders, as *Moshe* had commanded in accordance with the word of *Hashem*.

טו וַיִּשְׂאוּ בְנֵי־הַלְוִיִּם אֵת אֲרוֹן הָאֱלֹהִים כַּאֲשֶׁר צִוָּה מֹשֶׁה כִּדְבַר יְהוָה בִּכְתֵפָם בַּמֹּטוֹת עֲלֵיהֶם:

16 *David* ordered the officers of the *Leviim* to install their kinsmen, the singers, with musical instruments, harps, lyres, and cymbals, joyfully making their voices heard.

טז וַיֹּאמֶר דָּוִיד לְשָׂרֵי הַלְוִיִּם לְהַעֲמִיד אֶת־אֲחֵיהֶם הַמְשֹׁרְרִים בִּכְלֵי־שִׁיר נְבָלִים וְכִנֹּרוֹת וּמְצִלְתָּיִם מַשְׁמִיעִים לְהָרִים־בְּקוֹל לְשִׂמְחָה:

17 So the *Leviim* installed *Hayman* son of *Yoel* and, of his kinsmen, *Asaf* son of *Berechya*; and, of the sons of *Merari* their kinsmen, Ethan son of Kushaiah.

יז וַיַּעֲמִידוּ הַלְוִיִּם אֵת הֵימָן בֶּן־יוֹאֵל וּמִן־אֶחָיו אָסָף בֶּן־בֶּרֶכְיָהוּ וּמִן־בְּנֵי מְרָרִי אֲחֵיהֶם אֵיתָן בֶּן־קוּשָׁיָהוּ:

18 Together with them were their kinsmen of second rank, *Zecharya*, Ben, Jaaziel, Shemiramoth, *Yechiel*, Unni, *Eliav*, Benaiah, Maaseiah, Mattithiah, Eliphalehu, Mikneiah, *Oved Edom* and Jeiel the gatekeepers.

יח וְעִמָּהֶם אֲחֵיהֶם הַמִּשְׁנִים זְכַרְיָהוּ בֵּן וְיַעֲזִיאֵל וּשְׁמִירָמוֹת וִיחִיאֵל וְעֻנִּי אֱלִיאָב וּבְנָיָהוּ וּמַעֲשֵׂיָהוּ וּמַתִּתְיָהוּ וֶאֱלִיפְלֵהוּ וּמִקְנֵיָהוּ וְעֹבֵד אֱדֹם וִיעִיאֵל הַשֹּׁעֲרִים:

19 Also the singers *Hayman*, *Asaf*, and Ethan to sound the bronze cymbals,

יט וְהַמְשֹׁרְרִים הֵימָן אָסָף וְאֵיתָן בִּמְצִלְתַּיִם נְחֹשֶׁת לְהַשְׁמִיעַ:

2026

Divrei Hayamim I/I Chronicles
Chapter 16

דברי הימים א
פרק טז

20 and *Zecharya*, Aziel, Shemiramoth, *Yechiel*, Unni, *Eliav*, Maaseiah, and Benaiah with harps on alamoth;

כ וּזְכַרְיָה וַעֲזִיאֵל וּשְׁמִירָמוֹת וִיחִיאֵל וְעֻנִּי אֱלִיאָב וּמַעֲשֵׂיָהוּ וּבְנָיָהוּ בִּנְבָלִים עַל־עֲלָמוֹת׃

21 also Mattithiah, Eliphalehu, Mikneiah, Obededom, Jeiel, and Azaziah, with lyres to lead on the sheminith;

כא וּמַתִּתְיָהוּ וֶאֱלִיפְלֵהוּ וּמִקְנֵיָהוּ וְעֹבֵד אֱדֹם וִיעִיאֵל וַעֲזַזְיָהוּ בְּכִנֹּרוֹת עַל־הַשְּׁמִינִית לְנַצֵּחַ׃

22 also Chenaniah, officer of the *Leviim* in song; he was in charge of the song because he was a master.

כב וּכְנַנְיָהוּ שַׂר־הַלְוִיִּם בְּמַשָּׂא יָסֹר בַּמַּשָּׂא כִּי מֵבִין הוּא׃

23 *Berechya* and *Elkana* were gatekeepers for the *Aron*.

כג וּבֶרֶכְיָה וְאֶלְקָנָה שֹׁעֲרִים לָאָרוֹן׃

24 Shebaniah, Joshaphat, Nethanel, Amasai, *Zecharya*, Benaiah, and *Eliezer* the *Kohanim* sounded the trumpets before the *Aron* of *Hashem*, and Obededom and Jehiah were gatekeepers for the *Aron*.

כד וּשְׁבַנְיָהוּ וְיוֹשָׁפָט וּנְתַנְאֵל וַעֲמָשַׂי וּזְכַרְיָהוּ וּבְנָיָהוּ וֶאֱלִיעֶזֶר הַכֹּהֲנִים מַחְצְרִים [מַחְצְצרִים] בַּחֲצֹצְרוֹת לִפְנֵי אֲרוֹן הָאֱלֹהִים וְעֹבֵד אֱדֹם וִיחִיָּה שֹׁעֲרִים לָאָרוֹן׃

25 Then *David* and the elders of *Yisrael* and the officers of the thousands who were going to bring up the *Aron Brit Hashem* from the house of *Oved Edom* were joyful.

כה וַיְהִי דָוִיד וְזִקְנֵי יִשְׂרָאֵל וְשָׂרֵי הָאֲלָפִים הַהֹלְכִים לְהַעֲלוֹת אֶת־אֲרוֹן בְּרִית־יְהוָה מִן־בֵּית עֹבֵד־אֱדֹם בְּשִׂמְחָה׃

26 Since *Hashem* helped the *Leviim* who were carrying the *Aron Brit Hashem*, they sacrificed seven bulls and seven rams.

כו וַיְהִי בֶּעְזֹר הָאֱלֹהִים אֶת־הַלְוִיִּם נֹשְׂאֵי אֲרוֹן בְּרִית־יְהוָה וַיִּזְבְּחוּ שִׁבְעָה־פָרִים וְשִׁבְעָה אֵילִים׃

27 Now *David* and all the *Leviim* who were carrying the *Aron*, and the singers and Chenaniah, officer of song of the singers, were wrapped in robes of fine linen, and *David* wore a linen ephod.

כז וְדָוִיד מְכֻרְבָּל בִּמְעִיל בּוּץ וְכָל־הַלְוִיִּם הַנֹּשְׂאִים אֶת־הָאָרוֹן וְהַמְשֹׁרְרִים וּכְנַנְיָה הַשַּׂר הַמַּשָּׂא הַמְשֹׁרְרִים וְעַל־דָּוִיד אֵפוֹד בָּד׃

28 All *Yisrael* brought up the *Aron Brit Hashem* with shouts and with blasts of the *shofar*, with trumpets and cymbals, playing on harps and lyres.

כח וְכָל־יִשְׂרָאֵל מַעֲלִים אֶת־אֲרוֹן בְּרִית־יְהוָה בִּתְרוּעָה וּבְקוֹל שׁוֹפָר וּבַחֲצֹצְרוֹת וּבִמְצִלְתָּיִם מַשְׁמִעִים בִּנְבָלִים וְכִנֹּרוֹת׃

29 As the *Aron Brit Hashem* arrived at the City of *David*, *Michal* daughter of *Shaul* looked out of the window and saw King *David* leaping and dancing, and she despised him for it.

כט וַיְהִי אֲרוֹן בְּרִית יְהוָה בָּא עַד־עִיר דָּוִיד וּמִיכַל בַּת־שָׁאוּל נִשְׁקְפָה בְּעַד הַחַלּוֹן וַתֵּרֶא אֶת־הַמֶּלֶךְ דָּוִיד מְרַקֵּד וּמְשַׂחֵק וַתִּבֶז לוֹ בְּלִבָּהּ׃

16 1 They brought in the *Aron* of *Hashem* and set it up inside the tent that *David* had pitched for it, and they sacrificed burnt offerings and offerings of well-being before *Hashem*.

טז א וַיָּבִיאוּ אֶת־אֲרוֹן הָאֱלֹהִים וַיַּצִּיגוּ אֹתוֹ בְּתוֹךְ הָאֹהֶל אֲשֶׁר נָטָה־לוֹ דָּוִיד וַיַּקְרִיבוּ עֹלוֹת וּשְׁלָמִים לִפְנֵי הָאֱלֹהִים׃

2 When *David* finished sacrificing the burnt offerings and the offerings of well-being, he blessed the people in the name of *Hashem*.

ב וַיְכַל דָּוִיד מֵהַעֲלוֹת הָעֹלָה וְהַשְּׁלָמִים וַיְבָרֶךְ אֶת־הָעָם בְּשֵׁם יְהוָה׃

3 And he distributed to every person in *Yisrael* – man and woman alike – to each a loaf of bread, a cake made in a pan, and a raisin cake.

ג וַיְחַלֵּק לְכָל־אִישׁ יִשְׂרָאֵל מֵאִישׁ וְעַד־אִשָּׁה לְאִישׁ כִּכַּר־לֶחֶם וְאֶשְׁפָּר וַאֲשִׁישָׁה׃

Divrei Hayamim I / I Chronicles
Chapter 16

4 He appointed *Leviim* to minister before the *Aron* of *Hashem*, to invoke, to praise, and to extol God of *Yisrael*:

5 *Asaf* the chief, *Zecharya* second in rank, Jeiel, Shemiramoth, *Yechiel*, Mattithiah, *Eliav*, Benaiah, *Oved Edom*, and Jeiel, with harps and lyres, and *Asaf* sounding the cymbals,

6 and Benaiah and *Yachaziel* the *Kohanim*, with trumpets, regularly before the *Aron Brit Hashem*.

7 Then, on that day, *David* first commissioned *Asaf* and his kinsmen to give praise to *Hashem*:

8 "Praise *Hashem*; call on His name; proclaim His deeds among the peoples.

9 Sing praises unto Him; speak of all His wondrous acts.

10 Exult in His holy name; let all who seek *Hashem* rejoice.

11 Turn to *Hashem*, to His might; seek His presence constantly.

12 Remember the wonders He has done; His portents and the judgments He has pronounced,

13 O offspring of *Yisrael*, His servant, O descendants of *Yaakov*, His chosen ones.

14 He is *Hashem* our God; His judgments are throughout the earth.

15 Be ever mindful of His covenant, the promise He gave for a thousand generations,

16 that He made with *Avraham*, swore to *Yitzchak*,

17 and confirmed in a decree for *Yaakov*, for *Yisrael*, as an eternal covenant,

18 saying,'To you I will give the land of Canaan as your allotted heritage.'

lay-MOR l'-KHA e-TAYN E-retz k'-NA-an KHE-vel na-kha-lat-KHEM

19 You were then few in number, a handful, merely sojourning there,

20 wandering from nation to nation, from one kingdom to another.

21 He allowed no one to oppress them; He reproved kings on their account,

דברי הימים א
פרק טז

ד וַיִּתֵּן לִפְנֵי אֲרוֹן יְהֹוָה מִן־הַלְוִיִּם מְשָׁרְתִים וּלְהַזְכִּיר וּלְהוֹדוֹת וּלְהַלֵּל לַיהֹוָה אֱלֹהֵי יִשְׂרָאֵל׃

ה אָסָף הָרֹאשׁ וּמִשְׁנֵהוּ זְכַרְיָה יְעִיאֵל וּשְׁמִירָמוֹת וִיחִיאֵל וּמַתִּתְיָה וֶאֱלִיאָב וּבְנָיָהוּ וְעֹבֵד אֱדֹם וִיעִיאֵל בִּכְלֵי נְבָלִים וּבְכִנֹּרוֹת וְאָסָף בַּמְצִלְתַּיִם מַשְׁמִיעַ׃

ו וּבְנָיָהוּ וְיַחֲזִיאֵל הַכֹּהֲנִים בַּחֲצֹצְרוֹת תָּמִיד לִפְנֵי אֲרוֹן בְּרִית־הָאֱלֹהִים׃

ז בַּיּוֹם הַהוּא אָז נָתַן דָּוִיד בָּרֹאשׁ לְהֹדוֹת לַיהֹוָה בְּיַד־אָסָף וְאֶחָיו׃

ח הוֹדוּ לַיהֹוָה קִרְאוּ בִשְׁמוֹ הוֹדִיעוּ בָעַמִּים עֲלִילוֹתָיו׃

ט שִׁירוּ לוֹ זַמְּרוּ־לוֹ שִׂיחוּ בְּכָל־נִפְלְאֹתָיו׃

י הִתְהַלְלוּ בְּשֵׁם קָדְשׁוֹ יִשְׂמַח לֵב מְבַקְשֵׁי יְהֹוָה׃

יא דִּרְשׁוּ יְהֹוָה וְעֻזּוֹ בַּקְּשׁוּ פָנָיו תָּמִיד׃

יב זִכְרוּ נִפְלְאֹתָיו אֲשֶׁר עָשָׂה מֹפְתָיו וּמִשְׁפְּטֵי־פִיהוּ׃

יג זֶרַע יִשְׂרָאֵל עַבְדּוֹ בְּנֵי יַעֲקֹב בְּחִירָיו׃

יד הוּא יְהֹוָה אֱלֹהֵינוּ בְּכָל־הָאָרֶץ מִשְׁפָּטָיו׃

טו זִכְרוּ לְעוֹלָם בְּרִיתוֹ דָּבָר צִוָּה לְאֶלֶף דּוֹר׃

טז אֲשֶׁר כָּרַת אֶת־אַבְרָהָם וּשְׁבוּעָתוֹ לְיִצְחָק׃

יז וַיַּעֲמִידֶהָ לְיַעֲקֹב לְחֹק לְיִשְׂרָאֵל בְּרִית עוֹלָם׃

יח לֵאמֹר לְךָ אֶתֵּן אֶרֶץ־כְּנָעַן חֶבֶל נַחֲלַתְכֶם׃

יט בִּהְיוֹתְכֶם מְתֵי מִסְפָּר כִּמְעַט וְגָרִים בָּהּ׃

כ וַיִּתְהַלְּכוּ מִגּוֹי אֶל־גּוֹי וּמִמַּמְלָכָה אֶל־עַם אַחֵר׃

כא לֹא־הִנִּיחַ לְאִישׁ לְעָשְׁקָם וַיּוֹכַח עֲלֵיהֶם מְלָכִים׃

Divrei Hayamim I / I Chronicles
Chapter 16

דברי הימים א
פרק טז

22 'Do not touch My anointed ones; do not harm My *Neviim*.'

כב אַל־תִּגְּעוּ בִּמְשִׁיחָי וּבִנְבִיאַי אַל־תָּרֵעוּ:

23 "Sing to *Hashem*, all the earth. proclaim His victory day after day.

כג שִׁירוּ לַיהוָה כָּל־הָאָרֶץ בַּשְּׂרוּ מִיּוֹם־אֶל־יוֹם יְשׁוּעָתוֹ:

24 Tell of His glory among the nations, His wondrous deeds among all peoples.

כד סַפְּרוּ בַגּוֹיִם אֶת־כְּבוֹדוֹ בְּכָל־הָעַמִּים נִפְלְאֹתָיו:

25 For *Hashem* is great and much acclaimed, He is held in awe by all divine beings.

כה כִּי גָדוֹל יְהוָה וּמְהֻלָּל מְאֹד וְנוֹרָא הוּא עַל־כָּל־אֱלֹהִים:

26 All the gods of the peoples are mere idols, but *Hashem* made the heavens.

כו כִּי כָּל־אֱלֹהֵי הָעַמִּים אֱלִילִים וַיהוָה שָׁמַיִם עָשָׂה:

27 Glory and majesty are before Him; strength and joy are in His place.

כז הוֹד וְהָדָר לְפָנָיו עֹז וְחֶדְוָה בִּמְקֹמוֹ:

28 "Ascribe to *Hashem*, O families of the peoples, ascribe to *Hashem* glory and strength.

כח הָבוּ לַיהוָה מִשְׁפְּחוֹת עַמִּים הָבוּ לַיהוָה כָּבוֹד וָעֹז:

29 Ascribe to *Hashem* the glory of His name, bring tribute and enter before Him, bow down to *Hashem* majestic in holiness.

כט הָבוּ לַיהוָה כְּבוֹד שְׁמוֹ שְׂאוּ מִנְחָה וּבֹאוּ לְפָנָיו הִשְׁתַּחֲווּ לַיהוָה בְּהַדְרַת־קֹדֶשׁ:

30 Tremble in His presence, all the earth! The world stands firm; it cannot be shaken.

ל חִילוּ מִלְּפָנָיו כָּל־הָאָרֶץ אַף־תִּכּוֹן תֵּבֵל בַּל־תִּמּוֹט:

31 Let the heavens rejoice and the earth exult; let them declare among the nations, "*Hashem* is King!"

לא יִשְׂמְחוּ הַשָּׁמַיִם וְתָגֵל הָאָרֶץ וְיֹאמְרוּ בַגּוֹיִם יְהוָה מָלָךְ:

32 Let the sea and all within it thunder, the fields and everything in them exult;

לב יִרְעַם הַיָּם וּמְלוֹאוֹ יַעֲלֹץ הַשָּׂדֶה וְכָל־אֲשֶׁר־בּוֹ:

33 then shall all the trees of the forest shout for joy at the presence of *Hashem*, for He is coming to rule the earth.

לג אָז יְרַנְּנוּ עֲצֵי הַיָּעַר מִלִּפְנֵי יְהוָה כִּי־בָא לִשְׁפּוֹט אֶת־הָאָרֶץ:

34 Praise *Hashem* for He is good; His steadfast love is eternal.

לד הוֹדוּ לַיהוָה כִּי טוֹב כִּי לְעוֹלָם חַסְדּוֹ:

35 Declare: Deliver us, O *Hashem*, our deliverer, and gather us and save us from the nations, to acclaim Your holy name, to glory in Your praise.

לה וְאִמְרוּ הוֹשִׁיעֵנוּ אֱלֹהֵי יִשְׁעֵנוּ וְקַבְּצֵנוּ וְהַצִּילֵנוּ מִן־הַגּוֹיִם לְהֹדוֹת לְשֵׁם קָדְשֶׁךָ לְהִשְׁתַּבֵּחַ בִּתְהִלָּתֶךָ:

36 Blessed is *Hashem*, God of *Yisrael*, from eternity to eternity." And all the people said "*Amen*" and "Praise *Hashem*."

לו בָּרוּךְ יְהוָה אֱלֹהֵי יִשְׂרָאֵל מִן־הָעוֹלָם וְעַד הָעֹלָם וַיֹּאמְרוּ כָל־הָעָם אָמֵן וְהַלֵּל לַיהוָה:

37 He left *Asaf* and his kinsmen there before the *Aron Brit Hashem* to minister before the *Aron* regularly as each day required,

לז וַיַּעֲזָב־שָׁם לִפְנֵי אֲרוֹן בְּרִית־יְהוָה לְאָסָף וּלְאֶחָיו לְשָׁרֵת לִפְנֵי הָאָרוֹן תָּמִיד לִדְבַר־יוֹם בְּיוֹמוֹ:

38 as well as *Oved Edom* with their kinsmen – 68; also *Oved Edom* son of Jedithun and Hosah as gatekeepers;

לח וְעֹבֵד אֱדֹם וַאֲחֵיהֶם שִׁשִּׁים וּשְׁמוֹנָה וְעֹבֵד אֱדֹם בֶּן־יְדִיתוּן וְחֹסָה לְשֹׁעֲרִים:

Divrei Hayamim I / I Chronicles
Chapter 17

39 also *Tzadok* the *Kohen* and his fellow *Kohanim* before the *Mishkan* of *Hashem* at the shrine which was in *Givon*;

לט וְאֵת צָדוֹק הַכֹּהֵן וְאֶחָיו הַכֹּהֲנִים לִפְנֵי מִשְׁכַּן יְהֹוָה בַּבָּמָה אֲשֶׁר בְּגִבְעוֹן׃

40 to sacrifice burnt offerings to *Hashem* on the *Mizbayach* of the burnt offering regularly, morning and evening, in accordance with what was prescribed in the Teaching of *Hashem* with which He charged *Yisrael*.

מ לְהַעֲלוֹת עֹלוֹת לַיהֹוָה עַל־מִזְבַּח הָעֹלָה תָּמִיד לַבֹּקֶר וְלָעָרֶב וּלְכָל־הַכָּתוּב בְּתוֹרַת יְהֹוָה אֲשֶׁר צִוָּה עַל־יִשְׂרָאֵל׃

41 With them were *Hayman* and *Yedutun* and the other selected men designated by name to give praise to *Hashem*, "For His steadfast love is eternal."

מא וְעִמָּהֶם הֵימָן וִידוּתוּן וּשְׁאָר הַבְּרוּרִים אֲשֶׁר נִקְּבוּ בְּשֵׁמוֹת לְהֹדוֹת לַיהֹוָה כִּי לְעוֹלָם חַסְדּוֹ׃

42 *Hayman* and *Yedutun* had with them trumpets and cymbals to sound, and instruments for the songs of *Hashem*; and the sons of *Yedutun* were to be at the gate.

מב וְעִמָּהֶם הֵימָן וִידוּתוּן חֲצֹצְרוֹת וּמְצִלְתַּיִם לְמַשְׁמִיעִים וּכְלֵי שִׁיר הָאֱלֹהִים וּבְנֵי יְדוּתוּן לַשָּׁעַר׃

v'-i-ma-HEM hay-MAN vee-du-TUN kha-tzo-tz'-ROT um-tzil-TA-yim l'-mash-mee-EEM ukh-LAY SHEER ha-e-lo-HEEM uv-NAY y'-du-TUN la-SHA-ar

43 Then all the people went every one to his home, and *David* returned to greet his household.

מג וַיֵּלְכוּ כָל־הָעָם אִישׁ לְבֵיתוֹ וַיִּסֹּב דָּוִיד לְבָרֵךְ אֶת־בֵּיתוֹ׃

17

1 When *David* settled in his palace, *David* said to the *Navi Natan*, "Here I am dwelling in a house of cedar, while the *Aron Brit Hashem* is under tent-cloths."

יז א וַיְהִי כַּאֲשֶׁר יָשַׁב דָּוִיד בְּבֵיתוֹ וַיֹּאמֶר דָּוִיד אֶל־נָתָן הַנָּבִיא הִנֵּה אָנֹכִי יוֹשֵׁב בְּבֵית הָאֲרָזִים וַאֲרוֹן בְּרִית־יְהֹוָה תַּחַת יְרִיעוֹת׃

2 *Natan* said to *David*, "Do whatever you have in mind, for *Hashem* is with you."

ב וַיֹּאמֶר נָתָן אֶל־דָּוִיד כֹּל אֲשֶׁר בִּלְבָבְךָ עֲשֵׂה כִּי הָאֱלֹהִים עִמָּךְ׃

3 But that same night the word of *Hashem* came to *Natan*:

ג וַיְהִי בַּלַּיְלָה הַהוּא וַיְהִי דְּבַר־אֱלֹהִים אֶל־נָתָן לֵאמֹר׃

4 "Go and say to My servant *David*: Thus said *Hashem*: You are not the one to build a house for Me to dwell in.

ד לֵךְ וְאָמַרְתָּ אֶל־דָּוִיד עַבְדִּי כֹּה אָמַר יְהֹוָה לֹא אַתָּה תִּבְנֶה־לִּי הַבַּיִת לָשָׁבֶת׃

5 From the day that I brought out *Yisrael* to this day, I have not dwelt in a house, but have [gone] from tent to tent and from one *Mishkan* [to another].

ה כִּי לֹא יָשַׁבְתִּי בְּבַיִת מִן־הַיּוֹם אֲשֶׁר הֶעֱלֵיתִי אֶת־יִשְׂרָאֵל עַד הַיּוֹם הַזֶּה וָאֶהְיֶה מֵאֹהֶל אֶל־אֹהֶל וּמִמִּשְׁכָּן׃

16:42 Instruments for the songs of *Hashem* This verse describes how when *David* brought the Aron to *Yerushalayim*, he offered prayers of thanksgiving to God, accompanied by various musical instruments. The trumpets and cymbals mentioned in this verse, along with the lyres and harps mentioned in *Sefer Divrei Hayamim* I 15:16, were also used during worship in the *Beit Hamikdash*. The music of the Levitical choir and orchestra was an integral part of the divine service of the Holy Temple every day of the year, and was the sweetest music on earth, as it was the Levitical expression of the music of heaven. In today's Jerusalem, musicologists and expert craftsman work closely with the scholars at the Temple Institute to recreate the "musical instruments of *Hashem*" to be used when the Third Temple will be built.

Statue of a Levite blowing a trumpet, Temple Institute in Jerusalem

Divrei Hayamim I / I Chronicles
Chapter 17 — דברי הימים א · פרק יז

6 As I moved about wherever *Yisrael* went, did I ever reproach any of the judges of *Yisrael* whom I appointed to care for My people *Yisrael*: Why have you not built Me a house of cedar?

ו בְּכֹל אֲשֶׁר־הִתְהַלַּכְתִּי בְּכָל־יִשְׂרָאֵל הֲדָבָר דִּבַּרְתִּי אֶת־אַחַד שֹׁפְטֵי יִשְׂרָאֵל אֲשֶׁר צִוִּיתִי לִרְעוֹת אֶת־עַמִּי לֵאמֹר לָמָּה לֹא־בְנִיתֶם לִי בֵּית אֲרָזִים׃

7 "Further, say thus to My servant *David*: Thus said the Lord of Hosts: I took you from the pasture, from following the flock, to be ruler of My people *Yisrael*,

ז וְעַתָּה כֹּה־תֹאמַר לְעַבְדִּי לְדָוִיד כֹּה אָמַר יְהוָה צְבָאוֹת אֲנִי לְקַחְתִּיךָ מִן־הַנָּוֶה מִן־אַחֲרֵי הַצֹּאן לִהְיוֹת נָגִיד עַל עַמִּי יִשְׂרָאֵל׃

8 and I have been with you wherever you went, and have cut down all your enemies before you. Moreover, I will give you renown like that of the greatest men on earth.

ח וָאֶהְיֶה עִמְּךָ בְּכֹל אֲשֶׁר הָלַכְתָּ וָאַכְרִית אֶת־כָּל־אוֹיְבֶיךָ מִפָּנֶיךָ וְעָשִׂיתִי לְךָ שֵׁם כְּשֵׁם הַגְּדוֹלִים אֲשֶׁר בָּאָרֶץ׃

9 I will establish a home for My people *Yisrael* and will plant them firm, so that they shall dwell secure and shall tremble no more. Evil men shall not wear them down anymore as in the past,

ט וְשַׂמְתִּי מָקוֹם לְעַמִּי יִשְׂרָאֵל וּנְטַעְתִּיהוּ וְשָׁכַן תַּחְתָּיו וְלֹא יִרְגַּז עוֹד וְלֹא־יוֹסִיפוּ בְנֵי־עַוְלָה לְבַלֹּתוֹ כַּאֲשֶׁר בָּרִאשׁוֹנָה׃

10 ever since I appointed judges over My people *Yisrael*. I will subdue all your enemies. And I declare to you: *Hashem* will build a house for you.

י וּלְמִיָּמִים אֲשֶׁר צִוִּיתִי שֹׁפְטִים עַל־עַמִּי יִשְׂרָאֵל וְהִכְנַעְתִּי אֶת־כָּל־אוֹיְבֶיךָ וָאַגִּד לָךְ וּבַיִת יִבְנֶה־לְּךָ יְהוָה׃

11 When your days are done and you follow your fathers, I will raise up your offspring after you, one of your own sons, and I will establish his kingship.

יא וְהָיָה כִּי־מָלְאוּ יָמֶיךָ לָלֶכֶת עִם־אֲבֹתֶיךָ וַהֲקִימוֹתִי אֶת־זַרְעֲךָ אַחֲרֶיךָ אֲשֶׁר יִהְיֶה מִבָּנֶיךָ וַהֲכִינוֹתִי אֶת־מַלְכוּתוֹ׃

12 He shall build a house for Me, and I will establish his throne forever.

יב הוּא יִבְנֶה־לִּי בָּיִת וְכֹנַנְתִּי אֶת־כִּסְאוֹ עַד־עוֹלָם׃

HU yiv-neh LEE BA-yit v'-kho-nan-TEE et kis-O ad o-LAM

13 I will be a father to him, and he shall be a son to Me, but I will never withdraw My favor from him as I withdrew it from your predecessor.

יג אֲנִי אֶהְיֶה־לּוֹ לְאָב וְהוּא יִהְיֶה־לִּי לְבֵן וְחַסְדִּי לֹא־אָסִיר מֵעִמּוֹ כַּאֲשֶׁר הֲסִירוֹתִי מֵאֲשֶׁר הָיָה לְפָנֶיךָ׃

14 I will install him in My house and in My kingship forever, and his throne shall be established forever."

יד וְהַעֲמַדְתִּיהוּ בְּבֵיתִי וּבְמַלְכוּתִי עַד־הָעוֹלָם וְכִסְאוֹ יִהְיֶה נָכוֹן עַד־עוֹלָם׃

שלמה

17:12 He shall build a house for me King *David* wants to build the Holy Temple. However, *Hashem* tells him that his son, not he, will be the one to build the *Beit Hamikdash*. As the king who helps conquer the Land of Israel, fights Amalek and solidifies the monarchy, *David* plays an important part in the process of establishing the Israelites in their land. He is even able to make the preparations for the building of the Temple. however, as a warrior, he is not able to build the actual *Beit Hamikdash*, which is intended to promote peace and harmony among the Children of Israel as well as all the nations of the world. in contrast to *David*, his son *Shlomo* (שלמה) is a man of peace, as reflected in his name which derives from the Hebrew word for 'peace,' *shalom* (שלום). *Shlomo*, therefore, is God's choice for the king who will build the Temple. For this same reason, instruments of war and violence were not used in the construction of The *Beit Hamikdash*, so that peace would be built into its very foundation (I Kings 6:7).

Divrei Hayamim I / I Chronicles
Chapter 17

דברי הימים א
פרק יז

15 *Natan* spoke to *David* in accordance with all these words and all this prophecy.

טו כְּכֹל הַדְּבָרִים הָאֵלֶּה וּכְכֹל הֶחָזוֹן הַזֶּה כֵּן דִּבֶּר נָתָן אֶל־דָּוִיד:

16 Then King *David* came and sat before *Hashem*, and he said, "What am I, O *Hashem*, and what is my family, that You have brought me thus far?

טז וַיָּבֹא הַמֶּלֶךְ דָּוִיד וַיֵּשֶׁב לִפְנֵי יְהֹוָה וַיֹּאמֶר מִי־אֲנִי יְהֹוָה אֱלֹהִים וּמִי בֵיתִי כִּי הֲבִיאֹתַנִי עַד־הֲלֹם:

17 Yet even this, O *Hashem*, has seemed too little to You; for You have spoken of Your servant's house for the future. You regard me as a man of distinction, O *Hashem*.

יז וַתִּקְטַן זֹאת בְּעֵינֶיךָ אֱלֹהִים וַתְּדַבֵּר עַל־בֵּית־עַבְדְּךָ לְמֵרָחוֹק וּרְאִיתַנִי כְּתוֹר הָאָדָם הַמַּעֲלָה יְהֹוָה אֱלֹהִים:

18 What more can *David* add regarding the honoring of Your servant? You know Your servant.

יח מַה־יּוֹסִיף עוֹד דָּוִיד אֵלֶיךָ לְכָבוֹד אֶת־עַבְדֶּךָ וְאַתָּה אֶת־עַבְדְּךָ יָדָעְתָּ:

19 *Hashem*, for Your servant's sake, and of Your own accord, You have wrought this great thing, and made known all these great things.

יט יְהֹוָה בַּעֲבוּר עַבְדְּךָ וּכְלִבְּךָ עָשִׂיתָ אֵת כָּל־הַגְּדוּלָּה הַזֹּאת לְהֹדִיעַ אֶת־כָּל־הַגְּדֻלּוֹת:

20 *Hashem*, there is none like You, and there is no other God but You, as we have always heard.

כ יְהֹוָה אֵין כָּמוֹךָ וְאֵין אֱלֹהִים זוּלָתֶךָ בְּכֹל אֲשֶׁר־שָׁמַעְנוּ בְּאָזְנֵינוּ:

21 And who is like Your people *Yisrael*, a unique nation on earth, whom *Hashem* went and redeemed as His people, winning renown for Yourself for great and marvelous deeds, driving out nations before Your people whom You redeemed from Egypt.

כא וּמִי כְּעַמְּךָ יִשְׂרָאֵל גּוֹי אֶחָד בָּאָרֶץ אֲשֶׁר הָלַךְ הָאֱלֹהִים לִפְדּוֹת לוֹ עָם לָשׂוּם לְךָ שֵׁם גְּדֻלּוֹת וְנֹרָאוֹת לְגָרֵשׁ מִפְּנֵי עַמְּךָ אֲשֶׁר־פָּדִיתָ מִמִּצְרַיִם גּוֹיִם:

u-MEE k'-a-m'-KHA yis-ra-AYL GOY e-KHAD ba-A-retz a-SHER ha-LAKH ha-e-lo-HEEM lif-DOT LO AM la-SUM l'-KHA shaym g'-du-LOT v'-no-ra-OT l'-ga-RAYSH mi-p'-NAY a-m'-KHA a-sher pa-DEE-ta mi-mitz-RA-yim go-YIM

22 You have established Your people *Yisrael* as Your very own people forever; and You, *Hashem*, have become their God.

כב וַתִּתֵּן אֶת־עַמְּךָ יִשְׂרָאֵל לְךָ לְעָם עַד־עוֹלָם וְאַתָּה יְהֹוָה הָיִיתָ לָהֶם לֵאלֹהִים:

23 "And now, *Hashem*, let Your promise concerning Your servant and his house be fulfilled forever; and do as You have promised.

כג וְעַתָּה יְהֹוָה הַדָּבָר אֲשֶׁר דִּבַּרְתָּ עַל־עַבְדְּךָ וְעַל־בֵּיתוֹ יֵאָמֵן עַד־עוֹלָם וַעֲשֵׂה כַּאֲשֶׁר דִּבַּרְתָּ:

17:21 And who is like Your people *Yisrael* In this verse, Israel is referred to not only as a "people" but as a "singular nation on earth." Throughout history, the unique character of the Jewish people has been variously described, by friend and foe alike, as a people, a nation, a religion and even a race. It is hard to pin down the exact nature of the Jewish people, but it certainly seems to contain elements of both nationality and spirituality that deeply connect Jews with one another. During the first bloody week of the Yom Kippur War, a soldier stationed on the Golan Heights asked Prime Minister Golda Meir about the many casualties Israel had suffered, "I know we will win, but is all our sacrifice worthwhile?" The Prime Minister replied, "If our sacrifices are for ourselves, then no. But if for the sake of the whole Jewish people, then I believe with all my heart that any price is worthwhile." Her message was that the State of Israel would serve as a safe haven not only for Israelis, but for the entire People of Israel all over the world. Indeed, "who is like Your people *Yisrael*"?

Prime Minister Golda Meir (1898–1978)

Divrei Hayamim I/I Chronicles
Chapter 18

דברי הימים א
פרק יח

24 Let it be fulfilled that Your name be glorified forever, in that men will say, 'the Lord of Hosts, God of *Yisrael*, is *Yisrael*'s God'; and may the house of Your servant *David* be established before You.

כד וְיֵאָמֵן וְיִגְדַּל שִׁמְךָ עַד־עוֹלָם לֵאמֹר יְהֹוָה צְבָאוֹת אֱלֹהֵי יִשְׂרָאֵל אֱלֹהִים לְיִשְׂרָאֵל וּבֵית־דָּוִיד עַבְדְּךָ נָכוֹן לְפָנֶיךָ:

25 Because You, my God, have revealed to Your servant that You will build a house for him, Your servant has ventured to pray to You.

כה כִּי אַתָּה אֱלֹהַי גָּלִיתָ אֶת־אֹזֶן עַבְדְּךָ לִבְנוֹת לוֹ בָּיִת עַל־כֵּן מָצָא עַבְדְּךָ לְהִתְפַּלֵּל לְפָנֶיךָ:

26 And now, *Hashem*, You are *Hashem* and You have made this gracious promise to Your servant.

כו וְעַתָּה יְהֹוָה אַתָּה־הוּא הָאֱלֹהִים וַתְּדַבֵּר עַל־עַבְדְּךָ הַטּוֹבָה הַזֹּאת:

27 Now, it has pleased You to bless Your servant's house, that it abide before You forever; for You, *Hashem*, have blessed and are blessed forever."

כז וְעַתָּה הוֹאַלְתָּ לְבָרֵךְ אֶת־בֵּית עַבְדְּךָ לִהְיוֹת לְעוֹלָם לְפָנֶיךָ כִּי־אַתָּה יְהֹוָה בֵּרַכְתָּ וּמְבֹרָךְ לְעוֹלָם:

18 1 Sometime afterward, *David* attacked the Philistines and subdued them; and *David* took Gath and its dependencies from the Philistines.

יח א וַיְהִי אַחֲרֵי־כֵן וַיַּךְ דָּוִיד אֶת־פְּלִשְׁתִּים וַיַּכְנִיעֵם וַיִּקַּח אֶת־גַּת וּבְנֹתֶיהָ מִיַּד פְּלִשְׁתִּים:

2 He also defeated the Moabites; the Moabites became tributary vassals of *David*.

ב וַיַּךְ אֶת־מוֹאָב וַיִּהְיוּ מוֹאָב עֲבָדִים לְדָוִיד נֹשְׂאֵי מִנְחָה:

3 *David* defeated Hadadezer, king of Zobahhamath, who was on his way to set up his monument at the Euphrates River.

ג וַיַּךְ דָּוִיד אֶת־הֲדַדְעֶזֶר מֶלֶךְ־צוֹבָה חֲמָתָה בְּלֶכְתּוֹ לְהַצִּיב יָדוֹ בִּנְהַר־פְּרָת:

4 *David* captured 1,000 chariots and 7,000 horsemen and 20,000 foot soldiers of his force; and *David* hamstrung all the chariot horses except for 100, which he retained.

ד וַיִּלְכֹּד דָּוִיד מִמֶּנּוּ אֶלֶף רֶכֶב וְשִׁבְעַת אֲלָפִים פָּרָשִׁים וְעֶשְׂרִים אֶלֶף אִישׁ רַגְלִי וַיְעַקֵּר דָּוִיד אֶת־כָּל־הָרֶכֶב וַיּוֹתֵר מִמֶּנּוּ מֵאָה רָכֶב:

5 And when the Arameans of Damascus came to the aid of King Hadadezer of Zobah-hamath, *David* struck down 22,000 of the Arameans.

ה וַיָּבֹא אֲרַם דַּרְמֶשֶׂק לַעְזוֹר לַהֲדַדְעֶזֶר מֶלֶךְ צוֹבָה וַיַּךְ דָּוִיד בַּאֲרָם עֶשְׂרִים־וּשְׁנַיִם אֶלֶף אִישׁ:

6 *David* stationed [garrisons] in Aram of Damascus, and the Arameans became tributary vassals of *David*. *Hashem* gave *David* victory wherever he went.

ו וַיָּשֶׂם דָּוִיד בַּאֲרַם דַּרְמֶשֶׂק וַיְהִי אֲרָם לְדָוִיד עֲבָדִים נֹשְׂאֵי מִנְחָה וַיּוֹשַׁע יְהֹוָה לְדָוִיד בְּכֹל אֲשֶׁר הָלָךְ:

7 *David* took the gold shields carried by Hadadezer's retinue and brought them to *Yerushalayim*;

ז וַיִּקַּח דָּוִיד אֵת שִׁלְטֵי הַזָּהָב אֲשֶׁר הָיוּ עַל עַבְדֵי הֲדַדְעָזֶר וַיְבִיאֵם יְרוּשָׁלָ‍ִם:

8 and from Tibbath and Cun, towns of Hadadezer, *David* took a vast amount of copper, from which *Shlomo* made the bronze tank, the columns, and the bronze vessels.

ח וּמִטִּבְחַת וּמִכּוּן עָרֵי הֲדַדְעֶזֶר לָקַח דָּוִיד נְחֹשֶׁת רַבָּה מְאֹד בָּהּ עָשָׂה שְׁלֹמֹה אֶת־יָם הַנְּחֹשֶׁת וְאֶת־הָעַמּוּדִים וְאֵת כְּלֵי הַנְּחֹשֶׁת:

9 When King Tou of Hamath heard that *David* had defeated the entire army of King Hadadezer of Zobah,

ט וַיִּשְׁמַע תֹּעוּ מֶלֶךְ חֲמָת כִּי הִכָּה דָוִיד אֶת־כָּל־חֵיל הֲדַדְעֶזֶר מֶלֶךְ־צוֹבָה:

Divrei Hayamim I / I Chronicles
Chapter 19

10 he sent his son Hadoram to King *David* to greet him and to congratulate him on his military victory over Hadadezer – for Hadadezer had been at war with Tou; [he brought with him] all manner of gold, silver, and copper objects.

11 King *David* dedicated these to *Hashem*, along with the other silver and gold that he had taken from all the nations: from Edom, Moab, and Ammon; from the Philistines and the Amalekites.

12 Abshai son of *Tzeruya* struck down Edom in the Valley of Salt, 18,000 in all.

13 He stationed garrisons in Edom, and all the Edomites became vassals of *David*. *Hashem* gave *David* victory wherever he went.

14 *David* reigned over all *Yisrael*, and *David* executed true justice among all his people.

va-yim-LOKH da-VEED al kol yis-ra-AYL vai-HEE o-SEH mish-PAT utz-da-KAH l'-khol a-MO

15 *Yoav* son of *Tzeruya* was commander of the army; *Yehoshafat* son of *Achilud* was recorder;

16 *Tzadok* son of *Achituv* and *Avimelech* son of *Evyatar* were *Kohanim*; Shavsha was scribe;

17 Benaiah son of *Yehoyada* was commander of the Cherethites and the Pelethites; and *David*'s sons were first ministers of the king.

19

1 Sometime afterward, Nahash the king of the Ammonites died, and his son succeeded him as king.

2 *David* said, "I will keep faith with Hanun son of Nahash, since his father kept faith with me." *David* sent messengers with condolences to him over his father. But when *David*'s courtiers came to the land of Ammon to Hanun, with condolences,

---

18:14 ***David* executed true justice among all his people** King *David*'s rule over Israel is defined by justice and righteousness. As emphasized by the prophets, executing justice and righteousness is the charge of the Jewish people and their leaders in the Land of Israel (see Ezekiel 45:9). In this sense, *David* was an ideal king. While he did conduct several wars, his reign is ultimately defined not by violence, but justice. He was a just king, providing a model for all to follow. Following in King *David*'s path will bring the ultimate redemption, as the prophet *Yeshayahu* says, "*Tzion* shall be saved in the judgment, her repentant ones, in the retribution." (Isaiah 1:27).

Divrei Hayamim I / I Chronicles

Chapter 19

דברי הימים א
פרק יט

va-YO-mer da-VEED e-e-seh KHE-sed im kha-NUN ben na-KHASH kee a-SAH a-VEEV i-MEE KHE-sed va-yish-LAKH da-VEED mal-a-KHEEM l'-na-kha-MO al a-VEEV va-ya-vo-U av-DAY da-VEED el E-retz b'-NAY a-MON el kha-NUN l'-na-kha-MO

3 the Ammonite officials said to Hanun, "Do you think *David* is really honoring your father just because he sent you men with condolences? Why, it is to explore, to subvert, and to spy out the land that his courtiers have come to you."

ג וַיֹּאמְרוּ שָׂרֵי בְנֵי־עַמּוֹן לְחָנוּן הַמְכַבֵּד דָּוִיד אֶת־אָבִיךָ בְּעֵינֶיךָ כִּי־שָׁלַח לְךָ מְנַחֲמִים הֲלֹא בַּעֲבוּר לַחְקֹר וְלַהֲפֹךְ וּלְרַגֵּל הָאָרֶץ בָּאוּ עֲבָדָיו אֵלֶיךָ׃

4 So Hanun seized *David*'s courtiers, shaved them, and cut away half of their garments up to the buttocks, and sent them off.

ד וַיִּקַּח חָנוּן אֶת־עַבְדֵי דָוִיד וַיְגַלְּחֵם וַיִּכְרֹת אֶת־מַדְוֵיהֶם בַּחֵצִי עַד־הַמִּפְשָׂעָה וַיְשַׁלְּחֵם׃

5 When *David* was told about the men, he dispatched others to meet them, for the men were greatly embarrassed. And the king gave orders, "Stay in *Yericho* until your beards grow back; then you can return."

ה וַיֵּלְכוּ וַיַּגִּידוּ לְדָוִיד עַל־הָאֲנָשִׁים וַיִּשְׁלַח לִקְרָאתָם כִּי־הָיוּ הָאֲנָשִׁים נִכְלָמִים מְאֹד וַיֹּאמֶר הַמֶּלֶךְ שְׁבוּ בִירֵחוֹ עַד אֲשֶׁר־יְצַמַּח זְקַנְכֶם וְשַׁבְתֶּם׃

6 The Ammonites realized that they had incurred the wrath of *David*; so Hanun and the Ammonites sent 1,000 silver *kikarim* to hire chariots and horsemen from Aram-Naharaim, Aram-maacah, and Zobah.

ו וַיִּרְאוּ בְּנֵי עַמּוֹן כִּי הִתְבָּאֲשׁוּ עִם־דָּוִיד וַיִּשְׁלַח חָנוּן וּבְנֵי עַמּוֹן אֶלֶף כִּכַּר־כֶּסֶף לִשְׂכֹּר לָהֶם מִן־אֲרַם נַהֲרַיִם וּמִן־אֲרַם מַעֲכָה וּמִצּוֹבָה רֶכֶב וּפָרָשִׁים׃

7 They hired 32,000 chariots, the king of Maacah, and his army, who came and encamped before Medeba. The Ammonites were mobilized from their cities and came to do battle.

ז וַיִּשְׂכְּרוּ לָהֶם שְׁנַיִם וּשְׁלֹשִׁים אֶלֶף רֶכֶב וְאֶת־מֶלֶךְ מַעֲכָה וְאֶת־עַמּוֹ וַיָּבֹאוּ וַיַּחֲנוּ לִפְנֵי מֵידְבָא וּבְנֵי עַמּוֹן נֶאֶסְפוּ מֵעָרֵיהֶם וַיָּבֹאוּ לַמִּלְחָמָה׃

8 On learning this, *David* sent out *Yoav* and the whole army, [including] the professional fighters.

ח וַיִּשְׁמַע דָּוִיד וַיִּשְׁלַח אֶת־יוֹאָב וְאֵת כָּל־צָבָא הַגִּבּוֹרִים׃

9 The Ammonites marched out and took up their battle position at the entrance of the city, while the kings who came [took their stand] separately in the open.

ט וַיֵּצְאוּ בְּנֵי עַמּוֹן וַיַּעַרְכוּ מִלְחָמָה פֶּתַח הָעִיר וְהַמְּלָכִים אֲשֶׁר־בָּאוּ לְבַדָּם בַּשָּׂדֶה׃

10 *Yoav* saw that there was a battle line against him both front and rear. So he made a selection from all the picked men of *Yisrael* and arrayed them against the Arameans,

י וַיַּרְא יוֹאָב כִּי־הָיְתָה פְנֵי־הַמִּלְחָמָה אֵלָיו פָּנִים וְאָחוֹר וַיִּבְחַר מִכָּל־בָּחוּר בְּיִשְׂרָאֵל וַיַּעֲרֹךְ לִקְרַאת אֲרָם׃

11 and the rest of the troops he put under the command of his brother Abishai and arrayed them against the Ammonites.

יא וְאֵת יֶתֶר הָעָם נָתַן בְּיַד אַבְשַׁי אָחִיו וַיַּעַרְכוּ לִקְרַאת בְּנֵי עַמּוֹן׃

19:2 I will keep faith with Hanun son of Nahash *David* sends messages to comfort Hanun over the death of his father, even though he is a rival king. With this action, *David* shows that he understood that when it comes to relations between nations, there are considerations that go beyond mere politics. By disgracing *David*'s emissaries, though, Hanun shows that he does not believe in the possibility of friendship or gratitude between kings. *David*'s first instinct, however, is that statecraft doesn't nullify the necessity for kindness. By behaving in this manner, *David* shows what makes the kings of Israel who reign in *Yerushalayim* unique. After all, *Yerushalayim* is called "City of Righteousness, Faithful City" (Isaiah 1:26).

Divrei Hayamim I / I Chronicles
Chapter 20

דברי הימים א
פרק כ

12 *Yoav* said, "If the Arameans prove too strong for me, you come to my aid; and if the Ammonites prove too strong for you, I will come to your aid.

יב וַיֹּאמֶר אִם־תֶּחֱזַק מִמֶּנִּי אֲרָם וְהָיִיתָ לִּי לִתְשׁוּעָה וְאִם־בְּנֵי עַמּוֹן יֶחֶזְקוּ מִמְּךָ וְהוֹשַׁעְתִּיךָ:

13 Let us be strong and resolute for the sake of our people and the towns of our God; and *Hashem* will do what He deems right."

יג חֲזַק וְנִתְחַזְּקָה בְּעַד־עַמֵּנוּ וּבְעַד עָרֵי אֱלֹהֵינוּ וַיהֹוָה הַטּוֹב בְּעֵינָיו יַעֲשֶׂה:

14 *Yoav* and the troops with him marched into battle against the Arameans, who fled before him.

יד וַיִּגַּשׁ יוֹאָב וְהָעָם אֲשֶׁר־עִמּוֹ לִפְנֵי אֲרָם לַמִּלְחָמָה וַיָּנוּסוּ מִפָּנָיו:

15 And when the Ammonites saw that the Arameans had fled, they too fled before his brother Abishai, and withdrew into the city. So *Yoav* went to *Yerushalayim*.

טו וּבְנֵי עַמּוֹן רָאוּ כִּי־נָס אֲרָם וַיָּנוּסוּ גַּם־הֵם מִפְּנֵי אַבְשַׁי אָחִיו וַיָּבֹאוּ הָעִירָה וַיָּבֹא יוֹאָב יְרוּשָׁלָ͏ִם:

16 When the Arameans saw that they had been routed by *Yisrael*, they sent messengers to bring out the Arameans from across the Euphrates; Shophach, Hadadezer's army commander, led them.

טז וַיַּרְא אֲרָם כִּי נִגְּפוּ לִפְנֵי יִשְׂרָאֵל וַיִּשְׁלְחוּ מַלְאָכִים וַיּוֹצִיאוּ אֶת־אֲרָם אֲשֶׁר מֵעֵבֶר הַנָּהָר וְשׁוֹפַךְ שַׂר־צְבָא הֲדַדְעֶזֶר לִפְנֵיהֶם:

17 *David* was informed of it; he assembled all *Yisrael*, crossed the *Yarden*, and came and took up positions against them. *David* drew up his forces against Aram; and they fought with him.

יז וַיֻּגַּד לְדָוִיד וַיֶּאֱסֹף אֶת־כָּל־יִשְׂרָאֵל וַיַּעֲבֹר הַיַּרְדֵּן וַיָּבֹא אֲלֵהֶם וַיַּעֲרֹךְ אֲלֵהֶם וַיַּעֲרֹךְ דָּוִיד לִקְרַאת אֲרָם מִלְחָמָה וַיִּלָּחֲמוּ עִמּוֹ:

18 But the Arameans were put to flight by *Yisrael*. *David* killed 7,000 Aramean charioteers and 40,000 footmen; he also killed Shophach, the army commander.

יח וַיָּנָס אֲרָם מִלִּפְנֵי יִשְׂרָאֵל וַיַּהֲרֹג דָּוִיד מֵאֲרָם שִׁבְעַת אֲלָפִים רֶכֶב וְאַרְבָּעִים אֶלֶף אִישׁ רַגְלִי וְאֵת שׁוֹפַךְ שַׂר־הַצָּבָא הֵמִית:

19 And when all the vassals of Hadadezer saw that they had been routed by *Yisrael*, they submitted to *David* and became his vassals. And the Arameans would not help the Ammonites anymore.

יט וַיִּרְאוּ עַבְדֵי הֲדַדְעֶזֶר כִּי נִגְּפוּ לִפְנֵי יִשְׂרָאֵל וַיַּשְׁלִימוּ עִם־דָּוִיד וַיַּעַבְדֻהוּ וְלֹא־אָבָה אֲרָם לְהוֹשִׁיעַ אֶת־בְּנֵי־עַמּוֹן עוֹד:

20

1 At the turn of the year, the season when kings go out [to battle], *Yoav* led out the army force and devastated the land of Ammon, and then besieged Rabbah, while *David* remained in *Yerushalayim*; *Yoav* reduced Rabbah and left it in ruins.

כ א וַיְהִי לְעֵת תְּשׁוּבַת הַשָּׁנָה לְעֵת צֵאת הַמְּלָכִים וַיִּנְהַג יוֹאָב אֶת־חֵיל הַצָּבָא וַיַּשְׁחֵת אֶת־אֶרֶץ בְּנֵי־עַמּוֹן וַיָּבֹא וַיָּצַר אֶת־רַבָּה וְדָוִיד יֹשֵׁב בִּירוּשָׁלָ͏ִם וַיַּךְ יוֹאָב אֶת־רַבָּה וַיֶּהֶרְסֶהָ:

vai-HEE l'-AYT t'-shu-VAT ha-sha-NAH l'-AYT TZAYT ha-m'-la-KHEEM va-yin-HAG yo-AV et KHAYL ha-tza-VA va-yash-KHAYT et E-retz b'-NAY a-MON va-ya-VO va-YA-tzar et ra-BAH v'-da-VEED yo-SHAYV bee-ru-sha-LA-im va-YAKH yo-AV et ra-BAH va-ye-her-SE-ha

---

20:1 The turn of the year In this verse, the beginning of the year is called *teshuvat hashanah*, (תשובת השנה) which literally means "the turn of the year." The year is cyclical in nature, and the holidays, which are the focus of the Jewish year, are repeated at the same time each year. In a certain sense, the beginning of a new year is in fact a return to previous years, going back to the times of *Moshe* and the Exodus from Egypt which many of the holidays commemorate. Furthermore, the Jewish New Year focuses on God's judgement and man's

תשובת השנה

Divrei Hayamim I / I Chronicles
Chapter 21

דברי הימים א
פרק כא

2 *David* took the crown from the head of their king; he found that it weighed a *kikar* of gold, and in it were precious stones. It was placed on *David*'s head. He also carried off a vast amount of booty from the city.

ב וַיִּקַּ֣ח דָּוִ֣יד אֶת־עֲטֶרֶת־מַלְכָּם֩ מֵעַ֨ל רֹאשׁ֜וֹ וַיִּמְצָאָ֣הּ ׀ מִשְׁקַ֣ל כִּכַּר־זָהָ֗ב וּבָהּ֙ אֶ֣בֶן יְקָרָ֔ה וַתְּהִ֖י עַל־רֹ֣אשׁ דָּוִ֑יד וּשְׁלַ֥ל הָעִ֛יר הוֹצִ֖יא הַרְבֵּ֥ה מְאֹֽד׃

3 He led out the people who lived there and he hacked them with saws and iron threshing boards and axes; *David* did thus to all the towns of Ammon. Then *David* and all the troops returned to *Yerushalayim*.

ג וְאֶת־הָעָ֨ם אֲשֶׁר־בָּ֜הּ הוֹצִ֗יא וַיָּ֨שַׂר בַּמְּגֵרָ֜ה וּבַחֲרִיצֵ֤י הַבַּרְזֶל֙ וּבַמְּגֵר֔וֹת וְכֵן֙ יַעֲשֶׂ֣ה דָוִ֔יד לְכֹ֖ל עָרֵ֣י בְנֵי־עַמּ֑וֹן וַיָּ֧שָׁב דָּוִ֛יד וְכָל־הָעָ֖ם יְרוּשָׁלָֽ͏ִם׃

4 After this, fighting broke out with the Philistines at Gezer; that was when Sibbecai the Hushathite killed Sippai, a descendant of the Rephaim, and they were humbled.

ד וַיְהִי֙ אַחֲרֵיכֵ֔ן וַתַּעֲמֹ֧ד מִלְחָמָ֛ה בְּגֶ֖זֶר עִם־פְּלִשְׁתִּ֑ים אָ֣ז הִכָּ֞ה סִבְּכַ֣י הַחֻֽשָׁתִ֗י אֶת־סִפַּ֛י מִילִדֵ֥י הָרְפָאִ֖ים וַיִּכָּנֵֽעוּ׃

5 Again there was fighting with the Philistines, and *Elchanan* son of *Yair* killed Lahmi, the brother of Goliath the Gittite; his spear had a shaft like a weaver's beam.

ה וַתְּהִי־ע֥וֹד מִלְחָמָ֖ה אֶת־פְּלִשְׁתִּ֑ים וַיַּ֞ךְ אֶלְחָנָ֣ן בֶּן־*יעור* [יָעִ֗יר] אֶת־לַחְמִי֙ אֲחִי֙ גָּלְיָ֣ת הַגִּתִּ֔י וְעֵ֣ץ חֲנִית֔וֹ כִּמְנ֖וֹר אֹרְגִֽים׃

6 Once again there was fighting at Gath. There was a giant of a man who had twenty-four fingers [and toes], six [on each hand] and six [on each foot]; he too was descended from the Raphah.

ו וַתְּהִי־ע֥וֹד מִלְחָמָ֖ה בְּגַ֑ת וַיְהִ֣י ׀ אִ֣ישׁ מִדָּ֗ה וְאֶצְבְּעֹתָ֤יו שֵׁשׁ־וָשֵׁשׁ֙ עֶשְׂרִ֣ים וְאַרְבַּ֔ע וְגַם־ה֖וּא נוֹלַ֥ד לְהָרָפָֽא׃

7 When he taunted *Yisrael*, *Yehonatan* son of *David*'s brother Shimea killed him.

ז וַיְחָרֵ֖ף אֶת־יִשְׂרָאֵ֑ל וַיַּכֵּ֨הוּ֙ יְה֣וֹנָתָ֔ן בֶּן־שִׁמְעָ֖א אֲחִ֥י דָוִֽיד׃

8 These were descended from the Raphah in Gath, and they fell by the hands of *David* and his men.

ח אֵ֛ל נוּלְּד֥וּ לְהָרָפָ֖א בְּגַ֑ת וַיִּפְּל֥וּ בְיַד־דָּוִ֖יד וּבְיַד־עֲבָדָֽיו׃

21

1 Satan arose against *Yisrael* and incited *David* to number *Yisrael*.

א וַיַּעֲמֹ֥ד שָׂטָ֖ן עַל־יִשְׂרָאֵ֑ל וַיָּ֙סֶת֙ אֶת־דָּוִ֔יד לִמְנ֖וֹת אֶת־יִשְׂרָאֵֽל׃

2 *David* said to *Yoav* and to the commanders of the army, "Go and count *Yisrael* from *Be'er Sheva* to *Dan* and bring me information as to their number."

ב וַיֹּ֨אמֶר דָּוִ֜יד אֶל־יוֹאָ֣ב וְאֶל־שָׂרֵ֣י הָעָ֗ם לְכוּ֙ סִפְרוּ֙ אֶת־יִשְׂרָאֵ֔ל מִבְּאֵ֥ר שֶׁ֖בַע וְעַד־דָּ֑ן וְהָבִ֣יאוּ אֵלַ֔י וְאֵדְעָ֖ה אֶת־מִסְפָּרָֽם׃

3 *Yoav* answered, "May *Hashem* increase His people a hundredfold; my lord king, are they not all subjects of my lord? Why should my lord require this? Why should it be a cause of guilt for *Yisrael*?"

ג וַיֹּ֣אמֶר יוֹאָ֗ב יוֹסֵף֩ יְהֹוָ֨ה עַל־עַמּ֤וֹ ׀ כָּהֵם֙ מֵאָ֣ה פְעָמִ֔ים הֲלֹא֙ אֲדֹנִ֣י הַמֶּ֔לֶךְ כֻּלָּ֖ם לַאדֹנִ֣י לַעֲבָדִ֑ים לָ֣מָּה יְבַקֵּ֤שׁ זֹאת֙ אֲדֹנִ֔י לָ֛מָּה יִהְיֶ֥ה לְאַשְׁמָ֖ה לְיִשְׂרָאֵֽל׃

repentance. The word *teshuva* (תשובה), which means 'return', also means 'repentance'. Hence, the expression "*Teshuvat Hashanah*" also refers to the time of year when we are obligated to repent.

2037

Divrei Hayamim I / I Chronicles
Chapter 21

4 However, the king's command to *Yoav* remained firm, so *Yoav* set out and traversed all *Yisrael*; he then came to *Yerushalayim*.

5 *Yoav* reported to *David* the number of the people that had been recorded. All *Yisrael* comprised 1,100,000 ready to draw the sword, while in *Yehuda* there were 470,000 men ready to draw the sword.

6 He did not record among them *Levi* and *Binyamin*, because the king's command had become repugnant to *Yoav*.

7 *Hashem* was displeased about this matter and He struck *Yisrael*.

8 *David* said to *Hashem*, "I have sinned grievously in having done this thing; please remit the guilt of Your servant, for I have acted foolishly."

9 *Hashem* ordered *Gad*, *David*'s seer:

10 "Go and tell *David*: Thus said *Hashem*: I offer you three things; choose one of them and I will bring it upon you."

11 *Gad* came to *David* and told him, "Thus said *Hashem*: Select for yourself

12 a three-year famine; or that you be swept away three months before your adversaries with the sword of your enemies overtaking you; or three days of the sword of *Hashem*, pestilence in the land, the angel of *Hashem* wreaking destruction throughout the territory of *Yisrael*. Now consider what reply I shall take back to Him who sent me."

13 *David* said to *Gad*, "I am in great distress. Let me fall into the hands of *Hashem*, for His compassion is very great; and let me not fall into the hands of men."

14 *Hashem* sent a pestilence upon *Yisrael*, and 70,000 men fell in *Yisrael*.

15 *Hashem* sent an angel to *Yerushalayim* to destroy it, but as he was about to wreak destruction, *Hashem* saw and renounced further punishment and said to the destroying angel, "Enough! Stay your hand!" The angel of *Hashem* was then standing by the threshing floor of Ornan the Jebusite.

דברי הימים א
פרק כא

ד וּדְבַר־הַמֶּלֶךְ חָזַק עַל־יוֹאָב וַיֵּצֵא יוֹאָב וַיִּתְהַלֵּךְ בְּכָל־יִשְׂרָאֵל וַיָּבֹא יְרוּשָׁלָֽםִ:

ה וַיִּתֵּן יוֹאָב אֶת־מִסְפַּר מִפְקַד־הָעָם אֶל־דָּוִיד וַיְהִי כָל־יִשְׂרָאֵל אֶלֶף אֲלָפִים וּמֵאָה אֶלֶף אִישׁ שֹׁלֵף חֶרֶב וִיהוּדָה אַרְבַּע מֵאוֹת וְשִׁבְעִים אֶלֶף אִישׁ שֹׁלֵף חָֽרֶב:

ו וְלֵוִי וּבִנְיָמִן לֹא פָקַד בְּתוֹכָם כִּֽי־נִתְעַב דְּבַר־הַמֶּלֶךְ אֶת־יוֹאָֽב:

ז וַיֵּרַע בְּעֵינֵי הָאֱלֹהִים עַל־הַדָּבָר הַזֶּה וַיַּךְ אֶת־יִשְׂרָאֵֽל:

ח וַיֹּאמֶר דָּוִיד אֶל־הָאֱלֹהִים חָטָאתִי מְאֹד אֲשֶׁר עָשִׂיתִי אֶת־הַדָּבָר הַזֶּה וְעַתָּה הַעֲבֶר־נָא אֶת־עֲווֹן עַבְדְּךָ כִּי נִסְכַּלְתִּי מְאֹֽד:

ט וַיְדַבֵּר יְהוָה אֶל־גָּד חֹזֵה דָוִיד לֵאמֹֽר:

י לֵךְ וְדִבַּרְתָּ אֶל־דָּוִיד לֵאמֹר כֹּה אָמַר יְהוָה שָׁלוֹשׁ אֲנִי נֹטֶה עָלֶיךָ בְּחַר־לְךָ אַחַת מֵהֵנָּה וְאֶעֱשֶׂה־לָּֽךְ:

יא וַיָּבֹא גָד אֶל־דָּוִיד וַיֹּאמֶר לוֹ כֹּֽה־אָמַר יְהוָה קַבֶּל־לָֽךְ:

יב אִם־שָׁלוֹשׁ שָׁנִים רָעָב וְאִם־שְׁלֹשָׁה חֳדָשִׁים נִסְפֶּה מִפְּנֵֽי־צָרֶיךָ וְחֶרֶב אוֹיְבֶךָ ׀ לְמַשֶּׂגֶת וְאִם־שְׁלֹשֶׁת יָמִים חֶרֶב יְהוָה וְדֶבֶר בָּאָרֶץ וּמַלְאַךְ יְהוָה מַשְׁחִית בְּכָל־גְּבוּל יִשְׂרָאֵל וְעַתָּה רְאֵה מָֽה־אָשִׁיב אֶת־שֹׁלְחִי דָבָֽר:

יג וַיֹּאמֶר דָּוִיד אֶל־גָּד צַר־לִי מְאֹד אֶפְּלָה־נָּא בְיַד־יְהוָה כִּֽי־רַבִּים רַחֲמָיו מְאֹד וּבְיַד־אָדָם אַל־אֶפֹּֽל:

יד וַיִּתֵּן יְהוָה דֶּבֶר בְּיִשְׂרָאֵל וַיִּפֹּל מִיִּשְׂרָאֵל שִׁבְעִים אֶלֶף אִֽישׁ:

טו וַיִּשְׁלַח הָאֱלֹהִים ׀ מַלְאָךְ ׀ לִירוּשָׁלִַם לְהַשְׁחִיתָהּ וּכְהַשְׁחִית רָאָה יְהוָה וַיִּנָּחֶם עַל־הָרָעָה וַיֹּאמֶר לַמַּלְאָךְ הַמַּשְׁחִית רַב עַתָּה הֶרֶף יָדֶךָ וּמַלְאַךְ יְהוָה עֹמֵד עִם־גֹּרֶן אָרְנָן הַיְבוּסִֽי:

Divrei Hayamim I / I Chronicles
Chapter 21

16 David looked up and saw the angel of *Hashem* standing between heaven and earth, with a drawn sword in his hand directed against *Yerushalayim*. David and the elders, covered in sackcloth, threw themselves on their faces.

17 David said to *Hashem*, "Was it not I alone who ordered the numbering of the people? I alone am guilty, and have caused severe harm; but these sheep, what have they done? *Hashem* my God, let Your hand fall upon me and my father's house, and let not Your people be plagued!"

18 The angel of *Hashem* told *Gad* to inform David that David should go and set up a *Mizbayach* to *Hashem* on the threshing floor of Ornan the Jebusite.

19 David went up, following *Gad*'s instructions, which he had delivered in the name of *Hashem*.

20 Ornan too saw the angel; his four sons who were with him hid themselves while Ornan kept on threshing wheat.

21 David came to Ornan; when Ornan looked up, he saw David and came off the threshing floor and bowed low to David, with his face to the ground.

22 David said to Ornan, "Sell me the site of the threshing floor, that I may build on it a *Mizbayach* to *Hashem*. Sell it to me at the full price, that the plague against the people will be checked."

23 Ornan said to David, "Take it and let my lord the king do whatever he sees fit. See, I donate oxen for burnt offerings, and the threshing boards for wood, as well as wheat for a meal offering – I donate all of it."

24 But King David replied to Ornan, "No, I will buy them at the full price. I cannot make a present to God of what belongs to you, or sacrifice a burnt offering that has cost me nothing."

va-YO-mer ha-ME-lekh da-VEED l'-or-NAN LO kee ka-NOH ek-NEH b'-KHE-sef ma-LAY KEE lo e-SA a-sher l-KHA la-do-NAI v'-ha-a-LOT o-LAH khi-NAM

21:24 I will buy them at the full price King David refuses to receive the land upon which he would build the altar as a gift. Instead, he insists on paying full price for it. The first verse of the next chapter reveals that this land David purchased would become the permanent location of the *Beit Hamikdash*, the spiritual center of the Jewish people. As such, the ownership of the land must be beyond dispute. When something is given as a gift, the previous owner maintains some small moral claim to it, as he gave it without recompense. By buying the land, as *Avraham* had bought the Cave of Machpelah, David guarantees that the Jewish people's claim to the Temple Mount in *Yerushalayim* would be indisputable for all time.

Divrei Hayamim I / I Chronicles
Chapter 22

25 So *David* paid Ornan for the site 600 *shekalim* worth of gold.

כה וַיִּתֵּן דָּוִיד לְאָרְנָן בַּמָּקוֹם שִׁקְלֵי זָהָב מִשְׁקָל שֵׁשׁ מֵאוֹת׃

26 And *David* built there a *Mizbayach* to *Hashem* and sacrificed burnt offerings and offerings of well-being. He invoked *Hashem*, who answered him with fire from heaven on the *Mizbayach* of burnt offerings.

כו וַיִּבֶן שָׁם דָּוִיד מִזְבֵּחַ לַיהֹוָה וַיַּעַל עֹלוֹת וּשְׁלָמִים וַיִּקְרָא אֶל־יְהֹוָה וַיַּעֲנֵהוּ בָאֵשׁ מִן־הַשָּׁמַיִם עַל מִזְבַּח הָעֹלָה׃

27 *Hashem* ordered the angel to return his sword to its sheath.

כז וַיֹּאמֶר יְהֹוָה לַמַּלְאָךְ וַיָּשֶׁב חַרְבּוֹ אֶל־נְדָנָהּ׃

28 At that time, when *David* saw that *Hashem* answered him at the threshing floor of Ornan the Jebusite, then he sacrificed there –

כח בָּעֵת הַהִיא בִּרְאוֹת דָּוִיד כִּי־עָנָהוּ יְהֹוָה בְּגֹרֶן אָרְנָן הַיְבוּסִי וַיִּזְבַּח שָׁם׃

29 for the *Mishkan* of *Hashem*, which *Moshe* had made in the wilderness, and the *Mizbayach* of burnt offerings, were at that time in the shrine at *Givon*,

כט וּמִשְׁכַּן יְהֹוָה אֲשֶׁר־עָשָׂה מֹשֶׁה בַמִּדְבָּר וּמִזְבַּח הָעוֹלָה בָּעֵת הַהִיא בַּבָּמָה בְּגִבְעוֹן׃

30 and *David* was unable to go to it to worship *Hashem* because he was terrified by the sword of the angel of *Hashem*.

ל וְלֹא־יָכֹל דָּוִיד לָלֶכֶת לְפָנָיו לִדְרֹשׁ אֱלֹהִים כִּי נִבְעַת מִפְּנֵי חֶרֶב מַלְאַךְ יְהֹוָה׃

22

1 *David* said, "Here will be the House of *Hashem* and here the *Mizbayach* of burnt offerings for *Yisrael*."

א וַיֹּאמֶר דָּוִיד זֶה הוּא בֵּית יְהֹוָה הָאֱלֹהִים וְזֶה־מִזְבֵּחַ לְעֹלָה לְיִשְׂרָאֵל׃

2 *David* gave orders to assemble the aliens living in the land of *Yisrael*, and assigned them to be hewers, to quarry and dress stones for building the House of *Hashem*.

ב וַיֹּאמֶר דָּוִיד לִכְנוֹס אֶת־הַגֵּרִים אֲשֶׁר בְּאֶרֶץ יִשְׂרָאֵל וַיַּעֲמֵד חֹצְבִים לַחְצוֹב אַבְנֵי גָזִית לִבְנוֹת בֵּית הָאֱלֹהִים׃

3 Much iron for nails for the doors of the gates and for clasps did *David* lay aside, and so much copper it could not be weighed,

ג וּבַרְזֶל לָרֹב לַמִּסְמְרִים לְדַלְתוֹת הַשְּׁעָרִים וְלַמְחַבְּרוֹת הֵכִין דָּוִיד וּנְחֹשֶׁת לָרֹב אֵין מִשְׁקָל׃

4 and cedar logs without number – for the Sidonians and the Tyrians brought many cedar logs to *David*.

ד וַעֲצֵי אֲרָזִים לְאֵין מִסְפָּר כִּי הֵבִיאוּ הַצִּידֹנִים וְהַצֹּרִים עֲצֵי אֲרָזִים לָרֹב לְדָוִיד׃

5 For *David* thought, "My son *Shlomo* is an untried youth, and the House to be built for *Hashem* is to be made exceedingly great to win fame and glory throughout all the lands; let me then lay aside material for him." So *David* laid aside much material before he died.

ה וַיֹּאמֶר דָּוִיד שְׁלֹמֹה בְנִי נַעַר וָרָךְ וְהַבַּיִת לִבְנוֹת לַיהֹוָה לְהַגְדִּיל לְמַעְלָה לְשֵׁם וּלְתִפְאֶרֶת לְכָל־הָאֲרָצוֹת אָכִינָה נָּא לוֹ וַיָּכֶן דָּוִיד לָרֹב לִפְנֵי מוֹתוֹ׃

va-YO-mer da-VEED sh'-lo-MOH v'-NEE NA-ar va-RAKH v'-ha-BA-yit liv-NOT la-do-NAI l'-hag-DEEL l'-MA-lah l'-SHAYM ul-tif-E-ret l'-khol HA-a-ra-TZOT a-KHEE-nah NA LO va-YA-khen da-VEED la-ROV lif-NAY mo-TO

22:5 Let me then lay aside material for him Even though he has not been instructed to do so, King *David* begins preparations for the construction of the Temple. He feels that if he would leave all of the preparation to

Divrei Hayamim I / I Chronicles
Chapter 22

דברי הימים א
פרק כב

6 Then he summoned his son *Shlomo* and charged him with building the House for God of *Yisrael*.

ו וַיִּקְרָא לִשְׁלֹמֹה בְנוֹ וַיְצַוֵּהוּ לִבְנוֹת בַּיִת לַיהוָה אֱלֹהֵי יִשְׂרָאֵל׃

7 *David* said to *Shlomo*, "My son, I wanted to build a House for the name of *Hashem* my God.

ז וַיֹּאמֶר דָּוִיד לִשְׁלֹמֹה בנו [בְּנִי] אֲנִי הָיָה עִם־לְבָבִי לִבְנוֹת בַּיִת לְשֵׁם יְהוָה אֱלֹהָי׃

8 But the word of *Hashem* came to me, saying, 'You have shed much blood and fought great battles; you shall not build a House for My name for you have shed much blood on the earth in My sight.

ח וַיְהִי עָלַי דְּבַר־יְהוָה לֵאמֹר דָּם לָרֹב שָׁפַכְתָּ וּמִלְחָמוֹת גְּדֹלוֹת עָשִׂיתָ לֹא־תִבְנֶה בַיִת לִשְׁמִי כִּי דָּמִים רַבִּים שָׁפַכְתָּ אַרְצָה לְפָנָי׃

9 But you will have a son who will be a man at rest, for I will give him rest from all his enemies on all sides; *Shlomo* will be his name and I shall confer peace and quiet on *Yisrael* in his time.

ט הִנֵּה־בֵן נוֹלָד לָךְ הוּא יִהְיֶה אִישׁ מְנוּחָה וַהֲנִחוֹתִי לוֹ מִכָּל־אוֹיְבָיו מִסָּבִיב כִּי שְׁלֹמֹה יִהְיֶה שְׁמוֹ וְשָׁלוֹם וָשֶׁקֶט אֶתֵּן עַל־יִשְׂרָאֵל בְּיָמָיו׃

10 He will build a House for My name; he shall be a son to Me and I to him a father, and I will establish his throne of kingship over *Yisrael* forever.'

י הוּא־יִבְנֶה בַיִת לִשְׁמִי וְהוּא יִהְיֶה־לִּי לְבֵן וַאֲנִי־לוֹ לְאָב וַהֲכִינוֹתִי כִּסֵּא מַלְכוּתוֹ עַל־יִשְׂרָאֵל עַד־עוֹלָם׃

11 Now, my son, may *Hashem* be with you, and may you succeed in building the House of *Hashem* your God as He promised you would.

יא עַתָּה בְנִי יְהִי יְהוָה עִמָּךְ וְהִצְלַחְתָּ וּבָנִיתָ בֵּית יְהוָה אֱלֹהֶיךָ כַּאֲשֶׁר דִּבֶּר עָלֶיךָ׃

12 Only let *Hashem* give you sense and understanding and put you in charge of *Yisrael* and the observance of the Teaching of *Hashem* your God.

יב אַךְ יִתֶּן־לְךָ יְהוָה שֵׂכֶל וּבִינָה וִיצַוְּךָ עַל־יִשְׂרָאֵל וְלִשְׁמוֹר אֶת־תּוֹרַת יְהוָה אֱלֹהֶיךָ׃

13 Then you shall succeed, if you observantly carry out the laws and the rules that *Hashem* charged *Moshe* to lay upon *Yisrael*. Be strong and of good courage; do not be afraid or dismayed.

יג אָז תַּצְלִיחַ אִם־תִּשְׁמוֹר לַעֲשׂוֹת אֶת־הַחֻקִּים וְאֶת־הַמִּשְׁפָּטִים אֲשֶׁר צִוָּה יְהוָה אֶת־מֹשֶׁה עַל־יִשְׂרָאֵל חֲזַק וֶאֱמָץ אַל־תִּירָא וְאַל־תֵּחָת׃

14 See, by denying myself, I have laid aside for the House of *Hashem* one hundred thousand *kikarim* of gold and one million *kikarim* of silver, and so much copper and iron it cannot be weighed; I have also laid aside wood and stone, and you shall add to them.

יד וְהִנֵּה בְעָנְיִי הֲכִינוֹתִי לְבֵית־יְהוָה זָהָב כִּכָּרִים מֵאָה־אֶלֶף וְכֶסֶף אֶלֶף אֲלָפִים כִּכָּרִים וְלַנְּחֹשֶׁת וְלַבַּרְזֶל אֵין מִשְׁקָל כִּי לָרֹב הָיָה וְעֵצִים וַאֲבָנִים הֲכִינוֹתִי וַעֲלֵיהֶם תּוֹסִיף׃

15 An abundance of workmen is at your disposal – hewers, workers in stone and wood, and every kind of craftsman in every kind of material –

טו וְעִמְּךָ לָרֹב עֹשֵׂי מְלָאכָה חֹצְבִים וְחָרָשֵׁי אֶבֶן וָעֵץ וְכָל־חָכָם בְּכָל־מְלָאכָה׃

Shlomo, who was still young at the time, the building project would be delayed significantly. In addition, it is likely that *David* feels an overpowering urge to do whatever he can for God's glory. While he has been told that he will not be able to build the *Beit Hamikdash*, there is nothing stopping him from preparing for its construction. He simply cannot ignore his concern that God's honor is impugned by the lack of a permanent home.

Divrei Hayamim I/I Chronicles
Chapter 23

16 gold, silver, copper, and iron without limit. Go and do it, and may *Hashem* be with you."

17 *David* charged all the officers of *Yisrael* to support his son *Shlomo*,

18 "See, *Hashem* your God is with you, and He will give you rest on every side, for He delivered the inhabitants of the land into my hand so that the land lies conquered before *Hashem* and before His people.

19 Now, set your minds and hearts on worshiping *Hashem* your God, and go build the Sanctuary of *Hashem* your God so that you may bring the *Aron Brit Hashem* and the holy vessels of *Hashem* to the house that is built for the name of *Hashem*."

23

1 When *David* reached a ripe old age, he made his son *Shlomo* king over *Yisrael*.

2 Then *David* assembled all the officers of *Yisrael* and the *Kohanim* and the *Leviim*.

3 The *Leviim*, from the age of thirty and upward, were counted; the head-count of their males was 38,000:

4 of these there were 24,000 in charge of the work of the House of *Hashem*, 6,000 officers and magistrates,

5 4,000 gatekeepers, and 4,000 for praising *Hashem* "with instruments I devised for singing praises."

6 *David* formed them into divisions: The sons of *Levi*: *Gershon, Kehat,* and *Merari*.

7 The Gershonites: Ladan and *Shim'i*.

8 The sons of Ladan: *Yechiel* the chief, Zetham, and Yoel – 3.

9 The sons of *Shim'i*: Shelomith, Haziel, and Haran – 3. These were the chiefs of the clans of the Ladanites.

10 And the sons of *Shim'i*: Jahath, Zina, Jeush, and Beriah; these were the sons of *Shim'i* – 4.

11 Jahath was the chief and Zizah the second, but Jeush and Beriah did not have many children, so they were enrolled together as a single clan.

דברי הימים א
פרק כג

טז לַזָּהָב לַכֶּסֶף וְלַנְּחֹשֶׁת וְלַבַּרְזֶל אֵין מִסְפָּר קוּם וַעֲשֵׂה וִיהִי יְהֹוָה עִמָּךְ:

יז וַיְצַו דָּוִיד לְכָל־שָׂרֵי יִשְׂרָאֵל לַעְזֹר לִשְׁלֹמֹה בְנוֹ:

יח הֲלֹא יְהֹוָה אֱלֹהֵיכֶם עִמָּכֶם וְהֵנִיחַ לָכֶם מִסָּבִיב כִּי ׀ נָתַן בְּיָדִי אֵת יֹשְׁבֵי הָאָרֶץ וְנִכְבְּשָׁה הָאָרֶץ לִפְנֵי יְהֹוָה וְלִפְנֵי עַמּוֹ:

יט עַתָּה תְּנוּ לְבַבְכֶם וְנַפְשְׁכֶם לִדְרוֹשׁ לַיהֹוָה אֱלֹהֵיכֶם וְקוּמוּ וּבְנוּ אֶת־מִקְדַּשׁ יְהֹוָה הָאֱלֹהִים לְהָבִיא אֶת־אֲרוֹן בְּרִית־יְהֹוָה וּכְלֵי קֹדֶשׁ הָאֱלֹהִים לַבַּיִת הַנִּבְנֶה לְשֵׁם־יְהֹוָה:

כג א וְדָוִיד זָקֵן וְשָׂבַע יָמִים וַיַּמְלֵךְ אֶת־שְׁלֹמֹה בְנוֹ עַל־יִשְׂרָאֵל:

ב וַיֶּאֱסֹף אֶת־כָּל־שָׂרֵי יִשְׂרָאֵל וְהַכֹּהֲנִים וְהַלְוִיִּם:

ג וַיִּסָּפְרוּ הַלְוִיִּם מִבֶּן שְׁלֹשִׁים שָׁנָה וָמָעְלָה וַיְהִי מִסְפָּרָם לְגֻלְגְּלֹתָם לִגְבָרִים שְׁלֹשִׁים וּשְׁמוֹנָה אָלֶף:

ד מֵאֵלֶּה לְנַצֵּחַ עַל־מְלֶאכֶת בֵּית־יְהֹוָה עֶשְׂרִים וְאַרְבָּעָה אָלֶף וְשֹׁטְרִים וְשֹׁפְטִים שֵׁשֶׁת אֲלָפִים:

ה וְאַרְבַּעַת אֲלָפִים שֹׁעֲרִים וְאַרְבַּעַת אֲלָפִים מְהַלְלִים לַיהֹוָה בַּכֵּלִים אֲשֶׁר עָשִׂיתִי לְהַלֵּל:

ו וַיֶּחָלְקֵם דָּוִיד מַחְלְקוֹת לִבְנֵי לֵוִי לְגֵרְשׁוֹן קְהָת וּמְרָרִי:

ז לַגֵּרְשֻׁנִּי לַעְדָּן וְשִׁמְעִי:

ח בְּנֵי לַעְדָּן הָרֹאשׁ יְחִיאֵל וְזֵתָם וְיוֹאֵל שְׁלֹשָׁה:

ט בְּנֵי שִׁמְעִי שְׁלֹמוֹת [שְׁלוֹמִית] וַחֲזִיאֵל וְהָרָן שְׁלֹשָׁה אֵלֶּה רָאשֵׁי הָאָבוֹת לְלַעְדָּן:

י וּבְנֵי שִׁמְעִי יַחַת זִינָא וִיעוּשׁ וּבְרִיעָה אֵלֶּה בְנֵי־שִׁמְעִי אַרְבָּעָה:

יא וַיְהִי־יַחַת הָרֹאשׁ וְזִיזָה הַשֵּׁנִי וִיעוּשׁ וּבְרִיעָה לֹא־הִרְבּוּ בָנִים וַיִּהְיוּ לְבֵית אָב לִפְקֻדָּה אֶחָת:

Divrei Hayamim I / I Chronicles
Chapter 23

דברי הימים א
פרק כג

12 The sons of *Kehat*: *Amram*, Izhar, *Chevron*, and Uzziel – 4.

יב בְּנֵי קְהָת עַמְרָם יִצְהָר חֶבְרוֹן וְעֻזִּיאֵל אַרְבָּעָה:

13 The sons of *Amram*: *Aharon* and *Moshe*. *Aharon* was set apart, he and his sons, forever, to be consecrated as most holy, to make burnt offerings to *Hashem* and serve Him and pronounce blessings in His name forever.

יג בְּנֵי עַמְרָם אַהֲרֹן וּמֹשֶׁה וַיִּבָּדֵל אַהֲרֹן לְהַקְדִּישׁוֹ קֹדֶשׁ קָדָשִׁים הוּא־וּבָנָיו עַד־עוֹלָם לְהַקְטִיר לִפְנֵי יְהוָה לְשָׁרְתוֹ וּלְבָרֵךְ בִּשְׁמוֹ עַד־עוֹלָם:

14 As for *Moshe*, the man of *Hashem*, his sons were named after the tribe of *Levi*.

יד וּמֹשֶׁה אִישׁ הָאֱלֹהִים בָּנָיו יִקָּרְאוּ עַל־שֵׁבֶט הַלֵּוִי:

15 The sons of *Moshe*: *Gershom* and *Eliezer*.

טו בְּנֵי מֹשֶׁה גֵּרְשֹׁם וֶאֱלִיעֶזֶר:

16 The sons of *Gershom*: Shebuel the chief.

טז בְּנֵי גֵרְשׁוֹם שְׁבוּאֵל הָרֹאשׁ:

17 And the sons of *Eliezer* were: Rehabiah the chief. *Eliezer* had no other sons, but the sons of Rehabiah were very numerous.

יז וַיִּהְיוּ בְנֵי־אֱלִיעֶזֶר רְחַבְיָה הָרֹאשׁ וְלֹא־הָיָה לֶאֱלִיעֶזֶר בָּנִים אֲחֵרִים וּבְנֵי רְחַבְיָה רָבוּ לְמָעְלָה:

18 The sons of *Izhar*: Shelomith the chief.

יח בְּנֵי יִצְהָר שְׁלֹמִית הָרֹאשׁ:

19 The sons of *Chevron*: Jeriah the chief, Amariah the second, *Yachaziel* the third, and Jekameam the fourth.

יט בְּנֵי חֶבְרוֹן יְרִיָּהוּ הָרֹאשׁ אֲמַרְיָה הַשֵּׁנִי יַחֲזִיאֵל הַשְּׁלִישִׁי וִיקַמְעָם הָרְבִיעִי:

20 The sons of *Uzziel*: *Micha* the chief and Isshiah the second.

כ בְּנֵי עֻזִּיאֵל מִיכָה הָרֹאשׁ וְיִשִּׁיָּה הַשֵּׁנִי:

21 The sons of *Merari*: Mahli and Mushi. The sons of Mahli: *Elazar* and *Keesh*.

כא בְּנֵי מְרָרִי מַחְלִי וּמוּשִׁי בְּנֵי מַחְלִי אֶלְעָזָר וְקִישׁ:

22 *Elazar* died having no sons but only daughters; the sons of *Keesh*, their kinsmen, married them.

כב וַיָּמָת אֶלְעָזָר וְלֹא־הָיוּ לוֹ בָּנִים כִּי אִם־בָּנוֹת וַיִּשָּׂאוּם בְּנֵי־קִישׁ אֲחֵיהֶם:

23 The sons of Mushi: Mahli, Eder, and Jeremoth – 3.

כג בְּנֵי מוּשִׁי מַחְלִי וְעֵדֶר וִירֵמוֹת שְׁלֹשָׁה:

24 These are the sons of *Levi* by clans, with their clan chiefs as they were enrolled, with a list of their names by heads, who did the work of the service of the House of *Hashem* from the age of twenty and upward.

כד אֵלֶּה בְנֵי־לֵוִי לְבֵית אֲבֹתֵיהֶם רָאשֵׁי הָאָבוֹת לִפְקוּדֵיהֶם בְּמִסְפַּר שֵׁמוֹת לְגֻלְגְּלֹתָם עֹשֵׂה הַמְּלָאכָה לַעֲבֹדַת בֵּית יְהוָה מִבֶּן עֶשְׂרִים שָׁנָה וָמָעְלָה:

25 For *David* said, "God of *Yisrael* has given rest to His people and made His dwelling in *Yerushalayim* forever.

כה כִּי אָמַר דָּוִיד הֵנִיחַ יְהוָה אֱלֹהֵי־יִשְׂרָאֵל לְעַמּוֹ וַיִּשְׁכֹּן בִּירוּשָׁלִַם עַד־לְעוֹלָם:

26 Therefore the *Leviim* need not carry the *Mishkan* and all its various service vessels."

v'-GAM lal-vi-YIM ayn la-SAYT et ha-mish-KAN v'-et kol kay-LAV la-a-vo-da-TO

כו וְגַם לַלְוִיִּם אֵין־לָשֵׂאת אֶת־הַמִּשְׁכָּן וְאֶת־כָּל־כֵּלָיו לַעֲבֹדָתוֹ:

23:26 Therefore the *Leviim* need not carry the *Mishkan* In anticipation of the construction of the *Beit Hamikdash* in *Yerushalayim*, *David* counts the *Leviim* and assigns them a new role. Now that the house of God will find its permanent resting place in *Yerushalayim*, the job of carrying the *Mishkan* and the holy vessels, which had been assigned to the *Leviim* in the desert, is no longer relevant. They are therefore as-

Divrei Hayamim I / I Chronicles
Chapter 24

דברי הימים א
פרק כד

27 Among the last acts of *David* was the counting of the *Leviim* from the age of twenty and upward.

כז כִּי בְדִבְרֵי דָוִיד הָאַחֲרֹנִים הֵמָּה מִסְפַּר בְּנֵי־לֵוִי מִבֶּן עֶשְׂרִים שָׁנָה וּלְמָעְלָה:

28 For their appointment was alongside the Aaronites for the service of the House of *Hashem*, to look after the courts and the chambers, and the purity of all the holy things, and the performance of the service of the House of *Hashem*,

כח כִּי מַעֲמָדָם לְיַד־בְּנֵי אַהֲרֹן לַעֲבֹדַת בֵּית יְהֹוָה עַל־הַחֲצֵרוֹת וְעַל־הַלְּשָׁכוֹת וְעַל־טָהֳרַת לְכָל־קֹדֶשׁ וּמַעֲשֵׂה עֲבֹדַת בֵּית הָאֱלֹהִים:

29 and the rows of bread, and the fine flour for the meal offering, and the unleavened wafers, and the cakes made on the griddle and soaked, and every measure of capacity and length;

כט וּלְלֶחֶם הַמַּעֲרֶכֶת וּלְסֹלֶת לְמִנְחָה וְלִרְקִיקֵי הַמַּצּוֹת וְלַמַּחֲבַת וְלַמֻּרְבָּכֶת וּלְכָל־מְשׂוּרָה וּמִדָּה:

30 and to be present every morning to praise and extol *Hashem*, and at evening too,

ל וְלַעֲמֹד בַּבֹּקֶר בַּבֹּקֶר לְהֹדוֹת וּלְהַלֵּל לַיהֹוָה וְכֵן לָעָרֶב:

31 and whenever offerings were made to *Hashem*, according to the quantities prescribed for them, on *Shabbatot*, new moons and holidays, regularly, before *Hashem*;

לא וּלְכֹל הַעֲלוֹת עֹלוֹת לַיהֹוָה לַשַּׁבָּתוֹת לֶחֳדָשִׁים וְלַמֹּעֲדִים בְּמִסְפָּר כְּמִשְׁפָּט עֲלֵיהֶם תָּמִיד לִפְנֵי יְהֹוָה:

32 and so to keep watch over the Tent of Meeting, over the holy things, and over the Aaronites their kinsmen, for the service of the House of *Hashem*.

לב וְשָׁמְרוּ אֶת־מִשְׁמֶרֶת אֹהֶל־מוֹעֵד וְאֵת מִשְׁמֶרֶת הַקֹּדֶשׁ וּמִשְׁמֶרֶת בְּנֵי אַהֲרֹן אֲחֵיהֶם לַעֲבֹדַת בֵּית יְהֹוָה:

24

1 The divisions of the Aaronites were: The sons of *Aharon*: *Nadav* and *Avihu*, *Elazar* and *Itamar*.

כד א וְלִבְנֵי אַהֲרֹן מַחְלְקוֹתָם בְּנֵי אַהֲרֹן נָדָב וַאֲבִיהוּא אֶלְעָזָר וְאִיתָמָר:

2 *Nadav* and *Avihu* died in the lifetime of their father, and they had no children, so *Elazar* and *Itamar* served as *Kohanim*.

ב וַיָּמָת נָדָב וַאֲבִיהוּא לִפְנֵי אֲבִיהֶם וּבָנִים לֹא־הָיוּ לָהֶם וַיְכַהֲנוּ אֶלְעָזָר וְאִיתָמָר:

va-YA-mot na-DAV va-a-vee-HU lif-NAY a-vee-HEM u-va-NEEM lo ha-YU la-HEM vai-kha-ha-NU el-a-ZAR v'-ee-ta-MAR

---

signed other tasks; they are to assist the priests in the Temple service, serve as the gatekeepers for the Temple, and sing daily praises to the Lord. However, each *Levi* is to serve in the *Beit Hamikdash* for only one week out of every twenty-four (see chapter 25). The rest of their time, the members of the tribe of *Levi* have another highly significant job. They are to become the spiritual leaders of the Children of Israel by serving as officers, judges and teachers. As *Moshe* had blessed the tribe of *Levi* before his death, "They shall teach Your laws to *Yaakov* And Your instructions to *Yisrael*" (Deuteronomy 33:10). It is for this reason that they are not given their own portion in the Land of Israel, but instead are scattered among all the other tribes (see Joshua chapter 21). In this way, they are able to have an impact on the entire nation, providing the spiritual guidance essential for the Children of Israel to accurately represent God to the rest of the world.

24:2 *Nadav* and *Avihu* died in the lifetime of their father   The *Torah* tells us that *Nadav* and *Avihu* died during the joyous dedication ceremony of the *Mishkan*. After a heavenly fire descended and consumed the sacrificial offerings, revealing the Divine Presence, the verse states that these two of *Aharon's* sons "offered before *Hashem* alien fire, which He had not enjoined upon them" (Leviticus 10:1). The severe consequence of this act was that they were then consumed as well, also by heavenly fire. The *Netziv* suggests that their motivation for bringing the forbidden fire was the

Rabbi Naftali Z.Y. Berlin, the Netziv (1816–1893)

Divrei Hayamim I/I Chronicles
Chapter 24

דברי הימים א
פרק כד

3 *David*, *Tzadok* of the sons of *Elazar*, and *Achimelech* of the sons of *Itamar* divided them into offices by their tasks.

ג וַיֶּחָלְקֵם דָּוִיד וְצָדוֹק מִן־בְּנֵי אֶלְעָזָר וַאֲחִימֶלֶךְ מִן־בְּנֵי אִיתָמָר לִפְקֻדָּתָם בַּעֲבֹדָתָם׃

4 The sons of *Elazar* turned out to be more numerous by male heads than the sons of *Itamar*, so they divided the sons of *Elazar* into sixteen chiefs of clans and the sons of *Itamar* into eight clans.

ד וַיִּמָּצְאוּ בְנֵי־אֶלְעָזָר רַבִּים לְרָאשֵׁי הַגְּבָרִים מִן־בְּנֵי אִיתָמָר וַיַּחְלְקוּם לִבְנֵי אֶלְעָזָר רָאשִׁים לְבֵית־אָבוֹת שִׁשָּׁה עָשָׂר וְלִבְנֵי אִיתָמָר לְבֵית אֲבוֹתָם שְׁמוֹנָה׃

5 They divided them by lot, both on an equal footing, since they were all sanctuary officers and officers of *Hashem* – the sons of *Elazar* and the sons of *Itamar*.

ה וַיַּחְלְקוּם בְּגוֹרָלוֹת אֵלֶּה עִם־אֵלֶּה כִּי־הָיוּ שָׂרֵי־קֹדֶשׁ וְשָׂרֵי הָאֱלֹהִים מִבְּנֵי אֶלְעָזָר וּבִבְנֵי אִיתָמָר׃

6 *Shemaya* son of Nathanel, the scribe, who was of the *Leviim*, registered them under the eye of the king, the officers, and *Tzadok* the *Kohen*, and *Achimelech* son of *Evyatar*, and the chiefs of clans of the *Kohanim* and *Leviim* – one clan more taken for *Elazar* for each one taken of *Itamar*.

ו וַיִּכְתְּבֵם שְׁמַעְיָה בֶן־נְתַנְאֵל הַסּוֹפֵר מִן־הַלֵּוִי לִפְנֵי הַמֶּלֶךְ וְהַשָּׂרִים וְצָדוֹק הַכֹּהֵן וַאֲחִימֶלֶךְ בֶּן־אֶבְיָתָר וְרָאשֵׁי הָאָבוֹת לַכֹּהֲנִים וְלַלְוִיִּם בֵּית־אָב אֶחָד אָחֻז לְאֶלְעָזָר וְאָחֻז אָחֻז לְאִיתָמָר׃

7 The first lot fell on Jehoiarib; the second on Jedaiah;

ז וַיֵּצֵא הַגּוֹרָל הָרִאשׁוֹן לִיהוֹיָרִיב לִידַעְיָה הַשֵּׁנִי׃

8 the third on Harim; the fourth on Seorim;

ח לְחָרִם הַשְּׁלִישִׁי לִשְׂעֹרִים הָרְבִעִי׃

9 the fifth on Malchijah; the sixth on Mijamin;

ט לְמַלְכִּיָּה הַחֲמִישִׁי לְמִיָּמִן הַשִּׁשִּׁי׃

10 the seventh on Hakkoz; the eighth on *Aviya*;

י לְהַקּוֹץ הַשְּׁבִעִי לַאֲבִיָּה הַשְּׁמִינִי׃

11 the ninth on *Yeshua*; the tenth on *Shechanya*;

יא לְיֵשׁוּעַ הַתְּשִׁעִי לִשְׁכַנְיָהוּ הָעֲשִׂרִי׃

12 the eleventh on *Elyashiv*; the twelfth on Jakim;

יב לְאֶלְיָשִׁיב עַשְׁתֵּי עָשָׂר לְיָקִים שְׁנֵים עָשָׂר׃

13 the thirteenth on Huppah; the fourteenth on Jeshebeab;

יג לְחֻפָּה שְׁלֹשָׁה עָשָׂר לְיֶשֶׁבְאָב אַרְבָּעָה עָשָׂר׃

14 the fifteenth on Bilgah; the sixteenth on Immer;

יד לְבִלְגָּה חֲמִשָּׁה עָשָׂר לְאִמֵּר שִׁשָּׁה עָשָׂר׃

closeness that they felt to God at the moment of revelation; they were so overcome with this feeling that they desired to get even closer with an offering of their own, which they brought into the Holy of Holies. Though their intentions were pure, the offering was unauthorized and entry into the Holy sanctuary was forbidden, so they were punished. *Nadav* and *Avihu* were indeed close to God, as *Moshe* says of them "Through those near to Me I show Myself holy, and gain glory before all the people" (Leviticus 10:3), but such closeness does not grant a license to bend the rules. *Nadav* and *Avihu* teach us that holy places must be approached with awe and trepidation, and that holy people are held to a higher standard. One of the lessons for our generation is that the Children of Israel, living in the Land of Israel, must be especially careful to respect its sanctity and to behave in a way that will bring glory to God's name.

Divrei Hayamim I / I Chronicles
Chapter 24

דברי הימים א
פרק כד

15 the seventeenth on Hezir; the eighteenth on Happizzez;

16 the nineteenth on Pethahiah; the twentieth on Jehezkel;

17 the twenty-first on Jachin; the twenty-second on Gamul;

18 the twenty-third on Delaiah; the twenty-fourth on Maaziah.

19 According to this allocation of offices by tasks, they were to enter the House of *Hashem* as was laid down for them by *Aharon* their father, as God of *Yisrael* had commanded him.

20 The remaining *Leviim*: the sons of *Amram*: Shubael; the sons of Shubael: Jehdeiah;

21 Rehabiah. The sons of Rehabiah: Isshiah, the chief.

22 Izharites: Shelomoth. The sons of Shelomoth: Jahath

23 and Benai, Jeriah; the second, Amariah; the third, *Yachaziel*; the fourth, Jekameam.

24 The sons of Uzziel: *Micha*. The sons of *Micha*: Shamir.

25 The brother of *Micha*: Isshiah. The sons of Isshiah: Zecharya.

26 The sons of *Merari*: Mahli and Mushi. The sons of Jaazaiah, his son –

27 the sons of *Merari* by Jaazaiah his son: Shoham, Zakkur, and Ibri.

28 Mahli: *Elazar*; he had no sons.

29 *Keesh*: the sons of *Keesh*: Jerahmeel.

30 The sons of Mushi: Mahli, Eder, and Jerimoth. These were the sons of the *Leviim* by their clans.

31 These too cast lots corresponding to their kinsmen, the sons of *Aharon*, under the eye of King *David* and *Tzadok* and *Achimelech* and the chiefs of the clans of the *Kohanim* and *Leviim*, on the principle of "chief and youngest brother alike."

Divrei Hayamim I/I Chronicles
Chapter 25

דברי הימים א
פרק כה

25

1 *David* and the officers of the army set apart for service the sons of *Asaf*, of *Hayman*, and of *Yedutun*, who prophesied to the accompaniment of lyres, harps, and cymbals. The list of men who performed this work, according to their service, was:

א וַיַּבְדֵּל דָּוִיד וְשָׂרֵי הַצָּבָא לַעֲבֹדָה לִבְנֵי אָסָף וְהֵימָן וִידוּתוּן הַנִּבְּאִים [הַנִּבְּאִים] בְּכִנֹּרוֹת בִּנְבָלִים וּבִמְצִלְתָּיִם וַיְהִי מִסְפָּרָם אַנְשֵׁי מְלָאכָה לַעֲבֹדָתָם:

2 Sons of *Asaf*: Zaccur, *Yosef*, Nethaniah, and Asarelah – sons of *Asaf* under the charge of *Asaf*, who prophesied by order of the king.

ב לִבְנֵי אָסָף זַכּוּר וְיוֹסֵף וּנְתַנְיָה וַאֲשַׂרְאֵלָה בְּנֵי אָסָף עַל יַד־אָסָף הַנִּבָּא עַל־יְדֵי הַמֶּלֶךְ:

3 *Yedutun* – the sons of *Yedutun*: *Gedalia*, Zeri, Jeshaiah, Hashabiah, Mattithiah – 6, under the charge of their father *Yedutun*, who, accompanied on the harp, prophesied, praising and extolling *Hashem*.

ג לִידוּתוּן בְּנֵי יְדוּתוּן גְּדַלְיָהוּ וּצְרִי וִישַׁעְיָהוּ חֲשַׁבְיָהוּ וּמַתִּתְיָהוּ שִׁשָּׁה עַל יְדֵי אֲבִיהֶם יְדוּתוּן בַּכִּנּוֹר הַנִּבָּא עַל־הֹדוֹת וְהַלֵּל לַיהוָה:

4 *Hayman* – the sons of *Hayman*: Bukkiah, Mattaniah, Uzziel, Shebuel, Jerimoth, *Chananya*, Chanani, Eliathah, Giddalti, Romamti-ezer, Joshbekashah, Mallothi, Hothir, and Mahazioth;

ד לְהֵימָן בְּנֵי הֵימָן בֻּקִּיָּהוּ מַתַּנְיָהוּ עֻזִּיאֵל שְׁבוּאֵל וִירִימוֹת חֲנַנְיָה חֲנָנִי אֱלִיאָתָה גִּדַּלְתִּי וְרֹמַמְתִּי עֶזֶר יָשְׁבְּקָשָׁה מַלּוֹתִי הוֹתִיר מַחֲזִיאוֹת:

5 all these were sons of *Hayman*, the seer of the king, [who uttered] prophecies of *Hashem* for His greater glory. *Hashem* gave *Hayman* fourteen sons and three daughters;

ה כָּל־אֵלֶּה בָנִים לְהֵימָן חֹזֵה הַמֶּלֶךְ בְּדִבְרֵי הָאֱלֹהִים לְהָרִים קָרֶן וַיִּתֵּן הָאֱלֹהִים לְהֵימָן בָּנִים אַרְבָּעָה עָשָׂר וּבָנוֹת שָׁלוֹשׁ:

6 all these were under the charge of their father for the singing in the House of *Hashem*, to the accompaniment of cymbals, harps, and lyres, for the service of the House of *Hashem* by order of the king. *Asaf*, *Yedutun*, and *Hayman* –

ו כָּל־אֵלֶּה עַל־יְדֵי אֲבִיהֶם בַּשִּׁיר בֵּית יְהוָה בִּמְצִלְתַּיִם נְבָלִים וְכִנֹּרוֹת לַעֲבֹדַת בֵּית הָאֱלֹהִים עַל יְדֵי הַמֶּלֶךְ אָסָף וִידוּתוּן וְהֵימָן:

7 their total number with their kinsmen, trained singers of *Hashem* – all the masters, 288.

ז וַיְהִי מִסְפָּרָם עִם־אֲחֵיהֶם מְלֻמְּדֵי־שִׁיר לַיהוָה כָּל־הַמֵּבִין מָאתַיִם שְׁמוֹנִים וּשְׁמוֹנָה:

8 They cast lots for shifts on the principle of "small and great alike, like master like apprentice."

ח וַיַּפִּילוּ גּוֹרָלוֹת מִשְׁמֶרֶת לְעֻמַּת כַּקָּטֹן כַּגָּדוֹל מֵבִין עִם־תַּלְמִיד:

va-ya-PEE-lu go-ra-LOT mish-ME-ret l'-u-MAT ka-ka-TON ka-ga-DOL may-VEEN im tal-MEED

25:8 They cast lots The *Leviim* are to sing and prepare the sacrifices in the *Beit Hamikdash* in *Yerushalayim*. Just as the *Kohanim*, who actually perform the sacrificial order, are divided into twenty-four separate groups and then ordered by lot, so too the *Leviim*, who sing praises of God as accompaniment to the sacrifices, are also divided into twenty-four groups and ordered by lot. The Sages (*Rosh Hashana* 31a) enumerate the particular Psalms the *Leviim* would sing each day while the daily sacrifices were offered. As a remembrance of this recitation by the *Leviim*, Jews recite these same psalms, referred to as the "Song of the Day," at the conclusion of the morning prayers. The Sages (*Sofrim* 18:2) further teach that anyone one who mentions these verses on the proper day is considered as having built a new altar and offered a sacrifice on it.

Divrei Hayamim I / I Chronicles
Chapter 25

9 The first lot fell to *Asaf* – to *Yosef*; the second, to *Gedalia*, he and his brothers and his sons – 12;	ט וַיֵּצֵא הַגּוֹרָל הָרִאשׁוֹן לְאָסָף לְיוֹסֵף גְּדַלְיָהוּ הַשֵּׁנִי הוּא־וְאֶחָיו וּבָנָיו שְׁנֵים עָשָׂר:
10 the third, to Zaccur: his sons and his brothers – 12;	י הַשְּׁלִשִׁי זַכּוּר בָּנָיו וְאֶחָיו שְׁנֵים עָשָׂר:
11 the fourth, to Izri: his sons and his brothers – 12;	יא הָרְבִיעִי לַיִּצְרִי בָּנָיו וְאֶחָיו שְׁנֵים עָשָׂר:
12 the fifth, to Nethaniah: his sons and his brothers – 12;	יב הַחֲמִישִׁי נְתַנְיָהוּ בָּנָיו וְאֶחָיו שְׁנֵים עָשָׂר:
13 the sixth, to Bukkiah: his sons and his brothers – 12;	יג הַשִּׁשִּׁי בֻקִּיָּהוּ בָּנָיו וְאֶחָיו שְׁנֵים עָשָׂר:
14 the seventh, to Jesarelah: his sons and his brothers – 12;	יד הַשְּׁבִעִי יְשַׂרְאֵלָה בָּנָיו וְאֶחָיו שְׁנֵים עָשָׂר:
15 the eighth, to Jeshaiah: his sons and his brothers – 12;	טו הַשְּׁמִינִי יְשַׁעְיָהוּ בָּנָיו וְאֶחָיו שְׁנֵים עָשָׂר:
16 the ninth, to Mattaniah: his sons and his brothers – 12;	טז הַתְּשִׁיעִי מַתַּנְיָהוּ בָּנָיו וְאֶחָיו שְׁנֵים עָשָׂר:
17 the tenth, to *Shim'i*: his sons and his brothers – 12;	יז הָעֲשִׂירִי שִׁמְעִי בָּנָיו וְאֶחָיו שְׁנֵים עָשָׂר:
18 the eleventh to Azarel: his sons and his brothers – 12;	יח עַשְׁתֵּי־עָשָׂר עֲזַרְאֵל בָּנָיו וְאֶחָיו שְׁנֵים עָשָׂר:
19 the twelfth, to Hashabiah: his sons and his brothers – 12;	יט הַשְּׁנֵים עָשָׂר לַחֲשַׁבְיָה בָּנָיו וְאֶחָיו שְׁנֵים עָשָׂר:
20 the thirteenth, to Shubael: his sons and his brothers – 12;	כ לִשְׁלֹשָׁה עָשָׂר שׁוּבָאֵל בָּנָיו וְאֶחָיו שְׁנֵים עָשָׂר:
21 the fourteenth, to Mattithiah: his sons and his brothers – 12;	כא לְאַרְבָּעָה עָשָׂר מַתִּתְיָהוּ בָּנָיו וְאֶחָיו שְׁנֵים עָשָׂר:
22 the fifteenth, to Jeremoth: his sons and his brothers – 12;	כב לַחֲמִשָּׁה עָשָׂר לִירֵמוֹת בָּנָיו וְאֶחָיו שְׁנֵים עָשָׂר:
23 the sixteenth, to *Chananya*: his sons and his brothers – 12;	כג לְשִׁשָּׁה עָשָׂר לַחֲנַנְיָהוּ בָּנָיו וְאֶחָיו שְׁנֵים עָשָׂר:
24 the seventeenth, to Joshbekashah: his sons and his brothers – 12;	כד לְשִׁבְעָה עָשָׂר לְיָשְׁבְּקָשָׁה בָּנָיו וְאֶחָיו שְׁנֵים עָשָׂר:
25 the eighteenth, to *Chanani*: his sons and his brothers – 12;	כה לִשְׁמוֹנָה עָשָׂר לַחֲנָנִי בָּנָיו וְאֶחָיו שְׁנֵים עָשָׂר:
26 the nineteenth, to Mallothi: his sons and his brothers – 12;	כו לְתִשְׁעָה עָשָׂר לְמַלּוֹתִי בָּנָיו וְאֶחָיו שְׁנֵים עָשָׂר:
27 the twentieth, to Eliathah: his sons and his brothers – 12;	כז לְעֶשְׂרִים לֶאֱלִיָּתָה בָּנָיו וְאֶחָיו שְׁנֵים עָשָׂר:
28 the twenty-first, to Hothir: his sons and his brothers – 12;	כח לְאֶחָד וְעֶשְׂרִים לְהוֹתִיר בָּנָיו וְאֶחָיו שְׁנֵים עָשָׂר:

Divrei Hayamim I / I Chronicles
Chapter 26

דברי הימים א
פרק כו

29 the twenty-second, to Giddalti: his sons and his brothers – 12;

כט לִשְׁנַיִם וְעֶשְׂרִים לְגִדַּלְתִּי בָּנָיו וְאֶחָיו שְׁנֵים עָשָׂר:

30 the twenty-third, to Mahazioth: his sons and his brothers – 12;

ל לִשְׁלֹשָׁה וְעֶשְׂרִים לְמַחֲזִיאוֹת בָּנָיו וְאֶחָיו שְׁנֵים עָשָׂר:

31 the twenty-fourth, to Romamti-ezer: his sons and his brothers – 12.

לא לְאַרְבָּעָה וְעֶשְׂרִים לְרוֹמַמְתִּי עָזֶר בָּנָיו וְאֶחָיו שְׁנֵים עָשָׂר:

26

1 The divisions of the gatekeepers: Korahites: Meshelemiah son of Kore, of the sons of *Asaf*.

כו א לְמַחְלְקוֹת לְשֹׁעֲרִים לַקָּרְחִים מְשֶׁלֶמְיָהוּ בֶן־קֹרֵא מִן־בְּנֵי אָסָף:

l'-makh-l'-KOT l'-sho-a-REEM la-kor-KHEEM m'-she-lem-YA-hu ven ko-RAY min b'-NAY a-SAF

2 Sons of Meshelemiah: *Zecharya* the firstborn, Jediael the second, Zebadiah the third, Jathniel the fourth,

ב וְלִמְשֶׁלֶמְיָהוּ בָּנִים זְכַרְיָהוּ הַבְּכוֹר יְדִיעֲאֵל הַשֵּׁנִי זְבַדְיָהוּ הַשְּׁלִישִׁי יַתְנִיאֵל הָרְבִיעִי:

3 Elam the fifth, *Yehochanan* the sixth, Eliehoenai the seventh.

ג עֵילָם הַחֲמִישִׁי יְהוֹחָנָן הַשִּׁשִּׁי אֶלְיְהוֹעֵינַי הַשְּׁבִיעִי:

4 Sons of *Oved Edom*: *Shemaya* the first-born, Jehozabad the second, Joah the third, Sacar the fourth, Nethanel the fifth,

ד וּלְעֹבֵד אֱדֹם בָּנִים שְׁמַעְיָה הַבְּכוֹר יְהוֹזָבָד הַשֵּׁנִי יוֹאָח הַשְּׁלִשִׁי וְשָׂכָר הָרְבִיעִי וּנְתַנְאֵל הַחֲמִישִׁי:

5 Ammiel the sixth, *Yissachar* the seventh, Peullethai the eighth – for *Hashem* had blessed him.

ה עַמִּיאֵל הַשִּׁשִּׁי יִשָּׂשכָר הַשְּׁבִיעִי פְּעֻלְּתַי הַשְּׁמִינִי כִּי בֵרֲכוֹ אֱלֹהִים:

6 To his son *Shemaya* were born sons who exercised authority in their clans because they were men of substance.

ו וְלִשְׁמַעְיָה בְנוֹ נוֹלַד בָּנִים הַמִּמְשָׁלִים לְבֵית אֲבִיהֶם כִּי־גִבּוֹרֵי חַיִל הֵמָּה:

7 The sons of *Shemaya*: Othni, Rephael, Oved, Elzabad – his brothers, men of ability, were Elihu and Semachiah.

ז בְּנֵי שְׁמַעְיָה עָתְנִי וּרְפָאֵל וְעוֹבֵד אֶלְזָבָד אֶחָיו בְּנֵי־חָיִל אֱלִיהוּ וּסְמַכְיָהוּ:

8 All these, sons of Obededom; they and their sons and brothers, strong and able men for the service – 62 of Obededom.

ח כָּל־אֵלֶּה מִבְּנֵי עֹבֵד אֱדֹם הֵמָּה וּבְנֵיהֶם וַאֲחֵיהֶם אִישׁ־חַיִל בַּכֹּחַ לַעֲבֹדָה שִׁשִּׁים וּשְׁנַיִם לְעֹבֵד אֱדֹם:

9 Meshelemiah had sons and brothers, able men – 18.

ט וְלִמְשֶׁלֶמְיָהוּ בָּנִים וְאַחִים בְּנֵי־חָיִל שְׁמוֹנָה עָשָׂר:

26:1 The divisions of the gatekeepers In addition to their role as singers, the *Leviim* also served as gatekeepers; these were the two main tasks given to the *Leviim* in the *Beit Hamikdash*. Both of these jobs were considered significant and essential. The Book of *Ezra* lists both singers and gatekeepers among the exiles who returned to the Land of Israel to rebuild the Temple (Ezra 2:41–42). In fact, *Rambam* (Beit Habechira 8:1) writes that there is a positive biblical commandment to guard the *Beit Hamikdash* as a display of honor to the Temple, and to *Hashem*. He writes, "Even though there is no concern of enemies or robbers entering the *Beit Hamikdash*, guarding it is a show of honor. There is no comparison between a palace with guards to a palace without them." The Temple, and by extension all of *Eretz Yisrael*, is the King's palace, and we must treat it with the proper awe and respect.

Rambam (1135–1204)

Divrei Hayamim I / I Chronicles
Chapter 26

10 Hosah of the Merarites had sons: Shimri the chief (he was not the first-born, but his father designated him chief),

11 *Chilkiyahu* the second, Tebaliah the third, *Zecharya* the fourth. All the sons and brothers of Hosah – 13.

12 These are the divisions of the gatekeepers, by their chief men, [who worked in] shifts corresponding to their kinsmen, ministering in the House of *Hashem*.

13 They cast lots, small and great alike, by clans, for each gate.

14 The lot for the east [gate] fell to Shelemiah. Then they cast lots [for] *Zecharya* his son, a prudent counselor, and his lot came out to be the north [gate].

15 For *Oved Edom*, the south [gate], and for his sons, the vestibule.

16 For Shuppim and for Hosah, the west [gate], with the Shallecheth gate on the ascending highway. Watch corresponded to watch:

17 At the east – six *Leviim*; at the north – four daily; at the south – four daily; at the vestibule – two by two;

18 at the colonnade on the west – four at the causeway and two at the colonnade.

19 These were the divisions of the gatekeepers of the sons of *Korach* and the sons of *Merari*.

20 And the *Leviim*: *Achiya* over the treasuries of the House of *Hashem* and the treasuries of the dedicated things.

21 The sons of Ladan: the sons of the Gershonites belonging to Ladan; the chiefs of the clans of Ladan, the Gershonite – Yechieli.

22 The sons of Yechieli: Zetham and *Yoel*; his brother was over the treasuries of the House of *Hashem*.

23 Of the Amramites, the Izharites, the Chevronites, the Uzzielites:

24 Shebuel son of *Gershom* son of *Moshe* was the chief officer over the treasuries.

25 And his brothers: *Eliezer*, his son Rehabiah, his son Jeshaiah, his son *Yoram*, his son Zichri, his son Shelomith –

Divrei Hayamim I / I Chronicles
Chapter 27

26 that Shelomith and his brothers were over all the treasuries of dedicated things that were dedicated by King *David* and the chiefs of the clans, and the officers of thousands and hundreds and the other army officers;

27 they dedicated some of the booty of the wars to maintain the House of *Hashem*.

28 All that *Shmuel* the seer had dedicated, and *Shaul* son of *Keesh*, and *Avner* son of Ner, and *Yoav* son of *Tzeruya* – or [what] any other man had dedicated, was under the charge of Shelomith and his brothers.

29 The Izharites: Chenaniah and his sons were over *Yisrael* as clerks and magistrates for affairs outside [the sanctuary].

30 The Chevronites: Hashabiah and his brothers, capable men, 1,700, supervising *Yisrael* on the west side of the *Yarden* in all matters of *Hashem* and the service of the king.

31 The Chevronites: Jeriah, the chief of the Chevronites – they were investigated in the fortieth year of *David*'s reign by clans of all their lines, and men of substance were found among them in Jazer-gilead.

32 His brothers, able men, 2,700, chiefs of clans – *David* put them in charge of the Reubenites, the Gadites, and the half-tribe of *Menashe* in all matters of *Hashem* and matters of the king.

27

1 The number of Israelites – chiefs of clans, officers of thousands and hundreds and their clerks, who served the king in all matters of the divisions, who worked in monthly shifts during all the months of the year – each division, 24,000.

uv-NAY yis-ra-AYL l'-mis-pa-RAM ra-SHAY ha-a-VOT v'-sa-RAY ha-a-la-FEEM v'-ha-may-OT v'-shot'-ray-HEM ha-m'-sha-r'-TEEM et ha-ME-lekh l'-KHOL d'-VAR ha-makh-l'-KOT ha-ba-AH v'-ha-yo-TZAYT KHO-desh b'-KHO-desh l'-KHOL khod-SHAY ha-sha-NAH ha-ma-kha-LO-ket ha-a-KHAT es-REEM v'-ar-ba-AH A-lef

27:1 The number of Israelites After listing the jobs of the *Kohanim* and *Leviim*, we are told that the rest of the Children of Israel also have an important task: They must perform national army service. While the tribe of *Levi* is entrusted with the job of spiritually fortifying the nation, the rest of the people are charged with the responsibility of physical protection and defense. In contemporary Israel as well, every citizen is required to perform national army service in the IDF, except those engaged in full time *Torah* study. In the

Divrei Hayamim I / I Chronicles
Chapter 27

2 Over the first division for the first month – Jashobeam son of Zabdiel; his division had 24,000.

3 Of the sons of *Peretz*, he, the chief of all the officers of the army, [served] for the first month.

4 Over the division of the second month – Dodai the Ahohite; Mikloth was chief officer of his division; his division had 24,000.

5 The third army officer for the third month – Benaiah son of *Yehoyada*, the chief *Kohen*; his division had 24,000.

6 That was Benaiah, one of the warriors of the thirty and over the thirty; and [over] his division was Ammizabad his son.

7 The fourth, for the fourth month, *Asael* brother of *Yoav*, and his son Zebadiah after him; his division had 24,000.

8 The fifth, for the fifth month, the officer Shamhut the Izrahite; his division had 24,000.

9 The sixth, for the sixth month, Ira son of Ikkesh the Tekoite; his division had 24,000.

10 The seventh, for the seventh month, Helez the Pelonite, of the Ephraimites; his division had 24,000.

11 The eighth, for the eighth month, Sibbecai the Hushathite, of *Zerach*; his division had 24,000.

12 The ninth, for the ninth month, Abiezer the Anatotite, of *Binyamin*; his division had 24,000.

13 The tenth, for the tenth month, Mahrai the Netophathite, of *Zerach*; his division had 24,000.

---

early 1950s, Prime Minister David Ben Gurion reached an agreement with the leaders of the religious parties, exempting full time *Torah* scholars from serving in the IDF. Since its earliest days, Israel has affirmed the fact that just as the army strengthens the *Torah*, the *Torah* strengthens the army.

Divrei Hayamim I / I Chronicles
Chapter 27

14 The eleventh, for the eleventh month, Benaiah the Pirathonite, of the Ephraimites; his division had 24,000.

15 The twelfth, for the twelfth month, Heldai the Netophathite, of *Otniel*; his division had 24,000.

16 Over the tribes of *Yisrael*: *Reuven*: the chief officer, *Eliezer* son of Zichri. *Shimon*: Shephatiah son of Maaca.

17 *Levi*: Hashabiah son of Kemuel. *Aharon*: Tzadok.

18 *Yehuda*: Elihu, of the brothers of *David*. *Yissachar*: Omri son of *Michael*.

19 *Zevulun*: Ishmaiah son of *Ovadya*. *Naftali*: Jerimoth son of Azriel.

20 Ephraimites: *Hoshea* son of Azaziah. The half-tribe of *Menashe*: *Yoel* son of Pedaiah.

21 Half *Menashe* in *Gilad*: *Ido* son of *Zecharya*. *Binyamin*: Jaasiel son of *Avner*.

22 *Dan*: Azarel son of Jeroham. These were the officers of the tribes of *Yisrael*.

23 *David* did not take a census of those under twenty years of age, for *Hashem* had promised to make *Yisrael* as numerous as the stars of heaven.

24 *Yoav* son of *Tzeruya* did begin to count them, but he did not finish; wrath struck *Yisrael* on account of this, and the census was not entered into the account of the chronicles of King *David*.

25 Over the royal treasuries: Azmaveth son of Adiel. Over the treasuries in the country – in the towns, the hamlets, and the citadels: *Yehonatan* son of Uzziyahu.

26 Over the field laborers in agricultural work: Ezri son of Chelub.

27 Over the vineyards: *Shim'i* the Ramathite. And over the produce in the vineyards for wine cellars: Zabdi the Shiphmite.

28 Over the olive trees and the sycamores in the Shephelah: Baal-hanan the Gederite. Over the oil-stores: *Yoash*.

Divrei Hayamim I / I Chronicles
Chapter 28

דברי הימים א
פרק כח

29 Over the cattle pasturing in Sharon: Shirtai the Sharonite. And over the cattle in the valleys: *Shafat* son of Adlai.

30 Over the camels: Obil the Ishmaelite. And over the she-asses: Jehdeiah the Meronothite.

31 Over the flocks: Jaziz the Hagrite. All these were stewards of the property of King *David*.

32 *Yehonatan*, *David*'s uncle, was a counselor, a master, and a scribe: *Yechiel* son of Hachmoni was with the king's sons.

33 *Achitofel* was a counselor to the king. Hushai the Archite was the king's friend.

34 After *Achitofel* were *Yehoyada* son of Benaiah and *Evyatar*. The commander of the king's army was Yoav.

28 1 *David* assembled all the officers of *Yisrael* – the tribal officers, the divisional officers who served the king, the captains of thousands and the captains of hundreds, and the stewards of all the property and cattle of the king and his sons, with the eunuchs and the warriors, all the men of substance – to *Yerushalayim*.

2 King *David* rose to his feet and said, "Hear me, my brothers, my people! I wanted to build a resting-place for the *Aron Brit Hashem*, for the footstool of our God, and I laid aside material for building.

3 But *Hashem* said to me, 'You will not build a house for My name, for you are a man of battles and have shed blood.'

4 God of *Yisrael* chose me of all my father's house to be king over *Yisrael* forever. For He chose *Yehuda* to be ruler, and of the family of *Yehuda*, my father's house; and of my father's sons, He preferred to make me king over all *Yisrael*;

5 and of all my sons – for many are the sons *Hashem* gave me – He chose my son *Shlomo* to sit on the throne of the kingdom of *Hashem* over *Yisrael*.

כט וְעַל־הַבָּקָר הָרֹעִים בַּשָּׁרוֹן שִׁטְרַי [שִׁרְטַי] הַשָּׁרוֹנִי וְעַל־הַבָּקָר בָּעֲמָקִים שָׁפָט בֶּן־עַדְלָי:

ל וְעַל־הַגְּמַלִּים אוֹבִיל הַיִּשְׁמְעֵלִי וְעַל־הָאֲתֹנוֹת יֶחְדְּיָהוּ הַמֵּרֹנֹתִי:

לא וְעַל־הַצֹּאן יָזִיז הַהַגְרִי כָּל־אֵלֶּה שָׂרֵי הָרְכוּשׁ אֲשֶׁר לַמֶּלֶךְ דָּוִיד:

לב וִיהוֹנָתָן דּוֹד־דָּוִיד יוֹעֵץ אִישׁ־מֵבִין וְסוֹפֵר הוּא וִיחִיאֵל בֶּן־חַכְמוֹנִי עִם־בְּנֵי הַמֶּלֶךְ:

לג וַאֲחִיתֹפֶל יוֹעֵץ לַמֶּלֶךְ וְחוּשַׁי הָאַרְכִּי רֵעַ הַמֶּלֶךְ:

לד וְאַחֲרֵי אֲחִיתֹפֶל יְהוֹיָדָע בֶּן־בְּנָיָהוּ וְאֶבְיָתָר וְשַׂר־צָבָא לַמֶּלֶךְ יוֹאָב:

כח א וַיַּקְהֵל דָּוִיד אֶת־כָּל־שָׂרֵי יִשְׂרָאֵל שָׂרֵי הַשְּׁבָטִים וְשָׂרֵי הַמַּחְלְקוֹת הַמְשָׁרְתִים אֶת־הַמֶּלֶךְ וְשָׂרֵי הָאֲלָפִים וְשָׂרֵי הַמֵּאוֹת וְשָׂרֵי כָל־רְכוּשׁ־וּמִקְנֶה לַמֶּלֶךְ וּלְבָנָיו עִם־הַסָּרִיסִים וְהַגִּבּוֹרִים וּלְכָל־גִּבּוֹר חָיִל אֶל־יְרוּשָׁלָ͏ִם:

ב וַיָּקָם דָּוִיד הַמֶּלֶךְ עַל־רַגְלָיו וַיֹּאמֶר שְׁמָעוּנִי אַחַי וְעַמִּי אֲנִי עִם־לְבָבִי לִבְנוֹת בֵּית מְנוּחָה לַאֲרוֹן בְּרִית־יְהוָה וְלַהֲדֹם רַגְלֵי אֱלֹהֵינוּ וַהֲכִינוֹתִי לִבְנוֹת:

ג וְהָאֱלֹהִים אָמַר לִי לֹא־תִבְנֶה בַיִת לִשְׁמִי כִּי אִישׁ מִלְחָמוֹת אַתָּה וְדָמִים שָׁפָכְתָּ:

ד וַיִּבְחַר יְהוָה אֱלֹהֵי יִשְׂרָאֵל בִּי מִכֹּל בֵּית־אָבִי לִהְיוֹת לְמֶלֶךְ עַל־יִשְׂרָאֵל לְעוֹלָם כִּי בִיהוּדָה בָּחַר לְנָגִיד וּבְבֵית יְהוּדָה בֵּית אָבִי וּבִבְנֵי אָבִי בִּי רָצָה לְהַמְלִיךְ עַל־כָּל־יִשְׂרָאֵל:

ה וּמִכָּל־בָּנַי כִּי רַבִּים בָּנִים נָתַן לִי יְהוָה וַיִּבְחַר בִּשְׁלֹמֹה בְנִי לָשֶׁבֶת עַל־כִּסֵּא מַלְכוּת יְהוָה עַל־יִשְׂרָאֵל:

Divrei Hayamim I / I Chronicles
Chapter 28

דברי הימים א
פרק כח

6 He said to me, 'It will be your son *Shlomo* who will build My House and My courts, for I have chosen him to be a son to Me, and I will be a father to him.

א וַיֹּאמֶר לִי שְׁלֹמֹה בִנְךָ הוּא־יִבְנֶה בֵיתִי וַחֲצֵרוֹתָי כִּי־בָחַרְתִּי בוֹ לִי לְבֵן וַאֲנִי אֶהְיֶה־לּוֹ לְאָב:

va-YO-mer LEE sh'-lo-MOH vin-KHA hu yiv-NEH vay-TEE va-kha-tzay-ro-TAI kee va-KHAR-tee VO LEE v'-VAYN va-a-NEE eh-yeh LO l'-AV

7 I will establish his kingdom forever, if he keeps firmly to the observance of My commandments and rules as he does now.'

ז וַהֲכִינוֹתִי אֶת־מַלְכוּתוֹ עַד־לְעוֹלָם אִם־יֶחֱזַק לַעֲשׂוֹת מִצְוֺתַי וּמִשְׁפָּטַי כַּיּוֹם הַזֶּה:

8 And now, in the sight of all *Yisrael*, the congregation of *Hashem*, and in the hearing of our God, [I say:] Observe and apply yourselves to all the commandments of *Hashem* your God in order that you may possess this good land and bequeath it to your children after you forever.

ח וְעַתָּה לְעֵינֵי כָל־יִשְׂרָאֵל קְהַל־יְהֹוָה וּבְאָזְנֵי אֱלֹהֵינוּ שִׁמְרוּ וְדִרְשׁוּ כָּל־מִצְוֺת יְהֹוָה אֱלֹהֵיכֶם לְמַעַן תִּירְשׁוּ אֶת־הָאָרֶץ הַטּוֹבָה וְהִנְחַלְתֶּם לִבְנֵיכֶם אַחֲרֵיכֶם עַד־עוֹלָם:

9 "And you, my son *Shlomo*, know the God of your father, and serve Him with single mind and fervent heart, for *Hashem* searches all minds and discerns the design of every thought; if you seek Him He will be available to you, but if you forsake Him He will abandon you forever.

ט וְאַתָּה שְׁלֹמֹה־בְנִי דַּע אֶת־אֱלֹהֵי אָבִיךָ וְעָבְדֵהוּ בְּלֵב שָׁלֵם וּבְנֶפֶשׁ חֲפֵצָה כִּי כָל־לְבָבוֹת דּוֹרֵשׁ יְהֹוָה וְכָל־יֵצֶר מַחֲשָׁבוֹת מֵבִין אִם־תִּדְרְשֶׁנּוּ יִמָּצֵא לָךְ וְאִם־תַּעַזְבֶנּוּ יַזְנִיחֲךָ לָעַד:

10 See then, *Hashem* chose you to build a house as the sanctuary; be strong and do it."

י רְאֵה עַתָּה כִּי־יְהֹוָה בָּחַר בְּךָ לִבְנוֹת־בַּיִת לַמִּקְדָּשׁ חֲזַק וַעֲשֵׂה:

11 *David* gave his son *Shlomo* the plan of the porch and its houses, its storerooms and its upper chambers and inner chambers; and of the place of the *Aron*-cover;

יא וַיִּתֵּן דָּוִיד לִשְׁלֹמֹה בְנוֹ אֶת־תַּבְנִית הָאוּלָם וְאֶת־בָּתָּיו וְגַנְזַכָּיו וַעֲלִיֹּתָיו וַחֲדָרָיו הַפְּנִימִים וּבֵית הַכַּפֹּרֶת:

12 and the plan of all that he had by the spirit: of the courts of the House of *Hashem* and all its surrounding chambers, and of the treasuries of the House of *Hashem* and of the treasuries of the holy things;

יב וְתַבְנִית כֹּל אֲשֶׁר הָיָה בָרוּחַ עִמּוֹ לְחַצְרוֹת בֵּית־יְהֹוָה וּלְכָל־הַלְּשָׁכוֹת סָבִיב לְאֹצְרוֹת בֵּית הָאֱלֹהִים וּלְאֹצְרוֹת הַקֳּדָשִׁים:

28:6 For I have chosen him to be a son to Me, and I will be a father to him King *David's* son *Shlomo* is chosen by God as the heir to his father's throne and the eternal monarchy of the People of Israel. In addition to the name *Shlomo*, he is also known as *Yedidya*, which means 'beloved of God' (II Samuel 12:25). *Radak* suggests that *Hashem* wants his name to be *Shlomo* (שלמה), from the Hebrew word *shalom* (שלום), meaning 'peace,' because during his reign God would bless him and the People of Israel with peace. But *Shlomo* is also *Yedidya*, the beloved of God, as reflected in this verse. Indeed, both of his names accurately describe his accomplishments. During King *Shlomo's* reign, the Nation of Israel achieves the greatest heights, peace with the other nations, as well closeness to *Hashem* through service in the *Beit Hamikdash*.

Divrei Hayamim I/I Chronicles
Chapter 29

דברי הימים א
פרק כט

13 the divisions of *Kohanim* and *Leviim* for all the work of the service of the House of *Hashem* and all the vessels of the service of the House of *Hashem*;

יג וּלְמַחְלְקוֹת הַכֹּהֲנִים וְהַלְוִיִּם וּלְכָל־מְלֶאכֶת עֲבוֹדַת בֵּית־יְהֹוָה וּלְכָל־כְּלֵי עֲבוֹדַת בֵּית־יְהֹוָה:

14 and gold, the weight of gold for vessels of every sort of use; silver for all the vessels of silver by weight, for all the vessels of every kind of service;

יד לַזָּהָב בַּמִּשְׁקָל לַזָּהָב לְכָל־כְּלֵי עֲבוֹדָה וַעֲבוֹדָה לְכֹל כְּלֵי הַכֶּסֶף בְּמִשְׁקָל לְכָל־כְּלֵי עֲבוֹדָה וַעֲבוֹדָה:

15 the weight of the gold *menorah*s and their gold lamps, and the weight of the silver *menorah*s, each *menorah* and its silver lamps, according to the use of every *menorah*;

טו וּמִשְׁקָל לִמְנֹרוֹת הַזָּהָב וְנֵרֹתֵיהֶם זָהָב בְּמִשְׁקַל־מְנוֹרָה וּמְנוֹרָה וְנֵרֹתֶיהָ וְלִמְנֹרוֹת הַכֶּסֶף בְּמִשְׁקָל לִמְנוֹרָה וְנֵרֹתֶיהָ כַּעֲבוֹדַת מְנוֹרָה וּמְנוֹרָה:

16 and the weight of gold for the tables of the rows of bread, for each table, and of silver for the silver tables;

טז וְאֶת־הַזָּהָב מִשְׁקָל לְשֻׁלְחֲנוֹת הַמַּעֲרֶכֶת לְשֻׁלְחַן וְשֻׁלְחָן וְכֶסֶף לְשֻׁלְחֲנוֹת הַכָּסֶף:

17 and of the pure gold for the forks and the basins and the jars; and the weight of the gold bowls, every bowl; and the weight of the silver bowls, each and every bowl;

יז וְהַמִּזְלָגוֹת וְהַמִּזְרָקוֹת וְהַקְּשָׂוֹת זָהָב טָהוֹר וְלִכְפוֹרֵי הַזָּהָב בְּמִשְׁקָל לִכְפוֹר וּכְפוֹר וְלִכְפוֹרֵי הַכֶּסֶף בְּמִשְׁקָל לִכְפוֹר וּכְפוֹר:

18 the weight of refined gold for the incense *Mizbayach* and the gold for the figure of the chariot – the cherubs – those with outspread wings screening the *Aron Brit Hashem*.

יח וּלְמִזְבַּח הַקְּטֹרֶת זָהָב מְזֻקָּק בַּמִּשְׁקָל וּלְתַבְנִית הַמֶּרְכָּבָה הַכְּרֻבִים זָהָב לְפֹרְשִׂים וְסֹכְכִים עַל־אֲרוֹן בְּרִית־יְהֹוָה:

19 "All this that *Hashem* made me understand by His hand on me, I give you in writing – the plan of all the works."

יט הַכֹּל בִּכְתָב מִיַּד יְהֹוָה עָלַי הִשְׂכִּיל כֹּל מַלְאֲכוֹת הַתַּבְנִית:

20 *David* said to his son *Shlomo*, "Be strong and of good courage and do it; do not be afraid or dismayed, for *Hashem* my God is with you; He will not fail you or forsake you till all the work on the House of *Hashem* is done.

כ וַיֹּאמֶר דָּוִיד לִשְׁלֹמֹה בְנוֹ חֲזַק וֶאֱמַץ וַעֲשֵׂה אַל־תִּירָא וְאַל־תֵּחָת כִּי יְהֹוָה אֱלֹהִים אֱלֹהַי עִמָּךְ לֹא יַרְפְּךָ וְלֹא יַעַזְבֶךָּ עַד־לִכְלוֹת כָּל־מְלֶאכֶת עֲבוֹדַת בֵּית־יְהֹוָה:

21 Here are the divisions of the *Kohanim* and *Leviim* for all kinds of service of the House of *Hashem*, and with you in all the work are willing men, skilled in all sorts of tasks; also the officers and all the people are at your command."

כא וְהִנֵּה מַחְלְקוֹת הַכֹּהֲנִים וְהַלְוִיִּם לְכָל־עֲבוֹדַת בֵּית הָאֱלֹהִים וְעִמְּךָ בְכָל־מְלָאכָה לְכָל־נָדִיב בַּחָכְמָה לְכָל־עֲבוֹדָה וְהַשָּׂרִים וְכָל־הָעָם לְכָל־דְּבָרֶיךָ:

29

1 King *David* said to the entire assemblage, "*Hashem* has chosen my son *Shlomo* alone, an untried lad, although the work to be done is vast – for the temple is not for a man but for *Hashem*.

כט א וַיֹּאמֶר דָּוִיד הַמֶּלֶךְ לְכָל־הַקָּהָל שְׁלֹמֹה בְנִי אֶחָד בָּחַר־בּוֹ אֱלֹהִים נַעַר וָרָךְ וְהַמְּלָאכָה גְדוֹלָה כִּי לֹא לְאָדָם הַבִּירָה כִּי לַיהֹוָה אֱלֹהִים:

2 I have spared no effort to lay up for the House of my God gold for golden objects, silver for silver, copper for copper, iron for iron, wood for wooden, onyx-stone and inlay-stone, stone of antimony and variegated colors – every kind of precious stone and much marble.

ב וּכְכָל־כֹּחִי הֲכִינוֹתִי לְבֵית־אֱלֹהַי הַזָּהָב לַזָּהָב וְהַכֶּסֶף לַכֶּסֶף וְהַנְּחֹשֶׁת לַנְּחֹשֶׁת הַבַּרְזֶל לַבַּרְזֶל וְהָעֵצִים לָעֵצִים אַבְנֵי־שֹׁהַם וּמִלּוּאִים אַבְנֵי־פוּךְ וְרִקְמָה וְכֹל אֶבֶן יְקָרָה וְאַבְנֵי־שַׁיִשׁ לָרֹב:

Divrei Hayamim I/I Chronicles
Chapter 29

3 Besides, out of my solicitude for the House of my God, I gave over my private hoard of gold and silver to the House of my God – in addition to all that I laid aside for the holy House:

4 3,000 gold *kikarim* of Ophir gold, and 7,000 *kikarim* of refined silver for covering the walls of the houses

5 (gold for golden objects, silver for silver for all the work) – into the hands of craftsmen. Now who is going to make a freewill offering and devote himself today to *Hashem*?"

6 The officers of the clans and the officers of the tribes of *Yisrael* and the captains of thousands and hundreds and the supervisors of the king's work made freewill offerings,

7 giving for the work of the House of *Hashem*: 5,000 *kikarim* of gold, 10,000 darics, 10,000 *kikarim* of silver, 18,000 *kikarim* of copper, 100,000 *kikarim* of iron.

8 Whoever had stones in his possession gave them to the treasury of the House of *Hashem* in the charge of *Yechiel* the Gershonite.

9 The people rejoiced over the freewill offerings they made, for with a whole heart they made freewill offerings to *Hashem*; King *David* also rejoiced very much.

10 *David* blessed *Hashem* in front of all the assemblage; *David* said, "Blessed are You, *Hashem*, God of *Yisrael* our father, from eternity to eternity.

11 Yours, *Hashem*, are greatness, might, splendor, triumph, and majesty – yes, all that is in heaven and on earth; to You, *Hashem*, belong kingship and preeminence above all.

12 Riches and honor are Yours to dispense; You have dominion over all; with You are strength and might, and it is in Your power to make anyone great and strong.

13 Now, *Hashem*, we praise You and extol Your glorious name.

14 Who am I and who are my people, that we should have the means to make such a freewill offering; but all is from You, and it is Your gift that we have given to You.

דברי הימים א
פרק כט

ג וְעוֹד בִּרְצוֹתִי בְּבֵית אֱלֹהַי יֶשׁ־לִי סְגֻלָּה זָהָב וָכָסֶף נָתַתִּי לְבֵית־אֱלֹהַי לְמַעְלָה מִכָּל־הֲכִינוֹתִי לְבֵית הַקֹּדֶשׁ:

ד שְׁלֹשֶׁת אֲלָפִים כִּכְּרֵי זָהָב מִזְּהַב אוֹפִיר וְשִׁבְעַת אֲלָפִים כִּכַּר־כֶּסֶף מְזֻקָּק לָטוּחַ קִירוֹת הַבָּתִּים:

ה לַזָּהָב לַזָּהָב וְלַכֶּסֶף לַכֶּסֶף וּלְכָל־מְלָאכָה בְּיַד חָרָשִׁים וּמִי מִתְנַדֵּב לְמַלֹּאות יָדוֹ הַיּוֹם לַיהוָה:

ו וַיִּתְנַדְּבוּ שָׂרֵי הָאָבוֹת וְשָׂרֵי שִׁבְטֵי יִשְׂרָאֵל וְשָׂרֵי הָאֲלָפִים וְהַמֵּאוֹת וּלְשָׂרֵי מְלֶאכֶת הַמֶּלֶךְ:

ז וַיִּתְּנוּ לַעֲבוֹדַת בֵּית־הָאֱלֹהִים זָהָב כִּכָּרִים חֲמֵשֶׁת־אֲלָפִים וַאֲדַרְכֹנִים רִבּוֹ וְכֶסֶף כִּכָּרִים עֲשֶׂרֶת אֲלָפִים וּנְחֹשֶׁת רִבּוֹ וּשְׁמוֹנַת אֲלָפִים כִּכָּרִים וּבַרְזֶל מֵאָה־אֶלֶף כִּכָּרִים:

ח וְהַנִּמְצָא אִתּוֹ אֲבָנִים נָתְנוּ לְאוֹצַר בֵּית־יְהוָה עַל יַד־יְחִיאֵל הַגֵּרְשֻׁנִּי:

ט וַיִּשְׂמְחוּ הָעָם עַל־הִתְנַדְּבָם כִּי בְּלֵב שָׁלֵם הִתְנַדְּבוּ לַיהוָה וְגַם דָּוִיד הַמֶּלֶךְ שָׂמַח שִׂמְחָה גְדוֹלָה:

י וַיְבָרֶךְ דָּוִיד אֶת־יְהוָה לְעֵינֵי כָּל־הַקָּהָל וַיֹּאמֶר דָּוִיד בָּרוּךְ אַתָּה יְהוָה אֱלֹהֵי יִשְׂרָאֵל אָבִינוּ מֵעוֹלָם וְעַד־עוֹלָם:

יא לְךָ יְהוָה הַגְּדֻלָּה וְהַגְּבוּרָה וְהַתִּפְאֶרֶת וְהַנֵּצַח וְהַהוֹד כִּי־כֹל בַּשָּׁמַיִם וּבָאָרֶץ לְךָ יְהוָה הַמַּמְלָכָה וְהַמִּתְנַשֵּׂא לְכֹל לְרֹאשׁ:

יב וְהָעֹשֶׁר וְהַכָּבוֹד מִלְּפָנֶיךָ וְאַתָּה מוֹשֵׁל בַּכֹּל וּבְיָדְךָ כֹּחַ וּגְבוּרָה וּבְיָדְךָ לְגַדֵּל וּלְחַזֵּק לַכֹּל:

יג וְעַתָּה אֱלֹהֵינוּ מוֹדִים אֲנַחְנוּ לָךְ וּמְהַלְלִים לְשֵׁם תִּפְאַרְתֶּךָ:

יד וְכִי מִי אֲנִי וּמִי עַמִּי כִּי־נַעְצֹר כֹּחַ לְהִתְנַדֵּב כָּזֹאת כִּי־מִמְּךָ הַכֹּל וּמִיָּדְךָ נָתַנּוּ לָךְ:

Divrei Hayamim I / I Chronicles
Chapter 29

דברי הימים א
פרק כט

15 For we are sojourners with You, mere transients like our fathers; our days on earth are like a shadow, with nothing in prospect.

טו כִּי־גֵרִ֨ים אֲנַ֧חְנוּ לְפָנֶ֛יךָ וְתוֹשָׁבִ֖ים כְּכָל־אֲבֹתֵ֑ינוּ כַּצֵּ֧ל ׀ יָמֵ֛ינוּ עַל־הָאָ֖רֶץ וְאֵ֥ין מִקְוֶֽה׃

16 *Hashem* our God, all this great mass that we have laid aside to build You a House for Your holy name is from You, and it is all Yours.

טז יְהֹוָ֣ה אֱלֹהֵ֗ינוּ כֹּ֣ל הֶהָמ֤וֹן הַזֶּה֙ אֲשֶׁ֣ר הֲכִינֹ֔נוּ לִבְנֽוֹת־לְךָ֥ בַ֖יִת לְשֵׁ֣ם קׇדְשֶׁ֑ךָ מִיָּדְךָ֥ הִ֖יא [ה֥וּא] וּלְךָ֥ הַכֹּֽל׃

17 I know, *Hashem*, that You search the heart and desire uprightness; I, with upright heart, freely offered all these things; now Your people, who are present here – I saw them joyously making freewill offerings.

יז וְיָדַ֣עְתִּי אֱלֹהַ֔י כִּ֥י אַתָּ֖ה בֹּחֵ֣ן לֵבָ֑ב וּמֵֽישָׁרִ֖ים תִּרְצֶ֑ה אֲנִ֗י בְּיֹ֤שֶׁר לְבָבִי֙ הִתְנַדַּ֣בְתִּי כׇל־אֵ֔לֶּה וְעַתָּ֗ה עַמְּךָ֧ הַנִּמְצְאוּ־פֹ֛ה רָאִ֥יתִי בְשִׂמְחָ֖ה לְהִֽתְנַדֶּב־לָֽךְ׃

18 O God of *Avraham*, *Yitzchak*, and *Yisrael*, our fathers, remember this to the eternal credit of the thoughts of Your people's hearts, and make their hearts constant toward You.

יח יְהֹוָ֗ה אֱ֠לֹהֵ֠י אַבְרָהָ֨ם יִצְחָ֤ק וְיִשְׂרָאֵל֙ אֲבֹתֵ֔ינוּ שׇׁמְרָה־זֹּ֣את לְעוֹלָ֔ם לְיֵ֥צֶר מַחְשְׁב֖וֹת לְבַ֣ב עַמֶּ֑ךָ וְהָכֵ֥ן לְבָבָ֖ם אֵלֶֽיךָ׃

19 As to my son *Shlomo*, give him a whole heart to observe Your commandments, Your admonitions, and Your laws, and to fulfill them all, and to build this temple for which I have made provision."

יט וְלִשְׁלֹמֹ֣ה בְנִ֗י תֵּ֚ן לֵבָ֣ב שָׁלֵ֔ם לִשְׁמוֹר֙ מִצְוֺתֶ֔יךָ עֵדְוֺתֶ֖יךָ וְחֻקֶּ֑יךָ וְלַעֲשׂ֣וֹת הַכֹּ֔ל וְלִבְנ֖וֹת הַבִּירָ֥ה אֲשֶׁר־הֲכִינֽוֹתִי׃

20 *David* said to the whole assemblage, "Now bless *Hashem* your God." All the assemblage blessed God of their fathers, and bowed their heads low to *Hashem* and the king.

כ וַיֹּ֤אמֶר דָּוִיד֙ לְכׇל־הַקָּהָ֔ל בָּרְכוּ־נָ֖א אֶת־יְהֹוָ֣ה אֱלֹהֵיכֶ֑ם וַיְבָרְכ֣וּ כׇֽל־הַקָּהָ֗ל לַיהֹוָה֙ אֱלֹהֵ֣י אֲבֹתֵיהֶ֔ם וַיִּקְּד֧וּ וַיִּֽשְׁתַּחֲו֛וּ לַיהֹוָ֖ה וְלַמֶּֽלֶךְ׃

21 They offered sacrifices to *Hashem* and made burnt offerings to *Hashem* on the morrow of that day: 1,000 bulls, 1,000 rams, 1,000 lambs, with their libations; [they made] sacrifices in great number for all *Yisrael*,

כא וַיִּזְבְּח֣וּ לַיהֹוָ֣ה זְבָחִ֡ים וַיַּעֲל֣וּ עֹלוֹת֩ לַיהֹוָ֨ה לְֽמׇחֳרַ֜ת הַיּ֣וֹם הַה֗וּא פָּרִ֨ים אֶ֜לֶף אֵילִ֥ים אֶ֛לֶף כְּבָשִׂ֥ים אֶ֖לֶף וְנִסְכֵּיהֶ֑ם וּזְבָחִ֥ים לָרֹ֖ב לְכׇל־יִשְׂרָאֵֽל׃

22 and they ate and drank in the presence of *Hashem* on that day with great joy. They again proclaimed *Shlomo* son of *David* king, and they anointed him as ruler before *Hashem*, and *Tzadok* as *Kohen Gadol*.

כב וַיֹּאכְל֨וּ וַיִּשְׁתּ֜וּ לִפְנֵ֧י יְהֹוָ֛ה בַּיּ֥וֹם הַה֖וּא בְּשִׂמְחָ֣ה גְדוֹלָ֑ה וַיַּמְלִ֤יכוּ שֵׁנִית֙ לִשְׁלֹמֹ֣ה בֶן־דָּוִ֔יד וַיִּמְשְׁח֧וּ לַיהֹוָ֛ה לְנָגִ֖יד וּלְצָד֥וֹק לְכֹהֵֽן׃

va-yo-kh'-LU va-yish-TU lif-NAY a-do-NAI ba-YOM ha-HU b'-sim-KHAH g'-do-LAH va-yam-LEE-khu shay-NEET lish-lo-MOH ven da-VEED va-yim-sh'-KHU la-do-NAI l'-na-GEED ul-tza-DOK l'-kho-HAYN

29:22 *Tzadok* as *Kohen Gadol* The name *Tzadok* (צדוק) comes from the Hebrew word *tzedek* (צדק) which means 'justice' or 'righteousness'. *Tzadok* was a righteous priest who served in the times of King *David* and King *Shlomo*. After King *Shlomo* built the *Beit Hamikdash*, *Tzadok* was the first to serve as its High Priest. *Tzadok* and his descendants displayed loyalty and commitment to *Hashem*, and 'the house of *Tzadok*' is thus considered dear to God (see Ezekiel 44:15).

צדוק

Divrei Hayamim I / I Chronicles
Chapter 29

דברי הימים א
פרק כט

23 *Shlomo* successfully took over the throne of *Hashem* as king instead of his father *David*, and all went well with him. All *Yisrael* accepted him;

כג וַיֵּשֶׁב שְׁלֹמֹה עַל־כִּסֵּא יְהֹוָה לְמֶלֶךְ תַּחַת־דָּוִיד אָבִיו וַיַּצְלַח וַיִּשְׁמְעוּ אֵלָיו כָּל־יִשְׂרָאֵל׃

24 all the officials and the warriors, and the sons of King *David* as well, gave their hand in support of King *Shlomo*.

כד וְכָל־הַשָּׂרִים וְהַגִּבֹּרִים וְגַם כָּל־בְּנֵי הַמֶּלֶךְ דָּוִיד נָתְנוּ יָד תַּחַת שְׁלֹמֹה הַמֶּלֶךְ׃

25 *Hashem* made *Shlomo* exceedingly great in the eyes of all *Yisrael*, and endowed him with a regal majesty that no king of *Yisrael* before him ever had.

כה וַיְגַדֵּל יְהֹוָה אֶת־שְׁלֹמֹה לְמַעְלָה לְעֵינֵי כָּל־יִשְׂרָאֵל וַיִּתֵּן עָלָיו הוֹד מַלְכוּת אֲשֶׁר לֹא־הָיָה עַל־כָּל־מֶלֶךְ לְפָנָיו עַל־יִשְׂרָאֵל׃

26 Thus *David* son of *Yishai* reigned over all *Yisrael*;

כו וְדָוִיד בֶּן־יִשָׁי מָלַךְ עַל־כָּל־יִשְׂרָאֵל׃

27 the length of his reign over *Yisrael* was forty years: he reigned seven years in *Chevron* and thirty-three years in *Yerushalayim*.

כז וְהַיָּמִים אֲשֶׁר מָלַךְ עַל־יִשְׂרָאֵל אַרְבָּעִים שָׁנָה בְּחֶבְרוֹן מָלַךְ שֶׁבַע שָׁנִים וּבִירוּשָׁלַ͏ִם מָלַךְ שְׁלֹשִׁים וְשָׁלוֹשׁ׃

28 He died at a ripe old age, having enjoyed long life, riches and honor, and his son *Shlomo* reigned in his stead.

כח וַיָּמָת בְּשֵׂיבָה טוֹבָה שְׂבַע יָמִים עֹשֶׁר וְכָבוֹד וַיִּמְלֹךְ שְׁלֹמֹה בְנוֹ תַּחְתָּיו׃

29 The acts of King *David*, early and late, are recorded in the history of *Shmuel* the seer, the history of *Natan* the *Navi*, and the history of *Gad* the seer,

כט וְדִבְרֵי דָּוִיד הַמֶּלֶךְ הָרִאשֹׁנִים וְהָאַחֲרֹנִים הִנָּם כְּתוּבִים עַל־דִּבְרֵי שְׁמוּאֵל הָרֹאֶה וְעַל־דִּבְרֵי נָתָן הַנָּבִיא וְעַל־דִּבְרֵי גָּד הַחֹזֶה׃

30 together with all the mighty deeds of his kingship and the events that befell him and *Yisrael* and all the kingdoms of the earth.

ל עִם כָּל־מַלְכוּתוֹ וּגְבוּרָתוֹ וְהָעִתִּים אֲשֶׁר עָבְרוּ עָלָיו וְעַל־יִשְׂרָאֵל וְעַל כָּל־מַמְלְכוֹת הָאֲרָצוֹת׃

Divrei Hayamim II / II Chronicles
Chapter 1

דברי הימים ב
פרק א

א 1 Shlomo son of David took firm hold of his kingdom, for Hashem his God was with him and made him exceedingly great.

א וַיִּתְחַזֵּק שְׁלֹמֹה בֶן־דָּוִיד עַל־מַלְכוּתוֹ וַיהֹוָה אֱלֹהָיו עִמּוֹ וַיְגַדְּלֵהוּ לְמָעְלָה׃

2 Shlomo summoned all Yisrael – the officers of thousands and of hundreds, and the judges, and all the chiefs of all Yisrael, the heads of the clans.

ב וַיֹּאמֶר שְׁלֹמֹה לְכָל־יִשְׂרָאֵל לְשָׂרֵי הָאֲלָפִים וְהַמֵּאוֹת וְלַשֹּׁפְטִים וּלְכֹל נָשִׂיא לְכָל־יִשְׂרָאֵל רָאשֵׁי הָאָבוֹת׃

3 Then Shlomo, and all the assemblage with him, went to the shrine at Givon, for the Tent of Meeting, which Moshe the servant of Hashem had made in the wilderness, was there.

ג וַיֵּלְכוּ שְׁלֹמֹה וְכָל־הַקָּהָל עִמּוֹ לַבָּמָה אֲשֶׁר בְּגִבְעוֹן כִּי־שָׁם הָיָה אֹהֶל מוֹעֵד הָאֱלֹהִים אֲשֶׁר עָשָׂה מֹשֶׁה עֶבֶד־יְהֹוָה בַּמִּדְבָּר׃

4 But the Aron of Hashem David had brought up from Kiryat Ye'arim to the place which David had prepared for it; for he had pitched a tent for it in Yerushalayim.)

ד אֲבָל אֲרוֹן הָאֱלֹהִים הֶעֱלָה דָוִיד מִקִּרְיַת יְעָרִים בַּהֵכִין לוֹ דָּוִיד כִּי נָטָה־לוֹ אֹהֶל בִּירוּשָׁלָםִ׃

5 The bronze Mizbayach, which Betzalel son of Uri son of Chur had made, was also there before the Mishkan of Hashem, and Shlomo and the assemblage resorted to it.

ה וּמִזְבַּח הַנְּחֹשֶׁת אֲשֶׁר עָשָׂה בְּצַלְאֵל בֶּן־אוּרִי בֶן־חוּר שָׂם לִפְנֵי מִשְׁכַּן יְהֹוָה וַיִּדְרְשֵׁהוּ שְׁלֹמֹה וְהַקָּהָל׃

6 There Shlomo ascended the bronze Mizbayach before Hashem, which was at the Tent of Meeting, and on it sacrificed a thousand burnt offerings.

ו וַיַּעַל שְׁלֹמֹה שָׁם עַל־מִזְבַּח הַנְּחֹשֶׁת לִפְנֵי יְהֹוָה אֲשֶׁר לְאֹהֶל מוֹעֵד וַיַּעַל עָלָיו עֹלוֹת אָלֶף׃

7 That night, Hashem appeared to Shlomo and said to him, "Ask, what shall I grant you?"

ז בַּלַּיְלָה הַהוּא נִרְאָה אֱלֹהִים לִשְׁלֹמֹה וַיֹּאמֶר לוֹ שְׁאַל מָה אֶתֶּן־לָךְ׃

8 Shlomo said to Hashem, "You dealt most graciously with my father David, and now You have made me king in his stead.

ח וַיֹּאמֶר שְׁלֹמֹה לֵאלֹהִים אַתָּה עָשִׂיתָ עִם־דָּוִיד אָבִי חֶסֶד גָּדוֹל וְהִמְלַכְתַּנִי תַּחְתָּיו׃

9 Now, O Hashem, let Your promise to my father David be fulfilled; for You have made me king over a people as numerous as the dust of the earth.

ט עַתָּה יְהֹוָה אֱלֹהִים יֵאָמֵן דְּבָרְךָ עִם דָּוִיד אָבִי כִּי אַתָּה הִמְלַכְתַּנִי עַל־עַם רַב כַּעֲפַר הָאָרֶץ׃

10 Grant me then the wisdom and the knowledge to lead this people, for who can govern Your great people?"

י עַתָּה חָכְמָה וּמַדָּע תֶּן־לִי וְאֵצְאָה לִפְנֵי הָעָם־הַזֶּה וְאָבוֹאָה כִּי־מִי יִשְׁפֹּט אֶת־עַמְּךָ הַזֶּה הַגָּדוֹל׃

a-TAH khokh-MAH u-ma-DA ten LEE v'-AY-tz'-AH lif-NAY ha-am ha-ZEH v'-a-VO-ah kee MEE yish-POT et a-m'-KHA ha-ZEH ha-ga-DOL

1:10 For who can govern Your great people When given the opportunity to make a request of *Hashem*, *Shlomo* asks for wisdom and understanding to be able to judge the nation properly. Just as *David* his father "executed true justice among all his people" (I Chronicles 18:14) though he was "a man of battles and have shed blood" (Chronicles 28:3), *Shlomo's* reign will be similarly characterized by justice. While the wars to secure Israel's borders are significant, what personifies the Land of Israel in general, and the city of *Yerushalayim* in particular, is justice and righteousness (see, for example, Isaiah 33:5). Thus, *Eretz Yisrael* is inherited through justice (Deuter-

Supreme court in Jerusalem

Divrei Hayamim II / II Chronicles — Chapter 2

דברי הימים ב
פרק ב

11 Hashem said to Shlomo, "Because you want this, and have not asked for wealth, property, and glory, nor have you asked for the life of your enemy, or long life for yourself, but you have asked for the wisdom and the knowledge to be able to govern My people over whom I have made you king,

יא וַיֹּאמֶר־אֱלֹהִים לִשְׁלֹמֹה יַעַן אֲשֶׁר הָיְתָה זֹאת עִם־לְבָבֶךָ וְלֹא־שָׁאַלְתָּ עֹשֶׁר נְכָסִים וְכָבוֹד וְאֵת נֶפֶשׁ שֹׂנְאֶיךָ וְגַם־יָמִים רַבִּים לֹא שָׁאָלְתָּ וַתִּשְׁאַל־לְךָ חָכְמָה וּמַדָּע אֲשֶׁר תִּשְׁפּוֹט אֶת־עַמִּי אֲשֶׁר הִמְלַכְתִּיךָ עָלָיו:

12 wisdom and knowledge are granted to you, and I grant you also wealth, property, and glory, the like of which no king before you has had, nor shall any after you have."

יב הַחָכְמָה וְהַמַּדָּע נָתוּן לָךְ וְעֹשֶׁר וּנְכָסִים וְכָבוֹד אֶתֶּן־לָךְ אֲשֶׁר לֹא־הָיָה כֵן לַמְּלָכִים אֲשֶׁר לְפָנֶיךָ וְאַחֲרֶיךָ לֹא יִהְיֶה־כֵּן:

13 From the shrine at Givon, from the Tent of Meeting, Shlomo went to Yerushalayim and reigned over Yisrael.

יג וַיָּבֹא שְׁלֹמֹה לַבָּמָה אֲשֶׁר־בְּגִבְעוֹן יְרוּשָׁלִַם מִלִּפְנֵי אֹהֶל מוֹעֵד וַיִּמְלֹךְ עַל־יִשְׂרָאֵל:

14 Shlomo assembled chariots and horsemen; he had 1,400 chariots and 12,000 horses that he stationed in the chariot towns and with the king in Yerushalayim.

יד וַיֶּאֱסֹף שְׁלֹמֹה רֶכֶב וּפָרָשִׁים וַיְהִי־לוֹ אֶלֶף וְאַרְבַּע־מֵאוֹת רֶכֶב וּשְׁנֵים־עָשָׂר אֶלֶף פָּרָשִׁים וַיַּנִּיחֵם בְּעָרֵי הָרֶכֶב וְעִם־הַמֶּלֶךְ בִּירוּשָׁלִָם:

15 The king made silver and gold as plentiful in Yerushalayim as stones, and cedars as plentiful as the sycamores in the Shephelah.

טו וַיִּתֵּן הַמֶּלֶךְ אֶת־הַכֶּסֶף וְאֶת־הַזָּהָב בִּירוּשָׁלִַם כָּאֲבָנִים וְאֵת הָאֲרָזִים נָתַן כַּשִּׁקְמִים אֲשֶׁר־בַּשְּׁפֵלָה לָרֹב:

16 Shlomo's horses were imported from Egypt and from Que; the king's traders would buy them from Que at the market price.

טז וּמוֹצָא הַסּוּסִים אֲשֶׁר לִשְׁלֹמֹה מִמִּצְרָיִם וּמִקְוֵה סֹחֲרֵי הַמֶּלֶךְ מִקְוֵה יִקְחוּ בִמְחִיר:

17 A chariot imported from Egypt cost 600 shekalim of silver, and a horse 150. These in turn were exported by them to all the kings of the Hittites and the kings of the Arameans.

יז וַיַּעֲלוּ וַיּוֹצִיאוּ מִמִּצְרַיִם מֶרְכָּבָה בְּשֵׁשׁ מֵאוֹת כֶּסֶף וְסוּס בַּחֲמִשִּׁים וּמֵאָה וְכֵן לְכָל־מַלְכֵי הַחִתִּים וּמַלְכֵי אֲרָם בְּיָדָם יוֹצִיאוּ:

18 Then Shlomo resolved to build a House for the name of Hashem and a royal palace for himself.

יח וַיֹּאמֶר שְׁלֹמֹה לִבְנוֹת בַּיִת לְשֵׁם יְהוָה וּבַיִת לְמַלְכוּתוֹ:

2

1 Shlomo mustered 70,000 basket carriers and 80,000 quarriers in the hills, with 3,600 men supervising them.

ב א וַיִּסְפֹּר שְׁלֹמֹה שִׁבְעִים אֶלֶף אִישׁ סַבָּל וּשְׁמוֹנִים אֶלֶף אִישׁ חֹצֵב בָּהָר וּמְנַצְּחִים עֲלֵיהֶם שְׁלֹשֶׁת אֲלָפִים וְשֵׁשׁ מֵאוֹת:

---

onomy 16:20), justice allows for the land to flourish, and conversely, a lack of justice leads to its downfall and destruction. The *Beit Hamikdash*, built by *Shlomo*, is the seat of justice (Deuteronomy 17:8–10), and it is where the High Court would meet. In making this request of God, *Shlomo* sought to ensure that he would lead the Nation of Israel, in the Land of Israel, in justice and truth. Today, the State of Israel has an established judicial system which continues to pursue justice in the Holy Land, ensuring that the population is law-abiding and protecting the rights of its citizens. Like the High Court of old, Israel's Supreme Court is located in *Yerushalayim*.

Divrei Hayamim II/II Chronicles
Chapter 2

דברי הימים ב
פרק ב

2 *Shlomo* sent this message to King Huram of Tyre, "In view of what you did for my father *David* in sending him cedars to build a palace for his residence –

ב וַיִּשְׁלַח שְׁלֹמֹה אֶל־חוּרָם מֶלֶךְ־צֹר לֵאמֹר כַּאֲשֶׁר עָשִׂיתָ עִם־דָּוִיד אָבִי וַתִּשְׁלַח־לוֹ אֲרָזִים לִבְנוֹת־לוֹ בַיִת לָשֶׁבֶת בּוֹ:

3 see, I intend to build a House for the name of *Hashem* my God; I will dedicate it to Him for making incense offering of sweet spices in His honor, for the regular rows of bread, and for the morning and evening burnt offerings on *Shabbatot*, new moons, and festivals, as is *Yisrael*'s eternal duty.

ג הִנֵּה אֲנִי בוֹנֶה־בַּיִת לְשֵׁם יְהֹוָה אֱלֹהָי לְהַקְדִּישׁ לוֹ לְהַקְטִיר לְפָנָיו קְטֹרֶת סַמִּים וּמַעֲרֶכֶת תָּמִיד וְעֹלוֹת לַבֹּקֶר וְלָעֶרֶב לַשַּׁבָּתוֹת וְלֶחֳדָשִׁים וּלְמוֹעֲדֵי יְהֹוָה אֱלֹהֵינוּ לְעוֹלָם זֹאת עַל־יִשְׂרָאֵל:

hi-NAY a-NEE vo-neh BA-yit l'-SHAYM a-do-NAI e-lo-HAI l'-hak-DEESH LO l'-hak-TEER l'-fa-NAV k'-TO-ret sa-MEEM u-ma-a-RE-khet ta-MEED v'-o-LOT la-BO-ker v'-la-E-rev la-sha-ba-TOT v'-le-kho-da-SHEEM ul-mo-a-DAY a-do-NAI e-lo-HAY-nu l'-o-LAM ZOT al yis-ra-AYL

4 The House that I intend to build will be great, inasmuch as our God is greater than all gods.

ד וְהַבַּיִת אֲשֶׁר־אֲנִי בוֹנֶה גָּדוֹל כִּי־גָדוֹל אֱלֹהֵינוּ מִכָּל־הָאֱלֹהִים:

5 Who indeed is capable of building a House for Him! Even the heavens to their uttermost reaches cannot contain Him, and who am I that I should build Him a House – except as a place for making burnt offerings to Him?

ה וּמִי יַעֲצָר־כֹּחַ לִבְנוֹת־לוֹ בַיִת כִּי הַשָּׁמַיִם וּשְׁמֵי הַשָּׁמַיִם לֹא יְכַלְכְּלֻהוּ וּמִי אֲנִי אֲשֶׁר אֶבְנֶה־לּוֹ בַיִת כִּי אִם־לְהַקְטִיר לְפָנָיו:

6 Now send me a craftsman to work in gold, silver, bronze, and iron, and in purple, crimson, and blue yarn, and who knows how to engrave, alongside the craftsmen I have here in *Yehuda* and in *Yerushalayim*, whom my father *David* provided.

ו וְעַתָּה שְׁלַח־לִי אִישׁ־חָכָם לַעֲשׂוֹת בַּזָּהָב וּבַכֶּסֶף וּבַנְּחֹשֶׁת וּבַבַּרְזֶל וּבָאַרְגְּוָן וְכַרְמִיל וּתְכֵלֶת וְיֹדֵעַ לְפַתֵּחַ פִּתּוּחִים עִם־הַחֲכָמִים אֲשֶׁר עִמִּי בִּיהוּדָה וּבִירוּשָׁלַםִ אֲשֶׁר הֵכִין דָּוִיד אָבִי:

7 Send me cedars, cypress, and algum wood from the Lebanon, for I know that your servants are skilled at cutting the trees of Lebanon. My servants will work with yours

ז וּשְׁלַח־לִי עֲצֵי אֲרָזִים בְּרוֹשִׁים וְאַלְגּוּמִּים מֵהַלְּבָנוֹן כִּי אֲנִי יָדַעְתִּי אֲשֶׁר עֲבָדֶיךָ יוֹדְעִים לִכְרוֹת עֲצֵי לְבָנוֹן וְהִנֵּה עֲבָדַי עִם־עֲבָדֶיךָ:

8 to provide me with a great stock of timber; for the House that I intend to build will be singularly great.

ח וּלְהָכִין לִי עֵצִים לָרֹב כִּי הַבַּיִת אֲשֶׁר־אֲנִי בוֹנֶה גָּדוֹל וְהַפְלֵא:

2:3 New moons The Hebrew word for 'month' is *chodesh* (חודש), which comes from the word *chadash* (חדש), meaning 'new'. Sanctifying the new moon each month is the very first biblical commandment given collectively to the People of Israel (Exodus 12:2). As opposed to pagan worship, which requires a steady force such as the sun to venerate, the People of Israel were told to sanctify the moon which waxes and wanes on a monthly basis. The message is that no matter how dark life may seem, societies, nations and individuals can always change for the better. Our optimistic scanning of the black-blue skies for the first sliver of the new moon every month is our testimony to the possibility of growth, change and development. We must learn to sanctify that change.

חודש

Divrei Hayamim II/II Chronicles
Chapter 3

9 I have allocated for your servants, the wood-cutters who fell the trees, 20,000 *kor* of crushed wheat and 20,000 *kor* of barley, 20,000 *batim* of wine and 20,000 *batim* of oil."

10 Huram, king of Tyre, sent *Shlomo* this written message in reply, "Because *Hashem* loved His people, He made you king over them."

11 Huram continued, "Blessed is *Hashem*, God of *Yisrael*, who made the heavens and the earth, who gave King *David* a wise son, endowed with intelligence and understanding, to build a House for *Hashem* and a royal palace for himself.

12 Now I am sending you a skillful and intelligent man, my master Huram,

13 the son of a Danite woman, his father a Tyrian. He is skilled at working in gold, silver, bronze, iron, precious stones, and wood; in purple, blue, and crimson yarn and in fine linen; and at engraving and designing whatever will be required of him, alongside your craftsmen and the craftsmen of my lord, your father *David*.

14 As to the wheat, barley, oil, and wine which my lord mentioned, let him send them to his servants.

15 We undertake to cut down as many trees of Lebanon as you need, and deliver them to you as rafts by sea to Jaffa; you will transport them to *Yerushalayim*."

16 *Shlomo* took a census of all the aliens who were in the land of *Yisrael*, besides the census taken by his father *David*, and they were found to be 153,600.

17 He made 70,000 of them basket carriers, and 80,000 of them quarriers, with 3,600 supervisors to see that the people worked.

3 1 Then *Shlomo* began to build the House of *Hashem* in *Yerushalayim* on Mount *Moriah*, where [*Hashem*] had appeared to his father *David*, at the place which *David* had designated, at the threshing floor of Ornan the Jebusite.

2 He began to build on the second day of the second month of the fourth year of his reign.

Divrei Hayamim II/II Chronicles
Chapter 3

דברי הימים ב
פרק ג

3 These were the dimensions *Shlomo* established for building the House of *Hashem*: its length in *amot*, by the former measure, was 60, and its breadth was 20.

ג וְאֵלֶּה הוּסַד שְׁלֹמֹה לִבְנוֹת אֶת־בֵּית הָאֱלֹהִים הָאֹרֶךְ אַמּוֹת בַּמִּדָּה הָרִאשׁוֹנָה אַמּוֹת שִׁשִּׁים וְרֹחַב אַמּוֹת עֶשְׂרִים:

4 The length of the porch in front [was equal] to the breadth of the House – 20 *amot*, and its height was 120. Inside he overlaid it with pure gold.

ד וְהָאוּלָם אֲשֶׁר עַל־פְּנֵי הָאֹרֶךְ עַל־פְּנֵי רֹחַב־הַבַּיִת אַמּוֹת עֶשְׂרִים וְהַגֹּבַהּ מֵאָה וְעֶשְׂרִים וַיְצַפֵּהוּ מִפְּנִימָה זָהָב טָהוֹר:

5 The House itself he paneled with cypress wood. He overlaid it with fine gold and embossed on it palms and chains.

ה וְאֵת הַבַּיִת הַגָּדוֹל חִפָּה עֵץ בְּרוֹשִׁים וַיְחַפֵּהוּ זָהָב טוֹב וַיַּעַל עָלָיו תִּמֹרִים וְשַׁרְשְׁרוֹת:

6 He studded the House with precious stones for decoration; the gold was from Parvaim.

ו וַיְצַף אֶת־הַבַּיִת אֶבֶן יְקָרָה לְתִפְאָרֶת וְהַזָּהָב זְהַב פַּרְוָיִם:

7 He overlaid the House with gold – the beams, the thresholds, its walls and doors; he carved cherubim on the walls.

ז וַיְחַף אֶת־הַבַּיִת הַקֹּרוֹת הַסִּפִּים וְקִירוֹתָיו וְדַלְתוֹתָיו זָהָב וּפִתַּח כְּרוּבִים עַל־הַקִּירוֹת:

8 He made the Holy of Holies: its length was [equal to] the breadth of the house – 20 *amot*, and its breadth was 20 *amot*. He overlaid it with 600 *kikarim* of fine gold.

ח וַיַּעַשׂ אֶת־בֵּית־קֹדֶשׁ הַקֳּדָשִׁים אָרְכּוֹ עַל־פְּנֵי רֹחַב־הַבַּיִת אַמּוֹת עֶשְׂרִים וְרָחְבּוֹ אַמּוֹת עֶשְׂרִים וַיְחַפֵּהוּ זָהָב טוֹב לְכִכָּרִים שֵׁשׁ מֵאוֹת:

9 The weight of the nails was 50 *shekalim* of gold; the upper chambers he overlaid with gold.

ט וּמִשְׁקָל לְמִסְמְרוֹת לִשְׁקָלִים חֲמִשִּׁים זָהָב וְהָעֲלִיּוֹת חִפָּה זָהָב:

10 He made two sculptured cherubim in the Holy of Holies, and they were overlaid with gold.

י וַיַּעַשׂ בְּבֵית־קֹדֶשׁ הַקֳּדָשִׁים כְּרוּבִים שְׁנַיִם מַעֲשֵׂה צַעֲצֻעִים וַיְצַפּוּ אֹתָם זָהָב:

va-YA-as b'-VAYT KO-desh ha-ko-da-SHEEM k'-ru-VEEM sh'-NA-yim ma-a-SAY tza-a-tzu-EEM vai-tza-PU o-TAM za-HAV

11 The outspread wings of the cherubim were 20 *amot* across: one wing 5 *amot* long touching one wall of the House, and the other wing 5 *amot* long touching the wing of the other cherub;

יא וְכַנְפֵי הַכְּרוּבִים אָרְכָּם אַמּוֹת עֶשְׂרִים כְּנַף הָאֶחָד לְאַמּוֹת חָמֵשׁ מַגַּעַת לְקִיר הַבַּיִת וְהַכָּנָף הָאַחֶרֶת אַמּוֹת חָמֵשׁ מַגִּיעַ לִכְנַף הַכְּרוּב הָאַחֵר:

12 one wing of the other [cherub] 5 *amot* long extending to the other wall of the House, and its other wing 5 *amot* long touching the wing of the first cherub.

יב וּכְנַף הַכְּרוּב הָאֶחָד אַמּוֹת חָמֵשׁ מַגִּיעַ לְקִיר הַבָּיִת וְהַכָּנָף הָאַחֶרֶת אַמּוֹת חָמֵשׁ דְּבֵקָה לִכְנַף הַכְּרוּב הָאַחֵר:

3:10 He made two sculptured cherubim *Shlomo* builds two great cherubim in the Holy of Holies, paralleling the cherubim which God placed in front of the Garden of Eden "to guard the way to the tree of life" (Genesis 3:24). *Shlomo's* cherubim symbolize these guardians, showing that what lies behind them, the *Aron HaBrit*, holds the roots to the tree of life. The *Torah*, which is contained in the Ark, and the commandments therein are the pathway to life. As King *Shlomo* writes about the wisdom of the *Torah* "For they will bestow on you length of days, years of life and well-being," and, "she is a tree of life to those who grasp her" (Proverbs 3:2,18).

Divrei Hayamim II/II Chronicles
Chapter 4

דברי הימים ב
פרק ד

13 The wingspread of these cherubim was thus 20 *amot* across, and they were standing up facing the House.

יג כַּנְפֵי הַכְּרוּבִים הָאֵלֶּה פֹּרְשִׂים אַמּוֹת עֶשְׂרִים וְהֵם עֹמְדִים עַל־רַגְלֵיהֶם וּפְנֵיהֶם לַבָּיִת:

14 He made the curtain of blue, purple, and crimson yarn and fine linen, and he worked cherubim into it.

יד וַיַּעַשׂ אֶת־הַפָּרֹכֶת תְּכֵלֶת וְאַרְגָּמָן וְכַרְמִיל וּבוּץ וַיַּעַל עָלָיו כְּרוּבִים:

15 At the front of the House he made two columns 35 *amot* high; the capitals on top of them were 5 *amot* high.

טו וַיַּעַשׂ לִפְנֵי הַבַּיִת עַמּוּדִים שְׁנַיִם אַמּוֹת שְׁלֹשִׁים וְחָמֵשׁ אֹרֶךְ וְהַצֶּפֶת אֲשֶׁר־עַל־רֹאשׁוֹ אַמּוֹת חָמֵשׁ:

16 He made chainwork in the inner Sanctuary and set it on the top of the columns; he made a hundred pomegranates and set them into the chainwork.

טז וַיַּעַשׂ שַׁרְשְׁרוֹת בַּדְּבִיר וַיִּתֵּן עַל־רֹאשׁ הָעַמֻּדִים וַיַּעַשׂ רִמּוֹנִים מֵאָה וַיִּתֵּן בַּשַּׁרְשְׁרוֹת:

17 He erected the columns in front of the Great Hall, one to its right and one to its left; the one to the right was called Jachin, and the one to the left, Boaz.

יז וַיָּקֶם אֶת־הָעַמּוּדִים עַל־פְּנֵי הַהֵיכָל אֶחָד מִיָּמִין וְאֶחָד מֵהַשְּׂמֹאול וַיִּקְרָא שֵׁם־הַיְמָנִי [הַיְמִינִי] יָכִין וְשֵׁם הַשְּׂמָאלִי בֹּעַז:

4 1 He made a *Mizbayach* of bronze 20 *amot* long, 20 *amot* wide, and 10 *amot* high.

ד א וַיַּעַשׂ מִזְבַּח נְחֹשֶׁת עֶשְׂרִים אַמָּה אָרְכּוֹ וְעֶשְׂרִים אַמָּה רָחְבּוֹ וְעֶשֶׂר אַמּוֹת קוֹמָתוֹ:

2 He made the sea of cast metal 10 *amot* across from brim to brim, perfectly round; it was 5 *amot* high, and its circumference was 30 *amot*.

ב וַיַּעַשׂ אֶת־הַיָּם מוּצָק עֶשֶׂר בָּאַמָּה מִשְּׂפָתוֹ אֶל־שְׂפָתוֹ עָגוֹל סָבִיב וְחָמֵשׁ בָּאַמָּה קוֹמָתוֹ וְקָו שְׁלֹשִׁים בָּאַמָּה יָסֹב אֹתוֹ סָבִיב:

3 Beneath were figures of oxen set all around it, of 10 *amot*, encircling the sea; the oxen were in two rows, cast in one piece with it.

ג וּדְמוּת בְּקָרִים תַּחַת לוֹ סָבִיב סָבִיב סוֹבְבִים אֹתוֹ עֶשֶׂר בָּאַמָּה מַקִּיפִים אֶת־הַיָּם סָבִיב שְׁנַיִם טוּרִים הַבָּקָר יְצוּקִים בְּמֻצַקְתּוֹ:

4 It stood upon twelve oxen: three faced north, three faced west, three faced south, and three faced east, with the sea resting upon them; their haunches were all turned inward.

ד עוֹמֵד עַל־שְׁנֵים עָשָׂר בָּקָר שְׁלֹשָׁה פֹנִים צָפוֹנָה וּשְׁלוֹשָׁה פֹנִים יָמָּה וּשְׁלֹשָׁה פֹּנִים נֶגְבָּה וּשְׁלֹשָׁה פֹּנִים מִזְרָחָה וְהַיָּם עֲלֵיהֶם מִלְמָעְלָה וְכָל־אֲחֹרֵיהֶם בָּיְתָה:

5 It was a *tefach* thick, and its brim was made like that of a cup, like the petals of a lily. It held 3,000 *batim*.

ה וְעָבְיוֹ טֶפַח וּשְׂפָתוֹ כְּמַעֲשֵׂה שְׂפַת־כּוֹס פֶּרַח שׁוֹשַׁנָּה מַחֲזִיק בַּתִּים שְׁלֹשֶׁת אֲלָפִים יָכִיל:

6 He made ten bronze lavers for washing; he set five on the right and five on the left; they would rinse off in them the parts of the burnt offering; but the sea served the *Kohanim* for washing.

ו וַיַּעַשׂ כִּיּוֹרִים עֲשָׂרָה וַיִּתֵּן חֲמִשָּׁה מִיָּמִין וַחֲמִשָּׁה מִשְּׂמֹאול לְרָחְצָה בָהֶם אֶת־מַעֲשֵׂה הָעוֹלָה יָדִיחוּ בָם וְהַיָּם לְרָחְצָה לַכֹּהֲנִים בּוֹ:

7 He made ten *menorahs* of gold as prescribed, and placed them in the Great Hall, five on the right and five on the left.

ז וַיַּעַשׂ אֶת־מְנֹרוֹת הַזָּהָב עֶשֶׂר כְּמִשְׁפָּטָם וַיִּתֵּן בַּהֵיכָל חָמֵשׁ מִיָּמִין וְחָמֵשׁ מִשְּׂמֹאול:

Divrei Hayamim II/II Chronicles
Chapter 4

8 He made ten tables and placed them in the Great Hall, five on the right and five on the left. He made one hundred gold basins.

9 He built the court of the *Kohanim* and the great court, and doors for the great court; he overlaid the doors with bronze.

10 He set the sea on the right side, at the southeast corner.

11 Huram made the pails, the shovels, and the basins. With that Huram completed the work he had undertaken for King *Shlomo* in the House of *Hashem*:

12 the two columns, the globes, and the two capitals on top of the columns; and the two pieces of network to cover the two globes of the capitals on top of the columns;

13 the four hundred pomegranates for the two pieces of network, two rows of pomegranates for each network, to cover the two globes of the capitals on top of the columns;

14 he made the stands and the lavers upon the stands;

15 one sea with the twelve oxen beneath it;

16 the pails, the shovels, and the bowls. And all the vessels made for King *Shlomo* for the House of *Hashem* by Huram his master were of burnished bronze.

17 The king had them cast in molds dug out of the earth, in the plain of the *Yarden* between Succoth and Zeredah.

18 *Shlomo* made a very large number of vessels; the weight of the bronze used could not be reckoned.

19 And *Shlomo* made all the furnishings that were in the House of *Hashem*: the *Mizbayach* of gold; the tables for the bread of display;

20 the *menorah*s and their lamps, to burn as prescribed in front of the inner Sanctuary, of solid gold;

דברי הימים ב
פרק ד

ח וַיַּעַשׂ שֻׁלְחָנוֹת עֲשָׂרָה וַיַּנַּח בַּהֵיכָל חֲמִשָּׁה מִיָּמִין וַחֲמִשָּׁה מִשְּׂמֹאול וַיַּעַשׂ מִזְרְקֵי זָהָב מֵאָה:

ט וַיַּעַשׂ חֲצַר הַכֹּהֲנִים וְהָעֲזָרָה הַגְּדוֹלָה וּדְלָתוֹת לָעֲזָרָה וְדַלְתוֹתֵיהֶם צִפָּה נְחֹשֶׁת:

י וְאֶת־הַיָּם נָתַן מִכֶּתֶף הַיְמָנִית קֵדְמָה מִמּוּל נֶגְבָּה:

יא וַיַּעַשׂ חוּרָם אֶת־הַסִּירוֹת וְאֶת־הַיָּעִים וְאֶת־הַמִּזְרָקוֹת וַיְכַל חִירָם [חוּרָם] לַעֲשׂוֹת אֶת־הַמְּלָאכָה אֲשֶׁר עָשָׂה לַמֶּלֶךְ שְׁלֹמֹה בְּבֵית הָאֱלֹהִים:

יב עַמּוּדִים שְׁנַיִם וְהַגֻּלּוֹת וְהַכֹּתָרוֹת עַל־רֹאשׁ הָעַמּוּדִים שְׁתָּיִם וְהַשְּׂבָכוֹת שְׁתַּיִם לְכַסּוֹת אֶת־שְׁתֵּי גֻּלּוֹת הַכֹּתָרוֹת אֲשֶׁר עַל־רֹאשׁ הָעַמּוּדִים:

יג וְאֶת־הָרִמּוֹנִים אַרְבַּע מֵאוֹת לִשְׁתֵּי הַשְּׂבָכוֹת שְׁנַיִם טוּרִים רִמּוֹנִים לַשְּׂבָכָה הָאֶחָת לְכַסּוֹת אֶת־שְׁתֵּי גֻּלּוֹת הַכֹּתָרוֹת אֲשֶׁר עַל־פְּנֵי הָעַמּוּדִים:

יד וְאֶת־הַמְּכֹנוֹת עָשָׂה וְאֶת־הַכִּיֹּרוֹת עָשָׂה עַל־הַמְּכֹנוֹת:

טו אֶת־הַיָּם אֶחָד וְאֶת־הַבָּקָר שְׁנֵים־עָשָׂר תַּחְתָּיו:

טז וְאֶת־הַסִּירוֹת וְאֶת־הַיָּעִים וְאֶת־הַמִּזְלָגוֹת וְאֶת־כָּל־כְּלֵיהֶם עָשָׂה חוּרָם אָבִיו לַמֶּלֶךְ שְׁלֹמֹה לְבֵית יְהוָה נְחֹשֶׁת מָרוּק:

יז בְּכִכַּר הַיַּרְדֵּן יְצָקָם הַמֶּלֶךְ בַּעֲבִי הָאֲדָמָה בֵּין סֻכּוֹת וּבֵין צְרֵדָתָה:

יח וַיַּעַשׂ שְׁלֹמֹה כָּל־הַכֵּלִים הָאֵלֶּה לָרֹב מְאֹד כִּי לֹא נֶחְקַר מִשְׁקַל הַנְּחֹשֶׁת:

יט וַיַּעַשׂ שְׁלֹמֹה אֵת כָּל־הַכֵּלִים אֲשֶׁר בֵּית הָאֱלֹהִים וְאֵת מִזְבַּח הַזָּהָב וְאֶת־הַשֻּׁלְחָנוֹת וַעֲלֵיהֶם לֶחֶם הַפָּנִים:

כ וְאֶת־הַמְּנֹרוֹת וְנֵרֹתֵיהֶם לְבַעֲרָם כַּמִּשְׁפָּט לִפְנֵי הַדְּבִיר זָהָב סָגוּר:

Divrei Hayamim II / II Chronicles
Chapter 5

דברי הימים ב
פרק ה

v'-et ha-m'-no-ROT v'-nay-ro-tay-HEM l'-va-a-RAM ka-mish-PAT lif-NAY ha-d'-VEER za-HAV sa-GUR

21 and the petals, lamps, and tongs, of purest gold;

וְהַפֶּרַח וְהַנֵּרֹת וְהַמֶּלְקָחַיִם זָהָב הוּא מִכְלוֹת זָהָב: כא

22 the snuffers, basins, ladles, and fire pans, of solid gold; and the entrance to the House: the doors of the innermost part of the House, the Holy of Holies, and the doors of the Great Hall of the House, of gold.

וְהַמְזַמְּרוֹת וְהַמִּזְרָקוֹת וְהַכַּפּוֹת וְהַמַּחְתּוֹת זָהָב סָגוּר וּפֶתַח הַבַּיִת דַּלְתוֹתָיו הַפְּנִימִיּוֹת לְקֹדֶשׁ הַקֳּדָשִׁים וְדַלְתֵי הַבַּיִת לַהֵיכָל זָהָב: כב

5 1 When all the work that King *Shlomo* undertook for the House of *Hashem* was completed, *Shlomo* brought the things that his father *David* had consecrated – the silver, the gold, and the utensils – and deposited them in the treasury of the House of *Hashem*.

וַתִּשְׁלַם כָּל־הַמְּלָאכָה אֲשֶׁר־עָשָׂה שְׁלֹמֹה לְבֵית יְהוָה וַיָּבֵא שְׁלֹמֹה אֶת־קָדְשֵׁי דָּוִיד אָבִיו וְאֶת־הַכֶּסֶף וְאֶת־הַזָּהָב וְאֶת־כָּל־הַכֵּלִים נָתַן בְּאֹצְרוֹת בֵּית הָאֱלֹהִים: א

2 Then *Shlomo* convoked the elders of *Yisrael* – all the heads of the tribes and the ancestral chiefs of the Israelites – in *Yerushalayim*, to bring up the *Aron Brit Hashem* from the City of *David*, that is, *Tzion*.

אָז יַקְהֵיל שְׁלֹמֹה אֶת־זִקְנֵי יִשְׂרָאֵל וְאֶת־כָּל־רָאשֵׁי הַמַּטּוֹת נְשִׂיאֵי הָאָבוֹת לִבְנֵי יִשְׂרָאֵל אֶל־יְרוּשָׁלָ‍ִם לְהַעֲלוֹת אֶת־אֲרוֹן בְּרִית־יְהוָה מֵעִיר דָּוִיד הִיא צִיּוֹן: ב

3 All the men of *Yisrael* assembled before the king at the Feast, in the seventh month.

וַיִּקָּהֲלוּ אֶל־הַמֶּלֶךְ כָּל־אִישׁ יִשְׂרָאֵל בֶּחָג הוּא הַחֹדֶשׁ הַשְּׁבִעִי: ג

4 When all the elders of *Yisrael* had come, the *Leviim* carried the *Aron*.

וַיָּבֹאוּ כֹּל זִקְנֵי יִשְׂרָאֵל וַיִּשְׂאוּ הַלְוִיִּם אֶת־הָאָרוֹן: ד

5 They brought up the *Aron* and the Tent of Meeting and all the holy vessels that were in the Tent – the Levite *Kohanim* brought them up.

וַיַּעֲלוּ אֶת־הָאָרוֹן וְאֶת־אֹהֶל מוֹעֵד וְאֶת־כָּל־כְּלֵי הַקֹּדֶשׁ אֲשֶׁר בָּאֹהֶל הֶעֱלוּ אֹתָם הַכֹּהֲנִים הַלְוִיִּם: ה

6 Meanwhile, King *Shlomo* and the whole community of *Yisrael*, who had gathered to him before the *Aron*, were sacrificing sheep and oxen in such abundance that they could not be numbered or counted.

וְהַמֶּלֶךְ שְׁלֹמֹה וְכָל־עֲדַת יִשְׂרָאֵל הַנּוֹעָדִים עָלָיו לִפְנֵי הָאָרוֹן מְזַבְּחִים צֹאן וּבָקָר אֲשֶׁר לֹא־יִסָּפְרוּ וְלֹא יִמָּנוּ מֵרֹב: ו

Replica of the Temple menorah

4:20 To burn as prescribed The *menorah*, made of solid gold, was lit with pure olive oil and produced radiant light. The Talmud (*Menachot* 86b) states that the importance of the *menorah* in the *Beit Hamikdash* is that it showed that the Divine Presence rested among the People of Israel. As such, it was crucial that it be lit "as prescribed," a detail to which *Shlomo* attended. The light of the *menorah* is also symbolic of the Jewish Nation's duty to spread the light of *Torah* and God's will. The pure gold and olive oil are reflective of the pure intentions necessary to have a meaningful influence upon the entire world, for the sake of Heaven.

2067

Divrei Hayamim II / II Chronicles
Chapter 5

דברי הימים ב
פרק ה

7 The *Kohanim* brought the *Aron Brit Hashem* to its place in the inner Sanctuary of the House, in the Holy of Holies, beneath the wings of the cherubim;

ז וַיָּבִיאוּ הַכֹּהֲנִים אֶת־אֲרוֹן בְּרִית־יְהֹוָה אֶל־מְקוֹמוֹ אֶל־דְּבִיר הַבַּיִת אֶל־קֹדֶשׁ הַקֳּדָשִׁים אֶל־תַּחַת כַּנְפֵי הַכְּרוּבִים:

8 for the cherubim had their wings spread out over the place of the *Aron* so that the cherubim covered the *Aron* and its poles from above.

ח וַיִּהְיוּ הַכְּרוּבִים פֹּרְשִׂים כְּנָפַיִם עַל־מְקוֹם הָאָרוֹן וַיְכַסּוּ הַכְּרוּבִים עַל־הָאָרוֹן וְעַל־בַּדָּיו מִלְמָעְלָה:

9 The poles projected beyond the *Aron* and the ends of the poles were visible from the front of the inner Sanctuary, but they could not be seen from the outside; and there they remain to this day.

ט וַיַּאֲרִיכוּ הַבַּדִּים וַיֵּרָאוּ רָאשֵׁי הַבַּדִּים מִן־הָאָרוֹן עַל־פְּנֵי הַדְּבִיר וְלֹא יֵרָאוּ הַחוּצָה וַיְהִי־שָׁם עַד הַיּוֹם הַזֶּה:

10 There was nothing inside the *Aron* but the two tablets that *Moshe* placed [there] at Horeb, when *Hashem* made [a Covenant] with the Israelites after their departure from Egypt.

י אֵין בָּאָרוֹן רַק שְׁנֵי הַלֻּחוֹת אֲשֶׁר־נָתַן מֹשֶׁה בְּחֹרֵב אֲשֶׁר כָּרַת יְהֹוָה עִם־בְּנֵי יִשְׂרָאֵל בְּצֵאתָם מִמִּצְרָיִם:

11 When the *Kohanim* came out of the Sanctuary – all the *Kohanim* present had sanctified themselves, without keeping to the set divisions –

יא וַיְהִי בְּצֵאת הַכֹּהֲנִים מִן־הַקֹּדֶשׁ כִּי כׇּל־הַכֹּהֲנִים הַנִּמְצְאִים הִתְקַדָּשׁוּ אֵין לִשְׁמוֹר לְמַחְלְקוֹת:

12 all the Levite singers, *Asaf, Hayman, Yedutun,* their sons and their brothers, dressed in fine linen, holding cymbals, harps, and lyres, were standing to the east of the *Mizbayach*, and with them were 120 *Kohanim* who blew trumpets.

יב וְהַלְוִיִּם הַמְשֹׁרְרִים לְכֻלָּם לְאָסָף לְהֵימָן לִידֻתוּן וְלִבְנֵיהֶם וְלַאֲחֵיהֶם מְלֻבָּשִׁים בּוּץ בִּמְצִלְתַּיִם וּבִנְבָלִים וְכִנֹּרוֹת עֹמְדִים מִזְרָח לַמִּזְבֵּחַ וְעִמָּהֶם כֹּהֲנִים לְמֵאָה וְעֶשְׂרִים מַחְצְרִים [מַחְצְרִים] בַּחֲצֹצְרוֹת:

13 The trumpeters and the singers joined in unison to praise and extol *Hashem*; and as the sound of the trumpets, cymbals, and other musical instruments, and the praise of *Hashem*, "For He is good, for His steadfast love is eternal," grew louder, the House, the House of *Hashem*, was filled with a cloud.

יג וַיְהִי כְאֶחָד לַמְחַצְּרִים [לַמְחַצְּרִים] וְלַמְשֹׁרְרִים לְהַשְׁמִיעַ קוֹל־אֶחָד לְהַלֵּל וּלְהֹדוֹת לַיהֹוָה וּכְהָרִים קוֹל בַּחֲצֹצְרוֹת וּבִמְצִלְתַּיִם וּבִכְלֵי הַשִּׁיר וּבְהַלֵּל לַיהֹוָה כִּי טוֹב כִּי לְעוֹלָם חַסְדּוֹ וְהַבַּיִת מָלֵא עָנָן בֵּית יְהֹוָה:

14 The *Kohanim* could not stay and perform the service because of the cloud, for the glory of *Hashem* filled the House of *Hashem*.

יד וְלֹא־יָכְלוּ הַכֹּהֲנִים לַעֲמֹד לְשָׁרֵת מִפְּנֵי הֶעָנָן כִּי־מָלֵא כְבוֹד־יְהֹוָה אֶת־בֵּית הָאֱלֹהִים:

v'-lo ya-kh'-LU ha-ko-ha-NEEM la-a-MOD l'-sha-RAYT mi-p'-NAY he-a-NAN kee ma-LAY kh'-VOD a-do-NAI et BAYT ha-e-lo-HEEM

5:14 For the glory of *Hashem* filled the house of *Hashem* This description closely resembles that of the completion of the construction of the *Mishkan*: "*Moshe* could not enter the Tent of Meeting, because the cloud had settled upon it and the presence of *Hashem* filled the *Mishkan*" (Exodus 40:35). In both cases, a resting place for the Lord is built in the heart of the nation, and God's glory comes down to reside within it. In the desert, the *Mishkan* rests at the center of the Israelite camp. Here, the *Beit Hamikdash* is built on hallowed ground in the city of *Yerushalayim*. The concentration of His presence is a reminder that *Hashem* continuously dwells among His people.

2068

Divrei Hayamim II/II Chronicles
Chapter 6

6

1 Then *Shlomo* declared: "*Hashem* has chosen To abide in a thick cloud;

2 I have built for You A stately House, And a place where You May dwell forever."

3 Then, as the whole congregation of *Yisrael* stood, the king turned and blessed the whole congregation of *Yisrael*.

4 He said, "Blessed is God of *Yisrael*, who made a promise to my father *David* and fulfilled it. For He said,

5 'From the time I brought My people out of the land of Egypt, I never chose a city from among all the tribes of *Yisrael* to build a House where My name might abide; nor did I choose anyone to be the leader of my people *Yisrael*.

6 But then I chose *Yerushalayim* for My name to abide there, and I chose *David* to rule My people *Yisrael*.'

7 "Now my father *David* had wanted to build a House for the name of God of *Yisrael*.

8 But *Hashem* said to my father *David*, 'As for your wanting to build a House for My name, you do well to want that.

9 However, you shall not build the House; your son, the issue of your loins, he shall build the House for My name.'

10 Now *Hashem* has fulfilled the promise that He made. I have succeeded my father *David* and have ascended the throne of *Yisrael*, as *Hashem* promised. I have built the House for the name of God of *Yisrael*,

11 and there I have set the *Aron* containing the Covenant that *Hashem* made with the Israelites."

12 Then, standing before the *Mizbayach* of *Hashem* in front of the whole congregation of *Yisrael*, he spread forth his hands.

13 *Shlomo* had made a bronze platform and placed it in the midst of the Great Court; it was 5 *amot* long and 5 *amot* wide and 3 *amot* high. He stood on it; then, kneeling in front of the whole congregation of *Yisrael*, he spread forth his hands to heaven

דברי הימים ב
פרק ו

א אָז אָמַר שְׁלֹמֹה יְהוָה אָמַר לִשְׁכּוֹן בָּעֲרָפֶל:

ב וַאֲנִי בָּנִיתִי בֵית־זְבֻל לָךְ וּמָכוֹן לְשִׁבְתְּךָ עוֹלָמִים:

ג וַיַּסֵּב הַמֶּלֶךְ אֶת־פָּנָיו וַיְבָרֶךְ אֵת כָּל־קְהַל יִשְׂרָאֵל וְכָל־קְהַל יִשְׂרָאֵל עוֹמֵד:

ד וַיֹּאמֶר בָּרוּךְ יְהוָה אֱלֹהֵי יִשְׂרָאֵל אֲשֶׁר דִּבֶּר בְּפִיו אֵת דָּוִיד אָבִי וּבְיָדָיו מִלֵּא לֵאמֹר:

ה מִן־הַיּוֹם אֲשֶׁר הוֹצֵאתִי אֶת־עַמִּי מֵאֶרֶץ מִצְרַיִם לֹא־בָחַרְתִּי בְעִיר מִכֹּל שִׁבְטֵי יִשְׂרָאֵל לִבְנוֹת בַּיִת לִהְיוֹת שְׁמִי שָׁם וְלֹא־בָחַרְתִּי בְאִישׁ לִהְיוֹת נָגִיד עַל־עַמִּי יִשְׂרָאֵל:

ו וָאֶבְחַר בִּירוּשָׁלַ͏ִם לִהְיוֹת שְׁמִי שָׁם וָאֶבְחַר בְּדָוִיד לִהְיוֹת עַל־עַמִּי יִשְׂרָאֵל:

ז וַיְהִי עִם־לְבַב דָּוִיד אָבִי לִבְנוֹת בַּיִת לְשֵׁם יְהוָה אֱלֹהֵי יִשְׂרָאֵל:

ח וַיֹּאמֶר יְהוָה אֶל־דָּוִיד אָבִי יַעַן אֲשֶׁר הָיָה עִם־לְבָבְךָ לִבְנוֹת בַּיִת לִשְׁמִי הֱטִיבוֹתָ כִּי הָיָה עִם־לְבָבֶךָ:

ט רַק אַתָּה לֹא תִבְנֶה הַבָּיִת כִּי בִנְךָ הַיּוֹצֵא מֵחֲלָצֶיךָ הוּא־יִבְנֶה הַבַּיִת לִשְׁמִי:

י וַיָּקֶם יְהוָה אֶת־דְּבָרוֹ אֲשֶׁר דִּבֵּר וָאָקוּם תַּחַת דָּוִיד אָבִי וָאֵשֵׁב עַל־כִּסֵּא יִשְׂרָאֵל כַּאֲשֶׁר דִּבֶּר יְהוָה וָאֶבְנֶה הַבַּיִת לְשֵׁם יְהוָה אֱלֹהֵי יִשְׂרָאֵל:

יא וָאָשִׂים שָׁם אֶת־הָאָרוֹן אֲשֶׁר־שָׁם בְּרִית יְהוָה אֲשֶׁר כָּרַת עִם־בְּנֵי יִשְׂרָאֵל:

יב וַיַּעֲמֹד לִפְנֵי מִזְבַּח יְהוָה נֶגֶד כָּל־קְהַל יִשְׂרָאֵל וַיִּפְרֹשׂ כַּפָּיו:

יג כִּי־עָשָׂה שְׁלֹמֹה כִּיּוֹר נְחֹשֶׁת וַיִּתְּנֵהוּ בְּתוֹךְ הָעֲזָרָה חָמֵשׁ אַמּוֹת אָרְכּוֹ וְחָמֵשׁ אַמּוֹת רָחְבּוֹ וְאַמּוֹת שָׁלוֹשׁ קוֹמָתוֹ וַיַּעֲמֹד עָלָיו וַיִּבְרַךְ עַל־בִּרְכָּיו נֶגֶד כָּל־קְהַל יִשְׂרָאֵל וַיִּפְרֹשׂ כַּפָּיו הַשָּׁמָיְמָה:

Divrei Hayamim II / II Chronicles
Chapter 6

14 and said, "O God of *Yisrael*, there is no god like You in the heavens and on the earth, You who steadfastly maintain the Covenant with Your servants who walk before You with all their heart;

15 You who have kept the promises You made to Your servant, my father *David*; You made a promise and have fulfilled it – as is now the case.

16 And now, O God of *Yisrael*, keep that promise that You made to Your servant, my father *David*, 'You shall never lack a descendant in My sight sitting on the throne of *Yisrael* if only your children will look to their way and walk in the [path] of My teachings as you have walked before Me.'

17 Now, therefore, O God of *Yisrael*, let the promise that You made to Your servant, my father *David*, be confirmed.

18 "Does *Hashem* really dwell with man on earth? Even the heavens to their uttermost reaches cannot contain You; how much less this House that I have built!

19 Yet turn, *Hashem* my God, to the prayer and supplication of Your servant, and hear the cry and the prayer that Your servant offers to You.

20 May Your eyes be open day and night toward this House, toward the place where You have resolved to make Your name abide; may You heed the prayers that Your servant offers toward this place.

21 And when You hear the supplications that Your servant and Your people *Yisrael* offer toward this place, give heed in Your heavenly abode – give heed and pardon.

22 "If a man commits an offense against his fellow, and an oath is exacted from him, causing him to utter an imprecation against himself, and he comes with his imprecation before Your *Mizbayach* in this House,

23 may You hear in heaven and take action to judge Your servants, requiting him who is in the wrong by bringing down the punishment of his conduct on his head, vindicating him who is in the right by rewarding him according to his righteousness.

דברי הימים ב
פרק ו

יד וַיֹּאמֶר יְהֹוָה אֱלֹהֵי יִשְׂרָאֵל אֵין־כָּמוֹךָ אֱלֹהִים בַּשָּׁמַיִם וּבָאָרֶץ שֹׁמֵר הַבְּרִית וְהַחֶסֶד לַעֲבָדֶיךָ הַהֹלְכִים לְפָנֶיךָ בְּכָל־לִבָּם:

טו אֲשֶׁר שָׁמַרְתָּ לְעַבְדְּךָ דָּוִיד אָבִי אֵת אֲשֶׁר־דִּבַּרְתָּ לּוֹ וַתְּדַבֵּר בְּפִיךָ וּבְיָדְךָ מִלֵּאתָ כַּיּוֹם הַזֶּה:

טז וְעַתָּה יְהֹוָה אֱלֹהֵי יִשְׂרָאֵל שְׁמֹר לְעַבְדְּךָ דָוִיד אָבִי אֵת אֲשֶׁר דִּבַּרְתָּ לּוֹ לֵאמֹר לֹא־יִכָּרֵת לְךָ אִישׁ מִלְּפָנַי יוֹשֵׁב עַל־כִּסֵּא יִשְׂרָאֵל רַק אִם־יִשְׁמְרוּ בָנֶיךָ אֶת־דַּרְכָּם לָלֶכֶת בְּתוֹרָתִי כַּאֲשֶׁר הָלַכְתָּ לְפָנָי:

יז וְעַתָּה יְהֹוָה אֱלֹהֵי יִשְׂרָאֵל יֵאָמֵן דְּבָרְךָ אֲשֶׁר דִּבַּרְתָּ לְעַבְדְּךָ לְדָוִיד:

יח כִּי הַאֻמְנָם יֵשֵׁב אֱלֹהִים אֶת־הָאָדָם עַל־הָאָרֶץ הִנֵּה שָׁמַיִם וּשְׁמֵי הַשָּׁמַיִם לֹא יְכַלְכְּלוּךָ אַף כִּי־הַבַּיִת הַזֶּה אֲשֶׁר בָּנִיתִי:

יט וּפָנִיתָ אֶל־תְּפִלַּת עַבְדְּךָ וְאֶל־תְּחִנָּתוֹ יְהֹוָה אֱלֹהָי לִשְׁמֹעַ אֶל־הָרִנָּה וְאֶל־הַתְּפִלָּה אֲשֶׁר עַבְדְּךָ מִתְפַּלֵּל לְפָנֶיךָ:

כ לִהְיוֹת עֵינֶיךָ פְתֻחוֹת אֶל־הַבַּיִת הַזֶּה יוֹמָם וָלַיְלָה אֶל־הַמָּקוֹם אֲשֶׁר אָמַרְתָּ לָשׂוּם שִׁמְךָ שָׁם לִשְׁמוֹעַ אֶל־הַתְּפִלָּה אֲשֶׁר יִתְפַּלֵּל עַבְדְּךָ אֶל־הַמָּקוֹם הַזֶּה:

כא וְשָׁמַעְתָּ אֶל־תַּחֲנוּנֵי עַבְדְּךָ וְעַמְּךָ יִשְׂרָאֵל אֲשֶׁר יִתְפַּלְלוּ אֶל־הַמָּקוֹם הַזֶּה וְאַתָּה תִּשְׁמַע מִמְּקוֹם שִׁבְתְּךָ מִן־הַשָּׁמַיִם וְשָׁמַעְתָּ וְסָלָחְתָּ:

כב אִם־יֶחֱטָא אִישׁ לְרֵעֵהוּ וְנָשָׁא־בוֹ אָלָה לְהַאֲלֹתוֹ וּבָא אָלָה לִפְנֵי מִזְבַּחֲךָ בַּבַּיִת הַזֶּה:

כג וְאַתָּה תִּשְׁמַע מִן־הַשָּׁמַיִם וְעָשִׂיתָ וְשָׁפַטְתָּ אֶת־עֲבָדֶיךָ לְהָשִׁיב לְרָשָׁע לָתֵת דַּרְכּוֹ בְּרֹאשׁוֹ וּלְהַצְדִּיק צַדִּיק לָתֶת לוֹ כְּצִדְקָתוֹ:

Divrei Hayamim II/II Chronicles
Chapter 6

דברי הימים ב
פרק ו

24 "Should Your people *Yisrael* be defeated by an enemy because they have sinned against You, and then once again acknowledge Your name and offer prayer and supplication to You in this House,

כד וְאִם־יִנָּגֵף עַמְּךָ יִשְׂרָאֵל לִפְנֵי אוֹיֵב כִּי יֶחֶטְאוּ־לָךְ וְשָׁבוּ וְהוֹדוּ אֶת־שְׁמֶךָ וְהִתְפַּלְלוּ וְהִתְחַנְּנוּ לְפָנֶיךָ בַּבַּיִת הַזֶּה׃

25 may You hear in heaven and pardon the sin of Your people *Yisrael*, and restore them to the land that You gave to them and to their fathers.

כה וְאַתָּה תִּשְׁמַע מִן־הַשָּׁמַיִם וְסָלַחְתָּ לְחַטַּאת עַמְּךָ יִשְׂרָאֵל וַהֲשֵׁיבוֹתָם אֶל־הָאֲדָמָה אֲשֶׁר־נָתַתָּה לָהֶם וְלַאֲבֹתֵיהֶם׃

26 "Should the heavens be shut up and there be no rain because they have sinned against You, and then they pray toward this place and acknowledge Your name and repent of their sins, because You humbled them,

כו בְּהֵעָצֵר הַשָּׁמַיִם וְלֹא־יִהְיֶה מָטָר כִּי יֶחֶטְאוּ־לָךְ וְהִתְפַּלְלוּ אֶל־הַמָּקוֹם הַזֶּה וְהוֹדוּ אֶת־שְׁמֶךָ מֵחַטָּאתָם יְשׁוּבוּן כִּי תַעֲנֵם׃

27 may You hear in heaven and pardon the sin of Your servants, Your people *Yisrael*, when You have shown them the proper way in which they are to walk, and send down rain upon the land that You gave to Your people as their heritage.

כז וְאַתָּה תִּשְׁמַע הַשָּׁמַיִם וְסָלַחְתָּ לְחַטַּאת עֲבָדֶיךָ וְעַמְּךָ יִשְׂרָאֵל כִּי תוֹרֵם אֶל־הַדֶּרֶךְ הַטּוֹבָה אֲשֶׁר יֵלְכוּ־בָהּ וְנָתַתָּה מָטָר עַל־אַרְצְךָ אֲשֶׁר־נָתַתָּה לְעַמְּךָ לְנַחֲלָה׃

v'-a-TAH tish-MA ha-sha-MA-yim v'-SA-lakh-TA l'-kha-TAT a-va-DE-kha v'-a-m'-KHA yis-ra-AYL KEE to-RAYM el ha-DE-rekh ha-to-VAH a-SHER yay-l'-khu VAH v'-na-ta-TAH ma-TAR al ar-tz'-KHA a-sher na-TA-tah l'-a-m'-KHA l'-na-kha-LAH

28 So, too, if there is a famine in the land, if there is pestilence, blight, mildew, locusts, or caterpillars, or if an enemy oppresses them in any of the settlements of their land. "In any plague and in any disease,

כח רָעָב כִּי־יִהְיֶה בָאָרֶץ דֶּבֶר כִּי־יִהְיֶה שִׁדָּפוֹן וְיֵרָקוֹן אַרְבֶּה וְחָסִיל כִּי יִהְיֶה כִּי יָצַר־לוֹ אוֹיְבָיו בְּאֶרֶץ שְׁעָרָיו כָּל־נֶגַע וְכָל־מַחֲלָה׃

29 any prayer or supplication offered by any person among all Your people *Yisrael* – each of whom knows his affliction and his pain – when he spreads forth his hands toward this House,

כט כָּל־תְּפִלָּה כָל־תְּחִנָּה אֲשֶׁר יִהְיֶה לְכָל־הָאָדָם וּלְכֹל עַמְּךָ יִשְׂרָאֵל אֲשֶׁר יֵדְעוּ אִישׁ נִגְעוֹ וּמַכְאֹבוֹ וּפָרַשׂ כַּפָּיו אֶל־הַבַּיִת הַזֶּה׃

30 may You hear in Your heavenly abode, and pardon. Deal with each man according to his ways as You know his heart to be – for You alone know the hearts of all men –

ל וְאַתָּה תִּשְׁמַע מִן־הַשָּׁמַיִם מְכוֹן שִׁבְתֶּךָ וְסָלַחְתָּ וְנָתַתָּה לָאִישׁ כְּכָל־דְּרָכָיו אֲשֶׁר תֵּדַע אֶת־לְבָבוֹ כִּי אַתָּה לְבַדְּךָ יָדַעְתָּ אֶת־לְבַב בְּנֵי הָאָדָם׃

6:27 Pardon the sin of Your servants, Your people *Yisrael* In his prayer at the dedication of the *Beit Hamikdash*, *Shlomo* acknowledges that over time, the people will sin and will be punished, both as individuals and as a nation. He calls upon *Hashem* to bestow forgiveness on anyone who directs their prayers towards the *Beit Hamikdash* in *Yerushalayim*. The way to solve the problems of the Children of Israel and the Land of Israel is to face its spiritual center and pray to the true Owner of the land to forgive its inhabitants and inheritors. This is also the key to bringing salvation and redemption, as it says in verse 25, "restore them to the land that You gave to them and to their fathers." Throughout the ages, Jews have maintained the tradition of praying facing *Yerushalayim*, showing their eternal connection with their holy city and their belief in the fulfillment of *Shlomo's* prayer. God responds to *Shlomo* in the next chapter: "When My people, who bear My name, humble themselves, pray, and seek My favor and turn from their evil ways, I will hear in My heavenly abode and forgive their sins and heal their land" (7:14).

Divrei Hayamim II / II Chronicles
Chapter 6

31 so that they may revere You all the days that they live on the land that You gave to our fathers.

32 "Or if a foreigner who is not of Your people *Yisrael* comes from a distant land for the sake of Your great name, Your mighty hand, and Your outstretched arm, if he comes to pray toward this House,

33 may You hear in Your heavenly abode and grant whatever the foreigner appeals to You for. Thus all the peoples of the earth will know Your name and revere You, as does Your people *Yisrael*; and they will recognize that Your name is attached to this House that I have built.

34 "When Your people take the field against their enemies in a campaign on which You send them, and they pray to You in the direction of the city which You have chosen and the House which I have built to Your name,

35 may You hear in heaven their prayer and supplication and uphold their cause.

36 "When they sin against You – for there is no person who does not sin – and You are angry with them and deliver them to the enemy, and their captors carry them off to an enemy land, near or far;

37 and they take it to heart in the land to which they have been carried off, and repent and make supplication to You in the land of their captivity, saying, 'We have sinned, we have acted perversely, we have acted wickedly,'

38 and they turn back to You with all their heart and soul, in the land of their captivity where they were carried off, and pray in the direction of their land which You gave to their fathers and the city which You have chosen, and toward the House which I have built for Your name –

39 may You hear their prayer and supplication in Your heavenly abode, uphold their cause, and pardon Your people who have sinned against You.

40 Now My *Hashem*, may Your eyes be open and Your ears attentive to prayer from this place, and now,

דברי הימים ב
פרק ו

לא לְמַעַן יִירָאוּךָ לָלֶכֶת בִּדְרָכֶיךָ כָּל־הַיָּמִים אֲשֶׁר־הֵם חַיִּים עַל־פְּנֵי הָאֲדָמָה אֲשֶׁר נָתַתָּה לַאֲבֹתֵינוּ:

לב וְגַם אֶל־הַנָּכְרִי אֲשֶׁר לֹא מֵעַמְּךָ יִשְׂרָאֵל הוּא וּבָא מֵאֶרֶץ רְחוֹקָה לְמַעַן שִׁמְךָ הַגָּדוֹל וְיָדְךָ הַחֲזָקָה וּזְרוֹעֲךָ הַנְּטוּיָה וּבָאוּ וְהִתְפַּלְלוּ אֶל־הַבַּיִת הַזֶּה:

לג וְאַתָּה תִּשְׁמַע מִן־הַשָּׁמַיִם מִמְּכוֹן שִׁבְתֶּךָ וְעָשִׂיתָ כְּכֹל אֲשֶׁר־יִקְרָא אֵלֶיךָ הַנָּכְרִי לְמַעַן יֵדְעוּ כָל־עַמֵּי הָאָרֶץ אֶת־שְׁמֶךָ וּלְיִרְאָה אֹתְךָ כְּעַמְּךָ יִשְׂרָאֵל וְלָדַעַת כִּי־שִׁמְךָ נִקְרָא עַל־הַבַּיִת הַזֶּה אֲשֶׁר בָּנִיתִי:

לד כִּי־יֵצֵא עַמְּךָ לַמִּלְחָמָה עַל־אוֹיְבָיו בַּדֶּרֶךְ אֲשֶׁר תִּשְׁלָחֵם וְהִתְפַּלְלוּ אֵלֶיךָ דֶּרֶךְ הָעִיר הַזֹּאת אֲשֶׁר בָּחַרְתָּ בָּהּ וְהַבַּיִת אֲשֶׁר־בָּנִיתִי לִשְׁמֶךָ:

לה וְשָׁמַעְתָּ מִן־הַשָּׁמַיִם אֶת־תְּפִלָּתָם וְאֶת־תְּחִנָּתָם וְעָשִׂיתָ מִשְׁפָּטָם:

לו כִּי יֶחֱטְאוּ־לָךְ כִּי אֵין אָדָם אֲשֶׁר לֹא־יֶחֱטָא וְאָנַפְתָּ בָם וּנְתַתָּם לִפְנֵי אוֹיֵב וְשָׁבוּם שׁוֹבֵיהֶם אֶל־אֶרֶץ רְחוֹקָה אוֹ קְרוֹבָה:

לז וְהֵשִׁיבוּ אֶל־לְבָבָם בָּאָרֶץ אֲשֶׁר נִשְׁבּוּ־שָׁם וְשָׁבוּ וְהִתְחַנְּנוּ אֵלֶיךָ בְּאֶרֶץ שִׁבְיָם לֵאמֹר חָטָאנוּ הֶעֱוִינוּ וְרָשָׁעְנוּ:

לח וְשָׁבוּ אֵלֶיךָ בְּכָל־לִבָּם וּבְכָל־נַפְשָׁם בְּאֶרֶץ שִׁבְיָם אֲשֶׁר־שָׁבוּ אֹתָם וְהִתְפַּלְלוּ דֶּרֶךְ אַרְצָם אֲשֶׁר נָתַתָּה לַאֲבוֹתָם וְהָעִיר אֲשֶׁר בָּחַרְתָּ וְלַבַּיִת אֲשֶׁר־בָּנִיתִי לִשְׁמֶךָ:

לט וְשָׁמַעְתָּ מִן־הַשָּׁמַיִם מִמְּכוֹן שִׁבְתְּךָ אֶת־תְּפִלָּתָם וְאֶת־תְּחִנֹּתֵיהֶם וְעָשִׂיתָ מִשְׁפָּטָם וְסָלַחְתָּ לְעַמְּךָ אֲשֶׁר חָטְאוּ־לָךְ:

מ עַתָּה אֱלֹהַי יִהְיוּ־נָא עֵינֶיךָ פְּתֻחוֹת וְאָזְנֶיךָ קַשֻּׁבוֹת לִתְפִלַּת הַמָּקוֹם הַזֶּה:

Divrei Hayamim II / II Chronicles — Chapter 7

41 Advance, O *Hashem*, to your resting-place, You and Your mighty *Aron*. Your *Kohanim*, O *Hashem*, are clothed in triumph; Your loyal ones will rejoice in [Your] goodness.

42 O *Hashem*, do not reject Your anointed one; remember the loyalty of Your servant *David*."

7

1 When *Shlomo* finished praying, fire descended from heaven and consumed the burnt offering and the sacrifices, and the glory of *Hashem* filled the House.

2 The *Kohanim* could not enter the House of *Hashem*, for the glory of *Hashem* filled the House of *Hashem*.

3 All the Israelites witnessed the descent of the fire and the glory of *Hashem* on the House; they knelt with their faces to the ground and prostrated themselves, praising *Hashem*, "For He is good, for His steadfast love is eternal."

4 Then the king and all the people offered sacrifices before *Hashem*.

5 King *Shlomo* offered as sacrifices 22,000 oxen and 120,000 sheep; thus the king and all the people dedicated the House of *Hashem*.

6 The *Kohanim* stood at their watches; the *Leviim* with the instruments for *Hashem*'s music that King *David* had made to praise *Hashem*, "For His steadfast love is eternal," by means of the psalms of *David* that they knew. The *Kohanim* opposite them blew trumpets while all *Yisrael* were standing.

7 *Shlomo* consecrated the center of the court in front of the House of *Hashem*, because he presented there the burnt offerings and the fat parts of the offerings of well-being, since the bronze *Mizbayach* that *Shlomo* had made was not able to hold the burnt offerings, the meal offerings, and the fat parts.

8 At that time *Shlomo* kept the Feast for seven days – all *Yisrael* with him – a great assemblage from Lebo-hamath to the Wadi of Egypt.

9 On the eighth day they held a solemn gathering; they observed the dedication of the *Mizbayach* seven days, and the Feast seven days.

דברי הימים ב

פרק ז

מא וְעַתָּה קוּמָה יְהֹוָה אֱלֹהִים לְנוּחֶךָ אַתָּה וַאֲרוֹן עֻזֶּךָ כֹּהֲנֶיךָ יְהֹוָה אֱלֹהִים יִלְבְּשׁוּ תְשׁוּעָה וַחֲסִידֶיךָ יִשְׂמְחוּ בַטּוֹב:

מב יְהֹוָה אֱלֹהִים אַל־תָּשֵׁב פְּנֵי מְשִׁיחֶיךָ זָכְרָה לְחַסְדֵי דָּוִיד עַבְדֶּךָ:

א וּכְכַלּוֹת שְׁלֹמֹה לְהִתְפַּלֵּל וְהָאֵשׁ יָרְדָה מֵהַשָּׁמַיִם וַתֹּאכַל הָעֹלָה וְהַזְּבָחִים וּכְבוֹד יְהֹוָה מָלֵא אֶת־הַבָּיִת:

ב וְלֹא יָכְלוּ הַכֹּהֲנִים לָבוֹא אֶל־בֵּית יְהֹוָה כִּי־מָלֵא כְבוֹד־יְהֹוָה אֶת־בֵּית יְהֹוָה:

ג וְכֹל בְּנֵי יִשְׂרָאֵל רֹאִים בְּרֶדֶת הָאֵשׁ וּכְבוֹד יְהֹוָה עַל־הַבָּיִת וַיִּכְרְעוּ אַפַּיִם אַרְצָה עַל־הָרִצְפָה וַיִּשְׁתַּחֲווּ וְהוֹדוֹת לַיהֹוָה כִּי טוֹב כִּי לְעוֹלָם חַסְדּוֹ:

ד וְהַמֶּלֶךְ וְכָל־הָעָם זֹבְחִים זֶבַח לִפְנֵי יְהֹוָה:

ה וַיִּזְבַּח הַמֶּלֶךְ שְׁלֹמֹה אֶת־זֶבַח הַבָּקָר עֶשְׂרִים וּשְׁנַיִם אֶלֶף וְצֹאן מֵאָה וְעֶשְׂרִים אָלֶף וַיַּחְנְכוּ אֶת־בֵּית הָאֱלֹהִים הַמֶּלֶךְ וְכָל־הָעָם:

ו וְהַכֹּהֲנִים עַל־מִשְׁמְרוֹתָם עֹמְדִים וְהַלְוִיִּם בִּכְלֵי־שִׁיר יְהֹוָה אֲשֶׁר עָשָׂה דָּוִיד הַמֶּלֶךְ לְהֹדוֹת לַיהֹוָה כִּי־לְעוֹלָם חַסְדּוֹ בְּהַלֵּל דָּוִיד בְּיָדָם וְהַכֹּהֲנִים מַחְצְרִים [מַחְצְצְרִים] נֶגְדָּם וְכָל־יִשְׂרָאֵל עֹמְדִים:

ז וַיְקַדֵּשׁ שְׁלֹמֹה אֶת־תּוֹךְ הֶחָצֵר אֲשֶׁר לִפְנֵי בֵית־יְהֹוָה כִּי־עָשָׂה שָׁם הָעֹלוֹת וְאֵת חֶלְבֵי הַשְּׁלָמִים כִּי־מִזְבַּח הַנְּחֹשֶׁת אֲשֶׁר עָשָׂה שְׁלֹמֹה לֹא יָכוֹל לְהָכִיל אֶת־הָעֹלָה וְאֶת־הַמִּנְחָה וְאֶת־הַחֲלָבִים:

ח וַיַּעַשׂ שְׁלֹמֹה אֶת־הֶחָג בָּעֵת הַהִיא שִׁבְעַת יָמִים וְכָל־יִשְׂרָאֵל עִמּוֹ קָהָל גָּדוֹל מְאֹד מִלְּבוֹא חֲמָת עַד־נַחַל מִצְרָיִם:

ט וַיַּעֲשׂוּ בַּיּוֹם הַשְּׁמִינִי עֲצָרֶת כִּי חֲנֻכַּת הַמִּזְבֵּחַ עָשׂוּ שִׁבְעַת יָמִים וְהֶחָג שִׁבְעַת יָמִים:

Divrei Hayamim II / II Chronicles
Chapter 7

דברי הימים ב
פרק ז

10 On the twenty-third day of the seventh month he dismissed the people to their homes, rejoicing and in good spirits over the goodness that *Hashem* had shown to *David* and *Shlomo* and His people *Yisrael*.

י וּבְיוֹם עֶשְׂרִים וּשְׁלֹשָׁה לַחֹדֶשׁ הַשְּׁבִיעִי שִׁלַּח אֶת־הָעָם לְאָהֳלֵיהֶם שְׂמֵחִים וְטוֹבֵי לֵב עַל־הַטּוֹבָה אֲשֶׁר עָשָׂה יְהֹוָה לְדָוִיד וְלִשְׁלֹמֹה וּלְיִשְׂרָאֵל עַמּוֹ:

11 Thus *Shlomo* finished building the House of *Hashem* and the royal palace; *Shlomo* succeeded in everything he had set his heart on accomplishing with regard to the House of *Hashem* and his palace.

יא וַיְכַל שְׁלֹמֹה אֶת־בֵּית יְהֹוָה וְאֶת־בֵּית הַמֶּלֶךְ וְאֵת כָּל־הַבָּא עַל־לֵב שְׁלֹמֹה לַעֲשׂוֹת בְּבֵית־יְהֹוָה וּבְבֵיתוֹ הִצְלִיחַ:

12 *Hashem* appeared to *Shlomo* at night and said to him, "I have heard your prayer and have chosen this site as My House of sacrifice.

יב וַיֵּרָא יְהֹוָה אֶל־שְׁלֹמֹה בַּלָּיְלָה וַיֹּאמֶר לוֹ שָׁמַעְתִּי אֶת־תְּפִלָּתֶךָ וּבָחַרְתִּי בַּמָּקוֹם הַזֶּה לִי לְבֵית זָבַח:

13 If I shut up the heavens and there is no rain; if I command the locusts to ravage the land; or if I let loose pestilence against My people,

יג הֵן אֶעֱצֹר הַשָּׁמַיִם וְלֹא־יִהְיֶה מָטָר וְהֵן־אֲצַוֶּה עַל־חָגָב לֶאֱכוֹל הָאָרֶץ וְאִם־אֲשַׁלַּח דֶּבֶר בְּעַמִּי:

14 when My people, who bear My name, humble themselves, pray, and seek My favor and turn from their evil ways, I will hear in My heavenly abode and forgive their sins and heal their land.

יד וְיִכָּנְעוּ עַמִּי אֲשֶׁר נִקְרָא־שְׁמִי עֲלֵיהֶם וְיִתְפַּלְלוּ וִיבַקְשׁוּ פָנַי וְיָשֻׁבוּ מִדַּרְכֵיהֶם הָרָעִים וַאֲנִי אֶשְׁמַע מִן־הַשָּׁמַיִם וְאֶסְלַח לְחַטָּאתָם וְאֶרְפָּא אֶת־אַרְצָם:

v'-yi-ka-n'-U a-MEE a-SHER nik-ra sh'-MEE a-lay-HEM v'-yit-pa-l'-LU vee-vak-SHU fa-NAI v'-ya-SHU-vu mi-dar-khay-HEM ha-ra-EEM va-a-NEE esh-MA min ha-sha-MA-yim v'-es-LAKH l'-kha-ta-TAM v'-er-PA et ar-TZAM

15 Now My eyes will be open and My ears attentive to the prayers from this place.

טו עַתָּה עֵינַי יִהְיוּ פְתֻחוֹת וְאָזְנַי קַשֻּׁבוֹת לִתְפִלַּת הַמָּקוֹם הַזֶּה:

16 And now I have chosen and consecrated this House that My name be there forever. My eyes and My heart shall always be there.

טז וְעַתָּה בָּחַרְתִּי וְהִקְדַּשְׁתִּי אֶת־הַבַּיִת הַזֶּה לִהְיוֹת־שְׁמִי שָׁם עַד־עוֹלָם וְהָיוּ עֵינַי וְלִבִּי שָׁם כָּל־הַיָּמִים:

17 As for you, if you walk before Me as your father *David* walked before Me, doing all that I have commanded you, keeping My laws and rules,

יז וְאַתָּה אִם־תֵּלֵךְ לְפָנַי כַּאֲשֶׁר הָלַךְ דָּוִיד אָבִיךָ וְלַעֲשׂוֹת כְּכֹל אֲשֶׁר צִוִּיתִיךָ וְחֻקַּי וּמִשְׁפָּטַי תִּשְׁמוֹר:

18 then I will establish your royal throne over *Yisrael* forever, in accordance with the Covenant I made with your father *David*, saying, 'You shall never lack a descendant ruling over *Yisrael*.'

יח וַהֲקִימוֹתִי אֵת כִּסֵּא מַלְכוּתֶךָ כַּאֲשֶׁר כָּרַתִּי לְדָוִיד אָבִיךָ לֵאמֹר לֹא־יִכָּרֵת לְךָ אִישׁ מוֹשֵׁל בְּיִשְׂרָאֵל:

19 But if you turn away from Me and forsake My laws and commandments that I set before you, and go and serve other gods and worship them,

יט וְאִם־תְּשׁוּבוּן אַתֶּם וַעֲזַבְתֶּם חֻקּוֹתַי וּמִצְוֺתַי אֲשֶׁר נָתַתִּי לִפְנֵיכֶם וַהֲלַכְתֶּם וַעֲבַדְתֶּם אֱלֹהִים אֲחֵרִים וְהִשְׁתַּחֲוִיתֶם לָהֶם:

7:14 Forgive their sins and heal their land The Children of Israel are God's chosen people, and the Land of Israel is His chosen land. The people's conduct directly influences what happens in the land, since *Hashem* responds to them with reward or punishment as appropriate. As such, the people feel a great attachment to the land, since it is through the land that God communicates whether or not His people are following His will.

Divrei Hayamim II / II Chronicles
Chapter 8

20 then I will uproot them from My land that I gave them, and this House that I consecrated to My name I shall cast out of my sight, and make it a proverb and a byword among all peoples.

21 And as for this House, once so exalted, everyone passing by it shall be appalled and say, 'Why did *Hashem* do thus to this land and to this House?'

22 And the reply will be, 'It is because they forsook God of their fathers who freed them from the land of Egypt, and adopted other gods and worshiped them and served them; therefore He brought all this calamity upon them.'"

8

1 At the end of twenty years, during which *Shlomo* constructed the House of *Hashem* and his palace –

2 *Shlomo* also rebuilt the cities that Huram had given to him, and settled Israelites in them –

3 *Shlomo* marched against Hamath-zobah and overpowered it.

4 He built Tadmor in the desert and all the garrison towns that he built in Hamath.

5 He built Upper Beth-horon and Lower Beth-horon as fortified cities with walls, gates, and bars,

6 as well as Baalath and all of *Shlomo*'s garrison towns, chariot towns, and cavalry towns – everything that *Shlomo* desired to build in *Yerushalayim* and in the Lebanon, and throughout the territory that he ruled.

7 All the people that were left of the Hittites, Amorites, Perizzites, Hivites, and Jebusites, none of whom were of Israelite stock –

8 those of their descendants who were left after them in the land, whom the Israelites had not annihilated – these *Shlomo* subjected to forced labor, as is still the case.

9 But the Israelites, none of whom *Shlomo* enslaved for his works, served as soldiers and as his chief officers, and as commanders of his chariotry and cavalry.

Divrei Hayamim II / II Chronicles
Chapter 8

דברי הימים ב
פרק ח

10 These were King *Shlomo*'s prefects – 250 foremen over the people.

י וְאֵ֨לֶּה שָׂרֵ֧י הנציבים [הַנִּצָּבִ֛ים] אֲשֶׁר־לַמֶּ֥לֶךְ שְׁלֹמֹ֖ה חֲמִשִּׁ֣ים וּמָאתָ֑יִם הָרֹדִ֖ים בָּעָֽם׃

11 *Shlomo* brought up Pharaoh's daughter from the City of *David* to the palace that he had built for her, for he said, "No wife of mine shall dwell in a palace of King *David* of *Yisrael*, for [the area] is sacred since the *Aron* of *Hashem* has entered it."

יא וְאֶת־בַּת־פַּרְעֹ֗ה הֶעֱלָ֤ה שְׁלֹמֹה֙ מֵעִ֣יר דָּוִ֔יד לַבַּ֖יִת אֲשֶׁ֣ר בָּֽנָה־לָ֑הּ כִּ֣י אָמַ֗ר לֹא־תֵשֵׁ֨ב אִשָּׁ֥ה לִי֙ בְּבֵ֙ית֙ דָּוִ֣יד מֶֽלֶךְ־יִשְׂרָאֵ֔ל כִּי־קֹ֣דֶשׁ הֵ֔מָּה אֲשֶׁר־בָּ֥אָה אֲלֵיהֶ֖ם אֲר֥וֹן יְהֹוָֽה׃

12 At that time, *Shlomo* offered burnt offerings on the *Mizbayach* that he had built in front of the porch.

יב אָ֣ז הֶעֱלָ֧ה שְׁלֹמֹ֛ה עֹל֖וֹת לַיהֹוָ֑ה עַ֚ל מִזְבַּ֣ח יְהֹוָ֔ה אֲשֶׁ֥ר בָּנָ֖ה לִפְנֵ֥י הָאוּלָֽם׃

AZ he-e-LAH sh'-lo-MOH o-LOT la-do-NAI AL miz-BAKH a-do-NAI a-SHER ba-NAH lif-NAY ha-u-LAM

13 What was due for each day he sacrificed according to the commandment of *Moshe* for the *Shabbatot*, the new moons, and the thrice-yearly festivals – the festival of *Pesach*, the festival of *Shavuot*, and the festival of *Sukkot*.

יג וּבִדְבַר־י֣וֹם בְּי֗וֹם לְהַעֲלוֹת֙ כְּמִצְוַ֣ת מֹשֶׁ֔ה לַשַּׁבָּת֖וֹת וְלֶחֳדָשִׁ֑ים וְלַמּ֣וֹעֲד֔וֹת שָׁל֥וֹשׁ פְּעָמִ֖ים בַּשָּׁנָ֑ה בְּחַ֧ג הַמַּצּ֛וֹת וּבְחַ֥ג הַשָּׁבֻע֖וֹת וּבְחַ֥ג הַסֻּכּֽוֹת׃

14 Following the prescription of his father *David*, he set up the divisions of the *Kohanim* for their duties, and the *Leviim* for their watches, to praise and to serve alongside the *Kohanim*, according to each day's requirement, and the gatekeepers in their watches, gate by gate, for such was the commandment of *David*, the man of *Hashem*.

יד וַיַּעֲמֵ֣ד כְּמִשְׁפַּ֣ט דָּוִיד־אָ֠בִ֠יו אֶת־מַחְלְק֨וֹת הַכֹּהֲנִ֜ים עַל־עֲבֹדָתָ֗ם וְהַלְוִיִּ֣ם עַל־מִשְׁמְרוֹתָם֩ לְהַלֵּ֨ל וּלְשָׁרֵ֜ת נֶ֤גֶד הַכֹּהֲנִים֙ לִדְבַר־י֣וֹם בְּיוֹמ֔וֹ וְהַשּׁוֹעֲרִ֥ים בְּמַחְלְקוֹתָ֖ם לְשַׁ֣עַר וָשָׁ֑עַר כִּ֣י כֵ֔ן מִצְוַ֖ת דָּוִ֥יד אִישׁ־הָאֱלֹהִֽים׃

15 They did not depart from the commandment of the king relating to the *Kohanim* and the *Leviim* in all these matters and also relating to the treasuries.

טו וְלֹ֣א סָ֩רוּ֩ מִצְוַ֨ת הַמֶּ֜לֶךְ עַל־הַכֹּהֲנִ֧ים וְהַלְוִיִּ֛ם לְכָל־דָּבָ֖ר וְלָאֹצָרֽוֹת׃

16 And all of *Shlomo*'s work was well executed from the day the House of *Hashem* was founded until the House of *Hashem* was completed to perfection.

טז וַתִּכֹּן֙ כָּל־מְלֶ֣אכֶת שְׁלֹמֹ֔ה עַד־הַיּ֛וֹם מוּסַ֥ד בֵּית־יְהֹוָ֖ה וְעַד־כְּלֹת֑וֹ שָׁלֵ֖ם בֵּ֥ית יְהֹוָֽה׃

17 At that time *Shlomo* went to Ezion-geber and to Eloth on the seacoast of the land of Edom.

יז אָז֩ הָלַ֨ךְ שְׁלֹמֹ֜ה לְעֶצְיֽוֹן־גֶּ֧בֶר וְאֶל־אֵיל֛וֹת עַל־שְׂפַ֥ת הַיָּ֖ם בְּאֶ֥רֶץ אֱדֽוֹם׃

8:12 On the *Mizbayach* Once the construction of the *Beit Hamikdash* was completed, it became forbidden to offer sacrifices to the Lord anywhere else. Though the entire Land of Israel is holy, God desires that His people unite to serve him in one single center of worship. It is in *Yerushalayim* that the daily offerings, as well as individual offerings and the communal offerings of the *Shabbat* and festivals, are to be brought. According to Rabbi Yitzchak Abrabanel, having one central place of worship is a constant reminder of the unity of God. In his words, "The oneness of the altar and the Temple point to the oneness of *Hashem*, Who governs and watches over them." This was especially important in the ancient pagan world in which the Israelites lived. Indeed, when *Yerovam* established alternate places of worship to prevent his subjects in the northern Kingdom from worshipping in the *Beit Hamikdash*, this quickly led to idolatry (I Kings 12:28–30). Today, in the absence of the Temple, we may pray to *Hashem* wherever we find ourselves. But our prayers are always directed towards the *Har HaBayit*, the place where the *Beit Hamikdash* once stood and will again stand in the future.

The Temple Mount

Divrei Hayamim II/II Chronicles
Chapter 9

דברי הימים ב
פרק ט

18 Huram sent him, under the charge of servants, a fleet with a crew of expert seamen; they went with *Shlomo*'s men to Ophir, and obtained gold there in the amount of 450 *kikarim*, which they brought to King *Shlomo*.

יח וַיִּשְׁלַח־לוֹ חוּרָם בְּיַד־עֲבָדָיו אֳנִיּוֹת [אֳנִיּוֹת] וַעֲבָדִים יוֹדְעֵי יָם וַיָּבֹאוּ עִם־עַבְדֵי שְׁלֹמֹה אוֹפִירָה וַיִּקְחוּ מִשָּׁם אַרְבַּע־מֵאוֹת וַחֲמִשִּׁים כִּכַּר זָהָב וַיָּבִיאוּ אֶל־הַמֶּלֶךְ שְׁלֹמֹה׃

9

1 The queen of Sheba heard of *Shlomo*'s fame, and came to *Yerushalayim* to test *Shlomo* with hard questions, accompanied by a very large retinue, including camels bearing spices, a great quantity of gold, and precious stones. When she came to *Shlomo*, she spoke to him of all that she had on her mind.

א וּמַלְכַּת־שְׁבָא שָׁמְעָה אֶת־שֵׁמַע שְׁלֹמֹה וַתָּבוֹא לְנַסּוֹת אֶת־שְׁלֹמֹה בְחִידוֹת בִּירוּשָׁלַ͏ִם בְּחַיִל כָּבֵד מְאֹד וּגְמַלִּים נֹשְׂאִים בְּשָׂמִים וְזָהָב לָרֹב וְאֶבֶן יְקָרָה וַתָּבוֹא אֶל־שְׁלֹמֹה וַתְּדַבֵּר עִמּוֹ אֵת כָּל־אֲשֶׁר הָיָה עִם־לְבָבָהּ׃

u-mal-kat sh'-VA sha-m'-AH et SHAY-ma sh'-lo-MOH va-ta-VO l'-na-SOT et sh'-lo-MOH v'-khee-DOT bee-ru-sha-LA-im b'-KHA-yil ka-VAYD m'-OD ug-ma-LEEM no-s'-EEM b'-sa-MEEM v'-za-HAV la-ROV v'-E-ven y'-ka-RAH va-ta-VO el sh'-lo-MOH va-t'-da-BAYR i-MO AYT kol a-SHER ha-YAH im l'-va-VAH

2 *Shlomo* had answers for all her questions; there was nothing that *Shlomo* did not know, nothing to which he could not give her an answer.

ב וַיַּגֶּד־לָהּ שְׁלֹמֹה אֶת־כָּל־דְּבָרֶיהָ וְלֹא־נֶעְלַם דָּבָר מִשְּׁלֹמֹה אֲשֶׁר לֹא הִגִּיד לָהּ׃

3 When the queen of Sheba saw how wise *Shlomo* was and the palace he had built,

ג וַתֵּרֶא מַלְכַּת־שְׁבָא אֵת חָכְמַת שְׁלֹמֹה וְהַבַּיִת אֲשֶׁר בָּנָה׃

4 the fare of his table, the seating of his courtiers, the service and attire of his attendants, his butlers and their attire, and the procession with which he went up to the House of *Hashem*, it took her breath away.

ד וּמַאֲכַל שֻׁלְחָנוֹ וּמוֹשַׁב עֲבָדָיו וּמַעֲמַד מְשָׁרְתָיו וּמַלְבּוּשֵׁיהֶם וּמַשְׁקָיו וּמַלְבּוּשֵׁיהֶם וַעֲלִיָּתוֹ אֲשֶׁר יַעֲלֶה בֵּית יְהֹוָה וְלֹא־הָיָה עוֹד בָּהּ רוּחַ׃

5 She said to the king, "What I heard in my own land about you and your wisdom was true.

ה וַתֹּאמֶר אֶל־הַמֶּלֶךְ אֱמֶת הַדָּבָר אֲשֶׁר שָׁמַעְתִּי בְּאַרְצִי עַל־דְּבָרֶיךָ וְעַל־חָכְמָתֶךָ׃

6 I did not believe what they said until I came and saw with my own eyes that not even the half of your great wisdom had been described to me; you surpass the report that I heard.

ו וְלֹא־הֶאֱמַנְתִּי לְדִבְרֵיהֶם עַד אֲשֶׁר־בָּאתִי וַתִּרְאֶינָה עֵינַי וְהִנֵּה לֹא־הֻגַּד־לִי חֲצִי מַרְבִּית חָכְמָתֶךָ יָסַפְתָּ עַל־הַשְּׁמוּעָה אֲשֶׁר שָׁמָעְתִּי׃

9:1 The queen of Sheba heard of *Shlomo*'s fame King *Shlomo*'s reign can be described as the glory days of the Kingdom of Israel. *Shlomo* creates a kingdom that is characterized by peace and security, wealth and prosperity, wisdom and knowledge, justice and righteousness, spiritual devotion and international recognition. One of *Shlomo*'s goals in building the *Beit Hamikdash* is for the gentile nations of the world to also come to recognize the greatness and oneness of God, as he says "Thus all the peoples of the earth will know Your name and revere You, as does Your people *Yisrael*" (6:33). Perhaps this is why *Shlomo* made a point of making his kingdom so grand and establishing political connections and alliances. Indeed, in addition to his renowned reputation and vast impact, he succeeds in his mission to spread recognition of God, as demonstrated by the queen of Sheba's visit. She is so impressed with *Shlomo* and his kingdom, yet her reaction to her visit is, "Blessed is *Hashem* your God, who favored you and set you on His throne as a king before *Hashem*" (verse 8). The Nation of Israel continues to be charged with the same mission of spreading God's great name and His Oneness throughout the entire world.

Divrei Hayamim II / II Chronicles
Chapter 9

7 How fortunate are your men and how fortunate are these courtiers of yours who are always in attendance on you and can hear your wisdom!

8 Blessed is *Hashem* your God, who favored you and set you on His throne as a king before *Hashem*. It is because of your God's love for *Yisrael* and in order to establish them forever that He made you king over them to execute righteous justice."

9 She presented the king with 120 *kikarim* of gold, and a vast quantity of spices and precious stones. There were no such spices as those which the queen of Sheba gave to King *Shlomo* –

10 also, the servants of Huram and *Shlomo* who brought gold from Ophir brought algum-wood and precious stones.

11 The king made of the algum-wood ramps for the House of *Hashem* and for the royal palace, and lyres and harps for the musicians, whose like had never before been seen in the land of *Yehuda* –

12 King *Shlomo*, in turn, gave the queen of Sheba everything she expressed a desire for, exceeding a return for what she had brought to the king. Then she and her courtiers left and returned to her own land.

13 The gold that *Shlomo* received every year weighed 666 gold *kikarim*,

14 besides what traders and merchants brought, and the gold and silver that all the kings of Arabia and governors of the regions brought to *Shlomo*.

15 King *Shlomo* made 200 shields of beaten gold – 600 *shekalim* of beaten gold for each shield,

16 and 300 bucklers of beaten gold – 300 [*shekalim*] of gold for each buckler. The king placed them in the Lebanon Forest House.

17 The king also made a large throne of ivory, overlaid with pure gold.

18 Six steps led up to the throne; and the throne had a golden footstool attached to it, and arms on either side of the seat. Two lions stood beside the arms,

דברי הימים ב
פרק ט

ז אַשְׁרֵי אֲנָשֶׁיךָ וְאַשְׁרֵי עֲבָדֶיךָ אֵלֶּה הָעֹמְדִים לְפָנֶיךָ תָּמִיד וְשֹׁמְעִים אֶת־חָכְמָתֶךָ:

ח יְהִי יְהֹוָה אֱלֹהֶיךָ בָּרוּךְ אֲשֶׁר חָפֵץ בְּךָ לְתִתְּךָ עַל־כִּסְאוֹ לְמֶלֶךְ לַיהֹוָה אֱלֹהֶיךָ בְּאַהֲבַת אֱלֹהֶיךָ אֶת־יִשְׂרָאֵל לְהַעֲמִידוֹ לְעוֹלָם וַיִּתֶּנְךָ עֲלֵיהֶם לְמֶלֶךְ לַעֲשׂוֹת מִשְׁפָּט וּצְדָקָה:

ט וַתִּתֵּן לַמֶּלֶךְ מֵאָה וְעֶשְׂרִים כִּכַּר זָהָב וּבְשָׂמִים לָרֹב מְאֹד וְאֶבֶן יְקָרָה וְלֹא הָיָה כַּבֹּשֶׂם הַהוּא אֲשֶׁר־נָתְנָה מַלְכַּת־שְׁבָא לַמֶּלֶךְ שְׁלֹמֹה:

י וְגַם־עַבְדֵי חִירָם [חוּרָם] וְעַבְדֵי שְׁלֹמֹה אֲשֶׁר־הֵבִיאוּ זָהָב מֵאוֹפִיר הֵבִיאוּ עֲצֵי אַלְגּוּמִּים וְאֶבֶן יְקָרָה:

יא וַיַּעַשׂ הַמֶּלֶךְ אֶת־עֲצֵי הָאַלְגּוּמִּים מְסִלּוֹת לְבֵית־יְהֹוָה וּלְבֵית הַמֶּלֶךְ וְכִנֹּרוֹת וּנְבָלִים לַשָּׁרִים וְלֹא־נִרְאוּ כָהֵם לְפָנִים בְּאֶרֶץ יְהוּדָה:

יב וְהַמֶּלֶךְ שְׁלֹמֹה נָתַן לְמַלְכַּת־שְׁבָא אֶת־כָּל־חֶפְצָהּ אֲשֶׁר שָׁאָלָה מִלְּבַד אֲשֶׁר־הֵבִיאָה אֶל־הַמֶּלֶךְ וַתַּהֲפֹךְ וַתֵּלֶךְ לְאַרְצָהּ הִיא וַעֲבָדֶיהָ:

יג וַיְהִי מִשְׁקַל הַזָּהָב אֲשֶׁר־בָּא לִשְׁלֹמֹה בְּשָׁנָה אֶחָת שֵׁשׁ מֵאוֹת וְשִׁשִּׁים וָשֵׁשׁ כִּכְּרֵי זָהָב:

יד לְבַד מֵאַנְשֵׁי הַתָּרִים וְהַסֹּחֲרִים מְבִיאִים וְכָל־מַלְכֵי עֲרַב וּפַחוֹת הָאָרֶץ מְבִיאִים זָהָב וָכֶסֶף לִשְׁלֹמֹה:

טו וַיַּעַשׂ הַמֶּלֶךְ שְׁלֹמֹה מָאתַיִם צִנָּה זָהָב שָׁחוּט שֵׁשׁ מֵאוֹת זָהָב שָׁחוּט יַעֲלֶה עַל־הַצִּנָּה הָאֶחָת:

טז וּשְׁלֹשׁ־מֵאוֹת מָגִנִּים זָהָב שָׁחוּט שְׁלֹשׁ מֵאוֹת זָהָב יַעֲלֶה עַל־הַמָּגֵן הָאֶחָת וַיִּתְּנֵם הַמֶּלֶךְ בְּבֵית יַעַר הַלְּבָנוֹן:

יז וַיַּעַשׂ הַמֶּלֶךְ כִּסֵּא־שֵׁן גָּדוֹל וַיְצַפֵּהוּ זָהָב טָהוֹר:

יח וְשֵׁשׁ מַעֲלוֹת לַכִּסֵּא וְכֶבֶשׁ בַּזָּהָב לַכִּסֵּא מָאֳחָזִים וְיָדוֹת מִזֶּה וּמִזֶּה עַל־מְקוֹם הַשָּׁבֶת וּשְׁנַיִם אֲרָיוֹת עֹמְדִים אֵצֶל הַיָּדוֹת:

Divrei Hayamim II / II Chronicles
Chapter 9

19 and twelve lions stood on the six steps, six on either side. None such was ever made for any other kingdom.

20 All of King *Shlomo*'s drinking vessels were of gold, and all the utensils of the Lebanon Forest House were of pure gold; silver counted for nothing in *Shlomo*'s days.

21 The king's fleet traveled to Tarshish with Huram's servants. Once every three years, the Tarshish fleet came in, bearing gold and silver, ivory, apes, and peacocks.

22 King *Shlomo* surpassed all the kings of the earth in wealth and wisdom.

23 All the kings of the earth came to pay homage to *Shlomo* and to listen to the wisdom with which *Hashem* had endowed him.

24 Each brought his tribute – silver and gold objects, robes, weapons, and spices, horses and mules – in the amount due each year.

25 *Shlomo* had 4,000 stalls for horses and chariots, and 12,000 horsemen, which he stationed in the chariot towns and with the king in *Yerushalayim*.

26 He ruled over all the kings from the Euphrates to the land of the Philistines and to the border of Egypt.

27 The king made silver as plentiful in *Yerushalayim* as stones, and cedars as plentiful as sycamores in the Shephelah.

28 Horses were brought for *Shlomo* from Egypt and all the lands.

29 The other events of *Shlomo*'s reign, early and late, are recorded in the chronicle of the *Navi Natan* and in the prophecies of *Achiya* the Shilonite and in the visions of Jedo the seer concerning *Yerovam* son of Nebat.

30 *Shlomo* reigned forty years over all *Yisrael* in *Yerushalayim*.

31 *Shlomo* slept with his fathers and was buried in the city of his father *David*; his son *Rechovam* succeeded him as king.

Divrei Hayamim II/II Chronicles
Chapter 10

1 *Rechovam* went to *Shechem,* for all *Yisrael* had come to *Shechem* to acclaim him king.

2 *Yerovam* son of Nebat learned of it while he was in Egypt where he had fled from King *Shlomo,* and *Yerovam* returned from Egypt.

3 They sent for him; and *Yerovam* and all *Yisrael* came and spoke to *Rechovam* as follows:

4 "Your father made our yoke heavy. Now lighten the harsh labor and the heavy yoke that your father laid on us, and we will serve you."

5 He answered them, "Come back to me in three days." So the people went away.

6 King *Rechovam* took counsel with the elders who had served during the lifetime of his father *Shlomo.* He said, "What answer do you counsel to give these people?"

va-yi-va-ATZ ha-ME-lekh r'-khav-AM et ha-z'-kay-NEEM a-sher ha-YU o-m'-DEEM lif-NAY sh'-lo-MOH a-VEEV bih-yo-TO KHAI lay-MOR AYKH a-TEM no-a-TZEEM l'-ha-SHEEV la-AM ha-ZEH da-VAR

7 They answered him, "If you will be good to these people and appease them and speak to them with kind words, they will be your servants always."

8 But he ignored the counsel that the elders gave him, and took counsel with the young men who had grown up with him and were serving him.

9 "What," he asked, "do you counsel that we reply to these people who said to me, 'Lighten the yoke that your father laid on us'?"

10:6 Who had served during the lifetime of his father *Shlomo* Upon assuming the throne after his father's death, *Rechovam* is approached by representatives of the nation who request an easing of the tax burden that had been placed upon them by King *Shlomo.* *Rechovam* first consults the elders who had advised his father, but not liking the counsel they give, he instead turns to the younger people, his own contemporaries. This was a breach of the principle, "Ask your father, he will inform you, Your elders, they will tell you" (Deuteronomy 32:7). *Rechovam* follows the advice of his young friends, and this leads to the split in the kingdom, setting the ten tribes of the kingdom of *Yisrael* on a very negative path of idolatry and sin. Had *Rechovam* appreciated the meaning and importance of history and tradition, instead of trying to assert himself and his reign over the nation, much evil might have been averted.

Divrei Hayamim II/II Chronicles
Chapter 11

דברי הימים ב
פרק יא

10 And the young men who had grown up with him answered, "Speak thus to the people who said to you, 'Your father made our yoke heavy, now you make it lighter for us.' Say to them, 'My little finger is thicker than my father's loins.

י וַיְדַבְּרוּ אִתּוֹ הַיְלָדִים אֲשֶׁר גָּדְלוּ אִתּוֹ לֵאמֹר כֹּה־תֹאמַר לָעָם אֲשֶׁר־דִּבְּרוּ אֵלֶיךָ לֵאמֹר אָבִיךָ הִכְבִּיד אֶת־עֻלֵּנוּ וְאַתָּה הָקֵל מֵעָלֵינוּ כֹּה תֹּאמַר אֲלֵהֶם קָטָנִּי עָבָה מִמָּתְנֵי אָבִי:

11 My father imposed a heavy yoke on you, and I will add to your yoke; my father flogged you with whips, but I [will do so] with scorpions.'"

יא וְעַתָּה אָבִי הֶעְמִיס עֲלֵיכֶם עֹל כָּבֵד וַאֲנִי אֹסִיף עַל־עֻלְּכֶם אָבִי יִסַּר אֶתְכֶם בַּשּׁוֹטִים וַאֲנִי בָּעֲקְרַבִּים:

12 Yerovam and all the people came to Rechovam on the third day, since the king had told them, "Come back on the third day."

יב וַיָּבֹא יָרָבְעָם וְכָל־הָעָם אֶל־רְחַבְעָם בַּיּוֹם הַשְּׁלִשִׁי כַּאֲשֶׁר דִּבֶּר הַמֶּלֶךְ לֵאמֹר שׁוּבוּ אֵלַי בַּיּוֹם הַשְּׁלִשִׁי:

13 The king answered them harshly; thus King Rechovam ignored the elders' counsel.

יג וַיַּעֲנֵם הַמֶּלֶךְ קָשָׁה וַיַּעֲזֹב הַמֶּלֶךְ רְחַבְעָם אֵת עֲצַת הַזְּקֵנִים:

14 He spoke to them in accordance with the counsel of the young men, and said, "I will make your yoke heavy, and I will add to it; my father flogged you with whips, but I [will do so] with scorpions."

יד וַיְדַבֵּר אֲלֵהֶם כַּעֲצַת הַיְלָדִים לֵאמֹר אַכְבִּיד אֶת־עֻלְּכֶם וַאֲנִי אֹסִיף עָלָיו אָבִי יִסַּר אֶתְכֶם בַּשּׁוֹטִים וַאֲנִי בָּעֲקְרַבִּים:

15 The king did not listen to the people, for Hashem had brought it about in order that Hashem might fulfill the promise that He had made through Achiya the Shilonite to Yerovam son of Nebat.

טו וְלֹא־שָׁמַע הַמֶּלֶךְ אֶל־הָעָם כִּי־הָיְתָה נְסִבָּה מֵעִם הָאֱלֹהִים לְמַעַן הָקִים יְהוָה אֶת־דְּבָרוֹ אֲשֶׁר דִּבֶּר בְּיַד אֲחִיָּהוּ הַשִּׁלוֹנִי אֶל־יָרָבְעָם בֶּן־נְבָט:

16 When all Yisrael [saw] that the king had not listened to them, the people answered the king: "We have no portion in David, No share in Yishai's son! To your tents, O Yisrael! Now look to your own house, O David." So all Yisrael returned to their homes.

טז וְכָל־יִשְׂרָאֵל כִּי לֹא־שָׁמַע הַמֶּלֶךְ לָהֶם וַיָּשִׁיבוּ הָעָם אֶת־הַמֶּלֶךְ לֵאמֹר מַה־לָּנוּ חֵלֶק בְּדָוִיד וְלֹא־נַחֲלָה בְּבֶן־יִשַׁי אִישׁ לְאֹהָלֶיךָ יִשְׂרָאֵל עַתָּה רְאֵה בֵיתְךָ דָּוִיד וַיֵּלֶךְ כָּל־יִשְׂרָאֵל לְאֹהָלָיו:

17 But Rechovam continued to reign over the Israelites who lived in the towns of Yehuda.

יז וּבְנֵי יִשְׂרָאֵל הַיֹּשְׁבִים בְּעָרֵי יְהוּדָה וַיִּמְלֹךְ עֲלֵיהֶם רְחַבְעָם:

18 King Rechovam sent out Hadoram, who was in charge of the forced labor, but the Israelites pelted him to death with stones. Thereupon, King Rechovam hurriedly mounted his chariot and fled to Yerushalayim.

יח וַיִּשְׁלַח הַמֶּלֶךְ רְחַבְעָם אֶת־הֲדֹרָם אֲשֶׁר עַל־הַמַּס וַיִּרְגְּמוּ־בוֹ בְנֵי־יִשְׂרָאֵל אֶבֶן וַיָּמֹת וְהַמֶּלֶךְ רְחַבְעָם הִתְאַמֵּץ לַעֲלוֹת בַּמֶּרְכָּבָה לָנוּס יְרוּשָׁלָ͏ִם:

19 Yisrael has been in revolt against the house of David to this day.

יט וַיִּפְשְׁעוּ יִשְׂרָאֵל בְּבֵית דָּוִיד עַד הַיּוֹם הַזֶּה:

11 1 When Rechovam arrived in Yerushalayim, he mustered the house of Yehuda and Binyamin, 180,000 picked fighting men, to make war with Yisrael in order to restore the kingdom to Rechovam.

יא א וַיָּבֹא רְחַבְעָם יְרוּשָׁלַ͏ִם וַיַּקְהֵל אֶת־בֵּית יְהוּדָה וּבִנְיָמִן מֵאָה וּשְׁמוֹנִים אֶלֶף בָּחוּר עֹשֵׂה מִלְחָמָה לְהִלָּחֵם עִם־יִשְׂרָאֵל לְהָשִׁיב אֶת־הַמַּמְלָכָה לִרְחַבְעָם:

Divrei Hayamim II/II Chronicles
Chapter 11

דברי הימים ב
פרק יא

2 But the word of *Hashem* came to *Shemaya*, the man of *Hashem*:

ב וַיְהִי דְבַר־יְהֹוָה אֶל־שְׁמַעְיָהוּ אִישׁ־הָאֱלֹהִים לֵאמֹר׃

3 "Say to *Rechovam* son of *Shlomo* king of *Yehuda*, and to all *Yisrael* in *Yehuda* and *Binyamin*:

ג אֱמֹר אֶל־רְחַבְעָם בֶּן־שְׁלֹמֹה מֶלֶךְ יְהוּדָה וְאֶל כָּל־יִשְׂרָאֵל בִּיהוּדָה וּבִנְיָמִן לֵאמֹר׃

4 Thus said *Hashem*: You shall not set out to make war on your kinsmen. Let every man return to his home, for this thing has been brought about by Me." They heeded the words of *Hashem* and refrained from marching against *Yerovam*.

ד כֹּה אָמַר יְהֹוָה לֹא־תַעֲלוּ וְלֹא־תִלָּחֲמוּ עִם־אֲחֵיכֶם שׁוּבוּ אִישׁ לְבֵיתוֹ כִּי מֵאִתִּי נִהְיָה הַדָּבָר הַזֶּה וַיִּשְׁמְעוּ אֶת־דִּבְרֵי יְהֹוָה וַיָּשֻׁבוּ מִלֶּכֶת אֶל־יָרָבְעָם׃

KOH a-MAR a-do-NAI lo ta-a-LU v'-lo ti-LA-kha-MU im a-khay-KHEM SHU-vu EESH l'-vay-TO KEE may-i-TEE nih-YAH ha-da-VAR ha-ZEH va-yish-m'-U et div-RAY a-do-NAI va-ya-SHU-vu mi-LE-khet el ya-rov-AM

5 *Rechovam* dwelt in *Yerushalayim* and built fortified towns in *Yehuda*.

ה וַיֵּשֶׁב רְחַבְעָם בִּירוּשָׁלָ͏ִם וַיִּבֶן עָרִים לְמָצוֹר בִּיהוּדָה׃

6 He built up *Beit Lechem*, and Etam, and *Tekoa*,

ו וַיִּבֶן אֶת־בֵּית־לֶחֶם וְאֶת־עֵיטָם וְאֶת־תְּקוֹעַ׃

7 and Beth-zur, and Soco, and *Adulam*,

ז וְאֶת־בֵּית־צוּר וְאֶת־שׂוֹכוֹ וְאֶת־עֲדֻלָּם׃

8 and Gath, and Mareshah, and Ziph,

ח וְאֶת־גַּת וְאֶת־מָרֵשָׁה וְאֶת־זִיף׃

9 and Adoraim, and *Lachish*, and *Azeika*,

ט וְאֶת־אֲדוֹרַיִם וְאֶת־לָכִישׁ וְאֶת־עֲזֵקָה׃

10 and *Tzora*, and Aijalon, and *Chevron*, which are in *Yehuda* and in *Binyamin*, as fortified towns.

י וְאֶת־צָרְעָה וְאֶת־אַיָּלוֹן וְאֶת־חֶבְרוֹן אֲשֶׁר בִּיהוּדָה וּבְבִנְיָמִן עָרֵי מְצֻרוֹת׃

11 He strengthened the fortified towns and put commanders in them, along with stores of food, oil, and wine,

יא וַיְחַזֵּק אֶת־הַמְּצֻרוֹת וַיִּתֵּן בָּהֶם נְגִידִים וְאֹצְרוֹת מַאֲכָל וְשֶׁמֶן וָיָיִן׃

12 and shields and spears in every town. He strengthened them exceedingly; thus *Yehuda* and *Binyamin* were his.

יב וּבְכָל־עִיר וָעִיר צִנּוֹת וּרְמָחִים וַיְחַזְּקֵם לְהַרְבֵּה מְאֹד וַיְהִי־לוֹ יְהוּדָה וּבִנְיָמִן׃

13 The *Kohanim* and the *Leviim*, from all their territories throughout *Yisrael*, presented themselves to him.

יג וְהַכֹּהֲנִים וְהַלְוִיִּם אֲשֶׁר בְּכָל־יִשְׂרָאֵל הִתְיַצְּבוּ עָלָיו מִכָּל־גְּבוּלָם׃

11:4 You shall not set out to make war on your kinsmen Though the kingdom has split and ten tribes have rejected *Rechovam* and the house of *David*, God does not want there to be a war between the two kingdoms. He reminds the southern tribes of *Yehuda* and *Binyamin* that despite the rift, the members of both kingdoms are brothers, and they should therefore treat each other with peace and brotherhood. The split in the kingdom is not ideal, and it pains *Hashem* to see different members of the Nation of Israel at odds with each other. Instead, He longs for the time when once again "one king shall be king of them all. Never again shall they be two nations, and never again shall they be divided into two kingdoms" (Ezekiel 37:22). With the establishment of the State of Israel, the ingathering of the exiles and the return of some of the ten tribes, we are beginning to witness the miraculous fulfilment of the unity between the kingdom of *Yisrael* and the kingdom of *Yehuda*.

Divrei Hayamim II / II Chronicles
Chapter 12

דברי הימים ב
פרק יב

14 The *Leviim* had left their pasturelands and their holdings and had set out for *Yehuda* and *Yerushalayim*, for *Yerovam* and his sons had prevented them from serving *Hashem*,

יד כִּי־עָזְבוּ הַלְוִיִּם אֶת־מִגְרְשֵׁיהֶם וַאֲחֻזָּתָם וַיֵּלְכוּ לִיהוּדָה וְלִירוּשָׁלָ͏ִם כִּי־הִזְנִיחָם יָרָבְעָם וּבָנָיו מִכַּהֵן לַיהוָה׃

15 having appointed his own *Kohanim* for the shrines, goat-demons, and calves which he had made.

טו וַיַּעֲמֶד־לוֹ כֹּהֲנִים לַבָּמוֹת וְלַשְּׂעִירִים וְלָעֲגָלִים אֲשֶׁר עָשָׂה׃

16 From all the tribes of *Yisrael*, those intent on seeking God of *Yisrael* followed them to *Yerushalayim*, to sacrifice to God of their fathers.

טז וְאַחֲרֵיהֶם מִכֹּל שִׁבְטֵי יִשְׂרָאֵל הַנֹּתְנִים אֶת־לְבָבָם לְבַקֵּשׁ אֶת־יְהוָה אֱלֹהֵי יִשְׂרָאֵל בָּאוּ יְרוּשָׁלַ͏ִם לִזְבּוֹחַ לַיהוָה אֱלֹהֵי אֲבוֹתֵיהֶם׃

17 They strengthened the kingdom of *Yehuda*, and supported *Rechovam* son of *Shlomo* for three years, for they followed the ways of *David* and *Shlomo* for three years.

יז וַיְחַזְּקוּ אֶת־מַלְכוּת יְהוּדָה וַיְאַמְּצוּ אֶת־רְחַבְעָם בֶּן־שְׁלֹמֹה לְשָׁנִים שָׁלוֹשׁ כִּי הָלְכוּ בְּדֶרֶךְ דָּוִיד וּשְׁלֹמֹה לְשָׁנִים שָׁלוֹשׁ׃

18 *Rechovam* married Mahalath daughter of Jerimoth son of *David*, and *Avichayil* daughter of *Eliav* son of *Yishai*.

יח וַיִּקַּח־לוֹ רְחַבְעָם אִשָּׁה אֶת־מָחֲלַת בֶּן־[בַּת־]יְרִימוֹת בֶּן־דָּוִיד אֲבִיהַיִל בַּת־אֱלִיאָב בֶּן־יִשָׁי׃

19 She bore him sons: Jeush, Shemariah, and Zaham.

יט וַתֵּלֶד לוֹ בָּנִים אֶת־יְעוּשׁ וְאֶת־שְׁמַרְיָה וְאֶת־זָהַם׃

20 He then took Maacah daughter of *Avshalom*; she bore him *Aviya*, Attai, Ziza, and Shelomith.

כ וְאַחֲרֶיהָ לָקַח אֶת־מַעֲכָה בַת־אַבְשָׁלוֹם וַתֵּלֶד לוֹ אֶת־אֲבִיָּה וְאֶת־עַתַּי וְאֶת־זִיזָא וְאֶת־שְׁלֹמִית׃

21 *Rechovam* loved Maacah daughter of *Avshalom* more than his other wives and concubines – for he took eighteen wives and sixty concubines; he begot twenty-eight sons and sixty daughters.

כא וַיֶּאֱהַב רְחַבְעָם אֶת־מַעֲכָה בַת־אַבְשָׁלוֹם מִכָּל־נָשָׁיו וּפִילַגְשָׁיו כִּי נָשִׁים שְׁמוֹנֶה־עֶשְׂרֵה נָשָׂא וּפִילַגְשִׁים שִׁשִּׁים וַיּוֹלֶד עֶשְׂרִים וּשְׁמוֹנָה בָּנִים וְשִׁשִּׁים בָּנוֹת׃

22 *Rechovam* designated *Aviya* son of Maacah as chief and leader among his brothers, for he intended him to be his successor.

כב וַיַּעֲמֵד לָרֹאשׁ רְחַבְעָם אֶת־אֲבִיָּה בֶן־מַעֲכָה לְנָגִיד בְּאֶחָיו כִּי לְהַמְלִיכוֹ׃

23 He prudently distributed all his sons throughout the regions of *Yehuda* and *Binyamin* and throughout the fortified towns; he provided them with abundant food, and he sought many wives for them.

כג וַיָּבֶן וַיִּפְרֹץ מִכָּל־בָּנָיו לְכָל־אַרְצוֹת יְהוּדָה וּבִנְיָמִן לְכֹל עָרֵי הַמְּצֻרוֹת וַיִּתֵּן לָהֶם הַמָּזוֹן לָרֹב וַיִּשְׁאַל הֲמוֹן נָשִׁים׃

12 1 When the kingship of *Rechovam* was firmly established, and he grew strong, he abandoned the Teaching of *Hashem*, he and all *Yisrael* with him.

יב א וַיְהִי כְּהָכִין מַלְכוּת רְחַבְעָם וּכְחֶזְקָתוֹ עָזַב אֶת־תּוֹרַת יְהוָה וְכָל־יִשְׂרָאֵל עִמּוֹ׃

2 In the fifth year of King *Rechovam*, King Shishak of Egypt marched against *Yerushalayim* – for they had trespassed against *Hashem* –

ב וַיְהִי בַּשָּׁנָה הַחֲמִישִׁית לַמֶּלֶךְ רְחַבְעָם עָלָה שִׁישַׁק מֶלֶךְ־מִצְרַיִם עַל־יְרוּשָׁלָ͏ִם כִּי מָעֲלוּ בַּיהוָה׃

Divrei Hayamim II / II Chronicles
Chapter 12

3 with 1,200 chariots, 60,000 horsemen and innumerable troops who came with him from Egypt: Lybians, Sukkites, and Kushites.

4 He took the fortified towns of *Yehuda* and advanced on *Yerushalayim*.

5 The *Navi Shemaya* came to *Rechovam* and the officers of *Yehuda*, who had assembled in *Yerushalayim* because of Shishak, and said to them, "Thus said *Hashem*: You have abandoned Me, so I am abandoning you to Shishak."

6 Then the officers of *Yisrael* and the king humbled themselves and declared, "*Hashem* is in the right."

7 When *Hashem* saw that they had submitted, the word of *Hashem* came to *Shemaya*, saying, "Since they have humbled themselves, I will not destroy them but will grant them some measure of deliverance, and My wrath will not be poured out on *Yerushalayim* through Shishak.

8 They will be subject to him, and they will know the difference between serving Me and serving the kingdoms of the earth." King Shishak of Egypt marched against *Yerushalayim*.

9 He took away the treasures of the House of *Hashem* and the treasures of the royal palace; he took away everything; he took away the golden shields that *Shlomo* had made.

10 King *Rechovam* had bronze shields made in their place, and entrusted them to the officers of the guard who guarded the entrance to the royal palace.

11 Whenever the king entered the House of *Hashem*, the guards would carry them and then bring them back to the armory of the guards.

12 After he had humbled himself, the anger of *Hashem* was averted and He did not destroy him entirely; in *Yehuda*, too, good things were found.

13 King *Rechovam* grew strong in *Yerushalayim* and exercised kingship. *Rechovam* was forty-one years old when he became king, and he reigned seventeen years in *Yerushalayim* – the city *Hashem* had chosen out of all the tribes of *Yisrael* to establish His name there. His mother's name was Naamah the Ammonitess.

Divrei Hayamim II / II Chronicles
Chapter 13

va-yit-kha-ZAYK ha-ME-lekh r'-khav-AM bee-ru-sha-LA-im va-yim-LOKH KEE ven ar-ba-EEM v'-a-KHAT sha-NAH r'-khav-AM b'-mol-KHO ush-VA es-RAY sha-NAH ma-LAKH bee-ru-sha-LA-im ha-EER a-sher ba-KHAR a-do-NAI la-SUM et sh'-MO SHAM mi-KOL shiv-TAY yis-ra-AYL v'-SHAYM i-MO na-a-MAH ha-a-mo-NEET

14 He did what was wrong, for he had not set his heart to seek *Hashem*.

וַיַּעַשׂ הָרָע כִּי לֹא הֵכִין לִבּוֹ לִדְרוֹשׁ אֶת־יְהוָה׃

15 The deeds of *Rechovam*, early and late, are recorded in the chronicles of the *Navi Shemaya* and *Ido* the seer, in the manner of genealogy. There was continuous war between *Rechovam* and *Yerovam*.

וְדִבְרֵי רְחַבְעָם הָרִאשֹׁנִים וְהָאַחֲרוֹנִים הֲלֹא־הֵם כְּתוּבִים בְּדִבְרֵי שְׁמַעְיָה הַנָּבִיא וְעִדּוֹ הַחֹזֶה לְהִתְיַחֵשׂ וּמִלְחֲמוֹת רְחַבְעָם וְיָרָבְעָם כָּל־הַיָּמִים׃

16 *Rechovam* slept with his fathers and was buried in the City of *David*. His son *Aviya* succeeded him as king.

וַיִּשְׁכַּב רְחַבְעָם עִם־אֲבֹתָיו וַיִּקָּבֵר בְּעִיר דָּוִיד וַיִּמְלֹךְ אֲבִיָּה בְנוֹ תַּחְתָּיו׃

13

1 In the eighteenth year of King *Yerovam*, *Aviya* became king over *Yehuda*.

בִּשְׁנַת שְׁמוֹנֶה עֶשְׂרֵה לַמֶּלֶךְ יָרָבְעָם וַיִּמְלֹךְ אֲבִיָּה עַל־יְהוּדָה׃

2 He reigned three years in *Yerushalayim*; his mother's name was *Michaihu* daughter of Uriel of *Giva*. There was war between *Aviya* and *Yerovam*.

שָׁלוֹשׁ שָׁנִים מָלַךְ בִּירוּשָׁלִָם וְשֵׁם אִמּוֹ מִיכָיָהוּ בַת־אוּרִיאֵל מִן־גִּבְעָה וּמִלְחָמָה הָיְתָה בֵּין אֲבִיָּה וּבֵין יָרָבְעָם׃

3 *Aviya* joined battle with a force of warriors, 400,000 picked men. *Yerovam* arrayed for battle against him 800,000 picked men, warriors.

וַיֶּאְסֹר אֲבִיָּה אֶת־הַמִּלְחָמָה בְּחַיִל גִּבּוֹרֵי מִלְחָמָה אַרְבַּע־מֵאוֹת אֶלֶף אִישׁ בָּחוּר וְיָרָבְעָם עָרַךְ עִמּוֹ מִלְחָמָה בִּשְׁמוֹנֶה מֵאוֹת אֶלֶף אִישׁ בָּחוּר גִּבּוֹר חָיִל׃

4 *Aviya* stood on top of Mount Zemaraim in the hill country of *Efraim* and said, "Listen to me, *Yerovam* and all *Yisrael*.

וַיָּקָם אֲבִיָּה מֵעַל לְהַר צְמָרַיִם אֲשֶׁר בְּהַר אֶפְרָיִם וַיֹּאמַר שְׁמָעוּנִי יָרָבְעָם וְכָל־יִשְׂרָאֵל׃

5 Surely you know that God of *Yisrael* gave *David* kingship over *Yisrael* forever – to him and his sons – by a covenant of salt.

הֲלֹא לָכֶם לָדַעַת כִּי יְהוָה אֱלֹהֵי יִשְׂרָאֵל נָתַן מַמְלָכָה לְדָוִיד עַל־יִשְׂרָאֵל לְעוֹלָם לוֹ וּלְבָנָיו בְּרִית מֶלַח׃

6 *Yerovam* son of Nebat had been in the service of *Shlomo* son of *David*, but he rose up and rebelled against his master.

וַיָּקָם יָרָבְעָם בֶּן־נְבָט עֶבֶד שְׁלֹמֹה בֶן־דָּוִיד וַיִּמְרֹד עַל־אֲדֹנָיו׃

12:13 To establish His name there At an event celebrating Jerusalem Day in 2012, Prime Minister Benjamin Netanyahu stated: "Our generation had a great privilege – we saw the words of the prophets come true. We saw the rise of Zion, the return of Jewish sovereignty in the Land of Israel, the ingathering of exiles and our return to Jerusalem. We will make sure Jerusalem's golden light will shine on our people, and spread the light of Jerusalem to the whole world. We will protect Jerusalem, because Israel without Jerusalem is like a body without a heart." *Yerushalayim* is central to Israel, to Judaism and to the entire world, and this is not because any individual declared it special. It is so significant and beloved to man because, as this verse states, it is the place chosen by God "to establish His name there."

Prime Minister Benjamin Netanyahu (b. 1949)

Divrei Hayamim II/II Chronicles
Chapter 13

דברי הימים ב
פרק יג

7 Riff-raff and scoundrels gathered around him and pressed hard upon *Rechovam* son of *Shlomo*. *Rechovam* was inexperienced and fainthearted and could not stand up to them.

ז וַיִּקָּבְצוּ עָלָיו אֲנָשִׁים רֵקִים בְּנֵי בְלִיָּעַל וַיִּתְאַמְּצוּ עַל־רְחַבְעָם בֶּן־שְׁלֹמֹה וּרְחַבְעָם הָיָה נַעַר וְרַךְ־לֵבָב וְלֹא הִתְחַזַּק לִפְנֵיהֶם׃

8 Now you are bent on opposing the kingdom of *Hashem*, which is in the charge of the sons of *David*, because you are a great multitude and possess the golden calves that *Yerovam* made for you as gods.

ח וְעַתָּה אַתֶּם אֹמְרִים לְהִתְחַזֵּק לִפְנֵי מַמְלֶכֶת יְהֹוָה בְּיַד בְּנֵי דָוִיד וְאַתֶּם הָמוֹן רָב וְעִמָּכֶם עֶגְלֵי זָהָב אֲשֶׁר עָשָׂה לָכֶם יָרָבְעָם לֵאלֹהִים׃

v'-a-TAH a-TEM o-m'-REEM l'-hit-kha-ZAYK lif-NAY mam-LE-khet a-do-NAI b'-YAD b'-NAY da-VEED v'-a-TEM ha-MON RAV v'-i-ma-KHEM eg-LAY za-HAV a-SHER a-SAH la-KHEM ya-rov-AM lay-lo-HEEM

9 Did you not banish the *Kohanim* of *Hashem*, the sons of *Aharon* and the *Leviim*, and, like the peoples of the land, appoint your own *Kohanim*? Anyone who offered himself for ordination with a young bull of the herd and seven rams became a *Kohen* of no-gods!

ט הֲלֹא הִדַּחְתֶּם אֶת־כֹּהֲנֵי יְהֹוָה אֶת־בְּנֵי אַהֲרֹן וְהַלְוִיִּם וַתַּעֲשׂוּ לָכֶם כֹּהֲנִים כְּעַמֵּי הָאֲרָצוֹת כָּל־הַבָּא לְמַלֵּא יָדוֹ בְּפַר בֶּן־בָּקָר וְאֵילִם שִׁבְעָה וְהָיָה כֹהֵן לְלֹא אֱלֹהִים׃

10 As for us, *Hashem* is our God, and we have not forsaken Him. The *Kohanim* who minister to *Hashem* are the sons of *Aharon*, and the *Leviim* are at their tasks.

י וַאֲנַחְנוּ יְהֹוָה אֱלֹהֵינוּ וְלֹא עֲזַבְנֻהוּ וְכֹהֲנִים מְשָׁרְתִים לַיהֹוָה בְּנֵי אַהֲרֹן וְהַלְוִיִּם בַּמְלָאכֶת׃

11 They offer burnt offerings in smoke each morning and each evening, and the aromatic incense, the rows of bread on the pure table; they kindle the golden *menorah* with its lamps burning each evening, for we keep the charge of *Hashem* our God, while you have forsaken it.

יא וּמַקְטִרִים לַיהֹוָה עֹלוֹת בַּבֹּקֶר־בַּבֹּקֶר וּבָעֶרֶב־בָּעֶרֶב וּקְטֹרֶת־סַמִּים וּמַעֲרֶכֶת לֶחֶם עַל־הַשֻּׁלְחָן הַטָּהוֹר וּמְנוֹרַת הַזָּהָב וְנֵרֹתֶיהָ לְבָעֵר בָּעֶרֶב בָּעֶרֶב כִּי־שֹׁמְרִים אֲנַחְנוּ אֶת־מִשְׁמֶרֶת יְהֹוָה אֱלֹהֵינוּ וְאַתֶּם עֲזַבְתֶּם אֹתוֹ׃

12 See, *Hashem* is with us as our chief, and His *Kohanim* have the trumpets for sounding blasts against you. O children of *Yisrael*, do not fight God of your fathers, because you will not succeed."

יב וְהִנֵּה עִמָּנוּ בָרֹאשׁ הָאֱלֹהִים וְכֹהֲנָיו וַחֲצֹצְרוֹת הַתְּרוּעָה לְהָרִיעַ עֲלֵיכֶם בְּנֵי יִשְׂרָאֵל אַל־תִּלָּחֲמוּ עִם־יְהֹוָה אֱלֹהֵי־אֲבֹתֵיכֶם כִּי־לֹא תַצְלִיחוּ׃

13 *Yerovam*, however, had directed the ambush to go around and come from the rear, thus the main body was in front of *Yehuda*, while the ambush was behind them.

יג וְיָרָבְעָם הֵסֵב אֶת־הַמַּאְרָב לָבוֹא מֵאַחֲרֵיהֶם וַיִּהְיוּ לִפְנֵי יְהוּדָה וְהַמַּאְרָב מֵאַחֲרֵיהֶם׃

13:8 The kingdom of *Hashem*, which is in the charge of the sons of *David* *Aviya* understands that the reason he has arisen to the throne is to serve God. He tells *Yerovam* that he rules the "kingdom of *Hashem*," as the kings of *Yehuda* are from the line of *David*, and they maintain the service of God in the *Beit Hamikdash* in *Yerushalayim*. *Aviya* sees himself as the emissary of the Lord, the caretaker of His people who is expected to lead them in the service of *Hashem*. Because he understands this, God grants him victory; the triumph which was denied to his father *Rechovam*, who was motivated by pride, not piety. This is an example of how success in the Land of Israel is dependent upon recognition of *Hashem*, as *Asa* declares in the next chapter: "While the land is at our disposal because we turned to *Hashem* our God" (14:6).

Divrei Hayamim II / II Chronicles
Chapter 14

14 When *Yehuda* turned around and saw that the fighting was before and behind them, they cried out to *Hashem*, and the *Kohanim* blew the trumpets.

15 The men of *Yehuda* raised a shout; and when the men of *Yehuda* raised a shout, *Hashem* routed *Yerovam* and all *Yisrael* before *Aviya* and *Yehuda*.

16 The Israelites fled before *Yehuda*, and *Hashem* delivered them into their hands.

17 *Aviya* and his army inflicted a severe defeat on them; 500,000 men of *Yisrael* fell slain.

18 The Israelites were crushed at that time, while the people of *Yehuda* triumphed because they relied on God of their fathers.

19 *Aviya* pursued *Yerovam* and captured some of his cities – *Beit El* with its dependencies, Jeshanah with its dependencies, and Ephrain with its dependencies.

20 *Yerovam* could not muster strength again during the days of *Aviya*. *Hashem* struck him down and he died.

21 But *Aviya* grew powerful; he married fourteen wives and begat twenty-two sons and sixteen daughters.

22 The other events of *Aviya*'s reign, his conduct and his acts, are recorded in the story of the *Navi Ido*.

23 *Aviya* slept with his fathers and was buried in the City of *David*; his son *Asa* succeeded him as king. The land was untroubled for ten years.

14 1 *Asa* did what was good and pleasing to *Hashem* his God.

2 He abolished the alien altars and shrines; he smashed the pillars and cut down the sacred posts.

3 He ordered *Yehuda* to turn to God of their fathers and to observe the Teaching and the Commandment.

4 He abolished the shrines and the incense stands throughout the cities of *Yehuda*, and the kingdom was untroubled under him.

דברי הימים ב
פרק יד

יד וַיִּפְנוּ יְהוּדָה וְהִנֵּה לָהֶם הַמִּלְחָמָה פָּנִים וְאָחוֹר וַיִּצְעֲקוּ לַיהוָה וְהַכֹּהֲנִים מחצצרים [מַחְצְרִים] בַּחֲצֹצְרוֹת׃

טו וַיָּרִיעוּ אִישׁ יְהוּדָה וַיְהִי בְּהָרִיעַ אִישׁ יְהוּדָה וְהָאֱלֹהִים נָגַף אֶת־יָרָבְעָם וְכָל־יִשְׂרָאֵל לִפְנֵי אֲבִיָּה וִיהוּדָה׃

טז וַיָּנוּסוּ בְנֵי־יִשְׂרָאֵל מִפְּנֵי יְהוּדָה וַיִּתְּנֵם אֱלֹהִים בְּיָדָם׃

יז וַיַּכּוּ בָהֶם אֲבִיָּה וְעַמּוֹ מַכָּה רַבָּה וַיִּפְּלוּ חֲלָלִים מִיִּשְׂרָאֵל חֲמֵשׁ־מֵאוֹת אֶלֶף אִישׁ בָּחוּר׃

יח וַיִּכָּנְעוּ בְנֵי־יִשְׂרָאֵל בָּעֵת הַהִיא וַיֶּאֶמְצוּ בְּנֵי יְהוּדָה כִּי נִשְׁעֲנוּ עַל־יְהוָה אֱלֹהֵי אֲבוֹתֵיהֶם׃

יט וַיִּרְדֹּף אֲבִיָּה אַחֲרֵי יָרָבְעָם וַיִּלְכֹּד מִמֶּנּוּ עָרִים אֶת־בֵּית־אֵל וְאֶת־בְּנוֹתֶיהָ וְאֶת־יְשָׁנָה וְאֶת־בְּנוֹתֶיהָ וְאֶת־עפרון [עֶפְרַיִן] וּבְנֹתֶיהָ׃

כ וְלֹא־עָצַר כֹּחַ־יָרָבְעָם עוֹד בִּימֵי אֲבִיָּהוּ וַיִּגְּפֵהוּ יְהוָה וַיָּמֹת׃

כא וַיִּתְחַזֵּק אֲבִיָּהוּ וַיִּשָּׂא־לוֹ נָשִׁים אַרְבַּע עֶשְׂרֵה וַיּוֹלֶד עֶשְׂרִים וּשְׁנַיִם בָּנִים וְשֵׁשׁ עֶשְׂרֵה בָּנוֹת׃

כב וְיֶתֶר דִּבְרֵי אֲבִיָּה וּדְרָכָיו וּדְבָרָיו כְּתוּבִים בְּמִדְרַשׁ הַנָּבִיא עִדּוֹ׃

כג וַיִּשְׁכַּב אֲבִיָּה עִם־אֲבֹתָיו וַיִּקְבְּרוּ אֹתוֹ בְּעִיר דָּוִיד וַיִּמְלֹךְ אָסָא בְנוֹ תַּחְתָּיו בְּיָמָיו שָׁקְטָה הָאָרֶץ עֶשֶׂר שָׁנִים׃

יד א וַיַּעַשׂ אָסָא הַטּוֹב וְהַיָּשָׁר בְּעֵינֵי יְהוָה אֱלֹהָיו׃

ב וַיָּסַר אֶת־מִזְבְּחוֹת הַנֵּכָר וְהַבָּמוֹת וַיְשַׁבֵּר אֶת־הַמַּצֵּבוֹת וַיְגַדַּע אֶת־הָאֲשֵׁרִים׃

ג וַיֹּאמֶר לִיהוּדָה לִדְרוֹשׁ אֶת־יְהוָה אֱלֹהֵי אֲבוֹתֵיהֶם וְלַעֲשׂוֹת הַתּוֹרָה וְהַמִּצְוָה׃

ד וַיָּסַר מִכָּל־עָרֵי יְהוּדָה אֶת־הַבָּמוֹת וְאֶת־הַחַמָּנִים וַתִּשְׁקֹט הַמַּמְלָכָה לְפָנָיו׃

Divrei Hayamim II / II Chronicles

Chapter 14

דברי הימים ב
פרק יד

5 He built fortified towns in *Yehuda*, since the land was untroubled and he was not engaged in warfare during those years, for *Hashem* had granted him respite.

ה וַיִּבֶן עָרֵי מְצוּרָה בִּיהוּדָה כִּי־שָׁקְטָה הָאָרֶץ וְאֵין־עִמּוֹ מִלְחָמָה בַּשָּׁנִים הָאֵלֶּה כִּי־הֵנִיחַ יְהֹוָה לוֹ:

6 He said to *Yehuda*, "Let us build up these cities and surround them with walls and towers, gates and bars, while the land is at our disposal because we turned to *Hashem* our God – we turned [to Him] and He gave us respite on all sides." They were successful in their building.

ו וַיֹּאמֶר לִיהוּדָה נִבְנֶה אֶת־הֶעָרִים הָאֵלֶּה וְנָסֵב חוֹמָה וּמִגְדָּלִים דְּלָתַיִם וּבְרִיחִים עוֹדֶנּוּ הָאָרֶץ לְפָנֵינוּ כִּי דָרַשְׁנוּ אֶת־יְהֹוָה אֱלֹהֵינוּ דָּרַשְׁנוּ וַיָּנַח לָנוּ מִסָּבִיב וַיִּבְנוּ וַיַּצְלִיחוּ:

7 *Asa* had an army of 300,000 men from *Yehuda* bearing shields and spears, and 280,000 from *Binyamin* bearing bucklers and drawing the bow; all these were valiant men.

ז וַיְהִי לְאָסָא חַיִל נֹשֵׂא צִנָּה וָרֹמַח מִיהוּדָה שְׁלֹשׁ מֵאוֹת אֶלֶף וּמִבִּנְיָמִן נֹשְׂאֵי מָגֵן וְדֹרְכֵי קֶשֶׁת שְׁנַיִם מָאתַיִם וּשְׁמוֹנִים אָלֶף כָּל־אֵלֶּה גִּבּוֹרֵי חָיִל:

8 Zerah the Cushite marched out against them with an army of a thousand thousand and 300 chariots. When he reached Mareshah

ח וַיֵּצֵא אֲלֵיהֶם זֶרַח הַכּוּשִׁי בְּחַיִל אֶלֶף אֲלָפִים וּמַרְכָּבוֹת שְׁלֹשׁ מֵאוֹת וַיָּבֹא עַד־מָרֵשָׁה:

9 *Asa* confronted him, and the battle lines were drawn in the valley of Zephat by Mareshah.

ט וַיֵּצֵא אָסָא לְפָנָיו וַיַּעַרְכוּ מִלְחָמָה בְּגֵיא צְפַתָה לְמָרֵשָׁה:

10 *Asa* called to *Hashem* his God, and said, "*Hashem*, it is all the same to You to help the numerous and the powerless. Help us, *Hashem* our God, for we rely on You, and in Your name we have come against this great multitude. You are *Hashem* our God. Let no mortal hinder You."

י וַיִּקְרָא אָסָא אֶל־יְהֹוָה אֱלֹהָיו וַיֹּאמַר יְהֹוָה אֵין־עִמְּךָ לַעְזוֹר בֵּין רַב לְאֵין כֹּחַ עָזְרֵנוּ יְהֹוָה אֱלֹהֵינוּ כִּי־עָלֶיךָ נִשְׁעַנּוּ וּבְשִׁמְךָ בָאנוּ עַל־הֶהָמוֹן הַזֶּה יְהֹוָה אֱלֹהֵינוּ אַתָּה אַל־יַעְצֹר עִמְּךָ אֱנוֹשׁ:

va-yik-RA a-SA el a-do-NAI e-lo-HAV va-yo-MAR a-do-NAI ayn i-m'-KHA la-ZOR BAYN RAV l'-AYN KO-akh oz-RAY-nu a-do-NAI e-lo-HAY-nu kee a-LE-kha nish-A-nu uv-shim-KHA VA-nu al he-ha-MON ha-ZEH a-do-NAI e-lo-HAY-nu A-tah al ya-TZOR i-m'-KHA e-NOSH

11 So *Hashem* routed the Cushites before *Asa* and *Yehuda*, and the Cushites fled.

יא וַיִּגֹּף יְהֹוָה אֶת־הַכּוּשִׁים לִפְנֵי אָסָא וְלִפְנֵי יְהוּדָה וַיָּנֻסוּ הַכּוּשִׁים:

12 *Asa* and the army with him pursued them as far as Gerar. Many of the Cushites fell wounded beyond recovery, for they broke before *Hashem* and His camp. Very much spoil was taken.

יב וַיִּרְדְּפֵם אָסָא וְהָעָם אֲשֶׁר־עִמּוֹ עַד־לִגְרָר וַיִּפֹּל מִכּוּשִׁים לְאֵין לָהֶם מִחְיָה כִּי־נִשְׁבְּרוּ לִפְנֵי־יְהֹוָה וְלִפְנֵי מַחֲנֵהוּ וַיִּשְׂאוּ שָׁלָל הַרְבֵּה מְאֹד:

14:10 In Your name we have come against this great multitude Since the kingdom of *Yehuda* is the "kingdom of *Hashem*" (13:8), when it is attacked by a foreign enemy, it is fighting for God and His holy name. If the enemy wins, then in the enemy's mind, they have defeated not only the Nation of Israel but also *Hashem*. This is one reason why throughout Jewish history, so many empires sought to conquer the Land of Israel and the city of *Yerushalayim*. This is also why it was so important to foreign powers to destroy the *Beit Hamikdash*, as a sign that they had overpowered the God of Israel. Just as *Asa* fought to defend God's honor, so should we all.

Divrei Hayamim II / II Chronicles
Chapter 15

דברי הימים ב
פרק טו

13 All the cities in the vicinity of Gerar were ravaged, for a terror of *Hashem* seized them. All the cities were plundered, and they yielded much booty.

יג וַיַּכּוּ אֵת כָּל־הֶעָרִים סְבִיבוֹת גְּרָר כִּי־הָיָה פַחַד־יְהֹוָה עֲלֵיהֶם וַיָּבֹזּוּ אֶת־כָּל־הֶעָרִים כִּי־בִזָּה רַבָּה הָיְתָה בָהֶם:

14 They also ravaged the encampment of herdsmen, capturing much sheep and camels. Then they returned to *Yerushalayim*.

יד וְגַם־אָהֳלֵי מִקְנֶה הִכּוּ וַיִּשְׁבּוּ צֹאן לָרֹב וּגְמַלִּים וַיָּשֻׁבוּ יְרוּשָׁלָֽםִ:

15

1 The spirit of *Hashem* came upon *Azarya* son of *Oded*.

טו א וַעֲזַרְיָהוּ בֶּן־עוֹדֵד הָיְתָה עָלָיו רוּחַ אֱלֹהִים:

2 He came to *Asa* and said to him, "Listen to me, *Asa* and all *Yehuda* and *Binyamin*; *Hashem* is with you as long as you are with Him. If you turn to Him, He will respond to you, but if you forsake Him, He will forsake you.

ב וַיֵּצֵא לִפְנֵי אָסָא וַיֹּאמֶר לוֹ שְׁמָעוּנִי אָסָא וְכָל־יְהוּדָה וּבִנְיָמִן יְהֹוָה עִמָּכֶם בִּהְיֽוֹתְכֶם עִמּוֹ וְאִם־תִּדְרְשֻׁהוּ יִמָּצֵא לָכֶם וְאִם־תַּעַזְבֻהוּ יַעֲזֹב אֶתְכֶם:

3 *Yisrael* has gone many days without the true *Hashem*, without a *Kohen* to give instruction and without Teaching.

ג וְיָמִים רַבִּים לְיִשְׂרָאֵל לְלֹא אֱלֹהֵי אֱמֶת וּלְלֹא כֹּהֵן מוֹרֶה וּלְלֹא תוֹרָה:

4 But in distress it returned to God of *Yisrael*, and sought Him, and He responded to them.

ד וַיָּשָׁב בַּצַּר־לוֹ עַל־יְהֹוָה אֱלֹהֵי יִשְׂרָאֵל וַיְבַקְשֻׁהוּ וַיִּמָּצֵא לָהֶם:

5 At those times, no wayfarer was safe, for there was much tumult among all the inhabitants of the lands.

ה וּבָעִתִּים הָהֵם אֵין שָׁלוֹם לַיּוֹצֵא וְלַבָּא כִּי מְהוּמֹת רַבּוֹת עַל כָּל־יֹשְׁבֵי הָאֲרָצוֹת:

6 Nation was crushed by nation and city by city, for *Hashem* threw them into panic with every kind of trouble.

ו וְכֻתְּתוּ גוֹי־בְּגוֹי וְעִיר בְּעִיר כִּי־אֱלֹהִים הֲמָמָם בְּכָל־צָרָה:

7 As for you, be strong, do not be disheartened, for there is reward for your labor."

ז וְאַתֶּם חִזְקוּ וְאַל־יִרְפּוּ יְדֵיכֶם כִּי יֵשׁ שָׂכָר לִפְעֻלַּתְכֶם:

8 When *Asa* heard these words, the prophecy of *Oded* the *Navi*, he took courage and removed the abominations from the entire land of *Yehuda* and *Binyamin* and from the cities that he had captured in the hill country of *Efraim*. He restored the *Mizbayach* of *Hashem* in front of the porch of *Hashem*.

ח וְכִשְׁמֹעַ אָסָא הַדְּבָרִים הָאֵלֶּה וְהַנְּבוּאָה עֹדֵד הַנָּבִיא הִתְחַזַּק וַיַּעֲבֵר הַשִּׁקּוּצִים מִכָּל־אֶרֶץ יְהוּדָה וּבִנְיָמִן וּמִן־הֶעָרִים אֲשֶׁר לָכַד מֵהַר אֶפְרָיִם וַיְחַדֵּשׁ אֶת־מִזְבַּח יְהֹוָה אֲשֶׁר לִפְנֵי אוּלָם יְהֹוָה:

9 He assembled all the people of *Yehuda* and *Binyamin* and those people of *Efraim*, *Menashe*, and *Shimon* who sojourned among them, for many in *Yisrael* had thrown in their lot with him when they saw that *Hashem* his God was with him.

ט וַיִּקְבֹּץ אֶת־כָּל־יְהוּדָה וּבִנְיָמִן וְהַגָּרִים עִמָּהֶם מֵאֶפְרַיִם וּמְנַשֶּׁה וּמִשִּׁמְעוֹן כִּי־נָפְלוּ עָלָיו מִיִּשְׂרָאֵל לָרֹב בִּרְאֹתָם כִּי־יְהֹוָה אֱלֹהָיו עִמּוֹ:

10 They were assembled in *Yerushalayim* in the third month of the fifteenth year of the reign of *Asa*.

י וַיִּקָּבְצוּ יְרוּשָׁלַםִ בַּחֹדֶשׁ הַשְּׁלִשִׁי לִשְׁנַת חֲמֵשׁ־עֶשְׂרֵה לְמַלְכוּת אָסָא:

11 They brought sacrifices to *Hashem* on that day; they brought 700 oxen and 7,000 sheep of the spoil.

יא וַיִּזְבְּחוּ לַיהֹוָה בַּיּוֹם הַהוּא מִן־הַשָּׁלָל הֵבִיאוּ בָּקָר שְׁבַע מֵאוֹת וְצֹאן שִׁבְעַת אֲלָפִים:

Divrei Hayamim II/II Chronicles
Chapter 16

דברי הימים ב
פרק טז

12 They entered into a covenant to worship God of their fathers with all their heart and with all their soul.

יב וַיָּבֹאוּ בַבְּרִית לִדְרוֹשׁ אֶת־יְהֹוָה אֱלֹהֵי אֲבוֹתֵיהֶם בְּכָל־לְבָבָם וּבְכָל־נַפְשָׁם׃

13 Whoever would not worship God of *Yisrael* would be put to death, whether small or great, whether man or woman.

יג וְכֹל אֲשֶׁר לֹא־יִדְרֹשׁ לַיהֹוָה אֱלֹהֵי־יִשְׂרָאֵל יוּמָת לְמִן־קָטֹן וְעַד־גָּדוֹל לְמֵאִישׁ וְעַד־אִשָּׁה׃

14 So they took an oath to *Hashem* in a loud voice and with shouts, with trumpeting and blasts of the *shofar*.

יד וַיִּשָּׁבְעוּ לַיהֹוָה בְּקוֹל גָּדוֹל וּבִתְרוּעָה וּבַחֲצֹצְרוֹת וּבְשׁוֹפָרוֹת׃

15 All *Yehuda* rejoiced over the oath, for they swore with all their heart and sought Him with all their will. He responded to them and gave them respite on every side.

טו וַיִּשְׂמְחוּ כָל־יְהוּדָה עַל־הַשְּׁבוּעָה כִּי בְכָל־לְבָבָם נִשְׁבָּעוּ וּבְכָל־רְצוֹנָם בִּקְשֻׁהוּ וַיִּמָּצֵא לָהֶם וַיָּנַח יְהֹוָה לָהֶם מִסָּבִיב׃

va-yis-m'-KHU khol y'-hu-DAH al ha-sh'-vu-AH KEE v'-khol l'-va-VAM nish-BA-u uv-khol r'-tzo-NAM bik-SHU-hu va-yi-ma-TZAY la-HEM va-YA-nakh a-do-NAI la-HEM mi-sa-VEEV

16 He also deposed Maacah mother of King *Asa* from the rank of queen mother, because she had made an abominable thing for [the goddess] Asherah. *Asa* cut down her abominable thing, reduced it to dust, and burned it in the Wadi Kidron.

טז וְגַם־מַעֲכָה אֵם אָסָא הַמֶּלֶךְ הֱסִירָהּ מִגְּבִירָה אֲשֶׁר־עָשְׂתָה לַאֲשֵׁרָה מִפְלָצֶת וַיִּכְרֹת אָסָא אֶת־מִפְלַצְתָּהּ וַיָּדֶק וַיִּשְׂרֹף בְּנַחַל קִדְרוֹן׃

17 The shrines, indeed, were not abolished in *Yisrael*; however, *Asa* was wholehearted [with *Hashem*] all his life.

יז וְהַבָּמוֹת לֹא־סָרוּ מִיִּשְׂרָאֵל רַק לְבַב־אָסָא הָיָה שָׁלֵם כָּל־יָמָיו׃

18 He brought into the House of *Hashem* the things that he and his father had consecrated – silver, gold, and utensils.

יח וַיָּבֵא אֶת־קָדְשֵׁי אָבִיו וְקָדָשָׁיו בֵּית הָאֱלֹהִים כֶּסֶף וְזָהָב וְכֵלִים׃

19 There was no war until the thirty-fifth year of the reign of *Asa*.

יט וּמִלְחָמָה לֹא הָיָתָה עַד שְׁנַת־שְׁלֹשִׁים וְחָמֵשׁ לְמַלְכוּת אָסָא׃

16 ¹ In the thirty-sixth year of the reign of *Asa*, King *Basha* of *Yisrael* marched against *Yehuda* and built up *Rama* to block all movement of King *Asa* of *Yehuda*.

טז א בִּשְׁנַת שְׁלֹשִׁים וָשֵׁשׁ לְמַלְכוּת אָסָא עָלָה בַּעְשָׁא מֶלֶךְ־יִשְׂרָאֵל עַל־יְהוּדָה וַיִּבֶן אֶת־הָרָמָה לְבִלְתִּי תֵּת יוֹצֵא וָבָא לְאָסָא מֶלֶךְ יְהוּדָה׃

2 *Asa* took all the silver and gold from the treasuries of the House of *Hashem* and the royal palace, and sent them to King Ben-hadad of Aram, who resided in Damascus, with this message:

ב וַיֹּצֵא אָסָא כֶּסֶף וְזָהָב מֵאֹצְרוֹת בֵּית יְהֹוָה וּבֵית הַמֶּלֶךְ וַיִּשְׁלַח אֶל־בֶּן־הֲדַד מֶלֶךְ אֲרָם הַיּוֹשֵׁב בְּדַרְמֶשֶׂק לֵאמֹר׃

15:15 For they swore with all their heart *Asa* leads the people of *Yehuda* and *Binyamin* to recommit themselves wholeheartedly to God. They understand that to find *Hashem*, and for Him to remain with them, they must swear their absolute loyalty to Him. As such, *Asa* gathers the people together in *Yerushalayim* where they make an oath to serve *Hashem*, renewing the covenant first established by *Moshe* at Mount Sinai. In turn, God makes Himself available to them and grants them peace in the land.

Divrei Hayamim II/II Chronicles
Chapter 16

דברי הימים ב
פרק טז

3 "There is a pact between me and you, as there was between my father and your father. I herewith send you silver and gold; go and break your pact with King *Basha* of *Yisrael* so that he may withdraw from me."

ג בְּרִית בֵּינִי וּבֵינֶךָ וּבֵין אָבִי וּבֵין אָבִיךָ הִנֵּה שָׁלַחְתִּי לְךָ כֶּסֶף וְזָהָב לֵךְ הָפֵר בְּרִיתְךָ אֶת־בַּעְשָׁא מֶלֶךְ יִשְׂרָאֵל וְיַעֲלֶה מֵעָלָי:

4 Ben-hadad acceded to King *Asa*'s request; he sent his army commanders against the towns of *Yisrael* and ravaged Ijon, *Dan*, Abel-maim, and all the garrison towns of *Naftali*.

ד וַיִּשְׁמַע בֶּן הֲדַד אֶל־הַמֶּלֶךְ אָסָא וַיִּשְׁלַח אֶת־שָׂרֵי הַחֲיָלִים אֲשֶׁר־לוֹ אֶל־עָרֵי יִשְׂרָאֵל וַיַּכּוּ אֶת־עִיּוֹן וְאֶת־דָּן וְאֵת אָבֵל מָיִם וְאֵת כָּל־מִסְכְּנוֹת עָרֵי נַפְתָּלִי:

5 When *Basha* heard about it, he stopped building up *Rama* and put an end to the work on it.

ה וַיְהִי כִּשְׁמֹעַ בַּעְשָׁא וַיֶּחְדַּל מִבְּנוֹת אֶת־הָרָמָה וַיַּשְׁבֵּת אֶת־מְלַאכְתּוֹ:

6 Then King *Asa* mustered all *Yehuda*, and they carried away the stones and timber with which *Basha* had built up *Rama*; with these King *Asa* built up Geba and *Mitzpa*.

ו וְאָסָא הַמֶּלֶךְ לָקַח אֶת־כָּל־יְהוּדָה וַיִּשְׂאוּ אֶת־אַבְנֵי הָרָמָה וְאֶת־עֵצֶיהָ אֲשֶׁר בָּנָה בַּעְשָׁא וַיִּבֶן בָּהֶם אֶת־גֶּבַע וְאֶת־הַמִּצְפָּה:

7 At that time, *Chanani* the seer came to King *Asa* of *Yehuda* and said to him, "Because you relied on the king of Aram and did not rely on *Hashem* your God, therefore the army of the king of Aram has slipped out of your hands.

ז וּבָעֵת הַהִיא בָּא חֲנָנִי הָרֹאֶה אֶל־אָסָא מֶלֶךְ יְהוּדָה וַיֹּאמֶר אֵלָיו בְּהִשָּׁעֶנְךָ עַל־מֶלֶךְ אֲרָם וְלֹא נִשְׁעַנְתָּ עַל־יְהֹוָה אֱלֹהֶיךָ עַל־כֵּן נִמְלַט חֵיל מֶלֶךְ־אֲרָם מִיָּדֶךָ:

u-va-AYT ha-HEE BA kha-NA-nee ha-ro-EH el a-SA ME-lekh y'-hu-DAH va-YO-mer ay-LAV b'-hi-SHA-en-KHA al ME-lekh a-RAM v'-LO nish-AN-ta al a-do-NAI e-lo-HE-kha al KAYN nim-LAT KHAYL ME-lekh a-RAM mi-ya-DE-kha

8 The Cushites and Lybians were a mighty army with chariots and horsemen in very great numbers, yet because you relied on *Hashem* He delivered them into your hands.

ח הֲלֹא הַכּוּשִׁים וְהַלּוּבִים הָיוּ לְחַיִל לָרֹב לְרֶכֶב וּלְפָרָשִׁים לְהַרְבֵּה מְאֹד וּבְהִשָּׁעֶנְךָ עַל־יְהֹוָה נְתָנָם בְּיָדֶךָ:

9 For the eyes of *Hashem* range over the entire earth, to give support to those who are wholeheartedly with Him. You have acted foolishly in this matter, and henceforth you will be beset by wars."

ט כִּי יְהֹוָה עֵינָיו מְשֹׁטְטוֹת בְּכָל־הָאָרֶץ לְהִתְחַזֵּק עִם־לְבָבָם שָׁלֵם אֵלָיו נִסְכַּלְתָּ עַל־זֹאת כִּי מֵעַתָּה יֵשׁ עִמְּךָ מִלְחָמוֹת:

10 *Asa* was vexed at the seer and put him into the stocks, for he was furious with him because of that. *Asa* inflicted cruelties on some of the people at that time.

י וַיִּכְעַס אָסָא אֶל־הָרֹאֶה וַיִּתְּנֵהוּ בֵּית הַמַּהְפֶּכֶת כִּי־בְזַעַף עִמּוֹ עַל־זֹאת וַיְרַצֵּץ אָסָא מִן־הָעָם בָּעֵת הַהִיא:

16:7 Because you relied on the king of Aram *Asa* is criticized for the way he enlists assistance to help him defeat *Basha*, king of *Yisrael*. Instead of appealing to *Hashem* for help, he appeals to the king of Aram. In addition, he pays Aram with gold and silver taken from the treasuries of the *Beit Hamikdash*. While acting to protect oneself is praiseworthy, this is only true when it is accompanied by faith in God and prayer to *Hashem*.

Divrei Hayamim II / II Chronicles

Chapter 17

11 The acts of *Asa*, early and late, are recorded in the annals of the kings of *Yehuda* and *Yisrael*.

12 In the thirty-ninth year of his reign, *Asa* suffered from an acute foot ailment; but ill as he was, he still did not turn to *Hashem* but to physicians.

13 *Asa* slept with his fathers. He died in the forty-first year of his reign

14 and was buried in the grave that he had made for himself in the City of *David*. He was laid in his resting-place, which was filled with spices of all kinds, expertly blended; a very great fire was made in his honor.

17

1 His son *Yehoshafat* succeeded him as king, and took firm hold of *Yisrael*.

2 He stationed troops in all the fortified towns of *Yehuda*, and stationed garrisons throughout the land of *Yehuda* and the cities of *Efraim* which his father *Asa* had captured.

3 *Hashem* was with *Yehoshafat* because he followed the earlier ways of his father *David*, and did not worship the Baalim,

4 but worshiped the God of his father and followed His commandments – unlike the behavior of *Yisrael*.

5 So *Hashem* established the kingdom in his hands, and all *Yehuda* gave presents to *Yehoshafat*. He had wealth and glory in abundance.

6 His mind was elevated in the ways of *Hashem*. Moreover, he abolished the shrines and the sacred posts from *Yehuda*.

7 In the third year of his reign he sent his officers Ben-hail, *Ovadya*, *Zecharya*, Nethanel, and *Michaihu* throughout the cities of *Yehuda* to offer instruction.

8 With them were the *Leviim*, *Shemaya*, Nethaniah, Zebadiah, *Asael*, Shemiramoth, Jehonathan, *Adoniyahu*, Tobijah and Tob-*Adoniyahu* the *Leviim*; with them were Elishama and *Yehoram* the *Kohanim*.

דברי הימים ב

פרק יז

יא וְהִנֵּה דִּבְרֵי אָסָא הָרִאשׁוֹנִים וְהָאַחֲרוֹנִים הִנָּם כְּתוּבִים עַל־סֵפֶר הַמְּלָכִים לִיהוּדָה וְיִשְׂרָאֵל:

יב וַיֶּחֱלֶא אָסָא בִּשְׁנַת שְׁלוֹשִׁים וָתֵשַׁע לְמַלְכוּתוֹ בְּרַגְלָיו עַד־לְמַעְלָה חָלְיוֹ וְגַם־בְּחָלְיוֹ לֹא־דָרַשׁ אֶת־יְהֹוָה כִּי בָּרֹפְאִים:

יג וַיִּשְׁכַּב אָסָא עִם־אֲבֹתָיו וַיָּמָת בִּשְׁנַת אַרְבָּעִים וְאַחַת לְמָלְכוֹ:

יד וַיִּקְבְּרֻהוּ בְקִבְרֹתָיו אֲשֶׁר כָּרָה־לוֹ בְּעִיר דָּוִיד וַיַּשְׁכִּיבֻהוּ בַּמִּשְׁכָּב אֲשֶׁר מִלֵּא בְּשָׂמִים וּזְנִים מְרֻקָּחִים בְּמִרְקַחַת מַעֲשֶׂה וַיִּשְׂרְפוּ־לוֹ שְׂרֵפָה גְּדוֹלָה עַד־לִמְאֹד:

יז א וַיִּמְלֹךְ יְהוֹשָׁפָט בְּנוֹ תַּחְתָּיו וַיִּתְחַזֵּק עַל־יִשְׂרָאֵל:

ב וַיִּתֶּן־חַיִל בְּכָל־עָרֵי יְהוּדָה הַבְּצֻרוֹת וַיִּתֵּן נְצִיבִים בְּאֶרֶץ יְהוּדָה וּבְעָרֵי אֶפְרַיִם אֲשֶׁר לָכַד אָסָא אָבִיו:

ג וַיְהִי יְהֹוָה עִם־יְהוֹשָׁפָט כִּי הָלַךְ בְּדַרְכֵי דָּוִיד אָבִיו הָרִאשֹׁנִים וְלֹא דָרַשׁ לַבְּעָלִים:

ד כִּי לֵאלֹהֵי אָבִיו דָּרָשׁ וּבְמִצְוֺתָיו הָלָךְ וְלֹא כְּמַעֲשֵׂה יִשְׂרָאֵל:

ה וַיָּכֶן יְהֹוָה אֶת־הַמַּמְלָכָה בְּיָדוֹ וַיִּתְּנוּ כָל־יְהוּדָה מִנְחָה לִיהוֹשָׁפָט וַיְהִי־לוֹ עֹשֶׁר־וְכָבוֹד לָרֹב:

ו וַיִּגְבַּהּ לִבּוֹ בְּדַרְכֵי יְהֹוָה וְעוֹד הֵסִיר אֶת־הַבָּמוֹת וְאֶת־הָאֲשֵׁרִים מִיהוּדָה:

ז וּבִשְׁנַת שָׁלוֹשׁ לְמָלְכוֹ שָׁלַח לְשָׂרָיו לְבֶן־חַיִל וּלְעֹבַדְיָה וְלִזְכַרְיָה וְלִנְתַנְאֵל וּלְמִיכָיָהוּ לְלַמֵּד בְּעָרֵי יְהוּדָה:

ח וְעִמָּהֶם הַלְוִיִּם שְׁמַעְיָהוּ וּנְתַנְיָהוּ וּזְבַדְיָהוּ וַעֲשָׂהאֵל וּשְׁמִרִימוֹת [וּשְׁמִירָמוֹת] וִיהוֹנָתָן וַאֲדֹנִיָּהוּ וְטוֹבִיָּהוּ וְטוֹב אֲדוֹנִיָּה הַלְוִיִּם וְעִמָּהֶם אֱלִישָׁמָע וִיהוֹרָם הַכֹּהֲנִים:

Divrei Hayamim II / II Chronicles
Chapter 17

דברי הימים ב
פרק יז

9 They offered instruction throughout *Yehuda*, having with them the Book of the Teaching of *Hashem*. They made the rounds of all the cities of *Yehuda* and instructed the people.

ט וַיְלַמְּדוּ בִּיהוּדָה וְעִמָּהֶם סֵפֶר תּוֹרַת יְהֹוָה וַיָּסֹבּוּ בְּכָל־עָרֵי יְהוּדָה וַיְלַמְּדוּ בָּעָם׃

10 A terror of *Hashem* seized all the kingdoms of the lands around *Yehuda*, and they did not go to war with *Yehoshafat*.

י וַיְהִי ׀ פַּחַד יְהֹוָה עַל כָּל־מַמְלְכוֹת הָאֲרָצוֹת אֲשֶׁר סְבִיבוֹת יְהוּדָה וְלֹא נִלְחֲמוּ עִם־יְהוֹשָׁפָט׃

> vai-HEE PA-khad a-do-NAI AL kol mam-l'-KHOT ha-a-ra-TZOT a-SHER s'-vee-VOT y'-hu-DAH v'-LO nil-kha-MU im y'-ho-sha-FAT

11 From Philistia a load of silver was brought to *Yehoshafat* as tribute. The Arabs, too, brought him flocks: 7,700 rams and 7,700 he-goats.

יא וּמִן־פְּלִשְׁתִּים מְבִיאִים לִיהוֹשָׁפָט מִנְחָה וְכֶסֶף מַשָּׂא גַּם הָעַרְבִיאִים מְבִיאִים לוֹ צֹאן אֵילִים שִׁבְעַת אֲלָפִים וּשְׁבַע מֵאוֹת וּתְיָשִׁים שִׁבְעַת אֲלָפִים וּשְׁבַע מֵאוֹת׃

12 *Yehoshafat* grew greater and greater, and he built up fortresses and garrison towns in *Yehuda*.

יב וַיְהִי יְהוֹשָׁפָט הֹלֵךְ וְגָדֵל עַד־לְמָעְלָה וַיִּבֶן בִּיהוּדָה בִּירָנִיּוֹת וְעָרֵי מִסְכְּנוֹת׃

13 He carried out extensive works in the towns of *Yehuda*, and had soldiers, valiant men, in *Yerushalayim*.

יג וּמְלָאכָה רַבָּה הָיָה לוֹ בְּעָרֵי יְהוּדָה וְאַנְשֵׁי מִלְחָמָה גִּבּוֹרֵי חַיִל בִּירוּשָׁלָ͏ִם׃

14 They were enrolled according to their clans. *Yehuda*: chiefs of thousands, Adnah the chief, who had 300,000 valiant men;

יד וְאֵלֶּה פְקֻדָּתָם לְבֵית אֲבוֹתֵיהֶם לִיהוּדָה שָׂרֵי אֲלָפִים עַדְנָה הַשָּׂר וְעִמּוֹ גִּבּוֹרֵי חַיִל שְׁלֹשׁ מֵאוֹת אָלֶף׃

15 next to him was *Yehochanan* the captain, who had 280,000;

טו וְעַל־יָדוֹ יְהוֹחָנָן הַשָּׂר וְעִמּוֹ מָאתַיִם וּשְׁמוֹנִים אָלֶף׃

16 next to him was Amasiah son of Zichri, who made a freewill offering to *Hashem*. He had 200,000 valiant men.

טז וְעַל־יָדוֹ עֲמַסְיָה בֶן־זִכְרִי הַמִּתְנַדֵּב לַיהֹוָה וְעִמּוֹ מָאתַיִם אֶלֶף גִּבּוֹר חָיִל׃

17 *Binyamin*: Eliada, a valiant man, who had 200,000 men armed with bow and buckler;

יז וּמִן־בִּנְיָמִן גִּבּוֹר חַיִל אֶלְיָדָע וְעִמּוֹ נֹשְׁקֵי־קֶשֶׁת וּמָגֵן מָאתַיִם אָלֶף׃

18 next to him was Jehozabad, who had 180,000 armed men.

יח וְעַל־יָדוֹ יְהוֹזָבָד וְעִמּוֹ מֵאָה־וּשְׁמוֹנִים אֶלֶף חֲלוּצֵי צָבָא׃

19 These served the king, besides those whom the king assigned to the fortified towns throughout *Yehuda*.

יט אֵלֶּה הַמְשָׁרְתִים אֶת־הַמֶּלֶךְ מִלְּבַד אֲשֶׁר־נָתַן הַמֶּלֶךְ בְּעָרֵי הַמִּבְצָר בְּכָל־יְהוּדָה׃

17:10 A terror of *Hashem* seized all the kingdoms *Yehoshafat* is one of the greatest kings of the kingdom of *Yehuda*. He continues to remove idol worship from the kingdom and ensures that the people engage in *Torah* study. In response, the nations who surround *Yehuda* fear the God of Israel and do not wage war on His people. Furthermore, the Philistines even send gifts to *Yehoshafat*. This demonstrates that the combination of the People of Israel studying the *Torah* in the Land of Israel brings respect from their adversaries, and brings faith and peace to the world.

Divrei Hayamim II / II Chronicles
Chapter 18 · פרק יח · דברי הימים ב

18 ¹ So *Yehoshafat* had wealth and honor in abundance, and he allied himself by marriage to *Achav*.

א וַיְהִי לִיהוֹשָׁפָט עֹשֶׁר וְכָבוֹד לָרֹב וַיִּתְחַתֵּן לְאַחְאָב:

² After some years had passed, he came to visit *Achav* at *Shomron*. *Achav* slaughtered sheep and oxen in abundance for him and for the people with him, and persuaded him to march against Ramoth-gilead.

ב וַיֵּרֶד לְקֵץ שָׁנִים אֶל־אַחְאָב לְשֹׁמְרוֹן וַיִּזְבַּח־לוֹ אַחְאָב צֹאן וּבָקָר לָרֹב וְלָעָם אֲשֶׁר עִמּוֹ וַיְסִיתֵהוּ לַעֲלוֹת אֶל־רָמוֹת גִּלְעָד:

va-YAY-red l'-KAYTZ sha-NEEM el akh-AV l'-SHO-m'-RON va-yiz-bakh LO akh-AV TZON u-va-KAR la-ROV v'-la-AM a-SHER i-MO vai-see-TAY-hu la-a-LOT el ra-MOT gil-AD

³ King *Achav* of *Yisrael* said to King *Yehoshafat* of *Yehuda*, "Will you accompany me to Ramoth-gilead?" He answered him, "I will do what you do; my troops shall be your troops and shall accompany you in battle."

ג וַיֹּאמֶר אַחְאָב מֶלֶךְ־יִשְׂרָאֵל אֶל־יְהוֹשָׁפָט מֶלֶךְ יְהוּדָה הֲתֵלֵךְ עִמִּי רָמֹת גִּלְעָד וַיֹּאמֶר לוֹ כָּמוֹנִי כָמוֹךָ וּכְעַמְּךָ עַמִּי וְעִמְּךָ בַּמִּלְחָמָה:

⁴ *Yehoshafat* then said to the king of *Yisrael*, "But first inquire for the word of *Hashem*."

ד וַיֹּאמֶר יְהוֹשָׁפָט אֶל־מֶלֶךְ יִשְׂרָאֵל דְּרָשׁ־נָא כַיּוֹם אֶת־דְּבַר יְהוָה:

⁵ So the king of *Yisrael* gathered the *Neviim*, four hundred men, and asked them, "Shall I march upon Ramoth-gilead for battle, or shall I not?" "March," they said, "and *Hashem* will deliver it into the king's hands."

ה וַיִּקְבֹּץ מֶלֶךְ־יִשְׂרָאֵל אֶת־הַנְּבִאִים אַרְבַּע מֵאוֹת אִישׁ וַיֹּאמֶר אֲלֵהֶם הֲנֵלֵךְ אֶל־רָמֹת גִּלְעָד לַמִּלְחָמָה אִם־אֶחְדָּל וַיֹּאמְרוּ עֲלֵה וְיִתֵּן הָאֱלֹהִים בְּיַד הַמֶּלֶךְ:

⁶ Then *Yehoshafat* asked, "Is there not another *Navi* of *Hashem* here through whom we can inquire?"

ו וַיֹּאמֶר יְהוֹשָׁפָט הַאֵין פֹּה נָבִיא לַיהוָה עוֹד וְנִדְרְשָׁה מֵאֹתוֹ:

⁷ And the king of *Yisrael* answered *Yehoshafat*, "There is one more man through whom we can inquire of *Hashem*; but I hate him, because he never prophesies anything good for me but always misfortune. He is *Michaihu* son of Imlah." *Yehoshafat* replied, "Let the king not say such a thing."

ז וַיֹּאמֶר מֶלֶךְ־יִשְׂרָאֵל אֶל־יְהוֹשָׁפָט עוֹד אִישׁ־אֶחָד לִדְרוֹשׁ אֶת־יְהוָה מֵאֹתוֹ וַאֲנִי שְׂנֵאתִיהוּ כִּי־אֵינֶנּוּ מִתְנַבֵּא עָלַי לְטוֹבָה כִּי כָל־יָמָיו לְרָעָה הוּא מִיכָיְהוּ בֶן־יִמְלָא וַיֹּאמֶר יְהוֹשָׁפָט אַל־יֹאמַר הַמֶּלֶךְ כֵּן:

⁸ So the king of *Yisrael* summoned an officer and said, "Bring *Michaihu* son of Imlah at once."

ח וַיִּקְרָא מֶלֶךְ יִשְׂרָאֵל אֶל־סָרִיס אֶחָד וַיֹּאמֶר מַהֵר מִיכָהוּ [מִיכָיְהוּ] בֶּן־יִמְלָא:

18:2 After some years had passed, he came to visit Achav at Shomron *Yehoshafat* visits *Achav* in Samaria, known in Hebrew as *Shomron* (שומרון). The city of Samaria was purchased by *Achav's* father *Omri* to be the capital of the kingdom of *Yisrael* (I Kings 16:24), and is an important part of both the biblical heartLand of Israel and the modern State of Israel. Today, the area known as Samaria comprises over 11% of the modern State of Israel and is home to many vibrant communities including *Ariel*, *Karnei Shomron*, *Elon Moreh* and *Itamar*. Since it is located in the middle of Israel, Samaria plays a vital role in the spirituality, economics and security of the country. Though *Omri* sinned greatly in his religious conduct, his acquisition of the *Shomron* was of great national importance both in his time and today.

View of Shomron

Divrei Hayamim II / II Chronicles
Chapter 18

9 The king of *Yisrael* and King *Yehoshafat* of *Yehuda*, wearing their robes, were seated on their thrones situated in the threshing floor at the entrance of the gate of *Shomron*; and all the *Neviim* were prophesying before them.

10 *Tzidkiyahu* son of Chenaanah had provided himself with iron horns; and he said, "Thus said *Hashem*: With these you shall gore the Arameans till you make an end of them."

11 All the other *Neviim* were prophesying similarly, "March against Ramoth-gilead and be victorious! *Hashem* will deliver it into Your Majesty's hands."

12 The messenger who had gone to summon *Michaihu* said to him, "Look, the words of the *Neviim* are unanimously favorable to the king. Let your word be like that of the rest of them; speak a favorable word."

13 "By the life of *Hashem*," *Michaihu* answered, "I will speak only what my God tells me."

14 When he came before the king, the king said to him, "*Micha*, shall we march against Ramoth-gilead for battle or shall we not?" He answered him, "March and be victorious! They will be delivered into your hands."

15 The king said to him, "How many times must I adjure you to tell me nothing but the truth in the name of *Hashem*?"

16 Then he said, "I saw all *Yisrael* scattered over the hills like sheep without a shepherd; and *Hashem* said, 'These have no master; let everyone return to his home in safety.'"

17 The king of *Yisrael* said to *Yehoshafat*, "Did I not tell you that he would not prophesy good fortune for me, but only misfortune?"

18 Then [*Michaihu*] said, "Indeed, hear now the word of *Hashem*! I saw *Hashem* seated upon His throne, with all the host of heaven standing in attendance to the right and to the left of Him.

19 *Hashem* asked, 'Who will entice King *Achav* of *Yisrael* so that he will march and fall at Ramoth-gilead?' Then one said this and another said that,

20 until a certain spirit came forward and stood before *Hashem* and said, 'I will entice him.' 'How?' said *Hashem* to him.

דברי הימים ב
פרק יח

ט וּמֶ֣לֶךְ יִשְׂרָאֵ֡ל וִיהוֹשָׁפָ֣ט מֶלֶךְ־יְהוּדָ֡ה יוֹשְׁבִים֩ אִ֨ישׁ עַל־כִּסְא֜וֹ מְלֻבָּשִׁ֤ים בְּגָדִים֙ וְיֹשְׁבִ֣ים בְּגֹ֔רֶן פֶּ֖תַח שַׁ֣עַר שֹׁמְר֑וֹן וְכָ֨ל־הַנְּבִיאִ֔ים מִֽתְנַבְּאִ֖ים לִפְנֵיהֶֽם׃

י וַיַּ֥עַשׂ ל֛וֹ צִדְקִיָּ֥הוּ בֶן־כְּנַעֲנָ֖ה קַרְנֵ֣י בַרְזֶ֑ל וַיֹּ֙אמֶר֙ כֹּה־אָמַ֣ר יְהֹוָ֔ה בְּאֵ֛לֶּה תְּנַגַּ֥ח אֶת־אֲרָ֖ם עַד־כַּלּוֹתָֽם׃

יא וְכָ֨ל־הַנְּבִאִ֔ים נִבְּאִ֥ים כֵּ֖ן לֵאמֹ֑ר עֲלֵ֞ה רָמֹ֤ת גִּלְעָד֙ וְהַצְלַ֔ח וְנָתַ֥ן יְהֹוָ֖ה בְּיַ֥ד הַמֶּֽלֶךְ׃

יב וְהַמַּלְאָ֞ךְ אֲשֶׁר־הָלַ֣ךְ ׀ לִקְרֹ֣א לְמִיכָ֗יְהוּ דִּבֶּ֨ר אֵלָ֜יו לֵאמֹ֗ר הִנֵּ֞ה דִּבְרֵ֧י הַנְּבִאִ֛ים פֶּה־אֶחָ֥ד טוֹב֙ אֶל־הַמֶּ֔לֶךְ וִיהִי־נָ֧א דְבָרְךָ֛ כְּאַחַ֥ד מֵהֶ֖ם וְדִבַּ֥רְתָּ טּֽוֹב׃

יג וַיֹּ֖אמֶר מִיכָ֑יְהוּ חַי־יְהֹוָ֕ה כִּ֠י אֶת־אֲשֶׁר־יֹאמַ֥ר אֱלֹהַ֖י אֹת֥וֹ אֲדַבֵּֽר׃

יד וַיָּבֹא֮ אֶל־הַמֶּלֶךְ֒ וַיֹּ֨אמֶר הַמֶּ֜לֶךְ אֵלָ֗יו מִיכָה֙ הֲנֵלֵ֞ךְ אֶל־רָמֹ֥ת גִּלְעָ֛ד לַמִּלְחָמָ֖ה אִם־אֶחְדָּ֑ל וַיֹּ֙אמֶר֙ עֲל֣וּ וְהַצְלִ֔יחוּ וְיִנָּתְנ֖וּ בְּיֶדְכֶֽם׃

טו וַיֹּ֤אמֶר אֵלָיו֙ הַמֶּ֔לֶךְ עַד־כַּמֶּ֥ה פְעָמִ֖ים אֲנִ֣י מַשְׁבִּיעֶ֑ךָ אֲשֶׁ֧ר לֹא־תְדַבֵּ֛ר אֵלַ֥י רַק־אֱמֶ֖ת בְּשֵׁ֥ם יְהֹוָֽה׃

טז וַיֹּ֗אמֶר רָאִ֤יתִי אֶת־כָּל־יִשְׂרָאֵל֙ נְפוֹצִ֣ים עַל־הֶהָרִ֔ים כַּצֹּ֕אן אֲשֶׁ֥ר אֵין־לָהֶ֖ן רֹעֶ֑ה וַיֹּ֣אמֶר יְהֹוָ֗ה לֹא־אֲדֹנִים֙ לָאֵ֔לֶּה יָשׁ֥וּבוּ אִישׁ־לְבֵית֖וֹ בְּשָׁלֽוֹם׃

יז וַיֹּ֥אמֶר מֶֽלֶךְ־יִשְׂרָאֵ֖ל אֶל־יְהוֹשָׁפָ֑ט הֲלֹא֙ אָמַ֣רְתִּי אֵלֶ֔יךָ לֹא־יִתְנַבֵּ֥א עָלַ֛י ט֖וֹב כִּ֥י אִם־לְרָֽע׃

יח וַיֹּ֕אמֶר לָכֵ֖ן שִׁמְע֣וּ דְבַר־יְהֹוָ֑ה רָאִ֤יתִי אֶת־יְהֹוָה֙ יוֹשֵׁ֣ב עַל־כִּסְא֔וֹ וְכָל־צְבָ֤א הַשָּׁמַ֙יִם֙ עֹמְדִ֔ים עַל־יְמִינ֖וֹ וּשְׂמֹאלֽוֹ׃

יט וַיֹּ֣אמֶר יְהֹוָ֗ה מִ֤י יְפַתֶּה֙ אֶת־אַחְאָ֣ב מֶֽלֶךְ־יִשְׂרָאֵ֔ל וְיַ֕עַל וְיִפֹּ֖ל בְּרָמ֣וֹת גִּלְעָ֑ד וַיֹּ֕אמֶר זֶ֚ה אֹמֵ֣ר כָּ֔כָה וְזֶ֖ה אֹמֵ֥ר כָּֽכָה׃

כ וַיֵּצֵ֣א הָר֗וּחַ וַֽיַּעֲמֹד֙ לִפְנֵ֣י יְהֹוָ֔ה וַיֹּ֖אמֶר אֲנִ֣י אֲפַתֶּ֑נּוּ וַיֹּ֧אמֶר יְהֹוָ֛ה אֵלָ֖יו בַּמָּֽה׃

Divrei Hayamim II / II Chronicles
Chapter 18

21 And he replied, 'I will go forth and become a lying spirit in the mouth of all his *Neviim*.' Then He said, 'You will entice with success. Go forth and do it.'

22 Thus *Hashem* has put a lying spirit in the mouth of all these *Neviim* of yours; for *Hashem* has decreed misfortune for you."

23 Thereupon *Tzidkiyahu* son of Chenaanah came up and struck *Michaihu* on the cheek, and exclaimed, "However did the spirit of *Hashem* pass from me to speak with you!"

24 *Michaihu* replied, "You will see on the day when you try to hide in the innermost room."

25 Then the king of *Yisrael* said, "Take *Michaihu* and turn him over to *Amon*, the governor of the city, and to Prince *Yoash*,

26 and say, 'The king's orders are: Put this fellow in prison, and let his fare be scant bread and scant water until I come home safe.'"

27 To which *Michaihu* retorted, "If you ever come home safe, *Hashem* has not spoken through me." He said further, "Listen, all you peoples!"

28 The king of *Yisrael* and King *Yehoshafat* of *Yehuda* marched against Ramoth-gilead.

29 The king of *Yisrael* said to *Yehoshafat*, "I will disguise myself and go into the battle, but you, wear your robes." So the king of *Yisrael* disguised himself, and they went into the battle.

30 The king of Aram had given these instructions to his chariot officers: "Do not attack anyone, small or great, except the king of *Yisrael*."

31 When the chariot officers saw *Yehoshafat*, whom they took for the king of *Yisrael*, they wheeled around to attack him, and *Yehoshafat* cried out and *Hashem* helped him, and *Hashem* diverted them from him.

32 And when the chariot officers realized that he was not the king of *Yisrael*, they gave up the pursuit.

33 Then a man drew his bow at random and hit the king of *Yisrael* between the plates of the armor and he said to his charioteer, "Turn around and get me behind the lines; I am wounded."

דברי הימים ב
פרק יח

כא וַיֹּאמֶר אֵצֵא וְהָיִיתִי לְרוּחַ שֶׁקֶר בְּפִי כׇּל־נְבִיאָיו וַיֹּאמֶר תְּפַתֶּה וְגַם־תּוּכָל צֵא וַעֲשֵׂה־כֵן:

כב וְעַתָּה הִנֵּה נָתַן יְהֹוָה רוּחַ שֶׁקֶר בְּפִי נְבִיאֶיךָ אֵלֶּה וַיהֹוָה דִּבֶּר עָלֶיךָ רָעָה:

כג וַיִּגַּשׁ צִדְקִיָּהוּ בֶן־כְּנַעֲנָה וַיַּךְ אֶת־מִיכָיְהוּ עַל־הַלֶּחִי וַיֹּאמֶר אֵי זֶה הַדֶּרֶךְ עָבַר רוּחַ־יְהֹוָה מֵאִתִּי לְדַבֵּר אֹתָךְ:

כד וַיֹּאמֶר מִיכָיְהוּ הִנְּךָ רֹאֶה בַּיּוֹם הַהוּא אֲשֶׁר תָּבוֹא חֶדֶר בְּחֶדֶר לְהֵחָבֵא:

כה וַיֹּאמֶר מֶלֶךְ יִשְׂרָאֵל קְחוּ אֶת־מִיכָיְהוּ וַהֲשִׁיבֻהוּ אֶל־אָמוֹן שַׂר־הָעִיר וְאֶל־יוֹאָשׁ בֶּן־הַמֶּלֶךְ:

כו וַאֲמַרְתֶּם כֹּה אָמַר הַמֶּלֶךְ שִׂימוּ זֶה בֵּית הַכֶּלֶא וְהַאֲכִילֻהוּ לֶחֶם לַחַץ וּמַיִם לָחַץ עַד שׁוּבִי בְשָׁלוֹם:

כז וַיֹּאמֶר מִיכָיְהוּ אִם־שׁוֹב תָּשׁוּב בְּשָׁלוֹם לֹא־דִבֶּר יְהֹוָה בִּי וַיֹּאמֶר שִׁמְעוּ עַמִּים כֻּלָּם:

כח וַיַּעַל מֶלֶךְ־יִשְׂרָאֵל וִיהוֹשָׁפָט מֶלֶךְ־יְהוּדָה אֶל־רָמֹת גִּלְעָד:

כט וַיֹּאמֶר מֶלֶךְ יִשְׂרָאֵל אֶל־יְהוֹשָׁפָט הִתְחַפֵּשׂ וָבוֹא בַמִּלְחָמָה וְאַתָּה לְבַשׁ בְּגָדֶיךָ וַיִּתְחַפֵּשׂ מֶלֶךְ יִשְׂרָאֵל וַיָּבֹאוּ בַּמִּלְחָמָה:

ל וּמֶלֶךְ אֲרָם צִוָּה אֶת־שָׂרֵי הָרֶכֶב אֲשֶׁר־לוֹ לֵאמֹר לֹא תִּלָּחֲמוּ אֶת־הַקָּטֹן אֶת־הַגָּדוֹל כִּי אִם־אֶת־מֶלֶךְ יִשְׂרָאֵל לְבַדּוֹ:

לא וַיְהִי כִּרְאוֹת שָׂרֵי הָרֶכֶב אֶת־יְהוֹשָׁפָט וְהֵמָּה אָמְרוּ מֶלֶךְ יִשְׂרָאֵל הוּא וַיָּסֹבּוּ עָלָיו לְהִלָּחֵם וַיִּזְעַק יְהוֹשָׁפָט וַיהֹוָה עֲזָרוֹ וַיְסִיתֵם אֱלֹהִים מִמֶּנּוּ:

לב וַיְהִי כִּרְאוֹת שָׂרֵי הָרֶכֶב כִּי לֹא־הָיָה מֶלֶךְ יִשְׂרָאֵל וַיָּשֻׁבוּ מֵאַחֲרָיו:

לג וְאִישׁ מָשַׁךְ בַּקֶּשֶׁת לְתֻמּוֹ וַיַּךְ אֶת־מֶלֶךְ יִשְׂרָאֵל בֵּין הַדְּבָקִים וּבֵין הַשִּׁרְיָן וַיֹּאמֶר לָרַכָּב הֲפֹךְ יָדְךָ [יָדֶיךָ] וְהוֹצֵאתַנִי מִן־הַמַּחֲנֶה כִּי הׇחֳלֵיתִי:

Divrei Hayamim II/II Chronicles
Chapter 19

דברי הימים ב
פרק יט

34 The battle raged all day long, and the king remained propped up in the chariot facing Aram until dusk; he died as the sun was setting.

לד וַתַּעַל הַמִּלְחָמָה בַּיּוֹם הַהוּא וּמֶלֶךְ יִשְׂרָאֵל הָיָה מַעֲמִיד בַּמֶּרְכָּבָה נֹכַח אֲרָם עַד־הָעָרֶב וַיָּמָת לְעֵת בּוֹא הַשָּׁמֶשׁ:

19 1 King *Yehoshafat* of *Yehuda* returned safely to his palace, to *Yerushalayim*.

יט א וַיָּשָׁב יְהוֹשָׁפָט מֶלֶךְ־יְהוּדָה אֶל־בֵּיתוֹ בְּשָׁלוֹם לִירוּשָׁלָ͏ִם:

2 *Yehu* son of *Chanani* the seer went out to meet King *Yehoshafat* and said to him, "Should one give aid to the wicked and befriend those who hate *Hashem*? For this, wrath is upon you from *Hashem*.

ב וַיֵּצֵא אֶל־פָּנָיו יֵהוּא בֶן־חֲנָנִי הַחֹזֶה וַיֹּאמֶר אֶל־הַמֶּלֶךְ יְהוֹשָׁפָט הֲלָרָשָׁע לַעְזֹר וּלְשֹׂנְאֵי יְהֹוָה תֶּאֱהָב וּבָזֹאת עָלֶיךָ קֶּצֶף מִלִּפְנֵי יְהֹוָה:

3 However, there is some good in you, for you have purged the land of the sacred posts and have dedicated yourself to worship *Hashem*."

ג אֲבָל דְּבָרִים טוֹבִים נִמְצְאוּ עִמָּךְ כִּי־בִעַרְתָּ הָאֲשֵׁרוֹת מִן־הָאָרֶץ וַהֲכִינוֹתָ לְבָבְךָ לִדְרֹשׁ הָאֱלֹהִים:

4 *Yehoshafat* remained in *Yerushalayim* a while and then went out among the people from *Be'er Sheva* to the hill country of *Efraim*; he brought them back to God of their fathers.

ד וַיֵּשֶׁב יְהוֹשָׁפָט בִּירוּשָׁלָ͏ִם וַיָּשָׁב וַיֵּצֵא בָעָם מִבְּאֵר שֶׁבַע עַד־הַר אֶפְרַיִם וַיְשִׁיבֵם אֶל־יְהֹוָה אֱלֹהֵי אֲבוֹתֵיהֶם:

5 He appointed judges in the land in all the fortified towns of *Yehuda*, in each and every town.

ה וַיַּעֲמֵד שֹׁפְטִים בָּאָרֶץ בְּכָל־עָרֵי יְהוּדָה הַבְּצֻרוֹת לְעִיר וָעִיר:

va-ya-a-MAYD sho-f'-TEEM ba-A-ratz b'-khol a-RAY y'-hu-DAH ha-b'-tzu-ROT l'-EER va-EER

6 He charged the judges: "Consider what you are doing, for you judge not on behalf of man, but on behalf of *Hashem*, and He is with you when you pass judgment.

ו וַיֹּאמֶר אֶל־הַשֹּׁפְטִים רְאוּ מָה־אַתֶּם עֹשִׂים כִּי לֹא לְאָדָם תִּשְׁפְּטוּ כִּי לַיהֹוָה וְעִמָּכֶם בִּדְבַר מִשְׁפָּט:

7 Now let the dread of *Hashem* be upon you; act with care, for there is no injustice or favoritism or bribe-taking with *Hashem* our God."

ז וְעַתָּה יְהִי פַחַד־יְהֹוָה עֲלֵיכֶם שִׁמְרוּ וַעֲשׂוּ כִּי־אֵין עִם־יְהֹוָה אֱלֹהֵינוּ עַוְלָה וּמַשֹּׂא פָנִים וּמִקַּח־שֹׁחַד:

8 *Yehoshafat* also appointed in *Yerushalayim* some *Leviim* and *Kohanim* and heads of the clans of Israelites for rendering judgment in matters of *Hashem*, and for disputes. Then they returned to *Yerushalayim*.

ח וְגַם בִּירוּשָׁלַ͏ִם הֶעֱמִיד יְהוֹשָׁפָט מִן־הַלְוִיִּם וְהַכֹּהֲנִים וּמֵרָאשֵׁי הָאָבוֹת לְיִשְׂרָאֵל לְמִשְׁפַּט יְהֹוָה וְלָרִיב וַיָּשֻׁבוּ יְרוּשָׁלָ͏ִם:

19:5 He appointed judges in the land *Yehoshafat* understands the importance of justice in the land. As he has dedicated himself to worship *Hashem* (verse 3) he not only prays and offers sacrifices, but also places a strong emphasis on seeking justice. He appoints judges throughout the land to judge "on behalf of *Hashem*" (verse 6), and warns them about being honest and against taking bribes. He understands that part of serving God in the Land of Israel is pursuing justice and righteousness. In fact, the prophets emphasize that it was when the Jewish people stopped acting with justice that their troubles in the land, culminating with the destruction and exile, really began. Therefore, as part of the ultimate redemption, *Yeshayahu* teaches that *Hashem* "will restore your magistrates as of old, and your counselors as of yore. After that you shall be called City of Righteousness, Faithful City." He continues, "*Tzion* shall be saved in the judgment, her repentant ones, in the retribution" (Isaiah 1:26–27).

Divrei Hayamim II / II Chronicles
Chapter 20

9 He charged them, "This is how you shall act: in fear of *Hashem*, with fidelity, and with whole heart.

10 When a dispute comes before you from your brothers living in their towns, whether about homicide, or about ritual, or laws or rules, you must instruct them so that they do not incur guilt before *Hashem* and wrath be upon you and your brothers. Act so and you will not incur guilt.

11 See, Amariah the chief *Kohen* is over you in all cases concerning *Hashem*, and Zebadiah son of Ishmael is the commander of the house of *Yehuda* in all cases concerning the king; the Levitical officials are at your disposal; act with resolve and *Hashem* be with the good."

20 1 After that, Moabites, Ammonites, together with some Ammonites, came against *Yehoshafat* to wage war.

2 The report was brought to *Yehoshafat*: "A great multitude is coming against you from beyond the sea, from Aram, and is now in Hazazon-tamar" – that is, Ein-gedi.

3 *Yehoshafat* was afraid; he decided to resort to *Hashem* and proclaimed a fast for all *Yehuda*.

4 *Yehuda* assembled to beseech *Hashem*. They also came from all the towns of *Yehuda* to seek *Hashem*.

5 *Yehoshafat* stood in the congregation of *Yehuda* and *Yerushalayim* in the House of *Hashem* at the front of the new court.

6 He said, "God of our fathers, truly You are the God in heaven and You rule over the kingdoms of the nations; power and strength are Yours; none can oppose You.

7 O our God, you dispossessed the inhabitants of this land before Your people *Yisrael*, and You gave it to the descendants of Your friend *Avraham* forever.

8 They settled in it and in it built for You a House for Your name. They said,

9 'Should misfortune befall us – the punishing sword, pestilence, or famine, we shall stand before this House and before You – for Your name is in this House – and we shall cry out to You in our distress, and You will listen and deliver us.'

דברי הימים ב
פרק כ

ט וַיְצַו עֲלֵיהֶם לֵאמֹר כֹּה תַעֲשׂוּן בְּיִרְאַת יְהוָה בֶּאֱמוּנָה וּבְלֵבָב שָׁלֵם:

י וְכָל־רִיב אֲשֶׁר־יָבוֹא עֲלֵיכֶם מֵאֲחֵיכֶם הַיֹּשְׁבִים בְּעָרֵיהֶם בֵּין־דָּם לְדָם בֵּין־תּוֹרָה לְמִצְוָה לְחֻקִּים וּלְמִשְׁפָּטִים וְהִזְהַרְתֶּם אֹתָם וְלֹא יֶאְשְׁמוּ לַיהוָה וְהָיָה־קֶצֶף עֲלֵיכֶם וְעַל־אֲחֵיכֶם כֹּה תַעֲשׂוּן וְלֹא תֶאְשָׁמוּ:

יא וְהִנֵּה אֲמַרְיָהוּ כֹהֵן הָרֹאשׁ עֲלֵיכֶם לְכֹל דְּבַר־יְהוָה וּזְבַדְיָהוּ בֶן־יִשְׁמָעֵאל הַנָּגִיד לְבֵית־יְהוּדָה לְכֹל דְּבַר־הַמֶּלֶךְ וְשֹׁטְרִים הַלְוִיִּם לִפְנֵיכֶם חִזְקוּ וַעֲשׂוּ וִיהִי יְהוָה עִם־הַטּוֹב:

כ א וַיְהִי אַחֲרֵיכֵן בָּאוּ בְנֵי־מוֹאָב וּבְנֵי עַמּוֹן וְעִמָּהֶם מֵהָעַמּוֹנִים עַל־יְהוֹשָׁפָט לַמִּלְחָמָה:

ב וַיָּבֹאוּ וַיַּגִּידוּ לִיהוֹשָׁפָט לֵאמֹר בָּא עָלֶיךָ הָמוֹן רָב מֵעֵבֶר לַיָּם מֵאֲרָם וְהִנָּם בְּחַצְצוֹן תָּמָר הִיא עֵין גֶּדִי:

ג וַיִּרָא וַיִּתֵּן יְהוֹשָׁפָט אֶת־פָּנָיו לִדְרוֹשׁ לַיהוָה וַיִּקְרָא־צוֹם עַל־כָּל־יְהוּדָה:

ד וַיִּקָּבְצוּ יְהוּדָה לְבַקֵּשׁ מֵיְהוָה גַּם מִכָּל־עָרֵי יְהוּדָה בָּאוּ לְבַקֵּשׁ אֶת־יְהוָה:

ה וַיַּעֲמֹד יְהוֹשָׁפָט בִּקְהַל יְהוּדָה וִירוּשָׁלַםִ בְּבֵית יְהוָה לִפְנֵי הֶחָצֵר הַחֲדָשָׁה:

ו וַיֹּאמַר יְהוָה אֱלֹהֵי אֲבֹתֵינוּ הֲלֹא אַתָּה־הוּא אֱלֹהִים בַּשָּׁמַיִם וְאַתָּה מוֹשֵׁל בְּכֹל מַמְלְכוֹת הַגּוֹיִם וּבְיָדְךָ כֹּחַ וּגְבוּרָה וְאֵין עִמְּךָ לְהִתְיַצֵּב:

ז הֲלֹא אַתָּה אֱלֹהֵינוּ הוֹרַשְׁתָּ אֶת־יֹשְׁבֵי הָאָרֶץ הַזֹּאת מִלִּפְנֵי עַמְּךָ יִשְׂרָאֵל וַתִּתְּנָהּ לְזֶרַע אַבְרָהָם אֹהַבְךָ לְעוֹלָם:

ח וַיֵּשְׁבוּ־בָהּ וַיִּבְנוּ לְךָ בָּהּ מִקְדָּשׁ לְשִׁמְךָ לֵאמֹר:

ט אִם־תָּבוֹא עָלֵינוּ רָעָה חֶרֶב שְׁפוֹט וְדֶבֶר וְרָעָב נַעַמְדָה לִפְנֵי הַבַּיִת הַזֶּה וּלְפָנֶיךָ כִּי שִׁמְךָ בַּבַּיִת הַזֶּה וְנִזְעַק אֵלֶיךָ מִצָּרָתֵנוּ וְתִשְׁמַע וְתוֹשִׁיעַ:

Divrei Hayamim II/II Chronicles
Chapter 20

10 Now the people of Ammon, Moab, and the hill country of Seir, into whose [land] You did not let *Yisrael* come when they came from Egypt, but they turned aside from them and did not wipe them out,

11 these now repay us by coming to expel us from Your possession which You gave us as ours.

12 O our God, surely You will punish them, for we are powerless before this great multitude that has come against us, and do not know what to do, but our eyes are on You."

13 All *Yehuda* stood before *Hashem* with their little ones, their womenfolk, and their children.

14 Then in the midst of the congregation the spirit of *Hashem* came upon *Yachaziel* son of *Zecharya* son of Benaiah son of Jeiel son of Mattaniah the *Levi*, of the sons of *Asaf*,

15 and he said, "Give heed, all *Yehuda* and the inhabitants of *Yerushalayim* and King *Yehoshafat*; thus said *Hashem* to you, 'Do not fear or be dismayed by this great multitude, for the battle is *Hashem*'s, not yours.

16 March down against them tomorrow as they come up by the Ascent of Ziz; you will find them at the end of the wadi in the direction of the wilderness of Jeruel.

17 It is not for you to fight this battle; stand by, wait, and witness your deliverance by *Hashem*, O *Yehuda* and *Yerushalayim*; do not fear or be dismayed; go forth to meet them tomorrow and *Hashem* will be with you.'"

18 *Yehoshafat* bowed low with his face to the ground, and all *Yehuda* and the inhabitants of *Yerushalayim* threw themselves down before *Hashem* to worship *Hashem*.

19 *Leviim* of the sons of *Kehat* and of the sons of *Korach* got up to extol God of *Yisrael* at the top of their voices.

20 Early the next morning they arose and went forth to the wilderness of *Tekoa*. As they went forth, *Yehoshafat* stood and said, "Listen to me, O *Yehuda* and inhabitants of *Yerushalayim*: Trust firmly in *Hashem* your God and you will stand firm; trust firmly in His *Neviim* and you will succeed."

דברי הימים ב
פרק כ

י וְעַתָּה הִנֵּה בְנֵי־עַמּוֹן וּמוֹאָב וְהַר־שֵׂעִיר אֲשֶׁר לֹא־נָתַתָּה לְיִשְׂרָאֵל לָבוֹא בָהֶם בְּבֹאָם מֵאֶרֶץ מִצְרָיִם כִּי סָרוּ מֵעֲלֵיהֶם וְלֹא הִשְׁמִידוּם:

יא וְהִנֵּה־הֵם גֹּמְלִים עָלֵינוּ לָבוֹא לְגָרְשֵׁנוּ מִיְּרֻשָּׁתְךָ אֲשֶׁר הוֹרַשְׁתָּנוּ:

יב אֱלֹהֵינוּ הֲלֹא תִשְׁפָּט־בָּם כִּי אֵין בָּנוּ כֹּחַ לִפְנֵי הֶהָמוֹן הָרָב הַזֶּה הַבָּא עָלֵינוּ וַאֲנַחְנוּ לֹא נֵדַע מַה־נַּעֲשֶׂה כִּי עָלֶיךָ עֵינֵינוּ:

יג וְכָל־יְהוּדָה עֹמְדִים לִפְנֵי יְהֹוָה גַּם־טַפָּם נְשֵׁיהֶם וּבְנֵיהֶם:

יד וְיַחֲזִיאֵל בֶּן־זְכַרְיָהוּ בֶּן־בְּנָיָה בֶּן־יְעִיאֵל בֶּן־מַתַּנְיָה הַלֵּוִי מִן־בְּנֵי אָסָף הָיְתָה עָלָיו רוּחַ יְהֹוָה בְּתוֹךְ הַקָּהָל:

טו וַיֹּאמֶר הַקְשִׁיבוּ כָל־יְהוּדָה וְיֹשְׁבֵי יְרוּשָׁלַם וְהַמֶּלֶךְ יְהוֹשָׁפָט כֹּה־אָמַר יְהֹוָה לָכֶם אַתֶּם אַל־תִּירְאוּ וְאַל־תֵּחַתּוּ מִפְּנֵי הֶהָמוֹן הָרָב הַזֶּה כִּי לֹא לָכֶם הַמִּלְחָמָה כִּי לֵאלֹהִים:

טז מָחָר רְדוּ עֲלֵיהֶם הִנָּם עֹלִים בְּמַעֲלֵה הַצִּיץ וּמְצָאתֶם אֹתָם בְּסוֹף הַנַּחַל פְּנֵי מִדְבַּר יְרוּאֵל:

יז לֹא לָכֶם לְהִלָּחֵם בָּזֹאת הִתְיַצְּבוּ עִמְדוּ וּרְאוּ אֶת־יְשׁוּעַת יְהֹוָה עִמָּכֶם יְהוּדָה וִירוּשָׁלַם אַל־תִּירְאוּ וְאַל־תֵּחַתּוּ מָחָר צְאוּ לִפְנֵיהֶם וַיהֹוָה עִמָּכֶם:

יח וַיִּקֹּד יְהוֹשָׁפָט אַפַּיִם אָרְצָה וְכָל־יְהוּדָה וְיֹשְׁבֵי יְרוּשָׁלַם נָפְלוּ לִפְנֵי יְהֹוָה לְהִשְׁתַּחֲוֹת לַיהֹוָה:

יט וַיָּקֻמוּ הַלְוִיִּם מִן־בְּנֵי הַקְּהָתִים וּמִן־בְּנֵי הַקָּרְחִים לְהַלֵּל לַיהֹוָה אֱלֹהֵי יִשְׂרָאֵל בְּקוֹל גָּדוֹל לְמָעְלָה:

כ וַיַּשְׁכִּימוּ בַבֹּקֶר וַיֵּצְאוּ לְמִדְבַּר תְּקוֹעַ וּבְצֵאתָם עָמַד יְהוֹשָׁפָט וַיֹּאמֶר שְׁמָעוּנִי יְהוּדָה וְיֹשְׁבֵי יְרוּשָׁלַם הַאֲמִינוּ בַּיהֹוָה אֱלֹהֵיכֶם וְתֵאָמֵנוּ הַאֲמִינוּ בִנְבִיאָיו וְהַצְלִיחוּ:

Divrei Hayamim II / II Chronicles
Chapter 20

דברי הימים ב
פרק כ

21 After taking counsel with the people, he stationed singers to *Hashem* extolling the One majestic in holiness as they went forth ahead of the vanguard, saying, "Praise *Hashem*, for His steadfast love is eternal."

כא וַיִּוָּעַץ אֶל־הָעָם וַיַּעֲמֵד מְשֹׁרֲרִים לַיהוָה וּמְהַלְלִים לְהַדְרַת־קֹדֶשׁ בְּצֵאת לִפְנֵי הֶחָלוּץ וְאֹמְרִים הוֹדוּ לַיהוָה כִּי לְעוֹלָם חַסְדּוֹ:

22 As they began their joyous shouts and hymns, *Hashem* set ambushes for the men of Ammon, Moab, and the hill country of Seir, who were marching against *Yehuda*, and they were routed.

כב וּבְעֵת הֵחֵלּוּ בְרִנָּה וּתְהִלָּה נָתַן יְהוָה מְאָרְבִים עַל־בְּנֵי עַמּוֹן מוֹאָב וְהַר־שֵׂעִיר הַבָּאִים לִיהוּדָה וַיִּנָּגֵפוּ:

23 The Ammonites and Moabites turned against the men of the hill country of Seir to exterminate and annihilate them. When they had made an end of the men of Seir, each helped to destroy his fellow.

כג וַיַּעַמְדוּ בְּנֵי עַמּוֹן וּמוֹאָב עַל־יֹשְׁבֵי הַר־שֵׂעִיר לְהַחֲרִים וּלְהַשְׁמִיד וּכְכַלּוֹתָם בְּיוֹשְׁבֵי שֵׂעִיר עָזְרוּ אִישׁ־בְּרֵעֵהוּ לְמַשְׁחִית:

24 When *Yehuda* reached the lookout in the wilderness and looked for the multitude, they saw them lying on the ground as corpses; not one had survived.

כד וִיהוּדָה בָּא עַל־הַמִּצְפֶּה לַמִּדְבָּר וַיִּפְנוּ אֶל־הֶהָמוֹן וְהִנָּם פְּגָרִים נֹפְלִים אַרְצָה וְאֵין פְּלֵיטָה:

25 *Yehoshafat* and his army came to take the booty, and found an abundance of goods, corpses, and precious objects, which they pillaged, more than they could carry off. For three days they were taking booty, there was so much of it.

כה וַיָּבֹא יְהוֹשָׁפָט וְעַמּוֹ לָבֹז אֶת־שְׁלָלָם וַיִּמְצְאוּ בָהֶם לָרֹב וּרְכוּשׁ וּפְגָרִים וּכְלֵי חֲמֻדוֹת וַיְנַצְּלוּ לָהֶם לְאֵין מַשָּׂא וַיִּהְיוּ יָמִים שְׁלוֹשָׁה בֹּזְזִים אֶת־הַשָּׁלָל כִּי רַב־הוּא:

26 On the fourth day they assembled in the Valley of Blessing – for there they blessed *Hashem*; that is why that place is called the Valley of Blessing to this day.

כו וּבַיּוֹם הָרְבִעִי נִקְהֲלוּ לְעֵמֶק בְּרָכָה כִּי־שָׁם בֵּרֲכוּ אֶת־יְהוָה עַל־כֵּן קָרְאוּ אֶת־שֵׁם הַמָּקוֹם הַהוּא עֵמֶק בְּרָכָה עַד־הַיּוֹם:

u-va-YOM ha-r'-vi-EE nik-ha-LU l'-AY-mek b'ra-KHAH KEE SHAM bay-r'-KHU et a-do-NAI al KAYN ka-r'-U et SHAYM ha-ma-KOM ha-HU AY-mek b'ra-KHAH ad ha-YOM

27 All the men of *Yehuda* and *Yerushalayim* with *Yehoshafat* at their head returned joyfully to *Yerushalayim*, for *Hashem* had given them cause for rejoicing over their enemies.

כז וַיָּשֻׁבוּ כָּל־אִישׁ יְהוּדָה וִירוּשָׁלַםִ וִיהוֹשָׁפָט בְּרֹאשָׁם לָשׁוּב אֶל־יְרוּשָׁלַםִ בְּשִׂמְחָה כִּי־שִׂמְּחָם יְהוָה מֵאוֹיְבֵיהֶם:

28 They came to *Yerushalayim* to the House of *Hashem*, to the accompaniment of harps, lyres, and trumpets.

כח וַיָּבֹאוּ יְרוּשָׁלַםִ בִּנְבָלִים וּבְכִנֹּרוֹת וּבַחֲצֹצְרוֹת אֶל־בֵּית יְהוָה:

20:26 That place is called the Valley of Blessing to this day After God miraculously defeats his enemies, *Yehoshafat* gathers the people together to bless *Hashem*. The site of this blessing is named 'the Valley of Blessing,' or *Emek HaBeracha* (עמק ברכה) since *beracha* is the Hebrew word for blessing. Today, this valley is located in the Etzion region, and is surrounded by the Jewish towns of *Carmei Tzur, Bat Ayin, Kfar Etzion* and *Alon Shvut*. The land is truly blessed and is known for its fertile soil. The Gush Etzion Winery, located just outside the town of *Alon Shvut*, has a vineyard in the valley. The grapes grown there are used for their high-end blended red series of wines known as *Emek Beracha*.

The Gush Etzion Winery

Divrei Hayamim II/II Chronicles
Chapter 21

29 The terror of *Hashem* seized all the kingdoms of the lands when they heard that *Hashem* had fought the enemies of *Yisrael*.

30 The kingdom of *Yehoshafat* was untroubled, and his God granted him respite on all sides.

31 *Yehoshafat* reigned over *Yehuda*. He was thirty-five years old when he became king, and he reigned in *Yerushalayim* for twenty-five years. His mother's name was Azubah daughter of Shilhi.

32 He followed the course of his father *Asa* and did not deviate from it, doing what was pleasing to *Hashem*.

33 However, the shrines did not cease; the people still did not direct their heart toward the God of their fathers.

34 As for the other events of *Yehoshafat*'s reign, early and late, they are recorded in the annals of *Yehu* son of *Chanani*, which were included in the book of the kings of *Yisrael*.

35 Afterward, King *Yehoshafat* of *Yehuda* entered into a partnership with King *Achazyahu* of *Yisrael*, thereby acting wickedly.

36 He joined with him in constructing ships to go to Tarshish; the ships were constructed in Ezion-geber.

37 *Eliezer* son of Dodavahu of Mareshah prophesied against *Yehoshafat*, "As you have made a partnership with *Achazyahu*, *Hashem* will break up your work." The ships were wrecked and were unable to go to Tarshish.

21

1 *Yehoshafat* slept with his fathers and was buried with his fathers in the City of *David*; his son *Yehoram* succeeded him as king.

2 He had brothers, sons of *Yehoshafat*: *Azarya*, *Yechiel*, *Zecharya*, Azariahu, *Michael*, and Shephatiah; all these were sons of King *Yehoshafat* of *Yisrael*.

3 Their father gave them many gifts of silver, gold, and [other] presents, as well as fortified towns in *Yehuda*, but he gave the kingdom to *Yehoram* because he was the first-born.

דברי הימים ב
פרק כא

כט וַיְהִי פַּחַד אֱלֹהִים עַל כָּל־מַמְלְכוֹת הָאֲרָצוֹת בְּשָׁמְעָם כִּי נִלְחַם יְהוָה עִם אוֹיְבֵי יִשְׂרָאֵל:

ל וַתִּשְׁקֹט מַלְכוּת יְהוֹשָׁפָט וַיָּנַח לוֹ אֱלֹהָיו מִסָּבִיב:

לא וַיִּמְלֹךְ יְהוֹשָׁפָט עַל־יְהוּדָה בֶּן־שְׁלֹשִׁים וְחָמֵשׁ שָׁנָה בְּמָלְכוֹ וְעֶשְׂרִים וְחָמֵשׁ שָׁנָה מָלַךְ בִּירוּשָׁלִָם וְשֵׁם אִמּוֹ עֲזוּבָה בַּת־שִׁלְחִי:

לב וַיֵּלֶךְ בְּדֶרֶךְ אָבִיו אָסָא וְלֹא־סָר מִמֶּנָּה לַעֲשׂוֹת הַיָּשָׁר בְּעֵינֵי יְהוָה:

לג אַךְ הַבָּמוֹת לֹא־סָרוּ וְעוֹד הָעָם לֹא־הֵכִינוּ לְבָבָם לֵאלֹהֵי אֲבֹתֵיהֶם:

לד וְיֶתֶר דִּבְרֵי יְהוֹשָׁפָט הָרִאשֹׁנִים וְהָאַחֲרֹנִים הִנָּם כְּתוּבִים בְּדִבְרֵי יֵהוּא בֶן־חֲנָנִי אֲשֶׁר הֹעֲלָה עַל־סֵפֶר מַלְכֵי יִשְׂרָאֵל:

לה וְאַחֲרֵיכֵן אֶתְחַבַּר יְהוֹשָׁפָט מֶלֶךְ־יְהוּדָה עִם אֲחַזְיָה מֶלֶךְ־יִשְׂרָאֵל הוּא הִרְשִׁיעַ לַעֲשׂוֹת:

לו וַיְחַבְּרֵהוּ עִמּוֹ לַעֲשׂוֹת אֳנִיּוֹת לָלֶכֶת תַּרְשִׁישׁ וַיַּעֲשׂוּ אֳנִיּוֹת בְּעֶצְיוֹן גָּבֶר:

לז וַיִּתְנַבֵּא אֱלִיעֶזֶר בֶּן־דֹּדָוָהוּ מִמָּרֵשָׁה עַל־יְהוֹשָׁפָט לֵאמֹר כְּהִתְחַבֶּרְךָ עִם־אֲחַזְיָהוּ פָּרַץ יְהוָה אֶת־מַעֲשֶׂיךָ וַיִּשָּׁבְרוּ אֳנִיּוֹת וְלֹא עָצְרוּ לָלֶכֶת אֶל־תַּרְשִׁישׁ:

כא א וַיִּשְׁכַּב יְהוֹשָׁפָט עִם־אֲבֹתָיו וַיִּקָּבֵר עִם־אֲבֹתָיו בְּעִיר דָּוִיד וַיִּמְלֹךְ יְהוֹרָם בְּנוֹ תַּחְתָּיו:

ב וְלוֹ־אַחִים בְּנֵי יְהוֹשָׁפָט עֲזַרְיָה וִיחִיאֵל וּזְכַרְיָהוּ וַעֲזַרְיָהוּ וּמִיכָאֵל וּשְׁפַטְיָהוּ כָּל־אֵלֶּה בְּנֵי יְהוֹשָׁפָט מֶלֶךְ־יִשְׂרָאֵל:

ג וַיִּתֵּן לָהֶם אֲבִיהֶם מַתָּנוֹת רַבּוֹת לְכֶסֶף וּלְזָהָב וּלְמִגְדָּנוֹת עִם־עָרֵי מְצֻרוֹת בִּיהוּדָה וְאֶת־הַמַּמְלָכָה נָתַן לִיהוֹרָם כִּי־הוּא הַבְּכוֹר:

Divrei Hayamim II / II Chronicles
Chapter 21 / דברי הימים ב · פרק כא

4 *Yehoram* proceeded to take firm hold of his father's kingdom and put to the sword all his brothers, as well as some of the officers of *Yisrael*.

ד וַיָּקָם יְהוֹרָם עַל־מַמְלֶכֶת אָבִיו וַיִּתְחַזָּק וַיַּהֲרֹג אֶת־כָּל־אֶחָיו בֶּחָרֶב וְגַם מִשָּׂרֵי יִשְׂרָאֵל׃

5 *Yehoram* was thirty-two years old when he became king, and he reigned in *Yerushalayim* eight years.

ה בֶּן־שְׁלֹשִׁים וּשְׁתַּיִם שָׁנָה יְהוֹרָם בְּמָלְכוֹ וּשְׁמוֹנֶה שָׁנִים מָלַךְ בִּירוּשָׁלִָם׃

6 He followed the practices of the kings of *Yisrael* doing what the House of *Achav* had done, for he married a daughter of *Achav*; he did what was displeasing to *Hashem*.

ו וַיֵּלֶךְ בְּדֶרֶךְ מַלְכֵי יִשְׂרָאֵל כַּאֲשֶׁר עָשׂוּ בֵּית אַחְאָב כִּי בַּת־אַחְאָב הָיְתָה לּוֹ אִשָּׁה וַיַּעַשׂ הָרַע בְּעֵינֵי יְהוָה׃

7 However, *Hashem* refrained from destroying the House of *David* for the sake of the covenant he had made with *David*, and in accordance with his promise to maintain a lamp for him and his descendants for all time.

ז וְלֹא־אָבָה יְהוָה לְהַשְׁחִית אֶת־בֵּית דָּוִיד לְמַעַן הַבְּרִית אֲשֶׁר כָּרַת לְדָוִיד וְכַאֲשֶׁר אָמַר לָתֵת לוֹ נִיר וּלְבָנָיו כָּל־הַיָּמִים׃

8 During his reign, the Edomites rebelled against *Yehuda*'s rule and set up a king of their own.

ח בְּיָמָיו פָּשַׁע אֱדוֹם מִתַּחַת יַד־יְהוּדָה וַיַּמְלִיכוּ עֲלֵיהֶם מֶלֶךְ׃

9 *Yehoram* advanced [against them] with his officers and all his chariotry. He arose by night and attacked the Edomites, who surrounded him and the chariot commanders.

ט וַיַּעֲבֹר יְהוֹרָם עִם־שָׂרָיו וְכָל־הָרֶכֶב עִמּוֹ וַיְהִי קָם לַיְלָה וַיַּךְ אֶת־אֱדוֹם הַסּוֹבֵב אֵלָיו וְאֵת שָׂרֵי הָרָכֶב׃

10 Edom has been in rebellion against *Yehuda*, to this day; Libnah also rebelled against him at that time, because he had forsaken God of his fathers.

י וַיִּפְשַׁע אֱדוֹם מִתַּחַת יַד־יְהוּדָה עַד הַיּוֹם הַזֶּה אָז תִּפְשַׁע לִבְנָה בָּעֵת הַהִיא מִתַּחַת יָדוֹ כִּי עָזַב אֶת־יְהוָה אֱלֹהֵי אֲבֹתָיו׃

11 Moreover, he built shrines in the hill country of *Yehuda*; he led astray the inhabitants of *Yerushalayim* and made *Yehuda* wayward.

יא גַּם־הוּא עָשָׂה־בָמוֹת בְּהָרֵי יְהוּדָה וַיֶּזֶן אֶת־יֹשְׁבֵי יְרוּשָׁלִַם וַיַּדַּח אֶת־יְהוּדָה׃

12 A letter from *Eliyahu* the *Navi* came to him which read, "Thus says God of your father *David*: Since you have not followed the practices of your father *Yehoshafat* and the practices of King *Asa* of *Yehuda*,

יב וַיָּבֹא אֵלָיו מִכְתָּב מֵאֵלִיָּהוּ הַנָּבִיא לֵאמֹר כֹּה אָמַר יְהוָה אֱלֹהֵי דָּוִיד אָבִיךָ תַּחַת אֲשֶׁר לֹא־הָלַכְתָּ בְּדַרְכֵי יְהוֹשָׁפָט אָבִיךָ וּבְדַרְכֵי אָסָא מֶלֶךְ־יְהוּדָה׃

13 but have followed the practices of the kings of *Yisrael*, leading astray *Yehuda* and the inhabitants of *Yerushalayim* as the House of *Achav* led them astray, and have also killed your brothers of your father's house, who were better than you,

יג וַתֵּלֶךְ בְּדֶרֶךְ מַלְכֵי יִשְׂרָאֵל וַתַּזְנֶה אֶת־יְהוּדָה וְאֶת־יֹשְׁבֵי יְרוּשָׁלִַם כְּהַזְנוֹת בֵּית אַחְאָב וְגַם אֶת־אַחֶיךָ בֵית־אָבִיךָ הַטּוֹבִים מִמְּךָ הָרָגְתָּ׃

14 therefore, *Hashem* will inflict a great blow upon your people, your sons, and your wives and all your possessions.

יד הִנֵּה יְהוָה נֹגֵף מַגֵּפָה גְדוֹלָה בְּעַמֶּךָ וּבְבָנֶיךָ וּבְנָשֶׁיךָ וּבְכָל־רְכוּשֶׁךָ׃

15 As for you, you will be severely stricken with a disorder of the bowels year after year until your bowels drop out."

טו וְאַתָּה בָּחֳלָיִים רַבִּים בְּמַחֲלֵה מֵעֶיךָ עַד־יֵצְאוּ מֵעֶיךָ מִן־הַחֹלִי יָמִים עַל־יָמִים׃

Divrei Hayamim II/II Chronicles
Chapter 22

16 *Hashem* stirred up the spirit of the Philistines and the Arabs who were neighbors of the Cushites against *Yehoram*.

טז וַיָּעַר יְהוָה עַל־יְהוֹרָם אֵת רוּחַ הַפְּלִשְׁתִּים וְהָעַרְבִים אֲשֶׁר עַל־יַד כּוּשִׁים:

17 They marched against *Yehuda*, breached its defenses, and carried off all the property that was found in the king's palace, as well as his sons and his wives. The only son who remained was *Yehoachaz*, his youngest.

יז וַיַּעֲלוּ בִיהוּדָה וַיִּבְקָעוּהָ וַיִּשְׁבּוּ אֵת כָּל־הָרְכוּשׁ הַנִּמְצָא לְבֵית־הַמֶּלֶךְ וְגַם־בָּנָיו וְנָשָׁיו וְלֹא נִשְׁאַר־לוֹ בֵּן כִּי אִם־יְהוֹאָחָז קְטֹן בָּנָיו:

18 After this, *Hashem* afflicted him with an incurable disease of the bowels.

יח וְאַחֲרֵי כָּל־זֹאת נְגָפוֹ יְהוָה בְּמֵעָיו לָחֳלִי לְאֵין מַרְפֵּא:

19 Some years later, when a period of two years had elapsed, his bowels dropped out because of his disease, and he died a gruesome death. His people did not make a fire for him like the fire for his fathers.

יט וַיְהִי לְיָמִים מִיָּמִים וּכְעֵת צֵאת הַקֵּץ לְיָמִים שְׁנַיִם יָצְאוּ מֵעָיו עִם־חָלְיוֹ וַיָּמָת בְּתַחֲלֻאִים רָעִים וְלֹא־עָשׂוּ לוֹ עַמּוֹ שְׂרֵפָה כִּשְׂרֵפַת אֲבֹתָיו:

20 He was thirty-two years old when he became king, and he reigned in *Yerushalayim* eight years. He departed unpraised, and was buried in the City of *David*, but not in the tombs of the kings.

כ בֶּן־שְׁלֹשִׁים וּשְׁתַּיִם הָיָה בְמָלְכוֹ וּשְׁמוֹנֶה שָׁנִים מָלַךְ בִּירוּשָׁלָםִ וַיֵּלֶךְ בְּלֹא חֶמְדָּה וַיִּקְבְּרֻהוּ בְּעִיר דָּוִיד וְלֹא בְּקִבְרוֹת הַמְּלָכִים:

ben sh'-lo-SHEEM ush-TA-yim ha-YAH v'-mol-KHO ush-mo-NEH sha-NEEM ma-LAKH bee-ru-sha-LA-im va-YAY-lekh b'-LO khem-DAH va-yik-b'-RU-hu b'-EER da-VEED v'-LO b'-kiv-ROT ha-m'-la-KHEEM

22

1 The inhabitants of *Yerushalayim* made *Achazyahu*, his youngest son, king in his stead, because all the older ones had been killed by the troops that penetrated the camp with the Arabs. *Achazyahu* son of *Yehoram* reigned as king of *Yehuda*.

א וַיַּמְלִיכוּ יוֹשְׁבֵי יְרוּשָׁלַםִ אֶת־אֲחַזְיָהוּ בְנוֹ הַקָּטֹן תַּחְתָּיו כִּי כָל־הָרִאשֹׁנִים הָרַג הַגְּדוּד הַבָּא בָעַרְבִים לַמַּחֲנֶה וַיִּמְלֹךְ אֲחַזְיָהוּ בֶן־יְהוֹרָם מֶלֶךְ יְהוּדָה:

2 *Achazyahu* was forty-two years old when he became king, and he reigned in *Yerushalayim* one year; his mother's name was *Atalya* daughter of *Omri*.

ב בֶּן־אַרְבָּעִים וּשְׁתַּיִם שָׁנָה אֲחַזְיָהוּ בְמָלְכוֹ וְשָׁנָה אַחַת מָלַךְ בִּירוּשָׁלָםִ וְשֵׁם אִמּוֹ עֲתַלְיָהוּ בַּת־עָמְרִי:

3 He too followed the practices of the house of *Achav*, for his mother counseled him to do evil.

ג גַּם־הוּא הָלַךְ בְּדַרְכֵי בֵּית אַחְאָב כִּי אִמּוֹ הָיְתָה יוֹעַצְתּוֹ לְהַרְשִׁיעַ:

21:20 But not in the tombs of the kings *Yehoram* does not behave as his forefathers before him did. By marrying into the House of *Achav*, and bringing idol worship into the kingdom, he betrays God. As such, he is punished heavily for his sins, and though he is not stripped of his kingdom, it loses its prominence and power. Upon his death, the people bury him apart from his ancestors. They realize that though he is of the Davidic line, because of his actions he is not a true Davidic king. *Yehoram* teaches us that the Davidic line is not merely an inheritance; it demands a certain code of behavior. So too with all birthrights. The way a person behaves means more than who his ancestors were.

Divrei Hayamim II / II Chronicles
Chapter 22

דברי הימים ב
פרק כב

4 He did what was displeasing to *Hashem*, like the house of *Achav*, for they became his counselors after his father's death, to his ruination.

ד וַיַּ֧עַשׂ הָרַ֛ע בְּעֵינֵ֥י יְהֹוָ֖ה כְּבֵ֣ית אַחְאָ֑ב כִּי־הֵ֜מָּה הָֽיוּ־ל֣וֹ יֽוֹעֲצִ֗ים אַחֲרֵ֛י מ֥וֹת אָבִ֖יו לְמַשְׁחִ֥ית לֽוֹ׃

5 Moreover, he followed their counsel and marched with *Yehoram* son of King *Achav* of *Yisrael* to battle against King Hazael of Aram at Ramoth-gilead, where the Arameans wounded *Yoram*.

ה גַּ֣ם בַּעֲצָתָם֮ הָלַךְ֒ וַיֵּ֡לֶךְ אֶת־יְהוֹרָ֣ם בֶּן־אַחְאָב֩ מֶ֨לֶךְ יִשְׂרָאֵ֜ל לַמִּלְחָמָ֛ה עַל־חֲזָאֵ֥ל מֶֽלֶךְ־אֲרָ֖ם בְּרָמ֣וֹת גִּלְעָ֑ד וַיַּכּ֥וּ הָרַמִּ֖ים אֶת־יוֹרָֽם׃

6 He returned to *Yizrael* to recover from the wounds inflicted on him at *Rama* when he fought against King Hazael of Aram. King *Azarya* son of *Yehoram* of *Yehuda* went down to *Yizrael* to visit *Yehoram* son of *Achav* while he was ill.

ו וַיָּ֜שׇׁב לְהִתְרַפֵּ֣א בְיִזְרְעֶ֗אל כִּ֤י הַמַּכִּים֙ אֲשֶׁ֣ר הִכֻּ֣הוּ בָֽרָמָ֔ה בְּהִלָּ֣חֲמ֔וֹ אֶת־חֲזָהאֵ֖ל מֶ֣לֶךְ אֲרָ֑ם וַעֲזַרְיָ֨הוּ בֶן־יְהוֹרָ֜ם מֶ֣לֶךְ יְהוּדָ֗ה יָרַ֛ד לִרְא֛וֹת אֶת־יְהוֹרָ֥ם בֶּן־אַחְאָ֖ב בְּיִזְרְעֶ֥אל כִּי־חֹלֶ֥ה הֽוּא׃

7 *Hashem* caused the downfall of *Achazyahu* because he visited *Yoram*. During his visit he went out with *Yehoram* to *Yehu* son of Nimshi, whom *Hashem* had anointed to cut off the house of *Achav*.

ז וּמֵֽאֱלֹהִ֗ים הָֽיְתָה֙ תְּבוּסַ֣ת אֲחַזְיָ֔הוּ לָב֖וֹא אֶל־יוֹרָ֑ם וּבְבֹא֗וֹ יָצָ֤א עִם־יְהוֹרָם֙ אֶל־יֵה֣וּא בֶן־נִמְשִׁ֔י אֲשֶׁ֣ר מְשָׁח֣וֹ יְהֹוָ֔ה לְהַכְרִ֖ית אֶת־בֵּ֥ית אַחְאָֽב׃

8 In the course of bringing the house of *Achav* to judgment, *Yehu* came upon the officers of *Yehuda* and the nephews of *Achazyahu*, ministers of *Achazyahu*, and killed them.

ח וַיְהִ֕י כְּהִשָּׁפֵ֥ט יֵה֖וּא עִם־בֵּ֣ית אַחְאָ֑ב וַיִּמְצָא֙ אֶת־שָׂרֵ֣י יְהוּדָ֗ה וּבְנֵ֛י אֲחֵ֥י אֲחַזְיָ֖הוּ מְשָֽׁרְתִ֥ים לַאֲחַזְיָ֖הוּ וַיַּהַרְגֵֽם׃

9 He sent in search of *Achazyahu*, who was caught hiding in *Shomron*, was brought to *Yehu*, and put to death. He was given a burial, because it was said, "He is the son of *Yehoshafat* who worshiped *Hashem* wholeheartedly." So the house of *Achazyahu* could not muster the strength to rule.

ט וַיְבַקֵּשׁ֙ אֶת־אֲחַזְיָ֔הוּ וַֽיִּלְכְּדֻ֖הוּ וְה֣וּא מִתְחַבֵּ֣א בְשֹֽׁמְר֑וֹן וַיְבִאֻ֣הוּ אֶל־יֵה֗וּא וַיְמִתֻ֙הוּ֙ וַֽיִּקְבְּרֻ֔הוּ כִּ֣י אָמְר֔וּ בֶּן־יְהוֹשָׁפָ֣ט ה֔וּא אֲשֶׁר־דָּרַ֥שׁ אֶת־יְהֹוָ֖ה בְּכׇל־לְבָב֑וֹ וְאֵין֙ לְבֵ֣ית אֲחַזְיָ֔הוּ לַעְצֹ֥ר כֹּ֖חַ לְמַמְלָכָֽה׃

10 When *Atalya*, *Achazyahu*'s mother, learned that her son was dead, she promptly did away with all who were of the royal stock of the house of *Yehuda*.

י וַעֲתַלְיָ֙הוּ֙ אֵ֣ם אֲחַזְיָ֔הוּ רָאֲתָ֖ה כִּ֣י מֵ֣ת בְּנָ֑הּ וַתָּ֗קׇם וַתְּדַבֵּ֛ר אֶת־כׇּל־זֶ֥רַע הַמַּמְלָכָ֖ה לְבֵ֥ית יְהוּדָֽה׃

11 But *Yehoshavat*, daughter of the king, spirited away *Achazyahu*'s son *Yoash* from among the princes who were being slain, and put him and his nurse in a bedroom. *Yehoshavat*, daughter of King *Yehoram*, wife of the *Kohen Yehoyada* – she was the sister of *Achazyahu* – kept him hidden from *Atalya* so that he was not put to death.

יא וַתִּקַּח֩ יְהוֹשַׁבְעַ֨ת בַּת־הַמֶּ֜לֶךְ אֶת־יוֹאָ֣שׁ בֶּן־אֲחַזְיָ֗הוּ וַתִּגְנֹ֤ב אֹתוֹ֙ מִתּ֣וֹךְ בְּנֵֽי־הַמֶּ֙לֶךְ֙ הַמּ֣וּמָתִ֔ים וַתִּתֵּ֥ן אֹת֛וֹ וְאֶת־מֵינִקְתּ֖וֹ בַּחֲדַ֣ר הַמִּטּ֑וֹת וַתַּסְתִּירֵ֡הוּ יְהוֹשַׁבְעַ֣ת בַּת־הַמֶּ֣לֶךְ יְהוֹרָ֡ם אֵ֩שֶׁת֩ יְהוֹיָדָ֨ע הַכֹּהֵ֜ן כִּ֣י הִ֧יא הָיְתָ֣ה אֲח֣וֹת אֲחַזְיָ֗הוּ מִפְּנֵ֥י עֲתַלְיָ֖הוּ וְלֹ֥א הֱמִיתָֽתְהוּ׃

12 He stayed with them for six years, hidden in the House of *Hashem*, while *Atalya* reigned over the land.

יב וַיְהִ֤י אִתָּם֙ בְּבֵ֣ית הָאֱלֹהִ֔ים מִתְחַבֵּ֖א שֵׁ֣שׁ שָׁנִ֑ים וַעֲתַלְיָ֖ה מֹלֶ֥כֶת עַל־הָאָֽרֶץ׃

22:12 Hidden in the House of *Hashem* In her desire to rule, *Atalya* does the unthinkable: She wipes out the entire royal family including her own children and grandchildren. There is, however, one exception. Baby *Yoash* is hidden by his aunt, *Yehoshavat*, in the house of God, the *Beit Hamikdash* in *Yerushalayim*. It is this

Divrei Hayamim II / II Chronicles
Chapter 23

דברי הימים ב
פרק כג

vai-HEE i-TAM b'-VAYT ha-e-lo-HEEM mit-kha-BAY SHAYSH sha-NEEM va-a-tal-YAH mo-LE-khet al ha-A-retz

23 1 In the seventh year, *Yehoyada* took courage and brought the chiefs of the hundreds, *Azarya* son of Jeroham, Ishmael son of *Yehochanan*, *Azarya* son of Oved, Maaseiah son of Adaiah, and Elishaphat son of Zichri, into a compact with him.

א וּבַשָּׁנָה הַשְּׁבִעִית הִתְחַזַּק יְהוֹיָדָע וַיִּקַּח אֶת־שָׂרֵי הַמֵּאוֹת לַעֲזַרְיָהוּ בֶן־יְרֹחָם וּלְיִשְׁמָעֵאל בֶּן־יְהוֹחָנָן וְלַעֲזַרְיָהוּ בֶן־עוֹבֵד וְאֶת־מַעֲשֵׂיָהוּ בֶן־עֲדָיָהוּ וְאֶת־אֱלִישָׁפָט בֶּן־זִכְרִי עִמּוֹ בַבְּרִית:

2 They went through *Yehuda* and assembled the *Leviim* from all the towns of *Yehuda*, and the chiefs of the clans of *Yisrael*. They came to *Yerushalayim*

ב וַיָּסֹבּוּ בִּיהוּדָה וַיִּקְבְּצוּ אֶת־הַלְוִיִּם מִכָּל־עָרֵי יְהוּדָה וְרָאשֵׁי הָאָבוֹת לְיִשְׂרָאֵל וַיָּבֹאוּ אֶל־יְרוּשָׁלָ͏ִם:

3 and the entire assembly made a covenant with the king in the House of *Hashem*. He said to them, "The son of the king shall be king according to the promise *Hashem* made concerning the sons of *David*.

ג וַיִּכְרֹת כָּל־הַקָּהָל בְּרִית בְּבֵית הָאֱלֹהִים עִם־הַמֶּלֶךְ וַיֹּאמֶר לָהֶם הִנֵּה בֶן־הַמֶּלֶךְ יִמְלֹךְ כַּאֲשֶׁר דִּבֶּר יְהֹוָה עַל־בְּנֵי דָוִיד:

4 This is what you must do: One third of you, *Kohanim* and *Leviim*, who are on duty for the week, shall be gatekeepers at the thresholds;

ד זֶה הַדָּבָר אֲשֶׁר תַּעֲשׂוּ הַשְּׁלִשִׁית מִכֶּם בָּאֵי הַשַּׁבָּת לַכֹּהֲנִים וְלַלְוִיִּם לְשֹׁעֲרֵי הַסִּפִּים:

5 another third shall be stationed in the royal palace, and the other third at the Foundation Gate. All the people shall be in the courts of the House of *Hashem*.

ה וְהַשְּׁלִשִׁית בְּבֵית הַמֶּלֶךְ וְהַשְּׁלִשִׁית בְּשַׁעַר הַיְסוֹד וְכָל־הָעָם בְּחַצְרוֹת בֵּית יְהֹוָה:

6 Let no one enter the House of *Hashem* except the *Kohanim* and the ministering *Leviim*. They may enter because they are sanctified, but all the people shall obey the proscription of *Hashem*.

ו וְאַל־יָבוֹא בֵית־יְהֹוָה כִּי אִם־הַכֹּהֲנִים וְהַמְשָׁרְתִים לַלְוִיִּם הֵמָּה יָבֹאוּ כִּי־קֹדֶשׁ הֵמָּה וְכָל־הָעָם יִשְׁמְרוּ מִשְׁמֶרֶת יְהֹוָה:

7 The *Leviim* shall surround the king on every side, every man with his weapons at the ready; and whoever enters the House shall be killed. Stay close to the king in his comings and goings."

ז וְהִקִּיפוּ הַלְוִיִּם אֶת־הַמֶּלֶךְ סָבִיב אִישׁ וְכֵלָיו בְּיָדוֹ וְהַבָּא אֶל־הַבַּיִת יוּמָת וִהְיוּ אֶת־הַמֶּלֶךְ בְּבֹאוֹ וּבְצֵאתוֹ:

8 The *Leviim* and all *Yehuda* did just as *Yehoyada* the *Kohen* ordered: each took his men – those who were on duty that week and those who were off duty that week, for *Yehoyada* the *Kohen* had not dismissed the divisions.

ח וַיַּעֲשׂוּ הַלְוִיִּם וְכָל־יְהוּדָה כְּכֹל אֲשֶׁר־צִוָּה יְהוֹיָדָע הַכֹּהֵן וַיִּקְחוּ אִישׁ אֶת־אֲנָשָׁיו בָּאֵי הַשַּׁבָּת עִם יוֹצְאֵי הַשַּׁבָּת כִּי לֹא פָטַר יְהוֹיָדָע הַכֹּהֵן אֶת־הַמַּחְלְקוֹת:

9 *Yehoyada* the *Kohen* gave the chiefs of the hundreds King *David*'s spears and shields and quivers that were kept in the House of *Hashem*.

ט וַיִּתֵּן יְהוֹיָדָע הַכֹּהֵן לְשָׂרֵי הַמֵּאוֹת אֶת־הַחֲנִיתִים וְאֶת־הַמָּגִנּוֹת וְאֶת־הַשְּׁלָטִים אֲשֶׁר לַמֶּלֶךְ דָּוִיד אֲשֶׁר בֵּית הָאֱלֹהִים:

spiritual center of the Land of Israel, the house that *David* longed to build and that was constructed by his son *Shlomo*, which protects the rightful king and preserves the Davidic line. Through *Yehoshavat* and her husband *Yehoyada* the priest, *Hashem* fulfills His promise to *David* that "his line shall continue forever, his throne, as the sun before Me," (Psalms 89:37).

Divrei Hayamim II/II Chronicles
Chapter 23

10 He stationed the entire force, each man with his weapons at the ready, from the south end of the House to the north end of the House, at the *Mizbayach* and the House, to guard the king on every side.

וַיַּעֲמֵד אֶת־כָּל־הָעָם וְאִישׁ שִׁלְחוֹ בְיָדוֹ מִכֶּתֶף הַבַּיִת הַיְמָנִית עַד־כֶּתֶף הַבַּיִת הַשְּׂמָאלִית לַמִּזְבֵּחַ וְלַבָּיִת עַל־הַמֶּלֶךְ סָבִיב:

11 Then they brought out the king's son, and placed upon him the crown and the insignia. They proclaimed him king, and *Yehoyada* and his sons anointed him and shouted, "Long live the king!"

וַיּוֹצִיאוּ אֶת־בֶּן־הַמֶּלֶךְ וַיִּתְּנוּ עָלָיו אֶת־הַנֵּזֶר וְאֶת־הָעֵדוּת וַיַּמְלִיכוּ אֹתוֹ וַיִּמְשָׁחֻהוּ יְהוֹיָדָע וּבָנָיו וַיֹּאמְרוּ יְחִי הַמֶּלֶךְ:

va-yo-TZEE-u et ben ha-ME-lekh va-yi-t'-NU a-LAV et ha-NAY-zer v'et HA-ay-DUT va-yam-LEE-khu o-TO va-yim-sha-KHU-hu y'-ho-ya-DA u-va-NAV va-yo-m'-RU y'-KHEE ha-ME-lekh

12 When *Atalya* heard the shouting of the people and the guards and the acclamation of the king, she came out to the people, to the House of *Hashem*.

וַתִּשְׁמַע עֲתַלְיָהוּ אֶת־קוֹל הָעָם הָרָצִים וְהַמְהַלְלִים אֶת־הַמֶּלֶךְ וַתָּבוֹא אֶל־הָעָם בֵּית יְהֹוָה:

13 She looked about and saw the king standing by his pillar at the entrance, the chiefs with their trumpets beside the king, and all the people of the land rejoicing and blowing trumpets, and the singers with musical instruments leading the hymns. *Atalya* rent her garments and cried out, "Treason, treason!"

וַתֵּרֶא וְהִנֵּה הַמֶּלֶךְ עוֹמֵד עַל־עַמּוּדוֹ בַּמָּבוֹא וְהַשָּׂרִים וְהַחֲצֹצְרוֹת עַל־הַמֶּלֶךְ וְכָל־עַם הָאָרֶץ שָׂמֵחַ וְתוֹקֵעַ בַּחֲצֹצְרוֹת וְהַמְשֹׁרְרִים בִּכְלֵי הַשִּׁיר וּמוֹדִיעִים לְהַלֵּל וַתִּקְרַע עֲתַלְיָהוּ אֶת־בְּגָדֶיהָ וַתֹּאמֶר קֶשֶׁר קָשֶׁר:

14 Then the *Kohen Yehoyada* ordered out the army officers, the chiefs of hundreds, and said to them, "Take her out between the ranks, and if anyone follows her, put him to the sword." For the *Kohen* thought, "Let her not be put to death in the House of *Hashem*."

וַיּוֹצֵא יְהוֹיָדָע הַכֹּהֵן אֶת־שָׂרֵי הַמֵּאוֹת פְּקוּדֵי הַחַיִל וַיֹּאמֶר אֲלֵהֶם הוֹצִיאוּהָ אֶל־מִבֵּית הַשְּׂדֵרוֹת וְהַבָּא אַחֲרֶיהָ יוּמַת בֶּחָרֶב כִּי אָמַר הַכֹּהֵן לֹא תְמִיתוּהָ בֵּית יְהֹוָה:

15 They cleared a passage for her and she came to the entrance of the Horse Gate to the royal palace; there she was put to death.

וַיָּשִׂימוּ לָהּ יָדַיִם וַתָּבוֹא אֶל־מְבוֹא שַׁעַר־הַסּוּסִים בֵּית הַמֶּלֶךְ וַיְמִיתוּהָ שָׁם:

16 Then *Yehoyada* solemnized a covenant between himself and the people and the king that they should be the people of *Hashem*.

וַיִּכְרֹת יְהוֹיָדָע בְּרִית בֵּינוֹ וּבֵין כָּל־הָעָם וּבֵין הַמֶּלֶךְ לִהְיוֹת לְעָם לַיהֹוָה:

23:11 And placed upon him the crown and the insignia The Hebrew term for 'insignia' is *aydut* (עדות). According to *Rashi*, this is a reference to the *Torah*, which is called *aydut* or 'testimony' (see Psalms 78:5). Upon being declared king, young *Yoash* is given a *Torah* scroll, since a Jewish king must always carry a copy of the *Torah* with him. Appointing a king is one of the three commandments that the Israelites were instructed to perform after settling the Land of Israel. However, there is a risk that the king will forget the source of his strength and attribute his successes to his own wisdom and power. Therefore, kings were required to carry a *Torah* scroll with them at all times (Deuteronomy 17:14–20) as a constant reminder that all blessing and success in our lives comes not from man but from *Hashem*.

עדות

Divrei Hayamim II / II Chronicles
Chapter 24

דברי הימים ב
פרק כד

17 All the people then went to the temple of Baal; they tore it down and smashed its altars and images to bits, and they slew Mattan, the priest of Baal, in front of the altars.

יז וַיָּבֹאוּ כׇל־הָעָם בֵּית־הַבַּעַל וַיִּתְּצֻהוּ וְאֶת־מִזְבְּחֹתָיו וְאֶת־צְלָמָיו שִׁבֵּרוּ וְאֵת מַתָּן כֹּהֵן הַבַּעַל הָרְגוּ לִפְנֵי הַמִּזְבְּחוֹת׃

18 *Yehoyada* put the officers of the House of *Hashem* in the charge of Levite *Kohanim* whom *David* had assigned over the House of *Hashem* to offer up burnt offerings, as is prescribed in the Teaching of *Moshe*, accompanied by joyful song as ordained by *David*.

יח וַיָּשֶׂם יְהוֹיָדָע פְּקֻדֹּת בֵּית יְהֹוָה בְּיַד הַכֹּהֲנִים הַלְוִיִּם אֲשֶׁר חָלַק דָּוִיד עַל־בֵּית יְהֹוָה לְהַעֲלוֹת עֹלוֹת יְהֹוָה כַּכָּתוּב בְּתוֹרַת מֹשֶׁה בְּשִׂמְחָה וּבְשִׁיר עַל יְדֵי דָוִיד׃

19 He stationed the gatekeepers at the gates of the House of *Hashem* to prevent the entry of anyone unclean for any reason.

יט וַיַּעֲמֵד הַשּׁוֹעֲרִים עַל־שַׁעֲרֵי בֵּית יְהֹוָה וְלֹא־יָבֹא טָמֵא לְכׇל־דָּבָר׃

20 He took the chiefs of hundreds, the nobles, and the rulers of the people and all the people of the land, and they escorted the king down from the House of *Hashem* into the royal palace by the upper gate, and seated the king on the royal throne.

כ וַיִּקַּח אֶת־שָׂרֵי הַמֵּאוֹת וְאֶת־הָאַדִּירִים וְאֶת־הַמּוֹשְׁלִים בָּעָם וְאֵת כׇּל־עַם הָאָרֶץ וַיּוֹרֶד אֶת־הַמֶּלֶךְ מִבֵּית יְהֹוָה וַיָּבֹאוּ בְּתוֹךְ־שַׁעַר הָעֶלְיוֹן בֵּית הַמֶּלֶךְ וַיּוֹשִׁיבוּ אֶת־הַמֶּלֶךְ עַל כִּסֵּא הַמַּמְלָכָה׃

21 All the people of the land rejoiced, and the city was quiet. As for *Atalya*, she had been put to the sword.

כא וַיִּשְׂמְחוּ כׇל־עַם־הָאָרֶץ וְהָעִיר שָׁקָטָה וְאֶת־עֲתַלְיָהוּ הֵמִיתוּ בֶחָרֶב׃

24 1 *Yehoash* was seven years old when he became king, and he reigned in *Yerushalayim* forty years. His mother's name was Zibiah of *Be'er Sheva*.

כד א בֶּן־שֶׁבַע שָׁנִים יֹאָשׁ בְּמׇלְכוֹ וְאַרְבָּעִים שָׁנָה מָלַךְ בִּירוּשָׁלָ͏ִם וְשֵׁם אִמּוֹ צִבְיָה מִבְּאֵר שָׁבַע׃

2 All the days of the *Kohen Yehoyada*, *Yehoash* did what was pleasing to *Hashem*.

ב וַיַּעַשׂ יוֹאָשׁ הַיָּשָׁר בְּעֵינֵי יְהֹוָה כׇּל־יְמֵי יְהוֹיָדָע הַכֹּהֵן׃

3 *Yehoyada* took two wives for him, by whom he had sons and daughters.

ג וַיִּשָּׂא־לוֹ יְהוֹיָדָע נָשִׁים שְׁתָּיִם וַיּוֹלֶד בָּנִים וּבָנוֹת׃

4 Afterward, *Yoash* decided to renovate the House of *Hashem*.

ד וַיְהִי אַחֲרֵיכֵן הָיָה עִם־לֵב יוֹאָשׁ לְחַדֵּשׁ אֶת־בֵּית יְהֹוָה׃

5 He assembled the *Kohanim* and the *Leviim* and charged them as follows: "Go out to the towns of *Yehuda* and collect money from all *Yisrael* for the annual repair of the House of your God. Do it quickly." But the *Leviim* did not act quickly.

ה וַיִּקְבֹּץ אֶת־הַכֹּהֲנִים וְהַלְוִיִּם וַיֹּאמֶר לָהֶם צְאוּ לְעָרֵי יְהוּדָה וְקִבְצוּ מִכׇּל־יִשְׂרָאֵל כֶּסֶף לְחַזֵּק אֶת־בֵּית אֱלֹהֵיכֶם מִדֵּי שָׁנָה בְּשָׁנָה וְאַתֶּם תְּמַהֲרוּ לַדָּבָר וְלֹא מִהֲרוּ הַלְוִיִּם׃

6 The king summoned *Yehoyada* the chief and said to him, "Why have you not seen to it that the *Leviim* brought the tax imposed by *Moshe*, the servant of *Hashem*, and the congregation of *Yisrael* from *Yehuda* and *Yerushalayim* to the Tent of the Pact?"

ו וַיִּקְרָא הַמֶּלֶךְ לִיהוֹיָדָע הָרֹאשׁ וַיֹּאמֶר לוֹ מַדּוּעַ לֹא־דָרַשְׁתָּ עַל־הַלְוִיִּם לְהָבִיא מִיהוּדָה וּמִירוּשָׁלַ͏ִם אֶת־מַשְׂאַת מֹשֶׁה עֶבֶד־יְהֹוָה וְהַקָּהָל לְיִשְׂרָאֵל לְאֹהֶל הָעֵדוּת׃

7 For the children of the wicked *Atalya* had violated the House of *Hashem* and had even used the sacred things of the House of *Hashem* for the Baals.

ז כִּי עֲתַלְיָהוּ הַמִּרְשַׁעַת בָּנֶיהָ פָרְצוּ אֶת־בֵּית הָאֱלֹהִים וְגַם כׇּל־קׇדְשֵׁי בֵית־יְהֹוָה עָשׂוּ לַבְּעָלִים׃

Divrei Hayamim II / II Chronicles
Chapter 24

דברי הימים ב
פרק כד

8 The king ordered that a chest be made and placed on the outside of the gate of the House of *Hashem*.

ח וַיֹּ֣אמֶר הַמֶּ֔לֶךְ וַֽיַּעֲשׂ֖וּ אֲר֣וֹן אֶחָ֑ד וַֽיִּתְּנֻ֛הוּ בְּשַׁ֥עַר בֵּית־יְהֹוָ֖ה חֽוּצָה׃

9 A proclamation was issued in *Yehuda* and *Yerushalayim* to bring the tax imposed on *Yisrael* in the wilderness by *Moshe*, the servant of *Hashem*.

ט וַיִּתְּנוּ־ק֞וֹל בִּֽיהוּדָ֣ה וּבִירוּשָׁלַ֗͏ִם לְהָבִ֤יא לַֽיהֹוָה֙ מַשְׂאַ֞ת מֹשֶׁ֧ה עֶֽבֶד־הָאֱלֹהִ֛ים עַל־יִשְׂרָאֵ֖ל בַּמִּדְבָּֽר׃

10 All the officers and all the people gladly brought it and threw it into the chest till it was full.

י וַיִּשְׂמְח֥וּ כׇל־הַשָּׂרִ֖ים וְכׇל־הָעָ֑ם וַיָּבִ֛יאוּ וַיַּשְׁלִ֥יכוּ לָאָר֖וֹן עַד־לְכַלֵּֽה׃

11 Whenever the chest was brought to the royal officers by the *Leviim*, and they saw that it contained much money, the royal scribe and the agent of the chief *Kohen* came and emptied out the chest and carried it back to its place. They did this day by day, and much money was collected.

יא וַיְהִ֡י בְּעֵת֩ יָבִ֨יא אֶת־הָאָר֜וֹן אֶל־פְּקֻדַּ֣ת הַמֶּ֘לֶךְ֮ בְּיַ֣ד הַלְוִיִּם֒ וְכִרְאוֹתָ֞ם כִּי־רַ֣ב הַכֶּ֗סֶף וּבָ֨א סוֹפֵ֤ר הַמֶּ֙לֶךְ֙ וּפְקִיד֙ כֹּהֵ֣ן הָרֹ֔אשׁ וִיעָ֙רוּ֙ אֶת־הָ֣אָר֔וֹן וְיִשָּׂאֻ֖הוּ וִישִׁיבֻ֣הוּ אֶל־מְקֹמ֑וֹ כֹּ֤ה עָשׂוּ֙ לְי֣וֹם ׀ בְּי֔וֹם וַיַּאַסְפוּ־כֶ֖סֶף לָרֹֽב׃

12 The king and *Yehoyada* delivered the money to those who oversaw the tasks connected with the work of the House of *Hashem*. They hired masons and carpenters to renovate the House of *Hashem*, as well as craftsmen in iron and bronze to repair the House of *Hashem*.

יב וַיִּתְּנֵ֨הוּ הַמֶּ֜לֶךְ וִיהֽוֹיָדָ֗ע אֶל־עוֹשֵׂה֙ מְלֶ֙אכֶת֙ עֲבוֹדַ֣ת בֵּית־יְהֹוָ֔ה וַיִּֽהְי֤וּ שֹׂכְרִים֙ חֹצְבִ֣ים וְחָרָשִׁ֔ים לְחַדֵּ֖שׁ בֵּ֣ית יְהֹוָ֑ה וְ֠גַ֠ם לְחָרָשֵׁ֤י בַרְזֶל֙ וּנְחֹ֔שֶׁת לְחַזֵּ֖ק אֶת־בֵּ֥ית יְהֹוָֽה׃

13 The overseers did their work; under them the work went well and they restored the House of *Hashem* to its original form and repaired it.

יג וַֽיַּעֲשׂוּ֙ עֹשֵׂ֣י הַמְּלָאכָ֔ה וַתַּ֧עַל אֲרוּכָ֛ה לַמְּלָאכָ֖ה בְּיָדָ֑ם וַיַּעֲמִ֜ידוּ אֶת־בֵּ֧ית הָאֱלֹהִ֛ים עַל־מַתְכֻּנְתּ֖וֹ וַֽיְאַמְּצֻֽהוּ׃

14 When they had finished, they brought the money that was left over to the king and *Yehoyada*; it was made into utensils for the House of *Hashem*, service vessels: buckets and ladles, golden and silver vessels. Burnt offerings were offered up regularly in the House of *Hashem* all the days of *Yehoyada*.

יד וּכְכַלּוֹתָ֡ם הֵבִ֣יאוּ לִפְנֵי֩ הַמֶּ֨לֶךְ וִיהוֹיָדָ֜ע אֶת־שְׁאָ֣ר הַכֶּ֗סֶף וַיַּעֲשֵׂ֨הוּ כֵלִ֤ים לְבֵית־יְהֹוָה֙ כְּלֵ֣י שָׁרֵ֔ת וְהַעֲל֣וֹת וְכַפּ֔וֹת וּכְלֵ֥י זָהָ֖ב וָכָ֑סֶף וַ֠יִּהְי֠וּ מַעֲלִ֨ים עֹל֤וֹת בְּבֵית־יְהֹוָה֙ תָּמִ֔יד כֹּ֖ל יְמֵ֥י יְהוֹיָדָֽע׃

15 *Yehoyada* reached a ripe old age and died; he was one hundred and thirty years old at his death.

טו וַיִּזְקַ֧ן יְהוֹיָדָ֛ע וַיִּשְׂבַּ֥ע יָמִ֖ים וַיָּמֹ֑ת בֶּן־מֵאָ֧ה וּשְׁלֹשִׁ֛ים שָׁנָ֖ה בְּמוֹתֽוֹ׃

16 They buried him in the City of *David* together with the kings, because he had done good in *Yisrael*, and on behalf of *Hashem* and His House.

טז וַיִּקְבְּרֻ֤הוּ בְעִיר־דָּוִיד֙ עִם־הַמְּלָכִ֔ים כִּֽי־עָשָׂ֥ה טוֹבָ֖ה בְּיִשְׂרָאֵ֑ל וְעִ֥ם הָאֱלֹהִ֖ים וּבֵיתֽוֹ׃

va-yik-b'-RU-hu v'-EER da-VEED im ha-m'-la-KHEEM kee a-SAH to-VAH b'-yis-ra-AYL v'-im ha-e-lo-HEEM u-vay-TO

24:16 Because he had done good in *Yisrael* *Yehoyada* is buried "with the kings" even though he is not a member of the royal family. He is the only outsider recorded as being buried among the kingly descendants of *David*, something that even some of the actual kings, such as *Yehoram*, did not merit. *Metzudat David* explains that this is part of his reward for having "done good in *Yisrael*" in three ways. He appointed a king from the line of *David*, he brought the people back to *Hashem* and he restored the *Beit Hamikdash*. *Yehoyada* is buried with the kings because he acted in a manner expected of a king, even to the point of risking his own life, and the lives of his family members, for the sake of God and the Nation of Israel.

Divrei Hayamim II/II Chronicles
Chapter 24

17 But after the death of *Yehoyada*, the officers of *Yehuda* came, bowing low to the king; and the king listened to them.

18 They forsook the House of God of their fathers to serve the sacred posts and idols; and there was wrath upon *Yehuda* and *Yerushalayim* because of this guilt of theirs.

19 *Hashem* sent *Neviim* among them to bring them back to Him; they admonished them but they would not pay heed.

20 Then the spirit of *Hashem* enveloped *Zecharya* son of *Yehoyada* the *kohen*; he stood above the people and said to them, "Thus *Hashem* said: Why do you transgress the commandments of *Hashem* when you cannot succeed? Since you have forsaken *Hashem*, He has forsaken you."

21 They conspired against him and pelted him with stones in the court of the House of *Hashem*, by order of the king.

22 King *Yoash* disregarded the loyalty that his father *Yehoyada* had shown to him, and killed his son. As he was dying, he said, "May *Hashem* see and requite it."

23 At the turn of the year, the army of Aram marched against him; they invaded *Yehuda* and *Yerushalayim*, and wiped out all the officers of the people from among the people, and sent all the booty they took to the king of Damascus.

24 The invading army of Aram had come with but a few men, but *Hashem* delivered a very large army into their hands, because they had forsaken God of their fathers. They inflicted punishments on *Yoash*.

25 When they withdrew, having left him with many wounds, his courtiers plotted against him because of the murder of the sons of *Yehoyada* the *kohen*, and they killed him in bed. He died and was buried in the City of *David*; he was not buried in the tombs of the kings.

26 These were the men who conspired against him: Zabad son of Shimeath the Ammonitess, and Jehozabad son of Shimrith the Moabitess.

דברי הימים ב
פרק כד

יז וְאַחֲרֵי מוֹת יְהוֹיָדָע בָּאוּ שָׂרֵי יְהוּדָה וַיִּשְׁתַּחֲווּ לַמֶּלֶךְ אָז שָׁמַע הַמֶּלֶךְ אֲלֵיהֶם:

יח וַיַּעַזְבוּ אֶת־בֵּית יְהֹוָה אֱלֹהֵי אֲבוֹתֵיהֶם וַיַּעַבְדוּ אֶת־הָאֲשֵׁרִים וְאֶת־הָעֲצַבִּים וַיְהִי־קֶצֶף עַל־יְהוּדָה וִירוּשָׁלַםִ בְּאַשְׁמָתָם זֹאת:

יט וַיִּשְׁלַח בָּהֶם נְבִאִים לַהֲשִׁיבָם אֶל־יְהֹוָה וַיָּעִידוּ בָם וְלֹא הֶאֱזִינוּ:

כ וְרוּחַ אֱלֹהִים לָבְשָׁה אֶת־זְכַרְיָה בֶּן־יְהוֹיָדָע הַכֹּהֵן וַיַּעֲמֹד מֵעַל לָעָם וַיֹּאמֶר לָהֶם כֹּה אָמַר הָאֱלֹהִים לָמָה אַתֶּם עֹבְרִים אֶת־מִצְוֹת יְהֹוָה וְלֹא תַצְלִיחוּ כִּי־עֲזַבְתֶּם אֶת־יְהֹוָה וַיַּעֲזֹב אֶתְכֶם:

כא וַיִּקְשְׁרוּ עָלָיו וַיִּרְגְּמֻהוּ אֶבֶן בְּמִצְוַת הַמֶּלֶךְ בַּחֲצַר בֵּית יְהֹוָה:

כב וְלֹא־זָכַר יוֹאָשׁ הַמֶּלֶךְ הַחֶסֶד אֲשֶׁר עָשָׂה יְהוֹיָדָע אָבִיו עִמּוֹ וַיַּהֲרֹג אֶת־בְּנוֹ וּכְמוֹתוֹ אָמַר יֵרֶא יְהֹוָה וְיִדְרֹשׁ:

כג וַיְהִי לִתְקוּפַת הַשָּׁנָה עָלָה עָלָיו חֵיל אֲרָם וַיָּבֹאוּ אֶל־יְהוּדָה וִירוּשָׁלַםִ וַיַּשְׁחִיתוּ אֶת־כָּל־שָׂרֵי הָעָם מֵעָם וְכָל־שְׁלָלָם שִׁלְּחוּ לְמֶלֶךְ דַּרְמָשֶׂק:

כד כִּי בְמִצְעַר אֲנָשִׁים בָּאוּ חֵיל אֲרָם וַיהֹוָה נָתַן בְּיָדָם חַיִל לָרֹב מְאֹד כִּי עָזְבוּ אֶת־יְהֹוָה אֱלֹהֵי אֲבוֹתֵיהֶם וְאֶת־יוֹאָשׁ עָשׂוּ שְׁפָטִים:

כה וּבְלֶכְתָּם מִמֶּנּוּ כִּי־עָזְבוּ אֹתוֹ במחליים [בְּמַחֲלוּיִם] רַבִּים הִתְקַשְּׁרוּ עָלָיו עֲבָדָיו בִּדְמֵי בְּנֵי יְהוֹיָדָע הַכֹּהֵן וַיַּהַרְגֻהוּ עַל־מִטָּתוֹ וַיָּמֹת וַיִּקְבְּרֻהוּ בְּעִיר דָּוִיד וְלֹא קְבָרֻהוּ בְּקִבְרוֹת הַמְּלָכִים:

כו וְאֵלֶּה הַמִּתְקַשְּׁרִים עָלָיו זָבָד בֶּן־שִׁמְעָת הָעַמּוֹנִית וִיהוֹזָבָד בֶּן־שִׁמְרִית הַמּוֹאָבִית:

Divrei Hayamim II/II Chronicles
Chapter 25

דברי הימים ב
פרק כה

כז **27** As to his sons, and the many pronouncements against him, and his rebuilding of the House of *Hashem*, they are recorded in the story in the book of the kings. His son *Amatzya* succeeded him as king.

וּבָנָיו וְרֹב [יֶרֶב] הַמַּשָּׂא עָלָיו וִיסוֹד בֵּית הָאֱלֹהִים הִנָּם כְּתוּבִים עַל־מִדְרַשׁ סֵפֶר הַמְּלָכִים וַיִּמְלֹךְ אֲמַצְיָהוּ בְנוֹ תַּחְתָּיו:

25 **1** *Amatzya* was twenty-five years old when he became king, and he reigned twenty-nine years in *Yerushalayim*; his mother's name was Jehoaddan of *Yerushalayim*.

כה א בֶּן־עֶשְׂרִים וְחָמֵשׁ שָׁנָה מָלַךְ אֲמַצְיָהוּ וְעֶשְׂרִים וָתֵשַׁע שָׁנָה מָלַךְ בִּירוּשָׁלָ͏ִם וְשֵׁם אִמּוֹ יְהוֹעַדָּן מִירוּשָׁלָיִם:

2 He did what was pleasing to *Hashem*, but not with a whole heart.

ב וַיַּעַשׂ הַיָּשָׁר בְּעֵינֵי יְהֹוָה רַק לֹא בְּלֵבָב שָׁלֵם:

va-YA-as ha-ya-SHAR b'-ay-NAY a-do-NAI RAK LO b'-lay-VAV sha-LAYM

3 Once he had the kingdom firmly under control, he executed the courtiers who had assassinated his father the king.

ג וַיְהִי כַּאֲשֶׁר חָזְקָה הַמַּמְלָכָה עָלָיו וַיַּהֲרֹג אֶת־עֲבָדָיו הַמַּכִּים אֶת־הַמֶּלֶךְ אָבִיו:

4 But he did not put their children to death for [he acted] in accordance with what is written in the Teaching, in the Book of *Moshe*, where *Hashem* commanded, "Parents shall not die for children, nor shall children die for parents, but every person shall die only for his own crime."

ד וְאֶת־בְּנֵיהֶם לֹא הֵמִית כִּי כַכָּתוּב בַּתּוֹרָה בְּסֵפֶר מֹשֶׁה אֲשֶׁר־צִוָּה יְהֹוָה לֵאמֹר לֹא־יָמוּתוּ אָבוֹת עַל־בָּנִים וּבָנִים לֹא־יָמוּתוּ עַל־אָבוֹת כִּי אִישׁ בְּחֶטְאוֹ יָמוּתוּ:

5 *Amatzya* assembled the men of *Yehuda*, and he put all the men of *Yehuda* and *Binyamin* under officers of thousands and officers of hundreds, by clans. He mustered them from the age of twenty upward, and found them to be 300,000 picked men fit for service, able to bear spear and shield.

ה וַיִּקְבֹּץ אֲמַצְיָהוּ אֶת־יְהוּדָה וַיַּעֲמִידֵם לְבֵית־אָבוֹת לְשָׂרֵי הָאֲלָפִים וּלְשָׂרֵי הַמֵּאוֹת לְכָל־יְהוּדָה וּבִנְיָמִן וַיִּפְקְדֵם לְמִבֶּן עֶשְׂרִים שָׁנָה וָמַעְלָה וַיִּמְצָאֵם שְׁלֹשׁ־מֵאוֹת אֶלֶף בָּחוּר יוֹצֵא צָבָא אֹחֵז רֹמַח וְצִנָּה:

6 He hired 100,000 warriors from *Yisrael* for 100 *kikarim* of silver.

ו וַיִּשְׂכֹּר מִיִּשְׂרָאֵל מֵאָה אֶלֶף גִּבּוֹר חָיִל בְּמֵאָה כִכַּר־כָּסֶף:

7 Then a man of *Hashem* came to him and said, "O king! Do not let the army of *Yisrael* go with you, for *Hashem* is not with *Yisrael* – all these Ephraimites.

ז וְאִישׁ הָאֱלֹהִים בָּא אֵלָיו לֵאמֹר הַמֶּלֶךְ אַל־יָבֹא עִמְּךָ צְבָא יִשְׂרָאֵל כִּי אֵין יְהֹוָה עִם־יִשְׂרָאֵל כֹּל בְּנֵי אֶפְרָיִם:

25:2 But not with a whole heart Why is *Amatzya* hesitant in his service of *Hashem*? Perhaps he had learned idolatry as a child in his father's house. However, he notices that his father, like idolatrous kings before him, was struck down and reaches the conclusion that the worship of the one true God is the safest and most pragmatic course of action. However, when *Amatzya* obeys *Hashem*'s command and sends away his northern mercenaries, they sack his cities in disgust (verse 13). As such, he wonders if his original conclusion was wrong, and perhaps idolatry is the best course after all. We learn from here that it is not enough to serve God out of a desire for advancement. Worship of *Hashem* must be performed "with a whole heart."

Divrei Hayamim II / II Chronicles
Chapter 25

דברי הימים ב
פרק כה

8 But go by yourself and do it; take courage for battle, [else] *Hashem* will make you fall before the enemy. For in *Hashem* there is power to help one or make one fall!"

ח כִּי אִם־בֹּא אַתָּה עֲשֵׂה חֲזַק לַמִּלְחָמָה יַכְשִׁילְךָ הָאֱלֹהִים לִפְנֵי אוֹיֵב כִּי יֶשׁ־כֹּחַ בֵּאלֹהִים לַעְזוֹר וּלְהַכְשִׁיל:

9 *Amatzya* said to the man of *Hashem*, "And what am I to do about the 100 *kikarim* I gave for the Israelite force?" The man of *Hashem* replied, "*Hashem* has the means to give you much more than that."

ט וַיֹּאמֶר אֲמַצְיָהוּ לְאִישׁ הָאֱלֹהִים וּמַה־לַּעֲשׂוֹת לִמְאַת הַכִּכָּר אֲשֶׁר נָתַתִּי לִגְדוּד יִשְׂרָאֵל וַיֹּאמֶר אִישׁ הָאֱלֹהִים יֵשׁ לַיהוָה לָתֶת לְךָ הַרְבֵּה מִזֶּה:

10 So *Amatzya* detached the force that came to him from *Efraim*, [ordering them] to go back to their place. They were greatly enraged against *Yehuda* and returned to their place in a rage.

י וַיַּבְדִּילֵם אֲמַצְיָהוּ לְהַגְּדוּד אֲשֶׁר־בָּא אֵלָיו מֵאֶפְרַיִם לָלֶכֶת לִמְקוֹמָם וַיִּחַר אַפָּם מְאֹד בִּיהוּדָה וַיָּשׁוּבוּ לִמְקוֹמָם בָּחֳרִי־אָף:

11 *Amatzya* took courage and, leading his army, he marched to the Valley of Salt. He slew 10,000 men of Seir;

יא וַאֲמַצְיָהוּ הִתְחַזַּק וַיִּנְהַג אֶת־עַמּוֹ וַיֵּלֶךְ גֵּיא הַמֶּלַח וַיַּךְ אֶת־בְּנֵי־שֵׂעִיר עֲשֶׂרֶת אֲלָפִים:

12 another 10,000 the men of *Yehuda* captured alive and brought to the top of Sela. They threw them down from the top of Sela and every one of them was burst open.

יב וַעֲשֶׂרֶת אֲלָפִים חַיִּים שָׁבוּ בְּנֵי יְהוּדָה וַיְבִיאוּם לְרֹאשׁ הַסָּלַע וַיַּשְׁלִיכוּם מֵרֹאשׁ־הַסֶּלַע וְכֻלָּם נִבְקָעוּ:

13 The men of the force that *Amatzya* had sent back so they would not go with him into battle made forays against the towns of *Yehuda* from *Shomron* to Beth-horon. They slew 3,000 of them, and took much booty.

יג וּבְנֵי הַגְּדוּד אֲשֶׁר הֵשִׁיב אֲמַצְיָהוּ מִלֶּכֶת עִמּוֹ לַמִּלְחָמָה וַיִּפְשְׁטוּ בְּעָרֵי יְהוּדָה מִשֹּׁמְרוֹן וְעַד־בֵּית חוֹרוֹן וַיַּכּוּ מֵהֶם שְׁלֹשֶׁת אֲלָפִים וַיָּבֹזּוּ בִּזָּה רַבָּה:

14 After *Amatzya* returned from defeating the Edomites, he had the gods of the men of Seir brought, and installed them as his gods; he prostrated himself before them, and to them he made sacrifice.

יד וַיְהִי אַחֲרֵי בוֹא אֲמַצְיָהוּ מֵהַכּוֹת אֶת־אֲדוֹמִים וַיָּבֵא אֶת־אֱלֹהֵי בְּנֵי שֵׂעִיר וַיַּעֲמִידֵם לוֹ לֵאלֹהִים וְלִפְנֵיהֶם יִשְׁתַּחֲוֶה וְלָהֶם יְקַטֵּר:

15 *Hashem* was enraged at *Amatzya*, and sent a *Navi* to him who said to him, "Why are you worshiping the gods of a people who could not save their people from you?"

טו וַיִּחַר־אַף יְהוָה בַּאֲמַצְיָהוּ וַיִּשְׁלַח אֵלָיו נָבִיא וַיֹּאמֶר לוֹ לָמָה דָרַשְׁתָּ אֶת־אֱלֹהֵי הָעָם אֲשֶׁר לֹא־הִצִּילוּ אֶת־עַמָּם מִיָּדֶךָ:

16 As he spoke to him, [*Amatzya*] said to him, "Have we appointed you a counselor to the king? Stop, else you will be killed!" The *Navi* stopped, saying, "I see *Hashem* has counseled that you be destroyed, since you act this way and disregard my counsel."

טז וַיְהִי בְּדַבְּרוֹ אֵלָיו וַיֹּאמֶר לוֹ הַלְיוֹעֵץ לַמֶּלֶךְ נְתַנּוּךָ חֲדַל־לְךָ לָמָּה יַכּוּךָ וַיֶּחְדַּל הַנָּבִיא וַיֹּאמֶר יָדַעְתִּי כִּי־יָעַץ אֱלֹהִים לְהַשְׁחִיתֶךָ כִּי־עָשִׂיתָ זֹּאת וְלֹא שָׁמַעְתָּ לַעֲצָתִי:

17 Then King *Amatzya* of *Yehuda* took counsel and sent this message to *Yoash* son of *Yehoachaz* son of *Yehu*, king of *Yisrael*, "Come, let us confront each other!"

יז וַיִּוָּעַץ אֲמַצְיָהוּ מֶלֶךְ יְהוּדָה וַיִּשְׁלַח אֶל־יוֹאָשׁ בֶּן־יְהוֹאָחָז בֶּן־יֵהוּא מֶלֶךְ יִשְׂרָאֵל לֵאמֹר לך [לְכָה] נִתְרָאֶה פָנִים:

2111

Divrei Hayamim II/II Chronicles
Chapter 25

18 King *Yoash* of *Yisrael* sent back this message to King *Amatzya* of *Yehuda*, "The thistle in Lebanon sent this message to the cedar in Lebanon, 'Give your daughter to my son in marriage.' But a wild beast in Lebanon passed by and trampled the thistle.

19 You boast that you have defeated the Edomites and you are ambitious to get more glory. Now stay at home, lest, provoking disaster you fall, dragging *Yehuda* down with you."

20 But *Amatzya* paid no heed – it was *Hashem*'s doing, in order to deliver them up because they worshiped the gods of Edom.

21 King *Yoash* of *Yisrael* marched up, and he and King *Amatzya* of *Yehuda* confronted each other at *Beit Shemesh* in *Yehuda*.

22 The men of *Yehuda* were routed by *Yisrael*, and they all fled to their homes.

23 King *Yoash* of *Yisrael* captured *Amatzya* son of *Yoash* son of *Yehoachaz*, king of *Yehuda*, in *Beit Shemesh*. He brought him to *Yerushalayim* and made a breach of 400 *amot* in the wall of *Yerushalayim*, from the *Efraim* Gate to the Corner Gate.

24 Then, with all the gold and silver and all the utensils that were to be found in the House of *Hashem* in the custody of *Oved Edom*, and with the treasuries of the royal palace, and with the hostages, he returned to *Shomron*.

25 King *Amatzya* son of *Yoash* of *Yehuda* lived fifteen years after the death of King *Yoash* son of *Yehoachaz* of *Yisrael*.

26 The other events of *Amatzya*'s reign, early and late, are recorded in the book of the kings of *Yehuda* and *Yisrael*.

27 From the time that *Amatzya* turned from following *Hashem*, a conspiracy was formed against him in *Yerushalayim*, and he fled to *Lachish*; but they sent men after him to *Lachish* and they put him to death there.

28 They brought his body back on horses and buried him with his fathers in the city of *Yehuda*.

Divrei Hayamim II / II Chronicles
Chapter 26

26 1 Then all the people of *Yehuda* took *Uzziyahu*, who was sixteen years old, and proclaimed him king to succeed his father *Amatzya*.

2 It was he who rebuilt Eloth and restored it to *Yehuda* after King [*Amatzya*] slept with his fathers.

3 *Uzziyahu* was sixteen years old when he became king, and he reigned fifty-two years in *Yerushalayim*; his mother's name was Jecoliah of *Yerushalayim*.

4 He did what was pleasing to *Hashem* just as his father *Amatzya* had done.

5 He applied himself to the worship of *Hashem* during the time of *Zecharya*, instructor in the visions of *Hashem*; during the time he worshiped *Hashem*, *Hashem* made him prosper.

6 He went forth to fight the Philistines, and breached the wall of Gath and the wall of Jabneh and the wall of *Ashdod*; he built towns in [the region of] *Ashdod* and among the Philistines.

7 *Hashem* helped him against the Philistines, against the Arabs who lived in Gur-baal, and the Meunites.

8 The Ammonites paid tribute to *Uzziyahu*, and his fame spread to the approaches of Egypt, for he grew exceedingly strong.

9 *Uzziyahu* built towers in *Yerushalayim* on the Corner Gate and the Valley Gate and on the Angle, and fortified them.

10 He built towers in the wilderness and hewed out many cisterns, for he had much cattle, and farmers in the foothills and on the plain, and vine dressers in the mountains and on the fertile lands, for he loved the soil.

11 *Uzziyahu* had an army of warriors, a battle-ready force who were mustered by Jeiel the scribe and Maasseiah the adjutant under *Chananya*, one of the king's officers.

12 The clan chiefs, valiants, totaled 2,600;

13 under them was the trained army of 307,500, who made war with might and power to aid the king against the enemy.

דברי הימים ב
פרק כו

כו א וַיִּקְחוּ כָּל־עַם יְהוּדָה אֶת־עֻזִּיָּהוּ וְהוּא בֶּן־שֵׁשׁ עֶשְׂרֵה שָׁנָה וַיַּמְלִיכוּ אֹתוֹ תַּחַת אָבִיו אֲמַצְיָהוּ:

ב הוּא בָּנָה אֶת־אֵילוֹת וַיְשִׁיבֶהָ לִיהוּדָה אַחֲרֵי שְׁכַב־הַמֶּלֶךְ עִם־אֲבֹתָיו:

ג בֶּן־שֵׁשׁ עֶשְׂרֵה שָׁנָה עֻזִּיָּהוּ בְמָלְכוֹ וַחֲמִשִּׁים וּשְׁתַּיִם שָׁנָה מָלַךְ בִּירוּשָׁלִָם וְשֵׁם אִמּוֹ יְכִילְיָה [יְכָלְיָה] מִן־יְרוּשָׁלִָם:

ד וַיַּעַשׂ הַיָּשָׁר בְּעֵינֵי יְהוָה כְּכֹל אֲשֶׁר־עָשָׂה אֲמַצְיָהוּ אָבִיו:

ה וַיְהִי לִדְרֹשׁ אֱלֹהִים בִּימֵי זְכַרְיָהוּ הַמֵּבִין בִּרְאֹת הָאֱלֹהִים וּבִימֵי דָּרְשׁוֹ אֶת־יְהוָה הִצְלִיחוֹ הָאֱלֹהִים:

ו וַיֵּצֵא וַיִּלָּחֶם בַּפְּלִשְׁתִּים וַיִּפְרֹץ אֶת־חוֹמַת גַּת וְאֶת חוֹמַת יַבְנֶה וְאֵת חוֹמַת אַשְׁדּוֹד וַיִּבְנֶה עָרִים בְּאַשְׁדּוֹד וּבַפְּלִשְׁתִּים:

ז וַיַּעְזְרֵהוּ הָאֱלֹהִים עַל־פְּלִשְׁתִּים וְעַל־הָעַרְבִיִּים [הָעַרְבִים] הַיֹּשְׁבִים בְּגוּר־בָּעַל וְהַמְּעוּנִים:

ח וַיִּתְּנוּ הָעַמּוֹנִים מִנְחָה לְעֻזִּיָּהוּ וַיֵּלֶךְ שְׁמוֹ עַד־לְבוֹא מִצְרַיִם כִּי הֶחֱזִיק עַד־לְמָעְלָה:

ט וַיִּבֶן עֻזִּיָּהוּ מִגְדָּלִים בִּירוּשָׁלִַם עַל־שַׁעַר הַפִּנָּה וְעַל־שַׁעַר הַגַּיְא וְעַל־הַמִּקְצוֹעַ וַיְחַזְּקֵם:

י וַיִּבֶן מִגְדָּלִים בַּמִּדְבָּר וַיַּחְצֹב בֹּרוֹת רַבִּים כִּי מִקְנֶה־רַּב הָיָה לוֹ וּבַשְּׁפֵלָה וּבַמִּישׁוֹר אִכָּרִים וְכֹרְמִים בֶּהָרִים וּבַכַּרְמֶל כִּי־אֹהֵב אֲדָמָה הָיָה:

יא וַיְהִי לְעֻזִּיָּהוּ חַיִל עֹשֵׂה מִלְחָמָה יוֹצְאֵי צָבָא לִגְדוּד בְּמִסְפַּר פְּקֻדָּתָם בְּיַד יְעוּאֵל [יְעִיאֵל] הַסּוֹפֵר וּמַעֲשֵׂיָהוּ הַשּׁוֹטֵר עַל יַד־חֲנַנְיָהוּ מִשָּׂרֵי הַמֶּלֶךְ:

יב כֹּל מִסְפַּר רָאשֵׁי הָאָבוֹת לְגִבּוֹרֵי חָיִל אַלְפַּיִם וְשֵׁשׁ מֵאוֹת:

יג וְעַל־יָדָם חֵיל צָבָא שְׁלֹשׁ מֵאוֹת אֶלֶף וְשִׁבְעַת אֲלָפִים וַחֲמֵשׁ מֵאוֹת עוֹשֵׂי מִלְחָמָה בְּכֹחַ חָיִל לַעְזֹר לַמֶּלֶךְ עַל־הָאוֹיֵב:

Divrei Hayamim II / II Chronicles
Chapter 26

14 *Uzziyahu* provided them – the whole army – with shields and spears, and helmets and mail, and bows and slingstones.

יד וַיָּכֶן לָהֶם עֻזִּיָּהוּ לְכָל־הַצָּבָא מָגִנִּים וּרְמָחִים וְכוֹבָעִים וְשִׁרְיֹנוֹת וּקְשָׁתוֹת וּלְאַבְנֵי קְלָעִים׃

15 He made clever devices in *Yerushalayim*, set on the towers and the corners, for shooting arrows and large stones. His fame spread far, for he was helped wonderfully, and he became strong.

טו וַיַּעַשׂ בִּירוּשָׁלַ͏ִם חִשְּׁבֹנוֹת מַחֲשֶׁבֶת חוֹשֵׁב לִהְיוֹת עַל־הַמִּגְדָּלִים וְעַל־הַפִּנּוֹת לִירוֹא בַּחִצִּים וּבָאֲבָנִים גְּדֹלוֹת וַיֵּצֵא שְׁמוֹ עַד־לְמֵרָחוֹק כִּי־הִפְלִיא לְהֵעָזֵר עַד כִּי־חָזָק׃

16 When he was strong, he grew so arrogant he acted corruptly: he trespassed against his God by entering the Temple of *Hashem* to offer incense on the incense *Mizbayach*.

טז וּכְחֶזְקָתוֹ גָּבַהּ לִבּוֹ עַד־לְהַשְׁחִית וַיִּמְעַל בַּיהֹוָה אֱלֹהָיו וַיָּבֹא אֶל־הֵיכַל יְהֹוָה לְהַקְטִיר עַל־מִזְבַּח הַקְּטֹרֶת׃

17 The *kohen Azarya*, with eighty other brave *Kohanim* of *Hashem*, followed him in

יז וַיָּבֹא אַחֲרָיו עֲזַרְיָהוּ הַכֹּהֵן וְעִמּוֹ כֹּהֲנִים לַיהֹוָה שְׁמוֹנִים בְּנֵי־חָיִל׃

18 and, confronting King *Uzziyahu*, said to him, "It is not for you, *Uzziyahu*, to offer incense to *Hashem*, but for the Aaronite *Kohanim*, who have been consecrated, to offer incense. Get out of the Sanctuary, for you have trespassed; there will be no glory in it for you from *Hashem*."

יח וַיַּעַמְדוּ עַל־עֻזִּיָּהוּ הַמֶּלֶךְ וַיֹּאמְרוּ לוֹ לֹא־לְךָ עֻזִּיָּהוּ לְהַקְטִיר לַיהֹוָה כִּי לַכֹּהֲנִים בְּנֵי־אַהֲרֹן הַמְקֻדָּשִׁים לְהַקְטִיר צֵא מִן־הַמִּקְדָּשׁ כִּי מָעַלְתָּ וְלֹא־לְךָ לְכָבוֹד מֵיְהֹוָה אֱלֹהִים׃

19 *Uzziyahu*, holding the censer and ready to burn incense, got angry; but as he got angry with the *Kohanim*, leprosy broke out on his forehead in front of the *Kohanim* in the House of *Hashem* beside the incense *Mizbayach*.

יט וַיִּזְעַף עֻזִּיָּהוּ וּבְיָדוֹ מִקְטֶרֶת לְהַקְטִיר וּבְזַעְפּוֹ עִם־הַכֹּהֲנִים וְהַצָּרַעַת זָרְחָה בְמִצְחוֹ לִפְנֵי הַכֹּהֲנִים בְּבֵית יְהֹוָה מֵעַל לְמִזְבַּח הַקְּטֹרֶת׃

va-yiz-AF u-zi-YA-hu uv-ya-DO mik-TE-ret l'-hak-TEER uv-za-PO im ha-ko-ha-NEEM v'-ha-tza-RA-at za-r'-KHA v'-mitz-KHO lif-NAY ha-ko-ha-NEEM b'-VAYT a-do-NAI may-AL l'-miz-BAKH ha-k'-TO-ret

20 When the chief *kohen Azarya* and all the other *Kohanim* looked at him, his forehead was leprous, so they rushed him out of there; he too made haste to get out, for *Hashem* had struck him with a plague.

כ וַיִּפֶן אֵלָיו עֲזַרְיָהוּ כֹהֵן הָרֹאשׁ וְכָל־הַכֹּהֲנִים וְהִנֵּה־הוּא מְצֹרָע בְּמִצְחוֹ וַיַּבְהִלוּהוּ מִשָּׁם וְגַם־הוּא נִדְחַף לָצֵאת כִּי נִגְּעוֹ יְהֹוָה׃

26:19 Leprosy broke out on his forehead Emboldened by his success, *Uzziyahu* is not satisfied with being just a king; he wishes to be a *Kohen* as well. Since he is not a descendant of the house of *Levi*, he is barred from priesthood and his attempt to offer a sacrifice of incense defiles the *Beit Hamikdash*. Therefore, he contracts a form of ritual impurity even while attempting to bring a sacrifice in the Temple, a place in which ritual impurity is usually barred. *Rashi* (Isaiah 6:4) writes that this action causes the earthquake that shook the Land of Israel in the days of *Uzziyahu* (see Amos 1:1 and Zechariah 14:5). This shows the spiritual sensitivity of *Eretz Yisrael*. Not only is *Uzziyahu* punished, but the land itself reacts to the violation of God's command.

Rashi (1040–1105)

Divrei Hayamim II/II Chronicles
Chapter 27

דברי הימים ב
פרק כז

21 King *Uzziyahu* was a leper until the day of his death. He lived in isolated quarters as a leper, for he was cut off from the House of *Hashem* – while *Yotam* his son was in charge of the king's house and governed the people of the land.

כא וַיְהִי עֻזִּיָּהוּ הַמֶּלֶךְ מְצֹרָע עַד־יוֹם מוֹתוֹ וַיֵּשֶׁב בֵּית הַחָפְשׁוּת [הַחָפְשִׁית] מְצֹרָע כִּי נִגְזַר מִבֵּית יְהוָה וְיוֹתָם בְּנוֹ עַל־בֵּית הַמֶּלֶךְ שׁוֹפֵט אֶת־עַם הָאָרֶץ:

22 The other events of *Uzziyahu*'s reign, early and late, were recorded by the *Navi Yeshayahu* son of *Amotz*.

כב וְיֶתֶר דִּבְרֵי עֻזִּיָּהוּ הָרִאשֹׁנִים וְהָאַחֲרֹנִים כָּתַב יְשַׁעְיָהוּ בֶן־אָמוֹץ הַנָּבִיא:

23 *Uzziyahu* slept with his fathers in the burial field of the kings, because, they said, he was a leper; his son *Yotam* succeeded him as king.

כג וַיִּשְׁכַּב עֻזִּיָּהוּ עִם־אֲבֹתָיו וַיִּקְבְּרוּ אֹתוֹ עִם־אֲבֹתָיו בִּשְׂדֵה הַקְּבוּרָה אֲשֶׁר לַמְּלָכִים כִּי אָמְרוּ מְצוֹרָע הוּא וַיִּמְלֹךְ יוֹתָם בְּנוֹ תַּחְתָּיו:

27 1 *Yotam* was twenty-five years old when he became king, and he reigned sixteen years in *Yerushalayim*; his mother's name was Jerushah daughter of *Tzadok*.

כז א בֶּן־עֶשְׂרִים וְחָמֵשׁ שָׁנָה יוֹתָם בְּמָלְכוֹ וְשֵׁשׁ־עֶשְׂרֵה שָׁנָה מָלַךְ בִּירוּשָׁלָיִם וְשֵׁם אִמּוֹ יְרוּשָׁה בַּת־צָדוֹק:

2 He did what was pleasing to *Hashem* just as his father *Uzziyahu* had done, but he did not enter the Temple of *Hashem*; however, the people still acted corruptly.

va-YA-as ha-ya-SHAR b'-ay-NAY a-do-NAI k'-KHOL a-SHER a-SAH u-zi-YA-hu a-VEEV RAK lo VA el hay-KHAL a-do-NAI v'-OD ha-AM mash-khee-TEEM

ב וַיַּעַשׂ הַיָּשָׁר בְּעֵינֵי יְהוָה כְּכֹל אֲשֶׁר־עָשָׂה עֻזִּיָּהוּ אָבִיו רַק לֹא־בָא אֶל־הֵיכַל יְהוָה וְעוֹד הָעָם מַשְׁחִיתִים:

3 It was he who built the Upper Gate of the House of *Hashem*; he also built extensively on the wall of Ophel.

ג הוּא בָּנָה אֶת־שַׁעַר בֵּית־יְהוָה הָעֶלְיוֹן וּבְחוֹמַת הָעֹפֶל בָּנָה לָרֹב:

4 He built towns in the hill country of *Yehuda*, and in the woods he built fortresses and towers.

ד וְעָרִים בָּנָה בְּהַר־יְהוּדָה וּבֶחֳרָשִׁים בָּנָה בִּירָנִיּוֹת וּמִגְדָּלִים:

5 Moreover, he fought with the king of the Ammonites and overcame them; the Ammonites gave him that year 100 *kikarim* of silver and 10,000 *kor* of wheat and another 10,000 of barley; that is what the Ammonites paid him, and [likewise] in the second and third years.

ה וְהוּא נִלְחַם עִם־מֶלֶךְ בְּנֵי־עַמּוֹן וַיֶּחֱזַק עֲלֵיהֶם וַיִּתְּנוּ־לוֹ בְנֵי־עַמּוֹן בַּשָּׁנָה הַהִיא מֵאָה כִּכַּר־כֶּסֶף וַעֲשֶׂרֶת אֲלָפִים כֹּרִים חִטִּים וּשְׂעוֹרִים עֲשֶׂרֶת אֲלָפִים זֹאת הֵשִׁיבוּ לוֹ בְּנֵי עַמּוֹן וּבַשָּׁנָה הַשֵּׁנִית וְהַשְּׁלִשִׁית:

6 *Yotam* was strong because he maintained a faithful course before *Hashem* his God.

ו וַיִּתְחַזֵּק יוֹתָם כִּי הֵכִין דְּרָכָיו לִפְנֵי יְהוָה אֱלֹהָיו:

27:2 The people still acted corruptly While *Yotam* is remembered as a good and righteous king, he fails to influence the people in a significant way. In fact, the people continue their rebellions against *Hashem* and His worship. As is clear throughout *Tanakh*, a king is in a unique position to have significant impact on his subjects. Chizkiyahu, for example, is able to create positive change, bringing the nation to a spiritual state that they had not reached since the days of *Shlomo*. Menashe, on the other hand, leads the people to a spiritual low point. Therefore, though *Yotam* is considered a good king, he is remembered as a king who failed in his mission to cause the people to repent. Doing what is right is not enough; we must influence and inspire others to do so as well.

Divrei Hayamim II / II Chronicles
Chapter 28

דברי הימים ב
פרק כח

7 The other events of *Yotam*'s reign, and all his battles and his conduct, are recorded in the book of the kings of *Yisrael* and *Yehuda*.

ז וְיֶתֶר דִּבְרֵי יוֹתָם וְכָל־מִלְחֲמֹתָיו וּדְרָכָיו הִנָּם כְּתוּבִים עַל־סֵפֶר מַלְכֵי־יִשְׂרָאֵל וִיהוּדָה׃

8 He was twenty-five years old when he became king, and he reigned sixteen years in *Yerushalayim*.

ח בֶּן־עֶשְׂרִים וְחָמֵשׁ שָׁנָה הָיָה בְמָלְכוֹ וְשֵׁשׁ־עֶשְׂרֵה שָׁנָה מָלַךְ בִּירוּשָׁלָָם׃

9 *Yotam* slept with his fathers, and was buried in the City of *David*; his son *Achaz* succeeded him as king.

ט וַיִּשְׁכַּב יוֹתָם עִם־אֲבֹתָיו וַיִּקְבְּרוּ אֹתוֹ בְּעִיר דָּוִיד וַיִּמְלֹךְ אָחָז בְּנוֹ תַּחְתָּיו׃

28 1 *Achaz* was twenty years old when he became king, and he reigned sixteen years in *Yerushalayim*. He did not do what was pleasing to *Hashem* as his father *David* had done,

כח א בֶּן־עֶשְׂרִים שָׁנָה אָחָז בְּמָלְכוֹ וְשֵׁשׁ־עֶשְׂרֵה שָׁנָה מָלַךְ בִּירוּשָׁלָָם וְלֹא־עָשָׂה הַיָּשָׁר בְּעֵינֵי יְהוָה כְּדָוִיד אָבִיו׃

2 but followed the ways of the kings of *Yisrael*; he even made molten images for the Baals.

ב וַיֵּלֶךְ בְּדַרְכֵי מַלְכֵי יִשְׂרָאֵל וְגַם מַסֵּכוֹת עָשָׂה לַבְּעָלִים׃

3 He made offerings in the Valley of Ben-hinnom and burned his sons in fire, in the abhorrent fashion of the nations which *Hashem* had dispossessed before the Israelites.

ג וְהוּא הִקְטִיר בְּגֵיא בֶן־הִנֹּם וַיַּבְעֵר אֶת־בָּנָיו בָּאֵשׁ כְּתֹעֲבוֹת הַגּוֹיִם אֲשֶׁר הֹרִישׁ יְהוָה מִפְּנֵי בְּנֵי יִשְׂרָאֵל׃

v'-HU hik-TEER b'-GAY ven hi-NOM va-yav-AYR et ba-NAV ba-AYSH k'-to-a-VOT ha-go-YIM a-SHER ho-REESH a-do-NAI mi-p'-NAY b'-NAY yis-ra-AYL

4 He sacrificed and made offerings at the shrines, on the hills, and under every leafy tree.

ד וַיְזַבֵּחַ וַיְקַטֵּר בַּבָּמוֹת וְעַל־הַגְּבָעוֹת וְתַחַת כָּל־עֵץ רַעֲנָן׃

5 *Hashem* his God delivered him over to the king of Aram, who defeated him and took many of his men captive, and brought them to Damascus. He was also delivered over to the king of *Yisrael*, who inflicted a great defeat on him.

ה וַיִּתְּנֵהוּ יְהוָה אֱלֹהָיו בְּיַד מֶלֶךְ אֲרָם וַיַּכּוּ־בוֹ וַיִּשְׁבּוּ מִמֶּנּוּ שִׁבְיָה גְדוֹלָה וַיָּבִיאוּ דַּרְמָשֶׂק וְגַם בְּיַד־מֶלֶךְ יִשְׂרָאֵל נִתָּן וַיַּךְ־בּוֹ מַכָּה גְדוֹלָה׃

6 *Pekach* son of Remaliah killed 120,000 in *Yehuda* – all brave men – in one day, because they had forsaken God of their fathers.

ו וַיַּהֲרֹג פֶּקַח בֶּן־רְמַלְיָהוּ בִּיהוּדָה מֵאָה וְעֶשְׂרִים אֶלֶף בְּיוֹם אֶחָד הַכֹּל בְּנֵי־חָיִל בְּעָזְבָם אֶת־יְהוָה אֱלֹהֵי אֲבוֹתָם׃

7 Zichri, the champion of *Efraim*, killed Maaseiah the king's son, and Azrikam chief of the palace, and *Elkana*, the second to the king.

ז וַיַּהֲרֹג זִכְרִי גִּבּוֹר אֶפְרַיִם אֶת־מַעֲשֵׂיָהוּ בֶּן־הַמֶּלֶךְ וְאֶת־עַזְרִיקָם נְגִיד הַבָּיִת וְאֶת־אֶלְקָנָה מִשְׁנֵה הַמֶּלֶךְ׃

28:3 He made offerings in the Valley of Ben-hinnom Unlike his father and grandfather, *Achaz* was an evil king who reintroduces systematic idol worship and intentionally spreads it to every city in the kingdom (verse 25). In this verse, we are told that he worships *Baal* and burns his children in the Valley of Hinnom. In biblical times this cursed valley was known as the place where the sinful Israelites worshipped the false god *Baal* and offered their children as sacrifices to the fire god *Molech* (Jeremiah 32:35). Therefore, this valley, which is located just outside of the present-day Jerusalem Old City walls, was thought to be cursed. Figuratively, it became associated with hell. As the Sages teach (*Eiruvin* 19a), "The gate [to hell] lies between two palm trees in the valley of Hinnom, from which smoke is continually rising." The term 'Gehenna,' referring to hell, is derived from the Hebrew name for the valley, *Gei ben Hinnom* (גיא בן הנם).

Valley of Hinnom

Divrei Hayamim II / II Chronicles
Chapter 28

8 The Israelites captured 200,000 of their kinsmen, women, boys, and girls; they also took a large amount of booty from them and brought the booty to *Shomron*.

9 A *Navi* of *Hashem* by the name of *Oded* was there, who went out to meet the army on its return to *Shomron*. He said to them, "Because of the fury of God of your fathers against *Yehuda*, He delivered them over to you, and you killed them in a rage that reached heaven.

10 Do you now intend to subjugate the men and women of *Yehuda* and *Yerushalayim* to be your slaves? As it is, you have nothing but offenses against *Hashem* your God.

11 Now then, listen to me, and send back the captives you have taken from your kinsmen, for the wrath of *Hashem* is upon you!"

12 Some of the chief men of the Ephraimites – *Azarya* son of *Yehochanan*, *Berechya* son of Meshillemoth, Jehizkiah son of *Shalum*, and Amasa son of Hadlai – confronted those returning from the campaign

13 and said to them, "Do not bring these captives here, for it would mean our offending *Hashem*, adding to our sins and our offenses; for our offense is grave enough, and there is already wrath upon *Yisrael*."

14 So the soldiers released the captives and the booty in the presence of the officers and all the congregation.

15 Then the men named above proceeded to take the captives in hand, and with the booty they clothed all the naked among them – they clothed them and shod them and gave them to eat and drink and anointed them and provided donkeys for all who were failing and brought them to *Yericho*, the city of palms, back to their kinsmen. Then they returned to *Shomron*.

16 At that time, King *Achaz* sent to the king of Assyria for help.

17 Again the Edomites came and inflicted a defeat on *Yehuda* and took captives.

דברי הימים ב
פרק כח

ח וַיִּשְׁבּוּ בְנֵי־יִשְׂרָאֵל מֵאֲחֵיהֶם מָאתַיִם אֶלֶף נָשִׁים בָּנִים וּבָנוֹת וְגַם־שָׁלָל רָב בָּזְזוּ מֵהֶם וַיָּבִיאוּ אֶת־הַשָּׁלָל לְשֹׁמְרוֹן:

ט וְשָׁם הָיָה נָבִיא לַיהֹוָה עֹדֵד שְׁמוֹ וַיֵּצֵא לִפְנֵי הַצָּבָא הַבָּא לְשֹׁמְרוֹן וַיֹּאמֶר לָהֶם הִנֵּה בַּחֲמַת יְהֹוָה אֱלֹהֵי־אֲבוֹתֵיכֶם עַל־יְהוּדָה נְתָנָם בְּיֶדְכֶם וַתַּהַרְגוּ־בָם בְּזַעַף עַד לַשָּׁמַיִם הִגִּיעַ:

י וְעַתָּה בְּנֵי־יְהוּדָה וִירוּשָׁלַיִם אַתֶּם אֹמְרִים לִכְבֹּשׁ לַעֲבָדִים וְלִשְׁפָחוֹת לָכֶם הֲלֹא רַק־אַתֶּם עִמָּכֶם אֲשָׁמוֹת לַיהֹוָה אֱלֹהֵיכֶם:

יא וְעַתָּה שְׁמָעוּנִי וְהָשִׁיבוּ הַשִּׁבְיָה אֲשֶׁר שְׁבִיתֶם מֵאֲחֵיכֶם כִּי חֲרוֹן אַף־יְהֹוָה עֲלֵיכֶם:

יב וַיָּקֻמוּ אֲנָשִׁים מֵרָאשֵׁי בְנֵי־אֶפְרַיִם עֲזַרְיָהוּ בֶן־יְהוֹחָנָן בֶּרֶכְיָה בֶן־מְשִׁלֵּמוֹת וִיחִזְקִיָּהוּ בֶן־שַׁלֻּם וַעֲמָשָׂא בֶן־חַדְלָי עַל־הַבָּאִים מִן־הַצָּבָא:

יג וַיֹּאמְרוּ לָהֶם לֹא־תָבִיאוּ אֶת־הַשִּׁבְיָה הֵנָּה כִּי לְאַשְׁמַת יְהֹוָה עָלֵינוּ אַתֶּם אֹמְרִים לְהֹסִיף עַל־חַטֹּאתֵינוּ וְעַל־אַשְׁמָתֵינוּ כִּי־רַבָּה אַשְׁמָה לָנוּ וַחֲרוֹן אָף עַל־יִשְׂרָאֵל:

יד וַיַּעֲזֹב הֶחָלוּץ אֶת־הַשִּׁבְיָה וְאֶת־הַבִּזָּה לִפְנֵי הַשָּׂרִים וְכָל־הַקָּהָל:

טו וַיָּקֻמוּ הָאֲנָשִׁים אֲשֶׁר־נִקְּבוּ בְשֵׁמוֹת וַיַּחֲזִיקוּ בַשִּׁבְיָה וְכָל־מַעֲרֻמֵּיהֶם הִלְבִּישׁוּ מִן־הַשָּׁלָל וַיַּלְבִּשׁוּם וַיַּנְעִלוּם וַיַּאֲכִלוּם וַיַּשְׁקוּם וַיְסֻכוּם וַיְנַהֲלוּם בַּחֲמֹרִים לְכָל־כּוֹשֵׁל וַיְבִיאוּם יְרֵחוֹ עִיר־הַתְּמָרִים אֵצֶל אֲחֵיהֶם וַיָּשׁוּבוּ שֹׁמְרוֹן:

טז בָּעֵת הַהִיא שָׁלַח הַמֶּלֶךְ אָחָז עַל־מַלְכֵי אַשּׁוּר לַעְזֹר לוֹ:

יז וְעוֹד אֲדוֹמִים בָּאוּ וַיַּכּוּ בִיהוּדָה וַיִּשְׁבּוּ־שֶׁבִי:

Divrei Hayamim II / II Chronicles
Chapter 29

18 And the Philistines made forays against the cities of the Shephelah and the *Negev* of *Yehuda*; they seized *Beit Shemesh* and Aijalon and Gederoth, and Soco with its villages, and Timnah with its villages, and Gimzo with its villages; and they settled there.

19 Thus *Hashem* brought *Yehuda* low on account of King *Achaz* of *Yisrael*, for he threw off restraint in *Yehuda* and trespassed against *Hashem*.

20 Tillegath-pilneser, king of Assyria, marched against him and gave him trouble, instead of supporting him.

21 For *Achaz* plundered the House of *Hashem* and the house of the king and the officers, and made a gift to the king of Assyria – to no avail.

22 In his time of trouble, this King *Achaz* trespassed even more against *Hashem*,

23 sacrificing to the gods of Damascus which had defeated him, for he thought, "The gods of the kings of Aram help them; I shall sacrifice to them and they will help me"; but they were his ruin and that of all *Yisrael*.

24 *Achaz* collected the utensils of the House of *Hashem*, and cut the utensils of the House of *Hashem* to pieces. He shut the doors of the House of *Hashem* and made himself altars in every corner of *Yerushalayim*.

25 In every town in *Yehuda* he set up shrines to make offerings to other gods, vexing God of his fathers.

26 The other events of his reign and all his conduct, early and late, are recorded in the book of the kings of *Yehuda* and *Yisrael*.

27 *Achaz* slept with his fathers and was buried in the city, in *Yerushalayim*; his body was not brought to the tombs of the kings of *Yisrael*. His son *Chizkiyahu* succeeded him as king.

29

1 *Chizkiyahu* became king at the age of twenty-five, and he reigned twenty-nine years in *Yerushalayim*; his mother's name was *Aviya* daughter of *Zecharya*.

2 He did what was pleasing to *Hashem*, just as his father *David* had done.

Divrei Hayamim II/II Chronicles
Chapter 29

3 He, in the first month of the first year of his reign, opened the doors of the House of *Hashem* and repaired them.

4 He summoned the *Kohanim* and the *Leviim* and assembled them in the east square.

5 He said to them, "Listen to me, *Leviim*! Sanctify yourselves and sanctify the House of God of your fathers, and take the abhorrent things out of the holy place.

6 For our fathers trespassed and did what displeased *Hashem* our God; they forsook Him and turned their faces away from the dwelling-place of *Hashem*, turning their backs on it.

7 They also shut the doors of the porch and put out the lights; they did not offer incense and did not make burnt offerings in the holy place to the God of *Yisrael*.

8 The wrath of *Hashem* was upon *Yehuda* and *Yerushalayim*; He made them an object of horror, amazement, and hissing as you see with your own eyes.

9 Our fathers died by the sword, and our sons and daughters and wives are in captivity on account of this.

10 Now I wish to make a covenant with God of *Yisrael*, so that His rage may be withdrawn from us.

11 Now, my sons, do not be slack, for *Hashem* chose you to attend upon Him, to serve Him, to be His ministers and to make offerings to Him."

12 So the *Leviim* set to – Mahath son of Amasai and Yoel son of *Azarya* of the sons of *Kehat*; and of the sons of *Merari*, Keesh son of Abdi and *Azarya* son of Jehallelel; and of the Gershonites, Joah son of Zimmah and Eden son of Joah;

13 and of the sons of Elizaphan, Shimri and Jeiel; and of the sons of *Asaf*, *Zecharya* and Mattaniah

14 and of the sons of *Hayman*, *Yechiel* and *Shim'i*; and of the sons of *Yedutun*, *Shemaya* and Uzziel –

15 and, gathering their brothers, they sanctified themselves and came, by a command of the king concerning *Hashem*'s ordinances, to purify the House of *Hashem*.

דברי הימים ב
פרק כט

ג הוּא בַשָּׁנָה הָרִאשׁוֹנָה לְמָלְכוֹ בַּחֹדֶשׁ הָרִאשׁוֹן פָּתַח אֶת־דַּלְתוֹת בֵּית־יְהֹוָה וַיְחַזְּקֵם:

ד וַיָּבֵא אֶת־הַכֹּהֲנִים וְאֶת־הַלְוִיִּם וַיַּאַסְפֵם לִרְחוֹב הַמִּזְרָח:

ה וַיֹּאמֶר לָהֶם שְׁמָעוּנִי הַלְוִיִּם עַתָּה הִתְקַדְּשׁוּ וְקַדְּשׁוּ אֶת־בֵּית יְהֹוָה אֱלֹהֵי אֲבֹתֵיכֶם וְהוֹצִיאוּ אֶת־הַנִּדָּה מִן־הַקֹּדֶשׁ:

ו כִּי־מָעֲלוּ אֲבֹתֵינוּ וְעָשׂוּ הָרַע בְּעֵינֵי יְהֹוָה אֱלֹהֵינוּ וַיַּעַזְבֻהוּ וַיַּסֵּבּוּ פְנֵיהֶם מִמִּשְׁכַּן יְהֹוָה וַיִּתְּנוּ־עֹרֶף:

ז גַּם סָגְרוּ דַּלְתוֹת הָאוּלָם וַיְכַבּוּ אֶת־הַנֵּרוֹת וּקְטֹרֶת לֹא הִקְטִירוּ וְעֹלָה לֹא־הֶעֱלוּ בַקֹּדֶשׁ לֵאלֹהֵי יִשְׂרָאֵל:

ח וַיְהִי קֶצֶף יְהֹוָה עַל־יְהוּדָה וִירוּשָׁלָיִם וַיִּתְּנֵם לְזַעֲוָה [לְזַוָּעָה] לְשַׁמָּה וְלִשְׁרֵקָה כַּאֲשֶׁר אַתֶּם רֹאִים בְּעֵינֵיכֶם:

ט וְהִנֵּה נָפְלוּ אֲבוֹתֵינוּ בֶּחָרֶב וּבָנֵינוּ וּבְנוֹתֵינוּ וְנָשֵׁינוּ בַּשְּׁבִי עַל־זֹאת:

י עַתָּה עִם־לְבָבִי לִכְרוֹת בְּרִית לַיהֹוָה אֱלֹהֵי יִשְׂרָאֵל וְיָשֹׁב מִמֶּנּוּ חֲרוֹן אַפּוֹ:

יא בָּנַי עַתָּה אַל־תִּשָּׁלוּ כִּי־בָכֶם בָּחַר יְהֹוָה לַעֲמֹד לְפָנָיו לְשָׁרְתוֹ וְלִהְיוֹת לוֹ מְשָׁרְתִים וּמַקְטִרִים:

יב וַיָּקֻמוּ הַלְוִיִּם מַחַת בֶּן־עֲמָשַׂי וְיוֹאֵל בֶּן־עֲזַרְיָהוּ מִן־בְּנֵי הַקְּהָתִי וּמִן־בְּנֵי מְרָרִי קִישׁ בֶּן־עַבְדִּי וַעֲזַרְיָהוּ בֶּן־יְהַלֶּלְאֵל וּמִן־הַגֵּרְשֻׁנִּי יוֹאָח בֶּן־זִמָּה וְעֵדֶן בֶּן־יוֹאָח:

יג וּמִן־בְּנֵי אֱלִיצָפָן שִׁמְרִי וִיעוּאֵל [וִיעִיאֵל] וּמִן־בְּנֵי אָסָף זְכַרְיָהוּ וּמַתַּנְיָהוּ:

יד וּמִן־בְּנֵי הֵימָן יְחוּאֵל [יְחִיאֵל] וְשִׁמְעִי וּמִן־בְּנֵי יְדוּתוּן שְׁמַעְיָה וְעֻזִּיאֵל:

טו וַיַּאַסְפוּ אֶת־אֲחֵיהֶם וַיִּתְקַדְּשׁוּ וַיָּבֹאוּ כְמִצְוַת־הַמֶּלֶךְ בְּדִבְרֵי יְהֹוָה לְטַהֵר בֵּית יְהֹוָה:

Divrei Hayamim II / II Chronicles
Chapter 29

16 The *Kohanim* went into the House of *Hashem* to purify it, and brought all the unclean things they found in the Temple of *Hashem* out into the court of the House of *Hashem*; [there] the *Leviim* received them, to take them outside to Wadi Kidron.

17 They began the sanctification on the first day of the first month; on the eighth day of the month they reached the porch of *Hashem*. They sanctified the House of *Hashem* for eight days, and on the sixteenth day of the first month they finished.

18 Then they went into the palace of King *Chizkiyahu* and said, "We have purified the whole House of *Hashem* and the *Mizbayach* of burnt offering and all its utensils, and the table of the bread of display and all its utensils;

19 and all the utensils that King *Achaz* had befouled during his reign, when he trespassed, we have made ready and sanctified. They are standing in front of the *Mizbayach* of *Hashem*."

20 King *Chizkiyahu* rose early, gathered the officers of the city, and went up to the House of *Hashem*.

21 They brought seven bulls and seven rams and seven lambs and seven he-goats as a sin offering for the kingdom and for the Sanctuary and for *Yehuda*. He ordered the Aaronite *Kohanim* to offer them on the *Mizbayach* of *Hashem*.

22 The cattle were slaughtered, and the *Kohanim* received the blood and dashed it against the *Mizbayach*; the rams were slaughtered and the blood was dashed against the *Mizbayach*; the lambs were slaughtered and the blood was dashed against the *Mizbayach*.

23 The he-goats for the sin offering were presented to the king and the congregation, who laid their hands upon them.

24 The *Kohanim* slaughtered them and performed the purgation rite with the blood against the *Mizbayach*, to expiate for all *Yisrael*, for the king had designated the burnt offering and the sin offering to be for all *Yisrael*.

דברי הימים ב
פרק כט

טז וַיָּבֹאוּ הַכֹּהֲנִים לִפְנִימָה בֵית־יְהוָה לְטַהֵר וַיּוֹצִיאוּ אֵת כָּל־הַטֻּמְאָה אֲשֶׁר מָצְאוּ בְּהֵיכַל יְהוָה לַחֲצַר בֵּית יְהוָה וַיְקַבְּלוּ הַלְוִיִּם לְהוֹצִיא לְנַחַל־קִדְרוֹן חוּצָה:

יז וַיָּחֵלּוּ בְּאֶחָד לַחֹדֶשׁ הָרִאשׁוֹן לְקַדֵּשׁ וּבְיוֹם שְׁמוֹנָה לַחֹדֶשׁ בָּאוּ לְאוּלָם יְהוָה וַיְקַדְּשׁוּ אֶת־בֵּית־יְהוָה לְיָמִים שְׁמוֹנָה וּבְיוֹם שִׁשָּׁה עָשָׂר לַחֹדֶשׁ הָרִאשׁוֹן כִּלּוּ:

יח וַיָּבוֹאוּ פְנִימָה אֶל־חִזְקִיָּהוּ הַמֶּלֶךְ וַיֹּאמְרוּ טִהַרְנוּ אֶת־כָּל־בֵּית יְהוָה אֶת־מִזְבַּח הָעוֹלָה וְאֶת־כָּל־כֵּלָיו וְאֶת־שֻׁלְחַן הַמַּעֲרֶכֶת וְאֶת־כָּל־כֵּלָיו:

יט וְאֵת כָּל־הַכֵּלִים אֲשֶׁר הִזְנִיחַ הַמֶּלֶךְ אָחָז בְּמַלְכוּתוֹ בְּמַעֲלוֹ הֵכַנּוּ וְהִקְדָּשְׁנוּ וְהִנָּם לִפְנֵי מִזְבַּח יְהוָה:

כ וַיַּשְׁכֵּם יְחִזְקִיָּהוּ הַמֶּלֶךְ וַיֶּאֱסֹף אֵת שָׂרֵי הָעִיר וַיַּעַל בֵּית יְהוָה:

כא וַיָּבִיאוּ פָרִים־שִׁבְעָה וְאֵילִים שִׁבְעָה וּכְבָשִׂים שִׁבְעָה וּצְפִירֵי עִזִּים שִׁבְעָה לְחַטָּאת עַל־הַמַּמְלָכָה וְעַל־הַמִּקְדָּשׁ וְעַל־יְהוּדָה וַיֹּאמֶר לִבְנֵי אַהֲרֹן הַכֹּהֲנִים לְהַעֲלוֹת עַל־מִזְבַּח יְהוָה:

כב וַיִּשְׁחֲטוּ הַבָּקָר וַיְקַבְּלוּ הַכֹּהֲנִים אֶת־הַדָּם וַיִּזְרְקוּ הַמִּזְבֵּחָה וַיִּשְׁחֲטוּ הָאֵלִים וַיִּזְרְקוּ הַדָּם הַמִּזְבֵּחָה וַיִּשְׁחֲטוּ הַכְּבָשִׂים וַיִּזְרְקוּ הַדָּם הַמִּזְבֵּחָה:

כג וַיַּגִּישׁוּ אֶת־שְׂעִירֵי הַחַטָּאת לִפְנֵי הַמֶּלֶךְ וְהַקָּהָל וַיִּסְמְכוּ יְדֵיהֶם עֲלֵיהֶם:

כד וַיִּשְׁחָטוּם הַכֹּהֲנִים וַיְחַטְּאוּ אֶת־דָּמָם הַמִּזְבֵּחָה לְכַפֵּר עַל־כָּל־יִשְׂרָאֵל כִּי לְכָל־יִשְׂרָאֵל אָמַר הַמֶּלֶךְ הָעוֹלָה וְהַחַטָּאת:

Divrei Hayamim II / II Chronicles
Chapter 29

דברי הימים ב
פרק כט

25 He stationed the *Leviim* in the House of *Hashem* with cymbals and harps and lyres, as *David* and *Gad* the king's seer and *Natan* the *Navi* had ordained, for the ordinance was by *Hashem* through His *Neviim*.

כה וַיַּעֲמֵד אֶת־הַלְוִיִּם בֵּית יְהֹוָה בִּמְצִלְתַּיִם בִּנְבָלִים וּבְכִנֹּרוֹת בְּמִצְוַת דָּוִיד וְגָד חֹזֵה־הַמֶּלֶךְ וְנָתָן הַנָּבִיא כִּי בְיַד־יְהֹוָה הַמִּצְוָה בְּיַד־נְבִיאָיו:

26 When the *Leviim* were in place with the instruments of *David*, and the *Kohanim* with their trumpets,

כו וַיַּעַמְדוּ הַלְוִיִּם בִּכְלֵי דָוִיד וְהַכֹּהֲנִים בַּחֲצֹצְרוֹת:

27 *Chizkiyahu* gave the order to offer the burnt offering on the *Mizbayach*. When the burnt offering began, the song of *Hashem* and the trumpets began also, together with the instruments of King *David* of *Yisrael*.

כז וַיֹּאמֶר חִזְקִיָּהוּ לְהַעֲלוֹת הָעֹלָה לְהַמִּזְבֵּחַ וּבְעֵת הֵחֵל הָעוֹלָה הֵחֵל שִׁיר־יְהֹוָה וְהַחֲצֹצְרוֹת וְעַל־יְדֵי כְּלֵי דָּוִיד מֶלֶךְ־יִשְׂרָאֵל:

28 All the congregation prostrated themselves, the song was sung and the trumpets were blown – all this until the end of the burnt offering.

כח וְכָל־הַקָּהָל מִשְׁתַּחֲוִים וְהַשִּׁיר מְשׁוֹרֵר וְהַחֲצֹצְרוֹת מַחְצְצְרִים [מַחְצְרִים] הַכֹּל עַד לִכְלוֹת הָעֹלָה:

29 When the offering was finished, the king and all who were there with him knelt and prostrated themselves.

כט וּכְכַלּוֹת לְהַעֲלוֹת כָּרְעוּ הַמֶּלֶךְ וְכָל־הַנִּמְצְאִים אִתּוֹ וַיִּשְׁתַּחֲווּ:

u-kh'-kha-LOT l'-ha-a-LOT ka-r'-U ha-ME-lekh v'-khol ha-nim-tz'-EEM i-TO va-yish-ta-kha-VU

30 King *Chizkiyahu* and the officers ordered the *Leviim* to praise *Hashem* in the words of *David* and *Asaf* the seer; so they praised rapturously, and they bowed and prostrated themselves.

ל וַיֹּאמֶר יְחִזְקִיָּהוּ הַמֶּלֶךְ וְהַשָּׂרִים לַלְוִיִּם לְהַלֵּל לַיהֹוָה בְּדִבְרֵי דָוִיד וְאָסָף הַחֹזֶה וַיְהַלְלוּ עַד־לְשִׂמְחָה וַיִּקְּדוּ וַיִּשְׁתַּחֲווּ:

31 Then *Chizkiyahu* said, "Now you have consecrated yourselves to *Hashem*; come, bring sacrifices of well-being and thanksgiving to the House of *Hashem*." The congregation brought sacrifices of well-being and thanksgiving, and all who felt so moved brought burnt offerings.

לא וַיַּעַן יְחִזְקִיָּהוּ וַיֹּאמֶר עַתָּה מִלֵּאתֶם יֶדְכֶם לַיהֹוָה גֹּשׁוּ וְהָבִיאוּ זְבָחִים וְתוֹדוֹת לְבֵית יְהֹוָה וַיָּבִיאוּ הַקָּהָל זְבָחִים וְתוֹדוֹת וְכָל־נְדִיב לֵב עֹלוֹת:

32 The number of burnt offerings that the congregation brought was 70 cattle, 100 rams, 200 lambs – all these for burnt offerings to *Hashem*.

לב וַיְהִי מִסְפַּר הָעֹלָה אֲשֶׁר הֵבִיאוּ הַקָּהָל בָּקָר שִׁבְעִים אֵילִים מֵאָה כְּבָשִׂים מָאתָיִם לְעֹלָה לַיהֹוָה כָּל־אֵלֶּה:

29:29 Knelt and prostrated themselves *Chizkiyahu* institutes great reform in the kingdom of *Yehuda*. He abolishes the idolatry established by his father *Achaz*, reopens and cleanses the *Beit Hamikdash*, brings back the *Kohanim* and *Leviim* and reinstitutes the sacrificial offerings to *Hashem*. After the offerings are brought, the people "knelt and prostrated themselves" to *Hashem*. Once the *Beit Hamikdash* has been rededicated to the worship of God through true sacrifices offered with "a willing heart" (verse 31), *Hashem*'s presence returns to the *Beit Hamikdash*, necessitating prostration. Similarly, in our lives, God rests among those who are willing to sacrifice of themselves for Him.

Divrei Hayamim II/II Chronicles
Chapter 30

דברי הימים ב
פרק ל

33 The sacred offerings were 600 large cattle and 3,000 small cattle.

לג וְהַקֳּדָשִׁים בָּקָר שֵׁשׁ מֵאוֹת וְצֹאן שְׁלֹשֶׁת אֲלָפִים׃

34 The *Kohanim* were too few to be able to flay all the burnt offerings, so their kinsmen, the *Leviim*, reinforced them till the end of the work, and till the [rest of the] *Kohanim* sanctified themselves. (The *Leviim* were more conscientious about sanctifying themselves than the *Kohanim*.)

לד רַק הַכֹּהֲנִים הָיוּ לִמְעָט וְלֹא יָכְלוּ לְהַפְשִׁיט אֶת־כָּל־הָעֹלוֹת וַיְחַזְּקוּם אֲחֵיהֶם הַלְוִיִּם עַד־כְּלוֹת הַמְּלָאכָה וְעַד יִתְקַדְּשׁוּ הַכֹּהֲנִים כִּי הַלְוִיִּם יִשְׁרֵי לֵבָב לְהִתְקַדֵּשׁ מֵהַכֹּהֲנִים׃

35 For beside the large number of burnt offerings, there were the fat parts of the sacrifices of well-being and the libations for the burnt offerings; so the service of the House of *Hashem* was properly accomplished.

לה וְגַם־עֹלָה לָרֹב בְּחֶלְבֵי הַשְּׁלָמִים וּבַנְּסָכִים לָעֹלָה וַתִּכּוֹן עֲבוֹדַת בֵּית־יְהֹוָה׃

36 *Chizkiyahu* and all the people rejoiced over what *Hashem* had enabled the people to accomplish, because it had happened so suddenly.

לו וַיִּשְׂמַח יְחִזְקִיָּהוּ וְכָל־הָעָם עַל הַהֵכִין הָאֱלֹהִים לָעָם כִּי בְּפִתְאֹם הָיָה הַדָּבָר׃

30 1 *Chizkiyahu* sent word to all *Yisrael* and *Yehuda*; he also wrote letters to *Efraim* and *Menashe* to come to the House of *Hashem* in *Yerushalayim* to keep the *Pesach* for God of *Yisrael*.

ל א וַיִּשְׁלַח יְחִזְקִיָּהוּ עַל־כָּל־יִשְׂרָאֵל וִיהוּדָה וְגַם־אִגְּרוֹת כָּתַב עַל־אֶפְרַיִם וּמְנַשֶּׁה לָבוֹא לְבֵית־יְהֹוָה בִּירוּשָׁלָ͏ִם לַעֲשׂוֹת פֶּסַח לַיהֹוָה אֱלֹהֵי יִשְׂרָאֵל׃

2 The king and his officers and the congregation in *Yerushalayim* had agreed to keep the *Pesach* in the second month,

ב וַיִּוָּעַץ הַמֶּלֶךְ וְשָׂרָיו וְכָל־הַקָּהָל בִּירוּשָׁלָ͏ִם לַעֲשׂוֹת הַפֶּסַח בַּחֹדֶשׁ הַשֵּׁנִי׃

3 for at the time, they were unable to keep it, for not enough *Kohanim* had sanctified themselves, nor had the people assembled in *Yerushalayim*.

ג כִּי לֹא יָכְלוּ לַעֲשֹׂתוֹ בָּעֵת הַהִיא כִּי הַכֹּהֲנִים לֹא־הִתְקַדְּשׁוּ לְמַדַּי וְהָעָם לֹא־נֶאֶסְפוּ לִירוּשָׁלָ͏ִם׃

4 The king and the whole congregation thought it proper

ד וַיִּישַׁר הַדָּבָר בְּעֵינֵי הַמֶּלֶךְ וּבְעֵינֵי כָּל־הַקָּהָל׃

5 to issue a decree and proclaim throughout all *Yisrael* from *Be'er Sheva* to *Dan* that they come and keep the *Pesach* for God of *Yisrael* in *Yerushalayim* – not often did they act in accord with what was written.

ה וַיַּעֲמִידוּ דָבָר לְהַעֲבִיר קוֹל בְּכָל־יִשְׂרָאֵל מִבְּאֵר־שֶׁבַע וְעַד־דָּן לָבוֹא לַעֲשׂוֹת פֶּסַח לַיהֹוָה אֱלֹהֵי־יִשְׂרָאֵל בִּירוּשָׁלָ͏ִם כִּי לֹא לָרֹב עָשׂוּ כַּכָּתוּב׃

6 The couriers went out with the letters from the king and his officers through all *Yisrael* and *Yehuda*, by order of the king, proclaiming, "O you Israelites! Return to God of your fathers, *Avraham*,

ו וַיֵּלְכוּ הָרָצִים בָּאִגְּרוֹת מִיַּד הַמֶּלֶךְ וְשָׂרָיו בְּכָל־יִשְׂרָאֵל וִיהוּדָה וּכְמִצְוַת הַמֶּלֶךְ לֵאמֹר בְּנֵי יִשְׂרָאֵל שׁוּבוּ אֶל־יְהֹוָה אֱלֹהֵי אַבְרָהָם יִצְחָק וְיִשְׂרָאֵל

30:6 God of your fathers, *Avraham*, *Yitzchak*, and *Yisrael* *Chizkiyahu* invokes the God of *Avraham*, *Yitzchak* and *Yaakov*, the forefathers to whom the Land of Israel was first promised. He sends his messengers throughout the land to tell those who had inherited the land from their forefathers that if they renew their covenant with *Hashem* and rededicate themselves to His service, they can escape foreign domination. He calls on them to

2122

Divrei Hayamim II/II Chronicles
Chapter 30

דברי הימים ב
פרק ל

Yitzchak, and *Yisrael*, and He will return to the remnant of you who escaped from the hand of the kings of Assyria.

וְיָשֹׁב אֶל־הַפְּלֵיטָה הַנִּשְׁאֶרֶת לָכֶם מִכַּף מַלְכֵי אַשּׁוּר:

va-yay-l'-KHU ha-ra-TZEEM ba-i-g'-ROT mi-YAD ha-ME-lekh v'-sa-RAV b'-khol yis-ra-AYL vee-hu-DAH ukh-mitz-VAT ha-ME-lekh lay-MOR b'-NAY yis-ra-AYL SHU-vu el a-do-NAI e-lo-HAY av-ra-HAM yitz-KHAK v'-yis-ra-AYL v'-ya-SHOV el ha-p'-lay-TAH ha-nish-E-ret la-KHEM mi-KAF mal-KHAY a-SHUR

7 Do not be like your fathers and brothers who trespassed against God of their fathers and He turned them into a horror, as you see.

ז וְאַל־תִּהְיוּ כַּאֲבוֹתֵיכֶם וְכַאֲחֵיכֶם אֲשֶׁר מָעֲלוּ בַּיהוָה אֱלֹהֵי אֲבוֹתֵיהֶם וַיִּתְּנֵם לְשַׁמָּה כַּאֲשֶׁר אַתֶּם רֹאִים:

8 Now do not be stiffnecked like your fathers; submit yourselves to *Hashem* and come to His sanctuary, which He consecrated forever, and serve *Hashem* your God so that His anger may turn back from you.

ח עַתָּה אַל־תַּקְשׁוּ עָרְפְּכֶם כַּאֲבוֹתֵיכֶם תְּנוּ־יָד לַיהוָה וּבֹאוּ לְמִקְדָּשׁוֹ אֲשֶׁר הִקְדִּישׁ לְעוֹלָם וְעִבְדוּ אֶת־יְהוָה אֱלֹהֵיכֶם וְיָשֹׁב מִכֶּם חֲרוֹן אַפּוֹ:

9 If you return to *Hashem*, your brothers and children will be regarded with compassion by their captors, and will return to this land; for *Hashem* your God is gracious and merciful; He will not turn His face from you if you return to Him."

ט כִּי בְשׁוּבְכֶם עַל־יְהוָה אֲחֵיכֶם וּבְנֵיכֶם לְרַחֲמִים לִפְנֵי שׁוֹבֵיהֶם וְלָשׁוּב לָאָרֶץ הַזֹּאת כִּי־חַנּוּן וְרַחוּם יְהוָה אֱלֹהֵיכֶם וְלֹא־יָסִיר פָּנִים מִכֶּם אִם־תָּשׁוּבוּ אֵלָיו:

10 As the couriers passed from town to town in the land of *Efraim* and *Menashe* till they reached *Zevulun*, they were laughed at and mocked.

י וַיִּהְיוּ הָרָצִים עֹבְרִים מֵעִיר לָעִיר בְּאֶרֶץ־אֶפְרַיִם וּמְנַשֶּׁה וְעַד־זְבֻלוּן וַיִּהְיוּ מַשְׂחִיקִים עֲלֵיהֶם וּמַלְעִגִים בָּם:

11 Some of the people of *Asher* and *Menashe* and *Zevulun*, however, were contrite, and came to *Yerushalayim*.

יא אַךְ־אֲנָשִׁים מֵאָשֵׁר וּמְנַשֶּׁה וּמִזְּבֻלוּן נִכְנְעוּ וַיָּבֹאוּ לִירוּשָׁלִָם:

12 The hand of *Hashem* was on *Yehuda*, too, making them of a single mind to carry out the command of the king and officers concerning the ordinance of *Hashem*.

יב גַּם בִּיהוּדָה הָיְתָה יַד הָאֱלֹהִים לָתֵת לָהֶם לֵב אֶחָד לַעֲשׂוֹת מִצְוַת הַמֶּלֶךְ וְהַשָּׂרִים בִּדְבַר יְהוָה:

13 A great crowd assembled at *Yerushalayim* to keep the Festival of *Pesach* in the second month, a very great congregation.

יג וַיֵּאָסְפוּ יְרוּשָׁלִַם עַם־רָב לַעֲשׂוֹת אֶת־חַג הַמַּצּוֹת בַּחֹדֶשׁ הַשֵּׁנִי קָהָל לָרֹב מְאֹד:

14 They set to and removed the altars that were in *Yerushalayim*, and they removed all the incense stands and threw them into Wadi Kidron.

יד וַיָּקֻמוּ וַיָּסִירוּ אֶת־הַמִּזְבְּחוֹת אֲשֶׁר בִּירוּשָׁלִָם וְאֵת כָּל־הַמְקַטְּרוֹת הֵסִירוּ וַיַּשְׁלִיכוּ לְנַחַל קִדְרוֹן:

---

bring the *Pesach* sacrifice, which they first brought in Egypt, indelibly identifying them as *Hashem*'s people and symbolizing their freedom. The way to achieve freedom in their land is to renew their loyalty to their Father in Heaven.

Divrei Hayamim II / II Chronicles
Chapter 30

15 They slaughtered the paschal sacrifice on the fourteenth of the second month. The *Kohanim* and *Leviim* were ashamed, and they sanctified themselves and brought burnt offerings to the House of *Hashem*.

16 They took their stations, as was their rule according to the Teaching of *Moshe*, man of *Hashem*. The *Kohanim* dashed the blood [which they received] from the *Leviim*.

17 Since many in the congregation had not sanctified themselves, the *Leviim* were in charge of slaughtering the paschal sacrifice for everyone who was not clean, so as to consecrate them to *Hashem*.

18 For most of the people – many from *Efraim* and *Menashe*, *Yissachar* and *Zevulun* – had not purified themselves, yet they ate the paschal sacrifice in violation of what was written. *Chizkiyahu* prayed for them, saying, "*Hashem* will provide atonement for

19 everyone who set his mind on worshiping *Hashem*, God of his fathers, even if he is not purified for the sanctuary."

20 *Hashem* heard *Chizkiyahu* and healed the people.

21 The Israelites who were in *Yerushalayim* kept the Festival of *Pesach* seven days, with great rejoicing, the *Leviim* and the *Kohanim* praising *Hashem* daily with powerful instruments for *Hashem*.

22 *Chizkiyahu* persuaded all the *Leviim* who performed skillfully for *Hashem* to spend the seven days of the festival making offerings of well-being, and confessing to God of their fathers.

23 All the congregation resolved to keep seven more days, so they kept seven more days of rejoicing.

24 King *Chizkiyahu* of *Yehuda* contributed to the congregation 1,000 bulls and 7,000 sheep. And the officers contributed to the congregation 1,000 bulls and 10,000 sheep. And the *Kohanim* sanctified themselves in large numbers.

25 All the congregation of *Yehuda* and the *Kohanim* and the *Leviim* and all the congregation that came from *Yisrael*, and the resident aliens who came from the land of *Yisrael* and who lived in *Yehuda*, rejoiced.

דברי הימים ב
פרק ל

טו וַיִּשְׁחֲטוּ הַפֶּסַח בְּאַרְבָּעָה עָשָׂר לַחֹדֶשׁ הַשֵּׁנִי וְהַכֹּהֲנִים וְהַלְוִיִּם נִכְלְמוּ וַיִּתְקַדְּשׁוּ וַיָּבִיאוּ עֹלוֹת בֵּית יְהוָה:

טז וַיַּעַמְדוּ עַל־עָמְדָם כְּמִשְׁפָּטָם כְּתוֹרַת מֹשֶׁה אִישׁ־הָאֱלֹהִים הַכֹּהֲנִים זֹרְקִים אֶת־הַדָּם מִיַּד הַלְוִיִּם:

יז כִּי־רַבַּת בַּקָּהָל אֲשֶׁר לֹא־הִתְקַדָּשׁוּ וְהַלְוִיִּם עַל־שְׁחִיטַת הַפְּסָחִים לְכֹל לֹא טָהוֹר לְהַקְדִּישׁ לַיהוָה:

יח כִּי מַרְבִּית הָעָם רַבַּת מֵאֶפְרַיִם וּמְנַשֶּׁה יִשָּׂשכָר וּזְבֻלוּן לֹא הִטֶּהָרוּ כִּי־אָכְלוּ אֶת־הַפֶּסַח בְּלֹא כַכָּתוּב כִּי הִתְפַּלֵּל יְחִזְקִיָּהוּ עֲלֵיהֶם לֵאמֹר יְהוָה הַטּוֹב יְכַפֵּר בְּעַד:

יט כָּל־לְבָבוֹ הֵכִין לִדְרוֹשׁ הָאֱלֹהִים יְהוָה אֱלֹהֵי אֲבוֹתָיו וְלֹא כְּטָהֳרַת הַקֹּדֶשׁ:

כ וַיִּשְׁמַע יְהוָה אֶל־יְחִזְקִיָּהוּ וַיִּרְפָּא אֶת־הָעָם:

כא וַיַּעֲשׂוּ בְנֵי־יִשְׂרָאֵל הַנִּמְצְאִים בִּירוּשָׁלִַם אֶת־חַג הַמַּצּוֹת שִׁבְעַת יָמִים בְּשִׂמְחָה גְדוֹלָה וּמְהַלְלִים לַיהוָה יוֹם בְּיוֹם הַלְוִיִּם וְהַכֹּהֲנִים בִּכְלֵי־עֹז לַיהוָה:

כב וַיְדַבֵּר יְחִזְקִיָּהוּ עַל־לֵב כָּל־הַלְוִיִּם הַמַּשְׂכִּילִים שֵׂכֶל־טוֹב לַיהוָה וַיֹּאכְלוּ אֶת־הַמּוֹעֵד שִׁבְעַת הַיָּמִים מְזַבְּחִים זִבְחֵי שְׁלָמִים וּמִתְוַדִּים לַיהוָה אֱלֹהֵי אֲבוֹתֵיהֶם:

כג וַיִּוָּעֲצוּ כָּל־הַקָּהָל לַעֲשׂוֹת שִׁבְעַת יָמִים אֲחֵרִים וַיַּעֲשׂוּ שִׁבְעַת־יָמִים שִׂמְחָה:

כד כִּי חִזְקִיָּהוּ מֶלֶךְ־יְהוּדָה הֵרִים לַקָּהָל אֶלֶף פָּרִים וְשִׁבְעַת אֲלָפִים צֹאן וְהַשָּׂרִים הֵרִימוּ לַקָּהָל פָּרִים אֶלֶף וְצֹאן עֲשֶׂרֶת אֲלָפִים וַיִּתְקַדְּשׁוּ כֹהֲנִים לָרֹב:

כה וַיִּשְׂמְחוּ כָּל־קְהַל יְהוּדָה וְהַכֹּהֲנִים וְהַלְוִיִּם וְכָל־הַקָּהָל הַבָּאִים מִיִּשְׂרָאֵל וְהַגֵּרִים הַבָּאִים מֵאֶרֶץ יִשְׂרָאֵל וְהַיּוֹשְׁבִים בִּיהוּדָה:

Divrei Hayamim II/II Chronicles
Chapter 31

דברי הימים ב
פרק לא

26 There was great rejoicing in *Yerushalayim*, for since the time of King *Shlomo* son of *David* of *Yisrael* nothing like it had happened in *Yerushalayim*.

כו וַתְּהִי שִׂמְחָה־גְדוֹלָה בִּירוּשָׁלָ͏ִם כִּי מִימֵי שְׁלֹמֹה בֶן־דָּוִיד מֶלֶךְ יִשְׂרָאֵל לֹא כָזֹאת בִּירוּשָׁלָ͏ִם:

27 The Levite *Kohanim* rose and blessed the people, and their voice was heard, and their prayer went up to His holy abode, to heaven.

כז וַיָּקֻמוּ הַכֹּהֲנִים הַלְוִיִּם וַיְבָרְכוּ אֶת־הָעָם וַיִּשָּׁמַע בְּקוֹלָם וַתָּבוֹא תְפִלָּתָם לִמְעוֹן קָדְשׁוֹ לַשָּׁמָיִם:

31 1 When all this was finished, all *Yisrael* who were present went out into the towns of *Yehuda* and smashed the pillars, cut down the sacred posts, demolished the shrines and altars throughout *Yehuda* and *Binyamin*, and throughout *Efraim* and *Menashe*, to the very last one. Then all the Israelites returned to their towns, each to his possession.

לא א וּכְכַלּוֹת כָּל־זֹאת יָצְאוּ כָל־יִשְׂרָאֵל הַנִּמְצְאִים לְעָרֵי יְהוּדָה וַיְשַׁבְּרוּ הַמַּצֵּבוֹת וַיְגַדְּעוּ הָאֲשֵׁרִים וַיְנַתְּצוּ אֶת־הַבָּמוֹת וְאֶת־הַמִּזְבְּחֹת מִכָּל־יְהוּדָה וּבִנְיָמִן וּבְאֶפְרַיִם וּמְנַשֶּׁה עַד־לְכַלֵּה וַיָּשׁוּבוּ כָּל־בְּנֵי יִשְׂרָאֵל אִישׁ לַאֲחֻזָּתוֹ לְעָרֵיהֶם:

2 *Chizkiyahu* reconstituted the divisions of the *Kohanim* and *Leviim*, each man of the *Kohanim* and *Leviim* according to his office, for the burnt offerings, the offerings of well-being, to minister, and to sing hymns and praises in the gates of the courts of *Hashem*;

ב וַיַּעֲמֵד יְחִזְקִיָּהוּ אֶת־מַחְלְקוֹת הַכֹּהֲנִים וְהַלְוִיִּם עַל־מַחְלְקוֹתָם אִישׁ כְּפִי עֲבֹדָתוֹ לַכֹּהֲנִים וְלַלְוִיִּם לְעֹלָה וְלִשְׁלָמִים לְשָׁרֵת וּלְהֹדוֹת וּלְהַלֵּל בְּשַׁעֲרֵי מַחֲנוֹת יְהוָה:

3 also the king's portion, from his property, for the burnt offerings – the morning and evening burnt offering, and the burnt offerings for *Shabbatot*, and new moons, and festivals, as prescribed in the Teaching of *Hashem*.

ג וּמְנָת הַמֶּלֶךְ מִן־רְכוּשׁוֹ לָעֹלוֹת לְעֹלוֹת הַבֹּקֶר וְהָעֶרֶב וְהָעֹלוֹת לַשַּׁבָּתוֹת וְלֶחֳדָשִׁים וְלַמֹּעֲדִים כַּכָּתוּב בְּתוֹרַת יְהוָה:

4 He ordered the people, the inhabitants of *Yerushalayim*, to deliver the portions of the *Kohanim* and the *Leviim*, so that they might devote themselves to the Teaching of *Hashem*.

ד וַיֹּאמֶר לָעָם לְיוֹשְׁבֵי יְרוּשָׁלַ͏ִם לָתֵת מְנָת הַכֹּהֲנִים וְהַלְוִיִּם לְמַעַן יֶחֶזְקוּ בְּתוֹרַת יְהוָה:

5 When the word spread, the Israelites brought large quantities of grain, wine, oil, honey, and all kinds of agricultural produce, and tithes of all, in large amounts.

ה וְכִפְרֹץ הַדָּבָר הִרְבּוּ בְנֵי־יִשְׂרָאֵל רֵאשִׁית דָּגָן תִּירוֹשׁ וְיִצְהָר וּדְבַשׁ וְכֹל תְּבוּאַת שָׂדֶה וּמַעְשַׂר הַכֹּל לָרֹב הֵבִיאוּ:

v'-khif-ROTZ ha-da-VAR hir-BU v'-NAY yis-ra-AYL ray-SHEET da-GAN tee-ROSH v'-yitz-HAR ud-VASH v'-KHOL t'-vu-AT sa-DEH u-ma-SAR ha-KOL la-ROV hay-VEE-u

31:5 And tithes of all, in large amounts The gifts and tithes brought to the *Beit Hamikdash* and presented to the *Kohanim* and *Leviim* are examples of biblical commandments that apply only in the Land of Israel. A portion of the crops grown in the land is dedicated to the Creator before we eat from them ourselves, to remind us that no matter how hard we work the land, and despite the tremendous human effort required to produce it, our crops are really a gift from *Hashem*. Additionally, gifts are given to the religious leaders of Israel, to provide physical sustenance in exchange for the spiritual nourishment they offer the people. Since they have no portion of land of their own, the *Kohanim* and *Leviim* are dependent on the rest of the nation for their physical nourishment. In return, their contribution elevates everyone else's existence in the land. Such is life in *Eretz Yisrael* – the physical and spiritual are continuously intertwined.

Divrei Hayamim II/II Chronicles
Chapter 31

דברי הימים ב
פרק לא

6 The men of *Yisrael* and *Yehuda* living in the towns of *Yehuda* – they too brought tithes of cattle and sheep and tithes of sacred things consecrated to *Hashem* their God, piling them in heaps.

ו וּבְנֵ֤י יִשְׂרָאֵל֙ וִיהוּדָ֔ה הַיּוֹשְׁבִ֖ים בְּעָרֵ֣י יְהוּדָ֑ה גַּם־הֵ֗ם מַעְשַׂ֤ר בָּקָר֙ וָצֹ֔אן וּמַעְשַׂ֣ר קָֽדָשִׁ֗ים הַמְקֻדָּשִׁ֛ים לַיהֹוָ֥ה אֱלֹהֵיהֶ֖ם הֵבִ֑יאוּ וַֽיִּתְּנ֖וּ עֲרֵמ֥וֹת עֲרֵמֽוֹת׃

7 In the third month the heaps began to accumulate, and were finished in the seventh month.

ז בַּחֹ֙דֶשׁ֙ הַשְּׁלִשִׁ֔י הֵחֵ֥לּוּ הָעֲרֵמ֖וֹת לְיִסּ֑וֹד וּבַחֹ֥דֶשׁ הַשְּׁבִיעִ֖י כִּלּֽוּ׃

8 When *Chizkiyahu* and the officers came and saw the heaps, they blessed *Hashem* and his people *Yisrael*.

ח וַיָּבֹ֙אוּ֙ יְחִזְקִיָּ֣הוּ וְהַשָּׂרִ֔ים וַיִּרְא֖וּ אֶת־הָעֲרֵמ֑וֹת וַיְבָרֲכוּ֙ אֶת־יְהֹוָ֔ה וְאֵ֖ת עַמּ֥וֹ יִשְׂרָאֵֽל׃

9 *Chizkiyahu* asked the *Kohanim* and *Leviim* about the heaps.

ט וַיִּדְרֹ֣שׁ יְחִזְקִיָּ֗הוּ עַל־הַכֹּהֲנִ֛ים וְהַלְוִיִּ֖ם עַל־הָעֲרֵמֽוֹת׃

10 The chief *kohen* *Azarya*, of the house of *Tzadok*, replied to him, saying, "Ever since the gifts began to be brought to the House of *Hashem*, people have been eating to satiety and leaving over in great amounts, for *Hashem* has blessed His people; this huge amount is left over!"

י וַיֹּ֣אמֶר אֵלָ֗יו עֲזַרְיָ֧הוּ הַכֹּהֵ֛ן הָרֹ֖אשׁ לְבֵ֣ית צָד֑וֹק וַ֠יֹּ֠אמֶר מֵהָחֵ֨ל הַתְּרוּמָ֜ה לָבִ֣יא בֵית־יְהֹוָ֗ה אָכ֤וֹל וְשָׂבֹ֙ועַ֙ וְהוֹתֵ֣ר עַד־לָר֔וֹב כִּ֤י יְהֹוָה֙ בֵּרַ֣ךְ אֶת־עַמּ֔וֹ וְהַנּוֹתָ֖ר אֶת־הֶהָמ֥וֹן הַזֶּֽה׃

11 *Chizkiyahu* then gave orders to prepare store-chambers in the House of *Hashem*; and they were prepared.

יא וַיֹּ֣אמֶר יְחִזְקִיָּ֗הוּ לְהָכִ֧ין לְשָׁכ֛וֹת בְּבֵ֥ית יְהֹוָ֖ה וַיָּכִֽינוּ׃

12 They brought in the gifts and the tithes and the sacred things faithfully. Their supervisor was Conaniah the *Levi*, and *Shim'i* his brother was second in rank.

יב וַיָּבִ֨יאוּ אֶת־הַתְּרוּמָ֧ה וְהַֽמַּעֲשֵׂ֛ר וְהַקֳּדָשִׁ֖ים בֶּאֱמוּנָ֑ה וַעֲלֵיהֶ֤ם נָגִיד֙ כונניהו [כָּנַנְיָ֙הוּ֙] הַלֵּוִ֔י וְשִׁמְעִ֥י אָחִ֖יהוּ מִשְׁנֶֽה׃

13 *Yechiel* and *Azaziah* and *Nahath* and *Asael* and *Jerimoth* and *Yozavad* and *Eliel* and *Ismachiah* and *Mahath* and *Benaiah* were commissioners under Conaniah and *Shim'i* his brother by appointment of King *Chizkiyahu*; *Azarya* was supervisor of the House of *Hashem*.

יג וִיחִיאֵ֡ל וַ֠עֲזַזְיָ֠הוּ וְנַ֨חַת וַעֲשָׂהאֵ֜ל וִירִימ֤וֹת וְיוֹזָבָד֙ וֶאֱלִיאֵ֣ל וְיִסְמַכְיָ֔הוּ וּמַ֖חַת וּבְנָיָ֑הוּ פְּקִידִ֞ים מִיַּ֧ד כונניהו [כָּנַנְיָ֛הוּ] וְשִׁמְעִ֥י אָחִ֖יו בְּמִפְקַ֞ד יְחִזְקִיָּ֣הוּ הַמֶּ֗לֶךְ וַעֲזַרְיָ֖הוּ נְגִ֥יד בֵּית־הָאֱלֹהִֽים׃

14 Kore son of Imnah the *Levi*, the keeper of the East Gate, was in charge of the freewill offerings to *Hashem*, of the allocation of gifts to *Hashem*, and the most sacred things.

יד וְקוֹרֵ֨א בֶן־יִמְנָ֤ה הַלֵּוִי֙ הַשּׁוֹעֵ֣ר לַמִּזְרָ֔חָה עַ֖ל נִדְב֣וֹת הָאֱלֹהִ֑ים לָתֵת֙ תְּרוּמַ֣ת יְהֹוָ֔ה וְקָדְשֵׁ֖י הַקֳּדָשִֽׁים׃

15 Under him were Eden, Miniamin, *Yeshua*, *Shemaya*, Amariah, and *Shechanya*, in offices of trust in the priestly towns, making allocation to their brothers by divisions, to great and small alike;

טו וְעַל־יָד֡וֹ עֵ֣דֶן וּ֠מִנְיָמִ֠ן וְיֵשׁ֨וּעַ וּֽשְׁמַעְיָ֜הוּ אֲמַרְיָ֧הוּ וּשְׁכַנְיָ֛הוּ בְּעָרֵ֥י הַכֹּהֲנִ֖ים בֶּאֱמוּנָ֑ה לָתֵ֤ת לַאֲחֵיהֶם֙ בְּמַחְלְק֔וֹת כַּגָּד֖וֹל כַּקָּטָֽן׃

Divrei Hayamim II / II Chronicles
Chapter 32

16 besides allocating their daily rations to those males registered by families from three years old and up, all who entered the House of *Hashem* according to their service and their shift by division;

17 and in charge of the registry of *Kohanim* by clans, and of the *Leviim*, from twenty years old and up, by shifts, in their divisions;

18 and the registry of the dependents of their whole company – wives, sons, and daughters – for, relying upon them, they sanctified themselves in holiness.

19 And for the Aaronite *Kohanim*, in each and every one of their towns with adjoining fields, the above-named men were to allocate portions to every male of the *Kohanim* and to every registered *Levi*.

20 *Chizkiyahu* did this throughout *Yehuda*. He acted in a way that was good, upright, and faithful before *Hashem* his God.

21 Every work he undertook in the service of the House of *Hashem* or in the Teaching and the Commandment, to worship his God, he did with all his heart; and he prospered.

32 1 After these faithful deeds, King Sennacherib of Assyria invaded *Yehuda* and encamped against its fortified towns with the aim of taking them over.

2 When *Chizkiyahu* saw that Sennacherib had come, intent on making war against *Yerushalayim*,

3 he consulted with his officers and warriors about stopping the flow of the springs outside the city, and they supported him.

4 A large force was assembled to stop up all the springs and the wadi that flowed through the land, for otherwise, they thought, the king of Assyria would come and find water in abundance.

5 He acted with vigor, rebuilding the whole breached wall, raising towers on it, and building another wall outside it. He fortified the Millo of the City of *David*, and made a great quantity of arms and shields.

6 He appointed battle officers over the people; then, gathering them to him in the square of the city gate, he rallied them, saying,

דברי הימים ב
פרק לב

טז מִלְּבַד הִתְיַחְשָׂם לִזְכָרִים מִבֶּן שָׁלוֹשׁ שָׁנִים וּלְמַעְלָה לְכָל־הַבָּא לְבֵית־יְהֹוָה לִדְבַר־יוֹם בְּיוֹמוֹ לַעֲבוֹדָתָם בְּמִשְׁמְרוֹתָם כְּמַחְלְקוֹתֵיהֶם׃

יז וְאֵת הִתְיַחֵשׂ הַכֹּהֲנִים לְבֵית אֲבוֹתֵיהֶם וְהַלְוִיִּם מִבֶּן עֶשְׂרִים שָׁנָה וּלְמָעְלָה בְּמִשְׁמְרוֹתֵיהֶם בְּמַחְלְקוֹתֵיהֶם׃

יח וּלְהִתְיַחֵשׂ בְּכָל־טַפָּם נְשֵׁיהֶם וּבְנֵיהֶם וּבְנוֹתֵיהֶם לְכָל־קָהָל כִּי בֶאֱמוּנָתָם יִתְקַדְּשׁוּ־קֹדֶשׁ׃

יט וְלִבְנֵי אַהֲרֹן הַכֹּהֲנִים בִּשְׂדֵי מִגְרַשׁ עָרֵיהֶם בְּכָל־עִיר וָעִיר אֲנָשִׁים אֲשֶׁר נִקְּבוּ בְּשֵׁמוֹת לָתֵת מָנוֹת לְכָל־זָכָר בַּכֹּהֲנִים וּלְכָל־הִתְיַחֵשׂ בַּלְוִיִּם׃

כ וַיַּעַשׂ כָּזֹאת יְחִזְקִיָּהוּ בְּכָל־יְהוּדָה וַיַּעַשׂ הַטּוֹב וְהַיָּשָׁר וְהָאֱמֶת לִפְנֵי יְהֹוָה אֱלֹהָיו׃

כא וּבְכָל־מַעֲשֶׂה אֲשֶׁר־הֵחֵל בַּעֲבוֹדַת בֵּית־הָאֱלֹהִים וּבַתּוֹרָה וּבַמִּצְוָה לִדְרֹשׁ לֵאלֹהָיו בְּכָל־לְבָבוֹ עָשָׂה וְהִצְלִיחַ׃

לב א אַחֲרֵי הַדְּבָרִים וְהָאֱמֶת הָאֵלֶּה בָּא סַנְחֵרִיב מֶלֶךְ־אַשּׁוּר וַיָּבֹא בִיהוּדָה וַיִּחַן עַל־הֶעָרִים הַבְּצֻרוֹת וַיֹּאמֶר לְבִקְעָם אֵלָיו׃

ב וַיַּרְא יְחִזְקִיָּהוּ כִּי־בָא סַנְחֵרִיב וּפָנָיו לַמִּלְחָמָה עַל־יְרוּשָׁלָ͏ִם׃

ג וַיִּוָּעַץ עִם־שָׂרָיו וְגִבֹּרָיו לִסְתּוֹם אֶת־מֵימֵי הָעֲיָנוֹת אֲשֶׁר מִחוּץ לָעִיר וַיַּעְזְרוּהוּ׃

ד וַיִּקָּבְצוּ עַם־רָב וַיִּסְתְּמוּ אֶת־כָּל־הַמַּעְיָנוֹת וְאֶת־הַנַּחַל הַשּׁוֹטֵף בְּתוֹךְ־הָאָרֶץ לֵאמֹר לָמָּה יָבוֹאוּ מַלְכֵי אַשּׁוּר וּמָצְאוּ מַיִם רַבִּים׃

ה וַיִּתְחַזַּק וַיִּבֶן אֶת־כָּל־הַחוֹמָה הַפְּרוּצָה וַיַּעַל עַל־הַמִּגְדָּלוֹת וְלַחוּצָה הַחוֹמָה אַחֶרֶת וַיְחַזֵּק אֶת־הַמִּלּוֹא עִיר דָּוִיד וַיַּעַשׂ שֶׁלַח לָרֹב וּמָגִנִּים׃

ו וַיִּתֵּן שָׂרֵי מִלְחָמוֹת עַל־הָעָם וַיִּקְבְּצֵם אֵלָיו אֶל־רְחוֹב שַׁעַר הָעִיר וַיְדַבֵּר עַל־לְבָבָם לֵאמֹר׃

Divrei Hayamim II / II Chronicles
Chapter 32

דברי הימים ב
פרק לב

7 "Be strong and of good courage; do not be frightened or dismayed by the king of Assyria or by the horde that is with him, for we have more with us than he has with him.

ז חִזְק֣וּ וְאִמְצ֔וּ אַל־תִּֽירְא֣וּ וְאַל־תֵּחַ֗תּוּ מִפְּנֵי֙ מֶ֣לֶךְ אַשּׁ֔וּר וּמִלִּפְנֵ֖י כָּל־הֶהָמ֣וֹן אֲשֶׁר־עִמּ֑וֹ כִּֽי־עִמָּ֥נוּ רַ֖ב מֵעִמּֽוֹ׃

8 With him is an arm of flesh, but with us is *Hashem* our God, to help us and to fight our battles." The people were encouraged by the speech of King *Chizkiyahu* of *Yehuda*.

ח עִמּוֹ֙ זְר֣וֹעַ בָּשָׂ֔ר וְעִמָּ֜נוּ יְהֹוָ֤ה אֱלֹהֵ֙ינוּ֙ לְעָזְרֵ֔נוּ וּלְהִלָּחֵ֖ם מִלְחֲמֹתֵ֑נוּ וַיִּסָּמְכ֣וּ הָעָ֔ם עַל־דִּבְרֵ֖י יְחִזְקִיָּ֥הוּ מֶֽלֶךְ־יְהוּדָֽה׃

9 Afterward, King Sennacherib of Assyria sent his officers to *Yerushalayim* – he and all his staff being at *Lachish* – with this message to King *Chizkiyahu* of *Yehuda* and to all the people of *Yehuda* who were in *Yerushalayim*:

ט אַחַ֣ר זֶ֡ה שָׁלַח֩ סַנְחֵרִ֨יב מֶֽלֶךְ־אַשּׁ֜וּר עֲבָדָ֣יו יְרוּשָׁלַ֗יְמָה וְהוּא֙ עַל־לָכִ֔ישׁ וְכָל־מֶמְשַׁלְתּ֖וֹ עִמּ֑וֹ עַל־יְחִזְקִיָּ֙הוּ֙ מֶ֣לֶךְ יְהוּדָ֔ה וְעַל־כָּל־יְהוּדָ֖ה אֲשֶׁ֥ר בִּירוּשָׁלַ֖͏ִם לֵאמֹֽר׃

10 "Thus said King Sennacherib of Assyria: On what do you trust to enable you to endure a siege in *Yerushalayim*?

י כֹּ֣ה אָמַ֔ר סַנְחֵרִ֖יב מֶ֣לֶךְ אַשּׁ֑וּר עַל־מָה֙ אַתֶּ֣ם בֹּטְחִ֔ים וְיֹשְׁבִ֥ים בְּמָצ֖וֹר בִּירוּשָׁלָֽ͏ִם׃

11 *Chizkiyahu* is seducing you to a death of hunger and thirst, saying, '*Hashem* our God will save us from the king of Assyria.'

יא הֲלֹ֤א יְחִזְקִיָּ֙הוּ֙ מַסִּ֣ית אֶתְכֶ֔ם לָתֵ֣ת אֶתְכֶ֔ם לָמ֛וּת בְּרָעָ֥ב וּבְצָמָ֖א לֵאמֹ֑ר יְהֹוָ֣ה אֱלֹהֵ֔ינוּ יַצִּילֵ֕נוּ מִכַּ֖ף מֶ֥לֶךְ אַשּֽׁוּר׃

12 But is not *Chizkiyahu* the one who removed His shrines and His altars and commanded the people of *Yehuda* and *Yerushalayim* saying, 'Before this one *Mizbayach* you shall prostrate yourselves, and upon it make your burnt offerings'?

יב הֲלֹא־הוּא֙ יְחִזְקִיָּ֔הוּ הֵסִ֥יר אֶת־בָּמֹתָ֖יו וְאֶת־מִזְבְּחֹתָ֑יו וַיֹּ֨אמֶר לִיהוּדָ֜ה וְלִירוּשָׁלַ֗͏ִם לֵאמֹ֔ר לִפְנֵ֨י מִזְבֵּ֧חַ אֶחָ֛ד תִּֽשְׁתַּחֲו֖וּ וְעָלָ֥יו תַּקְטִֽירוּ׃

13 Surely you know what I and my fathers have done to the peoples of the lands? Were the gods of the nations of the lands able to save their lands from me?

יג הֲלֹ֣א תֵדְע֗וּ מֶ֤ה עָשִׂ֙יתִי֙ אֲנִ֣י וַאֲבוֹתַ֔י לְכֹ֖ל עַמֵּ֣י הָאֲרָצ֑וֹת הֲיָכ֣וֹל יָכְל֗וּ אֱלֹהֵי֙ גּוֹיֵ֣ הָאֲרָצ֔וֹת לְהַצִּ֥יל אֶת־אַרְצָ֖ם מִיָּדִֽי׃

14 Which of all the gods of any of those nations whom my fathers destroyed was able to save his people from me, that your God should be able to save you from me?

יד מִ֠י בְּֽכָל־אֱלֹהֵ֞י הַגּוֹיִ֤ם הָאֵ֙לֶּה֙ אֲשֶׁ֣ר הֶחֱרִ֣ימוּ אֲבוֹתַ֔י אֲשֶׁ֣ר יָכ֔וֹל לְהַצִּ֥יל אֶת־עַמּ֖וֹ מִיָּדִ֑י כִּ֤י יוּכַל֙ אֱלֹ֣הֵיכֶ֔ם לְהַצִּ֥יל אֶתְכֶ֖ם מִיָּדִֽי׃

15 Now then, do not let *Chizkiyahu* delude you; do not let him seduce you in this way; do not believe him. For no god of any nation or kingdom has been able to save his people from me or from my fathers – much less your God, to save you from me!"

טו וְעַתָּ֡ה אַל־יַשִּׁיא֩ אֶתְכֶ֨ם חִזְקִיָּ֜הוּ וְאַל־יַסִּ֨ית אֶתְכֶ֣ם כָּזֹאת֮ וְאַל־תַּאֲמִ֣ינוּ לוֹ֒ כִּי־לֹ֣א יוּכַ֗ל כָּל־אֱל֙וֹהַּ֙ כָּל־גּ֣וֹי וּמַמְלָכָ֔ה לְהַצִּ֥יל עַמּ֛וֹ מִיָּדִ֖י וּמִיַּ֣ד אֲבוֹתָ֑י אַ֚ף כִּ֣י אֱלֹֽהֵיכֶ֔ם לֹא־יַצִּ֥ילוּ אֶתְכֶ֖ם מִיָּדִֽי׃

16 His officers said still more things against *Hashem* and against His servant *Chizkiyahu*.

טז וְע֖וֹד דִּבְּר֣וּ עֲבָדָ֑יו עַל־יְהֹוָ֣ה הָאֱלֹהִ֔ים וְעַ֖ל יְחִזְקִיָּ֥הוּ עַבְדּֽוֹ׃

17 He also wrote letters reviling God of *Yisrael*, saying of Him, "Just as the gods of the other nations of the earth did not save their people from me, so the God of *Chizkiyahu* will not save his people from me."

יז וּסְפָרִ֣ים כָּתַ֔ב לְחָרֵ֕ף לַיהֹוָ֖ה אֱלֹהֵ֣י יִשְׂרָאֵ֑ל וְלֵֽאמֹ֨ר עָלָ֜יו לֵאמֹ֗ר כֵּאלֹהֵ֞י גּוֹיֵ֤ הָאֲרָצוֹת֙ אֲשֶׁ֨ר לֹא־הִצִּ֤ילוּ עַמָּם֙ מִיָּדִ֔י כֵּ֗ן לֹא־יַצִּ֛יל אֱלֹהֵ֥י יְחִזְקִיָּ֖הוּ עַמּ֥וֹ מִיָּדִֽי׃

2128

Divrei Hayamim II/II Chronicles
Chapter 32

דברי הימים ב
פרק לב

18 They called loudly in the language of *Yehuda* to the people of *Yerushalayim* who were on the wall, to frighten them into panic, so as to capture the city.

יח וַיִּקְרְאוּ בְקוֹל־גָּדוֹל יְהוּדִית עַל־עַם יְרוּשָׁלַםִ אֲשֶׁר עַל־הַחוֹמָה לְיָרְאָם וּלְבַהֲלָם לְמַעַן יִלְכְּדוּ אֶת־הָעִיר:

19 They spoke of the God of *Yerushalayim* as though He were like the gods of the other peoples of the earth, made by human hands.

יט וַיְדַבְּרוּ אֶל־אֱלֹהֵי יְרוּשָׁלָםִ כְּעַל אֱלֹהֵי עַמֵּי הָאָרֶץ מַעֲשֵׂה יְדֵי הָאָדָם:

20 Then King *Chizkiyahu* and the *Navi Yeshayahu* son of *Amotz* prayed about this, and cried out to heaven.

כ וַיִּתְפַּלֵּל יְחִזְקִיָּהוּ הַמֶּלֶךְ וִישַׁעְיָהוּ בֶן־אָמוֹץ הַנָּבִיא עַל־זֹאת וַיִּזְעֲקוּ הַשָּׁמָיִם:

21 *Hashem* sent an angel who annihilated every mighty warrior, commander, and officer in the army of the king of Assyria, and he returned in disgrace to his land. He entered the house of his god, and there some of his own offspring struck him down by the sword.

כא וַיִּשְׁלַח יְהוָה מַלְאָךְ וַיַּכְחֵד כָּל־גִּבּוֹר חַיִל וְנָגִיד וְשָׂר בְּמַחֲנֵה מֶלֶךְ אַשּׁוּר וַיָּשָׁב בְּבֹשֶׁת פָּנִים לְאַרְצוֹ וַיָּבֹא בֵּית אֱלֹהָיו וּמִיצִיאוֹ [וּמִיצִיאֵי] מֵעָיו שָׁם הִפִּילֻהוּ בֶחָרֶב:

22 Thus *Hashem* delivered *Chizkiyahu* and the inhabitants of *Yerushalayim* from King Sennacherib of Assyria, and from everyone; He provided for them on all sides.

כב וַיּוֹשַׁע יְהוָה אֶת־יְחִזְקִיָּהוּ וְאֵת יֹשְׁבֵי יְרוּשָׁלַםִ מִיַּד סַנְחֵרִיב מֶלֶךְ־אַשּׁוּר וּמִיַּד־כֹּל וַיְנַהֲלֵם מִסָּבִיב:

va-yo-SHA a-do-NAI et y'-khiz-ki-YA-hu v'-AYT yo-sh'-VAY y'-ru-sha-LA-im mi-YAD san-khay-REEV me-lekh a-SHUR u-mi-yad KOL vai-na-ha-LAYM mi-sa-VEEV

23 Many brought tribute to *Hashem* to *Yerushalayim*, and gifts to King *Chizkiyahu* of *Yehuda*; thereafter he was exalted in the eyes of all the nations.

כג וְרַבִּים מְבִיאִים מִנְחָה לַיהוָה לִירוּשָׁלַםִ וּמִגְדָּנוֹת לִיחִזְקִיָּהוּ מֶלֶךְ יְהוּדָה וַיִּנַּשֵּׂא לְעֵינֵי כָל־הַגּוֹיִם מֵאַחֲרֵי־כֵן:

24 At that time, *Chizkiyahu* fell deathly sick. He prayed to *Hashem*, who responded to him and gave him a sign.

כד בַּיָּמִים הָהֵם חָלָה יְחִזְקִיָּהוּ עַד־לָמוּת וַיִּתְפַּלֵּל אֶל־יְהוָה וַיֹּאמֶר לוֹ וּמוֹפֵת נָתַן לוֹ:

25 *Chizkiyahu* made no return for what had been bestowed upon him, for he grew arrogant; so wrath was decreed for him and for *Yehuda* and *Yerushalayim*.

כה וְלֹא־כִגְמֻל עָלָיו הֵשִׁיב יְחִזְקִיָּהוּ כִּי גָבַהּ לִבּוֹ וַיְהִי עָלָיו קֶצֶף וְעַל־יְהוּדָה וִירוּשָׁלָםִ:

32:22 **Hashem delivered Chizkiyahu and the inhabitants of Yerushalayim** *Chizkiyahu* was one of the greatest Jewish kings of all time. He abolished idolatry and improper worship and brought the people back to *Hashem*. The Sages teach that *Chizkiyahu* was so great that God considered making him the *Mashiach*, but decided not to, since *Chizkiyahu* failed to sing songs of praise to *Hashem* after being miraculously saved from Sennacherib's siege of *Yerushalayim*. Surely *Chizkiyahu* recognized and appreciated the miracle that God had done for him and the people. Yet his faith in *Hashem* was so strong, and he was so confident in God's salvation, that he was not surprised by the miracle and therefore not moved to sing songs of praise. This failure to sing to *Hashem* in praise of the great miracle was the reason he forfeited the possibility of becoming the Messiah. God performs miracles on a daily basis in the personal lives of every individual and for the Nation of Israel living in the Land of Israel. We must never take His blessings for granted.

Divrei Hayamim II / II Chronicles
Chapter 33

26 Then *Chizkiyahu* humbled himself where he had been arrogant, he and the inhabitants of *Yerushalayim*, and no wrath of *Hashem* came on them during the reign of *Chizkiyahu*.

27 *Chizkiyahu* enjoyed riches and glory in abundance; he filled treasuries with silver and gold, precious stones, spices, shields, and all lovely objects;

28 and store-cities with the produce of grain, wine, and oil, and stalls for all kinds of beasts, and flocks for sheepfolds.

29 And he acquired towns, and flocks of small and large cattle in great number, for *Hashem* endowed him with very many possessions.

30 It was *Chizkiyahu* who stopped up the spring of water of Upper *Gichon*, leading it downward west of the City of *David*; *Chizkiyahu* prospered in all that he did.

31 So too in the matter of the ambassadors of the princes of Babylon, who were sent to him to inquire about the sign that was in the land, when *Hashem* forsook him in order to test him, to learn all that was in his mind.

32 The other events of *Chizkiyahu*'s reign, and his faithful acts, are recorded in the visions of the *Navi Yeshayahu* son of *Amotz* and in the book of the kings of *Yehuda* and *Yisrael*.

33 *Chizkiyahu* slept with his fathers, and was buried on the upper part of the tombs of the sons of *David*. When he died, all the people of *Yehuda* and the inhabitants of *Yerushalayim* accorded him much honor. *Menashe*, his son, succeeded him.

33

1 *Menashe* was twelve years old when he became king, and he reigned fifty-five years in *Yerushalayim*.

2 He did what was displeasing to *Hashem*, following the abhorrent practices of the nations that *Hashem* had dispossessed before the Israelites.

va-YA-as ha-RA b'-ay-NAY a-do-NAI k'-to-a-VOT ha-go-YIM a-SHER ho-REESH a-do-NAI mi-p'-NAY b'-NAY yis-ra-AYL

33:2 Following the abhorrent practices of the nations Before entering the Land of Israel, *Hashem* tells the Children of Israel that remaining in the land is dependent upon their moral character. He warns them not to learn

Divrei Hayamim II/II Chronicles
Chapter 33

3 He rebuilt the shrines that his father *Chizkiyahu* had demolished; he erected altars for the Baals and made sacred posts. He bowed down to all the host of heaven and worshiped them,

4 and he built altars [to them] in the House of *Hashem*, of which *Hashem* had said, "My name will be in *Yerushalayim* forever."

5 He built altars for all the host of heaven in the two courts of the House of *Hashem*.

6 He consigned his sons to the fire in the Valley of Ben-hinnom, and he practiced soothsaying, divination, and sorcery, and consulted ghosts and familiar spirits; he did much that was displeasing to *Hashem* in order to vex Him.

7 He placed a sculptured image that he made in the House of *Hashem*, of which *Hashem* had said to *David* and to his son *Shlomo*, "In this House and in *Yerushalayim*, which I chose out of all the tribes of *Yisrael*, I will establish My name forever.

8 And I will never again remove the feet of *Yisrael* from the land that I assigned to their fathers, if only they observe faithfully all that I have commanded them – all the teaching and the laws and the rules given by *Moshe*."

9 *Menashe* led *Yehuda* and the inhabitants of *Yerushalayim* astray into evil greater than that done by the nations that *Hashem* had destroyed before the Israelites.

10 *Hashem* spoke to *Menashe* and his people, but they would not pay heed,

11 so *Hashem* brought against them the officers of the army of the king of Assyria, who took *Menashe* captive in manacles, bound him in fetters, and led him off to Babylon.

12 In his distress, he entreated *Hashem* his God and humbled himself greatly before the God of his fathers.

דברי הימים ב
פרק לג

ג וַיָּשָׁב וַיִּבֶן אֶת־הַבָּמוֹת אֲשֶׁר נִתַּץ יְחִזְקִיָּהוּ אָבִיו וַיָּקֶם מִזְבְּחוֹת לַבְּעָלִים וַיַּעַשׂ אֲשֵׁרוֹת וַיִּשְׁתַּחוּ לְכָל־צְבָא הַשָּׁמַיִם וַיַּעֲבֹד אֹתָם:

ד וּבָנָה מִזְבְּחוֹת בְּבֵית יְהוָה אֲשֶׁר אָמַר יְהוָה בִּירוּשָׁלַ͏ִם יִהְיֶה־שְּׁמִי לְעוֹלָם:

ה וַיִּבֶן מִזְבְּחוֹת לְכָל־צְבָא הַשָּׁמָיִם בִּשְׁתֵּי חַצְרוֹת בֵּית־יְהוָה:

ו וְהוּא הֶעֱבִיר אֶת־בָּנָיו בָּאֵשׁ בְּגֵי בֶן־הִנֹּם וְעוֹנֵן וְנִחֵשׁ וְכִשֵּׁף וְעָשָׂה אוֹב וְיִדְּעוֹנִי הִרְבָּה לַעֲשׂוֹת הָרַע בְּעֵינֵי יְהוָה לְהַכְעִיסוֹ:

ז וַיָּשֶׂם אֶת־פֶּסֶל הַסֶּמֶל אֲשֶׁר עָשָׂה בְּבֵית הָאֱלֹהִים אֲשֶׁר אָמַר אֱלֹהִים אֶל־דָּוִיד וְאֶל־שְׁלֹמֹה בְנוֹ בַּבַּיִת הַזֶּה וּבִירוּשָׁלַ͏ִם אֲשֶׁר בָּחַרְתִּי מִכֹּל שִׁבְטֵי יִשְׂרָאֵל אָשִׂים אֶת־שְׁמִי לְעֵילוֹם:

ח וְלֹא אוֹסִיף לְהָסִיר אֶת־רֶגֶל יִשְׂרָאֵל מֵעַל הָאֲדָמָה אֲשֶׁר הֶעֱמַדְתִּי לַאֲבוֹתֵיכֶם רַק אִם־יִשְׁמְרוּ לַעֲשׂוֹת אֵת כָּל־אֲשֶׁר צִוִּיתִים לְכָל־הַתּוֹרָה וְהַחֻקִּים וְהַמִּשְׁפָּטִים בְּיַד־מֹשֶׁה:

ט וַיֶּתַע מְנַשֶּׁה אֶת־יְהוּדָה וְיֹשְׁבֵי יְרוּשָׁלָ͏ִם לַעֲשׂוֹת רָע מִן־הַגּוֹיִם אֲשֶׁר הִשְׁמִיד יְהוָה מִפְּנֵי בְּנֵי יִשְׂרָאֵל:

י וַיְדַבֵּר יְהוָה אֶל־מְנַשֶּׁה וְאֶל־עַמּוֹ וְלֹא הִקְשִׁיבוּ:

יא וַיָּבֵא יְהוָה עֲלֵיהֶם אֶת־שָׂרֵי הַצָּבָא אֲשֶׁר לְמֶלֶךְ אַשּׁוּר וַיִּלְכְּדוּ אֶת־מְנַשֶּׁה בַּחֹחִים וַיַּאַסְרֻהוּ בַּנְחֻשְׁתַּיִם וַיּוֹלִיכֻהוּ בָּבֶלָה:

יב וּכְהָצֵר לוֹ חִלָּה אֶת־פְּנֵי יְהוָה אֱלֹהָיו וַיִּכָּנַע מְאֹד מִלִּפְנֵי אֱלֹהֵי אֲבֹתָיו:

---

from or mimic the abominations of the peoples already living there, since doing so will lead to expulsion from the land, just as the nations originally living there were expelled (Deuteronomy 18:9–12). King *Menashe* explicitly violates this command, causing the People of Israel to follow "the abhorrent practices of the nations." As such, God responds by declaring that He will send away the remainder of the Nation of Israel and allow their enemies to defeat them (II Kings 21:14).

Divrei Hayamim II / II Chronicles
Chapter 33

דברי הימים ב
פרק לג

13 He prayed to Him, and He granted his prayer, heard his plea, and returned him to *Yerushalayim* to his kingdom. Then *Menashe* knew that *Hashem* alone was *Hashem*.

יג וַיִּתְפַּלֵּל אֵלָיו וַיֵּעָתֶר לוֹ וַיִּשְׁמַע תְּחִנָּתוֹ וַיְשִׁיבֵהוּ יְרוּשָׁלַ͏ִם לְמַלְכוּתוֹ וַיֵּדַע מְנַשֶּׁה כִּי יְהֹוָה הוּא הָאֱלֹהִים:

14 Afterward he built the outer wall of the City of *David* west of *Gichon* in the wadi on the way to the Fish Gate, and it encircled Ophel; he raised it very high. He also placed army officers in all the fortified towns of *Yehuda*.

יד וְאַחֲרֵי־כֵן בָּנָה חוֹמָה חִיצוֹנָה ׀ לְעִיר־דָּוִיד מַעְרָבָה לְגִיחוֹן בַּנַּחַל וְלָבוֹא בְשַׁעַר הַדָּגִים וְסָבַב לָעֹפֶל וַיַּגְבִּיהֶהָ מְאֹד וַיָּשֶׂם שָׂרֵי־חַיִל בְּכָל־הֶעָרִים הַבְּצֻרוֹת בִּיהוּדָה:

15 He removed the foreign gods and the image from the House of *Hashem*, as well as all the altars that he had built on the Mount of the House of *Hashem* and in *Yerushalayim*, and dumped them outside the city.

טו וַיָּסַר אֶת־אֱלֹהֵי הַנֵּכָר וְאֶת־הַסֶּמֶל מִבֵּית יְהֹוָה וְכָל־הַמִּזְבְּחוֹת אֲשֶׁר בָּנָה בְּהַר בֵּית־יְהֹוָה וּבִירוּשָׁלָ͏ִם וַיַּשְׁלֵךְ חוּצָה לָעִיר:

16 He rebuilt the *Mizbayach* of *Hashem* and offered on it sacrifices of well-being and thanksgiving, and commanded the people of *Yehuda* to worship God of *Yisrael*.

טז וַיִּכֶן [וַיִּבֶן] אֶת־מִזְבַּח יְהֹוָה וַיִּזְבַּח עָלָיו זִבְחֵי שְׁלָמִים וְתוֹדָה וַיֹּאמֶר לִיהוּדָה לַעֲבוֹד אֶת־יְהֹוָה אֱלֹהֵי יִשְׂרָאֵל:

17 To be sure, the people continued sacrificing at the shrines, but only to *Hashem* their God.

יז אֲבָל עוֹד הָעָם זֹבְחִים בַּבָּמוֹת רַק לַיהֹוָה אֱלֹהֵיהֶם:

18 The other events of *Menashe*'s reign, and his prayer to his God, and the words of the seers who spoke to him in the name of God of *Yisrael* are found in the chronicles of the kings of *Yisrael*.

יח וְיֶתֶר דִּבְרֵי מְנַשֶּׁה וּתְפִלָּתוֹ אֶל־אֱלֹהָיו וְדִבְרֵי הַחֹזִים הַמְדַבְּרִים אֵלָיו בְּשֵׁם יְהֹוָה אֱלֹהֵי יִשְׂרָאֵל הִנָּם עַל־דִּבְרֵי מַלְכֵי יִשְׂרָאֵל:

19 His prayer and how it was granted to him, the whole account of his sin and trespass, and the places in which he built shrines and installed sacred posts and images before he humbled himself are recorded in the words of Hozai.

יט וּתְפִלָּתוֹ וְהֵעָתֶר־לוֹ וְכָל־חַטָּאתוֹ וּמַעְלוֹ וְהַמְּקֹמוֹת אֲשֶׁר בָּנָה בָהֶם בָּמוֹת וְהֶעֱמִיד הָאֲשֵׁרִים וְהַפְּסִלִים לִפְנֵי הִכָּנְעוֹ הִנָּם כְּתוּבִים עַל דִּבְרֵי חוֹזָי:

20 *Menashe* slept with his fathers and was buried on his palace grounds; his son *Amon* succeeded him as king.

כ וַיִּשְׁכַּב מְנַשֶּׁה עִם־אֲבֹתָיו וַיִּקְבְּרֻהוּ בֵּיתוֹ וַיִּמְלֹךְ אָמוֹן בְּנוֹ תַּחְתָּיו:

21 *Amon* was twenty-two years old when he became king, and he reigned two years in *Yerushalayim*.

כא בֶּן־עֶשְׂרִים וּשְׁתַּיִם שָׁנָה אָמוֹן בְּמָלְכוֹ וּשְׁתַּיִם שָׁנִים מָלַךְ בִּירוּשָׁלָ͏ִם:

22 He did what was displeasing to *Hashem*, as his father *Menashe* had done. *Amon* sacrificed to all the idols that his father *Menashe* had made and worshiped them.

כב וַיַּעַשׂ הָרַע בְּעֵינֵי יְהֹוָה כַּאֲשֶׁר עָשָׂה מְנַשֶּׁה אָבִיו וּלְכָל־הַפְּסִילִים אֲשֶׁר עָשָׂה מְנַשֶּׁה אָבִיו זִבַּח אָמוֹן וַיַּעַבְדֵם:

23 He did not humble himself before *Hashem*, as his father *Menashe* had humbled himself; instead, *Amon* incurred much guilt.

כג וְלֹא נִכְנַע מִלִּפְנֵי יְהֹוָה כְּהִכָּנַע מְנַשֶּׁה אָבִיו כִּי הוּא אָמוֹן הִרְבָּה אַשְׁמָה:

24 His courtiers conspired against him and killed him in his palace.

כד וַיִּקְשְׁרוּ עָלָיו עֲבָדָיו וַיְמִיתֻהוּ בְּבֵיתוֹ:

Divrei Hayamim II/II Chronicles
Chapter 34

דברי הימים ב
פרק לד

25 But the people of the land struck down all who had conspired against King *Amon*; and the people of the land made his son *Yoshiyahu* king in his stead.

כה וַיַּכּוּ עַם־הָאָרֶץ אֵת כָּל־הַקֹּשְׁרִים עַל־הַמֶּלֶךְ אָמוֹן וַיַּמְלִיכוּ עַם־הָאָרֶץ אֶת־יֹאשִׁיָּהוּ בְנוֹ תַּחְתָּיו:

34 1 *Yoshiyahu* was eight years old when he became king, and he reigned thirty-one years in *Yerushalayim*.

לד א בֶּן־שְׁמוֹנֶה שָׁנִים יֹאשִׁיָּהוּ בְמָלְכוֹ וּשְׁלֹשִׁים וְאַחַת שָׁנָה מָלַךְ בִּירוּשָׁלָםִ:

2 He did what was pleasing to *Hashem*, following the ways of his father *David* without deviating to the right or to the left.

ב וַיַּעַשׂ הַיָּשָׁר בְּעֵינֵי יְהוָה וַיֵּלֶךְ בְּדַרְכֵי דָּוִיד אָבִיו וְלֹא־סָר יָמִין וּשְׂמֹאול:

3 In the eighth year of his reign, while he was still young, he began to seek the God of his father *David*, and in the twelfth year he began to purge *Yehuda* and *Yerushalayim* of the shrines, the sacred posts, the idols, and the molten images.

ג וּבִשְׁמוֹנֶה שָׁנִים לְמָלְכוֹ וְהוּא עוֹדֶנּוּ נַעַר הֵחֵל לִדְרוֹשׁ לֵאלֹהֵי דָּוִיד אָבִיו וּבִשְׁתֵּים עֶשְׂרֵה שָׁנָה הֵחֵל לְטַהֵר אֶת־יְהוּדָה וִירוּשָׁלַםִ מִן־הַבָּמוֹת וְהָאֲשֵׁרִים וְהַפְּסִלִים וְהַמַּסֵּכוֹת:

4 At his bidding, they demolished the altars of the Baals, and he had the incense stands above them cut down; he smashed the sacred posts, the idols, and the images, ground them into dust, and strewed it onto the graves of those who had sacrificed to them.

ד וַיְנַתְּצוּ לְפָנָיו אֵת מִזְבְּחוֹת הַבְּעָלִים וְהַחַמָּנִים אֲשֶׁר־לְמַעְלָה מֵעֲלֵיהֶם גִּדֵּעַ וְהָאֲשֵׁרִים וְהַפְּסִלִים וְהַמַּסֵּכוֹת שִׁבַּר וְהֵדַק וַיִּזְרֹק עַל־פְּנֵי הַקְּבָרִים הַזֹּבְחִים לָהֶם:

5 He burned the bones of *Kohanim* on their altars and purged *Yehuda* and *Yerushalayim*.

ה וְעַצְמוֹת כֹּהֲנִים שָׂרַף עַל־מִזְבְּחוֹתִים [מִזְבְּחוֹתָם] וַיְטַהֵר אֶת־יְהוּדָה וְאֶת־יְרוּשָׁלָםִ:

6 In the towns of *Menashe* and *Efraim* and *Shimon*, as far as *Naftali*, [lying] in ruins on every side,

ו וּבְעָרֵי מְנַשֶּׁה וְאֶפְרַיִם וְשִׁמְעוֹן וְעַד־נַפְתָּלִי בהר בתיהם [בְּחַרְבֹתֵיהֶם] סָבִיב:

7 he demolished the altars and the sacred posts and smashed the idols and ground them into dust; and he hewed down all the incense stands throughout the land of *Yisrael*. Then he returned to *Yerushalayim*.

ז וַיְנַתֵּץ אֶת־הַמִּזְבְּחוֹת וְאֶת־הָאֲשֵׁרִים וְהַפְּסִלִים כִּתַּת לְהֵדַק וְכָל־הַחַמָּנִים גִּדַּע בְּכָל־אֶרֶץ יִשְׂרָאֵל וַיָּשָׁב לִירוּשָׁלָםִ:

8 In the eighteenth year of his reign, after purging the land and the House, he commissioned *Shafan* son of Azaliah, Maaseiah the governor of the city, and Joah son of Joahaz the recorder to repair the House of *Hashem* his God.

ח וּבִשְׁנַת שְׁמוֹנֶה עֶשְׂרֵה לְמָלְכוֹ לְטַהֵר הָאָרֶץ וְהַבָּיִת שָׁלַח אֶת־שָׁפָן בֶּן־אֲצַלְיָהוּ וְאֶת־מַעֲשֵׂיָהוּ שַׂר־הָעִיר וְאֵת יוֹאָח בֶּן־יוֹאָחָז הַמַּזְכִּיר לְחַזֵּק אֶת־בֵּית יְהוָה אֱלֹהָיו:

9 They came to the *Kohen Gadol Chilkiyahu* and delivered to him the silver brought to the House of *Hashem*, which the *Leviim*, the guards of the threshold, had collected from *Menashe* and *Efraim* and from all the remnant of *Yisrael* and from all *Yehuda* and *Binyamin* and the inhabitants of *Yerushalayim*.

ט וַיָּבֹאוּ אֶל־חִלְקִיָּהוּ הַכֹּהֵן הַגָּדוֹל וַיִּתְּנוּ אֶת־הַכֶּסֶף הַמּוּבָא בֵית־אֱלֹהִים אֲשֶׁר אָסְפוּ־הַלְוִיִּם שֹׁמְרֵי הַסַּף מִיַּד מְנַשֶּׁה וְאֶפְרַיִם וּמִכֹּל שְׁאֵרִית יִשְׂרָאֵל וּמִכָּל־יְהוּדָה וּבִנְיָמִן וישבי [וַיָּשֻׁבוּ] יְרוּשָׁלָםִ:

Divrei Hayamim II / II Chronicles
Chapter 34

10 They delivered it into the custody of the overseers who were in charge at the House of *Hashem*, and the overseers who worked in the House of *Hashem* spent it on examining and repairing the House.

11 They paid it out to the artisans and the masons to buy quarried stone and wood for the couplings and for making roof-beams for the buildings that the kings of *Yehuda* had allowed to fall into ruin.

12 The men did the work honestly; over them were appointed the *Leviim* Jahath and *Ovadya*, of the sons of *Merari*, and *Zecharya* and Meshullam, of the sons of *Kehat*, to supervise; while other *Leviim*, all the master musicians,

13 were over the porters, supervising all who worked at each and every task; some of the *Leviim* were scribes and officials and gatekeepers.

14 As they took out the silver that had been brought to the House of *Hashem*, the *Kohen Chilkiyahu* found a scroll of *Hashem*'s Teaching given by *Moshe*.

15 *Chilkiyahu* spoke up and said to the scribe *Shafan*, "I have found a scroll of the Teaching in the House of *Hashem*"; and *Chilkiyahu* gave the scroll to *Shafan*.

16 *Shafan* brought the scroll to the king and also reported to the king, "All that was entrusted to your servants is being done;

17 they have melted down the silver that was found in the House of *Hashem* and delivered it to those who were in charge, to the overseers."

18 The scribe *Shafan* also told the king, "The *Kohen Chilkiyahu* has given me a scroll"; and *Shafan* read from it to the king.

19 When the king heard the words of the Teaching, he tore his clothes.

20 The king gave orders to *Chilkiyahu*, and *Achikam* son of *Shafan*, and *Avdon* son of *Micha*, and the scribe *Shafan*, and Asaiah the king's minister, saying,

דברי הימים ב
פרק לד

י וַיִּתְּנוּ עַל־יַד עֹשֵׂה הַמְּלָאכָה הַמֻּפְקָדִים בְּבֵית יְהֹוָה וַיִּתְּנוּ אֹתוֹ עוֹשֵׂי הַמְּלָאכָה אֲשֶׁר עֹשִׂים בְּבֵית יְהֹוָה לִבְדּוֹק וּלְחַזֵּק הַבָּיִת:

יא וַיִּתְּנוּ לֶחָרָשִׁים וְלַבֹּנִים לִקְנוֹת אַבְנֵי מַחְצֵב וְעֵצִים לַמְחַבְּרוֹת וּלְקָרוֹת אֶת־הַבָּתִּים אֲשֶׁר הִשְׁחִיתוּ מַלְכֵי יְהוּדָה:

יב וְהָאֲנָשִׁים עֹשִׂים בֶּאֱמוּנָה בַּמְּלָאכָה וַעֲלֵיהֶם מֻפְקָדִים יַחַת וְעֹבַדְיָהוּ הַלְוִיִּם מִן־בְּנֵי מְרָרִי וּזְכַרְיָה וּמְשֻׁלָּם מִן־בְּנֵי הַקְּהָתִים לְנַצֵּחַ וְהַלְוִיִּם כָּל־מֵבִין בִּכְלֵי־שִׁיר:

יג וְעַל הַסַּבָּלִים וּמְנַצְּחִים לְכֹל עֹשֵׂה מְלָאכָה לַעֲבוֹדָה וַעֲבוֹדָה וּמֵהַלְוִיִּם סוֹפְרִים וְשֹׁטְרִים וְשׁוֹעֲרִים:

יד וּבְהוֹצִיאָם אֶת־הַכֶּסֶף הַמּוּבָא בֵּית יְהֹוָה מָצָא חִלְקִיָּהוּ הַכֹּהֵן אֶת־סֵפֶר תּוֹרַת־יְהֹוָה בְּיַד־מֹשֶׁה:

טו וַיַּעַן חִלְקִיָּהוּ וַיֹּאמֶר אֶל־שָׁפָן הַסּוֹפֵר סֵפֶר הַתּוֹרָה מָצָאתִי בְּבֵית יְהֹוָה וַיִּתֵּן חִלְקִיָּהוּ אֶת־הַסֵּפֶר אֶל־שָׁפָן:

טז וַיָּבֵא שָׁפָן אֶת־הַסֵּפֶר אֶל־הַמֶּלֶךְ וַיָּשֶׁב עוֹד אֶת־הַמֶּלֶךְ דָּבָר לֵאמֹר כֹּל אֲשֶׁר־נִתַּן בְּיַד־עֲבָדֶיךָ הֵם עֹשִׂים:

יז וַיַּתִּיכוּ אֶת־הַכֶּסֶף הַנִּמְצָא בְּבֵית־יְהֹוָה וַיִּתְּנוּהוּ עַל־יַד הַמֻּפְקָדִים וְעַל־יַד עוֹשֵׂי הַמְּלָאכָה:

יח וַיַּגֵּד שָׁפָן הַסּוֹפֵר לַמֶּלֶךְ לֵאמֹר סֵפֶר נָתַן לִי חִלְקִיָּהוּ הַכֹּהֵן וַיִּקְרָא־בוֹ שָׁפָן לִפְנֵי הַמֶּלֶךְ:

יט וַיְהִי כִּשְׁמֹעַ הַמֶּלֶךְ אֵת דִּבְרֵי הַתּוֹרָה וַיִּקְרַע אֶת־בְּגָדָיו:

כ וַיְצַו הַמֶּלֶךְ אֶת־חִלְקִיָּהוּ וְאֶת־אֲחִיקָם בֶּן־שָׁפָן וְאֶת־עַבְדּוֹן בֶּן־מִיכָה וְאֵת שָׁפָן הַסּוֹפֵר וְאֵת עֲשָׂיָה עֶבֶד־הַמֶּלֶךְ לֵאמֹר:

Divrei Hayamim II/II Chronicles
Chapter 34

דברי הימים ב
פרק לד

21 "Go, inquire of *Hashem* on my behalf and on behalf of those who remain in *Yisrael* and *Yehuda* concerning the words of the scroll that has been found, for great indeed must be the wrath of *Hashem* that has been poured down upon us because our fathers did not obey the word of *Hashem* and do all that is written in this scroll."

כא לְכוּ דִרְשׁוּ אֶת־יְהֹוָה בַּעֲדִי וּבְעַד הַנִּשְׁאָר בְּיִשְׂרָאֵל וּבִיהוּדָה עַל־דִּבְרֵי הַסֵּפֶר אֲשֶׁר נִמְצָא כִּי־גְדוֹלָה חֲמַת־יְהֹוָה אֲשֶׁר נִתְּכָה בָנוּ עַל אֲשֶׁר לֹא־שָׁמְרוּ אֲבוֹתֵינוּ אֶת־דְּבַר יְהֹוָה לַעֲשׂוֹת כְּכָל־הַכָּתוּב עַל־הַסֵּפֶר הַזֶּה:

22 *Chilkiyahu* and those whom the king [had ordered] went to the *Neviah Chulda*, wife of *Shalum* son of Tokhath son of Hasrah, keeper of the wardrobe, who was living in *Yerushalayim* in the Mishneh, and spoke to her accordingly.

כב וַיֵּלֶךְ חִלְקִיָּהוּ וַאֲשֶׁר הַמֶּלֶךְ אֶל־חֻלְדָּה הַנְּבִיאָה אֵשֶׁת שַׁלֻּם בֶּן־תּוֹקְהַת [תָּקְהַת] בֶּן־חַסְרָה שׁוֹמֵר הַבְּגָדִים וְהִיא יוֹשֶׁבֶת בִּירוּשָׁלַםִ בַּמִּשְׁנֶה וַיְדַבְּרוּ אֵלֶיהָ כָּזֹאת:

23 She responded to them: "Thus said God of *Yisrael*: Say to the man who sent you to Me,

כג וַתֹּאמֶר לָהֶם כֹּה־אָמַר יְהֹוָה אֱלֹהֵי יִשְׂרָאֵל אִמְרוּ לָאִישׁ אֲשֶׁר־שָׁלַח אֶתְכֶם אֵלָי:

24 'Thus said *Hashem*: I am going to bring disaster upon this place and its inhabitants – all the curses that are written in the scroll that was read to the king of *Yehuda* –

כד כֹּה אָמַר יְהֹוָה הִנְנִי מֵבִיא רָעָה עַל־הַמָּקוֹם הַזֶּה וְעַל־יוֹשְׁבָיו אֵת כָּל־הָאָלוֹת הַכְּתוּבוֹת עַל־הַסֵּפֶר אֲשֶׁר קָרְאוּ לִפְנֵי מֶלֶךְ יְהוּדָה:

25 because they forsook Me and made offerings to other gods in order to vex Me with all the works of their hands; My wrath shall be poured out against this place and not be quenched.'

כה תַּחַת אֲשֶׁר עֲזָבוּנִי וַיְקַטִּירוּ [וַיְקַטְּרוּ] לֵאלֹהִים אֲחֵרִים לְמַעַן הַכְעִיסֵנִי בְּכֹל מַעֲשֵׂי יְדֵיהֶם וְתִתַּךְ חֲמָתִי בַּמָּקוֹם הַזֶּה וְלֹא תִכְבֶּה:

26 But say this to the king of *Yehuda* who sent you to inquire of *Hashem*: 'Thus said God of *Yisrael*: As for the words which you have heard,

כו וְאֶל־מֶלֶךְ יְהוּדָה הַשֹּׁלֵחַ אֶתְכֶם לִדְרוֹשׁ בַּיהֹוָה כֹּה תֹאמְרוּ אֵלָיו כֹּה־אָמַר יְהֹוָה אֱלֹהֵי יִשְׂרָאֵל הַדְּבָרִים אֲשֶׁר שָׁמָעְתָּ:

27 since your heart was softened and you humbled yourself before *Hashem* when you heard His words concerning this place and its inhabitants, and you humbled yourself before Me and tore your clothes and wept before Me, I for My part have listened, declares *Hashem*.

כז יַעַן רַךְ־לְבָבְךָ וַתִּכָּנַע מִלִּפְנֵי אֱלֹהִים בְּשָׁמְעֲךָ אֶת־דְּבָרָיו עַל־הַמָּקוֹם הַזֶּה וְעַל־יֹשְׁבָיו וַתִּכָּנַע לְפָנַי וַתִּקְרַע אֶת־בְּגָדֶיךָ וַתֵּבְךְּ לְפָנָי וְגַם־אֲנִי שָׁמַעְתִּי נְאֻם־יְהֹוָה:

YA-an rakh l'-va-v'-KHA va-ti-ka-NA mi-lif-NAY e-lo-HEEM b'-shom-a-KHA et di-va-RAV al-ha-ma-KOM ha-ZEH v'-al yo-sh'-VAV va-ti-ka-NA l'-fa-NAI va-tik-RA et b'-ga-DE-kha va-TAYVK l'-fa-NAI v'-gam a-NEE sha-MA-tee n'-UM a-do-NAI

34:27 When you heard His words According to the Sages, the *Torah* scroll that was found during *Yoshiyahu's* reign was opened to the section in *Sefer* *Devarim* (28:15–68) which describes the punishments for idol worship and abandoning God in the Land of Israel. The *Radak* (II Kings 22:11) explains that *Yoshiyahu*

Divrei Hayamim II / II Chronicles
Chapter 35

28 Assuredly, I will gather you to your fathers, and you will be laid in your grave in peace; your eyes shall see nothing of the disaster that I will bring upon this place and its inhabitants.'" They reported this back to the king.

29 Then the king sent word and assembled all the elders of *Yehuda* and *Yerushalayim*.

30 The king went up to the House of *Hashem* with all the men of *Yehuda* and the inhabitants of *Yerushalayim* and the *Kohanim* and the *Leviim* – all the people, young and old – and he read to them the entire text of the covenant scroll that was found in the House of *Hashem*.

31 The king stood in his place and solemnized the covenant before *Hashem*: to follow *Hashem* and observe His commandments, His injunctions, and His laws with all his heart and soul, to fulfill all the terms of the covenant written in this scroll.

32 He obligated all the men of *Yerushalayim* and *Binyamin* who were present; and the inhabitants of *Yerushalayim* acted in accord with the Covenant of *Hashem*, God of their fathers.

33 *Yoshiyahu* removed all the abominations from the whole territory of the Israelites and obliged all who were in *Yisrael* to worship *Hashem* their God. Throughout his reign they did not deviate from following God of their fathers.

35

1 *Yoshiyahu* kept the *Pesach* for *Hashem* in *Yerushalayim*; the *Pesach* sacrifice was slaughtered on the fourteenth day of the first month.

2 He reinstated the *Kohanim* in their shifts and rallied them to the service of the House of *Hashem*.

---

understood this as a divine message: Even though he has put tremendous effort into abolishing idolatry, bringing the people closer to *Hashem* and renewing their covenant with their Creator, it seems that there is more work to be done, and *Hashem* is still angry with His people. Instead of giving up, *Yoshiyahu* is motivated to redouble his efforts to bring the people back to God. Hearing *Hashem*'s "words concerning this place and its inhabitants," meaning that God is still planning to punish the people and exile them from *Eretz Yisrael*, is enough to motivate *Yoshiyahu* to intensify his efforts and to humble himself before *Hashem*.

Open Torah scroll

Divrei Hayamim II/II Chronicles
Chapter 35

דברי הימים ב
פרק לה

3 He said to the *Leviim*, consecrated to *Hashem*, who taught all *Yisrael*, "Put the *Aron Kodesh* in the House that *Shlomo* son of *David*, king of *Yisrael*, built; as you no longer carry it on your shoulders, see now to the service of *Hashem* your God and His people *Yisrael*,

ג וַיֹּאמֶר לַלְוִיִּם הַמְּבוּנִים [הַמְּבִינִים] לְכׇל־יִשְׂרָאֵל הַקְּדוֹשִׁים לַיהֹוָה תְּנוּ אֶת־אֲרוֹן־הַקֹּדֶשׁ בַּבַּיִת אֲשֶׁר בָּנָה שְׁלֹמֹה בֶן־דָּוִיד מֶלֶךְ יִשְׂרָאֵל אֵין־לָכֶם מַשָּׂא בַּכָּתֵף עַתָּה עִבְדוּ אֶת־יְהֹוָה אֱלֹהֵיכֶם וְאֵת עַמּוֹ יִשְׂרָאֵל:

4 and dispose yourselves by clans according to your divisions, as prescribed in the writing of King *David* of *Yisrael* and in the document of his son *Shlomo*,

ד וְהִכּוֹנוּ לְבֵית־אֲבוֹתֵיכֶם כְּמַחְלְקוֹתֵיכֶם בִּכְתָב דָּוִיד מֶלֶךְ יִשְׂרָאֵל וּבְמִכְתַּב שְׁלֹמֹה בְנוֹ:

5 and attend in the Sanctuary, by clan divisions, on your kinsmen, the people – by clan divisions of the *Leviim*.

ה וְעִמְדוּ בַקֹּדֶשׁ לִפְלֻגּוֹת בֵּית הָאָבוֹת לַאֲחֵיכֶם בְּנֵי הָעָם וַחֲלֻקַּת בֵּית־אָב לַלְוִיִּם:

6 Having sanctified yourselves, slaughter the *Pesach* sacrifice and prepare it for your kinsmen, according to the word of *Hashem* given by *Moshe*."

ו וְשַׁחֲטוּ הַפָּסַח וְהִתְקַדְּשׁוּ וְהָכִינוּ לַאֲחֵיכֶם לַעֲשׂוֹת כִּדְבַר־יְהֹוָה בְּיַד־מֹשֶׁה:

7 *Yoshiyahu* donated to the people small cattle – lambs and goats, all for *Pesach* sacrifices for all present – to the sum of 30,000, and large cattle, 3,000 – these from the property of the king.

ז וַיָּרֶם יֹאשִׁיָּהוּ לִבְנֵי הָעָם צֹאן כְּבָשִׂים וּבְנֵי־עִזִּים הַכֹּל לַפְּסָחִים לְכׇל־הַנִּמְצָא לְמִסְפַּר שְׁלֹשִׁים אֶלֶף וּבָקָר שְׁלֹשֶׁת אֲלָפִים אֵלֶּה מֵרְכוּשׁ הַמֶּלֶךְ:

8 His officers gave a freewill offering to the people, to the *Kohanim*, and to the *Leviim*. *Chilkiyahu* and *Zecharya* and *Yechiel*, the chiefs of the House of *Hashem*, donated to the *Kohanim* for *Pesach* sacrifices 2,600 [small cattle] and 300 large cattle.

ח וְשָׂרָיו לִנְדָבָה לָעָם לַכֹּהֲנִים וְלַלְוִיִּם הֵרִימוּ חִלְקִיָּה וּזְכַרְיָהוּ וִיחִיאֵל נְגִידֵי בֵּית הָאֱלֹהִים לַכֹּהֲנִים נָתְנוּ לַפְּסָחִים אַלְפַּיִם וְשֵׁשׁ מֵאוֹת וּבָקָר שְׁלֹשׁ מֵאוֹת:

9 *Conaniah*, *Shemaya*, and *Nethanel*, his brothers, and *Hashabiah* and *Jeiel* and *Yozavad*, officers of the *Leviim*, donated 5,000 [small cattle] and 500 large cattle to the *Leviim* for *Pesach* sacrifices.

ט וְכָנַנְיָהוּ וּשְׁמַעְיָהוּ וּנְתַנְאֵל אֶחָיו וַחֲשַׁבְיָהוּ וִיעִיאֵל וְיוֹזָבָד שָׂרֵי הַלְוִיִּם הֵרִימוּ לַלְוִיִּם לַפְּסָחִים חֲמֵשֶׁת אֲלָפִים וּבָקָר חֲמֵשׁ מֵאוֹת:

10 The service was arranged well: the *Kohanim* stood at their posts and the *Leviim* in their divisions, by the king's command.

י וַתִּכּוֹן הָעֲבוֹדָה וַיַּעַמְדוּ הַכֹּהֲנִים עַל־עׇמְדָם וְהַלְוִיִּם עַל־מַחְלְקוֹתָם כְּמִצְוַת הַמֶּלֶךְ:

11 They slaughtered the *Pesach* sacrifice and the *Kohanim* [received its blood] from them and dashed it, while the *Leviim* flayed the animals.

יא וַיִּשְׁחֲטוּ הַפָּסַח וַיִּזְרְקוּ הַכֹּהֲנִים מִיָּדָם וְהַלְוִיִּם מַפְשִׁיטִים:

12 They removed the parts to be burnt, distributing them to divisions of the people by clans, and making the sacrifices to *Hashem*, as prescribed in the scroll of *Moshe*; they did the same for the cattle.

יב וַיָּסִירוּ הָעֹלָה לְתִתָּם לְמִפְלַגּוֹת לְבֵית־אָבוֹת לִבְנֵי הָעָם לְהַקְרִיב לַיהֹוָה כַּכָּתוּב בְּסֵפֶר מֹשֶׁה וְכֵן לַבָּקָר:

13 They roasted the *Pesach* sacrifice in fire, as prescribed, while the sacred offerings they cooked in pots, cauldrons, and pans, and conveyed them with dispatch to all the people.

יג וַיְבַשְּׁלוּ הַפֶּסַח בָּאֵשׁ כַּמִּשְׁפָּט וְהַקֳּדָשִׁים בִּשְּׁלוּ בַּסִּירוֹת וּבַדְּוָדִים וּבַצֵּלָחוֹת וַיָּרִיצוּ לְכׇל־בְּנֵי הָעָם:

Divrei Hayamim II / II Chronicles
Chapter 35

14 Afterward they provided for themselves and the *Kohanim*, for the Aaronite *Kohanim* were busy offering the burnt offerings and the fatty parts until nightfall, so the *Leviim* provided both for themselves and for the Aaronite *Kohanim*.

יד וְאַחַר הֵכִינוּ לָהֶם וְלַכֹּהֲנִים כִּי הַכֹּהֲנִים בְּנֵי אַהֲרֹן בְּהַעֲלוֹת הָעוֹלָה וְהַחֲלָבִים עַד־לָיְלָה וְהַלְוִיִּם הֵכִינוּ לָהֶם וְלַכֹּהֲנִים בְּנֵי אַהֲרֹן:

15 The Asaphite singers were at their stations, by command of *David* and *Asaf* and *Hayman* and *Yedutun*, the seer of the king; and the gatekeepers were at each and every gate. They did not have to leave their tasks, because their Levite brothers provided for them.

טו וְהַמְשֹׁרְרִים בְּנֵי־אָסָף עַל־מַעֲמָדָם כְּמִצְוַת דָּוִיד וְאָסָף וְהֵימָן וִידֻתוּן חוֹזֵה הַמֶּלֶךְ וְהַשֹּׁעֲרִים לְשַׁעַר וָשָׁעַר אֵין לָהֶם לָסוּר מֵעַל עֲבֹדָתָם כִּי־אֲחֵיהֶם הַלְוִיִּם הֵכִינוּ לָהֶם:

16 The entire service of *Hashem* was arranged well that day, to keep the *Pesach* and to make the burnt offerings on the *Mizbayach* of *Hashem*, according to the command of King *Yoshiyahu*.

טז וַתִּכּוֹן כָּל־עֲבוֹדַת יְהוָה בַּיּוֹם הַהוּא לַעֲשׂוֹת הַפֶּסַח וְהַעֲלוֹת עֹלוֹת עַל מִזְבַּח יְהוָה כְּמִצְוַת הַמֶּלֶךְ יֹאשִׁיָּהוּ:

17 All the Israelites present kept the *Pesach* at that time, and the festival of *Pesach* for seven days.

יז וַיַּעֲשׂוּ בְנֵי־יִשְׂרָאֵל הַנִּמְצְאִים אֶת־הַפֶּסַח בָּעֵת הַהִיא וְאֶת־חַג הַמַּצּוֹת שִׁבְעַת יָמִים:

18 Since the time of the *Navi Shmuel*, no *Pesach* like that one had ever been kept in *Yisrael*; none of the kings of *Yisrael* had kept a *Pesach* like the one kept by *Yoshiyahu* and the *Kohanim* and the *Leviim* and all *Yehuda* and *Yisrael* there present and the inhabitants of *Yerushalayim*.

יח וְלֹא־נַעֲשָׂה פֶסַח כָּמֹהוּ בְּיִשְׂרָאֵל מִימֵי שְׁמוּאֵל הַנָּבִיא וְכָל־מַלְכֵי יִשְׂרָאֵל לֹא־עָשׂוּ כַּפֶּסַח אֲשֶׁר־עָשָׂה יֹאשִׁיָּהוּ וְהַכֹּהֲנִים וְהַלְוִיִּם וְכָל־יְהוּדָה וְיִשְׂרָאֵל הַנִּמְצָא וְיוֹשְׁבֵי יְרוּשָׁלָיִם:

v'-LO na-a-SAH FE-sakh ka-MO-hu b'-yis-ra-AYL mee-MAY sh'-mu-AYL ha-na-VEE v'-khol mal-KHAY yis-ra-AYL lo a-SU ka-PE-sakh a-SHER a-SAH yo-shi-YA-hu v'-ha-ko-ha-NEEM v'-hal-vi-YIM v'-khol y'-hu-DAH v'-yis-ra-AYL ha-nim-TZA v'-yo-sh'-VAY y'-ru-sha-LA-im

19 That *Pesach* was kept in the eighteenth year of the reign of *Yoshiyahu*.

יט בִּשְׁמוֹנֶה עֶשְׂרֵה שָׁנָה לְמַלְכוּת יֹאשִׁיָּהוּ נַעֲשָׂה הַפֶּסַח הַזֶּה:

20 After all this furbishing of the Temple by *Yoshiyahu*, King Neco of Egypt came up to fight at Carchemish on the Euphrates, and *Yoshiyahu* went out against him.

כ אַחֲרֵי כָל־זֹאת אֲשֶׁר הֵכִין יֹאשִׁיָּהוּ אֶת־הַבַּיִת עָלָה נְכוֹ מֶלֶךְ־מִצְרַיִם לְהִלָּחֵם בְּכַרְכְּמִישׁ עַל־פְּרָת וַיֵּצֵא לִקְרָאתוֹ יֹאשִׁיָּהוּ:

35:18 No *Pesach* like that one Like his great-grandfather *Chizkiyahu*, *Yoshiyahu* incorporates the *Pesach* ritual into the process of renewing the covenant with *Hashem*. However, the verse implies that the *Pesach* celebration in the time of *Yoshiyahu* was even greater than that of *Chizkiyahu*, stating that there had not been a Passover celebration like it since the days of *Shmuel*. Radak suggests that what made *Yoshiyahu*'s celebration greater than *Chizkiyahu*'s was the fact that it was celebrated by "all *Yehuda* and *Yisrael* there present." Whereas many of the remaining members of the kingdom of *Yisrael* had scorned *Chizkiyahu*'s invitation to celebrate the *Pesach* holiday together with the kingdom of *Yehuda* in *Yerushalayim* (II Chronicles 30:10), in *Yoshiyahu*'s time, members of both kingdoms came together wholeheartedly in the service of *Hashem*. The unity of the Children of Israel is what enhanced the celebration beyond any that had taken place throughout the entire period of the kings.

Divrei Hayamim II / II Chronicles
Chapter 36

21 [Neco] sent messengers to him, saying, "What have I to do with you, king of *Yehuda*? I do not march against you this day but against the kingdom that wars with me, and it is *Hashem*'s will that I hurry. Refrain, then, from interfering with *Hashem* who is with me, that He not destroy you."

22 But *Yoshiyahu* would not let him alone; instead, he donned [his armor] to fight him, heedless of Neco's words from the mouth of *Hashem*; and he came to fight in the plain of Megiddo.

23 Archers shot King *Yoshiyahu*, and the king said to his servants, "Get me away from here, for I am badly wounded."

24 His servants carried him out of his chariot and put him in the wagon of his second-in-command, and conveyed him to *Yerushalayim*. There he died, and was buried in the grave of his fathers, and all *Yehuda* and *Yerushalayim* went into mourning over *Yoshiyahu*.

25 *Yirmiyahu* composed laments for *Yoshiyahu* which all the singers, male and female, recited in their laments for *Yoshiyahu*, as is done to this day; they became customary in *Yisrael* and were incorporated into the laments.

26 The other events of *Yoshiyahu*'s reign and his faithful deeds, in accord with the Teaching of *Hashem*,

27 and his acts, early and late, are recorded in the book of the kings of *Yisrael* and *Yehuda*.

36 1 The people of the land took *Yehoachaz* son of *Yoshiyahu* and made him king instead of his father in *Yerushalayim*.

2 *Yehoachaz* was twenty-three years old when he became king and he reigned three months in *Yerushalayim*.

3 The king of Egypt deposed him in *Yerushalayim* and laid a fine on the land of 100 silver *kikarim* and one gold *kikar*.

4 The king of Egypt made his brother Eliakim king over *Yehuda* and *Yerushalayim*, and changed his name to *Yehoyakim*; Neco took his brother Joahaz and brought him to Egypt.

Divrei Hayamim II / II Chronicles
Chapter 36

דברי הימים ב
פרק לו

5 *Yehoyakim* was twenty-five years old when he became king, and he reigned eleven years in *Yerushalayim*; he did what was displeasing to *Hashem* his God.

ה בֶּן־עֶשְׂרִים וְחָמֵשׁ שָׁנָה יְהוֹיָקִים בְּמָלְכוֹ וְאַחַת עֶשְׂרֵה שָׁנָה מָלַךְ בִּירוּשָׁלָ‍ִם וַיַּעַשׂ הָרַע בְּעֵינֵי יְהוָה אֱלֹהָיו:

6 King Nebuchadnezzar of Babylon marched against him; he bound him in fetters to convey him to Babylon.

ו עָלָיו עָלָה נְבוּכַדְנֶאצַּר מֶלֶךְ בָּבֶל וַיַּאַסְרֵהוּ בַּנְחֻשְׁתַּיִם לְהֹלִיכוֹ בָּבֶלָה:

7 Nebuchadnezzar also brought some vessels of the House of *Hashem* to Babylon, and set them in his palace in Babylon.

ז וּמִכְּלֵי בֵּית יְהוָה הֵבִיא נְבוּכַדְנֶאצַּר לְבָבֶל וַיִּתְּנֵם בְּהֵיכָלוֹ בְּבָבֶל:

8 The other events of *Yehoyakim*'s reign, and the abominable things he did, and what was found against him, are recorded in the book of the kings of *Yisrael* and *Yehuda*. His son *Yehoyachin* succeeded him as king.

ח וְיֶתֶר דִּבְרֵי יְהוֹיָקִים וְתֹעֲבֹתָיו אֲשֶׁר־עָשָׂה וְהַנִּמְצָא עָלָיו הִנָּם כְּתוּבִים עַל־סֵפֶר מַלְכֵי יִשְׂרָאֵל וִיהוּדָה וַיִּמְלֹךְ יְהוֹיָכִין בְּנוֹ תַּחְתָּיו:

9 *Yehoyachin* was eight years old when he became king, and he reigned three months and ten days in *Yerushalayim*; he did what was displeasing to *Hashem*.

ט בֶּן־שְׁמוֹנֶה שָׁנִים יְהוֹיָכִין בְּמָלְכוֹ וּשְׁלֹשָׁה חֳדָשִׁים וַעֲשֶׂרֶת יָמִים מָלַךְ בִּירוּשָׁלָ‍ִם וַיַּעַשׂ הָרַע בְּעֵינֵי יְהוָה:

10 At the turn of the year, King Nebuchadnezzar sent to have him brought to Babylon with the precious vessels of the House of *Hashem*, and he made his kinsman *Tzidkiyahu* king over *Yehuda* and *Yerushalayim*.

י וְלִתְשׁוּבַת הַשָּׁנָה שָׁלַח הַמֶּלֶךְ נְבוּכַדְנֶאצַּר וַיְבִאֵהוּ בָבֶלָה עִם־כְּלֵי חֶמְדַּת בֵּית־יְהוָה וַיַּמְלֵךְ אֶת־צִדְקִיָּהוּ אָחִיו עַל־יְהוּדָה וִירוּשָׁלָ‍ִם:

11 *Tzidkiyahu* was twenty-one years old when he became king, and he reigned eleven years in *Yerushalayim*.

יא בֶּן־עֶשְׂרִים וְאַחַת שָׁנָה צִדְקִיָּהוּ בְמָלְכוֹ וְאַחַת עֶשְׂרֵה שָׁנָה מָלַךְ בִּירוּשָׁלָ‍ִם:

12 He did what was displeasing to *Hashem* his God; he did not humble himself before the *Navi Yirmiyahu*, who spoke for *Hashem*.

יב וַיַּעַשׂ הָרַע בְּעֵינֵי יְהוָה אֱלֹהָיו לֹא נִכְנַע מִלִּפְנֵי יִרְמְיָהוּ הַנָּבִיא מִפִּי יְהוָה:

13 He also rebelled against Nebuchadnezzar, who made him take an oath by *Hashem*; he stiffened his neck and hardened his heart so as not to turn to God of *Yisrael*.

יג וְגַם בַּמֶּלֶךְ נְבוּכַדְנֶאצַּר מָרָד אֲשֶׁר הִשְׁבִּיעוֹ בֵּאלֹהִים וַיֶּקֶשׁ אֶת־עָרְפּוֹ וַיְאַמֵּץ אֶת־לְבָבוֹ מִשּׁוּב אֶל־יְהוָה אֱלֹהֵי יִשְׂרָאֵל:

14 All the officers of the *Kohanim* and the people committed many trespasses, following all the abominable practices of the nations. They polluted the House of *Hashem*, which He had consecrated in *Yerushalayim*.

יד גַּם כָּל־שָׂרֵי הַכֹּהֲנִים וְהָעָם הִרְבּוּ לִמְעָל־מַעַל כְּכֹל תֹּעֲבוֹת הַגּוֹיִם וַיְטַמְּאוּ אֶת־בֵּית יְהוָה אֲשֶׁר הִקְדִּישׁ בִּירוּשָׁלָ‍ִם:

15 God of their fathers had sent word to them through His messengers daily without fail, for He had pity on His people and His dwelling-place.

טו וַיִּשְׁלַח יְהוָה אֱלֹהֵי אֲבוֹתֵיהֶם עֲלֵיהֶם בְּיַד מַלְאָכָיו הַשְׁכֵּם וְשָׁלוֹחַ כִּי־חָמַל עַל־עַמּוֹ וְעַל־מְעוֹנוֹ:

16 But they mocked the messengers of *Hashem* and disdained His words and taunted His *Neviim* until the wrath of *Hashem* against His people grew beyond remedy.

טז וַיִּהְיוּ מַלְעִבִים בְּמַלְאֲכֵי הָאֱלֹהִים וּבוֹזִים דְּבָרָיו וּמִתַּעְתְּעִים בִּנְבִאָיו עַד עֲלוֹת חֲמַת־יְהוָה בְּעַמּוֹ עַד־לְאֵין מַרְפֵּא:

Divrei Hayamim II/II Chronicles
Chapter 36

דברי הימים ב
פרק לו

יז He therefore brought the king of the Chaldeans upon them, who killed their youths by the sword in their sanctuary; He did not spare youth, maiden, elder, or graybeard, but delivered all into his hands.

וַיַּעַל עֲלֵיהֶם אֶת־מֶלֶךְ כַּשְׂדִּיים [כַּשְׂדִּים] וַיַּהֲרֹג בַּחוּרֵיהֶם בַּחֶרֶב בְּבֵית מִקְדָּשָׁם וְלֹא חָמַל עַל־בָּחוּר וּבְתוּלָה זָקֵן וְיָשֵׁשׁ הַכֹּל נָתַן בְּיָדוֹ׃

יח All the vessels of the House of *Hashem*, large and small, and the treasures of the House of *Hashem* and the treasures of the king and his officers were all brought to Babylon.

וְכֹל כְּלֵי בֵּית הָאֱלֹהִים הַגְּדֹלִים וְהַקְּטַנִּים וְאֹצְרוֹת בֵּית יְהוָה וְאֹצְרוֹת הַמֶּלֶךְ וְשָׂרָיו הַכֹּל הֵבִיא בָבֶל׃

יט They burned the House of *Hashem* and tore down the wall of *Yerushalayim*, burned down all its mansions, and consigned all its precious objects to destruction.

וַיִּשְׂרְפוּ אֶת־בֵּית הָאֱלֹהִים וַיְנַתְּצוּ אֵת חוֹמַת יְרוּשָׁלָ͏ִם וְכָל־אַרְמְנוֹתֶיהָ שָׂרְפוּ בָאֵשׁ וְכָל־כְּלֵי מַחֲמַדֶּיהָ לְהַשְׁחִית׃

כ Those who survived the sword he exiled to Babylon, and they became his and his sons' servants till the rise of the Persian kingdom,

וַיֶּגֶל הַשְּׁאֵרִית מִן־הַחֶרֶב אֶל־בָּבֶל וַיִּהְיוּ־לוֹ וּלְבָנָיו לַעֲבָדִים עַד־מְלֹךְ מַלְכוּת פָּרָס׃

כא in fulfillment of the word of *Hashem* spoken by *Yirmiyahu*, until the land paid back its *Shabbatot*; as long as it lay desolate it kept *Shabbat*, till seventy years were completed.

לְמַלֹּאות דְּבַר־יְהוָה בְּפִי יִרְמְיָהוּ עַד־רָצְתָה הָאָרֶץ אֶת־שַׁבְּתוֹתֶיהָ כָּל־יְמֵי הָשַּׁמָּה שָׁבָתָה לְמַלֹּאות שִׁבְעִים שָׁנָה׃

כב And in the first year of King Cyrus of Persia, when the word of *Hashem* spoken by *Yirmiyahu* was fulfilled, *Hashem* roused the spirit of King Cyrus of Persia to issue a proclamation throughout his realm by word of mouth and in writing, as follows:

וּבִשְׁנַת אַחַת לְכוֹרֶשׁ מֶלֶךְ פָּרַס לִכְלוֹת דְּבַר־יְהוָה בְּפִי יִרְמְיָהוּ הֵעִיר יְהוָה אֶת־רוּחַ כֹּרֶשׁ מֶלֶךְ־פָּרַס וַיַּעֲבֶר־קוֹל בְּכָל־מַלְכוּתוֹ וְגַם־בְּמִכְתָּב לֵאמֹר׃

כג "Thus said King Cyrus of Persia: God of Heaven has given me all the kingdoms of the earth, and has charged me with building Him a House in *Yerushalayim*, which is in *Yehuda*. Any one of you of all His people, *Hashem* his God be with him and let him go up."

כֹּה־אָמַר כֹּרֶשׁ מֶלֶךְ פָּרַס כָּל־מַמְלְכוֹת הָאָרֶץ נָתַן לִי יְהוָה אֱלֹהֵי הַשָּׁמַיִם וְהוּא־פָקַד עָלַי לִבְנוֹת־לוֹ בַיִת בִּירוּשָׁלַ͏ִם אֲשֶׁר בִּיהוּדָה מִי־בָכֶם מִכָּל־עַמּוֹ יְהוָה אֱלֹהָיו עִמּוֹ וְיָעַל׃

koh a-MAR KO-resh ME-lekh pa-RAS kol mam-l'-KHOT ha-A-retz NA-tan LEE a-do-NAI e-lo-HAY ha-sha-MA-yim v'-HU fa-KAD a-LAI liv-NOT LO VA-yit bee-ru-sha-LA-im a-SHER bee-hu-DAH mee va-KHEM mi-kol a-MO a-do-NAI e-lo-HAV i-MO v'-YA-al

New immigrants at Ben Gurion airport

36:23 Let him go up The last verse in the *Tanakh* calls upon the Jewish people to ascend to *Eretz Yisrael*. After decades of Babylonian rule, Cyrus grants permission for the exiled Jews to return to their land and rebuild the *Beit Hamikdash* in *Yerushalayim*. This was a fulfillment of the prophecy of *Yirmiyahu*, that after seventy years *Hashem* would return the Jewish people home (Jeremiah 29:10). Just as He fulfilled His word to return the People of Israel to the Land of Israel after the first exile, today as well God has begun to fulfill His promise to gather the exiles from the four corners of the earth and to bring the ultimate redemption (Deuteronomy 30:3–5). Since the establishment of the State of Israel, millions of Jews have returned home from over one hundred different countries. How fortunate are we to witness the beginning stages of the tremendous miracle of the ingathering of the exiles. May we soon merit the final fulfillment of the complete redemption of Israel and the entire world.

Biographies of *The Israel Bible* Scholars

Ahuva Balofsky – Ahuva grew up in Toronto, Canada and obtained her B.A. Hons. and B.Ed. at York University. She taught Bible, Rabbinics and English at the Community Hebrew Academy of Toronto. After moving to Israel in 2004 with her family, she completed a Master's degree in Bible at Bar Ilan University.

Rabbi Avi Baumol – Rabbi Baumol, a pulpit Rabbi and Jewish educator, is currently serving the Jewish community of Krakow, Poland. He earned a B.A. from Yeshiva University and an M.A. in Jewish History from the Bernard Revel Graduate School. Rabbi Baumol is an alumnus of Yeshivat Har Etzion and received Rabbinic Ordination from Yeshiva University. He is the author of "The Poetry of Prayer; Tehillim in Tefillah," Gefen Publishing, Jerusalem 2009.

Rabbi Yaakov Beasley – Rabbi Beasley has been lecturing passionately on Bible in different venues in Israel and abroad for almost twenty years. His essays and articles on Bible study appear regularly in leading magazines. Rabbi Beasley is also the editor of the groundbreaking series on the Pentateuch, *Torah MiEtzion*, and is completing advanced Bible studies at Bar Ilan University. When not teaching, he enjoys the company of his family in their home in the Judean mountains.

Josh Even-Chen – Josh is a native of North Carolina, but has called Israel his home ever since immigrating to Israel with his family in 1978. Josh graduated from Bar-Ilan University and completed a teaching degree. He now works as a tour guide who is popular with diverse groups of varied ages and backgrounds. He lives in Ma'aleh Adumim with his wife Chana and their six children.

Rabbi Shmuel Jablon – Rabbi Jablon is a highly experienced Jewish educator, having served as an administrator and teacher in American Jewish day schools for over two decades. He is a rabbinic graduate of the Hebrew Theological College ("Skokie Yeshiva"), holds a Masters Degree in Education and is a member of the Rabbinical Council of America. In the summer of 5774 (2014), he fulfilled a life-long dream by making *aliyah* to Israel with his family.

Batya Markowitz – Batya is a two-time National Bible Contest winner. Growing up in Toronto, her dream was to make *aliyah* to Israel and become a Bible teacher. Today, Batya lives with her husband in the heart of Jerusalem, fulfilling both of those goals. Since receiving a degree in Jewish Education at Michlalah Jerusalem College, she has been teaching Jewish studies at the elementary, junior high and post high school levels.

Shira Schechter – Shira graduated from Stern College with a BA in Judaic studies and received masters' degrees in education and Bible from the Azrieli and the Bernard Revel graduate schools of Yeshiva University. Shira also studied at the Yeshiva University Graduate Program for women in Advanced Talmudic Studies, and was a teaching fellow at the Rabbi Soloveitchik Institute in Boston. Prior to making *aliyah* in 2013, Shira taught Bible to high school students in New Jersey.

Rabbi Noam Shapiro – Rabbi Shapiro studied at Yeshivat Har Etzion and has rabbinic ordination from Yeshiva University's Rabbi Isaac Elchanan Theological Seminary. Originally from Boston, Massachusetts, Rabbi Shapiro has taught *Torah* topics at high schools and Seminaries in the United States and Israel. Rabbi Shapiro also served as an editor for the Koren Talmud Bavli with commentary by Rabbi Adin Steinsaltz. He currently lives with his family in Gush Etzion, Israel.

Alexander Jacob Tsykin – Born in Melbourne, Rabbi Tsykin studied in Mount Scopus Memorial College for thirteen years before spending three years at Yeshivat Har Etzion pursuing advanced studies in Jewish law. He studied for two years in Monash University, Australia, and two years in Yeshiva University, New York, where he completed a degree in Jewish Studies focusing on Modern Jewish History. Alexander lives in Alon Shevut, Israel, with his wife and son.

Rabbi Naphtali ("Tuly") Weisz – Rabbi Weisz attended Yeshiva University (BA), the Rabbi Isaac Elchanan Theological Seminary (Rabbinic Ordination) and the Benjamin Cardozo School of Law (JD). He served as the Rabbi of the Beth Jacob Congregation in Columbus, Ohio before making *aliyah*. Rabbi Weisz founded Israel365 and the Yeshiva for the Nations and serves as the publisher of Breaking Israel News. He is also the editor of *The Israel Bible*.

Bibliography

This bibliography contains a short biography of the scholars and historical figures mentioned in the commentary of *The Israel Bible*.

Aaronsohn, Sarah (1890–1917) – Born in Zichron Yaakov, Aaronsohn and her siblings co-founded Nili, a Jewish, pro-British espionage group, established to help liberate Palestine from Ottoman rule. Aaronsohn was captured and tortured by the Turks, and killed herself before revealing anything to her torturers.

Abrabanel, Rabbi Yitzchak (1437–1508) – Born in Portugal, Abrabanel fled to Spain in 1483. He was a statesman, philosopher and Bible commentator. He tried to convince King Ferdinand to revoke the edict expelling the Jews from Spain in 1492 but was unsuccessful.

Agnon, Shmuel Yosef (1888–1970) – Born in Buczacz, Galicia, Agnon immigrated to Israel in 1908. An Israeli writer, his works are published under his initials S.Y. Agnon, and he is known in Hebrew by his acronym Shai (ש״י). One of the most admired Israeli authors of the 20th century, Agnon was awarded the Nobel Prize in Literature in 1966.

Albo, Rabbi Joseph (1380–1444) – Born in Spain, Albo was a Jewish rabbi and philosopher during the 15th century. He is best known for his philosophical work, *Book of the Principles*, in which he discusses the fundamental beliefs of Judaism.

Allon, Yigal (1918–1980) – Born in Kfar Tavor, Israel, Allon was a commander of the Palmach, a general in the IDF and an Israeli politician. He briefly served as interim Prime Minister of the State of Israel in 1969, following the death of Prime Minister Levi Eshkol.

Altschuler, Rabbi David (18th century) – Commonly known by the name of his commentary, *Metzudat David*, he lived in Galicia where he died a martyr's death. The *Metzudat David* commentary is considered basic for understanding the books of the prophets.

Aviner, Rabbi Shlomo (b. 1943) – Born in France, Aviner immigrated to Israel at age 23. He served in the Israeli Defense Forces and studied under Rabbi Tzvi Yehuda Kook. He is the Rabbi of Beit El and head of the Ateret

Yerushalayim seminary in the Old City of Jerusalem. He is the author of many books, including a commentary on the Book of Judges.

Barak, Ehud (b. 1942) – Born in Kibbutz Mishmar Hasharon, Barak is an Israeli politician who served as Israel's tenth Prime Minister from 1999–2001. He served in the IDF for 35 years and, along with two others, is the most decorated soldier in Israel's history.

Barbivai, Orna (b. 1962) – Born in Afula, Barbivai is a Major-General in the IDF and former head of its manpower directorate. She is the first woman to have been promoted to the rank of Major-General in the Israel Defense Forces.

Bar-Ilan, Rabbi Meir (1880–1949) – Born in Russia, Bar-Ilan moved to the United States in 1915 where he became an important leader of the Mizrachi Religious Zionist Movement. He moved to Israel in 1926 where he continued to lead Mizrachi and the struggle for a Jewish state. Bar Ilan University is named in his memory.

Barkat, Nir (b. 1959) – Born in Jerusalem, Barkat is an Israeli businessman and politician who has served as the mayor of Jerusalem since 2008.

Bazak, Rabbi Amnon (b. 1966) – Born in Jerusalem, Bazak is a teacher of Talmud at Yeshivat Har Etzion in Alon Shevut. He is an expert in the Bible, and teaches Bible classes at the Herzog teacher's college. He has published a number of books on the Bible.

Begin, Menachem (1913–1992) – Born in Belarus, Begin became an Israeli politician, founder of the Israeli political party Likud and 6th Prime Minister of the State of Israel. Before the establishment of the State, he headed the Zionist paramilitary organization called the Irgun. As Prime Minister, Begin signed a peace treaty with Egypt in 1979, for which he and Anwar Sadat were awarded the Nobel Peace Prize.

Ben-Gurion, David (1886–1973) – Born in Poland, Ben-Gurion immigrated to Israel in 1906. He is considered Israel's "founding father," as he formally declared the establishment of the State on May 14, 1948, and was the first to sign the Israeli Declaration of Independence which he helped write. Ben-Gurion served as the first Prime Minister of Israel.

Ben-Zvi, Yitzchak (1884–1963) – Born in the Ukraine, Ben-Zvi immigrated to the Land of Israel in 1907. He was a historian and a leader of the Labor Zionist movement. He served as the second president of the State of Israel from 1952 until his death in 1963.

Berlin, Rabbi Naftali Tzvi Yehuda (1816–1893) – Born in Belarus, Berlin is commonly known by his acronym *Netziv*. He was a *Torah* scholar and served as dean of the esteemed talmudical college of Volozhin from 1854 until it closed in 1892. Berlin authored a number of works on rabbinic literature as well as a commentary on the Bible.

Bialik, Chaim Nachman (1873–1934) – Born in the Ukraine, Bialik moved to Tel Aviv in 1924. He was one of the pioneers of Hebrew poetry and his works contributed to the revival of the Hebrew language. He became known as Israel's national poet.

Blech, Rabbi Benjamin (b. 1933) – Born in Zurich, Blech is a professor of Talmud at Yeshiva University in New York. He served as Rabbi of the Young Israel of Oceanside and has authored numerous books including *The Secrets of Hebrew Words*.

Braverman, Sarah (1919–2013) – Born in Romania, Braverman immigrated to Israel at a young age. She was a member of the Palmach, parachuted into Europe with the Jewish heroine Chana Senesh, and established the IDF Women's Corps. She is affectionately known as the "first lady of the IDF."

Carlebach, Rabbi Shlomo (1925–1994) – Born in Berlin, Carlebach moved to New York in 1939. He was a rabbi, religious teacher, composer and singer. He is known as one of the foremost Jewish religious songwriters of the century as well as a pioneer of the "baal teshuva movement," working to draw unaffiliated Jews back to Judaism.

Clorfene, Rabbi Chaim (b. 1939) – Born in Chicago, Illinois, Clorfene resides in Safed, Israel. He is a recognized authority on the Third Temple and the Messianic era, has authored numerous books, and produced multiple audio dramas and video presentations on the Third Temple and other Jewish topics.

Dayan, Moshe (1915–1981) – Born on Kibbutz Degania Alef, Dayan was the second child born on the first Israeli kibbutz. He was an Israeli military leader and politician, known for his role as Israeli Defense Minister during the 1967 Six-Day War as well as for his signature eye patch.

Eban, Abba (1915–2002) – Born in South Africa, Eban immigrated to Israel in 1940. He was a scholar of both Arabic and Hebrew as well as an Israeli diplomat and politician. Some of his different positions included Israeli Foreign Affairs Minister, Education Minister, Deputy Prime Minister, Ambassador to the United States and to the United Nations.

Eshkol, Levi (1895–1969) – Born in the Ukraine, Eshkol immigrated to the Land of Israel in 1914. He served as Israel's fourth Prime Minister from 1963 until his death in 1969.

Ginsberg, Asher (1856–1927) – Born in Russia, Ginsberg moved to Israel in 1922. He was a Hebrew essayist and is considered the founder of cultural Zionism. He is primarily known by his Hebrew pen name Achad Ha'am.

Glazerson, Rabbi Matityahu (b. 1937) – Born in K'far Saba, Glazerson is a rabbi, teacher, musician and composer. In his teaching, he focuses on the meaning behind the Hebrew letters and their numerical value. He has authored over 30 books.

Hakham, Rabbi Amos (1921–2012) – Born in Jerusalem, Hakham was a master of the Hebrew Bible and a scholar. He was the winner of the first International Bible Contest held in Israel in 1958. Hakham authored the commentary on a number of books for the Da'at Mikra Bible series, including the commentary on the Book of Psalms.

Halevi, Rabbi Judah (c. 1080 – c. 1145) – Born in Spain, Halevi was a physician, poet and philosopher. He wrote *The Kuzari* in defense of the teachings of Judaism. His is known to have had an intense yearning for the Holy land, and is famous for writing "My heart is in the east, and I in the uttermost west." He died shortly after arriving in Israel.

Hertz, Rabbi Joseph Herman (1872–1946) – Born in Hungary, Hertz was a rabbi and Bible scholar, and edited a notable commentary on the Pentateuch. He was the Chief Rabbi of the United Kingdom from 1913–1946.

Hirsch, Rabbi Samson Raphael (1808–1888) – Born in France, Hirsch was a rabbi in Frankfurt-Main and the leader of modern German-Jewish Orthodoxy. He wrote a six-volume commentary on the Pentateuch.

Horowitz, Rabbi Yeshaya (1565–1630) – Born in Prague, Horowitz immigrated to the Land of Israel in 1621. He was a prominent rabbi and kabbalist and is also known as the *Shelah ha-Kadosh* (the holy *Shelah*).

Ibn Ezra, Rabbi Abraham (1089–1164) – Born in Tuleda, Navarre, Ibn Ezra was a philosopher, poet, mathematician, astronomer, linguist and biblical exegete. His commentary is included in most common editions of the Hebrew Bible that contain rabbinic commentary.

Ickovitz, Rabbi Chaim (1749–1821) – Born in Volozhin, Ickovitz is commonly known as Rabbi Chaim of Volozhin. A rabbi, Talmudist and ethicist, he was the founder of the famed Volozhin talmudical college. He authored *Nefesh HaChaim*, a work of religious philosophy.

Jacob son of Asher (c. 1275–c. 1340) – Born in Germany, he was an influential medieval rabbi, often called the *Baal HaTurim*, after his main work on Jewish law, the *Arbaah Turim*, the Four Rows. He wrote two commentaries on the Pentateuch; a concise commentary of mystical and symbolic references in the *Torah*, and an exegetical commentary.

Kaplan, Rabbi Aryeh (1934–1983) – Born in the Bronx, New York, Kaplan was a rabbi, educator and author. He is considered an original thinker and was known for his knowledge of physics and kabbalah. Kaplan authored numerous works on a variety of topics including the Bible, Talmud, mysticism, Jewish beliefs and philosophy.

Keel, Yehuda (1916–2011) – Born in Saint Petersburg, Russia, Keel immigrated to Israel in 1936. He was an educator and Bible commentator and served as the head of the religious education department of the Israel Ministry of Education. He headed the Da'at Mikra biblical commentary project and was awarded the Israel Prize for Jewish studies in 1992.

Kimchi, Rabbi David (1160–1235) – Born in Provence, Kimchi is commonly known by his acronym Radak. A rabbi, philosopher and grammarian, he wrote a widely-studied commentary on the Bible.

Kook, Rabbi Abraham Isaac (1865–1935) – Born in Latvia, Kook immigrated to Israel in 1904. He was the first Ashkenazi Chief Rabbi of the Land of Israel, founder of the Mercaz HaRav academy and is viewed as one of the fathers of Religious Zionism. He was well known for his tremendous love for others and for his intellectual leadership helping to establish a Jewish State in the Land of Israel.

Kook, Rabbi Tzvi Yehuda (1891–1982) – Born in Lithuania, Kook immigrated to Israel in 1904. He was a Rabbi and leader of Religious Zionism and the only son of Rabbi Abraham Isaac Kook. He served as head of the Mercaz HaRav seminary as well as the editor of many of his late father's works. He continued in his father's path of Religious Zionism and was instrumental in encouraging Jews to settle in areas liberated during the Six Day War.

Kollek, Theodore (1911–2007) – Born in Hungary in 1911, Kollek immigrated to Israel in 1935. He served as mayor of Jerusalem for 28 years from 1965–1993, and dedicated himself to developing the city and was awarded the Israel Prize in 1988 for his contributions to society and the State of Israel.

Kremer, Rabbi Elijah (1720–1797) – Born in Lithuania, Kremer was a Talmudist, a master of Jewish law and a kabbalist. Because of his brilliance and mastery of text he is known as the "Genius of Vilna."

Leibowitz, Nechama (1905–1997) – Born in Riga, Latvia, Leibowitz immigrated to the Land of Israel in 1930. She was a Bible scholar and master educator who inspired many to study the Bible. She was known for her worksheets containing questions on the weekly *Torah* portion which she would personally review, correct and return.

Leibtag, Rabbi Menachem (b. 1958) – Born in Ohio, Leibtag immigrated to Israel where he is a Bible scholar, noted lecturer and pioneer of Jewish education on the internet. He teaches a thematic-analytic approach to biblical study, emphasizing biblical theme and structure, that combines traditional Jewish approaches with modern scholarship.

Levi ben Gershon (1288–1344) – Born in France, he is commonly known by his acronym Ralbag or Gersonides. He was a philosopher, mathematician, astronomer, Talmudist and Bible commentator.

Levin, Rabbi Aryeh (1885–1969) – Born in Poland, Levin was a rabbi and scholar known for his warmth, kindness, humility and love of every person. After immigrating to Israel, he became known as the "Father of the Prisoners" for his role as Jewish prison chaplain, bringing love, encouragement and hope to those behind bars.

Lichtman, Rabbi Moshe – Born in New Jersey, Lichtman immigrated to Israel in 1991. He is a rabbi, teacher and author, and is known for his translations of various Hebrew texts and for his work, *Eretz Yisrael in the Parshah* and *A Drop in the Ocean*.

Luntschitz, Rabbi Shlomo Ephraim (1550–1619) – Born in Poland, Luntschitz served as the Rabbi of Prague from 1604–1619 and was best known for his *Torah* commentary *Kli Yakar*.

Luria, Rabbi Isaac (1534–1572) – Born in Jerusalem, Luria is commonly known as the *Arizal* (the Ari of blessed memory). He became a rabbi and Jewish kabbalist in the mystical city of Safed. He is considered to be the father of contemporary Jewish mysticism.

Maimonides (1135–1204) – Born in Spain, Maimonides is commonly known as Rambam, the acronym of his name Rabbi Moshe ben (son of) Maimon. He was a preeminent Jewish legal scholar and philosopher, as well as a renowned physician. His numerous works include "The Guide for the Perplexed," the main source of his philosophical views, and the *"Mishneh Torah,"* his seminal codification of Jewish law. He is buried in Tiberias, Israel.

Meir, Golda (1898–1978) – Born in Kiev, Meir immigrated first to the United States and then to the Land of Israel in 1921. She served as Israel's fourth Prime Minister, the only woman to have held this position to date.

Meir Simcha of Dvinsk (1843–1926) – Born in Lithuania, he was a rabbi and prominent leader of the Orthodox Jewish community of Eastern Europe. He is known for his writings on Maimonides' work of Jewish law, called *Ohr Sameach*, as well as his commentary on the *Torah* called *Meshech Chochmah*.

Meiri, Rabbi Menachem (1249–c. 1310) – Born in Southern France, Meiri was a rabbi and Talmudic scholar. His commentary on the Talmud is considered one of the most monumental works on the Talmud.

Morgensztern, Rabbi Menachem Mendel (1787–1859) – Born in Poland, Morgensztern is also known as the Kotzker Rebbe. He was a Hasidic rabbi and leader, known for his sharp-witted sayings and down-to-earth philosophies.

Munk, Rabbi Michael (1905–1985) – Born in Berlin, Munk was an educator, author and activist. He founded the Adath Yisrael Synagogue of Hendon in London, and was the founding principal of the largest Orthodox Jewish school for girls in America.

Nahmanides (1194–1270) – Born in Spain, Rabbi Moshe ben (son of) Nachman is also known by his acronym the Ramban. He was one of the leading *Torah* scholars of the Middle Ages, and authored numerous works on *Torah* subjects, including a famed commentary on the Pentateuch.

Navon, Yitzchak (1921–2015) – Born in Jerusalem, Navon became an Israeli political and diplomat, author, and linguist. He served as the fifth president of the State of Israel from 1978–1983.

Netanyahu, Benjamin (b. 1949) – Born in Tel Aviv, Netanyahu is an Israeli politician, a veteran of an elite unit of the Israel Defense Forces, and a graduate of the Massachusetts Institute of Technology. In March 2015, he was elected to his fourth term as Prime Minister of the State of Israel.

Peres, Shimon (1923–2016) – Born in Poland, Peres immigrated to Israel in 1934. He was an Israeli politician who served as Prime Minister from 1984–1986, and from 1995–1996. He was also Israel's ninth president from 2007–2014.

Rabin, Yitzchak (1922–1995) – Born in Jerusalem, Rabin was an Israeli politician who served two terms as Prime Minister of the State of Israel, from 1974–1977 and again from 1992 until his assassination in 1995.

Riskin, Rabbi Shlomo (b. 1940) – Born in Brooklyn, Riskin served as a rabbi in New York before immigrating to Israel in 1983 to become the founding chief rabbi of Efrat. He is also the founder and chancellor of Ohr Torah Stone, a network of Jewish educational institutions in America and Israel.

Rivlin, Reuven (b. 1939) – Born in Jerusalem, Rivlin is an Israeli lawyer and politician who has been serving as Israel's 10th president since 2014.

Rosen, Rabbi Joseph (1858–1936) – Born in Rogachev, Belarus, Rosen was one of the most prominent Talmudic scholars of the early 20th century. He is known as the "Genius of Rogachev" because of his photographic memory and his ability to use seemingly unrelated Talmudic passages to elucidate a question or area of Jewish law under discussion.

Sacks, Rabbi Lord Jonathan (1948–2020) – Born in London, England, Sacks is a rabbi, scholar and philosopher, and has authored more than 25 books. Sacks served as the Chief Rabbi of the United Hebrew Congregations of the Commonwealth for 22 years.

Schneerson, Rabbi Menachem Mendel (1902–1994) – Born in Russia, Schneerson immigrated to the United States in 1941. He was the last leader of the Chabad-Lubavitch Hasidic movement and one of the most influential Jewish leaders of the 20th century.

Senesh, Chana (1921–1944) – Born in Hungary, Senesh immigrated to Israel in 1939. She was one of the 37 Jews from Mandatory Palestine parachuted into Yugoslavia by the British Army in an effort to save Jews from deportation to Auschwitz. She was ultimately caught and executed. She is remembered for her heroism as well as her poetry.

Sforno, Rabbi Ovadya (c. 1470–1550) – Born in Italy, Sforno was a rabbi, philosopher and physician. His commentary on the Bible often reflects his knowledge of natural sciences. His commentaries on Ecclesiastes and Song of Songs were dedicated to King Henry II of France, demonstrating a close relationship between them.

Shamir, Yitzchak (1915–2012) – Born in Ruzinoy, Poland, Shamir immigrated to the Land of Israel in 1935. He was an Israeli politician who served as both Israel's eighth and tenth Prime Minister, from 1983–1984 and 1986–1992.

Sharansky, Natan (b. 1948) – Born in the former Soviet Union, Sharansky is an Israeli politician and human rights activist and a former Russian refusenik. He immigrated to Israel following his release from Soviet prison in 1986, and has served as Chairman of the Executive of the Jewish Agency since 2009.

Sharett, Moshe (1894–1965) – Born in the Ukraine, Sharett immigrated to Israel in 1906. He was the second Prime Minister of the State of Israel, serving from 1954–1955, and also served as Israel's Foreign Minister from 1955–1956.

Sharon, Ariel (1928–2014) – Born in the Israeli agricultural community of Kfar Malal, Sharon was an Israeli general and politician. He served as Israel's eleventh Prime Minister from 2001–2006.

Shazar, Zalman (1889–1974) – Born in Belarus, Shazar immigrated to Israel in 1924. An Israeli politician, author and poet, he was the president of the State of Israel from 1963–1973.

Shemer, Naomi (1930–2004) – Born on Kibbutz Kvutzat Kinneret, Shemer became a well-known Israeli singer, songwriter and composer. Her most famous song, *Yerushalayim shel zahav*, Jerusalem of Gold, was written in 1967 and is considered by some to be an informal second Israeli national anthem.

Shlomo son of Yitzchak (1040–1105) – Born in France, he is commonly known by his acronym Rashi. He wrote extensive commentaries on the Bible and Talmud, and his comments are considered the most basic for understanding both the Pentateuch and the Talmud.

Shneur Zalman of Liadi (1745–1812) – Born in Belarus, he was the founder of the Chabad-Lubavitch dynasty of Hasidic Judaism. He is known as the *Baal Hatanya*, the Master of the Tanya, for his work on Hasidic Jewish philosophy and is author of various works on Jewish philosophy, law and prayer.

Slifkin, Rabbi Natan (b. 1975) – Born in England, Slifkin immigrated to Israel where he is a rabbi, educator and author popularly known as the "Zoo Rabbi." He has authored texts on zoology and science and their relationship to the *Torah*, and is the director of the Biblical Museum of Natural History in Beit Shemesh, Israel.

Soloveitchik, Rabbi Joseph B. (1903–1993) – Born in Poland, Soloveitchik was a renowned religious leader, Talmudic scholar, author and modern Jewish philosopher. He headed the rabbinical school of Yeshiva University in New York.

Sorotzkin, Rabbi Zalman (1881–1966) – Born in Lithuania, Sorotzkin was a Torah commentator who published a commentary on the Pentateuch known as *Oznaim L'Torah*.

Stavsky, Rabbi David (1930–2004) – Born in New York City, Stavsky was ordained at the Rabbi Isaac Elchanan Theological Seminary. He was a chaplain in the U.S. Army and the rabbi of Beth Jacob Congregation in Columbus, Ohio from 1957 until his death in 2004.

Teichman, Rabbi Zvi – Rabbi and head of the *Torah* study program at Ohel Moshe in Baltimore, Maryland. He has been involved in Jewish education for over 25 years and authored *Eretz HaTzvi*, a guide to the commandments that pertain specifically to the Land of Israel.

Weiser, Rabbi Meir Leibush (1809–1879) – Born in Volochisk, Volhynia, Weiser is known by his acronym, Malbim. He was a rabbi, master of Hebrew grammar and a Bible commentator. He is known for his principle that every word in the *Torah* carries its own meaning, even distinct from its synonyms.

Weizmann, Chaim (1874–1952) – Born in Belarus, Weizmann immigrated to Israel, settling in Rechovot in 1937, and served as the first president of the State of Israel from 1949–1952. A biochemist, he founded the Weizmann Institute of Science in Rechovot, Israel and helped establish the Hebrew University in Jerusalem.

Wiesel, Elie (1928–2016) – Born in Romania, Weisel was a professor, political activist and the author of 57 books. A Holocaust survivor, his writings are considered among the most significant in Holocaust literature.

Willig, Rabbi Mordechai (b. 1947) – Born in New York, Willig has been the rabbi and spiritual leader of the Young Israel of Riverdale synagogue since 1974. He is also a renowned scholar and professor of Talmud at Yeshiva University in New York.

Yadin, Yigael (1917–1984) – Born in Jerusalem, Yadin was an Israeli archeologist, politician and the second Chief of Staff of the Israel Defense Forces.

Yogev, Motti (b. 1956) – Born in Haifa, Yogev is an Israeli politician and member of the Israeli parliament. He previously served as secretary general of the Israeli branch of Bnei Akiva, the largest religious Zionist youth movement in the world, as well as deputy chairman of the Mateh Binyamin Regional Council.

List of Transliterated Words in *The Israel Bible*

The following is a list of nouns which have been transliterated into Hebrew in the English translation and commentary of *The Israel Bible*:

Hebrew Name	English Name	Pronunciation	Hebrew
Achan	Achan	a-KHAN	עָכָן
Achav	Ahab	akh-AV	אַחְאָב
Achaz	Ahaz	a-KHAZ	אָחָז
Achazyahu	Ahaziah	a-khaz-YA-hu	אֲחַזְיָהוּ
Achiezer	Ahiezer	a-khee-E-zer	אֲחִיעֶזֶר
Achihud	Ahihud	a-khee-HUD	אֲחִיהוּד
Achikam	Ahikam	a-khee-KAM	אֲחִיקָם
Achilud	Ahilud	a-khee-LUD	אֲחִילוּד
Achimelech	Ahimelech	a-khee-ME-lekh	אֲחִימֶלֶךְ
Achira	Ahira	a-khee-RA	אֲחִירַע
Achisamach	Ahisamach	a-khee-sa-MAKH	אֲחִיסָמָךְ
Achitofel	Ahithophel	a-khee-TO-fel	אֲחִיתֹפֶל
Achituv	Ahitub	a-khee-TUV	אֲחִיטוּב
Achiya	Ahijah	a-khi-YAH	אֲחִיָּה
Adam	Adam	a-DAM	אָדָם
Adar	Adar	a-DAR	אֲדָר
Adoniyahu	Adonijah	a-do-ni-YA-hu	אֲדֹנִיָּהוּ
Adulam	Adullam	a-du-LAM	עֲדֻלָּם
Agur	Agur	a-GUR	אָגוּר
Aharon	Aaron	a-ha-RON	אַהֲרֹן
Amasa	Amasa	a-ma-SA	עֲמָשָׂא
Amatzya	Amaziah	a-matz-YAH	אֲמַצְיָה
Amen	Amen	a-MAYN	אָמֵן
Amiel	Ammiel	a-mee-AYL	עַמִּיאֵל
Aminadav	Amminadab	a-mee-na-DAV	עַמִּינָדָב
Amitai	Amittai	a-mi-TAI	אֲמִתַּי

Hebrew Name	English Name	Pronunciation	Hebrew
Amnon	Amnon	am-NON	אַמְנוֹן
Amon	Amon	a-MON	אָמוֹן
Amos	Amos	a-MOS	עָמוֹס
Amotz	Amoz	a-MOTZ	אָמוֹץ
Amram	Amram	am-RAM	עַמְרָם
Anatot	Anathoth	a-na-TOT	עֲנָתוֹת
Aron	Ark	a-RON	אֲרוֹן
Aron HaBrit	Ark of the Covenant	a-RON ha-b'-REET	אֲרוֹן הַבְּרִית
Arpachshad	Arpachshad	ar-pakh-SHAD	אַרְפַּכְשָׁד
Asa	Asa	a-SA	אָסָא
Asael	Asahel	a-sah-AYL	עֲשָׂהאֵל
Asaf	Asaph	a-SAF	אָסָף
Ashdod	Ashdod	ash-DOD	אַשְׁדּוֹד
Asher	Asher	a-SHAYR	אָשֵׁר
Ashkelon	Ashkelon	ash-k'-LON	אַשְׁקְלוֹן
Atalya	Athaliah	a-tal-YAH	עֲתַלְיָה
Avdon	Abdon	av-DON	עַבְדּוֹן
Avichayil	Abihail	a-vee-KHA-yil	אֲבִיחַיִל
Avidan	Abidan	a-vee-DAN	אֲבִידָן
Avigail	Abigail	a-vee-GA-yil	אֲבִיגַיִל
Avihu	Abihu	a-vee-HU	אֲבִיהוּא
Avimelech	Abimelech	a-vee-ME-lekh	אֲבִימֶלֶךְ
Avinadav	Abinadab	a-vee-na-DAV	אֲבִינָדָב
Aviram	Abiram	a-vee-RAM	אֲבִירָם
Avishai	Abishai	a-vee-SHAI	אֲבִישַׁי
Aviya	Abijah	a-vi-YAH	אֲבִיָּה
Aviyam	Abijam	a-vi-YAM	אֲבִיָּם
Avner	Abner	av-NAYR	אַבְנֵר
Avraham	Abraham	av-ra-HAM	אַבְרָהָם
Avram	Abram	av-RAM	אַבְרָם
Avshalom	Absalom	av-sha-LOM	אַבְשָׁלוֹם
Azarya	Azariah	a-zar-YAH	עֲזַרְיָה
Azeika	Azekah	a-zay-KAH	עֲזֵקָה

Hebrew Name	English Name	Pronunciation	Hebrew
Azza	Gaza	a-ZAH	עַזָּה
B'nei Yisrael	The Children of Israel	b'-NAY yis-ra-AYL	בְּנֵי יִשְׂרָאֵל
Barak	Barak	ba-rakh-AYL	בָּרָק
Baruch	Baruch	ba-RUKH	בָּרוּךְ
Barzilai	Barzillai	bar-zi-LAI	בַּרְזִלַּי
Basha	Baasa	ba-SHA	בַּעְשָׁא
Batsheva	Bath-sheba	bat-SHE-va	בַּת־שֶׁבַע
Be'er Sheva	Beer-sheba	b'-AYR SHE-va	בְּאֵר שֶׁבַע
Be'eri	Beeri	b'-ay-REE	בְּאֵרִי
Beit Aven	Beth-aven	bayt A-ven	בֵּית אָוֶן
Beit El	Beth-el	bayt el	בֵּית אֵל
Beit Hamikdash	Temple	bayt ha-mik-DASH	בֵּית הַמִּקְדָּשׁ
Beit Lechem	Beth-lehem	bayt LE-khem	בֵּית לֶחֶם
Beit Shean	Beth-shean	bayt sh'-AN	בֵּית שְׁאָן
Beit Shemesh	Beth-shemesh	bayt SHE-mesh	בֵּית שֶׁמֶשׁ
Berechya	Berechiah	be-rekh-YAH	בֶּרֶכְיָה
Betzalel	Bezalel	b'-tzal-AYL	בְּצַלְאֵל
Bilha	Bilhah	bil-HAH	בִּלְהָה
Binyamin	Benjamin	bin-ya-MIN	בִּנְיָמִין
Boaz	Boaz	BO-az	בֹּעַז
Buki	Bukki	bu-KEE	בֻּקִּי
Buzi	Buzi	bu-ZEE	בּוּזִי
Carmel	Carmel	kar-MEL	כַּרְמֶל
Chachalya	Hacaliah	kha-khal-YAH	חֲכַלְיָה
Chagai	Haggai	kha-GAI	חַגַּי
Chana	Hannah	kha-NAH	חַנָּה
Chanamel	Hanamel	kha-nam-AYL	חֲנַמְאֵל
Chanani	Hanani	kha-NA-nee	חֲנָנִי
Chananya	Hananiah	kha-nan-YAH	חֲנַנְיָה
Chaniel	Hanniel	kha-nee-AYL	חַנִּיאֵל
Chanoch	Enoch	kha-NOKH	חֲנוֹךְ
Chava	Eve	kha-VAH	חַוָּה

Hebrew Name	English Name	Pronunciation	Hebrew
Chavakuk	Habakkuk	kha-va-KUK	חֲבַקּוּק
Chermon	Hermon	kher-MON	חֶרְמוֹן
Chetzron	Hezron	khetz-RON	חֶצְרוֹן
Chever	Heber	KHE-ver	חֶבֶר
Chevron	Hebron	khev-RON	חֶבְרוֹן
Chilkiyahu	Hilkiah	khil-ki-YA-hu	חִלְקִיָּהוּ
Chizkiyahu	Hezekiah	khiz-ki-YA-hu	חִזְקִיָּהוּ
Chofni	Hophni	khof-NEE	חָפְנִי
Chogla	Hoglah	khog-LAH	חָגְלָה
Chulda	Hulda	khul-DAH	חֻלְדָּה
Chur	Hur	Khur	חוּר
Dan	Dan	Dan	דָּן
Daniel	Daniel	da-ni-YAYL	דָּנִיֵּאל
Datan	Dathan	da-TAN	דָּתָן
David	David	da-VID	דָּוִד
Devora	Deborah	d'-vo-RAH	דְּבוֹרָה
Dina	Dinah	DEE-nah	דִּינָה
Doeg Ha'adomi	Doeg the Edomite	do-AYG ha-a-do-MEE	דּוֹאֵג הָאֲדֹמִי
Efraim	Ephraim	ef-RA-yim	אֶפְרַיִם
Efrat	Ephrat	ef-RAT	אֶפְרָתָה
Efrat	Ephrathah	ef-RA-tah	אֶפְרָתָה
Ehud	Ehud	ay-HUD	אֵהוּד
Eila	Elah	AY-lah	אֵלָה
Eilon	Elon	ay-LON	אֵילוֹן
Ein Gedi	En-gedi	ayn GE-dee	עֵין גֶּדִי
Elazar	Eleazar	el-a-ZAR	אֶלְעָזָר
Elchanan	Elhanan	el-kha-NAN	אֶלְחָנָן
Eli	Eli	ay-LEE	עֵלִי
Eliav	Eliab	e-lee-AV	אֱלִיאָב
Elidad	Elidad	e-lee-DAD	אֱלִידָד
Eliezer	Eliezer	e-lee-E-zer	אֱלִיעֶזֶר
Elimelech	Elimelech	e-lee-ME-lekh	אֱלִימֶלֶךְ
Elisha	Elisha	e-lee-SHA	אֱלִישָׁע

Hebrew Name	English Name	Pronunciation	Hebrew
Elishama	Elishama	e-lee-sha-MA	אֱלִישָׁמָע
Elisheva	Elisheba	e-lee-SHE-va	אֱלִישֶׁבַע
Elitzafan	Eli-zaphan	e-lee-tza-FAN	אֱלִיצָפָן
Elitzur	Elizur	e-lee-TZUR	אֱלִיצוּר
Eliyahu	Elijah	ay-li-YA-hu	אֵלִיָּהוּ
Elkana	Elkanah	el-ka-NAH	אֶלְקָנָה
Elyasaf	Eliasaph	el-ya-SAF	אֶלְיָסָף
Elyashiv	Eliashib	el-ya-SHEEV	אֶלְיָשִׁיב
Enosh	Enosh	e-NOSH	אֱנוֹשׁ
Er	Er	ayr	עֵר
Eshtaol	Eshtaol	esh-ta-OL	אֶשְׁתָּאֹל
Esther	Esther	es-TAYR	אֶסְתֵּר
Eved Melech	Ebed-melech	E-ved ME-lekh	עֶבֶד־מֶלֶךְ
Even Ha-Ezer	Eben-Ezer	E-ven ha-E-zer	אֶבֶן הָעֵזֶר
Ever	Eber	AY-ver	עֵבֶר
Evyatar	Abiathar	ev-ya-TAR	אֶבְיָתָר
Ezra	Ezra	ez-RA	עֶזְרָא
Gad	Gad	gad	גָּד
Gadi	Gaddi	ga-DEE	גַּדִּי
Gadiel	Gaddiel	ga-dee-AYL	גַּדִּיאֵל
Gamliel	Gamaliel	gam-lee-AYL	גַּמְלִיאֵל
Gedalia	Gedaliah	g'-dal-YA (hu)	גְּדַלְיָהוּ
Gedera	Gederah	g'-day-RAH	גְּדֵרָה
Gershom	Gershom	gay-r'-SHOM	גֵּרְשׁוֹם
Gershon	Gershon	gay-r'-SHON	גֵּרְשׁוֹן
Geshem	Geshem	GE-shem	גֶּשֶׁם
Geuel	Geuel	g'-u-AYL	גְּאוּאֵל
Gidon	Gideon	gid-ON	גִּדְעוֹן
Gilad	Gilead	gil-AD	גִּלְעָד
Gilgal	Gilgal	gil-GAL	גִּלְגָּל
Giva	Gibeah	giv-AH	גִּבְעָה
Givon	Gibeon	giv-ON	גִּבְעוֹן
Hadassa	Hadassah	ha-da-SAH	הֲדַסָּה

Hebrew Name	English Name	Pronunciation	Hebrew
Har Eival	Mount Ebal	ay-VAL	הַר עֵיבָל
Har Gerizim	Mount Gerizim	g'-ri-ZEEM	הַר גְּרִזִים
Har HaBayit	Temple Mount	har ha-BA-yit	הַר הַבַּיִת
Har HaZeitim	the Mount of Olives	har ha-zay-TEEM	הַר הַזֵּיתִים
Hashem	Lord/God		
Hayman	Heman	hay-MAN	הֵימָן
Hoshea	Hosea	ho-SHAY-a	הוֹשֵׁעַ
Ido	Iddo	i-DO	עִדּוֹ
Imanu-El	Immanuel	i-MA-nu ayl	עִמָּנוּ אֵל
Ish-boshet	Ish-bosheth	eesh BO-shet	אִישׁ־בֹּשֶׁת
Itamar	Ithamar	ee-ta-MAR	אִיתָמָר
Itiel	Ithiel	ee-tee-AYL	אִיתִיאֵל
Ivtzan	Ibzan	iv-TZAN	אִבְצָן
Iyov	Job	i-YOV	אִיּוֹב
Kadmiel	Kadmiel	kad-mee-AYL	קַדְמִיאֵל
Kalev	Caleb	ka-LAYV	כָּלֵב
Keesh	Kish	keesh	קִישׁ
Kehat	Kohath	k'-HAT	קְהָת
Keinan	Kenan	kay-NAN	קֵינָן
Kemuel	Kemuel	k'-mu-AYL	קְמוּאֵל
Keruvim	Cherubim	k'-ru-VEEM	כְּרוּבִים
Kilyon	Chilion	kil-YON	כִּלְיוֹן
Kiryat Arba	Kiriath-arba	keer-YAT AR-bah	קִרְיַת אַרְבַּע
Kiryat Sefer	Kiriath-sepher	keer-YAT SAY-fer	קִרְיַת־סֵפֶר
Kiryat Ye'arim	Kiriath-jearim	keer-YAT y'-a-REEM	קִרְיַת יְעָרִים
Kislev	Chislev	kis-LAYV	כִּסְלֵו
Kohanim	Priests	ko-ha-NEEM	כֹּהֲנִים
Kohelet	Koheleth	ko-HE-let	קֹהֶלֶת
Kohen	Priest	ko-HAYN	כֹּהֵן
Kohen Gadol	High Priest	ko-HAYN ga-DOL	כֹּהֵן גָּדוֹל
Korach	Korah	KO-rakh	קֹרַח
Kushi	Cushi	ku-SHEE	כּוּשִׁי
Lachish	Lachish	la-KHEESH	לָכִישׁ

Hebrew Name	English Name	Pronunciation	Hebrew
Leah	Leah	lay-AH	לֵאָה
Lemech	Lamech	LE-mekh	לֶמֶךְ
Lemuel	Lemuel	l'-mu-AYL	לְמוּאֵל
Levi	Levi	lay-VEE	לֵוִי
Leviim	Levites	l'-vee-IM	לְוִיִם
Machla	Mahlah	makh-LAH	מַחְלָה
Machlon	Mahlon	makh-LON	מַחְלוֹן
Machseya	Mahseiah	makh-say-YAH	מַחְסֵיָה
Malachi	Malachi	mal-a-KHEE	מַלְאָכִי
Manoach	Manoah	ma-NO-akh	מָנוֹחַ
Mashiach	Messiah	ma-SHEE-akh	מָשִׁיחַ
Mefiboshet	Mephibosheth	m'-fee-VO-shet	מְפִיבֹשֶׁת
Mehalalel	Mahalalel	ma-ha-lal-AYL	מַהֲלַלְאֵל
Menachem	Menahem	m'-na-KHAYM	מְנַחֵם
Menashe	Menasseh	m'-na-SHEH	מְנַשֶּׁה
Menorah	Candlestick	m'-no-RAH	מְנֹרָה
Merari	Merari	m'-ra-REE	מְרָרִי
Metushelach	Methusaleh	m'-tu-SHE-lakh	מְתוּשֶׁלַח
Micha	Micah	mee-KHAH	מִיכָה
Michael	Michael	mee-kha-AYL	מִיכָאֵל
Michaihu	Micaiah	mee-KHAI-hu	מִיכָיְהוּ
Michal	Michal	mee-KHAL	מִיכַל
Milka	Milcah	mil-KAH	מִלְכָּה
Miriam	Miriam	mir-YAM	מִרְיָם
Mishael	Mishael	mee-sha-AYL	מִישָׁאֵל
Mishkan	Tabernacle	mish-KAN	מִשְׁכָּן
Mitzpa	Mizpah	mitz-PAH	מִצְפָּה
Mizbayach	Altar	miz-BAY-akh	מִזְבֵּחַ
Mordechai	Mordecai	mor-d'-KHAI	מָרְדֳּכַי
Moriah	Moriah	mo-ri-YAH	מוֹרִיָּה
Moshe	Moses	mo-SHEH	מֹשֶׁה
Nachbi	Nahbi	nakh-BEE	נַחְבִּי
Nachor	Nahor	na-KHOR	נָחוֹר

Hebrew Name	English Name	Pronunciation	Hebrew
Nachshon	Nahshon	nakh-SHON	נַחְשׁוֹן
Nachum	Nahum	na-KHUM	נַחוּם
Nadav	Nadab	na-DAV	נָדָב
Naftali	Naphtali	naf-ta-LEE	נַפְתָּלִי
Naomi	Naomi	na-o-MEE	נָעֳמִי
Natan	Nathan	na-TAN	נָתָן
Naval	Nabal	na-VAL	נָבָל
Navi	Prophet	na-VEE	נָבִיא
Navot	Naboth	na-VAL	נָבֹל
Nechemya	Nehemiah	n'-khem-YAH	נְחֶמְיָה
Negev	Negeb	NE-gev	נֶגֶב
Nerya	Neriah	nay-ri-YAH	נֵרִיָּה
Netanel	Nethanel	n'-tan-AYL	נְתַנְאֵל
Neviah	Prophetess	n'-vee-AH	נְבִיאָה
Neviim	Prophets	n'-vee-EEM	נְבִיאִים
Nisan	Nisan	nee-SAN	נִיסָן
Noa	Noah	no-AH	נֹעָה
Noach	Noah	NO-akh	נֹחַ
Nov	Nob	nov	נֹב
Nun	Nun	nun	נוּן
Oded	Oded	o-DAYD	עוֹדֵד
Ohola	Oholah	a-ho-LAH	אָהֳלָה
Oholiav	Oholiab	o-ha-lee-AV	אָהֳלִיאָב
Oholiva	Oholibah	a-ho-lee-VAH	אָהֳלִיבָה
Omri	Omri	om-REE	עָמְרִי
Onan	Onan	o-NAN	אוֹנָן
Otniel	Othniel	ot-nee-AYL	עָתְנִיאֵל
Ovadya	Obadiah	o-vad-YAH	עֹבַדְיָה
Oved	Obed	o-VAYD	עוֹבֵד
Oved Edom	Obed Edom	o-VAYD e-DOM	עוֹבֵד אֱדוֹם
Pagiel	Pagiel	pag-ee-AYL	פַּגְעִיאֵל
Palti	Palti	pal-TEE	פַּלְטִי
Paltiel	Paltiel	pal-tee-AYL	פַּלְטִיאֵל

Hebrew Name	English Name	Pronunciation	Hebrew
Pekach	Pekah	PE-kakh	פֶּקַח
Pedael	Pedahel	p'-da-AYL	פְּדָהאֵל
Pekachya	Pekahiah	p'-kakh-YAH	פְּקַחְיָה
Peleg	Peleg	PE-leg	פֶּלֶג
Penina	Peninnah	p'-ni-NAH	פְּנִנָּה
Peretz	Perez	PE-retz	פֶּרֶץ
Petuel	Pethuel	p'-tu-AYL	פְּתוּאֵל
Pinchas	Phinehas	peen-KHAS	פִּינְחָס
Rachel	Rachel	ra-KHAYL	רָחֵל
Ram	Ram	ram	רָם
Rama	Ramah	ra-MAH	רָמָה
Re'u	Reu	r'-U	רְעוּ
Rechovam	Rehoboam	r'-khav-AM	רְחַבְעָם
Reuven	Reuben	r'-u-VAYN	רְאוּבֵן
Rivka	Rebecca	riv-KAH	רִבְקָה
Rut	Ruth	rut	רוּת
Salma	Salmon/Salmah	sal-MAH	שַׂלְמָה
Salmon	Salmon	sal-MON	שַׂלְמוֹן
Sara	Sarah	sa-RAH	שָׂרָה
Sarai	Sarai	sa-RAI	שָׂרַי
Selah	Selah	SE-lah	סֶלָה
Seraya	Seraiah	s'-ra-YAH	שְׂרָיָה
Serug	Serug	s'-RUG	שְׂרוּג
Setur	Sethur	s'-TUR	סְתוּר
Shaarayim	Shaaraim	sha-a-RA-yim	שַׁעֲרַיִם
Shabbat	Sabbath	sha-BAT	שַׁבָּת
Shabbatot	Sabbaths	sha-ba-TOT	שַׁבָּתוֹת
Shafan	Shaphan	sha-FAN	שָׁפָן
Shafat	Shaphat	sha-FAT	שָׁפָט
Shalem	Salem	sha-LAYM	שָׁלֵם
Shalum	Shallum	sha-LUM	שַׁלּוּם
Shamgar	Shamgar	sham-GAR	שַׁמְגַּר
Shamua	Shammua	sha-MU-a	שַׁמּוּעַ

Hebrew Name	English Name	Pronunciation	Hebrew
Shaul	Saul	sha-UL	שָׁאוּל
Shealtiel	Shealtiel	sh'-al-tee-AYL	שְׁאַלְתִּיאֵל
Shear Yashuv	Shear-Jashub	sh'-AR ya-SHUV	שְׁאָר יָשׁוּב
Shechanya	Shecaniah	sh'-khan-YAH	שְׁכַנְיָה
Shechem	Shechem	sh'-KHEM	שְׁכֶם
Sheila	Shelah	shay-LAH	שֵׁלָה
Shelach	Shelah	SHE-lakh	שֶׁלַח
Shelumiel	Shelumiel	sh'-lu-mee-AYL	שְׁלֻמִיאֵל
Shem	Shem	Shaym	שֵׁם
Shemaya	Shemaiah	sh'-ma-YAH	שְׁמַעְיָה
Sheshbatzar	Sheshbazzar	shaysh-ba-TZAR	שֵׁשְׁבַּצַּר
Shet	Seth	Shayt	שֵׁת
Shevat	Shebat	sh'-VAT	שְׁבָט
Shilo	Shiloh	shi-LOH	שִׁלֹה
Shim'i	Shimei	shim-EE	שִׁמְעִי
Shimon	Simeon	shim-ON	שִׁמְעוֹן
Shimshon	Samson	shim-SHON	שִׁמְשׁוֹן
Shlomo	Solomon	sh'-lo-MOH	שְׁלֹמֹה
Shmuel	Samuel	sh'-mu-AYL	שְׁמוּאֵל
Shofar	Horn	sho-FAR	שׁוֹפָר
Shofarot	Horns	sho-fa-ROT	שׁוֹפָרוֹת
Shomron	Samaria	sho-m'-RON	שֹׁמְרוֹן
Sivan	Sivan	see-VAN	סִיוָן
Tamar	Tamar	ta-MAR	תָּמָר
Tanakh	Hebrew Bible	ta-NAKH	תָּנַ"ךְ
Tapuach	Tappuah	ta-PU-akh	תַּפּוּחַ
Tavor	Tabor	ta-VOR	תָּבוֹר
Tekoa	Tekoa	t'-KO-a	תְּקוֹעָה
Terach	Terah	TE-rakh	תֶּרַח
Teveria	Tiberias	t'-ver-YAH	טְבֶרְיָה
Tevet	Tebeth	tay-VAYT	טֵבֵת
Tirtza	Tirzah	tir-TZAH	תִּרְצָה
Tola	Tola	to-LA	תּוֹלָע

Hebrew Name	English Name	Pronunciation	Hebrew
Tzadok	Zadok	tza-DOK	צָדוֹק
Tzefanya	Zephaniah	tz'-fan-YAH	צְפַנְיָה
Tzelofchad	Zelophehad	tz'-la-f'-KHAD	צְלָפְחָד
Tzeruya	Zeruiah	tz'-ru-YAH	צְרוּיָה
Tzfat	Safed	tz'-FAT	צְפַת
Tzidkiyahu	Zedekiah	tzid-ki-YA-hu	צִדְקִיָּהוּ
Tziklag	Ziklag	tzi-k'-LAG	צִקְלַג
Tzion	Zion	tzi-YON	צִיּוֹן
Tzipora	Zipporah	tzi-po-RAH	צִפֹּרָה
Tzora	Zorah	tzor-AH	צָרְעָה
Tzuriel	Zuriel	tzu-ree-AYL	צוּרִיאֵל
Ukal	Ucal	u-KAL	אֻכָל
Uri	Uri	u-REE	אוּרִי
Uriya	Uriah	u-ri-YAH	אוּרִיָּה
Utz	Uz	Utz	עוּץ
Uzziyahu	Uzziah	u-zi-YA-hu	עֻזִיָּהוּ
Yaakov	Jacob	ya-a-KOV	יַעֲקֹב
Yachaziel	Jahaziel	ya-kha-zee-AYL	יַחֲזִיאֵל
Yael	Jael	ya-AYL	יָעֵל
Yaffo	Joppa/Jaffa	ya-FO	יָפוֹ
Yair	Jair	ya-EER	יָאִיר
Yakeh	Jakeh	ya-KEH	יָקֶה
Yarden	Jordan	yar-DAYN	יַרְדֵּן
Yarmut	Jarmuth	yar-MUT	יַרְמוּת
Yechezkel	Ezekiel	y'-khez-KAYL	יְחֶזְקֵאל
Yechiel	Jehiel	y'-khee-AYL	יְחִיאֵל
Yechonya	Jeconiah	y'-khon-YAH	יְכָנְיָה
Yedutun	Jeduthun	y'-du-TUN	יְדוּתוּן
Yehoachaz	Jehoahaz	y'-ho-a-KHAZ	יְהוֹאָחָז
Yehoash	Jehoash	y'-ho-ASH	יְהוֹאָשׁ
Yehochanan	Jehohanan	y'-ho-kha-NAN	יְהוֹחָנָן
Yehonatan	Jonathan	y'-ho-na-TAN	יְהוֹנָתָן
Yehoram	Jehoram	y'-ho-RAM	יְהוֹרָם

Hebrew Name	English Name	Pronunciation	Hebrew
Yehoshafat	Jehoshaphat	y'-ho-sha-FAT	יְהוֹשָׁפָט
Yehoshavat	Jehoshabeath	y'-ho-shav-AT	יְהוֹשַׁבְעַת
Yehosheva	Jehosheba	y-ho-SHE-va	יְהוֹשֶׁבַע
Yehoshua	Joshua	y'-ho-SHU-a	יְהוֹשֻׁעַ
Yehotzadak	Jehozadak	y'-ho-tza-DAK	יְהוֹצָדָק
Yehoyachin	Jehoiachin	y'-ho-ya-KHEEN	יְהוֹיָכִין
Yehoyada	Jehoiada	y'-ho-ya-DA	יְהוֹיָדָע
Yehoyakim	Jehoiakim	y'-ho-ya-KEEM	יְהוֹיָקִים
Yehu	Jehu	yay-HU	יֵהוּא
Yehuda	Judah	y'-hu-DAH	יְהוּדָה
Yehudi	Jew	y'-hu-DEE	יְהוּדִי
Yehudim	Jews	y'-hu-DEEM	יְהוּדִים
Yered	Jared	YE-red	יֶרֶד
Yericho	Jericho	y'-ree-KHO	יְרִיחוֹ
Yerovam	Jeroboam	ya-rov-AM	יָרָבְעָם
Yerubaal	Jerubbaal	y'-ru-BA-al	יְרֻבַּעַל
Yerushalayim	Jerusalem	y'-ru-sha-LA-yim	יְרוּשָׁלַיִם
Yeshayahu	Isaiah	y'-sha-YA-hu	יְשַׁעְיָהוּ
Yeshua	Jeshua	yay-SHU-a	יֵשׁוּעַ
Yiftach	Jephthah	yif-TAKH	יִפְתָּח
Yigal	Igal	yig-AL	יִגְאָל
Yirmiyahu	Jeremiah	yir-m'-YA-hu	יִרְמִיָהוּ
Yishai	Jesse	yi-SHAI	יִשַׁי
Yisrael	Israel	yis-ra-AYL	יִשְׂרָאֵל
Yissachar	Issachar	yi-sa-KHAR	יִשָּׂשכָר
Yitzchak	Issac	yitz-KHAK	יִצְחָק
Yizrael	Jezreel	yiz-r'-EL	יִזְרְעֵאל
Yoash	Joash	yo-ASH	יוֹאָשׁ
Yoav	Joab	yo-AV	יוֹאָב
Yochanan	Johanan	yo-kha-NAN	יוֹחָנָן
Yocheved	Jochebed	yo-KHE-ved	יוֹכֶבֶד
Yoel	Joel	yo-AYL	יוֹאֵל
Yona	Jonah	yo-NAH	יוֹנָה

Hebrew Name	English Name	Pronunciation	Hebrew
Yonadav	Jonadab	yo-na-DAV	יוֹנָדָב
Yonatan	Jonathan	yo-na-TAN	יוֹנָתָן
Yoram	Joram	yo-RAM	יוֹרָם
Yosef	Joseph	yo-SAYF	יוֹסֵף
Yoshiyahu	Josiah	yo-shi-YA-hu	יֹאשִׁיָּהוּ
Yotam	Jotham	yo-TAM	יוֹתָם
Yotzadak	Jozadak	yo-tza-DAK	יוֹצָדָק
Yozavad	Jozabad	yo-za-VAD	יוֹזָבָד
Zanoach	Zanoah	za-NO-akh	זָנוֹחַ
Zecharya	Zechariah	z'-khar-YAH	זְכַרְיָה
Zerach	Zerah	ZE-rakh	זֶרַח
Zerubavel	Zerubbabel	z'-ru-ba-VEL	זְרֻבָּבֶל
Zevulun	Zebulun	z'-vu-LUN	זְבוּלֻן
Zilpa	Zilpah	zil-PAH	זִלְפָּה
Zimri	Zimri	zim-REE	זִמְרִי

Jewish Holidays

Chanukah	Hanukkah	kha-nu-KAH	חֲנוּכָּה
Pesach	Passover	PE-sakh	פֶּסַח
Purim	Purim	pu-REEM	פּוּרִים
Rosh Hashana	Jewish New Year	rosh ha-sha-NAH	רֹאשׁ הַשָּׁנָה
Shavuot	Feast of Weeks	sha-vu-OT	שָׁבוּעוֹת
Shemini Atzeret	Eight Day of Assembly	sh'-mee-NEE a-TZE-ret	שְׁמִינִי עֲצֶרֶת
Sukkot	Feast of Tabernacles	su-KOT	סֻכּוֹת
Yom Kippur	Day of Atonement	yom kee-PUR	יוֹם כִּיפּוּר

Biblical Measurements

Amah	Cubit	a-MAH	אַמָּה
Amot	Cubits	a-MOT	אַמּוֹת
Bat	Bath	bat	בַּת
Batim	Baths	ba-TEEM	בָּתִּים
Beka	half-shekel	BE-ka	בֶּקַע

Hebrew Name	English Name	Pronunciation	Hebrew
Chomarim	Homers	kho-ma-REEM	חֳמָרִים
Chomer	Homer	KHO-mer	חֹמֶר
Efah	Ephah	ay-FAH	אֵיפָה
Geira	Gerah	gay-RAH	גֵּרָה
Gomed	Gomed	GO-med	גֹּמֶד
Hin	Hin	heen	הִין
Kav	kab	kav	קַב
Kesita	kesitah	k'-see-TAH	קְשִׂיטָה
Kikar	talent	ki-KAR	כִּכָּר
Kikarim	talents	ki-ka-RIM	כִּכָּרִים
Kor	kor	kor	כֹּר
Letek	lethech	LE-tek	לֶתֶךְ
Log	Log	log	לֹג
Maneh	Mina	ma-NEH	מָנֶה
Manim	Minas	ma-NEEM	מָנִים
Omer	Omer	O-mer	עֹמֶר
Pim	Pim	peem	פִּים
Se'ah	Seah	say-AH	סְאָה
Se'eem	Seahs	s'-EEM	סְאִים
Shekalim	Shekels	sh'-ka-LEEM	שְׁקָלִים
Shekel	Shekel	SHE-kel	שֶׁקֶל
Tefach	Handbreadth	TE-fakh	טֶפַח
Zeret	Span	ZE-ret	זֶרֶת

Index

This index contains the names of people, places and concepts mentioned in the commentary of *The Israel Bible*.

Aaronsohn, Sarah, 695
Abrabanel, Rabbi Yitzchak, 108, 503, 1449, 1909, 1987
Achad Ha'am, 1730, 1818
Adam (Adam), 13, 61, 285, 995, 1401, 1639, 1987
Agnon, Shmuel Yosef, 1576
Aharon (Aaron), 308, 333, 338, 346, 352, 379, 1064, 1496, 1590, 1857
Allon, Yigal, 1421
Anatot (Anathoth), 1073, 1151, 1165
Arbel Valley, 1493
Archaeology, 541, 569, 659, 746, 1485, 1504, 1553, 1627, 1630, 1951, 2011
Aron (Ark), 338, 359, 657, 749, 829, 1632, 2003, 2023, 2025, 2030, 2064
Ashdod (Ashdod), 657, 669, 1005, 1186
Asher (Asher), 2009
Ashkelon (Ashkelon), 1186
Atlit, 1826
Avraham (Abraham), 5, 30, 31, 33, 35, 37, 47, 51, 53, 55, 61, 64, 118, 127, 133, 272, 392, 441, 461, 565, 569, 648, 738, 798, 829, 847, 953, 1026, 1496, 1552, 1635, 1857, 2039
Aviner, Rabbi Shlomo, 527, 539, 567, 594, 606, 647, 655, 675, 690, 778, 782, 821, 840, 935
Azza (Gaza), 1186
B'nei Yisrael (The Children of Israel), 213, 302, 386, 572
Balfour Declaration, 500, 1935
Bar Kochba, 954, 1811
Bar-Ilan, Rabbi Meir, 550
Barak, Ehud, 53

Barkat, Nir, 755
Bat Ayin, 1469, 1489, 2100
Batsheva (Bath-sheba), 693, 758, 762, 807, 1476, 1531, 1652
Be'er Sheva (Beer-sheba), 5, 51, 72, 648, 741
Begin, Menachem, 617, 1338, 1502, 1813
Beit El (Beth-el), 5, 72, 569, 847, 1187, 1365
Beit Hamikdash (Temple), 72, 187, 198, 241, 243, 254, 256, 261, 265, 289, 307, 327, 361, 480, 524, 553, 656, 677, 751, 798, 801, 818, 829, 832, 912, 948, 957, 969, 1211, 1304, 1314, 1433, 1437, 1442, 1504, 1521, 1567, 1575, 1818, 1859, 1911, 1935, 2031, 2068
Beit Lechem (Beth-lehem), 91, 679, 1402, 1632, 1798, 1801
Beit Shean (Beth-shean), 1639
Beit Shemesh (Beth-shemesh), 671
Ben Yehuda, Eliezer, 1932, 1983
Ben-Gurion, David, 294, 456, 550, 887, 1482, 1812, 1921, 1937, 2051
Ben-Zvi, Yitzchak, 828, 1254
Berlin, Rabbi Naftali Tzvi Yehuda, 516, 2044
Bialik, Chaim Nachman, 1420
Binyamin (Benjamin), 524, 654, 662, 1165, 1479, 1495, 1632, 1945, 2011
Braverman, Sarah, 47
Carmel (Carmel), 610, 865, 1625, 1784
Chagai (Haggai), 1331, 1433, 1439, 1858, 1920, 1932
Chana (Hannah), 655, 659, 661, 662, 1858
Chava (Eve), 61, 450, 1339, 1401, 1639
Chavakuk (Habakkuk), 1331, 1417, 1858
Chermon (Hermon), 777, 1473, 1521, 1579, 1625, 1633, 1784

Chevron (Hebron), 5, 55, 61, 324, 434, 565, 567, 656, 738, 898, 1552, 1812, 1974

Chizkiyahu (Hezekiah), 801, 804, 928, 934, 951, 970, 976, 990, 1003, 1015, 1020, 1022, 1136, 1332, 1395, 1561, 1627, 1979, 2121, 2129

Cohen, Eli, 730

Dan (Dan), 741, 777, 1187

Daniel (Daniel), 988, 1237, 1417, 1879, 1902, 1917

David (David), 98, 630, 655, 662, 675, 693, 697, 700, 1018, 1060, 1402, 1435, 1471, 1476, 1486, 1494, 1498, 1502, 1504, 1508, 1531, 1537, 1553, 1606, 1631, 1650

Dayan, Moshe, 609

Dead Sea, 7, 777, 1484, 1490

Declaration of Independence, 790, 1482, 1643

Devora (Deborah), 593, 595, 605, 608, 1549, 1858

Dona Gracia, 605

Eban, Abba, 1823

Efraim (Ephraim), 127, 578, 595, 617, 1946

Efrat (Ephrathah), 91, 1402, 1473, 1632

Ein Gedi (En-gedi), 1473, 1535, 1783, 1787

Elisha (Elisha), 867, 886, 1183, 1332, 1335, 1417, 1508, 1857

Eliyahu (Elijah), 802, 865, 867, 873, 883, 1332, 1470, 1857

Eshkol, Levi, 1534, 1813

Eshtaol (Eshtaol), 1293

Exile, 13, 14, 19, 22, 91, 204, 232, 297, 492, 578, 937, 947, 951, 992, 1074, 1105, 1137, 1188, 1207, 1215, 1231, 1294, 1627, 1637, 1731, 1809, 1839, 1856, 1861, 1879

Ezra (Ezra), 1463, 1625, 1919, 1937, 1942, 1985

First Lebanon War, 1813

Gad (Gad), 418, 420, 445, 560

Gichon (Gihon), 746, 1458

Gidon (Gideon), 595, 615, 617, 1043, 1496, 1572

Gilad (Gilead), 1096, 1473, 1605, 1784

Gilgal (Gilgal), 503, 539, 818, 1522

Ginsberg, Asher, 1730

Gush Etzion, 671, 766, 1489, 1827, 2100

Haganah, 47, 617, 1631

Halevi, Rabbi Judah, 16, 1142, 1738, 1772, 1880, 1943

Har HaBayit (Temple Mount), 175, 525, 677, 829, 1312, 1476, 1828, 2076

Har HaZeitim (the Mount of Olives), 772

Herzl, Theodore, 280

Hesder, 587

Hirsch, Rabbi Samson Raphael, 13, 38, 89, 104, 127, 164, 213, 1092, 1513, 1553, 1606, 1741

Holocaust, 425, 802, 1053, 1296, 1428

Hula Lake Park, 1473

Ibn Ezra, Rabbi Abraham, 195, 1041, 1361, 1465, 1629, 1637

Ingathering of the Exiles, 514, 527, 861, 995, 1254, 1275, 1289, 1298, 2141

Jordan River, 33, 437, 461, 531, 777, 891, 1473, 1521, 1546

Kaplan, Rabbi Aryeh, 1521

Keilah, 1469, 1506

Kimchi, Rabbi David, 47

Kiryat Arba (Kiriath-arba), 55, 436, 565

Kiryat Sefer (Kiriath-sepher), 598

Kiryat Ye'arim (Kiriath-jearim), 657

Knesset, 232, 503, 647, 1275, 1428, 1937

Kohanim (Priests), 187, 244, 298, 346, 372, 712, 1439, 1467, 1590, 1985, 2121

Kohen Gadol (High Priest), 285, 578, 714, 829, 1444, 1849, 2058

Kollek, Theodore, 1909

Kook, Rabbi Abraham Isaac, 611, 647, 674, 773, 823, 964, 996, 1144, 1173, 1672, 1739, 1920

Kook, Rabbi Tzvi Yehuda, 600, 631

Korach (Korah), 375, 379, 1744

Koren, Eliyahu, 1937

Kremer, Rabbi Elijah, 1050, 1861

Law of Return, 1275, 1815, 1826

Leah (Leah), 61, 738, 1148

Leibowitz, Nechama, 140

Levi (Levi), 321, 330, 333, 338, 381, 428, 563, 1528, 1542, 1556, 1625, 2003, 2030, 2043, 2047, 2049
Levin, Rabbi Aryeh, 897, 1637
Lichtman, Rabbi Moshe, 55, 191
Luria, Rabbi Isaac, 1707
Machpelah, 61, 565
Maimonides, 191, 908
Masada, 734, 1310
Mashiach (Messiah), 91, 98, 128, 175, 481, 611, 656, 802, 867, 883, 902, 926, 1009, 1385, 1453, 1797
Meir Simcha of Dvinsk, 514
Meir, Golda, 158, 280, 571, 1813, 1892, 2032
Meiri, Rabbi Menachem, 1516
Menashe (Menasseh), 127, 431, 560, 926, 1298, 1605, 2012
Menorah (Candlestick), 232, 308, 352, 361, 1103, 1314, 1445, 1446, 1630, 1967, 1974, 2067
Migdal Oz, 1469, 1542
Miriam (Miriam), 1858
Mishkan (Tabernacle), 135, 198, 208, 227, 234, 239, 243, 261, 265, 572, 584, 655, 659, 666, 818, 1522, 1566, 2043, 2068
Mizbayach (Altar), 256, 347, 2076
Mordechai (Mordecai), 228, 1856, 1861, 1866, 1877
Moriah (Moriah), 71, 1522, 1553
Moshe (Moses), 141, 164, 323, 333, 361, 363, 375, 386, 405, 418, 433, 437, 446, 519, 524, 541, 558, 644, 697, 1110, 1546, 1857
Mount of Olives, 56, 772, 1473, 1476
Naftali (Naphtali), 434, 529
Nahmanides, 317, 954
Navon, Yitzchak, 1438
Negev (Negeb), 169, 201, 303, 648, 1255, 1483, 1546
Netanyahu, Benjamin, 352, 391, 1814, 2085
NILI, 695
Noach (Noah), 22, 25, 1013, 1147, 1967, 1987
Noahide Laws, 908, 993
Olmert, Ehud, 1813

Omri (Omri), 803, 858, 1793, 2094
Operation Protective Edge, 1814
Peres, Shimon, 550, 1932
Pesach (Passover), 150, 224, 303, 355, 408, 495, 944, 1101, 1614, 1694, 1783, 1847, 2122, 2138
Pinchas (Phinehas), 399, 1857
Purim (Purim), 228, 1847, 1861, 1875
Rabin, Yitzchak, 184
Rachel (Rachel), 91, 679, 995, 1148, 1632
Reuven (Reuben), 97, 98, 418, 445, 1502
Revivim, 1230, 1546
Riskin, Rabbi Shlomo, 127, 511, 1632
Rivka (Rebecca), 56, 61, 738, 1991
Rivlin, Reuven, 737
Rosh Hanikra, 1469, 1585, 1590
Rosh Hashana (Jewish New Year), 165, 305, 514, 785, 1052, 1173, 1285, 1791
Rut (Ruth), 140, 630, 1482, 1671, 1797, 1800, 1807
Sacks, Rabbi Lord Jonathan, 1014, 1528, 1628
Sara (Sarah), 38, 47, 55, 565, 1652, 1780, 1858
Schneerson, Rabbi Menachem Mendel, 1453, 1755
Second Lebanon War, 640, 1813
Senesh, Chana, 64, 661
Sforno, Rabbi Obadiah, 1840, 1847
Shabbat (Sabbath), 175, 193, 216, 308, 361, 407, 542, 1147, 1707, 1818, 1958
Shamir, Yitzchak, 582
Sharansky, Natan, 514
Sharon, Ariel, 560
Shaul (Saul), 655, 662, 668, 675, 683, 693, 706, 718, 734, 737, 789, 803, 1479, 1495, 1496, 1506, 1532, 1537, 1539, 1606, 2016
Shavuot (Feast of Weeks), 224, 408, 1322, 1797, 1803
Shazar, Zalman, 503
Shechem (Shechem), 87, 125, 434, 503, 620, 1075
Shekel (Shekel), 213
Shemer, Naomi, 1057

Shemini Atzeret (Eight Day of Assembly), 412

Shilo (Shiloh), 128, 572, 584, 655, 657, 659, 677, 818, 1473, 1522, 1566

Shimon (Simeon), 529, 1999

Shimshon (Samson), 593, 631, 635, 640

Shlomo (Solomon), 241, 656, 741, 746, 751, 762, 801, 807, 810, 814, 817, 818, 823, 832, 839, 840, 1401, 1458, 1529, 1575, 1629, 1651, 1831, 1900, 2031, 2040, 2055, 2060, 2077

Shlomo son of Yitzchak (Rashi), 3, 10, 73, 77, 234, 302, 386, 668, 683, 868, 918, 1013, 1089, 1183, 1250, 1349, 1369, 1506, 1667, 1691, 1713, 1744, 1751, 1790, 1799, 1867, 1928, 1992, 2020, 2114

Shneur Zalman of Liadi, 19

Shofar (Horn), 542, 785, 1285, 1630

Shomron (Samaria), 858, 1003, 1075, 1261, 1371, 1374, 1395, 2094

Sinai War, 1812

Six-Day War, 631, 727, 730, 897, 934, 1057, 1576, 1813, 1823, 1921

Soloveitchik, Rabbi Joseph B., 489, 1609, 1627, 1733, 1792, 1817

Stavsky, Rabbi David, 71, 1064, 1100, 1385, 1556, 1731

Sukkot (Feast of Tabernacles), 224, 306, 307, 408, 412, 480, 832, 1322, 1377, 1461, 1832, 1967

Tamar (Tamar), 98, 1992

Tavor (Tabor), 606, 1340, 1473, 1579

Tekoa (Tekoa), 766

Timna Park, 265, 1473, 1485

Tiveria (Tiberias), 601, 1473, 1527, 1974

Truman, Harry, 1935

Twain, Mark, 317

Tzfat (Safed), 954, 1812, 1974

Tzidkiyahu (Zedekiah), 804, 1123, 1137, 1167, 1170, 1232, 1279

Tzion (Zion), 746, 749, 773, 969, 1038, 1059, 1084, 1383, 1384, 1530, 1576, 1628

War of Attrition, 1813

War of Independence, 687, 1576, 1812

Weizmann, Chaim, 1995

Western Wall, 469, 631, 832, 897, 1637, 1647, 1813, 1921

Wiesel, Elie, 1038

Wolfsohn, David, 330

Yaakov (Jacob), 569, 620, 648, 679, 738, 847, 1057, 1199, 1367, 1384, 1542, 1857, 1987, 2122

Yad Vashem, 1053

Yadin, Yigael, 541, 828

Yael (Jael), 607, 1549

Yaffo (Joppa/Jaffa), 1812

Yechezkel (Ezekiel), 154, 1207, 1211, 1218, 1220, 1237, 1314, 1858

Yehonatan (Jonathan), 690, 703, 706, 716, 734, 737

Yehoshua (Joshua), 366, 445, 516, 527, 550, 567, 578, 589, 1043, 1183

Yehuda (Judah), 97, 98, 258, 331, 529, 636

Yehudi (Jew), 258, 1930

Yericho (Jericho), 541, 542, 1473, 1630

Yerushalayim (Jerusalem), 35, 241, 243, 248, 321, 379, 481, 553, 584, 656, 749, 773, 836, 846, 853

Yeshayahu (Isaiah), 951, 966, 970, 1009, 1030, 1063

Yirmiyahu (Jeremiah), 91, 307, 1073, 1077, 1092, 1136, 1140, 1142, 1151, 1163, 1165, 1178, 1232, 1535, 1733, 1809, 1896, 1919, 2141

Yishai (Jesse), 1402, 1554, 1807

Yishi, 1469, 1499

Yissachar (Issachar), 129, 529

Yitzchak (Isaac), 4, 40, 63, 65, 648, 1857

Yizrael (Jezreel), 1335

Yom Hashoah (Holocaust Remembrance Day), 1296, 1428

Yom Kippur (Day of Atonement), 285, 829, 1444, 1483, 1849

Yom Kippur War, 1573, 1813, 2032

Yona (Jonah), 918, 1332, 1387, 1389, 1391, 1392, 1857

Yonatan (Jonathan), 687, 789, 1539

217

Yosef (Joseph), 77, 95, 97, 101, 108, 118, 125, 132, 142, 405, 1502, 1946

Yoshiyahu (Josiah), 801, 804, 847, 935, 940, 944, 1125, 1417, 1425, 2135, 2138

Zecharya (Zechariah), 481, 772, 1265, 1332, 1383, 1433, 1439, 1442, 1461

Zerubavel (Zerubbabel), 1921, 1986

Zevulun (Zebulun), 129, 529

Zionist Congress, 184, 330, 1275

Photo Credits

Book	Verse	Photo Credit
Genesis	1:01	Mark Neyman, GPO
Genesis	2:05	Mark Neyman, GPO
Genesis	7:19	Nathan Alpert, GPO
Genesis	8:09	Ryan Rodrick Beiler, Shutterstock.com
Genesis	13:10	Bill Rice, Wikimedia Commons
Genesis	14:18	Stefano Rocca, Shutterstock.com
Genesis	18:01	Eitan F., Wikimedia Commons
Genesis	21:31	Dr. Avishai Teicher, Wikimedia Commons
Genesis	22:18	Moshe Milner, GPO
Genesis	23:19	Avi Ohayon, GPO
Genesis	24:10	Elbud, Shutterstock.com
Genesis	25:09	David Rabkin, Shutterstock.com
Genesis	28:17	Andrew Shiva, Wikipedia
Genesis	28:19	Dvirraz, Wikimedia Commons
Genesis	33:19	Mark Neyman, GPO
Genesis	35:19	Wikimedia Commons
Genesis	37:02	Moshe Milner, GPO
Genesis	43:11	Moshe Milner, GPO
Genesis	46:04	Luis Villa del Campo, Wikimedia Commons
Genesis	47:30	Moshe Milner, GPO
Genesis	49:13	Mark Neyman, GPO
Exodus	6:08	Jewish Content Images, Shutterstock.com
Exodus	8:15	Mark Neyman, GPO
Exodus	9:01	To1490, Wikimedia Commons
Exodus	13:04	Mark Neyman, GPO
Exodus	13:05	Iusubov Nizami, Shutterstock.com
Exodus	14:19	Reut Gross, Wikimedia Commons
Exodus	16:35	Mark Neyman, GPO
Exodus	19:04	Teddy Brauner, GPO
Exodus	20:21	Moshe Milner, GPO
Exodus	26:15	Mark A. Wilson, Wikimedia Commons
Exodus	29:01	Ekaterina Lin, Shutterstock.com
Exodus	31:17	Zoltan Kluger, GPO
Exodus	34:24	Mark Neyman, GPO

Book	Verse	Photo Credit
Exodus	37:17	SA, Wikimedia Commons
Leviticus	3:01	Noam Chen, goisrael.com
Leviticus	6:05	David, Wikimedia Commons
Leviticus	9:23	Mboesch, Wikimedia Commons
Leviticus	12:03	Ya'akov Sa'ar, GPO
Leviticus	15:13	Avishai Teicher, Wikimedia Commons
Leviticus	16:02	Andrew Shiva, Wikipedia
Leviticus	17:04	Mark Neyman, GPO
Leviticus	23:10	Ya'akov Gefen, GPO
Leviticus	23:39	blueeyes, Shutterstock.com
Leviticus	23:43	Danny W, Wikimedia Commons
Leviticus	25:10	Avi Deror, Wikimedia Commons
Numbers	1:52	Zachi Evenor, goisrael.com
Numbers	2:03	Shlomo, Wikimedia Commons
Numbers	6:26	Mark Neyman, GPO
Numbers	8:02	Avi Ohayon, GPO
Numbers	9:05	Public Domain
Numbers	11;17	Ariely, Wikimedia Commons
Numbers	14:01	Amos Ben Gershom, GPO
Numbers	15:38	Blueeyes, Shutterstock.com
Numbers	17:23	Michal Levinsky, Wikimedia Commons
Numbers	21:05	Amos Ben Gershom, GPO
Numbers	22:11	Amos Ben Gershom, GPO
Numbers	26:02	Moshe Milner, GPO
Numbers	28:09	Tomer Tu, Shutterstock.com
Numbers	32:21	GPO
Numbers	33:53	Zoltan Kluger, GPO
Deuteronomy	1:25	Avi Ohayon, GPO
Deuteronomy	3:18	David 1, Wikimedia Commons
Deuteronomy	8:08	Moshe Milner, GPO
Deuteronomy	12:05	Avi Ohayon, GPO
Deuteronomy	13:05	Israel Defense Forces, Wikimedia Commons
Deuteronomy	16:16	Wikimedia Commons
Deuteronomy	22:07	Yossi Ezra, Pikiwiki
Deuteronomy	23:08	Kobi Gideon, GPO
Deuteronomy	24:20	Mark Neyman, GPO

Book	Verse	Photo Credit
Deuteronomy	26:01	Zoltan Kluger, GPO
Deuteronomy	27:05	Yuval Y, Wikimedia Commons
Deuteronomy	32:01	Mark Neyman, GPO
Deuteronomy	33:12	Flik47, Shutterstock.com
Joshua	1:02	Alefbet, Shutterstock.com
Joshua	4:20	Adam Zartal, Wikimedia Commons
Joshua	6:15	A. Sobkowski, via Wikimedia Commons
Joshua	9:27	Ar2332, via Wikimedia Commons
Joshua	14:13	David Rabkin, Shutterstock.com
Joshua	15:13	Mboesch, Wikimedia Commons
Joshua	16:02	Avi Deror, Wikimedia Commons
Joshua	18:01	Moshe Milner, GPO
Joshua	19:50	Shuki, Wikimedia Commons
Joshua	22:12	Beit Hashalom, Wikimedia Commons
Joshua	23:06	Yeshivat Shilo
Judges	4:06	Everett Historical, Shutterstock.com
Judges	9:01	Robert Hoetink, Shutterstock.com
Judges	19:30	Kobi Gideon, GPO
Judges	20:01	Irina Opachevsky, Shutterstock.com
I Samuel	1:10	Roman Yanushevsky, Shutterstock.com
I Samuel	5:01	Roman Yanushevsky, Shutterstock.com
I Samuel	6:09	Nina Mikryukova, Shutterstock.com
I Samuel	10:02	Irit Levi, Wikimedia Commons
I Samuel	13:19	Doron Talmi, Wikimedia Commons
I Samuel	16:11	Lerner Vadim, Shutterstock.com
I Samuel	17:26	Wilson44691, Wikimedia Commons
I Samuel	20:18	Zeev Veez, Wikimedia Commons
I Samuel	22:13	Avishai Teicher Pikiwiki, Wikimedia Commons
I Samuel	25:28	Reut Gross, Wikimedia Commons
I Samuel	28:03	Mosesr, Shutterstock.com
I Samuel	29:02	Irisphoto1, Shutterstock.com
I Samuel	31:04	Andrew Shiva, Wikimedia Commons
II Samuel	1:23	GPO
II Samuel	2:04	Ya'akov Sa'ar, GPO
II Samuel	5:07	Avi Ohayon, GPO
II Samuel	14:02	Ya'akov Sa'ar, GPO
II Samuel	15:30	Andrew Shiva, Wikimedia Commons
II Samuel	17:22	Chmee2, Wikimedia Commons
II Samuel	20:01	David Rubinger, GPO
II Samuel	22:03	Hans Pinn, GPO
II Samuel	23:01	Djampa, Wikimedia Commons
II Samuel	24:24	Classical Numismatic Group, Wikimedia Commons
I Kings	2:12	Israel Defense Forces, Wikimedia Commons
I Kings	9:15	Berthold Werner, Wikimedia Commons
I Kings	13:01	Dvirraz, Wikimedia Commons
I Kings	15:02	Andrew Shiva, Wikimedia Commons
I Kings	16:24	Alla Khananashvili, Shutterstock.com
I Kings	17:14	Haim Zach, GPO
I Kings	18:38	Netanel, Wikimedia Commons
II Kings	3:16	Netafim
II Kings	5:10	Bill Rice, Wikimedia Commons
II Kings	7:03	Arkady Mazor, Shutterstock.com
II Kings	11:12	Lawrie Cate, Wikimedia Commons
II Kings	16:06	StockStudio, Shutterstock.com
II Kings	17:23	Moshe Milner, GPO
II Kings	19:35	GPO
II Kings	22:11	Moshe Milner, GPO
Isaiah	4:02	Yuval Y, Wikimedia Commons
Isaiah	8:18	Andrew Shiva, Wikimedia Commons
Isaiah	11:12	Moshe Milner, GPO
Isaiah	22:11	Tamar Hayardeni, Wikimedia Commons
Isaiah	27:06	Amos Ben Gershom, GPO
Isaiah	28:25	Amos Ben Gershom, GPO
Isaiah	42:06	GPO
Isaiah	51:03	Protasov AN, Shutterstock.com
Isaiah	56:05	David Shankbone, Wikimedia Commons
Jeremiah	1:11	Mark Neyman, GPO
Jeremiah	2:13	Avishai Teicher, Wikimedia Commons

Book	Verse	Photo Credit
Jeremiah	4:06	Moshe Milner, GPO
Jeremiah	5:06	Ya'acov Sa'ar, GPO
Jeremiah	11:16	Britchi Mirela, Wikimedia Commons
Jeremiah	13:12	Yair Aronshtam, Wikimedia Commons
Jeremiah	19:02	Dror Feitelson, Wikimedia Commons
Jeremiah	24:02	Kvita Fabian, Shutterstock.com
Jeremiah	27:02	Slavoljub Pantelic, Shutterstock.com
Jeremiah	31:16	Moshe Milner, GPO
Jeremiah	32:07	Ya'acov Sa'ar, GPO
Jeremiah	36:22	Amos Ben Gershom, GPO
Jeremiah	39:05	Avishai Teicher, Wikimedia Commons
Ezekiel	3:15	StockStudio, Shutterstock.com
Ezekiel	13:04	Felagund, Wikimedia Commons
Ezekiel	15:06	Avi Ohayon, GPO
Ezekiel	20:06	Sergei25, Shutterstock.com
Ezekiel	21:02	Andrew Shiva, Wikimedia Commons
Ezekiel	28:25	Chaim, Wikimedia Commons
Ezekiel	32:02	Avi Ohayon, GPO
Ezekiel	33:03	Mark Neyman, GPO
Ezekiel	34:13	Mark Neyman, GPO
Ezekiel	36:08	Wikimedia Commons
Ezekiel	37:19	Moshe Milner, GPO
Ezekiel	41:18	Avishai Teicher, Wikimedia Commons
Ezekiel	43:11	Amos Ben Gershom, GPO
Hosea	1:04	Ori, Wikimedia Commons
Hosea	5:01	Moshe Milner, GPO
Hosea	10:01	Yehudit Garin, Wikimedia Commons
Hosea	13:08	Alexander Muvchin, Wikimedia Commons
Joel	1:04	Ya'akov Gefen, GPO
Amos	3:04	Ya'acov Sa'ar, GPO
Amos	5:24	Avi Ohayon, GPO
Amos	6:01	Shaliv, Wikimedia Commons
Obadiah	1:17	Avi Deror, Wikimedia Commons
Jonah	4:06	Eran Finkle, Wikimedia Commons
Mica	1:13	Wilson44691, Wikimedia Commons
Mica	4:04	SuperJew, Wikimedia Commons
Nahum	1:04	Mark Neyman, GPO
Zephaniah	1:15	Moshe Milner, GPO
Haggai	2:09	Stefano Rocca, Shutterstock.com
Zechariah	4:02	Amos Ben Gershom, GPO
Zechariah	4:11	GPO
Zechariah	9:09	GPO
Zechariah	13:01	Wilson44691, Wikimedia Commons
Zechariah	14:16	Wikimedia Commons
Psalms	3:01	Andrew Shiva, Wikimedia Commons
Psalms	8:09	Haim Zach, GPO
Psalms	9:09	Pinn Hans, GPO
Psalms	10:08	Netafim
Psalms	11:06	Tiia Monto, Wikimedia Commons
Psalms	12:07	Zairon, Wikimedia Commons
Psalms	13:06	Easy Sicha, Wikimedia Commons
Psalms	17:08	Yair Aronshtam, Wikimedia Commons
Psalms	18:08	irisphoto1, Shutterstock.com
Psalms	19:06	Protasov AN, Shutterstock.com
Psalms	20:07	Alefbet, Shutterstock.com
Psalms	21:04	Sir Shurf, Wikimedia Commons
Psalms	25:05	Ori, Wikimedia Commons
Psalms	30:01	Deror Avi, Wikimedia Commons
Psalms	34:13	Zoltan Kluger, GPO
Psalms	42:07	Amos Ben Gershom, GPO
Psalms	45:08	Alexander Sviridov, Shutterstock.com
Psalms	58:10	Eitan F, Wikimedia Commons
Psalms	65:11	Moshe Milner, GPO
Psalms	69:36	Djampa, Wikimedia Commons
Psalms	81:01	Avishai Teicher, Wikimedia Commons
Psalms	84:07	Oriaaaass, Wikimedia Commons
Psalms	87:02	Alefbet, Shutterstock.com
Psalms	89:13	Marc Tarlock, Wikimedia Commons
Psalms	92:13	Sergei25, Shutterstock.com
Psalms	93:04	Lerner Vadim, Shutterstock.com

Book	Verse	Photo Credit
Psalms	98:08	Michael Egenburg, Shutterstock.com
Psalms	108:09	Jim Greenhill, Wikimedia Commons
Psalms	116:14	Juan R. Cuadra, Wikimedia Commons
Psalms	121:01	Amos Ben Gershom, GPO
Psalms	124:07	Hanay, Wikimedia Commons
Psalms	128:06	Avishai Teicher, Wikimedia Commons
Psalms	130:06	GPO
Psalms	133:03	Mark Neyman, GPO
Psalms	139:14	GPO
Psalms	143:05	Wikimedia Commons
Psalms	147:14	Moshe Milner, GPO
Psalms	150:03	Alefbet, Shutterstock.com
Proverbs	3:09	Wikimedia Commons
Proverbs	6:23	James Emery, flickr
Proverbs	7:14	Andrew Shiva, Wikimedia Commons
Proverbs	10:22	Kobi Gideon, GPO
Proverbs	19:12	Mark Neyman, GPO
Proverbs	23:05	Mark Neyman, GPO
Job	28:18	Sararwut Jaimassiri, Shutterstock.com
Job	39:13	Avi Ohayon, GPO
Song of Songs	1:14	Einat Anker
Song of Songs	2:13	Avi Ohayon, GPO
Song of Songs	3:10	Stefano Rocca, Shutterstock.com
Song of Songs	4:13	Moshe Milner, GPO
Song of Songs	7:08	Oleg Zaslavsky, Shutterstcock.com
Ruth	2:17	Yaakov Gefen, GPO
Lamentations	1:02	Chaim, Wikimedia Commons
Lamentations	4:15	Bukvoed, Wikimedia Commons
Lamentations	4:19	Avishai Teicher, Wikimedia Commons
Ecclesiastes	7:11	Irit Gamlai, Wikimedia Commons
Esther	9:21	Mark Neyman, GPO
Daniel	6:11	John Theodor, Shutterstock.com
Daniel	10:02	Mark Neyman, GPO
Ezra		Moshe Milner, GPO
Ezra	6:14	Zoltan Kluger, GPO
Ezra	7:09	Zoltan Kluger, GPO
Ezra	8:31	Teddy Brauner, Wikimedia Commons
Nechemia	3:15	Itamar Babai, Wikimedia Commons
Nechemia	4:11	Moshe Milner, GPO
Nechemia	5:15	Great Siberia Studio, Shutterstock.com
Nechamia	6:01	Eitan F, Wikimedia Commons
Nehemiah	8:15	Ryan Rodrick Beiler, Shutterstock.com
Nehamiah	12:38	Rachel Lyra Hospodar, Wikimedia Commons
Nehemiah	13:19	Wilson44691, Wikimedia Commons
I Chronicles	7:31	Mark Neyman, GPO
I Chronicles	16:42	Faruk, Wikimedia Commons
II Chronicles	1:10	Israel Tourism, Wikimedia Commons
II Chronicles	4:20	Amos Ben Gershom, GPO
II Chronicles	8:12	Andrew Shiva, Wikimedia Commons
II Chronicles	18:02	Ori, Wikimedia Commons
II Chronicles	20:26	Michaeli, Wikimedia Commons
II Chronilces	28:03	Ron Almog, Wikimedia Commons
II Chronicles	34:27	Chameleons Eye, Shutterstock.com
II Chronicles	36:23	Mark Neyman, GPO

Chart of the Hebrew Months and their Holidays

Jewish Month	Approximate Secular Date	Holiday	Hebrew Date	Notes
		Rosh Chodesh (Head of the Month)	The first of every month	The Jewish Calendar is a lunar calendar, and each month begins when the moon re-appears in the sky. The beginning of each new month is called *Rosh Chodesh*, which literally means 'the head of the month.' *Rosh Chodesh* is celebrated as a mini-holiday on the first day of every Jewish month, and special prayers are added into the daily service. When a month is 30 days long, the 30th day is celebrated as *Rosh Chodesh* in addition to the first day of the following month.
Nisan	March–April	*Pesach* (Passover)	Begins on the 15th of *Nisan*	*Pesach* is a seven day holiday commemorating the Exodus from Egypt. Outside of Israel, an eighth day is observed.
		Yom Hashoa (Holocaust Memorial Day)	27th of *Nisan*	*Yom Hashoa* commemorates the 6 million Jews who perished in the Holocaust.
Iyar	April–May	*Yom Hazikaron* (Memorial Day)	4th of *Iyar*	*Yom Hazikaron* is Israel's memorial day, a day to remember Israel's fallen soldiers and victims of terror.
		Yom Haatzmaut (Israel's Independence Day)	5th of *Iyar*	*Yom Haatzmaut* celebrates Israel's declaration of independence in 1948.
		Lag Ba'Omer (33rd day of the Omer)	18th of *Iyar*	*Lag Ba'Omer* is a minor holiday celebrated on the 33rd day of the counting of the Omer
		Yom Yerushalayim (Jerusalem Day)	28th of *Iyar*	*Yom Yerushalayim*, Jerusalem Day, celebrates the re-unification of the city of Jerusalem following the 1967 Six-Day War.
Sivan	May–June	*Shavuot* (Feast of Weeks)	6th of *Sivan*	*Shavuot* celebrates the giving of the *Torah* at Mount Sinai. Outside of Israel it is observed for two days, the 6th and 7th of *Sivan*.

Jewish Month	Approximate Secular Date	Holiday	Hebrew Date	Notes
Tammuz	June–July	Fast of the Seventeenth of *Tammuz*	17th of *Tammuz*	The Fast of the Seventeenth of *Tammuz* commemorates the breeching of the walls of Jerusalem before the destruction of the Temple. It begins a three week mourning period over the destruction of the Temple, culminating with the fast of *Tisha B'Av*.
Av	July–August	*Tisha B'Av* (Fast of the 9th of *Av*)	9th of *Av*	*Tisha B'Av* is a fast day commemorating the destruction of the Temple in Jerusalem. It is the culmination of the three week mourning period over the destruction of the Temple which starts on the 17th of *Tammuz*.
Elul	August–September			
Tishrei	September–October	*Rosh Hashana* (Jewish New Year)	1st and 2nd of *Tishrei*	*Rosh Hashana* is the Jewish New Year.
		Tzom Gedalya (Fast of Gedaliah)	3rd of *Tishrei*	The Fast of Gedaliah commemorates the death of Gedaliah son of Ahikam, the governor of Judah following the destruction of the First Temple. His death marked the end of Jewish rule in the Land of Israel for many generations and led to the exile of the few remaining Jews who had not been taken to Babylonia.
		Yom Kippur (Day of Atonement)	10th of *Tishrei*	*Yom Kippur* is the Day of Atonement, the holiest day of the year.
		Sukkot (Feast of Tabernacles)	Begins on the 15th of *Tishrei*	*Sukkot* is a seven-day holiday celebrating God's protection of the Jews in the wilderness
		Shemini Atzeret/Simchat Torah (Eighth Day of Assembly)	22nd of *Tishrei*	*Shemini Atzeret* is a holiday that immediately follows *Sukkot* and celebrates the unique relationship between God and the Children of Israel. *Simchat Torah* celebrates the completion and renewal of the *Torah* reading cycle. In Israel, *Shemini Atzeret* and *Simchat Torah* are celebrated on the same day. Outside of Israel, they are celebrated on two consecutive days.
Cheshvan	October–November			

Jewish Month	Approximate Secular Date	Holiday	Hebrew Date	Notes
Kislev	November–December	Chanukah (Hanukkah)	Begins on the 25th of Kislev	Chanukah is an eight day festival which celebrates the defeat of the Syrian-Greeks, the re-dedication of the Temple in Jerusalem, and the miracles that God preformed to facilitate these events.
Tevet	December–January	The end of Chanukah (Hanukkah)	Chanukah ends on the 2nd or 3rd of Tevet depending on the year, since Kislev contains either 29 or 30 days	
		Fast of the 10th of Tevet	10th of Tevet	The Fast of the 10th of Tevet commemorates the Babylonian siege of Jerusalem prior to the destruction of the First Temple.
Shevat	January–February	Tu B'Shvat (15th of Shevat)	15th of Shevat	Tu B'Shvat marks the beginning of the new year for trees. It is when the first trees in the Land of Israel begin to blossom again after the winter season.
Adar*	February–March	Fast of Esther	13th of Adar	The Fast of Esther commemorates the fast observed by the Jewish people in Persia at the time of Mordechai and Esther.
		Purim	14th/15th of Adar	Purim celebrates God's salvation of the Jews from the evil Haman's plot to destroy them. In most places, this holiday is celebrated on the 14th of Adar. In Jerusalem, it is celebrated on the 15th of Adar.

* During a leap year, an extra month of Adar is added so that the Jewish lunar calendar remains aligned with the solar seasons. A leap year occurs 7 times in every 19 year cycle. When this happens, Purim is celebrated in the second Adar.

Map of Modern-Day Israel and its Neighbors

The following is a map of modern-day Israel and the surrounding countries

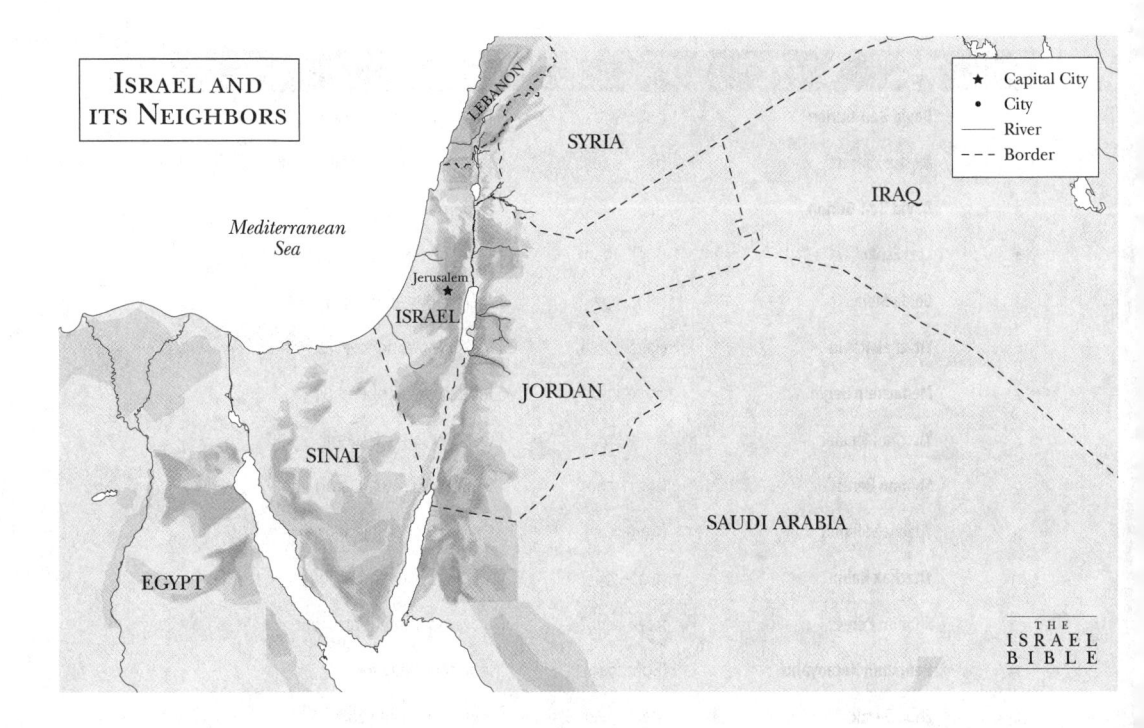

List of Prime Ministers of the State of Israel

Below is a list of the Prime Ministers of the State of Israel since the declaration of the State in 1948 until the present.

Number	Name	Years	Term
1	**David Ben-Gurion**	(1886–1973)	May 1948–January 1954
2	**Moshe Sharett**	(1894–1965)	January 1954–November 1955
3	**David Ben-Gurion**	(1886–1973)	November 1955–June 1963
4	**Levi Eshkol**	(1895–1969)	June 1963–February 1969
5	**Golda Meir**	(1898–1978)	March 1969–June 1974
6	**Yitzchak Rabin**	(1922–1995)	June 1974–June 1977
7	**Menachem Begin**	(1913–1992)	June 1977–October 1983
8	**Yitzchak Shamir**	(1915–2012)	October 1983–September 1984
9	**Shimon Peres**	(1923–2016)	September 1984–October 1986
10	**Yitzchak Shamir**	(1915–2012)	October 1986–July 1992
11	**Yitzchak Rabin**	(1922–1995)	July 1992–November 1995
12	**Shimon Peres**	(1923–2016)	November 1995–June 1996
13	**Benjamin Netanyahu**	(Born 1949)	June 1996–July 1999
14	**Ehud Barak**	(Born 1942)	July 1999–March 2001
15	**Ariel Sharon**	(1928–2014)	March 2001–April 2006
16	**Ehud Olmert**	(Born 1945)	April 2006–March 2009
17	**Benjamin Netanyahu**	(Born 1949)	March 2009–Present

Prayer for the State of Israel

Our Heavenly Father	a-VEE-nu she-ba-sha-MA-yim	אָבִינוּ שֶׁבַּשָּׁמַיִם
Israel's Rock and Redeemer	tzur yis-ra-AYL v'-go-a-LO	צוּר יִשְׂרָאֵל וְגוֹאֲלוֹ
Bless the State of Israel	ba-RAYKH et mi-dee-NAT yis-ra-AYL	בָּרֵךְ אֶת מְדִינַת יִשְׂרָאֵל
the first flowering of our redemption	ray-SHEET tz'-mee-KHAT g'-u-la-TAY-nu	רֵאשִׁית צְמִיחַת גְּאֻלָּתֵנוּ
Shield it under the wings of Your loving kindness	ha-GAYN a-LE-ha b'-ev-RAT khas-DE-kha	הָגֵן עָלֶיהָ בְּאֶבְרַת חַסְדֶּךָ
And spread over it the Tabernacle of Your peace	uf-ROS a-LE-ha su-KAT sh'-lo-ME-kha	וּפְרֹשׂ עָלֶיהָ סֻכַּת שְׁלוֹמֶךָ
Send Your light and truth	ush-LAKH o-r'-KHA va-a-mi-t'-KHA	וּשְׁלַח אוֹרְךָ וַאֲמִתְּךָ
to its leaders, ministers and officials	l'-ro-SHE-ha, sa-RE-ha v'-yo-a-TZE-ha	לְרָאשֶׁיהָ, שָׂרֶיהָ וְיוֹעֲצֶיהָ
And direct them with good counsel before You	v'-ta-k'-NAYM b'-ay-TZAH to-VAH m'-li-fa-NE-kha	וְתַקְּנֵם בְּעֵצָה טוֹבָה מִלְּפָנֶיךָ
Strengthen the hands of the defenders of our Holy Land	kha-ZAYK et y'-DAY m'-gi-NAY E-retz kod-SHAY-nu	חַזֵּק אֶת יְדֵי מְגִנֵּי אֶרֶץ קָדְשֵׁנוּ
Grant them deliverance, our God	v'-han-khee-LAYM e-lo-HAY-nu y'-shu-AH	וְהַנְחִילֵם אֱלֹהֵינוּ יְשׁוּעָה
And crown them with the crown of victory	va-a-TE-ret ni-tza-KHON t'-a-t'-RAYM	וַעֲטֶרֶת נִצָּחוֹן תְּעַטְּרֵם
Grant peace in the land	v'-na-ta-TA sha-LOM ba-A-retz	וְנָתַתָּ שָׁלוֹם בָּאָרֶץ
and everlasting joy to its inhabitants	v'-sim-KHAT o-LAM l'-yo-sh'-VE-ha	וְשִׂמְחַת עוֹלָם לְיוֹשְׁבֶיהָ

As for our brothers, the whole house of Israel	v'-ET a-KHAY-nu kol bayt yis-ra-AYL	וְאֶת אַחֵינוּ כָּל בֵּית יִשְׂרָאֵל
Remember them in all the lands of their dispersion	p'-KOD na b'-KHOL ar-TZOT p'-zu-ray-HEM	פְּקָד נָא בְּכָל אַרְצוֹת פְּזוּרֵיהֶם
And swiftly lead them upright	v'-to-lee-KHAYM m'-hay-RAH ko-m'-mi-YUT	וְתוֹלִיכֵם מְהֵרָה קוֹמְמִיּוּת
to *Zion* Your city	l'-TZI-yon ee-RE-kha	לְצִיּוֹן עִירֶךָ
And *Yerushalayim* Your dwelling place	v'-lee-ru-sha-LA-yim mish-KAN sh'-ME-kha	וְלִירוּשָׁלַיִם מִשְׁכַּן שְׁמֶךָ
As is written in the *Torah* of *Moses* Your servant (Deut. 30:4–5):	ka-ka-TUV b'-to-RAT mo-SHEH av-DE-kha:	כַּכָּתוּב בְּתוֹרַת מֹשֶׁה עַבְדֶּךָ (דברים ל:ד-ה):
"Even if you are scattered to the furthermost lands under the heavens	"im yih-YEH ni-da-kha-KHA bik-TZAY ha-sha-MA-yim	"אִם יִהְיֶה נִדַּחֲךָ בִּקְצֵה הַשָּׁמָיִם
From there the Lord your God will gather you	mi-SHAM yi-ka-betz-KHA a-do-NAI e-lo-HE-kha	מִשָּׁם יְקַבֶּצְךָ יְיָ אֱלֹהֶיךָ
and from there He will and take you back	u-mi-SHAM yi-ka-KHE-kha	וּמִשָּׁם יִקָּחֶךָ
The Lord your God will bring you to the land	ve-he-vee-a-KHA a-do-NAI e-lo-HE-kha el ha-A-retz	וֶהֱבִיאֲךָ יְיָ אֱלֹהֶיךָ אֶל הָאָרֶץ
That your ancestors possessed	a-SHER ya-r'-SHU a-vo-TE-khe	אֲשֶׁר יָרְשׁוּ אֲבֹתֶיךָ
and you will possess it	vee-rish-TAH	וִירִשְׁתָּהּ
And He will make you more prosperous and numerous than your ancestors"	v'-hay-tiv-KHA v'-hir-b'-KHA may-a-vo-TE-kha"	וְהֵיטִבְךָ וְהִרְבְּךָ מֵאֲבֹתֶיךָ"
Unite our hearts	v'-ya-KHAYD l'-va-VAY-nu	וְיַחֵד לְבָבֵנוּ
to love and revere Your name	l'-a-ha-VAH ul-yir-AH et sh'-ME-kha	לְאַהֲבָה וּלְיִרְאָה אֶת שְׁמֶךָ
And observe all the words of Your *Torah*	v'-lish-MOR et kol div-RAY to-ra-TE-kha	וְלִשְׁמֹר אֶת כָּל דִּבְרֵי תוֹרָתֶךָ

And swiftly send us	ush-LAKH LA-nu m'-hay-RAH	וּשְׁלַח לָנוּ מְהֵרָה
Your righteous anointed one of the house of *David*	ben da-VID m'-SHEE-akh tzid-KE-kha	בֶּן דָּוִד מְשִׁיחַ צִדְקֶךָ
To redeem those who long for Your salvation	lif-DOT m'-kha-KAY kaytz y'-shu-a-TE-kha	לִפְדּוֹת מְחַכֵּי קֵץ יְשׁוּעָתֶךָ
Appear in Your glorious majesty	ho-FA ba-ha-DAR g'-ON u-ZE-kha	הוֹפַע בַּהֲדַר גְּאוֹן עֻזֶּךָ
over all the dwellers on earth	al kol yo-sh'-VAY TAY-vayl ar-TZE-kha	עַל כָּל יוֹשְׁבֵי תֵבֵל אַרְצֶךָ
And let all who breathe declare:	v'-yo-MAR kol a-SHER n'-sha-MAH v'-a-PO	וְיֹאמַר כֹּל אֲשֶׁר נְשָׁמָה בְאַפּוֹ
The Lord God of Israel is King	a-do-NAI e-lo-HAY yis-ra-AYL ME-lekh	יְיָ אֱלֹהֵי יִשְׂרָאֵל מֶלֶךְ
And His kingship has dominion over all	u-mal-khu-TO ba-KOL ma-sha-LAH,	וּמַלְכוּתוֹ בַּכֹּל מָשָׁלָה
Amen, Selah	a-MAYN SE-lah	אָמֵן סֶלָה

Prayer for the Welfare of Israel's Soldiers

He Who blessed our forefathers	mee she-bay-RAKH a-vo-TAY-nu	מִי שֶׁבֵּרַךְ אֲבוֹתֵינוּ
Avraham, Yitzchak and Yaakov	av-ra-HAM yitz-KHAK v'-ya-a-KOV	אַבְרָהָם יִצְחָק וְיַעֲקֹב
may He bless the fighters of the Israel Defense Forces	hu y'-va-RAYKH et kha-ya-LAY tz'-VA ha-ha-ga-NAH l'-yis-ra-AYL	הוּא יְבָרֵךְ אֶת חַיָּלֵי צְבָא הַהֲגָנָה לְיִשְׂרָאֵל
and the security personnel	v'-an-SHAY ko-KHOT ha-bi-ta-KHON	וְאַנְשֵׁי כֹחוֹת הַבִּטָּחוֹן
who stand guard over our land	ha-o-m'-DEEM al mish-MAR ar-TZAY-nu	הָעוֹמְדִים עַל מִשְׁמַר אַרְצֵנוּ
and the cities of our God	v'-a-RAY e-lo-HAY-nu	וְעָרֵי אֱלֹהֵינוּ
from the border of the Lebanon to the desert of Egypt	mi-g'-VUL ha-l'-va-NON v'-AD mid-BAR mitz-RA-yim	מִגְּבוּל הַלְּבָנוֹן וְעַד מִדְבַּר מִצְרַיִם
and from the Great Sea unto the approach of the Aravah	u-MIN ha-YAM ha-ga-DOL ad l'-VO ha-a-ra-VAH	וּמִן הַיָּם הַגָּדוֹל עַד לְבוֹא הָעֲרָבָה
on the land, in the air, and on the sea	ba-ya-ba-SHAH ba-a-VEER u-va-YAM	בַּיַּבָּשָׁה בָּאֲוִיר וּבַיָּם
May the Almighty cause the enemies who rise up against us	yi-TAYN a-do-NAI et o-y'-VAY-nu ha-ka-MEEM a-LAY-nu	יִתֵּן יְיָ אֶת אוֹיְבֵינוּ הַקָּמִים עָלֵינוּ
to be struck down before them	ni-ga-FEEM lif-nay-HEM	נִגָּפִים לִפְנֵיהֶם
May the Holy One, Blessed is He	ha-ka-DOSH ba-RUKH hu	הַקָּדוֹשׁ בָּרוּךְ הוּא
preserve and rescue our fighters	yish-MOR v'-ya-TZEEL et kha-ya-LAY-nu	יִשְׁמֹר וְיַצִּיל אֶת חַיָּלֵינוּ
from every trouble and distress	mi-KOL tza-RAH v'-tzu-KAH	מִכָּל צָרָה וְצוּקָה

and from every plague and illness	u-mi-KOL NE-ga u-ma-kha-LAH	וּמִכָּל נֶגַע וּמַחֲלָה
and may He send blessing and success	v'-yish-LAKH b'-ra-KHAH v'-hatz-la-KHAH	וְיִשְׁלַח בְּרָכָה וְהַצְלָחָה
in their every endeavor	b'-KHOL ma-a-SAY y'-day-HEM	בְּכָל מַעֲשֵׂה יְדֵיהֶם
May He lead our enemies under our soldiers' sway	yad-BAYR so-n'-AY-nu takh-tay-HEM	יַדְבֵּר שׂוֹנְאֵינוּ תַּחְתֵּיהֶם
and glorify our forces with the crown of salvation	vee-a-t'-RAYM b'-KHE-ter y'-shu-AH	וִיעַטְּרֵם בְּכֶתֶר יְשׁוּעָה
and the mantle of victory	uv-a-TE-ret ni-tza-KHON	וּבַעֲטֶרֶת נִצָּחוֹן
And may there be fulfilled for them the verse (Deuteronomy 20:4):	vee-ku-YAM ba-HEM ha-ka-TUV:	וִיקֻיַּם בָּהֶם הַכָּתוּב (דברים כ,ד):
"For it is the Lord your God, Who goes with you	"kee a-do-NAI e-lo-hay-KHEM ha-ho-LAYKH i-ma-KHEM	"כִּי יְיָ אֱלֹהֵיכֶם הַהֹלֵךְ עִמָּכֶם
to battle your enemies for you	l'-hi-la-KHAYM la-KHEM im o-y'-vay-KHEM	לְהִלָּחֵם לָכֶם עִם אֹיְבֵיכֶם
to save you"	l'-ho-SHEE-a et-KHEM"	לְהוֹשִׁיעַ אֶתְכֶם"
Now let us say: Amen	v'-no-MAR "a-MAYN"	וְנֹאמַר: "אָמֵן"

Hatikvah

As long as in the heart, within	kol od ba-lay-VAV p'-NEE-mah	כֹּל עוֹד בַּלֵּבָב פְּנִימָה
A Jewish soul still yearns	NE-fesh y'-hu-DEE ho-mi-YAH	נֶפֶשׁ יְהוּדִי הוֹמִיָּה
And onward, towards the ends of the east	ul-fa-a-TAY miz-RAKH ka-DEE-mah	וּלְפַאֲתֵי מִזְרָח, קָדִימָה
An eye still gazes toward Zion	A-yin l'-tzi-YON tzo-fi-YAH	עַיִן לְצִיּוֹן צוֹפִיָּה
Our hope is not yet lost	od lo av-DAH tik-va-TAY-nu	עוֹד לֹא אָבְדָה תִּקְוָתֵנוּ
The hope two thousand years old	ha-tik-VAH bat sh'-NOT al-PA-yim	הַתִּקְוָה בַּת שְׁנוֹת אַלְפַּיִם
To be a free nation in our land	lih-YOT am khof-SHEE b'-ar-TZAY-nu	לִהְיוֹת עַם חָפְשִׁי בְּאַרְצֵנוּ
The Land of Zion and Yerushalayim	E-retz tzi-YON vee-ru-sha-LA-yim	אֶרֶץ צִיּוֹן וִירוּשָׁלַיִם

PRAISE FOR THE ISRAEL BIBLE

The Israel Bible is truly a magnificent gift to mankind at this time in history and I believe it will be an integral part of the "Tikkun Olam" or the repairing of the world in rectifying the breach between the nations of the world and the nation of Israel that all mankind may call upon Hashem in one accord.

– *Pastor Mark Biltz, El Shaddai Ministries*

The Bible is Israel's greatest export to the world, and so it is impossible to think of the Bible without connecting it to Israel, its land and its people. For many years it has been in my heart to see a publication that would prophetically chronicle the ongoing miraculous story of the Bible. Rabbi Tuly Weisz is helping to fulfill that dream with *The Israel Bible*.

– *Christine Darg, Co-founder, The Jerusalem Channel*

Christians as well as Jews will find much to learn from this excellent resource as they study God's word. I am confident that this special edition in honor of Israel's 70th anniversary will deepen the readers' spiritual relationship with God, strengthen their bonds with Israel – land and people – and deeply enrich their lives.

– *Rabbi Yechiel Eckstein, International Fellowship of Christian and Jews*

The Israel Bible not only highlights the centrality of the Land of Israel and the modern miracle of the State of Israel, but helps the Bible scholar and student alike, with helpful charts, study notes, professional essays and a relatable translation of the Hebrew text. What a beautiful and poignant way to celebrate the State of Israel's 70th birthday.

– *Rabbi Yehoshua Fass, Co-Founder of Nefesh B'Nefesh*

When you open *The Israel Bible* and see all 929 chapters containing lessons about Israel, you see that Israel is the Torah's main theme and begin to understand the major role that it plays.

The Israel Bible helps you understand that the whole Bible is all about the Land of Israel – and that is a message for all of humanity.

– *Rabbi Yehudah Glick, Member of Knesset*

The Israel Bible is a publication whose time has come. In these very critical and tempestuous times it is especially important to understand the inexplicable connection between the nation of Israel and the Land of Israel and this is precisely what Rabbi Tuly Weisz has succeeded in doing in this timely translation of the Bible.

– *Rabbi Shlomo Riskin, Chief Rabbi of Efrat*

The Israel Bible releases refreshing comprehension about words in scripture passages, and their origins. The creation of this work is brilliant. It will educate the educators, as well as the ordinary truth seeker. I believe it will help liberate many from the shackles of inaccurate theological interpretation and prepare them to meet the challenges that this understanding brings to the world.

– Sharon Sanders, Co-Founder Christian Friends of Israel &
Co-Founder Heart Beat for Israel

Thanks to Rabbi Tuly Weisz for reminding us that, at its core, the Hebrew bible is a description of a love story between a people and its land, the Jewish people and the land of Israel. From its earliest history, *Eretz Yisrael* has been central to Jewish living and Jewish destiny. The Jewish people dwelt in it, pined and yearned for it and, in our day, has miraculously merited to return to it.

– Rabbi Jacob J. Schacter,
Professor of Jewish History and Jewish Thought, Yeshiva University

I just received my copy of *The Israel Bible* and now see why Amazon Books is having a hard time keeping this majestic work in stock! Sorry to say my favorite Stone Edition *Tanach* may not be opened for a while. This is a *must* for every serious lover of the Word of God!

– Pastor Victor Styrsky, Eastern Regional Coordinator
for Christians United for Israel

After spending time studying *The Israel Bible*, I can say it gives much clarity to what the original Hebrew text was saying. This Bible is easy to follow and very informative. It makes my studies more enjoyable while reading the text, footnotes and quotes from many wise people. It is a great study Bible for all serious students of the Word.

– Pastor David Swaggerty, CharismaLife Ministries

Ever since I made my first trip to Israel, the words of the Bible have seemed to leap off the pages. Through reading *The Israel Bible*, I am now gaining a deeper understanding through inspiring Jewish insight, which has always connected the Bible to the People, Land, and God of Israel.

– Tommy Waller, President and Founder, HaYovel

This excellent work connects all the dots. It draws the reader closer to the Almighty, to the Torah, and to the Land of Israel. Rabbi Tuly Weisz and his colleagues are to be congratulated, and thanked, for this inspiring and informative gift to all who share our history and destiny.

– Rabbi Dr. Tzvi Hersh Weinreb,
Executive Vice President Emeritus, Orthodox Union

For more inspiring commentary,
interactive maps, educational videos,
vivid photographs and more,
please visit our website

www.TheIsraelBible.com

THE
ISRAEL
BIBLE